WHITAKER'S ALMANACK
2005

A & C BLACK

LONDON

AN

Almanack

For the Year of Our Lord

2005

ESTABLISHED 1868

BY

JOSEPH WHITAKER, FSA

CONTAINING AN ACCOUNT OF THE

ASTRONOMICAL AND OTHER PHENOMENA

AND

A vast Amount of INFORMATION respecting the GOVERNMENT, FINANCES, POPULATION, COMMERCE, and GENERAL STATISTICS of the various Nations of the WORLD with an INDEX containing nearly 10,000 References

LONDON

OFFICE: 37 SOHO SQUARE

LONDON W1D 3QZ

The traditional design of the title page for Whitaker's Almanack which has appeared in each edition since 1868

WHITAKER'S ALMANACK

2005

A & C BLACK

LONDON

A & C BLACK (PUBLISHERS) LTD
37 Soho Square, London W1D 3QZ

Whitaker's Almanack published annually since 1868

STANDARD EDITION
Hardback 0-7136-6995-0

CONCISE EDITION
Paperback 0-7136-6996-9

Designed by: Fiona Pike
Jacket photographs: © Corbis
Typeset in the EU by: RefineCatch Ltd, Bungay, Suffolk, Great Britain
Printed and bound in the EU by: William Clowes, Beccles, Suffolk, Great Britain

A CIP catalogue record for this book is available from the British Library.

A & C Black uses paper produced with elemental chlorine-free pulp harvested from managed sustainable forests.

Whitaker's Almanack was compiled with the assistance of: Christian Research; Military Balance 2003–4 published by Oxford University Press; People in Power © Cambridge International Reference on Current Affairs (CIRCA); The Diplomatic List © Crown Copyright; International Financial Statistics Year Book © International Monetary Fund; UK Hydrographic Office; The Met Office; Oxford Cartographers; The Business, Bloomsbury Publishing plc; CIA World Factbook; Keesings Worldwide

EDITORIAL STAFF
Editor-in-Chief: Lauren Simpson
Editor: Inna Ward
Editorial team: Ruth Northey; Anna Collishaw; Luke Block

CONTRIBUTORS
Vanessa White (Editorial); Elizabeth Holmes (Education); Gordon Taylor (Astronomy); Hemant Kanitkar (Hindu calendar); Isabelle Kenning (Mobile Communications); Karen Harries-Rees (Environment); Martin Miller (Information Technology); Clive Longhurst (Insurance); Roger Merrick (Mutual Societies); Duncan Murray, Chris Priestley (Legal Notes); Ken Tingley (Taxation); Dr Neil Faulkner, Dr Nadia Durrani (Archaeology); John Hitchman (Architecture); Ossian Ward (Art); Steve Clarke (Broadcasting); Peter Marren, Matthew Saunders (Conservation); Bridie Macmahon (Dance); Tom Charity (Film); Jon Ashworth (Business and Finance); Nicolette Jones (Literature); Pippa Murphy, Peter Nelson, Piers Martin (Music); Elizabeth Forbes (Opera); Patrick Robathan (Parliament); Erica Stary (Public Acts); Neil Bone (Science and Discovery); Jane Edwardes (Theatre); Edward Gibbes, Stan Greenberg (Sport), Kate Stenner, Toby Saul, Jill Laidlaw (Countries of the World)

INDEX
Colin Izat, Fiona Smith – IndX Ltd

CONTENTS

PREFACE

TO THE 137TH ANNUAL EDITION

Welcome to the 2005 edition of *Whitaker's Almanack*. Since the research and updating of this edition commenced, much has taken place on the global stage. The Madrid bombings in March 2004 indicate that the campaign against terror is far from over and allegations that US and UK troops tortured prisoners of war in Iraq caused widespread controversy during April and May. At home we countenanced higher-than-ever turnouts for the Mayoral, London Assembly and European elections and saw interest rates steadily increase following a 40-year low.

If there is one thing certain in the media it's that today's top stories rapidly become yesterday's news. No sooner do we finish reading a newspaper or watching a news broadcast when some other story develops to capture our attention. In such a fast-paced world, *Whitaker's Almanack* is invaluable because it summarises recent newsworthy events, outlines governmental and infrastructural developments and keeps one appraised of who's who and what's what in today's world while, at the same time, providing a unique, historical record for the future.

It is of vital importance that a reference book like *Whitaker's Almanack* goes further than merely reporting headline news. By providing such information as who runs our public offices, how our water and energy industries operate, how much it costs to send a child to an independent school or how to register a birth, death or marriage, *Whitaker's Almanack* gives a real insight into exactly which people, institutions and processes keep the modern world's cogs turning.

Furthermore, our expert coverage of the arts, science, sport, business and countries of the world is ideal for keeping one abreast of information that may not have received high-profile media coverage during the year. And, lest we forget, *Whitaker's Almanack*'s value as an all-round reference tool is enhanced by the inclusion of such stalwart sections as tidal data, astronomy and calendars.

As our world changes, it is important that *Whitaker's Almanack* evolves accordingly, and we included a readership survey in last year's edition to build a picture of what readers want from *Whitaker's Almanack* in the future. I'd like to take this opportunity to thank all those who took the time to fill in our questionnaire. We received some constructive feedback which will help us ensure that *Whitaker's Almanack* continues to improve year on year and that new content is added to give the publication a contemporary feel.

It was particularly refreshing to see from the results that over 90% of readers either 'liked' or 'strongly liked' the new page design. Other interesting findings included:

- The most frequently read sections are Countries of the World, Government and Parliament
- The least frequently read sections are Astronomy and Peerage
- The areas that readers would most like to see covered in future editions are travel and tourism, popular music, crime statistics, health statistics and household trends

In response to the readership survey, we are pleased to include information on travel and climate, popular music, crime and policing statistics, health statistics and household trends in this edition.

As always, this edition has been fully updated using only the most authoritative sources. Each year literally hundreds of people and organisations assist in the updating of *Whitaker's Almanack*. Without such help and support, *Whitaker's Almanack* would be but a shadow of its current form. To all of you, many thanks.

Lastly, I regret to inform you that one of our long-standing contributors and co-founder of the *Guinness Book of Records*, Norris McWhirter, sadly passed away on 19 April 2004. Norris compiled the World Geographical Statistics section of *Whitaker's Almanack* and many of you will remember him fondly as co-presenter of *Record Breakers* on BBC television in the 1970s and '80s. Our sincerest condolences to Norris's family and friends.

Lauren Simpson
Editor-in-Chief

Whitaker's Almanack
A & C Black Publishers Ltd
37 Soho Square
London
W1D 3QZ

Email: whitakers@acblack.com
Web: www.whitakersalmanack.com

THE YEAR 2005

CHRONOLOGICAL CYCLES AND ERAS

Dominical Letter	B
Golden Number (Lunar Cycle)	XI
Julian Period	6718
Roman Indiction	13
Solar Cycle	26

	Beginning
Japanese year Heisei 17	1 January
Chinese year of the Chicken or Rooster	9 February
Regnal year 54	6 February
Hindu new year	9 April
Indian (Saka) year 1927	9 April
Muslim year AH 1426	10 February
Sikh new year	14 March
Jewish year AM 5766	4 October
Roman year 2758 AUC	

RELIGIOUS CALENDARS

CHRISTIAN

Epiphany	6 January
Presentation of Christ in the Temple	2 February
Ash Wednesday	9 February
Maundy Thursday	24 March
The Annunciation	25 March
Good Friday	25 March
Easter Day (western churches)	27 March
Easter Day (Eastern Orthodox)	1 May
Rogation Sunday	1 May
Ascension Day	5 May
Pentecost (Whit Sunday)	15 May
Trinity Sunday	22 May
Corpus Christi	26 May
All Saints' Day	1 November
Advent Sunday	27 November
Christmas Day	25 December

HINDU

Makara Sankranti	14 January
Vasant Panchami (Sarasvati-puja)	13 February
Mahashivaratri	8 March
Holi	25 March
Chaitra (Hindu new year)	9 April
Ramanavami	18 April
Raksha-bandhan	19 August
Janmashtami	26 August
Ganesh Chaturthi, first day	7 September
Ganesh festival, last day	17 September
Durga-puja	4 October
Navaratri festival, first day	4 October
Sarasvati-puja	10 October
Dasara	12 October
Diwali, first day	30 October
Diwali, last day	3 November

JEWISH

Purim	25 March
Passover, first day	24 April
Feast of Weeks, first day	13 June
Jewish new year, first day	4 October
Yom Kippur (Day of Atonement)	13 October
Feast of Tabernacles, first day	18 October
Chanucah, first day	26 December

MUSLIM

Muslim new year	10 February
Ramadan, first day	4 October

SIKH

Birthday of Guru Gobind Singh Ji	5 January
Baisakhi Mela (Sikh new year)	14 March
Martyrdom of Guru Arjan Dev Ji	16 June
Birthday of Guru Nanak Dev Ji	15 November
Martyrdom of Guru Tegh Bahadur Ji	24 November

CIVIL CALENDAR

Accession of Queen Elizabeth II	6 February
Duke of York's birthday	19 February
St David's Day	1 March
Earl of Wessex birthday	10 March
Commonwealth Day	14 March
St Patrick's Day	17 March
Birthday of Queen Elizabeth II	21 April
St George's Day	23 April
Europe Day	9 May
Coronation of Queen Elizabeth II	2 June
Duke of Edinburgh's birthday	10 June
The Queen's Official Birthday	11 June
Princess Royal's birthday	15 August
Lord Mayor's Day	12 November
Remembrance Sunday	13 November
Prince of Wales's birthday	14 November
Wedding Day of Queen Elizabeth II	20 November
St Andrew's Day	30 November

LEGAL CALENDAR

LAW TERMS

Hilary Term	11 January to 23 March
Easter Term	5 April to 27 May
Trinity Term	7 June to 29 July
Michaelmas Term	1 October to 21 December

QUARTER DAYS

England, Wales and Northern Ireland

Lady	25 March
Midsummer	24 June
Michaelmas	29 September
Christmas	25 December

TERM DAYS

Scotland

Candlemas	28 February
Whitsunday	28 May
Lammas	28 August
Martinmas	28 November
Removal Terms	28 May, 28 November

2005

JANUARY

Sunday		2	9	16	23	30
Monday		3	10	17	24	31
Tuesday		4	11	18	25	
Wednesday		5	12	19	26	
Thursday		6	13	20	27	
Friday		7	14	21	28	
Saturday	1	8	15	22	29	

FEBRUARY

Sunday		6	13	20	27
Monday		7	14	21	28
Tuesday	1	8	15	22	
Wednesday	2	9	16	23	
Thursday	3	10	17	24	
Friday	4	11	18	25	
Saturday	5	12	19	26	

MARCH

Sunday		6	13	20	27
Monday		7	14	21	28
Tuesday	1	8	15	22	29
Wednesday	2	9	16	23	30
Thursday	3	10	17	24	31
Friday	4	11	18	25	
Saturday	5	12	19	26	

APRIL

Sunday		3	10	17	24
Monday		4	11	18	25
Tuesday		5	12	19	26
Wednesday		6	13	20	27
Thursday		7	14	21	28
Friday	1	8	15	22	29
Saturday	2	9	16	23	30

MAY

Sunday	1	8	15	22	29
Monday	2	9	16	23	30
Tuesday	3	10	17	24	31
Wednesday	4	11	18	25	
Thursday	5	12	19	26	
Friday	6	13	20	27	
Saturday	7	14	21	28	

JUNE

Sunday		5	12	19	26
Monday		6	13	20	27
Tuesday		7	14	21	28
Wednesday	1	8	15	22	29
Thursday	2	9	16	23	30
Friday	3	10	17	24	
Saturday	4	11	18	25	

JULY

Sunday		3	10	17	24	31
Monday		4	11	18	25	
Tuesday		5	12	19	26	
Wednesday		6	13	20	27	
Thursday		7	14	21	28	
Friday	1	8	15	22	29	
Saturday	2	9	16	23	30	

AUGUST

Sunday		7	14	21	28
Monday	1	8	15	22	29
Tuesday	2	9	16	23	30
Wednesday	3	10	17	24	31
Thursday	4	11	18	25	
Friday	5	12	19	26	
Saturday	6	13	20	27	

SEPTEMBER

Sunday		4	11	18	25
Monday		5	12	19	26
Tuesday		6	13	20	27
Wednesday		7	14	21	28
Thursday	1	8	15	22	29
Friday	2	9	16	23	30
Saturday	3	10	17	24	

OCTOBER

Sunday		2	9	16	23	30
Monday		3	10	17	24	31
Tuesday		4	11	18	25	
Wednesday		5	12	19	26	
Thursday		6	13	20	27	
Friday		7	14	21	28	
Saturday	1	8	15	22	29	

NOVEMBER

Sunday		6	13	20	27
Monday		7	14	21	28
Tuesday	1	8	15	22	29
Wednesday	2	9	16	23	30
Thursday	3	10	17	24	
Friday	4	11	18	25	
Saturday	5	12	19	26	

DECEMBER

Sunday		4	11	18	25
Monday		5	12	19	26
Tuesday		6	13	20	27
Wednesday		7	14	21	28
Thursday	1	8	15	22	29
Friday	2	9	16	23	30
Saturday	3	10	17	24	31

PUBLIC HOLIDAYS

PUBLIC HOLIDAYS	*England and Wales*	*Scotland*	*Northern Ireland*
New Year	†3 January	3, 4 January	†3 January
St Patrick's Day	–	–	‡17 March
*Good Friday	25 March	25 March	25 March
Easter Monday	28 March	–	28 March
Early May	†2 May	2 May	†2 May
Spring	30 May	†30 May	30 May
Battle of the Boyne	–	–	‡12 July
Summer	29 August	1 August	29 August
*Christmas	25, 26 December 27 taken in lieu	25, †26 December 27 taken in lieu	25, 26 December 27 taken in lieu

*In England, Wales and Northern Ireland, Christmas Day and Good Friday are common law holidays
In the Channel Islands, Liberation Day is a bank and public holiday
† Subject to royal proclamation
‡ Subject to proclamation by the Secretary of State for Northern Ireland

2006

JANUARY					
Sunday	1	8	15	22	29
Monday	2	9	16	23	30
Tuesday	3	10	17	24	31
Wednesday	4	11	18	25	
Thursday	5	12	19	26	
Friday	6	13	20	27	
Saturday	7	14	21	28	

FEBRUARY					
Sunday		5	12	19	26
Monday		6	13	20	27
Tuesday		7	14	21	28
Wednesday	1	8	15	22	
Thursday	2	9	16	23	
Friday	3	10	17	24	
Saturday	4	11	18	25	

MARCH					
Sunday		5	12	19	26
Monday		6	13	20	27
Tuesday		7	14	21	28
Wednesday	1	8	15	22	29
Thursday	2	9	16	23	30
Friday	3	10	17	24	31
Saturday	4	11	18	25	

APRIL						
Sunday		2	9	16	23	30
Monday		3	10	17	24	
Tuesday		4	11	18	25	
Wednesday		5	12	19	26	
Thursday		6	13	20	27	
Friday		7	14	21	28	
Saturday	1	8	15	22	29	

MAY					
Sunday		7	14	21	28
Monday	1	8	15	22	29
Tuesday	2	9	16	23	30
Wednesday	3	10	17	24	31
Thursday	4	11	18	25	
Friday	5	12	19	26	
Saturday	6	13	20	27	

JUNE					
Sunday		4	11	18	25
Monday		5	12	19	26
Tuesday		6	13	20	27
Wednesday		7	14	21	28
Thursday	1	8	15	22	29
Friday	2	9	16	23	30
Saturday	3	10	17	24	

JULY						
Sunday		2	9	16	23	30
Monday		3	10	17	24	31
Tuesday		4	11	18	25	
Wednesday		5	12	19	26	
Thursday		6	13	20	27	
Friday		7	14	21	28	
Saturday	1	8	15	22	29	

AUGUST					
Sunday		6	13	20	27
Monday		7	14	21	28
Tuesday	1	8	15	22	29
Wednesday	2	9	16	23	30
Thursday	3	10	17	24	31
Friday	4	11	18	25	
Saturday	5	12	19	26	

SEPTEMBER					
Sunday		3	10	17	24
Monday		4	11	18	25
Tuesday		5	12	19	26
Wednesday		6	13	20	27
Thursday		7	14	21	28
Friday	1	8	15	22	29
Saturday	2	9	16	23	30

OCTOBER					
Sunday	1	8	15	22	29
Monday	2	9	16	23	30
Tuesday	3	10	17	24	31
Wednesday	4	11	18	25	
Thursday	5	12	19	26	
Friday	6	13	20	27	
Saturday	7	14	21	28	

NOVEMBER					
Sunday		5	12	19	26
Monday		6	13	20	27
Tuesday		7	14	21	28
Wednesday	1	8	15	22	29
Thursday	2	9	16	23	30
Friday	3	10	17	24	
Saturday	4	11	18	25	

DECEMBER						
Sunday		3	10	17	24	31
Monday		4	11	18	25	
Tuesday		5	12	19	26	
Wednesday		6	13	20	27	
Thursday		7	14	21	28	
Friday	1	8	15	22	29	
Saturday	2	9	16	23	30	

PUBLIC HOLIDAYS	*England and Wales*	*Scotland*	*Northern Ireland*
New Year	†2 January	2, 3 January	†2 January
St Patrick's Day	–	–	‡17 March
*Good Friday	14 April	14 April	14 April
Easter Monday	17 April	–	17 April
Early May	†1 May	1 May	†1 May
Spring	29 May	†29 May	29 May
Battle of the Boyne	–	–	‡12 July
Summer	28 August	7 August	28 August
*Christmas	25, 26 December	25, †26 December	25, 26 December

*In England, Wales and Northern Ireland, Christmas Day and Good Friday are common law holidays
In the Channel Islands, Liberation Day is a bank and public holiday
† Subject to royal proclamation
‡ Subject to proclamation by the Secretary of State for Northern Ireland

FORTHCOMING EVENTS

* Provisional dates
† Venue not confirmed

JANUARY

6–16	Schroders London Boat Show, Excel, London Docklands
15–30	London International Mime Festival
19–23	London Art Fair, Business Design Centre, London

FEBRUARY

9	Chinese New Year Celebrations, London
11–13	Labour Party Spring Conference, Newcastle/Gateshead
26–6 March	Bath Literature Festival

MARCH

2–28	Ideal Home Exhibition, Earls Court, London
3	World Book Day
10–13	Crufts Dog Show, NEC, Birmingham
10–13	Liberal Democrat Party Spring Conference, Newcastle/ Gateshead
11–20	National Science Week
13–15	London Book Fair, London Olympia

APRIL

April–October	Pitlochry Festival Theatre season
21–24	Chelsea Art Fair, Chelsea Old Town Hall

MAY

19–28 August	Glyndebourne Festival Opera season
20–5 June	Bath International Music Festival
24–28	Chelsea Flower Show, Royal Hospital, Chelsea
27–5 June	The Hay Festival, Hay-on-Wye, Hereford
May–September	Chichester Festival Theatre season, Tayside

JUNE

June–August	Royal Academy of Arts Summer Exhibition
10–26	The Aldeburgh Festival of Music and the Arts
11	Trooping the Colour, Horseguards Parade, London

JULY

1–17	Cheltenham International Festival of Music
3–6	The Royal Show, National Agricultural Centre, Stoneleigh Park
5–10	Hampton Court Palace Flower Show, Surrey
8–17	York Early Music Festival
8–24	Buxton Festival, Derbyshire
Mid-July	The Welsh Proms, St David's Hall, Cardiff
15–10 September	BBC Promenade Concerts, Royal Albert Hall, London
20–24	RHS Flower Show, Tatton Park, Cheshire
30–6 August	Royal National Eisteddfod of Wales, Meifod, Powys

AUGUST

5–27	Edinburgh Military Tattoo, Edinburgh Castle
6–12	Three Choirs Festival, Worcester
14–4 September	Edinburgh International Festival
23–25	Wisley Flower Show, RHS Garden, Wisley
28–29	Notting Hill Carnival, Notting Hill, London
27–29	Town and Country Festival, National Agricultural Centre, Stoneleigh Park

SEPTEMBER

2–6 November	Blackpool Illuminations, Promenade
3	Braemar Royal Highland Gathering, Aberdeenshire
September	TUC Annual Congress
16–25	Southampton Boat Show, Mayflower Park, Southampton
18–22	Liberal Democrat Party Autumn Conference, Bournemouth
25–29	Labour Party Conference, Brighton

OCTOBER

3–6	Conservative Party Conference, Blackpool
6	National Poetry Day
October–January	Turner Prize Exhibition
*20 October–4 November	London Film Festival, NFT and other venues

NOVEMBER

6	London to Brighton Veteran Car Run
12	Lord Mayor's Procession and Show, City of London
18–27	Huddersfield Contemporary Music Festival
28–29	CBI Annual Conference

SPORTS EVENTS

FEBRUARY

13–20	Snooker: Masters, Wembley Conference Centre
5	Rugby Union: Six Nations Championship, France v. Scotland, Stade de France
5	Rugby Union: Six Nations Championship, Wales v. England, Millennium Stadium, Cardiff
6	Rugby Union: Six Nations Championship, Italy v. Ireland, Stadio Faliminio, Rome
12	Rugby Union: Six Nations Championship, Italy v. Wales, Stadio Faliminio, Rome
12	Rugby Union: Six Nations Championship, Scotland v. Ireland, Murrayfield

13	Rugby Union: Six Nations Championship, England v. France, Twickenham
26	Rugby Union: Six Nations Championship, Scotland v. Italy, Murrayfield
26	Rugby Union: Six Nations Championship, France v. Wales, Stade de France
27	Rugby Union: Six Nations Championship, Ireland v. England, Lansdowne Road
MARCH	
12	Rugby Union: Six Nations Championship, Ireland v. France, Lansdowne Road
12	Rugby Union: Six Nations Championship, England v. Italy, Twickenham
13	Rugby Union: Six Nations Championship, Scotland v. Wales, Murrayfield
19	Rugby Union: Six Nations Championship, Italy v. France, Stadio Faliminio, Rome
19	Rugby Union: Six Nations Championship, Wales v. Ireland, Millennium Stadium, Cardiff
19	Rugby Union: Six Nations Championship, England v. Scotland, Twickenham
27	Oxford and Cambridge Boat Race, Putney to Mortlake, London
APRIL	
16–2 May	Snooker: Embassy World Championship, Crucible Theatre, Sheffield
17	Athletics: Flora London Marathon
MAY	
5–8	Badminton Horse Trials, Badminton
8	Welsh FA Cup Final†
12–15	Royal Windsor Horse Show, Home Park, Windsor
21	The FA Cup Final, Millennium Stadium, Cardiff
28	Scottish FA Cup Final, Hampden Park, Glasgow
28–10 June	TT Motorcycle Races, Isle of Man
30–4 June	British Amateur Golf Championship, Royal Birkdale/Southport and Ainsdale Golf Clubs
JUNE	
20–3 July	Tennis: Wimbledon Championship, All England Lawn Tennis Club, Wimbledon
29–3 July	Rowing: Henley Royal Regatta, Henley-on-Thames
JULY	
*3	British Formula 1 Grand Prix, Silverstone, Northants
9–17	Sailing: The Admiral's Cup
14–17	Golf: The Open Championship, St Andrews Golf Club
14–23	Shooting: NRA Imperial Meeting, Bisley Camp, Surrey
28–31	Golf: The Women's British Open, Royal Birkdale Golf Club, Southport
30–6 August	Sailing: Cowes Week, Isle of Wight
AUGUST	
7	Sailing: The Rolex Fastnet Race
27	Rugby League: Challenge Cup Final, Millennium Stadium, Cardiff
SEPTEMBER	
1–4	Burghley Horse Trials, Burghley Park, Lincolnshire
9–11	Golf: The Solheim Cup, Indiana, USA
OCTOBER	
12–16	Horse of the Year Show, NEC, Birmingham

HORSE RACING

26 March	Lincoln Handicap, Doncaster
7–9 April	Grand National, Aintree, Liverpool
30 April	Two Thousand Guineas, Newmarket
1 May	One Thousand Guineas, Newmarket
3 June	The Oaks, Epsom
3 June	Coronation Cup, Epsom
4 June	The Derby, Epsom
14–18 June	Royal Ascot
22 July	King George VI and Queen Elizabeth Diamond Stakes
9 September	St Leger, Doncaster
29 September–1 October	Cambridgeshire Meeting, Newmarket
13–15 October	Champions Meeting, Newmarket

CRICKET

Npower Test Match Series

26–30 May	England v. Bangladesh, 1st, Lord's
3–7 June	England v. Bangladesh, 2nd, Durham
21–25 July	England v. Australia, 1st, Lord's
4–8 August	England v. Australia, 2nd, Edgbaston
11–15 August	England v. Australia, 3rd, Old Trafford, Manchester
25–29 August	England v. Australia, 4th, Trent Bridge, Nottingham
8–12 September	England v. Australia, 5th, The Oval

NatWest Series

16 June	England v. Bangladesh, The Oval
18 June	Australia v. Bangladesh, Cardiff
19 June	England v. Australia, Bristol
21 June	England v. Bangladesh, Trent Bridge, Nottingham
25 June	Australia v. Bangladesh, Old Trafford, Manchester
28 June	England v. Australia, Edgbaston
30 June	Australia v. Bangladesh, Canterbury
2 July	The Final, Lord's

CENTENARIES OF 2005

1305
23 August William Wallace, died

1405
14 February Timur, Mongol monarch and conqueror, died
18 October Pope Pius II, born

1505
27 October Ivan III, also known as Ivan the Great, died

1605
13 April Boris Godunov, tsar of Russia 1598–1605, died

1705
17 January John Ray, naturalist, died
13 July Titus Oates, Anglican priest, fabricated the Popish Plot in 1678, died
17 November Ninon de l'Enclos, French courtesan, died

1805
27 January Samuel Palmer, painter, born
2 April Hans Christian Andersen, novelist and writer of fairy tales, born
9 May Johann von Schiller, dramatist, died
28 May Luigi Boccherini, composer, died
21 October Lord Horatio Nelson, naval commander, died
23 October John Bartlett, lexicographer, born

1905
2 January Sir Michael Tippett, composer, born
21 January Christian Dior, dress designer and couturier, born
18 March Robert Donat, actor, born
24 March Jules Verne, writer, died
26 April Jean Vigo, film director, born
15 May Joseph Cotten, actor, born
16 May Henry Fonda, film actor, born
16 May H. E. Bates, novelist and playwright and short story writer born
21 June Jean-Paul Sartre, writer, born
25 July Elias Canetti, novelist and playwright; won Nobel Prize for Literature in 1981, born
5 September Arthur Koestler, political refugee and prisoner, born
18 September Agnes de Mille, dancer and choreographer, born
18 September Greta Garbo, film actress, born
19 September Thomas Barnardo, founder of the Barnardo's children's homes, died
15 October Sir Charles Snow, novelist, born
23 October Felix Bloch, physicist, Nobel prize winner 1952, born
21 December Anthony Powell, writer, born
24 December Howard Hughes, industrialist, pilot, film producer, born
31 December Jule Styne, composer, born

THE UNITED KINGDOM

THE UK IN FIGURES

The United Kingdom comprises Great Britain (England, Wales and Scotland) and Northern Ireland. The Isle of Man and the Channel Islands are Crown dependencies with their own legislative systems, and not a part of the United Kingdom.

POPULATION

The first official census of population in England, Wales and Scotland was taken in 1801 and a census has been taken every ten years since, except in 1941 when there was no census because of war. The last official census in the United Kingdom was taken on 29 April 2001 and the next is due in April 2011.

The first official census of population in Ireland was taken in 1841. However, all figures given below refer only to the area which is now Northern Ireland. Figures for Northern Ireland in 1921 and 1931 are estimates based on the censuses taken in 1926 and 1937 respectively.

Estimates of the population of England before 1801, calculated from the number of baptisms, burials and marriages, are:

1570	4,160,221	1670	5,773,646
1600	4,811,718	1700	6,045,008
1630	5,600,517	1750	6,517,035

For further details *see* www.statistics.gov.uk

CENSUS RESULTS 1801–2001

	United Kingdom			England and Wales			Scotland			Northern Ireland		
Thousands	*Total*	*Male*	*Female*	*Total*	*Male*	*Female*	*Total*	*Male*	*Female*	*Total*	*Male*	*Female*
1801	—	—	—	8,893	4,255	4,638	1,608	739	869	—	—	—
1811	13,368	6,368	7,000	10,165	4,874	5,291	1,806	826	980	—	—	—
1821	15,472	7,498	7,974	12,000	5,850	6,150	2,092	983	1,109	—	—	—
1831	17,835	8,647	9,188	13,897	6,771	7,126	2,364	1,114	1,250	—	—	—
1841	20,183	9,819	10,364	15,914	7,778	8,137	2,620	1,242	1,378	1,649	800	849
1851	22,259	10,855	11,404	17,928	8,781	9,146	2,889	1,376	1,513	1,443	698	745
1861	24,525	11,894	12,631	20,066	9,776	10,290	3,062	1,450	1,612	1,396	668	728
1871	27,431	13,309	14,122	22,712	11,059	11,653	3,360	1,603	1,757	1,359	647	712
1881	31,015	15,060	15,955	25,974	12,640	13,335	3,736	1,799	1,936	1,305	621	684
1891	34,264	16,593	17,671	29,003	14,060	14,942	4,026	1,943	2,083	1,236	590	646
1901	38,237	18,492	19,745	32,528	15,729	16,799	4,472	2,174	2,298	1,237	590	647
1911	42,082	20,357	21,725	36,070	17,446	18,625	4,761	2,309	2,452	1,251	603	648
1921	44,027	21,033	22,994	37,887	18,075	19,811	4,882	2,348	2,535	1,258	610	648
1931	46,038	22,060	23,978	39,952	19,133	20,819	4,843	2,326	2,517	1,243	601	642
1951	50,225	24,118	26,107	43,758	21,016	22,742	5,096	2,434	2,662	1,371	668	703
1961	52,709	25,481	27,228	46,105	22,304	23,801	5,179	2,483	2,697	1,425	694	731
1971	55,515	26,952	28,562	48,750	23,683	25,067	5,229	2,515	2,714	1,536	755	781
1981	55,848	27,104	28,742	49,155	23,873	25,281	5,131	2,466	2,664	*1,533	750	783
1991	56,467	27,344	29,123	49,890	24,182	25,707	4,999	2,392	2,607	1,578	769	809
2001	58,789	28,581	30,208	52,042	25,327	26,715	5,062	2,432	2,630	1,685	821	864

* Figure includes 44,500 non-enumerated persons

Source: ONS – Census Reports (Crown copyright)

RESIDENT POPULATION: 2002 ESTIMATES AND FUTURE PROJECTIONS (MID-YEAR)

	United Kingdom			England and Wales			Scotland			Northern Ireland		
Thousands	*Total*	*Male*	*Female*	*Total*	*Male*	*Female*	*Total*	*Male*	*Female*	*Total*	*Male*	*Female*
2002	59,229	28,911	30,318	52,478	25,651	26,827	5,055	2,432	2,623	1,697	829	868
2006	59,995	29,329	30,666	53,252	26,071	27,181	5,022	2,417	2,605	1,720	841	880
2011	61,022	29,853	31,169	54,287	26,600	27,687	4,984	2,398	2,586	1,751	855	896
2021	63,239	30,897	32,342	56,517	27,661	28,856	4,911	2,354	2,557	1,811	882	929
2026	64,178	31,297	32,880	57,492	28,088	29,404	4,854	2,319	2,535	1,831	890	941

Source: The Stationery Office – *Annual Abstract of Statistics 2004* (Crown copyright)

ISLANDS: CENSUS RESULTS 1901–2001

	Isle of Man			Jersey			*Guernsey		
	Total	*Male*	*Female*	*Total*	*Male*	*Female*	*Total*	*Male*	*Female*
1901	54,752	25,496	29,256	52,576	23,940	28,636	40,446	19,652	20,794
1911	52,016	23,937	28,079	51,898	24,014	27,884	41,858	20,661	21,197
1921	60,284	27,329	32,955	49,701	22,438	27,263	38,315	18,246	20,069
1931	49,308	22,443	26,865	50,462	23,424	27,038	40,643	19,659	20,984
1951	55,123	25,749	29,464	57,296	27,282	30,014	43,652	21,221	22,431
1961	48,151	22,060	26,091	57,200	27,200	30,000	45,068	21,671	23,397
1971	56,289	26,461	29,828	72,532	35,423	37,109	51,458	24,792	26,666
1981	64,679	30,901	33,778	77,000	37,000	40,000	53,313	25,701	27,612
1991	69,788	33,693	36,095	84,082	40,862	43,220	58,867	28,297	30,570
2001	76,315	37,372	38,943	87,186	42,485	44,701	59,807	29,138	30,669

* Population of Guernsey, Herm, Jethou and Lithou.

Figures for 1901–71 record all persons present on census night; census figures for 1981–2001 record all persons resident in the islands on census night. The 2001 population census also recorded the population of Alderney as 2,294 and an informal census of Sark gave its population as 591.

Source: Census 2001 (Crown copyright).

RESIDENT POPULATION

BY AGE AND SEX 2002

	Thousands	
Age Range	*Males*	*Females*
Under 1	338	322
1–4	1,406	1,341
5–9	1,885	1,795
10–14	2,002	1,903
15–19	1,926	1,826
20–29	3,685	3,703
30–44	6,681	6,795
45–59	5,597	5,704
60–64	1,413	1,475
65–74	2,325	2,640
75–84	1,337	2,004
85+	315	810

Source: The Stationery Office – *Annual Abstract of Statistics 2004* (Crown copyright)

BY ETHNIC GROUP AVERAGE SPRING 2002–WINTER 2002/3

Ethnic group	*Estimated population (thousands)*
White	
British*	51,010
Other*	1,946
Mixed	
White and Black Caribbean	234
White and Black African	72
White and Asian	129
Other Mixed	74
Asian	
Indian	1,016
Pakistani	718
Bangladeshi	273
Other Asian	302
Black	
Black Caribbean	584
Black African	541
Black Other	59
Chinese	199
Other	458
All†	59,330

*Data excludes Northern Ireland as detailed level ethnicity questions are not asked of the White group in Northern Ireland.

†Includes ethnic group not stated.

Source: The Stationery Office – *Annual Abstract of Statistics 2004* (Crown copyright).

IMMIGRATION

ACCEPTANCE FOR SETTLEMENT IN THE UK BY NATIONALITY

Region	*Number of persons*	
	2001	*2002*
Europe*	13,990	11,740
Americas: total	11,975	11,680
USA	4,385	4,355
Canada	1,320	1,300
Africa: total	31,925	39,165
Asia: total	44,155	46,585
Indian sub-continent	23,020	24,665
Middle East	4,830	5,345
Oceania: total	5,455	6,250
British Overseas Citizens	520	330
Stateless	390	215
All nationalities	108,410	115,965

* Excluding European Economic Area nationals

Source: The Stationery Office – *Annual Abstract of Statistics 2004* (Crown copyright)

BIRTHS

2002

	Live births	*Male*	*Female*	*Birth rate**
United Kingdom	669,000	343,000	327,000	11.3
England and Wales	596,000	306,000	290,000	11.4
Scotland	5,000	26,000	25,000	10.1
Northern Ireland	2,000	11,000	11,000	12.6

*Live births per 1,000 population

Source: The Stationery Office – *Annual Abstract of Statistics 2004* (Crown copyright)

LEGAL ABORTIONS

	1997	*2002*
England and Wales	170,145	175,569
Scotland	12,109	11,594

Source: The Stationery Office – *Annual Abstract of Statistics 2004* (Crown copyright)

DEATHS

2002

Males	*Deaths*	*Death Rate**
United Kingdom	287,837	10.0
England and Wales	253,144	
Scotland	27,743	
Northern Ireland	6,950	
Females		
United Kingdom	318,379	10.5
England and Wales	280,383	
Scotland	30,360	
Northern Ireland	7,636	

* Death rate per 1,000 population

Source: The Stationery Office – *Annual Abstract of Statistics 2004* (Crown copyright).

INFANT MORTALITY 2002

Deaths of infants under 1 year of age per 1,000 live births

	Number
United Kingdom	5.2
England and Wales	5.2
Scotland	5.3
Northern Ireland	4.7

Source: The Stationery Office – *Annual Abstract of Statistics 2004* (Crown copyright).

MARRIAGE AND DIVORCE

2002

	Marriages	*Divorces*
United Kingdom	286,129*	160,726
England and Wales	249,227*	147,735
Scotland	29,826	10,826
Northern Ireland	7,599	2,165

* 2001 Figures

Source: The Stationery Office – *Annual Abstract of Statistics 2004* (Crown copyright).

HOUSEHOLDS

BY TYPE OF HOUSEHOLD AND FAMILY IN GREAT BRITAIN 2003

Percentages

One Person	
Under state pension age	15
Over state pension age	14
Two or more unrelated adults	8
One family households	
Couple	
No children	28
1–2 dependent children	18
3 or more dependent children	4
Non-dependent children only	6
Lone parent	
Dependent children	5
Non-dependent children only	3
Multi-family households	1

Source: The Stationery Office – *Social Trends 2004* (Crown copyright).

HOUSEHOLDS BY SIZE 2003

Percentages

One person	29
Two people	35
Three people	15
Four people	14
Five people	5
Six or more people	2
All households (=100%) *(millions)*	24.5
Average household size (number of people)	2.4

Source: The Stationery Office – *Social Trends 2004* (Crown copyright).

PERCENTAGE OF DEPENDENT CHILDREN LIVING IN DIFFERENT FAMILY TYPES (GREAT BRITAIN)

	1992	*2001*	*2003*
Couple families			
1 child	18	17	17
2 children	39	38	37
3 or more children	27	25	24
Lone mother families			
1 child	4	6	6
2 children	5	7	8
3 or more children	4	5	6
Lone father families			
1 child	1	1	2
2 or more children	1	1	1

Source: The Stationery Office – *Social Trends 2004* (Crown copyright).

ADULTS LIVING WITH THEIR PARENTS BY AGE AND GENDER (ENGLAND)

Percentages

	1991	*2002*	*2003*
Males			
20–24	50	56	56
25–29	19	20	21
30–34	9	8	8
Females			
20–24	32	37	37
25–29	9	10	10
30–34	5	2	3

Source: The Stationery Office – *Social Trends 2004* (Crown copyright).

UK HOUSEHOLDS WITH INTERNET ACCESS BY HOUSEHOLD TYPE

Percentages

	1998/9	*2002/3*
One person		
Over state pension age	1	7
Under state pension age	8	36
Couple without children		
Over state pension age	2	21
Under state pension age	14	55
All other adults without children	16	57
Lone parent	5	35
Couple with children	16	69
All other adults with children	20	52

Source: The Stationery Office – *Social Trends 2004* (Crown copyright).

TENURE BY TYPE OF ACCOMODATION 2001 (ENGLAND AND WALES)
Percentages

	House or Bungalow			*Flat or Maisonette*	
	Detached	Semi-detached	Terraced	Purpose-built	Other
Owner-occupied					
Owned outright	35	35	22	6	2
Owned with mortgage	27	36	29	5	3
Shared ownership	6	34	33	21	5
Rented from social sector					
Council	4	31	26	37	3
Other	3	23	26	40	8
Rented privately					
Private landlord or letting agency	9	17	28	20	25
Employer of a household member	22	31	20	11	16
Relative or friend of a household member	14	26	34	13	13
Other	18	23	19	19	20
Living rent free	19	28	20	23	10
All tenures	23	32	26	13	5

Source: The Stationery Office – *Social Trends 2004* (Crown copyright).

HEALTH

DEATHS ANALYSED BY CAUSE 2002

	England and Wales	*Scotland*	*N. Ireland*
TOTAL DEATHS	533,527	58,103	14,586
Deaths from natural causes	515,262	55,689	13,949
Certain infectious and parasitic diseases	4,330	651	134
Intestinal infectious diseases	847	96	11
Respiratory & other tuberculosis	443	52	10
Meningococcal infection	115	13	7
Viral hepatitis	170	13	0
AIDS (HIV – disease)	198	33	3
Neoplasms	140,174	15,391	3,766
Malignant neoplasms	136,777	15,051	3,652
Malignant neoplasm of oesophagus	6,330	763	163
Malignant neoplasm of stomach	5,588	621	164
Malignant neoplasm of colon	9,504	975	270
Malignant neoplasm of rectum and anus	3,907	384	90
Malignant neoplasm of pancreas	6,142	562	194
Malignant neoplasm of trachea, bronchus and lung	28,806	4,039	802
Malignant neoplasm of skin	1,480	132	38
Malignant neoplasm of breast	11,557	1,110	278
Malignant neoplasm of cervix uteri	1,001	100	25
Malignant neoplasm of prostate	8,973	775	193
Leukaemia	3,911	330	93
Diseases of blood and blood-forming organs and certain disorders involving the immune mechanism	1,086	122	24
Endocrine, nutritional and metabolic diseases	7,897	902	238
Diabetes mellitus	6,192	676	187
Mental and behavioural disorders	14,444	2,446	411
Vascular and unspecified dementia	12,753	1,763	329
Alcohol abuse	435	339	74
Drug dependence and non-dependent abuse of drugs	882	294	6
Diseases of the nervous system and sense organs	14,796	1,317	531
Meningitis (including meningococcal)	173	6	5
Alzheimer's disease	4,771	388	246
Diseases of the circulatory system	209,433	22,688	5,729
Ischaemic heart diseases	102,833	11,692	2,948
Cerebrovascular diseases	59,068	6,722	1,573

Diseases of the respiratory system	69,900	6,806	1,883
Influenza	38	6	1
Pneumonia	32,631	2,466	951
Bronchitis, emphysema and other chronic obstructive pulmonary diseases	24,159	2,840	553
Asthma	1,264	131	36
Diseases of the digestive system	24,124	3,153	581
Gastric and duodenal ulcer	3,746	308	62
Chronic liver disease	5,376	1,128	166
Diseases of the skin and subcutaneous tissue	1,470	118	21
Diseases of the musculo-skeletal system and connective tissue	4,647	384	90
Rheumatoid arthritis and juvenile arthritis	966	133	21
Osteoporosis	1,605	59	19
Diseases of the genito-urinary system	8,452	1,013	333
Diseases of the kidney and ureter	4,072	627	246
Complications of pregnancy, childbirth and the puerperium	34	5	1
Certain conditions originating in the perinatal period (excluding neonatals)	208	155	62
Congenital malformations, deformations and chromasomal abnormalities (excluding neonatals)	1,233	168	53
Congenital malformations of the nervous system	127	31	7
Congenital malformations of the circulatory system	541	60	17
Symptons, signs and abnormal findings not classified elsewhere	13,034	370	92
Senility without mention of psychosis (old age)	11,645	191	63
Sudden infant death syndrome	137	32	0
Deaths from external causes	16,139	2,414	637
All accidents	10,382	1,315	424
Land transport accidents	2,929	321	144
Accidental falls	2,509	668	60
Accidental poisonings	814	37	30
Suicide and intentional self-harm	3,269	636	162
Homicide and assault	373	118	27
Event of undetermined intent	1,754	263	21

Source: The Stationery Office – *Annual Abstract of Statistics 2004* (Crown copyright).

NOTIFICATIONS OF INFECTIONS DISEASES (UK)

	2001	*2002*
Measles	2,661	3,675
Mumps	3,433	2,333
Rubella	1,782	2,002
Whooping cough	1,059	1,051
Scarlet fever	2,320	2,749
Dysentery	1,495	1,167
Food poisoning	95,752	81,562
Typhoid and paratyphoid fevers	254	183
Hepatitis	4,419	5,035
Tuberculosis	7,204	7,239
Malaria	1,118	866

Source: The Stationery Office – *Annual Abstract of Statistics 2004* (Crown copyright).

HIGH BLOOD PRESSURE BY AGE AND GENDER 2001 (ENGLAND)

Percentages

	16–44	*45–54*	*55–64*	*65–74*	*75+*	*All 16+*
Males†						
Treated	1	6	15	20	20	8
Untreated	19	32	37	41	42	29
Females						
Treated	1	6	13	23	28	9
Untreated	8	24	33	41	44	22

Source: The Stationery Office – *Social Trends 2004* (Crown copyright)

ADULTS EXCEEDING BENCHMARKS* OF ALCOHOL BY AGE AND GENDER 2001–2 (GREAT BRITAIN)

Percentages

	Males	*Females*
16–24	49	39
25–44	46	30
45–64	36	19
65+	18	5
All 16+	39	22

* On heaviest drinking day in the last week. Current Department of Health advice is that consumption of between three and four units a day for men and between 2 and 3 units a day for women should not lead to significant health risks. A unit of alcohol is 8 grams by weight or 10ml by volume of pure alcohol, i.e. the amount contained in half a pint of ordinary strength beer or lager, a single pub measure of spirits or a small glass of ordinary strength wine.

Source: The Stationery Office – *Social Trends 2004* (Crown copyright)

PREVALENCE OF DRUG MISUSE BY YOUNG ADULTS* BY DRUG CATEGORY AND GENDER 2001–2 (ENGLAND AND WALES)
Percentages

	Males	*Females*
Cannabis	33	21
Amphetamines	7	3
Ecstasy	9	4
Magic mushrooms or LSD	3	1
Cocaine	7	2
All Class 'A' drugs†	12	5
Any drug	35	24

* aged 16–24 years
† includes heroin, cocaine (powder and 'crack'), ecstasy, magic mushrooms, LSD and unprescribed use of methadone.
Source: The Stationery Office – *Social Trends 2004*

BODY MASS* BY GENDER 2001 (ENGLAND)
Percentages

	Males	*Females*
Underweight	4	6
Desirable	28	38
Overweight	47	33
Obese	21	23

* The Body Mass Index (BMI) standardised weight for height and is calculated as weight (kg)/height $(m)^2$. Underweight is defined as a BMI of 20 or less, desirable 20–25, overweight 25–30 and obese over 30.
Source: The Stationery Office – *Social Trends 2003*

AVERAGE DAILY PORTIONS OF FRUIT AND VEGETABLES CONSUMED* BY AGE AND GENDER 2000–1 (GREAT BRITAIN)
Percentages

	Average number of portions per day				
	None	*0–1*	*1–3*	*3–5*	*5+*
Males					
19–24	6	32	57	5	0
25–34	1	26	49	17	7
35–49	0	14	45	27	14
50–64	1	6	38	31	24
All males 19–64	1	17	46	23	13
Females					
19–24	2	34	47	13	4
25–34	1	18	52	20	9
35–49	1	15	45	22	17
50–64	0	7	37	34	22
All females 19–64	1	15	45	24	15

* The Department of Health recommends that a healthy diet should included a least five portions of a variety of fruit and vegetables (excluding potatoes) a day. All fruit juice, baked beans and other pulses are counted as one portion.
Source: The Stationery Office – *Social Trends 2004*

THE NATIONAL FLAG

The national flag of the United Kingdom is the Union Flag, generally known as the Union Jack.

The Union Flag is a combination of the cross of St George, patron saint of England, the cross of St Andrew, patron saint of Scotland, and a cross similar to that of St Patrick, patron saint of Ireland.

Cross of St George: cross Gules in a field Argent (red cross on a white ground)

Cross of St Andrew: saltire Argent in a field Azure (white diagonal cross on a blue ground)

Cross of St Patrick: saltire Gules in a field Argent (red diagonal cross on a white ground)

The Union Flag was first introduced in 1606 after the union of the kingdoms of England and Scotland under one sovereign. The cross of St Patrick was added in 1801 after the union of Great Britain and Ireland.

FLYING THE UNION FLAG

The correct orientation of the Union Flag when flying is with the broader diagonal band of white uppermost in the hoist (i.e. near the pole) and the narrower diagonal band of white uppermost in the fly (i.e. furthest from the pole).

It is the practice to fly the Union Flag daily on some customs houses. In all other cases, flags are flown on government buildings by command of The Queen. It is now customary for the Union Flag to be flown at Buckingham Palace, Windsor Castle and Sandringham when The Queen is not in residence.

The flying of the Union Flag on public buildings is decided by the Department for Culture, Media and Sport at The Queen's command. On the days appointed, the Union Flag is flown on government buildings in the United Kingdom from 8 a.m. to sunset.

FLAGS AT HALF-MAST

Flags are flown at half-mast (i.e. two-thirds up between the top and bottom of the flagstaff) on the following occasions:

(a) From the announcement of the death up to the funeral of the Sovereign, except on Proclamation Day, when flags are hoisted right up from 11 a.m. to sunset

(b) The funerals of members of the royal family, subject to special commands from The Queen in each case

(c) The funerals of foreign rulers, subject to special commands from The Queen in each case

(d) The funerals of prime ministers and ex-prime ministers of the UK, subject to special commands from The Queen in each case

(e) Other occasions by special command of The Queen

On occasions when days for flying flags coincide with days for flying flags at half-mast, the following rules are observed. Flags are flown:

(a) although a member of the royal family, or a near relative of the royal family, may be lying dead, unless special commands are received from The Queen to the contrary

(b) although it may be the day of the funeral of a foreign ruler

If the body of a very distinguished subject is lying at a government office, the flag may fly at half-mast on that office until the body has left (provided it is a day on which the flag would fly) and then the flag is to be hoisted right up. On all other government buildings the flag will fly as usual.

THE ROYAL STANDARD

The Royal Standard is hoisted only when The Queen is actually present in the building, and never when Her Majesty is passing in procession.

DAYS FOR FLYING FLAGS

Birthday of The Countess of Wessex	20 January
The Queen's Accession	6 February
Birthday of The Duke of York	19 February
*St David's Day (in Wales only)	1 March
Birthday of The Earl of Wessex	10 March
**Commonwealth Day (2005)	14 March
Birthday of The Queen	21 April
*St George's Day (in England only)	23 April
†Europe Day	9 May
Coronation Day	2 June
Birthday of The Duke of Edinburgh	10 June
The Queen's Official Birthday (2005)	11 June
Birthday of The Princess Royal	15 August
Remembrance Sunday (2005)	13 November
Birthday of The Prince of Wales	14 November
The Queen's Wedding Day	20 November
*St Andrew's Day (in Scotland only)	30 November
‡The opening of Parliament by The Queen	
‡The prorogation of Parliament by The Queen	

* Where a building has two or more flagstaffs, the appropriate national flag may be flown in addition to the Union Flag, but not in a superior position

** Commonwealth Day is always the second Monday in March

† The Union Flag should fly alongside the European flag. On government buildings that have only one flagpole, the Union Flag should take precedence

‡ Flags are flown whether or not The Queen performs the ceremony in person. Flags are flown only in the Greater London area

ROYAL FAMILY

THE SOVEREIGN

ELIZABETH II, by the Grace of God, of the United Kingdom of Great Britain and Northern Ireland and of her other Realms and Territories Queen, Head of the Commonwealth, Defender of the Faith
Her Majesty Elizabeth Alexandra Mary of Windsor, elder daughter of King George VI and of HM Queen Elizabeth the Queen Mother
Born 21 April 1926, at 17 Bruton Street, London W1
Ascended the throne 6 February 1952
Crowned 2 June 1953, at Westminster Abbey
Married 20 November 1947, in Westminster Abbey, HRH The Prince Philip, Duke of Edinburgh
Official residences: Buckingham Palace, London SW1A 1AA; Windsor Castle, Berks; Palace of Holyroodhouse, Edinburgh
Private residences: Sandringham, Norfolk; Balmoral Castle, Aberdeenshire

HUSBAND OF THE QUEEN

HRH THE PRINCE PHILIP, DUKE OF EDINBURGH, KG, KT, OM, GBE, AC, QSO, PC, Ranger of Windsor Park
Born 10 June 1921, son of Prince and Princess Andrew of Greece and Denmark, naturalised a British subject 1947, created Duke of Edinburgh, Earl of Merioneth and Baron Greenwich 1947

CHILDREN OF THE QUEEN

HRH THE PRINCE OF WALES (Prince Charles Philip Arthur George), KG, KT, GCB, OM and Great Master of the Order of the Bath, AK, QSO, PC, ADC(P)
Born 14 November 1948, created Prince of Wales and Earl of Chester 1958, succeeded as Duke of Cornwall, Duke of Rothesay, Earl of Carrick and Baron Renfrew, Lord of the Isles and Great Steward of Scotland 1952
Married 29 July 1981 Lady Diana Frances Spencer (Diana, Princess of Wales (1961–97), youngest daughter of the 8th Earl Spencer and the Hon. Mrs Shand Kydd), marriage dissolved 1996
Issue:
(1) HRH Prince William of Wales (Prince William Arthur Philip Louis), *born* 21 June 1982
(2) HRH Prince Henry of Wales (Prince Henry Charles Albert David), *born* 15 September 1984
Residences of the Prince of Wales: Clarence House, London SW1A 1BA; Highgrove, Doughton, Tetbury, Glos GL8 8TN; Birkhall, Ballater, Aberdeenshire

HRH THE PRINCESS ROYAL (Princess Anne Elizabeth Alice Louise), KG, GCVO
Born 15 August 1950, declared The Princess Royal 1987
Married (1) 14 November 1973 Captain Mark Anthony Peter Phillips, CVO (*born* 22 September 1948), marriage dissolved 1992; (2) 12 December 1992 Captain Timothy James Hamilton Laurence, MVO, RN (*born* 1 March 1955)
Issue:
(1) Peter Mark Andrew Phillips, *born* 15 November 1977
(2) Zara Anne Elizabeth Phillips, *born* 15 May 1981
Residence: Gatcombe Park, Minchinhampton, Glos GL6 9AT

HRH THE DUKE OF YORK (Prince Andrew Albert Christian Edward), KCVO, ADC(P)
Born 19 February 1960, created Duke of York, Earl of Inverness and Baron Killyleagh 1986
Married 23 July 1986 Sarah Margaret Ferguson, now Sarah, Duchess of York (*born* 15 October 1959, younger daughter of Major Ronald Ferguson and Mrs Hector Barrantes), marriage dissolved 1996
Issue:
(1) HRH Princess Beatrice of York (Princess Beatrice Elizabeth Mary), *born* 8 August 1988
(2) HRH Princess Eugenie of York (Princess Eugenie Victoria Helena), *born* 23 March 1990
Residences: Buckingham Palace, London SW1A 1AA; Sunninghill Park, Ascot, Berks SL5 7TH

HRH THE EARL OF WESSEX (Prince Edward Antony Richard Louis), KCVO
Born 10 March 1964, created Earl of Wessex, Viscount Severn 1999
Married 19 June 1999 Sophie Helen Rhys-Jones, now HRH The Countess of Wessex (*born* 20 January 1965, daughter of Mr and Mrs Christopher Rhys-Jones)
Issue:
(1) Lady Louise Windsor (Louise Alice Elizabeth), *born* 8 November 2003
Residence: Bagshot Park, Bagshot, Surrey GU19 5HS

NEPHEW OF THE QUEEN

DAVID ALBERT CHARLES ARMSTRONG-JONES, VISCOUNT LINLEY, *born* 3 November 1961, *married* 8 October 1993 the Hon. Serena Stanhope, and has issue, Hon. Charles Patrick Inigo Armstrong-Jones, *born* 1 July 1999; Hon. Margarita Elizabeth Alleyne Armstrong-Jones, *born* 14 May 2002

NIECE OF THE QUEEN

LADY SARAH CHATTO (Sarah Frances Elizabeth), *born* 1 May 1964, *married* 14 July 1994 Daniel Chatto, and has issue, Samuel David Benedict Chatto, *born* 28 July 1996; Arthur Robert Nathaniel Chatto, *born* 5 February 1999
Residence: Kensington Palace, London W8 4PU

AUNT OF THE QUEEN

HRH PRINCESS ALICE, DUCHESS OF GLOUCESTER (Alice Christabel), GCB, CI, GCVO, GBE, Grand Cordon of Al Kamal
Born 25 December 1901, third daughter of the 7th Duke of Buccleuch and Queensberry
Married 6 November 1935 (as Lady Alice Montagu-Douglas-Scott) Prince Henry, Duke of Gloucester, third son of King George V
Residence: Kensington Palace, London W8 4PU

COUSINS OF THE QUEEN

HRH THE DUKE OF GLOUCESTER (Prince Richard Alexander Walter George), KG, GCVO, Grand Prior of the Order of St John of Jerusalem
Born 26 August 1944
Married 8 July 1972 Birgitte Eva van Deurs, now HRH The Duchess of Gloucester, GCVO (*born* 20 June 1946, daughter of Asger Henriksen and Vivian van Deurs)
Issue:
(1) Earl of Ulster (Alexander Patrick Gregers Richard), *born* 24 October 1974 *married* 22 June 2002 Dr Claire Booth
(2) Lady Davina Lewis (Davina Elizabeth Alice Benedikte), *born* 19 November 1977 *married* 31 July 2004 Gary Lewis
(3) Lady Rose Windsor (Rose Victoria Birgitte Louise), *born* 1 March 1980
Residence: Kensington Palace, London W8 4PU

HRH THE DUKE OF KENT (Prince Edward George Nicholas Paul Patrick), KG, GCMG, GCVO, ADC(P)
Born 9 October 1935
Married 8 June 1961 Katharine Lucy Mary Worsley, now HRH The Duchess of Kent, GCVO (*born* 22 February 1933, daughter of Sir William Worsley, Bt.)
Issue:
(1) Earl of St Andrews (George Philip Nicholas), *born* 26 June 1962, *married* 9 January 1988 Sylvana Tomaselli, and has issue, Baron Downpatrick, (Edward Edmund Maximilian George) *born* 2 December 1988; Lady Marina-Charlotte Windsor (Marina-Charlotte Alexandra Katharine Helen), *born* 30 September 1992; Lady Amelia Windsor (Amelia Sophia Theodora Mary Margaret) *born* 24 August 1995
(2) Lady Helen Taylor (Helen Marina Lucy), *born* 28 April 1964, *married* 18 July 1992 Timothy Taylor, and has issue, Columbus George Donald Taylor, *born* 6 August 1994; Cassius Edward Taylor, *born* 26 December 1996; daughter Eloise Olivia Katharine Taylor, *born* 3 March 2003
(3) Lord Nicholas Windsor (Nicholas Charles Edward Jonathan), *born* 25 July 1970
Residence: Wren House, Palace Green, London W8 4PY

HRH PRINCESS ALEXANDRA, THE HON. LADY OGILVY (Princess Alexandra Helen Elizabeth Olga Christabel), KG, GCVO
Born 25 December 1936
Married 24 April 1963 The Rt. Hon. Sir Angus Ogilvy, KCVO (*born* 14 September 1928, second son of 12th Earl of Airlie)
Issue:
(1) James Robert Bruce Ogilvy, *born* 29 February 1964, *married* 30 July 1988 Julia Rawlinson, and has issue, Flora Alexandra Ogilvy, *born* 15 December 1994; Alexander Charles Ogilvy, *born* 12 November 1996
(2) Marina Victoria Alexandra, Mrs Mowatt, *born* 31 July 1966, *married* 2 February 1990 Paul Mowatt (marriage dissolved 1997), and has issue, Zenouska May Mowatt, *born* 26 May 1990; Christian Alexander Mowatt, *born* 4 June 1993
Residence: Thatched House Lodge, Richmond Park, Surrey TW10 5HP

HRH PRINCE MICHAEL OF KENT (Prince Michael George Charles Franklin), GCVO
Born 4 July 1942
Married 30 June 1978 Baroness Marie-Christine Agnes Hedwig Ida von Reibnitz, now HRH Princess Michael of Kent (*born* 15 January 1945, daughter of Baron Gunther von Reibnitz)
Issue:
(1) Lord Frederick Windsor (Frederick Michael George David Louis), *born* 6 April 1979
(2) Lady Gabriella Windsor (Gabriella Marina Alexandra Ophelia), *born* 23 April 1981
Residences: Kensington Palace, London W8 4PU; Nether Lypiatt Manor, Stroud, Glos GL6 7LS

ORDER OF SUCCESSION

1	HRH The Prince of Wales
2	HRH Prince William of Wales
3	HRH Prince Henry of Wales
4	HRH The Duke of York
5	HRH Princess Beatrice of York
6	HRH Princess Eugenie of York
7	HRH The Earl of Wessex
8	Lady Louise Windsor
9	HRH The Princess Royal
10	Peter Phillips
11	Zara Phillips
12	Viscount Linley
13	Hon. Charles Armstrong-Jones
14	Hon. Margarita Armstrong-Jones
15	Lady Sarah Chatto
16	Samuel Chatto
17	Arthur Chatto
18	HRH The Duke of Gloucester
19	Earl of Ulster
20	Lady Davina Lewis
21	Lady Rose Windsor
22	HRH The Duke of Kent
23	Lady Marina-Charlotte Windsor
24	Lady Amelia Windsor
25	Lady Helen Taylor
26	Columbus Taylor
27	Cassius Taylor
28	Eloise Taylor
29	Lord Frederick Windsor
30	Lady Gabriella Windsor
31	HRH Princess Alexandra, the Hon. Lady Ogilvy
32	James Ogilvy
33	Alexander Ogilvy
34	Flora Ogilvy
35	Marina, Mrs Paul Mowatt
36	Christian Mowatt
37	Zenouska Mowatt

HRH Prince Michael of Kent, and The Earl of St Andrews both lost the right of succession to the throne through marriage to a Roman Catholic. Lord Nicholas Windsor renounced his rights to the throne on converting to Roman Catholicism in 2001 and Baron Downpatrick in 2003. Any children remain in succession provided that they are in communion with the Church of England.

PRIVATE SECRETARIES TO THE ROYAL FAMILY

THE QUEEN

Office: Buckingham Palace, London SW1A 1AA
T 020-7930 4832
W www.royal.gov.uk
Private Secretary to The Queen, The Rt. Hon. Sir Robin Janvrin, KCB, KCVO

PRINCE PHILIP, THE DUKE OF EDINBURGH

Office: Buckingham Palace, London SW1A 1AA
T 020-7930 4832
Private Secretary, Brig. Sir Miles Hunt-Davis, KCVO, CBE

THE PRINCE OF WALES

Office: Clarence House, London SW1A 1BA
T 020-7930 4832
Private Secretary, Sir Michael Peat, KCVO

THE DUKE OF YORK

Office: Buckingham Palace, London SW1A 1AA
T 020-7930 4832
Private Secretary, Alistair Watson

THE EARL AND COUNTESS OF WESSEX

Office: Bagshot Park, Surrey GU19 5PJ
T 01276-707040
Private Secretary, Brig. J. Smedley

THE PRINCESS ROYAL

Office: Buckingham Palace, London SW1A 1AA
T 020-7930 4832
Private Secretary, Capt. N. P. Wright, LVO, RN

PRINCESS ALICE, DUCHESS OF GLOUCESTER AND THE DUKE OF GLOUCESTER

Office: Kensington Palace, London W8 4PU
T 020-7368 1000
Private Secretary, Sqn Ldr Lyn Johnson, MVO

THE DUKE OF KENT

Office: St James's Palace, London, SW1A 1BQ
T 020-7930 4872
Private Secretary, N. Adamson, LVO, OBE

THE DUCHESS OF KENT

Office: Wren House, Palace Green, London, W8 4PY
T 020-7937 2730
Personal Secretary, Miss V. Utley

PRINCE AND PRINCESS MICHAEL OF KENT

Office: Kensington Palace, London W8 4PU
T 020-7938 3519
Private Secretary, N. Chance

PRINCESS ALEXANDRA, THE HON. LADY OGILVY

Office: Buckingham Palace, London SW1A 1AA
T 020-7024 4270
Private Secretary, Col. Richard Macfarlane

ROYAL HOUSEHOLD

PRIVATE SECRETARY'S OFFICE

The Private Secretary, assisted by the two Assistant Private Secretaries, is responsible for:

- Informing and advising The Queen on constitutional, governmental and political matters in the UK, her other Realms and the wider Commonwealth, including communications with the Prime Minister and Government Departments
- Organising The Queen's domestic and overseas official programme, including the Presentation of Credentials by incoming foreign ambassadors from overseas countries
- The Queen's speeches and messages, The Queen's patronage, The Queen's photographs and official presents, portraits of The Queen and dedications and congratulatory messages
- Communications in connection with the role of the Royal Family and other members of the Royal Family and their households
- Dealing with correspondence to The Queen from members of the public
- Organising and co-ordinating Royal travel through the Royal Travel Office
- Co-ordinating and initiating research to support engagements by members of the Royal Family through the Co-ordination and Research Unit

The Private Secretary is also responsible for communications and media affairs. The Press Secretary is in charge of Buckingham Palace Press Office and reports to the Private Secretary. Assisted by the Deputy Press Secretary and three Assistant Press Secretaries, the Press Secretary is responsible for:

- Developing communications strategies to enhance the public understanding of the role of the Monarchy, including an education strategy, encompassing website development and other multi-media initiatives
- Briefing the British and international media on the role and duties of The Queen and issues relating to the royal family
- Responding to media enquiries
- Arranging media facilities in the United Kingdom and overseas to support royal functions and engagements
- The management of the Royal website

The Private Secretary is Keeper of the Royal Archives and is responsible for the care of the records of the Sovereign and the Royal Household from previous reigns. These papers are preserved in the Royal Archives at Windsor, where they are managed by the Registrar, reporting to the Assistant Keeper, and made available for historical research. As Keeper, it is the Private Secretary's responsibility to ensure the proper management of the records of the present reign with a view to their transfer to the archives as and when appropriate. The Private Secretary is an ex officio trustee of the Royal Collection Trust.

PRIVY PURSE AND TREASURER'S OFFICE

The Keeper of the Privy Purse and Treasurer to The Queen is responsible for:

- The Queen's Civil List, which is the money paid from the Government's Consolidated Fund to meet official expenditure relating to The Queen's duties as Head of State and Head of the Commonwealth
- Through the Director of Personnel, the identification, planning and management of personnel policy across the Household, the administration of all pension schemes provided for the Household and Private Estates employees, and the allocation of employee and pensioner housing
- Information technology systems for the Household
- Internal audit services
- Health and safety
- All insurance matters
- The Privy Purse, which is mainly financed by the net income of the Duchy of Lancaster, and which meets both official expenditure incurred by The Queen as Sovereign and private expenditure
- Liaison with other Members of the Royal Family and their Households on financial matters
- The Queen's private estates at Sandringham and Balmoral, The Queen's Racing Establishment and the Royal Studs and liaison with the Ascot Authority
- The Home Park at Windsor and liaison with the Crown Estate Commissioners concerning the Home Park and the Great Park at Windsor
- The Royal Philatelic Collection, which is managed by the Keeper of the Royal Philatelic Collection
- Administrative aspects of the Military Knights of Windsor and the Royal Almonry
- Administration of the Royal Victorian Order, of which the Keeper of the Privy Purse is Secretary, Long and Faithful Service Medals, and the Queen's Cups, Medals and Prizes, and policy on Commemorative Medals

The Keeper of the Privy purse is one of three Royal Trustees (in respect of his responsibilities for the Civil List) and is Receiver General of the Duchy of Lancaster and a member of the Duchy's Council. The Keeper of the Privy Purse is also responsible for property services for the Occupied Royal Palaces in England, which comprise Buckingham Palace, St James's Palace and Clarence House, Marlborough House Mews, the residential, office and general areas of Kensington Palace, Windsor Castle and related areas and buildings, Frogmore House, and Hampton Court Mews and Paddocks. The costs of property services for the Occupied Royal Palaces are met from a Grant-in-aid from the Department for Culture, Media and Sport. The Director of Property Services, assisted by the Deputy Treasurer has day-to-day responsibility for the Royal Household's Property Section, which is responsible for:

- Fire safety issues
- Repairs and refurbishment of buildings and new buildings work
- Utilities and telecommunications
- Putting up stages, tents and other work in connection with ceremonial occasions and official functions

The Property Section is also responsible, in effect on a sub-contract basis from the Department for Culture, Media and Sport, for the maintenance of Marlborough House. The Keeper of the Privy Purse also oversees Royal Communications and Information expenditure, which is met from the Property Services Grant-in-aid. The Keeper of the Privy Purse is responsible for the financial aspects of Royal Travel, which are overseen on a day-to-day basis by the Deputy Treasurer. The costs of official Royal Travel by aeroplane and train are met from a Grant-in-aid provided by the Department for Transport. The Keeper of the Privy Purse is an ex officio trustee of the Royal Collection Trust and is also chairman of its trading subsidiary Royal Collection Enterprises Limited. He is also an ex officio trustee of the Historic Royal Palaces Trust. The Queen's Civil List and the Grants-in-aid for property services and Royal Travel are provided by the Government in return for the surrender by the Sovereign of the net surplus from the Crown Estate and other hereditary revenues.
Keeper of the Privy Purse, Alan Reid

MASTER OF THE HOUSEHOLD'S DEPARTMENT

The Master of the Household is responsible for the staff and domestic arrangements at Buckingham Palace, Windsor Castle and the Palace of Holyroodhouse and at Balmoral Castle and Sandringham House when The Queen is in residence. These arrangements include:

- The provision of meals for The Queen and other members of the Royal Family, their guests and Royal Household employees
- Service by liveried staff at meals, receptions and other events
- Travel arrangements for employees and the movement of baggage between the Royal residences
- Cleaning and laundry
- Furnishings and the internal decorative appearance of the Occupied Royal Palaces in collaboration with the Director of the Royal Collection
- Liaison with the Royalty and Diplomatic Protection Department of the Metropolitan Police concerning security procedures at the Occupied Royal Palaces

The Master of the Household is responsible for The Queen's official entertaining, both at home and overseas, including preparation of guest lists, invitations and seating plans, and overseeing aspects of The Queen's private entertaining.
Master of the Household, Vice Adm. Tom Blackburn, KCVO, CB, LVO

LORD CHAMBERLAIN'S OFFICE

The Comptroller of the Lord Chamberlain's Office is responsible for:

- The organisation of all ceremonial engagements
- Garden Parties at Buckingham Palace and Palace at Holyroodhouse (except for catering and tents)
- The Crown Jewels, which are part of the Royal Collection, when they are in use on state occasions
- Co-ordination of the arrangements for The Queen to be represented at funerals and memorial services and at the arrival and departure of visiting Heads of State
- Advising on matters of precedence, style and titles, dress, flying of flags, gun salutes, mourning and other ceremonial questions

- Supervising the applications from tradesmen for Royal Warrants of Appointment
- Advising on the commercial use of royal emblems and contemporary royal photographs
- The Ecclesiastical Household, the Medical Household, the Body Guards and certain ceremonial appointments such as Gentlemen Ushers and Pages of Honour
- The Lords in Waiting, who represent The Queen on various occasions and escort the visiting Head of State during incoming state visits
- The Queen's Bargemaster and Watermen and The Queen's Swans

The Comptroller is also responsible for the Royal Mews, assisted by the Crown Equerry, who has day-to-day responsibility for:

- The provision of carriage processions for the State Opening of Parliament, State Visits, Trooping of the Colour, Royal Ascot, the Garter Ceremony, the Thistle Service, the Presentation of credentials to The Queen by incoming foreign Ambassadors and High Commissioners, and other state and ceremonial occasions
- The provision of chauffeur-driven cars
- Co-ordinating the travelling and transport arrangements by road in respect of The Queen's official engagements
- Supervision and administration of the Royal Mews at Buckingham Palace, Windsor Castle, Hampton Court and the Palace of Holyroodhouse

The Comptroller, Lord Chamberlain's Office also has overall responsibility for the Marshal of the Diplomatic Corps and the Secretary of the Central Chancery of the Orders of Knighthood.

Comptroller of the Lord Chamberlain's Office, Lt. Col. Sir Malcolm Ross, KCVO, OBE

ROYAL COLLECTION DEPARTMENT

The Royal Collection, which contains a large number of works of art of all kinds, is held by The Queen as Sovereign in trust for her successors and the nation and is not owned by her as an individual. The administration, conservation and presentation of the Royal Collection are funded by the Royal Collection Trust solely from income from visitors to Windsor Castle, Buckingham Palace and the Palace of Holyroodhouse in Edinburgh. The Royal Collection Trust is chaired by the Prince of Wales. The Lord Chamberlain, the Private Secretary and the Keeper of the Privy Purse are ex officio trustees and there are three external trustees appointed by The Queen.

The Director of the Royal Collection is responsible for:

- The administration and custodial control of the Royal Collection in all royal residences
- The care, display, conservation and restoration of items in the Collection
- Initiating and assisting research into the Collection and publishing catalogues and books on the Collection
- Making the Collection accessible to the public by display in places open to the public (including the unoccupied palaces), The Queen's Gallery at Buckingham Palace and the Queen's Gallery at the Palace of Holyroodhouse, by travelling exhibitions organised by museums and galleries in the United Kingdom and abroad
- Educating and informing the public about the Collection

The Director of the Royal Collection, who is at present also the Surveyor of The Queen's Works of Art, is assisted by the Surveyor of the Queen's Pictures, the Royal Librarian, the Deputy Surveyor of The Queen's Works of Art, the Managing Director, Royal Collection Enterprises, and the Finance Director, Royal Collection.

The Surveyor of the Queen's Pictures is responsible for pictures and miniatures, the Royal Librarian is responsible for all the books, manuscripts, coins and medals, insignia and works of art on paper including the watercolours, prints and drawings in the Print Room at Windsor Castle, and the Surveyor of the Queen's Works of art is responsible for furniture, ceramics and the other decorative arts in the Collection. The Director of the Royal Collection has overall responsibility for the trading activities that fund the Royal Collection Department. These are administered by Royal Collection Enterprises Limited, the trading subsidiary of The Royal Collection Trust, which is run by the Managing Director, Royal Collection Enterprises. The company, whose chairman is the Keeper of the Privy Purse, is responsible for:

- Managing access by the public to Windsor Castle (including Frogmore House), Buckingham Palace (including the Royal Mews and The Queen's Gallery) and the Palace of Holyroodhouse
- Running shops at each location
- Managing the images and intellectual property rights of the Royal Collection

The Director of the Royal Collection is also an ex officio trustee of the Historic Royal Palaces Trust.

ROYAL SALUTES

ENGLAND

The basic Royal Salute is 21 rounds with 41 rounds fired at Hyde Park because it is a Royal park. At the Tower of London 62 rounds are fired on Royal anniversaries (21 plus a further 20 because the Tower is a Royal Palace and a further 21 'for the City of London'). Gun salutes occur on the following Royal anniversaries:

- Accession Day
- The Queen's birthday
- Coronation Day
- The birthday of the Duke of Edinburgh
- The Queen's official birthday
- State Opening of Parliament

Gun salutes also occur when Parliament is prorogued by the Sovereign, on Royal births and when a visiting Head of State meets the Sovereign in London, Windsor or Edinburgh.

In London, salutes are fired at Hyde Park and The Tower of London although on some occasions (State visits, State Opening of Parliament and The Queen's Birthday Parade) Green Park is used instead.

Constable of the Royal Palace and Fortress of London, Gen. Sir Roger Wheeler, GCB, CBE

Lieutenant of the Tower of London, Lt.-Gen. Sir Hew Pike, KCB, MBE, DSO

Resident Governor and Keeper of the Jewel House, Maj.-Gen. Geoffrey Field, CB, OBE
Master Gunner of St James's Park, Gen. Sir Alex Harley, KBE, CB
Master Gunner within the Tower, Col. George Clarke, TD

SCOTLAND
Royal salutes are authorised at Edinburgh Castle and Stirling Castle, although in practice Edinburgh Castle is the only operating saluting station in Scotland.
A salute of 21 guns is fired on the following occasions:

- the anniversaries of the birth, accession and coronation of the Sovereign
- the anniversary of the birth of HRH Prince Philip, Duke of Edinburgh

A salute of 21 guns is fired in Edinburgh on the occasion of the opening of the General Assembly of the Church of Scotland. A salute of 21 guns may also be fired in Edinburgh on the arrival of HM The Queen or a member of the royal family who is a Royal Highness on an official visit.

Other Military saluting stations are at Cardiff and Belfast.

ROYAL FINANCES

FUNDING

CIVIL LIST
The Civil List dates back to the late 17th century. It was originally used by the sovereign to supplement hereditary revenues for paying the salaries of judges, ambassadors and other government officers as well as the expenses of the royal household. In 1760 on the accession of George III it was decided that the Civil List would be provided by Parliament to cover all relevant expenditure in return for the King surrendering the hereditary revenues of the Crown. At that time Parliament undertook to pay the salaries of judges, ambassadors, etc. In 1831 Parliament agreed also to meet the costs of the royal palaces in return for a reduction in the Civil List. Each sovereign has agreed to continue this arrangement.

The Civil List paid to The Queen is charged on the Consolidated Fund. Until 1972, the amount of money allocated annually under the Civil List was set for the duration of a reign. The system was then altered to a fixed annual payment for ten years but from 1975 high inflation made an annual review necessary. The system of payments reverted to the practice of a fixed annual payment of £7.9m for ten years from 1 January 1991. In 2001 the payments were further fixed until 31 December 2010. In June 2002 the annual accounts for the Civil List were published for the first time and are to continue to be published annually instead of at 10 yearly intervals.

The Civil List Acts provide for other members of the royal family to receive parliamentary annuities from government funds to meet the expenses of carrying out their official duties. Since 1975 The Queen has reimbursed the Treasury for the annuities paid to the Duke of Gloucester, the Duke of Kent and Princess Alexandra. Since 1993 The Queen has reimbursed all the annuities except those paid to herself, the late Queen Elizabeth the Queen Mother and the Duke of Edinburgh.

The Prince of Wales does not receive a parliamentary annuity. He derives his income from the revenues of the Duchy of Cornwall and these monies meet the official and private expenses of the Prince of Wales and his family.

The annual payments for the years 2001–11:

The Queen	£7,900,000
The Duke of Edinburgh	359,000
*The Duke of York	249,000
*The Earl of Wessex	141,000
*The Princess Royal	228,000
*Princess Alice, Duchess of Gloucester	87,000
*The Duke and Duchess of Gloucester	175,000
*The Duke and Duchess of Kent	236,000
*Princess Alexandra	225,000
	9,600,000
*Refunded to the Treasury	1,341,000
Total	8,259,000

GRANTS-IN-AID
The royal household receives grants-in-aid from two government departments to meet various official expenses. The Department for Culture, Media and Sport provides grant-in-aid to pay for the upkeep of English occupied royal palaces, the maintenance of Marlborough House and to meet the cost of royal media and information services. The Royal Travel grant-in-aid is provided by the Department for Transport to meet the cost of official royal travel by air and rail, using mainly aircraft from 32 (The Royal) Squadron, chartered commercial aircraft for major overseas state visits and the Royal Train.

Grants-in-aid voted by Parliament 2003–4:

Property Services, Royal Communications and Information and Maintenance of Marlborough House	£15,300,000 *(£16,050,000)**
Royal Travel	£5,942,000 *(£4,762,000)**

* Amount in parentheses is the total spent.

THE PRIVY PURSE
The funds received by the Privy Purse pay for official expenses incurred by The Queen as head of state and for some of The Queen's private expenditure. The revenues of the Duchy of Lancaster are the principal source of income for the Privy Purse.

FUNDING
The Queen's personal income derives mostly from investments, and is used to meet private expenditure.

EXPENDITURE MET BY GOVERNMENT DEPARTMENTS AND THE CROWN ESTATE
Administration of Honours
Equerries and orderlies
Maintenance of the Palace of Holyroodhouse
State visits to and by the Queen and Liaison with the Diplomatic Corps
Ceremonial occasions
Maintenance of Home Park, Windsor Castle

TAXATION

The sovereign is not legally liable to pay income tax or capital gains tax. After income tax was reintroduced in 1842, some income tax was paid voluntarily by the sovereign but over a long period these payments were phased out. In 1992 The Queen offered to pay tax on a voluntary basis from 6 April 1993, and the Prince of Wales offered to pay tax on a voluntary basis on his income from the Duchy of Cornwall. (He was already taxed in all other respects.)

The main provisions for The Queen and the Prince of Wales to pay tax, set out in a Memorandum of Understanding on Royal Taxation presented to Parliament on 11 February 1993, are that The Queen will pay income tax and capital gains tax in respect of her private income and assets, and on the proportion of the income and capital gains of the Privy Purse used for private purposes. Inheritance tax will be paid on The Queen's assets, except for those which pass to the next sovereign, whether automatically or by gift or bequest. The Prince of Wales will pay income tax on income from the Duchy of Cornwall used for private purposes.

The Prince of Wales has confirmed that he intends to pay tax on the same basis following his accession to the throne. Other members of the royal family are subject to tax as for any taxpayer.

MILITARY RANKS AND TITLES

THE QUEEN

ROYAL NAVY

Lord High Admiral of the United Kingdom

ARMY

Colonel-in-Chief

The Life Guards; The Blues and Royals (Royal Horse Guards and 1st Dragoons); The Royal Scots Dragoon Guards (Carabiniers and Greys); The Queen's Royal Lancers; Royal Tank Regiment; Corps of Royal Engineers; Grenadier Guards; Coldstream Guards; Scots Guards; Irish Guards; Welsh Guards; The Royal Welch Fusiliers; The Queen's Lancashire Regiment; The Argyll and Sutherland Highlanders (Princess Louise's); The Royal Green Jackets; Adjutant General's Corps; The Royal Mercian and Lancastrian Yeomanry; The Governor General's Horse Guards (of Canada); The King's Own Calgary Regiment (Royal Canadian Armoured Corps); Canadian Forces Military Engineers Branch; Royal 22e Regiment (of Canada); Governor General's Foot Guards (of Canada); The Canadian Grenadier Guards; Le Regiment de la Chaudiere (of Canada); 2nd Battalion Royal New Brunswick Regiment (North Shore); The 48th Highlanders of Canada; The Argyll and Sutherland Highlanders of Canada (Princess Louise's); The Calgary Highlanders; Royal Australian Engineers; Royal Australian Infantry Corps; Royal Australian Army Ordnance Corps; Royal Australian Army Nursing Corps; The Corps of Royal New Zealand Engineers; Royal New Zealand Infantry Regiment; The Malawi Rifles; The Royal Malta Artillery

Affiliated Colonel-in-Chief

The Queen's Gurkha Engineers

Captain General

Royal Regiment of Artillery; The Honourable Artillery Company; Combined Cadet Force; Royal Regiment of Canadian Artillery; Royal Regiment of Australian Artillery; Royal Regiment of New Zealand Artillery; Royal New Zealand Armoured Corps

Patron

Royal Army Chaplains' Department

ROYAL AIR FORCE

Air Commodore-in-Chief

Royal Auxiliary Air Force; Royal Air Force Regiment; Air Reserve of Canada; Royal Australian Air Force Reserve; Territorial Air Force (of New Zealand)

Commandant-in-Chief

Royal Air Force College, Cranwell

Royal Hon. Air Commodore

Royal Air Force Marham; 603 (City of Edinburgh) Squadron Royal Auxiliary Air Force

HRH THE PRINCE PHILIP, DUKE OF EDINBURGH

ROYAL NAVY

Admiral of the Fleet

Admiral of the Fleet, Royal Australian Navy

Admiral of the Fleet, Royal New Zealand Navy

Admiral of the Royal Canadian Sea Cadets

ROYAL MARINES

Captain General, Royal Marines

ARMY

Field Marshal

Field Marshal, Australian Military Forces

Field Marshal, New Zealand Army

Colonel-in-Chief

The Queen's Royal Hussars (Queen's Own and Royal Irish); The Royal Gloucestershire, Berkshire and Wiltshire Regiment; The Highlanders (Seaforth, Gordons and Camerons); Corps of Royal Electrical and Mechanical Engineers; Intelligence Corps; Army Cadet Force Association; The Royal Canadian Regiment; The Royal Hamilton Light Infantry (Wentworth Regiment of Canada); The Cameron Highlanders of Ottawa; The Queen's Own Cameron Highlanders of Canada; The Seaforth Highlanders of Canada; The Royal Canadian Army Cadets; The Royal Australian Corps of Electrical and Mechanical Engineers; The Australian Army Cadet Corps

Colonel
Grenadier Guards

Royal Hon. Colonel
City of Edinburgh University Officers' Training Corps; The Trinidad and Tobago Regiment

Member
Honourable Artillery Company

ROYAL AIR FORCE
Marshal of the Royal Air Force
Marshal of the Royal Australian Air Force
Marshal of the Royal New Zealand Air Force

Air Commodore-in-Chief
Air Training Corps; Royal Canadian Air Cadets

Royal Hon. Air Commodore
Royal Air Force Kinloss

HRH THE PRINCE OF WALES

ROYAL NAVY
Vice Admiral

ARMY
Lieutenant-General

Colonel-in-Chief
The Royal Dragoon Guards; The Cheshire (22nd) Regiment; The Royal Regiment of Wales (24th/41st Foot); The Parachute Regiment; The Royal Gurkha Rifles; Army Air Corps; The Royal Canadian Dragoons; Lord Strathcona's Horse (Royal Canadians); Royal Regiment of Canada (10th Royal Grenadiers); Royal Winnipeg Rifles; Royal Australian Armoured Corps; The Royal Pacific Islands Regiment; 1st The Queen's Dragoon Guards; The Black Watch (Royal Highland Regiment); The King's Regiment

Deputy Colonel-in-Chief
The Highlanders (Seaforth, Gordons and Camerons)

Colonel
Welsh Guards

Royal Hon. Colonel
The Queen's Own Yeomanry

ROYAL AIR FORCE
Air Marshal

Hon. Air Commodore
Royal Air Force Valley

Air Commodore-in-Chief
Royal New Zealand Air Force

Colonel-in-Chief
Air Reserve Group of Air Command (of Canada)

HRH THE DUKE OF YORK

ROYAL NAVY
Admiral of the Sea Cadet Corps

ARMY
Colonel-in-Chief
The Staffordshire Regiment (The Prince of Wales's); The Royal Irish Regiment (27th (Inniskilling), 83rd, 87th and The Ulster Defence Regiment); 9th/12th Royal Lancers; The Royal Highland Fusiliers; Small Arms School Corps; The Queen's York Rangers (First Americans); Royal New Zealand Army Logistics Regiment

ROYAL AIR FORCE
Royal Hon. Air Commodore
Royal Air Force Lossiemouth

HRH THE EARL OF WESSEX

ARMY
Colonel-in-Chief
Hastings and Prince Edward Regiment; Saskatchewan Dragoons
Royal Hon. Colonel
Royal Wessex Yeomanry

HRH THE PRINCESS ROYAL

ROYAL NAVY
Rear Admiral Chief Commandant for Women in the Royal Navy

ARMY
Colonel-in-Chief
The King's Royal Hussars; Royal Corps of Signals; Royal Logistic Corps; The Worcestershire and Sherwood Foresters Regiment (29th/45th Foot); The Royal Scots (The Royal Regiment); The Royal Army Veterinary Corps; 8th Canadian Hussars (Princess Louise's); Royal Newfoundland Regiment; Canadian Forces Communications and Electronics Branch; The Grey and Simcoe Foresters (Royal Canadian Armoured Corps); The Royal Regina Rifle Regiment; Canadian Forces Medical Branch; Royal Australian Corps of Signals; Royal New Zealand Corps of Signals; Royal New Zealand Nursing Corps

Affiliated Colonel-in-Chief
The Queen's Gurkha Signals; The Queen's Own Gurkha Transport Regiment

Colonel
The Blues and Royals (Royal Horse Guards and 1st Dragoons)

Royal Hon. Colonel
University of London Officers' Training Corps

Commandant
First Aid Nursing Yeomanry (Princess Royal's Volunteer Corps)

ROYAL AIR FORCE
Royal Hon. Air Commodore
Royal Air Force Lyneham; University of London Air Squadron

HRH PRINCESS ALICE, DUCHESS OF GLOUCESTER

ARMY
Colonel-in-Chief
The King's Own Scottish Borderers; The Royal Anglian Regiment; Royal Australian Corps of Transport

Deputy Colonel-in-Chief
The King's Royal Hussars

ROYAL AIR FORCE
Air Chief Marshal

Air Chief Commandant
Women, Royal Air Force

HRH THE DUKE OF GLOUCESTER

ARMY
Deputy Colonel-in-Chief
The Royal Gloucestershire, Berkshire and Wiltshire Regiment; The Royal Logistic Corps

Royal Hon. Colonel
Royal Monmouthshire Royal Engineers (Militia)

ROYAL AIR FORCE
Hon. Air Marshal

Royal Hon. Air Commodore
Royal Air Force Odiham; No 501 (County of Gloucester) Squadron Royal Auxiliary Air Force

HRH THE DUCHESS OF GLOUCESTER

ARMY
Colonel-in-Chief
Royal Army Dental Corps; Royal Australian Army Educational Corps; Royal New Zealand Army Educational Corps

Deputy Colonel-in-Chief
Adjutant-General's Corps

HRH THE DUKE OF KENT

ARMY
Field Marshal

Colonel-in-Chief
The Royal Regiment of Fusiliers; The Devonshire and Dorset Regiment; Lorne Scots (Peel, Dufferin and Hamilton Regiment)

Deputy Colonel-in-Chief
The Royal Scots Dragoon Guards (Carabiniers and Greys)

Colonel
Scots Guards

ROYAL AIR FORCE
Hon. Air Chief Marshal

Royal Hon. Air Commodore
Royal Air Force Leuchars

HRH THE DUCHESS OF KENT

ARMY
Hon. Major-General

Colonel-in-Chief
The Prince of Wales's Own Regiment of Yorkshire

Deputy Colonel-in-Chief
The Royal Dragoon Guards; Adjutant-General's Corps; The Royal Logistic Corps

HRH PRINCE MICHAEL OF KENT

ROYAL NAVY
Hon. Commodore Royal Naval Reserve

ARMY
Major (retd), The Royal Hussars (Prince of Wales's Own)

Colonel-in-Chief
Essex and Kent Scottish Regiment (Ontario)

ROYAL AIR FORCE
Royal Hon. Air Commodore
RAF Benson

HRH PRINCESS ALEXANDRA, THE HON. LADY OGILVY

ROYAL NAVY
Patron
Queen Alexandra's Royal Naval Nursing Service

ARMY
Colonel-in-Chief
The King's Own Royal Border Regiment; The Light Infantry; The Queen's Own Rifles of Canada; The Canadian Scottish Regiment (Princess Mary's)

Deputy Colonel-in-Chief
The Queen's Royal Lancers

Royal Hon. Colonel
The Royal Yeomanry

ROYAL AIR FORCE
Patron and Air Chief Commandant
Princess Mary's Royal Air Force Nursing Service

Royal Hon. Air Commodore
Royal Air Force Cottesmore

THE HOUSE OF WINDSOR

King George V assumed by royal proclamation (17 July 1917) for his House and family, as well as for all descendants in the male line of Queen Victoria who are subjects of these realms, the name of Windsor.

KING GEORGE V
(George Frederick Ernest Albert), second son of King Edward VII, *born* 3 June 1865; *married* 6 July 1893 HSH Princess Victoria Mary Augusta Louise Olga Pauline Claudine Agnes of Teck (Queen Mary, *born* 26 May 1867; *died* 24 March 1953); *succeeded* to the throne 6 May 1910; *died* 20 January 1936. *Issue:*

1. HRH PRINCE EDWARD Albert Christian George Andrew Patrick David, *born* 23 June 1894, *succeeded* to the throne as King Edward VIII, 20 January 1936; *abdicated* 11 December 1936; created *Duke of Windsor* 1937; *married* 3 June 1937, Mrs Wallis Simpson (Her Grace The Duchess of Windsor, *born* 19 June 1896; *died* 24 April 1986), *died* 28 May 1972

2. HRH PRINCE ALBERT Frederick Arthur George, *born* 14 December 1895, *created* Duke of York 1920; *married* 26 April 1923, Lady Elizabeth Bowes-Lyon, youngest daughter of the 14th Earl of Strathmore and Kinghorne (HM Queen Elizabeth the Queen Mother, *born* 4 August 1900; *died* 30 March 2002), *succeeded* to the throne as King George VI, 11 December 1936; *died* 6 February 1952, having had issue

3. HRH PRINCESS (Victoria Alexandra Alice) MARY, *born* 25 April 1897, *created* Princess Royal 1932; *married* 28 February 1922, Viscount Lascelles, later the 6th Earl of Harewood (1882–1947), *died* 28 March 1965. *Issue:*
(1) George Henry Hubert Lascelles, 7th Earl of Harewood, KBE, *born* 7 February 1923; *married* (1) 1949, Maria (Marion) Stein (marriage dissolved 1967); *issue, (a)* David Henry George, Viscount Lascelles, *born* 1950; *(b)* James Edward, *born* 1953; *(c)* (Robert) Jeremy Hugh, *born* 1955; (2) 1967, Mrs Patricia Tuckwell; *issue, (d)* Mark Hubert, *born* 1964
(2) Gerald David Lascelles (1924–98), *married* (1) 1952, Miss Angela Dowding (marriage dissolved 1978); *issue, (a)* Henry Ulick, *born* 1953; (2) 1978, Mrs Elizabeth Colvin; *issue, (b)* Martin David, *born* 1962

4. HRH PRINCE HENRY William Frederick Albert, *born* 31 March 1900, *created* Duke of Gloucester, Earl of Ulster and Baron Culloden 1928, *married* 6 November 1935, Lady Alice Christabel Montagu-Douglas-Scott, daughter of the 7th Duke of Buccleuch (HRH Princess Alice, Duchess of Gloucester); *died* 10 June 1974. *Issue:*
(1) HRH Prince William Henry Andrew Frederick, *born* 18 December 1941; *accidentally killed* 28 August 1972
(2) HRH Prince Richard Alexander Walter George (HRH The Duke of Gloucester)

5. HRH PRINCE GEORGE Edward Alexander Edmund, *born* 20 December 1902, *created* Duke of Kent, Earl of St Andrews and Baron Downpatrick 1934, *married* 29 November 1934, HRH Princess Marina of Greece and Denmark (*born* 30 November, 1906; *died* 27 August 1968); *killed on active service*, 25 August 1942. *Issue:*
(1) HRH Prince Edward George Nicholas Paul Patrick (HRH The Duke of Kent)
(2) HRH Princess Alexandra Helen Elizabeth Olga Christabel (HRH Princess Alexandra, the Hon. Lady Ogilvy)
(3) HRH Prince Michael George Charles Franklin (HRH Prince Michael of Kent)

6. HRH PRINCE JOHN Charles Francis, *born* 12 July 1905; *died* 18 January 1919

DESCENDANTS OF QUEEN VICTORIA

QUEEN VICTORIA
(Alexandrina Victoria), *born* 24 May 1819; *succeeded* to the throne 20 June 1837; *married* 10 February 1840 (Francis) Albert Augustus Charles Emmanuel, Duke of Saxony, Prince of Saxe-Coburg and Gotha (HRH Albert, Prince Consort, *born* 26 August 1819, *died* 14 December 1861); *died* 22 January 1901. *Issue:*

1. HRH PRINCESS VICTORIA Adelaide Mary Louisa (Princess Royal) (1840–1901), *m.* 1858, Friedrich III (1831–88), German Emperor March–June 1888. *Issue:*
(1) HIM Wilhelm II (1859–1941), German Emperor 1888–1918, *m.* (1) 1881 Princess Augusta Victoria of Schleswig-Holstein-Sonderburg-Augustenburg (1858–1921); (2) 1922 Princess Hermine of Reuss (1887–1947). *Issue:*
- *(a)* Prince Wilhelm (1882–1951), *Crown Prince* 1888–1918, *m.* 1905 Duchess Cecilie of Mecklenburg-Schwerin; *issue:* Prince Wilhelm (1906–40); Prince Louis Ferdinand (1907–94), *m.* 1938 Grand Duchess Kira; Prince Hubertus (1909–50); Prince Friedrich Georg (1911–66); Princess Alexandrine Irene (1915–80); Princess Cecilie (1917–75)
- *(b)* Prince Eitel-Friedrich (1883–1942), *m.* 1906 Duchess Sophie of Oldenburg (marriage dissolved 1926)
- *(c)* Prince Adalbert (1884–1948), *m.* 1914 Princess Adelheid of Saxe-Meiningen; *issue:* Princess Victoria Marina (1917–81); Prince Wilhelm Victor (1919–89)
- *(d)* Prince August Wilhelm (1887–1949), *m.* 1908 Princess Alexandra of Schleswig-Holstein-Sonderburg-Glücksburg (marriage dissolved 1920); *issue:* Prince Alexander (1912–85)
- *(e)* Prince Oskar (1888–1958), *m.* 1914 Countess von Ruppin; *issue:* Prince Oskar (1915–39); Prince Burchard (1917–88); Princess Herzeleide (1918–89); Prince Wilhelm-Karl (*b.* 1922)
- *(f)* Prince Joachim (1890–1920), *m.* 1916 Princess Marie of Anhalt; *issue:* Prince (Karl) Franz Joseph (1916–75), and has issue
- *(g)* Princess Viktoria Luise (1892–1980), *m.* 1913 Ernst, Duke of Brunswick 1913–18 (1887–1953); *issue:* Prince Ernst (1914–87); Prince Georg (*b.* 1915), *m.* 1946 Princess Sophie of Greece and has issue (two sons, one daughter); Princess Frederika (1917–81), *m.* 1938 Paul I, King of the

Hellenes; Prince Christian (1919–81); Prince Welf Heinrich (1923–97)

(2) Princess Charlotte (1860–1919), *m.* 1878 Bernhard, Duke of Saxe-Meiningen 1914 (1851–1928). *Issue:* Princess Feodora (1879–1945), *m.* 1898 Prince Heinrich XXX of Reuss

(3) Prince Heinrich (1862–1929), *m.* 1888 Princess Irene of Hesse. *Issue:*

- *(a)* Prince Waldemar (1889–1945), *m.* Princess Calixta Agnes of Lippe
- *(b)* Prince Sigismund (1896–1978), *m.* 1919 Princess Charlotte of Saxe-Altenburg; *issue:* Princess Barbara (1920–94); Prince Alfred (*b.* 1924)
- *(c)* Prince Heinrich (1900–4)

(4) Prince Sigismund (1864–6)

(5) Princess Victoria (1866–1929), *m.* (1) 1890, Prince Adolf of Schaumburg-Lippe (1859–1916); (2) 1927, Alexander Zubkov (1900–36)

(6) Prince Waldemar (1868–79)

(7) Princess Sophie (1870–1932), *m.* 1889 Constantine I (1868–1923), King of the Hellenes 1913–17, 1920–3. *Issue:*

- *(a)* George II (1890–1947), King of the Hellenes 1923–4 and 1935–47, *m.* 1921 Princess Elisabeth of Roumania (marriage dissolved 1935)
- *(b)* Alexander I (1893–1920), King of the Hellenes 1917–20, *m.* 1919 Aspasia Manos; *issue:* Princess Alexandra (1921–93), *m.* 1944 King Petar II of Yugoslavia
- *(c)* Princess Helena (1896–1982), *m.* 1921 King Carol of Roumania, (marriage dissolved 1928)
- *(d)* Paul I (1901–64), King of the Hellenes 1947–64, *m.* 1938 Princess Frederika of Brunswick; *issue:* King Constantine II (*b.* 1940), *m.* 1964 Princess Anne-Marie of Denmark, and has issue (three sons, two daughters); Princess Sophie (*b.* 1938), *m.* 1962 Juan Carlos I of Spain; Princess Irene (*b.* 1942)
- *(e)* Princess Irene (1904–74), *m.* 1939 4th Duke of Aosta; *issue:* Prince Amedeo, 5th Duke of Aosta (*b.* 1943)
- *(f)* Princess Katherine (Lady Katherine Brandram) (*b.* 1913), *m.* 1947 Major R. C. A. Brandram, MC, TD; *issue:* R. Paul G. A. Brandram (*b.* 1948)

(8) Princess Margarethe (1872–1954), *m.* 1893 Prince Friedrich Karl of Hesse (1868–1940). *Issue:*

- *(a)* Prince Friedrich Wilhelm (1893–1916)
- *(b)* Prince Maximilian (1894–1914)
- *(c)* Prince Philipp (1896–1980), *m.* 1925 Princess Mafalda of Italy; *issue:* Prince Moritz (*b.* 1926); Prince Heinrich (1927–99); Prince Otto (1937–98); Princess Elisabeth (*b.* 1940)
- *(d)* Prince Wolfgang (1896–1989), *m.* (1) 1924 Princess Marie Alexandra of Baden; (2) 1948 Ottilie Möller
- *(e)* Prince Richard (1901–69)
- *(f)* Prince Christoph (1901–43), *m.* 1930 Princess Sophie of Greece (*see* below) and has issue (two sons, three daughters)

2. HRH PRINCE ALBERT EDWARD (HM KING EDWARD VII), *b.* 9 November 1841, *m.* 1863 HRH Princess Alexandra of Denmark (1844–1925), *succeeded* to the throne 22 January 1901, *d.* 6 May 1910. *Issue:*

(1) Albert Victor, Duke of Clarence and Avondale (1864–92)

(2) George (HM KING GEORGE V) (1865–1936)

(3) Louise (1867–1931) Princess Royal 1905–31, *m.* 1889 1st Duke of Fife (1849–1912). *Issue:*

- *(a)* Princess Alexandra, Duchess of Fife (1891–1959), *m.* 1913 Prince Arthur of Connaught *(b)* Princess Maud (1893–1945), *m.* 1923 11th Earl of Southesk (1893–1992); *issue:* The Duke of Fife (*b.* 1929)

(4) Victoria (1868–1935)

(5) Maud (1869–1938), *m.* 1896 Prince Carl of Denmark (1872–1957), later King Haakon VII of Norway 1905–57. *Issue:*

- *(a)* Olav V (1903–91), King of Norway 1957–91, *m.* 1929 Princess Märtha of Sweden (1901–54); *issue:* Princess Ragnhild (*b.* 1930); Princess Astrid (*b.* 1932); Harald V, King of Norway (*b.* 1937)

(6) Alexander (6–7 April 1871)

3. HRH PRINCESS ALICE Maud Mary (1843–78), *m.* 1862 Prince Ludwig (1837–92), Grand Duke of Hesse 1877–92. *Issue:*

(1) Victoria (1863–1950), *m.* 1884 *Admiral of the Fleet* Prince Louis of Battenberg (1854–1921), *cr.* 1st Marquess of Milford Haven 1917. *Issue:*

- *(a)* Alice (1885–1969), *m.* 1903 Prince Andrew of Greece (1882–1944); *issue:* Princess Margarita (1905–81), *m.* 1931 Prince Gottfried of Hohenlohe-Langenburg (*see* below); Princess Theodora (1906–69), *m.* Prince Berthold of Baden (1906–63) and has issue (two sons, one daughter); Princess Cecilie (1911–37), *m.* George, Grand Duke of Hesse (*see* below); Princess Sophie (1914–2001), *m.* (1) 1930 Prince Christoph of Hesse (*see* above); (2) 1946 Prince Georg of Hanover; Prince Philip, Duke of Edinburgh (*b.* 1921)
- *(b)* Louise (1889–1965), *m.* 1923 Gustaf VI Adolf (1882–1973), King of Sweden 1950–73
- *(c)* George, 2nd Marquess of Milford Haven (1892–1938), *m.* 1916 Countess Nadejda, daughter of Grand Duke Michael of Russia; *issue:* Lady Tatiana (1917–88); David Michael, 3rd Marquess (1919–70)
- *(d)* Louis, 1st Earl Mountbatten of Burma (1900–79), *m.* 1922 Edwina Ashley, daughter of Lord Mount Temple; *issue:* Patricia, Countess Mountbatten of Burma (*b.* 1924), Pamela (*b.* 1929)

(2) Elizabeth (1864–1918), *m.* 1884 Grand Duke Sergius of Russia (1857–1905)

(3) Irene (1866–1953), *m.* 1888 Prince Heinrich of Prussia (4) Ernst Ludwig (1868–1937), Grand Duke of Hesse 1892–1918, *m.* (1) 1894 Princess Victoria Melita of Saxe-Coburg (*see* below) (marriage dissolved 1901); (2) 1905 Princess Eleonore of Solms-Hohensolmslich. *Issue:*

- *(a)* Princess Elizabeth (1895–1903)
- *(b)* George, Hereditary Grand Duke of Hesse (1906–37), *m.* Princess Cecilie of Greece (*see* above), and had issue, two sons, accidentally killed with parents, 1937
- *(c)* Ludwig, Prince of Hesse (1908–68), *m.* 1937 Margaret, daughter of 1st Lord Geddes

(5) Frederick William (1870–3)

(6) Alix (Tsaritsa of Russia) (1872–1918), *m.* 1894 Nicholas II (1868–1918) Tsar of All the Russias 1894–1917, assassinated 16 July 1918. *Issue:*

- *(a)* Grand Duchess Olga (1895–1918)
- *(b)* Grand Duchess Tatiana (1897–1918)
- *(c)* Grand Duchess Marie (1899–1918)
- *(d)* Grand Duchess Anastasia (1901–18)
- *(e)* Alexis, Tsarevich of Russia (1904–18)

(7) Marie (1874–8)

4. HRH PRINCE ALFRED Ernest Albert, Duke of

Edinburgh, *Admiral of the Fleet* (1844–1900), *m.* 1874 Grand Duchess Marie Alexandrovna of Russia (1853–1920); succeeded as Duke of Saxe-Coburg and Gotha 22 August 1893. *Issue:*
(1) Alfred, Prince of Saxe-Coburg (1874–99)
(2) Marie (1875–1938), *m.* 1893 Ferdinand (1865–1927), King of Roumania 1914–27. *Issue:*
- *(a)* Carol II (1893–1953), King of Roumania 1930–40, *m.* (2) 1921 Princess Helena of Greece (*see* above) (marriage dissolved 1928); *issue:* Michael (*b.* 1921), King of Roumania 1927–30, 1940–7, *m.* 1948 Princess Anne of Bourbon-Parma, and has issue (five daughters)
- *(b)* Elisabeth (1894–1956), *m.* 1921 George II, King of the Hellenes
- *(c)* Marie (1900–61), *m.* 1922 Alexander (1888–1934), King of Yugoslavia 1921–34; *issue:* Petar II (1923–70), King of Yugoslavia 1934–45, *m.* 1944 Princess Alexandra of Greece (*see* above) and has issue (Crown Prince Alexander, *b.* 1945); Prince Tomislav (1928–2000), *m.* (1) 1957 Princess Margarita of Baden (daughter of Princess Theodora of Greece and Prince Berthold of Baden, *see* above); (2) 1982 Linda Bonney; and has issue (three sons, one daughter); Prince Andrej (1929–90), *m.* (1) 1956 Princess Christina of Hesse (daughter of Prince Christoph of Hesse and Princess Sophie of Greece, *see* above); (2) 1963 Princess Kira-Melita of Leiningen (*see* below); and has issue (three sons, two daughters)
- *(d)* Prince Nicolas (1903–78)
- *(e)* Princess Ileana (1909–91), *m.* (1) 1931 Archduke Anton of Austria; (2) 1954 Dr Stefan Issarescu; *issue:* Archduke Stefan (1932–98); Archduchess Maria Ileana (1933–59); Archduchess Alexandra (*b.* 1935); Archduke Dominic (*b.* 1937); Archduchess Maria Magdalena (*b.* 1939); Archduchess Elisabeth (*b.* 1942)
- *(f)* Prince Mircea (1913–16)

(3) Victoria Melita (1876–1936), *m.* (1) 1894 Grand Duke Ernst Ludwig of Hesse (*see* above) (marriage dissolved 1901); (2) 1905 the Grand Duke Kirill of Russia (1876–1938). *Issue:*
- *(a)* Marie Kirillovna (1907–51), *m.* 1925 Prince Friedrich Karl of Leiningen; *issue:* Prince Emich (1926–91); Prince Karl (1928–90); Princess Kira-Melita (*b.* 1930), *m.* Prince Andrej of Yugoslavia (*see* above); Princess Margarita (1932–96); Princess Mechtilde (*b.* 1936); Prince Friedrich (1938–98)
- *(b)* Kira Kirillovna (1909–67), *m.* 1938 Prince Louis Ferdinand of Prussia; *issue:* Prince Friedrich Wilhelm (*b.* 1939); Prince Michael (*b.* 1940); Princess Marie (*b.* 1942); Princess Kira (*b.* 1943); Prince Louis Ferdinand (1944–77); Prince Christian (*b.* 1946); Princess Xenia (1949–92)
- *(c)* Vladimir Kirillovich (1917–92), *m.* 1948 Princess Leonida Bagration-Mukhransky; *issue:* Grand Duchess Maria (*b.* 1953), and has issue

(4) Alexandra (1878–1942), *m.* 1896 Ernst, Prince of Hohenlohe Langenburg. *Issue:*
- *(a)* Gottfried (1897–1960), *m.* 1931 Princess Margarita of Greece (*see* above); *issue:* Prince Kraft (1935–2004), Princess Beatrice (1936–97), Prince Georg Andreas (*b.* 1938), Prince Ruprecht (1944–76); Prince Albrecht (1944–92)
- *(b)* Maria (1899–1967), *m.* 1916 Prince Friedrich of Schleswig-Holstein-Sonderburg-Glücksburg; *issue:* Prince Peter (1922–80); Princess Marie (1927–2000)
- *(c)* Princess Alexandra (1901–63)
- *(d)* Princess Irma (1902–86)

(5) Princess Beatrice (1884–1966), *m.* 1909 Alfonso of Orleans, Infante of Spain. *Issue:*
- *(a)* Prince Alvaro (1910–97), *m.* 1937 Carla Parodi-Delfino; *issue:* Doña Gerarda (*b.* 1939); Don Alonso (1941–75); Doña Beatriz (*b.* 1943); Don Alvaro (*b.* 1947)
- *(b)* Prince Alonso (1912–36)
- *(c)* Prince Ataulfo (1913–74)

5. HRH PRINCESS HELENA Augusta Victoria (1846–1923), *m.* 1866 Prince Christian of Schleswig-Holstein-Sonderburg-Augustenburg (1831–1917). *Issue:*
(1) Prince Christian Victor (1867–1900)
(2) Prince Albert (1869–1931), Duke of Schleswig-Holstein 1921–31
(3) Princess Helena (1870–1948)
(4) Princess Marie Louise (1872–1956), *m.* 1891 Prince Aribert of Anhalt (marriage dissolved 1900)
(5) Prince Harold (12–20 May 1876)

6. HRH PRINCESS LOUISE Caroline Alberta (1848–1939), *m.* 1871 the Marquess of Lorne, afterwards 9th Duke of Argyll (1845–1914); without issue

7. HRH PRINCE ARTHUR William Patrick Albert, Duke of Connaught, *Field Marshal* (1850–1942), *m.* 1879 Princess Louisa of Prussia (1860–1917). *Issue:*
(1) Margaret (1882–1920), *m.* 1905 Crown Prince Gustaf Adolf (1882–1973), afterwards King of Sweden 1950–73. *Issue:*
- *(a)* Gustaf Adolf, Duke of Västerbotten (1906–47), *m.* 1932 Princess Sibylla of Saxe-Coburg-Gotha (*see* below); *issue:* Princess Margaretha (*b.* 1934); Princess Birgitta (*b.* 1937); Princess Désirée (*b.* 1938); Princess Christina (*b.* 1943); Carl XVI Gustaf, King of Sweden (*b.* 1946)
- *(b)* Count Sigvard Bernadotte (1907–2002), *m.* (1) 1934 Erika Patzeck; (2) 1943 Sonja Robbert; (3) 1961 Marianne Lindberg; *issue:* Count Michael (*b.* 1944)
- *(c)* Princess Ingrid (Queen Mother of Denmark) (1910–2000), *m.* 1935 Frederick IX (1899–1972), King of Denmark 1947–72; *issue:* Margrethe II, Queen of Denmark (*b.* 1940); Princess Benedikte (*b.* 1944); Princess Anne-Marie (*b.* 1946), *m.* 1964 Constantine II of Greece
- *(d)* Prince Bertil, Duke of Halland (1912–97), *m.* 1976 Mrs Lilian Craig
- *(e)* Count Carl Bernadotte (*b.* 1916), *m.* (1) 1946 Mrs Kerstin Johnson; (2) 1988 Countess Gunnila Bussler

(2) Arthur (1883–1938), *m.* 1913 HH the Duchess of Fife *Issue:*
Alastair Arthur, 2nd Duke of Connaught (1914–43)
(3) (Victoria) Patricia (1886–1974), *m.* 1919 Adm. Hon. Sir Alexander Ramsay. *Issue:*
- *(a)* Alexander Ramsay of Mar (1919–2000), *m.* 1956 Hon. Flora Fraser (Lady Saltoun)

8. HRH PRINCE LEOPOLD George Duncan Albert, Duke of Albany (1853–84), *m.* 1882 Princess Helena of Waldeck (1861–1922). *Issue:*
(1) Alice (1883–1981), *m.* 1904 Prince Alexander of Teck (1874–1957), *cr.* 1st Earl of Athlone 1917. *Issue:*
- *(a)* Lady May (1906–94), *m.* 1931 Sir Henry Abel-Smith, KCMG, KCVO, DSO; *issue:* Anne (*b.* 1932); Richard (*b.* 1933); Elizabeth (*b.* 1936)

(*b*) Rupert, Viscount Trematon (1907–28)
(*c*) Prince Maurice (March–September 1910)

(2) Charles Edward (1884–1954), Duke of Albany 1884 until title suspended 1917, Duke of Saxe-Coburg-Gotha 1900–18, *m.* 1905 Princess Victoria Adelheid of Schleswig-Holstein-Sonderburg-Glücksburg. *Issue:*
(*a*) Prince Johann Leopold (1906–72), and has issue
(*b*) Princess Sibylla (1908–72), *m.* 1932 Prince Gustav Adolf of Sweden (*see* above)
(*c*) Prince Dietmar Hubertus (1909–43)
(*d*) Princess Caroline (1912–83), and has issue
(*e*) Prince Friedrich Josias (1918–98), and has issue

9. HRH PRINCESS BEATRICE Mary Victoria Feodore (1857–1944), *m.* 1885 Prince Henry of Battenberg (1858–96). *Issue:*

(1) Alexander, 1st Marquess of Carisbrooke (1886–1960), *m.* 1917 Lady Irene Denison. *Issue:*
Lady Iris Mountbatten (1920–82), *m.*; *issue:* Robin A. Bryan (*b.* 1957)

(2) Victoria Eugénie (1887–1969), *m.* 1906 Alfonso XIII (1886–1941) King of Spain 1886–1931. *Issue:*
(*a*) Prince Alfonso (1907–38)
(*b*) Prince Jaime (1908–75), and has issue
(*c*) Princess Beatriz (1909–2002), and has issue
(*d*) Princess Maria (1911–96), and has issue
(*e*) Prince Juan (1913–93), Count of Barcelona; *issue:* Princess Maria (*b.* 1936); Juan Carlos I, King of Spain (*b.* 1938), *m.* 1962 Princess Sophie of Greece and has issue (one son, two daughters); Princess Margarita (*b.* 1939)
(*f*) Prince Gonzalo (1914–34)

(3) Major Lord Leopold Mountbatten (1889–1922)

(4) Maurice (1891–1914), died of wounds received in action

KINGS AND QUEENS

ENGLISH KINGS AND QUEENS 927 TO 1603

HOUSES OF CERDIC AND DENMARK

Reign

927–939 ÆTHELSTAN
Son of Edward the Elder, by Ecgwynn, and grandson of Alfred
Acceded to Wessex and Mercia *c.*924, established direct rule over Northumbria 927, effectively creating the Kingdom of England
Reigned 15 years

939–946 EDMUND I
Born 921, son of Edward the Elder, by Eadgifu
Married (1) Ælfgifu (2) Æthelflæd
Killed aged 25, *reigned* 6 years

946–955 EADRED
Son of Edward the Elder, by Eadgifu
Reigned 9 years

955–959 EADWIG
Born before 943, son of Edmund and Ælfgifu
Married Ælfgifu
Reigned 3 years

959–975 EDGAR I
Born 943, son of Edmund and Ælfgifu
Married (1) Æthelflæd (2) Wulfthryth (3) Ælfthryth
Died aged 32, *reigned* 15 years

975–978 EDWARD I (the Martyr)
*Born c.*962, son of Edgar and Æthelflæd
Assassinated aged *c.*16, *reigned* 2 years

978–1016 ÆTHELRED (the Unready)
*Born c.*968/969, son of Edgar and Ælfthryth
Married (1) Ælfgifu (2) Emma, daughter of Richard I, Count of Normandy
1013–14 dispossessed of kingdom by Swegn Forkbeard (King of Denmark 987–1014)
Died aged *c.*47, *reigned* 38 years

1016 EDMUND II (Ironside)
Born before 993, son of Æthelred and Ælfgifu
Married Ealdgyth
Died aged over 23, *reigned* 7 months (April–November)

1016–1035 CNUT (Canute)
*Born c.*995, son of Swegn Forkbeard, King of Denmark, and Gunhild
Married (1) Ælfgifu (2) Emma, widow of Æthelred the Unready
Gained submission of West Saxons 1015, Northumbrians 1016, Mercia 1016, King of all England after Edmund's death
King of Denmark 1019–35, King of Norway 1028–35
Died aged *c.*40, *reigned* 19 years

1035–1040 HAROLD I (Harefoot)
*Born c.*1016/17, son of Cnut and Ælfgifu
Married Ælfgifu
1035 recognised as regent for himself and his brother Harthacnut; 1037 recognised as king
Died aged *c.*23, *reigned* 4 years

1040–1042 HARTHACNUT
*Born c.*1018, son of Cnut and Emma
Titular king of Denmark from 1028
Acknowledged King of England 1035–7 with Harold I as regent; effective king after Harold's death
Died aged *c.*24, *reigned* 2 years

1042–1066 EDWARD II (the Confessor)
Born between 1002 and 1005, son of Æthelred the Unready and Emma
Married Eadgyth, daughter of Godwine, Earl of Wessex
Died aged over 60, *reigned* 23 years

1066 HAROLD II (Godwinesson)
*Born c.*1020, son of Godwine, Earl of Wessex, and Gytha
Married (1) Eadgyth (2) Ealdgyth
Killed in battle aged *c.*46, *reigned* 10 months (January – October)

THE HOUSE OF NORMANDY

1066–1087 WILLIAM I (the Conqueror)
Born 1027/8, son of Robert I, Duke of Normandy; obtained the Crown by conquest
Married Matilda, daughter of Baldwin, Count of Flanders
Died aged *c.*60, *reigned* 20 years

1087–1100 WILLIAM II (Rufus)
Born between 1056 and 1060, third son of William I; succeeded his father in England only
Killed aged *c.*40, *reigned* 12 years

1100–1135 HENRY I (Beauclerk)
Born 1068, fourth son of William I
Married (1) Edith or Matilda, daughter of Malcolm III of Scotland (2) Adela, daughter of Godfrey, Count of Louvain
Died aged 67, *reigned* 35 years

1135–1154 STEPHEN
Born not later than 1100, third son of Adela, daughter of William I, and Stephen, Count of Blois
Married Matilda, daughter of Eustace, Count of Boulogne
1141 (February – November) held captive by adherents of Matilda, daughter of Henry I, who contested the crown until 1153
Died aged over 53, *reigned* 18 years

THE HOUSE OF ANJOU (PLANTAGENETS)

1154–1189 HENRY II (Curtmantle)
Born 1133, son of Matilda, daughter of Henry I, and Geoffrey, Count of Anjou
Married Eleanor, daughter of William, Duke of Aquitaine, and divorced queen of Louis VII of France
Died aged 56, *reigned* 34 years

1189–1199 RICHARD I (Coeur de Lion)
Born 1157, third son of Henry II
Married Berengaria, daughter of Sancho VI, King of Navarre
Died aged 42, *reigned* 9 years

1199–1216 JOHN (Lackland)
Born 1167, fifth son of Henry II
Married (1) Isabella or Avisa, daughter of William, Earl of Gloucester (divorced) (2) Isabella, daughter of Aymer, Count of Angoulême
Died aged 48, *reigned* 17 years

1216–1272 HENRY III
Born 1207, son of John and Isabella of Angoulême
Married Eleanor, daughter of Raymond, Count of Provence
Died aged 65, *reigned* 56 years

1272–1307 EDWARD I (Longshanks)
Born 1239, eldest son of Henry III
Married (1) Eleanor, daughter of Ferdinand III, King of Castile (2) Margaret, daughter of Philip III of France
Died aged 68, *reigned* 34 years

1307–1327 EDWARD II
Born 1284, eldest surviving son of Edward I and Eleanor
Married Isabella, daughter of Philip IV of France
Deposed January 1327, *killed* September 1327 aged 43, *reigned* 19 years

1327–1377 EDWARD III
Born 1312, eldest son of Edward II
Married Philippa, daughter of William, Count of Hainault
Died aged 64, *reigned* 50 years

1377–1399 RICHARD II
Born 1367, son of Edward (the Black Prince), eldest son of Edward III
Married (1) Anne, daughter of Emperor Charles IV (2) Isabelle, daughter of Charles VI of France
Deposed September 1399, *killed* February 1400 aged 33, *reigned* 22 years

THE HOUSE OF LANCASTER

1399–1413 HENRY IV
Born 1366, son of John of Gaunt, fourth son of Edward III, and Blanche, daughter of Henry, Duke of Lancaster
Married (1) Mary, daughter of Humphrey, Earl of Hereford (2) Joan, daughter of Charles, King of Navarre, and widow of John, Duke of Brittany
Died aged *c*.47, *reigned* 13 years

1413–1422 HENRY V
Born 1387, eldest surviving son of Henry IV and Mary
Married Catherine, daughter of Charles VI of France
Died aged 34, *reigned* 9 years

1422–1471 HENRY VI
Born 1421, son of Henry V
Married Margaret, daughter of René, Duke of Anjou and Count of Provence
Deposed March 1461, *restored* October 1470
Deposed April 1471, *killed* May 1471 aged 49, *reigned* 39 years

THE HOUSE OF YORK

1461–1483 EDWARD IV
Born 1442, eldest son of Richard of York (grandson of Edmund, fifth son of Edward III, and son of Anne, great-granddaughter of Lionel, third son of Edward III)
Married Elizabeth Woodville, daughter of Richard, Lord Rivers, and widow of Sir John Grey
Acceded March 1461, *deposed* October 1470, *restored* April 1471
Died aged 40, *reigned* 21 years

1483 EDWARD V
Born 1470, eldest son of Edward IV
Deposed June 1483, *died* probably July – September 1483, aged 12, *reigned* 2 months (April – June)

1483–1485 RICHARD III
Born 1452, fourth son of Richard of York
Married Anne Neville, daughter of Richard, Earl of Warwick, and widow of Edward, Prince of Wales, son of Henry VI
Killed in battle aged 32, *reigned* 2 years

THE HOUSE OF TUDOR

1485–1509 HENRY VII
Born 1457, son of Margaret Beaufort (great-granddaughter of John of Gaunt, fourth son of Edward III) and Edmund Tudor, Earl of Richmond
Married Elizabeth, daughter of Edward IV
Died aged 52, *reigned* 23 years

1509–1547 HENRY VIII
Born 1491, second son of Henry VII
Married (1) Catherine, daughter of Ferdinand II, King of Aragon, and widow of his elder brother Arthur (divorced) (2) Anne, daughter of Sir Thomas Boleyn (executed) (3) Jane, daughter of Sir John Seymour (died in childbirth) (4) Anne, daughter of John, Duke of Cleves (divorced) (5) Catherine Howard, niece of the Duke of Norfolk (executed) (6) Catherine, daughter of Sir Thomas Parr and widow of Lord Latimer
Died aged 55, *reigned* 37 years

1547–1553 EDWARD VI
Born 1537, son of Henry VIII and Jane Seymour
Died aged 15, *reigned* 6 years

1553 JANE
Born 1537, daughter of Frances (daughter of Mary Tudor, the younger daughter of Henry VII) and Henry Grey, Duke of Suffolk
Married Lord Guildford Dudley, son of the Duke of Northumberland
Deposed July 1553, *executed* February 1554 aged 16, *reigned* 14 days

1553–1558 MARY I
Born 1516, daughter of Henry VIII and Catherine of Aragon
married Philip II of Spain
Died aged 42, *reigned* 5 years

1558–1603 ELIZABETH I
Born 1533, daughter of Henry VIII and Anne Boleyn
Died aged 69, *reigned* 44 years

BRITISH KINGS AND QUEENS SINCE 1603

THE HOUSE OF STUART

Reign

1603–1625 JAMES I (VI OF SCOTLAND)
Born 1566, son of Mary, Queen of Scots (granddaughter of Margaret Tudor, elder daughter of Henry VII), and Henry Stewart, Lord Darnley
Married Anne, daughter of Frederick II of Denmark
Died aged 58, *reigned* 22 years

1625–1649 CHARLES I
Born 1600, second son of James I
Married Henrietta Maria, daughter of Henry IV of France
Executed 1649 aged 48, *reigned* 23 years

COMMONWEALTH DECLARED 19 May 1649
1649–53 Government by a council of state
1653–8 Oliver Cromwell, *Lord Protector*
1658–9 Richard Cromwell, *Lord Protector*

1660–1685 CHARLES II
Born 1630, eldest son of Charles I
Married Catherine, daughter of John IV of Portugal
Died aged 54, *reigned* 24 years

1685–1688 JAMES II (VII OF SCOTLAND)
Born 1633, second son of Charles I
Married (1) Lady Anne Hyde, daughter of Edward, Earl of Clarendon (2) Mary, daughter of Alphonso, Duke of Modena
Reign ended with flight from kingdom December 1688
Died 1701 aged 67, *reigned* 3 years

INTERREGNUM
11 December 1688 to 12 February 1689

1689–1702 WILLIAM III
Born 1650, son of William II, Prince of Orange, and Mary Stuart, daughter of Charles I
Married Mary, elder daughter of James II
Died aged 51, *reigned* 13 years

1689–1694 MARY II
Born 1662, elder daughter of James II and Anne
Died aged 32, *reigned* 5 years

1702–1714 ANNE
Born 1665, younger daughter of James II and Anne
Married Prince George of Denmark, son of Frederick III of Denmark
Died aged 49, *reigned* 12 years

THE HOUSE OF HANOVER

1714–1727 GEORGE I (Elector of Hanover)
Born 1660, son of Sophia (daughter of Frederick, Elector Palatine, and Elizabeth Stuart, daughter of James I) and Ernest Augustus, Elector of Hanover
Married Sophia Dorothea, daughter of George William, Duke of Lüneburg-Celle
Died aged 67, *reigned* 12 years

1727–1760 GEORGE II
Born 1683, son of George I
Married Caroline, daughter of John Frederick, Margrave of Brandenburg-Anspach
Died aged 76, *reigned* 33 years

1760–1820 GEORGE III
Born 1738, son of Frederick, eldest son of George II
Married Charlotte, daughter of Charles Louis, Duke of Mecklenburg-Strelitz
Died aged 81, *reigned* 59 years

REGENCY 1811–20
Prince of Wales regent owing to the insanity of George III

1820–1830 GEORGE IV
Born 1762, eldest son of George III
Married Caroline, daughter of Charles, Duke of Brunswick-Wolfenbüttel
Died aged 67, *reigned* 10 years

1830–1837 WILLIAM IV
Born 1765, third son of George III
Married Adelaide, daughter of George, Duke of Saxe-Meiningen
Died aged 71, *reigned* 7 years

1837–1901 VICTORIA
Born 1819, daughter of Edward, fourth son of George III
Married Prince Albert of Saxe-Coburg and Gotha
Died aged 81, *reigned* 63 years

THE HOUSE OF SAXE-COBURG AND GOTHA

1901–1910 EDWARD VII
Born 1841, eldest son of Victoria and Albert
Married Alexandra, daughter of Christian IX of Denmark
Died aged 68, *reigned* 9 years

THE HOUSE OF WINDSOR

1910–1936 GEORGE V
Born 1865, second son of Edward VII
Married Victoria Mary, daughter of Francis, Duke of Teck
Died aged 70, *reigned* 25 years

1936 EDWARD VIII
Born 1894, eldest son of George V
Married (1937) Mrs Wallis Simpson
Abdicated 1936, *died* 1972 aged 77, *reigned* 10 months (20 January to 11 December)

1936–1952 GEORGE VI
Born 1895, second son of George V
Married Lady Elizabeth Bowes-Lyon, daughter of 14th Earl of Strathmore and Kinghorne
Died aged 56, *reigned* 15 years

1952– ELIZABETH II
Born 1926, elder daughter of George VI
Married Philip, son of Prince Andrew of Greece

KINGS AND QUEENS OF SCOTS 1016 TO 1603

Reign

1016–1034 MALCOLM II
Born c.954, son of Kenneth II
Acceded to Alba 1005, secured Lothian c.1016, obtained Strathclyde for his grandson Duncan c.1016, thus reigning over an area approximately the same as that governed by later rulers of Scotland
Died aged c.80, *reigned* 18 years

THE HOUSE OF ATHOLL

1034–1040 DUNCAN I
Son of Bethoc, daughter of Malcolm II, and Crinan, Mormaer of Atholl
Married a cousin of Siward, Earl of Northumbria
Reigned 5 years

1040–1057 MACBETH
Born c.1005, son of a daughter of Malcolm II and Finlaec, Mormaer of Moray
Married Gruoch, granddaughter of Kenneth III
Killed aged c.52, *reigned* 17 years

1057–1058 LULACH
Born c.1032, son of Gillacomgan, Mormaer of Moray, and Gruoch (and stepson of Macbeth)
Died aged c.26, *reigned* 7 months (August – March)

1058–1093 MALCOLM III (Canmore)
Born c.1031, elder son of Duncan I
Married (1) Ingibiorg (2) Margaret (St Margaret), granddaughter of Edmund II of England
Killed in battle aged c.62, *reigned* 35 years

1093–1097 DONALD III BÁN
Born c.1033, second son of Duncan I
deposed May 1094, *restored* November 1094, *deposed* October 1097, *reigned* 3 years

1094 DUNCAN II
Born c.1060, elder son of Malcolm III and Ingibiorg
Married Octreda of Dunbar
Killed aged c.34, *reigned* 6 months (May–November)

1097–1107 EDGAR
Born c.1074, second son of Malcolm III and Margaret
Died aged c.32, *reigned* 9 years

1107–1124 ALEXANDER I (The Fierce)
Born c.1077, fifth son of Malcolm III and Margaret
Married Sybilla, illegitimate daughter of Henry I of England
Died aged c.47, *reigned* 17 years

1124–1153 DAVID I (The Saint)
Born c.1085, sixth son of Malcolm III and Margaret
Married Matilda, daughter of Waltheof, Earl of Huntingdon
Died aged c.68, *reigned* 29 years

1153–1165 MALCOLM IV (The Maiden)
Born c.1141, son of Henry, Earl of Huntingdon, second son of David I
Died aged c.24, *reigned* 12 years

1165–1214 WILLIAM I (The Lion)
Born c.1142, brother of Malcolm IV
Married Ermengarde, daughter of Richard, Viscount of Beaumont
Died aged c.72, *reigned* 49 years

1214–1249 ALEXANDER II
Born 1198, son of William I
Married (1) Joan, daughter of John, King of England (2) Marie, daughter of Ingelram de Coucy
Died aged 50, *reigned* 34 years

1249–1286 ALEXANDER III
Born 1241, son of Alexander II and Marie
Married (1) Margaret, daughter of Henry III of England (2) Yolande, daughter of the Count of Dreux
Killed accidentally aged 44, *reigned* 36 years

1286–1290 MARGARET (The Maid of Norway)
Born 1283, daughter of Margaret (daughter of Alexander III) and Eric II of Norway
Died aged 7, *reigned* 4 years

FIRST INTERREGNUM 1290–2
Throne disputed by 13 competitors. Crown awarded to John Balliol by adjudication of Edward I of England

THE HOUSE OF BALLIOL

1292–1296 JOHN (Balliol)
Born c.1250, son of Dervorguilla, great-great-granddaughter of David I, and John de Balliol
Married Isabella, daughter of John, Earl of Surrey
Abdicated 1296, *died* 1313 aged c.63, *reigned* 3 years

SECOND INTERREGNUM 1296–1306
Edward I of England declared John Balliol to have forfeited the throne for contumacy in 1296 and took the government of Scotland into his own hands

THE HOUSE OF BRUCE

1306–1329 ROBERT I (Bruce)
Born 1274, son of Robert Bruce and Marjorie, countess of Carrick, and great-grandson of the second daughter of David, Earl of Huntingdon, brother of William I
Married (1) Isabella, daughter of Donald, Earl of Mar (2) Elizabeth, daughter of Richard, Earl of Ulster
Died aged 54, *reigned* 23 years

1329–1371 DAVID II
Born 1324, son of Robert I and Elizabeth
Married (1) Joanna, daughter of Edward II of England (2) Margaret Drummond, widow of Sir John Logie (divorced)
Died aged 46, *reigned* 41 years
1332 Edward Balliol, son of John Balliol, crowned King of Scots September, expelled December
1333–6 Edward Balliol restored as King of Scots

THE HOUSE OF STEWART

1371–1390	ROBERT II (Stewart) *Born* 1316, son of Marjorie (daughter of Robert I) and Walter, High Steward of Scotland *Married* (1) Elizabeth, daughter of Sir Robert Mure of Rowallan (2) Euphemia, daughter of Hugh, Earl of Ross *Died* aged 74, *reigned* 19 years
1390–1406	ROBERT III *Born* c.1337, son of Robert II and Elizabeth *Married* Annabella, daughter of Sir John Drummond of Stobhall *Died* aged *c.*69, *reigned* 16 years
1406–1437	JAMES I *Born* 1394, son of Robert III *Married* Joan Beaufort, daughter of John, Earl of Somerset *Assassinated* aged 42, *reigned* 30 years
1437–1460	JAMES II *Born* 1430, son of James I *Married* Mary, daughter of Arnold, Duke of Gueldres *Killed* accidentally aged 29, *reigned* 23 years
1460–1488	JAMES III *Born* 1452, son of James II *Married* Margaret, daughter of Christian I of Denmark *Assassinated* aged 36, *reigned* 27 years
1488–1513	JAMES IV *Born* 1473, son of James III *Married* Margaret Tudor, daughter of Henry VII of England *Killed* in battle aged 40, *reigned* 25 years
1513–1542	JAMES V *Born* 1512, son of James IV *Married* (1) Madeleine, daughter of Francis I of France (2) Mary of Lorraine, daughter of the Duc de Guise *Died* aged 30, *reigned* 29 years
1542–1567	MARY *Born* 1542, daughter of James V and Mary *Married* (1) the Dauphin, afterwards Francis II of France (2) Henry Stewart, Lord Darnley (3) James Hepburn, Earl of Bothwell *Abdicated* 1567, prisoner in England from 1568, *executed* 1587, *reigned* 24 years
1567–1625	JAMES VI (and I of England) *Born* 1566, son of Mary, Queen of Scots, and Henry, Lord Darnley Acceded 1567 to the Scottish throne, *reigned* 58 years Succeeded 1603 to the English throne, so joining the English and Scottish crowns in one person. The two kingdoms remained distinct until 1707 when the parliaments of the kingdoms became conjoined

WELSH SOVEREIGNS AND PRINCES

The title Prince of Wales is borne after individual conferment and is not inherited at birth, though some Princes have been declared and styled Prince of Wales but never formally so created (*s.*). The title was conferred on Prince Charles by The Queen on 26 July 1958. He was invested at Caernarvon on 1 July 1969.

INDEPENDENT PRINCES AD 844 TO 1282

844–878	Rhodri the Great
878–916	Anarawd, son of Rhodri
916–950	Hywel Dda, the Good
950–979	Iago ab Idwal (or Ieuaf)
979–985	Hywel ab Ieuaf, the Bad
985–986	Cadwallon, his brother
986–999	Maredudd ab Owain ap Hywel Dda
999–1008	Cynan ap Hywel ab Ieuaf
1018–1023	Llywelyn ap Seisyll
1023–1039	Iago ab Idwal ap Meurig
1039–1063	Gruffydd ap Llywelyn ap Seisyll
1063–1075	Bleddyn ap Cynfyn
1075–1081	Trahaern ap Caradog
1081–1137	Gruffydd ap Cynan ab Iago
1137–1170	Owain Gwynedd
1170–1194	Dafydd ab Owain Gwynedd
1194–1240	Llywelyn Fawr, the Great
1240–1246	Dafydd ap Llywelyn
1246–1282	Llywelyn ap Gruffydd ap Llywelyn

ENGLISH PRINCES SINCE 1301

1301	Edward (Edward II)
1343	Edward the Black Prince, son of Edward III
1376	Richard (Richard II), son of the Black Prince
1399	Henry of Monmouth (Henry V)
1454	Edward of Westminster, son of Henry VI
1471	Edward of Westminster (Edward V)
1483	Edward, son of Richard III (*d.* 1484)
1489	Arthur Tudor, son of Henry VII
1504	Henry Tudor (Henry VIII)
1610	Henry Stuart, son of James I (*d.* 1612)
1616	Charles Stuart (Charles I)
*c.*1638 (*s.*)	Charles Stuart (Charles II)
1688 (*s.*)	James Francis Edward Stuart (The Old Pretender), son of James II (*d.* 1766)
1714	George Augustus (George II)
1729	Frederick Lewis, son of George II (*d.* 1751)
1751	George William Frederick (George III)
1762	George Augustus Frederick (George IV)
1841	Albert Edward (Edward VII)
1901	George (George V)
1910	Edward (Edward VIII)
1958	Charles, son of Elizabeth II

PRINCESSES ROYAL

The style Princess Royal is conferred at the Sovereign's discretion on his or her eldest daughter. It is an honorary title, held for life, and cannot be inherited or passed on. It was first conferred on Princess Mary, daughter of Charles I, in approximately 1642.

*c.*1642	Princess Mary (1631–60), daughter of Charles I
1727	Princess Anne (1709–59), daughter of George II
1766	Princess Charlotte (1766–1828), daughter of George III
1840	Princess Victoria (1840–1901), daughter of Victoria
1905	Princess Louise (1867–1931), daughter of Edward VII
1932	Princess Mary (1897–1965), daughter of George V
1987	Princess Anne (b. 1950), daughter of Elizabeth II

PRECEDENCE

ENGLAND AND WALES

The Sovereign
The Prince Philip, Duke of Edinburgh
The Prince of Wales
The Sovereign's younger sons
The Sovereign's grandsons
The Sovereign's cousins
Archbishop of Canterbury
Lord High Chancellor
Archbishop of York
The Prime Minister
Lord President of the Council
Speaker of the House of Commons
Lord Privy Seal
Ambassadors and High Commissioners
Lord Great Chamberlain
Earl Marshal
Lord Chamberlain of the Household
Lord Steward of the Household
Master of the Horse
Dukes, according to their patent of creation:
(1) of England
(2) of Scotland
(3) of Great Britain
(4) of Ireland
(5) those created since the Union
Eldest sons of Dukes of the Blood Royal
Marquesses, according to their patent of creation:
(1) of England
(2) of Scotland
(3) of Great Britain
(4) of Ireland
(5) those created since the Union
Dukes' eldest sons
Earls, according to their patent of creation:
(1) of England
(2) of Scotland
(3) of Great Britain
(4) of Ireland
(5) those created since the Union
Younger sons of Dukes of Blood Royal
Marquesses' eldest sons
Dukes' younger sons
Viscounts, according to their patent of creation:
(1) of England
(2) of Scotland
(3) of Great Britain
(4) of Ireland
(5) those created since the Union
Earls' eldest sons
Marquesses' younger sons
Bishop of London
Bishop of Durham
Bishop of Winchester
Other English Diocesan Bishops according to seniority of consecration
Suffragan Bishops, according to seniority of consecration
Secretaries of State, if of the degree of a Baron
Barons, according to their patent of creation:
(1) of England
(2) of Scotland
(3) of Great Britain
(4) of Ireland
(5) those created since the Union, including Life Barons
Treasurer of the Household
Comptroller of the Household
Vice-Chamberlain of the Household
Secretaries of State under the degree of Baron
Viscounts' eldest sons
Earls' younger sons
Barons' eldest sons
Knights of the Garter
Privy Counsellors
Chancellor of the Exchequer
Chancellor of the Duchy of Lancaster
Lord Chief Justice of England
Master of the Rolls
President of the Family Division
Vice-Chancellor
Lords Justices of Appeal, according to seniority of appointment
Judges of the High Court, according to seniority of appointment
Viscounts' younger sons
Barons' younger sons
Sons of Life Peers and Lords of Appeal in Ordinary
Baronets, according to date of patent
Knights of the Thistle
Knights Grand Cross of the Bath
Knights Grand Commanders of the Star of India
Knights Grand Cross of St Michael and St George
Knights Grand Commanders of the Indian Empire
Knights Grand Cross of the Royal Victorian Order
Knights Grand Cross of the British Empire
Knights Commanders of the Bath
Knights Commanders of the Star of India
Knights Commanders of St Michael and St George
Knights Commanders of the Indian Empire
Knights Commanders of the Royal Victorian Order
Knights Commanders of the British Empire
Knights Bachelor
Vice-Chancellor of the County Palatine of Lancaster
Circuit Judges who held office as Official Referees to Supreme Court (immediately before 1 January 1972)
Recorder of London
Recorders of Liverpool and Manchester, according to priority of appointment
Common Serjeant
Circuit Judges who held office immediately before 1 January 1972, according to priority of appointment
Other Circuit Judges according to priority or order of their respective appointments
Companions of the Bath
Companions of the Star of India
Companions of St Michael and St George
Companions of the Indian Empire
Commanders of the Royal Victorian Order
Commanders of the British Empire
Companions of the Distinguished Service Order
Lieutenants of the Royal Victorian Order
Officers of the British Empire
Companions of the Imperial Service Order
Eldest sons of younger sons of Peers
Baronets' eldest sons
Eldest sons of Knights, in the same order as their fathers
Members of the Royal Victorian Order
Members of the British Empire
Younger sons of Baronets
Younger sons of Knights, in the same order as their fathers
Esquires
Gentlemen

SCOTLAND

The Sovereign
The Prince Philip, Duke of Edinburgh
The Lord High Commissioner to the General Assembly of the Church of Scotland (while that Assembly is sitting)
The Duke of Rothesay (eldest son of the Sovereign)
The Sovereign's younger sons
Grandsons of the Sovereign
The Sovereign's cousins
Lord-Lieutenants
Lord Provosts of Cities being *ex-officio* Lord-Lieutenants of those Cities during their term of office
Sheriffs Principal, successively, within their own localities and during holding of office
Lord Chancellor of Great Britain
Moderator of the General Assembly of the Church of Scotland
Keeper of the Great Seal of Scotland (the First Minister)
The Presiding Officer
The Secretary of State for Scotland
Hereditary High Constable of Scotland
Hereditary Master of the Household in Scotland
Dukes, in same order as in England
Eldest sons of Dukes of the Blood Royal
Marquesses, as in England
Eldest sons of Dukes
Earls, as in England
Younger sons of Dukes of Blood Royal
Eldest sons of Marquesses

Dukes' younger sons
Lord Justice General
Lord Clerk Register
Lord Advocate
The Advocate-General
Lord Justice Clerk
Viscounts, as in England
Eldest sons of Earls
Marquesses' younger sons
Lord-Barons, as in England
Eldest sons of Viscounts
Earls' younger sons
Lord-Barons' eldest sons
Knights of the Garter
Knights of the Thistle
Privy Counsellors
Senators of College of Justice (Lords of Session)
Viscounts' younger sons
Lord-Barons' younger sons
Baronets
Knights Grand Cross and Knights Grand Commanders of Orders, as in England
Knights Commanders of Orders, as in England
Solicitor-General for Scotland
Lord Lyon King of Arms
Sheriffs Principal, when not within own county
Knights Bachelor
Sheriffs
Companions of Orders, as in England
Commanders of the Royal Victorian Order
Commanders of the British Empire
Companions of the Distinguished Service Order
Lieutenants of the Royal Victorian Order
Officers of the British Empire
Companions of the Imperial Service Order
Eldest sons of younger sons of Peers
Eldest sons of Baronets
Eldest sons of Knights, as in England
Members of the Royal Victorian Order
Members of the British Empire
Baronets' younger sons
Knights' younger sons
Esquires
Gentlemen

WOMEN

Women take the same rank as their husbands or as their brothers; but the daughter of a peer marrying a commoner retains her title as Lady or Honourable. Daughters of peers rank next immediately after the wives of their elder brothers, and before their younger brothers' wives. Daughters of peers marrying peers of lower degree take the same order of precedence as that of their husbands; thus the daughter of a Duke marrying a Baron becomes of the rank of Baroness only, while her sisters married to commoners retain their rank and take precedence of the Baroness. Merely official rank on the husband's part does not give any similar precedence to the wife.

Peeresses in their own right take the same precedence as peers of the same rank, i.e. from their date of creation.

LOCAL PRECEDENCE

Scotland

The Lord Provosts of the city districts of Aberdeen, Dundee, Edinburgh and Glasgow are Lord Lieutenants for those districts *ex officio* and take precedence as such.

FORMS OF ADDRESS

It is only possible to cover here the forms of address for peers, baronets and knights, their wife and children, and Privy Counsellors. Greater detail should be sought in one of the publications devoted to the subject.

Both formal and social forms of address are given where usage differs; nowadays, the social form is generally preferred to the formal, which increasingly is used only for official documents and on very formal occasions.

F_ represents forename
S_ represents surname

BARON – *Envelope (formal)*, The Right Hon. Lord _; *(social)*, The Lord _. *Letter (formal)*, My Lord; *(social)*, Dear Lord _. *Spoken*, Lord _.

BARON'S WIFE – *Envelope (formal)*, The Right Hon. Lady _; *(social)*, The Lady _. *Letter (formal)*, My Lady; *(social)*, Dear Lady _. *Spoken*, Lady _.

BARON'S CHILDREN – *Envelope*, The Hon. F_ S_. *Letter*, Dear Mr/Miss/Mrs S_. *Spoken*, Mr/Miss/Mrs S_.

BARONESS IN OWN RIGHT – *Envelope*, may be addressed in same way as a Baron's wife or, if she prefers *(formal)*, The Right Hon. the Baroness _; *(social)*, The Baroness _. Otherwise as for a Baron's wife.

BARONET – *Envelope*, Sir F_ S_, Bt. *Letter (formal)*, Dear Sir; *(social)*, Dear Sir F_. *Spoken*, Sir F_.

BARONET'S WIFE – *Envelope*, Lady S_. *Letter (formal)*, Dear Madam; *(social)*, Dear Lady S_. *Spoken*, Lady S_.

COUNTESS IN OWN RIGHT – As for an Earl's wife.

COURTESY TITLES – The heir apparent to a Duke, Marquess or Earl uses the highest of his father's other titles as a courtesy title. (For a list, *see* the Peerage section.) The holder of a courtesy title is not styled The Most Hon. or The Right Hon., and in correspondence 'The' is omitted before the title. The heir apparent to a Scottish title may use the title 'Master' (*see* below).

DAME – *Envelope*, Dame F_ S_, followed by appropriate post-nominal letters. *Letter (formal)*, Dear Madam; *(social)*, Dear Dame F_. *Spoken*, Dame F_.

DUKE – *Envelope (formal)*, His Grace the Duke of _; *(social)*, The Duke of _. *Letter (formal)*, My Lord Duke; *(social)*, Dear Duke. *Spoken (formal)*, Your Grace; *(social)*, Duke.

DUKE'S WIFE – *Envelope (formal)*, Her Grace the Duchess of _; *(social)*, The Duchess of _. *Letter (formal)*, Dear Madam; *(social)*, Dear Duchess. *Spoken*, Duchess.

DUKE'S ELDEST SON – *see* Courtesy titles.

DUKE'S YOUNGER SONS – *Envelope*, Lord F_ S_. *Letter (formal)*, My Lord; *(social)*, Dear Lord F_. *Spoken (formal)*, My Lord; *(social)*, Lord F_.

DUKE'S DAUGHTER – *Envelope*, Lady F_ S_. *Letter (formal)*, Dear Madam; *(social)*, Dear Lady F_. *Spoken*, Lady F_.

EARL – *Envelope (formal)*, The Right Hon. the Earl (of) _; *(social)*, The Earl (of) _. *Letter (formal)*, My Lord; *(social)*, Dear Lord _. *Spoken (formal)*, My Lord; *(social)*, Lord _.

EARL'S WIFE – *Envelope (formal)*, The Right Hon. the Countess (of) _; *(social)*, The Countess (of) _. *Letter (formal)*, Madam; *(social)*, Lady _. *Spoken (formal)*, Madam; *(social)*, Lady _.

EARL'S CHILDREN – *Eldest son, see* Courtesy titles. *Younger sons*, The Hon. F_ S_ (for forms of address, *see* Baron's children). *Daughters*, Lady F_ S_ (for forms of address, *see* Duke's daughter).

KNIGHT (BACHELOR) – *Envelope*, Sir F_ S_. *Letter (formal)*, Dear Sir; *(social)*, Dear Sir F_. *Spoken*, Sir F_.

KNIGHT (ORDERS OF CHIVALRY) – *Envelope*, Sir F_ S_, followed by appropriate post-nominal letters. Otherwise as for Knight Bachelor.

KNIGHT'S WIFE – As for Baronet's wife.

LIFE PEER – As for Baron/Baroness in own right.

LIFE PEER'S WIFE – As for Baron's wife.

LIFE PEER'S CHILDREN – As for Baron's children.

MARQUESS – *Envelope (formal)*, The Most Hon. the Marquess of _; *(social)*, The Marquess of _. *Letter (formal)*, My Lord; *(social)*, Dear Lord _. *Spoken (formal)*, My Lord; *(social)*, Lord _.

MARQUESS'S WIFE – *Envelope (formal)*, The Most Hon. the Marchioness of _; *(social)*, The Marchioness of _. *Letter (formal)*, Madam; *(social)*, Dear Lady _. *Spoken*, Lady _.

MARQUESS'S CHILDREN – *Eldest son, see* Courtesy titles. *Younger sons*, Lord F_ S_ (for forms of address, *see* Duke's younger sons). *Daughters*, Lady F_ S_ (for forms of address, *see* Duke's daughter).

MASTER – The title is used by the heir apparent to a Scottish peerage, though usually the heir apparent to a Duke, Marquess or Earl uses his courtesy title rather than 'Master'. *Envelope*, The Master of _. *Letter (formal)*, Dear Sir; *(social)*, Dear Master of _. *Spoken (formal)*, Master, or Sir; *(social)*, Master, or Mr S_.

MASTER'S WIFE – Addressed as for the wife of the appropriate peerage style, otherwise as Mrs S_.

PRIVY COUNSELLOR – *Envelope*, The Right (or Rt.) Hon. F_ S_. *Letter*, Dear Mr/Miss/Mrs S_. *Spoken*, Mr/Miss/Mrs S_. It is incorrect to use the letters PC after the name in conjunction with the prefix The Right Hon., unless the Privy Counsellor is a peer below the rank of Marquess and so is styled The Right Hon. because of his rank. In this case only, the post-nominal letters may be used in conjunction with the prefix The Right Hon.

VISCOUNT – *Envelope (formal)*, The Right Hon. the Viscount _; *(social)*, The Viscount _. *Letter (formal)*, My Lord; *(social)*, Dear Lord _. *Spoken*, Lord _.

VISCOUNT'S WIFE – *Envelope (formal)*, The Right Hon. the Viscountess _; *(social)*, The Viscountess _. *Letter (formal)*, Madam; *(social)*, Dear Lady _. *Spoken*, Lady _.

VISCOUNT'S CHILDREN – As for Baron's children.

THE PEERAGE

The rules which govern the creation and succession of peerages are extremely complicated. There are, technically, five separate peerages, the Peerage of England, of Scotland, of Ireland, of Great Britain, and of the United Kingdom. The Peerage of Great Britain dates from 1707 when an Act of Union combined the two kingdoms of England and Scotland and separate peerages were discontinued. The Peerage of the United Kingdom dates from 1801 when Great Britain and Ireland were combined under an Act of Union. Some Scottish peers have received additional peerages of Great Britain or of the United Kingdom since 1707, and some Irish peers additional peerages of the United Kingdom since 1801.

The Peerage of Ireland was not entirely discontinued from 1801 but holders of Irish peerages, whether pre-dating or created subsequent to the Union of 1801, were not entitled to sit in the House of Lords if they had no additional English, Scottish, Great Britain or United Kingdom peerage. However, they are eligible for election to the House of Commons and to vote in parliamentary elections. An Irish peer holding a peerage of a lower grade which enabled him to sit in the House of Lords was introduced there by the title which enabled him to sit, though for all other purposes he was known by his higher title.

In the Peerage of Scotland there is no rank of Baron; the equivalent rank is Lord of Parliament, abbreviated to 'Lord' (the female equivalent is 'Lady'). All peers of England, Scotland, Great Britain or the United Kingdom who are 21 years or over, and of British, Irish or Commonwealth nationality were entitled to sit in the House of Lords until the House of Lords Act 1999, when hereditary peers lost the right to sit. Ninety-two hereditaries including the two Royal Office Holders, The Earl Marshal and the Lord Great Chamberlain, were allowed to remain, pending further reform. In the listings which follow, these peers are indicated by **.

HEREDITARY WOMEN PEERS

Most hereditary peerages pass on death to the nearest male heir, but there are exceptions, and several are held by women.

A woman peer in her own right retains her title after marriage, and if her husband's rank is the superior she is designated by the two titles jointly, the inferior one second. Her hereditary claim still holds good in spite of any marriage whether higher or lower. No rank held by a woman can confer any title or even precedence upon her husband but the rank of a hereditary woman peer in her own right is inherited by her eldest son (or in some cases daughter).

After the Peerage Act 1963, hereditary women peers in their own right were entitled to sit in the House of Lords, subject to the same qualifications as men, until the House of Lords Act 1999.

LIFE PEERS

Since 1876 non-hereditary or life peerages have been conferred on certain eminent judges to enable the judicial functions of the House of Lords to be carried out. These Lords are known as Lords of Appeal or law lords. In 2004, Baroness Hale of Richmond became the first female law lord.

Since 1958 life peerages have been conferred upon distinguished men and women from all walks of life, giving them seats in the House of Lords in the degree of Baron or Baroness. They are addressed in the same way as hereditary Lords and Barons, and their children have similar courtesy titles.

PEERAGES EXTINCT SINCE THE LAST EDITION

LIFE PEERAGES: Blake (cr. 1971); Brigstocke (cr. 1990); Bullock (cr. 1976); Constantine of Stanmore (cr. 1981); Diamond (cr. 1970); Dormand of Easington (cr. 1987); Gallacher (cr. 1982); Geraint (cr. 1992); Gibson (cr. 1975); Greene of Harrow Weald (cr. 1974); Hill-Norton (cr. 1979); Hardy of Wath (cr. 1997); Hobhouse of Woodborough (cr. 1998); Islwyn (cr. 1997); Jenkins of Putney (cr. 1981); Keith of Castleacre (cr. 1980); Murray of Epping Forest (cr. 1985); Pike (cr. 1974); Rayne (cr. 1976); Richardson (cr. 1979); Scanlon (cr. 1979); Walker of Doncaster (cr. 1997); Wallace of Coslany (cr. 1974); Wigoder (cr. 1974)

DISCLAIMER OF PEERAGES

The Peerage Act 1963 enables peers to disclaim their peerages for life. Peers alive in 1963 could disclaim within twelve months after the passing of the Act (31 July 1963); a person subsequently succeeding to a peerage may disclaim within 12 months (one month if an MP) after the date of succession, or of reaching 21, if later. The disclaimer is irrevocable but does not affect the descent of the peerage after the disclaimant's death, and children of a disclaimed peer may, if they wish, retain their precedence and any courtesy titles and styles borne as children of a peer. The disclaimer permitted the disclaimant to sit in the House of Commons if elected as an MP. As the House of Lords Act 1999 removed hereditary peers from the House of Lords, they are now entitled to sit in the House of Commons without having to disclaim their titles.

The following peerages are currently disclaimed:

EARLDOMS: Durham (1970); Selkirk (1994)
VISCOUNTCIES: Stansgate (1963)
BARONIES: Merthyr (1977); Reith (1972); Sanderson of Ayot (1971)

PEERS WHO ARE MINORS (i.e. under 21 years of age)
EARLS: Craven (*b.* 1989)
VISCOUNTS: Selby (*b.* 1993)

CONTRACTIONS AND SYMBOLS

S.	Scottish title
I.	Irish title
**	Hereditary peer remaining in the House of Lords for a transitional period
°	there is no 'of' in the title
b.	Born
s.	Succeeded
m.	Married
w.	widower or widow
M.	Minor
†	heir not ascertained at time of going to press

HEREDITARY PEERS

PEERS OF THE BLOOD ROYAL

Style, His Royal Highness The Duke of _/His Royal Highness the Earl of_
Style of address (formal) May it please your Royal Highness; *(informal)* Sir

Created	*Title, order of succession, name, etc.*	*Heir*
	Dukes	
1947	*Edinburgh* (1st), HRH The Prince Philip, Duke of Edinburgh	The Prince of Wales §
1337	*Cornwall,* Charles, Prince of Wales, *s.* 1952	‡
1398 S.	*Rothesay,* Charles, Prince of Wales, *s.* 1952	‡
1986	*York* (1st), The Prince Andrew, Duke of York	None
1999	*Wessex* (1st), The Prince Edward, Earl of Wessex	None
1928	*Gloucester* (2nd), Prince Richard, Duke of Gloucester, *s.* 1974	Earl of Ulster
1934	*Kent* (2nd), Prince Edward, Duke of Kent, *s.* 1942	Earl of St Andrews

§ In June 1999, Buckingham Palace revealed that the current Earl of Wessex will succeed to the Dukedom of Edinburgh after the title has returned to the crown. The Prince of Wales will only be able to confer the Dukedom on the Earl of Wessex when he succeeds his mother as King.
‡ The title is held by the Sovereign's eldest son from the moment of his birth or the Sovereign's accession.

DUKES

Coronet, Eight strawberry leaves
Style, His Grace the Duke of _
Wife's style, Her Grace the Duchess of _
Eldest son's style, Takes his father's second title as a courtesy title
Younger sons' style, 'Lord' before forename and family name
Daughters' style, 'Lady' before forename and family name
For forms of address, *see* page 43

Created		*Title, order of succession, name, etc.*	*Heir*
1868 I.		*Abercorn (5th),* James Hamilton, KG, *b.* 1934, *s.* 1979, *m., Lord Steward*	Marquess of Hamilton, *b.* 1969
1701 S.		*Argyll (13th),* Torquhil Ian Campbell, *b.* 1968, *s.* 2001	Lord Colin I. C., *b.* 1946
1703 S.		*Atholl (11th),* John Murray, *b.* 1929, *s.* 1996, *m.*	Marquis of Tullibardine, *b.* 1960
1682		*Beaufort (11th),* David Robert Somerset, *b.* 1928, *s.* 1984, *w.*	Marquess of Worcester, *b.* 1952
1694		*Bedford (15th),* Andrew Ian Henry Russell, *b.* 1962, *s.* 2003, *m.*	Lord Robin L. H. R., *b.* 1963
1663 S.		*Buccleuch (9th) and Queensberry (11th) (S. 1684),* Walter Francis John Montagu Douglas Scott, KT, VRD, *b.* 1923, *s.* 1973, *m.*	Earl of Dalkeith, KBE, *b.* 1954
1694		*Devonshire (12th),* Peregrine Andrew Morny Cavendish, *b.* 1944, *s.* 2004, *m.*	Marquess of Hartington, *b.* 1969
1900		*Fife (3rd),* James George Alexander Bannerman Carnegie, *b.* 1929, *s.* 1959	Earl of Southesk, *b.* 1961
1675		*Grafton (11th),* Hugh Denis Charles FitzRoy, KG, *b.* 1919, *s.* 1970, *m.*	Earl of Euston, *b.* 1947
1643 S.		*Hamilton (15th) and Brandon (12th) (1711),* Angus Alan Douglas Douglas-Hamilton, *b.* 1938, *s.* 1973 *Premier Peer of Scotland*	Marquis of Douglas and Clydesdale, *b.* 1978
1766 I.		*Leinster (8th),* Gerald FitzGerald, *b.* 1914, *s.* 1976, *m. Premier Duke and Marquess of Ireland*	Marquess of Kildare, *b.* 1948
1719		*Manchester (13th),* Alexander Charles David Drogo Montagu, *b.* 1962, *s.* 2002, *m.*	Viscount Mandeville, *b.* 1993
1702		*Marlborough (11th),* John George Vanderbilt Henry Spencer-Churchill, *b.* 1926, *s.* 1972, *m.*	Marquess of Blandford, *b.* 1955
1707 S.	**	*Montrose (8th),* James Graham, *b.* 1935, *s.* 1992, *m.*	Marquis of Graham, *b.* 1973
1483	**	*Norfolk (18th),* Edward Wiliam Fitzalan-Howard, *b.* 1956, *s.* 2002, *m. Premier Duke and Earl Marshal*	Earl of Arundel and Surrey, *b.* 1987
1766		*Northumberland (12th),* Ralph George Algernon Percy, *b.* 1956, *s.* 1995, *m.*	Earl Percy, *b.* 1984
1675		*Richmond (10th) and Gordon (5th) (1876)* Charles Henry Gordon Lennox, *b.* 1929, *s.* 1989, *m.*	Earl of March and Kinrara, *b.* 1955

Created	*Title, order of succession, name, etc.*	*Heir*
1707 S.	*Roxburghe (10th),* Guy David Innes-Ker, *b.* 1954, *s.* 1974, *m. Premier Baronet of Scotland*	Marquis of Bowmont and Cessford, *b.* 1981
1703	*Rutland (11th),* David Charles Robert Manners, *b.* 1959, *s.* 1999, *m.*	Marquess of Granby, *b.* 1999
1684	*St Albans (14th),* Murray de Vere Beauclerk, *b.* 1939, *s.* 1988, *m.*	Earl of Burford, *b.* 1965
1547	*Somerset (19th),* John Michael Edward Seymour, *b.* 1952, *s.* 1984, *m.*	Lord Seymour, *b.* 1982
1833	*Sutherland (7th),* Francis Ronald Egerton, *b.* 1940, *s.* 2000, *m.*	Marquess of Stafford, *b.* 1975
1814	*Wellington (8th),* Arthur Valerian Wellesley, KG, LVO, OBE, MC, *b.* 1915, *s.* 1972, *m.*	Marquess of Douro, *b.* 1945
1874	*Westminster (6th),* Gerald Cavendish Grosvenor, KG, OBE, *b.* 1951, *s.* 1979, *m.*	Earl Grosvenor, *b.* 1991

MARQUESSES

Coronet, Four strawberry leaves alternating with four silver balls
Style, The Most Hon. the Marquess (of) _ . In Scotland the spelling 'Marquis' is preferred for pre-Union creations
Wife's style, The Most Hon. the Marchioness (of) _
Eldest son's style, Takes his father's second title as a courtesy title
Younger sons' style, 'Lord' before forename and family name
Daughters' style, 'Lady' before forename and family name
For forms of address, *see* page 43

Created	*Title, order of succession, name, etc.*	*Heir*
1916	*Aberdeen and Temair (7th),* Alexander George Gordon, *b.* 1955, *s.* 2002, *m.*	Earl of Haddo, *b.* 1983
1876	*Abergavenny (6th) and 10th Earl, Abergavenny, 1784,* Christopher George Charles Nevill, *b.* 1955, *s.* 2000, *m.*	To Earldom only, David M. R. N., *b.* 1941
1821	*Ailesbury (8th),* Michael Sidney Cedric Brudenell-Bruce, *b.* 1926, *s.* 1974	Earl of Cardigan, *b.* 1952
1831	*Ailsa (8th),* Archibald Angus Charles Kennedy, *b.* 1956, *s.* 1994	Lord David Kennedy, *b.* 1958
1815	*Anglesey (7th),* George Charles Henry Victor Paget, *b.* 1922, *s.* 1947, *m.*	Earl of Uxbridge, *b.* 1950
1789	*Bath (7th),* Alexander George Thynn, *b.* 1932, *s.* 1992, *m.*	Viscount Weymouth, *b.* 1974
1826	*Bristol (8th),* Frederick William Augustus Hervey, *b.* 1979, *s.* 1999	Timothy H. H., *b.* 1960
1796	*Bute (7th),* John Colum Crichton-Stuart, *b.* 1958, *s.* 1993, *m.*	Lord Mount Stuart, *b.* 1989
1812	° *Camden (6th),* David George Edward Henry Pratt, *b.* 1930, *s.* 1983	Earl of Brecknock, *b.* 1965
1815	** *Cholmondeley (7th),* David George Philip Cholmondeley, *b.* 1960, *s.* 1990, *Lord Great Chamberlain*	Charles G. C., *b.* 1959
1816	° *Conyngham (7th),* Frederick William Henry Francis Conyngham, *b.* 1924, *s.* 1974, *m.*	Earl of Mount Charles, *b.* 1951
1791 I.	*Donegall (7th),* Dermot Richard Claud Chichester, LVO, *b.* 1916, *s.* 1975, *w.*	Earl of Belfast, *b.* 1952
1789 I.	*Downshire (9th),* (Arthur Francis) Nicholas Wills Hill, *b.* 1959, *s.* 2003, *m.*	Earl of Hillsborough, *b.* 1996
1801 I.	*Ely (8th),* Charles John Tottenham, *b.* 1913, *s.* 1969, *w.*	Viscount Loftus, *b.* 1943
1801	*Exeter (8th),* (William) Michael Anthony Cecil, *b.* 1935, *s.* 1988, *m.*	Lord Burghley, *b.* 1970
1800 I.	*Headfort (6th),* Thomas Geoffrey Charles Michael Taylour, *b.* 1932, *s.* 1960, *m.*	Earl of Bective, *b.* 1959
1793	*Hertford (9th),* Henry Jocelyn Seymour, *b.* 1958, *s.* 1997, *m.*	Earl of Yarmouth, *b.* 1993
1599 S.	*Huntly (13th),* Granville Charles Gomer Gordon, *b.* 1944, *s.* 1987, *m. Premier Marquess of Scotland*	Earl of Aboyne, *b.* 1973
1784	*Lansdowne (9th),* Charles Maurice Mercer Nairne Petty-Fitzmaurice, *b.* 1941, *s.* 1999, *m.*	Earl of Shelburne, *b.* 1970
1902	*Linlithgow (4th),* Adrian John Charles Hope, *b.* 1946, *s.* 1987, *m.*	Earl of Hopetoun, *b.* 1969
1816 I.	*Londonderry (9th),* Alexander Charles Robert Vane-Tempest-Stewart, *b.* 1937, *s.* 1955, *m.*	Viscount Castlereagh, *b.* 1972
1701 S.	*Lothian (12th),* Peter Francis Walter Kerr, KCVO, *b.* 1922, *s.* 1940, *m.*	Earl of Ancram, PC, MP, *b.* 1945
1917	*Milford Haven (4th),* George Ivar Louis Mountbatten, *b.* 1961, *s.* 1970, *m.*	Earl of Medina, *b.* 1991
1838	*Normanby (5th),* Constantine Edmund Walter Phipps, *b.* 1954, *s.* 1994, *m.*	Earl of Mulgrave, *b.* 1994

Created	*Title, order of succession, name, etc.*	*Heir*
1812	*Northampton (7th),* Spencer Douglas David Compton, *b.* 1946, *s.* 1978, *m.*	Earl Compton, *b.* 1973
1682 S.	*Queensberry (12th),* David Harrington Angus Douglas, *b.* 1929, *s.* 1954	Viscount Drumlanrig, *b.* 1967
1926	*Reading (4th),* Simon Charles Henry Rufus Isaacs, *b.* 1942, *s.* 1980, *m.*	Viscount Erleigh, *b.* 1986
1789	*Salisbury (7th) and Baron Gascoyne-Cecil (life peerage, 1999),* Robert Michael James Gascoyne-Cecil, PC, *b.* 1946, *s.* 2003, *m.*	Viscount Cranborne, *b.* 1970
1800 I.	*Sligo (11th),* Jeremy Ulick Browne, *b.* 1939, *s.* 1991, *m.*	Sebastian U. B., *b.* 1964
1787	° *Townshend (7th),* George John Patrick Dominic Townshend, *b.* 1916, *s.* 1921, *w.*	Viscount Raynham, *b.* 1945
1694 S.	*Tweeddale (13th),* Edward Douglas John Hay, *b.* 1947, *s.* 1979	Lord Charles D. M. H., *b.* 1947
1789 I.	*Waterford (8th),* John Hubert de la Poer Beresford, *b.* 1933, *s.* 1934, *m.*	Earl of Tyrone, *b.* 1958
1551	*Winchester (18th),* Nigel George Paulet, *b.* 1941, *s.* 1968, *m. Premier Marquess of England*	Earl of Wiltshire, *b.* 1969
1892	*Zetland (4th),* Lawrence Mark Dundas, *b.* 1937, *s.* 1989, *m.*	Earl of Ronaldshay, *b.* 1965

EARLS

Coronet, Eight silver balls on stalks alternating with eight gold strawberry leaves
Style, The Right Hon. the Earl (of) _
Wife's style, The Right Hon. the Countess (of) _
Eldest son's style, Takes his father's second title as a courtesy title
Younger sons' style, 'The Hon.' before forename and family name
Daughters' style, 'Lady' before forename and family name
For forms of address, *see* page 43

Created	*Title, order of succession, name, etc.*	*Heir*
1639 S.	*Airlie (13th),* David George Coke Patrick Ogilvy, KT, GCVO, PC, Royal Victorian Chain, *b.* 1926, *s.* 1968, *m.*	Lord Ogilvy, *b.* 1958
1696	*Albemarle (10th),* Rufus Arnold Alexis Keppel, *b.* 1965, *s.* 1979, *m.*	Crispian W. J. K., *b.* 1948
1952	° *Alexander of Tunis (2nd),* Shane William Desmond Alexander, *b.* 1935, *s.* 1969, *m.*	Hon. Brian J. A., *b.* 1939
1662	*Annandale and Hartfell (11th),* Patrick Andrew Wentworth Hope Johnstone, *b.* 1941, *s.* 1983, *m.* claim established 1985	Lord Johnstone, *b.* 1971
1789	° *Annesley (11th),* Philip Harrison Annesley, *b.* 1927, *s.* 2001, *m.*	*Hon.* Michael R. A., *b.* 1933
1785	*Antrim (9th),* Alexander Randal Mark McDonnell, *b.* 1935, *s.* 1977, *m.*	Viscount Dunluce, *b.* 1967
1762	** *Arran (9th),* Arthur Desmond Colquhoun Gore, *b.* 1938, *s.* 1983, *m.*	Paul A. G., CMG, CVO, *b.* 1921
1955	° ** *Attlee (3rd),* John Richard Attlee, *b.* 1956, *s.* 1991, *m.*	None
1714	*Aylesford (11th),* Charles Ian Finch-Knightley, *b.* 1918, *s.* 1958, *w.*	Lord Guernsey, *b.* 1947
1937	° ** *Baldwin of Bewdley (4th),* Edward Alfred Alexander Baldwin, *b.* 1938, *s.* 1976, *w.*	Viscount Corvedale, *b.* 1973
1922	*Balfour (5th),* Roderick Francis Arthur Balfour, *b.* 1948, *s.* 2003, *m.*	Charles G. Y. B., *b.* 1951
1772	° *Bathurst (8th),* Henry Allen John Bathurst, *b.* 1927, *s.* 1943, *m.*	Lord Apsley, *b.* 1961
1919	° *Beatty (3rd),* David Beatty, *b.* 1946, *s.* 1972, *m.*	Viscount Borodale, *b.* 1973
1797	*Belmore (8th),* John Armar Lowry-Corry, *b.* 1951, *s.* 1960, *m.*	Viscount Corry, *b.* 1985
1739 I.	*Bessborough (12th),* Myles Fitzhugh Longfield Ponsonby, *b.* 1941, *s.* 2002, *m.*	Viscount Duncannon, *b.* 1974
1815	*Bradford (7th),* Richard Thomas Orlando Bridgeman, *b.* 1947, *s.* 1981, *m.*	Viscount Newport, *b.* 1980
1469	*Buchan (17th),* Malcolm Harry Erskine, *b.* 1930, *s.* 1984, *m.*	Lord Cardross, *b.* 1960
1746	*Buckinghamshire (10th),* (George) Miles Hobart-Hampden, *b.* 1944, *s.* 1983, *m.*	Sir John Hobart, Bt., *b.* 1945
1800	° *Cadogan (8th),* Charles Gerald John Cadogan, *b.* 1937, *s.* 1997, *m.*	Viscount Chelsea, *b.* 1966
1878	° *Cairns (6th),* Simon Dallas Cairns, CVO, CBE, *b.* 1939, *s.* 1989, *m.*	Viscount Garmoyle, *b.* 1965
1455	** *Caithness (20th),* Malcolm Ian Sinclair, PC, *b.* 1948, *s.* 1965, *w.*	Lord Berriedale, *b.* 1981
1800	*Caledon (7th),* Nicholas James Alexander, *b.* 1955, *s.* 1980, *m.*	Viscount Alexander, *b.* 1990
1661	*Carlisle (13th),* George William Beaumont Howard, *b.* 1949, *s.* 1994	Hon. Philip C. W. H., *b.* 1963
1793	*Carnarvon (8th),* George Reginald Oliver Molyneux Herbert, *b.* 1956, *s.* 2001, *m.*	Lord Porchester, *b.* 1992
1748 I.	*Carrick (10th),* David James Theobald Somerset Butler, *b.* 1953, *s.* 1992, *m.*	Viscount Ikerrin, *b.* 1975

Created		*Title, order of succession, name, etc.*	*Heir*
1800 I.	°	*Castle Stewart (8th),* Arthur Patrick Avondale Stuart, *b.* 1928, *s.* 1961, *w.*	Viscount Stuart, *b.* 1953
1814	°	*Cathcart (7th),* Charles Alan Andrew Cathcart, *b.* 1952, *s.* 1999, *m.*	Lord Greenock, *b.* 1986
1647 I.		*Cavan,* The 12th Earl died in 1988.	†Roger C. Lambart, *b.* 1944
1827	°	*Cawdor (7th),* Colin Robert Vaughan Campbell, *b.* 1962, *s.* 1993, *m.*	Viscount Emlyn, *b.* 1998
1801		*Chichester (9th),* John Nicholas Pelham, *b.* 1944, *s.* 1944, *m.*	Richard A. H. P., *b.* 1952
1803 I.		*Clancarty (9th),* Nicholas Power Richard Le Poer Trench, *b.* 1952, *s.* 1995	None
1776 I.		*Clanwilliam (7th),* John Herbert Meade, *b.* 1919, *s.* 1989, *w.*	Lord Gillford, *b.* 1960
1776		*Clarendon (7th),* George Frederick Laurence Hyde Villiers, *b.* 1933, *s.* 1955, *m.*	Lord Hyde, *b.* 1976
1620 I.		*Cork and Orrery (15th),* John Richard Boyle, *b.* 1945, *s.* 2003, *m.*	Viscount Dungarvan, *b.* 1978
1850		*Cottenham (9th),* Mark John Henry Pepys, *b.* 1983, *s.* 2000	Hon. Sam R. P., *b.* 1986
1762 I.	**	*Courtown (9th),* James Patrick Montagu Burgoyne Winthrop Stopford, *b.* 1954, *s.* 1975, *m.*	Viscount Stopford, *b.* 1988
1697		*Coventry (13th),* Victor Gerald Coventry, *b.* 1917, *s.* 2004, *m.*	George W. C., *b.* 1939
1857	°	*Cowley (7th),* Garret Graham Wellesley, *b.* 1934, *s.* 1975, *m.*	Viscount Dangan, *b.* 1965
1892		*Cranbrook (5th),* Gathorne Gathorne-Hardy, *b.* 1933, *s.* 1978, *m.*	Lord Medway, *b.* 1968
1801 M.		*Craven (9th),* Benjamin Robert Joseph Craven, *b.* 1989, *s.* 1990	Rupert J. E. C., *b.* 1926
1398 S.		*Crawford (29th) and Balcarres (12th) (S. 1651) and Baron Balniel (life peerage, 1974),* Robert Alexander Lindsay, KT, GCVO, PC, *b.* 1927, *s.* 1975, *m. Premier Earl on Union Roll*	Lord Balniel, *b.* 1958
1861		*Cromartie (5th),* John Ruaridh Blunt Grant Mackenzie, *b.* 1948, *s.* 1989, *m.*	Viscount Tarbat, *b.* 1987
1901		*Cromer (4th),* Evelyn Rowland Esmond Baring, *b.* 1946, *s.* 1991, *m.*	Viscount Errington, *b.* 1994
1633 S.		*Dalhousie (17th),* James Hubert Ramsay, *b.* 1948, *s.* 1999, *m.*	Lord Ramsay, *b.* 1981
1725 I.		*Darnley (11th),* Adam Ivo Stuart Bligh, *b.* 1941, *s.* 1980, *m.*	Lord Clifton, *b.* 1968
1711		*Dartmouth (10th),* William Legge, *b.* 1949, *s.* 1997	Hon. Rupert L., *b.* 1951
1761	°	*De La Warr (11th),* William Herbrand Sackville, *b.* 1948, *s.* 1988, *m.*	Lord Buckhurst, *b.* 1979
1622		*Denbigh (12th) and Desmond (11th) (I. 1622),* Alexander Stephen Rudolph Feilding, *b.* 1970, *s.* 1995, *m.*	William D. F., *b.* 1939
1485		*Derby (19th),* Edward Richard William Stanley, *b.* 1962, *s.* 1994, *m.*	Lord Stanley, *b.* 1998
1553		*Devon (18th),* Hugh Rupert Courtenay, *b.* 1942, *s.* 1998, *m.*	Lord Courtenay, *b.* 1975
1800 I.		*Donoughmore (8th),* Richard Michael John Hely-Hutchinson, *b.* 1927, *s.* 1981, *w.*	Viscount Suirdale, *b.* 1952
1661 I.		*Drogheda (12th),* Henry Dermot Ponsonby Moore, *b.* 1937, *s.* 1989, *m.*	Viscount Moore, *b.* 1983
1837		*Ducie (7th),* David Leslie Moreton, *b.* 1951, *s.* 1991, *m.*	Lord Moreton, *b.* 1981
1860		*Dudley (4th),* William Humble David Ward, *b.* 1920, *s.* 1969, *m.*	Viscount Ednam, *b.* 1947
1660 S.	**	*Dundee (12th),* Alexander Henry Scrymgeour, *b.* 1949, *s.* 1983, *m.*	Lord Scrymgeour, *b.* 1982
1669 S.		*Dundonald (15th),* Iain Alexander Douglas Blair Cochrane, *b.* 1961, *s.* 1986, *m.*	Lord Cochrane, *b.* 1991
1686 S.		*Dunmore (12th),* Malcolm Kenneth Murray, *b.* 1946, *s.* 1995, *m.*	Hon. Geoffrey C. M., *b.* 1949
1822 I.		*Dunraven and Mount-Earl (7th),* Thady Windham Thomas Wyndham-Quin, *b.* 1939, *s.* 1965, *m.*	None
1833		*Durham (6th),* Antony Claud Frederick Lambton, *b.* 1922, *s.* 1970, *m.*, Disclaimed for life 1970	Hon. Edward R. L. (Baron Durham), *b.* 1961
1837		*Effingham (7th),* David Mowbray Algernon Howard, *b.* 1939, *s.* 1996, *m.*	Lord Howard of Effingham, *b.* 1971
1507 S.		*Eglinton (18th) and Winton (9th) (S. 1600),* Archibald George Montgomerie, *b.* 1939, *s.* 1966, *m.*	Lord Montgomerie, *b.* 1966
1733 I.		*Egmont (12th),* Thomas Frederick Gerald Perceval, *b.* 1934, *s.* 2001, *m.*	Hon. Donald W. P., *b.* 1954
1821		*Eldon (5th),* John Joseph Nicholas Scott, *b.* 1937, *s.* 1976, *m.*	Viscount Encombe, *b.* 1962
1633 S.		*Elgin (11th) and Kincardine (15th) (S. 1647),* Andrew Douglas Alexander Thomas Bruce, KT, *b.* 1924, *s.* 1968, *m.*	Lord Bruce, *b.* 1961
1789 I.		*Enniskillen (7th),* Andrew John Galbraith Cole, *b.* 1942, *s.* 1989, *m.*	Arthur G. C., *b.* 1920
1789 I.		*Erne (6th),* Henry George Victor John Crichton, *b.* 1937, *s.* 1940, *m.*	Viscount Crichton, *b.* 1971
1452 S.	**	*Erroll (24th),* Merlin Sereld Victor Gilbert Hay, *b.* 1948, *s.* 1978, *m. Hereditary Lord High Constable and Knight Marischal of Scotland*	Lord Hay, *b.* 1984
1661		*Essex (10th),* Robert Edward de Vere Capell, *b.* 1920, *s.* 1981, *m.*	Viscount Malden, *b.* 1944
1711	° **	*Ferrers (13th),* Robert Washington Shirley, PC, *b.* 1929, *s.* 1954, *m.*	Viscount Tamworth, *b.* 1952
1789	°	*Fortescue (8th),* Charles Hugh Richard Fortescue, *b.* 1951, *s.* 1993, *m.*	Hon. Martin D. F., *b.* 1924
1841		*Gainsborough (5th),* Anthony Gerard Edward Noel, *b.* 1923, *s.* 1927, *m.*	Viscount Campden, *b.* 1950
1623 S.		*Galloway (13th),* Randolph Keith Reginald Stewart, *b.* 1928, *s.* 1978, *w.*	Andrew C. S., *b.* 1949

Created	*Title, order of succession, name, etc.*	*Heir*
1703 S.	*Glasgow (10th),* Patrick Robin Archibald Boyle, *b.* 1939, *s.* 1984, *m.*	Viscount of Kelburn, *b.* 1978
1806 I.	*Gosford (7th),* Charles David Nicholas Alexander John Sparrow Acheson, *b.* 1942, *s.* 1966, *m.*	Hon. Patrick B. V. M. A., *b.* 1915
1945	*Gowrie (2nd),* Alexander Patrick Greysteil Hore-Ruthven, PC, *b.* 1939, *s.* 1955, *m.*	Viscount Ruthven of Canberra, *b.* 1964
1684 I.	*Granard (10th),* Peter Arthur Edward Hastings Forbes, *b.* 1957, *s.* 1992, *m.*	Viscount Forbes, *b.* 1981
1833	° *Granville (6th),* Granville George Fergus Leveson-Gower, *b.* 1959, *s.* 1996, *m.*	Lord Leveson, *b.* 1999
1806	° *Grey (6th),* Richard Fleming George Charles Grey, *b.* 1939, *s.* 1963, *m.*	Philip K. G., *b.* 1940
1752	*Guilford (10th),* Piers Edward Brownlow North, *b.* 1971, *s.* 1999, *m.*	Lord North, *b.* 2002
1619	*Haddington (13th),* John George Baillie-Hamilton, *b.* 1941, *s.* 1986, *m.*	Lord Binning, *b.* 1985
1919	° *Haig (2nd),* George Alexander Eugene Douglas Haig, OBE, *b.* 1918, *s.* 1928, *m.*	Viscount Dawick, *b.* 1961
1944	*Halifax (3rd),* Charles Edward Peter Neil Wood, *b.* 1944, *s.* 1980, *m.*	Lord Irwin, *b.* 1977
1898	*Halsbury (4th),* Adam Edward Giffard, *b.* 1934, *s.* 2000, *m.*	None
1754	*Hardwicke (10th),* Joseph Philip Sebastian Yorke, *b.* 1971, *s.* 1974	Charles E. Y., *b.* 1951
1812	*Harewood (7th),* George Henry Hubert Lascelles, KBE, *b.* 1923, *s.* 1947, *m.*	Viscount Lascelles, *b.* 1950
1742	*Harrington (11th),* William Henry Leicester Stanhope, *b.* 1922, *s.* 1929, *m.*	Viscount Petersham, *b.* 1945
1809	*Harrowby (7th),* Dudley Danvers Granville Coutts Ryder, TD, *b.* 1922, *s.* 1987, *m.*	Viscount Sandon, *b.* 1951
1605	** *Home (15th),* David Alexander Cospatrick Douglas-Home, CVO, CBE, *b.* 1943, *s.* 1995, *m.*	Lord Dunglass, *b.* 1987
1821	° ** *Howe (7th),* Frederick Richard Penn Curzon, *b.* 1951, *s.* 1984, *m.*	Viscount Curzon, *b.* 1994
1529	*Huntingdon (16th),* William Edward Robin Hood Hastings Bass, LVO, *b.* 1948, *s.* 1990, *m.*	Hon. Simon A. R. H. H. B., *b.* 1950
1885	*Iddesleigh (5th),* John Stafford Northcote, *b.* 1957, *s.* 2004, *m.*	Viscount St Cyres, *b.* 1985
1756	*Ilchester (9th),* Maurice Vivian de Touffreville Fox-Strangways, *b.* 1920, *s.* 1970, *m.*	Hon. Raymond G. F.-S., *b.* 1921
1929	*Inchcape (4th),* (Kenneth) Peter (Lyle) Mackay, *b.* 1943, *s.* 1994, *m.*	Viscount Glenapp, *b.* 1979
1919	*Iveagh (4th),* Arthur Edward Rory Guinness, *b.* 1969, *s.* 1992	Hon. Rory M. B. G., *b.* 1974
1925	° *Jellicoe (2nd) and Baron Jellicoe of Southampton (life peerage, 1999),* George Patrick John Rushworth Jellicoe, KBE, DSO, MC, PC, *b.* 1918, *s.* 1935, *m.*	Viscount Brocas, *b.* 1950
1697	*Jersey (10th),* George Francis William Child Villiers, *b.* 1976, *s.* 1998 *m.*	Hon. Jamie C. V., *b.* 1994
1822 I.	*Kilmorey (6th),* Richard Francis Needham, PC, *b.* 1942, *s.* 1977, *m.*, (does not use title)	Viscount Newry and Mourne, *b.* 1966
1866	*Kimberley (5th),* John Armine Wodehouse, *b.* 1951, *s.* 2002, *m.*	Lord Wodehouse, *b.* 1978
1768 I.	*Kingston (12th),* Robert Charles Henry King-Tenison, *b.* 1969, *s.* 2002, *m.*	Viscount Kingsborough, *b.* 2000
1633 S.	*Kinnoull (15th),* Arthur William George Patrick Hay, *b.* 1935, *s.* 1938, *m.*	Viscount Dupplin, *b.* 1962
1677 S.	*Kintore (13th),* Michael Canning William John Keith, *b.* 1939, *s.* 1989, *m.*	Lord Inverurie, *b.* 1976
1914	° *Kitchener of Khartoum (3rd),* Henry Herbert Kitchener, TD, *b.* 1919, *s.* 1937	None
1624	*Lauderdale (17th),* Patrick Francis Maitland, *b.* 1911, *s.* 1968, *w.*	Viscount Maitland, *b.* 1937
1837	*Leicester (7th),* Edward Douglas Coke, *b.* 1936, *s.* 1994, *m.*	Viscount Coke, *b.* 1965
1641 S.	*Leven (14th) and Melville (13th) (S. 1690),* Alexander Robert Leslie Melville, *b.* 1924, *s.* 1947, *m.*	Lord Balgonie, *b.* 1954
1831	*Lichfield (5th),* Thomas Patrick John Anson, *b.* 1939, *s.* 1960	Viscount Anson, *b.* 1978
1803 I.	*Limerick (7th),* Edmund Christopher Pery, *b.* 1963, *s.* 2003, *m.*	Viscount Glentworth, *b.* 1991
1572	*Lincoln (19th),* Robert Edward Fiennes-Clinton, *b.* 1972, *s.* 2001	Hon. William R. F.-C., *b.* 1980
1633 S.	** *Lindsay (16th),* James Randolph Lindesay-Bethune, *b.* 1955, *s.* 1989, *m.*	Viscount Garnock, *b.* 1990
1626	*Lindsey (14th) and Abingdon (9th) (1682),* Richard Henry Rupert Bertie, *b.* 1931, *s.* 1963, *m.*	Lord Norreys, *b.* 1958
1776 I.	*Lisburne (8th),* John David Malet Vaughan, *b.* 1918, *s.* 1965, *m.*	Viscount Vaughan, *b.* 1945
1822 I.	** *Listowel (6th),* Francis Michael Hare, *b.* 1964, *s.* 1997, *m.*	Hon. Timothy P. H., *b.* 1966
1905	** *Liverpool (5th),* Edward Peter Bertram Savile Foljambe, *b.* 1944, *s.* 1969, *m.*	Viscount Hawkesbury, *b.* 1972
1945	° *Lloyd George of Dwyfor (3rd),* Owen Lloyd George, *b.* 1924, *s.* 1968, *m.*	Viscount Gwynedd, *b.* 1951

Created		*Title, order of succession, name, etc.*	*Heir*
1785 I.		*Longford (8th),* Thomas Frank Dermot Pakenham, *b.* 1933, *s.* 2001, *m.*	Hon. Edward M. P., *b.* 1970
1807		*Lonsdale (7th),* James Hugh William Lowther, *b.* 1922, *s.* 1953, *m.*	Viscount Lowther, *b.* 1949
1633 S.		*Loudoun (14th),* Michael Edward Abney-Hastings, *b.* 1942, *s.* 2002, *m.*	Lord Mauchline, *b.* 1974
1838		*Lovelace (5th),* Peter Axel William Locke King, *b.* 1951, *s.* 1964, *m.*	None
1795 I.		*Lucan (7th),* Richard John Bingham, *b.* 1934, *s.* 1964, *m.* (missing since 8 November 1974)	Lord Bingham, *b.* 1967
1880		*Lytton (5th),* John Peter Michael Scawen Lytton, *b.* 1950, *s.* 1985, *m.*	Viscount Knebworth, *b.* 1989
1721		*Macclesfield (9th),* Richard Timothy George Mansfield Parker, *b.* 1943, *s.* 1992, *m.*	Hon. J. David G. P., *b.* 1945
1800		*Malmesbury (7th),* James Carleton Harris, *b.* 1946, *s.* 2000, *m.*	Viscount FitzHarris, *b.* 1970
1776		*Mansfield and Mansfield (8th) (1792),* William David Mungo James Murray, *b.* 1930, *s.* 1971, *m.*	Viscount Stormont, *b.* 1956
1565 S.		*Mar (14th) and Kellie (16th) (S. 1616) and Baron Erkine of Alloa Tower (life peerage, 2000),* James Thorne Erskine, *b.* 1949, *s.* 1994, *m.*	Hon. Alexander D. E., *b.* 1952
1785 I.		*Mayo (10th),* Terence Patrick Bourke, *b.* 1929, *s.* 1962	Lord Naas, *b.* 1953
1627 I.		*Meath (15th),* John Anthony Brabazon, *b.* 1941, *s.* 1998, *m.*	Lord Ardee, *b.* 1977
1766		*Mexborough (8th),* John Christopher George Savile, *b.* 1931, *s.* 1980, *m.*	Viscount Pollington, *b.* 1959
1813		*Minto (6th),* Gilbert Edward George Lariston Elliot-Murray-Kynynmound, OBE, *b.* 1928, *s.* 1975, *m.*	Viscount Melgund, *b.* 1953
1562 S.		*Moray (20th),* Douglas John Moray Stuart, *b.* 1928, *s.* 1974, *m.*	Lord Doune, *b.* 1966
1815		*Morley (6th),* John St Aubyn Parker, KCVO, *b.* 1923, *s.* 1962, *m.*	Viscount Boringdon, *b.* 1956
1458		*Morton (22nd),* John Charles Sholto Douglas, *b.* 1927, *s.* 1976, *m.*	Lord Aberdour, *b.* 1952
1789		*Mount Edgcumbe (8th),* Robert Charles Edgcumbe, *b.* 1939, *s.* 1982	Piers V. E., *b.* 1946
1805	°	*Nelson (9th),* Peter John Horatio Nelson, *b.* 1941, *s.* 1981, *m.*	Viscount Merton, *b.* 1971
1660 S.		*Newburgh (12th),* Don Filippo Giambattista Camillo Francesco Aldo Maria Rospigliosi, *b.* 1942, *s.* 1986, *m.*	Princess Donna Benedetta F. M. R., *b.* 1974
1827 I.		*Norbury (7th),* Richard James Graham-Toler, *b.* 1967, *s.* 2000	None
1806 I.		*Normanton (6th),* Shaun James Christian Welbore Ellis Agar, *b.* 1945, *s.* 1967, *m.*	Viscount Somerton, *b.* 1982
1647 S.	**	*Northesk (14th),* David John MacRae Carnegie, *b.* 1954, *s.* 1994, *m.*	Patrick C. C., *b.* 1940
1801	**	*Onslow (7th),* Michael William Coplestone Dillon Onslow, *b.* 1938, *s.* 1971, *m.*	Viscount Cranley, *b.* 1967
1696 S.		*Orkney (9th),* (Oliver) Peter St John, *b.* 1938, *s.* 1998, *m.*	Viscount Kirkwall, *b.* 1969
1328 I.		*Ormonde and Ossory (I. 1527),* The 25th/18th Earl (7th Marquess) died in 1988	†Viscount Mountgarret *b.* 1961 (*see* that title)
1925		*Oxford and Asquith (2nd),* Julian Edward George Asquith, KCMG, *b.* 1916, *s.* 1928, *w.*	Viscount Asquith, OBE, *b.* 1952
1929	° **	*Peel (3rd),* William James Robert Peel, *b.* 1947, *s.* 1969, *m.*	Viscount Clanfield, *b.* 1976
1551		*Pembroke (18th) and Montgomery (15th) (1605),* William Alexander Sidney Herbert, *b.* 1978, *s.* 2003	Earl of Carnarvon *b.* 1956 (*see* that title)
1605		*Perth (18th),* John Eric Drummond, *b.* 1935, *s.* 2002, *m.*	Viscount Strathallan, *b.* 1965
1905		*Plymouth (3rd),* Other Robert Ivor Windsor-Clive, *b.* 1923, *s.* 1943, *m.*	Viscount Windsor, *b.* 1951
1785		*Portarlington (7th),* George Lionel Yuill Seymour Dawson-Damer, *b.* 1938, *s.* 1959, *m.*	Viscount Carlow, *b.* 1965
1689		*Portland (12th),* Count Timothy Charles Robert Noel Bentinck, *b.* 1953, *s.* 1997, *m.*	Viscount Woodstock, *b.* 1984
1743		*Portsmouth (10th),* Quentin Gerard Carew Wallop, *b.* 1954, *s.* 1984, *m.*	Viscount Lymington, *b.* 1981
1804		*Powis (8th),* John George Herbert, *b.* 1952, *s.* 1993, *m.*	Viscount Clive, *b.* 1979
1765		*Radnor (8th),* Jacob Pleydell-Bouverie, *b.* 1927, *s.* 1968, *w.*	Viscount Folkestone, *b.* 1955
1831 I.		*Ranfurly (7th),* Gerald Françoys Needham Knox, *b.* 1929, *s.* 1988, *m.*	Viscount Northland, *b.* 1957
1771		*Roden (10th),* Robert John Jocelyn, *b.* 1938, *s.* 1993, *m.*	Viscount Jocelyn, *b.* 1989
1801		*Romney (8th),* Julian Charles Marsham, *b.* 1948, *s.* 2004, *m.*	Hon. David C. M., *b.* 1977
1703 S.		*Rosebery (7th),* Neil Archibald Primrose, *b.* 1929, *s.* 1974, *m.*	Lord Dalmeny, *b.* 1967
1806 I.		*Rosse (7th),* William Brendan Parsons, *b.* 1936, *s.* 1979, *m.*	Lord Oxmantown, *b.* 1969
1801	**	*Rosslyn (7th),* Peter St Clair-Erskine, *b.* 1958, *s.* 1977, *m.*	Lord Loughborough, *b.* 1986
1457 S.		*Rothes (21st),* Ian Lionel Malcolm Leslie, *b.* 1932, *s.* 1975, *m.*	Lord Leslie, *b.* 1958
1861	° **	*Russell (5th),* Conrad Sebastian Robert Russell, *b.* 1937, *s.* 1987, *m.*	Viscount Amberley, *b.* 1968
1915	°	*St Aldwyn (3rd),* Michael Henry Hicks Beach, *b.* 1950, *s.* 1992, *m.*	Hon. David S. H. B., *b.* 1955
1815		*St Germans (10th),* Peregrine Nicholas Eliot, *b.* 1941, *s.* 1988	Lord Eliot, *b.* 1966
1660	**	*Sandwich (11th),* John Edward Hollister Montagu, *b.* 1943, *s.* 1995, *m.*	Viscount Hinchingbrooke, *b.* 1969
1690		*Scarbrough (13th),* Richard Osbert Lumley, *b.* 1973, *s.* 2004	Hon. Thomas H. L., *b.* 1980

Created		*Title, order of succession, name, etc.*	*Heir*
1701 S.		*Seafield (13th),* Ian Derek Francis Ogilvie-Grant, *b.* 1939, *s.* 1969, *m.*	Viscount Reidhaven, *b.* 1963
1882	**	*Selborne (4th),* John Roundell Palmer, KBE, *b.* 1940, *s.* 1971, *m.*	Viscount Wolmer, *b.* 1971
1646 S.		*Selkirk,* Disclaimed for life 1994 (*see* Lord Selkirk of Douglas, page 70)	Hon. John A. D.-H., *b.* 1978
1672		*Shaftesbury (10th),* Anthony Ashley-Cooper, *b.* 1938, *s.* 1961, *m.*	Lord Ashley, *b.* 1977
1756 I.		*Shannon (9th),* Richard Bentinck Boyle, *b.* 1924, *s.* 1963	Viscount Boyle, *b.* 1960
1442	**	*Shrewsbury and Waterford (22nd),* Charles Henry John Benedict Crofton Chetwynd Chetwynd-Talbot, *b.* 1952, *s.* 1980, *m. Premier Earl of England and Ireland*	Viscount Ingestre, *b.* 1978
1961		*Snowdon (1st) and Baron Armstrong-Jones (life peerage, 1999),* Antony Charles Robert Armstrong-Jones, GCVO, *b.* 1930, *m.*	Viscount Linley, *b.* 1961
1765	°	*Spencer (9th),* Charles Edward Maurice Spencer, *b.* 1964, *s.* 1992, *m.*	Viscount Althorp, *b.* 1994
1703 S.		*Stair (14th),* John David James Dalrymple, *b.* 1961, *s.* 1996	Hon. David H. D., *b.* 1963
1984		*Stockton (2nd),* Alexander Daniel Alan Macmillan, MEP, *b.* 1943, *s.* 1986, *m.*	Viscount Macmillan of Ovenden, *b.* 1974
1821		*Stradbroke (6th),* Robert Keith Rous, *b.* 1937, *s.* 1983, *m.*	Viscount Dunwich, *b.* 1961
1847		*Strafford (8th),* Thomas Edmund Byng, *b.* 1936, *s.* 1984, *m.*	Viscount Enfield, *b.* 1964
1606 S.		*Strathmore and Kinghorne (18th) (S. 1677),* Michael Fergus Bowes Lyon, *b.* 1957, *s.* 1987, *m.*	Lord Glamis, *b.* 1986
1603		*Suffolk (21st) and Berkshire (14th) (1626),* Michael John James George Robert Howard, *b.* 1935, *s.* 1941, *m.*	Viscount Andover, *b.* 1974
1955		*Swinton (2nd),* David Yarburgh Cunliffe-Lister, *b.* 1937, *s.* 1972, *m.*	Hon. Nicholas J. C.-L., *b.* 1939
1714		*Tankerville (10th),* Peter Grey Bennet, *b.* 1956, *s.* 1980	Revd the Hon. George A. G. B., *b.* 1925
1822	°	*Temple of Stowe (8th),* (Walter) Grenville Algernon Temple-Gore-Langton, *b.* 1924, *s.* 1988, *m.*	Lord Langton, *b.* 1955
1815		*Verulam (7th),* John Duncan Grimston, *b.* 1951, *s.* 1973, *m.*	Viscount Grimston, *b.* 1978
1729	°	*Waldegrave (13th),* James Sherbrooke Waldegrave, *b.* 1940, *s.* 1995, *m.*	Viscount Chewton, *b.* 1986
1759		*Warwick (9th) and Brooke (9th) (1746),* Guy David Greville, *b.* 1957, *s.* 1996, *m.*	Lord Brooke, *b.* 1982
1633 S.		*Wemyss (12th) and March (8th),* Francis David Charteris, KT, *b.* 1912, *s.* 1937, *m.*	Lord Neidpath, *b.* 1948
1621 I.		*Westmeath (13th),* William Anthony Nugent, *b.* 1928, *s.* 1971, *m.*	Hon. Sean C. W. N., *b.* 1965
1624		*Westmorland (16th),* Anthony David Francis Henry Fane, *b.* 1951, *s.* 1993, *m.*	Hon. Harry St C. F., *b.* 1953
1876		*Wharncliffe (5th),* Richard Alan Montagu Stuart Wortley, *b.* 1953, *s.* 1987, *m.*	Viscount Carlton, *b.* 1980
1801		*Wilton (8th),* Francis Egerton Grosvenor, *b.* 1934, *s.* 1999, *m.*	Viscount Grey de Wilton, *b.* 1959
1628		*Winchilsea (17th) and Nottingham (12th) (1681),* Daniel James Hatfield Finch Hatton, *b.* 1967, *s.* 1999, *m.*	Viscount Maidstone, *b.* 1998
1766	°	*Winterton (8th),* (Donald) David Turnour, *b.* 1943, *s.* 1991, *m.*	Robert C. T., *b.* 1950
1956		*Woolton (3rd),* Simon Frederick Marquis, *b.* 1958, *s.* 1969, *m.*	None
1837		*Yarborough (8th),* Charles John Pelham, *b.* 1963, *s.* 1991, *m.*	Lord Worsley, *b.* 1990

COUNTESSES IN THEIR OWN RIGHT

Style, The Right Hon. the Countess (of) _
Husband, Untitled
Children's style, As for children of an Earl
For forms of address, *see* page 43

Created		*Title, order of succession, name, etc.*	*Heir*
1643 S.		*Dysart (12th in line),* Katherine Grant of Rothiemurchus, *b.* 1918, *s.* 2003	Lord Huntingtower, *b.* 1946
*c.*1115 S.	**	*Mar (31st in line),* Margaret of Mar, *b.* 1940, *s.* 1975, *m. Premier Earldom of Scotland*	Mistress of Mar, *b.* 1963
1947	°	*Mountbatten of Burma (2nd in line),* Patricia Edwina Victoria Knatchbull, CBE, *b.* 1924, *s.* 1979, *m.*	Lord Romsey, *b.* 1947
c..1235 S.		*Sutherland (24th in line),* Elizabeth Millicent Sutherland, *b.* 1921, *s.* 1963, *m.*	Lord Strathnaver, *b.* 1947

VISCOUNTS

Coronet, Sixteen silver balls
Style, The Right Hon. the Viscount _
Wife's style, The Right Hon. the Viscountess _
Children's style, 'The Hon.' before forename and family name
In Scotland, the heir apparent to a Viscount may be styled 'The Master of _ (title of peer)'
For forms of address, *see* page 43

Created		*Title, order of succession, name, etc.*	*Heir*
1945		*Addison (4th),* William Matthew Wand Addison, *b.* 1945, *s.* 1992, *m.*	Hon. Paul W. A., *b.* 1973
1946		*Alanbrooke (3rd),* Alan Victor Harold Brooke, *b.* 1932, *s.* 1972	None
1919	**	*Allenby (3rd),* Lt.-Col. Michael Jaffray Hynman Allenby, *b.* 1931, *s.* 1984, *m.*	Hon. Henry J. H. A., *b.* 1968
1911		*Allendale (4th),* Wentworth Peter Ismay Beaumont, *b.* 1948, *s.* 2002, *m.*	Hon. Wentworth A. I. B., *b.* 1979
1642 S.		*Arbuthnott (16th),* John Campbell Arbuthnott, KT, CBE, DSC, *b.* 1924, *s.* 1966, *m.*	Master of Arbuthnott, *b.* 1950
1751 I.		*Ashbrook (11th),* Michael Llowarch Warburton Flower, *b.* 1935, *s.* 1995, *m.*	Hon. Rowland F. W. F., *b.* 1975
1917	**	*Astor (4th),* William Waldorf Astor, *b.* 1951, *s.* 1966, *m.*	Hon. William W. A., *b.* 1979
1781 I.		*Bangor (8th),* William Maxwell David Ward, *b.* 1948, *s.* 1993, *m.*	Hon. E. Nicholas W., *b.* 1953
1925		*Bearsted (5th),* Nicholas Alan Samuel, *b.* 1950, *s.* 1996, *m.*	Hon. Harry R. S., *b.* 1988
1963		*Blakenham (2nd),* Michael John Hare, *b.* 1938, *s.* 1982, *m.*	Hon. Caspar J. H., *b.* 1972
1935	**	*Bledisloe (3rd),* Christopher Hiley Ludlow Bathurst, QC, *b.* 1934, *s.* 1979	Hon. Rupert E. L. B., *b.* 1964
1712		*Bolingbroke (7th) and St John (8th) (1716),* Kenneth Oliver Musgrave St John, *b.* 1927, *s.* 1974	Hon. Henry F. St J., *b.* 1957
1960		*Boyd of Merton (2nd),* Simon Donald Rupert Neville Lennox-Boyd, *b.* 1939, *s.* 1983, *m.*	Hon. Benjamin A. L.-B., *b.* 1964
1717 I.		*Boyne (11th),* Gustavus Michael Stucley Hamilton-Russell, *b.* 1965, *s.* 1995, *m.*	Hon. Gustavus A. E. H.-R., *b.* 1999
1929		*Brentford (4th),* Crispin William Joynson-Hicks, *b.* 1933, *s.* 1983, *m.*	Hon. Paul W. J.-H., *b.* 1971
1929	**	*Bridgeman (3rd),* Robin John Orlando Bridgeman, *b.* 1930, *s.* 1982, *m.*	Hon. Luke R. O. B., *b.* 1971
1868		*Bridport (4th) and 7th Duke, Bronte in Sicily, 1799,* Alexander Nelson Hood, *b.* 1948, *s.* 1969, *m.*	Hon. Peregrine A. N. H., *b.* 1974
1952	**	*Brookeborough (3rd),* Alan Henry Brooke, *b.* 1952, *s.* 1987, *m.*	Hon. Christopher A. B., *b.* 1954
1933		*Buckmaster (3rd),* Martin Stanley Buckmaster, OBE, *b.* 1921, *s.* 1974	Adrian C. B., *b.* 1949
1939		*Caldecote (3rd),* Piers James Hampden Inskip, *b.* 1947, *s.* 1999, *m.*	Hon. Thomas J. H. I., *b.* 1985
1941		*Camrose (4th),* Adrian Michael Berry, *b.* 1937, *s.* 2001, *m.*	Hon. Jonathan W. B., *b.* 1970
1954		*Chandos (3rd) and Baron Lyttelton of Aldershot (life peerage, 2000),* Thomas Orlando Lyttelton, *b.* 1953, *s.* 1980, *m.*	Hon. Oliver A. L., *b.* 1986
1665 I.		*Charlemont (15th),* John Dodd Caulfeild, *b.* 1966, *s.* 2001, *m.*	Hon. Shane A. C., *b.* 1996
1921		*Chelmsford (4th) and UK Baron Chelmsford, 1858,* Frederic Corin Piers Thesiger, *b.* 1962, *s.* 1999	To Barony only, Roderic M. D. T. *b.* 1915
1717 I.		*Chetwynd (10th),* Adam Richard John Casson Chetwynd, *b.* 1935, *s.* 1965, *m.*	Hon. Adam D. C., *b.* 1969
1911		*Chilston (4th),* Alastair George Akers-Douglas, *b.* 1946, *s.* 1982, *m.*	Hon. Oliver I. A.-D., *b.* 1973
1902		*Churchill (3rd) and 5th UK Baron Churchill, 1815,* Victor George Spencer, *b.* 1934, *s.* 1973	To Barony only, Richard H. R. S., *b.* 1926
1718		*Cobham (11th),* John William Leonard Lyttelton, *b.* 1943, *s.* 1977, *m.*	Hon. Christopher C. L., *b.* 1947
1902	**	*Colville of Culross (4th),* John Mark Alexander Colville, QC, *b.* 1933, *s.* 1945, *m.*	Master of Colville, *b.* 1959
1826		*Combermere (6th),* Thomas Robert Wellington Stapleton-Cotton, *b.* 1969, *s.* 2000	Hon. David P. D. S.-C., *b.* 1932
1917		*Cowdray (4th),* Michael Orlando Weetman Pearson, *b.* 1944, *s.* 1995, *m.*	Hon. Peregrine J. D. P., *b.* 1994
1927	**	*Craigavon (3rd),* Janric Fraser Craig, *b.* 1944, *s.* 1974	None
1886		*Cross (3rd),* Assheton Henry Cross, *b.* 1920, *s.* 1932	None
1943		*Daventry (4th),* James Edward FitzRoy Newdegate, *b.* 1960, *s.* 2000, *m.*	Hon. Humphrey J. F. N., *b.* 1995

Created		*Title, order of succession, name, etc.*	*Heir*
1937		*Davidson (2nd),* John Andrew Davidson, *b.* 1928, *s.* 1970, *m.*	Hon. Malcolm W. M. D., *b.* 1934
1956		*De L'Isle (2nd),* Philip John Algernon Sidney, MBE, *b.* 1945, *s.* 1991, *m.*	Hon. Philip W. E. S., *b.* 1985
1776 I.		*De Vesci (7th),* Thomas Eustace Vesey, *b.* 1955, *s.* 1983, *m.*	Hon. Oliver I. V., *b.* 1991
1917		*Devonport (3rd),* Terence Kearley, *b.* 1944, *s.* 1973	Chester D. H. K., *b.* 1932
1964		*Dilhorne (2nd),* John Mervyn Manningham-Buller, *b.* 1932, *s.* 1980, *m.*	Hon. James E. M.-B., *b.* 1956
1622 I.		*Dillon (22nd),* Henry Benedict Charles Dillon, *b.* 1973, *s.* 1982	Hon. Richard A. L. D., *b.* 1948
1785 I.		*Doneraile (10th),* Richard Allen St Leger, *b.* 1946, *s.* 1983, *m.*	Hon. Nathaniel W. R. St J. St L., *b.* 1971
1680 I.		*Downe (12th),* Richard Henry Dawnay, *b.* 1967, *s.* 2002	Thomas P. D., *b.* 1978
1959		*Dunrossil (3rd),* Andrew William Reginald Morrison, *b.* 1953, *s.* 2000, *m.*	Hon. Callum A. B. M., *b.* 1994
1964		*Eccles (2nd),* John Dawson Eccles, CBE, *b.* 1931, *s.* 1999, *m.*	Hon. William D. E., *b.* 1960
1897		*Esher (5th),* Christopher Gordon Baliol Brett, *b.* 1936, *s.* 2004, *m.*	Hon. Matthew C. A. B., *b.* 1963
1816		*Exmouth (10th),* Paul Edward Pellew, *b.* 1940, *s.* 1970, *m.*	Hon. Edward F. P., *b.* 1978
1620 S.	**	*Falkland (15th),* Lucius Edward William Plantagenet Cary, *b.* 1935, *s.* 1984, *m. Premier Scottish Viscount on the Roll*	Master of Falkland, *b.* 1963
1720		*Falmouth (9th),* George Hugh Boscawen, *b.* 1919, *s.* 1962, *m.*	Hon. Evelyn A. H. B., *b.* 1955
1720 I.		*Gage (8th),* (Henry) Nicolas Gage, *b.* 1934, *s.* 1993, *m.*	Hon. Henry W. G., *b.* 1975
1727 I.		*Galway (12th),* George Rupert Monckton-Arundell, *b.* 1922, *s.* 1980, *m.*	Hon. J. Philip M., *b.* 1952
1478 I.		*Gormanston (17th), 1868,* Jenico Nicholas Dudley Preston, *b.* 1939, *s.* 1940, *w. Premier Viscount of Ireland*	Hon. Jenico F. T. P., *b.* 1974
1816 I.		*Gort (9th),* Foley Robert Standish Prendergast Vereker, *b.* 1951, *s.* 1995, *m.*	Hon. Robert F. P. V., *b.* 1993
1900	**	*Goschen (4th),* Giles John Harry Goschen, *b.* 1965, *s.* 1977, *m.*	Hon. Alexander J. E. G., *b.* 2001
1849		*Gough (5th),* Shane Hugh Maryon Gough, *b.* 1941, *s.* 1951	None
1929		*Hailsham (3rd),* Douglas Martin Hogg, PC, QC, MP, *b.* 1945, *s.* 2001, *m.*	Hon. Quintin J. N. M. H., *b.* 1973
1891		*Hambleden (4th),* William Herbert Smith, *b.* 1930, *s.* 1948, *m.*	Hon. William H. B. S., *b.* 1955
1884		*Hampden (6th),* Anthony David Brand, *b.* 1937, *s.* 1975, *m.*	Hon. Francis A. B., *b.* 1970
1936		*Hanworth (3rd),* David Stephen Geoffrey Pollock, *b.* 1946, *s.* 1996, *m.*	Hon. Richard C. S. P., *b.* 1951
1791 I.		*Harberton (11th),* Henry Robert Pomeroy, *b.* 1958, *s.* 2004, *m.*	Hon. Patrick C. P., *b.* 1995
1846		*Hardinge (7th),* Andrew Hartland Hardinge, *b.* 1960, *s.* 2004, *m.*	Hon. Thomas H. de M. H., *b.* 1993
1791 I.		*Hawarden (9th),* (Robert) Connan Wyndham Leslie Maude, *b.* 1961, *s.* 1991, *m.*	Hon. Varian J. C. E. M., *b.* 1997
1960		*Head (2nd),* Richard Antony Head, *b.* 1937, *s.* 1983, *m.*	Hon. Henry J. H., *b.* 1980
1550		*Hereford (19th),* Charles Robin De Bohun Devereux, *b.* 1975, *s.* 2004, *Premier Viscount of England*	Hon. Edward M. de B. D., *b.* 1977
1842		*Hill (9th),* Peter David Raymond Charles Clegg-Hill, *b.* 1945, *s.* 2003	Paul A. R. C.-H., *b.* 1979
1796		*Hood (8th),* Henry Lyttleton Alexander Hood, *b.* 1958, *s.* 1999, *m.*	Hon. Archibald L. S. H., *b.* 1993
1956		*Ingleby (2nd),* Martin Raymond Peake, *b.* 1926, *s.* 1966, *w.*	None
1945		*Kemsley (3rd),* Richard Gomer Berry, *b.* 1951, *s.* 1999, *m.*	Hon. Luke G. B., *b.* 1998
1911		*Knollys (3rd),* David Francis Dudley Knollys, *b.* 1931, *s.* 1966, *m.*	Hon. Patrick N. M. K., *b.* 1962
1895		*Knutsford (6th),* Michael Holland-Hibbert, *b.* 1926, *s.* 1986, *m.*	Hon. Henry T. H.-H., *b.* 1959
1954		*Leathers (3rd),* Christopher Graeme Leathers, *b.* 1941, *s.* 1996, *m.*	Hon. James F. L., *b.* 1969
1781 I.		*Lifford (9th),* (Edward) James Wingfield Hewitt, *b.* 1949, *s.* 1987, *m.*	Hon. James T. W. H., *b.* 1979
1921		*Long (4th),* Richard Gerard Long, CBE, *b.* 1929, *s.* 1967, *m.*	Hon. James R. L., *b.* 1960
1957		*Mackintosh of Halifax (3rd),* (John) Clive Mackintosh, *b.* 1958, *s.* 1980, *m.*	Hon. Thomas H. G. M., *b.* 1985
1955		*Malvern (3rd),* Ashley Kevin Godfrey Huggins, *b.* 1949, *s.* 1978	Hon. M. James H., *b.* 1928
1945		*Marchwood (3rd),* David George Staveley Penny, *b.* 1936, *s.* 1979, *w.*	Hon. Peter G. W. P., *b.* 1965
1942		*Margesson (2nd),* Francis Vere Hampden Margesson, *b.* 1922, *s.* 1965, *m.*	Capt. Hon. Richard F. D. M., *b.* 1960
1660 I.		*Massereene (14th),* John David Clotworthy Whyte-Melville Foster Skeffington, *b.* 1940, *s.* 1992, *m.*	Hon. Charles J. C. W.-M. F. S., *b.* 1973
1802		*Melville (9th),* Robert David Ross Dundas, *b.* 1937, *s.* 1971, *m.*	Hon. Robert H. K. D., *b.* 1984
1916		*Mersey (4th),* Richard Maurice Clive Bigham, *b.* 1934, *s.* 1979, *m.*	Master of Nairne, *b.* 1966
1717 I.		*Midleton (12th),* Alan Henry Brodrick, *b.* 1949, *s.* 1988, *m.*	Hon. Ashley R. B., *b.* 1980
1962		*Mills (3rd),* Christopher Philip Roger Mills, *b.* 1956, *s.* 1988, *m.*	None
1716 I.		*Molesworth (12th),* Robert Bysse Kelham Molesworth, *b.* 1959, *s.* 1997	Hon. William J. C. M., *b.* 1960
1801 I.		*Monck (7th),* Charles Stanley Monck, *b.* 1953, *s.* 1982. Does not use title	Hon. George S. M., *b.* 1957

Created		*Title, order of succession, name, etc.*	*Heir*
1957		*Monckton of Brenchley (2nd),* Maj.-Gen. Gilbert Walter Riversdale Monckton, CB, OBE, MC, *b.* 1915, *s.* 1965, *m.*	Hon. Christopher W. M., *b.* 1952
1946		*Montgomery of Alamein (2nd),* David Bernard Montgomery, CBE, *b.* 1928, *s.* 1976, *m.*	Hon. Henry D. M., *b.* 1954
1550 I.		*Mountgarret (18th),* Piers James Richard Butler, *b.* 1961, *s.* 2004, *m.*	Hon. Edmund H. R. B., *b.* 1962
1952		*Norwich (2nd),* John Julius Cooper, CVO, *b.* 1929, *s.* 1954, *m.*	Hon. Jason C. D. B. C., *b.* 1959
1651 S.		*Oxfuird (14th),* Ian Arthur Alexander Makgill, *b.* 1969, *s.* 2003	Hon. Robert E. G. M., *b.* 1969
1873		*Portman (10th),* Christopher Edward Berkeley Portman, *b.* 1958, *s.* 1999, *m.*	Hon. Luke O. B. P., *b.* 1984
1743 I.		*Powerscourt (10th),* Mervyn Niall Wingfield, *b.* 1935, *s.* 1973, *m.*	Hon. Mervyn A. W., *b.* 1963
1900		*Ridley (4th),* Matthew White Ridley, KG, GCVO, TD, *b.* 1925, *s.* 1964, *m.*	Hon. Matthew W. R., *b.* 1958
1960		*Rochdale (2nd),* St John Durival Kemp, *b.* 1938, *s.* 1993, *m.*	Hon. Jonathan H. D. K., *b.* 1961
1919		*Rothermere (4th),* (Harold) Jonathan Esmond Vere Harmsworth, *b.* 1967, *s.* 1998, *m.*	Hon. Vere R. J. H. H., *b.* 1994
1937		*Runciman of Doxford (3rd),* Walter Garrison Runciman (Garry), CBE, *b.* 1934, *s.* 1989, *m.*	Hon. David W. R., *b.* 1967
1918		*St Davids (3rd),* Colwyn Jestyn John Philipps, *b.* 1939, *s.* 1991, *m.*	Hon. Rhodri C. P., *b.* 1966
1801		*St Vincent (7th),* Ronald George James Jervis, *b.* 1905, *s.* 1940, *m.*	Hon. Edward R. J. J., *b.* 1951
1937		*Samuel (3rd),* David Herbert Samuel, OBE, PHD, *b.* 1922, *s.* 1978, *m.*	Hon. Dan J. S., *b.* 1925
1911		*Scarsdale (4th),* Peter Ghislain Nathaniel Curzon, *b.* 1949, *s.* 2000, *m.*	Hon. David J. N. C., *b.* 1958
1905 M.		*Selby (6th),* Christopher Rolf Thomas Gully, *b.* 1993, *s.* 2001	Hon. (James) Edward H. G. G., *b.* 1945
1805		*Sidmouth (7th),* John Tonge Anthony Pellew Addington, *b.* 1914, *s.* 1976, *m.*	Hon. Jeremy F. A., *b.* 1947
1940	**	*Simon (3rd),* Jan David Simon, *b.* 1940, *s.* 1993, *m.*	None
1960	**	*Slim (2nd),* John Douglas Slim, OBE, *b.* 1927, *s.* 1970, *m.*	Hon. Mark W. R. S., *b.* 1960
1954		*Soulbury (2nd),* James Herwald Ramsbotham, *b.* 1915, *s.* 1971, *w.*	Hon. Sir Peter E. R., GCMG, GCVO, *b.* 1919
1776 I.		*Southwell (7th),* Pyers Anthony Joseph Southwell, *b.* 1930, *s.* 1960, *m.*	Hon. Richard A. P. S., *b.* 1956
1942		*Stansgate,* Anthony Neil Wedgwood Benn, *b.* 1925, *s.* 1960, *w.* Disclaimed for life 1963.	Stephen M. W. B., *b.* 1951
1959		*Stuart of Findhorn (3rd),* James Dominic Stuart, *b.* 1948, *s.* 1999, *m.*	Hon. Andrew M. S., *b.* 1957
1957	**	*Tenby (3rd),* William Lloyd George, *b.* 1927, *s.* 1983, *m.*	Hon. Timothy H. G. L. G., *b.* 1962
1952		*Thurso (3rd),* John Archibald Sinclair, MP, *b.* 1953, *s.* 1995, *m.*	Hon. James A. R. S., *b.* 1984
1721		*Torrington (11th),* Timothy Howard St George Byng, *b.* 1943, *s.* 1961, *m.*	John L. B., MC, *b.* 1919
1936		*Trenchard (3rd),* Hugh Trenchard, *b.* 1951, *s.* 1987, *m.*	Hon. Alexander T. T., *b.* 1978
1921	**	*Ullswater (2nd),* Nicholas James Christopher Lowther, PC, LVO, *b.* 1942, *s.* 1949, *m.*	Hon. Benjamin J. L., *b.* 1975
1621 I.		*Valentia (15th),* Richard John Dighton Annesley, *b.* 1929, *s.* 1983, *m.*	Hon. Francis W. D. A., *b.* 1959
1952	**	*Waverley (3rd),* John Desmond Forbes Anderson, *b.* 1949, *s.* 1990	Hon. Forbes A. R. A., *b.* 1996
1938		*Weir (3rd),* William Kenneth James Weir, *b.* 1933, *s.* 1975, *m.*	Hon. James W. H. W., *b.* 1965
1918		*Wimborne (4th),* Ivor Mervyn Vigors Guest, *b.* 1968, *s.* 1993	Hon. Julien J. G., *b.* 1945
1923		*Younger of Leckie (5th),* James Edward George Younger, *b.* 1955, *s.* 2003, *m.*	Hon. Alexander W. G. Y., *b.* 1993

BARONS/LORDS

Coronet, Six silver balls
Style, The Right Hon. the Lord _ . In the Peerage of Scotland there is no rank of Baron; the equivalent rank is Lord of Parliament (*see* page 44) and Scottish peers should always be styled 'Lord', never 'Baron'
Wife's style, The Right Hon. the Lady _
Children's style, 'The Hon.' before forename and family name
In Scotland, the heir apparent to a Lord may be styled 'The Master of _ (title of peer)'
For forms of address, *see* page 43

Created		*Title, order of succession, name, etc.*	*Heir*
1911		*Aberconway (4th)*, (Henry) Charles McLaren, *b.* 1948, *s.* 2003, *m.*	Hon. Charles S. M., *b.* 1984
1873	**	*Aberdare (4th)*, Morys George Lyndhurst Bruce, KBE, PC *b.* 1919, *s.* 1957, *m.*	Hon. Alastair J. L. B., *b.* 1947
1835		*Abinger (9th)*, James Harry Scarlett, *b.* 1959, *s.* 2002, *m.*	Hon. Peter R. S., *b.* 1961
1869		*Acton (4th) and Acton of Bridgnorth (life peerage, 2000)*, Richard Gerald Lyon-Dalberg-Acton, *b.* 1941, *s.* 1989, *m.*	Hon. John C. F. H. L.-D.-A., *b.* 1966
1887	**	*Addington (6th)*, Dominic Bryce Hubbard, *b.* 1963, *s.* 1982	Hon. Michael W. L. H., *b.* 1965
1896		*Aldenham (6th) and Hunsdon of Hunsdon (4th) (1923)*, Vicary Tyser Gibbs, *b.* 1948, *s.* 1986, *m.*	Hon. Humphrey W. F. G., *b.* 1989
1962		*Aldington (2nd)*, Charles Harold Stuart Low, *b.* 1948, *s.* 2000, *m.*	Hon. Philip T. A. L., *b.* 1990
1945		*Altrincham (3rd)*, Anthony Ulick David Dundas Grigg, *b.* 1934, *s.* 2001, *m.*	Hon. (Edward) Sebastian G., *b.* 1965
1929		*Alvingham (2nd)*, Maj.-Gen. Robert Guy Eardley Yerburgh, CBE, *b.* 1926, *s.* 1955, *m.*	Capt. Hon. Robert R. G. Y., *b.* 1956
1892		*Amherst of Hackney (4th)*, William Hugh Amherst Cecil, *b.* 1940, *s.* 1980, *m.*	Hon. H. William A. C., *b.* 1968
1881	**	*Ampthill (4th)*, Geoffrey Denis Erskine Russell, CBE, PC, *b.* 1921, *s.* 1973	Hon. David W. E. R., *b.* 1947
1947		*Amwell (3rd)*, Keith Norman Montague, *b.* 1943, *s.* 1990, *m.*	Hon. Ian K. M., *b.* 1973
1863		*Annaly (6th)*, Luke Richard White, *b.* 1954, *s.* 1990, *m.*	Hon. Luke H. W., *b.* 1990
1885		*Ashbourne (4th)*, Edward Barry Greynville Gibson, *b.* 1933, *s.* 1983, *m.*	Hon. Edward C. d'O. G., *b.* 1967
1835		*Ashburton (7th)*, John Francis Harcourt Baring, KG, KCVO, *b.* 1928, *s.* 1991, *m.*	Hon. Mark F. R. B., *b.* 1958
1892		*Ashcombe (4th)*, Henry Edward Cubitt, *b.* 1924, *s.* 1962, *m.*	Mark E. C., *b.* 1964
1911		*Ashton of Hyde (3rd)*, Thomas John Ashton, TD, *b.* 1926, *s.* 1983, *m.*	Hon. Thomas H. A., *b.* 1958
1800 I.		*Ashtown (7th)*, Nigel Clive Crosby Trench, KCMG, *b.* 1916, *s.* 1990, *m.*	Hon. Roderick N. G. T., *b.* 1944
1956	**	*Astor of Hever (3rd)*, John Jacob Astor, *b.* 1946, *s.* 1984, *m.*	Hon. Charles G. J. A., *b.* 1990
1789 I.		*Auckland (10th) and Auckland (10th) (1793)*, Robert Ian Burnard Eden, *b.* 1962, *s.* 1997, *m.*	Hon. Ronald J. E., *b.* 1931
1313		*Audley*, Barony in abeyance between three co-heiresses since 1997	
1900	**	*Avebury (4th)*, Eric Reginald Lubbock, *b.* 1928, *s.* 1971, *m.*	Hon. Lyulph A. J. L., *b.* 1954
1718 I.		*Aylmer (13th)*, Michael Anthony Aylmer, *b.* 1923, *s.* 1982, *m.*	Hon. A. Julian A., *b.* 1951
1929		*Baden-Powell (3rd)*, Robert Crause Baden-Powell, *b.* 1936, *s.* 1962, *m.*	Hon. David M. B.-P., *b.* 1940
1780		*Bagot (10th)*, (Charles Hugh) Shaun Bagot, *b.* 1944, *s.* 2001, *m.*	Richard C. V. B., *b.* 1941
1953		*Baillieu (3rd)*, James William Latham Baillieu, *b.* 1950, *s.* 1973, *m.*	Hon. Robert L. B., *b.* 1979
1607 S.		*Balfour of Burleigh (8th)*, Robert Bruce, *b.* 1927, *s.* 1967, *m.*	Hon. Victoria B., *b.* 1973
1945		*Balfour of Inchrye (2nd)*, Ian Balfour, *b.* 1924, *s.* 1988, *m.*	None
1924		*Banbury of Southam (3rd)*, Charles William Banbury, *b.* 1953, *s.* 1981, *m.*	None
1698		*Barnard (11th)*, Harry John Neville Vane, TD, *b.* 1923, *s.* 1964	Hon. Henry F. C. V., *b.* 1959
1887		*Basing (5th)*, Neil Lutley Sclater-Booth, *b.* 1939, *s.* 1983, *m.*	Hon. Stuart W. S.-B., *b.* 1969
1917		*Beaverbrook (3rd)*, Maxwell William Humphrey Aitken, *b.* 1951, *s.* 1985, *m.*	Hon. Maxwell F. A., *b.* 1977
1647 S.		*Belhaven and Stenton (13th)*, Robert Anthony Carmichael Hamilton, *b.* 1927, *s.* 1961, *m.*	Master of Belhaven, *b.* 1953
1848 I.		*Bellew (7th)*, James Bryan Bellew, *b.* 1920, *s.* 1981, *w.*	Hon. Bryan E. B., *b.* 1943
1856		*Belper (5th)*, Richard Henry Strutt, *b.* 1941, *s.* 1999, *m.*	Hon. Michael H. S., *b.* 1969
1938		*Belstead (2nd) and Ganzoni (life peerage, 1999)*, John Julian Ganzoni, PC, *b.* 1932, *s.* 1958	None

Created		*Title, order of succession, name, etc.*	*Heir*
1421		*Berkeley (18th) and Gueterbock (life peerage, 2000),* Anthony Fitzhardinge Gueterbock, OBE, *b.* 1939, *s.* 1992, *m.*	Hon. Thomas F. G., *b.* 1969
1922		*Bethell (4th),* Nicholas William Bethell, MEP, *b.* 1938, *s.* 1967, *m.*	Hon. James N. B., *b.* 1967
1938		*Bicester (3rd),* Angus Edward Vivian Smith, *b.* 1932, *s.* 1968	Hugh C. V. S., *b.* 1934
1903		*Biddulph (5th),* (Anthony) Nicholas Colin Maitland Biddulph, *b.* 1959, *s.* 1988, *m.*	Hon. Robert J. M. B., *b.* 1994
1938		*Birdwood (3rd),* Mark William Ogilvie Birdwood, *b.* 1938, *s.* 1962, *m.*	None
1958		*Birkett (2nd),* Michael Birkett, *b.* 1929, *s.* 1962, *w.*	Hon. Thomas B., *b.* 1982
1907		*Blyth (4th),* Anthony Audley Rupert Blyth, *b.* 1931, *s.* 1977, *m.*	Hon. James A. I. B., *b.* 1970
1797		*Bolton (8th),* Harry Algar Nigel Orde-Powlett, *b.* 1954, *s.* 2001, *m.*	Hon. Thomas O.-P., *b.* 1979
1452 S.		*Borthwick (24th),* John Hugh Borthwick, *b.* 1940, *s.* 1996, *m.*	Hon. James H. A. B. of Glengelt, *b.* 1940
1922		*Borwick (4th),* James Hugh Myles Borwick, MC, *b.* 1917, *s.* 1961, *m.*	(Geoffrey Robert) James B., *b.* 1955
1761		*Boston (10th),* Timothy George Frank Boteler Irby, *b.* 1939, *s.* 1978, *m.*	Hon. George W. E. B. I., *b.* 1971
1942	**	*Brabazon of Tara (3rd),* Ivon Anthony Moore-Brabazon, *b.* 1946, *s.* 1974, *m.*	Hon. Benjamin R. M.-B., *b.* 1983
1880		*Brabourne (7th),* John Ulick Knatchbull, CBE, *b.* 1924, *s.* 1943, *m.*	Lord Romsey, *b.* 1947
1925		*Bradbury (3rd),* John Bradbury, *b.* 1940, *s.* 1994, *m.*	Hon. John B., *b.* 1973
1962		*Brain (2nd),* Christopher Langdon Brain, *b.* 1926, *s.* 1966, *m.*	Hon. Michael C. B., *b.* 1928
1938		*Brassey of Apethorpe (3rd),* David Henry Brassey, OBE, *b.* 1932, *s.* 1967, *m.*	Hon. Edward B., *b.* 1964
1788		*Braybrooke (10th),* Robin Henry Charles Neville, *b.* 1932, *s.* 1990, *m.*	George N., *b.* 1943
1957	**	*Bridges (2nd),* Thomas Edward Bridges, GCMG, *b.* 1927, *s.* 1969, *m.*	Hon. Mark T. B., *b.* 1954
1945		*Broadbridge (4th),* Martin Hugh Broadbridge, *b.* 1929, *s.* 2000, *m.*	Hon. Richard J. M. B., *b.* 1959
1933		*Brocket (3rd),* Charles Ronald George Nall-Cain, *b.* 1952, *s.* 1967, *m.*	Hon. Alexander C. C. N.-C., *b.* 1984
1860	**	*Brougham and Vaux (5th),* Michael John Brougham, CBE, *b.* 1938, *s.* 1967	Hon. Charles W. B., *b.* 1971
1945		*Broughshane (3rd),* (William) Kensington Davison, DSO, DFC, *b.* 1914, *s.* 1995	None
1776		*Brownlow (7th),* Edward John Peregrine Cust, *b.* 1936, *s.* 1978, *m.*	Hon. Peregrine E. Q. C., *b.* 1974
1942		*Bruntisfield (2nd),* John Robert Warrender, OBE, MC, TD, *b.* 1921, *s.* 1993, *m.*	Hon. Michael J. V. W., *b.* 1949
1950		*Burden (3rd),* Andrew Philip Burden, *b.* 1959, *s.* 1995	Hon. Fraser W. E. B., *b.* 1964
1529		*Burgh (8th),* (Alexander) Gregory Disney Leith, *b.* 1958, *s.* 2001, *m.*	Hon. Alexander J. S. L., *b.* 1986
1903	**	*Burnham (6th),* Hugh John Frederick Lawson, *b.* 1931, *s.* 1993, *m.*	Hon. Harry F. A. L., *b.* 1968
1897		*Burton (3rd),* Michael Evan Victor Baillie, *b.* 1924, *s.* 1962, *m.*	Hon. Evan M. R. B., *b.* 1949
1643		*Byron (13th),* Robert James Byron, *b.* 1950, *s.* 1989, *m.*	Hon. Charles R. G. B., *b.* 1990
1937		*Cadman (3rd),* John Anthony Cadman, *b.* 1938, *s.* 1966, *m.*	Hon. Nicholas A. J. C., *b.* 1977
1945		*Calverley (3rd),* Charles Rodney Muff, *b.* 1946, *s.* 1971, *m.*	Hon. Jonathan E. M., *b.* 1975
1383		*Camoys (7th),* (Ralph) Thomas Campion George Sherman Stonor, GCVO, PC, *b.* 1940, *s.* 1976, *m.*	Hon. R. William R. T. S., *b.* 1974
1715 I.		*Carbery (11th),* Peter Ralfe Harrington Evans-Freke, *b.* 1920, *s.* 1970, *m.*	Hon. Michael P. E.-F., *b.* 1942
1834 I.		*Carew (7th) and Carew (7th) (1838),* Patrick Thomas Conolly-Carew, *b.* 1938, *s.* 1994, *m.*	Hon. William P. C.-C., *b.* 1973
1916		*Carnock (4th),* David Henry Arthur Nicolson, *b.* 1920, *s.* 1982	Nigel N., MBE, *b.* 1917
1796 I.		*Carrington (6th) and Carrington (6th) (1797) and Carington of Upton (life peerage, 1999),* Peter Alexander Rupert Carington, KG, GCMG, CH, MC, PC, *b.* 1919, *s.* 1938, *m.*	Hon. Rupert F. J. C., *b.* 1948
1812		*Castlemaine (8th),* Roland Thomas John Handcock, MBE, *b.* 1943, *s.* 1973, *m.*	Hon. Ronan M. E. H., *b.* 1989
1936		*Catto (3rd),* Innes Gordon Catto, *b.* 1950, *s.* 2001, *m.*	Hon. Alexander G. C., *b.* 1952
1918		*Cawley (4th),* John Francis Cawley, *b.* 1946, *s.* 2001, *m.*	Hon. William R. H. C., *b.* 1981
1937		*Chatfield (2nd),* Ernle David Lewis Chatfield, *b.* 1917, *s.* 1967, *m.*	None
1858		*Chesham (6th),* Nicholas Charles Cavendish, *b.* 1941, *s.* 1989, *m.*	Hon. Charles G. C. C., *b.* 1974
1945		*Chetwode (2nd),* Philip Chetwode, *b.* 1937, *s.* 1950, *m.*	Hon. Roger C., *b.* 1968
1945	**	*Chorley (2nd),* Roger Richard Edward Chorley, *b.* 1930, *s.* 1978, *m.*	Hon. Nicholas R. D. C., *b.* 1966
1858		*Churston (5th),* John Francis Yarde-Buller, *b.* 1934, *s.* 1991, *m.*	Hon. Benjamin F. A. Y.-B., *b.* 1974
1946		*Citrine (3rd),* Ronald Eric Citrine, *b.* 1919, *s.* 1997, *m.* Does not use title	None
1800		*Clanmorris (8th),* Simon John Ward Bingham, *b.* 1937, *s.* 1988, *m.*	Robert D. de B. B., *b.* 1942

Created		*Title, order of succession, name, etc.*	*Heir*
1672		*Clifford of Chudleigh (14th),* Thomas Hugh Clifford, *b.* 1948, *s.* 1988, *m.*	Hon. Alexander T. H. C., *b.* 1985
1299		*Clinton (22nd),* Gerard Nevile Mark Fane Trefusis, *b.* 1934, *s.* 1965, *m.*	Hon. Charles P. R. F. T., *b.* 1962
1955		*Clitheroe (2nd),* Ralph John Assheton, *b.* 1929, *s.* 1984, *m.*	Hon. Ralph C. A., *b.* 1962
1919		*Clwyd (3rd),* (John) Anthony Roberts, *b.* 1935, *s.* 1987, *m.*	Hon. J. Murray R., *b.* 1971
1948		*Clydesmuir (3rd),* David Ronald Colville, *b.* 1949, *s.* 1996, *m.*	Hon. Richard C., *b.* 1980
1960	**	*Cobbold (2nd),* David Antony Fromanteel Lytton Cobbold, *b.* 1937, *s.* 1987, *m.*	Hon. Henry F. L. C., *b.* 1962
1919		*Cochrane of Cults (4th),* (Ralph Henry) Vere Cochrane, *b.* 1926, *s.* 1990, *m.*	Hon. Thomas H. V. C., *b.* 1957
1954		*Coleraine (2nd),* (James) Martin (Bonar) Law, *b.* 1931, *s.* 1980, *m.*	Hon. James P. B. L., *b.* 1975
1873		*Coleridge (5th),* William Duke Coleridge, *b.* 1937, *s.* 1984, *m.*	Hon. James D. C., *b.* 1967
1946		*Colgrain (3rd),* David Colin Campbell, *b.* 1920, *s.* 1973, *m.*	Hon. Alastair C. L. C., *b.* 1951
1917	**	*Colwyn (3rd),* (Ian) Anthony Hamilton-Smith, CBE, *b.* 1942, *s.* 1966, *m.*	Hon. Craig P. H.-S., *b.* 1968
1956		*Colyton (2nd),* Alisdair John Munro Hopkinson, *b.* 1958, *s.* 1996, *m.*	Hon. James P. M. H., *b.* 1983
1841		*Congleton (8th),* Christopher Patrick Parnell, *b.* 1930, *s.* 1967, *m.*	Hon. John P. C. P., *b.* 1959
1927		*Cornwallis (3rd),* Fiennes Neil Wykeham Cornwallis, OBE, *b.* 1921, *s.* 1982, *m.*	Hon. F. W. Jeremy C., *b.* 1946
1874		*Cottesloe (5th),* Cdr. John Tapling Fremantle, *b.* 1927, *s.* 1994, *m.*	Hon. Thomas F. H. F., *b.* 1966
1929		*Craigmyle (4th),* Thomas Columba Shaw, *b.* 1960, *s.* 1998, *m.*	Hon. Alexander F. S., *b.* 1988
1899		*Cranworth (3rd),* Philip Bertram Gurdon, *b.* 1940, *s.* 1964, *w.*	Hon. Sacha W. R. G., *b.* 1970
1959	**	*Crathorne (2nd),* Charles James Dugdale, *b.* 1939, *s.* 1977, *m.*	Hon. Thomas A. J. D., *b.* 1977
1892		*Crawshaw (5th),* David Gerald Brooks, *b.* 1934, *s.* 1997, *m.*	Hon. John P. B., *b.* 1938
1940		*Croft (3rd),* Bernard William Henry Page Croft, *b.* 1949, *s.* 1997, *m.*	None
1797 I.		*Crofton (7th),* Guy Patrick Gilbert Crofton, *b.* 1951, *s.* 1989, *m.*	Hon. E. Harry P. C., *b.* 1988
1375		*Cromwell (7th),* Godfrey John Bewicke-Copley, *b.* 1960, *s.* 1982, *m.*	Hon. David G. B.-C., *b.* 1997
1947		*Crook (3rd),* Robert Douglas Edwin Crook, *b.* 1955, *s.* 2001, *m.*	Hon. Matthew R. C., *b.* 1990
1920		*Cullen of Ashbourne (3rd),* Edmund Willoughby Marsham Cokayne, *b.* 1916, *s.* 2000, *w.*	(Hon.) John O'B. M. C., *b.* 1920
1914		*Cunliffe (3rd),* Roger Cunliffe, *b.* 1932, *s.* 1963, *m.*	Hon. Henry C., *b.* 1962
1927		*Daresbury (4th),* Peter Gilbert Greenall, *b.* 1953, *s.* 1996, *m.*	Hon. Thomas E. G., *b.* 1984
1924		*Darling (3rd),* (Robert) Julian Henry Darling, *b.* 1944, *s.* 2003, *m.*	Hon. Robert J. C. D., *b.* 1972
1946		*Darwen (3rd),* Roger Michael Davies, *b.* 1938, *s.* 1988, *m.*	Hon. Paul D., *b.* 1962
1932		*Davies (3rd),* David Davies, *b.* 1940, *s.* 1944, *m.*	Hon. David D. D., *b.* 1975
1812 I.		*Decies (7th),* Marcus Hugh Tristram de la Poer Beresford, *b.* 1948, *s.* 1992, *m.*	Hon. Robert M. D. de la P. B., *b.* 1988
1299		*de Clifford (27th),* John Edward Southwell Russell, *b.* 1928, *s.* 1982, *m.*	Hon. William S. R., *b.* 1930
1851		*De Freyne (7th),* Francis Arthur John French, *b.* 1927, *s.* 1935, *m.*	Hon. Fulke C. A. J. F., *b.* 1957
1821		*Delamere (5th),* Hugh George Cholmondeley, *b.* 1934, *s.* 1979, *m.*	Hon. Thomas P. G. C., *b.* 1968
1838		*de Mauley (7th),* Rupert Charles Ponsonby, *b.* 1957, *s.* 2002, *m.*	Ashley G. P., *b.* 1959
1937	**	*Denham (2nd),* Bertram Stanley Mitford Bowyer, KBE, PC, *b.* 1927, *s.* 1948, *m.*	Hon. Richard G. G. B., *b.* 1959
1834		*Denman (5th),* Charles Spencer Denman, CBE, MC, TD, *b.* 1916, *s.* 1971, *w.*	Hon. Richard T. S. D., *b.* 1946
1885		*Deramore (6th),* Richard Arthur de Yarburgh-Bateson, *b.* 1911, *s.* 1964, *m.*	None
1887		*De Ramsey (4th),* John Ailwyn Fellowes, *b.* 1942, *s.* 1993, *m.*	Hon. Freddie J. F., *b.* 1978
1264		*de Ros (28th),* Peter Trevor Maxwell, *b.* 1958, *s.* 1983, *m. Premier Baron of England*	Hon. Finbar J. M., *b.* 1988
1881		*Derwent (5th),* Robin Evelyn Leo Vanden-Bempde-Johnstone, LVO, *b.* 1930, *s.* 1986, *m.*	Hon. Francis P. H. V.-B.-J., *b.* 1965
1831		*de Saumarez (7th),* Eric Douglas Saumarez, *b.* 1956, *s.* 1991, *m.*	Hon. Victor T. S., *b.* 1956
1910		*de Villiers (4th),* Alexander Charles de Villiers, *b.* 1940, *s.* 2001, *m.*	None
1930		*Dickinson (2nd),* Richard Clavering Hyett Dickinson, *b.* 1926, *s.* 1943, *m.*	Hon. Martin H. D., *b.* 1961
1620 I.		*Digby (12th) and Digby (5th) (1765),* Edward Henry Kenelm Digby, KCVO, *b.* 1924, *s.* 1964, *m.*	Hon. Henry N. K. D., *b.* 1954
1615		*Dormer (17th),* Geoffrey Henry Dormer, *b.* 1920, *s.* 1995, *m.*	Hon. William R. D., *b.* 1960
1943		*Dowding (3rd),* Piers Hugh Tremenheere Dowding, *b.* 1948, *s.* 1992	Hon. Mark D. J. D., *b.* 1949
1439		*Dudley (15th),* Jim Anthony Hill Wallace, *b.* 1930, *s.* 2002, *m.*	Hon. Jeremy W. G. W., *b.* 1964
1800 I.		*Dufferin and Clandeboye,* The 10th Baron died in 1991.	†Sir John Blackwood, Bt., *b.* 1944
1929		*Dulverton (3rd),* (Gilbert) Michael Hamilton Wills, *b.* 1944, *s.* 1992	Hon. Robert A. H. W., *b.* 1983
1800 I.		*Dunalley (7th),* Henry Francis Cornelius Prittie, *b.* 1948, *s.* 1992, *m.*	Hon. Joel H. P., *b.* 1981
1324 I.		*Dunboyne (29th),* John Fitzwalter Butler, *b.* 1951, *s.* 2004, *m.*	Hon. Richard P. T. B., *b.* 1983

Created		Title, order of succession, name, etc.	Heir
1892		*Dunleath (6th),* Brian Henry Mulholland, *b.* 1950, *s.* 1997, *m.*	Hon. Andrew H. M., *b.* 1981
1439 I.		*Dunsany (20th),* Edward John Carlos Plunkett, *b.* 1939, *s.* 1999, *m.*	Hon. Randal P., *b.* 1983
1780		*Dynevor (9th),* Richard Charles Uryan Rhys, *b.* 1935, *s.* 1962	Hon. Hugo G. U. R., *b.* 1966
1963		*Egremont (2nd) and Leconfield (7th) (1859),* John Max Henry Scawen Wyndham, *b.* 1948, *s.* 1972, *m.*	Hon. George R. V. W., *b.* 1983
1643		*Elibank (14th),* Alan D'Ardis Erskine-Murray, *b.* 1923, *s.* 1973, *w.*	Master of Elibank, *b.* 1964
1802		*Ellenborough (8th),* Richard Edward Cecil Law, *b.* 1926, *s.* 1945, *m.*	Maj. Hon. Rupert E. H. L., *b.* 1955
1509 S.		*Elphinstone (19th) and Elphinstone (5th) (1885),* Alexander Mountstuart Elphinstone, *b.* 1980, *s.* 1994	Hon. Angus J. E., *b.* 1982
1934	**	*Elton (2nd),* Rodney Elton, TD, *b.* 1930, *s.* 1973, *m.*	Hon. Edward P. E., *b.* 1966
1627 S.		*Fairfax of Cameron (14th),* Nicholas John Albert Fairfax, *b.* 1956, *s.* 1964, *m.*	Hon. Edward N. T. F., *b.* 1984
1961		*Fairhaven (3rd),* Ailwyn Henry George Broughton, *b.* 1936, *s.* 1973, *m.*	Maj. Hon. James H. A. B., *b.* 1963
1916		*Faringdon (3rd),* Charles Michael Henderson, *b.* 1937, *s.* 1977, *m.*	Hon. James H. H., *b.* 1961
1756		*Farnham (13th),* Simon Kenlis Maxwell, *b.* 1933, *s.* 2001, *m.*	Hon. Robin S. M., *b.* 1965
1856		*Fermoy (6th),* Patrick Maurice Burke Roche, *b.* 1967, *s.* 1984, *m.*	Hon. E. Hugh B. R., *b.* 1972
1826		*Feversham (6th),* Charles Antony Peter Duncombe, *b.* 1945, *s.* 1963, *m.*	Hon. Jasper O. S. D., *b.* 1968
1798 I.		*ffrench (8th),* Robuck John Peter Charles Mario ffrench, *b.* 1956, *s.* 1986, *m.*	Hon. John C. M. J. F. ff., *b.* 1928
1909		*Fisher (3rd),* John Vavasseur Fisher, DSC, *b.* 1921, *s.* 1955, *m.*	Hon. Patrick V. F., *b.* 1953
1295		*Fitzwalter (21st),* (Fitzwalter) Brook Plumptre, *b.* 1914, *s.* 1953, *m.*	Hon. Julian B. P., *b.* 1952
1776		*Foley (8th),* Adrian Gerald Foley, *b.* 1923, *s.* 1927, *m.*	Hon. Thomas H. F., *b.* 1961
1445		*Forbes (22nd),* Nigel Ivan Forbes, KBE, *b.* 1918, *s.* 1953, *m. Premier Lord of Scotland*	Master of Forbes, *b.* 1946
1821		*Forester (9th),* Charles Richard George Weld-Forester, *b.* 1975, *s.* 2003,	Wolstan W. W.-F., *b.* 1941
1922		*Forres (4th),* Alastair Stephen Grant Williamson, *b.* 1946, *s.* 1978, *m.*	Hon. George A. M. W., *b.* 1972
1917		*Forteviot (4th),* John James Evelyn Dewar, *b.* 1938, *s.* 1993, *w.*	Hon. Alexander J. E. D., *b.* 1971
1951	**	*Freyberg (3rd),* Valerian Bernard Freyberg, *b.* 1970, *s.* 1993	None
1917		*Gainford (3rd),* Joseph Edward Pease, *b.* 1921, *s.* 1971, *m.*	Hon. George P., *b.* 1926
1818		*Garvagh (5th),* (Alexander Leopold Ivor) George Canning, *b.* 1920, *s.* 1956, *m.*	Hon. Spencer G. S. de R. C., *b.* 1953
1942	**	*Geddes (3rd),* Euan Michael Ross Geddes, *b.* 1937, *s.* 1975, *m.*	Hon. James G. N. G., *b.* 1969
1876		*Gerard (5th),* Anthony Robert Hugo Gerard, *b.* 1949, *s.* 1992, *m.*	Hon. Rupert B. C. G., *b.* 1981
1824		*Gifford (6th),* Anthony Maurice Gifford, *b.* 1940, *s.* 1961, *m.*	Hon. Thomas A. G., *b.* 1967
1917		*Gisborough (3rd),* Thomas Richard John Long Chaloner, *b.* 1927, *s.* 1951, *m.*	Hon. T. Peregrine L. C., *b.* 1961
1960		*Gladwyn (2nd),* Miles Alvery Gladwyn Jebb, *b.* 1930, *s.* 1996	None
1899		*Glanusk (5th),* Christopher Russell Bailey, *b.* 1942, *s.* 1997, *m.*	Hon. Charles H. B., *b.* 1976
1918	**	*Glenarthur (4th),* Simon Mark Arthur, *b.* 1944, *s.* 1976, *m.*	Hon. Edward A. A., *b.* 1973
1911		*Glenconner (3rd),* Colin Christopher Paget Tennant, *b.* 1926, *s.* 1983, *m.*	Cody C. E. T., *b.* 1994
1964		*Glendevon (2nd),* Julian John Somerset Hope, *b.* 1950, *s.* 1996	Hon. Jonathan C. H., *b.* 1952
1922		*Glendyne (3rd),* Robert Nivison, *b.* 1926, *s.* 1967, *m.*	Hon. John N., *b.* 1960
1939	**	*Glentoran (3rd),* (Thomas) Robin (Valerian) Dixon, CBE, *b.* 1935, *s.* 1995, *m.*	Hon. Daniel G. D., *b.* 1959
1909		*Gorell (4th),* Timothy John Radcliffe Barnes, *b.* 1927, *s.* 1963, *m.*	Hon. Ronald A. H. B., *b.* 1931
1953	**	*Grantchester (3rd),* Christopher John Suenson-Taylor, *b.* 1951, *s.* 1995, *m.*	Hon. Jesse D. S.-T., *b.* 1977
1782		*Grantley (8th),* Richard William Brinsley Norton, *b.* 1956, *s.* 1995	Hon. Francis J. H. N., *b.* 1960
1794 I.		*Graves (10th),* Timothy Evelyn Graves, *b.* 1960, *s.* 2002	None
1445 S.		*Gray (23rd),* Andrew Godfrey Diarmid Stuart Campbell-Gray, *b.* 1964, *s.* 2003, *m.*	Master of Gray, *b.* 1996
1950		*Greenhill (3rd),* Malcolm Greenhill, *b.* 1924, *s.* 1989	None
1927	**	*Greenway (4th),* Ambrose Charles Drexel Greenway, *b.* 1941, *s.* 1975, *m.*	Hon. Nigel. P. G., *b.* 1944
1902		*Grenfell (3rd) and Grenfell of Kilvey (life peerage, 2000),* Julian Pascoe Francis St Leger Grenfell, *b.* 1935, *s.* 1976, *m.*	Francis P. J. G., *b.* 1938
1944		*Gretton (4th),* John Lysander Gretton, *b.* 1975, *s.* 1989	None
1397		*Grey of Codnor (6th),* Richard Henry Cornwall-Legh, *b.* 1936, *s.* 1996, *m.*	Hon. Richard S. C. C.-L., *b.* 1976
1955		*Gridley (3rd),* Richard David Arnold Gridley, *b.* 1956, *s.* 1996, *m.*	Hon. Carl R. G., *b.* 1981
1964		*Grimston of Westbury (3rd),* Robert John Sylvester Grimston, *b.* 1951, *s.* 2003, *m.*	Hon. Gerald C. W. G., *b.* 1953

Created		*Title, order of succession, name, etc.*	*Heir*
1886		*Grimthorpe (5th),* Edward John Beckett, *b.* 1954, *s.* 2003, *m.*	Hon. Harry M. B., *b.* 1993
1945		*Hacking (3rd),* Douglas David Hacking, *b.* 1938, *s.* 1971, *m.*	Hon. Douglas F. H., *b.* 1968
1950		*Haden-Guest (5th),* Christopher Haden-Guest, *b.* 1948, *s.* 1996, *m.*	Hon. Nicholas H.-G., *b.* 1951
1886		*Hamilton of Dalzell (4th),* James Leslie Hamilton, *b.* 1938, *s.* 1990, *m.*	Hon. Gavin G. H., *b.* 1968
1874		*Hampton (7th),* John Humphrey Arnott Pakington, *b.* 1964, *s.* 2003, *m.*	None
1939		*Hankey (3rd),* Donald Robin Alers Hankey, *b.* 1938, *s.* 1996, *m.*	Hon. Alexander M. A. H., *b.* 1947
1958		*Harding of Petherton (2nd),* John Charles Harding, *b.* 1928, *s.* 1989, *m.*	Hon. William A. J. H., *b.* 1969
1910		*Hardinge of Penshurst (4th),* Julian Alexander Hardinge, *b.* 1945, *s.* 1997	Hon. Hugh F. H., *b.* 1948
1876		*Harlech (6th),* Francis David Ormsby-Gore, *b.* 1954, *s.* 1985, *m.*	Hon. Jasset D. C. O.-G., *b.* 1986
1939		*Harmsworth (3rd),* Thomas Harold Raymond Harmsworth, *b.* 1939, *s.* 1990, *m.*	Hon. Dominic M. E. H., *b.* 1973
1815		*Harris (8th),* Anthony Harris, *b.* 1942, *s.* 1996, *m.*	Anthony J. T. H., *b.* 1915
1954		*Harvey of Tasburgh (2nd),* Peter Charles Oliver Harvey, *b.* 1921, *s.* 1968, *w.*	Charles J. G. H., *b.* 1951
1295		*Hastings (22nd),* Edward Delaval Henry Astley, *b.* 1912, *s.* 1956, *m.*	Hon. Delaval T. H. A., *b.* 1960
1835		*Hatherton (8th),* Edward Charles Littleton, *b.* 1950, *s.* 1985, *m.*	Hon. Thomas E. L., *b.* 1977
1776		*Hawke (11th),* Edward George Hawke, TD, *b.* 1950, *s.* 1992, *m.*	Hon. William M. T. H., *b.* 1995
1927		*Hayter (4th),* George William Michael Chubb, *b.* 1943, *s.* 2003, *m.*	Hon. Thomas F. F. C., *b.* 1986
1945		*Hazlerigg (3rd),* Arthur Grey Hazlerigg, *b.* 1951, *s.* 2002, *m.*	Hon. Arthur W. G. H., *b.* 1987
1943		*Hemingford (3rd),* (Dennis) Nicholas Herbert, *b.* 1934, *s.* 1982, *m.*	Hon. Christopher D. C. H., *b.* 1973
1906		*Hemphill (5th),* Peter Patrick Fitzroy Martyn Martyn-Hemphill, *b.* 1928, *s.* 1957, *m.*	Hon. Charles A. M. M.-H., *b.* 1954
1799 I.	**	*Henley (8th) and Northington (6th) (1885),* Oliver Michael Robert Eden, *b.* 1953, *s.* 1977, *m.*	Hon. John W. O. E., *b.* 1988
1800 I.		*Henniker (9th) and Hertsmere (5th) (1866),* Mark Ian Philip Chandos Henniker-Major, *b.* 1947, *s.* 2004, *m.*	Hon. Frederick J. C. H.-M., *b.* 1983
1461		*Herbert (19th),* David John Seyfried, *b.* 1952, *s.* 2002, *m.*	Hon. Oliver R. S. H., *b.* 1976
1886		*Herschell (3rd),* Rognvald Richard Farrer Herschell, *b.* 1923, *s.* 1929, *m.*	None
1935		*Hesketh (3rd),* Thomas Alexander Fermor-Hesketh, KBE, PC, *b.* 1950, *s.* 1955, *m.*	Hon. Frederick H. F.-H., *b.* 1988
1828		*Heytesbury (6th),* Francis William Holmes à Court, *b.* 1931, *s.* 1971, *m.*	Hon. James W. H. à. C., *b.* 1967
1886		*Hindlip (6th),* Charles Henry Allsopp, *b.* 1940, *s.* 1993, *m.*	Hon. Henry W. A., *b.* 1973
1950		*Hives (3rd),* Matthew Peter Hives, *b.* 1971, *s.* 1997	Hon. Michael B. H., *b.* 1926
1912		*Hollenden (4th),* Ian Hampden Hope-Morley, *b.* 1946, *s.* 1999, *m.*	Hon. Edward H.-M., *b.* 1981
1897		*Holm Patrick (4th),* Hans James David Hamilton, *b.* 1955, *s.* 1991, *m.*	Hon. Ion H. J. H., *b.* 1956
1797 I.		*Hotham (8th),* Henry Durand Hotham, *b.* 1940, *s.* 1967, *m.*	Hon. William B. H., *b.* 1972
1881		*Hothfield (6th),* Anthony Charles Sackville Tufton, *b.* 1939, *s.* 1991, *m.*	Hon. William S. T., *b.* 1977
1930		*Howard of Penrith (3rd),* Philip Esme Howard, *b.* 1945, *s.* 1999, *m.*	Hon. Thomas Philip H., *b.* 1974
1960		*Howick of Glendale (2nd),* Charles Evelyn Baring, *b.* 1937, *s.* 1973, *m.*	Hon. David E. C. B., *b.* 1975
1796 I.		*Huntingfield (7th),* Joshua Charles Vanneck, *b.* 1954, *s.* 1994, *m.*	Hon. Gerard C. A. V., *b.* 1985
1866	**	*Hylton (5th),* Raymond Hervey Jolliffe, *b.* 1932, *s.* 1967, *m.*	Hon. William H. M. J., *b.* 1967
1933		*Iliffe (3rd),* Robert Peter Richard Iliffe, *b.* 1944, *s.* 1996, *m.*	Hon. Edward R. I., *b.* 1968
1543 I.		*Inchiquin (18th),* Conor Myles John O'Brien, *b.* 1943, *s.* 1982, *m.*	Conor J. A. O'B., *b.* 1952
1962		*Inchyra (2nd),* Robert Charles Reneke Hoyer Millar, *b.* 1935, *s.* 1989, *m.*	Hon. C. James C. H. M., *b.* 1962
1964	**	*Inglewood (2nd),* (William) Richard Fletcher-Vane, MEP, *b.* 1951, *s.* 1989, *m.*	Hon. Henry W. F. F.-V., *b.* 1990
1919		*Inverforth (4th),* Andrew Peter Weir, *b.* 1966, *s.* 1982	Hon. John V. W., *b.* 1935
1941		*Ironside (2nd),* Edmund Oslac Ironside, *b.* 1924, *s.* 1959, *m.*	Hon. Charles E. G. I., *b.* 1956
1952		*Jeffreys (3rd),* Christopher Henry Mark Jeffreys, *b.* 1957, *s.* 1986, *m.*	Hon. Arthur M. H. J., *b.* 1989
1906		*Joicey (5th),* James Michael Joicey, *b.* 1953, *s.* 1993, *m.*	Hon. William J. J., *b.* 1990
1937		*Kenilworth (4th),* (John) Randle Siddeley, *b.* 1954, *s.* 1981, *m.*	Hon. William R. J. S., *b.* 1992
1935		*Kennet (2nd),* Wayland Hilton Young, *b.* 1923, *s.* 1960, *m.*	Hon. W. A. Thoby Y., *b.* 1957
1776 I.		*Kensington (8th) and Kensington (5th) (1886),* Hugh Ivor Edwardes, *b.* 1933, *s.* 1981, *m.*	Hon. W. Owen A. E., *b.* 1964
1951		*Kenswood (2nd),* John Michael Howard Whitfield, *b.* 1930, *s.* 1963, *m.*	Hon. Michael C. W., *b.* 1955
1788		*Kenyon (6th),* Lloyd Tyrell-Kenyon, *b.* 1947, *s.* 1993, *m.*	Hon. Lloyd N. T.-K., *b.* 1972
1947		*Kershaw (4th),* Edward John Kershaw, *b.* 1936, *s.* 1962, *m.*	Hon. John C. E. K., *b.* 1971
1943		*Keyes (2nd),* Roger George Bowlby Keyes, *b.* 1919, *s.* 1945, *w.*	Hon. Charles W. P. K., *b.* 1951

Created		*Title, order of succession, name, etc.*	*Heir*
1909		*Kilbracken (3rd),* John Raymond Godley, DSC, *b.* 1920, *s.* 1950	Hon. Christopher J. G., *b.* 1945
1900		*Killanin (4th),* (George) Redmond Fitzpatrick Morris, *b.* 1947, *s.* 1999, *m.*	Hon. Luke M. G. M., *b.* 1975
1943		*Killearn (3rd),* Victor Miles George Aldous Lampson, *b.* 1941, *s.* 1996, *m.*	Hon. Miles H. M. L., *b.* 1977
1789 I.		*Kilmaine (7th),* John David Henry Browne, *b.* 1948, *s.* 1978, *m.*	Hon. John F. S. B., *b.* 1983
1831		*Kilmarnock (7th),* Alastair Ivor Gilbert Boyd, *b.* 1927, *s.* 1975, *m.*	Hon. Robin J. B., *b.* 1941
1941		*Kindersley (3rd),* Robert Hugh Molesworth Kindersley, *b.* 1929, *s.* 1976, *m.*	Hon. Rupert J. M. K., *b.* 1955
1223 I.		*Kingsale (35th),* John de Courcy, *b.* 1941, *s.* 1969, *Premier Baron of Ireland*	Nevinson M. de C., *b.* 1958
1902		*Kinross (5th),* Christopher Patrick Balfour, *b.* 1949, *s.* 1985, *m.*	Hon. Alan I. B., *b.* 1978
1951		*Kirkwood (3rd),* David Harvie Kirkwood, PHD, *b.* 1931, *s.* 1970, *m.*	Hon. James S. K., *b.* 1937
1800 I.		*Langford (9th),* Col. Geoffrey Alexander Rowley-Conwy, OBE, *b.* 1912, *s.* 1953, *m.*	Hon. Owain G. R.-C., *b.* 1958
1942		*Latham (2nd),* Dominic Charles Latham, *b.* 1954, *s.* 1970	Anthony M. L., *b.* 1954
1431		*Latymer (9th),* Crispin James Alan Nevill Money-Coutts, *b.* 1955, *s.* 2003, *m.*	Hon. Drummond W. T. M.-C., *b.* 1986
1869		*Lawrence (5th),* David John Downer Lawrence, *b.* 1937, *s.* 1968	None
1947		*Layton (3rd),* Geoffrey Michael Layton, *b.* 1947, *s.* 1989, *m.*	Hon. David L., *b.* 1914
1839		*Leigh (6th),* Christopher Dudley Piers Leigh, *b.* 1960, *s.* 2003, *m.*	Hon. Rupert D. L., *b.* 1994
1962		*Leighton of St Mellons (3rd),* Robert William Henry Leighton Seager, *b.* 1955, *s.* 1998	Hon. Simon J. L. S., *b.* 1957
1797		*Lilford (7th),* George Vernon Powys, *b.* 1931, *s.* 1949, *m.*	Hon. Mark V. P., *b.* 1975
1945		*Lindsay of Birker (3rd),* James Francis Lindsay, *b.* 1945, *s.* 1994, *m.*	Alexander S. L., *b.* 1940
1758 I.		*Lisle (9th),* (John) Nicholas Geoffrey Lysaght, *b.* 1960, *s.* 2003	Hon. David J. L., *b.* 1963
1850		*Londesborough (9th),* Richard John Denison, *b.* 1959, *s.* 1968, *m.*	Hon. James F. D., *b.* 1990
1541 I.		*Louth (16th),* Otway Michael James Oliver Plunkett, *b.* 1929, *s.* 1950, *m.*	Hon. Jonathan O. P., *b.* 1952
1458 S.		*Lovat (16th) and Lovat (5th) (1837),* Simon Fraser, *b.* 1977, *s.* 1995	Hon. Jack F., *b.* 1984
1946		*Lucas of Chilworth (3rd),* Simon William Lucas, *b.* 1957, *s.* 2001, *m.*	Hon. John R. M. L., *b.* 1995
1663	**	*Lucas (11th) and Dingwall (14th) (S. 1609),* Ralph Matthew Palmer, *b.* 1951, *s.* 1991	Hon. Lewis E. P., *b.* 1987
1929	**	*Luke (3rd),* Arthur Charles St John Lawson-Johnston, *b.* 1933, *s.* 1996, *m.*	Hon. Ian J. St J. L.-J., *b.* 1963
1914	**	*Lyell (3rd),* Charles Lyell, *b.* 1939, *s.* 1943	None
1859		*Lyveden (7th),* Jack Leslie Vernon, *b.* 1938, *s.* 1999, *m.*	Hon. Colin R. V., *b.* 1967
1959		*MacAndrew (3rd),* Christopher Anthony Colin MacAndrew, *b.* 1945, *s.* 1989, *m.*	Hon. Oliver C. J. M., *b.* 1983
1776 I.		*Macdonald (8th),* Godfrey James Macdonald of Macdonald, *b.* 1947, *s.* 1970, *m.*	Hon. Godfrey E. H. T. M., *b.* 1982
1937		*McGowan (4th),* Harry John Charles McGowan, *b.* 1971, *s.* 2003, *m.*	Hon. Dominic J. W. McG., *b.* 1951
1922		*Maclay (3rd),* Joseph Paton Maclay, *b.* 1942, *s.* 1969, *m.*	Hon. Joseph P. M., *b.* 1977
1955		*McNair (3rd),* Duncan James McNair, *b.* 1947, *s.* 1989, *m.*	Hon. William S. A. M., *b.* 1958
1951		*Macpherson of Drumochter (2nd),* (James) Gordon Macpherson, *b.* 1924, *s.* 1965, *m.*	Hon. James A. M., *b.* 1979
1937	**	*Mancroft (3rd),* Benjamin Lloyd Stormont Mancroft, *b.* 1957, *s.* 1987, *m.*	Hon. Arthur L. S. M., *b.* 1995
1807		*Manners (5th),* John Robert Cecil Manners, *b.* 1923, *s.* 1972, *w.*	Hon. John H. R. M., *b.* 1956
1922		*Manton (4th),* Miles Ronald Marcus Watson, *b.* 1958, *s.* 2003, *m.*	Hon. Thomas N. C. D. W., *b.* 1985
1908		*Marchamley (4th),* William Francis Whiteley, *b.* 1968, *s.* 1994	None
1964		*Margadale (3rd),* Alastair John Morrison, *b.* 1958, *s.* 2003, *m.*	Hon. Declan J. M., *b.* 1993
1961		*Marks of Broughton (3rd),* Simon Richard Marks, *b.* 1950, *s.* 1998, *m.*	Hon. Michael M., *b.* 1989
1964		*Martonmere (2nd),* John Stephen Robinson, *b.* 1963, *s.* 1989	David A. R., *b.* 1965
1776 I.		*Massy (10th),* David Hamon Somerset Massy, *b.* 1947, *s.* 1995	Hon. John H. M., *b.* 1950
1935		*May (3rd),* Michael St John May, *b.* 1931, *s.* 1950, *m.*	Hon. Jasper B. St J. M., *b.* 1965
1928		*Melchett (4th),* Peter Robert Henry Mond, *b.* 1948, *s.* 1973	None
1925		*Merrivale (3rd),* Jack Henry Edmond Duke, *b.* 1917, *s.* 1951, *w.*	Hon. Derek J. P. D., *b.* 1948
1911		*Merthyr,* Trevor Oswin Lewis, CBE, *b.* 1935, *s.* 1977, *m.*	Disclaimed for life 1977. David T. L., *b.* 1977
1919		*Meston (3rd),* James Meston, *b.* 1950, *s.* 1984, *m.*	Hon. Thomas J. D. M., *b.* 1977
1838	**	*Methuen (7th),* Robert Alexander Holt Methuen, *b.* 1931, *s.* 1994, *m.*	James P. A. M.-C., *b.* 1952
1711		*Middleton (12th),* (Digby) Michael Godfrey John Willoughby, MC, *b.* 1921, *s.* 1970	Hon. Michael C. J. W., *b.* 1948
1939		*Milford (4th),* Guy Wogan Philipps, *b.* 1961, *s.* 1999, *m.*	Hon. Archie S. P., *b.* 1997

Created		*Title, order of succession, name, etc.*	*Heir*
1933		*Milne (2nd),* George Douglass Milne, TD, *b.* 1909, *s.* 1948, *m.*	Hon. George A. M., *b.* 1941
1951		*Milner of Leeds (3rd),* Richard James Milner, *b.* 1959, *s.* 2003, *m.*	None
1947		*Milverton (2nd),* Revd Fraser Arthur Richard Richards, *b.* 1930, *s.* 1978, *m.*	Hon. Michael H. R., *b.* 1936
1873		*Moncreiff (6th),* Rhoderick Harry Wellwood Moncreiff, *b.* 1954, *s.* 2002, *m.*	Hon. Harry J. W. M., *b.* 1986
1884		*Monk Bretton (3rd),* John Charles Dodson, *b.* 1924, *s.* 1933, *m.*	Hon. Christopher M. D., *b.* 1958
1885		*Monkswell (5th),* Gerard Collier, *b.* 1947, *s.* 1984, *m.*	Hon. James A. C., *b.* 1977
1728	**	*Monson (11th),* John Monson, *b.* 1932, *s.* 1958, *m.*	Hon. Nicholas J. M., *b.* 1955
1885	**	*Montagu of Beaulieu (3rd),* Edward John Barrington Douglas-Scott-Montagu, *b.* 1926, *s.* 1929, *m.*	Hon. Ralph D.-S.-M., *b.* 1961
1839		*Monteagle of Brandon (6th),* Gerald Spring Rice, *b.* 1926, *s.* 1946, *m.*	Hon. Charles J. S. R., *b.* 1953
1943	**	*Moran (2nd),* (Richard) John (McMoran) Wilson, KCMG, *b.* 1924, *s.* 1977, *m.*	Hon. James M. W., *b.* 1952
1918		*Morris (3rd),* Michael David Morris, *b.* 1937, *s.* 1975, *m.*	Hon. Thomas A. S. M., *b.* 1982
1950		*Morris of Kenwood (2nd),* Philip Geoffrey Morris, *b.* 1928, *s.* 1954, *m.*	Hon. Jonathan D. M., *b.* 1968
1831		*Mostyn (6th),* Llewellyn Roger Lloyd-Mostyn, *b.* 1948, *s.* 2000, *m.*	Hon. Gregory P. R. L.-M., *b.* 1984
1933		*Mottistone (4th),* David Peter Seely, CBE, *b.* 1920, *s.* 1966, *m.*	Hon. Peter J. P. S., *b.* 1949
1945		*Mountevans (3rd),* Edward Patrick Broke Evans, *b.* 1943, *s.* 1974, *m.*	Hon. Jeffrey de C. R. E., *b.* 1948
1283	**	*Mowbray (26th), Segrave (27th) (1295) and Stourton (23rd) (1448),* Charles Edward Stourton, CBE, *b.* 1923, *s.* 1965, *m.*	Hon. Edward W. S. S., *b.* 1953
1932		*Moyne (3rd),* Jonathan Bryan Guinness, *b.* 1930, *s.* 1992, *m.*	Hon. Jasper J. R. G., *b.* 1954
1929	**	*Moynihan (4th),* Colin Berkeley Moynihan, *b.* 1955, *s.* 1997, *m.*	Hon. Nicholas E. B. M., *b.* 1994
1781 I.		*Muskerry (9th),* Robert Fitzmaurice Deane, *b.* 1948, *s.* 1988, *m.*	Hon. Jonathan F. D., *b.* 1986
1627 S.		*Napier (14th) and Ettrick (5th) (1872),* Francis Nigel Napier, KCVO, *b.* 1930, *s.* 1954, *m.*	Master of Napier, *b.* 1962
1868		*Napier of Magdala (6th),* Robert Alan Napier, *b.* 1940, *s.* 1987, *m.*	Hon. James R. N., *b.* 1966
1940		*Nathan (2nd),* Roger Carol Michael Nathan, *b.* 1922, *s.* 1963, *m.*	Hon. Rupert H. B. N., *b.* 1957
1960		*Nelson of Stafford (3rd),* Henry Roy George Nelson, *b.* 1943, *s.* 1995, *m.*	Hon. Alistair W. H. N., *b.* 1973
1959		*Netherthorpe (3rd),* James Frederick Turner, *b.* 1964, *s.* 1982, *m.*	Hon. Andrew J. E. T., *b.* 1993
1946		*Newall (2nd),* Francis Storer Eaton Newall, *b.* 1930, *s.* 1963, *m.*	Hon. Richard H. E. N., *b.* 1961
1776 I.		*Newborough (8th),* Robert Vaughan Wynn, *b.* 1949, *s.* 1998, *m.*	Hon. Charles H. R. W., *b.* 1923
1892		*Newton (5th),* Richard Thomas Legh, *b.* 1950, *s.* 1992, *m.*	Hon. Piers R. L., *b.* 1979
1930		*Noel-Buxton (3rd),* Martin Connal Noel-Buxton, *b.* 1940, *s.* 1980, *m.*	Hon. Charles C. N.-B., *b.* 1975
1957		*Norrie (2nd),* (George) Willoughby Moke Norrie, *b.* 1936, *s.* 1977, *m.*	Hon. Mark W. J. N., *b.* 1972
1884	**	*Northbourne (5th),* Christopher George Walter James, *b.* 1926, *s.* 1982, *m.*	Hon. Charles W. H. J., *b.* 1960
1866	**	*Northbrook (6th),* Francis Thomas Baring, *b.* 1954, *s.* 1990, *m.*	To the Baronetcy, Peter B., *b.* 1939
1878		*Norton (8th),* James Nigel Arden Adderley, *b.* 1947, *s.* 1993, *m.*	Hon. Edward J. A. A., *b.* 1982
1906		*Nunburnholme (6th),* Stephen Charles Wilson, *b.* 1973, *s.* 2000	Hon. David M. W., *b.* 1954
1950		*Ogmore (2nd),* Gwilym Rees Rees-Williams, *b.* 1931, *s.* 1976, *m.*	Hon. Morgan R.-W., *b.* 1937
1870		*O'Hagan (4th),* Charles Towneley Strachey, *b.* 1945, *s.* 1961	Hon. Richard T. S., *b.* 1950
1868		*O'Neill (4th),* Raymond Arthur Clanaboy O'Neill, TD, *b.* 1933, *s.* 1944, *m.*	Hon. Shane S. C. O'N., *b.* 1965
1836 I.		*Oranmore and Browne (5th) and Mereworth (3rd) (1926),* Dominick Geoffrey Thomas Browne, *b.* 1929, *s.* 2002	Hon. Martin M. D. B., *b.* 1931
1933	**	*Palmer (4th),* Adrian Bailie Nottage Palmer, *b.* 1951, *s.* 1990, *m.*	Hon. Hugo B. R. P., *b.* 1980
1914		*Parmoor (4th),* (Frederick Alfred) Milo Cripps, *b.* 1929, *s.* 1977	Michael L. S. C., *b.* 1942
1937		*Pender (3rd),* John Willoughby Denison-Pender, *b.* 1933, *s.* 1965, *m.*	Hon. Henry J. R. D.-P., *b.* 1968
1866		*Penrhyn (7th),* Simon Douglas-Pennant, *b.* 1938, *s.* 2003, *m.*	Hon. Edward S. D.-P., *b.* 1966
1603		*Petre (18th),* John Patrick Lionel Petre, *b.* 1942, *s.* 1989, *m.*	Hon. Dominic W. P., *b.* 1966
1918		*Phillimore (5th),* Francis Stephen Phillimore, *b.* 1944, *s.* 1994, *m.*	Hon. Tristan A. S. P., *b.* 1977
1945		*Piercy (3rd),* James William Piercy, *b.* 1946, *s.* 1981	Hon. Mark E. P. P., *b.* 1953
1827		*Plunket (8th),* Robin Rathmore Plunket, *b.* 1925, *s.* 1975, *m.*	Hon. Shaun A. F. S. P., *b.* 1931
1831		*Poltimore (7th),* Mark Coplestone Bampfylde, *b.* 1957, *s.* 1978, *m.*	Hon. Henry A. W. B., *b.* 1985
1690 S.		*Polwarth (10th),* Henry Alexander Hepburne-Scott, TD, *b.* 1916, *s.* 1944, *m.*	Master of Polwarth, *b.* 1947
1930		*Ponsonby of Shulbrede (4th) and Ponsonby of Roehampton (life peerage, 2000),* Frederick Matthew Thomas Ponsonby, *b.* 1958, *s.* 1990	None
1958		*Poole (2nd),* David Charles Poole, *b.* 1945, *s.* 1993, *m.*	Hon. Oliver J. P., *b.* 1972

Created		*Title, order of succession, name, etc.*	*Heir*
1852		*Raglan (5th),* FitzRoy John Somerset, *b.* 1927, *s.* 1964	Hon. Geoffrey S., *b.* 1932
1932		*Rankeillour (4th),* Peter St Thomas More Henry Hope, *b.* 1935, *s.* 1967	Michael R. H., *b.* 1940
1953		*Rathcavan (3rd),* Hugh Detmar Torrens O'Neill, *b.* 1939, *s.* 1994, *m.*	Hon. François H. N. O'N., *b.* 1984
1916		*Rathcreedan (3rd),* Christopher John Norton, *b.* 1949, *s.* 1990, *m.*	Hon. Adam G. N., *b.* 1952
1868		*Rathdonnell (5th),* Thomas Benjamin McClintock-Bunbury, *b.* 1938, *s.* 1959, *m.*	Hon. William L. M.-B., *b.* 1966
1911		*Ravensdale (3rd),* Nicholas Mosley, MC, *b.* 1923, *s.* 1966, *m.*	Hon. Shaun N. M., *b.* 1949
1821		*Ravensworth (9th),* Thomas Arthur Hamish Liddell, *b.* 1954, *s.* 2004, *m.*	Hon. Henry A. T. L., *b.* 1987
1821		*Rayleigh (6th),* John Gerald Strutt, *b.* 1960, *s.* 1988, *m.*	Hon. John F. S., *b.* 1993
1937	**	*Rea (3rd),* John Nicolas Rea, MD, *b.* 1928, *s.* 1981, *m.*	Hon. Matthew J. R., *b.* 1956
1628 S.	**	*Reay (14th),* Hugh William Mackay, *b.* 1937, *s.* 1963, *m.*	Master of Reay, *b.* 1965
1902		*Redesdale (6th) and Mitford (life peerage 2000),* Rupert Bertram Mitford, *b.* 1967, *s.* 1991, *m.*	Hon. Bertram D. M., *b.* 2000
1940		*Reith,* Christopher John Reith, *b.* 1928, *s.* 1971, *m.* Disclaimed for life 1972.	Hon. James H. J. R., *b.* 1971
1928		*Remnant (3rd),* James Wogan Remnant, CVO, *b.* 1930, *s.* 1967, *m.*	Hon. Philip J. R., *b.* 1954
1806		*Rendlesham (9th),* Charles William Brooke Thellusson, *b.* 1954, *s.* 1999, *m.*	Hon. Peter R. T., *b.* 1920
1933		*Rennell (3rd),* (John Adrian) Tremayne Rodd, *b.* 1935, *s.* 1978, *m.*	Hon. James R. D. T. R., *b.* 1978
1964		*Renwick (2nd),* Harry Andrew Renwick, *b.* 1935, *s.* 1973, *m.*	Hon. Robert J. R., *b.* 1966
1885		*Revelstoke (6th),* James Cecil Baring, *b.* 1938, *s.* 2003, *m.*	Hon. Alexander R. B., *b.* 1970
1905		*Ritchie of Dundee (5th),* (Harold) Malcolm Ritchie, *b.* 1919, *s.* 1978, *m.*	Hon. C. Rupert R. R., *b.* 1958
1935		*Riverdale (3rd),* Anthony Robert Balfour, *b.* 1960, *s.* 1998	Hon. David R. B., *b.* 1938
1961		*Robertson of Oakridge (2nd),* William Ronald Robertson, *b.* 1930, *s.* 1974, *m.*	Hon. William B. E. R., *b.* 1975
1938		*Roborough (3rd),* Henry Massey Lopes, *b.* 1940, *s.* 1992, *m.*	Hon. Massey J. H. L., *b.* 1969
1931		*Rochester (2nd),* Foster Charles Lowry Lamb, *b.* 1916, *s.* 1955, *w.*	Hon. David C. L., *b.* 1944
1934		*Rockley (3rd),* James Hugh Cecil, *b.* 1934, *s.* 1976, *m.*	Hon. Anthony R. C., *b.* 1961
1782		*Rodney (10th),* George Brydges Rodney, *b.* 1953, *s.* 1992, *m.*	Hon. John G. B. R., *b.* 1999
1651 S.		*Rollo (14th) and Dunning (5th) (1869),* David Eric Howard Rollo, *b.* 1943, *s.* 1997, *m.*	Master of Rollo, *b.* 1972
1959		*Rootes (3rd),* Nicholas Geoffrey Rootes, *b.* 1951, *s.* 1992, *m.*	William B. R., *b.* 1944
1796 I.		*Rossmore (7th) and Rossmore (6th) (1838),* William Warner Westenra, *b.* 1931, *s.* 1958, *m.*	Hon. Benedict W. W., *b.* 1983
1939	**	*Rotherwick (3rd),* (Herbert) Robin Cayzer, *b.* 1954, *s.* 1996, *m.*	Hon. H. Robin C., *b.* 1989
1885		*Rothschild (4th),* (Nathaniel Charles) Jacob Rothschild, OM, GBE, *b.* 1936, *s.* 1990, *m.*	Hon. Nathaniel P. V. J. R., *b.* 1971
1911		*Rowallan (4th),* John Polson Cameron Corbett, *b.* 1947, *s.* 1993	Hon. Jason W. P. C. C., *b.* 1972
1947		*Rugby (3rd),* Robert Charles Maffey, *b.* 1951, *s.* 1990, *m.*	Hon. Timothy J. H. M., *b.* 1975
1919		*Russell of Liverpool (3rd),* Simon Gordon Jared Russell, *b.* 1952, *s.* 1981, *m.*	Hon. Edward C. S. R., *b.* 1985
1876		*Sackville (7th),* Robert Bertrand Sackville-West, *b.* 1958, *s.* 2004, *m.*	Hon. Arthur S.-W., *b.* 2000
1964		*St Helens (2nd),* Richard Francis Hughes-Young, *b.* 1945, *s.* 1980, *m.*	Hon. Henry T. H.-Y., *b.* 1986
1559	**	*St John of Bletso (21st),* Anthony Tudor St John, *b.* 1957, *s.* 1978, *m.*	Hon. Oliver B. St J., *b.* 1995
1887		*St Levan (4th),* John Francis Arthur St Aubyn, DSC, *b.* 1919, *s.* 1978, *w.*	Hon. O. Piers St. A., *b.* 1920
1885		*St Oswald (6th),* Charles Rowland Andrew Winn, *b.* 1959, *s.* 1999, *m.*	Hon. Rowland C. S. H. W., *b.* 1986
1960		*Sanderson of Ayot,* Alan Lindsay Sanderson, *b.* 1931, *s.* 1971, *m.* Disclaimed for life 1971.	Hon. Michael S., *b.* 1959
1945		*Sandford (2nd),* Revd John Cyril Edmondson, DSC, *b.* 1920, *s.* 1959, *m.*	Hon. James J. M. E., *b.* 1949
1871		*Sandhurst (6th),* Guy Rees John Mansfield, *b.* 1949, *s.* 2002, *m.*	Hon. Edward J. M., *b.* 1982
1802		*Sandys (7th),* Richard Michael Oliver Hill, *b.* 1931, *s.* 1961, *m.*	The Marquess of Downshire
1888		*Savile (3rd),* George Halifax Lumley-Savile, *b.* 1919, *s.* 1931	John A. T. L-S., *b.* 1947
1447		*Saye and Sele (21st),* Nathaniel Thomas Allen Fiennes, *b.* 1920, *s.* 1968, *m.*	Hon. Martin G. F., *b.* 1961
1826		*Seaford (6th),* Colin Humphrey Felton Ellis, *b.* 1946, *s.* 1999, *m.*	Hon. Benjamin F. T. E., *b.* 1976
1932	**	*Selsdon (3rd),* Malcolm McEacharn Mitchell-Thomson, *b.* 1937, *s.* 1963, *m.*	Hon. Callum M. M. M.-T., *b.* 1969
1489 S.		*Sempill (21st),* James William Stuart Whitemore Sempill, *b.* 1949, *s.* 1995, *m.*	Master of Sempill, *b.* 1979
1916		*Shaughnessy (4th),* Michael James Shaughnessy, *b.* 1946, *s.* 2003	Charles, G. P. S., *b.* 1955
1946		*Shepherd (3rd),* Graham George Shepherd, *b.* 1949, *s.* 2001, *m.*	Hon. Patrick M. S.
1964		*Sherfield (2nd),* Christopher James Makins, *b.* 1942, *s.* 1996, *m.*	Hon. Dwight W. M., *b.* 1951
1902		*Shuttleworth (5th),* Charles Geoffrey Nicholas Kay-Shuttleworth, *b.* 1948, *s.* 1975, *m.*	Hon. Thomas E. K.-S., *b.* 1976

Created		*Title, order of succession, name, etc.*	*Heir*
1950		*Silkin (3rd),* Christopher Lewis Silkin, *b.* 1947, *s.* 2001	Rory L. S., *b.* 1954
1963		*Silsoe (2nd),* David Malcolm Trustram Eve *b.* 1930, *s.* 1976, *m.*	Hon. Simon R. T. E., *b.* 1966
1947		*Simon of Wythenshawe (3rd),* Matthew Simon, *b.* 1955, *s.* 2002	Martin S., *b.* 1944
1449 S.		*Sinclair (18th),* Matthew Murray Kennedy St Clair, *b.* 1968, *s.* 2004	Malcolm A. J. St C., *b.* 1927
1957		*Sinclair of Cleeve (3rd),* John Lawrence Robert Sinclair, *b.* 1953, *s.* 1985	None
1919		*Sinha (6th),* Arup Kumar Sinha, *b.* 1966, *s.* 1999	Hon. Dilip K. S., *b.* 1967
1828	**	*Skelmersdale (7th),* Roger Bootle-Wilbraham, *b.* 1945, *s.* 1973, *m.*	Hon. Andrew B.-W., *b.* 1977
1916		*Somerleyton (3rd),* Savile William Francis Crossley, GCVO, *b.* 1928, *s.* 1959, *m.*	Hon. Hugh F. S. C., *b.* 1971
1784		*Somers (9th),* Philip Sebastian Somers Cocks, *b.* 1948, *s.* 1995	Alan B. C., *b.* 1930
1780		*Southampton (6th),* Charles James FitzRoy, *b.* 1928, *s.* 1989, *m.*	Hon. Edward C. F., *b.* 1955
1959		*Spens (4th),* Patrick Nathaniel George Spens, *b.* 1968, *s.* 2001, *m.*	Hon. Peter L. S., *b.* 2000
1640		*Stafford (15th),* Francis Melfort William Fitzherbert, *b.* 1954, *s.* 1986, *m.*	Hon. Benjamin J. B. F., *b.* 1983
1938		*Stamp (4th),* Trevor Charles Bosworth Stamp, MD, *b.* 1935, *s.* 1987, *m.*	Hon. Nicholas C. T. S., *b.* 1978
1839		*Stanley of Alderley (8th),* Sheffield (8th) (I. 1738) and Eddisbury (7th) (1848), Thomas Henry Oliver Stanley, *b.* 1927, *s.* 1971, *m.*	Hon. Richard O. S., *b.* 1956
1318	**	*Strabolgi (11th),* David Montague de Burgh Kenworthy, *b.* 1914, *s.* 1953, *m.*	Andrew D. W. K., *b.* 1967
1954		*Strang (2nd),* Colin Strang, *b.* 1922, *s.* 1978, *m.*	None
1955		*Strathalmond (3rd),* William Roberton Fraser, *b.* 1947, *s.* 1976, *m.*	Hon. William G. F., *b.* 1976
1936		*Strathcarron (2nd),* David William Anthony Blyth Macpherson, *b.* 1924, *s.* 1937, *m.*	Hon. Ian D. P. M., *b.* 1949
1955	**	*Strathclyde (2nd),* Thomas Galloway Dunlop du Roy de Blicquy Galbraith, PC, *b.* 1960, *s.* 1985, *m.*	Hon. Charles W. du R. de B. G., *b.* 1962
1900		*Strathcona and Mount Royal (4th),* Donald Euan Palmer Howard, *b.* 1923, *s.* 1959, *m.*	Hon. D. Alexander S. H., *b.* 1961
1836		*Stratheden (6th) and Campbell (6th) (1841),* Donald Campbell, *b.* 1934, *s.* 1987, *m.*	Hon. David A. C., *b.* 1963
1884		*Strathspey (6th),* James Patrick Trevor Grant of Grant, *b.* 1943, *s.* 1992, *m.*	Hon. Michael P. F. G., *b.* 1953
1838		*Sudeley (7th),* Merlin Charles Sainthill Hanbury-Tracy, *b.* 1939, *s.* 1941	D. Andrew J. H.-T., *b.* 1928
1786		*Suffield (11th),* Anthony Philip Harbord-Hamond, MC, *b.* 1922, *s.* 1951, *w.*	Hon. Charles A. A. H.-H., *b.* 1953
1893		*Swansea (4th),* John Hussey Hamilton Vivian, *b.* 1925, *s.* 1934, *m.*	Hon. Richard A. H. V., *b.* 1957
1907		*Swaythling (5th),* Charles Edgar Samuel Montagu, *b.* 1954, *s.* 1998, *m.*	Hon. Anthony T. S. M., *b.* 1931
1919	**	*Swinfen (3rd),* Roger Mynors Swinfen Eady, *b.* 1938, *s.* 1977, *m.*	Hon. Charles R. P. S. E., *b.* 1971
1935		*Sysonby (3rd),* John Frederick Ponsonby, *b.* 1945, *s.* 1956	None
1831 I.		*Talbot of Malahide (10th),* Reginald John Richard Arundell, *b.* 1931, *s.* 1987, *m.*	Hon. Richard J. T. A., *b.* 1957
1946		*Tedder (3rd),* Robin John Tedder, *b.* 1955, *s.* 1994, *m.*	Hon. Benjamin J. T., *b.* 1985
1884		*Tennyson (5th),* Cdr. Mark Aubrey Tennyson, DSC, *b.* 1920, *s.* 1991, *m.*	David H. A. T., *b.* 1960
1918		*Terrington (6th),* Christopher Richard James Woodhouse, MB, *b.* 1946, *s.* 2001, *m.*	Hon. Jack H. L. W., *b.* 1978
1940		*Teviot (2nd),* Charles John Kerr, *b.* 1934, *s.* 1968, *m.*	Hon. Charles R. K., *b.* 1971
1616		*Teynham (20th),* John Christopher Ingham Roper-Curzon, *b.* 1928, *s.* 1972, *m.*	Hon. David J. H. I. R.-C., *b.* 1965
1964		*Thomson of Fleet (2nd),* Kenneth Roy Thomson, *b.* 1923, *s.* 1976, *m.*	Hon. David K. R. T., *b.* 1957
1792		*Thurlow (8th),* Francis Edward Hovell-Thurlow-Cumming-Bruce, KCMG, *b.* 1912, *s.* 1971, *w.*	Hon. Roualeyn R. H.-T.-C.-B., *b.* 1952
1876		*Tollemache (5th),* Timothy John Edward Tollemache, *b.* 1939, *s.* 1975, *m.*	Hon. Edward J. H. T., *b.* 1976
1564 S.		*Torphichen (15th),* James Andrew Douglas Sandilands, *b.* 1946, *s.* 1975, *m.*	Robert P. S., *b.* 1950
1947	**	*Trefgarne (2nd),* David Garro Trefgarne, PC, *b.* 1941, *s.* 1960, *m.*	Hon. George G. T., *b.* 1970
1921		*Trevethin (4th) and Oaksey (2nd) (1947),* John Geoffrey Tristram Lawrence, OBE, *b.* 1929, *s.* 1971, *m.*	Hon. Patrick J. T. L., *b.* 1960
1880		*Trevor (5th),* Marke Charles Hill-Trevor, *b.* 1970, *s.* 1997, *m.*	Hon. Iain R. H.-T., *b.* 1971
1461 I.		*Trimlestown (21st),* Raymond Charles Barnewall, *b.* 1930, *s.* 1997	None
1940		*Tryon (3rd),* Anthony George Merrik Tryon, *b.* 1940, *s.* 1976	Hon. Charles G. B. T., *b.* 1976
1935		*Tweedsmuir (3rd),* William de l'Aigle Buchan, *b.* 1916, *s.* 1996, *m.*	Hon. John W. H. de l'A. B., *b.* 1950
1523		*Vaux of Harrowden (11th),* Anthony William Gilbey, *b.* 1940, *s.* 2002, *m.*	Hon. Richard H. G. G., *b.* 1965
1800 I.		*Ventry (8th),* Andrew Wesley Daubeny de Moleyns, *b.* 1943, *s.* 1987, *m.*	Hon. Francis W. D. de M., *b.* 1965
1762		*Vernon (11th),* Anthony William Vernon-Harcourt, *b.* 1939, *s.* 2000, *m.*	Hon. Simon A. V-H., *b.* 1969

Created	*Title, order of succession, name, etc.*	*Heir*
1922	*Vestey (3rd),* Samuel George Armstrong Vestey, *b.* 1941, *s.* 1954, *m.*	Hon. William G. V., *b.* 1983
1841	*Vivian (7th),* Charles Crespigny Hussey Vivian, *b.* 1966, *s.* 2004	Hon. Victor A. R. B. V., *b.* 1940
1934	*Wakehurst (3rd),* (John) Christopher Loder, *b.* 1925, *s.* 1970, *m.*	Hon. Timothy W. L., *b.* 1958
1723	** *Walpole (10th) and Walpole of Wolterton (8th) (1756),* Robert Horatio Walpole, *b.* 1938, *s.* 1989, *m.*	Hon. Jonathan R. H. W., *b.* 1967
1780	*Walsingham (9th),* John de Grey, MC, *b.* 1925, *s.* 1965, *m.*	Hon. Robert de. G., *b.* 1969
1936	*Wardington (2nd),* Christopher Henry Beaumont Pease, *b.* 1924, *s.* 1950, *m.*	Hon. William S. P., *b.* 1925
1792 I.	*Waterpark (7th),* Frederick Caryll Philip Cavendish, *b.* 1926, *s.* 1948, *m.*	Hon. Roderick A. C., *b.* 1959
1942	*Wedgwood (4th),* Piers Anthony Weymouth Wedgwood, *b.* 1954, *s.* 1970, *m.*	John W., *b.* 1919
1861	*Westbury (6th),* Richard Nicholas Bethell, MBE, *b.* 1950, *s.* 2001, *m.*	Hon. Alexander B., *b.* 1986
1944	*Westwood (3rd),* (William) Gavin Westwood, *b.* 1944, *s.* 1991, *m.*	Hon. W. Fergus W., *b.* 1972
1544/5	*Wharton (12th),* Myles Christopher David Robertson, *b.* 1964, *s.* 2000, *m.*	Hon. Christopher J. R., *b.* 1969
1935	*Wigram (2nd),* (George) Neville (Clive) Wigram, MC, *b.* 1915, *s.* 1960, *w.*	Maj. Hon. Andrew F. C. W., *b.* 1949
1491	** *Willoughby de Broke (21st),* Leopold David Verney, *b.* 1938, *s.* 1986, *m.*	Hon. Rupert G. V., *b.* 1966
1946	*Wilson (2nd),* Patrick Maitland Wilson, *b.* 1915, *s.* 1964, *w.*	None
1937	*Windlesham (3rd) and Hennesy (life peerage, 1999),* David James George Hennessy, CVO, PC, *b.* 1932, *s.* 1962, *w.*	Hon. James R. H., *b.* 1968
1951	*Wise (2nd),* John Clayton Wise, *b.* 1923, *s.* 1968, *m.*	Hon. Christopher J. C. W., *b.* 1949
1869	*Wolverton (7th),* Christopher Richard Glyn, *b.* 1938, *s.* 1988	Hon. Andrew J. G., *b.* 1943
1928	*Wraxall (3rd),* Eustace Hubert Beilby Gibbs, KCVO, CMG, *b.* 1929, *s.* 2001, *w.*	Hon. Anthony H. G., *b.* 1958
1915	*Wrenbury (3rd),* Revd John Burton Buckley, *b.* 1927, *s.* 1940, *m.*	Hon. William E. B., *b.* 1966
1838	*Wrottesley (6th),* Clifton Hugh Lancelot de Verdon Wrottesley, *b.* 1968, *s.* 1977, *m.*	Hon. Stephen J. W., *b.* 1955
1829	*Wynford (9th),* John Philip Robert Best, *b.* 1950, *s.* 2002, *m.*	Hon. Harry R. F. B., *b.* 1987
1308	*Zouche (18th),* James Assheton Frankland, *b.* 1943, *s.* 1965, *m.*	Hon. William T. A. F., *b.* 1984

BARONESSES/LADIES IN THEIR OWN RIGHT

Style, The Right Hon. the Lady _ , *or* The Right Hon. the Baroness _ , according to her preference. Either style may be used, except in the case of Scottish titles (indicated by S.), which are not baronies (*see* page 44) and whose holders are always addressed as Lady
Husband, Untitled
Children's style, As for children of a Baron
For forms of address, *see* page 43

Created	*Title, order of succession, name, etc.*	*Heir*
1664	*Arlington,* Jennifer Jane Forwood, *b.* 1939, *s.* 1999, *w.* Title called out of abeyance 1999	Hon. Patrick J. D. F., *b.* 1967
1455	*Berners (16th),* Pamela Vivien Kirkham, *b.* 1929, *s.* 1995, *m.*	Hon. Rupert W. T. K., *b.* 1953
1529	*Braye (8th),* Mary Penelope Aubrey-Fletcher, *b.* 1941, *s.* 1985, *m.*	Two co-heiresses
1321	*Dacre (27th),* Rachel Leila Douglas-Home, *b.* 1929, *s.* 1970, *w.*	Hon. James T. A. D.-H., *b.* 1952
1332	** *Darcy de Knayth (18th),* Davina Marcia Ingrams, DBE, *b.* 1938, *s.* 1943, *w.*	Hon. Caspar D. I., *b.* 1962
1490 S.	*Herries of Terregles (14th),* Anne Elizabeth Fitzalan-Howard, *b.* 1938, *s.* 1975, *w.*	Lady Mary Mumford, *b.* 1940
1597	*Howard de Walden (10th),* Mary Hazel Caridwen Czernin, *b.* 1935, *s.* 2004, *m.* Title called out of abeyance 2004	Hon. Peter J. J. C., *b.* 1966
1602 S.	*Kinloss (12th),* Beatrice Mary Grenville Freeman-Grenville, *b.* 1922, *s.* 1944, *m.*	Master of Kinloss, *b.* 1953
1445 S.	** *Saltoun (20th),* Flora Marjory Fraser, *b.* 1930, *s.* 1979, *w.*	Hon. Katharine I. M. I. F., *b.* 1957
1628	** *Strange (16th),* (Jean) Cherry Drummond of Megginch, *b.* 1928, *s.* 1986, *m.*	Hon. Adam H. D. of M., *b.* 1953
1313	*Willoughby de Eresby (27th),* (Nancy) Jane Marie Heathcote-Drummond-Willoughby, *b.* 1934, *s.* 1983	Two co-heiresses

LIFE PEERS

NEW LIFE PEERAGES *1 September 2003 to 31 August 2004:*

Sir David Alliance, CBE; Prof. Sir (Sushantha) Kumar Bhattacharyya, CBE; Jane Bonham Carter; Prof. Sir Alec (Nigel) Broers; Sir Simon Denis Brown, PC; Sir Ewen (James Hanning) Cameron; Sir Robert Douglas Carswell, PC; Patrick Robert Carter; Nicola Jane Chapman; Paul Rudd Drayson; Dr Frances Gertrude Claire D'Souza, CMG; Hugh John Maxwell Dykes; Kishwer Falkner; Sir Timothy Garden, KCB; Sir Edward (Alan John) George, GBE, PC; Prof. Anthony Giddens; Philip Gould; Revd. Dr Leslie John Griffiths; Dame Brenda Marjorie Hale, DBE, PC; Garry Richard Rushby Hart; Dr Edward Haughey; Alan Robert Haworth; Ruth Beatrice Henig; Greville Patrick Charles Howard; CBE; Sir Harold Stanley Kalms; Sir John (Olav) Kerr; Irvine Alan Stewart Laidlaw; Alexander Park Leitch; Margaret Josephine McDonagh; William David McKenzie; John Alston Maxton; Delyth Jane Morgan; Patricia Morris, OBE; Elaine Murphy; Dame Julia (Babette Sarah) Neuberger, DBE; Margaret Theresa Prosser, OBE; Dr. Diljit Singh Rana, MBE; Revd. John Roger Roberts; Richard Andrew Rosser; Edward Rowlands, CBE; Janet Anne Royall; Peter Charles Snape; Leonard Steinberg; David Maxim Triesman; Dr Peter Derek Truscott; Denis Tunnicliffe, CBE; Sir Iain Vallance; Margaret Mary Wall; Sir Anthony Young; Prof. Margaret Omolola Young, OBE

CREATED UNDER THE APPELLATE JURISDICTION ACT 1876 (AS AMENDED)

BARONS
Created

1986 *Ackner,* Desmond James Conrad Ackner, PC, *b.* 1920, *m.*
1980 *Bridge of Harwich,* Nigel Cyprian Bridge, PC, *b.* 1917, *m.*
1982 *Brightman,* John Anson, Brightman PC, *b.* 1911, *m.*
2004 *Brown of Eaton-under-Heywood,* Simon Denis Brown, PC, *b.* 1937, *m. Lord of Appeal in Ordinary*
1991 *Browne-Wilkinson,* Nicolas Christopher Henry Browne-Wilkinson, PC, *b.* 1930, *m.*
2004 *Carswell,* Robert Douglas Carswell, PC, *b.* 1934, *m. Lord of Appeal in Ordinary*
1996 *Clyde,* James John Clyde, PC, *b.* 1932, *m.*
1986 *Goff of Chieveley,* Robert Lionel Archibald Goff, PC, *b.* 1926, *m.*
1985 *Griffiths,* (William) Hugh Griffiths, MC, PC, *b.* 1923, *m.*
1995 *Hoffmann,* Leonard Hubert Hoffmann, PC, *b.* 1934, *m. Lord of Appeal in Ordinary*
1997 *Hutton,* (James) Brian (Edward) Hutton, PC, *b.* 1931, *m.*
1988 *Jauncey of Tullichettle,* Charles Eliot Jauncey, PC, *b.* 1925, *m.*
1979 *Lane,* Geoffrey Dawson Lane, AFC, PC, *b.* 1918, *m.*
1993 *Lloyd of Berwick,* Anthony John Leslie Lloyd, PC, *b.* 1929, *m.*
1998 *Millett,* Peter Julian Millett, PC, *b.* 1932, *m.*
1992 *Mustill,* Michael John Mustill, PC, *b.* 1931, *m.*
1994 *Nicholls of Birkenhead,* Donald James Nicholls, PC, *b.* 1933, *m. Second Senior Lord of Appeal in Ordinary*
1994 *Nolan,* Michael Patrick Nolan, PC, *b.* 1928, *m.*
1986 *Oliver of Aylmerton,* Peter Raymond Oliver, PC, *b.* 1921, *m.*
1999 *Phillips of Worth Matravers,* Nicholas Addison Phillips, b. 1938, *m. Master of the Rolls*
1997 *Saville of Newdigate,* Mark Oliver Saville, PC, *b.* 1936, *m. Lord of Appeal in Ordinary*
1977 *Scarman,* Leslie George Scarman, OBE, PC, *b.* 1911, *m.*
1992 *Slynn of Hadley,* Gordon Slynn, PC, *b.* 1930, *m.*
1995 *Steyn,* Johan van Zyl Steyn, PC, *b.* 1932, *m. Lord of Appeal in Ordinary*
1982 *Templeman,* Sydney William Templeman, MBE, PC, *b.* 1920, *m.*
1992 *Woolf,* Harry Kenneth Woolf, PC, *b.* 1933, *m. Lord Chief Justice of England and Wales*

BARONESSES

2004 *Hale of Richmond,* Brenda Marjorie Hale, DBE, PC, *b.* 1945, *m., Lord of Appeal in Ordinary*

CREATED UNDER THE LIFE PEERAGES ACT 1958

* Hereditary peer who has been granted a life peerage. For further details, please refer to the Hereditary Peers section, pages 44–64. For example, life peer *Balniel* can be found under his hereditary title *Earl of Crawford and Balcarres.*

BARONS
Created

2000 **Acton of Bridgnorth,* Lord Acton, *b.* 1941, *m.* (*see* Hereditary Peers)
2001 *Adebowale,* Victor Olufemi Adebowale, CBE, *b.* 1962
1998 *Ahmed,* Nazir Ahmed, *b.* 1957, *m.*
1996 *Alderdice,* John Thomas Alderdice, *b.* 1955, *m.*
1988 *Alexander of Weedon,* Robert Scott Alexander, QC, *b.* 1936, *m.*
1976 *Allen of Abbeydale,* Philip Allen, GCB, *b.* 1912, *w.*
1998 *Alli,* Waheed Alli, *b.* 1964
2004 *Alliance,* David Alliance, GBE, *b.* 1932
1997 *Alton of Liverpool,* David Patrick Paul Alton, *b.* 1951, *m.*
1992 *Archer of Sandwell,* Peter Kingsley Archer, PC, QC, *b.* 1926, *m.*
1992 *Archer of Weston-super-Mare,* Jeffrey Howard Archer, *b.* 1940, *m.*
1988 *Armstrong of Ilminster,* Robert Temple Armstrong, GCB, CVO, *b.* 1927, *m.*
1999 **Armstrong-Jones,* Earl of Snowdon, GCVO, *b.* 1930, *m.* (*see* Hereditary Peers)
2000 *Ashcroft,* Michael Anthony Ashcroft, KCMG,
2001 *Ashdown of Norton-sub-Hamdon,* Jeremy John Durham (Paddy) Ashdown, KBE, PC, *b.* 1941, *m.*
1992 *Ashley of Stoke,* Jack Ashley, CH, PC, *b.* 1922, *w.*
1993 *Attenborough,* Richard Samuel Attenborough, CBE, *b.* 1923, *m.*
1998 *Bach,* William Stephen Goulden Bach, *b.* 1946, *m.*
1997 *Bagri,* Raj Kumar Bagri, CBE, *b.* 1930, *m.*

1997 *Baker of Dorking,* Kenneth Wilfred Baker, CH, PC, *b.* 1934, *m.*
2004 *Ballyedmond,* Dr Edward Haughey, OBE, *b.* 1944, *m.*
1974 **Balniel,* The Earl of Crawford and Balcarres, *b.* 1927, *m.* (*see* Hereditary Peers)
1974 *Barber,* Anthony Perrinott Lysberg Barber, TD, PC, *b.* 1920, *m.*
1992 *Barber of Tewkesbury,* Derek Coates Barber, *b.* 1918, *m.*
1983 *Barnett,* Joel Barnett, PC, *b.* 1923, *m.*
1997 *Bassam of Brighton,* (John) Steven Bassam, *b.* 1953
1967 *Beaumont of Whitley,* Revd Timothy Wentworth Beaumont, *b.* 1928, *m.*
1998 *Bell,* Timothy John Leigh Bell, *b.* 1941, *m.*
2000 *Bernstein of Craigweil,* Alexander Bernstein, *b.* 1936, *m.*
2001 *Best,* Richard Stuart Best, OBE, *b.* 1945, *m.*
2001 *Bhatia,* Amirali Alibhai Bhatia, OBE, *b.* 1932, *m.*
2004 *Bhattacharyya,* Prof. (Sushantha) Kumar Bhattacharyya, CBE *b.* 1932, *m.*
1997 *Biffen,* (William) John Biffen, PC, *b.* 1930, *m.*
1996 *Bingham of Cornhill,* Thomas Henry Bingham, PC, *b.* 1933, *m. Senior Lord of Appeal in Ordinary*
2000 *Birt,* John Francis Hodgess Birt, *b.* 1944, *m.*
2001 *Black of Crossharbour,* Conrad Moffat Black, OC, PC, *b.* 1944, *m.*
1997 *Blackwell,* Norman Roy Blackwell, *b.* 1952, *m.*
1994 *Blaker,* Peter Allan Renshaw Blaker, KCMG, PC, *b.* 1922, *m.*
1978 *Blease,* William John Blease, *b.* 1914, *m.*
1995 *Blyth of Rowington,* James Blyth, *b.* 1940, *m.*
1996 *Borrie,* Gordon Johnson Borrie, QC, *b.* 1931, *m.*
1976 *Boston of Faversham,* Terence George Boston, QC, *b.* 1930, *m.*
1996 *Bowness,* Peter Spencer Bowness, CBE, *b.* 1943, *m.*
2003 *Boyce,* Michael Boyce, GCB, OBE, *b.* 1943
1999 *Bradshaw,* William Peter Bradshaw, *b.* 1936, *m.*
1998 *Bragg,* Melvyn Bragg, *b.* 1939, *m.*
1987 *Bramall,* Edwin Noel Westby Bramall, KG, GCB, OBE, MC, *b.* 1923, *m.*
2000 *Brennan,* Daniel Joseph Brennan, QC, *b.* 1942, *m.*
1999 *Brett,* William Henry Brett, *b.* 1942, *m.*
1976 *Briggs,* Asa Briggs, FBA, *b.* 1921, *m.*
2000 *Brittan of Spennithorne,* Leon Brittan, PC, QC, *b.* 1939, *m.*
2004 *Broers,* Prof. Alec (Nigel) Broers, *b.* 1938, *m.*
1997 *Brooke of Alverthorpe,* Clive Brooke, *b.* 1942, *m.*
2001 *Brooke of Sutton Mandeville,* Peter Leonard Brooke, CH, PC, *b.* 1934, *m.*
1998 *Brookman,* David Keith Brookman, *b.* 1937, *m.*
1979 *Brooks of Tremorfa,* John Edward Brooks, *b.* 1927, *m.*
2001 *Browne of Madingley,* Edmund John Phillip Browne, *b.* 1948
1974 *Bruce of Donington,* Donald William Trevor Bruce, *b.* 1912, *m.*
1997 *Burlison,* Thomas Henry Burlison, *b.* 1936, *m.*
1998 *Burns,* Terence Burns, GCB, *b.* 1944, *m.*
1998 *Butler of Brockwell,* (Frederick Edward) Robin Butler, KG, GCB, CVO, *b.* 1938, *m.*
1978 *Buxton of Alsa,* Aubrey Leland Oakes Buxton, KCVO, MC, *b.* 1918, *m.*
1987 *Callaghan of Cardiff,* (Leonard) James Callaghan, KG, PC, *b.* 1912, *m.*
2004 *Cameron of Dillington,* Ewen (James Hanning) Cameron, *b.* 1949, *m.*
1984 *Cameron of Lochbroom,* Kenneth John Cameron, PC, *b.* 1931, *m.*
1981 *Campbell of Alloway,* Alan Robertson Campbell, QC, *b.* 1917, *m.*
1974 *Campbell of Croy,* Gordon Thomas Calthrop Campbell, MC, PC, *b.* 1921, *m.*
2001 *Campbell-Savours,* Dale Norman Campbell-Savours, *b.* 1943, *m.*
2002 *Carey of Clifton,* Rt. Revd George Leonard Carey, PC, *b.* 1935, *m.*
1999 **Carington of Upton,* Lord Carrington, GCMG, *b.* 1919, *m.* (*see* Hereditary Peers)
1999 *Carlile of Berriew,* Alexander Charles Carlile, QC, *b.* 1948, *m.*
1987 *Carlisle of Bucklow,* Mark Carlisle, QC, PC, *b.* 1929, *m.*
1975 *Carr of Hadley,* (Leonard) Robert Carr, PC, *b.* 1916, *m.*
1987 *Carter,* Denis Victor Carter, PC, *b.* 1932, *m.*
2004 *Carter of Coles,* Patrick Robert Carter, *b.* 1946, *m.*
1990 *Cavendish of Furness,* (Richard) Hugh Cavendish, *b.* 1941, *m.*
1996 *Chadlington,* Peter Selwyn Gummer, *b.* 1942, *m.*
1964 *Chalfont,* (Alun) Arthur Gwynne Jones, OBE, MC, PC, *b.* 1919, *m.*
2001 *Chan,* Michael Chew Koon Chan, MBE, *b.* 1940, *m.*
1985 *Chapple,* Francis (Frank) Joseph Chapple, *b.* 1921, *w.*
1987 *Chilver,* (Amos) Henry Chilver, FRS, FREng, *b.* 1926, *m.*
1977 *Chitnis,* Pratap Chidamber Chitnis, *b.* 1936, *m.*
1998 *Christopher,* Anthony Martin Grosvenor Christopher, CBE, *b.* 1925, *m.*
1992 *Clark of Kempston,* William Gibson Haig Clark, PC, *b.* 1917, *m.*
2001 *Clark of Windermere,* David George Clark, PC, PHD, *b.* 1939, *m.*
1998 *Clarke of Hampstead,* Anthony James Clarke, CBE, *b.* 1932, *m.*
1998 *Clement-Jones,* Timothy Francis Clement-Jones, CBE, *b.* 1949, *m.*
1990 *Clinton-Davis,* Stanley Clinton Clinton-Davis, PC, *b.* 1928, *m.*
1978 *Cockfield,* (Francis) Arthur Cockfield, PC, *b.* 1916, *w.*
2000 *Coe,* Sebastian Newbold Coe, OBE, *b.* 1956, *m.*
2001 *Condon,* Paul Leslie Condon, QPM, *m.*
1992 *Cooke of Islandreagh,* Victor Alexander Cooke, OBE, *b.* 1920, *m.*
1996 *Cooke of Thorndon,* Robin Brunskill Cooke, KBE, PC, PHD, *b.* 1926, *m.*
1997 *Cope of Berkeley,* John Ambrose Cope, PC, *b.* 1937, *m.*
2001 *Corbett of Castle Vale,* Robin Corbett, *b.* 1933, *m.*
1991 *Craig of Radley,* David Brownrigg Craig, GCB, OBE, *b.* 1929, *m.*
1987 *Crickhowell,* (Roger) Nicholas Edwards, PC, *b.* 1934, *m.*
1978 *Croham,* Douglas Albert Vivian Allen, GCB, *b.* 1917, *w.*

2003 *Cullen,* William Douglas Cullen, PC, *b.* 1935, *m. Lord Justice General of Scotland and Lord President of the Court of Session*
1995 *Cuckney,* John Graham Cuckney, *b.* 1925, *w.*
1996 *Currie of Marylebone,* David Anthony Currie, *b.* 1946, *m.*
1993 *Dahrendorf,* Ralf Dahrendorf, KBE, PHD, DPHIL, FBA, *b.* 1929, *m.*
1997 *Davies of Coity,* (David) Garfield Davies, CBE, *b.* 1935, *m.*
1997 *Davies of Oldham,* Bryan Davies, *b.* 1939, *m.*
1993 *Dean of Harptree,* (Arthur) Paul Dean, PC, *b.* 1924, *m.*
1998 *Dearing,* Ronald Ernest Dearing, *b.* 1930, *m.*
1986 *Deedes,* William Francis Deedes, KBE MC, PC, *b.* 1913, *w.*
1991 *Desai,* Prof. Meghnad Jagdishchandra Desai, PHD, *b.* 1940, *m.*
1997 *Dholakia,* Navnit Dholakia, OBE, *b.* 1937, *m.*
1997 *Dixon,* Donald Dixon, PC, *b.* 1929, *m.*
1993 *Dixon-Smith,* Robert William Dixon-Smith, *b.* 1934, *m.*
1988 *Donaldson of Lymington,* John Francis Donaldson, PC, *b.* 1920, *m.*
1985 *Donoughue,* Bernard Donoughue, DPHIL, *b.* 1934
2004 *Drayson,* Paul Rudd Drayson, *b.* 1960, *m.*
1994 *Dubs,* Alfred Dubs, *b.* 1932, *m.*
2004 *Dykes,* Hugh John Maxwell Dykes, *b.* 1939, *m.*
1995 *Eames,* Robert Henry Alexander Eames, PHD, *b.* 1937, *m.*
1992 *Eatwell,* John Leonard Eatwell, PHD, *b.* 1945, *m.*
1983 *Eden of Winton,* John Benedict Eden, PC, *b.* 1925, *m.*
1999 *Elder,* Thomas Murray Elder, *b.* 1950
1992 *Elis-Thomas,* Dafydd Elis Elis-Thomas, *b.* 1946, *m.*
1985 *Elliott of Morpeth,* Robert William Elliott, *b.* 1920, *m.*
1981 *Elystan-Morgan,* Dafydd Elystan Elystan-Morgan, *b.* 1932, *m.*
2000 **Erskine of Alloa Tower,* Earl of Mar and Kellie, *b.* 1949, *m.* (*see* Hereditary Peers)
1997 *Evans of Parkside,* John Evans, *b.* 1930, *m.*
2000 *Evans of Temple Guiting,* Matthew Evans, CBE, *b.* 1941, *m.*
1998 *Evans of Watford,* David Charles Evans, *b.* 1942, *m.*
1992 *Ewing of Kirkford,* Harry Ewing, *b.* 1931, *m.*
1983 *Ezra,* Derek Ezra, MBE, *b.* 1919, *m.*
1997 *Falconer of Thoroton,* Charles Leslie Falconer, QC, *b.* 1951, *m.*
1999 *Faulkner of Worcester,* Richard Oliver Faulkner, *b.* 1946, *m.*
2001 *Fearn, Ronald Cyril Fearn,* OBE, *b.* 1931, *m.*
1996 *Feldman,* Basil Feldman, *b.* 1926, *m.*
1999 *Fellowes,* Robert Fellowes, GCB, GCVO, PC, *b.* 1941, *m.*
1999 *Filkin,* David Geoffrey Nigel Filkin, CBE, *b.* 1944
1983 *Fitt,* Gerard Fitt, *b.* 1926, *w.*
1979 *Flowers,* Brian Hilton Flowers, FRS, *b.* 1924, *m.*
1999 *Forsyth of Drumlean,* Michael Bruce Forsyth, *b.* 1954, *m.*
1982 *Forte,* Charles Forte, *b.* 1908, *m.*
1999 *Foster of Thames Bank,* Norman Robert Foster, OM, *b.* 1935, *m.*
2001 *Fowler,* (Peter) Norman Fowler, PC, *b.* 1938, *m.*
1989 *Fraser of Carmyllie,* Peter Lovat Fraser, PC, QC, *b.* 1945, *m.*
1997 *Freeman,* Roger Norman Freeman, PC, *b.* 1942, *m.*
2000 *Fyfe of Fairfield,* George Lennox Fyfe, *b.* 1941, *m.*
1999 **Ganzoni,* Lord Belstead, PC, *b.* 1932, (*see* Hereditary Peers)
2004 *Garden,* Timothy Garden, KCB, *b.* 1939, *m.*
1997 *Garel-Jones,* (William Armand) Thomas Tristan Garel-Jones, PC, *b.* 1941, *m.*
1999 **Gascoyne-Cecil,* The Marquess of Salisbury, PC , *b.* 1946, *m.* (see Hereditary Peers)
1999 *Gavron,* Robert Gavron, CBE, *b.* 1930, *m.*
2004 *George,* Edward (Alan John) George, GBE, PC, *b.* 1938, *m.*
2004 *Giddens,* Prof. Anthony Giddens, *b.* 1938, *m.*
1997 *Gilbert,* John William Gilbert, PC, PHD, *b.* 1927, *m.*
1992 *Gilmour of Craigmillar,* Ian Hedworth John Little Gilmour, PC, *b.* 1926, *m.*
1977 *Glenamara,* Edward Watson Short, CH, PC, *b.* 1912, *m.*
1999 *Goldsmith,* Peter Henry Goldsmith, QC, *b.* 1950, *m.*
1997 *Goodhart,* William Howard Goodhart, QC, *b.* 1933, *m.*
1997 *Gordon of Strathblane,* James Stuart Gordon, CBE, *b.* 1936, *m.*
2004 *Gould of Brookwood,* Philip Gould *b.* 1950 *m.*
1999 *Grabiner,* Anthony Stephen Grabiner, QC, *b.* 1945, *m.*
1983 *Graham of Edmonton,* (Thomas) Edward Graham, *b.* 1925, *m.*
1983 *Gray of Contin,* James (Hamish) Hector Northey Gray, PC, *b.* 1927, *m.*
2000 *Greaves,* Anthony Robert Greaves, *b.* 1942, *m.*
1975 *Gregson,* John Gregson, *b.* 1924
2000 **Grenfell of Kilvey,* Lord Grenfell, *b.* 1935, *m.* (*see* Hereditary Peers)
2004 *Griffiths of Burry Port,* Revd. Dr Leslie John Griffiths, *b.* 1942, *m.*
1991 *Griffiths of Fforestfach,* Brian Griffiths, *b.* 1941, *m.*
2001 *Grocott,* Bruce Joseph Grocott, PC, *b.* 1940, *m.*
2000 **Gueterbock,* Lord Berkley, OBE, *b.* 1939, *m.* (*see* Hereditary Peers)
2000 *Guthrie of Craigiebank,* Charles Ronald Llewelyn Guthrie, GCB, LVO, OBE, *b.* 1938, *m.*
1995 *Habgood,* Rt. Revd John Stapylton Habgood, PC, PHD, *b.* 1927, *m.*
2001 *Hannay of Chiswick,* David Hugh Alexander Hannay, GCMG, CH, *b.* 1935, *m.*
1998 *Hanningfield,* Paul Edward Winston White, *b.* 1940
1983 *Hanson,* James Edward Hanson, *b.* 1922, *w.*
1997 *Hardie,* Andrew Rutherford Hardie, QC, PC, *b.* 1946, *m.*
1998 *Harris of Haringey,* (Jonathan) Toby Harris, *b.* 1953, *m.*
1979 *Harris of High Cross,* Ralph Harris, *b.* 1924, *m.*
1996 *Harris of Peckham,* Philip Charles Harris, *b.* 1942, *m.*
1999 *Harrison,* Lyndon Henry Arthur Harrison, *b.* 1947, *m.*
2004 *Hart of Chilton,* Garry Richard Rushby Hart, *b.* 1940, *m.*
1993 *Haskel,* Simon Haskel, *b.* 1934, *m.*

1998 *Haskins,* Christopher Robin Haskins, *b.* 1937, *m.*
1997 *Hattersley,* Roy Sidney George Hattersley, PC, *b.* 1932, *m.*
2004 *Haworth,* Alan Robert Haworth, *b.* 1948, *m.*
1992 *Hayhoe,* Bernard John (Barney) Hayhoe, PC, *b.* 1925, *m.*
1992 *Healey,* Denis Winston Healey, CH, MBE, PC, *b.* 1917, *m.*
1999 **Hennessey,* Lord Windlesham, CVO, *b.* 1932, *m.* (*see* Hereditary Peers)
2001 *Heseltine,* Michael Ray Dibdin Heseltine, CH, PC, *b.* 1933, *m.*
1997 *Higgins,* Terence Langley Higgins, KBE, PC, *b.* 1928, *m.*
2000 *Hodgson of Astley Abbotts,* Robin Granville Hodgson, CBE, *b.* 1942, *m.*
1997 *Hogg of Cumbernauld,* Norman Hogg, *b.* 1938, *m.*
1991 *Hollick,* Clive Richard Hollick, *b.* 1945, *m.*
1990 *Holme of Cheltenham,* Richard Gordon Holme, CBE, *b.* 1936, *m.*
1979 *Hooson,* (Hugh) Emlyn Hooson, QC, *b.* 1925, *m.*
1995 *Hope of Craighead,* (James Arthur) David Hope, PC, *b.* 1938, *m. Lord of Appeal in Ordinary*
2004 *Howard of Rising,* Greville Patrick Charles Howard, *b.* 1941, *m.*
1992 *Howe of Aberavon,* (Richard Edward) Geoffrey Howe, CH, PC, QC, *b.* 1926, *m.*
1997 *Howell of Guildford,* David Arthur Russell Howell, PC, *b.* 1936, *m.*
1978 *Howie of Troon,* William Howie, *b.* 1924, *m.*
1997 *Hoyle,* (Eric) Douglas Harvey Hoyle, *b.* 1930, *w.*
1997 *Hughes of Woodside,* Robert Hughes, *b.* 1932, *m.*
2000 *Hunt of Chesterton,* Julian Charles Roland Hunt, CBE, *b.* 1941, *m.*
1997 *Hunt of Kings Heath,* Philip Alexander Hunt, OBE, *b.* 1949, *m.*
1980 *Hunt of Tanworth,* John Joseph Benedict Hunt, GCB, *b.* 1919, *m.*
1997 *Hunt of Wirral,* David James Fletcher Hunt, MBE, PC, *b.* 1942, *m.*
1997 *Hurd of Westwell,* Douglas Richard Hurd, CH, CBE, PC, *b.* 1930, *m.*
1996 *Hussey of North Bradley,* Marmaduke James Hussey, *b.* 1923, *m.*
1978 *Hutchinson of Lullington,* Jeremy Nicolas Hutchinson, QC, *b.* 1915, *m.*
1999 *Imbert,* Peter Michael Imbert, QPM, *b.* 1933, *m.*
1997 *Inge,* Peter Anthony Inge, KG, GCB, *b.* 1935, *m.*
1987 *Irvine of Lairg,* Alexander Andrew Mackay Irvine, PC, QC, *b.* 1940, *m.*
1997 *Jacobs,* (David) Anthony Jacobs, *b.* 1931, *m.*
1997 *Janner of Braunstone,* Greville Ewan Janner, QC, *b.* 1928, *w.*
1999 **Jellicoe of Southampton,* Earl Jellicoe, KBE, *b.* 1918, *w.* (*see* Hereditary Peers)
1987 *Jenkin of Roding,* (Charles) Patrick (Fleeming) Jenkin, PC, *b.* 1926, *m.*
2000 *Joffe,* Joel Goodman Joffe, CBE, *b.* 1932, *m.*
2001 *Jones,* (Stephen) Barry Jones, *b.* 1937, *m.*
1997 *Jopling,* (Thomas) Michael Jopling, PC, *b.* 1930, *m.*
2000 *Jordan,* William Brian Jordan, CBE, *b.* 1936, *m.*
1991 *Judd,* Frank Ashcroft Judd, *b.* 1935, *m.*
2004 *Kalms,* Harold Stanley Kalms, *b.* 1931 *m.*
1997 *Kelvedon,* (Henry) Paul Guinness Channon, PC, *b.* 1935, *m.*
2004 *Kerr of Kinlochard,* John (Olav) Kerr, GCMG, *b.* 1942, *m.*
2001 *Kilclooney,* John David Taylor, PC (NI), *b.* 1937, *m.*
1996 *Kilpatrick of Kincraig,* Robert Kilpatrick, CBE, *b.* 1926, *m.*
1985 *Kimball,* Marcus Richard Kimball, *b.* 1928, *m.*
2001 *King of Bridgwater,* Thomas Jeremy King, CH, PC, *b.* 1933, *m.*
1983 *King of Wartnaby,* John Leonard King, *b.* 1918, *m.*
1999 *King of West Bromwich,* Tarsem King, *b.* 1937
1993 *Kingsdown,* Robert (Robin) Leigh-Pemberton, KG, PC, *b.* 1927, *m.*
1994 *Kingsland,* Christopher James Prout, TD, PC, QC, *b.* 1942
1999 *Kirkham,* Graham Kirkham, *b.* 1944, *m.*
1975 *Kirkhill,* John Farquharson Smith, *b.* 1930, *m.*
1987 *Knights,* Philip Douglas Knights, CBE, QPM, *b.* 1920, *m.*
2004 *Laidlaw,* Irvine Alan Stewart Laidlaw, *b.* 1942, *m.*
1991 *Laing of Dunphail,* Hector Laing, *b.* 1923, *m.*
1999 *Laird,* John Dunn Laird, *b.* 1944, *m.*
1998 *Laming,* (William) Herbert Laming, CBE, *b.* 1936, *m.*
1998 *Lamont of Lerwick,* Norman Stewart Hughson Lamont, PC, *b.* 1942, *m.*
1990 *Lane of Horsell,* Peter Stewart Lane, *b.* 1925, *w.*
1997 *Lang of Monkton,* Ian Bruce Lang, PC, *b.* 1940, *m.*
1992 *Lawson of Blaby,* Nigel Lawson, PC, *b.* 1932, *m.*
2000 *Layard,* Peter Richard Grenville Layard, *b.* 1934, *m.*
1999 *Lea of Crondall,* David Edward Lea, OBE, *b.* 1937
2004 *Leitch,* Alexander Park Leitch, *b.* 1947, *m.*
1993 *Lester of Herne Hill,* Anthony Paul Lester, QC, *b.* 1936, *m.*
1997 *Levene of Portsoken,* Peter Keith Levene, KBE, *b.* 1941, *m.*
1997 *Levy,* Michael Abraham Levy, *b.* 1944, *m.*
1989 *Lewis of Newnham,* Jack Lewis, FRS, *b.* 1928, *m.*
1999 *Lipsey,* David Lawrence Lipsey, *b.* 1948, *m.*
2001 *Livsey of Talgarth,* Richard Arthur Lloyd Livsey, CBE, *b.* 1935, *m.*
1997 *Lloyd-Webber,* Andrew Lloyd Webber, *b.* 1948, *m.*
1997 *Lofthouse of Pontefract,* Geoffrey Lofthouse, *b.* 1925, *w.*
2000 *Luce,* Richard Napier Luce, GCVO, PC, *b.* 1936, *m.*
2000 **Lyttleton of Aldershot,* The Viscount Chandos, *b.* 1953, *m.* (*see* Hereditary Peers)
1984 *McAlpine of West Green,* (Robert) Alistair McAlpine, *b.* 1942, *m.*
1988 *Macaulay of Bragar,* Donald Macaulay, QC, *b.* 1933, *m.*
1975 *McCarthy,* William Edward John McCarthy, DPHIL, *b.* 1925, *m.*
1976 *McCluskey,* John Herbert McCluskey, *b.* 1929, *m.*
1989 *McColl of Dulwich,* Ian McColl, CBE, FRCS, FRCSE, *b.* 1933, *m.*
1998 *Macdonald of Tradeston,* Angus John Macdonald, CBE, *b.* 1940, *m.*
1991 *Macfarlane of Bearsden,* Norman Somerville Macfarlane, KT, FRSE, *b.* 1926, *m.*

2001 *MacGregor of Pulham Market,* John Roddick Russell MacGregor, CBE, PC, *b.* 1937, *m.*
1982 *McIntosh of Haringey,* Andrew Robert McIntosh, *b.* 1933, *m.*
1979 *Mackay of Clashfern,* James Peter Hymers Mackay, KT, PC, FRSE, *b.* 1927, *m.*
1995 *Mackay of Drumadoon,* Donald Sage Mackay, PC, *b.* 1946, *m.*
2004 *McKenzie of Luton,* William David McKenzie, *b.* 1946, *m.*
1999 *Mackenzie of Culkein,* Hector Uisdean MacKenzie, *b.* 1940
1998 *Mackenzie of Framwellgate,* Brian Mackenzie, OBE, *b.* 1943, *m.*
1974 *Mackie of Benshie,* George Yull Mackie, CBE, DSO, DFC, *b.* 1919, *m.*
1996 *MacLaurin of Knebworth,* Ian Charter MacLaurin, *b.* 1937, *m.*
2001 *Maclennon of Rogart,* Robert Adam Ross Maclennan, PC, *b.* 1936, *m.*
1995 *McNally,* Tom McNally, *b.* 1943, *m.*
2001 *Maginnis of Drumglass,* Kenneth Wiggins Maginnis, *b.* 1938, *m.*
1991 *Marlesford,* Mark Shuldham Schreiber, *b.* 1931, *m.*
1981 *Marsh,* Richard William Marsh, PC, *b.* 1928, *m.*
1998 *Marshall of Knightsbridge,* Colin Marsh Marshall, *b.* 1933, *m.*
1987 *Mason of Barnsley,* Roy Mason, PC, *b.* 1924, *m.*
2004 *Maxton,* John Alston Maxton, *b.* 1936, *m.*
2001 *May of Oxford,* Robert McCredie May, OM, *b.* 1936, *m.*
1997 *Mayhew of Twysden,* Patrick Barnabas Burke Mayhew, QC, PC, *b.* 1929, *m.*
1992 *Merlyn-Rees,* Merlyn Merlyn-Rees, PC, *b.* 1920, *m.*
1978 *Mishcon,* Victor Mishcon, QC, *b.* 1915, *m.*
2000 *Mitchell,* Parry Andrew Mitchell, *b.* 1943
2000 **Mitford,* Lord Redesdale, *b.* 1967, *m.* (*see* Hereditary Peers)
1997 *Molyneaux of Killead,* James Henry Molyneaux, KBE, PC, *b.* 1920
1997 *Monro of Langholm,* Hector Seymour Peter Monro, AE, PC, *b.* 1922, *m.*
1992 *Moore of Lower Marsh,* John Edward Michael Moore, PC, *b.* 1937, *m.*
1986 *Moore of Wolvercote,* Philip Brian Cecil Moore, GCB, GCVO, CMG, PC, *b.* 1921, *m.*
2000 *Morgan,* Kenneth Owen Morgan, *b.* 1934, *m.*
2001 *Morris of Aberavon,* John Morris, KG, QC, *b.* 1931, *m.*
1997 *Morris of Manchester,* Alfred Morris, PC, *b.* 1928, *m.*
2001 *Moser,* Claus Adolf Moser, KCB, CBE, *b.* 1922, *m.*
1979 *Murton of Lindisfarne,* (Henry) Oscar Murton, OBE, TD, PC, *b.* 1914, *m.*
1997 *Naseby,* Michael Wolfgang Laurence Morris, PC, *b.* 1936, *m.*
1997 *Neill of Bladen,* (Francis) Patrick Neill, QC, *b.* 1926, *m.*
1997 *Newby,* Richard Mark Newby, OBE, *b.* 1953, *m.*
1997 *Newton of Braintree,* Antony Harold Newton, OBE, PC, *b.* 1937, *m.*
1994 *Nickson,* David Wigley Nickson, KBE, FRSE, *b.* 1929, *m.*
1975 *Northfield,* (William) Donald Chapman, *b.* 1923
1998 *Norton of Louth,* Philip Norton, *b.* 1951
2000 *Oakeshott of Seagrove Bay,* Matthew Alan Oakeshott, *b.* 1947, *m.*
1997 *Orme,* Stanley Orme, PC, *b.* 1923, *m.*
2001 *Ouseley,* Herman George Ouseley, *b.* 1945, *m.*
1992 *Owen,* David Anthony Llewellyn Owen, CH, PC, *b.* 1938, *m.*
1999 *Oxburgh,* Ernest Ronald Oxburgh, KBE, FRS, PHD, *b.* 1934, *m.*
1991 *Palumbo,* Peter Garth Palumbo, *b.* 1935, *m.*
2000 *Parekh,* Bhikhu Chhotalal Parekh, *b.* 1935, *m.*
1992 *Parkinson,* Cecil Edward Parkinson, PC, *b.* 1931, *m.*
1975 *Parry,* Gordon Samuel David Parry, *b.* 1925, *m.*
1999 *Patel,* Narendra Babubhai Patel, *b.* 1938
2000 *Patel of Blackburn,* Adam Hafejee Patel, *b.* 1940
1997 *Patten,* John Haggitt Charles Patten, PC, *b.* 1945, *m.*
1996 *Paul,* Swraj Paul, *b.* 1931, *m.*
1990 *Pearson of Rannoch,* Malcolm Everard MacLaren Pearson, *b.* 1942, *m.*
2001 *Pendry,* Thomas Pendry, *b.* 1934, *m.*
1987 *Peston,* Maurice Harry Peston, *b.* 1931, *m.*
1983 *Peyton of Yeovil,* John Wynne William Peyton, PC, *b.* 1919, *m.*
1998 *Phillips of Sudbury,* Andrew Wyndham Phillips, OBE, *b.* 1939, *m.*
1996 *Pilkington of Oxenford,* Revd Canon Peter Pilkington, *b.* 1933, *w.*
1992 *Plant of Highfield,* Prof. Raymond Plant, PHD, *b.* 1945, *m.*
1987 *Plumb,* (Charles) Henry Plumb, *b.* 1925, *m.*
1981 *Plummer of St Marylebone,* (Arthur) Desmond (Herne) Plummer, TD, *b.* 1914, *m.*
2000 **Ponsonby of Roehampton,* Lord Ponsonby of Shulbrede, *b.* 1958 (*see* Hereditary Peers)
2000 *Powell of Bayswater,* Charles David Powell, KCMG, *b.* 1941
1987 *Prior,* James Michael Leathes Prior, PC, *b.* 1927, *m.*
1982 *Prys-Davies,* Gwilym Prys Prys-Davies, *b.* 1923, *m.*
1997 *Puttnam,* David Terence Puttnam, CBE, *b.* 1941, *m.*
1987 *Pym,* Francis Leslie Pym, MC, PC, *b.* 1922, *m.*
1982 *Quinton,* Anthony Meredith Quinton, FBA, *b.* 1925, *m.*
1994 *Quirk,* Prof. (Charles) Randolph Quirk, CBE, FBA, *b.* 1920, *m.*
2001 *Radice,* Giles Heneage Radice, PC, *b.* 1936
2004 *Rana,* Dr Diljit Singh Rana, MBE, *b.* 1938, *m.*
1997 *Randall of St Budeaux,* Stuart Jeffrey Randall, *b.* 1938, *m.*
1978 Rawlinson of Ewell, Peter Anthony Grayson Rawlinson, PC, QC, *b.* 1919, *m.*
1997 *Razzall,* (Edward) Timothy Razzall, CBE, *b.* 1943, *m.*
1987 *Rees,* Peter Wynford Innes Rees, PC, QC, *b.* 1926, *m.*
1988 *Rees-Mogg,* William Rees-Mogg, *b.* 1928, *m.*
1991 *Renfrew of Kaimsthorn,* (Andrew) Colin Renfrew, FBA, *b.* 1937, *m.*
1999 *Rennard,* Christopher John Rennard, MBE, *b.* 1960
1979 *Renton,* David Lockhart-Mure Renton, KBE, TD, PC, QC, *b.* 1908, *w.*
1997 *Renton of Mount Harry,* (Ronald) Timothy Renton, PC, *b.* 1932, *m.*

1997 *Renwick of Clifton,* Robin William Renwick, KCMG, *b.* 1937, *m.*
1990 *Richard,* Ivor Seward Richard, PC, QC, *b.* 1932, *m.*
1983 *Richardson of Duntisbourne,* Gordon William Humphreys Richardson, KG, MBE, TD, PC, *b.* 1915, *m.*
1992 *Rix,* Brian Norman Roger Rix, CBE, *b.* 1924, *m.*
2004 *Roberts of Llandudno,* Revd John Roger Roberts, *b.* 1935, *m.*
1997 *Roberts of Conwy,* (Ieuan) Wyn (Pritchard) Roberts, PC, *b.* 1930, *m.*
1999 *Robertson of Port Ellen,* George Islay MacNeill Robertson, PC, *b.* 1946, *m.*
1992 *Rodger of Earlsferry,* Alan Ferguson Rodger, PC, QC, FBA, *b.* 1944, *Lord of Appeal in Ordinary*
1992 *Rodgers of Quarry Bank,* William Thomas Rodgers, PC, *b.* 1928, *m.*
1999 *Rogan,* Dennis Robert David Rogan, *b.* 1942, *m.*
1996 *Rogers of Riverside,* Richard George Rogers, RA, RIBA, *b.* 1933, *m.*
1977 *Roll of Ipsden,* Eric Roll, KCMG, CB, *b.* 1907, *w.*
2001 *Rooker,* Jeffrey William Rooker, PC, *b.* 1941, *m.*
2000 *Roper,* John Francis Hodgess Roper, *b.* 1935, *m.*
2004 *Rosser,* Richard Andrew Rosser, *b.* 1944, *m.*
2004 *Rowlands,* Edward Rowlands, CBE, *b.* 1940, *m.*
1997 *Russell-Johnston,* (David) Russell Russell-Johnston, *b.* 1932, *m.*
1997 *Ryder of Wensum,* Richard Andrew Ryder, OBE, PC, *b.* 1949, *m.*
1996 *Saatchi,* Maurice Saatchi, *b.* 1946, *m.*
1989 *Sainsbury of Preston Candover,* John Davan Sainsbury, KG, *b.* 1927, *m.*
1997 *Sainsbury of Turville,* David John Sainsbury, *b.* 1940, *m.*
1987 *St John of Fawsley,* Norman Antony Francis St John-Stevas, PC, *b.* 1929
1997 *Sandberg,* Michael Graham Ruddock Sandberg, CBE, *b.* 1927, *m.*
1985 *Sanderson of Bowden,* Charles Russell Sanderson, *b.* 1933, *m.*
1998 *Sawyer,* Lawrence (Tom) Sawyer, *b.* 1943
2000 *Scott of Foscote,* Richard Rashleigh Folliott Scott, PC, *b.* 1934, *m. Lord of Appeal in Ordinary*
1997 *Selkirk of Douglas,* James Alexander Douglas-Hamilton, MSP, PC, QC, *b.* 1942, *m.*
1996 *Sewel,* John Buttifant Sewel, CBE, *b.* 1946
1999 *Sharman,* Colin Morven Sharman, OBE, *b.* 1943, *m.*
1994 *Shaw of Northstead,* Michael Norman Shaw, *b.* 1920, *m.*
2001 *Sheldon,* Robert Edward Sheldon, PC, *b.* 1923, *m.*
1994 *Sheppard of Didgemere,* Allan John George Sheppard, KCVO, *b.* 1932, *m.*
1998 *Sheppard of Liverpool,* David Stuart Sheppard, *b.* 1929, *m.*
2000 *Shutt of Greetland,* David Trevor Shutt, OBE, *b.* 1942
1971 *Simon of Glaisdale,* Jocelyn Edward Salis Simon, PC, *b.* 1911, *m.*
1997 *Simon of Highbury,* David Alec Gwyn Simon, CBE, *b.* 1939, *m.*
1997 *Simpson of Dunkeld,* George Simpson, *b.* 1942, *m.*
1991 *Skidelsky,* Robert Jacob Alexander Skidelsky, DPHIL, *b.* 1939, *m.*
1997 *Smith of Clifton,* Trevor Arthur Smith, *b.* 1937, *m.*
1999 *Smith of Leigh,* Peter Richard Charles Smith, *b.* 1945, *m.*
2004 *Snape,* Peter Charles Snape, *b.* 1942
1990 *Soulsby of Swaffham Prior,* Ernest Jackson Lawson Soulsby, PHD, *b.* 1926, *m.*
1983 *Stallard,* Albert William Stallard, *b.* 1921, *m.*
1997 *Steel of Aikwood,* David Martin Scott Steel, PC, KBE, MSP, *b.* 1938, *m.*
2004 *Steinberg,* Leonard Steinberg, *b.* 1936
1991 *Sterling of Plaistow,* Jeffrey Maurice Sterling, GCVO, CBE, *b.* 1934, *m.*
1987 *Stevens of Ludgate,* David Robert Stevens, *b.* 1936, *m.*
1999 *Stevenson of Coddenham,* Henry Dennistoun Stevenson, CBE, *b.* 1945, *m.*
1992 *Stewartby,* (Bernard Harold) Ian (Halley) Stewart, RD, PC, FBA, FRSE, *b.* 1935, *m.*
1983 *Stoddart of Swindon,* David Leonard Stoddart, *b.* 1926, *m.*
1969 *Stokes,* Donald Gresham Stokes, TD, FENG, *b.* 1914, *w.*
1997 *Stone of Blackheath,* Andrew Zelig Stone, *b.* 1942, *m.*
2001 *Sutherland of Houndwood,* Stewart Ross Sutherland, KT, *b.* 1941, *m.*
1971 *Tanlaw,* Simon Brooke Mackay, *b.* 1934, *m.*
1996 *Taverne,* Dick Taverne, QC, *b.* 1928, *m.*
1978 *Taylor of Blackburn,* Thomas Taylor, CBE, *b.* 1929, *m.*
1996 *Taylor of Warwick,* John David Beckett Taylor, *b.* 1952, *m.*
1992 *Tebbit,* Norman Beresford Tebbit, CH, PC, *b.* 1931, *m.*
2001 *Temple-Morris,* Peter Temple-Morris, *b.* 1938, *m.*
1996 *Thomas of Gresford,* Donald Martin Thomas, OBE, QC, *b.* 1937, *m.*
1987 *Thomas of Gwydir,* Peter John Mitchell Thomas, PC, QC, *b.* 1920, *w.*
1997 *Thomas of Macclesfield,* Terence James Thomas, CBE, *b.* 1937, *m.*
1981 *Thomas of Swynnerton,* Hugh Swynnerton Thomas, *b.* 1931, *m.*
1977 *Thomson of Monifieth,* George Morgan Thomson, KT, PC, *b.* 1921, *m.*
1990 *Tombs,* Francis Leonard Tombs, FENG, *b.* 1924, *m.*
1998 *Tomlinson,* John Edward Tomlinson, MEP, *b.* 1939
1994 *Tope,* Graham Norman Tope, CBE, *b.* 1943, *m.*
1981 *Tordoff,* Geoffrey Johnson Tordoff, *b.* 1928, *m.*
2004 *Triesman,* David Maxim Triesman, *b.* 1943
1999 *Trotman,* Alexander Trotman, *b.* 1933
2004 *Truscott,* Dr Peter Derek Truscott, *b.* 1959 *m.*
1993 *Tugendhat,* Christopher Samuel Tugendhat, *b.* 1937, *m.*
2004 *Tunnicliffe,* Denis Tunnicliffe, CBE, *b.* 1943, *m.*
2000 *Turnberg,* Leslie Arnold Turnberg, MD, *b.* 1934, *m.*
2004 *Vallance of Tummel,* Iain (David Thomas) Vallance, *b.* 1943, *m.*
1990 *Varley,* Eric Graham Varley, PC, *b.* 1932, *m.*
1996 *Vincent of Coleshill,* Richard Frederick Vincent, GBE, KCB, DSO, *b.* 1931, *m.*
1985 *Vinson,* Nigel Vinson, LVO, *b.* 1931, *m.*

1990 *Waddington,* David Charles Waddington, GCVO, PC, QC, *b.* 1929, *m.*
1990 *Wade of Chorlton,* (William) Oulton Wade, *b.* 1932, *m.*
1992 *Wakeham,* John Wakeham, PC, *b.* 1932, *m.*
1999 *Waldegrave of North Hill,* William Arthur Waldegrave, PC, *b.* 1946, *m.*
2003 *Walker of Gestingthorpe,* Robert Walker, PC, *b.* 1938, *m. Lord of Appeal in Ordinary*
1992 *Walker of Worcester,* Peter Edward Walker, MBE, PC, *b.* 1932, *m.*
1995 *Wallace of Saltaire,* William John Lawrence Wallace, PHD, *b.* 1941, *m.*
1989 *Walton of Detchant,* John Nicholas Walton, TD, FRCP, *b.* 1922, *m.*
1998 *Warner,* Norman Reginald Warner, *b.* 1940, *m.*
1997 *Watson of Invergowrie,* Michael Goodall Watson, MSP, *b.* 1949, *m.*
1999 *Watson of Richmond,* Alan John Watson, CBE, *b.* 1941, *m.*
1992 *Weatherill,* (Bruce) Bernard Weatherill, PC, *b.* 1920, *m.*
1977 *Wedderburn of Charlton,* (Kenneth) William Wedderburn, FBA, QC, *b.* 1927, *m.*
1976 *Weidenfeld,* (Arthur) George Weidenfeld, *b.* 1919, *m.*
1978 *Whaddon,* (John) Derek Page, *b.* 1927, *m.*
1996 *Whitty,* John Lawrence (Larry) Whitty, *b.* 1943, *m.*
1985 *Williams of Elvel,* Charles Cuthbert Powell Williams, CBE, *b.* 1933, *m.*
1999 *Williamson of Horton,* David (Francis) Williamson, GCMG, CB, *b.* 1934, *m.*
2002 *Wilson of Dinton,* Richard Thomas James Wilson, GCB, *b.* 1942, *m.*
1992 *Wilson of Tillyorn,* David Clive Wilson, KT, GCMG, PHD, *b.* 1935, *m.*
1995 *Winston,* Robert Maurice Lipson Winston, FRCOG, *b.* 1940, *m.*
1985 *Wolfson,* Leonard Gordon Wolfson, *b.* 1927, *m.*
1991 *Wolfson of Sunningdale,* David Wolfson, *b.* 1935, *m.*
1999 *Woolmer of Leeds,* Kenneth John Woolmer, *b.* 1940, *m.*
1994 *Wright of Richmond,* Patrick Richard Henry Wright, CGMC, *b.* 1931, *m.*
2004 *Young of Norwood Green,* Anthony (Ian) Young, *b.* 1942, *m.*
1984 *Young of Graffham,* David Ivor Young, PC, *b.* 1932, *m.*

BARONESSES
Created
1997 *Amos,* Valerie Ann Amos, *b.* 1954
2000 *Andrews,* Elizabeth Kay Andrews, OBE, *b.* 1943, *m.*
1996 *Anelay of St Johns,* Joyce Anne Anelay, DBE, *b.* 1947, *m.*
1999 *Ashton of Upholland,* Catherine Margaret Ashton, *b.* 1956, *m.*
1999 *Barker,* Elizabeth Jean Barker, *b.* 1961
2000 *Billingham,* Angela Theodora Billingham, DPHIL, *b.* 1939, *w.*
1987 *Blackstone,* Tessa Ann Vosper Blackstone, PHD, *b.* 1942
1987 *Blatch,* Emily May Blatch, CBE, PC, *b.* 1937, *m.*
1999 *Blood,* May Blood, MBE, *b.* 1938
2000 *Boothroyd,* Betty Boothroyd, PC, *b.* 1929
2004 *Bonham-Carter of Yarnbury,* Jane Bonham Carter, *b.* 1957, *w.*
1998 *Buscombe,* Peta Jane Buscombe, *b.* 1954, *m.*
1996 *Byford,* Hazel Byford, DBE, *b.* 1941, *m.*
1982 *Carnegy of Lour,* Elizabeth Patricia Carnegy of Lour, *b.* 1925
1992 *Chalker of Wallasey,* Lynda Chalker, PC, *b.* 1942, *m.*
2004 *Chapman of Leeds,* Nicola Jane Chapman, *b.* 1961
2000 *Cohen of Pimlico,* Janet Cohen, *b.* 1940, *m.*
1982 *Cox,* Caroline Anne Cox, *b.* 1937, *m.*
1998 *Crawley,* Christine Mary Crawley, MEP, *b.* 1950, *m.*
1990 *Cumberlege,* Julia Frances Cumberlege, CBE, *b.* 1943, *m.*
1978 *David,* Nora Ratcliff David, *b.* 1913, *w.*
1993 *Dean of Thornton-le-Fylde,* Brenda Dean, PC, *b.* 1943, *m.*
1974 *Delacourt-Smith of Alteryn,* Margaret Rosalind Delacourt-Smith, *b.* 1916, *m.*
2004 *D'Souza,* Dr Frances Gertrude Claire D'Souza, CMG, *b.* 1944 *m.*
1990 *Dunn,* Lydia Selina Dunn, DBE, *b.* 1940, *m.*
1990 *Eccles of Moulton,* Diana Catherine Eccles, *b.* 1933, *m.*
1972 *Elles,* Diana Louie Elles, *b.* 1921, *m.*
1997 *Emerton,* Audrey Caroline Emerton, DBE, *b.* 1935
1974 *Falkender,* Marcia Matilda Falkender, CBE, *b.* 1932
2004 *Falkner of Margravine,* Kishwer Falkner, *b.* 1955, *m.*
1994 *Farrington of Ribbleton,* Josephine Farrington, *b.* 1940, *m.*
2001 *Finlay of Llandaff,* Ilora Gillian Finlay, *b.* 1949, *m.*
1974 *Fisher of Rednal,* Doris Mary Gertrude Fisher, *b.* 1919, *w.*
1990 *Flather,* Shreela Flather, *m.*
1997 *Fookes,* Janet Evelyn Fookes, DBE, *b.* 1936
1999 *Gale,* Anita Gale, *b.* 1940
1981 *Gardner of Parkes,* (Rachel) Trixie (Anne) Gardner, *b.* 1927, *m.*
2000 *Gibson of Market Rasen,* Anne Gibson, OBE, *b.* 1940, *m.*
2001 *Golding,* Llinos Golding, *b.* 1933, *m.*
1998 *Goudie,* Mary Teresa Goudie, *b.* 1946, *m.*
1993 *Gould of Potternewton,* Joyce Brenda Gould, *b.* 1932, *m.*
2001 *Greenfield,* Susan Adele Greenfield, CBE, *b.* 1950, *m.*
2000 *Greengross,* Sally Ralea Greengross, OBE, *b.* 1935, *m.*
1991 *Hamwee,* Sally Rachel Hamwee, *b.* 1947
1999 *Hanham,* Joan Brownlow Hanham, CBE, *b.* 1939, *m.*
1999 *Harris of Richmond,* Angela Felicity Harris, *b.* 1944
1996 *Hayman,* Helene Valerie Hayman, PC, *b.* 1949, *m.*
2004 *Henig,* Ruth Beatrice Henig, CBE, *b.* 1943, *m.*
1991 *Hilton of Eggardon,* Jennifer Hilton, QPM, *b.* 1936
1995 *Hogg,* Sarah Elizabeth Mary Hogg, *b.* 1946, *m.*
1990 *Hollis of Heigham,* Patricia Lesley Hollis, DPHIL, *b.* 1941, *m.*

1985 *Hooper,* Gloria Dorothy Hooper, CMG, *b.* 1939
2001 *Howarth of Breckland,* Valerie Georgina Howarth, OBE, *b.* 1940
2001 *Howe of Idlicote,* Elspeth Rosamond Morton Howe, CBE, *b.* 1932, *m.*
1999 *Howells of St Davids,* Rosalind Patricia-Anne Howells, *b.* 1931, *m.*
1991 *James of Holland Park,* Phyllis Dorothy White (P. D. James), OBE, *b.* 1920, *w.*
1992 *Jay of Paddington,* Margaret Ann Jay, PC, *b.* 1939, *m.*
1979 *Jeger,* Lena May Jeger, *b.* 1915, *w.*
1997 *Kennedy of the Shaws,* Helena Ann Kennedy, QC, *b.* 1950, *m.*
1997 *Knight of Collingtree,* (Joan Christabel) Jill Knight, DBE, *b.* 1927, *w.*
1997 *Linklater of Butterstone,* Veronica Linklater, *b.* 1943, *m.*
1996 *Lloyd of Highbury,* Prof. June Kathleen Lloyd, DBE, FRCP, FRCPE, FRCGP, *b.* 1928
1978 *Lockwood,* Betty Lockwood, *b.* 1924, *w.*
1997 *Ludford,* Sarah Ann Ludford, MEP, *b.* 1951
2004 *McDonagh,* Margaret Josephine McDonagh
1979 *McFarlane of Llandaff,* Jean Kennedy McFarlane, *b.* 1926
1999 *McIntosh of Hudnall,* Genista Mary McIntosh, *b.* 1946
1997 *Maddock,* Diana Margaret Maddock, *b.* 1945, *m.*
1991 *Mallalieu,* Ann Mallalieu, QC, *b.* 1945, *m.*
1970 *Masham of Ilton,* Susan Lilian Primrose Cunliffe-Lister, *b.* 1935, *m.*
1999 *Massey of Darwen,* Doreen Elizabeth Massey, *b.* 1938, *m.*
2001 *Michie of Gallanach,* Janet Ray Michie, *b.* 1934, *m.*
1998 *Miller of Chilthorne Domer,* Susan Elizabeth Miller, *b.* 1954
1993 *Miller of Hendon,* Doreen Miller, MBE, *b.* 1933, *m.*
2004 *Morgan of Drefelin,* Delyth Jane Morgan *b.* 1961, *m.*
2001 *Morgan of Huyton,* Sally Morgan, *b.* 1959, *m.*
2004 *Morris of Bolton,* Patricia Morris, OBE, *b.* 1953
2004 *Murphy,* Elaine Murphy, *b.* 1947, *m.*
2004 *Neuberger,* Rabbi Julia (Babette Sarah), DBE, *b.* 1950, *m.*
1997 *Nicholson of Winterbourne,* Emma Harriet Nicholson, MEP, *b.* 1941, *m.*
1982 *Nicol,* Olive Mary Wendy Nicol, *b.* 1923, *m.*
2000 *Noakes,* Shiela Valerie Masters, DBE, *b.* 1949, *m.*
2000 *Northover,* Lindsay Patricia Granshaw, *b.* 1954
1991 *O'Cathain,* Detta O'Cathain, OBE, *b.* 1938, *m.*
1999 *O'Neill of Bengarve,* Onora Sylvia O'Neill, CBE, PHD, *b.* 1941
1989 *Oppenheim-Barnes,* Sally Oppenheim-Barnes, PC, *b.* 1930, *m.*
1990 *Park of Monmouth,* Daphne Margaret Sybil Désirée Park, CMG, OBE, *b.* 1921
1991 *Perry of Southwark,* Pauline Perry, *b.* 1931, *m.*
1997 *Pitkeathley,* Jill Elizabeth Pitkeathley, OBE, *b.* 1940
1981 *Platt of Writtle,* Beryl Catherine Platt, CBE, FENG, *b.* 1923, *m.*
1999 *Prashar,* Usha Kumari Prashar, CBE, *b.* 1948, *m.*
2004 *Prosser,* Margaret Theresa Prosser, OBE, *b.* 1937
1996 *Ramsay of Cartvale,* Margaret Mildred (Meta) Ramsay, *b.* 1936
1994 *Rawlings,* Patricia Elizabeth Rawlings, *b.* 1939
1997 *Rendell of Babergh,* Ruth Barbara Rendell, CBE, *b.* 1930, *m.*
1998 *Richardson of Calow,* Kathleen Margaret Richardson, OBE, *b.* 1938, *m.*
2004 *Royall of Blaisdon,* Janet Anne Royall, *b.* 1955, *m.*
1997 *Scotland of Asthal,* Patricia Janet Scotland, QC, *b.* 1955, *m.*
2000 *Scott of Needham Market,* Rosalind Carol Scott, *b.* 1957
1991 *Seccombe,* Joan Anna Dalziel Seccombe, DBE, *b.* 1930, *m.*
1998 *Sharp of Guildford,* Margaret Lucy Sharp, *b.* 1938, *m.*
1973 *Sharples,* Pamela Sharples, *b.* 1923, *m.*
1995 *Smith of Gilmorehill,* Elizabeth Margaret Smith, *b.* 1940, *w.*
1999 *Stern,* Vivien Helen Stern, CBE, *b.* 1941
1996 *Symons of Vernham Dean,* Elizabeth Conway Symons, *b.* 1951
1992 *Thatcher,* Margaret Hilda Thatcher, KG, OM, PC, FRS, *b.* 1925, *w.*
1994 *Thomas of Walliswood,* Susan Petronella Thomas, OBE, *b.* 1935, *m.*
1998 *Thornton,* (Dorothea) Glenys Thornton, *b.* 1952, *m.*
1980 *Trumpington,* Jean Alys Barker, PC, *b.* 1922, *w.*
1985 *Turner of Camden,* Muriel Winifred Turner, *b.* 1927, *m.*
1998 *Uddin,* Manzila Pola Uddin, *b.* 1959, *m.*
2004 *Wall of New Barnet,* Margaret Mary Wall, *b.* 1941, *m.*
2000 *Walmsley,* Joan Margaret Walmsley, *b.* 1943
1985 *Warnock,* Helen Mary Warnock, DBE, *b.* 1924, *w.*
1999 *Warwick of Undercliffe,* Diana Mary Warwick, *b.* 1945, *m.*
1999 *Whitaker,* Janet Alison Whitaker, *b.* 1936
1996 *Wilcox,* Judith Ann Wilcox, *b.* 1940, *w.*
1999 *Wilkins,* Rosalie Catherine Wilkins, *b.* 1946
1993 *Williams of Crosby,* Shirley Vivien Teresa Brittain Williams, PC, *b.* 1930, *m.*
2004 *Young of Hornsey,* Prof. Margaret Omolola Young, OBE, *b.* 1951, *m.*
1997 *Young of Old Scone,* Barbara Scott Young, *b.* 1948

LORDS SPIRITUAL

The Lords Spiritual are the Archbishops of Canterbury and York and 24 diocesan bishops of the Church of England. The Bishops of London, Durham and Winchester always have seats in the House of Lords; the other 21 seats are filled by the remaining diocesan bishops in order of seniority. The Bishop of Sodor and Man and the Bishop of Gibraltar are not eligible to sit in the House of Lords.

ARCHBISHOPS

Style, The Most Revd and Right Hon. the Lord Archbishop of _
Addressed as Archbishop, *or* Your Grace

INTRODUCED TO HOUSE OF LORDS

2003 *Canterbury* (104th), Rowan Douglas Williams, PC, DPHIL, *b.* 1950, *m.*, *cons.* 1992, *elected* 2002
1990 *York* (96th), David Michael Hope, KCVO, PC, DPHIL, LLD, *b.* 1940, *cons.* 1985, *elected* 1985, *trans.* 1995

BISHOPS

Style, The Right Revd the Lord Bishop of _
Addressed as My Lord
Elected date of confirmation as diocesan bishop

INTRODUCED TO HOUSE OF LORDS
(as at 31 August 2004)

1996 *London* (132nd), Richard John Carew Chartres, *b.* 1947, *m.*, *cons.* 1992, *elected* 1995
2003 *Durham* (71st), Nicholas Thomas Wright, DPHIL, *b.* 1948, *m.*, *cons.* 2003, *elected* 2003
1996 *Winchester* (96th), Michael Charles Scott-Joynt, *b.* 1943, *m.*, *cons.* 1987, *elected* 1995
1993 *Oxford* (41st), Richard Douglas Harries, *b.* 1936, *m.*, *cons.* 1987, *elected* 1987
1997 *Southwark* (9th), Thomas Frederick Butler, *b.* 1940, *m.*, *cons.* 1985, *elected* 1991, *trans.* 1998
1997 *Manchester* (11th), Nigel Simeon McCulloch, *b.* 1942, *m.*, *cons.* 1986, *elected* 1992, *trans.* 2002
1998 *Salisbury* (77th), David Stafffurth Stancliffe, *b.* 1942, *m.*, *cons.* 1993, *elected* 1993
1999 *Rochester* (106th), Michael James Nazir-Ali, PHD, *b.* 1949, *m.*, *cons.* 1984, *elected* 1994
1999 *Chelmsford* (9th) John Warren Gladwin, *b.* 1942, *m.*, *cons.* 1994, *elected* 1994, *trans.* 2003
1999 *Portsmouth* (8th), Kenneth William Stevenson, *b.* 1949, *m.*, *cons.* 1995, *elected* 1995
1999 *Derby* (6th), Jonathan Sansbury Bailey, *b.* 1940, *m.*, *cons.* 1992, *elected* 1995
1999 *St Albans* (9th), Christopher William Herbert, *b.* 1944, *m.*, *cons.* 1995, *elected* 1995
2001 *Peterborough* (37th), Ian Cundy, *b.* 1945, *m.*, *cons.* 1992, *elected* 1996
2001 *Chester* (40th), Peter Robert Forster, PHD, *b.* 1950, *cons.* 1996, *elected* 1996
2002 *St Edmundsbury and Ipswich* (9th), (John Hubert) Richard Lewis, *b.* 1943, *m.*, *cons.* 1992, *elected* 1997
2002 *Truro* (14th), William Ind, *b.* 1942, *m.*, *cons.* 1987, *elected* 1997
2002 *Worcester* (112th), Peter Stephen Maurice Selby, *b.* 1941, *cons.* 1984, *elected* 1997
2003 *Newcastle* (11th), (John) Martin Wharton, *b.* 1944, *m.*, *cons.* 1992, *elected* 1997
2003 *Sheffield* (6th), John Nicholls, *b.* 1943, *m.*, *cons.* 1990, *elected* 1997
2003 *Coventry* (8th), Colin J. Bennetts, *b.* 1940, *m.*, *cons.* 1994, *elected* 1998
2003 *Liverpool* (7th), James Jones, *b.* 1948, *m.*, *cons.* 1994, *elected* 1998
2003 *Leicester* (6th), Timothy John Stevens, *b.* 1946, *m.*, *cons.* 1995, *elected* 1999
2004 *Southwell* (10th), George Henry Cassidy, *b.* 1942, *m.*, *cons.* 1999, *elected* 1999
2004 *Norwich* (71st), Graham R. James, *b.* 1951, *m.*, *cons.* 1993, *elected* 1999

BISHOPS AWAITING SEATS, in order of seniority
(as at 31 August 2004)

Exeter (70th), Michael L. Langrish, *b.* 1946, *m.*, *cons.* 1993, *elected* 2000
Ripon and Leeds (12th), John R. Packer, *b.* 1946, *m.*, *cons.* 1996, *elected* 2000
Ely (68th) Dr. Anthony Russell, *b.* 1943, *m.*, *cons.* 1988, *elected* 2000
Carlisle (65th) Graham Dow, *b.* 1942, *m.*, *cons.* 1985, *elected* 2000
Chichester (102nd) John Hind, *b.* 1945, *cons.* 1991, *elected* 2001
Lincoln (71st) Dr John Saxbee, *b.* 1946, *cons.* 1994, *elected* 2001
Bath & Wells (77th) Peter Price, *b.* 1944, *m.*, *cons.* 1997, *elected* 2002
Birmingham (8th) Dr John Tucker Mugabi Sentamu, PHD, *b.* 1949, m., *cons.* 1996, *elected 2002*
Bradford (9th) David James, *b.* 1945, *cons.*1998, *elected* 2002
Wakefield (12th) Stephen G. Platten, *b.* 1947, *m.*, *cons.* 2003, *elected* 2003
Bristol (55th) Michael A. Hill, *b.* 1947, *m.*, *cons.* 1998, *elected* 2003
Lichfield (98th) Jonathan Gledhill, *b.* 1949, *m.*, *cons.* 1996, *elected* 2003
Blackburn (8th) Nicholas Reade, *b.* 1946, *m.*, *cons.* 2004, *elected* 2004
Hereford (104th), Anthony Martin Priddis, *b.* 1948, *m.*, *cons.* 1996, *elected* 2004
Gloucester (40th) Michael Francis Perham, *b.* 1947, *m.*, *cons.* 2004, *elected* 2004
Guildford (9th) *vacant*

COURTESY TITLES

From this list it will be seen that, for example, the Marquess of Blandford is heir to the Dukedom of Marlborough, and Viscount Amberley to the Earldom of Russell. Titles of second heirs (when in use) are also given, and the courtesy title of the father of a second heir is indicated by * e.g. Earl of Mornington, eldest son of *Marquess of Douro

For forms of address, *see* page 43

MARQUESSES

*Blandford – *Marlborough, D.*
Bowmont and Cessford – *Roxburghe, D.*
Douglas and Clydesdale – *Hamilton, D.*
*Douro – *Wellington, D.*
Graham – *Montrose, D.*
Hamilton – *Abercorn, D.*
Hartington – *Devonshire, D.*
Kildare – *Leinster, D.*
Stafford – *Sutherland, D.*
Tullibardine – *Atholl, D.*
*Worcester – *Beaufort, D.*
*Tyrone – *Waterford, M.*
Ulster – *Gloucester, D.*
*Uxbridge – *Anglesey, M.*
Wiltshire – *Winchester, M.*
Yarmouth – *Hertford, M.*

EARLS

Aboyne – *Huntly, M.*
Ancram – *Lothian, M.*
Arundel and Surrey – *Norfolk, D.*
*Bective – *Headfort, M.*
*Belfast – *Donegall, M.*
Brecknock – *Camden, M.*
Burford – *St Albans, D.*
*Cardigan – *Ailesbury, M.*
Compton – *Northampton, M.*
*Dalkeith – *Buccleuch, D.*
*Euston – *Grafton, D.*
Glamorgan – **Worcester, M.*
Grosvenor – *Westminster, D.*
Haddo – *Aberdeen and Temair, M.*
Hillsborough – *Downshire, M.*
Hopetoun – *Linlithgow, M.*
March and Kinrara – *Richmond, D.*
Medina – *Milford Haven, M.*
*Mount Charles – *Conyngham, M.*
Mornington – **Douro, M.*
Mulgrave – *Normanby, M.*
Percy – *Northumberland, D.*
Ronaldshay – *Zetland, M.*
*St Andrews – *Kent, D.*
Shelburne – *Lansdowne, M.*
*Southesk – *Fife, D.*
Sunderland – **Blandford, M.*

VISCOUNTS

Alexander – *Caledon, E.*
Althorp – *Spencer, E.*
Amberley – *Russell, E.*
Andover – *Suffolk and Berkshire, E.*
Anson – *Lichfield, E.*
Asquith – *Oxford and Asquith, E.*
Boringdon – *Morley, E.*
Borodale – *Beatty, E.*
Boyle – *Shannon, E.*
Brocas – *Jellicoe, E.*
Campden – *Gainsborough, E.*
Carlow – *Portarlington, E.*
Carlton – *Wharncliffe, E.*
Castlereagh – *Londonderry, M.*
Chelsea – *Cadogan, E.*
Chewton – *Waldegrave, E.*
Chichester – **Belfast, E.*
Clanfield – *Peel, E.*
Clive – *Powis, E.*
Coke – *Leicester, E.*
Corry – *Belmore, E.*
Corvedale – *Baldwin of Bewdley, E.*
Cranborne – *Salisbury, M.*
Cranley – *Onslow, E.*
Crichton – *Erne, E.*
Curzon – *Howe, E.*
Dangan – *Cowley, E.*
Dawick – *Haig, E.*
Drumlanrig – *Queensberry, M.*
Duncannon – *Bessborough, E.*
Dungarvan – *Cork and Orrery, E.*
Dunluce – *Antrim, E.*
Dunwich – *Stradbroke, E.*
Dupplin – *Kinnoull, E.*
Ednam – *Dudley, E.*
Emlyn – *Cawdor, E*
Encombe – *Eldon, E.*
Enfield – *Strafford, E.*
Erleigh – *Reading, M.*
Errington – *Cromer, E.*
FitzHarris – *Malmesbury, E.*
Folkestone – *Radnor, E.*
Forbes – *Granard, E.*
Garmoyle – *Cairns, E.*
Garnock – *Lindsay, E.*
Glenapp – *Inchcape, E.*
Glentworth – *Limerick, E.*
Grey de Wilton – *Wilton, E.*
Grimstone – *Verulam, E.*
Gwynedd – *Lloyd George of Dwyfor, E.*
Hawkesbury – *Liverpool, E.*
Hinchingbrooke – *Sandwich, E.*
Ikerrin – *Carrick, E.*
Ingestre – *Shrewsbury, E.*
Ipswich – **Euston, E.*
Jocelyn – *Roden, E.*
Kelburn – *Glasgow, E.*
Kingsborough – *Kingston, E.*
Kirkwall – *Orkney, E.*
Knebworth – *Lytton, E.*
Lascelles – *Harewood, E.*
Linley – *Snowdon, E.*
Loftus – *Ely, M.*
Lowther – *Lonsdale, E.*
Lymington – *Portsmouth, E.*
Macmillan of Ovenden – *Stockton, E.*
Maidstone – *Winchilsea, E*
Maitland – *Lauderdale, E.*
Malden – *Essex, E.*
Mandeville – *Manchester, D.*
Melgund – *Minto, E.*
Merton – *Nelson, E.*
Moore – *Drogheda, E.*
Newport – *Bradford, E.*
Northland – *Ranfurly, E*
Newry and Mourne – *Kilmorey, E.*
Petersham – *Harrington, E.*
Pollington – *Mexborough, E*
Raynham – *Townshend, M.*
Reidhaven – *Seafield, E.*
Ruthven of Canberra – *Gowrie, E.*
St Cyres – *Iddesleigh, E.*
Sandon – *Harrowby, E.*
Savernake – **Cardigan, E.*
Slane – **Mount Charles, E.*
Somerton – *Normanton, E.*
Stopford – *Courtown, E.*
Stormont – *Mansfield, E.*
Strathallan – *Perth, E.*
Stuart – *Castle Stewart, E.*
Suirdale – *Donoughmore, E.*
Tamworth – *Ferrers, E.*
Tarbat – *Cromartie, E.*
Vaughan – *Lisburne, E.*
Weymouth – *Bath, M.*
Windsor – *Plymouth, E.*
Wolmer – *Selborne, E.*
Woodstock – *Portland, E.*

BARONS (LORDS)

Aberdour – *Morton, E.*
Apsley – *Bathurst, E.*
Ardee – *Meath, E.*
Ashley – *Shaftesbury, E.*
Balgonie – *Leven and Melville, E.*
Balniel – *Crawford and Balcarres, E.*
Berriedale – *Caithness, E.*
Bingham – *Lucan, E.*
Binning – *Haddington, E.*
Brooke – *Warwick, E.*
Bruce – *Elgin, E.*
Buckhurst – *De La Warr, E*
Burghley – *Exeter, M.*
Cardross – *Buchan, E.*
Carnegie – **Southesk, E.*
Clifton – *Darnley, E.*
Cochrane – *Dundonald, E.*
Courtenay – *Devon, E.*
Dalmeny – *Rosebery, E.*
Doune – *Moray, E.*
Downpatrick – **St Andrews, E.*
Dunglass – *Home, E.*
Eliot – *St Germans, E.*
Eskdail – **Dalkeith, E.*
Formartine – **Haddo, E.*
Gillford – *Clanwilliam, E.*
Glamis – *Strathmore, E.*
Greenock – *Cathcart, E.*
Guernsey – *Aylesford, E.*
Hay – *Erroll, E.*
Howard of Effingham – *Effingham, E.*
Huntingtower – *Dysart, C.*
Hyde – *Clarendon, E.*
Inverurie – *Kintore, E.*
Irwin – *Halifax, E.*
Johnstone – *Annandale and Hartfell, E.*
Kenlis – **Bective, E.*
Langton – *Temple of Stowe, E.*
La Poer – **Tyrone, E.*
Leslie – *Rothes, E.*
Leveson – *Granville, E*
Loughborough – *Rosslyn, E.*
Mauchline – *Loudoun, C.*
Medway – *Cranbrook, E.*
Montgomerie – *Eglinton and Winton, E.*
Moreton – *Ducie, E.*
Mount Stuart – *Bute, M*
Naas – *Mayo, E.*
Neidpath – *Wemyss and March, E.*
Norreys – *Lindsey and Abingdon, E.*

North – *Guilford, E.*
Ogilvy – *Airlie, E.*
Oxmantown – *Rosse, E.*
Paget de Beaudesert – **Uxbridge, E.*
Porchester – *Carnarvon, E.*
Ramsay – *Dalhousie, E.*
Romsey – *Mountbatten of Burma, C.*
Scrymgeour – *Dundee, E.*
Seymour – *Somerset, D.*
Stanley – *Derby, E.*
Strathnaver – *Sutherland, C.*
Wodehouse – *Kimberley, E.*
Worsley – *Yarborough, E.*

PEERS' SURNAMES WHICH DIFFER FROM THEIR TITLES

The following symbols indicate the rank of the peer holding each title:

C. Countess
D. Duke
E. Earl
M. Marquess
V. Viscount
* Life Peer

Where no designation is given, the title is that of an hereditary Baron or Baroness

Abney-Hastings – *Loudoun, C.*
Acheson – *Gosford, E.*
Adderley – *Norton*
Addington – *Sidmouth, V.*
Adebowale – *A. of Thornes**
Agar – *Normanton, E.*
Aitken – *Beaverbrook*
Akers-Douglas – *Chilston, V.*
Alexander – *A. of Tunis, E.*
Alexander – *A. of Weedon**
Alexander – *Caledon, E.*
Allen – *A. of Abbeydale**
Allen – *Croham**
Allsopp – *Hindlip*
Alton – *A. of Liverpool**
Anderson – *Waverley, V.*
Anelay – *A. of St Johns**
Annesley – *Valentia, V.*
Anson – *Lichfield, E.*
Archer – *A. of Sandwell**
Archer – *A. of Weston-super-Mare**
Armstrong – *A. of Ilminster**
Armstrong-Jones – *Snowdon, E.*
Arthur – *Glenarthur*
Arundell – *Talbot of Malahide*
Ashdown – *A. of Norton-sub-Hamdon**
Ashley – *A. of Stoke**
Ashley-Cooper – *Shaftesbury, E.*
Ashton – *A. of Hyde*
Ashton – *A. of Upholland**
Asquith – *Oxford and Asquith, E.*
Assheton – *Clitheroe*
Astley – *Hastings*
Astor – *A. of Hever*
Aubrey-Fletcher – *Braye*
Bailey – *Glanusk*
Baillie – *Burton*
Baillie Hamilton – *Haddington, E.*
Baker – *B. of Dorking**
Baldwin – *B. of Bewdley, E.*
Balfour – *B. of Inchrye*
Balfour – *Kinross*
Balfour – *Riverdale*
Bampfylde – *Poltimore*
Banbury – *B. of Southam*
Barber – *B. of Tewkesbury**
Baring – *Ashburton*
Baring – *Cromer, E.*
Baring – *Howick of Glendale*
Baring – *Northbrook*
Baring – *Revelstoke*
Barker – *Trumpington**
Barnes – *Gorell*
Barnewall – *Trimlestown*
Bassam – *B. of Brighton**
Bathurst – *Bledisloe, V.*
Beauclerk – *St Albans, D.*
Beaumont – *Allendale, V.*
Beaumont – *B. of Whitley**
Beckett – *Grimthorpe*
Benn – *Stansgate, V.*
Bennet – *Tankerville, E.*
Bentinck – *Portland, E.*
Beresford – *Decies*
Beresford – *Waterford, M.*
Bernstein – *B. of Craigweil**
Berry – *Camrose, V.*
Berry – *Kemsley, V.*
Bertie – *Lindsey, E.*
Best – *Wynford*
Bethell – *Westbury*
Bewicke-Copley – *Cromwell*
Bigham – *Mersey, V.*
Bingham – *B. of Cornhill**
Bingham – *Clanmorris*
Bingham – *Lucan, E.*
Black – *B. of Crossharbour**
Bligh – *Darnley, E.*
Blyth – *B. of Rowington**
Bonham Carter – *B.-C. of Yarnbury**
Bootle-Wilbraham – *Skelmersdale*
Boscawen – *Falmouth, V.*
Boston – *B. of Faversham**
Bourke – *Mayo, E.*
Bowes Lyon – *Strathmore, E.*
Bowyer – *Denham*
Boyd – *Kilmarnock*
Boyle – *Cork and Orrery, E.*
Boyle – *Glasgow, E.*
Boyle – *Shannon, E.*
Brabazon – *Meath, E.*
Brand – *Hampden, V.*
Brassey – *B. of Apethorpe*
Brett – *Esher, V.*
Bridge – *B. of Harwich**
Bridgeman – *Bradford, E.*
Brittan – *B. of Spennithorne**
Brodrick – *Midleton, V.*
Brooke – *Alanbrooke, V.*
Brooke – *B. of Alverthorpe**
Brooke – *Brookeborough, V.*
Brooke – *B. of Sutton Mandeville**
Brooks – *B. of Tremorfa**
Brooks – *Crawshaw*
Brougham – *Brougham and Vaux*
Broughton – *Fairhaven*
Brown – *B. of Eaton-under-Heywood**
Browne – *Kilmaine*
Browne – *B. of Madingley**
Browne – *Oranmore and Browne*
Browne – *Sligo, M.*
Bruce – *Aberdare*
Bruce – *Balfour of Burleigh*
Bruce – *B. of Donington**
Bruce – *Elgin and Kincardine, E.*
Brudenell-Bruce – *Ailesbury, M.*
Buchan – *Tweedsmuir*
Buckley – *Wrenbury*
Butler – *B. of Brockwell**
Butler – *Carrick, E.*
Butler – *Dunboyne*
Butler – *Mountgarret, V.*
Buxton – *B. of Alsa**
Byng – *Strafford, E.*
Byng – *Torrington, V.*
Callaghan – *C. of Cardiff**
Cambell-Savours – *C.-S. of Allerdale**
Cameron – *C. of Dillington**
Cameron – *C. of Lochbroom**
Campbell – *Argyll, D.*
Campbell – *C. of Alloway**
Campbell – *C. of Croy**
Campbell – *Cawdor, E.*
Campbell – *Colgrain*
Campbell – *Stratheden and Campbell*
Campbell-Gray – *Gray*
Canning – *Garvagh*
Capell – *Essex, E.*
Carey – *C. of Clifton**
Carington – *Carrington*
Carlisle – *C. of Berriew**
Carlisle – *C. of Bucklow**
Carnegie – *Fife, D.*
Carnegie – *Northesk, E.*
Carr – *C. of Hadley**
Carter – *C. of Coles**
Cary – *Falkland, V.*
Caulfeild – *Charlemont, V.*
Cavendish – *C. of Furness**
Cavendish – *Chesham*
Cavendish – *Devonshire, D.*
Cavendish – *Waterpark*
Cayzer – *Rotherwick*
Cecil – *Amherst of Hackney*
Cecil – *Exeter, M.*
Cecil – *Rockley*
Czernin – *Howard de Walden*
Chalker – *C. of Wallasey**
Chaloner – *Gisborough*
Channon – *Kelvedon**
Chapman – *C. of Leeds**
Chapman – *Northfield**
Charteris – *Wemyss and March, E.*
Chetwynd-Talbot – *Shrewsbury, E.*
Chichester – *Donegall, M.*
Child Villiers – *Jersey, E.*
Cholmondeley – *Delamere*
Chubb – *Hayter*
Clark – *C. of Kempston**
Clarke – *C. of Hampstead**
Clegg-Hill – *Hill, V.*
Clifford – *C. of Chudleigh*
Cochrane – *C. of Cults*
Cochrane – *Dundonald, E.*
Cocks – *Somers*
Cohen – *C. of Pimlico**

Cokayne – *Cullen of Ashbourne*
Coke – *Leicester, E.*
Cole – *Enniskillen, E.*
Collier – *Monkswell*
Colville – *Clydesmuir*
Colville – *C. of Culross, V.*
Compton – *Northampton, M.*
Condon – *C. of Langdon Green**
Conolly-Carew – *Carew*
Cooke – *C. of Islandreagh**
Cooke – *C. of Thorndon**
Cooper – *Norwich, V*
Cope – *C. of Berkeley**
Corbett – *C. of Castle Vale**.
Corbett – *Rowallan*
Cornwall-Leigh – *Grey of Condor*
Courtenay – *Devon, E.*
Craig – *C. of Radley**
Craig – *Craigavon, V.*
Crichton – *Erne, E.*
Crichton-Stuart – *Bute, M.*
Cripps – *Parmoor*
Crossley – *Somerleyton*
Cubitt – *Ashcombe*
Cunliffe-Lister – *Masham of Ilton**
Cunliffe-Lister – *Swinton, E.*
Currie – *C. of Marylebone**
Curzon – *Howe, E.*
Curzon – *Scarsdale, V.*
Cust – *Brownlow*
Dalrymple – *Stair, E.*
Daubeny de Moleyns – *Ventry*
Davies – *D. of Coity**
Davies – *Darwen*
Davies – *D. of Oldham**
Davison – *Broughshane*
Dawnay – *Downe, V.*
Dawson-Damer – *Portarlington, E.*
Dean – *D. of Harptree**
Dean – *D. of Thornton-le-Fylde**
Deane – *Muskerry*
de Courcy – *Kingsale*
de Grey – *Walsingham*
Delacourt-Smith – *Delacourt Smith of Alteryn**
Denison – *Londesborough*
Denison-Pender – *Pender*
Devereux – *Hereford, V.*
Dewar – *Forteviot*
De Yarburgh-Bateson – *Deramore*
Dixon – *Glentoran*
Dodson – *Monk Bretton*
Donaldson – *D. of Lymington**
Douglas – *Morton, E.*
Douglas – *Queensberry, M.*
Douglas-Hamilton – *Hamilton, D.*
Douglas-Hamilton – *Selkirk, E.*
Douglas-Hamilton – *Selkirk of Douglas**
Douglas-Home – *Dacre*
Douglas-Home – *Home, E.*
Douglas-Pennant – *Penrhyn*
Douglas-Scott-Montagu – *Montagu of Beaulieu*
Drummond – *Perth, E.*
Drummond of Megginch – *Strange*
Dugdale – *Crathorne*
Duke – *Merrivale*
Duncombe – *Feversham*
Dundas – *Melville, V.*
Dundas – *Zetland, M.*
Eady – *Swinfen*
Eccles – *E. of Moulton**
Eden – *Auckland*
Eden – *E. of Winton**
Eden – *Henley*
Edgcumbe – *Mount Edgcumbe, E.*
Edmondson – *Sandford*
Edwardes – *Kensington*
Edwards – *Crickhowell**
Egerton – *Sutherland, D.*
Eliot – *St Germans, E.*
Elliott – *E. of Morpeth**
Elliot-Murray-Kynynmound – *Minto, E.*
Ellis – *Seaford*
Erskine – *Buchan, E.*
Erskine – *Mar and Kellie, E.*
Erskine-Murray – *Elibank*
Evans – *E. of Parkside**
Evans – *E. of Temple Guiting**
Evans – *E. of Watford**
Evans – *Mountevans*
Evans-Freke – *Carbery*
Eve – *Silsoe*
Ewing – *E. of Kirkford**
Fairfax – *F. of Cameron*
Falconer – *F. of Thoroton**
Falkner – *F. of Margravine**
Fane – *Westmorland, E.*
Farrington – *F. of Ribbleton**
Faulkner – *F. of Worcester**
Fearn – *F. of Southport**
Feilding – *Denbigh, E.*
Felton – *Seaford*
Fellowes – *De Ramsey*
Fermor-Hesketh – *Hesketh*
Fiennes – *Saye and Sele*
Fiennes-Clinton – *Lincoln, E.*
Finch Hatton – *Winchilsea, E.*
Finch-Knightley – *Aylesford, E.*
Finlay – *F. of Llandaff**
Fisher – *F. of Rednal**
Fitzalan-Howard – *Herries of Terregles*
Fitzalan-Howard – *Norfolk, D.*
FitzGerald – *Leinster, D.*
Fitzherbert – *Stafford*
FitzRoy – *Grafton, D.*
FitzRoy – *Southampton*
FitzRoy Newdegate – *Daventry, V.*
Fletcher-Vane – *Inglewood*
Flower – *Ashbrook, V.*
Foljambe – *Liverpool, E.*
Forbes – *Granard, E*
Forsyth – *F. of Drumlean**.
Forwood – *Arlington*
Foster – *F. of Thames Bank**
Fowler – *F. of Sutton Caulfield**
Fox-Strangways – *Ilchester, E.*
Frankland – *Zouche*
Fraser – *F. of Carmyllie**
Fraser – *F. of Kilmorack**
Fraser – *Lovat*
Fraser – *Saltoun*
Fraser – *Strathalmond*
Freeman-Grenville – *Kinloss*
Fremantle – *Cottesloe*
French – *De Freyne*
Fyfe – *F. of Fairfield**
Galbraith – *Strathclyde*
Ganzoni – *Belstead*
Gardner – *G. of Parkes**
Gascoyne-Cecil – *M. of Salisbury**
Gathorne-Hardy – *Cranbrook, E.*
Gibbs – *Aldenham*
Gibbs – *Wraxall*
Gibson – *Ashbourne*
Gibson – *G. of Market Rasen**
Giffard – *Halsbury, E.*
Gilbey – *Vaux of Harrowden*
Gilmour – *G. of Craigmillar**
Glyn – *Wolverton*
Godley – *Kilbracken*
Goff – *G. of Chieveley**
Golding – *G. of Newcastle-under-Lyme**
Gordon – *Aberdeen, M.*
Gordon – *G. of Strathblane**
Gordon – *Huntly, M.*
Gordon Lennox – *Richmond, D.*
Gore – *Arran, E.*
Gould – *G. of Brookwood**
Gould – *G. of Potternewton**
Graham – *G. of Edmonton**
Graham – *Montrose, D.*
Graham-Toler – *Norbury, E.*
Granshaw – *Northover**
Grant of Grant – *Strathspey*
Grant of Rothiemurchus – *Dysart, C.*
Granville – *G. of Eye**
Gray – *G. of Contin**
Greenall – *Daresbury*
Greville – *Warwick, E.*
Griffiths – *G. of Burry Port**
Griffiths – *G. of Fforestfach**
Grigg – *Altrincham*
Grimston – *G. of Westbury*
Grimston – *Verulam, E.*
Grosvenor – *Westminster, D.*
Grosvenor – *Wilton and Ebury, E*
Guest – *Wimborne, V*
Gueterbock – *Berkeley*
Guinness – *Iveagh, E.*
Guinness – *Moyne*
Gully – *Selby, V.*
Gummer – *Chadlington**
Gurdon – *Cranworth*
Guthrie – *G. of Craigiebank**
Gwynne Jones – *Chalfont**
Hale – *H. of Richmond**
Hamilton – *Abercorn, D.*
Hamilton – *Belhaven and Stenton*
Hamilton – *H. of Dalzell*
Hamilton – *Holm Patrick*
Hamilton-Russell – *Boyne, V.*
Hamilton-Smith – *Colwyn*
Hanbury-Tracy – *Sudeley*
Handcock – *Castlemaine*
Hannay – *H. of Chiswick**
Harbord-Hamond – *Suffield*
Harding – *H. of Petherton*
Hardinge – *H. of Penshurst*
Hare – *Blakenham, V.*
Hare – *Listowel, E.*
Harmsworth – *Rothermere, V.*
Harris – *H. of Haringey**
Harris – *H. of High Cross**
Harris – *H. of Peckham**
Harris – *H. of Richmond**
Harris – *Malmesbury, E.*
Hart – *H. of Chilton**
Harvey – *H. of Tasburgh*
Hastings Bass – *Huntingdon, E.*
Haughey – *Ballyedmond**
Hay – *Erroll, E.*
Hay – *Kinnoull, E.*
Hay – *Tweeddale, M.*

Heathcote-Drummond-Willoughby – *Willoughby de Eresby*
Hely-Hutchinson – *Donoughmore, E.*
Henderson – *Faringdon*
Hennessy – *Windlesham*
Henniker-Major – *Henniker*
Hepburne-Scott – *Polwarth*
Herbert – *Carnarvon, E.*
Herbert – *Hemingford*
Herbert – *Pembroke, E.*
Herbert – *Powis, E.*
Hervey – *Bristol, M.*
Heseltine – *H. of Thenford**
Hewitt – *Lifford, V.*
Hicks Beach – *St Aldwyn, E.*
Hill – *Downshire, M.*
Hill – *Sandys*
Hill-Trevor – *Trevor*
Hilton – *H. of Eggardon**
Hobart-Hampden – *Buckinghamshire, E.*
Hodgson – *H. of Astley Abbotts**
Hogg – *Hailsham, V.*
Hogg – *H. of Cumbernauld**
Holland-Hibbert – *Knutsford, V.*
Hollis – *H. of Heigham**
Holme – *H. of Cheltenham**
Holmes à Court – *Heytesbury*
Hood – *Bridport, V.*
Hope – *Glendevon*
Hope – *H. of Craighead**
Hope – *Linlithgow, M.*
Hope – *Rankeillour*
Hope Johnstone – *Annandale and Hartfell, E.*
Hope-Morley – *Hollenden*
Hopkinson – *Colyton*
Hore Ruthven – *Gowrie, E.*
Hovell-Thurlow-Cumming-Bruce – *Thurlow*
Howard – *Carlisle, E.*
Howard – *Effingham, E.*
Howard – *H. of Penrith*
Howard – *H. of Rising**
Howard – *Strathcona*
Howard – *Suffolk and Berkshire, E.*
Howarth – *H. of Breckland**
Howe – *H. of Aberavon**
Howe – *H. of Idlicote**
Howell – *H. of Guildford**
Howells – *H. of St. Davids**
Howie – *H. of Troon**
Hubbard – *Addington*
Huggins – *Malvern, V.*
Hughes – *H. of Woodside**
Hughes-Young – *St Helens*
Hunt – *H. of Chesterton**
Hunt – *H. of Kings Heath**
Hunt – *H. of Tanworth**
Hunt – *H. of Wirral**
Hurd – *H. of Westwell**
Hussey – *H. of North Bradley**
Hutchinson – *H. of Lullington**
Ingrams – *Darcy de Knayth*
Innes-Ker – *Roxburghe, D.*
Inskip – *Caldecote, V.*
Irby – *Boston*
Irvine – *I. of Lairg**
Isaacs – *Reading, M.*
James – *J. of Holland Park**
James – *Northbourne*
Janner – *J. of Braunstone**
Jauncey – *J. of Tullichettle**
Jay – *J. of Paddington**
Jebb – *Gladwyn*
Jenkin – *J. of Roding**
Jervis – *St Vincent, V.*
Jocelyn – *Roden, E.*
Jolliffe – *Hylton*
Jones – *J. of Deeside**
Joynson-Hicks – *Brentford, V.*
Kay-Shuttleworth – *Shuttleworth*
Kearley – *Devonport, V.*
Keith – *Kintore, E.*
Kemp – *Rochdale, V.*
Kennedy – *Ailsa, M*
Kennedy – *K. of the Shaws**.
Kenworthy – *Strabolgi*
Keppel – *Albemarle, E.*
Kerr – *K. of Kinlochard**
Kerr – *Lothian, M.*
Kerr – *Teviot*
Kilpatrick – *K. of Kincraig**
King – *Lovelace, E.*
King – *K. of Wartnaby**
King – *K. of West Bromwich**
King-Tenison – *Kingston, E.*
Kirkham – *Berners*
Kitchener – *K. of Khartoum, E.*
Knatchbull – *Brabourne*
Knatchbull – *Mountbatten of Burma, C.*
Knight – *K. of Collingtree**
Knox – *Ranfurly, E.*
Laing – *L. of Dunphail**
Lamb – *Rochester*
Lambton – *Durham, E.*
Lamont – *L. of Lerwick**
Lampson – *Killearn*
Lane – *L. of Horsell**
Lang – *L. of Monkton**
Lascelles – *Harewood, E.*
Law – *Coleraine*
Law – *Ellenborough*
Lawrence – *Trevethin and Oaksey*
Lawson – *Burnham*
Lawson – *L. of Blaby**
Lawson-Johnston – *Luke*
Lea – *L. of Crondall**
Legge – *Dartmouth, E.*
Legh – *Grey of Codnor*
Legh – *Newton*
Leigh-Pemberton – *Kingsdown**
Leith – *Burgh*
Lennox-Boyd – *Boyd of Merton, V.*
Le Poer Trench – *Clancarty, E.*
Leslie – *Rothes, E.*
Leslie Melville – *Leven and Melville, E.*
Lester – *L. of Herne Hill**
Levene – *L. of Portsoken**
Leveson-Gower – *Granville, E.*
Lewis – *L. of Newnham**
Lewis – *Merthyr*
Liddell – *Ravensworth*
Lindesay-Bethune – *Lindsay, E.*
Lindsay – *Crawford, E.*
Lindsay – *L. of Birker*
Linklater – *L. of Butterstone**
Littleton – *Hatherton*
Lloyd – *L. of Berwick**
Lloyd – *L. of Highbury**
Lloyd George – *Lloyd George of Dwyfor, E.*
Lloyd George – *Tenby, V.*
Lloyd-Mostyn – *Mostyn*
Loder – *Wakehurst*
Lofthouse – *L. of Pontefract**
Lopes – *Roborough*
Lour – *Carneggy of Lour**
Low – *Aldington*
Lowry-Corry – *Belmore, E.*
Lowther – *Lonsdale, E.*
Lowther – *Ullswater, V.*
Lubbock – *Avebury*
Lucas – *L. of Chilworth*
Lumley – *Scarbrough, E.*
Lumley-Savile – *Savile*
Lyon-Dalberg-Acton – *Acton*
Lysaght – *Lisle*
Lyttelton – *Chandos, V.*
Lyttelton – *Cobham, V.*
Lytton Cobbold – *Cobbold*
McAlpine – *M. of West Green**
Macaulay – *M. of Bragar**
McClintock-Bunbury – *Rathdonnell*
McColl – *M. of Dulwich**
Macdonald – *M. of Tradeston**
McDonnell – *Antrim, E.*
Macfarlane – *M. of Bearsden**
McFarlane – *M. of Llandaff**
MacGregor – *M. of Pulham Market**
McIntosh – *M. of Haringey**
McIntosh – *M. of Hudnall**
McKenzie – *M. of Luton**
Mackay – *Inchcape, E.*
Mackay – *M. of Clashfern**
Mackay – *M. of Drumadoon**
Mackay – *Reay*
Mackay – *Tanlaw**
MacKenzie – *M. of Culkein**
MacKenzie – *M. of Framwellgate**
Mackenzie – *Cromartie, E.*
Mackie – *M. of Benshie**
Mackintosh – *M. of Halifax, V.*
McLaren – *Aberconway*
MacLaurin – *M. of Knebworth**
MacLennan – *M. of Rogart**
Macmillan – *Stockton, E.*
Macpherson – *M. of Drumochter*
Macpherson – *Strathcarron*
Maffey – *Rugby*
Maginnis – *M. of Drumglass**
Maitland – *Lauderdale, E.*
Makgill – *Oxfuird, V.*
Makins – *Sherfield*
Manners – *Rutland, D.*
Manningham-Buller – *Dilhorne, V.*
Mansfield – *Sandhurst*
Marks – *M. of Broughton*
Marquis – *Woolton, E.*
Marshall – *M. of Knightsbridge**
Marsham – *Romney, E.*
Martyn-Hemphill – *Hemphill*
Mason – *M. of Barnsley**
Massey – *M. of Darwen**
Masters – *Noakes**
Maude – *Hawarden, V.*
Maxwell – *de Ros*
Maxwell – *Farnham*
May – *M. of Oxford**
Mayhew – *M. of Twysden**
Meade – *Clanwilliam, E.*
Mercer Nairne Petty-Fitzmaurice – *Lansdowne, M.*

Slynn – *S. of Hadley**
Smith – *Bicester*
Smith – *Hambleden, V.*
Smith – *Kirkhill**
Smith – *S. of Clifton**
Smith – *S. of Gilmorehill**
Smith – *S. of Leigh**
Somerset – *Beaufort, D.*
Somerset – *Raglan*
Soulsby – *S. of Swaffham Prior**
Spencer – *Churchill, V.*
Spencer-Churchill – *Marlborough, D.*
Spring Rice – *Monteagle of Brandon*
Stanhope – *Harrington, E.*
Stanley – *Derby, E.*
Stanley – *Stanley of Alderley and Sheffield*
Stapleton-Cotton – *Combermere, V.*
Steel – *S. of Aikwood**
Sterling – *S. of Plaistow**
Stevens – *S. of Ludgate**
Stevenson – *S. of Coddenham**
Stewart – *Galloway, E.*
Stewart – *Stewartby**
Stoddart – *S. of Swindon**
Stone – *S. of Blackheath**
Stonor – *Camoys*
Stopford – *Courtown, E.*
Stourton – *Mowbray*
Strachey – *O'Hagan*
Strutt – *Belper*
Strutt – *Rayleigh*
Stuart – *Castle Stewart, E.*
Stuart – *Moray, E.*
Stuart – *S. of Findhorn, V.*
Suenson-Taylor – *Grantchester*
Sutherland – *S. of Houndwood**
Symons – *S. of Vernham Dean**
Taylor – *Kilclooney**
Taylor – *T. of Blackburn**
Taylor – *T. of Warwick**
Taylour – *Headfort, M.*
Temple-Gore-Langton – *Temple of Stowe, E*
Temple-Morris – *Temple-Morris of Llandaff**
Tennant – *Glenconner*
Thellusson – *Rendlesham*
Thesiger – *Chelmsford, V.*
Thomas – *T. of Gresford**
Thomas – *T. of Gwydir**
Thomas – *T. of Macclesfield**
Thomas – *T. of Swynnerton**
Thomas – *T. of Walliswood**
Thomson – *T. of Fleet*
Thomson – *T. of Monifieth**
Thynn – *Bath, M.*
Tottenham – *Ely, M.*
Trefusis – *Clinton*
Trench – *Ashtown*
Tufton – *Hothfield*
Turner – *Netherthorpe*
Turner – *T. of Camden**
Turnour – *Winterton, E.*
Tyrell-Kenyon – *Kenyon*
Vanden-Bempde-Johnstone – *Derwent*
Vane – *Barnard*
Vane-Tempest-Stewart – *Londonderry, M.*
Vanneck – *Huntingfield*
Vaughan – *Lisburne, E.*
Vereker – *Gort, V.*
Verney – *Willoughby de Broke*
Vernon – *Lyveden*
Vesey – *De Vesci, V.*
Villiers – *Clarendon, E.*
Vincent – *V. of Coleshill**
Vivian – *Swansea*
Wade – *W. of Chorlton**
Waldegrave – *W. of North Hill**
Walker – *W. of Gestingthorpe**
Walker – *W. of Worcester**
Wall – *W. of New Barnett**
Wallace – *Dudley*
Wallace – *W. of Saltaire**
Wallace – *W. of Tummel**
Wallop – *Portsmouth, E.*
Walton – *W. of Detchant**
Ward – *Bangor, V.*
Ward – *Dudley, E.*
Warrender – *Bruntisfield*
Warwick – *W. of Undercliffe**
Watson – *W. of Invergowrie**
Watson – *Manton*
Watson – *W. of Richmond**
Webber – *Lloyd-Webber**
Wedderburn – *W. of Charlton**
Weir – *Inverforth*
Weld-Forester – *Forester*
Wellesley – *Cowley, E.*
Wellesley – *Wellington, D.*
Westenra – *Rossmore*
White – *Annaly*
White – *Hanningfield**
Whiteley – *Marchamley*
Whitfield – *Kenswood*
Williams – *W. of Crosby**
Williams – *W. of Elvel**
Williamson – *Forres*
Williamson – *W. of Horton**
Willoughby – *Middleton*
Wills – *Dulverton*
Wilson – *Moran*
Wilson – *Nunburnholme*
Wilson – *W. of Dinton**
Wilson – *W. of Tillyorn**
Windsor – *Gloucester, D.*
Windsor – *Kent, D.*
Windsor-Clive – *Plymouth, E.*
Wingfield – *Powerscourt, V.*
Winn – *St Oswald*
Wodehouse – *Kimberley, E.*
Wolfson – *W. of Sunningdale**
Wood – *Halifax, E.*
Woodhouse – *Terrington*
Woolmer – *W. of Leeds**
Wright – *W. of Richmond**
Wyndham – *Egremont and Leconfield*
Wyndham-Quin – *Dunraven, E.*
Wynn – *Newborough*
Yarde-Buller – *Churston*
Yerburgh – *Alvingham*
Yorke – *Hardwicke, E.*
Young – *Kennet*
Young – *Y. of Graffham**
Young – *Y. of Hornsey**
Young – *Y. of Norwood Green**
Young – *Y. of Old Scone**
Younger – *Y. of Leckie, V.*

ORDERS OF CHIVALRY

THE MOST NOBLE ORDER OF THE GARTER (1348)

KG
Ribbon, Blue
Motto, Honi soit qui mal y pense
(Shame on him who thinks evil of it)

The number of Knights Companions is limited to 24

SOVEREIGN OF THE ORDER
The Queen

LADIES OF THE ORDER
HRH The Princess Royal, 1994
HRH Princess Alexandra, The Hon. Lady Ogilvy, 2003

ROYAL KNIGHTS
HRH The Prince Philip, Duke of Edinburgh, 1947
HRH The Prince of Wales, 1958
HRH The Duke of Kent, 1985
HRH The Duke of Gloucester, 1997

EXTRA KNIGHTS COMPANIONS AND LADIES
Grand Duke Jean of Luxembourg, 1972
HM The Queen of Denmark, 1979
HM The King of Sweden, 1983
HM The King of Spain, 1988
HM The Queen of the Netherlands, 1989
HIM The Emperor of Japan, 1998
HM The King of Norway, 2001

KNIGHTS AND LADY COMPANIONS
The Duke of Grafton, 1976
The Lord Richardson of Duntisbourne, 1983
The Lord Carrington, 1985
The Lord Callaghan of Cardiff, 1987
The Duke of Wellington, 1990
Field Marshal the Lord Bramall, 1990
Sir Edward Heath, 1992
The Viscount Ridley, 1992
The Lord Sainsbury of Preston Candover, 1992
The Lord Ashburton, 1994
The Lord Kingsdown, 1994
Sir Ninian Stephen, 1994
The Baroness Thatcher, 1995
Sir Edmund Hillary, 1995
Sir Timothy Colman, 1996
The Duke of Abercorn, 1999
Sir William Gladstone, 1999
Field Marshal The Lord Inge, 2001
Sir Anthony Acland, 2001
The Duke of Westminster, 2003
The Lord Butler of Brockwell, 2003
The Lord Morris of Aberavon, 2003
Prelate, The Bishop of Winchester

Chancellor, The Lord Carrington, KG, GCMG, CH, MC
Register, The Dean of Windsor
Garter King of Arms, P. Gwynn-Jones, CVO
Gentleman Usher of the Black Rod, Lt.-Gen. Sir Michael Willcocks, KCB
Secretary, P. L. Dickinson

THE MOST ANCIENT AND MOST NOBLE ORDER OF THE THISTLE (REVIVED 1687)

KT
Ribbon, Green
Motto, Nemo me impune lacessit
(No one provokes me with impunity)

The number of Members is limited to 16

SOVEREIGN OF THE ORDER
The Queen

LADY OF THE THISTLE
HRH The Princess Royal, 2000

ROYAL KNIGHTS
HRH The Prince Philip, Duke of Edinburgh, 1952
HRH The Prince of Wales, Duke of Rothesay, 1977

KNIGHTS AND LADIES
The Earl of Wemyss and March, 1966
The Duke of Buccleuch and Queensberry, 1978
The Earl of Elgin and Kincardine, 1981
The Lord Thomson of Monifieth, 1981
The Earl of Airlie, 1985
Sir Iain Tennant, 1986
The Viscount of Arbuthnott, 1996
The Earl of Crawford and Balcarres, 1996
Lady Marion Fraser, 1996
The Lord Macfarlane of Bearsden, 1996
The Lord Mackay of Clashfern, 1997
The Lord Wilson of Tillyorn, 2000
The Lord Sutherland of Houndwood, 2002
Sir Eric Anderson, 2002

Chancellor, The Duke of Buccleuch and Queensberry, KT, VRD
Dean, The Very Revd G. I. Macmillan, CVO
Secretary and Lord Lyon King of Arms, R. O. Blair, LVO, WS
Usher of the Green Rod, Rear-Adm. C. H. Layman, CB, DSO, LVO

THE MOST HONOURABLE ORDER OF THE BATH (1725)

GCB *Military* GCE *Civil*

GCB	Knight (or Dame) Grand Cross
KCB	Knight Commander
DCB	Dame Commander
CB	Companion

Ribbon, Crimson
Motto, Tria juncta in uno
(Three joined in one)

Remodelled 1815, and enlarged many times since. The Order is divided into civil and military divisions. Women became eligible for the Order from 1 January 1971.

THE SOVEREIGN

GREAT MASTER AND FIRST OR PRINCIPAL KNIGHT GRAND CROSS
HRH The Prince of Wales, KG, KT, GCB, OM

Dean of the Order, The Dean of Westminster
Bath King of Arms, Gen. Sir Brian Kenny, GCB, CBE
Registrar and Secretary, Air Vice-Marshal Sir Richard Peirse, KCVO, CB
Genealogist, P. Gwynn-Jones, CVO
Gentleman Usher of the Scarlet Rod, Rear-Adm. I. R. Henderson, CB, CBE
Deputy Secretary, The Secretary of the Central Chancery of the Orders of Knighthood
Chancery, Central Chancery of the Orders of Knighthood, St James's Palace, London SW1A 1BH

THE ORDER OF MERIT (1902)

OM *Military*

OM *Civil*

OM
Ribbon, Blue and crimson

This Order is designed as a special distinction for eminent men and women without conferring a knighthood upon them. The Order is limited in numbers to 24, with the addition of foreign honorary members.

THE SOVEREIGN
HRH The Prince Philip, Duke of Edinburgh, 1968
Revd Prof. Owen Chadwick, KBE, 1983
Sir Andrew Huxley, 1983
Dr Frederick Sanger, 1986
Dame Cicely Saunders, 1989
The Baroness Thatcher, 1990
Dame Joan Sutherland, 1991
Sir Michael Atiyah, 1992
Lucian Freud, 1993
Sir Aaron Klug, 1995
The Lord Foster of Thames Bank, 1997
Sir Denis Rooke, 1997
Sir James Black, 2000
Sir Anthony Caro, 2000
Prof. Sir Roger Penrose, 2000
Sir Tom Stoppard, 2000
HRH The Prince of Wales, 2002
The Lord May of Oxford, 2002
The Lord Rothschild, 2002

Honorary Member, Nelson Mandela, 1995

Secretary and Registrar, The Lord Fellowes, GCB, GCVO, PC, QSO
Chancery, Central Chancery of the Orders of Knighthood, St James's Palace, London SW1A 1BH

THE MOST DISTINGUISHED ORDER OF ST MICHAEL AND ST GEORGE (1818)

GCMG

KCMG

GCMG	Knight (or Dame) Grand Cross
KCMG	Knight Commander
DCMG	Dame Commander
CMG	Companion

Ribbon, Saxon blue, with scarlet centre
Motto, Auspicium melioris aevi *(Token of a better age)*

THE SOVEREIGN

GRAND MASTER
HRH The Duke of Kent, KG, GCMG, GCVO, ADC

Prelate, The Rt. Revd Simon Barrington-Ward, KCMG
Chancellor, Sir Antony Acland, KG, GCMG, GCVO
Secretary, The Permanent Under-Secretary of State at the Foreign and Commonwealth Office and Head of the Diplomatic Service
Registrar, Lord Wilson of Tillyorn, KT, GCMG
King of Arms, Sir Ewen Fergusson, GCMG, GCVO
Gentleman Usher of the Blue Rod, Sir Anthony Figgis, KCVO, CMG
Dean, The Dean of St Paul's
Deputy Secretary, The Secretary of the Central Chancery of the Orders of Knighthood
Chancery, Central Chancery of the Orders of Knighthood, St James's Palace, London SW1A 1BH

THE MOST EMINENT ORDER OF THE INDIAN EMPIRE (1878)

GCIE	Knight Grand Commander
KCIE	Knight Commander
CIE	Companion

Ribbon, Imperial purple
Motto, Imperatricis auspiciis *(Under the auspices of the Empress)*

THE SOVEREIGN
Registrar, The Secretary of the Central Chancery of the Orders of Knighthood
No conferments have been made since 1947

THE IMPERIAL ORDER OF THE CROWN OF INDIA (1877) FOR LADIES

CI
Badge, the royal cipher in jewels within an oval, surmounted by an heraldic crown and attached to a bow of light blue watered ribbon, edged white

The honour does not confer any rank or title upon the recipient

No conferments have been made since 1947

HM The Queen, 1947
HRH Princess Alice, Duchess of Gloucester, 1937

THE ROYAL VICTORIAN ORDER (1896)

GCVO

KCVO

GCVO	Knight or Dame Grand Cross
KCVO	Knight Commander
DCVO	Dame Commander
CVO	Commander
LVO	Lieutenant
MVO	Member

Ribbon, Blue, with red and white edges
Motto, Victoria

THE SOVEREIGN

Chancellor, The Lord Chamberlain
Secretary, The Keeper of the Privy Purse
Registrar, The Secretary of the Central Chancery of the Orders of Knighthood
Chaplain, The Chaplain of the Queen's Chapel of the Savoy
Hon. Genealogist, D. H. B. Chesshyre, LVO

THE MOST EXCELLENT ORDER OF THE BRITISH EMPIRE (1917)

GBE

KBE

The Order was divided into military and civil divisions in December 1918

GBE	Knight or Dame Grand Cross
KBE	Knight Commander
DBE	Dame Commander
CBE	Commander
OBE	Officer
MBE	Member

Ribbon, Rose pink edged with pearl grey with vertical pearl stripe in centre (military division); without vertical pearl stripe (civil division)
Motto, For God and the Empire

THE SOVEREIGN

GRAND MASTER
HRH The Prince Philip, Duke of Edinburgh, KG, KT, OM, GBE, PC

Prelate, The Bishop of London
King of Arms, Air Chief Marshal Sir Patrick Hine, GCB, GBE
Registrar, The Secretary of the Central Chancery of the Orders of Knighthood
Secretary, The Secretary of the Cabinet and Head of the Home Civil Service
Dean, The Dean of St Paul's
Gentleman Usher of the Purple Rod, Sir Alexander Michael Graham, GBE, DCL
Chancery, Central Chancery of the Orders of Knighthood, St James's Palace, London SW1A 1BH

ORDER OF THE COMPANIONS OF HONOUR (1917)

CH

Ribbon, Carmine, with gold edges

This Order consists of one class only and carries with it no title. The number of awards is limited to 65 (excluding honorary members).

Anthony, Rt. Hon. John, 1981
Ashley of Stoke, The Lord, 1975
Attenborough, Sir David, 1995
Baker, Dame Janet, 1993
Baker of Dorking, The Lord, 1992
Birtwistle, Sir Harrison, 2000
Brenner, Sydney, 1986
Brook, Peter, 1998
Brooke of Sutton Mandeville, The Lord, 1992
Carrington, The Lord, 1983
Christie, Sir George, 2001
Davis, Sir Colin, 2001
De Chastelain, Gen. John, 1999
Doll, Prof. Sir Richard, 1995
Fraser, Rt. Hon. Malcolm, 1977
Freud, Lucian, 1983
Glenamara, The Lord, 1976
Hamilton, Richard, 1999
Hannay of Chiswick, The Lord, 2003
Hawking, Prof. Stephen, 1989
Healey, The Lord, 1979
Heseltine, The Lord, 1997
Hobsbawm, Prof. Eric, 1998
Hockney, David, 1997
Hodgkin, Sir Howard, 2002
Howard, Sir Michael, 2002
Howe of Aberavon, The Lord, 1996
Hurd of Westwell, The Lord, 1995
Jones, James, 1977
King of Bridgewater, The Lord, 1992
Lange, Rt. Hon. David, 1989
Lessing, Doris, 1999
Lovelock, James, 2002
McKenzie, Prof. Dan Peter, 2003
MacKerras, Sir Charles, 2003
Mahon, Sir Denis, 2002
Major, Rt. Hon. John, 1998
Owen, The Lord, 1994
Patten, Rt. Hon. Christopher, 1997
Pinter, Harold, 2002
Riley, Bridget, 1998
Sanger, Frederick, 1981
Scofield, Paul, 2000
Smith, Sir John, 1993
Somare, Rt. Hon. Sir Michael, 1978
Talboys, Rt. Hon. Sir Brian, 1981
Tebbit, The Lord, 1987
Varah, Revd Dr Chad, 1999

Honorary Members, Lee Kuan Yew, 1970; Prof. Amartya Sen, 2000; Bernard Haitink, 2002
Secretary and Registrar, The Secretary of the Central Chancery of the Orders of Knighthood

THE DISTINGUISHED SERVICE ORDER (1886)

DSO

Ribbon, Red, with blue edges

Bestowed in recognition of especial services in action of commissioned officers in the Navy, Army and Royal Air Force and (since 1942) Mercantile Marine. The members are Companions only. A Bar may be awarded for any additional act of service.

THE IMPERIAL SERVICE ORDER (1902)

ISO

Ribbon, Crimson, with blue centre

Appointment as Companion of this Order is open to members of the Civil Services whose eligibility is determined by the grade they hold. The Order consists of The Sovereign and Companions to a number not exceeding 1,900, of whom 1,300 may belong to the Home Civil Services and 600 to Overseas Civil Services. The then Prime Minister announced in March 1993 that he would make no further recommendations for appointments to the Order.

Secretary, The Secretary of the Cabinet and Head of the Home Civil Service
Registrar, The Secretary of the Central Chancery of the Orders of Knighthood

THE ROYAL VICTORIAN CHAIN (1902)

It confers no precedence on its holders

HM THE QUEEN

HM The King of Thailand, 1960
HM King Zahir Shah of Afghanistan, 1971
HM The Queen of Denmark, 1974
HM The King of Sweden, 1975
HM The Queen of the Netherlands, 1982
Gen. Antonio Eanes, 1985
HM The King of Spain, 1986
HM The King of Saudi Arabia, 1987
Dr Richard von Weizsäcker, 1992
HM The King of Norway, 1994
The Earl of Airlie, 1997
The Rt. Revd and Rt. Hon. Lord Carey of Clifton, 2002

BARONETAGE AND KNIGHTAGE

BARONETS

Style, 'Sir' before forename and surname, followed by 'Bt.'
Wife's style, 'Lady' followed by surname
For forms of address, *see* page 43

There are five different creations of baronetcies: Baronets of England (creations dating from 1611); Baronets of Ireland (creations dating from 1619); Baronets of Scotland or Nova Scotia (creations dating from 1625); Baronets of Great Britain (creations after the Act of Union 1707 which combined the kingdoms of England and Scotland); and Baronets of the United Kingdom (creations after the union of Great Britain and Ireland in 1801).

Badge of Baronets of the United Kingdom

Badge of Baronets of Nova Scotia

Badge of Ulster

The patent of creation limits the destination of a baronetcy, usually to male descendants of the first baronet, although special remainders allow the baronetcy to pass, if the male issue of sons fail, to the male issue of daughters of the first baronet. In the case of baronetcies of Scotland or Nova Scotia, a special remainder of 'heirs male and of tailzie' allows the baronetcy to descend to heirs general, including women. There are four existing Scottish baronets with such a remainder.

The Official Roll of the Baronetage is kept at the Department for Constitutional Affairs by the Registrar of the Baronetage. Anyone who considers that he is entitled to be entered on the Roll may petition the Crown through the Lord Chancellor. Every person succeeding to a baronetcy must exhibit proofs of succession to the Lord Chancellor. A person whose name is not entered on the Official Roll will not be addressed or mentioned by the title of baronet in any official document, nor will he be accorded precedence as a baronet.

BARONETCIES EXTINCT SINCE THE LAST EDITION
de Montmorency (cr. I.1631); Colyer-Fergusson (cr. 1866); Lewthwaite (cr. 1927)

Registrar of the Baronetage, Andrew McDonald
Assistant Registrar, Steven Johnson
Office, Department for Constitutional Affairs, Constitutional Policy Division, 6th Floor, Selborne House, 54 Victoria Street, London SW1E 6QW
T 020-7210 8564

KNIGHTS

Style, 'Sir' before forename and surname, followed by appropriate post-nominal initials if a Knight Grand Cross, Knight Grand Commander or Knight Commander
Wife's style, 'Lady' followed by surname
For forms of address, *see* page 43

The prefix 'Sir' is not used by knights who are clerics of the Church of England, who do not receive the accolade. Their wives are entitled to precedence as the wife of a knight but not to the style of 'Lady'.

ORDERS OF KNIGHTHOOD
Knight Grand Cross, Knight Grand Commander, and Knight Commander are the higher classes of the Orders of Chivalry (*see* page 80). Honorary knighthoods of these Orders may be conferred on men who are citizens of countries of which The Queen is not head of state. As a rule, the prefix 'Sir' is not used by honorary knights.

KNIGHTS BACHELOR

The Knights Bachelor do not constitute a Royal Order, but comprise the surviving representation of the ancient State Orders of Knighthood. The Register of Knights Bachelor, instituted by James I in the 17th century, lapsed, and in 1908 a voluntary association under the title of The Society of Knights (now The Imperial Society of Knights Bachelor by Royal Command) was formed with the primary objects of continuing the various registers dating from 1257 and obtaining the uniform registration of every created Knight Bachelor. In 1926 a design for a badge to be worn by Knights Bachelor was approved and adopted; in 1974 a neck badge and miniature were added.

Knight Principal, Sir Richard Gaskell
Prelate, Rt. Revd and Rt. Hon. The Bishop of London
Registrar, Sir Robert Balchin, DL
Hon. Treasurer, Sir Paul Judge
Clerk to the Council, R. L. Jenkins, LVO, TD
Office, 21 Old Buildings, Lincoln's Inn, London WC2A 3UJ

LIST OF BARONETS AND KNIGHTS

Revised to 31 August 2004
Peers are not included in this list

- † Not registered on the Official Roll of the Baronetage at the time of going to press
- ( ) The date of creation of the baronetcy is given in parenthesis
- I Baronet of Ireland
- NS Baronet of Nova Scotia
- S Baronet of Scotland

A full entry in italic type indicates that the recipient of a knighthood died during the year in which the honour was conferred. The name is included for purposes of record.

Abbott, Sir Albert Francis, Kt., CBE
Abbott, *Adm.* Sir Peter Charles, GBE, KCB
Abdy, Sir Valentine Robert Duff, Bt. (1850)
Acheson, *Prof.* Sir (Ernest) Donald, KBE
Ackers, Sir James George, Kt.
Ackers-Jones, Sir David, KBE, CMG
Ackroyd, Sir Timothy Robert Whyte, Bt. (1956)
Acland, Sir Antony Arthur, KG, GCMG, GCVO
Acland, *Lt.-Col.* Sir (Christopher) Guy (Dyke), Bt., MVO (1890)
Acland, Sir John Dyke, Bt. (1644)
Acland, *Maj.-Gen.* Sir John Hugh Bevil, KCB, CBE
Adam, Sir Christopher Eric Forbes, Bt. (1917)
Adam, Sir Kenneth Hugo, Kt., OBE
Adams, Sir William James, KCMG
Adsetts, Sir William Norman, Kt., OBE
Adye, Sir John Anthony, KCMG
Aga Khan IV, HH Prince Karim, KBE
Agnew, Sir Crispin Hamlyn, Bt. (S. 1629)
Agnew, Sir John Keith, Bt. (1895)
Agnew, Sir Rudolph Ion Joseph, Kt.
Agnew-Somerville, Sir Quentin Charles Somerville, Bt. (1957)
Aiken, *Air Chief Marshal* Sir John Alexander Carlisle, KCB
Aikens, *Hon.* Sir Richard John Pearson, Kt.
†Ainsworth, Sir Anthony Thomas Hugh, Bt. (1916)
Aird, *Capt.* Sir Alastair Sturgis, GCVO
Aird, Sir (George) John, Bt. (1901)
Airy, *Maj.-Gen.* Sir Christopher John, KCVO, CBE
Aitchison, Sir Charles Walter de Lancey, Bt. (1938)
Akehurst, *Gen.* Sir John Bryan, KCB, CBE
Alberti, *Prof.* Sir Kurt George Matthew Mayer, Kt.
Albu, Sir George, Bt. (1912)
Alcock, *Air Chief Marshal* Sir (Robert James) Michael, GCB, KBE
Aldous, *Rt. Hon.* Sir William, Kt.
Alexander, Sir Charles Gundry, Bt. (1945)
Alexander, Sir Douglas, Bt. (1921)
Allen, *Prof.* Sir Geoffrey, Kt., PHD, FRS
Allen, Sir John Derek, Kt., CBE
Allen, *Hon.* Sir Peter Austin Philip Jermyn, Kt.
Allen, Sir Thomas Boaz, Kt., CBE
Allen, *Hon.* Sir William Clifford, KCMG, MP
Allen, Sir William Guilford, Kt.
Alleyne, Sir George Allanmoore Ogarren, Kt.
Alleyne, *Revd* John Olpherts Campbell, Bt. (1769)
Allinson, Sir (Walter) Leonard, KCVO, CMG
Alliott, *Hon.* Sir John Downes, Kt.
Allison, *Air Chief Marshal* Sir John Shakespeare, KCB, CBE
Althaus, Sir Nigel Frederick, Kt.
Alun-Jones, Sir (John) Derek, Kt.
Ambo, *Rt. Revd* George, KBE
Amet, *Hon.* Sir Arnold Karibone, Kt.
Amory, Sir Ian Heathcoat, Bt. (1874)
Anderson, Sir John Anthony, KBE
Anderson, *Maj.-Gen.* Sir John Evelyn, KBE
Anderson, Sir John Muir, Kt., CMG
Anderson, Sir Leith Reinsford Steven, Kt., CBE
Anderson, *Vice-Adm.* Sir Neil Dudley, KBE, CB
Anderson, Sir (William) Eric Kinloch, KT
Anderson, *Prof.* Sir (William) Ferguson, Kt., OBE
Anderton, Sir (Cyril) James, Kt., CBE, QPM
Andrew, Sir Robert John, KCB
Andrews, Sir Derek Henry, KCB, CBE
Andrews, *Hon.* Sir Dormer George, Kt.
Angus, Sir Michael Richardson, Kt.
Annesley, Sir Hugh Norman, Kt., QPM
Anson, *Vice-Adm.* Sir Edward Rosebery, KCB
Anson, Sir John, KCB
Anson, *Rear-Adm.* Sir Peter, Bt., CB (1831)
Anstruther, Sir Ian Fife Campbell, Bt., (S. 1694)
Anstruther-Gough-Calthorpe, Sir Euan Hamilton, Bt. (1929)
Antico, Sir Tristan Venus, Kt.
Antrobus, Sir Edward Philip, Bt. (1815)
Appleyard, Sir Leonard Vincent, KCMG
Appleyard, Sir Raymond Kenelm, KBE
Arbib, Sir Martyn, Kt.
Arbuthnot, Sir Keith Robert Charles, Bt. (1823)
Arbuthnot, Sir William Reierson, Bt. (1964)
Arbuthnott, *Prof.* Sir John Peebles, Kt., PHD, FRSE
Archdale, *Capt.* Sir Edward Folmer, Bt., DSC, RN (1928)
Arculus, Sir Ronald, KCMG, KCVO
Armitage, *Air Chief Marshal* Sir Michael John, KCB, CBE
Armour, *Prof.* Sir James, Kt., CBE
Armstrong, Sir Christopher John Edmund Stuart, Bt., MBE (1841)
Armstrong, Sir Patrick John, Kt., CBE
Armstrong, Sir Richard, Kt., CBE
Armytage, Sir John Martin, Bt. (1738)
Arnold, *Rt. Hon.* Sir John Lewis, Kt.
Arnold, Sir Malcolm Henry, Kt., CBE
Arnold, Sir Thomas Richard, Kt.
Arnott, Sir Alexander John Maxwell, Bt. (1896)
Arrindell, Sir Clement Athelston, GCMG, GCVO, QC
Arthur, Sir Gavyn Farr, Kt.
Arthur, *Lt.-Gen.* Sir (John) Norman Stewart, KCB
Arthur, Sir Michael Anthony, KCMG
Arthur, Sir Stephen John, Bt. (1841)
Ash, *Prof.* Sir Eric Albert, Kt., CBE, FRS, FRENG
Ashburnham, Sir James Fleetwood, Bt. (1661)
Ashley, Sir Bernard Albert, Kt.
Ashmore, *Admiral of the Fleet* Sir Edward Beckwith, GCB, DSC
Aske, Sir Robert John Bingham, Bt. (1922)
Askew, Sir Bryan, Kt.
Asscher, Prof. Sir (Adolf) William, Kt., MD, FRCP
Astill, *Hon.* Sir Michael John, Kt.
Astley-Cooper, Sir Alexander Paston, Bt. (1821)
Aston, Sir Harold George, Kt., CBE
Astwood, *Hon.* Sir James Rufus, KBE
Atcherley, Sir Harold Winter, Kt.
Atiyah, Sir Michael Francis, Kt., OM, PHD, FRS
Atkins, *Rt. Hon.* Sir Robert James, Kt.
Atkinson, *Prof.* Sir Anthony Barnes, Kt.
Atkinson, *Air Marshal* Sir David William, KBE
Atkinson, Sir Frederick John, KCB
Atkinson, Sir John Alexander, KCB, DFC
Atkinson, Sir Robert, Kt., DSC, FRENG
Atopare, Sir Sailas, GCMG
Attenborough, Sir David Frederick, Kt., CH, CVO, CBE, FRS
Aubrey-Fletcher, Sir Henry Egerton, Bt. (1782)
Audland, Sir Christopher John, KCMG
Audley, Sir George Bernard, Kt.
Augier, *Prof.* Sir Fitz-Roy Richard, Kt.
Auld, *Rt. Hon.* Sir Robin Ernest, Kt.
Austin, Sir Anthony Leonard, Bt. (1894)
Austin, *Vice-Adm.* Sir Peter Murray, KCB
Austin, *Air Marshal* Sir Roger Mark, KCB, AFC
Austen-Smith, *Air Marshal* Sir Roy David, KBE, CB, CVO, DFC
Avei, Sir Moi, KBE
Axford, Sir William Ian, Kt.
Ayckbourn, Sir Alan, Kt., CBE
Aykroyd, Sir James Alexander Frederic, Bt. (1929)
Aykroyd, Sir William Miles, Bt., MC (1920)
Aylmer, Sir Richard John, Bt. (I. 1622)
Bacha, Sir Bhinod, Kt., CMG
Backhouse, Sir Jonathan Roger, Bt. (1901)
Bacon, Sir Nicholas Hickman Ponsonby, Bt. *Premier Baronet of England* (1611 and 1627)
Bacon, Sir Sidney Charles, Kt., CB, FRENG
Baddeley, Sir John Wolsey Beresford, Bt. (1922)

Baddiley, *Prof.* Sir James, Kt., PHD, DSC, FRS, FRSE
Badge, Sir Peter Gilmour Noto, Kt.
Baer, Sir Jack Mervyn Frank, Kt.
Bagge, Sir (John) Jeremy Picton, Bt. (1867)
Bagnall, *Air Chief Marshal* Sir Anthony, GBE, KCB
Bailey, Sir Alan Marshall, KCB
Bailey, Sir Brian Harry, Kt., OBE
Bailey, Sir Derrick Thomas Louis, Bt., DFC (1919)
Bailey, Sir John Bilsland, KCB
Bailey, Sir Richard John, Kt., CBE
Bailey, Sir Stanley Ernest, Kt., CBE, QPM
Bailhache, Sir Philip Martin, Kt.
Baillie, Sir Adrian Louis, Bt. (1823)
Bain, *Prof.* Sir George Sayers, Kt.
Baird, Sir Charles William Stuart, Bt. (1809)
†Baird, Sir James Andrew Gardiner, Bt. (S. 1695)
Baird, *Lt.-Gen.* Sir James Parlane, KBE, MD
Baird, *Air Marshal* Sir John Alexander, KBE
Baird, *Vice-Adm.* Sir Thomas Henry Eustace, KCB
Bairsto, *Air Marshal* Sir Peter Edward, KBE, CB
Baker, Sir Bryan William, Kt.
Baker, *Prof.* Sir John Hamilton, Kt., QC
Baker, *Rt. Hon.* Sir (Thomas) Scott (Gillespie), Kt.
Balchin, Sir Robert George Alexander, Kt.
Balderstone, Sir James Schofield, Kt.
Baldwin, *Prof.* Sir Jack Edward, Kt., FRS
Baldwin, Sir Peter Robert, KCB
Ball, *Air Marshal* Sir Alfred Henry Wynne, KCB, DSO, DFC
Ball, Sir Christopher John Elinger, Kt.
Ball, Sir Richard Bentley, Bt. (1911)
Ball, *Prof.* Sir Robert James, Kt., PHD
Ballantyne, *Dr* Sir Frederick Nathaniel, GCMG
Bamford, Sir Anthony Paul, Kt.
Band, *Adm.* Sir Jonathon, KCB
Banham, Sir John Michael Middlecott, Kt.
Bannerman, Sir David Gordon, Bt., OBE (S. 1682)
Bannister, Sir Roger Gilbert, Kt., CBE, DM, FRCP
Barber, Sir (Thomas) David, Bt. (1960)
Barbour, *Very Revd* Robert Alexander Stewart, KCVO, MC
Barclay, Sir Colville Herbert Sanford, Bt. (S. 1668)
Barclay, Sir David Rowat, Kt.
Barclay, Sir Frederick Hugh, Kt.
Barclay, Sir Peter Maurice, Kt., CBE
Barder, Sir Brian Leon, KCMG
Baring, Sir John Francis, Bt. (1911)
Barker, Sir Colin, Kt.
Barker, *Hon.* Sir (Richard) Ian, Kt.
Barlow, Sir Christopher Hilaro, Bt. (1803)
Barlow, Sir Frank, Kt., CBE
Barlow, Sir (George) William, Kt., FRENG
†Barlow, Sir James Alan, Bt. (1902)
Barlow, Sir John Kemp, Bt. (1907)
Barnard, Sir Joseph Brian, Kt.
Barnes, *The Most Revd.* Brian James, KBE
Barnes, Sir (James) David (Francis), Kt., CBE
Barnes, Sir Kenneth, KCB
Barnewall, Sir Reginald Robert, Bt. (I. 1623)
Baron, Sir Thomas, Kt., CBE
Barraclough, *Air Chief Marshal* Sir John, KCB, CBE, DFC, AFC
Barran, Sir John Napoleon Ruthven, Bt. (1895)
Barratt, Sir Lawrence Arthur, Kt.
Barratt, Sir Richard Stanley, Kt., CBE, QPM
Barratt-Boyes, Sir Brian Gerald, KBE
Barrett, Sir Stephen Jeremy, KCMG
Barrett-Lennard, *Revd* Hugh Dacre, Bt. (1801)
Barrington, Sir Benjamin, Bt. (1831)
Barrington, Sir Nicholas John, KCMG, CVO
Barrington-Ward, *Rt. Revd* Simon, KCMG
Barron, Sir Donald James, Kt.
Barrow, *Capt.* Sir Richard John Uniacke, Bt. (1835)
Barry, Sir (Lawrence) Edward (Anthony Tress), Bt. (1899)
Barter, Sir Peter Leslie Charles, Kt., OBE
†Bartlett, Sir Andrew Alan, Bt. (1913)
Barttelot, *Col.* Sir Brian Walter de Stopham, Bt., OBE (1875)
Batchelor, Sir Ivor Ralph Campbell, Kt., CBE
Bate, Sir David Lindsay, KBE
Bates, Sir Alan Arthur, Kt., CBE
Bates, Sir Geoffrey Voltelin, Bt., MC (1880)
Bates, Sir Malcolm Rowland, Kt.
Bates, Sir Richard Dawson Hoult, Bt. (1937)
Bateson, *Prof.* Sir Patrick, Kt.
Batho, Sir Peter Ghislain, Bt. (1928)
Bathurst, *Admiral of the Fleet* Sir (David) Benjamin, GCB
Bathurst, Sir Maurice Edward, Kt., CMG, CBE, QC
Batten, Sir John Charles, KCVO
Battersby, Prof. Sir Alan Rushton, Kt., FRS
Battishill, Sir Anthony Michael William, GCB
Baxendell, Sir Peter Brian, Kt., CBE, FRENG
Bayliss, Sir Richard Ian Samuel, KCVO, MD, FRCP
Bayne, Sir Nicholas Peter, KCMG
Baynes, Sir John Christopher Malcolm, Bt. (1801)
Bazley, Sir Thomas John Sebastian, Bt. (1869)
Beach, *Gen.* Sir (William Gerald) Hugh, GBE, KCB, MC
Beache, *Hon.* Sir Vincent Ian, KCMG
Beale, *Lt.-Gen.* Sir Peter John, KBE, FRCP
Beament, Sir James William Longman, Kt., SCD, FRS
Beamish, Sir Adrian John, KCMG
Beaumont, *Capt.* the Hon. Sir (Edward) Nicholas (Canning), KCVO
Beaumont, Sir George (Howland Francis), Bt. (1661)
Beaumont, Sir Richard Ashton, KCMG, OBE
Beaumont-Dark, Sir Anthony Michael, Kt.
Beatson, *Hon.* Sir Jack, Kt.
Beavis, *Air Chief Marshal* Sir Michael Gordon, KCB, CBE, AFC
Beck, Sir Edgar Philip, Kt.
Beckett, Sir Richard Gervase, Bt., QC (1921)
Beckett, Sir Terence Norman, KBE, FRENG
Beckwith, Sir John Lionel, Kt., CBE
Bedser, Sir Alec Victor, Kt., CBE
Beecham, Sir Jeremy Hugh, Kt.
Beecham, Sir John Stratford Roland, Bt. (1914)
Beetham, *Marshal of the Royal Air Force* Sir Michael James, GCB, CBE, DFC, AFC
Beevor, Sir Thomas Agnew, Bt. (1784)
Beldam, *Rt. Hon.* Sir (Alexander) Roy (Asplan), Kt.
Belich, Sir James, Kt.
Bell, Sir Brian Ernest, KBE
Bell, Sir David Charles Maurice, Kt.
Bell, Sir John Lowthian, Bt. (1885)
Bell, *Prof.* Sir Peter Robert Frank, Kt.
Bell, *Hon.* Sir Rodger, Kt.
Bell, Sir Stuart, Kt.
Bellamy, *Hon.* Sir Christopher William, Kt.
Bellingham, Sir Anthony Edward Norman, Bt. (1796)
Bender, Sir Brian Geoffrey, KCB
Bengough, *Col.* Sir Piers, KCVO, OBE
Benn, Sir (James) Jonathan, Bt. (1914)
Bennett, *Air Vice-Marshal* Sir Erik Peter, KBE, CB
Bennett, *Hon.* Sir Hugh Peter Derwyn, Kt.
Bennett, *Gen.* Sir Phillip Harvey, KBE, DSO
Bennett, Sir Richard Rodney, Kt., CBE
Bennett, Sir Ronald Wilfrid Murdoch, Bt. (1929)
Benson, Sir Christopher John, Kt.
Benyon, Sir William Richard, Kt.
Beresford, Sir (Alexander) Paul, Kt., MP
Beresford-Peirse, Sir Henry Grant de la Poer, Bt. (1814)
Berghuser, *Hon.* Sir Eric, Kt., MBE
Beringer, *Prof.* Sir John Evelyn, Kt., CBE
Berman, Sir Franklin Delow, KCMG

Berners-Lee, Sir Timothy John, KBE
Bernard, Sir Dallas Edmund, Bt. (1954)
Bernstein, Sir Howard, Kt.
Berney, Sir Julian Reedham Stuart, Bt. (1620)
Berridge, *Prof.* Sir Michael John, Kt., FRS
Berrill, Sir Kenneth Ernest, GBE, KCB
Berriman, Sir David, Kt.
Berry, *Prof.* Sir Colin Leonard, Kt., FRCPath.
Berry, *Prof.* Sir Michael Victor, Kt., FRS
Berthon, *Vice-Adm.* Sir Stephen Ferrier, KCB
Berthoud, Sir Martin Seymour, KCVO, CMG
Best, Sir Richard Radford, KCVO, CBE
Best-Shaw, Sir John Michael Robert, Bt. (1665)
Bethune, *Hon.* Sir (Walter) Angus, Kt.
Bett, Sir Michael, Kt., CBE
Bevan, Sir Martyn Evan Evans, Bt. (1958)
Bevan, Sir Nicolas, Kt., CB
Bevan, Sir Timothy Hugh, Kt.
Beverley, *Lt.-Gen.* Sir Henry York La Roche, KCB, OBE, RM
Bibby, Sir Michael James, Bt. (1959)
Bichard, Sir Michael George, KCB
Bickersteth, *Rt. Revd* John Monier, KCVO
Biddulph, Sir Ian D'Olier, Bt. (1664)
Bide, Sir Austin Ernest, Kt.
Bidwell, Sir Hugh Charles Philip, GBE
Biggam, Sir Robin Adair, Kt.
Biggs, Sir Norman Paris, Kt.
Bilas, Sir Angmai Simon, Kt., OBE
Billière, *Gen.* Sir Peter Edgar de la Cour de la, KCB, KBE, DSO, MC
Bingham, *Hon.* Sir Eardley Max, Kt.
Birch, Sir John Allan, KCVO, CMG
Birch, Sir Roger, Kt., CBE, QPM
Bird, Sir Richard Geoffrey Chapman, Bt. (1922)
Birkin, Sir John Christian William, Bt. (1905)
Birkin, Sir (John) Derek, Kt., TD
Birkmyre, Sir James, Bt. (1921)
Birrell, Sir James Drake, Kt.
Birtwistle, Sir Harrison, Kt., CH
Bischoff, Sir Winfried Franz Wilhelm, Kt.
Bishop, Sir Frederick Arthur, Kt., CB, CVO
Bishop, Sir Michael David, Kt., CBE
Bisson, *Rt. Hon.* Sir Gordon Ellis, Kt.
Bjelke-Petersen, Sir Johannes, KCMG
Black, Sir James Whyte, Kt., OM, FRCP, FRS
Black, *Adm.* Sir (John) Jeremy, GBE, KCB, DSO
Black, Sir Robert David, Bt. (1922)
Blackburn, *Vice-Adm.* Sir David Anthony James, KCVO, CB, LVO
Blackburne, *Hon.* Sir William Anthony, Kt.
Blacker, *Gen.* Sir (Anthony Stephen) Jeremy, KCB, CBE
Blackett, Sir Hugh Francis, Bt. (1673)
Blackham, *Vice-Adm.* Sir Jeremy Joe, KCB
Blacklock, *Surgeon Capt. Prof.* Sir Norman James, KCVO, OBE
Blackman, Sir Frank Milton, KCVO, OBE
Blackwood, Sir John Francis, Bt. (1814)
Blair, *Lt.-Gen.* Sir Chandos, KCVO, OBE, MC
Blair, Sir Edward Thomas Hunter, Bt. (1786)
Blair, Sir Ian Warwick, Kt., QPM
Blake, Sir Alfred Lapthorn, KCVO, MC
Blake, Sir Francis Michael, Bt. (1907)
Blake, Sir Peter Thomas, Kt., CBE
Blake, Sir (Thomas) Richard (Valentine), Bt. (I. 1622)
Blaker, Sir John, Bt. (1919)
Blakiston, Sir Ferguson Arthur James, Bt. (1763)
Blanch, Sir Malcolm, KCVO
Bland, Sir (Francis) Christopher (Buchan), Kt.
Bland, *Lt.-Col.* Sir Simon Claud Michael, KCVO
Blank, Sir Maurice Victor, Kt.
Blatherwick, Sir David Elliott Spiby, KCMG, OBE
Blelloch, Sir John Nial Henderson, KCB
Blennerhassett, Sir (Marmaduke) Adrian Francis William, Bt. (1809)
Blewitt, *Maj.* Sir Shane Gabriel Basil, GCVO
Blofeld, *Hon.* Sir John Christopher Calthorpe, Kt.
Blois, Sir Charles Nicholas Gervase, Bt. (1686)
Blom-Cooper, Sir Louis Jacques, Kt., QC
Blomefield, Sir Thomas Charles Peregrine, Bt. (1807)
Bloomfield, Sir Kenneth Percy, KCB
Blount, Sir Walter Edward Alpin, Bt., DSC (1642)
Blundell, Sir Thomas Leon, Kt., FRS
Blunden, Sir George, Kt.
Blunden, Sir Philip Overington, Bt. (I. 1766)
Blunt, Sir David Richard Reginald Harvey, Bt. (1720)
Blyth, Sir Charles (Chay), Kt., CBE, BEM
Boardman, *Prof.* Sir John, Kt., FSA, FBA
Bodey, *Hon.* Sir David Roderick Lessiter, Kt.
Bodmer, Sir Walter Fred, Kt., PHD, FRS
Body, Sir Richard Bernard Frank Stewart, Kt., MP
Bogan, Sir Nagora, KBE
Boileau, Sir Guy (Francis), Bt. (1838)
Boles, Sir Jeremy John Fortescue, Bt. (1922)
Boles, Sir John Dennis, Kt., MBE
Bolland, Sir Edwin, KCMG
Bollers, *Hon.* Sir Harold Brodie Smith, Kt.
Bolt, *Air Marshal* Sir Richard Bruce, KBE, CB, DFC, AFC
Bolton, Sir Frederic Bernard, Kt., MC
Bona, Sir Kina, KBE
Bonallack, Sir Michael Francis, Kt., OBE
Bond, Sir John Reginald Hartnell, Kt.
Bond, Sir Kenneth Raymond Boyden, Kt.
Bond, *Prof.* Sir Michael Richard, Kt., FRCPsych., FRCPGlas., FRCSE
Bondi, *Prof.* Sir Hermann, KCB, FRS
Bone, Sir Roger Bridgland, KCMG
Bonfield, Sir Peter Leahy, Kt., CBE, FRENG
Bonham, *Maj.* Sir Antony Lionel Thomas, Bt. (1852)
Bonington, Sir Christian John Storey, Kt., CBE
Bonsall, Sir Arthur Wilfred, KCMG, CBE
Bonsor, Sir Nicholas Cosmo, Bt. (1925)
Boolell, Sir Satcam, Kt.
Boord, Sir Nicolas John Charles, Bt. (1896)
Boorman, *Lt.-Gen.* Sir Derek, KCB
Booth, Sir Christopher Charles, Kt., MD, FRCP
Booth, Sir Douglas Allen, Bt. (1916)
Booth, Sir Gordon, KCMG, CVO
Boothby, Sir Brooke Charles, Bt. (1660)
Bore, Sir Albert, Kt.
Boreel, Sir Stephan Gerard, Bt. (1645)
†Borthwick, Sir Anthony Thomas, Bt. (1908)
Borysiewicz, *Prof.* Sir Leszek Krzysztof, Kt.
Bossom, *Hon.* Sir Clive, Bt. (1953)
Boswell, *Lt.-Gen.* Sir Alexander Crawford Simpson, KCB, CBE
Bosworth, Sir Neville Bruce Alfred, Kt., CBE
Booth, Sir Clive, Kt.
Bottoms, *Prof.* Sir Anthony Edward, Kt.
Bottomley, Sir James Reginald Alfred, KCMG
Boughey, Sir John George Fletcher, Bt. (1798)
Boulton, Sir Clifford John, GCB
Boulton, Sir William Whytehead, Bt., CBE, TD (1944)
Bourn, Sir John Bryant, KCB
Bowater, Sir Euan David Vansittart, Bt. (1939)
Bowater, Sir (John) Vansittart, Bt. (1914)
Bowden, Sir Andrew, Kt., MBE
Bowden, Sir Nicholas Richard, Bt. (1915)
Bowen, Sir Geoffrey Fraser, Kt.
Bowen, Sir Mark Edward Mortimer, Bt. (1921)
Bowett, *Prof.* Sir Derek William, Kt., CBE, QC, FBA
†Bowlby, Sir Richard Peregrine Longstaff, Bt. (1923)

Bowman, Sir Edwin Geoffrey, KCB
Bowman, Sir Jeffery Haverstock, Kt.
Bowman-Shaw, Sir (George) Neville, Kt.
Bowness, Sir Alan, Kt., CBE
Bowyer-Smyth, Sir Thomas Weyland, Bt. (1661)
Boyce, Sir Graham Hugh, KCMG
Boyce, Sir Robert Charles Leslie, Bt. (1952)
Boyd, Sir Alexander Walter, Bt. (1916)
Boyd, Sir John Dixon Iklé, KCMG
Boyd, *Prof.* Sir Robert David Hugh, Kt.
Boyd-Carpenter, Sir (Marsom) Henry, KCVO
Boyd-Carpenter, *Lt.-Gen. Hon.* Sir Thomas Patrick John, KBE
Boyle, Sir Stephen Gurney, Bt. (1904)
Boynton, Sir John Keyworth, Kt., MC
Boyson, *Rt. Hon.* Sir Rhodes, Kt.
Brabham, Sir John Arthur, Kt., OBE
Bracewell-Smith, Sir Charles, Bt. (1947)
Bradbeer, Sir John Derek Richardson, Kt., OBE, TD
Bradford, Sir Edward Alexander Slade, Bt. (1902)
Bradshaw, Sir Kenneth Anthony, KCB
Brady, *Prof.* Sir John Michael Kt. FRS
Braithwaite, Sir (Joseph) Franklin Madders, Kt.
Braithwaite, *Rt. Hon.* Sir Nicholas Alexander, Kt., OBE
Braithwaite, Sir Rodric Quentin, GCMG
Bramley, *Prof.* Sir Paul Anthony, Kt.
Branson, Sir Richard Charles Nicholas, Kt.
Bratza, *Hon.* Sir Nicolas Dušan, Kt.
Breckenridge, *Prof.* Sir Alasdair Muir, Kt. CBE
Brennan, *Hon.* Sir (Francis) Gerard, KBE
Brett, Sir Charles Edward Bainbridge, Kt., CBE
Brickwood, Sir Basil Greame, Bt. (1927)
Bridges, *Hon.* Sir Phillip Rodney, Kt., CMG
Brierley, Sir Ronald Alfred, Kt.
Bright, Sir Graham Frank James, Kt.
Bright, Sir Keith, Kt.
Brigstocke, *Adm.* Sir John Richard, KCB
Brinckman, Sir Theodore George Roderick, Bt. (1831)
†Brisco, Sir Campbell Howard, Bt. (1782)
Briscoe, Sir Brian Anthony, Kt.
Briscoe, Sir John Geoffrey James, Bt. (1910)
Brittan, Sir Samuel, Kt.
Britton, Sir Edward Louis, Kt., CBE
†Broadbent, Sir Andrew George, Bt. (1893)
Broadbent, Sir Richard John, KCB
Brocklebank, Sir Aubrey Thomas, Bt. (1885)
Brodie, Sir Benjamin David Ross, Bt. (1834)
Brodie-Hall, Sir Laurence Charles, Kt., AO, CMG
Bromhead, Sir John Desmond Gonville, Bt. (1806)
Bromley, Sir Michael Roger, KBE
Bromley, Sir Rupert Charles, Bt. (1757)
Brook, *Prof.* Sir Richard John, Kt. OBE
†Brooke, Sir Alistair Weston, Bt. (1919)
Brooke, Sir Francis George Windham, Bt. (1903)
Brooke, *Rt. Hon.* Sir Henry, Kt.
Brooke, Sir (Richard) David Christopher, Bt. (1662)
Brooking, Sir Trevor David, Kt., CBE
Brooks, Sir Timothy Gerald Martin, KCVO
Brooksbank, Sir (Edward) Nicholas, Bt. (1919)
Broomfield, Sir Nigel Hugh Robert Allen, KCMG
†Broughton, Sir David Delves, Bt. (1661)
Broun, Sir William Windsor, Bt. (S. 1686)
Brown, Sir (Austen) Patrick, KCB
Brown, *Adm.* Sir Brian Thomas, KCB, CBE
Brown, Sir (Cyril) Maxwell Palmer, KCB, CMG
Brown, Sir David, Kt.
Brown, *Vice-Adm.* Sir David Worthington, KCB
Brown, Sir Douglas Denison, Kt.
Brown, *Hon.* Sir Douglas Dunlop, Kt.
Brown, Sir George Francis Richmond, Bt. (1863)
Brown, Sir George Noel, Kt.
Brown, Sir Mervyn, KCMG, OBE
Brown, Sir Peter Randolph, Kt.
Brown, *Rt. Hon.* Sir Stephen, GBE
Brown, Sir Stephen David Reid, KCVO
Browne, Sir Nicholas Walker, KBE, CMG
Brownrigg, Sir Nicholas (Gawen), Bt. (1816)
Browse, *Prof.* Sir Norman Leslie, Kt., MD, FRCS
Bruce, Sir (Francis) Michael Ian, Bt. (S. 1628)
Bruce, Sir Hervey James Hugh, Bt. (1804)
Bruce-Gardner, Sir Robert Henry, Bt. (1945)
Bruce-Lockhart, Sir Alexander John (Sandy), Kt., OBE
Buckworth-Herne-Soame, Sir Charles John, Bt. (1697)
Brunner, Sir John Henry Kilian, Bt. (1895)
Brunton, Sir (Edward Francis) Lauder, Bt. (1908)
Brunton, Sir Gordon Charles, Kt.
Bryan, Sir Arthur, Kt.
Bryan, Sir Paul Elmore Oliver, Kt., DSO, MC
Bryson, *Adm.* Sir Lindsay Sutherland, KCB, FRENG
Buchan-Hepburn, Sir John Alastair Trant Kidd, Bt. (1815)
Buchanan, Sir Andrew George, Bt. (1878)
Buchanan, *Vice-Adm.* Sir Peter William, KBE
Buchanan, Sir (Ranald) Dennis, Kt., MBE
Buchanan, Sir Robert Wilson (Robin), Kt.
Buchanan-Jardine, *Maj.* Sir (Andrew) Rupert (John), Bt., MC (1885)
Buckland, Sir Ross, Kt.
Buckley, Sir Michael Sidney, Kt.
Buckley, *Lt.-Cdr.* Sir (Peter) Richard, KCVO
Buckley, *Hon.* Sir Roger John, Kt.
Budd, Sir Alan Peter, Kt.
Budd, Sir Colin Richard, KCMG
Bull, Sir George Jeffrey, Kt.
Bull, Sir Simeon George, Bt. (1922)
Bullard, Sir Julian Leonard, GCMG
Bultin, Sir Bato, Kt., MBE
Bunbury, Sir Michael William, Bt. (1681)
Bunch, Sir Austin Wyeth, Kt., CBE
Bunyard, Sir Robert Sidney, Kt., CBE, QPM
Burbidge, Sir Herbert Dudley, Bt. (1916)
Burden, Sir Anthony Thomas, Kt., QPM
Burdett, Sir Savile Aylmer, Bt. (1665)
Burgen, Sir Arnold Stanley Vincent, Kt., FRS
Burgess, *Gen.* Sir Edward Arthur, KCB, OBE
Burgess, Sir (Joseph) Stuart, Kt., CBE, PHD, FRSC
Burgh, Sir John Charles, KCMG, CB
Burke, Sir James Stanley Gilbert, Bt. (I. 1797)
Burke, Sir (Thomas) Kerry, Kt.
Burley, Sir Victor George, Kt., CBE
Burnell-Nugent, *Vice-Adm.* Sir James Michael, KCB, CBE, ADC
Burnet, Sir James William Alexander (Sir Alastair Burnet), Kt.
Burnett, *Air Chief Marshal* Sir Brian Kenyon, GCB, DFC, AFC
Burnett, Sir Charles David, Bt., (1913)
Burnett, Sir John Harrison, Kt.
Burnett, Sir Walter John, Kt.
Burney, Sir Nigel Dennistoun, Bt. (1921)
Burns, Sir (Robert) Andrew, KCMG
Burnton, *Hon.* Sir Stanley Jeffrey, Kt.
Burrell, Sir John Raymond, Bt. (1774)
Burridge, *Air Chief Marshal* Sir Brian Kevin, KCB, CBE, ADC
Burston, Sir Samuel Gerald Wood, Kt., OBE
Burt, Sir Peter Alexander, Kt.
Burton, Sir Carlisle Archibald, Kt., OBE
Burton, Sir George Vernon Kennedy, Kt., CBE

Burton, *Lt.-Gen.* Sir Edmund Fortescue Gerard, KBE
Burton, Sir Graham Stuart, KCMG
Burton, *Hon.* Sir Michael John, Kt.
Burton, Sir Michael St Edmund, KCVO, CMG
Bush, *Adm.* Sir John Fitzroy Duyland, GCB, DSC
Butler, *Rt. Hon.* Sir Adam Courtauld, Kt.
Butler, *Hon.* Sir Arlington Griffith, KCMG
Butler, Sir Michael Dacres, GCMG
Butler, Sir (Reginald) Michael (Thomas), Bt. (1922)
Butler, Sir Percy James, Kt., CBE, DL
Butler, *Hon.* Sir Richard Clive, Kt.
Butler, Sir Richard Pierce, Bt. (1628)
Butter, *Maj.* Sir David Henry, KCVO, MC
Butterfield, *Hon.* Sir Alexander Neil Logie, Kt.
Butterfill, Sir John Valentine, Kt., MP
Buxton, Sir Jocelyn Charles Roden, Bt. (1840)
Buxton, *Rt. Hon.* Sir Richard Joseph, Kt.
Buzzard, Sir Anthony Farquhar, Bt. (1929)
Byatt, Sir Hugh Campbell, KCVO, CMG
Byatt, Sir Ian Charles Rayner, Kt.
Byford, Sir Lawrence, Kt., CBE, QPM
Byron, Sir Charles Michael Dennis, Kt.
†Cable-Alexander, Sir Patrick Desmond William, Bt. (1809)
Cadbury, Sir (George) Adrian (Hayhurst), Kt.
Cadbury, Sir (Nicholas) Dominic, Kt.
Cadogan, *Prof.* Sir John Ivan George, Kt., CBE, FRS, FRSE
Cahn, Sir Albert Jonas, Bt. (1934)
Cain, Sir Henry Edney Conrad, Kt.
Caine, Sir Michael (Maurice Micklewhite), Kt., CBE
Caines, Sir John, KCB
Calderwood, Sir Robert, Kt.
Caldwell, Sir Edward George, KCB
Callan, Sir Ivan Roy, KCVO, CMG
Callaway, *Prof.* Sir Frank Adams, Kt., CMG, OBE
Calman, *Prof.* Sir Kenneth Charles, KCB, MD, FRCP, FRCS, FRSE
Calne, *Prof.* Sir Roy Yorke, Kt., FRS
Calvert-Smith, Sir David, Kt., QC
Cameron, Sir Hugh Roy Graham, Kt., QPM
Campbell, Sir Alan Hugh, GCMG
Campbell, *Prof.* Sir Colin Murray, Kt.
Campbell, *Prof.* Sir Donald, Kt., CBE, FRCS, FRCPGlas.
Campbell, Sir Ian Tofts, Kt., CBE, VRD
Campbell, Sir Ilay Mark, Bt. (1808)
Campbell, Sir James Alexander Moffat Bain, Bt. (S. 1668)
Campbell, Sir Lachlan Philip Kemeys, Bt. (1815)
†Campbell, Sir Roderick Duncan Hamilton, Bt. (1831)
Campbell, Sir Robin Auchinbreck, Bt. (S. 1628)
Campbell, *Rt. Hon.* Sir Walter Menzies, Kt., CBE, QC, MP
Campbell, *Rt. Hon.* Sir William Anthony, Kt.
Campbell-Orde, Sir John Alexander, Bt. (1790)
†Carden, Sir Christopher Robert, Bt. (1887)
Carden, Sir John Craven, Bt. (I. 1787)
Carew, Sir Rivers Verain, Bt. (1661)
Carey, Sir de Vic Graham, Kt.
Carey, Sir Peter Willoughby, GCB
Carleton-Smith, *Maj.-Gen.* Sir Michael Edward, Kt., CBE
Carlisle, Sir James Beethoven, GCMG
Carlisle, Sir John Michael, Kt.
Carlisle, Sir Kenneth Melville, Kt.
Carnegie, *Lt.-Gen.* Sir Robin Macdonald, KCB, OBE
Carnegie, Sir Roderick Howard, Kt.
Carnwath, *Rt. Hon.* Sir Robert John Anderson, Kt., CVO
Caro, Sir Anthony Alfred, Kt., OM, CBE
Carr, Sir (Albert) Raymond (Maillard), Kt.
Carr-Ellison, *Col.* Sir Ralph Harry, KCVO, TD
Carrick, *Hon.* Sir John Leslie, KCMG
Carrick, Sir Roger John, KCMG, LVO
Carruthers, Sir Ian James, Kt., OBE
Carsberg, *Prof.* Sir Bryan Victor, Kt.
Carter, *Prof.* Sir David Craig, Kt., FRCSE, FRCSGlas., FRCPE
Carter, Sir John, Kt., QC
Carter, Sir John Alexander, Kt.
Carter, Sir John Gordon Thomas, Kt.
Carter, Sir Philip David, Kt., CBE
Carter, Sir Richard Henry Alwyn, Kt.
Cartland, Sir George Barrington, Kt., CMG
Cartledge, Sir Bryan George, KCMG
Cary, Sir Roger Hugh, Bt. (1955)
Casey, *Rt. Hon.* Sir Maurice Eugene, Kt.
Cash, Sir Gerald Christopher, GCMG, GCVO, OBE
Cass, Sir Geoffrey Arthur, Kt.
Cassel, Sir Timothy Felix Harold, Bt. (1920)
Cassels, Sir John Seton, Kt., CB
Cassels, *Adm.* Sir Simon Alastair Cassillis, KCB, CBE
Cassidi, *Adm.* Sir (Arthur) Desmond, GCB
Castell, Sir William Martin, Kt.
Cater, Sir Jack, KBE
Catford, Sir (John) Robin, KCVO, CBE
Catherwood, Sir (Henry) Frederick (Ross), Kt.
Catling, Sir Richard Charles, Kt., CMG, OBE
Catto, *Prof.* Sir Graeme Robertson Dawson, Kt.
Cave, Sir John Charles, Bt. (1896)
Cave-Browne-Cave, Sir Robert, Bt. (1641)
Cayley, Sir Digby William David, Bt. (1661)
Cayzer, Sir James Arthur, Bt. (1904)
Cazalet, *Hon.* Sir Edward Stephen, Kt.
Cazalet, Sir Peter Grenville, Kt.
Cecil, *Rear-Adm.* Sir (Oswald) Nigel Amherst, KBE, CB
Chadwick, *Revd Prof.* Henry, KBE
Chadwick, *Rt. Hon.* Sir John Murray, Kt., ED
Chadwick, Sir Joshua Kenneth Burton, Bt. (1935)
Chadwick, *Revd Prof.* (William) Owen, OM, KBE, FBA
Chadwyck-Healey, Sir Charles Edward, Bt. (1919)
Chalmers, Sir Iain Geoffrey, Kt.
Chalmers, Sir Neil Robert, Kt.
Chalstrey, Sir (Leonard) John, Kt., MD, FRCS
Chan, *Rt. Hon.* Sir Julius, GCMG, KBE
Chance, Sir (George) Jeremy ffolliott, Bt. (1900)
Chandler, Sir Colin Michael, Kt.
Chandler, Sir Geoffrey, Kt., CBE
Chantler, *Prof.* Sir Cyril, Kt., MD, FRCP
Chaplin, Sir Malcolm Hilbery, Kt., CBE
Chapman, Sir David Robert Macgowan, Bt. (1958)
Chapman, Sir George Alan, Kt.
Chapman, Sir Sidney Brookes, Kt., MP
Chapple, *Field Marshal* Sir John Lyon, GCB, CBE
Charles, *Hon.* Sir Arthur William Hessin, Kt.
Charles, Sir George Frederick Lawrence, KCMG, CBE
Charlton, Sir Robert (Bobby), Kt., CBE
Charnley, Sir (William) John, Kt., CB, FRENG
Chataway, *Rt. Hon.* Sir Christopher, Kt.
Chatfield, Sir John Freeman, Kt., CBE
Chaytor, Sir George Reginald, Bt. (1831)
Checketts, *Sqn. Ldr.* Sir David John, KCVO
Checkland, Sir Michael, Kt.
Cheshire, *Air Chief Marshal* Sir John Anthony, KBE, CB
Chessells, Sir Arthur David (Tim), Kt.
Chesterton, Sir Oliver Sidney, Kt., MC
Chetwood, Sir Clifford Jack, Kt.
Chetwynd, Sir Arthur Ralph Talbot, Bt. (1795)
Cheyne, Sir Joseph Lister Watson, Bt., OBE (1908)
Chichester, Sir (Edward) John, Bt. (1641)
Chichester-Clark, Sir Robin, Kt.
Chilcot, Sir John Anthony, GCB
Child, Sir (Coles John) Jeremy, Bt. (1919)
Chilton, *Brig.* Sir Frederick Oliver, Kt., CBE, DSO

Chilwell, *Hon.* Sir Muir Fitzherbert, Kt.
Chinn, Sir Trevor Edwin, Kt., CVO
Chipperfield, Sir Geoffrey Howes, KCB
Chisholm, Sir John Alexander Raymond, Kt., FRENG
Chitty, Sir Thomas Willes, Bt. (1924)
Cholmeley, Sir Hugh John Frederick Sebastian, Bt. (1806)
Chow, Sir Chung Kong, Kt.
Chow, Sir Henry Francis, Kt., OBE
Christie, Sir George William Langham, Kt., CH
Christie, Sir William, Kt., MBE
Christopher, Sir Duncan Robin Carmichael, KBE, CMG
Chung, Sir Sze-yuen, GBE, FRENG
Clark, Sir Francis Drake, Bt. (1886)
Clark, Sir John Arnold, Kt.
Clark, Sir Jonathan George, Bt. (1917)
Clark, Sir Robert Anthony, Kt., DSC
Clark, Sir Terence Joseph, KBE, CMG, CVO
Clark, Sir Thomas Edwin, Kt.
Clarke, *Rt. Hon.* Sir Anthony Peter, Kt.
Clarke, Sir Arthur Charles, Kt., CBE
Clarke, Sir (Charles Mansfield) Tobias, Bt. (1831)
Clarke, *Hon.* Sir David Clive, Kt.
Clarke, Sir Ellis Emmanuel Innocent, GCMG
Clarke, Sir Jonathan Dennis, Kt.
Clarke, *Maj.* Sir Peter Cecil, KCVO
Clarke, Sir Robert Cyril, Kt.
Clarke, Sir Rupert William John, Bt., MBE (1882)
Clay, Sir Richard Henry, Bt. (1841)
Clayton, Sir David Robert, Bt. (1732)
Cleaver, Sir Anthony Brian, Kt.
Clementi, Sir David Cecil, Kt.
Cleminson, Sir James Arnold Stacey, KBE, MC
Clerk, Sir Robert Maxwell, Bt., OBE (1679)
Clerke, Sir John Edward Longueville, Bt. (1660)
Clifford, Sir Roger Joseph, Bt. (1887)
Clifford, Sir Timothy Peter Plint, Kt.
Clothier, Sir Cecil Montacute, KCB, QC
Clucas, Sir Kenneth Henry, KCB
Clutterbuck, *Vice-Adm.* Sir David Granville, KBE, CB
Coates, Sir Anthony Robert Milnes, Bt. (1911)
Coates, Sir David Frederick Charlton, Bt. (1921)
Coats, Sir Alastair Francis Stuart, Bt. (1905)
Coats, Sir William David, Kt.
Cobham, Sir Michael John, Kt., CBE
Cochrane, Sir (Henry) Marc (Sursock), Bt. (1903)
Cockburn, Sir John Elliot, Bt. (S. 1671)
Cockburn-Campbell, Sir Alexander Thomas, Bt. (1821)
Cockshaw, Sir Alan, Kt., FRENG
Codrington, Sir Simon Francis Bethell, Bt. (1876)
Codrington, Sir William Alexander, Bt. (1721)
Coghill, Sir Patrick Kendal Farley, Bt. (1778)
Coghlin, *Hon.* Sir Patrick, Kt.
Cohen, Sir Edward, Kt.
Cohen, Sir Ivor Harold, Kt., CBE, TD
Cohen, *Prof.* Sir Philip, Kt., PHD, FRS
Cohen, Sir Ronald, Kt.
Cole, Sir (Robert) William, Kt.
Coleridge, *Hon.* Sir Paul James Duke, Kt.
Coles, Sir (Arthur) John, GCMG
Colfox, Sir (William) John, Bt. (1939)
Collett, Sir Christopher, GBE
Collett, Sir Ian Seymour, Bt. (1934)
Collins, *Hon.* Sir Andrew David, Kt.
Collins, Sir Bryan Thomas Alfred, Kt., OBE, QFSM
Collins, Sir John Alexander, Kt.
Collins, Sir Kenneth Darlingston, Kt.
Collins, *Hon.* Sir Lawrence Antony, Kt.
Collum, Sir Hugh Robert, Kt.
Collyear, Sir John Gowen, Kt.
Colman, *Hon.* Sir Anthony David, Kt.
Colman, Sir Michael Jeremiah, Bt. (1907)
Colman, Sir Timothy, KG
Colquhoun of Luss, Sir Ivar Iain, Bt. (1786)
Colt, Sir Edward William Dutton, Bt. (1694)
Colthurst, Sir Charles St John, Bt. (1744)
Coltman, Sir (Arthur) Leycester Scott, KBE, CMG
Colvin, Sir Howard Montagu, Kt., CVO, CBE, FBA
Compton, *Rt. Hon.* Sir John George Melvin, KCMG
Conant, Sir John Ernest Michael, Bt. (1954)
Connell, *Hon.* Sir Michael Bryan, Kt.
Connery, Sir Sean, Kt.
Connor, Sir William Joseph, Kt.
Conran, Sir Terence Orby, Kt.
Cons, *Hon.* Sir Derek, Kt.
Constantinou, Sir Georkios, Kt., OBE
Cook, Sir Christopher Wymondham Rayner Herbert, Bt. (1886)
Cooke, *Col.* Sir David William Perceval, Bt. (1661)
Cooke, Sir Howard Felix Hanlan, GCMG, GCVO
Cooke, *Hon.* Sir Jeremy Lionel, Kt.
Cooke, *Prof.* Sir Ronald Urwick, Kt.
Cooksey, Sir David James Scott, Kt.
Cooper, *Gen.* Sir George Leslie Conroy, GCB, MC
Cooper, Sir Henry, Kt.
Cooper, Sir Richard Powell, Bt. (1905)
Cooper, Sir Robert George, Kt., CBE
Cooper, *Maj.-Gen.* Sir Simon Christie, GCVO
Cooper, Sir William Daniel Charles, Bt. (1863)
Coote, Sir Christopher John, Bt., *Premier Baronet of Ireland* (I. 1621)
Copas, *Most Revd* Virgil, KBE, DD
Copisarow, Sir Alcon Charles, Kt.
Corbett, *Maj.-Gen.* Sir Robert John Swan, KCVO, CB
Corby, Sir (Frederick) Brian, Kt.
Cordy-Simpson, *Lt.-Gen.* Sir Roderick Alexander, KBE, CB
Corfield, *Rt. Hon.* Sir Frederick Vernon, Kt.
Corfield, Sir Kenneth George, Kt., FRENG
Corley, Sir Kenneth Sholl Ferrand, Kt.
Cormack, Sir Patrick Thomas, Kt., MP
Corness, Sir Colin Ross, Kt.
Cornforth, Sir John Warcup, Kt., CBE, DPHIL, FRS
Corry, Sir James Michael, Bt. (1885)
Cortazzi, Sir (Henry Arthur) Hugh, GCMG
Cory, Sir (Clinton Charles) Donald, Bt. (1919)
Cory-Wright, Sir Richard Michael, Bt. (1903)
Cossons, Sir Neil, Kt., OBE
†Cotter, Sir Patrick Laurence Delaval Bt. (I. 1763)
Cotterell, Sir John Henry Geers, Bt. (1805)
Cotton, *Hon.* Sir Robert Carrington, KCMG
Cotton, Sir William Frederick, Kt., CBE
Cottrell, Sir Alan Howard, Kt., PHD, FRS, FRENG
†Cotts, Sir Richard Crichton Mitchell, Bt. (1921)
Couper, Sir James George, Bt. (1841)
Court, *Hon.* Sir Charles Walter Michael, KCMG, OBE
Courtenay, Sir Thomas Daniel, Kt.
Cousins, *Air Chief Marshal* Sir David, KCB, AFC
Coville, *Air Marshal* Sir Christopher Charles Cotton, KCB
Cowan, *Gen.* Sir Samuel, KCB, CBE
Coward, *Vice-Adm.* Sir John Francis, KCB, DSO
Cowen, *Rt. Hon. Prof.* Sir Zelman, GCMG, GCVO
Cowie, Sir Thomas (Tom), Kt., OBE
Cowper-Coles, Sir Sherard Louis, KCMG, LVO
Cowperthwaite, Sir John James, KBE, CMG
Cox, Sir Alan George, Kt., CBE
Cox, *Prof.* Sir David Roxbee, Kt.,
Cox, Sir Geoffrey Sandford, Kt., CBE
Cox, *Vice-Adm.* Sir John Michael Holland, KCB
Cradock, *Rt. Hon.* Sir Percy, GCMG
Craft, *Prof.* Sir Alan William, Kt.
Craig, Sir (Albert) James (Macqueen), GCMG
Craig-Cooper, Sir (Frederick Howard) Michael, Kt., CBE, TD
Crane, *Hon.* Sir Peter Francis, Kt.
Crane, *Prof.* Sir Peter Robert, Kt.
Craufurd, Sir Robert James, Bt. (1781)
Craven, Sir John Anthony, Kt.

Crawford, *Prof.* Sir Frederick William, Kt., FRENG
Crawley-Boevey, Sir Thomas Michael Blake, Bt. (1784)
Crew, Sir (Michael) Edward, Kt., QPM
Cresswell, *Hon.* Sir Peter John, Kt.
Crichton-Brown, Sir Robert, KCMG, CBE, TD
Crick, *Prof.* Sir Bernard, Kt.
Crill, Sir Peter Leslie, KBE
Crisp, Sir Edmund Nigel Ramsay, KCB
Crisp, Sir (John) Peter, Bt. (1913)
†Critchett, Sir Charles George Montague, Bt. (1908)
Crockett, Sir Andrew Duncan, Kt.
Croft, Sir Owen Glendower, Bt. (1671)
Croft, Sir Thomas Stephen Hutton, Bt. (1818)
†Crofton, Sir Hugh Denis, Bt. (1801)
Crofton, *Prof.* Sir John Wenman, Kt.
†Crofton, Sir Julian Malby, Bt. (1838)
Crompton, Sir Dan, Kt., CBE, QPM
Crossland, *Prof.* Sir Bernard, Kt., CBE, FRENG
Crossley, Sir Julian Charles, Bt. (1909)
Crowe, Sir Brian Lee, KCMG
Cruthers, Sir James Winter, Kt.
Cubbon, Sir Brian Crossland, GCB
Cubitt, Sir Hugh Guy, Kt., CBE
Cullen, Sir (Edward) John, Kt., FRENG
Culme-Seymour, Sir Michael Patrick, Bt. (1809)
Culpin, Sir Robert Paul, Kt.
Cummins, Sir Michael John Austin, Kt.
Cunliffe, Sir David Ellis, Bt. (1759)
Cunliffe-Owen, Sir Hugo Dudley, Bt. (1920)
Cunningham, *Lt.-Gen.* Sir Hugh Patrick, KBE
Cunynghame, Sir Andrew David Francis, Bt. (S. 1702)
†Currie, Sir Donald Scott, Bt. (1847)
Curry, Sir Donald Thomas Younger, Kt., CBE
Curtain, Sir Michael, KBE
Curtis, Sir Barry John, Kt.
Curtis, *Hon.* Sir Richard Herbert, Kt.
Curtis, Sir William Peter, Bt. (1802)
Curtiss, *Air Marshal* Sir John Bagot, KCB, KBE
Curwen, Sir Christopher Keith, KCMG
Cuschieri, *Prof.* Sir Alfred, Kt.
Cutler, Sir Charles Benjamin, KBE, ED
Dacie, *Prof.* Sir John Vivian, Kt., MD, FRS
Dain, Sir David John Michael, KCVO
Dales, Sir Richard Nigel, KCVO
Dalrymple-Hay, Sir James Brian, Bt. (1798)
Dalrymple-White, *Wg Cdr.* Sir Henry Arthur, Bt., DFC (1926)
Dalton, Sir Alan Nugent Goring, Kt., CBE
Dalton, *Vice-Adm.* Sir Geoffrey Thomas James Oliver, KCB
Dalyell, Sir Tam (Thomas), Bt., MP (NS 1685)
Daniel, Sir John Sagar, Kt., DSc
Dannatt, *Lt.-Gen.* Sir Francis Richard, KCB, CBE
Darby, Sir Peter Howard, Kt., CBE, QFSM
Darell, Sir Jeffrey Lionel, Bt., MC (1795)
Darling, Sir Clifford, GCVO
Darrington, Sir Michael John, Kt.
Dasgupta, *Prof.* Sir Partha Sarathi, Kt.
†Dashwood, Sir Edward John Francis, Bt., *Premier Baronet of Great Britain* (1707)
Dashwood, Sir Richard James, Bt. (1684)
Daunt, Sir Timothy Lewis Achilles, KCMG
Davenport-Handley, Sir David John, Kt., OBE
David, Sir Jean Marc, Kt., CBE, QC
David, *His Hon.* Sir Robin (Robert) Daniel George, Kt.,
Davidson, Sir Robert James, Kt., FRENG
Davies, Sir Alan Seymour, Kt.
Davies, *Hon.* Sir (Alfred William) Michael, Kt.
Davies, Sir (Charles) Noel, Kt.
Davies, *Prof.* Sir David Evan Naughton, Kt., CBE, FRS, FRENG
Davies, *Hon.* Sir (David Herbert) Mervyn, Kt., MC, TD
Davies, Sir David John, Kt.
Davies, Sir Frank John, Kt., CBE
Davies, *Prof.* Sir Graeme John, Kt., FRENG
Davies, Sir John Howard, Kt.
Davies, Sir John Michael, KCB
Davies, *Vice-Adm.* Sir Lancelot Richard Bell, KBE
Davies, Sir Peter Maxwell, Kt., CBE
Davies, Sir Rhys Everson, Kt., QC
Davis, Sir Andrew Frank, Kt., CBE
Davis, Sir Colin Rex, Kt., CH, CBE
Davis, Sir Crispin Henry Lamert, Kt.
Davis, Sir (Ernest) Howard, Kt., CMG, OBE
Davis, Sir John Gilbert, Bt. (1946)
Davis, *Hon.* Sir Nigel Anthony Lambert, Kt.
Davis, Sir Peter John, Kt.
Davis, *Hon.* Sir Thomas Robert Alexander Harries, KBE
Davis-Goff, Sir Robert (William), Bt. (1905)
Davison, *Rt. Hon.* Sir Ronald Keith, GBE, CMG
Davson, Sir Christopher Michael Edward, Bt. (1927)
Dawanincura, Sir John Norbert, Kt., OBE
Dawbarn, Sir Simon Yelverton, KCVO, CMG
Dawson, *Hon.* Sir Daryl Michael, KBE, CB
Dawson, Sir Hugh Michael Trevor, Bt. (1920)
Dawtry, Sir Alan (Graham), Kt., CBE, TD
Day, Sir Derek Malcolm, KCMG
Day, *Air Chief Marshal* Sir John Romney, KCB, OBE, ADC
Day, Sir (Judson) Graham, Kt.
Day, Sir Michael John, Kt., OBE
Day, Sir Simon James, Kt.
Deakin, Sir (Frederick) William (Dampier), Kt., DSO
Deane, *Hon.* Sir William Patrick, KBE
Dear, Sir Geoffrey James, Kt., QPM
Dearlove, Sir Richard Billing, KCMG, OBE
de Bellaigue, Sir Geoffrey, GCVO
†Debenham, Sir Thomas Adam, Bt. (1931)
de Deney, Sir Geoffrey Ivor, KCVO
de Hoghton, Sir (Richard) Bernard (Cuthbert), Bt. (1611)
De la Bère, Sir Cameron, Bt. (1953)
de la Rue, Sir Andrew George Ilay, Bt. (1898)
Dellow, Sir John Albert, Kt., CBE
Delves, *Lt.-Gen.* Sir Cedric Norman George, KBE
Denholm, Sir John Ferguson (Ian), Kt., CBE
Denison-Smith, *Lt.-Gen.* Sir Anthony Arthur, KBE
Denman, Sir (George) Roy, KCB, CMG
Denny, Sir Anthony Coningham de Waltham, Bt. (I. 1782)
Denny, Sir Charles Alistair Maurice, Bt. (1913)
Denton, *Prof.* Sir Eric James, Kt., CBE, FRS
Derbyshire, Sir Andrew George, Kt.
Derham, Sir Peter John, Kt.
de Trafford, Sir Dermot Humphrey, Bt. (1841)
Deverell, *Gen.* Sir John Freegard, KCB, OBE
Devesi, Sir Baddeley, GCMG, GCVO
De Ville, Sir Harold Godfrey Oscar, Kt., CBE
Devitt, Sir James Hugh Thomas, Bt. (1916)
de Waal, Sir (Constant Henrik) Henry, KCB, QC
Dewey, Sir Anthony Hugh, Bt. (1917)
Dewhurst, *Prof.* Sir (Christopher) John, Kt.
De Witt, Sir Ronald Wayne, Kt.
Dhenin, *Air Marshal* Sir Geoffrey Howard, KBE, AFC, GM, MD
Dhrangadhra, HH the Maharaja Raj Saheb of, KCIE
Dibela, *Hon.* Sir Kingsford, GCMG
Dick-Lauder, Sir Piers Robert, Bt. (S. 1690)
Dickinson, Sir Harold Herbert, Kt.
Dickinson, Sir Samuel Benson, Kt.
Dilke, Sir Charles John Wentworth, Bt. (1862)
Dillwyn-Venables-Llewelyn, Sir John Michael, Bt. (1890)
Dixon, Sir Jeremy, Kt.
Dixon, Sir Jonathan Mark, Bt. (1919)
Djanogly, Sir Harry Ari Simon, Kt., CBE

Dobson, *Vice-Adm.* Sir David Stuart, KBE
Dodds, Sir Ralph Jordan, Bt. (1964)
Dodds-Parker, Sir (Arthur) Douglas, Kt.
Doll, *Prof.* Sir (William) Richard (Shaboe), Kt., CH, OBE, FRS, DM, MD, DSC
Dollery, Sir Colin Terence, Kt.
Don-Wauchope, Sir Roger (Hamilton), Bt. (S. 1667)
Donald, Sir Alan Ewen, KCMG
Donald, *Air Marshal* Sir John George, KBE
Donaldson, *Prof.* Sir Liam Joseph, Kt.
Donne, *Hon.* Sir Gaven John, KBE
Donne, Sir John Christopher, Kt.
Donnelly, Sir Joseph Brian, KBE, CMG
Dookun, Sir Dewoonarain, Kt.
Dorey, Sir Graham Martyn, Kt.
Dorman, Sir Philip Henry Keppel, Bt. (1923)
Doughty, Sir Graham Martin, Kt.
Doughty, Sir William Roland, Kt.
Douglas, *Hon.* Sir Roger Owen, Kt.
Dover, *Prof.* Sir Kenneth James, Kt., DLitt, FBA, FRSE
Dowell, Sir Anthony James, Kt., CBE
Dowling, Sir Robert, Kt.
Down, Sir Alastair Frederick, Kt., OBE, MC, TD
Downes, Sir Edward Thomas, Kt., CBE
Downey, Sir Gordon Stanley, KCB
Downs, Sir Diarmuid, Kt., CBE, FRENG
Downward, *Maj.-Gen.* Sir Peter Aldcroft, KCVO, CB, DSO, DFC
Downward, Sir William Atkinson, Kt.
Dowson, Sir Philip Manning, Kt., CBE, PRA
Doyle, Sir Reginald Derek Henry, Kt., CBE
D'Oyly, Sir Hadley Gregory Bt. (1663)
Drake, *Hon.* Sir (Frederick) Maurice, Kt., DFC
Drewry, *Lt.-Gen.* Sir Christopher Francis, KCB, CBE
Drinkwater, Sir John Muir, Kt., QC
Driver, Sir Eric William, Kt.
Drummond, Sir John Richard Gray, Kt., CBE
Drury, Sir (Victor William) Michael, Kt., OBE
Dryden, Sir John Stephen Gyles, Bt. (1733 and 1795)
du Cann, *Rt. Hon.* Sir Edward Dillon Lott, KBE
†Duckworth, Sir Edward Richard Dyce, Bt. (1909)
du Cros, Sir Claude Philip Arthur Mallet, Bt. (1916)
Dudley-Williams, Sir Alastair Edgcumbe James, Bt. (1964)
Duff-Gordon, Sir Andrew Cosmo Lewis, Bt. (1813)
Duffell, *Lt.-Gen.* Sir Peter Royson, KCB, CBE, MC
Duffy, Sir (Albert) (Edward) Patrick, Kt., PHD
Dugdale, Sir William Stratford, Bt., MC (1936)
Duggin, Sir Thomas Joseph, Kt.
Dummett, *Prof.* Sir Michael Anthony Eardley, Kt., FBA
Dunbar, Sir Archibald Ranulph, Bt. (S. 1700)
Dunbar, Sir Robert Drummond Cospatrick, Bt. (S. 1698)
Dunbar, Sir James Michael, Bt. (S. 1694)
Dunbar of Hempriggs, Sir Richard Francis, Bt. (S. 1706)
Dunbar-Nasmith, *Prof.* Sir James Duncan, Kt., CBE
Duncan, Sir James Blair, Kt.
Dunlop, Sir Thomas, Bt. (1916)
Dunn, *Air Marshal* Sir Eric Clive, KBE, CB, BEM
Dunn, *Rt. Hon.* Sir Robin Horace Walford, Kt., MC
Dunne, Sir Thomas Raymond, KCVO
Dunning, Sir Simon William Patrick, Bt. (1930)
Dunnington-Jefferson, Sir Mervyn Stewart, Bt. (1958)
Dunstan, *Lt.-Gen.* Sir Donald Beaumont, KBE, CB
Dunt, *Vice-Adm.* Sir John Hugh, KCB
Duntze, Sir Daniel Evans Bt. (1774)
Dupre, Sir Tumun, Kt., MBE
Dupree, Sir Peter, Bt. (1921)
Durand, Sir Edward Alan Christopher David Percy, Bt. (1892)
Durant, Sir (Robert) Anthony (Bevis), Kt.
Durham, Sir Kenneth, Kt.
Durie, Sir David Robert Campbell, KCMG
Durrant, Sir William Alexander Estridge, Bt. (1784)
Duthie, *Prof.* Sir Herbert Livingston, Kt.
Duthie, Sir Robert Grieve (Robin), Kt., CBE
Dwyer, Sir Joseph Anthony, Kt.
Dyke, Sir David William Hart, Bt. (1677)
Dyson, *Rt. Hon.* Sir John Anthony, Kt.
Eady, *Hon.* Sir David, Kt.
Eardley-Wilmot, Sir Michael John Assheton, Bt. (1821)
Earle, Sir (Hardman) George (Algernon), Bt. (1869)
Easton, Sir Robert William Simpson, Kt., CBE
Eaton, *Adm.* Sir Kenneth John, GBE, KCB
Eberle, *Adm.* Sir James Henry Fuller, GCB
Ebrahim, Sir (Mahomed) Currimbhoy, Bt. (1910)
Echlin, Sir Norman David Fenton, Bt. (I. 1721)
Eckersley, Sir Donald Payze, Kt., OBE
Edge, *Capt.* Sir (Philip) Malcolm, KCVO
†Edge, Sir William, Bt. (1937)
Edmonstone, Sir Archibald Bruce Charles, Bt. (1774)
Edward, Sir David Alexander Ogilvy, KCMG
Edwardes, Sir Michael Owen, Kt.
Edwards, Sir Christopher John Churchill, Bt. (1866)
Edwards, Sir Llewellyn Roy, Kt.
Edwards, *Prof.* Sir Samuel Frederick, Kt., FRS
†Edwards-Moss, Sir David John, Bt. (1868)
Egan, Sir John Leopold, Kt.
Egerton, Sir Stephen Loftus, KCMG
Eichelbaum, *Rt. Hon.* Sir Thomas, GBE
Elias, *Hon.* Sir Patrick, Kt.
Eliott of Stobs, Sir Charles Joseph Alexander, Bt. (S. 1666)
Ellerton, Sir Geoffrey James, Kt., CMG, MBE
Elliot, Sir Gerald Henry, Kt.
Elliott, Sir Clive Christopher Hugh, Bt. (1917)
Elliott, Sir David Murray, KCMG, CB
Elliott, *Prof.* Sir John Huxtable, Kt., FBA
Elliott, Sir Randal Forbes, KBE
Elliott, *Prof.* Sir Roger James, Kt., FRS
Ellis, Sir Ronald, Kt., FRENG
Elphinstone, Sir John, Bt. (S. 1701)
Elphinstone, Sir John Howard Main, Bt. (1816)
Elsmore, Sir Lloyd, Kt., OBE
Elton, Sir Arnold, Kt., CBE
Elton, Sir Charles Abraham Grierson, Bt. (1717)
Elton, Sir Leslie, Kt.
Elwes, Sir Jeremy Vernon, Kt., CBE
Elwood, Sir Brian George Conway, Kt., CBE
Elworthy, Sir Peter Herbert, Kt.
Elworthy, *Air Cdre. Hon.* Sir Timothy Charles, KCVO, CBE
Emery, *Rt. Hon.* Sir Peter Frank Hannibal, Kt., MP
Empey, Sir Reginald Norman Morgan, Kt., OBE
Enderby, *Prof.* Sir John Edwin, Kt. CBE, FRS
Engle, Sir George Lawrence Jose, KCB, QC
English, Sir Terence Alexander Hawthorne, KBE, FRCS
Epstein, *Prof.* Sir (Michael) Anthony, Kt., CBE, FRS
Errington, *Col.* Sir Geoffrey Frederick, Bt., OBE (1963)
Errington, Sir Lancelot, KCB
Erskine, Sir (Thomas) David, Bt. (1821)
Erskine-Hill, Sir Alexander Rodger, Bt. (1945)
Esmonde, Sir Thomas Francis Grattan, Bt. (I. 1629)
Espie, Sir Frank Fletcher, Kt., OBE
Esplen, Sir John Graham, Bt. (1921)
Essenhigh, *Adm.* Sir Nigel Richard, GCB
Etherton, *Hon.* Sir Terence Michael Elkan Barnet, Kt.
Evans, Sir Anthony Adney, Bt. (1920)

Evans, *Rt. Hon.* Sir Anthony Howell Meurig, Kt., RD
Evans, *Prof.* Sir Christopher Thomas, Kt., OBE
Evans, *Air Chief Marshal* Sir David George, GCB, CBE
Evans, *Hon.* Sir David Roderick, Kt.
Evans, Sir Harold Matthew, Kt.
Evans, *Hon.* Sir Haydn Tudor, Kt.
Evans, *Prof.* Sir John Grimley, Kt., FRCP
Evans, Sir John Stanley, Kt., QPM
Evans, *Prof.* Sir Martin John, Kt., FRS
Evans, Sir Richard Harry, Kt., CBE
Evans, Sir Richard Mark, KCMG, KCVO
Evans, Sir Robert, Kt., CBE, FRENG
Evans, Sir (William) Vincent (John), GCMG, MBE, QC
Evans-Lombe, *Hon.* Sir Edward Christopher, Kt.
†Evans-Tipping, Sir David Gwynne, Bt. (1913)
Eveleigh, *Rt. Hon.* Sir Edward Walter, Kt., ERD
Everard, Sir Robin Charles, Bt. (1911)
Every, Sir Henry John Michael, Bt. (1641)
Ewans, Sir Martin Kenneth, KCMG
†Ewart, Sir William Michael, Bt. (1887)
Ewbank, *Hon.* Sir Anthony Bruce, Kt.
Eyre, Sir Reginald Edwin, Kt.
Eyre, Sir Richard Charles Hastings, Kt., CBE
Faber, Sir Richard Stanley, KCVO, CMG
Fagge, Sir John William Frederick, Bt. (1660)
Fairbairn, Sir (James) Brooke, Bt. (1869)
Fairhall, *Hon.* Sir Allen, KBE
Fairlie-Cuninghame, Sir Robert Henry, Bt. (S. 1630)
Fairweather, Sir Patrick Stanislaus, KCMG
Falconer, *Hon.* Sir Douglas William, Kt., MBE
†Falkiner, Sir Benjamin Simon Patrick, Bt. (I. 1778)
Fall, Sir Brian James Proetel, GCVO, KCMG
Falle, Sir Samuel, KCMG, KCVO, DSC
Fang, *Prof.* Sir Harry, Kt., CBE
Fareed, Sir Djamil Sheik, Kt.
Farmer, Sir Thomas, Kt., CBE
Farquhar, Sir Michael Fitzroy Henry, Bt. (1796)
Farquharson, *Rt. Hon.* Sir Donald Henry, Kt.
Farquharson, Sir James Robbie, KBE
Farrar-Hockley, *Gen.* Sir Anthony Heritage, GBE, KCB, DSO, MC
Farrell, Sir Terence, Kt., CBE
Farrer, Sir (Charles) Matthew, GCVO
†Farrington, Sir Henry William, Bt. (1818)
Fat, Sir (Maxime) Edouard (Lim Man) Lim, Kt.
Faulkner, Sir (James) Dennis (Compton), Kt., CBE, VRD
Fawkes, Sir Randol Francis, Kt.
Fay, Sir (Humphrey) Michael Gerard, Kt.
Fayrer, Sir John Lang Macpherson, Bt. (1896)
Fearn, Sir (Patrick) Robin, KCMG
Feilden, Sir Bernard Melchior, Kt., CBE
Feilden, Sir Henry Wemyss, Bt., (1846)
Fell, Sir David, KCB
Fender, Sir Brian Edward Frederick, Kt., CMG, PHD
Fenn, Sir Nicholas Maxted, GCMG
Fennell, *Hon.* Sir (John) Desmond Augustine, Kt., OBE
Fennessy, Sir Edward, Kt., CBE
Fergus, Sir Howard Archibald, KBE
Ferguson, Sir Alexander Chapman, Kt., CBE
†Ferguson-Davie, Sir Michael, Bt. (1847)
Fergusson of Kilkerran, Sir Charles, Bt. (S. 1703)
Fergusson, Sir Ewan Alastair John, GCMG, GCVO
Fermor, Sir Patrick Michael Leigh, Kt., DSO, OBE
Feroze, Sir Rustam Moolan, Kt., FRCS
Fersht, *Prof.* Sir Alan Roy, Kt., FRS
Ferris, *Hon.* Sir Francis Mursell, Kt., TD
ffolkes, Sir Robert Francis Alexander, Bt., OBE (1774)
Field, Sir Malcolm David, Kt.
Field, *Hon.* Sir Richard Alan, Kt.
Fielding, Sir Colin Cunningham, Kt., CB
Fielding, Sir Leslie, KCMG
Fieldsend, *Hon.* Sir John Charles Rowell, KBE
Fiennes, Sir Ranulph Twisleton-Wykeham, Bt., OBE (1916)
Figg, Sir Leonard Clifford William, KCMG
Figgis, Sir Anthony St John Howard, KCVO, CMG
Figures, Sir Colin Frederick, KCMG, OBE
Finlay, Sir David Ronald James Bell, Bt. (1964)
Finney, Sir Thomas, Kt., OBE
Fisher, Sir George Read, Kt., CMG
Fisher, *Hon.* Sir Henry Arthur Pears, Kt.
Fison, Sir (Richard) Guy, Bt., DSC (1905)
Fitzalan-Howard, *Maj.-Gen.* Lord Michael, GCVO, CB, CBE, MC
†Fitzgerald, *Revd* Daniel Patrick, Bt. (1903)
FitzGerald, Sir Adrian James Andrew, Bt. (1880)
FitzHerbert, Sir Richard Ranulph, Bt. (1784)
Fitzpatrick, *Air Marshal* Sir John Bernard, KBE, CB
Flanagan, Sir Ronald, GBE
Fletcher, Sir James Muir Cameron, Kt.
Floissac, *Hon.* Sir Vincent Frederick, Kt., CMG, OBE
Floyd, Sir Giles Henry Charles, Bt. (1816)
Foley, *Lt.-Gen.* Sir John Paul, KCB, OBE, MC
Foley, Sir (Thomas John) Noel, Kt., CBE
Follett, *Prof.* Sir Brian Keith, Kt., FRS
Foot, Sir Geoffrey James, Kt.
Foots, Sir James William, Kt.
Forbes, *Maj.* Sir Hamish Stewart, Bt., MBE, MC (1823)
Forbes, *Adm.* Sir Ian Andrew, KCB, CBE
Forbes of Craigievar, Sir John Alexander Cumnock, Bt. (S. 1630)
Forbes, *Vice-Adm.* Sir John Morrison, KCB
Forbes, *Hon.* Sir Thayne John, Kt.
Forbes-Leith, Sir George Ian David, Bt. (1923)
Ford, Sir Andrew Russell, Bt. (1929)
Ford, Sir David Robert, KBE, LVO
Ford, *Maj.* Sir Edward William Spencer, GCVO, KCB, ERD
Ford, *Air Marshal* Sir Geoffrey Harold, KBE, CB, FRENG
Ford, *Prof.* Sir Hugh, Kt., FRS, FRENG
Ford, Sir John Archibald, KCMG, MC
Ford, *Gen.* Sir Robert Cyril, GCB, CBE
Foreman, Sir Philip Frank, Kt., CBE, FRENG
Forestier-Walker, Sir Michael Leolin, Bt. (1835)
Forman, Sir John Denis, Kt., OBE
Forrest, *Prof.* Sir (Andrew) Patrick (McEwen), Kt.
Forrest, *Rear-Adm.* Sir Ronald Stephen, KCVO
Forte, Hon. Sir Rocco John Vincent, Kt.
Forwood, Sir Peter Noel, Bt. (1895)
Foster, Sir Andrew William, Kt.
Foster, *Prof.* Sir Christopher David, Kt.
Foster, Sir John Gregory, Bt. (1930)
Foster, Sir Robert Sidney, GCMG, KCVO
Foulkes, Sir Arther Alexander, KCMG
Foulkes, Sir Nigel Gordon, Kt.
Fountain, *Hon.* Sir Cyril Stanley Smith, Kt.
Fowden, Sir Leslie, Kt., FRS
Fowke, Sir David Frederick Gustavus, Bt. (1814)
Fowler, Sir (Edward) Michael Coulson, Kt.
Fox, *Rt. Hon.* Sir Michael John, Kt.
Fox, Sir Paul Leonard, Kt., CBE
France, Sir Christopher Walter, GCB
Francis, Sir Horace William Alexander, Kt., CBE, FRENG
Frank, Sir Douglas George Horace, Kt., QC
Frank, Sir Robert Andrew, Bt. (1920)
Franklin, Sir Michael David Milroy, KCB, CMG
Franks, Sir Arthur Temple, KCMG
Fraser, Sir Alasdair MacLeod, Kt.
Fraser, Sir Charles Annand, KCVO

Fraser, *Gen.* Sir David William, GCB, OBE
Fraser, Sir Iain Michael Duncan, Bt. (1943)
Fraser, Sir (James) Campbell, Kt.
Fraser, Sir James Murdo, KBE
Fraser, Sir William Kerr, GCB
Frayling, *Prof.* Sir Christopher John, Kt.
Frederick, Sir Christopher St John, Bt. (1723)
Freedman, *Prof.* Sir Lawrence David, KCMG, CBE
Freeland, Sir John Redvers, KCMG
Freeman, Sir James Robin, Bt. (1945)
Freer, *Air Chief Marshal* Sir Robert William George, GBE, KCB
French, *Air Marshal* Sir Joseph Charles, KCB, CBE
Frere, *Vice-Adm.* Sir Richard Tobias, KCB
Fretwell, Sir (Major) John (Emsley), GCMG
Freud, Sir Clement Raphael, Kt.
Friend *Prof.* Sir Richard Henry, Kt.
Froggatt, Sir Leslie Trevor, Kt.
Froggatt, Sir Peter, Kt.
Frossard, Sir Charles Keith, KBE
Frost, Sir David Paradine, Kt., OBE
Fry, Sir Peter Derek, Kt.
Fulford, *Hon.* Sir Adrian Bruce, Kt.
Fuller, Sir James Henry Fleetwood, Bt. (1910)
Fuller, *Hon.* Sir John Bryan Munro, Kt.
Furness, Sir Stephen Roberts, Bt. (1913)
Gadsden, Sir Peter Drury Haggerston, GBE, FRENG
Gage, *Hon.* Sir William Marcus, Kt.
Gains, Sir John Christopher, Kt.
Gainsford, Sir Ian Derek, Kt., DDS
Gaius, *Rt. Revd* Saimon, KBE
Galsworthy, Sir Anthony Charles, KCMG
Galway, Sir James, Kt., OBE
Gam, *Rt. Revd* Sir Getake, KBE
Gamble, Sir David Hugh Norman, Bt. (1897)
Gambon, Sir Michael John, Kt., CBE
Gardiner, Sir John Eliot, Kt., CBE
Gardner, Sir Roy Alan, Kt.
Garland, *Hon.* Sir Patrick Neville, Kt.
Garland, *Hon.* Sir Ransley Victor, KBE
Garlick, Sir John, KCB
Garner, Sir Anthony Stuart, Kt.
Garnett, *Adm.* Sir Ian David Graham, KCB
Garnier, *Rear-Adm.* Sir John, KCVO, CBE
Garrard, Sir David Eardley, Kt.
Garrett, Sir Anthony Peter, Kt., CBE
Garrick, Sir Ronald, Kt., CBE, FRENG
Garrioch, Sir (William) Henry, Kt.
Garrod, *Lt.-Gen.* Sir (John) Martin Carruthers, KCB, OBE
Garthwaite, Sir (William) Mark (Charles), Bt. (1919)
Gaskell, Sir Richard Kennedy Harvey, Kt.
Geno, Sir Makena Viora, KBE
Gent, Sir Christopher Charles, Kt.
George, Sir Arthur Thomas, Kt.
George, *Prof.* Sir Charles Frederick, MD, FRCP
George, Sir Richard William, Kt., CVO
Gerken, *Vice-Adm.* Sir Robert William Frank, KCB, CBE
Gershon, Sir Peter Oliver, Kt., CBE
Gethin, Sir Richard Joseph St Lawrence, Bt. (I. 1665)
Ghurburrun, Sir Rabindrah, Kt.
Gibb, Sir Francis Ross (Frank), Kt., CBE, FRENG
Gibbings, Sir Peter Walter, Kt.
Gibbons, Sir (John) David, KBE
Gibbons, Sir William Edward Doran, Bt. (1752)
Gibbs, *Rt. Hon.* Sir Harry Talbot, GCMG, KBE
Gibbs, *Hon.* Sir Richard John Hedley, Kt.
Gibbs, Sir Roger Geoffrey, Kt.
Gibbs, *Field Marshal* Sir Roland Christopher, GCB, CBE, DSO, MC
†Gibson, *Revd* Christopher Herbert, Bt. (1931)
Gibson, Sir Ian, Kt., CBE
Gibson, *Rt. Hon.* Sir Peter Leslie, Kt.
Gibson-Craig-Carmichael, Sir David Peter William, Bt. (S. 1702 and 1831)
Giddings, *Air Marshal* Sir (Kenneth Charles) Michael, KCB, OBE, DFC, AFC
Giffard, Sir (Charles) Sydney (Rycroft), KCMG
Gilbart-Denham, *Lt.-Col.* Sir Seymour Vivian, KCVO
Gilbert, *Air Chief Marshal* Sir Joseph Alfred, KCB, CBE
Gilbert, Sir Martin John, Kt., CBE
†Gilbey, Sir Walter Gavin, Bt. (1893)
Gill, Sir Anthony Keith, Kt.
Gill, Sir Arthur Benjamin Norman, Kt., CBE
Gillam, Sir Patrick John, Kt.
Gillen, *Hon.* Sir John de Winter, Kt.
Gillett, Sir Robin Danvers Penrose, Bt., GBE, RD (1959)
Gilmour, Sir John Edward, Bt., DSO, TD (1897)
Gina, Sir Lloyd Maepeza, KBE
Gingell, *Air Chief Marshal* Sir John, GBE, KCB, KCVO
Girolami, Sir Paul, Kt.
Girvan, *Hon.* Sir (Frederick) Paul, Kt.
Gladstone, Sir (Erskine) William, Bt., KG (1846)
Glenn, Sir (Joseph Robert) Archibald, Kt., OBE
Glidewell, *Rt. Hon.* Sir Iain Derek Laing, Kt.
Glover, Sir Victor Joseph Patrick, Kt.
Glyn, Sir Richard Lindsay, Bt. (1759 and 1800)
Goavea, Sir Sinaka Vakai, KBE
Gobbo, Sir James Augustine, Kt., AC
Godber, Sir George Edward, GCB, DM
Goldberg, *Prof.* Sir Abraham, Kt., MD, DSC, FRCP
Goldberg, *Prof.* Sir David Paul Brandes, Kt.
Goldman, Sir Samuel, KCB
Goldring, *Hon.* Sir John Bernard, Kt.
Gomersall, Sir Stephen John, KCMG
Gonsalves-Sabola, *Hon.* Sir Joaquim Claudino, Kt
†Gooch, Sir Miles Peter, Bt. (1866)
Gooch, Sir Timothy Robert, Bt., MBE (1746)
Goodall, Sir (Arthur) David Saunders, GCMG
Goodall, *Air Marshal* Sir Roderick Harvey, KBE, CB, AFC
Goode, Prof. Sir Royston Miles, Kt., CBE, QC
Goodenough, Sir Anthony Michael, KCMG
Goodenough, Sir William McLernon, Bt. (1943)
Goodhart, Sir Philip Carter, Kt.
Goodhart, Sir Robert Anthony Gordon, Bt. (1911)
Goodhew, Sir Victor Henry, Kt.
Goodison, Sir Alan Clowes, KCMG
Goodison, Sir Nicholas Proctor, Kt.
Goodlad, *Rt. Hon.* Sir Alastair Robertson, KCMG
Goodman, Sir Patrick Ledger, Kt., CBE
Goodson, Sir Mark Weston Lassam, Bt. (1922)
Goodwin, Sir Frederick, KBE
Goodwin, Sir Frederick Anderson, Kt.
Goodwin, Sir Matthew Dean, Kt., CBE
†Goold, Sir George William, Bt. (1801)
Gordon, Sir Charles Addison Somerville Snowden, KCB
Gordon, Sir Gerald Henry, Kt., CBE, QC
Gordon, Sir Keith Lyndell, Kt., CMG
Gordon, Sir Robert James, Bt. (S. 1706)
Gordon, Sir Sidney Samuel, Kt., CBE
Gordon-Cumming, Sir Alexander Penrose, Bt. (1804)
Gordon Lennox, Lord Nicholas Charles, KCMG, KCVO
†Gore, Sir Nigel Hugh St George, Bt. (I. 1622)
Gore-Booth, Hon. Sir David Alwyn, KCMG, KCVO
Gore-Booth, Sir Josslyn Henry Robert, Bt. (I. 1760)
Gorham, Sir Richard Masters, Kt., CBE, DFC
Goring, Sir William Burton Nigel, Bt. (1627)
Gorman, Sir John Reginald, Kt., CVO, CBE, MC
Gorst, Sir John Michael, Kt.
Goschen, Sir (Edward) Alexander, Bt. (1916)
Gosling, Sir (Frederick) Donald, KCVO
Goswell, Sir Brian Lawrence, Kt.
Gough, Sir Charles Brandon, Kt.
Goulden, Sir (Peter) John, GCMG
Goulding, Sir Marrack Irvine, KCMG

Goulding, Sir (William) Lingard Walter, Bt. (1904)
Gourlay, *Gen.* Sir (Basil) Ian (Spencer), KCB, OBE, MC, RM
Gourlay, Sir Simon Alexander, Kt.
Govan, Sir Lawrence Herbert, Kt.
Gow, *Gen.* Sir (James) Michael, GCB
Gowans, Sir James Learmonth, Kt., CBE, FRCP, FRS
†Graaff, Sir David de Villiers, Bt. (1911)
Grabham, Sir Anthony Henry, Kt.
Graham, Sir Alexander Michael, GBE
Graham, Sir James Bellingham, Bt. (1662)
Graham, Sir James Fergus Surtees, Bt. (1783)
Graham, Sir James Thompson, Kt., CMG
Graham, Sir John Alexander Noble, Bt., GCMG (1906)
Graham, Sir John Alistair, Kt.
Graham, Sir John Moodie, Bt. (1964)
Graham, Sir Norman William, Kt., CB
Graham, Sir Peter, KCB, QC
Graham, Sir Peter Alfred, Kt., OBE
Graham, *Lt.-Gen.* Sir Peter Walter, KCB, CBE
†Graham, Sir Ralph Stuart, Bt. (1629)
Graham-Moon, Sir Peter Wilfred Giles, Bt. (1855)
Graham-Smith, *Prof.* Sir Francis, Kt.
Grant, Sir Archibald, Bt. (S. 1705)
Grant, Sir Clifford, Kt.
Grant, Sir (John) Anthony, Kt.
Grant, Sir Patrick Alexander Benedict, Bt. (S. 1688)
Grant, *Lt.-Gen.* Sir Scott Carnegie, KCB
Grant-Suttie, Sir James Edward, Bt. (S. 1702)
Granville-Chapman, *Lt.-Gen.* Sir Timothy John, KCB, CBE
Gratton-Bellew, Sir Henry Charles, Bt. (1838)
Gray, *Hon.* Sir Charles Anthony St John, Kt.
Gray, *Prof.* Sir Denis John Pereira, Kt., OBE, FRCGP
Gray, Sir John Archibald Browne, Kt., SCD, FRS
Gray, *Lt.-Gen.* Sir Michael Stuart, KCB, OBE
Gray, Sir Robert McDowall (Robin), Kt.
Gray, Sir William Hume, Bt. (1917)
Graydon, *Air Chief Marshal* Sir Michael James, GCB, CBE
Grayson, Sir Jeremy Brian Vincent Harrington, Bt. (1922)
Green, Sir Allan David, KCB, QC
Green, Sir Andrew Fleming, KCMG
†Green, Sir Edward Patrick Lycett, Bt. (1886)
Green, Sir Gregory David, KCMG
Green, *Hon.* Sir Guy Stephen Montague, KBE
Green, Sir Kenneth, Kt.
Green, Sir Owen Whitley, Kt.
Green-Price, Sir Robert John, Bt. (1874)
Greenaway, Sir John Michael Burdick, Bt. (1933)
Greenbury, Sir Richard, Kt.
Greener, Sir Anthony Armitage, Kt.
Greengross, Sir Alan David, Kt.
Greening, *Rear-Adm.* Sir Paul Woollven, GCVO
Greenstock, Sir Jeremy Quentin, GCMG
Greenwell, Sir Edward Bernard, Bt. (1906)
Gregson, Sir Peter Lewis, GCB
Greig, Sir (Henry Louis) Carron, KCVO, CBE
Grenside, Sir John Peter, Kt., CBE
Grey, Sir Anthony Dysart, Bt. (1814)
Grey-Egerton, Sir (Philip) John (Caledon), Bt. (1617)
Grierson, Sir Michael John Bewes, Bt. (S. 1685)
Grierson, Sir Ronald Hugh, Kt.
Griffin, *Maj.* Sir (Arthur) John (Stewart), KCVO
Griffiths, Sir Eldon Wylie, Kt.
Grigson, *Hon.* Sir Geoffrey Douglas, Kt.
Grimshaw, Sir Nicholas Thomas, Kt., CBE
Grimwade, Sir Andrew Sheppard, Kt., CBE
Grindrod, *Most Revd* John Basil Rowland, KBE
Grinstead, Sir Stanley Gordon, Kt.
Grose, *Vice-Adm.* Sir Alan, KBE
Gross, *Hon.* Sir Peter Henry, Kt.
Grossart, Sir Angus McFarlane McLeod, Kt., CBE
Grotrian, Sir Philip Christian Brent, Bt. (1934)
Grove, Sir Charles Gerald, Bt. (1874)
Grove, Sir Edmund Frank, KCVO
Grugeon, Sir John Drury, Kt.
Guinness, Sir Howard Christian Sheldon, Kt., VRD
Guinness, Sir John Ralph Sidney, Kt., CB
Guinness, Sir Kenelm Ernest Lee, Bt. (1867)
Guise, Sir John Grant, Bt. (1783)
Gull, Sir Rupert William Cameron, Bt. (1872)
Gumbs, Sir Emile Rudolph, Kt.
Gun-Munro, Sir Sydney Douglas, GCMG, MBE
Gunn, Sir Robert Norman, Kt.
†Gunning, Sir Charles Theodore, Bt. (1778)
Gunston, Sir John Wellesley, Bt. (1938)
Gurdon, *Prof.* Sir John Bertrand, Kt., DPHIL, FRS
Guthrie, Sir Malcolm Connop, Bt. (1936)
Guy, *Gen.* Sir Roland Kelvin, GCB, CBE, DSO
Haddacks, *Vice-Adm.* Sir Paul Kenneth, KCB
Hadfield, Sir Ronald, Kt., QPM
Hadlee, Sir Richard John, Kt., MBE
Hagart-Alexander, Sir Claud, Bt. (1886)
Hague, *Prof.* Sir Douglas Chalmers, Kt., CBE
Halberg, Sir Murray Gordon, Kt., MBE
Hall, Sir Basil Brodribb, KCB, MC, TD
Hall, *Prof.* Sir David Michael Baldock, Kt.
Hall, Sir Ernest, Kt., OBE
Hall, Sir Graham Joseph, Kt.
Hall, Sir Iain Robert, Kt.
Hall, Sir (Frederick) John (Frank), Bt. (1923)
Hall, Sir John, Kt.
Hall, Sir John Bernard, Bt. (1919)
†Hall, Sir John Douglas Hoste, Bt. (S. 1687)
Hall, Sir Peter Edward, KBE, CMG
Hall, *Prof.* Sir Peter Geoffrey, Kt., FBA
Hall, Sir Peter Reginald Frederick, Kt., CBE
Hall, Sir Robert de Zouche, KCMG
Halliday, *Vice-Adm.* Sir Roy William, KBE, DSC
Halpern, Sir Ralph Mark, Kt.
Halsey, *Revd* John Walter Brooke, Bt. (1920)
Halstead, Sir Ronald, Kt., CBE
Hambling, Sir (Herbert) Hugh, Bt. (1924)
Hamer, *Hon.* Sir Rupert James, KCMG, ED
Hamilton, Sir Andrew Caradoc, Bt. (S. 1646)
Hamilton, *Rt. Hon.* Sir Archibald Gavin, Kt., MP
Hamilton, Sir Edward Sydney, Bt. (1776 and 1819)
Hamilton, Sir James Arnot, KCB, MBE, FRENG
Hamilton-Dalrymple, *Maj.* Sir Hew Fleetwood, Bt., GCVO (S. 1697)
Hamilton-Spencer-Smith, Sir John, Bt. (1804)
Hammick, Sir Stephen George, Bt. (1834)
Hammond, Sir Anthony Hilgrove, KCB, QC
Hampel, Sir Ronald Claus, Kt.
Hampson, Sir Stuart, Kt.
Hampton, Sir (Leslie) Geoffrey, Kt.
Hanbury-Tenison, Sir Richard, KCVO
Hancock, Sir David John Stowell, KCB
Hand, *Most Revd* Geoffrey David, KBE
Hanham, Sir Michael William, Bt., DFC (1667)
Hanley, *Rt. Hon.* Sir Jeremy James, KCMG
Hanmer, Sir John Wyndham Edward, Bt. (1774)
Hannam, Sir John Gordon, Kt.
Hanson, Sir (Charles) Rupert (Patrick), Bt. (1918)
Hanson, Sir John Gilbert, KCMG, CBE
Harcourt-Smith, *Air Chief Marshal* Sir David, GBE, KCB, DFC

Hardie, Sir Douglas Fleming, Kt., CBE
Hardie Boys, *Rt. Hon.* Sir Michael, GCMG
Harding, Sir George William, KCMG, CVO
Harding, *Marshal of the Royal Air Force* Sir Peter Robin, GCB
Harding, Sir Roy Pollard, Kt., CBE
Hardy, Sir David William, Kt.
Hardy, Sir James Gilbert, Kt., OBE
Hardy, Sir Richard Charles Chandos, Bt. (1876)
Hare, Sir David, Kt., FRSL
Hare, Sir Nicholas Patrick, Bt. (1818)
Harford, Sir (John) Timothy, Bt. (1934)
Hargroves, *Brig.* Sir Robert Louis, Kt., CBE
Harington, *Gen.* Sir Charles Henry Pepys, GCB, CBE, DSO, MC
Harington, Sir Nicholas John, Bt. (1611)
Harland, *Air Marshal* Sir Reginald Edward Wynyard, KBE, CB
Harley, *Gen.* Sir Alexander George Hamilton, KBE, CB
Harman, *Gen.* Sir Jack Wentworth, GCB, OBE, MC
Harman, *Hon.* Sir Jeremiah LeRoy, Kt.
Harman, Sir John Andrew, Kt.
Harmsworth, Sir Hildebrand Harold, Bt. (1922)
Harper, Sir Ewan William, Kt. CBE
Harper, *Prof.* Sir Peter Stanley, Kt., CBE
Harris, *Prof.* Sir Henry, Kt., FRCP, FRCPath., FRS
Harris, Sir Jack Wolfred Ashford, Bt. (1932)
Harris, *Air Marshal* Sir John Hulme, KCB, CBE
Harris, *Prof.* Sir Martin Best, Kt., CBE
Harris, Sir Thomas George, KBE, CMG
Harris, Sir William Gordon, KBE, CB, FRENG
Harrison, Sir David, Kt., CBE, FRENG
Harrison, Sir Ernest Thomas, Kt., OBE
Harrison, *Surgeon Vice-Adm.* Sir John Albert Bews, KBE
Harrison, *Hon.* Sir (John) Richard, Kt., ED
Harrison, *Hon.* Sir Michael Guy Vicat, Kt.
Harrison, Sir Michael James Harwood, Bt. (1961)
Harrison, Sir (Robert) Colin, Bt. (1922)
Harrison, Sir Terence, Kt., FREng
Harrop, Sir Peter John, KCB
Hart, Sir Graham Allan, KCB
Hart, *Hon.* Sir Michael Christopher Campbell, Kt.
Hartwell, Sir (Francis) Anthony Charles Peter, Bt. (1805)
Harvey, Sir Charles Richard Musgrave, Bt. (1933)
Harvey-Jones, Sir John Henry, Kt., MBE
Harvie, Sir John Smith, Kt., CBE
Harvie-Watt, Sir James, Bt. (1945)
Haselhurst, *Rt. Hon.* Sir Alan Gordon Barraclough, Kt., MP
Haskard, Sir Cosmo Dugal Patrick Thomas, KCMG, MBE
Haslam, *Rear-Adm.* Sir David William, KBE, CB
Hassett, *Gen.* Sir Francis George, KBE, CB, DSO, LVO
Hastings, Sir Max Macdonald, Kt.
Hastings, Sir Stephen Lewis Edmonstone, Kt., MC
Hatch, Sir David Edwin, Kt., CBE
Hatter, Sir Maurice, Kt.
Havelock-Allan, Sir (Anthony) Mark David, Bt. (1858)
Hawkins, Sir Richard Caesar, Bt. (1778)
Hawley, Sir Donald Frederick, KCMG, MBE
†Hawley, Sir Henry Nicholas, Bt. (1795)
Haworth, Sir Philip, Bt. (1911)
Hawthorne, *Prof.* Sir William Rede, Kt., CBE, SCD, FRS, FRENG
Hay, Sir David Osborne, Kt., CBE, DSO
Hay, Sir David Russell, Kt., CBE, FRCP, MD
Hay, Sir Hamish Grenfell, Kt.
Hay, Sir John Erroll Audley, Bt. (S. 1663)
†Hay, Sir Ronald Frederick Hamilton, Bt. (S. 1703)
Hayes, Sir Brian, Kt., CBE, QPM
Hayes, Sir Brian David, GCB
Hayman-Joyce, *Lt.-Gen.* Sir Robert John, KCB, CBE
Hayward, Sir Anthony William Byrd, Kt.
Hayward, Sir Jack Arnold, Kt., OBE
Haywood, Sir Harold, KCVO, OBE
Head, Sir Francis David Somerville, Bt. (1838)
Heap, Sir Peter William, KCMG
Heap, *Prof.* Sir Robert Brian, Kt., CBE, FRS
Hearne, Sir Graham James, Kt., CBE
Heath, *Rt. Hon.* Sir Edward Richard George, KG, MBE
Heath, Sir Mark Evelyn, KCVO, CMG
Heathcote, *Brig.* Sir Gilbert Simon, Bt., CBE (1733)
Heathcote, Sir Michael Perryman, Bt. (1733)
Heatley, Sir Peter, Kt., CBE
Hedley, *Hon.* Sir Mark, Kt.
Heiser, Sir Terence Michael, GCB
Henao, Revd Ravu, Kt., OBE
Henderson, Sir Denys Hartley, Kt.
Henderson, Sir (John) Nicholas, GCMG, KCVO
Henley, Sir Douglas Owen, KCB
Hennessy, Sir James Patrick Ivan, KBE, CMG
†Henniker, Sir Adrian Chandos, Bt. (1813)
Henniker-Heaton, Sir Yvo Robert, Bt. (1912)
Henriques, *Hon.* Sir Richard Henry Quixano, Kt.
Henry, *Rt. Hon.* Sir Denis Robert Maurice, Kt.
Henry, *Hon.* Sir Geoffrey Arama, KBE
†Henry, Sir Patrick Denis, Bt. (1923)
Henry, *Hon.* Sir Trevor Ernest, Kt.
Henshaw, Sir David George, Kt.
Hepple, *Prof.* Sir Bob Alexander, Kt.
Herbecq, Sir John Edward, KCB
Herbert, *Adm.* Sir Peter Geoffrey Marshall, KCB, OBE
Herbert, Sir Walter William, Kt.
Hermon, Sir John Charles, Kt., OBE, QPM
Heron, Sir Conrad Frederick, KCB, OBE
Heron, Sir Michael Gilbert, Kt.
Heron-Maxwell, Sir Nigel Mellor, Bt. (S. 1683)
Hervey, Sir Roger Blaise Ramsay, KCVO, CMG
Hervey-Bathurst, Sir Frederick John Charles Gordon, Bt. (1818)
Heseltine, *Rt. Hon.* Sir William Frederick Payne, GCB, GCVO
Hetherington, Sir Thomas Chalmers, KCB, CBE, TD, QC
Hewetson, Sir Christopher Raynor, Kt., TD
Hewett, Sir Richard Mark John, Bt. (1813)
Hewitt, Sir (Cyrus) Lenox (Simson), Kt., OBE
Hewitt, Sir Nicholas Charles Joseph, Bt. (1921)
Heygate, Sir Richard John Gage, Bt. (1831)
Heywood, Sir Peter, Bt. (1838)
Hezlet, *Vice-Adm.* Sir Arthur Richard, KBE, CB, DSO, DSC
Hibbert, Sir Jack, KCB
Hickey, Sir Justin, Kt.
Hickman, Sir (Richard) Glenn, Bt. (1903)
Hicks, Sir Robert, Kt.
Hidden, *Hon.* Sir Anthony Brian, Kt.
Hielscher, Sir Leo Arthur, Kt.
Higgins, *Hon.* Sir Malachy Joseph, Kt.
Higginson, Sir Gordon Robert, Kt., PHD, FRENG
Higgs, Sir Derek Alan, Kt.
Hill, Sir Arthur Alfred, Kt., CBE
Hill, Sir Brian John, Kt.
Hill, Sir James Frederick, Bt. (1917)
Hill, Sir John McGregor, Kt., PHD, FRENG
Hill, Sir John Alfred Rowley, Bt. (S. 1779)
Hill, *Vice-Adm.* Sir Robert Charles Finch, KBE, FRENG
Hill-Norton, *Vice-Adm. Hon.* Sir Nicholas John, KCB
Hill-Wood, Sir Samuel Thomas, Bt. (1921)
Hillary, Sir Edmund, KG, KBE
Hillhouse, Sir (Robert) Russell, KCB
Hills, Sir Graham John, Kt.
Hine, *Air Chief Marshal* Sir Patrick Bardon, GCB, GBE
Hirsch, *Prof.* Sir Peter Bernhard, Kt., PHD, FRS
Hirst, *Rt. Hon.* Sir David Cozens-Hardy, Kt.

Hirst, Sir Michael William, Kt.
Hoare, *Prof.* Sir Charles Anthony Richard, Kt., FRS
†Hoare, Sir David John, Bt. (1786)
Hoare, Sir Timothy Edward Charles, Bt., OBE (I. 1784)
Hobart, Sir John Vere, Bt. (1914)
Hobbs, *Maj.-Gen.* Sir Michael Frederick, KCVO, CBE
Hobday, Sir Gordon Ivan, Kt.
Hobhouse, Sir Charles John Spinney, Bt. (1812)
†Hodge, Sir Andrew Rowland, Bt. (1921)
Hodge, Sir James William, KCVO, CMG
Hodges, *Air Chief Marshal* Sir Lewis MacDonald, KCB, CBE, DSO, DFC
Hodgkin, Sir (Gordon) Howard (Eliot), Kt., CH, CBE
Hodgkinson, Sir Michael Stewart, Kt.
Hodgkinson, *Air Chief Marshal* Sir (William) Derek, KCB, CBE, DFC, AFC
Hodgson, Sir Maurice Arthur Eric, Kt., FRENG
Hodson, Sir Michael Robin Adderley, Bt. (I. 1789)
Hoffenberg, *Prof.* Sir Raymond, KBE
Hogg, Sir Christopher Anthony, Kt.
†Hogg, Sir Piers Michael James, Bt. (1846)
Holcroft, Sir Peter George Culcheth, Bt. (1921)
Holderness, Sir Martin William, Bt. (1920)
Holden, Sir Edward, Bt. (1893)
Holden, Sir John David, Bt. (1919)
Holden-Brown, Sir Derrick, Kt.
Holder, Sir John Henry, Bt. (1898)
Holdgate, Sir Martin Wyatt, Kt., CB, PHD
Holdsworth, Sir (George) Trevor, Kt., CVO
Holland, *Hon.* Sir Alan Douglas, Kt.
Holland, *Hon.* Sir Christopher John, Kt.
Holland, Sir Clifton Vaughan, Kt.
Holland, Sir Geoffrey, KCB
Holland, Sir John Anthony, Kt.
Holland, Sir Kenneth Lawrence, Kt., CBE, QFSM
Holland, Sir Philip Welsby, Kt.
Holliday, *Prof.* Sir Frederick George Thomas, Kt., CBE, FRSE
Hollings, *Hon.* Sir (Alfred) Kenneth, Kt., MC
Hollom, Sir Jasper Quintus, KBE
Holloway, *Hon.* Sir Barry Blyth, KBE
Holm, Sir Carl Henry, Kt., OBE
Holm, Sir Ian (Ian Holm Cuthbert), Kt., CBE
Holman, *Hon.* Sir (Edward) James, Kt.
Holmes, *Prof.* Sir Frank Wakefield, Kt.
Holmes, Sir John Eaton, GCVO, KBE, CMG
Holmes-Sellors, Sir Patrick John, KCVO
Holroyd, *Air Marshal* Sir Frank Martyn, KBE, CB
Holt, *Prof.* Sir James Clarke, Kt.
Holt, Sir Michael, Kt., CBE
Home, Sir William Dundas, Bt. (S. 1671)
Honeycombe, *Prof.* Sir Robert William Kerr, Kt., FRS, FRENG
Honywood, Sir Filmer Courtenay William, Bt. (1660)
Hood, Sir Harold Joseph, Bt., TD (1922)
Hookway, Sir Harry Thurston, Kt.
Hooper, *Hon.* Sir Anthony, Kt.
Hope, Sir Colin Frederick Newton, Kt.
Hope, *Rt. Revd and Rt. Hon.* David Michael, KCVO
Hope, Sir John Carl Alexander, Bt. (S. 1628)
Hope-Dunbar, Sir David, Bt. (S. 1664)
Hopkin, Sir (William Aylsham) Bryan, Kt., CBE
Hopkins, Sir Anthony Philip, Kt., CBE
Hopkins, Sir Michael John, Kt., CBE, RA, RIBA
Hopwood, *Prof.* Sir David Alan, Kt., FRS
Hordern, *Rt. Hon.* Sir Peter Maudslay, Kt.
Horlick, *Vice-Adm.* Sir Edwin John, KBE, FRENG
Horlick, Sir James Cunliffe William, Bt. (1914)
Horlock, *Prof.* Sir John Harold, Kt., FRS, FRENG
Horn, *Prof.* Sir Gabriel, Kt., FRS
Horn-Smith, Sir Julian Michael, Kt.
Hornby, Sir Derek Peter, Kt.
Hornby, Sir Simon Michael, Kt.
Horne, Sir Alan Gray Antony, Bt. (1929)
Horne, *Dr* Sir Alistair Allan, Kt. CBE
Horsbrugh-Porter, Sir John Simon, Bt. (1902)
Horsfall, Sir John Musgrave, Bt., MC, TD (1909)
†Hort, Sir Andrew Edwin Fenton, Bt. (1767)
Horton, Sir Robert Baynes, Kt.
Hosker, Sir Gerald Albery, KCB, QC
Hoskyns, Sir Benedict Leigh, Bt. (1676)
Hoskyns, Sir John Austin Hungerford Leigh, Kt.
Hotung, Sir Joseph Edward, Kt.
Houghton, Sir John Theodore, Kt., CBE, FRS
Houldsworth, Sir Richard Thomas Reginald, Bt. (1887)
Hourston, Sir Gordon Minto, Kt.
House, *Lt.-Gen.* Sir David George, GCB, KCVO, CBE, MC
Houssemayne du Boulay, Sir Roger William, KCVO, CMG
Houstoun-Boswall, Sir (Thomas) Alford, Bt. (1836)
Howard, Sir David Howarth Seymour, Bt. (1955)
Howard, *Prof.* Sir Michael Eliot, Kt., CH, CBE, MC
Howard-Dobson, *Gen.* Sir Patrick John, GCB
Howard-Lawson, Sir John Philip, Bt. (1841)
Howell, Sir Ralph Frederic, Kt.
Howells, Sir Eric Waldo Benjamin, Kt., CBE
Howes, Sir Christopher Kingston, KCVO, CB
Howlett, *Gen.* Sir Geoffrey Hugh Whitby, KBE, MC
Huggins, *Hon.* Sir Alan Armstrong, Kt.
Hugh-Jones, Sir Wynn Normington, Kt., LVO
Hugh-Smith, Sir Andrew Colin, Kt.
Hughes, *Hon.* Sir Anthony Philip Gilson, Kt.
Hughes, Hon. Sir Davis, Kt.
Hughes, Sir Jack William, Kt.
Hughes, Sir Thomas Collingwood, Bt. (1773)
Hughes, Sir Trevor Poulton, KCB
Hughes-Morgan, *His Hon. Maj.-Gen.* Sir David John, Bt., CB, CBE (1925)
Hull, *Prof.* Sir David, Kt.
Hulse, Sir Edward Jeremy Westrow, Bt. (1739)
Hum, Sir Christopher Owen, KCMG
Hume, Sir Alan Blyth, Kt., CB
Hunt, Sir John Leonard, Kt.
Hunt, *Adm.* Sir Nicholas John Streynsham, GCB, LVO
Hunt, *Hon.* Sir Patrick James, Kt.
Hunt, Sir Rex Masterman, Kt., CMG
Hunt-Davis, *Brig.* Sir Miles Garth, KCVO, CBE
Hunter, Sir Alistair John, KCMG
Hunter, *Prof.* Sir Laurence Colvin, Kt., CBE, FRSE
Huntington-Whiteley, Sir Hugo Baldwin, Bt. (1918)
Hurn, Sir (Francis) Roger, Kt.
Hurrell, Sir Anthony Gerald, KCVO, CMG
Hurst, Sir Geoffrey Charles, Kt., MBE
Husbands, Sir Clifford Straugh, GCMG
Hutchinson, *Hon.* Sir Ross, Kt., DFC
Hutchison, Sir James Colville, Bt. (1956)
Hutchison, *Rt. Hon.* Sir Michael, Kt.
Hutchison, Sir Robert, Bt. (1939)
Hutt, Sir Dexter Walter, Kt.
Huxley, *Prof.* Sir Andrew Fielding, Kt., OM, FRS
Huxtable, *Gen.* Sir Charles Richard, KCB, CBE
Ibbs, Sir (John) Robin, KBE
Imbert-Terry, Sir Michael Edward Stanley, Bt. (1917)
Imray, Sir Colin Henry, KBE, CMG
Ingham, Sir Bernard, Kt.
Ingilby, Sir Thomas Colvin William, Bt. (1866)
Inglefield-Watson, Sir John Forbes, Bt. (1895)
Inglis, Sir Brian Scott, Kt.
Inglis of Glencorse, Sir Roderick John, Bt. (S. 1703)

Ingram, Sir James Herbert Charles, Bt. (1893)
Ingram, Sir John Henderson, Kt., CBE
Inkin, Sir Geoffrey David, Kt., OBE
†Innes, Sir David Charles Kenneth Gordon, Bt. (NS 1686)
Innes of Edingight, Sir Malcolm Rognvald, KCVO
Innes, Sir Peter Alexander Berowald, Bt. (S. 1628)
Irvine, Sir Donald Hamilton, Kt., CBE, MD, FRCGP
Irving, *Prof.* Sir Miles Horsfall, Kt., MD, FRCS, FRCSE
Irwin, *Lt.-Gen.* Sir Alistair Stuart Hastings, KCB, CBE
Isaacs, Sir Jeremy Israel, Kt.
Isham, Sir Ian Vere Gyles, Bt. (1627)
Jack, *Hon.* Sir Alieu Sulayman, Kt.
Jack, Sir David, Kt., CBE, FRS, FRSE
Jack, Sir David Emmanuel, GCMG, MBE
Jack, *Hon.* Sir Raymond Evan, Kt.
Jackling, Sir Roger Tustin, KCB, CBE
Jackson, Sir Barry Trevor, Kt.
Jackson, Sir Kenneth Joseph, Kt.
Jackson, *Gen.* Sir Michael David, KCB, CBE
Jackson, Sir Michael Roland, Bt. (1902)
Jackson, Sir Nicholas Fane St George, Bt. (1913)
Jackson, Sir Keith Arnold, Bt. (1815)
Jackson, *Hon.* Sir Rupert Matthew, Kt.
†Jackson, Sir (William) Roland Cedric, Bt. (1869)
Jacob, *Hon.* Sir Robert Raphael Hayim (Robin), Kt.
Jacobi, Sir Derek George, Kt., CBE
Jacobi, *Dr* Sir James Edward, Kt., OBE
Jacobs, Sir Cecil Albert, Kt., CBE
Jacobs, *Hon.* Sir Kenneth Sydney, KBE
Jacomb, Sir Martin Wakefield, Kt.
Jaffray, Sir William Otho, Bt. (1892)
Jagger, Sir Michael Philip, Kt.
James, Sir Cynlais Morgan, KCMG
James, Sir Jeffrey Russell, KBE
James, Sir John Nigel Courtenay, KCVO, CBE
James, Sir Stanislaus Anthony, GCMG, OBE
Jamieson, *Air Marshal* Sir David Ewan, KBE, CB
Jansen, Sir Ross Malcolm, KBE
Janvrin, *Rt. Hon.* Sir Robin Berry, KCB, KCVO
Jardine of Applegirth, Sir Alexander Maule, Bt. (S. 1672)
Jardine, Sir Andrew Colin Douglas, Bt. (1916)
Jarman, *Prof.* Sir Brian, Kt., OBE
Jarratt, Sir Alexander Anthony, Kt., CB
Jarvis, Sir Gordon Ronald, Kt.
Jawara, *Hon.* Sir Dawda Kairaba, Kt.
Jay, Sir Antony Rupert, Kt., CVO
Jay, Sir Michael Hastings, KCMG
Jeewoolall, Sir Ramesh, Kt.
Jefferson, Sir George Rowland, Kt., CBE, FRENG
Jeffreys, *Prof.* Sir Alec John, Kt., FRS
Jeffries, *Hon.* Sir John Francis, Kt.
Jehangir, Sir Cowasji, Bt. (1908)
Jejeebhoy, Sir Jamsetjee, Bt. (1857)
Jenkins, Sir Brian Garton, GBE
Jenkins, Sir Elgar Spencer, Kt., OBE
Jenkins, Sir James Christopher, KCB, QC
Jenkins, Sir Michael Nicholas Howard, Kt., OBE
Jenkins, Sir Michael Romilly Heald, KCMG
Jenkins, Sir Simon, Kt.
Jenkinson, Sir John Banks, Bt. (1661)
Jenks, Sir Maurice Arthur Brian, Bt. (1932)
Jenner, *Air Marshal* Sir Timothy LVO, KCB
Jennings, Sir John Southwood, Kt., CBE, FRSE
Jennings, Sir Peter Neville Wake, Kt., CVO
Jephcott, Sir Neil Welbourn, Bt. (1962)
Jessel, Sir Charles John, Bt. (1883)
Jewkes, Sir Gordon Wesley, KCMG
Job, Sir Peter James Denton, Kt.
John, Sir David Glyndwr, KCMG
John, Sir Elton Hercules (Reginald Kenneth Dwight), Kt., CBE
Johns, *Air Chief Marshal* Sir Richard Edward, GCB, CBE, LVO
Johnson, Sir Colpoys Guy, Bt. (1755)
Johnson, *Gen.* Sir Garry Dene, KCB, OBE, MC
Johnson, Sir John Rodney, KCMG
†Johnson, Sir Patrick Eliot, Bt. (1818)
Johnson, *Hon.* Sir Robert Lionel, Kt.
Johnson, Sir Vassel Godfrey, Kt., CBE
Johnson-Ferguson, Sir Ian Edward, Bt. (1906)
Johnston, Sir John Baines, GCMG, KCVO
Johnston, *Lt.-Col.* Sir John Frederick Dame, GCVO, MC
Johnston, *Lt.-Gen.* Sir Maurice Robert, KCB, OBE
Johnston, Sir Thomas Alexander, Bt. (S. 1626)
Johnstone, Sir Geoffrey Adams Dinwiddie, KCMG
Johnstone, Sir (George) Richard Douglas, Bt. (S. 1700)
Johnstone, Sir (John) Raymond, Kt., CBE
Jolliffe, Sir Anthony Stuart, GBE
Jolly, Sir Aurthur Richard, KCMG
Jonas, Sir John Peter Jens, Kt., CBE
Jones, *Gen.* Sir (Charles) Edward Webb, KCB, CBE
Jones, *Air Marshal* Sir Edward Gordon, KCB, CBE, DSO, DFC
Jones, Sir Harry George, Kt., CBE
Jones, Sir John Francis, Kt.
Jones, Sir Keith Stephen, Kt.
Jones, Sir Lyndon, Kt.
Jones, Sir (Owen) Trevor, Kt.
Jones, Sir Richard Anthony Lloyd, KCB
Jones, Sir Robert Edward, Kt.
Jones, Sir Simon Warley Frederick Benton, Bt. (1919)
†Joseph, *Hon.* Sir James Samuel, Bt. (1943)
Jowitt, *Hon.* Sir Edwin Frank, Kt.
Judge, *Rt. Hon.* Sir Igor, Kt.
Judge, Sir Paul Rupert, Kt.
Jugnauth, *Rt. Hon.* Sir Anerood, KCMG
Jungius, *Vice-Adm.* Sir James George, KBE
Kaberry, *Hon.* Sir Christopher Donald, Bt. (1960)
Kakaraya, Sir Pato, KBE
Kalo, Sir Kwamala, Kt., MBE
Kan Yuet-Keung, Sir, GBE
Kapi, *Hon.* Sir Mari, Kt., CBE
Kaputin, Sir John Rumet, KBE, CMG
Kaufman, *Rt. Hon.* Sir Gerald Bernard, Kt., MP
Kausimae, Sir David Nanau, KBE
Kavali, Sir Thomas, Kt., OBE
Kawharu, *Prof.* Sir Ian Hugh, Kt.
Kay, *Prof.* Sir Andrew Watt, Kt.
Kay, *Hon.* Sir Maurice Ralph, Kt., PC
Kaye, Sir Paul Henry Gordon, Bt. (1923)
Keane, Sir Richard Michael, Bt. (1801)
Kearney, *Hon.* Sir William John Francis, Kt., CBE
Keeble, Sir (Herbert Ben) Curtis, GCMG
Keegan, Sir John Desmond Patrick, Kt., OBE
Keene, *Rt. Hon.* Sir David Wolfe, Kt.
Keith, *Hon.* Sir Brian Richard, Kt.
Keith, *Prof.* Sir James, KBE
†Kellett, Sir Stanley Charles, Bt. (1801)
Kelly, Sir Christopher William, KCB
Kelly, Sir David Robert Corbett, Kt., CBE
Kelly, *Rt. Hon.* Sir (John William) Basil, Kt.
Kemakeza, Sir Allan, Kt.
Kemball, *Air Marshal* Sir (Richard) John, KCB, CBE
Kemp, Sir (Edward) Peter, KCB
Kemp-Welch, Sir John, Kt.
Kenilorea, *Rt. Hon.* Sir Peter, KBE
Kennaway, Sir John Lawrence, Bt. (1791)
Kennedy, Sir Francis, KCMG, CBE
Kennedy, *Hon.* Sir Ian Alexander, Kt.
Kennedy, *Prof.* Sir Ian McColl, Kt.
Kennedy, Sir Ludovic Henry Coverley, Kt.
†Kennedy, Sir Michael Edward, Bt., (1836)
Kennedy, *Rt. Hon.* Sir Paul Joseph Morrow, Kt.
Kennedy, *Air Chief Marshal* Sir Thomas Lawrie, GCB, AFC
Kennedy-Good, Sir John, KBE
Kenny, Sir Anthony John Patrick, Kt. DPHIL, LITT, FBA
Kenny, *Gen.* Sir Brian Leslie Graham, GCB, CBE
Kentridge, Sir Sydney Woolf, KCMG, QC

Kenyon, Sir George Henry, Kt.
Kermode, Sir (John) Frank, Kt., FBA
Kermode, Sir Ronald Graham Quale, KBE
Kerr, *Hon.* Sir Brian Francis, Kt.
Kerr, *Adm.* Sir John Beverley, GCB
Kerry, Sir Michael James, KCB, QC
Kershaw, *Prof.* Sir Ian, Kt.
Kershaw, Sir (John) Anthony, Kt., MC
Keswick, Sir John Chippendale Lindley, Kt.
Kevau, *Prof.* Sir Isi Henao, Kt., CBE
Kikau, *Ratu* Sir Jone Latianara, KBE
Killen, *Hon.* Sir Denis James, KCMG
Kimber, Sir Charles Dixon, Bt. (1904)
King, *Prof.* Sir David Anthony, Kt., FRS
King, Sir John Christopher, Bt. (1888)
King, *Vice-Adm.* Sir Norman Ross Dutton, KBE
King, Sir Wayne Alexander, Bt. (1815)
Kingman, *Prof.* Sir John Frank Charles, Kt., FRS
Kingsland, Sir Richard, Kt., CBE, DFC
Kingsley, Sir Ben, Kt.
Kinloch, Sir David, Bt. (S. 1686)
Kinloch, Sir David Oliphant, Bt. (1873)
Kipalan, Sir Albert, Kt.
Kirkpatrick, Sir Ivone Elliott, Bt. (S. 1685)
Kirkwood, *Hon.* Sir Andrew Tristram Hammett, Kt.
Kirkwood, Sir Archibald Johnstone, Kt., MP
Kiszely, *Lt.-Gen.* Sir John Panton, KCB, MC
Kitcatt, Sir Peter Julian, Kt., CB
Kitson, *Gen.* Sir Frank Edward, GBE, KCB, MC
Kitson, Sir Timothy Peter Geoffrey, Kt.
Kleinwort, Sir Richard Drake, Bt. (1909)
Klug, Sir Aaron, Kt., OM
Kneller, Sir Alister Arthur, Kt.
Knight, Sir Harold Murray, KBE, DSC
Knight, *Air Chief Marshal* Sir Michael William Patrick, KCB, AFC
†Knill, Sir Thomas John Pugin Bartholomew, Bt. (1893)
Knowles, Sir Charles Francis, Bt. (1765)
Knowles, Sir Durward Randolph, Kt., OBE
Knowles, Sir Richard Marchant, Kt.
Knox, Sir David Laidlaw, Kt.
Knox, *Hon.* Sir John Leonard, Kt.
Knox, *Hon.* Sir William Edward, Kt.
Knox-Johnston, Sir William Robert Patrick (Sir Robin), Kt., CBE, RD
Koraea, Sir Thomas, Kt.
Kornberg, *Prof.* Sir Hans Leo, Kt., DSC, SCD, PHD, FRS
Korowi, Sir Wiwa, GCMG
Krebs, *Prof.* Sir John Richard, Kt., DPHIL, FRS
Kroto, *Prof.* Sir Harold Walter, Kt., FRS
Kulukundis, Sir Elias George (Eddie), Kt., OBE
Kurongku, *Most Revd* Peter, KBE
Lachmann, *Prof.* Sir Peter Julius, Kt.
Lacon, Sir Edmund Vere, Bt. (1818)
Lacy, Sir Patrick Brian Finucane, Bt. (1921)
Lacy, Sir John Trend, Kt., CBE
Laddie, *Hon.* Sir Hugh Ian Lang, Kt.
Laidlaw, Sir Christopher Charles Fraser, Kt.
Laing, Sir (John) Martin (Kirby), Kt., CBE
Laing, Sir (John) Maurice, Kt.
Laing, Sir (William) Kirby, Kt., FRENG
Laird, Sir Gavin Harry, Kt., CBE
Lake, Sir (Atwell) Graham, Bt. (1711)
Laker, Sir Frederick Alfred, Kt.
Lakin, Sir Michael, Bt. (1909)
Laking, Sir George Robert, KCMG
Lamb, Sir Albert Thomas, KBE, CMG, DFC
Lambert, Sir Anthony Edward, KCMG
Lambert, Sir John Henry, KCVO, CMG
†Lambert, Sir Peter John Biddulph, Bt. (1711)
Lampl, Sir Frank William, Kt.
Lampl, Sir Peter, Kt., OBE
Lamport, Sir Stephen Mark Jeffrey, KCVO
Landale, Sir David William Neil, KCVO
Landau, Sir Dennis Marcus, Kt.
Lander, Sir Stephen James, KCB
Lane, Prof. Sir David Philip, Kt.
†Langham, Sir John Stephen, Bt. (1660)
Langlands, Sir Robert Alan, Kt.
Langley, *Hon.* Sir Gordon Julian Hugh, Kt.
Langley, *Maj.-Gen.* Sir Henry Desmond Allen, KCVO, MBE
Langrishe, Sir James Hercules, Bt. (I. 1777)
Lankester, Sir Timothy Patrick, KCB
Lapli, Sir John Ini, GCMG
Lapun, *Hon.* Sir Paul, Kt.
Larcom, Sir (Charles) Christopher Royde, Bt. (1868)
Large, Sir Andrew McLeod Brooks, Kt.
Large, Sir Peter, Kt., CBE
Latham, *Rt. Hon.* Sir David Nicholas Ramsey, Kt.
Latham, Sir Michael Anthony, Kt.
Latham, Sir Richard Thomas Paul, Bt. (1919)
Latimer, Sir (Courtenay) Robert, Kt., CBE
Latimer, Sir Graham Stanley, KBE
Latour-Adrien, *Hon.* Sir Maurice, Kt.
Laughton, Sir Anthony Seymour, Kt.
Laurence, Sir Peter Harold, KCMG, MC
Laurie, Sir Robert Bayley Emilius, Bt. (1834)
Lauterpacht, Sir Elihu, Kt., CBE, QC
Lauti, *Rt. Hon.* Sir Toaripi, GCMG
Lavan, *Hon.* Sir John Martin, Kt.
Law, *Adm.* Sir Horace Rochfort, GCB, OBE, DSC
Lawes, Sir (John) Michael Bennet, Bt. (1882)
Lawler, Sir Peter James, Kt., OBE
†Lawrence, Sir Clive Wyndham, Bt. (1906)
Lawrence, Sir Henry Peter, Bt. (1858)
Lawrence, Sir Ivan John, Kt., QC
Lawrence, Sir John Patrick Grosvenor, Kt., CBE
Lawrence, Sir William Fettiplace, Bt. (1867)
Lawrence-Jones, Sir Christopher, Bt. (1831)
Laws, *Rt. Hon.* Sir John Grant McKenzie, Kt.
Lawson, Sir Christopher Donald, Kt.
Lawson, Sir Charles John Patrick, Bt. (1900)
Lawson, *Gen.* Sir Richard George, KCB, DSO, OBE
Lawson-Tancred, Sir Henry, Bt. (1662)
Layard, *Adm.* Sir Michael Henry Gordon, KCB, CBE
Lea, *Vice-Adm.* Sir John Stuart Crosbie, KBE
Lea, Sir Thomas William, Bt. (1892)
Leach, *Admiral of the Fleet* Sir Henry Conyers, GCB
Leahy, Sir Daniel Joseph, Kt.
Leahy, Sir John Henry Gladstone, KCMG
Leahy, Sir Terence Patrick, Kt.
Learmont, *Gen.* Sir John Hartley, KCB, CBE
Leather, Sir Edwin Hartley Cameron, KCMG, KCVO
Leaver, Sir Christopher, GBE
Le Bailly, *Vice-Adm.* Sir Louis Edward Stewart Holland, KBE, CB
Le Cheminant, *Air Chief Marshal* Sir Peter de Lacey, GBE, KCB, DFC
Lechmere, Sir Reginald Anthony Hungerford, Bt. (1818)
Ledger, Sir Philip Stevens, Kt., CBE, FRSE
Lee, Sir Arthur James, KBE, MC
Lee, *Brig.* Sir Leonard Henry, Kt., CBE
Lee, Sir Quo-wei, Kt., CBE
Leeds, Sir Christopher Anthony, Bt. (1812)
Lees, Sir David Bryan, Kt.
Lees, Sir Thomas Edward, Bt. (1897)
Lees, Sir Thomas Harcourt Ivor, Bt. (1804)
Lees, Sir (William) Antony Clare, Bt. (1937)
Le Fanu, *Maj.* Sir (George) Victor (Sheridan), KCVO
le Fleming, Sir David Kelland, Bt. (1705)
Legard, Sir Charles Thomas, Bt. (1660)
Legg, Sir Thomas Stuart, KCB, QC
Leggatt, *Rt. Hon.* Sir Andrew Peter, Kt.
Leggatt, Sir Hugh Frank John, Kt.

Leggett, *Prof.* Sir Anthony James, KBE
Leigh, Sir Geoffrey Norman, Kt.
Leigh, Sir Richard Henry, Bt. (1918)
Leighton, Sir Michael John Bryan, Bt. (1693)
Leitch, Sir George, KCB, OBE
Leith-Buchanan, Sir Charles Alexander James, Bt. (1775)
Le Marchant, Sir Francis Arthur, Bt. (1841)
Leng, *Gen.* Sir Peter John Hall, KCB, MBE, MC
Lennox-Boyd, The Hon. Sir Mark Alexander, Kt.
Leon, Sir John Ronald, Bt. (1911)
Leonard, *Rt. Revd Monsignor* and *Rt. Hon.* Graham Douglas, KCVO
Lepping, Sir George Geria Dennis, GCMG, MBE
Le Quesne, Sir (John) Godfray, Kt., QC
Lee-Steere, Sir Ernest Henry, KBE
Leslie, Sir Colin Alan Bettridge, Kt.
Leslie, Sir John Norman Ide, Bt. (1876)
Leslie, Sir Peter Evelyn, Kt.
Lester, Sir James Theodore, Kt.
Lethbridge, Sir Thomas Periam Hector Noel, Bt. (1804)
Lever, Sir Jeremy Frederick, KCMG, QC
Lever, Sir Paul, KCMG
Lever, Sir (Tresham) Christopher Arthur Lindsay, Bt. (1911)
Leveson, *Hon.* Sir Brian Henry, Kt.
Levey, Sir Michael Vincent, Kt., LVO
Levine, Sir Montague Bernard, Kt.
Levinge, Sir Richard George Robin, Bt. (I. 1704)
Lewinton, Sir Christopher, Kt.
Lewis, Sir David Courtenay Mansel, KCVO
Lewis, Sir John Anthony, Kt., OBE
Lewis, Sir Terence Murray, Kt., OBE, GM, QPM
Lewison, *Hon.* Sir Kim Martin Jordan, Kt.
Ley, Sir Ian Francis, Bt. (1905)
Li, Sir Ka-Shing, KBE
Lickiss, Sir Michael Gillam, Kt.
Liddington, Sir Bruce, Kt.
Liggins, *Prof.* Sir Graham Collingwood, Kt., CBE, FRS
Lightman, *Hon.* Sir Gavin Anthony, Kt.
Lighton, Sir Thomas Hamilton, Bt. (I. 1791)
Likierman, *Prof.* Sir John Andrew, Kt.
Lilleyman, *Prof.* Sir John Stuart, Kt.
Limon, Sir Donald William, KCB
Linacre, Sir (John) Gordon (Seymour), Kt., CBE, AFC, DFM
Lindop, Sir Norman, Kt.
Lindsay, Sir James Harvey Kincaid Stewart, Kt.
Lindsay, *Hon.* Sir John Edmund Frederic, Kt.
†Lindsay, Sir James Martin Evelyn, Bt., (1962)
†Lindsay-Hogg, Sir Michael Edward, Bt. (1905)
Lipton, Sir Stuart Anthony, Kt.
Lipworth, Sir (Maurice) Sydney, Kt.
Lister-Kaye, Sir John Phillip Lister, Bt. (1812)
Liston-Foulis, Sir Ian Primrose, Bt. (S. 1634)
Lithgow, Sir William James, Bt. (1925)
Little, *Most Revd* Thomas Francis, KBE
Littler, Sir (James) Geoffrey, KCB
Llewellyn, Sir David St Vincent, Bt. (1922)
Llewellyn-Smith, *Prof.* Sir Christopher Hubert, Kt.
Lloyd, *Prof.* Sir Geoffrey Ernest Richard, Kt., FBA
Lloyd, Sir Ian Stewart, Kt.
Lloyd, Sir Nicholas Markley, Kt.
Lloyd, *Rt. Hon.* Sir Peter Robert Cable, Kt., MP
Lloyd, Sir Richard Ernest Butler, Bt. (1960)
Lloyd, *Hon.* Sir Timothy Andrew Wigram, Kt.
Lloyd-Hughes, Sir Trevor Denby, Kt.
Lloyd-Jones, Sir (Peter) Hugh (Jefferd), Kt.
Loane, *Most Revd* Marcus Lawrence, KBE
Lobo, Sir Rogerio Hyndman, Kt., CBE
†Loder, Sir Edmund Jeune, Bt. (1887)
Logan, Sir David Brian Carleton, KCMG
Logan, Sir Donald Arthur, KCMG
Logan, Sir Raymond Douglas, Kt.
Lokoloko, Sir Tore, GCMG, GCVO, OBE
Longmore, *Rt. Hon.* Sir Andrew Centlivres, Kt.
Loram, *Vice-Adm.* Sir David Anning, KCB, CVO
Lord, Sir Michael Nicholson, Kt.
Lorimer, Sir (Thomas) Desmond, Kt.
Los, *Hon.* Sir Kubulan, Kt., CBE
Loughran, Sir Gerald Finbar, KCB
Lovell, Sir (Alfred Charles) Bernard, Kt., OBE, FRS
Lovelock, Sir Douglas Arthur, KCB
Loveridge, Sir John Warren, Kt.
Lovill, Sir John Roger, Kt., CBE
Lowe, *Air Chief Marshal* Sir Douglas Charles, GCB, DFC, AFC
Lowe, Sir Frank Budge, Kt.
Lowe, Sir Thomas William Gordon, Bt. (1918)
Lowson, Sir Ian Patrick, Bt. (1951)
Lowther, *Col.* Sir Charles Douglas, Bt. (1824)
Lowther, Sir John Luke, KCVO, CBE
Loyd, Sir Francis Alfred, KCMG, OBE
Loyd, Sir Julian St John, KCVO
Lu, Sir Tseng Chi, Kt.
Lucas, *Prof.* Sir Colin Renshaw, Kt.
Lucas, Sir Thomas Edward, Bt. (1887)
Lucas-Tooth, Sir (Hugh) John, Bt. (1920)
Lucy, Sir Edmund John William Hugh Cameron-Ramsay-Fairfax, Bt. (1836)
Luddington, Sir Donald Collin Cumyn, KBE, CMG, CVO
Lumsden, Sir David James, Kt.
Lush, *Hon.* Sir George Hermann, Kt.
Lushington, Sir John Richard Castleman, Bt. (1791)
Luttrell, *Col.* Sir Geoffrey Walter Fownes, KCVO, MC
Lyell, *Rt. Hon.* Sir Nicholas Walter, Kt., MP
Lygo, *Adm.* Sir Raymond Derek, KCB
Lyle, Sir Gavin Archibald, Bt. (1929)
Lynch-Blosse, *Capt.* Sir Richard Hely, Bt. (1622)
Lynch-Robinson, Sir Dominick Christopher, Bt. (1920)
Lyne, Sir Roderic Michael John, KBE, CMG
Lyons, Sir Edward Houghton, Kt.
Lyons, Sir James Reginald, Kt.
Lyons, Sir John, Kt.
Lyons, Sir Michael Thomas, Kt.
McAlpine, Sir William Hepburn, Bt. (1918)
Macara, Sir Alexander Wiseman, Kt., FRCP, FRCGP
†Macara, Sir Hugh Kenneth, Bt. (1911)
McAvoy, Sir (Francis) Joseph, Kt., CBE
McCaffrey, Sir Thomas Daniel, Kt.
McCallum, Sir Donald Murdo, Kt., CBE, FRENG
McCamley, Sir Graham Edward, KBE
McCartney, Sir (James) Paul, Kt., MBE
Macartney, Sir John Barrington, Bt. (I. 1799)
McClintock, Sir Eric Paul, Kt.
McColl, Sir Colin Hugh Verel, KCMG
McCollum, *Rt. Hon.* Sir William, Kt.
McCombe, *Hon.* Sir Richard George Bramwell, Kt.
McConnell, Sir Robert Shean, Bt. (1900)
McCorkell, *Col.* Sir Michael William, KCVO, OBE, TD
MacCormac, Sir Richard Cornelius, Kt., CBE
MacCormick, *Prof.* Sir Donald Neil, Kt., MEP, QC
†McCowan, Sir David William, Bt. (1934)
McCullough, *Hon.* Sir (Iain) Charles (Robert), Kt.
MacDermott, *Rt. Hon.* Sir John Clarke, Kt.
McDermott, Sir (Lawrence) Emmet, KBE
Macdonald of Sleat, Sir Ian Godfrey Bosville, Bt. (S. 1625)
Macdonald, Sir Kenneth Carmichael, KCB
McDonald, Sir Trevor, Kt., OBE
McDowell, Sir Eric Wallace, Kt., CBE
Mace, *Lt.-Gen.* Sir John Airth, KBE, CB
McEwen, Sir John Roderick Hugh, Bt. (1953)

McFarland, Sir John Talbot, Bt. (1914)
MacFarlane, *Prof.* Sir Alistair George James, Kt., CBE, FRS
Macfarlane, Sir (David) Neil, Kt.
Macfarlane, Sir George Gray, Kt., CB, FRENG
McFarlane, Sir Ian, Kt.
McGeoch, *Vice-Adm.* Sir Ian Lachlan Mackay, KCB, DSO, DSC
McGrath, Sir Brian Henry, GCVO
Macgregor, Sir Edwin Robert, Bt. (1828)
McGregor, Sir Ian Alexander, Kt., CBE
McGregor, Sir James David, Kt., OBE
MacGregor of MacGregor, Sir Malcolm Gregor Charles, Bt. (1795)
McGrigor, *Capt.* Sir Charles Edward, Bt. (1831)
McIntosh, Sir Neil William David, Kt., CBE
McIntosh, Sir Ronald Robert Duncan, KCB
McIntyre, Sir Donald Conroy, Kt., CBE
McIntyre, Sir Meredith Alister, Kt.
Mackay, *Hon.* Sir Colin Crichton, Kt.
MacKay, *Prof.* Sir Donald Iain, Kt.
MacKay, Sir Francis Henry, Kt.
McKay, Sir John Andrew, Kt., CBE
McKay, Sir William Robert, KCB
Mackay-Dick, *Maj.-Gen.* Sir Iain Charles, KCVO, MBE
Mackechnie, Sir Alistair John, Kt.
McKee, *Maj.* Sir (William) Cecil, Kt., ERD
McKellen, Sir Ian Murray, Kt., CBE
Mackenzie, Sir (James William) Guy, Bt. (1890)
Mackenzie, *Gen.* Sir Jeremy John George, GCB, OBE
†Mackenzie, Sir Peter Douglas, Bt. (S. 1673)
†Mackenzie, Sir Roderick McQuhae, Bt. (S. 1703)
McKenzie, Sir Roy Allan, KBE
Mackerras, Sir (Alan) Charles (MacLaurin), Kt., CH, CBE
Mackeson, Sir Rupert Henry, Bt. (1954)
McKillop, Sir Thomas Fulton Wilson, Kt.
McKinnon, Sir James, Kt.
McKinnon, *Hon.* Sir Stuart Neil, Kt.
Mackintosh, Sir Cameron Anthony, Kt.
Mackworth, Sir Digby (John), Bt. (1776)
McLaren, Sir Robin John Taylor, KCMG
McLaughlin, *Hon.* Mr Justice, Sir Richard, Kt.
Maclean of Dunconnell, Sir Charles Edward, Bt. (1957)
Maclean, Sir Donald Og Grant, Kt.
Maclean, Sir Lachlan Hector Charles, Bt. (NS 1631)
Maclean, Sir Murdo, Kt.
McLeod, Sir Charles Henry, Bt. (1925)
MacLeod, Sir (John) Maxwell Norman, Bt. (1924)
Macleod, Sir (Nathaniel William) Hamish, KBE
McLintock, Sir (Charles) Alan, Kt.
McLintock, Sir Michael William, Bt. (1934)
Maclure, Sir John Robert Spencer, Bt. (1898)
McMahon, Sir Brian Patrick, Bt. (1817)
McMahon, Sir Christopher William, Kt.
McMaster, Sir Brian John, Kt., CBE
Macmillan, Sir (Alexander McGregor) Graham, Kt.
MacMillan, *Lt.-Gen.* Sir John Richard Alexander, KCB, CBE
McMullin, *Rt. Hon.* Sir Duncan Wallace, Kt.
McMurtry, Sir David, Kt., CBE
Macnaghten, Sir Patrick Alexander, Bt. (1836)
McNair-Wilson, Sir Patrick Michael Ernest David, Kt.
McNamara, *Air Chief Marshal* Sir Neville Patrick, KBE
Macnaughton, *Prof.* Sir Malcolm Campbell, Kt.
McNee, Sir David Blackstock, Kt., QPM
McNulty, Sir (Robert William) Roy, Kt., CBE
MacPhail, Sir Bruce Dugald, Kt.
Macpherson, Sir Ronald Thomas Steward (Tommy), CBE, MC, TD
Macpherson of Cluny, *Hon.* Sir William Alan, Kt., TD
McQuarrie, Sir Albert, Kt.
MacRae, Sir (Alastair) Christopher (Donald Summerhayes), KCMG
Macready, Sir Nevil John Wilfrid, Bt. (1923)
MacSween, *Prof.* Sir Roderick Norman McIver, Kt.
Mactaggart, Sir John Auld, Bt. (1938)
Macwhinnie, Sir Gordon Menzies, Kt., CBE
McWilliam, Sir Michael Douglas, KCMG
McWilliams, Sir Francis, GBE
Madden, Sir David Christopher Andrew, KCMG
Madden, Sir Peter John, Bt. (1919)
Maddox, Sir John Royden, Kt.
Madel, Sir (William) David, Kt., MP
Magnus, Sir Laurence Henry Philip, Bt. (1917)
Mahon, Sir (John) Denis, Kt., CH, CBE
Mahon, Sir William Walter, Bt. (1819)
Maiden, Sir Colin James, Kt., DPHIL
Main, Sir Peter Tester, Kt., ERD
Maingard de la Ville ès Offrans, Sir Louis Pierre René, Kt., CBE
Maini, *Prof.* Sir Ravinder Nath, Kt.
Maino, Sir Charles, KBE
†Maitland, Sir Charles Alexander, Bt. (1818)
Maitland, Sir Donald James Dundas, GCMG, OBE
Malbon, *Vice-Adm.* Sir Fabian Michael, KBE
Malcolm, Sir James William Thomas Alexander, Bt. (S. 1665)
Malet, Sir Harry Douglas St Lo, Bt. (1791)
Mallaby, Sir Christopher Leslie George, GCMG, GCVO
Mallet, Sir William George, GCMG, CBE
Mallick, *Prof.* Sir Netar Prakash, Kt.
Mallinson, Sir William James, Bt. (1935)
Malpas, Sir Robert, Kt., CBE
Mamo, Sir Anthony Joseph, Kt., OBE
Mance, *Rt. Hon.* Sir Jonathan Hugh, Kt.
Mancham, Sir James Richard Marie, KBE
Manchester, Sir William Maxwell, KBE
Mander, Sir Charles Marcus, Bt. (1911)
Manduell, Sir John, Kt., CBE
Mann, *Hon.* Sir George Anthony, Kt.
Mann, *Rt. Revd* Michael Ashley, KCVO
Mann, Sir Rupert Edward, Bt. (1905)
Manning, Sir David Geoffrey, KCMG
Mansel, Sir Philip, Bt. (1622)
Mansfield, *Vice-Adm.* Sir (Edward) Gerard (Napier), KBE, CVO
Mansfield, *Prof.* Sir Peter, Kt.
Mantell, *Rt. Hon.* Sir Charles Barrie Knight, Kt.
Manton, Sir Edwin Alfred Grenville, Kt.
Manuella, Sir Tulaga, GCMG, MBE
Manzie, Sir (Andrew) Gordon, KCB
Margetson, Sir John William Denys, KCMG
Mark, Sir Robert, GBE
Markham, Sir Charles John, Bt. (1911)
Marling, Sir Charles William Somerset, Bt. (1882)
Marmot, Prof. Sir Michael Gideon, Kt.
Marr, Sir Leslie Lynn, Bt. (1919)
Marriner, Sir Neville, Kt., CBE
†Marsden, Sir Simon Neville Llewelyn, Bt. (1924)
Marsh, *Prof.* Sir John Stanley, Kt., CBE
Marshall, Sir Arthur Gregory George, Kt., OBE
Marshall, Sir Denis Alfred, Kt.
Marshall, *Prof.* Sir (Oshley) Roy, Kt., CBE
Marshall, Sir Peter Harold Reginald, KCMG
Marshall, Sir (Robert) Michael, Kt.
Martin, Sir Clive Haydon, Kt., OBE
Martin, Sir George Henry, Kt., CBE
Martin, *Vice-Adm.* Sir John Edward Ludgate, KCB, DSC
Martin, *Prof.* Sir Laurence Woodward, Kt.
Martin, Sir (Robert) Bruce, Kt., QC
Marychurch, Sir Peter Harvey, KCMG
Masefield, Sir Charles Beech Gordon, Kt.

Masefield, Sir Peter Gordon, Kt.
Mason, *Hon.* Sir Anthony Frank, KBE
Mason, Sir (Basil) John, Kt., CB, DSC, FRS
Mason, *Prof.* Sir David Kean, Kt., CBE
Mason, Sir Frederick Cecil, KCVO, CMG
Mason, Sir Gordon Charles, Kt., OBE
Mason, Sir John Charles Moir, KCMG
Mason, Sir John Peter, Kt., CBE
Mason, Sir Peter James, KBE
Mason, *Prof.* Sir Ronald, KCB, FRS
Massy-Greene, Sir (John) Brian, Kt.
Matane, Sir Paulias Nguna, Kt., CMG, OBE
Mather, Sir (David) Carol (Macdonell), Kt., MC
Mathers, Sir Robert William, Kt.
Matheson of Matheson, Sir Fergus John, Bt. (1882)
Mathewson, Sir George Ross, Kt., CBE, PHD, FRSE
Matthews, Sir Peter Alec, Kt.
Matthews, Sir Terence Hedley, Kt., OBE
Maud, *The Hon.* Sir Humphrey John Hamilton, KCMG
Maughan, Sir Deryck, Kt.
Mawer, Sir Philip John Courtney, Kt.
Mawhinney, *Rt. Hon.* Sir Brian Stanley, Kt., MP
Maxwell, Sir Michael Eustace George, Bt. (S. 1681)
Maxwell-Hyslop, Sir Robert John (Robin), Kt.
Maxwell-Scott, Sir Dominic James, Bt. (1642)
May, *Rt. Hon.* Sir Anthony Tristram Kenneth, Kt.
May, Sir Richard George, Kt.
Mayhew-Sanders, Sir John Reynolds, Kt.
Maynard, *Hon.* Sir Clement Travelyan, Kt.
Mayne, *Very Revd* Michael Clement Otway, KCVO
Meadow, *Prof.* Sir (Samuel) Roy, Kt., FRCP, FRCPE
Medlycott, Sir Mervyn Tregonwell, Bt. (1808)
Megarry, *Rt. Hon.* Sir Robert Edgar, Kt., FBA
Meldrum, Sir Graham, Kt., CBE, QFSM
Melhuish, Sir Michael Ramsay, KBE, CMG
Mellon, Sir James, KCMG
Melmoth, Sir Graham John, Kt.
Menter, Sir James Woodham, Kt., PHD, SCD, FRS
Merifield, Sir Anthony James, KCVO, CB
Meyer, Sir Anthony John Charles, Bt. (1910)
Meyer, Sir Christopher John Rome, KCMG
Meyjes, Sir Richard Anthony, Kt.
†Meyrick, Sir Timothy Thomas Charlton, Bt. (1880)
Miakwe, *Hon.* Sir Akepa, KBE
Michael, Sir Duncan, Kt.
Michael, Sir Peter Colin, Kt., CBE
Middleton, Sir John Maxwell, Kt.
Middleton, Sir Peter Edward, GCB
Miers, Sir (Henry) David Alastair Capel, KBE, CMG
Milbank, Sir Anthony Frederick, Bt. (1882)
Milborne-Swinnerton-Pilkington, Sir Thomas Henry, Bt. (S. 1635)
Milburn, Sir Anthony Rupert, Bt. (1905)
Miles, Sir Peter Tremayne, KCVO
Miles, Sir William Napier Maurice, Bt. (1859)
Millais, Sir Geoffrey Richard Everett, Bt. (1885)
Millar, Sir Oliver Nicholas, GCVO, FBA
Millard, Sir Guy Elwin, KCMG, CVO
Miller, Sir Albert Joel, KCMG, MVO, MBE, QPM, CPM
Miller, Sir Donald John, Kt., FRSE, FRENG
Miller, Sir Harry Holmes, Bt. (1705)
Miller, Sir Hilary Duppa (Hal), Kt.
Miller, *Lt.-Col.* Sir John Mansel, GCVO, DSO, MC
Miller, Sir Jonathan Wolfe, Kt., CBE
Miller, Sir Peter North, Kt.
Miller, Sir Robin Robert William, Kt.
Miller, Sir Ronald Andrew Baird, Kt., CBE
Miller of Glenlee, Sir Stephen William Macdonald, Bt. (1788)
Mills, *Vice-Adm.* Sir Charles Piercy, KCB, CBE, DSC
Mills, Sir Ian, Kt.
Mills, Sir Frank, KCVO, CMG
Mills, Sir John Lewis Ernest Watts, Kt., CBE
Mills, Sir Peter Frederick Leighton, Bt. (1921)
Milman, Sir David Patrick, Bt. (1800)
Milne, Sir John Drummond, Kt.
Milne-Watson, Sir Andrew Michael, Bt. (1937)
Milner, Sir Timothy William Lycett, Bt. (1717)
Milton-Thompson, *Surgeon Vice-Adm.* Sir Godfrey James, KBE
Mirrlees, *Prof.* Sir James Alexander, Kt., FBA
Mitchell, Sir David Bower, Kt.
Mitchell, Sir Derek Jack, KCB, CVO
Mitchell, *Rt. Hon.* Sir James FitzAllen, KCMG
Mitchell, *Very Revd* Patrick Reynolds, KCVO
Mitchell, *Hon.* Sir Stephen George, Kt.
Mitting, *Hon.* Sir John Edward, Kt.
Moate, Sir Roger Denis, Kt.
Mobbs, Sir (Gerald) Nigel, Kt.
Moberly, Sir Patrick Hamilton, KCMG
Moffat, Sir Brian Scott, Kt., OBE
Moffat, *Lt.-Gen.* Sir (William) Cameron, KBE
Mogg, Sir John Frederick, KCMG
Moir, Sir Christopher Ernest, Bt. (1916)
†Molesworth-St Aubyn, Sir William, Bt. (1689)
†Molony, Sir Thomas Desmond, Bt. (1925)
Monck, Sir Nicholas Jeremy, KCB
Money-Coutts, Sir David Burdett, KCVO
Montagu, Sir Nicholas Lionel John, KCB
Montagu-Pollock, Sir Giles Hampden, Bt. (1872)
Montague-Browne, Sir Anthony Arthur Duncan, KCMG, CBE, DFC
Montgomery, Sir (Basil Henry) David, Bt. (1801)
Montgomery, Sir (William) Fergus, Kt.
Montgomery-Cuninghame, Sir John Christopher Foggo, Bt. (NS 1672)
Moody-Stuart, Sir Mark, KCMG
Moollan, Sir Abdool Hamid Adam, Kt.
Moollan, *Hon.* Sir Cassam (Ismael), Kt.
†Moon, Sir Roger, Bt. (1887)
Moore, *Most Revd* Desmond Charles, KBE
Moore, Sir Francis Thomas, Kt.
Moore, *Maj.-Gen.* Sir (John) Jeremy, KCB, OBE, MC
Moore, Sir John Michael, KCVO, CB, DSC
Moore, *Vice Adm.* Sir Michael Antony Claës, KBE, LVO
Moore, *Prof.* Sir Norman Winfrid, Bt. (1919)
Moore, Sir Patrick Alfred Caldwell, Kt., CBE
Moore, Sir Patrick William Eisdell, Kt., OBE
Moore, Sir Roger George, KBE
Moore, Sir William Roger Clotworthy, Bt., TD (1932)
Moore-Bick, *Hon.* Sir Martin James, Kt.
Moores, Sir Peter, Kt., CBE
Morauta, Sir Mekere, Kt.
Mordaunt, Sir Richard Nigel Charles, Bt. (1611)
Moreton, Sir John Oscar, KCMG, KCVO, MC
Morgan, *Vice-Adm.* Sir Charles Christopher, KBE
Morgan, Sir Graham, Kt.
Morgan, Sir John Albert Leigh, KCMG
Morgan-Giles, *Rear-Adm.* Sir Morgan Charles, Kt., DSO, OBE, GM
Morison, *Hon.* Sir Thomas Richard Atkin, Kt.
Morland, *Hon.* Sir Michael, Kt.
Morland, Sir Robert Kenelm, Kt.
Morpeth, Sir Douglas Spottiswoode, Kt., TD
†Morris, Sir Allan Lindsay, Bt. (1806)
Morris, *Air Marshal* Sir Arnold Alec, KBE, CB
Morris, Sir Derek James, Kt.
Morris, Sir (James) Richard (Samuel), Kt., CBE

Morris, Sir Keith Elliot Hedley, KBE, CMG
Morris, *Prof.* Sir Peter John, Kt.
Morris, Sir Trefor Alfred, Kt., CBE, QPM
Morris, Sir William, Kt.
Morris, *Very Revd* William James, KCVO
Morrison, Sir (Alexander) Fraser, Kt., CBE
Morrison, *Hon.* Sir Charles Andrew, Kt.
Morrison, Sir Howard Leslie, Kt., OBE
Morrison, Sir Kenneth Duncan, Kt., CBE
Morrison-Bell, Sir William Hollin Dayrell, Bt. (1905)
Morrison-Low, Sir James Richard, Bt. (1908)
Morritt, *Rt. Hon.* Sir (Robert) Andrew, Kt., CVO
Morrow, Sir Ian Thomas, Kt.
Morse, Sir Christopher Jeremy, KCMG
Mortimer, Sir John Clifford, Kt., CBE, QC
Morton, *Adm.* Sir Anthony Storrs, GBE, KCB
Moseley, Sir George Walker, KCB
Moses, *Hon.* Sir Alan George, Kt.
Moss, Sir David Joseph, KCVO, CMG
Moss, Sir Stirling Craufurd, Kt., OBE
Mostyn, *Gen.* Sir (Joseph) David Frederick, KCB, CBE
Mostyn, Sir William Basil John, Bt. (1670)
Mott, Sir John Harmer, Bt. (1930)
Mottram, Sir Richard Clive, KCB
†Mount, Sir (William Robert) Ferdinand, Bt. (1921)
Mountain, Sir Denis Mortimer, Bt. (1922)
Mountfield, Sir Robin, KCB
Mowbray, Sir John, Kt.
Mowbray, Sir John Robert, Bt. (1880)
Muir, Sir Laurence Macdonald, Kt.
†Muir, Sir Richard James Kay, Bt. (1892)
Muir-Mackenzie, Sir Alexander Alwyne Henry Charles Brinton, Bt. (1805)
Mulcahy, Sir Geoffrey John, Kt.
Mullens, *Lt.-Gen.* Sir Anthony Richard Guy, KCB, OBE
Mummery, *Rt. Hon.* Sir John Frank, Kt.
Munby, *Hon.* Sir James Lawrence, Kt.
Munn, Sir James, Kt., OBE
Munro, Sir Alan Gordon, KCMG
†Munro, Sir Kenneth Arnold William, Bt. (S. 1634)
†Munro, Sir Keith Gordon, Bt. (1825)
Muria, *Hon.* Sir Gilbert John Baptist, Kt.
Murphy, Sir Leslie Frederick, Kt.
Murray, *Rt. Hon.* Sir Donald Bruce, Kt.
Murray, Sir James, KCMG
Murray, *Prof.* Sir Kenneth, Kt.
Murray, Sir Nigel Andrew Digby, Bt. (S. 1628)
Murray, Sir Patrick Ian Keith, Bt. (S. 1673)
†Murray, Sir Rowland William, Bt. (S. 1630)
Mursell, Sir Peter, Kt., MBE
Musgrave, Sir Christopher John Shane, Bt. (1782)
Musgrave, Sir Christopher Patrick Charles, Bt. (1611)
Musson, *Gen.* Sir Geoffrey Randolph Dixon, GCB, CBE, DSO
Myers, Sir Philip Alan, Kt., OBE, QPM
Myers, *Prof.* Sir Rupert Horace, KBE
Mynors, Sir Richard Baskerville, Bt. (1964)
Naipaul, Sir Vidiadhar Surajprasad, Kt.
Nairn, Sir Michael, Bt. (1904)
Nairne, *Rt. Hon.* Sir Patrick Dalmahoy, GCB, MC
Naish, Sir (Charles) David, Kt.
Nall, Sir Edward William Joseph Bt. (1954)
Namaliu, *Rt. Hon.* Sir Rabbie Langanai, KCMG
†Napier, Sir Charles Joseph, Bt. (1867)
Napier, Sir John Archibald Lennox, Bt. (S. 1627)
Napier, Sir Oliver John, Kt.
Naylor-Leyland, Sir Philip Vyvyan, Bt. (1895)
Neal, Sir Eric James, Kt., CVO
Neal, Sir Leonard Francis, Kt., CBE
Neale, Sir Gerrard Anthony, Kt.
Neave, Sir Paul Arundell, Bt. (1795)
Neill, *Rt. Hon.* Sir Brian Thomas, Kt.
Neill, Sir (James) Hugh, KCVO, CBE, TD
†Nelson, Sir Jamie Charles Vernon Hope, Bt. (1912)
Nelson, *Hon.* Sir Robert Franklyn, Kt.
Neuberger, *Hon.* Sir David Edmond, Kt., PC
Neubert, Sir Michael John, Kt.
Neville, Sir Roger Albert Gartside, Kt.
New, *Maj.-Gen.* Sir Laurence Anthony Wallis, Kt., CB, CBE
Newall, Sir Paul Henry, Kt., TD
Newby, *Prof.* Sir Howard Joseph, Kt., CBE
Newington, Sir Michael John, KCMG
Newman, Sir Francis Hugh Cecil, Bt. (1912)
Newman, Sir Geoffrey Robert, Bt. (1836)
Newman, *Hon.* Sir George Michael, Kt.
Newman, Sir Kenneth Leslie, GBE, QPM
Newman, *Vice-Adm.* Sir Roy Thomas, KCB
Newsam, Sir Peter Anthony, Kt.
†Newson-Smith, Sir Peter Frank Graham, Bt. (1944)
Newton, Sir (Charles) Wilfred, Kt., CBE
Newton, Sir (Harry) Michael (Rex), Bt. (1900)
Newton, Sir Kenneth Garnar, Bt., OBE, TD (1924)
Ngata, Sir Henare Kohere, KBE
Nichol, Sir Duncan Kirkbride, Kt., CBE
Nicholas, Sir David, Kt., CBE
Nicholas, Sir John William, KCVO, CMG
Nicholls, *Air Marshal* Sir John Moreton, KCB, CBE, DFC, AFC
Nicholls, Sir Nigel Hamilton, KCVO, CBE
Nichols, Sir Richard Everard, Kt.
Nicholson, Sir Bryan Hubert, Kt.
†Nicholson, Sir Charles Christian, Bt. (1912)
Nicholson, *Rt. Hon.* Sir Michael, Kt.
Nicholson, Sir Paul Douglas, Kt.
Nicholson, Sir Robin Buchanan, Kt., PHD, FRS, FRENG
Nicoll, Sir William, KCMG
Nightingale, Sir Charles Manners Gamaliel, Bt. (1628)
Nixon, Sir Simon Michael Christopher, Bt. (1906)
Nixon, Sir Edwin Ronald, Kt., CBE
Noble, Sir David Brunel, Bt. (1902)
Noble, Sir Iain Andrew, Bt., OBE (1923)
Nombri, Sir Joseph Karl, Kt., ISO, BEM
Noon, Sir Gulam Kaderbhoy, Kt., MBE
Norman, Sir Arthur Gordon, KBE, DFC
Norman, Sir Mark Annesley, Bt. (1915)
Norman, Sir Robert Henry, Kt., OBE
Norman, Sir Ronald, Kt., OBE
Norrington, Sir Roger Arthur Carver, Kt., CBE
Norris, Sir Eric George, KCMG
Norriss, Air Marshal Sir Peter Coulson, KBE, CB, AFC
North, Sir Peter Machin, Kt., CBE, QC, DCL, FBA
North, Sir Thomas Lindsay, Kt.
North, Sir (William) Jonathan (Frederick), Bt. (1920)
Norton-Griffiths, Sir John, Bt. (1922)
Nossal, Sir Gustav Joseph Victor, Kt., CBE
Nott, *Rt. Hon.* Sir John William Frederic, KCB
Nourse, *Rt. Hon.* Sir Martin Charles, Kt.
Nugent, Sir John Edwin Lavallin, Bt. (I. 1795)
Nugent, Sir Robin George Colborne, Bt. (1806)
†Nugent, Sir (Walter) Richard Middleton, Bt. (1831)
Nunn, Sir Trevor Robert, Kt., CBE
Nunneley, Sir Charles Kenneth Roylance, Kt.
Nursaw, Sir James, KCB, QC
Nurse, Sir Paul Maxime, Kt.
Nuttall, Sir Nicholas Keith Lillington, Bt. (1922)

Nutting, Sir John Grenfell, Bt., QC (1903)
Oakeley, Sir John Digby Atholl, Bt. (1790)
Oakes, Sir Christopher, Bt. (1939)
Oakshott, Hon. Sir Anthony Hendrie, Bt. (1959)
Oates, Sir Thomas, Kt., CMG, OBE
O'Brien, Sir Frederick William Fitzgerald, Kt.
O'Brien, Sir Richard, Kt., DSO, MC
O'Brien, Sir Timothy John, Bt. (1849)
O'Brien, *Adm.* Sir William Donough, KCB, DSC
O'Connell, Sir Bernard, Kt.
O'Connell, Sir Maurice James Donagh MacCarthy, Bt. (1869)
O'Dea, Sir Patrick Jerad, KCVO
Odell, Sir Stanley John, Kt.
Odgers, Sir Graeme David William, Kt.
O'Donnell, Sir Christopher John, Kt.
O'Dowd, Sir David Joseph, Kt., CBE, QPM
Ogden, Sir Robert, Kt., CBE
Ogilvy, *Rt. Hon.* Sir Angus James Bruce, KCVO
Ogilvy, Sir Francis Gilbert Arthur, Bt. (S. 1626)
Ogilvy-Wedderburn, Sir Andrew John Alexander, Bt. (1803)
Ognall, *Hon.* Sir Harry Henry, Kt.
Ohlson, Sir Brian Eric Christopher, Bt. (1920)
Oldham, *Dr* Sir John, Kt., OBE
Oliver, Sir James Michael Yorrick, Kt.
O'Loghlen, Sir Colman Michael, Bt. (1838)
Olver, Sir Stephen John Linley, KBE, CMG
Omand, Sir David Bruce, GCB
O'Nions, Prof. Sir Robert Keith, Kt., FRS, PHD
Ondaatje, Sir Christopher, Kt., CBE
Onslow, Sir John Roger Wilmot, Bt. (1797)
Oppenheimer, Sir Michael Bernard Grenville, Bt. (1921)
O'Regan, *Dr* Sir Stephen Gerard (Tipene), Kt.
O'Reilly, Sir Anthony John Francis, Kt.
Orr, Sir David Alexander, Kt., MC
Orr, Sir John, Kt., OBE
Orr-Ewing, Sir (Alistair) Simon, Bt. (1963)
Orr-Ewing, Sir Archibald Donald, Bt. (1886)
Osborn, Sir John Holbrook, Kt.
Osborn, Sir Richard Henry Danvers, Bt. (1662)
Osborne, Sir Peter George, Bt. (I. 1629)
Osmond, Sir Douglas, Kt., CBE
Osmotherly, Sir Edward Benjamin Crofton, Kt., CB
O'Sullevan, Sir Peter John, Kt., CBE
Oswald, *Admiral of the Fleet* Sir (John) Julian Robertson, GCB
Oswald, Sir (William Richard) Michael, KCVO
Otton, Sir Geoffrey John, KCB
Otton, *Rt. Hon.* Sir Philip Howard, Kt.
Oulton, Sir Antony Derek Maxwell, GCB, QC
Ouseley, *Hon.* Sir Brian Walter, Kt.
Outram, Sir Alan James, Bt. (1858)
Owen, Sir Geoffrey, Kt.
Owen, *Hon.* Sir John Arthur Dalziel, Kt.
Owen, *Hon.* Sir Robert Michael, Kt.
Pakenham, *Hon.* Sir Michael Aiden, KBE, CMG
Packer, Sir Richard John, KCB
Page, Sir (Arthur) John, Kt.
Page, Sir Frederick William, Kt., CBE, FRENG
Page, Sir John Joseph Joffre, Kt., OBE
Paget, Sir Julian Tolver, Bt., CVO (1871)
Paget, Sir Richard Herbert, Bt. (1886)
Pain, *Lt.-Gen.* Sir (Horace) Rollo (Squarey), KCB, MC
Paine, Sir Christopher Hammon, Kt., FRCP, FRCR
Palin, *Air Chief Marshal* Sir Roger Hewlett, KCB, OBE
Palliser, *Rt. Hon.* Sir (Arthur) Michael, GCMG
Palmar, Sir Derek James, Kt.
Palmer, Sir (Charles) Mark, Bt. (1886)
Palmer, Sir Geoffrey Christopher John, Bt. (1660)
Palmer, *Rt. Hon.* Sir Geoffrey Winston Russell, KCMG
Palmer, Sir John Edward Somerset, Bt. (1791)
Palmer, *Maj.-Gen.* Sir (Joseph) Michael, KCVO
Palmer, Sir Reginald Oswald, GCMG, MBE
Pantlin, Sir Dick Hurst, Kt., CBE
Paolozzi, Sir Eduardo Luigi, Kt., CBE, RA
Parbo, Sir Arvi Hillar, Kt.
Park, *Hon.* Sir Andrew Edward Wilson, Kt.
Parker, Sir Alan William, Kt., CBE
Parker, Sir Eric Wilson, Kt.
Parker, *Rt. Hon.* Sir Jonathan Frederic, Kt.
Parker, *Maj.* Sir Michael John, KCVO, CBE
Parker, Sir Richard (William) Hyde, Bt. (1681)
Parker, *Rt. Hon.* Sir Roger Jocelyn, Kt.
Parker, Sir (Thomas) John, Kt.
Parker, *Vice-Adm.* Sir (Wilfred) John, KBE, CB, DSC
Parker, Sir William Peter Brian, Bt. (1844)
Parkes, Sir Edward Walter, Kt., FRENG
Parry, Sir Emyr Jones, KCMG
Parry-Evans, *Air Chief Marshal* Sir David, GCB, CBE
Parsons, Sir John Christopher, KCVO
Parsons, Sir (John) Michael, Kt.
Parsons, Sir Richard Edmund (Clement Fownes), KCMG
Partridge, Sir Michael John Anthony, KCB
Pascoe, *Gen.* Sir Robert Alan, KCB, MBE
†Pasley, Sir Robert Killigrew Sabine, Bt. (1794)
Paston-Bedingfeld, *Capt.* Sir Edmund George Felix, Bt. (1661)
Paterson, Sir Dennis Craig, Kt.
Patnick, Sir (Cyril) Irvine, Kt., OBE
Patten, *Hon.* Mr Justice, Sir Nicholas John, Kt.
Pattie, *Rt. Hon.* Sir Geoffrey Edwin, Kt.
Pattinson, Sir (William) Derek, Kt.
Pattison, *Prof.* Sir John Ridley, Kt., DM, FRCPath.
Pattullo, Sir (David) Bruce, Kt., CBE
Pauncefort-Duncombe, Sir Philip Digby, Bt. (1859)
Payne, Sir Norman John, Kt., CBE, FRENG
Payne-Gallwey, Sir Philip Frankland, Bt. (1812)
Peach, Sir Leonard Harry, Kt.
Peacock, *Prof.* Sir Alan Turner, Kt., DSC
Pearce, Sir (Daniel Norton) Idris, Kt., CBE, TD
Pearse, Sir Brian Gerald, Kt.
Pearson, Sir Francis Nicholas Fraser, Bt. (1964)
Pearson, *Gen.* Sir Thomas Cecil Hook, KCB, CBE, DSO
Peart, *Prof.* Sir William Stanley, Kt., MD, FRS
Pease, Sir (Alfred) Vincent, Bt. (1882)
Pease, Sir Richard Thorn, Bt. (1920)
Peat, Sir Gerrard Charles, KCVO
Peat, Sir Michael Charles Gerrard, KCVO
Peck, Sir Edward Heywood, GCMG
Peckham, *Prof.* Sir Michael John, Kt.
Peek, *Vice-Adm.* Sir Richard Innes, KBE, CB, DSC
†Peek, Sir Richard Grenville, Bt. (1874)
Peel, Sir John Harold, KCVO
Peirse, *Air Vice-Marshal* Sir Richard Charles Fairfax, KCVO, CB
Pelgen, Sir Harry Friedrich, Kt., MBE
Peliza, Sir Robert John, KBE, ED
Pelly, Sir Richard John, Bt. (1840)
Pemberton, Sir Francis Wingate William, Kt., CBE
Pendry, *Prof.* Sir John Brian, Kt.
Penrose, *Prof.* Sir Roger, Kt., OM, FRS
Penry-Davey, *Hon.* Sir David Herbert, Kt.
Pereira, Sir (Herbert) Charles, Kt., DSC, FRS
Perowne, *Vice-Adm.* Sir James Francis, KBE
Perring, Sir John Raymond, Bt. (1963)
Perris, Sir David (Arthur), Kt., MBE
Perry, Sir David Howard, KCB
Perry, Sir (David) Norman, Kt., MBE
Perry, Sir Michael Sydney, GBE
Pervez, Sir Mohammed Anwar, Kt., OBE

Pestell, Sir John Richard, KCVO
Peters, *Prof.* Sir David Keith, Kt., FRCP
Petersen, Sir Jeffrey Charles, KCMG
Peterson, Sir Christopher Matthew, Kt., CBE, TD
†Petit, Sir Jehangir, Bt. (1890)
Peto, Sir Henry George Morton, Bt. (1855)
Peto, Sir Michael Henry Basil, Bt. (1927)
Peto, *Prof.* Sir Richard, Kt., FRS
Petrie, Sir Peter Charles, Bt., CMG (1918)
Pettigrew, Sir Russell Hilton, Kt.
Pettit, Sir Daniel Eric Arthur, Kt.
Pettitt, Sir Dennis, Kt.
Philips, *Prof.* Sir Cyril Henry, Kt.
Philipson-Stow, Sir Christopher, Bt., DFC (1907)
Phillips, Sir Fred Albert, Kt., CVO
Phillips, Sir (Gerald) Hayden, GCB
Phillips, Sir Henry Ellis Isidore, Kt., CMG, MBE
Phillips, Sir John David, Kt., QPM
Phillips, Sir Peter John, Kt., OBE
Phillips, Sir Robin Francis, Bt. (1912)
Phillis, Sir Robert Weston, Kt.
Pickard, Sir (John) Michael, Kt.
Pickthorn, Sir James Francis Mann, Bt. (1959)
Pidgeon, Sir John Allan Stewart, Kt.
†Piers, Sir James Desmond, Bt. (I. 1661)
Piggott-Brown, Sir William Brian, Bt. (1903)
Pigot, Sir George Hugh, Bt. (1764)
Pigott, *Lt.-Gen.* Sir Anthony David, KCB, CBE
Pigott, Sir Berkeley Henry Sebastian, Bt. (1808)
Pike, *Lt.-Gen.* Sir Hew William Royston, KCB, DSO, MBE
Pike, Sir Michael Edmund, KCVO, CMG
Pike, Sir Philip Ernest Housden, Kt., QC
Pilditch, Sir Richard Edward, Bt. (1929)
Pile, Sir Frederick Devereux, Bt., MC (1900)
Pill, *Rt. Hon.* Sir Malcolm Thomas, Kt.
Pilling, Sir Joseph Grant, KCB
Pinker, Sir George Douglas, KCVO
Pinsent, Sir Christopher Roy, Bt. (1938)
Pippard, *Prof.* Sir (Alfred) Brian, Kt., FRS
Pitakaka, Sir Moses Puibangara, GCMG
Pitcher, Sir Desmond Henry, Kt.
Pitchers, *Hon.* Sir Christopher (John), Kt.
Pitchford, *Hon.* Sir Christopher John, Kt.
Pitman, Sir Brian Ivor, Kt.
Pitoi, Sir Sere, Kt., CBE
Pitt, Sir Harry Raymond, Kt., PHD, FRS
Pitts, Sir Cyril Alfred, Kt.
Plastow, Sir David Arnold Stuart, Kt.
Platt, Sir Harold Grant, Kt.
Platt, Sir Martin Philip, Bt. (1959)
Pledger, *Air Chief Marshal* Sir Malcolm David, KCB, OBE, AFC
Plumbly, Sir Derek John, KCMG
Pogo, *Most Revd.* Ellison Leslie, KBE
Pohai, Sir Timothy, Kt., MBE
Pole, Sir (John) Richard (Walter Reginald) Carew, Bt. (1628)
Pole, Sir Peter Van Notten, Bt. (1791)
Polkinghorne, *Revd Canon* John Charlton, KBE, FRS
Pollard, Sir Charles, Kt.
†Pollen, Sir Richard John Hungerford, Bt. (1795)
Pollock, Sir George Frederick, Bt. (1866)
Pollock, *Admiral of the Fleet* Sir Michael Patrick, GCB, LVO, DSC
Ponsonby, Sir Ashley Charles Gibbs, Bt., KCVO, MC (1956)
Poole, *Hon.* Sir David Anthony, Kt.
Poore, Sir Herbert Edward, Bt. (1795)
Pope, Sir Joseph Albert, Kt., DSC, PHD
Popplewell, *Hon.* Sir Oliver Bury, Kt.
†Porritt, Sir Jonathon Espie, Bt. (1963)
Portal, Sir Jonathan Francis, Bt. (1901)
Porter, Sir Leslie, Kt.
Porter, Sir Robert Wilson, Kt., PC (NI)
Posnett, Sir Richard Neil, KBE, CMG
Potter, *Rt. Hon.* Sir Mark Howard, Kt.
Potter, *Maj.-Gen.* Sir (Wilfrid) John, KBE, CB
Potts, *Hon.* Sir Francis Humphrey, Kt.
Pound, Sir John David, Bt. (1905)
Povey, Sir Keith, Kt., QPM
Powell, Sir Nicholas Folliott Douglas, Bt. (1897)
Powell, Sir Richard Royle, GCB, KBE, CMG
Power, Sir Alastair John Cecil, Bt. (1924)
Power, *Hon.* Sir Noel Plunkett, Kt.
Prance, *Prof.* Sir Ghillean Tolmie, Kt., FRS
Prendergast, Sir (Walter) Kieran, KCVO, CMG
Prentice, *Hon.* Sir William Thomas, Kt., MBE
Prescott, Sir Mark, Bt. (1938)
†Preston, Sir Philip Charles Henry Hulton, Bt. (1815)
Prevost, Sir Christopher Gerald, Bt. (1805)
Price, Sir David Ernest Campbell, Kt.
Price, Sir Francis Caradoc Rose, Bt. (1815)
Price, Sir Frank Leslie, Kt.
Price, Sir Norman Charles, KCB
Prickett, *Air Chief Marshal* Sir Thomas Other, KCB, DSO, DFC
Prideaux, Sir Humphrey Povah Treverbian, Kt., OBE
†Primrose, Sir John Ure, Bt. (1903)
Prince-Smith, Sir (William) Richard, Bt. (1911)
Pringle, *Air Marshal* Sir Charles Norman Seton, KBE, FRENG
Pringle, *Hon.* Sir John Kenneth, Kt.
Pringle, *Lt.-Gen.* Sir Steuart (Robert), Bt., KCB, RM (S. 1683)
Pritchard, Sir Neil, KCMG
Prichard-Jones, Sir John, Bt. (1910)
†Proby, Sir William Henry, Bt. (1952)
Proctor-Beauchamp, Sir Christopher Radstock, Bt. (1745)
Prosser, Sir Ian Maurice Gray, Kt.
Pryke, Sir Christopher Dudley, Bt. (1926)
Puapua, *Rt. Hon.* Sir Tomasi, GCMG, KBE
Pugh, Sir Idwal Vaughan, KCB
Pumfrey, *Hon.* Sir Nicholas Richard, Kt.
Pumphrey, Sir (John) Laurence, KCMG
Purves, Sir William, Kt., CBE, DSO
Purvis, *Vice-Adm.* Sir Neville, KCB
Quan, Sir Henry (Francis), KBE
Quicke, Sir John Godolphin, Kt., CBE
Quigley, Sir (William) George (Henry), Kt., CB, PHD
Quilliam, *Hon.* Sir (James) Peter, Kt.
Quilter, Sir Anthony Raymond Leopold Cuthbert, Bt. (1897)
Quinlan, Sir Michael Edward, GCB
Quinton, Sir James Grand, Kt.
Radcliffe, Sir Sebastian Everard, Bt. (1813)
Radda, *Prof.* Sir George Karoly, Kt., CBE, FRS
Rae, *Hon.* Sir Wallace Alexander Ramsay, Kt.
Raeburn, Sir Michael Edward Norman, Bt. (1923)
Raikes, *Vice-Adm.* Sir Iwan Geoffrey, KCB, CBE, DSC
Raison, *Rt. Hon.* Sir Timothy Hugh Francis, Kt.
Ralli, Sir Godfrey Victor, Bt., TD (1912)
Ramdanee, Sir Mookteswar Baboolall Kailash, Kt.
Ramphal, Sir Shridath Surendranath, GCMG
Ramphul, Sir Baalkhristna, Kt.
Ramphul, Sir Indurduth, Kt.
Ramsay, Sir Alexander William Burnett, Bt. (1806)
Ramsay, Sir Allan John (Hepple), KBE, CMG
Ramsbotham, *Gen.* Sir David John, GCB, CBE
Ramsbotham, *Hon.* Sir Peter Edward, GCMG, GCVO
Ramsden, Sir John Charles Josslyn, Bt. (1689)
Randle, *Prof.* Sir Philip John, Kt.
Rankin, Sir Ian Niall, Bt. (1898)
Rasch, Sir Simon Anthony Carne, Bt. (1903)
Rashleigh, Sir Richard Harry, Bt. (1831)
Ratford, Sir David John Edward, KCMG, CVO
Rattee, *Hon.* Sir Donald Keith, Kt.

Rattle, Sir Simon Dennis, Kt., CBE
Rawlins, *Surgeon Vice-Adm.* Sir John Stuart Pepys, KBE
Rawlins, *Prof.* Sir Michael David, Kt., FRCP, FRCPED
Rawlinson, Sir Anthony Henry John, Bt. (1891)
Read, *Air Marshal* Sir Charles Frederick, KBE, CB, DFC, AFC
Read, Sir John Emms, Kt.
†Reade, Sir Kenneth Ray, Bt. (1661)
Reardon-Smith, Sir (William) Antony (John), Bt. (1920)
Reay, *Lt.-Gen.* Sir (Hubert) Alan John, KBE
Redgrave, *Maj.-Gen.* Sir Roy Michael Frederick, KBE, MC
Redgrave, Sir Steven Geoffrey, Kt., CBE
Redmayne, Sir Nicholas, Bt. (1964)
Redwood, Sir Peter Boverton, Bt. (1911)
Reece, Sir Charles Hugh, Kt.
Rees, Sir David Allan, Kt., PHD, DSC, FRS
Rees, *Prof.* Sir Martin John, Kt., FRS
Reeve, Sir Anthony, KCMG, KCVO
Reeves, *Most Revd* Paul Alfred, GCMG, GCVO
Reffell, *Adm.* Sir Derek Roy, KCB
Refshauge, *Maj.-Gen.* Sir William Dudley, Kt., CBE
Reid, Sir Alexander James, Bt. (1897)
Reid, Sir (Harold) Martin (Smith), KBE, CMG
Reid, Sir Hugh, Bt. (1922)
Reid, Sir Norman Robert, Kt.
Reid, Sir Robert Paul, Kt.
Reid, Sir William Kennedy, KCB
Reiher, Sir Frederick Bernard Carl, KBE, CMG
Reilly, *Lt.-Gen.* Sir Jeremy Calcott, KCB, DSO
Renals, Sir Stanley, Bt. (1895)
Renouf, Sir Clement William Bailey, Kt.
Renshaw, Sir John David Bine, Bt. (1903)
Renwick, Sir Richard Eustace, Bt. (1921)
Reporter, Sir Shapoor Ardeshirji, KBE
Reynolds, Sir David James, Bt. (1923)
Reynolds, Sir Peter William John, Kt., CBE
Rhodes, Sir John Christopher Douglas, Bt. (1919)
Rhodes, Sir Peregrine Alexander, KCMG
Rice, *Maj.-Gen.* Sir Desmond Hind Garrett, KCVO, CBE
Rice, Sir Timothy Miles Bindon, Kt.
Richard, Sir Cliff, Kt., OBE
Richards, Sir Brian Mansel, Kt., CBE, PHD
Richards, *Hon.* Sir David Anthony Stewart, Kt.
Richards, Sir Francis Neville, KCMG, CVO
Richards, *Lt.-Gen.* Sir John Charles Chisholm, KCB, KCVO, RM
Richards, Sir Rex Edward, Kt., DSC, FRS
Richards, *Hon.* Sir Stephen Price, Kt.
Richardson, Sir Anthony Lewis, Bt. (1924)
Richardson, *Rt. Hon.* Sir Ivor Lloyd Morgan, Kt.
Richardson, Sir (John) Eric, Kt., CBE
Richardson, *Lt.-Gen.* Sir Robert Francis, KCB, CVO, CBE
Richardson, Sir Thomas Legh, KCMG
Richardson-Bunbury, Sir (Richard David) Michael, Bt. (I. 1787)
Richmond, *Prof.* Sir Mark Henry, Kt., FRS
Ricketts, Sir Robert Cornwallis Gerald St Leger, Bt. (1828)
Riddell, Sir John Charles Buchanan, Bt., CVO (S. 1628)
Ridley, Sir Adam (Nicholas), Kt.
Ridley, Sir Michael Kershaw, KCVO
Rigby, Sir Anthony John, Bt. (1929)
Rigby, Sir Peter, Kt.
Rimer, *Hon.* Sir Colin Percy Farquharson, Kt.
†Ripley, Sir William Hugh, Bt. (1880)
Risk, Sir Thomas Neilson, Kt.
Ritako, Sir Thomas Baha, Kt., MBE
†Rivett-Carnac, Sir Miles James, Bt. (1836)
Rix, *Rt. Hon.* Sir Bernard Anthony, Kt.
Rix, Sir John, Kt., MBE, FRENG
Robati, Sir Pupuke, KBE
Robb, Sir John Weddell, Kt.
Roberts, *Hon.* Sir Denys Tudor Emil, KBE,
Roberts, Sir Derek Harry, Kt., CBE, FRS, FRENG
Roberts, *Prof.* Sir Edward Adam, KCMG
Roberts, Sir (Edward Fergus) Sidney, Kt., CBE
Roberts, *Prof.* Sir Gareth Gwyn, Kt., FRS
Roberts, Sir Gilbert Howland Rookehurst, Bt. (1809)
Roberts, Sir Hugh Ashley, KCVO
Roberts, Sir Ivor Anthony, KCMG
Roberts, Sir Samuel, Bt. (1919)
Roberts, Sir William James Denby, Bt. (1909)
Robertson, Sir Lewis, Kt., CBE, FRSE
Robins, Sir Ralph Harry, Kt., FRENG
Robinson, Sir Albert Edward Phineas, Kt.
†Robinson, Sir Christopher Philipse, Bt. (1854)
Robinson, Sir Gerrard Jude, Kt.
Robinson, Sir Ian, Kt.
Robinson, Sir John James Michael Laud, Bt. (1660)
Robinson, *Dr* Sir Kenneth, Kt.
Robinson, Sir Wilfred Henry Frederick, Bt. (1908)
Robson, *Prof.* Sir James Gordon, Kt., CBE
Robson, Sir John Adam, KCMG
Robson, Sir Stephen Arthur, Kt., CB
Robson, Sir Robert William, Kt., CBE
Roch, *Rt. Hon.* Sir John Ormond, Kt.
Roche, Sir David O'Grady, Bt. (1838)
Roche, Sir Henry John, Kt.
Rodgers, Sir (Andrew) Piers (Wingate Aikin-Sneath), Bt. (1964)
Rodley, *Prof.* Sir Nigel, KBE
Rodrigues, Sir Alberto Maria, Kt., CBE, ED
Rogers, Sir Frank Jarvis, Kt.
Rogers, *Air Chief Marshal* Sir John Robson, KCB, CBE
Rooke, Sir Denis Eric, Kt., OM, CBE, FRS, FRENG
Ropner, Sir John Bruce Woollacott, Bt. (1952)
†Ropner, Sir Robert Clinton, Bt. (1904)
Rose, *Rt. Hon.* Sir Christopher Dudley Roger, Kt.
Rose, Sir Clive Martin, GCMG
Rose, Sir David Lancaster, Bt. (1874)
Rose, *Gen.* Sir (Hugh) Michael, KCB, CBE, DSO, QGM
Rose, Sir John Edward Victor, Kt.
Rose, Sir Julian Day, Bt. (1872 and 1909)
Ross, *Maj.* Sir Andrew Charles Paterson, Bt. (1960)
Ross, *Lt.-Gen.* Sir Robert Jeremy, KCB, OBE
Ross, *Lt.-Col.* Sir Walter Hugh Malcolm, KCVO, OBE
Rossi, Sir Hugh Alexis Louis, Kt.
Rotblat, *Prof.* Sir Joseph, KCMG, CBE, FRS
Roth, *Prof.* Sir Martin, Kt., MD, FRCP
Rothschild, Sir Evelyn Robert Adrian de, Kt.
Rougier, *Hon.* Sir Richard George, Kt.
Rowe, *Rear-Adm.* Sir Patrick Barton, KCVO, CBE
Rowe-Beddoe, Sir David Sydney, Kt.
Rowe-Ham, Sir David Kenneth, GBE
Rowland, Sir (John) David, Kt.
Rowlands, *Air Marshal* Sir John Samuel, GC, KBE
Rowley, Sir Charles Robert, Bt. (1836) (1786)
Rowling, Sir John Reginald, Kt.
Rowlinson, *Prof.* Sir John Shipley, Kt., FRS
Royce, *Hon.* Sir Roger John, Kt.
Royden, Sir Christopher John, Bt. (1905)
Rudd, Sir (Anthony) Nigel (Russell), Kt.
Rudge, Sir Alan Walter, Kt., CBE, FRS
Rugge-Price, Sir James Keith Peter, Bt. (1804)
Ruggles-Brise, Sir John Archibald, Bt., CB, OBE, TD (1935)
Rumbold, Sir Henry John Sebastian, Bt. (1779)
Runchorelal, Sir (Udayan) Chinubhai Madhowlal, Bt. (1913)
Rusby, *Vice-Adm.* Sir Cameron, KCB, LVO
†Russell, Sir (Arthur) Mervyn, Bt. (1812)
Russell, Sir Charles Dominic, Bt. (1916)

Russell, Sir George, Kt., CBE
Russell, Sir Muir, KCB
Russell, *Prof.* Sir Peter Edward Lionel, Kt., DLitt, FBA
Russell, Sir (Robert) Mark, KCMG
Rutter, *Prof.* Sir Michael Llewellyn, Kt., CBE, MD, FRS
Ryan, Sir Derek Gerald, Bt. (1919)
Rycroft, Sir Richard John, Bt. (1784)
Ryder, *Hon.* Sir Ernest Nigel Ryder, Kt., TD
Ryrie, Sir William Sinclair, KCB
Sainsbury, *Rt. Hon.* Sir Timothy Alan Davan, Kt.
St Clair-Ford, Sir James Anson, Bt. (1793)
St George, Sir John Avenel Bligh, Bt. (I. 1766)
St John-Mildmay, Sir Walter John Hugh, Bt. (1772)
St Johnston, Sir Kerry, Kt.
Sainty, Sir John Christopher, KCB
Salisbury, Sir Robert William, Kt.
Salt, Sir Patrick MacDonnell, Bt. (1869)
Salt, Sir (Thomas) Michael John, Bt. (1899)
Salusbury-Trelawny, Sir John Barry, Bt. (1628)
Sampson, Sir Colin, Kt., CBE, QPM
Samuel, Sir John Michael Glen, Bt. (1898)
Samuelson, Sir (Bernard) Michael (Francis), Bt. (1884)
Samuelson, Sir Sydney Wylie, Kt., CBE
Sanders, Sir Robert Tait, KBE, CMG
Sanders, Sir Ronald Michael, KCMG
Sanderson, Sir Frank Linton, Bt. (1920)
Sarei, Sir Alexis Holyweek, Kt., CBE
Satchwell, Sir Kevin Joseph, Kt.
Savage, Sir Ernest Walter, Kt.
Savile, Sir James Wilson Vincent, Kt., OBE
Saxby, *Prof.* Sir Robin Keith, Kt.
Say, *Rt. Revd* Richard David, KCVO
Scheele, Sir Nicholas Vernon, KCMG
Schiemann, *Rt. Hon.* Sir Konrad Hermann Theodor, Kt.
Scholar, Sir Michael Charles, KCB
Scholey, Sir David Gerald, Kt., CBE
Scholey, Sir Robert, Kt., CBE, FRENG
Scholtens, Sir James Henry, KCVO
Schreier, Sir Bernard, Kt.
Schubert, Sir Sydney, Kt.
Scipio, Sir Hudson Rupert, Kt.
Scoon, Sir Paul, GCMG, GCVO, OBE
Scott, Sir Anthony Percy, Bt. (1913)
Scott, Sir David Aubrey, GCMG
Scott, Sir James Jervoise, Bt. (1962)
Scott, Sir Kenneth Bertram Adam, KCVO, CMG
Scott, *Rt. Hon.* Sir Nicholas Paul, KBE
Scott, Sir Oliver Christopher Anderson, Bt. (1909)
Scott, *Prof.* Sir Philip John, KBE
Scott, Sir Ridley, Kt.
Scott, Sir Robert David Hillyer, Kt.
Scott, Sir Walter John, Bt. (1907)
Scott, *Rear-Adm.* Sir (William) David (Stewart), KBE, CB
Seale, Sir Clarence David, Kt.
Seale, Sir John Henry, Bt. (1838)
Seaman, Sir Keith Douglas, KCVO, OBE
Sebastian, Sir Cuthbert Montraville, GCMG, OBE
†Sebright, Sir Rufus Hugo Giles, Bt. (1626)
Seccombe, Sir (William) Vernon Stephen, Kt.
Seconde, Sir Reginald Louis, KCMG, CVO
Sedley, *Rt. Hon.* Sir Stephen John, Kt.
Seely, Sir Nigel Edward, Bt. (1896)
Seeto, Sir Ling James, Kt., MBE
Seeyave, Sir Rene Sow Choung, Kt., CBE
Seligman, Sir Peter Wendel, Kt., CBE
Semple, Sir John Laughlin, KCB
Sergeant, Sir Patrick, Kt.
Series, Sir (Joseph Michel) Emile, Kt., CBE
Serota, Sir Nicholas Andrew, Kt.
Serpell, Sir David Radford, KCB, CMG, OBE
†Seton, Sir Charles Wallace, Bt. (S. 1683)
Seton, Sir Iain Bruce, Bt. (S. 1663)
Severne, *Air Vice-Marshal* Sir John de Milt, KCVO, OBE, AFC
Shackleton, *Prof.* Sir Nicholas John, Kt., PHD, FRS
Shaffer, Sir Peter Levin, Kt., CBE
Shakerley, Sir Geoffrey Adam, Bt. (1838)
Shakespeare, Sir Thomas William, Bt. (1942)
Sharp, Sir Adrian, Bt. (1922)
Sharp, Sir Kenneth Johnston, Kt., TD
Sharp, Sir Leslie, Kt., QPM
Sharp, Sir Sheridan Christopher Robin, Bt. (1920)
Sharples, Sir James, Kt., QPM
Shattock, Sir Gordon, Kt.
Shaw, Sir Brian Piers, Kt.
Shaw, Sir (Charles) Barry, Kt., CB, QC
Shaw, Sir Charles De Vere, Bt. (1821)
Shaw, *Prof.* Sir John Calman, Kt., CBE
Shaw, Sir Neil McGowan, Kt.
Shaw, Sir Roy, Kt.
Shaw, Sir Run Run, Kt., CBE
†Shaw-Stewart, Sir Ludovic Houston, Bt. (S. 1667)
Shebbeare, Sir Thomas Andrew, KCVO
Sheehy, Sir Patrick, Kt.
Sheen, *Hon.* Sir Barry Cross, Kt.
Sheffield, Sir Reginald Adrian Berkeley, Bt. (1755)
Shehadie, Sir Nicholas Michael, Kt., OBE
Sheil, *Hon.* Sir John, Kt.
Sheinwald, Sir Nigel Elton, KCMG
Shelley, Sir John Richard, Bt. (1611)
Shepherd, Sir Colin Ryley, Kt.
Shepherd, Sir John Alan, KCVO, CMG
Shepperd, Sir Alfred Joseph, Kt.
Sher, Sir Antony, KBE
Sherston-Baker, Sir Robert George Humphrey, Bt. (1796)
Sherman, Sir Alfred, Kt.
Shields, *Prof.* Sir Robert, Kt., MD
Shiffner, Sir Henry David, Bt. (1818)
Silber, *Hon.* Sir Stephen Robert, Kt.
Shinwell, Sir (Maurice) Adrian, Kt.
Shock, Sir Maurice, Kt.
Short, Sir Apenera Pera, KBE
Shortridge, Sir Jon Deacon, KCB
Shuckburgh, Sir Rupert Charles Gerald, Bt. (1660)
Siaguru, Sir Anthony Michael, KBE
Sieff, *Hon.* Sir David, Kt.
Silber, *Rt. Hon.* Sir Stephen Robert, Kt.
Simeon, Sir John Edmund Barrington, Bt. (1815)
Simmons, *Air Marshal* Sir Michael George, KCB, AFC
Simmons, Sir Stanley Clifford, Kt.
Simms, Sir Neville Ian, Kt., FRENG
Simon, *Hon.* Sir Peregrine Charles Hugh, Kt.
Simonet, Sir Louis Marcel Pierre, Kt., CBE
Simpson, *Hon.* Sir Alfred Henry, Kt.
Simpson, Sir William James, Kt.
Sims, Sir Roger Edward, Kt.
Sinclair, Sir Clive Marles, Kt.
Sinclair, Sir George Evelyn, Kt., CMG, OBE
Sinclair, Sir Ian McTaggart, KCMG, QC
Sinclair, Sir Patrick Robert Richard, Bt. (S. 1704)
Sinclair, Sir Robert John, Kt.
Sinclair-Lockhart, Sir Simon John Edward Francis, Bt. (S. 1636)
Sinden, Sir Donald Alfred, Kt., CBE
Singer, *Prof.* Sir Hans Wolfgang, Kt.
Singer, *Hon.* Sir Jan Peter, Kt.
Sione, Sir Tomu Malaefone, GCMG, OBE
Sitwell, Sir (Sacheverell) Reresby, Bt. (1808)
Skeggs, Sir Clifford George, Kt.
Skehel, Sir John James, Kt., FRS
Skingsley, *Air Chief Marshal* Sir Anthony Gerald, GBE, KCB
Skinner, Sir (Thomas) Keith (Hewitt), Bt. (1912)
Skipwith, Sir Patrick Alexander d'Estoteville, Bt. (1622)
Slack, Sir William Willatt, KCVO, FRCS
Slade, Sir Benjamin Julian Alfred, Bt. (1831)
Slade, *Rt. Hon.* Sir Christopher John, Kt.
Slaney, *Prof.* Sir Geoffrey, KBE
Slater, *Adm.* Sir John (Jock) Cunningham Kirkwood, GCB, LVO
Sleight, Sir Richard, Bt. (1920)
Sloan, Sir Andrew Kirkpatrick, Kt., QPM
Sloman, Sir Albert Edward, Kt., CBE
Smart, Sir Jack, Kt., CBE
Smedley, *Hon.* Sir (Frank) Brian, Kt.
Smiley, *Lt.-Col.* Sir John Philip, Bt. (1903)
Smith, Sir Alan, Kt., CBE, DFC
Smith, *Hon.* Sir Andrew Charles, Kt.

Smith, Sir Andrew Thomas, Bt. (1897)
Smith, Sir Christopher Sydney Winwood, Bt. (1809)
Smith, *Prof.* Sir Colin Stansfield, Kt., CBE
Smith, Sir Cyril, Kt., MBE
Smith, *Prof.* Sir David Cecil, Kt., FRS
Smith, Sir David Iser, KCVO
Smith, Sir Dudley (Gordon), Kt.
Smith, *Prof.* Sir Eric Brian, Kt., PHD
Smith, Sir Geoffrey Johnson, Kt., MP
Smith, Sir John Alfred, Kt., QPM
Smith, Sir John Lindsay Eric, Kt., CH, CBE
Smith, Sir Joseph William Grenville, Kt.
Smith, Sir Leslie Edward George, Kt.
Smith, Sir Michael John Llewellyn, KCVO, CMG
Smith, Sir (Norman) Brian, Kt., CBE, PHD
Smith, Sir Paul Brierley, Kt., CBE
Smith, *Hon.* Sir Peter (Winston), Kt.
Smith, Sir Robert Courtney, Kt., CBE
Smith, Sir Robert Haldane, Kt
Smith, Sir Robert Hill, Bt., MP (1945)
Smith, *Gen.* Sir Rupert Anthony, KCB, DSO, OBE, QGM
Smith-Dodsworth, Sir John Christopher, Bt. (1784)
Smith-Gordon, Sir (Lionel) Eldred (Peter), Bt. (1838)
Smith-Marriott, Sir Hugh Cavendish, Bt. (1774)
Smithers, Sir Peter Henry Berry Otway, Kt., VRD, DPHIL
Smyth, Sir Timothy John, Bt. (1955)
Soakimori, Sir Frederick Pa-Nukuanca, KBE, CPM
Sobers, Sir Garfield St Auburn, Kt.
Solomon, Sir Harry, Kt.
Somare, *Rt. Hon.* Sir Michael Thomas, GCMG, CH
Somerville, *Brig.* Sir John Nicholas, Kt., CBE
Sorrell, Sir Martin Stuart, Kt.
Soulsby, Sir Peter Alfred, Kt.
Soutar, *Air Marshal* Sir Charles John Williamson, KBE
South, Sir Arthur, Kt.
Southby, Sir John Richard Bilbe, Bt. (1937)
Southern, *Prof.* Sir Edwin Mellor, Kt.
Southgate, Sir Colin Grieve, Kt.
Southgate, Sir William David, Kt.
Southward, Sir Leonard Bingley, Kt., OBE
Southward, *Dr* Sir Nigel Ralph, KCVO
Southwood, *Prof.* Sir (Thomas) Richard (Edmund), Kt., FRS
Souyave, *Hon.* Sir (Louis) Georges, Kt.
Sowrey, *Air Marshal* Sir Frederick Beresford, KCB, CBE, AFC
Sparkes, Sir Robert Lyndley, Kt.
Sparrow, Sir John, Kt.
Spearman, Sir Alexander Young Richard Mainwaring, Bt. (1840)
Spedding, *Prof.* Sir Colin Raymond William, Kt., CBE
Speed, Sir (Herbert) Keith, Kt., RD
Speelman, Sir Cornelis Jacob, Bt. (1686)
Speight, *Hon.* Sir Graham Davies, Kt.
Spencer, Sir Derek Harold, Kt., QC
Spencer, *Vice-Adm.* Sir Peter, KCB
Spencer-Nairn, Sir Robert Arnold, Bt. (1933)
Spicer, Sir James Wilton, Kt.
Spicer, Sir Nicholas Adrian Albert, Bt., MB (1906)
Spicer, Sir (William) Michael Hardy, Kt., MP
Spiers, Sir Donald Maurice, Kt., CB, TD
Spooner, Sir James Douglas, Kt.
Spratt, *Col.* Sir Greville Douglas, GBE, TD
Spring, Sir Dryden Thomas, Kt.
Squire, *Air Chief Marshal* Sir Peter Ted, GCB, DFC, AFC, ADC
Stainton, Sir (John) Ross, Kt., CBE
Stamer, Sir (Lovelace) Anthony, Bt. (1809)
Standard, Sir Kenneth Livingstone, Kt., MD
Stanhope, *Adm.* Sir Mark, KCB, OBE
Stanier, Sir Beville Douglas, Bt. (1917)
Stanier, *Field Marshal* Sir John Wilfred, GCB, MBE
Stanley, *Rt. Hon.* Sir John Paul, Kt., MP
Staples, Sir Richard Molesworth, Bt. (I. 1628)
Stark, Sir Andrew Alexander Steel, KCMG, CVO
Starkey, Sir John Philip, Bt. (1935)
Staughton, *Rt. Hon.* Sir Christopher Stephen Thomas Jonathan Thayer, Kt.
Staveley, Sir John Malfroy, KBE, MC
Stear, *Air Chief Marshal* Sir Michael James Douglas, KCB, CBE
Steel, *Hon.* Sir David William, Kt.
Steer, Sir Alan William, Kt.
Stephen, *Rt. Hon.* Sir Ninian Martin, KG, GCMG, GCVO, KBE
Stephens, Sir (Edwin) Barrie, Kt.
Stephenson, Sir Henry Upton, Bt. (1936)
Stern, *Prof.* Sir Nicholas Herbert, Kt.
Sternberg, Sir Sigmund, Kt.
Stevens, Sir Jocelyn Edward Greville, Kt., CVO
Stevens, Sir John, Kt.
Stevens, Sir Laurence Houghton, Kt., CBE
Stevenson, Sir Simpson, Kt.
Stewart, Sir Alan, KBE
Stewart, Sir Alan d'Arcy, Bt. (I. 1623)
Stewart, Sir Brian John, Kt., CBE
Stewart, Sir David James Henderson, Bt. (1957)
Stewart, Sir David John Christopher, Bt. (1803)
Stewart, Sir Edward Jackson, Kt.
Stewart, Sir James Douglas, Kt.
Stewart, Sir James Moray, KCB
Stewart, Sir (John) Simon (Watson), Bt. (1920)
Stewart, Sir John Young, Kt., OBE
Stewart, *Lt.-Col.* Sir Robert Christie, KCVO, CBE, TD
Stewart, Sir Robertson Huntly, Kt., CBE
Stewart, Sir Robin Alastair, Bt. (1960)
Stewart, *Prof.* Sir William Duncan Paterson, Kt., FRS, FRSE
Stewart-Clark, Sir John, Bt., MEP (1918)
Stewart-Richardson, Sir Simon Alaisdair, Bt. (S. 1630)
Stewart-Wilson, *Lt.-Col.* Sir Blair Aubyn, KCVO
Stibbon, *Gen.* Sir John James, KCB, OBE
Stirling, Sir Alexander John Dickson, KBE, CMG
Stirling, Sir Angus Duncan Aeneas, Kt.
Stirling-Hamilton, Sir Malcolm William Bruce, Bt. (S. 1673)
Stirrup, *Air Chief Marshal* Sir Graham Eric, KCB, AFC
Stockdale, Sir Thomas Minshull, Bt. (1960)
Stoddart, *Wg Cdr.* Sir Kenneth Maxwell, KCVO, AE
Stoker, *Prof.* Sir Michael George Parke, Kt., CBE, FRCP, FRS, FRSE
Stones, Sir William Frederick, Kt., OBE
Stonhouse, *Revd* Michael Philip, Bt. (1628 and 1670)
Stonor, *Air Marshal* Sir Thomas Henry, KCB
Stoppard, Sir Thomas, Kt., OM, CBE
Storey, *Hon.* Sir Richard, Bt., CBE (1960)
Stothard, Sir Peter Michael, Kt.
Stott, Sir Adrian George Ellingham, Bt. (1920)
Stoute, Sir Michael Ronald, Kt.
Stowe, Sir Kenneth Ronald, GCB, CVO
Stracey, Sir John Simon, Bt. (1818)
Strachan, Sir Curtis Victor, Kt., CVO
Strachey, Sir Charles, Bt. (1801)
Strang Steel, Sir (Fiennes) Michael, Bt. (1938)
Strawson, *Prof.* Sir Peter Frederick, Kt., FBA
Street, *Hon.* Sir Laurence Whistler, KCMG
Streeton, Sir Terence George, KBE, CMG
Strickland-Constable, Sir Frederic, Bt. (1641)
Stringer, Sir Donald Edgar, Kt., CBE
Stringer, Sir Howard, Kt.
Strong, Sir Roy Colin, Kt., PHD, FSA
Stronge, Sir James Anselan Maxwell, Bt. (1803)
Stroud, *Prof.* Sir (Charles) Eric, Kt., FRCP
Stuart, Sir James Keith, Kt.
Stuart, Sir Kenneth Lamonte, Kt.
†Stuart, Sir Phillip Luttrell, Bt. (1660)
†Stuart-Forbes, Sir William Daniel, Bt. (S. 1626)

Stuart-Menteth, Sir James Wallace, Bt. (1838)
Stuart-Paul, *Air Marshal* Sir Ronald Ian, KBE
Stuart-Smith, *Rt. Hon.* Sir Murray, Kt.
Stuart-White, *Hon.* Sir Christopher Stuart, Kt.
Stubbs, Sir William Hamilton, Kt., PHD
Stucley, *Lt.* Sir Hugh George Coplestone Bampfylde, Bt. (1859)
Studd, Sir Edward Fairfax, Bt. (1929)
Studholme, Sir Henry William, Bt. (1956)
†Style, Sir William Frederick, Bt. (1627)
Sugar, Sir Alan Michael, Kt.
Sullivan, *Hon.* Sir Jeremy Mirth, Kt.
Sullivan, Sir Richard Arthur, Bt. (1804)
Sulston, Sir John Edward, Kt.
Sumner, *Hon.* Sir Christopher John, Kt.
Sutherland, Sir John Brewer, Bt. (1921)
Sutherland, Sir William George MacKenzie, Kt.
Sutton, Sir Frederick Walter, Kt., OBE
Sutton, *Air Marshal* Sir John Matthias Dobson, KCB
Sutton, Sir Richard Lexington, Bt. (1772)
Swaffield, Sir James Chesebrough, Kt., CBE, RD
Swaine, Sir John Joseph, Kt., CBE
Swan, Sir Conrad Marshall John Fisher, KCVO, PHD
Swan, Sir John William David, KBE
Swann, Sir Michael Christopher, Bt., TD (1906)
Swartz, *Hon.* Sir Reginald William Colin, KBE, ED
Sweeney, Sir George, Kt.
Sweeting, *Prof.* Sir Martin Nicholas, Kt., OBE, FRS
Sweetnam, Sir (David) Rodney, KCVO, CBE, FRCS
Swinburn, *Lt.-Gen.* Sir Richard Hull, KCB
Swinnerton-Dyer, *Prof.* Sir (Henry) Peter (Francis), Bt., KBE, FRS (1678)
Swinton, *Maj.-Gen.* Sir John, KCVO, OBE
Swire, Sir Adrian Christopher, Kt.
Swire, Sir John Anthony, Kt., CBE
Sykes, Sir David Michael, Bt. (1921)
Sykes, Sir Francis John Badcock, Bt. (1781)
Sykes, Sir Hugh Ridley, Kt.
Sykes, *Prof.* Sir (Malcolm) Keith, Kt.
Sykes, Sir Richard, Kt.
Sykes, Sir Tatton Christopher Mark, Bt. (1783)
Symington, *Prof.* Sir Thomas, Kt., MD, FRSE
Symons, *Vice-Adm.* Sir Patrick Jeremy, KBE
Synge, Sir Robert Carson, Bt. (1801)
Synnott, Sir Hilary Nicholas Hugh, KCMG
Tait, *Adm.* Sir (Allan) Gordon, KCB, DSC
Talboys, *Rt. Hon.* Sir Brian Edward, CH, KCB
Tangaroa, *Hon.* Sir Tangoroa, Kt., MBE
Tapps-Gervis-Meyrick, Sir George Christopher Cadafael, Bt. (1791)
Tapsell, Sir Peter Hannay Bailey, Kt., MP
Tate, Sir (Henry) Saxon, Bt. (1898)
Tavaiqia, *Ratu* Sir Josaia, KBE
Tavare, Sir John, Kt., CBE
Tavener, *Prof.* Sir John Kenneth, Kt.
Taylor, Sir (Arthur) Godfrey, Kt.
Taylor, Sir Cyril Julian Hebden, GBE
Taylor, Sir Edward Macmillan (Teddy), Kt., MP
Taylor, *Rt. Revd* John Bernard, KCVO
Taylor, *Dr.* Sir John Michael, Kt., OBE
Taylor, Sir Nicholas Richard Stuart, Bt. (1917)
Taylor, *Prof.* Sir William, Kt., CBE
Taylor, Sir William George, Kt.
Teagle, *Vice-Adm.* Sir Somerford Francis, KBE
Tebbit, Sir Donald Claude, GCMG
Tebbit, Sir Kevin Reginald, KCB, CMG
Telford, Sir Robert, Kt., CBE, FRENG
Temple, *Prof.* Sir John Graham, Kt.
Temple, *Maj.* Sir Richard Anthony Purbeck, Bt., MC (1876)
Templeton, Sir John Marks, Kt.
Tennant, Sir Anthony John, Kt.
Tennant, *Capt.* Sir Iain Mark, Kt.
Tennyson-D'Eyncourt, Sir Mark Gervais, Bt. (1930)
Terry, *Air Marshal* Sir Colin George, KBE, CB
Terry, *Air Chief Marshal* Sir Peter David George, GCB, AFC
Thatcher, Sir Mark, Bt. (1990)
Thomas, Sir David John Godfrey, Bt. (1694)
Thomas, Sir Derek Morison David, KCMG
Thomas, Sir Jeremy Cashel, KCMG
Thomas, Sir (John) Alan, Kt.
Thomas, *Prof.* Sir John Meurig, Kt., FRS
Thomas, Sir Keith Vivian, Kt.
Thomas, Sir Philip Lloyd, KCVO, CMG
Thomas, Sir Quentin Jeremy, Kt., CB
Thomas, Sir Robert Evan, Kt.
Thomas, *Hon.* Sir Roger John Laugharne, Kt.
Thomas, *Hon.* Sir Swinton Barclay, Kt.
Thomas, Sir William James Cooper, Bt., TD (1919)
Thomas, Sir (William) Michael (Marsh), Bt. (1918)
Thompson, Sir Christopher Peile, Bt. (1890)
Thompson, Sir Clive Malcolm, Kt.
Thompson, Sir David Albert, KCMG
Thompson, Sir Donald, Kt.
Thompson, Sir Gilbert Williamson, Kt., OBE
Thompson, *Prof.* Sir Michael Warwick, Kt., DSC
Thompson, Sir Nicholas Annesley, Bt. (1963)
Thompson, Sir Nigel Cooper, KCMG, CBE
Thompson, Sir Paul Anthony, Bt. (1963)
Thompson, Sir Peter Anthony, Kt.
Thompson, *Dr* Sir Richard Paul Hepworth, KCVO
Thompson, Sir Thomas d'Eyncourt John, Bt. (1806)
Thomson, Sir (Frederick Douglas) David, Bt. (1929)
Thomson, Sir John Adam, GCMG
Thomson, Sir John (Ian) Sutherland, KBE, CMG
Thomson, Sir Mark Wilfrid Home, Bt. (1925)
Thomson, Sir Thomas James, Kt., CBE, FRCP
Thorn, Sir John Samuel, Kt., OBE
Thorne, Sir Neil Gordon, Kt., OBE, TD
Thornton, Sir (George) Malcolm, Kt.
Thornton, Sir Peter Eustace, KCB
Thornton, Sir Richard Eustace, KCVO, OBE
†Thorold, Sir (Anthony) Oliver, Bt. (1642)
Thorpe, *Rt. Hon.* Sir Mathew Alexander, Kt.
Thouron, Sir John Rupert Hunt, KBE
Thwaites, Sir Bryan, Kt., PHD
Tickell, Sir Crispin Charles Cervantes, GCMG, KCVO
Tikaram, Sir Moti, KBE
Tilt, Sir Robin Richard, Kt.
Tiltman, Sir John Hessell, KCVO
Timmins, *Col.* Sir John Bradford, KCVO, OBE, TD
Tims, Sir Michael David, KCVO
Tindle, Sir Ray Stanley, Kt., CBE
Tippet, *Vice-Adm.* Sir Anthony Sanders, KCB
Tirvengadum, Sir Harry Krishnan, Kt.
Tod, *Vice-Adm.* Sir Jonathan James Richard, KCB, CBE
Todd, *Prof.* Sir David, Kt., CBE
Todd, Sir Ian Pelham, KBE, FRCS
Tollemache, Sir Lyonel Humphry John, Bt. (1793)
Tololo, Sir Alkan, KBE
Tomkins, Sir Edward Emile, GCMG, CVO
Tomkys, Sir (William) Roger, KCMG
Tomlinson, *Prof.* Sir Bernard Evans, Kt., CBE
Tomlinson, *Hon.* Sir Stephen Miles, Kt.
Tooley, Sir John, Kt.
ToRobert, Sir Henry Thomas, KBE
Torry, Sir Peter James, KCMG
Tory, Sir Geofroy William, KCMG
Touche, Sir Anthony George, Bt. (1920)
Touche, Sir Rodney Gordon, Bt. (1962)
Toulson, *Hon.* Sir Roger Grenfell, Kt.
Tovadek, Sir Martin, Kt. CMG

Tovey, Sir Brian John Maynard, KCMG
ToVue, Sir Ronald, Kt., OBE
Towneley, Sir Simon Peter Edmund Cosmo William, KCVO
Townsend, Sir Cyril David, Kt.
Traill, Sir Alan Towers, GBE
Trant, *Gen.* Sir Richard Brooking, KCB
Treacher, *Adm.* Sir John Devereux, KCB
Treacy, *Hon.* Sir Colman Maurice, Kt.
Treitel, *Prof.* Sir Guenter Heinz, Kt., FBA, QC
Trench, Sir Peter Edward, Kt., CBE, TD
Trescowthick, Sir Donald Henry, KBE
†Trevelyan, Sir Edward (Norman), Bt. (1662)
Trevelyan, Sir Geoffrey Washington, Bt. (1874)
Trezise, Sir Kenneth Bruce, Kt., OBE
Trippier, Sir David Austin, Kt., RD
Tritton, Sir Anthony John Ernest, Bt. (1905)
Trollope, Sir Anthony Simon, Bt. (1642)
Trotman-Dickenson, Sir Aubrey Fiennes, Kt.
Trotter, Sir Neville Guthrie, Kt.
Trotter, Sir Ronald Ramsay, Kt.
Troubridge, Sir Thomas Richard, Bt. (1799)
Troup, *Vice-Adm.* Sir (John) Anthony (Rose), KCB, DSC
Trousdell, *Lt.-Gen.* Sir Philip Charles Cornwallis, KBE, CB
Truscott, Sir George James Irving, Bt. (1909)
Tsang, Sir Donald Yam-keun, KBE
Tuck, Sir Bruce Adolph Reginald, Bt. (1910)
Tucker, *Hon.* Sir Richard Howard, Kt.
Tuckey, *Rt. Hon.* Sir Simon Lane, Kt.
Tugendhat, *Hon.* Sir Michael George, Kt.
Tuita, Sir Mariano Kelesimalefo, KBE
Tuite, Sir Christopher Hugh, Bt., PHD (1622)
Tuivaga, Sir Timoci Uluiburotu, Kt.
Tully, Sir William Mark, KBE
Tupper, Sir Charles Hibbert, Bt. (1888)
Turbott, Sir Ian Graham, Kt., CMG, CVO
Turing, Sir John Dermot, Bt. (S. 1638)
Turnbull, Sir Andrew, KCB, CVO
Turner, Sir Colin William Carstairs, Kt., CBE, DFC
Turner, *Hon.* Sir Michael John, Kt.
Turnquest, Sir Orville Alton, GCMG, QC
Tusa, Sir John, Kt.
Tuti, *Revd* Dudley, KBE
Tweedie, *Prof.* Sir David Philip, Kt.
Tyree, Sir (Alfred) William, Kt., OBE
Tyrwhitt, Sir Reginald Thomas Newman, Bt. (1919)
Unsworth, *Hon.* Sir Edgar Ignatius Godfrey, Kt., CMG
Unwin, Sir (James) Brian, KCB
Ure, Sir John Burns, KCMG, LVO
Urquhart, Sir Brian Edward, KCMG, MBE
Urwick, Sir Alan Bedford, KCVO, CMG
Usher, Sir Andrew John, Bt. (1899)
Utting, Sir William Benjamin, Kt., CB
Vai, Sir Mea, Kt., CBE, ISO
Vallat, Sir Francis Aimé, GBE, KCMG, QC
Vallings, *Vice-Adm.* Sir George Montague Francis, KCB
Vanderfelt, Sir Robin Victor, KBE
Vane, Sir John Robert, Kt., DPHIL, DSC, FRS
Vardy, Sir Peter, Kt.Vasquez, Sir Alfred Joseph, Kt., CBE, QC
Vassar-Smith, Sir John Rathbone, Bt. (1917)
Vavasour, Sir Eric Michael Joseph Marmaduke, Bt. (1828)
Veale, Sir Alan John Ralph, Kt., FRENG
Venner, Sir Kenneth Dwight Vincent, KBE
Vereker, Sir John Michael Medlicott, KCB
†Verney, Sir John Sebastian, Bt. (1946)
Verney, *Hon.* Sir Lawrence John, Kt., TD
†Verney, Sir Edmund Ralph, Bt. (1818)
Vernon, Sir Nigel John Douglas, Bt. (1914)
Vernon, Sir (William) Michael, Kt.
Vestey, Sir (John) Derek, Bt. (1921)
Vickers, *Lt.-Gen.* Sir Richard Maurice Hilton, KCB, CVO, OBE
Vincent, Sir William Percy Maxwell, Bt. (1936)
Vineall, Sir Anthony John Patrick, Kt.
Vinelott, *Hon.* Sir John Evelyn, Kt.
Vines, Sir William Joshua, Kt., CMG
von Schramek, Sir Eric Emil, Kt.
†Vyvyan, Sir Ralph Ferrers Alexander, Bt. (1645)
Wade-Gery, Sir Robert Lucian, KCMG, KCVO
Waine, *Rt. Revd* John, KCVO
Waite, *Rt. Hon.* Sir John Douglas, Kt.
Wake, Sir Hereward, Bt., MC (1621)
Wakefield, Sir (Edward) Humphry (Tyrell), Bt. (1962)
Wakefield, Sir Norman Edward, Kt.
Wakefield, Sir Peter George Arthur, KBE, CMG
Wakeford, Sir Geoffrey Michael Montgomery, Kt., OBE
Wakeford, *Air Marshal* Sir Richard Gordon, KCB, OBE, LVO, AFC
Wakeley, Sir John Cecil Nicholson, Bt., FRCS (1952)
†Wakeman, Sir Edward Offley Bertram, Bt. (1828)
Wakerley, *Hon.* Sir Richard MacLennon, Kt.
Wales, Sir Robert Andrew, Kt.
Waley-Cohen, Sir Stephen Harry, Bt. (1961)
Walford, Sir Christopher Rupert, Kt.
Walker, Sir Alfred Cecil, Kt.
Walker, *Gen.* Sir Antony Kenneth Frederick, KCB
Walker, Sir Baldwin Patrick, Bt. (1856)
Walker, Sir David Alan, Kt.
Walker, Sir Harold Berners, KCMG
Walker, *Maj.* Sir Hugh Ronald, Bt. (1906)
Walker, Sir James Graham, Kt., MBE
Walker, Sir John Ernest, Kt., DPHIL, FRS
Walker, *Air Marshal* Sir John Robert, KCB, CBE, AFC
Walker, *Gen.* Sir Michael John Dawson, GCB, CMG, CBE, ADC
Walker, Sir Miles Rawstron, Kt., CBE
Walker, Sir Patrick Jeremy, KCB
Walker, Sir Rodney Myerscough, Kt.
Walker, *Hon.* Sir Timothy Edward, Kt.
Walker, Sir Victor Stewart Heron, Bt. (1868)
Walker-Okeover, Andrew Peter Monro, Bt. (1886)
Walker-Smith, Sir John Jonah, Bt. (1960)
Wall, Sir John Anthony, Kt., CBE
Wall, Sir (John) Stephen, GCMG, LVO
Wall, *Hon.* Sir Nicholas Peter Rathbone, Kt., PC
Wall, Sir Robert William, Kt., OBE
Wallace, *Lt.-Gen.* Sir Christopher Brooke Quentin, KBE
Wallace, *Prof.* David James, Kt., CBE
Wallace, Sir Ian James, Kt., CBE
Waller, *Rt. Hon.* Sir (George) Mark, Kt.
Waller, Sir Robert William, Bt. (I. 1780)
Wallis, Sir Peter Gordon, KCVO
Wallis, Sir Timothy William, Kt.
Walmsley, *Vice-Adm.* Sir Robert, KCB
†Walsham, Sir Timothy John, Bt. (1831)
Walters, *Prof.* Sir Alan Arthur, Kt.
Walters, Sir Dennis Murray, Kt., MBE
Walters, Sir Frederick Donald, Kt.
Walters, Sir Peter Ingram, Kt.
Walters, Sir Roger Talbot, KBE, FRIBA
Wamiri, Sir Akapite, KBE
Wan, Sir Wamp, Kt., MBE
Ward, *Rt. Hon.* Sir Alan Hylton, Kt.
Ward, Sir John Devereux, Kt., CBE
Ward, *Prof.* Sir John MacQueen, Kt., CBE
Ward, Sir Joseph James Laffey, Bt. (1911)
Ward, Sir Timothy James, Kt.
Wardale, Sir Geoffrey Charles, KCB
Wardlaw, Sir Henry (John), Bt. (S. 1631)
Waring, Sir (Alfred) Holburt, Bt. (1935)
Warmington, Sir David Marshall, Bt. (1908)
Warner, Sir (Edward Courtenay) Henry, Bt. (1910)
Warner, *Prof.* Sir Frederick Edward, Kt., FRS, FRENG
Warner, Sir Gerald Chierici, KCMG

Warner, *Hon.* Sir Jean-Pierre Frank Eugene, Kt.
Warren, Sir (Frederick) Miles, KBE
Warren, Sir Kenneth Robin, Kt.
†Warren, Sir Michael Blackley, Bt. (1784)
Wass, Sir Douglas William Gretton, GCB
Waterhouse, *Hon.* Sir Ronald Gough, GBE
Waterlow, Sir Christopher Rupert, Bt. (1873)
Waterlow, Sir (James) Gerard, Bt. (1930)
Waters, *Gen.* Sir (Charles) John, GCB, CBE
Waters, Sir (Thomas) Neil (Morris), Kt.
Wates, Sir Christopher Stephen, Kt.
Watkins, *Rt. Hon.* Sir Tasker, VC, GBE
Watson, Sir Bruce Dunstan, Kt.
Watson, *Prof.* Sir David John, Kt., PHD
Watson, Sir (James) Andrew, Bt. (1866)
Watson, *Vice-Adm.* Sir Philip Alexander, KBE, LVO
Watson, Sir Ronald Matthew, Kt., CBE
Watt, *Lt.-Gen.* Sir Charles Redmond, KCVO, CBE
Watt, *Surgeon Vice-Adm.* Sir James, KBE, FRCS
Watts, Sir John Augustus Fitzroy, KCMG, CBE
Watts, Sir Arthur Desmond, KCMG
Watts, Sir Philip Beverley, KCMG
Weatherall, *Prof.* Sir David John, Kt., FRS
Weatherall, *Vice-Adm.* Sir James Lamb, KCVO, KBE
Weatherstone, Sir Dennis, KBE
Weatherup, *Hon.* Sir Ronald Eccles, Kt.
Webb, *Prof.* Sir Adrian Leonard, Kt.
Webb, Sir Thomas Langley, Kt.
Webb-Carter, *Gen.* Sir Evelyn John, KCVO, OBE
Webster, *Very Revd* Alan Brunskill, KCVO
Webster, *Vice-Adm.* Sir John Morrison, KCB
Webster, *Hon.* Sir Peter Edlin, Kt.
Wedgwood, Sir (Hugo) Martin, Bt. (1942)
Weekes, Sir Everton DeCourcey, KCMG, OBE
Weinberg, Sir Mark Aubrey, Kt.
Weir, Sir Michael Scott, KCMG
Weir, *Hon.* Sir Reginald George, Kt.
Weir, Sir Roderick Bignell, Kt.
Welby, Sir (Richard) Bruno Gregory, Bt. (1801)
Welch, Sir John Reader, Bt. (1957)
Weldon, Sir Anthony William, Bt. (I. 1723)
Weller, Sir Arthur Burton, Kt., CBE
Wellings, Sir Jack Alfred, Kt., CBE
†Wells, Sir Christopher Charles, Bt. (1944)
Wells, Sir John Julius, Kt.
Wells, Sir William Henry Weston, Kt., FRICS
West, *Adm.* Sir Alan William John, GCB, DSC, ADC
Westbrook, Sir Neil Gowanloch, Kt., CBE
Westmacott, Sir Peter John, KCMG
Weston, Sir Michael Charles Swift, KCMG, CVO
Weston, Sir (Philip) John, KCMG
Whalen, Sir Geoffrey Henry, Kt., CBE
Wheeler, Sir Harry Anthony, Kt., OBE
Wheeler, *Air Chief Marshal* Sir (Henry) Neil (George), GCB, CBE, DSO, DFC, AFC
Wheeler, *Rt. Hon.* Sir John Daniel, Kt.
Wheeler, Sir John Hieron, Bt. (1920)
Wheeler, *Gen.* Sir Roger Neil, GCB, CBE
Wheeler-Booth, Sir Michael Addison John, KCB
Wheler, Sir Edward Woodford, Bt. (1660)
Whishaw, Sir Charles Percival Law, Kt.
Whitaker, Sir John James Ingham (Jack), Bt. (1936)
White, *Prof.* Sir Christopher John, Kt., CVO
White, Sir Christopher Robert Meadows, Bt. (1937)
White, Sir David Harry, Kt.
White, *Hon.* Sir Frank John, Kt.
White, Sir George Stanley James, Bt. (1904)
White, *Adm.* Sir Hugo Moresby, GCB, CBE
White, *Hon.* Sir John Charles, Kt., MBE
White, Sir John Woolmer, Bt. (1922)
White, Sir Lynton Stuart, Kt., MBE, TD
White, Sir Nicholas Peter Archibald, Bt. (1802)
White, *Adm.* Sir Peter, GBE
White, Sir Willard Wentworth, Kt., CBE
Whitehead, Sir John Stainton, GCMG, CVO
Whitehead, Sir Rowland John Rathbone, Bt. (1889)
Whiteley, *Gen.* Sir Peter John Frederick, GCB, OBE, RM
Whitfield, Sir William, Kt., CBE
Whitmore, Sir Clive Anthony, GCB, CVO
Whitmore, Sir John Henry Douglas, Bt. (1954)
Whitney, Sir Raymond William, Kt., OBE, MP
Whitson, Sir Keith Roderick, Kt.
Wickerson, Sir John Michael, Kt.
Wicks, Sir Nigel Leonard, GCB, CVO, CBE
†Wigan, Sir Michael Iain, Bt. (1898)
Wiggin, Sir Alfred William (Jerry), Kt., TD
†Wiggin, Sir Charles Rupert John, Bt. (1892)
†Wigram, Sir John Woolmore, Bt. (1805)
Wilbraham, Sir Richard Baker, Bt. (1776)
Wiles, *Prof.* Sir Andrew John, KBE
Wilford, Sir (Kenneth) Michael, GCMG
Wilkes, *Prof.* Sir Maurice Vincent, Kt.
Wilkes, *Gen.* Sir Michael John, KCB, CBE
Wilkinson, Sir (David) Graham (Brook) Bt. (1941)
Wilkinson, *Prof.* Sir Denys Haigh, Kt., FRS
Wilkinson, Sir Philip William, Kt.
Willcocks, Sir David Valentine, Kt., CBE, MC
Willcocks, *Lt.-Gen.* Sir Michael Alan, KCB
Williams, Sir Alwyn, Kt., PHD, FRS, FRSE
Williams, Sir Arthur Dennis Pitt, Kt.
Williams, Sir (Arthur) Gareth Ludovic Emrys Rhys, Bt. (1918)
Williams, *Prof.* Sir Bruce Rodda, KBE
Williams, Sir Charles Othniel, Kt.
Williams, Sir Daniel Charles, GCMG, QC
Williams, *Adm.* Sir David, GCB
Williams, *Prof.* Sir David Glyndwr Tudor, Kt.
Williams, Sir David Innes, Kt.
Williams, Sir David Reeve, Kt., CBE
Williams, *Hon.* Sir Denys Ambrose, KCMG
Williams, Sir Donald Mark, Bt. (1866)
Williams, *Prof.* Sir (Edward) Dillwyn, Kt., FRCP
Williams, Sir Francis Owen Garbett, Kt., CBE
Williams, *Prof.* Sir Glanmor, Kt., CBE, FBA
Williams, Sir (John) Kyffin, Kt., OBE, DL, RA
Williams, Sir (Lawrence) Hugh, Bt. (1798)
Williams, Sir Leonard, KBE, CB
Williams, Sir Osmond, Bt., MC (1909)
Williams, Sir Peter Michael, Kt.
Williams, Sir (Robert) Philip Nathaniel, Bt. (1915)
Williams, Sir Robin Philip, Bt. (1953)
Williams, Sir (William) Maxwell (Harries), Kt.
Williams-Bulkeley, Sir Richard Thomas, Bt. (1661)
Williams-Wynn, Sir David Watkin, Bt. (1688)
Williamson, *Marshal of the Royal Air Force* Sir Keith Alec, GCB, AFC
Williamson, Sir Robert Brian, Kt., CBE
Willink, Sir Charles William, Bt. (1957)
Willis, *Vice-Adm.* Sir (Guido) James, KBE
Willis, *Air Chief Marshal* Sir John Frederick, GBE, KCB
Willison, *Lt.-Gen.* Sir David John, KCB, OBE, MC
Wills, Sir David James Vernon, Bt. (1923)

Wills, Sir David Seton, Bt. (1904)
Wilmot, Sir David, Kt., QPM
Wilmot, Sir Henry Robert, Bt. (1759)
Wilsey, *Gen.* Sir John Finlay Willasey, GCB, CBE
Wilshaw, Sir Michael, Kt.
Wilson, *Prof.* Sir Alan Geoffrey, Kt.
Wilson, *Lt.-Gen.* Sir (Alexander) James, KBE, MC
Wilson, Sir Anthony, Kt.
Wilson, *Vice-Adm.* Sir Barry Nigel, KCB
Wilson, *Prof.* Sir Colin Alexander St John, Kt., RA, FRIBA
Wilson, Sir David, Bt. (1920)
Wilson, Sir David Mackenzie, Kt.
Wilson, Sir James William Douglas, Bt. (1906)
Wilson, *Brig.* Sir Mathew John Anthony, Bt., OBE, MC (1874)
Wilson, *Hon.* Sir Nicholas Allan Roy, Kt.
Wilson, Sir Robert Peter, KCMG
Wilson, *Air Chief Marshal* Sir (Ronald) Andrew (Fellowes), KCB, AFC
Wilson, *Hon.* Sir Ronald Darling, KBE, CMG
Wilton, Sir (Arthur) John, KCMG, KCVO, MC
Wingate, *Capt.* Sir Miles Buckley, KCVO
Winkley, Sir David Ross, Kt.
Winnington, Sir Anthony Edward, Bt. (1755)
Winship, Sir Peter James Joseph, Kt., CBE
Winskill, *Air Cdre* Sir Archibald Little, KCVO, CBE, DFC
Winter, *Dr* Sir Gregory Winter, Kt., CBE
Winterton, Sir Nicholas Raymond, Kt.
Winton, Sir Nicholas George, Kt., MBE
Wisdom, Sir Norman, Kt., OBE
Wiseman, Sir John William, Bt. (1628)
Wolfendale, *Prof.* Sir Arnold Whittaker, Kt., FRS
Wolfson, Sir Brian Gordon, Kt.
Wolseley, Sir Charles Garnet Richard Mark, Bt. (1628)
†Wolseley, Sir James Douglas, Bt. (I. 1745)
†Wombell, Sir George Philip Frederick, Bt. (1778)
Womersley, Sir Peter John Walter, Bt. (1945)
Woo, Sir Leo Joseph, Kt.
Woo, Sir Po-Shing, Kt.
Wood, Sir Alan Marshall Muir, Kt., FRS, FRENG
Wood, Sir Andrew Marley, GCMG
Wood, Sir Anthony John Page, Bt. (1837)
Wood, Sir Ian Clark, Kt., CBE
Wood, *Hon.* Sir John Kember, Kt., MC
Wood, Sir Martin Francis, Kt., OBE
Wood, Sir Michael Charles, KCMG
Wood, *Hon.* Sir Roderic Lionel James, Kt.
Wood, Sir Russell Dillon, KCVO, VRD
Wood, Sir William Alan, KCVO, CB
Woodard, *Rear Adm.* Sir Robert Nathaniel, KCVO
Woodcock, Sir John, Kt., CBE, QPM
Woodhead, *Vice-Adm.* Sir (Anthony) Peter, KCB
Woodhouse, *Rt. Hon.* Sir (Arthur) Owen, KBE, DSC
Wooding, Sir Norman Samuel, Kt., CBE
Woodroffe, *Most Revd* George Cuthbert Manning, KBE
Woods, Sir Robert Kynnersley, Kt., CBE
Woodward, *Hon.* Sir (Albert) Edward, Kt., OBE
Woodward, Sir Clive Ronald, Kt., OBE
Woodward, *Adm.* Sir John Forster, GBE, KCB
Worsley, *Gen.* Sir Richard Edward, GCB, OBE
Worsley, Sir (William) Marcus (John), Bt. (1838)
Worsthorne, Sir Peregrine Gerard, Kt.
Wratten, *Air Chief Marshal* Sir William John, GBE, CB, AFC
Wraxall, Sir Charles Frederick Lascelles, Bt. (1813)
Wrey, Sir George Richard Bourchier, Bt. (1628)
Wrigglesworth, Sir Ian William, Kt.
Wright, Sir Allan Frederick, KBE
Wright, Sir David John, GCMG, LVO
Wright, Sir Denis Arthur Hepworth, GCMG
Wright, Sir Edward Maitland, Kt., DPHIL, LLD, DSC, FRSE
Wright, *Hon.* Sir (John) Michael, Kt.
Wright, Sir (John) Oliver, GCMG, GCVO, DSC
Wright, Sir Paul Hervé Giraud, KCMG, OBE
Wright, Sir Peter Robert, Kt., CBE
Wright, *Air Marshal* Sir Robert Alfred, KBE, AFC
Wrightson, Sir Charles Mark Garmondsway, Bt. (1900)
Wrigley, *Prof.* Sir Edward Anthony (Sir Tony), Kt., PHD, PBA
Wrixon-Becher, Sir John William Michael, Bt. (1831)
Wu, Sir Gordon Ying Sheung, KCMG
Wyldbore-Smith, *Maj.-Gen.* Sir (Francis) Brian, Kt., CB, DSO, OBE
Yacoub, *Prof.* Sir Magdi Habib, Kt., FRCS
Yaki, Sir Roy, KBE
Yang, *Hon.* Sir Ti Liang, Kt.
Yapp, Sir Stanley Graham, Kt.
Yardley, Sir David Charles Miller, Kt., LLD
Yarrow, Sir Eric Grant, Bt., MBE (1916)
Yellowlees, Sir Henry, KCB
Yocklunn, Sir John (Soong Chung), KCVO
Yoo Foo, Sir (François) Henri, Kt.
Young, Sir Brian Walter Mark, Kt.
Young, Sir Colville Norbert, GCMG, MBE
Young, Sir Dennis Charles, KCMG
Young, *Rt. Hon.* Sir George Samuel Knatchbull, Bt., MP (1813)
Young, *Hon.* Sir Harold William, KCMG
Young, Sir Jimmy Leslie Ronald, Kt., CBE
Young, Sir John Kenyon Roe, Bt. (1821)
Young, *Hon.* Sir John McIntosh, KCMG
Young, Sir John Robertson, GCMG
Young, Sir Leslie Clarence, Kt., CBE
Young, Sir Nicholas Charles, Kt.
Young, Sir Richard Dilworth, Kt.
Young, Sir Robin Urquhart, KCB
Young, Sir Roger William, Kt.
Young, Sir Stephen Stewart Templeton, Bt. (1945)
Young, Sir William Neil, Bt. (1769)
Younger, Sir Julian William Richard, Bt. (1911)
Yuwi, Sir Matiabe, KBE
Zeeman, *Prof.* Sir (Erik) Christopher, Kt., FRS
Zissman, Sir Bernard Philip, Kt.
Zochonis, Sir John Basil, Kt.
Zoleveke, Sir Gideon Pitabose, KBE
Zunz, Sir Gerhard Jacob (Jack), Kt., FRENG
Zurenuoc, Sir Zibang, KBE

THE ORDER OF ST JOHN

THE MOST VENERABLE ORDER OF THE HOSPITAL OF ST JOHN OF JERUSALEM (1888)

GCStJ	Bailiff/Dame Grand Cross
KStJ	Knight of Justice/Grace
DStJ	Dame of Justice/Grace
CStJ	Commander
OstJ	Officer
SBStJ	Serving Brother
SSStJ	Serving Sister
EsqStJ	Esquire

Mottoes, Pro Fide *and* Pro Utilitate Hominum
The Order of St John, founded in the early 12th century in Jerusalem, was a religious order with a particular duty to care for the sick. In Britain the Order was dissolved by Henry VIII in 1540 but the British branch was revived in the early 19th century. The branch was not accepted by the Grand Magistracy of the Order in Rome but its search for a role in the tradition of the Hospitallers led to the founding of the St John Ambulance Association in 1877 and later the St John Ambulance Brigade; in 1882 the St John Ophthalmic Hospital was founded in Jerusalem. A royal charter was granted in 1888 establishing the British Order of St John as a British Order of Chivalry with the Sovereign as its head. Since October 1999, a separate Priory of England and the Islands has governed the Order of England, the Channel Islands and the Isle of Man, with a Commandery in Northern Ireland.

The whole Order world-wide is now governed by a Grand Council including the representatives of all 8 Priories (England, Scotland, Wales, South Africa, New Zealand, Canada, Australia and the United States). There are also branches in about 30 other countries, mostly in the Commonwealth. Apart from the St John Ambulance Foundation, the Order is also responsible for the Jerusalem Eye Hospital.

Admission to the Order is conferred in recognition of service, usually in St John Ambulance or the Eye Hospital. Membership does not confer any rank, style, title or precedence on a recipient.

SOVEREIGN HEAD OF THE ORDER
HM The Queen

GRAND PRIOR
HRH The Duke of Gloucester, KD, GCVO

Lord Prior, Eric Barry
Prelate, The Rt Revd John Waine, KCVO
Deputy Lord Prior: Prof. Anthony Mellows, OBE, TD
Sub Prior, Mr John Strachan
Secretary General, Rear-Adm. Andrew Gough, CB
Headquarters, Priory House, 25 St John's Lane, London ECM 4PP

DAMES

DAMES GRAND CROSS AND DAMES COMMANDERS

Style, 'Dame' before forename and surname, followed by appropriate post-nominal initials. Where such an award is made to a lady already in possession of a higher title, the appropriate initials follow her name
Husband, Untitled
For forms of address, *see* page 43

Dame Grand Cross and Dame Commander are the higher classes for women of the Order of the Bath, the Order of St Michael and St George, the Royal Victorian Order, and the Order of the British Empire. Dames Grand Cross rank after the wives of Baronets and before the wives of Knights Grand Cross. Dames Commanders rank after the wives of Knights Grand Cross and before the wives of Knights Commanders.

Honorary Dames Commanders may be conferred on women who are citizens of countries of which The Queen is not head of state.

LIST OF DAMES
Revised to 31 August 2004

Women peers in their own right and life peers are not included in this list. Female members of the royal family are not included in this list; details of the orders they hold can be found within the Royal Family section.

If a dame has a double barrelled or hyphenated surname, she is listed under the first element of the name.

A full entry in italic type indicates that the recipient of an honour died during the year in which the honour was conferred. The name is included for the purposes of record.

Abaijah, Dame Josephine, DBE
Abel Smith, Lady, DCVO
Abergavenny, The Marchioness of, DCVO
Airlie, The Countess of, DCVO
Albemarle, The Countess of, DBE
Allen, *Prof.* Dame Ingrid Victoria, DBE
Anderson, *Brig. Hon.* Dame Mary Mackenzie (Mrs Pihl), DBE
Andrews, Dame Julie, DBE
Anglesey, The Marchioness of, DBE
Anson, Lady (Elizabeth Audrey), DBE
Anstee, Dame Margaret Joan, DCMG
Arden, *Rt. Hon.* Dame Mary Howarth (Mrs Mance), DBE
Atkins, Dame Eileen, DBE
Bainbridge, Dame Beryl, DBE
Baker, Dame Janet Abbott (Mrs Shelley), CH, DBE
Ballin, Dame Reubina Ann, DBE
Baron, *Hon.* Dame Florence Jacqueline, DBE
Barrow, Dame Jocelyn Anita (Mrs Downer), DBE
Barstow, Dame Josephine Clare (Mrs Anderson), DBE
Bassey, Dame Shirley, DBE
Beaurepaire, Dame Beryl Edith, DBE
Beer, *Prof.* Dame Gillian Patricia Kempster, DBE, FBA
Bergquist, *Prof.* Dame Patricia Rose, DBE
Bewley, Dame Beulah Rosemary, DBE
Bibby, Dame Enid, DBE
Black, *Hon.* Dame Jill Margaret, DBE
Blackadder, Dame Elizabeth Violet, DBE
Blaize, Dame Venetia Ursula, DBE
Blaxland, Dame Helen Frances, DBE
Booth, *Hon.* Dame Margaret Myfanwy Wood, DBE
Bowtell, Dame Ann Elizabeth, DCB
Boyd, Dame Vivienne Myra, DBE
Barbour, Dame Margaret (Mrs Ash), DBE
Bracewell, *Hon.* Dame Joyanne Winifred (Mrs Copeland), DBE
Brain, Dame Margaret Anne (Mrs Wheeler), DBE
Bridges, Dame Mary Patricia, DBE
Brittan, Dame Diana (Lady Brittan of Spennithorne), DBE
Browne, Lady Moyra Blanche Madeleine, DBE
Browne-Evans, Dame Lois Marie, DBE
Buckland, Dame Yvonne Helen Elaine, DBE
Burslem, Dame Alexandra Vivien, DBE
Butler-Sloss, *Rt. Hon.* Dame (Ann) Elizabeth (Oldfield), DBE
Buttfield, Dame Nancy Eileen, DBE
Byatt, Dame Antonia Susan, DBE, FRSL
Bynoe, Dame Hilda Louisa, DBE
Caldicott, Dame Fiona, DBE, FRCP, FRCPsych.
Campbell-Preston, Dame Frances Olivia, DCVO
Cartwright, Dame Silvia Rose, DBE
Charles, Dame (Mary) Eugenia, DBE
Clark, *Prof.* Dame Jill MacLeod, DBE
Clark, *Prof.* Dame (Margaret) June, DBE, PHD
Clay, Dame Marie Mildred, DBE
Clayton, Dame Barbara Evelyn (Mrs Klyne), DBE
Collarbone, Dame Patricia, DBE
Corsar, *The Hon.* Dame Mary Drummond, DBE
Coward, Dame Pamela Sarah, DBE
Cox, Dame Laura Mary (The Hon. Mrs Justice), DBE
Cropper, Dame Hilary Mary, DBE
Davies, Dame Wendy Patricia, DBE
Davis, Dame Karlene Cecile, DBE
Daws, Dame Joyce Margaretta, DBE
Dawson, *Prof.* Dame Sandra Jane Noble, DBE
Deech, Dame Ruth Lynn, DBE
Dell, Dame Miriam Patricia, DBE
Dench, Dame Judith Olivia (Mrs Williams), DBE
Descartes, Dame Marie Selipha Sesenne, DBE, BEM
Devonshire, The Duchess of, DCVO
Digby, Lady, DBE
Docherty, Dame Jacqueline, DBE
Duffield, Dame Vivien Louise, DBE
Dumont, Dame Ivy Leona, DCMG
Dyche, Dame Rachael Mary, DBE
Elcoat, Dame Catherine Elizabeth, DBE
Ellison, Dame Jill, DBE
Else, Dame Jean, DBE
Engel, Dame Pauline Frances (Sister Pauline Engel), DBE
Esteve-Coll, Dame Elizabeth Anne Loosemore, DBE
Evans, Dame Anne Elizabeth Jane, DBE
Evans, Dame Madeline Glynne Dervel, DBE, CMG
Evison, Dame Helen June Patricia, DBE
Fenner, Dame Peggy Edith, DBE
Fielding, Dame Pauline, DBE
Fort, Dame Maeve Geraldine, DCMG, DCVO

Fraser, Dame Dorothy Rita, DBE
Friend, Dame Phyllis Muriel, DBE
Fritchie, Dame Irene Tordoff (Dame Rennie Fritchie), DBE
Frost, Dame Phyllis Irene, DBE
Fry, Dame Margaret Louise, DBE
Gallagher, Dame Monica Josephine, DBE
Gardiner, Dame Helen Louisa, DBE, MVO
Giles, *Air Comdt.* Dame Pauline (Mrs Parsons), DBE, RRC
Glen-Haig, Dame Mary Alison, DBE
Gloster, *Hon.* Dame Elisabeth (Mrs Brodie), DBE
Glover, Dame Audrey Frances, DBE, CMG
Goodall, *Dr* Dame (Valerie) Jane, DBE
Goodman, Dame Barbara, DBE
Gordon, Dame Minita Elmira, GCMG, GCVO
Gordon, *Hon.* Dame Pamela Felicity, DBE
Gow, Dame Jane Elizabeth (Mrs Whiteley), DBE
Grafton, The Duchess of, GCVO
Grant, Dame Mavis, DBE
Green, Dame Pauline, DBE
Grey, Dame Beryl Elizabeth (Mrs Svenson), DBE
Grimthorpe, The Lady, DCVO
Guilfoyle, Dame Margaret Georgina Constance, DBE
Guthardt, *Revd Dr* Dame Phyllis Myra, DBE
Hallett, *Hon.* Dame Heather Carol, DBE
Harbison, Dame Joan Irene, DBE
Harper, Dame Elizabeth Margaret Way, DBE
Harris, Lady Pauline, DBE
Hedley-Miller, Dame Mary Elizabeth, DCVO, CB
Heilbron, *Hon.* Dame Rose, DBE
Herbison, Dame Jean Marjory, DBE, CMG
Hercus, *Hon.* Dame (Margaret) Ann, DCMG
Higgins, *Prof.* Dame Julia Stretton, DBE, FRS
Higgins, *Prof.* Dame Rosalyn, DBE, QC
Hill, *Air Cdre* Dame Felicity Barbara, DBE
Hine, Dame Deirdre Joan, DBE, FRCP
Hodgson, Dame Patricia Anne, DBE
Hogg, *Hon.* Dame Mary Claire (Mrs Koops), DBE
Hollows, Dame Sharon, DBE
Hoodless, Dame Elisabeth Anne, DBE
Hufton, *Prof.* Dame Olwen, DBE
Hussey, Dame Susan Katharine (Lady Hussey of North Bradley), DCVO
Hutton, Dame Deirdre Mary, DBE
Imison, Dame Tamsyn, DBE
Isaacs, Dame Albertha Madeline, DBE
James, Dame Naomi Christine (Mrs Haythorne), DBE
Jenkins, Dame (Mary) Jennifer (Lady Jenkins of Hillhead), DBE
Johnson, *Prof.* Dame Louise Napier, DBE, FRS
Jones, Dame Gwyneth (Mrs Haberfeld-Jones), DBE
Keegan, Dame Geraldine Mary Marcella, DBE
Kekedo, Dame Rosalina Violet, DBE
Kelleher, Dame Joan, DBE
Kellett-Bowman, Dame (Mary) Elaine, DBE
Kelly, Dame Lorna May Boreland, DBE
Kershaw, Dame Janet Elizabeth Murray (Dame Betty), DBE
Kettlewell, *Comdt.* Dame Marion Mildred, DBE
King, Dame Thea, DBE
Kirby, Dame Georgina Kamiria, DBE
Kramer, *Prof.* Dame Leonie Judith, DBE
Laine, Dame Cleo (Clementine) Dinah (Mrs Dankworth), DBE
Lamb, Dame Dawn Ruth, DBE
Legge-Schwarzkopf, Dame Elisabeth Friederike Marie Olga, DBE
Lewis, Dame Edna Leofrida (Lady Lewis), DBE
Lott, Dame Felicity Ann Emwhyla (Mrs Woolf), DBE
Louisy, Dame (Calliopa) Pearlette, GCMG
Lympany, Dame Moura, DBE
Lynn, Dame Vera (Mrs Lewis), DBE
McDonald, Dame Mavis, DCB
Mackinnon, Dame (Una) Patricia, DBE
McLaren, Dame Anne Laura, DBE, FRCOG, FRS
Macmillan of Ovenden, Katharine, Viscountess, DBE
Mayhew, Dame Judith, DBE
Major, Dame Malvina Lorraine (Mrs Fleming), DBE
Major, Dame Norma Christina Elizabeth, DBE
Markova, Dame Alicia, DBE
Metge, *Dr* Dame (Alice) Joan, DBE
Middleton, Dame Elaine Madoline, DCMG, MBE
Mills, Dame Barbara Jean Lyon, DBE, QC
Mirren, Dame Helen, DBE
Moores, Dame Yvonne, DBE
Morgan, *Dr* Dame Gillian Margaret, DBE
Morrison, *Hon.* Dame Mary Anne, DCVO
Muirhead, Dame Lorna Elizabeth Fox, DBE
Muldoon, Lady Thea Dale, DBE, QSO
Mumford, Lady Mary Katharine, DCVO
Munro, Dame Alison, DBE
Murdoch, Dame Elisabeth Joy, DBE
Murray, Dame (Alice) Rosemary, DBE, DPHIL
Neville, Dame Elizabeth, DBE, QPM
Neville-Jones, Dame (Lilian) Pauline, DCMG
Ogilvie, Dame Bridget Margaret, DBE, PHD, DSC
Oliver, Dame Gillian Frances, DBE
Ollerenshaw, Dame Kathleen Mary, DBE, DPHIL
Oxenbury, Dame Shirley Anne, DBE
Park, Dame Merle Florence (Mrs Bloch), DBE
Paterson, Dame Betty Fraser Ross, DBE
Pauffley, *Hon.* Dame Anna Evelyn Hamilton, DBE
Penhaligon, Dame Annette (Mrs Egerton), DBE
Peters, Dame Mary Elizabeth, DBE
Platt, Dame Denise, DBE
Plowright, Dame Joan Ann, DBE
Polak, *Prof.* Dame Julia Margaret, DBE
Poole, Dame Avril Anne Barker, DBE
Porter, Dame Shirley (Lady Porter), DBE
Powell, Dame Sally Ann Vickers, DBE
Prendergast, Dame Simone Ruth, DBE
Prentice, Dame Winifred Eva, DBE
Price, Dame Margaret Berenice, DBE
Purves, Dame Daphne Helen, DBE
Quinn, Dame Sheila Margaret Imelda, DBE
Rafferty, *Hon.* Dame Anne Judith, DBE
Rawson, *Prof.* Dame Jessica Mary, DBE
Rees, *Prof.* Dame Lesley Howard, DBE
Reeves, Dame Helen May, DBE
Richardson, Dame Mary, DBE
Riddelsdell, Dame Mildred, DCB, CBE
Ridley, Dame (Mildred) Betty, DBE
Ridsdale, Dame Victoire Evelyn Patricia (Lady Ridsdale), DBE
Rigg, Dame Diana, DBE
Rimington, Dame Stella, DCB
Ritterman, Dame Janet, DBE
Roberts, Dame Jane Elisabeth, DBE
Robins, Dame Ruth Laura, DBE
Robottom, Dame Marlene, DBE
Roddick, Dame Anita Lucia, DBE
Roe, Dame Marion Audrey, DBE
Roe, Dame Raigh Edith, DBE
Ronson, Dame Gail, DBE
Rothschild, Hon. Dame Miriam Louisa, DBE, FRS
Rue, Dame (Elsie) Rosemary, DBE
Rumbold, *Rt. Hon.* Dame Angela Claire Rosemary, DBE

Runciman of Doxford, The Viscountess, DBE
Salas, Dame Margaret Laurence, DBE
Salmond, *Prof.* Dame Mary Anne, DBE
Saunders, Dame Cicely Mary Strode, OM, DBE, FRCP
Sawyer, *Hon.* Dame Joan Augusta, DBE
Scardino, Dame Marjorie, DBE
Scott, Dame Catherine Margaret (Mrs Denton), DBE
Seward, Dame Margaret Helen Elizabeth, DBE
Shirley, Dame Stephanie, DBE
Shovelton, Dame Helena, DBE
Sibley, Dame Antoinette (Mrs Corbett), DBE
Smieton, Dame Mary Guillan, DBE
Smith, Dame Dela, DBE
Smith, *Rt. Hon.* Dame Janet Hilary (Mrs Mathieson), DBE
Smith, Dame Margaret Natalie (Maggie) (Mrs Cross), DBE
Smith, Dame Margot, DBE
Soames, Lady Mary, DBE
Southgate, *Prof.* Dame Lesley Jill, DBE
Spark, Dame Muriel Sarah, DBE
Spencer, Dame Rosemary Jane, DCMG
Steel, *Hon.* Dame (Anne) Heather (Mrs Beattie), DBE
Strachan, Dame Valerie Patricia Marie, DCB
Strathern, *Prof.* Dame Anne Marilyn, DBE
Sutherland, Dame Joan (Mrs Bonynge), OM, DBE
Sutherland, Dame Veronica Evelyn, DBE, CMG
Symmonds, Dame Olga Patricia, DBE
Taylor, Dame Elizabeth, DBE
Taylor, Dame Meg, DBE
Te Atairangikaahu, Te Arikinui, Dame, DBE
Te Kanawa, Dame Kiri Janette, DBE
Thomas, Dame Maureen Elizabeth (Lady Thomas), DBE
Thorneycroft, Lady Carla, DBE
Tinson, Dame Sue, DBE
Tizard, Dame Catherine Anne, GCMG, GCVO, DBE
Tokiel, Dame Rosa, DBE
Trotter, Dame Janet Olive, DBE
Turner-Warwick, Dame Margaret Elizabeth Harvey, DBE, FRCP, FRCPED
Uprichard, Dame Mary Elizabeth, DBE
Varley, Dame Joan Fleetwood, DBE
Wagner, Dame Gillian Mary Millicent (Lady Wagner), DBE
Wall, Dame (Alice) Anne, (Mrs Michael Wall), DCVO
Wallis, Dame Sheila Ann, DBE
Warburton, Dame Anne Marion, DCVO, CMG
Waterhouse, Dame Rachel Elizabeth, DBE, PHD
Webb, *Prof.* Dame Patricia, DBE
Weir, Dame Gillian Constance (Mrs Phelps), DBE
Weller, Dame Rita, DBE
Weston, Dame Margaret Kate, DBE
Wheldon, Dame Juliet Louise, DCB, QC
Wilson-Barnett, *Prof.* Dame Jenifer, DBE
Winstone, Dame Dorothy Gertrude, DBE, CMG
Wong Yick-ming, Dame Rosanna, DBE

DECORATIONS AND MEDALS

PRINCIPAL DECORATIONS AND MEDALS

In order of wear

VICTORIA CROSS (VC), 1856 (*see* below)
GEORGE CROSS (GC), 1940 (*see* below)

BRITISH ORDERS OF KNIGHTHOOD (*see* Orders of Chivalry)
BARONET'S BADGE
KNIGHT BACHELOR'S BADGE

INDIAN ORDER OF MERIT (MILITARY)

DECORATIONS
Conspicuous Gallantry Cross (CGC), 1995
Royal Red Cross Class I (RRC), 1883
Distinguished Service Cross (DSC), 1914. For all ranks for actions at sea
Military Cross (MC), December 1914. For all ranks for actions on land
Distinguished Flying Cross (DFC), 1918. For all ranks for acts of gallantry when flying in active operations against the enemy
Air Force Cross (AFC), 1918. For all ranks for acts of courage when flying, although not in active operations against the enemy
Royal Red Cross Class II (ARRC)
Order of British India
Kaisar-i-Hind Medal
Order of St John

MEDALS FOR GALLANTRY AND DISTINGUISHED CONDUCT
Union of South Africa Queen's Medal for Bravery, in Gold
Distinguished Conduct Medal (DCM), 1854
Conspicuous Gallantry Medal (CGM), 1874
Conspicuous Gallantry Medal (Flying)
George Medal (GM), 1940
Queen's Police Medal for Gallantry
Queen's Fire Service Medal for Gallantry
Royal West African Frontier Force Distinguished Conduct Medal
King's African Rifles Distinguished Conduct Medal
Indian Distinguished Service Medal
Union of South Africa Queen's Medal for Bravery, in Silver
Distinguished Service Medal (DSM), 1914
Military Medal (MM), 1916
Distinguished Flying Medal (DFM), 1918
Air Force Medal (AFM)
Constabulary Medal (Ireland)
Medal for Saving Life at Sea (Sea Gallantry Medal)
Indian Order of Merit (Civil)
Indian Police Medal for Gallantry
Ceylon Police Medal for Gallantry
Sierra Leone Police Medal for Gallantry
Sierra Leone Fire Brigades Medal for Gallantry
Colonial Police Medal for Gallantry (CPM)
Queen's Gallantry Medal (QGM), 1974
Royal Victorian Medal (RVM), Gold, Silver and Bronze
British Empire Medal (BEM)
Canada Medal
Queen's Police Medal for Distinguished Service (QPM)
Queen's Fire Service Medal for Distinguished Service (QFSM)
Queen's Volunteer Reserves Medal
Queen's Medal for Chiefs

CAMPAIGN MEDALS AND STARS
Including authorised United Nations, European Community/Union and North Atlantic Treaty Organisation medals (in order of date of campaign for which awarded)

POLAR MEDALS (in order of date)

IMPERIAL SERVICE MEDAL

POLICE MEDALS FOR VALUABLE SERVICE
Indian Police Medal for Meritorious Service
Ceylon Police Medal for Merit
Sierra Leone Police Medal for Meritorious Service
Sierra Leone Fire Brigades Medal for Meritorious Service
Colonial Police Medal for Meritorious Service

BADGE OF HONOUR

JUBILEE, CORONATION AND DURBAR MEDALS
King George V, King George VI, Queen Elizabeth II and Long and Faithful Service Medals

EFFICIENCY AND LONG SERVICE DECORATIONS AND MEDALS
Medal for Meritorious Service
Accumulated Campaign Service Medal
The Medal for Long Service and Good Conduct (Military)
Naval Long Service and Good Conduct Medal
Medal for Meritorious Service (Royal Navy 1918–28)
Indian Long Service and Good Conduct Medal
Indian Meritorious Service Medal
Royal Marines Meritorious Service Medal (1849–1947)
Royal Air Force Meritorious Service Medal (1918–1928)
Royal Air Force Long Service and Good Conduct Medal
Medal for Long Service and Good Conduct (Ulster Defence Regiment)
Indian Long Service and Good Conduct Medal
Royal West African Frontier Force Long Service and Good Conduct Medal
Royal Sierra Leone Military Forces Long Service and Good Conduct Medal
King's African Rifles and Long Service and Good Conduct Medal
Indian Meritorious Service Medal
Police Long Service and Good Conduct Medal
Fire Brigade Long Service and Good Conduct Medal
African Police Medal for Meritorious Service
Royal Canadian Mounted Police Long Service Medal
Ceylon Police Long Service Medal
Ceylon Fire Services Long Service Medal
Sierra Leone Police Long Service Medal
Colonial Police Long Service Medal
Sierra Leone Fire Brigades Long Service Medal
Mauritius Police Long Service and Good Conduct Medal

Mauritius Fire Services Long Service and Good Conduct Medal
Mauritius Prisons Service Long Service and Good Conduct Medal
Colonial Fire Brigades Long Service Medal
Colonial Prison Service Medal
Hong Kong Disciplined Services Medal
Army Emergency Reserve Decoration (ERD)
Volunteer Officers' Decoration (VD)
Volunteer Long Service Medal
Volunteer Officers' Decoration (for India and the Colonies)
Volunteer Long Service Medal (for India and the Colonies)
Colonial Auxiliary Forces Officers' Decoration
Colonial Auxiliary Forces Long Service Medal
Medal for Good Shooting (Naval)
Militia Long Service Medal
Imperial Yeomanry Long Service Medal
Territorial Decoration (TD), 1908
Ceylon Armed Services Long Service Medal
Efficiency Decoration (ED)
Territorial Efficiency Medal
Efficiency Medal
Special Reserve Long Service and Good Conduct Medal
Decoration for Officers of the Royal Navy Reserve (RD), 1910
Decoration for Officers of the Royal Naval Volunteer Reserve (VRD)
Royal Naval Reserve Long Service and Good Conduct Medal
Royal Naval Volunteer Reserve Long Service and Good Conduct Medal
Royal Naval Auxiliary Sick Berth Reserve Long Service and Good Conduct Medal
Royal Fleet Reserve Long Service and Good Conduct Medal
Royal Naval Wireless Auxiliary Reserve Long Service and Good Conduct Medal
Royal Naval Auxiliary Service Medal
Air Efficiency Award (AE), 1942
Volunteer Reserves Service Medal
Ulster Defence Regiment Medal
Northern Ireland Home Service Medal
Queen's Medal (for Champion Shots of the RN and RM)
Queen's Medal (for Champion Shots of the New Zealand Naval Forces)
Queen's Medal (for Champion Shots in the Military Forces)
Queen's Medal (for Champion Shots of the Air Forces)
Cadet Forces Medal, 1950
Coastguard Auxiliary Service Long Service Medal
Special Constabulary Long Service Medal
Canadian Forces Decoration
Royal Observer Corps Medal
Civil Defence Long Service Medal
Ambulance Service (Emergency Duties) Long Service and Good Conduct Medal
Royal Fleet Auxiliary Service Medal Rhodesia Medal
Royal Ulster Constabulary Service Medal
Northern Ireland Prison Service Medal
Union of South Africa Commemoration Medal
Indian Independence Medal
Pakistan Medal
Ceylon Armed Services Inauguration Medal
Ceylon Police Independence Medal (1948)
Sierra Leone Independence Medal
Jamaica Independence Medal
Uganda Independence Medal
Malawi Independence Medal
Fiji Independence Medal
Papua New Guinea Independence Medal
Solomon Islands Independence Medal
Service Medal of the Order of St John
Badge of the Order of the League of Mercy
Voluntary Medical Service Medal (1932)
Women's Voluntary Service Medal
South African Medal for War Services
Colonial Special Constabulary Medal

HONORARY MEMBERSHIP OF COMMONWEALTH ORDERS

OTHER COMMONWEALTH MEMBERS' ORDERS, DECORATIONS AND MEDALS

FOREIGN ORDERS

FOREIGN DECORATIONS

FOREIGN MEDALS

THE VICTORIA CROSS (1856)

FOR CONSPICUOUS BRAVERY

VC

Ribbon, Crimson, for all Services (until 1918 it was blue for the Royal Navy)

Instituted on 29 January 1856, the Victoria Cross was awarded retrospectively to 1854, the first being held by Lt. C. D. Lucas, RN, for bravery in the Baltic Sea on 21 June 1854 (gazetted 24 February 1857). The first 62 Crosses were presented by Queen Victoria in Hyde Park, London, on 26 June 1857.

The Victoria Cross is worn before all other decorations, on the left breast, and consists of a cross-pattée of bronze, one-and-a-half inches in diameter, with the Royal Crown surmounted by a lion in the centre, and beneath there is the inscription *For Valour*. Holders of the VC receive a tax-free annuity of £1,300, irrespective of need or other conditions. In 1911, the right to receive the Cross was extended to Indian soldiers, and in 1920 to matrons, sisters and nurses, and the staff of the Nursing Services and other services pertaining to hospitals and nursing, and to civilians of either sex regularly or temporarily under the orders, direction or supervision of the naval, military, or air forces of the Crown.

SURVIVING RECIPIENTS OF THE VICTORIA CROSS
as at August 2004

Annand, *Capt.* R. W. (Durham Light Infantry)
1940 *World War*
Bhan Bhagta Gurung, *Havildar* (2nd Gurkha Rifles)
1945 *World War*
Cruickshank, *Flt. Lt.* J. A. (RAFVR)
1944 *World War*
Fraser, *Lt.-Cdr.* I. E., DSC (RNR)
1945 *World War*
Kenna, *Pte.* E. (Australian Military Forces, 2/4th (NSW))
1945 *World War*
Lachhiman Gurung, *Havildar* (8th Gurkha Rifles)
1945 *World War*

Norton, *Capt.* G. R., MM (South African Forces, Kaffrarian Rifles)
1944 *World War*

Payne, *WO* K., DSC (USA) (Australian Army Training Team)
1969 *Vietnam*

Rambahadur Limbu, *Capt.*, MVO (10th Princess Mary's Gurkha Rifles)
1965 *Sarawak*

Smith, *Sgt.* E. A., CD (Seaforth Highlanders of Canada)
1944 *World War*

Speakman-Pitts, *Sgt.* W. (Black Watch, attached KOSB)
1951 *Korea*

Tulbahadur Pun, *Lt.* (6th Gurkha Rifles)
1944 *World War*

Umrao Singh, *Sub Major* (Royal Indian Artillery)
1944 *World War*

Watkins, *Maj. Rt. Hon.* Sir Tasker, GBE (Welch Regiment)
1944 *World War*

Wilson, *Lt.-Col.* E. C. T. (East Surrey Regiment)
1940 *World War*

THE GEORGE CROSS (1940)
FOR GALLANTRY

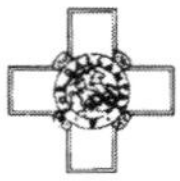

GC

Ribbon, Dark blue, threaded through a bar adorned with laurel leaves

Instituted 24 September 1940 (with amendments, 3 November 1942)

The George Cross is worn before all other decorations (except the VC) on the left breast (when worn by a woman it may be worn on the left shoulder from a ribbon of the same width and colour fashioned into a bow). It consists of a plain silver cross with four equal limbs, the cross having in the centre a circular medallion bearing a design showing St George and the Dragon. The inscription *For Gallantry* appears round the medallion and in the angle of each limb of the cross is the Royal cypher 'G VI' forming a circle concentric with the medallion. The reverse is plain and bears the name of the recipient and the date of the award. The cross is suspended by a ring from a bar adorned with laurel leaves on dark blue ribbon one-and-a-half inches wide.

The cross is intended primarily for civilians; awards to the fighting services are confined to actions for which purely military honours are not normally granted. It is awarded only for acts of the greatest heroism or of the most conspicuous courage in circumstances of extreme danger. From 1 April 1965, holders of the Cross have received a tax-free annuity, which is now £1,300. The cross has twice been awarded collectively rather than to an individual: to Malta (1942) and the Royal Ulster Constabulary (1999).

The royal warrant which ordained that the grant of the Empire Gallantry Medal should cease authorised holders of that medal to return it to the Central Chancery of the Orders of Knighthood and to receive in exchange the George Cross. A similar provision applied to posthumous awards of the Empire Gallantry Medal made after the outbreak of war in 1939. In October 1971 all surviving holders of the Albert Medal and the Edward Medal exchanged those decorations for the George Cross.

SURVIVING RECIPIENTS OF THE GEORGE CROSS
as at August 2004

If the recipient originally received the Empire Gallantry Medal (EGM), the Albert Medal (AM) or the Edward Medal (EM), this is indicated by the initials in parenthesis.

Archer, *Col.* B. S. T., GC, OBE, ERD, 1941
Bamford, J., GC, 1952
Beaton, J., GC, CVO, 1974
Bridge, *Lt.-Cdr.* J., GC, GM and bar, 1944
Butson, *Lt.-Col.* A. R. C., GC, CD, MD (AM), 1948
Bywater, R. A. S., GC, GM, 1944
Errington, H., GC, 1941
Farrow, K., GC (AM), 1948
Finney, Trooper C., GC, 2003
Flintoff, H. H., GC (EM), 1944
Gledhill, A. J., GC, 1967
Gregson, J. S., GC (AM), 1943
Johnson, *WO1 (SSM)* B., GC, 1990
Kinne, D. G., GC, 1954
Lowe, A. R., GC (AM), 1949
Lynch, J., GC, BEM (AM), 1948
Pratt, M. K., GC, 1978
Purves, Mrs M., GC (AM), 1949
Raweng, Awang anak, GC, 1951
Riley, G., GC (AM), 1944
Rowlands, *Air Marshal* Sir John, GC, KBE, 1943
Stevens, H. W., GC, 1958
Styles, *Lt.-Col.* S. G., GC, 1972
Walker, C., GC, 1972
Walker, C. H., GC (AM), 1942
Walton, E. W. K., GC (AM), DSO, 1948
Wilcox, C., GC (EM), 1949
Wooding, E. A., GC (AM), 1945

CHIEFS OF CLANS IN SCOTLAND

Only chiefs of whole Names or Clans are included, except certain special instances (marked *) who, though not chiefs of a whole name, were or are for some reason (e.g. the Macdonald forfeiture) independent. Under decision (*Campbell-Gray*, 1950) a bearer of a 'double or triple-barrelled' surname cannot be held chief of a part of such.

THE ROYAL HOUSE: HM THE QUEEN
AGNEW: **Sir Crispin Agnew of Lochnaw, Bt., QC**, 6 Palmerston Road, Edinburgh EH9 1TN
ANSTRUTHER: **Sir Ian Fife Campbell Anstruther, Bt.**, Barlavington, Petworth, West Sussex GU28 0LG
ARBUTHNOTT: **The Viscount of Arbuthnott, KT, CBE, DSC**, Arbuthnott House, Kincardineshire AB30 1PA
BANNERMAN: **Sir David Bannerman of Elsick, Bt.**, 3 St George's Road, St Margaret's, Twickenham, TW1 1QS
BARCLAY: **Peter C. Barclay of Towie Barclay and of that Ilk**, 69 Oakwood Court, Abbotsbury Road, London W14 8JF
BORTHWICK: **The Lord Borthwick**, Crookston, Heriot, Midlothian EH38 5YS
BOYD: **The Lord Kilmarnock, MBE**, 194 Regent's Park Road, London NW1 8XP
BOYLE: **The Earl of Glasgow**, Fairlie, Ayrshire KA29 0BE
BRODIE: **Alexander Brodie of Brodie**, 1 rue de Regrattier, Paris 75004
BROUN OF COLSTOUN: **Sir William Broun of Colstoun, Bt.**, 2–4 Reed Street, Cremorne, NSW 2090, Australia
BRUCE: **The Earl of Elgin and Kincardine, KT**, Broomhall, Dunfermline, Fife KY11 3DU
BUCHAN: **David Buchan of Auchmacoy**, Auchmacoy House, Ellon, Aberdeenshire
BURNETT: **J. C. A. Burnett of Leys**, Crathes Castle, Banchory, Kincardineshire
CAMERON: **Donald Cameron of Lochiel**, Achnacarry, Spean Bridge, Inverness-shire
CAMPBELL: **The Duke of Argyll**, Inveraray, Argyll PA32 8XF
CARMICHAEL: **Richard Carmichael of Carmichael**, Thankerton, Biggar, Lanarkshire
CARNEGIE: **The Duke of Fife**, Elsick House, Stonehaven, Kincardineshire AB3 2NT
CATHCART: **The Earl Cathcart**, 18 Smith Terrace, London SW3 4DL
CHARTERIS: **The Earl of Wemyss and March, KT**, Gosford House, East Lothian EH32 0PX
CLAN CHATTAN: **K. Mackintosh of Clan Chattan**, Fairburn, Felixburg, Zimbabwe
CHISHOLM: **Hamish Chisholm of Chisholm *(The Chisholm)***, Elmpine, Beck Row, Bury St Edmunds, IP28 8BT
COCHRANE: **The Earl of Dundonald**, Lochnell Castle, Ledaig, Argyllshire
COLQUHOUN: **Sir Ivar Colquhoun of Luss, Bt.**, Camstraddan, Luss, Dunbartonshire G83 8NX
CRANSTOUN: **David Cranstoun of that Ilk**, Corehouse, Lanark
CUMMING: **Sir Alastair Cumming of Altyre, Bt.**, Altyre, Forres, Moray
DARROCH: **Capt. Duncan Darroch of Gourock**, The Red House, Camberley, Surrey
DAVIDSON: **Alister Davidson of Davidston**, 21 Winscombe Street, Takapuna, Auckland, New Zealand
DEWAR: **Michael Dewar of that Ilk and Vogrie**, Rectory Farm House, Charlton Musgrove, Wincanton BA9 8ET
DRUMMOND: **The Earl of Perth**, Stobhall, Perth PH2 6DR
DUNBAR: **Sir James Dunbar of Mochrum, Bt.**, 211 Gardenville Drive, Yorktown, Va 23693, USA
DUNDAS: **David Dundas of Dundas**, 3 Crane Close, Tokai 7945, Cape Town, South Africa
DURIE: **Andrew Durie of Durie, CBE**, Finnich Malise, Croftamie, Stirlingshire G63 0HA
ELIOTT: **Mrs Margaret Eliott of Redheugh**, Redheugh, Newcastleton, Roxburghshire
ERSKINE: **The Earl of Mar and Kellie**, Erskine House, Kirk Wynd, Alloa, Clackmannan FK10 4JF
FARQUHARSON: **Capt. A. Farquharson of Invercauld, MC**, Invercauld, Braemar, Aberdeenshire AB35 5TT
FERGUSSON: **Sir Charles Fergusson of Kilkerran, Bt.**, Kilkerran, Maybole, Ayrshire
FORBES: **The Lord Forbes, KBE, Balforbes**, Alford, Aberdeenshire AB33 8DR
FORSYTH: **Alistair Forsyth of that Ilk**, Annfield Park, PO Box 175, Boyup Brook, Western Australia 6244
FRASER: **The Lady Saltoun**, Aberdeenshire AB35 5YB
*FRASER (OF LOVAT): **The Lord Lovat**, Beaufort Lodge, Beauly, Inverness-shire IV4 7AZ
GAYRE: **R. Gayre of Gayre and Nigg**, Minard Castle, Minard, Inverary, Argyll PA32 8YB
GORDON: **The Marquess of Huntly**, Aboyne Castle, Aberdeenshire AB34 5JP
GRAHAM: **The Duke of Montrose**, Drymen, Stirlingshire
GRANT: **The Lord Strathspey**, The School House, Lochbuie, Mull, Argyllshire PA62 6AA
GRIERSON: **Sir Michael Grierson of Lag, Bt.**, 40C Palace Road, London SW2 3NJ
GUTHRIE: **Alexander Guthrie of Guthrie**, 22 William Street, Shenton Park, Perth, Western Australia
HAIG: **The Earl Haig, OBE**, Melrose, Roxburghshire TD6 9DP
HALDANE: **Martin Haldane of Gleneagles**, Gleneagles, Auchterarder, Perthshire
HANNAY: **David Hannay of Kirkdale and of that Ilk**, Kirkdale, Carsluith, Dumfriesshire, DG8 7EA
HAY: **The Earl of Erroll**, Woodbury Hall, Sandy, Beds
HENDERSON: **John Henderson of Fordell**, 7 Owen Street, Toowoomba, Queensland, Australia
HUNTER: **Pauline Hunter of Hunterston**, Plover's Ridge, Lon Crecrist, Trearddur Bay, Anglesey LL65 2AZ
IRVINE OF DRUM: **David Irvine of Drum**, Holly Leaf Cottage, Banchory, Aberdeenshire AB31 4BR
JARDINE: **Sir Alexander Jardine of Applegirth, Bt.**, Ash House, Thwaites, Millom, Cumbria LA18 5HY
JOHNSTONE: **The Earl of Annandale and Hartfell**, Raehills, Lockerbie, Dumfriesshire
KEITH: **The Earl of Kintore**, The Stables, Keith Hall, Inverurie, Aberdeenshire AB51 0LD
KENNEDY: **The Marquess of Ailsa**, Cassillis House, Ayrshire
KERR: **The Marquess of Lothian, KCVO**, Ferniehurst Castle, Jedburgh, Roxburghshire TN8 6NX
KINCAID: **Arabella Kincaid of Kincaid**, Wood Farm, Caynton, Newport, Shropshire TF10 8NF
LAMONT: **Peter Lamont of that Ilk**, 40 Breakfast Road, Marayong, New South Wales, Australia
LEASK: **Madam Leask of Leask**, c/o 53 St Nicholas Street, Thetford IP24 1BG
LENNOX: **Edward Lennox of that Ilk**, Tods Top Farm, Downton on the Rock, Ludlow, Shropshire
LESLIE: **The Earl of Rothes**, Salisbury, Wilts SP5 1LX
LINDSAY: **The Earl of Crawford and Balcarres, KT, GCVO, PC, Balcarres**, Colinsburgh, Fife

LIVINGSTONE OF MACLEA: **Alastair Livingstone of Bachuil,** Bachuil, Isle of Lismore, Argyll PA34 5UL
LOCKHART: **Angus Lockhart of the Lee,** Newholme, Dunsyre, Lanark
LUMSDEN: **Gillem Lumsden of that Ilk and Blanerne,** Stapely Howe, Hoe Benham, Newbury, Berks
MACALESTER: **William St J. McAlester of Loup and Kennox,** 27 Durnham Road, Christchurch BH23 7ND
MACARTHUR; **John MacArthur of that Ilk,** Castle Kennedy House, Castle Kennedy, Stranraer, Wigtownshire DG9 8SJ
MCBAIN: **J. H. McBain of McBain,** 7025 North Finger Rock Place, Tucson, Arizona 85718, USA
MACDONALD: **The Lord Macdonald *(The Macdonald of Macdonald)*,** Kinloch Lodge, Sleat, Isle of Skye
*MACDONALD OF CLANRANALD: **Ranald Macdonald of Clanranald,** Mornish House, Killin, Perthshire FK21 8TX
*MACDONALD OF SLEAT (CLAN HUSTEAIN): **Sir Ian Macdonald of Sleat, Bt.,** Thorpe Hall, Driffield YO25 0JE
*MACDONELL OF GLENGARRY: **Ranald MacDonell of Glengarry,** 74 Haverhill Road, London SW12 0HB
MACDOUGALL: **Morag MacDougall of MacDougall,** Dunollie Castle, Oban, Argyll, PA34 5TT
MACDOWALL: **Fergus Macdowall of Garthland,** 16 Rowe Road, Ottawa, Ontario K29 2ZS
MACGREGOR: **Sir Malcolm MacGregor of MacGregor, Bt.,** Irvine House, Canonbie, Dumfriesshire DG14 0XF
MACINTYRE: **Donald MacIntyre of Glenoe,** 41 Temescal Terrace, San Francisco, California, USA
MACKAY: **The Lord Reay,** 98 Oakley Street, London SW3
MACKENZIE: **The Earl of Cromartie,** Castle Leod, Strathpeffer, Ross-shire IV14 9AA
MACKINNON: **Anne Mackinnon of Mackinnon,** 3 Anson Way, Bridgewater, Somerset TA6 3TB
MACKINTOSH: **John Mackintosh of Mackintosh *(The Mackintosh of Mackintosh)*,** Moy Hall, Inverness IV13 7YQ
MACLACHLAN: **Euan MacLachlan of MacLachlan,** Castle Lachlan, Strathlachlan, Strachur, Argyll PA27 8BU
MACLAREN: **Donald MacLaren of MacLaren and Achleskine,** Achleskine, Kirkton, Lochearnhead
MACLEAN: **The Hon. Sir Lachlan Maclean of Duart, Bt., CVO,** Arngask House, Glenfarg, Perthshire PH2 9QA
MACLENNAN: **Ruaraidh MacLennan of MacLennan,** Oldmill, Dores, Inverness-shire IV2 6R
MACLEOD: **John MacLeod of MacLeod,** Dunvegan Castle, Isle of Skye
MACMILLAN: **George MacMillan of MacMillan,** Finlaystone, Langbank, Renfrewshire
MACNAB: **J. C. Macnab of Macnab *(The Macnab)*,** Leuchars Castle Farmhouse, Leuchars, Fife KY16 0EY
MACNAGHTEN: **Sir Patrick Macnaghten of Macnaghten and Dundarave, Bt.,** Dundarave, Bushmills, Co. Antrim
MACNEACAIL: **John Macneacail of Macneacail and Scorrybreac,** PO Box 1172, Ballina, NSW 2478, Australia
MACNEIL OF BARRA: **Ian Macneil of Barra *(The Macneil of Barra)*,** 95/6 Grange Loan, Edinburgh
MACPHERSON: **The Hon. Sir William Macpherson of Cluny, TD,** Newton Castle, Blairgowrie, Perthshire
MACTAVISH: **E. S. Dugald MacTavish of Dunardry,** 3049 Vine Lane, Sebring, Florida 33870, USA
MACTHOMAS: **Andrew MacThomas of Finegand,** 25 Bradbourne Street, London SW6 3TF
MAITLAND: **The Earl of Lauderdale,** 12 St Vincent Street, Edinburgh
MAKGILL: **The Viscount of Oxfuird,** 28B Prince of Wales Mansions, Prince of Wales Drive, London SW11 4BQ
MALCOLM (MACCALLUM): **Robin N. L. Malcolm of Poltalloch,** Duntrune Castle, Lochgilphead, Argyll
MAR: **The Countess of Mar,** Great Witley, Worcs WR6 6JB
MARJORIBANKS: **Andrew Marjoribanks of that Ilk,** 10 Newark Street, Greenock
MATHESON: **Maj. Sir Fergus Matheson of Matheson, Bt.,** Old Rectory, Hedenham, Bungay, Suffolk NR35 2LD
MENZIES: **David Menzies of Menzies,** RMB 1220, Collie, Western Australia 6225
MOFFAT: **Madam Moffat of that Ilk,** St Jasual, Bullocks Farm Lane, Wheeler End Common, High Wycombe
MONCREIFFE: **The Hon. Peregrine Moncreiffe of that Ilk,** Easter Moncreiffe, Bridge of Earn, Perthshire
MONTGOMERIE: **The Earl of Eglinton and Winton,** Balhomie, Cargill, Perth PH2 6DS
MORRISON: **Dr Iain Morrison of Ruchdi,** Magnolia Cottage, The Street, Walberton, Sussex
MUNRO: **Hector Munro of Foulis,** Foulis Castle, Evanton, Ross-shire IV16 9UX
MURRAY: **The Duke of Atholl,** Blair Castle, Perthshire
NESBITT (or NISBET): **Mark Nesbitt of that Ilk,** 114 Cambridge Road, Teddington, Middlesex TW11 8DJ
NICOLSON: **The Lord Carnock,** 90 Whitehall Court, London SW1A 2EL
OGILVY: **The Earl of Airlie, KT, GCVO, PC,** Cortachy Castle, Kirriemuir, Angus
OLIPHANT: **Richard Oliphant of that Ilk,** 1B Kylerhea, Breaknish, Isle of Skye IV42 8NH
RAMSAY: **The Earl of Dalhousie,** Brechin Castle, Angus DD7 6SH
RATTRAY: **James Rattray of Rattray,** Rattray, Perthshire
RIDDELL: **Sir John Riddell of Riddell, CB, CVO,** Hepple, Morpeth, Northumberland
ROBERTSON: **Alexander Robertson of Struan *(Struan-Robertson)*,** The Breach Farm, Goudhurst Road, Kent
ROLLO: **The Lord Rollo,** Pitcairns, Dunning, Perthshire
ROSE: **Miss Elizabeth Rose of Kilravock,** Kilravock Castle, Croy, Inverness
ROSS: **David Ross of that Ilk and Balnagowan,** Shandwick, Perth Road, Stanley, Perthshire
RUTHVEN: **The Earl of Gowrie, PC,** 34 King Street, Covent Garden, London WC2
SCOTT: **The Duke of Buccleuch and Queensberry, KT, VRD,** Bowhill, Selkirk
SCRYMGEOUR: **The Earl of Dundee,** Cupar, Fife
SEMPILL: **The Lord Sempill,** Edinburgh, EH6 8AE
SHAW: **John Shaw of Tordarroch,** East Craig an Ron, 22 Academy Mead, Fortrose IV10 8TW
SINCLAIR: **The Earl of Caithness,** 137 Claxton Grove, London W6 8HB
SKENE: **Danus Skene of Skene,** Orwell House, Manse Road, Milnathort, Fife KY13 9YQ
STIRLING: **Fraser Stirling of Cader,** 44A Oakley Street, London SW3 5HA
STRANGE: **Maj. Timothy Strange of Balcaskie,** Little Holme, Porton Road, Amesbury, Wilts
SUTHERLAND: **The Countess of Sutherland,** House of Tongue, Brora, Sutherland
SWINTON: **John Swinton of that Ilk,** Alberta, Canada
TROTTER: **Alexander Trotter of Mortonhall,** Charterhall, Duns, Berwickshire
URQUHART: **Kenneth Urquhart of Urquhart,** 507 Jefferson Park Avenue, Jefferson, New Orleans, La. 70121, USA
WALLACE: **Ian Wallace of that Ilk,** 5 Lennox Street, Edinburgh EH4 1QB
WEDDERBURN OF THAT ILK: **The Master of Dundee,** Birkhill, Cupar, Fife
WEMYSS: **David Wemyss of that Ilk,** Invermay, Perthshire

THE PRIVY COUNCIL

The Sovereign in Council, or Privy Council, was the chief source of executive power until the system of Cabinet government developed in the 18th century. Now the Privy Council's main functions are to advise the Sovereign and to exercise its own statutory responsibilities independent of the Sovereign in Council.

Membership of the Privy Council is automatic upon appointment to certain government and judicial positions in the United Kingdom, e.g. Cabinet ministers must be Privy Counsellors and are sworn in on first assuming office. Membership is also accorded by The Queen to eminent people in the UK and independent countries of the Commonwealth of which Her Majesty is Queen, on the recommendation of the British Prime Minister. Membership of the Council is retained for life, except for very occasional removals.

The administrative functions of the Privy Council are carried out by the Privy Council Office under the direction of the President of the Council, who is always a member of the Cabinet.

President of the Council, The Rt. Hon. Baroness Amos
Clerk of the Council, A. Galloway

MEMBERS *as at August 2004*

HRH The Duke of Edinburgh, 1951
HRH The Prince of Wales, 1977

Aberdare, Lord, 1974
Ackner, Lord, 1980
Airlie, Earl of, 1984
Aldous, Sir William, 1995
Alebua, Ezekiel, 1988
Amos, Baroness, 2003
Ampthill, Lord, 1995
Ancram, Michael, 1996
Anderson, Donald, 2000
Anthony, Douglas, 1971
Arbuthnot, James, 1998
Archer of Sandwell, Lord, 1977
Arden, Dame Mary, 2000
Armstrong, Hilary, 1999
Arnold, Sir John, 1979
Arthur, *Hon.* Owen, 1995
Ashdown of Norton-sub-Hamdon, Lord, 1989
Ashley of Stoke, Lord, 1979
Atkins, Sir Robert, 1995
Auld, Sir Robin, 1995
Baker, Sir Thomas, 2002
Baker of Dorking, Lord, 1984
Barber, Lord, 1963
Barnett, Lord, 1975
Barron, Kevin, 2001
Battle, John, 2002
Beckett, Margaret, 1993
Beith, Alan, 1992
Beldam, Sir Roy, 1989
Belstead, Lord, 1983 (also known as Lord Ganzoni)
Benn, Anthony, 1964
Benn, Hilary, 2003
Biffen, Lord, 1979
Bingham of Cornhill, Lord, 1986
Birch, William, 1992
Bisson, Sir Gordon, 1987
Blackstone, Baroness, 2001
Blair, Tony, 1994
Blaker, Lord, 1983
Blanchard, Peter, 1998
Blatch, Baroness, 1993
Blunkett, David, 1997
Boateng, Paul, 1999
Bolger, James, 1991
Booth, Albert, 1976
Boothroyd, Baroness, 1992
Boscawen, *Hon.* Robert, 1992
Bottomley, Virginia, 1992
Boyd, Colin, 2000
Boyson, Sir Rhodes, 1987
Bradley, Keith, 2001
Brathwaite, Sir Nicholas, 1991
Bridge of Harwich, Lord, 1975
Brightman, Lord, 1979
Brittan of Spennithorne, Lord, 1981
Brook, Sir Henry, 1996
Brooke of Sutton Mandeville, Lord, 1988
Brown, Gordon, 1996
Brown, Nicholas, 1997
Brown, Sir Stephen, 1983
Brown of Eaton-under-Heywood, Lord, 1992
Browne-Wilkinson, Lord, 1983
Butler, Sir Adam, 1984
Butler of Brockwell, Lord, 2004
Butler-Sloss, Dame Elizabeth, 1988
Buxton, Sir Richard, 1997
Byers, Stephen, 1998
Caborn, Richard, 1999
Caithness, Earl of, 1990
Callaghan of Cardiff, Lord, 1964
Cameron of Lochbroom, Lord, 1984
Camoys, Lord, 1997
Campbell of Croy, Lord, 1970
Campbell, Sir Walter Menzies, 1999
Campbell, Sir William, 1999
Canterbury, The Archbishop of, 2002
Carey of Clifton, Lord, 1991
Carlisle of Bucklow, Lord, 1979
Carnwath, Sir Robert, 2002
Carr of Hadley, Lord, 1963
Carrington, Lord, 1959 (also known as Lord Carrington of Upton)
Carswell, Lord, 1993
Carter, Lord, 1997
Casey, Sir Maurice, 1986
Chadwick, Sir John, 1997
Chalfont, Lord, 1964
Chalker of Wallasey, Baroness, 1987
Chan, Sir Julius, 1981
Chataway, Sir Christopher, 1970
Chilcot, Sir John, 2004
Christie, Perry, 2004
Clark of Windermere, Lord, 1997
Clark, Helen, 1990
Clark of Kempston, Lord, 1990
Clarke, Sir Anthony, 1998
Clarke, Charles, 2001
Clarke, Kenneth, 1984
Clarke, Thomas, 1997
Clinton-Davis, Lord, 1998
Clyde, Lord, 1996
Cockfield, Lord, 1982
Colman, Fraser, 1986
Compton, Sir John, 1983
Cook, Robin, 1996
Cooke of Thorndon, Lord, 1977
Cope of Berkeley, Lord, 1988
Corfield, Sir Frederick, 1970
Corston, Jean, 2003
Cosgrove, Lady, 2003
Coulsfield, Lord, 2000
Cowen, Sir Zelman, 1981
Cradock, Sir Percy, 1993
Crawford and Balcarres, Earl of, 1972
Creech, *Hon.* Wyatt, 1999
Crickhowell, Lord, 1979
Croom-Johnson, Sir David, 1984
Cullen, *Hon.* Lord, 1997
Cunningham, Jack, 1993
Curry, David, 1996
Darling, Alistair, 1997
Davies, Denzil, 1978
Davies, Ronald, 1997
Davis, David, 1997
Davis, Terence, 1999
Davison, Sir Ronald, 1978
Dean of Harptree, Lord, 1991
Dean of Thornton-le-Fylde, Baroness, 1998
Deedes, Lord, 1962
Denham, John, 2000
Denham, Lord, 1981
Dixon, Lord, 1996
Dobson, Frank, 1997
Donaldson of Lymington, Lord, 1979
Dorrell, Stephen, 1994
du Cann, Sir Edward, 1964
Duncan Smith, Iain, 2001
Dunn, Sir Robin, 1980
Dyson, Sir John, 2001
East, Paul, 1998
Eden of Winton, Lord, 1972
Eggar, Timothy, 1995
Eichelaum, Sir Thomas, 1989
Elias, *Hon.* Dame, Sian, 1999
Emery, Sir Peter, 1993
Esquivel, Manuel, 1986
Evans, Sir Anthony, 1992
Eveleigh, Sir Edward, 1977
Falconer of Thoroton, Lord, 2003
Farquharson, Sir Donald, 1989
Fellowes, Lord, 1990
Ferrers, Earl, 1982

Field, Frank, 1997
Floissac, Sir Vincent, 1992
Foot, Michael, 1974
Forsyth of Drumlean, The Lord, 1995
Forth, Eric, 1997
Foster, Derek, 1993
Foulkes, George, 2002
Fowler, Lord, 1979
Fox, Sir Michael, 1981
Fraser, Malcolm, 1976
Fraser of Carmyllie, Lord, 1989
Freeman, John, 1966
Freeman, Lord, 1993
Freeson, Reginald, 1976
Garel-Jones, Lord, 1992
Gault, Thomas, 1992
George, Bruce, 2000
George, Lord, 1999
Georges, Telford, 1986
Gibbs, Sir Harry, 1972
Gibson, Sir Peter, 1993
Gilbert, Lord, 1978
Gill, Lord, 2002
Gilmour of Craigmillar, Lord, 1973
Glenamara, Lord, 1964
Glidewell, Sir Iain, 1985
Goff of Chieveley, Lord, 1982
Goldsmith, Lord, 2002
Goodlad, Sir Alastair, 1992
Gowrie, Earl of, 1984
Graham, Sir Douglas, 1998
Graham of Edmonton, Lord, 1998
Gray of Contin, Lord, 1982
Griffiths, Lord, 1980
Grocott, Lord, 2002
Gummer, John, 1985
Habgood, Rt. Revd Lord, 1983
Hague, William, 1995
Hain, Peter, 2001
Hale of Richmond, Baroness, 1999
Hamilton, Sir Archie, 1991
Hamilton, Lord, 2002
Hanley, Sir Jeremy, 1994
Hardie, Lord, 1997
Hardie Boys, Sir Michael, 1989
Harman, Harriet, 1997
Harrison, Walter, 1977
Haselhurst, Sir Alan, 1999
Hattersley, Lord, 1975
Hayhoe, Lord, 1985
Hayman, Baroness, 2000
Healey, Lord, 1964
Heath, Sir Edward, 1955
Heathcoat-Amory, David, 1996
Henry, Sir Denis, 1993
Henry, John, 1996
Heseltine, Lord, 1979
Heseltine, Sir William, 1986
Hesketh, Lord, 1991
Hewitt, Patricia, 2001
Higgins, Lord, 1979
Hill, Keith, 2003
Hirst, Sir David, 1992
Hodge, Margaret, 2003
Hoffmann, Lord, 1992
Hogg, *Hon.* Douglas, 1992
Hollis of Heigham, Baroness, 1999
Holme of Cheltenham, Lord, 2000
Hoon, Geoffrey, 1999
Hope of Craighead, Lord, 1989
Hordern, Sir Peter, 1993
Howard, Michael, 1990
Howarth, Alan, 2000
Howe of Aberavon, Lord, 1972
Howell of Guildford, Lord, 1979
Hughes, Beverley, 2004
Hunt, Jonathan, 1989
Hunt of Wirral, Lord, 1990
Hurd of Westwell, Lord, 1982
Hutchison, Sir Michael, 1995
Hutton, Lord, 1988
Hutton, John, 2001
Inge, Lord, 2004
Ingraham, Hubert, 1993
Ingram, Adam, 1999
Irvine of Lairg, Lord, 1997
Jack, Michael, 1997
Jacob, Lord, 2004
Janvrin, Sir Robin, 1998
Jauncey of Tullichettle, Lord, 1988
Jay of Paddington, Baroness, 1998
Jellicoe, Earl, 1963 (also known as Lord Jellicoe of Southampton)
Jenkin of Roding, Lord, 1973
Johnson, Alan, 2003
Johnson Smith, Sir Geoffrey, 1996
Jones, Lord, 1999
Jopling, Lord, 1979
Jowell, Tessa, 1998
Judge, Sir Igor, 1996
Jugnauth, Sir Anerood, 1987
Kaufman, Sir Gerald, 1978
Kay, Lord, 2004
Keene, Sir David, 2000
Keith, Sir Kenneth, 1998
Kelly, Sir Basil, 1984
Kelvedon, Lord, 1980
Kenilorea, Sir Peter, 1979
Kennedy, Charles, 1999
Kennedy, Jane, 2003
Kennedy, Sir Paul, 1992
Kerr, Lord, 2004
King of Bridgwater, Lord, 1979
Kingsdown, Lord, 1987
Kingsland, Lord, 1994
Kinnock, Neil, 1983
Kirkwood, Lord, 2000
Knight, Gregory, 1995
Lamont of Lerwick, Lord, 1986
Lane, Lord, 1975
Lang of Monkton, Lord, 1990
Lange, David, 1984
Latasi, Kamuta, 1996
Latham, Sir David, 2000
Lauti, Sir Toaripi, 1979
Laws, Sir John, 1999
Lawson of Blaby, Lord, 1981
Lawton, Sir Frederick, 1972
Leggatt, Sir Andrew, 1990
Leonard, Rt. Revd Graham, 1981
Letwin, Oliver, 2002
Liddell, Mrs Helen, 1998
Lilley, Peter, 1990
Lloyd of Berwick, Lord, 1984
Lloyd, Sir Peter, 1994
London, The Bishop of, 1995
Longmore, Sir Andrew, 2001
Louisy, Allan, 1981
Luce, Lord, 1986
Lyell, Sir Nicholas, 1990
Mabon, Dickson, 1977
McAvoy, Thomas, 2003
McCartney, Ian, 1999
McCollum, Sir Liam, 1997
McConnell, Jack, 2001
McCowan, Sir Anthony, 1989
MacDermott, Sir John, 1987
Macdonald of Tradeston, Lord, 1999
Macfadyen, Lord, 2002
MacGregor of Pulham Market, Lord, 1985
MacIntyre, Duncan, 1980
Mackay, Andrew, 1998
McIntosh of Haringey, Lord, 2002
McKay, Ian, 1992
Mackay of Clashfern, Lord, 1979
Mackay of Drumadoon, Lord, 1996
McKinnon, Donald, 1992
Maclean, David, 1995
Maclean, Lord, 2001
McLeish, Henry, 2000
Maclennan of Rogart, Lord, 1997
McMullin, Sir Duncan, 1980
Major, John, 1987
Mance, Sir Jonathan, 1999
Mandelson, Peter, 1998
Mantell, Sir Charles, 1997
Marnoch, Lord, 2001
Marsh, Lord, 1966
Martin, Michael, 2000
Mason of Barnsley, Lord, 1968
Mates, Michael, 2004
Maude, *Hon.* Francis, 1992
Mawhinney, Sir Brian, 1994
May, Sir Anthony, 1998
May, Theresa, 2003
Mayhew of Twysden, Lord, 1986
Meacher, Michael, 1997
Megarry, Sir Robert, 1978
Mellor, David, 1990
Merlyn-Rees, Lord, 1974
Michael, Alun, 1998
Milburn, Alan, 1998
Millan, Bruce, 1975
Millett, Lord, 1994
Milligan, Lord, 2000
Mitchell, Sir James, 1985
Mitchell, Dr Keith, 2004
Molyneaux of Killead, Lord, 1983
Monro of Langholm, Lord, 1995
Moore, Michael, 1990
Moore of Lower Marsh, Lord, 1986
Moore of Wolvercote, Lord, 1977
Morgan, Rhodri, 2000
Morris, Charles, 1978
Morris, Estelle, 1999
Morris of Aberavon, Lord, 1970
Morris of Manchester, Lord, 1979
Morritt, Sir Robert, 1994
Mowlam, Marjorie, 1997
Moyle, Roland, 1978
Mummery, Sir John, 1996
Murphy, Paul, 1999
Murray, *Hon.* Lord, 1974
Murray, Sir Donald, 1989
Murton of Lindisfarne, Lord, 1976
Mustill, Lord, 1985
Nairne, Sir Patrick, 1982
Namaliu, Sir Rabbie, 1989
Naseby, Lord, 1994
Needham, Sir Richard, 1994
Neill, Sir Brian, 1985
Neuberger, Lord, 2004
Newton of Braintree, Lord, 1988
Nicholls of Birkenhead, Lord, 1995
Nicholson, Sir Michael, 1995
Nolan, Lord, 1991
Nott, Sir John, 1979
Nourse, Sir Martin, 1985
Oakes, Gordon, 1979
O'Connor, Sir Patrick, 1980
O'Donnell, Turlough, 1979
Ogilvy, Sir Angus, 1997
Oliver of Aylmerton, Lord, 1980
Oppenheim-Barnes, Baroness, 1979
Orme, Lord, 1974
Osbourne, Lord, 2001
Otton, Sir Philip, 1995
Owen, Lord, 1976
Paeniu, Bikenibeu, 1991

Palliser, Sir Michael, 1983
Palmer, Sir Geoffrey, 1986
Parker, Sir Jonathan, 2000
Parker, Sir Roger, 1983
Parkinson, Lord, 1981
Patten, Christopher, 1989
Patten, Lord, 1990
Patterson, Percival, 1993
Pattie, Sir Geoffrey, 1987
Pendry, Lord, 2000
Penrose, Lord, 2000
Peters, Winston, 1998
Peyton of Yeovil, Lord, 1970
Phillips of Worth Matravers, Lord, 1995
Pill, Sir Malcolm, 1995
Pindling, Sir Lynden, 1976
Portillo, Michael, 1992
Potter, Sir Mark, 1996
Prescott, John, 1994
Price, George, 1982
Primarolo, Dawn, 2002
Prior, Lord, 1970
Prosser, Lord, 2000
Puapua, Sir Tomasi, 1982
Pym, Lord, 1970
Quin, Ms Joyce, 1998
Radice, Lord, 1999
Raison, Sir Timothy, 1982
Ramsden, James, 1963
Rawlinson of Ewell, Lord, 1964
Raynsford, Nick, 2001
Redwood, John, 1993
Rees, Lord, 1983
Reid, John, 1998
Renton, Lord, 1962
Renton of Mount Harry, Lord, 1989
Richard, Lord, 1993
Richardson, Sir Ivor, 1978
Richardson of Duntisbourne, Lord, 1976
Rix, Sir Bernard, 2000
Roberts of Conwy, Lord, 1991
Robertson of Port Ellen, Lord, 1997
Roch, Sir John, 1993
Rodger of Earlsferry, Lord, 1992
Rodgers of Quarry Bank, Lord, 1975
Rooker, Lord, 1999
Rose, Sir Christopher, 1992
Ross, *Hon.* Lord, 1985
Rumbold, Dame Angela, 1991
Ryder of Wensum, Lord, 1990
Sainsbury, Sir Timothy, 1992
St John of Fawsley, Lord, 1979
Salisbury, Marquess of, 1994
Sandiford, Erskine, 1989
Saville of Newdigate, Lord, 1994
Scarman, Lord, 1973
Schiemann, Sir Konrad, 1995
Scotland of Asthal, Baroness, 2001
Scott, Sir Nicholas, 1989
Scott of Foscote, Lord, 1991
Seaga, Edward, 1981
Sedley, Sir Stephen, 1999
Selkirk of Douglas, Lord, 1996
Shearer, Hugh, 1969
Sheldon, Lord, 1977
Shephard, Gillian, 1992
Shipley, Jennifer, 1998
Short, Clare, 1997
Simmonds, Kennedy, 1984
Simon of Glaisdale, Lord, 1961
Sinclair, Ian, 1977
Slade, Sir Christopher, 1982
Slynn of Hadley, Lord, 1992
Smith, Andrew, 1997
Smith, Christopher, 1997
Smith, Dame Janet, 2002
Smith, Jacqueline, 2003
Somare, Sir Michael, 1977
Spellar, John, 2001
Stanley, Sir John, 1984
Staughton, Sir Christopher, 1988
Steel of Aikwood, Lord, 1977
Stephen, Sir Ninian, 1979
Stewartby, Lord, 1989
Steyn, Lord, 1992
Strang, Gavin, 1997
Strathclyde, Lord, 1995
Straw, Jack, 1997
Stuart-Smith, Sir Murray, 1988
Sutherland, Lord, 2000
Symons of Vernham Dean, Baroness, 2001
Talboys, Sir Brian, 1977
Taylor, Ann, 1997
Tebbit, Lord, 1981
Templeman, Lord, 1978
Thatcher, Baroness, 1970
Thomas, Edmund, 1996
Thomas of Gwydir, Lord, 1964
Thomas, Sir Roger, 2003
Thomas, Sir Swinton, 1994
Thomson of Monifieth, Lord, 1966
Thorpe, Jeremy, 1967
Thorpe, Sir Matthew, 1995
Tipping, Andrew, 1998
Tizard, Robert, 1986
Trefgarne, Lord, 1989
Trimble, David, 1997
Trumpington, Baroness, 1992
Tuckey, Sir Simon, 1998
Ullswater, Viscount, 1994
Upton, Simon, 1999
Varley, Lord, 1974
Waddington, Lord, 1987
Waite, Sir John, 1993
Wakeham, Lord, 1983
Waldegrave of North Hill, Lord, 1990
Walker of Gestingthorpe, Lord, 1997
Walker of Worcester, Lord, 1970
Wall, Lord, 2004
Wallace, James, 2000
Waller, Sir Mark, 1996
Ward, Sir Alan, 1995
Watkins, Sir Tasker, 1980
Weatherill, Lord, 1980
Wheeler, Sir John, 1993
Widdecombe, Ann, 1997
Wigley, Dafydd, 1997
Williams, Alan, 1977
Williams of Crosby, Baroness, 1974
Wilson, Brian, 2003
Windlesham, Lord, 1973 (also known as Lord Hennessy)
Winti, Paias, 1987
Withers, Reginald, 1977
Woodhouse, Sir Owen, 1974
Woolf, Lord, 1986
Wylie, *Hon.* Lord, 1970
York, The Archbishop of, 1991
Young, Sir George, 1993
Young of Graffham, Lord, 1984
Zacca, Edward, 1992

THE PRIVY COUNCIL OF NORTHERN IRELAND

The Privy Council of Northern Ireland had responsibilities in Northern Ireland similar to those of the Privy Council in Great Britain until the Northern Ireland Act 1974 instituted direct rule and a UK Cabinet minister became responsible for the functions previously exercised by the Northern Ireland government.

Membership of the Privy Council of Northern Ireland is retained for life. Since the Northern Ireland Constitution Act 1973 no further appointments have been made. The postnominal initials PC (NI) are used to differentiate its members from those of the Privy Council.

MEMBERS *as at August 2004*

Bailie, Robin, 1971
Bleakley, David, 1971
Craig, William, 1963
Dobson, John, 1969
Kelly, Sir Basil, 1969
Kilclooney, Lord, 1970
Kirk, Herbert, 1962
Long, William, 1966
McIvor, Basil, 1971
Porter, Sir Robert, 1969

PARLIAMENT

The United Kingdom constitution is not contained in any single document but has evolved over time, formed partly by statute, partly by common law and partly by convention. A constitutional monarchy, the United Kingdom is governed by Ministers of the Crown in the name of the Sovereign, who is head both of the state and of the government.

The organs of government are the legislature (Parliament), the executive and the judiciary. The executive consists of HM Government (Cabinet and other Ministers), government departments, local authorities (*see* Local Government, Government Departments and Public Offices). The judiciary (*see* Law Courts and Offices) pronounces on the law, both written and unwritten, interprets statutes and is responsible for the enforcement of the law; the judiciary is independent of both the legislature and the executive.

THE MONARCHY

The Sovereign personifies the state and is, in law, an integral part of the legislature, head of the executive, head of the judiciary, commander-in-chief of all armed forces of the Crown and 'Supreme Governor' of the Church of England. The seat of the monarchy is in the United Kingdom. In the Channel Islands and the Isle of Man, which are Crown dependencies, the Sovereign is represented by a Lieutenant-Governor. In the member states of the Commonwealth of which the Sovereign is head of state, her representative is a Governor-General; in UK dependencies the Sovereign is usually represented by a Governor, who is responsible to the British Government.

Although in practice the powers of the monarchy are now very limited, restricted mainly to the advisory and ceremonial, there are important acts of government which require the participation of the Sovereign. These include summoning, proroguing and dissolving Parliament, giving royal assent to bills passed by Parliament, appointing important office-holders, e.g. government ministers, judges, bishops and governors, conferring peerages, knighthoods and other honours, and granting pardon to a person wrongly convicted of a crime. The Sovereign appoints the Prime Minister; by convention this office is held by the leader of the political party which enjoys, or can secure, a majority of votes in the House of Commons. In international affairs the Sovereign as head of state has the power to declare war and make peace, to recognise foreign states and governments, to conclude treaties and to annex or cede territory. However, as the Sovereign entrusts executive power to Ministers of the Crown and acts on the advice of her Ministers, which she cannot ignore, royal prerogative powers are in practice exercised by Ministers, who are responsible to Parliament.

Ministerial responsibility does not diminish the Sovereign's importance to the smooth working of government. She holds meetings of the Privy Council (*see* below), gives audiences to her Ministers and other officials at home and overseas, receives accounts of Cabinet decisions, reads dispatches and signs state papers; she must be informed and consulted on every aspect of national life; and she must show complete impartiality.

COUNSELLORS OF STATE

In the event of the Sovereign's absence abroad, it is necessary to appoint Counsellors of State under letters patent to carry out the chief functions of the Monarch, including the holding of Privy Councils and giving royal assent to acts passed by Parliament. The normal procedure is to appoint as Counsellors three or four members of the royal family among those remaining in the UK.

In the event of the Sovereign on accession being under the age of 18 years, or at any time unavailable or incapacitated by infirmity of mind or body for the performance of the royal functions, provision is made for a regency.

THE PRIVY COUNCIL

The Sovereign in Council, or Privy Council, was the chief source of executive power until the system of Cabinet government developed. Its main function is to advise the Sovereign to approve Orders in Council and to advise on the issue of royal proclamations. The Council's own statutory responsibilities (independent of the powers of the Sovereign in Council) include powers of supervision over the registering bodies for the medical and allied professions. A full Council is summoned only on the death of the Sovereign or when the Sovereign announces his or her intention to marry. (For a full list of Privy Counsellors, *see* The Privy Council section.)

There are a number of advisory Privy Council committees, whose meetings the Sovereign does not attend. Some are prerogative committees, such as those dealing with legislative matters submitted by the legislatures of the Channel Islands and the Isle of Man or with applications for charters of incorporation; and some are provided for by statute, e.g. those for the universities of Oxford and Cambridge and the Scottish universities.

The Judicial Committee of the Privy Council is the court of final appeal from courts of the UK dependencies, courts of independent Commonwealth countries which have retained the right of appeal and courts of the Channel Islands and the Isle of Man.

It also has certain jurisdiction within the United Kingdom, the most important of which is that it is the court of final appeal for 'devolution issues,' i.e. issues as to the legal competences and functions of the legislative and executive authorities established in Scotland, Wales and Northern Ireland by the devolution legislation of 1998.

The Committee is composed of Privy Counsellors who hold, or have held, high judicial office, although usually only three or five hear each case.

Administrative work is carried out by the Privy Council Office under the direction of the Lord President of the Council, a Cabinet Minister.

PARLIAMENT

Parliament is the supreme law-making authority and can legislate for the UK as a whole or for any parts of it separately (the Channel Islands and the Isle of Man are Crown dependencies and not part of the UK). The main functions of Parliament are to pass laws, to provide (by voting taxation) the means of carrying on the work of government and to scrutinise government policy and administration, particularly proposals for expenditure. International treaties and agreements are by custom presented to Parliament before ratification.

Parliament emerged during the late 13th and early 14th centuries. The officers of the King's household and the King's judges were the nucleus of early Parliaments, joined by such ecclesiastical and lay magnates as the King might summon to form a prototype 'House of Lords', and occasionally by the knights of the shires, burgesses and proctors of the lower clergy. By the end of Edward III's reign a 'House of Commons' was beginning to appear; the first known Speaker was elected in 1377.

Parliamentary procedure is based on custom and precedent, partly formulated in the Standing Orders of both Houses of Parliament, and each House has the right to control its own internal proceedings and to commit for contempt. The system of debate in the two Houses is similar; when a motion has been moved, the Speaker proposes the question as the subject of a debate. Members speak from wherever they have been sitting. Questions are decided by a vote on a simple majority. Draft legislation is introduced, in either House, as a bill. Bills can be introduced by a Government Minister or a private Member, but in practice the majority of bills which become law are introduced by the Government. To become law, a bill must be passed by each House (for parliamentary stages, *see* Bill, page 130) and then sent to the Sovereign for the royal assent, after which it becomes an Act of Parliament.

Proceedings of both Houses are public, except on extremely rare occasions. The minutes (called *Votes and Proceedings in the Commons*, and *Minutes of Proceedings in the Lords*) and the speeches (*The Official Report of Parliamentary Debates*, Hansard) are published daily. Proceedings are also recorded for transmission on radio and television and stored in the Parliamentary Recording Unit before transfer to the National Sound Archive. Television cameras have been allowed into the House of Lords since 1985 and into the House of Commons since 1989; committee meetings may also be televised.

By the Parliament Act of 1911, the maximum duration of a Parliament is five years (if not previously dissolved), the term being reckoned from the date given on the writs for the new Parliament. The maximum life has been prolonged by legislation in such rare circumstances as the two world wars (31 January 1911 to 25 November 1918; 26 November 1935 to 15 June 1945). Dissolution and writs for a general election are ordered by the Sovereign on the advice of the Prime Minister. The life of a Parliament is divided into sessions, usually of one year in length, beginning and ending most often in October or November.

DEVOLUTION

The Scottish Parliament has legislative power over all devolved matters, i.e. matters not reserved to Westminster or otherwise outside its powers. The National Assembly for Wales has power to make secondary legislation in the areas where executive functions have been transferred to it. The Northern Ireland Assembly has legislative authority in the fields previously administered by the Northern Ireland departments. The Assembly was suspended in October 2002 and dissolved in April 2003. For further information, *see* the Regional Government section.

THE HOUSE OF LORDS

London SW1A 0PW
T 020-7219 3000 **Information Office** 020-7219 3107
E hlinfo@parliament.uk
W www.parliament.uk

The House of Lords is the second chamber, or 'Upper House' of the UK's bi-cameral parliament. Until the beginning of the twentieth century, the House of Lords had considerable power, being able to veto any bill submitted to it by the House of Commons. Today the main functions of the House of Lords are to revise legislation, to act as a check on the Government, to provide a forum of independent expertise and to act as a final court of appeal.

The House of Lords has a number of Select Committees. Some relate to the internal affairs of the House – such as its management and administration – while others carry out important investigative work on matters of public interest. There are four main areas of work – Europe, Science, the Economy and the Constitution. House of Lords investigative committees look at broader issues and do not mirror Government Departments as do Select Committees in the Commons.

The House of Lords has judicial powers as the ultimate court of appeal for courts in Great Britain and Northern Ireland, except for criminal cases in Scotland. These powers are exercised by the Lords of Appeal in Ordinary (the Law Lords) (*see* Law Courts and Officers section). On 12 June 2003 the Government announced reforms affecting the role of the Lord Chancellor as a judge and Speaker of the House of Lords and establishing a separate Supreme Court (*see* Government Departments section).

Members of the House of Lords comprise life peers created under the Life Peerages Act 1958, 92 hereditary peers under the House of Lords Act 1999 and Lords of Appeal in Ordinary, i.e. Law Lords, under the Appellate Jurisdiction Act 1876. The Archbishops of Canterbury and York, the Bishops of London, Durham and Winchester, and the 21 senior diocesan bishops of the Church of England are also members.

The House of Lords Act provides for 90 elected hereditary peers to remain in the House of Lords until longer-term reform of the House has been carried out. Elections for each of the party groups and crossbenches were held in October and November 1999; 42 Conservative, 28 crossbench, three Liberal Democrat and two Labour. Fifteen office holders were elected by the Whole House. Two Hereditary Peers, the Earl Marshal and the Lord Great Chamberlain are also members.

Peers are disqualified from sitting in the House if they are:

- aliens, i.e. any peer who is not a British citizen, a Commonwealth citizen (under the British Nationality Act 1981) or a citizen of the Republic of Ireland
- under the age of 21
- undischarged bankrupts or, in Scotland, those whose estate is sequestered
- convicted of treason

Bishops retire at the age of 70 and cease to be members of the house at that time.

Peers who do not wish to attend sittings of the House of Lords may apply for Leave of Absence for the duration of a Parliament.

Members of the House of Lords are unpaid but are entitled to allowances for attendance at sittings of the House. The daily maxima are £128.00 for overnight subsistence, £64.00 for day subsistence and incidental travel, and £53.50 for secretarial costs (as at August 2004).

COMPOSITION *as at 1 August 2004*
Archbishops and Bishops, 26
Life peers under the Appellate Jurisdiction Act 1876, 29 (1 woman)
Life peers under the Life Peerages Act 1958, 567 (120 women)
Peers under the House of Lords Act 1999, 92 (4 women)
Total 714

STATE OF THE PARTIES *as at 1 August 2004**
Conservative, 206
Labour, 191
Liberal Democrats, 66
Crossbench, 179
Archbishops and Bishops, 26
Other, 35**
Total: 703

* Excluding 11 peers on leave of absence from the House
** Includes 24 newly created Life Peers who had not been introduced as at 1 July 2004

OFFICERS

The House is presided over by the Lord Chancellor, who is *ex officio* Speaker of the House. (On 12 June 2003 the Government announced proposals to end the role of the Lord Chancellor as a judge and Speaker of the House of Lords, *see* description of Lord Chancellor's role below and Government Departments section).

A panel of deputy Speakers is appointed by Royal Commission. The first deputy Speaker is the Chairman of Committees, appointed at the beginning of each session, who is a salaried officer of the House. He takes the chair when the whole House is in Committee and in some select committees. He is assisted by a panel of deputy chairmen, headed by the salaried Principal Deputy Chairman of Committees, who is also chairman of the European Communities Committee of the House.

The Clerk of the Parliaments is the Accounting Officer and the chief permanent official responsible for the administration of the House. The Gentleman Usher of the Black Rod is responsible for security and other services and also has royal duties as secretary to the Lord Great Chamberlain.

Secretary of State for Constitutional Affairs and Lord Chancellor (The Lord Chancellor's salary is paid by the Department for Constitutional Affairs and no salary is claimed as Lord Chancellor or Speaker of the House of Lords), The Rt. Hon. Lord Falconer of Thoroton, QC
Private Secretary, Mrs S. Albon
Chairman of Committees (£77,220), The Lord Brabazon of Tara
Principal Deputy Chairman of Committees (£72,243), The Lord Grenfell

HOUSE OF LORDS MANAGEMENT BOARD
Staff are placed in the following pay bands according to their level of responsibility and taking account of other factors such as experience and marketability.

Judicial Group 4	£150,878
Senior Band 3	£90,867–£129,352
Senior Band 2	£73,762–£119,303
Senior Band 1A	£62,004–£100,061
Senior Band 1	£53,541–£89,156
Band A1	£45,911–£65,533
Band A2	£37,861–£54,219

Clerk of the Parliaments (Judicial Group 4), P. D. G. Hayter, LVO
Clerk Assistant (Senior Band 3), M. G. Pownall
Reading Clerk and Clerk of the Journals (Senior Band 2), D. R. Beamish
Clerk of the Committees and Clerk of the Overseas Office (Senior Band 2), Dr R. H. Walters
Principal Finance Officer (Senior Band 1A), E. C. Ollard
Head of Human Resources (Senior Band 1A), Dr F. P. Tudor
Clerk of the Judicial Office and Registrar of Lords Interests (Senior Band 1A), B. P. Keith
Librarian (Senior Band 1A), D. L. Jones
Clerk of Public and Private Bill Office and Examiner of Petitions for Private Bills in the House of Lords (Senior Band 1), T. V. Mohan
Editor of the Official Report (Senior Band 1), Miss J. A. Bradshaw
Clerk of the Records (Senior Band 1), S. K. Ellison
Financial Adviser (Senior Band 1), M. J. Barram
Accountant (Senior Band 1), A. D. Underwood
Director of Public Information (Band A1), Miss M. L. Morgan
Counsel to the Chairman of Committees (Senior Band 2), D. W. Saunders, CB; A. Roberts
Second Counsel to the Chairman of Committees (Senior Band 2), Dr C. S. Kerse, CB
Legal Adviser to the Human Rights Committee (Senior Band 2), M. Hunt
Clerk of the Procedure Committee (Senior Band 1), M. E. Ollard
Clerks of Select Committees (Senior Band 1), S. P. Burton; J. A. Vaughan

DEPARTMENT OF THE GENTLEMAN USHER OF THE BLACK ROD
Gentleman Usher of the Black Rod and Serjeant-at-Arms (Senior Band 2), Lt.-Gen. Sir Michael Willcocks, KCB
Yeoman Usher of the Black Rod and Deputy Serjeant-at-Arms (Band A2), Brig. H. D. C. Duncan, MBE

SELECT COMMITTEES
The main House of Lords select committees, as at June 2004, are as follows:
European Union – Chair, The Lord Grenfell; *Clerk*, S. Burton
European Union – Sub-committees:
- *A (Economic and Financial Affairs and International Trade) – Chair*, The Lord Radice; *Clerk*, J. Brooke
- *B (Internal Market) – Chair*, The Lord Woolmer of Leeds; *Clerk*, P. Wogan
- *C (Foreign Affairs, Defence and Development Policy) – Chair*, The Lord Bowness; *Clerk*, A. Nelson
- *D (Agriculture and the Environment) – Chair*, The Lord Renton of Mount Harry; *Clerk*, N. Besly

E (Law and Institutions) – *Chair*, The Lord Scott of Foscote; *Clerk*, S. Todd
F (Home Affairs) – *Chair*, The Baroness Harris of Richmond; *Clerk*, T. Rawsthorne
G (Social and Consumer Affairs) – *Chair*, The Lord Williamson of Horton; *Clerk*, G. Baker
Constitution Committee – *Chair*, The Lord Norton of Louth; *Clerk*, I. Mackley
Delegated Powers and Regulatory Reform – *Chair*, The Lord Dahrendorf; *Clerk*, C. Salmon
Economic Affairs – *Chair*, The Lord Peston; *Clerk*, R. Graham-Harrison
Science and Technology – *Chair*, The Lord Oxburgh, FRCOG; *Clerk*, Dr C. S. Johnson
I – *Chair*, The Lord Mitchell; *Clerk*, M. Collon
II – *Chair*, The Lord Oxburgh; *Clerk*, Dr C. S. Johnson
Human Rights Joint Committee – *Chair*, Jean Corston, MP; *Lords Clerk*, N. Besly
House of Lords Reform Joint Committee – *Chair*, Dr Jack Cunningham, MP; *Lords Clerk*, D. Beamish

THE HOUSE OF COMMONS

London SW1A 0AA
T 020-7219 3000
Information Office 020-7219 4272
Forthcoming business 020-7219 5532
E hcinfo@parliament.uk
W www.parliament.uk

The members of the House of Commons are elected by universal adult suffrage. For electoral purposes, the United Kingdom is divided into constituencies, each of which returns one member to the House of Commons, the member being the candidate who obtains the largest number of votes cast in the constituency. To ensure equitable representation, the four Boundary Commissions keep constituency boundaries under review and recommend any redistribution of seats which may seem necessary because of population movements, etc. The number of seats was raised to 640 in 1945, reduced to 625 in 1948, and subsequently rose to 630 in 1955, 635 in 1970, 650 in 1983, 651 in 1992 and 659 in 1997. Of the present 659 seats, there are 529 for England, 40 for Wales, 72 for Scotland and 18 for Northern Ireland. The number of Scottish MPs at Westminster is likely to be cut by approximately 12 by 2007.

An electoral reform commission headed by Lord Jenkins of Hillhead proposed in October 1998 that the 'first-past-the-post' system of electing members of the House of Commons should be replaced by an alternative vote top-up system, under which 80–85 per cent of MPs would be elected by an alternative vote method and the remaining 15–20 per cent by an open-list system of proportional representation.

ELECTIONS

Elections are by secret ballot, each elector casting one vote; voting is not compulsory. For entitlement to vote in parliamentary elections, *see* Legal Notes section. When a seat becomes vacant between general elections, a by-election is held.

British subjects and citizens of the Irish Republic can stand for election as Members of Parliament (MPs) provided they are 21 or over and not subject to disqualification. Those disqualified from sitting in the House include:

- undischarged bankrupts
- people sentenced to more than one year's imprisonment
- members of the House of Lords (but hereditary peers not sitting in the Lords are eligible)
- holders of certain offices listed in the House of Commons Disqualification Act 1975, e.g. members of the judiciary, civil service, regular armed forces, police forces, some local government officers and some members of public corporations and government commissions.

A candidate does not require any party backing but his or her nomination for election must be supported by the signatures of ten people registered in the constituency. A candidate must also deposit with the returning officer £500, which is forfeit if the candidate does not receive more than 5 per cent of the votes cast. All election expenses at a general election, except the candidate's personal expenses, are subject to a statutory limit of £5,483, plus 4.6 pence for each elector in a borough constituency or 6.2 pence for each elector in a county constituency. These figures are due to be updated before the next General Election.

See pages 137–181 for an alphabetical list of MPs, results of the last general election and results of by-elections since the general election.

STATE OF THE PARTIES *as at 1 August 2004*

Conservative, 163 (14 women)
Labour, 407 (94 women)
Liberal Democrats, 55 (6 women)
Plaid Cymru, 4
Scottish National Party, 5 (1 woman)
Sinn Fein (have not taken their seats), 4 (1 woman)
Social Democratic Labour, 3
Democratic Unionist Party, 6 (1 woman)
Ulster Unionist, 5 (1 woman)
Independent, 3
The Speaker and three Deputy Speakers, 4 (1 woman)
Total, 659 (119 women)

BUSINESS

The week's business of the House is outlined each Thursday by the Leader of the House, after consultation between the Chief Government Whip and the Chief Opposition Whip. A quarter to a third of the time will be taken up by the Government's legislative programme and the rest by other business. As a rule, bills likely to raise political controversy are introduced in the Commons before going on to the Lords, and the Commons claims exclusive control in respect of national taxation and expenditure. Bills such as the Finance Bill, which imposes taxation, and the Consolidated Fund Bills, which authorise expenditure, must begin in the Commons. A bill of which the financial provisions are subsidiary may begin in the Lords; and the Commons may waive its rights in regard to Lords' amendments affecting finance.

The Commons has a public register of MPs' financial and certain other interests; this is published annually as a House of Commons paper. Members must also disclose any relevant financial interest or benefit in a matter before the House when taking part in a debate, in certain other proceedings of the House, or in consultations with other MPs, with Ministers or with civil servants.

MEMBERS' PAY AND ALLOWANCES

Since 1911 members of the House of Commons have received salary payments; facilities for free travel were introduced in 1924. Annual salary rates since 1911 are as follows:

1911	£400	1985 Jan	£16,904
1931	360	1986 Jan	17,702
1934	380	1987 Jan	18,500
1935	400	1988 Jan	22,548
1937	600	1989 Jan	24,107
1946	1,000	1990 Jan	26,701
1954	1,250	1991 Jan	28,970
1957	1,750	1992 Jan	30,854
1964	3,250	1994 Jan	31,687
1972 Jan	4,500	1995 Jan	33,189
1975 June	5,750	1996 Jan	34,085
1976 June	6,062	1996 July	43,000
1977 July	6,270	1997 April	43,860
1978 June	6,897	1998 April	45,066
1979 June	9,450	1999 April	47,008
1980 June	11,750	2000 April	48,371
1981 June	13,950	2001 April	49,822
1982 June	14,510	2002 April	55,118
1983 June	15,308	2003 April	56,358
1984 Jan	16,106	2004 April	57,485

In 1969 MPs were granted an allowance for secretarial and research expenses, revised in July 2001. From April 2004 Members receive an Incidental Expenses Provision (£19,325) and a staffing allowance (between £66,458 and £77,534).

Since 1972 MPs have been able to claim reimbursement for the additional cost of staying overnight away from their main residence while on parliamentary business; this is known as the Additional Costs Allowance and from April 2004 is £20,902 a year.

Members of staff who are paid out of the allowances can benefit from a sum not exceeding 10 per cent of their gross salary which is paid into the Portcullis Pension Plan. This sum comes from a central budget.

MEMBERS' PENSIONS

Pension arrangements for MPs were first introduced in 1964. The arrangements currently provide a pension of one-fiftieth of salary for each year of pensionable service with a maximum of two-thirds of salary at age 65. Pension is payable normally at age 65, for men and women, or on later retirement. Pensions may be paid earlier, e.g. on retirement due to ill health or at age 60 after 20 years' service. The widow/widower of a former MP receives a pension of five-eighths of the late MP's pension. Pensions are index-linked. Members currently contribute six or nine per cent of salary to the pension fund; there is an Exchequer contribution, currently 24 per cent of an MPs salary.

The House of Commons Members' Fund provides for annual or lump sum grants to ex-MPs, their widows or widowers, and children whose incomes are below certain limits or who are experiencing severe hardship. Members contribute £24 a year and the Exchequer £215,000 a year to the fund.

HOUSE OF COMMONS PAY BANDS

Staff are placed in the following Senior Civil Service pay bands. These pay bands apply to the most senior staff in departments and agencies.

Pay Band 1	£53,451–£112,248
Pay Band 2	£73,762–£155,008
Pay Band 3	£90,867–£192,424

* 2003 Pay Bands

OFFICERS AND OFFICIALS

The House of Commons is presided over by the Speaker, who has considerable powers to maintain order in the House. A Deputy Speaker, called the Chairman of Ways and Means, and two Deputy Chairmen may preside over sittings of the House of Commons; they are elected by the House, and, like the Speaker, neither speak nor vote other than in their official capacity.

The staff of the House are employed by a Commission chaired by the Speaker. The heads of the six House of Commons departments are permanent officers of the House, not MPs. The Clerk of the House is the principal adviser to the Speaker on the privileges and procedures of the House, the conduct of the business of the House, and committees. The Serjeant-at-Arms is responsible for security, ceremonial, and for accommodation in the Commons part of the Palace of Westminster.

Speaker (£130,347), The Rt. Hon. Michael J. Martin, MP (Glasgow Springburn)
Chairman of Ways and Means (£95,281), Sir Alan Haselhurst, MP (Saffron Walden)
First Deputy Chairman of Ways and Means (£90,703), Sylvia Heal, MP (Halesowen and Rowley Regis)
Second Deputy Chairman of Ways and Means (£90,703), Sir Michael Lord, MP (Suffolk Central and Ipswich North)

OFFICES OF THE SPEAKER AND CHAIRMAN OF WAYS AND MEANS

Speaker's Secretary (*£60,788–£98,099), R. K. Daw
Chaplain to the Speaker, Revd Canon R. Wright
Secretary to the Chairman of Ways and Means (£39,302–£53,600), J. Whatley

DEPARTMENT OF THE CLERK OF THE HOUSE

Clerk of the House of Commons (*£143,258), R. B. Sands
Clerk Assistant (*£89,085–£126,816), D. G. Millar
Clerk of Committees (*£89,085–£126,816), G. Cubie, CB
Clerk of Legislation (*£89,085–£126,816), Dr M. R. Jack
Principal Clerks (*£72,316–£116,964)
Table Office, Ms H. E. Irwin
Journals, W. A. Proctor
Principal Clerk and Deputy Head of Committee Office, R. W. G. Wilson
Principal Clerks (*£60,788–£98,099)
Overseas Office, Ms J. Sharpe
Bills, F. A. Cranmer
Clerk of Domestic Committees/Secretary to the Commission, R. J. Rogers
Select Committees, D. L. Natzler; D. W. N. Doig
Delegated Legislation, L. C. Laurence Smyth
Deputy Principal Clerks (*£52,403–£87,408), Dr C. R. M. Ward; A. Sandall; A. R. Kennon; S. J. Patrick; D. J. Gerhold; C. J. Poyser; D. F. Harrison; S. J. Priestley; A. H. Doherty; P. A. Evans; R. I. S. Phillips; Dr R. G. James; D. R. Lloyd; B. M. Hutton; J. S. Benger, DPHIL; Ms E. C. Samson; N. P. Walker; Mrs E. J. Flood; C. G. Lee; C. D. Stanton; Miss L. M. Gardner; F. J. Reid; C. A. Shaw; P. G. Moon; T. W. P. Healey; Mrs S. A. R. Davies; Mrs J. N. St J. Mulley; M. Hennessy; P. Aylett
Senior Clerks (*£34,979–£50,770), M. Clark; J. D. Whatley; K. C. Fox; J. D. W. Rhys; Mrs E. S. Hunt; Miss S. McGlashan; Mrs C. Oxborough;T. Goldsmith; H. A. Yardley; Ms K. Emms; N. P. Wright; M. Hillyard; J. H. Davies; M. P. Atkins; S. Mark; T. Jarvis; G.K. Clarke; G. F. J. Farrar; J. Patterson; C. Porro; M. Etherton; Ms C. A. Littleboy; Miss T. S. Garralty; Miss F. McLean; R. C. A.

Cooke; J. Gearson; G. McKee; D. Bates; Ms L. Spiers; I. Rogers; D. H. Griffiths ; D. Lees; A. Kidner; T. Byrne; Sir Edward Osmotherly; P. Harborne
Examiners of Petitions for Private Bills, F. A. Cranmer; T. Mohan
Registrar of Members' Interests (*£53,534–£87,598), Ms A. Barry
Taxing Officer, F. A. Cranmer

VOTE OFFICE
Deliverer of the Vote (£53,451–£112,248), J. F. Collins
Deputy Deliverers of the Vote (*£34,979–£50,770), O. B. T. Sweeney *(Parliamentary)*; R. Brook *(Development)*; Ms J. Pitt *(Production)*; A. Powell *(Systems)*

LEGAL SERVICES OFFICE
Speaker's Counsel and Head of Legal Services Office (£73,762–£155,008), J. E. G. Vaux
Counsel for European Legislation (£73,762–£155,008), M. Carpenter
Counsel for Legislation, A. D. Preston
Assistant Counsel (£53,451–£112,248), A. Akbar; P. Brooksbank

DEPARTMENT OF THE SERJEANT-AT-ARMS
Serjeant-at-Arms (£73,762–£155,008), M. J. A. Cummins
Deputy Serjeant-at-Arms (£53,451–£112,248), R. M. Morton
Assistant Serjeants-at-Arms, P. A. J. Wright; J. M. Robertson; M. Harvey

DEPARTMENT OF THE LIBRARY
Librarian (£73,762–£119,303), Miss P. J. Baines
Directors (£53,451–£89,156), K. G. Cuninghame *(Resources)*; R. Clements *(Research Services)*; Miss E. M. McInnes *(PIMS Project Director)*; B. Twigger *(Parliamentary and Reference Services)*; E. Wood *(Information Services)*
Heads of Sections (£47,667–£64,989), Dr C. Pond; Mrs C. Andrews; Ms F. Whittle; Ms D. Clark; C. Barclay; Mrs C. Gillie; Ms P. J. Strickland; R. Cracknell; P. Ryan T. Edmonds; B. Morgan
Senior Library Clerks (£39,302–£53,600), A. Seely; Ms F. Poole; Ms J. Lourie; D. Webb; Ms A. Thorp; Ms L. Conway; P. Ward; Ms S. Broadbridge; P. Bowers; T. Youngs; V. Miller; C. Sear; O. Gay; R. Kelly; Ms I. White; Ms H. Holden; K. Parry; Ms B. Brevitt; Ms D. Gore; Ms E. Downing; S. McGinnes; Ms J. Roll; S. Kennedy; T. Jarret; Ms W. Wilson

DEPARTMENT OF FINANCE AND ADMINISTRATION
Director of Finance and Administration (£73,762–£119,303), A. J. Walker
Director of Operations (£62,004–£100,061), A. A. Cameron
Director of Human Resource Management (£53,451–£89,156) Ms S. Craig
Director of Finance Policy (£53,451–£89,156), C. Ridley
Director of Internal Review Services (£47,667–£64,989), R. Russell

DEPARTMENT OF THE OFFICIAL REPORT
Editor, W. G. Garland (£73,762–£155,008)
Deputy Editors (£53,451–£112,248), V. A. Widgery; Miss L. Sutherland; Ms C. Fogarty

REFRESHMENT DEPARTMENT
Director of Catering Services (£62,004–£100,061), Mrs S. Harrison
Catering Operations Manager (Outbuildings) (£39,302–£53,600), Ms D. Herd
Food and Beverage Operations Manager, Palace of Westminster (£39,302–£53,600), R. Gibbs
Executive Chef (£34,979–£50,770), D. Dorricott
Business Development Manager (£34,797–£50,770), Mrs J. Rissen
Retail Manager (£34,979–£57,770), Mrs M. DeSouza
Human Resources and Development Manager (£39,302–£53,600), J. van den Broek

SELECT COMMITTEES
The more significant committees, as at 1 August 2004:

DEPARTMENTAL COMMITTEES
Accommodation and Works – Chair, Derek Conway, MP; *Clerk,* Tim Jarvis
Administration – Chair, Mrs M. Roe, MP; *Clerk,* Tim Jarvis
Constitutional Affairs – Chair, The Rt. Hon. Alan Beith, MP; *Clerk,* Roger Phillips
Culture, Media and Sport – Chair, The Rt. Hon. Gerald Kaufman, MP; *Clerks,* Fergus Reid; Olivia Davidson
Defence – Chair, The Rt. Hon. Bruce George, MP; *Clerks,* Steven Mark; Mark Hutton
Education and Skills – Chair, Barry Sheerman, MP, *Clerks,* David Lloyd; Susan Griffiths
Environment, Food and Rural Affairs – Chair, The Rt. Hon. Michael Jack, MP; *Acting Clerk,* Fiona McLean
Foreign Affairs – Chair, The Rt. Hon. Donald Anderson, MP; *Clerks,* Steve Priestley; Geoffrey Farrar
Health – Chair, David Hinchliffe, MP; *Clerks,* Dr John Benger; Keith Neary
Home Affairs – Chair, The Rt. Hon. John Denham, MP; *Clerks,* Dr Robin James; Mark Etherton
Information – Chair, Robert Key, MP; *Clerk,* Gordon Clarke
International Development – Chair, Tony Baldry, MP; *Clerks,* Alistair Doherty; Sarah Hartwell
Northern Ireland Affairs – Chair, Michael Mates, MP; *Clerk,* Dr John Patterson
Office of the Deputy Prime Minister: Housing, Planning, Local Government and the Regions – Chair, Andrew Bennett, MP; *Clerks,* Kate Emms; Libby Preston
Scottish Affairs – Chair, Mrs I. Adams, MP; *Clerk,* Mike Clark
Trade and Industry – Chair, Martin O'Neill, MP; *Clerks,* Mrs Elizabeth Flood; David Lees
Transport – Chair, Gwyneth Dunwoody, MP; *Clerks,* Eve Samson; David Bates
Treasury – Chair, The Rt. Hon. John McFall, MP; *Clerks,* Crispin Poyser; Alex Kidner
Welsh Affairs – Chair, Martyn Jones, MP; *Clerk,* James Davies
Work and Pensions – Chair, Sir Archy Kirkwood, MP; *Clerks,* Phillip Moon; Mick Hillyard

NON-DEPARTMENTAL COMMITTEES
Environmental Audit – Chair, Peter Ainsworth, MP; *Clerks,* Mike Hennessy; Lynne Spiers
European Scrutiny – Chair, Jimmy Hood, MP; *Clerks,* Dorian Gerhold; Jane Fox
Finance and Services – Chair, Sir Stuart Bell, MP; *Clerks,* Robert Rogers; Shona McGlashan
House of Lords Reform (Joint Committee) – Chair, The Rt.

Hon. Jack Cunningham, MP; *Clerks*, Malcolm Jack; David Beamish
Human Rights (Joint Committee) – *Chair*, The Rt. Hon. Jean Corston, MP; *Clerks*, Paul Evans; Nicolas Besly
Intelligence and Security (Cabinet Office) – *Chair*, The Rt. Hon. Ann Taylor, MP; *Clerks*, Alistair Corbett; Martin Sterling
Modernisation of the House of Commons – *Chair*, The Rt. Hon. Peter Hain, MP; *Clerks*, George Cubie; Tom Healey
Procedure – *Chair*, Sir Nicholas Winterton, MP; *Clerks*, Simon Patrick; Jenny McCullough
Public Accounts – *Chair*, Edward Leigh, MP; *Clerk*, Nick Wright
Public Administration – *Chair*, Tony Wright, MP; *Clerks*, Phillip Aylett; Clive Porro
Regulatory Reform – *Chair*, Peter Pike, MP; *Clerk*, Martyn Atkins
Science and Technology – *Chair*, Dr Ian Gibson, MP; *Clerks*, Chris Shaw; Emily Commander
Statutory Instruments (Joint Committee) – *Chair*, David Tredinnick, MP; *Clerks*, Martyn Atkins; Anna Murphy

PARLIAMENTARY INFORMATION

The following is a short glossary of aspects of the work of Parliament. Unless otherwise stated, references are to House of Commons procedures.

BILL – Proposed legislation is termed a bill. The stages of a public bill (for private bills, *see* page 131) in the House of Commons are as follows:
First Reading: This stage merely constitutes an order to have the bill printed.
Second Reading: The debate on the principles of the bill.
Committee Stage: The detailed examination of a bill, clause by clause. In most cases this takes place in a standing committee, or the whole House may act as a committee. A special standing committee may take evidence before embarking on detailed scrutiny of the bill. Very rarely, a bill may be examined by a select committee.
Report Stage: Detailed review of a bill as amended in committee.
Third Reading: Final debate on a bill. Public bills go through the same stages in the House of Lords, except that in almost all cases the committee stage is taken in committee of the whole House.

A bill may start in either House, and has to pass through both Houses to become law. Both Houses have to agree the same text of a bill, so that the amendments made by the second House are then considered in the originating House, and if not agreed, sent back or themselves amended, until agreement is reached.

CHILTERN HUNDREDS – A nominal office of profit under the Crown, the acceptance of which requires an MP to vacate his/her seat. The Manor of Northstead is similar. These are the only means by which an MP may resign.

CONSOLIDATED FUND BILL – A bill to authorise issue of money to maintain Government services. The bill is dealt with without debate.

EARLY DAY MOTION – A motion put on the notice paper by an MP without in general the real prospect of its being debated. Such motions are expressions of back-bench opinion.

FATHER OF THE HOUSE – The Member whose continuous service in the House of Commons is the longest. The present Father of the House is the Rt. Hon. Tam Dalyell.

HOURS OF MEETING – The House of Commons normally meets on Tuesdays, Wednesdays and Thursdays at 11.30 a.m., Mondays at 2.30 p.m. and some Fridays at 9.30 a.m. There are ten Fridays without sittings in each session. (*See also* Westminster Hall Sittings, below.) The House of Lords normally meets at 2.30 p.m. Monday to Wednesday and at 3 p.m. on Thursday. In the latter part of the session, the House of Lords sometimes sits on Fridays at 11 a.m.

LEADER OF THE OPPOSITION – In 1937 the office of Leader of the Opposition was recognised and a salary was assigned to the post. Since April 2003 this has been £121,840 (including parliamentary salary of £56,358). The present leader of the Opposition is Michael Howard.

THE LORD CHANCELLOR – The Lord High Chancellor of Great Britain is (*ex officio*) the Speaker of the House of Lords. Unlike the Speaker of the House of Commons, he is a member of the Government, takes part in debates and votes in divisions. He has none of the powers to maintain order that the Speaker in the Commons has, these powers being exercised in the Lords by the House as a whole. The Lord Chancellor sits in the Lords on one of the Woolsacks, couches covered with red cloth and stuffed with wool. If he wishes to address the House in any way except formally as Speaker, he leaves the Woolsack.

On 12 June 2003 the Prime Minister announced the creation of the Department for Constitutional Affairs, which will incorporate most of the responsibilities of the Lord Chancellor's department. The post of Lord Chancellor and the Department of the Lord Chancellor will eventually be abolished. Other changes announced include the replacement of the law lords with a Supreme Court as the final court of appeal, and the creation of a new Judicial Appointments Commission.

The current Lord Chancellor is Lord Falconer of Thoroton who will continue in the post until his powers are transferred to his new post of Secretary of State for Constitutional Affairs. Lord Falconer currently operates as a conventional Cabinet Minister and head of department, and is located together with his permanent secretary and departmental officials in the offices of the Lord Chancellor's department. For further information on the new Department for Constitutional Affairs *see* the Government section.

NORTHERN IRELAND GRAND COMMITTEE – The Northern Ireland Grand Committee consists of all MPs representing constituencies in Northern Ireland, together with not more than 25 other MPs nominated by the Committee of Selection. The business of the committee includes questions, short debates, ministerial statements, bills, legislative proposals and other matters relating exclusively to Northern Ireland, and delegated legislation.

The Northern Ireland Affairs Committee is one of the departmental select committees, empowered to examine the expenditure, administration and policy of the Northern Ireland Office and the administration and expenditure of the Crown Solicitor's Office.

OPPOSITION DAY – A day on which the topic for debate is chosen by the Opposition. There are 20 such days in a normal session. On 17 days, subjects are chosen by the Leader of the Opposition; on the remaining three days by the leader of the next largest opposition party.

PARLIAMENT ACTS 1911 AND 1949 – Under these

Acts, bills may become law without the consent of the Lords, though the House of Lords has the power to delay a public bill for 13 months from its first second reading in the House of Commons.

PRIME MINISTER'S QUESTIONS – The Prime Minister answers questions from 12.00 to 12.30 p.m. on Wednesdays.

PRIVATE BILL – A bill promoted by a body or an individual to give powers additional to, or in conflict with, the general law, and to which a special procedure applies to enable people affected to object.

PRIVATE MEMBER'S BILL – A public bill promoted by a Member who is not a member of the Government.

PRIVATE NOTICE QUESTION – A question adjudged of urgent importance on submission to the Speaker (in the Lords, the Leader of the House), answered at the end of oral questions, usually at 3.30 p.m.

PRIVILEGE – The following are covered by the privilege of Parliament:

(i) freedom of speech in parliamentary proceedings

(iii) the printing and publishing of anything relating to the proceedings of the two Houses is subject to privilege

(iv) each House is the guardian of its dignity and may punish any insult to the House as a whole

QUESTION TIME – Oral questions are answered by Ministers in the Commons from 2.30 to 3.30 p.m. Monday to Wednesday and 11.30 a.m. to 12.30 p.m. on Thursdays. Questions are also taken at the start of the Lords sittings, with a daily limit of four oral questions.

ROYAL ASSENT – The royal assent is signified by letters patent to such bills and measures as have passed both Houses of Parliament (or bills which have been passed under the Parliament Acts 1911 and 1949). The Sovereign has not given royal assent in person since 1854. On occasion, for instance in the prorogation of Parliament, royal assent may be pronounced to the two Houses by Lords Commissioners. More usually royal assent is notified to each House sitting separately in accordance with the Royal Assent Act 1967. The old French formulae for royal assent are then endorsed on the acts by the Clerk of the Parliaments.

The power to withhold assent resides with the Sovereign but has not been exercised in the UK since 1707.

SELECT COMMITTEES – Consisting usually of ten to fifteen members of all parties, select committees are a means used by both Houses in order to investigate certain matters.

Most select committees in the House of Commons are tied to departments: each committee investigates subjects within a government department's remit. There are other select committees dealing with public accounts (i.e. the spending by the Government of money voted by Parliament) and European legislation, and also domestic committees dealing, for example, with privilege and procedure. Major select committees usually take evidence in public; their evidence and reports are published by The Stationery Office. House of Commons select committees are reconstituted after a general election. For main committees, *see* page 129.

The principal select committee in the House of Lords is that on the European Communities, which has, at present, six sub-committees dealing with all areas of Community policy. The House of Lords also has a select committee on science and technology, which appoints sub-committees to deal with specific subjects, and a select committee on delegated powers and deregulation. For committees, *see* page 126. In addition, *ad hoc* select committees have been set up from time to time to investigate specific subjects. There are also some joint committees of the two Houses, e.g. the committees on statutory instruments and on parliamentary privilege.

THE SPEAKER – The Speaker of the House of Commons is the spokesman and chairman of the Chamber. He or she is elected by the House at the beginning of each Parliament or when the previous Speaker retires or dies. The Speaker neither speaks in debates nor votes in divisions except when the voting is equal.

VACANT SEATS – When a vacancy occurs in the House of Commons during a session of Parliament, the writ for the by-election is moved by a Whip of the party to which the member whose seat has been vacated belonged. If the House is in recess, the Speaker can issue a warrant for a writ, should two members certify to him that a seat is vacant.

WELSH AFFAIRS COMMITTEE – The Welsh Affairs Committee, one of the departmental select committees, was empowered to examine the expenditure, administration and policy of the Welsh Office. Following devolution, the role of the select committee has been questioned. If it continues, it will be concerned with the role and responsibilities of the relevant Secretary of State and on occasion the policy of the UK departments as it affects Wales.

WESTMINSTER HALL SITTINGS – Following a report by the Modernisation of the House of Commons Select Committee, the Commons decided in May 1999 to set up a second debating forum. It is known as 'Westminster Hall' and sittings are in the Grand Committee Room on Tuesdays from 10 a.m. to 1 p.m., Wednesdays from 9.30 a.m. to 2 p.m. and Thursdays from 2.30 p.m. for up to three hours. Sittings will be open to the public at the times indicated.

WHIPS – In order to secure the attendance of Members of a particular party in Parliament, particularly on the occasion of an important vote, Whips (originally known as 'Whippers-in') are appointed. The written appeal or circular letter issued by them is also known as a 'whip', its urgency being denoted by the number of times it is underlined. Failure to respond to a three-line whip is tantamount in the Commons to secession (at any rate temporarily) from the party. Whips are provided with office accommodation in both Houses, and Government and some Opposition Whips receive salaries from public funds.

PARLIAMENTARY EDUCATION UNIT

Norman Shaw Building (North), London SW1A 2TT
T 020-7219 2105
E edunit@parliament.uk
W www.explore.parliament.uk

GOVERNMENT OFFICE

The Government is the body of Ministers responsible for the administration of national affairs, determining policy and introducing into Parliament any legislation necessary to give effect to government policy. The majority of Ministers are members of the House of Commons but members of the House of Lords or of neither House may also hold ministerial responsibility. The Lord Chancellor is always a member of the House of Lords. The Prime Minister is, by current convention, always a member of the House of Commons.

THE PRIME MINISTER

The office of Prime Minister, which had been in existence for nearly 200 years, was officially recognised in 1905 and its holder was granted a place in the table of precedence. The Prime Minister, by tradition also First Lord of the Treasury and Minister for the Civil Service, is appointed by the Sovereign and is usually the leader of the party which enjoys, or can secure, a majority in the House of Commons. Other Ministers are appointed by the Sovereign on the recommendation of the Prime Minister, who also allocates functions amongst Ministers and has the power to obtain their resignation or dismissal individually.

The Prime Minister informs the Sovereign of state and political matters, advises on the dissolution of Parliament, and makes recommendations for important Crown-appointments, the award of honours, etc.

As the chairman of Cabinet meetings and leader of a political party, the Prime Minister is responsible for translating party policy into government activity. As leader of the Government, the Prime Minister is responsible to Parliament and to the electorate for the policies and their implementation.

The Prime Minister also represents the nation in international affairs, e.g. summit conferences.

THE CABINET

The Cabinet developed during the 18th century as an inner committee of the Privy Council, which was the chief source of executive power until that time. The Cabinet is composed of about 20 Ministers chosen by the Prime Minister, usually the heads of government departments (generally known as Secretaries of State unless they have a special title, e.g. Chancellor of the Exchequer), the leaders of the two Houses of Parliament, and the holders of various traditional offices.

The Cabinet's functions are the final determination of policy, control of government and co-ordination of government departments. The exercise of its functions is dependent upon enjoying majority support in the House of Commons. Cabinet meetings are held in private, taking place once or twice a week during parliamentary sittings and less often during a recess. Proceedings are confidential, the members being bound by their oath as Privy Counsellors not to disclose information about the proceedings.

The convention of collective responsibility means that the Cabinet acts unanimously even when Cabinet Ministers do not all agree on a subject. The policies of departmental Ministers must be consistent with the policies of the Government as a whole, and once the Government's policy has been decided, each Minister is expected to support it or resign.

The convention of ministerial responsibility holds a Minister, as the political head of his or her department, accountable to Parliament for the department's work. Departmental Ministers usually decide all matters within their responsibility, although on matters of political importance they normally consult their colleagues collectively. A decision by a departmental Minister is binding on the Government as a whole.

POLITICAL PARTIES

Before the reign of William and Mary the principal officers of state were chosen by and were responsible to the Sovereign alone and not to Parliament or the nation at large. Such officers acted sometimes in concert with one another but more often independently, and the fall of one did not, of necessity, involve that of others, although all were liable to be dismissed at any moment.

In 1693 the Earl of Sunderland recommended to William III the advisability of selecting a ministry from the political party which enjoyed a majority in the House of Commons and the first united ministry was drawn in 1696 from the Whigs, to which party the King owed his throne. This group became known as the Junto and was regarded with suspicion as a novelty in the political life of the nation, being a small section meeting in secret apart from the main body of Ministers. It may be regarded as the forerunner of the Cabinet and in the course of time it led to the establishment of the principle of joint responsibility of Ministers, so that internal disagreement caused a change of personnel or resignation of the whole body of Ministers.

The accession of George I, who was unfamiliar with the English language, led to a disinclination on the part of the Sovereign to preside at meetings of his Ministers and caused the appearance of a Prime Minister, a position first acquired by Robert Walpole in 1721 and retained by him without interruption for 20 years and 326 days.

DEVELOPMENT OF PARTIES

In 1828 the Whigs became known as Liberals, a name originally given to it by its opponents to imply laxity of principles, but gradually accepted by the party to indicate its claim to be pioneers and champions of political reform and progressive legislation. In 1861 a Liberal Registration Association was founded and Liberal Associations became widespread. In 1877 a National Liberal Federation was formed, with headquarters in London. The Liberal Party was in power for long periods during the second half of the 19th-century and for several years during the first quarter of the 20th-century, but after a split in the party the numbers elected were small from 1931. In 1988, a majority of the Liberals agreed on a merger with the Social Democratic Party under the title Social and Liberal Democrats; since 1989 they have been known as the Liberal Democrats. A minority continue separately as the Liberal Party.

Soon after the change from Whig to Liberal the Tory Party became known as Conservative, a name believed to have been invented by John Wilson Croker in 1830 and to have been generally adopted about the time of the passing of the Reform Act of 1832 to indicate that the preservation of national institutions was the leading principle of the party. After the Home Rule crisis of 1886 the dissentient Liberals entered into a compact with the Conservatives, under which the latter undertook not to contest their seats, but a separate Liberal Unionist organisation was maintained until 1912, when it was united with the Conservatives.

Labour candidates for Parliament made their first appearance at the general election of 1892, when there were 27 standing as Labour or Liberal-Labour. In 1900 the Labour Representation Committee was set up in order to establish a distinct Labour group in Parliament, with its own whips, its own policy, and a readiness to co-operate with any party which might be engaged in promoting legislation in the direct interest of labour. In 1906 the LRC became known as the Labour Party.

The Council for Social Democracy was announced by four former Labour Cabinet Ministers in January 1981 and in March 1981 the Social Democratic Party was launched. Later that year the SDP and the Liberal Party formed an electoral alliance. In 1988 a majority of the SDP agreed on a merger with the Liberal Party but a minority continued as a separate party under the SDP title. In 1990 it was decided to wind up the party organisation and its three sitting MPs were known as independent social democrats. None were returned at the 1992 general election.

Plaid Cymru was founded in 1926 to provide an independent political voice for Wales and to campaign for self-government in Wales.

The Scottish National Party was founded in 1934 to campaign for independence for Scotland.

The Social Democratic and Labour Party was founded in 1970, emerging from the civil rights movement of the 1960s, with the aim of promoting reform, reconciliation and partnership across the sectarian divide in Northern Ireland and of opposing violence from any quarter.

The Democratic Unionist Party was founded in 1971 to resist moves by the Ulster Unionist Party which were considered a threat to the Union. Its aim is to maintain Northern Ireland as an integral part of the UK.

The Ulster Unionist Council first met formally in 1905. Its objectives are to maintain Northern Ireland as an integral part of the UK and to promote the aims of the Ulster Unionist Party.

GOVERNMENT AND OPPOSITION

The government of the day is formed by the party which wins the largest number of seats in the House of Commons at a general election, or which has the support of a majority of members in the House of Commons. By tradition, the leader of the majority party is asked by the Sovereign to form a government, while the largest minority party becomes the official Opposition with its own leader and a 'Shadow Cabinet.' Leaders of the Government and Opposition sit on the front benches of the Commons with their supporters (the back-benchers) sitting behind them.

FINANCIAL SUPPORT

Financial support for Opposition parties in the House of Commons was introduced in 1975 and is commonly known as Short Money, after Edward Short, the Leader of the House at that time, who introduced the scheme. Short money allocation for 2004–5 is:

Conservative	£3,666,801.46
Liberal Democrats	£1,244,855.74
Plaid Cymru	£74,087.32
SNP	£119,875.41
SDLP	£58,416.99
Democratic Unionists	£84,812.59
Ulster Unionists	£101,576.31

A specific allocation for the Leader of the Opposition's office was introduced in April 1999 and has been set at £563,448.50 for the years 2004–5.

Financial support for Opposition parties in the House

of Lords was introduced in 1996 and is commonly known as Cranborne Money.

The parties included here are those with MPs sitting in the House of Commons in the present Parliament.

CONSERVATIVE PARTY

Conservative Central Office, 32 Smith Square, London SW1P 3HH
T 020-7222 9000 F 020-7222 1135
E ccoffice@conservatives.com
W www.conservatives.com

SHADOW CABINET *as at September 2004*
Leader of the Opposition, The Rt. Hon. Michael Howard, QC, MP
Deputy Leader and Secretary of State for International Affairs, The Rt. Hon. Michael Ancram, QC, MP
Chancellor of the Exchequer, The Rt. Hon. Oliver Letwin, MP
Secretary of State for Home Affairs, The Rt. Hon. David Davis, MP
Party Chairmen, Dr Liam Fox, MP; Lord Maurice Saatchi, MP
Chief Whip, The Rt. Hon. David Maclean, MP
Secretary of State for Defence, Hon. Nicholas Soames, MP
Secretary of State for Deregulation, The Rt. Hon. John Redwood, MP
Secretary of State for Education, Tim Collins, MP
Secretary of State for Environment and Transport, The Rt. Hon. Tim Yeo, MP
Secretary of State for the Family, The Rt. Hon. Theresa May, MP
Secretary of State for Health, Andrew Lansley, MP
Leader in the House of Lords, The Rt. Hon. Lord Strathclyde
Secretary of State for Local and Devolved Government Affairs, Caroline Spelman, MP
Secretary of State for Work and Pensions, David Willetts, MP

SCOTTISH CONSERVATIVE AND UNIONIST PARTY

83 Princes Street, Edinburgh EH2 2ER
T 0131-247 6890 F 0131-247 6891
E central.office@scottishtories.org.uk
W www.scottishtories.org.uk
Chairman, David Mitchell, CBE
Deputy Chairman, Mrs M. Goodman
Hon. Treasurer, Mrs J. Slater
Campaigns and Operations, Mark McInnes

LABOUR PARTY

16 Old Queen Street, London SW1H 9HP
T 0870-590 0200 F 020-7802 1234
E info@new.labour.org.uk
W www.labour.org.uk
Parliamentary Party Leader, The Rt. Hon. Tony Blair, MP
Deputy Party Leader, The Rt. Hon. John Prescott, MP
Leader in the Lords, The Rt. Hon. Baroness Amos
Chair, The Rt. Hon. Ian McCartney, MP
General Secretary, Matt Carter
General Secretary, Scottish Labour Party, L. Quinn

LIBERAL DEMOCRATS

4 Cowley Street, London SW1P 3NB
T 020-7222 7999 F 020-7799 2170
E info@libdems.org.uk
W www.libdems.org.uk
President, Lord Dholakia
Hon. Treasurer, Reg Clark
Chief Executive, Lord Chris Rennard
Parliamentary Party Leader, The Rt. Hon. Charles Kennedy, MP
Leader in the House of Commons, Paul Tyler, MP
Leader in the Lords, Baroness Williams of Grosby

LIBERAL DEMOCRAT SPOKESMEN *as at July 2004*
Deputy Leader and Foreign Secretary, The Rt. Hon. Menzies Campbell, QC, MP
Chancellor, Dr Vincent Cable, MP
Culture, Media and Sport, Don Foster, MP
Defence, Paul Keetch, MP
Education and Skills, Phil Willis, MP
Environment, Norman Baker, MP
Food and Rural Affairs, Andrew George, MP
Foreign Affairs, Michael Moore, MP
Health, Paul Burstow, MP
Home Affairs, Mark Oaten, MP
International Development, Tom Brake, MP
Office of the Deputy Prime Minister, Edward Davey, MP
Scotland and Transport, John Thurso, MP
Spokesperson for London, Simon Hughes, MP
Trade and Industry, Malcolm Bruce, MP
Treasury, David Laws, MP
Wales and Northern Ireland, Lembit Opik, MP
Women and Older People, Sandra Gidley, MP
Work and Pensions, Prof. Steve Webb, MP
Chair of the Parliamentary Party, Matthew Taylor, MP
Chair of Campaigns and Communications Committee, Lord Razzall

LIBERAL DEMOCRAT WHIPS
House of Lords, The Lord Roper of Thorney Island
House of Commons, Andrew Stunell, MP *(Chief Whip)*

SCOTTISH LIBERAL DEMOCRATS

4 Clifton Terrace, Edinburgh EH12 5DR
T 0131-337 2314 F 0131-337 3566
E administration@scotlibdems.org.uk
W www.scotlibdems.org.uk
Party President, Malcolm Bruce, MP
Party Leader, Jim Wallace, MSP
Convener, Judy Hayman
Vice-Convener, Keith Raffan, MSP; Karen Freel; Robert Brown
Treasurer, Douglas Herbison
Chief of Staff, Dr Derek Barrie

WELSH LIBERAL DEMOCRATS

Bay View House, 102 Bute Street, Cardiff CF10 5AD
T 029-2031 3400 F 029-2031 3401
E ldwales@cix.co.uk
W www.welshlibdems.org.uk
Party President, Rob Humphreys
Party Leader, Lembit Opik, MP
Chairman, Rob Humphreys
Treasurer, Phylip Hobson
Secretary, vacant
Administrative Officer, Abigail Hughes
Chief Executive, Chris Lines

PLAID CYMRU – THE PARTY OF WALES

18 Park Grove, Cardiff CF10 3BN
T 029-2064 6000 F 029-2064 6001
E post@plaidcymru.org
W www.plaidcymru.org
Party President, Dafydd Iwan
Chairman, John Dixon
Hon. Treasurer, Jeff Canning
Chief Executive/General Secretary, Dafydd Trystan

SCOTTISH NATIONAL PARTY

107 McDonald Road, Edinburgh EH7 4NW
T 0131-525 8900 F 0131-525 8901
E snp.hq@snp.org W www.snp.org
Parliamentary Party Leader, Alex Salmond, MSP
Chief Whip, Bruce Crawford, MSP
National Convener, Alex Salmond, MSP
Senior Vice-Convener, Nicola Sturgeon, MSP
National Treasurer, Jim Mather, MSP
National Secretary, Alasdair Allan
Chief Executive, Peter Murrell

NORTHERN IRELAND DEMOCRATIC UNIONIST PARTY

91 Dundela Avenue, Belfast BT4 3BU
T 028-9047 1155 F 028-9047 1797
E info@dup.org.uk W www.dup2win.com
Parliamentary Party Leader, Ian Paisley, MP, MEP, MLA
Deputy Leader, Peter Robinson, MP, MLA
Chairman, Maurice Morrow, MLA
Chief Executive, Allan Ewart
Hon. Treasurer, Gregory Campbell, MP, MLA
Party Secretary, Nigel Dodds, MP, MLA

SINN FEIN

53 Falls Road, Belfast BT12 4PD
T 028-9022 3000 F 028-9022 3001
E sfadmin@eircom.net W www.sinnfein.ie
Party President, Gerry Adams, MP, MLA
Vice-President, Pat Doherty, MP, MLA
Chief Negotiator, Martin McGuinness, MP, MLA
General Secretary, Robbie Smyth

SOCIAL DEMOCRATIC AND LABOUR PARTY

121 Ormeau Road, Belfast BT7 1SH
T 028-9024 7700 F 028-9023 6699
E sdlp@indigo.ie W www.sdlp.ie
Parliamentary Party Leader, Mark Durkan, MLA
Deputy Leader, Dr Alasdair McDonnell, MLA
Chief Whip, John Dallat, MLA
Chairperson, Patricia Lewsley, MLA
Hon. Treasurer, Berna McIvor
General Secretary, Geraldine Cosgrove

ULSTER UNIONIST PARTY

429 Holywood Road, Belfast BT4 2LN
T 028-9076 5500 F 028-9076 9419
E uup@uup.org W www.uup.org
Party Leader, The Rt. Hon. David Trimble, MP
Chief Whip, Ald. Roy Beggs, MP

ULSTER UNIONIST COUNCIL
President, Lord Rogan of Lower Iveagh
Leader, The Rt. Hon. David Trimble, MP, MLA
Chairman of the Executive Committee, James Cooper
Hon. Treasurer, Jack Allen, OBE
Vice-Chairman, David Campbell
Vice-Presidents, Lord Maginnis of Drumglass; Jim Nicholson, MEP; Cllr. Jim Rodgers, OBE; Mrs May Steele, MBE
Hon. Secretaries, Mrs Joan Carson; Cllr. Danny Kennedy, MLA; Cllr. Michael McGimpsey, MLA; Dermot Nesbitt, MLA
Assistant Honorary Treasurer, Edward Keown

SPEAKERS OF THE COMMONS

This list comprises Speakers of the House of Commons since 1708. The date of appointment given is the day on which the Speaker was first elected by the House of Commons. The appointment requires royal approbation before it is confirmed and this is usually given within a few days. The present Speaker is the 156th.

PARLIAMENT OF GREAT BRITAIN

Sir Richard Onslow *(Lord Onslow)*, 16 November 1708
William Bromley, 25 November 1710
Sir Thomas Hanmer, 16 February 1714
Spencer Compton *(Earl of Wilmington)*, 17 March 1715
Arthur Onslow, 23 January 1728
Sir John Cust, 3 November 1761
Sir Fletcher Norton *(Lord Grantley)*, 22 January 1770
Charles Cornwall, 31 October 1780
Hon. William Grenville *(Lord Grenville)*, 5 January 1789
Henry Addington *(Viscount Sidmouth)*, 8 June 1789

PARLIAMENT OF THE UNITED KINGDOM

Sir John Mitford *(Lord Redesdale)*, 11 February 1801
Charles Abbot *(Lord Colchester)*, 10 February 1802
Charles Manners-Sutton *(Viscount Canterbury)*, 2 June 1817
James Abercromby *(Lord Dunfermline)*, 19 February 1835
Charles Shaw-Lefevre *(Viscount Eversley)*, 27 May 1839
J. Evelyn Denison *(Viscount Ossington)*, 30 April 1857
Sir Henry Brand *(Viscount Hampden)*, 9 February 1872
Arthur Wellesley Peel *(Viscount Peel)*, 26 February 1884
William Gully *(Viscount Selby)*, 10 April 1895
James Lowther *(Viscount Ullswater)*, 8 June 1905
John Whitley, 27 April 1921
Hon. Edward Fitzroy, 20 June 1928
Douglas Clifton-Brown *(Viscount Ruffside)*, 9 March 1943
William Morrison *(Viscount Dunrossil)*, 31 October 1951
Sir Harry Hylton-Foster, 20 October 1959
Horace King *(Lord Maybray-King)*, 26 October 1965
Selwyn Lloyd *(Lord Selwyn-Lloyd)*, 12 January 1971
George Thomas *(Viscount Tonypandy)*, 2 February 1976
Bernard Weatherill *(Lord Weatherill)*, 15 June 1983
Betty Boothroyd, 27 April 1992
Michael Martin, 23 October 2000

MEMBERS OF PARLIAMENT *as at 1 September 2004*

*__Abbott,__ Ms Diane (*b.* 1953) *Lab., Hackney North and Stoke Newington,* Maj. 13,651
*__Adams,__ Gerard (Gerry) (*b.* 1948) *SF, Belfast West,* Maj. 19,342
*__Adams,__ Mrs K. Irene, JP (*b.* 1948) *Lab., Paisley North,* Maj. 9,321
*__Ainger,__ Nicholas R. (*b.* 1949) *Lab., Carmarthen West and Pembrokeshire South,* Maj. 4,538
*__Ainsworth,__ Peter M. (*b.* 1956) *C., Surrey East,* Maj. 13,203
*__Ainsworth,__ Robert W. (*b.* 1952) *Lab., Coventry North East,* Maj. 15,751
*__Alexander,__ Douglas G. (*b.* 1967) *Lab., Paisley South,* Maj. 11,910
Allan, Richard B. (*b.* 1966) *LD, Sheffield Hallam,* Maj. 9,347
*__Allen,__ Graham W. (*b.* 1953) *Lab., Nottingham North,* Maj. 12,240
*__Amess,__ David A. A. (*b.* 1952) *C., Southend West,* Maj. 7,941
*__Ancram,__ Rt. Hon. Michael A. F. J. K. (Earl of Ancram) (*b.* 1945) *C., Devizes,* Maj. 11,896
*__Anderson,__ Rt. Hon. Donald (*b.* 1939) *Lab., Swansea East,* Maj. 16,148
*__Anderson,__ Mrs Janet (*b.* 1949) *Lab., Rossendale and Darwen,* Maj. 5,223
*__Arbuthnot,__ Rt. Hon. James N. (*b.* 1952) *C., Hampshire North East,* Maj. 13,257
*__Armstrong,__ Rt. Hon. Hilary J. (*b.* 1945) *Lab., Durham North West,* Maj. 16,333
Atherton, Ms Candy K. (*b.* 1955) *Lab., Falmouth and Camborne,* Maj. 4,527
Atkins, Ms Charlotte (*b.* 1950) *Lab., Staffordshire Moorlands,* Maj. 5,838
*__Atkinson,__ David A. (*b.* 1940) *C., Bournemouth East,* Maj. 3,434
*__Atkinson,__ Peter L. (*b.* 1943) *C., Hexham,* Maj. 2,529
*__Austin,__ John E. (*b.* 1944) *Lab., Erith and Thamesmead,* Maj. 11,167
Bacon, Richard (*b.* 1962) *C., Norfolk South,* Maj. 6,893
*__Bailey,__ Adrian (*b.* 1945) *Lab. Co-op., West Bromwich West,* Maj. 11,355
Baird, Vera (*b.* 1950) *Lab., Redcar,* Maj. 13,443
*__Baker,__ Norman (*b.* 1957) *LD, Lewes,* Maj. 9,710
*__Baldry,__ Anthony B. (*b.* 1950) *C., Banbury,* Maj. 5,219
*__Banks,__ Anthony L. (*b.* 1943) *Lab., West Ham,* Maj. 15,645
Barker, Gregory (*b.* 1966) *C., Bexhill and Battle,* Maj. 10,503
*__Barnes,__ Harold (*b.* 1936) *Lab., Derbyshire North East,* Maj. 12,258
Baron, John (*b.* 1959) *C., Billericay,* Maj. 5,013
Barrett, John (*b.* 1954) *LD, Edinburgh West,* Maj. 7,589
*__Barron,__ Rt. Hon. Kevin J. (*b.* 1946) *Lab., Rother Valley,* Maj. 14,882
*__Battle,__ John D. (*b.* 1951) *Lab., Leeds West,* Maj. 14,935
*__Bayley,__ Hugh (*b.* 1952) *Lab., City of York,* Maj. 13,779
Beard, Nigel C. (*b.* 1936) *Lab., Bexleyheath and Crayford,* Maj. 1,472
*__Beckett,__ Rt. Hon. Margaret (*b.* 1943) *Lab., Derby South,* Maj. 13,855
Begg, Ms Anne (*b.* 1955) *Lab., Aberdeen South,* Maj. 4,388
*__Beggs,__ Roy (*b.* 1936) *UUP, Antrim East,* Maj. 128
*__Beith,__ Rt. Hon. Alan J. (*b.* 1943) *LD, Berwick upon Tweed,* Maj. 8,458
*__Bell,__ Stuart (*b.* 1938) *Lab., Middlesbrough,* Maj. 16,330
Bellingham, Henry (*b.* 1955) *Lab., Norfolk North West,* Maj. 3,485
*__Benn,__ Hilary J. (*b.* 1953) *Lab., Leeds Central,* Maj. 14,381
*__Bennett,__ Andrew F. (*b.* 1939) *Lab., Denton and Reddish,* Maj. 15,330
*__Benton,__ Joseph E. (*b.* 1933) *Lab., Bootle,* Maj. 19,043
Bercow, John S. (*b.* 1963) *C., Buckingham,* Maj. 13,325
*__Beresford,__ Sir Paul (*b.* 1946) *C., Mole Valley,* Maj. 10,153
*__Berry,__ Dr Roger (*b.* 1948) *Lab., Kingswood,* Maj. 13,962
*__Best,__ Harold (*b.* 1939) *Lab., Leeds North West,* Maj. 5,236
*__Betts,__ Clive J. C. (*b.* 1950) *Lab., Sheffield Attercliffe,* Maj. 18,844
Blackman, Ms Elizabeth M. (*b.* 1949) *Lab., Erewash,* Maj. 6,932
*__Blair,__ Rt. Hon. Tony C. L. (*b.* 1953) *Lab., Sedgefield,* Maj. 17,713
Blears, Hazel A. (*b.* 1956) *Lab., Salford,* Maj. 11,012
Blizzard, Robert J. (*b.* 1950) *Lab., Waveney,* Maj. 8,553
*__Blunkett,__ Rt. Hon. David (*b.* 1947) *Lab., Sheffield Brightside,* Maj. 17,049
*__Blunt,__ Crispin J. R. (*b.* 1960) *C., Reigate,* Maj. 8,025
*__Boateng,__ Rt. Hon. Paul Y. (*b.* 1951) *Lab., Brent South,* Maj. 17,380
Borrow, David S. (*b.* 1952) *Lab., Ribble South,* Maj. 3,792
*__Boswell,__ Timothy E. (*b.* 1942) *C., Daventry,* Maj. 9,649
*__Bottomley,__ Peter J. (*b.* 1944) *C., Worthing West,* Maj. 9,037
*__Bottomley,__ Rt. Hon. Virginia H. B. M. (*b.* 1948) *C., Surrey South West,* Maj. 861
*__Bradley,__ Rt. Hon. Keith (*b.* 1950) *Lab., Manchester Withington,* Maj. 11,524
Bradley, Peter C. S. (*b.* 1953) *Lab., The Wrekin,* Maj. 3,587
Bradshaw, Benjamin P. J. (*b.* 1960) *Lab., Exeter,* Maj. 11,759
*__Brady,__ Graham (*b.* 1967) *C., Altrincham and Sale West,* Maj. 2,941
Brake, Thomas A. (*b.* 1962) *LD, Carshalton and Wallington,* Maj. 4,547
*__Brazier,__ Julian W. H., TD (*b.* 1953) *C., Canterbury,* Maj. 2,069
Breed, Colin E. (*b.* 1947) *LD, Cornwall South East,* Maj. 5,375
Brennan, Kevin (*b.* 1959) *Lab., Cardiff West,* Maj. 11,321
Brooke, Annette (*b.* 1947) *LD, Dorset Mid and Poole North,* Maj. 384
*__Brown,__ Rt. Hon. J. Gordon, PHD (*b.* 1951) *Lab., Dunfermline East,* Maj. 15,063
*__Brown,__ Rt. Hon. Nicholas H. (*b.* 1950) *Lab., Newcastle upon Tyne East and Wallsend,* Maj. 14,223
Brown, Russell L. (*b.* 1951) *Lab., Dumfries,* Maj. 8,834
Browne, Desmond (*b.* 1952) *Lab., Kilmarnock and Loudoun,* Maj. 10,334
*__Browning,__ Mrs Angela F. (*b.* 1946) *C., Tiverton and Honiton,* Maj. 6,284
*__Bruce,__ Malcolm G. (*b.* 1944) *LD, Gordon,* Maj. 7,879
Bryant, Chris (*b.* 1962) *Lab., Rhondda,* Maj. 16,047
Buck, Ms Karen P. (*b.* 1958) *Lab., Regent's Park and Kensington North,* Maj. 10,266
*__Burden,__ Richard H. (*b.* 1954) *Lab., Birmingham Northfield,* Maj. 7,798

Burgon, Colin (*b.* 1948) *Lab., Elmet,* Maj. 4,171
Burnett, John P. A. (*b.* 1945) *LD, Devon West and Torridge,* Maj. 1,194
***Burnham,** Andy (*b.* 1970) *Lab., Leigh,* Maj. 16,362
***Burns,** Simon H. M. (*b.* 1952) *C., Chelmsford West,* Maj. 6,261
Burnside, David (*b.* 1952) *UUP, Antrim South,* Maj. 1,011
Burstow, Paul K. (*b.* 1962) *LD, Sutton and Cheam,* Maj. 4,304
Burt, Alistair (*b.* 1955) *C., Bedfordshire North East,* Maj. 8,577
***Butterfill,** John V. (*b.* 1941) *C., Bournemouth West,* Maj. 4,718
***Byers,** Rt. Hon. Stephen J. (*b.* 1953) *Lab., Tyneside North,* Maj. 20,668
Byrne, Liam (*b.* 1970) *Lab., Birmingham Hodge Hill,* Maj. 460
Cable, Dr J. Vincent (*b.* 1943) *LD, Twickenham,* Maj. 7,655
***Caborn,** Rt. Hon. Richard G. (*b.* 1943) *Lab., Sheffield Central,* Maj. 12,544
Cairns, David (*b.* 1966) *Lab., Greenock and Inverclyde,* Maj. 9,890
Calton, Patsy (*b.* 1948) *LD, Cheadle,* Maj. 33
Cameron, David (*b.* 1966) *C., Witney,* Maj. 7,973
Campbell, Alan (*b.* 1957) *Lab., Tynemouth,* Maj. 8,678
***Campbell,** Mrs Anne (*b.* 1940) *Lab., Cambridge,* Maj. 8,579
Campbell, Gregory (*b.* 1953) *DUP, Londonderry East,* Maj. 1,901
***Campbell,** Ronald (*b.* 1943) *Lab., Blyth Valley,* Maj. 12,188
***Campbell,** Rt. Hon. W. Menzies, CBE, QC (*b.* 1941), *LD, Fife North East,* Maj. 9,736
***Caplin,** Ivor K. (*b.* 1958) *Lab., Hove,* Maj. 3,171
Carmichael, Alistair (*b.* 1965) *LD, Orkney and Shetland,* Maj. 3,475
Casale, Roger M. (*b.* 1960) *Lab., Wimbledon,* Maj. 3,744
***Cash,** William N. P. (*b.* 1940) *C., Stone,* Maj. 6,036
Caton, Martin P. (*b.* 1951) *Lab., Gower,* Maj. 7,395
***Cawsey,** Ian A. (*b.* 1960) *Lab., Brigg and Goole,* Maj. 3,961
Challen, Colin (*b.* 1953) *Lab., Morley and Rothwell,* Maj. 12,090
***Chapman,** J. K. (Ben) (*b.* 1940) *Lab., Wirral South,* Maj. 5,049
***Chapman,** Sir Sydney (*b.* 1935) *C., Chipping Barnet,* Maj. 2,701
***Chaytor,** David M. (*b.* 1949) *Lab., Bury North,* Maj. 6,532
***Chidgey,** David W. G. (*b.* 1942) *LD, Eastleigh,* Maj. 3,058
***Chope,** Christopher R., OBE (*b.* 1947) *C., Christchurch,* Maj. 13,544
***Clapham,** Michael (*b.* 1943) *Lab., Barnsley West and Penistone,* Maj. 12,352
***Clappison,** W. James (*b.* 1956) *C., Hertsmere,* Maj. 4,902
Clark, Mrs Helen R. (*b.* 1954) *Lab., Peterborough,* Maj. 384
Clark, Dr Lynda M., QC (*b.* 1949) *Lab., Edinburgh Pentlands,* Maj. 1,742
Clark, Paul G. (*b.* 1957) *Lab., Gillingham,* Maj. 2,272
Clarke, Anthony R. (*b.* 1963) *Lab., Northampton South,* Maj. 885
***Clarke,** Rt. Hon. Charles R. (*b.* 1950) *Lab., Norwich South,* Maj. 8,816
***Clarke,** Rt. Hon. Kenneth H., QC (*b.* 1940) *C., Rushcliffe,* Maj. 7,357
***Clarke,** Rt. Hon. Thomas, CBE (*b.* 1941) *Lab., Coatbridge and Chryston,* Maj. 15,314
***Clelland,** David G. (*b.* 1943) *Lab., Tyne Bridge,* Maj. 14,889
***Clifton-Brown,** Geoffrey R. (*b.* 1953) *C., Cotswold,* Maj. 11,983
***Clwyd,** Ann (*b.* 1937) *Lab., Cynon Valley,* Maj. 12,998
***Coaker,** Vernon R. (*b.* 1953) *Lab., Gedling,* Maj. 5,598
***Coffey,** Ms M. Ann (*b.* 1946) *Lab., Stockport,* Maj. 11,569
***Cohen,** Harry M. (*b.* 1949) *Lab., Leyton and Wanstead,* Maj. 12,904
Coleman, Iain (*b.* 1958) *Lab., Hammersmith and Fulham,* Maj. 2,015
Collins, Timothy W. G., CBE (*b.* 1964) *C., Westmorland and Lonsdale,* Maj. 3,147
Colman, Anthony (*b.* 1943) *Lab., Putney,* Maj. 2,771
***Connarty,** Michael (*b.* 1947) *Lab., Falkirk East,* Maj. 10,712
Conway, Derek (*b.* 1953) *C., Old Bexley and Sidcup,* Maj. 3,345
***Cook,** Frank (*b.* 1935) *Lab., Stockton North,* Maj. 14,647
***Cook,** Rt. Hon. R. F. (Robin) (*b.* 1946) *Lab., Livingston,* Maj. 10,616
Cooper, Ms Yvette (*b.* 1969) *Lab., Pontefract and Castleford,* Maj. 16,378
***Corbyn,** Jeremy B. (*b.* 1949) *Lab., Islington North,* Maj. 12,958
***Cormack,** Sir Patrick, FSA (*b.* 1939) *C., Staffordshire South,* Maj. 6,881
***Corston,** Ms Jean A. (*b.* 1942) *Lab., Bristol East,* Maj. 13,392
Cotter, Brian J. (*b.* 1938) *LD, Weston-super-Mare,* Maj. 338
***Cousins,** James M. (*b.* 1944) *Lab., Newcastle upon Tyne Central,* Maj. 11,605
***Cox,** Thomas M. (*b.* 1930) *Lab., Tooting,* Maj. 10,400
***Cran,** James D. (*b.* 1944) *C., Beverley and Holderness,* Maj. 781
Cranston, Ross F., QC (*b.* 1948) *Lab., Dudley North,* Maj. 6,800
***Crausby,** David A. (*b.* 1946) *Lab., Bolton North East,* Maj. 8,422
Cruddas, Jon (*b.* 1965) *Lab., Dagenham,* Maj. 8,693
Cryer, Mrs C. Ann (*b.* 1939) *Lab., Keighley,* Maj. 4,005
Cryer, John R. (*b.* 1964) *Lab., Hornchurch,* Maj. 1,482
***Cummings,** John S. (*b.* 1943) *Lab., Easington,* Maj. 21,949
***Cunningham,** Rt. Hon. Dr. J. A. (Jack), PHD (*b.* 1939) *Lab., Copeland,* Maj. 4,964
***Cunningham,** James D. (*b.* 1941) *Lab., Coventry South,* Maj. 8,279
Cunningham, Tony (*b.* 1952) *Lab., Workington,* Maj. 10,850
***Curry,** Rt. Hon. David M. (*b.* 1944) *C., Skipton and Ripon,* Maj. 12,930
Curtis-Thomas, Ms Claire (*b.* 1958) *Lab., Crosby,* Maj. 8,353
***Dalyell,** Tam (*b.* 1932) *Lab., Linlithgow,* Maj. 9,129
***Darling,** Rt. Hon. Alistair M. (*b.* 1953) *Lab., Edinburgh Central,* Maj. 8,142
Davey, Edward J. (*b.* 1965) *LD, Kingston and Surbiton,* Maj. 15,676
Davey, Ms Valerie (*b.* 1940) *Lab., Bristol West,* Maj. 4,426
David, Wayne (*b.* 1957) *Lab., Caerphilly,* Maj. 14,425

*__Davidson,__ Ian G. (*b.* 1950) *Lab. Co-op., Glasgow Pollok,* Maj. 11,268
*__Davies,__ Rt. Hon. D. J. Denzil (*b.* 1938) *Lab., Llanelli,* Maj. 6,403
Davies, Geraint R. (*b.* 1960) *Lab., Croydon Central,* Maj. 3,984
*__Davies,__ J. Quentin (*b.* 1944) *C., Grantham and Stamford,* Maj. 4,518
*__Davis,__ Rt. Hon. David M. (*b.* 1948) *C., Haltemprice and Howden,* Maj. 1,903
Dawson, T. Hilton (*b.* 1953) *Lab., Lancaster and Wyre,* Maj. 481
Dean, Ms Janet E. A. (*b.* 1949) *Lab., Burton,* Maj. 4,849
*__Denham,__ Rt. Hon. John Y. (*b.* 1953) *Lab., Southampton Itchen,* Maj. 11,223
*__Dhanda,__ Parmjit (*b.* 1971) *Lab., Gloucester,* Maj. 3,880
*__Dismore,__ Andrew H. (*b.* 1954) *Lab., Hendon,* Maj. 7,417
Djanogly, Jonathan (*b.* 1965) *C., Huntingdon,* Maj. 12,792
Dobbin, James (*b.* 1941) *Lab. Co-op., Heywood and Middleton,* Maj. 11,670
*__Dobson,__ Rt. Hon. Frank G. (*b.* 1940) *Lab., Holborn and St Pancras,* Maj. 11,175
Dodds, Nigel, MLA (*b.* 1958) *DUP, Belfast North,* Maj. 6,387
Doherty, Pat (*b.* 1945) *SF, Tyrone West,* Maj. 5,040
Donaldson, Jeffrey M. (*b.* 1962) *UUP, Lagan Valley,* Maj. 18,342
*__Donohoe,__ Brian H. (*b.* 1948) *Lab., Cunninghame South,* Maj. 11,230
Doran, Frank (*b.* 1949) *Lab., Aberdeen Central,* Maj. 6,646
*__Dorrell,__ Rt. Hon. Stephen J. (*b.* 1952) *C., Charnwood,* Maj. 7,739
Doughty, Sue (*b.* 1955) *LD, Guildford,* Maj. 538
*__Dowd,__ James P. (*b.* 1951) *Lab., Lewisham West,* Maj. 11,920
Drew, David E. (*b.* 1952) *Lab. Co-op., Stroud,* Maj. 5,039
Drown, Ms Julia K. (*b.* 1962) *Lab., Swindon South,* Maj. 7,341
*__Duncan,__ Alan J. C. (*b.* 1957) *C., Rutland and Melton,* Maj. 8,612
Duncan, Peter (*b.* 1965) *C., Galloway and Upper Nithsdale,* Maj. 74
*__Duncan Smith,__ G. Iain (*b.* 1954) *C., Chingford and Woodford Green,* Maj. 5,487
*__Dunwoody,__ Hon. Mrs Gwyneth P. (*b.* 1930) *Lab., Crewe and Nantwich,* Maj. 9,906
*__Eagle,__ Ms Angela (*b.* 1961) *Lab., Wallasey,* Maj. 12,276
Eagle, Ms Maria (*b.* 1961) *Lab., Liverpool Garston,* Maj. 12,494
Edwards, Huw W. E. (*b.* 1953) *Lab., Monmouth,* Maj. 384
Efford, Clive S. (*b.* 1958) *Lab., Eltham,* Maj. 6,996
*__Ellman,__ Mrs Louise J. (*b.* 1945) *Lab. Co-op., Liverpool Riverside,* Maj. 13,950
*__Ennis,__ Jeffrey (*b.* 1952) *Lab., Barnsley East and Mexborough,* Maj. 16,789
*__Etherington,__ William (*b.* 1941) *Lab., Sunderland North,* Maj. 13,354
*__Evans,__ Nigel M. (*b.* 1957) *C., Ribble Valley,* Maj. 11,238
Ewing, Annabelle (*b.* 1960) *SNP, Perth,* Maj. 48
*__Fabricant,__ Michael L. D. (*b.* 1950) *C., Lichfield,* Maj. 4,426
*__Fallon,__ Michael C. (*b.* 1952) *C., Sevenoaks,* Maj. 10,154
Farrelly, Paul (*b.* 1962) *Lab., Newcastle under Lyme,* Maj. 9,986
*__Field,__ Rt. Hon. Frank (*b.* 1942) *Lab., Birkenhead,* Maj. 15,591
*__Field,__ Mark (*b.* 1934) *C., Cities of London and Westminster,* Maj. 4,499
*__Fisher,__ Mark (*b.* 1944) *Lab., Stoke-on-Trent Central,* Maj. 11,845
*__Fitzpatrick,__ James (*b.* 1952) *Lab., Poplar and Canning Town,* Maj. 14,104
*__Fitzsimons,__ Mrs Lorna (*b.* 1967) *Lab., Rochdale,* Maj. 5,655
*__Flight,__ Howard E. (*b.* 1948) *C., Arundel and South Downs,* Maj. 13,704
*__Flint,__ Ms Caroline L. (*b.* 1961) *Lab., Don Valley,* Maj. 9,520
Flook, Adrian (*b.* 1963) *C., Taunton,* Maj. 235
*__Flynn,__ Paul P. (*b.* 1935) *Lab., Newport West,* Maj. 9,304
Follett, Ms D. Barbara (*b.* 1942) *Lab., Stevenage,* Maj. 8,566
*__Forth,__ Rt. Hon. Eric (*b.* 1944) *C., Bromley and Chislehurst,* Maj. 9,037
*__Foster,__ Rt. Hon. Derek (*b.* 1937) *Lab., Bishop Auckland,* Maj. 13,926
*__Foster,__ Donald M. E. (*b.* 1947) *LD, Bath,* Maj. 9,894
Foster, Michael (*b.* 1963) *Lab., Worcester,* Maj. 5,766
*__Foster,__ Michael J. (*b.* 1946) *Lab., Hastings and Rye,* Maj. 4,308
*__Foulkes,__ Rt. Hon. George (*b.* 1942) *Lab. Co-op., Carrick, Cumnock and Doon Valley,* Maj. 14,856
*__Fox,__ Dr Liam (*b.* 1961) *C., Woodspring,* Maj. 8,798
Francis, Dr David Hywel (*b.* 1946) *Lab., Aberavon,* Maj. 16,108
Francois, Mark, PHD (*b.* 1965) *C., Rayleigh,* Maj. 8,290
*__Gale,__ Roger J. (*b.* 1943) *C., Thanet North,* Maj. 6,650
*__Galloway,__ George (*b.* 1954) *Ind. Lab., Glasgow Kelvin,* Maj. 7,260
*__Gapes,__ Michael J. (*b.* 1952) *Lab. Co-op., Ilford South,* Maj. 13,997
Gardiner, Barry S. (*b.* 1957) *Lab., Brent North,* Maj. 10,205
*__Garnier,__ Edward H., QC (*b.* 1952) *C., Harborough,* Maj. 5,252
George, Andrew H. (*b.* 1958) *LD, St Ives,* Maj. 10,053
*__George,__ Rt. Hon. Bruce T. (*b.* 1942) *Lab., Walsall South,* Maj. 9,931
*__Gerrard,__ Neil F. (*b.* 1942) *Lab., Walthamstow,* Maj. 15,181
*__Gibb,__ Nicholas J. (*b.* 1960) *C., Bognor Regis and Littlehampton,* Maj. 5,643
*__Gibson,__ Dr Ian (*b.* 1938) *Lab., Norwich North,* Maj. 5,863
*__Gidley,__ Sandra (*b.* 1957) *LD, Romsey,* Maj. 2,370
Gildernew, Michelle (*b.* 1970) *SF, Fermanagh and South Tyrone,* Maj. 53
Gill, Parmjit Singh (*b.* 1966) *LD, Leicester South,* Maj. 1,654
*__Gillan,__ Mrs Cheryl E. K. (*b.* 1952) *C., Chesham and Amersham,* Maj. 11,882
Gilroy, Mrs Linda (*b.* 1949) *Lab. Co-op., Plymouth Sutton,* Maj. 7,517
*__Godsiff,__ Roger D. (*b.* 1946) *Lab., Birmingham Sparkbrook and Small Heath,* Maj. 16,246
Goggins, Paul G. (*b.* 1953) *Lab., Wythenshawe and Sale East,* Maj. 12,608
Goodman, Paul (*b.* 1960) *C., Wycombe,* Maj. 3,168
Gray, James W. (*b.* 1954) *C., Wiltshire North,* Maj. 3,878
Grayling, Chris (*b.* 1962) *C., Epsom and Ewell,* Maj. 10,080
Green, Damian H. (*b.* 1956) *C., Ashford,* Maj. 7,359
Green, Matthew (*b.* 1970) *LD, Ludlow,* Maj. 1,630
*__Greenway,__ John R. (*b.* 1946) *C., Ryedale,* Maj. 4,875

*__Grieve__, Dominic C. R. (*b.* 1956) *C., Beaconsfield,* Maj. 11,065
*__Griffiths__, Ms Jane P. (*b.* 1954) *Lab., Reading East,* Maj. 5,588
*__Griffiths__, Nigel (*b.* 1955) *Lab., Edinburgh South,* Maj. 5,499
*__Griffiths__, Winston J. (*b.* 1943) *Lab., Bridgend,* Maj. 10,045
Grogan, John T. (*b.* 1961) *Lab., Selby,* Maj. 2,138
*__Gummer__, Rt. Hon. John S. (*b.* 1939) *C., Suffolk Coastal,* Maj. 4,326
*__Hague__, Rt. Hon. William J. (*b.* 1961) *C., Richmond,* Maj. 16,319
*__Hain__, Rt. Hon. Peter G. (*b.* 1950) *Lab., Neath,* Maj. 14,816
*__Hall__, Michael T. (*b.* 1952) *Lab., Weaver Vale,* Maj. 9,637
Hall, Patrick (*b.* 1951) *Lab., Bedford,* Maj. 6,157
Hamilton, David (*b.* 1950) *Lab., Midlothian,* Maj. 9,014
*__Hamilton__, Fabian (*b.* 1955) *Lab., Leeds North East,* Maj. 7,089
Hammond, Philip (*b.* 1955) *C., Runnymede and Weybridge,* Maj. 8,360
*__Hancock__, Michael T., CBE (*b.* 1946) *LD, Portsmouth South,* Maj. 6,094
*__Hanson__, David G. (*b.* 1957) *Lab., Delyn,* Maj. 8,065
*__Harman__, Rt. Hon. Harriet, QC (*b.* 1950) *Lab., Camberwell and Peckham,* Maj. 14,123
*__Harris__, Dr Evan (*b.* 1965) *LD, Oxford West and Abingdon,* Maj. 9,185
Harris, Tom (*b.* 1964) *Lab., Glasgow Cathcart,* Maj. 10,816
*__Harvey__, Nicholas B. (*b.* 1961) *LD, Devon North,* Maj. 2,984
*__Haselhurst__, Rt. Hon. Sir Alan (*b.* 1937) *C., Saffron Walden,* Maj. 12,004
Havard, Dai (*b.* 1949) *Lab., Merthyr Tydfil and Rhymney,* Maj. 14,923
Hawkins, Nick (*b.* 1957) *C., Surrey Heath,* Maj. 10,819
Hayes, John H. (*b.* 1958) *C., South Holland and the Deepings,* Maj. 11,099
*__Heal__, Mrs Sylvia L. (*b.* 1942) *Lab., Halesowen and Rowley Regis,* Maj. 7,359
*__Heald__, Oliver (*b.* 1954) *C., Hertfordshire North East,* Maj. 3,444
Healey, John (*b.* 1960) *Lab., Wentworth,* Maj. 16,449
Heath, David W., CBE (*b.* 1954) *LD, Somerton and Frome,* Maj. 668
*__Heathcoat-Amory__, Rt. Hon. David P. (*b.* 1949) *C., Wells,* Maj. 2,796
*__Henderson__, Douglas J. (*b.* 1949) *Lab., Newcastle upon Tyne North,* Maj. 14,450
Henderson, Ivan J. (*b.* 1958) *Lab., Harwich,* Maj. 2,596
*__Hendrick__, Mark (*b.* 1958) *Lab.Co-op., Preston,* Maj. 12,268
Hendry, Charles (*b.* 1959) *C., Wealden,* Maj. 13,772
Hepburn, Stephen (*b.* 1959) *Lab., Jarrow,* Maj. 17,595
*__Heppell__, John (*b.* 1948) *Lab., Nottingham East,* Maj. 10,320
Hermon, Lady Sylvia (*b.* 1956) *UUP, Down North,* Maj. 7,324
Hesford, Stephen (*b.* 1957) *Lab., Wirral West,* Maj. 4,035
Hewitt, Rt. Hon. Patricia H. (*b.* 1948) *Lab., Leicester West,* Maj. 9,639
Heyes, David (*b.* 1946) *Lab., Ashton under Lyne,* Maj. 15,518
*__Hill__, Rt. Hon. Keith T. (*b.* 1943) *Lab., Streatham,* Maj. 14,270
*__Hinchliffe__, David M. (*b.* 1948) *Lab., Wakefield,* Maj. 7,954
Hoban, Mark (*b.* 1964) *C., Fareham,* Maj. 7,009
*__Hodge__, Rt. Hon. Mrs Margaret E., MBE (*b.* 1944) *Lab., Barking,* Maj. 9,534
*__Hoey__, Ms Catharine (Kate) L. (*b.* 1946) *Lab., Vauxhall,* Maj. 13,018
*__Hogg__, Rt. Hon. Douglas M., QC (*b.* 1945) *C., Sleaford and North Hykeham,* Maj. 8,622
Holmes, Paul (*b.* 1957) *LD, Chesterfield,* Maj. 2,586
*__Hood__, James (*b.* 1948) *Lab., Clydesdale,* Maj. 7,794
*__Hoon__, Rt. Hon. Geoffrey W. (*b.* 1953) *Lab., Ashfield,* Maj. 13,268
Hope, Philip I. (*b.* 1955) *Lab. Co-op., Corby,* Maj. 5,700
Hopkins, Kelvin P. (*b.* 1941) *Lab., Luton North,* Maj. 9,977
*__Horam__, John R. (*b.* 1939) *C., Orpington,* Maj. 269
*__Howard__, Rt. Hon. Michael, QC (*b.* 1941) *C., Folkestone and Hythe,* Maj. 5,907
*__Howarth__, Rt. Hon. Alan, CBE (*b.* 1944) *Lab., Newport East,* Maj. 9,874
*__Howarth__, George E. (*b.* 1949) *Lab., Knowsley North and Sefton East,* Maj. 18,927
Howarth, J. Gerald D. (*b.* 1947) *C., Aldershot,* Maj. 6,564
*__Howells__, Dr Kim S., PHD (*b.* 1946) *Lab., Pontypridd,* Maj. 17,684
Hoyle, Lindsay H. (*b.* 1957) *Lab., Chorley,* Maj. 8,444
*__Hughes__, Rt. Hon. Beverley J. (*b.* 1950) *Lab., Stretford and Urmston,* Maj. 13,239
*__Hughes__, Kevin M. (*b.* 1952) *Lab., Doncaster North,* Maj. 15,187
*__Hughes__, Simon H. W. (*b.* 1951) *LD, Southwark North and Bermondsey,* Maj. 9,632
Humble, Mrs Jovanka (Joan) (*b.* 1951) *Lab., Blackpool North and Fleetwood,* Maj. 5,721
*__Hume__, John, MEP (*b.* 1937) *SDLP, Foyle,* Maj. 11,550
*__Hunter__, Andrew R. F. (*b.* 1943) *Ind. C., Basingstoke,* Maj. 880
Hurst, Alan A. (*b.* 1945) *Lab., Braintree,* Maj. 358
*__Hutton__, Rt. Hon. John M. P. (*b.* 1955) *Lab., Barrow and Furness,* Maj. 9,889
Iddon, Dr Brian (*b.* 1940) *Lab., Bolton South East,* Maj. 12,871
*__Illsley__, Eric E. (*b.* 1955) *Lab., Barnsley Central,* Maj. 15,130
*__Ingram__, Rt. Hon. Adam P. (*b.* 1947) *Lab., East Kilbride,* Maj. 12,755
*__Irranca-Davies__, Huw (*b.* 1963) *Lab., Ogmore,* Maj. 5,721
*__Jack__, Rt. Hon. J. Michael (*b.* 1946) *C., Fylde,* Maj. 9,610
*__Jackson__, Ms Glenda M., CBE (*b.* 1936) *Lab., Hampstead and Highgate,* Maj. 7,876
*__Jackson__, Mrs Helen M. (*b.* 1939) *Lab., Sheffield Hillsborough,* Maj. 14,569
*__Jackson__, Robert V. (*b.* 1946) *C., Wantage,* Maj. 5,600
*__Jamieson__, David C. (*b.* 1947) *Lab., Plymouth Devonport,* Maj. 13,033
*__Jenkin__, Bernard C. (*b.* 1959) *C., Essex North,* Maj. 7,186
*__Jenkins__, Brian D. (*b.* 1942) *Lab., Tamworth,* Maj. 4,598
*__Johnson__, Rt. Hon. Alan A. (*b.* 1950) *Lab., Kingston upon Hull West and Hessle,* Maj. 10,951
Johnson, Boris (*b.* 1964) *C., Henley,* Maj. 8,458
Johnson, Ms Melanie J. (*b.* 1955) *Lab., Welwyn Hatfield,* Maj. 1,196
Jones, Ms Helen M. (*b.* 1954) *Lab., Warrington North,* Maj. 15,156
*__Jones__, Jonathan O. (*b.* 1954) *Lab. Co-op., Cardiff Central,* Maj. 659
Jones, Kevan (*b.* 1964) *Lab., Durham North,* Maj. 18,683

*__Jones,__ Dr Lynne M., PHD (*b.* 1951) *Lab., Birmingham Selly Oak,* Maj. 10,339
*__Jones,__ Martyn D. (*b.* 1947) *Lab., Clwyd South,* Maj. 8,898
*__Jones,__ Nigel D. (*b.* 1948) *LD, Cheltenham,* Maj. 5,255
*__Jowell,__ Rt. Hon. Tessa J. H. D. (*b.* 1947) *Lab., Dulwich and West Norwood,* Maj. 12,310
*__Joyce,__ Eric (*b.* 1960) *Lab., Falkirk West,* Maj. 8,532
*__Kaufman,__ Rt. Hon. Sir Gerald B. (*b.* 1930) *Lab., Manchester Gorton,* Maj. 11,304
Keeble, Ms Sally C. (*b.* 1951) *Lab., Northampton North,* Maj. 7,893
*__Keen,__ D. Alan (*b.* 1937) *Lab. Co-op., Feltham and Heston,* Maj. 12,657
Keen, Mrs Ann L. (*b.* 1948) *Lab. Co-op., Brentford and Isleworth,* Maj. 10,318
*__Keetch,__ Paul S. (*b.* 1961) *LD, Hereford,* Maj. 968
*__Kelly,__ Ms Ruth M. (*b.* 1968) *Lab., Bolton West,* Maj. 5,518
*__Kemp,__ Fraser (*b.* 1958) *Lab., Houghton and Washington East,* Maj. 19,818
*__Kennedy,__ Rt. Hon. Charles P. (*b.* 1959) *LD, Ross, Skye and Inverness West,* Maj. 12,952
*__Kennedy,__ Rt. Hon. Jane E. (*b.* 1958) *Lab., Liverpool Wavertree,* Maj. 12,319
*__Key,__ S. Robert (*b.* 1945) *C., Salisbury,* Maj. 8,703
*__Khabra,__ Piara S. (*b.* 1922) *Lab., Ealing Southall,* Maj. 13,683
*__Kidney,__ David N. (*b.* 1955) *Lab., Stafford,* Maj. 5,032
*__Kilfoyle,__ Peter (*b.* 1946) *Lab., Liverpool Walton,* Maj. 17,996
King, Andrew (*b.* 1948) *Lab., Rugby and Kenilworth,* Maj. 2,877
*__King,__ Ms Oona T. (*b.* 1967) *Lab., Bethnal Green and Bow,* Maj. 10,057
*__Kirkbride,__ Miss Julie (*b.* 1960) *C., Bromsgrove,* Maj. 8,138
*__Kirkwood,__ Archibald J. (*b.* 1946) *LD, Roxburgh and Berwickshire,* Maj. 7,511
*__Knight,__ Rt. Hon. Greg (*b.* 1949) *C., Yorkshire East,* Maj. 4,682
Knight, Jim (*b.* 1965) *Lab., Dorset South,* Maj. 153
*__Kumar,__ Dr Ashok (*b.* 1956) *Lab., Middlesbrough South and Cleveland East,* Maj. 9,351
*__Ladyman,__ Dr Stephen J. (*b.* 1952) *Lab., Thanet South,* Maj. 1,792
Laing, Mrs Eleanor F. (*b.* 1958) *C., Epping Forest,* Maj. 8,426
*__Lait,__ Ms Jacqueline A. H. (*b.* 1947) *C., Beckenham,* Maj. 4,959
Lamb, Norman (*b.* 1957) *LD, Norfolk North,* Maj. 483
*__Lammy,__ David (*b.* 1972) *Lab., Tottenham,* Maj. 16,916
*__Lansley,__ Andrew D., CBE (*b.* 1956) *C., Cambridgeshire South,* Maj. 8,403
*__Lawrence,__ Mrs Jacqueline R. (*b.* 1948) *Lab., Preseli Pembrokeshire,* Maj. 2,946
Laws, David (*b.* 1965) *LD, Yeovil,* Maj. 3,928
*__Laxton,__ Robert (*b.* 1944) *Lab., Derby North,* Maj. 6,982
Lazarowicz, Mark (*b.* 1953) *Lab., Edinburgh North and Leith,* Maj. 8,817
*__Leigh,__ Edward J. E. (*b.* 1950) *C., Gainsborough,* Maj. 8,071
*__Lepper,__ David (*b.* 1945) *Lab. Co-op., Brighton Pavilion,* Maj. 9,643
Leslie, Christopher M. (*b.* 1972) *Lab., Shipley,* Maj. 1,428
Letwin, Rt. Hon. Oliver (*b.* 1956) *C., Dorset West,* Maj. 1,414
*__Levitt,__ Tom (*b.* 1954) *Lab., High Peak,* Maj. 4,489
*__Lewis,__ Ivan (*b.* 1967) *Lab., Bury South,* Maj. 12,772
*__Lewis,__ Dr Julian M. (*b.* 1951) *C., New Forest East,* Maj. 3,829
*__Lewis,__ Terence (*b.* 1935) *Lab., Worsley,* Maj. 11,787
*__Liddell,__ Rt. Hon. Helen (*b.* 1950) *Lab., Airdrie and Shotts,* Maj. 12,340
Liddell-Grainger, Ian (*b.* 1959) *C., Bridgwater,* Maj. 4,987
*__Lidington,__ David R., PHD (*b.* 1956) *C., Aylesbury,* Maj. 10,009
*__Lilley,__ Rt. Hon. Peter B. (*b.* 1943) *C., Hitchin and Harpenden,* Maj. 6,663
Linton, J. Martin (*b.* 1944) *Lab., Battersea,* Maj. 5,053
*__Lloyd,__ Anthony J. (*b.* 1950) *Lab., Manchester Central,* Maj. 13,742
*__Llwyd,__ Elfyn (*b.* 1951) *PC, Meirionnydd nant Conwy,* Maj. 5,684
*__Lord,__ Sir Michael N. (*b.* 1938) *C., Suffolk Central and Ipswich North,* Maj. 3,469
*__Loughton,__ Timothy P. (*b.* 1962) *C., Worthing East and Shoreham,* Maj. 6,139
*__Love,__ Andrew (*b.* 1949) *Lab. Co-op., Edmonton,* Maj. 9,772
Lucas, Ian (*b.* 1960) *Lab., Wrexham,* Maj. 9,188
*__Luff,__ Peter J. (*b.* 1955) *C., Worcestershire Mid,* Maj. 10,627
Luke, Iain (*b.* 1951) *Lab., Dundee East,* Maj. 4,475
Lyons, John (*b.* 1950) *Lab., Strathkelvin and Bearsden,* Maj. 11,717
*__McAvoy,__ Thomas M. (*b.* 1943) *Lab. Co-op., Glasgow Rutherglen,* Maj. 12,625
*__McCabe,__ Stephen J. (*b.* 1955) *Lab., Birmingham Hall Green,* Maj. 6,648
*__McCafferty,__ Ms Christine (*b.* 1945) *Lab., Calder Valley,* Maj. 3,094
*__McCartney,__ Rt. Hon. Ian (*b.* 1951) *Lab., Makerfield,* Maj. 17,750
*__McDonagh,__ Ms Siobhain A. (*b.* 1960) *Lab., Mitcham and Morden,* Maj. 13,785
*__MacDonald,__ Calum A., PHD (*b.* 1956) *Lab., Western Isles,* Maj. 1,074
McDonnell, John M. (*b.* 1951) *Lab., Hayes and Harlington,* Maj. 13,466
*__MacDougall,__ John (*b.* 1947) *Lab., Fife Central,* Maj. 10,075
*__McFall,__ Rt. Hon. John (*b.* 1944) *Lab. Co-op., Dumbarton,* Maj. 9,575
*__McGrady,__ Edward K. (*b.* 1935) *SDLP, Down South,* Maj. 13,858
McGuinness, Martin (*b.* 1950) *SF, Ulster Mid,* Maj. 9,953
McGuire, Mrs Anne (*b.* 1949) *Lab., Stirling,* Maj. 6,274
*__McIntosh,__ Miss Anne C. B. (*b.* 1954) *C., Vale of York,* Maj. 12,517
McIsaac, Ms Shona (*b.* 1960) *Lab., Cleethorpes,* Maj. 5,620
*__Mackay,__ Rt. Hon. Andrew J. (*b.* 1949) *C., Bracknell,* Maj. 6,713
McKechin, Ann (*b.* 1961) *Lab., Glasgow Maryhill,* Maj. 9,888
McKenna, Ms Rosemary, CBE (*b.* 1941) *Lab., Cumbernauld and Kilsyth,* Maj. 7,520
*__Mackinlay,__ Andrew S. (*b.* 1949) *Lab., Thurrock,* Maj. 9,997
*__Maclean,__ Rt. Hon. David J. (*b.* 1953) *C., Penrith and the Border,* Maj. 14,677
*__McLoughlin,__ Patrick A. (*b.* 1957) *C., Derbyshire West,* Maj. 7,370

***McNamara,** J. Kevin (*b.* 1934) *Lab., Hull North,* Maj. 10,721
***McNulty,** Anthony J. (*b.* 1958) *Lab., Harrow East,* Maj. 11,124
***MacShane,** Dr Denis, PHD (*b.* 1948) *Lab., Rotherham,* Maj. 13,077
Mactaggart, Ms Fiona M. (*b.* 1953) *Lab., Slough,* Maj. 12,508
***McWalter,** Tony (*b.* 1945) *Lab. Co-op., Hemel Hempstead,* Maj. 3,742
***McWilliam,** John D. (*b.* 1941) *Lab., Blaydon,* Maj. 7,809
Mahmood, Khalid (*b.* 1961) *Lab., Birmingham Perry Barr,* Maj. 8,753
***Mahon,** Mrs Alice (*b.* 1937) *Lab., Halifax,* Maj. 6,129
Malins, Humfrey J., CBE (*b.* 1945) *C., Woking,* Maj. 6,759
***Mallaber,** Ms C. Judith (*b.* 1951) *Lab., Amber Valley,* Maj. 7,227
***Mallon,** Seamus (*b.* 1936) *SDLP, Newry and Armagh,* Maj. 3,575
†***Mandelson,** Rt. Hon. Peter B. (*b.* 1953) *Lab., Hartlepool,* Maj. 14,571
Mann, John (*b.* 1960) *Lab., Bassetlaw,* Maj. 9,748
***Maples,** John C. (*b.* 1943) *C., Stratford-upon-Avon,* Maj. 11,802
Marris, Robert (*b.* 1955) *Lab., Wolverhampton South West,* Maj. 3,487
***Marsden,** Gordon (*b.* 1953) *Lab., Blackpool South,* Maj. 8,262
***Marsden,** Paul W. B. (*b.* 1968) *Lab., Shrewsbury and Atcham,* Maj. 3,579
***Marshall,** David, PHD (*b.* 1941) *Lab., Glasgow Shettleston,* Maj. 9,818
***Marshall-Andrews,** Robert G., QC (*b.* 1944) *Lab., Medway,* Maj. 3,780
***Martin,** Rt. Hon. Michael J. (*b.* 1945) *The Speaker, Glasgow Springburn,* Maj. 11,378
***Martlew,** Eric A. (*b.* 1949) *Lab., Carlisle,* Maj. 5,702
***Mates,** Rt. Hon. Michael J. (*b.* 1934) *C., Hampshire East,* Maj. 8,890
***Maude,** Rt. Hon. Francis A. A. (*b.* 1953) *C., Horsham,* Maj. 13,666
***Mawhinney,** Rt. Hon. Sir Brian, PHD (*b.* 1940) *C., Cambridgeshire North West,* Maj. 8,101
***May,** Rt. Hon. Theresa M. (*b.* 1956) *C., Maidenhead,* Maj. 3,284
***Meacher,** Rt. Hon. Michael H. (*b.* 1939) *Lab., Oldham West and Royton,* Maj. 13,365
***Meale,** J. Alan (*b.* 1949) *Lab., Mansfield,* Maj. 11,038
Mercer, Patrick, OBE (*b.* 1956) *C., Newark,* Maj. 4,073
***Merron,** Ms Gillian J. (*b.* 1959) *Lab., Lincoln,* Maj. 8,420
***Michael,** Rt. Hon. Alun E. (*b.* 1943) *Lab. Co-op., Cardiff South and Penarth,* Maj. 12,287
***Milburn,** Rt. Hon. Alan (*b.* 1958) *Lab., Darlington,* Maj. 9,529
Miliband, David (*b.* 1966) *Lab., South Shields,* Maj. 14,090
***Miller,** Andrew P. (*b.* 1949) *Lab., Ellesmere Port and Neston,* Maj. 10,861
Mitchell, Andrew (*b.* 1956) *C., Sutton Coldfield,* Maj. 10,104
***Mitchell,** Austin V., DPHIL (*b.* 1934) *Lab., Great Grimsby,* Maj. 11,484
***Moffatt,** Mrs Laura J. (*b.* 1954) *Lab., Crawley,* Maj. 6,770
***Mole,** Chris (*b.* 1958) *Lab., Ipswich,* Maj. 4,087
***Moonie,** Dr Lewis (*b.* 1947) *Lab. Co-op., Kirkcaldy,* Maj. 8,963
***Moore,** Michael (*b.* 1965) *LD, Tweeddale, Ettrick and Lauderdale,* Maj. 5,157
***Moran,** Ms Margaret (*b.* 1955) *Lab., Luton South,* Maj. 10,133
Morgan, Ms Julie (*b.* 1944) *Lab., Cardiff North,* Maj. 6,165
***Morley,** Elliot A. (*b.* 1952) *Lab., Scunthorpe,* Maj. 10,372
***Morris,** Rt. Hon. Estelle (*b.* 1952) *Lab., Birmingham Yardley,* Maj. 2,578
***Moss,** Malcolm D. (*b.* 1943) *C., Cambridgeshire North East,* Maj. 6,373
Mountford, Ms Kali C. J. (*b.* 1954) *Lab., Colne Valley,* Maj. 4,639
***Mudie,** George E. (*b.* 1945) *Lab., Leeds East,* Maj. 12,643
***Mullin,** Christopher J. (*b.* 1947) *Lab., Sunderland South,* Maj. 13,667
Munn, Meg (*b.* 1959) *Lab. Co-op., Sheffield Heeley,* Maj. 11,704
Murphy, Denis (*b.* 1948) *Lab., Wansbeck,* Maj. 13,101
Murphy, Jim (*b.* 1967) *Lab., Eastwood,* Maj. 9,141
***Murphy,** Rt. Hon. Paul P. (*b.* 1948) *Lab., Torfaen,* Maj. 16,280
Murrison, Andrew (*b.* 1961) *C., Westbury,* Maj. 5,294
Naysmith, Dr J. Douglas (*b.* 1941) *Lab. Co-op., Bristol North West,* Maj. 11,087
Norman, Archibald J. (*b.* 1954) *C., Tunbridge Wells,* Maj. 9,730
Norris, Dan (*b.* 1960) *Lab., Wansdyke,* Maj. 5,113
***Oaten,** Mark (*b.* 1964) *LD, Winchester,* Maj. 9,634
***O'Brien,** Michael (*b.* 1954) *Lab., Warwickshire North,* Maj. 9,639
***O'Brien,** Stephen (*b.* 1957) *C., Eddisbury,* Maj. 4,568
***O'Brien,** William (*b.* 1929) *Lab., Normanton,* Maj. 9,937
***O'Hara,** Edward (*b.* 1937) *Lab., Knowsley South,* Maj. 21,316
***Olner,** William J. (*b.* 1942) *Lab., Nuneaton,* Maj. 7,535
***O'Neill,** Martin J. (*b.* 1945) *Lab., Ochil,* Maj. 5,349
Öpik, Lembit (*b.* 1965) *LD, Montgomeryshire,* Maj. 6,234
***Organ,** Ms Diana M. (*b.* 1952) *Lab., Forest of Dean,* Maj. 2,049
Osborne, George (*b.* 1971) *C., Tatton,* Maj. 8,611
Osborne, Mrs Sandra C. (*b.* 1956) *Lab., Ayr,* Maj. 2,545
***Ottaway,** Richard G. J. (*b.* 1945) *C., Croydon South,* Maj. 8,697
***Owen,** Albert (*b.* 1960) *Lab., Ynys Môn,* Maj. 800
***Page,** Richard L. (*b.* 1941) *C., Hertfordshire South West,* Maj. 8,181
***Paice,** James E. T. (*b.* 1949) *C., Cambridgeshire South East,* Maj. 8,990
***Paisley,** Revd Ian R. K., MEP (*b.* 1926) *DUP, Antrim North,* Maj. 14,224
Palmer, Dr Nicholas D. (*b.* 1950) *Lab., Broxtowe,* Maj. 5,873
***Paterson,** Owen W. (*b.* 1956) *C., Shropshire North,* Maj. 6,241
***Pearson,** Ian P., PHD (*b.* 1959) *Lab., Dudley South,* Maj. 6,817
***Perham,** Ms Linda (*b.* 1947) *Lab., Ilford North,* Maj. 2,115
Picking, Anne (*b.* 1958) *Lab., East Lothian,* Maj. 10,830
***Pickles,** Eric J. (*b.* 1952) *C., Brentwood and Ongar,* Maj. 2,821
***Pickthall,** Colin (*b.* 1944) *Lab., Lancashire West,* Maj. 9,643

*__Pike__, Peter L. (*b.* 1937) *Lab., Burnley,* Maj. 10,498
*__Plaskitt__, James A. (*b.* 1954) *Lab., Warwick and Leamington,* Maj. 5,953
Pollard, Kerry P. (*b.* 1944) *Lab., St Albans,* Maj. 4,466
*__Pond__, Christopher R. (*b.* 1952) *Lab., Gravesham,* Maj. 4,862
*__Pope__, Gregory J. (*b.* 1960) *Lab., Hyndburn,* Maj. 8,219
*__Portillo__, Rt. Hon. Michael (*b.* 1953) *C., Kensington and Chelsea,* Maj. 8,771
Pound, Stephen P. (*b.* 1948) *Lab., Ealing North,* Maj. 11,837
*__Prentice__, Ms Bridget T. (*b.* 1952) *Lab., Lewisham East,* Maj. 8,959
*__Prentice__, Gordon (*b.* 1951) *Lab., Pendle,* Maj. 4,275
*__Prescott__, Rt. Hon. John L. (*b.* 1938) *Lab., Hull East,* Maj. 15,325
Price, Adam (*b.* 1968) *PC, Carmarthen East and Dinefwr,* Maj. 2,590
*__Primarolo__, Rt. Hon. Dawn (*b.* 1954) *Lab., Bristol South,* Maj. 14,181
*__Prisk__, Mark (*b.* 1962) *C., Hertford and Stortford,* Maj. 5,603
*__Prosser__, Gwynfor M. (*b.* 1943) *Lab., Dover,* Maj. 5,199
Pugh, Dr John (*b.* 1949) *LD, Southport,* Maj. 3,007
*__Purchase__, Kenneth (*b.* 1939) *Lab. Co-op., Wolverhampton North East,* Maj. 9,965
Purnell, James (*b.* 1970) *Lab., Stalybridge and Hyde,* Maj. 8,859
*__Quin__, Rt. Hon. Joyce G. (*b.* 1944) *Lab., Gateshead East and Washington West,* Maj. 17,904
*__Quinn__, Lawrence W. (*b.* 1956) *Lab., Scarborough and Whitby,* Maj. 3,585
*__Rammell__, William E. (*b.* 1959) *Lab., Harlow,* Maj. 5,228
*__Randall__, A. John (*b.* 1955) *C., Uxbridge,* Maj. 2,098
Rapson, Sydney N. J. (*b.* 1942) *Lab., Portsmouth North,* Maj. 5,134
*__Raynsford__, Rt. Hon. W. R. N. (Nick) (*b.* 1945) *Lab., Greenwich and Woolwich,* Maj. 13,433
*__Redwood__, Rt. Hon. John A., DPHIL (*b.* 1951) *C., Wokingham,* Maj. 5,994
Reed, Andrew J. (*b.* 1964) *Lab., Loughborough,* Maj. 6,378
Reid, Alan (*b.* 1954) *LD, Argyll and Bute,* Maj. 1,653
*__Reid__, Rt. Hon. John, PHD (*b.* 1947) *Lab., Hamilton North and Bellshill,* Maj. 13,561
*__Rendel__, David D. (*b.* 1949) *LD, Newbury,* Maj. 2,415
*__Robathan__, Andrew R. G. (*b.* 1951) *C., Blaby,* Maj. 6,209
Robertson, Angus (*b.* 1969) *SNP, Moray,* Maj. 1,744
Robertson, Hugh (*b.* 1962) *C., Faversham and Mid Kent,* Maj. 4,183
*__Robertson__, John (*b.* 1952) *Lab., Glasgow Anniesland,* Maj. 11,054
Robertson, Laurence A. (*b.* 1958) *C., Tewkesbury,* Maj. 8,663
*__Robinson__, Geoffrey (*b.* 1938) *Lab., Coventry North West,* Maj. 10,874
Robinson, Iris, MLA (*b.* 1949) *DUP, Strangford,* Maj. 1,110
*__Robinson__, Peter D. (*b.* 1948) *DUP, Belfast East,* Maj. 7,117
*__Roche__, Mrs Barbara M. R. (*b.* 1954) *Lab., Hornsey and Wood Green,* Maj. 10,614
*__Roe__, Dame Marion A., DBE (*b.* 1936) *C., Broxbourne,* Maj. 8,993
*__Rooney__, Terence H. (*b.* 1950) *Lab., Bradford North,* Maj. 8,969
Rosindell, Andrew (*b.* 1966) *C., Romford,* Maj. 5,977
*__Ross__, Ernest (*b.* 1942) *Lab., Dundee West,* Maj. 6,800
*__Roy__, Frank (*b.* 1958) *Lab., Motherwell and Wishaw,* Maj. 10,956
*__Ruane__, Christopher S. (*b.* 1958) *Lab., Vale of Clwyd,* Maj. 5,761
*__Ruddock__, Mrs Joan M. (*b.* 1943) *Lab., Lewisham Deptford,* Maj. 15,293
Ruffley, David L. (*b.* 1962) *C., Bury St Edmunds,* Maj. 2,503
Russell, Ms Christine M. (*b.* 1945) *Lab., City of Chester,* Maj. 6,894
*__Russell__, Robert E. (*b.* 1946) *LD, Colchester,* Maj. 5,553
*__Ryan__, Ms Joan M. (*b.* 1955) *Lab., Enfield North,* Maj. 2,291
*__Salmond__, Alexander E. A. (*b.* 1954) *SNP, Banff and Buchan,* Maj. 10,503
Salter, Martin J. (*b.* 1954) *Lab., Reading West,* Maj. 8,849
*__Sanders__, Adrian M. (*b.* 1959) *LD, Torbay,* Maj. 6,708
*__Sarwar__, Mohammad (*b.* 1952) *Lab., Glasgow Govan,* Maj. 6,400
*__Savidge__, Malcolm K. (*b.* 1946) *Lab., Aberdeen North,* Maj. 4,449
*__Sawford__, Philip A. (*b.* 1950) *Lab., Kettering,* Maj. 665
*__Sayeed__, Jonathan (*b.* 1948) *C., Bedfordshire Mid,* Maj. 8,066
*__Sedgemore__, Brian C. J. (*b.* 1937) *Lab., Hackney South and Shoreditch,* Maj. 15,049
Selous, Andrew (*b.* 1962) *C., Bedfordshire South West,* Maj. 776
*__Shaw__, Jonathan R. (*b.* 1966) *Lab., Chatham and Aylesford,* Maj. 4,340
*__Sheerman__, Barry J. (*b.* 1940) *Lab. Co-op., Huddersfield,* Maj. 10,046
*__Shephard__, Rt. Hon. Gillian P. (*b.* 1940) *C., Norfolk South West,* Maj. 9,366
*__Shepherd__, Richard C. S. (*b.* 1942) *C., Aldridge-Brownhills,* Maj. 3,768
Sheridan, Jim (*b.* 1952) *Lab., Renfrewshire West,* Maj. 8,575
*__Shipley__, Ms Debra A. (*b.* 1957) *Lab., Stourbridge,* Maj. 3,812
*__Short__, Rt. Hon. Clare (*b.* 1946) *Lab., Birmingham Ladywood,* Maj. 18,143
Simmonds, Mark (*b.* 1964) *C., Boston and Skegness,* Maj. 515
Simon, Siôn (*b.* 1969) *Lab., Birmingham Erdington,* Maj. 9,962
*__Simpson__, Alan J. (*b.* 1948) *Lab., Nottingham South,* Maj. 9,989
*__Simpson__, Keith (*b.* 1949) *C., Norfolk Mid,* Maj. 4,562
Singh, Marsha (*b.* 1954) *Lab., Bradford West,* Maj. 4,165
*__Skinner__, Dennis E. (*b.* 1932) *Lab., Bolsover,* Maj. 18,777
*__Smith__, Rt. Hon. Andrew D. (*b.* 1951) *Lab., Oxford East,* Maj. 10,344
*__Smith__, Ms Angela E. (*b.* 1959) *Lab. Co-op., Basildon,* Maj. 7,738
*__Smith__, Rt. Hon. Christopher R., PHD (*b.* 1951) *Lab., Islington South and Finsbury,* Maj. 7,280
*__Smith__, Ms Geraldine (*b.* 1961) *Lab., Morecambe and Lunesdale,* Maj. 5,092
*__Smith__, Rt. Hon. Jacqui (*b.* 1962) *Lab., Redditch,* Maj. 2,484
*__Smith__, John W. P. (*b.* 1951) *Lab., Vale of Glamorgan,* Maj. 4,700
*__Smith__, Llewellyn T. (*b.* 1944) *Lab., Blaenau Gwent,* Maj. 19,313

***Smith,** Sir Robert, Bt. (*b.* 1958) *LD, Aberdeenshire West and Kincardine,* Maj. 4,821
***Smyth,** Revd W. Martin (*b.* 1931) *UUP, Belfast South,* Maj. 5,399
***Soames,** Hon. A. Nicholas W. (*b.* 1948) *C., Sussex Mid,* Maj. 6,898
***Soley,** Clive S. (*b.* 1939) *Lab., Ealing, Acton and Shepherd's Bush,* Maj. 10,789
Southworth, Ms Helen M. (*b.* 1956) *Lab., Warrington South,* Maj. 7,387
***Spellar,** Rt. Hon. John F. (*b.* 1947) *Lab., Warley,* Maj. 11,850
Spelman, Mrs Caroline A. (*b.* 1958) *C., Meriden,* Maj. 3,784
***Spicer,** Sir Michael (*b.* 1943) *C., Worcestershire West,* Maj. 5,374
Spink, Dr Robert (*b.* 1948) *C., Castle Point,* Maj. 985
***Spring,** Richard J. G. (*b.* 1946) *C., Suffolk West,* Maj. 4,295
***Squire,** Ms Rachel A. (*b.* 1954) *Lab., Dunfermline West,* Maj. 10,980
***Stanley,** Rt. Hon. Sir John (*b.* 1942) *C., Tonbridge and Malling,* Maj. 8,250
Starkey, Dr Phyllis M. (*b.* 1947) *Lab., Milton Keynes South West,* Maj. 6,978
***Steen,** Anthony (*b.* 1939) *C., Totnes,* Maj. 3,597
***Steinberg,** Gerald N. (*b.* 1945) *Lab., City of Durham,* Maj. 13,441
***Stevenson,** George W. (*b.* 1938) *Lab., Stoke-on-Trent South,* Maj. 10,489
***Stewart,** David J. (*b.* 1956) *Lab., Inverness East, Nairn and Lochaber,* Maj. 4,716
***Stewart,** Ian (*b.* 1950) *Lab., Eccles,* Maj. 14,528
***Stinchcombe,** Paul D. (*b.* 1962) *Lab., Wellingborough,* Maj. 2,355
***Stoate,** Dr Howard G. A. (*b.* 1954) *Lab., Dartford,* Maj. 3,306
***Strang,** Rt. Hon. Dr Gavin (*b.* 1943) *Lab., Edinburgh East and Musselburgh,* Maj. 12,168
***Straw,** Rt. Hon. J. W. (Jack) (*b.* 1946) *Lab., Blackburn,* Maj. 9,249
***Streeter,** Gary N. (*b.* 1955) *C., Devon South West,* Maj. 7,144
***Stringer,** Graham E. (*b.* 1950) *Lab., Manchester Blackley,* Maj. 14,464
***Stuart,** Mrs Gisela G. (*b.* 1955) *Lab., Birmingham Edgbaston,* Maj. 4,698
***Stunell,** Andrew (*b.* 1942) *LD, Hazel Grove,* Maj. 8,435
***Sutcliffe,** Gerard (*b.* 1953) *Lab., Bradford South,* Maj. 9,662
Swayne, Desmond A. (*b.* 1956) *C., New Forest West,* Maj. 13,191
Swire, Hugo (*b.* 1959) *C., Devon East,* Maj. 8,195
***Syms,** Robert A. R. (*b.* 1956) *C., Poole,* Maj. 7,166
Tami, Mark (*b.* 1963) *Lab., Alyn and Deeside,* Maj. 9,222
***Tapsell,** Sir Peter (*b.* 1930) *C., Louth and Horncastle,* Maj. 7,554
***Taylor,** Rt. Hon. Ann (*b.* 1947) *Lab., Dewsbury,* Maj. 7,449
***Taylor,** Ms Dari J. (*b.* 1944) *Lab., Stockton South,* Maj. 9,086
Taylor, David L. (*b.* 1946) *Lab. Co-op., Leicestershire North West,* Maj. 8,157
***Taylor,** Sir Edward (Teddy) (*b.* 1937) *C., Rochford and Southend East,* Maj. 7,034
***Taylor,** Ian C., MBE (*b.* 1945) *C., Esher and Walton,* Maj. 11,538
***Taylor,** John M. (*b.* 1941) *C., Solihull,* Maj. 9,407
***Taylor,** Matthew O. J. (*b.* 1963) *LD, Truro and St Austell,* Maj. 8,065
Taylor, Dr Richard (*b.* 1935) *KHHC, Wyre Forest,* Maj. 17,630
Teather, Sarah (*b.* 1974) *LD, Brent East,* Maj. 1,118
Thomas, Gareth (*b.* 1954) *Lab., Clwyd West,* Maj. 1,115
***Thomas,** Gareth R. (*b.* 1967) *Lab., Harrow West,* Maj. 6,156
***Thomas,** Simon (*b.* 1963) *PC, Ceredigion,* Maj. 3,944
***Thurso,** John (*b.* 1953) *LD, Caithness, Sutherland and Easter Ross,* Maj. 2,744
***Timms,** Stephen C. (*b.* 1955) *Lab., East Ham,* Maj. 21,032
***Tipping,** S. P. (Paddy) (*b.* 1949) *Lab., Sherwood,* Maj. 9,373
Todd, Mark W. (*b.* 1954) *Lab., Derbyshire South,* Maj. 7,851
Tonge, Dr Jennifer L. (*b.* 1941) *LD, Richmond Park,* Maj. 4,964
***Touhig,** J. Donnelly (Don) (*b.* 1947) *Lab. Co-op., Islwyn,* Maj. 15,309
***Tredinnick,** David A. S. (*b.* 1950) *C., Bosworth,* Maj. 2,280
***Trend,** Hon. Michael St J., CBE (*b.* 1952) *C., Windsor,* Maj. 8,889
***Trickett,** Jon H. (*b.* 1950) *Lab., Hemsworth,* Maj. 15,636
***Trimble,** Rt. Hon. W. David (*b.* 1944) *UUP, Upper Bann,* Maj. 2,058
Truswell, Paul A. (*b.* 1955) *Lab., Pudsey,* Maj. 5,626
Turner, Andrew (*b.* 1953) *C., Isle of Wight,* Maj. 2,826
***Turner,** Dennis (*b.* 1942) *Lab. Co-op., Wolverhampton South East,* Maj. 12,464
Turner, Dr Desmond S. (*b.* 1939) *Lab., Brighton Kemptown,* Maj. 4,922
***Turner,** Neil (*b.* 1945) *Lab., Wigan,* Maj. 13,743
***Twigg,** J. Derek (*b.* 1959) *Lab., Halton,* Maj. 17,428
***Twigg,** Stephen (*b.* 1966) *Lab., Enfield Southgate,* Maj. 5,546
***Tyler,** Paul A., CBE (*b.* 1941) *LD, Cornwall North,* Maj. 9,832
***Tynan,** Bill (*b.* 1940) *Lab., Hamilton South,* Maj. 10,775
***Tyrie,** Andrew G. (*b.* 1957) *C., Chichester,* Maj. 11,355
***Vaz,** N. Keith A. S. (*b.* 1956) *Lab., Leicester East,* Maj. 13,422
***Viggers,** Peter J. (*b.* 1938) *C., Gosport,* Maj. 2,621
***Vis,** Dr R. J. (Rudi) (*b.* 1941) *Lab., Finchley and Golders Green,* Maj. 3,716
***Walley,** Ms Joan L. (*b.* 1949) *Lab., Stoke-on-Trent North,* Maj. 11,784
***Walter,** Robert J. (*b.* 1948) *C., Dorset North,* Maj. 3,797
***Ward,** Ms Claire M. (*b.* 1972) *Lab., Watford,* Maj. 5,555
***Wareing,** Robert N. (*b.* 1930) *Lab., Liverpool West Derby,* Maj. 15,853
***Waterson,** Nigel C. (*b.* 1950) *C., Eastbourne,* Maj. 2,154
Watkinson, Angela (*b.* 1941) *C., Upminster,* Maj. 1,241
***Watson,** Tom (*b.* 1967) *Lab., West Bromwich East,* Maj. 9,763
Watts, David L. (*b.* 1951) *Lab., St Helens North,* Maj. 15,901
Webb, Prof. Steven J. (*b.* 1965) *LD, Northavon,* Maj. 9,877
Weir, Michael (*b.* 1957) *SNP, Angus,* Maj. 3,611
White, Brian A. R. (*b.* 1957) *Lab., Milton Keynes North East,* Maj. 1,829
***Whitehead,** Dr Alan P. V. (*b.* 1950) *Lab., Southampton Test,* Maj. 11,207
***Whittingdale,** John F. L., OBE (*b.* 1959) *C., Maldon and Chelmsford East,* Maj. 8,462

*__Wicks,__ Malcolm H. (*b.* 1947) *Lab., Croydon North,* Maj. 16,858
*__Widdecombe,__ Rt. Hon. Ann N. (*b.* 1947) *C., Maidstone and the Weald,* Maj. 10,318
Wiggin, Bill (*b.* 1966) *C., Leominster,* Maj. 10,367
*__Wilkinson,__ John A. D. (*b.* 1940) *C., Ruislip-Northwood,* Maj. 7,537
*__Willetts,__ David L. (*b.* 1956) *C., Havant,* Maj. 4,207
*__Williams,__ Rt. Hon. Alan J. (*b.* 1930) *Lab., Swansea West,* Maj. 9,550
*__Williams,__ Betty (*b.* 1944) *Lab., Conwy,* Maj. 6,219
Williams, Hywel (*b.* 1953) *PC, Caernarfon,* Maj. 3,511
Williams, Roger (*b.* 1948) *LD, Brecon and Radnorshire,* Maj. 751
*__Willis,__ G. Philip (*b.* 1941) *LD, Harrogate and Knaresborough,* Maj. 8,845
Wills, Michael D. (*b.* 1952) *Lab., Swindon North,* Maj. 8,105
*__Wilshire,__ David (*b.* 1943) *C., Spelthorne,* Maj. 3,262
*__Wilson,__ Rt. Hon. Brian D. H. (*b.* 1948) *Lab., Cunninghame North,* Maj. 8,398
*__Winnick,__ David J. (*b.* 1933) *Lab., Walsall North,* Maj. 9,391
*__Winterton,__ Mrs J. Ann (*b.* 1941) *C., Congleton,* Maj. 7,134
*__Winterton,__ Sir Nicholas R. (*b.* 1938) *C., Macclesfield,* Maj. 7,200

*Sitting MP
† A by-election for Hartlepool was held on 30 September 2004 following the resignation of Peter Mandelson. *See* Stop Press.
For by-elections since 2001 *see* page 181

Winterton, Ms Rosalie (*b.* 1958) *Lab., Doncaster Central,* Maj. 11,999
Wishart, Peter (*b.* 1962) *SNP, Tayside North,* Maj. 3,283
*__Wood,__ Michael R. (*b.* 1946) *Lab., Batley and Spen,* Maj. 5,064
Woodward, Shaun (*b.* 1958) *Lab., St Helens South,* Maj. 8,985
*__Woolas,__ Philip J. (*b.* 1959) *Lab., Oldham East and Saddleworth,* Maj. 2,726
*__Worthington,__ Anthony (*b.* 1941) *Lab., Clydebank and Milngavie,* Maj. 10,724
*__Wray,__ James (*b.* 1938) *Lab., Glasgow Baillieston,* Maj. 9,839
Wright, Anthony D., DPHIL (*b.* 1954) *Lab., Great Yarmouth,* Maj. 4,564
*__Wright,__ Dr Anthony W. (*b.* 1948) *Lab., Cannock Chase,* Maj. 10,704
Wright, David (*b.* 1967) *Lab., Telford,* Maj. 8,383
*__Wyatt,__ Derek M. (*b.* 1949) *Lab., Sittingbourne and Sheppey,* Maj. 3,509
*__Yeo,__ Timothy S. K. (*b.* 1945) *C., Suffolk South,* Maj. 5,081
*__Young,__ Rt. Hon. Sir George, Bt. (*b.* 1941) *C., Hampshire North West,* Maj. 12,009
Younger-Ross, Richard (*b.* 1953) *LD, Teignbridge,* Maj. 3,011

GENERAL ELECTION STATISTICS

PARLIAMENTS SINCE 1970

Assembled	*Dissolved*	*yr*	*m.*	*d.*
29 June 1970	8 February 1974	3	7	10
6 March 1974	20 September 1974	0	6	14
22 October 1974	7 April 1979	4	5	16
9 May 1979	13 May 1983	4	0	4
15 June 1983	18 May 1987	3	11	3
17 June 1987	16 March 1992	4	8	28
27 April 1992	8 April 1997	4	11	12
7 May 1997	14 May 2001	4	0	7
13 June 2001				

GENERAL ELECTION TURNOUT

	2001	1997
England	59.4	71.4
Wales	61.6	73.5
Scotland	58.2	71.3
Northern Ireland	68.0	67.1

VOTES CAST 1997 AND 2001

	1997	2001
Conservative	9,600,940	8,357,622
Labour	13,517,911	10,724,895
Liberal Democrats	5,243,440	4,812,833
Scottish Nationalist	622,260	464,305
Plaid Cymru	161,030	195,892
N. Ireland parties	780,920	635,735
Others	1,361,701	1,177,516
Total	31,287,702	26,368,798

PARLIAMENTARY CONSTITUENCIES AS AT 7 JUNE 2001

The results of voting in each parliamentary division at the general election of 7 June 2001 are given below. The majority in the 1997 general election and any by-election between 1997 and 2001, is given below the 2001 result.

Key
*Sitting MP
†Previously MP in another seat
E. Electorate
T. Turnout

Abbreviations

AL	Asian League
Alliance	Alliance
Anti-Corrupt	Anti-Corruption Forum
BNP	British National Party
Bean	New Millennium Bean
CPA	Christian Peoples Alliance
Ch. D.	Christian Democrat
Choice	People's Choice
Comm.	Communist Party
Community	Independent Community Candidate Empowering Change
C.	Conservative
Country	Countryside Party
Customer	Direct Customer Service Party
Def Welfare	Defend the Welfare State Against Blairism
DUP	Democratic Unionist Party
EIP	English Independence Party
Elvis	Church of the Militant Elvis Party
Ext. Club	Extinction Club
FDP	Fancy Dress Party
Free	Freedom Party
Green	Green Party
Grey	Grey Party
Ind.	Independent
Ind. UU	Independent United Unionist
Ind. Vote	Independent – Vote for Yourself Party
IOW	Isle of Wight Party
JLD P	John Lillburne Democratic Party
JP	Justice Party
KHHC	Kidderminster Hospital and Health Concern
Lab.	Labour
Lab. Co-op	Labour and Co-operative
LCA	Legalise Cannabis Alliance
LD	Liberal Democrat
LP	Liberated Party
Left All	All Left Alliance
Lib.	Liberal
Loony	Monster Raving Loony Party
Low Excise	Lower Excise Duty Party
Marxist	Marxist Party
Meb. Ker.	Mebyon Kernow
Muslim	Muslim Party
NBP	New Britain Party
NF	National Front
NI Unionist	Northern Ireland Unionist
NI WC	Northern Ireland Women's Coalition
PC	Plaid Cymru
PF	Pathfinders
PJP	People's Justice Party
PUP	Progressive Unionist Party
Pacifist	Pacifist for Peace, Justice, Cooperation, Environment
Pensioner	Pensioner Coalition
Pro Euro C	Pro Euro Conservative Party
ProLife	ProLife Alliance
Prog Dem	Progress Democratic Party Members Decide Policy
Qari	Qari
R & R Loony	Rock & Roll Loony Party
RP	Rate Payer
Ref. UK	Reform UK
Reform	Reform 2000
Res. Motor	Motor Residents and Motorists of Great Britain
SDLP	Social Democratic and Labour Party
SF	Sinn Fein
SNP	Scottish National Party
SSP	Scottish Socialist Party
Scot. Ref.	Scottish Freedom Referendum Party
Scot. U.	Scottish Unionist
Soc.	Socialist Party
Soc. All.	Socialist Alliance
Soc. Alt.	Socialist Alternative Party
Soc. Lab.	Socialist Labour Party
Socialist	Socialist
Speaker	The Speaker
Stuck	Stuckist
Sunrise	Chairman of Sunrise Radio
Tatton	Tatton Group Independent
Third	Third Way
Truth	Truth Party
UK Ind.	UK Independence Party
UKU	United Kingdom Unionist
UUP	Ulster Unionist Party
Unrep.	Unrepresented People's Party
WSA	Welsh Socialist Alliance
Wessex Reg.	Wessex Regionalist
WFLOE	Women for Life on Earth
Women's Co.	Women's Coalition
WP	Workers' Party
WRP	Workers' Revolutionary Party
Wrestling	Jam Wrestling Party

ENGLAND

ALDERSHOT
E. 78,262 T. 45,315 (57.90%) C. hold
*Gerald Howarth, C. 19,106
Adrian Collett, LD 12,542
Luke Akehurst, Lab. 11,391
Derek Rumsey, UK Ind. 797
Adam Stacey, Green 630
Arthur Pendragon, Ind. 459
Alan Hope, Loony 390
C. majority 6,564 (14.49%)
1.13% swing LD to C.
(1997: C. maj. 6,621 (12.22%))

ALDRIDGE-BROWNHILLS
E. 62,388 T. 37,810 (60.60%) C. hold
*Richard Shepherd, C. 18,974
Ian Geary, Lab. 15,206
Mrs Monica Howes, LD 3,251
John Rothery, Soc. All. 379
C. majority 3,768 (9.97%)
2.26% swing Lab. to C.
(1997: C. maj. 2,526 (5.44%))

ALTRINCHAM & SALE WEST
E. 71,820 T. 43,568 (60.66%) C. hold
*Graham Brady, C. 20,113
Ms Janet Baugh, Lab. 17,172
Christopher Gaskell, LD 6,283
C. majority 2,941 (6.75%)
1.92% swing Lab. to C.
(1997: C. maj. 1,505 (2.91%))

AMBER VALLEY
E. 73,798 T. 44,513 (60.32%) Lab. hold
*Ms Judy Mallaber, Lab. 23,101
Ms Gillian Shaw, C. 15,874
Ms Kate Smith, LD 5,538
Lab. majority 7,227 (16.24%)
2.49% swing Lab. to C.
(1997: Lab. maj. 11,613 (21.21%))

ARUNDEL & SOUTH DOWNS
E. 70,956 T. 45,889 (64.67%) C. hold
*Howard Flight, C. 23,969
Derek Deedman, LD 10,265
Charles Taylor, Lab. 9,488
Robert Perrin, UK Ind. 2,167
C. majority 13,704 (29.86%)
1.26% swing LD to C.
(1997: C. maj. 14,035 (27.34%))

ASHFIELD
E. 73,428 T. 39,350 (53.59%) Lab. hold
*Rt. Hon. G. Hoon, Lab. 22,875
Julian Leigh, C. 9,607
Bill Smith, LD 4,428
Melvin Harby, Ind. 1,471
George Watson, Soc. All. 589
Ms Katrina Howse, Soc. Lab. 380
Lab. majority 13,268 (33.72%)
5.60% swing Lab. to C.
(1997: Lab. maj. 22,728 (44.91%))

ASHFORD
E. 76,699 T. 47,937 (62.50%) C. hold
*Damien Green, C. 22,739
John Adams, Lab. 15,380
Keith Fitchett, LD 7,236
Richard Boden, Green 1,353
David Waller, UK Ind. 1,229
C. majority 7,359 (15.35%)
2.84% swing Lab. to C.
(1997: C. maj. 5,355 (9.68%))

ASHTON UNDER LYNE
E. 72,820 T. 35,764 (49.11%) Lab. hold
David Heyes, Lab. 22,340
Tim Charlesworth, C. 6,822
Mrs Kate Fletcher, LD 4,237
Roger Woods, BNP 1,617
Nigel Rolland, Green 748
Lab. majority 15,518 (43.39%)
2.59% swing Lab. to C.
(1997: Lab. maj. 22,965 (48.57%))

AYLESBURY
E. 80,002 T. 49,087 (61.36%) C. hold
*David Lidington, C. 23,230
Peter Jones, LD 13,221
Keith White, Lab. 11,388
Justin Harper, UK Ind. 1,248
C. majority 10,009 (20.39%)
2.88% swing LD to C.
(1997: C. maj. 8,419 (14.63%))

BANBURY
E. 83,392 T. 51,515 (61.77%) C. hold
*Tony Baldry, C. 23,271
Leslie Sibley, Lab. 18,052
Tony Worgan, LD 8,216
Bev Cotton, Green 1,281
Stephen Harris, UK Ind. 695
C. majority 5,219 (10.13%)
1.02% swing Lab. to C.
(1997: C. maj. 4,737 (8.10%))

BARKING
E. 55,229 T. 25,126 (45.49%) Lab. hold
*Mrs Margaret Hodge, Lab. 15,302
Mike Weatherley, C. 5,768
Anura Keppetipola, LD 2,450
Mark Toleman, BNP 1,606
Lab. majority 9,534 (37.94%)
5.14% swing Lab. to C.
(1997: Lab. maj. 15,896 (48.22%))

BARNSLEY CENTRAL
E. 60,086 T. 27,543 (45.84%) Lab. hold
*Eric Illsley, Lab. 19,181
Alan Hartley, LD 4,051
Ian McCord, C. 3,608
Henry Rajch, Soc. All. 703
Lab. majority 15,130 (54.93%)
6.26% swing Lab. to LD
(1997: Lab. maj. 24,501 (67.15%))

BARNSLEY EAST & MEXBOROUGH
E. 65,655 T. 32,509 (49.51%) Lab. hold
*Jeff Ennis, Lab. 21,945
Mrs Sharron Brook, LD 5,156
Matthew Offord, C. 4,024
Terry Robinson, Soc. Lab. 722
George Savage, UK Ind. 662
Lab. majority 16,789 (51.64%)
5.57% swing Lab. to LD
(1997: Lab. maj. 26,763 (61.76%))

BARNSLEY WEST & PENISTONE
E. 65,291 T. 34,564 (52.94%) Lab. hold
*Michael Clapham, Lab. 20,244
William Rowe, C. 7,892
Miles Crompton, LD 6,428
Lab. majority 12,352 (35.74%)
2.59% swing Lab. to C.
(1997: Lab. maj. 17,267 (40.91%))

BARROW & FURNESS
E. 64,746 T. 39,020 (60.27%) Lab. hold
*Rt. Hon. J. Hutton, Lab. 21,724
James Airey, C. 11,835
Barry Rabone, LD 4,750
John Smith, UK Ind. 711
Lab. majority 9,889 (25.34%)
2.36% swing Lab. to C.
(1997: Lab. maj. 14,497 (30.06%))

BASILDON
E. 74,121 T. 40,875 (55.15%)
Lab. Co-op hold
*Ms Angela Smith, Lab. Co-op 21,551
Dominic Schofield, C. 13,813
Ms Jane Smithard, LD 3,691
Frank Mallon, UK Ind. 1,397
Dick Duane, Soc. All. 423
Lab. Co-op majority 7,738 (18.93%)
3.04% swing Lab. Co-op to C.
(1997: Lab. maj. 13,280 (25.02%))

BASINGSTOKE
E. 79,110 T. 47,995 (60.67%) C. hold
*Andrew Hunter, C. 20,490
Jon Hartley, Lab. 19,610
Steve Sollitt, LD 6,693
Mrs Kim-Elisbeth Graham, UK Ind. 1,202
C. majority 880 (1.83%)
1.18% swing C. to Lab.
(1997: C. maj. 2,397 (4.19%))

BASSETLAW
E. 68,302 T. 38,895 (56.95%) Lab. hold
John Mann, Lab. 21,506
Mrs Alison Holley, C. 11,758
Neil Taylor, LD 4,942
Kevin Meloy, Soc. Lab. 689
Lab. majority 9,748 (25.06%)
5.68% swing Lab. to C.
(1997: Lab. maj 17,460 (36.43%))

BATH
E. 71,372 T. 46,296 (64.87%) LD hold
*Don Foster, LD 23,372
Ashley Fox, C. 13,478
Ms Marilyn Hawkings, Lab. 7,269
Mike Boulton, Green 1,469
Andrew Tettenborn, UK Ind. 708
LD majority 9,894 (21.37%)
2.06% swing C. to LD
(1997: LD maj. 9,319 (17.26%))

BATLEY & SPEN
E. 63,665 T. 38,542 (60.54%) Lab. hold
*Mike Wood Lab. 19,224
Mrs Elizabeth Peacock C. 14,160
Ms Kath Pinnock, LD 3,989
Clive Lord, Green 595
Allen Burton, UK Ind. 574
Lab. majority 5,064 (13.14%)
0.03% swing C. to Lab.
(1997: Lab. maj. 6,141 (13.08%))

BATTERSEA
E. 67,495 T. 36,804 (54.53%) Lab. hold
*Martin Linton, Lab. 18,498
Mrs Lucy Shersby, C. 13,445
Ms Siobhan Vitelli, LD 4,450
Thomas Barber, Ind. 411
Lab. majority 5,053 (13.73%)
1.21% swing C. to Lab.
(1997: Lab. maj. 5,360 (11.31%))

BEACONSFIELD
E. 68,378 T. 42,044 (61.49%) C. hold
*Dominic Grieve, C. 22,233
Stephen Lathrope, Lab. 9,168
Stephen Lloyd, LD 9,017
Andrew Moffatt, UK Ind. 1,626
C. majority 13,065 (31.07%)
0.95% swing Lab. to C.
(1997: C. maj. 13,987 (27.86%))

BECKENHAM
E. 72,241 T. 45,562 (63.07%) C. hold
*Mrs Jacqui Lait, C. 20,618
Richard Watts, Lab. 15,659
Alex Feakes, LD 7,308
Ms Karen Moran, Green 961
Christopher Pratt, UK Ind. 782
Rif Winfield, Lib. 234
C. majority 4,959 (10.88%)
0.89% swing Lab. to C.
(1997 Nov. by-election: C. maj. 1,227 (3.85%); (1997: C. maj. 4,953 (9.11%))

BEDFORD
E. 67,763 T. 40,579 (59.88%) Lab. hold
*Patrick Hall, Lab. 19,454
Mrs Nicky Attenborough, C. 13,297
Michael Headley, LD 6,425
Dr Richard Rawlins, Ind. 973
Mrs Jennifer Lo Bianco, UK Ind. 430
Lab. majority 6,157 (15.17%)
0.89% swing Lab. to C.
(1997: Lab. maj. 8,300 (16.96%))

BEDFORDSHIRE MID
E. 70,594 T. 46,638 (66.07%) C. hold
*Jonathan Sayeed, C. 22,109
James Valentine, Lab. 14,043
Graham Mabbutt, LD 9,205
Christopher Laurence, UK Ind. 1,281
C. majority 8,066 (17.29%)
1.89% swing Lab. to C.
(1997: C. maj. 7,090 (13.51%))

BEDFORDSHIRE NORTH EAST
E. 69,451 T. 45,246 (65.15%) C. hold
Alastair Burt, C. 22,586
Philip Ross, Lab. 14,009
Dan Rogerson, LD 7,409
Ms Ros Hill, UK Ind. 1,242
C. majority 8,577 (18.96%)
3.64% swing Lab. to C.
(1997: C. maj. 5,883 (11.68%))

BEDFORDSHIRE SOUTH WEST
E. 72,126 T. 43,854 (60.80%) C. hold
Andrew Selous, C. 18,477
Andrew Date, Lab. 17,701
Martin Pantling, LD 6,473
Tom Wise, UK Ind. 1,203
C. majority 776 (1.77%)
0.76% swing Lab. to C.
(1997: C. maj. 132 (0.24%))

BERWICK-UPON-TWEED
E. 56,918 T. 36,308 (63.79%) LD hold
*Rt. Hon. A. Beith, LD 18,651
Glen Sanderson, C. 10,193
Martin Walker, Lab. 6,435
John Pearson, UK Ind. 1,029
LD majority 8,458 (23.30%)
0.94% swing C. to LD
(1997: LD maj. 8,042 (19.24%))

BETHNAL GREEN & BOW
E. 79,192 T. 38,470 (48.58%) Lab. hold
*Ms Oona King, Lab. 19,380
Shahagir Faruk, C. 9,323
Ms Janet Ludlow, LD 5,946
Ms Anna Bragga, Green 1,666
Michael Davidson, BNP 1,267
Dennis Delderfield, NBP 888
Lab. majority 10,057 (26.14%)
0.44% swing C. to Lab.
(1997: Lab. maj. 11,285 (25.26%))

BEVERLEY & HOLDERNESS
E. 75,146 T. 46,375 (61.71%) C. hold
*James Cran, C. 19,168
Ms Pippa Langford, Lab. 18,387
Stewart Willie, LD 7,356
Stephen Wallis, UK Ind. 1,464
C. majority 781 (1.68%)
0.08% swing Lab. to C.
(1997: C. maj. 811 (1.53%))

BEXHILL & BATTLE
E. 69,010 T. 44,783 (64.89%) C. hold
Greg Barker, C. 21,555
Stephen Hardy, LD 11,052
Ms Anne Moore-Williams, Lab. 8,702
Nigel Farage, UK Ind. 3,474
C. majority 10,503 (23.45%)
0.40% swing LD to C.
(1997: C. maj. 11,100 (22.66%))

BEXLEYHEATH & CRAYFORD
E. 63,580 T. 40,378 (63.51%) Lab. hold
*Nigel Beard, Lab. 17,593
David Evennett, C. 16,121
Nickolas O'Hare, LD 4,476
Colin Smith, BNP 1,408
John Dunford, UK Ind. 780
Lab. majority 1,472 (3.65%)
1.72% swing Lab. to C.
(1997: Lab. maj. 3,415 (7.08%))

BILLERICAY
E. 78,528 T. 45,598 (58.07%) C. hold
John Baron, C. 21,608
Ms Amanda Campbell, Lab. 16,595
Frank Bellard, LD 6,323
Nick Yeomans, UK Ind. 1,072
C. majority 5,013 (10.99%)
4.27% swing Lab. to C.
(1997: C. maj. 1,356 (2.45%))

BIRKENHEAD
E. 60,726 T. 28,967 (47.70%) Lab. hold
*Rt. Hon. F. Field, Lab. 20,418
Brian Stewart, C. 4,827
Roy Wood, LD 3,722
Lab. majority 15,591 (53.82%)
0.86% swing Lab. to C.
(1997: Lab. maj. 21,843 (55.55%))

BIRMINGHAM EDGBASTON
E. 67,405 T. 37,749 (56.00%) Lab. hold
*Ms Gisela Stuart, Lab. 18,517
Nigel Hastilow, C. 13,819
Ms Nicola Davies, LD 4,528
John Gretton, Pro Euro C 454
Sam Brackenbury, Soc. Lab. 431
Lab. majority 4,698 (12.45%)
1.23% swing C. to Lab.
(1997: Lab. maj. 4,842 (9.99%))

BIRMINGHAM ERDINGTON
E. 65,668 T. 30,604 (46.60%) Lab. hold
Sion Llewelyn Simon, Lab. 17,375
Oliver Lodge, C. 7,413
Ms Sandra Johnson, LD 3,602
Michael Shore, NF 681
Steve Goddard, Soc. All. 669
Mark Nattrass, UK Ind. 521
Ms Judith Sambrook-Marshall, Soc. Lab. 343
Lab. majority 9,962 (32.55%)
0.62% swing C. to Lab.
(1997: Lab. maj. 12,657 (31.32%))

BIRMINGHAM HALL GREEN
E. 57,563 T. 33,084 (57.47%) Lab. hold
*Stephen McCabe, Lab. 18,049
Chris White, C. 11,401
Punjab Singh, LD 2,926
Peter Johnson, UK Ind. 708
Lab. majority 6,648 (20.09%)
0.02% swing Lab. to C.
(1997: Lab. maj. 8,420 (20.14%))

BIRMINGHAM HODGE HILL
E. 55,254 T. 26,465 (47.90%) Lab. hold
*Rt. Hon. T. Davis, Lab. 16,901
Mrs Debbie Lewis, C. 5,283
Alistair Dow, LD 2,147
Lee Windridge, BNP 889
Parwez Hussain, PJP 561
Dennis Cridge, Soc. Lab. 284
Harvey Vivian, UK Ind. 275
Ayub Khan, Muslim 125
Lab. majority 11,618 (43.90%)
1.16% swing C. to Lab.
(1997: Lab. maj. 14,200 (41.58%))

BIRMINGHAM LADYWOOD
E. 71,113 T. 31,493 (44.29%) Lab. hold
*Rt. Hon. Ms C. Short, Lab. 21,694
Benjamin Prentice, C. 3,551
Mahmood Chaudhry, LD 2,586
Allah Ditta, PJP 2,112
Surinder Virdee, Soc. Lab. 443
Mahmood Hussain, Muslim 432
James Caffery, ProLife 392
Dr Anneliese Nattrass, UK Ind. 283
Lab. majority 18,143 (57.61%)
1.59% swing Lab. to C.
(1997: Lab. maj. 23,082 (60.78%))

BIRMINGHAM NORTHFIELD
E. 55,922 T. 29,534 (52.81%) Lab. hold
*Richard Burden, Lab. 16,528
Nils Purser, C. 8,730
Trevor Sword, LD 3,322
Stephen Rogers, UK Ind. 550
Clive Walder, Soc. All. 193
Zane Carpenter, Soc. Lab. 151
Andrew Chaffer, Comm. 60
Lab. majority 7,798 (26.40%)
1.53% swing Lab. to C.
(1997: Lab. maj. 11,443 (29.46%))

BIRMINGHAM PERRY BARR
E. 71,121 T. 37,417 (52.61%) Lab. hold
Khalid Mahmood, Lab. 17,415
David Binns, C. 8,662
Jon Hunt, LD 8,566
Avtar Singh Jouh, Soc. Lab. 1,544
Ms Caroline Johnson, Soc. All. 465
Ms Natalya Nattrass, UK Ind. 352
Michael Roche, Marxist 221
Robert Davidson, Muslim 192
Lab. majority 8,753 (23.39%)
8.96% swing Lab. to C.
(1997: Lab. maj. 18,957 (41.32%))

BIRMINGHAM SELLY OAK
E. 71,237 T. 40,100 (56.29%) Lab. hold
*Dr Lynne Jones, Lab. 21,015
Ken Hardeman, C. 10,676
David Osborne, LD 6,532
Barney Smith, Green 1,309
Mrs Beryl Williams, UK Ind. 568
Lab. majority 10,339 (25.78%)
1.04% swing Lab. to C.
(1997: Lab. maj. 14,088 (27.87%))

BIRMINGHAM SPARKBROOK & SMALL HEATH
E. 74,358 T. 36,647 (49.28%) Lab. hold
*Roger Godsiff, Lab. 21,087
Qassim Afzal, LD 4,841
Shafaq Hussain, PJP 4,770
Iftkhar Hussain, C. 3,948
Gul Mohammed, Ind. 662
Wayne Vincent, UK Ind. 634
Abdul Aziz, Muslim 401
Salman Mirza, Soc. All. 304
Lab. majority 16,246 (44.33%))
5.31% swing Lab. to LD
(1997: Lab. maj. 19,526 (46.76%)

BIRMINGHAM YARDLEY
E. 52,444 T. 30,013 (57.23%) Lab. hold
*Rt. Hon. Ms E. Morris, Lab. 14,085
John Hemming, LD 11,507
Barrie Roberts, C. 3,941
Alan Ware, UK Ind. 329
Colin Wren, Soc. Lab. 151
Lab. majority 2,578 (8.59%)
2.74% swing Lab. to LD
(1997: Lab. maj. 5,315 (14.07%))

BISHOP AUCKLAND
E. 67,377 T. 38,559 (57.23%) Lab. hold
*Rt. Hon. D. Foster, Lab. 22,680
Mrs Fiona McNish, C. 8,754
Chris Foote-Wood, LD 6,073
Carl Bennett, Green 1,052
Lab. majority 13,926 (36.12%)
4.85% swing Lab. to C.
(1997: Lab. maj. 21,064 (45.82%))

BLABY
E. 73,907 T. 47,642 (64.46%) C. hold
*Andrew Robathan, C. 22,104
David Morgan, Lab. 15,895
Geoff Welsh, LD 8,286
Edward Scott, BNP 1,357
C. majority 6,209 (13.03%)
0.48% swing Lab. to C.
(1997: C. maj. 6,474 (12.08%))

BLACKBURN
E. 72,621 T. 40,484 (55.75%) Lab. hold
*Rt. Hon. J. Straw, Lab. 21,808
John Cotton, C. 12,559
Imtiaz Patel, LD 3,264
Mrs Dorothy Baxter, UK Ind. 1,185
Paul Morris, Ind. 577
Terence Cullen, Soc. Lab. 559
Frederick Nichol, Socialist 532
Lab. majority 9,249 (22.85%)
3.79% swing Lab. to C.
(1997: Lab. maj. 14,451 (30.43%))

BLACKPOOL NORTH & FLEETWOOD
E. 74,456 T. 42,581 (57.19%) Lab. hold
*Ms Joan Humble, Lab. 21,610
Alan Vincent, C. 15,889
Steven Bate, LD 4,132
Colin Porter, UK Ind. 950
Lab. majority 5,721 (13.44%)
1.60% swing Lab. to C.
(1997: Lab. maj. 8,946 (16.64%))

BLACKPOOL SOUTH
E. 74,311 T. 38,792 (52.20%) Lab. hold
*Gordon Marsden, Lab. 21,060
David Morris, C. 12,798
Ms Doreen Holt, LD 4,115
Mrs Val Cowell, UK Ind. 819
Lab. majority 8,262 (21.30%)
0.67% swing Lab. to C.
(1997: Lab. maj. 11,616 (22.63%))

BLAYDON
E. 64,574 T. 37,086 (57.43%) Lab. hold
*John McWilliam, Lab. 20,340
Peter Maughan, LD 12,531
Mark Watson, C. 4,215
Lab. majority 7,809 (21.06%)
7.55% swing Lab. to LD
(1997: Lab. maj. 16,605 (36.16%))

BLYTH VALLEY
E. 63,274 T. 34,550 (54.60%) Lab. hold
*Ronnie Campbell, Lab. 20,627
Jeff Reid, LD 8,439
Wayne Daley, C. 5,484
Lab. majority 12,188 (35.28%)
3.24% swing Lab. to LD
(1997: Lab. maj. 17,736 (41.75%))

BOGNOR REGIS & LITTLEHAMPTON
E. 66,903 T. 38,968 (58.25%) C. hold
*Nick Gibb, C. 17,602
George O'Neill, Lab. 11,959
Ms Pamela Peskett, LD 6,846
George Stride, UK Ind. 1,779
Ms Lilias Rider Haggard Cheyne, Green 782
C. majority 5,643 (14.48%)
0.64% swing C. to Lab.
(1997: C. maj. 7,321 (15.76%))

BOLSOVER
E. 67,537 T. 38,271 (56.67%) Lab. hold
*Dennis Skinner, Lab. 26,249
Simon Massey, C. 7,472
Ms Marie Bradley, LD 4,550
Lab. majority 18,777 (49.06%)
4.10% swing Lab. to C.
(1997: Lab. maj. 27,149 (57.26%))

BOLTON NORTH EAST
E. 69,514 T. 38,950 (56.03%) Lab. hold
*David Crausby, Lab. 21,166
Michael Winstanley, C. 12,744
Tim Perkins, LD 4,004
Kenneth McIvor, Green 629
Ms Lynne Lowe, Soc. Lab. 407
Lab. majority 8,422 (21.62%)
2.06% swing Lab. to C.
(1997: Lab. maj. 12,669 (25.74%))

BOLTON SOUTH EAST
E. 68,140 T. 34,154 (50.12%) Lab. hold
*Dr Brian Iddon, Lab. 21,129
Haroon Rashid, C. 8,258
Frank Harasiwka, LD 3,941
Dr William John Kelly, Soc. Lab. 826
Lab. majority 12,871 (37.69%)
5.74% swing Lab. to C.
(1997: Lab. maj. 21,311 (49.16%))

BOLTON WEST
E. 66,033 T. 41,214 (62.41%) Lab. hold
*Ms Ruth Kelly, Lab. 19,381
James Stevens, C. 13,863
Ms Barbara Ronson, LD 7,573
David Toomer, Soc. All. 397
Lab. majority 5,518 (13.39%)
0.50% swing Lab. to C.
(1997: Lab. maj. 7,072 (14.39%))

BOOTLE
E. 56,320 T. 27,594 (49.00%) Lab. hold
*Joe Benton, Lab. 21,400
Jim Murray, LD 2,357
Miss Judith Symes, C. 2,194
Dave Flynn, Soc. Lab. 971
Peter Glover, Soc. All. 672
Lab. majority 19,043 (69.01%)
4.05% swing Lab. to LD
(1997: Lab. maj. 28,421 (74.36%))

BOSTON & SKEGNESS
E. 69,010 T. 40,313 (58.42%) C. hold
Mark Simmonds, C. 17,298
Ms Elaine Bird, Lab. 16,783
Duncan Moffatt, LD 4,994
Cyril Wakefield, UK Ind. 717
Martin Harrison, Green 521
C. majority 515 (1.28%)
0.06% swing C. to Lab.
(1997: C. maj. 647 (1.39%))

BOSWORTH
E. 69,992 T. 45,106 (64.44%) C. hold
*David Tredinnick, C. 20,030
Andrew Furlong, Lab. 17,750
Jon Ellis, LD 7,326
C. majority 2,280 (5.05%)
1.54% swing Lab. to C.
(1997: C. maj. 1,027 (1.97%))

BOURNEMOUTH EAST
E. 60,454 T. 35,799 (59.22%) C. hold
*David Atkinson, C. 15,501
Andrew Garratt, LD 12,067
Paul Nicholson, Lab. 7,107
George Chamberlaine, UK Ind. 1,124
C. majority 3,434 (9.59%)
0.21% swing C. to LD
(1997: C. maj. 4,346 (10.01%))

BOURNEMOUTH WEST
E. 62,038 T. 33,648 (54.24%) C. hold
*John Butterfill, C. 14,417
David Stokes, Lab. 9,699
Ms Fiona Hornby, LD 8,468
Mrs Cynthia Blake, UK Ind. 1,064
C. majority 4,718 (14.02%)
1.54% swing C. to Lab.
(1997: C. maj. 5,710 (13.90%))

BRACKNELL
E. 81,118 T. 49,225 (60.68%) C. hold
*Rt. Hon. A. Mackay, C. 22,962
Ms Janet Keene, Lab. 16,249
Ray Earwicker, LD 8,424
Lawrence Boxall, UK Ind. 1,266
Ms Dominica Roberts, (ProLife) 324
C. majority 6,713 (13.64%)
1.97% swing C. to Lab.
(1997: C. maj. 10,387 (17.58%))

BRADFORD NORTH
E. 66,454 T. 35,017 (52.69%) Lab. hold
*Terry Rooney, Lab. 17,419
Zahid Iqbal, C. 8,450
David Ward, LD 6,924
John Brayshaw, BNP 1,613
Steven Schofield, Green 611
Lab. majority 8,969 (25.61%)
2.44% swing Lab. to C.
(1997: Lab. maj. 12,770 (30.49%))

BRADFORD SOUTH
E. 68,450 T. 35,137 (51.33%) Lab. hold
*Gerry Sutcliffe, Lab. 19,603
Graham Tennyson, C. 9,941
Alexander Wilson-Fletcher, LD 3,717
Peter North, UK Ind. 783
Tony Kelly, Soc. Lab. 571
Ateeq Siddique, Soc. All. 302
George Riseborough, Def Welfare 220
Lab. majority 9,662 (27.50%)
0.61% swing Lab. to C.
(1997: Lab. maj. 12,936 (28.71%))

BRADFORD WEST
E. 71,620 T. 38,370 (53.57%) Lab. hold
*Marsha Singh, Lab. 18,401
Mohammed Riaz, C. 14,236
John Robinson, Green 2,672
Abdul Rauf Khan, LD 2,437
Imran Hussain, UK Ind. 427
Farhan Khokhar, AL 197
Lab. majority 4,165 (10.85%)
1.17% swing C. to Lab.
(1997: Lab. maj. 3,877 (8.51%))

BRAINTREE
E. 79,157 T. 50,315 (63.56%) Lab. hold
*Alan Hurst, Lab. 21,123
Brooks Newmark, C. 20,765
Peter Turner, LD 5,664
James Abbott, Green 1,241
Michael Nolan, LCA 774
Charles Cole, UK Ind. 748
Lab. majority 358 (0.71%)
0.95% swing Lab. to C.
(1997: Lab. maj. 1,451 (2.61%))

BRENT EAST
E. 58,095 T. 28,992 (49.90%) Lab. hold
Paul Daisley, Lab. 18,325
David Gauke, C. 5,278
Ms Nowsheen Bhatti, LD 3,065
Ms Simone Aspis, Green 1,361
Ms Sarah Macken, ProLife 392
Ms Iris Cremer, Soc. Lab. 383
Ashwin Tanna, UK Ind. 188
Lab. majority 13,047 (45.00%)
0.01% swing Lab. to C.
(1997: Lab. maj. 15,882 (45.03%))

BRENT NORTH
E. 58,789 T. 33,939 (57.73%) Lab. hold
*Barry Gardiner, Lab. 20,149
Philip Allott, C. 9,944
Paul Lorber, LD 3,846
Lab. majority 10,205 (30.07%)
9.77% swing C. to Lab.
(1997: Lab. maj. 4,019 (10.53%))

BRENT SOUTH
E. 55,891 T. 28,637 (51.24%) Lab. hold
*Rt. Hon. P. Boateng, Lab. 20,984
Carupiah Selvarajah, C. 3,604
Havard Hughes, LD 3,098
Mick McDonnell, Soc. All. 491
Thomas Mac Stiofain, Res. Motor 460
Lab. majority 17,380 (60.69%)
1.81% swing C. to Lab.
(1997: Lab. maj. 19,691 (57.08%))

BRENTFORD & ISLEWORTH
E. 84,049 T. 44,514 (52.96%) Lab. hold
*Ms Ann Keen, Lab. 23,275
Tim Mack, C. 12,957
Gareth Hartwell, LD 5,994
Nic Ferriday, Green 1,324
Gerald Ingram, UK Ind. 412
Danny Faith, Soc. All. 408
Asa Khaira, Ind. 144
Lab. majority 10,318 (23.18%)
1.26% swing Lab. to C.
(1997: Lab. maj. 14,424 (25.70%))

BRENTWOOD & ONGAR
E. 64,695 T. 43,542 (67.30%) C. hold
*Eric Pickles, C. 16,558
†Martin Bell, Ind Bell 13,737
David Kendall, LD 6,772
Ms Diana Johnson, Lab. 5,505
Ken Gulleford, UK Ind. 611
Peter Pryke, Ind. 239
David Bishop, Elvis 68
Tony Appleton, Ind. 52
C. majority 2,821 (6.48%)
(1997: C. maj. 9,690 (19.10%))

BRIDGWATER
E. 74,079 T. 47,847 (64.59%) C. hold
Ian Liddell-Grainger, C. 19,354
Ian Thorn, LD 14,367
William Monteith, Lab. 12,803
Ms Vicky Gardner, UK Ind. 1,323
C. majority 4,987 (10.42%)
3.57% swing LD to C.
(1997: C. maj. 1,796 (3.28%))

BRIGG & GOOLE
E. 63,536 T. 41,054 (64.62%) Lab. hold
*Ian Cawsey, Lab. 20,066
Don Stewart, C. 16,105
David Nolan, LD 3,796
Godfrey Bloom, UK Ind. 688
Michael Kenny, Soc. Lab. 399
Lab. majority 3,961 (9.65%)
2.00% swing Lab. to C.
(1997: Lab. maj. 6,389 (13.65%))

BRIGHTON KEMPTOWN
E. 67,621 T. 39,203 (57.97%) Lab. hold
*Dr Desmond Turner, Lab. 18,745
Geoffrey Theobald, C. 13,823
Ms Jan Marshall, LD 4,064
Hugh Miller, Green 1,290
Dr James Chamberlain-Webber, UK Ind. 543
John McLeod, Soc. Lab. 364
Dave Dobbs, Free 227
Ms Elaine Cook, ProLife 147
Lab. majority 4,922 (12.56%)
2.45% swing C. to Lab.
(1997: Lab. maj. 3,534 (7.66%))

BRIGHTON PAVILION
E. 69,200 T. 40,723 (58.85%) Lab. Co-op hold
*David Lepper, Lab. Co-op 19,846
David Gold, C. 10,203
Ms Ruth Berry, LD 5,348
Keith Taylor, Green 3,806
Ian Fyvie, Soc. Lab. 573
Bob Dobbs, Free 409
Stuart Hutchin, UK Ind. 361
Ms Marie Paragallo, ProLife 177
Lab. Co-op majority 9,643 (23.68%)
1.63% swing Lab. Co-op to C.
(1997: Lab. maj. 13,181 (26.93%))

BRISTOL EAST
E. 70,279 T. 40,334 (57.39%) Lab. hold
*Ms Jean Corston, Lab. 22,180
Jack Lo-Presti, C. 8,788
Brian Niblett, LD 6,915
Geoff Collard, Green 1,110
Roger Marsh, UK Ind. 572
Mike Langley, Soc. Lab. 438
Andy Pryor, Soc. All. 331
Lab. majority 13,392 (33.20%)
0.16% swing Lab. to C.
(1997: Lab. maj. 16,159 (33.52%))

BRISTOL NORTH WEST
E. 76,756 T. 46,692 (60.83%) Lab. Co-op hold
*Doug Naysmith, Lab. Co-op 24,436
Charles Hansard, C. 13,349
Peter Tyzack, LD 7,387
Miss Diane Carr, UK Ind. 1,149
Vince Horrigan, Soc. Lab. 371
Lab. Co-op majority 11,087 (23.74%)
1.57% swing C. to Lab. Co-op
(1997: Lab. maj. 11,382 (20.60%))

BRISTOL SOUTH
E. 72,490 T. 40,970 (56.52%) Lab. hold
*Ms Dawn Primarolo, Lab. 23,299
Richard Eddy, C. 9,118
James Main, LD 6,078
Glenn Vowles, Green 1,233
Brian Drummond, Soc. All. 496
Chris Prasad, UK Ind. 496
Giles Shorter, Soc. Lab. 250
Lab. majority 14,181 (34.61%)
2.08% swing Lab. to C.
(1997: Lab. maj. 19,328 (38.77%))

BRISTOL WEST
E. 84,821 T. 55,665 (65.63%) Lab. hold
*Ms Valerie Davey, Lab. 20,505
Stephen Williams, LD 16,079
Mrs Pamela Chesters, C. 16,040
John Devaney, Green 1,961
Bernard Kennedy, Soc. Lab. 590
Simon Muir, UK Ind. 490
Lab. majority 4,426 (7.95%)
0.37% swing LD to Lab.
(1997: Lab. maj. 1,493 (2.38%))

BROMLEY & CHISLEHURST
E. 68,763 T. 43,231 (62.87%) C. hold
*Rt. Hon. E. Forth, C. 21,412
Ms Sue Polydorou, Lab. 12,375
Geoff Payne, LD 8,180
Rob Bryant, UK Ind. 1,264
C. majority 9,037 (20.90%)
0.09% swing C. to Lab.
(1997: C. maj. 11,118 (21.08%))

BROMSGROVE
E. 68,115 T. 45,684 (67.07%) C. hold
*Miss Julie Kirkbride, C. 23,640
Peter McDonald, Lab. 15,502
Mrs Margaret Rowley, LD 5,430
Ian Gregory, UK Ind. 1,112
C. majority 8,138 (17.81%)
4.22% swing Lab. to C.
(1997: C. maj. 4,895 (9.38%))

BROXBOURNE
E. 68,982 T. 37,845 (54.86%) C. hold
*Mrs Marion Roe, C. 20,487
David Prendergast, Lab. 11,494
Ms Julia Davies, LD 4,158
Martin Harvey, UK Ind. 858
John Cope, BNP 848
C. majority 8,993 (23.76%)
4.80% swing Lab. to C.
(1997: C. maj. 6,653 (14.16%))

BROXTOWE
E. 73,675 T. 49,004 (66.51%) Lab. hold
*Nick Palmer, Lab. 23,836
Mrs Pauline Latham, C. 17,963
David Watts, LD 7,205
Lab. majority 5,873 (11.98%)
1.20% swing C. to Lab.
(1997: Lab. maj. 5,575 (9.59%))

BUCKINGHAM
E. 65,270 T. 45,272 (69.36%) C. hold
*John Bercow, C. 24,296
Mark Seddon, Lab. 10,971
Ms Isobel Wilson, LD 9,037
Christopher Silcock, UK Ind. 968
C. majority 13,325 (29.43%)
2.18% swing Lab. to C.
(1997: C. maj. 12,386 (25.08%))

BURNLEY
E. 66,393 T. 36,884 (55.55%) Lab. hold
*Peter Pike, Lab. 18,195
Robert Frost, C. 7,697
Paul Wright, LD 5,975
Steven Smith, BNP 4,151
Richard Buttrey, UK Ind. 866
Lab. majority 10,498 (28.46%)
4.62% swing Lab. to C.
(1997: Lab. maj. 17,062 (37.71%))

BURTON
E. 75,194 T. 46,457 (61.78%) Lab. hold
*Ms Janet Dean, Lab. 22,783
Mrs Maggie Punyer, C. 17,934
David Fletcher, LD 4,468
Ian Crompton, UK Ind. 984
John Taylor, ProLife 288
Lab. majority 4,849 (10.44%)
0.59% swing Lab. to C.
(1997: Lab. Maj. 6,330 (11.62%))

BURY NORTH
E. 71,108 T. 44,788 (62.99%) Lab. hold
*David Chaytor, Lab. 22,945
John Walsh, C. 16,413
Bryn Hackley, LD 5,430
Lab. majority 6,532 (14.58%)
0.15% swing C. to Lab.
(1997: Lab. maj. 7,866 (14.29%))

BURY SOUTH
E. 67,276 T. 39,539 (58.77%) Lab. hold
*Ivan Lewis, Lab. 23,406
Mrs Nicola Le Page, C. 10,634
Tim Pickstone, LD 5,499
Lab. majority 12,772 (32.30%)
3.80% swing C. to Lab.
(1997: Lab. maj. 12,433 (24.70%))

BURY ST EDMUNDS
E. 76,146 T. 50,257 (66.00%) C. hold
*David Ruffley, C. 21,850
Mark Ereira, Lab. 19,347
Richard Williams, LD 6,998
John Howlett, UK Ind. 831
Mike Brundle, Ind. 651
Michael Benwell, Soc. Lab. 580
C. majority 2,503 (4.98%)
2.16% swing Lab. to C.
(1997: C. maj. 368 (0.66%))

CALDER VALLEY
E. 75,298 T. 47,425 (62.98%) Lab. hold
*Mrs Christine McCafferty, Lab. 20,244
Mrs Sue Robson-Catling, C. 17,150
Michael Taylor, LD 7,596
Steve Hutton, Green 1,034
John Nunn, UK Ind. 729
Philip Lockwood, LCA 672
Lab. majority 3,094 (6.52%)
2.27% swing Lab. to C.
(1997: Lab. maj. 6,255 (11.07%))

CAMBERWELL & PECKHAM
E. 53,694 T. 25,104 (46.75%) Lab. hold
*Rt. Hon. Ms H. Harman, Lab. 17,473
Donnachadh McCarthy, LD 3,350
Jonathan Morgan, C. 2,740
Storm Poorun, Green 805
John Mulrenan, Soc. All. 478
Robert Adams, Soc. Lab. 188
Frank Sweeney, WRP 70
Lab. majority 14,123 (56.26%)
0.91% swing Lab. to LD
(1997: Lab. maj. 16,351 (57.43%))

CAMBRIDGE
E. 70,663 T. 42,836 (60.62%) Lab. hold
*Ms Anne Campbell, Lab. 19,316
David Howarth, LD 10,737
Graham Stuart, C. 9,829
Stephen Lawrence, Green 1,413
Howard Senter, Soc. All. 716
Len Baynes, UK Ind. 532
Ms Clare Underwood, ProLife 232
Ms Margaret Courtney, WRP 61
Lab. majority 8,579 (20.03%)
8.64% swing Lab. to LD
(1997: Lab. maj. 14,137 (27.54%))

CAMBRIDGESHIRE NORTH EAST
E. 79,891 T. 48,051 (60.15%) C. hold
*Malcolm Moss, C. 23,132
Dil Owen, Lab. 16,759
Richard Renaut, LD 6,733
John Stevens, UK Ind. 1,189
Tony Hoey, ProLife 238
C. majority 6,373 (13.26%)
2.03% swing Lab. to C.
(1997: C. maj. 5,101 (9.20%))

CAMBRIDGESHIRE NORTH WEST
E. 70,569 T. 43,956 (62.29%) C. hold
*Rt. Hon. Sir B. Mawhinney, C. 21,895
Ms Anthea Cox, Lab. 13,794
Alastair Taylor, LD 6,957
Barry Hudson, UK Ind. 881
David Hall, Ind. 429
C. majority 8,101 (18.43%)
1.27% swing Lab. to C.
(1997: C. maj. 7,754 (15.88%))

CAMBRIDGESHIRE SOUTH
E. 72,095 T. 48,341 (67.05%) C. hold
*Andrew Lansley, C. 21,387
Ms Amanda Taylor, LD 12,984
Dr Joan Herbert, Lab. 11,737
Simon Saggers, Green 1,182
Mrs Helene Davies, UK Ind. 875
Ms Beata Klepacka, ProLife 176
C. majority 8,403 (17.38%)
0.58% swing LD to C.
(1997: C. maj. 8,712 (16.23%))

CAMBRIDGESHIRE SOUTH EAST
E. 81,663 T. 51,886 (63.54%) C. hold
*James Paice, C. 22,927
Ms Sal Brinton, LD 13,937
Andrew Inchley, Lab. 13,714
Neil Scarr, UK Ind. 1,308
C. majority 8,990 (17.33%)
0.27% swing C. to LD
(1997: C. maj. 9,349 (16.46%))

CANNOCK CHASE
E. 73,423 T. 41,064 (55.93%) Lab. hold
*Dr Tony Wright, Lab. 23,049
Gavin Smithers, C. 12,345
Stewart Reynolds, LD 5,670
Lab. majority 10,704 (26.07%)
0.79% swing Lab. to C.
(1997: Lab. maj. 14,478 (27.65%))

CANTERBURY
E. 74,159 T. 45,132 (60.86%) C. hold
*Julian Brazier, C. 18,711
Ms Emily Thornberry, Lab. 16,642
Peter Wales, LD 8,056
Ms Hazel Dawe, Green 920
Ms Lisa Moore, UK Ind. 803
C. majority 2,069 (4.58%)
1.37% swing C. to Lab.
(1997: C. maj. 3,964 (7.33%))

CARLISLE
E. 58,811 T. 34,909 (59.36%) Lab. hold
*Eric Martlew, Lab. 17,856
Mike Mitchelson, C. 12,154
John Guest, LD 4,076
Colin Paisley, LCA 554
Paul Wilcox, Soc. All. 269
Lab. majority 5,702 (16.33%)
6.04% swing Lab. to C.
(1997: Lab. maj. 12,390 (28.41%))

CARSHALTON & WALLINGTON
E. 67,337 T. 40,612 (60.31%) LD hold
*Tom Brake, LD 18,289
Ken Andrew, C. 13,742
Ms Margaret Cooper, Lab. 7,466
Simon Dixon, Green 614
Martin Haley, UK Ind. 501
LD majority 4,547 (11.20%)
3.26% swing C. to LD
(1997: LD maj. 2,267 (4.68%))

CASTLE POINT
E. 68,108 T. 39,763 (58.38%) C. gain
Dr Robert Spink, C. 17,738
*Ms Christine Butler, Lab. 16,753
Billy Boulton, LD 3,116
Ron Hurrell, UK Ind. 1,273
Douglas Roberts, Ind. 663
Nik Searle, Truth 220
C. majority 985 (2.48%)
2.39% swing Lab. to C.
(1997: Lab. maj. 1,116 (2.30%)

CHARNWOOD
E. 74,836 T. 48,265 (64.49%) C. hold
*Rt. Hon. S. Dorrell, C. 23,283
Sean Sheahan, Lab. 15,544
Ms Susan King, LD 7,835
Jamie Bye, UK Ind. 1,603
C. majority 7,739 (16.03%)
2.77% swing Lab. to C.
(1997: C. maj. 5,900 (10.50%))

CHATHAM & AYLESFORD
E. 69,759 T. 39,735 (56.96%) Lab. hold
*Jonathan Shaw, Lab. 19,180
Sean Holden, C. 14,840
David Lettington, LD 4,705
Gregory Knopp, UK Ind. 1,010
Lab. majority 4,340 (10.92%)
2.62% swing C. to Lab.
(1997: Lab. maj. 2,790 (5.68%))

CHEADLE
E. 69,002 T. 43,606 (63.20%) LD gain
Ms Patsy Calton, LD 18,477
*Stephen Day, C. 18,444
Howard Dawber, Lab. 6,086
Vincent Cavanagh, UK Ind. 599
LD majority, 33 (0.08%)
3.07% swing C. to LD
(1997: C. maj. 3,189 (6.07%))

CHELMSFORD WEST
E. 78,291 T. 48,143 (61.49%) C. hold
*Simon Burns, C. 20,446
Adrian Longden, Lab. 14,185
Stephen Robinson, LD 11,197
Mrs Eleanor Burgess, Green 837
Ken Wedon, UK Ind. 785
Christopher Philbin, LCA 693
C. majority 6,261 (13.01%)
0.62% swing C. to Lab.
(1997: C. maj. 6,691 (11.42%))

CHELTENHAM
E. 67,563 T. 41,835 (61.92%) LD hold
*Nigel Jones, LD 19,970
Rob Garnham, C. 14,715
Andy Erlam, Lab. 5,041
Keith Bessant, Green 735
Dancing Ken Hanks, Loony 513
Jim Carver, UK Ind. 482
Anthony Gates, ProLife 272
Roger Everest, Ind. 107
LD majority 5,255 (12.56%)
0.32% swing LD to C.
(1997: LD maj. 6,645 (13.21%))

CHESHAM & AMERSHAM
E. 70,021 T. 45,283 (64.67%) C. hold
*Mrs Cheryl Gillan, C. 22,867
John Ford, LD 10,985
Ken Hulme, Lab. 8,497
Ian Harvey, UK Ind. 1,367
Nick Wilkins, Green 1,114
Ms Gillian Duval, ProLife 453
C. majority 11,882 (26.24%)
0.16% swing C. to LD
(1997: C. maj. 13,859 (26.55%))

CHESTER, CITY OF
E. 70,382 T. 44,877 (63.76%) Lab. hold
*Ms Christine Russell, Lab. 21,760
David Jones, C. 14,866
Tony Dawson, LD 6,589
Allan Weddell, UK Ind. 899
George Rogers, Ind. 763
Lab. majority 6,894 (15.36%)
1.70% swing Lab. to C.
(1997: Lab. maj. 10,553 (18.76%))

CHESTERFIELD
E. 73,252 T. 44,441 (60.67%) LD gain
Paul Holmes, LD 21,249
Reg Race, Lab. 18,663
Simon Hitchcock, C. 3,613
Ms Jeannie Robinson, Soc. All. 437
Bill Harrison, Soc. Lab. 295
Christopher Rawson, Ind. 184
LD majority 2,586 (5.82%)
8.53% swing Lab. to LD
(1997: Lab. maj. 5,775 (11.24%))

CHICHESTER
E. 77,703 T. 49,512 (63.72%) C. hold
*Andrew Tyrie, C. 23,320
Ms Lynne Ravenscroft, LD 11,965
Ms Celia Barlow, Lab. 10,627
Douglas Denny, UK Ind. 2,308
Gavin Graham, Green 1,292
C. majority 11,355 (22.93%)
2.74% swing LD to C.
(1997: C. maj. 9,734 (17.45%))

CHINGFORD & WOODFORD GREEN
E. 63,252 T. 36,982 (58.47%) C. hold
*Iain Duncan Smith, C. 17,834
Ms Jessica Webb, Lab. 12,347
John Beanse, LD 5,739
Ms Jean Griffin, BNP 1,062
C. majority 5,487 (14.84%)
0.99% swing Lab. to C.
(1997: C. maj. 5,714 (12.85%))

CHIPPING BARNET
E. 70,217 T. 42,456 (60.46%) C. hold
*Sir Sydney Chapman, C. 19,702
Damien Welfare, Lab. 17,001
Sean Hooker, LD 5,753
C. majority 2,701 (6.36%)
2.14% swing Lab. to C.
(1997: C. maj. 1,035 (2.09%))

CHORLEY
E. 77,036 T. 47,952 (62.25%) Lab. hold
*Lindsay Hoyle, Lab. 25,088
Peter Booth, C. 6,644
Stephen Fenn, LD 5,372
Graham Frost, UK Ind. 848
Lab. majority 18,444 (17.61%)
0.25% swing C. to Lab.
(1997: Lab. maj. 9,870 (17.10%))

CHRISTCHURCH
E. 73,503 T. 49,567 (67.44%) C. hold
*Christopher Chope, C. 27,306
Ms Dorothy Webb, LD 13,762
Ms Judith Begg, Lab. 7,506
Ms Margaret Strange, UK Ind. 993
C. majority 13,544 (27.32%)
11.74% swing LD to C.
(1997: C. maj. 2,165 (3.85%))

CITIES OF LONDON & WESTMINSTER
E. 71,935 T. 33,975 (47.23%) C. hold
Mark Field, C. 15,737
Michael Katz, Lab. 11,238
Martin Horwood, LD 5,218
Hugo Charlton, Green 1,318
Colin Merton, UK Ind. 464
C. majority 4,499 (13.24%)
0.54% swing Lab. to C.
(1997: C. maj. 4,881 (12.16%))

CLEETHORPES
E. 68,392 T. 42,418 (62.02%) Lab. hold
*Ms Shona McIsaac, Lab. 21,032
Stephen Howd, C. 15,412
Gordon Smith, LD 5,080
Ms Janet Hatton, UK Ind. 894
Lab. majority 5,620 (13.25%)
2.47% swing Lab. to C.
(1997: Lab. maj. 9,176 (18.18%))

COLCHESTER
E. 78,955 T. 43,736 (55.39%) LD hold
*Bob Russell, LD 18,627
Kevin Bentley, C. 13,074
Chris Fegan, Lab. 10,925
Roger Lord, UK Ind. 631
Leonard Overy-Owen, Grey 479
LD maj 5,553 (12.70%)
4.83% swing C. to LD
(1997: LD maj. 1,581 (3.04%))

COLNE VALLEY
E. 74,192 T. 46,987 (63.33%) Lab. hold
*Ms Kali Mountford, Lab. 18,967
Philip Davies, C. 14,328
Gordon Beever, LD 11,694
Richard Plunkett, Green 1,081
Dr Arthur Quarmby, UK Ind. 917
Lab. majority 4,639 (9.87%)
0.65% swing C. to Lab.
(1997: Lab. maj. 4,840 (8.58%))

CONGLETON
E. 71,941 T. 45,083 (62.67%) C. hold
*Mrs Ann Winterton, C. 20,872
John Flanagan, Lab. 13,738
David Lloyd-Griffiths, LD 9,719
Bill Young, UK Ind. 754
C. majority 7,134 (15.82%)
1.08% swing Lab. to C.
(1997: C. maj. 6,130 (11.48%))

COPELAND
E. 53,526 T. 34,750 (64.92%) Lab. hold
*Rt. Hon. Dr J. Cunningham, Lab. 17,991
Mike Graham, C. 13,027
Mark Gayler, LD 3,732
Lab. majority 4,964 (14.28%)
7.30% swing Lab. to C.
(1997: Lab. maj. 11,944 (28.89%))

CORBY
E. 72,304 T. 47,222 (65.31%)
Lab. Co-op hold
*Phil Hope, Lab. Co-op 23,283
Andrew Griffith, C. 17,583
Kevin Scudder, LD 4,751
Ian Gillman, UK Ind. 855
Andrew Dickson, Soc. Lab. 750
Lab. Co-op majority 5,700 (12.07%)
4.95% swing Lab. Co-op to C.
(1997: Lab. maj. 11,860 (21.98%))

CORNWALL NORTH
E. 84,662 T. 53,983 (63.76%) LD hold
*Paul Tyler, LD 28,082
John Weller, C. 18,250
Mike Goodman, Lab. 5,257
Steve Protz, UK Ind. 2,394
LD majority 9,832 (18.21%)
2.79% swing LD to C.
(1997: LD maj. 13,933 (23.79%))

CORNWALL SOUTH EAST
E. 79,090 T. 51,753 (65.44%) LD hold
*Colin Breed, LD 23,756
Ashley Gray, C. 18,381
Bill Stevens, Lab. 6,429
Graham Palmer, UK Ind. 1,978
Dr Ken George, Meb. Ker. 1,209
LD majority 5,375 (10.39%)
0.45% swing LD to C.
(1997: LD maj. 6,480 (11.28%))

COTSWOLD
E. 68,154 T. 45,981 (67.47%) C. hold
*Geoffrey Clifton-Brown, C. 23,133
Ms Angela Lawrence, LD 11,150
Richard Wilkins, Lab. 10,383
Mrs Jill Stopps, UK Ind. 1,315
C. majority 11,983 (26.06%)
1.33% swing LD to C.
(1997: C. maj. 11,965 (23.41%))

COVENTRY NORTH EAST
E. 73,998 T. 37,265 (50.36%) Lab. hold
Bob Ainsworth, Lab. 22,739
Gordon Bell, C. 6,988
Geoffrey Sewards, LD 4,163
Dave Nellist, Soc. All. 2,638
Edward Sheppard, BNP 737
Lab. majority 15,751 (42.27%)
2.34% swing Lab. to C.
(1997: Lab. maj. 22,569 (46.94%))

COVENTRY NORTH WEST
E. 76,652 T. 42,551 (55.51%) Lab. hold
*Geoffrey Robinson, Lab. 21,892
Andrew Fairburn, C. 11,018
Napier Penlington, LD 5,832
Ms Christine Oddy, Ind. 3,159
Mark Benson, UK Ind. 650
Lab. majority 10,874 (25.56%)
2.50% swing Lab. to C.
(1997: Lab. maj. 16,601 (30.56%))

COVENTRY SOUTH
E. 72,527 T. 40,096 (55.28%) Lab. hold
*Jim Cunningham, Lab. 20,125
Ms Heather Wheeler, C. 11,846
Vincent McKee, LD 5,672
Rob Windsor, Soc. All. 1,475
Ms Irene Rogers, Ind. 564
Timothy Logan, Soc. Lab. 414
Lab. majority 8,279 (20.65%)
0.61% swing Lab. to C.
(1997: Lab. maj. 10,953 (21.86%))

CRAWLEY
E. 71,626 T. 39,522 (55.18%) Lab. hold
*Ms Laura Moffatt, Lab. 19,488
Henry Smith, C. 12,718
Ms Linda Seekings, LD 5,009
Brian Galloway, UK Ind. 1,137
Ms Claire Staniford, Loony 388
Arshad Khan, JP 271
Karl Stewart, Soc. Lab. 260
Ms Muriel Hirsch, Soc. All. 251
Lab. majority 6,770 (17.13%)
3.05% swing Lab. to C.
(1997: Lab. maj. 11,707 (23.22%))

CREWE & NANTWICH
E. 69,040 T. 41,547 (60.18%) Lab. hold
*Mrs Gwyneth Dunwoody, Lab. 22,556
Donald Potter, C. 12,650
David Cannon, LD 5,595
Roger Croston, UK Ind. 746
Lab. majority 9,906 (23.84%)
3.69% swing Lab. to C.
(1997: Lab. maj. 15,798 (31.22%))

CROSBY
E. 57,375 T. 36,866 (64.25%) Lab. hold
*Ms Claire Curtis-Thomas, Lab. 20,327
Robert Collinson, C. 11,974
Tim Drake, LD 4,084
Mark Holt, Soc. Lab. 481
Lab. majority 8,353 (22.66%)
3.19% swing C. to Lab.
(1997: Lab. maj. 7,182 (16.27%))

CROYDON CENTRAL
E. 77,567 T. 45,860 (59.12%) Lab. hold
*Geraint Davies, Lab. 21,643
David Congdon, C. 17,659
Paul Booth, LD 5,156
James Feisenberger, UK Ind. 545
Ms Lynda Miller, BNP 449
John Cartwright, Loony 408
Lab. majority 3,984 (8.69%)
0.85% swing C. to Lab.
(1997: Lab. maj. 3,897 (6.99%))

CROYDON NORTH
E. 76,600 T. 41,882 (54.68%) Lab. hold
*Malcolm Wicks, Lab. 26,610
Simon Allison, C. 9,752
Ms Sandra Lawman, LD 4,375
Alan Smith, UK Ind. 606
Don Madgwick, Soc. All. 539
Lab. majority 16,858 (40.25%)
2.63% swing C. to Lab.
(1997: Lab. maj. 18,398 (35.00%))

CROYDON SOUTH
E. 73,402 T. 45,060 (61.39%) C. hold
*Richard Ottaway, C. 22,169
Gerry Ryan, Lab. 13,472
Ms Anne Gallop, LD 8,226
Mrs Kathleen Garner, UK Ind. 998
Mark Samuel, Choice 195
C. majority 8,697 (19.30%))
1.35% swing C. to Lab.
(1997: C. maj. 11,930 (22.01%))

DAGENHAM
E. 59,340 T. 27,580 (46.48%) Lab. hold
Jon Cruddas, Lab. 15,784
Michael White, C. 7,091
Adrian Gee-Turner, LD 2,820
David Hill, BNP 1,378
Berlyne Hamilton, Soc. All. 262
Robert Siggins, Soc. Lab. 245
Lab. majority 8,693 (31.52%)
7.82% swing Lab. to C.
(1997: Lab. maj. 17,054 (47.16%))

DARLINGTON
E. 64,328 T. 40,754 (63.35%) Lab. hold
*Rt. Hon. A. Milburn, Lab. 22,479
Tony Richmond, C. 12,950
Robert Adamson, LD 4,358
Alan Docherty, Soc. All. 469
Craig Platt, Ind. 269
Ms Amanda Rose, Soc. Lab. 229
Lab. majority 9,529 (23.38%)
4.94% swing Lab. to C.
(1997: Lab. maj. 16,025 (33.27%))

DARTFORD
E. 72,258 T. 44,740 (61.92%) Lab. hold
*Howard Stoate, Lab. 21,466
Bob Dunn, C. 18,160
Graham Morgan, LD 3,781
Mark Croucher, UK Ind. 989
Keith Davenport, FDP 344
Lab. majority 3,306 (7.39%)
0.47% swing Lab. to C.
(1997: Lab. maj. 4,328 (8.32%))

DAVENTRY
E. 86,537 T. 56,684 (65.50%) C. hold
*Tim Boswell, C. 27,911
Kevin Quigley, Lab. 18,262
Jamie Calder, LD 9,130
Peter Baden, UK Ind. 1,381
C. majority 9,649 (17.02%)
2.54% swing Lab. to C.
(1997: C. maj. 7,378 (11.95%))

DENTON & REDDISH
E. 69,236 T. 33,593 (48.52%) Lab. hold
*Andrew Bennett, Lab. 21,913
Paul Newman, C. 6,583
Roger Fletcher, LD 4,152
Alan Cadwallender, UK Ind. 945
Lab. majority 15,330 (45.63%)
0.78% swing C. to Lab.
(1997: Lab. maj. 20,311 (44.08%))

DERBY NORTH
E. 76,489 T. 44,054 (57.60%) Lab. hold
*Bob Laxton, Lab. 22,415
Barrie Holden, C. 15,433
Robert Charlesworth, LD 6,206
Lab. majority 6,982 (15.85%)
1.53% swing Lab. to C.
(1997: Lab. maj. 10,615 (18.91%))

DERBY SOUTH
E. 77,366 T. 43,075 (55.68%) Lab. hold
*Rt. Hon. Mrs M. Beckett, Lab. 24,310
Simon Spencer, C. 10,455
Anders Hanson, LD 8,310
Lab. majority 13,855 (32.16%)
0.54% swing C. to Lab.
(1997: Lab. maj. 16,106 (31.08%))

DERBYSHIRE NORTH EAST
E. 71,527 T. 42,124 (58.89%) Lab. hold
*Harry Barnes, Lab. 23,437
James Hollingsworth, C. 11,179
Mark Higginbottom, LD 7,508
Lab. majority 12,258 (29.10%)
3.08% swing Lab. to C.
(1997: Lab. maj. 18,321 (35.25%))

DERBYSHIRE SOUTH
E. 81,010 T. 51,945 (64.12%) Lab. hold
*Mark Todd, Lab. 26,338
James Hakewill, C. 18,487
Russell Eagling, LD 5,233
John Blunt, UK Ind. 1,074
Paul Liversuch, Soc. Lab. 564
James Taylor, Ind. 249
Lab. majority 7,851 (15.11%)
4.09% swing Lab. to C.
(1997: Lab. maj. 13,967 (23.29%))

DERBYSHIRE WEST
E. 75,067 T. 50,589 (67.39%) C. hold
*Patrick McLoughlin, C. 24,280
Stephen Clamp, Lab. 16,910
Jeremy Beckett, LD 7,922
Stuart Bavester, UK Ind. 672
Nick Delves, Loony 472
Robert Goodall, Ind. 333
C. majority 7,370 (14.57%)
2.99% swing Lab. to C.
(1997: C. maj. 4,885 (8.59%))

DEVIZES
E. 83,655 T. 53,249 (63.65%) C. hold
*Rt. Hon. M. Ancram, C. 25,159
Jim Thorpe, Lab. 13,263
Ms Helen Frances, LD 11,756
Alan Wood, UK Ind. 1,521
Ludovic Kennedy, Ind. 1,078
Ms Vanessa Potter, Loony 472
C. majority 11,896 (22.34%)
1.88% swing Lab. to C.
(1997: C. maj. 9,782 (16.29%))

DEVON EAST
E. 70,278 T. 47,837 (68.07%) C. hold
Hugo Swire, C 22,681
Tim Dumper, LD 14,486
Phil Starr, Lab. 7,974
David Wilson, UK Ind. 2,696
C. majority 8,195 (17.13%)
1.44% swing LD to C.
(1997: C. maj. 7,489 (14.25%))

DEVON NORTH
E. 72,100 T. 49,254 (68.31%) LD hold
*Nick Harvey, LD 21,784
Clive Allen, C. 18,800
Ms Viv Gale, Lab. 4,995
Roger Knapman, UK Ind. 2,484
Tony Bown, Green 1,191
LD majority 2,984 (6.06%)
2.61% swing LD to C.
(1997: LD maj. 6,181 (11.27%))

DEVON SOUTH WEST
E. 70,922 T. 46,904 (66.13%) C. hold
*Gary Streeter, C. 21,970
Christopher Mavin, Lab. 14,826
Phil Hutty, LD 8,616
Roger Bullock, UK Ind. 1,492
C. majority 7,144 (15.23%)
0.58% swing Lab. to C.
(1997: C. maj. 7,433 (14.07%))

DEVON WEST & TORRIDGE
E. 78,976 T. 55,684 (70.51%) LD hold
*John Burnett, LD 23,474
Geoffrey Cox, C. 22,280
David Brenton, Lab. 5,959
Bob Edwards, UK Ind. 2,674
Martin Quinn, Green 1,297
LD majority 1,194 (2.14%)
0.58% swing LD to C.
(1997: LD maj. 1,957 (3.31%))

DEWSBURY
E. 62,344 T. 36,651 (58.79%) Lab. hold
*Rt. Hon. Mrs A. Taylor, Lab. 18,524
Robert Cole, C. 11,075
Ian Cuthbertson, LD 4,382
Russell Smith, BNP 1,632
Ms Brenda Smithson, Green 560
David Peace, UK Ind. 478
Lab. majority 7,449 (20.32%)
0.50% swing C. to Lab.
(1997: Lab. maj. 8,323 (19.33%))

DON VALLEY
E. 66,244 T. 36,630 (55.30%) Lab. hold
*Ms Caroline Flint, Lab. 20,009
James Browne, C. 10,489
Phillip Smith, LD 4,089
Tony Wilde, Ind. 800
David Cooper, UK Ind. 777
Nigel Ball, Soc. Lab. 466
Lab. majority 9,520 (25.99%)
3.84% swing Lab. to C.
(1997: Lab. maj. 14,659 (33.66%))

DONCASTER CENTRAL
E. 65,087 T. 33,902 (52.09%) Lab. hold
*Ms Rosie Winterton, Lab. 20,034
Gary Meggitt, C. 8,035
Michael Southcombe, LD 4,390
David Gordon, UK Ind. 926
Ms Janet Terry, Soc. All. 517
Lab. majority 11,999 (35.39%)
2.85% swing Lab. to C.
(1997: Lab. maj. 17,856 (41.10%))

DONCASTER NORTH
E. 62,124 T. 31,363 (50.48%) Lab. hold
*Kevin Hughes, Lab. 19,788
Mrs Anita Kapoor, C. 4,601
Colin Ross, LD 3,323
Martin Williams, Ind. 2,926
John Wallis, UK Ind. 725
Lab. majority 15,187 (48.42%)
3.28% swing Lab. to C.
(1997: Lab. maj. 21,937 (54.99%))

DORSET MID & POOLE NORTH
E. 66,675 T. 43,718 (65.57%) LD gain
Ms Annette Brooke, LD 18,358
*Christopher Fraser, C. 17,974
James Selby-Bennett, Lab. 6,765
Jeff Mager, UK Ind. 621
LD majority 384 (0.88%)
1.11% swing C. to LD
(1997: C. maj. 681 (1.34%))

DORSET NORTH
E. 72,140 T. 47,821 (66.29%) C. hold
*Robert Walter, C. 22,314
Miss Emily Gasson, LD 18,517
Mark Wareham, Lab. 5,334
Peter Jenkins, UK Ind. 1,019
Joseph Duthie, Low Excise 391
Mrs Cora Bone, Ind. 246
C. majority 3,797 (7.94%)
1.36% swing LD to C.
(1997: C. maj. 2,746 (5.23%))

DORSET SOUTH
E. 69,233 T. 45,345 (65.50%) Lab. gain
Jim Knight, Lab. 19,027
*Ian Cameron Bruce, C. 18,874
Andrew Canning, LD 6,531
Laurence Moss, UK Ind. 913
Lab. majority 153 (0.34%)
0.25% swing C. to Lab.
(1997: C. maj. 77 (0.16%))

DORSET WEST
E. 74,016 T. 49,571 (66.97%) C. hold
*Oliver Letwin, C. 22,126
Simon Green, LD 20,712
Richard Hyde, Lab. 6,733
C. majority 1,414 (2.85%)
0.29% swing C. to LD
(1997: C. maj. 1,840 (3.44%))

DOVER
E. 69,025 T. 44,960 (65.14%) Lab. hold
*Gwyn Prosser, Lab. 21,943
Paul Watkins, C. 16,744
Antony Hook, LD 5,131
Lee Speakman, UK Ind. 1,142
Lab. majority 5,199 (11.56%)
5.05% swing Lab. to C.
(1997: Lab. maj. 11,739 (21.66%))

DUDLEY NORTH
E. 68,964 T. 38,564 (55.92%) Lab. hold
*Ross Cranston, Lab. 20,095
Andrew Griffiths, C. 13,295
Richard Burt, LD 3,352
Simon Darby, BNP 1,822
Lab. majority 6,800 (17.63%)
1.08% swing Lab. to C.
(1997: Lab. maj. 9,457 (19.79%))

DUDLEY SOUTH
E. 65,578 T. 36,344 (55.42%) Lab. hold
*Ian Pearson, Lab. 18,109
Jason Sugarman, C. 11,292
Ms Lorely Burt, LD 5,421
John Westwood, UK Ind. 859
Ms Angela Thompson Soc. All. 663
Lab. majority 6,817 (18.76%)
4.22% swing Lab. to C.
(1997: Lab. maj. 13,027 (27.19%))

DULWICH & WEST NORWOOD
E. 70,497 T. 38,247 (54.25%) Lab. hold
*Rt. Hon. Ms T. Jowell, Lab. 20,999
Nick Vineall, C. 8,689
Ms Caroline Pidgeon, LD 5,806
Ms Jenny Jones, Green 1,914
Brian Kelly, Soc. All. 839
Lab. majority 12,310 (32.19%)
2.29% swing Lab. to C.
(1997: Lab. maj. 16,769 (36.76%))

DURHAM NORTH
E. 67,610 T. 38,568 (57.04%) Lab. hold
Kevan Jones, Lab. 25,920
Matthew Palmer, C. 7,237
Ms Carole Field, LD 5,411
Lab. majority 18,683 (48.44%)
3.65% swing Lab. to C.
(1997: Lab. maj. 26,299 (55.75%))

DURHAM NORTH WEST
E. 67,062 T. 39,226 (58.49%) Lab. hold
*Rt. Hon. Ms H. Armstrong, Lab. 24,526
William Clouston, C. 8,193
Alan Ord, LD 5,846
Ms Joan Hartnell, Soc. Lab. 661
Lab. majority 16,333 (41.64%)
5.90% swing Lab. to C.
(1997: Lab. maj. 24,754 (53.44%))

DURHAM, CITY OF
E. 69,633 T. 41,486 (59.58%) Lab. hold
*Gerry Steinberg, Lab. 23,254
Ms Carol Woods, LD 9,813
Nick Cartmell, C. 7,167
Mrs Chris Williamson, UK Ind. 1,252
Lab. majority 13,441 (32.40%)
7.82% swing Lab. to LD
(1997: Lab. maj. 22,504 (45.80%))

EALING ACTON & SHEPHERD'S BUSH
E. 70,697 T. 37,201 (52.62%) Lab. hold
*Clive Soley, Lab. 20,144
Miss Justine Greening, C. 9,355
Martin Tod, LD 6,171
Nick Grant, Soc. All. 529
Andrew Lawrie, UK Ind. 476
Carlos Rule, Soc. Lab. 301
Ms Rebecca Ng, ProLife 225
Lab. majority 10,789 (29.00%)
1.77% swing Lab. to C.
(1997: Lab. maj. 15,647 (32.55%))

EALING NORTH
E. 77,524 T. 44,957 (57.99%) Lab. hold
*Stephen Pound, Lab. 25,022
Charles Walker, C. 13,185
Francesco Fruzza, LD 5,043
Ms Astra Seibe, Green 1,039
Daniel Moss, UK Ind. 668
Lab. majority 11,837 (26.33%)
4.94% swing C. to Lab.
(1997: Lab. maj. 9,160 (16.44%))

EALING SOUTHALL
E. 82,373 T. 46,828 (56.85%) Lab. hold
*Piara Khabra, Lab. 22,239
Daniel Kawczynski, C. 8,556
Avtar Lit, Sunrise 5,764
Baldev Sharma, LD 4,680
Ms Jane Cook, Green 2,119
Salvinder Dhillon, Community 1,214
Mushtaq Choudhry, Ind. 1,166
Harpal Brar, Soc,. Lab. 921
Mohammed Bhutta, Qari 169
Lab. majority 13,683 (29.22%)
5.00% swing Lab. to C.
(1997: Lab. maj. 21,423 (39.21%))

EASINGTON
E. 61,532 T. 33,010 (53.65%) Lab. hold
*John Cummings, Lab. 25,360
Philip Lovel, C. 3,411
Christopher Ord, LD 3,408
Dave Robinson, Soc. Lab. 831
Lab. majority 21,949 (66.49%)
2.57% swing Lab. to C.
(1997: Lab. maj. 30,012 (71.64%))

EAST HAM
E. 71,255 T. 37,277 (52.31%) Lab. hold
*Stephen Timms, Lab. 27,241
Peter Campbell, C. 6,209
Ms Bridget Fox, LD 2,600
Rod Finlayson, Soc. Lab. 783
Ms Johinda Pandhal, UK Ind. 444
Lab. majority 21,032 (56.42%)
3.95% swing C. to Lab.
(1997: Lab. maj. 19,358 (48.53%))

EASTBOURNE
E. 73,784 T. 44,770 (60.68%) C. hold
*Nigel Waterson, C. 19,738
Chris Berry, LD 17,584
Ms Gillian Roles, Lab. 5,967
Barry Jones, UK, Ind. 907
Ms Theresia Williamson, Lib. 574
C. majority 2,154 (4.81%)
0.51% swing LD to C.
(1997: C. maj. 1,994 (3.79%))

EASTLEIGH
E. 74,603 T. 47,573 (63.77%) LD hold
*David Chidgey, LD 19,360
Conor Burns, C. 16,302
Sam Jaffa, Lab. 10,426
Stephen Challis, UK Ind. 849
Ms Martha Lyn, Green 636
LD majority 3,058 (6.43%)
2.54% swing C. to LD
(1997: LD maj. 754 (1.35%))

ECCLES
E. 68,764 T. 33,182 (48.25%) Lab. hold
*Ian Stewart, Lab. 21,395
Peter Caillard, C. 6,867
Bob Boyd, LD 4,920
Lab. majority 14,528 (43.78%)
2.09% swing Lab. to C.
(1997: Lab. maj. 21,916 (47.96%))

EDDISBURY
E. 69,181 T. 44,387 (64.16%) C. hold
*Stephen O'Brien, C. 20,556
Bill Eyres, Lab. 15,988
Paul Roberts, LD 6,975
David Carson, UK Ind. 868
C. majority 4,568 (10.29%)
3.95% swing Lab. to C.
1999 Jul. by-election: C. maj. 1,606
(1997: C. maj. 1,185 (2.39%))

EDMONTON
E. 62,294 T. 34,774 (55.82%)
Lab. Co-op hold
*Andy Love, Lab. Co-op 20,481
David Burrowes, C. 10,709
Douglas Taylor, LD 2,438
Miss Gwyneth Rolph, UK Ind. 406
Erol Basarik, Reform 344
Howard Medwell, Soc. All. 296
Dr Ram Saxena, Ind. 100
Lab. Co-op majority 9,772 (28.10%)
0.97% swing Lab. Co-op to C.
(1997: Lab. maj. 13,472 (30.04%)

ELLESMERE PORT & NESTON
E. 68,147 T. 41,528 (60.94%) Lab. hold
*Andrew Miller, Lab. 22,964
Gareth Williams, C. 12,103
Stuart Kelly, LD 4,828
Henry Crocker, UK Ind. 824
Geoff Nicholls, Green 809
Lab. majority 10,861 (26.15%)
2.18% swing Lab. to C.
(1997: Lab. maj. 16,036 (30.51%))

ELMET
E. 70,041 T. 45,937 (65.59%) Lab. hold
*Colin Burgon, Lab. 22,038
Andrew Millard, C. 17,867
Ms Madeleine Kirk, LD 5,001
Andrew Spence, UK Ind. 1,031
Lab. majority 4,171 (9.08%)
3.57% swing Lab. to C.
(1997: Lab. maj. 8,779 (16.22%))

ELTHAM
E. 57,519 T. 33,792 (58.75%) Lab. hold
*Clive Efford, Lab. 17,855
Mrs Sharon Massey, C. 10,859
Martin Morris, LD 4,121
Terry Jones, UK Ind. 706
Andrew Graham, Ind. 251
Lab. majority 6,996 (20.70%)
1.37% swing Lab. to C.
(1997: Lab. maj. 10,182 (23.45%))

ENFIELD NORTH
E. 67,756 T. 38,143 (56.29%) Lab. hold
*Ms Joan Ryan, Lab. 17,888
Nick De Bois, C. 15,597
Ms Hilary Leighter, LD 3,355
Ramon Johns, BNP 605
Brian Hall, UK Ind. 247
Michael Akerman, ProLife 241
Richard Course, Ind. 210
Lab. majority 2,291 (6.01%)
4.15% swing Lab. to C.
(1997: Lab. maj. 6,822 (14.31%))

ENFIELD SOUTHGATE
E. 66,418 T. 41,908 (63.10%) Lab. hold
*Stephen Twigg, Lab. 21,727
John Flack, C. 16,181
Wayne Hoban, LD 2,935
Ms Elaine Graham-Leigh, Green 662
Roy Freshwater, UK Ind. 298
Andrew Malakouna, Ind. 105
Lab. majority 5,546 (13.23%)
5.08% swing C. to Lab.
(1997: Lab. maj. 1,433 (3.08%))

EPPING FOREST
E. 72,645 T. 42,414 (58.39%) C. hold
*Mrs Eleanor Laing, C. 20,833
Christopher Naylor, Lab. 12,407
Michael Heavens, LD 7,884
Andrew Smith, UK Ind. 1,290
C. majority 8,426 (19.87%)
4.98% swing Lab. to C.
(1997: C. maj. 5,252 (9.91%))

EPSOM & EWELL
E. 74,266 T. 46,643 (62.81%) C. hold
Chris Grayling, C. 22,430
Charles Mansell, Lab. 12,350
John Vincent, LD 10,316
G. Webster-Gardiner, UK Ind. 1,547
C. majority 10,080 (21.61%)
0.17% swing Lab. to C.
(1997: C. maj. 11,525 (21.27%))

EREWASH
E. 78,484 T. 48,596 (61.92%) Lab. hold
*Ms Liz Blackman, Lab. 23,915
Gregor MacGregor, C. 16,983
Martin Garnett, LD 5,586
Ms Louise Smith, UK Ind. 692
Steven Belshaw, BNP 591
R U Seerius, Loony 428
Peter Waldock, Soc. Lab. 401
Lab. majority 6,932 (14.26%)
0.44% swing Lab. to C.
(1997: Lab. maj. 9,135 (15.14%))

ERITH & THAMESMEAD
E. 66,371 T. 33,351 (50.25%) Lab. hold
*John Austin, Lab. 19,769
Mark Brooks, C. 8,602
James Kempton, LD 3,800
Hardev Dhillon, Soc. Lab. 1,180
Lab. majority 11,167 (33.48%)
4.21% swing Lab. to C.
(1997: Lab. maj. 17,424 (41.90%))

ESHER & WALTON
E. 73,541 T. 45,531 (61.91%) C. hold
*Ian Taylor, C. 22,296
Joe McGowan, Lab. 10,758
Mark Marsh, LD 10,241
Bernard Collignon, UK Ind. 2,236
C. majority 11,538 (25.34%)
0.86% swing C. to Lab.
(1997: C. maj. 14,528 (27.07%))

ESSEX NORTH
E. 71,680 T. 44,944 (62.70%) C. hold
*Bernard Jenkin, C. 21,325
Philip Hawkins, Lab. 14,139
Trevor Ellis, LD 7,867
George Curtis, UK Ind. 1,613
C. majority 7,186 (15.99%)
2.65% swing Lab. to C.
(1997: C. maj. 5,476 (10.69%))

EXETER
E. 81,942 T. 52,616 (64.21%) Lab. hold
*Ben Bradshaw, Lab. 26,194
Mrs Anne Jobson, C. 14,435
Richard Copus, LD 6,512
David Morrish, Lib. 2,596
Paul Edwards, Green 1,240
John Stuart, UK Ind. 1,109
Francis Choules, Soc. All. 530
Lab. majority 11,759 (22.35%)
1.71% swing C. to Lab.
(1997: Lab. maj. 11,705 (18.92%))

FALMOUTH & CAMBORNE
E. 72,833 T. 46,820 (64.28%) Lab. hold
*Ms Candy Atherton, Lab. 18,532
Nick Serpell, C. 14,005
Julian Brazil, LD 11,453
John Browne, UK Ind. 1,328
Ms Hilda Wasley, Meb. Ker. 853
Paul Holmes, Lib. 649
Lab. majority 4,527 (9.67%)
2.33% swing C. to Lab.
(1997: Lab. maj. 2,688 (5.01%))

FAREHAM
E. 72,678 T. 45,447 (62.53%) C. hold
Mark Hoban, C. 21,389
James Carr, Lab. 14,380
Hugh Pritchard, LD 8,503
William O'Brien, UK Ind. 1,175
C. majority 7,009 (15.42%)
2.21% swing C. to Lab.
(1997: C. maj. 10,358 (19.85%))

FAVERSHAM & KENT MID
E. 67,995 T. 41,051 (60.37%) C. hold
Hugh Robertson, C. 18,739
Grahame Birchall, Lab. 14,556
Mike Sole, LD 5,529
Jim Gascoyne, UK Ind. 828
Ms Penny Kemp, Green 799
Norman Davidson, R & R Loony 600
C. majority 4,183 (10.19%)
0.89% swing Lab. to C.
(1997: C. maj. 4,173 (8.41%))

FELTHAM & HESTON
E. 73,229 T. 36,177 (49.40%)
Lab. Co-op hold
*Alan Keen, Lab. Co-op 21,406
Mrs Liz Mammatt, C. 8,749
Andy Darley, LD 4,998
Surinder Cheema, Soc. Lab. 651
Warwick Prachar, Ind. 204
Asa Khaira, Ind. 169
Lab. Co-op majority 12,657 (34.99%)
1.11% swing C. to Lab. Co-op
(1997: Lab. maj. 15,273 (32.76%))

FINCHLEY & GOLDERS GREEN
E. 76,175 T. 43,675 (57.34%) Lab. hold
*Rudi Vis, Lab. 20,205
John Marshall, C. 16,489
Ms Sarah Teather, LD 5,266
Ms Miranda Dunn, Green 1,385
John de Roeck, UK Ind. 330
Lab. majority 3,716 (8.51%)
1.08% swing C. to Lab.
(1997: Lab. maj. 3,189 (6.34%))

FOLKESTONE & HYTHE
E. 71,503 T. 45,855 (64.13%) C. hold
*Rt. Hon. M. Howard, C. 20,645
Peter Carroll, LD 14,738
Albert Catterall, Lab. 9,260
John Baker, UK Ind. 1,212
C. majority 5,907 (12.88%)
0.36% swing LD to C.
(1997: C. maj. 6,332 (12.17%))

FOREST OF DEAN
E. 66,240 T. 44,607 (67.34%) Lab. hold
*Ms Diana Organ, Lab. 19,350
Mark Harper, C. 17,301
David Gayler, LD 5,762
Simon Pickering, Green 1,254
Allen Prout, UK Ind. 661
Gerald Morgan, Ind. 279
Lab. majority 2,049 (4.59%)
4.02% swing Lab. to C.
(1997: Lab. maj. 6,343 (12.64%))

FYLDE
E. 72,207 T. 44,737 (61.96%) C. hold
*Rt. Hon. M. Jack, C. 23,383
John Stockton, Lab. 13,773
John Begg, LD 6,599
Mrs Lesley Brown, UK Ind. 982
C. majority 9,610 (21.48%)
2.13% swing Lab. to C.
(1997: C. maj. 8,963 (17.22%))

GAINSBOROUGH
E. 65,871 T. 42,319 (64.25%) C. hold
*Edward Leigh, C. 19,555
Alan Rhodes, Lab. 11,484
Steve Taylor, LD 11,280
C. majority 8,071 (19.07%)
2.39% swing Lab. to C.
(1997: C. maj. 6,826 (14.29%))

GATESHEAD EAST & WASHINGTON WEST
E. 64,041 T. 33,615 (52.49%) Lab. hold
*Rt. Hon. Ms J. Quin, Lab. 22,903
Ron Beadle, LD 4,999
Ms Elizabeth Campbell, C. 4,970
Martin Rouse, UK Ind. 743
Lab. majority 17,904 (53.26%)
4.04% swing Lab. to LD
(1997: Lab. maj. 24,950 (57.92%))

GEDLING
E. 68,540 T. 43,816 (63.93%) Lab. hold
*Vernon Coaker, Lab. 22,383
Jonathan Bullock, C. 16,785
Tony Gillam, LD 4,648
Lab. majority 5,598 (12.78%)
2.74% swing C. to Lab.
(1997: Lab. maj. 3,802 (7.29%))

GILLINGHAM
E. 70,898 T. 42,212 (59.54%) Lab. hold
*Paul Clark, Lab. 18,782
Tim Butcher, C. 16,510
Jonathan Hunt, LD 5,755
Tony Scholefield, UK Ind. 933
Wynford Vaughan, Soc. All. 232
Lab. majority 2,272 (5.38%)
0.74% swing C. to Lab.
(1997: Lab. maj. 1,980 (3.91%))

GLOUCESTER
E. 81,144 T. 48,223 (59.43%) Lab. hold
Parmjit Dhanda, Lab. 22,067
Paul James, C. 18,187
Tim Bullamore, LD 6,875
Terry Lines, UK Ind. 822
Stewart Smyth, Soc. All. 272
Lab. majority 3,880 (8.05%)
3.11% swing Lab. to C.
(1997: Lab. maj. 8,259 (14.26%))

GOSPORT
E. 69,626 T. 39,789 (57.15%) C. hold
*Peter Viggers, C. 17,364
Richard Williams, Lab. 14,743
Roger Roberts, LD 6,011
John Bowles, UK Ind. 1,162
Kevin Chetwynd, Soc. Lab. 509
C. majority 2,621 (6.59%)
3.18% swing C. to Lab.
(1997: C. maj. 6,258 (12.94%))

GRANTHAM & STAMFORD
E. 74,459 T. 46,289 (62.17%) C. hold
*Quentin Davies, C. 21,329
John Robinson, Lab. 16,811
Ms Jane Carr, LD 6,665
Miss Marilyn Swain, UK Ind. 1,484
C. majority 4,518 (9.76%)
2.34% swing Lab. to C.
(1997: C. maj. 2,692 (5.08%))

GRAVESHAM
E. 69,590 T. 43,639 (62.71%) Lab. hold
*Chris Pond, Lab. 21,773
Jacques Arnold, C. 16,911
Bruce Parmenter, LD 4,031
William Jenner, UK Ind. 924
Lab. majority 4,862 (11.14%)
0.15% swing C. to Lab.
(1997: Lab. maj. 5,779 (10.85%))

GREAT GRIMSBY
E. 63,157 T. 33,017 (52.28%) Lab. hold
*Austin Mitchell, Lab. 19,118
James Cousins, C. 7,634
Andrew de Freitas, LD 6,265
Lab. majority 11,484 (34.78%)
1.46% swing Lab. to C.
(1997: Lab. maj. 16,244 (37.70%))

GREAT YARMOUTH
E. 69,131 T. 40,366 (58.39%) Lab. hold
*Tony Wright, Lab. 20,344
Charles Reynolds, C. 15,780
Maurice Leeke, LD 3,392
Bertie Poole, UK Ind. 850
Lab. majority 4,564 (11.31%)
3.21% swing Lab. to C.
(1997: Lab. maj. 8,668 (17.73%))

GREENWICH & WOOLWICH
E. 62,530 T. 32,536 (52.03%) Lab. hold
*Rt. Hon. N. Raynsford, Lab. 19,691
Richard Forsdyke, C. 6,258
Russell Pyne, LD 5,082
Stan Gain, UK Ind. 672
Miss Kirstie Paton, Soc. All. 481
Ms Margaret Sharkey, Soc. Lab. 352
Lab. majority 13,433 (41.29%)
1.79% swing Lab. to C.
(1997: Lab. maj. 18,128 (44.87%))

GUILDFORD
E. 76,046 T. 47,842 (62.91%) LD gain
Ms Sue Doughty, LD 20,358
*Nick St Aubyn, C. 19,820
Ms Joyce Still, Lab. 6,558
Ms Sonya Porter, UK Ind. 736
John Morris, Pacifist 370
LD majority 538 (1.12%)
4.77% swing C. to LD
(1997: C. maj. 4,791 (8.41%))

HACKNEY NORTH & STOKE NEWINGTON
E. 60,444 T. 29,621 (49.01%) Lab. hold
*Ms Diane Abbott, Lab. 18,081
Mrs Pauline Dye, C. 4,430
Ms Meral Ece, LD 4,170
Chit Yen Chong, Green 2,184
Sukant Chandan, Soc. Lab. 756
Lab. majority 13,651 (46.09%)
0.74% swing Lab. to C.
(1997: Lab. maj. 15,627 (47.57%))

HACKNEY SOUTH & SHOREDITCH
E. 63,990 T. 30,347 (47.42%) Lab. hold
*Brian Sedgemore, Lab. 19,471
Tony Vickers, LD 4,422
Paul White, C. 4,180
Ms Cecilia Prosper, Soc. All. 1,401
Saim Kokshal, Reform 471
Ivan Beavis, Comm. 259
William Rogers, WRP 143
Lab. majority 15,049 (49.59%)
2.60% swing LD to Lab.
(1997: Lab. maj. 14,980 (44.39%))

HALESOWEN & ROWLEY REGIS
E. 65,683 T. 39,274 (59.79%) Lab. hold
*Ms Sylvia Heal, Lab. 20,804
Les Jones, C. 13,445
Patrick Harley, LD 4,089
Alan Sheath, UK Ind. 936
Lab. majority 7,359 (18.74%)
1.23% swing Lab. to C.
(1997: Lab. maj. 10,337 (21.20%))

HALIFAX
E. 69,870 T. 40,390 (57.81%) Lab. hold
*Ms Alice Mahon, Lab. 19,800
James Walsh, C. 13,671
John Durkin, LD 5,878
Mrs Helen Martinek, UK Ind. 1,041
Lab. majority 6,129 (15.17%)
3.50% swing Lab. to C.
(1997: Lab. maj. 11,212 (22.18%))

HALTEMPRICE & HOWDEN
E. 67,055 T. 43,928 (65.51%) C. hold
*Rt. Hon. D. Davis, C. 18,994
John Neal, LD 17,091
Leslie Howell, Lab. 6,898
Ms Joanne Robinson, UK Ind. 945
C. majority 1,903 (4.33%)
5.41% swing C. to LD
(1997: C. maj. 7,514 (15.16%))

HALTON
E. 63,673 T. 34,470 (54.14%) Lab. hold
*Derek Twigg, Lab. 23,841
Chris Davenport, C. 6,413
Peter Walker, LD 4,216
Lab. majority 17,428 (50.56%)
1.33% swing Lab. to C.
(1997: Lab. maj. 23,650 (53.22%))

HAMMERSMITH & FULHAM
E. 79,302 T. 44,700 (56.37%) Lab. hold
*Iain Coleman, Lab. 19,801
Matthew Carrington, C. 17,786
Jon Burden, LD 5,294
Daniel Lopez Dias, Green 1,444
Gerald Roberts, UK Ind. 375
Lab. majority 2,015 (4.51%)
1.30% swing Lab. to C.
(1997: Lab. maj. 3,842 (7.11%))

HAMPSHIRE EAST
E. 78,802 T. 50,289 (63.82%) C. hold
*Michael Mates, C. 23,950
Robert Booker, LD 15,060
Ms Barbara Burfoot, Lab. 9,866
Stephen Coles, UK Ind. 1,413
C. majority 8,890 (17.68%)
1.13% swing C. to LD
(1997: C. maj. 11,590 (19.93%))

HAMPSHIRE NORTH EAST
E. 71,323 T. 43,947 (61.62%) C. hold
*Rt. Hon. J. Arbuthnot, C. 23,379
Mike Plummer, LD 10,122
Barry Jones, Lab. 8,744
Graham Mellstrom, UK Ind. 1,702
C. majority 13,257 (30.17%)
1.00% swing LD to C.
(1997: C. maj. 14,398 (28.17%))

HAMPSHIRE NORTH WEST
E. 76,359 T. 48,631 (63.69%) C. hold
*Rt. Hon. Sir G. Young, C. 24,374
Mick Mumford, Lab. 12,365
Alex Bentley, LD 10,329
Stanley Oram, UK Ind. 1,563
C. majority 12,009 (24.69%)
1.53% swing Lab. to C.
(1997: C. maj. 11,551 (21.13%))

HAMPSTEAD & HIGHGATE
E. 65,309 T. 35,407 (54.21%) Lab. hold
*Ms Glenda Jackson, Lab. 16,601
Andrew Mennear, C. 8,725
Jonathan Simpson, LD 7,273
Andrew Cornwell, Green 1,654
Ms Helen Cooper, Soc. All. 559
Thomas McDermott, UK Ind. 316
Ms Sister Xnunoftheabove, Ind. 144
Ms Mary Teale, ProLife 92
Amos Klein, Ind. 43
Lab. majority 7,876 (22.24%)
3.96% swing Lab. to C.
(1997: Lab. maj. 13,284 (30.17%))

HARBOROUGH
E. 73,300 T. 46,427 (63.34%) C. hold
*Edward Garnier, C. 20,748
Ms Jill Hope, LD 15,496
Raj Jethwa, Lab. 9,271
David Knight, UK Ind. 912
C. majority 5,252 (11.31%)
0.49% swing C. to LD
(1997: C. maj. 6,524 (12.30%))

HARLOW
E. 67,074 T. 40,115 (59.81%) Lab. hold
*Bill Rammell, Lab. 19,169
Robert Halfon, C. 13,941
Ms Lorna Spenceley, LD 5,381
Tony Bennett, UK Ind. 1,223
John Hobbs, Soc. All. 401
Lab. majority 5,228 (13.03%)
4.48% swing Lab. to C.
(1997: Lab. maj. 10,514 (21.99%))

HARROGATE & KNARESBOROUGH
E. 65,185 T. 42,179 (64.71%) LD hold
*Phil Willis, LD 23,445
Andrew Jones, C. 14,600
Alastair MacDonald, Lab. 3,101
Bill Brown, UK Ind. 761
John Cornforth, ProLife 272
LD majority 8,845 (20.97%)
3.94% swing C. to LD
(1997: LD maj. 6,236 (13.09%))

HARROW EAST
E. 81,575 T. 48,077 (58.94%) Lab. hold
*Tony McNulty, Lab. 26,590
Peter Wilding, C. 15,466
George Kershaw, LD 6,021
Lab. majority 11,124 (23.14%)
3.02% swing C. to Lab.
(1997: Lab. maj. 9,738 (17.09%))

HARROW WEST
E. 73,505 T. 46,648 (63.46%) Lab. hold
*Gareth Thomas, Lab. 23,142
Danny Finkelstein, C. 16,986
Christopher Noyce, LD 5,995
Peter Kefford, UK Ind. 525
Lab. majority 6,156 (13.20%)
5.42% swing C. to Lab.
(1997: Lab. maj. 1,240 (2.36%))

HARTLEPOOL
E. 67,652 T. 38,051 (56.25%) Lab. hold
*Rt. Hon. P. Mandelson, Lab. 22,506
Gus Robinson, C. 7,935
Nigel Boddy, LD 5,717
Arthur Scargill, Soc. Lab. 912
Ian Cameron, Ind. 557
John Booth, Ind. 424
Lab. majority 14,571 (38.29%)
0.54% swing Lab. to C.
(1997: Lab. maj. 17,508 (39.38%))

HARWICH
E. 77,539 T. 48,115 (62.05%) Lab. hold
*Ivan Henderson, Lab. 21,951
Ian Sproat, C. 19,355
Peter Wilcock, LD 4,099
Tony Finnegan-Butler, UK Ind. 2,463
Clive Lawrance, Ind. 247
Lab. majority 2,596 (5.40%)
1.56% swing C. to Lab.
(1997: Lab. maj. 1,216 (2.28%))

HASTINGS & RYE
E. 70,632 T. 41,218 (58.36%) Lab. hold
*Michael Foster, Lab. 19,402
Mark Coote, C. 15,094
Graem Peters, LD 4,266
Alan Coomber, UK Ind. 911
Ms Sally Phillips, Green 721
Mrs Gillian Bargery, Ind. 486
John Ord-Clarke, Loony 198
Brett McLean, R & R Loony 140
Lab. majority 4,308 (10.45%)
2.62% swing C. to Lab.
(1997: Lab. maj. 2,560 (5.21%))

HAVANT
E. 70,246 T. 40,437 (57.56%) C. hold
*David Willetts, C. 17,769
Peter Guthrie, Lab. 13,562
Ms Helena Cole, LD 7,508
Kevin Jacks, Green 793
Tim Cuell, UK Ind. 561
Roy Stanley, Ind. 244
C. majority 4,207 (10.40%)
1.34% swing Lab. to C.
(1997: C. maj. 3,729 (7.72%))

HAYES & HARLINGTON
E. 57,561 T. 32,403 (56.29%) Lab. hold
*John McDonnell, Lab. 21,279
Robert McLean, C. 7,813
Ms Nahid Boethe, LD 1,958
Gary Burch, BNP 705
Wally Kennedy, Soc. Alt. 648
Lab. majority 13,466 (41.56%)
3.39% swing C. to Lab.
(1997: Lab. maj. 14,291 (34.78%))

HAZEL GROVE
E. 65,107 T. 38,478 (59.10%) LD hold
*Andrew Stunell, LD 20,020
Ms Nadine Bargery, C. 11,585
Martin Miller, Lab. 6,230
Gerald Price, UK Ind. 643
LD majority 8,435 (21.92%)
1.01% swing LD to C.
(1997: LD maj. 11,814 (23.95%))

HEMEL HEMPSTEAD
E. 72,086 T. 45,833 (63.58%)
Lab. Co-op hold
*Tony McWalter, Lab. Co-op 21,389
Paul Ivey, C. 17,647
Neil Stuart, LD 5,877
Barry Newton, UK Ind. 920
Lab.Co-opmajority3,742(8.16%)
0.78% swing C. to Lab. Co-op
(1997: Lab. maj. 3,636 (6.60%))

HEMSWORTH
E. 67,948 T. 35,227 (51.84%) Lab. hold
*Jon Trickett, Lab. 23,036
Mrs Elizabeth Truss, C. 7,400
Ed Waller, LD 3,990
Paul Turek, Soc. Lab. 801
Lab. majority 15,636 (44.39%)
4.19% swing Lab. to C.
(1997: Lab. maj. 23,992 (52.76%))

HENDON
E. 78,212 T. 40,851 (52.23%) Lab. hold
*Andrew Dismore, Lab. 21,432
Richard Evans, C. 14,015
Wayne Casey, LD 4,724
Craig Crosbie, UK Ind. 409
Ms Stella Taylor, WRP 164
Michael Stewart, Prog Dem 107
Lab. majority 7,417 (18.16%)
2.93% swing C. to Lab.
(1997: Lab. maj. 6,155 (12.30%))

HENLEY
E. 69,081 T. 44,401 (64.27%) C. hold
Boris Johnson, C. 20,466
Ms Catherine Bearder, LD 12,008
Ms Janet Mathews, Lab. 9,367
Philip Collings, UK Ind. 1,413
Oliver Tickell, Green 1,147
C. majority 8,458 (19.05%)
1.31% swing C. to LD
(1997: C. maj. 11,167 (21.66%))

HEREFORD
E. 70,305 T. 44,624 (63.47%) LD hold
*Paul Keetch, LD 18,244
Mrs Virginia Taylor, C. 17,276
David Hallam, Lab. 6,739
Clive Easton, UK Ind. 1,184
David Gillett, Green 1,181
LD majority 968 (2.17%)
5.24% swing LD to C.
(1997: LD maj. 6,648 (12.65%))

HERTFORD & STORTFORD
E. 75,141 T. 47,176 (62.78%) C. hold
Mark Prisk, C. 21,074
Simon Speller, Lab. 15,471
Ms Mione Gold Spink, LD 9,388
Stuart Rising, UK Ind. 1,243
C. majority 5,603 (11.88%)
0.37% swing C. to Lab.
(1997: C. maj. 6,885 (12.62%))

HERTFORDSHIRE NORTH EAST
E. 68,790 T. 44,645 (64.90%) C. hold
*Oliver Heald, C. 19,695
Ivan Gibbons, Lab. 16,251
Ms Alison Kingman, LD 7,686
Michael Virgo, UK Ind. 1,013
C. majority 3,444 (7.71%)
0.89% swing Lab. to C.
(1997: C. maj. 3,088 (5.94%))

HERTFORDSHIRE SOUTH WEST
E. 73,367 T. 47,269 (64.43%) C. hold
*Richard Page, C. 20,933
Graham Dale, Lab. 12,752
Ed Featherstone, LD 12,431
Colin Dale-Mills, UK Ind. 847
Ms Julia Goffin, ProLife 306
C. majority 8,181 (17.31%)
0.39% swing C. to Lab.
(1997: C. maj. 10,021 (18.08%))

HERTSMERE
E. 68,780 T. 41,505 (60.34%) C. hold
*James Clappison, C. 19,855
Ms Hilary Broderick, Lab. 14,953
Paul Thompson, LD 6,300
James Dry, Soc. Lab. 397
C. majority 4,902 (11.81%)
2.85% swing Lab. to C.
(1997: C. maj. 3,075 (6.11%))

HEXHAM
E. 59,807 T. 42,413 (70.92%) C. hold
*Peter Atkinson, C. 18,917
Paul Brannen, Lab. 16,388
Philip Latham, LD 6,380
Alan Patterson, UK Ind. 728
C. majority 2,529 (5.96%)
2.74% swing Lab. to C.
(1997: C. maj. 222 (0.49%))

HEYWOOD & MIDDLETON
E. 73,005 T. 38,779 (53.12%)
Lab. Co-op hold
*Jim Dobbin, Lab. Co-op 22,377
Mrs Marilyn Hopkins, C. 10,707
Ian Greenhalgh, LD 4,329
Philip Burke, Lib. 1,021
Ms Christine West, Ch. D. 345
Lab. Co-op majority 11,670 (30.09%)
2.30% swing Lab. Co-op to C.
(1997: Lab. maj. 17,542 (34.70%))

HIGH PEAK
E. 73,774 T. 48,114 (65.22%) Lab. hold
*Tom Levitt, Lab. 22,430
Simon Chapman, C. 17,941
Peter Ashenden, LD 7,743
Lab. majority 4,489 (9.33%)
3.03% swing Lab. to C.
(1997: Lab. maj. 8,791 (15.38%))

HITCHIN & HARPENDEN
E. 67,196 T. 44,924 (66.86%) C. hold
*Rt. Hon. P. Lilley, C. 21,271
Alan Amos, Lab. 14,608
John Murphy, LD 8,076
John Saunders, UK Ind. 606
Peter Rigby, Ind. 363
C. majority 6,663 (14.83%)
1.06% swing Lab. to C.
(1997: C. maj. 6,671 (12.72%))

HOLBORN & ST PANCRAS
E. 62,813 T. 31,129 (49.56%) Lab. hold
*Rt. Hon. F. Dobson, Lab. 16,770
Nathaniel Green, LD 5,595
Mrs Roseanne Serelli, C. 5,258
Rob Whitley, Green 1,875
Ms Candy Udwin, Soc. All. 971
Joti Brar, Soc. Lab. 359
Magnus Nielsen, UK Ind. 301
Lab. majority 11,175 (35.90%)
8.31% swing Lab. to LD
(1997: Lab. maj. 17,903 (47.11%))

HORNCHURCH
E. 61,008 T. 35,557 (58.28%) Lab. hold
*John Cryer, Lab. 16,514
Robin Squire, C. 15,032
Ms Sarah Lea, LD 2,928
Lawrence Webb, UK Ind. 893
Mr David Durant, Third 190
Lab. majority 1,482 (4.17%)
4.38% swing Lab. to C.
(1997: Lab. maj. 5,680 (12.93%))

HORNSEY & WOOD GREEN
E. 75,967 T. 44,063 (58.00%) Lab. hold
*Ms Barbara Roche, Lab. 21,967
Ms Lynne Featherstone, LD 11,353
Jason Hollands, C. 6,921
Ms Jayne Forbes, Green 2,228
Ms Louise Christian, Soc. All. 1,106
Ms Ella Rule, Soc. Lab. 294
Erdil Ataman, Reform 194
Lab. majority 10,614 (24.09%)
13.21% swing Lab. to LD
(1997: Lab. maj. 20,499 (39.82%))

HORSHAM
E. 79,604 T. 50,770 (63.78%) C. hold
*Rt. Hon. F. Maude, C. 26,134
Hubert Carr, LD 12,468
Ms Janet Sully, Lab. 10,267
Hugo Miller, UK Ind. 1,472
Jim Duggan, Ind. 429
C. majority 13,666 (26.92%)
0.46% swing LD to C.
(1997: C. maj. 14,862 (26.00%))

HOUGHTON & WASHINGTON EAST
E. 67,946 T. 33,641 (49.51%) Lab. hold
*Fraser Kemp, Lab. 24,628
Tony Devenish, C. 4,810
Richard Ormerod, LD 4,203
Lab. majority 19,818 (58.91%)
2.29% swing Lab. to C.
(1997: Lab. maj. 26,555 (63.49%))

HOVE
E. 70,889 T. 41,988 (59.23%) Lab. hold
*Ivor Caplin, Lab. 19,253
Mrs Jenny Langston, C. 16,082
Harold de Souza, LD 3,823
Ms Anthea Ballam, Green 1,369
Andy Richards, Soc. All. 531
Richard Franklin, UK Ind. 358
Nigel Donovan, Lib. 316
Simon Dobbshead, Free 196
Thomas Major, Ind. 60
Lab. majority 3,171 (7.55%)
0.34% swing Lab. to C.
(1997: Lab. maj. 3,959 (8.23%))

HUDDERSFIELD
E. 64,349 T. 35,383 (54.99%)
Lab. Co-op hold
*Barry Sheerman, Lab. Co-op 18,840
Paul Baverstock, C. 8,794
Neil Bentley, LD 5,300
John Phillips, Green 1,254
Mrs Judith Longman, UK Ind. 613
Graham Hellawell, Soc. All. 374
George Randall, Soc. Lab. 208
Lab. Co-op majority 10,046 (28.39%)
3.59% swing Lab. Co-op to C.
(1997: Lab. maj. 15,848 (35.57%))

HULL EAST
E. 66,473 T. 30,875 (46.45%) Lab. hold
*Rt. Hon. J. Prescott, Lab. 19,938
Ms Jo Swinson, LD 4,613
Ms Sandip Verma, C. 4,276
Ms Jeanette Jenkinson, UK Ind. 1,218
Ms Linda Muir, Soc. Lab. 830
Lab. majority 15,325 (49.64%)
5.94% swing Lab. to LD
(1997: Lab. maj. 23,318 (57.60%))

HULL NORTH
E. 63,022 T. 28,633 (45.43%) Lab. hold
*Kevin McNamara, Lab. 16,364
Ms Simone Butterworth, LD 5,643
Paul Charlson, C. 4,902
Ms Tineka Robinson, UK Ind. 655
Roger Smith, Soc. All. 490
Carl Wagner, LCA 478
Christopher Veasey, Ind. 101
Lab. majority 10,721 (37.44%)
6.89% swing Lab. to LD
(1997: Lab. maj. 19,705 (50.79%))

HULL WEST & HESSLE
E. 63,077 T. 28,916 (45.84%) Lab. hold
*Alan Johnson, Lab. 16,880
John Sharp, C. 5,929
Ms Angela Wastling, LD 4,364
John Cornforth, UK Ind. 878
David Harris, Ind. 512
David Skinner, Soc. Lab. 353
Lab. majority 10,951 (37.87%)
1.38% swing Lab. to C.
(1997: Lab. maj. 15,525 (40.48%))

HUNTINGDON
E. 78,604 T. 49,089 (62.45%) C. hold
Jonathan Djanogly, C. 24,507
Michael Pope, LD 11,715
Takki Sulaiman, Lab. 11,211
Derek Norman, UK Ind. 1,656
C. majority 12,792 (26.06%)
7.26% swing C. to LD
(1997: C. maj. 18,140 (31.84%))

HYNDBURN
E. 66,445 T. 38,243 (57.56%) Lab. hold
*Greg Pope, Lab. 20,900
Peter Britcliffe, C. 12,681
Bill Greene, LD 3,680
John Tomlin, UK Ind. 982
Lab. majority 8,219 (21.49%)
1.11% swing Lab. to C.
(1997: Lab. maj. 11,448 (23.71%))

ILFORD NORTH
E. 68,893 T. 40,234 (58.40%) Lab. hold
*Ms Linda Perham, Lab. 18,428
Vivian Bendall, C. 16,313
Gavin Stollar, LD 4,717
Martin Levin, UK Ind. 776
Lab. majority 2,115 (5.26%)
0.67% swing Lab. to C.
(1997: Lab. maj. 3,224 (6.60%))

ILFORD SOUTH
E. 76,025 T. 41,295 (54.32%)
Lab. Co-op hold
*Mike Gapes, Lab. Co-op 24,619
Suresh Kuma, C. 10,622
Ralph Scott, LD 4,647
Harun Khan, UK Ind. 1,407
Lab. Co-op majority 13,997 (33.90%)
2.75% swing C. to Lab. Co-op
(1997: Lab. maj. 14,200 (28.39%))

IPSWICH
E. 68,198 T. 38,873 (57.00%) Lab. hold
*Jamie Cann, Lab. 19,952
Edward Wild, C. 11,871
Terry Gilbert, LD 5,904
William Vinyard, UK Ind. 624
Peter Leach, Soc. All. 305
Shaun Gratton, Soc. Lab. 217
Lab. majority 8,081 (20.79%)
0.40% swing Lab. to C.
(1997: Lab. maj. 10,439 (21.58%))

ISLE OF WIGHT
E. 106,305 T. 63,482 (59.72%) C. gain
Andrew Turner, C. 25,223
*Dr Peter Brand, LD 22,397
Ms Deborah Gardiner, Lab. 9,676
David Lott, UK Ind. 2,106
David Holmes, Ind. 1,423
Paul Scivier, Green 1,279
Philip Murray, IOW 1,164
James Spensley, Soc. Lab. 214
C. majority 2,826 (4.45%)
6.61% swing LD to C.
(1997: LD maj. 6,406 (8.76%))

ISLINGTON NORTH
E. 61,970 T. 30,216 (48.76%) Lab. hold
*Jeremy Corbyn, Lab. 18,699
Ms Laura Willoughby, LD 5,741
Neil Rands, C. 3,249
Chris Ashby, Green 1,876
Steve Cook, Soc. Lab. 512
Emine Hassan, Reform 139
Lab. majority 12,958 (42.88%)
6.38% swing Lab. to LD
(1997: Lab. maj. 19,955 (55.64%))

ISLINGTON SOUTH & FINSBURY
E. 59,515 T. 28,206 (47.39%) Lab. hold
*Rt. Hon. C. Smith, Lab. 15,217
Keith Sharp, LD 7,937
Mrs Nicky Morgan, C. 3,860
Ms Janine Booth, Soc. All. 817
Thomas McCarthy, Ind. 267
Charles Thomson, Stuck 108
Lab. majority 7,280 (25.81%)
7.71% swing Lab. to LD
(1997: Lab. maj. 14,563 (41.24%))

JARROW
E. 63,172 T. 34,479 (54.58%) Lab. hold
*Stephen Hepburn, Lab. 22,777
James Selby, LD 5,182
Donald Wood, C. 5,056
Alan Badger, UK Ind. 716
Alan Le Blond, Ind. 391
John Bissett, Soc. 357
Lab. majority 17,595 (51.03%)
1.37% swing Lab. to LD
(1997: Lab. maj. 21,933 (49.91%))

KEIGHLEY
E. 68,349 T. 43,333 (63.40%) Lab. hold
*Ms Ann Cryer, Lab. 20,888
Simon Cooke, C. 16,883
Mike Doyle, LD 4,722
Michael Cassidy, UK Ind. 840
Lab. majority 4,005 (9.24%)
2.30% swing Lab. to C.
(1997: Lab. maj. 7,132 (13.85%))

KENSINGTON & CHELSEA
E. 62,007 T. 28,038 (45.22%) C. hold
*Rt. Hon. M. Portillo, C. 15,270
Simon Stanley, Lab. 6,499
Ms Kishwer Falkner, LD 4,416
Ms Julia Stephenson, Green 1,158
Nicholas Hockney, UK Ind. 416
Ms Josephine Quintavalle, ProLife 179
Ginger Crab, Wrestling 100
C. majority 8,771 (31.28%)
2.81% swing Lab. to C.
(1999 Nov. by-election: C. maj. 6,706 (34.37%); 1997: C. maj. 9,519 (25.66%))

KETTERING
E. 79,697 T. 53,752 (67.45%) Lab. hold
*Philip Sawford, Lab. 24,034
Philip Hollobone, C. 23,369
Roger Aron, LD 5,469
Barry Mahoney, UK Ind. 880
Lab. majority 665 (1.24%)
0.45% swing C. to Lab.
(1997: Lab. Maj. 189 (0.33%))

KINGSTON & SURBITON
E. 72,687 T. 49,093 (67.54%) LD hold
*Edward Davey, LD 29,542
David Shaw, C. 13,866
Phil Woodford ,Lab. 4,302
Chris Spruce, Green 572
Miss Amy Burns, UK Ind. 438
John Hayball, Soc. Lab. 319
Jeremy Middleton, Unrep. 54
LD majority 15,676 (31.93%)
15.92% swing C. to LD
(1997: LD maj. 56 (0.10%))

KINGSWOOD
E. 80,531 T. 52,676 (65.41%) Lab. hold
*Dr Roger Berry, Lab. 28,903
Robert Marven, C. 14,941
Christopher Greenfield, LD 7,747
David Smith, UK Ind. 1,085
Lab. majority 13,962 (26.51%)
1.35% swing C. to Lab.
(1997: Lab. Maj. 14,253 (23.80%))

KNOWSLEY NORTH & SEFTON EAST
E. 70,781 T. 37,517 (53.00%) Lab. hold
*George Howarth, Lab. 25,035
Keith Chapman, C. 6,108
Richard Roberts, LD 5,173
Ron Waugh, Soc. Lab. 574
Thomas Rossiter, Ind. 356
David Jones, Ind. 271
Lab. majority 18,927 (50.45%)
1.08% swing Lab. to C.
(1997: Lab. maj. 26,147 (52.61%))

KNOWSLEY SOUTH
E. 70,681 T. 36,590 (51.77%) Lab. hold
*Eddie O'Hara, Lab. 26,071
David Smithson, LD 4,755
Paul Jemetta, C. 4,250
Alan Fogg, Soc. Lab. 1,068
Ms Mona McNee, Ind. 446
Lab. majority 21,316 (58.26%)
5.27% swing Lab. to LD
(1997: Lab. maj. 30,708 (64.53%))

LANCASHIRE WEST
E. 72,858 T. 42,971 (58.98%) Lab. hold
*Colin Pickthall, Lab. 23,404
Jeremy Myers, C. 13,761
John Thornton, LD 4,966
David Hill, Ind. 523
David Braid, Ind. 317
Lab. majority 9,643 (22.44%)
4.42% swing Lab. to C.
(1997: Lab. maj. 17,119 (31.28%))

LANCASTER & WYRE
E. 78,964 T. 52,350 (66.30%) Lab. hold
*Hilton Dawson, Lab. 22,556
Steve Barclay, C. 22,075
Ms Liz Scott, LD 5,383
Prof John Whitelegg, Green 1,595
Dr John Whittaker, UK Ind. 741
Lab. majority 481 (0.92%)
0.64% swing Lab. to C.
(1997: Lab. maj. 1,295 (2.20%))

LEEDS CENTRAL
E. 65,497 T. 27,306 (41.69%) Lab. hold
*Hilary Benn, Lab. 18,277
Miss Victoria Richmond, C. 3,896
Stewart Arnold, LD 3,607
David Burgess, UK Ind. 775
Steve Johnson, Soc. All. 751
Lab. majority 14,381 (52.67%)
1.62% swing Lab. to C.
(1999 Jun. by-election: Lab. maj. 2,293 (17.39%); 1997: Lab. maj. 20,689 (55.90%))

LEEDS EAST
E. 56,400 T. 29,055 (51.52%) Lab. hold
*George Mudie, Lab. 18,290
Barry Anderson, C. 5,647
Brian Jennings, LD 3,923
Raymond Northgreaves, UK Ind. 634
Mark King, Soc. Lab. 419
Peter Socrates, Ind. 142
Lab. majority 12,643 (43.51%)
2.64% swing Lab. to C.
(1997: Lab. maj. 17,466 (48.80%))

LEEDS NORTH EAST
E. 64,123 T. 39,773 (62.03%) Lab. hold
*Fabian Hamilton, Lab. 19,540
Owain Rhys, C. 12,451
Jonathan Brown, LD 6,325
Ms Celia Foote, Left All 770
Jeffrey Miles, UK Ind. 382
Colin Muir, Soc. Lab. 173
Mohammed Zaman, Ind. 132
Lab. majority 7,089 (17.82%)
1.27% swing C. to Lab.
(1997: Lab. maj. 6,959 (15.29%))

LEEDS NORTH WEST
E. 72,945 T. 42,451 (58.20%) Lab. hold
*Harold Best, Lab. 17,794
Adam Pritchard, C. 12,558
David Hall-Matthews, LD 11,431
Simon Jones, UK Ind. 668
Lab. majority 5,236 (12.33%)
2.27% swing C. to Lab.
(1997: Lab. maj. 3,844 (7.79%))

LEEDS WEST
E. 64,218 T. 32,094 (49.98%) Lab. hold
*John Battle, Lab. 19,943
Kris Hopkins, C. 5,008
Darren Finlay, LD 3,350
David Blackburn, Green 2,573
William Finley, UK Ind. 758
Noel Nowosielski, Lib. 462
Lab. majority 14,935 (46.54%)
1.31% swing Lab. to C.
(1997: Lab. maj. 19,771 (49.16%))

LEICESTER EAST
E. 65,527 T. 40,661 (62.05%) Lab. hold
*Keith Vaz, Lab. 23,402
John Mugglestone, C. 9,960
Ms Harpinder Athwal, LD 4,989
Dave Roberts, Soc. Lab. 837
Clive Potter, BNP 772
Shirley Bennett, Ind. 701
Lab. majority 13,442 (33.06%)
4.22% swing Lab. to C.
(1997: Lab. maj. 18,422 (41.49%))

LEICESTER SOUTH
E. 72,671 T. 42,142 (57.99%) Lab. hold
*Jim Marshall, Lab. 22,958
Richard Hoile, C. 9,715
Parmjit Singh Gill, LD 7,243
Ms Margaret Layton, Green 1,217
Arnold Gardner, Soc. Lab. 676
Kirti Ladwa, UK Ind. 333
Lab. majority 13,243 (31.42%)
1.43% swing Lab. to C.
(1997: Lab. maj. 16,493 (34.28%))

LEICESTER WEST
E. 65,267 T. 33,219 (50.90%) Lab. hold
*Rt. Hon. Ms P. Hewitt, Lab. 18,014
Chris Shaw, C. 8,375
Andrew Vincent, LD 5,085
Matthew Gough, Green 1,074
Sean Kirkpatrick, Soc. Lab. 350
Steve Score, Soc. All. 321
Lab. majority 9,639 (29.02%)
1.21% swing Lab. to C.
(1997: Lab. maj. 12,864 (31.44%))

LEICESTERSHIRE NORTH WEST
E. 68,414 T. 45,009 (65.79%)
Lab. Co-op hold
*David Taylor, Lab. Co-op 23,431
Nick Weston, C. 15,274
Charlie Fraser-Fleming, LD 4,651
William Nattrass, UK Ind. 1,021
Robert Nettleton, Ind. 632
Lab. Co-op majority 8,157 (18.12%)
3.64% swing Lab. Co-op to C.
(1997: Lab. maj. 13,219 (25.41%))

LEIGH
E. 71,054 T. 35,298 (49.68%) Lab. hold
Andrew Burnham, Lab. 22,783
Andrew Oxley, C. 6,421
Ray Atkins, LD 4,524
William Kelly, Soc. Lab. 820
Chris Best, UK Ind. 750
Lab. majority 16,362 (46.35%)
3.50% swing Lab. to C.
(1997: Lab. maj. 24,496 (53.35%))

LEOMINSTER
E. 68,695 T. 46,729 (68.02%) C. gain
Bill Wiggin, C. 22,879
Ms Celia Downie, LD 12,512
Stephen Hart, Lab. 7,872
Ms Pippa Bennett, Green 1,690
Christopher Kingsley, UK Ind. 1,590
John Haycock, Ind. 186
C. majority 10,367 (22.19%)
2.35% swing LD to C.
(1997: C. maj. 8,835 (17.48%))

LEWES
E. 66,332 T. 45,433 (68.49%) LD hold
*Norman Baker, LD 25,588
Simon Sinnatt, C. 15,878
Paul Richards, Lab. 3,317
John Harvey, UK Ind. 650
LD majority 9,710 (21.37%)
9.36% swing C. to LD
(1997: LD maj. 1,300 (2.65%))

LEWISHAM DEPTFORD
E. 62,869 T. 29,107 (46.30%) Lab. hold
*Joan Ruddock, Lab. 18,915
Ms Cordelia McCartney, C. 3,622
Andrew Wiseman, LD 3,409
Darren Johnson, Green 1,901
Ian Page, Soc. All. 1,260
Lab. majority 15,293 (52.54%)
1.78% swing Lab. to C.
(1997: Lab. maj. 18,878 (56.11%))

LEWISHAM EAST
E. 58,302 T. 30,040 (51.52%) Lab. hold
*Ms Bridget Prentice, Lab. 16,116
David McInnes, C. 7,157
David Buxton, LD 4,937
Barry Roberts, BNP 1,005
Ms Jean Kysow, Soc. All. 464
Maurice Link, UK Ind. 361
Lab. majority 8,959 (29.82%)
1.30% swing Lab. to C.
(1997: Lab. maj. 12,127 (32.42%))

LEWISHAM WEST
E. 60,947 T. 30,815 (50.56%) Lab. hold
*Jim Dowd, Lab. 18,816
Gary Johnson, C. 6,896
Richard Thomas, LD 4,146
Frederick Pearson, UK Ind. 485
Nick Long, Ind. 472
Lab. majority 11,920 (38.68%)
0.25% swing C. to Lab.
(1997: Lab. maj. 14,337 (38.19%))

LEYTON & WANSTEAD
E. 61,549 T. 33,718 (54.78%) Lab. hold
*Harry Cohen, Lab. 19,558
Edward Heckels, C. 6,654
Alex Wilcock, LD 5,389
Ashley Gunstock, Green 1,030
Ms Sally Labern, Soc. All. 709
M. Skaife D'Ingerthorp, UK Ind. 378
Lab. majority 12,904 (38.27%)
0.17% swing Lab. to C.
(1997: Lab. maj. 15,186 (38.62%))

LICHFIELD
E. 63,794 T. 41,680 (65.34%) C. hold
*Michael Fabricant, C. 20,480
Martin Machray, Lab. 16,054
Phillip Bennion, LD 4,462
John Phazey, UK Ind. 684
C. majority 4,426 (10.62%)
5.06% swing Lab. to C.
(1997: C. maj. 238 (0.49%))

LINCOLN
E. 66,299 T. 37,125 (56.00%) Lab. hold
*Ms Gillian Merron, Lab. 20,003
Mrs Christine Talbot, C. 11,583
Ms Lisa Gabriel, LD 4,703
Roger Doughty, UK Ind. 836
Lab. majority 8,420 (22.68%)
0.61% swing Lab. to C.
(1997: Lab. maj. 11,130 (23.91%))

LIVERPOOL GARSTON
E. 65,094 T. 32,651 (50.16%) Lab. hold
*Ms Maria Eagle, Lab. 20,043
Ms Paula Keaveney, LD 7,549
Miss Helen Sutton, C. 5,059
Lab. majority 12,494 (38.27%)
2.05% swing Lab. to LD
(1997: Lab. maj. 18,417 (42.36%))

LIVERPOOL RIVERSIDE
E. 74,827 T. 25,503 (34.08%)
Lab. Co-op hold
*Ms Louise Ellman, Lab. Co-op 18,201
Richard Marbrow, LD 4,251
Miss Judith Edwards, C. 2,142
Ms Cathy Wilson, Soc. All. 909
Lab. Co-op majority 13,950 (54.70%)
1.23% swing Lab. Co-op to LD
(1997: Lab. maj. 21,799 (57.16%))

LIVERPOOL WALTON
E. 66,237 T. 28,458 (42.96%) Lab. hold
*Peter Kilfoyle, Lab. 22,143
Kiron Reid, LD 4,147
Stephen Horgan, C. 1,726
Paul Forrest, UK Ind. 442
Lab. majority 17,996 (63.24%)
2.00% swing Lab. to LD
(1997: Lab. maj. 27,038 (67.24%))

LIVERPOOL WAVERTREE
E. 72,555 T. 32,138 (44.29%) Lab. hold
*Ms Jane Kennedy, Lab. 20,155
Christopher Newby, LD 7,836
Geoffrey Allen, C. 3,091
Michael Lane, Soc. Lab. 359
Mark O'Brien, Soc. All. 349
Neil Miney, UK Ind. 348
Lab. majority 12,319 (38.33%)
2.29% swing Lab. to LD
(1997: Lab. maj. 19,701 (42.91%))

LIVERPOOL WEST DERBY
E. 67,921 T. 30,907 (45.50%) Lab. hold
*Robert Wareing, Lab. 20,454
Steve Radford, Lib. 4,601
Patrick Moloney, LD 3,366
Bill Clare, C. 2,486
Lab. majority 15,853 (51.29%)
5.15% swing Lab. to Lib.
(1997: Lab. maj. 25,965 (61.59%))

LOUGHBOROUGH
E. 70,077 T. 44,254 (63.15%)
Lab. Co-op hold
*Andy Reed, Lab. Co-op 22,016
Neil Lyon, C. 15,638
Ms Julie Simons, LD 5,667
John Bigger, UK Ind. 933
Lab. Co-op majority 6,378 (14.41%)
1.75% swing C. to Lab. Co-op
(1997: Lab. maj. 5,712 (10.91%))

LOUTH & HORNCASTLE
E. 71,556 T. 44,460 (62.13%) C. hold
*Sir Peter Tapsell, C. 21,543
David Bolland, Lab. 13,989
Ms Fiona Martin, LD 8,928
C. majority 7,554 (16.99%)
1.59% swing Lab. to C.
(1997: C. maj. 6,900 (13.81%))

LUDLOW
E. 63,053 T. 43,124 (68.39%) LD gain
Matthew Green, LD 18,620
Martin Taylor-Smith, C. 16,990
Nigel Knowles, Lab. 5,785
Jim Gaffney, Green 871
Phil Gutteridge, UK Ind. 858
LD majority 1,630 (3.78%)
8.27% swing C. to LD
(1997: C. maj. 5,909 (12.77%))

LUTON NORTH
E. 65,998 T. 39,126 (59.28%) Lab. hold
*Kelvin Hopkins, Lab. 22,187
Mrs Amanda Sater, C. 12,210
Dr Bob Hoyle, LD 3,795
Colin Brown, UK Ind. 934
Lab. majority 9,977 (25.50%)
2.58% swing C. to Lab.
(1997: Lab. maj. 9,626 (20.34%))

LUTON SOUTH
E. 68,985 T. 39,351 (57.04%) Lab. hold
*Ms Margaret Moran, Lab. 21,719
Gordon Henderson, C. 11,586
Rabi Martins, LD 4,292
Marc Scheimann, Green 798
Charles Lawman, UK Ind. 578
Joe Hearne, Soc. All. 271
Robert Bolton, WRP 107
Lab. majority 10,133 (25.75%)
1.13% swing C. to Lab.
(1997: Lab. maj. 11,319 (23.49%))

MACCLESFIELD
E. 73,123 T. 45,585 (62.34%) C. hold
*Nicholas Winterton, C. 22,284
Stephen Carter, Lab. 15,084
Mike Flynn, LD 8,217
C. majority 7,200 (15.79%)
0.09% swing C. to Lab.
(1997: C. maj. 8,654 (15.97%))

MAIDENHEAD
E. 68,130 T. 43,318 (63.58%) C. hold
*Mrs Theresa May, C. 19,506
Ms Kathryn Newbound, LD 16,222
John O'Farrell, Lab. 6,577
Dr Denis Cooper, UK Ind. 741
Lloyd Clarke, Loony 272
C. majority 3,284 (7.58%)
7.98% swing C. to LD
(1997: C. maj. 11,981 (23.54%))

MAIDSTONE & THE WEALD
E. 74,002 T. 45,577 (61.59%) C. hold
*Rt. Hon. Miss A. Widdecombe, C. 22,621
Mark Davis, Lab. 12,303
Ms Allison Wainman, LD 9,064
John Botting, UK Ind. 978
Neil Hunt, Ind. 611
C. majority 10,318 (22.64%)
2.36% swing Lab. to C.
(1997: C. maj. 9,603 (17.91%))

MAKERFIELD
E. 68,457 T. 34,856 (50.92%) Lab. hold
*Rt. Hon. Ian McCartney, Lab. 23,879
Mrs Jane Brooks, C. 6,129
David Crowther, LD 3,990
Malcolm Jones, Soc. All. 858
Lab. majority 17,750 (50.92%)
3.61% swing Lab. to C.
(1997: Lab. maj. 26,177 (58.15%))

MALDON & CHELMSFORD EAST
E. 69,201 T. 44,100 (63.73%) C. hold
*John Whittingdale, C. 21,719
Russell Kennedy, Lab. 13,257
Ms Jane Jackson, LD 7,002
Geoffrey Harris, UK Ind. 1,135
Walter Schwarz, Green 987
C. majority 8,462 (19.19%)
0.37% swing C. to Lab.
(1997: C. maj. 10,039 (19.92%))

MANCHESTER BLACKLEY
E. 59,111 T. 26,523 (44.87%) Lab. hold
*Graham Stringer, Lab. 18,285
Lance Stanbury, C. 3,821
Gary Riding, LD 3,015
Kevin Barr, Soc. Lab. 485
Ms Karen Reissmann, Soc. All. 461
Aziz Bhatti, Anti-Corrupt 456
Lab. majority 14,464 (54.53%)
0.13% swing Lab. to C.
(1997: Lab. maj. 19,588 (54.79%))

MANCHESTER CENTRAL
E. 66,268 T. 25,928 (39.13%) Lab. hold
*Tony Lloyd, Lab. 17,812
Philip Hobson, LD 4,070
Aaron Powell, C. 2,328
Ms Vanessa Hall, Green 1,018
Ron Sinclair, Soc. Lab. 484
Ms Terrenia Brosnan, ProLife 216
Lab. majority 13,742 (53.00%)
2.84% swing Lab. to LD
(1997: Lab. maj. 19,682 (58.69%))

MANCHESTER GORTON
E. 63,834 T. 27,229 (42.66%) Lab. hold
*Rt. Hon. G. Kaufman, Lab. 17,099
Ms Jackie Pearcey, LD 5,795
Christopher Causer, C. 2,705
Bruce Bingham, Green 835
Rashid Bhatti, UK Ind. 462
Ms Kirsty Muir, Soc. Lab. 333
Lab. majority 11,304 (41.51%)
3.12% swing Lab. to LD
(1997: Lab. maj. 17,342 (47.76%))

MANCHESTER WITHINGTON
E. 67,480 T. 35,050 (51.94%) Lab. hold
*Rt. Hon. K. Bradley, Lab. 19,239
Ms Yasmin Zalzala, LD 7,715
Julian Samways, C. 5,349
Ms Michelle Valentine, Green 1,539
John Clegg, Soc. All. 1,208
Lab. majority 11,524 (32.88%)
7.53% swing Lab. to LD
(1997: Lab. maj. 18,581 (42.20%))

MANSFIELD
E. 66,748 T. 36,852 (55.21%) Lab. hold
*Alan Meale, Lab. 21,050
William Wellesley, C. 10,012
Tim Hill, LD 5,790
Lab. majority 11,038 (29.95%)
6.65% swing Lab. to C.
(1997: Lab. maj. 20,518 (43.26%))

MEDWAY
E. 64,930 T. 38,610 (59.46%) Lab. hold
*Robert Marshall-Andrews, Lab. 18,914
Mark Reckless, C. 15,134
Geoffrey Juby, LD 3,604
Ms Nikki Sinclaire, UK Ind. 958
Lab. majority 3,780 (9.79%)
1.08% swing Lab. to C.
(1997: Lab. maj. 5,354 (11.96%))

MERIDEN
E. 74,439 T. 44,559 (59.86%) C. hold
*Mrs Caroline Spelman, C. 21,246
Ms Christine Shawcroft, Lab. 17,462
Nigel Hicks, LD 4,941
Richard Adams, UK Ind. 910
C. majority 3,784 (8.49%)
3.71% swing Lab. to C.
(1997: C. maj. 582 (1.07%))

MIDDLESBROUGH
E. 67,659 T. 33,717 (49.83%) Lab. hold
*Stuart Bell, Lab. 22,783
Alex Finn, C. 6,453
Keith Miller, LD 3,512
Geoff Kerr-Morgan, Soc. All. 577
Kai Andersen, Soc. Lab. 392
Lab. majority 16,330 (48.43%)
2.92% swing Lab. to C.
(1997: Lab. maj. 25,018 (54.28%))

MIDDLESBROUGH SOUTH & CLEVELAND EAST
E. 71,485 T. 43,991 (61.54%) Lab. hold
*Dr Ashok Kumar, Lab. 24,321
Mrs Barbara Harpham, C. 14,970
Ms Linda Parrish, LD 4,700
Lab. majority 9,351 (21.26%)
0.73% swing C. to Lab.
(1997: Lab. maj. 10,607 (19.79%))

MILTON KEYNES NORTH EAST
E. 75,526 T. 47,094 (62.35%) Lab. hold
*Brian White, Lab. 19,761
Mrs Marion Rix, C. 17,932
David Yeoward, LD 8,375
Michael Phillips, UK Ind. 1,026
Lab. majority 1,829 (3.88%)
1.71% swing C. to Lab.
(1997: Lab. maj. 240 (0.47%))

MILTON KEYNES SOUTH WEST
E. 76,607 T. 45,384 (59.24%) Lab. hold
*Dr Phyllis Starkey, Lab. 22,484
Iain Stewart, C. 15,506
Nazar Mohammad, LD 4,828
Alan Francis, Green 957
Clive Davies, UK Ind. 848
Patrick Denning, LCA 500
Dave Bradbury, Soc. All. 261
Lab. majority 6,978 (15.38%)
2.45% swing Lab. to C.
(1997: Lab. maj. 10,292 (20.28%))

MITCHAM & MORDEN
E. 65,671 T. 37,961 (57.80%) Lab. hold
*Ms Siobhain McDonagh, Lab. 22,936
Harry Stokes, C. 9,151
Nicholas Harris, LD 3,820
Tom Walsh, Green 926
John Tyndall, BNP 642
Adrian Roberts, UK Ind. 486
Lab. majority 13,785 (36.31%)
3.83% swing C. to Lab.
(1997: Lab. maj. 13,741 (28.66%))

MOLE VALLEY
E. 67,770 T. 47,072 (69.46%) C. hold
*Sir Paul Beresford, C. 23,790
Ms Celia Savage, LD 13,637
Dan Redford, Lab. 7,837
Ron Walters, UK Ind. 1,333
William Newton, ProLife 475
C. majority 10,153 (21.57%)
1.41% swing LD to C.
(1997: C. maj. 10,221 (18.74%))

MORECAMBE & LUNESDALE
E. 68,607 T. 41,655 (60.72%) Lab. hold
*Ms Geraldine Smith, Lab. 20,646
David Nuttall, C. 15,554
Chris Cotton, LD 3,817
Gregg Beaman, UK Ind. 935
Ms Cherith Adams, Green 703
Lab. majority 5,092 (12.22%)
0.05% swing C. to Lab.
(1997: Lab. maj. 5,965 (12.12%))

MORLEY & ROTHWELL
E. 71,815 T. 38,442 (53.53%) Lab. hold
Colin Challen, Lab. 21,919
David Schofield, C. 9,829
Stewart Golton, LD 5,446
John Bardsley, UK Ind. 1,248
Lab. majority 12,090 (31.45%)
0.35% swing Lab. to C.
(1997: Lab. maj. 14,750 (32.14%))

NEW FOREST EAST
E. 66,767 T. 42,178 (63.17%) C. hold
*Dr Julian Lewis, C. 17,902
Brian Dash, LD 14,073
Alan Goodfellow, Lab. 9,141
William Howe, UK Ind. 1,062
C. majority 3,829 (9.08%)
0.78% swing C. to LD
(1997: C. maj. 5,215 (10.63%))

NEW FOREST WEST
E. 67,806 T. 44,087 (65.02%) C. hold
*Desmond Swayne, C. 24,575
Mike Bignell, LD 11,384
Ms Crada Onuegbu, Lab. 6,481
Michael Clark, UK Ind. 1,647
C. majority 13,191 (29.92%)
3.57% swing LD to C.
(1997: C. maj. 11,332 (22.78%))

NEWARK
E. 71,089 T. 45,147 (63.51%) C. gain
Patrick Mercer, C. 20,983
*Ms Fiona Jones, Lab. 16,910
David Harding-Price, LD 5,970
Donald Haxby, Ind. 822
Ian Thomson, Soc. All. 462
C. majority 4,073 (9.02%)
7.41% swing Lab. to C.
(1997: Lab. maj. 3,016 (5.80%))

NEWBURY
E. 75,490 T. 50,807 (67.30%) LD hold
*David Rendel, LD 24,507
Richard Benyon, C. 22,092
Steve Billcliffe, Lab. 3,523
Ms Delphine Gray-Fisk, UK Ind. 685
LD majority 2,415 (4.75%)
5.16% swing LD to C.
(1997: LD maj. 8,517 (15.08%)

NEWCASTLE UPON TYNE CENTRAL
E. 67,970 T. 34,870 (51.30%) Lab. hold
*Jim Cousins, Lab. 19,169
Stephen Psallidas, LD 7,564
Aidan Ruff, C. 7,414
Gordon Potts, Soc. Lab. 723
Lab. majority 11,605 (33.28%)
5.44% swing Lab. to LD
(1997: Lab. maj. 16,480 (35.75%))

NEWCASTLE UPON TYNE EAST & WALLSEND
E. 61,494 T. 32,694 (53.17%) Lab. hold
*Rt. Hon. N. Brown, Lab. 20,642
David Ord, LD 6,419
Tim Troman, C. 3,873
Andrew Gray, Green 651
Dr Harash Narang, Ind. 563
Ms Blanch Carpenter, Soc. Lab. 420
Martin Levy, Comm. 126
Lab. majority 14,223 (43.50%)
8.53% swing Lab. to LD
(1997: Lab. maj. 23,811 (57.25%))

NEWCASTLE UPON TYNE NORTH
E. 63,208 T. 36,368 (57.54%) Lab. hold
*Doug Henderson, Lab. 21,874
Phillip Smith, C. 7,424
Graham Soult, LD 7,070
Lab. majority 14,450 (39.73%)
1.50% swing Lab. to C.
(1997: Lab. maj. 19,332 (42.74%))

NEWCASTLE-UNDER-LYME
E. 65,739 T. 38,674 (58.83%) Lab. hold
Paul Farrelly, Lab. 20,650
Mike Flynn, C. 10,664
Jerry Roodhouse, LD 5,993
Robert Fyson, Ind. 773
Paul Godfrey, UK Ind. 594
Lab. majority 9,986 (25.82%)
4.60% swing Lab. to C.
(1997: Lab. maj. 17,206 (35.02%))

NORFOLK MID
E. 74,911 T. 52,548 (70.15%) C. hold
*Keith Simpson, C. 23,519
Daniel Zeichner, Lab. 18,957
Ms V. Clifford-Jackson, LD 7,621
John Agnew, UK Ind. 1,333
Peter Reeve, Green 1,118
C. majority 4,562 (8.68%)
3.18% swing Lab. to C.
(1997: C. maj. 1,336 (2.33%))

NORFOLK NORTH
E. 80,061 T. 56,220 (70.22%) LD gain
Norman Lamb, LD 23,978
*David Prior, C. 23,495
Michael Gates, Lab. 7,490
Mike Sheridan, Green 649
Paul Simison, UK Ind. 608
LD majority 483 (0.86%)
1.53% swing C. to LD
(1997: C. maj. 1,293 (2.20%))

NORFOLK NORTH WEST
E. 77,387 T. 51,203 (66.16%) C. gain
Henry Bellingham, C. 24,846
*Dr George Turner, Lab. 21,361
Dr Ian Mack, LD 4,292
Ian Durrant, UK Ind. 704
C. majority 3,485 (6.81%)
4.57% swing Lab. to C.
(1997: Lab. maj. 1,339 (2.33%))

NORFOLK SOUTH
E. 82,710 T. 55,929 (67.62%) C. hold
Richard Bacon, C. 23,589
Dr Anne Lee, LD 16,696
Mark Wells, Lab. 13,719
Ms Stephanie Ross-Wagenknecht, Green 1,069
Joseph Neal, UK Ind. 856
C. majority 6,893 (12.32%)
0.22% swing LD to C.
(1997: C. maj. 7,378 (11.88%))

NORFOLK SOUTH WEST
E. 83,903 T. 52,949 (63.11%) C. hold
*Rt. Hon. Mrs G. Shephard, C. 27,633
Ms Anne Hanson, Lab. 18,267
Gordon Dean, LD 5,681
Ian Smith, UK Ind. 1,368
C. majority 9,366 (17.69%)
6.75% swing Lab. to C.
(1997: C. maj. 2,464 (4.19%))

NORMANTON
E. 65,392 T. 34,155 (52.23%) Lab. hold
*William O'Brien, Lab. 19,152
Graham Smith, C. 9,215
Stephen Pearson, LD 4,990
Mick Appleyard, Soc. Lab. 798
Lab. majority 9,937 (29.09%)
3.93% swing Lab. to C.
(1997: Lab. maj. 15,893 (36.96%))

NORTHAMPTON NORTH
E. 74,124 T. 41,494 (55.98%) Lab. hold
*Ms Sally Keeble, Lab. 20,507
John Whelan, C. 12,614
Richard Church, LD 7,363
Dusan Torbica, UK Ind. 596
Gordon White, Soc. All. 414
Lab. majority 7,893 (19.02%)
0.16% swing Lab. to C.
(1997: Lab. maj. 10,000 (19.34%))

NORTHAMPTON SOUTH
E. 85,271 T. 51,029 (59.84%) Lab. hold
*Tony Clarke, Lab. 21,882
Shailesh Vara, C. 20,997
Andrew Simpson, LD 6,355
Derek Clark, UK Ind. 1,237
Miss Tina Harvey, LP 362
Ms Clare Johnson, ProLife 196
Lab. majority 885 (1.73%)
0.22% swing C. to Lab.
(1997: Lab. maj. 744 (1.30%))

NORTHAVON
E. 78,841 T. 55,758 (70.72%) LD hold
*Steve Webb, LD 29,217
Dr Carrie Ruxton, C. 19,340
Robert Hall, Lab. 6,450
Mrs Carmen Carver, UK Ind. 751
LD majority 9,877 (17.71%)
7.15% swing C. to LD
(1997: LD maj. 2,137 (3.42%))

NORWICH NORTH
E. 74,911 T. 45,614 (60.89%) Lab. hold
*Dr Ian Gibson, Lab. 21,624
Ms Kay Mason, C. 15,761
Ms Moira Toye, LD 6,750
Robert Tinch, Green 797
Guy Cheyney, UK Ind. 471
Michael Betts, Ind. 211
Lab. majority 5,863 (12.85%)
2.17% swing Lab. to C.
(1997: Lab. maj. 9,470 (17.20%))

NORWICH SOUTH
E. 65,792 T. 42,592 (64.74%) Lab. hold
*Rt. Hon. C. Clarke, Lab. 19,367
Andrew French , C. 10,551
Andrew Aalders-Dunthorne, LD 9,640
Adrian Holmes, Green 1,434
Alun Buffrey, LCA 620
Edward Manningham, Soc. All. 507
Tarquin Mills, UK Ind. 473
Lab. majority 8,816 (20.70%)
3.67% swing Lab. to C.
(1997: Lab. maj. 14,239 (28.03%))

NOTTINGHAM EAST
E. 65,339 T. 29,731 (45.50%) Lab. hold
*John Heppell, Lab. 17,530
Richard Allan, C. 7,210
Tim Ball, LD 3,874
Pete Radcliff, Soc. All. 1,117
Lab. majority 10,320 (34.71%)
2.04% swing Lab. to C.
(1997: Lab. maj. 15,419 (38.80%))

NOTTINGHAM NORTH
E. 64,281 T. 30,042 (46.74%) Lab. hold
*Graham Allen, Lab. 19,392
Martin Wright, C. 7,152
Rob Lee, LD 3,177
Andrew Botham, Soc. Lab. 321
Lab. majority 12,240 (40.74%)
2.34% swing Lab. to C.
(1997: Lab. maj. 18,801 (45.42%))

NOTTINGHAM SOUTH
E. 73,049 T. 36,605 (50.11%) Lab. hold
*Alan Simpson, Lab. 19,949
Mrs Wendy Manning, C. 9,960
Kevin Mulloy, LD 6,064
David Bartrop, UK Ind. 632
Lab. majority 9,989 (27.29%)
0.13% swing Lab. to C.
(1997: Lab. maj. 13,364 (27.55%))

NUNEATON
E. 72,101 T. 43,312 (60.07%) Lab. hold
*Bill Olner, Lab. 22,577
Mark Lancaster, C. 15,042
Tony Ferguson, LD 4,820
Brian James, UK Ind. 873
Lab. majority 7,535 (17.40%)
3.95% swing Lab. to C.
(1997: Lab. maj. 13,540 (25.30%))

OLD BEXLEY & SIDCUP
E. 67,841 T. 42,133 (62.11%) C. hold
Derek Conway, C. 19,130
Jim Dickson, Lab. 15,785
Ms Belinda Ford, LD 5,792
Mrs Janice Cronin, UK Ind. 1,426
C. majority 3,345 (7.94%)
0.49% swing Lab. to C.
(1997: C. maj. 3,569 (6.95%))

OLDHAM EAST & SADDLEWORTH
E. 74,511 T. 45,420 (60.96%) Lab. hold
*Phil Woolas, Lab. 17,537
Howard Sykes, LD 14,811
Craig Heeley, C. 7,304
Michael Treacy, BNP 5,091
Ms Barbara Little, UK Ind. 677
Lab. majority 2,726 (6.00%)
0.13% swing Lab. to LD
(1997: Lab. maj. 3,389 (6.26%))

OLDHAM WEST & ROYTON
E. 69,409 T. 39,962 (57.57%) Lab. hold
*Rt. Hon. M. Meacher, Lab. 20,441
Duncan Reed, C. 7,076
Nick Griffin, BNP 6,552
Marc Ramsbottom, LD 4,975
David Roney, Green 918
Lab. majority 13,365 (33.44%)
0.99% swing Lab. to C.
(1997: Lab. maj. 16,201 (35.42%))

ORPINGTON
E. 74,423 T. 50,912 (68.41%) C. hold
*John Horam, C. 22,334
Chris Maines, LD 22,065
Chris Purnell, Lab. 5,517
John Youles, UK Ind. 996
C. majority 269 (0.53%)
2.19% swing C. to LD
(1997: C. maj. 2,952 (4.91%))

OXFORD EAST
E. 74,421 T. 39,848 (53.54%) Lab. hold
*Rt. Hon. A. Smith, Lab. 19,681
Steve Goddard, LD 9,337
Ms Cheryl Potter, C. 7,446
Pritam Singh, Green 1,501
John Lister, Soc. All. 708
Peter Gardner, UK Ind. 570
Fahim Ahmed, Soc. Lab. 274
Ms Linda Hodge, ProLife 254
Pathmanathan Mylvaganan, Ind. 77
Lab. majority 10,344 (25.96%)
8.08% swing Lab. to LD
(1997: Lab. maj. 16,665 (34.81%))

OXFORD WEST & ABINGDON
E. 79,915 T. 51,568 (64.53%) LD hold
*Dr Evan Harris, LD 24,670
Ed Matts, C. 15,485
Ms Gillian Kirk, Lab. 9,114
Mike Woodin, Green 1,423
Marcus Watney, UK Ind. 451
Ms Sigrid Shreeve, Ind. 332
Robert Twigger, Ext. Club 93
LD majority 9,185 (17.81%)
3.77% swing C. to LD
(1997: LD maj. 6,285 (10.27%))

PENDLE
E. 62,870 T. 39,732 (63.20%) Lab. hold
*Gordon Prentice, Lab. 17,729
Rasjid Skinner, C. 13,454
David Whipp, LD 5,479
Christian Jackson, BNP 1,976
Graham Cannon, UK Ind. 1,094
Lab. majority 4,275 (10.76%)
6.13% swing Lab. to C.
(1997: Lab. maj. 10,824 (23.02%))

PENRITH & THE BORDER
E. 67,776 T. 44,249 (65.29%) C. hold
*Rt. Hon. D. Maclean, C. 24,302
Kenneth Geyve Walker, LD 9,625
Michael Boaden, Lab. 8,177
Thomas Lowther, UK Ind. 938
Mark Gibson, LCA 870
John Moffat, Ind. 337
C. majority 14,677 (33.17%)
6.13% swing LD to C.
(1997: C. maj. 10,233 (20.90%))

PETERBOROUGH
E. 64,918 T. 39,812 (61.33%) Lab. hold
*Mrs Helen Brinton, Lab. 17,975
Stewart Jackson, C. 15,121
Nick Sandford, LD 5,761
Julian Fairweather, UK Ind. 955
Lab. majority 2,854 (7.17%)
3.98% swing Lab. to C.
(1997: Lab. maj. 7,323 (15.12%))

PLYMOUTH DEVONPORT
E. 73,666 T. 41,719 (56.63%) Lab. hold
*David Jamieson, Lab. 24,322
John Glen, C. 11,289
Keith Baldry, LD 4,513
Michael Parker, UK Ind. 958
Tony Staunton, Soc. All. 334
Rob Hawkins, Soc. Lab. 303
Lab. majority 13,033 (31.24%)
2.73% swing Lab. to C.
(1997: Lab. maj. 19,067 (36.70%))

PLYMOUTH SUTTON
E. 68,438 T. 39,073 (57.09%)
Lab. Co-op hold
*Mrs Linda Gilroy, Lab. Co-op 19,827
Oliver Colvile, C. 12,310
Alan Connett, LD 5,605
Alan Whitton, UK Ind. 970
Henry Leary, Soc. Lab. 361
Lab. Co-op majority 7,517 (19.24%)
0.29% swing Lab. Co-op to C.
(1997: Lab. maj. 9,440 (19.81%))

PONTEFRACT & CASTLEFORD
E. 63,181 T. 31,391 (49.68%) Lab. hold
*Ms Yvette Cooper, Lab. 21,890
Ms Pamela Singleton, C. 5,512
Wesley Paxton, LD 2,315
John Burdon, UK Ind. 739
Trevor Bolderson, Soc. Lab. 605
John Gill, Soc. All. 330
Lab. majority 16,378 (52.17%)
4.99% swing Lab. to C.
(1997: Lab. maj. 25,725 (62.15%))

POOLE
E. 64,644 T. 39,233 (60.69%) C. hold
*Robert Syms, C. 17,710
David Watt, Lab. 10,544
Nick Westbrook, LD 10,011
John Bass, UK Ind. 968
C. majority 7,166 (18.27%)
1.15% swing C. to Lab.
(1997: C. maj. 5,298 (11.32%))

POPLAR & CANNING TOWN
E. 75,173 T. 34,108 (45.37%) Lab. hold
*Jim Fitzpatrick, Lab. 20,862
Robert Marr, C. 6,758
Ms Alexi Sugden, LD 3,795
Paul Borg, BNP 1,743
Dr Kambiz Boomla, Soc. All. 950
Lab. majority 14,104 (41.35%)
3.41% swing Lab. to C.
(1997: Lab. maj. 18,915 (48.17%))

PORTSMOUTH NORTH
E. 64,256 T. 36,866 (57.37%) Lab. hold
*Syd Rapson, Lab. 18,676
Chris Day, C. 13,542
Darren Sanders, LD 3,795
William McCabe, UK Ind. 559
Brian Bundy, Ind. 294
Lab. majority 5,134 (13.93%)
2.19% swing C. to Lab.
(1997: Lab. maj. 4,323 (9.55%))

PORTSMOUTH SOUTH
E. 77,095 T. 39,215 (50.87%) LD hold
*Mike Hancock, LD 17,490
Philip Warr, C. 11,396
Graham Heaney, Lab. 9,361
John Molyneux, Soc. All. 647
Michael Tarrant, UK Ind. 321
LD majority 6,094 (15.54%)
3.58% swing C. to LD
(1997: LD maj. 4,327 (8.37%))

PRESTON
E. 72,077 T. 36,041 (50.00%)
Lab. Co-op hold
*Mark Hendrick, Lab. Co-op 20,540
Graham O'Hare, C. 8,272
Bill Chadwick, LD 4,746
Bilal Patel, Ind. 1,241
Richard Merrick, Green 1,019
The Rev David Braid, Ind. 223
Lab. Co-op majority 12,268 (34.04%)
2.41% swing Lab. Co-op to C.
(2000 Nov. by-election: Lab. maj. 4,426)
(1997: Lab. majority 18,680 (38.86%))

PUDSEY
E. 71,405 T. 45,175 (63.27%) Lab. hold

*Paul Truswell, Lab.	21,717
John Procter, C.	16,091
Stephen Boddy, LD	6,423
David Sewards, UK Ind.	944

Lab. majority 5,626 (12.45%)
0.34% swing C. to Lab.
(1997: Lab. maj. 6,207 (11.77%))

PUTNEY
E. 60,643 T. 34,254 (56.48%) Lab. hold

*Tony Colman, Lab.	15,911
Michael Simpson, C.	13,140
Tony Burrett, LD	4,671
Ms Pat Wild, UK Ind.	347
Ms Yvonne Windsor, ProLife	185

Lab. majority 2,771 (8.09%)
0.66% swing C. to Lab.
(1997: Lab. maj. 2,976 (6.76%))

RAYLEIGH
E. 70,073 T. 42,773 (61.04%) C. hold

Mark Francois, C.	21,434
Paul Clark, Lab.	13,144
Geoff Williams, LD	6,614
Colin Morgan, UK Ind.	1,581

C. majority 8,290 (19.38%)
0.72% swing C. to Lab.
(1997: C. maj. 10,684 (20.83%))

READING EAST
E. 74,637 T. 43,618 (58.44%) Lab. hold

*Ms Jane Griffiths, Lab.	19,531
Barry Tanswell, C.	13,943
Tom Dobrashian, LD	8,078
Ms Miriam Kennett, Green	1,053
Miss Amy Thornton, UK Ind.	525
Darren Williams, Soc. All.	394
Peter Hammerson, Ind.	94

Lab. majority 5,588 (12.81%)
2.63% swing C. to Lab.
(1997: Lab. maj. 3,795 (7.55%))

READING WEST
E. 71,688 T. 41,986 (58.57%) Lab. hold

*Martin Salter, Lab.	22,300
Stephen Reid, C.	13,451
Ms Polly Martin, LD	5,387
David Black, UK Ind.	848

Lab. maj 8,849 (21.08%)
7.44% swing C. to Lab.
(1997: Lab. maj. 2,997 (6.20%))

REDCAR
E. 66,179 T. 38,198 (57.72%) Lab. hold

Ms Vera Baird, Lab.	23,026
Chris Main, C.	9,583
Stan Wilson, LD	4,817
John Taylor, Soc. Lab.	772

Lab. majority 13,443 (35.19%)
4.53% swing Lab. to C.
(1997: Lab. maj. 21,664 (44.25%))

REDDITCH
E. 62,543 T. 37,032 (59.21%) Lab. hold

*Ms Jacqui Smith, Lab.	16,899
Mrs Karen Lumley, C.	14,415
Michael Ashall, LD	3,808
George Flynn, UK Ind.	1,259
Richard Armstrong, Green	651

Lab. majority 2,484 (6.71%)
3.49% swing Lab. to C.
(1997: Lab. maj. 6,125 (13.69%))

REGENT'S PARK & KENSINGTON NORTH
E. 75,886 T. 37,052 (48.83%) Lab. hold

*Ms Karen Buck, Lab.	20,247
Peter Wilson, C.	9,981
David Boyle, LD	4,669
Dr Paul Miller, Green	1,268
China Mieville, Soc. All.	459
Alan Crisp, UK Ind.	354
Ms Charlotte Regan, Ind.	74

Lab. majority 10,266 (27.71%)
1.63% swing Lab. to C.
(1997: Lab. maj. 14,657 (30.96%))

REIGATE
E. 65,023 T. 39,474 (60.71%) C. hold

*Crispin Blunt, C.	18,875
Simon Charleton, Lab.	10,850
Ms Jane Kulka, LD	8,330
Stephen Smith, UK Ind.	1,062
Harold Green, Ref. UK	357

C. majority 8,025 (20.33%)
2.13% swing Lab. to C.
(1997: C. maj. 7,741 (16.07%))

RIBBLE SOUTH (SOUTH RIBBLE)
E. 73,794 T. 46,130 (62.51%) Lab. hold

*David Borrow, Lab.	21,386
Adrian Owens, C.	17,594
Mark Alcock, LD	7,150

Lab. majority 3,792 (8.22%)
0.49% swing Lab. to C.
(1997: Lab. maj. 5,084 (9.20%))

RIBBLE VALLEY
E. 74,319 T. 49,171 (66.16%) C. hold

*Nigel Evans, C.	25,308
Mike Carr, LD	14,070
Marcus Johnstone, Lab.	9,793

C. majority 11,238 (22.85%)
5.63% swing LD to C.
(1997: C. maj. 6,640 (11.60%))

RICHMOND (YORKS)
E. 65,360 T. 44,034 (67.37%) C. hold

*Rt. Hon. W. Hague, C.	25,951
Ms Fay Tinnion, Lab.	9,632
Edward Forth, LD	7,890
Mrs Melodie Staniforth, Loony	561

C. majority 16,319 (37.06%)
8.00% swing Lab. to C.
(1997: C. maj. 10,051 (21.05%))

RICHMOND PARK
E. 72,663 T. 49,151 (67.64%) LD hold

*Dr Jenny Tonge, LD	23,444
Tom Harris, C.	18,480
Barry Langford, Lab.	5,541
James Page, Green	1,223
Peter St John Howe, UK Ind.	348
Raymond Perrin, Ind.	115

LD majority 4,964 (10.10%)
2.45% swing C. to LD
(1997: LD maj. 2,951 (5.19%))

ROCHDALE
E. 69,506 T. 39,412 (56.70%) Lab. hold

*Ms Lorna Fitzsimons, Lab.	19,406
Paul Rowen, LD	13,751
Ms Elaina Cohen, C.	5,274
Nick Harvey, Green	728
Mohammed Salim, Ind.	253

Lab. majority 5,655 (14.35%)
2.45% swing LD to Lab.
(1997: Lab. maj. 4,545 (9.45%))

ROCHFORD & SOUTHEND EAST
E. 69,991 T. 37,452 (53.51%) C. hold

*Sir Teddy Taylor, C.	20,058
Chris Dandridge, Lab.	13,024
Stephen Newton, LD	2,780
Adrian Hedges, Green	990
Brian Lynch, Lib.	600

C. majority 7,034 (18.78%)
4.86% swing Lab. to C.
(1997: C. maj. 4,225 (9.07%))

ROMFORD
E. 59,893 T. 35,701 (59.61%) C. gain

Andrew Rosindell, C.	18,931
*Ms Eileen Gordon, Lab.	12,954
Nigel Meyer, LD	2,869
Stephen Ward, UK Ind.	533
Frank McAllister, BNP	414

C. majority 5,977 (16.74%)
9.14% swing Lab. to C.
(1997: Lab. maj. 649 (1.54%))

ROMSEY
E. 70,584 T. 48,459 (68.65%) LD hold

*Mrs Sandra Gidley, LD	22,756
Paul Raynes, C.	20,386
Stephen Roberts, Lab.	3,986
Anthony McCabe, UK Ind.	730
Derrick Large, LCA	601

LD majority 2,370 (4.89%)
10.73% swing C. to LD
(2000 May by-election: LD maj. 3,311 (8.55%); 1997: C. maj. 8,585 (16.56%))

ROSSENDALE & DARWEN
E. 70,280 T. 41,358 (58.85%) Lab. hold

*Ms Janet Anderson, Lab.	20,251
George Lee, C.	15,028
Brian Dunning, LD	6,079

Lab. majority 5,223 (12.63%)
4.38% swing Lab. to C.
(1997: Lab. maj. 10,949 (21.38%))

ROTHER VALLEY
E. 69,174 T. 36,803 (53.20%) Lab. hold

*Rt. Hon. K. Barron, Lab.	22,851
James Duddridge, C.	7,969
Ms Win Knight, LD	4,603
David Cutts, UK Ind.	1,380

Lab. majority 14,882 (40.44%)
5.22% swing Lab. to C.
(1997: Lab. maj. 23,485 (50.88%))

ROTHERHAM
E. 57,931 T. 29,354 (50.67%) Lab. hold

*Denis MacShane, Lab.	18,759
Richard Powell, C.	5,682
Charles Hall, LD	3,117
Peter Griffith, UK Ind.	730
Dick Penycate, Green	577
Ms Freda Smith, Soc. All.	352
Geoffrey Bartholomew, JLDP	137

Lab. majority 13,077 (44.55%)
6.24% swing Lab. to C.
(1997: Lab. maj. 21,469 (57.02%))

RUGBY & KENILWORTH
E. 79,764 T. 53,796 (67.44%) Lab. hold

*Andy King, Lab.	24,221
David Martin, C.	21,344
Ms Gwen Fairweather, LD	7,444
Paul Garratt, UK Ind.	787

Lab. maj 2,877 (5.35%)
2.27% swing C. to Lab.
(1997: Lab. maj. 495 (0.81%))

RUISLIP-NORTHWOOD
E. 60,788 T. 37,141 (61.10%) C. hold
*John Wilkinson, C. 18,115
Ms Gillian Travis, Lab. 10,578
Mike Cox, LD 7,177
Graham Lee, Green 724
Ian Edward, BNP 547
C. majority 7,537 (20.29%)
1.46% swing Lab. to C.
(1997: C. maj. 7,794 (17.38%))

RUNNYMEDE & WEYBRIDGE
E. 75,569 T. 42,426 (56.14%) C. hold
*Philip Hammond, C. 20,646
Ms Jane Briginshaw, Lab. 12,286
Chris Bushill, LD 6,924
Christopher Browne, UK Ind. 1,332
Charles Gilman, Green 1,238
C. majority 8,360 (19.70%)
0.27% swing Lab. to C.
(1997: C. maj. 9,875 (19.16%))

RUSHCLIFFE
E. 81,839 T. 54,446 (66.53%) C. hold
*Rt. Hon. K. Clarke, C. 25,869
Paul Fallon, Lab. 18,512
Jeremy Hargreaves, LD 7,395
Ken Browne, UK Ind. 1,434
Ashley Baxter, Green 1,236
C. majority 7,357 (13.51%)
2.69% swing Lab. to C.
(1997: C. maj. 5,055 (8.14%))

RUTLAND & MELTON
E. 72,448 T. 47,056 (64.95%) C. hold
*Alan Duncan, C. 22,621
Matthew O'Callaghan, Lab. 14,009
Kim Lee, LD 8,386
Peter Baker, UK Ind. 1,223
Christopher Davies, Green 817
C. majority 8,612 (18.30%)
0.76% swing Lab. to C.
(1997: C. maj. 8,836 (16.78%))

RYEDALE
E. 66,543 T. 43,899 (65.97%) C. hold
*John Greenway, C. 20,711
Keith Orrell, LD 15,836
David Ellis, Lab. 6,470
Stephen Feaster, UK Ind. 882
C. majority 4,875 (11.11%)
0.37% swing LD to C.
(1997: C. maj. 5,058 (10.37%))

SAFFRON WALDEN
E. 76,724 T. 50,040 (65.22%) C. hold
*Rt. Hon. Sir A. Haselhurst, C. 24,485
Mrs E. Tealby-Watson, LD 12,481
Ms Tania Rogers, Lab. 11,305
Richard Glover, UK Ind. 1,769
C. majority 12,004 (23.99%)
2.73% swing LD to C.
(1997: C. maj. 10,573 (18.53%))

SALFORD
E. 54,152 T. 22,514 (41.58%) Lab. hold
*Ms Hazel Blears, Lab. 14,649
Norman Owen, LD 3,637
Chris King, C. 3,446
Peter Grant, Soc. All. 414
Ms Hazel Wallace, Ind. 216
Roy Masterson, Ind. 152
Lab. majority 11,012 (48.91%)
4.89% swing Lab. to LD
(1997: Lab. maj. 17,069 (51.53%))

SALISBURY
E. 80,538 T. 52,603 (65.31%) C. hold
*Robert Key, C. 24,527
Ms Yvonne Emmerson-Peirce, LD 15,824
Ms Sue Mallory, Lab. 9,199
Malcolm Wood, UK Ind. 1,958
Hamish Soutar, Green 1,095
C. majority 8,703 (16.54%)
2.88% swing LD to C.
(1997: C. maj. 6,276 (10.78%))

SCARBOROUGH & WHITBY
E. 75,213 T. 47,523 (63.18%) Lab. hold
*Lawrie Quinn, Lab. 22,426
John Sykes, C. 18,841
Tom Pearce, LD 3,977
Jonathan Dixon, Green 1,049
John Jacob, UK Ind. 970
Ms Theresa Murray, ProLife 260
Lab. maj 3,585 (7.54%)
0.94% swing Lab. to C.
(1997: Lab. maj. 5,124 (9.43%))

SCUNTHORPE
E. 59,689 T. 33,625 (56.33%) Lab. hold
*Elliot Morley, Lab. 20,096
Bernard Theobald, C. 9,724
Bob Tress, LD 3,156
John Cliff, UK Ind. 347
David Patterson, Ind. 302
Lab. majority 10,372 (30.85%)
1.62% swing Lab. to C.
(1997: Lab. maj. 14,173 (34.09%))

SEDGEFIELD
E. 64,925 T. 40,258 (62.01%) Lab. hold
*Rt. Hon. T. Blair, Lab. 26,110
Douglas Carswell, C. 8,397
Andrew Duffield, LD 3,624
Andrew Spence, UK Ind. 974
Brian Gibson, Soc. Lab. 518
Christopher Driver, R & R Loony 375
Ms Helen John, WFLOE 260
Lab. majority 17,713 (44.00%)
4.69% swing Lab. to C.
(1997: Lab. maj. 25,143 (53.37%))

SELBY
E. 77,924 T. 50,272 (64.51%) Lab. hold
*John Grogan, Lab. 22,652
Michael Mitchell, C. 20,514
Jeremy Wilcock, LD 5,569
Ms Helen Kenwright, Green 902
Bob Lewis, UK Ind. 635
Lab. majority 2,138 (4.25%)
1.28% swing Lab. to C.
(1997: Lab. maj. 3,836 (6.81%))

SEVENOAKS
E. 66,648 T. 42,614 (63.94%) C. hold
*Michael Fallon, C. 21,052
Ms Caroline Humphreys, Lab. 10,898
Clive Gray, LD 9,214
Mrs Lisa Hawkins, UK Ind. 1,155
Mark Ellis, PF 295
C. majority 10,154 (23.83%)
1.48% swing Lab. to C.
(1997: C. maj. 10,461 (20.86%))

SHEFFIELD ATTERCLIFFE
E. 68,386 T. 35,824 (52.38%) Lab. hold
*Clive Betts, Lab. 24,287
John Perry, C. 5,443
Ms Gail Smith, LD 5,092
Ms Pauline Arnott, UK Ind. 1,002
Lab. majority 18,844 (52.60%)
1.69% swing C. to Lab.
(1997: Lab. maj. 21,818 (49.23%))

SHEFFIELD BRIGHTSIDE
E. 54,711 T. 25,552 (46.70%) Lab. hold
*Rt. Hon. D. Blunkett, Lab. 19,650
Matthew Wilson, C. 2,601
Ms Alison Firth, LD 2,238
Brian Wilson, Soc. All. 361
Robert Morris, Soc. Lab. 354
Mark Suter, UK Ind. 348
Lab. majority 17,049 (66.72%)
0.81% swing C. to Lab.
(1997: Lab. maj. 19,954 (58.92%))

SHEFFIELD CENTRAL
E. 62,018 T. 30,069 (48.48%) Lab. hold
Rt. Hon. R. Caborn, Lab. 18,477
Ali Qadar, LD 5,933
Miss Noelle Brelsford, C. 3,289
Bernard Little, Green 1,008
Nick Riley, Soc. All. 754
David Hadfield, Soc. Lab. 289
Ms Charlotte Schofield, UK Ind. 257
Michael Driver, WRP 62
Lab. majority 12,544 (41.72%)
2.36% swing Lab. to LD
(1997: Lab. maj. 16,906 (46.43%))

SHEFFIELD HALLAM
E. 60,288 T. 38,246 (63.44%) LD hold
*Richard Allan, LD 21,203
John Harthman, C. 11,856
Ms Gillian Furniss, Lab. 4,758
Leslie Arnott, UK Ind. 429
LD majority 9,347 (24.44%)
3.12% swing C. to LD
(1997: LD maj. 8,271 (18.19%))

SHEFFIELD HEELEY
E. 62,758 T. 34,139 (54.40%) Lab. hold
Ms Meg Munn, Lab. 19,452
David Willis, LD 7,748
Ms Carolyn Abbott, C. 4,864
Rob Unwin, Green 774
Brian Fischer, Soc. Lab. 667
David Dunn, UK Ind. 634
Lab. majority 11,704 (34.28%)
2.60% swing Lab. to LD
(1997: Lab. maj. 17,078 (39.48%))

SHEFFIELD HILLSBOROUGH
E. 75,097 T. 42,536 (56.64%) Lab. hold
*Ms Helen Jackson, Lab. 24,170
John Commons, LD 9,601
Graham King, C. 7,801
Peter Webb, UK Ind. 964
Lab. majority 14,569 (34.25%)
1.62% swing LD to Lab.
(1997: Lab. maj. 16,451 (31.02%))

SHERWOOD
E. 75,670 T. 45,900 (60.66%) Lab. hold
*Paddy Tipping, Lab. 24,900
Brandon Lewis, C. 15,527
Peter Harris, LD 5,473
Lab. majority 9,373 (20.42%)
4.66% swing Lab. to C.
(1997: Lab. maj. 16,812 (29.74%))

SHIPLEY
E. 69,577 T. 46,020 (66.14%) Lab. hold

*Christopher Leslie, Lab.	20,243
David Senior, C.	18,815
Ms Helen Wright, LD	4,996
Martin Love, Green	1,386
Walter Whitacker, UK Ind.	580

Lab. majority 1,428 (3.10%)
1.28% swing Lab. to C.
(1997: Lab. maj. 2,996 (5.67%))

SHREWSBURY & ATCHAM
E. 74,964 T. 49,909 (66.58%) Lab. hold

*Paul Marsden, Lab.	22,253
Miss Anthea McIntyre, C.	18,674
Jonathan Rule, LD	6,173
Henry Curteis, UK Ind.	1,620
Ms Emma Bullard, Green	931
James Gollins, Ind.	258

Lab. majority 3,579 (7.17%)
2.08% swing C. to Lab.
(1997: Lab. maj. 1,670 (3.02%))

SHROPSHIRE NORTH
E. 73,716 T. 46,520 (63.11%) C. hold

*Owen Paterson, C.	22,631
Michael Ion, Lab.	16,390
Ben Jephcott, LD	5,945
David Trevanion, UK Ind.	1,165
Russell Maxfield, Ind.	389

C. majority 6,241 (13.42%)
4.58% swing Lab. to C.
(1997: C. maj. 2,195 (4.26%))

SITTINGBOURNE & SHEPPEY
E. 65,825 T. 37,858 (57.51%) Lab. hold

*Derek Wyatt, Lab.	17,340
Adrian Lee, C.	13,831
Ms Elvie Lowe, LD	5,353
Michael Young, R & R Loony	673
Robert Oakley, UK Ind.	661

Lab. majority 3,509 (9.27%)
2.54% swing C. to Lab.
(1997: Lab. maj. 1,929 (4.18%))

SKIPTON & RIPON
E. 75,201 T. 49,126 (65.33%) C. hold

*Rt. Hon. D. Curry, C.	25,736
Bernard Bateman, LD	12,806
Michael Dugher, Lab.	8,543
Mrs Nancy Holdsworth, UK Ind.	2,041

C. majority 12,930 (26.32%)
2.47% swing LD to C.
(1997: C. maj. 11,620 (21.38%))

SLEAFORD & NORTH HYKEHAM
E. 74,561 T. 48,719 (65.34%) C. hold

*Rt. D. Hogg, C.	24,190
Ms Elizabeth Donnelly, Lab.	15,568
Robert Arbon, LD	7,894
Michael Ward-Barrow, UK Ind.	1,067

C. majority 8,622 (17.70%)
4.03% swing Lab. to C.
(1997: C. maj. 5,123 (9.64%))

SLOUGH
E. 72,429 T. 38,998 (53.84%) Lab. hold

*Ms Fiona Mactaggart, Lab.	22,718
Mrs Diana Coad, C.	10,210
Keith Kerr, LD	4,109
Michael Haines, Ind.	859
John Lane, UK Ind.	738
Choudry Nazir, Ind.	364

Lab. majority 12,508 (32.07%)
2.34% swing C. to Lab.
(1997: Lab. maj. 13,071 (27.39%))

SOLIHULL
E. 77,094 T. 48,271 (62.61%) C. hold

*John Taylor, C.	21,935
Ms Jo Byron, LD	12,528
Brendan O'Brien, Lab.	12,373
Andy Moore, UK Ind.	1,061
Ms Stephanie Pyne, ProLife	374

C. majority 9,407 (19.49%)
0.07% swing LD to C.
(1997: C. maj. 11,397 (19.35%))

SOMERTON & FROME
E. 74,991 T. 52,684 (70.25%) LD hold

*David Heath, LD	22,983
Jonathan Marland, C.	22,315
Andrew Perkins, Lab.	6,113
Peter Bridgwood, UK Ind.	919
Ms Jean Pollock, Lib.	354

LD majority 668 (1.27%)
0.52% swing C. to LD
(1997: LD maj. 130 (0.23%))

SOUTH HOLLAND & THE DEEPINGS
E. 73,880 T. 46,202 (62.54%) C. hold

*John Hayes, C.	25,611
Graham Walker, Lab.	14,512
Ms Grace Hill, LD	4,761
Malcolm Charlesworth, UK Ind.	1,318

C. majority 11,099 (24.02%)
4.04% swing Lab. to C.
(1997: C. maj. 7,991 (15.94%))

SOUTH SHIELDS
E. 61,802 T. 30,448 (49.27%) Lab. hold

David Miliband, Lab.	19,230
Miss Joanna Gardner, C.	5,140
Marshall Grainger, LD	5,127
Alan Hardy, UK Ind.	689
Roger Nettleship, Ind.	262

Lab. majority 14,090 (46.28%)
5.28% swing Lab. to C.
(1997: Lab. maj. 22,153 (56.84%))

SOUTHAMPTON ITCHEN
E. 76,603 T. 41,373 (54.01%) Lab. hold

*Rt. Hon. J. Denham, Lab.	22,553
Mrs Caroline Nokes, C.	11,330
Mark Cooper, LD	6,195
Kim Rose, UK Ind.	829
Gavin Marsh, Soc. All.	241
Michael Holmes, Soc. Lab.	225

Lab. majority 11,223 (27.13%)
0.37% swing C. to Lab.
(1997: Lab. maj. 14,209 (26.38%))

SOUTHAMPTON TEST
E. 73,893 T. 41,575 (56.26%) Lab. hold

*Alan Whitehead, Lab.	21,824
Richard Gueterbock, C.	10,617
John Shaw, LD	7,522
Garry Rankin-Moore, UK Ind.	792
Mark Abel, Soc. All.	442
Paramjit Bahia, Soc. Lab.	378

Lab. majority 11,207 (26.96%)
0.43% swing C. to Lab.
(1997: Lab. maj. 13,684 (26.10%))

SOUTHEND WEST
E. 64,116 T. 37,375 (58.29%) C. hold

*David Amess, C.	17,313
Paul Fisher, Lab.	9,372
Richard de Ste Croix, LD	9,319
Brian Lee, UK Ind.	1,371

C. majority 7,941 (21.25%)
2.64% swing Lab. to C.
(1997: C. maj. 2,615 (5.62%))

SOUTHPORT
E. 70,785 T. 41,153 (58.14%) LD hold

John Pugh, LD	18,011
Laurence Jones, C.	15,004
Paul Brant, Lab.	6,816
David Green, Lib.	767
Gerry Kelley, UK Ind.	555

LD majority 3,007 (7.31%)
2.44% swing LD to C.
(1997: LD maj. 6,160 (12.18%))

SOUTHWARK NORTH & BERMONDSEY
E. 73,527 T. 36,862 (50.13%) LD hold

*Simon Hughes, LD	20,991
Kingsley Abrams, Lab.	11,359
Ewan Wallace, C.	2,800
Ms Ruth Jenkins, Green	752
Ms Lianne Shore, NF	612
Rob McWhirter, UK Ind.	271
John Davies, Ind.	77

LD majority 9,632 (26.13%)
8.91% swing Lab. to LD
(1997: LD maj. 3,387 (8.30%))

SPELTHORNE
E. 68,731 T. 41,794 (60.81%) C. hold

*David Wilshire, C.	18,851
Andrew Shaw, Lab.	15,589
Martin Rimmer, LD	6,156
Richard Squire, UK Ind.	1,198

C. majority 3,262 (7.80%)
0.56% swing Lab. to C.
(1997: C. maj. 3,473 (6.69%))

ST ALBANS
E. 66,040 T. 43,761 (66.26%) Lab. hold

*Kerry Pollard, Lab.	19,889
Charles Elphicke, C.	15,423
Nick Rijke, LD	7,847
Christopher Sherwin, UK Ind.	602

Lab. majority 4,466 (10.21%)
0.71% swing C. to Lab.
(1997: Lab. maj. 4,459 (8.78%))

ST HELENS NORTH
E. 70,545 T. 37,601 (53.30%) Lab. hold

Dave Watts, Lab.	22,977
Simon Pearce, C.	7,076
John Beirne, LD	6,609
Stephen Whatham, Soc. Lab.	939

Lab. majority 15,901 (42.29%)
2.64% swing Lab. to C.
(1997: Lab. maj. 23,417 (47.57%))

ST HELENS SOUTH
E. 65,122 T. 33,804 (51.91%) Lab. hold

†Shaun Woodward, Lab.	16,799
Brian Spencer, LD	7,814
Dr Lee Rotherham, C.	4,675
Neil Thompson, Soc. All.	2,325
Mike Perry, Soc. Lab.	1,504
Bryan Slater, UK Ind.	336
Michael Murphy, Ind.	271
David Braid, Ind.	80

Lab. majority 8,985 (26.58%)
14.33% swing Lab. to LD
(1997: Lab. maj. 23,739 (53.63%))

ST IVES
E. 74,256 T. 49,266 (66.35%) LD hold
*Andrew George, LD 25,413
Miss Joanna Richardson, C. 15,360
William Morris, Lab. 6,567
Mick Faulkner, UK Ind. 1,926
LD majority 10,053 (20.41%)
3.55% swing C. to LD
(1997: LD maj. 7,170 (13.30%))

STAFFORD
E. 67,934 T. 44,366 (65.31%) Lab. hold
*David Kidney, Lab. 21,285
Philip Cochrane, C. 16,253
Ms Jeanne Pinkerton, LD 4,205
Earl of Bradford, UK Ind. 2,315
Michael Hames, R & R Loony 308
Lab. maj 5,032 (11.34%)
1.50% swing C. to Lab.
(1997: Lab. maj. 4,314 (8.34%))

STAFFORDSHIRE MOORLANDS
E. 66,760 T. 42,658 (63.90%) Lab. hold
*Ms Charlotte Atkins, Lab. 20,904
Marcus Hayes, C. 15,066
John Redfern, LD 5,928
Paul Gilbert, UK Ind. 760
Lab. maj 5,838 (13.69%)
2.99% swing Lab. to C.
(1997: Lab. maj. 10,049 (19.66%))

STAFFORDSHIRE SOUTH
E. 69,925 T. 42,180 (60.32%) C. hold
*Sir Patrick Cormack, C. 21,295
Paul Kalinauckas, Lab. 14,414
Ms Jo Harrison, LD 4,891
Mike Lynch, UK Ind. 1,580
C. majority 6,881 (16.31%)
0.51% swing Lab. to C.
(1997: C. maj. 7,821 (15.30%))

STALYBRIDGE & HYDE
E. 66,265 T. 32,046 (48.36%) Lab. hold
James Purnell, Lab. 17,781
Andrew Reid, C. 8,922
Brendon Jones, LD 4,327
Frank Bennett, UK Ind. 1,016
Lab. majority 8,859 (27.64%)
3.36% swing Lab. to C.
(1997: Lab. maj. 14,806 (34.36%))

STEVENAGE
E. 69,203 T. 42,453 (61.35%) Lab. hold
*Ms Barbara Follett, Lab. 22,025
Graeme Quar, C. 13,459
Harry Davies, LD 6,027
Steve Glennon, Soc. All. 449
Antal Losonczi, Ind. 320
Ms Sarah Bell, ProLife 173
Lab. majority 8,566 (20.18%)
1.18% swing Lab. to C.
(1997: Lab. maj. 11,582 (22.54%))

STOCKPORT
E. 66,397 T. 35,383 (53.29%) Lab. hold
*Ms Ann Coffey, Lab. 20,731
John Allen, C. 9,162
Mark Hunter, LD 5,490
Lab. majority 11,569 (32.70%)
3.91% swing Lab. to C.
(1997: Lab. maj. 18,912 (40.52%))

STOCKTON NORTH
E. 65,192 T. 35,427 (54.34%) Lab. hold
*Frank Cook, Lab. 22,470
Ms Amanda Vigar, C. 7,823
Ms Mary Wallace, LD 4,208
Bill Wennington, Green 926
Lab. majority 14,647 (41.34%)
3.34% swing Lab. to C.
(1997: Lab. maj. 21,357 (48.02%))

STOCKTON SOUTH
E. 71,026 T. 44,209 (62.24%) Lab. hold
*Ms Dari Taylor, Lab. 23,414
Tim Devlin, C. 14,328
Mrs Suzanne Fletcher, LD 6,012
Lawrie Coombes, Soc. All. 455
Lab. majority 9,086 (20.55%)
0.84% swing Lab. to C.
(1997: Lab. maj. 11,585 (22.23%))

STOKE-ON-TRENT CENTRAL
E. 59,750 T. 28,300 (47.36%) Lab. hold
*Mark Fisher, Lab. 17,170
Ms Jill Clark, C. 5,325
Gavin Webb, LD 4,148
Richard Wise, Ind. 1,657
Lab. majority 11,845 (41.86%)
3.83% swing Lab. to C.
(1997: Lab. maj. 19,924 (49.51%))

STOKE-ON-TRENT NORTH
E. 57,998 T. 30,115 (51.92%) Lab. hold
*Ms Joan Walley, Lab. 17,460
Benjamin Browning, C. 5,676
Henry Jebb, LD 3,580
Lee Wanger, Ind. 3,399
Lab. maj 11,784 (39.13%)
2.92% swing Lab. to C.
(1997: Lab. maj. 17,392 (44.98%))

STOKE-ON-TRENT SOUTH
E. 70,032 T. 36,028 (51.45%) Lab. hold
*George Stevenson, Lab. 19,366
Philip Bastiman, C. 8,877
Christopher Coleman, LD 4,724
Adrian Knapper, Ind. 1,703
Steven Batkin, BNP 1,358
Lab. majority 10,489 (29.11%)
5.23% swing Lab. to C.
(1997: Lab. maj. 18,303 (39.58%))

STONE
E. 68,847 T. 45,642 (66.29%) C. hold
*William Cash, C. 22,395
John Palfreyman, Lab. 16,359
Brendan McKeown, LD 6,888
C. majority 6,036 (13.22%)
3.01% swing Lab. to C.
(1997: C. maj. 3,818 (7.20%))

STOURBRIDGE
E. 64,610 T. 39,924 (61.79%) Lab. hold
*Ms Debra Shipley, Lab. 18,823
Stephen Eyre, C. 15,011
Chris Bramall, LD 4,833
John Knotts, UK Ind. 763
Mick Atherton, Soc. Lab. 494
Lab. majority 3,812 (9.55%)
0.91% swing Lab. to C.
(1997: Lab. maj. 5,645 (11.36%))

STRATFORD-ON-AVON
E. 85,241 T. 54,914 (64.42%) C. hold
*John Maples, C. 27,606
Dr Susan Juned, LD 15,804
Mushtaq Hussain, Lab. 9,164
Ronald Mole, UK Ind. 1,184
Mick Davies, Green 1,156
C. majority 11,802 (21.49%)
0.61% swing C. to LD
(1997: C. maj. 14,106 (22.72%))

STREATHAM
E. 76,021 T. 36,998 (48.67%) Lab. hold
*Keith Hill, Lab. 21,041
Roger O'Brien, LD 6,771
Stephen Hocking, C. 6,639
Mohammed Sajid, Green 1,641
Greg Tucker, Soc. All. 906
Lab. majority 14,270 (38.57%)
5.33% swing Lab. to LD
(1997: Lab. maj. 18,423 (41.04%))

STRETFORD & URMSTON
E. 70,924 T. 38,973 (54.95%) Lab. hold
*Ms Beverley Hughes, Lab. 23,804
Jonathan Mackie, C. 10,565
John Bridges, LD 3,891
Ms Katie Price, Ind. 713
Lab. majority 13,239 (33.97%)
2.98% swing C. to Lab.
(1997: Lab. maj. 13,640 (28.01%))

STROUD
E. 78,878 T. 55,175 (69.95%)
Lab. Co-op hold
*David Drew, Lab. Co-op 25,685
Neil Carmichael, C. 20,646
Ms Janice Beasley, LD 6,036
Kevin Cranston, Green 1,913
Adrian Blake, UK Ind. 895
Lab.Co-opmajority5,039(9.13%)
2.24% swing C. to Lab. Co-op
(1997: Lab. maj. 2,910 (4.66%))

SUFFOLK CENTRAL & IPSWICH NORTH
E. 74,200 T. 47,104 (63.48%) C. hold
*Michael Lord, C. 20,924
Ms Carole Jones, Lab. 17,455
Mrs Ann Elvin, LD 7,593
Jonathan Wright, UK Ind. 1,132
C. majority 3,469 (7.36%)
0.33% swing Lab. to C.
(1997: C. maj. 3,538 (6.70%))

SUFFOLK COASTAL
E. 75,963 T. 50,407 (66.36%) C. hold
*Rt. Hon. J. Gummer, C. 21,847
Nigel Gardner, Lab. 17,521
Tony Schur, LD 9,192
Michael Burn, UK Ind. 1,847
C. majority 4,326 (8.58%)
1.40% swing Lab. to C.
(1997: C. maj. 3,254 (5.79%))

SUFFOLK SOUTH
E. 68,408 T. 45,293 (66.21%) C. hold
*Tim Yeo, C. 18,748
Marc Young, Lab. 13,667
Mrs Tessa Munt, LD 11,296
Derek Allen, UK Ind. 1,582
C. majority 5,081 (11.22%)
1.59% swing Lab. to C.
(1997: C. maj. 4,175 (8.03%))

SUFFOLK WEST
E. 71,220 T. 42,445 (59.60%) C. hold
*Richard Spring, C. 20,201
Michael Jeffreys, Lab. 15,906
Robin Martlew, LD 5,017
Will Burrows, UK Ind. 1,321
C. majority 4,295 (10.12%)
3.16% swing Lab. to C.
(1997: C. maj. 1,867 (3.80%))

SUNDERLAND NORTH
E. 60,846 T. 29,820 (49.01%) Lab. hold
*Bill Etherington, Lab. 18,685
Michael Harris, C. 5,331
John Lennox, LD 3,599
Neil Herron, Ind. 1,518
David Guynan, BNP 687
Lab. majority 13,354 (44.78%)
3.38% swing Lab. to C.
(1997: Lab. maj. 19,697 (51.55%))

SUNDERLAND SOUTH
E. 64,577 T. 31,187 (48.29%) Lab. hold
*Chris Mullin, Lab. 19,921
Jim Boyd, C. 6,254
Mark Greenfield, LD 3,675
Joseph Dobbie, BNP 576
Joseph Moore, UK Ind. 470
Ms Rosalyn Warner, Loony 291
Lab. maj 13,667 (43.82%)
2.68% swing Lab. to C.
(1997: Lab. maj. 19,638 (49.18%))

SURREY EAST
E. 75,049 T. 47,049 (62.69%) C. hold
*Peter Ainsworth, C. 24,706
Jeremy Pursehouse, LD 11,503
Ms Jo Tanner, Lab. 8,994
Anthony Stone, UK Ind. 1,846
C. majority 13,203 (28.06%)
0.23% swing LD to C.
(1997: C. maj. 15,093 (27.61%))

SURREY HEATH
E. 75,858 T. 45,102 (59.46%) C. hold
*Nicholas Hawkins, C. 22,401
Mark Lelliott, LD 11,582
James Norman, Lab. 9,640
Nigel Hunt, UK Ind. 1,479
C. majority 10,819 (23.99%)
2.89% swing C. to LD
(1997: C. maj. 16,287 (29.76%))

SURREY SOUTH WEST
E. 74,127 T. 49,592 (66.90%) C. hold
*Rt. Hon. Mrs V. Bottomley, C. 22,462
Simon Cordon, LD 21,601
Martin Whelton, Lab. 4,321
Timothy Clark, UK Ind. 1,208
C. majority 861 (1.74%)
1.52% swing C. to LD
(1997: C. maj. 2,694 (4.77%))

SUSSEX MID
E. 70,632 T. 45,822 (64.87%) C. hold
*Nicholas Soames, C. 21,150
Ms Lesley Wilkins, LD 14,252
Paul Mitchell, Lab. 8,693
Petrina Holsworth, UK Ind. 1,126
Peter Berry, Loony 601
C. majority 6,898 (15.05%)
1.12% swing LD to C.
(1997: C. maj. 6,854 (12.82%))

SUTTON & CHEAM
E. 63,648 T. 39,723 (62.41%) LD hold
*Paul Burstow, LD 19,382
Lady Olga Maitland, C. 15,078
Ms Lisa Homan, Lab. 5,263
LD majority 4,304 (10.84%)
3.19% swing C. to LD
(1997: LD maj. 2,097 (4.45%))

SUTTON COLDFIELD
E. 71,856 T. 43,452 (60.47%) C. hold
Andrew Mitchell, C. 21,909
Robert Pocock, Lab. 11,805
Martin Turner, LD 8,268
Mike Nattrass, UK Ind. 1,186
Ian Robinson, Ind. 284
C. majority 10,104 (23.25%)
2.58% swing C. to Lab.
(1997: C. maj. 14,885 (28.41%))

SWINDON NORTH
E. 69,335 T. 42,328 (61.05%) Lab. hold
*Michael Wills, Lab. 22,371
Nick Martin, C. 14,266
David Nation, LD 4,891
Brian Lloyd, UK Ind. 800
Lab. majority 8,105 (19.15%)
1.61% swing C. to Lab.
(1997: Lab. maj. 7,688 (15.93%))

SWINDON SOUTH
E. 71,080 T. 43,384 (61.04%) Lab. hold
*Ms Julia Drown, Lab. 22,260
Simon Coombs, C. 14,919
Geoff Brewer, LD 5,165
Mrs Vicki Sharp, UK Ind. 713
Roly Gillard, R & R Loony 327
Lab. majority 7,341 (16.92%)
2.94% swing C. to Lab.
(1997: Lab. maj. 5,645 (11.04%))

TAMWORTH
E. 69,596 T. 40,250 (57.83%) Lab. hold
*Brian Jenkins, Lab. 19,722
Ms Luise Gunter, C. 15,124
Ms Jennifer Pinkett, LD 4,721
Paul Sootheran, UK Ind. 683
Lab. majority 4,598 (11.42%)
1.81% swing Lab. to C.
(1997: Lab. maj. 7,496 (15.04%))

TATTON
E. 64,954 T. 41,278 (63.55%) C. gain
George Osborne, C. 19,860
Steve Conquest, Lab. 11,249
Mike Ash, LD 7,685
Mark Sheppard, UK Ind. 769
Peter Sharratt, Ind. 734
Mrs Viviane Allinson, Tatton 505
John Batchelor, Ind. 322
Jonathan Boyd Hunt, Ind. 154
C. majority 8,611 (20.86%)
(1997: Ind. maj. 11,077 (22.70%))

TAUNTON
E. 81,651 T. 55,225 (67.64%) C. gain
Adrian Flook, C. 23,033
*Mrs Jackie Ballard, LD 22,798
Andrew Govier, Lab. 8,254
Michael Canton, UK Ind. 1,140
C. majority 235 (0.43%)
2.21% swing LD to C.
(1997: LD maj. 2,443 (4.00%))

TEIGNBRIDGE
E. 85,533 T. 59,310 (69.34%) LD gain
Richard Younger-Ross, LD 26,343
*Patrick Nicholls, C. 23,332
Christopher Bain, Lab. 7,366
Paul Viscount Exmouth, UK Ind. 2,269
LD majority 3,011 (5.08%)
2.76% swing C. to LD
(1997: C. maj. 281 (0.45%))

TELFORD
E. 59,486 T. 30,875 (51.90%) Lab. hold
David Wright, Lab. 16,854
Andrew Henderson, C. 8,471
Ms Sally Wiggin, LD 3,983
Ms Nicola Brookes, UK Ind. 1,098
Mike Jeffries, Soc. All. 469
Lab. majority 8,383 (27.15%)
1.63% swing Lab. to C.
(1997: Lab. maj. 11,290 (30.42%))

TEWKESBURY
E. 70,276 T. 45,195 (64.31%) C. hold
*Laurence Robertson, C. 20,830
Keir Dhillon, Lab. 12,167
Stephen Martin, LD 11,863
Charles Vernall, Ind. 335
C. majority 8,663 (19.17%)
0.19% swing C. to Lab.
(1997: C. maj. 9,234 (17.71%))

THANET NORTH
E. 70,581 T. 41,868 (59.32%) C. hold
*Roger Gale, C. 21,050
James Stewart Laing, Lab. 14,400
Seth Proctor, LD 4,603
John Moore, UK Ind. 980
David Shortt, Ind. 440
Thomas Holmes, NF 395
C. majority 6,650 (15.88%)
5.12% swing Lab. to C.
(1997: C. maj. 2,766 (5.65%))

THANET SOUTH
E. 61,462 T. 39,431 (64.16%) Lab. hold
*Dr Stephen Ladyman, Lab. 18,002
Mark Macgregor, C. 16,210
Guy Voizey, LD 3,706
William Baldwin, Ind. 770
Terry Eccott, UK Ind. 501
Bernard Franklin, NF 242
Lab. majority 1,792 (4.54%)
0.92% swing Lab. to C.
(1997: Lab. maj. 2,878 (6.39%))

THURROCK
E. 76,524 T. 37,362 (48.82%) Lab. hold
*Andrew Mackinlay, Lab. 21,121
Mike Penning, C. 11,124
John Lathan, LD 3,846
Christopher Sheppard, UK Ind. 1,271
Lab. majority 9,997 (26.76%)
4.90% swing Lab. to C.
(1997: Lab. maj. 17,256 (36.55%))

TIVERTON & HONITON
E. 80,646 T. 55,784 (69.17%) C. hold
*Mrs Angela Browning, C. 26,258
Jim Barnard, LD 19,974
Ms Isabel Owen, Lab. 6,647
Alan Langmaid, UK Ind. 1,281
Matthew Burgess, Green 1,030
Mrs Jennifer Roach, Lib. 594
C. majority 6,284 (11.26%)
4.23% swing LD to C.
(1997: C. maj. 1,653 (2.80%))

TONBRIDGE & MALLING
E. 65,939 T. 42,436 (64.36%) C. hold
*Rt. Hon. Sir J. Stanley, C. 20,956
Ms Victoria Hayman, Lab. 12,706
Ms Merilyn Canet, LD 7,605
Ms Lynn Croucher, UK Ind. 1,169
C. majority 8,250 (19.44%)
0.67% swing C. to Lab.
(1997: C. maj. 10,230 (20.78%))

TOOTING
E. 68,447 T. 37,591 (54.92%) Lab. hold
*Tom Cox, Lab. 20,332
Alexander Nicoll, C. 9,932
Simon James, LD 5,583
Matthew Ledbury, Green 1,744
Lab. majority 10,400 (27.67%)
2.45% swing Lab. to C.
(1997: Lab. maj. 15,011 (32.56%))

TORBAY
E. 72,409 T. 47,569 (65.69%) LD hold
*Adrian Sanders, LD 24,015
Christian Sweeting, C. 17,307
John McKay, Lab. 4,484
Graham Booth, UK Ind. 1,512
Ms Pam Neale, Ind. 251
LD majority 6,708 (14.10%)
7.04% swing C. to LD
(1997: LD maj. 12 (0.02%))

TOTNES
E. 72,548 T. 49,246 (67.88%) C. hold
*Anthony Steen, C. 21,914
Ms Rachel Oliver, LD 18,317
Thomas Wildy, Lab. 6,005
Craig Mackinlay, UK Ind. 3,010
C. majority 3,597 (7.30%)
2.84% swing LD to C.
(1997: C. maj. 877 (1.63%))

TOTTENHAM
E. 65,567 T. 31,601 (48.20%) Lab. hold
*David Lammy, Lab. 21,317
Ms Uma Fernandes, C. 4,401
Ms Meher Khan, LD 3,008
Peter Budge, Green 1,443
Weyman Bennett, Soc. All. 1,162
Unver Shefki, Reform 270
Lab. maj 16,916 (53.53%)
0.03% swing Lab. to C.
(2000 Jun. by-election: Lab. maj. 5,646 (34.39%); 1997: Lab. Maj. 20,200 (53.58%))

TRURO & ST AUSTELL
E. 79,219 T. 50,295 (63.49%) LD hold
*Matthew Taylor, LD 24,296
Tim Bonner, C. 16,231
David Phillips, Lab. 6,889
James Wonnacott, UK Ind. 1,664
Conan Jenkin, Meb. Ker. 1,137
John Lee, Ind. 78
LD majority 8,065 (16.04%)
3.00% swing LD to C.
(1997: LD maj. 12,501 (22.03%))

TUNBRIDGE WELLS
E. 64,534 T. 40,201 (62.29%) C. hold
*Archie Norman, C. 19,643
Keith Brown, LD 9,913
Ian Carvell, Lab. 9,332
Victor Webb, UK Ind. 1,313
C. majority 9,730 (24.20%)
4.34% swing LD to C.
(1997: C. maj. 7,506 (15.52%))

TWICKENHAM
E. 74,135 T. 49,938 (67.36%) LD hold
*Dr Vincent Cable, LD 24,344
Nick Longworth, C. 16,689
Dean Rogers, Lab. 6,903
Ms Judy Maciejowska, Green 1,423
Ray Hollebone, UK Ind. 579
LD majority 7,655 (15.33%)
3.98% swing C. to LD
(1997: LD maj. 4,281 (7.36%))

TYNE BRIDGE
E. 58,900 T. 26,032 (44.20%) Lab. hold
*David Clelland, Lab. 18,345
James Cook, C. 3,456
Jonathan Wallace, LD 3,213
James Fitzpatrick, Soc. Lab. 533
Samuel Robson, Soc. All. 485
Lab. majority 14,889 (57.19%)
4.27% swing Lab. to C.
(1997: Lab. maj. 22,906 (65.73%))

TYNEMOUTH
E. 65,184 T. 43,903 (67.35%) Lab. hold
*Alan Campbell, Lab. 23,364
Karl Poulsen, C. 14,686
Ms Penny Reid, LD 5,108
Michael Rollings, UK Ind. 745
Lab. majority 8,678 (19.77%)
1.14% swing Lab. to C.
(1997: Lab. maj. 11,273 (22.04%))

TYNESIDE NORTH
E. 64,914 T. 37,569 (57.88%) Lab. hold
*Rt. Hon. S. Byers, Lab. 26,127
Mark Ruffell, C. 5,459
Simon Reed, LD 4,649
Alan Taylor, UK Ind. 770
Pete Burnett, Soc. All. 324
Ken Capstick, Soc. Lab. 240
Lab. majority 20,668 (55.01%)
2.02% swing Lab. to C.
(1997: Lab. maj. 26,643 (59.05%))

UPMINSTER
E. 56,829 T. 33,851 (59.57%) C. gain
Mrs Angela Watkinson, C. 15,410
*Keith Darvill, Lab. 14,169
Peter Truesdale, LD 3,183
Terry Murray, UK Ind. 1,089
C. majority 1,241 (3.67%)
5.18% swing Lab. to C.
(1997: Lab. maj. 2,770 (6.70%))

UXBRIDGE
E. 58,066 T. 33,418 (57.55%) C. hold
*John Randall, C. 15,751
David Salisbury-Jones, Lab. 13,653
Ms Catherine Royce, LD 3,426
Paul Cannons, UK Ind. 588
C. majority 2,098 (6.28%)
2.26% swing Lab. to C.
(1997 Jul. by-election: C. maj. 3,766 (11.82%); 1997: C. maj. 724 (1.75%))

VALE OF YORK
E. 73,335 T. 48,490 (66.12%) C. hold
*Miss Anne McIntosh, C. 25,033
Christopher Jukes, Lab. 12,516
Greg Stone, LD 9,799
Peter Thornber, UK Ind. 1,142
C. majority 12,517 (25.81%)
3.78% swing Lab. to C.
(1997: C. maj. 9,721 (18.25%))

VAUXHALL
E. 74,474 T. 33,392 (44.84%) Lab. hold
*Ms Kate Hoey, Lab. 19,738
Anthony Bottrall, LD 6,720
Gareth Compton, C. 4,489
Shane Collins, Green 1,485
Ms Theresa Bennett, Soc. All. 853
Martin Boyd, Ind. 107
Lab. majority 13,018 (38.99%)
4.39% swing Lab. to LD
(1997: Lab. maj. 18,660 (47.77%))

WAKEFIELD
E. 75,750 T. 41,254 (54.46%) Lab. hold
*David Hinchcliffe, Lab. 20,592
Mrs Thelma Karran, C. 12,638
Douglas Dale, LD 5,097
Ms Sarah Greenwood, Green 1,075
Ms Janice Cannon, UK Ind. 677
Abdul Aziz, Soc. Lab. 634
Mick Griffiths, Soc. All. 541
Lab. majority 7,954 (19.28%)
4.82% swing Lab. to C.
(1997: Lab. maj. 14,604 (28.93%))

WALLASEY
E. 64,889 T. 37,346 (57.55%) Lab. hold
*Ms Angela Eagle, Lab. 22,718
Mrs Lesley Rennie, C. 10,442
Peter Reisdorf, LD 4,186
Lab. majority 12,276 (32.87%)
3.92% swing Lab. to C.
(1997: Lab. maj. 19,074 (40.72%))

WALSALL NORTH
E. 66,020 T. 32,312 (48.94%) Lab. hold
*David Winnick, Lab. 18,779
Melvin Pitt, C. 9,388
Michael Heap, LD 2,923
Mrs Jenny Mayo, UK Ind. 812
Dave Church, Soc. All. 410
Lab. majority 9,391 (29.06%)
(1997: Lab. maj. 12,588 (29.07%))

WALSALL SOUTH
E. 62,657 T. 34,899 (55.70%) Lab. hold
*Rt. Hon. B. George, Lab. 20,574
Mike Bird, C. 10,643
Bill Tomlinson, LD 2,365
Derek Bennett, UK Ind. 974
Peter Smith, Soc. All. 343
Lab. majority 9,931 (28.46%)
1.15% swing C. to Lab.
(1997: Lab. maj. 11,312 (26.16%))

WALTHAMSTOW
E. 64,403 T. 34,429 (53.46%) Lab. hold
*Neil Gerrard, Lab. 21,402
Nick Boys Smith, C. 6,221
Peter Dunphy, LD 5,024
Simon Donovan, Soc. Alt. 806
William Phillips, BNP 389
Ms Gerda Mayer, UK Ind. 298
Ms Barbara Duffy, ProLife 289
Lab. majority 15,181 (44.09%)
0.64% swing C. to Lab.
(1997: Lab. maj. 17,149 (42.81%))

WANSBECK
E. 62,989 T. 37,419 (59.41%) Lab. hold
*Denis Murphy, Lab. 21,617
Alan Thompson, LD 8,516
Mrs Rachael Lake, C. 4,774
Michael Kirkup, Ind. 1,076
Dr Nic Best, Green 954
Gavin Attwell, UK Ind. 482
Lab. majority 13,101 (35.01%)
7.25% swing Lab. to LD
(1997: Lab. maj. 22,367 (49.52%))

WANSDYKE
E. 70,728 T. 49,047 (69.35%) Lab. hold
*Dan Norris, Lab. 22,706
Chris Watt, C. 17,593
Ms Gail Coleshill, LD 7,135
Francis Hayden, Green 958
Peter Sandell, UK Ind. 655
Lab. majority 5,113 (10.42%)
0.83% swing C. to Lab.
(1997: Lab. maj. 4,799 (8.77%))

WANTAGE
E. 76,129 T. 49,129 (64.53%) C. hold
*Robert Jackson, C. 19,475
Stephen Beer, Lab. 13,875
Neil Fawcett, LD 13,776
David Brooks-Saxl, Green 1,062
Count Nichola Tolstoy, UK Ind. 941
C. majority 5,600 (11.40%)
0.31% swing Lab. to C.
(1997: C. maj. 6,039 (10.77%))

WARLEY
E. 58,071 T. 31,415 (54.10%) Lab. hold
*Rt. Hon. J. Spellar, Lab. 19,007
Mark Pritchard, C. 7,157
Ron Cockings, LD 3,315
Harbhajan Dardi, Soc. Lab. 1,936
Lab. majority 11,850 (37.72%)
1.00% swing Lab. to C.
(1997: Lab. maj. 15,451 (39.73%))

WARRINGTON NORTH
E. 72,445 T. 38,910 (53.71%) Lab. hold
*Ms Helen Jones, Lab. 24,026
James Usher, C. 8,870
Roy Smith, LD 5,232
Jack Kirkham, UK Ind. 782
Lab. majority 15,156 (38.95%)
0.43% swing C. to Lab.
(1997: Lab. maj. 19,527 (38.10%))

WARRINGTON SOUTH
E. 74,283 T. 45,487 (61.23%) Lab. hold
*Ms Helen Southworth, Lab. 22,409
Ms Caroline Mosley, C. 15,022
Roger Barlow, LD 7,419
Mrs Joan Kelley, UK Ind. 637
Lab. majority 7,387 (16.24%)
1.69% swing Lab. to C.
(1997: Lab. maj. 10,807 (19.62%))

WARWICK & LEAMINGTON
E. 81,405 T. 53,539 (65.77%) Lab. hold
*James Plaskitt, Lab. 26,108
David Campbell Bannerman, C. 20,155
Ms Linda Forbes, LD 5,964
Ms Clare Kime, Soc. All. 664
Greville Warwick, UK Ind. 648
Lab. majority 5,953 (11.12%)
2.73% swing C. to Lab.
(1997: Lab. maj. 3,398 (5.65%))

WARWICKSHIRE NORTH
E. 73,828 T. 44,409 (60.15%) Lab. hold
*Mike O'Brien, Lab. 24,023
Geoff Parsons, C. 14,384
William Powell, LD 5,052
John Flynn, UK Ind. 950
Lab. majority 9,639 (21.71%)
2.76% swing Lab. to C.
(1997: Lab. maj. 14,767 (27.23%))

WATFORD
E. 75,724 T. 46,372 (61.24%) Lab. hold
*Ms Claire Ward, Lab. 20,992
Michael McManus, C. 15,437
Duncan Hames, LD 8,088
Ms Denise Kingsley, Green 900
Edmund Stewart-Mole, UK Ind. 535
Jon Berry, Soc. All. 420
Lab. majority 5,555 (11.98%)
0.75% swing C. to Lab.
(1997: Lab. maj. 5,792 (10.48%))

WAVENEY
E. 76,585 T. 47,167 (61.59%) Lab. hold
*Bob Blizzard, Lab. 23,914
Lee Scott, C. 15,361
David Young, LD 5,370
Brian Aylett, UK Ind. 1,097
Graham Elliot, Green 983
Rupert Mallin, Soc. All. 442
Lab. majority 8,553 (18.13%)
1.93% swing Lab. to C.
(1997: Lab. maj. 12,453 (21.99%))

WEALDEN
E. 83,066 T. 52,756 (63.51%) C. hold
Charles Hendry, C. 26,279
Steve Murphy, LD 12,507
Ms Kathy Fordham, Lab. 10,705
Keith Riddle, UK Ind. 1,539
Julian Salmon, Green 1,273
Cyril Thornton, Pensioner 453
C. majority 13,772 (26.11%)
1.03% swing LD to C.
(1997: C. maj. 14,204 (24.04%))

WEAVER VALE
E. 68,236 T. 39,271 (57.55%) Lab. hold
*Mike Hall, Lab. 20,611
Carl Cross, C. 10,974
Nigel Griffiths, LD 5,643
Michael Cooksley, Ind. 1,484
Jim Bradshaw, UK Ind. 559
Lab. majority 9,637 (24.54%)
1.65% swing Lab. to C.
(1997: Lab. maj. 13,448 (27.84%))

WELLINGBOROUGH
E. 77,389 T. 51,006 (65.91%) Lab. hold
*Paul Stinchcombe, Lab. 23,867
Peter Bone, C. 21,512
Peter Gaskell, LD 4,763
Anthony Ellwood, UK Ind. 864
Lab. majority 2,355 (4.62%)
2.14% swing C. to Lab.
(1997: Lab. maj. 187 (0.33%))

WELLS
E. 74,189 T. 51,314 (69.17%) C. hold
*Rt. Hon. D. Heathcoat-Amory, C. 22,462
Graham Oakes, LD 19,666
Andy Merryfield, Lab. 7,915
Steve Reed, UK Ind. 1,104
Colin Bex, Wessex Reg. 167
C. majority 2,796 (5.45%)
2.25% swing LD to C.
(1997: C. maj. 528 (0.94%))

WELWYN HATFIELD
E. 67,004 T. 42,821 (63.91%) Lab. hold
*Ms Melanie Johnson, Lab. 18,484
Grant Shapps, C. 17,288
Daniel Cooke, LD 6,021
Malcolm Biggs, UK Ind. 798
Ms Fiona Pinto, ProLife 230
Lab. majority 1,196 (2.79%)
3.89% swing Lab. to C.
(1997: Lab. maj. 5,595 (10.57%))

WENTWORTH
E. 64,033 T. 33,778 (52.75%) Lab. hold
*John Healey, Lab. 22,798
Mike Roberts, C. 6,349
David Wildgoose, LD 3,652
John Wilkinson, UK Ind. 979
Lab. majority 16,449 (48.70%)
4.32% swing Lab. to C.
(1997: Lab. maj. 23,959 (57.34%))

WEST BROMWICH EAST
E. 61,198 T. 32,664 (53.37%) Lab. hold
Tom Watson, Lab. 18,250
David MacFarlane, C. 8,487
Ian Garrett, LD 4,507
Steven Grey, UK Ind. 835
Sheera Johal, Soc. Lab. 585
Lab. majority 9,763 (29.89%)
1.43% swing Lab. to C.
(1997: Lab. maj. 13,584 (32.74%))

WEST BROMWICH WEST
E. 66,777 T. 31,840 (47.68%)
Lab. Co-op hold
*Adrian Bailey, Lab. Co-op 19,352
Mrs Karen Bissell, C. 7,997
Mrs Sadie Smith, LD 2,168
John Salvage, BNP 1,428
Kevin Walker, UK Ind. 499
Baghwant Singh, Soc. Lab. 396
Lab. Co-op majority 11,355
(35.66%)
(2000 Nov. by-election: Lab. maj. 3,232 (17.12%); 1997: Speaker maj. 15,423 (42.03%))

WEST HAM
E. 59,828 T. 29,273 (48.93%) Lab. hold
*Tony Banks, Lab. 20,449
Syed Kamall, C. 4,804
Paul Fox, LD 2,166
Ms Jackie Chandler Oatts, Green 1,197
Gerard Batten, UK Ind. 657
Lab. majority 15,645 (53.45%)
2.24% swing Lab. to C.
(1997: Lab. maj. 19,494 (57.92%))

WESTBURY
E. 75,911 T. 50,628 (66.69%) C. hold
Dr Andrew Murrison, C. 21,299
David Vigar, LD 16,005
Ms Sarah Cardy, Lab. 10,847
Charles Booth-Jones, UK Ind. 1,261
Bob Gledhill, Green 1,216
C. majority 5,294 (10.46%)
0.12% swing C. to LD
(1997: C. maj. 6,068 (10.69%))

WESTMORLAND & LONSDALE
E. 70,637 T. 47,903 (67.82%) C. hold
*Tim Collins, C. 22,486
Tim Farron, LD 19,339
John Bateson, Lab. 5,234
Robert Gibson, UK Ind. 552
Tim Bell, Ind. 292
C. majority 3,147 (6.57%)
1.17% swing C. to LD
(1997: C. maj. 4,521 (8.90%))

WESTON-SUPER-MARE
E. 74,343 T. 46,680 (62.79%) LD hold
*Brian Cotter, LD 18,424
John Penrose, C. 18,086
Derek Kraft, Lab. 9,235
Bill Lukins, UK Ind. 650
John Peverelle, Ind. 206
Richard Sibley, Ind. 79
LD majority 338 (0.72%)
0.83% swing LD to C.
(1997: LD maj. 1,274 (2.39%))

WIGAN
E. 64,040 T. 33,591 (52.45%) Lab. hold
*Neil Turner, Lab. 20,739
Mark Page, C. 6,996
Trevor Beswick, LD 4,970
Dave Lowe, Soc. All. 886
Lab. majority 13,743 (40.91%)
5.38% swing Lab. to C.
(1999 Sept. by-election: Lab. maj 6,729)
(1997: Lab. maj. 22,643 (51.67%))

WILTSHIRE NORTH
E. 79,524 T. 52,948 (66.58%) C. hold
*James Gray, C. 24,090
Hugh Pym, LD 20,212
Ms Jo Garton, Lab. 7,556
Neil Dowdney, UK Ind. 1,090
C. majority 3,878 (7.32%)
0.67% swing LD to C.
(1997: C. maj. 3,475 (5.99%))

WIMBLEDON
E. 63,930 T. 41,109 (64.30%) Lab. hold
*Roger Casale, Lab. 18,806
Stephen Hammond, C. 15,062
Martin Pierce, LD 5,341
Rajeev Thacker, Green 1,007
Roger Glencross, CPA 479
Ms Mariana Bell, UK Ind. 414
Lab. majority 3,744 (9.11%)
1.47% swing C. to Lab.
(1997: Lab. maj. 2,980 (6.17%))

WINCHESTER
E. 81,852 T. 59,158 (72.27%) LD hold
*Mark Oaten, LD 32,282
Andrew Hayes, C. 22,648
Stephen Wyeth, Lab. 3,498
Ms Joan Martin, UK Ind. 664
Ms Henrietta Rouse, Wessex Reg. 66
LD majority 9,634 (16.29%)
8.14% swing C. to LD
(1997 Nov. by-election: LD maj 21,556 (39.64%))
(1997: LD maj. 2 (0.00%)

WINDSOR
E. 69,136 T. 42,110 (60.91%) C. hold
*Michael Trend, C. 19,900
Nick Pinfield, LD 11,011
Mark Muller, Lab. 10,137
John Fagan, UK Ind. 1,062
C. majority 8,889 (21.11%)
0.79% swing LD to C.
(1997: C. maj. 9,917 (19.53%))

WIRRAL SOUTH
E. 60,653 T. 39,818 (65.65%) Lab. hold
*Ben Chapman, Lab. 18,890
Anthony Millard, C. 13,841
Phillip Gilchrist, LD 7,087
Lab. majority 5,049 (12.68%)
0.94% swing Lab. to C.
(1997: Lab. maj. 7,004 (14.56%))

WIRRAL WEST
E. 62,294 T. 40,475 (64.97%) Lab. hold
*Stephen Hesford, Lab. 19,105
Chris Lynch, C. 15,070
Simon Holbrook, LD 6,300
Lab. majority 4,035 (9.97%)
2.06% swing C. to Lab.
(1997: Lab. maj. 2,738 (5.84%))

WITNEY
E. 74,624 T. 49,203 (65.93%) C. gain
David Cameron, C. 22,153
Michael Bartlet, Lab. 14,180
Gareth Epps, LD 10,000
Mark Stevenson, Green 1,100
Barry Beadle, Ind. 1,003
Kenneth Dukes, UK Ind. 767
C. majority 7,973 (16.20%)
1.87% swing Lab. to C.
(1997: C. maj. 7,028 (12.46%))

WOKING
E. 71,163 T. 42,910 (60.30%) C. hold
*Humfrey Malins, C. 19,747
Alan Hilliar, LD 12,988
Sabir Hussain, Lab. 8,714
Michael Harvey, UK Ind. 1,461
C. majority 6,759 (15.75%)
2.30% swing LD to C.
(1997: C. maj. 5,678 (11.15%))

WOKINGHAM
E. 68,430 T. 43,848 (64.08%) C. hold
*Rt. Hon. J. Redwood, C. 20,216
Dr Royce Longton, LD 14,222
Matthew Syed, Lab. 7,633
Franklin Carstairs, UK Ind. 897
Peter "Top Cat" Owen, Loony 880
C. majority 5,994 (13.67%)
2.51% swing C. to LD
(1997: C. maj. 9,365 (18.69%))

WOLVERHAMPTON NORTH EAST
E. 60,486 T. 31,494 (52.07%) Lab. Co-op hold
*Ken Purchase, Lab. Co-op 18,984
Ms Maria Miller, C. 9,019
Steven Bourne, LD 2,494
Thomas McCartney, UK Ind. 997
Lab. Co-op majority 9,965 (31.64%)
0.14% swing C. to Lab. Co-op
(1997: Lab. maj. 12,987 (31.37%))

WOLVERHAMPTON SOUTH EAST
E. 53,931 T. 27,297 (50.61%) Lab. Co-op hold
*Dennis Turner, Lab. Co-op 18,409
Adrian Pepper, C. 5,945
Peter Wild, LD 2,389
James Barry, NF 554
Lab. Co-op majority 12,464 (45.66%)
1.04% swing C. to Lab. Co-op
(1997: Lab. maj. 15,182 (43.58%))

WOLVERHAMPTON SOUTH WEST
E. 67,171 T. 40,897 (60.88%) Lab. hold
Robert Marris, Lab. 19,735
David Chambers, C. 16,248
Mike Dixon, LD 3,425
Ms Wendy Walker, Green 805
Doug Hope, UK Ind. 684
Lab. majority 3,487 (8.53%)
0.97% swing Lab. to C.
(1997: Lab. maj. 5,118 (10.46%))

WOODSPRING
E. 71,023 T. 48,758 (68.65%) C. hold
*Dr Liam Fox, C. 21,297
Chanel Stevens, Lab. 12,499
Colin Eldridge, LD 11,816
David Shopland, Ind. 1,412
Dr Richard Lawson, Green 1,282
Fraser Crean, UK Ind. 452
C. majority 8,798 (18.04%)
2.86% swing C. to Lab.
(1997: C. maj. 7,734 (14.08%))

WORCESTER
E. 71,255 T. 44,210 (62.04%) Lab. hold
*Michael Foster, Lab. 21,478
Richard Adams, C. 15,712
Paul Chandler, LD 5,578
Richard Chamings, UK Ind. 1,442
Lab. majority 5,766 (13.04%)
0.67% swing Lab. to C.
(1997: Lab. maj. 7,425 (14.38%))

WORCESTERSHIRE MID
E. 71,985 T. 44,897 (62.37%) C. hold
*Peter Luff, C. 22,937
David Bannister, Lab. 12,310
R. Woodthorpe-Browne, LD 8,420
Tony Eaves, UK Ind. 1,230
C. majority 10,627 (23.67%)
2.57% swing Lab. to C.
(1997: C. maj. 9,412 (18.52%))

WORCESTERSHIRE WEST
E. 66,769 T. 44,807 (67.11%) C. hold
*Sir Michael Spicer, C. 20,597
Mike Hadley, LD 15,223
Waquar Azmi, Lab. 6,275
Ian Morris, UK Ind. 1,574
Malcolm Victory, Green 1,138
C. majority 5,374 (11.99%)
2.10% swing LD to C.
(1997: C. maj. 3,846 (7.80%))

WORKINGTON
E. 65,965 T. 41,822 (63.40%) Lab. hold
Tony Cunningham, Lab. 23,209
Tim Stoddart, C. 12,359
Ian Francis, LD 5,214
John Peacock, LCA 1,040
Lab. majority 10,850 (25.94%)
6.93% swing Lab. to C.
(1997: Lab. maj. 19,656 (39.81%))

WORSLEY
E. 69,300 T. 35,363 (51.03%) Lab. hold
*Terry Lewis, Lab. 20,193
Tobias Ellwood, C. 8,406
Robert Bleakley, LD 6,188
Ms Dorothy Entwistle, Soc. Lab. 576
Lab. majority 11,787 (33.33%)
2.30% swing Lab. to C.
(1997: Lab. maj. 17,741 (37.93%))

WORTHING EAST & SHOREHAM
E. 71,890 T. 43,068 (59.91%) C. hold
*Tim Loughton, C. 18,608
Daniel Yates, Lab. 12,469
Paul Elgood, LD 9,876
Jim McCulloch, UK Ind. 1,195
Christopher Baldwin, LCA 920
C. majority 6,139 (14.25%)
1.14% swing C. to Lab.
(1997: C. maj. 5,098 (9.89%))

WORTHING WEST
E. 72,419 T. 43,209 (59.67%) C. hold
*Peter Bottomley, C. 20,508
James Walsh, LD 11,471
Alan Butcher, Lab. 9,270
Tim Cross, UK Ind. 1,960
C. majority 9,037 (20.91%)
2.96% swing LD to C.
(1997: C. maj. 7,713 (15.00%))

WREKIN, THE
E. 65,837 T. 41,490 (63.02%) Lab. hold
*Peter Bradley, Lab. 19,532
Jacob Rees-Mogg, C. 15,945
Ian Jenkins, LD 4,738
Denis Brookes, UK Ind. 1,275
Lab. majority 3,587 (8.65%)
0.98% swing C. to Lab.
(1997: Lab. maj. 3,025 (6.69%))

WYCOMBE
E. 74,647 T. 44,974 (60.25%) C. hold
Paul Goodman, C. 19,064
Chauhdry Shafique, Lab. 15,896
Ms Dee Tomlin, LD 7,658
Christopher Cooke, UK Ind. 1,059
John Laker, Green 1,057
David Fitton, Ind. 240
C. majority 3,168 (7.04%)
1.26% swing Lab. to C.
(1997: C. maj. 2,370 (4.53%))

WYRE FOREST
E. 72,152 T. 49,062 (68.00%) KHHC gain
Dr Richard Taylor, KHHC 28,487
*David Lock, Lab. 10,857
Mark Simpson, C. 9,350
James Millington, UK Ind. 368
KHHC majority 17,630 (35.93%)
(1997: Lab. maj. 6,946 (12.62%))

WYTHENSHAWE & SALE EAST
E. 72,127 T. 35,055 (48.60%) Lab. hold
*Paul Goggins, Lab. 21,032
Mrs Susan Fildes, C. 8,424
Ms Vanessa Tucker, LD 4,320
Lance Crookes, Green 869
Fred Shaw, Soc. Lab. 410
Lab. majority 12,608 (35.97%)
1.49% swing C. to Lab.
(1997: Lab. maj. 15,019 (32.99%))

YEOVIL
E. 75,977 T. 48,132 (63.35%) LD hold
David Laws, LD 21,266
Marco Forgione, C. 17,338
Joe Conway, Lab. 7,077
Neil Boxall, UK Ind. 1,131
Alex Begg, Green 786
Tony Prior, Lib. 534
LD majority 3,928 (8.16%)
6.47% swing LD to C.
(1997: LD maj. 11,403 (21.10%))

YORK, CITY OF
E. 80,431 T. 47,980 (59.65%) Lab. hold
*Hugh Bayley, Lab. 25,072
Michael McIntyre, C. 11,293
Andrew Waller, LD 8,519
Bill Shaw, Green 1,465
Frank Ormston, Soc. All. 674
Richard Bate, UK Ind. 576
Graham Cambridge, Loony 381
Lab. majority 13,779 (28.72%)
3.23% swing Lab. to C.
(1997: Lab. maj. 20,523 (35.17%))

YORKSHIRE EAST
E. 72,342 T. 43,314 (59.87%) C. hold
Rt. Hon. G. Knight, C. 19,861
Ms Tracey Simpson-Laing, Lab. 15,179
Ms Mary-Rose Hardy, LD 6,300
Trevor Pearson, UK Ind. 1,661
Paul Dessoy, Ind. 313
C. majority 4,682 (10.81%)
1.99% swing Lab. to C.
(1997: C. maj. 3,337 (6.82%))

WALES

ABERAVON
E. 49,660 T. 30,190 (60.79%) Lab. hold
Hywel Francis, Lab. 19,063
Ms Lisa Turnbull, PC 2,955
Chris Davies, LD 2,933
Ali Miraj, C. 2,296
Andrew Tutton, RP 1,960
Captain Beany, Bean 727
Mr Martin Chapman, Soc. All. 256
Lab. majority 16,108 (53.36%)
6.08% swing Lab. to PC
(1997: Lab. maj. 21,571 (59.98%))

ALYN & DEESIDE
E. 60,478 T. 35,421 (58.57%) Lab. hold
Mark Tami, Lab. 18,525
Mark Isherwood, C. 9,303
Derek Burnham, LD 4,585
Richard Coombs, PC 1,182
Klaus Armstrong-Braun, Green 881
William Crawford, UK Ind. 481
Max Cooksey, Ind. 253
Glyn Davies, Comm. 211
Lab. majority 9,222 (26.04%)
6.53% swing Lab. to C.
(1997: Lab. maj. 16,403 (39.10%))

BLAENAU GWENT
E. 53,353 T. 31,725 (59.46%) Lab. hold
*Llew Smith, Lab. 22,855
Adam Rykala, PC 3,542
Edward Townsend, LD 2,945
Huw Williams, C. 2,383
Lab. majority 19,313 (60.88%)
6.68% swing Lab. to PC
(1997: Lab. maj. 28,035 (70.74%))

BRECON & RADNORSHIRE
E. 52,247 T. 37,516 (71.81%) LD hold
Roger Williams, LD 13,824
Dr Felix Aubel, C. 13,073
Huw Irranca-Davis, Lab. 8,024
Brynach Parri, PC 1,301
Ian Mitchell, Ind. 762
Mrs Elizabeth Phillips, UK Ind. 452
Robert Nicholson, Ind. 80
LD majority 751 (2.00%)
4.94% swing LD to C.
(1997: LD maj. 5,097 (11.89%))

BRIDGEND
E. 61,496 T. 37,004 (60.17%) Lab. hold
*Win Griffiths, Lab. 19,422
Ms Tania Brisby, C. 9,377
Ms Jean Barraclough, LD 5,330
Ms Monica Mahoney, PC 2,652
Ms Sara Jeremy, ProLife 223
Lab. majority 10,045 (27.15%)
4.05% swing Lab. to C.
(1997: Lab. maj. 15,248 (35.24%))

CAERNARFON
E. 47,354 T. 29,053 (61.35%) PC hold
Hywel Williams, PC 12,894
Martin Eaglestone, Lab. 9,383
Ms Bronwen Naish, C. 4,403
Melab Owain, LD 1,823
Ifor Lloyd, UK Ind. 550
PC majority 3,511 (12.08%)
4.75% swing PC to Lab
(1997: PC maj. 7,449 (21.59%))

CAERPHILLY
E. 67,593 T. 38,831 (57.45%) Lab. hold
Wayne David, Lab. 22,597
Lindsay Whittle, PC 8,172
David Simmonds, C. 4,413
Rob Roffe, LD 3,649
Lab. majority 14,425 (37.15%)
10.49% swing Lab. to PC
(1997: Lab. maj. 25,839 (57.08%))

CARDIFF CENTRAL
E. 59,785 T. 34,842 (58.28%) Lab. Co-op hold
*Jon Owen Jones, Lab. Co-op 13,451
Ms Jenny Willott, LD 12,792
Gregory Walker, C. 5,537
Richard Grigg, PC 1,680
Stephen Bartley, Green 661
Julian Goss, Soc. All. 283
Frank Hughes, UK Ind. 221
Ms Madeleine Jeremy, ProLife 217
Lab. Co-op majority 659 (1.89%)
8.43% swing Lab. Co-op to LD
(1997: Lab. maj. 7,923 (18.75%))

CARDIFF NORTH
E. 62,634 T. 43,240 (69.04%) Lab. hold
*Ms Julie Morgan, Lab. 19,845
Alastair Watson, C. 13,680
John Dixon, LD 6,631
Sion Jobbins, PC 2,471
Don Hulston, UK Ind. 613
Lab. majority 6,165 (14.26%)
1.25% swing Lab. to C.
(1997: Lab. maj. 8,126 (16.76%))

CARDIFF SOUTH & PENARTH
E. 62,125 T. 35,751 (57.55%)
Lab. Co-op hold
*Rt. Hon. A. Michael, Lab. Co-op 20,094
Ms Maureen Kelly Owen, C. 7,807
Dr Rodney Berman, LD 4,572
Ms Lila Haines, PC 1,983
Justin Callan, UK Ind. 501
Dave Bartlett, Soc. All. 427
Ms Anne Savoury, ProLife 367
Lab. Co-op majority 12,287 (34.37%)
0.81% swing C. to Lab. Co-op
(1997: Lab. maj. 13,881 (32.74%))

CARDIFF WEST
E. 58,348 T. 34,083 (58.41%) Lab. hold
Kevin Brennan, Lab. 18,594
Andrew Davies, C. 7,273
Ms Jacqui Gasson, LD 4,458
Delme Bowen, PC 3,296
Ms Joyce Jenking, UK Ind. 462
Lab. majority 11,321 (33.22%)
2.79% swing Lab. to C.
(1997: Lab. maj. 15,628 (38.80%))

CARMARTHEN EAST & DINEFWR
E. 54,035 T. 38,053 (70.42%) PC gain
Adam Price, PC 16,130
*Alan Williams, Lab. 13,540
David N Thomas, C. 4,912
Doiran Evans, LD 2,815
Mike Squires, UK Ind. 656
PC majority 2,590 (6.81%)
7.54% swing Lab. to PC
(1997: Lab. maj. 3,450 (8.27%))

CARMARTHEN WEST & PEMBROKESHIRE SOUTH
E. 56,518 T. 36,916 (65.32%) Lab. hold
*Nick Ainger, Lab. 15,349
Robert Wilson, C. 10,811
Llyr Hughes Griffiths, PC 6,893
William Jeremy, LD 3,248
Ian Phillips, UK Ind. 537
Nick Turner, Customer 78
Lab. majority 4,538 (12.29%)
5.14% swing Lab. to C.
(1997: Lab. maj. 9,621 (22.57%))

CEREDIGION
E. 56,118 T. 34,606 (61.67%) PC hold
*Simon Thomas, PC 13,241
Mark Williams, LD 9,297
Paul Davies, C. 6,730
David Grace, Lab. 5,338
PC majority 3,944 (11.40%)
6.89% swing PC to LD
(2000 Feb. by-election: PC maj. 4,948 (19.74%); 1997: PC maj. 6,961 (17.33%))

CLWYD SOUTH
E. 53,680 T. 33,496 (62.40%) Lab. hold
*Martyn Jones, Lab. 17,217
Tom Biggins, C. 8,319
Dyfed Edwards, PC 3,982
David Griffiths, LD 3,426
Mrs Edwina Theunissen, UK Ind. 552
Lab. majority 8,898 (26.56%)
4.25% swing Lab. to C.
(1997: Lab. maj. 13,810 (35.07%))

CLWYD WEST
E. 53,960 T. 34,600 (64.12%) Lab. hold
*Gareth Thomas, Lab. 13,426
Jimmy James, C. 12,311
Elfed Williams, PC 4,453
Ms Bobbie Feeley, LD 3,934
Matthew Guest, UK Ind. 476
Lab. majority 1,115 (3.22%)
0.68% swing Lab. to C.
(1997: Lab. maj. 1,848 (4.59%))

CONWY
E. 54,751 T. 34,366 (62.77%) Lab. hold
*Mrs Betty Williams, Lab. 14,366
David Logan, C. 8,147
Ms Vicky Macdonald, LD 5,800
Ms Ann Owen, PC 5,665
Alan Barham, UK Ind. 388
Lab. majority 6,219 (18.10%)
3.66% swing C. to Lab
(1997: Lab. maj. 1,596 (3.84%))

CYNON VALLEY
E. 48,591 T. 26,958 (55.48%) Lab. hold
*Ms Ann Clwyd, Lab. 17,685
Steven Cornelius, PC 4,687
Ian Parry, LD 2,541
Julian Waters, C. 2,045
Lab. majority 12,998 (48.22%)
5.44% swing Lab. to PC
(1997: Lab. maj. 19,755 (59.10%))

DELYN
E. 54,732 T. 34,636 (63.28%) Lab. hold
*David Hanson, Lab. 17,825
Paul Brierley, C. 9,220
Tudor Jones, LD 5,329
Paul Rowlinson, PC 2,262
Lab. majority 8,605 (24.84%)
2.29% swing Lab. to C.
(1997: Lab. maj. 11,693 (29.42%))

GOWER
E. 58,943 T. 37,353 (63.37%) Lab. hold
*Martin Caton, Lab. 17,676
John Bushell, C. 10,281
Ms Sheila Waye, LD 4,507
Ms Sian Caiach, PC 3,865
Ms Tina Shrewsbury, Green 607
Darran Hickery, Soc. Lab. 417
Lab. majority 7,395 (19.80%)
5.11% swing Lab. to C.
(1997: Lab. maj. 13,007 (30.02%))

ISLWYN
E. 51,230 T. 31,691 (61.86%)
Lab. Co-op hold
*Don Touhig, Lab. Co-op 19,505
Kevin Etheridge, LD 4,196
Leigh Thomas, PC 3,767
Philip Howells, C. 2,543
Paul Taylor, Ind. 1,263
Ms Mary Millington, Soc. Lab. 417
Lab. Co-op majority 15,309 (48.31%)
8.71% swing Lab. Co-op to LD
(1997: Lab. maj. 23,931 (65.73%))

LLANELLI
E. 58,148 T. 36,198 (62.25%) Lab. hold
*Rt. Hon. D. Davies, Lab. 17,586
Dyfan Jones, PC 11,183
Simon Hayes, C. 3,442
Ken Rees, LD 3,065
Ms Jan Cliff, Green 515
John Willock, Soc. Lab. 407
Lab. majority 6,403 (17.69%)
10.62% swing Lab. to PC
(1997: Lab. maj. 16,039 (38.92%))

MEIRIONNYDD NANT CONWY
E. 33,175 T. 21,068 (63.51%) PC hold
*Elfyn Llwyd, PC 10,459
Ms Denise Idris Jones, Lab. 4,775
Ms Lisa Francis, C. 3,962
Dafydd Raw-Rees, LD 1,872
PC majority 5,684 (26.98%)
0.36% swing PC to Lab.
(1997: PC maj. 6,805 (27.69%))

MERTHYR TYDFIL & RHYMNEY
E. 55,368 T. 31,684 (57.22%) Lab. hold
Dai Havard, Lab. 19,574
Robert Hughes, PC 4,651
Keith Rogers, LD 2,385
Richard Cuming, C. 2,272
Jeff Edwards, Ind. 1,936
Ken Evans, Soc. Lab. 692
Anthony Lewis, ProLife 174
Lab. majority 14,923 (47.10%)
11.80% swing Lab. to PC
(1997: Lab. maj. 27,086 (69.20%))

MONMOUTH
E. 62,202 T. 44,462 (71.48%) Lab. hold
*Huw Edwards, Lab. 19,021
Roger Evans, C. 18,637
Neil Parker, LD 5,080
Marc Hubbard, PC 1,068
David Rowlands, UK Ind. 656
Lab. majority 384 (0.86%)
3.83% swing Lab. to C.
(1997: Lab. maj. 4,178 (8.52%))

MONTGOMERYSHIRE
E. 44,243 T. 28,983 (65.51%) LD hold
*Lembit Opik, LD 14,319
David Jones, C. 8,085
Paul Davies, Lab. 3,443
David Senior, PC 1,969
David William Rowlands, UK Ind. 786
Miss Ruth Davies, ProLife 210
Reg Taylor, Ind. 171
LD majority 6,234 (21.51%)
0.88% swing C. to LD
(1997: LD maj. 6,303 (19.74%))

NEATH
E. 56,107 T. 35,020 (62.42%) Lab. hold
*Rt. Hon. P. Hain, Lab. 21,253
Alun Llywelyn, PC 6,437
David Davies, LD 3,335
David Devine, C. 3,310
Huw Pudner, Soc. All. 483
Gerardo Brienza, ProLife 202
Lab. majority 14,816 (42.31%)
11.56% swing Lab. to PC
(1997: Lab. maj. 26,741 (64.84%))

NEWPORT EAST
E. 56,118 T. 31,282 (55.74%) Lab. hold
*Rt. Hon. A. Howarth, Lab. 17,120
Ian Oakley, C. 7,246
Alistair Cameron, LD 4,394
Madoc Batcup, PC 1,519
Ms Liz Screen, Soc. Lab. 420
Neal Reynolds, UK Ind. 410
Robert Griffiths, Comm. 173
Lab. majority 9,874 (31.56%)
2.36% swing Lab. to C.
(1997: Lab. maj. 13,523 (36.29%))

NEWPORT WEST
E. 59,742 T. 35,063 (58.69%) Lab. hold
*Paul Flynn, Lab. 18,489
Dr William Morgan, C. 9,185
Ms Veronica Watkins, LD 4,095
Anthony Salkeld, PC 2,510
Hugh Moelwyn-Hughes, UK Ind. 506
Terry Cavill, BNP 278
Lab. majority 9,304 (26.54%)
4.81% swing Lab. to C.
(1997: Lab. maj. 14,537 (36.16%))

OGMORE
E. 52,185 T. 30,353 (58.16%) Lab. hold
*Sir Ray Powell, Lab. 18,833
Ms Angela Pulman, PC 4,259
Ian Lewis, LD 3,878
Richard Hill, C. 3,383
Lab. majority 14,574 (48.02%)
9.46% swing Lab. to PC
(1997: Lab. maj. 24,447 (64.22%))

PONTYPRIDD
E. 66,105 T. 38,309 (57.95%) Lab. hold
*Dr Kim Howells, Lab. 22,963
Bleddyn Hancock, PC 5,279
Ms Prudence Dailey, C. 5,096
Eric Brooke, LD 4,152
Ms Sue Warry, UK Ind. 603
Joseph Biddulph, ProLife 216
Lab. majority 17,684 (46.16%)
5.61% swing Lab. to PC
(1997: Lab. maj. 23,129 (50.44%))

PRESELI PEMBROKESHIRE
E. 54,283 T. 36,777 (67.75%) Lab. hold
*Ms Jackie Lawrence, Lab. 15,206
Stephen Crabb, C. 12,260
Rhys Sinnet, PC 4,658
Alexander Dauncey, LD 3,882
Ms Trish Bowen, Soc. Lab. 452
Hugh Jones, UK Ind. 319
Lab. majority 2,946 (8.01%)
6.29% swing Lab. to C.
(1997: Lab. maj. 8,736 (20.60%))

RHONDDA
E. 56,059 T. 34,002 (60.65%) Lab. hold
Chris Bryant, Lab. 23,230
Ms Leanne Wood, PC 7,183
Peter Hobbins, C. 1,557
Gavin Cox, LD 1,525
Glyndwr Summers, Ind. 507
Lab. majority 16,047 (47.19%)
6.95% swing Lab. to PC
(1997: Lab. maj. 24,931 (61.09%))

SWANSEA EAST
E. 57,273 T. 30,072 (52.51%) Lab. hold
*Rt. Hon. D. Anderson, Lab. 19,612
John Ball, PC 3,464
Robert Speht, LD 3,064
Paul Morris, C. 3,026
Tony Young, Green 463
Tim Jenkins, UK Ind. 443
Lab. majority 16,148 (53.70%)
9.15% swing Lab. to PC
(1997: Lab. maj. 25,569 (66.12%))

SWANSEA WEST
E. 57,074 T. 32,100 (56.24%) Lab. hold
*Rt. Hon. A. Williams, Lab. 15,644
Ms Margaret Harper, C. 6,094
Mike Day, LD 5,313
Ian Titherington, PC 3,404
Richard Lewis, UK Ind. 653
Martyn Shrewsbury, Green 626
Alec Thraves, Soc. All. 366
Lab. majority 9,550 (29.75%)
2.99% swing Lab. to C.
(1997: Lab. maj. 14,459 (35.73%))

TORFAEN
E. 61,110 T. 35,242 (57.67%) Lab. hold
*Rt. Hon. P. Murphy, Lab. 21,883
Jason Evans, C. 5,603
Alan Masters, LD 3,936
Stephen Smith, PC 2,720
Mrs Brenda Vipass, UK Ind. 657
Steve Bell, Soc. All. 443
Lab. majority 16,280 (46.19%)
5.27% swing Lab. to C.
(1997: Lab. maj. 24,536 (56.74%))

VALE OF CLWYD
E. 51,247 T. 32,346 (63.12%) Lab. hold
*Chris Ruane, Lab. 16,179
Brendan Murphy, C. 10,418
Graham Rees, LD 3,058
John Penri Williams, PC 2,300
William Campbell, UK Ind. 391
Lab. majority 5,761 (17.81%)
2.54% swing Lab. to C.
(1997: Lab. maj. 8,955 (22.89%))

VALE OF GLAMORGAN
E. 67,071 T. 45,184 (67.37%) Lab. hold
*John Smith, Lab. 20,524
Lady Susan Inkin, C. 15,824
Dewi Smith, LD 5,521
Chris Franks, PC 2,867
Niall Warry, UK Ind. 448
Lab. majority 4,700 (10.40%)
4.57% swing Lab. to C.
(1997: Lab. maj. 10,532 (19.54%))

WREXHAM
E. 50,465 T. 30,048 (59.54%) Lab. hold
Ian Lucas, Lab. 15,934
Ms Felicity Elphick, C. 6,746
Ron Davies, LD 5,153
Malcolm Evans, PC 1,783
Mrs Jane Brookes, UK Ind. 432
Lab. majority 9,188 (30.58%)
0.86% swing Lab. to C.
(1997: Lab. maj. 11,762 (32.30%))

YNYS MON
E. 53,117 T. 34,018 (64.04%) Lab. gain
Albert Owen, Lab. 11,906
Eilian Williams, PC 11,106
Albie Fox, C. 7,653
Nick Bennett, LD 2,772
Francis Wykes, UK Ind. 359
Ms Nona Donald, Ind. 222
Lab. majority 800 (2.35%)
4.28% swing PC to Lab
(1997: PC maj. 2,481 (6.21%))

SCOTLAND

ABERDEEN CENTRAL
E. 50,098 T. 26,429 (52.75%) Lab. hold
*Frank Doran, Lab. 12,025
Wayne Gault, SNP 5,379
Ms Eleanor Anderson, LD 4,547
Stewart Whyte, C. 3,761
Andy Cumbers, SSP 717
Lab. majority 6,646 (25.15%)
4.24% swing Lab. to SNP
(1997: Lab. maj. 10,801 (30.32%))

ABERDEEN NORTH
E. 52,746 T. 30,357 (57.55%) Lab. hold
*Malcolm Savidge, Lab. 13,157
Dr Allan Alasdair, SNP 8,708
Jim Donaldson, LD 4,991
Richard Cowling, C. 3,047
Ms Shona Forman, SSP 454
Lab. majority 4,449 (14.66%)
5.70% swing Lab. to SNP
(1997: Lab. maj. 10,010 (26.06%))

ABERDEEN SOUTH
E. 58,907 T. 36,890 (62.62%) Lab. hold
*Ms Anne Begg, Lab. 14,696
Ian Yuill, LD 10,308
Moray Macdonald, C. 7,098
Ian Angus, SNP 4,293
David Watt, SSP 495
Lab. majority 4,388 (11.89%)
2.13% swing LD to Lab.
(1997: Lab. maj. 3,365 (7.64%))

ABERDEENSHIRE WEST & KINCARDINE
E. 61,180 T. 37,914 (61.97%) LD hold
*Sir Robert Smith, LD 16,507
Tom Kerr, C. 11,686
Kevin Hutchens, Lab. 4,669
John Green, SNP 4,634
Alan Manley, SSP 418
LD majority 4,821 (12.72%)
3.28% swing C. to LD
(1997: LD maj. 2,662 (6.16%))

AIRDRIE & SHOTTS
E. 58,349 T. 31,736 (54.39%) Lab. hold
*Rt. Hon. Ms H. Liddell, Lab. 18,478
Ms Alison Lindsay, SNP 6,138
John Love, LD 2,376
Gordon McIntosh, C. 1,960
Ms Mary Dempsey, Scot. U. 1,439
Kenny McGuigan, SSP 1,171
Chris Herriot, Soc. Lab. 174
Lab. majority 12,340 (38.88%)
0.73% swing SNP to Lab.
(1997: Lab. maj. 15,412 (37.42%))

ANGUS
E. 59,004 T. 35,013 (59.34%) SNP hold
Michael Weir, SNP 12,347
Marcus Booth, C. 8,736
Ian McFatridge, Lab. 8,183
Peter Nield, LD 5,015
Bruce Wallace, SSP 732
SNP majority 3,611 (10.31%)
6.67% swing SNP to C.
(1997: SNP maj. 10,189 (23.66%))

ARGYLL & BUTE
E. 49,175 T. 30,957 (62.95%) LD hold
Alan Reid, LD 9,245
Hugh Raven, Lab. 7,592
David Petrie, C. 6,436
Ms Agnes Samuel, SNP 6,433
Des Divers, SSP 1,251
LD majority 1,653 (5.34%)
9.60% swing LD to Lab.
(1997: LD maj. 6,081 (17.03%))

AYR
E. 55,630 T. 38,560 (69.32%) Lab. hold
*Ms Sandra Osborne, Lab. 16,801
Phil Gallie, C. 14,256
Jim Mather, SNP 4,621
Stuart Ritchie, LD 2,089
James Stewart, SSP 692
Joseph Smith, UK Ind. 101
Lab. majority 2,545 (6.60%)
4.01% swing Lab. to C.
(1997: Lab. maj. 6,543 (14.62%))

BANFF & BUCHAN
E. 56,496 T. 30,806 (54.53%) SNP hold
*Alex Salmond, SNP 16,710
Alexander Wallace, C. 6,207
Edward Harris, Lab. 4,363
Douglas Herbison, LD 2,769
Ms Alice Rowan, SSP 447
Eric Davidson, UK Ind. 310
SNP majority 10,503 (34.09%)
1.06% swing C. to SNP
(1997: SNP maj. 12,845 (31.97%))

CAITHNESS, SUTHERLAND & EASTER ROSS
E. 41,225 T. 24,867 (60.32%) LD hold
Viscount Thurso, LD 9,041
Michael Meighan, Lab. 6,297
John Macadam, SNP 5,273
Robert Rowantree, C. 3,513
Ms Karn Mabon, SSP 544
Gordon Campbell, Ind. 199
LD majority 2,744 (11.03%)
1.64% swing Lab. to LD
(1997: LD maj. 2,259 (7.75%))

CARRICK, CUMNOCK & DOON VALLEY
E. 64,919 T. 40,107 (61.78%) Lab. Co-op hold
*George Foulkes, Lab. Co-op 22,174
Gordon Miller, C. 7,318
Tom Wilson, SNP 6,258
Ms Amy Rogers, LD 2,932
Ms Amanda McFarlane, SSP 1,058
James McDaid, Soc. Lab. 367
Lab. Co-op majority 14,856 (37.04%)
2.90% swing Lab. Co-op to C.
(1997: Lab. maj. 21,062 (42.84%))

CLYDEBANK & MILNGAVIE
E. 52,534 T. 32,491 (61.85%) Lab. hold
*Tony Worthington, Lab. 17,249
Jim Yuill, SNP 6,525
Rod Ackland, LD 3,909
Dr Catherine Pickering, C. 3,514
Ms Dawn Brennan, SSP 1,294
Lab. majority 10,724 (33.01%)
0.54% swing Lab. to SNP
(1997: Lab. maj. 13,320 (34.08%))

CLYDESDALE
E. 64,423 T. 38,222 (59.33%) Lab. hold
*Jimmy Hood, Lab. 17,822
Jim Wright, SNP 10,028
Kevin Newton, C. 5,034
Ms Moira Craig, LD 4,111
Paul Cockshott, SSP 974
Donald MacKay, UK Ind. 253
Lab. majority 7,794 (20.39%)
5.01% swing Lab. to SNP
(1997: Lab. maj. 13,809 (30.41%))

COATBRIDGE & CHRYSTON
E. 52,178 T. 30,311 (58.09%) Lab. hold
*Rt. Hon. T. Clarke, Lab. 19,807
Peter Kearney, SNP 4,493
Alistair Tough, LD 2,293
Patrick Ross-Taylor, C. 2,171
Ms Lynne Sheridan, SSP 1,547
Lab. majority 15,314 (50.52%)
0.39% swing Lab. to SNP
(1997: Lab. maj. 19,295 (51.30%))

CUMBERNAULD & KILSYTH
E. 49,739 T. 29,699 (59.71%) Lab. hold
*Ms Rosemary McKenna, Lab. 16,144
David McGlashan, SNP 8,624
John O'Donnell, LD 1,934
Ms Alison Ross, C. 1,460
Kenny McEwan, SSP 1,287
Thomas Taylor, Scot. Ref. 250
Lab. majority 7,520 (25.32%)
2.78% swing Lab. to SNP
(1997: Lab. maj. 11,128 (30.89%))

CUNNINGHAME NORTH
E. 54,993 T. 33,816 (61.49%) Lab. hold
*Brian Wilson, Lab. 15,571
Campbell Martin, SNP 7,173
Richard Wilkinson, C. 6,666
Ross Chmiel, LD 3,060
Sean Scott, SSP 964
Ms Louise McDaid, Soc. Lab. 382
Lab. majority 8,398 (24.83%)
3.51% swing Lab. to SNP
(1997: Lab. maj. 11,039 (26.84%))

CUNNINGHAME SOUTH
E. 49,982 T. 28,009 (56.04%) Lab. hold
*Brian Donohoe, Lab. 16,424
Bill Kidd, SNP 5,194
Mrs Pam Paterson, C. 2,682
John Boyd, LD 2,094
Ms Rosemary Byrne, SSP 1,233
Bobby Cochrane, Soc. Lab. 382
Lab. majority 11,230 (40.09%)
0.93% swing Lab. to SNP
(1997: Lab. maj. 14,869 (41.95%))

DUMBARTON
E. 56,267 T. 33,994 (60.42%) Lab. Co-op hold
*John McFall, Lab. Co-op 16,151
Iain Robertson, SNP 6,576
Eric Thompson, LD 5,265
Peter Ramsay, C. 4,648
Les Robertson, SSP 1,354
Lab. Co-op majority 9,575 (28.17%)
0.89% swing SNP to Lab. Co-op
(1997: Lab. maj. 10,883 (26.38%))

DUMFRIES
E. 62,931 T. 42,586 (67.67%) Lab. hold
*Russell Brow, Lab. 20,830
John Charteris, C. 11,996
John Ross Scott, LD 4,955
Gerry Fisher, SNP 4,103
John Dennis, SSP 702
Lab. majority 8,834 (20.74%)
0.64% swing C. to Lab.
(1997: Lab. maj. 9,643 (19.47%))

DUNDEE EAST
E. 56,535 T. 32,358 (57.24%) Lab. hold
Iain Luke, Lab. 14,635
Stewart Hosie, SNP 10,160
Alan Donnelly, C. 3,900
Raymond Lawrie, LD 2,784
Harvey Duke, SSP 879
Lab. majority 4,475 (13.83%)
5.38% swing Lab. to SNP
(1997: Lab. maj. 9,961 (24.58%))

DUNDEE WEST
E. 53,760 T. 29,242 (54.39%) Lab. hold
*Ernie Ross, Lab. 14,787
Gordon Archer, SNP 7,987
Ian Hail, C. 2,656
Ms Elizabeth Dick, LD 2,620
Jim McFarlane, SSP 1,192
Lab. majority 6,800 (23.25%)
3.65% swing Lab. to SNP
(1997: Lab. maj. 11,859 (30.56%))

DUNFERMLINE EAST
E. 52,811 T. 30,086 (56.97%) Lab. hold
*Rt. Hon. G. Brown, Lab. 19,487
John Mellon, SNP 4,424
Stuart Randall, C. 2,838
John Mainland, LD 2,281
Andy Jackson, SSP 770
Tom Dunsmore, UK Ind. 286
Lab. majority 15,063 (50.07%)
0.60% swing Lab. to SNP
(1997: Lab. maj. 18,751 (51.26%))

DUNFERMLINE WEST
E. 54,293 T. 30,975 (57.05%) Lab. hold
*Ms Rachel Squire, Lab. 16,370
Brian Goodall, SNP 5,390
Russell McPhate, LD 4,832
James Mackie, C. 3,166
Ms Kate Stewart, SSP 746
Alastair Harper, UK Ind. 471
Lab. majority 10,980 (35.45%)
0.77% swing SNP to Lab.
(1997: Lab. maj. 12,354 (33.91%))

EAST KILBRIDE
E. 66,572 T. 41,690 (62.62%) Lab. hold
*Rt. Hon. A. Ingram, Lab. 22,205
Archie Buchanan, SNP 9,450
Ewan Hawthorn, LD 4,278
Mrs Margaret McCulloch, C. 4,238
David Stevenson, SSP 1,519
Lab. majority 12,755 (30.59%)
2.52% swing Lab. to SNP
(1997: Lab. maj. 17,384 (35.63%))

EAST LOTHIAN
E. 58,987 T. 36,871 (62.51%) Lab. hold
Mrs Anne Picking, Lab. 17,407
Hamish Mair, C. 6,577
Ms Judy Hayman, LD 6,506
Ms Hilary Brown, SNP 5,381
Derrick White, SSP 624
Jake Herriot, Soc. Lab. 376
Lab. majority 10,830 (29.37%)
1.68% swing Lab. to C.
(1997: Lab. maj. 14,221 (32.74%))

EASTWOOD
E. 68,378 T. 48,368 (70.74%) Lab. hold
*Jim Murphy, Lab. 23,036
Raymond Robertson, C. 13,895
Allan Steele, LD 6,239
Stewart Maxwell, SNP 4,137
Peter Murray, SSP 814
Dr Manar Tayan, Ind. 247
Lab. majority 9,141 (18.90%)
6.35% swing C. to Lab.
(1997: Lab. maj. 3,236 (6.19%))

EDINBURGH CENTRAL
E. 66,089 T. 34,390 (52.04%) Lab. hold
*Rt. Hon. A. Darling, Lab. 14,495
Andrew Myles, LD 6,353
Alastair Orr, C. 5,643
Dr Ian McKee, SNP 4,832
Graeme Farmer, Green 1,809
Kevin Williamson, SSP 1,258
Lab. majority 8,142 (23.68%)
5.15% swing Lab. to LD
(1997: Lab. maj. 11,070 (25.90%))

EDINBURGH EAST & MUSSELBURGH
E. 59,241 T. 34,454 (58.16%) Lab. hold
*Rt. Hon. Dr G. Strang, Lab. 18,124
Rob Munn, SNP 5,956
Gary Peacock, LD 4,981
Peter Finnie, C. 3,906
Derek Durkin, SSP 1,487
Lab. majority 12,168 (35.32%)
0.41% swing SNP to Lab.
(1997: Lab. maj. 14,530 (34.50%))

EDINBURGH NORTH & LEITH
E. 62,475 T. 33,234 (53.20%) Lab. hold
Mark Lazarowicz, Lab. 15,271
Sebastian Tombs, LD 6,454
Ms Kaukab Stewart, SNP 5,290
Iain Mitchell, C. 4,626
Ms Catriona Grant, SSP 1,334
Don Jacobsen, Soc. Lab. 259
Lab. majority 8,817 (26.53%)
3.67% swing Lab. to LD
(1997: Lab. maj. 10,978 (26.81%))

EDINBURGH PENTLANDS
E. 59,841 T. 38,932 (65.06%) Lab. hold
*Dr Lynda Clark, Lab. 15,797
Sir Malcolm Rifkind, C. 14,055
David Walker, LD 4,210
Stewart Gibb, SNP 4,210
James Mearns, SSP 555
William McMurdo, UK Ind. 105
Lab. majority 1,742 (4.47%)
3.08% swing Lab. to C.
(1997: Lab. maj. 4,862 (10.63%))

EDINBURGH SOUTH
E. 64,012 T. 37,166 (58.06%) Lab. hold
*Nigel Griffiths, Lab. 15,671
Ms Marilyne MacLaren, LD 10,172
Geoffrey Buchan, C. 6,172
Ms Heather Williams, SNP 3,683
Colin Fox, SSP 933
Ms Linda Hendry, LCA 535
Lab. majority 5,499 (14.80%)
7.19% swing Lab. to LD
(1997: Lab. maj. 11,452 (25.54%))

EDINBURGH WEST
E. 61,895 T. 39,478 (63.78%) LD hold
John Barrett, LD 16,719
Ms Elspeth Alexandra, Lab. 9,130
Iain Whyte, C. 8,894
Alyn Smith, SNP 4,047
Bill Scott, SSP 688
LD majority 7,589 (19.22%)
2.59% swing LD to Lab.
(1997: LD maj. 7,253 (15.22%))

FALKIRK EAST
E. 57,633 T. 33,702 (58.48%) Lab. hold
*Michael Connarty, Lab. 18,536
Ms Isabel Hutton, SNP 7,824
Bill Stevenson, C. 3,252
Ms Karen Utting, LD 2,992
Tony Weir, SSP 725
Raymond Stead, Soc. Lab. 373
Lab. majority 10,712 (31.78%)
0.20% swing Lab. to SNP
(1997: Lab. maj. 13,385 (32.18%))

FALKIRK WEST
E. 53,583 T. 30,891 (57.65%) Lab. hold
*Eric Joyce, Lab. 16,022
David Kerr, SNP 7,490
Simon Murray, C. 2,321
Hugh O'Donnell, LD 2,203
William Buchanan, Ind. 1,464
Ms Mhairi McAlpine, SSP 707
Hugh Lynch, Ind. 490
Ronnie Forbes, Soc. Lab. 194
Lab. majority 8,532 (27.62%)
4.15% swing Lab. to SNP
(2000 Dec. by-election: Lab. maj. 705 (3.61%))
(1997: Lab. maj. 13,783 (35.92%))

FIFE CENTRAL
E. 59,597 T. 32,512 (54.55%) Lab. hold
John MacDougall, Lab. 18,310
David Alexander, SNP 8,235
Ms Elizabeth Riches, LD 2,775
Jeremy Balfour, C. 2,351
Ms Morag Balfour, SSP 841
Lab. majority 10,075 (30.99%)
1.33% swing Lab. to SNP
(1997: Lab. maj. 13,713 (33.64%))

FIFE NORTH EAST
E. 61,900 T. 34,692 (56.05%) LD hold
*Rt. Hon. M. Campbell, LD 17,926
Mike Scott-Hayward, C. 8,190
Ms Claire Brennan, Lab. 3,950
Ms Kris Murray-Browne, SNP 3,596
Keith White, SSP 610
Mrs Leslie Von Goetz, LCA 420
LD majority 9,736 (28.06%)
1.66% swing C. to LD
(1997: LD maj. 10,356 (24.75%))

GALLOWAY & UPPER NITHSDALE
E. 52,756 T. 35,914 (68.08%) C. gain
Peter Duncan, C. 12,222
Malcolm Fleming, SNP 12,148
Thomas Sloan, Lab. 7,258
Neil Wallace, LD 3,698
Andy Harvey, SSP 588
C. majority 74 (0.21%)
6.80% swing SNP to C.
(1997: SNP maj. 5,624 (13.39%))

GLASGOW ANNIESLAND
E. 53,290 T. 26,722 (50.14%) Lab. hold
*John Robertson, Lab. 15,102
Grant Thoms, SNP 4,048
Christopher McGinty, LD 3,244
Stewart Connell, C. 2,651
Charlie McCarthy, SSP 1,486
Ms Katherine McGavigan, Soc. Lab. 191
Lab. majority 11,054 (41.37%)
1.68% swing Lab. to SNP
(2000 Nov. by-election: Lab. maj. 6,337 (31.35%))
(1997: Lab. maj. 15,154 (44.73%))

GLASGOW BAILLIESTON
E. 49,268 T. 23,261 (47.21%) Lab. hold
*Jimmy Wray, Lab. 14,200
Lachlan McNeill, SNP 4,361
David Comrie, C. 1,580
Jim McVicar, SSP 1,569
Charles Dundas, LD 1,551
Lab. majority 9,839 (42.30%)
2.15% swing Lab. to SNP
(1997: Lab. maj. 14,840 (46.59%))

GLASGOW CATHCART
E. 52,094 T. 27,386 (52.57%) Lab. hold
Tom Harris, Lab. 14,902
Mrs Josephine Docherty, SNP 4,086
Richard Cook, C. 3,662
Tom Henery, LD 3,006
Ronnie Stevenson, SSP 1,730
Lab. majority 10,816 (39.49%)
1.80% swing SNP to Lab.
(1997: Lab. maj. 12,245 (35.90%))

GLASGOW GOVAN
E. 54,068 T. 25,284 (46.76%) Lab. hold
*Mohammad Sarwar, Lab. 12,464
Ms Karen Neary, SNP 6,064
Bob Stewart, LD 2,815
Mark Menzies, C. 2,167
Willie McGartland, SSP 1,531
John Foster, Comm. 174
Badar Mirza, Ind. 69
Lab. majority 6,400 (25.31%)
8.14% swing SNP to Lab.
(1997: Lab. maj. 2,914 (9.04%))

GLASGOW KELVIN
E. 61,534 T. 26,802 (43.56%) Lab. hold
*George Galloway, Lab. 12,014
Ms Tamsin Mayberry, LD 4,754
Frank Rankin, SNP 4,513
Miss Davina Rankin, C. 2,388
Ms Heather Ritchie, SSP 1,847
Tim Shand, Green 1,286
Lab. majority 7,260 (27.09%)
4.85% swing Lab. to LD
(1997: Lab. maj. 9,665 (29.60%))

GLASGOW MARYHILL
E. 55,431 T. 22,231 (40.11%) Lab. hold
Ms Ann McKechin, Lab. 13,420
Alex Dingwall, SNP 3,532
Stuart Callison, LD 2,372
Gordon Scott, SSP 1,745
Gawain Towler, C. 1,162
Lab. majority 9,888 (44.48%)
1.76% swing Lab. to SNP
(1997: Lab. maj. 14,264 (47.99%))

GLASGOW POLLOK
E. 49,201 T. 25,277 (51.37%) Lab. Co-op hold
*Ian Davidson, Lab. Co-op 15,497
David Ritchie, SNP 4,229
Keith Baldssara, SSP 2,522
Ms Isabel Nelson, LD 1,612
Rory O'Brien, C. 1,417
Lab. Co-op majority 11,268 (44.58%)
1.27% swing SNP to Lab. Co-op

GLASGOW RUTHERGLEN
E. 51,855 T. 29,213 (56.34%) Lab. Co-op hold
*Tommy McAvoy, Lab. Co-op 16,760
Ms Anne McLaughlin, SNP 4,135
David Jackson, LD 3,689
Malcolm Macaskill, C. 3,301
Bill Bonnar, SSP 1,328
Lab. Co-op majority 12,625 (43.22%)
0.48% swing SNP to Lab. Co-op
(1997: Lab. maj. 15,007 (42.25%))

GLASGOW SHETTLESTON
E. 51,557 T. 20,465 (39.69%) Lab. hold
*David Marshall, Lab. 13,235
Jim Byrne, SNP 3,417
Ms Rosie Kane, SSP 1,396
Lewis Hutton, LD 1,105
Campbell Murdoch, C. 1,082
Murdo Ritchie, Soc. Lab. 230
Lab. majority 9,818 (47.97%)
5.60% swing Lab. to SNP
(1997: Lab. maj. 15,868 (59.18%))

GLASGOW SPRINGBURN
E. 55,192 T. 24,104 (43.67%) Speaker hold
*Rt. Hon. M. Martin, Speaker 16,053
Sandy Bain, SNP 4,675
Ms Carolyn Leckie, SSP 1,879
Daniel Houston, Scot. U. 1,289
Richard Silvester, Ind. 208
Speaker majority 11,378 (47.20%)
(1997: Lab. maj. 17,326 (54.87%))

GORDON
E. 59,996 T. 35,001 (58.34%) LD hold
*Malcolm Bruce, LD 15,928
Mrs Nanette Milne, C. 8,049
Mrs Rhona Kemp, SNP 5,760
Ellis Thorpe, Lab. 4,730
John Sangster, SSP 534
LD majority 7,879 (22.51%)
2.97% swing C. to LD
(1997: LD maj. 6,997 (16.57%))

GREENOCK & INVERCLYDE
E. 47,884 T. 28,419 (59.35%) Lab. hold
David Cairns, Lab. 14,929
Chic Brodie, LD 5,039
Andrew Murie, SNP 4,248
Alistair Haw, C. 3,000
Davey Landels, SSP 1,203
Lab. majority 9,890 (34.80%)
3.77% swing Lab. to LD
(1997: Lab. maj. 13,040 (37.59%))

HAMILTON NORTH & BELLSHILL
E. 53,539 T. 30,404 (56.79%) Lab. hold
*Rt. Hon. Dr J. Reid, Lab. 18,786
Chris Stephens, SNP 5,225
Bill Frain Bell, C. 2,649
Keith Legg, LD 2,360
Ms Shareen Blackall, SSP 1,189
Steve Mayes, Soc. Lab. 195
Lab. majority 13,561 (44.60%)
0.16% swing Lab. to SNP
(1997: Lab. maj. 17,067 (44.92%))

HAMILTON SOUTH
E. 46,665 T. 26,750 (57.32%) Lab. hold
*Bill Tynan, Lab. 15,965
John Wilson, SNP 5,190
John Oswald, LD 2,381
Neil Richardson, C. 1,876
Ms Gena Mitchell, SSP 1,187
Ms Janice Murdoch, UK Ind. 151
Lab. majority 10,775 (40.28%)
3.85% swing Lab. to SNP
1999 Sep. by-election: Lab. maj 556 (2.86%)
(1997: Lab. maj. 15,878 (47.98%))

INVERNESS EAST, NAIRN & LOCHABER
E. 67,139 T. 42,461 (63.24%) Lab. hold
*David Stewart, Lab. 15,605
Angus MacNeil, SNP 10,889
Ms Patsy Kenton, LD 9,420
Richard Jenkins, C. 5,653
Steve Arnott, SSP 894
Lab. majority 4,716 (11.11%)
3.10% swing SNP to Lab.
(1997: Lab. maj. 2,339 (4.90%))

KILMARNOCK & LOUDOUN
E. 61,049 T. 37,665 (61.70%) Lab. hold
*Des Browne, Lab. 19,926
John Brady, SNP 9,592
Donald Reece, C. 3,943
John Stewart, LD 3,177
Jason Muir, SSP 1,027
Lab. majority 10,334 (27.44%)
6.07% swing SNP to Lab.
(1997: Lab. maj. 7,256 (15.30%))

KIRKCALDY
E. 51,559 T. 28,157 (54.61%) Lab. Co-op hold
*Dr Lewis Moonie, Lab. Co-op 15,227
Ms Shirley-Anne Somerville, SNP 6,264
Scott Campbell, C. 3,013
Andrew Weston, LD 2,849
Dougie Kinnear, SSP 804
Lab. Co-op majority 8,963 (31.83%)
0.60% swing SNP to Lab. Co-op
(1997: Lab. maj. 10,710 (30.63%))

LINLITHGOW
E. 54,599 T. 31,655 (57.98%) Lab. hold
*Tam Dalyell, Lab. 17,207
Jim Sibbald, SNP 8,078
Gordon Lindhurst, C. 2,836
Martin Oliver, LD 2,628
Eddie Cornoch, SSP 695
Ms Helen Cronin, R & R Loony 211
Lab. majority 9,129 (28.84%)
0.75% swing SNP to Lab.
(1997: Lab. maj. 10,838 (27.33%))

LIVINGSTON
E. 64,850 T. 36,033 (55.56%) Lab. hold
*Rt. Hon. R. Cook, Lab. 19,108
Graham Sutherland, SNP 8,492
Gordon Mackenzie, LD 3,969
Ian Mowat, C. 2,995
Ms Wendy Milne, SSP 1,110
Robert Kingdon, UK Ind. 359
Lab. majority 10,616 (29.46%)
1.02% swing SNP to Lab.
(1997: Lab. maj. 11,747 (27.43%))

MIDLOTHIAN
E. 48,625 T. 28,724 (59.07%) Lab. hold
David Hamilton, Lab. 15,145
Ian Goldie, SNP 6,131
Ms Jacqueline Bell, LD 3,686
Robin Traquair, C. 2,748
Bob Goupillot, SSP 837
Terence Holden, ProLife 177
Lab. majority 9,014 (31.38%)
1.69% swing SNP to Lab.
(1997: Lab. maj. 9,870 (28.00%))

MORAY
E. 58,008 T. 33,223 (57.27%) SNP hold
Angus Robertson, SNP 10,076
Mrs Catriona Munro, Lab. 8,332
Frank Spencer-Nairn, C. 7,677
Ms Linda Gorn, LD 5,224
Ms Norma Anderson, SSP 821
Bill Jappy, Ind. 802
Nigel Kenyon, UK Ind. 291
SNP majority 1,744 (5.25%)
8.25% swing SNP to Lab.
(1997: SNP maj. 5,566 (14.00%))

MOTHERWELL & WISHAW
E. 52,418 T. 29,673 (56.61%) Lab. hold
*Frank Roy, Lab. 16,681
Jim McGuigan, SNP 5,725
Mark Nolan, C. 3,155
Iain Brown, LD 2,791
Stephen Smellie, SSP 1,260
Ms Claire Watt, Soc. Lab. 61
Lab. majority 10,956 (36.92%)
1.00% swing SNP to Lab.
(1997: Lab. maj. 12,791 (34.93%))

OCHIL
E. 57,554 T. 35,303 (61.34%) Lab. hold
*Martin O'Neill, Lab. 16,004
Keith Brown, SNP 10,655
Alasdair Campbell, C. 4,235
Paul Edie, LD 3,253
Ms Pauline Thompson, SSP 751
Flash Gordon Approaching, Loony 405
Lab. majority 5,349 (15.15%)
2.26% swing SNP to Lab.
(1997: Lab. maj. 4,652 (10.63%))

ORKNEY & SHETLAND
E. 31,909 T. 16,733 (52.44%) LD hold
Alistair Carmichael, LD 6,919
Robert Mochrie, Lab. 3,444
John Firth, C. 3,121
John Mowat, SNP 2,473
Peter Andrews, SSP 776
LD majority 3,475 (20.77%)
6.48% swing LD to Lab.
(1997: LD maj. 6,968 (33.72%))

PAISLEY NORTH
E. 47,994 T. 27,153 (56.58%) Lab. hold
*Ms Irene Adams, Lab. 15,058
George Adam, SNP 5,737
Ms Jane Hook, LD 2,709
Craig Stevenson, C. 2,404
Jim Halfpenny, SSP 982
Robert Graham, ProLife 263
Lab. majority 9,321 (34.33%)
1.61% swing Lab. to SNP
(1997: Lab. maj. 12,814 (37.54%))

PAISLEY SOUTH
E. 53,351 T. 30,536 (57.24%) Lab. hold
*Douglas Alexander, Lab. 17,830
Brian Lawson, SNP 5,920
Brian O'Malley, LD 3,178
Andrew Cossar, C. 2,301
Ms Frances Curran, SSP 835
Ms Patricia Graham, ProLife 346
Terence O'Donnell, Ind. 126
Lab. majority 11,910 (39.00%)
2.44% swing SNP to Lab.
(1997 Nov. by-election: Lab. maj. 2,731)
(1997: Lab. maj. 12,750 (34.13%))

PERTH
E. 61,497 T. 37,816 (61.49%) SNP hold
Ms Annabelle Ewing, SNP 11,237
Miss Elizabeth Smith, C. 11,189
Ms Marion Dingwall, Lab. 9,638
Ms Vicki Harris, LD 4,853
Frank Byrne, SSP 899
SNP majority 48 (0.13%)
3.46% swing SNP to C.
(1997: SNP maj. 3,141 (7.05%))

RENFREWSHIRE WEST
E. 52,889 T. 33,497 (63.33%) Lab. gain
James Sheridan, Lab. 15,720
Ms Carol Puthucheary, SNP 7,145
David Sharpe, C. 5,522
Ms Clare Hamblen, LD 4,185
Ms Arlene Nunnery, SSP 925
Lab. majority 8,575 (25.60%)
2.77% swing SNP to Lab.
(1997: Lab. maj. 7,979 (20.05%))

ROSS, SKYE & INVERNESS WEST
E. 56,522 T. 34,812 (61.59%) LD hold
*Rt. Hon. C. Kennedy, LD 18,832
Donald Crichton, Lab. 5, 880
Ms Jean Urquhart, SNP 4,901
Angus Laing, C. 3,096
Dr Eleanor Scott, Green 699
Stuart Topp, SSP 683
Philip Anderson, UK Ind. 456
James Crawford, Country 265
LD majority 12,952 (37.21%)
13.57% swing Lab. to LD
(1997: LD maj. 4,019 (10.06%))

ROXBURGH & BERWICKSHIRE
E. 47,059 T. 28,797 (61.19%) LD hold
*Archy Kirkwood, LD 14,044
George Turnbull, C. 6,533
Ms C. Maxwell-Stuart, Lab. 4,498
Roderick Campbell, SNP 2,806
Ms Amanda Millar, SSP 463
Peter Neilson, UK Ind. 453
LD majority 7,511 (26.08%)
1.73% swing C. to LD
(1997: LD maj. 7,906 (22.63%))

STIRLING
E. 53,097 T. 35,930 (67.67%) Lab. hold
*Ms Anne McGuire, Lab. 15,175
Geoff Mawdsley, C. 8,901
Ms Fiona Macaulay, SNP 5,877
Clive Freeman, LD 4,208
Dr Clarke Mullen, SSP 1,012
Mark Ruskell, Green 757
Lab. majority 6,274 (17.46%)
1.27% swing C. to Lab.
(1997: Lab. maj. 6,411 (14.93%))

STRATHKELVIN & BEARSDEN
E. 62,729 T. 41,486 (66.14%) Lab. hold
John Lyons, Lab. 19,250
Gordon Macdonald, LD 7,533
Calum Smith, SNP 6,675
Murray Roxburgh, C. 6,635
Willie Telfer, SSP 1,393
Lab. majority 11,717 (28.24%)
7.44% swing Lab. to LD
(1997: Lab. maj. 16,292 (32.77%))

TAYSIDE NORTH
E. 61,645 T. 38,517 (62.48%) SNP hold
Peter Wishart, SNP 15,441
Murdo Fraser, C. 12,158
Thomas Docherty, Lab. 5,715
Ms Julia Robertson, LD 4,363
Ms Rosie Adams, SSP 620
Ms Tina MacDonald, Ind. 220
SNP majority 3,283 (8.52%)
0.30% swing SNP to C.
(1997: SNP maj. 4,160 (9.13%))

TWEEDDALE, ETTRICK & LAUDERDALE
E. 51,966 T. 33,217 (63.92%) LD hold
*Michael Moore, LD 14,035
Keith Geddes, Lab. 8,878
Andrew Brocklehurst, C. 5,118
Richard Thomson, SNP 4,108
Norman Lockhart, SSP 695
John Hein, Lib. 383
LD majority 5,157 (15.53%)
5.86% swing Lab. to LD
(1997: LD maj. 1,489 (3.81%))

WESTERN ISLES
E. 21,807 T. 13,159 (60.34%) Lab. hold
*Calum MacDonald, Lab. 5,924
Alasdair Nicholson, SNP 4,850
Douglas Taylor, C. 1,250
John Horne, LD 849
Ms Joanne Telfer, SSP 286
Lab. maj 1,074 (8.16%)
7.02% swing Lab. to SNP
(1997: Lab. maj. 3,576 (22.20%))

NORTHERN IRELAND

ANTRIM EAST
E. 60,897 T. 36,000 (59.12%) UUP hold
*Roy Beggs, UUP 13,101
Sammy Wilson, DUP 12,973
John Mathews, Alliance 4,483
Danny O'Connor, SDLP 2,641
Robert Mason, Ind. 1,092
Ms Jeanette Graffin, SF 903
Alan Greer, C. 807
UUP majority 128 (0.36%)
9.48% swing UUP to DUP
(1997: UUP maj. 6,389 (18.60%))

ANTRIM NORTH
E. 74,451 T. 49,217 (66.11%) DUP hold
*Revd Ian Paisley, DUP 24,539
Lexie Scott, UUP 10,315
Sean Farren, SDLP 8,283
John Kelly, SF 4,822
Miss Jayne Dunlop, Alliance 1,258
DUP majority 14,224 (28.90%)
3.01% swing UUP to DUP
(1997: DUP maj. 10,574 (22.89%))

ANTRIM SOUTH
E. 70,651 T. 44,158 (62.50%) UUP gain
David Burnside, UUP 16,366
*Revd Robert McCrea, DUP 15,355
Sean McKee, SDLP 5,336
Martin Meehan, SF 4,160
David Ford, Alliance 1,969
Norman Boyd, NI Unionist 972
UUP majority 1,011 (2.29%)
10.21% swing UUP to DUP
(2000 Sep. by-election: DUP maj. 822)
(1997: UUP maj. 16,611 (41.33%))

BELFAST EAST
E. 58,455 T. 36,829 (63.00%) DUP hold
*Peter Robinson, DUP 15,667
Tim Lemon, UUP 8,550
Dr David Alderdice, Alliance 5,832
David Ervine, PUP 3,669
Joe O'Donnell, SF 1,237
Ms Ciara Farren, SDLP 880
Terry Dick, C. 800
Joe Bell, WP 123
Rainbow George Weiss, Ind. Vote 71
DUP majority 7,117 (19.32%)
1.01% swing UUP to DUP
(1997: DUP maj. 6,754 (17.30%))

BELFAST NORTH
E. 60,941 T. 40,932 (67.17%) DUP gain
Nigel Dodds, DUP 16,718
Gerry Kelly, SF 10,331
Alban Maginness, SDLP 8,592
*Cecil Walker, UUP 4,904
Ms Marcella Delaney, WP 253
Rainbow George Weiss, Ind. Vote 134
DUP maj 6,387 (15.60%)
(1997: UUP maj. 13,024 (31.42%))

BELFAST SOUTH
E. 59,436 T. 37,952 (63.85%) UUP hold
*Revd M. Smyth, UUP 17,008
Dr Alasdair McDonnell, SDLP 11,609
Prof Monica McWilliams, Women's Co. 2,968
Alex Maskey, SF 2,894
Ms Geraldine Rice, Alliance 2,042
Ms Dawn Purvis, PUP 1,112
Paddy Lynn, WP 204
Rainbow George Weiss, Ind. Vote 115
UUP majority 5,399 (14.23%)
1.29% swing SDLP to UUP
(1997: UUP maj. 4,600 (11.65%))

BELFAST WEST
E. 59,617 T. 40,982 (68.74%) SF hold
*Gerry Adams, SF 27,096
Alex Attwood, SDLP 7,754
The Revd Eric Smyth, DUP 2,641
Chris McGimpsey, UUP 2,541
John Lowry, WP 736
Mr David Kerr, Third 116
Rainbow George Weiss, Ind. Vote 98
SF majority 19,342 (47.20%)
14.98% swing SDLP to SF
(1997: SF maj. 7,909 (17.24%))

DOWN NORTH
E. 63,212 T. 37,189 (58.83%) UUP gain
Lady Sylvia Hermon, UUP 20,833
*Robert McCartney, UKU 13,509
Ms Marietta Farrell, SDLP 1,275
Julian Robertson, C. 815
Chris Carter, Ind. 444
Eamon McConvey, SF 313
UUP majority 7,324 (19.69%)
11.83% swing UKU to UUP
(1997: UKU maj. 1,449 (3.96%))

DOWN SOUTH
E. 73,519 T. 52,074 (70.83%) SDLP hold
*Eddie McGrady, SDLP 24,136
Mick Murphy, SF 10,278
Dermot Nesbitt, UUP 9,173
Jim Wells, DUP 7,802
Ms Betty Campbell, Alliance 685
SDLP majority 13,858 (26.61%)
7.97% swing SDLP to SF
(1997: SDLP maj. 9,933 (20.08%))

FERMANAGH & SOUTH TYRONE
E. 66,640 T. 51,974 (77.99%) SF gain
Ms Michelle Gildernew, SF 17,739
James Cooper, UUP 17,686
Tommy Gallagher, SDLP 9,706
Jim Dixon, Ind. UU 6,843
SF majority 53 (0.10%)
14.22% swing UUP to SF
(1997: UUP maj. 13,688 (28.34%))

FOYLE
E. 70,943 T. 48,879 (68.90%) SDLP hold
*John Hume, SDLP 24,538
Mitchel McLaughlin, SF 12,988
William Hay, DUP 7,414
Andrew Davidson, UUP 3,360
Colm Cavanagh, Alliance 579
SDLP majority 11,550 (23.63%)
2.47% swing SDLP to SF
(1997: SDLP maj. 13,664 (28.57%))

LAGAN VALLEY
E. 72,671 T. 45,941 (63.22%) UUP hold
*Jeffrey Donaldson, UUP 25,966
Seamus Close, Alliance 7,624
Edwin Poots, DUP 6,164
Ms Patricia Lewsley, SDLP 3,462
Paul Butler, SF 2,725
UUP majority 18,342 (39.93%)
0.86% swing Alliance to UUP
(1997: UUP maj. 16,925 (38.20%))

LONDONDERRY EAST
E. 60,276 T. 39,869 (66.14%) DUP gain
Gregory Campbell, DUP 12,813
*William Ross, UUP 10,912
John Dallat, SDLP 8,298
Francie Brolly, SF 6,221
Mrs Yvonne Boyle, Alliance 1,625
DUP maj 1,901 (4.77%)
7.36% swing UUP to DUP
(1997: UUP maj. 3,794 (9.95%))

NEWRY & ARMAGH
E. 72,466 T. 55,621 (76.75%) SDLP hold
*Seamus Mallon, SDLP 20,784
Conor Murphy, SF 17,209
Paul Berry, DUP 10,795
Mrs Sylvia McRoberts, UUP 6,833
SDLP majority 3,575 (6.43%)
7.75% swing SDLP to SF
(1997: SDLP maj. 4,889 (9.17%))

STRANGFORD
E. 72,192 T. 43,254 (59.92%) DUP gain
Mrs Iris Robinson, DUP 18,532
*David McNarry, UUP 17,422
Kieran McCarthy, Alliance 2,902
Danny McCarthy, SDLP 2,646
Liam Johnstone, SF 930
Cedric Wilson, NI Unionist 822
DUP majority 1,110 (2.57%)
8.32% swing UUP to DUP
(1997: UUP maj. 5,852 (14.07%))

TYRONE WEST
E. 60,739 T. 48,530 (79.90%) SF gain
Pat Doherty, SF 19,814
*William Thompson, UUP 14,774
Ms Brid Rodgers, SDLP 13,942
SF majority 5,040 (10.39%)
7.05% swing UUP to SF
(1997: UUP maj. 1,161 (2.51%))

ULSTER MID
E. 61,390 T. 49,936 (81.34%) SF hold
*Martin McGuinness, SF 25,502
Ian McCrea, DUP 15,549
Ms Eilis Haughey, SDLP 8,376
Francie Donnelly, WP 509
SF majority 9,953 (19.93%)
8.11% swing DUP to SF
(1997: SF maj. 1,883 (3.71%))

UPPER BANN
E. 72,574 T. 51,036 (70.32%) UUP hold
*Rt. Hon. D. Trimble, UUP 17,095
David Simpson, DUP 15,037
Dr Dara O'Hagan, SF 10,770
Ms Dolores Kelly, SDLP 7,607
Tom French, WP 527
UUP majority 2,058 (4.03%)
14.05% swing UUP to DUP
(1997: UUP maj. 9,252 (19.36%))

BY-ELECTIONS SINCE THE 2001 GENERAL ELECTION

BIRMINGHAM HODGE HILL
(15 July 2004)
E. 53,940 T. 37.9%

Liam Byrne, Lab.	7,451
Nicola Davies, LD	6,991
Stephen Eyre, C.	3,543
John Rees, Respect	1,282
James Starkey, NF	805
Mark Wheatley, EDP	277
James Hargreaves, OCV	90
Lab. majority	460

LEICESTER SOUTH
(15 July 2004)
E. 72,514 T. 40.6%

Parmjit Singh Gill, LD	10,274
Peter Soulsby, Lab.	8,620
Chris Heaton-Harris, C.	5,796
Yvonne Ridley, Respect	3,724
David Roberts, Soc. Lab.	263
RU Seerious, Loony	225
Patrick Kennedy, Ind.	204
Paul Lord, Ind.	186
Mark Benson, Ind.	55
Jiten Bardwaj, Ind.	36
Alan Barrett, Ind.	25
LD majority	1,654

BRENT EAST
(18 September 2003)
E. 57,778 T. 36.2%

Sarah Teather, LD	8,158
Robert Evans, Lab.	7,040
Uma Fernandes, C.	3,368
Noel Lynch, Green	638
Brian Butterworth, Soc. All.	361
Khidori Fawzi Ibrahim, Public Services Not War	219
Winston McKenzie, Ind.	197
Kelly McBride, Ind.	189
Harold Immanuel, Ind. Lab.	188
Brian Hall, UK Ind.	140
Iris Cremer, Soc. Lab.	111
Neil Walsh, Ind.	101
Alan Howling Lord Hope, Loony	59
Aaron Barschack, No Description	37
Jiten Bardwaj, No Description	35
Rainbow George Weiss, www.xat.org.	11
LD majority	1,118

OGMORE
(14 February 2002)
E. 52,209 T. 35.2%

Huw Irranca-Davies, Lab.	9,548
Bleddyn Hancock, PC	3,827
Veronica Watkins, LD	1,608
Guto Bebb, C.	1,377
Christopher Herriot, Soc. Lab.	1,152
Jonathan Spink, Green	250
Jeff Hurford, WSA	205
Leslie Edwards, Loony	187
Captain Beany, Bean	122
Revd David Braid, Ind.	100
Lab. majority	5,721

IPSWICH
(22 November 2001)
E. 68,244 T. 40.2%

Chris Mole, Lab.	11,881
Paul West, C.	7,794
Ms Tessa Munt, LD	6,146
Dave Cooper, CPA	581
Jonathan Wright, UK Ind.	276
Tony Slade, Green	255
John Ramirez, LCA	236
Peter Leech, Soc. All.	152
Nicholas Winskill, EIP	84
Lab. majority	4,087

A by-election for Hartlepool was held on 30 September 2004 following the resignation of Peter Mandelson. *See* Stop Press.

PRIME MINISTERS

Over the centuries there has been some variation in the determination of the dates of appointment of Prime Ministers. Where possible, the date given is that on which a new Prime Minister kissed the Sovereign's hands and accepted the commission to form a ministry. However, until the middle of the 19th century the dating of a commission or transfer of seals could be the date of taking office. Where the composition of the Government changed, e.g. became a coalition, but the Prime Minister remained the same, the date of the change of government is given.

YEAR APPOINTED	
1721	Sir Robert Walpole, Whig
1742	The Earl of Wilmington, Whig
1743	Henry Pelham, Whig
1754	The Duke of Newcastle, Whig
1756	The Duke of Devonshire, Whig
1757	The Duke of Newcastle, Whig
1762	The Earl of Bute, Tory
1763	George Grenville, Whig
1765	The Marquess of Rockingham, Whig
1766	The Earl of Chatham, Whig
1767	The Duke of Grafton, Whig
1770	Lord North, Tory
1782 March	The Marquess of Rockingham, Whig
1782 July	The Earl of Shelburne, Whig
1783 April	The Duke of Portland, Coalition
1783 Dec.	William Pitt, Tory
1801	Henry Addington, Tory
1804	William Pitt, Tory
1806	The Lord Grenville, Whig
1807	The Duke of Portland, Tory
1809	Spencer Perceval, Tory
1812	The Earl of Liverpool, Tory
1827 April	George Canning, Tory
1827 Aug.	Viscount Goderich, Tory
1828	The Duke of Wellington, Tory
1830	The Earl Grey, Whig
1834 July	The Viscount Melbourne, Whig
1834 Nov.	The Duke of Wellington, Tory
1834 Dec.	Sir Robert Peel, Tory
1835	The Viscount of Melbourne, Whig
1841	Sir Robert Peel, Tory
1846	Lord John Russell (later The Earl Russell), Whig
1852 Feb.	The Earl of Derby, Tory
1852 Dec.	The Earl of Aberdeen, Peelite
1855	The Viscount Palmerston, Liberal
1858	The Earl of Derby, Conservative
1859	The Viscount Palmerston, Liberal
1865	The Earl Russell, Liberal
1866	The Earl of Derby, Conservative
1868 Feb.	Benjamin Disraeli, Conservative
1868 Dec.	William Gladstone, Liberal
1874	Benjamin Disraeli, Conservative
1880	William Gladstone, Liberal
1885	The Marquess of Salisbury, Conservative
1886 Feb.	William Gladstone, Liberal
1886 July	The Marquess of Salisbury, Conservative
1892	William Gladstone, Liberal
1894	The Earl of Rosebery, Liberal
1895	The Marquess of Salisbury, Conservative
1902	Arthur Balfour, Conservative
1905	Sir Henry Campbell-Bannerman, Liberal
1908	Herbert Asquith, Liberal
1915	Herbert Asquith, Coalition
1916	David Lloyd-George, Coalition
1922	Andrew Bonar Law, Conservative
1923	Stanley Baldwin, Conservative
1924 Jan.	Ramsay MacDonald, Labour
1924 Nov.	Stanley Baldwin, Conservative
1929	Ramsay MacDonald, Labour
1931	Ramsay MacDonald, Coalition
1935	Stanley Baldwin, Coalition
1937	Neville Chamberlain, Coalition
1940	Winston Churchill, Coalition
1945 May	Winston Churchill, Conservative
1945 July	Clement Attlee, Labour
1951	Sir Winston Churchill, Conservative
1955	Sir Anthony Eden, Conservative
1957	Harold Macmillan, Conservative
1963	Sir Alec Douglas-Home, Conservative
1964	Harold Wilson, Labour
1970	Edward Heath, Conservative
1974	Harold Wilson, Labour
1976	James Callaghan, Labour
1979	Margaret Thatcher, Conservative
1990	John Major, Conservative
1997	Anthony Blair, Labour

LEADERS OF THE OPPOSITION

The office of Leader of the Opposition was officially recognised in 1937 and a salary was assigned to the post.

YEAR APPOINTED	
1916	Herbert Asquith, Liberal
1918	William Adamson, Labour
1921	John Clynes, Labour
1922	Ramsay MacDonald, Labour (leader of official Opposition)
1924	Stanley Baldwin, Conservative
1929	Stanley Baldwin, Conservative
1931	Arthur Henderson, Labour (leader of Labour Opposition)
1931	George Lansbury, Labour
1935	Clement Attlee, Labour
1945	Clement Attlee, Labour
1945	Winston Churchill, Conservative
1951	Clement Attlee, Labour
1955	Hugh Gaitskell, Labour
1963	Harold Wilson, Labour
1965	Edward Heath, Conservative
1974	Edward Heath, Conservative
1970	Harold Wilson, Labour
1975	Margaret Thatcher, Conservative
1979	James Callaghan, Labour
1980	Michael Foot, Labour
1983	Neil Kinnock, Labour
1992	John Smith, Labour
1994	Anthony Blair, Labour
1997	William Hague, Conservative
2001	Iain Duncan Smith, Conservative
2003	Michael Howard, Conservative

THE GOVERNMENT

THE CABINET AS AT 10 SEPTEMBER 2004

Prime Minister, First Lord of the Treasury and Minister for the Civil Service
The Rt. Hon. Tony Blair, MP (since May 1997)
Deputy Prime Minister and First Secretary of State
The Rt. Hon. John Prescott, MP, *Deputy Prime Minister* (since May 1997) and *First Secretary of State* (since June 2001)
Chancellor of the Exchequer
The Rt. Hon. Gordon Brown, MP (since May 1997)
Leader of the House of Commons, Lord Privy Seal and Secretary of State for Wales
The Rt. Hon. Peter Hain, MP (since June 2003)
Secretary of State for Constitutional Affairs and Lord Chancellor
The Rt. Hon. The Lord Falconer of Thoroton, QC (since June 2003)
Secretary of State for Foreign and Commonwealth Affairs
The Rt. Hon. Jack Straw, MP (since June 2001)
Secretary of State for the Home Department
The Rt. Hon. David Blunkett, MP (since June 2001)
Secretary of State for Environment, Food and Rural Affairs
The Rt. Hon. Margaret Beckett, MP (since June 2001)
Secretary of State for International Development (since October 2003)
The Rt. Hon. Hilary Benn, MP
Secretary of State for Transport (since May 2002) *and Secretary of State for Scotland* (since June 2003)
The Rt. Hon. Alistair Darling, MP
Secretary of State for Health
The Rt. Hon. John Reid, MP (since June 2003)
Secretary of State for Northern Ireland
The Rt. Hon. Paul Murphy (since October 2002)
Secretary of State for Defence
The Rt. Hon. Geoff Hoon, MP (since October 1999)
Secretary of State for Work and Pensions
The Rt. Hon. Alan Johnson, MP (since September 2004)
Leader of the House of Lords and Lord President of the Council (since October 2003)
The Rt. Hon. Baroness Amos
Secretary of State for Trade and Industry
The Rt. Hon. Patricia Hewitt, MP (since June 2001)
Secretary of State for Education and Skills
The Rt. Hon. Charles Clarke, MP (since October 2002)
Secretary of State for Culture, Media and Sport
The Rt. Hon. Tessa Jowell, MP (since June 2001)
Parliamentary Secretary to the Treasury (Chief Whip)
The Rt. Hon. Hilary Armstrong, MP (since June 2001)
Minister Without Portfolio and Party Chair
The Rt. Hon. Ian McCartney, MP (since June 2003)
Chief Secretary to the Treasury
The Rt. Hon. Paul Boateng, MP (since May 2002)

The Minister of State at the Department for Work and Pensions with responsibility for Work, and the Government Chief Whip in the House of Lords attend Cabinet meetings although they are not members of the Cabinet.

LAW OFFICERS

Attorney-General
The Rt. Hon. Lord Goldsmith, QC (since June 2001)
Lord Advocate
Colin Boyd, QC (since February 2000)
Solicitor-General
The Rt. Hon. Harriet Harman, MP QC (since June 2001)
Solicitor-General for Scotland
Mrs Elish Angiolini, QC (since November 2001)
Advocate-General for Scotland
Dr Lynda Clark, QC, MP (since May 1999)

MINISTERS OF STATE

Cabinet Office
The Rt. Hon. Alan Milburn, MP *(Chancellor of the Duchy of Lancaster)*
Ruth Kelly, MP *(Cabinet Office)*
Culture, Media and Sport
The Rt. Hon. Richard Caborn, MP *(Sport and Tourism)*
The Rt. Hon. Estelle Morris, MP *(Arts)*
Defence
The Rt. Hon. Adam Ingram, MP *(Armed Forces)*
Office of the Deputy Prime Minister
The Rt. Hon. Keith Hill, MP *(Housing and Planning)*
The Rt. Hon. Nick Raynsford, MP *(Local Government and the Regions)*
The Rt. Hon. Lord Rooker *(Regeneration and Regional Development)*
Education and Skills
David Miliband, MP *(School Standards)*
The Rt. Hon. Margaret Hodge, MBE, MP *(Children)*
Dr Kim Howells, MP *(Universities)*
Environment, Food and Rural Affairs
Elliot Morley, MP *(Environment and Agri-Environment)*
The Rt. Hon. Alun Michael, MP *(Rural Affairs)*
Foreign and Commonwealth Office
Dr Denis MacShane, MP *(Europe)*
The Rt. Hon. The Baroness Symons of Vernham Dean *(Middle East)*
Douglas Alexander, MP *(Trade)*
Health
The Rt. Hon. John Hutton, MP
Rosie Winterton, MP
Home Office
The Rt. Hon. Baroness Scotland of Asthal, QC *(Criminal Justice System and Law Reform)*
Hazel Blears, MP *(Crime Reduction, Policing and Community Safety)*
Des Browne, MP *(Citizenship, Immigration and Counter-Terrorism)*
Northern Ireland Office
The Rt. Hon. John Spellar, MP
Trade and Industry
Mike O'Brien, MP *(E-Commerce, Energy and Competitiveness)*
Douglas Alexander, MP *(Trade)*
The Rt. Hon. Jacqui Smith, MP *(Industry and the Regions and Deputy Minister for Women)*

Transport
Tony McNulty, MP
Treasury
The Rt. Hon. Dawn Primarolo, MP *(Paymaster-General)*
Stephen Timms, MP *(Financial Secretary)*
John Healey, MP *(Economic Secretary)*
Work and Pensions
The Rt. Hon. Jane Kennedy, MP *(Work)*
Malcolm Wicks, MP *(Pensions)*

UNDER-SECRETARIES OF STATE

Constitutional Affairs
Baroness Ashton of Upholland
David Lammy, MP
Christopher Leslie, MP
Anne McGuire, MP *(Scotland)*
Don Touhig, MP *(Wales)*
Culture, Media and Sport
The Rt. Hon. Lord McIntosh of Haringey *(Media and Heritage)*
Defence
Ivor Caplin, MP *(Veterans)*
The Lord Bach *(Defence Procurement)*
Office of the Deputy Prime Minister
Yvette Cooper, MP
Phil Hope, MP
Education and Skills
The Lord Filkin, CBE
Ivan Lewis, MP *(Skills and Vocational Education)*
Stephen Twigg, MP *(Schools)*
Environment, Food and Rural Affairs
Ben Bradshaw, MP *(Nature, Conservation and Fisheries)*
The Lord Whitty of Camberwell *(Food, Farming and Sustainable Energy)*
Foreign and Commonwealth Office
Bill Rammell, MP
Chris Mullin, MP
Health
Melanie Johnson, MP
Lord Warner of Brockley
Dr Stephen Ladyman, MP
Home Office
Paul Goggins, MP *(Correctional Services and Reducing Re-offending)*
Caroline Flint, MP *(Anti-Drugs Co-ordination, Reducing Organised Crime and International and European Issues)*
Fiona Mactaggart, MP *(Race Equality, Community Policy and Civil Renewal)*
International Development
Gareth Thomas, MP
Northern Ireland Office
Barry Gardiner, MP
Ian Pearson, MP
Angela Smith, MP
Trade and Industry
The Lord Sainsbury of Turville, KG *(Science and Innovation)*
Gerry Sutcliffe, MP *(Employment Relations, Competition and Consumers)*
Nigel Griffiths, MP *(Small Business)*
Transport
David Jamieson, MP
Charlotte Atkins, MP
Work and Pensions
The Rt. Hon. The Baroness Hollis of Heigham *(Lords)*
Chris Pond, MP
Ms Maria Eagle, MP *(Disabled People)*

GOVERNMENT WHIPS

HOUSE OF LORDS
Captain of the Honourable Corps of the Gentlemen-at-Arms (Chief Whip)
The Rt. Hon. The Lord Grocott
Captain of The Queen's Bodyguard of the Yeomen of the Guard (Deputy Chief Whip)
The Lord Davies of Oldham
Lords-in-Waiting
The Lord Evans of Temple Guiting
The Lord Bassam of Brighton
The Lord Triesman
Baronesses-in-Waiting
The Baroness Farrington of Ribbleton
The Baroness Andrews, OBE
The Baroness Crawley

HOUSE OF COMMONS
Parliamentary Secretary to the Treasury (Chief Whip)
The Rt. Hon. Hilary Armstrong, MP
Treasurer of HM Household (Deputy Chief Whip)
Bob Ainsworth, MP
Comptroller of HM Household
The Rt. Hon. Thomas McAvoy, MP
Vice-Chamberlain of HM Household
Jim Fitzpatrick, MP
Lords Commissioners of HM Treasury
John Heppell, MP; Nick Ainger, MP; Jim Murphy, MP; Joan Ryan, MP; Derek Twigg, MP
Assistant Whips
Fraser Kemp, MP; Charlotte Atkins, MP; Paul Clark, MP; Vernon Coaker, MP; Gillian Merron, MP; Margaret Moran, MP; Bridget Prentice, MP; Tom Watson, MP

GOVERNMENT DEPARTMENTS

THE CIVIL SERVICE

Under the Next Steps programme, launched in 1988, many semi-autonomous executive agencies were established to carry out much of the work of the Civil Service. Executive agencies operate within a framework set by the responsible minister which specifies policies, objectives and available resources. All executive agencies are set annual performance targets by their Minister. Each agency has a chief executive, who is responsible for the day-to-day operations of the agency and who is accountable to the minister for the use of resources and for meeting the agency's targets. The minister accounts to Parliament for the work of the agency. Nearly 80 per cent of civil servants now work in executive agencies. In April 2003 there were about 542,770 permanent civil servants.

The Senior Civil Service was created in 1996 and on 1 April 2002 comprised 4,020 staff from Permanent Secretary to the former Grade 5 level, including all agency chief executives. All Government departments and executive agencies are now responsible for their own pay and grading systems for civil servants outside the Senior Civil Service.

SALARIES 2004–5

MINISTERIAL SALARIES *from 1 April 2004*

Ministers who are Members of the House of Commons receive a parliamentary salary (£57,485) in addition to their ministerial salary.

Prime Minister	£121,437
Cabinet minister (Commons)	£72,862
Cabinet minister (Lords)	£98,899
Minister of State (Commons)	£37,796
Minister of State (Lords)	£77,220
Parliamentary Under-Secretary (Commons)	£28,688
Parliamentary Under-Secretary (Lords)	£67,255

SPECIAL ADVISERS' SALARIES *from 1 April 2004*

Special advisers to Government Ministers are paid out of public funds; their salaries are negotiated individually, but are usually in the range £36,347 to £96,213.

CIVIL SERVICE SALARIES *from 1 April 2004*

Senior Civil Servants

Permanent Secretary	£121,100–£256,550
Band 3	£90,867–£192,424
Band 2	£73,762–£155,008
Band 1A	£62,004–£122,938
Band 1	£53,451–£112,248

Staff are placed in pay bands according to their level of responsibility and taking account of other factors such as experience and marketability. Movement within and between bands is based on performance. Following the delegation of responsibility for pay and grading to Government departments and agencies from 1 April 1996, it is no longer possible to show service-wide pay rates for staff outside the Senior Civil Service.

GOVERNMENT DEPARTMENTS

CABINET OFFICE

70 Whitehall, London SW1A 2AS
Switchboard 020-7276 3000 T 020-7276 1234
W www.cabinet-office.gov.uk

The Cabinet Office has four main roles: to support the Prime Minister in leading the Government; to support the Government in transacting its business; to lead and support the reform and delivery programme and to co-ordinate security and intelligence. The Department is headed by the Chancellor of the Duchy of Lancaster and has one Minister of State. The Cabinet Office has two Executive Agencies: The Government Car and Despatch Agency (GCDA) and the Central Office of Information (COI Communications) which is a department in its own right and operates as a Trading Fund.

Prime Minister and Minister for the Civil Service, The Rt. Hon. Tony Blair, MP
Principal Private Secretary to the Prime Minister and Head of Policy Directorate, Ivan Rogers
Chancellor of the Duchy of Lancaster, The Rt. Hon. Alan Milburn, MP
Parliamentary Private Secretary, Kevin Brennan, MP
Principal Private Secretary, Tony Sampson
Assistant Private Secretaries, Helen Gahir; Michelle Duncan
Minister for the Cabinet Office, Ruth Kelly, MP
Private Secretary, Georgia Hutchinson
Secretary of the Cabinet and Head of the Home Civil Service, Sir Andrew Turnbull, KCB, CVO
Principal Private Secretary, Penny Ciniewicz
Private Secretary, Sue Pither
Assistant Private Secretaries, Rebecca Mupita; Jeanne Bilbrough
Security and Intelligence Co-ordinator and Permanent Secretary, Sir David Omand, GCB
Principal Private Secretary, Dominic Fagan
Private Secretary, Lisa Harlow
Minister without Portfolio and Party Chair, The Rt. Hon. Ian McCartney, MP
Parliamentary Private Secretary, Gareth Thomas, MP

CEREMONIAL SECRETARIAT
Great Smith Street, London SW1P 3BQ
T 020-7276 2777
Ceremonial Officer, Mrs Gay Catto

CIVIL CONTINGENCIES SECRETARIAT
10 Great George Street, London SW1P 3AE
Head, Susan Scholefield, CMG

DEFENCE AND OVERSEAS AFFAIRS SECRETARIAT
Prime Minister's Foreign Policy Adviser and Head of Secretariat, Sir Nigel Sheinwald, KCMG
Deputy Head, Desmond Bowen, CMG

ECONOMIC AND DOMESTIC SECRETARIAT
Director, Paul Britton, CB
Deputy Head, Robin Fellgett

EUROPEAN SECRETARIAT
Prime Minister's European Policy Adviser and Head of Secretariat, Kim Darroch, CMG
Deputy Head, Katrina Williams

INTELLIGENCE AND SECURITY SECRETARIAT
Director, Security and Intelligence, Chris Wright
Chief of the Assessments Staff, Tim Dowse

OFFICE OF THE COMMISSIONER FOR PUBLIC APPOINTMENTS (OCPA)
35 Great Smith Street, London SW1P 3BQ
T 020-7276 2625
The Commissioner for Public Appointments is responsible for monitoring, regulating and providing advice to departments on 12,000 ministerial appointments to public bodies. The Commissioner publishes a Code of Practice, guidance for departments and an annual report. The Commissioner can investigate complaints about the way in which appointments were made or applicants treated.
Commissioner for Public Appointments, Dame Rennie Fritchie, DBE
Senior Policy Adviser, Alistair Howie
Secretary to the Commissioner and Head of the Office, Jim Barron

OFFICE OF THE CIVIL SERVICE COMMISSIONERS (OCSC)
35 Great Smith Street, London SW1P 3BQ
T 020-7276 2615
The independent Civil Service Commissioners are the custodians of the principle of selection on merit by fair and open competition; they publish a Recruitment Code and audit departments' and agencies' performance against it. When the most senior posts are opened to people from outside the Service, the Commissioners normally chair the recruitment process. The Commissioners also act as an independent appeals body under the Civil Service Code.
First Commissioner, Baroness Usha Prashar, CBE
Commissioners (part-time), D. Bell; P. Bounds; J. Boyle; Ms B. Curtis; Ms S. Forbes, CBE; Dame Rennie Fritchie, DBE; Prof. E. Gallagher, CBE; H. Hamill, CB; G. Lemos, CMG; A. MacDonald, CB; G. Maddrell; Dr M. Semple, OBE
Secretary to the Commissioners and Head of the Office, Jim Barron

REGULATORY IMPACT UNIT (RIU)
22 Whitehall, London SW1A 2WH
T 020-7276 2193
The Regulatory Impact Unit (RIU) works with other Government departments, agencies and regulators to help ensure that regulations are fair and effective, and helps reduce bureaucracy. The RIU also examines the impact on the voluntary sector, charities and the public sector and supports the work of the Better Regulation Task Force.
Director, Simon Virley
Deputy Directors, M. Courtney; Ms J. Cruickshank; I. Morfett; Ms K. Hill; Dr P. Rushbrook; P. Clarke

THE PRIME MINISTER'S DELIVERY UNIT
1 Horse Guards Road, London SW1A 2HQ
T 020-7270 5811
The Prime Minister's Delivery Unit was established in June 2001. Its main role is to ensure the delivery of the Prime Minister's top priority outcomes in the public services sector by 2005. The Unit reports to the Prime Minister through the Head of the Civil Service and the Minister for the Cabinet Office. Following the Spending Review 2002 the Delivery Unit now shares responsibility with the Treasury for the joint Public Service Agreement (PSA) target to improve public services by working with departments to help them meet their PSA targets consistently with the fiscal rules. The Unit's work is carried out by a team of around 40 people drawn from the public and private sectors. The Unit also draws on the expertise of a wider group of Associates with experience of successful delivery in the public, private and voluntary sectors.
Prime Minister's Chief Adviser on Delivery, Prof. Michael Barber
Deputy Directors, William Jordan; Peter Thomas

E-GOVERNMENT UNIT
Stockley House, 130 Wilton Road, Victoria, London SW1V 1LQ
T 020-7276 3283
The e-Government Unit works with departments to efficiently deliver public services by joining up electronic government services with the needs of customers. It also provides sponsorship of Information Assurance. The e-Government Unit takes on the work previously undertaken by the Office of the e-Envoy.
Head of e-Government, Ian Watmore

STRATEGY UNIT (SU)
Admiralty Arch, The Mall, London SW1A 2WH
T 020-7277 1881
The Strategy Unit (SU) is the result of a merger of the Performance and Innovation Unit (PIU) and the Prime Minister's Forward Strategy Unit (PMFSU). The Strategy Unit carries out long-term strategic reviews and policy analysis which can take several forms: reviews of major areas of policy; studies of cross-cutting policy issues; and strategic audit. The Unit undertakes work on a wide range of policy areas, including: e-commerce; rural policy; modernising central government; the future of the Post Office; recovery of criminal assets; adoption; resource productivity; workforce development; ethnic minorities; GM crops and alcohol misuse.
Executive Director, Jamie Rentoul
Deputy Directors, S. Aldridge; Ms P. Greer; Ms C. Laing

THE PRIME MINISTER'S OFFICE OF PUBLIC SERVICES REFORM
22 Whitehall, London SW1A 2WH
T 020-7276 3600
W www.pm-gov.uk/opsr
To strengthen the Government's ability to improve public services, the Prime Minister established the Office of Public Services Reform in 2001, based within the Cabinet Office. The Unit reports directly to the Prime Minister through the Cabinet Secretary. Its role is to advise and work with the Prime Minister and departments in order to implement the following four principles of reform and deliver customer-focused public services. The principles of reform are: to provide standards within a framework of clear accountability; to give local leaders responsibility and accountability for delivery; to meet the diversity of customer needs, to reduce bureaucracy and to offer greater incentives and rewards for staff; and to provide different ways for users to receive services.

The Unit works on local service projects within health, education, the criminal justice system and local government. It also leads work on understanding customers.

Prime Minister's Adviser on Public Services Reform, Dr Wendy Thomson

CENTRAL SPONSOR FOR INFORMATION ASSURANCE (CSIA)
Stockley House, 130 Wilton Road, London SW1V 1LQ
T 020-7276 3267

The CSIA was established on 1 April 2003 to assure the Government that risks to the national information infrastructure are managed appropriately. It works with partners in the public and private sectors, as well as its international counterparts, to help safeguard the nation's IT and telecommunications services.

Director, Dr Steve Marsh

CORPORATE DEVELOPMENT GROUP (CDG)
Admiralty Arch, The Mall, London SW1A 2WH
T 020-7276 1566 F 020-7276 1404

Director-General, Ms A. Perkins, CB
Directors, David Spencer; Anne-Marie Lawlor; Tim Kemp; Richard Furlong

GOVERNMENT INFORMATION AND COMMUNICATION SERVICE (GICS)
10 Great George St, London SW1P 3AE
T 020-7276 5090

The Office of the Head of the Government Information and Communication Service is responsible for the standards of the service provided by the GICS to Whitehall departments and their agencies. It supports the Head of the Civil Service's work and provides guidance on the strategic development of the GICS, its professional practice, recruitment and promotion. Its focus is on cross-departmental communication and management of the central GICS units.

Deputy Head of GICS (Corporate and HR Strategy), Ms S. Jenkins
Director of GICS Development Centre, T. Dunmore
Director of Operations, Ms L. Salisbury
Head of GICS Operating Unit, Ms C. McCall
Director, Media Monitoring Unit, Ms E. Thwaites
Head of Government News Network, R. Haslam
Regional Director, Eastern, Ms M. Basham, 2nd Floor, Block A1, Westbrook Centre, Milton Road, Cambridge CB4 1YG
Regional Director, East Midlands, P. Smith, The Belgrave Centre, Talbot Street, Nottingham NG1 5GG
Regional Director, West Midlands, B. Garner, Five Ways House, Islington Row, Middleway, Edgbaston, Birmingham B15 1SH
Regional Director, North East, C. Child, Wellbar House, Gallowgate, Newcastle upon Tyne NE1 4TB
Regional Director, North West, Ms E. Jones, Sunley Tower, Piccadilly Plaza, Manchester M1 4BE
Regional Director, London and South East, Ms V. Burdon, Hercules Road, London SE1 7DU
Regional Director, South West, P. Whitbread, The Pithay, Bristol BS1 2PB
Regional Director, Yorkshire and the Humber, Ms W. Miller, City House, New Station Street, Leeds LS1 4JG

CORPORATE MANAGEMENT
Managing Director Accounting Officer, Colin Balmer
Director of Finance, Jerry Page
Director, Business Development, John Sweetman
Director, Human Resources, Claudette Francis
Deputy Director, Histories and Records, Tessa Stirling
Deputy Director, Infrastructure, Eric Hepburn

HER MAJESTY'S STATIONERY OFFICE
St Clements House, 2–16 Colegate, Norwich NR3 1BQ
T 01603-621000

Controller, Carol Tullo

COMMUNICATION GROUP
70 Whitehall, London SW1A 2AS
T 020-7270 3000

Advises on presentation of departmental policy and activity. Handles media and public relations activities other than recruitment publicity and advertising.

Director of Communication, Melanie Leech
Head of News, John Bretherton

EXECUTIVE AGENCIES

GOVERNMENT CAR AND DESPATCH AGENCY
46 Ponton Road, London SW8 5AX
T 020-7217 3839 F 020-7217 3840

The Agency provides secure transport and mail distribution to Government and the public sector.

Chief Executive, N. Matheson

COI COMMUNICATIONS
Hercules Road, London SE1 7DU
T 020-7928 2345 F 020-7928 5037

COI Communications (The Central Office of Information) is a Government agency which offers consultancy, procurement and project management services to central Government. Administrative responsibility for the COI rests with the Minister for the Cabinet Office.

Chief Executive, A. Bishop
Deputy Chief Executive, P. Buchanan
Senior Personal Secretary, Mrs I. MacMull

MANAGEMENT BOARD
Members, I. Hamilton; Mrs S. Whetton; G. Beasant; A. Wade; Ms E. Lochhead
Secretary, Mrs I. MacMull

PRIME MINISTER'S OFFICE
10 Downing Street, London SW1A 2AA
T 020-7270 3000 F 020-7925 0918
W www.number-10.gov.uk

Prime Minister, The Rt. Hon Tony Blair, MP
Chief of Staff, Jonathan Powell
Principal Private Secretary and Head of Policy Directorate, Ivan Rogers
Parliamentary Private Secretary, David Hanson, MP
Personal Assistant to Prime Minister (Diary), Katie Kay
Director of Political Operations, Pat McFadden
Head of Policy, Geoff Mulgan
Policy Directorate, Carey Oppenheim; Simon Morys; Geoffrey Norris; Arnab Banerji; Sarah Hunter; Simon Stevens; Justin Russell; Clare Sumner; Alasdair McGowan; Matthew Elson; Martin Hurst; Matthew Taylor; Liz Lloyd
Foreign Policy, Matthew Rycroft; David Quarrey; Roger Liddle
Head of Delivery Unit, Prof. Michael Barber
Head of the Office of Public Services Reform, Wendy Thomson
Head of Strategy Unit, Geoff Mulgan

Research and Information Unit, Catherine Rimmer
Director of Communications and Strategy, David Hill
Strategic Communications Unit, Godric Smith
Direct Communications Unit, Jan Taylor
Prime Minister's Official Spokesman, Tom Kelly
Director of Events and Visits, Jo Gibbons
Director of Government Relations, The Baroness Margaret Morgan of Huyton
Secretary for Appointments, William Chapman
Advisor on Education, Public Services and Constitutional Reform, Andrew Adonis
Advisor on Foreign Policy and Head of the Overseas and Defence Secretariat, Nigel Sheinwald
Advisor on European Union Affairs and Head of the European Secretariat, Sir Stephen Wall
Parliamentary Clerk, Nicholas Howard

OFFICE OF THE DEPUTY PRIME MINISTER

26 Whitehall, London SW1A 2WH
T 020-7944 4400
W www.odpm.gov.uk

The Office of the Deputy Prime Minister (ODPM) was created in May 2002 taking on responsibility for policy areas from both the Department for Transport, Local Government and the Regions and the Cabinet Office. The ODPM brings together regional and local government (including the Regional Government Offices), housing, planning and regeneration, social exclusion and neighbourhood renewal.

Regional and local government and the Government's cross-cutting agenda for neighbourhood renewal and social inclusion are administered by a single department under the Deputy Prime Minister, who also has responsibility for implementing regional government and local government white papers. The Deputy Prime Minister will continue to act as the Prime Minister's deputy across the full range of domestic and international business, chairing a range of key Cabinet committees.

Deputy Prime Minister and First Secretary of State, The Rt. Hon. John Prescott, MP
Private Secretary, Peter Betts
Minister of State, The Rt. Hon. Nick Raynsford, MP *(Local Government and the Regions)*
Private Secretary, Angela Kerr
Minister of State, The Rt. Hon. Lord Rooker *(Regeneration and Regional Development)*
Private Secretary, Jenny Mainland
Minister of State, Keith Hill, MP *(Housing and Planning)*
Private Secretary, Mark Livesey
Parliamentary Under-Secretary, Phil Hope, MP
Private Secretary, Karen Abbott
Parliamentary Under-Secretary, Yvette Cooper, MP
Private Secretary, Patrick Owen
Permanent Secretary, Mavis McDonald
Private Secretary, Andrew Vaughan
Chief Scientist, David Fisk

DIRECTORATE OF COMMUNICATION
Director of Communication Directorate, Derek Plews
Deputy Director of Communications, Jane Groom

CORPORATE STRATEGY AND RESOURCES GROUP
Director-General, Corporate Strategy and Resources Group, Peter Unwin
Director, Mike Bailey *(HR and Workplace Services)*; Andrew Lean *(Finance)*; Michael Kell *(Analysis and Research)*; vacant *(Business Change and Delivery)*
Heads of Departments, David Buttress; Caroline Cousin; Janet Fortune: Andree Kerr; David Smith; Helen Edwards; Su Bonfanti; Alan Beard; Amanda McFeeters; Steve Simmonds; Chris Smith; Jan White; Peter Capell; Andrew Morrison; Bruce Oelman; Shona Dunn; Steph Coster; Cath Shaw

LEGAL DIRECTORATE
Director of Legal Directorate, Sandra Unerman
Heads of Departments, Pamela Conlan; Fred Croft; Gloria Hedley-Dent; David Jordan; Judith-Anne MacKenzie; Donatella Phillips; John Wright

LOCAL GOVERNMENT AND FIRE GROUP
Director-General, Local Government and Fire Group, Neil Kinghan
Directors, Lindsay Bell *(Local Government Finance)*; Clive Norris *(Fire and Rescue Service)*; John O'Brien *(Local Government Performance and Practice)*; David Prout *(Local Government Policy)*
Heads of Departments, Pam Williams; Stephen Claughton; Robert Davies; Meg Green; Andrew Allberry; Terry Crossley; Richard Gibson; Kevin Lloyd; Paul Rowsell; Geoff Tierney; Paul Downie; Sarah Sturrock; Sir Graham Meldrum; Dr David Peace; Diana Kahn; Dave Lawrence; Marie Winckler; Shelagh Prosser; Mandy Skinner

REGIONAL DEVELOPMENT GROUP
Director-General, Regional Development Group, Rob Smith
Directors, Richard Allan *(Regional Policy)*; Andrew Campbell *(Regional Co-ordination Unit)*; Alun Evans *(Civil Resilience)*
Heads of Departments, Nick Dexter; Ian Jones; Julie Anderson; Vince Brady; Christopher Bowden; Mike Reed; Richard Bruce; Philip Cox; Ian Scotter; Mitesh Dhanak

SUSTAINABLE COMMUNITIES GROUP
Director-General, Sustainable Communities Group, Richard McCarthy
Directors, Jeff Channing *(Thames Gateway)*; Brian Hackland *(Planning)*; David Lunts *(Urban Policy)*; Neil McDonald *(Housing)*; Andrew Wells *(Sustainable Communities)*
Heads of Departments, Mark Coulshed; Henry Cleary; Duncan Campbell; Michelle Banks; Peter Ruback; David Liston-Jones; Peter Matthew; David Edwards; Keith Thorpe; Pam Temple; Paul Everall; Richard Footitt; Dawn Eastmead; Anne Kirkham; Carol Sweetenham; Hilary Bartle; Helen Giles; Mike Ash; Lester Hicks; Joan Bailey; John Stambollouian; Lisette Simcock; Bob Ledsome; Joanna Key

TACKLING DISADVANTAGE GROUP
Director-General, Tackling Disadvantage Group, Joe Montgomery
Directors, Terrie Alafat *(Homelessness and Housing Support)*; Alan Davis *(Neighbourhood Strategy)*; Alan Riddell *(Neighbourhood Operations)*
Director, Social Exclusion Unit, Claire Tyler
Heads of Departments, John Bright; Carol Hayden; Allan Bowman; Patrick Allen; Martin Joseph; Teresa Vokes; Gordon Campbell; Ashley Horsey; Neil O'Connor; Wendy Jarvis; Marcus Bell; Sally Burlington; Vanessa Scarborough; Bert Provan; Ruth Stainer; Rosie Seymour

REGIONAL CO-ORDINATION UNIT
River Walk House, Millbank, London SW1P 4RR
T 020-7217 3550
Director-General, Rob Smith
Director, Teresa Vokes

CIVIL RESILIENCE DIRECTORATE
Director-General, Rob Smith
Regional Directors, Caroline Bowdler *(Government Office for the East)*; Jane Todd *(Government Office for the East Midlands)*; Liz Meek *(Government Office for London)*; Jonathon Blackie *(Government Office for the North East)*; Keith Barnes *(Government Office for the North West)*; Paul Martin *(Government Office for the South East)*; Jane Henderson *(Government Office for the South West)*; Graham Garbutt *(Government Office for the West Midlands)*; Felicity Everiss *(Government Office for Yorkshire and the Humber)*

EXECUTIVE AGENCIES

FIRE SERVICE COLLEGE
Moreton-in-Marsh, Gloucestershire, GL56 0RH
T 01608-650831 F 01608-651788
W www.fireservicecollege.ac.uk
The Fire Service College provides unique facilities for both practical and theoretical fire fighting, fire safety and accident and emergency training, including urban search and rescue and community safety.
Acting Chief Executive, Anne Frost

ORDNANCE SURVEY
Romsey Road, Southampton SO16 4GU
T 08456-050505 F 023-8079 2615
W www.ordnancesurvey.co.uk
The Ordnance Survey department carries out official surveying and definitive mapping of Great Britain.
Chief Executive, V. Lawrence

PLANNING INSPECTORATE
Temple Quay House, 2 The Square, Temple Quay, Bristol BS1 6PN T 0117-372 6372
Crown Buildings, Cathays Park, Cardiff CF10 3NQ
T 029-2082 3866 F 029-2082 5150
W www.planning-inspectorate.gov.uk
The Inspectorate deals with appeals against the decisions of local authorities on planning applications and appeals against local authority enforcement notices. It also provides inspectors who hold inquiries into objections to local authority planning.
Chief Executive, Katrine Sporle

THE QUEEN ELIZABETH II CONFERENCE CENTRE
Broad Sanctuary, London SW1P 3EE
T 020-7222 5000 F 020-7798 4200
W www.qeiicc.co.uk
The Centre provides secure conference facilities for national and international government and private sector use.
Chief Executive, John McCarthy

THE RENT SERVICE
5 Welbeck Street, London W1G 9YQ
T 020-7023 6000 F 020-7023 6222
W www.therentservice.gov.uk
The Agency combines 77 independent units previously administered by local authorities.
Chief Executive, Ms C. Copeland

DEPARTMENT FOR CONSTITUTIONAL AFFAIRS (DCA)

Selbourne House, 54–60 Victoria Street, London SW1E 6QW
T 020-7210 8500
W www.dca.gov.uk

The Department for Constitutional Affairs was created on 12 June 2003, as part of the Government's drive to modernise the constitution. It brings together most of the Lord Chancellor's Department, the UK devolution settlements and, for administrative purposes only, the staff of the Scotland Office and the Wales Office. The new department is charged with building fair, effective and accessible justice services, which contribute towards a safe and secure society and protect the rights of citizens; and to modernise the law and constitution. Its principal responsibilities include: in partnership with the Home Office and the Crown Prosecution Service to deliver an effective criminal justice system; in partnership with the Home Office to improve the effectiveness of the asylum system; to reform the constitution, in particular establishing a Supreme Court, and a Judicial Appointments Commission; to effectively manage the courts and many tribunals; until the appointment of the Commission, to undertake the appointment and training of the judiciary; to provide legal aid and legal services to help tackle social exclusion; to oversee the legal services market, including regulation and competition; to reform and revise English civil law particularly in the fields of freedom of information, privacy and data sharing, human rights, reform of the House of Lords, the constitutional relationship with the Channel Islands and the Isle of Man, royal, church and hereditary issues, electoral law and policy, referenda and Party funding.

The department employs over 11,500 civil servants, over 10,000 of whom work in courts and tribunals throughout the country. It includes a number of related bodies: the Law Commission; the Judicial Studies Board; the Official Solicitor and Public Trustee; the Legal Services Ombudsman; the Judge Advocate General's Office; the Magistrates' Court Service Inspectorate; the Commission for Judicial Appointments; the Information Commissioner's Office and the Council on Tribunals. It is the sponsor department for the Legal Services Commission. The Secretary of State for Constitutional Affairs is also responsible for the Land Registry, the Public Record Office, and the Court Service in Northern Ireland. The Scotland and Wales Offices continue to exist under the umbrella of the Department for Constitutional Affairs but report to the Secretaries of State for Scotland and Wales respectively.

Secretary of State for Constitutional Affairs and Lord Chancellor, The Rt. Hon. The Lord Falconer of Thoroton, QC
Principal Private Secretary, Mike Anderson
Special Adviser, Philip Bassett
Parliamentary Clerk, Ann Nixon
Parliamentary Under-Secretary, David Lammy, MP
Private Secretary, Edward Bowles
Parliamentary Under-Secretary, Christopher Leslie, MP
Private Secretary, Grant Morris
Parliamentary Under-Secretary, Baroness Ashton of Upholland
Private Secretary, Nicola Westmore
Permanent Secretary, Alex Allan
Private Secretary, Jade Cortes

PERMANENT SECRETARY'S OFFICE
Permanent Secretary and Clerk of the Crown in Chancery, Alex Allan
Clerk of the Chamber and Head of the Crown Office, C. I. P. Denyer

COMMUNICATIONS GROUP
T 020-7210 2022
Head of Communications, Lucian Hudson
Head of Corporate Communications and Projects, Mike Wicksteed

CLIENTS AND POLICY GROUP
T 020-7210 2022
Director-General, Dr J. Spencer
Director, Civil Justice and Legal Services Directorate, A. Finlay
Director, Asylum and Diversity, N. Smedley
Director, Constitution, A. McDonald
Heads of Divisions, Kay Birch; Keith Budgen; Ms S. Field; Ms S. Johnson; Judith Simpson; E. Adams; John Sills; Edwin Kilby; Belinda Crowe; A. Frazer; A. Maultby; Ms M. Shaw

FINANCE
T 020-7210 2801
Director-General, S. Ball
Director of Facilities Management, C. Lyne
Principal Finance Officer, A. Cogbill
Head of Internal Audit, A. Rummins

LEGAL AND JUDICIAL SERVICES
T 020-7210 2810
Directors-General, John Lyon; P. Jenkins
Heads of Divisions, A. Shaw *(Courts Policy)*; J. Powell *(Competitions (Courts))*; P. Farmer *(Information and Planning)*; R. Sams *(Competitions, Tribunals)*; D. Staff *(Pay, Pensions and Terms and Conditions)*; Ms M. Pigott and Ms J. Killick *(Policy and Correspondence)*; R. Heaton *(The Legal Adviser)*; Ms C. Johnston *(Family and Criminal)*; E. Robinson *(Asylum, Civil and Administrative Justice and Public Legal Services)*; A. Wallace *(Civil Law, Legal Services, EU and Devolution)*

CHIEF EXECUTIVE OPERATIONS
T 020-7210 8001
Chief Executive Operations and Second Permanent Secretary, Ian Magee

CHIEF EXECUTIVE AND DIRECTOR FIELD SERVICES
T 020-7210 1373
Acting Chief Executive, Sir Ron De Witt
Director, Kevin Pogson

ECCLESIASTICAL PATRONAGE
10 Downing Street, London SW1S 2AA
T 020-7930 4433

CROWN OFFICE
House of Lords, London SW1A 0PW
T 020-7219 4713

SUPREME COURT GROUP
Strand, London WC2A 2LL
T 020-7947 6000

EXECUTIVE AGENCIES

THE COURT SERVICE
Southside, 105 Victoria Street, London SW1E 6QT
T 020-7210 1646 F 020-7210 2059
W www.courtservice.gov.uk
The Court Service provides administrative support to the Supreme Court, the Crown Court, county courts and a number of tribunals in England and Wales.
Chief Executive (Acting), P. Handcock
Director of Human Resources (Acting), Ms H. Dudley
Director of Information Services, Communications Technologies and e-Delivery, Ms A. Vernon
Director of Programmes and Projects, D. Barr
Director of Purchasing and Contract Management, C. Lyne
Director of Tribunals, S. Smith
Head of Magistrates' Courts Administrative Division, N. Haighton
Programme Director Magistrates' Courts IT Division and LIBRA Project, N. Haighton

HM LAND REGISTRY
32 Lincoln Inn Fields, London WC2A 3PH
T 020-7917 8888

NATIONAL ARCHIVES
Ruskin Avenue, Kew, Surrey TW9 4DU
T 020-8876 3444

PUBLIC GUARDIANSHIP OFFICE
Archway Tower, 2 Junction Road, London N19 5SZ
T 0845-330 2900

DEPARTMENT FOR CULTURE, MEDIA AND SPORT

2–4 Cockspur Street, London SW1Y 5DH
T 020-7211 6200 F 020-7211 6032
W www.culture.gov.uk
The Department for Culture, Media and Sport was established in July 1997 and is responsible for Government policy relating to the arts, broadcasting, press freedom and regulation, the film and music industries, museums and galleries, libraries, architecture and the historic environment, sport and recreation, tourism, the National Lottery, gambling, and alcohol and entertainment licensing.
Secretary of State for Culture, Media and Sport, The Rt. Hon. Tessa Jowell, MP
Principal Private Secretary, Heather Rogers
Special Advisers, Bill Bush; Nick Bent
Parliamentary Private Secretary, Gordon Marsden, MP
Minister of State, The Rt. Hon. Estelle Morris, MP *(Arts)*
Private Secretary, David McLaren
Parliamentary Private Secretary, Dr Howard Stoate, MP
Minister of State, The Rt. Hon. Richard Caborn, MP *(Sport and Tourism)*
Private Secretary, Graeme Cornell
Parliamentary Private Secretary, Ben Chapman, MP
Parliamentary Under-Secretary, The Rt. Hon. The Lord McIntosh of Haringey *(Media and Heritage)*
Private Secretary, Gareth Maybury
Permanent Secretary, Sue Street
Director-General, Children, Young People and Communities, Jeff Jacobs

STRATEGY AND COMMUNICATIONS DIRECTORATE
Head of Group, Siobhan Kenny
Head of News, Paddy Feeny
Head of Promotions and Publicity, Penny Dolby
Head of Strategy, Policy, and Delivery, David Roe

CORPORATE SERVICES DIRECTORATE
Head of Group, Nicholas Kroll
Head, Analytical Services, vacant
Head, Finance and Planning Division, Keith Smith
Head, Internal Audit, Michael Kirk
Head, Personnel and Central Services Division, Shaun Cove

ARTS AND CULTURE DIRECTORATE
Head of Group, Alan Davey
Director, Government Art Collection, Penny Johnson
Head, Architecture and Historic Environment Division, vacant
Head, Arts Division, Phil Clapp
Head, Museums and Cultural Property, Nigel Pittman
Head, Museums and Libraries Sponsorship, Richard Hartman
Head, Public Appointments, Honours and Modernisation, Janet Evans

CREATIVE INDUSTRIES, BROADCASTING, GAMBLING AND LOTTERY DIRECTORATE
Head of Group, Andrew Ramsay
Head, Broadcasting Division, Jon Zeff
Head, Creative Industries Division, Mark Ferrero
Head, Gambling and National Lottery Licensing, Elliot Grant
Head, National Lottery Distribution and Communities, Simon Broadley

TOURISM, LIBRARIES AND COMMUNITIES DIRECTORATE
Head of Group, Brian Leonard
Head, Alcohol and Entertainment Licensing, Andrew Cunningham
Head, Libraries and Communities, Vanessa Brand
Head, Tourism Division, Harry Reeves

SPORT DIRECTORATE
Head of Group, Nicky Roche
Head, Olympic Games Unit, Paul Bolt
Head, Sports Division, Paul Heron

EXECUTIVE AGENCY

ROYAL PARKS AGENCY
The Old Police House, Hyde Park, London W2 2UH
T 020-7298 2000 F 020-7298 2005
The agency is responsible for maintaining and developing the royal parks.
Chief Executive, William Weston, MVO

DEPARTMENT FOR EDUCATION AND SKILLS

Sanctuary Buildings, Great Smith Street, London SW1P 3BT
Caxton House, Tothill Street, London SW1H 9NA
Castle View House, East Lane, Runcorn, WA7 2GJ
Mowden Hall, Staindrop Road, Darlington DL3 9BG
Moorfoot, Sheffield S1 4PQ
T 08700-012345 **Public Enquiries** 08700-002288
E info@dfes.gsi.gov.uk W www.dfes.gov.uk

The Department for Education and Skills aims to help build a competitive economy and inclusive society by creating opportunities for everyone to develop their learning potential and achieve excellence in standards of education and levels of skills. The department's main objectives are to give children an excellent start in education and to enable young people and adults to develop and equip themselves with the skills, knowledge and personal qualities needed for life and work. The department also sponsors eleven non-departmental public bodies across a variety of professional disciplines and educational services.

Secretary of State for Education and Skills, The Rt. Hon. Charles Clarke, MP
Principal Private Secretary, Mela Watts
Private Secretary, Jenny Loosley
Special Advisers, Hannah Pawlby; Robert Hill
Parliamentary Private Secretary, Michael John Foster, MP
Minister of State for School Standards, David Miliband, MP
Private Secretary, Nick Carson
Parliamentary Private Secretary, Ian Cawsey, MP
Minister of State for Universities, Dr Kim Howells, MP
Private Secretary, Jo Ware
Parliamentary Private Secretary, David Borrow, MP
Minister of State for Children, The Rt. Hon. Margaret Hodge, MBE, MP
Private Secretary, Claire Carroll
Parliamentary Private Secretary, Meg Munn, MP
Parliamentary Under-Secretary of State for Schools, Stephen Twigg, MP
Private Secretary, Charles Deighton-Fox
Parliamentary Under-Secretary of State, The Lord Filkin, CBE
Private Secretary, Rebecca Beeton
Parliamentary Under-Secretary of State for Skills and Vocational Education, Ivan Lewis, MP
Private Secretary, Jo Bewley
Permanent Secretary, David Normington, CB
Private Secretary, Paul Price
Parliamentary Clerk, Jonathan Duff
Spokesman in the House of Lords, The Lord Filkin, CBE

STRATEGY AND COMMUNICATIONS DIRECTORATE
Director, Michael Stevenson
Heads of Divisions, Trevor Cook *(Press Office)*; D.-J. Collins *(News)*
Divisional Managers, Yasmin Diamond *(Corporate Communications)*; Mel Brown *(Marketing and Publicity)*; Mohammad Haroon *(Regions, Delivery Support and Regeneration)*; Diana Laurillard *(e-Learning Strategy Unit)*

SCHOOLS DIRECTORATE
Director-General, Peter Housden

SECONDARY EDUCATION GROUP
Director, Peter Wanless
Divisional Managers, Susanna Todd *(School Diversity)*; Neil Flint *(Academies Division)*; Barnaby Shaw *(School Improvement and Excellence)*; Jon Coles *(London Challenge Programme)*

STANDARDS AND EFFECTIVENESS UNIT
Directors, David Hopkins; Andrew McCully
Director of Innovation Unit, Mike Gibbons
Divisional Managers, Andrew McCully *(Pupil Standards)*; Hilary Emery *(Schools Directorate Adviser)*; Caroline Macready *(School Performance and Accountability)*
Leadership and Teacher Development, Richard Harrison

RESOURCES, INFRASTRUCTURE AND GOVERNANCE GROUP
Director, Stephen Crowne
Divisional Managers, Shan Scott *(School Admissions, Organisation and Governance)*; Andrew Wye; Lorraine Chapman *(School and LEA Funding)*; Sally Brooks *(Schools Capital and Buildings)*; Mukund Patel *(Schools Building and Design Unit)*; Penny Jones *(School Transport, Safety and Independent Schools)*

SCHOOL WORKFORCE UNIT
Director, Stephen Hillier
Deputy Directors, Stuart Edwards *(SWU Infrastructure)*; Ian Whitehouse *(SWU Pay and Performance Management)*; Heath Monk *(School Workforce Remodelling)*
SWU Team Leader, Pensions and Medical Fitness to Teach, Paul Bleasdale

PRIMARY EDUCATION AND E-LEARNING GROUP
Director, Helen Williams
Divisional Managers, Mela Watts *(Curriculum)*; Doug Brown *(ICT in Schools)*; Matthew Conway *(PE and School Sport and Club Links Project, Joint with Department for Culture, Media and Sport)*; Annabel Burns *(Ethnic Minority Achievement Project)*; Nick Baxter *(Improving Behaviour and Attendance)*

CHILDREN, YOUNG PEOPLE AND FAMILIES DIRECTORATE
Director-General, Tom Jeffery

SURE START UNIT
Director, Naomi Eisenstadt
Divisional Managers, David Jeffrey *(Quality and Standards)*, Jackie Doughty *(Programme Delivery)*; Nick Tooze *(Infrastructure)*; Sue Lewis *(Planning and Performance)*

SAFEGUARDING CHILDREN AND SUPPORTING FAMILIES GROUP
Director, Althea Efunshile
Divisional Managers, Colin Green *(Child Protection)*; David Holmes *(Looked After Children)*; Bruce Clark *(Vulnerable Children)*; Ann Gross *(Special Educational Needs and Disability)*; Ruth Kennedy *(Families)*

SUPPORTING CHILDREN AND YOUNG PEOPLE GROUP
Chief Executive, Anne Weinstock
Divisional Managers, Gordon McKenzie *(Cross Policy Group)*; Steve Jackson *(Connexions and the Regions)*; Jane Haywood *(Children and Youth)*; Marcus Bell *(Cross Whitehall)*; Kathy Bundred *(Children's Fund)*

CHILDREN'S WORKFORCE UNIT
Director, Jeanette Pugh
Divisional Managers, Chris Wells *(Children's Workforce Strategy)*; Peter Mucklow *(Information Sharing and Assessment)*

SCHOOLS DIRECTORATE AND CHILDREN, YOUNG PEOPLE AND FAMILIES DIRECTORATE JOINT COMMANDS
Divisional Manager, Policy and Performance, Christina Bienkowska

LOCAL TRANSFORMATION GROUP
Director, Sheila Scales
Divisional Managers, Robert Wood *(Local Authority Performance)*; Andrew Sargent *(Local Partnerships)*; Jenny Wright *(Change and Innovation)*; Richard Blows *(Local Implementation)*

STRATEGY GROUP
Director, Anne Jackson
Divisional Managers, Janet Grauberg *(Finance)*; Anne Jackson *(Children's Bill and Strategy)*

LIFELONG LEARNING DIRECTORATE
Director-General, Janice Shiner
Divisional Managers, Chris Barnham *(Offenders Learning and Skills Unit)*; John Temple *(Strategy and Funding)*

ADULT BASIC SKILLS STRATEGY UNIT
Director, Susan Pember
Deputy Directors, Mark Dawe *(Planning and Delivery)*; Barry Brooks *(Standards and Achievement)*

ADULT LEARNING GROUP
Director, Stephen Marston
Divisional Managers, Tim Down *(Adult Learner Support)*; Margaret Bennett *(Engaging Adults in Learning)*; Simon Perryman *(Sector Skills)*; Hugh Tollyfield *(Skills for Success)*; Madeleine Durie *(Strategic Policy and Programme Support)*; Jane Mark-Lawson and Heidi Adcock *(National and Regional Skills)*

LEARNING DELIVERY AND STANDARDS GROUP
Director, Peter Lauener
Divisional Managers, Trevor Tucknutt *(FE Strategy)*; James Turner *(Learning and Skills Unit)*; Jon Ashe *(Quality Improvement)*; Norman White *(ILA Project)*

STANDARDS UNIT
Director for Teaching and Learning, Jane Williams
Divisional Managers, David Taylor *(Teaching and Learning)*; Barbara Roberts *(Workforce Development)*

QUALIFICATIONS AND YOUNG PEOPLE
Director, Rob Hull
Divisional Managers, Sara Marshall *(Qualifications for Work)*; Celia Johnson *(School and College Qualifications)*; Trevor Fellowes *(Young People Learner Support)*; Alan Davies *(Young People's Policy)*; Jane Benham *(Examinations System)*; Carol Hunter *(14–19 Programmes)*

JOINT INTERNATIONAL UNIT
Director, Clive Tucker
Divisional Managers, Jane Evans *(European Union)*; Gordon Pursglove *(European Social Fund)*; Marie Niven *(International Relations)*

HIGHER EDUCATION DIRECTORATE
Director-General, Sir Alan Wilson
HE Adviser to Director-General, Nick Sanders
Head of HE Strategy Performance Unit, Elaine Hendry
Divisional Manager, HE Bill Team, Lesley Longstone

STRATEGY AND IMPLEMENTATION GROUP
Director, Ruth Thompson
Divisional Managers, Steve Geary *(Foundation Degrees, Employability and Progression Division)*; Linda Dale *(Quality and Participation)*; Rachel Green *(Funding and Research)*; Martin Williams *(Access and Modernisation)*

STUDENT FINANCE GROUP
Director, Michael Hipkins
Divisional Managers, Peter Swift *(Student Finance Policy)*; Ian Morrison *(Student Finance Delivery)*; Noreen Graham *(Student Finance Modernisation)*

CORPORATE SERVICES AND DEVELOPMENT DIRECTORATE
Director-General, Susan Thomas
Divisional Managers, Graham Archer *(Leadership and Personnel)*; Mike Daly *(Change)*; Graham Holley *(Learning Academy)*; Colin Moore *(Information Services)*; Paul Neill *(Commercial Services)*; Jan Stockwell and Dawn Jarvis *(Equality and Diversity Unit)*; Katie Driver *(e-Delivery)*

LEGAL ADVISER'S OFFICE
Legal Adviser, Jonathan Jones
Divisional Managers, Dudley Aries *(Lifelong Learning and School Workforce)*; Francis Clarke *(Effectiveness and Admissions)*; Penny Halnan *(Governance and Finance)*; Nic Ash *(Special Needs and Curriculum)*; Carol Davies *(Equality, Establishment and European Commission)*; Carola Geist-Divver *(Higher Education and Student Support)*; Sandra Walker *(Children's Services)*

FINANCE AND ANALYTICAL SERVICES DIRECTORATE
Director-General, Peter Makeham
Divisional Managers, Suzanne Orr *(Internal Audit)*; Ray Hinchcliffe *(Programme and Project Management Unit)*

FINANCE
Director, Stephen Kershaw
Divisional Managers, Peter Houten *(Finance Strategy)*; Marion Maddox *(Corporate Planning and Performance)*; Peter Connor, CBE *(Financial Accounting)*

ANALYTICAL SERVICES
Director, Paul Johnson
Divisional Managers, Audrey Brown *(Schools 1)*; Richard Bartholomew *(Children and Families)*; Tony Moody *(Youth)*; Karen Hancock *(Higher Education)*; Bob Butcher *(Adults)*; John Elliot *(Central Economics and International)*; Malcolm Britton *(Qualifications, Pupil Assessment and IT)*; Alan Cranston *(Data Agency Project)*

DEPARTMENT FOR ENVIRONMENT, FOOD AND RURAL AFFAIRS

Nobel House, 17 Smith Square, London SW1P 3JR
T 020-7238 3000 F 020-7238 6591
W www.defra.gov.uk

The Department for Environment, Food, and Rural Affairs is responsible for Government policies on agriculture, horticulture and fisheries in England and for policies relating to the food chain. In association with the agriculture departments of the Scottish Executive, the National Assembly for Wales and the Northern Ireland Office, and with the Intervention Board, the department is responsible for negotiations in the EU on the common agricultural and fisheries policies, and for single European market questions relating to its responsibilities. Its remit includes international agricultural and food trade policy.

The department exercises responsibilities for policies on climate change and international negotiations on sustainable development. It is also responsible for a range of pollution issues relating to waste and recycling, the protection and enhancement of the countryside and the marine environment, flood defence, GM crops, hunting, rural development and other rural issues. It is the licensing authority for veterinary medicines and the registration authority for pesticides. It administers policies relating to the control of animal, plant and fish diseases. It provides scientific, technical and professional services and advice to farmers, growers and ancillary industries, and commissions research to assist in the formulation and assessment of policy and to underpin applied research and development work done by industry. Responsibility for food safety and standards was transferred to the Food Standards Agency in April 2000.

Secretary of State for Environment, Food and Rural Affairs, The Rt. Hon. Margaret Beckett, MP
Principal Private Secretary, Gavin Ross
Private Secretaries, Robin Healey; Janice Kerr; Marianne Jenner
Special Advisers, Sheila Watson; Hazell Phillips
Minister of State (Environment and Agri-Environment), Elliot Morley, MP
Senior Private Secretary, Bradley Bates
Private Secretary, Emma Webbon
Minister of State (Rural Affairs and Urban Quality of Life), The Rt. Hon. Alun Michael, MP
Private Secretaries, Mike Burbridge; Rory Wallace
Assistant Private Secretaries, Louise Parry; Lewis Mortimer
Parliamentary Private Secretary, Peter Bradley, MP
Parliamentary Under-Secretary (Nature, Conservation and Fisheries), Ben Bradshaw, MP
Principal Private Secretary, Kathleen Cameron
Private Secretary, Jodie Tremelling
Parliamentary Under-Secretary (Farming, Food and Sustainable Energy), The Lord Whitty of Camberwell
Senior Private Secretary, Charlotte Middleton
Private Secretary, Emily Garner
Assistant Private Secretaries, Fiona Tranter; Mark Bainbridge
Permanent Secretary, Brian Bender, CB
Private Secretary, Claire Lewis
Assistant Private Secretary, Simon Huish

SUSTAINABLE FARMING, FOOD AND FISHERIES
T 020-7238 3000
Director-General, Andrew Lebrecht

FOOD CHAIN ANALYSIS AND FARMING
Director, vacant
Heads of Division, Ray Anderson; Andrea Young

EU AND INTERNATIONAL POLICY
Director, David Hunter
Heads of Division, Sarah Thomas; Andrew Lawrence

SUSTAINABLE AGRICULTURE AND LIVESTOCK PRODUCTS DIRECTORATE
Director, Sonia Phippard
Heads of Division, Nigel Atkinson; Dr Mike Segal; Andrew Slade

FOOD INDUSTRY AND CROPS DIRECTORATE
Director, John Robbs
Heads of Division, Andrew Perrins; Jeremy Cowper; David Jones; Andrew Kuyk; Callton Young; Heather Hamilton; Dr Stephen Hunter

FISHERIES DIRECTORATE
Fisheries Director, Rodney Anderson
Heads of Division, Peter Boyling; Richard Cowan; Barry Edwards; Linsay Harris; Terence Ilott; James Bradley
Chief Inspector, Sea Fisheries Inspectorate, Nigel Gooding

ECONOMICS AND STATISTICS DIRECTORATE
East Block, Whitehall Place, London SW1A 2HH
T 020-7270 6000
Director, David Thompson
Heads of Division, Simon Harding; Peter Helm; Peter Muriel; Stuart Platt; John Watson

NATURAL RESOURCES AND RURAL AFFAIRS DIRECTORATE GENERAL
T 020-7238 3000
Director-General, Ursula Brennan

NATURAL RESOURCES RURAL AFFAIRS
Director, Jane Brown
Heads of Division, Martin Nesbit; John Osmond; Alan Taylor; Mike Blackburn

RURAL POLICIES AND COMMUNITIES
Director, John Mills
Heads of Division, David Coleman; Graham Cory; Katheryn Packer; Richard Pullen; Peter Cleasby; Robin Mortimer

MODERNISING RURAL DELIVERY PROGRAMME
Director, Oona Muirhead
Heads of Division, Clare Hawley; Andrew Robinson

WILDLIFE, COUNTRYSIDE AND FLOOD MANAGEMENT DIRECTORATE
Director, Brian Harding
Heads of Division, Martin Brasher; Martin Capstick; Susan Carter; Linsay Harris; Terry Bird; Sheila McCabe; Peter Costigan

ANIMAL HEALTH AND WELFARE DIRECTORATE GENERAL
1A Page Street, London SW1P 4PQ T 020-7904 6000
Chief Veterinary Officer and Director-General, Debby Reynolds
Deputy Chief Veterinary Officer, vacant
Heads of Division, Nigel Gibbens; Fred Landeg; Ruth Lysons; David Pritchard; Alick Simmons; Peter Soul; David Bench; Nick Coulson

ANIMAL HEALTH AND WELFARE DIRECTORATE
Director, David Dawson
Heads of Division, Malcolm Hunt; Diana Linksey; Alison Reeves; John Bourne; Simon Hewitt

TSE GROUP
Director, Peter Nash
Heads of Division, Mandy Bailey; Catharine Boyle; Sue Eades; Francis Marlow

ENVIRONMENT PROTECTION DIRECTORATE GENERAL
Ashdown House, 123 Victoria Street, London SW1E 6DE
T 020-7238 6000
Director-General, Bill Stow, CB

ENVIRONMENT QUALITY AND WASTE DIRECTORATE
Director, Neil Thornton
Heads of Division, Sue Ellis; Bob Ryder; Martin Williams; Lindsay Cornish; Ivor Llewelyn; John Burns

CLIMATE, ENERGY AND ENVIRONMENTAL RISK DIRECTORATE
Director, Henry Derwent
Heads of Division, Colin Church; Jeremy Eppel; Sarah Hendry; Chris Leigh; Chris De Grouchy; Stephen De Souza

ENVIRONMENTAL PROTECTION STRATEGY DIRECTORATE
Director, Robert Lowson
Heads of Division, Scott Ghagan; John Custance; Bob Davies; Helen Marquard; Bob Davies; Roy Hathaway

WATER AND LAND DIRECTORATE
Director, Richard Bird
Heads of Division, Daniel Instone; John Roberts; Prof. Jeni Colbourne; Sarah Nason; Richard Wood

STRATEGY AND SUSTAINABLE DEVELOPMENT
Director, Jill Rutter
Heads of Division, Bronwen Jones; Andy Taylor

SOLICITOR AND LEGAL SERVICES DIRECTORATE GENERAL
Solicitor and Director-General Legal Services, Donald Macrae
Directors, Clare Sylvester; vacant
Heads of Division, Charles Allen; Chris Burke; Ian Corbett; Peter Davis; Brian Dickinson; Nigel Lefton; Alistair McGlone; Jonathan Robinson; Sue Spence; Anne Werbicki; Gisela Davis; Anne Sachs; Linda Dann
Chief Investigation Officer, Jan Panting

SCIENCE DIRECTORATE
Cromwell House, Dean Stanley Street, London SW1P 3JH
T 020-7238 6000
Chief Scientific Adviser and Head of Directorate, Prof. Howard Dalton, FRS
Deputy Chief Scientific Adviser, Miles Parker
Heads of Division, Dr Tony Burne; Dr John Sherlock; Michael Harrison

OPERATIONS AND SERVICE DELIVERY DIRECTORATE GENERAL
T 020-7238 3000
Director-General, Mark Addison

VETERINARY SERVICES
1A Page Street, London SW1P 4PQ T 020-7904 6000
Deputy Chief Veterinary Officer (Services), Martin Atkinson
Heads of Veterinary Services, Linda Smith *(West)*; Robert Paul *(North)*; Gareth Jones *(East)*; Derick McIntosh *(Scotland)*
Chief Veterinary Officer (Scotland), Charles Milne
Assistant Veterinary Officer (Wales), Tony Edwards
Service Delivery, Richard Drummond
Contingency Planning, Ann Waters

CORPORATE SERVICES DIRECTORATE
East Block, Whitehall Place, London SW1A 2HH
T 020-7270 6000
Director, Richard Allen
Heads of Division, Wendy Cartwright; Neil MacIntosh; Tony Nickson; Caroline Smith; John Nodder; Mike Watkind

COMMUNICATIONS DIRECTORATE
Director of Communications, Lucian Hudson
Head of Corporate Communications, Kelly Freeman
Head of News, Martyn Smith

E-BUSINESS DIRECTORATE
Government Buildings, Epsom Road, Guildford, Surrey GU1 2LD
T 01483-568121
Director, David Myers
Director of IT, Shaun Soper
Heads of Division, Peter Barber; David Brown; Pearl Scrivener; Ray Boguslawski; Denise McDonagh

DELIVERY STRATEGY TEAM
1A Page Street, London SW1P 4PQ T 020-7904 6000
Head, George Trevelyan

GOVERNMENT OFFICES, RURAL DIRECTORS
East of England, Building A, Westbrook Centre, Milton Road, Cambridge, CB4 1YG T 01223-372759
Rural Director, J. Rabagliati
East Midlands, The Belgrave Centre, Talbot Street, Nottingham, NG1 5GG T 0115-971 9971
Rural Director, G. Norbury
North East, Welbar House, Gallowgate, Newcastle-upon-Tyne, NE1 4TD T 0191-201 3300
Rural Director, J. Bainton
North West, Sunley Tower, Piccadilly Plaza, Manchester, M1 4BE T 0161-952 4000
Regional Director, N. Cumberlidge
South East, Bridge House, 1 Walnut Tree Close, Guildford, Surrey, GU1 4GA T 01483-882255
Regional Director, Ms A. Parker
South West, 4th and 5th Floors, The Pithay, Bristol, BS1 2PB T 0117-900 1700
Regional Director, T. Render
West Midlands, 77 Paradise Circus, Queensway, Birmingham, B1 2DT T 0121-212 5000
Regional Director, B. Davies
Yorkshire and the Humberside, PO Box 213, City House, New Station Street, Leeds, LS1 4US T 0113-280 0600
Regional Director, G. Kingston

RURAL DEVELOPMENT SERVICE
T 020-7238 3000
Head of Group, John Adams
Head of Technical Advice, Alan Hooper
Business Process Director, Jeff Robinson
ERDPIT Programme Director, Ann Tarran
Strategy Delivery and Implementation, Paul Egginton

RURAL DEVELOPMENT CENTRES AND MANAGERS
East, Block B, Government Buildings, Brooklands Avenue, Cambridge, CB2 2DR T 01223-462727
Regional Manager, Martin Edwards
East Midlands, Block 7, Government Buildings, Chalfont Drive, Nottingham, NG8 3SN T 0115-929 1191
Regional Manager, Sue Buckenham
North East, Government Buildings, Kenton Bar, Newcastle-upon-Tyne, NE5 3EW T 0191-214 1800
Regional Manager, Fiona Gough
North West, Electra Way, Crewe Business Park, Crewe, Cheshire, CW1 6GJ T 01270-754000
Regional Manager, Tony Percival
South East, Block A, Government Buildings, Coley Park, Reading, Berkshire, RG1 6DT T 0118-958 1222
Regional Manager, Nick Beard
South West, Block 3, Government Buildings, Burghill Road, Westbury-on-Trym, Bristol, BS10 6NJ T 0117-959 1000
Regional Manager, David Sisson
West Midlands, Block C, Government Buildings, Whittington Road, Worcester, WR5 2LQ T 01905-763355
Regional Manager, Geoff Sansome
Yorkshire and The Humber, Government Buildings, Otley Road, Lawnswood, Leeds, LS16 5QT T 0113-230 3750
Regional Manager, Mark Watson

FINANCE, PLANNING AND RESOURCES DIRECTORATE
East Block, Whitehall Place, London SW1A 2HH
T 020-7270 6000
Finance Director, Andrew Burchell
Deputy Director, Ian Grattidge
Heads of Division, Roger Atkinson; Julie Flint; David Rabey; Richard Wilkinson; Andrew Cox; Lee McDonough; David Littler

IMPROVEMENT AND DELIVERY GROUP
Cromwell House, Dean Bradley Street, London SW1P 3JH
T 020-7238 6000
Director and Secretary to the Management Board, Francesca Okosi
Heads of Division, Marcus Nisbet; Angela Evans; Richard Chalk

EXECUTIVE AGENCIES

CENTRE FOR ENVIRONMENT, FISHERIES AND AQUACULTURE SCIENCE
Pakefield Road, Lowestoft, Suffolk NR33 0HT
T 01502-562244 F 01502-513865
The Agency, established in April 1997, provides research and consultancy services in fisheries science and management, aquaculture, fish health and hygiene, environmental impact assessment, and environmental quality assessment.
Chief Executive, Dr P. Greig-Smith

CENTRAL SCIENCE LABORATORY (CSL)
Sand Hutton, York YO41 1LZ
T 01904-462000 F 01904-462111
The Central Science Laboratory (CSL) provides advice, technical and enforcement support, underpinned by appropriate research, to meet both the statutory and policy objectives of DEFRA. It provides research and development and advice on a commercial basis to other government departments and to public and private sector organisations both overseas and UK-based. CSL's main work areas are: safeguarding food supplies through the identification and control of invertebrate pests, plant pests and diseases; the management of vertebrate wildlife, food

and consumer safety with the emphasis on the microbiological and chemical safety, and the quality and nutritional value of food. CSL is also concerned with environmental protection through the investigation of the impact of agriculture on the environment, and the promotion of biodiversity in agricultural habitats.
Chief Executive, Prof. M. Roberts

PESTICIDES SAFETY DIRECTORATE
Mallard House, Kings Pool, 3 Peasholme Green, York YO1 7PX
T 01904-640500 F 01904-455733
The Pesticides Safety Directorate is responsible for the evaluation and approval of agricultural pesticides and the development of policies relating to them, in order to protect consumers, users and the environment.
Chief Executive, Dr H. K. Wilson
Director (Approvals), R. Davis
Director (Finance, IT, and Corporate Services), Ms K. Dyson
Director (Policy), Dr S. Popple

RURAL PAYMENTS AGENCY
Kings House, 33 Kings Road, Reading RG1 3BU
T 0118-958 3626 F 0118-959 7736
The Rural Payments Agency (RPA) is an executive agency of the Department for Environment, Food and Rural Affairs. It is the single paying agency responsible for Common Agricultural Policy (CAP) schemes in England and for certain schemes throughout the UK.
Chief Executive, J. McNeill
Director (Business), S. Vry
Director (CAP), A. Sutton
Director (Finance), A. Kerr
Director (Human Resources), R. Gregg
Director (IS), A. McDermott
Director (Operations), H. MacKinnon

VETERINARY LABORATORIES AGENCY
Woodham Lane, New Haw, Addlestone, Surrey KT15 3NB
T 01932-341111 F 01932-347046
The Veterinary Laboratories Agency safeguards public and animal health through world class veterinary research and surveillance of farmed livestock and wildlife.
Chief Executive, Prof. S. Edwards
Director of Finance, C. Morrey
Director of Research (Acting), Prof. C. J. Thorns
Director of Science Strategy, Prof. J. A. Morris
Director of Surveillance and Laboratory Services, R. D. Hancock
Laboratory Secretary, C. Edwards

VETERINARY MEDICINES DIRECTORATE
Woodham Lane, New Haw, Addlestone, Surrey KT15 3LS
T 01932-336911 F 01932-336618
The Veterinary Medicines Directorate is responsible for all aspects of the authorisation and control of veterinary medicines, including post-authorisation surveillance of residues in animals and animal products, and the provision of policy advice to Ministers.
Chief Executive, S. Dean
Director (Corporate Business), C. Bean
Director (Licensing), J. O'Brien
Director (Policy), J. Fitzgerald

FOREIGN AND COMMONWEALTH OFFICE

King Charles Street, London SW1A 2AH
T 020-7008 1500 W www.fco.gov.uk
The Foreign and Commonwealth Office provides, through its staff in the UK and through its diplomatic missions abroad, the means of communication between the British Government and other governments and international governmental organisations on all matters falling within the field of international relations.

It is responsible for alerting the British Government to the implications of developments overseas; for promoting British interests overseas; for protecting British citizens abroad; for explaining British policies to, and cultivating relationships with, governments overseas; for the discharge of British responsibilities to the overseas territories; for entry clearance UK Visas, with the Home Office and for promoting British business overseas (jointly with the Department of Trade and Industry through UK Trade and Investment).
Secretary of State for Foreign and Commonwealth Affairs, The Rt. Hon. Jack Straw, MP
Principal Private Secretary, Geoffrey Adams, CMG
Special Advisers, Dr Michael Williams; Ed Owen
Team Parliamentary Private Secretary, Roger Casale, MP
Minister of State, Dr Denis MacShane, MP *(Europe)*
Private Secretary, Peter Boxer
Parliamentary Private Secretary, Phyllis Starkey, MP
Minister of State, The Rt. Hon. The Baroness Symons of Vernham Dean *(Middle East)*
Private Secretary, Emma Wade
Parliamentary Private Secretary, Mark Todd, MP
Minister of State, Douglas Alexander, MP *(Trade, Investment and Foreign Affairs)*
Private Secretary, Peter Elder
Parliamentary Private Secretary, Lawrie Quinn, MP
Parliamentary Under-Secretary of State, Bill Rammell, MP
Private Secretary, David Whineray
Parliamentary Under-Secretary of State, Chris Mullin, MP
Private Secretary, Bharat Joshi
Permanent Under-Secretary of State and Head of HM Diplomatic Service, Sir Michael Jay, KCMG
Private Secretary, Menna Rawlings
Group Chief Executive, UK Trade and Investment, Sir Stephen Brown, KCVO
Directors-General, Dickie Stagg, CMG *(Corporate Affairs)*; John Sawers, CMG *(Political)*; Nicola Brewer, CMG *(EU Policy)*; William Ehrman, CMG *(Defence/Intelligence)*; Martin Donnelly *(Economic)*

DIRECTORS
Africa, James Bevan
Americas/Overseas Territories, Robert Culshaw, MVO
Asia Pacific, Nigel Cox
Chief Executive FCO Services, Stephen Sage
Communications, John Williams
Consular Services, Paul Sizeland
Finance, Ric Todd
EU Bilateral, Resources and Mediterranean, Dominick Chilcott
Global Issues, Philippa Drew
Human Resources, Darren Warren
International Security, David Richmond
Iraq, vacant
Middle East and North Africa, Simon Fraser
South Asia, Tom Phillips, CMG
Strategy and Information, Anne Pringle, CMG
UK Visas, Robin Barnett

SPECIAL REPRESENTATIVES
Afghanistan, Tom Phillips, CMG
Georgia, Sir Brian Fall, KCMG
Sudan, Alan Goulty, CMG

HEADS OF DEPARTMENTS
Afghanistan Unit, Jan Thompson
Africa Department (Equatorial), Tim Hitchens
Africa Department (Southern), Andrew Lloyd
Association of South East Asian Nations and Oceania Group, Michael Reilly
Commonwealth Co-ordination, Asif Ahmad
Consular Assistance Group, Janet Douglas
Consular Crisis Group, Ralph Publicover
Consular Resources Group, David Popplestone
Counter-Proliferation, David Landsman
Counter-Terrorism Policy Department, Philip Parham
Diplomatic Service Families Association, Emilie Salvesen
Drugs and International Crime Department, Lesley Pallett
Eastern Department, Simon Smith
Eastern Adriatic Department, Karen Pierce, CVO
Economic Policy, Creon Butler
Energy and Climate Change Group, Simon Banks (Deputy Head)
Environment Policy Department, Valerie Caton
Estate Strategy Unit, Julian Metcalfe
European Union Assistant Directorate (External), Tim Barrow, LVO, MBE
EU Common Foreign and Security Policy Team, James Morrison
EU Enlargement and Wider Europe Team, Charles Garrett
EU Northern Europe and International Team, Andrew Key
European Union Department (Internal), David Frost
European Union Mediterranean, Rob Fenn (Eastern); Wendy Wyver (Western)
Far East Group, Denis Keefe
Financial Planning and Performance Department, Tristan Price
FCO Services, Stephen Sage *(Chief Executive)*; Joy Herring *(Client Services)*; Nigel Morris *(Facilities Service Delivery)*; Patrick Cullen *(ICT Service Delivery)*; Dr Vanessa L. Davies *(People and Best Practice Service Delivery)*; John Elgie *(Positive Image UK Service Delivery)*; Rod Peters *(Supply Chain Service Delivery)*; Kerry Simmonds *(Finance)*; Elaine Kennedy *(Human Resources)*
Human Resources Directorate, David Warren *(Head of HR Directorate)*; Andrew Heyn *(HR Direct)*; Andrew George *(Health and Welfare Policy Team)*; Diane Corner; Carole Sweeney *(Legal Policy Team)*; David Powell *(Pay and Benefits Policy Team)*; Howard Drake *(Career Development and Senior Management)*; Richard Tauwhare *(Learning and Development)*; Gerry Reffo *(Performance Assessment and Development)*; Simon Pease *(Workforce Planning Team)*
Human Rights Policy, Jon Benjamin
Information Management, Heather Yasamee
Internal Audit (FCO/DFID), Jon Hews
IT Strategy Unit, Nick Westcott
Latin America and Caribbean Department, Stephen Williams
Legal Adviser, Sir Michael Wood, KCMG
Middle East Department, Charles Gray, CMG
Near East and North Africa Department, Nicholas Archer
North America Department, Martin Rickerd, OBE, MVO
Online Communications Department, Richard Codrington
Organisation for Security Co-operation in Europe and the Council of Europe Department, Peter January
Overseas Territories Department, Tony Crombie, OBE
Parliamentary Relations and Devolution, Matthew Hamlyn
Partnership and Networks Development Unit, Fraser Wheeler
Passports and Documentary Services Group, David Clegg, MVO
Policy, Communication and Training Group, Tim Flear, MVO
Press Office, John Williams *(Press Secretary)*; Peter Reid *(Head of News Room)*
Prism Programme, Andy Tucker
Procurement Policy, Michael Gower
Protocol Division, Charles de Chassiron, CVO
Public Diplomacy Policy Department, Paul Madden
Research Analysts, Robin Hoggard
Resource Accounting, Iain Morgan
Science and Technology Unit, Fiona Clouder Richards
Security Policy, Paul Johnston
Security Strategy Unit, Peter Millett
South Asian Department, Stephen Smith
Sudan Unit, Dr Alastair McPhail
Trade Union Side, Stephen Watson *(TUS Chair)*; Pam Chapman *(TUS Secretary)*
UK Visas (Joint FCO/Home Office Directorate), Robin Barnett
United Nations Department, Alistair Harrison, CVO
Whitehall Liaison Department, Matthew Kidd

UK TRADE AND INVESTMENT
Group Chief Executive, Sir Stephen Brown, KCVO
Deputy Group Chief Executive, Ian Jones

INTERNATIONAL SECTORS GROUP
Group Director, Peter Tibber

INTERNATIONAL TRADE DEVELOPMENT GROUP
Group Director, Ian Fletcher

STRATEGY AND COMMUNICATIONS GROUP
Group Director, John Reynolds

EXECUTIVE AGENCIES

CORPS OF QUEEN'S MESSENGERS
Support Group, Foreign and Commonwealth Office, London SW1A 2AH **T** 020-7270 2779
Superintendent of the Corps of Queen's Messengers, A. C. Brown
Queen's Messengers, P. Allen; R. Allen; Maj. A. N. D. Bols; Maj. P. C. H. Dening-Smitherman; Sqn. Ldr. J. S. Frizzell; Maj. D. A. Griffiths; Sqn Ldr A. Hill; R. Long; Maj. K. J. Rowbottom; Maj. M. R. Senior; Maj. J. E. A. Andre; W. Lisle; Maj. J. H. Steele; J. A. Hatfield; Sqn Ldr P. J. Hearn; S. J. Addy; Lt.-Col. R. I. S. Burgess

WILTON PARK CONFERENCE CENTRE
Wiston House, Steyning, W. Sussex BN44 3DZ
T 01903-815020 **F** 01903-816373
Wilton Park organises international affairs conferences and is hired out to Government departments and commercial users.
Chief Executive, Colin Jennings

DEPARTMENT OF HEALTH

Richmond House, 79 Whitehall, London SW1A 2NL
T 020-7210 3000
W www.doh.gov.uk

The Department of Health is responsible for the provision of the National Health Service in England and for social care. The department's aims are to support, protect, promote and improve the nation's health; to secure the provision of comprehensive, high quality care for all those who need it, regardless of their ability to pay, where they live or their age; and to provide responsive social care and child protection for those who lack the support they need.

The Department of Health is responsible for setting health and social care policy in England. The department's work sets standards and drives modernisation across all areas of the NHS, social care and public health.

Secretary of State for Health, The Rt. Hon. Dr John Reid, MP
Principal Private Secretary, Dominic Hardy
Private Secretaries, Helena Feinstein; Nicola Hewer
Assistant Private Secretaries, Susanne Rowe; Rachel Robertson
Parliamentary Private Secretary, Mike Hall, MP
Minister of State for Health, The Rt. Hon. John Hutton, MP
Private Secretary, Sally Warren
Parliamentary Private Secretary, Claire Ward, MP
Minister of State, Rosie Winterton, MP
Private Secretary, Alistair Finney
Parliamentary Private Secretary, Jim Knight, MP
Parliamentary Under-Secretary of State (Community), Stephen Ladyman, MP
Private Secretary, Wendy Brown
Parliamentary Under-Secretary of State (Lords), Lord Warner of Brockley
Private Secretary, Frances Smethurst
Parliamentary Under-Secretary of State (Public Health), Melanie Johnson, MP
Acting Private Secretary, Anna Norris
Parliamentary Clerk, Neil Townley
Permanent Secretary, Sir Nigel Crisp, KCB
Head of Sir Nigel Crisp's Office, David McNeil
Private Secretaries, Yvonne Coghill; Andrew Larter
Assistant Private Secretaries, Lesley Whitehead; Clare Osborne

MANAGEMENT BOARD
Permanent Secretary and Chief Executive of the NHS, Sir Nigel Crisp KCB
Director of User Experience and Involvement and Chief Nursing Officer, Sarah Mullally
Group Director and Chief Medical Officer of Standards & Quality, Prof. Sir Liam Donaldson
Group Director of Delivery, John Bacon
Group Director, Strategy & Business Development, Hugh Taylor, CB
Director of Communications, Sian Jarvis
Director of Finance and Investment, Richard Douglas
Director of Strategy, Stephen O'Brien

HEALTH AND SOCIAL CARE STANDARDS AND QUALITY GROUP
Group Director, Prof. Sir Liam Donaldson
Director, Care Services Directorate, Anthony Sheehan
Director, Children and Mental Health, Mark Davies
Director, Group Business Team, Alan Doran
Director, Health Protection, International Health and Scientific Development, Dr David Harper, CB
Director, Older People & Disability, Craig Muir
Director, Regional Public Health, vacant
Director, Research and Development, Prof. Sir John Pattison
Deputy Director, Maggie King
Deputy Director, Delivery, Sally Davies
Deputy Director, Research Policy Strategy, Russell Hamilton
Division Head, Health Improvement & Prevention, Imogen Sharp
Division Head, Quality Strategy, Ron Cullen
Division Head, Sexual Health and Substance Misuse, Cathy Hamlyn
Division Head, Standards & Investigation, Ann Stephenson
Division Heads, Penny Bevan; Gerard Hetherington; Nick Boyd; Liz Woodeson Dr David Harper, CB
Chief Dental Officer, Professor Raman Bedi
Health Improvement, Deputy Chief Medical Officer, Dr Fiona Adshead
Healthcare Quality, Deputy Chief Medical Officer for Healthcare Quality, Prof. Aidan Halligan

STRATEGY AND BUSINESS DEVELOPMENT GROUP
Group Director, Hugh Taylor
Director of Development, Kate Barnard
Director, Communications, Sian Jarvis
Director, Corporate Management and Development, Hugh Taylor
Director, Strategy, Stephen O'Brien
Director, User Experience and Involvement, Sarah Mullally
Deputy Director, Flora Goldhill
Head of Campaign Management, Wynn Roberts
Head of News, Jon Hibbs
Head of Policy Unit, Tim Baxter
Head of Statistics, Dr John Fox
Head of Strategic Communications, John Worne
Head, Employee Reward, Sue Fathers
Head, Equality and Human Rights Group, Elisabeth Al-Khalifa
Head, Group Business Team, Peter Allanson
Head, Legislation, Richard Carter
Head, Operational Research for Leeds, Dr Geoff Royston
Head, Operational Research for London, Andre Hare
Head, Policy and Dissemination, Population and Lifestyles, Patsy Bailey *(Acting)*
Head, Social Care, Population Groups and Surveys, Anne Custance *(Acting)*
Branch Heads, Alan Angilley; Shaun Gallagher; Kevin Guinness; Mike Brownlee
Branch Heads, Equality and Human Rights Group, Melanie Field; Barry Mussenden; Lydia Yee
Branch Heads, Jim Allwood; Chris Horsey; Sue Lake; Linda Wishart; Judith Dainty; Adrian McNeil
Career Management, John Middleton
Change Management and Development, Anne Rainsberry
Change Management Team, Ruth Carnall
Chief Economic Adviser, Economics and Operational Research, Prof. Barry McCormick
Chief Health Professions Officer, Kay East
Chief Pharmaceutical Officer for England, Dr Jim Smith
Chief Scientific Officer, Sue Hill
Customer Services Centre, Linda Percival
Dental, Optical, Pharmacy and Prescription, Jim Stokoe
Deputy Chief Nursing Officer, Improving Patient Experience Programme, Kate Billingham
Deputy Chief Pharmacist, Jeanette Howe
DH Policy Collaborative Programme, Sue Gallagher
DH Security Unit, Joseph Neanor
Employee Relations and Support, vacant
Information Services, Dr Andrew Holt, CBE
Medicines, Pharmacy and Industry, Dr Felicity Harvey
NHS Workforce and General Practice, Andy Sutherland
Patients and the Public, Harry Cayton
Performance Management and Improvement, Marion Furr
Project Leader, Andrea Humphrey
Public Health, Disease, Hospital Care and Quality, Richard Willmer
Secretariat, Heather Gwynn, CBE
Senior Economic Advisers, Dr Donald Franklin; Richard Murray
Senior Medical Officer, Dr Peter Clappison

Strategic Human Resources, Pip Parr
System Reform Programme Manager, Steve Barnsley
Workstream Manager, Self Care, David Mowat

HEALTH AND SOCIAL CARE SERVICES DELIVERY GROUP
Group Director, John Bacon
Director, Access, Margaret Edwards
Director, Counter Fraud and Security Management, Jim Gee
Director, Finance and Investment, Richard Douglas
Director, Programmes and Performance, Duncan Selbie
Director, Recovery and Support Unit, John Wilderspin
Director, Workforce, Andrew Foster
Director-General, Information Systems and National Programme Delivery, Richard Granger
Deputy Director, Accounting and Governance, Anne-Marie Miller
Deputy Director, Investment, Peter Coates
Deputy Director, NHS and Social Care, Phil Taylor
Deputy Director, Recovery and Support Unit, Richard Gleave
Deputy Director, Martin Staniforth
Head of Group Business Team, Julie Taylor
Head of Primary Care, Gary Belfield
Head of Secondary Care, Matthew Coats
Head, Business Improvement, Richard Mundon
Head, Delivery and Programmes, Ivan Ellul
Deputy Account Managers, Ian Dodge; Chris Garrett; Helen Robinson; Tim Young
Access Policy Development and Capacity Planning, Bob Ricketts
Branch Heads, Carl Vincent; Martin Campbell; Liz Eccles; Jeff Tomlinson; Peter Kendall; Alistair MacLellan; John Holden; Jeff Peers; Amanda Phillips; Keith Smith; Ben Dyson; Mike Walker; Andrew Griffiths; Pat Kelsey; Helen Pedley; Paul Loveland; Richard Armstrong; Debbie Mellor, OBE; Dean Royles; Steve Catling; Philip Leech
Chief Programme Officer, Gordon Hextall
Commercial Director, Ken Anderson
National Clinical Director of Primary Care, David Colin-Thome
Performance Policy and Delivery, Giles Wilmore
Workforce Capacity Portfolio Director, Rob Webster

MODERNISATION AGENCY
Director of Modernisation Agency, David Fillingham
Director, Corporate and External Affairs, Dr Valerie Day
Director, Finance, Martin Gore
Director, Health and Social Care Leadership Programmes, Penny Humphris
Director, Human Resources & Organisational Development, Caroline Corrigan
Director, Innovation and Knowledge, Pursuing Perfection, Helen Bevan
Director, New Ways of Working, Judy Hargadon
Director, Service Improvement, Michael Scott
Director, Strategic Communications, Jeremy Mooney
Director, Technologies in Health, Mark Outhwaite
Assistant Directors, Partnership Development, Tony Baldasera; Cathy Green; Jasbir Sunner; Anne O'Brien
Head, National Clinical Governance Support Team, Ron Cullen
National Director, National Institute for Mental Health in England, Philip Sculthorpe
Partnership Development Director, Prof. Christine Beasley

HER MAJESTY'S INSPECTOR OF ANATOMY
Branch Head, Dr Jeremy Metters, CB

SOLICITOR'S OFFICE, DEPARTMENT FOR WORK AND PENSIONS
Solicitor, Ms Marilynne Morgan, CB
Director of Legal Services, Mrs Greer Kerrigan

ADVISORY COMMITTEES

ADVISORY COMMITTEE ON THE MICROBIOLOGICAL SAFETY OF FOOD
Aviation House, 125 Kingsway, London WC2B 6NH
T 030-7276 8946

COMMITTEE ON THE SAFETY OF MEDICINES
Market Towers, 1 Nine Elms Lane, London SW8 5NQ
T 020-7084 2000 **W** www.mhra.gov.uk

SPECIAL HEALTH AUTHORITIES

DENTAL VOCATIONAL TRAINING AUTHORITY
Master's House, Temple Grove, Compton Place Road, Eastbourne BN20 8AD **T** 01323-431189

FAMILY HEALTH SERVICES APPEAL AUTHORITY
30 Victoria Avenue, Harrogate HG1 5PR
T 01423-530280

HEALTH DEVELOPMENT AGENCY
Holborn Gate, 330 High Holborn, London WC1V 7BA
T 020-7430 0850

NATIONAL BLOOD SERVICE
Oak House, Reeds Crescent, Watford WD24 4QN
T 020-8258 2700 **W** www.blood.co.uk

NATIONAL INSTITUTE OF ClINICAL EXCELLENCE
71 High Holborn, London WC1V 6NA
T 020-7067 5800

NHS INFORMATION AUTHORITY
Aqueous II, Aston Cross, Rocky Lane, Birmingham B6 5RQ
T 0121-333 0333

NHS LITIGATION AUTHORITY
Napier House, 24 High Holborn, London WC1V 6AZ
T 020-7430 8700

PRESCRIPTION PRICING AUTHORITY
Bridge House, 152 Pilgrim Street, Newcastle-upon-Tyne NE1 6SN **T** 0191-232 5371

UK TRANSPLANT
Fox Den Road, Stoke Gifford, Bristol BS34 8RR
T 0117-975 7575

EXECUTIVE AGENCIES

MEDICINES AND HEALTHCARE PRODUCTS REGULATORY AGENCY (MHRA)
Market Towers, 1 Nine Elms Lane, London SW8 5NQ
T 020-7273 2000 **F** 020-7273 2353
The MHRA is responsible for protecting and promoting public and patient safety by ensuring that medicines, healthcare products and medical equipment meet appropriate standards of safety, quality, performance and effectiveness, and are used safely.

Chairman, Prof. Alasdair Breckenridge
Chief Executive, Prof. K. Woods

NHS ESTATES
1 Trevelyan Square, Boar Lane, Leeds LS1 6AE
T 0113-254 7000 F 0113-254 7299
NHS Estates provides advice and guidance in the area of health care estate and facilities management to the NHS and the health care industry.
Chief Executive, Peter Wearmouth

NHS PENSIONS AGENCY
Hesketh House, 200–220 Broadway, Fleetwood, Lancs FY7 8LG
T 01253-774774 F 01253-774860
NHS Pensions administers the NHS occupational pension scheme and the NHS Bursary Scheme for students.
Chief Executive, Alan Stuttard

NHS PURCHASING AND SUPPLY AGENCY
Premier House 60 Caversham Road, Reading, Berks RG1 7EB
T 0118-980 8600
The agency is responsible for ensuring that the NHS makes the most effective use of its resources by getting the best value for money possible when purchasing goods and services.
Chief Executive, Duncan Eaton

HOME OFFICE

Home Office, 50 Queen Anne's Gate, London SW1H 9AT
T 0870-000 1585 F 020-7273 2065
W www.homeoffice.gov.uk

The Home Office deals with those internal affairs in England and Wales which have not been assigned to other Government departments. The Home Secretary is the link between The Queen and the public and exercises certain powers on her behalf, including that of the royal pardon.

The Home Office's objectives are: to build a safe, just and tolerant society and to maintain and enhance public security and protection; to support and mobilise communities so that they are able to shape policy and improvement for their locality, overcome nuisance and anti-social behaviour, maintain and enhance social cohesion and enjoy their homes and public spaces peacefully; to deliver departmental policies and responsibilities fairly, effectively and efficiently; and to make the best use of resources. These objectives reflect the priorities of the Government and the Home Secretary in areas of crime, citizenship and communities, namely: to reduce crime and the fear of crime; to reduce organised and international crime; to combat terrorism and other threats to national security; to ensure the effective delivery of justice; to deliver effective custodial and community sentences; to reduce re-offending and protect the public; to reduce the availability and abuse of dangerous drugs; to regulate entry to, and settlement in, the UK in the interests of sustainable growth and social inclusion; and to support strong, active communities in which people of all races and backgrounds are valued and participate on equal terms.

The Home Office delivers these aims through the prison, probation and immigration services; its agencies and non-departmental public bodies, and by working with partners in private, public and voluntary sectors, individuals and communities. The Home Secretary is also the link between the UK Government and the governments of the Channel Islands and the Isle of Man.

Secretary of State for the Home Department, The Rt. Hon. David Blunkett, MP
Principal Private Secretary, Jonathan Sedgwick
Private Secretaries, Gareth Redmond; Kevin O'Connor; Nicola Thomas; Alice Reynolds; Dan Hartropp
Special Advisers, Katherine Raymond; Matthew Seward; Huw Evans; Matt Cavanagh
Minister of State, Hazel Blears, MP *(Crime Reduction, Policing, Community Safety)*
Private Secretary, Richard Austin
Minister of State, Des Browne, MP *(Citizenship, Immigration and Counter-Terrorism)*
Private Secretary, Neil Roberts
Minister of State, The Rt. Hon. Baroness Scotland of Asthal, QC *(Criminal Justice System and Law Reform)*
Private Secretary, Joanne Drean
Parliamentary Under-Secretary of State, Caroline Flint, MP *(Anti-Drugs Co-ordination and Organised and International Crime)*
Private Secretary, Jill Wanliss
Parliamentary Under-Secretary of State, Paul Goggins, MP *(Correctional Services and Reducing Re-Offending)*
Private Secretary, Dr Samantha Milton
Parliamentary Under-Secretary of State, Fiona Mactaggart, MP *(Race Equality, Community Policy, and Civil Renewal)*
Private Secretary, Graham Johnston
Permanent Secretary of State, John Gieve
Private Secretary, Diana Luchford
Parliamentary Clerk, Tony Strutt

COMMUNICATION DIRECTORATE
Director of Communications, Julia Simpson
Assistant Director and Head of Direct Communications Unit, Geoff Sampher
Customer Communications Manager, Katie Kerr
Deputy Director and Head of News (Press Office), John Toker
Deputy Director of Communications and Head of Marketing and Strategic Communications, Anne Nash
Head of Internal Communications Unit, Bill Reay
Head of Information Services Unit, Peter Griffiths

COMMUNITIES GROUP
Director-General, Helen Edwards
Director, Active Community Unit, vacant
Chairman, Commission for Racial Equality, Trevor Phillips
Heads of Units, Animal Procedures and Coroners Unit, Dr Jon Richmond; *Community Cohesion Unit*, Judith Lempriere; *Race Equality Unit*, Bruce Gill; *Regions and Renewals Unit*, Betty Moxon and John Curtis; *Identity Cards Programme Director*, Katherine Courtney; *Service Delivery Workstrand Assistant Director*, Richard Jenkins

CORPORATE DEVELOPMENT AND SERVICES DIRECTORATE
Director, Charles Everett
Heads of Units, Andrew Hyslop and David Palmer *(Agreement and Service Delivery)*; Tony Edwards *(Building and Estate Management)*; Nigel Arkle *(Commercial and Procurement Unit)*; Tony Fitzpatrick *(Home Office Pay and Pensions Service)*; Carol Anderson *(Programme Project Management Support Services)*; Peter Lowe *(Information Management Technology Unit)*
President of HO Sports and Social Association, John Gieve

CRIME REDUCTION AND COMMUNITY SAFETY GROUP
Director-General, Mark Neale
Directors, Margaret O'Mara *(Organised Crime)*; Peter Storr *(International)*; Sue Killen *(Drugs)*
Heads of Units, Vic Hogg *(Communities and Law Enforcement Drugs Unit)*; Paul Regan *(Extradition Bill*

Team); Lesley Pallett *(European and International Unit)*; Jim Bradley *(Financial Crime Team)*; Clive Welsh *(Judicial Co-operation Unit)*; Stephen Webb *(Policing and Organised Crime Unit)*; Judy Youell *(Strategic Co-ordination and Planning Unit)*; Judith Lempriere *(Treatment, Young People and Local Delivery Drugs Unit)*

CRIMINAL JUSTICE GROUP
Director-General, Moira Wallace, OBE
Director-General, Criminal Justice System IT, Jo Wright
Director, James Quinault *(Strategic Planning and Analysis)*
Heads of Units, Anne Reece *(Claims Assessment Team)*; David Evans *(Confidence and Communications Team)*; David Reardon *(Criminal Justice System Race Unit)*; Deborah Grice *(Criminal Law Policy Unit)*; vacant *(Criminal Procedure and Evidence Unit)*; Catherine Lee *(Justice and Witnesses)*; Ann-Marie Field *(Local Performance and Delivery Support)*; Henry Cohen *(Programme Management)*; Paul A. David *(Resources, Planning and Communication)*; James Quinault *(Strategic Planning and Analysis)*; Frances Flaxington *(Victims Unit)*; *Chairman, Youth Justice Board*, Rod Morgan

HUMAN RESOURCES DIRECTORATE
Director, David Spencer
Personnel Director, Deborah Louden
Heads of Units, Tony Williams *(Human Resources Operations)*; Nigel Benger *(Corporate Support Services Unit)*; David McDonough *(Departmental Security Unit)*; Jill Douglas *(Personnel Management and Administration)*

IMMIGRATION AND NATIONALITY DIRECTORATE
Director-General, Bill Jeffrey
Senior Directors, Ken Sutton *(Asylum Support, Casework and Appeals)*; Mark Tanzer *(Change and Reform Strategy)*; David Stephens *(Finance and Services)*; Steven Barnett *(Human Resources)*; Paula Higson *(Managed Migration)*; Brodie Clark *(Operations and Projects)*; Nick Baird *(Policy)*
Directors, Joyce Irvine *(Appeals Directorate)*; Terry Neale *(Asylum Casework Directorate)*; Dave Roberts *(Border Control)*; Stephen Calvard *(Business Information Systems and Technology Directorate)*; Mary Shaw *(Department for Constitutional Affairs Asylum Division)*; Peter Topping *(Head of Correspondence Delivery Project)*; Brian Pollett *(Detention Services)*; Mark Goulding *(E-Border)*; Colin Allars *(Enforcement and Removals)*; Tony Arber *(Finance)*; Christina Parry *(General Group, Managed Migration)*; Ros McCool *(Human Resources Services)*; Lorraine Rogerson *(Immigration and Nationality Policy Directorate)*; Don Ingham *(Immigration Service Major Projects)*; Stacy Thornton *(Immigration Service Regions)*; David Wilson *(Intelligence)*; Susannah Simon *(International Policy Directorate)*; Emma de-la-Haye *(Joint Delivery Programme)*; Freda Chaloner *(National Asylum Support Service)*; Digby Griffith *(National Asylum Support Service: Accommodation)*; Jeremy Oppenheim *(National Asylum Support Service: Casework and Regions)*; Chris Hudson *(Operations Manager, Managed Migration)*

WORK PERMITS UK
Director, Kevin Faulkner
Heads of Units, Neil Hughes *(Customer Relations, Intelligence and Post Issue Checking)*; Roy Saxby *(Managed Migration)*; Steve Lamb *(Operations Manager)*; Mick Seals *(Policy, Reviews, Sector Schemes Evaluation)*

LEGAL ADVISORS' BRANCH
Senior Legal Advisor, David Seymour
Deputy Legal Advisor, Clive Osborne
Assistant Legal Advisors, Richard Clayton; Jim O'Meara; Anne Morris; Harry Carter; Sally Weston; Kevan Norris; Peter Fish; Rosemary Davies; Andrew Dodsworth; Robert Messenger; Sara Sternberg

PERFORMANCE AND FINANCE DIRECTORATE
Director, William Rye
Heads of Units, Tim Hurdle *(Audit and Assurance Unit)*; Carl Moynehan *(Accounting and Finance Unit)*; Alison Barnett *(Performance and Finance Support)*

RESEARCH, DEVELOPMENT AND STATISTICS DIRECTORATE
Director, Prof. Paul Wiles
Directors, Jon Simmons *(Analysing Crime Programme)*; Carol Hedderman *(Offending and Crime Justice Group)*
Assistant Directors, David Pyle; Carole F. Willis *(Crime and Policing Group)*; Gary Raw *(Immigration and Community Group)*
Heads of Units, Mark Greenhorn *(Corporate Management Unit)*

CENTRAL POLICE TRAINING AND DEVELOPMENT AUTHORITY (CENTREX)
Chief Executive, Chris Mould
Directors, Andy Humphreys *(Performance and Service Delivery)*; Valerie Vaughan-Dick *(Resources)*

EXECUTIVE AGENCIES

UK PASSPORT SERVICE
Globe House, 89 Eccleston Square, London SW1V 1PN
Advice Line 0870-521 0410
Chief Executive, Bernard Herdan

CRIMINAL RECORDS BUREAU
Horton House, Exchange Flags, Liverpool L2 3YL
T 0870-909 0811
Chief Executive, Vincent Gaskill

FORENSIC SCIENCE SERVICE
Operational Headquarters, Priory House, Gooch Street North, Birmingham B5 6QQ **T** 0121-607 6800
Chief Executive, David Werrett

HM PRISON SERVICE
Cleland House, Page Street, London SW1P 4LN
Director-General, Phil Wheatley

PAROLE BOARD FOR ENGLAND AND WALES
see Prison Service section

PRISONS AND PROBATIONS OMBUDSMAN FOR ENGLAND AND WALES
see Prison Service section

DEPARTMENT FOR INTERNATIONAL DEVELOPMENT

1 Palace Street, London SW1 5HE
T 020-7023 0000 **F** 020-7023 0016
E enquiry@dfid.gov.uk
W www.dfid.gov.uk
Abercrombie House, Eaglesham Road, East Kilbride, Glasgow G75 8EA
T 01355-844000 **F** 01355-844099
Public Enquiries 0845-300 4100

The Department for International Development (DFID) is responsible for promoting sustainable development and reducing poverty. The central focus of the Government's policy, based on the 1997 and 2000 White Papers on International Development, is a commitment to the internationally agreed Millennium Development Goals, to be achieved by 2015. These seek to eradicate extreme poverty and hunger; achieve universal primary education; promote gender equality and empower women; reduce child mortality; improve maternal health; combat HIV/AIDS, malaria and other diseases; ensure environmental sustainability; and encourage a global partnership for development.

DFID's assistance is concentrated in the poorest countries of sub-Saharan Africa and Asia, but also contributes to poverty reduction and sustainable development in middle-income countries, including those in Latin America and Eastern Europe. DFID works in partnership with governments committed to the Millennium Development Goals, and with the private sector and the research community. It also works with multilateral institutions, including the World Bank, United Nations agencies, and the European Commission. DFID has headquarters in London and East Kilbride, offices in many developing countries, and staff based in British embassies and high commissions around the world.

Secretary of State for International Development, Hilary Benn, MP
Principal Private Secretary, Moazzam Malik
Private Secretary, Steven Sabey
Special Advisers, Alex Evans; Beatrice Stern
Parliamentary Private Secretaries, Tom Levitt, MP; Dr Ashok Kumar, MP
Parliamentary Clerk, Peter Gordon
Parliamentary Under-Secretary of State, Gareth R. Thomas, MP
Private Secretary, Alison Cochrane
Assistant Private Secretary, Hamid Kennedy
House of Lords Spokespeople, Baroness Amos; Lord Triesman
Liaison Peer, Baroness Whitaker
Permanent Secretary, Suma Chakrabarti
Private Secretary, Charlie Whetham
Director-General, Corporate Performance and Knowledge Sharing, Mark Lowcock
Director-General, Policy and International, Masood Ahmed
Director-General, Regional Programmes, Minouche Safix
Non-Executive Directors, Nemat Shafik; Bill Griffiths

REGIONAL PROGRAMMES

AFRICA DIVISION

Director of Division, Dave Fish
Director of Africa Policy, Graham Teskey
East and Central Africa, Heads of Departments, David Batt *(Deputy Director);* Desmond Curran *(Africa Great Lakes and Horn)*
East and Central Africa, Heads of Offices, Peter Kerby *(Ethiopia)*; vacant *(Kenya)*; Dr Colin Kirk *(Rwanda)*; Caroline Sergeant *(Tanzania)*; Eric Hawthorne *(Uganda)*
East and Central Africa, Heads of Field Offices, Martin Johnston *(Angola)*; Georgina Yates *(Burundi)*; Paul Godfrey *(Democratic Republic of Congo)*; David Bell *(Somalia)*
Southern Africa, Head of Department, Anthony Smith *(Deputy Director)*
Southern Africa, Heads of Offices, Roger Wilson *(Malawi)*; Eamon Cassidy *(Mozambique)*; Helen Mealins *(Zambia)*; John Barrett *(Zimbabwe)*
Southern Africa, Heads of Field Offices, Sue Wardell *(South Africa, SACU, SADC)*; John Riley *(Botswana)*; Ish Thorn *(Lesotho)*; Kathy Wells *(Swaziland)*
West Africa, Sudan, Conflict and Humanitarian Policy, Heads of Departments, Brian Thomson *(Deputy Director)*
West Africa, Heads of Offices, John Winter *(Ghana)*; William Kingsmill *(Nigeria)*
West Africa, Heads of Field Offices, Jim Maund *(Sierra Leone)*; Louise Thomas *(Sudan)*; Rob Shooter *(West Africa, including Liberia)*; Bernard Harbone *(Conflict and Humanitarian Policy)*

ASIA AND PACIFIC DIVISION

Director of Division, Martin Dinham, CBE
Heads of Departments, Marcus Manuel *(Asia Directorate and Deputy Director, Asia and Pacific Division)*; Pam Jenkins *(Director's Cabinet)*; Howard Taylor *(County Programmes Unit)*; Jeremy Clarke *(Asia Policy and Strategy)*; John Gordon *(Regional Policy Unit)*; Joy Hutcheon *(Western Asia Department)*
Heads of Offices, Paul Ackroyd *(Bangladesh)*; Charlotte Seymour-Smith *(India)*; David Wood *(Nepal)*; Desmond Woode *(Pacific)*; Marshall Elliot *(South East Asia)*; Bela Bird *(Vietnam)*; Adrian Davis *(China)*; Dr Richard Hogg *(Afghanistan)*; Dr Daniel Arghiros *(Cambodia)*; vacant *(Indonesia)*; Penny Thorpe *(Sri Lanka);* Gareth Aicken *(Pakistan)*

EUROPE, MIDDLE EAST AND AMERICAS DIVISION

Director of Division, Carolyn Miller
Heads of Departments, Brenda Killen *(Europe, Middle East and Americas)*; Jessica Irvine *(Europe and Central Asia)*; Richard Teuten *(Latin America)*; Alistair Fernie *(Middle East and North Africa)*; Clive Warren *(Overseas Territories)*
Heads of Offices, Sam Bickersteth *(Bolivia)*; vacant *(Brazil)*; Joanne Alston *(Caribbean)*; Gregory Briffa *(Guyana)*; Vic Heard *(Honduras)*; Elizabeth Carrire *(Jamaica)*; Georgia Taylor *(Nicaragua)*; Mark Lewis *(Peru)*; Simon Bland *(Russia)*; Doug Houston *(Ukraine)*
UK Delegation to the European Bank of Reconstruction and Development, Simon Ray

POLICY AND INTERNATIONAL

POLICY DIVISION

Director of Division, Sharon White
Deputy Directors, Marshall Elliott, Susanna Moorehead, Dr Michael Schultz

OFFICE OF THE CHIEF ADVISERS

Heads of Profession, Adrian Wood *(Economics)*; Roger Edmunds *(Statistics)*; Martin Sergeant *(Infrastructure and Urban Development)*; Jim Harvey *(Rural Livelihoods)*; John Warburton *(Environment)*; Desmond Bermingham *(Education)*
Chief Advisers, David Stanton *(Enterprise Development)*; Steve Bass *(Environment)*; Dr Julian Lob-Levyt *(Human Development)*; Sue Unsworth *(Governance)*; Dr Andrew Norton *(Social Development)*
Deputy Heads of Profession, John Burton *(Economics)*; Stewart Tyson *(Health)*; Max Everest-Phillips *(Governance)*; Pat Holden *(Social Development)*

INTERNATIONAL DIVISION
Director of Division, Peter Grant
Heads of Departments, Michael Mosselmans *(Conflict and Humanitarian Affairs)*; Nick Dyer *(European Union)*; Margaret Cund *(International Financial Institutions)*; Dianna Melrose *(International Trade)*; Carol Robson *(United Nations and Commonwealth)*
Team Leader, Rachel Turner *(International Division Advisory Team)*
UK Permanent Representative, Anthony Beattie *(FAO)*
UK Permanent Delegate, David Leslie Stanton *(UNESCO)*

CORPORATE PERFORMANCE AND KNOWLEDGE SHARING

CORPORATE PERFORMANCE AND KNOWLEDGE SHARING DIVISION
Heads of Departments, Mike Hammond *(Evaluation)*; Gavin McGillivray *(Private Sector Infrastructure/CDC)*; Paul Spray *(Policy Research)*

FINANCE AND CORPORATE PERFORMANCE DIVISION
Director of Division, Richard Calvert
Heads of Departments, Kevin Sparkhall *(Strategy and Finance)*; Mike Smithson *(Accounts)*; Mike Noronha *(Internal Audit)*; Stephen Chard *(Programme Guidance and Support)*; Gordon Alexander *(ARIES)*

HUMAN RESOURCES DIVISION
Director, Liz Davies
Heads of Departments, John Anning *(Human Resources Operations)*; Ian McKendry *(Human Resources Policy)*; Peter Brough *(Overseas Pensions)*

INFORMATION, KNOWLEDGE AND COMMUNICATIONS DIVISION
Director of Division, Owen Barder
Heads of Departments, Michael Green *(Information and Civil Society)*; Simon Jones *(Information Systems and Services)*; Gary James *(Office Services and Security)*; David Gillett *(Special Projects)*

OFFICE OF THE LEADER OF THE HOUSE OF COMMONS

2 Carlton Gardens, London SW1Y 5AA
W www.commonsleader.gov.uk

The Office of the Leader of the House of Commons is responsible for the arrangement of government business in the House of Commons and for planning and supervising the Government's legislative programme. The Leader upholds the rights and privileges of the House and acts as a spokesperson for the Government as a whole.

The Leader reports regularly to Cabinet on parliamentary business and the legislative programme. In his capacity as Leader of the House, he is a member of the Public Accounts Commission and of the House of Commons Commission, and also chairs the Select Committee on Modernisation of the House and the Electoral Policy Committee. As Lord Privy Seal, he is trustee of the Chevening Estate.

The Deputy Leader of the House of Commons supports the Leader in handling the Government's business in the House of Commons. He is responsible for monitoring MPs' and Peers' correspondence and is a member of several Committees including, the Cabinet Committee for the Legislative Programme, Parliamentary Modernisation, Electoral Policy, Local Government Strategy, and the Criminal Justice Review Cabinet Committee.

Leader of the House of Commons, The Rt. Hon. Peter Hain, MP
Principal Private Secretary, Glynne Jones
Private Secretaries, Stephen Hillcoat; James Newman; Mike Newman
Deputy Leader of the House of Commons, Phil Woolas, MP
Private Secretary, Frances Slee

LORD CHANCELLOR'S DEPARTMENT

see Department for Constitutional Affairs

NORTHERN IRELAND OFFICE

11 Millbank, London SW1P 4PN
T 020-7210 3000
Castle Buildings, Stormont, Belfast BT4 3SG
T 028-9052 0700
W www.nio.gov.uk

The Northern Ireland Office was established in 1972, when the Northern Ireland (Temporary Provisions) Act transferred the legislative and executive powers of the Northern Ireland Parliament and Government to the UK Parliament and a Secretary of State.

The Northern Ireland Office is responsible primarily for security issues, law and order and prisons, and for matters relating to the political and constitutional future of the province. It also deals with international issues as they affect Northern Ireland.

Under the terms of the 1998 Good Friday Agreement, power was devolved to the Northern Ireland Assembly in 1999. The Assembly took on responsibility for the relevant areas of work previously undertaken by the departments of the Northern Ireland Office covering agriculture and rural development, the environment, regional development, social development, education, higher education, training and employment, enterprise, trade and investment, culture, arts and leisure, health, social services, public safety and finance and personnel. On 14 October 2002 the Northern Ireland Assembly was suspended and Northern Ireland returned to direct rule. For further details, *see* Regional Government section.

Secretary of State for Northern Ireland, The Rt. Hon. Paul Murphy, MP
Parliamentary Private Secretary, Gareth Thomas, MP
Minister of State, The Rt. Hon. John Spellar, MP
Parliamentary Private Secretary, Tom Harris, MP
Parliamentary Under-Secretaries of State, Ian Pearson, MP; Angela Smith, MP; Barry Gardiner, MP
Permanent Under-Secretary of State, Sir Joseph Pilling, KCB
Head of the Northern Ireland Civil Service, Nigel Hamilton

NORTHERN IRELAND INFORMATION SERVICE
Stormont Castle, Stormont Estate, Belfast BT4 3TT
T 028-9052 0700

EXECUTIVE AGENCIES

COMPENSATION AGENCY, Royston House, Upper Queen Street, Belfast BT1 6FD T 028-9024 9944
FORENSIC SCIENCE NORTHERN IRELAND, Seapark, 151 Belfast Road, Carrickfergus, Co. Antrim BT38 8PL T 028-9036 5744
YOUTH JUSTICE AGENCY, Corporate Headquarters, 4143 Waring Street, Belfast BT1 2DY T 028-9031 6 400
NORTHERN IRELAND PRISON SERVICE

SCOTLAND OFFICE

Dover House, Whitehall, London SW1A 2AU
T 020-7270 6754 F 020-7270 6812
1 Melville Crescent, Edinburgh, EH3 7HW
T 0131-244 9010 F 0131-244 9028
E scottish.secretary@scotland.gov.uk
W www.scottishsecretary.gov.uk

The Scotland Office is the department of the Secretary of State for Scotland, who represents Scottish interests in the Cabinet on matters reserved to the UK Parliament, i.e. constitutional matters, financial and economic matters, defence and international relations, immigration, social security, various matters relating to the single market with the UK (energy, transport, consumer protection) and employment. It also supports the Advocate-General, the legal adviser to the UK Government on Scottish law. *See* also Regional Government section and Department for Constitutional Affairs.

Secretary of State for Scotland, The Rt. Hon. Alistair Darling, MP
Private Secretary, Ms J. Colquhoun
Parliamentary Under-Secretary of State, Anne McGuire, MP
Private Secretary, Chloe Squires
Parliamentary Private Secretary, David Stewart, MP
Advocate-General for Scotland, Dr Lynda Clark, QC, MP
Private Secretary, James Johnston
Spokesperson in the House of Lords, Lord Evans of Temple Guiting, CBE

DEPARTMENT OF TRADE AND INDUSTRY

1 Victoria Street, London SW1H 0ET
T 020-7215 5000 F 020-7215 0105
W www.dti.gov.uk

The Department of Trade and Industry works with businesses, employees and consumers to increase UK productivity and competitiveness. The department's aim is to make the UK a more prosperous country and close the gap with its international competitors by making it easier and more attractive to start and grow new businesses in the UK. The DTI focuses on innovation to help more firms to grow and capture new markets, ensuring fair and open markets at home and overseas to support successful UK businesses and the creation of jobs, and better support for scientific excellence.

Secretary of State for Trade and Industry, Minister for Women and e-Minister, The Rt. Hon. Patricia Hewitt, MP
Principal Private Secretary, Matthew Hilton
Private Secretaries, Ian Gibbons; Shantha Shanmugalingam; Louise Proudlove; Joanne Edwards
Parliamentary Private Secretaries, Oona King, MP; Jackie Lawrence, MP
Minister of State, Douglas Alexander, MP *(Trade)*
Private Secretary, Peter Elder
Parliamentary Private Secretary, Lawrie Quinn, MP
Minister of State, Mike O'Brien, MP *(E-Commerce, Energy and Competitiveness)*
Private Secretary, Brian Payne
Parliamentary Private Secretary, Eric Joyce, MP
Minister of State, The Rt. Hon. Jacqui Smith, MP *(Industry, Regions, Deputy Minister for Women and Equality)*
Private Secretary, Spencer Mahoney
Parliamentary Private Secretary, Andy Love, MP
Parliamentary Under-Secretary of State, Gerry Sutcliffe, MP *(Employment Relations, Competition and Consumers)*
Private Secretary, Sam Myers
Parliamentary Under-Secretary of State, The Lord Sainsbury of Turville *(Science and Innovation)*
Private Secretary, Joe Burns
Parliamentary Under-Secretary of State, Nigel Griffiths, MP *(Small Business)*
Private Secretary, Claire Ball
Permanent Secretary, Sir Robin Young, KCB
Private Secretary, Tom Ridge
Parliamentary Clerk, Tim Williams
Chief Scientific Adviser and Head of Office of Science and Technology, Prof. Sir David King, KB
Director-General, Research Councils, Sir Keith O'Nions
Chief Executive UK Trade and Investment, Sir Stephen Brown, KCVO

STRATEGY UNIT
Director of Communications, Sheree Dodd
Director of Strategy Unit, Geoff Dart
Chief Economic Adviser, Vicky Pryce

INNOVATION GROUP
Director-General, David Hughes
Directors, Jonathan Startup *(Sustainable Development)*; Peter Burke *(Business Planning and Strategy)*; John Rhodes *(Facilitating Innovation)*; vacant *(Technical Innovation and Sustainable Development)*; David Reed *(Standards and Technical Regulations)*

BRITISH NATIONAL SPACE CENTRE
Director-General, Dr Colin Hicks
Deputy Director-General, David Leadbeater
Director, Space Applications and Programmes, Paula Freedman

NATIONAL WEIGHTS AND MEASURES LABORATORY
Director and Chief Executive, Jeffrey Llewellyn

PATENT OFFICE
Chief Executive, Ron Marchant

ENERGY GROUP
Director-General, Joan MacNaughton
Heads of Units, Jim Campbell *(Licensing and Consents Unit)*; Peter Waller *(Nuclear and Coal Liabilities Unit)*; Claire Durkin *(Energy Innovation and Business Unit)*; Neil Hirst *(Energy Markets Unit)*; Paul McIntyre *(British Energy Team)*; Rob Wright *(Energy Strategy Unit)*
Directors, Simon Toole *(Licensing Exploration and Development)*; Richard Mellish *(Electricity Consents and Agency Project Management)*; Alan Edwards *(Liabilities Management Unit)*; Stephen Spivey *(Nuclear Reform Bill)*; Ian Gregory *(Nuclear Business Relations)*; Ann Taylor *(Coal Health Claims)*; Iain Todd *(Energy Industries Business Unit and Oil and Gas Industry Development)*; Patrick Robinson *(Nuclear Safety and Security)*; Peter Fenwick *(Engineering Inspectorate)*; Ian Downing *(International Nuclear Policy and Programmes)*; Michael Buckland-Smith *(Civil Nuclear Security)*; Liz Baker *(Domestic and European Energy)*; Ann Eggington *(International and Infrastructure)*; Graham White *(Social Issues and Information)*; Ruth Hannant *(British Energy)*; David Hayes *(Strategic Issues)*; Adrian Gault *(Strategy Development, Research and Analysis)*; Rob Wright *(Energy MSU)*

BUSINESS GROUP
Director-General, Mark Gibson
Deputy Director-General, Regions, Katharine Elliott

BUSINESS RELATIONS
Director of Business Relations, John Alty
Directors, David Hendon *(Business Relations 2)*; David Saunders *(Business Support)*; Mark Higson *(Postal Services)*; Rachel Jenkinson *(Business Group, Change Management Team)*; Sheila Morris *(Business Relations Strategic Management)*; Rosa Wilkinson *(Policy, Business Relations)*; Martin Berry *(Industry Sponsorship Support)*

AEROSPACE AND DEFENCE INDUSTRIES TECHNOLOGY
Director, David Way

AUTOMOTIVE
Director, Sarah Chambers

BIOSCIENCE
Director, Monica Darnbrough

CHEMICALS
Director, Dr David Jennings

CONSTRUCTION INDUSTRIES
Director, Elizabeth Whatmore

CONSUMER GOODS AND SERVICES
Director, Jane Swift

MARINE UNIT
Director, Chris North

MATERIALS AND ENGINEERING
Director, Simon Edmonds

REGIONS
Directors, Tony Medawar *(RDA Sponsorship and Finance)*; Peter Bunn *(Regional Policy)*; John Neve *(Regional European Funds and Devolution)*; Andrew Steele *(Regional Assistance)*; vacant *(Social Enterprise Unit)*

SMALL BUSINESS SERVICE
Chief Executive, Martin Wyn-Griffith
Deputy Chief Executive, Stephen Lyle Smythe
Directors, Dr Ken Poulter *(Business Services)*; Mandy Mayer *(Strategy, Governance and Learning)*; Howard Capelin *(Channel Management)*; Peter Bentley *(Finance Director)*

SERVICES GROUP
Director-General, Dr Catherine Bell

EXPORT CONTROL AND NON PROLIFERATION
Director of Export Control and Non Proliferation, Mike O'Shea

FINANCE AND RESOURCE MANAGEMENT
Director of Finance and Resource Management, David Evans

HUMAN RESOURCES AND CHANGE MANAGEMENT
Director of Human Resources and Change Management, Shirley Pointer

INFORMATION AND WORKPLACE SERVICES
Director, Yvonne Gallagher
Directors, Jon Whitfield; David Evans *(Internal Audit)*; Peter Mason *(Finance)*; Curtis Juman *(Resource Accounting and Budgeting)*; Adam Jackson *(Business Planning and Performance Management)*; Tim Soane *(Change and Knowledge Management Unit)*; Rosemary Heyhoe *(HR Operations)*; Christine Hewitt, Jan Dixon *(HR Strategy and Terms of Employment)*; Howard Ewing *(People Deployment and Development)*; Andrew Matthew *(E-Strategy and Major Projects)*; Liz Maclachlan *(Information Policy and Services)*; Glyn Williams *(Export Control Organisation)*

FAIR MARKETS GROUP
Director-General, Stephen Haddrill

CORPORATE LAW AND GOVERNANCE
Director of Corporate Law and Governance, Bernadette Kelly
Directors, Robert Burns, Keith Masson, Rachel Clark, Richard Carter *(Company Law)*; John Grewe *(Financial Reporting Policy)*; Andrew Watchman *(Accountancy Advisor)*; Anne Willcocks *(Joint Head of Companies Bill Team)*; vacant *(Policy and Resources)*; Robert Burns *(Investigations and Inspector of Companies)*

CONSUMER AND COMPETITION POLICY
Director of Consumer and Competition Policy, Jonathan Rees
Directors, Pat Sellers *(Specific Market Interventions)*; Andrew Rees *(Research, Analysis and Evidence Database)*; Thoss Shearer *(Economic Regulation and Reform)*; Katherine Wright *(Strategy and Delivery)*; Tony Sims *(Europe and International)*; Adrian Walker-Smith *(Consumer Credit)*; Fiona Price *(Cross-Market Intervention)*

EMPLOYMENT RELATIONS
Director of Employment Relations, Janice Munday
Directors, Sarah Rhodes *(Dispute Resolution)*; Ros McCarthy-Ward *(Selected Employment Rights)*; Grant Fitzner *(Employment Market Analysis and Research)*; Jane Whewell *(European Strategy and Labour Market Flexibility)*; Julie Carney *(Participation and Skills)*

LOW PAY COMMISSION
Secretary, Kate Harre

WOMEN AND EQUALITY UNIT
35 Great Smith Street, London SW1P 3BJ
T 020-7273 8802
Director, Angela Mason
Directors, Liz Chennells *(Gender Equality and Social Justice)*; vacant *(Productivity and Diversity)*; Kate Allan *(Equality Co-Ordination)*

EUROPEAN AND WORLD TRADE POLICY
Director, World Trade, Edmund Hosker
Director, Europe, Jo Durning
Directors, Dr Elaine Drage *(EC Trade Policy)*; Julian Farrel *(EU Economic Reform)*; Tim Abraham *(Co-ordination World Trade)*; David Andrews *(Market Access)*; Matthew Cocks *(Future of Europe)*; Peter Dodd *(International Economies)*; vacant *(State Aid)*

LEGAL SERVICES GROUP
The Solicitor and Director-General, Anthony Inglese
Director of Legal Resource Management and Business Law, Carl Warren
Director of Legal Services A (Business and Consumers), Tessa Dunstan
Director of Legal Services B (Employment Discrimination, Equality and Intellectual Property), vacant

Director of Legal Services C (Energy, Communications, EC and Overseas Trade), Deborah Collins
Director of Legal Services D (Law Enforcement), Scott Milligan
Director of Legal Services E (Company Law and British Energy), Philip Bovey

UK TRADE AND INVESTMENT
Kingsgate House, 66–74 Victoria Street, London SW1E 6SW
T 020-7215 8000
UK Trade and Investment is the government organisation that supports both companies in the UK trading internationally and overseas enterprises seeking to locate in the UK. The organisation brings together the work of the DTI and the FCO.
Group Chief Executive, Sir Stephen Brown
Chief Executive, Inward Investment, William Pedder
Deputy Group Chief Executive, Director Corporate Resources, Susan Haird
Group Director, International Trade Development, David Warren
Group Director, Strategy and Communication, John Reynolds
Director, International Sectors Group, Peter Tibber

EXECUTIVE AGENCIES
COMPANIES HOUSE
Crown Way, Cardiff CF14 3UZ
T 0870-333 3636 F 029-2038 0900
E enquiries@companieshouse.gov.uk
W www.companieshouse.gov.uk
London Information Centre, 21 Bloomsbury Street, London WC1B 3XD T 0870-333 3636 F 029-2038 0517
Edinburgh, 37 Castle Terrace, Edinburgh EH1 2EB
T 0870-333 3636 F 0131-535 5820
Companies House incorporates companies, registers company documents and provides company information.
Registrar of Companies for England and Wales, Claire Clancy
Registrar for Scotland, Jim Henderson

EMPLOYMENT TRIBUNALS SERVICE
19–29 Woburn Place, London WC1H 0LU
T 020-7273 8666 F 020-7273 8686
The Service became an executive agency in 1997 and brought together the administrative support for the employment tribunals and the Employment Appeal Tribunal.
Chief Executive, Roger Heathcote

THE INSOLVENCY SERVICE
PO Box 203, 21 Bloomsbury Street, London WC1B 3QW
T 020-7637 1110 F 020-7291 6731
The Service administers and investigates the affairs of bankrupts and companies in compulsory liquidation; deals with the disqualification of directors in all corporate failures; regulates insolvency practitioners and their professional bodies; provides banking and investment services for bankruptcy and liquidation estates; and advises Ministers on insolvency policy issues.
Inspector-General and Chief Executive, Desmond Flynn
Deputy Inspectors-General, G. Horne; L. T. Cramp

NATIONAL WEIGHTS AND MEASURES LABORATORY
Stanton Avenue, Teddington, Middx TW11 0JZ
T 020-8943 7272 F 020-8943 7270
W www.nwml.gov.uk
The Laboratory administers weights and measures legislation, carries out type examination, calibration and testing, and runs courses on legal metrology.
Chief Executive, Dr Jeff Llewellyn

PATENT OFFICE
see Intellectual Property section

DEPARTMENT FOR TRANSPORT
Great Minster House, 76 Marsham Street, London SW1P 4DR
Ashdown House, 123 Victoria Street, London SW1E 6DE
T 020-7944 8300/020-7944 4873
W www.dft.gov.uk
The Department for Transport was established in May 2002 following the de-merger of the Department of Transport, Local Government and the Regions.

The department's main responsibilities are aviation, freight, health and safety, integrated and local transport, London Underground, maritime, mobility and inclusion, railways, roads and road safety, shipping and vehicles.
Secretary of State for Transport, The Rt. Hon Alistair Darling, MP
Principal Private Secretary, Scott McPherson
Minister of State, Tony McNulty, MP *(Transport)*
Private Secretary, Deborah Heenan
Parliamentary Under-Secretary of State, David Jamieson, MP *(Transport)*
Private Secretary, Naomi Hunt
Parliamentary Under-Secretary of State, Charlotte Atkins, MP *(Transport)*
Private Secretary, Emma Cliffe
Permanent Secretary, David Rowlands
Private Secretary, Dr Ben Still

BUSINESS DELIVERY SERVICES DIRECTORATE
Director, Michael Herron

DRIVER, VEHICLE AND OPERATOR GROUP
Director-General, Stephen Hickey

DRIVER, VEHICLE AND OPERATOR DIRECTORATE
Director, Andrew Stott

LEGAL SERVICES DIRECTORATE
Director, Christopher Muttukumaru
Divisional Managers, Alan Jones *(Aviation)*; Stephen Rock *(Driving and Road Safety)*; Hussein Kaya *(Highways)*; Elizabeth Walsh *(Railways, Operations and Construction)*; Robert Caune *(Railways, Track and Safety)*; Julie Murnane *(Road Vehicles)*; Martin Bedford *(Employment and Corporate Services)*; Ginny Harrison *(Marine)*; David Ingham *(Secondary Legislation)*

RAILWAYS, AVIATION, LOGISTICS, MARITIME AND SECURITY GROUP
Director-General, Sue Killen
Directors, David McMillan *(Aviation Directorate)*; Brian Wadsworth *(Logistics and Maritime Transport Directorate)*; Mark Lambirth *(Rail Directorate)*; Mike Fuhr *(Major Projects Directorate)*; Stephen Bligh *(Maritime and Coastguard Agency)*; Niki Tompkinson *(Transport Security Directorate)*; Vivien Bodnar *(Rail Performance Directorate)*
Deputy Director, John Grubb *(Transport Security Division)*
Chief Inspectors, Ken Smart *(Air Accidents Investigation Branch)*; Stephen Meyer *(Marine Accidents Investigation Branch)*
Principal Investigator of Rail Accidents, Carolyn Griffiths *(Rail Accidents Investigation Branch)*

ROADS, REGIONAL AND LOCAL TRANSPORT GROUP
Director-General, Robert Devereux
Directors, Bob Linnard *(Integrated and Local Transport Directorate)*; Steve Gooding *(Roads and Vehicle Directorate)*; Bronwyn Hill *(Regional Transport Directorate)*

STRATEGY, FINANCE AND DELIVERY GROUP
Director-General, Willy Rickett
Directors, Charles Skinner *(Communication Directorate)*; vacant *(Strategy and Delivery Directorate)*; Chris Riley *(Transport Analysis and Economics Directorate)*; Ken Beeton *(Transport Finance Directorate)*; Ann Frye *(Mobility and Inclusion Unit)*
Chair, Trade Union Side, Chris Hickey

EXECUTIVE AGENCIES

DRIVER AND VEHICLE LICENSING AGENCY
Longview Road, Morriston, Swansea SA6 7JL
T 01792-782341 **F** 01792-782793
W www.dvla.gov.uk
The Agency is responsible for registering and licensing drivers and vehicles, and the collection and enforcement of vehicle exercise duty.
Chief Executive, C. Bennett

DRIVING STANDARDS AGENCY
Stanley House, Talbot Street, Nottingham NG1 5GU
T 0115-901 2500 **F** 0115-901 2940
W www.dsa.gov.uk
The Agency is responsible for carrying out theory and practical driving tests for car drivers, motorcyclists, bus and lorry drivers and for maintaining the registers of Approved Driving Instructors and Large Goods Vehicle Instructors, as well as supervising Compulsory Basic Training (CBT) for learner motorcyclists. There are five area offices, which manage over 430 practical test centres across Britain.
Chief Executive, G. Austin

HIGHWAYS AGENCY
123 Buckingham Palace Road, London SW1W 9HA
T 08459-556575 **F** 020-7921 4592
W www.highways.gov.uk
The Agency is responsible for delivering the Transport Department's road programme and for maintaining the national road network in England.
Chief Executive, Archie Robertson

MARITIME AND COASTGUARD AGENCY
Spring Place, 105 Commercial Road, Southampton SO15 1EG
T 023-8032 9100 **F** 023-8032 9298
W www.mcga.gov.uk
The agency's aim is to prevent loss of life, continuously improve maritime safety and protect the marine environment.
Chief Executive, Capt. Stephen Bligh
Chief Coastguard, J. Astbury

VEHICLE CERTIFICATION AGENCY
1 Eastgate Office Centre, Eastgate Road, Bristol BS5 6XX
T 0117-951 5151 **F** 0117-952 4103
W www.vca.gov.uk
The agency is the UK authority responsible for ensuring that vehicles and vehicle parts have been designed and constructed to meet internationally agreed standards of safety and environmental protection.
Chief Executive, P. Markwick

VEHICLE AND OPERATOR SERVICES AGENCY
Berkeley House, Croydon Street, Bristol BS5 0DA
T 0117-954 3200 **F** 0117-954 3212
W www.vosa.gov.uk
The Vehicle and Operator Services Agency was formed on 1 April 2003 from the merger of the Vehicle Inspectorate and the Traffic Area Network. The agency is responsible for processing applications for licences to operate heavy goods and public service vehicles and registering bus services; operating and administering testing schemes for all vehicles including statutory annual testing of commercial vehicles, single vehicle approval of imported vehicles and vehicle identity checks; supervision of the MOT scheme; enforcement checks of vehicle safety, drivers' hours and emissions; supporting the independent Traffic Commissioners in carrying out their responsibilities for operator licensing, vocational drivers and bus registration; providing training and advice for commercial operators and MOT testers; investigating vehicle accidents, defects and recalls.
Chief Executive, Maurice R. Newey

HM TREASURY

1 Horse Guards Road, London SW1A 2HQ
T 020–7270 5000
E public.enquiries@hm-treasury.gov.uk
W www.hm-treasury.gov.uk
The Office of the Lord High Treasurer has been continuously in commission for well over 200 years. The Lord High Commissioners of HM Treasury are the First Lord of the Treasury (who is also the Prime Minister), the Chancellor of the Exchequer and five junior Lords. This Board of Commissioners is assisted at present by the Chief Secretary, the Parliamentary Secretary (who is also the Government Chief Whip in the House of Commons), the Paymaster-General, the Financial Secretary, and the Economic Secretary. The Prime Minister as First Lord is not primarily concerned with the day-to-day aspects of Treasury business; neither are the Parliamentary Secretary and the Junior Lords as Government Whips. Treasury business is managed by the Chancellor of the Exchequer and the other Treasury Ministers, assisted by the Permanent Secretary.

The Chief Secretary is responsible for public expenditure planning and control; public sector pay; value for money in the public services; public service agreements; public/private partnerships and procurement policy; strategic oversight of banking, financial services and insurance; departmental investment strategies; including the Capital Modernisation Fund and Invest to Save Budget; welfare reform; devolution; and resource accounting and budgeting.

The Paymaster-General is responsible for the Inland Revenue and the Valuation Office, with overall responsibility for the Finance Bill. She leads on personal taxation, business taxation, European and international tax issues.

The Economic Secretary is responsible for Customs and Excise; growth and productivity; science, research and development; competition and deregulation policy; export credit; VAT and road and fuel duties; and parliamentary financial business (Public Accounts Committee, National Audit Office).

The Financial Secretary is responsible for National Savings and Investments, the Debt Management Office, the Office of National Statistics, the Royal Mint, and the Government Actuary's Department; banking, financial services and insurance; foreign exchange reserves; debt management policy; financial services tax issues and charity taxation. She provides support to the Chancellor on EU issues.

Prime Minister and First Lord of the Treasury, The Rt. Hon. Tony Blair, MP
Chancellor of the Exchequer, The Rt. Hon. Gordon Brown, MP
Principal Private Secretary, Mark Bowman
Private Secretaries, Beth Russell; John-Christophe Gray
Parliamentary Private Secretary, Ann Keen, MP
Chief Economic Adviser to the Treasury, Michael Ellam
Special Advisers, Ian Austin; Spencer Livermore; Shriti Vadera; Stewart Wood; Paul Gregg; Chris Wales
Chief Secretary to the Treasury, The Rt. Hon. Paul Boateng, MP
Private Secretary, Dan Rosenfield
Parliamentary Private Secretary, Helen Southworth, MP
Special Adviser, Nicola Murphy
Paymaster-General, The Rt. Hon. Dawn Primarolo, MP
Private Secretary, Kathryn Morgan
Parliamentary Private Secretary, Chris Pond, MP
Financial Secretary to the Treasury, Stephen Timms, MP
Private Secretary, Guy Davison
Parliamentary Private Secretary, James Purnell, MP
Economic Secretary to the Treasury, John Healey, MP
Private Secretary, Sam Woods
Permanent Secretary to the Treasury, Gus O'Donnell, CB
Private Secretary, Cairan Martin
Parliamentary Secretary to the Treasury and Government Chief Whip, The Rt. Hon. Hilary Armstrong, MP
Private Secretary, Roy Stone, MP
Treasurer of HM Household and Deputy Chief Whip, Bob Ainsworth, MP
Comptroller of HM Household, The Rt. Hon. Thomas McAvoy, MP
Vice-Chamberlain of HM Household, Jim Fitzpatrick, MP
Lords Commissioners of HM Treasury (Whips), John Heppel, MP; Nick Ainger, MP; Jim Murphy, MP; Derek Twigg, MP; Joan Ryan, MP
Assistant Whips, Fraser Kemp, MP; Gillian Merron, MP; Charlotte Atkins, MP; Vernon Coaker, MP; Paul Clark, MP; Margaret Moran, MP; Bridget Prentice, MP; Tom Watson, MP

DIRECTORATES

Head of Ministerial Support Team, M. Bowman
Head of Communications and Strategy Team, M. Ellam

MACROECONOMIC POLICY AND INTERNATIONAL FINANCE

Managing Director, Jon Cunliffe
Directors, Simon Brooks; Stephen Pickford; Sue Owen; Melanie Dawes

BUDGET AND PUBLIC FINANCE

Managing Director, Nick Macpherson
Directors, Nick Holgate; Dave Ramsden; Edward Troup; Mike Williams

PUBLIC SERVICES

Managing Director, Jonathan Stephens
Directors, Ray Shostak; Paul Johnson; Anita Charlesworth

CORPORATE SERVICES AND DEVELOPMENT

Managing Director, Hilary Douglas

FINANCIAL MANAGEMENT, REPORTING AND AUDIT

Managing Director, Andrew Likierman
Director, Brian Glicksman

FINANCE, REGULATION AND INDUSTRY

Managing Director, James Sassoon
Directors, John Kingman; Phil Wynn Owen

EXECUTIVE AGENCIES

NATIONAL SAVINGS AND INVESTMENTS

see Finance section

OFFICE FOR NATIONAL STATISTICS

see Public Bodies section

ROYAL MINT

see Public Bodies section

UK DEBT MANAGEMENT OFFICE

Eastcheap Court, 11 Philpot Lane, London, EC3M 8UD
T 020-7862 6500 F 020-7862 6509

The UK Debt Management Office was launched as an executive agency of HM Treasury in April 1998. The office has two main functions: it is the Government's debt manager (issuing gilts, managing the gilt market); and the Government's cash manager (balancing the Exchequer's cash flow on a daily basis). On 1 July 2002 the operations of the Public Works Loan Board (PWLB), and the Commissioners for the Reduction of the National Debt (CRND) were integrated with the DMO.

Chief Executive, R. Stheeman

OTHER BODIES

OFFICE OF GOVERNMENT COMMERCE (OGC)

Trevelyan House, 26–30 Great Peter Street, London SW1P 2BY
T 0845-000 4999 W www.ogc.gov.uk

The Office of Government Commerce was set up on the 1 April 2000. It is a unique body within government, overseen by a supervisory board of Ministers and officials from across the departments of Government. Its aim is to achieve the best value for money for the Government's commercial relationships and coherence of purchasing activity across 200 Government departments, non-governmental bodies and agencies. The OGC is an office of HM Treasury.

Chief Executive, John Oughton

OGC BUYING SOLUTIONS
Royal Liver Building, Pier Head, Liverpool L3 1PE
T 0870-268 2222 F 0151-227 3315
W www.ogcbuyingsolutions.gov.uk
The Agency provides a professional purchasing service to Government departments and other public bodies. From April 2000 it became part of the Office of Government Commerce reporting to the Chief Secretary to the Treasury.
Chief Executive, Hugh Barrett

DEPARTMENT OF HM PROCURATOR-GENERAL AND TREASURY SOLICITOR
Queen Anne's Chambers, 28 Broadway, London SW1H 9JS
T 020-7210 3000 F 020-7210 3004
The Treasury Solicitor's Department, which became an executive agency in 1996, provides legal services for many Government departments. Those without their own lawyers are provided with legal advice, and both they and other departments are provided with litigation services. The Treasury Solicitor is also the Queen's Proctor, and is responsible for collecting Bona Vacantia on behalf of the Crown.
HM Procurator-General and Treasury Solicitor (SCS), Dame Juliet Wheldon, DCB, QC

LITIGATION DIVISION
Head of Division, D. Pearson

QUEEN'S PROCTOR DIVISION
Queen's Proctor, Juliet Wheldon
Assistant Queen's Proctor, Ravi Sampanthar

DIRECTORATE OF CORPORATE STRATEGY
Director of Corporate Strategy, Hilary Jackson

BONA VACANTIA DIVISION
Head of Division, Valerie Cain

EUROPEAN DIVISION
Legal Adviser, Frances Nash

CULTURE, MEDIA AND SPORT DIVISION
Head of Division, Ms I. Letwin

CABINET OFFICE AND CENTRAL ADVISORY DIVISION
Head of Division, Ms R. Jeffreys

MINISTRY OF DEFENCE ADVISORY DIVISION
Head of Division, M. J. Hemming

DEPARTMENT FOR EDUCATION AND SKILLS DIVISION
Head of Division, J. Jones

HM TREASURY ADVISORY DIVISION
Legal Adviser, S. Parker

WALES OFFICE
Gwydyr House, Whitehall, London SW1A 2ER
T 020-7270 0549 F 020-7270 0568
E walesoffice@walesoffice.gsi.gov.uk
W www.walesoffice.gov.uk
The Wales Office is the department of the Secretary of State for Wales, who represents Welsh interests in the Cabinet. *See* also Regional Government section and Department for Constitutional Affairs.
Secretary of State for Wales, The Rt. Hon. Peter Hain, MP
Principal Private Secretary, Simon Morris
Parliamentary Private Secretary, Chris Ruane, MP
Parliamentary Under-Secretary, Don Touhig, MP
Head of Office, Alison Jackson

DEPARTMENT FOR WORK AND PENSIONS
Richmond House, 79 Whitehall, London SW1A 2NS
T 020-7238 0800 F 020-7238 0763
E ministers@dwp.gsi.gov.uk
W www.dwp.gov.uk
The Department for Work and Pensions was formed on 8 June 2001 from parts of the former Department of Social Security and Department for Education and Employment and the Employment Service. The department helps unemployed people of working age into work, helps employers to fill their vacancies and provides financial support to people unable to help themselves through back to work programmes. The department also administers the Child Support system, social security benefits and the social fund. In addition, the department has reciprocal social security arrangements with other countries.

In April 2002 the Benefits Agency and the Employment Service was replaced by the Jobcentre Plus network (responsible for helping people to find jobs and paying benefits to people of working age), and the Pension Service which administers the Benefits Agency's pension-related services.
Secretary of State for Work and Pensions, The Rt. Hon. Alan Johnson, MP
Principal Private Secretary, Susan Park
Private Secretaries, Georgina Hill; Paul Todd; Matt Adams; Tammy Fevrier
Special Advisers, Chris Norton; Tom Clark
Parliamentary Private Secretary, Bob Laxton, MP
Minister of State, The Rt. Hon. Jane Kennedy, MP
Parliamentary Private Secretary, Kali Mountford, MP
Private Secretary, Caroline Crowther
Minister of State, Malcolm Wicks, MP *(Pensions)*
Private Secretary, Sara Protheroe
Assistant Private Secretary, Helen Hutchings
Parliamentary Private Secretary, David Cairns, MP
Parliamentary Under-Secretary of State, Chris Pond, MP
Private Secretary, Helen Daniels
Parliamentary Under-Secretary of State (Lords), The Rt. Hon. The Baroness Hollis of Heigham, DL
Private Secretary, Lucy Vause
Parliamentary Under-Secretary of State, Maria Eagle, MP *(Disabled People)*
Private Secretary, Paul McCourt
Permanent Secretary, Sir Richard Mottram, KCB
Private Secretary, Judith Tunstall
Parliamentary Clerk, Tim Elms

WORKING AGE AND CHILDREN GROUP
Group Director, Adam Sharples
Director, Fraud, Planning and Presentation Strategy, R. Clark
Director, National Employment Panel, Ms C. Stratton
Director, Work and Welfare Strategy, M. Richardson
Divisional Manager, Family Poverty and Employment Division, Julia Sweeney

PENSIONS AND DISABILITY GROUP
Managing Director, P. Gray
Director, Disability and Carers Service, Terry Moran
Director, Disability and Carers, Bruce Calderwood
Director, Information and Analysis Directorate, Robert Laslett
Director, Joint International Unit, C. Tucker
Director, Pensions Reform Division, Christopher Evans
Director, Pensions Stewardship Division, Richard d'Souza
Director, Private Pensions Centre, Policy Implementation Division, Charles Ramsden
Director, Private Pensions Policy Design Division, Tracy Gale
Director, Private Pensions Programme, Ms Hilary Reynolds
Divisional Manager, Pensions Strategy, Chris Capella
Head of Division, Private Pensions, Pension Protection Team, Charlie Massey

CORPORATE AND SHARED SERVICES GROUP FINANCE
Group Director and Principal Finance Officer, J. Codling
Director, Commercial, D. Smith
Director, Corporate Management Information, Sue Rice
Director, Financial Management, M. Davison
Director, Financial Services, P. Robinson
Director, Internal Assurance Services, C. Turner

PROGRAMME AND SYSTEMS DELIVERY GROUP
Group Director, Joe Harley
Head, Programme and Systems Delivery, Stephen Holt
Director, Digital Infrastructure, Debbie Heigh
Director, External Supply, John Priest
Director, Planning and Finance Strategy, Keith Palmer

HUMAN RESOURCES GROUP
Group Director, Kevin White
Diversity Director, Dr Barbara Burford
Head of Department, Development, Dawn Brodick
Head of Department, HR Services, G. Adey
Head of Department, Occupational Psychology, Dr M. Dalgliesh
Head of Department, Senior Civil Service, Kim Archer
Head of Department, Training Services, Mick Holbrook
Head of Department, Workforce Planning, Clarissa Poulson

MEDICAL POLICY AND CORPORATE MEDICAL GROUP
Chief Medical Adviser and Medical Director, Dr M. Aylward
Contractorisation of Medical Services (IMPACT) Project, Dr M. Henderson
EU of Medical Advisers in Social Security (UEMASS), Dr P. Stidolph
Policy Manager, Disability and Carer Benefits, Dr R. Thomas
Policy Manager, State Incapacity Benefits, Dr P. Sawney

LAW AND SPECIAL POLICY GROUP
Head of Group, Paul Jenkins
Director of Legal Services, J. Catlin
Assistant Director, Commercial Branch, R. Powell
Assistant Director, SOL Litigation, Ms A. James
Assistant Director, SOL Prosecutions, Amanda de Blaquiere

INFORMATION AND ANALYSIS DIRECTORATE
Director, Nick Dyson
Policy Manager, Ajudicational and Constitutional Reform, J. Griffiths
Policy Manager, Pension Provision Group, G. Fiegehen
Policy Manager, Welfare to Work Strategy, Jonathan Portes

COMMUNICATIONS DIRECTORATE
Group Director, Simon MacDowall
Head of Corporate Communications, Ken Young
Head of Marketing, Steve O'Neill
Head of Media Relations and News, Lindsey French

EXECUTIVE AGENCIES

APPEALS SERVICE AGENCY
see Tribunals Section

CHILD SUPPORT AGENCY
Long Benton, Benton Park Road, Newcastle upon Tyne NE98 1YX
CSA Helpline 08457-133133
The Agency was set up in April 1993. It is responsible for the administration of the Child Support Act and for the assessment, collection and enforcement of maintenance payments for all new cases.
Chief Executive, D. Smith
Non-Executive Directors, Dorit Braun; Mary Hay; Barbara Moorhouse; John Cross
Deputy Chief Executive and Director of Operations, M. Isaac
Directors, Ms E. Fox; John Oliver; Jim Edgar; Michael Foley; Sheila Bird; Ron Eagle

JOBCENTRE PLUS
Richmond House, 79 Whitehall, London SW1A 2NS
T 020-7238 0800 **F** 020-7238-0763
W www.jobcentreplus.gov.uk
Jobcentre Plus was formed in April 2002 following the merger of the Employment Service and some parts of the Benefits Agency. The agency administers claims for and payment of social security benefits to help people gain employment or improve their prospects for work as well as helping employers to fill their vacancies.
Chief Executive, D. Anderson

THE PENSION SERVICE
Trevelyan House, 30 Great Peter Street, London SW1P 2BY
Public Enquiries 0113-232 2414
The Pension Service was launched in April 2002 as an organisation dedicated to understanding the wishes and needs of today's and future pensioners, and providing State financial support for pensioners.
Chief Executive, Ms A. Cleveland

VETERANS AGENCY
Norcross, Blackpool, Lancs FY5 3WP
T 0800-169 2277
E help@veteransagency.gsi.gov.uk
W www.veteransagency.mod.uk
The Veterans Agency provides information and advice on issues of concern to veterans and their families. The Agency also administers the War Pension Scheme and provides welfare support to war pensioners and war widow(er)s and is responsible for the management of the Ilford Park Polish Home.
Chief Executive, A. Burnham

PUBLIC OFFICES

ADJUDICATOR'S OFFICE

Haymarket House, 28 Haymarket, London SW1Y 4SP
T 020-7930 2292 F 020-7930 2298
W www.adjucatorsoffice.gov.uk

The Adjudicator's Office opened in 1993 and investigates complaints about the way the Inland Revenue (including the Valuation Office Agency), Customs and Excise and the Public Guardianship Office have handled a person's affairs.

The Adjudicator, Dame Barbara Mills, DBE, QC
Head of Office, C. Gordon

ADVISORY, CONCILIATION AND ARBITRATION SERVICE

Brandon House, 180 Borough High Street, London SE1 1LW
T 020-7210 3613 F 020-7210 3708
W www.acas.org.uk

The Advisory, Conciliation and Arbitration Service (ACAS) was set up under the Employment Protection Act 1975 (the provisions now being found in the Trade Union and Labour Relations (Consolidation) Act 1992).

ACAS is directed by a Council consisting of a full-time chairman and part-time employer, trade union and independent members, all appointed by the Secretary of State for Trade and Industry. The functions of the Service are to promote the improvement of industrial relations in general, to provide facilities for conciliation, mediation and arbitration as means of avoiding and resolving industrial disputes, and to provide advisory and information services on industrial relations matters to employers, employees and their representatives.

ACAS has regional offices in Birmingham, Bury St Edmonds, Bristol, Cardiff, Glasgow, Kent, Leeds, Liverpool, London, Manchester, Newcastle upon Tyne and Nottingham.

Chair, R. Donaghy, OBE
Chief Executive, J. Taylor

ANCIENT MONUMENTS BOARD FOR WALES (CADW)

Crown Buildings, Cathays Park, Cardiff CF10 3NQ
T 029-2050 0200 F 029-2082 6375
E cadw@wales.gsi.gov.uk
W www.cadw.wales.gov.uk

The Ancient Monuments Board for Wales advises the Welsh Assembly on its statutory functions in respect of ancient monuments and historic buildings.

Chairman, Prof. R. R. Davies, CBE, FBA, DPHIL
Members, R. G. Keen; M. J. Garner; Prof. R. A. Griffiths, DLITT; R. Brewer, FSA; Prof. A. Whittle, FBA, DPHIL; C. Musson, MBE, FSA; Prof. M. Aldhouse-Green, FSA; Dr E. Plunkett Dillon; Dr N. Edwards
Secretary, Mrs J. Booker

ART GALLERIES

NATIONAL GALLERIES OF SCOTLAND

The Mound, Edinburgh EH2 2EL
T 0131-624 6200 F 0131-623 7126

The National Galleries of Scotland comprise the National Gallery of Scotland, the Scottish National Portrait Gallery, the Scottish National Gallery of Modern Art, the Dean Gallery and the Royal Scottish Academy Building. There are also outstations at Paxton House, Berwickshire, and Duff House, Banffshire. Total Government grant-in-aid for 2003–4 was £12.54 million.

TRUSTEES

Chairman of the Trustees, Mr B. Ivory, CBE
Trustees, Ms V. Atkinson; Ms A. Bonnar; Bailie E. Cameron; G. J. N. Gemmell, CBE; M. Ellington; Dr I. McKenzie Smith, OBE; Prof. R. Thomson; G. Weaver; Dr Ruth Wishart

OFFICERS

Director-General, Sir T. Clifford, FRSE
Director, National Gallery of Scotland, M. Clarke
Director, Scottish National Portrait Gallery, J. Holloway
Director, Scottish National Gallery of Modern Art and Dean Gallery, R. Calvocoressi

NATIONAL GALLERY

Trafalgar Square, London WC2N 5DN
T 020-7747 2885 F 020-7747 2423
W www.nationalgallery.org.uk

The National Gallery, which houses a permanent collection of western painting from the 13th to the 20th century, was founded in 1824, following a parliamentary grant of £60,000 for the purchase and exhibition of the Angerstein collection of pictures. The present site was first occupied in 1838; an extension to the north of the building with a public entrance in Orange Street was opened in 1975, and the Sainsbury wing was opened in 1991. Total Government grant-in-aid for 2004–5 is £21.227 million.

BOARD OF TRUSTEES

Chairman, P. Scott, QC
Trustees, Prof. D. Ades; S. Burke; J. Fenton; M. Getty; Prof. J. Higgins; Lady Hopkins; Sir John Kerr; J. Lessore; D. A. Moore; Lady Normanby; J. Snow; R. Sondhi; Sir Colin Southgate

OFFICERS

Director, Dr C. Saumarez Smith
Director of Administration, J. MacAuslan
Director of Conservation, M. H. Wyld, CBE
Director of Communications, Clare Gough
Director of Collections and Media, Dr S. Foister
Director of Education, K. Adler
Director of Scientific Research, Dr A. Roy
Senior Curator, D. Jaffé

NATIONAL PORTRAIT GALLERY

St Martin's Place, London WC2H 0HE
T 020-7306 0055 F 020-7306 0056
W www.npg.org.uk

A grant was made in 1856 to form a gallery of the portraits of the most eminent persons in British history. The present building was opened in 1896 and the Ondaatje Wing; including a new Balcony Gallery, Tudor Gallery, IT Gallery, Lecture Theatre and roof-top restaurant opened in May 2000. There are three regional partnerships displaying portraits at Montacute House, Beningbrough Hall and Bodelwyddan Castle. Total Government grant-in-aid for 2004-5 is £6.108 million.

BOARD OF TRUSTEES
Chairman, Sir David Scholey, CBE
Trustees, Prof. P. King, CBE, PRA; Ms F. Fraser; Sir M. Hastings; T. Phillips, CBE, RA; Prof. The Earl Russell, FBA; Mrs A. Shulman; Sir John Weston, KCMG; Baroness Willoughby de Eresby, DL; Prof. D. Cannadine; Prof. L. Jordanova; Dr C. Ondaatje, CBE, OC; Sara Selwood; Prof. R. Boucher, CBE, FRENG; Ms A. Fawcett, CBE; The Rt. Hon. Baroness Amos
Director, S. Nairne

ROYAL FINE ART COMMISSION FOR SCOTLAND

Bakehouse Close, 146 Canongate, Edinburgh EH8 8DD
T 0131-556 6699 F 0131-556 6633
W www.futurescotland.org

The Commission was established in 1927 and advises Ministers and local authorities on the visual impact and quality of design of construction projects. It is an independent body and gives its opinions impartially.
Chairman, The Rt. Hon. The Lord Cameron of Lochbroom, PC, FRSE
Commissioners, Ms J. Malvenan; R. G. Maund; M. Murray; D. Page; Ms B. Rae, CBE; Prof. R. Russell; M. Turnbull; A. Wright, OBE; Ms K. Anderson; Mrs M. Hickish; P. Stallan
Secretary, C. Prosser

TATE BRITAIN

Millbank, London SW1P 4RG
T 020-7887 8008 F 020-7887 8007
W www.tate.org.uk

Tate Britain displays the national collection of British art. The gallery opened in 1897, the cost of building (£80,000) being defrayed by Sir Henry Tate, who also contributed the nucleus of the present collection. The Turner wing was opened in 1910, and further galleries and a new sculpture hall followed in 1937. In 1979 a further extension was built, and the Clore Gallery, for the Turner collection, was opened in 1987. The Centenary Development was opened in 2001. There are four Tate galleries: Tate Britain and Tate Modern in London, Tate Liverpool and Tate St Ives.

BOARD OF TRUSTEES
Chairman, D. Verey
Trustees, Prof. D. Ades; Ms H. Alexander; Ms V. Barnsley; Prof. J. Latto; J. Snow; J. Studzinski; Ms G. Wearing; C. Ofili; J. Opie; Sir Howard Davies; P. Myners, CBE

OFFICERS
Director, Sir Nicholas Serota
Deputy Director, Alex Beard
Director of Collections, Jan Debbaut
Director, Tate Britain, S. Deuchar
Director, Tate Liverpool, C. Gruneberg
Director, Tate Modern, V. Todoli
Director, Tate St Ives, S. Daniel-McElvoy

TATE MODERN

Bankside, London SE1 9TG
T 020-7887 8008 Booking 020-7887 8888
W www.tate.org.uk

Opened on 11 May 2000, Tate Modern displays the Tate collection of international modern art dating from 1900 to the present day. It includes works by Dalí, Picasso, Matisse and Warhol as well as many contemporary works. It is housed in the former Bankside Power Station in London, which was redesigned by the Swiss architects Herzog & de Meuron.
Director, V. Todoli

WALLACE COLLECTION

Hertford House, Manchester Square, London W1M 3BN
T 020-7563 9500 F 020-7224 2155
W www.wallacecollection.org

The Wallace Collection was bequeathed to the nation by the widow of Sir Richard Wallace, in 1897, and Hertford House was subsequently acquired by the Government. Total Government grant-in-aid for 2003–4 was £2.2 million.
Director, Miss R. J. Savill
Head of Finance and Administration (acting), Simon Pink

ARTS COUNCILS

ARTS COUNCIL ENGLAND

14 Great Peter Street, London SW1P 3NQ
T 0845-300 6200 F 020-7973 6590
E enquiries@artscouncil.org.uk
W www.artscouncil.org.uk

Arts Council England is the national development agency for the arts in England, distributing public money from Government and the National Lottery. Between 2003 and 2006 Arts Council England will invest £2 billion of public funds in the arts in England. Arts Council Grants for the arts are for individuals, arts organisations, national touring and other people who use the arts in their work.

On 1 April 2002, the Arts Council of England and nine regional arts boards joined together to form a single development organisation for the arts. The nine regions are East, East Midlands, London, North East, North West, South East, South West, West Midlands and Yorkshire.
Chairman, Sir Christopher Frayling
Members, Sir Norman Adsetts, OBE; T. Bloxham, MBE; Ms D. Bull, CBE; P. Collard; Ms D. Grubb; Lady Sue Woodford Hollick; Prof. A. Livingston; S. Lowe; B. McMaster, CBE; Ms E. Owusu; W. Sieghart; Prof. S. Timperley; Ms D. Wilson
Chief Executive, P. Hewitt

ARTS COUNCIL OF NORTHERN IRELAND

MacNeice House, 77 Malone Road, Belfast BT9 6AQ
T 028-9038 5200 **F** 028-9066 1715
E publicaffairs@artscouncil-ni.org
W www.artscouncil-ni.org

The Arts Council of Northern Ireland is the prime distributor of Government funds in support of the arts in Northern Ireland. It is funded by the Department of Culture, Arts and Leisure, and the grant for 2003–4 was over £7 million.
Chair, Ms R. Kelly
Vice-Chair, M. Bradley
Members, Mrs E. M. Benson; Mrs K. Bond; W. Chamberlain; Ms L. Finnegan; Ms J. A. Holmes; A. Kennedy; T. Kerr; B. J. Milligan; W. H. C. Montgomery; Ms S. M. O'Connor; G. O'Heara; P. Spratt
Chief Executive, Ms R. McDonough

ARTS COUNCIL OF WALES

9 Museum Place, Cardiff CF10 3NX
T 029-2037 6500 **F** 029-2022 1447
E info@artswales.org.uk
W www.artswales.org.uk

The Arts Council of Wales is the development body for the arts in Wales. It funds arts organisations with funding from the National Assembly for Wales and is the distributor of National Lottery funds to the arts in Wales. The grant for 2003–4 was £34,445,801.
Chairman, Geraint Talfan Davies
Members, D. Davies; H. James; D. W. Walters; R. Till; S. Dancey; Dr F. Rhydderch; C. O'Neil; M. Elis; R. Wyn Hughes; D. Vokes; H. Roberts; J. Metcalf; J. Robert; Prof. D. Smith
Chief Executive, P. Tyndall

SCOTTISH ARTS COUNCIL

12 Manor Place, Edinburgh EH3 7DD
T 0131-226 6051 **F** 0131-225 9833
E help.desk@scottisharts.org.uk
W www.scottisharts.org.uk

The Scottish Arts Council is the main arts development agency in Scotland. It is a non-departmental public body, accountable to Scottish Ministers. The Scottish Arts Council investing funds from the Scottish Executive and National Lottery and working with partners to support and develop artistic excellence and creativity throughout Scotland.
Acting Chairman, D. Idiens
Members, Cllr E. Cameron; J. Scott Moncrieff; W. Speirs; Ms J. Baker; Ms L. Mitchell; J. Mulgrew; A. Cormack; S. Grimmond; Ms J. Hawksworth; A. Herman; R. McEwan; Ms A. Marrs; R. Smith; B. Twist
Director, G. Berry

ASSEMBLY OMBUDSMAN FOR NORTHERN IRELAND AND NORTHERN IRELAND COMMISSIONER FOR COMPLAINTS

Progressive House, 33 Wellington Place, Belfast BT1 6HN
T 028-9023 3821 **F** 028-9023 4912
E ombudsman@ni-ombudsman.org.uk
W www.ni-ombudsman.org.uk

The Ombudsman is appointed under legislation with powers to investigate complaints by people claiming to have sustained injustice in consequence of maladministration arising from action taken by a Northern Ireland Government department, or any other public body within his remit. Staff are presently seconded from the Northern Ireland Civil Service.
Ombudsman, T. Frawley
Deputy Ombudsman, J. MacQuarrie
Directors, C. O'Hare; R. Doherty; H. Mallon; P. Gibson

AUDIT COMMISSION FOR LOCAL AUTHORITIES AND THE NATIONAL HEALTH SERVICE IN ENGLAND AND WALES

1 Vincent Square, London SW1P 2PN
T 020-7828 1212 **F** 020-7976 6187
E enquiries@audit-commission.gov.uk
W www.audit-commission.gov.uk

The Audit Commission was set up in 1983 and is responsible for appointing external auditors to local authorities, including the Greater London Authority, and local National Health Service bodies in England and Wales. It is also responsible for promoting the proper stewardship of public finances and value for money in the services provided by local authorities and health bodies.

The Commission has a chairman, a deputy chairman and up to 18 members who are appointed by the Office of the Deputy Prime Minister in consultation with the Secretary of State for Wales and the Health Secretaries in England and Wales.
Chair, J. Strachan
Members, Dr. P. Lane; G. Lemos; D. Moss; J. Bowen; R. Hoyle; S. Bundred; Dr J. Dixon; Ms S. Drew Smith; P. Jones; Sir Michael Lyons; B. Pomeroy; Cllr. Baroness Scott; Prof. P. C. Smith
Chief Executive, Steve Bundred

AUDIT SCOTLAND

110 George Street, Edinburgh EH2 4LH
T 0131-477 1234 **F** 0131-477 4567
W www.audit–scotland.gov.uk

Audit Scotland was set up on 1 April 2000 to provide services to the Accounts Commission and the Auditor General for Scotland. Together they help to ensure that the Scottish Executive and public sector bodies in Scotland are held accountable for the proper, efficient and effective use of around £18 billion of public funds.

Audit Scotland's work covers over 200 bodies including local authorities, police and fire boards; NHS boards and trusts; further education colleges; the water authority; departments of the Scottish Executive; executive agencies such as the Prison Service and non-departmental public bodies such as Scottish Enterprise.

Audit Scotland carries out financial and regularity

audits to ensure that public sector bodies adhere to the highest standards of financial management and governance. It also performs audits to ensure that these bodies achieve the best value for money. All of Audit Scotland's work in connection with local authorities, fire and police boards is carried out for the Accounts Commission while its other work is undertaken for the Auditor General.
Auditor General, R. W. Black
Accounts Commission Chairman, A. MacNish
Secretary, W. F. Magee

BANK OF ENGLAND

Threadneedle Street, London EC2R 8AH
T 020-7601 4444 F 020-7601 4771
E enquiries@bankofengland.co.uk
W www.bankofengland.co.uk

The Bank of England was incorporated in 1694 under royal charter. It is the banker of the Government and it manages the issue of banknotes. Since May 1997 it has been operationally independent and its Monetary Policy Committee has had responsibility for setting short-term interest rates to meet the Government's inflation target. As the central reserve bank of the country, the Bank keeps the accounts of British banks, which maintain with it a proportion of their cash resources, and of most overseas central banks. The Bank has three main areas of activity: monetary stability, market operations and financial stability. Its responsibility for banking supervision has been transferred to the Financial Services Authority.
Governor, M. A. King
Deputy Governors, Sir Andrew Large; Ms R. Lomax
Non-Executive Directors, Sir David Cooksey; Sir Ian Gibson, CBE; Ms K. A. O'Donovan; Dr D. Julius, CBE; Sir. John Bond; Ms B. Blow; Sir Brian Moffat, OBE; Mrs L. Powers-Freeling; B. Barber; The Hon. Peter Jay; Dr D. Potter, CBE; Ms H. Rabbatts, CBE; Mrs M. Francis, LVO; Sir Graham Hall; C. McCarthy; Sir William Morris
Monetary Policy Committee, The Governor; the Deputy Governors; Prof. S. Nickell; C. Bean; Ms K. Barker; Ms M. Bell; P. Tucker; R. Lambert
Advisers to the Governor, M. Glover; C. Goodhart; A. Clark
Chief Cashier and Executive Director, Banking Services, A. Bailey
Chief Registrar, G. P. Sparkes
Secretary, A. Wardlow
The Auditor, Mrs C. Brady

BOUNDARY COMMISSIONS

The Commissions are constituted under the Parliamentary Constituencies Act 1986. The Speaker of the House of Commons is *ex officio* chairman of all four commissions in the UK. Each of the four commissions is required by law to keep the parliamentary constituencies in their part of the UK under review. The latest Boundary Commission report for England was completed in April 1995 and its proposals took effect at the 1997 general election. The next report must be submitted before April 2006. The latest Scottish report was completed in December 1994, with the European constituencies completed in April 1996.

ENGLAND

1 Drummond Gate, London SW1V 2QQ
T 020-7533 5177 F 020-7533 5176
Deputy Chairman, The Hon. Mr Justice Harrison
Joint Secretaries, R. Farrance; M. Barnett

WALES

1st Floor, Caradog House, 1–6 St Andrews Place, Cardiff CF10 3BE
T 029-2039 5031 F 029-2039 5250
Deputy Chairman, The Hon. Mr Justice Richards
Joint Secretaries, E. H. Lewis; M. Barnett

SCOTLAND

3 Drumsheugh Gardens, Edinburgh EH3 7QJ
T 0131-538 7200 F 0131-538 7240
Deputy Chairman, The Rt. Hon. Lady Cosgrove
Secretary, R. Smith

NORTHERN IRELAND

2nd Floor, Forestview, Purdy's Lane, Newtownbreda, Belfast BT8 7AR
T 028-9069 4800 F 028-9069 4801
Deputy Chairman, The Hon. Mr Justice Coghlin
Secretary, J. R. Fisher

BRITISH BROADCASTING CORPORATION

Broadcasting House, Portland Place, London W1A 1AA
T 020-7580 4468 BBC Information Line 0870-010 0222
W www.bbc.co.uk
Television Centre, Wood Lane, London W12 7RJ

The BBC was incorporated under royal charter in 1926 as successor to the British Broadcasting Company Ltd. The BBC's current charter came into force on 1 May 1996 and extends to 31 December 2006. The chairman, vice-chairman and other governors are appointed by The Queen-in-Council. The BBC is financed by revenue from receiving licences for the home services and by grant-in-aid from Parliament for the World Service (radio).

BOARD OF GOVERNORS
Chairman, M. Grade
Vice-Chairman, Anthony Salz
National Governors, Prof. F. Monds *(N. Ireland)*; Prof. M. Jones *(Wales)*; Sir Robert Smith *(Scotland)*; R. Sondhi, CBE
Governors, D. Gleeson; Dame Pauline Neville-Jones, DCMG; Dame Ruth Deech; Angela Sarkis, CBE; Deborah Bull, CBE; R.Tait

BOARD OF MANAGEMENT

EXECUTIVE COMMITTEE
Director-General and Editor-in-Chief, M. Thompson
Deputy Director-General, M. Byford
Directors, Ms J. Bennett *(Television)*; Ms J. Abramsky *(Radio and Music)*; Ms H. Boaden *(News)*; J. Willis *(Factual and Learning)*; A. Yentob *(Drama, Entertainment and Children)*; P. Loughrey *(Nations and Regions)*; J. Smith *(Chief Operating Officer)*; S. Dando *(Human Resources and Internal)*; A. Duncan *(Marketing, Communications and Audiences)*; P. Salmon *(Sport)*; Ms C. Thomson *(Policy and Legal)*; Ms C. Fairbairn *(Strategy and Distribution)*; A. Highfield *(New Media)*; vacant *(Chief Executive, BBC Worldwide)*

OTHER SENIOR STAFF
Controller, BBC1, L. Heggessey
Controller, BBC2, R. Keating
Controller, BBC3, S. Murphy
Controller, BBC4, R. Keating
Controller, Factual, G. Benson
Controller, BBC Daytime, Ms A. Sharman
Controller, Radio 1, A. Parfitt
Controller, Radio 2, L. Douglas
Controller, Radio 3, R. Wright
Controller, Radio 4, D. Damazer
Controller, Radio 5 Live, B. Shennan
Controller, BBC Proms, Live Events and Television Classical Music, N. Kenyon
Controller, Network Development, Nations and Regions, C. Cameron

BRITISH COUNCIL

10 Spring Gardens, London SW1A 2BN
T 020-7930 8466 F 020-7389 6347
Bridgewater House, 58 Whitworth Street, Manchester M1 6BB
T 0161-957 7000

The British Council was established in 1934, incorporated by Royal Charter in 1940 and granted a supplemental charter in 1993. It is an independent, non-political organisation which promotes Britain abroad and is the UK's international organisation for educational and cultural relations. The British Council is represented in 216 towns and cities in 109 countries. Turnover in 2004–5, including Foreign and Commonwealth Office grants and contracted money, is expected to be £485.5 million.
Chairman, The Baroness Kennedy of The Shaws, QC
Director-General, D. Green, CMG

BRITISH FILM INSTITUTE

21 Stephen Street, London W1T 1LN
T 020-7255 1444 F 020-7436 0439
W www.bfi.org.uk

The British Film Institute (BFI) offers opportunities for people throughout the UK to experience, learn and discover more about the world of film and moving image culture. The BFI incorporates the BFI National Library, the monthly magazine *Sight and Sound*, the BFI National Film Theatre, the annual London Film Festival and the BFI London IMAX, and provides advice and support for regional cinemas and film festivals across the UK. The BFI also undertakes the preservation of, and promotes access to films, television programmes, computer games, museum collections, stills, posters and designs, and other special collections.
Chairman, Anthony Minghella, CBE
Director, Amanda Nevill

BRITISH PHARMACOPOEIA COMMISSION

Market Towers, 1 Nine Elms Lane, London SW8 5NQ
T 020-7084 2561 F 020-7084 0566

The British Pharmacopoeia Commission sets standards for medicinal products used in human and veterinary medicines and is responsible for publication of the British Pharmacopoeia (a publicly available statement of the standard that a product must meet throughout its shelf-life), the British Pharmacopoeia (Veterinary) and the selection of British Approved Names. It has 15 members who are appointed by the Secretary of State for Health, the Minister for Environment, Food and Rural Affairs, the Scottish Ministers, the National Assembly for Wales, and the relevant Northern Ireland departments.
Chairman, Prof. D. Calam, OBE, DPHIL
Vice-Chairman, Prof. J. A. Goldsmith
Secretary and Scientific Director, Dr M. G. Lee

BRITISH STANDARDS INSTITUTION, BSI GROUP

389 Chiswick High Road, London W4 4AL
T 020-8996 9000 F 020-8996 7001
E cservices@bsi-global.com W www.bsi-global.com

British Standards – a part of the BSI Group – is the recognised authority in the UK for the preparation and publication of national standards, both for products and the service sector. About 90 per cent of its standards work is internationally linked. British Standards are issued for voluntary adoption, though in some cases compliance with a British Standard is required by legislation. Industrial and consumer products and services certified as complying with the relevant British Standard and operating an assessed quality management system are eligible to carry BSI's certification trade mark, known as the 'Kitemark'.
Chairman, Sir David John, KCMG
Chief Executive, Stevan Breeze

BRITISH WATERWAYS

Willow Grange, Church Road, Watford, Herts WD17 4QA
T 01923-226422 F 01923-201400
E enquiries.hq@britishwaterways.co.uk
W www.britishwaterways.co.uk

British Waterways conserves and manages over 2,000 miles of canals and rivers in England, Scotland and Wales. It is responsible to the Secretary of State for Environment, Food and Rural Affairs.

Its responsibilities include maintaining the waterways and structures on and around them; looking after wildlife and the waterway environment; and ensuring that canals and rivers are safe and enjoyable places to visit.
Chairman, Dr G. Greener
Vice-Chairman of the Board, Sir P. Soulsby
Board Members, D. Langslow; I. Darling; Ms H. Gordon; C. Christie; Ms S. Achmatowicz; G. Fleming; Ms J. Lewis-Jones; Ms A. Malik; T. Tricker
Chief Executive, R. Evans

BROADS AUTHORITY

18 Colegate, Norwich NR3 1BQ
T 01603-610734 F 01603-765710
E broads@broads-authority.gov.uk
W www.broads-authority.gov.uk

The Broads Authority is a special statutory authority set up under the Norfolk and Suffolk Broads Act 1988. The functions of the Authority are to conserve and enhance the natural beauty of the Broads; to provide integrated management of the land and water space of the area; to promote the enjoyment of the Broads by the public; and to protect the interests of navigation. The Authority comprises 35 members, appointed by the local authorities in the area covered, environmental conservation bodies, the Environment Agency, and the Great Yarmouth Port Authority.
Chairman, Prof. K. Turner
Chief Executive, Dr J. Packman

CENTRAL ARBITRATION COMMITTEE

Third Floor, Discovery House, 28–42 Banner Street, London, EC1Y 8QE
T 020-7251 9747 F 020-7251 3114
E enquiries@cac.gov.uk W www.cac.gov.uk

The Central Arbitration Committee is a permanent independent body which determines claims for statutory recognition and de-recognition of trade unions under the Employment Relations Act 1999, it also adjudicates on disclosure of information cases, issues relating to the European Works Council Directive and arbitrates on trade disputes.

Chairman, Sir Michael Burton
Secretary and Chief Executive, G. Charles

CERTIFICATION OFFICE FOR TRADE UNIONS AND EMPLOYERS' ASSOCIATIONS

Brandon House, 180 Borough High Street, London SE1 1LW
T 020-7210 3734/5 F 020-7210 3612
E info@certoffice.org W www.certoffice.org

The Certification Office is an independent statutory authority. The Certification Officer is appointed by the Secretary of State for Trade and Industry and is responsible for receiving and scrutinising annual returns from trade unions and employers' associations; for determining complaints concerning trade union elections, certain ballots and certain breaches of trade union rules; for ensuring observance of statutory requirements governing mergers between trade unions and employers' associations; for overseeing the political funds and finances of trade unions and employers' associations; and for certifying the independence of trade unions.

Certification Officer, David Cockburn

SCOTLAND

54–66 Frederick Street, Edinburgh EH2 1NB
T 0131-200 1200
Certification Officer for Scotland, Christine Stuart

CHARITY COMMISSION

Harmsworth House, 13–15 Bouverie Street, London EC4Y 8DP
T 0870-333 0123 F 020-7674 2310
2nd Floor, 20 King's Parade, Queen's Dock, Liverpool L3 4DQ
T 0870-333 0123 F 0151-703 1555
Woodfield House, Tangier, Taunton, Somerset TA1 4BL
T 0870-333 0123 F 01823-345003
W www.charitycommission.gov.uk

The Charity Commission for England and Wales is the Government Department whose aim is to give the public confidence in the integrity of charities. It also carries out the functions of the registration, monitoring and support of charities and the investigation of alleged wrong-doing. The Commission maintains a computerised register of some 187,000 charities. It is accountable to the courts and, for its efficiency, to the Home Secretary. There are five Commissioners appointed by the Home Office for a fixed term and the Commission has Offices in London, Liverpool, Taunton and Newport.

Chief Commissioner, J. Stoker
Acting Legal Commissioner, K. M. Dibble
Commissioners (part-time), D. Taylor; D. Unwin; Ms G. Peacock
Director of Operations, S. Gillespie
Heads of Legal Section, G. S. Goodchild; K. M. Dibble; J. Kilby
Head of Human Resources, Ms S. Bailey
Head of Policy Division, Ms R. Chapman
Information Systems Controller, K. Chown

REGIONAL OFFICES

SCOTLAND – Scottish Charities Office, Crown Office, 25 Chambers Street, Edinburgh EH1 1LA T 0131-226 2626
NORTHERN IRELAND – Department for Social Development, Charities Branch, 5th Floor, Churchill House, Victoria Square, Belfast BT1 4SD
WALES – 8th Floor, Clarence House, Clarence Place, Newport, South Wales NP19 7AA T 0870-333 0123

CHURCH COMMISSIONERS

1 Millbank, London SW1P 3JZ
T 020-7898 1000 F 020-7898 1131
E commissioners.enquiry@c-of-e.org
W www.churchcommissioners.org

The Church Commissioners were established in 1948 by the amalgamation of Queen Anne's Bounty (established 1704) and the Ecclesiastical Commissioners (established 1836). They are responsible for the management of the majority of the Church of England's assets, the income from which is predominantly used to help pay for the stipend and pension of the clergy. The Commissioners own over 120,000 acres of agricultural land, a number of residential estates in central London, and commercial property across Great Britain. They also carry out administrative duties in connection with pastoral reorganisation and redundant churches.

The Commissioners are: the Archbishops of Canterbury and of York; four bishops, three clergy and four lay persons elected by the respective houses of the General Synod; two deans or provosts elected by all the deans and provosts; three persons nominated by The Queen; three persons nominated by the Archbishops of Canterbury and York; three persons nominated by the Archbishops after consultation with others including the lord mayors of London and York and the vice-chancellors of the universities of Oxford and Cambridge; the First Lord of the Treasury; the Lord President of the Council; the Home Secretary; the Lord Chancellor; the Secretary of State for Culture, Media and Sport; and the Speaker of the House of Commons.

CHURCH ESTATES COMMISSIONERS

First, A. Whittam Smith
Second, Sir Stuart Bell, MP
Third, The Viscountess Brentford

OFFICERS

Secretary, A. C. Brown
Deputy Secretary (Finance and Investment), C. W. Daws

ASSISTANT SECRETARIES

Chief Surveyor, P. Clark
Chief Investments Manager, M. Chaloner
Pastoral and Redundant Churches, M. D. Elengorn
Official Solicitor, S. Jones

CIVIL AVIATION AUTHORITY

CAA House, 45–59 Kingsway, London WC2B 6TE
T 020-7379 7311
W www.caa.co.uk

The CAA is responsible for the economic regulation of UK airlines and for the safety regulation of UK civil aviation by the certification of airlines and aircraft and by licensing aerodromes, flight crew and aircraft engineers.

The CAA advises the Government on aviation issues, represents consumer interests, conducts economic and scientific research, produces statistical data, and provides specialist services and other training and consultancy services to clients world-wide. It also regulates UK airspace and runs the ATOL flight and air holiday protection scheme.

Chairman, Sir Roy McNulty
Secretary and Legal Adviser, R. J. Britton

COAL AUTHORITY

200 Lichfield Lane, Mansfield, Notts NG18 4RG
T 01623-427162 F 01623-622072
E thecoalauthority@coal.gov.uk
W www.coal.gov.uk

The Coal Authority was established under the Coal Industry Act 1994 to manage certain functions previously undertaken by British Coal, including ownership of unworked coal. It is responsible for licensing coal mining operations and for providing information on coal reserves and past and future coal mining. It settles subsidence claims not falling on coal mining operators. It deals with the management and disposal of property, and with surface hazards such as abandoned coal mine shafts.

Chairman, J. Harris
Chief Executive, Dr I. Roxburgh

COLLEGE OF ARMS (HERALDS' COLLEGE)

Queen Victoria Street, London EC4V 4BT
T 020-7248 2762 F 020-7248 6448
E enquiries@college-of-arms.gov.uk
W www.college-of-arms.gov.uk

The Sovereign's Officers of Arms (Kings, Heralds and Pursuivants of Arms) were first incorporated by Richard III. The powers vested by the Crown in the Earl Marshal (the Duke of Norfolk) with regard to state ceremonial are largely exercised through the College. The College is also the official repository of the arms and pedigrees of English, Welsh, Northern Irish and Commonwealth (except Canadian) families and their descendants, and its records include official copies of the records of Ulster King of Arms, the originals of which remain in Dublin. The 13 officers of the College specialise in genealogical and heraldic work for their respective clients.

Arms have always been, and still are, granted by letters patent from the Kings of Arms. A right to arms can only be established by the registration in the official records of the College of Arms of a pedigree showing direct male line descent from an ancestor already appearing therein as being entitled to arms, or by making application through the College of Arms for a grant of arms. Grants are made to corporations as well as to individuals.

Earl Marshal, The Duke of Norfolk

KINGS OF ARMS
Garter, P. L. Gwynn-Jones, CVO, FSA
Clarenceux, D. H. B. Chesshyre, LVO, FSA
Norroy and Ulster, T. Woodcock, LVO, FSA

HERALDS
Richmond (and Earl Marshal's Secretary), P. L. Dickinson
York, H. E. Paston-Bedingfeld
Chester (and Registrar), T. H. S. Duke
Lancaster, R. J. B. Noel
Windsor, W. G. Hunt, TD

PURSUIVANTS
Rouge Croix, D. V. White
Rouge Dragon, C. E. A. Cheesman

COMMISSION FOR ARCHITECTURE AND THE BUILT ENVIRONMENT

The Tower Building, 11 York Road, London SE1 7NX
T 020-7960 2400 F 020-7960 2444
E enquiries@cabe.org.uk W www.cabe.org.uk

The Commission for Architecture and the Built Environment (CABE) is responsible for promoting the importance of high quality architecture and urban design and encouraging the understanding of architecture through educational and regional initiatives. CABE offers free advice to local authorities, public sector clients and others embarking on building projects of any size or purpose.

Interim Chairman, Paul Finch
Chief Executive, R. Simmons

COMMISSION FOR INTEGRATED TRANSPORT

2nd Floor, 12 St James's Square, London SW1Y 4RB
E cfit@dft.gsi.gov.uk
W www.cfit.gov.uk

The Commission for Integrated Transport was proposed in the 1998 Transport White Paper and was set up in June 1999. Its role is to provide independent expert advice to the Government in order to achieve a transport system that supports sustainable development. Members of the Commission are appointed by the Secretary of State for Transport.

Chairman, Prof. D. Begg
Vice-Chairman, Sir Trevor Chinn
Members, L. Christensen, CBE; S. Francis; S. Joseph; D. Leeder; Ms L. Matson; W. Morris; Ms H. Holland; N. Scales; M. Parker; Baroness Scott; Sir Michael Hodgkinson; Sir Roy McNulty, CBE; R. Bowker; N. Betteridge; S. Hickey; M. Roberts

COMMISSION FOR LOCAL ADMINISTRATION IN ENGLAND

10th Floor, Millbank Tower, Millbank, London SW1P 4QP
T 020-7217 4620 F 020-7217 4621
Enquiry line 0845-602 1983

Local Commissioners (local government ombudsmen) are responsible for investigating complaints from members of the public against local authorities (but not town and parish councils); English Partnerships (planning matters only); Housing Action Trusts; education appeal panels; police authorities and certain other authorities. The Commissioners are appointed by the Crown on the recommendation of the Deputy Prime Minister.

Certain types of action are excluded from investigation, including personnel matters and commercial transactions unless they relate to the purchase or sale of land. Complaints can be sent direct to the Local Government Ombudsman or through a councillor, although the Local Government Ombudsman will not consider a complaint unless the council has had an opportunity to investigate and reply to a complainant.

A free leaflet *Complaint about the council? How to complain to the Local Government Ombudsman* is available from the Commission's offices.

Chairman and Chief Executive of the Commission and Local Commissioner (£147,198), T. Redmond
Vice-Chairman and Local Commissioner (£111,361), Mrs P. A. Thomas
Local Commissioner (£110,361), J. R. White
Member (*ex officio*), *The Parliamentary Commissioner for Administration*
Deputy Chief Executive and Secretary (£73,869), N. J. Karney

COMMISSION FOR RACIAL EQUALITY

St Dunstan's House, 201–211 Borough High Street, London SE1 1GZ
T 020-7939 0000 F 020-7939 0001
E info@cre.gov.uk W www.cre.gov.uk

The Commission for Racial Equality was set up under the 1976 Race Relations Act. It receives an annual grant from the Home Office but works independently of Government. The CRE is run by commissioners appointed by the Home Secretary, and has support from all the main political parties.

The CRE has three main duties: to work towards the elimination of racial discrimination and to promote equality of opportunity; to encourage good relations between people from different racial backgrounds; and to monitor the way the Race Relations Act is working and recommend ways in which it can be improved.

The CRE is the only Government-appointed body with statutory power to enforce the Race Relations Act. It also has a reference library which is open to the public (by appointment only).

Chairman, Trevor Phillips
Chief Executive, Sheila Rogers

COMMITTEE ON STANDARDS IN PUBLIC LIFE

35 Great Smith Street, London SW1P 3BQ
T 020-7276 2595 F 020-7276 2585
W www.public-standards.gov.uk

The Committee on Standards in Public Life was set up in October 1994. It is a standing body whose chairman and members are appointed by the Prime Minister; three members are nominated by the leaders of the three main political parties. The Committee's remit is to examine concerns about standards of conduct of all holders of public office, including arrangements relating to financial and commercial activities, and to make recommendations as to any changes in present arrangements which might be required to ensure the highest standards of propriety in public life. It is also charged with reviewing issues in relation to the funding of political parties. The Committee does not investigate individual allegations of misconduct.

Chair, Sir Alistair Graham
Members, The Rt. Hon. Chris Smith, MP; Rita Donaghy, OBE; Prof. Hazel Genn, CBE; Dame Patricia Hodgson, DBE; Baroness Maddock; The Rt. Hon. Gillian Shephard, MP; Dr Elizabeth Vallance; Dr Brian Woods-Scawen
Secretary, Robert Behrens

COMMONWEALTH INSTITUTE

Kensington High Street, London W8 6NQ
T 020-7603 4535 F 020-7602 4525
E information@commonwealth.org.uk
W www.commonwealth.org.uk

The Commonwealth Institute is an educational trust. Its members are the member states of the Commonwealth who elect a Board of Trustees responsible to them. The Trustees have entered a joint venture with Cambridge University to create a Centre for Commonwealth Education.

Chairman, Miss J. Hanratty, OBE
Vice-Chairman, The Rt. Hon. Lord Fellowes, GCB, GCVO
Company Secretary, Ms J. Curry

COMMONWEALTH WAR GRAVES COMMISSION

2 Marlow Road, Maidenhead, Berks SL6 7DX
T 01628-634221 F 01628-771208
E general.enq@cwgc.org
W www.cwgc.org

The Commonwealth War Graves Commission (formerly Imperial War Graves Commission) was founded by royal charter in 1917. It is responsible for the commemoration of 1,694,783 members of the forces of the Commonwealth who lost their lives in the two world wars. More than one million graves are maintained in 23,292 burial grounds throughout the world. Over three-quarters of a million men and women who have no known grave or who were cremated are commemorated by name on memorials built by the Commission.

The funds of the Commission are derived from the six participating governments, i.e. the UK, Canada, Australia, New Zealand, South Africa and India.

President, HRH The Duke of Kent, KG, GCMG, GCVO, ADC
Chairman, The Secretary of State for Defence (UK)
Vice-Chairman, Gen. Sir John Wilsey, GCB, CBE, DL
Members, The High Commissioners in London for Australia, Canada, South Africa, New Zealand and India; Dame Susan Tinson, DBE; Sir John Keegan, OBE; Adm. Sir Peter Abbott, GBE, KCB; Alan Meale, MP; Ian Henderson, CBE, FRICS; Air Chief Marshal Sir Peter Squire, GCB, DFC, AFC, ADC; The Hon. Nicholas Soames, MP; Sir Rob Young, GCMG
Director-General and Secretary to the Commission, R. E. Kellaway
Deputy Director-General, M. S. Johnson, OBE
Legal Adviser and Solicitor, G. C. Reddie
Directors, D. R. Parker *(Information and Secretariat)*; B. Davidson, MBE *(Works)*; D. C. Parker *(Horticulture)*; Ms C. Cecil *(Personnel)*; P. J. Haysom *(Finance)*

IMPERIAL WAR GRAVES ENDOWMENT FUND

Trustees, A. C. Barker *(Chairman)*; C. G. Clarke; Gen. Sir John Wilsey, GCB, CBE
Secretary to the Trustees, P. J. Haysom

COMMUNITIES SCOTLAND

Thistle House, 91 Haymarket Terrace, Edinburgh EH12 5HE
T 0131-313 0044 F 0131-313 2680
W www.communitiesscotland.gov.uk

Communities Scotland is a Scottish Executive agency, reporting directly to Ministers. The agency's overall aim is to improve the quality of life for people in Scotland by working with others to create sustainable, healthy and attractive communities. They do this by regenerating neighbourhoods, empowering communities and improving the effectiveness of investment.
Chief Executive, Angiolina Foster

COMMUNITY FUND

1 Plough Place, London EC4A 1DE
T 020-7211 1800 Enquiries 020-7211 3737 F 020-7211 1750
W www.community-fund.org.uk

The Fund was set up under the National Lottery Act 1993 to distribute funds from the Lottery to support charitable, benevolent and philanthropic organisations. The chair and members are appointed by the Secretary of State for Culture, Media and Sport. The Fund's aim is to meet the needs of those at greatest disadvantage in society and also to improve the quality of life in the community.

It has UK-wide, county and regional priorities for its general grants programmes and runs two specialist programmes for research and international grants. So far the fund has distributed £2.4 billion to 54,000 charities and community groups.
Chair, Lady Brittan, CBE
Deputy Chairman, Dame Valerie Strachan, DCB
Members, E. Appelbee, MBE; S. Burkeman; J. Carroll; P. Cavanagh; D. Graham; K. Hampton; Prof. J. Kearney, OBE; S. Malley; R. Martineau; Ms E. Watkins; B. Whitaker, CBE; Ms C. Tongue; T. Idris
Director of Operations, Adriènne Kelbie
Director of Planning and Performance, Gerald Oppenheim

COMPETITION COMMISSION

Victoria House, Southampton Row, London WC1B 4AD
T 020-7271 0100 F 020-7271 0367
E info@competition-commission.gsi.gov.uk
W www.competition-commission.org.uk

The Commission was established in 1948 as the Monopolies and Restrictive Practices Commission (later the Monopolies and Mergers Commission); it became the Competition Commission in April 1999 under the Competition Act 1998. The Commission conducts in-depth inquiries into mergers (anticipated and completed); markets; and the regulation of major industries. Every inquiry the Commission undertakes is in response to a reference made to it by another authority, usually the Office of Fair Trading, but in certain circumstances by a Minister or by the regulators under sector-specific legislative provisions relating to regulated industries. The Commission has no power to conduct inquiries on its own initiative.

The Commission has a full-time chairman and three deputy chairmen. There are usually around 50 Commission members to carry out investigations. All are appointed by the Secretary of State for Trade and Industry for single eight-year terms.
Chairman, Prof P. A. Geroski
Deputy Chairman, P. J. Freeman
President, Appeal Tribunals, His Hon. Sir Christopher Bellamy, QC
Members, S. Ahmed; Prof. J. Baillie; R. D. D. Bertram; Mrs S. E. Brown, OBE; Miss L. I. Christmas; C. Clarke; Dr J. Collings; Dr D. Coyle; C. Darke; L. D. Elks; N. Garthwaite; W. Gibson; C. F. W. Goodall; Prof. C. Graham; Prof. A. Gregory; Mrs D. Guy; A. Hadfield; G. H. Hadley; Prof. A. Hamlin; Prof. J. Haskel; P. F. Hazell; C. E. Henderson, CB; G. L. Holbrook, MBE; R. N. Holroyd; Mrs M. J. Hopkirk; Prof. P. D. Klemperer; Prof. B. Lyons; N. C. L. Macdonald; Dame Barbara Mills, DBE, QC; Prof. P. Moizer; Dr E. M. Monck; Sir Derek Morris; Prof. D. Parker; Ms E. Pollard; R. A. Rawlinson; J. B. K. Rickford, CBE; E. J. Seddon; Dame Helena Shovelton, DBE; C. R. Smallwood; J. D. S. Stark; P. Stoddart; Prof. D. G. Trelford; R. Turgoose; Prof. C. Waddams; S. D. Walzer; M. R. Webster; Prof. S. R. M. Wilks; C. Wilson; A. M. Young
Non-Executive Directors, A. P. Foster; Dame Patricia Hodgson, DBE
Chief Executive and Secretary, R. Foster

COMPETITION SERVICE

Victoria House, Bloomsbury Place, London WC1A 2EB
T 020-7979 7979 F 020-7979 7978
E info@catribunal.org.uk
W www.catribunal.org.uk

The Enterprise Act 2002 created the Competition Service, a non-departmental public body whose purpose is to fund and provide support services to the Competition Appeal Tribunal. Support services include everything necessary to facilitate the carrying out by the Competition Appeal Tribunal of its statutory functions such as administration, accommodation and office equipment.
Director, Operations, Jeremy Straker

COUNCIL ON TRIBUNALS

81 Chancery Lane, London WC2A 1BQ
T 020-7855 5200 F 020-7855 5201
E enquiries@cot.gsi.gov.uk
W www.council-on-tribunals.gov.uk

The Council on Tribunals is an independent body that operates under the Tribunals and Inquiries Act 1992. It consists of 15 members appointed by the Lord Chancellor/Secretary of State for Constitutional Affairs and the Scottish Ministers; one member is appointed to represent the interests of people in Wales. The Scottish Committee of the Council generally considers Scottish tribunals and matters relating only to Scotland. The Parliamentary Commissioner for administration is an *ex officio* member of the Council and the Scottish Committee.

The Council advises on and keeps under review the constitution and working of the tribunals listed in the Tribunals and Inquiries Act, and considers and reports on administrative procedures relating to statutory inquiries. Some 80 tribunals are currently under the Council's supervision. It is consulted by and advises Government departments on a wide range of subjects relating to adjudicative procedures.
Chairman, The Rt. Hon. The Lord Newton of Braintree, OBE
Members, The Parliamentary Commissioner *(ex officio)*; J. Elliot, DKS *(Chairman of the Scottish Committee)*; Mrs C. Berkeley; Mrs E. C. Cameron; Miss J. C. Edwards; Ms Y. N. Genn; Mrs R. Hepplewhite; Mrs S. R. Howdle; Ms P.

Letts; B. Quoroll; Prof. G. Richardson; S. D. Mannion, QPM; A. W. Russell, CB; Dr A. V. Stokes; Ms H. Wilcox
Acting Secretary, R. B. Burningham

SCOTTISH COMMITTEE OF THE COUNCIL ON TRIBUNALS
44 Palmerston Place, Edinburgh EH12 5BJ
T 0131-220 1236 F 0131-225 4271
E sccot@gtnet.gov.uk
Chairman, R. J. Elliot, WS
Members, The Parliamentary Commissioner for Administration *(ex officio)*; Mrs B. Bruce; D. Graham; Mrs. M. Wood; Mrs E. Cameron; Mr S. Mannion; Mrs A. Watson
Secretary, Mrs E. M. MacRae

COUNTRYSIDE AGENCY

John Dower House, Crescent Place, Cheltenham, Glos GL50 3RA
T 01242-521381 F 01242-584270
W www.countryside.gov.uk

The Countryside Agency was set up in April 1999 by the merger of the Countryside Commission with parts of the Rural Development Commission. It is a statutory body which promotes the conservation and enhancement of the countryside in England and undertakes activities aimed at stimulating job creation and the provision of essential services in the countryside. The Agency is funded by an annual grant from the Department for Environment, Food and Rural Affairs and board members are appointed by the Secretary of State.
Chair, Ms P. Warhurst
Members, Ms K. Ashbrook; Rt. Revd Bishop of Norwich; Sir Martin Doughty; P. Fane; A. Hams, OBE; Prof. P. Lowe; Ms F. Rowe; J. Varley; Norman Glass; Dr Tayo Adebowale
Chief Executive, R. G. Wakeford
Directors, Miss M. A. Clark, OBE; Tim Lunel; S. Sleet; Tracey Slaven

COUNTRYSIDE COUNCIL FOR WALES/ CYNGOR CEFN GWLAD CYMRU

Maes y Ffynnon, Penrhosgarnedd, Bangor, Gwynedd LL57 2DW
T 0845-130 6229 F 01248-355782

The Countryside Council for Wales is the Government's statutory adviser on sustaining natural beauty, wildlife and the opportunity for outdoor enjoyment in Wales and its inshore waters. It is funded by the National Assembly for Wales and accountable to the First Secretary, who appoints its members.
Chairman, J. Lloyd Jones, OBE
Chief Executive, R. Thomas
Director, Corporate Services, L. Warmington
Director, Countryside Policy, Dr J. Taylor
Director of Science, Dr D. Parker

COURT OF THE LORD LYON

HM New Register House, Edinburgh EH1 3YT
T 0131-556 7255 F 0131-557 2148
W www.lyon-court.com

The Court of the Lord Lyon is the Scottish Court of Chivalry (including the genealogical jurisdiction of the *Ri-Sennachie* of Scotland's Celtic Kings). The Lord Lyon King of Arms has jurisdiction, subject to appeal to the Court of Session and the House of Lords, in questions of heraldry and the right to bear arms. The Court also administers the Scottish Public Register of All Arms and Bearings and the Public Register of All Genealogies. Pedigrees are established by decrees of Lyon Court and by letters patent. As Royal Commissioner in Armory, the Lord Lyon grants patents of arms (which constitute the grantee and heirs noble in the Noblesse of Scotland) to virtuous and well-deserving Scotsmen and to petitioners (personal or corporate) in The Queen's overseas realms of Scottish connection, and issues birthbrieves.
Lord Lyon King of Arms, R. O. Blair, LVO, WS

HERALDS
Albany, J. A. Spens, MVO, RD, WS
Rothesay, Sir Crispin Agnew of Lochnaw, BT, QC
Ross, C. J. Burnett, FSA SCOT

PURSUIVANTS
Unicorn, Alastair Campbell of Airds
Carrick, Mrs C. G. W. Roads, MVO, FSA SCOT
Bute, W. D. H. Sellar
Orkney Herald Extraordinary, Sir Malcolm Innes of Edingight, KCVO, WS
Linlithgow Pursuivant Extraordinary, J. C. G. George
Lyon Clerk and Keeper of Records, Mrs C. G. W. Roads, MVO, FSA SCOT
Procurator-Fiscal, George Way of Plean, SSC
Herald Painter, Mrs J. Phillips
Macer, H. M. Love

COVENT GARDEN MARKET AUTHORITY

Covent House, New Covent Garden Market, London SW8 5NX
T 020-7720 2211 F 020-7622 5307
E info@cgma.gov.uk
W www.cgma.gov.uk

The Covent Garden Market Authority is constituted under the Covent Garden Market Acts 1961 to 1977, the members being appointed by the Minister of Environment, Food and Rural Affairs. The Authority owns and operates the 56-acre New Covent Garden Markets (fruit, vegetables, flowers) which have been trading since 1974.
Chairman (part-time), L. Mills, CBE
General Manager, Dr P. M. Liggins
Secretary, C. Farey

CRIMINAL CASES REVIEW COMMISSION

Alpha Tower, Suffolk Street, Queensway, Birmingham B1 1TT
T 0121-633 1800 F 0121-633 1823/1804
E info@ccrc.gov.uk W www.ccrc.gov.uk

The Criminal Cases Review Commission is an independent body set up under the Criminal Appeal Act 1995. It is a non-departmental public body reporting to Parliament via the Home Secretary. It is responsible for investigating suspected miscarriages of justice in England, Wales and Northern Ireland, and deciding whether or not to refer cases back to an appeal court. Membership of the Commission is by royal appointment; the senior executive staff are appointed by the Commission.
Chairman, Prof. Graham Zellick
Members, B. Capon; L. Elks; A. Foster; I. Nicholl; D. Kyle; Prof. L. Leigh; J. MacKeith; K. Singh; B. Skitt; D. Jessel; M. Allen; M. Emerton; J. Weeden
Chief Executive, Ms J. Courtney
Director of Finance, C. Albert
Head of Human Resources, P. Wilkinson

Head of Communications, B. Worrall
Legal Advisers, J. Wagstaff; Ms F. Barrie
Police Adviser, R. Barrington

CRIMINAL INJURIES COMPENSATION APPEALS PANEL (CICAP)

11th Floor, Cardinal Tower, 12 Farringdon Road, London EC1M 3HS
T 020-7549 4600 F 020-7549 4643
E info@cicap.gsi.gov.uk W www.cicap.gov.uk
Chairman, R. Goodier
Chief Executive and Secretary to the Panel, R. Burke

CRIMINAL INJURIES COMPENSATION AUTHORITY (CICA)

Morley House, 26–30 Holborn Viaduct, London EC1A 2JQ
T 020-7842 6800 F 020-7436 0804
W www.cica.gov.uk
Tay House, 300 Bath Street, Glasgow G2 4LN
T 0141-331 2726 F 0141-331 2287
Freephone 0800-358 3601

All applications for compensation for personal injury arising from crimes of violence in England, Scotland and Wales are dealt with at the above locations. (Separate arrangements apply in Northern Ireland.) Applications received up to 31 March 1996 are assessed on the basis of common law damages under the 1990 compensation scheme. Applications received on or after 1 April 1996 are assessed under a tariff-based scheme, made under the Criminal Injuries Compensation Act 1995, by the Criminal Injuries Compensation Authority (CICA). There is a separate avenue of appeal to the Criminal Injuries Compensation Appeals Panel (CICAP).
Chief Executive, Howard Webber
Deputy Chief Executive, Edward McKeown
Head of Legal Services, Anne Johnstone

CROFTERS COMMISSION

4–6 Castle Wynd, Inverness IV2 3EQ
T 01463-663450 F 01463-711820
E info@crofterscommission.org.uk
W www.crofterscommission.org.uk

The Crofters Commission, established in 1955 under the Crofters (Scotland) Act is a government funded organisation whose overall objective is the promotion of thriving and sustainable crofting communities. It works with communities to develop, reorganise and regulate crofting, and advises Scottish Ministers on crofting matters. The Commission administers the Crofting Counties Agricultural Grants Scheme, the Croft Entrant Scheme, the Livestock Improvement Schemes and the Crofting Community Development Scheme. It also provides a free enquiry service.
Chairman, David Green
Chief Executive, Shane Rankin

CROWN ESTATE

16 Carlton House Terrace, London SW1Y 5AH
T 020-7210 4377 F 020-7930 8187
W www.crownestate.co.uk

The Crown Estate includes substantial blocks of urban property, primarily in London, almost 120,000 hectares of agricultural land, almost half the foreshore, and the sea bed out to the twelve mile territorial limit throughout the United Kingdom. The Crown Estate is part of the hereditary possessions of the Sovereign 'in right of the Crown', managed under the provisions of the Crown Estate Act 1961 by the Crown Estate Commissioners who have a duty to maintain and enhance the capital value of estate and the income obtained from it.
Chairman, Ian Grant, CBE
Chief Executive, Roger Bright
Commissioners, Sir Donald Curry, KB, CBE; Hugh Duberly, CBE; Martin Moore; Dinah Nichols, CB; Ronald Spinney, FRICS; Jenefer Greenwood, FRICS
Director of Urban Estates, Tony Bickmore, FRICS

HEADS OF DEPARTMENTS

Asset Management, Dr Tony Murray
Communications, Irene Belcher
Corporate Planning and Human Resources, Martin Gravestock
Customer Management, Elspeth Miller
Development Management, Liam Colgan
Finance and Information Systems, John Lelliott
Internal Audit, John Ford
Legal Adviser and Head of Legal Services, David Harris
Marine Estates, Frank Parrish
Office Portfolio, Alan Meakin
Regional Portfolio, Mal Dillon
Residential Portfolio, Giles Clarke
Retail Portfolio, David Shaw
Rural Estates, Chris Bourchier
Valuation, Roland Spence

EDINBURGH OFFICE

6 Bell's Brae, Edinburgh EH4 3BJ
T 0131-260 6070 F 0131-260 6090
Edinburgh Office Manager, Ian Pritchard

WINDSOR ESTATE

The Crown Estate Office, The Great Park, Windsor, Berks SL4 2HT
T 01753-860222 F 01753-859617
Deputy Ranger, P. Everett

DEER COMMISSION FOR SCOTLAND

Knowsley, 82 Fairfield Road, Inverness IV3 5LH
T 01463-231751 F 01463-712931
E enquiries@deercom.com
W www.dcs.gov.uk

The Deer Commission for Scotland has the general functions of furthering the conservation and control of deer in Scotland. It has the statutory duty, with powers, to prevent damage to agriculture, forestry and the habitat by deer. It is funded by the Scottish Executive.
Chairman (part-time), A. Raven
Director, N. Reiter
Technical Director, D. Balharry

DESIGN COUNCIL

34 Bow Street, London WC2E 7DL
T 020-7420 5200 F 020-7420 5300

The Design Council is a campaigning and lobbying organisation which works with partners in business, education and Government to promote the effective use of good design. It is a registered charity with a Royal Charter and is funded by grant-in-aid from the Department of Trade and Industry.
Chairman, George Cox
Chief Executive, D. Kester

DISABILITY RIGHTS COMMISSION (DRC)

Stratford upon Avon CV37 9BR
T 0845-762 2633
W www.drc-gb.org

The Commission is an executive non-departmental public body established in April 2000. Its role is to advise Government on issues of discrimination against disabled people and the operation of the Disability Discrimination Act 1995. It promotes good practice to employers and service providers and provides advice, information and legal support to disabled people.

Chair, B. Massie, CBE
Chief Executive, B. Niven
Commissioners, S. Alam; M. Burton; Ms J. Campbell, MBE; Ms S. Daniels; M. Devenney; R. Exell, OBE; Dr K. Fitzpatrick; C. Holmes, MBE; Mrs E. Noad; Ms E. Rank-Petruzziello

DUCHY OF CORNWALL

10 Buckingham Gate, London SW1E 6LA
T 020-7834 7346 F 020-7931 9541
W www.princeofwales.gov.uk

The Duchy of Cornwall was created by Edward III in 1337 for the support of his eldest son Edward, later known as the Black Prince. It is the oldest of the English duchies. The duchy is acquired by inheritance by the sovereign's eldest son either at birth or on the accession of his parent to the throne, whichever is the later. The primary purpose of the estate remains to provide an income for the Prince of Wales. The estate is mainly agricultural and based in the south-west of England. A recent purchase has increased the landholding to approximately 150,000 acres in 26 counties. The duchy also has some residential property, a number of shops and offices, and a Stock Exchange portfolio. Prince Charles is the 24th Duke of Cornwall.

THE PRINCE'S COUNCIL
Chairman, HRH The Prince of Wales, KG, KT, GCB, OM
Lord Warden of the Stannaries, The Earl Peel
Receiver-General, The Rt. Hon. J. H. Leigh-Pemberton
Attorney-General to the Prince of Wales, N. Underhill, QC
Secretary and Keeper of the Records, W. R. A. Ross
Other members, R. Broadhurst; J. Coode; W. N. Hood, CBE; Sir Christopher Howes, CB; Sir Michael Peat; J. E. Pugsley; The Duke of Westminster

DUCHY OF LANCASTER

Lancaster Place, Strand, London WC2E 7ED
T 020-7269 1700 F 020-7267 1711
E info@duchyoflancaster.co.uk W www.duchyoflancaster.co.uk

The estates and jurisdiction known as the Duchy of Lancaster have belonged to the reigning monarch since 1399 when John of Gaunt's son came to the throne as Henry IV. As the Lancaster Inheritance it goes back as far as 1265 when Henry III granted his youngest son Edmund lands and possessions following the Baron's war. In 1267 Henry gave Edmund the County, Honor and Castle of Lancaster and created him the first Earl of Lancaster. In 1351 Edward III created Lancaster a County Palatine.

The Chancellor of the Duchy of Lancaster is responsible for the administration of the Duchy, the appointment of justices of the peace in Lancashire, Greater Manchester and Merseyside and ecclesiastical patronage in the Duchy gift.

Chancellor of the Duchy of Lancaster (and Minister for the Cabinet Office), D. G. Alexander, MP
Chairman of the Duchy Council, Sir Michael Bunbury, BT
Attorney-General, M. T. F. Briggs, QC
Receiver-General, A. Reid
Clerk of the Council and Chief Executive, P. R. Clarke

ECGD (EXPORT CREDITS GUARANTEE DEPARTMENT)

PO Box 2200, Exchange Tower, Harbour Exchange Square, London E14 9GS
T 020-7512 7000 F 020-7512 7649
W www.ecgd.gov.uk

ECGD, the Export Credits Guarantee Department is the UK's export credit agency. A separate government department reporting to the Secretary of State for Trade and Industry, it has more than 80 years' experience of working closely with exporters, project sponsors, banks and buyers to help UK exporters of capital equipment and project-related goods and services. ECGD does this by providing: help in arranging finance packages for buyers of UK goods by guaranteeing bank loans; insurance against non-payment to UK exporters; and, overseas investment insurance – a facility that gives UK investors up to 15 years' insurance against political risks such as war, expropriation and restrictions on remittances.

EXECUTIVE COMMITTEE
Chief Executive and Accounting Officer, P. Crawford
Group Directors, V. P. Lunn-Rockliffe *(Portfolio Asset Management)*; J. R. Weiss *(Business)*; T. M. Jaffray *(Risk Management Group)*; J. Ormerod *(Strategy and Communications Division)*; I. Dickson *(Finance Division)*; S. R. Dodgson *(Central Services Division)*; D. N. Ridley *(General Counsel)*

NON-EXECUTIVE DIRECTORS
D. Harrison; J. Wright; T. Davies

DIRECTORS
Business Divisions, G. G. Welsh; R. Gotts; M. D. Pentecost
Capital and Pricing Division, J. Croall
Country Risk and Economics Division, P. J. Radford
Operational Research and Portfolio Risk Analysis Division, Ms R. A. Kaufman
International Debt and Development Division, E. J. Walsby
Recovery Division, R. F. Lethbridge
Guarantee Management Division, A. C. Faulkner
Portfolio Management Division, J. Cross
Information Services Division Ms L. Woods
Internal Audit and Assurance, G. Cassell

EXPORT GUARANTEES ADVISORY COUNCIL
Chairman, E. P. Airey
Other Members, Sir S. Brown; J. Elkington; Prof. J. Kydd; A. Shepherd; Dr R. Thamotheram; M. Roberts; P. Talbot

ENGLISH HERITAGE (HISTORIC BUILDINGS AND MONUMENTS COMMISSION FOR ENGLAND)

23 Savile Row, London W1S 2ET
T 020-7973 3000 F 020-7973 3001
W www.english-heritage.org.uk

English Heritage was established under the National Heritage Act 1983. On 1 April 1999 it merged with the Royal Commission on the Historical Monuments of England to become the new lead body for England's historic environment. Its duties are to carry out and sponsor archaeological, architectural and scientific surveys and research designed to increase the understanding of England's past and its changing condition; to offer expert advice and skills and give grants to secure the preservation of listed buildings, cathedrals, churches, archaeological sites, ancient monuments and historic houses of England; to encourage the imaginative re-use of historic buildings to aid regeneration of the centres of cities, towns and villages; to manage the historic monuments and historic buildings in England; and to curate and make publicly accessible the National Monuments Record, whose records of over one million historic sites and buildings, and collections of more than 12 million photographs, maps, drawings and reports constitute the central database and archive of England's historic environment.

Chairman, Sir Neil Cossons, OBE
Commissioners, M. Cairns; Prof. D. Cannadine; Mrs G. Drummond; P. Gough, CBE; Ms J. Grenville; M. Jolly, CBE; The Earl of Leicester; R. Morris, OBE, FSA; L. Sparks, OBE; Miss M. Adebowale; Mrs J. Bridges, CBE; B. Bryson; M. Chande; Marquess of Douro, OBE; Hon. D. Des, FRSA; Ms E. Williamson
Chief Executive, Dr S. Thurley
NATIONAL MONUMENTS RECORD, National Monuments Record Centre, Kemble Drive, Swindon SN2 2GZ T 01793-414600 F 01793-414606
LONDON SEARCH ROOM, 55 Blandford Street, London SW1H 3AF T 020-7208 8200 F 020-7224 5333

ENGLISH NATURE

Northminster House, Peterborough PE1 1UA
T 01733-455000 F 01733-568834
Enquiry Service 01733-455100
E enquiries@english-nature.org.uk
W www.english-nature.org.uk

English Nature was established in 1991 and is responsible for advising the Department of the Environment, Food and Rural Affairs on nature conservation in England. It promotes, directly and through others, the conservation of England's wildlife and natural features. It selects, establishes and manages National Nature Reserves and identifies and notifies Sites of Special Scientific Interest. It provides advice and information about nature conservation, and supports and conducts research relevant to these functions. Through the Joint Nature Conservation Committee, it works with its sister organisations in Scotland and Wales on UK and international nature conservation issues. Free publications are available by contacting the Enquiry Service.

Chairman, M. Doughty
Chief Executive, Dr A. Brown
Directors, Dr K. L. Duff; Miss C. E. M. Wood; Ms S. Collins; A. Clements; P. Newby

ENVIRONMENT AGENCY

Rio House, Waterside Drive, Aztec West, Almondsbury, Bristol BS32 4UD
T 01454-624400 F 01454-624409
E enquiries@environment-agency.gov.uk
W www.environment-agency.gov.uk

The Environment Agency was established in 1996 under the Environment Act 1995 and is a non-departmental public body sponsored by the Department of the Environment, Food and Rural Affairs and the National Assembly for Wales. The Agency is responsible for pollution prevention and control in England and Wales, and for the management and use of water resources, including flood defences, fisheries and navigation. It has head offices in London and Bristol and eight regional offices.

THE BOARD
Chairman, Sir John Harman
Members, T. Cantle; A. Dare, CBE; Prof. P. Matthews; Ms S. Parkin; Prof. D. Ritchie; Prof. L. Warren; K. Twitchen; P. Bye; J. Edmonds; Prof. R. Macrory; R. Percy; G. Wardell; Dr L. Stanton

THE EXECUTIVE
Chief Executive, B. Young
Director of Corporate Affairs, H. McCallum
Director of Environmental Protection, A. Skinner
Director of Finance, N. Reader
Director of Legal Services, R. Navarro
Director of Operations, Dr P. Leinster
Director of Personnel, G. Duncan
Director of Water Management, D. King

EQUAL OPPORTUNITIES COMMISSION

Arndale House, Arndale Centre, Manchester M4 3EQ
T 0845-601 5901 F 0161-838 1733
E info@eoc.org.uk
W www.eoc.org.uk
Media Enquiries, 36 Broadway, London SW1H 0BH
T 020-7222 0004
Other Offices, St Stephens House, 279 Bath Street, Glasgow G2 4JL
T 0845-601 5901
Windsor House, Windsor Lane, Cardiff CF10 3GE
T 029-2034 3552

The Equal Opportunities Commission was established under the Sex Discrimination Act in 1975. It was set up as an independent statutory body with the following powers: to work towards the elimination of discrimination on the grounds of sex or marriage; to promote equality of opportunity for women and men; to keep under review the Sex Discrimination Act and the Equal Pay Act; and to provide legal advice and assistance to individuals who have been discriminated against.

Chair, Ms J. Mellor
Deputy Chair, Ms J. Watson
Commissioners, Ms T. Akpeki; Ms S. Ashtiany; Ms K. Carberry; Ms F. Cannon; Ms J. Drake; Ms S. Pierce; S. Sharma; D. Smith; Ms T. Woodcraft; Ms D. Mattinson; Ms R. Arshad; N. Rhys Wooding
Chief Executive, C. Slocock

EQUALITY COMMISSION FOR NORTHERN IRELAND

Equality House, 7–9 Shaftesbury Square, Belfast, BT2 7DP
T 028-9050 0600 F 028-9024 8687
E information@equalityni.org
W www.equalityni.org

The Equality Commission was set up in 1999 under the Northern Ireland Act 1998 and is responsible for promoting equality, eliminating discrimination on the grounds of race, disability, gender, religion and political opinion and for overseeing the statutory duty on public authorities to promote equality of opportunity.
Chief Commissioner, Mrs J. Harbison
Deputy Chief Commissioner, Ms A. O'Reilly
Chief Executive, Ms E. Collins

FOOD STANDARDS AGENCY (UK)

Aviation House, 125 Kingsway, London, WC2B 6NH
T 020-7276 8000 F 020-7276 8004
W www.food.gov.uk

The Food Standards Agency (FSA) was established in April 2000 to protect public health from risks arising in connection with the consumption of food, and otherwise to protect the interests of consumers in relation to food. The Agency has the general function of developing policy in these areas and provides information and advice to the Government, other public bodies and consumers. It also sets standards for and monitors food law enforcement by local authorities. The Agency is a UK-wide non-ministerial Government body led by a board which has been appointed to act in the public interest. It has executive offices in Scotland, Wales and Northern Ireland. It is advised by advisory committees on food safety matters of special interest to each of these areas.
Chairman, Prof. Sir John Krebs, FRC
Deputy Chair, Julia Unwin, OBE
Chief Executive, Dr Jon Bell

EXECUTIVE AGENCY

MEAT HYGIENE SERVICE
Kings Pool, Peasholme Green, York YO1 7PR
T 01904-455500 F 01904-455502

The Meat Hygiene Service was launched on 1 April 1995 as an agency of the former Ministry of Agriculture, Fisheries and Food, and became an Executive Agency of the Food Standards Agency on 1 April 2000. It protects public health and animal welfare at slaughter through veterinary supervision and meat inspection in licensed fresh meat premises in Great Britain.
Chief Executive, C. J. Lawson

FOOD STANDARDS AGENCY NORTHERN IRELAND

10c Clarendon Road, Belfast, BT1 3BG
T 028-9041 7700 F 028-9041 7726
E infofsani@foodstandards.gsi.gov.uk
W www.food.gov.uk

FOOD STANDARDS AGENCY SCOTLAND

St Magnus House, 6th Floor, 25 Guild Street, Aberdeen, AB11 6NJ
T 01224-285100 F 01224-285167
E scotland@foodstandards.gsi.gov.uk
W www.food.gov.uk

FOOD STANDARDS AGENCY WALES

11th Floor, Southgate House, Wood Street, Cardiff CF10 1EW
T 029-2067 8999 F 029-2067 8919
E wales@foodstandards.gsi.gov.uk
W www.food.gov.uk

FOREIGN COMPENSATION COMMISSION

Room SG/111, Old Admiralty Building, Whitehall, London, SW1A 2PA
T 020-7008 1321 F 020-7008 0160

The Commission was set up by the Foreign Compensation Act 1950 primarily to distribute, under Orders in Council, funds received from other governments in accordance with agreements to pay compensation for expropriated British property and other losses sustained by British nationals.
Chairman, Dr John H. Bancer
Secretary, vacant

FORESTRY COMMISSION

Silvan House, 231 Corstorphine Road, Edinburgh EH12 7AT
T 0845-367 3787 F 0131-334 3047
E enquiries@forestry.gsi.gov.uk
W www.forestry.gov.uk

The Forestry Commission is the Government department responsible for forestry policy in Great Britain. It reports directly to forestry Ministers (i.e. the Minister of Environment, Food and Rural Affairs, the Scottish Ministers and the National Assembly for Wales), to whom it is responsible for advice on forestry policy and for the implementation of that policy.

The Commission's principal objectives are to protect Britain's forests and woodlands; expand Britain's forest area; enhance the economic value of forest resources; conserve and improve the biodiversity, landscape and cultural heritage of forests and woodlands; develop opportunities for woodland recreation; and increase public understanding of and community participation in forestry. Forest Enterprise, an executive agency of the Forestry Commission, ceased to exist on 1 April 2003. Three new bodies, one each for England, Scotland and Wales have been created in its place.
Chairman (part-time), The Rt. Hon. Lord Clark of Windermere
Director-General and Deputy Chairman, T. Rollinson

FORESTRY COMMISSION ENGLAND, Great Eastern House, Tenison Road, Cambridge CB1 2BU T 01223-314546
FORESTRY COMMISSION SCOTLAND, 231 Corstorphine Road, Edinburgh EH12 7AT T 9131-334 0303
FORESTRY COMMISSION WALES, Victoria Terrace, Aberystwyth, Ceredigion SY23 2DQ T 01970-625866
FOREST RESEARCH, Alice Holt Lodge, Wrecclesham, Farnham, Surrey GU10 4LU T 01420-222555
NORTHERN RESEARCH STATION, Roslin, Midlothian EH25 9SY T 0131-445 2176

GAMING BOARD FOR GREAT BRITAIN

Berkshire House, 168–173 High Holborn, London WC1V 7AA
T 020-7306 6200 F 020-7306 6266
E enqs@gbgb.org.uk
W www.gbgb.org.uk

The Board was established in 1968 and is responsible to the Secretary of State for Culture, Media and Sport. It is the regulatory body for casinos, bingo clubs, gaming machines and all local authority lotteries in Great Britain. Its functions are to ensure that those involved in organising gaming and lotteries are fit and proper to do so and to keep gaming free from criminal infiltration; to ensure that gaming and lotteries are run fairly and in accordance with the law; and to advise the Secretary of State on developments in gaming and lotteries.
Chairman, P. Dean, CBE
Secretary, T. Kavanagh, CBE

GOVERNMENT ACTUARY'S DEPARTMENT

Finlaison House, 15/17 Furnival Street, London EC4A 1AB
T 020-7211 2601 F 020-7211 2640/2650
E enquiries@gad.gov.uk
W www.gad.gov.uk

The Government Actuary's Department provides a consulting service to Government departments, the public sector, and overseas governments. The actuaries advise on social security schemes and superannuation arrangements in the public sector at home and abroad, on population and other statistical studies, and on supervision of insurance companies and pension funds.
Government Actuary, C. D. Daykin, CB
Directing Actuaries, A. G. Young; A. I. Johnston
Chief Actuaries, E. I. Battersby; I. A. Boonin; S. R. Humphrey; D. Lewis; G. T. Russell

GOVERNMENT HOSPITALITY

Lancaster House, Stable Yard, St James's, London SW1A 1BB
T 020-7008 8517 F 020-7008 8526

The Government Hospitality Fund was instituted in 1908 for the purpose of organising official hospitality on a regular basis with a view to the promotion of international goodwill.

Government Hospitality is now incorporated as part of the Foreign and Commonwealth Office's Services Directorate.
Minister, B. Rammell
Manager of Government Hospitality, R. Alexander

GOVERNMENT OFFICES FOR THE REGIONS

The nine Government Offices for the Regions (GOs) are the primary means by which a wide range of Government policies are delivered in the English regions. The Government Offices bring together the activities and interests of ten 'sponsor' government departments: the Office of the Deputy Prime Minister; the Department for Education and Skills; the Department of Trade and Industry; the Department for Environment, Food and Rural Affairs; the Home Office; the Department for Culture, Media and Sport; the Department for Work and Pensions; the Department for Transport; the Department of Health; and the Cabinet Office.

GOs contribute to the delivery of over forty Public Service Agreements (PSAs) on behalf of their sponsor departments. These PSAs cover a diverse range of tasks including regenerating communities, fighting crime, tackling housing needs, improving public health, raising standards in education and skills, tackling countryside issues, and reducing unemployment. GOs also manage European funds.

GOs directly manage the spending programmes of the government departments listed above. They oversee budgets and contracts delegated to regional organisations, as well as carrying out regulatory functions and sponsoring Regional Development Agencies. As part of central government, their role also includes providing a regional perspective to inform the development and evaluation of policy. In 2002–3, the GOs were responsible for approximately £9 billion of government expenditure.

The Government Office Network comprises the nine regional Government Offices, and the Regional Co-ordination Unit.

REGIONAL CO-ORDINATION UNIT

Riverwalk House, 157–161 Millbank, London SW1P 4RR
T 020-7217 3595 F 020-7217 3590
W www.rcu.gov.uk
Director-General, Rob Smith
Director, A. Campbell
Directors, Ian Jones *(Corporate Communications)*; Nick Dexter *(Strategy)*; Julie Anderson *(Business Development)*; Vince Brady *(Human Resources)*

EAST MIDLANDS

The Belgrave Centre, Stanley Place, Talbot Street, Nottingham NG1 5GG
T 0115-971 9971 F 0115-971 2404
E enquiries.goem@go-regions.gov.uk
W www.go-em.gov.uk
Regional Director, Jane Todd

EAST OF ENGLAND

Eastbrook, Shaftesbury Road, Cambridge CB2 2DF
T 01223-372500 F 01223-372501
W www.go-east.gov.uk
Regional Director, Caroline Bowdler

LONDON

Riverwalk House, 157–161 Millbank, London SW1P 4RR
T 020-7217 3111 F 020-7217 3450
W www.go-london.gov.uk
Regional Director, Liz Meek

NORTH-EAST

Citygate, Gallowgate, Newcastle upon Tyne NE1 4WH
T 0191-201 3300 F 0191-202 3998
W www.go-ne.gov.uk
Regional Director, Jonathan Blackie

NORTH-WEST

City Tower, Piccadilly Plaza, Manchester M1 4BE
T 0161-952 4000 F 0161-952 4099
W www.go-nw.gov.uk
Regional Director, Keith Barnes

SOUTH-EAST

Bridge House, 1 Walnut Tree Close, Guildford, Surrey GU1 4GA
T 01483-882255 F 01483-882259
W www.go-se.gov.uk
Regional Director, Paul Martin

SOUTH-WEST
2 Rivergate, Temple Quay, Bristol BS1 6ED
T 0117-900 1700 F 0117-900 1900
W www.gosw.gov.uk
Regional Director, Jane Henderson

WEST MIDLANDS
77 Paradise Circus, Queensway, Birmingham B1 2DT
T 0121-212 5050 F 0121-212 1010
E enquiries.gowm@go-regions.gsi.gov.uk
W www.go-wm.gov.uk
Regional Director, Graham Garbutt

YORKSHIRE AND THE HUMBER
PO Box 213, City House, New Station Street, Leeds LS1 4US
T 0113-283 8301 F 0113-283 6394
E enquiries.goyh@go-regions.gsi.gov.uk W www.goyh.gov.uk
Regional Director, Felicity Everiss

HEALTH AND SAFETY COMMISSION

Rose Court, 2 Southwark Bridge, London SE1 9HS
T 020-7717 6000 F 020-7717 6644
E hseinformationservices@natbrit.com
W www.hse.gov.uk

The Health and Safety Commission was created under the Health and Safety at Work etc. Act 1974, with duties to reform health and safety law, to propose new regulations, and generally to promote the protection of people at work and the public from hazards arising from industrial and commercial activity, including major industrial accidents and the transportation of hazardous materials.

Its members are nominated by organisations representing employers, employees, local authorities and others.

Chairman, B. Callaghan
Members, Ms J. Donovan; Ms J. Edmond-Smith; G. Brumwell; Ms M. Burns; A. Chowdry; J. Longworth; Ms J. Hackitt; H. Robertson; Ms E. Snape

HEALTH AND SAFETY EXECUTIVE

Rose Court, 2 Southwark Bridge, London SE1 9HS
T 020-7717 6000 F 020-7717 6717

The Health and Safety Executive is the Health and Safety Commission's major instrument. Through its inspectorates it enforces health and safety law in the majority of industrial premises. The Executive advises the Commission in its major task of laying down safety standards through regulations and practical guidance for many industrial processes. The Executive is also the licensing authority for nuclear installations, the reporting officer on the severity of nuclear incidents in Britain, and it is responsible for the Channel Tunnel Safety Authority.

Director-General, T. Walker
Deputy Director-General, Operations, J. McCracken
Deputy Director-General, Policy, K. Timms
Director and HM Chief Inspector of the Nuclear Installations Inspectorate, L. Williams
Director of Rail Safety, A. Sefton
Director, Corporate Science and Analytical Service Directorate and Chief Scientist, Dr P. Davies
Director, Field Operations Directorate, S. Caldwell
Director, Hazardous Installations Directorate, C. Willby
Director, Health Directorate, J. Willis
Director, Resource and Planning Directorate, V. Dews
Director, Safety Policy, N. Starling

HEALTH PROTECTION AGENCY

Central Office: Level 11, The Adelphi, 10–11 John Adam Street, London WC2N 6HT
T 020-7339 1300 F 020-7339 1302
E firstname.surname@ hpa.org.uk
W www.hpa.org.uk

The Health Protection Agency (HPA) was set up on 1 April 2003 to provide an integrated approach to protecting public health and reducing the impact of infections, chemicals, poisons and radiation hazards on human health. It brings together the functions and expertise from the Public Health Laboratory Service, including the Communicable Disease Surveillance Centre, the Centre for Applied Microbiology and Research, the National Focus for Chemical Incidents, the Regional Service Provider Units that support the management of chemical incidents, the National Poisons Information Service, and the NHS public health staff responsible for control of infectious disease, emergency planning and other protection support.

Chairman, Sir William Stewart
Chief Executive, Prof. Pat Troop
Directors, Prof. Roger Gilmour *(Business)*; Prof. Stephen Palmer *(Chemical Hazards and Poisons)*; Dr A. Nicoll *(Communicable Disease Surveillance Centre)*; Dr Nigel Lightfoot *(Emergency Response)*; Dr Mary O'Mahony *(Local and Regional Services)*; Prof. Pete Borriello *(Specialist and Reference Microbiology)*

HIGHLANDS AND ISLANDS ENTERPRISE

Cowan House, Inverness Retail and Business Park, Inverness, Scotland IV2 7GF
T 01463-234171 F 01463-244469
E hie.general@hient.co.uk
W www.hie.co.uk

Highlands and Islands Enterprise (HIE) was set up under the Enterprise and New Towns (Scotland) Act 1991. Its role is to design, direct and deliver enterprise development, training and environmental and social projects and services. HIE is made up of a strategic core body and ten Local Enterprise Companies (LECs) to which many of its individual functions are delegated.

Chairman, Dr J. Hunter
Chief Executive, I. J. R. S. Cumming

HISTORIC ENVIRONMENT ADVISORY COUNCIL FOR SCOTLAND

Longmore House, Salisbury Place, Edinburgh EH9 1SH
T 0131-668 8810 F 0131-668 8788
E heacs@scotland.gsi.gov.uk W www.heacs.org.uk

The Historic Environment Advisory Council for Scotland is the advisory body set up to provide Scottish Ministers with advice on issues affecting the historic environment and how the functions of the Scottish Ministers may be exercised effectively for the benefit of the historic environment. In this context the historic environment means any or all structures and places in Scotland of historical, archaeological or architectural interest or importance.

Chair, Mrs Elizabeth Burns, OBE
Secretary, Dr Malcolm Bangor-Jones

HISTORIC ROYAL PALACES

Hampton Court Palace, Surrey KT8 9AU
T 0870-751 5172 F 020-8781 9754
W www.hrp.org.uk

Historic Royal Palaces is a non-departmental public body with charitable status. The Secretary of State for Culture, Media and Sport is still accountable to Parliament for the care, conservation and presentation of the palaces, which are owned by the Sovereign in right of the Crown. The chairman of the trustees is appointed by The Queen on the advice of the Secretary of State. Historic Royal Palaces is responsible for the Tower of London, Hampton Court Palace, Kensington Palace State Apartments, the Royal Ceremonial Dress Collection, Kew Palace, Queen Charlotte's Cottage, and the Banqueting House, Whitehall.

TRUSTEES
Chairman, Sir Nigel Mobbs
Appointed by The Queen, A. Reid; Sir Hugh Roberts, KCVO, FSA; Field Marshal The Lord Inge, KG, GCB
Appointed by the Secretary of State, Ms A. Heylin, OBE; S. Jones, LVO; Mrs G. Woolfe, MBE; Dr B. Cherry, FSA
Ex officio, Sir Roger Wheeler, GCB, CBE *(Constable of the Tower of London)*

OFFICERS
Chief Executive, M. Day
Director of Conservation, J. Barnes
Director of Finance, Ms S. O'Neill
Director of Human Resources, G. Josephs
Director, Palaces Group, R. Giddins
Marketing Director, D. Homan
Resident Governor, HM Tower of London, Maj.-Gen. G. Field, CB, OBE
Retail Director, Ms A. Boyes

HOME-GROWN CEREALS AUTHORITY

Caledonia House, 223 Pentonville Road, London N1 9HY
T 020-7520 3904 F 020-7520 3954

Set up under the Cereals Marketing Act 1965, the HGCA Board consists of seven members representing UK cereal growers, seven representing dealers in, or processors of, grain and two independent members. HGCA's functions are to improve the production and marketing of UK-grown cereals and oilseeds through a research and development programme, to provide a market information service and to promote UK cereals in export markets.
Chairman, J. Page
Chief Executive, P. V. Biscoe

HONOURS SCRUTINY COMMITTEE

35 Great Smith Street, London SW1P 3BQ
T 020-7276 2770 F 020-7276 2766

The Honours Scrutiny Committee is a committee of Privy Counsellors. The Prime Minister submits certain particulars to the Committee about persons recommended for honour at any level other than a peerage for their political services, or for an honour at the level of Knight or Dame for non-political services. The Committee, after such enquiry as it thinks fit, reports to the Prime Minister whether, so far as it believes, the political candidates are fit and proper persons to be recommended and for any non-political candidate, who may have made a political donation, whether this was a factor in the recommendation for an honour.
Chairman, The Lord Thomson of Monifieth, KT
Members, The Baroness Dean of Thornton-le-Fylde; The Lord Hurd of Westwell, CH, CBE
Secretary, Mrs P. G. W. Catto

HORSERACE TOTALISATOR BOARD

Tote House, 74 Upper Richmond Road, London SW15 2SU
T 020-8874 6411 F 020-8874 6107
W www.tote.co.uk

The Horserace Totalisator Board (the Tote) was established by the Betting, Gaming and Lotteries Act 1963. Its function is to operate totalisators on approved racecourses in Great Britain, and it also provides on and off-course cash and credit offices. Under the Horserace Totalisator and Betting Levy Board Act 1972, it is further empowered to offer bets at starting price (or other bets at fixed odds) on any sporting event, and under the Horserace Totalisator Board Act 1997 to take bets on any event, except the National Lottery. The chairman and members of the Board are appointed by the Secretary of State, Department of Culture, Media and Sport.

The Government announced in March 2001 that the Tote would eventually be sold to a racing trust, subject to the necessary legislation going through Parliament. The privatisation of the Tote was expected to be completed by the end of 2004.
Chairman, P. I. Jones
Chief Operating Officer, T. Phillips

HOUSING CORPORATION

Maple House, 149 Tottenham Court Road, London W1T 7BN
T 020-7393 2000 F 020-7393 2111
E enquiries@housingcorp.gsx.gov.uk
W www.housingcorp.gov.uk

Established by Parliament in 1964, the Housing Corporation regulates and funds registered social landlords which are non-profit making bodies run by voluntary committees. There are over 2,000 registered social landlords, most of which are housing associations, who provide homes for more than 1.5 million people. Under the Housing Act 1996, the Corporation's regulatory role was widened to embrace new types of landlords, in particular local housing companies. The Corporation is funded by the Office of the Deputy Prime Minister.
Chairman, Peter Dixon
Deputy Chairman, E. Armitage, OBE
Chief Executive, Jon Rouse

HOUSING OMBUDSMAN SERVICE

Norman House, 105–109 Strand, London WC2R 0AA
T 020-7836 3630 F 020-7836 3900
E ombudsman@ihos.org.uk
W www.ihos.org.uk

The Housing Ombudsman Service deals with complaints and disputes involving landlords and tenants. The Ombudsman has a statutory jurisdiction over all registered social landlords in England. Private and other landlords can join the Service on a voluntary basis.
Ombudsman, M. Biles
Chair of Board, G. Lewis
Director of Corporate Services, Wilma Jarvie

HUMAN FERTILISATION AND EMBRYOLOGY AUTHORITY

21 Bloomsbury Street, London WC1B 3HF
T 020-7291 8200 F 020-7291 8201
E admin@hfea.gov.uk
W www.hfea.gov.uk

The Human Fertilisation and Embryology Authority (HFEA) was established under the Human Fertilisation and Embryology Act 1990. Its function is to licence the following activities: the creation or use of embryos outside the body in the provision of infertility treatment services; the use of donated gametes in infertility treatment; the storage of gametes or embryos; and research on human embryos. It maintains a confidential database of all such treatments and of egg and sperm donors, and provides information to patients, clinics and the public. The HFEA also keeps under review information about embryos and, when requested to do so, gives advice to the Secretary of State for Health.

Chairman, S. Leather
Deputy Chairman, Prof. T. Baldwin
Members, Prof. D. Barlow; Prof. C. Barratt; Prof. P. Braude; I. Brecker; Ms C. Brown; Prof. I. Cameron; Prof. N. Haites; Dr M. Jamieson; S. Jenkins; W. Merricks; Ms S. Nathan; Ms S. Nebhrajani; The Right Hon. Bishop D. Harries; Ms E. Jackson; Ms J. Hunt
Director of Sub-Committees, Mrs J. Denton

HUMAN GENETICS COMMISSION

Area 652C, Skipton House, 80 London Road, London SE1 6LH
T 020-7972 1518 F 020-7972 1717
E hgc@doh.gov.uk
W www.hgc.gov.uk

The Human Genetics Commission was established in 1999, subsuming three previous advisory committees. Its remit is to give Ministers strategic advice on how developments in human genetics will impact on people and health care, focusing in particular on the special and ethical implications.

Chairman, Baroness H. Kennedy of the Shaws, QC
Members, Dr W. Albert, Prof. E. Anionwu; Dr S. Bain; Prof. J. Burn; Dr H. Harris; Prof. J. Harris; Ms S. Leather; Ms H. Newiss; Prof. M. Richards; Dr S. Singleton; Mr G. Watts; Mr P. Webb; Prof. V. van Heyningen; Dr Patrick Morrison; Dr R. Skinner; Emeritius Prof. Brenda Almond; Mrs C. Patch; P. Sayers; Sir John Sueston; Dr Celia Brazell; A. Kent
Head of Secretariat, M. Bale

INDEPENDENT INTERNATIONAL COMMISSION ON DECOMMISSIONING

Dublin Castle, Block M, Ship Street, Dublin 2
T 00 353 1-478 0111 F 00 353 1-478 0600
Rosepark House, Upper Newtownards Road, Belfast BT4 3NX
T 028-9048 8600 F 028-9048 8601

The Commission was established by agreement between the British and Irish Governments in August 1997. Its objective is to facilitate the decommissioning of illegally-held firearms and explosives in accordance with the relevant legislation in both jurisdictions. Its members are appointed jointly by the two Governments; staff are appointed by the Commission. All are drawn from countries other than the UK and the Republic of Ireland.

Commissioners, Gen. J. de Chastelain *(Chairman, Canada)* A. D. Sens *(USA)*
Staff Director, A. Suonio *(Finland)*
Admin/Finances, K. Juntunen; R. Schoen; J. Mladinich

INDEPENDENT POLICE COMPLAINTS COMMISSION (IPCC)

90 High Holborn, London WC1V 6BH
T 0845-300 2002 F 020-7404 0430
E enquiries@ipcc.gsi.gov.uk
W www.ipcc.gov.uk

The Independent Police Complaints Commission succeeded the Police Complaints Authority on 1 April 2004. It was established under the Police Reform Act 2002 following responses to the government document *Complaints against Police; Framework for a New System*, published in December 2000. The IPCC is an independent public body and is not part of any government department. The IPCC has teams of investigators headed by Regional Directors in each of its regions to assist with supervision and management of some police investigations. They also carry out independent investigations into serious incidents or allegations of misconduct by persons serving with the police. The 18 commissioners of the IPCC must not previously have worked for the police.

Chairman, N. Hardwick
Deputy Chairs, Ms C. Gilham; J. Wadham
Commissioners, I. Bynoe; J. Crawley; T. Davies; M. Franklin; G. Garland; Ms D. Glass; L. Jackson; N. Long; L. Lustgarten; N. Malik; Ms R. Marsh; D. Petch; M. Mian Pritchard; A. Somal; Ms N. Williams
Chief Executive, Susan Atkins

INDEPENDENT REVIEW SERVICE FOR THE SOCIAL FUND

4th Floor, Centre City Podium, 5 Hill Street, Birmingham B5 4UB
T 0845-300 1960 F 0121-606 2180
E sfc@irs-review.org.uk
W www.irs-review.org.uk

The Social Fund Commissioner is appointed by the Secretary of State for Work and Pensions. The Commissioner appoints Social Fund Inspectors, who provide an independent review of decisions made by Social Fund Officers in the Department of Work and Pensions.

Social Fund Commissioner, Sir Richard Tilt

INFORMATION COMMISSIONER'S OFFICE

Wycliffe House, Water Lane, Wilmslow, Cheshire SK9 5AF
T 01625-545745 F 01625-524510
E mail@ico.gsi.gov.uk
W www.informationcommissioner.gov.uk

The Information Commissioner Office oversees and enforces the Freedom of Information Act 2000 and the Data Protection Act 1998, with the objective of promoting public access to official information and protecting personal information.

The Data Protection Act 1998 sets out rules for the processing of personal information and applies to records held on computers and some paper files. It works in two ways; it dictates that those who record and use personal information (data controllers) must be open about how the information is used and must follow the eight principles of 'good information handling' and; it gives individuals certain rights to access their personal information.

The Freedom of Information Act 2000 is designed to help end the culture of unnecessary secrecy and open up the inner working of the public sector to citizens and businesses. Under the Freedom of Information Act, public authorities must publish a publication scheme that sets out what information the public authority is obliged publish by law.

The Information Commissioner reports annually to parliament on the performance of his functions under the Acts and has obligations to assess breaches of the Acts.

Commissioner, Richard Thomas

INDUSTRIAL INJURIES ADVISORY COUNCIL

6th Floor, The Adelphi, 1–11 John Adam Street, London WC2N 6HT
T 020-7962 8066 **F** 020-7712 2255
E iiac@dial.pipex.com **W** www.iiac.org.uk

The Industrial Injuries Advisory Council was established under the Social Security Administration Act 1992, with statutory provisions governing its work set out in section 171 of the Act. The Council has three roles: to advise on the proscription of diseases; to advise on matters referred to the Council by the Secretary of State or proposals concerning the Industrial Injuries Benefit Scheme; and to advise on any other matter relating to industrial injuries benefit or its administration.

Chairman, Prof. A. J. Newman Taylor, OBE, FRCP
Administrative Secretary, N. Davidson

JOINT NATURE CONSERVATION COMMITTEE

Monkstone House, City Road, Peterborough PE1 1JY
T 01733-562626 **F** 01733-555948

The Committee was established under the Environmental Protection Act 1990. It advises the Government and others on UK and international nature conservation issues and disseminates knowledge on these subjects. It establishes common standards for the monitoring of nature conservation and research, and provides guidance to English Nature, Scottish Natural Heritage, the Countryside Council for Wales and the Department of the Environment for Northern Ireland.

Acting Chairman, Prof. David Ingram
Director of Resources and External Affairs, M. Yeo
Director of Science, Dr M. A. Vincent
Managing Director, D. Steer

LAND REGISTRIES

LAND REGISTRY

32 Lincoln's Inn Fields, London WC2A 3PH
T 020-7919 8888 **F** 020-7955 0110
E enquiries.pic@landregistry.gov.uk
W www.landregistry.gov.uk

The registration of title to land was first introduced in England and Wales by the Land Registry Act 1862; the Land Registry operates today under the Land Registration Acts 1925 to 2002. The object of registering title to land is to create and maintain a register of landowners whose title is guaranteed by the state and so to simplify the transfer, mortgage and other dealings with real property. Registration on sale is now compulsory throughout England and Wales. The register has been open to inspection by the public since 1990.

The Land Registry is an executive agency and Trading Fund administered by the Chief Land Registrar.

HEADQUARTERS OFFICE

Chief Land Registrar and Chief Executive, P. Collis
Director of Legal Services, J. V. Timothy
Director of Finance, Ms H. Jackson
Director of Business Development and Deputy Chief Executive, E. G. Beardsall
Director of Education and Training, Mrs L. Chamberlain
Director of Facilities, A. Elston
Director of Geographic Information, R. Ashwin
Director of Information Systems, I. Johnson
Director of Marketing and Communication, Mrs D. Reynolds
Director of Operations, A. Howarth
Director of Personnel, Mrs L. Daniels
Director of Service Development, P. Norman
Director of Strategy, A. Pemberton

INFORMATION SYSTEMS DIRECTORATE

Burrington Way, Plymouth PL5 3LP
T 01752-635600
Head of IT Services/Head of Strategy Division, P. A. Maycock/C. Bitton
Head of IT Development Division, J. Formby
Head of IT Directorate Services, K. Deards

LAND CHARGES CREDITS DEPARTMENT

Plumer House, Tailyour Road, Crownhill, Plymouth PL6 5HY
T 01752-636666
Superintendent, Ms M. Telfer

LAND REGISTRY OFFICES

BIRKENHEAD (OLD MARKET) – Old Market House, Hamilton Street, Birkenhead CH41 5FL **T** 0151-473 1110 *Land Registrar*, P. J. Brough
BIRKENHEAD (ROSEBRAE) – Rosebrae Court, Woodside Ferry Approach, Birkenhead CH41 6DU **T** 0151-472 6666 *Land Registrar*, M. J. Garwood
COVENTRY – Leigh Court, Torrington Avenue, Tile Hill, Coventry CV4 9XZ **T** 024-7686 0860 *Land Registrar*, Mrs D. M. Weaver
CROYDON – Sunley House, Bedford Park, Croydon CR9 3LE **T** 020-8781 9103 *Acting Land Registrar*, C. H. Johnson
DURHAM (BOLDON HOUSE) – Boldon House, Wheatlands Way, Pity Me, Durham DH1 5GJ **T** 0191-301 2345 *Land Registrar*, R. B. Fearnley
DURHAM (SOUTHFIELD HOUSE) – Southfield House, Southfield Way, Durham DH1 5TR **T** 0191-301 3500 *Land Registrar*, P. J. Timothy
GLOUCESTER – Twyver House, Bruton Way, Gloucester GL1 1DQ **T** 01452-511111 *Land Registrar*, Mrs J. Jenkins
HARROW – Lyon House, Lyon Road, Harrow, Middx HA1 2EU **T** 020-8235 1181 *Land Registrar*, C. Tate
KINGSTON UPON HULL – Earle House, Colonial Street, Hull HU2 8JN **T** 01482-223244 *Land Registrar*, S. R. Coveney
LANCASHIRE – Wrea Brook Court, Lytham Road, Warton, Preston, PR4 1TE **T** 01772-836700 *Land Registrar*, Mrs L. Wallwork
LEICESTER – Westbridge Place, Leicester LE3 5DR **T** 0116-265 4000 *Land Registrar*, Mrs J. A. Goodfellow
LYTHAM – Birkenhead House, East Beach, Lytham St Annes, Lancs FY8 5AB **T** 01253-849849 *Acting Land Registrar*, Mrs L. Wallwork
NOTTINGHAM (EAST) – Robins Wood Road, Nottingham NG8 3RQ **T** 0115-906 5353 *Land Registrar*, Ms A. M. Goss

NOTTINGHAM (WEST) – Chalfont Drive, Nottingham NG8 3RN T 0115-935 1166 *Land Registrar*, P. A. Brown

PETERBOROUGH – Touthill Close, City Road, Peterborough PE1 1XN T 01733-288288 *Land Registrar*, C. W. Martin

PLYMOUTH – Plumer House, Tailyour Road, Crownhill, Plymouth PL6 5HY T 01752-636000 *Land Registrar*, A. J. Pain

PORTSMOUTH – St Andrew's Court, St Michael's Road, Portsmouth PO1 2JH T 023-9276 8888 *Land Registrar*, S. R. Sehrawat

STEVENAGE – Brickdale House, Swingate, Stevenage, Herts SG1 1XG T 01438-788889 *Land Registrar*, M. Croker

SWANSEA – Tŷ Bryn Glas, High Street, Swansea SA1 1PW T 01792-458877 *Land Registrar*, G. A. Hughes

TELFORD – Parkside Court, Hall Park Way, Telford TF3 4LR T 01952-290355 *Land Registrar*, A. M. Lewis

TUNBRIDGE WELLS – Forest Court, Forest Road, Tunbridge Wells, Kent TN2 5AQ T 01892-510015 *Land Registrar*, G. R. Tooke

WALES – Tŷ Cwm Tawe, Phoenix Way, Llansamlet, Swansea SA7 9FQ T 01792-355000 *Land Registrar*, T. M. Lewis

WEYMOUTH – Melcombe Court, 1 Cumberland Drive, Weymouth, Dorset DT4 9TT T 01305-363636 *Land Registrar*, J. Pownall

YORK – James House, James Street, York YO10 3YZ T 01904-450000 *Land Registrar*, Mrs R. F. Lovel

REGISTERS OF SCOTLAND

Meadowbank House, 153 London Road, Edinburgh EH8 7AU
T 0131-659 6111 F 0131-479 3688
Customer Service Centre 0845-607 0161
E customer.services@ros.gov.uk
W www.ros.gov.uk

Registers of Scotland is the executive agency responsible for framing and maintaining records relating to property and other legal documents in Scotland. The agency holds 16 registers: two property registers (General Register of Sasines and Land Register of Scotland) and the remainder grouped under the Chancery and Judicial registers (Register of Deeds in the Books of Council and Session; Register of Protests; Register of Judgements; Register of Service of Heirs; Register of the Great Seal; Register of the Quarter Seal; Register of the Prince's Seal; Register of Crown Grants; Register of Sheriffs' Commissions; Register of the Cachet Seal; Register of Inhibitions and Adjudications; Register of Entails; Register of Hornings; and Register of Community Interests in Land).

Chief Executive and Keeper of the Registers of Scotland, J. Meldrum
Deputy Keeper, B. Beveridge
Managing Director, F. Manson

LAW COMMISSION

Conquest House, 37–38 John Street, London WC1N 2BQ
T 020-7453 1220 F 020-7453 1297
W www.lawcom.gov.uk

The Law Commission was set up in 1965, under the Law Commissions Act 1965, to make proposals to the Government for the examination of the law in England and Wales and for its revision where it is unsuited for modern requirements, obscure, or otherwise unsatisfactory. It recommends to the Lord Chancellor programmes for the examination of different branches of the law and suggests whether the examination should be carried out by the Commission itself or by some other body. The Commission is also responsible for the preparation of Consolidation and Statute Law (Repeals) Bills.

Chairman, The Hon. Mr Justice Toulson
Commissioners, Judge A. Wilkie, QC; Prof. H. Beale, QC; Prof. M. Partington, CBE; S. Bridge
Chief Executive, S. Humphreys

LAW OFFICERS' DEPARTMENTS

Legal Secretariat to the Law Officers, Attorney-General's Chambers, 9 Buckingham Gate, London SW1E 6JP
T 020-7271 2422 F 020-7271 2430
E lslo@gtnet.gov.uk
W www.lslo.gov.uk
Attorney-General's Chambers, Royal Courts of Justice, Belfast BT1 3JY
T 028-9054 6082 F 028-9054 6049

The Law Officers of the Crown for England and Wales are the Attorney-General and the Solicitor-General. The Attorney-General, assisted by the Solicitor-General, is the chief legal adviser to the Government and is also ultimately responsible for all Crown litigation. He has overall responsibility for the work of the Law Officers' Departments (the Treasury Solicitor's Department, the Crown Prosecution Service, the Serious Fraud Office and the Legal Secretariat to the Law Officers). He has a specific statutory duty to superintend the discharge of their duties by the Director of Public Prosecutions (who heads the Crown Prosecution Service) and the Director of the Serious Fraud Office. The Director of Public Prosecutions for Northern Ireland is also responsible to the Attorney-General for the performance of his functions. The Attorney-General has additional responsibilities in relation to aspects of the civil and criminal law.

Attorney-General, The Rt. Hon. The Lord Goldsmith, QC
Private Secretary, C. Bartlett
Parliamentary Private Secretary, M. Foster, MP
Solicitor-General, The Rt. Hon. Harriet Harman, QC, MP
Legal Secretary, D. Brummell
Deputy Legal Secretary, S. Parkinson

LEARNING AND SKILLS COUNCIL

Cheylesmore House, Quinton Road, Coventry, West Midlands, CV1 2WT
T 0845-019 4170 F 024-7649 3600
E info@lsc.gov.uk W www.lsc.gov.uk

The Learning and Skills Council (LSC) was established in April 2001 to replace the Further Education Funding and the Training and Enterprise Councils. It is a non-departmental public body responsible for the planning and funding of post-16 education and training. Its annual budget for 2003–4 was £8 billion. Its remit is to ensure that high quality post-16 provision is available to meet the needs of employers, individuals and communities. The LSC operates through a national office based in Coventry and 47 local departments, which work to promote the equality of opportunity in the workplace, aiming to ensure that the needs of the most disadvantaged people in the labour market are met. These local departments in most cases have coterminous boundaries with Small Business Service franchises.

Chairman, Chris Banks
Chief Executive, Mark Haysom

LEGAL SERVICES COMMISSION

85 Gray's Inn Road, London WC1X 8TX
T 020-7759 0000 Directory Information line 0845-608 1122
W www.legalservices.gov.uk

The Legal Services Commission was created under the Access to Justice Act 1999 and replaced the Legal Aid Board in April 2000. It is a non-departmental public body which is accountable to the Department for Constitutional Affairs.

The Commission's four core objectives are: to fund legal and advice services in England and Wales; to identify unmet legal needs; to develop those providing legal aid; and to develop innovative services to meet priority legal needs. It also runs the Community Legal Service which provides advice and legal representation for people involved in civil cases, and the Criminal Defence Service, which provides advice and legal representation for people facing criminal charges.

The Commission produces free information leaflets which are available from solicitors' and advisory offices and on the Commission's websites.

Chief Executive, Clare Dodgson
Members, A. Edwards; Ms J. Herzog; Ms Y. Mosquito; J. Shearer; Ms M. Richards; A. Andrew; D. Edmonds; T. Jones
Secretary, Anne-Marie Roberts

LIBRARIES

BRITISH LIBRARY

96 Euston Road, London NW1 2DB
T 020-7412 7000
E visitor-services@bl.uk W www.bl.uk

The British Library was established in 1973. It is the UK's national library and occupies a key position in the library and information network. The Library aims to serve scholarship, research, industry, commerce and all other major users of information. Its services are based on collections which include over 16 million volumes, 1 million discs, and 55,000 hours of tape recordings. The Library is now based at two sites: London (St Pancras and Colindale) and Boston Spa, W. Yorks. The Library's sponsoring department is the Department for Culture, Media and Sport.

Access to the reading rooms at St Pancras is limited to holders of a British Library Reader's Pass; information about eligibility is available from the Reader Admissions Office. The exhibition galleries and public areas are open to all, free of charge.

Opening hours of services vary and should be checked by telephone.

BRITISH LIBRARY BOARD

Chairman, Lord Eatwell of Stratton
Chief Executive and Deputy Chairman, Mrs L. Brindley
Members, H. Boyd-Carpenter, KCVO; S. Olswang; Prof. R. Burgess; Ms S. Forbes, CBE; D. Lewis; Sir Colin Lucas; Ms E. Mackay; R. S. Broadhurst, CBE; Dr G. W. Roberts

BRITISH LIBRARY, BOSTON SPA

Boston Spa, Wetherby, W. Yorks LS23 7BQ
T 01937-546000

BRITISH LIBRARY, ST PANCRAS

96 Euston Road, London NW1 2DB
T 020-7412 7000
Press and Public Relations, T 020-7412 7111
Visitor Services, T 020-7412 7332
Education Service, T 020-7412 7797

SCHOLARSHIP AND COLLECTIONS

Reader Services, T 020-7412 7676
Asia, Pacific and Africa Collections, T 020-7412 7873
British Collections, T 020-7412 7676
Western Manuscripts, T 020-7412 7513
Map Library, T 020-7412 7702
Music Library, T 020-7412 7772
Philatelic Collections, T 020-7412 7635
British Library Sound Archive, T 020-7412 7440
British Library Newspapers, Colindale Avenue, London NW9 5HE T 020-7412 7353
European and American Collections, T 020-7412 7676

OPERATIONS AND SERVICES

Reader Admissions, T 020-7412 7677

SCIENCE, TECHNOLOGY AND INNOVATION

Science and Technology, T 020-7412 7494/7289
Patents, T 020-7412 7919/7920
Business, T 020-7412 7454
Social Policy Information Service, T 020-7412 7536
National Preservation Office, T 020-7412 7612

NATIONAL LIBRARY OF SCOTLAND

George IV Bridge, Edinburgh EH1 1EW
T 0131-226 4531 F 0131-622 4803
E enquiries@nls.uk W www.nls.uk

The Library, which was founded as the Advocates' Library in 1682, became the National Library of Scotland in 1925. It is funded by the Scottish Executive. It contains about eight million books and pamphlets, 20,000 current periodicals, 350 newspaper titles and 120,000 manuscripts. It has an unrivalled Scottish collection.

The Reading Room is for reference and research which cannot conveniently be pursued elsewhere. Admission is by ticket.

Chairman of the Trustees, Prof. Michael Anderson, OBE, FBA, FRSE
National Librarian and Secretary to the Trustees, M. Wade
Director of Collection Development, C. Newton
Director of Corporate Services, D. Campbell
Director of Customer Services, G. Hunt
Director of Development and Marketing, A. Miller

NATIONAL LIBRARY OF WALES/ LLYFRGELL GENEDLAETHOL CYMRU

Aberystwyth SY23 3BU
T 01970-632800 F 01970-615709
W www.llgc.org.uk

The National Library of Wales was founded by royal charter in 1907, and is funded by the National Assembly for Wales. It contains about four million printed books, 40,000 manuscripts, four million deeds and documents, numerous maps, prints and drawings, and a sound and moving image collection. It specialises in manuscripts and books relating to Wales and the Celtic peoples. It is the repository for pre-1858 Welsh probate records, manorial records and tithe documents, and certain legal records. Admission is by reader's ticket to the Reading Rooms but

entry to the exhibition programme is free.
President, Dr R. Brinley Jones
Heads of Departments, M. W. Mainwaring *(Corporate Services)*; G. Jenkins *(Collection Services)*; Dr W. R. M. Griffiths *(Public Services)*
Librarian, A. M. W. Green

LIGHTHOUSE AUTHORITIES

CORPORATION OF TRINITY HOUSE

Trinity House, Tower Hill, London EC3N 4DH
T 020-7481 6900 F 020-7480 7662
W www.trinityhouse.co.uk

Trinity House, the first general lighthouse and pilotage authority in the kingdom, was granted its first charter by Henry VIII in 1514. The Corporation is the general lighthouse authority for England, Wales and the Channel Islands and maintains 72 lighthouses, 13 major floating aids to navigation (e.g. light vessels) and more than 420 buoys. The Corporation also has certain statutory jurisdiction over aids to navigation maintained by local harbour authorities and is responsible for dealing with wrecks dangerous to navigation, except those occurring within port limits or wrecks of HM ships.

The Trinity House Lighthouse Service is maintained out of the General Lighthouse Fund which is provided from light dues levied on ships calling at ports of the UK and the Republic of Ireland. The Corporation is also a deep-sea pilotage authority and a charitable organisation.

The affairs of the Corporation are controlled by a board of Elder Brethren and the Secretary. A separate board, which comprises Elder Brethren, senior staff and outside representatives, currently controls the Lighthouse Service. The Elder Brethren also act as nautical assessors in marine cases in the Admiralty Division of the High Court of Justice.

ELDER BRETHREN
Master, HRH The Prince Philip, Duke of Edinburgh, KG, KT, PC
Deputy Master and Executive Chairman, Rear-Adm. J. M. de Halpert, CB
Wardens, Capt. C. M. C. Stewart *(Rental)*; Cdre. P. J. Melson, CBE, RN; *(Nether)*
Elder Brethren, HRH The Prince of Wales, KG, KT; HRH The Duke of York, KCVO, ADC; Sir Brian Shaw; Capt. J. E. Bury; Capt. D. J. Cloke; Capt. Sir Miles Wingate, KCVO; The Rt. Hon. Sir Edward Heath, KG, MBE; Capt. P. F. Mason, CBE; Capt.T. Woodfield, OBE; The Rt. Hon. The Lord Simon of Glaisdale, DL; Capt. D. T. Smith, OBE, RN; Cdr. Sir Robin Gillett, BT, GBE, RD, RNR; Capt. Sir Malcolm Edge, KCVO; The Rt. Hon. The Lord Cuckney of Millbank; Capt. D. J. Orr; The Rt. Hon. The Lord Carrington, KG, GCMG, CH, MC, PC; The Rt. Hon. The Lord Mackay of Clashfern, KT; Sir Adrian Swire; The Rt. Hon. The Lord Sterling of Plaistow, CBE, GCVO; Cdr. M. J. Rivett-Carnac, RN, DL; Adm. Sir Jock Slater, GCB, LVO, DL; Capt. J. R. Burton-Hall, RD; Capt. I. Gibb; Capt. D. C. Glass; D. F. Potter; Capt. D. P. Richards, RD, RNR; S. P. Sherard; The Lord Brown of Madingley; The Rt. Hon. The Lord Robertson of Port Ellen, GCMG; Rear-Adm. Sir Patrick Rowe, KCVO, CBE; The Hon. C. C. Lyttelton; Capt. N. R. Pryke, MCIT

OFFICERS
Secretary, P. Galloway
Director of Finance, J. S. Wedge
Director of Operations and Asset Management, Cdre. P. J. Melson, CBE, RN
Head of Human Resources, P. F. Morgan
Legal and Risk Manager, J. D. Price
Navigation Manager, Mrs K. Hossain
Marketing and PR Manager , S. J. W. Dunning
Media and Communication Officer, H. L. Cooper

NORTHERN LIGHTHOUSE BOARD

84 George Street, Edinburgh EH2 3DA
T 0131-473 3100 F 0131-220 2093
E enquiries@nlb.org.uk W www.nlb.org.uk

The Lighthouse Board is the general lighthouse authority for Scotland and the Isle of Man and owes its origin to an Act of Parliament passed in 1786. At present there are 19 Commissioners who operate under the Merchant Shipping Act 1995.

The Commissioners control 199 lighthouses and many lighted and unlighted buoys and a DGPS system.

COMMISSIONERS
The Lord Advocate; the Solicitor-General for Scotland; the Lord Provosts of Edinburgh, Glasgow and Aberdeen; the Provost of Inverness; the Convener of Argyll and Bute Council; the Sheriffs-Principal of North Strathclyde, Tayside, Central and Fife, Grampian, Highlands and Islands, South Strathclyde, Dumfries and Galloway, Lothians and Borders and Glasgow and Strathkelvin; P. MacKay, CB; Capt. K. MacLeod; Dr A. Cubie, CBE; R. Quayle; A. Whyte

OFFICERS
Chief Executive, Capt. J. B. Taylor, RN
Director of Finance, D. Gorman
Director of Engineering, M. Waddell
Director of Operations and Navigational Requirements, G. Platten

LOCAL GOVERNMENT OMBUDSMAN FOR WALES

Derwen House, Court Road, Bridgend CF31 1BN
T 01656-661325 F 01656-673279
E enquiries@ombudsman-wales.org
W www.ombudsman-wales.org

The Local Government Ombudsman for Wales has similar powers to the Local Commissioners in England, but since the end of 2001 he has also had additional powers (similar to the Standards Board for England) to investigate allegations made against local authority members of misconduct. The Ombudsman is appointed by the Crown on the recommendation of the Secretary of State for Wales. A free leaflet *Your Local Government Ombudsman in Wales* is available from the Ombudsman's office.
Public Services and Local Government Ombudsman for Wales, Adam Peat
Member (*ex officio*), The Parliamentary Commissioner for Administration

LORD GREAT CHAMBERLAIN'S OFFICE

House of Lords, London SW1A 0PW
T 020-7219 3100 F 020-7219 2500

The Lord Great Chamberlain is a Great Officer of State, the office being hereditary since the grant of Henry I to the family of De Vere, Earls of Oxford. It is now a joint hereditary office rotating on the death of the Sovereign between the Cholmondeley, Carington and the Ancaster families. The Lord Great Chamberlain is responsible for the royal apartments in the Palace of Westminster, i.e. the Sovereign's Robing Room, the Royal Gallery, the administration of the Chapel of St Mary Undercroft and, in conjunction with the Lord Chancellor and the Speaker, Westminster Hall. The Lord Great Chamberlain has the right to perform specific services at a Coronation, he carries out ceremonial duties in the Palace of Westminster when the Sovereign visits the Palace and has particular responsibility for the internal administrative arrangements within the House of Lords for State Openings of Parliament.

Lord Great Chamberlain, The Marquess of Cholmondeley
Secretary to the Lord Great Chamberlain, Lt.-Gen. Sir Michael Willcocks, KCB
Clerks to the Lord Great Chamberlain, Ms J. Perodeau; Ms Rebecca Russel Ponte

LORD PRIVY SEAL'S OFFICE

Cabinet Office, 70 Whitehall, London SW1A 2AT
T 020-7270 3000
W www.cabinetoffice.gov.uk

The Lord Privy Seal is a member of the Cabinet and Leader of the House of Lords. He has no departmental portfolio, but is a member of a number of Cabinet committees. He is responsible to the Prime Minister for the organisation of Government business in the House and has a responsibility to the House itself to advise it on procedural matters and other difficulties which arise. He is the Lords' spokesperson on Northern Ireland issues.

Lord Privy Seal, Leader of the House of Lords, The Rt. Hon. Baroness Amos
Principal Private Secretary, Christopher Jacobs
Private Secretary (House of Lords), Andrew Makower

MENTAL HEALTH ACT COMMISSION

Maid Marian House, 56 Hounds Gate, Nottingham NG1 6BG
T 0115-943 7100 F 0115-943 7101
E chiefexec@mhac.trent.nhs.uk W www.mhac.trent.nhs.uk

The Mental Health Act Commission was established in 1983. Its functions are to keep under review the operation of the Mental Health Act 1983; to visit and meet patients detained under the Act; to investigate complaints falling within the Commission's remit; to operate the consent to treatment safeguards in the Mental Health Act; to publish a biennial report on its activities; to monitor the implementation of the Code of Practice; and to advise Ministers. Commissioners are appointed by the Secretary of State for Health.

Chairman, Prof. K. Patel
Vice-Chairman, Ms D. Jenkins
Chief Executive, C. Heginbotham

MILLENNIUM COMMISSION

Portland House, Stag Place, London SW1E 5EZ
T 020-7880 2001 F 020-7880 2000
E info@millennium.gov.uk

The Millennium Commission was established in February 1994 and is accountable to the Department for Culture, Media and Sport. It is an independent body which distributes money from National Lottery proceeds to projects to mark the millennium. The Commission expects all its grant-giving work to be complete by 2006.

Chair, The Rt. Hon. Tessa Jowell, MP
Members, Dr H. Couper, FRAS; Ms F. Benjamin, OBE; Lord Heseltine, MP, PC; Mrs J. Donovan, CBE; M. d'Ancona; Lord Glentoran, CBE; The Rt. Hon. R. Caborn, MP
Director, M. O'Connor, CBE

MUSEUMS

BRITISH MUSEUM

Great Russell Street, London WC1B 3DG
T 020-7323 8000 F 020-7323 8616
E information@thebritishmuseum.ac.uk
W www.thebritishmuseum.ac.uk

The British Museum houses the national collection of antiquities, ethnography, coins and paper money, medals, prints and drawings. The British Museum may be said to date from 1753, when Parliament approved the holding of a public lottery to raise funds for the purchase of the collections of Sir Hans Sloane and the Harleian manuscripts, and for their proper housing and maintenance. The building (Montagu House) was opened in 1759. The present buildings were erected between 1823 and the present day, and the original collection has increased to its present dimensions by gifts and purchases. Total government grant-in-aid for 2004–5 is £37,999 million.

BOARD OF TRUSTEES

Appointed by the Sovereign, HRH The Duke of Gloucester, KG, GCVO
Appointed by the Prime Minister, C. Allen-Jones; Hasan Askari; Nicholas Barber; Prof. Barry Cunliffe; The Rt. Hon. Countess of Dalkeith; Sir Michael Hopkins; Sir Joseph Hotung; Prof. Martin Kemp; David Lindsell; Christopher McCall; Tom Phillips; Anna Ritchie; Eric Salama; Prof. Jean Thomas; Sir Keith Thomas; Richard Lambert
Appointed by the Trustees of the British Museum, Sir John Boyd *(Chair)*; The Hon. Phillip Lader; Lord Powell of Bayswater, KCMG; J. Tusa *(Deputy Chair)*; Lord Browne of Madingley *(Deputy Chair)*

OFFICERS

Director, Neil MacGregor
Deputy Director, Andrew Burnett
Deputy Director, Dawn Austwick, OBE
Director of Marketing and Public Affairs, vacant
Director of Operations, Chris Rofe
Director of Resources, D. Austwick, OBE
Acting Head of Communications, Joanna Mackle
Head of Building and Estates, K. T. Stannard
Head of Education, J. F. Reeve
Head of Finance, Chris Herring
Head of Membership Development, Ms M. Fenn
Secretary, T. Doubleday
Visitor Operations Manager, Kerry Foster

KEEPERS
Keeper of Ancient Near East Antiquities, Dr John Curtis
Keeper of Coins and Medals, Andrew Burnett
Keeper of Department of Asia, Robert Knox
Keeper of Egyptian Antiquities, Vivian Davies
Keeper of Ethnography, John Mack
Keeper of Greek and Roman Antiquities, Dr Dyfri Williams
Keeper of Prehistory and Europe, Leslie Webster
Keeper, Presentation, Ian Jenkins
Keeper of Prints and Drawings, Antony Griffiths
Conservation, Documentation and Science, Sheridan Bowman

IMPERIAL WAR MUSEUM

Lambeth Road, London SE1 6HZ
T 020-7416 5320 F 020-7416 5374

The Museum, founded in 1917, illustrates and records all aspects of the two world wars and other military operations involving Britain and the Commonwealth since 1914. It was opened in its present home, formerly Bethlem Hospital, in 1936. The Museum is a multi-branch organisation which also includes: the Cabinet War Rooms in Whitehall, HMS Belfast in the Pool of London, Imperial War Museum Duxford in Cambridgeshire and Imperial War Museum North in Trafford.

The total grant-in-aid (including grants for special projects) for 2004–5 is £17.491 million.

OFFICERS
Chairman of Trustees, Adm. Sir Jock Slater, GCB, LVO
Director-General, R. W. K. Crawford, CBE
Director of Collections, M. Whitmore
Director of Corporate Services, A. Stoneman
Director of Development, Ms V. Cornwall
Director of HMS Belfast, B. King
Director of Public Services, Miss A. Godwin
Director, Cabinet War Rooms, P. Reed
Director, Imperial War Museum, Duxford, E. Inman, OBE
Director, Imperial War Museum, North, J. Forrester
Secretary and Director of Finance, J. Card

MUSEUM OF LONDON

London Wall, London EC2Y 5HN
T 0870-444 3852 F 0870-444 3853
E info@museumoflondon.org.uk
W www.museumoflondon.org.uk

The Museum of London illustrates the history of London from prehistoric times to the present day. It opened in 1976 and is based on the amalgamation of the former Guildhall Museum and London Museum. The Museum is controlled by a Board of Governors, appointed (nine each) by the Government and the Corporation of London. The Museum is currently funded by grants from the Department for Culture, Media and Sport and the Corporation of London. The total grant-in-aid for 2004–5 is £6.506 million.
Chairman of Board of Governors, R. Hambro
Director, Prof. J. Lohman

MUSEUMS, LIBRARIES AND ARCHIVES COUNCIL

16 Queen Anne's Gate, London SW1H 9AA
T 020-7273 1444 F 020-7273 1404
E info@mla.gov.uk W www.resource.gov.uk

The Museums, Libraries and Archives Council (MLA) was launched in April 2000 in order to provide strategic guidance, advice and advocacy across the whole of Government on museum, archive and library matters. It is a non-departmental public body sponsored by the Department for Culture, Media and Sport. The MLA replaced the Museums and Galleries Commission (MGC) and the Library and Information Commission (LIC), and now includes archives within its portfolio.
Chairman, Mark Wood
Chief Executive, C. Batt, OBE
Board Members, L. Grossman; V. Gray; A. Chowdhury; Dr M. Crozier; M. Jones; N. MacGregor; M. Stevenson; A. Watkin; D. Barrie; Ms L. Brindley; B. MacNaught; B. McKee; D. Henshaw; Sir Geoffrey Holland; N. Kingsley; Ms V. Tandy

NATIONAL ARMY MUSEUM

Royal Hospital Road, London SW3 4HT
T 020-7730 0717 F 020-7823 6573
E info@national-army-museum.ac.uk
W www.national-army-museum.ac.uk

The National Army Museum covers the history of five centuries of the British Army. It was established by royal charter in 1960.
Assistant Directors, D. K. Smurthwaite; Dr A. J. Guy; P. B. Boyden

NATURAL HISTORY MUSEUM

Cromwell Road, London SW7 5BD
T 020-7942 5000

The Natural History Museum originates from the natural history departments of the British Museum, which grew extensively during the 19th century; in 1860 the natural history collection was moved from Bloomsbury to a new location. Part of the site of the 1862 International Exhibition in South Kensington was acquired for the new museum, and the Museum opened to the public in 1881. In 1963 the Natural History Museum became completely independent with its own board of trustees. The Walter Rothschild Zoological Museum, Tring, bequeathed by the second Lord Rothschild, has formed part of the Museum since 1938. The Geological Museum merged with the Natural History Museum in 1985. Total Government grant-in-aid for 2004–5 is £39.367 million.
Trustees, Prof. Sir Keith O'Nions, FRS *(Chairman)*; Sir Richard Sykes, FRS; Dame Judith Mayhew, DBE; Prof. M. Hassell, CBE, FRS; O. Stocken; Prof. J. McGlade; Prof. Dianne Edwards, CBE, FRS, Prof. C. Leaver, CBE, FRS; The Lord Palumbo; Prof. Linda Partridge, FRS, FRSE; Prof. Georgina Mace, OBE; Sir William Castell

SENIOR STAFF
Director, Dr Michael Dixon
Director of Communications and Development, Ms S. Ament
Director of Estates, K. Rellis
Director of Finance, N. Greenwood
Director of Human Resources, D. Hill
Director of Science, R. Lane
Director, Tring Zoological Museum, Mrs T. Wild

Head of Audit and Review, D. Thorpe
Head of Library and Information Services, G. Higley
Head of Visitor and Operational Services, D. Candlin
Keeper of Botany, Dr J. Vogel
Keeper of Entomology, Dr R. Vane-Wright
Keeper of Mineralogy, Prof. A. Fleet
Keeper of Palaeontology, Dr N. MacLeod
Keeper of Zoology, Prof. P. Rainbow

NATIONAL MARITIME MUSEUM

Park Row, Greenwich, London SE10 9NF
T 020-8858 4422 F 020-8312 6632

Established by Act of Parliament in 1934, the National Maritime Museum illustrates the maritime history of Great Britain in the widest sense, underlining the importance of the sea and its influence on the nation's power, wealth, culture, technology and institutions. The Museum is in three groups of buildings in Greenwich Park the main building, the Queen's House (built by Inigo Jones, 1616–35) and the Royal Observatory (including Wren's Flamsteed House). In May 1999, a £20 million Heritage Lottery supported project opened 16 new galleries in a glazed courtyard in the Museum's west wing. Total Government grant-in-aid for 2004–5 is £15.731 million.
Director, R. Clare
Chairman, Sir David Hardy

NATIONAL MUSEUMS LIVERPOOL

PO Box 33, 127 Dale Street, Liverpool L69 3LA
T 0151-207 0001 F 0151-478 4790
W www.liverpoolmuseums.org.uk

The Board of Trustees of the National Museums Liverpool (formerly National Museums and Galleries on Merseyside) is responsible for the Liverpool Museum, the Merseyside Maritime Museum (incorporating HM Customs and Excise National Museum), the Museum of Liverpool Life, the Lady Lever Art Gallery, the Walker, Sudley House and the Conservation Centre. Total Government grant-in-aid for 2004–5 was £17.333 million.
Chairman of the Board of Trustees, D. McDonnell
Director, Dr David Fleming
Keeper of Art Galleries, J. Treuherz
Keeper of Conservation, A. Durham
Keeper, Liverpool Museum, J. Millard
Keeper, Merseyside Maritime Museum and Museum of Liverpool Life, T. Tibbles

NATIONAL MUSEUMS AND GALLERIES OF WALES

Cathays Park, Cardiff CF10 3NP
T 029-2039 7951 F 029-2057 3321
E post@nmgw.ac.uk W www.nmgw.ac.uk

The National Museums and Galleries of Wales comprise the National Museum and Gallery Cardiff, the Museum of Welsh Life, St Fagans, Big Pit National Museum of Wales, Blaenafon, the Roman Legionary Museum Caerleon, Turner House Gallery Penarth, the Welsh Slate Museum Llanberis, the Segontium Roman Museum Caernarfon and the Museum of the Welsh Woollen Industry Dre-fach, Felindre. Total funding from the Welsh Assembly Government for 2003–4 was £20.536 million.
President, Paul E. Loveluck, CBE
Vice-President, Dr Susan J. Davies
Treasurer, Gwyn Howells, ACIB

OFFICERS
Director-General, Michael Houlihan
Directors, Dr E. Wiliam *(Collections and Education and Deputy Director)*; J. Williams-Davies *(Museum of Welsh Life)*; M. Tooby *(National Museum and Gallery)*; R. Gwyn *(Strategic Communications)*; M. Richards *(Operations)*; J. Sheppard *(Finance and IT)*
Council Members, M.C. T. Prichard, CBE; Dr Brian Willott; M. A. J. Salter; J. E. Peirson Jones; Prof. Colin L. Jones, OBE; Dr Iolo ap Gwynn; D. Bowen Lewis; J. Wynford Evans, CBE; Dr Peter Warren, CBE; Prof. J. W. Last, CBE; Prof. D. Egan; H. R. C. Williams; Rhiannon Wyn Hughes, MBE

NATIONAL MUSEUMS OF SCOTLAND

Chambers Street, Edinburgh EH1 1JF
T 0131-247 4422 F 0131-220 4819
E info@nms.ac.uk W www.nms.ac.uk

The National Museums of Scotland comprise the Royal Museum of Scotland, the National War Museum of Scotland, the Museum of Scottish Country Life, the Museum of Flight, Shambellie House Museum of Costume and the Museum of Scotland. Total funding from the Scottish Executive is an annual grant of £16 million.

BOARD OF TRUSTEES
Chairman, The Lord Wilson of Tillyorn, KT, GCMG, PHD, FRSE
Members, G. S. Johnston, OBE, TD, KCSG, DL, CA; Ms C. Macaulay; Sir Neil McIntosh, CBE, DL; Mrs N. Mahal, DCG; Prof. A. Manning, OBE, DPHIL, FRSE, FIBIOL; Prof. J. Murray, CENG; I. Ritchie, CBE, FRENG, FRSE; A. J. C. Smith, FCIA; J. A. G. Fiddes, OBE; Prof. M. Lynch, PHD, FRSE, FSA (SCOT); Miss A. MacLean; Mrs L. Hart, MBE

OFFICERS
Director, Dr G. Rintoul, PHD
Director of Collections, Jane Carmichael
Director of Facilities Management and Projects, S. Elson, FSA SCOT
Director of Finance and Resources, A. Patience
Director of Marketing and Development, Catherine Holden
Director of Public Programmes, Mary Bryden, FRSA
Head of Corporate Policy and Performance, Sheila McClure
Managing Director of NMS Enterprises, P. Williamson

ROYAL AIR FORCE MUSEUM

Grahame Park Way, London NW9 5LL
T 020-8205 2266 F 020-8200 1751
W www.rafmuseum.com

Situated on the former airfield at RAF Hendon, the Museum illustrates the development of aviation from before the Wright brothers to the present-day RAF. Total Government grant-in-aid for 2003–4, including funding for the outstation at Cosford, is £6.798 million.
Director-General, Dr M. A. Fopp
Directors, J. Kitchen; S. Garman; K. Ifould
Senior Keeper, P. Elliott

SCIENCE MUSEUM

Exhibition Road, London SW7 2DD
T 0870-870 4868 F 020-7942 4447

The Science Museum, part of the National Museum of Science and Industry, houses the national collections of science, technology, industry and medicine. The Museum began as the science collection of the South Kensington Museum and first opened in 1857. In 1883 it acquired the collections of the Patent Museum and in 1909 the science collections were transferred to the new Science Museum, leaving the art collections with the Victoria and Albert Museum. The Wellcome Wing was opened in July 2000.

Some of the Museum's commercial aircraft, agricultural machinery, and road and rail transport collections are at Wroughton, Wilts. The National Museum of Science and Industry also incorporates the National Railway Museum, York, the National Museum of Photography, Film and Television, Bradford, and Locomotion: the National Railway Museum at Shildon.

Total Government grant-in-aid for 2004–5 is £32,494 million.

BOARD OF TRUSTEES
Chairman, The Rt. Hon. Lord Waldegrave of North Hill
Members, Prof. Sir Ron U. Cooke, DSC; Prof. A. Dowling, CBE, FRENG; G. Dyke; Dr A. Grocock; Dr D. Gurr; R. Haythornthwaite; D. E. Rayner, CBE; Prof. Sir Martin Rees; Dr Maggie Semple, OBE; S. Singh, MBE; M. G. Smith; Prof. R. A. Smith, PHD, FRENG; Prof. Kathy Sykes; Sir William Wells

OFFICERS
Director, Dr. L. Sharp
Head of Corporate Communications, M. Pudney
Head of Design, T. Molloy
Head of Estates, J. Bevin
Head of Finance, Ms A. Caine
Interim Head of Human Resources, Ms B. Halikowa
Head of IT, Ms M. Burns
Head of National Museum of Photography, Film and Television, C. Philpott
Managing Director, NMSI Trading Ltd, Ms M. Jackson
Head of National Railway Museum, A. Scott
Head of Planning and Development, A. Leitch
Head of Science Museum, J. Tucker
Head of Sustainable Development and Master Planning, C. Gordon

VICTORIA AND ALBERT MUSEUM

Cromwell Road, London SW7 2RL
T 020-7942 2000 W www.vam.ac.uk

The Victoria and Albert Museum is the national museum of fine and applied art and design. It descends directly from the Museum of Manufactures, which opened in Marlborough House in 1852 after the Great Exhibition of 1851. The Museum was moved in 1857 to become part of the South Kensington Museum. It was renamed the Victoria and Albert Museum in 1899. It also houses the National Art Library and Print Room.

The Museum administers two branch museums: the Museum of Childhood at Bethnal Green and the Theatre Museum in Covent Garden. The museum in Bethnal Green was opened in 1872 and the building is the most important surviving example of the type of glass and iron construction used by Paxton for the Great Exhibition.

Total Government grant-in-aid for 2004–5 is £36.1 million.

BOARD OF TRUSTEES
Chairman, Paula Ridley
Members, J. Altaras; Prof. M. Buck; R. Dickins; Prof. Sir Christopher Frayling, PHD; Prof. Lisa Jardine, PHD; Mrs J. Gordon Clark; R. Mather; P. Rogers; P. Ruddock; The Rt. Hon. Sir Timothy Sainsbury; Dame Marjorie Scardino, DBE
Secretary to the Board of Trustees, J. F. Rider

OFFICERS
Director, M. Jones
Director of Collections and Keeper of Asian Department, Dr D. Swallow
Director of Collections Services, N. Umney
Director of Finance and Resources, I. Blatchford
Director of Learning and Interpretation, D. Anderson, OBE
Director of Personnel and Visitor Services, L. Stracey
Director of Projects and Estate, Mrs G. F. Miles
Director of Public Affairs, D. Whitmore
Director of Development, J. McCaffrey
Director of the Museum of Childhood, Ms D. Lees
Director of the Theatre Museum, G. Marsh
Head of Conservation, Ms S. Smith
Head of Exhibitions, Mrs L. Lloyd Jones
Head of Photographic Services, J. Stevenson
Head of Records and Collections Services, A. Seal
Head of Regional Liaison and Purchase Grant Fund, Miss J. Davies
Head of Research Department, Ms C. Sargentson
Keeper of Furniture, Textiles and Fashion Department, C. Wilk
Keeper of Sculpture, Metalwork, Ceramics and Glass Department, Dr P. E. D. Williamson
Keeper of Word and Image Department, Ms S. B. Lambert
Managing Director of V&A Enterprises Ltd (Acting), Ms J. Prosser

---

NATIONAL AUDIT OFFICE

157–197 Buckingham Palace Road, London SW1W 9SP
T 020-7798 7000 F 020-7798 7070
3–4 Park Place, Cardiff CF10 3DP
T 029-2067 8500 F 029-2067 8501
E enquiries@nao.gsi.gov.uk
W www.nao.org.uk

The National Audit Office came into existence under the National Audit Act 1983 to replace and continue the work of the former Exchequer and Audit Department. The Act reinforced the Office's total financial and operational independence from the Government and brought its head, the Comptroller and Auditor-General, into a closer relationship with Parliament as an officer of the House of Commons.

The National Audit Office provides independent information, advice and assurance to Parliament and the public about all aspects of the financial operations of Government departments and many other bodies receiving public funds. It does this by examining and certifying the accounts of these organisations and by regularly publishing reports to Parliament on the results of its value for money investigations of the economy, efficiency and effectiveness with which public resources have been used. The National Audit Office is also the auditor by agreement of the accounts of certain international and other organisations. In addition, the Office authorises the issue of public funds to Government departments.

Comptroller and Auditor-General, Sir John Bourne, KCB
Private Secretary, N. Sayers
Deputy Comptroller and Auditor-General, T. Burr
Assistant Auditors-General, J. Colman; Miss C. Mawhood; M. Sinclair; Ms W. Kenway-Smith; M. Whitehouse; J. Rickleton

NATIONAL CONSUMER COUNCIL

20 Grosvenor Gardens, London SW1W 0DH
T 020-7730 3469 F 020-7730 0191
E info@ncc.org.uk W www.ncc.org.uk

The National Consumer Council (NCC) was set up by the Government in 1975 to give an independent voice to consumers in the UK. Its role is to advocate the consumer interest to decision-makers in national and local government, industry and regulatory bodies, business and the professions. It does this through a combination of research and campaigning. NCC is a non-profit making company limited by guarantee and is largely funded by grant-in-aid from the Department of Trade and Industry. The Council is not a consumer advice or complaints body.

Chair, Deirdre Hutton, CBE
Chief Executive, Ed Mayo

NATIONAL ENDOWMENT FOR SCIENCE, TECHNOLOGY AND THE ARTS (NESTA)

Fishmongers' Chambers, 110 Upper Thames Street, London EC4R 3TW
T 020-7645 9500 F 020-7645 9501
W www.nesta.org.uk

The National Endowment for Science, Technology and the Arts (NESTA) was established under the National Lottery Act 1998 with a £200 million endowment from the proceeds of the National Lottery. It runs four funding programmes: *Invention and Innovation* takes original ideas with commercial or social potential and helps them get to market; *Fellowship* supports exceptionally talented and innovative people, and enables them to pursue a tailor-made programme of personal creative development; *Learning* researches and pioneers initiatives, which will drive education and encourage public engagement with science, technology and the arts; and the *Graduate Pioneer Programme* supports recent graduates from the creative industries.

Chairman, Chris Powell
Chief Executive, J. Newton

NATIONAL HERITAGE MEMORIAL FUND

7 Holbein Place, London SW1W 8NR
T 020-7591 6000 F 020-7591 6001
W www.hlf.org.uk

The National Heritage Memorial Fund was set up under the National Heritage Act 1980 in memory of people who have given their lives for the United Kingdom. The Fund provides grants (and sometimes loans) to organisations based in the United Kingdom, mainly so they can buy items of outstanding interest and of importance to the national heritage. These must either be at risk or have a memorial character. The Fund is administered by 14 trustees who are appointed by the Prime Minister.

The National Lottery etc Act 1993 designated the Fund as distributor of the heritage share of proceeds from the National Lottery. As a result, the Fund now operates two funds: the National Heritage Memorial Fund and the Heritage Lottery Fund. The National Heritage Memorial Fund receives an annual grant from the Department for Culture, Media and Sport.

Chair, L. Forgan
Trustees, Prof. C. Baines; N. Dodd; Sir Angus Grossart, CBE; G. Waterfield; Ms P. Wilson; Earl of Dalkeith; Prof. T. Pritchard; J. Wright, CBE; Dr M. Phillips; Dr D. Langslow; Madhu Anjali; Catherine Graham-Harrison; M. Emmerich
Director, Ms C. Souter

NATIONAL LOTTERY COMMISSION

101 Wigmore Street, London W1U 1QU
T 020-7016 3400 F 020-7016 3401
W www.natlotcomm.gov.uk

The National Lottery Commission replaced the Office of the National Lottery (OFLOT) in April 1999 under the National Lottery Act 1998. The Commission is responsible for the granting, varying and enforcing of licences to run the National Lottery. Its duties are to ensure that the National Lottery is run with all due propriety, that the interests of players are protected, and, subject to these two objectives, that returns to the 'good causes' are maximised.

Gaming and lotteries in the UK are officially regulated and may only be run by licensed operators or in licensed premises.

The Department of Culture, Media and Sport is responsible for gaming and lottery policy and laws. The National Lottery is the most heavily regulated part of the gaming market. Empowered by the National Lottery Act 1993, the Department of Culture, Media and Sport directs the National Lottery Commission, who in turn regulates Camelot, the lottery operator. Camelot, a private company wholly owned by five shareholders, was granted a second seven-year licence to run the Lottery, which began on 27 January 2002. The main National Lottery draw was relaunched as Lotto in spring 2002. Total sales of Lottery products in 2002–3 were almost £4,600 million – this represented a fall of 5.4 per cent on the previous year. Lotto sales dropped by 12.1 per cent, making up just under 74 per cent of total sales revenue. A total of £3,387 million was spent on Lotto tickets alone during 2002–3, and £2,238 million was paid out in prizes.

Chair, Moira Black
Chief Executive, M. Harris
Commissioners, Ms H. Spicer; T. Hornsby; Ms J. Valentine; B. Pomeroy
Director of Compliance, Ms M. Phillips
Director of Licensing, K. Jones
Director of Performance and Communications, Ms C. Forrester
Director of Resources, Ms C. McCullough

NATIONAL PHYSICAL LABORATORY

Queens Road, Teddington, Middx TW11 0LW
T 020-8977 3222 F 020-8943 6458

The Laboratory is the UK's national standards laboratory. It develops, maintains and disseminates national measurement standards for physical quantities such as mass, length, time, temperature, voltage, force and

pressure. It also conducts underpinning research on engineering materials and information technology and disseminates good measurement practice. It is Government-owned but contractor-operated.
Managing Director, Dr B. McGuiness
Director of Business Development, D. C. Richardson

NATIONAL RADIOLOGICAL PROTECTION BOARD

Chilton, Didcot, Oxon OX11 0RQ
T 01235-831600 F 01235-833891
E nrpb@nrpb.org
W www.nrpb.org

The National Radiological Protection Board is an independent statutory body created by the Radiological Protection Act 1970. It is the national point of authoritative reference on radiological protection for both ionising and non-ionising radiations, and has issued recommendations on limiting human exposure to electromagnetic fields and radiation from a range of sources, including X-rays, the Sun, base stations and mobile phones. Its sponsoring department is the Department of Health. The National Radiological Protection Board also works in partnership with the Health Protection Agency.
Chairman, Sir William Stewart, FRS, FRSE
Director, Prof. R. Cox

NATIONAL SAVINGS AND INVESTMENTS

375 Kensington High Street, London W14 8SD
T 020-7348 9200 F 020-7048 9698
W www.nsandi.com

National Savings and Investments came into being in 1861 when the Palmerston government set up the Post Office Savings Bank, a savings scheme which aimed to encourage ordinary wage earners 'to provide for themselves against adversity and ill health'. National Savings and Investments was established as a Government department in 1969. It became an executive agency of the Treasury in 1996 and is responsible for the design, marketing and administration of savings and investment products for personal savers and investors. In April 1999 Siemens Business Services took over all the back office functions at National Savings and Investments.
Chief Executive, A. Cook
Finance Director, T. Bayley
Marketing Director, G. Cattanach
Partnerships and Operations Director, S. Owen
Sales Director, J. Prout

NEW OPPORTUNITIES FUND

1 Plough Place, London EC4A 1DE
T 020-7211 1800 F 020-7211 1750
E enquiries@nof.org.uk
W www.nof.org.uk

The New Opportunities Fund provides lottery funding for health, education and environment projects in order to help create lasting improvements to the quality of life, particularly in disadvantaged communities.

The Fund works with national, regional and local partners from the public, private and voluntary sectors to fund initiatives, with particular focus on the needs of those who are most disadvantaged in society.
Chair of the Board, Sir Clive Booth
Members of the Board, G. Oppenheim *(Director, Performance and Planning)*; Ms V. Potter *(Director, Policy and External Relations)*; M. Cooke *(Director, Finance and Corporate Services)*; Ms A. Kelbie *(Director, Operations)*; W. Rader *(Director, Northern Ireland)*; Ms C. Doyle *(Director, Wales)*; vacant *(Director, Scotland)*
Chief Executive, S. Dunmore

NORTHERN IRELAND AUDIT OFFICE

106 University Street, Belfast BT7 1EU
T 028-9025 1000 F 028-9025 1106
E info@niauditoffice.gov.uk
W www.niauditoffice.gov.uk

The primary aim of the Northern Ireland Audit Office is to provide independent assurance, information and advice to the Northern Ireland Assembly on the proper accounting for Northern Ireland departmental and certain other public expenditure, revenue, assets and liabilities; on regularity and propriety; and on the economy, efficiency and effectiveness of the use of resources.
Comptroller and Auditor-General for Northern Ireland, J. M. Dowdall, CB

NORTHERN IRELAND AUTHORITY FOR ENERGY REGULATION

Brookmount Buildings, 42 Fountain Street, Belfast BT1 5EE
T 028-9031 1575 F 028-9031 1740
E ofreg@nics.gov.uk
W www.ofreg.nics.gov.uk

The Northern Ireland Authority for Energy Regulation operating as The Office for the Regulation of Electricity & Gas (Ofreg) is the regulatory body for the electricity and gas supply industries in Northern Ireland.
Chairman and Chief Executive, Douglas McIldoon

NORTHERN IRELAND HUMAN RIGHTS COMMISSION

Temple Court, 39 North Street, Belfast BT1 1NA
T 028-9024 3987 F 028-9024 7844
E information@nihrc.org
W www.nihrc.org

The Northern Ireland Human Rights Commission was set up in March 1999. Its main functions are to keep under review the law and practice relating to human rights in Northern Ireland, to advise the Government and to promote an awareness of human rights in Northern Ireland. It can also take cases to court. The Commission currently consists of one full-time commissioner and six part-time commissioners, all appointed by the Secretary of State for Northern Ireland.
Chief Commissioner, Prof. B. Dickson
Commissioners, Mrs M. A. Dinsmore, QC; T. Donnelly, MBE; Lady Christine Eames; Prof. T. Hadden; Ms P. Kelly; K. McLaughlin

OCCUPATIONAL PENSIONS REGULATORY AUTHORITY

Invicta House, Trafalgar Place, Brighton BN1 4DW
T 01273-627600 F 01273-627688
E helpdesk@opra.gov.uk
W www.opra.gov.uk

The Occupational Pensions Regulatory Authority (OPRA) was set up under the Pensions Act 1995 and became fully operational on 6 April 1997. It is the UK

regulator of pension arrangements offered by employers. It maintains a register of stakeholder pensions and regulates payments into stakeholder and personal pensions.
Chairman, Harriet Maunsell, OBE
Chief Executive, Anthony Hobman

OFFICE FOR NATIONAL STATISTICS

1 Drummond Gate, London SW1V 2QQ
T 0845-601 3034
E info@statistics.gov.uk
W www.statistics.gov.uk

The Office for National Statistics was created in 1996 by the merger of the Central Statistical Office and the Office of Population Censuses and Surveys. It is both a Government department and an executive agency of the Treasury and is responsible for preparing, interpreting and publishing key statistics on the government, economy and society of the UK. Its key responsibilities include: the provision of population estimates and projections and statistics on health and other demographic matters in England and Wales; the production of the UK National Accounts and other key economic indicators; the organisation of population censuses in England and Wales and surveys for Government departments and public bodies; and the promotion of these functions within the UK, the European Union and internationally to provide a statistical service to meet European Union and international requirements.

The General Register Office is part of the ONS and is responsible for administering marriage laws, and for local registration of births, marriages and deaths in England and Wales.

The National Statistics initiative was launched in June 2000, headed by the National Statistician, with an independent Statistics Commission, providing assurance to Parliament about the integrity of official statistics and statistical practice. The National Statistics brand encompasses the statistical output of the ONS, plus many of the key public interest statistics produced by other Government departments.

National Statistician, Registrar General for England and Wales, Len Cook
Executive Directors, Karen Dunnell *(Surveys and Administrative Sources)*; Colin Mowl *(Macroeconomics and Labour Market)*; John Pullinger *(Economic and Social Reporting)*; Peter Walton *(Organisational Development and Resources)*; vacant *(Methodology)*; Dennis Roberts *(Registration Services)*
Corporate Directors, Mike Hughes *(National Statistics and Planning)*; Dayantha Joshua *(Information Management)*; Peter Murphy *(Finance and Procurement)*; Helena Rafalowska *(Communications)*; Susan Young *(Human Resources)*
National Statistician's Private Office, Jackie Orme; Timothy Stamp; Brigid Keenan
Parliamentary Clerks, Robert Smith; Alex Elton-Wall

OFFICE FOR STANDARDS IN EDUCATION (OFSTED)

Alexandra House, 33 Kingsway, London WC2B 6SE
T 020-7421 6800 Early Years **Helpline** 0845-601 4771
F 020-7421 6707
E geninfo@ofsted.gov.uk
W www.ofsted.gov.uk

OFSTED is a non-ministerial Government department established under the Education (Schools Act) 1992. Since April 2001 OFSTED has been responsible for inspecting all educational provision for 16–19 year olds to establish and monitor an independent inspection system for maintained schools in England. Its inspection role also includes the inspection of local education authorities, teacher training institutions and youth work. In September 2001, OFSTED took over the regulation of childcare providers, from 150 local authorities.
HM Chief Inspector, D. Bell
Directorate of Education, Ms M. Rosen
Director of Corporate Services, R. Knight
Director of Early Years, M. Smith
Director of Finance, P. Jolly
Director of Strategy and Resources, R. Green

OFFICE OF COMMUNICATIONS (OFCOM)

Riverside House, 2A Southwark Bridge Road, London, SE1 9HA
T 020-7981 3000 F 020-7981 3333
E wwwenq@ofcom.org.uk
W www.ofcom.org.uk

The Office of Communications (Ofcom) was established in 2003 under the Office of Communications Act 2002 as the independent regulator for the UK communications industries with responsibility for television, radio, telecommunications and wireless communications services. It merged the functions of five regulatory bodies: the Independent Television Commission (ITC), The Broadcasting Standards Commission (BSC), the Office of Telecommunications (Oftel), the Radio Authority (RAu) and the Radiocommunications Agency (RA). Ofcom's duties include: promoting choice, quality and value in electronic communications services; ensuring the most efficient use of the radiocommunications spectrum; ensuring a wide range of electronic communications services, including broadband, is available across the UK; ensuring the availability of a wide range of high quality TV and radio programmes; maintaining plurality in the media by ensuring a sufficiently broad range of ownership; and protecting audiences against offensive or harmful material, unfairness or the infringement of privacy on TV and radio. Members of the Board are appointed by the Secretaries of State for Trade and Industry and for Culture, Media and Sport.
Chief Executive, S. Carter
Chairman, D. Currie
Deputy Chairman, R. Hooper
Members, Ms M. Banerjee; D. Edmonds; I. Hargreaves; Ms K. Meek; Ms S. Nathan; E. Richards

OFFICE OF FAIR TRADING

Fleetbank House, 2–6 Salisbury Square, London EC4Y 8JX
T 020-7211 8000 F 020-7211 8800
E enquiries@oft.gov.uk
W www.oft.gov.uk

The Office of Fair Trading is a non-ministerial Government department established as a corporate body. It pursues its primary goal of making markets work better for consumers through enforcement of competition and consumer legislation, market studies and communication.

The Consumer Regulation Enforcement Division pursues the Office's consumer protection duties principally through the Enterprise Act 2002, the Consumer Credit Act 1974, the Estate Agents Act 1979, the Control of Misleading Advertisements Regulations

Act 1988, the Consumer Protection (Distance Selling) Regulations 2000 and the Unfair Terms in Consumer Contracts Regulations 1999.

The Competition Enforcement Division is responsible for investigating and taking action against agreements that restrict competition and conduct abusing a dominant position under both the UK Competition Act 1998, as amended by the Enterprise Act 2002, and European competition legislation. The Division also reviews mergers under the UK and EC merger control regimes. It has additional responsibilities for competition matters arising under other legislation, including the Financial Services and Markets Act 2000 and the Transport Act 2000.

The Markets and Policy Initiatives Division conducts market studies, which are made public, helping the Office assess whether action is needed to make markets work better for consumers. It negotiates and reviews undertakings following certain Competition Commission reports, provides advice to Government departments on the potential effects of new policy and legislation on competition and consumers, co-ordinates the Office's overall relationships with government departments, devolved administrations and other bodies, and leads on payment systems work.

The Communications Division's work entails the empowerment of consumers through campaigns, advice and education. It also informs businesses of their rights and duties under competition and consumer laws giving an opportunity for law-abiding businesses to complain about anti-competitive behaviour of others.

The Office of Fair Trading also liaises with the European Commission on competition and consumer protection initiatives.

Chairman, John Vickers
Executive Director, Penny Boys
Non-Executive Directors, Allan Asher, Lord Blackwell, Christine Farnish, Richard Whish, Rosalind Wright

COMMUNICATIONS DIVISION
Director of Communications, Mike Ricketts

COMPETITION ENFORCEMENT DIVISION
Divisional Director, Vincent Smith
Branch Directors, Ali Nikpay, Neil Feinson, Simon Priddis, Beckett McGrath, Justin Coombs, Alan Williams, Christiane Kent, Simon Williams

CONSUMER REGULATION ENFORCEMENT DIVISION
Divisional Director, Christine Wade
Branch Directors, Colin Brown, Steven Wood, Ray Hall, Ray Watson

LEGAL DIVISION
Solicitor , Brian McHenry
Branch Directors, Frances Barr, Simon Brindley, Louis Christofides, Jessica Farry, Paul Gurowich

MARKETS AND POLICIES INITIATIVES DIVISION
Divisional Director, Jonathan May
Branch Directors, Amelia Fletcher, Daniel Gordon, Chris Rawlins, Graham Winton

RESOURCES AND SERVICES
Director of Resources and Services, David Fisher

OFFICE OF GAS AND ELECTRICITY MARKETS (OFGEM)

9 Millbank, London, SW1P 3GE
T 020-7901 7000 F 020-7901 7066
Regents Court, 70 West Regent Street, Glasgow G2 2QZ
T 0141-331 2678 F 0141-331 2777
W www.ofgem.gov.uk

The Office of Gas and Electricity Markets (Ofgem) supports the Gas and Electricity Markets Authority, the regulator of the gas and electricity industries in Great Britain.

Ofgem aims to bring choice and value to all gas and electricity customers by promoting competition and regulating monopolies. The Authority's powers are provided for under the Gas Act 1986, the Electricity Act 1989 and the Utilities Act 2000.

Chief Executive, A. Buchanan
Managing Directors, J. Neilson *(Corporate Affairs)*; Dr B. Moselle *(Corporate Strategy)*; D. Gray *(Networks)*; S. Smith *(Markets)*
Chief Operating Officer, R. Field

OFFICE OF THE LEGAL SERVICES OMBUDSMAN

3rd Floor, Sunlight House, Quay Street, Manchester M3 3JZ
T 0161-839 7262; 0845-601 0794 F 0161-832 5446
E lso@olso.gsi.gov.uk
W www.olso.org

The Legal Services Ombudsman is appointed by the Lord Chancellor under the Courts and Legal Services Act 1990 to oversee the handling of complaints against solicitors, barristers, licensed conveyancers, legal executives and patent agents by their professional bodies. A complainant must first complain to the relevant professional body before raising the matter with the Ombudsman. The Ombudsman is independent of the legal profession and her services are free of charge.

Legal Services Ombudsman, Ms Zahida Manzoor, CBE
Operations Director, S. Lees

OFFICE OF THE LEGAL SERVICES OMBUDSMAN (SCOTTISH)

17 Waterloo Place, Edinburgh, EH1 3DL
T 0131-556 9123 F 0131-556 9292
E ombudsman@slso.org.uk
W www.slso.org.uk

The Ombudsman investigates complaints about the way in which Scottish professional bodies have handled a complaint against a practitioner.

The Ombudsman also examines complaints about the unwillingness of a professional body to investigate a complaint against a practitioner.

Scottish Legal Services Ombudsman, Mrs L. Costelloe Baker

OFFICE OF THE LORD ADVOCATE

Crown Office, 25 Chambers Street, Edinburgh EH1 1LA
T 0131-226 2626 F 0131-226 6910
E scottish.ministers@scotland.gsi.gov.uk
W www.crownoffice.gov.uk

The Law Officers for Scotland are the Lord Advocate and the Solicitor-General for Scotland.

Lord Advocate, The Rt. Hon. Colin Boyd, QC
Solicitor-General for Scotland, Ms E. Angiolini, QC

Private Secretary to the Lord Advocate, Miss S. McGuire
Private Secretary to the Solicitor General, R. Kent
Assistant Private Secretary, C. Orman

OFFICE OF MANPOWER ECONOMICS

8th Floor, Oxford House, 76 Oxford Street, London W1D 1BS
T 020-7467 7244 F 020-7467 7248
W www.ome.uk.com

The Office of Manpower Economics was set up in 1971. It is an independent non-statutory organisation which is responsible for servicing independent review bodies which advise on the pay of various public service groups, the Pharmacists' Review Panel and the Police Negotiating and Police Advisory (England and Wales) Boards. The Office is also responsible for servicing *ad hoc* bodies of inquiry and for undertaking research into pay and associated matters as requested by the Government.

OME Director, Dr R. A. Wright
Director, Health Secretariats and OME Deputy Director, D. A. Miner
Director, Armed Forces' Secretariat, Mrs C. Haworth
Director, Senior Salaries Secretariat, N. D. Peace
Director, School Teachers' Secretariat, D. J. T. Wilson
Director, Prison Service Secretariat and Police Negotiating and Police Advisory (England and Wales) Boards Secretariat, M. C. Cahill
Press Liaison Officer, C. P. Jordan

OFFICE OF THE PENSIONS OMBUDSMAN

6th Floor, 11 Belgrave Road, London SW1V 1RB
T 020-7834 9144 F 020-7821 0065
E enquiries@pensions-ombudsman.org.uk
W www.pensions-ombudsman.org.uk

The Pensions Ombudsman is appointed under the Pension Schemes Act 1993 as amended by the Pensions Act 1995. He independently investigates and decides complaints and disputes concerning pension schemes.

Pensions Ombudsman, D. Laverick

OFFICE OF RAIL REGULATION

1 Waterhouse Square, 138–142 Holborn, London EC1N 2TQ
T 020-7282 2000 F 020-7282 2047
E orr@dial.pipex.com W www.rail-reg.gov.uk

The Office of the Rail Regulator was set up under the Railways Act 1993. It became the Office of Rail Regulation on 5 July 2004, under the provisions of the Railways and Transport Safety Act 2003. The Office's principal function is to regulate Network Rail's stewardship of the national network and to provide the economic regulation of the monopoly and dominant elements of the rail industry. The Office also licenses operators of railway assets, approves agreements for access by those operators to track, stations and light maintenance depots, and enforces domestic competition law. The International Rail Regulator is a statutory office separate from that of the Office of Rail Regulation. The International Rail Regulator licenses the operation of certain international rail services in the European Economic Area, and access to railway infrastructure in Great Britain for the purpose of the operation of such services. The Office of The International Rail Regulator is co-located with the Office of Rail Regulation, which fulfils both functions.

Chairman, C. Bolt
Chief Executive, Ms S. McCarthy
Director of Corporate Affairs, K. Webb
Director of Infrastructure and Economic Regulation, T. Martin

OFFICE OF WATER SERVICES

Centre City Tower, 7 Hill Street, Birmingham B5 4UA
T 0121-625 1300 F 0121-625 1400
E enquiries@ofwat.gsi.gov.uk
W www.ofwat.gov.uk

The Office of Water Services (Ofwat) was set up under the Water Act 1989 and is a non-ministerial Government department headed by the Director-General of Water Services. It is the independent economic regulator of the water and sewerage companies in England and Wales. Ofwat's main duties are to ensure that the companies can finance and carry out the functions specified in the Water Industry Act 1991 and to protect the interests of water customers. There are ten WaterVoice committees which are concerned solely with the interests of water customers. Representation of customer interests at national and European level is the responsibility of the WaterVoice Council.

Director-General of Water Services, P. Fletcher
Chairman, WaterVoice Council, M. Terry

ORDNANCE SURVEY

Romsey Road, Maybush, Southampton SO16 4GU
T 023-8030 5030 **Helpline** 0845-605 0505 F 023-8079 2615
E customerservices@ordnancesurvey.co.uk

Ordnance Survey is the national mapping agency for Great Britain. It is a Government department and executive agency operating as a Trading Fund and reporting to the Office of the Deputy Prime Minister.

Director-General and Chief Executive, Ms V. Lawrence

PARADES COMMISSION

Windsor House, 9–15 Bedford Street, Belfast BT2 7EL
T 028-9089 5900 F 028-9032 2988
E info@paradescommissionni.org
W www.paradescommission.org

The Parades Commission was set up under the Public Processions (Northern Ireland) Act 1998. Its function is to encourage and facilitate local accommodation on contentious parades; where this is not possible, the Commission is empowered to make legal determinations about such parades, which may include imposing conditions on aspects of the notified parade.

The chairman and members are appointed by the Secretary of State for Northern Ireland; the membership must, as far as is practicable, be representative of the community in Northern Ireland.

Chairman, Sir Anthony Holland
Members, J. Cousins; Revd R. Magee; W. Martin; P. Osborne; Sir John Pringle; P. Quinn

PARLIAMENTARY AND HEALTH SERVICE OMBUDSMAN

Millbank Tower, Millbank, London SW1P 4QP
T 0845-015 4033 F 020-7217 4160
E opca.enquiries@ombudsman.org.uk
W www.ombudsman.org.uk
Health Service Ombudsman T 0845-015 4033
F 020-7217 4000
E ohsc.enquiries@ombudsman.gsi.gov.uk

The Parliamentary Ombudsman (also known as the Parliamentary Commissioner for Administration) is independent of Government and is an officer of Parliament. She is responsible for investigating complaints referred to her by MPs from members of the public who claim to have sustained injustice in consequence of maladministration by or on behalf of Government departments and certain non-departmental public bodies. In March 1999 an additional 158 public bodies were brought within the jurisdiction of the Parliamentary Ombudsman. Certain types of action by Government departments or bodies are excluded from investigation. The Parliamentary Ombudsman is also responsible for investigating complaints, referred by MPs, alleging that access to official information has been wrongly refused under the Code of Practice on Access to Government Information 1994.

The Health Service Ombudsman (also known as the Health Service Commissioner) for England and for Wales is responsible for investigating complaints against National Health Service authorities and trusts that are not dealt with by those authorities to the satisfaction of the complainant. Complaints can be referred direct by the member of the public who claims to have sustained injustice or hardship in consequence of the failure in a service provided by a relevant body, failure of that body to provide a service or in consequence of any other action by that body. The Ombudsman's jurisdiction now covers complaints about family doctors, dentists, pharmacists and opticians, and complaints about actions resulting from clinical judgement.

The Health Service Ombudsman is also responsible for investigating complaints that information has been wrongly refused under the Code of Practice on Openness in the National Health Service 1995. The two offices are presently held by the Parliamentary Ombudsman.

Parliamentary Ombudsman and Health Service Ombudsman, Ms A. Abraham
Deputy Parliamentary Commissioner, Ms T. Longdon
Directors, Parliamentary Commissioner, Ms C. Corrigan; N. Jordan
Directors, Health Service Commissioners, D. R. G. Pinchin; L. Charlton
Finance and Establishment Officer, I. Walker

PARLIAMENTARY COMMISSIONER FOR STANDARDS

House of Commons, London SW1A 0AA
T 020-7219 0320 F 020-7219 0490

Following the recommendations of the Committee on Standards in Public Life, the House of Commons agreed to the appointment of an independent Parliamentary Commissioner for Standards with effect from November 1995. The Commissioner has responsibility for maintaining and monitoring the operation of the Register of Members' Interests; advising Members of Parliament and the Select Committee on Standards and Privileges; interpreting the rules on disclosure and advocacy, and on other questions of propriety. The Commissioner also receives and investigates complaints about the conduct of MPs.

Parliamentary Commissioner for Standards, Sir Philip Mawer

PARLIAMENTARY COUNSEL

36 Whitehall, London SW1A 2AY
T 020-7210 6611 F 020-7210 6632
W www.parliamentary-counsel.gov.uk

Parliamentary Counsel draft all Government bills (i.e. primary legislation) except those relating exclusively to Scotland. They also advise on all aspects of parliamentary procedure in connection with such bills and draft Government amendments to them as well as any motions (including financial resolutions) necessary to secure their introduction into, and passage through, Parliament.

First Parliamentary Counsel, E. G. Bowman, CB
Counsel, Sir E. G. Caldwell; D. W. Saunders, CB; G. B. Sellers, CB; P. F. A. Knowles, CB; S. C. Laws, CB; R. S. Parker, CB; Miss C. E. Johnston, CB; P. J. Davies, CB; J. M. Sellers; A. J. Hogarth; Mrs H. J. Caldwell; D. I. Greenberg; Mrs E. A. F. Gardiner; D. J. Cook; Mrs L. A. McLaughlin; D. J. Ramsay

PAROLE BOARD FOR ENGLAND AND WALES

Abell House, John Islip Street, London SW1P 4LH
T 020-7217 5314 F 020-7217 5793
E info@paroleboard.gov.uk
W www.paroleboard.gov.uk

The duty of the Parole Board is to advise the Home Secretary with respect to matters referred to it by him which are connected with the early release or recall of prisoners. Its functions include giving directions concerning the release on licence of prisoners serving discretionary life sentences and of certain prisoners serving long-term determinate sentences.

Chairman, Prof. Sir Duncan Nichol, CBE
Vice-Chairman, The Hon. Mr Justice Gage
Chief Executive, C. Glenn

PAROLE BOARD FOR SCOTLAND

Saughton House, Broomhouse Drive, Edinburgh EH11 3XD
T 0131-244 8373 F 0131-244 6974

The Board directs and advises the Scottish Ministers on the release of prisoners on licence, and related matters.

Chairman, Prof. J. J. McManus
Vice-Chairman, Mrs M. Casserly
Secretary, H. P. Boyce

PATENT OFFICE

Concept House, Cardiff Road, Newport NP10 8QQ
T 0845-950 0505 F 01633-813600
E enquiries@patent.gov.uk
W www.patent.gov.uk

The Patent Office is an executive agency of the Department of Trade and Industry. The duties of the Patent Office are to administer the Patent Acts, the Registered Designs Act and the Trade Marks Act, and to deal with questions relating to the Copyright, Designs and Patents Act 1988. The Search and Advisory Service

carries out commercial searches through patent information.
Comptroller-General and Chief Executive, R. Marchant
Director, Finance, Dr K. Woodrow
Director, Intellectual Property and Innovation, P. Lawrence
Director, IT and Corporate Services, Mrs C. Fullerton
Director, Patents, S. Dennehey
Director, Trade Marks and Designs, R. Webb

PENSIONS COMPENSATION BOARD

11 Belgrave Road, London SW1V 1RB
T 020-7828 9794 F 020-7931 7239

The Pensions Compensation Board was established under the Pensions Act 1995 and is funded by a levy paid by all eligible occupational pension schemes. Its function is to compensate occupational pension schemes for losses due to dishonesty where the employer is insolvent.
Chairman, Sir Bryan Carsberg
Secretary, M. Lydon

POLICE OMBUDSMAN FOR NORTHERN IRELAND

New Cathedral Buildings, St Anne's Square, Belfast BT1 1PG
T 028-9082 8600 F 028-9082 8659
E info@policeombudsman.org
W www.policeombudsman.org

Founded in November 2000 under the Police (Northern Ireland) Act 1998, the function of the Office of the Police Ombudsman for Northern Ireland is to investigate complaints against the police in an impartial, efficient, effective and (as far as is possible) transparent way, to win the confidence of the public and the police. It must report on trends in complaints and react to incidents involving the police, where it is in the public interest, even if no individual complaint has been made.
Police Ombudsman, N. O'Loan

PORT OF LONDON AUTHORITY

Bakers' Hall, 7 Harp Lane, London EC3R 6LB
T 020-7743 7900 F 020-7743 7999
W www.portoflondon.co.uk

The Port of London Authority (PLA) is the port authority for the 93 miles of the tidal River Thames from the Estuary to Teddington. It provides navigational and pilotage services for ships using the Port of London, including the maintenance of shipping channels. The PLA is also actively engaged in the promotion of the Port of London. The Port of London is one of the UK's main three ports, handling over 50 million tonnes of cargo each year. The port comprises over 80 independently owned terminals and port facilities, which handle a wide range of cargoes.

The PLA is a public trust constituted under the Port of London Act 1908 and subsequent legislation.
Chairman, S. P. Sherrard
Chief Executive, S. C. Cuthbert
Secretary, D. Cartlidge

POSTAL SERVICES COMMISSION

Hercules House, Hercules Road, London SE1 7DB
T 020-7593 2100

The Postal Services Commission (Postcomm) is an independent regulator set up by the Postal Services Act 2000 to ensure that postal operators, including Royal Mail, meet the needs of their customers throughout the UK. Postcomm monitors the network of post offices in the UK and makes annual reports to the DTI.
Chairman, Nigel Stapleton

PRISONS AND PROBATION OMBUDSMAN FOR ENGLAND AND WALES

Ashley House, 2 Monck Street, London SW1P 2BQ
T 020-7035 2876 F 020-7035 2860
E mail@ppo.gsi.gov.uk
W www.ppo.gov.uk

The Ombudsman is appointed by the Home Secretary. He provides a free and independent adjudication service for prisoners and those under probation supervision who have been unable to resolve their grievances with the Prison and Probation Services. He also conducts independent investigations into the deaths of prisoners, residents of probation hostels and people detained by the immigration authorities.
Ombudsman, S. Shaw

PRIVY COUNCIL OFFICE

2 Carlton Gardens, London SW1Y 5AA
T 020-7210 1033 F 020-7210 1071
W www.privycouncil.gov.uk

The Office is responsible for the arrangements leading to the making of all royal proclamations and Orders in Council; for certain formalities connected with ministerial changes; for considering applications for the granting (or amendment) of royal charters; for the scrutiny and approval of by-laws and statutes of chartered bodies; and for the appointment of high sheriffs and many Crown and Privy Council appointments to governing bodies.
Lord President of the Council (and Leader of the House of Lords), The Rt. Hon. Baroness Amos, PC
Principal Private Secretary, Chris Jacobs
Private Secretary, Nicki Daniels
Clerk of the Council, Alex Galloway
Deputy Clerk of the Council and Director of Corporate Services, Graham Donald
Senior Clerk, Meriel McCullagh
Registrar of the Judicial Committee, John Watherston

PUBLIC GUARDIANSHIP OFFICE

Archway Tower, 2 Junction Road, London N19 5SZ
T 020-7664 7000 F 020-7664 7705
E custserv@guardianship.gov.uk
W www.guardianship.gov.uk

The Public Guardianship Office (PGO) is the administrative arm of the Court of Protection and is part of the Department for Constitutional Affairs.

Established on the 1 April 2001, it has taken over the mental health functions previously undertaken by the Public Trust Office (PTO), which also provides services that promote the financial and social well-being of people with mental incapacity.
Acting Chief Executive and Director of Operations, D. Thompson
Acting Director of Finance, S. Taylor
Assistant Director of Client Services, G. Bradshaw
Assistant Director of Strategy and Finance, C. McIlwrath
Director of Business Strategy and Innovation, G. Dalton
Manager of Complaints Handling Team, N. Ross

RAIL SAFETY AND STANDARDS BOARD

Evergreen House, 160 Euston Road, London NW1 2DX
T 020-7904 7777 F 020-7557 7791
E enquiries@rssb.co.uk
W www.rssb.co.uk

The Rail Safety and Standards Board was established on 1 April 2003 to help focus the rail industry on the continuous improvement in the safety performance of Britain's railways through facilitating the reduction in risk to passengers and railway workers. Its objectives include: the development of a long-term industry safety strategy; the effective representation of the UK rail industry in the development of EU legislation and standards that impact on the safe interworking of trains and infrastructure; and the facilitation of a research and development programme, education and awareness of safety issues. The Rail Safety and Standards Board is a not-for-profit organisation.
Chief Executive, Len Porter

RECORD OFFICES

ADVISORY COUNCIL ON NATIONAL RECORDS AND ARCHIVES

Secretariat: The National Archives, Kew, Surrey TW9 4DU
T 020-8392 5381 F 020-8392 5286

Following the bringing together of the Public Record Office and the Historical Manuscripts Commission to form the National Archives, the Advisory Council advises on all matters relating to the preservation, use of, and access to historical manuscripts, records and archives of all kinds. The new Advisory Council on National Records and Archives encompasses the statutory Advisory Council on Public Records, and advises on public records issues as before.
Chairman, The Rt. Hon. Lord Phillips, Master of the Rolls
Secretary, T. R. Padfield

CORPORATION OF LONDON RECORDS OFFICE

PO Box 270, Guildhall, London EC2P 2EJ
T 020-7332 1251 F 020-7710 8682
E clro@corpoflondon.gov.uk
W www.cityoflondon.gov.uk/archives/clro

The Corporation of London Records Office contains the municipal archives of the City of London which are regarded as the most complete collection of ancient municipal records in existence. The collection includes charters of William the Conqueror, Henry II, and later kings and queens to 1957; ancient custumals: Liber Horn, Dunthorne, Custumarum, Ordinacionum, Memorandorum and Albus, Liber de Antiquis Legibus, and collections of statutes; continuous series of judicial rolls, books from 1252 and Council minutes from 1275; records of the Old Bailey and Guildhall sessions from 1603; financial records from the 16th century; the records of London Bridge from the 12th century; and numerous subsidiary series and miscellanea of historical interest.
Head Archivist, D. Jenkins, PHD
City Archives Manager, J. M. Bankes

HOUSE OF LORDS RECORD OFFICE (THE PARLIAMENTARY ARCHIVES)

House of Lords, London SW1A 0PW
T 020-7219 3074 F 020-7219 2570
E hlro@parliament.uk W www.parliament.uk

Since 1497, the records of Parliament have been kept within the Palace of Westminster. They are in the custody of the Clerk of the Parliaments. In 1946 the Record Office was established to supervise their preservation and their availability to the public.

Some three million documents are preserved, including Acts of Parliament from 1497, journals of the House of Lords from 1510, minutes and committee proceedings from 1610, and papers laid before Parliament from 1531. Amongst the records are the Petition of Right, the Death Warrant of Charles I, the Declaration of Breda, and the Bill of Rights. The House of Lords Record Office also has charge of the journals of the House of Commons (from 1547), and other surviving records of the Commons (from 1572), including documents relating to private bill legislation from 1818. Among other documents are the records of the Lord Great Chamberlain, the political papers of certain members of the two Houses, and documents relating to Parliament acquired on behalf of the nation. The Record Office makes the records available through a public search room and answers enquiries concerning the archives and history of Parliament.
Clerk of the Records, S. K. Ellison
Assistant Clerks of the Records, D. L. Prior; Dr C. Shenton; Ms F. P. Grey *(Freedom of Information Officer)*

NATIONAL ARCHIVES

Kew, Richmond, Surrey TW9 4DU
T 020-8876 3444 F 020-8878 8905
W www.nationalarchives.gov.uk

The National Archives, a government department and an executive agency reporting to the Lord Chancellor/ Secretary of State for Constitutional Affairs, was formed in April 2003 by bringing together the Public Record Office (founded in 1838) and the Historical Manuscripts Commission (founded in 1869).

The National Archives for England, Wales and the United Kingdom acts as the custodian of the nation's collective memory as revealed in the records of government. It also collects and disseminates information about archives relating to British history wherever they are held.

Its aims are: to assist and promote the study of the past through the public records and other archives in order to inform the present and the future; to act as chief source of authoritative advice and guidance on records management, archive policy and related information policy matters within government; to provide impartial advice to custodians of records and papers throughout the public and private sectors on records and archives management.

The National Archives administers the UK's public records system under the Public Records Acts of 1958 and 1967. The records it holds span 1,000 years – from the Domesday Book to the latest government papers to be released – and fill more than 100 miles of shelving. The records held by the National Archives are available to the public, without charge, in the reading rooms.

The National Archives also provides free expert advice to owners, custodians and users of archives throughout the UK. They include central and local government,

universities, business and industry, many other individuals and institutions, and a range of public and private grant-awarding bodies.
Chief Executive, Mrs S. Tyacke, CB
Director of National Advisory and Public Services, Dr E. Hallam-Smith
Director of Government and Technology Group, Dr D. Thomas
Director of Strategy, Finance and Resources, Mrs W. Jones
Head of Online Services and Strategic Marketing, J. Strachan

NATIONAL ARCHIVES OF SCOTLAND

HM General Register House, Edinburgh EH1 3YY
T 0131-535 1314 **F** 0131-535 1360
E enquiries@nas.gov.uk **W** www.nas.gov.uk

The history of the national archives of Scotland can be traced back to the 13th century. The National Archives of Scotland (formerly the Scottish Record Office) is an executive agency of the Scottish Executive and keeps the administrative records of pre-Union Scotland, the registers of central and local courts of law, the public registers of property rights and legal documents, and many collections of local and church records and private archives. Certain groups of records, mainly the modern records of Government departments in Scotland, the Scottish railway records, the plans collection, and private archives of an industrial or commercial nature, are preserved in the branch repository at West Register House in Charlotte Square. The National Register of Archives for Scotland is based in the West Register House.
Keeper of the Records of Scotland, G. P. MacKenzie
Deputy Keepers, Dr P. D. Anderson; D. Brownlee

PUBLIC RECORD OFFICE OF NORTHERN IRELAND

66 Balmoral Avenue, Belfast BT9 6NY
T 028-9025 5905 **F** 028-9025 5999
E proni@dcalni.gov.uk **W** www.proni.gov.uk

The Public Record Office of Northern Ireland is responsible for identifying and preserving Northern Ireland's archival heritage and making it available to the public. It is an executive agency of the Department of Culture, Arts and Leisure.
Chief Executive, Dr G. Slater

REGISTRAR OF PUBLIC LENDING RIGHT

Richard House, Sorbonne Close, Stockton on Tees TS17 6DA
T 01642-604699 **F** 01642-615641
E jim.parker@plr.uk.com
W www.plr.uk.com

Under the Public Lending Right system, in operation since 1983, payment is made from public funds to authors whose books are lent out from public libraries. Payment is made once a year and the amount each author receives is proportionate to the number of times (established from a sample) that each registered book has been lent out during the previous year. The Registrar of PLR, who is appointed by the Secretary of State for Culture, Media and Sport, compiles the register of authors and books. Authors resident in all EC countries are eligible to apply. (The term 'author' covers writers, illustrators, translators, and some editors/compilers.)

A payment of 4.85 pence was made in 2003–4 for each estimated loan of a registered book, up to a top limit of £6,000 for the books of any one registered author; the money for loans above this level is used to augment the remaining PLR payments. In 2004, the sum of £6.4 million was paid out to 18,763 registered authors and assignees as the annual payment of PLR.
Registrar, Dr J. G. Parker
Chairman of Advisory Committee, S. Brett

SCOTTISH RECORDS ADVISORY COUNCIL

HM General Register House, Edinburgh EH1 3YY
T 0131-535 1403 **F** 0131-535 1430
W www.nas.gov.uk

The Council was established under the Public Records (Scotland) Act 1937. Its members are appointed by the First Minister and it may submit proposals or make representations to the First Minister, the Lord Justice General or the Lord President of the Court of Session on questions relating to the public records of Scotland.
Chairman, Prof. H. MacQueen
Secretary, Dr A. Rosie

HM REVENUE AND CUSTOMS

Board of Inland Revenue, Somerset House, Strand, London WC2R 1LB
T 020-7438 6622 **F** 020-7438 7562
E library.ir.sh@gtnet.gov.uk
W www.inlandrevenue.gov.uk
HM Customs and Excise, New King's Beam House, 5th Floor East, 22 Upper Ground, London SE1 9PJ
T 020-7620 1313 **National Advice Service** 0845-010 900
W www.hmce.gov.uk

The Board of Inland Revenue and HM Customs and Excise merged on 1 September 2004 to become HM Revenue and Customs. The Board of Inland Revenue was constituted under the Inland Revenue Board Act 1849. The Board administers and collects direct taxes – income tax, corporation tax, capital gains tax, inheritance tax, stamp duty, and petroleum revenue tax – and advises the Chancellor of the Exchequer on policy questions involving them.

The Valuation Office is an executive agency responsible for valuing property for tax purposes. The Contributions Agency of the Department for Work and Pensions which is responsible for the collection of contributions under the National Insurance scheme, became part of the Inland Revenue in April 1999 and is now an executive office called the National Insurance Contributions Office. The Contributions Unit of the Social Security Agency in Northern Ireland also transferred to the Inland Revenue in April 1999.

HM Customs and Excise is responsible for collecting and administering customs and excise duties and VAT, and advises the Chancellor of the Exchequer on any matters connected with them.

THE BOARD OF INLAND REVENUE
Chairman, David Varney
Deputy Chairman, Paul Gray
Head of Revenue Policy, D. Hartnett
Chief Executive, Valuation Office Agency, M. Johns

THE BOARD OF HM CUSTOMS AND EXCISE
Chairman, Mike Eland

VALUATION OFFICE AGENCY
New Court, 48 Carey Street, London WC2A 2JE
T 020-7506 1700 F 020-7506 1998
W www.voa.gov.uk
50 Frederick Street, Edinburgh EH2 1NG
T 0131-465 0700 F 0131-465 0799
Chief Executive, A. Hudson
Chief Valuer, Scotland, A. Ainslie
Chief Valuer, Wales, C. R. Danigls

REVIEW BODIES

The secretariat for these bodies is provided by the Office of Manpower Economics

THE ARMED FORCES' PAY REVIEW BODY

The Review Body on Armed Forces Pay was appointed in 1971. It advises the Prime Minister and Government on the pay and allowances of members of naval, military and air forces of the Crown.
Chairman, Prof. D. Greenaway
Members, N. Sherlock; Vice-Adm. Sir Peter Woodhead; Dr A. Wright; J. Davies; Prof. The Lord Patel of Dunkeld; M. Ward; R. Burgin; Dr P. Knight

THE REVIEW BODY ON DOCTORS' AND DENTISTS' REMUNERATION

The Review Body on Doctors' and Dentists' Remuneration was set up in 1971. It advises the Prime Minister and the Secretaries of State for Health, Scotland and Wales on the remuneration of doctors and dentists taking any part in the National Health Service.
Chairman, M. Blair, QC
Members, Prof. F. Burchill; H. Donaldson; Dr G. Jones; Prof. J. Beath; Dr M. Collingwood

THE REVIEW BODY FOR NURSING AND OTHER HEALTH PROFESSIONS

The Review Body for nursing staff, midwives, health visitors and professions allied to medicine was set up in 1983. Following the Agenda for Change the review body changed its name. It advises the Prime Minister and the Secretaries of State for Health, Scotland and Wales on the remuneration of nursing staff and other health professions employed in the National Health Service.
Chairman, Prof. Sir C. Booth
Members, W. MacPherson; Prof. P. Weetman; Prof. R. Disney; S. Whitlam

POLICE ADVISORY BOARD FOR ENGLAND AND WALES

The Police Advisory Board for England and Wales provides advice to the Secretary of State on general questions affecting the police in England and Wales and considers draft regulations which the Secretary of State proposes to make with respect to matters other than hours of duty, leave, pay and allowances or the issue, use and return of police clothing, personal equipment and other effects.
Independent Chair, John Randall
Independent Deputy Chair, Mark Baker, CBE

POLICE NEGOTIATING BOARD

The Police Negotiating Board (PNB) was established by Act of Parliament in 1980 to negotiate pay, allowances, hours of duty, leave and pensions of United Kingdom police officers and to make recommendations on these matters to the Home Secretary, Secretary of State for Northern Ireland, and Scottish Ministers.
Independent Chair, John Randall
Independent Deputy Chair, Mark Baker, CBE

THE PRISON SERVICE PAY REVIEW BODY

The Prison Service Pay Review Body (PSPRB) was set up in 2001. It makes independent recommendations on the pay of prison governors, prison officers and related grades for the Prison Service in England and Wales and for the Northern Ireland Prison Service.
Chairman, Sir Toby Frere, KCB
Members, J. Abrams; D. Bourn; B. Brewer; P. Heard; F. Horisk; P. Tett

THE SCHOOL TEACHERS' REVIEW BODY

The School Teachers' Review Body (STRB) was set up under the School Teachers' Pay and Conditions Act 1991. It is required to examine and report on such matters relating to the statutory conditions of employment of school teachers in England and Wales as may be referred to it by the Secretary of State for Education and Skills.
Chairman, W. Cockburn, CBE, TD
Members, R. Gardner; Dr B. Roberts; J. Singh; R. East; M. Goodridge; J. Stephens; M. Chatterji; B. Warman

THE SENIOR SALARIES REVIEW BODY

The Senior Salaries Review Body (formerly the Top Salaries Review Body) was set up in 1971 to advise the Prime Minister on the remuneration of the judiciary, senior civil servants and senior officers of the armed forces. In 1993 its remit was extended to cover the pay, pensions and allowances of MPs, Ministers and others whose pay is determined by a Ministerial and Other Salaries Order and the allowances of peers. It also advises on the pay of officers and members of the devolved Parliament and Assemblies.
Chairman, J. Baker, CBE
Members, D. Clayman; J. Rubin; M. Sim Lei; J. McKenna; M. Galbraith; Prof. D. Greenaway; R. Pearson

---

ROYAL BOTANIC GARDEN EDINBURGH

20A Inverleith Row, Edinburgh EH3 5LR
T 0131-552 7171 F 0131-248 2901
E info@rbge.org.uk
W www.rbge.org.uk

The Royal Botanic Garden Edinburgh (RBGE) originated as the Physic Garden, established in 1670 beside the Palace of Holyroodhouse. The Garden moved to its present 28-hectare site at Inverleith, Edinburgh, in 1821. There are also three Regional Gardens: Benmore Botanic Garden, near Dunoon, Argyll; Logan Botanic Garden, near Stranraer, Wigtownshire; and Dawyck Botanic Garden, near Stobo, Peeblesshire. Since 1986 RBGE has been administered by a board of trustees established under the National Heritage (Scotland) Act 1985. It receives an annual grant from the Environment and Rural Affairs Department of the Scottish Executive.

RBGE is an international centre for scientific research on plant diversity and for horticulture education and conservation. It has an extensive library, a herbarium with

over two million preserved plant specimens, and over 16,500 species in the living collections.
Chairman of the Board of Trustees, Dr P. Nicholson
Regius Keeper, Prof. S. Blackmore, FRSE

ROYAL BOTANIC GARDENS KEW

Richmond, Surrey TW9 3AB
T 020-8332 5000 F 020-8332 5197
Wakehurst Place, Ardingly, nr Haywards Heath, W. Sussex RH17 6TN
T 01444-89000 F 01444-894069
W www.kew.org

The Royal Botanic Gardens (RBG) Kew were originally laid out as a private garden for Kew House for George III's mother, Princess Augusta, in 1759. The gardens were much enlarged in the 19th century, notably by the inclusion of the grounds of the former Richmond Lodge. In 1965 the garden at Wakehurst Place was acquired; it is owned by the National Trust and managed by RBG Kew. Under the National Heritage Act 1983 a board of trustees was set up to administer the gardens, which in 1984 became an independent body supported by grant-in-aid from the Department of Environment, Food and Rural Affairs.

The functions of RBG Kew are to carry out research into plant sciences, to disseminate knowledge about plants and to provide the public with the opportunity to gain knowledge and enjoyment from the gardens' collections. There are extensive national reference collections of living and preserved plants and a comprehensive library and archive. The main emphasis is on plant conservation and bio-diversity.

BOARD OF TRUSTEES
Chairman, The Lord Selbourne
Members, Baroness Hayman; A. Cahn, CMG; Ms T. Burman; D. Norman; R. Lapthorne, CBE; I. Oag; Prof. C. Payne; Ms M. Regan; R. Deverell; D. Bradley; Sir Richard Sykes
Director, Prof. P. Crane, FRS

ROYAL COMMISSION FOR THE EXHIBITION OF 1851

Sherfield Building, Imperial College, London SW7 2AZ
T 020-7594 8790 F 020-7594 8794
E royalcom1851@ic.ac.uk
W www.royalcommission1851.org.uk

The Royal Commission was incorporated by supplemental charter as a permanent commission after winding up the affairs of the Great Exhibition of 1851. Its object is to promote scientific and artistic education by means of funds derived from its Kensington estate, purchased with the surplus left over from the Great Exhibition. Annual charitable expenditure on educational grants is about £1 million.
President, HRH The Prince Philip, Duke of Edinburgh, KG, KT, PC
Chairman, Board of Management, Sir Alan Rudge, CBE, FRS, FRENG
Secretary to Commissioners, M. C. Shirley

ROYAL COMMISSION ON ENVIRONMENTAL POLLUTION

3rd Floor, The Sanctuary, Westminster, London SW1P 3JS
T 020-7799 8970 F 020-7799 8971
E enquiries@rcep.org.uk W www.rcep.org.uk

The Commission was set up in 1970 to advise on national and international matters concerning the pollution of the environment.
Chairman, Prof. Sir Tom Blundell, FRS
Members, Dr I. Graham-Bryce, CBE; Prof. R. Clift, OBE, FRENG; Sir Brian Follett, FRS; Prof. B. Hoskins, CBE, FRS; Dr S. Owens, OBE; Prof. J. Plant, CBE; Prof. P. Ekins; Prof. S. Holgate; J. Speirs; Prof. J. Sprent; Prof. J. Jowell; Prof. S. Rayner
Secretary, T. Eddy

ROYAL COMMISSION ON THE ANCIENT AND HISTORICAL MONUMENTS OF SCOTLAND

John Sinclair House, 16 Bernard Terrace, Edinburgh EH8 9NX
T 0131-662 1456 F 0131-662 1499
E nmrs@rcahms.gov.uk W www.rcahms.gov.uk

The Royal Commission was established in 1908 and is appointed to provide for the survey and recording of ancient and historical monuments connected with the culture, civilisation and conditions of life of the people in Scotland from the earliest times. It is funded by the Scottish Executive. The Commission compiles and maintains the National Monuments Record of Scotland as the national record of the archaeological and historical environment.
Chairman, Mrs K. Dalyell
Commissioners, Dr B. E. Crawford, FSA; Miss A. C. Riches, OBE, FSA; J. W. T. Simpson; Dr M. A. Mackay; Dr J. Murray; Dr A. Macdonald; Prof. C. D. Morris, FSA, FRSE; Dr S. Nenadic; G. Masterton, CENG
Secretary, R. J. Mercer, FSA, FRSE

ROYAL COMMISSION ON THE ANCIENT AND HISTORICAL MONUMENTS OF WALES

Crown Building, Plas Crug, Aberystwyth SY23 1NJ
T 01970-621200 F 01970-627701
E nmr.wales@rcahmw.gov.uk
W www.rcahmw.org.uk

The Royal Commission was established in 1908 and is currently empowered by a Royal Warrant of 2001 to survey, record, publish and maintain a database of ancient and historical and maritime sites and structures, and landscapes in Wales. The Commission is funded by the National Assembly for Wales and is also responsible for the National Monuments Record of Wales, which is open daily for public reference, for the supply of archaeological information to the Ordnance Survey, for the co-ordination of archaeological aerial photography in Wales, and for sponsorship of the regional Sites and Monuments Records.
Chairman, Prof. R. A. Griffiths, DLITT
Commissioners, Prof. A. D. Carr, FSA; D. W. Crossley, FSA; N. Harries; J. W. Lloyd, CB; J. Newman, FSA; Prof. P. Sims-Williams, FBA; Dr L. O. W. Smith
Secretary, P. R. White, FSA

ROYAL MAIL GROUP PLC

148 Old Street, London EC1V 9HQ
T 020-7250 2888
W www.royalmailgroup.com

Crown services for the carriage of Government dispatches were set up in about 1516. The conveyance of public correspondence began in 1635 and the mail service was made a parliamentary responsibility with the setting up of a Post Office in 1657. Telegraphs came under Post Office control in 1870 and the Post Office Telephone Service began in 1880. The National Girobank service of the Post Office began in 1968. The Post Office ceased to be a Government department in 1969 when responsibility for the running of the postal, telecommunications, giro and remittance services was transferred to a public authority called The Post Office.

The 1981 British Telecommunications Act separated the functions of the Post Office, making it solely responsible for postal services and Girobank. Girobank was privatised in 1990. The Postal Services Act 2000 turned The Post Office into a wholly owned public limited company establishing a regulatory regime under the Postal Service Commission. The Post Office Group changed its name to Consignia plc on 26 March 2001 when its new corporate structure took effect. On 4 November the name was changed to Royal Mail Group plc.

The chairman, chief executive and members of the Board are appointed by the Secretary of State for Trade and Industry but responsibility for the running of Royal Mail Group plc as a whole rests with the Board in its corporate capacity.

BOARD
Chairman, A. Leighton
Chief Executive, A. Crozier
Members, M. Cassoni *(Group Finance Director)*; E. Toime *(Executive Deputy Chairman)*; T. McCarthy *(Group Director, People and Organisational Development)*; D. Mills *(Chief Executive, Post Office Ltd)*
Non Executive Directors, Ms R. Thorne; D. Fish; R. Handover; J. Neill; B. Wigley
Secretary, J. Evans

ROYAL MINT

Llantrisant, Pontyclun CF72 8YT
T 01443-222111 F 01443-623148
E information.office@royalmint.gov.uk
W www.royalmint.com

The prime responsibility of the Royal Mint is the provision of United Kingdom coinage but it actively competes in world markets for a share of the available circulating coin business and about half of the coins and blanks it produces annually are exported. The Mint also manufactures special proof and uncirculated quality coins in gold, silver and other metals; military and civil decorations and medals; commemorative and prize medals; and royal and official seals. It also markets a range of gifts and collectible items.

The Royal Mint became an executive agency of the Treasury in 1990. The Government announced in July 1999 that the Royal Mint would be given greater commercial freedom to expand its business into new areas and develop partnerships with the private sector.
Master of the Mint, The Chancellor of the Exchequer *(ex officio)*
Chief Executive, G. Sheehan

ROYAL NATIONAL THEATRE

South Bank, London, SE1 9PX
T 020-7452 3333 F 020-7452 3344
W www.nationaltheatre.org.uk
Chairman, Sir Christopher Hogg
Members, B. Okri; The Rt. Hon. Chris Smith, MP; E. Walker-Arnott; A. Ptaszynski; Ms R. Lomax; N. Wright; J. Hill; Ms N. Horlick; Ms C. Merrick; Ms C. Newling; G. Morris
Company Secretary, Mrs M. McGregor
Director, Nicholas Hytner
Executive Director, Nick Starr

RURAL PAYMENTS AGENCY (RPA)

Kings House, Kings Road, Reading, Berkshire RG1 3BU
T 0118-958 3626 F 0118-959 7736
E enquiries@rpa.gsi.gov.uk
W www.rpa.gov.uk

The Rural Payments Agency (RPA) is as an executive agency of the Department for Environment, Food and Rural Affairs. It is the single paying agency responsible for Common Agricultural Policy (CAP) schemes in England and for certain schemes throughout the UK.
Chief Executive, J. McNeill
Directors, H. MacKinnon *(Operations)*; A. Kerr, *(Finance)*; R. Gregg *(Human Resources)*; A. MacDermott *(Information Systems)*; S. Vry *(Business Development)*; I. Corbett *(Legal Director)*

SCOTTISH CRIMINAL CASES REVIEW COMMISSION

5th Floor, Portland House, 17 Renfield Street, Glasgow G2 5AH
T 0141-270 7030 F 0141-270 7040/23
E info@sccrc.org.uk
W www.sccrc.org.uk

The Commission is a non-departmental public body which started operating on 1 April 1999. It took over from the Secretary of State for Scotland powers to consider alleged miscarriages of justice in Scotland and refer cases meeting the relevant criteria to the High Court for determination. Members are appointed by Her Majesty The Queen on the recommendation of the First Minister; senior executive staff are appointed by the Commission.
Chairperson, The Very Revd G. Forbes, CBE
Members, Prof. P. Duff; Sir Gerald Gordon, CBE, QC; R. Anderson, QC; D. Belfall; J. Mackay, QPM; A. Wylie, QC; G. Bell, QC
Chief Executive, Gerard Sinclair

SCOTTISH ENTERPRISE

5 Atlantic Quay, 150 Broomielaw, Glasgow G2 8LU
T 0141-248 2700 Helpline 0845-607 8787 F 0141-221 3217
E network.helpline@scotent.co.uk
W www.scottish-enterprise.com

Scottish Enterprise was established in 1991 and its purpose is to create jobs and prosperity for the people of Scotland. It is funded largely by the Scottish Executive and is responsible to the Scottish Ministers. Working in partnership with the private and public sectors, Scottish Enterprise aims to further the development of Scotland's economy, to enhance the skills of the Scottish workforce and to promote Scotland's international competitiveness. Scottish Enterprise is concerned with attracting firms to Scotland and, through Scottish Trade International, it

helps Scottish companies to compete in world export markets. Scottish Enterprise has a network of Local Enterprise Companies that deliver economic development services at local level.
Chairman, Sir John Ward, CBE
Chief Executive, Jack Perry

SCOTTISH ENVIRONMENT PROTECTION AGENCY

Erskine Court, The Castle Business Park, Stirling FK9 4TR
T 01786-457700 **Hotline** 0800 80 70 60
F 01786-446885 **W** www.sepa.org.uk

The Scottish Environment Protection Agency (SEPA) is the public body responsible for environmental protection in Scotland. It regulates potential pollution to land, air and water, the storage, transport and disposal of controlled waste and the safe keeping and disposal of radioactive materials. It does this within a complex legislative framework of Acts of Parliament, EC Directives and Regulations, granting licenses to operations of industrial processes and waste disposal. SEPA also operates Floodline, 0845-988 1188, a public service providing information on possible risk of flooding 24 hours a day, 365 days a year.
Chairman, Sir Ken Collins
Chief Executive, Campbell Gemmell
Director of Environmental Regulation and Improvement, Colin Bayes
Director of Environmental and Organisational Development, Calum MacDonald
Director of Environmental Science, Chris Spray
Head of Human Resources and Organisational Development, Richard Claughton

SCOTTISH LAW COMMISSION

140 Causewayside, Edinburgh EH9 1PR
T 0131-668 2131 **F** 0131-662 4900
E info@scotlawcom.gov.uk
W www.scotlawcom.gov.uk

The Commission keeps the law in Scotland under review and makes proposals for its development and reform. It is responsible to the Scottish Ministers through the Scottish Executive Justice Department.
Chairman (part-time), The Hon. Lord Eassie
Chief Executive, Miss J. McLeod
Commissioners, Prof. G. Maher, QC; Prof. K. G. C. Reid; Prof. J. M. Thomson; C. J. Tyre, QC

SCOTTISH LEGAL AID BOARD

44 Drumsheugh Gardens, Edinburgh EH3 7SW
T 0131-226 7061 **F** 0131-220 4878
E general@slab.org.uk
W www.slab.org.uk

The Scottish Legal Aid Board was set up under the Legal Aid (Scotland) Act 1986 to manage legal aid in Scotland. Board members are appointed by Scottish Ministers.
Chairman, Mrs J. Couper
Members, W. Gallagher; G. McKinstry; D. J. C. Nicol; Prof. J. P. Percy, CBE; Mrs Y. Osman; Mrs M. Scanlan; M. C. Thomson, QC; P. Gray, QC; Mrs E. Morton; S. Singh; Sheriff K. Ross
Chief Executive, L. Montgomery

SCOTTISH NATURAL HERITAGE

12 Hope Terrace, Edinburgh EH9 2AS
T 0131-447 4784 **F** 0131-446 2277
E enquiries@snh.gov.uk
W www.snh.org.uk

Scottish Natural Heritage was established in 1992 under the Natural Heritage (Scotland) Act 1991. It provides advice on nature conservation to all those whose activities affect wildlife, landforms and features of geological interest in Scotland, and seeks to develop and improve facilities for the enjoyment and understanding of the Scottish countryside. It is funded by the Scottish Executive.
Chairman, Dr J. Markland, CBE
Chief Executive, I. Jardine
Chief Scientific Adviser, C. Galbraith
Directors of Operations, J. Thomson *(West)*; A. Bachell *(East)*; J. Watson *(North)*
Director of Corporate Services, I. Edgeler

SCOTTISH PRISONS COMPLAINTS COMMISSION

Government Buildings, Broomhouse Drive, Edinburgh EH11 3XD
T 0131-244 8423 **F** 0131-244 8430
E spcc@scotland.gsi.gov.uk **W** www.scotland.gov.uk/spcc

The Commission was established in 1994. It is an independent body to which prisoners in Scottish prisons can make application in relation to any matter where they have failed to obtain satisfaction from the Scottish Prison Service's internal grievance procedures. Clinical judgements made by medical officers, matters which are the subject of legal proceedings and matters relating to sentence, conviction and parole decision-making are excluded from the Commission's jurisdiction. The Commissioner is appointed by the Scottish Ministers.
Commissioner, V. Barrett

SCOTTISH PUBLIC SERVICES OMBUDSMAN

4 Melville Street, Edinburgh, EH3 7NS
T 0870-011 5378 **F** 0870-011 5379
E enquiries@scottishombudsman.org.uk
W www.scottishombudsman.org.uk

The Scottish Public Services Ombudsman was established in 2002. The Ombudsman investigates complaints about Scottish government departments, councils, housing associations, the national health service and other public bodies. The public bodies which the Scottish Public Services Ombudsman may consider investigating are taken from a list of such bodies outlined in the Scottish Public Services Ombudsman Act 2002. Complaints considered by the Ombudsman can range from complaints about poor service, failure to provide a service, administrative failure and complaints about the NHS including hospital staff, GPs, dentists and other health professionals.
Scottish Public Services Ombudsman, Prof. A. Brown

SEAFISH INDUSTRY AUTHORITY

18 Logie Mill, Logie Green Road, Edinburgh EH7 4HG
T 0131-558 3331 F 0131-558 1442
E seafish@seafish.co.uk
W www.seafish.org.uk

Established under the Fisheries Act 1981, Seafish works with the seafood industry to satisfy consumers, raise standards, improve efficiency and secure a sustainable future. It is sponsored by the four UK fisheries departments.
Chairman, A. Dewar-Durie
Chief Executive, J. Rutherford

SECURITY AND INTELLIGENCE SERVICES

Under the Intelligence Services Act 1994, the Intelligence and Security Committee of Parliamentarians was established to oversee the work of GCHQ, MI5 and MI6; in 1999 an Investigator was appointed to the committee in order to reinforce the authority of its findings and establish public confidence in the system. The Act also established the Intelligence Services Tribunal, which hears complaints made against GCHQ and MI6. The Security Service Tribunal and Commissioner (*see* below) investigate complaints about MI5.

GOVERNMENT COMMUNICATIONS HEADQUARTERS (GCHQ)

Priors Road, Cheltenham, Glos GL52 5AJ
T 01242-221491 F 01242-574349

GCHQ produces signals intelligence in support of national security and the UK's economic wellbeing, and in the prevention or detection of serious crime. Additionally, GCHQ Communications-Electronics Security Group (CESG) provides advice and assistance to Government departments, the armed forces and other national infrastructure bodies on the security of their communications and information systems. GCHQ was placed on a statutory footing by the Intelligence Services Act 1994 and is headed by a director who is directly accountable to the Foreign Secretary.
Director, D. E. Pepper

INTELLIGENCE SERVICES COMMISSIONER

c/o PO Box 33220, London SW1H 9ZQ
T 020-7273 4514

The Commissioner is appointed by the Prime Minister. He keeps under review the issue of warrants by the Secretaries of State as detailed under the Regulation of Investigatory Powers Act (RIPA) 2000. The Commissioner is also required to submit an annual report on the discharge of his functions to the Prime Minister.
Commissioner, The Rt. Hon. Lord Justice Simon Brown
Private Secretary, D. Payne

INTERCEPTION OF COMMUNICATIONS COMMISSIONER

c/o PO Box 33220, London SW1H 9ZQ
T 020-7273 4514

The Interception of Communications Commissioner is appointed by the Prime Minister for a period of three years. The Commissioner's job is to keep under review the issue of interception warrants and the adequacy of the arrangements for ensuring the product of interception is properly handled. He does this by reviewing the warrant applications that the intercepting agencies have made to the Secretary of State, in order to make sure that the Secretary of State was right to sign the warrants. He also visits the Security Service and other agencies to examine his selection of interception warrants with the officers responsible for the relevant investigations. At the end of each reporting year, the Commissioner submits a report to the Prime Minister which is subsequently laid before Parliament and published.
Commissioner, Sir Swinton Thomas
Private Secretary, D. Payne

INVESTIGATORY POWERS TRIBUNAL

PO Box 33220, London, SW1H 9ZQ
T 020-7273 4514

The Investigatory Powers Tribunal replaced the Interception of Communications Tribunal, the Intelligence Services Tribunal, the Security Services Tribunal and the complaints function of the Commissioner appointed under the Police Act 1997.

The Regulation of Investigatory Powers Act 2000 provides for a Tribunal made up of senior members of the legal profession, independent of the Government and appointed by The Queen, to consider all complaints against the intelligence services and those against public authorities in respect of powers covered by RIPA; and to consider proceedings brought under section 7 of the Human Rights Act 1998 against the intelligence services and law enforcement agencies in respect of these powers.
President, The Rt. Hon. Lord Justice John Mummery
Vice-President, Mr Justice Michael Burton
Members, W. Carmichael; Sir David Calcutt, QC; Sir Richard Gaskell; Sheriff Principal J. McInnes, QC; Sir John Pringle, QC; P. Scott, QC; R. Seabrook, QC
Secretary, Mr D. Payne

NCIS NATIONAL CRIMINAL INTELLIGENCE SERVICE

PO Box 8000, London SE11 5EN
T 020-7238 8000 W www.ncis.gov.uk

The National Criminal Intelligence Service (NCIS) provides intelligence about serious and organised crime to law enforcement, government and other relevant national and international agencies.
Director-General, P. Hampson, QPM, CBE
Deputy Director-General, D. Bolt
Director, Finance, Ms M. Ashworth
Director, Intelligence Services Division, N. Bailey
Director, International Division, R. Wainwright
Director, Resources Division, N. Beard
Director, UK Division, K. Bristow

SERVICE AUTHORITY

PO Box 2600, London SW1V 2WG
T 020-7238 2600

The Service Authority for NCIS is responsible for ensuring its effective operation. It operates with the Service Authority for the National Crime Squad. There are 26 members of the authorities, of whom the chairman and nine others serve as 'core members' on both authorities.
Chairman, D. Lock
Clerk, T. Simmons
Treasurer, P. Derrick

SECRET INTELLIGENCE SERVICE (MI6)

PO Box 1300, London SE1 1BD

The Secret Intelligence Service produces secret intelligence in support of the Government's security, defence, foreign and economic policies. It was placed on a statutory footing by the Intelligence Services Act 1994 and is headed by a chief, known as 'C', who is directly accountable to the Foreign Secretary.

Chief, J. M. Scarlett, OBE, CMG

SECURITY SERVICE (MI5)

PO Box 3255, London SW1P 1AE
T 020-7930 9000
W www.mi5.gov.uk

The Security Service is responsible for security intelligence work against covertly organised threats to the UK. These include terrorism, espionage and the proliferation of weapons of mass destruction. The Service also supports the police and other law enforcement agencies in their work against serious crime and provides security advice to a wide range of organisations to help reduce vulnerability to threats from individuals, groups or countries hostile to UK interests.

Director-General, Ms E. Manningham-Buller

SENTENCE REVIEW COMMISSIONERS

5th Floor, Windsor House, 12–16 Bedford Street, Belfast BT2 7SR
T 028-9054 9412 F 028-9054 9427
E sentrev@belfast.org.uk
W www.sentencereview.org.uk

The Sentence Review Commissioners are appointed by the Secretary of State for Northern Ireland to consider applications from prisoners serving sentences in Northern Ireland for declarations that they are entitled to early release in accordance with the provisions of the Northern Ireland (Sentences) Act 1998. The commissioners have been appointed until 31 July 2005 and are served by staff seconded from the Northern Ireland Office.

Joint Chairmen, Sir John Belloch, KCB; B. Currin
Commissioners, Dr S. Casale; Dr P. Curran; I. Dunbar, CB; Mrs M. Gilpin; Dr A. Grounds; Ms C. McGrory; Dr D. Morrow
Secretary, Dr M. Power

SERIOUS FRAUD OFFICE

Elm House, 10–16 Elm Street, London WC1X 0BJ
T 020-7239 7272 F 020-7837 1689
E public.enquiries@sfo.gsi.gov.uk

The Serious Fraud Office is an independent government department that investigates and prosecutes serious or complex fraud. It is part of the UK Criminal Justice System. The Office is headed by the Director who is appointed by and accountable to the Attorney General. The SFO has jurisdiction over England, Wales and Northern Ireland but not Scotland, the Isle of Man or the Channel Islands.

Director, Robert Wardle

SMALL BUSINESS COUNCIL

6th Floor, Kingsgate House, 66–74 Victoria Street, London SW1E 6SW
T 020-7215 8519
E sbcsecretariat@sbs.gsi.gov.uk
W www.sbs.gov.uk/sbc

The Small Business Council was set up in May 2000. It is a non-departmental public body reporting to the Secretary of State for Trade and Industry on the needs of small businesses.

Chairman, W. Sargent
Members, G. Burton; Ms E. Caleb; P. Donaldson; Ms L. Gradwell; Mrs T. Graham, OBE; P. Harrod; Ms C. Hughes; A. Ive; S. Johnson; Mrs S. Brownson, OBE; M. Robinson; S. Topman; Prof. M. Ram; Mrs L. Shafar; J. McLaren-Stewart; I. Patel; Ms S. Preston; Ms F. Price; Dr J. Reynolds; S. Taggart; Miss J. Ward; Mrs C. Whitmill

SMALL BUSINESS SERVICE

Kingsgate House, 66–74 Victoria Street, London SW1E 6SW
T 020-7215 5000 Enquiries 0845-001 0031
W www.sbs.gov.uk
Business Link T 0845-600 9006 W www.businesslink.gov.uk

The Small Business Service was set up in March 2000 as an agency of the Department of Trade and Industry. The Service works with the public, private and voluntary sectors. Working through the Business Link network, the Small Business Service provides information, advice or access to experts for small businesses.

Chairman, Nigel Griffiths, MP
Chief Executive, Martin Wyn Griffith
Strategy Board Members, M. Gibson; S. Haddrill; S. Lyle Smythe; R. Price; R. Buse; Ms T. Graham, OBE; A. Summers

STATISTICS COMMISSION

10 Great George Street, London SW1P 3AE
T 020-7273 8008
E statscom@statscom.org.uk
W www.statscom.org.uk

The Statistics Commission has been set up to advise on the quality, quality assurance and priority-setting for official statistics, and on the procedures designed to deliver statistical integrity, to help ensure official statistics are trustworthy and responsive to public needs. It is independent of both Ministers and the producers of National Statistics. It operates in a transparent way with the minutes of its meetings, correspondence and evidence it receives, and advice it gives, all normally publicly available for scrutiny.

Chairman, Prof. D. Rhind, CBE, FRS, FBA
Members, Miss C. Bowe; Sir Kenneth Calman, KCB; Ms P. Hodgson; Mrs J. Trewsdale; D. Wanless; M. Weale

STRATEGIC RAIL AUTHORITY

55 Victoria Street, London SW1H 0EU
T 020-7654 6000 F 020-7654 6010
W www.sra.gov.uk

The Strategic Rail Authority (SRA) formally came into being on 1 February 2001 following the introduction of the Transport Act 2000. On 14 January 2002 it published its Strategic Plan, setting out the strategic priorities for Britain's railways over the next ten years.

As well as providing overall strategic direction for Britain's railways, the SRA has responsibility for consumer protection, the development of rail freight and administering freight grants, and for steering forward investment projects aimed at opening up bottlenecks and expanding network capacity. It is directly responsible for letting and managing passenger rail franchises.

The SRA manages all public sector expenditure in the rail industry and operates under directions and guidance issued by the Secretary of State for Transport. In Scotland it is also subject to directions and guidance from the Scottish Minister for Transport, and to directions and guidance from the Mayor of London in respect of services operating within the capital.

In January 2004 the Secretary of State for Transport announced a fundamental review of the rail industry. In July 2004 a white paper was published highlighting the main proposals, one of which is that the SRA will eventually be wound up. Its strategic responsibilities and financial obligations will ultimately transfer to the Secretary of State for Transport.

Chairman and Chief Executive, R. Bowker
Non-executive members, L. D. Adams, OBE; D. A. Begg; W. Gallagher; D. Grayson, CBE; P. H. Kent, CBE; J. Mayhew; D. A. Quarmby, CBE; M. Banerjee, CBE; J. Lewis-Jones; D. Norgrove
Secretary, P. Trewin

TOURISM BODIES

Visit Britain, Visit Scotland, the Wales Tourist Board and the Northern Ireland Tourist Board are responsible for developing and marketing the tourist industry in their respective countries.

VISIT BRITAIN

Thames Tower, Black's Road, London W6 9EL **T** 020-8846 9000
F 020-8563-0302 **W** www.visitbritain.com
Chief Executive, T. Wright

VISIT SCOTLAND

23 Ravelston Terrace, Edinburgh EH4 3TP **T** 0131-332 2433
Thistle House, Beechwood Park North, Inverness IV2 3ED
T 01463-716996 **W** www.visitscotland.com
Chairman, P. Lederer; *Chief Executive*, P. Riddle

WALES TOURIST BOARD

Brunel House, 2 Fitzalan Road, Cardiff CF24 0UY
T 029-2049 9909 **F** 029-2048 5031
E info@tourism.wales.gov.uk **W** www.visitwales.com
Chief Executive, Jonathan Jones

NORTHERN IRELAND TOURIST BOARD

St Anne's Court, 59 North Street, Belfast BT1 1NB
T 028-9023 1221 **F** 028-9024 0960 **E** info@nitb.com
W www.discovernorthernireland.com
Chief Executive, A. Clarke

TRANSPORT FOR LONDON

Windsor House, 42–50 Victoria Street, London SW1H 0TL
T 020-7941 4500 **Travel Line** 020-7222 1234
E travinfo@tfl.gov.uk **W** www.tfl.gov.uk/tfl/

Transport for London (TfL) is responsible for the capital's transport system. Its role is to implement the Mayor of London's Transport Strategy and manage the transport services across London for which the Mayor has responsibility.

Chairman, Ken Livingstone
Vice-Chairman, Dave Wetzel
Commissioner of Transport for London, Bob Kiley

UK FILM COUNCIL

10 Little Portland Street, London W1W 7JG
T 020-7861 7861 **F** 020-7861 7862
E info@ukfilmcouncil.org.uk **W** www.ukfilmcouncil.org.uk

The Council was created in April 2000 by the Department for Culture, Media and Sport to develop a strategy for the development and leadership of film culture and the film industry. It is responsible for the majority of the Department for Culture, Media and Sport funding for film as well as lottery and grant-in-aid (with the exception of the National Film and Television School).

Chairman, A. Parker
Deputy Chairman, S. Till
Chief Executive, J. Woodward

UK FILM COUNCIL INTERNATIONAL

10 Little Portland Street, London W1W 7JG
T 020-7861 7860 **F** 020-7861 7864
E internationalinfo@ukfilmcouncil.org.uk
W www.ukfilmcouncil.org.uk

UK Film Council International (formerly the British Film Commission) was originally established in 1991. Its remit is to attract inward investment by promoting the UK as an international production centre to the film and television industries and encouraging the use of British locations, services, facilities and personnel. Working with the UK Screen Agencies, UK Film Council International also provides overseas producers with a bespoke information service and offers practical help and advice to those filming in the UK.

British Film Commissioner, S. Norris
Director, Ms C. Wise

UNITED KINGDOM SPORTS COUNCIL (UK SPORT)

40 Bernard Street, London WC1N 1ST
T 020-7211 5100 **F** 020-7211 5246
W www.uksport.gov.uk

The UK Sports Council (UK Sport) was established by Royal Charter in January 1997. Its role is to lead the UK to sporting excellence by supporting winning athletes, world class events, world class standards and ethically fair and drug-free sport.

Chairman, Sue Campbell, CBE
Acting Chief Executive, Liz Nicholl

UNRELATED LIVE TRANSPLANT REGULATORY AUTHORITY

c/o Department of Health, Room 339, Wellington House, 133–155 Waterloo Road, London SE1 8UG
T 020-7972 4812 **F** 020-7972 4852
E dhmail@doh.gsi.gov.uk/ultra
W www.advisorybodies.doh.gov.uk/ultra

The Unrelated Live Transplant Regulatory Authority (ULTRA) is a statutory body established in 1990. In every case where the transplant of an organ within the definition of the Human Organ Transplants Act 1989 is proposed between a living donor and a recipient who are not genetically related, the proposal must be referred to ULTRA. Applications must be made by registered medical practitioners.

The Authority comprises a chairman and ten members appointed by the Secretary of State for Health. The secretariat is provided by Department of Health officials.

Chairman, Prof. Sir Roddy MacSween
Members, Prof. J. A. Bradley; Ms D. Bowman; Dr J. F. Douglas; Dr S. Fuggle; Dr R. Gokal; A. J. Hooker; Ms A. Keogh; Prof. A. Rees; Mrs S. Roff; Mrs S. J. Sullivan
Administrative Secretary, E. Scarlett
Medical Secretary, Dr P. Doyle

UK ATOMIC ENERGY AUTHORITY

Harwell, Didcot, Oxon OX11 0RA
T 01235-820220 F 01235-436401
W www.ukaea.org.uk

The UKAEA was established by the Atomic Energy Authority Act 1954 and took over responsibility for the research and development of the civil nuclear power programme. The Authority's commercial arm, AEA Technology PLC, was privatised in 1996. UKAEA is now responsible for the safe management and decommissioning of its radioactive plant and for maximising the income from the buildings and land on its sites. UKAEA also undertakes the UK's contribution to the international fusion programme.

Acting Chairman, Hon Mrs Barbara Thomas
Chief Executive, Dipesh Shah

WALES YOUTH AGENCY

Leslie Court, Lon-y-Llyn, Caerphilly CF83 1BQ
T 029-2085 5700 F 029-2085 5701
E wya@wya.org.uk
W www.wya.org.uk

The Wales Youth Agency is an independent organisation funded by the National Assembly for Wales to support the youth service in Wales. Its functions include the encouragement and development of the partnership between statutory and voluntary agencies relating to young people; the promotion of staff development and training; and the extension of marketing and information services in the relevant fields. The board of directors does not receive a salary.

Acting Chairman of the Board of Directors, Dr H. William
Chief Executive, Huw Jones
Assistant Chief Executive, John Rose

WELSH ADMINISTRATION OMBUDSMAN

5th Floor, Capital Tower, Greyfriars Road, Cardiff CF10 3AG
T 0845-601 0987 F 029-2022 6909
E wao.enquiries@ombudsman.gsi.gov.uk
W www.ombudsman.org.uk

The Welsh Administration Ombudsman was appointed in July 1999 to investigate complaints by members of the public who have suffered an injustice through maladministration by the National Assembly for Wales and certain public bodies involved in devolved Welsh affairs.

Welsh Administration Ombudsman, Adam Peat

WELSH DEVELOPMENT AGENCY

Plas Glyndwr, Kingsway, Cardiff CF10 3AH
T 01443-845500 F 01443-845589
E enquiries@wda.co.uk W www.wda.co.uk

The Agency was established under the Welsh Development Agency Act 1975. Its remit is to help further the regeneration of the economy and improve the environment in Wales. Under the Government of Wales Act 1998, the Land Authority for Wales and the Development Board for Rural Wales merged with the Welsh Development Agency. The Agency is sponsored by the National Assembly for Wales.

The Agency's priorities are to create new businesses and to encourage existing small firms to grow. Its main activities include promoting Wales as a location for inward investment, helping to boost the growth, profitability and competitiveness of indigenous Welsh companies, providing investment capital for industry, encouraging investment by the private sector in property development, grant-aiding land reclamation, and stimulating quality urban and rural development.

Chairman, R. Jones, OBE
Chief Executive, G. Hawker, CBE

WOMEN'S NATIONAL COMMISSION

35 Great Smith Street, London SW1 3BQ
T 020-7276 2555 F 020-7276 2563
E wnc@dti.gsi.gov.uk
W www.thewnc.org.uk

The Women's National Commission was established in 1969 as an independent advisory committee to the Government. Its remit is to ensure that the informed opinions of women are given their due weight in the deliberations of the Government and in public debate on matters of public interest including those of special interest to women. The Commission is based within the Department of Trade and Industry alongside the Women and Equality Unit.

Chair, Baroness Margaret Prosser
Director, Ms J. Veitch

REGIONAL GOVERNMENT

LONDON

GREATER LONDON AUTHORITY (GLA)

City Hall, The Queen's Walk, London SE1 2AA
T 020-7983 4000
Press Office 020-7983 4071/4072/4090/4067/4228
E mayor@london.gov.uk W www.london.gov.uk

On 7 May 1998 London voted in favour of the formation of the Greater London Authority. The first elections to the GLA took place on 4 May 2000 and the new Authority took over its responsibilities on 3 July 2000. On 15 July 2002 the GLA moved to one of London's most spectacular buildings, built on a brownfield site on the south bank of the river Thames, adjacent to Tower Bridge. The second elections to the GLA took place on 10 June 2004.

The structure and objectives of the GLA stem from its eight main areas of responsibility. These are transport, planning, economic development and regeneration, the environment, police, fire and emergency planning, culture and health. The bodies that co-ordinate these functions and report to the GLA are: Transport for London (TfL), the London Development Agency (LDA), the Metropolitan Police Authority (MPA) and the London Fire and Emergency Planning Authority (LFEPA). The GLA also absorbed a number of other London bodies, such as the London Planning Advisory Committee, the London Ecology Unit and the London Research Centre.

The GLA consists of a directly elected Mayor, the Mayor of London, and a separately elected assembly, the London Assembly. The Mayor has the key role of decision making with the Assembly performing the tasks of regulating and scrutinising these decisions. In addition, the GLA has around 600 permanent staff to support the activities of the Mayor and the Assembly, which are overseen by a Head of Paid Service. The Mayor may appoint two political advisors but he may not appoint the Chief Executive, the Monitoring Officer or the Chief Finance Officer. These must be appointed by the Assembly.

Every aspect of the Assembly and its activities must be open to public scrutiny and therefore accountable. The Assembly holds the Mayor to account through scrutiny of his strategies, decisions and actions. This is carried out by direct questioning at Assembly meetings and by conducting detailed investigations in committee.

People's Question Time gives Londoners the chance to question the Mayor and the London Assembly about plans, priorities and policies for London. It is held twice a year in different areas of London. A People's Question Time meeting was scheduled to take place in October 2004.

The role of the Mayor can be broken down into a number of key areas: to represent and promote London at home and abroad and speak up for Londoners; to devise strategies and plans to tackle London-wide issues, such as transport, economic development and regeneration, air quality, noise, waste, bio-diversity, planning and culture; to set budgets for Transport for London, the London Development Agency, the Metropolitan Police Authority and the London Fire and Emergency Planning Authority; to control new transport and economic development bodies and appoint their members; to make appointments to the new police and fire authorities; and to publish regular reports on the state of the environment in London.

The role of the Assembly can be broken down into a number of key areas:

- to provide a check and balance on the Mayor
- to have the power to amend the Mayor's budget by a majority of two-thirds
- to investigate issues of London-wide significance and make proposals to the Mayor
- to provide the Deputy Mayor and the members serving on the police, fire and emergency planning authorities with advice

Mayor, Ken Livingstone
Deputy Mayor, Nicky Gavron
Chair of the London Assembly, Brian Coleman
Deputy Chair of the Assembly, Sally Hamwee

ELECTIONS AND THE VOTING SYSTEMS

The Assembly is elected every four years at the same time as the Mayor and consists of 25 members. There is one member from each of the 14 GLA constituencies topped up with 11 London members who are representatives of political parties or individuals standing as independent candidates. The next election will be in May 2008.

The GLA constituencies are: Barnet and Camden; Bexley and Bromley; Brent and Harrow; City and East, covering Barking and Dagenham, the City of London, Newham and Tower Hamlets; Croydon and Sutton; Ealing and Hillingdon; Enfield and Haringey; Greenwich and Lewisham; Havering and Redbridge; North East, covering Hackney, Islington and Waltham Forest; Lambeth and Southwark; West Central, covering Hammersmith and Fulham, Kensington and Chelsea and Westminster; South West, covering Hounslow, Kingston upon Thames and Richmond upon Thames; Merton and Wandsworth.

Two distinct voting systems are used to appoint the existing Mayor and the Assembly. The Mayor is elected using the Supplementary Vote System (SVS). With SVS electors have two votes; one to give a first choice for Mayor and one to give a second choice. Electors cannot vote twice for the same candidate. If one candidate gets more than half of all the first choice votes, he or she becomes Mayor. If no candidate gets more than half the first choice votes, the two candidates with the most first choice votes remain in the election and all the other candidates drop out. The second choice votes on the ballot papers of the candidates who drop out are then counted. Where these second choice votes are for the two remaining candidates they are added to the first choice votes these candidates already have. The candidate with the most first and second choice votes combined becomes the Mayor of London.

The Assembly is appointed using the Additional Member System (AMS). Under AMS, electors have two votes. The first vote is for a constituency candidate. The second vote is for a party list or individual candidate contesting the London-wide Assembly seats. The 14 constituency members are elected under the first-past-the-post system, the same system used in general and local elections. Electors vote for one candidate and the candidate with the most votes wins. The Additional (London) Members are drawn from party lists or are independent candidates who stand as London Members.

The Greater London Returning Officer (GLRO) is the independent official responsible for running the first election in London. The GLRO has overall responsibility for running a free, fair and efficient election. He is supported in this by Returning Officers in each of the 14 London Constituencies.

GLRO, Anthony Mayer
Deputy GLRO, John Bennett
Deputy Regional Returning Officer, David Weschler

TRANSPORT FOR LONDON (TfL)

TfL is the integrated body responsible for London's transport system. Its role is to implement the Mayor's transport strategy for London and manage transport services across the capital for which the Mayor has reponsibility. TfL is directed by a management board whose members are chosen for their understanding of transport matters and are appointed by the Mayor, who chairs the board. TfL's role is:

- to manage the Underground, buses, Croydon Tramlink and the Docklands Light Railway (DLR)
- to manage a 580 km network of main roads and all of London's 4,600 traffic lights
- to regulate taxis and minicabs
- to run the London River Services, Victoria Coach Station and London's Transport Museum
- to help to co-ordinate the Dial-a-Ride and Taxicard schemes for door-to-door services for transport users with mobility problems

The London Borough Councils maintain the role of highway and traffic authorities for 95 per cent of London's roads. A £5 congestion charge for motorists driving into central London between the hours of 7a.m. and 6.30p.m., Monday to Friday (excluding public holidays) was introduced on 17 February 2003.

Transport Commissioner for London, Robert Kiley

LONDON DEVELOPMENT AGENCY (LDA)

The LDA promotes economic development and regeneration. It is one of the nine regional development agencies set up around the country to perform this task. It is managed by a board of 14 members appointed by the Mayor.

The key aspects of the LDA's role are:

- to promote business efficiency, investment and competitiveness
- to promote employment
- to enhance the skills of local people
- to create sustainable development

The London Boroughs retain powers to promote economic development in their local areas.

Chair, Mary Reilly

THE ENVIRONMENT

The Mayor is required to formulate strategies to tackle London's environmental issues including the quality of water, air and land; the use of energy and London's contribution to climate change targets; ground water levels and traffic emissions; and municipal waste management.

METROPOLITAN POLICE AUTHORITY (MPA)

This body, which oversees the policing of London, consists of 12 members of the assembly, including the Deputy Mayor, four magistrates and seven independents. One of the independents is appointed directly by the Home Secretary. The role of the MPA is:

- to maintain an efficient and effective police force
- to publish an annual policing plan
- to set police targets and monitor performance
- to be part of the appointment, discipline and removal of senior officers
- to be responsible for the performance budget
- to oversee formal inquiries and the implementation of their recommendations

The boundaries of the metropolitan police districts have been changed to be in line with the 32 London boroughs. Areas beyond the GLA remit have been incorporated into the Surrey, Hertfordshire and Essex police areas. The City of London has its own police force.

Chair, Len Duvall

LONDON FIRE AND EMERGENCY PLANNING AUTHORITY (LFEPA)

On 3 July 2000 the London Fire and Civil Defence Authority became the London Fire and Emergency Planning Authority. It consists of 17 members, 9 drawn from the assembly and 8 from the London Boroughs. The role of LFEPA is:

- to set the strategy for the provision of fire services
- to ensure that the fire brigade can meet all the normal requirements efficiently
- to ensure that effective arrangements are made for the fire brigade to receive emergency calls and deal with them promptly
- to ensure that information useful to the development of the fire brigades is gathered
- to assist the boroughs with their emergency planning training and exercises

Chair, Valerie Shawcross

SALARIES *as at July 2004*

Mayor	£112,639
Deputy Mayor	£70,034
Assembly Member	£47,924

LONDON ASSEMBLY COMMITTEES

Chair, 2004 Elections Review Committee, Brian Coleman
Chair, Audit Panel, Peter Hulme Cross
Chair, Budget Committee, Andrew Pelling
Chair, Business Management and Appointments Committee, Sally Hamwee
Chair, Economic Development and Planning Committee, Dee Doocey
Chair, Environment Committee, Darren Johnson
Chair, Health and Public Services Committee, Joanne McCartney
Chair, Safer London Committee, Richard Barnes
Chair, Transport Committee, Lynne Featherstone
Commission on London Governance (Advisory Committee)
Standards Committee

LONDON ASSEMBLY ORGANISATIONAL STRUCTURE

MAYOR'S OFFICE

Public Affairs (International and European Relations, London Stakeholders, Government and Parliamentary Liaison, Public Consultation, Public Affairs Publications)
Best Value Partnership (Borough Liaison)

Economic and Business Policy (Private Sector, Strategic Evaluation Unit)
Equalities and Policing
Environment
Tourism and Creative Industries
London House (Brussels)
Administration Manager

SECRETARIAT
Assembly Support
Scrutiny and Investigations
Committee Services
Assembly's Media Relations

CHIEF EXECUTIVE'S OFFICE
Governance
Marketing
Mayor's Media Relations

POLICY AND PARTNERSHIPS
Spatial Development Strategy
Planning Decisions
Architecture and Urbanism Unit
Environment
Culture
Policy Support (Health, Housing and Homelessness, Social Inclusion, Sustainable Development)
Business Support

CORPORATE SERVICES
GLA Economics
Information and Communication Technology
Legal
HR and Administration (Facilities Management and Internal Communications)
Research Library
Data Management
Public Liaison
Business Support

FINANCE AND PERFORMANCE
Core Performance and Project Management
Strategic Performance
Core Finance
Strategic Finance

LONDON ASSEMBLY MEMBERS *as at 10 June 2004*
The Mayor, Ken Livingstone *(Lab.)*
Arbour, Anthony *(C.), South West,* Maj. 4,067
Arnold, Jennette *(Lab.), North East,* Maj. 13,338
Barnes, Richard Michael *(C.), Ealing and Hillingdon,* Maj. 11,016
Biggs, John Robert *(Lab.), City and East,* Maj. 14,336
Blackman, Robert *(C.), Brent and Harrow,* Maj. 4,686
Bray, Angela Lavinia *(C.), West Central,* Maj. 29,944
Coleman, Brian *(C.), Barnet and Camden,* Maj. 11,519
Cross, Peter Kenneth Hulme *(UKIP), London List*
Doocey, Dee *(LD), London List*
Duvall, Leonard Lloyd *(Lab.), Greenwich and Lewisham,* Maj. 14,083
Evans, Jeremy Roger *(C.), Havering and Redbridge,* Maj. 16,706
Featherstone, Lynne Choona *(LD), London List*
Gavron, Felicia Nicolette *(Lab.), London List*
Hamwee, Sally Rachel *(LD), London List*
Hockney, Nicholas Damian *(UKIP), London List*
Howlett, Elizabeth *(C.), Merton and Wandsworth,* Maj. 16,878
Johnson, Darren *(Green), London List*
Jones, Jenny *(Green), London List*
McCartney, Joanne *(Lab.), Enfield and Haringey,* Maj. 1,574
Neill, Robert James Macgillivray *(C.), Bexley and Bromley,* Maj. 34,254
Pelling, Andrew John *(C.), Croydon and Sutton,* Maj. 23,694
Qureshi, Murad *(Lab.), London List*
Shawcross, Valerie *(Lab.), Lambeth and Southwark,* Maj. 5,475
Tope, Graham Norman *(LD), London List*
Tuffrey, Michael William *(LD), London List*

STATE OF THE PARTIES *as at 10 June 2004*

Party	*Seats*	*Gain/Loss*
Conservative	9	0
Labour	7	–2
Liberal Democrats	5	+1
Green	2	–1
UK Independence	2	+2

MAYORAL ELECTION RESULTS

10 June 2004
E. 5,197,647 *T.* 1,920,533 (36.95%)
Change in turnout from 2000: +2.52%
Good votes: 1st choice 1,863,671 (97.04%); 2nd choice 1,591,443 (82.86%)
Rejected votes: 1st choice 56,862 (2.96%); 2nd choice 329,090 (17.14%)

First Choice	*Party*	*Votes*	*%*
Ken Livingstone	Lab.	685,541	35.70
Steven Norris	C.	542,423	28.24
Simon Hughes	LD	284,645	14.82
Frank Maloney	UKIP	115,665	6.02
Lindsey German	Respect	61,731	3.21
Julian Leppert	BNP	58,405	3.04
Darren Johnson	Green	57,331	2.99
Ram Gidoomal	CPA	41,696	2.17
Lorna Reid	Ind. Working Class	9,542	0.50
Tammy Nagalingam	Ind.	6,692	0.35

Second Choice	*Party*	*Votes*	*%*
Simon Hughes	LD	465,704	24.25
Ken Livingstone	Lab.	250,517	13.04
Steven Norris	C.	222,559	11.59
Darren Johnson	Green	208,686	10.87
Frank Maloney	UKIP	193,157	10.06
Julian Leppert	BNP	70,736	3.68
Lindsey German	Respect	63,294	3.30
Ram Gidoomal	CPA	56,721	2.95
Lorna Reid	Ind. Working Class	39,678	2.07
Tammy Nagalingam	Ind.	20,391	1.06

LONDON ASSEMBLY ELECTION RESULTS

10 June 2004

CONSTITUENCIES

BARNET AND CAMDEN
E. 371,186, *T.* 38.41%

Brian Coleman, C.	47,640
Lucy Anderson, Lab.	36,121
Jonathan Simpson, LD	23,603
Miranda Dunn, Green	11,921
Magnus Nielsen, UKIP	8,685
Elisabeth Wheatley, Respect	5,150
Humberto Heliotrope, CPA	1,914

C. majority 11,519

BEXLEY AND BROMLEY
E. 397,075, *T.* 41.48%

Robert Neill, C.	64,246
Duncan Borrowman, LD	29,992
Heather Bennett, UKIP	26,703
Charles Mansell, Lab.	24,848
Ann Garrett, Green	8,069
Miranda Suit, CPA	3,397
Alun Morinan, Respect	1,673

C. majority 34,254

BRENT AND HARROW
E. 332,723, *T.* 38.03%

Robert Blackman, C.	39,900
Toby Harris, Lab.	35,214
Havard Hughes, LD	20,782
Daniel Moss, UKIP	7,199
Mohammad Ali, Green	6,975
Albert Harriott, Respect	4,586
Gladstone Macaulay, CPA	2,734

C. majority 4,686

CITY AND EAST
E. 437,298, *T.* 33.43%

John Biggs, Lab.	38,085
Shafi Choudhury, C.	23,749
Oliur Rahman, Respect	19,675
Guy Burton, LD	18,255
Christopher Pratt, UKIP	17,997
Terry McGrenera, Green	8,687
Christopher Gill, CPA	4,461

Lab. majority 14,336

CROYDON AND SUTTON
E. 376,175, *T.* 37.82%

Andrew Pelling, C.	52,330
Steven Gauge, LD	28,636
Sean Fitzsimons, Lab.	25,861
James Feisenberger, UKIP	15,203
Shasha Khan, Green	6,175
David Campanale, CPA	4,234
Waqas Hussain, Respect	3,108

C. majority 23,694

EALING AND HILLINGDON
E. 397,564, *T.* 37.28%

Richard Barnes, C.	45,230
Gurcharan Singh, Lab.	34,214
Michael Cox, LD	23,440
David Malindine, UKIP	14,698
Sarah Edwards, Green	9,395
Dalawar Chaudhry, Ind.	5,285
Salvinder Dhillon, Respect	4,229
Genevieve Hibbs, CPA	3,024

C. majority 11,016

ENFIELD AND HARINGEY
E. 343,617, *T.* 36.14%

Joanne McCartney, Lab.	33,955
Peter Forrest, C.	32,381
Wayne Hoban, LD	19,720
Brian Hall, UKIP	10,652
Jayne Forbes, Green	10,310
Sait Akgul, Respect	6,855
Peter Wolstenholme, CPA	2,365

Lab. majority 1,574

GREENWICH AND LEWISHAM
E. 329,450, *T.* 35.10%

Leonard Duvall, Lab.	36,251
Gareth Bacon, C.	22,168
Alexander Feakes, LD	19,183
Timothy Reynolds, UKIP	13,454
Susan Luxton, Green	11,271
Stephen Hammond, CPA	3,619
Ian Page, Respect/Soc. Alt.	2,825

Lab. majority 14,083

HAVERING AND REDBRIDGE
E. 350,652, *T.* 38.96%

Jeremy Evans, C.	44,723
Keith Darvill, Lab.	28,017
Lawrence Webb, UKIP	18,297
Matthew Lake, LD	13,646
Malvin Brown, Residents Assn. of London	6,925
Ashley Gunstock, Green	6,009
Abdurahman Jafar, Respect	5,185
Juliet Hawkins, CPA	2,917
David Stephens, Third Way	2,031
Peter Thorogood, Ind.	1,597

C. majority 16,706

LAMBETH AND SOUTHWARK
E. 373,293, *T.* 33.38%

Valerie Shawcross, Lab.	36,280
Caroline Pidgeon, LD	30,805
Bernard Gentry, C.	17,379
Shane Collins, Green	11,900
Frank Maloney, UKIP	8,776
Janet Noble, Respect	4,930
Simisola Lawanson, CPA	3,655
Navindh Baburam, Ind.	608

Lab. majority 5,475

MERTON AND WANDSWORTH
E. 340,792, *T.* 38.55%

Elizabeth Howlett, C.	48,295
Kathryn Smith, Lab.	31,417
Andrew Martin, LD	17,864
Roy Vickery, Green	10,163
Adrian Roberts, UKIP	8,327
Ruairidh Maclean, Respect	4,291
Ellen Greco, CPA	2,782
Rathy Alagaratnam, Ind.	1,240

C. majority 16,878

NORTH EAST
E. 410,719, *T.* 33.93%

Jennette Arnold, Lab.	37,380
Terry Stacy, LD	24,042
Andrew Boff, C.	23,264
Jon Nott, Green	16,739
Robert Selby, UKIP	11,459
Dean Ryan, Respect	11,184
Andrew Otchie, CPA	3,219
James Beavis, Comm.	1,378

Lab. majority 13,338

SOUTH WEST
E. 384,450, *T.* 40.31%

Tony Arbour, C.	48,858
Dee Doocey, LD	44,791
Seema Malhotra, Lab.	25,225
Alan Hindle, UKIP	12,477
Judy Maciejowska, Green	9,866
Omar Waraich, Respect	3,785
Peter Flower, CPA	3,008

C. majority 4,067

WEST CENTRAL
E. 352,653, *T.* 35.28%

Angela Bray, C.	51,884
Ansuya Sodha, Lab.	21,940
Francesco Fruzza, LD	17,478
Julia Stephenson, Green	10,762
Nicholas Hockney, UKIP	7,219
Kevin Cobham, Respect	4,825
Jillian McLachlan, CPA	1,993

C. majority 29,944

WALES

NATIONAL ASSEMBLY FOR WALES

Cathays Park, Cardiff CF1 3NQ
T 029-2082 5111
National Assembly Information Line 029-2089 8200
E webmaster@wales.gov.uk
W www.wales.gov.uk

In July 1997 the Government announced plans to establish a National Assembly for Wales. In a referendum on 18 September 1997 about 50 per cent of the electorate voted, of whom 50.3 per cent voted in favour of the Assembly. Elections are to be held every four years. The first elections were held on 6 May 1999 when approximately 46 per cent of the electorate voted. On 1 May 2003 the second Welsh Assembly elections took place. The next election will take place in May 2007.

The Assembly has 60 members (including the Presiding Officer), comprising 40 constituency members and 20 additional regional members from party lists. It can introduce only secondary legislation and has no power to raise or lower income tax.

The National Assembly for Wales has responsibility in Wales for ministerial functions relating to health and personal social services; education, except for terms and conditions of service and student awards; training; the Welsh language, arts and culture; the implementation of the Citizen's Charter in Wales; local government; housing; water and sewerage; environmental protection; sport; agriculture and fisheries; forestry; land use, including town and country planning and countryside and nature conservation; new towns; non-departmental public bodies and appointments in Wales; ancient monuments and historic buildings and the Welsh Arts Council; roads; tourism; financial assistance to industry; the Strategic Development Scheme in Wales and the Programme for the Valleys; and the operation of the European Regional Development Fund in Wales and other European Union matters.

SALARIES *as at 1 April 2004*

†First Minister	£72,863
†Minister/Presiding Officer	£37,797
Assembly Members	£43,283*

* Reduced by two-thirds if the member is already an MP or an MEP

† First Minister, Ministers and Presiding Officer also receive the Assembly Member salary

THE PRESIDING OFFICER

Lord Daffydd Elis-Thomas

WELSH ASSEMBLY GOVERNMENT

First Minister of the Assembly, Rhodri Morgan, AM
Principal Private Secretary, Lawrence Conway
Special Advisers, Paul Griffiths; Mark Drakeford; Dr Rachel Jones; Cathy Owens; Martin Mansfield; Jane Runeckles
Minister for Business, Karen Sinclair, AM
Minister for Culture, Welsh Language and Sport, Alun Pugh, AM
Minister for Economic Development and Transport, Andrew Davies, AM
Minister for Education and Lifelong Learning, Jane Davidson, AM
Minister for Environment, Planning and Countryside, Carwyn Jones, AM
Minister for Finance, Local Government and Public Services, Sue Essex, AM
Minister for Health and Social Services, Jane Hutt, AM
Minister for Social Justice and Regeneration, Edwina Hart, AM
Deputy Minister for Communities, Huw Lewis
Deputy Minister for Older People, John Griffiths
Deputy Minister for Transport, Brian Gibbons
Permanent Secretary, Sir Jon Shortridge
Clerk to the Assembly, Paul Silk

EXECUTIVE BOARD

Senior Director, Policy, Derek Jones
Director, Business and Information Management, Bryan Mitchell
Director, Economic Development and Transport, David Pritchard
Director, Education and Training, Richard Davies
Director, Environment, Planning and Countryside, Gareth Jones
Director, Health and Social Care, Ann Lloyd
Director, Human Resources, Bernard Galton
Director, Local Government, Public Service and Culture, Hugh Rawlings
Director, Public Service Development, Barbara Wilson
Director, Regulation/Inspection Review, Helen Thomas
Director, Social Justice and Regeneration, John Bader
Director, Spending Review, Martin Evans
Director, Strategy and Communications, Huw Brodie
Chief Medical Officer, Dr Ruth Hall
Principal Finance Officer, David Richards
Non-executive Directors, Adrian Webb; Kathryn Bishop

DEPARTMENTS AND OFFICES

Agriculture and Rural Affairs Department
Communications Directorate
Economic Development Department
Finance Group
Health Protection and Improvement Directorate
Local Government Group
NHS Directorate
Office of the Counsel General
Office of the Presiding Officer
Social Services and Communities Group
Strategic Policy Unit
Training and Education Department
Transport, Planning and Environment Group

EXECUTIVE AGENCIES

Cadw: Welsh Historic Monuments
Planning Inspectorate
Welsh European Funding Office

COMMITTEES

SUBJECT COMMITTEES

Culture, Welsh Language and Sport
Economic Development and Transport
Education and Lifelong Learning
Environment, Planning and Countryside
Health and Social Services
Local Government and Public Services
Social Justice and Regeneration

STANDING COMMITTEES
Audit
Business
Equality of Opportunity
European and External Affairs
House
Legislation
Standards of Conduct

MEMBERS OF THE WELSH ASSEMBLY *as at July 2004*

Andrews, Leighton, *Lab., Rhondda*, Maj. 7,954
Barrett, Ms Lorraine Jayne, *Lab., Cardiff South and Penarth*, Maj. 4,114
Bates, Michael, *LD, Montgomeryshire*, Maj. 12,297
Black, Peter, *LD, South Wales West region*
Bourne, Prof. Nicholas, *C., Mid and West Wales region*
Burnham, Mrs Eleanor, *LD, North Wales region*
Butler, Mrs Rosemary Janet Mair, *Lab., Newport West*, Maj. 3,752
Cairns, Alun, *C., South Wales West region*
Chapman, Ms Christine, *Lab., Cynon Valley*, Maj. 7,117
Cuthbert, Jeffrey, *Lab., Caerphilly*, Maj. 4,974
Davidson, Ms Jane Elizabeth, *Lab., Pontypridd*, Maj. 6,920
Davies, Andrew David, *Lab., Swansea West*, Maj. 2,562
Davies, David Thomas Charles, *C., Monmouth*, Maj. 8,510
Davies, Edward, *C., Mid and West Wales region*
Davies, Ms Janet, *PC, South Wales West region*
Davies, Ms Jocelyn, *PC, South Wales East region*
Dunwoody-Kneafsey, Moyra Tamsin, *Lab., Preseli Pembrokeshire*, Maj. 1,326
Elis-Thomas, Lord Dafydd, *PC, Meirionnydd Nant Conwy*, Maj. 8,742
Essex, Ms Susan Linda, *Lab., Cardiff North*, Maj. 540
Francis, Elizabeth Ann (Lisa), *C., Mid and West Wales region*
German, Michael, *LD, South Wales East region*
Gibbons, Brian, *Lab., Aberavon*, Maj. 7,813
Graham, William, *C., South Wales East region*
Gregory, Ms Janice, *Lab., Ogmore*, Maj. 6,504
Griffiths, Albert John, *Lab., Newport East*, Maj. 3,464
Gwyther, Ms Christine Margery, *Lab., Carmarthen West and South Pembrokeshire*, Maj. 515
Hart, Ms Edwina, *Lab., Gower*, Maj. 5,688
Hutt, Ms Jane, *Lab., Vale of Glamorgan*, Maj. 2,653
Idris Jones, Ms Denise, *Lab., Conwy*, Maj. 72
Isherwood, Mark, *C., North Wales region*
James, Ms Irene, *Lab., Islwyn*, Maj. 7,320
Jones, Alun, *PC, Caernarfon*, Maj. 5,905
Jones, Carwyn Howell, *Lab., Bridgend*, Maj. 2,421
Jones, Ms Elin, *PC, Ceredigion*, Maj. 4,618
Jones, Ms Helen, *PC, Mid and West Wales region*
Jones, Ms Laura Anne, *C., South Wales East region*
Jones, Ms Margaret Ann (known as Ann), *Lab., Vale of Clwyd*, Maj. 3,341
Law, Peter, *Lab., Blaenau Gwent*, Maj. 11,736
Lewis, Huw, *Lab., Merthyr Tydfil and Rhymney*, Maj. 8,160
Lloyd, Dr David, *PC, South Wales West region*
Lloyd, Mrs Val, *Lab., Swansea East*, Maj. 3,997
Marek, Dr John, *Forward Wales, Wrexham*, Maj. 973
Melding, David, *C., South Wales Central region*
Mewies, Mrs Sandra Elaine, *Lab., Delyn*, Maj.1,624
Morgan, Hywel Rhodri, *Lab., Cardiff West*, Maj. 6,837
Morgan, Jonathan, *C., South Wales Central region*
Neagle, Mrs Lynne, *Lab., Torfaen*, Maj. 6,964
Pugh, Alun John, *Lab., Clwyd West*, Maj. 436
Randerson, Ms Jennifer Elizabeth, *LD, Cardiff Central*, Maj. 7,156
Ryder, Mrs Janet, *PC, North Wales region*
Sergeant, Carl, *Lab., Alyn and Deeside*, Maj. 3,503
Sinclair, Ms Karen, *Lab., Clwyd South*, Maj. 2,891
Thomas, Ms Catherine, *Lab., Llanelli*, Maj. 21
Thomas, Ms Gwenda, *Lab., Neath*, Maj. 4,946
Thomas, Owen, *PC, South Wales Central region*
Thomas, Rhodri, *PC, Carmarthen East and Dinefwr*, Maj. 4,614
Williams, Byrnle, *C., North Wales region*
Williams, Ms Kirsty, *LD, Brecon and Radnorshire*, Maj. 5,308
Wood, Ms Leanne, *PC, South Wales Central region*
Wyn Jones, Ieuan, *PC, Ynys Mon*, Maj. 2,255

STATE OF THE PARTIES *as at July 2004*

	Constituency AM	*Regional AMs*	*AM Total*
Labour	30	0	30
Plaid Cymru	4†	7	11†
Conservative	1	10	11
Liberal Democrats	3	3	6
Others	1	0	1
The Presiding Officer	1	0	1

† Excludes the Presiding Officer, who has no party allegiance while in post

WELSH ASSEMBLY ELECTION RESULTS

1 May 2003

CONSTITUENCIES

ABERAVON
(S. Wales West)
E. 50,208, *T.* 37.6%

Brian Gibbons, *Lab.*	11,137
Geraint Owen, *PC*	3,324
Ms Claire Waller, *LD*	1,840
Myr Boult, *C.*	1,732
Robert Williams, *Soc. Alt.*	608
Gwenno Saunders, *Ind. Wales*	114

Lab. majority 7,813

ALYN AND DEESIDE
(Wales N.)
E. 60,518, *T.* 25.1%

Carl Sergeant, *Lab.*	7,036
Matthew Wright, *C.*	3,533
Paul Brighton, *LD*	2,509
Richard Coombs, *PC*	1,160
William Crawford, *UK Ind.*	826

Lab. majority 3,503

BLAENAU GWENT
(S. Wales East)
E. 52,927, *T.* 37.8%

Peter Law, *Lab.*	13,884
Stephen Bard, *LD*	2,148
Rhys Ab Elis, *PC*	1,889
Barrie O'Keefe, *C.*	1,131
Roger Thomas, *UK Ind.*	719

Lab. majority 11,736

BRECON AND RADNORSHIRE
(Wales Mid and W.)
E. 53,739, *T.* 50.0%

Ms Kirsty Williams, *LD*	13,325
Nicholas Bourne, *C.*	8,017
David Rees, *Lab.*	3,130
Brynach Parri, *PC*	1,329
Ms Elizabeth Phillips, *UK Ind.*	1,042

LD majority 5,308

BRIDGEND
(S. Wales West)
E. 62,540, *T.* 35.4%

Carwyn Howell Jones, *Lab.*	9,487
Alun Hugh Cairns, *C.*	7,066
Ms Cheryl Anne Green, *LD*	2,980
Keith Parry, *PC*	1,939
Timothy Charles Jenkins, *UK Ind.*	677

Lab. majority 2,421

CAERNARFON
(Wales N.)
E. 47,173, *T.* 45.0%

Alun Ffred Jones, *PC*	11,675
Martin Robert Eaglestone, *Lab.*	5,770
Goronwy Owen Edwards, *C.*	2,402
Stephen William Churchman, *LD*	1,392

PC majority 5,905

CAERPHILLY
(S. Wales East)
E. 68,152, *T.* 37.3%

Jeffrey Cuthbert, *Lab.*	11,893
Lindsay Whittle, *PC*	6,919
Ms Laura Jones, *C.*	2,570
Rob Roffe, *LD*	1,281
Ms Anne Blackman, *Ind.*	1,204
Revd Avril, Dafydd-Lewis, *Ind.*	930
Ms Brenda Vipass, *UK Ind.*	590

Lab. majority 4,974

CARDIFF CENTRAL
(S. Wales Central)
E. 62,470, *T.* 33.7%

Ms Jennifer Elizabeth Randerson, *LD*	11,256
Geoff Miles Mungham, *Lab.*	4,100
Craig Stuart Piper, *C.*	2,378
Owen John Thomas, *PC*	1,795
Raja Gul Raiz, *Soc. All.*	541
Captain Beany, *Bean*	289
Ms Madeleine Elise Jeremy, *ProLife,*	239

LD majority 7,156

CARDIFF NORTH
(S. Wales Central)
E. 64,528, *T.* 43.9%

Ms Susan Linda Essex, *Lab.*	10,413
Jonathan Morgan, *C.*	9,873
John Leslie Dixon, *LD*	3,474
Hewel William Wyn Jones, *PC*	2,679
Donald Edwin Hulston, *UK Ind.*	1,295

Lab. majority 540

CARDIFF SOUTH AND PENARTH
(S. Wales Central)
E. 65,505, *T.* 31.0%

Ms Lorraine Jayne Barrett, *Lab.*	8,978
Ms Dianne Elizabeth Rees, *C.*	4,864
Rodney Simon Berman, *LD*	3,154
Richard Rhys Grigg, *PC*	2,538
David Charles Bartlett, *Soc. Alt.*	585

Lab. majority 4,114

CARDIFF WEST
(S. Wales Central)
E. 60,523, *T.* 35.4%

Hywel Rhodri Morgan, *Lab.*	10,420
Ms Heather Douglas, *C.*	3,583
Ms Jacqueline-Anne Gasson, *LD*	2,914
Ms Eluned Mary Bush, *PC*	2,859
Frank Roger Wynne Hughes, *UK Ind.*	929

Lab. majority 6,837

CARMARTHEN EAST AND DINEFWR
(Wales Mid and W.)
E. 54,110, *T.* 49.5%

Rhodri Thomas, *PC*	12,969
Anthony Cooper, *Lab.*	8,355
Harri Lloyd-Davies, *C.*	3,576
Steffan John, *LD*	1,866

PC majority 4,614

CARMARTHEN WEST AND SOUTH PEMBROKESHIRE
(Wales Mid and W.)
E. 56,403, *T.* 43.0%

Ms Christine Margery Gwyther, *Lab.*	8,384
Llyr Hughes Griffiths, *PC*	7,869
David Nicholas Thomas, *C.*	4,917
Ms Mary Kathleen Megarry, *LD*	2,222
Arthur Ronald Williams, *Ind.*	580

Lab. majority 515

CEREDIGION
(Wales Mid and W.)
E. 52,940, *T.* 50.0%

Ms Elin Jones, *PC*	11,883
John Davies, *LD*	7,265
Ms Rhianon Passmore, *Lab.*	3,308
Owen Williams *C.*	2,923
Ian Sheldon, *UK Ind.*	940

PC majority 4,618

CLWYD SOUTH
(Wales N.)
E. 53,452, *T.* 35.1%

Ms Karen Sinclair, *Lab.*	6,814
Dyfed Edwards, *PC*	3,923
Albert Fox, *C.*	3,548
Marc Jones, *John Marek Ind.*	2,210
Derek Burnham, *LD*	1,666
Ms Edwina Theunissen, *UK Ind.*	501

Lab. majority 2,891

CLWYD WEST
(Wales N.)
E. 54,463, *T.* 40.6%

Alun John Pugh, *Lab.*	7,693
Brynle Williams *C.*	7,257
Ms Janet Ryder, *PC*	4,715
Ms Eleanor Burnham, *LD*	1,743
Peter Murray, *UK Ind.*	715

Lab. majority 436

CONWY
(Wales N.)
E. 54,443, *T.* 38.7%

Ms Denise Idris Jones, *Lab.*	6,467
Gareth Jones, *PC*	6,395
Guto ap Owain Bebb, *C.*	5,152
Graham Rees, *LD*	2,914

Lab. majority 72

CYNON VALLEY
(S. Wales Central)
E. 44,473, *T.* 37.5%

Ms Christine Chapman, *Lab.*	10,841
David Alun Walters, *PC*	3,724
Robert Owen Humphreys, *LD*	1,120
Daniel Clive Byron Thomas, *C.*	984

Lab. majority 7,117

DELYN
(Wales N.)
E. 54,426, *T.* 31.4%

Ms Sandra Elaine Mewies, *Lab.*	6,520
Mark Isherwood, *C.*	4,896
David Lloyd, *LD*	2,880
Paul Rowlinson, *PC*	2,588

Lab. majority 1,624

GOWER
(S. Wales West)
E. 60,523, *T.* 39.9%

Ms Edwina Hart, *Lab.*	10,334
Stephen James, *C.*	4,646
Ms Sian Caiach, *PC*	3,502
Nicholas Tregoning, *LD*	2,775
Richard Lewis, *UK Ind.*	2,444

Lab. majority 5,688

ISLWYN
(S. Wales East)
E. 51,170, *T.* 40.3%

Ms Irene James, *Lab.*	11,246
Brian Hancock, *PC*	3,926
Paul Taylor, *Tinker against the Assembly*	2,201
Ms Terri-Anne Matthews, *C.*	1,848
Huw Price, *LD*	1,268

Lab. majority 7,320

LLANELLI
(Wales Mid and W.)
E. 57,428, *T.* 40.9%

Ms Catherine Thomas, *Lab.*	9,916
Ms Helen Mary Jones, *PC*	9,895
Gareth Jones, *C.*	1,712
Kenneth Rees, *LD*	1,644

Lab. majority 21

MEIRIONYDD NANT CONWY
(Wales Mid and W.)
E. 33,742, *T.* 45.5%

Lord Dafydd Elis-Thomas, *PC*	8,717
Edwin Woodward, *Lab.*	2,891
Lisa Francis, *C.*	2,485
Kenneth Harris, *LD*	1,100

PC majority 5,826

MERTHYR TYDFIL AND RHYMNEY
(S. Wales East)
E. 55,768, *T.* 33.5%

Huw Lewis, *Lab.*	11,148
Alun Cox, *PC*	2,988
John Prosser, *C.*	1,539
Neil Greer, *Ind.*	1,423
John Ault, *LD*	1,324

Lab. majority 8,160

MONMOUTH
(S. Wales East)
E. 62,451, *T.* 44.9%

David Thomas Charles Davies, *C.*	15,989
Ms Sian Catherine James, *Lab.*	7,479
Ms Alison Leyland Willott, *LD*	2,973
Stephen Vaughan Thomas, *PC*	1,355

C. majority 8,510

MONTGOMERYSHIRE
(Wales Mid and W.)
E. 45,598, *T.* 43.0%

Michael Bates, *LD*	7,869
Edward Davies, *C.*	5,572
Ms Rina Clarke, *Lab.*	2,039
David Senior, *PC*	1,918
David Rowlands, *UK Ind.*	1,107
Robert Mills, *Ind.*	985

LD majority 2,297

NEATH
(S. Wales West)
E. 56,759, *T.* 39.4%

Ms Gwenda Thomas, *Lab.*	11,332
Alun Llewelyn, *PC*	6,386
Ms Helen Jones, *LD*	2,048
Chris Smart, *C.*	2,011
Huw Pudner, *WSA*	410

Lab. majority 4,946

NEWPORT EAST
(S. Wales East)
E. 56,563, *T.* 30.4%

Albert John Griffiths, *Lab.*	7,621
Matthew Robert Hatton Evans, *C.*	4,157
Charles Edward Townsend, *LD*	2,768
Mohammad Asghar, *PC*	1,555
Neal John Reynolds, *UK Ind.*	987

Lab. majority 3,464

NEWPORT WEST
(S. Wales East)
E. 61,238, *T.* 35.3%

Ms Rosemary Janet Mair Butler, *Lab.*	10,053
William Graham, *C.*	6,301
Phylip Andrew David Hobson, *LD*	2,094
Anthony Michael Salkeld, *PC*	1,678
Hugh Moelwyn Hughes, *UK Ind.*	1,102
Richard Morse, *WSA*	198

Lab. majority 3,752

OGMORE
(S. Wales West)
E. 49,565, *T.* 34.3%

Ms Janice Gregory, *Lab.*	9,874
Ms Janet Marion Davies, *PC*	3,370
Ms Jacqueline Radford, *LD*	1,567
Richard John Hill, *C.*	1,532
Christopher Herriott, *Soc. Lab.*	410

Lab. majority 6,504

PONTYPRIDD
(S. Wales Central)
E. 63,204, *T.* 38.8%

Ms Jane Elizabeth Davidson, *Lab.*	12,206
Delme Ifor Bowen, *PC*	5,286
Michael John Powell, *LD*	3,443
Ms Jayne Louise Cowan, *C.*	2,438
Peter Manuel Gracia, *UK Ind.*	1,025

Lab. majority 6,920

PRESELI PEMBROKESHIRE
(Wales Mid and W.)
E. 55,195, *T.* 41.7%

Moyra Tamsin Dunwoody-Kneafsey, *Lab.*	8,067
Paul Windsor Davies, *C.*	6,741
Sion Tomos Jobbins, *PC*	5,227
Michael Ian Warden, *LD*	2,799

Lab. majority 1,326

RHONDDA
(S. Wales Central)
E. 50,463, *T.* 46.0%

Leighton Andrews, *Lab.*	14,170
Geraint Davies, *PC*	6,216
Jeff Gregory, *Ind.*	909
Ms Veronica Watkins, *LD*	680
Dr K. T. Rajan, *UK Ind.*	524
Paul Williams, *C.*	504

Lab. majority 7,954

SWANSEA EAST
(S. Wales West)
E. 57,252, *T.* 30.7%

Ms Val Lloyd, *Lab.*	8,221
Peter Black, *LD*	4,224
Dr Dewi Evans, *PC*	2,223
David Alan Robinson, *UK Ind.*	1,474
Peter Morris, *C.*	1,135
Alan Thomson, *WSA*	133

Lab. majority 3,997

SWANSEA WEST
(S. Wales West)
E. 58,749, *T.* 33.3%

Andrew David Davies, *Lab.*	7,023
Dr David Rees Lloyd, *PC*	4,461
Arthur Michael Day, *LD*	3,510
Dorian Rowbottom, *C.*	3,106
David Charles Evans, *UK Ind.*	1,040
David Leigh Richards, *WSA*	272

Lab. majority 2,562

TORFAEN
(S. Wales East)
E. 61,264, *T.* 32.1%

Ms Lynne Neagle, *Lab.*	10,152
Nicholas Ramsay, *C.*	3,188
Michael German, *LD*	2,746
Aneurin Preece, *PC*	2,092
David Rowlands, *UK Ind.*	1,377

Lab. majority 6,964

VALE OF CLWYD
(Wales N.)
E. 49,319, *T.* 36.5%

Ms Margaret Ann Jones, *Lab.*	8,256
Darren Millar, *C.*	5,487
Malcom Evans, *PC*	2,516
Ms Robina Feeley, *LD*	1,630

Lab. majority 2,769

VALE OF GLAMORGAN
(S. Wales Central)
E. 68,947, *T.* 40.7%

Ms Jane Hutt, *Lab.*	12,267
David Melding, *C.*	9,614
Christopher Franks, *PC*	3,921
Ms Nilmini de Silva, *LD*	2,049

Lab. majority 2,653

WREXHAM
(Wales N.)
E. 50,508, *T.* 34.5%

Dr John Marek, *John Marek Ind.*	6,539
Ms Susan Lesley Griffiths, *Lab.*	5,566
Ms Janet Finch-Saunders, *C.*	2,228
Tom Ripperth, *LD*	1,701
Peter Ryder, *PC*	1,329

John Marek Ind. majority 973

YNYS MON
(Wales N.)
E. 49,998, *T.* 51.0%

Ieuan Wyn Jones, *PC*	9,452
Peter Rogers, *C.*	7,197
William Jones, *Lab.*	6,024
Nicholas Bennett, *LD*	2,089
Francis Charles Wykes, *UK Ind.*	481

PC majority 2,255

REGIONS

MID AND WEST WALES
E. 409,155 *T.* 184,198

PC	51,874 (28.2%)
Lab.	46,451 (25.2%)
C.	35,566 (19.3%)
LD	30,177 (16.4%)
Green	7,794 (4.2%)
UK Ind.	5,945 (3.2%)
Mid and West Wales Pensioners	3,968 (2.2%)
Ind. Wales	1,324 (0.7%)
Vote 2 Stop The War	716 (0.4%)
ProLife	383 (0.2%)

PC majority 5,423
(May 1999 PC Majority 30,712)
Additional Members: Prof. N. Bourne, *C.*, G. Davies, *C.*, L. Francis, *C.*, H. Jones, *PC*

NORTH WALES
E. 474,300 *T.* 175,028

Lab.	55,250 (31.6%)
PC.	41,640 (23.8%)
C.	38,543 (22.0%)
LD	17,503 (10.0%)
John Marek Ind.	11,008 (6.3%)
UK Ind.	4,500 (2.6%)
Green	4,200 (2.4%)
Ind. Wales	1,552 (0.9%)
Comm.	522 (0.3%)
ProLife	310 (0.2%)

Lab. majority 13,610
(May 1999 Lab. Majority 4,155)
Additional Members: E. Burnham, *LD*, M. Isherwood, *C.*, J. Ryder, *PC*, B. Williams, *C.*

SOUTH WALES CENTRAL
E. 480,113 *T.* 181,047

Lab.	74,369 (41.1%)
C.	33,404 (18.5%)
PC	27,956 (15.4%)
LD	24,926 (13.8%)
UK Ind.	6,920 (3.8%)
Green	6,047 (3.3%)
Soc. Lab.	3,217 (1.8%)
Bean	1,027 (0.6%)
Ind. Wales	1,018 (0.6%)
Vote 2 Stop The War	1,013 (0.6%)
Comm.	577 (0.3%)
ProLife	573 (0.3%)

Lab. majority 40,965
(May 1999 Lab. Majority 21,484)
Additional Members: D. Melding, *C.*, J. Morgan, *C.*, O. Thomas, *PC*, L. Wood, *PC*

SOUTH WALES EAST
E. 469,533 *T.* 169,731

Lab.	76,522 (45.1%)
C.	34,231 (20.2%)
PC	21,384 (12.6%)
LD	17,661 (10.4%)
UK Ind.	5,949 (3.5%)
Green	5,291 (3.1%)
Soc. Lab.	3,695 (2.2%)
BNP	3,210 (1.9%)
Ind Wales	1,226 (0.7%)
ProLife	562 (0.3%)

Lab. majority 42,291
(May 1999 Lab. Majority 34,814)
Additional Members: J. Davies, *PC*, M. German, *LD*, W. Graham, *C.*, L. A. Jones, *C.*

SOUTH WALES WEST
E. 395,596 *T.* 23,541

Lab.	58,066 (41.6%)
PC	24,799 (17.8%)
C.	20,981 (15.0%)
LD	17,746 (12.7%)
Green	6,696 (4.8%)
UK Ind.	6,113 (4.4%)
Soc. Lab.	3,446 (2.5%)
Ind. Wales	1,346 (1.0%)
ProLife	355 (0.3%)

Lab. majority 33,267
(May 1999 Lab. Majority 19,868)
Additional Members: P. Black, *LD*, A. Cairns, *C.*, J. Davies, *PC*, D. Lloyd, *PC*

NORTHERN IRELAND

NORTHERN IRELAND ASSEMBLY

Parliament Buildings, Stormont, Belfast BT4 3XX
T 028-9052 1333 F 028-9052 1961
W www.ni-assembly.gov.uk

The Assembly was suspended from midnight on 14 October 2002 and was dissolved on 28 April 2003. On 26 November 2003 elections to the Assembly were held but the Assembly remains suspended at the time of going to press (August 2004). The Secretary of State assumed responsibility for the direction of the Northern Ireland departments. The following is an overview of the organisation and structure of the Assembly, which applied when it was operational. Talks to discuss the future of the Assembly are ongoing.

The Assembly has 108 members elected by single transferable vote (six from each of the 18 Westminster constituencies). The first elections took place on 25 June 1998 and members met for the first time on 1 July. Safeguards ensure that key decisions have cross-community support. The executive powers of the Assembly are discharged by an Executive Committee comprising a First Minister and Deputy First Minister (jointly elected by the Assembly on a cross-community basis) and up to ten ministers with departmental responsibilities. Ministerial posts are allocated on the basis of the number of seats each party holds. Ministers receive 70 per cent of full pay during suspension of the Assembly.

The Assembly met in shadow form, pending the establishment of an Executive and the transfer of powers from Parliament. Following devolution it has executive and legislative authority over those areas formerly the responsibility of the Northern Ireland government departments.

Power was initially due to be transferred to the new Executive on 10 March 1999, but disagreements emerged over whether Sinn Fein should be allowed to enter the Executive before IRA weapons had been decommissioned. Further deadlines of 2 April and 30 June were also missed. On 15 July the Assembly met to nominate ministers, with the transfer of power to follow on 18 July. However, as the decommissioning issue had still not been resolved, Unionists failed to nominate ministers (the UUP boycotting the meeting itself) and the process collapsed. On 20 July the two prime ministers announced a review of the implementation of the Good Friday Agreement to be facilitated by Senator George Mitchell. The timing of the review dove-tailed with the inevitably sensitive publication of the Patten Commission's report on policing.

Following a series of meetings involving the parties in London, Mitchell's interim report of 15 November stated that he was increasingly more confident that the parties could find a way through the impasse.

On 18 November, following statements from the UUP, Sinn Fein and the IRA, Senator Mitchell concluded the review indicating that he now believed there was a basis for devolution to occur, for the institutions to be established and for decommissioning to take place as soon as possible. He concluded that devolution should take effect, the Executive Committee should meet and paramilitary organisations should appoint their authorised representatives to the Independent International Commission on Decommissioning (IICD) in that order and all in the same day. On 20 November the Secretary of State announced support for the Mitchell proposals and stated that the Assembly should meet on 29 November for the purpose of running the d'Hondt procedure for appointing shadow ministers and devolution should take effect after the necessary Parliamentary procedures had been completed on 2 December 1999.

Powers were devolved to Assembly and other institutions established on 2 December on a basis agreed by the parties during the Mitchell review. The Mitchell review created the expectation that the establishment of the institutions and the appointment of authorised representatives produced conditions in which Sinn Fein could influence bringing about the start of decommissioning. But it was a matter of political reality that if decommissioning did not occur by the end of January it would be very difficult for David Trimble to continue as leader of the Ulster Unionist Party beyond this. In late November the Council of the UUP had endorsed the Mitchell outcome but, reflecting the political reality, also recommended that progress on the timing and modalities of decommissioning be reviewed at the end of January 2000 through reports presented to the two governments by the IICD.

Devolution and the institutions were able to flourish on the basis of sufficient cross-community support. Unfortunately that support began to ebb when the anticipated progress on decommissioning failed to materialise at the end of January. The two Governments took receipt of General de Chastelain's 31 January report but held back publication in order to explore any hope of credible progress on decommissioning. Both governments tried further efforts to gain clarity on the decommissioning issue.

The Secretary of State announced the suspension legislation on 3 February and warned publicly that it would come into effect on 11 February. On the morning of 11 February, there was some sign that a new IRA proposal was emerging. The Irish Government presented a new position from its leadership. There were still only words and no timescale, but it did include clearer and less equivocal words than before. Unfortunately this was not enough to avert the collapse of the institutions.

Suspension meant that the Assembly could not meet or conduct any business. Parliament Buildings remained open for use by Assembly Members for the purpose of carrying out constituency work and they continued to be paid salaries and allowances – set at the lower pre-devolution shadow rate to reflect the suspension of Assembly business.

Following a period of intensive discussions with pro-Agreement parties during 4 and 5 May at Hillsborough, the Prime Minister and Taoiseach issued a joint statement committing both Government's proposals. On May 6, the IRA responded with a significant and forthcoming statement in which they recognised that:

- the implementation of what the Governments had agreed would provide a new context in which Republicans could pursue their political objectives peacefully
- in that new context the IRA leadership would initiate a process that would completely and verifiably put arms beyond use
- the IRA would renew contact with the Decommissioning Commission
- agreed, as a confidence building measure, to open a number of arms dumps to independent inspectors reporting to the Decommissioning Commission on a regular basis to verify that arms remain secure

The pro-Agreement parties welcomed these developments. The UUP leader, David Trimble said that the IRA statement 'appeared to break new ground'. The Prime Minister and the Taoiseach announced on 8 May that they would ask the former Finnish President Martti Ahtisaari and Cyril Ramaphosa, the ANC negotiator, to become the independent inspectors. On 9 May, the Chief Constable of the RUC recognised that the IRA statement marked a significant reduction in the overall threat and announced a number of measures, spread across Northern Ireland, designed as a return to more normal policing.

The Government published the Police Bill on 16 May and gave assurances to Unionists that the legal description of the new police service would incorporate the RUC, while the operational and working name would change to Police Service of Northern Ireland. The Government also took an enabling power to resolve the flying of flags over Government buildings if the devolved Executive could not.

A week later than originally envisaged the Ulster Unionist Council endorsed the Government's proposals on 27 May and devolved government was restored to Northern Ireland with effect from midnight on 29 May 2000.

Following considerable political unrest, David Trimble resigned as Northern Ireland First Minister on 1 July 2001, followed on 18 October by other UUP Ministers. His resignation was an ultimatum to encourage the IRA to start decommissioning their weapons. The administrative elements of his post passed to Sir Reg Empey.

To allow time to resolve this situation the Secretary of State for Northern Ireland ordered 24-hour suspensions of the Assembly on 10 August and 22 September 2001. On 5 November 2001 this period was concluded when David Trimble was elected as First Minister and Mark Durkan was elected as Deputy First Minister to replace Seamus Mallon who had retired.

SALARIES *as at December 2003**

Assembly Member £31,817

*In 2004 the salaries were frozen at 2003 level until the Assembly is reinstated.

NORTHERN IRELAND EXECUTIVE

Castle Buildings, Stormont, Belfast BT4 3SG
T 028-9052 0700 **F** 028-9052 8195
W www.northernireland.gov.uk

During suspension the following departments fall under the control of the Secretary of State for Northern Ireland and his Northern Ireland Office ministerial team.

Secretary of State for Northern Ireland, The Rt. Hon. Paul Murphy, MP

Under-Secretary of State, Ian Pearson *(Security and Policing, Finance and Personnel, Agriculture and Regional Development and Office of the First Minister and Deputy First Minister)*

Minister of State, John Spellar *(Social Development, Regional Development and Office of the First Minister and Deputy First Minister)*

Parliamentary Under-Secretary, Barry Gardiner *(Employment and Learning, Education and Enterprise, Trade and Investment)*

Parliamentary Under-Secretary, Angela Smith *(Health, Social Services and Public Safety, Environment and Culture, Arts and Leisure)*

OFFICE OF THE FIRST MINISTER AND DEPUTY MINISTER

Castle Buildings, Stormont Estate, Belfast BT4 3SR
T 028-9052 8400 **W** www.ofmdfmni.gov.uk

DEPARTMENT OF AGRICULTURE AND RURAL DEVELOPMENT

Dundonald House, Upper Newtownards Road, Belfast BT4 3SB
T 028-9052 4999 **F** 028-9052 5546 **W** www.dardni.gov.uk

EXECUTIVE AGENCIES

RIVERS AGENCY, 4 Hospital Road, Belfast BT8 8JP
T 028-9025 3355

FOREST SERVICE, Dundonald House, Belfast BT4 3SB
T 028-9052 4822

DEPARTMENT OF CULTURE, ARTS AND LEISURE

3rd Floor, Interpoint, 20–24 York Street, Belfast BT15 1AQ
T 028-9025 8825 **F** 028-9025 8906 **W** www.dcalni.gov.uk

EXECUTIVE AGENCIES

THE PUBLIC RECORD OFFICE OF NORTHERN IRELAND, 66 Balmoral Avenue, Belfast BT9 6NY **T** 028-9025 1318 **F** 028-9025 5999

THE ORDNANCE SURVEY OF NORTHERN IRELAND, Colby House, Stranmillis Court, Belfast BT9 5BJ **T** 028-9025 5755 **F** 028-9025 5700

DEPARTMENT OF EDUCATION

Rathgael House, 43 Balloo Road, Bangor, Co. Down BT19 7PR
T 028-9127 9279 **F** 028-9127 9100 **W** www.deni.gov.uk

DEPARTMENT FOR EMPLOYMENT AND LEARNING

39/49 Adelaide House, Adelaide Street, Belfast BT2 8FD
T 028-9025 7793 **W** www.delni.gov.uk

DEPARTMENT OF ENTERPRISE, TRADE AND INVESTMENT

Netherleigh, Massey Avenue, Belfast BT4 2JP **T** 028-9052 9900 **F** 028-9052 9550

DEPARTMENT OF THE ENVIRONMENT

Clarence Court, 10–18 Adelaide Street, Belfast BT2 8GB
T 028-9054 0540 **W** www.doeni.gov.uk

EXECUTIVE AGENCIES

Driver and Vehicle Licensing Agency (Northern Ireland)
Driver and Vehicle Testing Agency (Northern Ireland)
Environment and Heritage Service
Planning Service

DEPARTMENT OF FINANCE AND PERSONNEL

Rathgael House, Balloo Road, Bangor BT19 7NA
T 028-9127 9279 **W** www.dfpni.gov.uk

EXECUTIVE AGENCIES

BUSINESS DEVELOPMENT SERVICE, Craigantlet Buildings, Stoney Road, Belfast BT4 3SX **T** 028-9052 0444

LAND REGISTERS OF NORTHERN IRELAND, Lincoln Building, 27–45 Great Victoria Street, Belfast BT2 7SL **T** 028-9025 1515

NORTHERN IRELAND STATISTICS AND RESEARCH AGENCY*, McAuley House, 2–14 Castle Street, Belfast BT1 1SA
T 028-9034 8100

RATE COLLECTION AGENCY, Oxford House, 49–55 Chichester Street, Belfast BT1 4HH **T** 028-9025 2252

VALUATION AND LANDS AGENCY, Queen's Court, 56–66 Upper Queen Street, Belfast BT1 6FD **T** 028-9025 0700

*Incorporates the General Register Office (Northern Ireland), Oxford House, 49–55 Chichester Street, Belfast BT1 4HH
T 028-9025 2000

DEPARTMENT OF HEALTH, SOCIAL SERVICES AND PUBLIC SAFETY
Castle Buildings, Stormont, Belfast BT4 3SJ **T** 028-9052 0500 **F** 028-9052 0572 **W** www.dhsspsni.gov.uk

EXECUTIVE AGENCIES
Northern Ireland Health and Social Services Estates Agency

DEPARTMENT FOR REGIONAL DEVELOPMENT
Clarence Court, 10–18 Adelaide Street, Belfast BT2 8GB
T 028-9054 0540 **F** 028-9054 0064 **W** www.drdni.gov.uk

DEPARTMENT FOR SOCIAL DEVELOPMENT
Churchill House, Victoria Square, Belfast BT1 4SD
T 028-9056 9100 **W** www.dsdni.gov.uk

NORTHERN IRELAND ASSEMBLY MEMBERS
as at 2 August 2004
Adams, Gerry, *(SF), Belfast West*
Armstrong, Billy, *(UUP), Ulster Mid*
Attwood, Alex, *(SDLP), Belfast West*
***Beare**, Norah, *(DUP), Lagan Valley*
Beggs, Roy, *(UUP), Antrim East*
Bell, Billy, *(UUP), Lagan Valley*
Bell, Eileen, *(All.), Down North*
Berry, Paul, *(DUP), Newry and Armagh*
Birnie, Dr Esmond, *(UUP), Belfast South*
Bradley, Dominic, *(SDLP), Newry and Armagh*
Bradley, Mary, *(SDLP), Foyle*
Bradley, P. J., *(SDLP), Down South*
Brolly, Francis, *(SF), East Londonderry*
Buchanan, Thomas, *(DUP), Tyrone West*
Burns, Thomas, *(SDLP), Antrim South*
Burnside, David, *(UUP), Antrim South*
Campbell, Gregory, *(DUP), Londonderry East*
Clarke, Willie, *(SF), Down South*
Close, Seamus, *(All.), Lagan Valley*
Clyde, Wilson, *(DUP), Antrim South*
Cobain, Fred, *(UUP), Belfast North*
Copeland, Michael, *(UUP), Belfast East*
Coulter, Revd Robert, *(UUP), Antrim North*
Cree, Leslie, *(UUP), Down North*
Dallat, John, *(SDLP), Londonderry East*
Dawson, George, *(DUP), Antrim East*
De Brun, Ms Bairbre, *(SF), Belfast West*
Deeny, Kieran, *(Ind.), Tyrone West*
Dodds, Diane, *(DUP), Belfast West*
Dodds, Nigel, *(DUP), Belfast North*
Doherty, Pat, *(SF), Tyrone West*
***Donaldson**, Jeffrey, *(DUP), Lagan Valley*
Dougan, Geraldine, *(SF), Ulster Mid*
Durkan, Mark, *(SDLP), Foyle*
Easton, Alex, *(DUP), Down North*
Elliot, Tom, *(UUP), Fermanagh and South Tyrone*
Empey, Sir Reg, *(UUP), Belfast East*
Ennis, George, *(DUP), Strangford*
Ervine, David, *(PUP), Belfast East*
Farren, Dr Sean, *(SDLP), Antrim North*
Ferguson, Michael, *(SF), Belfast West*
Ford, David, *(All.), Antrim South*
***Foster**, Arlene, *(DUP), Fermanagh and South Tyrone*
Gallagher, Tommy, *(SDLP), Fermanagh and South Tyrone*
Gardiner, Samuel, *(UUP), Upper Bann*
Gildernew, Michelle, *(SF), Fermanagh and South Tyrone*
Girvan, Paul, *(DUP), Antrim South*
Hanna, Carmel, *(SDLP), Belfast South*
Hay, William, *(DUP), Foyle*
Hilditch, David, *(DUP), Antrim East*
Hillis, Norman, *(UUP), Londonderry East*
Hussey, Derek, *(UUP), Tyrone West*
Hyland, Davy, *(SF), Newry and Armagh*
Kelly, Dolores, *(SDLP), Upper Bann*
Kelly, Gerry, *(SF), Belfast North*
Kennedy, Danny, *(UUP), Newry and Armagh*
Kilclooney, Lord, *(UUP), Strangford*
Lewsley, Patricia, *(SDLP), Lagan Valley*
Long, Naomi, *(All.), Belfast East*
Maginness, Alban, *(SDLP), Belfast North*
Maskey, Alex, *(SF), Belfast South*
McCann, Fra, *(SF), Belfast West*
McCarthy, Kieran, *(All.), Strangford*
†**McCartney**, Raymond, *(SF), Foyle*
McCartney, Robert, *(UKUP), Down North*
McCausland, Nelson, *(DUP), Belfast North*
McClarty, David, *(UUP), Londonderry East*
McCrea, Revd William, *(DUP), Ulster Mid*
McDonnell, Dr Alasdair, *(SDLP), Belfast South*
McElduff, Barry, *(SF), Tyrone West*
McFarland, Alan, *(UUP), Down North*
McGimpsey, Michael, *(UUP), Belfast South*
McGlone, Patsy, *(SDLP), Ulster Mid*
McGuigan, Philip, *(SF), Antrim North*
McGuinness, Martin, *(SF), Ulster Mid*
McLaughlin, Mitchel, *(SF), Foyle*
McMenamin, Eugene, *(SDLP), Tyrone West*
McNarry, David, *(UUP), Strangford*
Molloy, Francis, *(SF), Ulster Mid*
Morrow, Maurice, *(DUP), Fermanagh and South Tyrone*
Moutray, Stephen, *(DUP), Upper Bann*
Murphy, Conor, *(SF), Newry and Armagh*
Neeson, Sean, *(All.), Antrim East*
Nesbitt, Dermot, *(UUP), Down South*
Newton, Robin, *(DUP), Belfast East*
O'Dowd, John, *(SF), Upper Bann*
O'Rawe, Patricia, *(SF), Newry and Armagh*
O'Reilly, Tom, *(SF), Fermanagh and South Tyrone*
Paisley, Revd Dr Ian, *(DUP), Antrim North*
Paisley, Ian Jnr., *(DUP), Antrim North*
Poots, Edwin, *(DUP), Lagan Valley*
Ramsey, Pat, *(SDLP), Foyle*
Ritchie, Margaret, *(SDLP), Down South*
Robinson, George, *(DUP), East Londonderry*
Robinson, Iris, *(DUP), Strangford*
Robinson, Ken, *(UUP), Antrim East*
Robinson, Mark, *(DUP), Belfast South*
Robinson, Peter, *(DUP), Belfast East*
Ruane, Caitriona, *(SF), Down South*
Shannon, Jim, *(DUP), Strangford*
Simpson, David, *(DUP), Upper Bann*
Stanton, Kathy, *(SF), Belfast North*
Storey, Mervyn, *(DUP), Antrim North*
Trimble, The Rt. Hon. David, *(UUP), Upper Bann*
Weir, Peter, *(DUP), Down North*
Wells, Jim, *(DUP), Down South*
Wilson, Jim, *(UUP), Antrim South*
Wilson, Sammy, *(DUP), Antrim East*

* Elected as UUP candidate, became a member of the DUP with effect from 15 January 2004

† Mrs Mary Nelis resigned from the Northern Ireland Assembly and was replaced by Mr Raymond McCartney whose appointment was notified by the Chief Electoral Officer with effect from 15 July 2004

POLITICAL COMPOSITION

DUP	Democratic Unionist Party	33
SF	Sinn Fein	24
UUP	Ulster Unionist Party	24
SDLP	Social Democratic and Labour Party	18
All.	Alliance Party	6
PUP	Progressive Unionist Party	1
UKUP	UK Unionist Party	1
Ind.	Independent	1

NORTHERN IRELAND ASSEMBLY ELECTION RESULTS

26 November 2003

* Indicates those who were elected

ANTRIM EAST
E. 55,473, *T.* 56.50%
Total Valid Poll: 30,952
Quota: 4,422
*Roy Beggs, *UUP*
*Sammy Wilson, *DUP*
*George Dawson, *DUP*
*David Hilditch, *DUP*
Daniel O'Connor, *SDLP*
*Sean Neeson, *All.*
*Ken Robinson, *UUP*
Roy McCune, *UUP*
Jack McKee, *Ind.*
Stewart Dickson, *All.*
Roger Hutchinson, *Ind.*
Oliver McMullan, *SF*
Tom Robinson, *UKUP*
Carolyn Howarth, *PUP*
Robert Mason, *Ind.*
John Anderson, *Ind.*
Anne Monaghan, *NIWC*
Alan Greer, *C.*
Andrew Frew, *Green*

ANTRIM NORTH
E. 70,489, *T.* 63.32%
Total Valid Poll: 44,099
Quota: 6,300
*Revd Dr Ian Paisley, *DUP*
*Ian Paisley Jnr., *DUP*
*Revd Robert Coulter, *UUP*
*Philip McGuigan, *SF*
*Sean Farren, *SDLP*
*Mervyn Storey, *DUP*
James Currie, *UUP*
Declan O'Loan, *SDLP*
Jayne Dunlop, *All.*
Kane Gardiner, *Ind.*
Nathaniel Small, *UKUP*
Billy McCaughey, *PUP*

ANTRIM SOUTH
E. 63,640, *T.* 59.49%
Total Valid Poll: 37,421
Quota: 5,346
*David Burnside, *UUP*
*Wilson Clyde, *DUP*
*Paul Girvan, *DUP*
Martin Meehan, *SF*
*David Ford, *All.*
*Jim Wilson, *UUP*
*Thomas Burns, *SDLP*
Donovan McClelland, *SDLP*
John Smyth, *DUP*
Adrian Cochrane-Watson, *UUP*
Norman Boyd, *NIUP*
Joan Cosgrove, *NIWC*
Ken Wilkinson, *PUP*
Jason Docherty, *C.*

BELFAST EAST
E. 51,937 *T.* 60.70%
Total Valid Poll: 30,965
Quota: 4,424
*Peter Robinson, *DUP*
*Sir Reg Empey, *UUP*
*David Ervine, *PUP*
*Naomi Long, *All.*
*Michael Copeland, *UUP*
Jim Rodgers, *UUP*
*Robin Newton, *DUP*
Harry Toan, *DUP*
Joe O'Donnell, *SF*
Leo Van Es, *SDLP*
Terry Dick, *C.*
Thomas Black, *Soc.*
Joseph Bell, *WP*
John McBlain, *Ind.*
George Weiss, *VFY*

BELFAST NORTH
E. 51,353, *T.* 62.31%
Total Valid Poll: 31,532
Quota: 4,505
*Nigel Dodds, *DUP*
*Gerry Kelly, *SF*
*Alban Maginness, *SDLP*
*Kathy Stanton, *SF*
*Fred Cobain, *UUP*
Pat Convery, *SDLP*
*Nelson McCausland, *DUP*
William Hutchinson, *PUP*
Fraser Agnew, *UUC*
Frank McCoubrey, *Ind.*
Eliz Byrne McCullough, *NIWC*
Marjorie Hawkins, *All.*
Peter Emerson, *Green*
Raymond McCord, *Ind.*
Marcella Delaney, *WP*
John Gallagher, *VFYP*

BELFAST SOUTH
E. 50,707, *T.* 62.59%
Total Valid Poll: 31,330
Quota: 4,476
*Michael McGimpsey, *UUP*
*Mark Robinson, *DUP*
*Alex Maskey, *SF*
*Carmel Hanna, *SDLP*
*Alasdair McDonnell, *SDLP*
Ruth Patterson, *DUP*
*Esmond Birnie, *UUP*
Monica McWilliams, *NIWC*
Geraldine Rice, *All.*
John Hiddleston, *UUP*
Tom Ekin, *All.*
Thomas Morrow, *PUP*
John Wright, *Green*
James Barbour, *SP*
Roger Lomas, *C.*
Patrick Lynn, *WP*
Linsay Steven, *VFYP*

BELFAST WEST
E. 50,861, *T.* 65.92%
Total Valid Poll: 32,854
Quota: 4,694
*Gerry Adams, *SF*
*Fra McCann, *SF*
*Bairbre De Brun, *SF*
*Michael Ferguson, *SF*
*Alex Attwood, *SDLP*
Sue Ramsey, *SF*
Joe Hendron, *SDLP*
*Diane Dodds, *DUP*
Chris McGimpsey, *UUP*
Hugh Smyth, *PUP*
John Lowry, *WP*
John MacVicar, *Ind.*
Kathryn Ayers, *All.*
David Kerr, *Ulster Third Way*

DOWN NORTH
E. 57,422, *T.* 54.54%
Total Valid Poll: 30,835
Quota: 4,406
*Leslie Cree, *UUP*
*Peter Weir, *DUP*
*Alex Easton, *DUP*
*Alan McFarland, *UUP*
*Robert McCartney, *UKUP*
Diana Peacocke, *UUP*
*Eileen Bell, *All.*
Liam Logan, *SDLP*
Brian Wilson, *Ind.*
Jane Morrice, *NIWC*
Ann Chambers, *Ind. Unionist*
John Barry, *Green*
Stephen Farry, *All.*
Julian Robertson, *C.*
Alan Field, *Ind.*
David Rose, *PUP*
Maria George, *SF*
Tom Sheridan, *UKUP*
Chris Carter, *Ind.*

DOWN SOUTH
E. 70,149, *T.* 65.59%
Total Valid Poll: 45,346
Quota: 6,479
*Jim Wells, *DUP*
*Dermot Nesbitt, *UUP*
*P. J. Bradley, *SDLP*
*Catriona Ruane, *SF*
*Margaret Ritchie, *SDLP*
*Willie Clarke, *SF*
Eamonn O'Neill, *SDLP*
Jim Donaldson, *UUP*
Eamonn McConvey, *SF*
Marian Fitzpatrick, *SDLP*
Raymond Blaney, *Green*
Trudy Miller, *NIWC*
Neil Powell, *All.*
Nelson Wharton, *UKUP*
Malachi Curran, *Ind.*
Desmond O'Hagan, *WP*

FERMANAGH AND SOUTH TYRONE
E. 64,336, *T.* 72.86%
Total Valid Poll: 46,160
Quota: 6,595
*Michelle Gildernew, *SF*
*Tom Elliot, *UUP*
*Maurice Morrow, *DUP*
*Tom O'Reilly, *SF*
*Arlene Foster, *UUP*†
*Tommy Gallagher, *SDLP*
Gerry McHugh, *SF*
Bert Johnston, *DUP*
Frank Britton, *SDLP*
Robert Mulligan, *UUP*
Eithne McNulty, *NIWC*
Linda Cleland, *All.*
†elected as UUP candidate, became a member of the DUP with effect from 15 January 2004

FOYLE
E. 65,303, *T.* 63.45%
Total Valid Poll: 40,806
Quota: 5,830
*Mark Durkan, *SDLP*
*William Hay, *DUP*
*Mitchel McLaughlin, *SF*
Raymond McCartney, *SF*
*Mary Nelis, *SF*†
*Mary Bradley, *SDLP*
Mary Hamilton, *UUP*
*Pat Ramsey, *SDLP*
Eamonn McCann, *SEA*
Gerard Diver, *SDLP*
Annie Courtney, *Ind.*
Alan Castle, *All.*
Danny McBrearty, *Ind.*
†Mary Nelis resigned from the Northern Ireland Assembly and was replaced by Raymond McCartney whose appointment was notified by the Chief Electoral Officer with effect from 15 July 2004

LAGAN VALLEY
E. 67,910, *T.* 61.44%
Total Valid Poll: 41,254
Quota: 5,894
*Jeffrey Donaldson, *UUP*†
*Edwin Poots, *DUP*
*Seamus Close, *All.*
Andrew Hunter, *DUP*
Paul Butler, *SF*
*Patricia Lewsley, *SDLP*
*Billy Bell, *UUP*
Ivan Davis, *Ind.*
*Norah Beare, *UUP*
Jim Kirkpatrick, *UUP*
Joanne Johnston, *C.*
Andrew Park, *PUP*
Frances McCarthy, *WP*
†elected as UUP candidate, became a member of the DUP with effect from 15 January 2004

LONDONDERRY EAST
E. 56,203, *T.* 61.75%
Total Valid Poll: 34,273
Quota: 4,897
*Gregory Campbell, *DUP*
*David McClarty, *UUP*
*Francis Brolly, *SF*
*George Robinson, *DUP*
*John Dallat, *SDLP*
Maurice Bradley, *DUP*
Michael Coyle, *SDLP*
*Norman Hillis, *UUP*
Cliona O'Kane, *SF*
Boyd Douglas, *UUC*
Edwin Stevenson, *UUP*
Pauline Armitage, *UKUP*
Yvonne Boyle, *All.*
Marion Baur, *SEA*

NEWRY AND ARMAGH
E. 68,731, *T.* 70.18%
Total Valid Poll: 47,378
Quota: 6,769
* Paul Berry, *DUP*
* Conor Murphy, *SF*
* Danny Kennedy, *UUP*
* Davy Hyland, *SF*
* Patricia O'Rawe, *SF*
Jim Lennon, *SDLP*
* Dominic Bradley, *SDLP*
John Fee, *SDLP*
William Frazer, *Ind.*
Freda Donnelly, *DUP*
Peter Whitcroft, *All.*

STRANGFORD
E. 66,308, *T.* 57.06%
Total Valid Poll: 37,250
Quota: 5,322
*Iris Robinson, *DUP*
*Lord Kilclooney, *UUP*
*Jim Shannon, *DUP*
*George Ennis, *DUP*
*David McNarry, *UUP*
Joe Boyle, *SDLP*
*Kieran McCarthy, *All.*
Bob Little, *UUP*
Dermot Kennedy, *SF*
Cedric Wilson, *NIUP*
Colin Neill, *PUP*
Philip Orr, *Green*
Danny McCarthy, *Ind.*

TYRONE WEST
E. 57,795, *T.* 73.24%
Total Valid Poll: 41,729
Quota: 5,962
*Dr Kieran Deeny, *Ind.*
*Pat Doherty, *SF*
*Barry McElduff, *SF*
*Thomas Buchanan, *DUP*
Brian McMahon, *SF*
*Derek Hussey, *UUP*
*Eugene McMenamin, *SDLP*
Joe Byrne, *SDLP*
Derek Reaney, *DUP*
Bert Wilson, *UUP*
Roy Reid, *PUP*
Steven Alexander, *All.*

ULSTER MID
E. 60,095, *T.* 74.92%
Total Valid Poll: 44,362
Quota: 6,338
*Revd Dr William McCrea, *DUP*
*Martin McGuinness, *SF*
*Geraldine Dougan, *SF*
*Francie Molloy, *SF*
*Billy Armstrong, *UUP*
*Patsy McGlone, *SDLP*
Dennis Haughey, *SDLP*
Trevor Wilson, *UUP*
Alan Miller, *DUP*
Cora Groogan, *SF*
Francis Donnelly, *WP*
James Holmes, *All.*

UPPER BANN
E. 68,814, *T.* 64.15%
Total Valid Poll: 43,482
Quota: 6,212
*David Trimble, *UUP*
*David Simpson, *DUP*
*John O'Dowd, *SF*
*Stephen Moutray, *DUP*
Dara O'Hagan, *SF*
*Dolores Kelly, *SDLP*
Kieran Corr, *SDLP*
*Samuel Gardiner, *UUP*
Denis Watson, *DUP*
George Savage, *UUP*
David Jones, *Ind.*
Sidney Anderson, *Ind.*
Francis McQuaid, *All.*
Tom French, *WP*

SCOTLAND

SCOTTISH PARLIAMENT

Edinburgh EH99 1SP
T 0131-348 5000/0845-278 1999 **F** 0131-348 5601
Textphone 0131-348 5415/0845-270 0152
E sp.info@scottish.parliament.uk
W www.scottish.parliament.uk

In July 1997 the Government announced plans to establish a Scottish Parliament. In a referendum on 11 September 1997 about 60 per cent of the electorate voted. Of those who voted, 74.3 per cent voted in favour of the Parliament and 63.5 in favour of its having tax-raising powers. Elections are to be held every four years. The first elections were held on 6 May 1999 when about 59 per cent of the electorate voted. The first meeting was held on 12 May 1999 and the Scottish Parliament was officially opened on 1 July 1999 at the Assembly Hall, Edinburgh. A new building to house Parliament opened at Holyrood on 7 September 2004. On 1 May 2003 the second elections to the Scottish Parliament took place.

The Scottish Parliament has 129 members (including the Presiding Officer), comprising 73 constituency members and 56 additional regional members mainly from party lists. It can introduce primary legislation and has the power to raise or lower the basic rate of income tax by up to three pence in the pound.

The areas for which the Scottish Parliament is responsible include: education, health, law, environment, economic development, local government, housing, police, fire services, planning, financial assistance to industry, tourism, some transport, heritage and the arts, agriculture, forestry and food standards.

SALARIES *as at 1 April 2004*

First Minister	£72,862*
Ministers	£37,798*
Lord Advocate	£49,382*
Solicitor-General for Scotland	£35,707*
Junior Ministers	£23,675*
MSPs	£50,300†
Presiding Officer	£37,798*
Deputy Presiding Officers	£23,675*

* In addition to the MSP salary
† Reduced by two-thirds if the member is already an MP or an MEP

SCOTTISH EXECUTIVE

St Andrew's House, Regent Road,
Edinburgh EH1 3DG
T 0845-774 1741 **Enquiry Line** 0131-556 8400
E ceu@scotland.gov.uk
W www.scotland.gov.uk

The Scottish Executive is the devolved government for Scotland. It is responsible for most of the issues of day-to-day concern to the people of Scotland, including health, education, justice, rural affairs and transport, and manages an annual budget of around £20 billion.

The Executive was established in 1999, following the first elections to the Scottish Parliament. It is a coalition between the Scottish Labour Party and the Scottish Liberal Democrats.

The Executive is led by a First Minister who is nominated by the Parliament and in turn appoints the other Scottish Ministers.

Scottish Executive civil servants are accountable to Scottish Ministers, who are themselves accountable to the Scottish Parliament.

First Minister, The Rt. Hon. Jack McConnell, MSP *(Lab.)*
Deputy First Minister and Minister for Enterprise and Lifelong Learning, The Rt. Hon. Jim Wallace, QC, MSP *(LD)*
Minister for Communities, Margaret Curran, MSP *(Lab.)*
Minister for Education and Young People, Peter Peacock, MSP *(Lab.)*
Minister for Environment and Rural Development, Ross Finnie, MSP *(LD)*
Minister for Finance and Public Services, Andy Kerr, MSP *(Lab.)*
Minister for Health and Community Care, Malcolm Chisholm, MSP *(Lab.)*
Minister for Justice, Cathy Jamieson, MSP *(Lab.)*
Minister for Parliamentary Business, Patricia Ferguson, MSP *(Lab.)*
Minister for Tourism, Culture and Sport, Frank McAveety, MSP *(Lab.)*
Minister for Transport, Nicol Stephen, MSP *(LD)*
Lord Advocate, The Rt. Hon. Colin Boyd, QC

JUNIOR MINISTERS (NOT MEMBERS OF THE SCOTTISH EXECUTIVE)

Deputy Minister for Communities, Mary Mulligan, MSP *(Lab.)*
Deputy Minister for Education and Young People, Euan Robson, MSP *(LD)*
Deputy Minister for Enterprise, and Lifelong Learning, Lewis Macdonald, MSP *(Lab.)*
Deputy Minister for Environment and Rural Development, Allan Wilson, MSP *(Lab.)*
Deputy Minister for Finance and Parliamentary Business, Tavish Scott, MSP *(LD)*
Deputy Minister for Health and Community Care, Tom McCabe, MSP *(Lab.)*
Deputy Minister for Justice, Hugh Henry, MSP *(Lab.)*
Solicitor-General for Scotland, Elish Angiolini, QC

CHANGE AND CORPORATE SERVICES

Saughton House, Broomhouse Drive, Edinburgh EH11 3XD
T 0845-774 1741
Director of Change and Corporate Services, vacant

FINANCE AND CENTRAL SERVICES DEPARTMENT (FCSD)

Victoria Quay, Edinburgh EH6 6QQ
T 0845-774 1741/0131-556 8400
Acting Head of Department, Dr A. Goudie

EXECUTIVE AGENCY
Scottish Public Pensions Agency

ENVIRONMENT AND RURAL AFFAIRS DEPARTMENT

Pentland House, 47 Robb's Loan, Edinburgh EH14 1TY
T 0845-774 1741/0131-556 8400 F 0131 244 6116
Head of Department, J. S. Graham

EXECUTIVE AGENCIES
Animal Health Veterinary Unit
Fisheries Research Services
Scottish Agricultural Science Agency
Scottish Fisheries Protection Agency

DEVELOPMENT DEPARTMENT
Victoria Quay, Edinburgh EH6 6QQ
T 0131-244 0763
Head of Department, Mrs Nicola Munro

EXECUTIVE AGENCY
Communities Scotland

EDUCATION DEPARTMENT
Victoria Quay, Edinburgh EH6 6QQ
T 0845-774 1741/0131-556 8400
Head of Department, M. Ewart

EXECUTIVE AGENCIES
Historic Scotland
HM Inspectorate of Education

ENTERPRISE, TRANSPORT AND LIFELONG LEARNING DEPARTMENT
Meridian Court, Cadogan Street, Glasgow G2 7AB
T 0131-556 8400 F 0131-244 8240
Head of Department, E. W. Frizzell, CB

EXECUTIVE AGENCY
Student Awards Agency for Scotland

HEALTH DEPARTMENT
St Andrew's House, Edinburgh EH1 3DG
T 0131-244 2440
Chief Executive, T. Jones

JUSTICE DEPARTMENT
St Andrew's House, Regent Road, Edinburgh EH1 3DG
T 0131-244 2120 F 0131-244 2121
Head of Department, J. D. Gallagher

EXECUTIVE AGENCIES
Accountant in Bankruptcy
General Register Office for Scotland
Registers of Scotland
Scottish Court Service
Scottish Prison Service

LEGAL AND PARLIAMENTARY SERVICES
25 Chambers Street, Edinburgh EH1 1LA
T 0845-774 1741 F 0131-225 7473
Head of Department, Robert Gordon

OFFICE OF THE PERMANENT SECRETARY
St Andrew's House, Regent Road, Edinburgh EH1 3DG
T 0131-244 2120 F 0131-244 2121
Head of Department, John Elvidge

MEMBERS OF THE SCOTTISH PARLIAMENT *as at August 2004*
***Adam**, Brian, *SNP, Glasgow, Aberdeen North*, Maj. 457
***Aitken**, Bill, *C., Glasgow region*
***Alexander**, Wendy, *Lab., Paisley North*, Maj. 4,310
***Baillie**, Jackie, *Lab., Dumbarton*, Maj. 6,612
Baird, Shiona, *Green, North East Scotland region*
Baker, Richard, *Lab., North East Scotland region*
Ballance, Chris, *Green, South of Scotland region*
Ballard, Mark, *Green, Lothians region*
***Barrie**, Scott, *Lab., Dunfermline West*, Maj. 4,080
***Boyack**, Sarah, *Lab., Edinburgh Central*, Maj. 2,666
***Brankin**, Rhona, *Lab. Co-op, Midlothian*, Maj. 5,542
Brocklebank, Ted, *C., Mid Scotland and Fife region*
***Brown**, Robert E., *LD, Glasgow region*
***Butler**, Bill, *Lab., Glasgow Anniesland*, Maj. 6,253
Byrne, Rosemary, *SSP, South of Scotland region*
***Canavan**, Dennis, *Ind., Falkirk West*, Maj. 10,000
***Chisholm**, Malcolm, *Lab., Edinburgh North and Leith*, Maj. 5,414
***Craigie**, Cathie, *Lab., Cumbernauld and Kilsyth*, Maj. 520
***Crawford**, Bruce, *SNP, Mid Scotland and Fife region*
***Cunningham**, Roseanna, *SNP, Perth*, Maj. 727
Curran, Frances, *SSP, West of Scotland region*
***Curran**, Margaret, *Lab., Glasgow Baillieston*, Maj. 6,178
***Davidson**, David, *C., North East Scotland region*
***Deacon**, Susan, *Lab., Edinburgh East and Musselburgh*, Maj. 6,158
***Douglas-Hamilton**, James, *C., Lothians region*
***Eadie**, Helen, *Lab. Co-op*, Dunfermline East, Maj. 7,290
***Ewing**, Fergus, *SNP, Inverness East, Nairn and Lochaber*, Maj. 1,046
***Ewing**, Margaret, *SNP, Moray*, Maj. 5,312
***Fabiani**, Linda, *SNP, Central Scotland region*
***Ferguson**, Patricia, *Lab., Glasgow Maryhill*, Maj. 5,368
***Fergusson**, Alex, *C., Galloway and Upper Nithsdale*, Maj. 99
***Finnie**, Ross, *LD, West of Scotland region*
Fox, Colin, *SSP, Lothians region*
***Fraser**, Murdo, *C., Mid Scotland and Fife region*
***Gallie**, Phil, *C., South of Scotland region*
Gibson, Rob, *SNP, Highlands and Islands region*
***Gillon**, Karen, *Lab., Clydesdale*, Maj. 6,671
Glen, Marlyn, *Lab., North East Scotland region*
***Godman**, Trish, *Lab., Renfrewshire West*, Maj. 2,492
***Goldie**, Annabel, *C., West of Scotland region*
***Gorrie**, Donald, *LD, Central Scotland region*
***Grahame**, Christine, *SNP, South of Scotland region*
***Harper**, Robin, *Green, Lothians region*
Harvie, Patrick, *Green, Glasgow region*
***Henry**, Hugh, *Lab., Paisley South*, Maj. 2,453
***Home Robertson**, John, *Lab., East Lothian*, Maj. 8,175
***Hughes**, Janis, *Lab., Glasgow Rutherglen*, Maj. 6,303
***Hyslop**, Fiona, *SNP, Lothians region*
***Ingram**, Adam, *SNP, South of Scotland region*
***Jackson**, Gordon, *Lab., Glasgow Govan*, Maj. 1,235
***Jackson**, Dr Sylvia, *Lab., Stirling*, Maj. 2,880
***Jamieson**, Cathy, *Lab. Co-op, Carrick, Cumnock and Doon Valley*, Maj. 7,454
***Jamieson**, Margaret, *Lab., Kilmarnock and Loudoun*, Maj. 1,210
***Johnstone**, Alex, *C., North East Scotland region*
Kane, Rosie, *SSP, Glasgow region*
***Kerr**, Andy, *Lab., East Kilbride*, Maj. 5,281
***Lamont**, Johann, *Lab. Co-op, Glasgow Pollok*, Maj. 3,341
Leckie, Carolyn, *SSP, Central Scotland region*
***Livingstone**, Marilyn, *Lab., Kirkcaldy*, Maj. 4,824
***Lochhead**, Richard, *SNP, North East Scotland region*
***Lyon**, George, *LD, Argyll and Bute*, Maj. 4,196
***MacAskill**, Kenny, *SNP, Lothians region*
***Macdonald**, Lewis, *Lab., Aberdeen Central*, Maj. 1,242
***MacDonald**, Margo, *Ind., Lothians region*
***Macintosh**, Kenneth, *Lab., Eastwood*, Maj. 3,702
***Maclean**, Kate, *Lab., Dundee West*, Maj. 1,066
***Macmillan**, Maureen, *Lab., Highlands and Islands region*
Martin, Campbell, *SNP, West of Scotland region*
***Martin**, Paul, *Lab., Glasgow Springburn*, Maj. 8,007
***Marwick**, Tricia, *SNP, Mid Scotland and Fife region*
Mather, Jim, *SNP, Highlands and Islands region*
***Matheson**, Michael, *SNP, Central Scotland region*
Maxwell, Stewart, *SNP, West of Scotland*
May, Christine, *Lab. Co-op, Fife Central*, Maj. 2,762
***McAveety**, Frank, *Lab., Glasgow Shettleston*, Maj. 6,347

***McCabe**, Tom, *Lab., Hamilton South,* Maj. 4,824
***McConnell**, Jack, *Lab., Motherwell and Wishaw,* Maj. 9,259
McFee, Bruce, *SNP, West of Scotland region*
***McGrigor**, Jamie, *C., Highlands and Islands region*
***McLetchie**, David, *C., Edinburgh Pentlands,* Maj. 2,111
***McMahon**, Michael, *Lab., Hamilton North and Bellshill,* Maj. 7,905
***McNeil**, Duncan, *Lab., Greenock and Inverclyde,* Maj. 3,009
***McNeill**, Pauline, *Lab., Glasgow Kelvin,* Maj. 3,289
***McNulty**, Des, *Lab., Clydebank and Milngavie,* Maj. 4,534
Milne, Nanette, *C., North East Scotland region*
Mitchell, Margaret, *C., Central Scotland region*
***Monteith**, Brian, *C., Mid Scotland and Fife region*
***Morgan**, Alasdair, *SNP, South of Scotland region*
***Morrison**, Alasdair, *Lab., Western Isles,* Maj. 720
***Muldoon**, Bristow, *Lab., Livingston,* Maj. 3,670
***Mulligan**, Mary, *Lab., Linlithgow,* Maj. 1,970
***Mundell**, David, *C., South of Scotland region*
Munro, John F., *LD, Ross, Skye and Inverness West,* Maj. 6,848
***Murray**, Dr Elaine, *Lab., Dumfries,* Maj. 1,096
***Neil**, Alex, *SNP, Central Scotland region*
***Oldfather**, Irene, *Lab., Cunninghame South,* Maj. 6,076
***Peacock**, Peter, *Lab., Highlands and Islands region*
***Peattie**, Cathy, *Lab., Falkirk East,* Maj. 6,659
Pringle, Mike, *LD, Edinburgh South,* Maj. 158
Purvis, Jeremy, *LD, Tweeddale, Ettrick and Lauderdale,* Maj. 538
***Radcliffe**, Nora, *LD, Gordon,* Maj. 4,071
***Raffan**, Keith, *LD, Mid Scotland and Fife region*
***Reid**, George, *SNP, Ochil,* Maj. 296
***Robison**, Shona, *SNP, Dundee East,* Maj. 90
***Robson**, Euan, *LD, Roxburgh and Berwickshire,* Maj. 2,490
***Rumbles**, Mike, *LD, Aberdeenshire West Kincardine,* Maj. 5,399
Ruskell, Mark, *Green, Mid Scotland and Fife region*
***Scanlon**, Mary, *C., Highlands and Islands region*
Scott, Eleanor, *Green, Highlands and Islands region*
***Scott**, John, *C., Ayr,* Maj. 1,890
***Scott**, Tavish, *LD, Shetland,* Maj. 2,260
***Sheridan**, Tommy, *SSP, Glasgow region*
***Smith**, Elaine, *Lab., Coatbridge and Chryston,* Maj. 8,571
***Smith**, Iain, *LD, Fife North East,* Maj. 5,055
***Smith**, Margaret, *LD, Edinburgh West,* Maj. 5,914
***Stephen**, Nicol, *LD, Aberdeen South,* Maj. 8,016
***Stevenson**, Stewart, *SNP, Banff and Buchan,* Maj. 8,364
***Stone**, Jamie, *LD, Caithness, Sutherland and Easter Ross,* Maj. 2,092
***Sturgeon**, Nicola, *SNP, Glasgow region*
Swinburne, John, *SSCUP, Central Scotland region*
***Swinney**, John, *SNP, North Tayside,* Maj. 4,503
***Tosh**, Murray, *C., West of Scotland region*
Turner, Dr Jean, *Ind., Strathkelvin and Bearsden,* Maj. 38
***Wallace**, Jim, *LD, Orkney,* Maj. 1,755
***Watson**, Mike (Lord Watson of Invergowrie), *Lab., Glasgow Cathcart,* Maj. 5,112
***Welsh**, Andrew, *SNP, Angus,* Maj. 6,687
***White**, Sandra, *SNP, Glasgow region*
***Whitefield**, Karen, *Lab., Airdrie and Shotts,* Maj. 8,977
***Wilson**, Allan, *Lab., Cunninghame North,* Maj. 3,387
*Sitting MSP

STATE OF THE PARTIES *as at August 2004†*

	Constituency MSPs	*Regional MSPs*	*Total*
Scottish Labour Party	46	4	50
Scottish National Party	9‡	18	27‡
Scottish Conservative and Unionist Party	3	15	18
Scottish Liberal Democrats	13	4	17
Scottish Green Party	0	7	7
Scottish Socialist Party	0	6	6
Scottish Senior Citizens' Unity Party	0	1	1
Independent†	2	1	3
Total	73	56	129

† Independents are: Dennis Canavan, Margo MacDonald and Dr Jean Turner
‡ The Presiding Officer was elected as a constituency member for the SNP but has no party allegiance while in post
The Presiding Officer, George Reid, MSP
Deputy Presiding Officers, Trish Godman, MSP *(Lab.)*; Murray Tosh, MSP *(C.)*

SCOTTISH PARLIAMENT ELECTION RESULTS

1 May 2003

ABERDEEN CENTRAL
(Scotland North East Region)
E. 49,477 *T.* 20,964 (42.37%)

Lewis Macdonald *(Lab.)*	6,835
Richard Lochhead *(SNP)*	5,593
Eleanor Anderson *(LD)*	4,744
Alan Butler *(C.)*	2,616
Andy Cumbers, *(SSP)*	1,176

Lab. Maj. 1,242 (5.92%)
2.13% swing Lab. to SNP

ABERDEEN NORTH
(Scotland North East Region)
E. 52,898 *T.* 25,027 (47.31%)

Brian Adam *(SNP)*	8,381
Elaine Thomson *(Lab.)*	7,924
John Reynolds *(LD)*	5,767
Jim Gifford *(C.)*	2,311
Katrine Trolle *(SSP)*	644

SNP Maj. 457 (1.83%)
1.63% swing Lab. to SNP

ABERDEEN SOUTH
(Scotland North East Region)
E. 58,204 *T.* 30,124 (51.76%)

Nicol Stephen *(LD)*	13,821
Richard Baker *(Lab.)*	5,805
Ian Duncan *(C.)*	5,230
Maureen Watt *(SNP)*	4,315
Keith Farnsworth *(SSP)*	953

LD Maj. 8,016 (26.61%)
10.77% swing Lab. to LD

ABERDEENSHIRE WEST AND KINCARDINE
(Scotland North East Region)
E. 62,542 *T.* 31,636 (50.58%)

Mike Rumbles *(LD)*	14,553
David Davidson *(C.)*	9,154
Ian Angus *(SNP)*	4,489
Kevin Hutchens *(Lab.)*	2,727
Alan Manley *(SSP)*	713

LD Maj. 5,399 (17.07%)
5.33% swing C. to LD

AIRDRIE AND SHOTTS
(Scotland Central Region)
E. 56,680 *T.* 25,086 (44.26%)

Karen Whitefield *(Lab.)*	14,209
Gil Paterson *(SNP)*	5,232
Alan Melville *(C.)*	2,203
Fraser Coats *(SSP)*	2,096
Kevin Lang *(LD)*	1,346

Lab. Maj. 8,977 (35.78%)
4.37% swing SNP to Lab.

ANGUS
(Scotland North East Region)
E. 60,608 *T.* 29,789 (49.15%)

Andrew Welsh *(SNP)*	13,251
Alex Johnstone *(C.)*	6,564
John Denning *(Lab.)*	4,871
Dick Speirs *(LD)*	3,802
Bruce Wallace *(SSP)*	1,301

SNP Maj. 6,687 (22.45%)
1.66% swing SNP to C.

ARGYLL AND BUTE
(Highlands and Islands Region)
E. 48,330 *T.* 27,948 (57.83%)

George Lyon *(LD)*	9,817
David Petrie *(C.)*	5,621
Jim Mather *(SNP)*	5,485
Hugh Raven *(Lab.)*	5,107
Des Divers *(SSP)*	1,667
David Walker *(SPA)*	251

LD Maj. 4,196 (15.01%)
1.68% swing LD to C.

AYR
(Scotland South Region)
E. 55,523 *T.* 31,591 (56.90%)

John Scott *(C.)*	12,865
Rita Miller *(Lab.)*	10,975
James Dornan *(SNP)*	4,334
Stuart Ritchie *(LD)*	1,769
James Stewart *(SSP)*	1,648

C. Maj. 1,890 (5.98%)
3.02% swing Lab. to C.

BANFF AND BUCHAN
(Scotland North East Region)
E. 55,358 *T.* 26,149 (47.24%)

Stewart Stevenson *(SNP)*	13,827
Stewart Whyte *(C.)*	5,463
Ian Brotchie *(Lab.)*	2,885
Debra Storr *(LD)*	2,227
Alan Buchan *(SPA)*	907
Alice Rowan *(SSP)*	840

SNP Maj. 8,364 (31.99%)
1.80% swing SNP to C.

CAITHNESS, SUTHERLAND AND EASTER ROSS
(Highlands and Islands Region)
E. 40,462 *T.* 21,127 (52.21%)

Jamie Stone *(LD)*	7,742
Deirdre Steven *(Lab.)*	5,650
Rob Gibson *(SNP)*	3,692
Alan McLeod *(C.)*	2,262
Gordon Campbell *(Ind.)*	953
Frank Ward *(SSP)*	828

LD Maj. 2,092 (9.90%)
3.48% swing LD to Lab.

CARRICK, CUMNOCK AND DOON VALLEY
(Scotland South Region)
E. 65,102 *T.* 34,366 (52.79%)

Cathy Jamieson *(Lab. Co-op)*	16,484
Phil Gallie *(C.)*	9,030
Adam Ingram *(SNP)*	5,822
Murray Steele *(SSP)*	1,715
Caron Howden *(LD)*	1,315

Lab. Co-op Maj. 7,454 (21.69%)
3.20% swing Lab. Co-op to C.

CLYDEBANK AND MILNGAVIE
(Scotland West Region)
E. 51,327 *T.* 26,514 (51.66%)

Des McNulty *(Lab.)*	10,585
Jim Yuill *(SNP)*	6,051
Rod Ackland *(LD)*	3,224
Mary Leishman *(C.)*	2,885
Dawn Brennan *(SSP)*	1,902
Danny McCafferty *(Ind.)*	1,867

Lab. Maj. 4,534 (17.10%)
1.49% swing SNP to Lab.

CLYDESDALE
(Scotland South Region)
E. 63,675 *T.* 32,442 (50.95%)

Karen Gillon *(Lab.)*	14,800
John Brady *(SNP)*	8,129
Alastair Campbell *(C.)*	5,174
Fraser Grieve *(LD)*	2,338
Owen Meharry *(SSP)*	1,422
David Morrison *(SPA)*	579

Lab. Maj. 6,671 (20.56%)
5.30% swing SNP to Lab.

COATBRIDGE AND CHRYSTON
(Scotland Central Region)
E. 51,521 *T.* 23,862 (46.32%)

Elaine Smith *(Lab.)*	13,422
James Gribben *(SNP)*	4,851
Donald Reece *(C.)*	2,041
Gordon Martin *(SSP)*	1,911
Doreen Nisbet *(LD)*	1,637

Lab. Maj. 8,571 (35.92%)
0.73% swing SNP to Lab.

CUMBERNAULD AND KILSYTH
(Scotland Central Region)
E. 48,667 *T.* 24,404 (50.14%)

Cathie Craigie *(Lab.)*	10,146
Andrew Wilson *(SNP)*	9,626
Kenny McEwan *(SSP)*	1,823
Hugh O'Donnell *(LD)*	1,264
Margaret McCulloch *(C.)*	978
Christopher Donohue *(Ind.)*	567

Lab. Maj. 520 (2.13%)
5.89% swing Lab. to SNP

CUNNINGHAME NORTH
(Scotland West Region)
E. 55,319 *T.* 28,631 (51.76%)

Allan Wilson *(Lab.)*	11,142
Campbell Martin *(SNP)*	7,755
Peter Ramsay *(C.)*	5,542
John Boyd *(LD)*	2,333
Sean Scott *(SSP)*	1,859

Lab. Maj. 3,387 (11.83%)
1.25% swing Lab. to SNP

CUNNINGHAME SOUTH
(Scotland South Region)
E. 49,877 *T.* 22,772 (45.66%)

Irene Oldfather *(Lab.)*	11,165
Michael Russell *(SNP)*	5,089
Rosemary Byrne *(SSP)*	2,677
Andrew Brocklehurst *(C.)*	2,336
Iain Dale *(LD)*	1,505

Lab. Maj. 6,076 (26.68%)
1.78% swing SNP to Lab.

DUMBARTON
(Scotland West Region)
E. 55,575 *T.* 28,823 (51.86%)

Jackie Baillie *(Lab.)*	12,154
Iain Docherty *(SNP)*	5,542
Eric Thompson *(LD)*	4,455
Murray Tosh *(C.)*	4,178
Les Robertson *(SSP)*	2,494

Lab. Maj. 6,612 (22.94%)
4.61% swing SNP to Lab.

DUMFRIES
(Scotland South Region)
E. 61,517 *T.* 32,110 (52.20%)

Elaine Murray *(Lab.)*	12,834
David Mundell *(C.)*	11,738
Andrew Wood *(SNP)*	3,931
Clare Hamblen *(LD)*	2,394
John Dennis *(SSP)*	1,213

Lab. Maj. 1,096 (3.41%)
3.05% swing Lab. to C.

DUNDEE EAST
(Scotland North East Region)
E. 53,876 *T.* 26,348 (48.90%)

Shona Robison *(SNP)*	10,428
John McAllion *(Lab.)*	10,338
Edward Prince *(C.)*	3,133
Clive Sneddon *(LD)*	1,584
James Gourlay *(Ind.)*	865

SNP Maj. 90 (0.34%)
4.68% swing Lab. to SNP

DUNDEE WEST
(Scotland North East Region)
E. 51,387 *T.* 25,003 (48.66%)

Kate McLean *(Lab.)*	8,234
Irene McGugan *(SNP)*	7,168
Ian Borthwick *(Ind.)*	4,715
Shona Ferrier *(LD)*	1,878
Jim McFarland *(SSP)*	1,501
Victoria Roberts *(C.)*	1,376
Morag MacLachlan *(SPA)*	131

Lab. Maj. 1,066 (4.26%)
1.92% swing SNP to Lab.

DUNFERMLINE EAST
(Scotland Mid and Fife Region)
E. 51,220 *T.* 23,154 (45.20%)

Helen Eadie *(Lab. Co-op)*	11,552
Janet Law *(SNP)*	4,262
Stuart Randall *(C.)*	2,485
Brian Stewart *(Local Hospital)*	1,890
Linda Graham *(SSP)*	1,537
Rodger Spillane *(LD)*	1,428

Lab. Co-op Maj. 7,290 (31.48%)
1.08% swing SNP to Lab. Co-op

DUNFERMLINE WEST
(Scotland Mid and Fife Region)
E. 53,915 *T.* 25,240 (46.81%)

Scott Barrie *(Lab.)*	8,664
David Wishart *(Local Hospital)*	4,584
Brian Goodall *(SNP)*	4,392
Jim Tolson *(LD)*	3,636
Jim Mackie *(C.)*	1,868
Andy Jackson *(SSP)*	923
Alastair Harper *(Ind.)*	714
Damien Quigg *(Ind. Q)*	459

Lab. Maj. 4,080 (16.16%)

EAST KILBRIDE
(Scotland Central Region)
E. 65,472 *T.* 34,087 (52.06%)

Andy Kerr *(Lab.)*	13,825
Linda Fabiani *(SNP)*	8,544
Grace Campbell *(C.)*	3,785
Carolyn Leckie *(SSP)*	2,736
Colin McCartney *(Ind.)*	2,597
Alex Mackie *(LD)*	2,181
John Houston *(Ind. Houston)*	419

Lab. Maj. 5,281 (15.49%)
0.08% swing Lab. to SNP

EAST LOTHIAN
(Scotland South Region)
E. 59,227 *T.* 31,204 (52.69%)

John Home Robertson *(Lab.)*	13,683
Judy Hayman *(LD)*	5,508
Stewart Thomson *(C.)*	5,459
Tom Roberts *(SNP)*	5,174
Hugh Kerr *(SSP)*	1,380

Lab. Maj. 8,175 (26.20%)
6.95% swing Lab. to LD

EASTWOOD
(Scotland West Region)
E. 67,051 *T.* 38,889 (58.00%)

Ken Macintosh *(Lab.)*	13,946
Jackson Carlaw *(C.)*	10,244
Allan Steele *(LD)*	5,056
Stewart Maxwell *(SNP)*	4,736
Margaret Hinds *(Local Health)*	3,163
Steve Oram *(SSP)*	1,504
Martyn Greene *(SPA)*	240

Lab. Maj. 3,702 (9.52%)
2.42% swing C. to Lab.

EDINBURGH CENTRAL
(Lothians Region)
E. 60,824 *T.* 28,014 (46.06%)

Sarah Boyack *(Lab.)*	9,066
Andy Myles *(LD)*	6,400
Kevin Pringle *(SNP)*	4,965
Peter Finnie *(C.)*	4,802
Catriona Grant *(SSP)*	2,552
James O'Neill *(SPA)*	229

Lab. Maj. 2,666 (9.52%)
5.98% swing Lab. to LD

EDINBURGH EAST AND MUSSELBURGH
(Lothians Region)
E. 57,704 *T.* 29,044 (50.33%)

Susan Deacon *(Lab.)*	12,655
Kenny MacAskill *(SNP)*	6,497
John Smart *(C.)*	3,863
Gary Peacock *(LD)*	3,582
Derek Durkin *(SSP)*	2,447

Lab. Maj. 6,158 (21.20%)
1.53% swing SNP to Lab.

EDINBURGH NORTH AND LEITH
(Lothians Region)
E. 60,501 *T.* 28,734 (47.49%)

Malcolm Chisholm *(Lab.)*	10,979
Anne Dana *(SNP)*	5,565
Ian Mowat *(C.)*	4,821
Sebastian Tombs *(LD)*	4,785
Bill Scott *(SSP)*	2,584

Lab. Maj. 5,414 (18.84%)
1.13% swing Lab. to SNP

EDINBURGH PENTLANDS
(Lothians Region)
E. 58,534 *T.* 33,382 (57.03%)

David McLetchie *(C.)*	12,420
Iain Gray *(Lab.)*	10,309
Ian McKee *(SNP)*	5,620
Simon Clark *(LD)*	3,943
Frank O'Donnell *(SSP)*	1,090

C. Maj. 2,111 (6.32%)
6.80% swing Lab. to C.

EDINBURGH SOUTH
(Lothians Region)
E. 60,366 *T.* 31,196 (51.68%)

Mike Pringle *(LD)*	10,005
Angus Mackay *(Lab.)*	9,847
Gordon Buchan *(C.)*	5,180
Alex Orr *(SNP)*	4,396
Shirley Gibb *(SSP)*	1,768

LD Maj. 158 (0.51%)
7.61% swing Lab. to LD

EDINBURGH WEST
(Lothians Region)
E. 60,136 *T.* 33,301 (55.38%)

Margaret Smith *(LD)*	14,434
James Douglas-Hamilton *(C.)*	8,520
Carol Fox *(Lab.)*	5,046
Alyn Smith *(SNP)*	4,133
Pat Smith *(SSP)*	993
Bruce Skivington *(SPA)*	175

LD Maj. 5,914 (17.76%)
3.37% swing C. to LD

FALKIRK EAST
(Scotland Central Region)
E. 56,175 *T.* 27,559 (49.06%)

Cathy Peattie *(Lab.)*	14,235
Keith Brown *(SNP)*	7,576
Thomas Calvert *(C.)*	2,720
Karen Utting *(LD)*	1,651
Mhairi McAlpine *(SSP)*	1,377

Lab. Maj. 6,659 (24.16%)
6.20% swing SNP to Lab.

FALKIRK WEST
(Scotland Central Region)
E. 52,122 *T.* 26,400 (50.65%)

Dennis Canavan *(Falkirk W)*	14,703
Michael Matheson *(SNP)*	4,703
Lee Whitehill *(Lab.)*	4,589
Iain Mitchell *(C.)*	1,657
Jacqueline Kelly *(LD)*	748

Falkirk W Maj. 10,000 (37.88%)
0.34% swing SNP to Falkirk W

FIFE CENTRAL
(Scotland Mid and Fife Region)
E. 57,633 *T.* 25,597 (44.41%)

Christine May *(Lab. Co-op)*	10,591
Tricia Marwick *(SNP)*	7,829
Andrew Rodger *(Ind.)*	2,258
James North *(C.)*	1,803
Elizabeth Riches *(LD)*	1,725
Morag Balfour *(SSP)*	1,391

Lab. Co-op Maj. 2,762 (10.79%)
7.81% swing Lab. Co-op to SNP

FIFE NORTH EAST
(Scotland Mid and Fife Region)
E. 58,695 *T.* 29,282 (49.89%)

Iain Smith *(LD)*	13,479
Ted Brocklebank *(C.)*	8,424
Capre Ross-Williams *(SNP)*	3,660
Gregor Poynton *(Lab.)*	2,353
Carlo Morelli *(SSP)*	1,366

LD Maj. 5,055 (17.26%)
1.59% swing C. to LD

GALLOWAY AND UPPER NITHSDALE
(Scotland South Region)
E. 51,651 *T.* 29,635 (57.38%)

Alex Fergusson *(C.)*	11,332
Alasdair Morgan *(SNP)*	11,233
Norma Hart *(Lab.)*	4,299
Neil Wallace *(LD)*	1,847
Joy Cherkaoui *(SSP)*	709
Graham Brockhouse *(SPA)*	215

C. Maj. 99 (0.33%)
4.70% swing SNP to C.

GLASGOW ANNIESLAND
(Glasgow Region)
E. 50,795 *T.* 22,165 (43.64%)

Bill Butler *(Lab. Co-op)*	10,141
Bill Kidd *(SNP)*	3,888
Bill Aitken *(C.)*	3,186
Charlie McCarthy *(SSP)*	2,620
Iain Brown *(LD)*	2,330

Lab. Co-op Maj. 6,253 (28.21%)
5.19% swing Lab. Co-op to SNP

GLASGOW BAILLIESTON
(Glasgow Region)
E. 46,346 *T.* 18,270 (39.42%)

Margaret Curran *(Lab.)*	9,657
Lachlan McNeill *(SNP)*	3,479
Jim McVicar *(SSP)*	2,461
Janette McAlpine *(C.)*	1,472
David Jackson *(LD)*	1,201

Lab. Maj. 6,178 (33.81%)
10.43% swing SNP to Lab.

GLASGOW CATHCART
(Glasgow Region)
E. 49,017 *T.* 22,307 (45.51%)

Mike Watson *(Lab.)*	8,742
David Ritchie *(SNP)*	3,630
Richard Cook *(C.)*	2,888
Malcolm Wilson *(SSP)*	2,819
Pat Lally *(Local Health)*	2,419
Tom Henery *(LD)*	1,741
Robert Wilson *(Parent Ex)*	68

Lab. Maj. 5,112 (22.92%)
1.50% swing SNP to Lab.

GLASGOW GOVAN
(Glasgow Region)
E. 48,635 *T.* 21,136 (43.46%)

Gordon Jackson *(Lab.)*	7,834
Nicola Sturgeon *(SNP)*	6,599
Jimmy Scott *(SSP)*	2,369
Faisal Butt *(C.)*	1,878
Paul Graham *(LD)*	1,807
Razaq Dean *(Ind.)*	226
John Foster *(CPPDS)*	215
Asif Nasir *(SPA)*	208

Lab. Maj. 1,235 (5.84%)
0.41% swing Lab. to SNP

GLASGOW KELVIN
(Glasgow Region)
E. 56,038 *T.* 22,080 (39.40%)

Pauline McNeill *(Lab.)*	7,880
Sandra White *(SNP)*	4,591
Douglas Herbison *(LD)*	3,334
Andy Harvey *(SSP)*	3,159
Gawain Towler *(C.)*	1,816
Alistair McConnachie *(Ind. Green)*	1,300

Lab. Maj. 3,289 (14.90%)
0.32% swing Lab. to SNP

GLASGOW MARYHILL
(Glasgow Region)
E. 49,119 *T.* 18,243 (37.14%)

Patricia Ferguson *(Lab.)*	8,997
Bill Wilson *(SNP)*	3,629
Donnie Nicolson *(SSP)*	2,945
Arthur Sanderson *(LD)*	1,785
Robert Erskine *(C.)*	887

Lab. Maj. 5,368 (29.42%)
5.31% swing SNP to Lab.

GLASGOW POLLOK
(Glasgow Region)
E. 47,134 *T.* 21,538 (45.70%)

Johann Lamont *(Lab. Co-op)*	9,357
Tommy Sheridan *(SSP)*	6,016
Kenneth Gibson *(SNP)*	4,118
Ashraf Anjum *(C.)*	1,012
Isabel Nelson *(LD)*	962
Robert Ray *(Parent Ex)*	73

Lab. Co-op Maj. 3,341 (15.51%)
3.35% swing Lab. Co-op to SSP

GLASGOW RUTHERGLEN
(Glasgow Region)
E. 49,512 *T.* 23,554 (47.57%)

Janis Hughes *(Lab.)*	10,794
Robert Brown *(LD)*	4,491
Anne McLaughlin *(SNP)*	3,511
Gavin Brown *(C.)*	2,499
Bill Bonnar *(SSP)*	2,259

Lab. Maj. 6,303 (26.76%)
0.21% swing LD to Lab.

GLASGOW SHETTLESTON
(Glasgow Region)
E. 46,730 *T.* 16,547 (35.41%)

Francis McAveety *(Lab. Co-op)*	9,365
Jim Byrne *(SNP)*	3,018
Rosie Kane *(SSP)*	2,403
Dorothy Luckhurst *(C.)*	982
Lewis Hutton *(LD)*	779

Lab. Co-op Maj. 6,347 (38.36%)
5.87% swing SNP to Lab. Co-op

GLASGOW SPRINGBURN
(Glasgow Region)
E. 49,551 *T.* 18,573 (37.48%)

Paul Martin *(Lab.)*	10,963
Frank Rankin *(SNP)*	2,956
Margaret Bean *(SSP)*	2,653
Alan Rodger *(C.)*	1,233
Charles Dundas *(LD)*	768

Lab. Maj. 8,007 (43.11%)
5.36% swing SNP to Lab.

GORDON
(Scotland North East Region)
E. 60,686 *T.* 28,798 (47.45%)

Nora Radcliffe *(LD)*	10,963
Nanette Milne *(C.)*	6,892
Alasdair Allan *(SNP)*	6,501
Ellis Thorpe *(Lab.)*	2,973
John Sangster *(SSP)*	780
Steven Mathers *(Ind.)*	689

LD Maj. 4,071 (14.14%)
1.48% swing LD to C.

GREENOCK AND INVERCLYDE
(Scotland West Region)
E. 46,045 *T.* 23,781 (51.65%)

Duncan McNeil *(Lab.)*	9,674
Ross Finnie *(LD)*	6,665
Tom Chalmers *(SNP)*	3,532
Tricia McCafferty *(SSP)*	2,338
Charles Dunlop *(C.)*	1,572

Lab. Maj. 3,009 (12.65%)
1.20% swing Lab. to LD

HAMILTON NORTH AND BELLSHILL
(Scotland Central Region)
E. 51,965 *T.* 24,195 (46.56%)

Michael McMahon *(Lab.)*	12,812
Alex Neil *(SNP)*	4,907
Charles Ferguson *(C.)*	2,625
Shareen Blackhall *(SSP)*	1,932
Siobhan Mathers *(LD)*	1,477
Gordon McIntosh *(SPA)*	442

Lab. Maj. 7,905 (32.67%)
7.36% swing SNP to Lab.

HAMILTON SOUTH
(Scotland Central Region)
E. 45,749 *T.* 20,518 (44.85%)

Tom McCabe *(Lab.)*	9,546
John Wilson *(SNP)*	4,722
Margaret Mitchell *(C.)*	2,601
Willie O'Neil *(SSP)*	1,893
John Oswald *(LD)*	1,756

Lab. Maj. 4,824 (23.51%)
2.09% swing Lab. to SNP

INVERNESS EAST, NAIRN AND LOCHABER
(Highlands and Islands Region)
E. 66,694 *T.* 34,795 (52.17%)

Fergus Ewing *(SNP)*	10,764
Rhoda Grant *(Lab.)*	9,718
Mary Scanlon *(C.)*	6,205
Patsy Kenton *(LD)*	5,622
Steve Arnott *(SSP)*	1,661
Thomas Lamont *(Ind.)*	825

SNP Maj. 1,046 (3.01%)
0.98% swing Lab. to SNP

KILMARNOCK AND LOUDOUN
(Scotland Central Region)
E. 61,055 *T.* 31,520 (51.63%)

Margaret Jamieson *(Lab.)*	12,633
Danny Coffey *(SNP)*	11,423
Robin Traquair *(C.)*	3,295
Ian Gibson *(LD)*	1,571
Colin Rutherford *(SSP)*	1,421
May Anderson *(Ind. Anderson)*	404
Matthew Donnelly *(Ind.)*	402
Lyndsay McIntosh *(SPA)*	371

Lab. Maj. 1,210 (3.84%)
1.59% swing Lab. to SNP

KIRKCALDY
(Scotland Mid and Fife Region)
E. 49,653 *T.* 21,939 (44.18%)

Marilyn Livingstone *(Lab. Co-op)*	10,235
Colin Welsh *(SNP)*	5,411
Alex Cole-Hamilton *(LD)*	2,417
Mike Scott-Hayward *(C.)*	2,332
Rudi Vogels *(SSP)*	1,544

Lab. Co-op Maj. 4,824 (21.99%)
3.10% swing SNP to Lab. Co-op

LINLITHGOW
(Lothians Region)
E. 54,113 *T.* 27,645 (51.09%)

Mary Mulligan *(Lab.)*	11,548
Fiona Hyslop *(SNP)*	9,578
Gordon Lindhurst *(C.)*	3,059
Martin Oliver *(LD)*	2,093
Steve Nimmo *(SSP)*	1,367

Lab. Maj. 1,970 (7.13%)
0.77% swing Lab. to SNP

LIVINGSTON
(Lothians Region)
E. 65,421 *T.* 30,557 (46.71%)

Bristow Muldoon *(Lab.)*	13,327
Peter Johnston *(SNP)*	9,657
Lindsay Paterson *(C.)*	2,848
Paul McGreal *(LD)*	2,714
Robert Richard *(SSP)*	1,640
Stephen Milburn *(SPA)*	371

Lab. Maj. 3,670 (12.01%)
0.67% swing SNP to Lab.

MIDLOTHIAN
(Lothians Region)
E. 48,319 *T.* 23,556 (48.75%)

Rhona Brankin *(Lab. Co-op)*	11,139
Graham Sutherland *(SNP)*	5,597
Jacqui Bell *(LD)*	2,700
Rosemary MacArthur *(C.)*	2,557
Bob Goupillot *(SSP)*	1,563

Lab. Co-op Maj. 5,542 (23.53%)
2.48% swing SNP to Lab. Co-op

MORAY
(Highlands and Islands Region)
E. 58,242 *T.* 26,981 (46.33%)

Margaret Ewing *(SNP)*	11,384
Tim Wood *(C.)*	6,072
Peter Peacock *(Lab.)*	5,157
Linda Gorn *(LD)*	3,283
Norma Anderson *(SSP)*	1,085

SNP Maj. 5,312 (19.69%)
3.24% swing C. to SNP

MOTHERWELL AND WISHAW
(Scotland Central Region)
E. 51,785 *T.* 25,388 (49.03%)

Jack McConnell *(Lab.)*	13,739
Lloyd Quinan *(SNP)*	4,480
Mark Nolan *(C.)*	2,542
John Milligan *(SSP)*	1,961
John Swinburne *(SSCUP)*	1,597
Keith Legg *(LD)*	1,069

Lab. Maj. 9,259 (36.47%)
9.92% swing SNP to Lab.

OCHIL
(Scotland Mid and Fife Region)
E. 55,596 *T.* 30,416 (54.71%)

George Reid *(SNP)*	11,659
Richard Simpson *(Lab.)*	11,363
Malcolm Parkin *(C.)*	2,946
Catherine Whittingham *(LD)*	2,536
Felicity Garvie *(SSP)*	1,102
Flash Gordon Approaching *(Loony)*	432
William Whyte *(ND)*	378

SNP Maj. 296 (0.97%)
2.25% swing Lab. to SNP

ORKNEY
(Highlands and Islands Region)
E. 15,487 *T.* 8,004 (51.68%)

Jim Wallace *(LD)*	3,659
Christopher Zawadski *(C.)*	1,904
John Mowat *(SNP)*	1,056
John Aberdein *(SSP)*	914
Richard Meade *(Lab.)*	471

LD Maj. 1,755 (21.93%)
14.93% swing LD to C.

PAISLEY NORTH
(Scotland West Region)
E. 44,999 *T.* 22,206 (49.35%)

Wendy Alexander *(Lab.)*	10,631
George Adam *(SNP)*	6,321
Allison Cook *(C.)*	1,871
Brian O'Malley *(LD)*	1,705
Sean Hurl *(SSP)*	1,678

Lab. Maj. 4,310 (19.41%)
1.39% swing SNP to Lab.

PAISLEY SOUTH
(Scotland West Region)
E. 49,818 *T.* 24,984 (50.15%)

Hugh Henry *(Lab.)*	10,190
Bill Martin *(SNP)*	7,737
Eileen McCartin *(LD)*	3,517
Mark Jones *(C.)*	1,775
Frances Curran *(SSP)*	1,765

Lab. Maj. 2,453 (9.82%)
2.42% swing Lab. to SNP

PERTH
(Scotland and Mid Fife Region)
E. 61,957 *T.* 31,614 (51.03%)

Roseanna Cunningham *(SNP)*	10,717
Alexander Stewart *(C.)*	9,990
Robert Ball *(Lab.)*	5,629
Gordon Campbell *(LD)*	3,530
Philip Stott *(SSP)*	982
Thomas Burns *(Ind.)*	509
Ken Buchanan *(SPA)*	257

SNP Maj. 727 (2.30%)
1.56% swing SNP to C.

RENFREWSHIRE WEST
(Scotland West Region)
E. 50,963 *T.* 28,302 (55.53%)

Trish Godman *(Lab.)*	9,671
Bruce McFee *(SNP)*	7,179
Annabel Goldie *(C.)*	6,867
Alison King *(LD)*	2,902
Gerry MaCartney *(SSP)*	1,683

Lab. Maj. 2,492 (8.81%)
0.15% swing SNP to Lab.

ROSS, SKYE AND INVERNESS WEST
(Highlands and Islands Region)
E. 55,777 *T.* 28,971 (51.94%)

John Farquhar Munro *(LD)*	12,495
David Thompson *(SNP)*	5,647
Maureen MacMillan *(Lab.)*	5,464
Jamie McGrigor *(C.)*	3,772
Anne McLeod *(SSP)*	1,593

LD Maj. 6,848 (23.64%)
6.66% swing SNP to LD

ROXBURGH AND BERWICKSHIRE
(Scotland South Region)
E. 45,625 *T.* 22,511 (49.34%)

Euan Robson *(LD)*	9,280
Sandy Scott *(C.)*	6,790
Roderick Campbell *(SNP)*	2,816
Sam Held *(Lab.)*	2,802
Graeme McIver *(SSP)*	823

LD Maj. 2,490 (11.06%)
0.90% swing LD to C.

SHETLAND
(Highlands and Islands Region)
E. 16,677 *T.* 8,645 (51.84%)

Tavish Scott *(LD)*	3,989
Willie Ross *(SNP)*	1,729
John Firth *(C.)*	1,281
Peter Hamilton *(Lab.)*	880
Peter Andrews *(SSP)*	766

LD Maj. 2,260 (26.14%)
7.00% swing LD to SNP

STIRLING
(Scotland and Mid Fife Region)
E. 52,087 *T.* 29,647 (56.92%)

Sylvia Jackson *(Lab.)*	10,661
Brian Monteith *(C.)*	7,781
Bruce Crawford *(SNP)*	5,645
Kenyon Wright *(LD)*	3,432
Margaret Stewart *(SSP)*	1,486
Keith Harding *(SPA)*	642

Lab. Maj. 2,880 (9.71%)
1.25% swing Lab. to C.

STRATHKELVIN AND BEARSDEN
(Scotland West Region)
E. 61,905 *T.* 35,736 (57.73%)

Jean Turner *(Ind.)*	10,988
Brian Fitzpatrick *(Lab.)*	10,950
Jo Swinson *(LD)*	4,950
Fiona McLeod *(SNP)*	4,846
Rory O'Brien *(C.)*	4,002

Ind. Maj. 38 (0.11%)

TAYSIDE NORTH
(Scotland Mid and Fife Region)
E. 62,697 *T.* 33,343 (53.18%)

John Swinney *(SNP)*	14,969
Murdo Fraser *(C.)*	10,466
Gordon MacRae *(Lab.)*	3,527
Bob Forrest *(LD)*	3,206
Rosie Adams *(SSP)*	941
George Ashe *(SPA)*	234

SNP Maj. 4,503 (13.51%)
1.24% swing C. to SNP

TWEEDDALE, ETTRICK AND LAUDERDALE
(Scotland South Region)
E. 50,912 *T.* 26,700 (52.44%)

Jeremy Purvis *(LD)*	7,197
Christine Grahame *(SNP)*	6,659
Catherine Maxwell Stuart *(Lab.)*	5,757
Derek Brownlee *(C.)*	5,686
Norman Lockhart *(SSP)*	1,055
Alex Black *(SPA)*	346

LD Maj. 538 (2.01%)
5.63% swing LD to SNP

WESTERN ISLES
(Highlands and Islands Region)
E. 21,205 *T.* 12,387 (58.42%)

Alasdair Morrison *(Lab.)*	5,825
Alasdair Nicholson *(SNP)*	5,105
Frank Warren *(C.)*	612
Conor Snowden *(LD)*	498
Joanne Telfer *(SSP)*	347

Lab. Maj. 720 (5.81%)
4.59% swing Lab. to SNP

REGIONS

GLASGOW
E. 492,877 *T.* 39.42%

Lab.	77,040	(39.65%)
SNP	34,894	(17.96%)
SSP	31,116	(16.02%)
C.	15,299	(7.87%)
LD	14,839	(7.64%)
Green	14,570	(7.50%)
SSCUP	4,750	(2.44%)
Soc. Lab.	3,091	(1.59%)
ProLife	2,477	(1.27%)
SUP	2,349	(1.21%)
BNP	2,344	(1.21%)
SPA	612	(0.32%)
UK Ind.	552	(0.28%)
CPPDS	345	(0.18%)
Lab. majority	42,146	(21.69%)

1.64% swing *SNP* to *Lab.*

ADDITIONAL MEMBERS

Bill Aitken	*(C.)*
Robert Brown	*(LD)*
Ms Sandra White	*(SNP)*
Ms Nicola Sturgeon	*(SNP)*
Patrick Harvie	*(Green)*
Tommy Sheridan	*(SSP)*
Ms Rosie Kane	*(SSP)*

HIGHLANDS AND ISLANDS
E. 322,874 *T.* 52.22%

SNP	39,497	(23.43%)
Lab.	37,605	(22.30%)
LD	31,655	(18.78%)
C.	26,989	(16.01%)
Green	13,935	(8.27%)
SSP	9,000	(5.34%)
UK Ind.	1,947	(1.15%)
SASSDR	1,822	(1.08%)
CPFRI	1,768	(1.05%)
Soc. Lab.	1,617	(0.96%)
PRSP	1,438	(0.85%)
SPA	793	(0.47%)
Ind.	353	(0.21%)
Rural	177	(0.10%)
SNP majority	1,892	(1.12%)

0.57% swing *SNP* to *Lab.*

ADDITIONAL MEMBERS

Jamie McGrigor	*(C.)*
Mrs Mary Scanlon	*(C.)*
Peter Peacock	*(Lab.)*
Ms Maureen MacMillan	*(Lab.)*
Jim Mather	*(SNP)*
Rob Gibson	*(SNP)*
Ms Eleanor Scott	*(Green)*

LOTHIANS
E. 525,918 *T.* 50.52%

Lab.	65,102	(24.50%)
SNP	43,142	(16.24%)
C.	40,173	(15.12%)
Green	31,908	(12.01%)
LD	29,237	(11.01%)
Ind.	27,144	(10.22%)
SSP	14,448	(5.44%)
PP	5,609	(2.11%)
Lib	2,573	(0.97%)
Soc. Lab.	2,181	(0.82%)
UK Ind.	1,057	(0.40%)
Witchery	964	(0.36%)
SPA	879	(0.33%)
ProLife	608	(0.23%)
Ind. C.	383	(0.14%)
Ind. A.	184	(0.07%)
Ind. Gatensbury	78	(0.03%)
Lab. majority	21,960	(8.27%)

1.89% swing *SNP* to *Lab.*

ADDITIONAL MEMBERS

Lord James Douglas-Hamilton	*(C.)*
Kenny MacAskill	*(SNP)*
Ms Fiona Hyslop	*(SNP)*
Robin Harper	*(Green)*
Mark Ballard	*(Green)*
Ms Margo MacDonald	*(Ind.)*
Colin Fox	*(SSP)*

SCOTLAND CENTRAL
E. 541,191 *T.* 48.61%

Lab.	106,318	(40.41%)
SNP	59,274	(22.53%)
C.	24,121	(9.17%)
SSP	19,016	(7.23%)
SSCUP	17,146	(6.52%)
LD	15,494	(5.89%)
Green	12,248	(4.66%)
Soc. Lab.	3,855	(1.47%)
SUP	2,147	(0.82%)
Ind.	1,265	(0.48%)
SPA	1,192	(0.45%)
UK Ind.	1,009	(0.38%)
Lab. majority	47,044	(17.88%)

3.19% swing *SNP* to *Lab.*

ADDITIONAL MEMBERS

Mrs Margaret Mitchell	*(C.)*
Donald Gorrie	*(LD)*
Alex Neil	*(SNP)*
Michael Matheson	*(SNP)*
Ms Linda Fabiani	*(SNP)*
John Swinburne	*(SSCUP)*
Ms Carolyn Leckie	*(SSP)*

SCOTLAND MID AND FIFE
E. 503,453 *T.* 49.68%

Lab.	63,239	(25.29%)
SNP	57,631	(23.04%)
C.	43,941	(17.57%)
LD	30,112	(12.04%)
Green	17,147	(6.86%)
SSP	11,401	(4.56%)
PP	8,380	(3.35%)
FHC	5,064	(2.02%)
SLH	4,662	(1.86%)
UK Ind.	2,355	(0.94%)
Soc. Lab.	2,273	(0.91%)
SPA	1,191	(0.48%)
Christian	1,064	(0.43%)
Ind. Gray	996	(0.40%)
Ind.	637	(0.25%)
Lab. majority	5,608	(2.24%)

1.22% swing *Lab.* to *SNP*

ADDITIONAL MEMBERS

Murdo Fraser	*(C.)*
Brian Monteith	*(C.)*
Ted Brocklebank	*(C.)*
Keith Raffan	*(LD)*
Bruce Crawford	*(SNP)*
Ms Tricia Marwick	*(SNP)*
Mark Ruskell	*(Green)*

SCOTLAND NORTH EAST
E. 505,036 *T.* 48.25%

SNP	66,463	(27.28%)
Lab.	49,189	(20.19%)
LD	45,831	(18.81%)
C.	42,318	(17.37%)
Green	12,724	(5.22%)
SSP	10,226	(4.20%)
PP	5,584	(2.29%)
Fishing	5,566	(2.28%)
Soc. Lab.	2,431	(1.00%)
UK Ind.	1,498	(0.61%)
SPA	941	(0.39%)
Ind.	902	(0.37%)
SNP majority	17,274	(7.09%)

0.10% swing *Lab.* to *SNP*

ADDITIONAL MEMBERS

David Davidson	*(C.)*
Alex Johnstone	*(C.)*
Mrs Nanette Milne	*(C.)*
Ms Marlyn Glen	*(Lab.)*
Richard Baker	*(Lab.)*
Richard Lochhead	*(SNP)*
Ms Shiona Baird	*(Green)*

SCOTLAND SOUTH
E. 503,109 *T.* 52.33%

Lab.	78,955	(29.99%)
C.	63,827	(24.24%)
SNP	48,371	(18.37%)
LD	27,026	(10.26%)
Green	15,062	(5.72%)
SSP	14,228	(5.40%)
PP	9,082	(3.45%)
Soc. Lab.	3,054	(1.16%)
UK Ind.	1,889	(0.72%)
SPA	1,436	(0.55%)
Rural	355	(0.13%)
Lab. majority	15,128	(5.75%)

1.83% swing *Lab.* to *C.*

ADDITIONAL MEMBERS

Phil Gallie	*(C.)*
David Mundell	*(C.)*
Ms Christine Grahame	*(SNP)*
Alasdair Morgan	*(SNP)*
Adam Ingram	*(SNP)*
Chris Ballance	*(Green)*
Ms Rosemary Byrne	*(SSP)*

SCOTLAND WEST
E. 483,002 *T.* 61.53%

Lab.	83,931	(28.24%)
LD	71,580	(24.09%)
SNP	50,387	(16.96%)
C.	40,261	(13.55%)
SSP	18,591	(6.26%)
Green	14,544	(4.89%)
SSCUP	7,100	(2.39%)
ProLife	3,674	(1.24%)
Soc. Lab.	3,155	(1.06%)
UK Ind.	1,662	(0.56%)
SUP	1,617	(0.54%)
SPA	674	(0.23%)
Lab. majority	12,351	(4.16%)

11.70% swing *Lab.* to *LD*

ADDITIONAL MEMBERS

Miss Annabel Goldie	*(C.)*
Murray Tosh	*(C.)*
Ross Finnie	*(LD)*
Campbell Martin	*(SNP)*
Bruce McFee	*(SNP)*
Stewart Maxwell	*(SNP)*
Ms Frances Curran	*(SSP)*

LOCAL GOVERNMENT

Major changes in local government were introduced in England and Wales in 1974 and in Scotland in 1975 by the Local Government Act 1972 and the Local Government (Scotland) Act 1973. Further significant alterations were made in England by the Local Government Acts of 1985, 1992 and 2000.

The structure in England was based on two tiers of local authorities (county councils and district councils) in the non-metropolitan areas; and a single tier of metropolitan councils in the six metropolitan areas of England and London borough councils in London.

Following reviews of the structure of local government in England by the Local Government Commission, 46 unitary (all-purpose) authorities were created between April 1995 and April 1998 to cover certain areas in the non-metropolitan counties. The remaining county areas continue to have two tiers of local authorities. The county and district councils in the Isle of Wight were replaced by a single unitary authority on 1 April 1995; the former counties of Avon, Cleveland, Humberside and Berkshire have been replaced by unitary authorities; and Hereford and Worcester was replaced by a new county council for Worcestershire (with district councils) and a unitary authority for Herefordshire.

The Local Government (Wales) Act 1994 and the Local Government etc. (Scotland) Act 1994 abolished the two-tier structure in Wales and Scotland with effect from 1 April 1996, replacing it with a single tier of unitary authorities.

ELECTIONS

Local elections are normally held on the first Thursday in May, although in 2004 they were held on the 10 June to coincide with the European Parliament elections. Generally, all British subjects, citizens of the Republic of Ireland, Commonwealth and other European Union citizens who are 18 years or over and resident on the qualifying date in the area for which the election is being held, are entitled to vote at local government elections. A register of electors is prepared and published annually by local electoral registration officers.

A returning officer has the overall responsibility for an election. Voting takes place at polling stations, arranged by the local authority and under the supervision of a presiding officer specially appointed for the purpose. Candidates, who are subject to various statutory qualifications and disqualifications designed to ensure that they are suitable persons to hold office, must be nominated by electors for the electoral area concerned.

In England, the Boundary Commission for England is responsible for carrying out periodic reviews of electoral arrangements and making recommendations to the Electoral Commission. Following the Deputy Prime Minister's announcement on 16 June 2003 that referendums would be held on the establishment of three elected regional assemblies in the North East, North West and Yorkshire and the Humber, the Boundary Committee for England commenced a major review of local government structure in these areas. Final recommendations were submitted to the Deputy Prime Minister on 25 May 2004 and provide for a minimum of two different options for the establishment of unitary authorities in each county area. A referendum in the North East region was set to be held on 4 November 2004.

In Wales and Scotland these matters are the responsibility of the Local Government Boundary Commission for Wales and the Boundary Commission for Scotland respectively. The Local Government Act 2000 provided for the Secretary of State to change the frequency and phasing of elections. *See* Public Offices section.

INTERNAL ORGANISATION

The council as a whole is the final decision-making body within any authority. Councils are free to a great extent to make their own internal organisational arrangements. The Local Government Act, given Royal assent on 28 July 2000, allows councils to adopt one of three broad categories of a new constitution which include a separate executive.

These three categories are:

- A directly elected mayor with a cabinet selected by that mayor
- A cabinet, either elected by the council or appointed by its leader
- A directly elected mayor and council manager

Normally, questions of policy are settled by the full council, while the administration of the various services is the responsibility of committees of councillors. Day-to-day decisions are delegated to the council's officers, who act within the policies laid down by the councillors.

FINANCE

Local government in England, Wales and Scotland is financed from four sources: the council tax, non-domestic rates, government grants, and income from fees and charges for services.

COUNCIL TAX

Under the Local Government Finance Act 1992, from 1 April 1993 the council tax replaced the community charge (which had been introduced in April 1989 in Scotland and April 1990 in England and Wales in place of domestic rates).

The council tax is a local tax levied by each local council. Liability for the council tax bill usually falls on the owner-occupier or tenant of a dwelling which is their sole or main residence. Council tax bills may be reduced because of the personal circumstances of people resident in a property, and there are discounts in the case of dwellings occupied by fewer than two adults.

In England, each county council, each district council and each police authority sets its own council tax rate. The district councils collect the combined council tax, and the county councils and police authorities claim their share from the district councils' collection funds. In Wales, each unitary authority and each police authority sets its own council tax rate. The unitary authorities collect the combined council tax and the police authorities claim their share from the funds. In Scotland, each local authority sets its own rate of council tax.

The tax relates to the value of the dwelling. Each dwelling is placed in one of eight valuation bands, ranging from A to H, based on the property's estimated market value as at 1 April 1991. Wales is currently undergoing a revaluation of bands based on the estimated market value of property as at 1 April 2003. The new band structure will take effect from 1 April 2005 and will be used to calculate council tax bills in Wales for the financial year 2005–6 onwards. The existing bands have been used to calculate council tax for 2004–5.

The valuation bands and ranges of values in England, Wales and Scotland are:

England

A	Up to £40,000	E	£88,001–£120,000
B	£40,001–£52,000	F	£120,001–£160,000
C	£52,001–£68,000	G	£160,001–£320,000
D	£68,001–£88,000	H	Over £320,000

Wales (up to 1 April 2005)

A	Up to £30,000	E	£66,001–£90,000
B	£30,001–£39,000	F	£90,001–£120,000
C	£39,001–£51,000	G	£120,001–£240,000
D	£51,001–£66,000	H	Over £240,000

Wales (from 1 April 2005)

A	Up to £44,000	F	£162,001–£223,000
B	£44,001–£65,000	G	£223,001–£324,000
C	£65,001–£91,000	H	£324,001–£424,000
D	£91,001–£123,000	I	Over £424,000
E	£123,001–£162,000		

Scotland

A	Up to £27,000	E	£58,001–£80,000
B	£27,001–£35,000	F	£80,001–£106,000
C	£35,001–£45,000	G	£106,001–£212,000
D	£45,001–£58,000	H	Over £212,000

The council tax within a local area varies between the different bands according to proportions laid down by law. The charge attributable to each band as a proportion of the Band D charge set by the council is approximately:

A	67%	E	122%
B	78%	F	144%
C	89%	G	167%
D	100%	H	200%

The Band D rate is given in the tables on the following pages. There may be variations from the given figure within each district council area because of different parish or community precepts being levied.

NON-DOMESTIC RATES

Non-domestic (business) rates are collected by billing authorities; these are the district councils in those areas of England with two tiers of local government and unitary authorities in other parts of England, in Wales and in Scotland. In respect of England and Wales, the Local Government Finance Act 1988 provides for liability for rates to be assessed on the basis of a poundage (multiplier) tax on the rateable value of property (hereditaments). Separate multipliers are set by the Office of the Deputy Prime Minister in England, the National Assembly for Wales and the Scottish Executive, and rates are collected by the billing authority for the area where a property is located. Rate income collected by billing authorities is paid into a national non-domestic rating (NNDR) pool and redistributed to individual authorities on the basis of the adult population figure as prescribed by the Office of the Deputy Prime Minister, the National Assembly for Wales or the Scottish Executive. The rates pools are maintained separately in England, Wales and Scotland. Actual payment of rates in certain cases is subject to transitional arrangements, to phase in the larger increases and reductions in rates resulting from the effects of the latest revaluation.

Rates are levied in Scotland in accordance with the Local Government (Scotland) Act 1975. For 1995–6, the Secretary of State for Scotland prescribed a single non-domestic rates poundage to apply throughout the country at the same level as the uniform business rate (UBR) in England. Rate income is pooled and redistributed to local authorities on a per capita basis.

Rateable values for the 2005 rating lists come into effect on 1 April 2005. They are derived from the rental value of property as at 1 April 2003 and determined on certain statutory assumptions by the Valuation Office Agency in England and Wales, and by Regional Assessors in Scotland. New property which is added to the list, and significant changes to existing property, necessitate amendments to the rateable value on the same basis. Rating lists (valuation rolls in Scotland) remain in force until the next general revaluation. Such revaluations take place every five years, the next being in 2010. Certain types of property are exempt from rates, or benefit from a reduced rate.

COMPLAINTS

Local Government Ombudsmen are responsible for investigating complaints from members of the public who claim to have suffered as a consequence of maladministration in local government or in certain local bodies.

The Northern Ireland Commissioner for Complaints fulfils a similar function in Northern Ireland, investigating complaints about local authorities and certain public bodies.

Complaints are made to the relevant local authority in the first instance and complainants may approach the Ombudsmen or Commissioners if not satisfied. Complaints may also be made directly to the Ombudsmen or Commissioners.

The Local Government Act 2000 established a Standards Board and Adjudication Panel in England. The Standards Board investigates any allegations that councillors have breached the council's Code of Conduct and if there is evidence of wrongdoing the Adjudication Panel will consider the report of investigations and if it is upheld, impose a penalty. In Wales the Commission for Local Administration in Wales undertakes the role of the Standards Board.

THE QUEEN'S REPRESENTATIVES

The Lord-Lieutenant of a county is the permanent local representative of the Crown in that county. The appointment of Lords-Lieutenant is now regulated by the Lieutenancies Act 1997. They are appointed by the Sovereign on the recommendation of the Prime Minister.

The retirement age is 75. The office of Lord-Lieutenant dates from 1551, and its holder was originally responsible for the maintenance of order and for local defence in the county. The duties of the post include attending on royalty during official visits to the county, performing certain duties in connection with armed forces of the Crown (and in particular the reserve forces), and making presentations of honours and awards on behalf of the Crown. In England, Wales and Northern Ireland, the Lord-Lieutenant usually also holds the office of *Custos Rotulorum*. As such, he or she acts as head of the county's commission of the peace (which recommends the appointment of magistrates).

The office of Sheriff (from the Old English shire-reeve) of a county was created in the tenth century. The Sheriff was the special nominee of the Sovereign, and the office reached the peak of its influence under the Norman kings. The Provisions of Oxford (1258) laid down a yearly tenure of office. Since the mid-16th century the office has been purely civil, with military duties taken over by the Lord-Lieutenant of the county. The Sheriff (commonly known as 'High Sheriff') attends on royalty during official visits to the county, acts as the returning officer during parliamentary elections in county constituencies, attends the opening ceremony when a High Court judge goes on circuit, executes High Court writs, and appoints under-sheriffs to act as deputies. The appointments and duties of the High Sheriffs in England and Wales are laid down by the Sheriffs Act 1887.

The serving High Sheriff submits a list of names of possible future sheriffs to a tribunal which chooses three names to put to the Sovereign. The tribunal nominates the High Sheriff annually on 12 November and the Sovereign picks the name of the Sheriff to succeed in the following year. The term of office runs from 25 March to the following 24 March (the civil and legal year before 1752). No person may be chosen twice in three years if there is any other suitable person in the county.

CIVIC DIGNITIES

District councils in England may petition for a royal charter granting borough or 'city' status to the district. Local councils in Wales may petition for a royal charter granting county borough or 'city' status to the council.

In England and Wales the chairman of a borough or county borough council may be called a mayor, and the chairman of a city council may be called a Lord Mayor if Lord Mayoralty has been conferred on that city. Parish councils in England and community councils in Wales may call themselves 'town councils', in which case their chairman is the town mayor.

In Scotland the chairman of a local council may be known as a convenor; a provost is the equivalent of a mayor. The chairmen of the councils for the cities of Aberdeen, Dundee, Edinburgh and Glasgow are Lord Provosts.

ENGLAND

There are currently 34 counties; all are divided into districts. In addition, there are 46 unitary authorities and 238 district councils. The populations of most of the unitary authorities are in the range of 100,000 to 300,000. The district councils have populations broadly in the range of 60,000 to 100,000; some, however, have larger populations, because of the need to avoid dividing large towns, and some in mainly rural areas have smaller populations.

The main conurbations outside Greater London – Tyne and Wear, West Midlands, Merseyside, Greater Manchester, West Yorkshire and South Yorkshire – are divided into 36 metropolitan boroughs, most of which have a population of over 200,000.

There are also about 10,000 parishes, in 219 of the district councils and 18 of the metropolitan boroughs.

ELECTIONS

For districts, counties and for about 8,000 parishes, there are elected councils, consisting of directly elected councillors. The councillors elect annually one of their number as chairman.

Generally, councillors serve four years and there are no elections of district and parish councillors in county election years. In metropolitan boroughs, one-third of the councillors for each ward are elected each year except in the year when county elections take place elsewhere. District councils can choose whether to have elections by thirds or whole council elections. In the former case, one-third of the council, as nearly as may be, is elected in each year of metropolitan borough elections. If whole council elections are chosen, these are held in the year midway between county elections.

FUNCTIONS

In non-metropolitan areas, functions are divided between the districts and counties, those requiring the larger area or population are generally the responsibility of the county. The metropolitan councils, with the larger population in their areas, already had wider functions than non-metropolitan councils, and following abolition of the metropolitan county councils were also given most of their functions.

The allocation of functions is as follows:

County councils: education; strategic planning; traffic, transport and highways; fire service; consumer protection; refuse disposal; smallholdings; social services; libraries

District councils: local planning; housing; highways (maintenance of certain urban roads and off-street car parks); building regulations; environmental health; refuse collection; cemeteries and crematoria

Unitary and Metropolitan councils: their functions are all those listed above, except that the fire service is exercised by a joint body

Concurrently by county and district councils: recreation (parks, playing fields, swimming pools); museums; encouragement of the arts, tourism and industry

The Police and Magistrates Court Act 1994 set up police authorities in England and Wales separate from the local authorities.

PARISH COUNCILS

Parishes with 200 or more electors must generally have parish councils, which means that over three-quarters of the parishes have councils. A parish council comprises at least five members, the number being fixed by the district council. Elections are held every four years, at the time of the election of the district councillor for the ward including the parish. All parishes have parish meetings, comprising the electors of the parish. Where there is no council, the meeting must be held at least twice a year.

Parish council functions include: allotments; encouragement of arts and crafts; community halls, recreational facilities (e.g. open spaces, swimming pools), cemeteries and crematoria; and many minor functions. They must also be given an opportunity to comment on planning applications. They may, like county and district councils, spend limited sums for the general benefit of the parish. They levy a precept on the district councils for their funds.

FINANCE

Aggregate external finance for 2004–5 has been determined at £54,208 million. Of this, specific grants were estimated at £12,240 million; £26,964 million was in respect of Revenue Support Grant and £15,004 million was support from the national non-domestic rate pool.

In England, the average council tax per dwelling for 2004–5 is £967, an increase from £908 in 2003–4. The average council tax for 2004–5 is £1,005 in shire areas, £1,035 in London and £813 in metropolitan areas. In England, the average council tax bill for a band D dwelling (occupied by two adults) for 2004–5 is £1,167, an average increase of 5.9 per cent from 2003–4. The average band D council tax is £1,186 in shire areas, £1,119 in London and £1,143 in metropolitan areas. The assumed council tax yield for 2004–5 is £20,302 million.

The provisional amount estimated to be raised from national non-domestic rates from central and local lists is £17,400 million. The amount of national non-domestic rates to be redistributed to authorities from the pool in 2004–5 is £15,004 million. The national non-domestic rate multiplier, or poundage, for 2004–5 is 45.6p.

Under the Local Government and Housing Act 1989, local authorities have four main ways of paying for capital expenditure: borrowing and other forms of extended credit; capital grants from central government towards some types of capital expenditure; 'usable' capital receipts from the sale of land, houses and other assets; and revenue.

The amount of capital expenditure which a local authority can finance by borrowing (or other forms of credit) is effectively limited by the credit approvals issued to it by central government. Most credit approvals can be used for any kind of local authority capital expenditure; these are known as basic credit approvals. Others (supplementary credit approvals) can be used only for the kind of expenditure specified in the approval, and so are often given to fund particular projects or services.

Local authorities can use all capital receipts from the sale of property or assets for capital spending, except in the case of sales of council houses. Generally, the 'usable' part of a local authority's capital receipts consists of 25 per cent of receipts from the sale of council houses and 50 per cent of other housing assets such as shops or vacant land. The balance has to be set aside as provision for repaying debt and meeting other credit liabilities.

EXPENDITURE

Local authority budgeted net revenue expenditure for 2004–5 is:

Service	*£m*
Central services (including administration & emergency planning)	3,142
Education	32,509
Social Services	15,585
Police	9,739
Highways and Transport	5,367
Fire	2,025
Planning	1,532
Courts services	398
Mandatory rent allowances	6,642
Mandatory rent rebates	601
Non-housing revenue account housing	2,425
Rent rebates granted to housing revenue account tenants	2,895
Cultural services (including sport & recreation)	2,819
Environment	3,785
Other services	313
Net current expenditure	89,777
Capital financing	2,577
Capital expenditure charged to revenue account	524
Council tax benefit	2,747
Discretionary non-domestic rate relief	24
Flood defence payments to Environment Agency	28
Locally funded council tax discounts	1
Pension interest costs	57
Less interest receipts	(717)
Less specific grants outside AEF	(15,623)
Gross revenue expenditure	79,395
Less specific grants inside AEF	(12,240)
Net Revenue expenditure	67,155
Less appropriations from reserves	(589)
Less adjustments	(2)
BUDGET REQUIREMENT	66,564

AEF = aggregate external finance

LONDON

The Greater London Council was abolished in 1986 and London is divided into 32 borough councils, which have a status similar to the metropolitan borough councils in the rest of England, and the Corporation of the City of London.

In March 1998 the Government announced proposals for a Greater London Authority (GLA) covering the area of the 32 London boroughs and the City of London, which would comprise a directly elected mayor and a 25-member assembly. A referendum was held in London on 7 May 1998; the turnout was approximately 34 per cent, and 72 per cent of electors voted in favour of the GLA. The independent candidate for London Mayor, Ken Livingstone, was elected on 4 May 2000 and the Authority assumed its responsibilities on 3 July 2000. He was re-elected on 10 June 2004 as a Labour candidate.

The GLA is responsible for transport, economic development, strategic planning, culture, health, the environment, the police and fire and emergency planning. The separately elected assembly scrutinise the mayor's activities and approve plans and budgets. There are 14 Constituency Assembly members, each representing a separate area of London (each constituency is made up of two or three complete London boroughs). Eleven additional members, making up the total Assembly complement of 25 members, are elected on a London-wide basis, either as independents or from party political lists on the basis of proportional representation. Parties or independent candidates must secure at least five per cent of the vote to be entitled to additional seats.

LONDON BOROUGH COUNCILS

The London boroughs have whole council elections every four years, in the year immediately following the county council election year. The most recent elections took place on 2 May 2002.

The borough councils have responsibility for the following functions: building regulations; cemeteries and crematoria; consumer protection; education; youth employment; environmental health; electoral registration; food; drugs; housing; leisure services; libraries; local planning; local roads; museums; parking; recreation (parks, playing fields, swimming pools); refuse collection and street cleansing; social services; town planning; and traffic management.

CORPORATION OF LONDON

The Corporation of London is the local authority for the City of London. Its legal definition is 'The Mayor and Commonalty and Citizens of the City of London'. It is governed by the Court of Common Council, which consists of the Lord Mayor, 25 other aldermen, and about 100 common councilmen. The Lord Mayor and two sheriffs are nominated annually by the City guilds (the livery companies) and elected by the Court of Aldermen. Aldermen and councilmen are elected from the 25 wards into which the City is divided; councilmen must stand for re-election annually. The Council is a legislative assembly, and there are no political parties.

The Corporation has the same functions as the London borough councils. In addition, it runs the City of London Police; is the health authority for the Port of London; has health control of animal imports throughout Greater London, including at Heathrow airport; owns and manages public open spaces throughout Greater London; runs the Central Criminal Court; and runs Billingsgate, Smithfield and Spitalfields markets.

THE CITY GUILDS (LIVERY COMPANIES)

The livery companies of the City of London grew out of early medieval religious fraternities and began to emerge as trade and craft guilds, retaining their religious aspect, in the 12th century. From the early 14th century, only members of the trade and craft guilds could call themselves citizens of the City of London. The guilds began to be called livery companies, because of the distinctive livery worn by the most prosperous guild members on ceremonial occasions, in the late 15th century.

By the early 19th century the power of the companies within their trades had begun to wane, but those wearing the livery of a company continued to play an important role in the government of the City of London. Liverymen still have the right to nominate the Lord Mayor and sheriffs, and most members of the Court of Common Council are liverymen.

WALES

The Local Government (Wales) Act 1994 abolished the two-tier structure of eight county and 37 district councils which had existed since 1974, and replaced it, from 1 April 1996, with 22 unitary authorities. The new authorities were elected in May 1995. Each unitary authority has inherited all the functions of the previous county and district councils, except fire services (which are provided by three combined fire authorities, composed of representatives of the unitary authorities) and National Parks (which are the responsibility of three independent National Park Authorities).

COMMUNITY COUNCILS

In Wales community councils are the equivalent of parishes in England. Unlike England, where many areas are not in any parish, communities have been established for the whole of Wales, approximately 865 communities in all. Community meetings may be convened as and when desired.

Community councils exist in 737 communities and further councils may be established at the request of a community meeting.

FINANCE

Non-hypothecated funding for 2004–5 is £3,313.5 million. This comprises revenue support grant of £2,591 million, support from the national non-domestic rate pool of £672 million, Deprivation Grant of £20.5 million and Performance Incentive Grant of £30 million. The non-domestic rating multiplier or poundage for Wales for 2004–5 is 45.2p. The average Band D council tax levied in Wales for 2004–5 is £887, comprising unitary authorities £734, police authorities £133 and community councils £20.

EXPENDITURE

Local authority budgeted net revenue expenditure for 2004–5 is:

Service	*£m*
Education	2,005.1
Personal social services	1,014.5
Local Environmental services	298.6
Roads and transport	248.4
Libraries, culture, heritage, sport and recreation	161.2
Council tax benefit and administration	13.3
Non-housing revenue account housing, including housing benefit	372.8
Rent rebates granted to housing revenue account tenants	266.5
Debt financing costs	269.5
Other services	376.4
Police	548.5
Fire	126.7
Other law, order and protective services	30.1
National Parks	16.6
Gross Revenue Expenditure	5,748.0
Less specific government grants	(1,286.7)
Net revenue expenditure	4,461.4

SCOTLAND

The Local Government etc. (Scotland) Act 1994 abolished the two-tier structure of nine regional and 53 district councils which had existed since 1975 and replaced it, from 1 April 1996, with 29 unitary authorities on the mainland; the three islands councils remained. The new authorities were elected in April 1995.

In July 1999 the Scottish Parliament assumed responsibility for legislation on local government. The Government had established a Commission on Local Government and the Scottish Parliament (the McIntosh Commission) to make recommendations on the relationship between local authorities and the new Parliament and on increasing local authorities' accountability. The Commission published its reports in July 1999.

Following this report, the Scottish Executive established the 'Renewing Local Democracy' working group to consider ways in which to make council membership more attractive and councils more representative of their communities. The group would also advise on appropriate membership levels for each council, looking at modernising management practices and local concerns. They also investigated which method of election would be most appropriate, taking account of the following criteria; proportionality and the councillor-ward link, fair provision for independents, allowance for geographical diversity and a close fit between council wards and natural communities, and advise on an appropriate system of remuneration for councillors, taking account of available resources.

The Scottish Executive also set up the Leadership Advisory Panel in August 1999 following the recommendations of the McIntosh Report. The panel worked closely with Scottish local authorities helping them to conduct a self-review of their political management structures and to implement its recommendations.

The Local Government in Scotland Bill was introduced to the Scottish Parliament in May 2002. This Bill centres on three integrated core elements:

- A power for local authorities to promote and improve well-being of their area and/or persons in it
- Statutory underpinning for community planning through the introduction of a duty on local authorities and key partners, including police, health boards and enterprise agencies
- A duty to secure best value.

ELECTIONS

The unitary authorities consist of directly elected councillors. The Scottish Local Government (Elections) Act 2002 moved elections from a three-year to a four-year cycle; the last elections took place in May 2003. The 2004 register showed 3,857,997 electors in Scotland.

FUNCTIONS

The functions of the councils and islands councils are: education; social work; strategic planning; the provision of infrastructure such as roads; consumer protection; flood prevention; coast protection; valuation and rating; the police and fire services; civil defence; electoral registration; public transport; registration of births, deaths and marriages; housing; leisure and recreation; development and building control; environmental health; licensing; allotments; public conveniences; and the administration of district courts.

COMMUNITY COUNCILS

Scottish community councils differ from those in England and Wales. Their purpose as defined in statute is to ascertain and express the views of the communities they represent, and to take in the interests of their communities such action as appears to be expedient or practicable. Over 1,100 community councils have been established under schemes drawn up by local authorities in Scotland.

FINANCE

Budgeted aggregate external finance for 2004–5 is £7,669 million, comprising; £5,118 million revenue support grant, non-domestic rate income of £1,896 million and specific grants of £656 million. The non-domestic rate multiplier or poundage for 2004–5 is 48.8p. In 2003–4 a single owned property with a rateable value of £5,000 is eligible for 20 per cent small business rate relief. The average Band D council tax for 2004–5 is £1,053.

EXPENDITURE

The 2004–5 net expenditure budget estimates for local authorities in Scotland were:

Service	*£m*
Education	3,869.6
Cultural and related services	505.6
Social Work Services	1,867.1
Police	937.6
Roads and transport	496.9
Environmental services	441.4
Fire	248.6
Total planning and development services	146.0
Total	8,512.8

NORTHERN IRELAND

For the purpose of local government Northern Ireland has a system of 26 single-tier district councils.

ELECTIONS

Council members are elected for periods of four years at a time on the principle of proportional representation.

FUNCTIONS

The district councils have three main roles. These are:

Executive: responsibility for a wide range of local services including building regulations; community services; consumer protection; cultural facilities; environmental health; miscellaneous licensing and registration provisions, including dog control; litter prevention; recreational and social facilities; refuse collection and disposal; street cleansing; and tourist development

Representative: nominating representatives to sit as members of the various statutory bodies responsible for the administration of regional services such as drainage, education, fire, health and personal social services, housing, and libraries

Consultative: acting as the medium through which the views of local people are expressed on the operation in their area of other regional services, notably conservation (including water supply and sewerage services), planning and roads, provided by those departments of central government which have an obligation, statutory or otherwise, to consult the district councils about proposals affecting their areas

FINANCE

Local government in Northern Ireland is funded by a system of rates. The ratepayer receives a combined tax bill consisting of the Regional Rate and the District Rate, which is set by each district council. The Regional and District Rates are both collected by the Rate Collection Agency. The product of the District Rates is paid over to each council whilst the product of the Regional Rate supports expenditure by the departments of the Executive and Assembly. Rate bills are calculated by multiplying the property's Net Annual Value (NAV) by the Regional and District Rate poundages respectively. A general revaluation of non domestic properties became effective from 1 April 2003, based on 2001 rental values, however the values of domestic properties continue to be based on 1976 rental values.

For 2004–5 the overall average domestic poundage is 294.02p and the overall average non-domestic rate poundage is 43.94p.

POLITICAL COMPOSITION OF LOCAL COUNCILS

AS AT JUNE 2004

Abbreviations

All.	Alliance
BNP	British National Party
C.	Conservative
CU	Conservative and Unionist
DUP	Democratic Unionist
Green	Green
Ind.	Independent
Ind. All.	Independent Alliance
Ind. UU	Independent Unionist
IKHHC	Independent Kidderminster Hospital and Health Concern
IF	Island First
Lab.	Labour
LD	Liberal Democrat
Lib.	Liberal
NP	Non-Political/Non-Party
PC	Plaid Cymru
R.	Residents Association/Ratepayers
SD	Social Democrat
SDLP	Social Democratic and Labour Party
SF	Sinn Fein
SNP	Scottish National Party
Soc.	Socialist
Soc. Dem.	Social Democratic
SSP	Scottish Socialist Party
UKIP	UK Independence Party
UUP	Ulster Unionist Party
v.	Vacant

Total no. of seats is given in brackets after council name

ENGLAND

COUNTY COUNCILS

Bedfordshire (49)	C. 26; Lab. 13; LD 9; Ind. 1
Buckinghamshire (54)	C. 40; LD 9; Lab. 5
Cambridgeshire (59)	C. 34; LD 17; Lab. 8
Cheshire (51)	C. 28; Lab. 16; LD 6; Ind. 1
Cornwall (79)	LD 35; Ind. 25; C. 10; Lab. 9
Cumbria (84)	Lab. 38; C. 33; LD 11; Ind. 1; v. 1
Derbyshire (64)	Lab. 41; C. 13; LD 7; Other 2; Ind. 1
Devon (54)	LD 22; C. 22; Lab. 5; Ind. 5
Dorset (42)	C. 23; LD 13; Lab. 4; Ind. 1; v. 1
Durham (61)	Lab. 52; LD 4; Ind. 3; C. 2
East Sussex (44)	C. 24; LD 13; Lab. 7
Essex (79)	C. 49; Lab. 18; LD 10; Ind. 2
Gloucestershire (63)	C. 27; Lab. 19; LD 16; Ind. 1
Hampshire (74)	C. 46; LD 20; Lab. 8
Hertfordshire (77)	C. 41; Lab. 24; LD 11; Ind. 1
Kent (84)	C. 52; Lab. 22; LD 10
Lancashire (78)	Lab. 44; C. 27; LD 5; Green 1; Other 1
Leicestershire (54)	C. 29; Lab. 15; LD 10
Lincolnshire (77)	C. 48; Lab. 21; LD 4; Ind. 3; Other 1
Norfolk (84)	C. 47; Lab. 26; LD 11
North Yorkshire (74)	C. 42; LD 17; Lab. 12; Ind. 1; Other 2
Northamptonshire (73)	Lab. 39; C. 33; LD 1
Northumberland (67)	Lab. 38; C. 17; LD 9; Ind. 3
Nottinghamshire (63)	Lab. 39; C. 21; LD 3
Oxfordshire (69)	C. 24; Lab. 24; LD 20; Green 1; v. 1
Shropshire (44)	C. 19; Lab. 11; LD 8; Ind. Other 4; Ind. 2
Somerset (58)	LD 29; C. 24; Lab. 5
Staffordshire (62)	Lab. 36; C. 22; LD 4
Suffolk (80)	Lab. 33; C. 32; LD 12; Ind. 2; Other 1
Surrey (76)	C. 51; LD 13; Lab. 6; R. 4; Ind. 2
Warwickshire (62)	Lab. 27; C. 20; LD 13; Ind. 1; Other 1
West Sussex (71)	C. 41; LD 19; Lab. 11
Wiltshire (47)	C. 27; LD 13; Ind. 4; Lab. 3
Worcestershire (57)	C. 26; Lab. 14; LD 8; IKHHC 6; Lib. 2; Ind. 1

DISTRICT COUNCILS

Adur (29)	C. 24; Lab. 2; R. 2; LD 1
Allerdale (56)	Lab. 27; C. 16; LD 4; Other 6; Ind. 3
Alnwick (30)	Ind. 11; LD 10; Other 4; C. 3; Lab. 2
Amber Valley (45)	C. 24; Lab. 21
Arun (56)	C. 36; LD 11; Lab. 8; Ind. 1
Ashfield (33)	Lab. 18; Ind. 12; C. 1; Green 2
Ashford (43)	C. 25; Other 7; LD 5; Lab. 4; Ind. 2
Aylesbury Vale (59)	C. 30; LD 25; Ind. 4
Babergh (43)	LD 18; C. 11; Ind. 7; Lab. 6; Other 1
Barrow-in-Furness (38)	Lab. 24; C. 12; Ind. 2
Basildon (42)	C. 25; Lab. 14; LD 3
Basingstoke and Deane (60)	C. 28; LD 16; Lab. 12; Ind. 4
Bassetlaw (48)	C. 24; Lab. 18; Ind. 5; LD 1
Bedford (54)	C. 16; Lab. 15; LD 13; Ind. 10
Berwick-upon-Tweed (29)	C. 13; LD 8; Ind. 6; Other 2
Blaby (39)	C. 25; LD 9; Lab. 4; Ind. 1
Blyth Valley (50)	Lab. 35; LD 9; Ind. 3; C. 3
Bolsover (37)	Lab. 31; Ind. 4; R. 2
Boston (32)	C. 12; Lab. 11; Ind. 5; LD 4
Braintree (60)	C. 26; Lab. 20; Ind 7; LD 5; Green 2
Breckland (54)	C. 42; Lab. 8; Ind. 4
Brentwood (37)	C. 21; LD 13; Lab. 3
Bridgnorth (34)	C. 17; LD 8; Ind. 7; Lab. 2
Broadland (47)	C. 31; LD 11; Ind. 5
Bromsgrove (39)	C. 21; Lab. 8; Ind. 6; R. 4
Broxbourne (38)	C. 34; Lab. 2; Ind. 1; BNP 1
Broxtowe (44)	Lab. 15; C. 13; LD 13; Ind. 2; UKIP 1
Burnley (45)	Lab. 21; LD 11; BNP 6; C. 4; Ind. 3
Cambridge (42)	LD 28; Lab. 13; C. 1
Cannock Chase (41)	Lab. 17; LD 14; C. 10
Canterbury (50)	C. 24; LD 19; Lab. 7
Caradon (42)	Ind. 22; LD 14; C. 4; Lab. 1; v. 1
Carlisle (52)	Lab. 24; C. 20; LD 7; Ind. 1
Carrick (47)	LD 29; C. 11; Ind. 7

Castle Morpeth (33)	Lab. 10; C. 9; Ind. 7; LD 6; Green 1
Castle Point (41)	C. 35; R. 5; Ind. 1
Charnwood (52)	C. 24; Lab. 21; LD 7
Chelmsford (57)	C. 35; LD 20; Lab. 2
Cheltenham (40)	LD 18; C. 15; Ind. 5; Lab. 2
Cherwell (50)	C. 36; Lab. 10; LD 4
Chester (60)	LD 22; C. 20; Lab 17; Ind. 1
Chester-le-Street (32)	Lab. 27; Ind. 4; C. 1
Chesterfield (48)	LD 36; Lab. 12
Chichester (48)	C. 25; LD 21; Ind. 2
Chiltern (40)	C. 27; LD 12; R. 1
Chorley (47)	Lab. 21; C. 20; LD 3; Ind. 3
Christchurch (24)	C. 14; LD 8; Ind. 2
Colchester (60)	C. 28; LD 23; Lab. 6; Ind. 3
Congleton (48)	C. 25; LD 14; Ind. 7; Lab. 2
Copeland (51)	Lab. 30; C. 16; Ind. 4; LD 1
Corby (29)	Lab. 18; C. 9; LD 2
Cotswolds (44)	C. 26; Ind. 10; LD 8
Craven (30)	C. 13; Ind. 11; LD 6
Crawley (37)	Lab. 19; C. 16; LD 2
Crewe and Nantwich (56)	Lab. 22; C. 22; Ind. 6; LD 6
Dacorum (52)	C. 32; Lab. 14; LD 6
Dartford (44)	C. 21; Lab. 16; Other 7
Daventry (38)	C. 34; Lab. 3; LD 1
Derbyshire Dales (39)	C. 24; LD 9; Lab. 5; Ind. 1
Derwentside (55)	Lab. 38; Ind. 15; LD 1; Ind. Other 1
Dover (45)	C. 22; Lab. 20; LD 3
Durham (50)	LD 30; Lab. 17; Ind. 3
Easington (51)	Lab. 44; Ind. 5; LD 2
East Cambridgeshire (39)	LD 17; C. 15; Ind. 7
East Devon (59)	C. 35; LD 18; Ind. 6
East Dorset (36)	C. 24; LD 11; Ind. 1
East Hampshire (44)	C. 26; LD 17; v. 1
East Hertfordshire (50)	C. 41; LD 5; Ind. 4
East Lindsey (60)	Ind. 27; C. 14; Lab. 12; LD 6; Other 1
East Northamptonshire (36)	C. 33; Lab. 3
East Staffordshire (39)	C. 22; Lab. 16; LD 1
Eastbourne (27)	C. 14; LD 13
Eastleigh (44)	LD 32; C. 9; Lab. 3
Eden (38)	Ind. 27; C. 7; LD 4
Ellesmere Port and Neston (43)	Lab. 29; C. 12; LD 2
Elmbridge (60)	R. 31; C. 21; LD 8
Epping Forest (58)	C. 23; LD 15; R. 9; Lab. 4; Ind. 4; BNP 3
Epsom and Ewell (38)	R. 27; LD 6; Lab. 3; C. 2
Erewash (51)	C. 26; Lab. 19; LD 3; Ind. 2; v. 1
Exeter (40)	Lab. 19; LD 12; C. 5; Lib. 4
Fareham (31)	C. 22; LD 9
Fenland (40)	C. 35; Lab. 3; Ind. 1; v. 1
Forest Heath (27)	C. 22; Ind. 5
Forest of Dean (48)	C. 17; Lab. 16; Ind. 11; LD 4
Fylde (51)	C. 27; Ind. 11; R. 7; Ind. Other 4; LD 2
Gedling (50)	C. 21; Lab. 21; LD 7; Ind. 1
Gloucester (36)	C. 16; LD 12; Lab. 8
Gosport (34)	C. 15; Lab. 11; LD 6; Ind. 2
Gravesham (44)	Lab. 23; C. 21
Great Yarmouth (39)	C. 26; Lab. 13
Guildford (48)	C. 25; LD 20; Lab. 2; Ind. 1
Hambleton (44)	C. 36; Ind. 4; LD 3; Lab. 1
Harborough (37)	LD 18; C. 16; Ind. 2; Lab. 1

Harlow (33)	C. 13; Lab. 11; LD 9
Harrogate (54)	C. 29; LD 21; Ind. 4
Hart (35)	C. 18; LD 12; Ind. 3; R. 2
Hastings (32)	Lab 15; C. 13; LD 4
Havant (38)	C. 27; Lab 6; LD 5
Hertsmere (39)	C. 25; Lab. 7; LD 7
High Peak (43)	Lab. 18; C. 12; LD 7; Ind. 6
Hinckley and Bosworth (34)	C. 19; LD 8; Lab. 6; v. 1
Horsham (44)	C. 22; LD 19; Ind. 2; v. 1
Huntingdonshire (52)	C. 40; LD 10; Ind. 2
Hyndburn (35)	C. 20; Lab. 15
Ipswich (48)	Lab. 23; C. 18; LD 7
Kennet (43)	C. 27; Ind. 8; Other 4; LD 3; Lab. 1
Kerrier (44)	Ind. 21; LD 10; Lab. 5; C. 4; Other 4
Kettering (45)	C. 30; Lab. 13; Ind. 2
King's Lynn and West Norfolk (62)	C. 36; Lab. 14; LD 7; Ind. 5
Lancaster (60)	Lab. 20; Ind. 12; C. 11; LD 8; Green 7; Ind. Other 2
Lewes (41)	LD 27; C. 11; Ind. 3
Lichfield (56)	C. 35; Lab. 16; LD 5
Lincoln City (33)	Lab. 25; C. 7; LD 1
Macclesfield (60)	C. 35; LD 14; Lab. 6; R. 3; Ind. 2
Maidstone (55)	C. 23; LD 20; Lab. 9; Ind. 3
Maldon (31)	C. 21; Ind. 4; Other 4; Lab. 2
Malvern Hills (38)	LD 19; C. 13; Ind. 5; Green 1
Mansfield (46)	Ind. 26; Lab. 15; LD 4; C. 1
Melton (28)	C. 19; Ind. 5; Lab. 4
Mendip (46)	C. 31; LD 11; Ind. 4
Mid Bedfordshire (53)	C. 38; LD 11; Ind. 4
Mid Devon (42)	Ind. Other 20; C. 12; LD 8; Green 1; v. 1
Mid Suffolk (40)	C. 21; LD 11; Ind. 5; Lab. 2; Green 1
Mid Sussex (54)	C. 28; LD 24; Lab. 2
Mole Valley (41)	C. 19; LD 17; Ind. 5
New Forest (60)	C. 32; LD 27; Ind. 1
Newark and Sherwood (46)	C. 23; Lab. 12; Ind. 5; LD 4; Ind. Other 1; Other 1
Newcastle-under-Lyme (60)	Lab. 31; LD 14; C. 14; Ind 1
North Cornwall (36)	Ind. 19; LD 12; C. 3; Other 1; v. 1
North Devon (43)	LD 22; C. 10; Ind. 5; Ind. Other 4; Other 2
North Dorset (33)	C. 15; LD 12; Ind. 5; v. 1
North East Derbyshire (53)	Lab. 36; C. 9; LD 5; Ind. 3
North Hertfordshire (49)	C. 28; Lab. 14; LD 7
North Kesteven (40)	C. 17; UKIP 8; LD 5; Lab. 4; Ind. 3; Ind. Other 2; v. 1
North Norfolk (48)	LD 29; Other 16; Ind. 3
North Shropshire (40)	Ind. 21; C. 15; Lab. 4
North Warwickshire (35)	Lab. 16; C. 15; LD 4
North West Leicestershire (38)	Lab. 21; C. 12; LD 3; Ind. 2
North Wiltshire (53)	LD 26; C. 25; Lab. 1; Ind. 1
Northampton (47)	C. 19; LD 17; Lab. 11
Norwich (39)	LD 18; Lab. 15; Green 5; C. 1
Nuneaton and Bedworth (34)	Lab. 22; C. 11; LD 1
Oadby and Wigston (26)	LD 17; C. 9

Oswestry (29)	C. 10; Ind. Other 8; LD 7; Ind. 3; Lab. 1
Oxford (48)	Lab. 20; LD 18; Green 7; Ind. 3
Pendle (49)	LD 30; C. 11; Lab. 8
Penwith (35)	LD 14; C. 12; Ind. 8; Lab. 1
Preston (57)	Lab. 24; C. 18; LD 10; Ind. 4; Soc. All. 1
Purbeck (24)	C. 13; LD 8; Ind. 3
Redditch (29)	Lab. 16; C. 10; LD 3
Reigate and Banstead (51)	C. 37; R 6; LD 5; Lab. 3
Restormel (45)	LD 22; Ind. 13; C. 9; Other 1
Ribble Valley (40)	C. 22; LD 15; Ind. 2; Lab. 1
Richmondshire (34)	C. 11; Ind. 9; LD 8; Ind. Other 5; SD 1
Rochford (39)	C. 32; LD 4; Ind. 1; Lab. 1; R 1
Rossendale (36)	C. 25; Lab. 9; LD 1; Ind. 1
Rother (38)	C. 25; LD 7; Lab. 3; Ind. 3
Rugby (48)	C. 21; Lab. 14; LD 10; Ind. 3
Runnymede (42)	C. 33; Ind. 6; Lab. 3
Rushcliffe (50)	C. 34; LD 10; Lab. 4; Ind. Other 1; Green 1
Rushmoor (42)	C. 24; LD 12; Lab. 5; Ind. 1
Ryedale (30)	C. 11; LD 8; Ind. 7; Lib. 2; Ind Other 1; v. 1
St Albans (58)	LD 29; C. 17; Lab. 11; Ind. 1
St Edmundsbury (45)	C. 28; Lab. 12; Ind. 3; LD 2
Salisbury (55)	C. 31; LD 9; Lab. 11; Ind. 4
Scarborough (50)	C. 27; Ind. 14; Lab. 7; LD 2
Sedgefield (50)	Lab. 34; Ind. 7; LD 7; C. 1
Sedgemoor (50)	C. 35; Lab. 14; LD 1
Selby (41)	Lab. 14; C. 23; Ind. 3; LD 1
Sevenoaks (54)	C. 32; Lab. 10; LD 8; Ind. 3; v. 1
Shepway (46)	LD 26; C. 17; Lab. 1; Green 1; Ind. 1
Shrewsbury and Atcham (40)	C. 20; Lab. 10; LD 6; Ind. 3; v. 1
South Bedfordshire (50)	C. 34; LD 12; Lab. 4
South Bucks (40)	C. 33; Ind. 6; LD 1
South Cambridgeshire (57)	C. 23; LD 19; Ind. 13; Lab. 2
South Derbyshire (36)	Lab. 21; C. 14; Ind. 1
South Hams (40)	C. 28; LD 7; Lab. 3; Ind. 2
South Holland (38)	C. 26; Ind. 11; Other 1
South Kesteven (58)	C. 30; Ind. 12; Lab. 10; LD 5; v. 1
South Lakeland (52)	LD 22; C. 20; Lab. 8; Ind. 2
South Norfolk (46)	LD 28; C. 18
South Northants (42)	C. 30; Ind. 8; Lab. 4
South Oxfordshire (48)	C. 28; LD 9; Lab. 4; Other 4; Ind. 3
South Ribble (55)	C. 18; Lab. 16; LD 15; Other 3; Ind. 2; v. 1
South Shropshire (34)	LD 14; C. 10; Ind. 8; Other 2
South Somerset (60)	LD 36; C. 17; Ind. 7
South Staffordshire (49)	C. 35; Lab. 8; Ind. 4; Other 1; LD 1
Spelthorne (39)	C. 35; LD 4
Stafford (59)	C. 40; Lab. 14; LD 5
Staffordshire Moorlands (56)	C. 20; R. 13; LD 11; Lab. 7; Ind. 4; v. 1
Stevenage (39)	Lab. 32; C. 3; LD 4
Stratford-on-Avon (53)	C. 30; LD 20; Ind. 3
Stroud (51)	C. 27; Lab. 11; LD 6; Green 4; Ind. 3
Suffolk Coastal (55)	C. 43; LD 10; Lab. 2
Surrey Heath (40)	C. 22; LD 13; Lab. 3; Ind. 2
Swale (47)	C. 26; Lab. 11; LD 10
Tamworth (30)	C. 16; Lab. 13; Ind. 1
Tandridge (42)	C. 28; LD 11; Lab. 2; Ind. 1
Taunton Deane (54)	C. 31; LD 15; Lab. 5; Ind. 3
Teesdale (32)	Ind. 12; Lab. 9; Ind. Other 8; C. 3
Teignbridge (46)	LD 17; Ind. 15; C. 14
Tendring (60)	C. 25; LD 13; Lab. 11; Ind. 7; Other 4
Test Valley (48)	C. 30; LD 16; Ind. 2
Tewkesbury (38)	C. 18; LD 9; Ind. Other 7; Lab. 3; Ind. 1
Thanet (56)	C. 30; Lab. 23; LD 1; Ind. 1; v. 1
Three Rivers (48)	LD 29; C. 12; Lab. 7
Tonbridge and Malling (53)	C. 33; LD 13; Lab. 7
Torridge (36)	Ind. 27; LD 7; Green 1; C. 1
Tunbridge Wells (48)	C. 35; LD 12; Lab. 1
Tynedale (52)	C. 27; LD 11; Lab. 9; Ind. 5
Uttlesford (44)	LD 31; C. 10; Ind. 3
Vale of White Horse (51)	LD 29; C. 21; Ind. 1
Vale Royal (57)	C. 22; Lab. 21; LD 12; Ind. 2
Wansbeck (45)	Lab. 37; LD 8
Warwick (46)	Lab. 14; C. 16; LD 10; Ind. 6
Watford (36)	LD 26; Lab. 4; C. 4; Green 2
Waveney (48)	C. 24; Lab. 14; Ind. 7; LD 3
Waverley (57)	C. 28; LD 29
Wealden (55)	C. 35; LD 13; Ind. 6; v. 1
Wear Valley (40)	Lab. 25; LD 9; Ind. 6
Wellingborough (36)	C. 26; Lab. 9; v. 1
Welwyn & Hatfield (48)	C. 31; Lab. 15; LD 2
West Devon (31)	C. 12; Ind. 10; LD 8; UKIP 1
West Dorset (48)	C. 26; LD 12; Ind. 10
West Lancashire (54)	C. 29; Lab. 25
West Lindsey (37)	C. 19; LD 16; Ind. 2
West Oxfordshire (49)	C. 29; LD 13; Ind. 6; Lab. 1
West Somerset (31)	C. 18; Ind. 9; Lab. 2; LD 2
West Wiltshire (44)	LD 19; C. 18; Ind. 4; Lab. 3
Weymouth and Portland (36)	LD 14; Lab. 9; C. 8; Ind. 5
Winchester (58)	LD 26; C. 22; Ind. 5; Lab. 5
Woking (36)	C. 17; LD 15; Lab. 4
Worcester (35)	C. 18; Lab. 10; LD 3; Ind. Other 3; Ind. 1
Worthing (37)	C. 26; LD 11
Wychavon (45)	C. 31; LD 12; Lab. 2
Wycombe (60)	C. 46; Lab. 9; LD 2; Ind. 3
Wyre (55)	C. 33; Lab. 21; LD 1
Wyre Forest (42)	C. 19; IKHHC 8; Lib. 8; Lab. 4; LD 2; Ind. 1

LONDON BOROUGH COUNCILS

Barking and Dagenham (51)	Lab. 42; R. 3; LD 3; C. 3
Barnet (63)	C. 33; Lab. 24; LD 6
Bexley (63)	Lab. 32; C. 30; LD 1
Brent (63)	Lab. 35; C. 18; LD 10
Bromley (60)	LD 41; C. 13; Lab. 6
Camden (54)	Lab. 35; C. 11; LD 8
Croydon (70)	Lab. 37; C. 31; LD 1; Ind. 1
Ealing (69)	Lab. 48; C. 17; LD 4
Enfield (63)	C. 39; Lab. 24
Greenwich (51)	Lab. 38; C. 9; LD 4
Hackney (57)	Lab. 45; C. 8; LD 3; v. 1
Hammersmith and Fulham (46)	Lab. 29; C. 17

Haringey (57)	Lab. 42; LD 15
Harrow (63)	Lab. 30; C. 28; LD 3; Ind. 2
Havering (53)	C. 26; R. 17; Lab. 10
Hillingdon (65)	C. 30; Lab. 27; LD 8
Hounslow (59)	Lab. 36; C. 14; LD 5; Ind. 4
Islington (48)	LD 36; Lab. 10; Ind. 2
Kensington and Chelsea (54)	C. 42; Lab. 12
Kingston upon Thames (48)	LD 30; C. 15; Lab. 3
Lambeth (63)	Lab. 28; LD 28; C. 7
Lewisham (54)	Lab. 42; LD 6; C. 2; Soc. 2; Ind. 1; Green 1
Merton (60)	Lab. 33; C. 24; R. 3
Newham (60)	Lab. 59; Ind. 1
Redbridge (63)	C. 34; Lab. 20; LD 9
Richmond upon Thames (54)	C. 37; LD 16; v. 1
Southwark (63)	LD 29; Lab. 28; C. 6
Sutton (54)	LD 43; C. 8; Lab. 3
Tower Hamlets (51)	Lab. 34; LD 16; Other 1
Waltham Forest (60)	Lab. 27; C. 18; LD 15
Wandsworth (60)	C. 50; Lab. 10
Westminster (60)	C. 48; Lab. 12

METROPOLITAN BOROUGH COUNCILS

Barnsley (63)	Lab. 33; Ind. 22; C. 5; LD 3
Birmingham (120)	Lab. 53; C. 39; LD 28
Bolton (60)	LD 21; Lab. 20; C. 19
Bradford (90)	C. 38; Lab. 29; LD 15; BNP 4; Green 4
Bury (51)	Lab. 27; C. 19; LD 5
Calderdale (51)	C. 21; LD 15; Lab. 9; Ind 3; BNP 3
Coventry (54)	C. 27; Lab. 22; LD 3; Other 2
Doncaster (63)	Lab. 27; Ind. 14; LD 13; C. 9
Dudley (72)	C. 40; Lab. 25; LD 7
Gateshead (66)	Lab. 43; LD 22; Lib. 1
Kirklees (69)	LD 25; C. 22; Lab. 17; Green 3; Ind. 1; BNP 1
Knowsley (63)	Lab. 52; LD 11
Leeds (99)	Lab. 40; LD 26; C. 24; Green 3; Ind. 6
Liverpool (90)	LD 60; Lab 27; Lib. 3
Manchester (96)	Lab. 56; LD 39; Green 1
Newcastle-upon-Tyne (78)	LD 48; Lab. 30
North Tyneside (60)	C. 27; Lab. 26; LD 7
Oldham (60)	Lab. 32; LD 25; C. 2; Ind. 1
Rochdale (60)	LD 25; Lab. 24; C. 11
Rotherham (63)	Lab. 53; C. 7; Ind. 3
St Helens (48)	Lab. 24; LD 18; C. 6
Salford (60)	Lab. 44; LD 8; C. 8
Sandwell (72)	Lab. 52; C. 13; LD 6; BNP 1
Sefton (66)	LD 27; Lab. 20; C. 19
Sheffield (84)	Lab. 44; LD 37; C. 2; Green 1
Solihull (51)	C. 27; LD 15; Lab. 8; Ind 1
South Tyneside (54)	Lab. 35; Ind. 12; LD 4; C. 3
Stockport (63)	LD 35; Lab. 14; C. 10; Ind. 4
Sunderland (75)	Lab. 61; C. 12; LD 2
Tameside (57)	Lab. 45; C. 7; LD 3; Ind. 2
Trafford (63)	C. 40; Lab. 20; LD 3
Wakefield (63)	Lab. 43; C. 11; Ind. 6; LD 3
Walsall (60)	C. 35; Lab. 18; LD 6; Other 1
Wigan (75)	Lab. 42; Ind. 18; LD 8; C. 7
Wirral (66)	Lab. 26; C. 21; LD 19
Wolverhampton (60)	Lab. 41; C. 16; LD 3

UNITARY COUNCILS

Bath and North East Somerset (65)	LD 29; C. 26; Lab. 6; Ind. 4
Blackburn with Darwen (64)	Lab. 33; C. 17; LD 12; v. 2
Blackpool (42)	Lab. 25; C. 13; LD 4
Bournemouth (54)	LD 32; C. 17; Lab. 3; Ind. 2
Bracknell Forest (42)	C. 34; Lab. 6; LD 1; Ind. 1
Brighton and Hove (54)	Lab. 24; C. 20; Green 6; LD 3; Ind. 1
Bristol (70)	Lab. 31; LD 27; C. 11; Ind. 1
Darlington (53)	Lab. 35; C. 16; LD 2
Derby (51)	Lab. 24; LD 14; C. 11; UKIP 1; v. 1
East Riding of Yorkshire (64)	C. 28; LD 20; Lab. 8; Ind. 6; SDP 2
Halton (56)	Lab. 35; LD 14; C. 7
Hartlepool (46)	Lab. 25; LD 9; Ind. 9; C. 4
Herefordshire (58)	C. 21; Ind. 17; LD 16; Lab. 4
Isle of Wight (48)	IF 27; C. 13; Other 5; Lab. 3
Kingston-upon-Hull (59)	Lab. 27; LD 24; Ind. 5; C. 2; UKIP 1
Leicester (54)	LD 25; Lab. 20; C. 8; v. 1
Luton (48)	Lab. 23; LD 20; C. 4; Ind. 1
Medway (55)	C. 30; Lab. 17; LD 6; Ind. 2
Middlesbrough (48)	Lab. 32; C. 7; LD 5; Ind. 4
Milton Keynes (51)	LD 27; Lab. 16; C. 7; Ind. 1
North East Lincolnshire (42)	LD 16; C. 15; Lab. 7; Ind. 4
North Lincolnshire (43)	Lab. 21; C. 22
North Somerset (61)	C. 24; LD 23; Lab. 10; Ind. 3; Green 1
Nottingham (55)	Lab. 36; LD 11; C. 8
Peterborough (57)	C. 33; Ind. 9; Lab. 7; Lib. 4; LD 4
Plymouth (57)	Lab. 35; C. 19; LD 2; Ind. 1
Poole (42)	C. 26; LD 16
Portsmouth (42)	LD 20; C. 15; Lab. 7
Reading (46)	Lab. 35; C. 6; LD 5
Redcar and Cleveland (59)	Lab. 22; LD 15; C. 13; Ind. 9
Rutland (26)	C. 15; Ind. 6; LD 5
Slough (41)	Lab. 15; C. 8; Ind. 6; LD 6; R 3; Lib. 3
South Gloucestershire (70)	LD 33; C. 21; Lab 16
Southampton (48)	LD 19; Lab. 15; C. 14
Southend-on-Sea (51)	C. 33; Lab. 9; LD 7; Ind. 2
Stockton-on-Tees (55)	Lab. 28; C. 13; Ind. 8; LD 6
Stoke-on-Trent (60)	Lab. 34; Ind. 13; LD 5; C. 5; BNP 2; v. 1
Swindon (59)	C. 33; Lab. 19; LD 7
Telford and Wrekin (54)	Lab. 29; C. 13; Ind. 6; LD 6
Thurrock (49)	C. 28; Lab. 19; Ind. 2
Torbay (36)	LD 27; C. 9
Warrington (57)	Lab. 30; LD 21; C. 6
West Berkshire (52)	LD 26; C. 26
Windsor and Maidenhead (57)	LD 34; C. 15; Ind 7; Lab. 1
Wokingham (54)	C. 33; LD 20; v. 1
York (47)	Lab. 15; LD 29; Green 2; Ind. 1

WALES

Blaenau Gwent (42)	Lab. 31; Ind. 8; LD 3
Bridgend (54)	Lab. 21; LD 13; Ind. 10; C. 8; PC 1; v. 1
Caerphilly (73)	Lab. 39; PC 26; Ind. 8
Cardiff (75)	LD 33; Lab. 27; C. 12; PC 3
Carmarthenshire (74)	Ind. 32; Lab. 25; PC 16; C. 1
Ceredigion (42)	Ind. 16; PC 16; LD 9; Lab. 1
Conwy (59)	Ind. 19; Lab. 12; C. 12; PC 9; LD 6; v. 1
Denbighshire (47)	Ind. 19; Lab. 8; C. 8; PC 7; Other 3; LD 2
Flintshire (70)	Lab. 37; Ind. 18; LD 10; C. 4; PC 1
Gwynedd (83)	PC 41; Ind. 17: Lab. 10; LD 7
Merthyr Tydfil (33)	Lab. 17; Ind. 16
Monmouthshire (43)	C. 24; Lab. 8; Ind. 5; LD 4; PC 2
Neath Port Talbot (64)	Lab. 36; PC 10; R 9; Ind. 7; LD 2
Newport (50)	Lab. 31; C. 11; LD 6; PC 1; Ind. 1
Pembrokeshire (60)	Ind. 40; Lab. 12; PC 5; LD 3
Powys (73)	Ind. 53; LD 16; Lab. 4
Rhondda Cynon Taff (75)	Lab. 57; PC 13; Ind. 3; LD 2
Swansea (72)	Lab. 32; LD 19; Ind. 12; PC 5; C. 4
Torfaen (44)	Lab. 34; Ind. 7; LD 2; C. 1
Vale of Glamorgan (47)	C. 20; Lab. 16; PC 8; Ind. 3
Wrexham (52)	Ind. 20; Lab. 19; LD 10; C. 3
Ynys Mon (Isle of Anglesey) (40)	Ind. 28; PC 8; C. 2; Lab. 1; LD 1

SCOTLAND

Aberdeen (43)	LD 20; Lab. 14; SNP 6; C. 3
Aberdeenshire (68)	LD 28; SNP 18; Ind. 11; C. 11
Angus (29)	SNP 17; Ind. 6; LD 3; C. 2; Lab. 1
Argyll and Bute (36)	Ind. 22; LD 8; SNP 3; C. 3
Clackmannanshire (18)	SNP 6; Lab. 10; C. 1; Ind. 1
Dumfries and Galloway (47)	Lab. 14; Ind. 12; CU 9; LD 5; SNP 5; v. 2
Dundee (29)	SNP 11; Lab. 10; C. 5; LD 2; Ind. 1
East Ayrshire (32)	Lab. 23; SNP 8; C. 1
East Dunbartonshire (24)	LD 12; Lab. 9; C. 3
East Lothian (23)	Lab. 16; C. 4; SNP 1; LD 1; Ind. 1
East Renfrewshire (20)	Lab. 8; C. 7; LD 3; Ind. 2
Edinburgh (58)	Lab. 30; LD 15; C. 13
Eilean Siar (Western Isles) (31)	Ind. 22; Lab. 5; SNP 3; v. 1
Falkirk (32)	Lab. 14; SNP 9; Ind. 7; C. 2
Fife (78)	Lab. 36; LD 23; SNP 11; Other 6; C. 2
Glasgow (79)	Lab. 71; SNP 3; LD 3; C. 1; SSP 1
Highland (80)	Ind. 57; LD 9; Lab. 8; SNP 6
Inverclyde (20)	LD 13; Lab. 6; Ind. 1
Midlothian (18)	Lab. 15; LD 2; Ind. 1
Moray (26)	Ind. 15; Lab. 5; SNP 3; CU 1; LD 1; v. 1
North Ayrshire (30)	Lab. 20; C. 5; SNP 3; Ind. 2
North Lanarkshire (70)	Lab. 54; SNP 11; Ind. 5
Orkney Islands (21)	Ind. 21
Perth and Kinross (41)	SNP 15; C. 10; LD 9; Lab. 5; Ind. 2
Renfrewshire (40)	Lab. 21; SNP 15; LD 3; C. 1
Scottish Borders (34)	CU 11; Ind. 11; LD 8; NP 3; SNP 1
Shetland Islands (22)	Ind. 17; LD 5
South Ayrshire (30)	Lab. 15; C. 15
South Lanarkshire (67)	Lab. 51; SNP 9; Ind. 3; C. 2; LD 2
Stirling (22)	Lab. 12; C. 10
West Dunbartonshire (22)	Lab. 17; SNP 3; SSP 1; Ind. 1
West Lothian (32)	Lab. 18; SNP 11; Ind. 2; C. 1

NORTHERN IRELAND

Antrim (19)	UUP 8; DUP 5; SDLP 4; SF 2
Ards (23)	DUP 9; UUP 8; All. 4; Ind. 2
Armagh City (22)	UUP 7; SDLP 6; SF 5; DUP 4
Ballymena (24)	DUP 11; UUP 7; SDLP 4; Ind. 2
Ballymoney (16)	DUP 8; UUP 5; SDLP 2; SF 1
Banbridge (17)	UUP 6; DUP 6; SDLP 3; All. 1; Ind. 1
Belfast (51)	SF 14; UUP 11; DUP 10; SDLP 9; Other 4; All. 3
Carrickfergus (17)	DUP 6; All. 5; UUP 4; Ind. 2
Castlereagh (24)	DUP 10; UUP 5; All. 4; SDLP 2; Ind. 2
Coleraine (22)	UUP 9; DUP 7; SDLP 3; Ind. 1; SF 1; Other 1
Cookstown (16)	SF 6; SDLP 4; UUP 3; DUP 2; Ind. 1
Craigavon (26)	UUP 7; SDLP 7; DUP 6; SF 4; Ind. UU 2
Derry City (30)	SDLP 13; SF 10; DUP 4; UUP 2; Ind. 1
Down (23)	SDLP 9; UUP 6; SF 4; DUP 2; Ind. 2
Dungannon and South Tyrone (22)	SF 8; UUP 6; SDLP 4; DUP 3; Ind. 1
Fermanagh (23)	UUP 9; SF 7; SDLP 4; DUP 2; Ind. 1
Larne (15)	DUP 5; UUP 4; All. 2; SDLP 2; Ind. 2
Limavady (15)	SDLP 4; SF 4; UUP 3; DUP 2; Other 2
Lisburn (30)	UUP 12; DUP 6; Other 5; SF 4; SDLP 3
Magherafelt (16)	SF 7; DUP 3; SDLP 3; UUP 2; Ind. 1
Moyle (15)	SDLP 5; Ind. 3; UUP 3; DUP 2; SF 2
Newry and Mourne (30)	SDLP 10; SF 13; UUP 4; Ind. 2; DUP 1
Newtownabbey (25)	UUP 9; DUP 7; Other 6; SDLP 2; SF 1
North Down (25)	UUP 8; Ind. 7; All 5; DUP 5
Omagh (21)	SF 8; SDLP 6; UUP 3; DUP 2; Ind. 2
Strabane (16)	SF 7; SDLP 4; DUP 3; UUP 2

ENGLAND

The Kingdom of England lies between 55° 46′ and 49° 57′ 30″ N. latitude (from a few miles north of the mouth of the Tweed to the Lizard), and between 1° 46′ E. and 5° 43′ W. (from Lowestoft to Land's End). England is bounded on the north by the Cheviot Hills; on the south by the English Channel; on the east by the Straits of Dover (Pas de Calais) and the North Sea; and on the west by the Atlantic Ocean, Wales and the Irish Sea. It has a total area of 50,351 sq. miles (130,410 sq. km): land 50,058 sq. miles (129,652 sq. km); inland water 293 sq. miles (758 sq. km).

POPULATION

The population at the 2001 census was 49,138,831. The average density of the population in 2001 was 3.8 persons per hectare.

FLAG

The flag of England is the cross of St George, a red cross on a white field (cross gules in a field argent). The cross of St George, the patron saint of England, has been used since the 13th century.

RELIEF

There is a marked division between the upland and lowland areas of England. In the extreme north the Cheviot Hills (highest point, The Cheviot, 2,674 ft) form a natural boundary with Scotland. Running south from the Cheviots, though divided from them by the Tyne Gap, is the Pennine range (highest point, Cross Fell, 2,930 ft), the main orological feature of the country. The Pennines culminate in the Peak District of Derbyshire (Kinder Scout, 2,088 ft). West of the Pennines are the Cumbrian mountains, which include Scafell Pike (3,210 ft), the highest peak in England, and to the east are the Yorkshire Moors, their highest point being Urra Moor (1,490 ft).

In the west, the foothills of the Welsh mountains extend into the bordering English counties of Shropshire (the Wrekin, 1,334 ft; Long Mynd, 1,694 ft) and Hereford and Worcester (the Malvern Hills – Worcestershire Beacon, 1,394 ft). Extensive areas of highland and moorland are also to be found in the south-western peninsula formed by Somerset, Devon and Cornwall: principally Exmoor (Dunkery Beacon, 1,704 ft), Dartmoor (High Willhays, 2,038 ft) and Bodmin Moor (Brown Willy, 1,377 ft). Ranges of low, undulating hills run across the south of the country, including the Cotswolds in the Midlands and south-west, the Chilterns to the north of London, and the North (Kent) and South (Sussex) Downs of the south-east coastal areas.

The lowlands of England lie in the Vale of York, East Anglia and the area around the Wash. The lowest-lying are the Cambridgeshire Fens in the valleys of the Great Ouse and the River Nene, which are below sea-level in places. Since the 17th century extensive drainage has brought much of the Fens under cultivation. The North Sea coast between the Thames and the Humber, low-lying and formed of sand and shingle for the most part, is subject to erosion and defences against further incursion have been built along many stretches.

HYDROGRAPHY

The Severn is the longest river in Great Britain, rising in the north-eastern slopes of Plynlimon (Wales) and entering England in Shropshire with a total length of 220 miles (354 km) from its source to its outflow into the Bristol Channel, where it receives on the east the Bristol Avon, and on the west the Wye, its other tributaries being the Vyrnwy, Tern, Stour, Teme and Upper (or Warwickshire) Avon. The Severn is tidal below Gloucester, and a high bore or tidal wave sometimes reverses the flow as high as Tewkesbury (13½ miles above Gloucester). The scenery of the greater part of the river is very picturesque and beautiful, and the Severn is a noted salmon river, some of its tributaries being famous for trout. Navigation is assisted by the Gloucester and Berkeley Ship Canal (16¼ miles), which admits vessels of 350 tons to Gloucester. The Severn Tunnel was begun in 1873 and completed in 1886 at a cost of £2 million and after many difficulties caused by flooding. It is 4 miles 628 yards in length (of which 2¼ miles are under the river). The Severn road bridge between Haysgate, Gwent, and Almondsbury, Glos, with a centre span of 3,240 ft, was opened in 1966.

The longest river wholly in England is the Thames, with a total length of 215 miles (346 km) from its source in the Cotswold hills to the Nore, and is navigable by ocean-going ships to London Bridge. The Thames is tidal to Teddington (69 miles from its mouth) and forms county boundaries almost throughout its course; on its banks are situated London, Windsor Castle, Eton College and Oxford University. Of the remaining English rivers, those flowing into the North Sea are the Tyne, Wear, Tees, Ouse and Trent from the Pennine Range, the Great Ouse (160 miles), which rises in Northamptonshire, and the Orwell and Stour from the hills of East Anglia. Flowing into the English Channel are the Sussex Ouse from the Weald, the Itchen from the Hampshire Hills, and the Axe, Teign, Dart, Tamar and Exe from the Devonian hills. Flowing into the Irish Sea are the Mersey, Ribble and Eden from the western slopes of the Pennines and the Derwent from the Cumbrian mountains.

The English Lakes, noteworthy for their picturesque scenery and poetic associations, lie in Cumbria, the largest being Windermere (10 miles long), Ullswater and Derwent Water.

ISLANDS

The Isle of Wight is separated from Hampshire by the Solent. The capital, Newport, stands at the head of the estuary of the Medina, Cowes (at the mouth) being the chief port. Other centres are Ryde, Sandown, Shanklin, Ventnor, Freshwater, Yarmouth, Totland Bay, Seaview and Bembridge.

Lundy (the name means Puffin Island), 11 miles north-west of Hartland Point, Devon, is about three miles long and about half a mile wide on average, with a total area of about 1,116 acres, and a population of about 18. It became the property of the National Trust in 1969 and is now principally a bird sanctuary.

The Isles of Scilly consist of about 140 islands and skerries (total area, 6 sq. miles/10 sq. km) situated 28 miles south-west of Land's End in Cornwall. Only five are inhabited: St Mary's, St Agnes, Bryher, Tresco and St Martin's. The population at the 2001 census was 2,153. The entire group has been designated a Conservation Area, a Heritage Coast, and an Area of Outstanding Natural Beauty, and has been given National Nature

Reserve status by the Nature Conservancy Council because of its unique flora and fauna. Tourism and the winter/spring flower trade for the home market form the basis of the economy of the Isles. The island group is a recognised rural development area.

EARLY HISTORY

Archaeological evidence suggests that England has been inhabited since at least the Palaeolithic period, though the extent of the various Palaeolithic cultures was dependent upon the degree of glaciation. The succeeding Neolithic and Bronze Age cultures have left abundant remains throughout the country, the best-known of these being the henges and stone circles of Stonehenge (ten miles north of Salisbury, Wilts) and Avebury (Wilts), both of which are believed to have been of religious significance. In the latter part of the Bronze Age the Goidels, a people of Celtic race, and in the Iron Age other Celtic races of Brythons and Belgae, invaded the country and brought with them Celtic civilisation and dialects, place names in England bear witness to the spread of the invasion over the whole kingdom.

THE ROMAN CONQUEST

The Roman conquest of Gaul (57–50 BC) brought Britain into close contact with Roman civilisation, but although Julius Caesar raided the south of Britain in 55 BC and 54 BC, conquest was not undertaken until nearly 100 years later. In AD 43 the Emperor Claudius dispatched Aulus Plautius, with a well-equipped force of 40,000, and himself followed with reinforcements in the same year. Success was delayed by the resistance of Caratacus (Caractacus), the British leader from AD 48–51, who was finally captured and sent to Rome, and by a great revolt in AD 61 led by Boudicca (Boadicea), Queen of the Iceni; but the south of Britain was secured by AD 70, and Wales and the area north to the Tyne by about AD 80.

In AD 122, the Emperor Hadrian visited Britain and built a continuous rampart, since known as Hadrian's Wall, from Wallsend to Bowness (Tyne to Solway). The work was entrusted by the Emperor Hadrian to Aulus Platorius Nepos, legate of Britain from AD 122 to 126, and it was intended to form the northern frontier of the Roman Empire.

The Romans administered Britain as a province under a Governor, with a well-defined system of local government, each Roman municipality ruling itself and its surrounding territory, while London was the centre of the road system and the seat of the financial officials of the Province of Britain. Colchester, Lincoln, York, Gloucester and St Albans stand on the sites of five Roman municipalities, and Wroxeter, Caerleon, Chester, Lincoln and York were at various times the sites of legionary fortresses. Well-preserved Roman towns have been uncovered at or near Silchester *(Calleva Atrebatum)*, ten miles south of Reading, Wroxeter *(Viroconium Cornoviorum)*, near Shrewsbury, and St Albans *(Verulamium)* in Hertfordshire.

Four main groups of roads radiated from London, and a fifth (the Fosse) ran obliquely from Lincoln through Leicester, Cirencester and Bath to Exeter. Of the four groups radiating from London, one ran south-east to Canterbury and the coast of Kent, a second to Silchester and thence to parts of western Britain and south Wales, a third (later known as Watling Street) ran through Verulamium to Chester, with various branches, and the fourth reached Colchester, Lincoln, York and the eastern counties.

In the fourth century Britain was subject to raids along the east coast by Saxon pirates, which led to the establishment of a system of coastal defences from the Wash to Southampton Water, with forts at Brancaster, Burgh Castle (Yarmouth), Walton (Felixstowe), Bradwell, Reculver, Richborough, Dover, Lympne, Pevensey and Porchester (Portsmouth). The Irish (Scoti) and Picts in the north were also becoming more aggressive; from about AD 350 incursions became more frequent and more formidable. As the Roman Empire came under attack increasingly towards the end of the fourth century, many troops were removed from Britain for service in other parts of the empire. The island was eventually cut off from Rome by the Teutonic conquest of Gaul, and with the withdrawal of the last Roman garrison early in the fifth century, the Romano-British were left to themselves.

SAXON SETTLEMENT

According to legend, the British King Vortigern called in the Saxons to defend him against the Picts, the Saxon chieftains being Hengist and Horsa, who landed at Ebbsfleet, Kent, and established themselves in the Isle of Thanet; but the events during the one-and-a-half centuries between the final break with Rome and the re-establishment of Christianity are unclear. However, it would appear that in the course of this period the raids turned into large-scale settlement by invaders traditionally known as Angles (England north of the Wash and East Anglia), Saxons (Essex and southern England) and Jutes (Kent and the Weald), which pushed the Romano-British into the mountainous areas of the north and west. Celtic culture outside Wales and Cornwall survives only in topographical names. Various kingdoms established at this time attempted to claim overlordship of the whole country, hegemony finally being achieved by Wessex (capital, Winchester) in the ninth century. This century also saw the beginning of raids by the Vikings (Danes), which were resisted by Alfred the Great (871–899), who fixed a limit to the advance of Danish settlement by the Treaty of Wedmore (878), giving them the area north and east of Watling Street, on condition that they adopt Christianity.

In the tenth century the kings of Wessex recovered the whole of England from the Danes, but subsequent rulers were unable to resist a second wave of invaders. England paid tribute *(Danegeld)* for many years, and was invaded in 1013 by the Danes and ruled by Danish kings from 1016 until 1042, when Edward the Confessor was recalled from exile in Normandy. On Edward's death in 1066 Harold Godwinson (brother-in-law of Edward and son of Earl Godwin of Wessex) was chosen King of England. After defeating (at Stamford Bridge, Yorkshire, 25 September) an invading army under Harald Hadraada, King of Norway (aided by the outlawed Earl Tostig of Northumbria, Harold's brother), Harold was himself defeated at the Battle of Hastings on 14 October 1066, and the Norman conquest secured the throne of England for Duke William of Normandy, a cousin of Edward the Confessor.

CHRISTIANITY

Christianity reached the Roman province of Britain from Gaul in the third century (or possibly earlier); Alban, traditionally Britain's first martyr, was put to death as a Christian during the persecution of Diocletian (22 June 303), at his native town *Verulamium*; and the Bishops of

Londinium, *Eboracum* (York), and *Lindum* (Lincoln) attended the Council of Arles in 314. However, the Anglo-Saxon invasions submerged the Christian religion in England until the sixth century when conversion was undertaken in the north from 563 by Celtic missionaries from Ireland led by St Columba, and in the south by a mission sent from Rome in 597 which was led by St Augustine, who became the first archbishop of Canterbury. England appears to have been converted again by the end of the seventh century and followed, after the Council of Whitby in 663, the practices of the Roman Church, which brought the kingdom into the mainstream of European thought and culture.

PRINCIPAL CITIES

There are 50 cities in England and space constraints prevent us from including profiles of them all. The profiles below represent just a selection of England's principal cities (with date city status conferred). Other cities are: Brighton and Hove (2000), Chichester (pre-1900), Derby (1977), Ely (pre-1900), Gloucester (pre-1900), Hereford (pre-1900), Lichfield (pre-1900), London (pre-1900), Peterborough (pre-1900), Plymouth (1928), Portsmouth (1926), Preston (2002), Ripon (pre-1900), Salford (1926), Southampton (1964), Sunderland (1992), Truro (pre-1900), Wakefield (pre-1900), Wells (pre-1900), Westminster (pre-1900), Wolverhampton (2000) and Worcester (pre-1900).

Certain cities have also been granted a Lord Mayoralty – this grant confers no additional powers or functions and is purely honorific. Cities with Lord Mayors are: Birmingham, Bradford, Bristol, Canterbury, Chester, Coventry, Exeter, Kingston-upon-Hull, Leeds, Leicester, Liverpool, London, Manchester, Newcastle-upon-Tyne, Norwich, Nottingham, Oxford, Plymouth, Portsmouth, Sheffield and Stoke-on-Trent.

BATH (PRE-1900)

Bath stands on the River Avon between the Cotswold Hills to the North and the Mendips to the south. In the early eighteenth century, Bath became England's premier spa town where the rich and celebrated members of fashionable society gathered to 'take the waters' and enjoy the town's theatres and concert rooms. During this period the architect John Wood laid the foundations for a new Georgian city to be built using the honey-coloured stone that Bath is famous for today.

Today Bath is a thriving tourist destination and remains a leading cultural, religious and historical centre with many art galleries and historic sites including; the Pump Room (1790), The Royal Crescent (1767), the Circus (1754), the 18th-century Assembly Rooms (housing the Museum of Costume), Pulteney Bridge (1771), the Guildhall and the Abbey, now over 500 years old, which is built on the site of the Saxon monastery.

BIRMINGHAM (PRE-1900)

Birmingham is Britain's second largest city with a population of nearly one million. The generally accepted derivation of 'Birmingham' is the *ham* (dwelling-place) of the *ing* (family) of *Beorma*, presumed to have been Saxon. During the Industrial Revolution the town grew into a major manufacturing centre and in 1889 was granted city status.

Recent developments include the Millennium Point, incorporating the science museum, Thinktank and Brindleyplace. On 4 September 2003 the Bullring shopping centre was officially opened as part of the city's urban regeneration programme.

The principal buildings are the Town Hall (1834–50), the Council House (1879), Victoria Law Courts (1891), Birmingham University (1906–9), the 13th-century Church of St Martin-in-the-Bull-Ring (rebuilt 1873), Our Lady, Help of Christians Church, the Cathedral (formerly St Philip's Church) (1711), the Roman Catholic Cathedral of St Chad (1839–41), the assay office (1773) and the National Exhibition Centre (1976). There is also the Birmingham Museum and Art Gallery including the Waterhall Gallery which opened in 2001.

BRADFORD (PRE-1900)

During the Industrial Revolution of the 18th and 19th centuries Bradford expanded rapidly and a great deal of wealth was generated by the wool industry.

Bradford city centre has a host of buildings with historical and cultural interest, including: City Hall, with its 19th-century Lord Mayor's rooms and Victorian law court; Bradford Cathedral; The Priestly, a theatre and arts centre originally established as the Bradford Civic Playhouse by J. B. Priestly and friends; the Colour Museum; the National Museum of Photography, Film and Television which houses five floors of interactive displays and three cinemas; and Piece Hall Yard which incorporates the Bradford Club, a Victorian Gothic style club dating from 1837, and the Peace Museum.

BRISTOL (PRE-1900)

Bristol was a Royal Borough before the Norman Conquest. The earliest form of the name is *Bricgstow*. In 1373 Edward III granted Bristol county status.

The chief buildings include the 12th-century Cathedral (with later additions), with Norman chapter house and gateway, the 14th-century Church of St Mary Redcliffe, Wesley's Chapel, Broadmead, the Merchant Venturers' Almshouses, the Council House (1956), Guildhall, Exchange (erected from the designs of John Wood in 1743), Cabot Tower, the University and Clifton College. The Roman Catholic Cathedral at Clifton was opened in 1973.

The Clifton Suspension Bridge, with a span of 702 feet over the Avon, was projected by Brunel in 1836 but was not completed until 1864. Brunel's SS *Great Britain*, the first ocean-going propeller-driven ship, is now being restored in the City Docks from where she was launched in 1843. The docks themselves have been extensively restored and redeveloped; the 19th-century two-storey former tea warehouse is now the Arnolfini centre for contemporary arts, and an 18th-century sail loft houses the Architecture Centre. Behind the baroque-domed facade of the former 'E' Shed are shops, cafes, restaurants and the Watershed Media Centre, and on Princes Wharf disused transit sheds house the Industrial Museum.

CAMBRIDGE (1951)

Cambridge, a settlement far older than its ancient University, lies on the River Cam or Granta. The city is a county town and regional headquarters. Its industries include technology research and development, and biotechnology. Among its open spaces are Jesus Green, Sheep's Green, Coe Fen, Parker's Piece, Christ's Pieces, the University Botanic Garden, and the 'Backs' – lawns and gardens through which the Cam winds behind the principal line of college buildings. Historical sites east of the Cam include; King's Parade, Great St Mary's Church, Gibbs' Senate House and King's College Chapel.

University and college buildings provide the outstanding features of Cambridge's architecture but several churches (especially St Benet's, the oldest building in the city, and St Sepulchre's, the Round Church) are also notable. The Guildhall (1937) stands on a site of which at least part has held municipal buildings since 1224.

CANTERBURY (PRE-1900)
Canterbury, the Metropolitan City of the Anglican Communion, dates back to prehistoric times. It was the Roman *Durovernum Cantiacorum* and the Saxon *Cant-wara-byrig* (stronghold of the men of Kent). Here in 597 St Augustine began the conversion of the English to Christianity, when Ethelbert, King of Kent, was baptised.

Of the Benedictine St Augustine's Abbey, burial place of the Jutish Kings of Kent, only ruins remain. St Martin's Church, on the eastern outskirts of the city, is stated by Bede to have been the place of worship of Queen Bertha, the Christian wife of King Ethelbert, before the advent of St Augustine.

In 1170 the rivalry of Church and State culminated in the murder in Canterbury Cathedral, by Henry II's knights, of Archbishop Thomas Becket. His shrine became a great centre of pilgrimage, as described in Chaucer's *Canterbury Tales.* After the Reformation pilgrimages ceased, but the prosperity of the city was strengthened by an influx of Huguenot refugees, who introduced weaving. The poet and playwright Christopher Marlowe was born and reared in Canterbury, and there are also literary associations with Defoe, Dickens, Joseph Conrad and Somerset Maugham.

The Cathedral, with architecture ranging from the 11th to the 15th centuries, is world famous. Modern pilgrims are attracted particularly to the Martyrdom, the Black Prince's Tomb, the Warriors' Chapel and the many examples of medieval stained glass.

The medieval city walls are built on Roman foundations and the 14th-century West Gate is one of the finest buildings of its kind in the country.

The 1,000-seat Marlowe Theatre is a centre for the Canterbury Arts Festival each autumn.

CARLISLE (PRE-1900)
Carlisle is situated at the confluence of the River Eden and River Caldew, 309 miles north-west of London and about ten miles from the Scottish border. It was granted a charter in 1158.

The city stands at the western end of Hadrian's Wall and dates from the original Roman settlement of *Luguvalium.* Granted to Scotland in the tenth century, Carlisle is not included in the Domesday Book. William Rufus reclaimed the area in 1092 and the castle and city walls were built to guard Carlisle and the western border; the citadel is a Tudor addition to protect the south of the city. Border disputes were common until the problem of the Debateable Lands was settled in 1552. During the Civil War the city remained Royalist; in 1745 Carlisle was besieged for the last time by the Young Pretender (Bonnie Prince Charlie).

The Cathedral, originally a 12th-century Augustinian priory, was enlarged in the 13th and 14th centuries after the diocese was created in 1133. To the south is a restored Tithe Barn and nearby the 18th-century church of St Cuthbert, the third to stand on a site dating from the seventh century.

Carlisle is the major shopping, commercial and agricultural centre for the area, and industries include the manufacture of metal goods, biscuits and textiles. However, the largest employer is the services sector, most notably in central and local government, retailing and transport. The city has an important communications position at the centre of a network of major roads, as a stage on the main west coast rail services, and with its own airport at Crosby-on-Eden.

CHESTER (PRE-1900)
Chester is situated on the River Dee. Its recorded history dates from the first century when the Romans founded the fortress of *Deva.* The city's name is derived from the Latin *castra* (a camp or encampment). During the Middle Ages, Chester was the principal port of north-west England but declined with the silting of the Dee estuary and competition from Liverpool. The city was also an important military centre, notably during Edward I's Welsh campaigns and the Elizabethan Irish campaigns. During the Civil War, Chester supported the King and was besieged from 1643 to 1646. Chester's first charter was granted *c.* 1175 and the city was incorporated in 1506. The office of Sheriff is the earliest created in the country (*c.* 1120s), and in 1992 the Mayor was granted the title of Lord Mayor. He/she also enjoys the title 'Admiral of the Dee'.

The city's architectural features include the city walls (an almost complete two-mile circuit), the unique 13th-century Rows (covered galleries above the street-level shops), the Victorian Gothic Town Hall (1869), the Castle (rebuilt 1788 and 1822) and numerous half-timbered buildings. The Cathedral was a Benedictine abbey until the Dissolution. Remaining monastic buildings include the chapter house, refectory and cloisters and there is a modern free-standing bell tower. The Norman church of St John the Baptist was a cathedral church in the early Middle Ages.

COVENTRY (PRE-1900)
Coventry is an important industrial centre, producing vehicles, machine tools, agricultural machinery, man-made fibres, aerospace components and telecommunications equipment. New investment has come from financial services, power transmission, professional services, leisure and education.

The city owes its beginning to Leofric, Earl of Mercia, and his wife Godiva who, in 1043, founded a Benedictine monastery. The guildhall of St Mary dates from the 14th century, three of the city's churches date from the 14th and 15th centuries, and 16th-century almshouses may still be seen. Coventry's first cathedral was destroyed at the Reformation, its second in the 1940 blitz (the walls and spire remain) and the new cathedral designed by Sir Basil Spence, consecrated in 1962, now draws numerous visitors.

Coventry is the home of the University of Warwick, Coventry University, the Westwood Business Park, the Cable and Wireless Technical Training College, the Museum of British Road Transport and the Skydome Arena.

DURHAM (PRE-1900)
The city of Durham is a major tourist attraction and its prominent Norman Cathedral and Castle are set high on a wooded peninsula overlooking the River Wear. The Cathedral was founded as a shrine for the body of St Cuthbert in 995. The present building dates from 1093

and among its many treasures is the tomb of the Venerable Bede (673–735). Durham's Prince Bishops had unique powers up to 1836, being lay rulers as well as religious leaders. As a palatinate, Durham could have its own army, nobility, coinage and courts. The Castle was the main seat of the Prince Bishops for nearly 800 years; it is now used as a college by the University. The University, founded on the initiative of Bishop William Van Mildert, is England's third oldest.

Among other buildings of interest is the Guildhall in the Market Place which dates originally from the 14th century. Work has been carried out to conserve this area as part of the city's contribution to the Council of Europe's Urban Renaissance Campaign. Annual events include Durham's Regatta in June (claimed to be the oldest rowing event in Britain) and the Annual Gala (formerly Durham Miners' Gala) in July.

The economy has undergone a significant change with the replacement of mining as the dominant industry by 'white collar' employment. Although still a predominantly rural area, the industrial and commercial sector is growing and a wide range of manufacturing and service industries are based on industrial estates in and around the city. A research and development centre, linked to the University, also plays an important role in the local economy.

EXETER (PRE-1900)

Exeter lies on the River Exe ten miles from the sea and was granted a charter by Henry II. The Romans founded *Isca Dumnoniorum* in the first century AD as a legionary fortress, and in the third century a stone wall (much of which remains) was built, providing protection against Saxon, and then Danish invasions. After the Conquest, the city led a resistance to William in the west until reduced by siege. The Normans built the ringwork castle of Rougemont, the gatehouse and towers remain, although the rest was pulled down in 1784. The first bridge across the Exe was built in the early 13th century. The city's main port was situated downstream at Topsham until the construction in the 1560s of the first true canal in England. The redevelopment of the canal in 1700 brought seaborne trade directly into the city. Exeter was the Royalist headquarters in the west during the Civil War.

The diocese of Exeter was established by Edward the Confessor in 1050, although a minster existed near the Cathedral site from the late seventh century. A new cathedral was built in the 12th century but the present building, incorporating the Norman Towers, was begun *c.* 1275 and completed about a century later. The Guildhall dates from the 12th century and there are many other medieval buildings in the city, as well as architecture in the Georgian and Regency styles, and the Custom House (1680). Damage suffered by bombing in 1942 led to the redevelopment of the city centre.

Exeter's prosperity from medieval times was based on trade in wool, commemorated by Tuckers Hall. The wool trade flourished until the late 18th century when export trade was hit by the French wars. Subsequently Exeter has developed as an administrative and commercial centre, notably in the distributive trades, light manufacturing industries and tourism.

KINGSTON-UPON-HULL (PRE-1900)

Hull (officially Kingston-upon-Hull) lies at the junction of the River Hull with the Humber, 22 miles from the North Sea. It is one of the major seaports of the United Kingdom. The port provides a wide range of cargo services, including ro-ro and container traffic, and handles an estimated million passengers annually on daily sailings to Rotterdam and Zeebrugge. There is a variety of manufacturing and service industries.

The city, restored after heavy air raid damage during the Second World War, has good educational facilities with both the University of Hull and the University of Lincoln being within its boundaries. Hull is home to the world's only submarium, The Deep, a £45.5 million project which opened in March 2002, and the Kingston Communications Stadium, with a seating capacity for 25,000, which was completed in December 2002. A £25 million BBC regional centre based at Queen's Gardens was due to open at the end of 2004.

Tourism is a major growth industry and the old town area has been renovated and includes Museums, a marina and shopping complex. Just west of the city is the Humber Bridge, until recently the world's longest single-span suspension bridge.

Kingston-upon-Hull was so named by Edward I. City status was accorded in 1897 and the office of Mayor raised to the dignity of Lord Mayor in 1914.

LANCASTER (1937)

Lancaster was originally a Roman fort and in Anglo-Saxon times a church was built within the ruins of the fort.

In the late 17th century, Lancaster began to trade with the West Indies and the new American colonies. This trade meant the 18th century was an age of great prosperity for the city and there are many splendid buildings dating from this period, including the complete port facility of St George's Quay, with the Custom House and numerous warehouses.

In the Victorian age, Lancaster began to specialise in textiles and two major manufacturing firms, Storeys and Williamsons, dominated the industry, the latter having a world reputation for the production of linoleum.

Lancaster was originally a market town and a borough, gaining its first charter in 1193. In 1937 Lancaster was awarded city status on King George VI's Coronation Day. Today, Lancaster has mainly technology and service industries and is an important centre for education.

LEEDS (PRE-1900)

Leeds, situated in the lower Aire Valley, is a junction for road, rail, canal and air services and an important manufacturing and commercial centre.

The principal buildings are the Civic Hall (1933), the Town Hall (1858), the Municipal Buildings and Art Gallery (1884) with the Henry Moore Gallery (1982), the Corn Exchange (1863) and the University. The Parish Church (St Peter's) was rebuilt in 1841; the 17th-century St John's Church has a fine interior with a famous English Renaissance screen; the last remaining 18th-century church in the city is Holy Trinity in Boar Lane (1727). Kirkstall Abbey (about three miles from the centre of the city), founded by Henry de Lacy in 1152, is one of the most complete examples of Cistercian houses now remaining. Temple Newsam, birthplace of Lord Darnley, was acquired by the Council in 1922. The present house was largely rebuilt by Sir Arthur Ingram in about 1620. Adel Church, about five miles from the centre of the city, is a fine Norman structure. The new Royal Armouries Museum houses the collection of antique arms and armour formerly held at the Tower of London.

Leeds was first incorporated by Charles I in 1626. The earliest forms of the name are *Loidis* or *Ledes*, the origins of which are obscure.

LEICESTER (1919)
Leicester is situated geographically in the centre of England. The city was an important Roman settlement and also one of the five Danish boroughs of Danelaw. In 1485 Richard III was buried in Leicester following his death at the nearby Battle of Bosworth. In 1589 Queen Elizabeth I granted a charter to the city and the ancient title was confirmed by letters patent in 1919.

The textile industry, responsible for Leicester's early expansion, has declined in recent years, although the city still maintains a strong manufacturing base. Cotton mills and factories are now undergoing extensive regeneration and are being converted into offices, apartments, bars and restaurants. The principal buildings include the two universities, the University of Leicester and De Montfort University, as well as the Town Hall, the 13th-century Guildhall, De Montfort Hall, Leicester Cathedral, the Jewry Wall (the UK's highest standing Roman wall), St Nicholas Church and St Mary de Castro church. The motte and Great Hall of Leicester can be seen from the castle gardens, situated next to the ancient River Soar.

LINCOLN (PRE-1900)
Situated 40 miles inland on the River Witham, Lincoln derives its name from a contraction of *Lindum Colonia*, the settlement founded in AD 48 by the Romans to command the crossing of Ermine Street and Fosse Way. Sections of the third-century Roman city wall can be seen, including an extant gateway (Newport Arch), and excavations have discovered traces of a sewerage system unique in Britain. The Romans also drained the surrounding fenland and created a canal system, laying the foundations of Lincoln's agricultural prosperity and also the city's importance in the medieval wool trade as a port and Staple town.

As one of the Five Boroughs of Danelaw, Lincoln was an important trading centre in the ninth and tenth centuries and medieval prosperity from the wool trade lasted until the 14th century. This wealth enabled local merchants to build parish churches, of which three survive, and there are also remains of a 12th century Jewish community (Jew's House and Court, Aaron's House). However, the removal of the Staple to Boston in 1369 heralded a decline, from which the city only recovered fully in the 19th century, when improved fen drainage made Lincoln agriculturally important. Improved canal and rail links led to industrial development, mainly in the manufacture of machinery, components and engineering products.

The castle was built shortly after the Conquest and is unusual in having two mounds; on one motte stands a Keep (Lucy's Tower) added in the 12th century. It currently houses one of the four surviving copies of the Magna Carta. The Cathedral was begun *c.* 1073 when the first Norman bishop moved the see of Lindsey to Lincoln, but was mostly destroyed by fire and earthquake in the 12th century. Rebuilding was begun by St Hugh and completed over a century later. Other notable architectural features are the 12th-century High Bridge, the oldest in Britain still to carry buildings, and the Guildhall situated above the 15th–16th-century Stonebow gateway.

LIVERPOOL (PRE-1900)
Liverpool, on the north bank of the River Mersey, three miles from the Irish Sea, is the United Kingdom's foremost port for Atlantic trade. Tunnels link Liverpool with Birkenhead and Wallasey.

There are 2,100 acres of dockland on both sides of the river and the Gladstone and Royal Seaforth Docks can accommodate tanker-sized vessels. Liverpool Free Port was opened in 1984.

Liverpool was created a free borough in 1207 and a city in 1880. From the early 18th century it expanded rapidly with the growth of industrialisation and the Atlantic trade. Surviving buildings from this period include the Bluecoat Chambers (1717, formerly the Bluecoat School), the Town Hall (1754, rebuilt to the original design 1795), and buildings in Rodney Street, Canning Street and the suburbs. Notable from the 19th and 20th centuries are the Anglican Cathedral, built from the designs of Sir Giles Gilbert Scott (the foundation stone was laid in 1904, and the building was completed only in 1980); the Catholic Metropolitan Cathedral (designed by Sir Frederick Gibberd, consecrated 1967) and St George's Hall (1842), regarded as one of the finest modern examples of classical architecture. The refurbished Albert Dock (designed by Jesse Hartley) contains the Merseyside Maritime Museum and Tate Gallery, Liverpool.

In 1852 an Act was obtained for establishing a public library, museum and art gallery; as a result Liverpool had one of the first public libraries in the country. The Brown, Picton and Hornby libraries form one of the country's major collections. The Victoria Building of Liverpool University, the Royal Liver, Cunard and Mersey Docks & Harbour Company buildings at the Pier Head, the Municipal Buildings and the Philharmonic Hall are other examples of the city's fine architecture.

MANCHESTER (PRE-1900)
Manchester (the *Mamucium* of the Romans, who occupied it in AD 79) is a commercial and industrial centre with a population engaged in the engineering, chemical, clothing, food processing and textile industries and in education. Banking, insurance and a growing leisure industry are among the prime commercial activities. The city is connected with the sea by the Manchester Ship Canal, opened in 1894, 35.5 miles long, and accommodating ships up to 15,000 tons. In 2003 Manchester Airport handled just over 19.5 million terminal, transit, scheduled and charter passengers.

The principal buildings are: the Town Hall, erected in 1877 from the designs of Alfred Waterhouse, with a large extension of 1938; the Royal Exchange (1869, enlarged 1921); the Central Library (1934); Heaton Hall; the 17th-century Chetham Library; the Rylands Library (1900), which includes the Althorp collection; the University precinct; the 15th-century Cathedral (formerly the parish church) and G-MEX exhibition centre. Recent developments include the Manchester Arena, the largest indoor arena in Europe, and the Bridgewater Hall. Manchester is the home of the Hallé Orchestra, the Royal Northern College of Music, the Royal Exchange Theatre and seven public art galleries. Metrolink, the light rail system, opened in 1992.

To accommodate the Commonwealth Games held in Manchester in 2002, new sports facilities were built including a stadium, swimming pool complex and the National Cycling Centre.

The town received its first charter of incorporation in 1838 and was created a city in 1853.

NEWCASTLE UPON TYNE (PRE-1900)

Newcastle upon Tyne, on the north bank of the River Tyne, is eight miles from the North Sea. A cathedral and university city, it is the administrative, commercial and cultural centre for north-east England and the principal port. It is an important manufacturing centre with a wide variety of industries.

The principal buildings include the Castle Keep (12th century), Black Gate (13th century), Blackfriars (13th century), West Walls (13th century), St Nicholas's Cathedral (15th century, fine lantern tower), St Andrew's Church (12th–14th century), St John's (14th–15th century), All Saints (1786 by Stephenson), St Mary's Roman Catholic Cathedral (1844), Trinity House (17th century), Sandhill (16th-century houses), Guildhall (Georgian), Grey Street (1834–9), Central Station (1846–50), Laing Art Gallery (1904), University of Newcastle Physics Building (1962) and Medical Building (1985), Civic Centre (1963), Central Library (1969) and Eldon Square Shopping Development (1976). Open spaces include the Town Moor (927 acres) and Jesmond Dene. Ten bridges span the Tyne at Newcastle.

The city's name is derived from the 'new castle' (1080) erected as a defence against the Scots. In 1400 it was made a county, and in 1882 a city.

NORWICH (PRE-1900)

Norwich grew from an early Anglo-Saxon settlement near the confluence of the Rivers Yare and Wensum, and now serves as provincial capital for the predominantly agricultural region of East Anglia. The name is thought to relate to the most northerly of a group of Anglo-Saxon villages or *wics*. The city's first known charter was granted in 1158 by Henry II.

Norwich serves its surrounding area as a market town and commercial centre, banking and insurance being prominent among the city's businesses. From the 14th century until the Industrial Revolution, Norwich was the regional centre of the woollen industry, but now the biggest single industry is financial services and principal trades are engineering, printing, shoemaking, double glazing, the production of chemicals and clothing, food processing and technology. Norwich is accessible to seagoing vessels by means of the River Yare, entered at Great Yarmouth, 20 miles to the east.

Among many historic buildings are the Cathedral (completed in the 12th century and surmounted by a 15th-century spire 315 feet in height); the keep of the Norman castle (now a museum and art gallery); the 15th-century flint-walled Guildhall; some thirty medieval parish churches; St Andrew's and Blackfriars' Halls; the Tudor houses preserved in Elm Hill and the Georgian Assembly House. The University of East Anglia is on the city's western boundary.

NOTTINGHAM (PRE-1900)

Nottingham stands on the River Trent. *Snotingaham* or *Notingeham*, literally the homestead of the people of Snot, is the Anglo-Saxon name for the Celtic settlement of *Tigguocobauc*, or the house of caves. In 878, Nottingham became one of the Five Boroughs of Danelaw. William the Conqueror ordered the construction of Nottingham Castle, while the town itself developed rapidly under Norman rule. Its laws and rights were later formally recognised by Henry II's charter in 1155. The Castle became a favoured residence of King John. In 1642 King Charles I raised his personal standard at Nottingham Castle at the start of the Civil War.

Nottingham is home to Notts County FC (the world's oldest football league side), Nottingham Forest FC, Nottingham Racecourse, Trent Bridge cricket ground and the National Watersports Centre. The principal industries include textiles, pharmaceuticals, food manufacturing, engineering and telecommunications. There are two universities within the city boundaries.

Architecturally, Nottingham has a wealth of notable buildings, particularly those designed in the Victorian era by T. C. Hine and Watson Fothergill. The City Council owns the Castle, of Norman origin but restored in 1878, Wollaton Hall (1580–8), Newstead Abbey (home of Lord Byron), the Guildhall (1888) and Council House (1929). St Mary's, St Peter's and St Nicholas's Churches are of interest, as is the Roman Catholic Cathedral (Pugin, 1842–4). Nottingham was granted city status in 1897.

OXFORD (PRE-1900)

Oxford is a university city, an important industrial centre, and a market town. Industry played a minor part in Oxford until the motor industry was established in 1912.

Oxford is known for its architecture, its oldest specimens being the reputedly Saxon tower of St Michael's church, the remains of the Norman castle and city walls, and the Norman church at Iffley. It also has many Gothic buildings, such as the Divinity Schools, the Old Library at Merton College, William of Wykeham's New College, Magdalen College and Christ Church and many other college buildings. Later centuries are represented by the Laudian quadrangle at St John's College, the Renaissance Sheldonian Theatre by Wren, Trinity College Chapel, and All Saints Church, Hawksmoor's mock-Gothic at All Souls College, and the 18th-century Queen's College. In addition to individual buildings, High Street and Radcliffe Square both form interesting architectural compositions. Most of the Colleges have gardens, those of Magdalen, New College, St John's and Worcester being the largest.

ST ALBANS (PRE-1900)

The origins of St Albans, situated on the River Ver, stem from the Roman town of *Verulamium*. Named after the first Christian martyr in Britain, who was executed here, St Albans has developed around the Norman Abbey and Cathedral Church (consecrated 1115), built partly of materials from the old Roman city. The museums house Iron Age and Roman artefacts and the Roman Theatre, unique in Britain, has a stage as opposed to an amphitheatre. Archaeological excavations in the city centre have revealed evidence of pre-Roman, Saxon and medieval occupation.

The town's significance grew to the extent that it was a signatory and venue for the drafting of the Magna Carta. It was also the scene of riots during the Peasants' Revolt, the French King John was imprisoned there after the Battle of Poitiers, and heavy fighting took place there during the Wars of the Roses.

Previously controlled by the Abbot, the town achieved a charter in 1553 and city status in 1877. The street market, first established in 1553, is still an important feature of the city, as are many hotels and inns, surviving from the days when St Albans was an important coach stop. Tourist attractions include historic churches and houses, and a 15th-century clock tower.

The city is now home to a wide range of firms, with special emphasis on information and legal services. In addition, it is the home of the Royal National Rose Society, and of Rothamsted Park agricultural research centre.

SALISBURY (PRE-1900)
The history of Salisbury centres around the Cathedral and Cathedral Close. The city evolved from an Iron Age camp a mile to the north of its current position which was strengthened by the Romans and called *Serviodunum*. The Normans built a castle and cathedral on the site and renamed it Sarum. In AD 1220, Bishop Richard Poore and the architect Elias de Derham decided to build a new Gothic style cathedral. The cathedral was completed 38 years later and a community known as New Sarum, now called Salisbury, grew around it. Originally the cathedral had a squat tower. The 404 ft spire that makes the cathedral the tallest medieval structure in the world was added *c.* 1315. A walled Close with houses for the clergy was built around the cathedral, the Medieval Hall still stands today, alongside buildings dating from the 13th to the 20th century; including some designed by Sir Christopher Wren.

A prosperous wool and cloth trade allowed Salisbury to flourish until the 17th century. When the wool trade declined new crafts were established including cutlery, leather and basket work, saddlery, lacemaking, joinery and malting. By 1750 it had become an important road junction and coaching centre and in the Victorian era the railways created a new age of expansion and prosperity. Today Salisbury is a thriving tourist centre.

SHEFFIELD (PRE-1900)
Sheffield is situated at the junction of the Sheaf, Porter, Rivelin and Loxley valleys with the River Don. Though its cutlery, silverware and plate have long been famous, Sheffield has other and now more important industries: special and alloy steels, engineering, tool-making, medical equipment and media-related industries (in its new Cultural Industries Quarter). Sheffield has two universities and is an important research centre.

The parish church of St Peter and St Paul, founded in the 12th century, became the Cathedral Church of the Diocese of Sheffield in 1914. The Roman Catholic Cathedral Church of St Marie (founded 1847) was created Cathedral for the new diocese of Hallam in 1980. Parts of the present building date from *c.* 1435. The principal buildings are the Town Hall (1897), the Cutlers' Hall (1832), City Hall (1932), Graves Art Gallery (1934), Mappin Art Gallery, the Crucible Theatre and the restored 19th-century Lyceum theatre, which dates from 1897 and was reopened in 1990. Three major sports venues were opened in 1990 to 1991. These are Sheffield Arena, Don Valley Stadium and Pond's Forge. The Millennium Galleries opened in 2001. Sheffield was created a city in 1893.

STOKE-ON-TRENT (1925)
Stoke-on-Trent, standing on the River Trent and familiarly known as The Potteries, is the main centre of employment for the population of north Staffordshire. The city is the largest clayware producer in the world (china, earthenware, sanitary goods, refractories, bricks and tiles) and also has a wide range of other manufacturing industry, including steel, chemicals, engineering and tyres. Extensive reconstruction has been carried out in recent years.

The city was formed by the federation of the separate municipal authorities of Tunstall, Burslem, Hanley, Stoke, Fenton, and Longton in 1910 and received its city status in 1925.

WINCHESTER (PRE-1900)
Winchester, the ancient capital of England, is situated on the River Itchen. The city is rich in architecture of all types but the Cathedral takes pride of place. The cathedral was built in 1079–93 and exhibits examples of Norman, Early English and Perpendicular styles. The author Jane Austen is buried in the Cathedral. Winchester College, founded in 1382, is one of the most famous public schools, the original building (1393) remaining largely unaltered. St Cross Hospital, another great medieval foundation, lies one mile south of the city. The almshouses were founded in 1136 by Bishop Henry de Blois, and Cardinal Henry Beaufort added a new almshouse of 'Noble Poverty' in 1446. The chapel and dwellings are of great architectural interest, and visitors may still receive the 'Wayfarer's Dole' of bread and ale.

Excavations have done much to clarify the origins and development of Winchester. Part of the forum and several of the streets from the Roman town have been discovered. Excavations in the Cathedral Close have uncovered the entire site of the Anglo-Saxon cathedral (known as the Old Minster) and parts of the New Minster which was built by Alfred's son, Edward the Elder, and is the burial place of the Alfredian dynasty. The original burial place of St Swithun, before his remains were translated to a site in the present cathedral, was also uncovered.

Excavations in other parts of the city have thrown much light on Norman Winchester, notably on the site of the Royal Castle (adjacent to which the new Law Courts have been built) and in the grounds of Wolvesey Castle, where the great house built by Bishops Giffard and Henry de Blois in the 12th century has been uncovered. The Great Hall, built by Henry III between 1222 and 1236, survives and houses the Arthurian Round Table.

YORK (PRE-1900)
The city of York is an archiepiscopal seat. Its recorded history dates from AD 71, when the Roman Ninth Legion established a base under Petilius Cerealis later becoming the fortress of *Eboracum*. In Anglo-Saxon times the city was the royal and ecclesiastical centre of Northumbria, and after capture by a Viking army in AD 866 it became the capital of the Viking kingdom of Jorvik. By the 14th century the city had become a great mercantile centre, mainly because of its control of the wool trade, and was used as the chief base against the Scots. Under the Tudors its fortunes declined, though Henry VIII made it the headquarters of the Council of the North. Excavations on many sites, including Coppergate, have greatly expanded knowledge of Roman, Viking and medieval urban life.

With its development as a railway centre in the 19th century the commercial life of York expanded. The principal industries are the manufacture of chocolate, scientific instruments and sugar.

The city is rich in examples of architecture of all periods. The earliest church was built in AD 627 and, in the 12th to 15th centuries, the present Minster was built in a succession of styles. Other examples within the city are the medieval city walls and gateways, churches and guildhalls. Domestic architecture includes the Georgian mansions of The Mount, Micklegate and Bootham.

ENGLISH COUNTIES AND SHIRES

LORDS-LIEUTENANT AND HIGH SHERIFFS

County/Shire	*Lord-Lieutenant*	*High Sheriff, 2004–5*
Bedfordshire	S. C. Whitbread	C. Ibbett
Berkshire	P. L. Wroughton	J. West
Bristol	J. Tidmarsh	Lady Kingman
Cambridgeshire	Archibald Hugh Duberly	Sir Charles Chadwyck-Healey, Bt
Cheshire	W. A. Bromley-Davenport	S. Sherrard
Cornwall	Lady Mary Holborow	James Southwell
Cumbria	J. A. Cropper	Frederick Markham
Derbyshire	J. K. Bather	J. Olivier
Devon	E. Dancer, CBE	The Countess of Devon
Dorset	Capt. M. Fulford-Dobson	A. Simmons
Durham	Sir Paul Nicholson	Richard Coad
East Riding of Yorkshire	R. Marriott, TD	S. Booth
East Sussex	Mrs P. Stewart-Roberts	J. Avery
Essex	The Lord Petre	A. Streeter
Gloucestershire	H. W. G. Elwes	S. Preston
Greater London	The Lord Imbert, QPM	Frances Cairncross
Greater Manchester	Col. J. B. Timmins, OBE, TD	Robert Hough
Hampshire	Mrs F. M. Fagan	Sir James Scott, Bt.
Herefordshire	Sir Thomas Dunne, KCVO	James Nicholas
Hertfordshire	S. A. Bowes Lyon	Lady Nichols
Isle of Wight	C. D. J. Bland	A. Goddard
Kent	A. Willett, CBE	J. Loudon
Lancashire	The Lord Shuttleworth	Gail Stanley
Leicestershire	Lady Gretton	F. Hussain, MBE
Lincolnshire	Mrs B. K. Cracroft-Eley	C. Welby
Merseyside	A. W. Waterworth	Stuart Christie
Norfolk	Richard Jewson	J. Alston
North Yorkshire	The Lord Crathorne	Mrs C. Thornton-Berry
Northumberland	Sir John Riddell, CVO	Mrs S. Burnell
Nottinghamshire	Sir Andrew Buchanan, Bt.	H. Machin
Oxfordshire	H. L. J. Brunner	Mrs A. Kelaart
Rutland	Dr Laurence Howard	M. Taylor
Shropshire	A. E. H. Heber-Percy	H. Salwey
Somerset	Lady Gass	S. Evans
South Yorkshire	David Moody	Pamela Edwards Liversidge, OBE
Staffordshire	J. A. Hawley, TD	Mrs D. Carver
Suffolk	The Lord Tollemache	The Countess of Euston
Surrey	Mrs S. J. F. Goad	Dr G. Dowling
Tyne and Wear	N. Sherlock	Sir Neville Guthrie Trotter
Warwickshire	M. Dunne	Mrs G. Jefferson
West Midlands	R. R. Taylor, OBE	J. Andrews
West Sussex	H. Wyatt	R. Reed
West Yorkshire	Dr Ingrid Roscoe	J. Barker
Wiltshire	John Bush, OBE	Lt.-Col. J. Arkell, TD
Worcestershire	M. Brinton	James Nicholas

COUNTY COUNCILS: CONTACT DETAILS, AREA

Council	*Administrative Headquarters*	*Telephone*	*Area (Hectares)*
Bedfordshire	County Hall, Bedford	01234-363222	119,220
Buckinghamshire	County Hall, Aylesbury	01296-395000	156,509
Cambridgeshire	Shire Hall, Cambridge	01223-717111	304,357
Cheshire	County Hall, Chester	01244-602424	208,344
Cornwall	County Hall, Truro	01872-322000	354,810
Cumbria	The Courts, Carlisle	01228-606060	676,780
Derbyshire	County Hall, Matlock	01629-580000	255,000
Devon	County Hall, Exeter	01392-382000	656,085
Dorset	County Hall, Dorchester	01305-251000	254,181
Durham	County Hall, Durham	0191-383 3000	223,181
East Sussex	County Hall, Lewes	01273-481000	179,530
Essex	County Hall, Chelmsford	01245-492211	345,619
Gloucestershire	Shire Hall, Gloucester	01452-425000	279,875
Hampshire	The Castle, Winchester	01962-841841	367,896
Hertfordshire	County Hall, Hertford	01992-555555	163,416
Kent	County Hall, Maidstone	01622-671411	373,063
Lancashire	County Hall, Preston	01772-254868	289,780
Leicestershire	County Hall, Leicester	0116-232 3232	208,300
Lincolnshire	County Offices, Lincoln	01522-552222	591,470
Norfolk	County Hall, Norwich	0844-800 8020	537,234
Northamptonshire	County Hall, Northampton	01604-236236	235,966
Northumberland	County Hall, Morpeth	01670-533000	502,594
North Yorkshire	County Hall, Northallerton	01609-780780	803,741
Nottinghamshire	County Hall, Nottingham	0115-982 3823	208,519
Oxfordshire	County Hall, Oxford	01865-792422	260,595
Shropshire	The Shirehall, Shrewsbury	01743-251000	318,761
Somerset	County Hall, Taunton	01823-355455	345,233
Staffordshire	County Buildings, Stafford	01785-223121	262,355
Suffolk	County Hall, Ipswich	01473-583000	380,207
Surrey	County Hall, Kingston upon Thames	020-8541 8800	167,011
Warwickshire	Shire Hall, Warwick	01926-410410	197,854
West Sussex	County Hall, Chichester	01243-777100	198,936
Wiltshire	County Hall, Trowbridge	01225-713000	325,548
Worcestershire	County Hall, Worcester	01905-763763	173,529

COUNTY COUNCILS: POPULATION, BAND D COUNCIL TAX, CHIEF EXECUTIVES

Council	*Population*	*Band D Charge**	*Chief Executive*
Bedfordshire	382,100	£943	Dick Wilkinson
Buckinghamshire	479,020	£858	Chris Williams
Cambridgeshire	556,800	£813	Ian Stewart
Cheshire	674,200	£887	Jeremy Taylor
Cornwall	502,000	£838	Peter Stethridge
Cumbria	488,513	£928	John Harwood
Derbyshire	739,300	£897	Nick Hodgson
Devon	710,500	£900	Philip Jenkinson
Dorset	391,517	£918	David Jenkins
Durham	489,700	£884	Kingsley Smith
East Sussex	498,800	£920	Cheryl Miller
Essex	1,310,922	£892	Stewart Ashurst
Gloucestershire	564,841	£889	Joyce Redfearn
Hampshire	1,244,400	£840	Peter Robertson
Hertfordshire	1,011,000	£895	Caroline Tapster
Kent	1,353,000	£846	Michael Pitt
Lancashire	1,429,400	£927	Chris Trinick
Leicestershire	610,300	£867	J. Sinnott
Lincolnshire	612,000	£858	David Bowles
Norfolk	797,900	£930	Tim Byles
North Yorkshire	570,100	£817	Jeremy Walker
Northamptonshire	629,676	£833	Peter Gould
Northumberland	307,000	£1,023	Mark Henderson
Nottinghamshire	748,800	£994	Roger Latham
Oxfordshire	607,500	£925	Richard Shaw
Shropshire	283,300	£848	Carolyn Downs
Somerset	503,400	£907	Alan Jones
Staffordshire	810,697	£823	N. Pursey
Suffolk	671,100	£924	Mike More
Surrey	1,059,500	£889	Paul Coen
Warwickshire	506,200	£922	Ian Caulfield
West Sussex	750,000	£910	Mark Hammond
Wiltshire	432,973	£852	Dr Keith Robinson
Worcestershire	542,238	£825	Rob Sykes

* Average Band D council tax in the county area exclusive of precepts for fire and police

DISTRICT COUNCILS

District Council	*Telephone*	*Population*	*Band D Charge**	*Chief Executive*
Adur	01273-263000	59,627	£1,241	Ian Lowrie
Allerdale	01900-326333	93,000	£1,222	P. Leonard
Alnwick	01665-510505	31,400	£1,259	Bill Batey
Amber valley	01773-570222	118,000	£1,226	Peter Carney
Arun	01903-737500	140,759	£1,191	Ian Sumnall
Ashfield	01623-450000	109,800	£1,320	Alan Mellor
Ashford	01233-637311	102,661	£1,126	David Hill
Aylesbury vale	01296-585858	165,749	£1,172	Richard Carr
Babergh	01473-822801	82,310	£1,206	Patricia Rockall
Barrow-in-Furness	01229-894900	71,980	£1,259	Tom Campbell
Basildon	01268-533333	165,668	£1,256	John Robb
Basingstoke and Deane	01256-844844	152,800	£1,103	Gordon Hoadcroft
Bassetlaw	01909-533533	107,831	£1,319	James Molloy
Bedford	01234-267422	149,200	£1,263	Shaun Field
Berwick-upon-Tweed	01289-330044	27,000	£1,254	Jane Pannell
Blaby	0116-275 0555	91,600	£1,192	Philip Dolan
Blyth valley	01670-542322	80,000	£1,234	Geoff Paul
Bolsover	01246-240000	72,482	£1,272	W. Lumley
Boston	01205-314200	57,000	£1,124	Nicola Bulbeck
Braintree	01376-552525	132,468	£1,202	Allan Reid
Breckland	01362-695333	121,418	£1,165	Rob Garnett
Brentwood	01277-261111	71,502	£1,198	R. McLintock
Bridgnorth	01746-713100	52,497	£1,200	John Harmeston
Broadland	01603-431133	118,513	£1,206	Colin Bland
Bromsgrove	01527-873232	84,900	£1,183	Sue Nixon
Broxbourne	01992-785555	87,500	£1,098	Mike Walker
Broxtowe	0115-917 7777	108,000	£1,321	M. Brown
Burnley	01282-425011	89,000	£1,290	Dr Gillian Taylor
CAMBRIDGE CITY	01223-457000	120,650	£1,120	R. Hammond
Cannock Chase	01543-462621	92,127	£1,186	Stephen Brown
CANTERBURY CITY	01227-862000	165,000	£1,158	Colin Carmichael
Caradon	01579-341000	79,679	£1,135	B. Davies
CARLISLE CITY	01228-817000	100,734	£1,248	Peter Stybelski
Carrick	01872-224400	88,900	£1,136	John Winskill
Castle Morpeth	01670-535000	50,000	£1,292	Ken Dunbar
Castle Point	01268-882200	84,800	£1,237	B. Rollinson
Charnwood	01509-263151	158,300	£1,175	Brian Hayes
Chelmsford	01245-606606	157,072	£1,201	Steve Packham
Cheltenham	01242-262626	110,000	£1,201	Christine Laird
Cherwell	01295-252535	137,500	£1,215	G. Handley
CHESTER CITY	01244-324324	118,000	£1,198	Paul Durham
Chester-le-Street	0191-387 1919	55,000	£1,212	Roy Templeman
Chesterfield	01246-345345	100,000	£1,192	D. Shaw
Chichester	01243-785166	106,450	£1,159	John Marsland
Chiltern	01494-729000	71,013	£1,194	Alan Goodrum
Chorley	01257-515151	100,239	£1,244	Jeff Davies
Christchurch	01202-495000	44,908	£1,236	Mike Turvey
Colchester	01206-282222	159,600	£1,204	Adrian Pritchard
Congleton	01270-763231	90,758	£1,200	Glyn Chambers
Copeland	01946-852585	69,200	£1,241	J. Stanforth
Corby	01536-464000	52,000	£1,129	Chris Mallender
Cotswolds	01285-623000	81,402	£1,206	R. Austin
Craven	01756-700600	53,555	£1,199	Gill Dixon
Crawley	01293-438000	99,744	£1,178	Michael Coughlin
Crewe and Nantwich	01270-537777	114,900	£1,182	Alan Wenham
Dacorum	01442-228000	132,240	£1,149	Daniel Zammit
Dartford	01322-343434	85,911	£1,150	G. Harris
Daventry	01327-871100	73,521	£1,130	Steve Atkinson
Derbyshire Dales	01629-761100	69,469	£1,251	David Wheatcroft
Derwentside	01207-218000	85,065	£1,294	Mike Clark
Dover	01304-821199	104,566	£1,159	Nadeem Aziz

District Council	*Telephone*	*Population*	*Band D Charge**	*Chief Executive*
DURHAM CITY	0191-386 6111	87,656	£1,235	B. Spears
Easington	0191-527 0501	93,981	£1,349	Janet Johnson
East Cambridgeshire	01353-665555	68,900	£1,138	John Hill
East Devon	01395-516551	125,520	£1,189	Mark Williams
East Dorset	01202-886201	83,788	£1,272	Alan Breakwell
East Hampshire	01730-266551	111,750	£1,161	Will Godfrey
East Hertfordshire	01279-655261	126,000	£1,174	Miranda Steward; Rachel Stopard
East Lindsey	01507-601111	130,500	£1,085	Rachel Mann, *acting*
East Northamptonshire	01832-742000	78,511	£1,132	Stephen Baker
East Staffordshire	01283-508000	103,000	£1,192	William Saunders
Eastbourne	01323-410000	89,800	£1,279	Martin Ray
Eastleigh	023-8068 8000	117,000	£1,163	Chris Tapp
Eden	01768-864671	49,880	£1,227	Ian Bruce
Ellesmere Port and Neston	0151-356 6789	81,400	£1,197	S. Ewbank
Elmbridge	01372-474474	124,300	£1,211	Michael Lockwood
Epping Forest	01992-564000	120,896	£1,217	John Burgess
Epsom and Ewell	01372-732000	66,800	£1,164	David Smith
Erewash	0115-907 2244	108,000	£1,215	John Rice
EXETER CITY	01392-277888	111,189	£1,172	Philip Bostock
Fareham	01329-236100	109,407	£1,123	A. Davies
Fenland	01354-654321	82,500	£1,210	Tim Pilsbury
Forest Heath	01638-719000	55,514	£1,212	David Burnip
Forest of Dean	01594-810000	80,000	£1,227	Tim Perrin
Fylde	01253-721222	73,217	£1,219	Ken Lee
Gedling	0115-901 3901	110,200	£1,300	Peter Murdoch
GLOUCESTER CITY	01452-522232	109,300	£1,198	Paul Smith
Gosport	023-9258 4242	76,415	£1,174	Malcolm Crocker
Gravesham	01474-564422	92,000	£1,138	David Williams
Great Yarmouth	01493-856100	89,900	£1,192	Richard Packham
Guildford	01483-505050	129,701	£1,180	David Willams
Hambleton	01609-779977	84,111	£1,128	P. Simpson
Harborough	01858-821100	75,200	£1,196	Michael Wilson
Harlow	01279-446611	83,000	£1,263	Malcolm Morley
Harrogate	01423-500600	150,588	£1,224	P. Walsh
Hart	01252-622122	87,806	£1,168	Jules Samuels
Hastings	01424-781066	84,000	£1,285	Roy Mawford
Havant	023-9247 4174	120,500	£1,152	Gwen Andrews
Hertsmere	020-8207 2277	94,947	£1,153	Ron Higgins
High Peak	0845-129 7777	89,300	£1,233	Peter Sloman
Hinckley and Bosworth	01455-238141	100,141	£1,146	*vacant*
Horsham	01403-215100	125,700	£1,158	Martin Pearson
Huntingdonshire	01480-388388	157,000	£1,133	David Monks
Hyndburn	01254-388111	81,800	£1,259	David Welsby
Ipswich	01473-432000	114,000	£1,313	J. Hehir
Kennet	01380-724911	74,833	£1,171	Mark Boden
Kerrier	01209-614000	90,990	£1,144	Barry Manning
Kettering	01536-410333	82,000	£1,140	David Cook
King's Lynn and West Norfolk	01553-616200	135,600	£1,203	Ray Harding, *acting*
LANCASTER CITY	01524-582000	133,914	£1,232	Mark Cullinan
Lewes	01273-471600	93,000	£1,292	John Crawford
Lichfield	01543-308000	93,835	£1,155	Nina Dawes
LINCOLN CITY	01522-881188	82,750	£1,154	Andrew Taylor
Macclesfield	01625-500500	150,144	£1,189	Vivien Horton
Maidstone	01622-602000	139,000	£1,198	David Petford
Maldon	01621-854477	57,300	£1,215	Avril Spencer, *acting*
Malvern Hills	01684-892700	72,182	£1,183	Chris Bocock
Mansfield	01623-463463	98,500	£1,337	Richard Goad
Melton	01664-502502	47,488	£1,185	Delwyn Burbidge
Mendip	01749-343399	103,865	£1,192	David Thomson
Mid Bedfordshire	01525-402051	121,300	£1,271	Jaki Salisbury
Mid Devon	01884-255255	69,883	£1,240	Paul Edwards
Mid Suffolk	01449-720711	86,000	£1,205	Andrew Good
Mid Sussex	01444-458166	127,400	£1,177	John Jory
Mole Valley	01306-885001	80,300	£1,165	Heather Kerswell
New Forest	02380-285000	172,319	£1,179	David Yates
Newark and Sherwood	01636-650000	105,800	£1,367	Richard Dix

District Council	*Telephone*	*Population*	*Band D Charge**	*Chief Executive*
Newcastle-Under-Lyme	01782-717717	122,075	£1,164	Felix Harley
North Cornwall	01208-893333	81,000	£1,144	David Brown
North Devon	01271-327711	87,508	£1,234	John Sunderland
North Dorset	01258-454111	61,360	£1,223	Liz Goodall
North East Derbyshire	01246-231111	97,000	£1,273	Carole Gilby
North Hertfordshire	01462-474000	116,400	£1,175	John Campbell
North Kesteven	01529-414155	96,852	£1,128	Ruth Marlow
North Norfolk	01263-513811	100,500	£1,206	Philip Burton
North Shropshire	01939-232771	54,581	£1,228	R. Hughes
North Warwickshire	01827-715341	60,000	£1,263	Jerry Hutchinson
North West Leicestershire	01530-454545	88,800	£1,210	M. Diaper
North Wiltshire	01249-706111	125,370	£1,204	R. Marshall
Northampton	01604-837837	196,300	£1,158	Mairi McLean
NORWICH CITY	01603-622233	121,700	£1,251	Anne Seex
Nuneaton and Bedworth	02476-376376	119,132	£1,232	Christine Kerr
Oadby and Wigston	0116-288-8961	55,800	£1,197	R. Hyde
Oswestry	01691-671111	37,000	£1,266	Paul Shevlin
OXFORD CITY	01865-249811	134,248	£1,261	Caroline Bull
Pendle	01282-661661	89,248	£1,291	Stephen Barnes
Penwith	01736-362341	63,000	£1,101	J. McKenna
PRESTON CITY	01772-906000	135,000	£1,286	J. Carr
Purbeck	01929-556561	44,130	£1,260	P. Croft
Redditch	01527-64252	76,747	£1,192	Christopher Smith
Reigate and Banstead	01737-276000	119,000	£1,196	Nigel Clifford
Restormel	01726-223300	95,800	£1,104	P. Crowson
Ribble Valley	01200-425111	53,161	£1,206	David Morris
Richmondshire	01748-829100	47,846	£1,219	Harry Tabiner
Rochford	01702-546366	78,489	£1,229	Paul Warren
Rossendale	01706-217777	65,000	£1,296	O. Williams
Rother	01424-787878	85,000	£1,248	Derek Stevens
Rugby	01788-533533	88,900	£1,210	Diane Colley
Runnymede	01932-838383	78,048	£1,137	Tim Williams
Rushcliffe	0115-981 9911	106,301	£1,300	Keith Beaumont
Rushmoor	01252-398398	86,000	£1,152	Andrew Lloyd
Ryedale	01653-600666	50,800	£1,215	H. Mosley
ST ALBANS CITY	01727-866100	130,000	£1,184	Peter Learner
St Edmundsbury	01284-763233	98,000	£1,214	D. Cadman
SALISBURY	01722-336272	85,803	£1,155	Richard Sheard
Scarborough	01723-232323	108,000	£1,222	John Trebble
Sedgefield	01388-816166	87,206	£1,376	N. Vaulks
Sedgemoor	01278-435435	104,000	£1,160	Kerry Rickards
Selby	01757-705101	76,468	£1,207	M. Connor
Sevenoaks	01732-227000	109,305	£1,195	Robin Hales
Shepway	01303-850388	99,265	£1,230	R. Thompson
Shrewsbury and Atcham	01743-281000	95,425	£1,192	Robin Hooper
South Bedfordshire	01582-472222	111,100	£1,332	John Ruddick
South Bucks	01753-533333	61,945	£1,168	Chris Furness
South Cambridgeshire	01223-443000	132,000	£1,099	John Ballantyne
South Derbyshire	01283-221000	76,000	£1,208	Frank McArdle
South Hams	01803-861234	81,846	£1,207	Ruth Bagley
South Holland	01775-761161	79,125	£1,118	Terry Huggins
South Kesteven	01476-406080	120,000	£1,096	Duncan Kerr
South Lakeland	01539-733333	103,000	£1,237	Mike Jones, *acting*
South Norfolk	01508-533633	104,334	£1,221	Geoffrey Rivers
South Northamptonshire	01327-322322	79,293	£1,154	Rob Tinlin
South Oxfordshire	01491-823000	128,177	£1,213	David Buckle
South Ribble	01772-421491	103,900	£1,252	Jean Hunter
South Shropshire	01584-813000	40,000	£1,264	Graham Biggs
South Somerset	01935-462462	155,770	£1,200	Philip Dolan
South Staffordshire	01902-696000	105,600	£1,134	Les Barnfield
Spelthorne	01784-451499	89,600	£1,171	Karen Satterford
Stafford	01785-619000	120,000	£1,153	David Rawlings
Staffordshire Moorlands	01538-483483	94,390	£1,171	Simon Baker
Stevenage	01438-242242	79,177	£1,167	Ian Paske
Stratford-on-Avon	01789-267575	111,536	£1,190	Paul Lankester
Stroud	01453-766321	110,000	£1,247	David Hagg

District Council	*Telephone*	*Population*	*Band D Charge**	*Chief Executive*
Suffolk Coastal	01394-383789	115,200	£1,193	Jan Ormodroyd
Surrey Heath	01276-707100	85,900	£1,198	Barry Catchpole
Swale	01795-424341	123,000	£1,143	J. Edwards
Tamworth	01827-709709	80,000	£1,129	David Weatherley
Tandridge	01883-722000	80,000	£1,198	Philip Thomas
Taunton Deane	01823-356356	100,800	£1,158	S. Fletcher
Teesdale	01833-690000	24,457	£1,242	Charles Anderson
Teignbridge	01626-361101	120,958	£1,222	Howard Davis
Tendring	01255-425501	138,555	£1,189	John Hawkins
Test Valley	01264-368000	113,352	£1,119	Roger Tetstall
Tewkesbury	01684-295010	77,321	£1,150	Teri Turner
Thanet	01843-577000	126,702	£1,182	Richard Samuel
Three Rivers	01923-776611	85,000	£1,181	S. Halls
Tonbridge and Malling	01732-844522	107,800	£1,167	David Hughes
Torridge	01237-428700	56,000	£1,203	Roger Heath, *acting*
Tunbridge Wells	01892-526121	103,000	£1,144	R. Stone
Tynedale	01434-652200	59,000	£1,268	Richard Robson
Uttlesford	01799-510510	70,300	£1,206	Alasdair Bovaird
Vale of White Horse	01235-520202	112,900	£1,173	Terry Stock
Vale Royal	01606-862862	122,300	£1,197	Anne Bingham-Holmes
Wansbeck	01670-532200	61,138	£1,249	R. Stephenson
Warwick	01926-450000	125,931	£1,178	Janie Barrett
Watford	01923-226400	80,400	£1,239	Alastair Robertson
Waveney	01502-562111	110,000	£1,173	*vacant*
Waverley	01483-523333	115,976	£1,202	Christine Pointer
Wealden	01892-653311	142,700	£1,286	Charles Lant
Wear Valley	01388-765555	61,339	£1,238	Iain Phillips
Wellingborough	01933-229777	70,000	£1,104	T. McArdle
Welwyn Hatfield	01707-357000	97,553	£1,201	Michel Saminaden
West Devon	01822-813600	50,689	£1,255	David Incoll
West Dorset	01305-251010	92,360	£1,254	David Clarke
West Lancashire	01695-577177	108,378	£1,246	William Taylor
West Lindsey	01427-676676	81,161	£1,152	Robert Nelsey
West Oxfordshire	01993-861000	99,000	£1,154	G. Bonner
West Somerset	01984-632291	35,075	£1,177	Tim Howes
West Wiltshire	01225-776655	112,000	£1,194	Andrew Pate
Weymouth and Portland	01305-838000	63,000	£1,315	Tom Grainger
WINCHESTER CITY	01962-840222	107,274	£1,147	S. Eden
Woking	01483-755855	89,431	£1,203	Paul Russell
WORCESTER CITY	01905-723471	95,363	£1,159	D. Wareing
Worthing	01903-239999	100,000	£1,185	Sheryl Grady
Wychavon	01386-565000	112,949	£1,146	Jack Hegarty
Wycombe	01494-461000	161,850	£1,163	Richard Cummins
Wyre	01253-891000	106,826	£1,224	Jim Corry
Wyre Forest	01562-820505	96,981	£1,200	W. Delin

*Average Band D council tax
Councils in CAPITAL LETTERS have city status

METROPOLITAN BOROUGH COUNCILS

Metropolitan Borough Councils	*Telephone*	*Population*	*Band D Charge**	*Chief Executive*
Barnsley	01226-770770	218,000	£1,104	Phil Coppard
BIRMINGHAM CITY	0121-303 9944	977,000	£1,106	Lin Homer
Bolton	01204-333333	267,400	£1,162	B. Knight
BRADFORD CITY	01274-432001	467,665	£1,061	Philip Robinson, *acting*
Bury	0161-253 5000	181,000	£1,117	Mark Sanders
Calderdale	01422-357257	192,400	£1,181	Paul Sheehan
COVENTRY CITY	02476-833333	301,000	£1,210	Stella Manzie
Doncaster	01302-734444	289,897	£1,094	Susan Law
Dudley	01384-818181	305,155	£1,034	Andrew Sparke
Gateshead	0191-433 3000	200,000	£1,300	Roger Kelly
Kirklees	01484-221000	392,000	£1,134	A. Elson
Knowsley	0151-489 6000	153,094	£1,151	Steve Gallagher
LEEDS CITY	0113-247 4554	726,757	£1,040	P. Rogerson
LIVERPOOL CITY	0151-233 3000	439,476	£1,223	David Henshaw
MANCHESTER CITY	0161-234 5000	439,549	£1,133	Howard Bernstein
NEWCASTLE UPON TYNE CITY	0191-232 8520	283,000	£1,302	Ian Stratford
North Tyneside	0191-200 6565	192,000	£1,228	John Marsden
Oldham	0161-911 3000	218,680	£1,283	Andrew Kilburn
Rochdale	01706-647474	208,950	£1,152	Roger Ellis
Rotherham	01709-382121	253,706	£1,143	Mike Cuff
SALFORD CITY	0161-794 4711	220,000	£1,285	John Willis
Sandwell	0121-569 2200	282,900	£1,125	Nigel Summers
Sefton	0151-922 4040	287,700	£1,188	Graham Haywood
SHEFFIELD CITY	0114-272 6444	530,300	£1,216	Bob Kerslake
Solihull	0121-704 6000	205,600	£1,045	Katherine Kerswell
South Tyneside	0191-427 1717	152,710	£1,184	Irene Lucas
St Helens	01744-456000	178,854	£1,178	Carole Hudson
Stockport	0161-480 4949	291,500	£1,198	John Schultz
SUNDERLAND CITY	0191-553 1000	280,800	£1,101	Jed Fitzgerald
Tameside	0161-342 8355	213,043	£1,124	Janet Orchard
Trafford	0161-912 1212	225,000	£990	Dr Gary Pickering, *acting*
WAKEFIELD CITY	01924-306090	319,600	£1,048	John Foster
Walsall	01922-650000	261,599	£1,233	Anne Shepperd
Wigan	01942-244991	310,000	£1,136	Frank Costello
Wirral	0151-638 7070	312,289	£1,175	Stephen Maddox
WOLVERHAMPTON CITY	01902-556556	240,500	£1,174	D. Anderson

*Average Band D council tax
Councils in CAPITAL LETTERS have city status

UNITARY COUNCILS

Unitary Councils	*Telephone*	*Population*	*Band D Charge**	*Chief Executive*
Bath and North East Somerset	01225-477000	165,000	£1,140	John Everitt
Blackburn with Darwen	01254-585585	137,600	£1,212	Philip Watson
Blackpool	01253-477477	153,600	£1,179	S. Weaver
Bournemouth	01202-451451	163,444	£1,186	Paul Godier
Bracknell Forest	01344-424642	109,617	£1,048	Timothy Wheadon
BRIGHTON AND HOVE CITY	01273-290000	247,817	£1,162	David Panter
BRISTOL CITY	0117-922 2000	380,615	£1,235	N. Gurney
Darlington	01325-380651	97,838	£1,099	Barry Keel
DERBY CITY	01332-293111	236,429	£1,079	Ray Cowlishaw
East Riding of Yorkshire	01482-887700	314,113	£1,183	D. Stephenson
Halton	0151-424 2061	118,200	£1,070	M. Cuff
Hartlepool	01429-266522	91,200	£1,297	Paul Walker
Herefordshire	01432-260000	167,000	£1,185	Neil Pringle
Isle of Wight	01983-821000	132,938	£1,195	M. Fisher
KINGSTON UPON HULL CITY	01482-609100	241,443	£1,094	Jan Didrichsen
LEICESTER CITY	0116-254 9922	296,000	£1,144	R. Green
Luton	01582-546000	184,356	£1,073	Darra Singh
Medway	01634-306000	249,502	£1,014	Judith Armitt
Middlesbrough	01642-245432	142,300	£1,173	Brian Dinsdale
Milton Keynes	01908-691691	210,980	£1,097	John Best
North East Lincolnshire	01472-313131	156,000	£1,265	Jim Leivers
North Lincolnshire	01724-296296	162,000	£1,237	Michael Garnett
North Somerset	01934-888888	188,500	£1,161	Graham Turner
NOTTINGHAM CITY	0115-915 5555	267,000	£1,259	Gordon Mitchell
PETERBOROUGH CITY	01733-563141	158,500	£1,117	Gillian Beasley
PLYMOUTH CITY	01752-668000	255,000	£1,121	Sohail Faruqi
Poole	01202-633633	140,940	£1,138	John McBride
PORTSMOUTH CITY	023-9282 2251	186,700	£1,070	N. Gurney
Reading	0118-939 0900	150,000	£1,212	Trish Haines
Redcar and Cleveland	01642-444000	139,200	£1,214	Colin Moore
Rutland	01572-722577	34,600	£1,344	K. Franklin
Slough	01753-552288	119,000	£1,055	Cheryl Coppell
South Gloucestershire	01454-868686	245,640	£1,193	Mike Robinson
SOUTHAMPTON CITY	023-8022 3855	216,000	£1,176	Brad Roynon
Southend-on-Sea	01702-215000	164,400	£1,016	J. Krawiec
Stockton-on-Tees	01642-393939	178,000	£1,165	George Garlick
STOKE-ON-TRENT CITY	01782-234567	253,200	£1,093	Ita O'Donovan
Swindon	01793-463000	182,600	£1,131	Simon Birch
Telford and Wrekin	01952-202100	158,285	£1,144	Michael Frater
Thurrock	01375-390000	134,806	£1,060	Eric Nath
Torbay	01803-201201	123,000	£1,168	R. Painter
Warrington	01925-444400	191,200	£1,053	Bernice Law
West Berkshire	01635-42400	144,483	£1,229	Jim Graham
Windsor and Maidenhead	01628-798888	133,626	£1,061	David Lunn
Wokingham	0118-974 6000	148,869	£1,195	Doug Patterson
YORK CITY	01904-613161	181,326	£1,078	David Atkinson

*Average Band D council tax
Councils in CAPITAL LETTERS have city status

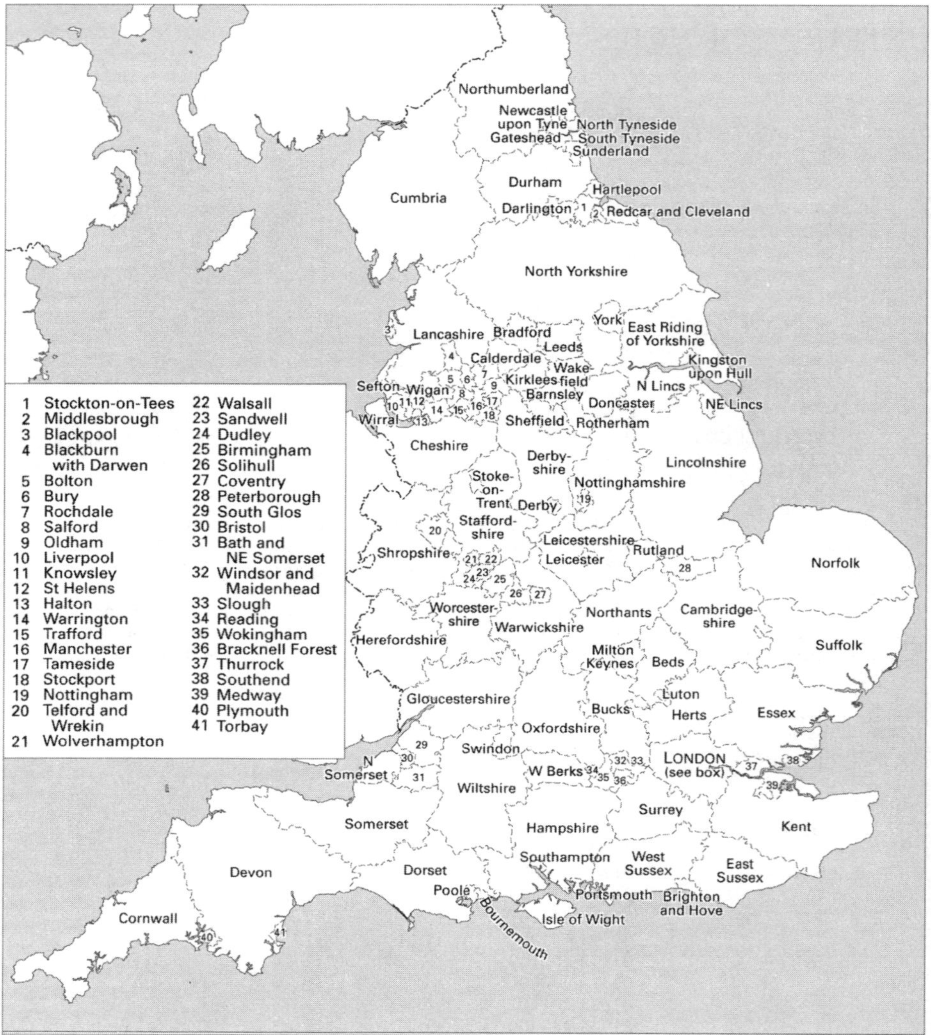

1 Hillingdon
2 Harrow
3 Barnet
4 Enfield
5 Waltham Forest
6 Redbridge
7 Barking and Dagenham
8 Havering
9 Ealing
10 Brent
11 Camden
12 Haringey
13 Islington
14 Hackney
15 Newham
16 Hounslow
17 Hammersmith and Fulham
18 Kensington and Chelsea
19 City of Westminster
20 City of London
21 Tower Hamlets
22 Richmond upon Thames
23 Wandsworth
24 Lambeth
25 Southwark
26 Lewisham
27 Greenwich
28 Bexley
29 Kingston upon Thames
30 Merton
31 Sutton
32 Croydon
33 Bromley

LONDON

THE CORPORATION OF LONDON

The City of London is the historic centre at the heart of London known as 'the square mile' around which the vast metropolis has grown over the centuries. The City's residential population at census day 2001 was 7,186. The civic government is carried on by the Corporation of London through the Court of Common Council.

The City is an international financial centre, generating over £20 billion a year for the British economy. It includes the head offices of the principal banks, insurance companies and mercantile houses, in addition to buildings ranging from the historic Roman Wall and the 15th-century Guildhall, to the massive splendour of St Paul's Cathedral and the architectural beauty of Wren's spires.

The City of London was described by Tacitus in AD 62 as 'a busy emporium for trade and traders'. Under the Romans it became an important administration centre and hub of the road system. Little is known of London in Saxon times, when it formed part of the kingdom of the East Saxons. In 886 Alfred recovered London from the Danes and reconstituted it a burgh under his son-in-law. In 1066 the citizens submitted to William the Conqueror who in 1067 granted them a charter, which is still preserved, establishing them in the rights and privileges they had hitherto enjoyed.

THE MAYORALTY

The Mayoralty was probably established about 1189, the first Mayor being Henry Fitz Ailwyn who filled the office for 23 years and was succeeded by Fitz Alan (1212–14). A new charter was granted by King John in 1215, directing the Mayor to be chosen annually, which has been done ever since, though in early times the same individual often held the office more than once. A familiar instance is that of 'Whittington, thrice Lord Mayor of London' (in reality four times, 1397, 1398, 1406, 1419); and many modern cases have occurred. The earliest instance of the phrase 'Lord Mayor' in English is in 1414. It was used more generally in the latter part of the 15th century and became invariable from 1535 onwards. At Michaelmas the liverymen in Common Hall choose two Aldermen who have served the office of Sheriff for presentation to the Court of Aldermen, and one is chosen to be Lord Mayor for the following mayoral year.

LORD MAYOR'S DAY

The Lord Mayor of London was previously elected on the feast of St Simon and St Jude (28 October), and from the time of Edward I, at least, was presented to the King or to the Barons of the Exchequer on the following day, unless that day was a Sunday. The day of election was altered to 16 October in 1346, and after some further changes was fixed for Michaelmas Day in 1546, but the ceremonies of admittance and swearing-in of the Lord Mayor continued to take place on 28 and 29 October respectively until 1751. In 1752, at the reform of the calendar, the Lord Mayor was continued in office until 8 November, the 'new style' equivalent of 28 October. The Lord Mayor is now presented to the Lord Chief Justice at the Royal Courts of Justice on the second Saturday in November to make the final declaration of office, having been sworn in at Guildhall on the preceding day. The procession to the Royal Courts of Justice is popularly known as the Lord Mayor's Show.

REPRESENTATIVES

Aldermen are mentioned in the 11th century and their office is of Saxon origin. They were elected annually between 1377 and 1394, when an Act of Parliament of Richard II directed them to be chosen for life.

The Common Council, elected annually on the first Friday in December, was, at an early date, substituted for a popular assembly called the *Folkmote*. At first only two representatives were sent from each ward, but the number has since been greatly increased. The City of London (Ward Elections) Act gained Royal Assent in November 2002 and allowed for new voting arrangements. These include the introduction of periodic re-elections for the 25 Aldermen, a reduction in the number of Councilmen and a comprehensive review of the 25 electoral ward boundaries.

OFFICERS

Sheriffs were Saxon officers; their predecessors were the *wic-reeves* and *portreeves* of London and Middlesex. At first they were officers of the Crown, and were named by the Barons of the Exchequer; but Henry I (in 1132) gave the citizens permission to choose their own Sheriffs, and the annual election of Sheriffs became fully operative under King John's charter of 1199. The citizens lost this privilege, as far as the election of the Sheriff of Middlesex was concerned, by the Local Government Act 1888; but the liverymen continue to choose two Sheriffs of the City of London, who are appointed on Midsummer Day and take office at Michaelmas.

The office of Chamberlain is an ancient one, the first contemporary record of which is 1237. The Town Clerk (or Common Clerk) is first mentioned in 1274.

ACTIVITIES

The work of the Corporation is assigned to a number of committees which present reports to the Court of Common Council. These Committees are: Barbican Centre; Barbican Residential; Board of Governors of the City of London Freeman's School, the City of London School, London School for Girls, the Guildhall School of Music and Drama and the Museum of London; Bridge House Trust; City Lands and Bridge House Estates; Managers of West Ham Park; Community Services; Education; Epping Forest and Open Spaces; Establishment; Finance; Gresham (city side); Guildhall Yard East Building; Hampstead Heath Management; Libraries; Guildhall Art Galleries and Archives; Livery; Markets; Planning and Transportation; Police; Policy and Resources; Port Health and Environmental Services; Queen's Park and Highgate Wood Management and Standards Committees.

The City's estate, in the possession of which the Corporation of London differs from other municipalities, is managed by the City Lands and Bridge House Estates Committee, the chairmanship of which carries with it the title of Chief Commoner.

The Honourable the Irish Society, which manages the Corporation's estates in Ulster, consists of a Governor and five other Aldermen, the Recorder, and 19 Common Councilmen, of whom one is elected Deputy Governor.

THE LORD MAYOR 2004–5
The Rt. Hon. the Lord Mayor, Alderman Rt. Hon. Michael Savory
Private Secretary, P. Tribe

THE SHERIFFS 2004–5
David Bilsland; John Hughesdon *(Alderman Billingsgate)*

OFFICERS, ETC.
Town Clerk, Chris Duffield
Chamberlain, P. Derrick
Chief Commoner (2004), Tom Jackson
Clerk, The Honourable the Irish Society, S. Waley, 75 Watling Street, London EC4M 9BJ T 020-7489 7777

THE ALDERMEN
with office held and date of appointment to that office

Name and Ward	*CC*	*Ald.*	*Shff*	*Lord Mayor*
Sir Alan Towers-Traill, GBE, *Langbourn*	1970	1975	1982	1984
Sir David Rowe-Ham, GBE, *Bridge* and *Bridge Wt.*	–	1976	1984	1986
Sir Brian Jenkins, GBE, *Cordwainer*	–	1980	1987	1991
Sir Paul Newall, TD, *Walbrook*	1980	1981	1989	1993
Sir Richard Nichols, *Candlewick*	1983	1984	1994	1997
Lord Levene of Portsoken, KBE, *Portsoken*	1983	1984	1995	1998
Sir Clive Martin, OBE, *Aldgate*	–	1985	1996	1999
Sir David Howard, Bt.	1972	1986	1997	2000
Sir Michael Oliver, *Bishopsgate Out*	1980	1987	1997	2001
Gavyn Arthur, *Cripplegate*	1988	1991	1998	2002
Robert Finch, *Coleman Street*	–	1992	1999	2003

All the above have passed the Civic Chair

Michael Savory, *Bread Street*	1980	1996	2001
Richard Agutter, *Castle Baynard*	–	1995	2000
David Brewer, *Bassishaw*	1992	1996	2002
Nicholas Anstee, *Aldersgate*	1987	1996	
John Hughesdon, *Billingsgate*	1991	1997	
Simon Walsh, *Farringdon Wt.*	1989	2000	
John Stuttard, *Lime Street*	–	2001	
Dr Andrew Parmley, *Vintry*	1992	2001	
David Lewis, *Broad Street*	–	2001	
Robert Hall, *Farringdon Wn.*	1995	2002	
Mrs Alison Gowman, *Dowgate*	1991	2002	
Richard Walduck, OBE, *Tower*	–	2003	
Gordon Haines, *Queenhithe*	–	2004	
Colin Hart, *Cheap*	–	2004	

THE COMMON COUNCIL
Deputy: Each Common Councilman so described serves as deputy to the Alderman of her/his ward.

Abrahams, G. (2000)	*Farringdon Wt.*
Absalom, J. D. (1994)	*Farringdon Wt.*
Altman, L. P., CBE (1996)	*Cripplegate Wn.*
Angell, E. H. (1991)	*Cripplegate Wt.*
Ayers, K. E. (1996)	*Bassishaw*
Barker, *Deputy* J. A. (1981)	*Cripplegate Wn.*
Beale, *Deputy* M. J. (1979)	*Lime Street*
Bear, M. D. (2003)	*Portsoken*
Bird, J. L., OBE (1977)	*Bridge*
Boleat, M. J. (2002)	*Cordwainer*
Bradshaw, D. J. (1991)	*Cripplegate Wn.*
Branson, N. A. C. (2002)	*Langbourn*
Brewster, J. W., OBE (1994)	*Bassishaw*
Caspi, D. R. (1994)	*Bridge*
Cassidy, *Deputy* M. J. (1989)	*Coleman Street*
Catt, R. M. (2004)	*Castle Baynard*
Cenci Di Bello, Mrs P. J. (2004)	*Farringdon Wn.*
Chadwick, R. A. H. (1994)	*Tower*
Cohen, Mrs C. M., OBE (1986)	*Lime Street*
Cotgrove, D. (1991)	*Lime Street*
Currie, *Deputy* Miss S. E. M. (1985)	*Cripplegate Wt.*
Dove, W. H., MBE (1993)	*Bishopsgate*
Duckworth, S. (2000)	*Bishopsgate*
Dudley, The Revd Dr M. R. (2002)	*Aldersgate*
Duffield, R. W. (2004)	*Farringdon Wn.*
Eskenzi, *Deputy* A. N., CBE (1970)	*Farringdon Wn.*
Eve, R. A. (1980)	*Cheap*
Everett, K. M. (1984)	*Candlewick*
Falk, F. A., TD (1997)	*Broad Street*
Farr, M. C. (1998)	*Walbrook*
Farrow, *Deputy* M. W. W. (1996)	*Farringdon Wt.*
Farthing, R. B. C. (1981)	*Aldgate*
FitzGerald, *Deputy* R. C. A. (1981)	*Bread Street*
Fraser, S. J. (1993)	*Coleman Street*
Fraser, *Deputy* W. B. (1981)	*Vintry*
Galloway, *Deputy* A. D. (1981)	*Broad Street*
Gillon, G. M. F. (1995)	*Cordwainer*
Ginsburg, S. (1990)	*Bishopsgate*
Graves, A. C. (1985)	*Bishopsgate*
Halliday, *Deputy* Mrs P. (1992)	*Walbrook*
Hardwick, Dr P. B. (1987)	*Aldgate*
Harris-Jones, Dr R. D. L. (2001)	*Farringdon Wt.*
Haynes, J. E. H. (1986)	*Cornhill*
Henderson-Begg, M. (1977)	*Coleman Street*
Hoffman, T. (2002)	*Vintry*
Holland, *Deputy* J., CBE (1972)	*Aldgate*
Hughes-Penney, R. C. (2004)	*Farringdon Wn.*
Hunt, W. G. (2004)	*Castle Baynard*
Jackson, L. St J. T. (1978)	*Bread Street*
Jones, H. L. M. (2004)	*Portsoken*
Kellett, Mrs M. W. F. (1986)	*Tower*
Kemp, D. L. (1984)	*Coleman Street*
King, A. (1999)	*Queenhithe*
Knowles, *Deputy* S. K. (1984)	*Candlewick*
Lawrence, G. A. (2003)	*Farringdon Wt.*
Leck, P. (1998)	*Aldersgate*
Lee, The Revd Dr B. J. (2001)	*Portsoken*
Lord, C. E. (2000)	*Coleman Street*
Luder, I. D. (1998)	*Castle Baynard*
McGuinness, C. (1997)	*Castle Baynard*
Malins, J. H., QC (1981)	*Farringdon Wt.*
Martinelli, *Deputy* P. J. (1994)	*Bassishaw*
Mayhew, J. P. (1996)	*Aldersgate*
Mead, Mrs W. (1997)	*Farringdon Wt.*
Millner, E. P. (2004)	*Portsoken*
Mitchell, *Deputy* C. R. (1971)	*Castle Baynard*
Mobsby, *Deputy* D. J. L. (1985)	*Billingsgate*
Mooney, B. D. F. (1998)	*Queenhithe*
Moss, A. D. (1989)	*Tower*
Moys, Mrs S. (2000)	*Aldgate*

Nash, *Deputy* Mrs J. C. (1983)	*Aldersgate*
Newman, Mrs P. B. (1989)	*Aldersgate*
Nove, P. R. (2004)	*Castle Baynard*
Owen, Mrs J. (1975)	*Langbourn*
Owen-Ward, J. R. (1983)	*Bridge*
Page, M. (2002)	*Farringdon Wn.*
Pembroke, *Deputy* Mrs A. M. F. (1978)	*Cheap*
Pointon, G. N. (2004)	*Billingsgate*
Pollard, J. H. G. (2002)	*Dowgate*
Price, E. E. (1996)	*Farringdon Wt.*
Pulman, *Deputy* G. A. G. (1983)	*Tower*
Punter, C. (1993)	*Cripplegate Wn.*
Quilter, S. D. (1998)	*Cripplegate Wt.*
Regan, R. D. (1998)	*Farringdon Wn.*
Robinson, Mrs D. C. (1989)	*Bishopsgate*
Roney, *Deputy* E. P. T., CBE (1974)	*Bishopsgate*
Scott, J. (1999)	*Broad Street*
Shalit, *Deputy* D. M. (1972)	*Farringdon Wn.*
Sherlock, *Deputy* M. R. C. (1992)	*Dowgate*
Simons, J. L. (2004)	*Castle Baynard*
Snyder, *Deputy* M. J. (1986)	*Cordwainer*
Spanner, J. H., TD (2001)	*Farringdon Wt.*
Stevenson, F. P. (1994)	*Cripplegate Wn.*
Streeter, P. T. (2004)	*Bishopsgate*
Thompson, D. J. (2004)	*Aldgate*
Tomlinson, J. (2004)	*Cripplegate*
Twogood, M. (2004)	*Farringdon Wt.*
Wang, Mrs C. A. M. (2004)	*Cornhill*
Willoughby, *Deputy* P. J. (1985)	*Bishopsgate*
Wooten, D. H. (2002)	*Farringdon Wn.*

THE CITY GUILDS (LIVERY COMPANIES)

The constitution of the livery companies has been unchanged for centuries. There are three ranks of membership: freemen, liverymen and assistants. A person can become a freeman by patrimony (through a parent having been a freeman); by servitude (through having served an apprenticeship to a freeman); or by redemption (by purchase).

Election to the livery is the prerogative of the company, who can elect any of its freemen as liverymen. Assistants are usually elected from the livery and form a Court of Assistants which is the governing body of the company. The Master (in some companies called the Prime Warden) is elected annually from the assistants.

The register for 2004–5 listed 24,336 liverymen of the guilds entitled to vote at elections at Common Hall.

The order of precedence, omitting extinct companies, is given in parenthesis after the name of each company in the list below. In certain companies the election of Master or Prime Warden for the year does not take place until the autumn. In such cases the Master or Prime Warden for 2003–4 is given.

THE TWELVE GREAT COMPANIES

In order of civic precedence

MERCERS *(1)*. *Hall,* Mercers' Hall, Ironmonger Lane, London EC2V 8HE *Livery,* 233. *Clerk,* C. H. Parker *Master,* C. C. Scott

GROCERS *(2)*. *Hall,* Grocers' Hall, Princes Street, London EC2R 8AD *Livery,* 323. *Clerk,* Brig. P. P. Rawlins, MBE *Master,* Vice-Adm. Sir Toby Frere, KCB

DRAPERS *(3)*. *Hall,* Drapers' Hall, Throgmorton Avenue, London EC2N 2DQ *Livery,* 282. *Clerk,* Rear-Adm. A. B. Ross, CB, CBE; *Master,* Martin Sankey

FISHMONGERS *(4)*. *Hall,* Fishmongers' Hall, London Bridge, London EC4R 9EL *Livery,* 353. *Clerk,* K. S. Waters *Prime Warden,* Sir Angus Stirling

GOLDSMITHS *(5)*. *Hall,* Goldsmiths' Hall, Foster Lane, London EC2V 6BN *Livery,* 275. *Clerk,* R. I. Talbot *Prime Warden,* B. E. Toye

SKINNERS *(6/7)*. *Hall,* Skinners' Hall, 8 Dowgate Hill, London EC4R 2SP *Livery,* 393. *Clerk,* Maj.-Gen. Brian Plummer, CBE; *Master,* A. B. E. Hudson, MBE

MERCHANT TAYLORS *(6/7)*. Hall, 30 Threadneedle Street, London EC2R 8JB *Livery,* 325. *Clerk,* D. A. Peck *Master,* M. W. G. Skinner

HABERDASHERS *(8)*. *Hall,* 18 West Smithfield, London EC1A 9HQ *Livery,* 288. *Clerk,* Capt. R. J. Fisher, RN *Master,* Julien Prevett

SALTERS *(9)*. *Hall,* Salters' Hall, 4 Fore Street, London EC2Y 5DE *Livery,* 168. *Clerk,* Col. M. P. Barneby *Master,* J. A. Goodeve

IRONMONGERS *(10)*. *Hall,* Ironmongers' Hall, Shaftesbury Place, Barbican, London EC2Y 8AA *Livery,* 133. *Clerk,* J. A. Oliver; *Master,* A. R. P. Carden

VINTNERS *(11)*. *Hall,* Vintners' Hall, Upper Thames Street, London EC4V 3BG *Livery,* 308. *Clerk,* Brig. M. Smythe, OBE, *Master,* F. J. Avery

CLOTHWORKERS *(12)*. *Hall,* Clothworkers' Hall, Dunster Court, Mincing Lane, London EC3R 7AH *Livery,* 215. *Clerk,* A. C. Blessley; *Master,* Peter Rawson

OTHER CITY GUILDS

In alphabetical order

ACTUARIES *(91)*. *Hall,* The Cote, Old Gloucester Road, Alveston, Bristol BS35 3LQ *Livery,* 200. *Clerk,* M. J. Turner *Master,* A. J. Frost

AIR PILOTS AND AIR NAVIGATORS *(81)*. *Hall,* Cobham House, 9 Warwick Court, Gray's Inn, London WC1R 5DJ *Livery,* 500. *Grand Master,* HRH The Duke of York, KCVO, ADC; *Clerk,* Paul Tacon *Master,* Capt. Richard Feux, LVO, FRAES

APOTHECARIES, SOCIETY OF *(58)*. *Hall,* Apothecaries' Hall, 14 Black Friars Lane, London EC4V 6EJ *Livery,* 1,758. *Clerk,* A. M. Wallington Smith; *Master,* W. S. Shand

ARBITRATORS *(93)*. 13 Hall Gardens, Colney Heath, St Albans, Herts AL4 0QF *Livery,* 150. *Clerk,* Mrs G. Duffy *Master,* A. W. Drysdale

ARMOURERS AND BRASIERS *(22)*. *Hall,* Armourers' Hall, 81 Coleman Street, London EC2R 5BJ *Livery,* 120. *Clerk,* Cdr. T. J. K. Sloane, OBE, RN; *Master,* A. M. R. Pontifex

BAKERS *(19)*. *Hall,* Bakers' Hall, Harp Lane, London EC3R 6DP *Livery,* 370. *Clerk,* J. W. Tompkins *Master,* Richard E. B. Sawyer

BARBERS *(17)*. *Hall,* Barber-Surgeons' Hall, Monkwell Square, Wood Street, London EC2Y 5BL *Livery,* 200. *Clerk,* Col. P. J. Durrant, MBE; *Master,* C. W. Sprague

BASKETMAKERS *(52)*. 29 Ingram House, Park Road, Hampton Wick, Surrey KT1 4BA *Livery,* 308. *Clerk,* R. de Pilkyngton; *Prime Warden,* R. Bartle

BLACKSMITHS *(40)*. 48 Upwood Road, London SE12 8AN *Livery,* 229. *Clerk,* C. Jeal; *Prime Warden,* John Shreeves

BOWYERS *(38)*. 5 Archer House, Vicarage Crescent, London SW11 3LF *Livery,* 102. *Clerk,* Richard Wilkinson *Master,* P. Seaton

BREWERS *(14)*. *Hall,* Brewers Hall, Aldermanbury Square, London EC2V 7HR *Livery,* 170. *Clerk,* Brig. D. J. Ross, CBE; *Master,* R. A. S. Everard

BRODERERS *(48)*. Ember House, 35–37 Creek Road, East Molesey, Surrey KT8 9BE *Livery,* 173. *Clerk,* P. J. C. Crouch; *Master,* M. A. Hissey

BUILDERS MERCHANTS *(88)*. 4 College Hill, London EC4R 2RB *Livery*, 200. *Clerk*, Miss S. M. Robinson, TD *Master*, S. J. Somerville

BUTCHERS *(24)*. *Hall*, Butchers' Hall, 87 Bartholomew Close, London EC1A 7EB *Livery*, 594. *Clerk*, A. J. C. Morrow, CVO; *Master*, Colin Cullimore, CBE

CARMEN *(77)*. 8 Little Trinity Lane, London EC4V 2AN *Livery*, 469. *Clerk*, Walter Gill; *Master*, R. N. Cullimore

CARPENTERS *(26)*. *Hall*, Carpenters' Hall, 1 Throgmorton Avenue, London EC2N 2JJ *Livery*, 150. *Clerk*, Maj.-Gen. P. T. Stevenson, OBE; *Master*, J. A. C. Wheeler

CHARTERED ACCOUNTANTS *(86)*. The Rustlings, Valley Close, Studham, Dunstable LU6 2QN *Livery*, 334. *Clerk*, C. Bygrave; *Master*, G. Acher, CBE, LVO

CHARTERED ARCHITECTS *(98)*. 82A Muswell Hill Road, London N10 3JR *Livery*, 172. *Clerk*, D. Cole-Adams *Master*, Nigel Thomson

CHARTERED SECRETARIES AND ADMINISTRATORS *(87)*. 3rd Floor, Saddlers' House, 40 Gutter Lane, London EC2V 6BR *Livery*, 224. *Clerk*, Col. M. J. Dudding, OBE, TD, FCIS; *Master*, D. H. Kirkham, CBE, FCIS

CHARTERED SURVEYORS *(85)*. 75 Meadway Drive, Horsell, Woking, Surrey GU21 4TF *Livery*, 350. *Clerk*, Mrs A. L. Jackson; *Master*, T. G. Knight

CLOCKMAKERS *(61)*. Salters' Hall, 4 Fore Street, London EC2Y 5DE *Livery*, 230. *Clerk*, Gp Capt. P. H. Gibson, MBE; *Master*, Mrs D. M. Uff

COACHMAKERS AND COACH-HARNESS MAKERS *(72)*. Woodlands House, The Clump, Chorleywood, Hertfordshire WD3 4BB *Livery*, 385. *Clerk*, Gp Capt. G. Bunn, CBE *Master*, Michael Limb, OBE

CONSTRUCTORS *(99)*. Forge Farmhouse, Glassenbury, Cranbrook, Kent TN17 2QE *Livery*, 130. *Clerk*, Tim Nicholson; *Master*, Peter Knight

COOKS *(35)*. Registry Chambers, The Old Deanery, Deans Court, London EC4V 5AA *Livery*, 75. *Clerk*, M. C. Thatcher; *Master*, G. A. V. Rees

COOPERS *(36)*. *Hall*, Coopers' Hall, 13 Devonshire Square, London EC2M 4TH *Livery*, 260. *Clerk*, A. G. R. Carroll *Master*, John Newton

CORDWAINERS *(27)*. 8 Warwick Court, Gray's Inn, London WC1R 5DJ *Livery*, 164. *Clerk*, Lt.-Col. J. R. Blundell, RM *Master*, L. J. E. Chamberlain

CURRIERS *(29)*. Hedgerley, 10 The Leaze, Ashton Keynes, Wiltshire SN6 6PE *Livery*, 88. *Clerk*, D. M. Moss *Master*, W. N. Bagshawe

CUTLERS *(18)*. *Hall*, Cutlers' Hall, Warwick Lane, London EC4M 7BR *Livery*, 100. *Clerk*, J. P. Allen *Master*, M. W. Roberts

DISTILLERS *(69)*. 71 Lincoln's Inn Fields, London WC2A 3JF *Livery*, 270. *Clerk*, C. V. Hughes *Master*, D. N. V. Churton, MBE

DYERS *(13)*. *Hall*, Dyers' Hall, 10 Dowgate Hill, London EC4R 2ST *Livery*, 127. *Clerk*, J. R. Chambers, FCA *Prime Warden*, M. Bird

ENGINEERS *(94)*. Wax Chandlers' Hall, Gresham Street, London EC2V 7AD *Livery*, 289. *Clerk*, Air Vice-Marshal G. Skinner, CBE *Master*, Maj.-Gen. E. G. Wilmott, CB, OBE

ENVIRONMENTAL CLEANERS *(97)*. 6 Grange Meadows, Elmswell, Bury St Edmunds, Suffolk IP30 9GE *Livery*, 258. *Clerk*, M. A. Bizley; *Master*, Paul R. Michael

FAN MAKERS *(76)*. Skinners' Hall, 8 Dowgate Hill, London EC4R 2SP *Livery*, 210. *Clerk*, K. J. Patterson *Master*, J. R. G. Thomas

FARMERS *(80)*. *Hall*, 3 Cloth Street, London EC1 *Livery*, 300. *Clerk*, Miss M. L. Winter *Master*, N. J. Fiske

FARRIERS *(55)*. 19 Queen Street, Chipperfield, Kings Langley, Herts WD4 9BT *Livery*, 345. *Clerk*, Mrs C. C. Clifford *Master*, Brig. P. G. H. Jepson

FELTMAKERS *(63)*. The Old Post House, Upton Grey, Basingstoke, Hampshire RG25 2RL *Livery*, 170. *Clerk*, Maj. J. T. H. Coombs *Master*, D. N. Bedford

FIREFIGHTERS *(103)*. The Insurance Hall, 20 Aldermanbury, London EC2V 7GF *Livery*, 65. *Clerk*, Mrs M. Holland Prior; *Master*, R. Dunley

FLETCHERS *(39)*. *Hall*, The Farmers' and Fletchers' Hall, 3 Cloth Street, London EC1A 7LD *Livery*, 140. *Clerk*, M. Johnson; *Master*, F. A. Neal, CMG

FOUNDERS *(33)*. *Hall*, Founders' Hall, Number One, Cloth Fair, London EC1A 7JQ *Livery*, 165. *Clerk*, A. J. Gillett *Master*, Richard J. Martin

FRAMEWORK KNITTERS *(64)*. 86 Park Drive, Upminster, Essex RM14 3AS *Livery*, 275. *Clerk*, A. J. Clark *Master*, D. A. Buswell

FRUITERERS *(45)*. Chapelstones, 84 High Street, Codford St Mary, Warminster BA12 0ND *Livery*, 284. *Clerk*, Lt.-Col. L. G. French; *Master*, H. H. Bryant

FUELLERS *(95)*. 26 Merrick Square, London SE1 4JB *Livery*, 95. *Clerk*, Sir W. Anthony J. Reardon Smith, Bt. *Master*, David Port

FURNITURE MAKERS *(83)*. Painters' Hall, 9 Little Trinity Lane, London EC4V 2AD *Livery*, 294. *Clerk*, Mrs J. A. Wright; *Master*, D. L. Burbidge, OBE

GARDENERS *(66)*. 25 Luke Street, London EC2A 4AR *Livery*, 269. *Clerk*, Col. N. G. S. Gray *Master*, C. R. G. Shewell-Cooper

GIRDLERS *(23)*. *Hall*, Girdlers' Hall, Basinghall Avenue, London EC2V 5DD *Livery*, 80. *Clerk*, Lt.-Col. R. Sullivan *Master*, O. C. S. Swann

GLASS-SELLERS *(71)*. 57 Witley Court, Coram Street, London WC1N 1MD *Livery*, 230. *Hon. Clerk*, A. J. Smith *Master*, Prof. J. R. Whiteman, PHD, FIMA, FRSA

GLAZIERS AND PAINTERS OF GLASS *(53)*. *Hall*, Glaziers' Hall, 9 Montague Close, London SE1 9DD *Livery*, 244. *Clerk*, Col. D. W. Eking *Master*, Ms P. Shaw

GLOVERS *(62)*. 73 Clapham Manor Street, London SW4 6DS *Livery*, 260. *Clerk*, Mrs M. Hood *Master*, William Loach

GOLD AND SILVER WYRE DRAWERS *(74)*. 'Twizzletwig', The Ballands South, Fetcham, Leatherhead, Surrey KT22 9EP *Livery*, 310. *Clerk*, T. J. Waller *Master*, Michael C. Roberts

GUNMAKERS *(73)*. The Proof House, 48–50 Commercial Road, London E1 1LP *Livery*, 265. *Clerk*, Col. W. F. Chesshyre; *Master*, C. D. Price

HACKNEY CARRIAGE DRIVERS *(104)*. 25 The Grove, Parkfield, Latimer, Buckinghamshire HP5 1UE *Livery*, 90. *Clerk*, Mary Whitworth; *Master*, John Rennie

HORNERS *(54)*. c/o Clergy House, Hide Place, London SW1P 4NJ *Livery*, 235. *Clerk*, A. R. Layard *Master*, I. A. McColl

INFORMATION TECHNOLOGISTS *(100)*. *Hall*, Information Technologists' Hall, 39A Bartholomew Close, London EC1A 7JN *Livery*, 293. *Clerk*, Mrs G. Wilson *Master*, Roger Graham, OBE

INNHOLDERS *(32)*. *Hall*, Innholders' Hall, 30 College Street, London EC4R 2RH *Livery*, 143. *Clerk*, D. E. Bulger *Master*, W. R. Spouse

INSURERS *(92)*. The Hall, 20 Aldermanbury, London EC2V 7HY *Livery*, 370. *Clerk*, L. J. Walters *Master*, M. K. Bewes

JOINERS AND CEILERS *(41)*. 75 Meadway Drive, Horsell, Woking, Surrey GU21 4TF *Livery*, 124. *Clerk*, Mrs A. L. Jackson; *Master*, John Christopher

LAUNDERERS *(89)*. *Hall*, Launderers Hall, 9 Montague Close, London Bridge, London SE1 9DD *Livery*, 250. *Clerk*, Mrs J. Polek; *Master*, Alec Kennedy

LEATHERSELLERS *(15)*. *Hall*, Leathersellers' Hall, 15 St Helen's Place, London EC3A 6DQ *Livery*, 150. *Clerk*, Capt. J. G. F. Cooke, OBE, RN; *Master*, Tony Lister

LIGHTMONGERS *(96)*. Crown Wharf, 11a Coldharbour, Blackwall Reach, London E14 9NS *Livery*, 194. *Clerk*, D. B. Wheatley; *Master*, Ian Crosby

LORINERS *(57)*. 8 Portland Square, London E1W 2QR *Livery*, 358. *Clerk*, G. B. Forbes; *Master*, John W. Owen, CMG, MBE

MAKERS OF PLAYING CARDS *(75)*. 42 Warnford Court, Throgmorton Street, London EC2N 2AT *Livery*, 147. *Clerk*, Paul Bowen; *Master*, Graeme Living

MANAGEMENT CONSULTANTS *(105)*. Ladymead, 23 Hilltop Road, Earley, Reading RG6 1BY *Livery*, 150. *Clerk*, Claire Dyer; *Master*, Alan Broomhead

MARKETORS *(90)*. 13 Hall Gardens, Colney Heath, St Albans, Herts AL4 0QF *Livery*, 240. *Clerk*, Mrs G. Duffy; *Master*, David Hanger

MASONS *(30)*. 22 Cannon Hill, Southgate, London N14 6LG *Livery*, 122. *Clerk*, P. F. Clark; *Master*, M. J. Peachey

MASTER MARINERS *(78)*. *Hall*, HQS Wellington, Temple Stairs, Victoria Embankment, London WC2R 2PN *Livery*, 215. *Admiral*, HRH The Prince Philip, Duke of Edinburgh, KG, KT, OM, GBE, PC; *Clerk*, Cdr. I. S. Gregory, RN; *Master*, Capt. C. R. Smiley

MUSICIANS *(50)*. 6th Floor, 2 London Wall Building, London EC2M 5PP *Livery*, 374. *Clerk*, Col. T. P. B. Hoggarth *Master*, J. Rennert

NEEDLEMAKERS *(65)*. 5 Staple Inn, London WC1V 7QH *Livery*, 230. *Clerk*, M. G. Cook; *Master*, Graham Born

PAINTER-STAINERS *(28)*. *Hall*, Painters' Hall, 9 Little Trinity Lane, London EC4V 2AD *Livery*, 320. *Clerk*, Chris Twyman; *Master*, D. R. Clover

PATTENMAKERS *(70)*. 3 The High Street, Sutton Valence, Kent ME17 3AG *Livery*, 200. *Clerk*, Col. R. W. Murfin, TD; *Master*, Donald Newell

PAVIORS *(56)*. 3 Ridgemount Gardens, Enfield, Middx EN2 8QL *Livery*, 234. *Clerk*, J. L. White *Master*, John Edward Mills

PEWTERERS *(16)*. *Hall*, Pewterers' Hall, Oat Lane, London EC2V 7DE *Livery*, 125. *Clerk*, Lt. Col. T. M. Reeve-Tucker, OBE; *Master*, R. G. Wildash

PLAISTERERS *(46)*. *Hall*, Plaisterers' Hall, 1 London Wall, London EC2Y 5JU *Livery*, 210. *Clerk*, Mrs. H. Machtus *Master*, D. R. Measom

PLUMBERS *(31)*. Wax Chandlers' Hall, 6 Greesham Street, London EC2V 7AD *Livery*, 332. *Clerk*, Lt.-Col. R. J. A. Paterson-Fox; *Master*, M. S. Samuel, CENG

POULTERS *(34)*. The Old Butchers, Station Road, Groombridge, Kent TN3 9QX *Livery*, 197. *Clerk*, Mrs G. W. Butcher; *Master*, R. G. T. Hulbert

SADDLERS *(25)*. *Hall*, Saddlers' Hall, 40 Gutter Lane, London EC2V 6BR *Livery*, 70. *Clerk*, Gp Capt. W. S. Brereton Martin, CBE; *Master*, H. S. Dyson-Laurie

SCIENTIFIC INSTRUMENT MAKERS *(84)*. 9 Montague Close, London SE1 9DD *Livery*, 240. *Clerk*, N. J. Watson *Master*, Prof. R. W. Hartley

SCRIVENERS *(44)*. HQS Wellington, Temple Stairs, Victoria Embankment, London WC2R 2PN *Livery*, 194. *Clerk*, A. Hill; *Master*, R. D. Millett

SHIPWRIGHTS *(59)*. Ironmongers Hall, Barbican, London EC2Y 8AA *Livery*, 414. *Grand Master*, HRH The Prince Philip, Duke of Edinburgh, KG, KT, OM, GBE, PC *Clerk*, Rear Adm. Derek Anthony, MBE *Prime Warden*, Peter Buckley

SOLICITORS *(79)*. 4 College Hill, London EC4R 2RB *Livery*, 354. *Clerk*, N. Cameron; *Master*, A. J. C. Collett

SPECTACLE MAKERS *(60)*. Apothecaries' Hall, Black Friars Lane, London EC4V 6EL *Livery*, 353. *Clerk*, Lt.-Col. J. A. B. Salmon, OBE, LLB; *Master*, N. H. Wingate

STATIONERS AND NEWSPAPER MAKERS *(47)*. *Hall*, Stationers' Hall, Ave Maria Lane, London EC4M 7DD *Livery*, 416. *Clerk*, Brig. D. G. Sharp, AFC; *Master*, J. G. Benn

TALLOW CHANDLERS *(21)*. *Hall*, Tallow Chandlers' Hall, 4 Dowgate Hill, London EC4R 2SH *Livery*, 200. *Clerk*, Brig. R. W. Wilde, CBE; *Master*, D. A. K. Simmonds

TIN PLATE WORKERS (ALIAS WIRE WORKERS) *(67)*. Bartholomew House, 66 Westbury Road, New Malden, Surrey KT3 5AS *Livery*, 200. *Clerk*, Michael Henderson-Begg; *Master*, Henry Edmonds

TOBACCO PIPE MAKERS AND TOBACCO BLENDERS *(82)*. Hackhurst Farm, Lower Dicker, Hailsham, E. Sussex BN27 4BP *Livery*, 153. *Clerk*, N. J. Hallings-Pott *Master*, D. Glynn-Jones

TURNERS *(51)*. 182 Temple Chambers, Temple Avenue, London EC4Y 0HP *Livery*, 169. *Clerk*, E. A. Windsor Clive *Master*, R. J. Levy

TYLERS AND BRICKLAYERS *(37)*. 30 Shelley Avenue, Tiptree CO5 0SF *Livery*, 150. *Clerk*, Barry Blumson *Master*, Sandy Angus

UPHOLDERS *(49)*. Hall in the Wood, 46 Quail Gardens, Selsdon Vale, Croydon CR2 8TF *Livery*, 210. *Clerk*, Mrs J. R. Cody; *Master*, M. A. Brecknell

WATER CONSERVATORS *(102)*. 22 Broadfields, Headstone Lane, Hatch End, Middlesex HA2 6NH *Livery*, 185. *Clerk*, R. A. Riley; *Master*, Dr Marion J. Carter

WAX CHANDLERS *(20)*. *Hall*, Wax Chandlers' Hall, 6 Gresham Street, London EC2V 7AD *Livery*, 129. *Clerk*, R. J. Percival; *Master*, A. G. McKay

WEAVERS *(42)*. Saddlers' House, Gutter Lane, London EC2V 6BR *Livery*, 125. *Clerk*, Mr. J. Snowdon *Upper Bailiff*, J. F. M. Monkhouse

WHEELWRIGHTS *(68)*. Ember House, 35–37 Creek Road, East Molesey, Surrey KT8 9BE *Livery*, 217. *Clerk*, P. J. C. Crouch; *Master*, D. N. Legg

WOOLMEN *(43)*. 22 Broomfields, Headstone Lane, Hatch End, Middlesex HAZ 6WH *Livery*, 137. *Clerk*, Ralph Riley *Master*, John Townend

WORLD TRADERS *(101)*. 36 Ladbroke Grove, London W11 2PA *Livery*, 175. *Clerk*, N. R. Pullman *Master*, Eric Stobart

INTERNATIONAL BANKERS *(No Livery)*. 1 Bengal Court, London EC3V 9DD *Freemen*, 502. *Clerk*, Tim Woods *Master*, Lord George of St Tudy, PC, GBE

TAX ADVISERS *(No Livery)*. 504 Bryer Court, Barbican, London EC2Y 8DE *Freemen*, 130. *Clerk*, John Jeffrey-Cook; *Master*, M. B. Squires

SECURITY PROFESSIONALS *(No Livery)*. 1 Wallis Mews, Guildford Road, Leatherhead, Surrey KT22 9DQ *Freemen, 240 Clerk*, John Maddock *Master*, Wg Cdr. Michael Welply

PARISH CLERKS *(No Livery*)*. Acreholt, 33 Medstead Road, Beech, Alton, Hampshire GU34 4AD *Members*, 96. *Clerk*, Lt.-Col. B. J. N. Coombes; *Master*, M. R. C. Sherlock

WATERMEN AND LIGHTERMEN*(No Livery*)*. *Hall*, Watermen's Hall, 16 St Mary-at-Hill, London EC3R 8EF *Craft Owning Freemen*, 326. *Clerk*, C. Middlemiss *Master*, Robert E. Lupton

* Parish Clerks and Watermen and Lightermen have requested to remain with no livery.

LONDON BOROUGH COUNCILS

Council	*Administrative Headquarters*	*Telephone*	*Population*	*Band D charge* *	*Chief Executive*
Barking and Dagenham	Dagenham, RM10 7BN	020-8592 4500	156,696	£1,110	Graham Farrant
Barnet	Hendon, NW4 4BG	020-8359 2000	314,564	£1,214	Leo Boland
Bexley	Bexleyheath, DA6 7LB	020-8303 7777	220,458	£1,186	Nick Johnson
Brent	Wembley, HA9 9HD	020-8937 1234	263,466	£1,141	Gareth Daniel
Bromley	Bromley, BR1 3UH	020-8464 3333	300,000	£1,040	David Bartlett
Camden	Judd Street, WC1H 9JE	020-7278 4444	210,000	£1,200	Moira Gibb
CORPORATION OF LONDON	Guildhall, EC2P 2EJ	020-7332 1902	6,700	£773	Chris Duffield
Croydon	Park Lane, Croydon, CR9 3JS	020-8686 4433	330,700	£1,165	David Wechsler
Ealing	New Broadway, W5 2BY	020-8825 5000	311,000	£1,192	Gillian Guy
Enfield	Silver Street, EN1 3XA	020-8379 1000	273,559	£1,193	Robert Leak
Greenwich	Wellington Street, SE18 6PW	020-8854 8888	214,403	£1,141	Mary Ney
Hackney	Mare Street, E8 1EA	020-8356 5000	202,824	£1,221	Max Caller
Hammersmith and Fulham	King Street, W6 9JU	020-8748 3020	157,470	£1,131	Geoff Alltimes
Haringey	High Road, N22 8LE	020-8489 0000	213,000	£1,259	David Warwick
Harrow	Harrow, HA1 2UJ	020-8863 5611	206,814	£1,275	Joyce Markham
Havering	Romford, RM1 3BD	01708-434343	224,250	£1,284	S. Evans
Hillingdon	Uxbridge, UB8 1UW	01895-250111	243,006	£1,215	Dorian Leatham
Hounslow	Lampton Road, TW3 4DN	020-8583 2000	240,397	£1,262	Mark Gilks
Islington	Upper Street, N1 2UD	020-7527 2000	175,797	£1,107	Helen Bailey
Kensington and Chelsea	Hornton Street, W8 7NX	020-7937 5464	190,300	£954	Derek Myers
Kingston upon Thames	Kingston upon Thames, KT1 1EU	020-8546 2121	147,273	£1,309	Bruce McDonald
Lambeth	Brixton, SW2 1RW	020-7926 1000	267,500	£1,050	Faith Boardman
Lewisham	Catford Road, SE6 4RU	020-8314 6000	250,000	£1,141	Barry Quirk
Merton	London Road, Morden SM4 5DX	020-8543 2222	179,000	£1,209	Ged Curran
Newham	Barking Road, East Ham, E6 2RP	020-8430 2000	254,041	£1,059	Dave Burbage
Redbridge	Ilford, IG1 1DD	020-8554 5000	238,635	£1,142	Roger Hampson
Richmond upon Thames	Twickenham, TW1 3BZ	020-8891 1411	182,766	£1,339	Gillian Norton
Southwark	Peckam Road, SE5 8UB	020-7525 5000	240,000	£1,071	Robert Coomber
Sutton	St. Nicholas Way, SM1 1EA	020-8770 5000	179,768	£1,180	Joanna Simons
Tower Hamlets	Clove Crescent, E14 2BG	020-7364 5000	181,251	£1,008	Christine Gilbert
Waltham Forest	Forest Road, E17 4JF	020-8496 4201	218,341	£1,245	Simon White
Wandsworth	Wandsworth High Street, SW18 2PU	020-8871 6000	266,600	£601	Gerald Jones
WESTMINSTER	Victoria Street, SW1E 6QP	020-7641 6000	181,000	£605	Peter Rogers

*Average Band D council tax
Councils in CAPITAL LETTERS have City Status

WALES

The Principality of Wales (Cymru) occupies the extreme west of the central southern portion of the island of Great Britain, with a total area of 8,015 sq. miles (20,758 sq. km): land 7,965 sq. miles (20,628 sq. km); inland water 50 sq. miles (130 sq. km). It is bounded on the north by the Irish Sea, on the south by the Bristol Channel, on the east by the English counties of Cheshire, Shropshire, Herefordshire and Gloucestershire, and on the west by St George's Channel.

Across the Menai Straits is the island of Anglesey (Ynys Môn) (276 sq. miles), communication with which is facilitated by the Menai Suspension Bridge (1,000 ft long) built by Telford in 1826, and by the tubular railway bridge (1,100 ft long) built by Stephenson in 1850. Holyhead harbour, on Holy Isle (north-west of Anglesey), provides accommodation for ferry services to Dublin (70 miles).

POPULATION

The population at the 2001 census was 2,903,085 (males 1,403,782; females 1,499,303). The average density of population in 2001 was 1.4 persons per hectare.

RELIEF

Wales is a country of extensive tracts of high plateau and shorter stretches of mountain ranges deeply dissected by river valleys. Lower-lying ground is largely confined to the coastal belt and the lower parts of the valleys. The highest mountains are those of Snowdonia in the north-west (Snowdon, 3,559 ft), Berwyn (Aran Fawddwy, 2,971 ft), Cader Idris (Pen y Gadair, 2,928 ft), Dyfed (Plynlimon, 2,467 ft), and the Black Mountain, Brecon Beacons and Black Forest ranges in the south-east (Carmarthen Van, 2,630 ft, Pen y Fan, 2,906 ft, Waun Fâch, 2,660 ft).

HYDROGRAPHY

The principal river in Wales is the Severn, which flows from the slopes of Plynlimon to the English border. The Wye (130 miles) also rises in the slopes of Plynlimon. The Usk (56 miles) flows into the Bristol Channel, through Gwent. The Dee (70 miles) rises in Bala Lake and flows through the Vale of Llangollen, where an aqueduct (built by Telford in 1805) carries the Pontcysyllte branch of the Shropshire Union Canal across the valley. The estuary of the Dee is the navigable portion, 14 miles in length and about five miles in breadth, and the tide rushes in with dangerous speed over the 'Sands of Dee'. The Towy (68 miles), Teifi (50 miles), Taff (40 miles), Dovey (30 miles), Taf (25 miles) and Conway (24 miles), the last named broad and navigable, are wholly Welsh rivers.

The largest natural lake is Bala (Llyn Tegid) in Gwynedd, nearly four miles long and about one mile wide. Lake Vyrnwy is an artificial reservoir, about the size of Bala, and forms the water supply of Liverpool; Birmingham is supplied from reservoirs in the Elan and Claerwen valleys.

WELSH LANGUAGE

According to the 2001 census results, the lowest estimate of percentage of persons aged three years and over able to speak Welsh is:

Blaenau Gwent	9.1	Neath Port Talbot	17.8
Bridgend	10.6	Newport	9.6
Caerphilly	10.9	Pembrokeshire	21.5
Cardiff	10.9	Powys	20.8
Carmarthenshire	50.1	Rhondda Cynon Taf	12.3
Ceredigion	51.8	Swansea	13.2
Conwy	29.2	Torfaen	10.7
Denbighshire	26.1	Vale of Glamorgan	11.1
Flintshire	14.1	Wrexham	14.4
Gwynedd	68.7	Ynys Mon (Isle of Anglesey)	59.8
Merthyr Tydfil	10.0		
Monmouthshire	9.0		
Wales	20.5		

FLAG

The flag of Wales, the Red Dragon (Y Ddraig Goch), is a red dragon on a field divided white over green (per fess argent and vert a dragon passant gules). The flag was augmented in 1953 by a royal badge on a shield encircled with a riband bearing the words *Ddraig Goch Ddyry Cychwyn* and imperially crowned, but this augmented flag is rarely used.

EARLY HISTORY

The earliest inhabitants of whom there is any record appear to have been subdued or exterminated by the Goidels (a people of Celtic race) in the Bronze Age. A further invasion of Celtic Brythons and Belgae followed in the ensuing Iron Age. The Roman conquest of southern Britain and Wales was for some time successfully opposed by Caratacus (Caractacus or Caradog), chieftain of the Catuvellauni and son of Cunobelinus (Cymbeline). South-east Wales was subjugated and the legionary fortress at Caerleon-on-Usk established by about AD 75–77; the conquest of Wales was completed by Agricola about AD 78. Communications were opened up by the construction of military roads from Chester to Caerleon-on-Usk and Caerwent, and from Chester to Conwy (and thence to Carmarthen and Neath). Christianity was introduced during the Roman occupation, in the fourth century.

ANGLO-SAXON ATTACKS

The Anglo-Saxon invaders of southern Britain drove the Celts into the mountain stronghold of Wales, and into Strathclyde (Cumberland and south-west Scotland) and Cornwall, giving them the name of *Waelisc* (Welsh), meaning 'foreign'. The West Saxons' victory of Deorham (AD 577) isolated Wales from Cornwall and the battle of Chester (AD 613) cut off communication with Strathclyde and northern Britain. In the eighth century the boundaries of the Welsh were further restricted by the annexations of Offa, King of Mercia, and counter-attacks were largely prevented by the construction of an artificial boundary from the Dee to the Wye (Offa's Dyke).

In the ninth century Rhodri Mawr (844–878) united the country and successfully resisted further incursions of the Saxons by land and raids of Norse and Danish pirates by sea, but at his death his three provinces of Gwynedd (north), Powys (mid) and Deheubarth (south) were divided among his three sons, Anarawd, Mervyn and Cadell. Cadell's son Hywel Dda ruled a large part of Wales and codified its laws but the provinces were not united again until the rule of Llewelyn ap Seisyllt (husband of the heiress of Gwynedd) from 1018 to 1023.

THE NORMAN CONQUEST

After the Norman conquest of England, William I created palatine counties along the Welsh frontier, and the Norman barons began to make encroachments into Welsh territory. The Welsh princes recovered many of their losses during the civil wars of Stephen's reign and in the early 13th century Owen Gruffydd, prince of Gwynedd, was the dominant figure in Wales. Under Llywelyn ap Iorwerth (1194–1240) the Welsh united in powerful resistance to English incursions and Llywelyn's privileges and *de facto* independence were recognised in the Magna Carta. His grandson, Llywelyn ap Gruffydd, was the last native prince; he was killed in 1282 during hostilities between the Welsh and English, allowing Edward I of England to establish his authority over the country. On 7 February 1301, Edward of Caernarvon, son of Edward I, was created Prince of Wales, a title subsequently borne by the eldest son of the sovereign.

Strong Welsh national feeling continued, expressed in the early 15th century in the rising led by Owain Glyndwr, but the situation was altered by the accession to the English throne in 1485 of Henry VII of the Welsh House of Tudor. Wales was politically assimilated to England under the Act of Union of 1535, which extended English laws to the Principality and gave it parliamentary representation for the first time.

EISTEDDFOD

The Welsh are a distinct nation, with a language and literature of their own, and the national bardic festival (Eisteddfod), instituted by Prince Rhys ap Griffith in 1176, is still held annually. These *Eisteddfodau* (sessions) form part of the *Gorsedd* (assembly) and are believed to date from the time of Prydian, a ruling prince in an age many centuries before the Christian era.

PRINCIPAL CITIES

There are five cities in Wales (with date city status conferred); Bangor (pre-1900), Cardiff (1905), St David's (1994), Newport (2002) and Swansea (1969).

Cardiff and Swansea have also been granted Lord Mayoralities.

CARDIFF

Cardiff, at the mouth of the Rivers Taff, Rhymney and Ely, is the capital city of Wales and at the 2001 census had a population of 305,353. The city has changed dramatically in recent years following the regeneration of Cardiff Bay and construction of a barrage, which has created a permanent freshwater lake and waterfront for the city. As the capital city of Wales, Cardiff is home to the National Assembly for Wales and is a major administrative, retail, business and cultural centre.

The civic centre, is home to many fine buildings including, the City Hall, Castell Coch, Cardiff Castle, Llandaff Cathedral, the National Museum of Wales, University Buildings, Law Courts and the Temple of Peace and Health. The Millennium Stadium opened in 1999.

SWANSEA

Swansea *(Abertawe)* is a city and a seaport and at the 2001 census had a population of 223,293. The Gower peninsula was brought within the city boundary under local government reform in 1974.

The principal buildings are the Norman Castle (rebuilt *c.* 1330), the Royal Institution of South Wales, founded in 1835 (including Library), the University of Wales Swansea at Singleton, and the Guildhall, containing Frank Brangwyn's British Empire panels. The Dylan Thomas Centre, formerly the old Guildhall, was restored in 1995. More recent buildings include the County Hall, the new Maritime Quarter Marina and leisure centre.

Swansea was chartered by the Earl of Warwick, *c.* 1158–84, and further charters were granted by King John, Henry III, Edward II, Edward III and James II, Cromwell (two) and the Marcher Lord William de Breos. It was formally invested with city status in 1969 by HRH The Prince of Wales.

LOCAL COUNCILS

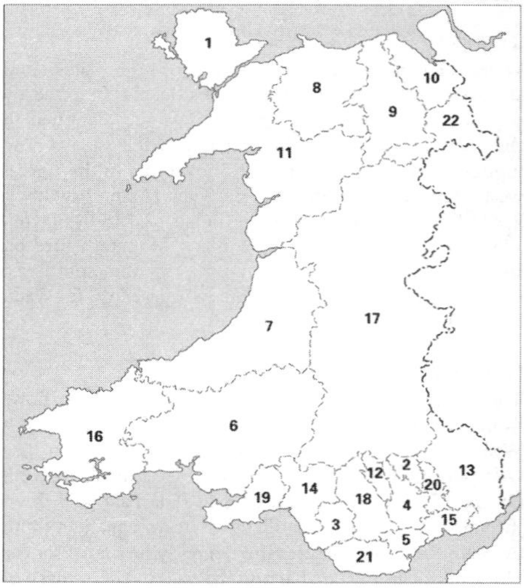

Key	*County*		
1	Anglesey	12	Merthyr Tydfil
2	Blaenau Gwent	13	Monmouthshire
3	Bridgend	14	Neath Port Talbot
4	Caerphilly	15	Newport
5	Cardiff	16	Pembrokeshire
6	Carmarthenshire	17	Powys
7	Ceredigion	18	Rhondda, Cynon, Taff
8	Conwy	19	Swansea
9	Denbighshire	20	Torfaen
10	Flintshire	21	Vale of Glamorgan
11	Gwynedd	22	Wrexham

LORDS-LIEUTENANT AND HIGH SHERIFFS

County/Shire	*Lord-Lieutenant*	*High Sheriff, 2004–5*
Clwyd	T. Jones, CBE	Dr J. O'Hara
Dyfed	The Rt. Hon. Baron Morris of Aberavon, QC	Mrs N. Drew
Gwent	S. Boyle	Brian Watkins, CMG
Gwynedd	Prof. E. Sunderland, OBE	J. Williams-Ellis
Mid Glamorgan	Kate Thomas	Mrs B. Williams
Powys	The Hon. Mrs E. S. Legge-Bourke, LVO	Lady Davies
S. Glamorgan	Capt. N. Lloyd-Edwards	Mrs F. Peel
W. Glamorgan	R. C. Hastie, CBE	David Lewis

LOCAL COUNCILS

Council	*Administrative Headquarters*	*Telephone*	*Population*	*Band D charge**	*Chief Executive*
Blaenau Gwent	Ebbw Vale	01495-350555	73,000	£1,038	R. Morrison
Bridgend	Bridgend	01656-643643	129,000	£949	Keri Lewis
Caerphilly	Hengoed	01443-815588	170,000	£862	Malgwyn Davies
CARDIFF CITY	Cardiff	029-2087 2000	327,500	£872	Byron Davies
Carmarthenshire	Carmarthen	01267-234567	173,000	£907	Mark James
Ceredigion	Aberaeron	01545-570881	77,202	£883	Owen Watkin
Conwy	Conwy	01492-574000	110,500	£777	C. Barker
Denbighshire	Ruthin	01824-706000	93,065	£1,007	Ian Miller
Flintshire	Mold	01352-752121	148,565	£881	Philip McGreevy
Gwynedd	Caernarfon	01286-672255	116,000	£890	Harry Thomas
Merthyr Tydfil	Merthyr Tydfil	01685-725000	54,000	£1,049	Alistair Neill
Monmouthshire	Cwmbran	01633-644644	84,885	£917	Colin Berg *(Acting)*
Neath Port Talbot	Port Talbot	01639-763333	137,954	£1,087	Ken Sawyers
NEWPORT	Newport	01633-244491	138,500	£732	Chris Freegard
Pembrokeshire	Haverfordwest	01437-764551	114,700	£707	Bryn Parry-Jones
Powys	Llandrindod Wells	01597-826000	123,000	£868	Jacky Tonge
Rhondda Cynon Taff	Tonypandy	01443-424000	340,000	£955	Kim Ryley
SWANSEA	Swansea	01792-636000	231,180	£880	Tim Thorogood
Torfaen	Pontypool	01495-762200	90,500	£892	Meg Holborow
Vale of Glamorgan	Barry	01446-700111	119,281	£829	John Maitland-Evans
Wrexham	Wrexham	01978-292000	125,000	£911	I. Garner
Ynys Mon (Isle of Anglesey)	Ynys Mon	01248-750057	67,863	£843	Geraint Edwards

* Average Band D council tax rounded to the nearest £, without discounts and inclusive of precepts
Councils in CAPITAL LETTERS have City Status

SCOTLAND

The Kingdom of Scotland occupies the northern portion of the main island of Great Britain and includes the Inner and Outer Hebrides, Orkney, Shetland, and many other islands. It lies between 60° 51′ 30″ and 54° 38′ N. latitude and between 1° 45′ 32″ and 6° 14′ W. longitude, with England to the south, the Atlantic Ocean on the north and west, and the North Sea on the east.

The greatest length of the mainland (Cape Wrath to the Mull of Galloway) is 274 miles, and the greatest breadth (Buchan Ness to Applecross) is 154 miles. The customary measurement of the island of Great Britain is from the site of John o' Groats house, near Duncansby Head, Caithness, to Land's End, Cornwall, a total distance of 603 miles in a straight line and approximately 900 miles by road.

The total area of Scotland is 30,420 sq. miles (78,789 sq. km); land 29,767 sq. miles (77,097 sq. km), inland water 653 sq. miles (1,692 sq. km).

POPULATION

The population at the 2001 census was 5,062,011 (males 2,432,494; females 2,629,517). The average density of the population in 2001 was 0.65 persons per hectare.

RELIEF

There are three natural orographic divisions of Scotland. The southern uplands have their highest points in Merrick (2,766 ft), Rhinns of Kells (2,669 ft), and Cairnsmuir of Carsphairn (2,614 ft), in the west; and the Tweedsmuir Hills in the east (Hartfell 2,651 ft, Dollar Law 2,682 ft, Broad Law 2,756 ft).

The central lowlands, formed by the valleys of the Clyde, Forth and Tay, divide the southern uplands from the northern Highlands, which extend almost from the extreme north of the mainland to the central lowlands, and are divided into a northern and a southern system by the Great Glen.

The Grampian Mountains, which entirely cover the southern Highland area, include in the west Ben Nevis (4,406 ft), the highest point in the British Isles, and in the east the Cairngorm Mountains (Cairn Gorm 4,084 ft, Braeriach 4,248 ft, Ben Macdui 4,296 ft). The north-western Highland area contains the mountains of Wester and Easter Ross (Carn Eige 3,880 ft, Sgurr na Lapaich 3,775 ft).

Created, like the central lowlands, by a major geological fault, the Great Glen (60 miles long) runs between Inverness and Fort William, and contains Loch Ness, Loch Oich and Loch Lochy. These are linked to each other and to the north-east and south-west coasts of Scotland by the Caledonian Canal, providing a navigable passage between the Moray Firth and the Inner Hebrides.

HYDROGRAPHY

The western coast is fragmented by peninsulas and islands, and indented by fjords (sea-lochs), the longest of which is Loch Fyne (42 miles long) in Argyll. Although the east coast tends to be less fractured and lower, there are several great drowned inlets (firths), e.g. Firth of Forth, Firth of Tay, Moray Firth, as well as the Firth of Clyde in the west.

The lochs are the principal hydrographic feature. The largest in Scotland and in Britain is Loch Lomond (27 sq. miles), in the Grampian valleys; the longest and deepest is Loch Ness (24 miles long and 800 ft deep), in the Great Glen; and Loch Shin (20 miles long) and Loch Maree in the Highlands.

The longest river is the Tay (117 miles), noted for its salmon. It flows into the North Sea, with Dundee on the estuary, which is spanned by the Tay Bridge (10,289 ft) opened in 1887 and the Tay Road Bridge (7,365 ft) opened in 1966. Other noted salmon rivers are the Dee (90 miles) which flows into the North Sea at Aberdeen, and the Spey (110 miles), the swiftest flowing river in the British Isles, which flows into Moray Firth. The Tweed, which gave its name to the woollen cloth produced along its banks, marks in the lower stretches of its 96-mile course the border between Scotland and England.

The most important river commercially is the Clyde (106 miles), formed by the junction of the Daer and Portrail water, which flows through the city of Glasgow to the Firth of Clyde. During its course it passes over the picturesque Falls of Clyde, Bonnington Linn (30 ft), Corra Linn (84 ft), Dundaff Linn (10 ft) and Stonebyres Linn (80 ft), above and below Lanark. The Forth (66 miles), upon which stands Edinburgh, the capital, is spanned by the Forth Railway Bridge (1890), which is 5,330 ft long, and the Forth Road Bridge (1964), which has a total length of 6,156 ft (over water) and a single span of 3,000 ft.

The highest waterfall in Scotland, and the British Isles, is Eas a'Chùal Aluinn with a total height of 658 ft, which falls from Glas Bheinn in Sutherland. The Falls of Glomach, on a head-stream of the Elchaig in Wester Ross, have a drop of 370 ft.

GAELIC LANGUAGE

According to the 2001 census, 1.2 per cent of the population of Scotland, mainly in Western Isles, were able to speak the Scottish form of Gaelic.

LOWLAND SCOTTISH LANGUAGE

Several regional Lowland Scottish dialects, known variously as Scots, Scotch, Lallans or Doric, are widely spoken. The General Register Office (Scotland) estimated in 1996 that 1.5 million people, or 30 per cent of the population, are Scots speakers. A question on Scots was not included in the 2001 census.

FLAG

The flag of Scotland is known as the Saltire. It is a white diagonal cross on a blue field (saltire argent in a field azure) and represents St Andrew, the patron saint of Scotland.

THE SCOTTISH ISLANDS

ORKNEY

The Orkney Islands (total area 375.5 sq. miles) lie about six miles north of the mainland, separated from it by the Pentland Firth. Of the 90 islands and islets (holms and skerries) in the group, about one-third are inhabited.

The total population at the 2001 census was 19,245;

the 2001 populations of the islands shown here include those of smaller islands forming part of the same council district.

Mainland, 15,339	Rousay, 267
Burray, 357	Sanday, 478
Eday, 121	Shapinsay, 300
Flotta, 81	South Ronaldsay, 854
Hoy, 392	Stronsay, 358
North Ronaldsay, 70	Westray, 563
Papa Westray, 65	

The islands are rich in prehistoric and Scandinavian remains, the most notable being the Stone Age village of Skara Brae, the burial chamber of Maeshowe, the many brochs (towers) and the 12th-century St Magnus Cathedral. Scapa Flow, between the Mainland and Hoy, was the war station of the British Grand Fleet from 1914 to 1919 and the scene of the scuttling of the surrendered German High Seas Fleet (21 June 1919).

Most of the islands are low-lying and fertile, and farming (principally beef cattle) is the main industry. Flotta, to the south of Scapa Flow, is the site of the oil terminal for the Piper, Claymore and Tartan fields in the North Sea.

The capital is Kirkwall (population 6,206) situated on Mainland.

SHETLAND

The Shetland Islands have a total area of 551 sq. miles and a population at the 2001 census of 21,988. They lie about 50 miles north of the Orkneys, with Fair Isle about half-way between the two groups. Out Stack, off Muckle Flugga, one mile north of Unst, is the most northerly part of the British Isles (60° 51′ 30″ N. lat.).

There are over 100 islands, of which 16 are inhabited. Populations at the 2001 census were:

Mainland, 17,575	Muckle Roe, 104
Bressay, 384	Trondra, 133
East Burra, 66	Unst, 720
Fair Isle, 69	West Burra, 784
Fetlar, 86	Whalsay, 1,034
Housay, 76	Yell, 957

Shetland's many archaeological sites include Jarlshof, Mousa and Clickhimin, and its long connection with Scandinavia has resulted in a strong Norse influence on its place-names and dialect.

Industries include fishing, knitwear and farming. In addition to the fishing fleet there are fish processing factories, and the traditional handknitting of Fair Isle and Unst is supplemented now with machine-knitted garments. Farming is mainly crofting, with sheep being raised on the moorland and hills of the islands. Latterly the islands have become a centre of the North Sea oil industry, with pipelines from the Brent and Ninian fields running to the terminal at Sullom Voe, the largest of its kind in Europe. Lerwick is the main centre for supply services for offshore oil exploration and development.

The capital is Lerwick (population 6,830) situated on Mainland.

THE HEBRIDES

Until the late 13th century the Hebrides included other Scottish islands in the Firth of Clyde, the peninsula of Kintyre (Argyll), the Isle of Man, and the (Irish) Isle of Rathlin. The origin of the name is stated to be the Greek *Eboudai*, latinised as *Hebudes* by Pliny, and corrupted to its present form. The Norwegian name *Sudreyjar* (Southern Islands) was latinised as *Sodorenses*, a name that survives in the Anglican bishopric of Sodor and Man.

There are over 500 islands and islets, of which about 100 are inhabited, though mountainous terrain and extensive peat bogs mean that only a fraction of the total area is under cultivation. Stone, Bronze and Iron Age settlement has left many remains, including those at Callanish on Lewis, and Norse colonisation influenced language, customs and place-names. Occupations include farming (mostly crofting and stock-raising), fishing and the manufacture of tweeds and other woollens. Tourism is also an important factor in the economy.

The Inner Hebrides lie off the west coast of Scotland and relatively close to the mainland. The largest and best-known is Skye (area 643 sq. miles; pop. 9,251; chief town, Portree), which contains the Cuillin Hills (Sgurr Alasdair 3,257 ft), the Red Hills (Beinn na Caillich 2,403 ft), Bla Bheinn (3,046 ft) and The Storr (2,358 ft). Other islands in the Highland council area include Raasay (pop. 194), Rum, Eigg (pop. 131) and Muck.

Further south the Inner Hebridean islands include Arran (pop. 5,058) containing Goat Fell (2,868 ft); Coll and Tiree (pop. 934); Colonsay and Oronsay (pop. 113); Easdale (pop. 58); Gigha (pop. 110); Islay (area 235 sq. miles; pop. 3,457); Jura (area 160 sq. miles; pop. 188) with a range of hills culminating in the Paps of Jura (Beinn-an-Oir, 2,576 ft, and Beinn Chaolais, 2,477 ft); Lismore (pop. 146); Luing (pop. 220); and Mull (area 367 sq. miles; pop. 2,696; chief town Tobermory) containing Ben More (3,171 ft).

The Outer Hebrides, separated from the mainland by the Minch, now form the Eilean Siar Western Isles Islands Council area (area 1,119 sq. miles; population at the 2001 census 26,502). The main islands are Lewis with Harris (area 770 sq. miles, pop. 19,918), whose chief town, Stornoway, is the administrative headquarters; North Uist (pop. 1,320); South Uist (pop. 1,818); Benbecula (pop. 1,249) and Barra (pop. 1,078). Other inhabited islands include Bernera (233), Berneray (136), Eriskay (133), Grimsay (201), Scalpay (322) and Vatersay (94).

EARLY HISTORY

There is evidence of human settlement in Scotland dating from the third millennium BC, the earliest settlers being Middle Stone Age hunters and fishermen. Early in the second millennium BC, New Stone Age farmers began to cultivate crops and rear livestock; their settlements were on the west coast and in the north, and included Skara Brae and Maeshowe (Orkney). Settlement by the Early Bronze Age 'Beaker folk', so-called from the shape of their drinking vessels, in eastern Scotland dates from about 1800 BC. Further settlement is believed to have occurred from 700 BC onwards, as tribes were displaced from further south by new incursions from the Continent and the Roman invasions from AD 43.

Julius Agricola, the Roman governor of Britain AD 77–84, extended the Roman conquests in Britain by advancing into Caledonia, culminating with a victory at Mons Graupius, probably in AD 84; he was recalled to Rome shortly afterwards and his forward policy was not pursued. Hadrian's Wall, mostly completed by AD 30, marked the northern frontier of the Roman empire except for the period between about AD 144 and 190 when the frontier moved north to the Forth-Clyde isthmus and a turf wall, the Antonine Wall, was manned.

After the Roman withdrawal from Britain, there were centuries of warfare between the Picts, Scots, Britons, Angles and Vikings. The Picts, believed to be a non-Indo-European race, occupied the area north of the Forth. The Scots, a Gaelic-speaking people of northern Ireland, colonised the area of Argyll and Bute (the kingdom of Dalriada) in the fifth century AD and then expanded eastwards and northwards. The Britons, speaking a Brythonic Celtic language, colonised Scotland from the south from the first century BC; they lost control of south-eastern Scotland (incorporated into the kingdom of Northumbria) to the Angles in the early seventh century but retained Strathclyde (south-western Scotland and Cumbria). Viking raids from the late eighth century were followed by Norse settlement in the western and northern isles, Argyll, Caithness and Sutherland from the mid-ninth century onwards.

UNIFICATION

The union of the areas which now comprise Scotland began in AD 843 when Kenneth mac Alpin, king of the Scots from *c.*834, became also king of the Picts, joining the two lands to form the kingdom of Alba (comprising Scotland north of a line between the Forth and Clyde rivers). Lothian, the eastern part of the area between the Forth and the Tweed, seems to have been leased to Kenneth II of Alba (reigned 971–995) by Edgar of England *c.*973/4, and Scottish possession was confirmed by Malcolm II's victory over a Northumbrian army at Carham *c.*1016. At about this time Malcolm II (reigned 1005–34) placed his grandson Duncan on the throne of the British kingdom of Strathclyde, bringing under Scots rule virtually all of what is now Scotland.

The Norse possessions were incorporated into the kingdom of Scotland from the 12th century onwards. An uprising in the mid-12th century drove the Norse from most of mainland Argyll. The Hebrides were ceded to Scotland by the Treaty of Perth in 1266 after a Norwegian expedition in 1263 failed to maintain Norse authority over the islands. Orkney and Shetland fell to Scotland in 1468–9 as a pledge for the unpaid dowry of Margaret of Denmark, wife of James III, though Danish claims of suzerainty were relinquished only with the marriage of Anne of Denmark to James VI in 1590.

From the 11th century, there were frequent wars between Scotland and England over territory and the extent of England's political influence. The failure of the Scottish royal line with the death of Margaret of Norway in 1290 led to disputes over the throne which were resolved by the adjudication of Edward I of England. He awarded the throne to John Balliol in 1292 but Balliol's refusal to be a puppet king led to war. Balliol surrendered to Edward I in 1296 and Edward attempted to rule Scotland himself. Resistance to Scotland's loss of independence was led by William Wallace, who defeated the English at Stirling Bridge (1297), and Robert Bruce, crowned in 1306, who held most of Scotland by 1311 and routed Edward II's army at Bannockburn (1314). England recognised the independence of Scotland in the Treaty of Northampton in 1328. Subsequent clashes include the disastrous battle of Flodden (1513) in which James IV and many of his nobles fell.

THE UNION

In 1603 James VI of Scotland succeeded Elizabeth I on the throne of England (his mother, Mary Queen of Scots, was the great-granddaughter of Henry VII), his successors reigning as sovereigns of Great Britain. Political union of the two countries did not occur until 1707.

THE JACOBITE REVOLTS

After the abdication (by flight) in 1688 of James VII and II, the crown devolved upon William III (grandson of Charles I) and Mary II (elder daughter of James VII and II). In 1689 Graham of Claverhouse roused the Highlands on behalf of James VII and II, but died after a military success at Killiecrankie.

After the death of Anne (younger daughter of James VII and II), the throne devolved upon George I (great-grandson of James VI and I). In 1715, armed risings on behalf of James Stuart (the Old Pretender, son of James VII and II) led to the indecisive battle of Sheriffmuir, and the Jacobite movement died down until 1745, when Charles Stuart (the Young Pretender) defeated the Royalist troops at Prestonpans and advanced to Derby (1746). From Derby, the adherents of 'James VIII and III' (the title claimed for his father by Charles Stuart) fell back on the defensive and were finally crushed at Culloden (16 April 1746).

PRINCIPAL CITIES

ABERDEEN

Aberdeen, 130 miles north-east of Edinburgh, received its charter as a Royal Burgh in 1124. Scotland's third largest city, Aberdeen lies between two rivers, the Dee and the Don facing the North Sea, the city has a strong maritime history and today is a main centre for offshore oil exploration and production. It is also an ancient university town and distinguished research centre. Other industries include engineering, food processing, textiles, paper manufacturing and chemicals.

Places of interest include King's College, St Machar's Cathedral, Brig o' Balgownie, Duthie Park and Winter Gardens, Hazlehead Park, the Kirk of St Nicholas, Mercat Cross, Marischal College and Marischal Museum, Provost Skene's House, Art Gallery, Gordon Highlanders Museum, Satrosphere Hands-On Discovery Centre, and Aberdeen Maritime Museum.

DUNDEE

The Royal Burgh of Dundee is situated on the north bank of the Tay estuary. The city's port and dock installations are important to the offshore oil industry and the airport also provides servicing facilities. Principal industries include textiles, biotechnology and digital media, lasers, printing, tyre manufacture, food processing, engineering, and tourism.

The unique City Churches – three churches under one roof, together with the 15th-century St Mary's Tower – are the most prominent architectural feature. Dundee has two historic ships: the Dundee-built RRS *Discovery* which took Capt. Scott to the Antarctic lies alongside Discovery Quay, and the frigate *Unicorn*, the only British-built wooden warship still afloat, is moored in Victoria Dock. Places of interest include Mills Public Observatory, the Tay road and rail bridges, Dundee Contemporary Arts Centre, McManus Galleries, Claypotts Castle, Broughty Castle, Verdant Works (Textile Heritage Centre) and the Sensation science centre.

EDINBURGH

Edinburgh is the capital city and seat of government in Scotland. The city is built on a group of hills and contains in Princes Street one of the most beautiful thoroughfares in the world.

The principal buildings are the Castle, which now houses the Stone of Scone and also includes St Margaret's Chapel, the oldest building in Edinburgh, and near it, the Scottish National War Memorial; the Palace of Holyroodhouse; Parliament House, the present seat of the judicature; three universities (Edinburgh, Heriot-Watt, Napier); St Giles' Cathedral; St Mary's (Scottish Episcopal) Cathedral (Sir George Gilbert Scott); the General Register House (Robert Adam); the National and the Signet Libraries; the National Gallery of Scotland; the Royal Scottish Academy; the Scottish National Portrait Gallery; and the Edinburgh International Conference Centre.

GLASGOW

Glasgow, a Royal Burgh, is Scotland's largest city and its principal commercial and industrial centre. The city occupies the north and south banks of the Clyde, formerly one of the chief commercial estuaries in the world. The main industries include engineering, electronics, finance, chemicals and printing. The city is also a key tourist and conference destination.

The chief buildings are the 13th-century Gothic Cathedral, the University (Sir George Gilbert Scott), the City Chambers, the Royal Concert Hall, St Mungo Museum of Religious Life and Art, Pollok House, the School of Art (Mackintosh), Kelvingrove Art Galleries, the Gallery of Modern Art, the Burrell Collection museum and the Mitchell Library. The city is home to the Scottish National Orchestra, Scottish Opera, Scottish Ballet and BBC Scotland and Scottish Television.

INVERNESS

Inverness was granted city status in 2000. The city's name is derived from the Gaelic for 'the mouth of the Ness', referring to the river on which it lies. Inverness is recorded as being at the junction of the old trade routes since 565AD. Today the city is the main administrative centre for the north of Scotland and is the capital of the Highlands. Tourism is one of the city's main industries.

Among the city's most notable buildings is Abertarff House, built in 1593 and the oldest secular building remaining in Inverness. Balnain House, built as a town house in 1726 is a fine example of early Georgian architecture. Once a hospital for Hanoverian soldiers after the battle of Culloden and as billets for the Royal Engineers when completing the 1st Ordnance Survey, today Balnain House is the National Trust for Scotland's regional HQ. The Old High Church, on St Michael's Mount, is the original Parish Church of Inverness and is built on the sight of the earliest Christian church in the city. Parts of the church date back to the 14th century.

Stirling was granted city status in 2002. Aberdeen, Dundee, Edinburgh and Glasgow have also been granted Lord Mayoralty/Lord Provostship.

LORDS-LIEUTENANT

Stirling was granted city status in 2002. Aberdeen, Dundee, Edinburgh and Glasgow have also been granted Lord Mayoralty/Lord Provostship.

Title	*Name*
Aberdeenshire	A. D. M. Farquharson, OBE
Angus	Mrs G. L. Osborne
Argyll and Bute	K. A. Mackinnon
Ayrshire and Arran	Maj. R. Y. Henderson, TD
Banffshire	Mrs Clare Russell
Berwickshire	Maj. A. R. Trotter
Caithness	M. A. G. Dunnett
Clackmannan	Mrs S. C. Cruickshank
Dumfries	Capt. R. C. Cunningham-Jardine
Dunbartonshire	Brig. D. D. G. Hardie, TD
East Lothian	W. Garth Morrison, CBE
Eilean Siar/Western Isles	A. Matheson, OBE
Fife	Mrs C. M. Dean
Inverness	Donald Angus Cameron of Lochiel, KT, CVO
Kincardineshire	J. D. B. Smart
Lanarkshire	G. K. Cox, MBE
Midlothian	Patrick Robert Prenter, CBE
Moray	Air Vice-Marshal G. A. Chesworth, CB, OBE, DFC
Nairn	E. J. Brodie
Orkney	G. R. Marwick
Perth and Kinross	Sir David Montgomery, Bt.
Renfrewshire	C. H. Parker, OBE
Ross and Cromarty	Capt. R. W. K. Stirling of Fairburn, TD
Roxburgh, Ettrick and Lauderdale	Dr June Paterson-Brown, CBE
Shetland	J. H. Scott
Stirling and Falkirk	Lt.-Col. J. Stirling of Garden, CBE, TD
Sutherland	vacant
The Stewartry of Kirkcudbright	Lt.-Gen. Sir Norman Arthur, KCB
Tweeddale	Capt. D. Younger
West Lothian	Mrs I. G. Brydie, MBE
Wigtown	Maj. E. S. Orr-Ewing

The Lord Provosts of the four city districts of Aberdeen, Dundee, Edinburgh and Glasgow are Lords-Lieutenant for those districts *ex officio*.

LOCAL COUNCILS

Council	*Administrative Headquarters*	*Telephone*	*Population*	*Band D charge* *	*Chief Executive*
ABERDEEN	Aberdeen	01224-522000	211,250	£1,107	Douglas Paterson
Aberdeenshire	Aberdeen	01467-620981	226,940	£1,014	Alan Campbell
Angus	Forfar	01307-461460	109,000	£985	Sandy Watson
Argyll and Bute	Lochgilphead	01546-602127	89,000	£1,075	James McLellan
Clackmannanshire	Alloa	01259-452000	47,930	£1,043	Keir Bloomer
Dumfries and Galloway	Dumfries	01387-260000	147,000	£964	Philip Jones
DUNDEE	Dundee	01382-434000	145,663	£1,135	Alex Stephen
East Ayrshire	Kilmarnock	01563-576000	120,300	£1,064	Fiona Lees
East Dunbartonshire	Kirkintilloch	0141-578 8000	108,243	£1,033	Sue Bruce
East Lothian	Haddington	01620-827827	90,180	£1,042	John Lindsay
East Renfrewshire	Giffnock	0141-577 3000	89,790	£1,003	Peter Daniels
EDINBURGH	Edinburgh	0131-200 2000	444,020	£1,083	Tom Aitchison
Eilean Siar (Western Isles)	Stornoway	01851-703773	27,940	£911	Bill Howat
Falkirk	Falkirk	01324-506070	145,270	£951	Mary Pitcaithly
Fife	Glenrothes	01592-414141	349,200	£1,015	Douglas Sinclair
GLASGOW	Glasgow	0141-287 2000	609,370	£1,185	George Black
Highland	Inverness	01463-702000	208,900	£1,039	Arthur McCourt
Inverclyde	Greenock	01475-717171	82,930	£1,143	Robert Cleary
Midlothian	Dalkeith	0131-270 7500	82,200	£1,126	Trevor Muir
Moray	Elgin	01343-543451	86,940	£996	Alastair Keddie
North Ayrshire	Irvine	01294-324100	140,000	£1,025	Bernard Devine
North Lanarkshire	Motherwell	01698-302222	321,820	£1,006	Gavin Whitefield
Orkney	Kirkwall	01856-873535	19,245	£940	Alistair Buchan
Perth and Kinross	Perth	01738-475000	134,949	£1,037	Bernadette Malone
Renfrewshire	Paisley	0141-842 5000	172,867	£1,039	Tom Scholes
Scottish Borders	Melrose	01835-824000	106,764	£985	David Hume
Shetland	Lerwick	01595-744511	21,940	£936	Morgan Goodlad
South Ayrshire	Ayr	01292-612000	113,960	£1,012	Tom Cairns
South Lanarkshire	Hamilton	01698-454444	302,216	£1,005	Michael Docherty
STIRLING	Stirling	0845-277700	84,700	£1,105	Keith Yates
West Dumbarton	Dunbartonshire	01389-737000	93,378	£1,089	Tim Huntingford
West Lothian	Livingston	01506-777000	153,086	£1,028	Alex Linkston

* Average Band D council tax without discounts and inclusive of any precepts. Councils in CAPITAL LETTERS have City Status

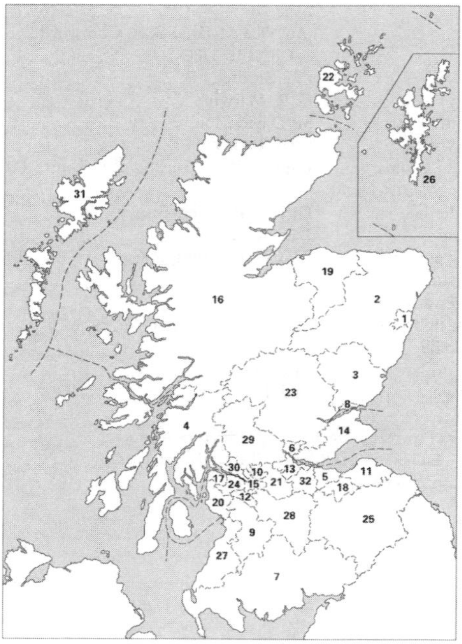

Key	*Council*		
1	Aberdeen City	17	Inverclyde
2	Aberdeenshire	18	Midlothian
3	Angus	19	Moray
4	Argyll and Bute	20	North Ayrshire
5	City of Edinburgh	21	North Lanarkshire
6	Clackmannanshire	22	Orkney
7	Dumfries and Galloway	23	Perth and Kinross
8	Dundee City	24	Renfrewshire
9	East Ayrshire	25	Scottish Borders
10	East Dunbartonshire	26	Shetland
11	East Lothian	27	South Ayrshire
12	East Renfrewshire	28	South Lanarkshire
13	Falkirk	29	Stirling
14	Fife	30	West Dunbartonshire
15	Glasgow City	31	Western Isles (Eilean Siar)
16	Highland	32	West Lothian

NORTHERN IRELAND

Northern Ireland has a total area of 5,467 sq. miles (14,144 sq. km): land, 5,225 sq. miles (13,532 sq. km); inland water and tideways, 249 sq. miles (628 sq. km).

The population of Northern Ireland at the 2001 census was 1,685,267 (males, 821,449; females, 863,818).

In 2001 the number of persons in the various religious denominations (expressed as percentages of the total population) were: Catholic, 40.26; Presbyterian, 20.69; Church of Ireland, 15.30; Methodist Church in Ireland, 3.51; other Christian (including Christian related) 6.07; other religions and philosophies, 0.3; no religion or religion not stated, 13.88.

FLAG

The official national flag of Northern Ireland is now the Union Flag. The flag formerly in use (a white, six-pointed star in the centre of a red cross on a white field, enclosing a red hand and surmounted by a crown) has not been used since the imposition of direct rule.

PRINCIPAL CITIES

BELFAST

Belfast, the administrative centre of Northern Ireland, is situated at the mouth of the River Lagan at its entrance to Belfast Lough. The city grew, owing to its easy access by sea to Scottish coal and iron, to be a great industrial centre.

The principal buildings are of a relatively recent date and include the Parliament Buildings at Stormont, the City Hall, Waterfront Hall, the Law Courts, the Public Library and the Museum and Art Gallery.

Belfast received its first charter of incorporation in 1613 and was created a city in 1888; the title of Lord Mayor was conferred in 1892.

LONDONDERRY

Londonderry (originally Derry) is situated on the River Foyle, and has important associations with the City of London. The Irish Society was created by the City of London in 1610, and under its royal charter of 1613 it fortified the city and was for a long time closely associated with its administration. Because of this connection the city was incorporated in 1613 under the new name of Londonderry.

The city is famous for the great siege of 1688–9, when for 105 days the town held out against the forces of James II. The city walls are still intact and form a circuit of almost a mile around the old city.

Interesting buildings are the Protestant Cathedral of St Columb's (1633) and the Guildhall, reconstructed in 1912 and containing a number of beautiful stained glass windows, many of which were presented by the livery companies of London.

Three other places in Northern Ireland have been granted city status: Armagh (1994), Newry (2002) and Lisburn (2002).

CONSTITUTIONAL DEVELOPMENTS

Northern Ireland is subject to the same fundamental constitutional provisions which apply to the rest of the United Kingdom. It had its own parliament and government from 1921 to 1972, but after increasing civil unrest the Northern Ireland (Temporary Provisions) Act 1972 transferred the legislative and executive powers of the Northern Ireland parliament and government to the UK Parliament and a Secretary of State. The Northern Ireland Constitution Act 1973 provided for devolution in Northern Ireland through an assembly and executive, but a power-sharing executive formed by the Northern Ireland political parties in January 1974 collapsed in May 1974. Since then Northern Ireland has been governed by direct rule under the provisions of the Northern Ireland Act 1974. This allows Parliament to approve all laws for Northern Ireland and places the Northern Ireland department under the direction and control of the Secretary of State for Northern Ireland.

Attempts were made by successive governments to find a means of restoring a widely acceptable form of devolved government to Northern Ireland. In 1985 the governments of the United Kingdom and the Republic of Ireland signed the Anglo-Irish Agreement, establishing an intergovernmental conference in which the Irish government may put forward views and proposals on certain aspects of Northern Ireland affairs.

Discussions between the British and Irish governments and the main Northern Ireland parties began in 1991. It was agreed that any political settlement would need to address relationships within Northern Ireland, within the island of Ireland (north/south) and between the British and Irish governments (east/west). Although round table talks ended in 1992 the process continued from September 1993 as separate bilateral discussions with three of the Northern Ireland parties (the DUP declined to participate).

In December 1993 the British and Irish governments published the Joint Declaration complementing the political talks, and making clear that any settlement would need to be founded on principles of democracy and consent. The declaration also stated that all democratically mandated parties could be involved in political talks as long as they permanently renounced paramilitary violence.

The provisional IRA and loyalist paramilitary groups announced cease-fires on 31 August and 13 October 1994 respectively. The Government initiated exploratory meetings with Sinn Fein and loyalist representatives in December 1994.

In February 1995 the then Prime Minister (John Major) launched *A Framework for Accountable Government in Northern Ireland* and, with the Irish Prime Minister, *A New Framework for Agreement.* These outlined what a comprehensive political settlement might look like. The ideas were intended to facilitate multilateral dialogue involving the Northern Ireland parties and the British government.

In autumn 1995 the Prime Minister said that Sinn Fein would not be invited to all-party talks until the IRA had decommissioned its arms; the IRA ruled out any decommissioning of weapons in advance of a political settlement. An international body chaired by a former US senator, George Mitchell, reported in January 1996 that no weapons would be decommissioned before the start of all-party talks and that a compromise agreement was necessary under which weapons would be decommissioned during negotiations. The Prime Minister accepted the report and proposed the election of representatives to conduct all-party talks. On 9 February 1996 the IRA called off its cease-fire.

PEACE TALKS

Following elections on 30 May 1996, all-party talks opened at Stormont Castle on 10 June 1996 which included nine of the ten parties returned at the election; Sinn Fein representatives were turned away because the IRA had failed to reinstate its cease-fire. On 29 July 1996 the all-party talks were suspended after disagreements over the issue of decommissioning arms. An opening agenda for the talks was agreed in October 1996.

On 25 June 1997 the newly-elected Labour Government said that substantive negotiations should begin in September 1997 with a view to reaching conclusions by May 1998. The British and Irish governments issued a joint paper outlining their proposals for resolving the decommissioning issue. The Government also indicated that if the IRA were to call a cease-fire, it would assess whether it was genuine over a period of six weeks, and if satisfied that it was so, would then invite Sinn Fein to the talks. An IRA cease-fire was declared on 20 July 1997.

When the UK Government announced in August 1997 that Sinn Fein would be present when the substantive talks opened on 15 September, the unionist and loyalist parties, unhappy at the terms on which Sinn Fein had been admitted, boycotted the opening session. The Ulster Unionist Party, the Progressive Unionist Party and the Ulster Democratic Party re-entered the negotiations on 17 September. Full-scale peace talks began on 7 October. The parties had agreed to concentrate on constitutional issues, with the issue of decommissioning terrorist weapons to be handled by a new independent commission.

On 12 January 1998 the British and Irish governments issued a joint document, *Propositions on Heads of Agreement*, proposing the establishment of various new cross-border bodies; further proposals were presented on 27 January. A draft peace settlement was issued by the talks' chairman, Sen. George Mitchell, on 6 April 1998 but was rejected by the Unionists the following day. On 10 April agreement was reached between the British and Irish governments and the eight Northern Ireland political parties still involved in the talks (the Good Friday Agreement). The agreement provided for an elected New Northern Ireland Assembly; a North/South Ministerial Council, and a British-Irish Council comprising representatives of the British, Irish, Channel Islands and Isle of Man governments and members of the new assemblies for Scotland, Wales and Northern Ireland. Further points included the abandonment of the Republic of Ireland's constitutional claim to Northern Ireland; the decommissioning of weapons; the release of paramilitary prisoners; and changes in policing.

Referendums on the agreement were held in Northern Ireland and the Republic of Ireland on 22 May 1998. In Northern Ireland the turnout was 81 per cent, of which 71.12 per cent voted in favour of the agreement. In the Republic of Ireland, the turnout was about 55 per cent, of which 94.4 per cent voted in favour of both the agreement and the necessary constitutional change. In the UK, the Northern Ireland Act 1998, enshrining the provisions of the Agreement, received Royal Assent in November 1998.

For details of the Northern Ireland Assembly and further political developments in Northern Ireland, *see* the Regional Government section.

OTHER BODIES

Consultations between the First Minister and Deputy First Minister, the British and Irish Governments and the political parties concluded in early 1999 with an agreement to establish six areas for cross-border bodies and a further six areas for co-operation. Treaties between the British and Irish governments establishing the bodies and parallel domestic legislation to underpin them are now in place.

The Good Friday Agreement also provided for a British-Irish Intergovernmental Conference to promote bilateral co-operation at all levels on matters of mutual interest, with a particular focus on non-devolved Northern Ireland matters, and supported by a joint standing Secretariat.

The British-Irish Council operates on the basis of consensus and may reach agreements on common policies in areas of mutual interest. Since its formation in 1999, the Council has met five times at summit level. The last meeting was in Wales in November 2003.

FINANCE

Northern Ireland's expenditure is funded by the Northern Ireland Consolidated Fund (NICF). Up until devolution on 2 December 1999, the NICF was largely financed by Northern Ireland's attributed share of UK taxation and supplemented by a grant-in-aid. From devolution, these separate elements have been subsumed into a single Block Grant. The Northern Ireland Departmental Expenditure Limit for 2004–5 is £7,135.7 million.

LORDS-LIEUTENANT

County	*Area (sq. miles)*	*Lord-Lieutenant*
Antrim	1,093	The Lord O'Neill, TD
Armagh	484	The Earl of Caledon
Belfast City	25	Lady Carswell, OBE
Down	945	Maj. William Hall
Fermanagh	647	The Earl of Erne
Londonderry	798	Denis Desmond, CBE
Londonderry City	3.4	Dr Donal Keegan, OBE
Tyrone	1,211	The Duke of Abercorn

DISTRICT COUNCILS

Council	*Telephone*	*Population*	*Chief Executive*
Antrim, Co. Down	028-9446 3113	48,366	David McCammick
Ards, Co. Down	028-9182 4000	73,244	Ashley Boreland
ARMAGH CITY, Co. Armagh	028-3752 9600	54,263	Victor Brownlees
Ballymena, Co. Antrim	028-2566 0300	58,610	Mervyn Rankin
Ballymoney, Co. Antrim	028-2766 0200	26,894	John Dempsey
Banbridge, Co. Down	028-4066 0600	41,392	Robert Gilmore
BELFAST CITY, Co. Antrim and Co. Down	028-9032 0202	277,391	Peter McNaney
Carrickfergus, Co. Antrim	028-9335 1604	37,659	Alan Cardwell
Castlereagh, Co. Down	028-9049 4500	66,488	Adrian Donaldson
Coleraine, Co. Londonderry	028-7034 7034	56,315	Wavell Moore
Cookstown, Co. Tyrone	028-8676 2205	32,581	Michael McGuckin
Craigavon, Co. Armagh	028-3831 2400	80,671	Francis Rock
DERRY CITY, Co. Londonderry	028-7136 5151	105,066	Anthony McGurk
Down, Co. Down	028-4461 0800	63,828	John McGrillen
Dungannon, Co. Tyrone	028-8772 0300	47,735	William Beattie
Fermanagh, Co. Fermanagh	028-6632 5050	57,527	Rodney Connor
Larne, Co. Antrim	028-2827 2313	30,832	Colm McGarry
Limavady, Co. Londonderry	028-7772 2226	32,422	John Stevenson
LISBURN CITY, Co. Antrim	028-9250 9250	108,694	Norman Davidson
Magherafelt, Co. Londonderry	028-7939 7979	39,780	John McLaughlin
Moyle, Co. Antrim	028-2076 2225	15,933	Richard Lewis
NEWRY and Mourne, Co. Down and Co. Armagh	028-3031 3031	87,058	Thomas McCall
Newtownabbey, Co. Antrim	028-9034 0000	79,995	Norman Dunn
North Down, Co. Down	028-9127 0371	76,323	Trevor Polley
Omagh, Co. Tyrone	028-8224 5321	47,952	Daniel McSorley
Strabane, Co. Tyrone	028-7138 2204	38,248	Philip Faithfull

Councils in CAPITAL LETTERS have City Status

THE ISLE OF MAN

Ellan Vannin

The Isle of Man is an island situated in the Irish Sea, in latitude 54° 3'–54° 25' N. and longitude 4° 18'–4° 47' W., nearly equidistant from England, Scotland and Ireland. Although the early inhabitants were of Celtic origin, the Isle of Man was part of the Norwegian Kingdom of the Hebrides until 1266, when this was ceded to Scotland. Subsequently granted to the Stanleys (Earls of Derby) in the 15th century and later to the Dukes of Atholl, it was brought under the administration of the Crown in 1765. The island forms the bishopric of Sodor and Man.

The total land area is 221 sq. miles (572 sq. km). The report on the 2001 census showed a resident population of 76,315. The main language in use is English. There are no remaining native speakers of Manx Gaelic but 1,527 people are able to speak the language.

CAPITAL ΨDouglas; population (2001), 25,347. ΨCastletown (3,100) is the ancient capital; the other towns are ΨPeel (3,785) and ΨRamsey (7,322)

FLAG – A red flag charged with three conjoined armoured legs in white and gold

TYNWALD DAY – 5 July

GOVERNMENT

The Isle of Man is a self-governing Crown dependency, having its own parliamentary, legal and administrative system. The British Government is responsible for international relations and defence. Under the UK Act of Accession, Protocol 3, the island's relationship with the European Union is limited to trade alone and does not extend to financial aid. The Lieutenant-Governor is The Queen's personal representative on the island.

The legislature, Tynwald, is the oldest parliament in the world in continuous existence. It has two branches: the Legislative Council and the House of Keys. The Council consists of the President of Tynwald, the Bishop of Sodor and Man, the Attorney-General (who does not have a vote) and eight members elected by the House of Keys. The House of Keys has 24 members, elected by universal adult suffrage. The branches sit separately to consider legislation and sit together, as Tynwald Court, for most other parliamentary purposes.

The presiding officer of Tynwald Court is the President of Tynwald, elected by the members, who also presides over sittings of the Legislative Council. The presiding officer of the House of Keys is Mr Speaker, who is elected by members of the House.

The principal members of the Manx Government are the Chief Minister and nine departmental ministers, who comprise the Council of Ministers.

Lieutenant-Governor, HE Air-Marshal I. MacFadyen, CB, OBE
ADC to the Lieutenant-Governor, C. J. Tummon
President of Tynwald, The Hon. Noel Cringle
Speaker, House of Keys, The Hon. James Brown, SHK
The First Deemster and Clerk of the Rolls, John Michael Kerruish
Clerk of Tynwald, Secretary to the House of Keys and Counsel to the Speaker, Mr Malachy Cornwell-Kelly
Clerk of the Legislative Council and Deputy Clerk of Tynwald, Mrs M. Cullen
Attorney-General, W. J. H. Corlett, QC
Chief Minister, The Hon. Richard Corkill, MHK
Chief Secretary, Mrs M. Williams

ECONOMY

Most of the income generated in the island is earned in the services sector with financial and professional services accounting for just over half of the national income. Tourism and manufacturing are also major generators of income whilst the island's other traditional industries of agriculture and fishing now play a smaller role in the economy. Under the terms of Protocol 3, the island has tariff-free access to EU markets for its goods.

The island's unemployment rate is approximately 0.6 per cent and price inflation is around 3.6 per cent per annum.

FINANCE

The budget for 2004–5 provides for net revenue expenditure of £448 million. The principal sources of government revenue are taxes on income and expenditure. Income tax is payable at a rate of 10 per cent on the first £10,000 of taxable income for single resident individuals and 18 per cent on the balance, after personal allowances of £8,225. These bands are doubled for married couples. The rate of income tax is 10 per cent on the first £100 million of taxable income of trading companies, rising to 15 per cent on the balance. By agreement with the British Government, the island keeps most of its rates of indirect taxation (VAT and duties) the same as those in the United Kingdom. However, VAT on tourist accommodation, property, repairs and renovations is charged at 5 per cent. A reciprocal agreement on national insurance benefits and pensions exists between the governments of the Isle of Man and the United Kingdom. Taxes are also charged on property (rates), but these are comparatively low.

The major government expenditure items are health, social security and education, which account for 58 per cent of the government budget. The island makes an annual contribution to the United Kingdom for defence and other external services.

The island has a special relationship with the European Union and neither contributes money to nor receives funds from the EU budget.

THE ISLES OF SCILLY

The Isles of Scilly are a cluster of small islands, set 28 miles of the coast of Cornwall in the Atlantic Ocean. There are five inhabited islands; St Mary's, Tresco, St Martin's. Bryher and St. Agnes. The islands are administered by the Council of the Isles of Scilly; a 21-member body, of which 13 are elected by St Mary's residents and 2 by each of the remaining islands.

Administrative Headquarters, Town Hall, St Mary's, Isles of Scilly, TR21 0LW T 01720-422537
Chief Executive, Philip Hygate

THE CHANNEL ISLANDS

The Channel Islands, situated off the north-west coast of France (at distances from ten to 30 miles), are the only portions of the Dukedom of Normandy still belonging to the Crown, to which they have been attached since the Norman Conquest of 1066. They were the only British territory to come under German occupation during the Second World War, following invasion on 30 June to 1 July 1940. The islands were relieved by British forces on 9 May 1945, and 9 May (Liberation Day) is now observed as a bank and public holiday.

The islands consist of Jersey (28,717 acres/11,630 ha), Guernsey (15,654 acres/6,340 ha), and the dependencies of Guernsey: Alderney (1,962 acres/795 ha), Brecqhou (74/30), Great Sark (1,035/419), Little Sark (239/97), Herm (320/130), Jethou (44/18) and Lihou (38/15) – a total of 48,083 acres/19,474 ha, or 75 sq. miles/194 sq. km. The 2001 census showed the population of Jersey as 87,186; Guernsey, 59,807 and Alderney, 2,294. Sark did not complete the same census but a recent informal census gave its population figure as 591. The official languages are English and French.

GOVERNMENT

The islands are Crown dependencies with their own legislative assemblies (the States in Jersey, Guernsey and Alderney, and the Court of Chief Pleas in Sark), and systems of local administration and of law, and their own courts. Acts passed by the States require the sanction of The Queen-in-Council. The British Government is responsible for defence and international relations. The Channel Islands have trading rights alone within the European Union; these rights do not include financial aid.

In both Bailiwicks the Lieutenant-Governor and Commander-in-Chief, who is appointed by the Crown, is the personal representative of The Queen and the channel of communication between the Crown (via the Privy Council) and the island's government.

In 2001 the States of Jersey moved to a ministerial system of government combined with a system of scrutiny. This system is expected to be fully implemented by the end of December 2005. On 1 May 2004 Guernsey also introduced a ministerial governance system consisting of a Policy Council comprising a chief minister and ten departmental ministers. There are also five specialist committees. Justice is administered by the Royal Courts of Jersey and Guernsey, each consisting of the Bailiff and 12 elected Jurats. The Bailiffs of Jersey and Guernsey, appointed by the Crown, are President of the States and of the Royal Courts of their respective islands.

Each Bailiwick constitutes a deanery under the jurisdiction of the Bishop of Winchester.

ECONOMY

A mild climate and good soil have led to the development of intensive systems of agriculture and horticulture, which form a significant part of the economy. Equally important are invisible earnings, principally from tourism and banking and finance, the low rate of income tax (20p in the £ in Jersey and Guernsey; no tax of any kind in Sark) and the absence of super-tax and death duties, making the islands an important offshore financial centre.

Principal exports are agricultural produce and flowers; imports are chiefly machinery, manufactured goods, food, fuel and chemicals. Trade with the UK is regarded as internal.

JERSEY

Lieutenant-Governor and Commander-in-Chief of Jersey, Air Chief Marshal Sir John Cheshire, KBE, CB, *apptd* 2001
Secretary and ADC, Lt.-Col. A. J. C. Woodrow, OBE, MC
Bailiff of Jersey, Sir Philip Bailhache, Kt.
Deputy Bailiff, M. C. St J. Birt
Attorney-General, W. J. Bailhache, QC
Receiver-General, P. Lewin
Solicitor-General, Miss S. C. Nicolle, QC
Greffier of the States, M. N. de la Haye
States Treasurer, Mr I. Black

FINANCE

Year to 31 December	*2002*	*2003*
Revenue income	£572,179,000	£568,005,000
Revenue expenditure	£500,654,000	£526,837,000
Capital expenditure	£89,303,000	£62,730,000
Public debt	0	0

CHIEF TOWN – ΨSt Helier, on the south coast of Jersey
FLAG – A white field charged with a red saltire cross, and the arms of Jersey in the upper centre

GUERNSEY AND DEPENDENCIES

Lieutenant-Governor and Commander-in-Chief of the Bailiwick of Guernsey and its Dependencies, HE Lieutenant-General Sir John Foley, KCB, OBE, MC, *apptd 2000*
Secretary and ADC, Colonel R. H. Graham, MBE
Bailiff of Guernsey, Sir de Vic Graham Carey
Deputy Bailiff, G. R. Rowland, QC
HM Procureur and Receiver-General, J. N. van Leuven, QC
HM Comptroller, H. E. Roberts, QC
Chief Executive, States of Guernsey, M. J. Brown
Chief Minister, Deputy Laurie Morgan

FINANCE

Year to 31 Dec.	*2002*	*2003*
Revenue	£288,320,000	£287,969,000
Expenditure	£239,727,000	£254,390,000

CHIEF TOWNS – ΨSt Peter Port, on the east coast of Guernsey; St Anne on Alderney
FLAG – White, bearing a red cross of St George, with a gold cross overall in the centre

ALDERNEY

President of the States, Sir Norman Browse

SARK

Seigneur of Sark, J. M. Beaumont, OBE

OTHER DEPENDENCIES

Herm and Lihou are owned by the States of Guernsey; Herm is leased. Jethou is leased by the Crown to the States of Guernsey and is sub-let by the States. Brecqhou is within the legislative and judicial territory of Sark.

EUROPEAN PARLIAMENT

European Parliament elections take place at five-yearly intervals; the first direct elections to the Parliament were held in 1979. In mainland Britain MEPs were elected in all constituencies on a first-past-the-post basis until the elections of June 1999 when a regional system of proportional representation was introduced (*see* below); in Northern Ireland three MEPs have been elected by the single transferable vote system of proportional representation since 1979. From 1979 to 1994 the number of seats held by the UK in the European Parliament was 81. At the June 1994 election the number of seats increased to 87. Following EU enlargement in May 2004, the number of seats at the June 2004 election decreased to 78 (England 64, Wales 4, Scotland 7, Northern Ireland 3).

At the European Parliament elections held on 10 June 2004, all British MEPs were elected under a 'closed-list' regional system of proportional representation, with England being divided into nine regions and Scotland and Wales each constituting a region. Parties submitted a list of candidates for each region in their own order of preference. Voters voted for a party or an independent candidate, and the first seat in each region was allocated to the party or candidate with the highest number of votes. The rest of the seats in each region were then allocated broadly in proportion to each party's share of the vote. Each region returned the following number of members: East Midlands, 6; Eastern, 7; London, 9; North East, 3; North West, 9; South East, 10; South West, 7; West Midlands, 7; Yorkshire and the Humber, 6; Wales, 4; Scotland, 7.

If a vacancy occurs due to the resignation or death of an MEP, the vacancy is filled by the next available person on that party's list. If an independent MEP resigns or dies, a by-election is held. Where an MEP leaves the party on whose list he/she was elected, there is no requirement to resign and he/she can remain in office until the next election.

British subjects and nationals of member states of the European Union are eligible for election to the European Parliament provided they are 21 or over and not subject to disqualification. Since 1994, eligible citizens have had the right to vote in elections to the European Parliament in the UK as long as they are entered on the electoral register.

MEPs currently receive a salary from the parliaments or governments of their respective member states, set at the level of the national parliamentary salary and subject to national taxation. British MEPs receive a salary of £57,485. MPs who are also MEPs do not receive both salaries in full. Instead they receive the full MPs' salary plus a 'duality rate' equal to one third of the MEPs' salary. Thus their total salary is £76,646 (comprising £57,485 plus £19,161).

A proposal that all MEPs should be paid the same rate of salary out of the EU budget, and be subject to the EU tax rate, is under negotiation between the European Parliament and the Council of Ministers but has yet to be agreed.

The next elections to the European Parliament will take place in June 2009.

UK MEMBERS *as at 10 June 2004*

*Denotes membership of the last European Parliament

Allister, James (*b.* 1953), *DUP, Northern Ireland*
Ashworth, Richard (*b.* 1947), *C., South East*
***Atkins**, Rt. Hon. Sir Robert (*b.* 1946), *C., North West*
***Attwooll**, Ms Elspeth M. A. (*b.* 1943), *LD, Scotland*
Batten, Gerard (*b.* 1972), *UKIP, London*
***Beazley**, Christopher J. P. (*b.* 1952), *C., Eastern*
Bloom, Godfrey (*b.* 1949), *UKIP, Yorkshire and the Humber*
***Booth**, Graham (*b.* 1940), *UKIP, South West*
***Bowis**, John C., OBE (*b.* 1945), *C., London*
***Bradbourn**, Philip, OBE (*b.* 1951), *C., West Midlands*
***Bushill-Matthews**, Philip (*b.* 1943), *C., West Midlands*
***Callanan**, Martin (*b.* 1961), *C., North East*
***Cashman**, Michael (*b.* 1950), *Lab., West Midlands*
***Chichester**, Giles B. (*b.* 1946), *C., South West*
Clark, Derek (*b.* 1933), *UKIP, East Midlands*
***Corbett**, Richard (*b.* 1955), *Lab., Yorkshire and the Humber*
***Davies**, Christopher G. (*b.* 1954), *LD, North West*
de Brun, Bairbre Ms (*b.* 1954), *SF, Northern Ireland*
***Deva**, Niranjan J. A. (Nirj), FRSA (*b.* 1948), *C., South East*
***Dover**, Densmore (*b.* 1938), *C., North West*
***Duff**, Andrew N. (*b.* 1950), *LD, Eastern*
***Elles**, James E. M. (*b.* 1949), *C., South East*
***Evans**, Ms Jillian R. (*b.* 1959), *PC, Wales*
***Evans**, Jonathan P., FRSA (*b.* 1950), *C., Wales*
***Evans**, Robert J. E. (*b.* 1956), *Lab., London*
***Farage**, Nigel P. (*b.* 1964), *UKIP, South East*
***Ford**, Glyn J. (*b.* 1950), *Lab., South West*
***Gill**, Ms Neena (*b.* 1956), *Lab., West Midlands*
Hall, Fiona (*b.* 1955), *LD, North East*
***Hannan**, Daniel J. (*b.* 1971), *C., South East*
***Harbour**, Malcolm (*b.* 1947), *C., West Midlands*
***Heaton-Harris**, Christopher (*b.* 1967), *C., East Midlands*
***Helmer**, Roger (*b.* 1944), *C., East Midlands*
***Honeyball**, Mary Mrs (*b.* 1952), *Lab., London*
***Howitt**, Richard (*b.* 1961), *Lab., Eastern*
***Hudghton**, Ian (*b.* 1951), *SNP, Scotland*
***Hughes**, Stephen (*b.* 1952), *Lab., North East*
***Huhne**, Christopher M. P., OBE (*b.* 1954), *LD, South East*
***Jackson**, Mrs Caroline F., DPHIL (*b.* 1946), *C., South West*
Karim, Sajjad (*b.* 1970), *LD, North West*
Kilroy-Silk, Robert (*b.* 1942), *UKIP, East Midlands*
***Kinnock**, Mrs Glenys (*b.* 1944), *Lab., Wales*
***Kirkhope**, Timothy J. R. (*b.* 1945), *C., Yorkshire and the Humber*
Knapman, Roger (*b.* 1944), *UKIP, South West*
***Lambert**, Ms Jean D. (*b.* 1950), *Green, London*
***Lucas**, Dr Caroline (*b.* 1960), *Green, South East*
***Ludford**, Sarah Ms (*b.* 1951), *LD, London*
***Lynne**, Elizabeth Ms (*b.* 1948), *LD, West Midlands*
***McAvan**, Linda Ms (*b.* 1962), *Lab., Yorkshire and the Humber*
***McCarthy**, Arlene Ms (*b.* 1960), *Lab., North West*
***McMillan-Scott**, Edward H. C. (*b.* 1949), *C., Yorkshire and the Humber*
***Martin**, David W. (*b.* 1954), *Lab., Scotland*
***Moraes**, Claude (*b.* 1965), *Lab., London*
***Morgan**, Eluned Ms (*b.* 1967), *Lab., Wales*

Mote, Ashley (*b.* 1936), *UKIP, South East*
Nattrass, Mike (*b.* 1945), *UKIP, West Midlands*
***Newton Dunn**, William F. (Bill) (*b.* 1941), *LD, East Midlands*
***Nicholson**, Emma Ms (*b.* 1941), *LD, South East*
***Nicholson**, James (*b.* 1945), *UUP, Northern Ireland*
***Parish**, Neil (*b.* 1956), *C., South West*
***Purvis**, John R., CBE (*b.* 1938), *C., Scotland*
***Skinner**, Peter W. (*b.* 1959), *Lab., South East*
Smith, Alyn (*b.* 1973), *SNP, Scotland*
***Stevenson**, Struan (*b.* 1948), *C., Scotland*
***Stihler**, Catherine D. (*b.* 1973), *Lab., Scotland*
***Sturdy**, Robert W. (*b.* 1944), *C., Eastern*
***Sumberg**, David (*b.* 1941), *C., North West*
***Tannock**, Dr Charles (*b.* 1957), *C., London*
***Titford**, Jeffrey (*b.* 1933), *UKIP, Eastern*
***Titley**, Gary (*b.* 1950), *Lab., North West,*
***van Orden**, Geoffrey (*b.* 1945), *C., Eastern*
***Villiers**, Theresa Ms (*b.* 1968), *C., London*
***Wallis**, Diana Ms (*b.* 1954), *LD, Yorkshire and the Humber*
***Watson**, Graham R. (*b.* 1956), *LD, South West*
***Whitehead**, Phillip (*b.* 1937), *Lab., East Midlands*
Whittaker, John (*b.* 1945), *UKIP, North West*
Wise, Tom (*b.* 1948), *UKIP, Eastern*
***Wynn**, Terence (Terry) (*b.* 1946), *Lab., North West*

UK REGIONS *as at 10 June 2004*

Abbreviations

AGS	Alliance for Green Socialism
Common	The Common Good
ED	English Democrats
EFP	English Freedom Party
FW	Forward Wales
OCV	Operation Christian Vote
Peace	Peace Party
PPBG	People's Party for Better Government
Respect	Respect – Unity Coalition
SEA	Socialist Environmental Alliance
Senior	Senior Citizens
Soc. All.	Socialist Alliance
SSP	Scottish Socialist Party
SWW	Scottish Wind Watch

For other abbreviations, *see* UK General Election Results

EASTERN

(Bedfordshire, Cambridgeshire, Essex, Hertfordshire, Luton, Norfolk, Peterborough, Southend-on-Sea, Suffolk, Thurrock)

E. 4,137,210	*T.* 36.63%
C.	465,526 (30.8%)
UKIP	296,160 (19.6%)
Lab.	244,929 (16.2%)
LD	211,378 (14.0%)
Ind.	93,028 (6.2%)
Green	84,068 (5.6%)
BNP	65,557 (4.3%)
ED	26,807 (1.8%)
Respect	13,094 (0.9%)
Ind.	5,137 (0.3%)
ProLife	3,730 (0.3%)
C. majority	169,366

(June 1999, C. maj. 174,959)

MEMBERS ELECTED
*G. van Orden, *C.*
*J. Titford, *UKIP*
*R. Howitt, *Lab.*
*R. Sturdy, *C.*
A. Duff, *LD*
*C. Beazley, *C.*
T. Wise, *UKIP*

EAST MIDLANDS

(Derby, Derbyshire, Leicester, Leicestershire, Northamptonshire, Nottingham, Nottinghamshire, Rutland)

E. 3,220,019	*T.* 44.59%
C.	371,362 (26.4%)
UKIP	366,498 (26.1%)
Lab.	294,918 (21.0%)
LD	181,964 (12.9%)
BNP	91,860 (6.5%)
Green	76,633 (5.5%)
Respect	20,009 (1.4%)
Ind.	2,615 (0.2%)
Ind.	847 (0.1%)
C. majority	4,864

(June 1999, C. maj. 78,906)

MEMBERS ELECTED
*R. Helmer, *C.*
R. Kilroy-Silk, *UKIP*
*P. Whitehead, *Lab.*
*C. Heaton-Harris, *C.*
D. Clark, *UKIP*
*W. Newton Dunn, *LD*

LONDON

E. 5,054,957	*T.* 37.65%
C.	504,941 (26.53%)
Lab.	466,584 (24.51%)
LD	288,790 (15.17%)
UKIP	232,633 (12.22%)
Green	158,986 (8.35%)
Respect	91,175 (4.79%)
BNP	76,152 (4.00%)
CPA	45,038 (2.37%)
ED	15,945 (0.84%)
PPBG	5,205 (0.27%)
C. majority	38,357

(June 1994, Lab. maj. 26,477)

MEMBERS ELECTED
*Miss T. Villiers, *C.*
*C. Moraes, *Lab.*
*Ms S. Ludford, *LD*
*J. Bowis, *C.*
Ms M. Honeyball, *Lab.*
G. Batten, *UKIP*
*C. Tannock, *C.*
*Ms J. Lambert, *Green*
*R. Evans, *Lab.*

NORTH EAST

(Co. Durham, Darlington, Hartlepool, Middlesbrough, Northumberland, Redcar and Cleveland, Stockton-on-Tees, Tyne and Wear)

E. 1,905,132	*T.* 41.51%
Lab.	266,057 (34.1%)
C.	144,969 (18.6%)
LD	138,791 (17.8%)
UKIP	94,887 (12.2%)
BNP	50,249 (6.4%)
Ind.	39,658 (5.1%)
Green	37,247 (4.8%)
Respect	8,633 (1.1%)
Lab. majority	121,088

(June 1999, Lab. maj. 57,000)

MEMBERS ELECTED
*S. Hughes, *Lab.*
*M. Callanan, *C.*
Ms F. Hall, *LD*

NORTHERN IRELAND

(Northern Ireland forms a three-member seat with a single transferable vote system)

E. 1,191,307	*T.* 46.53%
First Count	
Jim Allister, *DUP*	175,761 (31.9%)
Bairbre de Brun, *SF*	144,541 (26.3%)
Jim Nicholson, *UUP*	91,164 (16.6%)
Martin Morgan, *SDLP*	87,559 (15.9%)
John Gilliland, *Ind.*	36,270 (6.6%)
Eamonn McCann, *SEA*	9,172 (1.6%)
Lindsay Whitcroft, *Green*	4,810 (0.9%)

MEMBERS ELECTED
J. Allister, *DUP*
B. de Brun, *SF*
*J. Nicholson, *UUP*

NORTH WEST

(Blackburn-with-Darwen, Blackpool, Cheshire, Cumbria, Greater Manchester, Halton, Lancashire, Merseyside, Warrington)

E. 5,151,488	*T.* 41.46%
Lab.	576,388 (27.3%)
C.	509,446 (24.1%)
LD	335,063 (15.8%)
UKIP	257,158 (12.2%)
BNP	134,958 (6.4%)
Green	117,393 (5.6%)
Lib.	96,325 (4.6%)
ED	34,110 (1.6%)
Respect	24,636 (1.2%)
Country	11,283 (0.5%)
ProLife	10,084 (0.5%)
Ind.	8,318 (0.4%)
Lab. majority	66,942

(June 1999, C. maj. 9,516)

MEMBERS ELECTED
*G. Titley, *Lab.*
*D. Dover, *C.*
*C. Davies, *LD*
*Ms A. McCarthy, *Lab.*
J. Whittaker, *UKIP*
*D. Sumberg, *C.*
*T. Wynn, *Lab.*
*Sir Robert Atkins, *C.*
S. Karim, *LD*

SCOTLAND

E. 3,807,521	*T.* 30.91%
Lab.	310,865 (26.40%)
SNP	231,505 (19.67%)
C.	209,028 (17.80%)
LD	154,178 (13.10%)
Green	79,695 (6.77%)
UKIP	78,828 (6.70%)
SSP	61,356 (5.20%)
OCV	21,056 (1.79%)
BNP	19,427 (1.65%)
SWW	7,255 (0.62%)
Ind.	3,624 (0.31%)
Lab. majority	79,360

(June 1999, Lab. maj. 14,962)

MEMBERS ELECTED
*D. Martin, *Lab.*
*I. Hudghton, *SNP*
*S. Stevenson, *C.*
*Ms C. Stihler, *Lab.*
*Ms E. Attwooll, *LD*
A. Smith, *SNP*
*J. Purvis, *C.*

SOUTH EAST

(Bracknell Forest, Brighton and Hove, Buckinghamshire, East Sussex, Hampshire, Isle of Wight, Kent, Medway, Milton Keynes, Oxfordshire, Portsmouth, Reading, Slough, Southampton, Surrey, West Berkshire, West Sussex, Windsor and Maidenhead, Wokingham)

E. 6,048,349	*T.* 36.78%
C.	776,370 (35.2%)
UKIP	431,111 (19.5%)
LD	338,342 (15.3%)
Lab.	301,398 (13.7%)
Green	173,351 (7.9%)
BNP	64,877 (2.9%)
Senior	42,681 (1.9%)
ED	29,126 (1.3%)
Respect	13,426 (0.9%)
Peace	12,572 (0.6%)
CPA	11,733 (0.5%)
ProLife	6,579 (0.3%)
Ind.	5,671 (0.3%)
C. majority	345,259

(June 1999, C. maj. 369,785)

MEMBERS ELECTED
*D. Hannan, *C.*
*N. Farage, *UKIP*
*N. Deva, *C.*
*C. Huhne, *LD*
*P. Skinner, *Lab.*
*J. Elles, *C.*
A. Mote, *UKIP*
R. Ashworth, *C.*
*Dr Caroline Lucas, *Green*
Ms E. Nicholson, *LD*

SOUTH WEST

(Bath and North East Somerset, Bournemouth, Bristol, Cornwall, Devon, Dorset, Gloucestershire, North Somerset, South Gloucestershire, Swindon, Torbay, Wiltshire)

E. 3,845,210	*T.* 44.59%
C.	457,371 (31.6%)
UKIP	326,684 (22.6%)
LD	265,619 (18.3%)
Lab.	209,908 (14.5%)
Green	103,821 (7.2%)
BNP	43,653 (3.0%)
Country	30,824 (2.1%)
Respect	10,437 (0.7%)
C. majority	130,687

(June 1999, C. maj. 246,283)

MEMBERS ELECTED
*N. Parish, *C.*
G. Booth, *UKIP*
*G. Watson, *LD*
*Dr Caroline Jackson, *C.*
*G. Ford, *Lab.*
R. Knapman, *UKIP*
*G. Chichester, *C.*

WALES

E. 2,218,649	*T.* 41.9%
Lab.	297,810 (32%)
C.	177,771 (19%)
PC	159,888 (17%)
UKIP	96,677 (10.5%)
LD	96,116 (10%)
Green	32,761 (3.6%)
BNP	27,135 (3.0%)
FW	17,280 (1.9%)
Ch. D	6,821 (0.7%)
Respect	5,427 (0.6%)
Lab. majority	120,039

(June 1999, Lab. maj. 14,455)

MEMBERS ELECTED
*Ms G. Kinnock, *Lab.*
*J. Evans, *C.*
*Ms J. Evans, *PC*
*Ms E. Morgan, *Lab.*

WEST MIDLANDS

(Herefordshire, Shropshire, Staffordshire, Stoke-on-Trent, Telford and Wrekin, Warwickshire, West Midlands Metropolitan area, Worcestershire)

E. 3,957,848	*T.* 36.63%
C.	392,937 (27.3%)
Lab.	336,613 (23.4%)
UKIP	251,366 (17.5%)
LD	197,479 (13.7%)
BNP	107,794 (7.5%)
Green	73,991 (5.2%)
Respect	34,704 (2.4%)
Pensioner	33,501 (2.3%)
Common	8,650 (0.6%)
C. majority	56,324

(June 1999, C. Maj. 84,048)

MEMBERS ELECTED
*P. Bushill-Matthews, *C.*
*M. Cashman, *Lab.*
M. Nattrass, *UKIP*
*Ms E. Lynne, *LD*
*P. Bradbourn, *C.*
*Ms N. Gill, *Lab.*
*M. Harbour, *C.*

YORKSHIRE AND THE HUMBER

(East Riding of Yorkshire, Kingston upon Hull, North East Lincolnshire, North Lincolnshire, North Yorkshire, South Yorkshire, West Yorkshire, York)

E. 3,719,717	*T.* 42.93%
Lab.	413,213 (26.3%)
C.	387,369 (24.6%)
LD	244,607 (15.6%)
UKIP	228,666 (14.0%)
BNP	126,538 (8.0%)
Green	90,337 (5.7%)
Respect	29,865 (1.9%)
ED	24,068 (1.5%)
Ind.	14,762 (0.9%)
AGS	13,776 (0.9%)
Lab. majority	25,844

(June 1999, C. maj. 39,629)

MEMBERS ELECTED
*Ms Linda McAvan, *Lab.*
*T. Kirkhope, *C.*
*Ms D. Wallis, *LD*
G. Bloom, *UKIP*
*R. Corbett, *Lab.*
*E. McMillan-Scott, *C.*

For further information about the European Parliament, visit www.europarl.org.uk

The county and unitary authority areas listed after each European parliamentary constituency name are a guide to the areas covered by each constituency.

For detailed information about which areas of the country are covered by a particular region, please contact the Home Office.

LAW COURTS AND OFFICES

THE JUDICIAL COMMITTEE OF THE PRIVY COUNCIL

The Judicial Committee of the Privy Council is the final court of appeal for the United Kingdom overseas territories and Crown dependencies and those independent Commonwealth countries which have retained this avenue of appeal (Antigua and Barbuda, The Bahamas, Barbados, Belize, Brunei, Dominica, Grenada, Jamaica, Kiribati, Mauritius, St Christopher and Nevis, St Lucia, St Vincent and the Grenadines, Trinidad and Tobago, and Tuvalu). The Committee also hears appeals against pastoral schemes under the Pastoral Measure 1983.

Under the devolution legislation enacted in 1998, the Judicial Committee of the Privy Council is the final arbiter in disputes as to the legal competence of things done or proposed by the devolved legislative and Executive authorities in Scotland, Wales and Northern Ireland.

In 2003 the Judicial Committee dealt with a total of 99 appeals and 49 petitions for special leave to appeal.

The members of the Judicial Committee include past and present Lord Chancellors and Lords of Appeal in Ordinary, and other Privy Counsellors who hold or have held high judicial office in the United Kingdom and in certain designated courts of Commonwealth countries from which appeals lie to the Judicial Committee.

JUDICIAL COMMITTEE OF THE PRIVY COUNCIL
Downing Street, London SW1A 2AJ
T 020-7276 0483/5
Registrar of the Privy Council, J. A. C. Watherston
Chief Clerk, Mrs J. Lindsay

THE JUDICATURE OF ENGLAND AND WALES

The legal system of England and Wales is separate from those of Scotland and Northern Ireland and differs from them in law, judicial procedure and court structure, although there is a common distinction between civil law (disputes between individuals) and criminal law (acts harmful to the community).

The supreme judicial authority for England and Wales is the House of Lords, which is the ultimate court of appeal from all courts in Great Britain and Northern Ireland (except criminal courts in Scotland) for all cases except those concerning the interpretation and application of European Community law, including preliminary rulings requested by British courts and tribunals, which are decided by the European Court of Justice (*see* European Union section). Under the Human Rights Act 1998, which came into force on 2 October 2000, the European Convention on Human Rights is incorporated into British law; unresolved cases are still referred to the European Court of Human Rights. As a Court of Appeal the House of Lords consists of the Lord Chancellor and the Lords of Appeal in Ordinary (law lords).

SUPREME COURT OF JUDICATURE

The Supreme Court of Judicature comprises the Court of Appeal, the High Court of Justice and the Crown Court. The High Court of Justice is the superior civil court and is divided into three divisions. The Chancery Division is concerned mainly with equity, bankruptcy and contentious probate business. The Queen's Bench Division deals with commercial and maritime law, serious personal injury and medical negligence cases, cases involving a breach of contract and professional negligence actions. The Family Division deals with matters relating to family law. Sittings are held at the Royal Courts of Justice in London or at 126 District Registries outside the capital. High Court judges sit alone to hear cases at first instance. The Technology and Construction Court, which deals with cases that require expert evidence on technical and other issues concerning mainly the construction industry, is also currently part of the High Court. Appeals from the High Court are heard in the Court of Appeal (Civil Division), presided over by the Master of the Rolls, and may go on to the House of Lords.

In December 1999 the Lord Chancellor began a wide-ranging, independent review of the criminal courts in England and Wales. Lord Justice Auld lead the review into how the criminal courts work at every level. The report *Review of the Criminal Courts of England and Wales* was published in October 2001 and assesses what should be done to modernise and improve the criminal justice system so that its aims can be achieved more effectively.

CRIMINAL CASES

In criminal matters the decision to prosecute in the majority of cases rests with the Crown Prosecution Service, the independent prosecuting body in England and Wales. The Service is headed by the Director of Public Prosecutions, who works under the superintendence of the Attorney-General. Certain categories of offence continue to require the Attorney-General's consent for prosecution.

The Crown Court sits in about 90 centres, divided into six circuits, and is presided over by High Court judges, full-time circuit judges, and part-time recorders, sitting with a jury in all trials which are contested. Since 12 April 2000, the distinction between assistant recorders and recorders has changed. Consequently, there are now only full recorders. The post of assistant recorder remains on the statute book but appointments are no longer made. There were 1,325 full recorders at 1 June 2002. The Crown Court deals with trials of the more serious criminal offences, the sentencing of offenders committed for sentence by magistrates' courts (when magistrates consider their own power of sentence inadequate), and appeals from magistrates' courts. Magistrates usually sit with a circuit judge or recorder to deal with appeals and committals for sentence. Appeals from the Crown Court, either against sentence or conviction, are made to the Court of Appeal (Criminal Division), presided over by the Lord Chief Justice. A further appeal from the Court of Appeal to the House of Lords can be brought if a point of law of general public importance is considered to be involved.

Minor criminal offences (summary offences) are dealt with in magistrates' courts, which usually consist of three unpaid lay magistrates (justices of the peace) sitting without a jury, who are advised on points of law and procedure by a legally-qualified clerk to the justices. There were 24,520 justices of the peace at 1 April 2002. In busier courts a full-time, salaried and legally-qualified stipendiary magistrate presides alone. Cases involving people under 18 are heard in youth courts, specially constituted magistrates' courts. Preliminary proceedings in a serious case to decide whether there is evidence to justify committal for trial in the Crown Court are also dealt with in the magistrates' courts. Appeals from magistrates' courts against sentence or conviction are made to the Crown Court. Appeals upon a point of law are made to the High Court, and may go on to the House of Lords.

CIVIL CASES

Most minor civil cases are dealt with by the county courts, of which there are around 222 (*see* the Court Service website, www.courtservice.gov.uk for further details). Cases are heard by circuit judges, courts or district judges (magistrates' courts). There were 411 district judges and 107 District Judges (magistrates' courts) at 1 September 2003. For cases involving small claims there are special simplified procedures. Where there are financial limits on county court jurisdiction, claims which exceed those limits may be tried in the county courts with the consent of the parties, subject to the Court's agreement, or in certain circumstances on transfer from the High Court. Outside London, bankruptcy proceedings can be heard in designated county courts. Magistrates' courts can deal with certain classes of civil case and committees of magistrates license public houses, clubs and betting shops. For the implementation of the Children Act 1989, a new structure of hearing centres was set up in 1991 for family proceedings cases, involving magistrates' courts (family proceedings courts), divorce county courts, family hearing centres and care centres. Appeals in family matters heard in the family proceedings courts go to the Family Division of the High Court; affiliation appeals and appeals from decisions of the licensing committees of magistrates go to the Crown Court. Appeals from county courts may be heard in the High Court of Appeal (civil division) and may go on to the House of Lords.

CORONERS' COURT

Coroners' courts investigate violent and unnatural deaths or sudden deaths where the cause is unknown. Cases may be brought before a local coroner (a senior lawyer or doctor) by doctors, the police, various public authorities or members of the public. Where a death is sudden and the cause is unknown, the coroner may order a post-mortem examination to determine the cause of death rather than hold an inquest in court.

Judicial appointments are made by The Queen; the most senior appointments are made on the advice of the Prime Minister and other appointments on the advice of the Lord Chancellor.

Under the provisions of the Criminal Appeal Act 1995, a Commission was set up to direct and supervise investigations into possible miscarriages of justice and to refer cases to the courts on the grounds of conviction and sentence; these functions were formerly the responsibility of the Home Secretary.

THE HOUSE OF LORDS

AS FINAL COURT OF APPEAL

The Lord High Chancellor and Secretary of State for Constitutional Affairs (£207,742, this is the statutory entitlement, however, Lord Falconer currently receives only a salary equivalent to that received by other Secretaries of State in the House of Lords), The Rt. Hon. the Lord Falconer of Thoroton, *born* 1951, *apptd* 2003

LORDS OF APPEAL IN ORDINARY *as at 26 August 2004* (each £179,431)

Style, The Rt. Hon. Lord/Lady–

Rt. Hon. Lord Bingham of Cornhill, *born* 1933, *apptd* 2000
Rt. Hon. Lord Nicholls of Birkenhead, *born* 1933, *apptd* 1994
Rt. Hon. Lord Steyn, *born* 1932, *apptd* 1995
Rt. Hon. Lord Hoffmann, *born* 1934, *apptd* 1995
Rt. Hon. Lord Hope of Craighead, *born* 1938, *apptd* 1996
Rt. Hon. Lord Saville of Newdigate, *born* 1936, *apptd* 1997
Rt. Hon. Lord Scott Foscote, *born* 1934, *apptd* 2000
Rt. Hon. Lord Rodger of Earlsferry, *born* 1944, *apptd* 2001
Rt. Hon. Lord Walker of Gestingthorpe, *born* 1938, *apptd* 2002
Lady Hale of Richmond, *born* 1945, *apptd* 2004
Lord Carswell, *born* 1934, *apptd* 2004
Lord Brown of Eaton-under-Heywood, *born* 1937, *apptd* 2004

JUDICIAL OFFICE OF THE HOUSE OF LORDS, House of Lords, London SW1A 0PW T 020-7219 3111

Registrar, The Clerk of the Parliaments

SUPREME COURT OF JUDICATURE

COURT OF APPEAL

The Master of the Rolls (£185,705), The Rt. Hon. Lord Phillips of Worth Matravers, *born* 1938, *apptd* 2000
Secretary, Mrs L. Francis
Clerk, Miss L. Turvey

LORDS JUSTICES OF APPEAL *as at 26 August 2004* (each £170,554)

Style, The Rt. Hon. Lord/Lady Justice [surname]

Rt. Hon. Sir Paul Kennedy, *born* 1935, *apptd* 1992
Rt. Hon. Sir Christopher Rose, *born* 1937, *apptd* 1992
Rt. Hon. Sir Peter Gibson, *born* 1934, *apptd* 1993
Rt. Hon. Sir Robin Auld, *born* 1937, *apptd* 1995
Rt. Hon. Sir Malcolm Pill, *born* 1938, *apptd* 1995
Rt. Hon. Sir Alan Ward, *born* 1938, *apptd* 1995
Rt. Hon. Sir Mathew Thorpe, *born* 1938, *apptd* 1995
Rt. Hon. Sir Mark Potter, *born* 1937, *apptd* 1996
Rt. Hon. Sir Henry Brooke, *born* 1936, *apptd* 1996
Rt. Hon. Sir Igor Judge, *born* 1941, *apptd* 1996
Rt. Hon. Sir George Waller, *born* 1940, *apptd* 1996
Rt. Hon. Sir John Mummery, *born* 1938, *apptd* 1996
Rt. Hon. Sir John Chadwick, ED, *born* 1941, *apptd* 1997
Rt. Hon. Sir Richard Buxton, *born* 1938, *apptd* 1997

Rt. Hon. Sir Anthony May, *born* 1940, *apptd* 1997
Rt. Hon. Sir Simon Tuckey, *born* 1941, *apptd* 1998
Rt. Hon. Sir Anthony Clarke, *born* 1943, *apptd* 1998
Rt. Hon. Sir John Laws, *born* 1945, *apptd* 1999
Rt. Hon. Sir Stephen Sedley, *born* 1939, *apptd* 1999
Rt. Hon. Sir Jonathan Mance, *born* 1943, *apptd* 1999
Rt. Hon. Sir David Latham, *born* 1942, *apptd* 2000
Rt. Hon. Sir Bernard Anthony Rix, *born* 1943, *apptd* 2000
Rt. Hon. Sir Jonathan Parker, *born* 1937, *apptd* 2000
Rt. Hon. Dame Mary Howarth Arden, DBE, *born* 1947, *apptd* 2000
Rt. Hon. Sir David Wolfe Keene, *born* 1941, *apptd* 2000
Rt. Hon. Sir John Anthony Dyson, *born* 1943, *apptd* 2001
Rt. Hon. Sir Andrew Centlivres Longmore, *born* 1944, *apptd* 2001
Rt. Hon. Sir Robert John Carnwath, CVO, *born* 1945, *apptd* 2002
Rt. Hon. Sir Thomas Baker, *born* 1937, *apptd* 2002
Rt. Hon. Dame Janet Hilary Smith, DBE, *born* 1940, *apptd* 2002
Rt. Hon. Sir Roger Laugharne Thomas, *born* 1947, *apptd* 2003
Rt. Hon. Sir Robin Jacob, *born* 1941, *apptd* 2003
Rt. Hon. Sir Nicholas Wall, *born* 1945, *apptd* 2004
Rt. Hon. Sir David Neuberger, *born* 1948, *apptd* 2004
Rt. Hon. Sir Maurice Ralph Kay, *born* 1942, *apptd* 2004
Rt. Hon. Sir Anthony Hooper, *born* 1937, *apptd* 2004

Ex officio Judges, The Lord High Chancellor and Secretary of State for Constitutional Affairs; the Lord Chief Justice of England and Wales; the Master of the Rolls; the President of the Family Division; and the Vice-Chancellor

COURT OF APPEAL (CIVIL DIVISION)
Vice-President, The Rt. Hon. Lord Justice Henry Brooke

COURT OF APPEAL (CRIMINAL DIVISION)
Vice-President, The Rt. Hon. Lord Justice Rose
Judges, The Lord Chief Justice of England; the Master of the Rolls; Lords Justices of Appeal; and Judges of the High Court of Justice

COURTS-MARTIAL APPEAL COURT
Judges, The Lord Chief Justice of England; the Master of the Rolls; Lords Justices of Appeal; and Judges of the High Court of Justice

HIGH COURT OF JUSTICE

CHANCERY DIVISION
President, The Lord High Chancellor and Secretary of State for Constitutional Affairs
The Vice-Chancellor (£179,431), The Rt. Hon. Sir Andrew Moritt, CVO, *born,* 1938 *apptd* 2000
Secretary, Miss E. Harbert
Clerk, Mrs A. Serfaty

JUDGES (each £150,878)
Style, The Hon. Mr/Mrs Justice [surname]

Hon. Sir John Lindsay, *born* 1935, *apptd* 1992
Hon. Sir Edward Evans-Lombe, *born* 1937, *apptd* 1993
Hon. Sir William Blackburne, *born* 1944, *apptd* 1993
Hon. Sir Gavin Lightman, *born* 1939, *apptd* 1994
Hon. Sir Colin Rimer, *born* 1944, *apptd* 1994
Hon. Sir Hugh Laddie, *born* 1946, *apptd* 1995
Hon. Sir Timothy Lloyd, *born* 1946, *apptd* 1996
Hon. Sir Andrew Park, *born* 1939, *apptd* 1997
Hon. Sir Nicholas Pumfrey, *born* 1951, *apptd* 1997
Hon. Sir Michael Hart, *born* 1948, *apptd* 1998
Hon. Sir Lawrence Collins, *born* 1941, *apptd* 2000
Hon. Sir Nicholas John Patten, *born* 1950, *apptd* 2000
Hon. Sir Terrence Michael Barnet Etherton, *born* 1951, *apptd* 2001
Hon. Sir Peter Winston Smith, *born* 1952, *apptd* 2002
Hon. Sir Kim Lewison, *born* 1952, *apptd* 2003
Hon. Sir David Richards, *born* 1951, *apptd* 2003
Hon. Sir George Anthony Mann, *born* 1951, *apptd* 2004

HIGH COURT OF JUSTICE IN BANKRUPTCY
Judges, The Vice-Chancellor and Judges of the Chancery Division of the High Court

COMPANIES COURT
Judges, The Vice-Chancellor and Judges of the Chancery Division of the High Court

PATENT COURT (APPELLATE SECTION)
Judge, The Hon. Mr Justice Jacob

QUEEN'S BENCH DIVISION
The Lord Chief Justice of England and Wales (£205,242)
The Rt. Hon. the Lord Woolf, *born* 1933, *apptd* 2000
Private Secretary, Miss M. Souris
Clerk, Ms J. Jones
Vice-President, The Rt. Hon. Lord Justice May, *born* 1940, *apptd* 2002

JUDGES *as at 26 August 2004* (each £150,878)
Style, The Hon. Mr/Mrs Justice [surname]

Hon. Sir Stuart McKinnon, *born* 1938, *apptd* 1988
Hon. Sir Douglas Dunlop Brown, *born* 1931, *apptd* 1996
Hon. Sir Roger Buckley, *born* 1939, *apptd* 1989
Hon. Sir Peter Cresswell, *born* 1944, *apptd* 1991
Hon. Sir Christopher Holland, *born* 1937, *apptd* 1992
Hon. Sir Richard Curtis, *born* 1933, *apptd* 1992
Hon. Sir Anthony Colman, *born* 1938, *apptd* 1992
Hon. Sir Thayne Forbes, *born* 1938, *apptd* 1993
Hon. Sir Rodger Bell, *born* 1939, *apptd* 1993
Hon. Sir Michael Harrison, *born* 1939, *apptd* 1993
Hon. Sir William Gage, *born* 1938, *apptd* 1993
Hon. Sir Thomas Morison, *born* 1939, *apptd* 1993
Hon. Sir Andrew Collins, *born* 1942, *apptd* 1994
Hon. Sir Alexander Butterfield, *born* 1942, *apptd* 1995
Hon. Sir George Newman, *born* 1941, *apptd* 1995
Hon. Sir David Poole, *born* 1938, *apptd* 1995
Hon. Sir Martin Moore-Bick, *born* 1946, *apptd* 1995
Hon. Sir Gordon Langley, *born* 1943, *apptd* 1995
Hon. Sir Robert Nelson, *born* 1942, *apptd* 1996
Hon. Sir Roger Toulson, *born* 1946, *apptd* 1996
Hon. Sir Michael Astill, *born* 1938, *apptd* 1996
Hon. Sir Alan Moses, *born* 1945, *apptd* 1996
Hon. Sir David Eady, *born* 1943, *apptd* 1997
Hon. Sir Jeremy Sullivan, *born* 1945, *apptd* 1997
Hon. Sir David Penry-Davey, *born* 1942, *apptd* 1997
Hon. Sir Stephen Richards, *born* 1950, *apptd* 1997
Hon. Sir David Steel, *born* 1943, *apptd* 1998
Hon. Sir Charles Gray, *born* 1942, *apptd* 1998
Hon. Sir Nicolas Bratza, *born* 1945, *apptd* 1998
Hon. Sir Michael Burton, *born* 1946, *apptd* 1998
Hon. Sir Rupert Jackson, *born* 1948, *apptd* 1999
Hon. Dame Heather Hallett, DBE, *born* 1949, *apptd* 1999

Hon. Sir Patrick Elias, *born* 1947, *apptd* 1999
Hon. Sir Richard Aikens, *born* 1948, *apptd* 1999
Hon. Sir Stephen Silber, *born* 1944, *apptd* 1999
Hon. Sir John Goldring, *born* 1944, *apptd* 1999
Hon. Sir Peter Crane, *born* 1940, *apptd* 2000
Hon. Dame Anne Rafferty, DBE, *born* 1950, *apptd* 2000
Hon. Sir Geoffrey Grigson, *born* 1944, *apptd* 2000
Hon. Sir Richard Gibbs, *born* 1941, *apptd* 2000
Hon. Sir Richard Henriques, *born* 1943, *apptd* 2000
Hon. Sir Stephen Tomlinson, *born* 1952, *apptd* 2000
Hon. Sir Andrew Smith, *born* 1947, *apptd* 2000
Hon. Sir Stanley Burnton, *born* 1942, *apptd* 2000
Hon. Sir Patrick Hunt, *born* 1943, *apptd* 2000
Hon. Sir Christopher Pitchford, *born* 1947, *apptd* 2000
Hon. Sir Brian Leveson, *born* 1949, *apptd* 2000
Hon. Sir Duncan Ouseley, *born* 1950, *apptd* 2000
Hon. Sir Raymond Jack, *born* 1942, *apptd* 2001
Hon. Sir Richard McCombe, *born* 1952, *apptd* 2001
Hon. Sir Robert Owen, *born* 1944, *apptd* 2001
Hon. Sir Colin Mackay, *born* 1943, *apptd* 2001
Hon. Sir John Mitting, *born* 1947, *apptd* 2001
Hon. Sir David Evans, *born* 1946, *apptd* 2001
Hon. Sir Nigel Davis, *born* 1951, *apptd* 2001
Hon. Sir Peter Gross, *born* 1952, *apptd* 2001
Hon. Sir Brian Keith, *born* 1944, *apptd* 2001
Hon. Sir Jeremy Cooke, *born* 1949, *apptd* 2001
Hon. Sir Richard Field, *born* 1947, *apptd* 2002
Hon. Sir Christopher Pitchers, *born* 1942, *apptd* 2002
Hon. Sir Adrian Fulford, *born* 1953, *apptd* 2002
Hon. Sir Colman Treacy, *born* 1949, *apptd* 2002
Hon. Sir Peregrine Simon, *born* 1950, *apptd* 2002
Hon. Sir Roger Royce, *born* 1944, *apptd* 2002
Hon. Dame Laura Cox, DBE, *born* 1951, *apptd* 2002
Hon. Sir Jack Beatson, *born* 1948, *apptd* 2003
Hon. Sir Michael Tugendhat, *born* 1944, *apptd* 2003
Hon. Sir David Clarke, *born* 1942, *apptd* 2003
Hon. Sir Richard Wakerley, *born* 1942, *apptd* 2003
Hon. Dame Elizabeth Gloster, DBE, *born* 1949, *apptd* 2004
Hon. Sir David Bean, *born* 1954, *apptd* 2004
Hon. Sir Anthony Hughes, *born* 1948, *apptd* 2004

FAMILY DIVISION

President (£179,431), The Rt. Hon. Dame Elizabeth Butler-Sloss, DBE, *born* 1933, *apptd* 1999
Secretary, Mrs S. Leung
Clerk, R. Smith

JUDGES *as at 26 August 2004* (each £150,878)
Style, The Hon. Mr/Mrs Justice [surname]

Hon. Dame Joyanne Bracewell, DBE, *born* 1934, *apptd* 1990
Hon. Sir Peter Singer, *born* 1944, *apptd* 1993
Hon. Sir Nicholas Wilson, *born* 1945, *apptd* 1993
Hon. Sir Andrew Kirkwood, *born* 1944, *apptd* 1993
Hon. Sir Hugh Bennett, *born* 1943, *apptd* 1995
Hon. Sir Edward Holman, *born* 1947, *apptd* 1995
Hon. Dame Mary Hogg, DBE, *born* 1947, *apptd* 1995
Hon. Sir Christopher Sumner, *born* 1939, *apptd* 1996
Hon. Sir Arthur Charles, *born* 1948, *apptd* 1998
Hon. Sir David Bodey, *born* 1947, *apptd* 1999
Hon. Dame Jill Black, DBE, *born* 1954, *apptd* 1999
Hon. Sir James Munby, *born* 1948, *apptd* 2000
Hon. Sir Paul Coleridge, *born* 1949, *apptd* 2000
Hon. Sir Mark Hedley, *born* 1946, *apptd* 2002
Hon. Dame Anna Hamilton Pauffley, DBE, *born* 1956, *apptd* 2003
Hon. Sir Roderic Wood, *born* 1951, *apptd* 2004
Hon. Dame Florence Baron, DBE, *born* 1952, *apptd* 2004
Hon. Sir Ernest Ryder, *born* 1957, *apptd* 2004

TECHNOLOGY AND CONSTRUCTION COURT

St Dunstan's House, 133–137 Fetter Lane, London EC4A 1HD
T 020-7947 6022

JUDGES (each £122,139, Presiding Judge, £150,878)
The Hon. Mr Justice Jackson *(Presiding Judge)*
His Hon. Judge Havery, QC
His Hon. Judge Lloyd, QC
His Hon. Judge Thornton, QC
His Hon. Judge Wilcox
His Hon. Judge Toulmin, CMG, QC
His Hon. Judge Seymour, QC
His Hon. Judge Coulson, QC

Court Manager, Kevin Johnson

LORD CHANCELLOR'S DEPARTMENT

see Government Departments section

SUPREME COURT DEPARTMENTS AND OFFICES

Royal Courts of Justice, London WC2A 2LL
T 020-7947 6000

DIRECTOR'S OFFICE
T 020-7947 6159
Director, Mark Camley
Group Manager and Deputy Director, J. Selch
Group Manager, Probate Service, R. P. Knight
Group Manager, Family Proceedings, J. Miller
Finance and Performance Officer, K. Richardson

ADMIRALTY AND COMMERCIAL REGISTRY AND MARSHAL'S OFFICE
T 020-7947 6112
Registrar, P. Miller
Admiralty Marshal and Court Manager, K. Houghton

BANKRUPTCY AND COMPANIES COURT
T 020-7947 6444
Chief Registrar, S. Baister
Bankruptcy Registrars, G. W. Jaques; J. A. Simmonds; P. J. S. Rawson; C. Derrett; W. Nicholls
Court Manager, Jane O'Connor

CENTRAL OFFICE OF THE SUPREME COURT
Senior Master of the Supreme Court (QBD), and Queen's Remembrancer, R. L. Turner
Masters of the Supreme Court (QBD), M. Tennant; P. Miller; I. H. Foster; G. H. Rose; P. G. A. Eyre; H. J. Leslie; J. G. G. Ungley; S. Whittaker; B. Yoxall; B. J. F. Fontaine
Court Manager, M. A. Brown

CHANCERY CHAMBERS
T 020-7947 7785
Chief Master of the Supreme Court, J. I. Winegarten
Masters of the Supreme Court, J. A. Moncaster; R. A. Bowman; N. W. Bragge; T. J. Bowles; N. S. Price
Court Manager, G. Robinson

COURT OF APPEAL CIVIL DIVISION
T 020-7947 6533
Head of the Civil Appeals Office, David Gladwell
Court Manager, Judy Anckorn

COURT OF APPEAL CRIMINAL DIVISION
T 020-7947 6011
Registrar, R. A. Venne
Deputy Registrar, Mrs L. G. Knapman
Group Manager, Helen Smith

ADMINISTRATIVE OFFICE OF THE SUPREME COURT
T 020-7947 6655
Master of the Crown Office, and Queen's Coroner and Attorney, R. A. Venne
Head of Crown Office, Mrs L. G. Knapman
Group Manager, Helen Smith

EXAMINERS OF THE COURT
Empowered to take examination of witnesses in all Divisions of the High Court.
Examiners, A. G. Dyer; A. W. Hughes; Mrs G. M. Kenne; R. M. Planterose; M. W. M. Chism

SUPREME COURT COSTS OFFICE
T 020-7947 7314
Senior Cost Judge, P. T. Hurst
Masters of the Supreme Court, T. H. Seager-Berry; C. C. Wright; P. R. Rogers; J. E. O'Hare; C. D. N. Campbell; J. Simons; A. Gordon-Saker
Court Manager, Geoff Waterhouse

COURT OF PROTECTION
Archway Towers, 11th Floor, 2 Junction Road,
London N19 5SZ
T 020-7664 7317
Master, D. A. Lush

ELECTION PETITIONS OFFICE
Room E113, Royal Courts of Justice, Strand,
London WC2A 2LL T 020-7947 6131
The office accepts petitions and deals with all matters relating to the questioning of parliamentary, European Parliament and local government elections, and with applications for relief under the Representation of the People legislation.
Prescribed Officer, R. L. Turner
Chief Clerk, Mrs A. J. Burns

OFFICE OF THE LORD CHANCELLOR'S VISITORS
Archway Towers, 11th Floor, 2 Junction Road,
London N19 5SZ T 020-7664 7317
Legal Visitor, A. R. Tyrrell
Medical Visitors, S. B. Mahapatra; A. Bailey; T. Heads; J. Waite; P. Hettiaratchy; R. Lucas; N. Choudry; P. Saleem

OFFICIAL RECEIVERS' DEPARTMENT
21 Bloomsbury Street, London WC1B 3QW
T 020-7637 1110
Inspector-General, D. Flynn
Deputies, L. Gramp; G. Horna

OFFICIAL SOLICITOR'S DEPARTMENT
81 Chancery Lane, London WC2B 6HD
T 020-7911 7127
Official Solicitor to the Supreme Court, L. C. Oates
Deputy Official Solicitor, E. Solomons
Chief Clerk, Edward Bloomfield

PRINCIPAL REGISTRY (FAMILY DIVISION)
First Avenue House, 42–49 High Holborn,
London WC1V 6NP
T 020-7947 6000
Senior District Judge, G. B. N. A. Angel
District Judges, A. R. S. Bassett-Cross; M. C. Berry; H. Black; Miss S. M. Bowman; Miss H. C. Bradley; G. C. Brasse; Miss P. Cushing; K. E. Green; R. Harper; Maple; C. Million; Mrs K. T. Moorhouse; Redgrave; Miss L. D. Roberts; Robinson; M. J. Segal; K. J. White; P. Waller
Family and Probate Service Group Manager, R. P. Knight
District Probate Registrars:
Birmingham and Stoke-on-Trent, Miss P. Walbeoff
Brighton and Maidstone, P. Ellwood
Bristol, Exeter and Bodmin, R. H. P. Joyce
Cardiff, Bangor and Carmarthen, P. Curran (*Deputy*)
Ipswich, Norwich and Peterborough, Miss H. Whitby
Leeds, Lincoln and Sheffield, A. P. Dawson
Liverpool, Lancaster and Chester, C. Fox
Manchester and Nottingham, P. Burch
Newcastle, Carlisle, York and Middlesborough, P. Sanderson
Oxford, Gloucester and Leicester, R. R. Da Costa
Winchester, A. K. Biggs

JUDGE ADVOCATES

THE JUDGE ADVOCATE OF THE FLEET
c/o Chichester Combined Court, Southgate, Chichester
PO19 1SX T 01243-520741

Judge Advocate of the Fleet (£113,000), His Hon. Judge Sessions

OFFICE OF THE JUDGE ADVOCATE-GENERAL OF THE FORCES
(Joint Service for the Army and the Royal Air Force)
81 Chancery Lane, London WC2A IBQ
T 020-7218 8089

Judge Advocate-General (£113,121), vacant
Vice-Judge Advocate-General (£108,850), E. G. Moelwyn-Hughes
Judge Advocates *(£94,760), M. A. Hunter; J. P. Camp; C. R. Burn; R. C. C. Seymour; I. H. Pearson; J. F. T. Bayliss; M. R. Elsom
Style for Judge Advocates, Judge Advocate [surname]
*salary includes £4,000 inner London weighting

HIGH COURT AND CROWN COURT CENTRES

First-tier centres deal with both civil and criminal cases and are served by High Court and circuit judges. Second-tier centres deal with criminal cases only and are served by High Court and circuit judges. Third-tier centres deal with criminal cases only and are served only by circuit judges.

MIDLAND CIRCUIT
First-tier – Birmingham, Lincoln, Nottingham, Stafford, Warwick
Second-tier – Leicester, Northampton, Shrewsbury, Worcester, Wolverhampton
Third-tier – Coventry, Derby, Hereford, Stoke-on-Trent
Circuit Administrator, Mrs D. Ponsonby, The Priory Courts, 6th Floor, 33 Bull Street, Birmingham B4 6DW
T 0121-681 3201

Group Managers: Mrs J. Grosvenor *(Acting), West Midlands*; R. Perry *(Acting), Warwickshire Group*; D. Bennett, *Staffordshire/West Mercia Group*; A. Phillips, *East Midlands Group*

NORTH-EASTERN CIRCUIT
First-tier – Leeds, Newcastle upon Tyne, Sheffield, Teesside
Second-tier – Bradford, York
Third-tier – Doncaster, Durham, Kingston-upon-Hull, Great Grimsby
Circuit Administrator, S. Proudlock, 18th Floor, West Riding House, Albion Street, Leeds LS1 5AA T 0113-251 1200
Group Managers: Linda Mayhew *(Acting), North and West Yorkshire Group*; David Keane, *Tyne Tees Group*; Sarah Greenhough *(Acting), Humberside and South Yorkshire Group*

NORTHERN CIRCUIT
First-tier – Carlisle, Liverpool, Manchester (Crown Square), Preston
Third-tier – Barrow-in-Furness, Bolton, Burnley, Lancaster; Manchester (Minshull Street)
Regional Director, North West, C. A. Mayer, 15 Quay Street, Manchester M60 9FD T 0161-833 1005
Group Managers: Miss G. Hague, *Lancashire Group*; R. Knott, *Greater Manchester Group*; S. McNally, *Merseyside Group*; S. Evans, *Cumbria Group*

SOUTH-EASTERN CIRCUIT
First-tier – Chelmsford, Lewes, Norwich
Second-tier – Ipswich, London (Central Criminal Court), Luton, Maidstone, Reading, St Albans
Third-tier – Aylesbury, Basildon, Bury St Edmunds, Cambridge, Canterbury, Chichester, Croydon, Guildford, King's Lynn, London (Blackfriars, Harrow, Inner London Sessions House, Isleworth, Kingston, Middlesex Guildhall, Snaresbrook, Southwark, Wood Green, Woolwich), Southend
Circuit Administrator, D. Ryan, CBE, New Cavendish House, 18 Maltravers Street, London WC2R 3EU T 020-7947 7232
Group Managers: D. Weston *(London Crown)*; L. Lennon *(London County)*; J. Cave *(Kent and Sussex)*; M. Littlewood *(East Anglia, Bedfordshire and Hertfordshire)*; S. Townley *(Thames Valley, Surrey and Oxford)*

The High Court in Greater London sits at the Royal Courts of Justice.

WALES AND CHESTER CIRCUIT
First-tier – Caernarfon, Cardiff, Chester, Mold, Swansea
Second-tier – Carmarthen, Merthyr Tydfil, Newport, Welshpool
Third-tier – Dolgellau, Haverfordwest, Knutsford, Warrington
Circuit Administrator, N. Chibnall, Churchill House, Churchill Way, Cardiff CF10 4HH T 029-2041 5500
Group Managers: G. Pickett, *South Wales Group*; G. Kenney, *North Wales and Cheshire Group*

WESTERN CIRCUIT
First-tier – Bristol, Exeter, Truro, Winchester
Second-tier – Dorchester, Gloucester, Plymouth, Weymouth
Third-tier – Barnstaple, Bournemouth, Newport (IOW), Portsmouth, Salisbury, Southampton, Swindon, Taunton
Circuit Administrator, Peter Risk, 5th Floor, Greyfriars, Lewins Mead, Bristol BS1 2NR T 0117-910 3600
Group Managers: N. Jeffery, *Wiltshire*; D. Gentry, *Devon and Cornwall*; R. White, *Avon and Somerset*; R. Brummitt, *Dorset*; M. Speller, *Gloucestershire*; S. Williamson, *Hampshire and Isle of Wight*; P. Downton, *Regional Transition Manager*

CIRCUIT JUDGES

**Senior Circuit Judges*, each £122,139
Circuit Judges at the Central Criminal Court, London (Old Bailey Judges), each £122,139
Circuit Judges, each £113,121
Style, His/Her Hon. Judge [surname]
Senior Presiding Judge, The Rt. Hon. Lord Justice Judge

MIDLAND CIRCUIT
Presiding Judges, The Hon. Mr Justice Goldring; The Hon. Mr Justice Gibbs

I. D. G. Alexander, QC; Miss C. Alton; D. Bennett; R. Bray; D. Brunning; J. Burgess; Miss J. Butler, QC; J. Cavell; M. Challinor; *F. Chapman; P. Clark; M. Coates; R. Cole; N. B. Coles, QC; I. Collis; T. Corrie; P. De Mille (shared with South-Eastern Circuit); Miss P. Deeley; M. J. Dudley; M. R. Eades; P. Eccles, QC; T. Faber; Miss E. Fisher; J. Fletcher; A. Geddes; P. Glenn; J. Milmo, QC; R. Griffith-Jones; A. Hamilton; D. Hamilton; S. Hammond; Miss A. W. Hampton; C. Harris, QC (shared with South-Eastern Circuit); M. Heath; E. Hindley, QC; C. Hodson; H. Hughes; R. Inglis; R. Jenkins; F. Kirkham; A. MacDuff, QC; P. McCahill, QC; D. McCarthy; A. McCreath; D. McEvoy, QC; M. McKenna; J. Machin; W. D. Matthews; H. R. Mayor, QC; C. Metcalf; A. Mitchell; N. Mitchell; P. Morrell; I. Morris; M. Mott; A. H. Norris, QC; R. O'Rorke; S. Oliver-Jones, QC; R. Onions; R. Orme; J. Orrell; D. Perrett, QC; M. Pert, QC; *R. Pollard; D. Pugsley; J. Pyke; J. Rubery; R. Rundell; J. H. B. Saunders, QC *(Recorder of Birmingham)*; J. Shand; D. Stanley; M. Stokes, QC; G. Styler; A. Taylor; J. Teare; S. Tonking; S. Waine; J. Wait; J. Warner; N. Webb; C. Wide, QC; W. Wood, QC

NORTH-EASTERN CIRCUIT
Presiding Judges, The Hon. Mr Justice Henriques; The Hon. Mr Justice Andrew Smith

NORTH AND WEST YORKSHIRE GROUP
R. Adams; G. N. Barr Young; J. E. Barry; R. Bartfield; C. O. J. Behrens; P. Benson; B. Bush; G. Cliffe; P. J. Cockroft; J. Dobkin; A. C. Finnerty; R. A. Grant; S. P. Grenfell; S. J. Gullick; T. S. A. Hawkesworth, QC; P. M. L. Hoffman; P. Hunt; R. Ibbotson; N. H. Jones, QC; G. H. Kamil; T. D. Kent-Jones, TD; P. Langan, QC; K. M. P. Macgill; A. G. McCallum; R. M. Scott; J. Spencer, QC; S. M. Spencer, QC, J. S. H. Stewart, QC; L. Sutcliffe; T. Walsh; J. S. Wolstenholme

TYNE TEES GROUP
P. J. B. Armstrong; B. Bolton; P. H. Bowers; A. N. J. Briggs; D. M. A. Bryant; M. C. Carr; M. L. Cartlidge; E. J. Faulks; P. J. Fox, QC; T. Hewitt; D. Hodson; A. T. Lancaster; P. R. Lowden; J. T. Milford, QC; J. P. Moir; M. G. C. Moorhouse; L. Spittle; M. Taylor; C. T. Walton; J. De G. Walford; G. Whitburn, QC; D. R. Wood

HUMBERSIDE AND SOUTH YORKSHIRE GROUP
T. W. Barber; D. R. Bentley, QC; J. W. Bullimore; A. C. Carr; M. T. Cracknell; J. Davies; J. Dowse; A. R. Goldsack, QC; L. Hull; S. Jack; P. Jones; K. R. Keen, QC; S. W. Lawler, QC; M. K. Mettyear; R. J. Moore; M. J. A. Murphy, QC; J. H. Reddihough; P. E. Robertshaw; J. Shipley; J. A. Swanson

NORTHERN CIRCUIT
Presiding Judges, The Hon. Mr Justice McCombe; The Hon. Mr Justice Leveson

M. P. Allweis; J. M. Appleby; J. F. Appleton; E. K. Armitage, QC; R. K. Atherton; Miss P. H. Badley; S. W. Baker; P. Batty; R. C. W. Bennett; A. N. H. Blake; C. Bloom, QC; D. Boulton; L. F. M. Brown; R. Brown; J. K. Burke, QC; M. D. Byrne; B. I. Caulfield; D. Clark; G. M. Clifton; C. J. Cornwall; I. W. Crompton; Miss J. M. P. Daley; B. R. Duckworth; S. B. Duncan; Miss D. B. Eaglestone; T. K. Earnshaw; G. A. Ensor; P. S. Fish; Miss B. A. Forrester; J. R. Foster, QC; J. R. B. Geake; D. S. Gee; H. Gee, QC; W. George; A. J. Gilbart, QC; *J. A. D. Gilliland, QC; N. B. D. Gilmour, QC; *H. B. Globe, QC *(Recorder of Liverpool)*; C. L. Goldstone, QC; I. M. Hamilton; J. A. Hammond; D. Harris, QC; *T. B. Hegarty, QC; M. J. Henshell; F. R. B. Holloway; *R. C. Holman; A. D. Hope; *N. J. G. Howarth; C. James; *M. Kershaw, QC *(Commercial Circuit Judge)*; E. M. Knopf; Miss L. J. Kushner, QC; P. M. Lakin; B. L. Lever; B. Lewis; J. Lewis; A. C. Lowcock; D. Lynch; A. P. Lyon; D. I. Mackay; J. B. Macmillan; *D. G. Maddison *(Recorder of Manchester)*; *B. C. Maddocks; C. J. Mahon; W. P. Morris; T. J. Mort; L. A. Newton; *C. P. L. Openshaw, QC *(Recorder of Preston)*; F. D. Owen; J. A. Phillips; J. C. Phipps; P. R. Raynor, QC; J. H. Roberts; Miss M. Roddy; Miss G. D. Ruaux; M. W. Rudland; A. A. Rumbelow, QC; E. Slinger; A. Smith; P. Smith; Miss E. M. Steel; M. T. Steiger, QC; *S. Stewart, QC; D. R. Swift; P. Sycamore; C. B. Tetlow; I. J. C. Trigger; A. R. Warnock; Miss B. J. Watson; K. Wilkinson; B. Woodward

SOUTH-EASTERN CIRCUIT
Presiding Judges, The Hon. Mr Justice Aikens; The Hon. Mrs Justice Rafferty; The Hon. Mr Justice Bell

M. F. Addison; P. C. Ader; J. Altman; Mrs S. C. Andrew; A. R. L. Ansell; M. G. Anthony; S. A. Anwyl, QC; Charles Atkins; E. H. Bailey; F. Baker, QC; C. G. Ball, QC; A. F. Balston; G. S. Barham; B. J. Barker, QC; S. Barnes; W. E. Barnett, QC; R. A. Barratt, QC; *G. A. Bathurst-Norman; P. J. L. Beaumont, QC *(Common Serjeant)*; R. V. M. E. Behar; J. Bevan, QC; Mrs C. V. Bevington; N. C. van der Bijl; I. G. Bing; M. G. Binning; W. J. Birtles; B. M. B. Black; H. O. Blacksell, QC; J. G. Boal, QC; A. V. Bradbury; G. B. Breen; M. Brooke, QC; R. G. Brown; J. M. Bull, QC; J. P. Burke; L. S. Burn, QC; The Hon. C. W. Byers; D. Caddick; A. Campbell; Ms A. Campbell; J. Q. Campbell; J. Carey; M. J. Carroll; M. T. Catterson; R. Chapple; P. C. Clegg; Miss S. Coates; N. J. Coleman; S. H. Colgan; *P. H. Collins, CBE; S. S. Coltart; C. D. Compston; T. A. C. Coningsby, QC; J. G. Connor; R. D. Connor; R. A. Cooke; A. Cooper; P. E. Copley; T. G. E. Corrie; Dr E. Cotran; P. Coulson, QC; P. R. Cowell; K. Cox; R. C. Cox; M. L. S. Cripps; C. A. Critchlow; J. F. Crocker; D. L. Croft, QC; D. M. Cryan; P. Curl; Mrs P. M. T. Dangor; A. M. Darroch; M. Dean, QC; P. G. Dedman; J. E. Devaux; P. Dodgson; P. H. Downes; W. H. Dunn, QC; C. M. Edwards; D. R. Ellis; R. C. Elly; C. Elwen; Fabyan Evans; Miss D. Faber; J. D. Farnworth; P. Fingret; P. E. J. Focke, QC; G. C. F. Forrester; R. Foster; Ms D. A. Freedman; M. Fysh, QC; C. A. H. Gibson; Miss A. F. Goddard, QC; A. Goldstaub, QC; D. N. Goodin; C. G. M. Gordon; J. B. Gosschalk; A. A. Goymer; C. Gratwicke; A. E. Greenwood; P. Grobel; TD, VRD; G. H. Gypps; J. Hall; Miss G. Hallon; J. Hamilton; Miss S. Hamilton, QC; C. R. H. Hardy; C. Harris, QC; M. F. Harris; W. G. Hawkesworth; R. G. Hawkins, QC; J. M. Haworth; R. J. Haworth; R. M. Hayward; R. Hayward-Smith, QC; D. E. A. Higgins; A. N. Hitching; H. E. G. Hodge, OBE; K. M. J. Hollis; J. F. Holt; K. A. D. Hornby; M. Horowitz, QC; M. Hucker; J. C. A. Hughes, QC; M. J. Hyam *(Recorder of London)*; D. A. Inman; A. B. Issard-Davies; Dr P. J. E. Jackson; G. Jones Nicholas; T. J. C. Joseph; I. G. F. Karsten, QC; S. S. Katkhuda; C. J. B. Kemp; W. A. Kennedy; G. M. P. F. Khayat, QC; A. W. P. King; T. R. King; B. J. Knight, QC; P. E. Knowles; Stephen Kramer; Capt. J. B. R. Langdon, RN; P. H. Latham; T. Lawrence; D. M. Levy, QC; C. C. D. Lindsay, QC; S. H. Lloyd; F. R. Lockhart; N. G. E. Loraine-Smith; J. A. M. Lowen; Mrs C. M. Ludlow; Capt. S. Lyons; A. G. McDowall; R. J. McGregor-Johnson; B. M. McIntyre; R. G. McKinnon; W. N. McKinnon; N. A. McKittrick; J. McMullen, QC; D. Mackie, QC, CBE; K. C. Macrae; N. Madge; T. Maher; F. J. M. Marr-Johnson; D. N. N. Martineau; D. Matheson, QC; Ms S. Matthews, QC; V. Mayer; N. A. Medawar, QC; D. J. Mellor; G. D. Mercer; P. N. De Mille; Miss A. E. Mitchell; C. R. Mitchell; D. C. Mitchell; F. I. Mitchell; H. M. Morgan; A. P. Morris; D. Morton Jack; C. J. Moss, QC; P. Moss; R. T. Moss; Miss M. J. S. Mowat; G. S. Murdoch, QC; T. M. E. Nash; M. H. D. Neligan; A. I. Niblett; Mrs M. F. Norrie-Walker; Brig. A. P. Norris, OBE; P. W. O'Brien; J. O'Mahony; M. A. Oppenheimer; M. O'Sullivan; D. C. J. Paget, QC; A. Pardoe, QC; A. Patience, QC; W. Pawlak; Mrs N. Pearce; Prof. D. S. Pearl; Miss V. A. Pearlman; N. A. J. Philpot; T. D. Pillay; A. B. Pitts; D. C. Pitman; J. R. Platt; J. R. Playford, QC; Miss I. M. Plumstead; T. G. Pontius; S. Pratt; R. J. C. V. Prendergast; J. Price; D. W. Radford; D. J. Rennie; J. R. Reid, QC; M. P. Reynolds; M. S. Rich, QC; J. Richards; D. J. Richardson; N. P. Riddell; G. Rivlin, QC; S. D. Robbins; J. Roberts, QC; J. M. Roberts; W. M. Rose; J. Rylance; T. R. G. Ryland; J. E. A. Samuels, QC; R. B. Sanders; A. R. G. Scott-Gall; J. S. Sennitt; D. Serota, QC; J. L. Sessions; A. G. Simmons; K. T. Simpson; P. R. Simpson; S. P. Sleeman; C. M. Smith, QC; S. A. R. Smith; Miss Z. P. Smith; E. Southwell; S. B. Spence; S. M. Stephens, QC; P. R. Statman; Mrs L. J. Stern, QC; N. A. Stewart; D. M. A. Stokes, QC; G. Stone, QC; T. M. F. Stow, QC; J. B. C. Tanzer, QC; A. M. Tapping; P. Testar; C. Thomas; P. J. Thompson; A. G. Y. Thorpe; C. H. Tilling; D. Turner; C. J. M. Tyrer; J. E. van der Werff; T. L. Viljoen; J. P. Wadsworth, QC; Miss A. P. Wakefield; R. Wakefield; R. Walker; S. P. Waller; A. R. Webb; C. S. Welchman; A. F. Wilkie, QC; S. R. Wilkinson; Miss J. A. Williams; Ms S. Williams; R. J. Winstanley; S. E. Woollam; D. Worsley; P. Wulwik; M. P. Yelton; M. K. Zeidman, QC; K. H. Zucker, QC

WALES AND CHESTER CIRCUIT
Presiding Judges, The Hon. Mr Justice Roderick Evans; The Hon. Mr Justice Pitchford

K. Barnett; M. R. Burr; J. R. Case; N. M. Chambers, QC; S. Clarke; J. Curran; D. L. Daniel; D. Davies; R. L. Denyer, QC; J. B. S. Diehl, QC; R. Dutton; E. Edwards; G. O. Edwards, QC; M. Farmer, QC; M. Furness; W. Gaskell; D. Halbert; D. Hale; J. D. Durham Hall, QC; G. R. Hickinbottom; S. Hopkins, QC; R. P. Hughes; T. M.

Hughes, QC; G. Jones; C. Llewellyn-Jones, QC; C. Masterman; D. W. Morgan; D. G. Morris; D. C. Morton; I. C. Parry; G. A. L. Price, QC; P. Price, QC; E. M. Rees; D. W. Richards; P. Richards; J. M. T. Rogers, QC; K. Thomas; *J. G. Williams, QC; W. Williams, QC; N. F. Woodward

WESTERN CIRCUIT
Presiding Judges, The Hon. Mrs Justice Hallett; The Hon. Mr Justice David Steel

P. R. Barclay; A. J. Barnett; J. F. Beashel; R. Bond; J. G. Boggis, QC; G. Boney, QC; J. Bonvin; *M. J. L. Brodrick; J. M. Burford, QC; *R. D. Bursell, QC; G. W. A. Cottle; M. G. Cotterill; T. G. Cowling; *T. Crowther, QC; K. C. Cutler; P. Darlow; Susan P. Darwall Smith; Mrs L. Davies; J. W. Dixon; J. Foley; F. Gilbert, QC; D. L. Griffiths; J. D. Griggs; C. M. A. Hagen; J. M. Harrow; A. M. Havelock-Allan, QC; P. J. Hooton; M. K. Harington; R. Rooke Hetherington; I. Hughes, QC; G. Hume Jones; J. R. Jarvis; P. Lambert; C. Leigh, QC; T. Longbotham; T. Mackean; I. S. McKintosh; J. G. McNaught; The Lord Meston, QC; T. J. Milligan; J. O. Neligan; S. K. O'Malley; S. K. Overend; R. Price; M. W. Roach; R. Rucker; J. Rudd; A. Rutherford; R. M. Shawcross; D. Smith, QC; G. Tabor, QC; W. E. M. Taylor; D. K. Ticehurst, QC; D. I. H. Tyzack, QC; N. Vincent; R. C. B. Wade; P. Wassall; J. H. Weeks, QC; J. S. Wiggs

DISTRICT JUDGES
District Judges (each £90,760)

MIDLAND CIRCUIT
M. Anson; S. W. Arnold; M. Asokan; P. Atkinson; C. Beale; A. Brown; A. Butler; M. Cardinal; D. Cernik; R. Chapman; A. Cleary; R. Cole; D. J. Cooke; T. Cotterill; T. Davies; E. Dickinson; D. D. Douce; P. Dowling; L. Eaton; M. Ellery; A. Elliott; S. Gailey; F. Goddard; R. Hearne; R. L. Hudson; J. Ilsley; J. Jack; A. Jenkins; A. Jones; P. Kesterton; K. Lacy; I. Lettall; D. Lipman; P. McHale; P. Mackenzie; A. Marston; A. Maw; R. Merriman; D. Millard; A. Mithani; R. J. Morton; D. O'Regan; B. Oliver; D. Owen; M. Parry; P. Rank; F. Reeson; P. Richmond; T. Ridgway; S. Rogers; P. Sanghera; R. Savage; L. H. Schroeder; V. Sehdev; S. C. W. Smith; V. Stamenkovich; A. F. Suckling; P. Thompson; R. J. Toombs; Ms K. A. Venables; W. A. Vincent; P. Waterworth; R. Whitehurst

NORTH-EASTERN CIRCUIT
S. T. Alderson; H. Anderson; C. A. Arkless; I. D. Atherton; A. M. Babbington; H. J. Bailey; R. Barraclough; C. W. Bellamy; I. P. Besford; C. M. Birkby; J. Bower; J. A. Buchan; P. E. Bullock; I. L. Buxton; S. Chesterfield; P. Cuthbertson; G. J. Edwards; I. S. Fairwood; J. Flanagan; P. R. Giles; M. M. Glentworth; N. W. Goudie; S. J. Greenwood; M. F. Handley; R. V. M. Hall; J. E. Harrison; H. F. Heath; N. G. Hickinbottom; R. N. Hill; T. W. Hill; J. R. A. Howard; R. A. Jordan; C. Khan; D. Kirkham; A. M. Large; D. E. Lascelles; P. E. Lawton; G. Y. Lingard; R. Loomba; G. Lord; J. E. Mainwaring-Taylor; G. M. Marley; P. C. Mort; D. A. Oldham; A. P. Powell; M. F. Rhodes; D. M. Robertson; J. S. Robinson; S. Rodgers; D. Scott-Phillips; I. F. Slim; S. E. Spencer; B. D. Stapely; D. M. Stocken; J. A. Taylor; P. W. J. Traynor; D. J. R. Weston; P. J. E. Wildsmith; J. S. Wilson; H. P. Wood; M. J. Young

NORTHERN CIRCUIT
G. R. Ashton; R. R. P. Ackroyd; I. Bennett; P. H. Berkson; Ms A. J. C. Brazier; R Bryce; M. E. Buckley; Ms V. Buckley; D. B. Chapman; J L. Clark; J. R. Clegg; J. F. Coffey; P. St J. Dignan; E. Donnelly; J. F. Duerden; C. R. Fairclough; G. J. Fitzgerald; R. M. Forrester; C. R. Fox; C. E. Freeman; B. N. Gaunt; J. M. Geedes; M. Gosnell; M. J. Gregory; M. Griffiths; A. J. J. Harrison; N. Harrison; L. Henthorn; J. D. Heyworth; J. Horan; M. A. Hovington; G. A. Humphreys-Roberts; S. C. Jackson; J. A. James; E. Johnson; A. Jones; E. R. Jones; G. A. Needham; G. Nuttall; N. A. Law; R. A. McCullagh; B. V. McGrath; Ms M. A. Mornington; L. C. Osborne; J. K. Park; M. I. Peake; I. J. Pickup; J. J. B. Rawkins; A. M. Saffman; D. J. Shannon; Ms J. Shaw; M. J. Simpson; R. Smedley; G. D. Smith; W. H. Stansfield; L. S. Stephens; Ms P. S. Stockton; L. G. Sykes; C. M. Swindley; R. Talbot; B. W. Travers; M. W. Turner; M. J. Wilby; P. T. Wilby; S. Wright

SOUTH-EASTERN CIRCUIT
J. L. Allen; I. Avent; P. R. Ayers; J. D. Banks; S. Batcup; P. W. Bazley-White; J. L. Beattie; D. Beck; R. H. L. Blomfield; A. J. Blundson, M. Birchall; G. Brett; G. H. Burgess; L. M. Burgess; P. R. Carr; C. B. Chandler; J. H.G. Chrispin; E. Cohen; L. Cohen; J. I. Collier; B. R. J. Cole; A. J. Coni; C. N. Darbyshire; C. Dabezies; R. A. Davis; S. A. F. Davies; J. R. Davidson; I. M. Diamond; R. D. Dudley; C. M. Edwards; I. Evans; D. Eynon; M. Fawcett; G. B. Field; Ms R. Fine; S. H. D. Fink; N. G. Freeborough; J. M. Fortgang; V. W. Gatter; P. Gamba; S. M. Gerlis; M. C. Gilchrist; P. S. Gill; J. Gittens; P. M. L. Glover; S. G. Gold; G. A. Green; N. J. Gregory; E. J. Habershon; D. F. Hallett; C. Hamilton; S. Hasan; M. J. Haselgrove; D. N. Hayes; R. M. Henry; S. Henson; P. F. Hewetson-Brown; M. Hickman; R. S. Hicks; R. M. Jacey; N. E. Jackson; S. G. Jackson; W. Jackson; T. H. N. Jenkins; Ms H. Johns; S. V. Jones; J. I. Karet; J. L. C. Kirby; H. E. Kemp; D. C. Lamdin; M. Langley; I. H. Lay; Lee; C. J. Letham; H. A. J. Letts; A. Levey; S. E. Levinson; B. G. Lightman; W. N. McKinnon; H. L. Manners; M. J. Marin; R. Matthews; T. McLoughlin; J. S. Merrick; L. D. Millard; A. J. Mills; E. C. Millward; R. J. Mitchell; S. R. Mitchell; C. B. Molle; S. I. Morley; A. Morris; P. Mostyn; B. Mullis; R. M. Naqvi; M. J. Parker; T. Parker; M. J. Payne; G. L. Pearl; P. Pearl; P. H. Pelly; P. R. Pescod; S. Plaskow; Polden; K. A. Price; A. L. Raeside; M. A. Read; J. M. Rhodes; J. T. Robinson; P. Rogers; M. Royall; B. I. Rutland; S. Sethi; F. W. Shanks; I. Sheratte; G. Silverman; H. Silverman; M. N. Skerratt; E. J. Silverwood-Cope; M. M. Short; R. Southcombe; R. G. Sparrow; E. Stary; G. M. Stephenson; D. Steel; P. A. Sturdy; J. E. Taylor; J. R. K. Taylor; A. K. Taylor; E. R. W. Temple; R. C. Tetlow; A. D. Thomas; I. G. Tilbury; M. Trent; C. Vokes; M. Walker; A. S. Wharton; A. N. Wicks; G. K. Wilding; F. J. Wilkinson; E. Willers; J. E. Wright; A. J. Worthington; M. Zimmels

WALES AND CHESTER CIRCUIT
D. J. Asplin; C. F. Beattie; G. H. F. Carson; J. L. Davies; C. R. Dawson; Mrs H. Dawson; J. M. Doel; P. M. Evans; Miss R. Evans; Mrs J. E. Garland-Thomas; W. H. Godwin; S. G. Harrison; R. L. Hendicott; R. A. Hoffman; D. L. Hughes; D. P. Jenkins; T. A. John; T. J. Lewis; P. H. Llewellyn, OBE; C. W. Newman; A. T. North; Mrs C. E. O'Leary; C. G. Perry; D. Wyn Rees; V. Reeves; J. E. Regan; S. Rogers; R. Singh, CBE; J. G. Thomas; A. A. Wallace; A. J. P. Weaver; O. W. Williams

WESTERN CIRCUIT
C. M. Ackner; C. E. H. Ackroyd; R. D. I. Adam; J D. Ainsworth; R. C. Bird; D. Carney; B. R. Carron; G. F. Cawood; M. T. Cooper; P. W. Corrigan; J. P. Crosse; M. Dancey; M. P. H. Daniel; J. M. R. Dowell; Ms J. Exton; D.

J. Field; J. Freeman; J. W. Frenkel; C. Fuller; F. Goodard; R. A. F. Griggs; A. M. Harvey; J. Hurley; R. D. S. James; P. D. Jolly; B. G. Meredith; P. Mildred; P. Mitchell; A. D. Moon; N. J. Murphy; R. F. D. Naylor; M. Rutherford; A. L. Simons; P. N. Singleton; B. J. A. Smith; J. Sparrow; Mrs G. Stuart Brown; M. H. Tennant; A. B. Thomas; J. L. Thomas; C. J. Tromans; J. Turner; A. J. Wainwright; A. Walker; I. E. Weintroub; D. R. White; R. A. Wilson

DISTRICT JUDGES (MAGISTRATES' COURTS)

The Provisional and Metropolitan Division has been changed; all former Provincial and Metropolitan Stipendiary Magistrates can serve nationally within any district and are now called District Judges (Magistrates' Courts).

District Judges (each £94,760) salary includes £4,000 inner London weighting

M. A. Abelson; Mrs J. H. Alderson; R. W. Anderson; Mrs A. Arnold; G. B. Babington-Browne; A. Berg; J. S. Bennett; A. Bopa-Rai; J. A. Browne; P. H. R. Browning; N. R. Cadbury; A. L. Callaway; G. Chalk; J. J. Charles; T. M. Chatelier; D. J. Chinery; R. F. S. Clancy; D. A. Cooper; M. Cooper; S. N. Cooper; C. R. Darnton; Mrs S. E. Driver; S. Earl; R. Elsey; P. R. Farmer; J. Finestein; P. J. Firth; D. R. Fletcher; J. G. Foster; M. J. Friel; I. Gillespie; C. Goulborn; R. House; M. L. R. Harris; R. Holland; J. A. Jellema; R. D. Kitson; Ms B. A. Knight; N. Leigh-Smith; I. S. Lomax; C. M. McColl; D. V. Manning-Davies; D. M. Meredith; B. Morgan; Mrs L. Morgan; M. C. Morris; P. T. Nuttall; D. Parsons; J. B. Prowse; S. Qureshi; P. B. Richardson; P. G. G. Richards; M. A. Rosenberg; F. J. Rutherford; N. Sanders; A. Shaw; Mrs E. M. Shelvey; P. C. Tain; D. R. G. Tapp; D. L. Thomas; W. D. Thomas; M. J. Walker; P. Ward; G. R. Watkins; Miss P. J. Watkins; R. E. H. Williams; M. Wood; J. I. Woollard; R. J. Zara

METROPOLITAN DISTRICTS

Bow Street, T. H. Workman *(Senior District Judge)*; C. L. Pratt; H. N. Evans; Miss D. E. Wickham
Brent Magistrates' Court, Mrs K. J. Marshall
Camberwell Green, A. C. Baldwin; Miss S. V. Green; Ms A. L. Sawetz; P. Wain; J. A. Zani
Croydon Magistrates' Court, A. P. Carr; M. Hunter
East Central Division, Miss D. Quick; I. M. Baker; P. A. M. Clark; J. V. Perkins; R. A. McPhee
Essex, K. A. Gray
Greenwich/Woolwich, M. Kelly; H. C. F. Riddle; P. S. Wallis; D. Lynch
Feltham Magistrates' Court, S. N. Day
Hendon Magistrates' Court, C. S. Wiles
Highbury Corner, I. M. Baker; J. Henderson; R. A. McPhee; Miss D. Quick; J. V. Perkins; P. A. M. Clark
Horseferry Road, A. R. Davies; A. T. Evans; Miss C. S. R. Tubbs; M. Snow; Q. A. Purdy
Inner London and City, N. Crichton
Marylebone, Miss E. J. Roscoe; G. Parsons
Middlesex, S. N. Day; C. Wiles; K. Marshall; B. Barnes
North East London, G. E. Cawdron
South-Western, K. I. Grant; S. Bayne; P. M. Gillibrand
Stratford Magistrates' Court, H. Gott; Miss S. L. Sims; C. A. Dawson
Thames, Mrs J. R. Comyns; S. E. Dawson; Miss A. M. Rose; M. J. Read; Miss F. J. McIvor
Thames Valley, T. English; B. Loosley; A. Vickers
Tower Bridge, G. S. F. Black; S. Somjee; T. R. Stone
West London Magistrates' Court, J. B. Coleman; D. K. Lachlar; J. R. D. Philips; D. Simpson; Miss S. F. Williams; A. Sweet

GREATER LONDON MAGISTRATES' COURTS AUTHORITY
185 Marylebone Road, London, NW1 5QL T 0845 601 3600

Justices' Chief Executive and Clerk to the Committee (Acting), Michael Heap
Training Manager, Rosemary Marsh
Director of Human Resources, Sandra Campbell
Director of Finance, Tony Summers
Director of Legal Operations, Mark Eldridge

CROWN PROSECUTION SERVICE

50 Ludgate Hill, London EC4M 7EX
T 020-7796 8000
E enquiries@cps.gov.uk
W www.cps.gov.uk

The Crown Prosecution Service (CPS) is responsible for the independent review and conduct of criminal proceedings instituted by police forces in England and Wales, with the exception of cases conducted by the Serious Fraud Office and certain minor offences.

The Service is headed by the Director of Public Prosecutions (DPP), who works under the superintendence of the Attorney General, and a Chief Executive. The Service comprises a headquarters and 42 areas, each area corresponding to a police area in England and Wales. Each area is headed by a Chief Crown Prosecutor, supported by an Area Business Manager.

Director of Public Prosecutions, Ken Macdonald, QC
Chief Executive , R. Foster
Directors, C. Newell *(Casework)*; G. Patten *(Policy)*; J. Graham *(Finance)*; Ms C. Hamon *(Business Information Systems)*; Ms A. O'Connor *(Human Resources)*
Head of Communications, Mrs S. Cunningham
Head of Management Audit Services, R. Capstick

CPS AREAS ENGLAND

AVON AND SOMERSET, 2nd Floor, Froomsgate House, Rupert Street, Bristol BS1 2QJ T 0117-930 2800
Chief Crown Prosecutor, D. Archer
BEDFORDSHIRE, Sceptre House, 7–9 Castle Street, Luton LU1 3AJ T 01582-816600
Chief Crown Prosecutor, R. Newcombe
CAMBRIDGESHIRE, Justinian House, Spitfire Close, Ermine Business Park, Huntingdon, Cambs PE29 6XY T 01480-825200
Chief Crown Prosecutor, R. Crowley
CHESHIRE, 2nd Floor, Windsor House, Pepper Street, Chester CH1 1TD T 01244-408600
Chief Crown Prosecutor, B. Hughes
CLEVELAND, 5 Linthorpe Road, Middlesbrough, Cleveland TS1 1TX T 01642-204500
Chief Crown Prosecutor, M. Goldman
CUMBRIA, 1st Floor, Stocklund House, Castle Street, Carlisle CA3 8SY T 01228-882900
Chief Crown Prosecutor, D. Farmer
DERBYSHIRE, 7th Floor, St Peter's House, Gower Street, Derby DE1 1SB T 01332-614000
Chief Crown Prosecutor, B. Gunn
DEVON AND CORNWALL, Hawkins House, Pynes Hill, Rydon Lane, Exeter EX2 5SS T 01392-288000
Chief Crown Prosecutor, A. Cresswell

DORSET, 1st Floor, Oxford House, Oxford Road, Bournemouth BH8 8HA T 01202-498700
Chief Crown Prosecutor, J. Revell
DURHAM, Elvet House, Hallgarth Street, Durham DH1 3AT T 0191-383 5800
Chief Crown Prosecutor, Ms P. Ragnauth
ESSEX, County House, 100 New London Road, Chelmsford CM2 0RG T 01245-455800
Chief Crown Prosecutor, J. Bell
GLOUCESTERSHIRE, 2 Kimbrose Way, Gloucester GL1 2DB T 01452-872400
Chief Crown Prosecutor, R. Coe Salazar
GREATER MANCHESTER, PO Box 237, 8th Floor, Sunlight House, Quay Street, Manchester M60 3PS T 0161-827 4700
Chief Crown Prosecutor, J. Holt
HAMPSHIRE AND ISLE OF WIGHT, 3rd Floor, Black Horse House, 8–10 Leigh Road, Eastleigh, Hants SO50 9FH T 02380-673800
Chief Crown Prosecutor, N. Hawkins
HERTFORDSHIRE, Queen's House, 58 Victoria Street, St Albans, Herts AL1 3HZ T 01727-798700
Chief Crown Prosecutor, C. Ingham
HUMBERSIDE, Citadel House, 58 High Street, Kingston-upon-Hull HU1 1QD T 01482-621000
Chief Crown Prosecutor, N. Cowgill
KENT, Priory Gate, 29 Union Street, Maidstone, Kent ME14 1PT T 01622-356300
Chief Crown Prosecutor, Ms E. Howe
LANCASHIRE, 1st Floor, Guildhall House, Guildhall Street, Preston PR1 3NU T 01772-208100
Chief Crown Prosecutor, R. Marshall
LEICESTERSHIRE, Princes Court, 34 York Road, Leicester LE1 5TU T 0116-204 6700
Chief Crown Prosecutor, M. Howard
LINCOLNSHIRE, Crosstrend House, 10A Newport, Lincoln LN1 3DF T 01522-585900
Chief Crown Prosecutor, Ms A. Kerr
LONDON, 7th Floor, CPS HQ, 50 Ludgate Hill, London EC4M 7EX T 020-7796 8000
Chief Crown Prosecutor, Ms D. Sharpling
MERSEYSIDE, 7th Floor (South), Royal Liver Building, Pier Head, Liverpool L3 1HN T 0151-239 6400
Chief Crown Prosecutor, J. Holt
NORFOLK, Haldin House, Old Bank of England Court, Queen Street, Norwich NR2 4SX T 01603-693000
Chief Crown Prosecutor, P. Tidey
NORTH YORKSHIRE, 6th Floor, Ryedale Building, 60 Piccadilly, York YO1 1NS T 01904-731700
Chief Crown Prosecutor, R. Turnbull
NORTHAMPTONSHIRE, Beaumont House, Cliftonville, Northampton NN1 5BE T 01604-823600
Chief Crown Prosecutor, C. Chapman
NORTHUMBRIA, St Ann's Quay, 122 Quayside, Newcastle upon Tyne NE1 3BD T 0191-260 4200
Chief Crown Prosecutor, Ms N. Reasbeck
NOTTINGHAMSHIRE, 2 King Edward Court, King Edward Street, Nottingham NG1 1EL T 0115-852 3300
Chief Crown Prosecutor, Ms K. Carty
SOUTH YORKSHIRE, Greenfield House, 32 Scotland Street, Sheffield S3 7DQ T 0114-229 8600
Chief Crown Prosecutor, Mrs J. Walker
STAFFORDSHIRE, 11a Princes Street, Stafford ST16 2EU T 01785-272200
Chief Crown Prosecutor, H. Ireland
SUFFOLK, Saxon House, 1 Cromwell Square, Ipswich IP1 1TS T 01473-282100
Chief Crown Prosecutor, C. Yule
SURREY, One Onslow Street, Guildford, Surrey GU1 4YA T 01483-468200
Chief Crown Prosecutor, Ms S. Hebblethwaite
SUSSEX, City Gates, 185 Dyke Road, Brighton BN3 1TL T 01273-765600
Chief Crown Prosecutor, Mrs S. J. Gallagher
THAMES VALLEY, The Courtyard, Lombard Street, Abingdon, Oxon OX14 5SE T 01235-551900
Chief Crown Prosecutor, B. Ubhey
WARWICKSHIRE, Rossmore House, 10 Newbold Terrace, Leamington Spa, Warks CV32 4EA T 01926-455000
Chief Crown Prosecutor, M. Lynn
WEST MERCIA, Artillery House, Heritage Way, Droitwich, Worcester WR9 8YB T 01905-825000
Chief Crown Prosecutor, J. England
WEST MIDLANDS, 14th Floor, Colmore Gate, 2 Colmore Row, Birmingham B3 2QA T 0121-262 1300
Chief Crown Prosecutor, D. Blundell
WEST YORKSHIRE, Oxford House, Oxford Row, Leeds LS1 3BE T 0113-290 2700
Chief Crown Prosecutor, N. Franklin
WILTSHIRE, 2nd Floor, Fox Talbot House, Bellinger Close, Malmesbury Road, Chippenham, Wilts SN15 1BN T 01249-766100
Chief Crown Prosecutor, Ms K. Harold

CPS AREAS WALES

DYFED POWYS, Heol Penlanffos, Tanerdy, Carmarthen, Dyfed SA31 2EZ T 01267-242100
Chief Crown Prosecutor, S. Rowlands
GWENT, 6th Floor, Chartist Tower, Upper Dock Street, Newport, Gwent NP20 1DW T 01633-261100
Chief Crown Prosecutor, vacant
NORTH WALES, Bromfield House, Ellice Way, Wrexham LL13 7YW T 01978-346000
Chief Crown Prosecutor, E. Beltrami
SOUTH WALES, 20th Floor, Capital House, Greyfriars Road, Cardiff CF1 3PL T 029-2080 3900
Chief Crown Prosecutor, C. Woolley

THE SCOTTISH JUDICATURE

Scotland has a legal system separate from and differing greatly from the English legal system in enacted law, judicial procedure and the structure of courts.

In Scotland the system of public prosecution is headed by the Lord Advocate and is independent of the police, who have no say in the decision to prosecute. The Lord Advocate, discharging his functions through the Crown Office in Edinburgh, is responsible for prosecutions in the High Court, sheriff courts and district courts. Prosecutions in the High Court are prepared by the Crown Office and conducted in court by one of the law officers, by an advocate-depute, or by a solicitor advocate. In the inferior courts the decision to prosecute is made and prosecution is preferred by procurators fiscal, who are lawyers and full-time civil servants subject to the directions of the Crown Office. A permanent legally-qualified civil servant known as the Crown Agent is responsible for the running of the Crown Office and the organisation of the Procurator Fiscal Service, of which he is the head.

Scotland is divided into six sheriffdoms, each with a full-time sheriff principal. The sheriffdoms are further divided into sheriff court districts, each of which has a legally-qualified resident sheriff or sheriffs, who are the judges of the court.

In criminal cases sheriffs principal and sheriffs have the same powers; sitting with a jury of 15 members, they may try more serious cases on indictment, or, sitting alone, may try lesser cases under summary procedure. Minor summary offences are dealt with in district courts which are administered by the district and the islands local government authorities and presided over by lay justices of the peace (of whom there are about 4,000) and, in Glasgow only, by district judges (magistrates' courts). Juvenile offenders (children under 16) may be brought before an informal children's hearing comprising three local lay people. The superior criminal court is the High Court of Justiciary which is both a trial and an appeal court. Cases on indictment are tried by a High Court judge, sitting with a jury of 15, in Edinburgh and on circuit in other towns. Appeals from the lower courts against conviction or sentence are heard also by the High Court, which sits as an appeal court only in Edinburgh. There is no further appeal to the House of Lords in criminal cases.

In civil cases the jurisdiction of the sheriff court extends to most kinds of action. Appeal against decisions of the sheriff may be made to the sheriff principal and thence to the Court of Session, or direct to the Court of Session, which sits only in Edinburgh. The Court of Session is divided into the Inner and the Outer House. The Outer House is a court of first instance in which cases are heard by judges sitting singly, sometimes with a jury of 12. The Inner House, itself subdivided into two divisions of equal status, is mainly an appeal court. Appeals may be made to the Inner House from the Outer House as well as from the sheriff court. An appeal may be made from the Inner House to the House of Lords.

The judges of the Court of Session are the same as those of the High Court of Justiciary, the Lord President of the Court of Session also holding the office of Lord Justice General in the High Court. Senators of the College of Justice are Lords Commissioners of Justiciary as well as judges of the Court of Session. On appointment, a Senator takes a judicial title, which is retained for life. Although styled The Hon./Rt. Hon. Lord, the Senator is not a peer.

The office of coroner does not exist in Scotland. The local procurator fiscal inquires privately into sudden or suspicious deaths and may report findings to the Crown Agent. In some cases a fatal accident inquiry may be held before the sheriff.

COURT OF SESSION AND HIGH COURT OF JUSTICIARY

The Lord President and Lord Justice General (£185,705)
The Rt. Hon. the Lord Cullen of Whitekirk, *born* 1935, *apptd* 2001
Private Secretary, A. Maxwell

INNER HOUSE

Lords of Session (each £170,554)

FIRST DIVISION
The Lord President

Rt. Hon. Lord Marnoch (Michael Bruce), *born* 1938, *apptd* 1990
Rt. Hon. Lord Penrose, (George Penrose), *born* 1938, *apptd* 1990
Rt. Hon. Lord Hamilton (Arthur Hamilton), *born* 1942, *apptd* 1995
Rt. Hon. Lady Cosgrove (Hazel Aronson), *born* 1946, *apptd* 1996

SECOND DIVISION
Lord Justice Clerk (£179,431), The Rt. Hon. Lord Gill (Brian Gill), *born* 1942, *apptd* 2001
Rt. Hon. Lord Kirkwood (Ian Kirkwood), *born* 1932, *apptd* 1987
Rt. Hon. Lord MacLean (Ranald MacLean), *born* 1938, *apptd* 1990
Rt. Hon. Lord Osborne (Kenneth Osborne), *born* 1937, *apptd* 1990
Rt. Hon. Lord MacFadyen (Donald MacFadyen), *born* 1945, *apptd* 1995

OUTER HOUSE

Lords of Session (each £150,878)

Hon. Lord Abernethy (Alistair Cameron), *born* 1938, *apptd* 1992
Hon. Lord Johnston (Alan Johnston), *born* 1942, *apptd* 1994
Hon. Lord Dawson (Thomas Dawson), *born* 1948, *apptd* 1995
Hon. Lord Nimmo Smith (William Nimmo Smith), *born* 1942, *apptd* 1996
Hon. Lord Philip (Alexander Philip), *born* 1942, *apptd* 1996
Hon. Lord Kingarth (Derek Emslie), *born* 1949, *apptd* 1997
Hon. Lord Eassie (Ronald Mackay), *born* 1945, *apptd* 1997
Hon. Lord Reed (Robert Reed), *born* 1956, *apptd* 1998
Hon. Lord Wheatley (John Wheatley), *born* 1941, *apptd* 2000
Hon. Lady Paton (Ann Paton), *born* 1952, *apptd* 2000
Hon. Lord Carloway (Colin Sutherland), *born* 1954, *apptd* 2000
Hon. Lord Clarke (Matthew Clarke), *born* 1947, *apptd* 2000
Rt. Hon. The Lord Hardie (Andrew Hardie), *born* 1946, *apptd* 2000
Rt. Hon. The Lord Mackay of Drumadoon (Donald Mackay), *born* 1946, *apptd* 2000
Hon. Lord McEwan (Robin McEwan), *born* 1943, *apptd* 2000
Hon. Lord Menzies (Duncan Menzies), *born* 1953, *apptd* 2001
Hon. Lord Drummond Young (James Drummond Young), *born* 1950, *apptd* 2001
Hon. Lord Emslie (Nigel Emslie), *born* 1947, *apptd* 2001
Hon. Lady Smith (Anne Smith), *born* 1955, *apptd* 2001
Hon. Lord Brodie (Philip Brodie), *born* 1950, *apptd* 2002
Hon. Lord Bracadale (Alastair Campbell), *born* 1949, *apptd* 2003

COURT OF SESSION AND HIGH COURT OF JUSTICIARY

Parliament House, Parliament Square, Edinburgh EH1 1HQ
T 0131-225 2595

Principal Clerk of Session and Justiciary, J. L. Anderson
Deputy Principal Clerk of Justiciary, N. Dowie
Deputy Principal Clerk of Session and Principal Extractor, R. Cockburn
Deputy in Charge of Offices of Court, Y. Anderson
Deputy Principal Clerk (Keeper of the Rolls), A. Moffat
Deputy Clerks of Session and Justiciary, N. Dowie; I. Smith; Q. Oliver; W. Dunn; A. Finlayson; J. McLean; M. Weir; R. Sinclair; I. Martin; N. McGinley; J. Lynn; E. Dickson; Mr G. Combe; R. MacPherson; D. Bruton;

D. MacLeod; A. McKay; L. Maclachlan; A. Thompson; J. Moyes; J. O'Donnell; L. McFarlane; C. Reid; Mr T. Cruickshank

SCOTTISH EXECUTIVE JUSTICE DEPARTMENT

Hayweight House, 23 Lauriston Street, Edinburgh EH3 9DQ
T 0131-229 9200

The Judicial Appointments and Finance Division is responsible for the provision of sufficient Judges and Sheriffs to meet the needs of the business of the supreme and Sheriffs Court in Scotland. It is also responsible for providing the Secretariat for the independent Judicial Appointments Board for Scotland as well as providing resources for the efficient administration of a number of specialist courts and tribunals.
Head of Judicial Appointments and Finance Division, D. Stewart

SCOTTISH COURT SERVICE

Hayweight House, 23 Lauriston Street, Edinburgh EH3 9DQ
T 0131-229 9200

The Scottish Court Service is an executive agency within the Scottish Executive Justice Department. It is responsible to the Scottish Ministers for the provision of staff, court houses and associated services for the Supreme and Sheriff Courts.
Chief Executive, J. Ewing

SHERIFF COURT OF CHANCERY

27 Chambers Street, Edinburgh EH1 1LB
T 0131-225 2525

The Court deals with service of heirs and completion of title in relation to heritable property.
Sheriff of Chancery, I. D. Macphail, QC

HM COMMISSARY OFFICE

27 Chambers Street, Edinburgh EH1 1LB
T 0131-225 2525

The Office is responsible for issuing confirmation, a legal document entitling a person to execute a deceased person's will, and other related matters.
Commissary Clerk, David Shand

SCOTTISH LAND COURT

1 Grosvenor Crescent, Edinburgh EH12 5ER
T 0131-225 3595

The court deals with disputes relating to agricultural and crofting land in Scotland.
Chairman (£122,139), The Hon. Lord McGhie (James McGhie), QC
Members, D. J. Houston; A. Macdonald *(part-time)*; J. Kinloch *(part-time)*
Principal Clerk, K. H. R. Graham, WS

SHERIFFDOMS

SALARIES

Sheriff Principal	£122,139
Sheriff	£113,121

*Floating Sheriff

GLASGOW AND STRATHKELVIN

Sheriff Principal, E. F. Bowen, QC
Area Director West, I. Scott

SHERIFFS AND SHERIFF CLERKS

Glasgow, B. Kearney; B. A. Lockhart; Mrs A. L. A. Duncan; A. C. Henry; J. K. Mitchell; A. G. Johnston; Miss S. A. O. Raeburn, QC; D. Convery; I. A. S. Peebles, QC; C. W. McFarlane, QC; H. Matthews, QC; J. A. Baird; *Mrs P. M. M. Bowman; Miss R. E. A. Rae, QC; A. W. Noble; J. D. Friel; Mrs D. M. MacNeill, QC; J. A. Taylor; C. A. L. Scott; S. Cathcart; *Ms L. M. Ruxton; I. H. L. Miller; Mrs F. L. Reith, QC; W. J. Totten; *M. G. O' Grady, QC; A. C. Normand; W. H. Holligan
Sheriff Clerk, C. Binning

GRAMPIAN, HIGHLANDS AND ISLANDS

Sheriff Principal, Sir Stephen S. T. Young, Bt., QC
Area Director North, J. Robertson

SHERIFFS AND SHERIFF CLERKS

Aberdeen and Stonehaven, A. S. Jessop; Mrs A. M. Cowan; C. J. Harris, QC; G. K. Buchanan; J. K. Tierney; K. A. Mchernan; D. J. Cusine; *P. P. Davies; *K. M. Stewart; *Sheriff Clerks*, Mrs E. Laing *(Aberdeen)*; A. Hempseed *(Stonehaven)*
Elgin, I. A. Cameron; *Sheriff Clerk*, M. McBey
Fort William, W. D. Small *(also Oban)*; *Sheriff Clerk Depute*, S. McKenna
Inverness, Portree, Stornoway, Dingwall, Tain, Wick and Dornoch, D. Booker-Milburn; A. Pollock; D. O. Sutherland; A. L. MacFadyen; *Sheriff Clerks*, A. Bayliss *(Inverness)*; M. McBey *(Dingwall)*; *Sheriff Clerks Depute*, Miss M. Campbell *(Lochmaddy and Portree)*; Miss A. B. Armstrong *(Stornoway)*; L. MacLachlan *(Tain)*; Mrs J. McEwan *(Wick)*; K. Kerr *(Dornoch)*
Kirkwall and Lerwick, G. Napier; *Sheriff Clerks Depute*, A. Moore *(Kirkwall)*; M. Flanagan *(Lerwick)*
Peterhead, *M. Garden; *Sheriff Clerk, (Peterhead)*; *Sheriff Clerk Depute*, Mrs F. L. MacPherson *(Banff)*
Lochmaddy/Banff, *P. P. Davies; A. L. MacFadyen

LOTHIAN AND BORDERS

Sheriff Principal, I. D. Macphail, QC
Area Director East, M. Bonar

SHERIFFS AND SHERIFF CLERKS

Edinburgh, R. G. Craik, QC *(also Peebles)*; Miss I. A. Poole; A. M. Bell; J. M. S. Horsburgh, QC; G. W. S. Presslie *(also Haddington)*; J. A. Farrell; A. Lothian; C. N. Stoddart; M. McPartlin; J. D. Allan; K. M. MacIver; N. M. P. Morrison, QC; G. W. M. Liddle; Miss M. M. Stephen; Mrs M. L. E. Jarvie, QC; *Mrs K. E. C. Mackie; *N. J. MacKinnon; *J. P. Scott; *D. W. M. McIntyre; *J. C. C. McSherry; *Sheriff Clerk*, J. Ross
Linlithgow, G. R. Fleming; P. Gillam; W. D. Muirhead; *M. G. R. Edington; *Sheriff Clerk*, R. D. Sinclair
Haddington, G. W. S. Presslie *(also Edinburgh)*; *Sheriff Clerk*, J. O'Donnell
Jedburgh and Duns, T. A. K. Drummond, QC; *Sheriff Clerk*, I. W. Williamson
Peebles, R. G. Craik, QC *(also Edinburgh)*; *Sheriff Clerk Depute*, M. L. Kubeczka
Selkirk, T. A. K. Drummond, QC; *Sheriff Clerk Depute*, L. McFarlane

NORTH STRATHCLYDE

Sheriff Principal, B. A. Kerr, QC
Area Director West, I. Scott

SHERIFFS AND SHERIFF CLERKS
Campbeltown, *W. Dunlop *(also Paisley)*; *Sheriff Clerk Depute*, Miss E. Napier
Dumbarton, J. T. Fitzsimons; T. Scott; S. W. H. Fraser; *Sheriff Clerk*, S. Bain
Dunoon, Mrs C. M. A. F. Gimblett; *Sheriff Clerk Depute*, J. McGraw
Greenock, J. Herald *(also Rothesay)*; V. J. Canavan; *Mrs R. Swanney; *Sheriff Clerk*, J. Tannahill
Kilmarnock, T. M. Croan; C. G. McKay; Mrs I. S. McDonald; *Sheriff Clerk*, G. Waddell
Oban, W. D. Small *(also Fort William)*; *Sheriff Clerk Depute*, D. Irwin
Paisley, J. Spy; N. Douglas; D. J. Pender; *W. Dunlop; *(also Campbeltown)* G. C. Kavanagh; Ms S. M. Sinclair; *C. W. Pettigrew; *Ms S. A. Waldron; *A. M. Cubie; *Sheriff Clerk*, Miss S. Hindes
Rothesay, J. Herald *(also Greenock)*; *Sheriff Clerk Depute*, Mrs C. K. McCormick

SOUTH STRATHCLYDE, DUMFRIES AND GALLOWAY

Sheriff Principal, J. C. McInnes, QC
Area Director West, I. Scott

SHERIFFS AND SHERIFF CLERKS
Airdrie, R. H. Dickson; J. C. Morris, QC; A. D. Vannet; Mrs M. M. Galbraith *(also Lanark)* *Sheriff Clerk*, D. Forrester
Ayr, N. Gow, QC; C. B. Miller; J. McGowan; *Sheriff Clerk*, Miss C. D. Cockburn
Dumfries, K. G. Barr; K. A. Ross; *Sheriff Clerk*, P. McGonigle
Hamilton, W. E. Gibson; J. H. Stewart; Miss J. Powrie; H. S. Neilson; T. Welsh, QC; D. M. Bicket; Mrs M. Smart; H. K. Small; *J. Montgomery; *Ms C. A. Kelly; *W. S. S. Ireland; *Sheriff Clerk*, P. Feeney
Lanark, Ms N. C. Stewart; Mrs M. M. Galbraith *(also Airdrie)*; *Sheriff Clerk*, Mrs M. McLean
Stranraer and Kirkcudbright, J. R. Smith; *Sheriff Clerks*, W. McIntosh *(Stranraer)*; B. Lindsay *(Kirkcudbright)*

TAYSIDE, CENTRAL AND FIFE

Sheriff Principal, R. A. Dunlop, QC
Area Director East, M. Bonar

SHERIFFS AND SHERIFF CLERKS
Alloa, W. M. Reid; *Sheriff Clerk*, R. G. McKeand
Arbroath, C. N. R. Stein; *Sheriff Clerks*, M. Herbertson *(Arbroath)*; S. Munro *(Forfar)*
Cupar, G. J. Evans; *Sheriff Clerk*, A. Nicol
Dundee, R. A. Davidson; I. D. Dunbar; F. R. Crowe; A. J. M. Duff; A. G. McCulloch; *L. Wood; *Sheriff Clerk*, D. Nicoll
Dunfermline, I. C. Simpson; Mrs I. G. McColl; *D. M. Mackie; *Sheriff Clerk*, W. McCulloch
Falkirk, A. V. Sheehan; A. J. Murphy; *C. Caldwell; *Sheriff Clerk*, R. McMillan
Forfar, K. A. Veal
Kirkcaldy, B. G. Donald; R. J. MacLeod; *Sheriff Clerk*, W. Jones
Perth, M. J. Fletcher; L. D. R. Foulis; R. A. McCreadie, QC; *D. C. W. Pyle; *Sheriff Clerk*, J. Murphy
Stirling, The Hon. R. E. G. Younger; A. W. Robertson

STIPENDIARY MAGISTRATES

GLASGOW
R. Hamilton, *apptd* 1984; J. B. C. Nisbet, *apptd* 1984; R. B. Christie, *apptd* 1985; Mrs J. A. M. MacLean, *apptd* 1990

CROWN OFFICE AND PROCURATOR FISCAL SERVICE

CROWN OFFICE
25 Chambers Street, Edinburgh EH1 1LA
T 0131-226 2626 W www.crownoffice.gov.uk

Crown Agent (£104,581), N. McFadyen
Deputy Crown Agent (£86,364), W. A. Gilchrist

PROCURATORS FISCAL

SALARIES

Area Fiscals	£53,451–£192,424
District Procurator Fiscal	£38,500–£56,600

GRAMPIAN AREA
Area Procurator Fiscal, J. Watt *(Aberdeen)*
Procurators Fiscal, Miss C. Frame; A. B. Hutchinson; S. Ralph

HIGHLAND AND ISLANDS AREA
Area Procurator Fiscal, A. Laing *(Inverness)*
Procurators Fiscal, R. W. Urquhart; Ms A. Wyllie; Ms S. Foard; D. S. Teale; G. Aitken; A. MacDonald

LANARKSHIRE AREA
Area Procurator Fiscal, J. Brisbane *(Hamilton)*
Procurators Fiscal, D. Spiers; Mrs A. C. Donaldson; S. Houston

CENTRAL AREA
Area Procurator Fiscal, Mrs G. M. Watt *(Stirling)*
Procurators Fiscal, R. McQuaid; M. Bell

TAYSIDE AREA
Area Procurator Fiscal, D. Howdle *(Dundee)*
Procurators Fiscal, J. I. Craigen; D. Griffiths; B. Bott

FIFE AREA
Area Procurator Fiscal, C. Ritchie *(Kirkcaldy)*
Procurators Fiscal, E. B. Russell; J. Robertson

LOTHIAN AND BORDERS AREA
Area Procurator Fiscal, D. Brown *(Edinburgh)*
Procurators Fiscal, A. R. G. Fraser; A. J. P. Reith; R. Stott; W. Gallacher; M. Paterson

AYRSHIRE AREA
Area Procurator Fiscal, Mrs J. E. Cameron *(Kilmarnock)*
Procurators Fiscal, I. L. Murray

ARGYLL AREA
Area Procurator Fiscal, J. Miller *(Paisley)*
Procurators Fiscal, D. L. Webster; W. S. Carnegie; B. R. Maguire; G. F. Williams; M. Ramage

DUMFRIES AND GALLOWAY
Area Procurator Fiscal, T. Dysart *(Dumfries)*
Procurators Fiscal, J. Service; N. Patrick

GLASGOW AREA
Area Procurator Fiscal, C. Dyer *(Glasgow)*

NORTHERN IRELAND JUDICATURE

In Northern Ireland the legal system and the structure of courts closely resemble those of England and Wales; there are, however, often differences in enacted law.

The Supreme Court of Judicature of Northern Ireland comprises the Court of Appeal, the High Court of Justice and the Crown Court. The practice and procedure of these courts is similar to that in England. The superior civil court is the High Court of Justice, from which an appeal lies to the Northern Ireland Court of Appeal; the House of Lords is the final civil appeal court.

The Crown Court, served by High Court and county court judges, deals with criminal trials on indictment. Cases are heard before a judge and, except those involving offences specified under emergency legislation, a jury. Appeals from the Crown Court against conviction or sentence are heard by the Northern Ireland Court of Appeal; the House of Lords is the final court of appeal.

The decision to prosecute in cases tried on indictment and in summary cases of a serious nature rests in Northern Ireland with the Director of Public Prosecutions, who is responsible to the Attorney-General. Minor summary offences are prosecuted by the police.

Minor criminal offences are dealt with in magistrates' courts by a legally qualified resident magistrate and, where an offender is under 17, by juvenile courts each consisting of a resident magistrate and two lay members specially qualified to deal with juveniles (at least one of whom must be a woman). On 19 August 2002 there were 878 justices of the peace in Northern Ireland. Appeals from magistrates' courts are heard by the county court, or by the Court of Appeal on a point of law or an issue as to jurisdiction.

Magistrates' courts in Northern Ireland can deal with certain classes of civil case but most minor civil cases are dealt with in county courts. Judgments of all civil courts are enforceable through a centralised procedure administered by the Enforcement of Judgments Office.

SUPREME COURT OF JUDICATURE

The Royal Courts of Justice, Belfast BT1 3JF
T 028-9023 5111

Lord Chief Justice of Northern Ireland (£185,705), The Rt. Hon. Sir Brian Kerr, *born* 1948, *apptd* 2004
Principal Secretary, S. T. A. Rogers

LORDS JUSTICES OF APPEAL (each £170,554)
Style, The Rt. Hon. Lord Justice [surname]

Rt. Hon. Sir Michael Nicholson, *born* 1933, *apptd* 1995
Rt. Hon. Sir William McCollum, *born* 1933, *apptd* 1997
Rt. Hon. Sir Anthony Campbell, *born* 1936, *apptd* 1998

PUISNE JUDGES (each £150,878)
Style, The Hon. Mr Justice [surname]

Hon. Sir John Sheil, *born* 1938, *apptd* 1989
Hon. Sir Brian Kerr, *born* 1948, *apptd* 1993
Hon. Sir Malachy Higgins, *born* 1944, *apptd* 1993
Hon. Sir Paul Girvan, *born* 1948, *apptd* 1995
Hon. Sir Patrick Coghlin, *born* 1945, *apptd* 1997
Hon. Sir John Gillen, *born* 1947, *apptd* 1998
Hon. Sir Richard McLaughlin, *born* 1947, *apptd* 1999
Hon. Sir Ronald Weatherup, *born* 1947, *apptd* June 2001
Hon. Sir Reginald Weir, *born* 1947, *apptd* 2003
Hon. Sir Declan Morgan, *born* 1952, *apptd* 2004

MASTERS OF THE SUPREME COURT (each £90,760)
Master, Queen's Bench and Appeals and Clerk of the Crown, J. W. Wilson, QC
Master, High Court, C. J. McCorry
Master, Office of Care and Protection, F. B. Hall
Master, Chancery Office, R. A. Ellison
Master, Bankruptcy and Companies Office, C. W. G. Redpath
Master, Probate and Matrimonial Office, Miss M. McReynolds
Master, Taxing Office, J. C. Napier

OFFICIAL SOLICITOR
Official Solicitor to the Supreme Court of Northern Ireland, Miss B. M. Donnelly

COUNTY COURTS

JUDGES (each £113,121)
Style, His/Her Hon. Judge [surname]

Judge Burgess, Judge Curran, QC; Judge Finnegan; Judge Gibson, QC; Judge Kennedy; Judge Lockie; Judge McFarland; Judge McKay, QC; Judge Markey, QC; Judge Marriman, QC; Judge Martin *(Chief Social Security and Child Support Commissioner)*; Judge Rodgers; Judge Smyth, QC

RECORDERS
Belfast (£131,910), Judge Hart, QC
Londonderry, Her Hon. Judge Philpott, QC

MAGISTRATES' COURTS

RESIDENT MAGISTRATES (each £90,760)
There are 19 resident magistrates in Northern Ireland.

CROWN SOLICITORS' OFFICE
PO Box 410, Royal Courts of Justice, Belfast BT1 3JY
T 028-9054 2555
Crown Solicitor, O. G. Paulin

DEPARTMENT OF THE DIRECTOR OF PUBLIC PROSECUTIONS
93 Chichester Street, Belfast BT1 3TR
T 028-9054 2444
Director of Public Prosecutions, Sir Alasdair Fraser, CB, QC
Deputy Director of Public Prosecutions, W. R. Junkin

NORTHERN IRELAND COURT SERVICE
Windsor House, Bedford Street, Belfast BT2 7LT
T 028-9032 8594
Director, D. A. Lavery

LORD CHANCELLORS SINCE 1900

Year appointed	*Name*
1895	Lord Halsbury
1905	Lord Loreburn
1912	Lord Haldane
1915	Lord Buckmaster
1916	Lord Finlay
1919	Lord Birkenhead
1922	Viscount Cave
1924 *Jan.*	Viscount Haldane
1924 *Nov.*	Viscount Cave
1928	Lord Hailsham
1929	Lord Sankey
1935	Viscount Hailsham
1938	Lord Maugham
1939	Viscount Caldecote
1940	Viscount Simon
1945	Lord Jowitt
1951	Lord Simonds
1954	Viscount Kilmuir
1962	Lord Dilhorne
1964	Lord Gardiner
1970	Lord Hailsham of St Marylebone
1974	Lord Elwyn-Jones
1979	Lord Hailsham of St Marylebone
1987 *June*	Lord Havers
1987 *Oct.*	Lord Mackay of Clashfern
1997	Lord Irvine of Lairg
2003	Lord Falconer of Thoroton

TRIBUNALS

AGRICULTURAL LAND TRIBUNALS

c/o DEFRA, Ergon House, Horseferry Road, London SW1P 2AL
T 020-7238 6523 F 020-7238 6553

Agricultural Land Tribunals settle disputes and other issues between agricultural landlords and tenants, and drainage disputes between neighbours.

There are seven tribunals covering England and one covering Wales. For each tribunal the Lord Chancellor* appoints a chairman and one or more deputies (barristers or solicitors of at least seven years standing). The Lord Chancellor also appoints lay members to three statutory panels: the 'landowners' panel, the 'farmers' panel and the 'drainage' panel.

Each tribunal is an independent statutory body with jurisdiction only within its own area. A separate tribunal is constituted for each case, and consists of a chairman and two lay members nominated by the chairman.

Chairmen (England), G. L. Newsom; W. D. M. Wood; P. A. de la Piquerie; N. Thomas; His Hon. Judge Robert Taylor; J. H. Weatherill; His Hon. Judge Machin, QC
Deputy Chairmen, Ms A. M. Seifert; T. D. Bowles; J. E. Mitting; P. Bleasdale; W. M. Kingston; M. E. Heywood; Mrs S. Evans; His Hon. Judge W. H. R. Crawford; M. O. Rodger; P. Morgan, QC; A. R. Gore; J. G. Orme, TD
Chairman (Wales), W. J. Owen
Deputy Chairman (Wales), B. L. Y. Richards

APPEALS SERVICE

14 Grays Inn Road, Fox Court, London WC1X 8HN
T 020-7712 2600
W www.appeals-service.gov.uk

The Appeals Service arranges and hears appeals on decisions concerned with social security, child support, housing benefit, council tax benefit, vaccine damage, tax credits and compensation recovery.

Judicial authority for the Service rests with the president, while administrative responsibility is exercised by the Appeals Service Agency, which is an executive agency of the Department for Work and Pensions.

President, His Hon. Judge Michael Harris
Chief Executive, Appeals Service Agency, Christina Townsend

CARE STANDARDS TRIBUNAL

18 Pocock Street, London SE1 0BW
T 020-7960 0660 F 020-7960 0661/0662
E cst@cst.gsi.gov.uk W www.carestandardstribunal.gov.uk

The Tribunal considers appeals in relation to decisions made about the inclusion of individuals' names on the list of those considered unsuitable to work with children, restrictions from teaching, and general registration decisions made about care homes, children's homes, nurses agencies, residential family centres and fostering agencies. The Tribunal's President appoints the panels for each case and each appeal is heard by a legally qualified chairman and two lay members with expertise in the field.

President, Judge David Pearl
Secretary to the Tribunal, Barbara Erne

COMMONS COMMISSIONERS

Room Zone 1/05b, Temple Quay House, 2 The Square, Temple Quay, Bristol BS1 6EB
T 0117-372 8973 F 0117-372 8250

The Commons Commissioners are responsible for deciding disputes arising under the Commons Registration Act 1965. They also enquire into the ownership of unclaimed common land and village greens. Commissioners are appointed by the Lord Chancellor*.

Chief Commons Commissioner (part-time), E. F. Cousins
Clerk, N. Wilson

COMPETITION APPEAL TRIBUNAL

Victoria House, Bloomsbury Place, London WC1A 2EB
T 020-7979 7979 F 020-7979 7978
E info@catribunal.org.uk
W www.catribunal.org.uk

The Competition Appeal Tribunal (CAT) is a specialist tribunal established to hear certain cases in the sphere of UK competition and economic regulatory law. The CAT hears appeals against decisions of the Office of Fair Trading and the regulators in the electricity, gas, water, railways and air traffic services sectors under the Competition Act 1998, and the Competition Commission under the merger control and market investigation provisions of the Enterprise Act 2002. The CAT also has jurisdiction under the Competition Act 1998 to award damages in respect of infringements of EC or UK competition law and to hear appeals against decisions of OFCOM under the Communications Act 2003. The CAT is headed by the President and has a panel of 19 members with backgrounds in law, economics, business, accountancy and regulation.

President, Sir Christopher Bellamy
Chairman, Marion Simmons, QC
Registrar, Charles Dhanowa
Members, Prof. A. Bain, OBE; M. Blair, QC; P. Clayton; B. Colgate; M. Davey; P. Grant-Hutchison; Prof. P. Grinyer; Ms S. Hewitt; Ms A. Kelly; Hon. A. Lewis; G. Mather; Prof. J. Pickering; R. Prosser, OBE; Dr A. Pryor, CB; Ms P. Quigley, WS; A. Scott, TD; Ms V. Smith-Hillman; Prof. P. Stoneman; D. Summers

COPYRIGHT TRIBUNAL

Harmsworth House, 13–15 Bouverie Street, London EC4Y 8DP
T 020-7596 6510 Minicom: 0845-922 2250 F 020-7596 6526
E copyright.tribunal@patent.gov.uk
W www.patent.gov.uk/copy/tribunal/index.htm

The Copyright Tribunal resolves disputes over copyright licences, principally where there is collective licensing.

The chairman and two deputy chairmen are appointed by the Lord Chancellor*. Up to eight ordinary members are appointed by the Secretary of State for Trade and Industry.

Chairman, C. P. Tootal
Secretary, Miss J. E. M. Durdin

EMPLOYMENT TRIBUNALS (ENGLAND AND WALES)

Ground Floor, 19–29 Woburn Place, London WC1H 0LU
T 020-7273 8603 Enquiry line 0845-795 9775
F 020-7273 8686
W www.employmenttribunals.gov.uk

Employment Tribunals for England and Wales sit in 12 regions. The tribunals deal with matters of employment law, redundancy, dismissal, contract disputes, sexual, racial and disability discrimination and related areas of dispute which may arise in the workplace. A public register of applications and decisions is held at Southgate Street, Bury St Edmunds, Suffolk IP33 2AQ. The tribunals are funded by the Department of Trade and Industry; administrative support is provided by the Employment Tribunals Service.

Chairmen, who may be full-time or part-time, are legally qualified. They are appointed by the Lord Chancellor*. Tribunal members are appointed by the Secretary of State for Trade and Industry.
President, G. Meeran

CENTRAL OFFICE OF THE EMPLOYMENT TRIBUNALS (SCOTLAND)

Eagle Building, 215 Bothwell Street, Glasgow G2 7TS
T 0141-204 0730 F 0141-204 0732

Tribunals in Scotland have the same remit as those in England and Wales. Chairmen are appointed by the Lord President of the Court of Session and lay members by the Secretary of State for Trade and Industry.
President, C. M. Milne
Regional Chairman, Shona Simon

EMPLOYMENT APPEAL TRIBUNAL

Central Office: Audit House, 58 Victoria Embankment, London EC4Y 0DS
T 020-7273 1040 F 020-7273 1045
Divisional Office: 52 Melville Street, Edinburgh EH3 7HS
T 0131-225 3963 F 0131-220 6694
W www.employmentappeals.gov.uk

The Employment Appeal Tribunal hears appeals on a question of law arising from any decision of an employment tribunal. A tribunal consists of a judge and two lay members. They are appointed by The Queen on the recommendation of the Lord Chancellor* and the Secretary of State for Trade and Industry. Administrative support is provided by the Employment Tribunals Service.
President, The Hon. Mr Justice Burton
Scottish Chairman, The Hon. Lord Johnson
Registrar, P. Donleavy

GENERAL COMMISSIONERS OF INCOME TAX

Department for Constitutional Affairs, Selborne House, 54–60 Victoria Street, London SW1E 6QW
T 020-7210 8990 F 020-7210 0660

General Commissioners of Income Tax operate under the Taxes Management Act 1970. They are unpaid judicial officers who sit in some 407 Divisions throughout the United Kingdom to hear appeals against decisions by the Inland Revenue on a variety of taxation matters. The Commissioners' jurisdiction was extended in 1999 to hear National Insurance appeals. The Lord Chancellor* appoints General Commissioners (except in Scotland, where they are appointed by the Scottish Executive). There are approximately 2,300 General Commissioners appointed throughout the United Kingdom. In each Division, Commissioners appoint a Clerk, who is normally legally qualified, who makes the administrative arrangements for appeal hearings and advises the Commissioners on points of law and procedure. The Department for Constitutional Affairs pays the Clerks' remuneration. Appeals from the General Commissioners are by way of case stated, on a point of law, to the High Court (the Court of Session in Scotland or the Court of Appeal in Northern Ireland). In 2003, approximately 29,500 cases were listed before the General Commissioners.

IMMIGRATION APPELLATE AUTHORITY

Arnhem Support Centre, PO Box 6987, Leicester LE1 6ZX
T 0845-6000 877 W www.iaa.gov.uk

The Immigration Appellate Authority (IAA) is a tribunal which hears appeals against decisions made by the Home Secretary (and his officials) and its powers are derived from the Immigration and Asylum Act 1999. Immigration Adjudicators hear appeals from immigration decisions concerning the need for, and the refusal of, leave to enter or remain in the UK, refusals to grant asylum, decisions to make deportation orders and directions to remove persons subject to immigration control from the UK. An appeal against a decision by the Home Secretary will normally go to the first tier (the Immigration Adjudicators) where the person making the appeal, his/her representative and a representative from the Home Office will usually attend a hearing before an Immigration Adjudicator, who will determine whether or not to uphold the original Home Office decision.

The Immigration Appeal Tribunal provides a second appellate level for those dissatisfied with an Adjudicator's decision. Leave to appeal needs to be obtained. An appeal will usually require a hearing at which all sides attend before a panel of three people. The panel is normally comprised of a legally qualified chairman and two lay members, who decide whether to uphold or overturn the Adjudicator's determination. From the Tribunal there is an appeal to the Court of Appeal on a point of law only.

IMMIGRATION APPEAL TRIBUNAL

Field House, 15 Breams Buildings, Chancery Lane, London EC4A 1DZ T 020-7073 4200

The Immigration Appeal Tribunal comprises 26 full-time vice-presidents, 50 part-time legally qualified chairpersons and 60 lay members.
President, The Hon. Mr Justice Ouseley
Deputy President, C. M. G. Ockelton

IMMIGRATION APPEAL ADJUDICATORS

Chief Adjudicator, His Hon. Judge H. Hodge, OBE
Deputy Chief Adjudicator, E. Arfon-Jones

IMMIGRATION SERVICES TRIBUNAL

Procession House, 55 Ludgate Hill, London EC4M 7JW
T 020-7029 9780 F 020-7029 9782
E imset@dca.gsi.gov.uk
W www.immigrationservicestribunal.gov.uk

The Immigration Services Tribunal is an independent judicial body set up to provide a forum in which appeals against decisions of the Immigration Services Commissioner and complaints made by the Immigration

Services Commissioner can be heard and determined. The cases exclusively concern people providing advice and representation services in connection with immigration matters.

The Tribunal forms part of the Court Service. It is the responsibility of the Lord Chancellor*. There is a president, who is the judicial head; other judicial members, who must be legally qualified; lay members who must have substantial experience in immigration services or in the law and procedure relating to immigration; and a secretary who is responsible for administration. The tribunal can sit anywhere in the UK.

President, Hon. Judge Seddon Cripps
Judicial Members, D. Bean, QC; G. Marriott; Judge Burgess; B. Kennedy, QC; D. W. Hunter, QC
Members, P. Barnett; O. Conway; M. Hoare; S. Maguire; A. Montgomery; I. Newton; M. Quayum; S. Rowlands
Tribunal Manager, G. Evans

INDUSTRIAL TRIBUNALS AND THE FAIR EMPLOYMENT TRIBUNAL (NORTHERN IRELAND)

Long Bridge House, 20–24 Waring Street, Belfast BT1 2EB
T 028-9032 7666 F 028-9023 0184
W www.industrialfairemploymenttribunalsni.gov.uk

The industrial tribunal system in Northern Ireland was set up in 1965 and has a similar remit to the employment tribunals in the rest of the UK. There is also a Fair Employment Tribunal, which hears and determines individual cases of alleged religious or political discrimination in employment. Employers can appeal to the Fair Employment Tribunal if they consider the directions of the Equality Commission to be unreasonable, inappropriate or unnecessary, and the Equality Commission can make application to the Tribunal for the enforcement of undertakings or directions with which an employer has not complied.

The president, vice-president and part-time chairmen of the Fair Employment Tribunal are appointed by the Lord Chancellor*. The full-time chairman and the part-time chairmen of the industrial tribunals and the panel members to both the industrial tribunals and the Fair Employment Tribunal are appointed by the Department for Employment and Learning.

President of the Industrial Tribunals and the Fair Employment Tribunal, J. Maguire, CBE
Vice-President of the Industrial Tribunals and the Fair Employment Tribunal, Mrs M. P. Price
Secretary, Miss A. Loney

INFORMATION TRIBUNAL

Room 4.01, MWB Business Exchange, 10 Greycoat Place, London SW1P 1SB
T 020-7654 3465 F 020-7654 3583

The Information Tribunal determines appeals against notices issued by the Information Commissioner. The chairman and deputy chairman are appointed by the Lord Chancellor* and must be legally qualified. Lay members are appointed by the Lord Chancellor to represent the interests of data users or data subjects. A tribunal consists of a chairman sitting with equal numbers of the lay members. There is a separate panel of the tribunal which hears national security appeals; the president of this panel is the Rt. Hon. Sir Anthony Evans, RD.

Chairman, David Marks
Secretary, Charlotte Mercer

LANDS TRIBUNAL

Procession House, 55 Ludgate Hill, London EC4M 7JW
T 020-7029 9780 F 020-7029 9781
E lands@dca.gsi.gov.uk W www.landstribunal.gov.uk

The Lands Tribunal is an independent judicial body which determines questions relating to the valuation of land, rating appeals from valuation tribunals, appeals from leasehold valuation tribunals, the discharge or modification of restrictive covenants, and compulsory purchase compensation. The tribunal may also arbitrate under references by consent. The president and members are appointed by the Lord Chancellor*. Cases are usually heard by a single member but they may sometimes be heard by two members.

President, G. R. Bartlett, QC
Members, P. H. Clarke, FRICS; N. J. Rose, FRICS; P. R. Francis, FRICS
Member (part-time), His Hon. Judge Rich, QC
Tribunal Section Manager, J. Clottey

LANDS TRIBUNAL FOR SCOTLAND

1 Grosvenor Crescent, Edinburgh EH12 5ER
T 0131-225 7996 F 0131-226 4812
W www.lands-tribunal-scotland.org.uk

The Lands Tribunal for Scotland has the same remit as the tribunal for England and Wales but also covers questions relating to tenants' rights to buy their homes under the Housing (Scotland) Act 1987. The president is appointed by the Lord President of the Court of Session.

President, The Hon. Lord McGhie, QC
Members, A. R. MacLeary, FRICS
Members (part-time), J. N. Wright, QC, I. M. Darling, FRICS
Clerk, N. M. Tainsh

MENTAL HEALTH REVIEW TRIBUNALS

Secretariat: Health Service Directorate, Room LG02 Wellington House, 133–155 Waterloo Road, London SE1 8UG
T 020-7972 4577 F 020-7972 4884

The Mental Health Review Tribunals are independent judicial bodies which review the cases of patients compulsorily detained under the provisions of the Mental Health Act 1983. They have the power to discharge the patient, to recommend leave of absence, delayed discharge, transfer to another hospital or that a guardianship order be made, to reclassify both restricted and unrestricted patients, and to recommend consideration of a supervision application. There are four tribunals in England, each headed by a regional chairman who is appointed by the Lord Chancellor* on a part-time basis. Each tribunal is made up of at least three members, and must include a lawyer, who acts as president, a medical member and a lay member.

There are five regional offices:

LIVERPOOL, 3rd Floor, Cressington House, 249 St Mary's Road, Garston, Liverpool L19 0NF T 0151-728 5400
LONDON (NORTH), Spur 3, Block 1, Government Buildings, Honeypot Lane, Stanmore, Middx HA7 1AY
T 020-7972 1000
LONDON (SOUTH), Block 3, Crown Offices, Kingston Bypass Road, Surbiton, Surrey KT6 5QN T 020-8268 4549
NOTTINGHAM, Spur A, Block 5, Government Buildings, Chalfont Drive, Western Boulevard, Nottingham NG8 3RZ
T 0115-942 8308
WALES, 4th Floor, Crown Buildings, Cathays Park, Cardiff CF1 3NQ T 029-2082 5328

NATIONAL HEALTH SERVICE TRIBUNAL (SCOTLAND)

40 Craiglockhart Road North, Edinburgh EH14 1BT
T/F 0131-443 2575

The Scottish National Health Service Tribunal considers representations that the continued inclusion of a doctor, dentist, optometrist or pharmacist on a health board's list would be prejudicial to the efficiency of the service concerned. The tribunal sits when required and is composed of a chairman, one lay member, and one practitioner member drawn from a representative professional panel. The chairman is appointed by the Lord President of the Court of Session, and the lay member and the members of the professional panel are appointed by the Scottish Ministers.
Chairman, M. G. Thomson, QC
Lay member, J. D. M. Robertson, CBE
Clerk to the Tribunal, W. Bryden

PENSIONS APPEAL TRIBUNAL

Central Office (England and Wales), 55 Ludgate Hill, London EC4M 7JW
T 020-7029 9800 F 020-7029 9801
W www.pensionsappealtribunal.gov.uk

The Pensions Appeal Tribunals are responsible for hearing appeals from ex-servicemen or women and widows who have had their claims for a war pension rejected by the Secretary of State for Work and Pensions. The Entitlement Appeal Tribunals hear appeals in cases where the Secretary of State has refused to grant a war pension. The Assessment Appeal Tribunals hear appeals against the Secretary of State's assessment of the degree of disablement caused by an accepted condition. The tribunal members are appointed by the Secretary of State for Constitutional Affairs.
President, Dr H. M. G. Concannon
Tribunal Manager, Ms J. White

PENSIONS APPEAL TRIBUNALS FOR SCOTLAND
20 Walker Street, Edinburgh EH3 7HS
T 0131-220 1404
President, C. N. McEachran, QC

OFFICE OF THE SOCIAL SECURITY AND CHILD SUPPORT COMMISSIONERS

3rd Floor, Procession House, 55 Ludgate Hill, London EC4A 7JW
T 020-7029 9850 F 020-7029 9819
23 Melville Street, Edinburgh EH3 7PW
T 0131-225 2201
W www.osscsc.gov.uk

The Social Security Commissioners are the final statutory authority to decide appeals relating to entitlement to social security benefits. The Child Support Commissioners are the final statutory authority to decide appeals relating to child support. Appeals may be made in relation to both matters only on a point of law. The Commissioners' jurisdiction covers England, Wales and Scotland. There are 18 commissioners; they are all qualified lawyers.
Chief Social Security Commissioner and Chief Child Support Commissioner, His Hon. Judge Gary Hickinbottom
Secretary, Ms L. Armes *(London)*; S. Niven *(Edinburgh)*

OFFICE OF THE SOCIAL SECURITY COMMISSIONERS AND CHILD SUPPORT COMMISSIONERS FOR NORTHERN IRELAND

1st Floor, Headline Building, 10–14 Victoria Street, Belfast BT1 3GG
T 028-9033 2344 F 028-9031 3510
E socialsecuritycommissioners@courtsni.gov.uk
W www.courtsni.gov.uk

The role of Northern Ireland Social Security Commissioners and Child Support Commissioners is similar to that of the Commissioners in Great Britain. There are two commissioners for Northern Ireland.
Chief Commissioner, His Hon. Judge Martin, QC
Commissioner, Mrs M. F. Brown
Registrar of Appeals, W. R. Brown

SOLICITORS' DISCIPLINARY TRIBUNAL

3rd Floor, Gate House, 1 Farringdon Street, London EC4M 7NS
T 020-7329 4808 F 020-7329 4833
E enquiries@solicitorsdt.com
W www.solicitorstribunal.org.uk

The Solicitors' Disciplinary Tribunal is an independent statutory body whose members are appointed by the Master of the Rolls. The tribunal considers applications made to it alleging either professional misconduct and/or a breach of the statutory rules by which solicitors are bound against an individually named solicitor, former solicitor, registered foreign lawyer, or solicitor's clerk. The Tribunal has around 30 members, two thirds are solicitor members and one third lay members. The president and solicitor members do not receive remuneration and lay members are remunerated by the Department for Constitutional Affairs.
President, A. Isaacs
Clerk to the Tribunal, Mrs S. C. Elson

SOLICITORS' DISCIPLINE TRIBUNAL (SCOTTISH)

Unit 3.5, The Granary Business Centre, Coal Road, Cupar, Fife KY15 5YQ
T 01334-659088 F 01334-659099

The Scottish Solicitors' Discipline Tribunal is an independent statutory body with a panel of 18 members, ten of whom are solicitors; members are appointed by the Lord President of the Court of Session. Its principal function is to consider complaints of misconduct against solicitors in Scotland.
Chairman, G. F. Ritchie
Clerk, J. V. Lea, WS

SPECIAL COMMISSIONERS

15–19 Bedford Avenue, London WC1B 3AS
T 020-7612 9649 F 020-7436 4151
W www.financeandtaxtribunals.gov.uk

The Special Commissioners are an independent body appointed by the Lord Chancellor* to hear complex appeals against decisions of the Board of Inland Revenue and its officials.
Presiding Special Commissioner, His Hon. Stephen Oliver, QC
Clerk, R. P. Lester

SPECIAL EDUCATIONAL NEEDS AND DISABILITY TRIBUNAL

Central Office, Procession House, 55 Ludgate Hill, London EC4M 7JW
T 0870-241 2555 F 020-7029 9726
Darlington Office, Ground Floor, Mowden Hall, Staindrop Road DL3 9BG
W www.sendist.gov.uk

The Special Educational Needs and Disability Tribunal considers parents' appeals against the decisions of Local Education Authorities (LEAs) about children's special educational needs if parents cannot reach agreement with the LEA. The President and Chairmen are appointed by the Lord Chancellor* and the Secretaries of State for Education and Employment and Wales appoint the lay members.

President, Lady Rosemary Hughes
Tribunal Secretary, Kevin Mullany

SPECIAL IMMIGRATION APPEALS COMMISSION

15 Breams Buildings, London EC4A 1DZ
T 020-7073 4200

The Commission was set up under the Special Immigration Appeals Commission Act 1997. Its main function is to consider appeals against orders for deportations in cases which involve, in the main, considerations of national security. Members are appointed by the Lord Chancellor*.

Chairman, The Hon. Mr Justice Ouseley

TRAFFIC COMMISSIONERS

c/o Scottish Traffic Area, Argyle House, 3 Lady Lawson Street, Edinburgh EH3 9SE
T 0131-200 4955 F 0131-229 0682
W www.vosa.gov.uk

The Traffic Commissioners are responsible for licensing operators of heavy goods and public service vehicles. There are seven Commissioners in the eight traffic areas covering Britain. Each Traffic Commissioner constitutes a tribunal for the purposes of the Tribunals and Inquiries Act 1992.

Traffic Commissioner, Miss J. N. Aitken

TRANSPORT TRIBUNAL

Procession House, 55 Ludgate Hill, London EC4M 7JW
T 020-7029 9780 F 020-7029 9782
E transport@dca.gsi.gov.uk
W www.transporttribunal.gov.uk

The Transport Tribunal has three jurisdictions; it hears appeals against decisions made by Traffic Commissioners at public inquiries as well as hearing appeals against decisions of the Registrar of Approved Driving Instructors and is able to resolve disputes under the Postal Services Act 2000. The tribunal consists of a legally qualified president, other judicial members, and lay members. The president and legal members are appointed by the Lord Chancellor* and the lay members by the Secretary of State for Transport. Members of the Transport Tribunal also act as the London Service Permit Appeals Panel.

President, H. B. H. Carlisle, QC
Judicial members, His Hon. Judge Brodrick; J. Beech; F. Burton
Lay members, D. Yeomans; P. Steel; L. Milliken; G. Inch; S. James; J. Robinson
Tribunal Manager, E. Castle

VALUATION TRIBUNALS

Chief Executive's Office, Block 1, Angel Square, 1 Torrens Street, London EC1V 1NY
T 020-7841 8700 F 020-7837 6131
W www.valuation-tribunals.gov.uk

The Valuation Tribunals hear appeals concerning the council tax, non-domestic rating and land drainage rates in England and Wales. There are 56 tribunals in England and four in Wales; those in England are funded by the Office of the Deputy Prime Minister and those in Wales by the National Assembly for Wales. A separate tribunal is constituted for each hearing, and normally consists of a chairman and two other members. Members are appointed by a representative of the local authorities and the Valuation Tribunal president and serve on a voluntary basis. The Valuation Tribunal Management Board considers all matters affecting valuation tribunals in England, and the Council of Wales Valuation Tribunals performs the same function in Wales.

Chairman, Valuation Tribunal Management Board, N. Galbraith
Valuation Tribunals Chief Executive Officer, Laurence Barnes
President, Council of Wales Valuation Tribunals, J. H. Owens

VAT AND DUTIES TRIBUNALS

15–19 Bedford Avenue, London WC1B 3AS
T 020-7612 9700 F 020-7436 4151
W www.financeandtaxtribunals.gov.uk

VAT and Duties Tribunals are administered by the Department for Constitutional Affairs in England and Wales, and by the First Minister in Scotland. They are independent and decide disputes between taxpayers and Customs and Excise. In England and Wales, the president and chairmen are appointed by the Lord Chancellor* and members by the Treasury. Chairmen in Scotland are appointed by the Lord President of the Court of Session.

President, His Hon. Stephen Oliver, QC
Vice-President, England and Wales, J. D. Demack
Vice-President, Scotland, T. G. Coutts, QC
Vice-President, Northern Ireland, His Hon. J. McKee, QC
Registrar, R. P. Lester

TRIBUNAL CENTRES

EDINBURGH, 44 Palmerston Place, Edinburgh EH12 5BJ
T 0131-226 3551
LONDON (including Belfast), 15–19 Bedford Avenue, London WC1B 3AS T 020-7612 9700
MANCHESTER, 9th Floor, Westpoint, 501 Chester Road, Manchester M16 5HU T 0161-868 6600

* The Lord Chancellor's Department was abolished and replaced with the Department for Constitutional Affairs in June 2003. The Secretary of State for Constitutional Affairs, the Rt. Hon. The Lord Falconer of Thoroton, is also the Lord Chancellor.

THE POLICE SERVICE

There are 52 police forces in the United Kingdom. Most forces' area is coterminous with one or more local authority areas. Policing in London is carried out by the Metropolitan Police and the City of London Police; in Northern Ireland by the Police Service of Northern Ireland; and by the Isle of Man, States of Jersey and Guernsey forces in their respective islands and bailiwicks. National services include the National Crime Squad and the National Criminal Intelligence Service (NCIS).

Police Authorities are independent bodies, responsible for the oversight of local policing. There are five police authorities in England and Wales, each with nineteen members comprising ten local councillors, three magistrates and six independent members. In Scotland, six of the forces are maintained by joint police boards, made up of local councillors from each council in the force area; the other two constabularies (Dumfries & Galloway and Fife) are directly administered by their respective local councils. In London the Metropolitan Police Authority oversees police operations and has twenty-three members; twelve drawn from the Greater London Authority (GLA), four magistrates and seven independent members. A committee of the Corporation of London including councillors and magistrates oversees the City of London Police. In Northern Ireland the policing board is made up of nineteen political and independent members.

Police authorities in England, Scotland and Wales are financed by central and local government grants and a precept on the council tax. The Northern Ireland Policing Board is wholly funded by central government. The police authorities, subject to the approval of the Home Secretary (in England and Wales), the Secretary of State for Northern Ireland and to regulations, are responsible for appointing the Chief Constable. In England and Wales they are responsible for publishing annual policing plans and reports, setting local objectives and a budget, and levying the precept. The police authorities in Scotland are responsible for setting a budget, providing the resources necessary to police the area adequately, appointing officers of the rank of Assistant Chief Constable and above, and determining the number of officers and civilian staff in the force. The Northern Ireland Policing Board exercises these functions in Northern Ireland.

The Home Secretary, the Secretary of State for Northern Ireland and the Scottish Executive are responsible for the organisation, administration and operation of the police service. They make regulations covering matters such as police ranks, discipline, hours of duty and pay and allowances. All police forces are subject to inspection by HM Inspectors of Constabulary, who report to the Home Secretary, Scottish Executive or Secretary of State for Northern Ireland.

COMPLAINTS

The Independent Police Complaints Commission (IPCC) has overall responsibility for the system for complaints against the police, taking over from the Police Complaints Authority (PCA) which ceased to exist on 31 March 2004. The IPCC has the power to initiate, carry out and oversee investigations and is also responsible for the way complaints are handled by local police forces. An officer who is dismissed, required to resign or reduced in rank, whether as a result of a complaint or not, may appeal to a police appeals tribunal established by the relevant police authority. In Scotland, Chief Constables are obliged to investigate a complaint against one of their officers; if there is a suggestion of criminal activity, the complaint is investigated by an independent public prosecutor. In Northern Ireland complaints are investigated by the Police Ombudsman.

RATES OF PAY

BASIC RATES OF PAY *at 1 April 2004*

Chief Constable of Police Service of Northern Ireland	
No fixed term	£123,660–£132,912
Fixed term appointment	£130,020–£139,740
Chief Constables of Greater Manchester, Strathclyde and West Midlands	£147,501–£150,000
Chief Constable	£105,000–£140,001
Deputy Chief Constable	£90,000–£115,002
Assistant Chief Constable	£75,000–£87,501
Chief Superintendent*	£59,988–£63,456
Superintendent*	£50,550–£58,965
Chief Inspector†	£42,810–£46,998
Inspector†	£38,679–£43,659
Sergeant	£30,186–£33,927
Constable	£19,227–£30,186

*The rank of Chief Superintendent was re-introduced on 1 January 2002. Superintendents who were not given the rank of Chief Superintendent on its re-introduction receive full protection of their existing Superintendent range 2 salary (£58,965–£62,751).

†Includes London salary range, applicable only to officers in the Metropolitan and City of London polices forces.

Metropolitan Police

Commissioner	£168,198–£180,777
Deputy Commissioner	£136,638–£146,853
Assistant Commissioner	£116,151–£130,020
Deputy Assistant Commissioner	£92,922–£104,016
Commander	£72,948–£83,736

City of London Police

Commissioner	£99,984–£116,151
Assistant Commissioner	80% of the basic salary of the commissioner or £83,736, whichever is higher

POLICE FORCES

Strength: size of force as known at February 2004
Source: Hazell & Co. Police and Constabulary Almanac 2004

ENGLAND

AVON AND SOMERSET CONSTABULARY, PO Box 37, Portishead, Bristol BS20 8QJ **T** 01275-818181
Strength, 3,185
Chief Constable, S. Pilkington, QPM

BEDFORDSHIRE POLICE, Police Headquarters, Woburn Road, Kempston, Bedford MK43 9AX **T** 01234-841212
Strength, 1,184
Chief Constable, P. Hancock, QPM

CAMBRIDGESHIRE CONSTABULARY, Hinchingbrooke Park, Huntingdon PE29 6NP **T** 01480-456111
Strength, 1,415
Chief Constable, T. Lloyd, QPM

CHESHIRE CONSTABULARY, Clemonds Hey, Oakmere Road, Winsford CW7 2UA **T** 01244-350000
Strength, 2,146
Chief Constable, P. Fahy, QPM

CLEVELAND POLICE, PO Box 70, Ladgate Lane, Middlesbrough TS8 9EH **T** 01642-326326
Strength, 1,656
Chief Constable, Sean Price

CUMBRIA CONSTABULARY, Carleton Hall, Penrith, Cumbria CA10 2AU **T** 01768-891999
Strength, 1,203
Chief Constable, Michael Baxter

DERBYSHIRE CONSTABULARY, Butterley Hall, Ripley, Derbyshire DE5 3RS **T** 01773-570100
Strength, 2,118
Chief Constable, D. F. Coleman

DEVON AND CORNWALL CONSTABULARY, Middlemoor, Exeter EX2 7HQ **T** 08452-777444
Strength, 3,287
Chief Constable, Maria Wallis, QPM

DORSET POLICE HEADQUARTERS, Winfrith, Dorchester, Dorset DT2 8DZ **T** 01929-462727
Strength, 1,402
Chief Constable, Mrs J. Stichbury, QPM

DURHAM CONSTABULARY, Aykley Heads, Durham DH1 5TT **T** 0191-386 4929 **W** www.durham.police.uk
Strength, 1,685
Chief Constable, P. Garvin

ESSEX POLICE, PO Box 2, Springfield, Chelmsford, Essex CM2 6DA **T** 01245-491491 **W** www.essex.police.uk
Strength, 3,189
Chief Constable, D. F. Stevens, QPM

GLOUCESTERSHIRE CONSTABULARY, Holland House, Lansdown Road, Cheltenham, Glos GL51 6QH **T** 0845-0901234 **W** www.gloucestershire.police.uk
Strength, 1,174
Chief Constable, T. Brain, QPM, PHD

GREATER MANCHESTER POLICE, PO Box 22 (S West PDO), Chester House, Boyer Street, Manchester M16 0RE **T** 0161-872 5050
Strength, 7,111
Chief Constable, Michael J. Todd, QPM, MPHIL

HAMPSHIRE CONSTABULARY, West Hill, Winchester, Hants SO22 5DB **T** 0845-045 4545
Strength, 3,500
Chief Constable, Paul Kernaghan, QPM

HERTFORDSHIRE CONSTABULARY, Stanborough Road, Welwyn Garden City, Herts AL8 6XF **T** 01707-354200
Strength, 1,851
Chief Constable, Paul Acres, QPM

HUMBERSIDE POLICE, Priory Road Police Station, Priory Road, Hull HU1 5SF **T** 01482-326111
Strength, 2,207
Chief Constable, D. Westwood, QPM, PHD

KENT CONSTABULARY, Sutton Road, Maidstone, Kent ME15 9BZ **T** 01622-690690
Strength, 3,555
Chief Constable, M. Fuller

LANCASHIRE CONSTABULARY, PO Box 77, Hutton, Nr. Preston, Lancs PR4 5SB
T 01772-614444 **W** www.lancashire.police.uk
Strength, 3,451
Chief Contstable, Paul Stephenson, QPM

LEICESTERSHIRE CONSTABULARY, St John's, Enderby, Leicester LE19 2BX **T** 0116-222 2222
Strength, 2,211
Chief Constable, Matthew Baggott

LINCOLNSHIRE POLICE, PO Box 999, Lincoln LN5 7PH **T** 01522-532222 **W** www.lincs.police.uk
Strength, 1,266
Chief Constable, Tony Lake

MERSEYSIDE POLICE, PO Box 59, Liverpool L69 1JD **T** 0151-709 6010
Strength, 4,257
Chief Constable, N. Bettison, QPM

NORFOLK CONSTABULARY, Operations and Communications Centre, Falconers Chase, Wymondham, Norfolk NR18 0WW
T 01953-424242
Strength, 1,580
Chief Constable, A. Hayman

NORTHAMPTONSHIRE POLICE, Wootton Hall, Northampton NN4 0JQ **T** 01604-700700
Strength, 1,258
Chief Constable, Peter Maddison

NORTHUMBRIA POLICE, Ponteland, Newcastle upon Tyne NE20 0BL **T** 01661-872555
Strength, 4,031
Chief Constable, Crispian Strachan, QPM

NORTH YORKSHIRE POLICE, Newby Wiske Hall, Northallerton, N. Yorks DL7 9HA
T 01609-783131 **W** www.northyorkshire.police.uk
Strength, 1,427
Chief Constable, Ms. D. Cannings

NOTTINGHAMSHIRE POLICE, Sherwood Lodge, Arnold, Nottingham NG5 8PP **T** 0115-967 0999
Strength, 2,458
Chief Constable, S. Green, QPM

SOUTH YORKSHIRE POLICE, Snig Hill, Sheffield S3 8LY **T** 0114-220 2020
Strength, 3,223
Chief Constable, M. Hedges, QPM

STAFFORDSHIRE POLICE, Cannock Road, Stafford ST17 0QG **T** 01785-257717
Strength, 2,218
Chief Constable, John Giffard, CBE, QPM

SUFFOLK CONSTABULARY, Martlesham Heath, Ipswich IP5 3QS **T** 01473-613500
Strength, 1,309
Chief Constable, A. McWhirter, QPM

SURREY POLICE, Mount Browne, Sandy Lane, Guildford, Surrey GU3 1HG **T** 0845-125 2222 **W** www.surrey.police.uk
Strength, 1,995
Chief Constable, Denis O'Connor, CBE, QPM

SUSSEX POLICE, Malling House, Lewes, Sussex BN7 2DZ **T** 0845-607 0999
Strength, 3,140
Chief Constable, Ken Jones, QPM

THAMES VALLEY POLICE, Kidlington, Oxon OX5 2NZ
T 0845-8505 505
Strength, 3,821
Chief Constable, Peter Neyroud, QPM

WARWICKSHIRE POLICE, Leek Wootton, Warwick CV35 7QB
T 01926-415000
Strength, 1,008
Chief Constable, John Burbeck, QPM

WEST MERCIA CONSTABULARY, Hindlip Hall, Hindlip, PO Box 55, Worcester WR3 8SP
T 01905-723000 W www.westmercia.police.uk
Strength, 2,395
Chief Constable, P. West

WEST MIDLANDS POLICE, PO Box 52, Lloyd House, Colmore Circus, Queensway, Birmingham B4 6NQ T 0845-113 5000
Strength, 7,573
Chief Constable, Paul Scott-Lee, QPM

WEST YORKSHIRE POLICE, PO Box 9, Wakefield, W. Yorks WF1 3QP T 01924-375222
Strength, 4,927
Chief Constable, C. Cramphorn

WILTSHIRE CONSTABULARY, London Road, Devizes, Wilts SN10 2DN T 01380-722341
Strength, 1,238
Chief Constable, Dame Elizabeth Neville, DBE, QPM, PHD

WALES

DYFED-POWYS POLICE, PO Box 99, Llangunnor, Carmarthen, Carmarthenshire SA31 2PF T 01267-222020
Strength, 1,161
Chief Constable, T. Grange, QPM

GWENT POLICE, Croesyceiliog, Cwmbran, Torfaen NP44 2XJ
T 01633-838111 W www.gwent.police.uk
Strength, 1,261
Chief Constable, K. Turner, QPM

NORTH WALES POLICE, Colwyn Bay, Conwy LL29 8AW
T 01492-517171
Strength, 1,528
Chief Constable, R. Brunstrom

SOUTH WALES POLICE, Cowbridge Road, Bridgend CF31 3SU T 01656-655555
Strength, 3,157
Chief Constable, Barbara Wilding, QPM

SCOTLAND

CENTRAL SCOTLAND POLICE, Police Headquarters, Randolphfield, Stirling FK8 2HD
T 01786-456000 W www.centralscotland.police.uk
Strength, 751
Chief Constable, Andrew Cameron, QPM

DUMFRIES AND GALLOWAY CONSTABULARY, Police Headquarters, Cornwall Mount, Dumfries DG1 1PZ
T 01387-252112 W www.dumfriesandgalloway.police.uk
Strength, 462
Chief Constable, D. Strang, QPM

FIFE CONSTABULARY, Detroit Road, Glenrothes, Fife KY6 2RJ
T 01592-418888 W www.fife.police.uk
Strength, 953
Chief Constable, Peter Wilson, QPM

GRAMPIAN POLICE, Queen Street, Aberdeen AB10 1ZA
T 0845-600 5700 W www.grampian.police.uk
Strength, 1,308
Chief Constable, Andrew Brown, CBE, QPM

LOTHIAN AND BORDERS POLICE, Fettes Avenue, Edinburgh EH4 1RB T 0131-311 3131
Strength, 2,602
Chief Constable, Paddy Tomkins

NORTHERN CONSTABULARY, Old Perth Road, Inverness IV2 3SY T 01463-715555
Strength, 680
Chief Constable, Ian Latimer

STRATHCLYDE POLICE, Police Headquarters, 173 Pitt Street, Glasgow G2 4JS
T 0141-532 2000 W www.strathclyde.police.uk
Strength, 7,889
Chief Constable, William Rae, QPM

TAYSIDE POLICE, PO Box 59, West Bell Street, Dundee DD1 9JU T 01382-223200 W www.tayside.police.uk
Strength, 1,161
Chief Constable, John Vine, QPM

NORTHERN IRELAND

POLICE SERVICE OF NORTHERN IRELAND, Brooklyn, Knock Road, Belfast BT5 6LE
T 028-9065 0222 W www.psni.police.uk
Strength, 9,851
Chief Constable, H. Orde

ISLANDS

GUERNSEY POLICE, Police Headquarters, Hospital Lane, St Peter Port, Guernsey GY1 2QN T 01481-725111
Strength, 177
Chief Officer, G. LePage

ISLE OF MAN CONSTABULARY, Police Headquarters, Glencrutchery Road, Douglas, Isle of Man IM2 4RG
T 01624-631212
Strength, 236
Chief Constable, M. Culverhouse

STATES OF JERSEY POLICE, PO Box 789, St Helier, Jersey JE4 3ZD T 01534-612612
Strength, 241
Chief Officer, Graham Power, QPM

METROPOLITAN POLICE SERVICE

NEW SCOTLAND YARD, 8–10 Broadway, London SW1H 0BG
T 020-7230 1212
Strength (February 2004), 28,477

Commissioner, Sir John Stevens, QPM, LLD
Deputy Commissioner, Sir Ian Blair, QPM
Chief of Staff, Deputy Assistant Commissioner, Carole Howlett

TERRITORIAL POLICING
Assistant Commissioner, Tim Godwin, OBE
Deputy Assistant Commissioner, Stephen House

SPECIALIST OPERATIONS
Assistant Commissioner, David Veness, CBE, QPM
Deputy Assistant Commissioner, Peter Clarke, CVO, QPM

SPECIALIST CRIME
Assistant Commissioner, Tarique Ghaffur, QPM
Deputy Assistant Commissioners, Bill Griffiths; Mike Fuller

HUMAN RESOURCES
Assistant Commissioner, Bernard Hogan-Howe
Director, Martin Tiplady

CITY OF LONDON POLICE

37 Wood Street, London EC2P 2NQ
T 020-7601 2222
Strength (February 2004), 720

Though small, the City of London has one of the most important financial centres in the world and the force has particular expertise in areas such as fraud investigation as

well as the areas required of any police force. The force has a wholly elected police authority, the police committee of the Corporation of London, which appoints the Commissioner.
Commissioner, James Hart, QPM, PHD
Assistant Commissioner, Mike Bowron
Commander, Frank Armstrong

BRITISH TRANSPORT POLICE

15 Tavistock Place, London WC1H 9SJ T 020-7388 7541
Strength (February 2004), 2,206

British Transport Police is the national police force for the railways in England, Wales and Scotland, including the London Underground system, Docklands Light Railway, Midland Metro Tram system and Croydon Tramlink. The Chief Constable reports to the British Transport Police Authority. The members of the Authority are appointed by the Secretary of State for Transport and include representatives from the rail industry as well as independent members. Officers are paid the same as other police forces.
Chief Constable, Ian Johnston, CBE, QPM
Deputy Chief Constable, Andy Trotter, QPM

MINISTRY OF DEFENCE POLICE

MDP Wethersfield, Braintree, Essex CM7 4AZ T 01371-854000
Strength (March 2004), 3,281

The Ministry of Defence Police is a civilian police force with specific responsibility for meeting the requirements of the MOD and associated customers, including visiting forces and the Royal Mint. Other specialist services include marine policing, dogs, firearms and Police Search Teams. The Force also has its own Criminal Investigation Department with specialist officers working in the field of fraud investigation and can also offer crime prevention advice. MDP officers are also serving as a part of the British contingent of police officers supporting the United Nations policing operations.
Chief Constable, D. L. Clarke, QPM
Deputy Chief Constable, D. A. Ray, QPM, MA, LLM
Head of Secretariat, S. Beedle
Assistant Chief Constables, (Personnel & Training) vacant; *(Operational Support)* J. P. Bligh; *(Divisional Operations)* G. P. McAuley

ROYAL PARKS CONSTABULARY

Police Station, Hyde Park, London W2 2UH T 020-7298 2000
Strength (February 2004), 139

The Royal Parks Constabulary (RPC) is part of the Royal Parks, an executive agency of the Department for Culture, Media and Sport. It is responsible for policing 17 Royal Parks, Gardens and open spaces in and around London, comprising an area of around 6,000 acres. Officers of the force are appointed under the Parks Regulations Act 1872 (as amended).

On 1 April 2004 the RPC began a merger with the Metropolitan Police Service (MPS). The MPS established a Royal Parks Operational Command Unit and will co-police the Parks with the RPC until the two units become fully merged in 2005. The MPS Operational Command Unit is also based at Hyde Park Station.
Chief Officer RPC, Supt. D. Pollock
Deputy Chief Officer, Chief Inspector Kevin Quinn
Occupational Command Unit Commander MPS, Supt. H. Ball

UNITED KINGDOM ATOMIC ENERGY AUTHORITY CONSTABULARY

Building E6, Culham Science Centre, Abingdon, Oxon OX14 3DB
T 01235-463760
Strength (February 2004), 583

The Constabulary is responsible for policing the United Kingdom Atomic Energy Authority, URENCO (Uranium Enrichment Services Worldwide) and British Nuclear Fuels PLC establishments and for escorting nuclear material between establishments within the UK and worldwide. The Chief Constable is responsible, through the United Kingdom Atomic Energy Authority Police Authority, to the President of the Board of Trade.
Chief Constable, W. F. Pryke
Deputy Chief Constable, P. P. Crossan

NATIONAL POLICE BODIES

THE SPECIAL CONSTABULARY

Each police force has its own special constabulary, made up of volunteers who work in their spare time. Special Constables have full police powers. Visit www.specialconstables.gov.uk

NATIONAL CRIME SQUAD

Headquarters: PO Box 2500, London SW1V 2WF
T 020-7238 2500

The National Crime Squad was established on 1 April 1998, replacing the six regional crime squads in England and Wales. It investigates national and international organised and serious crime. It also supports police forces investigating serious crime. The Squad is accountable to the National Crime Squad Service Authority.
Director-General, William Hughes, QPM

NCS AND NCIS SERVICE AUTHORITIES

Headquarters: PO Box 2600, London SW1V 2WG
T 020-7238 2600

The Service Authorities are responsible for ensuring the effective operation of the National Crime Squad and National Criminal Intelligence Service. Each Authority has eleven members, of whom eight sit on both Authorities as core members. The Service Authorities are non-departmental public bodies.
Chairman, Paul Lever
Clerk, Andrew Mulholland

NATIONAL MISSING PERSONS BUREAU

Headquarters: New Scotland Yard, Broadway, London SW1H 0BG
T 0207-230 4029

The Police National Missing Persons Bureau (PNMPB) acts as a central clearing house of information, receiving reports about vulnerable missing persons that are still outstanding after 14 days and details of unidentified persons or remains within 48 hours of being found from all forces in England and Wales. Reports are also received from Scottish police forces, the Police Services of Northern Ireland and foreign police forces via Interpol. The Bureau also manages the Missing Kids website, http://uk.missingkids.com
Director, G. Pugh

NATIONAL INFORMATION TECHNOLOGY ORGANISATION
Headquarters: New Kings Beam House, 22 Upper Ground, London SE1 9QY
T 020-8358 5555

The Police Information Technology Organisation (PITO) is a non-departmental public body funded by grant-in-aid from central Government and by charges from the services provided. It provides information technology, communications systems and services to the police and other criminal justice organisations in the UK and also has a role in the purchasing of goods and services for the police.
Chairman, Lt.-Gen. Sir Edmund Burton, KBE
Chief Executive, Phillip Webb

FORENSIC SCIENCE SERVICE
Headquarters: Trident Court, 2920 Solihull Parkway, Birmingham Business Park B37 3YN
T 0121-329 5200

The Forensic Science Service (FSS) is an executive agency of the Home Office providing forensic science services to the police forces in England and Wales. It employs over 2,500 people, including over 1,600 trained scientists and has seven laboratories throughout the country.
Chief Executive, David Werrett, PHD

STAFF ASSOCIATIONS

Police officers are not permitted to join a trade union or to take strike action. All ranks have their own staff associations.

ASSOCIATION OF CHIEF POLICE OFFICERS OF ENGLAND, WALES AND NORTHERN IRELAND, 7th Floor, 25 Victoria Street, London SW1H 0EX T 020-7227 3434
Negotiating Secretary, N. Yeo

POLICE SUPERINTENDENTS' ASSOCIATION OF ENGLAND AND WALES, 67A Reading Road, Pangbourne, Reading RG8 7JD T 0118-984 4005
National Secretary, Chief Supt. Philip Aspey

POLICE FEDERATION OF ENGLAND AND WALES, 15–17 Langley Road, Surbiton, Surrey KT6 6LP T 020-8335 1000
General Secretary, C. E. Elliott

ASSOCIATION OF CHIEF POLICE OFFICERS IN SCOTLAND, Police Headquarters, 173 Pitt Street, Glasgow G2 4JS T 0141-532 2052
Hon. Secretary, William Rae, QPM

ASSOCIATION OF SCOTTISH POLICE SUPERINTENDENTS, Secretariat, 173 Pitt Street, Glasgow G2 4JS T 0141-221 5796
General Secretary, Carol Forfar

SCOTTISH POLICE FEDERATION, 5 Woodside Place, Glasgow G3 7QF T 0141-332 5234
General Secretary, Douglas Keil, QPM

SUPERINTENDENTS' ASSOCIATION OF NORTHERN IRELAND, 77–79 Garnerville Road, Belfast BT4 2NX T 028-909 22201
Hon. Secretary, Supt. M. L. Allen

POLICE FEDERATION FOR NORTHERN IRELAND, 77–79 Garnerville Road, Belfast BT4 2NX T 028-9076 4200
Secretary, T. Spence

THE PRISON SERVICE

The prison services in the United Kingdom are the responsibility of the Home Secretary, the Scottish Executive Justice Department and the Secretary of State for Northern Ireland. The chief director generals (Chief Executive in Scotland), officers of the Prison Service, the Scottish Prison Service and the Northern Ireland Prison Service are responsible for the day-to-day running of the system.

There are 139 prison establishments in England and Wales, 20 in Scotland and three in Northern Ireland. Convicted prisoners are classified according to their assessed security risk and are housed in establishments appropriate to that level of security. There are no open prisons in Northern Ireland. Female prisoners are housed in women's establishments or in separate wings of mixed prisons. Remand prisoners are, where possible, housed separately from convicted prisoners. Offenders under the age of 21 are usually detained in a young offender institution, which may be a separate establishment or part of a prison.

Eleven prisons are now run by the private sector, and in England and Wales all escort services have been contracted out to private companies. In Scotland, one prison (Kilmarnock) was built and financed by the private sector and is being operated by private contractors.

There are independent prison inspectorates in England and Wales and Scotland which report annually on conditions and the treatment of prisoners. HM Chief Inspector of Prisons for England and Wales also performs an inspectorate role for prisons in Northern Ireland. Every prison establishment also has an independent board of visitors or visiting committee made up of local volunteers.

Any prisoner whose complaint is not satisfied by the internal complaints procedures may complain to the Prisons Ombudsman for England and Wales or the Scottish Prisons Complaints Commission. There is no Prisons Ombudsman for Northern Ireland, but complaints by prisoners regarding maladministration may be made to the Parliamentary Commissioner for Administration.

From May 2003, the 11 private sector prisons in England and Wales became the direct responsibility of the Commissioner for Correctional Services, a new post in the Home Office with overall responsibility for HM Prison Service, the National Probation Service and the Youth Justice Board. The Commissioner also has responsibility for correctional services policy, the prisons and probation inspectorates, the Prisons Ombudsman and the Board of Visitors. Martin Narey was appointed Commissioner in March 2003, with Phil Wheatley taking over as Director-General of the Prison Service.

In January 2004, Martin Narey was appointed Chief Executive of the National Offender Management Service, a new service announced in the Government report, *Reducing Crime, Changing Lives*. This new service integrates prisons and probation in a system which will ensure end-to-end management of offenders and is expected to reduce re-offending and cut the rate of growth in the prison population.

AVERAGE PRISON POPULATION (UK)
as at March 2004

	Remand	*Sentenced*	*Other*
ENGLAND AND WALES			
Male	11,737	57,882	1,044
Female	1,019	3,562	51
Total	12,756	61,444	1,095
*SCOTLAND			
Male	—	—	—
Female	—	—	—
Total	1,018	5,168	—
N. IRELAND			
Male	443	818	—
Female	8	14	—
Total	451	832	—
UK TOTAL	27,432	129,720	2,190

The projected prison population for 2007 in England and Wales is 78,100 if custody rates and sentence lengths remain at 2001 levels.

* Figures for Scotland are for 2003

Sources: Home Office – *Research Development Statistics*; Scottish Prison Service – *Annual Report and Accounts*; Northern Ireland Prison Service – *Annual Report* 2003–4

SENTENCED PRISON POPULATION BY SEX AND OFFENCE (ENGLAND AND WALES)
as at 31 March 2004

	Male	*Female*
Violence against the person	13,305	578
Sexual offences	5,664	22
Burglary	8,543	251
Robbery	7,930	375
Theft, handling	4,382	513
Fraud and forgery	1,022	136
Drugs offences	9,069	1,262
Other offences	7,079	374
Offence not known	818	46
In default of payment of a fine	70	5
*Total	57,882	3,562

*Figures do not include civil (non-criminal) prisoners

Source: Home Office – *Research Development Statistics*

SENTENCED POPULATION BY LENGTH OF SENTENCE (ENGLAND AND WALES) *as at 31 March 2004*

	Adults	*Young Offenders*
Less than 12 months	6,660	2,019
12 months to less than 4 years	17,105	4,402
4 years to less than life	23,816	1,889
Life	5,393	160
*Total	52,974	8,470

*Figures include fine defaulters

Source: Home Office – *Research Development Statistics*

AVERAGE DAILY SENTENCED POPULATION BY LENGTH OF SENTENCE 2002–3 (SCOTLAND)

	Adults	*Young Offenders*
Less than 4 years	2,120	433
4 years or over (including life)	2,506	169
Total	4,626	602

Source: Scottish Prison Service – *Annual Report and Accounts 2002–3*

PRISON SUICIDES APRIL 2003 – MARCH 2004 (ENGLAND AND WALES)

Males	83
Females	10
Total	93
Rate per 100,000 prisoners in custody	126

Source: Safer Custody Group

OPERATING COSTS OF PRISON SERVICE IN ENGLAND AND WALES 2003–4

	£
Staff costs	1,364,193,000
Other administrative costs	969,138,000
Operating income	400,046,000
Net operating costs for the year	2,105,189,000
Average cost per prisoner place *(reflecting establishment costs only)*	27,320

Source: HM Prison Service – *Annual Report and Accounts 2003–4*

OPERATING COSTS OF SCOTTISH PRISON SERVICE 2002–3

	£
Total income	2,290,000
Total expenditure	20,214,000
Staff costs	121,912,000
Running costs	63,939,000
Other current expenditure	23,363,000
Operating cost	206,224,000
Cost of capital charges	23,264,000
Interest payable and similar charges	7,000
Interest receivable	68,000
Net operating costs for the year	229,427,000
Lockerbie Trial Costs	0
Cost for financial year	229,427,000

Source: Scottish Prison Service – *Annual Report and Accounts 2002–3*

OPERATING COSTS OF NORTHERN IRELAND PRISON SERVICE 2003–4

	£
Income	187,000
Staff Costs	77,635,000
Depreciation and other charges	7,065,000
Other Operating Costs	20,817,000
Total Expenditure	105,677,000
Net operating costs for the year	112,461,000

Source: Northern Ireland Prison Service – *Annual Report and Accounts 2003–4*

THE PRISON SERVICES

HM PRISON SERVICE

Cleland House, Page Street, London SW1P 4LN
T 0870-000 1397 W www.hmprisonservice.gov.uk

SALARIES *from 1 April 2004*

Senior Manager A	£47,780–£69,455
Senior Manager B	£45,911–£66,406
Senior Manager C	£40,937–£59,803
Senior Manager D	£36,500–£54,667
Manager E	£25,873–£41,141
Manager F	£22,389–£34,898
Manager G	£20,159–£28,587

THE PRISON SERVICE MANAGEMENT BOARD

Director-General (SCS), P. Wheatley
Deputy Director-General (SCS), Director of High Security Prisons (SCS), P. Atherton
Director of Operations (SCS), M. Spurr
Director of Personnel (SCS), G. Hadley
Director of Finance (SCS), A. Beasley
Director of Corporate Affairs (SCS), M. Manisty
Director of Resettlement (SCS), P. Wrench
Head of the Prison Health Policy Unit (SCS), J. Boyington
Board Secretary and Head of Secretariat (SMB), K. Everett
Race Equality Advisor, B. Thompson
Legal Adviser, H. Carter

AREA MANAGERS

Eastern, D. McAllister; *East Midlands (North),* N. Clifford; *East Midlands (South),* B. Perry; *High Security Prisons,* P. Atherton; *London,* B. Duff; *North East,* M. Egan; *North West,* I. Lockwood; *South East (Thames Valley and Hampshire),* N. Pascoe; *South East (Kent),* A. Smith; *South West,* J. Petherick; *(Surrey and Sussex),* S. Moore; *Wales,* J. May; *West Midlands,* B.Payling; *Yorkshire and Humberside,* S. Wagstaffe
Head of Women's Estate, N. Clifford
Operational Manager for Women's Estate, H. Banks
Operational Manager for Juvenile Estate, S. McEwan

PRISON ESTABLISHMENTS – ENGLAND AND WALES

Prisoners as at 31 March 2004, 75,295
Adult Prisoners as at 31 March 2004, 64,211
Young Offenders as at 31 March 2004, 11,084

ACKLINGTON, Morpeth, Northumberland NE65 9XF *Prisoners,* 869 *Governor,* N. Flinders
ALBANY, Newport, Isle of Wight PO30 5RS *Prisoners,* 512 *Governor,* M. Jones
†‡ALTCOURSE (private prison), Higher Lane, Fazakerley, Liverpool L9 7LH *Prisoners,* 990 *Director,* W. MacGowan
†‡ASHFIELD (private prison), Shortwood Road, Pucklechurch, Bristol BS16 9QT *Prisoners,* 289 *Director,* Ms V. O'Dea
ASHWELL, Oakham, Leics LE15 7LF *Prisoners,* 528 *Governor,* C. Di Paolo
*ASKHAM GRANGE, Askham Richard, York YO26 5RF *Prisoners,* 134 *Governor,* Miss D. Elaine
†AYLESBURY, Bierton Road, Aylesbury, Bucks HP20 1EH *Prisoners,* 359 *Governor,* D. Kennedy
†BEDFORD, St Loyes Street, Bedford MK40 1HG *Prisoners,* 491 *Governor,* G. Baulf
†BELMARSH, Western Way, Thamesmead, London SE28 0EB *Prisoners,* 909 *Governor,* G. Hughes

†BIRMINGHAM, Winson Green Road, Birmingham B18 4AS *Prisoners*, 1,396 *Governor*, M. Shann
†BLAKENHURST, Hewell Lane, Redditch, Worcs B97 6QS *Prisoners*, 873 *Governor*, F. Parker
BLANTYRE HOUSE, Goudhurst, Cranbrook, Kent TN17 2NH *Prisoners*, 119 *Governor*, J. Wilson
BLUNDESTON, Lowestoft, Suffolk NR32 5BG *Prisoners*, 457 *Governor*, Ms T. Clarke
†‡BRINSFORD, New Road, Featherstone, Wolverhampton WV10 7PY *Prisoners*, 463 *Governor*, T. Watson
†BRISTOL, Cambridge Road, Bristol BS7 8PS *Prisoners*, 586 *Governor*, M. Bell
†BRIXTON, PO Box 369, Jebb Avenue, London SW2 5XF *Prisoners*, 811 *Governor*, J. Podmore
*†‡BROCKHILL, Redditch, Worcester B97 6RD *Prisoners*, 140 *Governor*, B. Treen
†BRONZEFIELD (private prison), Woodthorpe Road, Ashford, Middlesex, TW15 3JX *Prisoners*, 450 *Director*, J. McDowell
*†‡BUCKLEY HALL (private prison), Buckley Farm Lane, Rochdale, Lancs OL12 9DP *Prisoners*, 327 *Governor*, S. Morrison
†BULLINGDON, PO Box 50, Bicester, Oxon OX25 1WD *Prisoners*, 953 *Governor*, S. Saunders
*‡BULLWOOD HALL, High Road, Hockley, Essex SS5 4TE *Prisoners*, 155 *Governor*, T. Hassall
CAMP HILL, Newport, Isle of Wight PO30 5PB *Prisoners*, 574 *Governor*, B. Bennett
CANTERBURY, 46 Longport, Canterbury CT1 1PJ *Prisoners*, 309 *Governor*, H. Rinaldi
†CARDIFF, Knox Road, Cardiff CF24 1UG *Prisoners*, 671 *Governor*, P. Tidball
‡CASTINGTON, Morpeth, Northumberland NE65 9XG *Prisoners*, 313 *Governor*, M. Spencer
CHANNINGS WOOD, Denbury, Newton Abbott, Devon TQ12 6DW *Prisoners*, 661 *Governor*, N. Evans
†‡CHELMSFORD, 200 Springfield Road, Chelmsford, Essex CM2 6LQ *Prisoners*, 593 *Governor*, S. Rodford
COLDINGLEY, Bisley, Woking, Surrey GU24 9EX *Prisoners*, 385 *Governor*, P. McDowell
*COOKHAM WOOD, Rochester, Kent ME1 3LU *Prisoners*, 138 *Governor*, E. Tullet
DARTMOOR, Princetown, Yelverton, Devon PL20 6RR *Prisoners*, 616 *Governor*, C. Sturt
‡DEERBOLT, Bowes Road, Barnard Castle, Co. Durham DL12 9BG *Prisoners*, 479 *Governor*, A. Tallentire
†‡DONCASTER (private prison), Off North Bridge, Marshgate, Doncaster DN5 8UX *Prisoners*, 1,099 *Director*, R. MacFarquar
†DORCHESTER, North Square, Dorchester DT1 1JD *Prisoners*, 234 *Governor*, S. Holland
DOVEGATE (Private prison), Uttoxeter, ST14 8XR *Prisoners*, 858 *Director*, K. Rogers
§DOVER, The Citadel, Western Heights, Dover CT17 9DR *Prisoners*, 280 *Governor*, V. Whitecross
*DOWNVIEW, Sutton Lane, Sutton, Surrey SM2 5PD *Prisoners*, 220 *Governor*, P. Dawson
*DRAKE HALL, Eccleshall, Staffs ST21 6LQ *Prisoners*, 300 *Governor*, J. Huntington
*†DURHAM, Old Elvet, Durham DH1 3HU *Prisoners*, 729 *Governor*, M. Newell
*EAST SUTTON PARK, Sutton Valence, Maidstone, Kent ME17 3DF *Prisoners*, 101 *Governor*, R. Carter
*†‡EASTWOOD PARK, Falfield, Wotton-under-Edge, Glos GL12 8DB *Prisoners*, 336 *Governor*, T. Beeston
*EDMUNDS HILL, Stradishall, Newmarket, Suffolk CB8 9YG *Prisoners*, 288 *Governor*, Sue Doolan
†‡ELMLEY, Church Road, Eastchurch, Sheerness, Kent ME12 4DZ *Prisoners*, 986 *Governor*, C. Bartlett
ERLESTOKE, Devizes, Wilts SN10 5TU *Prisoners*, 417 *Governor*, C. Broom
EVERTHORPE, Brough, E. Yorks HU15 1RB *Prisoners*, 466 *Governor*, A. Rice
†EXETER, New North Road, Exeter EX4 4EX *Prisoners*, 530 *Governor*, I. Mulholland
FEATHERSTONE, New Road, Wolverhampton WV10 7PU *Prisoners*, 611 *Governor*, M. Bolton
†‡FELTHAM, Bedfont Road, Feltham, Middx TW13 4ND *Prisoners*, 674 *Governor*, A. Cross
FORD, Arundel, W. Sussex BN18 0BX *Prisoners*, 515 *Governor*, F. Radford
FOREST BANK (private prison), Agecroft Road, Pendlebury, Manchester M27 8UE *Prisoners*, 991 *Governor*, I. Woods
*FOSTON HALL, Foston, Derbys DE65 5DN *Prisoners*, 231 *Governor*, P. Scriven
FRANKLAND, Brasside, Durham DH1 5YD *Prisoners*, 657 *Governor*, P. Copple
FULL SUTTON, Full Sutton, York YO41 1PS *Prisoners*, 602 *Governor*, B. Mullen
GARTH, Ulnes Walton Lane, Leyland, Preston PR5 3NE *Prisoners*, 662 *Governor*, B. McColm
GARTREE, Gallow Field Road, Market Harborough, Leics LE16 7RP *Prisoners*, 412 *Governor*, R. Daly
†‡GLEN PARVA, Tigers Road, Wigston, Leicester LE18 4TN *Prisoners*, 780 *Governor*, B. Edwards
†GLOUCESTER, Barrack Square, Gloucester GL1 2JN *Prisoners*, 315 *Governor*, D. Chalmers
GRENDON, Grendon Underwood, Aylesbury, Bucks HP18 0TL *Prisoners*, 225 *Governor*, P. Bennett
‡GUYS MARSH, Shaftesbury, Dorset SP7 0AH *Prisoners*, 558 *Governor*, B. Greenbury
§HASLAR, Dolphin Way, Gosport, Hampshire, PO12 2AW *Prisoners*, 116 *Manager*, C. Draper
‡HATFIELD, Thorne Road, Hatfield, Doncaster DN7 6EL *Prisoners*, 180 *Governor*, T. Watson
HAVERIGG, Millom, Cumbria LA18 4NA *Prisoners*, 555 *Governor*, S. McCullagh
HEWELL GRANGE, Redditch, Worcs B97 6QQ *Prisoners*, 168 *Governor*, A. Gomme
†‡HIGH DOWN, Sutton Lane, Sutton, Surrey SM2 5PJ *Prisoners*, 752 *Governor*, S. West
*†‡HIGHPOINT (NORTH AND SOUTH), Stradishall, Newmarket, Suffolk CB8 9YG *Prisoners*, 812 *Governor*, R. Haley
†HINDLEY, Gibson Street, Bickershaw, Wigan, Lancs WN2 5TH *Prisoners*, 512 *Governor*, J. Blake
‡HOLLESLEY BAY COLONY, Woodbridge, Suffolk IP12 3JW *Prisoners*, 299 *Governor*, M. Wood
*†‡HOLLOWAY, Parkhurst Road, London N7 0NU *Prisoners*, 467 *Governor*, E. Willetts
HOLME HOUSE, Holme House Road, Stockton-on-Tees TS18 2QU *Prisoners*, 968 *Governor*, M. Lees
†HULL, Hedon Road, Hull HU9 5LS *Prisoners*, 1,078 *Governor*, M. Read
‡HUNTERCOMBE, Huntercombe Place, Nuffield, Henley-on-Thames RG9 5SB *Prisoners*, 361 *Governor*, E. Jones
KINGSTON, 122 Milton Road, Portsmouth PO3 6AS *Prisoners*, 137 *Governor*, J. Robinson
KIRKHAM, Freckleton Road, Preston PR4 2RN *Prisoners*, 551 *Governor*, S. Lawrence
KIRKLEVINGTON GRANGE, Yarm, Cleveland TS15 9PA *Prisoners*, 223 *Governor*, A. Richer
LANCASTER, The Castle, Lancaster LA1 1YL *Prisoners*, 233 *Governor*, D. Harrison

‡LANCASTER FARMS, Far Moor Lane, Stone Row Head, off Quernmore Road, Lancaster LA1 3QZ
Prisoners, 510 *Governor*, T. Williams
LATCHMERE HOUSE, Church Road, Ham Common, Richmond, Surrey TW10 5HH
Prisoners, 197 *Governor*, T. Hinchliffe
†LEEDS, Armley, Leeds LS12 2TJ
Prisoners, 1,254 *Governor*, I. Blakeman
LEICESTER, Welford Road, Leicester LE2 7AJ
Prisoners, 379 *Governor*, S. Turner
†‡LEWES, Brighton Road, Lewes, E. Sussex BN7 1EA
Prisoners, 486 *Governor*, E. McLennan-Murray
LEYHILL, Wotton-under-Edge, Glos GL12 8BT
Prisoners, 499 *Governor*, R. Booty
†LINCOLN, Greetwell Road, Lincoln LN2 4BD
Prisoners, 460 *Governor*, L. Saunders
§LINDHOLME, Bawtry Road, Hatfield Woodhouse, Doncaster DN7 6EE *Prisoners*, 664 *Governor*, M. Ward
LITTLEHEY, Perry, Huntingdon, Cambs PE28 0SR
Prisoners, 698 *Governor*, J. Morgan
†LIVERPOOL, 68 Hornby Road, Liverpool L9 3DF
Prisoners, 1,427 *Governor*, C. James
LONG LARTIN, South Littleton, Evesham, Worcs WR11 8TZ
Prisoners, 434 *Governor*, N. Leader
LOWDHAM GRANGE (private prison), Lowdham, Notts NG14 7DA *Prisoners*, 519 *Director*, P. Wright
*†‡LOW NEWTON, Brasside, Durham DH1 5AD
Prisoners, 351 *Governor*, D. Thompson
MAIDSTONE, 36 County Road, Maidstone ME14 1UZ
Prisoners, 543 *Governor*, J. Glabally
MANCHESTER, Southall Street, Manchester M60 9AH
Prisoners, 1,223 *Governor*, C. Sheffield
‡MOORLAND CLOSED, Bawtry Road, Hatfield Woodhouse, Doncaster DN7 6BW *Prisoners*, 762 *Governor*, J. Tilley
‡MOORLAND OPEN, Thorne Road, Hatfield, Doncaster DN7 6EL *Prisoners*, 249 *Governor*, J. Tilley
*MORTON HALL, Swinderby, Lincoln LN6 9PT
Prisoners, 368 *Governor*, D. Evans
THE MOUNT, Molyneaux Avenue, Bovingdon, Hemel Hempstead HP3 0NZ *Prisoners*, 753 *Governor*, P. Wailen
*†‡NEW HALL, Dial Wood, Flockton, Wakefield WF4 4AX
Prisoners, 365 *Governor*, S. Snell
‡NORTHALLERTON, 15A East Road, Northallerton, N. Yorks DL6 1NW *Prisoners*, 216 *Governor*, B. Shaw
NORTH SEA CAMP, Freiston, Boston, Lincs PE22 0QX
Prisoners, 296 *Governor*, K. Beaumont
†NORWICH, Mousehold, Norwich NR1 4LU
Prisoners, 738 *Governor*, J. Knight
†NOTTINGHAM, Perry Road, Sherwood, Nottingham NG5 3AG *Prisoners*, 493 *Governor*, A. Beck
‡ONLEY, Willoughby, Rugby, Warks CV23 8AP
Prisoners, 490 *Governor*, A. Perry
†‡PARC (private prison), Heol Hopcyn John, Bridgend CF35 6AR *Prisoners*, 1,030 *Director*, R. Woolford
†PARKHURST, Newport, Isle of Wight PO30 5NX
Prisoners, 498 *Governor*, S. Metcalf
†PENTONVILLE, Caledonian Road, London N7 8TT
Prisoners, 1,190 *Governor*, R. Kringle
‡PORTLAND, Easton, Portland, Dorset DT5 1DL
Prisoners, 467 *Governor*, S. Twinn
†PRESTON, 2 Ribbleton Lane, Preston PR1 5AB
Prisoners, 674 *Governor*, A. Brown
RANBY, Ranby, Retford, Notts DN22 8EU
Prisoners, 858 *Governor*, P. Wragg
†‡READING, Forbury Road, Reading RG1 3HY
Prisoners, 263 *Governor*, P. Bryant
*RISLEY, Risley, Warrington WA3 6BP *Prisoners*, 1,059. *Governor*, P. Norbury
†‡ROCHESTER, 1 Fort Road, Rochester, Kent ME1 3QS
Prisoners, 281 *Governor*, C. Kershaw
RYE HILL (private prison), Onley, Rugby CV23 8AM
Prisoners, 661 *Director*, S. Mitson
*SEND, Ripley Road, Send, Woking, Surrey GU23 7LJ
Prisoners, 211 *Governor*, B. Ritchie
SHEPTON MALLET, Cornhill, Shepton Mallet, Somerset BA4 5LU *Prisoners*, 186 *Governor*, S. Dymond-White
†SHREWSBURY, The Dana, Shrewsbury SY1 2HR
Prisoners, 329 *Governor*, M. Boulton
SPRING HILL, Grendon Underwood, Aylesbury, Bucks, HP18 0TH *Prisoners*, 330 *Governor*, P. Bennett
STAFFORD, 54 Gaol Road, Stafford ST16 3AW
Prisoners, 632 *Governor*, P. L. J. Taylor
STANDFORD HILL, Church Road, Eastchurch, Isle of Sheppey, Kent ME12 4AA
Prisoners, 453 *Governor*, T. Robson
STOCKEN, Stocken Hall Road, Stretton, nr Oakham, Leics LE15 7RD *Prisoners*, 619 *Governor*, M. Bartlett
‡STOKE HEATH, Stoke Heath, Market Drayton, Shropshire TF9 2JL *Prisoners*, 667 *Governor*, P. Small
*†‡STYAL, Wilmslow, Cheshire SK9 4HR
Prisoners, 408 *Governor*, S. Hall
SUDBURY, Ashbourne, Derbys DE6 5HW
Prisoners, 554 *Governor*, C. Davidson
SWALESIDE, Brabazon Road, Eastchurch, Isle of Sheppey, Kent ME12 4AX *Prisoners*, 771 *Governor*, M. Conway
†SWANSEA, 200 Oystermouth Road, Swansea SA1 3SR
Prisoners, 335 *Governor*, P. Taylor
‡SWINFEN HALL, Lichfield, Staffs WS14 9QS
Prisoners, 306 *Governor*, P. Knapton
‡THORN CROSS, Arley Road, Appleton Thorn, Warrington WA4 4RL *Prisoners*, 259 *Governor*, M. Moulden
‡USK, 47 Maryport Street, Usk, Gwent NP5 1XP
Prisoners, 248 *Governor*, P. Morgan
THE VERNE, Portland, Dorset DT5 1EQ
Prisoners, 582 *Governor*, M. Cook
WAKEFIELD, 5 Love Lane, Wakefield WF2 9AG
Prisoners, 559 *Governor*, J. Slater
†WANDSWORTH, Heathfield Road, London SW18 3HS
Prisoners, 1,431 *Governor*, J. Heavens
‡WARREN HILL, Hollesley, Woodbridge, Suffolk IP12 3JW
Prisoners, 202 *Governor*, S. Robinson
WAYLAND, Griston, Thetford, Norfolk IP25 6RL
Prisoners, 693 *Governor*, J. Shanley
WEALSTUN, Wetherby, W. Yorks LS23 7AZ
Prisoners, 593 *Governor*, S. Tilley
WEARE, Portland Dock, Castletown, Portland, Dorset DT5 1PZ
Prisoners, 380 *Governor*, D. Calvert
WELLINGBOROUGH, Millers Park, Doddington Road, Wellingborough, Northants NN8 2NH
Prisoners, 522 *Governor*, J. Lewis
‡WERRINGTON, Werrington, Stoke-on-Trent ST9 0DX
Prisoners, 137 *Governor*, F. Flynn
‡WETHERBY, York Road, Wetherby, W. Yorks LS22 5ED
Prisoners, 313 *Governor*, P. Foweather
WHATTON, 14 Cromwell Road, Nottingham NG13 9FQ
Prisoners, 351 *Governor*, V. Hart
WHITEMOOR, Longhill Road, March, Cambs PE15 0PR
Prisoners, 425 *Governor*, M. Lomas
*WINCHESTER, Romsey Road, Winchester SO22 5DF
Prisoners, 639 *Governor*, C. Allison
WOLDS (private prison), Everthorpe, Brough, E. Yorks HU15 2JZ *Prisoners*, 355 *Director*, D. McDonnell
†‡§WOODHILL, Tattenhoe Street, Milton Keynes MK4 4DA
Prisoners, 779 *Governor*, P. Haley
WORMWOOD SCRUBS, PO Box 757, Du Cane Road, London W12 0AE *Prisoners*, 1,227 *Governor*, K. Munns

WYMOTT, Ulnes Walton Lane, Leyland, Preston PR5 3LW
Prisoners, 906 *Governor*, A. Scott

SCOTTISH PRISON SERVICE

Calton House, 5 Redheughs Rigg, Edinburgh EH12 9HW
T 0131-556 8400 **W** www.sps.gov.uk

SALARIES 2003–4

The following pay bands have applied since 1 October 2002 and were scheduled for review by the end of 2004. Senior managers in the Scottish Prison Service, including governors and deputy governors of prisons, are paid across three pay bands:

Band I	£48,000–£58,000
Band H	£38,100–£48,100
Band G	£30,000–£40,000

STAFF

Chief Executive of Scottish Prison Service, T. Cameron
Director, Human Resources, B. Allison
Director, Finance and Information Systems, W. Pretswell
Director, Strategy and Business Performance, K. Thomson
Director, Rehabilitation and Care, A. Spencer
Director of Prisons, M. Duffy
Director of Prison Services, P. Withers
Head of Training, Scottish Prison Service College, W. Rattray
Head of Communications, T. Fox

PRISON ESTABLISHMENTS

Average prisoners numbers *as at 21 May 2004*

*ABERDEEN, Craiginches, 4 Grampian Place, Aberdeen AB1 8FN *Prisoners*, 223 *Governor*, A. Mooney
BARLINNIE, Barlinnie, Glasgow G33 2QX
Prisoners, 1,202 *Governor*, W. McKinlay
CASTLE HUNTLY, Castle Huntly, Longforgan, nr Dundee DD2 5HL *Prisoners*, 155 *Governor*, I. Whitehead
*†CORNTON VALE, Cornton Road, Stirling FK9 5NU
Prisoners, 247 *Governor*, S. Brookes
*DUMFRIES, Terregles Street, Dumfries DG2 9AX
Prisoners, 183 *Governor*, C. McGeever
EDINBURGH, 33 Stenhouse Road, Edinburgh EH11 3LN
Prisoners, 728 *Governor*, D. Croft
GLENOCHIL, King O'Muir Road, Tullibody, Clackmannanshire FK10 3AD *Prisoners*, 484 *Governor*, K. Donegan
GREENOCK, Gateside, Greenock PA16 9AH
Prisoners, 354 *Governor*, S. Swan
*INVERNESS, Porterfield, Duffy Drive, Inverness IV2 3HH
Prisoners, 142 *Governor*, A. MacDonald
KILMARNOCK (private prison), Bowhouse, Mauchline Road, Kilmarnock KA1 5JH
Prisoners, 588 *Governor*, N. Cameron
LOW MOSS, Low Moss, Bishopbriggs, Glasgow G64 2QB
Prisoners, 285 *Governor*, E. Fairbairn
NORANSIDE, Noranside, Fern, by Forfar, Angus DD8 3QY
Prisoners, 136 *Governor*, I. Whitehead
PERTH, 3 Edinburgh Road, Perth PH2 8AT
Prisoners, 704 *Governor*, W. Millar
PETERHEAD, Salthouse Head, Peterhead, Aberdeenshire AB42 2YY *Prisoners*, 295 *Governor*, I. Gunn
†POLMONT, Brightons, Falkirk, Stirlingshire FK2 0AB
Prisoners, 657 *Governor*, D. Gunn
SHOTTS, Shotts ML7 4LE *Prisoners*, 500 *Governor*, A. Park

NORTHERN IRELAND PRISON SERVICE

Dundonald House, Upper Newtownards Road, Belfast BT4 3SU
T 028-9052 2922 **F** 028-9052 5100
E info@niprisonservice.gov.uk
W www.niprisonservice.gov.uk

SALARIES 2004–5

Governor 1	£60,010–£64,673
Governor 2	£54,312–£57,950
Governor 3	£46,763–£50,145
Governor 4	£39,276–£42,962
Governor 5	£33,986–£38,501

A Northern Ireland allowance is also payable

PRISON ESTABLISHMENTS

Average number of prisoners/young offenders *as at September 2004*

‡HYDEBANK WOOD YOC, Hospital Road, Belfast BT8 8NA
Young Offenders, 238
*§MAGHABERRY, Old Road, Ballinderry Upper, Lisburn, Co. Antrim BT28 2PT *Prisoners*, 659
MAGILLIGAN, Point Road, Limavady, Co. Londonderry BT49 0LR *Prisoners*, 328

* Women's establishment or establishment with units for women
† Remand Centre or establishment with units for remand prisoners
‡ Young Offender Institution or establishment with units for young offenders
§ Immigration Removal Centre

DEFENCE

The armed forces of the United Kingdom comprise the Royal Navy, the Army and the Royal Air Force. The Queen is Commander-in-Chief of all the armed forces. The Secretary of State for Defence is responsible for the formulation and content of defence policy and for providing the means by which it is conducted. The formal legal basis for the conduct of defence in the UK rests on a range of powers vested by statute and Letters Patent in the Defence Council, chaired by the Secretary of State for Defence. Beneath the Ministers lies the top management of the Ministry of Defence, headed jointly by the Permanent Secretary and the Chief of Defence Staff. The Permanent Secretary is the Government's principal civilian adviser on defence and has the primary responsibility for policy, finance, management and administration. He is also personally accountable to Parliament for the expenditure of all public money voted for defence purposes. The Chief of the Defence Staff is the professional head of the Armed Forces in the UK and the principal military adviser to the Secretary of State and the Government.

The Defence Management Board (DMB) is the executive board of the Defence Council. Chaired by the Permanent Secretary, it acts as the main executive board of the Ministry of Defence, providing senior level leadership and strategic management of defence.

The Central Staff, headed by the Vice-Chief of the Defence Staff and the Second Permanent Under-Secretary of State is the policy core of the Department. The Defence Procurement Agency is responsible for purchasing equipment. The Defence Logistics Organisation has responsibility for logistic support.

A permanent Joint Headquarters for the conduct of joint operations was set up at Northwood in 1996. The Joint Headquarters connects the policy and strategic functions of the MoD Head Office with the conduct of operations and is intended to strengthen the policy/executive division.

Britain pursues its defence and security policies through its membership of NATO (to which most of its armed forces are committed), the European Union, the Organisation for Security and Co-operation in Europe and the UN (*see* International Organisations section).

ARMED FORCES STRENGTH *as at 1 July 2004*

All Services	205,140
Men	186,800
Women	18,340
Royal Naval Services	40,510
Army	111,500
Royal Air Force	53,130

Source: Ministry of Defence

SERVICE PERSONNEL *as at 1 July 2004*

	Royal Navy	*Army*	*RAF*	*All Services*
1975 strength	76,200	167,100	95,000	338,300
1990 strength	63,210	152,810	89,680	305,700
1999 strength	43,700	109,720	55,210	208,630
2001 strength	42,420	109,530	53,700	205,650
2002 strength	41,630	110,050	53,000	204,680
2003 strength	41,550	112,130	53,240	206,920
2004 strength	40,510	111,500	53,130	205,140

Figures are for UK Regular Forces (including both trained and untrained personnel), and exclude Gurkhas, full-time Reserve Service personnel, the Home Service battalions of the Royal Irish Regiment, mobilised reservists and Naval Activated Reservists.

Source: Ministry of Defence

CIVILIAN PERSONNEL

1993 level	159,600
1999 level	123,000
2000 level	121,300
2001 level	118,200
2002 level	110,100
2003 level	107,600
2004 level	108,990

As of 1 April 2004 the definition of the civilian workforce changed to include permanent and casual personnel, Royal Fleet Auxiliaries, Trading Funds and Locally Engaged civilians. Figures above reflect the revised definition.

Source: *UK Defence Statistics 2004*

DEPLOYMENT OF UK PERSONNEL *as at 1 July 2003**

	England	*Wales*	*Scotland*	*N. Ireland*	*Other*
All Services	139,010	2,100	13,870	5,160	8,580
Officers	23,380	300	1,850	580	1,270
Other Ranks	115,630	1,800	12,020	4,580	7,310
Army‡	69,950	920	3,040	4,620	4,710
Officers	9,770	110	550	490	380
Other Ranks	60,180	810	2,490	4,130	4,330
Navy†‡	31,950	20	4,890	150	660
Officers	6,310	10	570	10	160
Other Ranks	25,640	10	4,320	140	500
RAF‡	37,100	1,160	5,950	390	3,210
Officers	7,290	180	730	80	740
Other Ranks	29,810	980	5,220	310	2,470

*Figures are for UK Regular Forces, both Trained and Untrained, located in the UK. They exclude Gurkhas, full-time Reserve Service personnel, the Home Service battalions of the Royal Irish Regiment and mobilised reservists. These are the most recent figures available from the Ministry of Defence at the time of going to press.

† Naval Service personnel on sea service in home waters are included against the local authority containing the home port of their ship.

‡ The titles Naval Service, Army and Royal Air Force include nursing services.

Source: Ministry of Defence

SERVICE PERSONNEL OVERSEAS *as at 1 October 2002*

	Breakdown	*Total*
All Services		41,980
Officers	5,740	
Other Ranks	36,240	
Army		33,070
Officers	3,840	
Ranks	29,230	
Royal Navy		3,840
Officers	760	
Ranks	3,080	
RAF		5,080
Officers	1,140	
Ranks	3,940	

Source: Ministry of Defence. These are the most recent figures available at the time of going to press.

NUCLEAR FORCES

Britain's nuclear forces comprise four ballistic missile submarines carrying Trident missiles and equipped with nuclear warheads. All nuclear free-fall bombs have been taken out of service.

ARMS CONTROL

The 1990 Conventional Armed Forces in Europe (CFE) Treaty, which commits all NATO and former Warsaw Pact members to limiting their holdings of five major classes of conventional weapons, has been adapted to reflect the changed geo-strategic environment and negotiations continue for its implementation. The Open Skies Treaty, which the UK signed in 1992 and entered into force in 2002, allows for the overflight of States Parties by other States Parties using unarmed observation aircraft.

In 1968 the UK signed and ratified the Nuclear Non-Proliferation Treaty, which came into force in 1970 and was indefinitely and unconditionally extended in 1995. In 1996 the UK signed the Comprehensive Nuclear Test Ban Treaty and ratified it in 1998. The UK is a party to the 1972 Biological and Toxin Weapons Convention, which provides for a world-wide ban on biological weapons, and the 1993 Chemical Weapons Convention, which came into force in 1997 and provides for a verifiable world-wide ban on chemical weapons.

DEFENCE BUDGET (DEPARTMENTAL EXPENDITURE LIMIT PLANS)

Projection	*£ billion*
2003–4	30.8
2004–5	31.5
2005–6	32.3

Source: The Budget 2003

MINISTRY OF DEFENCE

Old War Office, Whitehall, London SW1A 2EU
T 020-7218 9000 Public Enquiry Office 020-7218 6645
W www.mod.uk

Officers promoted in an acting capacity to a more senior rank are listed under the more senior rank. Promotion to five-star rank is no longer usual in peacetime.

GRADE EQUIVALENTS

Grade 1 equivalents: (5*) Admiral of the Fleet, (5*) Field Marshal, (5*) Marshal of the RAF, (4*) Admiral, (4*) General, (4*) Air Chief Marshal

Grade 2 equivalents: (3*) Vice Admiral, (3*) Lieutenant-General, (3*) Air Marshal

Secretary of State for Defence, The Rt. Hon. Geoffrey Hoon, MP
Private Secretary, C. Baker
Special Advisers, R. Taylor; M. Dogher
Parliamentary Private Secretary, Liz Blackman, MP
Minister of State for the Armed Forces, The Rt. Hon. Adam Ingram, MP
Parliamentary Private Secretary, Alan Campbell, MP
Team PPS, Syd Rapson, MP
Private Secretary, G. Dean
Parliamentary Under-Secretary of State for Defence and Minister for Defence Procurement, Lord Bach
Private Secretary, B. Palmer
Parliamentary Under-Secretary of State for Defence and Minister for Veterans, Ivor Caplin, MP
Private Secretary, A. Cruttwell
Permanent Under-Secretary of State, Sir Kevin Tebbit, KCB, CMG
Chief of Defence Staff, Gen. Sir Michael Walker GCB, CMG, CBE, ADC, Gen
Second Permanent Under-Secretary, Ian Andrews, CBE, TD

THE DEFENCE COUNCIL

The Defence Council is the Senior Committee of the Ministry of Defence, which was established by Royal Prerogative under the Letters Patent in April 1964. The Letters Patent confer on the Defence Council the command over all of the Armed Forces and charge the Council with such matters relating to the administration of the Armed Forces as the Secretary of State for Defence should direct them to execute. It is chaired by the Secretary of State for Defence and consists of: the Minister of State for the Armed Forces, the Parliamentary Under-Secretary of State for Defence and Minister for Defence Procurement, the Parliamentary Under-Secretary of State for Defence and Minister for Veterans; the Permanent Under-Secretary of State, the Chief of the Defence Staff; the Chief of the Naval Staff and First Sea Lord, the Chief of the General Staff, the Chief of the Air Staff; the Vice-Chief of the Defence Staff, the Second Permanent Under-Secretary of State, the Chief Scientific Advisor, the Chief of Defence Procurement and the Chief of Defence Logistics.

CHIEFS OF STAFF

CHIEF OF THE NAVAL STAFF

First Sea Lord and Chief of the Naval Staff (4)*, Adm. Sir Alan West, GCB, DSC, ADC
Asst Chief of the Naval Staff (2)*, Rear-Adm. A. J. Johns, CBE

CHIEF OF GENERAL STAFF

Chief of the General Staff (4)*, Gen. Sir Mike Jackson, KCB, CBE, DSO, ADC
Asst Chief of the General Staff (2)*, Maj.-Gen. D. J. Richards, CBE, DSO

CHIEF OF THE AIR STAFF

Chief of the Air Staff (4)*, Air Chief Marshal Sir Jock Stirrup, KCB, AFC, ADC
Asst Chief of the Air Staff (2)*, Air Vice-Marshal, D. Walker, CBE, AFC

CENTRAL STAFFS

Vice-Chief of the Defence Staff, Air Chief Marshal Sir Anthony Bagnall, GBE, KCB
Second Permanent Under-Secretary, Ian Andrews, CBE, TD

DEFENCE INTELLIGENCE STAFF

Old War Office, Whitehall, London SW1A 2EU
T 020-7218 6645 F 020-7218 1562
Chief of Defence Intelligence (3)*, Lt.-Gen. A. P. Ridgway, CBE
Deputy Chief of Defence Intelligence, Martin Howard

DEFENCE SCIENTIFIC STAFF

Chief Scientific Adviser, Prof. Sir Keith O'Nions, FRS
Science and Technology Director and Director-General of Research and Technology, M. Markin, OBE

COMMANDER-IN-CHIEF FLEET

C.-in-C. Fleet, Adm. Sir Jonathon Band, KCB
Deputy C.-in-C. Fleet, Vice-Adm. T. McClement, OBE

SECOND SEA LORD/COMMANDER-IN-CHIEF NAVAL HOME COMMAND

Second Sea Lord and C.-in-C. Naval Home Command, Vice-Adm. Sir James Burnell-Nugent, KCB, CBE, ADC
Chief of Staff to Second Sea Lord and C.-in-C. Naval Home Command, Rear-Adm. R. Melly

ADJUTANT-GENERAL'S DEPARTMENT

Adjutant-General, Lt.-Gen. Sir Alistair Irwin, KCB, CBE
Deputy Adjutant-General and Director-General Service Conditions, Maj.-Gen. Currie

COMMANDER-IN-CHIEF LAND COMMAND

C.-in-C., Land Command, Gen. Sir Timothy Granville-Chapman, KCB, CBE, ADC
Chief of Staff, HQ Land Command, Maj.-Gen. A. R. D. Shirreff, CBE

HQ STRIKE COMMAND

Air Officer Commanding-in-Chief, Air Chief Marshal Brian Burridge, KCB, CBE, ADC
Deputy Commander-in-Chief Strike Command, Air Marshal C. R. Loader, OBE

HQ PERSONNEL AND TRAINING COMMAND

Air Member for Personnel and Commander-in-Chief Personnel and Training Command, Air Marshal Sir Joe French, KCB, CBE
Chief of Staff and Deputy Commander-in-Chief Personnel and Training Command, Air Vice-Marshal J. A. Collier, CBE

DEFENCE PROCUREMENT AGENCY

215 MOD Abbey Wood, Bristol BS34 8JH
T 0117-913 0000 F 0117-913 0902
W www.mod.uk/dpa
Chief of Defence Procurement and Chief Executive, DPA, Vice-Adm. Sir Peter Spencer, KCB

EXECUTIVE AGENCIES

DEFENCE LOGISTICS ORGANISATION (DLO)

DLO Headquarters, Spur 4, E Block, Ensleigh, Bath BA1 5AB
Chief of Defence Logistics, Air Chief Marshal Sir Malcolm Pledger, KCB, OBE, AFC

DLO'S BUSINESS UNITS

ARMY BASE REPAIR ORGANISATION (ABRO), Building 203, Portway, Monxton Road, Andover, Hampshire SP11 8HT T 01264-383295
BRITISH FORCES POST OFFICE (BFPO), Inglis Barracks, Mill Hill, London NW7 1PX T 08457-697978
CORPORATE TECHNICAL SERVICES (CTS), DLO, Monxton Road, Andover SP11 8HT T 01264-382515
DEFENCE CATERING GROUP, Spur 12, Beckford, Ensleigh, Bath BA1 5AB T 01225-467943
DEFENCE COMMUNCATIONS SERVICES AGENCY (DCSA), Building 111, Basil Hill Site, Park Lane, Corsham, Wilts SN13 9NR T 01225-467733
DEFENCE FUELS GROUP, West Moors, Wimborne, Dorset BH21 6QS T 01202-654351
DEFENCE STORAGE AND DISTRIBUTION AGENCY, Ploughley Road, Lower Arncott, Bicester, Oxon OX25 2LD T 01869-256840
DEFENCE TRANSPORT AND MOVEMENTS AGENCY (DTMA), Building 400, DLO Andover, Monxton Road, Andover, Hampshire SP11 8HJ T 01264-381125
EQUIPMENT SUPPORT (AIR AND LAND), DLO Secretariat (Strike), Room J103, Cranswick House, RAF Wyton, Huntingdon, Cambs PE28 2EA T 01480-452451
PAYD PROJECT, Building 209, DLO Andover, Monxton Road, Andover, Hants SP11 8HT T 01264-348051
WARSHIP SUPPORT AGENCY, MOD Abbey Wood, Bristol, BS34 8SH T 0117-913 7505

OTHER EXECUTIVE AGENCIES

ARMED FORCES PERSONNEL ADMINISTRATION AGENCY (AFPAA), Building 182, RAF Innsworth, Gloucester GL3 1HW T 01452-712612, ext. 7347
ARMY PERSONNEL CENTRE (APC), Kentigern House, 65 Brown Street, Glasgow G2 8EX T 0141-244 2023
ARMY TRAINING AND RECRUITING AGENCY, Building 370, Trenchard Lines, Upavon, Pewsey, Wilts SN9 6BE T 01980-618009
DEFENCE ANALYTICAL SERVICES AGENCY (DASA), Room 711 St Giles Court, 1–13 St Giles High Street, London WC2H 8LD T 020-7218 0390
DEFENCE AVIATION REPAIR AGENCY (DARA), Head Office, Building 145, St Athan, Barry, Vale of Glamorgan CF62 4WA T 01446-798834
DEFENCE BILLS AGENCY (DBA), Room 410, Mersey House, Drury Lane, Liverpool L2 7PX T 0151-242 2225
DEFENCE DENTAL AGENCY (DDA), RAF Halton, Aylesbury, Bucks HP22 5PG T 01296-623535
DEFENCE ESTATES, St George's House, Blakemore Drive, Sutton Coldfield, W. Midlands B75 7RL T 0121-311 2140
DEFENCE GEOGRAPHIC AND IMAGERY INTELLIGENCE AGENCY, Watson Building, Elmwood Avenue, Feltham TW13 7AH T 020-8818 2119
DEFENCE HOUSING EXECUTIVE, 6th Floor, Ibex House, 42–47 Minories, London EC3N 1DY T 020-7423 4815

DEFENCE INTELLIGENCE AND SECURITY CENTRE (DISC), Chicksands, Shefford, Beds SG17 5PR T 01462-752181

DEFENCE MEDICAL EDUCATION AND TRAINING AGENCY (DMETA), MacKenzie Building, Fort Blockhouse, Gosport, Hampshire PO12 2AB T 023-9276 5141

DEFENCE PROCUREMENT AGENCY (DPA), Maple 2120, MOD Abbey Wood, Bristol BS34 8JH T 0117-913 0000

DEFENCE SCIENCE AND TECHNOLOGY LABORATORY (DSTL), Porton Down, Salisbury, Wiltshire SP4 OJQ T 01980-613121

DEFENCE VETTING AGENCY, Building 107, Imphal Barracks, Fulford Road, York YO10 4AS T 01904-662444

DISPOSAL SERVICES AGENCY, St George's Court, 2–12 Bloomsbury Way, London WC1A 2SH T 020-7305 2588

THE DUKE OF YORK'S ROYAL MILITARY SCHOOL (DYRMS), Dover, Kent CT15 5EQ T 01304-245029

MEDICAL SUPPLIES AGENCY, Drummond Barracks, Ludgershall, Andover, Hants SP11 9RU T 01264-798622

MET OFFICE, Fitzroy Road, Exeter, EX1 3PB T 0870-900 0100

MINISTRY OF DEFENCE POLICE, Wethersfield, Braintree, Essex CM7 4AZ T 01371-854000

NAVAL MANNING AGENCY, Victory Building, HM Naval Base, Portsmouth PO1 3LS T 023-9272 7422

NAVAL RECRUITING AND TRAINING AGENCY (NRTA), Victory Building, HM Naval Base, Portsmouth PO1 3LS T 023-9272 7603

PAY AND PERSONNEL AGENCY, PO Box 99, Bath BA1 5AA T 01225-828105

QUEEN VICTORIA SCHOOL, Dunblane, Perthshire FK15 0JY T 01786-822288

QINETIQ, Ively Road, Farnborough, Hampshire GU14 0LX T 01980-613121

RAF PERSONNEL MANAGEMENT AGENCY, Building 248, RAF Innsworth, Gloucester GL3 1EZ T 01452-712612

RAF TRAINING GROUP DEFENCE AGENCY, RAF Innsworth, Gloucester GL3 1EZ T 01452-712612, ext. 5302

SERVICE CHILDREN'S EDUCATION, HQ UKSCE, Building 5, Wegberg Military Complex, BFPO 40

UNITED KINGDOM HYDROGRAPHIC OFFICE, Admiralty Way, Taunton, Somerset TA1 2DN T 01823-337900

VETERANS AGENCY, Tomlinson House, Norcross, Blackpool, FY5 3WP T 0800-169 2277

THE ROYAL NAVY

LORD HIGH ADMIRAL OF THE UNITED KINGDOM
HM The Queen

ADMIRALS OF THE FLEET
HRH The Prince Philip, Duke of Edinburgh, KG, KT, OM, GBE, AC, QSO, PC, *apptd* 1953
Sir Michael Pollock, GCB, LVO, DSC, *apptd* 1974
Sir Edward Ashmore, GCB, DSC, *apptd* 1977
Sir Henry Leach, GCB, *apptd* 1982
Sir Julian Oswald, GCB, *apptd* 1993
Sir Benjamin Bathurst, GCB, *apptd* 1995

ADMIRALS
West, Sir Alan, GCB, DSC, ADC *(First Sea Lord and Chief of Naval Staff)*
Garnett, Sir Ian, KCB *(Chief of Staff Supreme Headquarters Allied Powers Europe)*
Forbes, Sir Ian, KCB, CBE *(Former Deputy Supreme Allied Commander Transformation)*
Band, Sir Jonathon, KCB *(C.-in-C. Fleet, C.-in-C. East Atlantic, and Commander Allied Naval Forces North)*
Stanhope, Sir Mark, KCB, OBE *(Deputy Supreme Allied Commander Transformation)*

VICE-ADMIRALS
Haddacks, Sir Paul, KCB *(Director of International Military Staff, NATO)*
Burnell-Nugent, Sir James Michael, KCB, CBE, ADC *(Second Sea Lord and C.-in-C. Naval Home Command)*
Dunt, Peter Arthur, CB *(Chief Executive Defence Estate Agency)*
McClement, Timothy, OBE *(Deputy C.-in-C. Fleet)*

REAR-ADMIRALS
HRH The Princess Royal, KG, KT, GCVO *(Chief Commandant for Women in the Royal Navy)*
Stevens, Robert Patrick, CB *(Chief of Staff to Commander Allied Naval Forces, Southern Europe)*
Ward, Rees Graham John, CB *(Chief Executive, Defence Communications Services Agency)*
Guild, Nigel Charles Forbes, CB *(Director-General Capability (Carrier Strike) Chief Naval Engineer Officer)*
Dymock, Anthony Knox, CB *(Head of British Defence Staff, Washington)*
Reeve, Jonathon, CB *(Deputy Chief Executive, Warship Support Agency and Navy Member for Logistics)*
Lockwood, Roger Graham *(Senior Naval Member of the Directing Staff Royal College of Defence Studies)*
McLean, Rory Alistair Ian, CB, OBE *(Asst Chief of the Defence Staff (Resources and Planning))*
Davies, Peter Roland, CBE *(Flag Officer Training and Recruiting and Chief Executive, Naval Recruiting and Training Agency)*
Kilgour, Niall Stuart Roderick *(Commander (Operations) to C.-in-C. Fleet and Rear-Adm. Submarines)*
Style, Charles Rodney, CBE *(Commander, UK Maritime Force)*
Kerr, Mark William Graham *(Naval Secretary and Chief Executive, Naval Manning Agency)*
Boissier, Robin Paul *(Deputy Commander Strike Force South)*
Cheadle, Richard Frank *(Defence Procurement Agency Executive Director 4, Controller of the Navy)*
Goodall, Simon Richard James, CBE *(Director-General Training and Education)*
Snelson, David George, CB *(Chief of Staff (Warfare) to C.-in-C. Fleet)*
Harris, Nicholas Henry Linton, MBE *(Flag Officer Scotland, N. England and N. Ireland, and Naval Base Commander Clyde)*
Johns, Adrian James, CBE *(Assistant Chief of Naval Staff)*
Chittenden, Timothy Clive *(Chief of Staff (Support) to C.-in-C. Fleet)*
Spires, Trevor Allan *(Chief Executive Armed Forces Personnel Administration Agency)*
Melly, Richard Graham *(Chief of Staff to Second Sea Lord and Commander-in-Chief Naval Home Command)*
Wilcocks, Philip Lawrence *(Deputy Chief of Joint Operations (Operational Support))*
Ainsley, Roger Stewart *(Flag Officer Sea Training)*
Soar, Trevor Alan, OBE *(Capability Manager (Precision Attack))*
Lambert, Paul *(Commander (Operations) Fleet, Rear-Adm. Submarines (as Head of Fighting ARM), Commander Submarine Allied Naval Forces)*

HM FLEET *as at 1 September 2004*

SUBMARINES	
Vanguard Class	Vanguard, Vengeance, Victorious, Vigilant
Swiftsure Class	Sceptre, Sovereign, Spartan, Superb
Trafalgar Class	Talent, Tireless, Torbay, Trafalgar, Trenchant, Triumph, Turbulent
AIRCRAFT CARRIERS	Ark Royal, Illustrious, Invincible
AMPHIBIOUS ASSAULT SHIP	Ocean, Albion
DESTROYERS	
Type 42 Batch 1	Cardiff, Glasgow, Newcastle
Type 42 Batch 2	Exeter, Liverpool, Nottingham, Southampton
Type 42 Batch 3	Edinburgh, Gloucester, Manchester, York
FRIGATES	
Type 23	Argyll, Grafton, Iron Duke, Kent, Lancaster, Marlborough, Monmouth, Montrose, Norfolk, Northumberland, Portland, Richmond, St Albans, Somerset, Sutherland, Westminster
Type 22	Campbeltown, Chatham, Cornwall, Cumberland
MINEHUNTERS	
Hunt Class	Atherstone, Brecon, Brocklesby, Cattistock, Chiddingfold, Cottesmore, Dulverton, Hurworth, Ledbury, Middleton, Quorn
Sandown Class	Bangor, Blyth, Bridport, Grimsby, Inverness, Pembroke, Penzance, Ramsey, Sandown, Shoreham, Walney

PATROL CRAFT	
Archer Class P2000 Fast Training Boats	Archer, Biter, Blazer, Charger, Dasher, Example, Exploit, Explorer, Express, Puncher, Pursuer, Raider, Smiter, Tracker, Ranger, Trumpeter
Gibraltar Squadron 16m Fast Patrol Class	Sabre, Scimitar
Castle Class Patrol Vessels	Leeds Castle, Dumbarton Castle
River Class Patrol Vessels	Tyne, Mersey, Severn
SURVEY VESSELS	
Antarctic Patrol Ship	Endurance
Ocean Survey Vessels	Scott
Coastal Survey Vessels	Roebuck, Gleaner
Multi-Role Survey Vessels	HMS Echo, HMS Enterprise

OTHER PARTS OF THE NAVAL SERVICE

ROYAL MARINES

The Royal Marines were formed in 1664 and are part of the Naval Service. Their primary purpose is to conduct amphibious and land warfare. The principal operational units are 3 Commando Brigade Royal Marines, an amphibious all-arms brigade trained to operate in arduous environments, which is a core element of the UK's Joint Rapid Reaction Force; Fleet Protection Group Royal Marines, which is responsible for the security of nuclear weapon facilities; and Special Boat Service, the maritime special forces. The Royal Marines also provide detachments for warships and land-based naval parties as required. The headquarters of the Royal Marines is at Portsmouth and principal bases are at Plymouth, Arbroath, Poole, Taunton and Chivenor. The Corps of Royal Marines is about 6,500 strong.

Representative Colonel Commandant, Royal Marines, Lt.-Gen. R. H. G. Fulton
Deputy Commander, NATO Rapid Deployable Corps Italy, Maj.-Gen. R. G. T. Lane, CBE
Commandant-General, Royal Marines, Maj.-Gen. J. B. Dutton, CBE

ROYAL MARINES RESERVES (RMR)

The Royal Marines Reserve is a commando-trained volunteer force with the principal role, when mobilised, of supporting the Royal Marines. The current strength of the RMR is about 1,000.

Commanding Officer, RMR, Lt.-Col. E. C. Musto

ROYAL FLEET AUXILIARY SERVICE (RFA)

The Royal Fleet Auxiliary Service is a civilian-manned flotilla of 20 ships. Its primary role is to supply the Royal Navy at sea with fuel, ammunition, food and stores, enabling it to maintain operations away from its home ports. It also provides secure logistic support and amphibious operations for the Army and Royal Marines, and forward ship maintenance and repair and sea-borne aviation training facilities for the Royal Navy.

FLEET AIR ARM

The Fleet Air Arm (FAA) provides the Royal Navy with a multi-role aviation combat capability able to operate autonomously at short notice world-wide in all environments, over the sea and land. The FAA has some 6,200 people, which comprises 11.5 per cent of the total Royal Naval strength. It operates some 200 combat aircraft and more than 50 support/training aircraft.

ROYAL NAVAL RESERVE (RNR)

The Royal Naval Reserve is an integral part of the Naval Service. It comprises up to 3,850 men and women nationwide who volunteer to train in their spare time to enable the Royal Navy to meet its operational commitments, at sea and ashore, in crisis or war.

The standard annual training commitment is 24 days, including 12 days' continuous operational training.

Director, Naval Reserves, Capt. S. J. Timms, OBE

QUEEN ALEXANDRA'S ROYAL NAVAL NURSING SERVICE

The first nursing sisters were appointed to naval hospitals in 1884 and the Queen Alexandra's Royal Naval Nursing Service (QARNNS) gained its current title in 1902. Nursing ratings were introduced in 1960 and men were integrated into the Service in 1982; QARNNS recruits qualified nurses as both officers and ratings and student nurse training can be undertaken in the Service.

Patron, HRH Princess Alexandra, the Hon. Lady Ogilvy, GCVO
Matron-in-Chief and Director of Naval Nursing Services, Capt. L. Gibbon

THE ARMY

THE QUEEN

FIELD MARSHALS
HRH The Prince Philip, Duke of Edinburgh, KG, KT, OM, GBE, AC, QSO, PC, *apptd* 1953
HRH The Duke of Kent, KG, GCMG, GCVO, ADC, *apptd* 1993
Sir Roland Gibbs, GCB, CBE, DSO, MC, *apptd* 1979
The Lord Bramall, KG, GCB, OBE, MC, *apptd* 1982
The Lord Vincent of Coleshill, GBE, KCB, DSO, *apptd* 1991
Sir John Stanier, GCB, MBE, *apptd* 1985
Sir John Chapple, GCB, CBE, *apptd* 1992
The Lord Inge, KG, GCB, DL, *apptd* 1994

GENERALS
Walker, Sir Michael, GCB, CMG, CBE, ADC, Gen *(Chief of the Defence Staff)*
Jackson, Sir Mike, KCB, CBE, DSO, ADC, Col. Cmdt. Parachute Regiment, Col. Cmdt. AG Corps, Hon. Col. The Rifle Volunteers *(Chief of the General Staff)*
Granville-Chapman, Sir Timothy, KCB, CBE, ADC, Gen *(C-in-C. Land Command)*

LIEUTENANT-GENERALS
Irwin, Sir Alistair, KCB, CBE, *(Adjutant-General)*
McColl, J. C., CBE, DSO *(Senior British Military Representative – Iraq)*
Delves, Sir Cedric, KBE, DSO *(Held Strength)*
O'Donoghue, K., CBE *(Deputy Chief of the Defence Staff (Health))*
Reith, Sir John, KCB, CBE *(Chief of Joint Operations Permanent Joint Headquarters)*
Kiszely, Sir John, KCB, MC *(Commander Regional Forces Land Command)*
Palmer, A. M. D., CBE *(Deputy Chief of the Defence Staff (Personnel))*
HRH The Prince of Wales, KG, KT, GCB and Great Master of the Order of the Bath, OM, QSO, PC, ADC(P)
Trousdell, P. C. C., KBE, CB *(General Officer Commanding Northern Ireland)*
Ridgway, A. P., CB, CBE *(Chief of Defence Intelligence)*
Dannatt, F. R., KCB, CBE, MC *(Commander Allied Rapid Reaction Corps)*
Watt, Sir Redmond, KVCO, CBE *(Commander Field Army Land Command)*
Judd, D. L., CB *(Deputy Commander in Chief, North Europe)*

MAJOR-GENERALS
Raper, A. J., CBE *(Defence Logistics Transformation Team Leader/Quartermaster General)*
Viggers, F. R., MBE *(Military Secretary)*
Moore-Bick, J. D., CBE, *(GOC United Kingdom Support Command Germany)*
Gordon, R. D. S., CBE *(Force Commander UN Mission to Ethiopia and Eritrea)*
Brims, R. V., CBE, *(Deputy Chief Joint Operations (Operations) Permanent Joint Headquarters)*
Gilchrist, P. *(Technical Director, Defence Procurement Agency/Master General of the Ordnance)*
Cross, T., CBE *(End to End Implementation Team Leader)*
Figgures, A. C., CBE *(Technical Director, Defence Procurement Agency)*
Gamon, J. A., CBE, QHDS *(Chief Executive of the Defence Dental Agency)*
Richards, D. J., CBE, DSO *(Assistant Chief to the General Staff)*
Shaw, J. M., MBE *(GOC Theatre Troops Land Command)*
Baxter, R., CBE *(Commandant Royal Military College of Science)*
Ritchie, A.S., CBE *(Commandant Royal Military Academy, Sandhurst)*
Bailey, J. B. A., MBE *(Director-General Development and Doctrine)*
Cima, K. H., *(Senior Army Member, Royal College of Defence Studies)*
Williams, P. G., OBE *(Head of NATO Military Liaison Mission Moscow)*
Short, J. H. T., OBE, *(Chief of Staff Joint Headquarters (North)*
Lamb, G. C. M., CMG, OBE, DSO *(GOC 3rd (UK) Division)*
Rollo, W. R., CBE *(GOC (Designate) Multi-National Division (South East))*
Leakey, A. D., CBE *(Director-General Army Training and Recruiting)*
Wood, M. D., CBE *(Director-General Logistics (Supply Chain))*
Huntley, M., *(Director-General Logistics (Land))*
Wall, P. A., CBE *(GOC 1st (UK) Armoured Division)*
Cottam, N. J., OBE *(GOC 5th Division)*
Shirreff, A. R. D., CBE *(Chief of Staff HQ, Land Command)*
Duncan, A. D. A., DSO, OBE *(Director-General Training Support (Land))*
Houghton, J. N. R., CBE *(Assistant Chief of the Defence Staff (Operations))*
Pearson, P. T. C., CBE *(Commander British Forces Cyprus)*
Howell, D. M., OBE *(Director Army Legal Services)*
Lillywhite, L. P., MBE, QHS *(Director-General Army Medical Services)*
HRH The Duke of Westminster, KG, OBE, TD, DL *(Assistant Chief of the Defence Staff (Reserves and Cadets))*
Applegate, R. A. D., OBE *(Capability Manager (Battlefield Manouvre))*
Tyler, T. N. *(Deputy Adjutant-General and Director-General Service Conditions (Army))*
Loudon, W. E. B., OBE *(GOC 2nd Division)*
Kerr, J. S., CBE *(GOC 4th Division)*
Roberts, S. J. L., OBE *(GOC London District)*
Bill, D. R. *(GOC United Kingdom Support Command (Germany))*
Whitley, A. E., CBE, CMG *(Senior British Loan Service Officer, Oman)*
Fleet, A. R., OBE *(Kosovo Protection Corps Co-ordinator)*
Graham, A. J. N., CBE *(Deputy Commanding General Multi-National Corps, Iraq)*
Stewart, A. R. E. de C., CBE *(GOC Multi-National Division (South-East))*
Cooper, J., DSO *(Deputy Commander Combined Force Command, Afghanistan)*
Brown, C. C., OBE *(Chief of Staff Allied Rapid Reaction Corps)*
Wilkes, Revd D. E., QHC *(Chaplain General)*

CONSTITUTION OF THE ARMY

The regular forces include the following arms, branches and corps. They are listed in accordance with the order of precedence within the British Army. All enquiries with regard to records of serving personnel (Regular and Territorial Army) should be directed to: Relations with the Public, Army Personnel Office, Kentigern House, 65 Brown Street, Glasgow G2 8EX T 0141–224 2023/3303

THE ARMS

HOUSEHOLD CAVALRY – The Household Cavalry Regiment (The Life Guards and The Blues and Royals)

ROYAL ARMOURED CORPS – Cavalry Regiments: 1st The Queen's Dragoon Guards; The Royal Scots Dragoon Guards (Carabiniers and Greys); The Royal Dragoon Guards; The Queen's Royal Hussars (The Queen's Own and Royal Irish); 9th/12th Royal Lancers (Prince of Wales's); The King's Royal Hussars; The Light Dragoons; The Queen's Royal Lancers; Royal Tank Regiment, comprising two regular regiments

ARTILLERY – Royal Regiment of Artillery

ENGINEERS – Corps of Royal Engineers

SIGNALS – Royal Corps of Signals

THE INFANTRY

The Foot Guards and regiments of Infantry of the Line are grouped in divisions as follows:

GUARDS DIVISION – Grenadier, Coldstream, Scots, Irish and Welsh Guards. *Divisional Office*, HQ Infantry, Warminster Training Centre, Warminster, Wilts. *Training Centre*, Infantry Training Centre, Vimy Barracks, Catterick, N. Yorks

SCOTTISH DIVISION – The Royal Scots (The Royal Regiment); The Royal Highland Fusiliers (Princess Margaret's Own Glasgow and Ayrshire Regiment); The King's Own Scottish Borderers; The Black Watch (Royal Highland Regiment); The Highlanders (Seaforth, Gordons and Camerons); The Argyll and Sutherland Highlanders (Princess Louise's). *Divisional Office*, HQ Infantry, Warminster Training Centre, Warminster, Wilts. *Training Centre*, Infantry Training Centre, Vimy Barracks, Catterick, N. Yorks

QUEEN'S DIVISION – The Princess of Wales's Royal Regiment (Queen's and Royal Hampshire's); The Royal Regiment of Fusiliers; The Royal Anglian Regiment. *Divisional Office*, HQ Infantry, Warminster Training Centre, Warminster, Wilts. *Training Centre*, Infantry Training Centre, Vimy Barracks, Catterick, N. Yorks

KING'S DIVISION – The King's Own Royal Border Regiment; The King's Regiment; The Prince of Wales's Own Regiment of Yorkshire; The Green Howards (Alexandra, Princess of Wales's Own Yorkshire Regiment); The Queen's Lancashire Regiment; The Duke of Wellington's Regiment (West Riding). *Divisional Office*, HQ Infantry, Warminster Training Centre, Warminster, Wilts. *Training Centre*, Infantry Training Centre, Vimy Barracks, Catterick, N. Yorks

PRINCE OF WALES'S DIVISION – The Devonshire and Dorset Regiment; The Cheshire Regiment; The Royal Welch Fusiliers; The Royal Regiment of Wales (24th/41st Foot); The Royal Gloucestershire, Berkshire and Wiltshire Regiment; The Worcestershire and Sherwood Foresters Regiment (29th/45th Foot); The Staffordshire Regiment (The Prince of Wales's). *Divisional Office*, HQ Infantry, Warminster Training Centre, Warminster, Wilts. *Training Centre*, Infantry Training Centre, Vimy Barracks, Catterick, N. Yorks

LIGHT DIVISION – The Light Infantry; The Royal Green Jackets. *Divisional Office*, HQ Infantry, Warminster Training Centre, Warminster, Wilts. *Training Centre*, Infantry Training Centre, Vimy Barracks, Catterick, N. Yorks

THE ROYAL IRISH REGIMENT (one general service and three home service battalions) (27th (Inniskilling), 83rd, 87th and the Ulster Defence Regiment). *Regimental HQ* and *Training Centre*, St Patrick's Barracks, BFPO 808

BRIGADE OF GURKHAS – The Royal Gurkha Rifles; The Queen's Gurkha Engineers; Queen's Gurkha Signals; The Queen's Own Gurkha Logistic Regiment. *Regimental HQ*, Airfield Camp, Netheravon, Wilts. *Gurkha Company*, Infantry Training Centre, Vimy Barracks, Catterick, N. Yorks

THE PARACHUTE REGIMENT (three regular battalions) – *Regimental HQ*, Flagstaff House, Colchester, Essex. *Training Centre*, Infantry Training Centre, Vimy Barracks, Catterick, N. Yorks

SPECIAL AIR SERVICE REGIMENT – Stirling Lines, Hereford

ARMY AIR CORPS – *Regimental HQ* and *Training Centre*, Middle Wallop, Stockbridge, Hants

SERVICES

Royal Army Chaplains' Department – *Regimental HQ*, HQ AG, Upavon, Pewsey, Wilts. *Training Centre*, Armed Forces Chaplaincy Centre, Amport House, Amport, Andover, Hants

The Royal Logistic Corps – *Regimental HQ*, Blackdown Barracks, Deepcut, Camberley, Surrey. *Training Centre*, Princess Royal Barracks, Deepcut, Camberley, Surrey

Royal Army Medical Corps – *Regimental HQ*, former Army Staff College, Slim Road, Camberley, Surrey and *Training Centre*, Defence Medical Services Keogh Barracks, Ash Vale, Aldershot, Hants

Corps of Royal Electrical and Mechanical Engineers – *Regimental HQ* and *Training Centre*, Hazebrouck Barracks, Isaac Newton Road, Arborfield, Reading, Berks

Adjutant-General's Corps – Staff and Personnel Support Branch (SPS), Provost Branch (Royal Military Police and Military Provost Staff Corps (RMP and MPS), Educational and Training Services Branch (ETS), Army Legal Services Branch (ALS), Regimental HQ, Worthy Down, Winchester, Hants. *Training Centres*, SPS and ETS Worthy Down, Winchester, Hants; RMP and MPS, Roussillon Barracks, Chichester, West Sussex

Royal Army Veterinary Corps – *Regimental HQ*, former Army Staff College, Slim Road, Camberley, Surrey, *Training Centre*, Defence Animal Centre, Melton Mowbray, Leics

Royal Army Dental Corps – *Regimental HQ*, former Army Staff College, Slim Road, Camberley, Surrey, *Training Centre*, Evelyn Woods Road, Aldershot, Hants

Intelligence Corps – *Directorate HQ* and *Training Centre*, Chicksands, Shefford, Beds

Army Physical Training Corps – *Regimental HQ*, Trenchard Lines, Upavon, Pewsey, Wilts, *Training Centre*, Army School of Physical Training, Fox Lines, Queen's Avenue, Aldershot, Hants

Queen Alexandra's Royal Army Nursing Corps – *Regimental HQ*, former Army Staff College, Slim Road, Camberley, *Training Centres*, Army Nursing Training is carried out at Universities of Birmingham and Portsmouth

Corps of Army Music – *Directorate HQ* and *Training Centre,* Army School of Music, Kneller Hall, Kneller Road, Twickenham, Middx

ARMY EQUIPMENT HOLDINGS *as at August 2003*

Tanks	560
Armoured combat vehicles	2,361
Artillery pieces	441
Combat Aircraft	502
Helicopters	254

THE TERRITORIAL ARMY (TA)

The Territorial Army provides formed units and individuals as an essential part of the Army's order of battle for operations across all military tasks in order to ensure that the Army is capable of mounting and sustaining operations at nominated states of readiness. It also provides a basis for regeneration, while at the same time maintaining links with the local community and society at large. Since 1 December 2002 its established strength has been 41,893.

Inspector-General, Lt.-Gen. Sir J. P. Kiszely, KCB, MC

QUEEN ALEXANDRA'S ROYAL ARMY NURSING CORPS

The Queen Alexandra's Royal Army Nursing Corps (QARANC) was founded in 1902 as Queen Alexandra's Imperial Military Nursing Service (QAIMNS) and gained its present title in 1949. The QARANC has trained nurses for the register since 1950 and also trains and employs Health Care Assistants to Level 3 NVQ. The Corps recruits qualified nurses as Officers and other ranks and in 1992 male nurses already serving in the Army were transferred to the QARANC.

Director of Army Nursing Services (DANS) and Matron in Chief Army, Col. K. George

THE ROYAL AIR FORCE

THE QUEEN

MARSHALS OF THE ROYAL AIR FORCE
HRH The Prince Philip, Duke of Edinburgh, KG, KT, OM, GBE, AC, QSO, PC, *apptd* 1953
Sir Michael Beetham, GCB, CBE, DFC, AFC, *apptd* 1982
Sir Keith Williamson, GCB, AFC, *apptd* 1985
The Lord Craig of Radley, GCB, OBE, *apptd* 1988

AIR CHIEF MARSHALS
HRH Princess Alice, Duchess of Gloucester, GCB, CI, GCVO, GBE
Stirrup, Sir Jock, KCB, AFC, ADC *(Chief of the Air Staff)*
Bagnall, Sir Anthony, KCB, GBE *(Vice-Chief of Defence Staff)*
Burridge, Sir Brian, KCB,CBE, ADC *(C.-in-C. RAF Strike Command)*
Pledger, Sir Malcolm, KCB, OBE, AFC *(Chief of Defence Logistics)*

AIR MARSHALS
French, Sir Joe, KCB, CBE *(Air Member for Personnel and C.-in-C. Personnel and Training Command)*
Loader, C. R., OBE *(Deputy C.-in-C. Strike Command)*
Miller, G. A., CBE *(Deputy Commander Joint Force Command, Naples)*
Sturley, P. O., CB, MBE *(Chief of Staff, HQ Component Command Air North)*
Torpy, G. L., CBE, DSO *(Chief of Joint Operations, JHQ)*
Wright, Sir Robert, KBE, AFC *(UK Military Representative to NATO and the EU)*
HRH The Prince of Wales, KG, KT, GCB and Great Master of the Order of the Bath, OM, QSO, PC, ADC(P)

AIR VICE-MARSHALS
Charles, R. A. *(Director Legal Services, RAF)*
Chisnall, S., *(Senior Directing Staff (Air), Royal College of Defence Studies)*
Cliffe, J. A., OBE *(Chief of Staff (Operations) Strike Command)*
Collier, J. A., CBE *(Chief of Staff to Air Member for Personnel and Deputy C.-in-C. Personnel and Training Command)*
Dalton, S. G. G. *(Capability Manager (Information Superiority), MOD)*
Dougherty, S. R. C., QHP *(Director-General, Medical Services (RAF))*
Heath, M. C., CBE *(Senior British Military Adviser, US Central Command)*
The Ven. Hesketh, R. D. *(Chaplain-in-Chief to the Royal Air Force) (Holds rank relative to Air Vice-Marshal)*
Jones, G., CBE, MBE *(Assistant Chief of Staff (Resources), Regional Headquarters, Allied Forces Southern Europe)*
Luker, P. D., OBE *(Commander Joint Helicopter Command)*
Maddox, N. D. A., CBE *(Air Officer Commanding No 2 Group)*
McNicoll, I. W., CBE *(Director-General Joint Doctrine and Concepts Centre)*
Moore, R. C., MBE *(Air Officer Administration and Air Officer Commanding Directly Administered Units)*
Moran, C. H., OBE, MVO *(Air Officer Commanding No 1 Group)*
Ness, C. W. *(Harrier Integrated Project Team Leader)*
Peach, S. W., CBE *(Director-General Intelligence Collection, MOD)*
Pocock, D. J. *(Defence Services Secretary)*
Rennison, D. R. G. *(Chief of Staff (Support) Strike Command)*
Ruddock, P. W. D., CBE *(Air Secretary)*
Smith, A. J., OBE *(Assistant Chief of the Defence Staff (Logistics Operations)*
Thompson, J. H., CB *(Director-General, Saudi Arabia Armed Forces Project)*
Thornton, B. M., CB *(Director-General Logistics (Strike))*
Thornton, E. J., QHP *(Director-General Healthcare)*
Vallance, A. G. B., CB, OBE *(Executive Assistant Chief of Staff Command Structure Implementation, SHAPE)*
Walker, D., CBE, AFC *(Assistant Chief of the Air Staff)*
Walker, D. A., OBE, MVO *(Air Officer Commanding Training Group)*
Walker, P. B., CBE *(Assistant Chief of Staff Policy and Requirements, SHAPE)*
White, A. D., CB *(Air Officer Commanding No 3 Group)*

CONSTITUTION OF THE ROYAL AIR FORCE

The RAF consists of two commands, Strike Command and Personnel and Training Command. Three RAF stations – Aldergrove, Benson and Odiham – are part of Joint Helicopter Command.

Strike Command's mission is to deliver, sustain and develop air power in the most effective manner to meet the UK's Foreign and Security Policy. Consisting of three groups, each organised around specific operational duties, the Command is responsible for all the RAF's front line forces. No 1 Group comprises the tactical fast-jet forces responsible for attack, offensive support and air defence operations. No 2 Group provides air combat support and includes enabling forces such as Air Transport and Air Refuelling, and the RAF Regiment. No 3 Group is the Air Battle management group and includes Airborne Early Warning, Maritime Patrol, and Search and Rescue aircraft.

Personnel and Training Command (PTC) is responsible for recruiting, training, supporting and retaining the servicemen and women needed to sustain the Royal Air Force. The Command consists of two agencies. The RAF Training Group Defence Agency deals with the recruitment and selection of all RAF personnel, as well as providing RAF non-operational flying and ground training. The RAF Personnel Management Agency (RAF PMA), is responsible for managing the careers of uniformed personnel serving in the Regular and Reserve Air Forces. It also assigns and deploys personnel to meet the military tasks in times of war, crisis and peace.

RAF EQUIPMENT *as at 1 February 2004**

AIRCRAFT	
BAe 125	5
BAe 146	2
Beech 200	7
Canberra	5
C17 Globemaster	4
Dominie	9
Harrier	60
Hawk	102
Hercules	50
Islander	1
Jaguar	46
Nimrod	23
Sentry E-3D	6

HELICOPTERS	
Chinook	31
Griffin	9
Merlin	18
Puma	33
Sea King	21
Squirrel	26
Twin Squirrel	3
GLIDERS	
Vigilant	61
Viking	87
BATTLE OF BRITAIN MEMORIAL FLIGHT	
Chipmunk	2
Dakota	1
Hurricane	2
Lancaster	1
Spitfire	5

*All figures shown relate to the Required Operating Fleet. The actual number of aircraft will, in many cases, vary from the figure given due to reasons such as operational commitments and engineering programmes.

ROYAL AUXILIARY AIR FORCE (RAuxAF)

The Auxiliary Air Force was formed in 1924 to train an elite corps of civilians to serve their country in flying squadrons in their spare time. In 1947 the Force was awarded the prefix 'Royal' in recognition of its distinguished war service and The Sovereign's Colour for the Royal Auxiliary Air Force was presented in 1989. The RAuxAF continues to recruit civilians who undertake military training in their spare time to support the Royal Air Force in times of emergency or war.

Air Commodore-in-Chief, HM The Queen

Honorary Inspector-General Royal Auxiliary Air Force, AVM. B. H. Newton, CB, CVO, OBE

Inspector Royal Auxiliary Air Force, Gp. Capt. R. G. Kemp, QVRM, AE, ADC, FRIN, RAUXAF

PRINCESS MARY'S ROYAL AIR FORCE NURSING SERVICE

The Princess Mary's Royal Air Force Nursing Service (PMRAFNS) was formed on 1 June 1918 as the Royal Air Force Nursing Service. In June 1923, His Majesty King George V gave his Royal Assent for the Royal Air Force Nursing Service to be known as the Princess Mary's Royal Air Force Nursing Service. Men were integrated into the PMRAFNS in 1980 and now serve as officers and other ranks.

Patron and Air Chief Commandant, HRH Princess Alexandra, The Hon. Lady Ogilvy, GCVO

Director of Nursing Services and Matron-in-Chief, Gp Capt. R. A. Reid, OBE, ARRC, QHNS

SERVICE SALARIES

The following rates of pay apply from 1 April 2004.

The pay rates shown are for Army personnel. The rates apply also to personnel of equivalent rank and pay band in the other services (*see* below for table of relative ranks).

Rank	*Daily*	*Annual*
SECOND LIEUTENANT	£56.66	£20,680.90
LIEUTENANT		
On appointment	£68.11	£24,860.15
After 1 year in rank	£69.90	£25,513.50
After 2 years in rank	£71.69	£26,166.85
After 3 years in rank	£73.48	£26,820.20
After 4 years in rank	£75.27	£27,473.55
CAPTAIN		
On appointment	£87.27	£31,853.55
After 1 year in rank	£89.61	£32,707.65
After 2 years in rank	£91.98	£33,572.70
After 3 years in rank	£94.35	£34,437.75
After 4 years in rank	£96.70	£35,295.50
After 5 years in rank	£99.07	£36,160.55
After 6 years in rank	£101.42	£37,018.30
After 7 years in rank	£102.61	£37,452.65
After 8 years in rank	£103.79	£37,883.35
MAJOR		
On appointment	£109.93	£40,124.45
After 1 year in rank	£112.65	£41,117.25
After 2 years in rank	£115.35	£42,102.75
After 3 years in rank	£118.08	£43,099.20
After 4 years in rank	£120.79	£44,088.35
After 5 years in rank	£123.51	£45,081.15
After 6 years in rank	£126.23	£46,073.95
After 7 years in rank	£128.94	£47,063.10
After 8 years in rank	£131.66	£48,055.90
LIEUTENANT-COLONEL		
On appointment	£154.29	£56,315.85
After 1 year in rank	£156.34	£57,064.10
After 2 years in rank	£158.37	£57,805.05
After 3 years in rank	£160.39	£58,542.35
After 4 years in rank	£162.42	£59,283.30
After 5 years in rank	£164.45	£60,024.25
After 6 years in rank	£166.48	£60,765.20
After 7 years in rank	£168.51	£61,506.15
After 8 years in rank	£170.56	£62,254.40
COLONEL		
On appointment	£178.68	£65,218.20
After 1 year in rank	£181.03	£66,075.95
After 2 years in rank	£183.38	£66,933.70
After 3 years in rank	£185.73	£67,791.45
After 4 years in rank	£188.08	£68,649.20
After 5 years in rank	£190.43	£69,506.95
After 6 years in rank	£192.77	£70,361.05
After 7 years in rank	£195.13	£71,222.45
After 8 years in rank	£197.49	£72,083.85
BRIGADIER		
On appointment	£214.32	£78,226.80
After 1 year in rank	£216.60	£79,059.00
After 2 years in rank	£218.88	£79,891.20
After 3 years in rank	£221.16	£80,723.40
After 4 years in rank	£223.46	£81,562.90

PAY SYSTEM FOR SENIOR OFFICERS

Revised pay rates effective from 1 April 2004 for all military officers of 2* rank and above (excluding medical and dental officers).

MAJOR-GENERAL (2*)

	Daily	*Annual*
Scale 1	£239.89	£87,559
Scale 2	£244.68	£89,310
Scale 3	£249.48	£91,060
Scale 4	£254.28	£92,812
Scale 5	£259.07	£94,562
Scale 6	£263.87	£96,313
Scale 7	£268.67	£98,063

LIEUTENANT-GENERAL (3*)

	Daily	*Annual*
Scale 1	£280.07	£102,227
Scale 2	£287.07	£104,781
Scale 3	£294.07	£107,336
Scale 4	£301.06	£109,888
Scale 5	£308.06	£112,442
Scale 6	£315.05	£114,995
Scale 7	n/a	n/a

GENERAL (4*)

	Daily	*Annual*
Scale 1	£344.88	£125,882
Scale 2	£353.82	£129,146
Scale 3	£362.77	£132,411
Scale 4	£371.71	£135,675
Scale 5	£380.66	£138,940
Scale 6	£389.60	£142,205
Scale 7	n/a	n/a

Field Marshal – appointments to this rank will not usually be made in peacetime. The salary for holders of the rank is equivalent to the salary of a 5-Star General, a salary created only in times of war. In peacetime, the equivalent rank to Field Marshal is the Chief of the Defence Staff. From 1 April 2004, the annual salary for the Chief of the Defence Staff is £189,000.

OFFICERS COMMISSIONED FROM THE SENIOR RANKS

Rank	*Daily*	*Annual*
Level 15	£116.66	£42,580.90
Level 14	£115.89	£42,299.85
Level 13	£115.09	£42,007.85
Level 12	£113.53	£41,438.45
Level 11	£111.99	£40,876.35
Level 10	£110.43	£40,306.95
Level 9	£108.87	£39,737.55
Level 8	£107.31	£39,168.15
Level 7*	£105.37	£38,460.05
Level 6	£104.17	£38,022.05
Level 5	£102.96	£37,580.40
Level 4**	£100.55	£36,700.75
Level 3	£99.36	£36,266.40
Level 2	£98.14	£35,821.10
Level 1***	£95.74	£34,945.10

*Minimum entry point for SUY, SCCs and LEs with over 15 years' service

**Minimum entry point for SUY, SCCs and LEs with between 12–15 years' service

***Minimum entry point for SUY, SCCs and LEs with under 12 years' service

SOLDIERS' SALARIES

The pay structure below officer level is divided into pay bands. Jobs at each rank are allocated to bands according to their score in the job evaluation system. Length of service is from age 18.
Scale A: committed to serve for less than 6 years, or those with less than 9 years' service who are serving on Open Engagement
Scale B: committed to serve for 6 years but less than 9 years
Scale C: committed to serve for 9 years or more, or those with more than 9 years' service who are serving on Open Engagement

Rates of pay effective from 1 April 2004 are:

	Lower Band		Higher Band	
	Daily	*Annual*	*Daily*	*Annual*
PRIVATE				
Level 1	£36.88	£13,461.20	£36.88	£13,461.20
Level 2	£39.05	£14,253.25	£42.22	£15,410.30
Level 3	£41.21	£15,041.65	£46.61	£17,012.65
Level 4	£44.83	£16,362.95	£50.12	£18,293.80
LANCE CORPORAL (levels 5–7 also applicable to Privates)				
Level 5	£47.23	£17,238.95	£55.42	£20,228.30
Level 6	£49.21	£17,961.65	£58.11	£21,210.15
Level 7	£51.32	£18,731.80	£60.78	£22,184.70
Level 8	£53.67	£19,589.55	£63.51	£23,181.15
Level 9	£55.61	£20,297.65	£66.61	£24,312.65

	Lower Band		Higher Band	
	Daily	*Annual*	*Daily*	*Annual*
CORPORAL				
Level 1	£60.78	£22,184.70	£63.51	£23,181.15
Level 2	£63.51	£23,181.15	£66.61	£24,312.65
Level 3	£66.61	£24,312.65	£69.87	£25,502.55
Level 4	£67.13	£24,502.45	£71.50	£26,097.50
Level 5	£67.65	£24,692.25	£73.23	£26,728.95
Level 6	£68.18	£24,885.70	£74.75	£27,283.75
Level 7	£68.69	£25,071.85	£76.38	£27,878.70

	Lower Band		Higher Band	
	Daily	*Annual*	*Daily*	*Annual*
SERGEANT				
Level 1	£69.09	£25,217.85	£75.40	£27,521.00
Level 2	£70.89	£25,874.85	£77.35	£28,232.75
Level 3	£72.67	£26,524.55	£79.31	£28,948.15
Level 4	£73.41	£26,794.65	£80.31	£29,313.15
Level 5	£75.32	£27,491.80	£81.87	£29,882.55
Level 6	£77.92	£28,440.80	£83.44	£30,455.60
Level 7	£78.51	£28,656.15	£85.00	£31,025.00

	Lower Band		Higher Band	
	Daily	*Annual*	*Daily*	*Annual*
STAFF SERGEANT				
Level 1	£76.48	£27,915.20	£85.06	£31,046.90
Level 2	£77.48	£28,280.20	£87.12	£31,798.80
Level 3	£79.99	£29,196.35	£89.19	£32,554.35
Level 4	£81.86	£29,878.90	£91.26	£33,309.90
WARRANT OFFICER II (levels 5–7 also applicable to staff Sergeants)				
Level 5	£82.98	£30,287.70	£93.34	£34,069.10
Level 6	£86.73	£31,656.45	£95.40	£34,821.00
Level 7	£88.06	£32,141.90	£96.78	£35,324.70
Level 8	£89.19	£32,554.35	£98.16	£35,828.40
Level 9	£91.21	£33,291.65	£99.55	£36,335.75

	Lower Band		Higher Band	
	Daily	*Annual*	*Daily*	*Annual*
WARRANT OFFICER I				
Level 1	£88.84	£32,426.60	£96.86	£35,353.90
Level 2	£90.57	£33,058.05	£98.77	£36,051.05
Level 3	£92.40	£33,726.00	£100.47	£36,671.55
Level 4	£94.23	£34,393.95	£102.31	£37,343.15
Level 5	£96.07	£35,065.55	£104.14	£38,011.10
Level 6	£98.77	£36,051.05	£105.99	£38,686.35
Level 7	£101.55	£37,065.75	£107.61	£39,277.65

RELATIVE RANK – ARMED FORCES

Royal Navy	*Army*	*Royal Air Force*
1 Admiral of the Fleet	1 Field Marshal	1 Marshal of the RAF
2 Admiral (Adm.)	2 General (Gen.)	2 Air Chief Marshal
3 Vice-Admiral (Vice-Adm.)	3 Lieutenant-General (Lt.-Gen.)	3 Air Marshal
4 Rear-Admiral (Rear-Adm.)	4 Major-General (Maj.-Gen.)	4 Air Vice-Marshal
5 Commodore (Cdre)	5 Brigadier (Brig.)	5 Air Commodore (Air Cdre)
6 Captain (Capt.)	6 Colonel (Col.)	6 Group Captain (Gp Capt.)
7 Commander (Cdr.)	7 Lieutenant-Colonel (Lt.-Col.)	7 Wing Commander (Wg Cdr.)
8 Lieutenant-Commander (Lt. Cdr.)	8 Major (Maj.)	8 Squadron Leader (Sqn Ldr)
9 Lieutenant (Lt.)	9 Captain (Capt.)	9 Flight Lieutenant (Flt. Lt.)
10 Sub-Lieutenant (Sub-Lt.)	10 Lieutenant (Lt.)	10 Flying Officer (FO)
11 Acting Sub-Lieutenant (Acting Sub-Lt.)	11 Second Lieutenant (2nd Lt.)	11 Pilot Officer (PO)

SERVICE RETIRED PAY

on compulsory retirement

Those who leave the services having served at least five years, but not long enough to qualify for the appropriate immediate pension, now qualify for a preserved pension and terminal grant, both of which are payable at age 60. The tax-free resettlement grants shown below are payable on release to those who qualify for a preserved pension and who have completed nine years service from age 21 (officers) or 12 years from age 18 (other ranks).

The annual rates for army personnel are given. The rates apply also to personnel of equivalent rank in the other services, including the nursing services.

OFFICERS

Applicable to officers who give full pay service on the active list on or after 31 March 2004. Pensionable earnings for senior officers (*) is defined as the total amount of basic pay received during the year ending on the day prior to retirement, or the amount of basic pay received during any 12 month period within 3 years prior to retirement, whichever is the higher. Figures for Senior Officers are percentage rates of pensionable earnings on final salary arrangements on or after 31 March 2004.

No. of years reckonable service over age 21	*Capt. and below*	*Major*	*Lt.-Col.*	*Colonel*	*Brigadier*	*Major-General**	*Lieutenant-General**	*General**
16	£10,550	£12,565	£16,474	£19,076	£22,769	—	—	—
17	£11,036	£13,162	£17,237	£19,959	£23,657	—	—	—
18	£11,523	£13,759	£17,999	£20,841	£24,544	—	—	—
19	£12,009	£14,356	£18,761	£21,724	£25,432	—	—	—
20	£12,495	£14,952	£19,523	£22,606	£26,320	—	—	—
21	£12,981	£15,549	£20,285	£23,488	£27,207	—	—	—
22	£13,468	£16,146	£21,047	£24,371	£28,095	—	—	—
23	£13,954	£16,743	£21,810	£25,253	£28,983	—	—	—
24	£14,440	£17,339	£22,572	£26,136	£29,870	38.5%	—	—
25	£14,927	£17,936	£23,334	£27,018	£30,758	39.7%	—	—
26	£15,413	£18,533	£24,096	£27,901	£31,646	40.8%	—	—
27	£15,899	£19,130	£24,858	£28,783	£32,533	42.0%	42.0%	—
28	£16,385	£19,726	£25,620	£29,666	£33,421	43.1%	43.1%	—
29	£16,872	£20,323	£26,383	£30,548	£34,309	44.3%	44.3%	—
30	£17,358	£20,920	£27,145	£31,431	£35,197	45.4%	45.4%	45.4%
31	£17,844	£21,517	£27,907	£32,313	£36,084	46.6%	46.6%	46.6%
32	£18,330	£22,114	£28,669	£33,196	£36,972	47.7%	47.7%	47.7%
33	£18,817	£22,710	£29,431	£34,078	£37,860	48.9%	48.9%	48.9%
34	£19,303	£23,307	£30,193	£34,961	£38,747	50.0%	50.0%	50.0%

WARRANT OFFICERS, NCOS AND PRIVATES

(Applicable to soldiers who give full pay service on or after 31 March 2004)

No. of years reckonable service	*Below Corporal*	*Corporal*	*Sergeant*	*Staff Sergeant*	*Warrant Officer Level II*	*Warrant Officer Level I*
22	£6,235	£8,054	£8,829	£10,057	£10,581	£11,418
23	£6,452	£8,335	£9,138	£10,409	£10,950	£11,817
24	£6,670	£8,616	£9,446	£10,760	£11,320	£12,215
25	£6,888	£8,897	£9,754	£11,111	£11,689	£12,614
26	£7,105	£9,178	£10,062	£11,462	£12,058	£13,012
27	£7,323	£9,459	£10,370	£11,813	£12,428	£13,411
28	£7,541	£9,740	£10,678	£12,164	£12,797	£13,809
29	£7,758	£10,022	£10,987	£12,515	£13,166	£14,208
30	£7,976	£10,303	£11,295	£12,866	£13,535	£14,606
31	£8,193	£10,584	£11,603	£13,217	£13,905	£15,005
32	£8,411	£10,865	£11,911	£13,568	£14,274	£15,404
33	£8,629	£11,146	£12,219	£13,919	£14,643	£15,802
34	£8,846	£11,427	£12,528	£14,270	£15,013	£16,201
35	£9,064	£11,708	£12,836	£14,621	£15,382	£16,599
36	£9,282	£11,989	£13,144	£14,972	£15,751	£16,998
37	£9,499	£12,270	£13,452	£15,323	£16,121	£17,396

RESETTLEMENT GRANTS

Terminal grants are in each case three times the rate of retired pay or pension. There are special rates of retired pay for certain other ranks not shown above. Lower rates are payable in cases of voluntary retirement.

A gratuity of £3,590 is payable for officers with short service commissions for each year completed. Resettlement grants are: officers £12,339 non-commissioned ranks £8,433.

EDUCATION

Responsibility for education in England lies with the Secretary of State for Education and Skills; in Wales, with the Welsh Assembly; in Scotland, with the Scottish Executive; and in Northern Ireland with the Education Minister and the Minister for Employment and Learning.

The main concerns of the education departments are the formulation of national policies for education and the maintenance of consistency in educational standards. They are responsible for the broad allocation of revenue and capital resources for education, and for the supply and training of teachers. The Secretary of State is responsible for determining the rates of pay and conditions of employment of teachers in England and in Wales. In Scotland and Northern Ireland these are matters for the respective ministers. The Teacher Training Agency in England promotes teaching as a career on behalf of the Secretary of State and the Welsh Assembly.

EXPENDITURE

In the UK in 2002–3, total expenditure on education and training was:

	2002–3 *outturn accruals* £m	2003–4 *estimated outturn accruals* £m
Under fives	3,203	3,693
Primary schools	14,658	16,191
Secondary schools	15,870	17,479
Higher education	6,632	7,056
Further education	6,560	7,328
Student support	1,661	1,664
Training	1,496	1,527
Other education and training	5,232	6,098
Total education and training	55,312	61,036

Total managed expenditure on education and training in real terms from 1994–5 to 2003–4 in £ billion was:

	£bn		£bn
1994–5	44.7	1999–2000	45.4
1995–6	44.3	2000–1	48.6
1996–7	43.8	2001–2	52.7
1997–8	43.7	2002–3	55.3
1998–9	44.0	2003–4 (estimated)	59.4

Of which: education

	£bn		£bn
1994–5	43.1	1999–2000	43.9
1995–6	42.9	2000–1	47.1
1996–7	42.2	2001–2	51.4
1997–8	42.3	2002–3	53.8
1998–9	42.7	2003–4 (estimated)	57.9

Most of this expenditure, except that for higher and further education in England, Wales and Scotland (which is met by the respective funding agencies), is incurred by local authorities, which make their own expenditure decisions according to their local situations and needs. Expenditure on education by central government and local authorities in the UK in 2002–3 (£m) was:

	2002–3
Local education authorities	
Current	32,888
Capital	2,298
Total	35,186
Central government	
Current	17,490
Capital	1,140
Total	18,630
All public authorities	
Current	50,378
Capital	3,438
Total	53,816

The following table shows total managed expenditure on education and training as a percentage of GDP:

	2001–2 *outturn*	2002–3 *outturn*	2003–4 *estimated outturn*
Education and training	5.1	5.2	5.5
Of which: education	4.9	5.1	5.3

The bulk of direct expenditure by the Department for Education and Skills (DfES), the Welsh Assembly and the Scottish Executive is directed towards supporting post-16 education. Funding for higher education in universities and colleges is channelled through the Higher Education Funding Councils (HEFCs). Funding for further education, sixth form provision, and adult and community education is channelled through the funding councils for that sector and, in Wales, through the National Council for Education and Training (ELWA). In addition, the DfES currently funds student support in England and Wales (although Wales will be taking over responsibility for student support in Wales at a future date, still to be agreed), the City Technology Colleges, the City College for the Technology of the Arts, and pays grants under the specialist schools programme.

In Wales the Assembly also funds curriculum development, educational services and research. In Scotland the main elements of central government expenditure, in addition to those outlined above, are grant-aided special schools, student awards and bursaries (through the Student Awards Agency for Scotland), teachers, curriculum development, special educational needs and community education. In Northern Ireland the Department of Education also administers the teachers' superannuation scheme, pays teachers' salaries and funds grant-maintained integrated and voluntary grammar schools. The Department for Employment and Learning directly funds higher education, student awards and further education.

LOCAL EDUCATION ADMINISTRATION

In England and Wales the school education service is administered by Local Education Authorities (LEAs), which have day-to-day responsibility for providing most state primary and secondary education in their areas. They share with the appropriate funding bodies the duty to provide adult education to meet local needs. The LEAs own and maintain most schools and some colleges, build new ones and provide equipment. LEAs are financed largely from the council tax and aggregate external finance from the Office of the Deputy Prime Minister in England and the Welsh Assembly in Wales. LEA-maintained schools usually manage their own budgets. The LEA allocates funds to the school, largely on the basis of pupil numbers, and the school governing body is responsible for overseeing spending and for most aspects of staffing, including appointments and dismissals. LEAs also have intervention powers to add additional governors, take back a school's delegated budget or replace the governing body of a school with an interim executive when a school is placed in special measures, is judged to have serious weaknesses or is causing concern and has not complied with a formal warning from the LEA. The duty of providing education locally in Scotland rests with the education authorities. They are responsible for the construction of buildings, the employment of teachers and other staff, and the provision of equipment and materials. Devolved School Management is in place for all primary, secondary and special schools. Education authorities are required to establish school boards consisting of parents and teachers as well as co-opted members, responsible, among other things, for the appointment of staff.

Education, with the exception of further and higher education, is administered locally in Northern Ireland by five education and library boards, which fund controlled and maintained schools and whose costs are met in full by the Northern Ireland Executive. All grant-aided schools include elected parents and teachers on their boards of governors. Provision has been made for schools wishing to provide integrated education to have grant-maintained integrated status, funded directly by the Department of Education. All schools and colleges of further education have full responsibility for their own budgets, including staffing costs.

THE INSPECTORATE

ENGLAND

The Office for Standards in Education (Ofsted) is a non-ministerial government department in England headed by HM Chief Inspector of Schools (HMCI). Ofsted's remit is to help improve the quality and standards of childcare through regular independent inspection and regulation. It must also provide advice to the Secretary of State based on inspection evidence. Ofsted must report on all maintained schools in England, Local Education Authorities (supported by the Audit Commission), initial teacher training courses, the private, voluntary and independent nursery sector (including childminders and day-care establishments), independent schools, (including independent special schools), youth services, service children's education, and all education and training for people aged 16–19 in sixth form and further education colleges. Ofsted also reports on the impact of government initiatives such as the national numeracy and literacy strategies.

A new inspection framework, Framework 2003 – Inspecting Schools, came into effect in September 2003. Schools are inspected at least once every six years. There are 238 HMIs and 946 Childcare Inspectors on Ofsted's permanent staff. W www.ofsted.gov.uk

WALES

Estyn: Arolygiaeth Ei Mawrhydi dros Addysg a Hyfforddiant yng Nghymru (Her Majesty's Inspectorate for Education and Training in Wales) is responsible for inspecting early years provision in the non-maintained sector, primary schools, secondary schools, special schools (including independent special schools), pupil referral units, independent schools, further education, youth support services, local education authorities, teacher education and training, work-based learning, Careers Wales companies, the education, guidance and training elements of the New Deal, and adult community based learning. Its remit also includes providing advice to the Welsh Assembly on a wide range of education and training matters. W www.estyn.gov.uk

SCOTLAND

HM Inspectorate of Education (HMIE) is an executive agency of the Scottish Executive. HM Inspectors (HMI) inspect or review and report on education provision in primary, secondary and special schools, further education institutions (under contract to the Scottish Further Education Funding Council), initial teacher education, community learning and development, the care and welfare of pupils, the education functions of local authorities, prison education, children's services, and in other contexts as necessary. They work in collaboration with the Care Commission in integrated inspection of pre-school education centres and residential schools. They work with Audit Scotland on the inspection of education authorities and on behalf of the Scottish Further Education Funding Council in the review of Scotland's 43 further education colleges. HMIs work in teams alongside lay members (who are volunteer members of the public) and associate assessors (who are practising teachers or senior educationalists seconded for the inspection). HMIE is led by the senior chief inspector, supported by six chief inspectors (five of whom head inspectorates) and twelve assistant chief inspectors. There are approximately 80 HMI in Scotland. The inspection of higher education is the responsibility of inspectors appointed to the Higher Education Funding Council for Scotland. W www.hmie.gov.uk

NORTHERN IRELAND

Inspection is carried out in Northern Ireland by the Education and Training Inspectorate, which provides inspection services for the Department of Education, the Department for Employment and Learning and the Department of Culture, Arts and Leisure. Schools are currently inspected once every five to seven years. In further education and training, extended inspections are carried out once every eight years and focused inspections at least every four years. In addition, the Inspectorate provides evidence-based advice to ministers and departments to assist in the formulation and evaluation of policies in education, training and youth. The Inspectorate comprises one chief inspector, four assistant chief inspectors, 10 managing inspectors and 52 inspectors. W www.deni.gov.uk/inspection_services

SCHOOLS AND PUPILS

Full-time education is compulsory in Great Britain for all children between five and 16 years and between four and 16 years in Northern Ireland. About 93 per cent of children receive free education from public funds and the rest attend fee-paying schools or are educated at home. Provision is being increased for pre-school children and many pupils remain at school after the minimum leaving age. No fees are charged in any publicly maintained school in England, Wales or Scotland. In Northern Ireland, fees may be charged by voluntary schools and are paid by pupils in preparatory departments of grammar schools, but pupils admitted to the secondary departments of grammar schools, unless they come from outside Northern Ireland, do not pay fees. Students under 19 years of age attending courses at further education colleges are not charged course fees.

PUPIL NUMBERS

In the maintained sector in the UK in 2003 there were:

Primary pupils	5,178,200
Secondary pupils	3,995,000
Pupils in special schools	111,500
Pupils in pupil referral units	12,400
Total pupils in all maintained schools	10,100,400

ENGLAND AND WALES

There are two main types of school in England and Wales: schools maintained by the state, which charge no fees; and independent schools, which charge fees. Schools maintained by the state, with the exception in England of Academies and City Technology Colleges, are maintained by Local Education Authorities (LEAs).

Schools maintained by the state are classified as community, voluntary or foundation schools. Community schools are owned by LEAs and wholly funded by them (although sixth forms have separate funding arrangements). They are non-denominational and provide primary and secondary education. Schools in the voluntary category provide primary and secondary education and many have a particular religious ethos. Although the buildings are in many cases provided by the voluntary body, the LEA maintains them financially. There are two subdivisions in the voluntary category: voluntary controlled, and voluntary aided. In the case of voluntary controlled schools, the LEA bears all the costs. In voluntary aided schools, although the managers or governors are responsible for repairs, improvements and alterations to the building, central government may reimburse up to 90 per cent of approved capital expenditure (85 per cent in Wales), while the LEA pays for internal maintenance and other running costs. Foundation schools provide primary and secondary education. They can have a religious character, although most do not. They are funded by the LEA, and by the relevant funding bodies in respect of sixth form provision, although the land and buildings will be owned by a foundation or by the governors.

The number of schools by category in 2003 was:

	England	*Wales*
Maintained nursery schools (inc two Direct Grant for England)	477	37
Maintained primary and secondary schools: total	21,297	1,829
Of which:		
Community	13,401	1,544
Voluntary aided	4,280	162
Voluntary controlled	2,741	111
Foundation	875	12
Pupil Referral Units	360	29
Maintained special schools	1,088	43
Non-maintained special schools	72	–
CTCs and CCTAs (England only)	15	–
Academies	3	–
Independent schools	2,160	59
Total	25,472	1,997

LEAs are required to provide the schools that they maintain with a delegated budget to cover their running costs, including staffing costs. LEAs can retain funding of various centrally provided services, including transport and some special educational needs. The LEA acts as the admission authority for most community and some voluntary schools.

Governing bodies – All publicly maintained schools have a governing body, usually made up of a number of parent and local community representatives, governors appointed by the LEA if the school is LEA-maintained, the head teacher (unless he or she chooses otherwise), and serving teachers and other staff. Schools can appoint up to two sponsor governors; sponsor governors are persons who give substantial assistance to the school, financially or in kind, or who provide services to the school. Governing bodies are responsible for the overall policies of schools and their academic aims and objectives.

City Technology Colleges (CTCs) and City Colleges for the Technology of the Arts (CCTAs) are found in England only, and are state-aided but independent of LEAs. Their aim is to widen the choice of secondary education in disadvantaged urban areas and to teach a broad curriculum with an emphasis on science, technology, business understanding and arts technologies. Capital costs are shared by government and business sponsors, and running costs are covered by a per capita grant from the DfES in line with an average of the comparable costs in LEA-maintained schools in the areas where CTCs are located.

The Specialist Schools Programme is open to all state secondary schools, including special schools with secondary age pupils, in England that wish to develop a curriculum specialism in one of ten specialist areas: arts, business and enterprise, engineering, humanities, languages, mathematics and computing, music, science, sports, and technology. Schools can also combine two specialisms. Schools must raise £50,000 in unconditional private/business sponsorship, except smaller schools (schools with 500 pupils or fewer) which must raise at least £20,000 depending on pupil numbers. There are two application rounds a year. Schools must prepare four-year development plans. These must include measurable targets for how they intend to raise attainment and extend opportunities for pupils in the specialist area, improve teaching and learning and thereby secure improvement across the whole school. Schools must also share expertise, resources and good practice with other schools and the wider community. Specialist schools receive additional recurrent funding to support the targets within their plan. This is based on £129 for every additional pupil above 1,200 up to 1,400 pupils. In addition, specialist schools receive a one-off capital grant of £100,000 supplemented by sponsorship raised, to improve their specialist facilities. Specialist schools are encouraged to include sponsors and local businesses on their Governing Body. All maintained schools are able to appoint two sponsor governors, and specialist schools will be expected to appoint some sponsor/business/employer governors. Specialist schools can apply for redesignation at the end of the phase to extend the status for a further four-year period. In July 2004 there were 1,954 designated specialist schools.

Academies – Academies are schools open to all abilities. They are usually in disadvantaged areas and are established by sponsors from business or faith or voluntary groups. Sponsors and the DfES provide capital costs, and running costs are met in full by the DfES. Academies either replace seriously failing schools or are established to meet a demand for places. The first three academies opened in September 2002 and a further nine opened in September 2003. Five more academies were due to open in September 2004.

Excellence in Cities (EiC) is a programme of support designed to raise school standards and pupil expectations in disadvantaged urban communities. Excellence Clusters bring the core strands of the EiC programme to smaller pockets of deprivation elsewhere.

Federations are groups of two or more schools with a formal agreement to work together to raise standards.

The Beacon Schools programme was set up to help raise standards across primary and secondary education by sharing and spreading locally and nationally the good practice identified in successful schools. The programme is currently being phased out and the last contracts will end by August 2005. A new programme at secondary level, the *Leading Edge Partnership Programme,* builds on the success of the Beacon Schools programme and supports innovative approaches to addressing critical learning challenges; 103 partnerships began in September 2003 and a further 102 partnerships were announced in early 2004. In addition, a *Leading Practice* programme is currently being developed to recognise and spread best practice.

Independent/State School Partnerships were launched in 1998 and forge links between independent and state schools to enhance the opportunities on offer to pupils. From September 2004, a £1.4 million government package will fund 46 new partnership projects.

Education Action Zones (EAZs) were established from 1997 to develop local partnerships between schools, parents, the community, businesses and local authorities to find solutions to educational underachievement. They were set up as statutory bodies with a maximum five-year lifespan. After five years EAZs in rural areas will transform into Excellence Clusters and those in Excellence in Cities (EiC) areas will transform into EiC Action Zones. The last EAZs to transform will do so in May 2005.

SCOTLAND

Education authority schools (known as public schools) are financed by local government, partly through revenue support grants from central government, and partly from local taxation. Devolved management from the local authority to the school is in place for more than 88 per cent of all school-level expenditure. A small number of grant-aided schools, mainly in the special sector, are conducted by boards of managers and receive grants direct from the Scottish Executive Education Department. Independent schools charge fees and receive no direct grant, but are subject to inspection and registration. The number of schools by category in September 2003 was:

Publicly funded schools	2,826
Independent schools	150
Total	2,976

NORTHERN IRELAND

Controlled schools are managed by the Education and Library Boards (ELBs) through boards of governors consisting of representatives of transferors (mainly the Protestant churches), parents, teachers and the ELB. Within the controlled sector there is a small number of controlled integrated and Irish-medium schools. Voluntary maintained schools are managed by boards of governors consisting of members nominated by trustees (mainly Roman Catholic) with representatives of teachers, parents and the ELB. Voluntary schools receive grants towards capital costs and running costs in whole or in part. A majority are entitled to capital grants at 100 per cent. Voluntary non-maintained schools are mainly voluntary grammar schools managed by boards of governors consisting of representatives of parents, teachers and, in most cases, the Department of Education and the ELB, as well as those appointed as provided in each school's scheme of management. Integrated schools exist to educate Protestant and Roman Catholic children, as well as those of other creeds, together. Latest figures show that there are currently 57 integrated schools, comprising 19 integrated second level colleges and 38 integrated primary schools. There are a number of schools and units that provide education entirely through the medium of the Irish language. Latest figures show that there are 16 Irish-medium schools and 12 Irish-medium units attached to schools in the English language sector. Of the 16 schools, 15 are Irish-medium primary schools. There are also 3 Irish-medium nursery units. The number of schools in Northern Ireland by type in 2003–4 was:

Grant Aided Mainstream	
Nursery*	100
Primary	892
Secondary: total	233
grammar	70
other	163
Non-maintained mainstream	17
Special (maintained)	47
Total	1,289

*Excludes voluntary and private pre-school education centres

THE STATE SYSTEM

SURE START

All early years services in England, including pre-school education, now come under the Sure Start banner. Sure Start programmes increase the availability of childcare for all children; improve health, education and emotional development for young people; and support parents in their role by increasing their opportunity to work, train and study. Its remit is usually confined to the under 5s, but in the case of childcare it is responsible for ensuring that accessible and affordable care is available for all children up to the age of 14, or 16 for children with a special need.
W www.surestart.gov.uk

PRE-SCHOOL EDUCATION

Pre-school education is for children from three to five years. It is not compulsory, although a free place is available for every three and four-year-old whose parents want one. In Wales, a free part-time place in a maintained or non-maintained setting is available for each child from the term following their third birthday. The Early Years Advisory Panel is responsible for making recommendations to the Minister for Education and Lifelong Learning on the strategy for expanding early years provision in Wales. In Scotland, pre-school education places are available for all three- and four-year-olds whose parents want one. Northern Ireland has a compulsory school-starting age of four, and since March 2003 sufficient places have been available for each child in its' immediate pre-school year whose parents wish it.

Free, part-time, pre-school, or early education is funded by the Government via local authorities but takes place variously in nursery schools, nursery classes in primary schools, private schools, voluntary sector groups and some childminder networks in England. All providers, whatever their sector, can receive Government funding through local authorities to provide free places if they can show through Ofsted inspections that curricular goals are being met. In Northern Ireland approximately 30 per cent of pre-school education takes place in voluntary/private sector playgroups funded by the Department of Education. The proportion of all three- and four-year-olds in the UK enrolled in pre-school education as at January 2003, by sector, was:

	Public Sector	*Private and voluntary Sector*	*All Providers*
	%	%	%
UK	65	34	99
England	64	38	102
Wales	80	–	80
Scotland	65	26	91
Northern Ireland	59	13	71

PRIMARY EDUCATION

Primary education begins at five years of age in Great Britain and four years of age in Northern Ireland. In England, Wales and Northern Ireland the transfer to secondary school is generally made at 11 years of age. In Scotland, the primary school course lasts for seven years and pupils transfer to secondary courses at about the age of 12.

Primary schools consist mainly of infant schools for children aged five to seven, junior schools for those aged seven to 11, and combined junior and infant schools for both age groups. First schools in some parts of England cater for ages five to ten as the first stage of a three-tier system of first, middle and secondary schools. Scotland has only primary schools and not infant and junior schools.

PRIMARY SCHOOLS (UK) 2002–3

No. of primary schools	22,638
No. of pupils (including nursery classes)	5,178,200
No. of pupils (excluding nursery classes)	4,855,100

Pupil-teacher ratios in public sector mainstream primary schools were:

	2000–1	2001–2	2002–3
UK	22.3	22.0	22.0
England	22.9	22.5	22.6
Wales	21.5	21.0	21.0
Scotland	19.0	18.9	18.0
Northern Ireland	20.1	19.8	19.6

The average size of classes 'as taught' was 26.0 in 2002–3, the same as in 2001–2. (Figures refer to 'all classes' rather than 'one-teacher classes' only.)

MIDDLE SCHOOLS

Middle schools take children from first schools, mostly in England, cover varying age ranges between eight and 14 and usually lead on to comprehensive upper schools.

SECONDARY EDUCATION

Secondary schools are for children aged 11 to 16 and for those who choose to stay on to 18. At 16, many students prefer to move on to tertiary or sixth form colleges or into further education colleges or work-based training. Most secondary schools in England, Wales and Scotland are co-educational. The largest secondary schools have over 1,500 pupils, but only 5.2 per cent of schools in the United Kingdom take over 1,000 pupils.

SECONDARY SCHOOLS 2002–3

	England	*Wales*	*Scotland*	*N. Ireland*
No. of pupils (000s)	3,308.0	214.3	316.9	155.7
Average class size	21.9	20.5	n/a	n/a
Pupil–teacher ratio	17.0	16.4	12.7	14.4

In England and Wales the main types of maintained secondary schools are: comprehensive schools, whose admission arrangements are without reference to ability or aptitude; deemed middle schools, for children aged between eight and 14 years who then move on to senior comprehensive schools at 12, 13 or 14; and (in England) secondary grammar schools, with selective intake, providing an academic course from 11 to 16–18 years.

In Scotland all pupils in education authority secondary schools attend schools with a comprehensive intake. Most of these schools provide a full range of courses appropriate to all levels of ability from first to sixth year.

In most areas of Northern Ireland there is a selective system of secondary education with pupils transferring either to grammar schools (35 per cent of pupils in 2003) or secondary schools (65 per cent of pupils in 2003) at 10–11 years of age. Grammar schools provide an academic type of secondary education with A-levels at the end of the seventh year, while secondary non-grammar schools follow a curriculum suited to a wider range of aptitudes and abilities.

SPECIAL EDUCATION

Wherever possible, taking parents' wishes into account, children with special educational needs (SEN) are educated in ordinary schools, which are required to publish their policy for pupils with such needs. Local Education Authorities in England and Wales and Education and Library Boards in Northern Ireland are required to identify and secure provision for children with special educational needs and to involve the parents in any decision.

In Scotland, school placing is a matter of agreement between education authorities and parents. Parents have the right to say which school they want their child to attend, and a right of appeal if their wishes are not being met.

Maintained special schools are run by education authorities which pay all the costs of maintenance, but under the terms of local management, those able and wishing to manage their own budgets may choose to do so. Non-maintained special schools are run by voluntary bodies; they may receive some grant from central government for capital expenditure and for equipment but their current expenditure is met primarily from the fees charged to education authorities for pupils placed in the schools. Some independent schools provide education wholly or mainly for children with special educational needs. The number of pupils in maintained schools with statements of special needs in 2002–3 was:

	No.	*%*
UK	296,900	2.9
England	250,500	3.0
Wales	16,000	3.1
Scotland	20,000	2.3
Northern Ireland	10,300	3.0

ALTERNATIVE PROVISION

There is no legal obligation on parents in the UK to educate their children at school provided that the local education authority is satisfied that the child is receiving full-time education suited to its age, abilities and aptitudes. The education authority need not be informed that a child is being educated at home unless the child is already registered at a state school. In that case the parents must arrange for the child's name to be removed from the school's register (by writing to the head teacher) before education at home can begin. Failure to do so leaves the parents liable to prosecution for condoning non-attendance. There are no official figures on the numbers of pupils educated outside school but estimates suggest that between 100,000 and 170,000 children are being educated at home.

INDEPENDENT SCHOOLS

Independent schools charge fees and are owned and managed under special trusts, with profits being used for the benefit of the schools concerned. There are 2,300 independent schools in Britain, educating over 630,000 pupils, or seven per cent of the total school-age population. The number of pupils at independent schools in 2003 was:

UK	630,000
England	580,000
Wales	9,600
Scotland	31,400
Northern Ireland	9,200

The annual survey carried out by the Independent Schools Council (ISC) shows that 0.1 per cent more pupils were being educated in ISC accredited independent schools in 2004 than in 2003. The Independent Schools Council, formed in 1974, acts on behalf of seven independent schools' associations. These associations are: the Headmasters' and Headmistresses' Conference, the Girls' Schools Association, the Independent Schools Association, the Society of Headmasters and Headmistresses of Independent Schools, the Incorporated Association of Preparatory Schools, the Association of Governing Bodies of Independent Schools and the Independent Schools Bursars Association. There are 1,279 schools in membership of the ISC, responsible for 80 per cent of all children educated outside the state sector. Most of the schools outside ISC membership are likely to be privately owned. The ISC has overall responsibility for the Independent Schools Inspectorate (ISI), which works under a framework agreed with the DfES and Ofsted. A school must pass an ISI accreditation inspection to qualify for membership of an association within ISC. Schools are evaluated on their educational standards (including attainment, learning and behaviour), quality of teaching, assessment and recording, curriculum, staffing, premises and resources, links with parents and the community, pupils' personal development and pastoral care, management, efficiency, aims and ethos. ISC schools are subject to inspection every six years. In 2003 over half of the 11-year-olds who took national curriculum Key Stage 2 tests at preparatory schools achieved the level expected of 14-year-olds. At GCSE, 54.6 per cent of all exams taken by independent school candidates achieve either an A* or A grade (compared to the national average of 16.7 per cent) and at A-level, about 69 per cent of entries were awarded an A or B grade (national average, 44.5 per cent). In 2003, over 116,000 pupils at ISC schools received help with their fees in the form of bursaries and scholarships from the schools. In 2003, ISC member schools spent £523 million (an average of £1,034 per pupil) on new and improved buildings and equipment. W www.iscis.uk.net

THE CURRICULUM

ENGLAND

The national curriculum was introduced in primary and secondary schools between autumn 1989 and autumn 1996, for the period of compulsory schooling from five to 16. It is mandatory in all maintained schools. Following a review in 1999, a revised curriculum was introduced in schools from September 2000.

The Foundation Stage was introduced in September 2000 for children aged 3–5. It sets out six areas of learning:

- Personal, social and emotional development
- Communication
- Mathematical development
- Knowledge and understanding of the world
- Physical development
- Creative development

The Education Act 2002 extended the national curriculum to include the Foundation Stage. This Act also established a single national assessment system for the Foundation Stage called the Foundation Stage Profile.

The statutory subjects in the national curriculum are:

Core subjects	*Foundation subjects*
English	Design and Technology
Mathematics	Information and Communication Technology
Science	History
	Geography
	Art and Design
	Music
	Physical Education

At Key Stage 3 (11- to 14-year-olds) a modern foreign language is introduced. At Key Stage 4 (14- to 16-year-olds) pupils are required to continue to study the core subjects, plus physical education, design and technology, a modern foreign language, and information and communication technology. Citizenship is a compulsory subject for secondary pupils. Other foundation subjects are optional and other subjects, such as drama, dance and classical languages, are taught when the resources of individual schools permit. Religious education must be taught across all key stages.

Statutory assessment takes place on entry to primary school and national tests and tasks in English and mathematics at Key Stage 1 (five- to seven-year-olds), with the addition of science at Key Stages 2 (seven- to 11-year-olds) and 3 (11- to 14-year-olds), are in place. Teachers make their own assessments of their pupils' progress to set alongside the test results. At Key Stage 4, the GCSE and vocational equivalents are the main form of assessment.

The DfES in England publishes tables showing pupils' performance in A-level, AS-level, GCSE, GNVQ and Vocational A-level examinations school by school. LEAs are required to publish similar information in November each year showing the results of national curriculum tests and teacher assessments for seven, 11- and 14-year-olds.

The Qualifications and Curriculum Authority (QCA) is

an independent government agency funded by the DfES. It is responsible for ensuring that the curriculum and qualifications available to young people and adults are of high quality, coherent and flexible and its remit ranges from the under-fives to higher level vocational qualifications. W www.qca.org.uk

WALES

The national curriculum was introduced simultaneously in Wales and, although it is broadly similar, has separate and distinctive characteristics which are reflected, where appropriate, in the programmes of study. Following a review of the curriculum in Wales, changes were introduced from September 2000. Welsh is compulsory for pupils at all key stages, either as a first or as a second language. According to the January 2002 schools' census and the 2002 national curriculum assessment results, 20 per cent of primary school pupils are taught in classes where Welsh is used as a medium of teaching to some degree. In November 2002, additional funding of £9.5 million was announced for Welsh language education; £7 million will be used to support bilingual nursery education in 2004–6. The percentage of children speaking Welsh fluently in primary school has increased from 13.2 per cent in 1988 to 16.8 per cent in 2002.

Schools perform tests and tasks in all the national curriculum subjects except at Key Stage 1, where teacher assessment is the sole means of assessing attainment. Approximately 38,000 pupils in each of the Key Stages 2 and 3 take the tests each year.

In 2003, the percentage of pupils reaching or exceeding the expected standards at each key stage (teacher assessment results in parenthesis) in England and Wales were (figures for England are provisional):

	England		*Wales*	
	Boys	*Girls*	*Boys*	*Girls*
Key Stage 1				
7 year olds				
level 2 or above				
English				
Reading	80 (81)	88 (89)		
Writing	76 (78)	87 (87)		
Welsh	-	-	- (82)	- (91)
Reading	-	-	- (75)	- (85)
Writing	-	-	- (70)	- (82)
Maths	89 (87)	91 (90)	- (85)	-(89)
Science	- (88)	- (91)	- (86)	- (90)
Key Stage 2				
11 year olds				
level 4 or above				
English	70 (67)	80 (78)	74 (71)	84 (82)
Welsh	-	-	72 (70)	83 (81)
Maths	73 (74)	72 (75)	74 (75)	76 (78)
Science	86 (81)	87 (83)	87 (83)	88 (86)
Key Stage 3				
14 year olds				
level 5 or above				
English	61 (60)	75 (75)	55 (56)	72 (74)
Welsh	-	-	66 (65)	81 (81)
Maths	69 (70)	72 (74)	67 (67)	69 (70)

Awdurdod Cymwysterau, Cwricwlwm ac Asesu Cymru (ACCAC)/the Qualifications, Curriculum and Assessment Authority for Wales advises government on the matters within its remit. ACCAC is funded by the National Assembly for Wales. W www.accac.org.uk

SCOTLAND

The content and management of the curriculum in Scotland are not prescribed by statute but are the responsibility of education authorities and individual head teachers. Advice and guidance are provided by the Scottish Executive Education Department and Learning and Teaching Scotland, which also has a developmental role. These bodies have produced guidelines on the structure and balance of the curriculum as well as for each of five broad curriculum areas for the five to 14 age group. There are also guidelines on assessment across the whole curriculum, on reporting to parents, and on the use of national tests for reading, writing and mathematics at six levels. Testing is carried out by the school when the teacher judges that a pupil has completed a level; most pupils are expected to move from one level to the next at roughly 18-month to two-year intervals. Guidance on the curriculum for 14- to 16-year-olds recommends study within each of eight modes: language and communication; mathematical studies; science; technology; social studies; creative activities; physical education; and religious and moral education. There is also a recommended percentage of time to be devoted to each area over the two years. Provision is also made for teaching in Gaelic in many parts of Scotland and the number of pupils, at all levels from nursery to secondary, in Gaelic-medium education is growing. Local authorities must ensure that local education provision meets demand and consider whether they need a Gaelic-medium class, school or unit. For 16- to 18-year-olds, National Qualifications, a unified framework of courses and awards which brings together both academic and vocational courses, was introduced in 1999. The Scottish Qualifications Authority awards the certificates. W www.sqa.org.uk

NORTHERN IRELAND

The statutory Northern Ireland curriculum is made up of religious education and five broad areas of study at primary level and six at secondary level. Provided the requirements of the statutory curriculum are met, it is for each school to decide what additional subjects should be made available for pupils. Pupils at Key Stages 1 and 2 study religious education, English, mathematics, science, history and geography (known as the environment and society area of study), art and design, music and PE (the creative and expressive area of study), Irish (in Irish-speaking schools only) and four educational cross-curricular themes (education for mutual understanding, cultural heritage, health education and information technology). At Key Stage 3, pupils also study technology and design, plus a foreign language (pupils in Irish-speaking schools can study a foreign language or continue studying Irish) and two extra cross-curricular themes (economic awareness and careers education). At Key Stage 4, pupils can drop technology and design, art and design, and music and can choose one subject from history, geography, business studies, home economics, economics, political studies or social and environmental studies. The Northern Ireland Council for the Curriculum, Examinations and Assessment (CCEA) is currently reviewing the curriculum. The necessary legislation to implement the revised curriculum will be in place by September 2006, however, in practice the new curriculum will be phased in over a number of years to allow schools to plan for and implement the changes. Initially there is likely to be an increased level of piloting from September 2004. The assessment of pupils is broadly in line with practice in England and Wales and takes place at the ages of eight, 11 and 14. The GCSE is used to assess 16-year-olds. The CCEA monitors and advises the Department of Education and teachers on all matters relating to the curriculum, assessment arrangements and examinations in grant-aided schools. It conducts GCSE, A- and AS-level examinations, pupil assessment at Key Stages 1, 2 and 3 and administers the transfer procedure tests. W www.ccea.org.uk

PUBLIC EXAMINATIONS AND QUALIFICATIONS

ENGLAND, WALES AND NORTHERN IRELAND

In 1988 a single system of examinations, the General Certificate of Secondary Education (GCSE), which is usually taken after five years of secondary education was introduced. The GCSE is the main method of assessing the performance of pupils at age 16 in all national curriculum subjects required to be assessed at the end of compulsory schooling. The structure of the examination reflects national curriculum requirements where these apply. GCSE short-course qualifications are available in some subjects. As a rule the syllabus comprises half the content of a full GCSE course. In September 2002 eight GCSEs in vocational subjects were introduced and they are: applied art and design, applied business, engineering, health and social care, applied ICT, leisure and tourism, manufacturing, and applied science.

The GCSE differs from its predecessors in that there are syllabuses based on national criteria covering course objectives, content and assessment methods; differentiated assessment (i.e. different papers or questions for different ranges of ability) and grade-related criteria (i.e. grades awarded on absolute rather than relative performance). The GCSE certificates are awarded on an eight-point scale, A* to G. All GCSE syllabuses, assessments and grading procedures are monitored by the Qualifications and Curriculum Authority to ensure that they conform to the national criteria. In 2003, 52.9 per cent of 15 to 16-year olds gained at least five results at grade C or better at GCSE or General National Vocational Qualification (GNVQ) equivalent. Students are increasingly encouraged to continue their education post-16. For those who do so, in addition to the vocational qualifications outlined below, there are General Certificate of Education (GCE) and Vocational Certificate of Education (VCE) Advanced (A-level) examinations. A-level courses usually last two years and have traditionally provided the foundation for entry to higher education. Following extensive consultations in 1996 and 1997 which indicated the need to broaden the post-16 curriculum, new A-level qualifications were introduced in September 2000. The new Advanced Subsidiary (AS) level examinations represents the first half of a full A-level, and is assessed accordingly. The new A-level qualification consists of six units (three AS units and three A2 units). Students who go on to complete the full A-level will be assessed on their attainment in all six units, which may be taken either in stages or at the end of the course. A-levels and AS-levels are marked on a scale from A to E. There is also the opportunity for A-level candidates to take additional papers known as Advanced Extension Awards (which replaced Special papers). The awards are designed to stretch the most able A-level students. Many maintained schools offer BTEC Firsts and an increasing number offer BTEC Nationals. National Vocational Qualifications (NVQs) in the form of General NVQs (GNVQs) are also available to students in schools. The Advanced Vocational Certificate of Education (AVCE) exists in three, six and 12-unit forms.

The City & Guilds Diploma of Vocational Education is intended for a wide ability range. Within guidelines and to meet specified criteria, schools and colleges design their own courses. These stress activity-based learning, core skills (which include application of number, communication and information technology), and work experience. The diploma is of value to those who want to find out what aptitudes they may have and to prepare themselves for work but who may not yet be committed to a particular occupation. It can be taken alongside GCSEs and can provide a context for the introduction of GNVQ units into the Key Stage 4 curriculum.

The various examining boards in England have combined into three unitary awarding bodies (UABs), which offer both academic and vocational qualifications: GNVQs, GCSEs, AS- and A-levels. The bodies are the Assessment and Qualifications Alliance (AQA), Edexcel, and Oxford, Cambridge and RSA Examinations (OCR). The Joint Council for General Qualifications (JCGQ) comprises the three English UABs, the Welsh Joint Education Committee and the Northern Ireland Council for the Curriculum, Examinations and Assessment.

SCOTLAND

Scotland has its own system of public examinations, and in 1999 a new system of National Qualifications was introduced. Five levels of study are offered: Access, Intermediate 1, Intermediate 2, Higher and Advanced Higher. The new Higher National course and Advanced Higher National course are direct replacements for the old SCE Higher grade and the Certificate of Sixth Year Studies respectively. National Qualifications are included on the Scottish Credit and Qualifications Framework (see below), with Access equating to levels 1 to 3, Intermediate 1 to level 4, Intermediate 2 to level 5, Higher to level 6 and Advanced Higher to level 7.

National Courses consist of blocks of study called National Units. A unit usually consists of around 40 hours of study and there are three units in a course. Unit awards demonstrate that a learner has achieved competence in a particular area of study. National Course awards are graded by external assessment, which consists of an examination, coursework or performance, or a combination of two or more of these. National Course awards also require candidates to pass all unit assessments of the course. A typical National Course external assessment requires candidates to demonstrate long-term retention of knowledge, high levels of problem solving, integration of knowledge across a whole course and an ability to apply knowledge and skills in novel situations. The range of subjects has been expanded to include vocational qualifications.

A number of schools use the new National Qualifications system for pupils in their fourth year of secondary education, but the majority of this lower age group still take the traditional Standard Grade examinations take place at the end of a two-year course. Awards at Standard Grade are set at three levels: Credit (leading to awards at grade 1 or 2); General (leading to awards at grade 3 or 4); and Foundation (leading to awards at grade 5 or 6). Grade 7 is awarded to those who, although they have completed the course, have not attained any of these levels. Normally pupils will take examinations covering two pairs of grades, either grades 1–4 or grades 3–6. Most candidates take seven or eight Standard Grade examinations. The three levels of Standard Grade equate to levels 3 to 5 of the SCQF.

THE INTERNATIONAL BACCALAUREATE DIPLOMA

The International Baccalaureate Organisation is a non-profit, Swiss educational foundation established in 1968. The Diploma Programme for which it is best known was developed by a group of schools seeking to establish a common curriculum and a university entry credential for geographically mobile students. They believed that an education emphasising critical thinking and exposure to a variety of points of view would encourage intercultural understanding. Today the IBO offers three programmes to schools. The Diploma Programme is for students in the final two years of secondary school. The Middle Years Programme, adopted in 1994, is for students aged 11–16, and the Primary Years Programme, adopted in 1997, is for students aged 3–12. There are 59 schools in the UK offering the IB Diploma. W www.ibo.org

PROGRESS FILE

Progress File is the successor to the National Record of Achievement which ceased to be available in July 2004. Progress File is an interactive set of guides designed to help young people and adults identify their skills. It enables individuals to manage their learning through promoting ongoing reviewing, planning and development, and recording achievement as part of lifelong learning. The Progress File objectives are to equip people to plan and manage their learning and make effective transitions; to increase motivation and confidence to achieve; and to stimulate learning to gain knowledge and skills, including where these are not recognised in national qualifications.
W www.dfes.gov.uk/progressfile/

TEACHERS

ENGLAND AND WALES

All teachers working in maintained primary, special and secondary schools, non-maintained special schools and pupil referral units are required to register with the General Teaching Council for England (GTCE) in England and the General Teaching Council for Wales (GTCW) in Wales. W www.gtce.org.uk and www.gtcw.org.uk

New entrants to the teaching profession in state primary and secondary schools are required to be graduates and to have Qualified Teacher Status (QTS). QTS is achieved by successfully completing a course of initial teacher training (ITT), traditionally either a Bachelor of Education (BEd) degree, BA with QTS, BSc with QTS or the Postgraduate Certificate of Education (PGCE) at an accredited institution. New entrants are statutorily required to serve a one-year induction period during which they will have a structured programme of support. All initial teacher training has a strong element of practical school-based work, with student teachers spending significant periods of their training in the classroom.

In addition to the traditional routes, in recent years various employment-based routes to QTS have been developed. The Graduate Teacher Programme (GTP) is designed for mature, well-qualified people who can quickly take on teaching responsibilities and who need to earn a living while they train. Trainees are paid a salary and undergo up to a year of school-based training. The Registered Teacher Programme (RTP) is designed for people without a degree or formal teaching qualification but with at least two years of higher education; entrants are paid a salary and complete a degree while undergoing training for up to two years. Employment-based training routes account for about 10 per cent of all teacher training places.

Teachers in further education are not required to have QTS, though roughly half have a teaching qualification and most have industrial, commercial or professional experience. As from July 2002, all new entrants to FE teaching in Wales are required to have, or to be working towards, a specified FE teaching qualification. A qualification for aspiring head teachers, the National Professional Qualification for Headship (NPQH), has been introduced. The National College for School Leadership administers this qualification and others and acts as a focus for development and support. In Wales, the NPQH and other headship programmes are administered by the Welsh Assembly Government and consideration is being given to establishing a similar scheme in respect of FE principals, in association with powers under the Education Act 2002 allowing the making of regulations requiring FE principals to have a specified qualification.

The Department for Education and Skills and the Welsh Assembly have introduced various financial incentives to encourage people to train as teachers. A tax-free training bursary of £6,000 is available to most people on post-graduate teacher training courses. Teachers who successfully gain QTS in a priority subject on a PGCE course and who then go on to teach that subject may receive a further £4,000 'Golden Hello' after completing their first year of work. The priority subjects are: English (including drama), Welsh (in Wales), design and technology, information technology, mathematics, modern foreign languages and science. In Wales a similar scheme operates, on a pilot basis, for those undertaking the full-time PGCE (FE) or PGCE (PcET) (Post-compulsory Education and Training). Eligible students receive a bursary of £6,000 (£7,000 for mathematics and science courses from September 2005), paid in instalments whilst studying. In England, other training awards may be available through the Secondary Shortage Subject Scheme (SSSS). This is an additional, means-tested hardship fund from the TTA. The subjects currently included are: design and technology, geography, information technology, mathematics, modern languages, music, religious education and science.

In Wales, placement grants supported by the Higher Education Funding Council for Wales (HEFCW) provide £1,000 per funded student on undergraduate priority courses – the same subjects that attract the £4,000 training grant – and £600 to students on other undergraduate courses.

The TTA administers a returners' programme for qualified teachers who wish to refresh their skills before returning to the profession. Participants are entitled to a bursary of up to £150 a week to a total of £1,500 and additional childcare support. The TTA supports the sharing of good practice in teacher training, encourages schools to offer placements for trainee teachers, and approves organisations to offer training and assessment for higher level teaching assistant (HLTA) status. The Secretary of State announced on 29 March 2004 that he is extending the TTA's remit to include training for school support staff, and aspects of continuing professional development for teachers.

The TTA funds all types of teacher training in England, whether run by universities, colleges or schools. In Wales funding is undertaken by the HEFCW. On an integrated England and Wales basis the TTA also acts as a central source of information and advice about entry to teaching. The General Teaching Council, an independent professional council, acts as a disciplinary body dealing with cases of misconduct and incompetence. It is also responsible for promoting the profession and professional standards and for advising the Secretary of State. The separate General Teaching Council for Wales operates on a similar basis.

The Specialist Teacher Assistant (STA) scheme provides trained support to qualified teachers in the teaching of reading, writing and arithmetic to young pupils.
W www.useyourheadteach.gov.uk and www.teachernet.gov.uk/management/professionaldevelopment/npqh

SCOTLAND

The General Teaching Council (GTC) for Scotland advises central government on matters relating to teacher supply and the professional suitability of all teacher training courses. The GTC is also the body responsible for disciplinary procedures in cases of professional misconduct. All teachers in maintained schools must be registered with the GTC. Only graduates are accepted as entrants to the profession; primary school teachers undertake either a four-year vocational degree course or a one-year postgraduate course, while teachers of academic subjects in secondary schools undertake the latter. There is also a combined degree sometimes known as a concurrent degree.

The Scottish Qualification for Headship has been introduced for aspiring head teachers. The colleges of education provide both in-service and pre-service training for teachers which is subject to inspection by HM Inspectorate of Education. The colleges are funded by the Scottish Higher Education Funding Council, which also sets intake levels for teacher education courses.
W www.gtcs.org.uk and www.sqh.ed.ac.uk

NORTHERN IRELAND

All new entrants to teaching in grant-aided schools are graduates and hold an approved teaching qualification. A fully integrated programme of Initial Teacher Education (ITE), induction and early professional development as well as the Professional Qualification for Headship (PQH(NI)) programme, is in place in Northern Ireland. ITE is provided by Queen's University, Belfast, University of Ulster, Stranmillis University College, St Mary's University College and the Open University (NI). The university colleges are concerned with teacher education mainly for the primary school sector and the universities mainly for the post-primary sector. The General Teaching Council for Northern Ireland advises government on professional issues, maintains a register of professional teachers and acts as a disciplinary body.

QUALIFIED TEACHERS 2001–2
(full-time) (thousands)*

	E&W	*Scotland*	*NI*	*Total UK*
Maintained nursery and primary schools	181.5	21.5	8.6	211.6
Maintained secondary schools	194.2	22.7	9.7	226.6
Non-maintained mainstream schools	50.2	2.5	0.1	52.8
All special schools	13.5	2.1	0.8	16.3
Total	439.4	48.8	19.1	507.3

*Provisional

SALARIES

Qualified teachers in England, Wales and Northern Ireland, other than the leadership group (which includes head teachers, deputy head teachers and advanced skills teachers) are paid on a six point main pay scale. Good quality performers have the opportunity to be assessed against national standards and moving to the three point upper scale. An 'Excellent Teacher' scheme is being developed now which, subject to consideration by the School Teachers' review Body, would allow further salary progression. Entry points and placement depend on relevant experience. There are additional cash allowances for management responsibilities, special needs work and recruitment and retention factors which may be awarded at the discretion of the relevant body, i.e. the governing body or the LEA. The 'advanced skills teacher' grade was introduced to enhance prospects in the classroom for the most able teachers; this grade does not apply in Northern Ireland. Experienced teachers are assessed against national standards to move onto the upper pay scale, after which they receive performance-related pay increases. There is a statutory superannuation scheme. Teachers working in the London area are paid on separate pay scales. Salary scales for teachers in England, Wales and Northern Ireland as at 2004 are:

Head teacher	£36,432–£90,360+
Principal (Northern Ireland) (2003 figures)	£31,416–£88,155
Deputy head/Vice-principal (Northern Ireland) (2003 figures)	from £31,416
Advanced skills teacher	£30,501–£48,657
Teacher	£18,558–£31,602
Inner London	
Head teacher	£42,525–£96,450+
Deputy head teacher	from £38,292
Advanced skills teacher	£36,594–£54,747
Teacher	£22,059–£37,692

Teachers in Scotland are paid on a seven-point scale. The entry point depends on type of qualification and additional allowances are payable under a range of circumstances. Salary scales for teachers in Scotland from 1 August 2004 are:

Head teacher/Depute head teacher	£36,531–£71,310
Principal teacher	£32,208–£41,574
Chartered teacher	£30,459–£36,219
Main grade	£18,522–£29,541

POST-16 EDUCATION

In the United Kingdom in 2001–2, 79 per cent of 16-year-olds and 68 per cent of 17-year-olds were in post-compulsory education, either at school or in full-time further education or in Government supported training. There were over 5.3 million further education students in the UK during the academic year 2001–2, of which 80 per cent were part-time. The number of students by country of study in 2001–2 was (in thousands):

	Full-time	*Part-time*
UK	1,128.2	4,227.1
England	1,016.7	3,613.6
Wales	45.0	210.0
Scotland*	45.1	345.0
Northern Ireland†	21.4	58.4

* Enrolments, not head count
† Provisional

In 2002–3, there were 467 further education colleges in the UK of which 103 were sixth form colleges. In 2001–2, there were 57,000 full-time academic staff in further education institutions.

ENGLAND AND WALES

Further education and sixth form colleges are funded directly through the Learning and Skills Council in England, which operates through 47 local offices, and the National Council for Education and Training in Wales. Further education colleges are controlled by autonomous further education corporations, which include substantial representation from industry and commerce, and which own assets and employ staff. Their funding is determined in part by the number of students enrolled and their level of achievement.

Much further education tends to be broadly vocational in purpose and employers are often involved in designing courses. It ranges from lower-level technical and commercial courses and government-sponsored training, through courses for those aiming at higher-level posts in industry, commerce and administration, to professional courses. Facilities exist for GCE A- and AS-levels, GCSEs, GNVQs and a full range of vocational qualifications. These courses can form the foundation for progress to higher education qualifications. Many students attend part-time, either through day or block release from employment, or in the evenings. Adult learners usually form the largest proportion of students in further education colleges, often studying part-time in the evening or at weekends. The main courses and examinations in the vocational field, all of which link in with the National Vocational Qualification (NVQ) framework, are offered by the following bodies, but there are also many others. Edexcel resulted from the merger of the Business and Technology Education Council (BTEC) and London Examinations. It provides programmes of study across a wide range of subject areas. Qualifications offered include GNVQs, NVQs, GCSEs, AS- and A-levels, National and Higher National diplomas and certificates, and other BTEC qualifications. City & Guilds specialise in developing qualifications and assessments for work-related and leisure qualifications. They offer nationally and internationally recognised certificates in over 500 vocational qualifications. The progressive structure of awards spans seven levels, from foundation to the highest level of professional competence.

Oxford, Cambridge and RSA Examinations cover the full range of academic and vocational qualifications. The latter include accounting, business administration, customer service, management, language schemes, information technology and teaching qualifications. A wide range of NVQs and GNVQs are offered and a policy operates of credit accumulation, so that candidates can take a single unit or complete qualifications.
W www.lsc.gov.uk and www.elwa.ac.uk

WORK-BASED LEARNING

Apprenticeships are a way for young people aged 16–24 to get hands-on experience and on-the-job training while gaining nationally recognised qualifications. The Learning and Skills Council contributes towards the cost of training and assessment. The National Council for Education and Training Wales (ELWa) provides financial assistance in Wales. Apprenticeships normally last between one and three years and there are two levels: Apprenticeships and Advanced Apprenticeships at Levels 2 and 3 respectively. Both of these lead to:

- National Vocational Qualifications
- Key Skills qualifications – transferable work-related skills like IT and communication, problem solving, application of mathematics, improving learning, and performance and teamwork
- Technical certificates – vocationally related qualifications that provide the basic knowledge of the NVQ

There are approximately 255,500 young people aged between 16 to 24 on Apprenticeships in England alone, with similar programmes in place in Scotland, Northern Ireland and Wales.

From January 2004 the Apprenticeship programmes in Wales were opened to all people irrespective of age and who have left full-time statutory education.
W www.realworkrealpay.info

SCOTLAND

The Scottish Further Education Funding Council is the statutory body responsible for funding the 46 further education colleges. The Scottish Qualifications Authority (SQA) is the statutory awarding body for qualifications in the national education and training system in Scotland. It is both the main awarding body for qualifications for work including Scottish Vocational Qualifications (SVQs) and is also their accrediting body. The SQA is by statute required clearly to separate its awarding and accrediting functions. There are three main qualification 'families' in Scottish further education: National Qualifications; Higher National Qualifications (HNC and HND); and SVQs. In addition to Standard Grade qualifications, National Qualifications are available at five levels: Access, Intermediate 1, Intermediate 2, Higher and Advanced Higher. Another feature of the qualifications system is the Scottish Group Award (SGA). SGAs are built up unit by unit and allow opportunity for credit transfer from other qualifications (such as Standard Grade or SVQ), providing a further option for learners, especially adult learners. SVQs are competence-based qualifications suitable for work-place delivery but they can also be taken in further education colleges and other centres where work-place conditions can be simulated. The Scottish Credit and Qualifications Framework (SCQF) includes qualifications across academic and vocational sectors in a single credit-based framework. It comprises 12 levels, covering all mainstream qualifications from Access level in National Qualifications to postgraduate qualifications, and including SVQs. In the academic year 2001–2 there were 514,877 student enrolments on vocational and non-vocational courses in further education colleges. Of this total, higher educational courses accounted for 64,089 enrolments.
W www.sfefc.ac.uk and www.sqa.org.uk

NORTHERN IRELAND

All further education colleges are independent corporate bodies like their counterparts in the rest of the UK. Responsibility for the sector lies with the Department for Employment and Learning, which funds the colleges directly. The colleges own their own property, are responsible for their own services and employ their own staff.

The governing bodies of the colleges must include at least 50 per cent membership who are engaged or employed in business, industry, or any profession.

Northern Ireland has 16 institutions of further education, and in 2001–2 there were 21,422 full-time and 58,445 part-time enrolments on vocational further education courses.

W www.delni.gov.uk

STUDENT SUPPORT

Education Maintenance Allowance (EMA) is a means tested allowance to support young people in post-16 education. It became available across England from September 2004. It consists of a weekly payment of up to £30, plus periodic bonus payments. EMA is available to students who are 16 by 31 August and staying on at school or college (and to older students in EMA pilot areas for the academic year 2004–5). Also available to students in England in that age group are Learner Support Funds. These funds, which are targeted at those students in greatest need, have four separate strands: Transport, Childcare (Care2Learn), Residential and General funding. Whilst the funding for both transport and childcare are universal, the discretionary nature of the other funds allows local learning institutions to provide targeted help and support where it is most needed. In England, the Adult Learning Grant is currently being piloted in the North East and South East regions, plus a further nine Learning and Skills Council areas: Bedfordshire and Luton, Devon and Cornwall, Humberside, Lancashire, Leicestershire, London West, Shropshire, South Yorkshire, and the Black Country. It offers an allowance of up to £30 per week to adults on low incomes studying full time for a first full Level 2 qualification (five GCSEs or equivalent) or for young adults studying full time for a first Level 3 qualification (two A-levels or equivalent). Eligible Welsh-domiciled students aged over 18 on further education courses, whether full-time or part-time (subject to a minimum contact requirement), receive a means-tested non-repayable Assembly Learning Grant. The grant is administered by LEAs. Discretionary Financial Contingency Funds are also available to all students suffering hardship and are administered by the institutions themselves. In addition, Individual Learning Accounts are available in Wales, which provide adults with means-tested support of up to £200 to undertake a wide range of learning. Eligible Scottish-domiciled further education students can apply to their college for discretionary support in the form of bursaries. These can include allowances for maintenance, travel, study, two homes, dependants and special educational needs. College students receiving EMAs may also be eligible for the non-maintenance elements. In addition, colleges administer discretionary funds in the form of hardship, childcare and young students' retention funds.

Full-time students over 19 years of age and resident in Northern Ireland, on certain vocational courses, may benefit from discretionary non-repayable Access Bursaries. The bursaries are administered by the Education and Library Boards. Support for further education students in Northern Ireland includes free tuition to all full-time students up to age 18 and to all full-time students over 18 undertaking a vocational course at Level 3 or below. In addition, financial help is provided by colleges through a discretionary support fund for both full-time and part-time students whose access to and participation in further education is inhibited by financial considerations.

VOCATIONAL QUALIFICATIONS

National Vocational Qualifications (NVQs) are work-related competence-based qualifications. They are designed to reflect the skills and knowledge needed to do a job effectively, and represent national standards recognised by employers. General National Vocational Qualifications (GNVQs) provide a vocational alternative to academic qualifications in colleges and schools for 16–19 year olds. Each GNVQ is related to a broad area of work and is a unit-based qualification assessed through a combination of continuous assessment and short test papers. They are available in 14 vocational areas at two levels: Foundation and Intermediate.

The Vocational Certificate of Education (VCE), sometimes known as the Vocational A-level, replaced Advanced GNVQs. It is available in different forms: the three-unit VCE Advanced Subsidiary (equivalent to one GCE AS-level), the six-unit VCE Advanced Level (equivalent to one GCE A-level), and the 12-unit VCE Double Award (equivalent to two GCE A-levels). The timetable for the withdrawal of the individual six-unit GNVQ titles was issued by the Qualifications and Curriculum Authority in November 2003. The withdrawal is taking place in three stages from 2005 to 2007, starting with titles with extremely low numbers of candidate entries. The withdrawal of the six-unit GNVQ is the end of a process, first announced in 2000, whereby all elements of the GNVQ qualification (Part One, six-unit, and Advanced Level) were to be withdrawn. The QCA has identified and advised schools and colleges of alternative qualifications for each of the GNVQ subject areas.

HIGHER EDUCATION

The term higher education is used to describe education above A-level, Higher and Advanced Higher Grade and their equivalent, which is provided in universities, colleges of higher education and in some further education colleges.

A White Paper, *The Future of Higher Education*, published in January 2003, sets out the Government's plans for reform and investment in universities and higher education colleges, and includes proposals for changes in the student finance system.

STUDENT NUMBERS IN THE UK

Higher Education student numbers in the UK in 2002–3 were:

	Total	*Full-time*	*Part-time*
Total HE students in the UK	2,175,115	–	–
Total post-graduate students	497,500	206,755	290,745
Total undergraduate students	1,677,615	1,111,310	566,305

Higher Education qualifications obtained in the UK in 2002–3 were:

	Total HE qualifications obtained	*Total first degrees*	*Total higher degrees*	*Total other postgraduate*	*Total other undergraduate*
Full-time	398,855	250,625	68,055	35,360	44,815
Part-time	158,935	31,755	30,830	30,105	66,245

Advice to government on matters relating to higher education is provided by the Higher Education Funding Councils for England, Wales and Scotland, and by the Higher Education Council in Northern Ireland. The former receive a block grant from central government which is allocated to the universities and colleges. In Northern Ireland the grant is allocated directly to institutions by the Department for Employment and Learning. W www.hefc.ac.uk, www.hefcw.ac.uk, www.shefc.ac.uk, www.delni.gov.uk

TYPES OF HIGHER EDUCATION INSTITUTION

The Further and Higher Education Act 1992 and parallel legislation in Scotland removed the distinction between higher education provided by the universities and that provided in England and Wales by the former polytechnics and colleges of higher education and in Scotland by the former central institutions and others. It allowed all polytechnics, and other higher education institutions which satisfy the necessary criteria, to award their own taught course and research degrees and to adopt the title of university. All the polytechnics, and some colleges of higher education have since done so. The change of name does not affect the legal constitution of the institutions. Funding is by the Higher Education Funding Councils for England, Wales and Scotland and directly by the Department for Employment and Learning in Northern Ireland. There are now 89 universities in the UK whereas only 48 existed prior to the Further and Higher Education Acts 1992. Of the 89, 72 are in England (including the University of London, which has a federal structure), two in Wales (one a federal institution comprising six constituent institutions and two university colleges), 14 in Scotland (15 including the Open University Scotland) and two in Northern Ireland. There are also 64 colleges of higher education, some of which are multidisciplinary while others specialise, for example, in teacher training.

GOVERNANCE OF UNIVERSITIES AND COLLEGES

The pre-1992 universities each have their own system of internal governance but broad similarities exist. Most are run by two main bodies: the senate, which deals primarily with academic issues and consists of members elected from within the university; and the council, which is the executive governing body and is responsible for all appointments and promotions, and bidding for and allocation of financial resources. At least half the members of the council are drawn from outside the university. Many of the council's functions are carried out through committees. Joint committees of senate and council are common. The 1992 Act, and the Education reform Act 1988, set out the system of governance for universities which were formerly polytechnics or other higher education institutions and for the colleges of higher education. Each institution also has articles of government that are approved by the Privy Council. These post-1992 institutions are run by boards of governors, which are responsible for the mission, finances and all appointments. Much of the board's business is delegated to committees. In particular, there is usually an academic board that deals with all matters related to teaching and research.

OPEN UNIVERSITY AND THE UNIVERSITY FOR INDUSTRY

The non-residential Open University provides a modular programme of courses throughout the UK leading to first and higher degrees, diplomas and certificates. Students are taught through distance learning, using written and audio-visual materials and the Internet, supported by tutorials and short residential courses. No qualifications are needed for entry. The Open University received £164.7 million in public funding 2002–3. In 2002–3, 158,000 undergraduates were registered. The University for Industry (UfI) promotes learning ranging from basic skills to specialised technological and management skills. It aims to help individuals to improve their chances of employment, improve their career prospects and boost business competitiveness. It works as a public-private partnership in England, Wales and Northern Ireland. UfI's services are delivered through Learndirect, which provides access to courses, over 80 per cent of which are online. There are over 2000 Learndirect centres. There is one private university in England, the University of Buckingham, which receives no public funding.

SCOTLAND

The Scottish Higher Education Funding Council (SHEFC) funds 20 institutions of higher education, including 14 universities. The universities are broadly managed as described above and the remaining colleges are managed by independent governing bodies which include representatives of industrial, commercial, professional and educational interests. Most of the courses outside the universities have a vocational orientation and a substantial number are sandwich courses.

NORTHERN IRELAND

In Northern Ireland higher education is provided in the 16 colleges of further education, the two universities and the two university colleges. These institutions offer a range of courses, including first and postgraduate degrees, PGCEs, undergraduate diplomas and certificates, and professional qualifications.

ACADEMIC STAFF

Each university and college appoints its own academic staff. The Universities and Colleges Employers Association (UCEA) is the employers' association for subscribing universities and other higher education institutions in the UK. It provides a framework within which representatives of institutions can discuss salaries, conditions of service, employee relations and all matters connected with the employment of staff and employees. The services of the UCEA include collective bargaining and an annual salary survey. Teaching staff in higher education require no formal teaching qualification. However, the Institute for Learning and Teaching in Higher Education, funded by the funding councils, was set up to establish an accreditation scheme and continuing professional development for higher education teachers and to encourage innovation in teaching and learning. The funding councils also fund the Learner and Teaching Support Network to develop and share good practice. In April 2004 both organisations were incorporated into a new national body: the Higher Education Academy.

Teacher trainers are required to spend a certain amount of time in schools to ensure that they have sufficient recent practical experience.

The number of full-time academic staff in all UK institutions in 2002–3 was:

	Total	*Male*	*Female*
UK	120,800	78,385	42,410
England	97,345	63,025	34,315
Wales	5,825	3,835	1,990
Scotland	14,585	9,545	5,040
Northern Ireland	3,045	1,980	1,065

Lecturers' Common Interest Group Higher Education Pay Scales effective from 1 August 2004 are given below. However, for many institutions these scales will be phased in between August 2004 and July 2006.

Grade Lecturer	£ p.a.
9	24,886
10	24,886
11	25,633
12	27,194
13	28,009
14	28,850
15	29,715
Senior lecturer	
0	28,850
1	29,715
2	30,607
3	31,544
4	32,471
5	33,445
6	34,448
7	35,482
8	36,546
Principal lecturer	
0	37,643
1	37,643
2	37,643
3	37,643
4	38,772
5	39,935
6	41,133
7	42,367
8	42,367
9	43,638
Researcher A	
1	12,987
2	14,192
3	15,056
4	15,973
5	16,946
6	17,978
Researcher B	
1	19,645
2	19,645
3	20,842
4	22,111
5	22,774
6	24,161
7	24,868
8	25,633
9	27,194
10	28,009
11	28,850

Part-time hourly rates	
I/II/III	32.42
IV	26.77
V	19.59

FINANCE

The total income of institutions of higher education in the UK in 2002–3 was:

	£	% *of total*
Funding Council grants	6,054,559	38.9
Tuition fees, education grants and contracts	3,743,094	24.1
Research grants and contracts	2,595,445	16.7
Other income	2,938,382	18.9
Endowment and investment income	230,491	1.5
Total	15,561,971	100

COURSES

In the UK all universities and some colleges award their own degrees and other qualifications and may act as awarding and validating bodies for colleges. The power to award degrees is regulated by law and it is an offence to purport to award a UK degree unless authorised to do so. The Quality Assurance Agency for Higher Education (QAA) advises government on applications for degree-awarding powers.

Facilities exist for full-time and part-time study, day release, sandwich or block release. Credit accumulation and transfer systems (CATS) allow a student to achieve a final qualification by accumulating credits for courses of study successfully achieved, or even professional experience, over a period.

Higher education courses comprise: first degree and postgraduate (including research); Diploma in Higher Education (DipHE); BTEC Higher National Diplomas (HND) and Higher National Certificates (HNC); and preparation for professional examinations.

The DipHE is commonly a two-year diploma usually intended to serve as a stepping stone to a degree course or other further study. The DipHE is awarded by the institution itself if it is accredited; by an accredited institution of its choice if not. The HNCs are awarded after two years' part-time study. The HNDs are awarded after two years' full-time, or three years' sandwich-course or part-time study.

The foundation degree, launched in 2001, is a two-year vocational higher education qualification which forms either a self-contained qualification or a basis for further study leading to an honours degree or further professional qualifications.

Undergraduate courses lead to the title of Bachelor, Bachelor of Arts (BA) and Bachelor of Science (BSc) being the most common, except in certain Scottish universities where Master is sometimes used for a first degree in arts subjects. For a higher degree the titles are Master of Arts (MA), Master of Science (MSc) and the research degrees of Master of Philosophy (MPhil) and Doctor of Philosophy (PhD or, at a few universities, DPhil).

Most undergraduate courses at universities and colleges of higher education run for three years, but some take four years or longer. Postgraduate studies vary in length.

Post-experience short courses form a significant part of higher education provision, reflecting the demand for

professional and technical training. Most of these courses fund themselves.
W www.qaa.ac.uk

ADMISSIONS

The target proportion of 18- to 30-year-olds entering full-time higher education by 2010 is set in England at 50 per cent. Institutions suffer financial penalties if the number of students laid down for them by the funding councils is exceeded, but the individual university or college decides which students to accept. The formal entry requirements to most degree courses are two or more A-levels at grade E or above (or equivalent), and to HND courses one A-level (or equivalent). In practice, most offers of places require qualifications in excess of this, higher requirements usually reflecting the popularity of a course or institution. These requirements do not, however, exclude applications from students with a variety of non-GCSE qualifications or unquantified experience and skills. For admission to a degree, DipHE or HND, potential students apply through the Universities and Colleges Admission Service (UCAS). UCAS operates an online application system. The aim is that by 2006, 100 per cent of applications will be received electronically. At present it is still possible to submit paper-based applications. Applicants can also fill in their applications using the CD-based electronic application system (EAS). UCAS handles over 450,000 applications a year as the UK's only central admissions service for full-time higher education courses. The only exception among universities is the Open University, which conducts its own admissions. Applications for undergraduate teacher training courses are made through UCAS and for postgraduate teacher training, through the Graduate Teacher Training Registry. Details of initial teacher training courses in Scotland can be obtained from colleges of education and those universities offering such courses, and from Universities Scotland. For 2005, applications for postgraduate social work will also be though UCAS. For admission as a postgraduate student, universities and colleges normally require a good first degree in a subject related to the proposed course of study or research. Most applications are made to individual institutions, except for teaching and social work. W www.ucas.ac.uk

FEES

Entrants to undergraduate courses domiciled in England, Wales and Northern Ireland pay, directly to the institution, an annual contribution to their fees (up to £1,150 in 2004–5) depending on their own level of income or that of their spouse or parents. Those whose parents' residual income is less than £21,475 pay nothing and those whose parents have a residual income of £31,973 or more pay the full £1,150. The fee contribution represents some 25 per cent of the average cost of a higher education course in the UK and the balance is paid by the student's LEA or, in Northern Ireland, by the student's regional Education and Library Board. Students from EU member countries pay fees at home student rates and, if studying at institutions in England, Wales and Northern Ireland, are liable to make an annual contribution to fees assessed against family income. Among the classes of students exempt from payment are: Scottish-domiciled and EU students at Scottish institutions; students from England, Wales and Northern Ireland in the fourth year of a four-year degree course at a Scottish institution; existing students with mandatory awards (see below), for whom the grant-awarding body pays; students on certain courses of initial teacher training; medical students in the fifth year of their course; health professionals on National Health Service bursaries; and full-time or part-time students on benefit or low incomes. For students on an access course, fees start from about £200; financial help with this is available. For part-time or flexible learning tuition fees vary, and tuition is free for those on a low income or for those who receive certain benefits.

STUDENT SUPPORT

LOANS

Since September 1998, the means-tested loan has been the main form of support for most undergraduate students in the UK on full-time or sandwich undergraduate courses of higher education. Students apply through LEAs in England and Wales, education and library boards in Northern Ireland and the Students Awards Agency in Scotland. Of the maximum loan, 75 per cent is available to all eligible students regardless of income; the remaining 25 per cent is means tested by the LEA. The loan rates for 2004–5 are:

Living in college/lodgings in London area	£5,050
Living in college/lodgings elsewhere	£4,095
Living in parental home	£3,240

Extra income assessed loans are available to students whose courses last more than 30 term-time weeks or who need to study abroad in certain high-cost countries. Loans of up to £500 are available in 2003–4 to part-time students on low incomes or with dependent children.

Loans are available to students on designated courses. Certain residency conditions also apply. In 2002–3, 836,800 loans were taken up, to the value of £2,621.3 million.

Repayment of income contingent loans begins in the April following the end of the course. Those who pay tax through PAYE have repayments deducted from their salaries once they earn more than £10,000 a year. This amount will increase to £15,000 from April 2005. The self-employed make repayments through their tax returns. Repayments are calculated at 9 per cent of income over the threshold. If income falls below the threshold, repayments cease until income rises above it.

NON-REPAYABLE GRANTS AND ALLOWANCES

Eligible students, such as single parents, others with dependants or those leaving care, are entitled to apply for various additional means-tested supplementary grants for help in meeting certain living and other costs, for childcare and for each child at school. Disabled students are eligible for non means-tested Disabled Students' Allowances.

From the academic year 2004–5, Higher Education Grants of £1,000 will be available to students whose family income is £15,200 or less. Partial grants are available to those whose family income is between £15,201 and £21,185. Eligible Welsh-domiciled undergraduates from low-income families, whether on full-time or part-time courses, receive a means-tested non-repayable Assembly Learning Grant of up to £1,500 per year. The grant is administered by local education authorities. Eligible Scottish-domiciled students from low income families at institutions in Scotland may apply for a Young Students' Bursary. The maximum available in 2003–4 is £2,100. Full-time students on a low income who are resident in Northern Ireland may benefit from discretionary non-repayable Access Bursaries of up to £2,000. The award of a bursary carries a reduction in student loan entitlement. The bursaries are administered by the education and library boards.

LEARNER SUPPORT AND ACCESS FUNDS

Funds, variously known as hardship or access funds (Financial Contingency Funds in Wales and Support Funds in Northern Ireland) are allocated by central government to the appropriate funding councils in England and Wales and to the Student Awards Agency in Scotland, and are administered by further and higher education institutions. In Northern Ireland they are allocated by central government directly to the institution. Their purpose is to provide help for individual students facing financial difficulties. All students, whether full- or part-time, undergraduate or postgraduate, may apply. Universities and colleges set their own criteria and manage their own procedures within the national framework. The amount payable depends on individual circumstances and on the amount the institution has available. Some colleges offer non-repayable bursaries from hardship funds, i.e. a payment for each year of the course, to students who might be prevented from completing their studies due to financial problems. Individual colleges and universities may also offer emergency funds.

POSTGRADUATE AWARDS

Most postgraduates have to pay large contributions towards their tuition fees as the only mandatory funding for postgraduate study is for students taking the Postgraduate Certificate in Education (PGCE). Postgraduate students, with the exception of students in England, Wales and Northern Ireland on loan-bearing diploma courses such as teacher training, are not eligible to apply for student loans. The Research Councils and the Arts and Humanities Research Board are the biggest providers of postgraduate funding. Grants for postgraduate study are discretionary and competition for them is fierce. They comprise maintenance grants for students undertaking doctoral research or taught masters degrees, are not means-tested and are dependent on the class of first degree (especially for research degrees); and flat-rate maintenance grants. There are additional allowances for disabled students, those with dependants and for fieldwork expenses.

Awards are funded by the British Academy, the Higher Education Funding Councils for England and Wales, the Scottish Higher Education Funding Council and the Department for Employment and Learning for Northern Ireland, among others. Employers may also offer financial support.

ADULT AND CONTINUING EDUCATION

In the UK, the duty of securing adult and continuing education leading to academic or vocational qualifications is statutory. The Learning and Skills Council in England, the National Council for Education and Training in Wales and the Further Education Funding Council in Scotland are responsible for and fund those courses which take place in their sector and lead to academic and vocational qualifications, prepare students to undertake further or higher education courses, or confer basic skills; the Higher Education Funding Councils fund advanced courses of continuing education. The LEAs have the power, although not the duty, to provide those courses which do not fall within the remit of the funding bodies. In Northern Ireland the Department for Employment and Learning is responsible for the funding of the statutory further education sector.

The involvement of universities in adult education and continuing education has diversified considerably. Birkbeck College in the University of London offers a range of degree and other courses designed specifically to meet the needs of mature students. The post-1992 universities and the colleges of higher education, because of their range of courses and flexible patterns of student attendance, provide opportunities in the field of adult and continuing education. The Forum for the Advancement of Continuing Education promotes collaboration between institutions of higher education active in this area. The Open University, in partnership with the BBC, provides distance teaching leading to first degrees, and also offers post-experience and higher degree courses. Of the voluntary bodies providing adult education, the biggest is the Workers' Educational Association (WEA), which operates throughout the UK and provides over 10,000 courses each year, reaching more than 110,000 adults. The WEA is a charity supported by funding from the Learning and Skills Council in England and by the Scottish Executive and local authorities in Scotland. NIACE, the National Institute of Adult Continuing Education, has a broad remit to promote lifelong learning opportunities for adults. NIACE works to develop increased participation in education and training in England and Wales, particularly for those currently under-represented. It does this through research and project work, conferences, publications and the provision of an information service to educational providers. NIACE and the Basic Skills Agency together manage the Community Learning Fund on behalf of the DfES. NIACE Dysgu Cymru, the Welsh committee, receives financial support from the National Assembly for Wales, support in kind from local authorities, and advises government, voluntary bodies and education providers on adult continuing education and training matters in Wales. In Scotland, advice on adult and community education, and promotion thereof, is provided by Community Learning Scotland; in April 2002 Community Learning Scotland ceased to be a non-departmental public body and some of its functions transferred to the Communities Scotland agency. In Northern Ireland, those functions are undertaken by the Department for Employment and Learning.
W www.niace.org.uk

The Adult Learning Inspectorate (ALI) is a non-departmental government-funded public body established under the Learning and Skills Act 2000 with the responsibility of raising the standards of education and training for young people and adults in England. It inspects and reports on the quality of education and training and can also be commissioned to inspect private training provision in the UK. W www.ali.gov.uk

The Universities' Association for Continuing Education (UACE) represents and promotes the interests of continuing education and lifelong learning providers within higher education. W www.uace.org.uk

EDUCATION DIRECTORY

LOCAL EDUCATION AUTHORITIES

ENGLAND

COUNTY COUNCILS

BEDFORDSHIRE County Hall, Cauldwell Street, Bedford MK42 9AP **T** 01234-363222 **W** www.bedfordshire.gov.uk
Director, David Doran

BUCKINGHAMSHIRE County Hall, Walton Street, Aylesbury HP20 1UA **T** 01296-395000 **W** www.buckscc.gov.uk
Chief Education Officer, P. J. Mooney

CAMBRIDGESHIRE Box ELH 1505, Shire Hall, Castle Hill, Cambridge CB3 0AF **T** 01223-717111 **W** www.cambridgeshire.gov.uk
Director, A. Baxter

CHESHIRE County Hall, Chester CH1 1SQ **T** 01244-602424 **W** www.cheshire.gov.uk
Director of Education and Community, D. Cracknell

CORNWALL County Hall, Truro TR1 3AY **T** 01872-322000 **W** www.cornwall.gov.uk
Director, G. Aver

CUMBRIA 5 Portland Square, Carlisle CA1 1PU **T** 01228-606877 **W** www.cumbria.gov.uk/education
Director of Education, V. Ashfield

DERBYSHIRE County Hall, Matlock DE4 3AG **T** 01629-585814 **W** www.derbyshire.gov.uk
Chief Education Officer, R. V. Taylor

DEVON County Hall, Topsham Road, Exeter EX2 4QG **T** 01392-382059 **W** www.devon.gov.uk
Director, P. Norrey

DORSET County Hall, Colliton Park, Dorchester DT1 1XJ **T** 01305-224110 **W** www.dorsetcc.gov.uk
Director, D. Goddard

DURHAM County Hall, Durham DH1 5UJ **T** 0191-386 4411 **W** www.durham.gov.uk
Director, K. Mitchell

EAST SUSSEX PO Box 4, County Hall, St Anne's Crescent, Lewes BN7 1SG **T** 01273-481000 **W** www.eastsussexcc.gov.uk
Director of Education, Ms D. Stokoe

ESSEX PO Box 47, Chelmsford CM2 6WN **T** 01245-492211 **W** www.essexcc.gov.uk
Director of Learning Services, P. Lincoln

GLOUCESTERSHIRE Shire Hall, Westgate Street, Gloucester GL1 2TG **T** 01452-425302 **W** www.gloscc.gov.uk
Chief Education Officer, Roger Crouch

HAMPSHIRE County Office, Education Department, The Castle, Winchester SO23 8UG **T** 01962-846452 **W** www.hants.gov.uk/education
County Education Officer, A. J. Seber

HERTFORDSHIRE County Hall, Pegs Lane, Hertford SG13 8DE **T** 01438-737500 **W** www.hertsdirect.org
Director, J. Hariss

ISLE OF WIGHT County Hall, High Street, Newport PO30 1UD **T** 01983-823400 **W** www.iwight.com
Director of Education, D. Pettitt

KENT Sessions House, County Hall, Maidstone ME14 1XG **T** 01622-671411 **W** www.kent.gov.uk
Strategic Director, Nick Henwood

LANCASHIRE PO Box 61, County Hall, Preston PR1 8RJ **T** 01772-254868 **W** www.lancashire.gov.uk
Director, S. Mulvany

LEICESTERSHIRE County Hall, Glenfield, Leicester LE3 8RF **T** 0116-265 6631 **W** www.leics.gov.uk
Director, Mrs J. A. M. Strong

LINCOLNSHIRE County Offices, Newland, Lincoln LN1 1YQ **T** 01522-552222 **W** www.lincolnshire.gov.uk
Director, Dr C. Berry

NORFOLK County Hall, Martineau Lane, Norwich NR1 2DL **T** 01603-222146 **W** www.norfolk.gov.uk
Director, Dr B. C. Slater

NORTHAMPTONSHIRE PO Box 216, John Dryden House, 8–10 The Lakes, Northampton NN4 7DD **T** 01604-236252 **W** www.northamptonshire.gov.uk
Corporate Director, A. Sortwell

NORTHUMBERLAND County Hall, Morpeth NE61 2EF **T** 01670-533001
Director, B. Edwards

NORTH YORKSHIRE County Hall, Northallerton, N. Yorks DL7 8AE **T** 01609-780780 **W** www.northyorks.gov.uk
Director, Cynthia Welbourn

NOTTINGHAMSHIRE County Hall, West Bridgford, Nottingham NG2 7QP **T** 0115-982 3823 **W** www.nottinghamshire.gov.uk
Director, P. Tulley

OXFORDSHIRE Macclesfield House, New Road, Oxford OX1 1NA **T** 01865-815449 **W** www.oxfordshire.gov.uk
Director for Learning and Culture, Keith Bartley

SHROPSHIRE The Shirehall, Abbey Foregate, Shrewsbury SY2 6ND **T** 01743-254307 **W** www.shropshireonline.gov.uk
Corporate Director, Mrs E. Nicholson

SOMERSET County Hall, Taunton TA1 4DY **T** 01823-355455 **W** www.somerset.gov.uk
Executive Director – Lifelong Learning, J. Rose *(acting)*

STAFFORDSHIRE Tipping Street, Stafford ST16 2DH **T** 01785-223121 **W** www.staffordshire.gov.uk
Director, Peter Traves

SUFFOLK St Andrew House, County Hall, Ipswich IP4 1LJ **T** 01473-584631 **W** www.suffolkcc.gov.uk
Director, D. J. Peachey

SURREY County Hall, Penrhyn Road, Kingston-upon-Thames KT1 2DJ **T** 0845-600 9009 **W** www.surreycc.gov.uk
Director, Dr P. Gray

WARWICKSHIRE 22 Northgate Street, Warwick CV34 4SP **T** 01926-410410 **W** www.warwickshire.gov.uk
County Education Officer, E. Wood

WEST SUSSEX County Hall, Chichester PO19 1RF **T** 01243-777750 **W** www.westsussex.gov.uk
Director, R. Back

WILTSHIRE County Hall, Bythesea Road, Trowbridge BA14 8JB **T** 01225-713000 **W** www.wiltshire.gov.uk
Director of Children, Education and Libraries, R. W. Wolfson

WORCESTERSHIRE Educational Services Directorate, PO Box 73, Worcester WR5 2YA **T** 01905-766859 **W** www.worcestershire.gov.uk
Director, J. Kramer

UNITARY AND METROPOLITAN BOROUGH COUNCILS

BARNSLEY Berneslai Close, Barnsley S70 2HS **T** 01226-773500 **W** www.barnsley.gov.uk
Executive Director, Education, E. Sutton

BATH AND NORTH EAST SOMERSET PO Box 25, Riverside, Temple Street, Keynsham, Bristol BS31 1DN **T** 01225-477000 **W** www.bathnes.gov.uk
Education Director, M. Young

BIRMINGHAM Education Offices, Margaret Street, Birmingham B3 3BU **T** 0121-303 2550 **W** www.bgfl.org
Chief Education Officer, Tony Howell

BLACKBURN WITH DARWEN Town Hall, Blackburn BB1 7DY **T** 01254-477477 **W** www.blackburn.gov.uk
Director, Peter Morgan

BLACKPOOL Progress House, Clifton Road, Blackpool FY4 4US **T** 01253-477477
Director of Education, Leisure and Cultural Services, D. Lund

BOLTON Paderborn House, Civic Centre, Bolton BL1 1JW **T** 01204-333333
Director, Mrs M. Blenkinsop

BOURNEMOUTH Dorset House, 20–22 Christchurch Road, Bournemouth BH1 3NL **T** 01202-456191
Director, P. Deshpande

BRACKNELL FOREST Seymour House, 38 Broadway, Bracknell, Berks RG12 1AU **T** 01344-424642 **W** www.bracknell-forest.gov.uk
Director of Education, T. Eccleston

BRADFORD Flockton House, Flockton Road, Bradford BD4 7EB **T** 01274-751700 **W** www.educationbradford.com
Director of Education and Schools, P. Green

BRIGHTON AND HOVE PO Box 2503, Kings House, Grand Avenue, Hove BN3 2SU **T** 01273-290000 **W** www.brighton-hove.gov.uk
Strategic Director, David Hawker

BRISTOL The Council House, College Green, Bristol BS99 7EB **T** 0117-903 7962 **W** www.bristol-lea.org.uk
Director of Education, Heather Tomlinson

BURY Athenaeum House, Market Street, Bury BL9 0BN **T** 0161-253 5652
Chief Education Officer, H. Williams

CALDERDALE Northgate House, Northgate, Halifax HX1 1UN **T** 01422-357257 **W** www.calderdale.gov.uk
Group Director, C. A. Gruen

COVENTRY Council Offices, Earl Street, Coventry CV1 5RS **T** 024-7683 1511 **W** www.coventry.gov.uk
Strategic Director, Roger Edwardson

DARLINGTON Town Hall, Darlington DL1 5QT **T** 01325-380651 **W** www.darlington.gov.uk
Director, G. Pennington

DERBY Middleton House, 27 St Mary's Gate, Derby DE1 3NN **T** 01332-716924 **W** www.derby.gov.uk
Director, A. Flack

DONCASTER PO Box 266, The Council House, College Road, Doncaster DN1 3AD **T** 01302-737103
Executive Director, M. Eales

DUDLEY Westox House, 1 Trinity Road, Dudley DY1 1JQ **T** 01384-818181 **W** www.dudley.gov.uk
Director, John Freeman

EAST RIDING OF YORKSHIRE County Hall, Beverley HU17 9BA **T** 01482-392020 **W** www.eastriding.gov.uk
Director of Lifelong Learning, Jon Mager

GATESHEAD Civic Centre, Regent Street, Gateshead NE8 1HH **T** 0191-433 3000 **W** www.gateshead.gov.uk
Director, Brian H. Edwards

HALTON Grosvenor House, Halton Lea, Runcorn WA7 2WD **T** 0151-424 2061
Director, G. Talbot

HARTLEPOOL Civic Centre, Victoria Road, Hartlepool TS24 8AY **T** 01429-266522 **W** www.hartlepool.gov.uk
Director, J. J. Fitt

HEREFORDSHIRE PO Box 185, Hereford HR4 9ZR **T** 01432-260900 **W** www.education.herefordshire.gov.uk
Director, Dr E. Oram

KINGSTON UPON HULL Essex House, Manor Street, Kingston upon Hull HU1 1YD **T** 01482-613007
Corporate Director, Helen McMullen

KIRKLEES Oldgate House, 2 Oldgate, Huddersfield HD1 6QW **T** 01484-225242 **W** www.kirkleesmc.gov.uk
Director of Lifelong Learning, G. Tonkin

KNOWSLEY Education Offices, Huyton Hey Road, Huyton, Knowsley L36 5YH **T** 0151-443 3232 **W** www.knowsley.gov.uk
Director, S. Munby

LEEDS Merrion House, 110 Merrion Centre, Leeds LS2 8DT **T** 0113-247 5590 **W** www.educationleeds.co.uk
Chief Executive, Chris Edwards

LEICESTER Marlborough House, 38 Welford Road, Leicester LE2 7AA **T** 0116-252 7807 **W** www.leicester.gov.uk
Corporate Director of Education and Lifelong Learning, S. Andrews

LIVERPOOL 4th Floor, Lewis Buildings, 4 Renshaw Street, Liverpool L1 4AD **T** 0151-233 3006 **W** www.liverpool.gov.uk
Executive Director, Colin Hilton

LUTON Unity House, 111 Stuart Street, Luton LU1 5NP **T** 01582-548001 **W** www.luton.gov.uk
Corporate Director Lifelong Learning, T. Dessent

MANCHESTER Overseas House, Quay Street, Manchester M3 3BB **T** 0161-234 5000
Chief Education Officer, M. Waters

MEDWAY Civic Centre, Strood, Rochester, Kent ME2 4AY **T** 01634-306000 **W** www.medway.gov.uk
Director of Education, R. Collinson

MIDDLESBROUGH PO Box 99, Town Hall, Middlesbrough TS1 2QQ **T** 01642-245432
Corporate Director, Terry Redmayne

MILTON KEYNES Civic Offices, Saxon Court, 505 Avebury Boulevard, Milton Keynes MK9 3HS **T** 01908-691691 **W** www.mkweb.co.uk
Head of Education, J. McElligott

NEWCASTLE UPON TYNE Civic Centre, Newcastle upon Tyne NE1 8PU **T** 0191-232 8520 **W** www.newcastle.gov.uk
Director, P. Turner

NORTH EAST LINCOLNSHIRE 7 Eleanor Street, Grimsby DN32 9DU **T** 01472-323021 **W** www.nelincs.gov.uk
Director, Geoff Hill

NORTH LINCOLNSHIRE PO Box 35, Hewson House, Station Road, Brigg DN20 8XJ **T** 01724-297240 **W** www.northlincs.gov.uk
Head of Education, Learning and Achievement, D. Lea

NORTH SOMERSET PO Box 51, Town Hall, Weston-super-Mare BS23 1ZZ **T** 01934-888888 **W** www.n-somerset.gov.uk
Director, Colin Diamond

NORTH TYNESIDE Stephenson House, Stephenson Street, North Shields NE30 1QA T 0191-200 6565 W www.northtyneside.gov.uk
Education Director, Gill Alexander

NOTTINGHAM Sandfield Centre, Sandfield Road, Lenton, Nottingham NG7 1QH T 0115-915 5555 W www.nottinghamschools.co.uk
Director, Heather Tomlinson

OLDHAM PO Box 40, Civic Centre, West Street, Oldham OL1 1XJ T 0161-911 4260 W www.oldham.gov.uk
Executive Director of Education and Culture (acting), P. Makin

PETERBOROUGH Bayard Place, Broadway, Peterborough PE1 1FB T 01733-748444 W www.peterborough.gov.uk
Director, J. Evans

PLYMOUTH Plymouth PL1 2AA T 01752-307400 W www.pgfl.plymouth.gov.uk
Director, Bronwen Lacey

POOLE Civic Centre, Poole, Dorset BH15 2RU T 01202-633633 W www.boroughofpoole.com
Policy Director – Education, John Nash

PORTSMOUTH Civic Offices, Guildhall Square, Portsmouth PO1 2AL T 023-9282 2251 W www.portsmouthcc.gov.uk
Director of Education and Lifelong Learning, Linda Fisher

READING Civic Centre, PO Box 2623, Reading RG1 7WA T 0118-939 0900 W www.reading.gov.uk
Director, Andrew Daykin

REDCAR AND CLEVELAND Council Offices, Kirkleatham Street, Redcar TS10 1YA T 01642-444121 W www.redcar-cleveland.gov.uk
Director, Jenny Lewis

ROCHDALE PO Box 70, Municipal Offices, Smith Street, Rochdale OL16 1YD T 01706-647474
Director of Education, T. Piggott

ROTHERHAM Education Office, Norfolk House, Walker Place, Rotherham S65 1AS T 01709-382121 W www.rotherham.gov.uk
Director of Education, A. Bedford *(acting)*

RUTLAND Catmose, Oakham, Rutland LE15 6HP T 01572-758481 W www.rutnet.co.uk
Director, Ms C. Chambers

SALFORD Minerva House, Pendlebury Road, Swinton, Manchester T 0161-778 0123 W www.salford.gov.uk
Director, Mrs J. Baker

SANDWELL PO Box 41, Shaftesbury House, 402 High Street, West Bromwich, West Midlands B70 9LT T 0121-569 2200 W www.lea.sandwell.gov.uk
Executive Director, E. Griffiths

SEFTON Town Hall, Oriel Road, Bootle, Merseyside L20 7AE T 0151-922 4040 W www.sefton.gov.uk/education
Strategic Director, Bryn Marsh

SHEFFIELD Education Directorate, Town Hall, Pinstone Street, Sheffield S1 2HH T 0114-273 5722 W www.sheffield.gov.uk
Executive Director, Jonathan Crossley-Holland

SLOUGH Town Hall, Bath Road, Slough SL1 3UQ T 01753-875700
Director of Learning and Cultural Services, Christopher Spencer

SOLIHULL PO Box 20, Council House, Solihull B91 3QU T 0121-704 6000 W www.solihull.gov.uk
Director of Education and Children's Services, K. Crompton

SOUTHAMPTON 5th Floor, Frobisher House, Nelson Gate, Southampton SO15 1BZ T 023-8083 2771 W www.southampton.gov.uk
Executive Director, I. Sandbrook

SOUTHEND Civic Centre, Victoria Avenue, Southend-on-Sea SS2 6ER T 01702-215000
Director, Lorraine O'Reilly

SOUTH GLOUCESTERSHIRE Bowling Hill, Chipping Sodbury, S. Glos BS37 6JX T 01454-868686 W www.southglos.gov.uk
Director of Education, Ms T. Gillespie

SOUTH TYNESIDE Town Hall and Civic Offices, Westoe Road, South Shields NE33 2RL T 0191-427 1717
Director, Barbara Hughes

ST HELENS Rivington Centre, Rivington Road, St Helens WA10 4ND T 01744-456000 W www.sthelens.gov.uk
Director, Mrs S. Richardson

STOCKPORT Town Hall, Stockport SK1 3XE T 0161-474 3813 W www.stockport.gov.uk
Director for Education, Ed Blundell

STOCKTON-ON-TEES Municipal Buildings, PO Box 228, Church Road, Stockton-on-Tees TS18 1XE T 01642-393939 W www.stockton.gov.uk
Director, S. T. Bradford

STOKE-ON-TRENT Floor 2, Civic Centre, Glebe Street, Stoke-on-Trent ST4 1HH T 01782-232014 W www.stoke.gov.uk/education
Director, N. Rigby

SUNDERLAND PO Box 101, Civic Centre, Sunderland SR2 7DN T 0191-553 1000 W www.sunderland.gov.uk
Director of Education, Barbara Comiskey

SWINDON Sanford House, Sanford Street, Swindon SN1 1QH T 01793-463069 W www.swindon.gov.uk
Director of Education, Hilary Pitts

TAMESIDE Council Offices, Wellington Road, Ashton under Lyne, Lancs OL6 6DL T 0161-342 8355 W www.tameside.gov.uk
Chief Education Officer, I. Smith

TELFORD AND WREKIN PO Box 440, Civic Offices, Telford, Shropshire TF3 4WF T 01952-202100 W www.telford.gov.uk
Corporate Director, Mrs C. Davies

THURROCK PO Box 118, Grays, Essex RM17 6GF T 01375-652652 W www.thurrock.gov.uk/education
Corporate Director – Education, Steve Beynon

TORBAY Oldway Mansion, Paignton, Devon TQ3 2TE T 01803-208208
Chief Executive of Children's Services, Frank Weeple

TRAFFORD PO Box 40, Trafford Town Hall, Talbot Road, Stretford, Trafford, Greater Manchester M32 OEL T 0161-912 2000 W www.trafford.gov.uk
Chief Executive, Chris Pratt

WAKEFIELD County Hall, Bond Street, Wakefield WF1 2QL T 01924-306090 W www.wakefield.gov.uk
Corporate Director (Education), J. McLeod

WALSALL Civic Centre, Darwall Street, Walsall WS1 1TP T 01922-652301 W www.walsall.gov.uk
Chief Education Officer, D. McNulty

WARRINGTON New Town House, Buttermarket Street, Warrington, Cheshire WA1 2NJ T 01925-444400
Director, M. L. Roxburgh

WEST BERKSHIRE Avonbank House, West Street, Newbury, Berks RG14 1BZ T 01635-42400 W www.westberks.gov.uk
Corporate Director, Richard Hubbard

WIGAN Gateway House, Standishgate, Wigan, Lancs WN1 1AE T 01942-828891 W www.wiganmbc.gov.uk
Director, G. Rowney

WINDSOR AND MAIDENHEAD Town Hall, St Ives Road, Maidenhead, Berks SL6 1RF T 01628-798888 W www.rbwm.gov.uk
Director, M. D. Peckham

WIRRAL Hamilton Building, Conway Street, Birkenhead, Wirral CH41 4FD **T** 0151-666 2121
Director, Howard Cooper

WOKINGHAM Shute End, Wokingham, Berks RG40 1WN **T** 0118-974 6100
W www.wokingham.gov.uk
Assistant Chief Executive, Jackie Harrop

WOLVERHAMPTON St Peter's Square, Wolverhampton WV1 1RR **T** 01902-556556
W www.wolverhampton.gov.uk
Co-ordinating Director, Roy Lockwood

YORK Mill House, North Street, York YO1 6JD
T 01904-613161 **W** www.york.gov.uk
Director, Patrick Scott

LONDON

*Inner London borough

BARKING AND DAGENHAM Town Hall, Barking, Essex IG11 7LU **T** 020-8227 3181/3662 **W** www.bardaglea.org.uk
Director, R. Luxton

BARNET Building 4, North London Business Park, Oakleigh Road South, London N11 1NP **T** 020-8359 2000
W www.barnet.gov.uk
Director of Education, G. Palmer

BEXLEY Hill View, Hill View Drive, Welling, Kent DA16 3RY **T** 020-8303 7777 **W** www.bexley.gov.uk
Director of Education, D. Absalom

BRENT Chesterfield House, 9 Park Lane, Wembley, Middx HA9 7RW **T** 020-8937 3000 **W** www.brent.gov.uk
Director, John Christie

BROMLEY Civic Centre, Stockwell Close, Bromley BR1 3UH
T 020-8464 3333 **W** bk.bromley.gov.uk
Director, Ken Davis

*CAMDEN Crowndale Centre, 218–220 Eversholt Street, London NW1 1BD **T** 020-7911 1525
Director, R. Litchfield

*CITY OF LONDON PO Box 270, Guildhall, London EC2P 2EJ
T 020-7332 1750
City Education Officer, I. Canfort

*CITY OF WESTMINSTER City Hall, 64 Victoria Street, London SW1E 6QP **T** 020-7641 6000
W www.westminster.gov.uk
Director of Education, Mrs Phyl Crawford

CROYDON Taberner House, Park Lane, Croydon CR9 1TP
T 020-8760 5452 **W** www.croydon.gov.uk
Director, P. Wylie

EALING Perceval House, 14–16 Uxbridge Road, London W5 2HL **T** 020-8579 2424 **W** www.ealing.gov.uk
Director, Dr Caroline Whalley

ENFIELD PO Box 56, Civic Centre, Silver Street, Enfield, Middx EN1 3XQ **T** 020-8366 6565
Director, P. Lewis

*GREENWICH Riverside House, Woolwich High Street, London SE18 6DF **T** 020-8921 8238
W www.greenwich.gov.uk
Director, P. Burnett

*HACKNEY 1 Reading Lane, London E8 1GQ
T 020-8820 7000
W www.learningtrust.co.uk
Chief Executive, Alan Wood

*HAMMERSMITH AND FULHAM Town Hall, King Street, London W6 9JU **T** 020-8748 3020 **W** www.lbhf.gov.uk
Director, Sandy Adamson

HARINGEY Civic Centre, High Road, London N22 8LE
T 020-8489 0000 **W** www.haringey.gov.uk
Director of Education, D. Warwick

HARROW PO Box 22, Civic Centre, Station Road, Harrow HA1 2UW **T** 020-8863 5611 **W** www.harrow.gov.uk
Director of Learning and Community Development, Javed Khan

HAVERING Town Hall, Main Road, Romford RM1 3BC
T 01708-434343
Executive Director of Lifelong Learning, S. Evans

HILLINGDON Civic Centre, High Street, Uxbridge UB8 1UW
T 01895-250529
Corporate Director, P. O'Hear

HOUNSLOW Civic Centre, Lampton Road, Hounslow, Middx TW3 4DN **T** 020-8583 2000 **W** www.hounslow.gov.uk
Director, Robert Garnett

*ISLINGTON Laycock Street, Islington, London N1 1TH
T 020-7527 5566 **W** www.islington.gov.uk
Director of Regeneration and Education, Mohammed Mehmet

*KENSINGTON AND CHELSEA Town Hall, Hornton Street, London W8 7NX **T** 020-7361 3334
W www.rbkc.gov.uk
Executive Director, Jacky Griffin

KINGSTON UPON THAMES Guildhall 2, Kingston upon Thames KT1 1EU **T** 020-8546 2121
W www.kingston.gov.uk
Director, P. Leeson

*LAMBETH International House, Canterbury Crescent, London SW9 7QE **T** 020-7926 1000 **W** www.lambeth.gov.uk
Executive Director of Education, Phyllis Dunipace

*LEWISHAM 3rd Floor, Laurence House, 1 Catford Road, London SE6 4RU **T** 020-8314 6200
W www.lewisham.gov.uk
Executive Director, Ms F. Sulke

MERTON Civic Centre, London Road, Morden, Surrey SM4 5DX **T** 020-8543 2222 **W** www.merton.gov.uk
Director of Education, Leisure and Libraries, Mrs Sue Evans

NEWHAM Broadway House, 322 High Street, Stratford, London E15 1AJ **T** 020-8430 2000
Director of Education and Community Learning, Ms P. Maddison

REDBRIDGE Lynton House, 255–259 High Road, Ilford, Essex IG1 1NN **T** 020-8478 3020 **W** www.redbridge.gov.uk
Director, E. Grant

RICHMOND UPON THAMES 1st Floor, Regal House, London Road, Twickenham TW1 3QB
T 020-8891 1411
W www.richmond.gov.uk
Director of Education and Leisure Services, Anji Phillips

*SOUTHWARK John Smith House, 144–152 Walworth Road, London SE17 1JE **T** 020-7525 5050/5001
W www.southwark.lgfl.net
Director of Education and Culture, Dr Roger Smith

SUTTON The Grove, Carshalton, Surrey SM5 3AL
T 020-8770 5000 **W** www.sutton.gov.uk
Strategic Director, Dr I. Birnbaum

*TOWER HAMLETS Town Hall, Mulberry Place, 5 Clove Crescent, London E14 2BG **T** 020-7364 5000
W www.towerhamlets-pdc.org.uk
Corporate Director – Education, Stephen Grix

WALTHAM FOREST Education Centre, 97 Queens Road, Walthamstow, London E17 8QS **T** 020-8496 5900
Chief Executive, Graham Moss

*WANDSWORTH Town Hall, Wandsworth High Street, London SW18 2PU **T** 020-8871 8013
W www.wandsworth.gov.uk
Director, P. Robinson

WALES

ANGLESEY Ffordd Glanhwfa, Llangefni, Anglesey LL7 7EY T 01248-752900 W www.ynysmon.gov.uk
Director, R. P. Jones

BLAENAU GWENT Festival House, Victoria Business Park, Ebbw Vale, Blaenau Gwent NP23 6ER T 01495-355337
Director of Lifelong Learning and Strategic Partnerships, J. Pearce

BRIDGEND Sunnyside, Bridgend CF31 4AR T 01656-642600 W www.bridgend.gov.uk
Director, D. Matthews

CAERPHILLY Council Offices, Caerphilly Road, Ystrad Mynach, Hengoed CF82 7EP T 01443-815588
Director, David Hopkins

CARDIFF County Hall, Atlantic Wharf, Cardiff CF10 4UW T 029-2087 2700 W www.cardiff.gov.uk
Head of Service, H. Knight

CARMARTHENSHIRE Pibwrlwyd, Carmarthen SA31 2NH T 01267-224532 W www.carmarthenshire.gov.uk
Director, Alun G. Davies

CEREDIGION Swyddfa'r Sir, Marine Terrace, Aberystwyth SY23 2DE T 01970-633600
Director, R. J. Williams

CONWY Government Buildings, Dinerth Road, Colwyn Bay LL28 4UL T 01492-575031 W www.conwy.gov.uk
Director, R. E. Williams

DENBIGHSHIRE Caledfryn, Smithfield Road, Denbigh, Denbighshire LL16 3RJ T 01824-706777 W www.denbighshire.gov.uk
Director, S. Bowen

FLINTSHIRE County Hall, Mold CH7 6ND T 01352-704023 W www.flintshire.gov.uk
Director, John R. Clutton

GWYNEDD Cyngor Gwynedd, Council Offices, Caernarfon LL55 1SH T 01286-679456 W www.gwynedd.gov.uk
Director, D. Whittall

MERTHYR TYDFIL Ty Keir Hardie, Riverside Court, Avenue De Clichy, Merthyr Tydfil CF47 8XD T 01685-724600 W www.mnet2000.org.uk
Director of Integrated Children's Services, W. V. Morgan

MONMOUTHSHIRE Floor 5, County Hall, Cwmbran NP44 2XH T 01633-644487 W www.monmouthshire.gov.uk
Director, P. Cooke

NEATH PORT TALBOT Civic Centre, Port Talbot SA13 1PJ T 01639-763298 W www.neath-porttalbot.gov.uk
Director, K. Napieralla

NEWPORT Civic Centre, Newport NP20 4UR T 01633-232257 W www.newport.gov.uk
Chief Education Officer, D. Griffiths

PEMBROKESHIRE County Hall, Haverfordwest SA61 1TP T 01437-764551 W www.pembrokeshire.gov.uk
Director, G. Davies

POWYS County Hall, Llandrindod Wells LD1 5LG T 01597-826422 W www.education.powys.gov.uk
Group Director, M. Barker

RHONDDA CYNON TAFF Ty Trevithick, Abercynon, Mountain Ash, CF45 4UQ T 01443-744000
Group Director, D. Jones

SWANSEA County Hall, Oystermouth Road, Swansea SA1 3SN T 01792-636351 W www.swansea.gov.uk/education
Director, R. Parry

TORFAEN County Hall, Croesyceiliog, Cwmbran, Torfaen NP44 2WN T 01495-762200 W www.torfaen.gov.uk
Director, M. de Val

VALE OF GLAMORGAN Civic Offices, Holton Road, Barry CF63 4RU T 01446-709138 W www.valeofglamorgan.gov.uk
Director, B. Jeffreys

WREXHAM, Ty Henblas, Queen's Square, Wrexham LL13 8AZ T 01978-297401 W www.wrexham.gov.uk
Director, Terry Garner

SCOTLAND

ABERDEEN Summerhill Education Centre, Stronsay Drive, Aberdeen AB15 6JA T 01224-522000 W www.aberdeen-education.org.uk
Corporate Director, J. Stodter

ABERDEENSHIRE Woodhill House, Westburn Road, Aberdeen AB16 5GJ T 01224-664630 W www.aberdeenshire.gov.uk
Director, H. Vernal

ANGUS County Buildings, Market Street, Forfar DD8 3WE T 01307-461460 W www.angus.gov.uk
Director of Education, Jim Anderson

ARGYLL AND BUTE Argyll House, Alexandra Parade, Dunoon, Argyll PA23 8AJ T 01369-704000 W www.argyll-bute.gov.uk
Strategic Director, A. Law

CLACKMANNANSHIRE Lime Tree House, Castle Street, Alloa FK10 1EX T 01259-450000 W www.clacksweb.org.uk
Director, Dave Jones

DUMFRIES AND GALLOWAY Education Department, 30 Edinburgh Road, Dumfries DG1 1NW T 01387-260427
Director of Education and Community Services, F. Sanderson

DUNDEE Floor 8, Tayside House, Crichton Street, Dundee DD1 3RJ T 01382-433111 W www.dundeecity.gov.uk
Director of Education, Mrs A. Wilson

EAST AYRSHIRE Council Headquarters, London Road, Kilmarnock KA3 7BU T 01563-576017 W www.east-ayrshire.gov.uk
Director, J. Mulgrew

EAST DUNBARTONSHIRE Boclair House, 100 Milngavie Road, Bearsden, Glasgow G61 2TQ T 0141-578 8000 W www.eastdunbarton.gov.uk
Strategic Director - Community, Ms S. Bruce

EAST LOTHIAN John Muir House, Haddington EH413HA T 01620-827827 W www.eastlothian.gov.uk
Director of Education and Community Services, A. Blackie

EAST RENFREWSHIRE Council Offices, Eastwood Park, Rouken Glen Road, Giffnock G46 6UG T 0141-577 3000 W www.eastrenfrewshire.gov.uk
Director, John Wilson

EDINBURGH Wellington Court, 10 Waterloo Place, Edinburgh EH1 3EG T 0131-469 3000
Director, Education, R. Jobson

EILEAN SIAR/WESTERN ISLES Council Offices, Sandwick Road, Stornoway, Isle of Lewis HS1 2BW T 01851-703773
Director of Education, Murdo Macleod

FALKIRK McLaren House, Marchmont Avenue, Polmont, Falkirk FK2 0NZ T 01324-506600 W www.falkirk.gov.uk
Director, Dr G. Young

FIFE Fife House, North Street, Glenrothes KY7 5PN T 01592-414141 W www.fife.gov.uk
Head of Education, Roger Stewart

GLASGOW Nye Bevan House, 20 India Street, Glasgow G2 4PF T 0141-287 6898 W www.glasgow.gov.uk
Director, Ronnie O'Connor

HIGHLAND Council Buildings, Glenurquhart Road, Inverness IV3 5NX T 01463-702802 W www.highland.gov.uk
Director, B. Robertson
INVERCLYDE 105 Dalrymple Street, Greenock PA15 1HT T 01475-712824
Director, B. McLeary
MIDLOTHIAN Fairfield House, 8 Lothian Road, Dalkeith EH22 3ZG T 0131-270 7500 W www.midlothian.gov.uk
Director, D. MacKay
MORAY Council Offices, High Street, Elgin IV30 1BX T 01343-563001 W www.moray.gov.uk
Director, Donald Duncan
NORTH AYRSHIRE Cunninghame House, Irvine KA12 8EE T 01294-324100 W www.north-ayrshire.gov.uk
Corporate Director, J. Travers
NORTH LANARKSHIRE Municipal Buildings, Kildonan Street, Coatbridge ML5 3BT T 01236-812222 W www.northlan.gov.uk
Director, Michael O'Neill
ORKNEY ISLANDS Council Offices, School Place, Kirkwall, Orkney KW15 1NY T 01856-873535 W www.orkney.gov.uk
Director, Leslie Manson
PERTH AND KINROSS Pullar House, 35 Kinnoull Street, Perth PH1 5GD T 01738-476200
Executive Director, George Waddell
RENFREWSHIRE Council Headquarters, South Building, Cotton Street, Paisley PA1 1LE T 0141-8425663 W www.renfrewshire.gov.uk
Director of Education of Leisure, Ms S. Rae
SCOTTISH BORDERS Council Headquarters, Newtown St Boswells, Melrose, Roxburghshire TD6 0SA T 01835-824000 W www.scottishborders.gov.uk
Director, G. Roger
SHETLAND ISLANDS Hayfield House, Hayfield Lane, Lerwick, Shetland ZE1 0QD T 01595-744000 W www.shetland.gov.uk
Head of Education, Alex Jamieson
SOUTH AYRSHIRE County Buildings, Wellington Square, Ayr KA7 1DR T 01292-612201 W www.south-ayrshire.gov.uk
Director, Mike McCabe
SOUTH LANARKSHIRE Council Headquarters, Almada Street, Hamilton ML3 0AE T 01698-454545 W www.southlanarkshire.gov.uk
Executive Director, Ms M. Allan
STIRLING Viewforth, Stirling FK8 2ET T 01786-442666 W www.stirling.gov.uk
Director, Gordon Jeyes
WEST DUNBARTONSHIRE Council Offices, Garshake Road, Dumbarton G82 3PU T 01389-737301
Director, I. McMurdo
WEST LOTHIAN Lindsay House, South Bridge Street, Bathgate EH48 1TS T 01506-776000
Director of Education and Cultural Services, Ms K. Reid

NORTHERN IRELAND

BELFAST 40 Academy Street, Belfast BT1 2NQ T 028-9056 4000 W www.belb.org.uk
Chief Executive, David Cargo
NORTH EAST County Hall, 182 Galgorm Road, Ballymena, Co. Antrim BT42 1HN T 028-2565 3333 W www.neelb.org.uk
Chief Executive, G. Topping
SOUTH 3 Charlemont Place, The Mall, Armagh BT61 9AX T 028-3751 2200 W www.selb.org
Chief Executive, Mrs H. McClenagahan
SOUTH EAST Headquarters Offices, Grahamsbridge Road, Dundonald, Belfast BT16 2HS T 028-9056 6200 W www.seelb.org.uk
Chief Executive, J. B. Fitzsimons
WEST 1 Hospital Road, Omagh, Co. Tyrone BT79 0AW T 028-8241 1411 W www.welbni.org
Chief Executive, B. Mulholland

ISLANDS

GUERNSEY The Grange, St Peter Port, Guernsey GY1 1RQ T 01481-710821
Director, D. T. Neale
ISLE OF MAN St. George's Court, Upper Church Street, Douglas, Isle of Man IM1 2SG T 01624-685820 W www.gov.im
Director, John Cain
ISLES OF SCILLY Town Hall, St Mary's, Isles of Scilly TR21 0LW T 01720-422537 W www.scilly.gov.uk
Secretary for Education, P. S. Hygate
JERSEY PO Box 142, Jersey JE4 8QJ T 01534-509500
Director of Education, Sport and Culture, T. W. McKeon

ADVISORY BODIES

SCHOOLS

BRITISH EDUCATIONAL COMMUNICATIONS AND TECHNOLOGY AGENCY Milburn Hill Road, Science Park, Coventry CV4 7JJ T 024-7641 6994 E becta@becta.org.uk W www.becta.org.uk
Chief Executive, Owen Lynch
EDUCATION OTHERWISE PO Box 7420, London N9 9SG T 0870-730 0074 E enquiries@education-otherwise.org W www.education-otherwise.org
INTERNATIONAL BACCALAUREATE ORGANISATION Peterson House, Malthouse Avenue, Cardiff Gate, Cardiff CF23 8GL T 029-2054 7777 E ibca@ibo.org W www.ibo.org
Academic Director, Prof. Jeff Thompson
LEARNING AND SKILLS COUNCIL Cheylesmore House, Quinton Road, Coventry CV1 2WT T 0845-019 4170 E info@lsc.gov.uk W www.lsc.gov.uk
Chief Executive, Mark Haysom
SPECIAL EDUCATIONAL NEEDS AND DISABILITY TRIBUNAL 7th Floor, Windsor House, 50 Victoria Street, London SW1H 0NW T 01325-392555 E tribunalqueries@sendist.gsi.gov.uk W www.sendist.gov.uk
President, Lady Rosemary Hughes

INDEPENDENT SCHOOLS

ASSOCIATION OF GOVERNING BODIES OF INDEPENDENT SCHOOLS Field House, Newton Tony, Salisbury, Wilts SP4 0HF W www.agbis.org.uk
Secretary, Shane Ruther-Jerome
INDEPENDENT SCHOOLS COUNCIL Grosvenor Gardens House, 35–37 Grosvenor Gardens, London SW1W 0BS T 020-7798 1500 E info@isis.org.uk W www.isis.org.uk
General Secretary, Jonathan Shephard
INDEPENDENT SCHOOLS EXAMINATIONS BOARD Jordan House, Christchurch Road, New Milton, Hants BH25 6QJ T 01425-621111 E ce@iseb.co.uk W www.iseb.co.uk
General Secretary, Mrs J. Williams

FURTHER EDUCATION

ACER (ASSOCIATION OF COLLEGES IN THE EASTERN REGION) Suite 1, Lancaster House, Meadow Lane, St Ives, Huntingdon, Cambs PE27 4LG T 01480-468198 E general@acer.ac.uk W www.acer.ac.uk
Chief Executive, Veronica Windmill

AOSEC (ASSOCIATION OF SOUTH EAST COLLEGES) Building 33, The University of Reading, London Road, Reading RG1 5AQ T 0118-378 6319 W www.aosec.org.uk
Chief Executive, Breyan Knowles

CENTRA (EDUCATION AND TRAINING SERVICES) LTD Duxbury Park, Duxbury Hall Road, Chorley, Lancs PR7 4AT T 01257-241428 E enquiries@centra.org.uk W www.centra.org.uk
Chief Executive, P. Wren

EMFEC (EAST MIDLAND FURTHER EDUCATION COUNCIL) Robins Wood House, Robins Wood Road, Aspley, Nottingham NG8 3NH T 0115-854 1616 E enquiries@emfec.co.uk W www.emfec.co.uk
Chief Executive, Ms J. Gardiner

LEARNING AND SKILLS DEVELOPMENT AGENCY Regent Arcade House, 19–25 Argyll Street, London W1F 7LS T 020-7297 9000 W www.lsda.org.uk
Chief Executive, Chris Hughes

LEARNING SOUTH WEST Bishops Hull House, Bishops Hull, Taunton, Somerset TA1 5EP T 01823-335491 W www.learning-southwest.org.uk
Chief Executive, Liz McGrath

NCFE Citygate, St James Boulevard, Newcastle upon Tyne NE1 4JE T 0191-239 8000 E info@ncfe.org.uk W www.ncfe.org.uk
Chief Executive, Isabel Sutcliffe

WELSH JOINT EDUCATION COMMITTEE 245 Western Avenue, Cardiff CF5 2YX T 029-2026 5000 E exams@wjec.co.uk W www.wjec.co.uk
Chief Executive, Wyn G. Roberts

HIGHER EDUCATION

ASSOCIATION OF COMMONWEALTH UNIVERSITIES John Foster House, 36 Gordon Square, London WC1H 0PF T 020-7380 6700 E info@acu.ac.uk W www.acu.ac.uk
Secretary-General, Prof. Michael Gibbons

NORTHERN IRELAND HIGHER EDUCATION COUNCIL 4th Floor, Room 407, Adelaide House, 39–49 Adelaide Street, Belfast BT2 8FD T 02890-257400 E tony.hopkins@delni.gov.uk
Chairman, Tony Hopkins CBE

QUALITY ASSURANCE AGENCY FOR HIGHER EDUCATION Southgate House, Southgate Street, Gloucester GL1 1UB T 01452-557000 E comms@qaa.ac.uk W www.qaa.ac.uk
Chief Executive, Peter Williams

UNIVERSITIES SCOTLAND 53 Hanover Street, Edinburgh EH2 2PJ T 0131-226 1111 E info@universities-scotland.ac.uk W www.universities-scotland.ac.uk
Director, David Caldwell

UNIVERSITIES UK Woburn House, 20 Tavistock Square, London WC1H 9HQ T 020-7419 4111 E info@universitiesuk.ac.uk W www.universitiesuk.ac.uk
Chief Executive, Baroness Diana Warwick

CURRICULUM COUNCILS

ACCAC Castle Buildings, Womanby Street, Cardiff CF10 1SX T 029-2037 5400 E info@accac.org.uk W www.accac.org.uk
Chief Executive, John Valentine Williams

COUNCIL FOR THE CURRICULUM, EXAMINATIONS AND ASSESSMENT 29 Clarendon Road, Clarendon Dock, Belfast BT1 3BG T 028-9026 1200 E info@ccea.org.uk W www.ccea.org.uk
Chief Executive, Gavin Boyd

LEARNING AND TEACHING SCOTLAND Gardyne Road, Dundee DD5 1NY T 01382-443600 E enquiries@ltscotland.com W www.ltscotland.com
Chief Executive, M. Baughan

QUALIFICATIONS AND CURRICULUM AUTHORITY 83 Piccadilly, London W1Y 8QA T 020-7509 5555 E info@qca.org.uk W www.qca.org.uk
Chairman, Dr Ken Boston

EXAMINING BODIES

ENGLAND

ASSESSMENT AND QUALIFICATIONS ALLIANCE (AQA) Devas Street, Manchester M15 6EX T 0161-953 1180 E mailbox@aqa.org.uk W www.aqa.org.uk
Director-General, Dr Mike Cresswell

EDEXCEL Stewart House, 32 Russell Square, London WC1B 5DN T 0870-240 9800 E enquiries@edexcel.org.uk W www.edexcel.org.uk
Chief Executive, John Kerr

OCR (OXFORD CAMBRIDGE AND RSA EXAMINATIONS) Head Office, 1 Regent Street, Cambridge CB2 1GG T 01223-552552 E helpdesk@ocr.org.uk W www.ocr.org.uk
Chief Executive, Greg Watson

SCOTLAND

SCOTTISH QUALIFICATIONS AUTHORITY Hanover House, 24 Douglas Street, Glasgow G2 7NQ T 0141-242 2214 E helpdesk@sqa.org.uk W www.sqa.org.uk
Chief Executive, Anton Colella

WALES

WELSH JOINT EDUCATION COMMITTEE 245 Western Avenue, Cardiff CF5 2YX T 029-2026 5000 E exams@wjec.co.uk W www.wjec.co.uk
Chief Executive, Wyn G. Roberts

NORTHERN IRELAND

NORTHERN IRELAND COUNCIL FOR THE CURRICULUM, EXAMINATIONS AND ASSESSMENT 29 Clarendon Road, Belfast, County Antrim BT1 3BG T 028-9026 1200 E info@ccea.org.uk W www.ccea.org.uk
Chief Executive, Gavin Boyd

GCSE AND A-LEVEL

See above: AQA, EDEXCEL, NORTHERN IRELAND COUNCIL FOR THE CURRICULUM, EXAMINATIONS AND ASSESSMENT, WELSH JOINT EDUCATION COMMITTEE

FURTHER EDUCATION
CITY & GUILDS 1 Giltspur Street, London EC1A 9DD
T 020-7294 2468 E enquiry@city-and-guilds.co.uk
W www.city-and-guilds.co.uk
Director-General, C. Humphries CBE
EDEXEL, OCR, *see* above

FUNDING COUNCILS

FURTHER EDUCATION
LEARNING AND SKILLS COUNCIL Cheylesmore House, Quinton Road, Coventry CV1 2WT T 0845-019 4170
E info@lsc.gov.uk W www.lsc.gov.uk
Chief Executive, Mark Haysom
NATIONAL COUNCIL – ELWA Linden Court, The Orchards, Ilex Close, Cardiff CF14 5DZ T 029-2076 1861
E info@elwa.org.uk W www.elwa.org.uk
Chief Executive, Elizabeth Raikes
SCOTTISH FUNDING COUNCILS FOR FURTHER AND HIGHER EDUCATION Donaldson House, 97 Haymarket Terrace, Edinburgh EH12 5HD T 0131-313 6500
E info@sfc.ac.uk W www.shefc.ac.uk
Chief Executive, Roger McClure

HIGHER EDUCATION
HIGHER EDUCATION COUNCIL – ELWA Linden Court, The Orchards, Ilex Close, Cardiff CF14 5DZ T 029-2076 1861
E info@elwa.org.uk W www.elwa.org.uk
Chief Executive, S. Martin
HIGHER EDUCATION FUNDING COUNCIL FOR ENGLAND Northavon House, Coldharbour Lane, Bristol BS16 1QD T 0117-931 7317 E hefce@hefce.ac.uk
W www.hefce.ac.uk
Chief Executive, Sir Howard Newby
SCOTTISH FUNDING COUNCILS FOR FURTHER AND HIGHER EDUCATION Donaldson House, 97 Haymarket Terrace, Edinburgh EH12 5HD T 0131-313 6500
E info@sfc.ac.uk W www.sfc.ac.uk
Chief Executive, Roger McClure
STUDENT AWARDS AGENCY FOR SCOTLAND Gyleview House, 3 Redheughs Rigg, Edinburgh EH12 9HH
T 0131-476 8212 E saas.geu@scotland.gov.uk
W www.saas.gov.uk
Chief Executive, D. Stephen
STUDENT LOANS COMPANY LTD 100 Bothwell Street, Glasgow G2 7JD T 0141-306 2000 W www.slc.co.uk
Chief Executive, C. Ward
TEACHER TRAINING AGENCY Portland House, Stag Place, London SW1E 5TT T 020-7925 3700
E enquiry@teach-tta.gov.uk W www.teach-tta.gov.uk
Chief Executive, R. Tabberer

ADMISSIONS AND COURSE INFORMATION

CAREERS RESEARCH AND ADVISORY CENTRE Sheraton House, Castle Park, Cambridge CB3 0AX T 01223-460277
E enquiries@crac.org.uk W www.crac.org.uk
Chief Executive, David Thomas
GRADUATE TEACHER TRAINING REGISTRY Rosehill, New Barn Lane, Cheltenham, Glos GL52 3LZ
T 0870-1122205 E enquiries@gttr.ac.uk W www.gttr.ac.uk
GTTR Unit Manager, Miss Houston
SOCIAL WORK ADMISSIONS SYSTEM Rosehill, New Barn Lane, Cheltenham, Glos GL52 3LZ T 0870-112 2207
SWAS Unit Manager, Janet Pearce
UNIVERSITIES AND COLLEGES ADMISSIONS SERVICE Rosehill, New Barn Lane, Cheltenham, Glos GL52 3LZ
T 01242-222444 E enquiries@ucas.ac.uk W www.ucas.com
Chief Executive, Anthony Maclaran
UNIVERSITIES SCOTLAND 53 Hanover Street, Edinburgh EH2 2PJ T 0131-226 1111
E info@universities-scotland.ac.uk
W www.universities-scotland.ac.uk
Director, David Caldwell

UNIVERSITIES

The following is a list of universities which have been granted degree awarding powers by either a Royal Charter or an Act of Parliament. There are other recognised bodies in the UK with degree awarding powers, as well as institutions offering courses leading to a degree of a recognised body. For further information please visit www.dfes.gov.uk.

UNIVERSITY OF ABERDEEN (1495)
King's College, Aberdeen AB24 3FX T 01224-272000
E pubrel@abdn.ac.uk W www.abdn.ac.uk
Full-time students (2003–4), 10,727
Chancellor, Lord Wilson of Tillyhorn, KCMG
Vice-Chancellor and Principal, Prof. Duncan C Rice
Academic Registrar, Dr T. Webb

UNIVERSITY OF ABERTAY DUNDEE (1994)
Bell Street, Dundee DD1 1HG T 01382-308000
E sro@abertay.ac.uk W www.abertay.ac.uk
Full-time students (2003–4), 4,386
Chancellor, The Rt. Hon. Earl of Airlie, KT, GCVO, PC
Vice-Chancellor, Prof. Bernard King
Registrar, Philip Henry

ANGLIA POLYTECHNIC UNIVERSITY (1992)
Rivermead Campus, Bishop Hall Lane, Chelmsford, Essex CM1 1SQ T 01245-493131 E info@anglia.ac.uk
W www.anglia.ac.uk
Full-time students (2003–4), 20,000
Chancellor, Lord Ashcroft, KCMG
Vice-Chancellor, Prof. David Tichmarsh
Secretary and Clerk, Stephen Bennett

ASTON UNIVERSITY (1895)
Aston Triangle, Birmingham B4 7ET T 0121-359 3611
W www.aston.ac.uk
Full-time students (2003–4), 5,657
Chancellor, Sir Adrian Cadbury
Vice-Chancellor, Prof. Mike Wright
Registrar, David Packham

UNIVERSITY OF BATH (1966)
Claverton Down, Bath BA2 7AY T 01225-388388
W www.bath.ac.uk
Full-time students (2003–4), 9,210
Chancellor, Lord Tugenhat
Vice-Chancellor, Prof. Glynis Breakwell
Registrar, Jonathan Bursey

UNIVERSITY OF BIRMINGHAM (1900)
Edgbaston, Birmingham BH15 2TT T 0121-414 3344
W www.bham.ac.uk
Full-time students (2003–4), 24,900
Chancellor, Sir Dominic Cadbury
Vice-Chancellor, Prof. Michael Sterling, FRENG
Registrar and Secretary, Jonathan Nicholls

BOURNEMOUTH UNIVERSITY (1992)
Fern Barrow, Poole, Dorset BH12 5BB T 01202-524111
E marketing@bournemouth.ac.uk W www.bournemouth.ac.uk
Full-time students (2003–4), 14,407
Chancellor, Lord John Taylor of Warwick
Vice-Chancellor, Prof. Gillian Slater
Registrar, Noel Richardson

UNIVERSITY OF BRADFORD (1966)
Richmond Building, Richmond Road, Bradford, W. Yorks
BD7 1DP T 01274-232323 W www.brad.ac.uk
Full-time students (2003–4), 7,816
Chancellor, Baroness Lockwood of Dewsbury
Vice-Chancellor, Prof. Chris Taylor
Registrar and Secretary, N. J. Andrew

UNIVERSITY OF BRIGHTON (1992)
Mithras House, Lewes Road, Brighton BN2 4AT
T 01273-600900 E postmaster@bton.ac.uk W www.bton.ac.uk
Full-time students (2003–4), 15,000
Chairman of the Board, Sir Michael Checkland
Director, Prof. Sir David Watson
Registrar and Secretary, Ms C. E. Moon

UNIVERSITY OF BRISTOL (1876)
Senate House, Tyndall Avenue, Bristol BS8 1TH
T 0117-928 9000 W www.bristol.ac.uk
Full-time students (2003–4), 14,500
Chancellor, Rt. Hon. Dame Brenda Hale, DBE, PC
Vice-Chancellor, Prof. Eric Thomas
Registrar, D. W. M. Pretty

BRUNEL UNIVERSITY (1966)
Uxbridge, Middx UB8 3PH T 01895-274000
W www.brunel.ac.uk
Full-time students (2003–4), 12,000
Chancellor, The Rt. Hon. Lord Wakeham, PC
Vice-Chancellor, Prof. Stephen Schwartz
Secretary and Registrar, Ms J. Weale

UNIVERSITY OF BUCKINGHAM (1983)
Buckingham MK18 1EG T 01280-814080
E reception@buckingham.ac.uk W www.buckingham.ac.uk
Full-time students (2003–4), 720
Chancellor, Sir Martin Jacomb
Vice-Chancellor, Dr Terence Kealey
Secretary, Prof. John Clarke

UNIVERSITY OF CAMBRIDGE (1209)
The Old Schools, Trinity Lane, Cambridge CB2 1TN
T 01223-337733 W www.cam.ac.uk
Undergraduates (2003–4), 17,600
Chancellor, HRH The Prince Phillip, Duke of Edinburgh, KG, KT, OM, GBE, PC (1977)
Vice-Chancellor, Prof. Alison Richard (Newnham) (2003)
Deputy High Steward, The Lord Richardson of Duntisbourne, MBE, TD, PC (1983)
Commissary, The Lord Mackay of Clashfern, KT, PC, FRSE (2002)
Orator, A. J. Bowen (Jesus) (1993)
Registrary, T. J. Mead, PHD (Wolfson) (1997)
Librarian, P. K. Fox (Selwyn) (1994)
Director of the Fitzwilliam Museum, D. D. Robinson (Magdalene) (1995)
High Steward, Dame Bridget Ogilvie FRS (Girton) (2001)
Academic Secretary, G. P. Allen (Wolfson)

COLLEGES AND HALLS *with dates of foundation*
CHRIST'S (1505) *Master,* Prof. Malcolm Bowie, DPHIL, FBA (2002)
CHURCHILL (1960) *Master,* Sir John Boyd, KCMG (1996)
CLARE (1326) *Master,* Prof. A. J. Badger, PHD (2003)
CLARE HALL (1966) *President,* Prof. E. Salje, PHD, FRS (2001)
CORPUS CHRISTI (1352) *Master,* Prof. H. Ahmed, FRENG (2000)
DARWIN (1964) *Master,* Prof. W. A. Brown, CBE
DOWNING (1800) *Master,* Prof. B. J. Everitt, PHD (2003)
EMMANUEL (1584) *Master,* Lord Wilson of Dinton, GCB, LLB (2002)
FITZWILLIAM (1966) *Master,* Prof. B. F. G. Johnson, PHD, FRS (1999)
GIRTON (1869) *Mistress,* Prof. Dame Marylin Strathern, PHD, FBA (1998)
GONVILLE AND CAIUS (1348) *Master,* N. McKendrick (1996)
HOMERTON (1824) *Principal,* Dr K. B. Pretty
HUGHES HALL (1985) *President,* Prof. P. Richards, MD, PHD (1998)
JESUS (1496) *Master,* Prof. R. Mair, PHD, FRENG (2001)
KING'S (1441) *Provost,* Prof. P. P. G. Bateson
LUCY CAVENDISH COLLEGE (1965) *President,* Dame Veronica Sutherland, CMG (2001)
MAGDALENE (1542) *Master,* D. D. Robinson (2002)
NEW HALL (1954) *President,* Mrs A. Lonsdale (1996)
NEWNHAM (1871) *Principal,* Baroness O'Neill of Bengarve, CBE (1992)
PEMBROKE (1347) *Master,* Sir Richard Dearlove, KCMG, OBE (2004)
PETERHOUSE (1284) *Master,* Lord Wilson of Tillyorn, KT, GCMG (2002)
QUEENS' (1448) *President,* Lord Eatwell, (1997)
ROBINSON (1977) *Warden,* A. D. Yates, (2001)
ST CATHARINE'S (1473) *Master,* Prof. D. S. Ingram, (2000)
ST EDMUND'S (1896) *Master,* Prof. Brian Heap, FRS (1996)
ST JOHN'S (1511) *Master,* Prof. R. N. Perham, SCD, FRS (2004)
SELWYN (1882) *Master,* Prof. R. J. Bowring, LITTD (2000)
SIDNEY SUSSEX (1596) *Master,* Prof. Dame Sandra Dawson, (1999)
TRINITY (1546) *Master,* Prof. Sir Martin Rees, FRS (2004)
TRINITY HALL (1350) *Master,* Prof. M. J. Daunton, FBA (2004)
WOLFSON (1965) *President,* Prof. G. Johnson, PHD (1994)

UNIVERSITY OF CENTRAL ENGLAND IN BIRMINGHAM (1992)
Perry Barr, Birmingham B42 2SU T 0121-331 5000
E info@ucechoices.com W www.uce.ac.uk
Full-time students (2003–4), 24,000
Chancellor, Cllr John Alden
Vice-Chancellor, Dr Peter Knight
Secretary and Registrar, Maxine Penlington

UNIVERSITY OF CENTRAL LANCASHIRE (1992)
Preston PR1 2HE T 01772-201201 W www.uclan.ac.uk
Full-time students (2003–4), 34,000
Chancellor, Sir Richard Evans, CBE
Vice-Chancellor, Dr Malcolm McVicar
Director of Student Affairs, Ian McMillan

CITY UNIVERSITY (1966)
Northampton Square, London EC1V 0HB T 020-7040 5060
E registry@city.ac.uk W www.city.ac.uk
Full-time students (2003–4), 12,814
Chancellor, The Rt. Hon. Lord Mayor of London
Vice-Chancellor, Prof. D.W. Rhind, PHD, DSC
Registrar, Eamon Martin

COVENTRY UNIVERSITY (1992)
Priory Street, Coventry CV1 5FB T 024-7688 7688
E cor002@coventry.ac.uk W www.coventry.ac.uk
Full-time students (2003–4), 17,000
Chancellor, The Lord Plumb (1995)
Vice-Chancellor, Dr Michael Goldstein, CBE
Academic Registrar, Ms Kate Quantrell

CRANFIELD UNIVERSITY (1969)
Cranfield, Beds MK43 0AL T 01234-750111
E info@cranfield.ac.uk W www.cranfield.ac.uk
Full-time students (2003–4), 2,149
Chancellor, The Lord Vincent of Coleshill, GBE, KCB, DSO
Vice-Chancellor, Prof. Frank Hartley, DSC
Academic Registrar and Secretary, David Buck

DE MONTFORT UNIVERSITY (1992)
The Gateway, Leicester LE1 9BH T 08459-454647
E enquiry@dmu.ac.uk W www.dmu.ac.uk
Full-time students (2003–4),17,000
Chancellor, The Baroness Usha Prasher of Runnymede, CBE
Chief Executive and Vice-Chancellor, Prof. Philip Turner, PHD
Registrar, Eugene Critchlow

UNIVERSITY OF DERBY (1992)
Kedleston Road, Derby DE22 1GB T 01332-590500
W www.derby.ac.uk
Full-time students (2003–4), 25,000
Chancellor, Sir Christopher Ball
Vice-Chancellor, Prof. Roger Waterhouse
Registrar, Jennifer Fry

UNIVERSITY OF DUNDEE (1967)
Dundee DD1 4HN T 01382-344000 E secretary@dundee.ac.uk
W www.dundee.ac.uk
Full-time students (2003–4), 9,271
Chancellor, Sir James Black, FRCP, FRS
Vice-Chancellor, Sir Alan Langlands
Academic Secretary, Dr David Duncan

UNIVERSITY OF DURHAM (1832)
The University Office, Durham DH1 3HP T 0191-334 2000
W www.dur.ac.uk
Full-time students (2003–4), 13,700
Chancellor, vacant
Vice-Chancellor and Warden, Prof. Sir Kenneth Calman, KCB, MD, PHD
Registrar and Secretary, L. Sanders

COLLEGES
COLLINGWOOD, *Principal,* Prof. Jane H. M. Taylor, DPHIL (2001)
GEORGE STEPHENSON, *Principal,* Prof. A. C. Darnell, (2001)
GREY, *Master,* Prof. J. M. Chamberlain, DPHIL (2004)
HATFIELD, *Acting Master,* Angel B. Scott, (2002)
JOHN SNOW, *Principal,* Prof. H. M. Evans, PHD (2002)
ST AIDAN'S, *Principal,* J. S. Ashworth, (1998)
ST CHAD'S, *Principal,* Revd J. P. M. Cassidy, PHD (1997)
ST CUTHBERT'S SOCIETY, *Principal,* Prof. R.D. Boyne, PHD (2004)
ST HILD AND ST BEDE, *Principal,* J. A. Pearson, PHD (2000)
ST JOHN'S, *Principal,* Rt. Revd Prof. S.W. Sykes, (1999)
ST MARY'S, *Principal,* Miss J. L. Hobbs, (1999)
TREVELYAN, *Principal,* N. Martin, PHD (2000)
UNIVERSITY, *Master,* Prof. M. E. Tucker, PHD (2000)
USHAW, *Rector,* Revd T. Drainey (2004)
USTINOV COLLEGE, *Principal,* Susan J. Scott (2003)
VAN MILDERT, *Principal,* G. Patterson (2000)

UNIVERSITY OF EAST ANGLIA (1963)
Norwich NR4 7TJ T 01603-456161 E press@uea.ac.uk
W www.uea.ac.uk
Full-time students (2003–4), 13,000
Chancellor, Sir Brandon Gough
Vice-Chancellor, Professor David Eastwood
Registrar and Secretary, Brian Summers

UNIVERSITY OF EAST LONDON (1898)
Longbridge Road, Dagenham, Essex RM8 2AS T 020-8223 3000
E publicity@uel.ac.uk W www.uel.ac.uk
Full-time students (2003–4), 15,000
Chancellor, Lord Rix
Vice-Chancellor, Prof. Michael Thorne
Registrar and Secretary, Alan Ingle

UNIVERSITY OF EDINBURGH (1583)
Old College, South Bridge, Edinburgh EH8 9YL
T 0131-650 1000 E communications.office@ed.ac.uk
W www.ed.ac.uk
Full-time students (2003–4), 20,000
Chancellor, HRH The Prince Philip, Duke of Edinburgh, KG, KT, OM
Principle and Vice-Chancellor, Prof. Tim O'Shea
Secretary, Melvyn Cornish

UNIVERSITY OF ESSEX (1964)
Wivenhoe Park, Colchester C04 3SQ T 01206-873333
E admit@essex.ac.uk W www.essex.ac.uk
Full-time students (2003–4), 7,273
Chancellor, Lord Phillips of Sudbury
Vice-Chancellor, Prof. Ivor Crewe
Registrar and Secretary, Dr Tony Rich

UNIVERSITY OF EXETER (1955)
Northcote House, The Queen's Drive, Exeter EX4 4QJ
T 01392-661000 E s.d.franklin@exeter.ac.uk
W www.exeter.ac.uk
Full-time students (2003–4), 11,278
Chancellor, The Lord Alexander of Weedon
Vice Chancellor, Prof. Steve Smith
Registrar and Secretary, David J. Allen

UNIVERSITY OF GLAMORGAN (1992)
Pontypridd CF37 1DL
T 0800-716925
W www.glam.ac.uk
Full-time students (2003–4), 19,820
Chancellor, The Rt. Hon. Lord Morris of Aberavon
Vice-Chancellor, Sir Adrian Webb
Secretary, Leigh Bracegirdle

UNIVERSITY OF GLASGOW (1451)
Gilbert Scott Building, University Avenue, Glasgow G12 8QQ
T 0141-339 8855 E publicity.services@gla.ac.uk
W www.gla.ac.uk
Full-time students (2003–4), 19,521
Chancellor, Sir William Kerr Fraser, GCB, LLD
Vice-Chancellor, Sir Muir Russell, KCB, FRSE
Head of Registry, Christine Lowther

GLASGOW CALEDONIAN UNIVERSITY (1993)
City Campus, 70 Cowcaddens Road, Glasgow G4 0BA
T 0141-331 3000 E helpline@gcal.ac.uk
W www.caledonian.ac.uk
Full-time students (2003–4), 14,000
Chancellor, Magnus Magnusson, MBE
Vice-Chancellor, Dr Ian Johnston, CB
Secretary, Brian Murray

UNIVERSITY OF GLOUCESTERSHIRE (2001)
Cheltenham GL50 2QF T 01242-532700 W www.glos.ac.uk
Full-time students (2003–4), 6,063
Chancellor, Lord Carey of Clifton
Vice-Chancellor, Dame Janet Trotter
Academic Registrar, Peter Griffiths

UNIVERSITY OF GREENWICH (1992)
Old Royal Naval College, Park Row, Greenwich, London SE10 9LS T 020-8331 8000 E courseinfo@gre.ac.uk
W www.gre.ac.uk
Full-time students (2003–4), 13,747
Chancellor, The Rt. Hon. Lord Holme of Cheltenham, CBE
Vice-Chancellor, Baroness Blackstone
Academic Registrar, Christine Rose

HERIOT-WATT UNIVERSITY (1966)
Edinburgh EH14 4AS T 0131-449 5111 W www.hw.ac.uk
Full-time students (2003–4) 6,300
Chancellor, The Lord Mackay of Clashfern, KT, PC
Vice-Chancellor, Prof. John Archer, FRENG
Secretary, P. L. Wilson

UNIVERSITY OF HERTFORDSHIRE (1992)
College Lane, Hatfield, Herts AL10 9AB T 01707-284000
W www.herts.ac.uk
Full-time students (2003–4), 16,656
Chancellor, Lord Maclaren of Knebworth
Vice-Chancellor, Prof. R. J. J. Wilson
Registrar and Secretary, P. E. Waters

UNIVERSITY OF HUDDERSFIELD (1992)
Queensgate, Huddersfield HD1 3DH T 01484-422288
E prospectus@hud.ac.uk W www.hud.ac.uk
Full-time students (2003–4), 18,432
Chancellor, Patrick Stewart
Vice-Chancellor, Prof. John Tarrant
Secretary, Tony Mears

UNIVERSITY OF HULL (1927)
Cottingham Road, Hull HU6 7RX T 01482-346311
W www.hull.ac.uk
Full-time students (2003–4), 10,390
Chancellor, Lord Armstrong of Ilminster
Vice-Chancellor, Prof. David Drewy
Registrar, David Lock

KEELE UNIVERSITY (1962)
Keele, Staffs ST5 5BG T 01782-621111 W www.keele.ac.uk
Full-time students (2003–4), 5,636
Chancellor, Prof. Sir David Weatherall, KT, DL, MB
Vice-Chancellor, Prof. Janet Finch, CBE
Secretary and Registrar, Simon Morris

UNIVERSITY OF KENT AT CANTERBURY (1965)
Canterbury, Kent CT2 7NZ T 01227-764000
W www.kent.ac.uk
Full-time students (2003–4), 8,411
Chancellor, Sir Crispin Tickle, GCMG, KCVO
Vice-Chancellor, Prof. David Melville
Registrar and Secretary, Nick McHard

KINGSTON UNIVERSITY (1992)
River House, 53–57 High Street, Kingston upon Thames, Surrey KT1 1LQ T 020-8547 2000 E admissions-info@kingston.ac.uk
W www.kingston.ac.uk
Full-time students (2003–4), 12,776
Chancellor, Sir Peter Hall
Vice-Chancellor, Prof. Peter Scott
Senior Secretary, Ann Pohan

UNIVERSITY OF LANCASTER (1964)
Bailrigg, Lancaster LA1 4YW T 01524-65201
W www.lancs.ac.uk
Full-time students (2003–4), 9,386
Chancellor, HRH Princess Alexandra
Vice-Chancellor, Prof. Paul Wellings
Secretary, Fiona Aiken

UNIVERSITY OF LEEDS (1904)
Leeds LS2 9JT T 0113-243 1751 E pressoffice@leeds.ac.uk
W www.leeds.ac.uk
Full-time students (2003–4), 29,000
Chancellor, Lord Bragg of Wigton
Vice-Chancellor, Prof. Michael Arthur
Secretary, J. Roger Gair

LEEDS METROPOLITAN UNIVERSITY (1992)
City Campus, Leeds LS1 3HE T 0113-283 2600
E course-enquiries@lmu.ac.uk W www.lmu.ac.uk
Full-time students (2003–4), 15,505
Chancellor, Leslie Silver, OBE
Vice-Chancellor, Prof. Simon Lee
Secretary, Steve Denton

UNIVERSITY OF LEICESTER (1957)
University Road, Leicester LE1 7RH T 0116-252 2522
E pressoffice@le.ac.uk W www.le.ac.uk
Full-time students (2003–4), 10,462
Chancellor, Sir Michael Atiyah, OM, FRS, PHD
Vice-Chancellor, Prof. R. Burgess, PHD
Registrar and Secretary, K. J. Julian

UNIVERSITY OF LINCOLN (1992)
Brayford Pool, Lincoln, LN6 7TS T 01522-882000
E marketing@lincoln.ac.uk W www.ulh.ac.uk
Full-time students (2003–4), 7,531
Chancellor, Dame Elizabeth Esteve-Coll
Vice-Chancellor, Prof. David Chiddick
Registrar, Edmund Fitzpatrick

UNIVERSITY OF LIVERPOOL (1903)
Senate House, Abercromby Square, Liverpool L69 3BX
T 0151-794 2000 W www.liv.ac.uk
Full-time students (2003–4), 17,229
Chancellor, The Rt. Hon. Lord Owen, CH
Vice-Chancellor, Prof. J. D. Bone
Registrar and Secretary, M. D. Carr

LIVERPOOL JOHN MOORES UNIVERSITY (1992)
Egerton Court, 2 Rodaney Street, Liverpool L3 5UX
T 0151-231 2121 W www.livjm.ac.uk
Full-time students (2003–4), 14,623
Chancellor, Cherie Booth, QC
Vice-Chancellor, Prof. M. Brown
Registrar and Secretary, Alison Wild

UNIVERSITY OF LONDON (1836)
Senate House, Malet Street, London WC1E 7HU
T 020-7862 8000 E enquiries@lon.ac.uk
W www.lon.ac.uk
Full-time students (2003–4), 88,000
Visitor, HM the Queen in Council
Chancellor, HRH The Princess Royal, KG, GCVO, FRS
Vice-Chancellor, Prof. Sir Graeme Davies (2003)
Chairman of the Council, The Rt. Hon. The Lord Brooke of Sutton Mandeville, CH, PC
Academic Registrar, Mrs G. F. Roberts
Director of Administration, Ms Catherine Swarbrick

COLLEGES AND INSTITUTES

BIRKBECK COLLEGE Malet Street, London WC1E 7HX
Master, Prof. D. Latchman (2003)

BRITISH INSTITUTE IN PARIS 9–11 rue de Constantine, 75340 Paris, Cedex 07
Director, Prof. Robert Lethbridge (2003)

COURTAULD INSTITUTE OF ART North Block, Somerset House, Strand, London WC2R 0RN
Director, Prof. J. Cuno (2003)

GOLDSMITHS COLLEGE Lewisham Way, New Cross, London SE14 6NW
Warden, Prof. B. Pimlott (1998)

HEYTHROP COLLEGE Kensington Square, London W8 5HQ
Principal, Revd Dr J. McDade, SJ, BD (1999)

IMPERIAL COLLEGE OF SCIENCE, TECHNOLOGY AND MEDICINE (includes Imperial College Schools of Medicine at Charing Cross, Hammersmith and St Mary's hospitals and at the National Heart and Lung Institute), South Kensington, London SW7 2AZ
Rector, Prof. Sir Richard Sykes, FRS (2001)

INSTITUTE OF CANCER RESEARCH Royal Cancer Hospital, Chester Beatty Laboratories, 237 Fulham Road, London SW3 6JB
Chief Executive, Prof. P. Rigby (1999)

INSTITUTE OF EDUCATION 20 Bedford Way, London WC1H 0AL
Director, Prof. G. Whitty (2000)

KING'S COLLEGE LONDON (includes Guy's, King's and St Thomas's Schools of Medicine, Dentistry and Biomedical Sciences), Strand, London WC2R 2LS
Principal, Prof. R. Trainor (2004)

LONDON BUSINESS SCHOOL Sussex Place, Regent's Park, London NW1 4SU
Principal, Prof. L. D'Andrea Tyson (2002)

LONDON SCHOOL OF ECONOMICS AND POLITICAL SCIENCE Houghton Street, London WC2A 2AE
Director, Sir Howard Davies (2003)

LONDON SCHOOL OF HYGIENE AND TROPICAL MEDICINE Keppel Street, London WC1E 7HT
Dean, Prof. A. Haines, 2001

QUEEN MARY AND WESTFIELD COLLEGE (incorporating St Bartholomew's and the Royal London School of Medicine and Dentistry), Mile End Road, London E1 4NS
Principal, Prof. A. Smith, FRS (1998)

ROYAL ACADEMY OF MUSIC Marylebone Road, London NW1 5HT
Principal, Prof. Curtis Price (1995)

ROYAL HOLLOWAY Egham Hill, Egham, Surrey TW20 0EX
Principal, Prof. S. Hill, MPHIL (2002)

ROYAL VETERINARY COLLEGE Royal College Street, London NW1 0TU
Principal and Dean, Prof. Q. McKellar (2004)

SCHOOL OF ADVANCED STUDY Senate House, Malet Street, London WC1E 7HU
Dean, Prof. T. C. Daintith

INSTITUTE FOR THE STUDY OF THE AMERICAS 31 Tavistock Square, London WC1H 9HA
Director, Prof. J. Dunkerley (1998)

INSTITUTE OF ADVANCED LEGAL STUDIES Charles Clore House, 17 Russell Square, London WC1B 5DR
Director, Prof. Avrom Sherr

INSTITUTE OF CLASSICAL STUDIES Senate House, Malet Street, London WC1E 7HU
Director, Prof. G. B. Waywell, FSA (1996)

INSTITUTE OF COMMONWEALTH STUDIES 27–28 Russell Square, London WC1B 5DS
Director, Prof. T. Shaw (2001)

INSTITUTE OF ENGLISH STUDIES Senate House, Malet Street, London WC1E 7HU
Director, Prof. W. Gould (2000)

INSTITUTE OF GERMANIC STUDIES 29 Russell Square, London WC1B 5DP
Director, Prof. R. Görner, (1999)

INSTITUTE OF HISTORICAL RESEARCH Senate House, Malet Street, London WC1E 7HU
Director, Prof. David Bates

INSTITUTE OF ROMANCE STUDIES Senate House, Malet Street, London WC1E 7HU
Director, Prof. J. Still (2002)

WARBURG INSTITUTE Woburn Square, London WC1H 0AB
Director, Prof. C. Hope

SCHOOL OF ORIENTAL AND AFRICAN STUDIES Thornhaugh Street, Russell Square, London WC1H1AX
Director, Prof. C. Bundy (2001)

SCHOOL OF PHARMACY 29–39 Brunswick Square, London WC1N 1AX
Dean, Prof. A. T. Florence, CBE, PHD, FRSE (1989)

ST GEORGE'S HOSPITAL MEDICAL SCHOOL Cranmer Terrace, London SW17 0RE
Principal, Prof. Michael Farthing (2003), FRCP

UNIVERSITY COLLEGE LONDON (including UCL Medical School), Gower Street, London WC1E 6BT
Provost and President, Prof. Malcolm Grant (2003)

UNIVERSITY MARINE BIOLOGICAL STATION Millport, Isle of Cumbrae KA28 0EG
Director, Dr Rupert Ormond

EXTERNAL PROGRAMME Senate House, Malet Street, London WC1E 7HU
Director, Prof. J. M. McConnell (1992)

PHILOSOPHY PROGRAMME Senate House, Malet Street, London WC1E 7HU
Director, Prof. T. Crane

LONDON METROPOLITAN UNIVERSITY (2002)
London City Campus, 31 Jewry Street, London EC3N 2EY
T 020-7320 1000 W www.londonmet.ac.uk
Full-time students (2003–4), 18,200
President, Prof. Roderick Floud
Vice-Chancellor and Chief Executive, Brian Roper
Secretary, John MacParland

LOUGHBOROUGH UNIVERSITY (1966)
Ashby Road, Loughborough, Leics LE11 3TU T 01509-263171
W www.lboro.ac.uk
Full-time students (2003–4), 12,000
Chancellor, Sir John Jennings, CBE
Vice-Chancellor, Prof. David Wallace, CBE, FRS, FRENG
Registrar and Secretary, John Town

UNIVERSITY OF LUTON (1993)
Park Square, Luton LU1 3JU T 01582-734111
E admissions@luton.ac.uk W www.luton.ac.uk
Full-time students (2003–4), 11,500
Chancellor, Sir Robin Biggam
Vice-Chancellor, Dr Dai John

UNIVERSITY OF MANCHESTER (1824)
Oxford Road, Manchester M13 9PL T 0161-275 2000
E enquiry@manchester.ac.uk W www.man.ac.uk
Full-time students (2003–4), 34,000
Co-Chancellors, Anna Ford and Sir Terry Leahy
Vice-Chancellor, Prof. Alan Gilbert
Registrar and Secretary, Dugald Mackie

MANCHESTER METROPOLITAN UNIVERSITY (1992)
All Saints, Manchester M15 6BH T 0161-247 2000
E enquiries@mmu.ac.uk W www.mmu.ac.uk
Full-time students (2003–4), 26,000
Chancellor, Dame Janet Smith, OBE
Vice-Chancellor, Alexandra V. Burslem, OBE
Registrar, Janusz Karczewski-Slowikowski

MIDDLESEX UNIVERSITY (1992)
North London Business Park, Oakleigh Road, London N11 1QS
T 020-8411 5000 E admissions@mdx.ac.uk W www.mdx.ac.uk
Full-time students (2003–4), 25,000
Chancellor, The Rt. Hon. Lord Sheppard of Didgemere, KCVO, KT
Vice-Chancellor, Prof. Michael Driscoll
Registrar, Colin Davis

NAPIER UNIVERSITY (1992)
Craighouse Campus, Craighouse Road, Edinburgh EH10 5LG
T 0500-353570 E info@napier.ac.uk W www.napier.ac.uk
Full-time students (2003–4), 12,000
Principal and Vice-Chancellor, Prof. Joan Stringer
Secretary, Dr Gerry Webby

UNIVERSITY OF NEWCASTLE UPON TYNE (1963)
6 Kensington Terrace, Newcastle upon Tyne NE17 7RU
T 0191-222 6000 W www.ncl.ac.uk
Full-time students (2003–4), 14,667
Chancellor, The Rt. Hon. Christopher Patten
Vice-Chancellor, Prof. Christopher Edwards
Registrar, Dr John Hogan

NORTHUMBRIA UNIVERSITY AT NEWCASTLE (1992)
Ellison Building, Ellison Place, Newcastle upon Tyne NE1 8ST
T 0191-232 6002 E ca.marketing@northumbria.ac.uk
W www.northumbria.ac.uk
Full-time students (2003–4), 23,912
Chancellor, Lord Glenamara
Vice-Chancellor, Prof. Kel Fidler
Registrar, Mrs Cheryl Penna

UNIVERSITY OF NOTTINGHAM (1948)
University Park, Nottingham NG7 2RD T 0115-951 5151
E university-profile@nottingham.ac.uk
W www.nottingham.ac.uk
Full-time students (2003–4), 24,500
Chancellor, Prof. F. Yang, LITTD
Vice-Chancellor, Prof. Sir Colin Campbell
Registrar, K. H. Jones

NOTTINGHAM TRENT UNIVERSITY (1992)
Burton Street, Nottingham NG1 4BU T 0115-941 8418
E cor.web@ntu.ac.uk W www.ntu.ac.uk
Full-time students (2003–4), 18,546
Chairman, John Peace
Vice-Chancellor, Prof. Neil Gorman
Registrar, David Samson

OPEN UNIVERSITY (1969)
Walton Hall, Milton Keynes MK7 6AA T 01908-274066
E general-enquiries@open.ac.uk W www.open.ac.uk
Full-time students (2003–4), 79,262
Chancellor, Rt. Hon. Betty Boothroyd
Vice-Chancellor, Prof. Brenda Gourley
Registrar, Helen Niven

UNIVERSITY OF OXFORD (*c.* 12th century)
University Offices, Wellington Square, Oxford OX1 2JD
T 01865-270000 E information.officer@admin.ox.ac.uk
W www.ox.ac.uk
Students in residence 2003–4, 17,097
Chancellor, The Rt. Hon. Chris Patten, CH, elected 2003
High Steward, The Rt Hon. Lord Bingham of Cornhill (Balliol, Nuffield), elected 2002
Vice-Chancellor, Dr J. A. Hood, elected 2004
Pro-Vice-Chancellors, Dr Bill Macmillan, Prof. Paul Slack, Prof. Susan Iversen
Registrar, D. R. Holmes (St John's), elected 1998
Secretary of the Faculties and Academic Registrar, A. P. Weale (Worcester), elected 1984
Proctors, Dr J. F. Wheater (University), Revd Dr J. D. Maltby (Corpus Christi)
Assessor, Dr D. J. Walker (St Hugh's) elected 2004
Public Orator, R. H. A. Jenkyns
Director of University Library Services and Bodley's Librarian, R. P. Carr (Balliol), appointed 1997
Director of the Ashmolean Museum, Dr C. Brown (Worcester), elected 1998
Keeper of Archives, S. Bailey, appointed 2000
Surveyor to the University, Ms J. Wood, appointed 2004
Secretary of the Chest, J. R. Clements (Merton), elected 1995

COLLEGES AND HALLS *with dates of foundation*
ALL SOULS (1438) *Warden,* Prof. J. Davis, FBA, PHD (1995)
BALLIOL (1263) *Master,* A. Graham (1998)
BLACKFRIARS (1221) *Regent,* Revd F. G. Kerr (1998)

BRASENOSE (1509) *Principal,* Prof. R. Cashmore, FRS (2003)
CAMPION HALL (1896) *Master,* Revd Dr G. J. Hughes (1998)
CHRIST CHURCH (1546) *Dean,* Very Revd C. A. Lewis (2003)
CORPUS CHRISTI (1517) *President,* Timothy Lankester, KCB (2001)
EXETER (1314) *Rector,* Ms Frances Cairncross, CBE (2004)
GREEN (1979) *Warden,* Sir John Hanson, KCMG, CBE (1997)
GREYFRIARS (1910) *Warden,* Revd Dr T. G. Weinandy (1996)
HARRIS MANCHESTER (1786) *Principal,* Revd R. Waller, PHD (1988)
HERTFORD (1974) *Principal,* Sir Walter Bodmer, FRS, FRCPATH (1996)
JESUS (1571) *Principal,* Sir Peter North, CBE, FBA (1984)
KEBLE (1868) *Warden,* Prof. A. Cameron, CBE, PHD, FBA (1994)
KELLOGG (1990) *President,* Dr G. P. Thomas (1990)
LADY MARGARET HALL (1878) *Principal,* Dr Frances Lannon, FRHIST (2002)
LINACRE (1962) *Principal,* Prof. P. A. Slack, FBA (1996)
LINCOLN (1427) *Rector,* Prof. P. Langford (2000)
MAGDALEN (1458) *President,* A. D. Smith, CBE (1998)
MANSFIELD (1886) *Principal,* Dr. D. Walford, FRCPATH, FRCP, FFPHM (1996)
MERTON (1264) *Warden,* Prof. Dame J. Rawson, CBE, FBA (1994)
NEW COLLEGE (1379) *Warden,* Prof. A. J. Ryan, FBA (1996)
NUFFIELD (1958) *Warden,* Sir Tony Atkinson, FBA (1994)
ORIEL (1326) *Provost,* Sir Derek Morris (2004)
PEMBROKE (1624) *Master,* Giles Henderson, CBE (2001)
QUEEN'S (1340) *Provost,* Sir Alan Budd (1999)
REGENT'S PARK (1820) *Principal,* Revd Dr P. S. Fiddes (1989)
ST ANNE'S (1952) *Principal,* vacant
ST ANTONY'S (1953) *Warden,* Sir Marrack Goulding, KCMG (1997)
ST BENET'S HALL (1897) *Master,* Father Leo Chamberlain (2004)
ST CATHERINE'S (1963) *Master,* Prof. Roger Ainsworth (2003)
ST CROSS (1965) *Master,* Prof. Andrew Goudie (2003)
ST EDMUND HALL (c.1278) *Principal,* Prof. D. M. P. Mingos, FRS, FRSC (1999)
ST HILDA'S (1893) *Principal,* Lady Judith English (2001)
ST HUGH'S (1886) *Principal,* A. Dilnot, CBE (2002)
ST JOHN'S (1555) *President,* Sir Michael Scholar, KCB (2001)
ST PETER'S (1929) *Master,* Prof. Bernard Silverman, FRS (2003)
SOMERVILLE (1879) *Principal,* Dame Fiona Caldicott, DBE, FRCP, FRCPSYCH (1996)
TEMPLETON (1965) *President,* Sir David Rowland (1998)
TRINITY (1554) *President,* The Hon. Michael J. Beloff, FRSA (1996)
UNIVERSITY (1249) *Master,* Lord Butler of Brockwell, GCB, CVO (1998)
WADHAM (1610) *Warden,* Sir Neil Chalmers, CBE (2003)
WOLFSON (1966) *President,* Prof. Sir Gareth Roberts, FRS, PHD (2000)
WORCESTER (1714) *Provost,* R. G. Smethurst (1991)
WYCLIFFE HALL (1877) *Principal,* Revd Dr A. E. McGrath (1995)

OXFORD BROOKES UNIVERSITY (1992)

Gipsy Lane, Oxford OX3 0BP **T** 01865-484848
E query@brookes.ac.uk **W** www.brookes.ac.uk
Full-time students (2003–4), 15,570
Chancellor, Jon Snow
Vice-Chancellor, Prof. Graham Upton
Academic Registrar, Stephen Marshall

UNIVERSITY OF PAISLEY (1992)

Paisley PA1 2BE **T** 0141-848 3000 **E** uni-direct@paisley.ac.uk
W www.paisley.ac.uk
Full-time students (2003–4), 7,500
Chancellor, Sir Robert Smith
Principal and Vice-Chancellor, Prof. John Macklin
Registrar, David Rigg

UNIVERSITY OF PLYMOUTH (1992)

Drake Circus, Plymouth PL4 8AA **T** 01752-600600
E admissions@plymouth.ac.uk **W** www.plymouth.ac.uk
Full-time students (2003–4), 17,328
Vice-Chancellor, Prof. R. Levinsky
Academic Registrar and Secretary, Miss J. Hopkinson

UNIVERSITY OF PORTSMOUTH (1992)

University House, Winston Churchill Avenue, Portsmouth PO1 2UP **T** 023-9284 8484 **E** info.centre@port.ac.uk
W www.port.ac.uk
Full-time students (2003–4), 17,710
Chancellor, Lord Palumbo
Vice-Chancellor, Prof. John Craven
Registrar, Andy Rees

QUEEN'S UNIVERSITY OF BELFAST (1908)

Belfast BT7 1NN **T** 028-9024 5133 **E** comms.office@qub.ac.uk
W www.qub.ac.uk
Full-time students (2003–4), 16,000
Chancellor, Senator George Mitchell
Vice-Chancellor, Prof. Sir George Bain
Registrar, James O'Kane

UNIVERSITY OF READING (1926)

Whiteknights, PO Box 217, Reading RG6 6AH **T** 0118-987 5123
E communications@reading.ac.uk **W** www.reading.ac.uk
Full-time students (2003–4), 10,750
Chancellor, Lord Carrington, KG, GCMG, CH
Vice-Chancellor, Prof. R. G. Marshall, CBE
Director of Student Services, W.P. Watts

ROBERT GORDON UNIVERSITY (1992)

Schoolhill, Aberdeen AB10 1FR **T** 01224-262000
E admissions@rgu.ac.uk **W** www.rgu.ac.uk
Full-time students (2003–4), 8,230
Chancellor, Sir Bob Reid
Vice-Chancellor, Prof. William Stevely
Registrar, Hilary Douglas

UNIVERSITY OF ST ANDREWS (1411)

College Gate, St Andrews, Fife KY16 9AJ **T** 01334-476161
E secretary@st-and.ac.uk **W** www.st-and.ac.uk
Full-time students (2003–4), 6,700
Chancellor, Sir Kenneth Dover
Principal and Vice-Chancellor, Dr Brian Lang
Registrar, Alastair Work

UNIVERSITY OF SALFORD (1896)
Salford, Greater Manchester M5 4WT **T** 0161-295 5000
E marketing@salford.ac.uk **W** www.salford.ac.uk
Full-time students (2003–4), 15,000
Chancellor, Sir Walter Bodmer
Vice-Chancellor, Prof. Michael Harloe
Registrar, Dr Malcolm Winton

UNIVERSITY OF SHEFFIELD (1905)
Western Bank, Sheffield S10 2TN **T** 0114-222 2000
E proffice@sheffield.ac.uk **W** www.shef.ac.uk
Full-time students (2003–4), 21,403
Chancellor, Sir Peter Middleton
Vice-Chancellor, Prof. R. F. Boucher
Registrar and Secretary, Dr D. E. Fletcher

SHEFFIELD HALLAM UNIVERSITY (1992)
City Campus, Howard Street, Sheffield S1 1WB
T 0114-225 5555 **W** www.shu.ac.uk
Full-time students (2003–4), 21,000
Chancellor, Prof. The Lord Winston
Vice-Chancellor, Prof. Diana Green

UNIVERSITY OF SOUTHAMPTON (1952)
Highfield, Southampton SO17 1BJ **T** 023-8059 5000
E external@soton.ac.uk **W** www.soton.ac.uk
Full-time students (2003–4), 17,119
Chancellor, The Lord Selbourne
Vice-Chancellor, Prof. Bill Wakeham
Secretary and Registrar, John Lauwerys

SOUTH BANK UNIVERSITY (1992)
103 Borough Road, London SE1 0AA **T** 020-7928 8989
W www.sbu.ac.uk
Full-time students (2003–4), 15,940
Chancellor, Prof. Deian Hopkin
Vice-Chancellors, Dr Peter McCaffery, Dr Mike Wilkinson
Secretary, Dr Ruth Farwell

STAFFORDSHIRE UNIVERSITY (1992)
College Road, Stoke-on-Trent ST4 2DE **T** 01782-294000
E admissions@staffs.ac.uk **W** www.staffs.ac.uk
Full-time students (2003–4), 18,500
Chief Executive, Prof. Christine King
Dean of Students, Francesca Francis
Secretary, Ken Sproston

UNIVERSITY OF STIRLING (1967)
Stirling FK9 4LA **T** 01786-473171 **E** c&d@stir.ac.uk
W www.stir.ac.uk
Full-time students (2003–4), 6,800
Chancellor, Dame Diana Rigg
Vice-Chancellor (acting), Prof. Christine Hallet
Registrar, Douglas Wood

UNIVERSITY OF STRATHCLYDE (1796)
McCance Building, John Anderson Campus, Glasgow G1 1XQ
T 0141-552 4400 **W** www.strath.ac.uk
Full-time students (2003–4), 15,136
Chancellor, The Lord Hope of Craighead
Vice-Chancellor and Principal, Prof. Andrew Hamnett
Secretary, Dr Peter West

UNIVERSITY OF SUNDERLAND (1992)
Langham Tower, Ryhope Road, Sunderland SR2 7EE
T 0191-515 2000 **E** student-helpline@sunderland.ac.uk
W www.sunderland.ac.uk
Full-time students (2003–4), 8,500
Chancellor, The Lord Puttnam of Queensgate, CBE
Vice-Chancellor, Prof. P. Fidler, MBE
Secretary, J. D. Pacey

UNIVERSITY OF SURREY (1966)
Guildford, Surrey GU2 7XH **T** 01483-300800
E information@surrey.ac.uk **W** www.surrey.ac.uk
Full-time students (2003–4), 10,612
Chancellor, HRH The Duke of Kent, KG
Vice-Chancellor, Prof. P. J. Dowling, CBE, FRENG
Registrar, P. W. Beardsley

UNIVERSITY OF SUSSEX (1961)
Sussex House, Falmer, Brighton BN1 9RH **T** 01273-606755
E information@sussex.ac.uk **W** www.sussex.ac.uk
Full-time students (2003–4), 9,200
Chancellor, Lord Attenborough, CBE
Vice-Chancellor, Prof. Alasdair Smith
Registrar and Secretary, Neil Gershon

UNIVERSITY OF TEESSIDE (1992)
Middlesbrough, Tees Valley TS1 3BA **T** 01642-218121
E m.white@tees.ac.uk **W** www.tees.ac.uk
Full-time students (2003–4), 9,000
Chancellor, Lord Leon Brittan of Spennithorn
Vice-Chancellor, Prof. D. Fraser
University Secretary, J. M. McClintock

THAMES VALLEY UNIVERSITY (1992)
St Mary's Road, Ealing, London W5 5RF **T** 020-8579 5000
E learning.advice@tvu.ac.uk **W** www.tvu.ac.uk
Full-time students (2003–4), 12,948
Vice-Chancellor, Prof. Geoff Crispin
Secretary, Ann Marie Dalton

UNIVERSITY OF ULSTER (1984)
Cromore Road, Coleraine, Co. Londonderry BT52 1SA
T 08700 400 700 **E** online@ulster.ac.uk **W** www.ulster.ac.uk
Full-time students (2003–4), 16,479
Chancellor, Sir Richard Nichols, DCL, LLD
Vice-Chancellor, Prof. P. G. McKenna, PHD
Pro-Chancellor, Dr G. Butus

UNIVERSITY OF WALES (1893)
King Edward VII Avenue, Cathays Park, Cardiff CF10 3NS
T 029-2038 2656 **E** uniwales@wales.ac.uk **W** www.wales.ac.uk
Full-time students (2003–4), 62,000
Chancellor, HRH The Prince of Wales, KG, KT, GCB, OM, PC
Senior Vice-Chancellor, Prof. A. J. Chapman
Secretary-General, Dr L. E. Williams

MEMBER INSTITUTES
UNIVERSITY OF WALES, ABERYSTWYTH Old College, King Street, Aberystwyth SY23 2AX **T** 01970-623111
Vice-Chancellor, Prof. N. G. Lloyd
UNIVERSITY OF WALES, BANGOR Bangor, Gwynedd LL57 2DG **T** 01248-351151
Vice-Chancellor, Prof. R. M. Jones
UNIVERSITY OF WALES COLLEGE, NEWPORT Caerleon Campus, PO Box 179, Newport NP6 1YG **T** 01633-430088
Vice-Chancellor, Prof. J. R. Lusty, PHD, FRSC (2002)

UNIVERSITY OF WALES INSTITUTE, CARDIFF Llandaff Centre, Western Avenue, Cardiff CF5 2SG
T 01222-506070
Vice-Chancellor, A. J. Chapman
UNIVERSITY OF WALES, LAMPETER Lampeter SA48 7ED
T 01570-422351
Vice-Chancellor, Prof. R. A. Pearce
UNIVERSITY OF WALES, SWANSEA Singleton Park, Swansea SA2 8PP T 01792-205678
Vice-Chancellor, Prof. R. B. Davies

UNIVERSITY OF WARWICK (1965)
Coventry CV4 7AL T 024-7652 3523 W www.warwick.ac.uk
Full-time students (2003–4), 15,536
Chancellor, Sir Nicholas Scheele
Vice-Chancellor, Prof. V. D. Vandelinde, FRS
Secretary, C. E. Charlton

UNIVERSITY OF WESTMINSTER (1992)
309 Regent Street, London W1B 2UW T 020-7911 5000
E admissions@wmin.ac.uk W www.wmin.ac.uk
Full-time students (2003–4), 12,647
Chairman of the Board of Governors, Sir Alan Thomas
Vice-Chancellor and Rector, Dr Geoffrey Copland
Academic Registrar, Evelyn Rugg

UNIVERSITY OF THE WEST OF ENGLAND (1992)
Frenchay Campus, Coldharbour Lane, Bristol BS16 1QY
T 0117-965 6261 E enquiries@uwe.ac.uk W www.uwe.ac.uk
Full-time students (2003—4), 18,519
Chancellor, The Rt. Hon. Dame Elizabeth Butler-Sloss, DBE
Vice-Chancellor, A. C. Morris, CBE
Academic Secretary, Carole Webb

UNIVERSITY OF WOLVERHAMPTON (1992)
Wulfruna Street, Wolverhampton WV1 1SB T 01902-321000
W www.wlv.ac.uk
Full-time students (2003–4), 14,223
Chancellor, The Lord Paul of Marylebone
Vice-Chancellor, Prof. John Brooks, PHD, DSC
Registrar, J. Nelson

UNIVERSITY OF YORK (1963)
Heslington, York YO10 5DD T 01904-430000
W www.york.ac.uk
Full-time students (2003–4), 10,000
Chancellor, Dame Janet Barker, CH, DBE
Vice-Chancellor, Prof. B. Cantor, PHD, FRENG
Registrar and Secretary, D. J. Foster

PROFESSIONAL EDUCATION

The organisations listed below are those which, by providing specialist training or conducting examinations, control entry into a profession, or are responsible for maintaining a register of those with professional qualifications in their sector.

EU RECOGNITION
It is possible for those with professional qualifications obtained in the UK to have these recognised in other European Countries. A booklet, *Europe Open for Professions,* is available at www.dfes.gov.uk/europeopen. Further information can be obtained from:

DEPARTMENT FOR EDUCATION AND SKILLS Room E3B, Moorfoot, Sheffield S1 4PQ T 0870-0012345
W www.dfes.gov.uk

ACCOUNTANCY

The main bodies granting membership on examination after a period of practical work are:

ASSOCIATION OF CHARTERED CERTIFIED ACCOUNTANTS (ACCA) 29 Lincoln's Inn Fields, London WC2A 3EE T 020-7396 7000 W www.accaglobal.com
Chief Executive, Anthea Rose
CIMA (THE CHARTERED INSTITUTE OF MANAGEMENT ACCOUNTANTS) 26 Chapter Street, London SW1P 4NP
T 020-7663 5441 W www.cimaglobal.com
Chief Executive, Charles Tilley
INSTITUTE OF CHARTERED ACCOUNTANTS IN ENGLAND AND WALES Chartered Accountants' Hall, PO Box 433, Moorgate Place, London EC2P 2BJ
T 020-7920 8100 W www.icaew.co.uk
Secretary-General, Peter Owen
INSTITUTE OF CHARTERED ACCOUNTANTS OF SCOTLAND CA House, 21 Haymarket Yards, Edinburgh EH12 5BH T 0131-347 0100 W www.icas.org.uk
Chief Executive, David Brew

ACTUARIAL SCIENCE

The UK actuarial profession is controlled by the Institute of Actuaries in London and the Faculty of Actuaries in Edinburgh. The Faculty and Institute together set professional codes, disciplinary standards and examinations continuing professional development. UK qualified actuaries may be Fellows of either organisation. Practising certificates are issued on certain actuaries for their statutory role in the financial management of life offices and most pension schemes.

FACULTY OF ACTUARIES IN SCOTLAND Maclaurin House, 18 Dublin Street, Edinburgh EH1 3PP T 0131-240 1300
W www.actuaries.org.uk
Secretary, Richard Machonachie
INSTITUTE OF ACTUARIES Staple Inn Hall, High Holborn, London WC1V 7QJ T 020-7632 2100
W www.actuaries.org.uk
Secretary-General, Caroline Instance

ARCHITECTURE

The Education Committee of the Royal Institute of British Architects sets standards and guides the whole system of architectural education throughout the UK. The Architects Registration Board is the independent regulator for the architects' profession in the UK. It was established to simultaneously protect the interests of consumers and to safeguard the reputation of architects. RIBA recognises courses at 36 schools of architecture in the UK for exemption from their own examinations as well as courses at 56 overseas schools.

ARCHITECTS REGISTRATION BOARD 8 Weymouth Street, London W1W 5BU T 020-7580 5861 W www.arb.org.uk
Chief Executive and Registrar, Robin Vaughan
ARCHITECTURAL ASSOCIATION 34–36 Bedford Square, London WC1B 3ES T 020-7887 4000
W www.aaschool.ac.uk
Chief Executive, Mohsen Mostafavi
ROYAL INSTITUTE OF BRITISH ARCHITECTS 66 Portland Place, London W1N 4AD T 020-7580 5533
W www.architecture.com

BANKING

Professional organisations granting qualifications after examination are:

CHARTERED INSTITUTE OF BANKERS IN SCOTLAND Drumsheugh House, 38b Drumsheugh Gardens, Edinburgh EH3 7SW **T** 0131-473 7777 **W** www.ciobs.org.uk
Chief Executive, Prof. Charles Munn

INSTITUTE OF FINANCIAL SERVICES IFS House, 4/9 Burgate Lane, Canterbury CT1 2XJ **T** 01227-818609 **W** www.ifslearning.com
Chief Executive Officer, G. Shreeve

BUILDING

CHARTERED INSTITUTE OF BUILDING Englemere, Kings Ride, Ascot, Berks SL5 7TB **T** 01344-630700 **W** www.ciob.org.uk
Chief Executive, Chris Blythe

INSTITUTE OF CLERKS OF WORKS OF GREAT BRITAIN Equinox, 28 Commerce Road, Lynch Wood, Peterborough PE2 6LR **T** 01733-405160

RICS (ROYAL INSTITUTION OF CHARTERED SURVEYORS) 12 Great George Street, Parliament Square, London SW1P 3AD **T** 020-7222 7000 **W** www.rics.org.uk
Chief Executive, J. Armstrong

BUSINESS MANAGEMENT AND ADMINISTRATION

ASSOCIATION OF MBAS 25 Hosier Lane, London EC1A 9LQ **T** 020-7246 2686 **W** www.mba.org.uk
Director-General, M. A. Jones

CAM FOUNDATION Moor Hall, Cookham, Maidenhead, Berks SL6 9QH **T** 01628-427180 **W** www.camfoundation.com

CHARTERED INSTITUTE OF HOUSING Octavia House, Westwood Business Park, Westwood Way, Coventry CV4 8JP **T** 024-7685 1700 **W** www.cih.org
Chief Executive, D. Butler

CHARTERED INSTITUTE OF PERSONNEL AND DEVELOPMENT CIPD House, Camp Road, London SW19 4UX **T** 020-8971 9000 **W** www.cipd.co.uk
Director-General, G. Armstrong

CHARTERED INSTITUTE OF PURCHASING AND SUPPLY (1932) Easton House, Easton on the Hill, Stamford, Lincs PE9 3NZ **T** 01780-756777 **W** www.cips.org
Chief Executive, K. James

CHARTERED MANAGEMENT INSTITUTE Management House, Cottingham Road, Corby, Northants NN17 1TT **T** 01536-204222 **W** www.managers.org.uk
Chief Executive, Ms M. Chapman

HENLEY MANAGEMENT COLLEGE Greenlands, Henley on Thames, Oxon RG9 3AU **T** 01491-571454 **W** www.henleymc.ac.uk

INSTITUTE OF ADMINISTRATIVE MANAGEMENT 16 Park Crescent, London, W1B 1BA **T** 020-7612 7099 **W** www.instam.org
Chief Executive, David Woodgate

INSTITUTE OF CHARTERED SECRETARIES AND ADMINISTRATORS 16 Park Crescent, London W1B 1AH **T** 020-7580 4741 **W** www.icsa.org.uk
Chief Executive, M. J. Ainsworth

INSTITUTE OF CHARTERED SHIPBROKERS 85 Gracechurch Street London EC3V 0AA **T** 020-7623 1111 **W** www.ics.org.uk
Director-General, Alan Phillips

INSTITUTE OF EXPORT Export House, Minerva Business Park, Lynch Wood, Peterborough PE2 6FT **T** 01733-404400 **W** www.export.org.uk
Chief Executive, Hugh Allen

INSTITUTE OF HEALTHCARE MANAGEMENT 46 Grosvenor Gardens, London SW1W 0EB **T** 020-7881 9235 **W** www.ihm.org.uk
Chief Executive, Rosey Foster *(acting)*

INSTITUTE OF QUALITY ASSURANCE 12 Grosvenor Crescent, London SW1X 7EE **T** 020-7245 6722 **W** www.iqa.org

CHIROPRACTIC

The General Chiropractic Council (GCC) is the statutory regulatory body for chiropractors and its role and remit is defined in the Chiropractors Act 1994. It is illegal for anyone in the UK to use the title 'chiropractor' unless registered with the GCC.

BRITISH CHIROPRACTIC ASSOCIATION Blagrave House, Blagrave Street, Reading, Berks RG1 1QB **T** 0118-950 5950 **W** www.chiropractic-uk.co.uk

GENERAL CHIROPRACTIC COUNCIL 44 Wicklow Street, London WC1X 9HL **T** 020-7713 5155 **W** www.gcc-uk.org

SCOTTISH CHIROPRACTIC ASSOCIATION Laigh Hatton Farm, Old Greenock Road, Bishopton, Renfrewshire PA7 5PB **T** 01505-863151 **W** www.sca-chiropractic.org

DANCE

The Council for Dance Education and Training (CDET) accredits courses at the following: ArtsEdLondon; Arts Education Tring Park; Central School of Ballet; Bird College of Performing Arts; Elmhurst – The School for Dance and Performing Arts; The Hammond School; The Italia Conti Academy of Theatre Arts Limited; Laban; Laine Theatre Arts Ltd; London Contemporary Dance School; London Studio Centre; Midlands Academy of Dance and Drama Centre; Northern Ballet School, Performers College; Stella Mann College; Studios la Pointe; The Urdang Academy.

The accreditation of a course in a school does not neccessarily imply that other courses of a different type or duration in the same school are also accredited. CDET has approved the teacher registration systems of a number of other dance organisations in the UK. Contact CDET for further information.

CDET Toynbee Hall, 28 Commercial Street, London E1 6LS **T** 020-7247 4030 **W** www.cdet.org.uk

IMPERIAL SOCIETY OF TEACHERS OF DANCING Imperial House, 22–26 Paul Street, London EC2A 4QE **T** 020-7377 1577 **W** www.istd.org
Chief Executive, Michael J. Browne

INTERNATIONAL DANCE TEACHERS' ASSOCIATION International House, 76 Bennett Road, Brighton BN2 5JL **T** 01273-685652 **W** www.idta.co.uk

ROYAL ACADEMY OF DANCE 36 Battersea Square, London SW11 3RA **T** 020-7326 8000 **W** www.rad.org.uk
Chief Executive, L. Rittner

ROYAL BALLET SCHOOL 46 Floral Street, London WC2E 9DA **T** 020-7836 8899 **W** www.royalballetschool.co.uk
Director, Ms G. Stock, AM

DEFENCE

JOINT SERVICES COMMAND AND STAFF COLLEGE Faringdon Road, Watchfield, Swindon, Wilts SN6 8TS **T** 01793-788000 **W** www.jscsc.org.uk
Commandant, Maj.-Gen. J. C. McColl, CBE

ROYAL COLLEGE OF DEFENCE STUDIES Seaford House, 37 Belgrave Square, London SW1X 8NS **T** 020-7915 4800 **W** www.da.mod.uk/rcds
Commandant, Lt.-Gen. (Retd) Sir Christopher Wallace, KBE

ROYAL NAVAL COLLEGE

BRITANNIA ROYAL NAVAL COLLEGE Dartmouth, Devon TQ6 0HJ T 01803-677108
Commodore, Cdre C. A. Johnstone-Burt, OBE, ADC

MILITARY COLLEGES

DIRECTORATE OF EDUCATIONAL AND TRAINING SERVICES (ARMY) Trenchard Lines, Upavon, Pewsey, Wilts SN9 6BE T 01980-618719/618701 W www.agc-ets.co.uk
Director, Brig. M. St. J. Filler

ROYAL MILITARY ACADEMY SANDHURST Camberley, Surrey GU15 4PQ T 01276-63344 W www.sandhurst.mod.uk
Commandant, Maj.-Gen. A. S. Ritchie, CBE

ROYAL MILITARY COLLEGE OF SCIENCE Cranfield University, RMCS Shrivenham, Swindon SN6 8LA T 01793-782551 W www.rmcs.cranfield.ac.uk

ROYAL AIR FORCE COLLEGES

ROYAL AIR FORCE COLLEGE Cranwell, Sleaford, Lincs NG34 8HB T 01400-261201 W www.cranwell.raf.mod.uk
Air Officer Commanding and Commandant,

TRAINING DEVELOPMENT WING RAF Halton, Aylesbury, Bucks HP22 5PG T 01296-623535 ext. 6363

DENTISTRY

In order to practise in the UK, a dentist must be registered with the General Dental Council. To be registered a person must be qualified in one of the following ways: hold the degree or diploma in dental surgery of a university in the UK or hold the licentiate in dental surgery awarded by one of the Royal Surgical Colleges in the UK; have completed the Council's International Qualifying Examination (IQE); be a European Community or European Economic Area national holding an appropriate European diploma; hold a registered overseas diploma or be an EEA national holding a primary dental qualification from outside the EEA but having acquired the right to practise in the EEA. The holder of a dental degree or diploma other than those referred to above may be eligible for temporary registration to enable him or her to practice dentistry in the United Kingdom for a limited period and in specificied posts without the need to take further examinations. The Dentists Register and Rolls of Dental Auxiliaries are maintained by:

GENERAL DENTAL COUNCIL 37 Wimpole Street, London W1G 8DQ T 020-7887 3800 W www.gdc-uk.org

DIETETICS

The professional association is the British Dietetic Association. Full membership is open to dieticians holding a recognised qualification, who must also be registered with the Health Professions Council (*see* Professions Supplementary to Medicine).

BRITISH DIETETIC ASSOCIATION 5th Floor, Charles House, 148–149 Great Charles Street Queensway, Birmingham B3 3HT T 0121-200 8080 W www.bda.uk.com

DRAMA

The national validating body for courses providing training in drama for the professional theatre is the National Council for Drama Training (NCDT). NCDT accredits courses at 21 drama schools in England, Scotland and Wales. It also sponsers annual seminars on graduate showcases, television training and skills needs in the small sector. There are two useful guides for students entering drama school: *A Practical Guide to Vocational Training in Dance and Drama* and *An Applicant's Guide to Auditioning and Interviewing at Dance and Drama.* These publications and numerous information sheets and useful links are available on the NCDT's website (*see* below).

NATIONAL COUNCIL FOR DRAMA TRAINING 1–7 Woburn Walk, London WC1H 0JJ T 020-7387 3650 W www.ncdt.co.uk

ENGINEERING

Engineering Council (UK) sets the standards for the accreditation for academic courses in universities and colleges and the practical training in industry. The Council also runs the National Register of Chartered Engineers, Incorporated Engineers and Engineering Technicians.

The principal qualifying bodies are:

BRITISH COMPUTER SOCIETY 1 Sanford Street, Swindon SN1 1HJ T 01793-417417 W www.bcs.org
Chief Executive, David Clarke

CHARTERED INSTITUTE OF BUILDING SERVICES ENGINEERS 222 Balham High Road, London SW12 9BS T 020-8675 5211 W www.cibse.org
Chief Executive, Julian Amey

ENGINEERING AND TECHNOLOGY BOARD 10 Maltravers Street, London WC2R 3ER T 020-7240 7333 W www.etechb.co.uk

INSTITUTE OF MARINE ENGINEERING, SCIENCE AND TECHNOLOGY 80 Coleman Street, London EC2R 5BJ T 020-7382 2600 W www.imarest.org
Director-General, K. F. Read

INSTITUTE OF MATERIALS, MINERALS AND MINING 1 Carlton House Terrace, London SW1Y 5DB T 020-7451 7300 W www.iom3.org
Chief Executive, Dr B. Rickinson

INSTITUTE OF MEASUREMENT AND CONTROL 87 Gower Street, London WC1E 6AF T 020-7387 4949 W www.instmc.org.uk
Secretary, M. J. Yates

INSTITUTE OF PHYSICS 76 Portland Place, London W1B 1NT T 020-7470 4800 W www.iop.org
Chief Executive, Julia King

INSTITUTION OF CHEMICAL ENGINEERS Davis Building, 165–189 Railway Terrace, Rugby, Warks CV21 3HQ T 01788-578214 W www.icheme.org
Chief Executive, Dr Trevor Evans

INSTITUTION OF CIVIL ENGINEERS 1 Great George Street, London SW1P 3AA T 020-7222 7722 W www.ice.org.uk
Acting Chief Executive, Amar Bhogal

INSTITUTION OF ELECTRICAL ENGINEERS Savoy Place, London WC2R 0BL T 020-7240 1871 W www.iee.org.uk
Chief Executive, Dr Alf Roberts

INSTITUTION OF GAS ENGINEERS AND MANAGERS 12 York Gate, London NW1 4QG T 020-7487 0650 W www.igaseng.com
Chief Executive Officer, G. Davies

INSTITUTION OF MECHANICAL ENGINEERS 1 Birdcage Walk, London SW1H 9JJ T 020-7222 7899 W www.imeche.org.uk
Director-General, Sir Michael Moore, KBE, LVO

INSTITUTION OF STRUCTURAL ENGINEERS 11 Upper Belgrave Street, London SW1X 8BH T 020-7235 4535 W www.istructe.org.uk
Chief Executive and Secretary, Dr K. J. Eaton

INSTITUTION OF STRUCTURAL ENGINEERS (Scottish Branch), 15 Beresford Place, East Trinity Road, Edinburgh EH5 3SL T 0131-552 8852 W www.istructe.org.uk
Chief Executive and Secretary, Dr K. J. Eaton

ROYAL AERONAUTICAL SOCIETY 4 Hamilton Place, London W1J 7BQ T 020-7670 4300 W www.raes.org.uk
Director, K. Mans

ROYAL INSTITUTION OF NAVAL ARCHITECTS 10 Upper Belgrave Street, London SW1X 8BQ T 020-7235 4622 W www.rina.org.uk
Chief Executive, T. Blakeley

FILM AND TELEVISION

Postgraduate training for those intending to make a career in film, television and new media production is provided by the National Film and Television School, which offers MA courses in animation direction, documentary direction, fiction direction, producing, screenwriting, cinematography, production design, editing, sound post-production and composing for film and television. The school also offers a Diploma course in sound recording and a script development Executive Diploma, run in association with the Script Factory. Five-week feature development workshops run at intervals during the year. Short courses enabling professionals to update or expand their skills are run by the National Short Course Training Programme.

NATIONAL FILM AND TELEVISION SCHOOL Beaconsfield Studios, Station Road, Beaconsfield, Bucks HP9 1LJ T 01494-671234 W www.nftsfilm-tv.ac.uk
Director, Nick Powell

FORESTRY AND TIMBER STUDIES

Professional organisations include:

COMMONWEALTH FORESTRY ASSOCIATION PO 142, Bicester, Oxon OX26 6ZJ T 01865-271037 W www.cfa-international.org
Chairman, Dr J. S. Maini

INSTITUTE OF CHARTERED FORESTERS 7a St Colme Street, Edinburgh EH3 6AA T 0131-225 2705 W www.charteredforesters.org
Executive Director, Mrs M. W. Dick, FRSA, OBE

ROYAL FORESTRY SOCIETY OF ENGLAND, WALES AND NORTHERN IRELAND 102 High Street, Tring, Herts HP23 4AF T 01442-822028 W www.rfs.org.uk
Director, Dr J. E. Jackson

ROYAL SCOTTISH FORESTRY SOCIETY Hagg-on-Esk, Canonbie, Dumfriesshire DG14 0BE T 01387-371518 W www.rsfs.org
President, P. J. Fothergill

FUEL AND ENERGY SCIENCE

The principal professional body is:

INSTITUTE OF PETROLEUM 61 New Cavendish Street, London W1G 7AR T 020-7467 7100 W www.intertek-cb.com
Director-General, Mrs L. Kingham

HOTELKEEPING, CATERING AND INSTITUTIONAL MANAGEMENT

See also, DIETETICS

The qualifying professional body in these areas is:

HOTEL AND CATERING INTERNATIONAL MANAGEMENT ASSOCIATION Trinity Court, 34 West Street, Sutton, Surrey SM1 1SH T 020-8661 4900 W www.hcima.org.uk
Chief Executive, Philippe Rossiter

INSURANCE

Organisations conducting examinations and awarding diplomas are:

ASSOCIATION OF AVERAGE ADJUSTERS The Baltic Exchange, St Mary Axe, London EC3A 8BH T 020-7623 5501 W www.average-adjusters.com
Chairman, Tim Madge

CHARTERED INSTITUTE OF LOSS ADJUSTERS Peninsular House, 36 Monument Street, London EC3R 8LJ T 020-7337 9960 W www.cila.co.uk
Executive Director, Graham Cave

CHARTERED INSURANCE INSTITUTE 20 Aldermanbury, London EC2V 7HY T 020-8989 8464 W www.cii.co.uk
Director-General, Dr Sandy Scott

JOURNALISM

Courses for trainee newspaper journalists are available at 30 centres. One-year full time courses are available for selected students, three-year degree programmes and 18-week courses for graduates. Particulars for all these courses are available from the National Council for the Training of Journalists. Short courses for mid-career development are available, as are various distance learning courses.

For periodical journalists, there are twelve centres running courses approved by the Periodicals Training Council (PTC). The PTC also provides career information for people wishing to join the industry.

NATIONAL COUNCIL FOR THE TRAINING OF JOURNALISTS Latton Bush Centre, Southern Way, Harlow, Essex CM18 7BL T 01279-430009 W www.nctj.com

PERIODICALS TRAINING COUNCIL 28 Kingsway, London WC2B 6JR T 020-7404 4168 W www.ppa.co.uk/ptc

LAW

THE BAR

The governing body of the Bar of England and Wales is the General Council of the Bar (also known as the Bar Council). All practising barrisers pay an annual subscription fee to support the Bar Council. Its functions include dealing with disciplinary matters, acting as the public voice of the profession, and regulating the education and training requirements for those wishing to enter the profession.

Those intending to practise at the Bar of England and Wales must complete three main stages of training: the academic stage (the law degree, or non-law degree plus conversion course), the vocational stage (the Bar Vocational Course/BVC), and pupillage (a period of in-service training). There are also Continuing Professional Development (CPD) requirements on barristers, and a minimum number of hours of CPD must be completed each year. Training at the vocational stage takes place at one of eight validated institutions around the country; pupillage can take place in any approved legal environment, usually a set of barristers' chambers, but it can also be in an employed legal environment, such as the government legal service. All barristers must be members of one of the four Inns of Court. Students are currently Called to the Bar by their Inn after completion of the vocational stage, but from 2008 Call will take place after a period of pupillage. Call to the Bar does not entitle a person to practise as a barrister, successful completion of pupillage is now a pre-requisite. Further information can be found on the Bar Council's website.

Admission to the Bar of Northern Ireland by the Honorable Society of the Inn of Court of Northern Ireland and admission as an Advocate of the Scottish Bar is controlled by the Faculty of Advocates.

BVCONLINE The General Council of the Bar, 2–3 Curistor Street, London EC4A 1NE T 020-7440 4000
W www.bvconline.co.uk
Chief Executive, N. Morison

FACULTY OF ADVOCATES Advocates Library, Parliament House, Edinburgh EH1 1RF T 0131-226 5071
W www.advocates.org.uk
Dean, G. N. H. Emslie, QC

GENERAL COUNCIL OF THE BAR 3 Bedford Row, London WC1R 4DB T 020-7242 0082 W www.barcouncil.org.uk

HONORABLE SOCIETY OF THE INN OF COURT OF NORTHERN IRELAND The Under-treasurer's Office, Royal Courts of Justice, Belfast BT1 3JF T 028-9072 4699

INNS OF COURT SCHOOL OF LAW 4 Gray's Inn Place, Gray's Inn, London WC1R 5DX T 020-7404 5787
W www.city.ac.uk/icsl

The Inns of Court

GRAY'S INN 8 South Square, London WC1R 5ET
T 020-7458 7800 W www.graysinn.org.uk
Treasurer, The Rt. Hon. Sir Paul Kennedy, QC

HONOURABLE SOCIETY OF LINCOLN'S INN Treasury Office, Lincoln's Inn, London WC2A 3TL T 020-7405 1393
W www.lincolnsinn.org.uk
Under-Treasurer, Col. D. Hills, MBE

INNER TEMPLE London EC4Y 7HL T 020-7797 8250
W www.innertemple.org.uk
Treasurer, Richard Southwell, QC

MIDDLE TEMPLE Middle Temple Lane, London EC4Y 9AT
T 020-7427 4800 W www.middletemple.org.uk
Treasurer, Rt. Hon. Lord Justice Rose, QC

SOLICITORS

The College of Law is the oldest and largest provider of vocational legal education and training for students wishing to become solicitors and barristers in England and Wales. It also offers training after qualification and a wide range of distance-learning courses. There are a number of other institutions offering the neccesary courses, namely the Legal Practice Course and the Common Professional Examination (conversion course for non-law graduates). The Law Society of England and Wales, the Law Society of Scotland and the Law Society of Northern Ireland control the education and examination of trainee solicitors and the admission of solicitors.

COLLEGE OF LAW Braboeuf Manor, Portsmouth Road, St Catherine's, Guildford, Surrey GU3 1HA T 01483-460200
W www.lawcol.org.uk

LAW SOCIETY OF ENGLAND AND WALES 113 Chancery Lane, London WC2A 1PL T 020-7242 1222
W www.lawsociety.org.uk

LAW SOCIETY OF NORTHERN IRELAND Law Society House, 98 Victoria Street, Belfast BT1 3JZ T 028-9023 1614
W www.lawsoc-ni.org
Chief Executive and Secretary, J. W. Bailie

LAW SOCIETY OF SCOTLAND 26 Drumsheugh Gardens, Edinburgh EH3 7YR T 0131-226 7411
W www.lawscot.org.uk

LIBRARIANSHIP AND INFORMATION SCIENCE

The Chartered Institute of Library and Information Professionals accredits degree and postgraduate courses in library and information science which are offered by 17 universities in the UK. A full list of accredited degree and postgraduate courses is available from the Institute's Membership, Careers and Qualifications Department and on its website.

CHARTERED INSTITUTE OF LIBRARY AND INFORMATION PROFESSIONALS 7 Ridgmount Street, London WC1E 7AE
T 020-7255 0500 Text phone 020-7255 0505
W www.cilip.org.uk

MEDICINE

All doctors must be registered with the General Medical Council (GMC), which is responsible for protecting the public by setting standards for professional practice, overseeing medical education, keeping a register of qualified doctors and taking action where a doctor's fitness to practice is in doubt. A doctor not registered with the GMC is not a 'legally qualified' medical practitioner for the purpose of the Medical Act 1983. In order to be eligible for registration, doctors must obtain a primary medical qualification recognised by the GMC and have satisfactorily completed a year of general medical training. Special arrangements apply to doctors qualified outside the UK. Once registered, doctors undertake general professional and basic specialist training as senior house officers. Further specialist training is provided by the royal colleges, faculties and societies listed below.

The United Examining Board holds qualifying examinations for candidates who have trained overseas. These candidates must also have spent a period at a UK medical school.

FACULTY OF PHARMACEUTICAL MEDICINE 1 St Andrew's Place, Regents Park, London NW1 4LB
T 020-7224 0343 W www.fpm.org.uk
Faculty Administrator, Mrs Kathryn Swanston

GENERAL MEDICAL COUNCIL 178 Great Portland Street, London W1N 6JE T 020-7580 7642 W www.gmc-uk.org

ROYAL COLLEGE OF GENERAL PRACTITIONERS 14 Princes Gate, London SW7 1PU T 020-7581 3232
W www.rcgp.org.uk
Hon. Secretary, Dr M. Baker

SCOTTISH COUNCIL FOR POSTGRADUATE MEDICAL AND DENTAL EDUCATION 2nd Floor, Hanover Buildings, 66 Rose Street, Edinburgh EH2 2NN T 0131-225 4365

UNITED EXAMINING BOARD Apothecaries Hall, Black Friars Lane, London EC4V 6EJ T 020-7236 1180
Chairman, Prof J. S. P. Lumley

COLLEGES/SOCIETIES HOLDING POSTGRADUATE MEMBERSHIP AND DIPLOMA

FACULTY OF ACCIDENT AND EMERGENCY MEDICINE 35–43 Lincoln's Inn Fields, London WC2A 3PE
T 020-7405 7071 W www.faem.org.uk
President, I. W. R. Anderson

FACULTY OF PUBLIC HEALTH MEDICINE 4 St Andrews Place, London NW1 4LB T 020-7935 0243
W www.fphm.org.uk
Faculty Secretary, P. Scourfield

ROYAL COLLEGE OF ANAESTHETISTS 48–49 Russell Square, London WC1B 4JY T 020-7813 1900 W www.rcoa.ac.uk
The College Secretary, Kevin Story

ROYAL COLLEGE OF OBSTETRICIANS AND GYNAECOLOGISTS 27 Sussex Place, Regent's Park, London NW1 4RG T 020-7772 6200 W www.rcog.org.uk
College Secretary, P. A. Barnett

ROYAL COLLEGE OF PAEDIATRICS AND CHILD HEALTH 50 Hallam Street, London W1W 6DE T 020-7307 5600 W www.rcpch.ac.uk
College Secretary, Len Tyler

ROYAL COLLEGE OF PATHOLOGISTS 2 Carlton House Terrace, London SW1Y 5AF T 020-7451 6700 W www.rcpath.org
Chief Executive, D. Ross

ROYAL COLLEGE OF PHYSICIANS 11 St Andrews Place, Regent's Park, London NW1 4LE T 020-7935 1174 W www.rcplondon.ac.uk
President, Prof. Sir George Alberti

ROYAL COLLEGE OF PHYSICIANS AND SURGEONS OF GLASGOW 232–242 St Vincent Street, Glasgow G2 5RJ T 0141-221 6072 W www.rcpsglasg.ac.uk
President, Prof. A. R. Lorimer

ROYAL COLLEGE OF PHYSICIANS OF EDINBURGH 9 Queen Street, Edinburgh EH2 1JQ T 0131-225 7324 W www.rcpe.ac.uk
President, Dr N. D. C. Finlayson, OBE

ROYAL COLLEGE OF PSYCHIATRISTS 17 Belgrave Square, London SW1X 8PG T 020-7235 2351 W www.rcpsych.ac.uk
President, Dr Mike Shooter

ROYAL COLLEGE OF RADIOLOGISTS 38 Portland Place, London W1B 1JQ T 020-7636 4432 W www.rcr.ac.uk
President, Dr Dan Ash

ROYAL COLLEGE OF SURGEONS OF EDINBURGH Nicolson Street, Edinburgh EH8 9DW T 0131-527 1600 W www.rcsed.ac.uk
Chief Executive, J. R. C. Foster

ROYAL COLLEGE OF SURGEONS OF ENGLAND 35–43 Lincoln's Inn Fields, London WC2A 3PE T 020-7405 3474 W www.rcseng.ac.uk
Chief Executive, Craig Duncan

SOCIETY OF APOTHECARIES OF LONDON 14 Black Friars Lane, London EC4V 6EJ T 020-7236 1189 W www.apothecaries.org
The Clerk, R. J. Stringer

PROFESSIONS SUPPLEMENTARY TO MEDICINE

The standard of professional education in art, drama and music therapies, biomedical sciences, chiropody, dietetics, occupational therapy, orthoptics, prosthetics, othotics, physiotherapy and radiography is regulated by the Health Professional Council. It also ensures that the registration of professionals is linked to continual professional development.

HEALTH PROFESSIONS COUNCIL TO MEDICINE Park House, 184 Kennington Park Road, London SE11 4BU T 020-7582 0866 W www.hpc-uk.org

ART, DRAMA AND MUSIC THERAPIES

A Postgraduate qualification in the relevant therapy is required. Details of accredited training programes in the UK can be obtained from the following organisations:

ASSOCIATION OF PROFESSIONAL MUSIC THERAPIES 26 Hamlyn Road, Glastonbury, Somerset BA6 8HT T 01458-834919 W www.apmt.org.uk
Administrator, Mrs D. Asbridge

BRITISH ASSOCIATION OF ART THERAPISTS Mary Ward House, 5 Tavistock Place, London WC1H 9SN T 020-7383 3774 W www.baat.org

BRITISH ASSOCIATION OF DRAMA THERAPISTS 41 Broomhouse Lane, London SW6 3DP T 020-7731 0160 W www.badth.demon.co.uk

BIOMEDICAL SCIENCES

Qualifications from higher education establishments and training in medical laboratories are required for membership of the Institute of Biomedical Science.

INSTITUTE OF BIOMEDICAL SCIENCE 12 Coldbath Square, London EC1R 5HL T 020-7713 0214 W www.ibms.org

CHIROPODY

Professional Recognition is granted by the Society of Chiropodists and Podiatrists to students who are awarded BSc degrees in Podiatry or Podiatric Medicine after attending a course of full-time training for three or four years at one of the 13 recognised schools in the UK (ten in England and Wales, two in Scotland and one in Northern Ireland). Qualifications granted and degrees recognised by the Society are approved for the purpose of State Registration, which is a condition of employment within the National Health Service.

SOCIETY OF CHIROPODISTS AND PODIATRISTS 1 Fellmongers Path, Tower Bridge Road, London SE1 3LY T 020-7234 8620 W www.feetforlife.org
Chief Executive, Ms Hilary De Lyon

COMPLEMENTARY MEDICINE

Professional courses are validated by:

INSTITUTE FOR COMPLEMENTARY MEDICINE PO Box 194, London SE16 7QZ T 020-7237 5165 W www.icmedicine.co.uk

OCCUPATIONAL THERAPY

The professional qualification and eligibility for registration may be obtained upon successful completion of a validated course in any of the institutions approved by the College of Occupational Therapists. The courses are normally degree-level courses based in higher education institutions. For further information please visit the websites below.

COLLEGE OF OCCUPATIONAL THERAPISTS 106–114 Borough High Street, London SE1 1LB T 020-7357 6480 W www.cot.org.uk

FACULTY OF OCCUPATIONAL MEDICINE 6 St Andrew's Place, London NW1 4LB T 020-7317 5890 W www.facoccmed.ac.uk
President, Dr W J Gunnyeon

ORTHOPTICS

Orthoptists undertake the diagnosis and treatment of all types of squint and other anomalies of binocular vision, working in close collaboration with ophthalmologists. The training and maintenance of professional standards are the responsibility of the Health Professions Council (*see* Professions Supplementary to Medicine). The professional body is the British and Irish Orthoptic Society and training is at degree level.

BRITISH AND IRISH ORTHOPTIC SOCIETY Tavistock House North, Tavistock Square, London WC1H 9HX T 020-7387 7992 W www.orthoptics.org.uk
Hon. Chairman, June Carpenter

PHYSIOTHERAPY
Full-time three- or four-year degree courses are available at 30 higher education institutions in the UK. Information about courses leading to eligibility for Membership of the Chartered Society of Physiotherapy and to State Registration is available from the Chartered Society of Physiotherapy.

CHARTERED SOCIETY OF PHYSIOTHERAPY 14 Bedford Row, London WC1R 4ED **T** 020-7306 6666 **W** www.csp.org.uk

PROSTHETICS AND ORTHOTICS
Prosthetists provide artificial limbs, while orthotists provide devices to support or control a part of the body. It is neccessary to obtain an honours degree to become a prosthetist or orthotist. Training is centred at two UK universities, University of Salford and University of Strathclyde.

BRITISH ASSOCIATION OF PROSTHETISTS AND ORTHOTISTS Sir James Clark Building, Abbey Mill Business Centre, Paisley PA1 1TJ **T** 0141-561 7217 **W** www.bapo.com

RADIOGRAPHY AND RADIOTHERAPY
In order to practise both diagnostic and therapeutic radiography in the UK, it is necessary to have successfully completed a course of education and training recognised by the Privy Council. Such courses are offered by universities throughout the UK and lead to the award of a degree in radiography. Further information is available from the Society and College of Radiographers.

SOCIETY AND COLLEGE OF RADIOGRAPHERS 207 Providence Square, Mill Street, London SE1 2EW **T** 020-7740 7200 **W** www.sor.org

MERCHANT NAVY TRAINING

OFFICERS

WARSASH MARITIME CENTRE Southampton Institute, Newtown Road, Warsash, Southampton SO31 9ZL **T** 01489-576161 **W** www.solent.ac.uk/wmc/
Head, John Milligan

SEAFARERS

NATIONAL SEA TRAINING CENTRE North West Kent College, Dering Way, Gravesend, Kent DA12 2JJ **T** 01322-629600 **W** www.nwkcollege.ac.uk
Director of Faculty - NSTC, I. R. Goodwin

MUSIC

Education and training for a career in musical performance and composition are provided by the institutions and conservatoires listed below. Professional organisations granting qualifications after examination are the Associated Board of the Royal Schools of Music and the Trinity College Examination Board.

ASSOCIATED BOARD OF THE ROYAL SCHOOLS OF MUSIC 24 Portland Place, London W1B 1LU **T** 020-7636 5400 **W** www.abrsm.org

BIRMINGHAM CONSERVATOIRE University of Central England in Birmingham, Paradise Place, Birmingham B3 3HG **T** 0121-331 5901 **W** www.conservatoire.uce.ac.uk
Principal, Prof. George Caird

GUILDHALL SCHOOL OF MUSIC & DRAMA Silk Street, Barbican, London EC2Y 8DT **T** 020-7628 2571 **W** www.gsmd.ac.uk
Principal, Baroness McIntosh of Hudnall

LEEDS COLLEGE OF MUSIC 3 Quarry Hill, Leeds LS2 7PD **T** 0113-222 3400 **W** www.lcm.ac.uk

LONDON COLLEGE OF MUSIC AND MEDIA Thames Valley University, St Mary's Road, London W5 5RF **T** 020-8231 2304 **W** elgar.tvu.ac.uk

NATIONAL OPERA STUDIO 2 Chapel Yard, Wandsworth High Street, London SW18 4HZ **T** 0208-874 8811 **W** www.nationaloperastudio.org.uk

ROYAL ACADEMY OF MUSIC Marylebone Road, London NW1 5HT **T** 020-7873 7373 **W** www.ram.ac.uk
Principal, Prof. Curtis Price

ROYAL COLLEGE OF MUSIC Prince Consort Road, London SW7 2BS
Director, Ms J. Ritterman

ROYAL COLLEGE OF ORGANISTS 7 St Andrew Street, London EC4A 3LQ **T** 020-7936 3606 **W** www.rco.org.uk
The Registrar, Gordon St. J. Clarke

ROYAL NORTHERN COLLEGE OF MUSIC 124 Oxford Road, Manchester M13 9RD **T** 0161-907 5200 **W** www.rncm.ac.uk
Principal, Prof. E. Gregson

ROYAL SCOTTISH ACADEMY OF MUSIC AND DRAMA 100 Renfrew Street, Glasgow G2 3DB **T** 0141-332 4101 **W** www.rsamd.ac.uk
Principal, John Wallace, OBE

ROYAL WELSH COLLEGE OF MUSIC AND DRAMA Castle Grounds, Cathays Park, Cardiff CF10 3ER **T** 029-2034 2854 **W** www.rwcmd.ac.uk

TRINITY COLLEGE OF MUSIC King Charles Court, Old Royal Naval College, London SE10 9JF **T** 020-8305 4444 **W** www.tcm.ac.uk
Principal, G. Henderson

NURSING

All nurses and midwives must be registered with the Nursing and Midwifery Council (NMC). Courses leading to registration as a nurse or midwife are at least three years in length. Most courses are at diploma level, but some are at degree level. Students study in colleges of nursing or in institutions of higher education. Different courses lead to different types of registration, including Registered Nurse (RN), Registered Mental Nurse (RMN), Registered Learning Disability Nurse (RLDN), Registered Sick Children's Nurse (RSCN), Registered Midwife (RM) and Registered Health Visitor (RHV). The NMC is responsible for validating courses in nursing and midwifery.

The Royal College of Nursing is the largest professional union representing nurses and provides higher education through its Institute.

ROYAL COLLEGE OF NURSING 20 Cavendish Square, London W1G 0RN **T** 020-7409 3333 **W** www.rcn.org.uk
General Secretary, Dr Beverly Malone

UK CENTRAL COUNCIL FOR NURSING, MIDWIFERY AND HEALTH VISITING 23 Portland Place, London W1N 4JT **T** 020-7637 7181 **W** www.nmc-uk.org

OPHTHALMIC AND DISPENSING OPTICS

Professional bodies are:

ASSOCIATION OF BRITISH DISPENSING OPTICIANS Godmersham Park Mansion, Godmersham, Kent CT4 7DT **T** 01227-738829 **W** www.abdo.org.uk
General Secretary, Sir Anthony Garrett, CBE

COLLEGE OF OPTOMETRISTS 42 Craven Street, London WC2N 5NG **T** 020-7839 6000 **W** www.college-optometrists.org
Chief Executive, P. D. Leigh

OSTEOPATHY

Osteopathy is the first of the professions previously outside conventional medical services to achieve statutory recognition under a new body the General Osteopathic Council (GOC). Since May 2000 all practising osteopaths have to be registered with the GOC and the title 'osteopath' is protected by law. To gain entry to the register, all newly qualified osteopaths have to be in possession of a recognised qualification from a course of training accredited by the GOC. The GOC is also responsible for the regulation, promotion and development of the profession.

GENERAL OSTEOPATHIC COUNCIL Osteopathy House, 176 Tower Bridge Road, London SE1 3LU T 020-7357 6655 W www.osteopathy.org.uk
Chief Executive & Registrar, Miss M. J. Craggs

PHARMACY

The Royal Pharmaceutical Society of Great Britain is the regulatory and professional body for pharmicists in all aspects of practice. It has a statutory duty to maintain the registers of pharmacists and pharmacy premises. In order to register students must have a degree in pharmacy followed by one year pre-registration training at a premises recognised by the Society and must pass an entrance examination.

ROYAL PHARMACEUTICAL SOCIETY OF GREAT BRITAIN 1 Lambeth High Street, London SE1 7JN T 020-7735 9141 W www.rpsgb.org.uk
Secretary and Registrar, Ms A. M Lewis

PHOTOGRAPHY

The professional body is:

BRITISH INSTITUTE OF PROFESSIONAL PHOTOGRAPHY Fox Talbot House, Amwell End, Ware, Herts SG12 9HN T 01920-464011 W www.bipp.com
Chief Executive, Alex Mair

PRINTING

Details of training courses in printing can be obtained from the Institute of Printing and the British Printing Industries Federation. Examinations are also held by various independent further education examining boards.

BRITISH PRINTING INDUSTRIES FEDERATION Farringdon Point, 29–35 Farringdon Rd, London EC1M 3JF T 020-7915 8300 W www.britishprint.com
Chief Executive, Michael Johnson

INSTITUTE OF PRINTING The Mews, Hill House, Clanricarde Road, Tunbridge Wells, Kent TN1 1PJ T 01892-538118 W www.instituteofprinting.org

SCIENCE

Professional qualifications are awarded by:

INSTITUTE OF BIOLOGY 20–22 Queensberry Place, London SW7 2DZ T 020-7581 8333 W www.iob.org
Chief Executive, Prof. Alan Malcolm

ROYAL SOCIETY OF CHEMISTRY Burlington House, Piccadilly, London W1J 0BA T 020-7437 8656 W www.rsc.org
Secretary-General and Chief Executive, Dr D. Giachardi

SPEECH AND LANGUAGE THERAPY

The Royal College of Speech and Language Therapists accredits education and training courses leading to qualification.

ROYAL COLLEGE OF SPEECH AND LANGUAGE THERAPISTS 2 White Hart Yard, London SE1 1NX T 020-7378 1200 W www.rcslt.org
Chief Executive, Kamini Gadhok

SURVEYING

The qualifying professional bodies include:

ASSOCIATION OF BUILDING ENGINEERS Lutyens House, Billing Brook Road, Weston Favell, Northampton NN3 8NW T 01604-404121 W www.abe.org.uk
Chief Executive, David Gibson

INSTITUTE OF REVENUES, RATING AND VALUATION 41 Doughty Street, London WC1N 2LF T 020-7831 3505 W www.irrv.org.uk
Director, David Magor

ROYAL INSTITUTION OF CHARTERED SURVEYORS 12 Great George Street, Parliament Square, London SW1P 3AD T 020-7222 7000 W www.rics.org
Chief Executive, J. H. A. J. Armstrong

TEACHING

To work as a qualified teacher in a school in England and Wales, Qualified Teacher Status (QTS) must be acquired by completing a programme of Initial Teacher Training. Teaching is an all-graduate profession. Those without a first degree may take a Bachelor of Education (BEd) or a Bachelor of Arts/Science (BA/BSc) with QTS, full-time for three or four years, depending on the programme followed. These degrees combine subject and professional studies with teaching practice.

For those who already have a first degree, the most common route is through a one-year Postgraduate Certificate in Education (PGCE). This may be taken full-time or part-time, or as a distance learning programme. Postgraduates may also gain QTS through training in a school (School-Centred Initial Teacher Training). Graduates aged 24 or above can apply to train through the Graduate Teacher Programme, which offers a salary while employed in a school as a trainee teacher, usually for one year.

Further information on how to become a teacher in England and Wales is available on the Teacher Training Agency's website (*see* below) or in *The Initial Teacher Training Handbook* (£9.99 plus p&p) available from UCAS on 01242-544610. Further personal advice is available from the Teaching Information Line, 0845-600 0991. The Higher Education Funding Council (ELWA) funds initial teacher training and accredits providers of initial teacher training in Wales. They also produce Performance Information on Initial Teacher Training Providers in Wales. Details on courses in Scotland can be obtained from universities and the Graduate Teacher Training Registry (GTTR). Details of the courses in Northern Ireland can be obtained from the Department of Education for Northern Ireland.

TEACHER TRAINING AGENCY Portland House, Stag Place, London SW1E 5TT T 020-7925 3700 W www.useyourheadteach.gov.uk

TEXTILES

TEXTILE INSTITUTE 1st Floor, St James's Buildings, Oxford Street, Manchester M1 6FQ T 0161-237 1188 W www.texi.org
Membership Director, Steven Kirkwood

VETERINARY MEDICINE

The regulatory body for veterinary medicine is the Royal College of Veterinary Surgeons, which keeps the register of those entitled to practice veterinary medicine. Holders of recognised degrees from any of the six UK university veterinary schools or from certain EU or overseas universities are entitled to be registered, and holders of certain other degrees may take a statutory membership examination.

The British Veterinary Association is the professional body representing veterinary surgeons. The British Veterinary Nursing Association is the professional body representing veterinary nurses.

BRITISH VETERINARY NURSING ASSOCIATION Level 15, Terminus House, Terminus Street, Harlow, Essex CM20 1XA
T 01279-450567 **W** www.bvna.org.uk

ROYAL COLLEGE OF VETERINARY SURGEONS Belgravia House, 62–64 Horseferry Road, London SW1P 2AF
T 020-7222 2001 **W** www.rcvs.org.uk

INDEPENDENT SCHOOLS

The following pages list those independent schools in the UK and Europe whose head is a member of the Headmasters and Headmistresses' Conference (HMC), the Society of Headmasters and Headmistresses of Independent Schools (SHMIS) or the Girls' School Association (GSA). This list contains the name of the school, location, date founded, number of pupils, termly fees (day and board), the name of the head and details of which of the above associations the school is a member. This section has been compiled with the help of Klaus Boehm and Jenny Lees-Spalding, editors of the *Guide to Independent Schools 2005*.

School	*Date founded*	*No. of pupils*	*Termly fees Day*	*Board*	*Head (with association affliation)*
ENGLAND					
The Abbey School, Reading	1887	990	£2,800	–	Mrs Barbara E. Stanley (GSA)
Abbey Gate College, Cheshire	1977	410	£2,393	–	Edward W. Mitchell (SHMIS)
Abbots Bromley School for Girls, Staffs	1921	285	£3,450	£5,915	Mrs Mary Steel (GSA)
Abbotsholme School, Uttoxeter	1889	252	£4,095	£5,995	Stephen Fairclough (SHMIS)
Abingdon School, Abingdon	1256	796	£3,354	£6,776	Mark Turner (HMC)
Ackworth School, Pontefract	1779	540	£2,971	£5,093	Martin Dickinson (HMC, SHMIS)
Aldenham School, Hertfordshire	1597	463	£4,484	£6,499	Richard Harman (HMC)
Alderley Edge School for Girls, Cheshire	1876	610	£2,268	–	Mrs Kathy Mills (GSA)
The Alice Ottley School, Worcester	1883	610	£2,731	–	Mrs Morag Chapman (GSA)
Alleyn's School, London	1619	942	£3,350	–	Colin Diggory (HMC)
Ampleforth College, York	1802	548	£3,650	£6,840	Revd Gabriel Everitt (HMC)
Ardingly College, Haywards Heath	1858	731	£4,880	£6,515	John Franklin (HMC)
Arnold School, Blackpool	1896	1,133	£2,200	–	Barry M. Hughes (HMC)
The Arts Educational School, Herts	1945	276	£5,850	£7,270	Stefan Anderson (SHMIS)
Ashford School, Kent	1898	575	£3,480	£6,043	Mrs Paula Holloway (GSA)
Ashville College, Harrogate	1877	840	£2,789	£5,229	A. Fleck (HMC)
The Atherley School Southampton	1926	450	£2,638	–	Mrs Maureen Bradley (GSA)
Austin Friars St Monica's, Cumbria	1951	471	£2,666	–	Christopher Lumb (SHMIS)
Bablake School, Coventry	1344	1,000	£2,212	–	Dr S. Nuttall (HMC)
Badminton School, Bristol	1858	399	£3,885	£6,910	Mrs Jan Scarrow (GSA)
Bancroft's School, Woodford Green	1737	965	£3,140	–	Dr Peter Scott (HMC)
Barnard Castle School, Durham	1883	691	£2,838	£4,795	David Ewart (HMC)
Batley Grammar School, W. Yorkshire	1612	407	£2,344	–	Brian Battye (HMC)
Battle Abbey School, E. Sussex	1912	287	£3,459	£5,557	Roger Clark (SHMIS)
Bearwood College, Wokingham	1827	342	£4,070	£6,315	S. G. G. Aiano (SHMIS)
Bedales School, Hampshire	1893	412	£5,698	£7,454	Keith Budge (HMC, SHMIS)
Bedford School, Bedford	1552	1,100	£4,010	£6,305	Dr I. Philip Evans OBE (HMC)
Bedford High School, Bedford	1882	874	£2,955	£5,417	Mrs Gina Piotrowska (GSA)
Bedford Modern School, Bedford	1566	1,170	£2,786	–	Stephen Smith (HMC)
Bedgebury School, Cranbrook, Kent	1860	350	£3,880	£6,245	Mrs Hilary Moriarty (GSA)
Bedstone College, Shropshire	1948	275	£3,090	£5,740	Michael S. Symonds (SHMIS)
Beechwood School, Tunbridge Wells	1915	350	£3,475	£5,625	Nicholas Beesley (GSA)
The Belvedere School GDST, Liverpool	1880	550	£2,310	–	Mrs Gillian Richards (GSA)
Benenden School, Kent	1923	470	–	£7,450	Mrs Claire Oulton (GSA)
Berkhamsted Collegiate School, Herts	1541	1,460	£3,939	£6,266	Dr P. Chadwick (HMC, GSA)
Bethany School, Kent	1866	340	£3,598	£5,597	Nicholas Dorey (SHMIS)
Birkdale School, Sheffield	1915	800	£2,577	–	Robert J. Court (HMC)
Birkenhead School, Wirral	1860	737	£2,339	–	John Clark (HMC)
Birkenhead High School GDST, Wirral	1901	830	£2,310	–	Mrs Carole Evans (GSA)
Bishop's Stortford College, Herts	1868	402	£3,804	£5,277	John G. Trotman (HMC)
Blackheath High School GDST, London	1880	590	£2,883	–	Mrs Elizabeth Laws (GSA)
Bloxham School, Oxfordshire	1860	410	£5,425	£6,995	Mark Allbrook (HMC)
Blundell's School, Devon	1604	553	£4,140	£6,485	Jonathan Leigh (HMC)
Bolton School Boys' Division, Lancs	1524	1,095	£2,498	–	Mervyn Brooker (HMC)
Bolton School Girls' Division, Lancs	1877	1,315	£2,498	–	Miss E. J. Panton (GSA)
Bootham School, York	1823	420	£3,660	£5,675	Jonathan Taylor (HMC)
Box Hill School, Dorking	1959	350	£3,520	£5,800	Mark Eagers (SHMIS)
Bradfield College, Reading	1850	600	£5,640	£7,050	Peter Roberts (HMC)
Bradford Girls' Grammar School, W. Yorks	1875	809	£2,643	–	Mrs L. J. Warrington (GSA)
Bradford Grammar School, W. Yorks	1548	1,077	£2,755	–	Stephen Davidson (HMC)

School	*Date founded*	*No. of pupils*	*Termly fees Day*	*Board*	*Head (with association affliation)*
Brentwood School, Essex	1557	1,117	£3,482	£6,032	Ian Davies (HMC)
Brighton and Hove High School GDST, Brighton	1876	752	£2,310	–	Mrs Ann Greatorex (GSA)
Brighton College, E. Sussex	1845	700	£4,401	£6,822	Dr Anthony Seldon (HMC)
Brigidine School, Windsor	1948	274	£3,045	–	Mrs Janet Dunn (GSA)
Bristol Cathedral School, Bristol	1542	440	£2,496	–	K. J. Riley (HMC)
Bristol Grammar School, Bristol	1532	1,249	£2,505	–	David Mascord (HMC)
Bromley High School GDST, Kent	1883	912	£2,883	–	Mrs Lorna Duggleby (GSA)
Bromsgrove School, Worcestershire	1548	1,102	£3,415	£6,030	T. M. Taylor (HMC)
Bruton School for Girls, Somerset	1900	450	£2,985	£5,090	Mrs Barbara Bates (GSA)
Bryanston School, Dorset	1928	651	£5,815	£7,269	Tom Wheare (HMC)
Burgess Hill School for Girls, W. Sussex	1906	720	£3,170	£5,500	Mrs Susan Gorham (GSA)
Bury Grammar School, Lancashire	1726	826	£2,120	–	Keith Richards (HMC)
Bury Grammar School (Girls), Lancashire	1884	1,016	£2,120	–	Mrs R. S. Georghiou (GSA)
Canford School, Wimbourne	1923	600	£5,315	£7,085	John D. Lever (HMC)
Casterton School, Cumbria	1823	340	£3,308	£5,529	A. F. Thomas (GSA)
Caterham School, Surrey	1811	987	£3,469	£6,471	Rob Davey (HMC)
Central Newcastle High School GDST, Newcastle upon Tyne	1895	997	£2,310	–	Mrs Lindsey Jane Griffin (GSA)
Channing School, London	1885	536	£3,250	–	Mrs Elizabeth Radice (GSA)
Charterhouse, Godalming	1611	723	£6,112	£7,394	Revd John Witheridge (HMC)
Cheadle Hulme School, Cheshire	1855	1,394	£2,377	–	Paul Dixon (HMC)
Cheltenham College, Glos	1841	582	£5,360	£7,150	P. A. Chamberlain (HMC)
The Cheltenham Ladies' College, Glos	1853	867	£4,637	£6,906	Mrs Vicky Tuck (GSA)
Chetham's School of Music, Manchester	1653	292	£5,667	£7,321	Mrs Claire Moreland (HMC)
Chetwynde School, Barrow-in-Furness	1938	536	£1,533	–	Mrs I. Nixon (SHMIS)
Chigwell School, Essex	1629	726	£3,355	£5,099	David Gibbs (HMC)
Christ's Hospital, W. Sussex	1552	832	–	£5,966	Dr Peter Southern (HMC)
Churcher's College, Hampshire	1722	802	£2,795	–	J. M. L. Williams (HMC, SHMIS)
City of London School, London	1442	895	£3,507	–	David Levin (HMC)
City of London Freemen's School, Surrey	1854	840	£3,651	£5,805	D. C. Haywood (HMC)
City of London School for Girls, London	1894	668	£3,363	–	Dr Yvonne Burne (GSA)
Claremont Fan Court School, Surrey	1922	600	£3,285	–	Mrs Patricia Farrar (SHMIS)
Clayesmore School, Dorset	1896	340	£4,660	£6,459	Martin Cooke (SHMIS)
Clifton College, Bristol	1862	660	£4,500	£6,600	Stephen Spurr (HMC)
Clifton High School, Bristol	1877	740	£2,605	–	Mrs M. C. Culligan (GSA)
Cobham Hall School, Kent	1962	220	£4,450	£6,450	Helen Davy (GSA)
Cokethorpe School, Oxfordshire	1957	570	£3,750	–	Damian J. Ettinger (SHMIS)
Colfe's School, London	1652	1,078	£3,174	–	Andrew Chicken (HMC)
Colston's Collegiate School, Bristol	1710	929	£2,370	£5,015	D. G. Crawford (HMC, SHMIS)
Colston's Girls' School, Bristol	1891	443	£2,278	–	Mrs Lesley Jones (GSA)
Combe Bank School, Sevenoaks	1924	420	£3,720	–	Mrs Rosemary Martin (GSA)
Concord College, Shrewsbury	1949	326	£2,300	£6,068	Anthony Morris (SHMIS)
Cranleigh School, Surrey	1865	604	£5,700	£7,110	Guy Waller (HMC)
Croham Hurst School, Croydon	1899	558	£2,920	–	Miss Sue Budgen (GSA)
Croydon High School for Girls GDST, Croydon	1874	828	£2,883	–	Miss Lorna M. Ogilvie (GSA)
Culford School, Bury St Edmunds	1881	680	£4,095	£6,283	Julian Johnson-Munday (HMC)
The Dame Alice Harpur School, Bedford	1882	952	£2,767	–	Mrs Jill Berry (GSA)
Dame Allan's Boys' School, Newcastle upon Tyne	1705	470	£2,276	–	John Hind (HMC)
Dame Allan's Girls' School, Newcastle upon Tyne	1705	423	£2,276	–	John Hind (GSA)
Dauntsey's School, Wiltshire	1542	688	£3,790	£6,345	S. B. Roberts (HMC)
Dean Close School, Cheltenham	1886	466	£4,995	£7,095	Revd T. M. Hastie-Smith (HMC)
Denstone College, Uttoxeter	1868	456	£3,100	£4,863	David Derbyshire (HMC)
Derby High School, Derby	1892	600	£2,395	–	Colin Callaghan (GSA)
Dover College, Kent	1871	354	£2,995	£5,995	Howard Blackett (SHMIS)
Downe House, Newbury	1907	537	£5,210	£7,200	Mrs Emma McKendrick (GSA)
Downside School, Bath	1606	320	£3,230	£6,190	D. L. Maidlow Davis (HMC)
Duke of York Royal Military School, Dover	1803	500	–	£650	John Cummings (SHMIS)
Dulwich College, London	1619	1,450	£3,580	£7,210	Graham G. Able (HMC)
Dunottar School, Reigate	1926	425	£3,050	–	Mrs Jeanne Hobson (GSA)
Durham School, Durham	1414	360	£3,832	£5,832	N. G. Kern (HMC)

School	*Date founded*	*No. of pupils*	*Termly fees Day*	*Board*	*Head (with association affliation)*
Durham High School for Girls, Durham	1884	578	£2,435	–	Mrs Ann J. Templeman (GSA)
Eastbourne College, E. Sussex	1867	580	£4,390	£6,695	Charles M. P. Bush (HMC)
Edgbaston High School for Girls, Birmingham	1876	930	£2,370	–	Miss E. Mullinger (GSA)
Ellesmere College, Shropshire	1884	482	£3,866	£4,995	B. J. Wignall (HMC)
Elmhurst in Association with Birmingham Royal Ballet, Birmingham	1910	186	£4,200	£5,400	John McNamara (SHMIS)
Eltham College, London	1842	785	£3,302	–	Paul Henderson (HMC)
Emanuel School, London	1594	692	£3,387	–	Mark Hanley-Browne (HMC)
Embley Park School, Romsey	1946	450	£3,280	£5,370	David Chapman (SHMIS)
Epsom College, Surrey	1855	680	£5,015	£7,108	Stephen Borthwick (HMC)
Eton College, Windsor	1440	1,287	–	£7,460	Anthony R. M. Little (HMC)
Ewell Castle School, Surrey	1926	510	£2,780	–	A. J. Tibble (SHMIS)
Exeter School, Devon	1633	850	£2,465	–	Bob Griffin (HMC)
Farlington School, W. Sussex	1896	478	£3,325	£5,105	Mrs Trina Mawer (GSA)
Farnborough Hill, Hampshire	1889	500	£2,640	–	Miss Jacqueline Thomas (GSA)
Farringtons and Stratford House, Kent	1911	502	£2,950	£5,420	Mrs Catherine James (GSA)
Felsted School, Essex	1564	450	£4,918	£6,615	Stephen Roberts (HMC)
Forest School, London	1834	1,175	£3,377	£5,294	A. G. Boggis (HMC)
Framlingham College, Suffolk	1864	710	£3,753	£5,839	Mrs Gwen Randall (HMC)
Francis Holland School, London NW1	1878	395	£3,450	–	Mrs Vivienne Durham (GSA)
Francis Holland School, London SW1	1881	480	£3,575	–	Miss S. Pattenden (GSA)
Frensham Heights School, Farnham	1925	480	£4,130	£6,460	Andrew Fisher (HMC)
Friends' School, Essex	1702	376	£3,428	£5,715	Andy Waters (SHMIS)
Fulneck School, W. Yorkshire	1753	426	£2,640	£4,850	T. Kernohan (SHMIS)
Gateways School, Leeds	1941	560	£2,463	–	Mrs Denise Davidson (GSA)
Giggleswick School, N. Yorkshire	1512	498	£4,400	£6,557	Geoffrey Boult (HMC)
The Godolphin School, Salisbury	1726	410	£3,995	£6,300	Miss Jill Horsburgh (GSA)
Godolphin and Latymer School, London	1905	700	£3,490	–	Miss Margaret Rudland (GSA)
The Grange School, Cheshire	1933	1,116	£2,100	–	Jennifer Stephen (HMC)
Greenacre School for Girls, Surrey	1933	430	£2,720	–	Mrs Pat Wood (GSA)
Grenville College, Devon	1954	410	£2,690	£5,432	Dr S. Wormleighton (SHMIS)
Gresham's School, Norfolk	1555	508	£5,045	£6,505	A. R. Clark (HMC)
Guildford High School, Guildford	1888	920	£3,117	–	Mrs Fiona Boulton (GSA)
The Haberdashers' Aske's Boys' School, Hertfordshire	1690	1,300	£3,420	–	Peter Hamilton (HMC)
The Haberdashers' Aske's School for Girls, Hertfordshire	1690	1,135	£2,800	–	Mrs Penelope Penney (GSA)
Haileybury, Hertfordshire	1862	720	£5,245	£6,985	Stuart Westley (HMC)
Halliford School, London	1921	350	£2,750	–	Philip V. Cottam (SHMIS)
Hampton School, Middlesex	1556	1,065	£3,330	–	Barry Martin (HMC)
Harrogate Ladies' College, N. Yorkshire	1893	360	£3,330	£5,600	Dr Margaret J. Hustler (GSA)
Harrow School, Middlesex	1572	785	–	£7,345	Barnaby Lenon (HMC)
Headington School, Oxford	1915	962	£3,060	£5,835	Mrs Anne Coutts (GSA)
Heathfield School, Ascot	1899	220	–	£7,270	Mrs Frances King (GSA)
Heathfield School GDST, Middlesex	1900	632	£2,883	–	Miss Christine Juett (GSA)
Hereford Cathedral School, Hereford	1384	900	£2,650	–	Dr Howard Tomlinson (HMC)
Hethersett Old Hall School, Norwich	1928	274	£2,785	£5,500	Mrs Janet Mark (GSA)
Highclare School, Birmingham	1934	866	£2,395	–	Mrs Margaret Viles (GSA)
Highgate School, London	1565	1,100	£4,035	–	Richard Kennedy (HMC)
Hipperholme Grammar School, Halifax,	1648	300	£2,170	–	C. C. Robinson (SHMIS)
Holy Trinity College, Bromley	1886	520	£3,013	–	Mrs Pauline Lightfoot (GSA)
Holy Trinity School, Kidderminster	1903	406	£2,420	–	Mrs Y. Wilkinson (GSA)
Hull High School, Hull	1890	425	£2,240	–	Mrs A. V. Wood (GSA)
Hulme Grammar School for Boys, Oldham,	1611	720	£2,099	–	Ken Jones (HMC)
Hulme Grammar School for Girls, Oldham	1895	598	£2,099	–	Miss M. S. Smolenski (GSA)
Hurstpierpoint College, W. Sussex	1849	385	£4,910	£6,340	Tim Manly (HMC)
Hymers College, Hull	1893	968	£2,151	–	John Morris (HMC)
Immanuel College, Hertfordshire	1990	545	£3,317	–	Philip Skelker (SHMIS)
Ipswich School, Suffolk	1390	703	£2,878	£5,007	Ian Galbraith (HMC)
Ipswich High School GDST, Suffolk	1878	700	£2,310	–	Miss Valerie MacCuish (GSA)
James Allen's Girls' School, London	1741	770	£3,275	–	Mrs Marion Gibbs (GSA)
The John Lyon School, Middlesex	1876	550	£3,395	–	Kevin Riley (HMC)
Kelly College, Devon	1877	360	£4,050	£6,600	Mark Steed (HMC)
Kent College, Canterbury	1885	680	£3,615	£6,175	G. G. Carminati (HMC)

School	*Date founded*	*No. of pupils*	*Termly fees Day*	*Board*	*Head (with association affliation)*
Kent College, Tunbridge Wells	1886	575	£3,880	£6,265	Mrs Anne E. Upton (GSA)
Kimbolton School, Huntingdon	1600	1,111	£3,040	£5,140	Jonathan Belbin (HMC)
King Edward VII and Queen Mary School, Lytham St Anne's	1908	800	£2,115	–	Robert Karling (HMC)
King Edward's School, Bath	1552	990	£2,832	–	Miss C. Thompson (HMC)
King Edward's School, Birmingham	1552	860	£2,460	–	Roger Dancey (HMC)
King Edward VI High School for Girls, Birmingham	1883	550	£2,420	–	Miss Sarah Evans (GSA, SHMIS)
King Edward VI School, Southampton	1553	950	£2,807	–	Julian Thould (HMC)
King Edward's School, Surrey	1553	474	£4,150	£5,850	Kerr Fulton-Peebles (HMC)
King Henry VIII School, Coventry	1545	1,122	£2,212	–	G. Fisher (HMC, GSA)
King's School, Somerset	1519	343	£4,630	£6,230	N. M. Lashbrook (HMC)
The King's School, Canterbury	597	791	£5,420	£7,320	Keith Wilkinson (HMC)
The King's School, Chester	1541	746	£2,475	–	Timothy J. Turvey (HMC)
The King's School, Cambridgshire	970	920	£4,295	£6,220	Mrs Susan Freestone (HMC)
The King's School, Gloucester	1541	515	£3,865	–	Peter Lacey (HMC)
The King's School in Macclesfield, Cheshire	1502	1,400	£2,332	–	S. Coyne (HMC)
King's School, Rochester	1541	720	£4,125	£6,850	Dr I. R. Walker (HMC)
King's College, Taunton	1522	420	£4,210	£6,320	Christopher Ramsey (HMC)
The King's School, Tynemouth	1860	850	£2,326	–	Philip Cantwell (HMC)
King's High School for Girls, Warwick	1879	550	£2,534	–	Elizabeth Surber (GSA)
The King's School, Worcester	1541	1,300	£2,906	–	T. H. Keyes (HMC)
King's College School, London	1829	762	£4,105	–	Tony Evans (HMC)
Kingham Hill School, Oxfordshire	1886	250	£4,131	£6,249	Martin J Morris (SHMIS)
The Kingsley School, Leamington Spa	1884	620	£2,530	–	Mrs Christine A. Mannion Watson (GSA)
Kingston Grammar School, Kingston upon Thames	1561	620	£3,376	–	C. D. Baxter (HMC)
Kingswood School, Bath	1748	636	£2,884	£6,109	Gary M. Best (HMC)
Kirkham Grammar School, Preston	1549	975	£2,065	£3,800	Douglas Walker (HMC) (SHMIS)
La Sagesse School, Newcastle upon Tyne	1912	260	£2,450	–	Miss Linda Clark (GSA)
The Lady Eleanor Holles School, Middlesex	1711	880	£3,224	–	Mrs Gillian Lowe (GSA)
Lancing College, W. Sussex	1848	488	£4,785	£6,880	P. M. Tinniswood (HMC)
Langley School, Norwich	1910	450	£2,725	£5,425	J. G. Malcolm (SHMIS)
Latymer Upper School, London	1624	970	£3,785	–	Peter Winter (HMC)
Lavant House Rosemead, Chichester	1919	150	£3,175	£5,030	Mrs M. Scott (GSA)
Leeds Grammar School, Leeds	1552	1,380	£2,685	–	Dr Mark Bailey (HMC)
Leeds Girls' High School, Leeds	1876	995	£2,602	–	Ms Sue Fishburn (GSA)
Leicester Grammar School, Leicester	1981	700	£2,510	–	Christopher King (HMC)
Leicester High School for Girls, Leicester	1906	435	£2,410	–	Mrs J. Burns (GSA)
Leighton Park School, Reading	1890	427	£4,484	£6,619	John Dunston (HMC, SHMIS)
The Leys School, Cambridge	1875	540	£4,260	£6,655	Mark Slater (HMC, GSA)
Licensed Victuallers' School, Ascot	1803	839	£3,390	£5,480	Ian Mullins (SHMIS)
Lincoln Minster School, Lincoln	1996	687	£2,675	£5,062	Clive Rickart (SHMIS)
Liverpool College, Liverpool	1840	920	£2,440	–	Brian Christian (HMC)
Lodge School, Surrey	1916	258	£2,750	–	Miss Pamela A. Maynard (GSA)
Longridge Towers School, Berwick upon Tweed	1983	322	£2,310	£4,750	Dr Michael Barron (SHMIS)
Lord Wandsworth College, Hants	1920	510	£4,545	£6,100	Ian Power (HMC, SHMIS)
Loughborough Grammar School, Loughborough	1495	1,040	£2,589	£4,626	Paul Fisher (HMC)
Loughborough High School, Loughborough	1849	605	£2,355	–	Miss Bridget O'Connor (GSA)
Luckley-Oakfield School, Wokingham	1918	350	£3,186	£5,438	Miss V. Davis (GSA)
Magdalen College School, Oxford	1480	630	£3,078	–	A. D. Halls (HMC)
Malvern College, Worcs	1865	539	£4,740	£7,330	Hugh Carson (HMC)
Malvern Girls' College, Worcs	1893	360	£4,800	£7,845	Mrs P. M. C. Leggate (GSA)
The Manchester Grammar School, Manchester	1515	1,440	£2,276	–	Dr Christopher Ray (HMC)
Manchester High School for Girls, Manchester	1874	920	£2,275	–	Mrs Christine Lee-Jones (GSA)
The Marist Senior School, Ascot	1870	308	£2,660	–	Karl McCloskey (GSA)
Marlborough College, Wilts	1843	860	£5,475	£7,300	Nicholas Sampson (HMC)

School	*Date founded*	*No. of pupils*	*Termly fees Day*	*Board*	*Head (with association affliation)*
Marymount International School, Kingston upon Thames	1955	230	£4,317	£7,300	Cliff Canning (GSA)
The Maynard School, Exeter	1658	478	£2,544	–	Dr Daphne West (GSA)
Merchant Taylors' School, Liverpool	1620	850	£2,184	–	Simon Dawkins (HMC)
Merchant Taylors' School, Middlesex	1561	800	£3,755	–	Stephen Wright (HMC)
Merchant Taylors' School for Girls, Liverpool	1888	920	£2,052	–	Miss J. Brandreth (GSA)
Mill Hill School, London	1807	610	£4,195	£6,580	William R. Winfield (HMC)
Millfield School, Somerset	1935	1,253	£4,725	£7,145	Peter M. Johnson (HMC)
Milton Abbey School, Dorset	1954	225	£5,295	£7,060	W. J. Hughes-D'Aeth (SHMIS)
Moira House School, Eastbourne	1875	420	£3,455	£5,885	Mrs Ann Harris (GSA, SHMIS)
Monkton Combe School, Bath	1868	350	£4,635	£6,700	Michael Cuthbertson (HMC)
More House School, London	1953	220	£3,260	–	Mrs Lesley Falconer (GSA)
Moreton Hall, Oswestry	1913	310	£4,860	£6,650	J. Forster (GSA)
Mount School, London	1925	360	£2,493	–	Mrs J. Kirsten Jackson (GSA)
The Mount School, York	1785	463	£3,565	£5,535	Mrs Diana Gant (GSA)
Mount St Mary's College, Derbyshire	1842	321	£2,770	£4,995	Philip MacDonald (HMC)
New Hall School, Chelmsford	1642	700	£3,970	£5,970	Mrs K. A. Jeffrey (GSA)
Newcastle upon Tyne Church High School, Newcastle upon Tyne	1885	560	£2,400	–	Mrs Lesley Smith (GSA)
Newcastle-under-Lyme School, Staffordshire	1602	1,080	£2,136	–	Robert Dillow (HMC)
North Cestrian Grammar School, Altrincham	1951	320	£1,945	–	David G. Vanstone (SHMIS)
North London Collegiate School, Middlesex	1850	1009	£3,180	–	Mrs Bernice McCabe (GSA)
Northampton High School, Northampton	1878	844	£2,440	–	Mrs L. A. Mayne (GSA)
Northamptonshire Grammar School, Northampton	1989	360	£2,838	–	Simon Larter (SHMIS)
Northwood College, Middlesex	1878	770	£3,019	–	Mrs Ruth Mercer (GSA)
Norwich School, Norwich	1547	785	£2,667	–	J. B. Hawkins (HMC)
Norwich High School for Girls GDST, Norwich	1875	895	£2,310	–	Mrs Valerie Bidwell (GSA)
Notre Dame Senior School, Surrey	1937	375	£2,800	–	Mrs Bridget Williams (GSA)
Notting Hill and Ealing High School GDST, London	1873	830	£2,883	–	Mrs Susan Whitfield (GSA)
Nottingham High School for Girls GDST, Nottingham	1875	1,117	£2,310	–	Mrs Angela Rees (GSA)
Nottingham High School, Nottingham	1513	820	£2,690	–	C. Parker, CBE (HMC)
Oakham School, Rutland	1584	1,037	£4,040	£6,760	Dr Joseph A. F. Spence (HMC)
Ockbrook School, Derbyshire	1799	500	£2,246	£4,152	Denise P. Bolland (GSA)
Old Palace School of John Whitgift, Croydon	1889	850	£2,698	–	Mrs Joy Hancock (GSA)
The Oratory School, Woodcote, Reading	1859	400	£4,930	£6,835	Clive Dytor MC (HMC)
Oswestry School, Shropshire	1407	436	£3,310	£5,570	Paul Stockdale (SHMIS)
Oundle School, Peterborough	1556	1,067	£3,632	£6,632	Dr Ralph Townsend (HMC)
Our Lady of Sion School, Sussex	1862	520	£2,585	–	M. Scullion (SHMIS)
Our Lady's Convent Senior School, Oxon	1860	390	£2,380	–	Mrs Glynne Butt (GSA)
Oxford High School GDST, Oxford	1875	916	£2,310	–	Miss Felicity Lusk (GSA)
Pangbourne College, Berkshire	1917	362	£4,590	£6,545	Dr Kenneth Greig (HMC)
Parsons Mead School, Surrey	1897	302	£3,175	–	Mrs Patricia Taylor (GSA)
The Perse School, Cambridge	1615	650	£3,277	–	Nigel Richardson (HMC)
The Perse School for Girls, Cambridge	1881	680	£3,055	–	Miss Tricia Kelleher (GSA)
Peterborough High School, Peterborough	1895	370	£2,794	£5,090	Mrs Sarah Dixon (GSA)
Pipers Corner School, High Wycombe	1930	450	£3,215	£5,315	Mrs Valerie Stattersfield (GSA)
Plymouth College, Devon	1877	640	£2,711	£5,191	Alan Morsley (HMC, GSA)
Pocklington School, York	1514	622	£2,911	£5,073	Nicholas Clements (HMC)
Polam Hall School, Durham	1854	480	£2,690	£5,235	Miss Marie Green (GSA)
Portland Place School, London	1996	300	£3,550	–	Richard Walker (SHMIS)
The Portsmouth Grammar School, Hants	1732	940	£2,761	–	Dr Timothy Hands (HMC)
Portsmouth High School GDST, Hants	1882	629	£2,310	–	Miss P. Hulse (GSA)
The Princess Helena College, Herts	1820	190	£4,045	£5,895	Anne-Marie Hodgkiss (GSA)
Princethorpe College, Rugby	1958	655	£2,295	–	John M Shinkwin (SHMIS)
Prior Park College, Bath	1830	545	£3,310	£5,968	Giles Mercer (HMC)
Prior's Field School, Surrey	1902	310	£3,595	£5,695	Mrs Jenny Dwyer (GSA)
Priory School, Birmingham	1933	320	£2,415	–	Mrs Elaine Brook (GSA)

School	*Date founded*	*No. of pupils*	*Termly fees Day*	*Board*	*Head (with association affliation)*
The Purcell School, Hertfordshire	1962	177	£6,434	£8,229	John Tolputt (SHMIS)
Putney High School GDST, London	1893	800	£2,883	–	Dr Denise V. Lodge (GSA)
Queen Anne's School, Reading	1894	332	£4,445	£6,580	Mrs Deborah Forbes (GSA)
Queen Elizabeth's Grammar School, Blackburn	1509	825	£2,445	–	Dr David Hempsall (HMC)
Queen Elizabeth Grammar School, Wakefield	1591	1,000	£2,497	–	Michael Gibbons (HMC)
Queen Elizabeth's Hospital, Bristol	1590	570	£2,444	£4,504	Stephen Holliday (HMC)
Queen Margaret's School, York	1901	369	£3,695	£5,831	Dr G. A. H. Chapman (GSA)
The Queen's School, Chester	1878	611	£2,495	–	Mrs C. M. Buckley (GSA)
Queen's College London, London	1848	380	£3,710	–	Miss M. M. Connell (GSA)
Queen's College, Somerset	1843	721	£3,597	£5,421	Christopher J. Alcock (HMC)
Queen's Gate School, London	1891	400	£3,250	–	Mrs Angela Holyoak (GSA)
Queenswood, Hertfordshire	1894	401	£5,120	£6,820	Clarissa Farr (GSA)
Radley College, Oxfordshire	1847	628	–	£7,120	Angus McPhail (HMC)
Ratcliffe College, Leicester	1847	616	£3,371	£5,077	Peter Farrar (HMC)
Read School, N. Yorkshire	1667	280	£2,125	£4,600	Richard Hadfield (SHMIS)
Reading Blue Coat School, Berkshire	1646	650	£3,085	–	S. J. W. McArthur (HMC, SHMIS)
The Red Maids' School, Bristol	1634	400	£2,340	–	Mrs Isobel Tobias (GSA)
Redland High School for Girls, Bristol	1882	672	£2,470	–	Dr Ruth A. Weeks (GSA)
Reed's School, Surrey	1813	460	£4,604	£6,090	D. W. Jarrett (HMC, SHMIS)
Reigate Grammar School, Surrey	1675	1,050	£3,085	–	David Thomas (HMC)
Rendcomb College, Cirencester	1920	350	£4,585	£5,787	Gerry Holden (HMC, SHMIS)
Repton School, Derby	1557	555	£4,955	£6,675	R. A. Holroyd (HMC)
Rishworth School, W. Yorkshire	1724	560	£2,645	£5,190	Richard Baker (SHMIS)
RNIB New College Worcester, Worcester	–	115	£8,450	£12,175	Nick Ratcliffe (HMC)
Roedean School, Brighton	1885	396	£4,130	£7,400	Mrs Carolyn Shaw (GSA)
Rossall School, Lancashire	1844	415	£2,782	£7,003	Tim Wilbur (HMC)
The Royal Ballet School, London	1929	205	£5,545	£7,639	Gailene Stock (SHMIS)
The Royal Grammar School, Guildford	1509	863	£3,305	–	Timothy Young (HMC)
Royal Grammar School, Newcastle upon Tyne	1510	1,135	£2,283	–	James F. X. Miller (HMC)
Royal Grammar School, Worcester	1291	1,069	£2,520	–	W. A. Jones (HMC)
The Royal High School GDST, Bath	1864	900	£2,310	£4,531	James Graham-Brown (GSA)
Royal Hospital School, Ipswich	1712	680	£3,380	£5,317	Howard Blackett (HMC, SHMIS)
The Royal Masonic School, Herts	1788	751	£2,947	£4,843	Mrs Diana Rose (GSA)
Royal Russell School, Croydon	1853	810	£3,220	£6,410	Dr John Jennings (HMC, SHMIS)
The Royal School Haslemere, Surrey	1840	356	£3,663	£5,816	Mrs L. Taylor-Gooby (GSA)
Royal Wolverhampton School, Wolverhampton	1850	310	£2,885	£5,940	T. Waters (SHMIS)
Rugby School, Warwickshire	1567	793	£4,600	£7,250	Patrick Derham (HMC)
Ryde School, Isle of Wight	1921	720	£2,470	£5,045	Dr Nick J. England (HMC, SHMIS)
Rye St Antony School, Oxford	1930	400	£2,885	£4,900	Miss Alison Jones (GSA)
St Albans School, Abbey Gateway, St Albans	1100	730	£3,331	–	Andrew Grant (HMC)
St Albans High School for Girls, St Albans	1889	950	£2,790	–	Mrs Carol Y. Daly (GSA)
St Antony's Leweston School, Dorset	1891	252	£3,925	£5,925	Henry J. MacDonald (GSA)
St Bede's Senior School, E. Sussex	1978	707	£3,860	£6,280	Stephen Cole (SHMIS)
St Bede's College, Manchester	1879	1,448	£2,028	–	John Byrne (HMC)
St Bees School, Cumbria	1583	300	£3,822	£6,377	Philip J. Capes (HMC)
St Benedict's School, London	1902	605	£3,040	–	Christopher J. Cleugh (HMC)
St Catherine's School, Guildford	1885	740	£3,465	£5,700	Mrs A. Phillips (GSA)
St Christopher School, Hertfordshire	1915	611	£3,585	£6,300	Donald Wilkinson (SHMIS)
St Columba's College, St Albans	1955	865	£2,570	–	D. S. Darlington (HMC)
St David's School, Middlesex	1716	437	£2,891	£5,341	Ms P. A. Bristow (GSA)
St Dominic's Priory School, Staffordshire	1934	300	£2,151	–	Andrew Egan (GSA)
St Dunstan's College, London	1446	925	£3,420	–	Fiona Cordeaux (HMC)
St Edmund's School, Canterbury	1749	561	£4,311	£6,677	A. Nicholas Ridley (HMC)
St Edmund's College, Hertfordshire	1568	680	£3,595	£5,825	Chris Long (HMC)
St Edward's School, Cheltenham	1987	450	£3,025	–	Dr Andrew J. Nash (SHMIS)
St Edward's School, Oxford	1863	640	£5,694	£7,208	Andrew Trotman (HMC)

School	*Date founded*	*No. of pupils*	*Termly fees Day*	*Board*	*Head (with association affliation)*
St Elphin's School, Derbyshire	1844	210	£2,995	£4,985	Dr Deborah Mouat (GSA)
St Felix and St George's School, Suffolk	1897	340	£3,500	£5,500	David A. T. Ward (SHMIS)
St Francis' College, Hertfordshire	1933	500	£2,890	£5,685	Miss Mairin Hegarty (GSA)
St Gabriel's School, Newbury	1929	530	£2,950	–	Alun S. Jones (GSA)
St George's School, Ascot	1900	313	£4,350	£6,750	Mrs Joanna Grant-Peterkin (GSA)
St George's School, Birmingham	1999	380	£2,450	–	Miss Hilary Phillips (SHMIS)
St George's College, Surrey	1869	850	£3,540	–	Joseph A. Peake (HMC, SHMIS)
The School of St Helen and St Katharine, Abingdon	1903	616	£2,664	–	Mrs Cynthia Hall (GSA)
St Helen's School, Middlesex	1899	1,048	£3,040	£5,634	Mrs Mary Morris (GSA)
St James School, Grimsby	1880	235	£2,656	£4,431	Susan M. Isaac (SHMIS)
St James Independent School for Boys (Senior), Surrey	1975	295	£2,820	£3,920	David Boddy (SHMIS)
St James Independent School for Girls (Senior), London	1975	239	£2,820		Mrs L. Hyde (GSA)
St James's School, Worcestershire	1896	145	£3,998	£6,660	Rosalind Hayes (GSA)
St John's School, Surrey	1851	445	£4,650	£6,600	N. Haddock, MBE (HMC)
St John's College, Hampshire	1908	633	£2,260	£5,300	N. W. Thorne (SHMIS)
St Joseph's College, Ipswich	1937	588	£2,850	£4,895	Mrs S. Grant (SHMIS)
St Joseph's Convent School, Reading	1910	408	£2,700	–	Mrs M. Sheridan (GSA)
St Lawrence College, Kent	1879	482	£4,190	£6,780	Revd Mark Aitken (HMC)
St Leonards-Mayfield School, E. Sussex	1863	380	£4,020	£6,170	Mrs Julia Dalton (GSA)
St Margaret's School for Girls, Exeter	1902	386	£2,414	–	Miss R. Edbrooke (GSA)
St Margaret's School, Hertfordshire	1749	450	£3,395	£5,995	Miss Marlene de Villiers (GSA)
St Martin's, Malvern Hall, W. Midlands	1941	580	£2,510	–	Mrs Jennifer R. Taylor (GSA)
St Mary's School, Wiltshire	1873	290	£4,800	£7,100	Mrs Helen Wright (GSA)
St Mary's School, Cambridge	1898	485	£2,990	£5,990	Mrs Jayne Triffitt (GSA)
St Mary's College, Merseyside	1919	978	£2,113	–	Jean Marsh (HMC)
St Mary's School, Buckinghamshire	1872	300	£3,090	–	Mrs Fanny Balcombe (GSA)
St Mary's School, Dorset	1945	340	£4,105	£6,085	Mrs M. McSwiggan (GSA)
St Mary's School, Oxfordshire	1872	225	£4,650	£6,950	Mrs Susan Sowden (GSA)
St Mary's Convent School, Worcester	1934	330	£2,260	–	Mrs Susan Cookson (GSA)
St Mary's School Ascot, Berkshire	1885	360	£4,770	£6,900	Mrs Mary Breen (GSA)
St Mary's Hall, Brighton	1836	380	£3,369	£5,508	Mrs Susan M. Meek (GSA)
St Paul's School, London	1509	830	£4,500	£6,695	Dr. G. M. Stephen (HMC)
St Paul's Girls' School, London	1509	680	£3,724	–	Miss Elizabeth Diggory (GSA)
St Peter's School, York	627	500	£3,462	£5,813	Richard Smyth (HMC)
St Swithun's School, Winchester	1884	480	£3,760	£6,200	Dr Helen L. Harvey (GSA)
St Teresa's School, Surrey	1928	330	£3,455	£5,470	Mrs Mary Prescott (GSA)
Scarborough College, Scarborough	1898	530	£2,574	£3,833	T. L. Kirkup (SHMIS)
Seaford College, W. Sussex	1884	401	£3,955	£6,020	Toby J. Mullins (SHMIS)
Sedbergh School, Cumbria	1525	420	£4,900	£6,580	Christopher Hirst (HMC)
Sevenoaks School, Kent	1432	977	£4,179	£7,333	Mrs Katy Ricks (HMC)
Shebbear College, Devon	1841	290	£2,640	£4,930	R. S. Barnes (SHMIS)
Sheffield High School GDST, Sheffield	1878	962	£2,310	–	Mrs Valerie Dunsford (GSA)
Sherborne School, Dorset	1550	560	£5,635	£7,225	S. F. Eliot (HMC)
Sherborne School for Girls, Dorset	1899	360	£5,270	£7,195	Mrs G. Kerton-Johnson (GSA)
Shiplake College, Oxfordshire	1959	300	£4,235	£6,280	N. V. Bevan (HMC, SHMIS)
Shrewsbury School, Shrewsbury	1552	687	£5,045	£7,180	Jeremy Goulding (HMC)
Shrewsbury High School GDST, Shrewsbury	1885	647	£2,310	–	Mrs Marilyn Cass (GSA)
Sibford School, Banbury	1842	392	£2,817	£5,579	Michael Goodwin (SHMIS)
Sidcot School, Somerset	1808	484	£2,995	£6,525	John Walmsley (SHMIS)
Silcoates School, Wakefield	1820	750	£2,952	–	A. Paul Spillane (HMC)
Sir William Perkins's School, Surrey	1725	560	£2,838	–	Miss Susan Ross (GSA)
Solihull School, Solihull	1560	964	£2,515	–	John Claughton (HMC)
South Hampstead High School GDST, London	1876	907	£2,883	–	Jennifer Stephen (GSA)
Stafford Grammar School, Stafford	1982	363	£2,232	–	Michael R. Darley (SHMIS)
Stamford School, Lincolnshire	1532	648	£2,808	£5,328	Dr Peter Mason (HMC)
Stamford High School, Lincolnshire	1877	642	£2,808	£5,328	Dr Peter Mason (GSA)
Stanbridge Earls School, Hampshire	1952	199	£5,000	£6,745	Nicholas Hall (SHMIS)
Stockport Grammar School, Cheshire	1487	1,410	£2,205	–	I. Mellor (HMC)

School	*Date founded*	*No. of pupils*	*Termly fees Day*	*Board*	*Head (with association affliation)*
Stonar School, Wiltshire	1895	450	£2,950	£5,250	Mrs Clare Osborne (GSA)
Stonyhurst College, Lancashire	1593	410	£3,844	£6,636	Adrian Aylward (HMC)
Stover School, Devon	1932	510	£2,495	£5,245	Thomas A. Packer (GSA, SHMIS)
Stowe School, Buckingham	1923	600	£5,445	£7,260	Dr A. Wallersteiner (HMC)
Streatham Hill and Clapham High School GDST, London	1887	830	£2,883	–	Mrs Susan Mitchell (GSA)
Sunderland High School, Sunderland	1884	600	£2,191	–	Dr Angela Slater (SHMIS)
Surbiton High School, Kingston upon Thames	1884	1,258	£2,987	–	Dr Jennifer Longhurst (GSA)
Sutton High School GDST, Surrey	1884	743	£2,883	–	Stephen Callaghan (GSA)
Sutton Valence School, Kent	1576	471	£4,220	£6,680	Joe Davies (HMC)
Sydenham High School for Girls GDST, London	1887	710	£2,883	–	Mrs Kathryn Pullen (GSA)
Talbot Heath, Bournemouth	1886	617	£2,750	£4,580	Mrs Christine Dipple (GSA)
Taunton School, Somerset	1850	480	£3,940	£6,130	Julian Whiteley (HMC)
Teesside High School, Stockton-on-Tees	1970	470	£2,412	–	Mrs Hilary French (GSA)
Tettenhall College, Wolverhampton	1863	492	£2,841	£4,937	Dr P. C. Bodkin (HMC, SHMIS)
Thetford Grammar School, Norfolk	1060	300	£2,455	–	J. R. Weeks (SHMIS)
Tonbridge School, Kent	1553	735	£5,210	£7,374	J. M. Hammond (HMC)
Tormead School, Guildford	1905	740	£2,900	–	Mrs Susan Marks (GSA)
Trent College, Nottingham	1866	1,030	£3,566	£5,375	Jonathan S. Lee (HMC)
Trinity School of John Whitgift, Croydon	1596	885	£3,175	–	Christopher Tarrant (HMC)
Truro School, Truro	1880	817	£2,678	£5,223	Paul K. Smith (HMC)
Truro High School, Truro	1880	450	£2,550	£4,785	Michael McDowell (GSA)
Tudor Hall School, Banbury	1850	275	£3,942	£6,117	Miss Wendy Griffiths (GSA)
University College School, London	1830	1,059	£4,015	–	Kenneth Durham (HMC)
Uppingham School, Rutland	1584	722	£4,972	£7,102	Dr Stephan Winkley (HMC)
Wakefield Girls' High School, Wakefield	1878	712	£2,497	–	Mrs Patricia Langham (GSA)
Walthamstow Hall, Sevenoaks	1838	450	£3,765	–	Mrs Jill Milner (GSA)
Warminster School, Wiltshire	1707	650	£3,045	£5,300	David Dowdles (SHMIS)
Warwick School, Warwick	c 914	1,086	£2,737	£5,841	Edward Halse (HMC)
Welbeck College, Loughborough	1953	220	–	£2,122	Tony Halliwell (SHMIS)
Wellingborough School, Northants	1595	836	£2,997	–	Garry Bowe (HMC)
Wellington College, Berkshire	1853	775	£5,840	£7,300	A. Hugh Munro (HMC)
Wellington School, Somerset	1837	800	£2,636	£4,910	A. J. Rogers (HMC)
Wells Cathedral School, Somerset	c 1150	713	£3,730	£6,230	Elizabeth Cairncross (HMC)
Wentworth College, Bournemouth	1871	235	£3,055	£4,920	Miss Sandra D. Coe (GSA)
West Buckland School, Devon	1858	700	£2,890	£5,040	John Vick (HMC)
Westfield School, Newcastle upon Tyne	1959	370	£2,385	–	Mrs Marion Farndale (GSA)
Westholme School, Lancashire	1923	1,095	£1,969	–	Mrs Lillian Croston (GSA)
Westminster School, London	1560	705	£5,068	£7,316	Tristram Jones-Parry (HMC)
Westonbirt School, Glos	1928	230	£4,470	£6,410	Mrs Mary Henderson (GSA)
Whitgift School, Croydon	1596	1,193	£3,574	–	Dr Christopher Barnett (HMC)
William Hulme's Grammar School, Manchester	1887	570	£2,372	–	Stephen R. Patriarca (HMC)
Wimbledon High School GDST, London	1880	900	£2,883	–	Mrs Pamela Wilkes (GSA)
Winchester College, Winchester	1382	700	£7,016	£7,385	Tommy Cookson (HMC)
Windermere St Anne's School, Cumbria	1863	405	£3,020	£5,460	Miss W. A. Ellis (SHMIS)
Wisbech Grammar School, Cambridgeshire	1379	720	£2,620	–	Robert S. Repper (HMC)
Wispers School, Surrey	1946	120	£3,700	£5,870	L. Henry Beltran (GSA)
Withington Girls' School, Manchester	1890	635	£2,215	–	Mrs Janet Pickering (GSA)
Woldingham School, Surrey	1842	530	£4,010	£6,710	Miss Diana Vernon (GSA)
Wolverhampton Grammar School, Wolverhampton	1512	730	£2,764	–	Dr Bernard Trafford (HMC)
Woodbridge School, Suffolk	1577	904	£3,264	£5,684	Stephen H. Cole (HMC)
Woodhouse Grove School, Bradford	1812	670	£2,760	£4,960	David Humphreys (HMC)
Worksop College, Nottinghamshire	1890	400	£3,945	£5,765	Roy A. Collard (HMC)
Worth School, W. Sussex	1933	440	£5,025	£6,783	Peter Armstrong (HMC)
Wrekin College, Shropshire	1880	450	£3,745	£6,195	Stephen Drew (HMC)
Wychwood School, Oxford	1897	150	£2,750	£4,480	S. Wingfield Digby (GSA)
Wycliffe College, Glos	1882	800	£4,415	£6,570	Dr Tony Collins (HMC)

School	*Date founded*	*No. of pupils*	*Termly fees Day*	*Board*	*Head (with association affliation)*
Wycombe Abbey School, High Wycombe	1896	538	£5,475	£7,300	Mrs Pauline Davies (GSA)
Yarm School, Cleveland	1978	930	£2,666	–	David M. Dunn (HMC, SHMIS)
The Yehudi Menuhin School, Surrey	1963	61	£9,662	£9,924	Nicolas Chisholm (SHMIS)
WALES					
Christ College, Brecon	1541	320	£4,350	£5,605	D. P. Jones (HMC)
Haberdashers' Monmouth School for Girls, Monmouth	1892	675	£2,940	£5,082	Dr Brenda Despontin (GSA)
Howell's School, Denbighshire	1540	340	£2,990	£4,590	Mrs Louise Robinson (GSA)
Howell's School GDST, Cardiff	1860	734	£2,310	–	Mrs Jane Fitz (GSA)
Llandovery College, Carmarthenshire	1847	312	£3,370	£5,085	Peter Hogan (HMC)
Monmouth School, Monmouth	1614	676	£2,989	£4,983	Tim Haynes (HMC)
Rougemont School, Gwent	1920	739	£2,373	–	Dr Jonathan Tribbick (HMC)
Ruthin School, North Wales	1284	245	£3,210	£5,170	John Rowlands (SHMIS)
Rydal Penrhos School, North Wales	1885	394	£3,541	£5,935	Michael S. James (HMC) (SHMIS)
St David's College, North Wales	1965	250	£3,384	£5,883	William G. Seymour (SHMIS)
SCOTLAND					
Albyn School for Girls, Aberdeen	1867	390	£2,520	–	Dr John Halliday (GSA)
Craigholme School, Glasgow	1894	551	£2,380	–	Mrs Gillian Burt (GSA)
Dollar Academy, Dollar	1818	1,200	£2,412	£5,466	John Robertson (HMC)
High School of Dundee, Dundee	1239	1,042	£2,330	–	A. Michael Duncan (HMC)
The Edinburgh Academy, Edinburgh	1824	840	£2,901	£5,952	John Light (HMC)
Fernhill School, Glasgow	1972	165	£2,019	–	Mrs Louisa M. McLay (GSA)
Fettes College, Edinburgh	1870	581	£4,629	£6,733	Michael Spens (HMC)
George Heriot's School, Edinburgh	1628	1,547	£2,348	–	Alistair Hector (HMC)
George Watson's College, Edinburgh	1741	2,271	£2,496	–	Gareth Edwards (HMC)
The Glasgow Academy, Glasgow	1846	1,096	£2,460	–	David Comins (HMC)
The High School of Glasgow, Glasgow	1124	1,050	£2,502	–	Colin Mair (HMC)
Glenalmond College, Perthshire	1841	395	£4,575	£6,720	Gordon Woods (HMC)
Hutchesons' Grammar School, Glasgow	1641	2,086	£2,289	–	John Knowles (HMC)
Kelvinside Academy, Glasgow	1878	640	£2,673	–	John Broadfoot (HMC)
Kilgraston School, Perthshire	1920	225	£3,500	£5,930	Michael Farmer (GSA)
Lomond School, Argyll and Bute	1845	535	£2,446	£5,232	Angus Macdonald (SHMIS)
Loretto School, Midlothian	1827	416	£4,455	£6,676	Michael Mavor (HMC)
The Mary Erskine School, Edinburgh	1694	699	£2,418	£4,823	David Gray (GSA)
Merchiston Castle School, Edinburgh	1833	415	£4,690	£6,600	Andrew Hunter (HMC)
Morrison's Academy, Perthshire	1860	517	£2,427	£5,919	Simon Pengelley (HMC)
Robert Gordon's College, Aberdeen	1732	1,451	£2,410	–	Brian Lockhart (HMC)
St Aloysius' College, Glasgow	1859	1,300	£2,233	–	John Stoer (HMC)
St Columba's School, Renfrewshire	1897	720	£2,400	–	David G. Girdwood (HMC)
St George's School for Girls, Edinburgh	1888	1,020	£2,350	£5,075	Dr Judith McClure (GSA)
St Margaret's School for Girls, Aberdeen	1846	376	£2,409	–	Mrs Lyn McKay (GSA)
St Margaret's School, Edinburgh	1855	580	£2,327	£4,862	Mrs Eileen Davis (GSA)
Stewart's Melville College, Edinburgh	1832	710	£2,543	£4,823	David Gray (HMC)
Strathallan School, Perth	1913	450	£4,396	£6,504	Bruce K. Thompson (HMC)
NORTHERN IRELAND					
Bangor Grammar School, Bangor	1856	1,010	£95	–	Stephen Connolly (HMC)
Belfast Royal Academy, Belfast	1785	1,566	£80	–	W. S. F. Young (HMC)
Campbell College, Belfast	1894	724	£575	£2,775	Dr Ivan Pollock (HMC)
Coleraine Academical Institution, Londonderry	1860	702	£75	–	Leonard F. Quigg (HMC)
The Methodist College, Belfast	1868	2,370	£27-£1,610	£3,663	Dr Wilfred Mulryne (HMC)
Portora Royal School, Enniskillen	1608	500	£25	–	J. Neill Morton (HMC)
The Royal Belfast Academical Institution, Belfast	1810	1,050	£230	–	Michael Ridley (HMC)
The Royal School, Dungannon	1614	660	£40	£3083	P. D. Hewitt (SHMIS)
BELGIUM					
The British School of Brussels, 3080 Tervuren	1969	1,129	€7560	–	Roland S. Chant (HMC)

School	*Date founded*	*No. of pupils*	*Termly fees Day*	*Board*	*Head (with association affliation)*
FRANCE					
International School of Paris, 75016 Paris	1964	450	€5,800	–	Gareth Jones (HMC)
ITALY					
St George's British International School, 00123 Rome	1958	610	€4,600	–	Nicholas Johnson (HMC)
Sir James Henderson School, 20134 Milan	1969	670	€3,100	–	Trevor Church (HMC)
NETHERLANDS					
The British School in the Netherlands, 2252 BG Voorschoten	1935	1,991	€4,300	–	Trevor Rowell (HMC)
PORTUGAL					
St Julian's School, 2776-601 Carcavelos	1932	914	€5,045	–	David Smith (HMC)
SPAIN					
King's College, 28761 Madrid	1969	1,352	€2,827	€4,963	Christopher T. Gill Leech (HMC)
SWITZERLAND					
Aiglon College, 1885 Chesieres-Villars	1949	333	14,167 SFr	21,467 SFr	Revd Dr Jonathan Long (HMC)
CHANNEL ISLANDS					
Elizabeth College, Guernsey	1563	740	£1,750	–	Dr N. D. Argent (HMC)
Ladies' College, Guernsey	1872	550	£1,170	–	Miss M. E. Macdonald (GSA)
Victoria College, Jersey	1852	900	£1,150	–	Robert Cook (HMC)

NATIONAL ACADEMIES OF SCHOLARSHIP

BRITISH ACADEMY (1902)

10 Carlton House Terrace, London SW1Y 5AH
T 020-7969 5200 F 020-7969 5300
W www.britac.ac.uk

The British Academy is an independent, self-governing learned society for the promotion of the humanities and social sciences. It supports advanced academic research and is a channel for the Government's support of research in those disciplines.

The Fellows are scholars who have attained distinction in one of the branches of study that the Academy exists to promote. Candidates must be nominated by existing Fellows. There are 770 Ordinary Fellows, 15 Honorary Fellows and 306 Corresponding Fellows overseas.

President, The Viscount Runciman, PBA
Treasurer, Prof. R. J. P. Kain, FBA
Foreign Secretary, Prof. C. N. J. Mann, FBA
Publications Secretary, Dr D. J. McKitterick, FBA
Secretary, P. W. H. Brown, CBE

ROYAL ACADEMY OF ARTS (1768)

Burlington House, Piccadilly, London W1J OBD
T 020-7300 8000 F 020-7300 8001
W www.royalacademy.org.uk

The Royal Academy of Arts is an independent, self-governing society devoted to the encouragement and promotion of the fine arts.

Membership of the Academy is limited to 80 Royal Academicians, all being painters, engravers, sculptors or architects. Candidates are nominated and elected by the existing Academicians. There is also a limited class of honorary membership and there were 20 honorary members as at June 2004.

President, Prof. P. King, CBE, PRA
Treasurer, Prof. P. Huxley, RA
Keeper, Prof. B. Neiland, RA
Secretary, Miss L. Fitt

ROYAL ACADEMY OF ENGINEERING (1976)

29 Great Peter Street, London SW1P 3LW
T 020-7222 2688 F 020-7233 0054
W www.raeng.org.uk

The Royal Academy of Engineering was established as the Fellowship of Engineering in 1976. It was granted a royal charter in 1983 and its present title in 1992. It is an independent, self-governing body whose object is the pursuit, encouragement and maintenance of excellence in the whole field of engineering, in order to promote the advancement of the science, art and practice of engineering for the benefit of the public.

Election to the Fellowship is by invitation only, from nominations supported by the body of Fellows. At June 2004 there were 1,324 Fellows. The Duke of Edinburgh is the Senior Fellow and the Duke of Kent is a Royal Fellow.

President, Sir Alec Broers, FRS, FRENG
Senior Vice-President, Sir Duncan Michael, FRENG
Vice-Presidents, G. A. Campbell, FRENG; P. Saraga, OBE, FRENG; Dr S. E. Ion, OBE, FRENG; P. C. Ruffles, CBE, FRS, FRENG; Dr S. Steedman, FRENG; Sir Peter Williams, CBE, FRS, FRENG
Hon. Treasurer, C. Price, FRENG
Hon. Secretaries, P. Saraga, OBE, FRENG *(International Activities)*; Dr Julia King, CBE, FRENG *(Education and Training)*
Chief Executive, J. Burch

ROYAL SCOTTISH ACADEMY (1838)

The Mound, Edinburgh EH2 2EL
T 0131-225 6671 W www.royalscottishacademy.org

The Scottish Academy was founded in 1826 to arrange exhibitions of contemporary paintings and to establish a society of fine art in Scotland. The Academy was granted a royal charter in 1838.

Members are elected from the disciplines of painting, sculpture, architecture and printmaking. Elections are from nominations put forward by the existing membership. At mid-2004 there were four Senior Academicians, five Senior Associates, 36 Academicians, 46 Associates, four non-resident Associates and 20 Honorary Members.

President, I. McKenzie Smith, OBE, PRSA
Secretary, W. Scott, RSA
Treasurer, I. Metzstein, RSA
Administrative Secretary, B. Laidlaw, ACIS

ROYAL SOCIETY (1660)

6–9 Carlton House Terrace, London SW1Y 5AG
T 020-7839 5561 F 020-7930 2170
W www.royalsoc.ac.uk

The Royal Society is an independent academy promoting the natural and applied sciences. Founded in 1660, the Society has three roles, as the UK academy of science, as a learned Society and as a funding agency. It is an independent, self-governing body under a royal charter, promoting and advancing all fields of physical and biological sciences, of mathematics and engineering, medical and agricultural sciences and their application.

Fellows are elected for their contributions to science, both in fundamental research resulting in greater understanding, and also in leading and directing scientific and technological progress in industry and research establishments. A maximum of 42 new Fellows, who must be citizens or residents of the British Commonwealth countries or Ireland, may be elected annually.

Up to six Foreign Members, who are selected from those not eligible to become Fellows because of citizenship or residency, are elected annually for their contributions to science.

One Honorary Fellow may be elected each year from those not eligible for election as Fellows or Foreign members. There are approximately 1,300 Fellows and Foreign Members covering all scientific disciplines.

President, Lord May of Oxford, Kt., AC
Treasurer, Prof. D. Wallace, CBE, FRS
Biological Secretary, Prof. D. Read, FRS
Physical Secretary, Prof. J. Enderby, CBE, FRS

Foreign Secretary, Prof. Dame J. Higgins, DBE, FRS
Executive Secretary, S. Cox, CVO

ROYAL SOCIETY OF EDINBURGH (1783)

22–26 George Street, Edinburgh EH2 2PQ
T 0131-240 5000 **F** 0131-240 5024
W www.royalsoced.org.uk

The Royal Society of Edinburgh (RSE) is Scotland's National Academy. A wholly independent, non party-political body with charitable status, the RSE provides a forum for broadly-based interdisciplinary activity in Scotland. This includes organising conferences and lectures both for the specialist and for the general public; providing independent, expert advice to key decision making bodies, including Government and Parliament; strengthening links between academia and industry and boosting wealth generation at home. The Society's Research Awards programme annually awards nearly half a million pounds to exceptionally talented young academics and potential entrepreneurs in Scotland.

Fellows are elected by ballot after being nominated by at least four existing Fellows. Elections are held annually, on the first Monday in March.

At June 2004 there were 1,280 Ordinary Fellows, 71 Honorary Fellows and 24 Corresponding Fellows.

President, Lord Sutherland of Houndwood, Kt., FBA, FRSE
Vice-Presidents, Prof. J. Coggins, FRSE; Prof. A. C. Walker, FRSE; Prof. Gavin McCrone, CB, FRSE
Treasurer, Prof. Sir Laurence Hunter, CBE, FRSE
General Secretary, Prof. A. Miller, CBE, FRSE

THE RESEARCH COUNCILS

The Government funds basic and applied civil science research, mostly through the seven research councils, which are supported by the Department of Trade and Industry. The councils support research and training in universities and other higher education establishments. They also receive income for research commissioned by Government departments and the private sector. A total of £356 million of resource is being added to the science budget over three years from 2002 to increase basic research. Of this, £252 million, (including £12 million of capital) will be directed to cross-council research programmes in genomics, e-science and basic technology. The remaining £104 million of resource is added to the science budget, mainly to provide an uplift to existing council programmes. In July 2000, the Chancellor announced a further £1 billion of investment in science infrastructure over the years 2002–4, comprising £755 million from Government and £225 million from the Wellcome Trust.

The Government science budget for 2004–5 includes the following allocations:

	2004–5 *£m*
BBSRC	285.007
ESRC	102.694
EPSRC	490.519
MRC	435.088
NERC	266.687
PPARC	259.180
*CLRC	8.113
Pensions	31.140
Royal Society	31.045
Royal Academy of Engineering	5.600
Diamond	10.081
Higher Education Innovation Fund	60.305
Science Research Investment Fund	296.570
Cambridge/MIT	14.000
Exchange Rate and Contingency	25.000
OST Managed Funds	58.364
Exploitation of Discoveries at PSREs	4.655

*partially funded by the European Union

BIOTECHNOLOGY AND BIOLOGICAL SCIENCES RESEARCH COUNCIL (BBSRC)

Polaris House, North Star Avenue, Swindon SN2 1UH
T 01793-413200

The BBSRC promotes and supports research and post-graduate training relating to the understanding and exploitation of biological systems; advances knowledge and technology; provides trained scientists to meet the needs of biotechnological-related industries; and provides advice, disseminates knowledge, and promotes public understanding of biotechnology and the biological sciences.
Chairman, Dr P. Ringrose
Chief Executive, Prof. J. Goodfellow, CBE

INSTITUTES

BABRAHAM INSTITUTE, Babraham Hall, Babraham, Cambridge CB2 4AT T 01223-496000
Director, Dr R. G. Dyer,

INSTITUTE FOR ANIMAL HEALTH, Compton Laboratory, Compton, Newbury, Berks RG20 7NN T 01635-578411
Director, Prof. P. P. Pastoret

BBSRC/MRC NEUROPATHOGENESIS UNIT, Ogston Building, West Mains Road, Edinburgh EH9 3JF
T 0131-667 5204

PIRBRIGHT LABORATORY, Ash Road, Pirbright, Woking, Surrey GU24 0NF T 01483-232441
Director, Dr A. I. Donaldson

ROTHAMSTED RESEARCH, Rothamsted, Harpenden, Herts AL5 2JQ T 01582-763133 *Director*, Prof. I. R. Crute

BROOM'S BARN, Higham, Bury St Edmunds, Suffolk IP28 6NP T 01284-812200 *Director*, Dr J. D. Pidgeon

INSTITUTE OF FOOD RESEARCH, Norwich Research Park, Colney Lane, Norwich NR4 7UA T 01603-255000
Director, Prof. D. White

INSTITUTE OF GRASSLAND AND ENVIRONMENTAL RESEARCH, Aberystwyth Research Centre, Plas Gogerddan, Aberystwyth, SY23 3EB
T 01970-823000 *Director*, Prof. C. Pollock, OBE

NORTH WYKE RESEARCH STATION, Okehampton, Devon EX20 2SB T 01837-883500 *Head*, Prof. S. Jarvis

JOHN INNES CENTRE, Norwich Research Park, Colney, Norwich NR4 7UH T 01603-452571
Director, Prof. C. Lamb

ROSLIN INSTITUTE, Roslin, Midlothian EH25 9PS
T 0131-527 4200 *Director*, Prof. John Clarke

SILSOE RESEARCH INSTITUTE, Wrest Park, Silsoe, Bedford MK45 4HS T 01525-860000 *Director*, Prof. B. Day

SCOTTISH EXECUTIVE ENVIRONMENT AND RURAL AFFAIRS DEPARTMENT

BIOMATHEMATICS AND STATISTICS SCOTLAND BioSS (administered by SCRI), University of Edinburgh, James Clerk Maxwell Building, The King's Buildings, Mayfield Road, Edinburgh EH9 3JZ T 0131-650 4900
Acting Director, David Elstan
HANNAH RESEARCH INSTITUTE, Hannah Research Park, Ayr KA6 5HL T 01292-674000
Director, Prof. Chris Knight
MACAULAY LAND USE RESEARCH INSTITUTE, Craigiebuckler, Aberdeen AB15 8QH T 01224-498200
Director, Prof. E. M. Gill
MOREDUN RESEARCH INSTITUTE, Pentlands Science Park, Bush Loan, Penicuik, Midlothian EH26 0PZ
T 0131-445 5111 *Director*, Prof. Julie Fitzpatrick

ROWETT RESEARCH INSTITUTE, Greenburn Road, Bucksburn, Aberdeen AB21 9SB T 01224-712751
Director, Prof. P. J. Morgan
SCOTTISH CROP RESEARCH INSTITUTE (SCRI), Invergowrie, Dundee DD2 5DA T 01382-562731
Director, Prof. J. Hillman, FRSE

COUNCIL FOR THE CENTRAL LABORATORY OF THE RESEARCH COUNCILS (CCLRC)

Rutherford Appleton Laboratory, Chilton, Didcot, Oxon OX11 0QX
T 01235-445553 F 01235-446665
W www.cclrc.ac.uk

The CCLRC is a non-departmental body of the Office of Science and Technology, which is part of the Department of Trade and Industry. It is the national portal and centre for key, large-scale research facilities in support of science and engineering research. In particular, the CCLRC has strategic and operational roles in respect of neutron scattering, synchrotron radiation and high power laser facilities. These will enable UK researchers to carry out world-leading science. As well as providing strategic advice, the CCLRC also provides facilities for scientists to research a broad spectrum of applications, from the molecular structure of drugs enabling them to be targeted to maximise efficiency and minimise side effects, to the discovery of planets in distant galaxies.

The CCLRC operates the Rutherford Appleton Laboratory in Oxfordshire, the Daresbury Laboratory in Cheshire and the Chilbolton Observatory in Hampshire.
Chairman, Prof. Sir Graeme Davies
Chief Executive, Prof. J. Wood

CHILBOLTON OBSERVATORY, Stockbridge, Hampshire SO20 6BJ T 01264-860391
DARESBURY LABORATORY, Daresbury, Warrington, Cheshire WA4 4AD T 01925-603000
RUTHERFORD APPLETON LABORATORY, Chilton, Didcot, Oxon OX11 0QX T 01235-445000

ECONOMIC AND SOCIAL RESEARCH COUNCIL (ESRC)

Polaris House, North Star Avenue, Swindon SN2 1UJ
T 01793-413000
E comms@esrc.ac.uk W www.esrc.ac.uk

The purpose of the ESRC is to promote and support research and postgraduate training in the social sciences; to advance knowledge and provide trained social scientists; to provide advice on, and disseminate knowledge and promote public understanding of the social sciences.
Chairman, F. Cairncross, CBE
Chief Executive, I. Diamond

RESEARCH CENTRES

CENTRE FOR ANALYSIS OF RISK AND RELEGATION, London School of Economics and Political Science, Houghton Street, London WC2A 2AE T 020-7955 6577
Directors, Prof. M. Power; Prof. B. Hutter
CENTRE FOR THE ANALYSIS OF SOCIAL EXCLUSION, London School of Economics, Houghton Street, London WC2A 2AE T 020-7955 7419 *Director*, Prof. J. Hills
CENTRE FOR BUSINESS RELATIONSHIPS, ACCOUNTABILITY, SUSTAINABILITY AND SOCIETY, Cardiff University, 54 Park Place, Cardiff CF10 3AT T 029-7955 6577, *Director*, Prof. K. Peattie
CENTRE FOR BUSINESS RESEARCH, Department of Applied Economics, University of Cambridge, Sidgwick Avenue, Cambridge CB3 9DE T 01223-335248
Director, Prof. A. Hughes
CENTRE FOR ECONOMIC AND SOCIAL ASPECTS OF GENOMICS, Lancaster University, Furness College, Lancaster, RA1 4YG T 01524-592503
Director, Prof. R. Chadwick
CENTRE FOR ECONOMIC LEARNING AND SOCIAL EVOLUTION, Department of Economics, University College London, Gower Street, London WC1E 6BT T 020-7387 7050
Research Director, Prof. T. Börgers
CENTRE FOR ECONOMIC PERFORMANCE, London School of Economics, Houghton Street, London WC2A 2AE T 020-7955 7048
Directors, Prof. R. Layard; Prof. R. Freeman
CENTRE FOR GENOMICS IN SOCIETY, University of Exeter, Amory Building, Rennes Drive, Exeter, Devon, EX4 4RJ T 01392-262053 *Director*, J. Dupré
CENTRE FOR MICROECONOMIC ANALYSIS OF PUBLIC POLICY (CMAPP), Institute for Fiscal Studies, 7 Ridgmount Street, London WC1E 7AE T 020-7636 3784
Director, Prof. R. Blundell
CENTRE FOR ORGANISATION AND INNOVATION, Institute of Work Psychology, University of Sheffield, Sheffield S10 2TN T 0114-222 3287 *Director*, Prof. T. Wall
CENTRE FOR RESEARCH ON INNOVATION AND COMPETITION, Faculty of Economic and Social Studies, University of Manchester M13 9PL T 0161-275 2000
Directors, Prof. S. Metcalfe; Prof. R. Coombs
CENTRE FOR SKILLS, KNOWLEDGE AND ORGANISATIONAL PERFORMANCE (SKOPE), University of Oxford, Department of Economics, Manor Road, Oxford, OX1 3UP T 01865-271087
Director, K. Mayhews
CENTRE FOR SOCIAL AND ECONOMIC RESEARCH ON INNOVATION IN GENOMICS, The University of Edinburgh, Old Surgeon's Hall, High School Yards, Edinburgh, EH1 1LZ T 0131-650 9113
Director, Prof. J. Tait
CENTRE FOR SOCIAL AND ECONOMIC RESEARCH ON THE GLOBAL ENVIRONMENT, School of Environmental Sciences, University of East Anglia, Norwich NR4 7TJ T 01603-593176 *Director*, Prof. R. K. Turner
CENTRE FOR THE STUDY OF GLOBALISATION AND REGIONALISATION, Department of Political Science, University of Warwick, Coventry CV4 7AL T 024-7652 3916
Directors, Prof. R. Higgott; J. Whalley
CENTRE ON MICRO-SOCIAL CHANGE, University of Essex, Wivenhoe Park, Colchester, Essex CO4 3SQ T 01206-872957 *Director*, Prof. J. Ermisch
CENTRE ON MIGRATION, POLICY AND SOCIETY, University of Oxford, 58 Banbury Road, Oxford OX2 6QS T 01865-274711, *Director*, Dr S. Vertovec
COMPLEX PRODUCT SYSTEMS INNOVATION CENTRE, SPRU, Mantell Building, University of Sussex, Brighton BN1 9RF T 01273-686758 *Director*, Prof. M. Hobday
FINANCIAL MARKETS CENTRE, London School of Economics, Houghton Street, London WC2A 2AE T 020-7955 7002 *Director*, Prof. D. Webb
TRANSPORT STUDIES UNIT, Centre for Transport Studies, University College London, Gower Street, London WC1E 6BT T 020-7380 7009 *Director*, Prof. P. Goodwin

RESOURCE CENTRES

CENTRE FOR APPLIED SOCIAL SURVEYS, Social and Community Planning Research, 35 Northampton Square, London EC1V 0AX T 020-7250 1866 *Director*, R. Thomas

CENTRE FOR ECONOMIC POLICY RESEARCH, 90–98 Goswell Road, London EC1V 7DB T 020-7878 2900
Director, Prof. R. Portes

ESRC DATA ARCHIVE, University of Essex, Wivenhoe Park, Colchester, Essex CO4 3SQ T 01206-872001
Director, K. Schurer

ESRC UK CENTRE FOR EVIDENCE BASED POLICY, Queen Mary and Westfield College, Department of Politics, Mile End Road, London E1 4NS
Director, Prof. K. Young

INTERNATIONAL BIBLIOGRAPHY OF THE SOCIAL SCIENCES, British Library of Political and Economic Science, London School of Economics, Houghton Street, London WC2A 2AE T 020-7955 7000
Director, Ms J. Sykes

INTERNATIONAL BIBLIOGRAPHY OF THE SOCIAL SCIENCES: ON-LINE RESOURCE CENTRE, LSE, 10 Portugal Street, London WC2A 2HD T 020-7955 7455
Director, Ms. L. Brindley

QUALITATIVE DATA ARCHIVAL RESOURCE CENTRE, Department of Sociology, University of Essex, Colchester, Essex CO4 3SQ T 01206-873058
Director, Prof. P. Thompson

RESOURCE CENTRE FOR ACCESS TO DATA IN EUROPE, Department of Geography, University of Durham, Durham DH1 3HP T 0191-374 7350 *Director*, Prof. R. Hudson

ENGINEERING AND PHYSICAL SCIENCES RESEARCH COUNCIL (EPSRC)

Polaris House, North Star Avenue, Swindon SN2 1ET
T 01793-444000 W www.epsrc.ac.uk

The EPSRC is the largest of the UK Research Councils and funds research and postgraduate training in engineering, the physical sciences and basic technology in universities and other organisations throughout the UK. It also provides advice, disseminates knowledge and promotes public understanding in these areas.
Chairman, Prof. Dame Julia Higgins, FRS, FRENG
Chief Executive, Prof. J. O'Reilly, FRENG, CENG

MEDICAL RESEARCH COUNCIL (MRC)

20 Park Crescent, London W1B 1AL
T 020-7636 5422 F 020-7436 2663 W www.mrc.ac.uk

The purpose of the MRC is to promote medical and related biological research. The council employs its own research staff and funds research by other institutions and individuals, complementing the research resources of the universities and hospitals.
Chairman, Sir Anthony Cleaver
Chief Executive, Prof. Colin Blakemore
Chairman, Neurosciences and Mental Health Board, Prof. A. North
Chairman, Molecular and Cellular Medicine Board, Prof. M. Wakelam
Chairman, Infections and Immunity Board, Prof. A. McMichael
Chairman, Health Services and Public Health Research Board, Dr D. Armstrong
Chairman, Physiological and Clinical Sciences Board, Prof. John Savill

MRC RESEARCH CENTRES

Biostatistics Unit W www.mrc-bsu.cam.ac.uk
Cambridge Centre for Behavioural and Clinical Neuroscience T 01223-333558
Cancer Cell Unit W www.hutchison-mrc.cam.ac.uk
Cell Biology Unit W www.ucl.ac.uk/lmcb
MRC/UCl Centre Development for Medical Molecular Virology T 020-7679 9119 W www.ucl.ac.uk/windeyer-institute/institute/mrc.htm
MRC/University of Newcastle Centre Development in Clinical Brain Ageing W www.ncl.ac.uk/iah/cdcba.htm
Centre for Developmental Neurobiology W www.kcl.ac.uk/depsta/biomedical/mrcdevbiol
MRC/University of Edinburgh Centre for Inflammation Research W www.med.ed.ac.uk/idg/inflamrs.htm
Centre for Protein Engineering W www.mrc-cpe.cam.ac.uk
MRC/University of Bristol Centre for Synaptic Plasticity W www.bris.ac.uk/depts/synaptic
Clinical Sciences Centre W www.csc.mrc.ac.uk
Clinical Trials Unit W www.ctu.mrc.ac.uk
Cognition and Brain Sciences Unit W www.mrc-cbu.cam.ac.uk
Dunn Human Nutrition Unit W www.mrc-dunn.cam.ac.uk
Epidemiology Unit T 01223-330315
Epidemiology Resource Centre T 023-8077 7624
Functional Genetics Unit W www.mrcfgu.ox.ac.uk
MRC/University of Sussex Genome Damage and Stability Centre W www.biols.susx.ac.uk/gdsc/frameset
Health Services Research Collaboration W www.hsrc.ac.uk
Human Genetics Unit W www.hgu.mrc.ac.uk
Human Immunology Unit W www.jr2.ox.ac.uk/mrc-hiu/pages.home.htm
Human Reproductive Sciences Unit W www.hrsu.mrc.ac.uk
Immunochemistry Unit W www.bioch.ox.ac.uk/immunoch
MRC/University of Birmingham Centre for Immune Regulation W www.bham.ac.uk/mrcbcir/home.htm
Institute for Environment and Health W www.le.ac.uk/ieh
Institute of Hearing Research W www.ihr.mrc.ac.uk
Laboratories Fajara, The Gambia W www.extra.mrc.ac.uk/gambia
Laboratory of Molecular Biology T 01223-248011 W www2.mrc-lmb.cam.ac.uk
MRC/UCL Laboratory for Molecular Virology T 020-7679 9119
Mammalian Genetics Unit T 01235-841000 W www.mgu.har.mrc.ac.uk
Molecular Haemotology Unit T 01865-222443 W www.imm.ox.ac.uk/groups/mrc_molhaem
National Institute for Medical Research W www.nimr.mrc.ac.uk
Prion Unit W www.prion.ucl.ac.uk
Protein Phosphorylation Unit W www.dundee.ac.uk/lifesciences/mrcppu
Radiation and Genome Stability Unit W www.ragsu.har.mrc.ac.uk
Resource Centre for Human Nutrition Research W www.mrc-hnr.cam.ac.uk
Rosalind Franklin Centre for Genomics Research W www.hgmp.mrc.ac.uk
Social and Public Health Sciences Unit W www.msoc-mrc.gla.ac.uk

Social, Genetic and Developmental Psychiatry Centre W www.iop.kcl.ac.uk/iopweb/departments/home/default.aspx?locator=10
Toxicology Unit W www.le.ac.uk/cmht
Virology Unit W www.vir.gla.ac.uk

NATURAL ENVIRONMENT RESEARCH COUNCIL (NERC)

Polaris House, North Star Avenue, Swindon SN2 1EU
T 01793-411500 F 01793-411501
W www.nerc.ac.uk

The UK's Natural Environment Research Council (NERC) funds and carries out impartial scientific research in the sciences of the environment. Its work covers the full range of atmospheric, earth, terrestrial and aquatic sciences, from the depth of the oceans to the upper atmosphere. Its mission is to gather and apply knowledge, create understanding and predict the behaviour of the natural environment and its resources.
Chairman, R. Margetts, CBE, FRENG
Chief Executive, Prof. J. Lawton, CBE, FRS

RESEARCH CENTRES

BRITISH ANTARCTIC SURVEY, High Cross, Madingley Road, Cambridge, CB3 OET T 01223-221400 *Director*, Prof. C. Rapley
BRITISH GEOLOGICAL SURVEY, Kingsley Dunham Centre, Keyworth, Nottingham, NG12 5GG T 0115-936 3100 *Executive Director*, Dr D. Falvey
CENTRE FOR ECOLOGY AND HYDROLOGY (CEH), Corporate Planning Office, Polaris House, North Star Avenue, Swindon, SN2 1EU T 01793-442524 *Director*, Prof. P. Nuttall, OBE
PROUDMAN OCEANOGRAPHIC LABORATORY, Joseph Proudman Building, 6 Brownlow Street, Liverpool L3 5DA T 0151-795 4800 *Director*, Dr E. Hill

COLLABORATIVE CENTRES

CENTRE OF OBSERVATION OF AIR-SEA INTERACTIONS AND FLUXES, PLYMOUTH MARINE LABORATORY, Prospect Place, Plymouth, PL1 3DH *Director*, Prof. J. Aiken
CENTRE FOR OBSERVATION AND MODELLING OF EARTHQUAKES AND TECTONICS, COMET Centre of Excellence, Department of Earth Sciences, University of Oxford, Parks Road, Oxford OX1 3PR T 01865-272030 *Head of Department*, Prof. J. Woodhouse
CENTRE FOR POLAR OBSERVATION AND MODELLING, Department of Space and Climate Physics, Pearson Building, University College London, Gower Street, London WC1E 6BT T 020-7679 3031 *Director*, Prof. Duncan Wingham
CENTRE FOR POPULATION BIOLOGY, Imperial College, Silwood Park, Ascot, SL5 7PY T 0200-7594 2474 *Director*, Prof. J. Godfray
CLIMATE AND LAND SURFACE SYSTEMS INTERACTION CENTRE, University of Wales Swansea, Singleton Park, Swansea, SA2 8PP T 01792-295647 *Director*, Prof. M. Barnsley
DATA ASSIMILATION RESEARCH CENTRE, Department of Meteorology, University of Reading, Reading RG6 6BB T 0118-931 6981 *Director*, Prof. A. O'Neill
ENVIRONMENTAL SYSTEMS SCIENCE CENTRE, University of Reading, PO Box 238, Reading, RG6 6AL T 0118-931 8741 *Director*, Prof. R. Gurney
NATIONAL INSTITUTE FOR ENVIRONMENTAL E-SCIENCE, Centre for Mathematical Science, Wilberforce Road, Cambridge, CB3 0WA T 01223-764289 *Director*, Dr M. Dove
NERC CENTRES FOR ATMOSPHERIC SCIENCE, University of Reading, Earley Gate, PO Box 243, Reading RG6 6BB T 0118-378 6452 *Director*, Prof. A. Thorpe
NCAS ATMOSPHERIC CHEMISTRY MODELLING SUPPORT UNIT, Dept of Chemistry, University of Cambridge, Lensfield Road, Cambridge CB2 1EW T 01223-336473 *Director*, Prof. J. Pyle
NCAS BRITISH ATMOSPHERIC DATA CENTRE, Rutherford Appleton Laboratory, Chilton, Didcot, OX11 0QX T 01235-446432 *Director*, Dr B. Lawrence
NCAS CENTRE FOR GLOBAL ATMOSPHERIC MODELLING, Department of Meteorology, University of Reading, PO Box 243, Earley Gate, Reading, RG6 6BB T 0118-378 8315 *Director*, Prof. J. Slingo
NCAS DISTRIBUTED INSTITUTE FOR ATMOSPHERIC COMPOSITION, School of Chemistry, University of Leeds, Leeds, LS2 9JT T 0113-343 6450 *Director*, Prof. M. Pilling
NCAS FACILITY FOR AIRBORNE ATMOSPHERIC MEASUREMENTS, Physics Dept, UMIST, PO Box 88, Manchester, M60 1QD T 0161-200 3936 *Director*, Prof. P. Jonas
NCAS UNIVERSITIES FACILITY FOR ATMOSPHERIC MEASUREMENTS, School of Environment, University of Leeds, Leeds, LS2 9JT T 0113-343 1632 *Director*, Dr A. Blyth
NCAS UNIVERSITIES WEATHER RESEARCH NETWORK, Dept of Meteorology, University of Reading, PO Box 243, Earley Gate, Reading, RG6 6BB T 0118-931 6311 *Director*, Prof. P. Mason
NERC CENTRE FOR TERRESTRIAL CARBON DYNAMICS, University of Sheffield, Hicks Building, Hounsfield Road, Sheffield S3 7RH T 0114-222 3803
PLYMOUTH MARINE LABORATORY, Prospect Place, West Hoe, Plymouth, PL1 3DH T 01752-633100 *Director*, Prof. N. Owens
SCOTTISH ASSOCIATION FOR MARINE SCIENCE, Dunstaffnage Marine Laboratory, by Dunbeg, Oban, Argyll, PA37 1QA T 01631-559000 *Director*, Prof. G. Shimmield
SEA MAMMAL RESEARCH UNIT, Gatty Marine Laboratory, University of St Andrews, Fife, KY16 8LB T 01334-462630 *Director*, Prof. I. Boyd
SOUTHAMPTON OCEANOGRAPHY CENTRE, University of Southampton, European Way, Southampton, SO14 3ZH T 023-8059 6666 *Director*, Prof. H. Roe
TYNDALL CENTRE, School of Environmental Sciences, University of East Anglia, Norwich, Norfolk NR4 7TJ T 01603-593900 *Director*, Dr M. Hulme

PARTICLE PHYSICS AND ASTRONOMY RESEARCH COUNCIL (PPARC)

Polaris House, North Star Avenue, Swindon SN2 1SZ
T 01793-442000 F 01793-442125
E pr.pus@pparc.ac.uk

The Particle Physics and Astronomy Research Centre (PPARC) is the UK's strategic science investment agency. It funds research, education and public understanding in four broad areas of science – particle physics, astronomy, cosmology and space sciences.

PPARC is government funded and provides research grants and studentships to scientists in British universities, gives researchers access to world-class facilities and funds the UK membership of international bodies such as the European Laboratory for Particle Physics (CERN), the

European Space Agency (ESA) and The European Southern Observatory (ESO). It also contributes money to the UK telescopes overseas on La Palma, Hawaii, Australia and in Chile, the UK Astronomy Technology Centre at the Royal Observatory, Edinburgh and the MERLIN/VLBI National Facility.
Chairman, P. Warry
Chief Executive, Prof. I. Halliday, FRSE, FINSTP

ISAAC NEWTON GROUP OF TELESCOPES, Apartado de Coreos 321, Santa Cruz de la Palma, Tenerife 38780, Canary Islands T +34 922-42500 *Director*, R. Rutten
JOINT ASTRONOMY CENTRE, 660 N A'ohoku Place, University Park, Hilo, Hawaii, USA T +808 96720
Director, Prof. G. Davies
UK ASTRONOMY TECHNOLOGY CENTRE, Blackford Hill, Edinburgh EH9 3HJ T 0131-668 8100
Director, Dr A. Russell

RESEARCH AND TECHNOLOGY ORGANISATIONS

The following industrial and technological research bodies are members of the Applied Industrial Research Trading Organisations (AIRTO). Members' activities span a wide range of disciplines from life sciences to engineering. Their work includes basic research, development and design of innovative products or processes, instrumentation testing and certification, and technology and management consultancy. AIRTO publishes a directory to help clients identify the organisations that might be able to assist them.

AIRTO, c/o CCFRA, Station Road, Chipping Campden, Gloucestershire, GL55 6LD T 01386-842247
President, Prof. R. Brook
ADVANCED MANUFACTURING TECHNOLOGY RESEARCH INSTITUTE, Hulley Road, Macclesfield, Cheshire SK10 2NE T 01625-425421
Managing Director, P. Sholl
AIRCRAFT RESEARCH ASSOCIATION LTD, Manton Lane, Bedford MK41 7PF T 01234-350681
Chief Executive, B. Timmins
BLC (THE LEATHER TECHNOLOGY CENTRE), Leather Trade House, Kings Park Road, Moulton Park, Northants NN3 6JD T 01604-679999 *Chief Executive*, M. Parsons
BRE (BUILDING RESEARCH ESTABLISHMENT), Garston, Watford, Hertfordshire WD2 7JR T 01923-664000
Chief Executive, Dr M. Wyatt
BREWING RESEARCH INTERNATIONAL, Lyttel Hall, Coopers Hill Road, Nutfield, Surrey RH1 4HY T 01737-822272
Director-General, Dr M. Kierstan
BRITISH MARITIME TECHNOLOGY LTD, Orlando House, 1 Waldegrave Road, Teddington, Middx TW11 8LZ T 020-8943 5544 *Chief Executive*, R. Swann
BRITISH TEXTILE TECHNOLOGY GROUP, Wira House, West Park Ring Road, Leeds LS16 6QL T 0113-259 1999; Shirley House, Wilmslow Road, Didsbury, Manchester M20 2RB T 0161-445 8141 *Chief Executive*, A. King
BUILDING SERVICES RESEARCH AND INFORMATION ASSOCIATION, Old Bracknell Lane West, Bracknell, Berks RG12 7AH T 01344-465526 *Chief Executive*, A. Eastwell
CAMPDEN AND CHORLEYWOOD FOOD RESEARCH ASSOCIATION, Chipping Campden, Glos GL55 6LD T 01386-842000 *Director-General*, Prof. C. Dennis
CENTRAL LABORATORY OF THE RESEARCH COUNCILS, Chilton, Didcot, Oxfordshire, OX11 0QX T 01235-821900 *Chief Executive*, Prof. J. Wood
CERAM RESEARCH (BRITISH CERAMIC RESEARCH LTD), Queen's Road, Penkhull, Stoke-on-Trent ST4 7LQ T 01782-764444 *Chief Executive*, Dr N. E. Sanderson
CIRIA (CONSTRUCTION INDUSTRY RESEARCH AND INFORMATION ASSOCIATION), Classic House, 174–180 Old St., London EC1V 9BP T 020-7549 3300
Director-General, Dr T. Broyd
CRL (Specialist products, technology licences, research and development), Dawley Road, Hayes, Middx UB3 1HH T 020-8848 9779 *Managing Director*, Dr B. Holcroft
FIRA INTERNATIONAL LTD (FURNITURE INDUSTRY RESEARCH ASSOCIATION), Maxwell Road, Stevenage, Herts SG1 2EW T 01438-777700
Managing Director, H. Davies
HR WALLINGFORD GROUP LTD (Hydroinformatics and engineering), Howbery Park, Wallingford, Oxon OX10 8BA T 01491-835381 *Chief Executive*, Dr S. W. Huntington
ITRI LIMITED (Tin and chemicals), Kingston Lane, Uxbridge, Middlesex UB8 3PJ T 01895-272 406
Chief Executive, D. Bishop
LGC, Queens Road, Teddington, Middx TW11 0LY T 020-8943 7000
Chief Executive and Government Chemist, Dr R. Worswick
LEATHERHEAD FOOD INTERNATIONAL, Randalls Road, Leatherhead, Surrey KT22 7RY T 01372-376761
Director, J. Bevington
MATERIALS ENGINEERING RESEARCH LABORATORY LTD, Tamworth Road, Hertford SG13 7DG T 01992-500120
Managing Director, Dr. R. H. Martin
MOTOR INDUSTRY RESEARCH ASSOCIATION, Watling Street, Nuneaton, Warks CV10 0TU T 024-7635 5000
Managing Director, J. R. Wood
MOTOR INSURANCE REPAIR RESEARCH CENTRE, Colthorp Lane, Thatcham, Berks RG19 4NP T 01635-868855 *Chief Executive*, P. Roberts
NATIONAL COMPUTING CENTRE LTD, Oxford House, Oxford Road, Manchester M1 7ED T 0161-242 2499
Chief Executive, M. Gough
NATIONAL PHYSICAL LABORATORY, Queens Road, Teddington, Middx TW11 0LW T 020-8977 3222
Chief Executive, Dr B. McGuiness
NCIMB LIMITED (Microbiological supply and bacterial culture collection), 23 St Machar Drive, Aberdeen, AB24 3RY T 01224-273332 *Chief Executive*, Dr A. Syms
PAINT RESEARCH ASSOCIATION, 8 Waldegrave Road, Teddington, Middx TW11 8LD T 020-8614 4800
Acting Managing Director, Company Secretary and Finance Director, J. Marshall
PERA GROUP (Multi-disciplinary research, design, development and consultancy), Pera Innovation Park, Melton Mowbray, Leicestershire LE13 0PB T 01664-501501
Chief Executive, Dr P. Davies, CBE
QINETIQ (Science Consultancy), Cody Building, Ively Road, Farnborough, Hants GU14 0LX T 08700-100942
Chief Executive, Sir John Chisholm, FENG
RAPRA TECHNOLOGY LTD (Rubber and plastics), Shawbury, Shrewsbury SY4 4NR T 01939-250383; North East Centre, 18 Belasis Court, Belasis Technology Park, Billingham TS23 4AZ T 01642-370406
Managing Director, A. Ward
SATRA TECHNOLOGY CENTRE (Footwear, apparel, safety products and furniture), Satra House, Rockingham Road, Kettering, Northants NN16 9JH T 01536-410000
Chief Executive, Dr R. E. Whittaker

SCOTCH WHISKY RESEARCH INSTITUTE, The Robertson Trust Building, Research Park North, Riccarton, Edinburgh, EH14 4AP T 0131 449-8900 *Director*, Dr G. M. Steele

SIRA LTD (Measurement, instrumentation, control and optical systems technology), South Hill, Chislehurst, Kent BR7 5EH T 020-8467 2636
Managing Director, Prof. R. A. Brook

SMITH INSTITUTE (Mathematics and computing), PO Box 183, Guildford, Surrey GU2 5GG T 01483-579108
Chairman of the Council, Dr B. Smith, CBE

SPORTS TURF RESEARCH INSTITUTE, St Ives Estate, Bingley, W. Yorks BD16 1AU T 01274-565131
Chief Executive, Dr G. McKillop

STEEL CONSTRUCTION INSTITUTE, Silwood Park, Ascot, Berks SL5 7QN T 01344-623345 *Director*, Dr G. Owens

TNO BIBRA INTERNATIONAL LTD, Woodmansterne Road, Carshalton, Surrey SM5 4DS T 020-8652 1000
Director, Dr G. van der Veek

TRADA TECHNOLOGY LTD (Timber and wood-based products), Chiltern House, Stocking Lane, Hughenden Valley, High Wycombe, Bucks HP14 4ND T 01494-563091
Managing Director, A. Abbott

TWI, Abington Hall, Abington, Cambridge CB1 6AL T 01223-891162
Chief Executive, A. B. M. Braithwaite, OBE

SOCIAL WELFARE

NATIONAL HEALTH SERVICE

The National Health Service (NHS) came into being on 5 July 1948 under the National Health Service Act 1946, covering England and Wales and, under separate legislation, Scotland and Northern Ireland. The NHS is now administered by the Secretary of State for Health (in England), the National Assembly for Wales, the Scottish Executive and the Secretary of State for Northern Ireland.

The function of the NHS is to provide a comprehensive health service designed to secure improvement in the physical and mental health of the people and to prevent, diagnose and treat illness. It was founded on the principle that treatment should be provided according to clinical need rather than ability to pay, and should be free at the point of delivery.

Hospital, mental, dental, nursing, ophthalmic and ambulance services and facilities for the care of expectant and nursing mothers and young children are provided by the NHS to meet all reasonable requirements. Rehabilitation services such as occupational therapy, physiotherapy, speech therapy and surgical and medical appliances are supplied where appropriate. Specialists and consultants who work in NHS hospitals can also engage in private practice, including the treatment of their private patients in NHS hospitals.

STRUCTURE

The structure of the NHS remained relatively stable for the first 30 years of its existence. In 1974, a three-tier management structure comprising Regional Health Authorities, Area Health Authorities and District Management Teams was introduced in England, and the NHS became responsible for community health services. In 1979 Area Health Authorities were abolished and District Management Teams were replaced by District Health Authorities.

The National Health Service and Community Care Act 1990 provided for more streamlined Regional Health Authorities and District Health Authorities, and for the establishment of Family Health Services Authorities (FHSAs) and NHS Trusts. The concept of the 'internal market' was introduced into health care, whereby care was provided through NHS contracts where health authorities or boards and GP fundholders (the purchasers) were responsible for buying health care from hospitals, non-fundholding GPs, community services and ambulance services (the providers). The Act also paved the way for the Community Care reforms, which were introduced in April 1993, and changed the way care is administered for older people, the mentally ill, the physically handicapped and people with learning disabilities.

ENGLAND

Regional Health Authorities in England were abolished in April 1996 and replaced by eight regional offices which, together with the headquarters in Leeds, formed the NHS Executive (which has since been merged with the Department of Health). In April 2002, as an interim arrangement, the eight regional offices were replaced by four Directorates of Health and Social Care (DsHSC). In April 2003, the DsHSCs were abolished.

STRATEGIC HEALTH AUTHORITIES

In April 1996 the District Health Authorities and Family Health Service Authorities were merged to form 100 unified Health Authorities (HAs) in England. In April 2002, 28 new health authorities were formed from the existing HAs. In October 2002, as part of the new arrangements set out in the NHS Reform and Health Care Professions Act 2002, these new health authorities were renamed Strategic Health Authorities (SHAs) and charged with creating a strategic framework for managing the performance of Primary Care Trusts and building the capacity of health services locally.

PRIMARY CARE TRUSTS

The first 17 Primary Care Trusts (PCTs) became operational in England on 1 April 2000. As at 1 April 2004 a total of 304 PCTs covered all areas of England. PCTs were created to give primary care professionals greater control over how resources are best used to benefit patients. PCTs are responsible for tackling health inequalities, developing primary and community health services and commissioning secondary care services. They are free-standing statutory bodies undertaking many of the functions previously exercised by former Health Authorities, such as securing the provision of services and integrating health and social care.

Each PCT is overseen by a lay board, comprising a chairman and non-executive directors who are appointed by the NHS Appointments Commission and who are members of the local community to be served by the PCT. The Board's role is to provide strategic oversight and verification to the work of the Executive, which is made up of health professionals.

FOUNDATION TRUSTS

The first ten NHS foundation trusts were established on 1 April 2004 with a further ten established on 1 July 2004. NHS foundation trusts are NHS hospitals, they are part of the NHS but have their own accountabilty and governance systems, which function outside of the Department of Health's framework, giving them greater freedom to run their own affairs. NHS foundation trusts treat patients according to NHS principles and standards and are inspected by the Healthcare Commission. The Government's aim is that by 2008, all NHS trusts will have reached a standard which will enable them to apply for NHS foundation trust status.

Contact details for all the SHAs, PCTs and other NHS organisations in England can be found in the *NHS England, Authorities and Trusts* section on the NHS website: www.nhs.uk or by calling the Department of Health Public Enquiry Office on 020-7210 4850.

WALES

In Wales there were five HAs which replaced the former 17 HAs and FHSAs in April 1996. The HAs set up 22 Local Health Groups (LHGs), coterminous with local authority areas (*see* Local Government Section), which began work in April 1999. Originally they advised HAs, but in March 2003 the five HAs were abolished and the LHGs, were renamed Local Health Boards (LHBs) and took up a role similar to PCTs; assuming responsibility for commissioning services and devising strategies for improving health. They also integrate the delivery of primary and community care. Each Local Health Board has a governing body made up of local doctors, a nurse, other health professionals, members of the local authority and voluntary organisations and others to represent the interests of patients. There is also a small executive team to take action on decisions and provide services for the public.

Contact details for the LHBs and other NHS organisations in Wales are available in the *NHS Wales Directory* section on the Welsh NHS website. W www.wales.nhs.uk

SCOTLAND

In Scotland, the Scottish Executive Health Department leads the central management of the NHS, heading a Management Executive which oversees the work of 15 area Health Boards responsible for planning health services for their area, and 28 self-governing NHS Trusts responsible for providing services to patients and the community. At a local level there are currently Local Health Care Co-operatives (LHCCs) which are voluntary associations of primary health care professionals and local authority representatives. There are plans to replace the LHCCs with Community Health Partnerships (CHPs) to give more consistency to the planning, development and delivery of local services across Scotland.

FOUNDATION TRUSTS

ARGYLL AND CLYDE, Ross House, Hawkhead Road, Paisley PA2 7BN T 0141-842 7200 W www.show.scot.nhs.uk/achb

AYRSHIRE AND ARRAN, Boswell House, 10 Arthur Street, Ayr KA7 1QJ T 01292-611040 W www.nhsayrshireandarran.com

BORDERS, Newstead, Melrose, Roxburghshire TD6 9BD T 01896-825500 W www.nhsborders.org.uk

DUMFRIES AND GALLOWAY, Mid North, The Crichton, Glencaple Road, Dumfries DG1 4TG T 01387-272700 W www.show.scot.nhs.uk/dghb

FIFE, Springfield House, Cupar KY15 5UP T 01334-656200 W www.show.scot.nhs.uk/fhb

FORTH VALLEY, 33 Spittal Street, Stirling FK8 1DX T 01786-463031 W www.show.scot.nhs.uk/nhsfv

GRAMPIAN, Summerfield House, 2 Eday Road, Aberdeen AB15 6RE T 01224-663456 W www.ghb.uk.com

GREATER GLASGOW, Dalian House, 350 St Vincent Street, Glasgow G3 8YZ T 0141-201 4444 W www.nhsgg.org.uk

HIGHLAND, Assynt House, Beechwood Park, Inverness IV2 3HG T 01463-717123 W www.show.scot.nhs.uk/hhb

LANARKSHIRE, 14 Beckford Street, Hamilton, Lanarkshire ML3 0TA T 01698-281313 W www.show.scot.nhs.uk/nhslanarkshire

LOTHIAN, Deaconess House, 148 Pleasance, Edinburgh EH8 9RS T 0131-536 9000 W www.nhslothian.scot.nhs.uk

ORKNEY, Garden House, New Scapa Road, Kirkwall, Orkney KW15 1BQ T 01856-885400 W www.show.scot.nhs.uk/ohb

SHETLAND, Brevik House, South Road, Lerwick ZE1 0TG T 01595-696767 W www.show.scot.nhs.uk/shb

TAYSIDE, Kings Cross, Clepington Road, Dundee DD3 8EA T 01382-818479 W www.nhstayside.scot.nhs.uk

WESTERN ISLES, 37 South Beach Street, Stornoway, Isle of Lewis HS1 2BB T 01851-702997 W www.show.scot.nhs.uk/wihb

NORTHERN IRELAND

In Northern Ireland there are four Health and Social Services Boards responsible for commissioning services to meet the needs of their respective populations. They are also responsible for assessing the needs of that population, establishing objectives and developing policies and priorities to meet these objectives. There are 15 Local Health and Social Care Groups (LHSCGs) responsible for the planning and delivery of primary and community care and to represent local interests to their respective Health and Social Services Board.

EASTERN, Champion House, 12–22 Linenhall Street, Belfast BT2 8BS T 028-9032 1313 W www.ehssb.n-i.nhs.uk

NORTHERN, County Hall, 182 Galgorm Road, Ballymena BT42 1QB T 028-2565 3333 W www.nhssb.n-i.nhs.uk

SOUTHERN, Tower Hill, Armagh BT61 7DR T 028-3741 0041 W www.shssb.n-i.nhs.uk

WESTERN, 15 Gransha Park, Clooney Road, Londonderry BT47 6FN T 028-7186 0086 W www.whssb.n-i.nhs.uk

PATIENT AND PUBLIC INVOLVEMENT FORUMS

There are Patient and Public Involvement (PPI) Forums throughout the UK; their role is to represent the interests of the public to NHS Trusts, PCTs and SHAs and their equivalents in Wales and Scotland.

There is a PPI Forum for every NHS Trust and PCT in England. PPI Forums are made up of local people and play an active role in health-related decision-making within their communities. They have a number of primary roles which include:

- Obtaining views from local communities on the range and day to day delivery of health services and making recommendations and reports
- Influencing the design of and access to NHS services
- Providing advice and information to patients and their carers about services
- Monitoring the effectiveness of local Patient Advice and Liaison Services (PALS)

THE NHS PLAN

In July 2000 the government launched the NHS Plan, a ten year strategy to modernise the health service. In June 2004 the Government launched the NHS Improvement Plan, which set out the next stage of NHS reform, moving the focus from access to services towards the broader issues of public health and chronic disease management. The core aims are to sustain increased levels of investment in the NHS and to continue to focus on the improvements outlined in the NHS Plan, while delivering greater levels of choice and information to patients. In July 2004, the Department of Health published *National Standards, Local Action: Health and Social Care Standards and Planning Framework 2005/6–2007/8* which cut the number of national targets that NHS providers must comply from 62 to 20. These national targets, which cover areas such as waiting times for accident and emergency treatment, will become national core standards which all providers of care must maintain from April 2005. Alongside, NHS providers will be given power to set more locally relevant targets.

FINANCE

The NHS is still funded mainly through general taxation, although in recent years more reliance has been placed on the NHS element of National Insurance contributions, patient charges and other sources of income.

In the April 2002 Budget, the Chancellor announced a five-year spending plan for the NHS. Over the years 2003–4 to 2007–8, these plans mean that expenditure on the NHS in the UK will increase on average by 7.2 per cent a year over and above inflation, 7.4 per cent a year for England. The spending plans are set out in the table below:

£ millions	*UK*	*% real terms increase**	*England*	*% real terms increase**
2003–4	74,800	7.0	61,300	7.1
2004–5	82,200	7.1	67,400	7.2
2005–6	90,500	7.4	74,400	7.6
2006–7	99,400	7.2	81,800	7.3
2007–8	109,400	7.4	90,200	7.5

* calculated using GDP deflator at 27 June 2003
Source: Department of Health

NATIONAL HEALTH SERVICE EXPENDITURE 2002–3 OUTTURN (ENGLAND)

	£ million
Hospitals, community health, family health (discretionary) and related services and NHS Trusts	51,053
Family health services (non-discretionary)	2,023
Central and other services*	966
Total	54,042

* includes: environmental health, health promotion, support to the voluntary sector and expenditure on the administration of the Department of Health
Source: Department of Health

GOVERNMENT EXPENDITURE ON WELFARE SERVICES 2001–2

	£ million
Central government	52
Local authorities running expenses	13,279
Capital expenditure	137
Total	13,472

Source: The Stationery Office – *Annual Abstract of Statistics 2004* (Crown copyright)

PRIVATE FINANCE INITIATIVE

The Private Finance Initiative (PFI) was launched in 1992, and involves the private sector in designing, building, financing and operating new hospitals and primary care premises, which are then leased to the NHS. The NHS Plan committed the NHS to entering into a new public private partnership, Partnerships for Health, a joint venture between the Department of Health and Partnerships UK plc (PUK) established in September 2001. Its role is to support the development of NHS Local Improvement Finance Trusts (LIFT) by implementing a standard approach to procurement as well as providing some equity. LIFTs are set up as limited companies with the local NHS, Partnerships for Health and the private sector as shareholders. LIFT schemes build and refurbish primary care premises, which the schemes own and then rent to GPs on a lease basis (as well as other parties such as chemists, opticians, dentists etc). There are 42 LIFT schemes covering more than 100 PCTs, with up to £1,000 million investment supported by £195 million of public money.

EMPLOYEES AND SALARIES

EMPLOYEES

NHS HOSPITAL AND COMMUNITY HEALTH SERVICE STAFF *(Great Britain) 2002*
Full-time equivalent

Hospital medical staff	76,122
Community health medical staff	1,902
Hospital dental staff	1,944
Community health dental staff	1,413
Nursing and midwifery staff	455,361
General medical practitioners	38,649
General dental practitioners	22,194

Source: National Statistics – *Annual Abstract of Statistics 2004* (Crown copyright)

SALARIES

General Practitioners (GPs), dentists, optometrists and pharmacists are self-employed, and are employed by the NHS under contract. On 20 June 2003 GPs accepted a new practice-based contract which rewards practices for delivering quality and a wider range of services. Dentists receive payment for items of treatment for individual adult patients and, in addition, a continuing care payment for those registered with them. Optometrists receive approved fees for each sight test they carry out. Pharmacists receive professional fees from the NHS and are refunded the cost of prescriptions supplied. Doctors in training receive additional supplements reflecting the intensity and out-of-hours elements of their duties, these can range from 20–100 per cent of the basic salary.

SALARIES
As at 1 April 2004 for Hospital Medical and Dental Staff and Nurses (these figures do not include merit awards, discretionary points or banding supplements):

Consultant	£55,699–£72,483
Specialist Registrar	£27,483–£41,733
Registrar	£27,483–£33,337
Senior House Officer	£24,587–£34,477
House Officer	£19,703–£22,240
Nursing Grades H–I (Modern Matron)	£26,650–£34,920
Nursing Grades G–I (Senior Ward Sister)	£23,860–£34,920
Nursing Grade F (Ward Sister)	£20,220–£25,250
Nursing Grade E (Senior Staff Nurse)	£18,230–£22,015
Nursing Grade D (Staff Nurse)	£17,060–£18,830
Nursing Grade C (Enrolled Nurse and some Nursing auxiliary staff)	£13,900–£17,060
Nursing Grades A–B	£10,375–£13,025

HEALTH SERVICES

PRIMARY AND COMMUNITY HEALTH CARE

Primary and community health care services comprise the family health services (i.e. the general medical, personal medical, pharmaceutical, dental, and ophthalmic services) and community services (including preventive activities such as vaccination, immunisation and fluoridation). Nursing services including practice nurses, community nurses and health visitors and ante- and post-natal care.

PRIMARY MEDICAL SERVICES

In England, Primary Medical Services are the responsibility of Primary Care Trusts (PCTs) who contract with GPs to provide the service to the NHS. They do so in one of two ways: by providing general medical services (GMS) under national rules or by successfully applying to become a personal medical service (PMS) pilot, with a contract that is largely locally determined. As at 1 October 2003, just over 40 per cent of GPs were in PMS.

In Wales, responsibility for primary medical services rests with Local Health Boards (LHBs) and in Scotland with the NHS Trusts (*see* Structure section).

Any vocationally trained doctor may provide general or personal medical services. The average number of patients on a doctor's list in the UK as at September 2002 was 1,838. GPs may also have private fee-paying patients, but not if that patient is already an NHS patient on that doctor's patient list.

A person who is ordinarily resident in the UK is eligible to register with a GP (or PMS provider) for free primary care treatment. Should a patient have difficulty in registering with a doctor, he or she should contact the local PCT for help. When a person is away from home he/she can still access primary care treatment from a GP if they ask to be treated as a temporary resident. In an emergency any doctor in the service will give treatment and advice.

GPs are responsible for the care of their patients 24 hours a day, seven days a week, but can fulfil the terms of their contract by delegating or transferring responsibility for out-of-hours (OOH) care to an accredited provider. Under the new GMS contract, practices will be able to opt out of responsibility for patient care during the OOH period. When they do so, it will become a Primary Care Trust (PCT) responsibility. PCTs will be able to provide the OOH cover themselves or commission the service from an OOH provider.

Increasingly, some secondary care services, such as minor operations and consultations can be provided in a primary care setting. The number of such practitioners is growing and the new GMS contract provides a platform for further expansion.

In addition, drop-in services are being developed. A total of 42 NHS Walk-in Centres are operational across the country, with further centres planned to open over the next few years. They are nurse-led and provide treatment for minor ailments and injuries, health information and self-help advice with extended opening hours (normally every day of the year from 7a.m.-10p.m. Monday to Friday, and 9a.m.-10p.m. Saturday and Sunday).

HEALTH COSTS

Some people are exempt or entitled to help with health costs such as prescription charges, ophthalmic and dental costs, and in some cases help towards travel costs to and from hospital.

The following list is intended as a general guide to those who are entitled to help or are exempt:

- children under 16 and young people in full time education who are under 19
- people aged 60 or over
- pregnant women and women who have had a baby in the last 12 months
- people receiving Income Support and/or Jobseeker's Allowance
- people receiving Tax Credits
- people with a specified medical condition
- people with impaired hearing
- patients of a genito-urinary medicine clinic
- people who need help to go out or live in residential care or a nursing home
- people supported by a Local Authority after leaving care
- NHS in-patients
- NHS out-patients for all medication given at the hospital
- patients of the Community Dental Service
- people registered blind or partially sighted
- people who need complex lenses
- war pensioners

People in other circumstances may also be eligible for help; Booklet HC11, available from main post offices or local social security offices, gives further details. Or visit: www.dh.gov.uk

PHARMACEUTICAL SERVICES

Patients may obtain medicines and appliances under the NHS from any pharmacy whose owner has entered into arrangements with the PCT to provide this service; the number of these pharmacies in England and Wales as at March 2003 was 10,452. There are also some suppliers who only provide special appliances. In rural areas, where access to a pharmacy may be difficult, patients may be able to obtain medicines, etc., from a dispensing doctor.

Except for contraceptives (for which there is no charge), a charge of £6.40 is payable for each item supplied unless the patient is exempt and the declaration on the back of the prescription form is completed. Prepayment certificates (£33.40 valid for four months, £91.80 valid for a year) may be purchased by those patients not entitled to exemption who require frequent prescriptions.

DENTAL SERVICES

Dentists, like doctors, may take part in the NHS and also have private patients. Over 18,000 dentists in England provide NHS general dental services. They are responsible to the PCTs in whose areas they provide services. Patients may go to any dentist who is taking part in the NHS and is willing to accept them. Patients are required to pay 80 per cent of the cost of NHS dental treatment. Since 1 April 2003 the maximum charge allowed for an NHS course of treatment has been £372. There is no charge for arrest of bleeding or repairs to dentures; home visits by the dentist or re-opening a surgery in an emergency are charged for as treatment given in the normal way.

In July 2004 the government announced a £368 million funding injection for NHS dentistry. The Department of Health plans to recruit the equivalent of an extra 1,000 dentists by October 2005, of which around 650 will be new recruits. This funding was accompanied by a package of reforms to modernise the dentistry profession and ensure continued local expenditure on dentistry through PCTs.

GENERAL DENTAL SERVICE 2002–3 (ENGLAND)

Number of dentists	18,500
Number of patients registered	
Adults	16,600,000
Children	6,700,000
Number of courses of treatment	
Adults	26,300,000
Expenditure (£ million)	
Gross expenditure	1,770
Paid by patients	500
Paid out of public funds	1,270

Source: Department of Health

GENERAL OPHTHALMIC SERVICES

General Ophthalmic Services are administered by PCTs. Testing of sight may be carried out by any ophthalmic medical practitioner or ophthalmic optician (optometrist). The optician must give the prescription to the patient, who can take this to any supplier of glasses to have them dispensed. Only registered opticians can supply glasses to children and to people registered as blind or partially sighted. At the end of December 2002 there were 8,096 ophthalmic practitioners under contract to provide NHS sight tests. An estimated 16.9 million sight tests were carried out in 2002–3 in Great Britain.

The NHS sight test costs £16.72. Free eyesight tests and help towards the cost are available to people in certain circumstances. Help is also available for the purchase of glasses. (*see* Health Costs section or booklet HC11)

COMMUNITY CHILD HEALTH SERVICE

Pre-school services at GP surgeries or child health clinics provide regular monitoring of children's physical, mental and emotional health and development, and advice to parents on their children's health and welfare.

The School Health Service provides for the medical and dental examination of schoolchildren, and advises the local education authority, the school, the parents and the pupil of any health factors which may require special consideration during the pupil's school life. GPs are increasingly undertaking child health monitoring in order to improve the preventive health care of children.

All Primary Care Trusts (PCTs) are working with Local Authorities under accredited local health and education partnerships to recruit more schools into the Healthy Schools Programme which was established in 1999 as a joint initiative between the Department of Health and the Department for Education and Skills.

NHS DIRECT

NHS Direct is a telephone service staffed by nurses which gives patients advice on how to look after themselves as well as directing them to the appropriate part of the NHS for treatment if necessary. T 0845-4647

SECONDARY CARE AND OTHER SERVICES

HOSPITALS

NHS hospitals provide acute and specialist care services, treating conditions which normally cannot be dealt with by primary care specialists and medical emergencies.

NUMBER OF BEDS AND PATIENT ACTIVITY 2002

	England	*Wales*
In-patients:		
Average daily available beds	184,000	14,300
Average daily occupation of beds	157,000	11,800
Persons waiting for admission at 31 March	992,000	74,600
Day-case admissions	3,592,000*	109,400
Ordinary admissions	8,761,000*	493,000
Out-patient attendances:		
New patients	13,032,000	747,300
Total attendances	44,598,000	2,842,500
Accident and emergency:		
New cases	12,945,000	888,700
Total attendances	14,046,000	1,004,700
Ward attendances	1,179,000	–

* 2001 figures

SCOTLAND

In-patients:	
Average available staffed beds	30,900
Average occupied beds	25,100
Out-patient attendances:	
New patients	2,743,000
Total attendances	6,291,000

NORTHERN IRELAND

In-patients:	
Beds available	8,301
Average daily occupation of beds	6,973
Out-patients:	
New cases	992,000
Total attendances	2,122,000

Source: The Stationery Office – *Annual Abstract of Statistics 2004* (Crown copyright)

CHARGES

NHS trusts can provide accommodation in single rooms or small wards, if not required for patients who need privacy for medical reasons. The patient is still an NHS patient, but there may be a charge for these additional facilities. NHS trusts can charge for certain patient services that are considered to be additional treatments over and above the normal service provision. There is no blanket policy to cover this and each case is considered in the light of the patient's clinical need. However, if an item or service is considered to be an integral part of a patient's treatment by their clinician, then a charge should not be made.

In some NHS hospitals, accommodation and services are available for the treatment of private patients where it does not interfere with care for NHS patients. Income generated by treating private patients is then put back into the local NHS services. Private patients undertake to pay the full costs of medical treatment, accommodation, medication and other related services. Charges for private patients are set locally.

WAITING LISTS

At the end of March 2004 the total number of patients waiting to be admitted to NHS hospitals in England was 906,000, a decrease of 8.7 per cent on the previous year. The number of patients in England and Wales who had been waiting more than nine months was 48, a decrease of 99.9 per cent on the previous year, when the total was 53,183. No patients had been waiting longer than 12 months at the end of March 2004 and the average wait was 10.2 weeks. Under the charter *Your Guide to the NHS*, patients are guaranteed admission within 18 months of being placed on a waiting list. In July 2004 a new target was set of an 18 week maximum wait from start time (i.e. seeing a GP) to treatment by 2008.

AMBULANCE SERVICE

The NHS provides emergency ambulance services free of charge via the 999 emergency telephone service. Air ambulances, provided through local charities and partially funded by the NHS, are used throughout the UK. They assist with cases where access may be difficult or heavy traffic could hinder road progress. Non-emergency ambulance services are provided free of charge to patients who are deemed to require them on medical grounds.

In 2003–4 in England approximately 5.3 million emergency calls were made to the ambulance service, an increase of 8 per cent on the previous year. There were about 3.4 million emergency patient journeys. Since 1

April 2001 all services have had a system of call prioritisation. The prioritisation procedures require all emergency calls to be classified as either immediately life threatening (category A) or other emergency (category B/C). Services are expected to reach 75 per cent of Category A (life threatening) calls within eight minutes and 95 per cent of category B/C calls within 19 minutes in rural areas and 14 minutes in urban areas. In 2003–4, 75.7 per cent of life threatening calls resulted in emergency response arriving at the scene of the incident within 8 minutes (74.6 per cent in 2002–3). Twenty-two services met or exceeded the 75 per cent target. For category B/C calls, 11 services responded to 95 per cent or more calls within 14 or 19 minutes.

BLOOD SERVICES

There are four national bodies which co-ordinate the blood donor programme in the UK. Donors give blood at local centres on a voluntary basis.

NATIONAL BLOOD SERVICE, Oak House, Reeds Crescent, Watford, Herts WD24 4QN **T** 01923-486800 **W** www.blood.co.uk

SCOTTISH NATIONAL BLOOD TRANSFUSION SERVICE, 21 Ellens Glen Road, Edinburgh EH17 7QT **T** 0131-536 5700 **W** www.scotblood.co.uk

WELSH BLOOD SERVICE, Ely Valley Road, Talbot Green, Pontyclun CF72 9WB **T** 01443-622000 **W** www.welsh-blood.org.uk

NORTHERN IRELAND BLOOD TRANSFUSION SERVICE, Belfast City Hospital Complex, Lisburn Road, Belfast BT9 7TS **T** 028-9032 1414 **W** www.nibts.org

HOSPICES

Hospice or palliative care may be available for patients with life-threatening illnesses. It may be provided at the patient's home or in a voluntary or NHS hospice or in hospital, and is intended to ensure the best possible quality of life for the patient during their illness, and to provide help and support to both the patient and the patient's family. The National Council for Hospices and Specialist Palliative Care Services co-ordinates NHS and voluntary services in England, Wales and Northern Ireland; the Scottish Partnership Agency for Palliative and Cancer Care performs the same function in Scotland.

NATIONAL COUNCIL FOR HOSPICE AND SPECIALIST PALLIATIVE CARE SERVICES, 1st Floor, 34–44 Britannia Street, London WC1X 9JG **T** 020-7520 8299 **W** www.hospiceinformation.info

SCOTTISH PARTNERSHIP FOR PALLIATIVE CARE, 1A Cambridge Street, Edinburgh EH1 2DY **T** 0131-229 0538 **W** www.palliativecarescotland.org.uk

NHS CHARTERS

The original Patient's Charter was published in 1991 and came into force in 1992; an expanded version was published in 1995. The Charter set out the rights of patients in relation to the standards of service they should expect to receive at all times and standards of service that the NHS aimed to provide.

The Patient's Charter was replaced nationally in 2001 with *Your Guide to the NHS,* which provided information on how to get treatment and gave specific details on minimum standards for patients, targets for the NHS and improvements in the NHS Plan. It also detailed what patients had a right to expect from the NHS and what is expected from patients.

Information for patients about all aspects of the NHS has now been reorganised and is available on the NHS website. **W** www.nhs.uk

COMPLAINTS

There are three levels to the NHS complaints procedure: the first level involves resolution of a complaint locally, following a direct approach to the Patients Advice and Liaison Service (PALS) at the relevant NHS service provider; the second level involves an independent review procedure by the local PCT if the complaint is not resolved locally. As a final resort, patients may approach the Health Service Ombudsman (in Northern Ireland, the Commissioner for Complaints) if they are dissatisfied with the response of the NHS to a complaint.

RECIPROCAL ARRANGEMENTS

Citizens of countries in the European Economic Area (EEA – *see* European Union section) who are resident in the UK are entitled to receive emergency health care either free of charge or for a reduced charge when they are temporarily visiting other member states of the EEA. Form E111, available at post offices, should be obtained before travelling (to be replaced by the European Health Insurance Card from December 2005). There are also bilateral agreements with several other countries, including Australia and New Zealand, for the provision of urgent medical treatment free of charge.

EEA nationals visiting the UK and visitors from other countries with which the UK has bilateral health care agreements, are entitled to receive emergency health care on the NHS on the same terms as it is available to UK residents.

PERSONAL SOCIAL SERVICES

The Secretary of State for Health (in England), the National Assembly for Wales, the Scottish Executive and the Secretary of State for Northern Ireland are responsible, under the Local Authority Social Services Act 1970, for the provision of social services for older people, disabled people, families and children, and those with mental disorders. Personal Social Services are administered by local authorities according to policies with standards set by central and devolved government. Each authority has a Director of Social Services and a Social Services Committee responsible for the social services functions placed upon them. Local authorities provide, enable and commission care after assessing the needs of their population. The private and voluntary sectors also play an important role in the delivery of social services, and an estimated six million people in Great Britain provide substantial regular care for a member of their family.

Under the Care Standards Act 2000, the National Care Standards Commission (NCSC) was set up on 1 April 2002 to regulate social, private and voluntary care services throughout England. In April 2004, under the Health and Social Care (Community Health and Standards) Act 2003, the NCSC was replaced by the Commission for Social Care Inspection (CSCI). The CSCI was established as a single, regulatory authority, incorporating the work formerly carried out by the the Social Services Inspectorate (SSI), the SSI/Audit Commission Joint Review Team and the NCSC. Services such as care homes and children's homes managed by local authorities, domiciliary care services, independent fostering agencies and residential family centres, that were previously regulated by the NCSC, are now registered and inspected by the CSCI. The CSCI ensures that care services are run in accordance with national minimum standards and regulations that have been set by the Government. As well as regulating care services, the CSCI assesses all areas of care services provided by the 150 local authorities in England against a national agenda, ensuring they meet their social services responsibilities through a system of inspections and self-assessment. The CSCI collates information on local services from May to July each year and makes this information available to the public.

COMMISSION FOR SOCIAL CARE INSPECTION (CSCI), 33 Greycoat Street, London SW1P 2QF T 020-7979 2000 W www.csci.org.uk

FINANCE

The Personal Social Services programme is financed partly by central government, with decisions on expenditure allocations being made at local authority level. Spending on personal social services in 2001–2 by central government was £52 million with £13,416 million allocated by local authorities.

STAFF

PERSONAL SOCIAL SERVICES STAFF 2002 (ENGLAND)

Full-time equivalent

Home help service	37,300
Field social workers	35,800
Residential care staff	51,400
Day care establishments staff	29,300
All other staff (including management and administration and ancillary staff)	54,500
Total staff	208,300

Source: National Statistics – Annual Abstract of Statistics 2004 (Crown copyright)

OLDER PEOPLE

Services for older people are designed to enable them to remain living in their own homes for as long as possible. Local authority services include advice, domestic help, meals in the home, alterations to the home to aid mobility, emergency alarm systems, day and/or night attendants, laundry services and the provision of day centres and recreational facilities. Charges may be made for these services. Respite care may also be provided in order to allow carers temporary relief from their responsibilities.

Local authorities and the private sector also provide 'sheltered housing' for older people, sometimes with resident wardens.

If an older person is admitted to a residential home, charges are made according to a means test; if the person cannot afford to pay, the costs are met by the local authority.

In March 2001 a National Service Framework for Older People was published. The framework set national standards and service models of care across health and social service for older people whether they live at home, in residential care or are being cared for in hospital.

DISABLED PEOPLE

Services for disabled people are designed to enable them to remain living in their own homes wherever possible. Local authority services include advice, adaptations to the home, meals in the home, help with personal care, occupational therapy, educational facilities and recreational facilities. Respite care may also be provided in order to allow carers temporary relief from their responsibilities.

Special housing may be available for disabled people who can live independently, and residential accommodation for those who cannot.

FAMILIES AND CHILDREN

Local authorities are required to provide services aimed at safeguarding the welfare of children in need and, wherever possible, allowing them to be brought up by their families. Services include advice, counselling, help in the home and the provision of family centres. Many authorities also provide short-term refuge accommodation for women and children.

DAY CARE

In allocating day care places to children, local authorities give priority to children with special needs, whether in terms of their health, learning abilities or social needs. Since September 2001 the Office for Standards in Education (OFSTED) has been responsible for the regulation and registration of all early years childcare and education provision in England (previously the responsibility of the local authorities). All day care and childminding services which care for children under 8 years of age for more than two hours a day must register with OFSTED and are inspected at least every two years. In March 2003 there were over 1.3 million childcare places and almost 100,000 childcare providers in England.

In Wales, Scotland and Northern Ireland local authorities have responsibility for registration and inspection of day care facilities.

CHILD PROTECTION

Children considered to be at risk of physical injury, neglect or sexual abuse are placed on the local authority's child protection register. Local authority social services staff, schools, health visitors and other agencies work together to prevent and detect cases of abuse. In England as of 31 March 2003 there were 26,600 children on child protection registers, a 3.5 per cent increase from March 2002. Of the children registered during 2002–3, 11,700 were at risk of neglect, 5,700 of physical abuse, 3,000 of sexual abuse and 5,400 of emotional abuse. On 31 March 2003 there were 2,239 children on child protection registers in Wales and 1,608 in Northern Ireland. In Scotland as of 31 March 2002*, there were 2,018 children on local child protection registers.

* 2003 figures for Scotland were not available at the time of going to press.

LOCAL AUTHORITY CARE

Local authorities are required to provide accommodation for children who have no parents or guardians or whose parents or guardians are unable or unwilling to care for them. A family proceedings court may also issue a care order where a child is being neglected or abused, or is not attending school; the court must be satisfied that this would positively contribute to the well-being of the child.

The welfare of children in local authority care must be properly safeguarded. Children may be placed with foster families, who receive payments to cover the expenses of caring for the child or children, or in residential care.

Children's homes may be run by the local authority or by the private or voluntary sectors; all homes are subject to inspection procedures. In England as of 31 March 2002,

59,700 children were in the care of local authorities. Of these, 39,200 were in foster placements.

ADOPTION

Local authorities are required to provide an adoption service, either directly or via approved voluntary societies. In the UK, in 2002, 6,239 children (under 18 years of age) were entered onto the Adopted Children Register; 5,680 in England and Wales, 385 in Scotland and 174 in Northern Ireland.

PEOPLE WITH LEARNING DISABILITIES

Services for people with learning disabilities are designed to enable them to remain living in the community wherever possible. Local authority services include short-term care, support in the home, the provision of day care centres, and help with other activities outside the home. Residential care is provided for the severely or profoundly disabled.

MENTALLY ILL PEOPLE

Under the Care Programme Approach, mentally ill people should be assessed by specialist services and receive a care plan, and a key worker should be appointed for each patient. Regular reviews of the patient's progress should be conducted. Local authorities provide help and advice to mentally ill people and their families, and places in day centres and social centres. Social workers can apply for a mentally disturbed person to be compulsorily detained in hospital. Where appropriate, mentally ill people are provided with accommodation in special hospitals, local authority accommodation, or homes run by private or voluntary organisations. Patients who have been discharged from hospitals may be placed on a supervision register. A Mental Health National Service Framework was published in September 1999 setting national standards on how to prevent and treat mental illness.

NATIONAL INSURANCE

The National Insurance (NI) scheme operates under the Social Security Contributions and Benefits Act 1992 and the Social Security Administration Act 1992, and orders and regulations made thereunder. The scheme is financed by contributions payable by earners, employers and others (*see* below) and by a Treasury grant. Money collected under the scheme is used to finance the National Insurance Fund (from which contributory benefits are paid) and to contribute to the cost of the National Health Service.

NATIONAL INSURANCE FUND

Estimated receipts and payments of the National Insurance Fund for 2004–5:

Receipts	*£000s*
Net National Insurance contributions	62,239,000
Compensation from Consolidated Fund for Statutory Sick Pay and Statutory Maternity Pay recoveries	1,284,000
Income from investments	1,375,000
State scheme premiums	149,000
Other receipts	68,000
Total receipts	65,115,000

Payments	*£000s*
Benefits	55,290,000
Benefits increase due to proposed changes	1,536,000
Personal and stakeholder pensions contracted-out rebates	3,793,000
Age-related rebates for contracted-out money purchase schemes	295,000
Transfers to Northern Ireland	255,000
Administration	1,321,000
Redundancy fund payments (net)	248,000
Other payments	20,000
Total receipts	62,759,000

Balances	*£000s*
Opening balance	27,264,000
Excess of receipts over payments	2,369,000
Balance at end of year	29,633,000

CONTRIBUTIONS

There are six classes of National Insurance contributions (NICs):

Class 1	paid by employees and their employers
Class 1A	paid by employers who provide employees with certain benefits in kind for private use, such as company cars
Class 1B	paid by employers who enter into a Pay As You Earn (PAYE) Settlement Agreement with the Inland Revenue
Class 2	paid by self-employed people
Class 3	voluntary contributions paid to protect entitlement to the State Pension and who do not pay enough NI contributions in another class
Class 4	paid by the self-employed on their taxable profits over a set limit. These are normally paid by self-employed people in addition to Class 2 contributions. Class 4 contributions do not count towards benefits.

The lower and upper earnings limits and the percentage rates referred to below apply from April 2004 to April 2005.

CLASS 1

Class 1 contributions are paid where a person:

- is an employed earner (employee), office holder (e.g. company director) or employed under a contract of service in Great Britain or Northern Ireland
- is 16 or over and under state pension age
- earns at or above the earnings threshold of £91.00 per week (including overtime pay, bonus, commission, etc., without deduction of superannuation contributions)

Class 1 contributions are made up of primary and secondary contributions. Primary contributions are those paid by the employee and these are deducted from earnings by the employer. Since 6 April 2001 the employee's and employer's earnings thresholds have been the same and are referred to as the earnings threshold. Primary contributions are not paid on earnings below the earnings threshold of £91.00. Contributions are payable at the rate of eleven per cent on earnings between the earnings threshold and the upper earnings limit of £610.00 per week (9.4 per cent for contracted-out employment). Above the upper earnings limit one per cent is payable.

Some married women or widows pay a reduced rate of 4.85 per cent on earnings between the earnings threshold and upper earnings limits and one per cent above this. It is no longer possible to elect to pay the reduced rate but those who had reduced liability before 12 May 1977 may retain it so long as certain conditions are met. *See* leaflet CA09 (widows) or leaflet CA13 (married women).

Secondary contributions are paid by employers of employed earners at the rate of 12.8 per cent on all earnings above the earnings threshold of £91.00 per week. There is no upper earnings limit for employers' contributions. Employers operating contracted-out salary related schemes pay reduced contributions of 9.3 per cent; those with contracted-out money-purchase schemes pay 11.8 per cent. The contracted-out rate applies only to that portion of earnings between the earnings threshold and the upper earnings limits. Employers' contributions below and above those respective limits are assessed at the appropriate not contracted-out rate.

CLASS 2

Class 2 contributions are paid where a person is self-employed and is 16 or over and under state pension age. Contributions are paid at a flat rate of £2.05 per week regardless of the amount earned. However, those with earnings of less than £4,215 a year can apply for Small Earnings Exception, e.g. exemption from liability to pay Class 2 contributions. Those granted exemption from Class 2 contributions may pay Class 2 or Class 3 contributions voluntarily. Self-employed earners (whether or not they pay Class 2 contributions) may also be liable to pay Class 4 contributions based on profits. There are special rules for those who are concurrently employed and self-employed.

Married women and widows can no longer choose not to pay Class 2 contributions but those who elected not to pay Class 2 contributions before 12 May 1977 may retain the right so long as certain conditions are met.

Class 2 contributions are collected by the National Insurance Contributions Office (NICO), an executive agency of the Inland Revenue, by direct debit or quarterly bills. *See* leaflets CWL2 and CA02.

CLASS 3

Class 3 contributions are voluntary flat-rate contributions of £7.15 per week payable by persons over the age of 16 who would otherwise be unable to qualify for retirement pension and certain other benefits because they have an insufficient record of Class 1 or Class 2 contributions. This may include those who are not working, those not liable for Class 1 or Class 2 contributions or those excepted from Class 2 contributions. Married women and widows who on or before 11 May 1977 elected not to pay Class 1 (full rate) or Class 2 contributions cannot pay Class 3 contributions while they retain this right. Class 3 contributions are collected by the NICO by quarterly bills or direct debit. *See* leaflet CA08.

CLASS 4

Self-employed people whose profits and gains are over £4,745 a year pay Class 4 contributions in addition to Class 2 contributions. This applies to self-employed earners over 16 and under the state pension age. Class 4 contributions are calculated at eight per cent of annual profits or gains between £4,745 and £31,720 and one per cent above. Class 4 contributions are assessed and collected by the Inland Revenue together with Schedule D tax. It is possible, in some circumstances, to apply for exceptions from liability to pay Class 4 contributions or to have the amount of contribution reduced (where Class 1 contributions are payable on earnings assessed for Class 4 contributions). *See* leaflet CWL2.

PENSIONS

The Social Security Pensions Act (1975) came into force in 1978. It aimed to:

- reduce reliance on means-tested benefit in old age, widowhood and chronic ill-health
- ensure that occupational pension schemes which are contracted out of the state scheme fulfil the conditions of a good scheme
- ensure that pensions are adequately protected against inflation
- ensure that men and women are treated equally in State and occupational schemes

Legislation and regulations introduced since 1978 go further towards fulfilling these aims and more changes came into effect in April 1997. One of the changes is to equalise the state pension age for men (currently 65 years) and women (currently 60 years) from 6 April 2020. The change will be phased in over the ten years leading up to 6 April 2020. As a result the state pension age is as follows:

- the pension age for men remains at 65
- the pension age for women born on or before 5 October 1950 remains at 60
- the pension age for women born on or between 6 October 1950 and 5 October 1951 is 61
- the pension age for women born on or between 6 October 1951 and 5 October 1952 is 62
- the pension age for women born on or between 6 October 1952 and 5 October 1953 is 63
- the pension age for women born on or between 6 October 1953 and 5 October 1954 is 64
- the pension age for women born on 6 October 1954 or later is 65

STATE PENSION SCHEME

The state pension scheme consists of the basic State Pension and the State Second Pension, also known as the Additional Pension, which reformed the State Earnings-Related Pension Scheme (SERPS) from 6 April 2002.

The amount of basic State Pension paid is dependent on the number of 'qualifying years' a person has in their 'working life'. A 'qualifying year' is a tax year in which a person pays enough Class 1 National Insurance contributions (NICs) at the standard rate or class 2 or 3 NICs for the whole year (*see* National Insurance section) for it to count towards their basic State Pension. Those in receipt of Carer's Allowance, Working Tax Credit (with a disability element), Jobseeker's Allowance, Incapacity Benefit, Statutory Sick Pay or Statutory Maternity Pay may have Class 1 NICs credited to them. Persons undertaking certain training courses or jury service or who have been wrongly imprisoned for a conviction which is quashed on appeal may also get class 1 credits for each week they receive benefit or fulfil certain conditions. Class 1 credits count toward all future contributory benefits. A Class 3 credit for basic State Pension and bereavement benefit purposes is awarded, where required, for each week the Working Tax Credit (without a disability element) has been received.

'Working life' is counted from the start of the tax year in which a person reaches 16 to the end of the tax year before the one in which they reach pensionable age: for men this is normally 49 years and for women this varies between 44 and 49 years depending on birth date (*see above*). To get the full rate (100 per cent) basic pension a person must have qualifying years for about 90 per cent of their working life. To get the minimum basic pension (25 per cent) a person will need ten or eleven qualifying years. Married women who are not entitled to a pension on their own NICs may get a pension on their husband's NICs. It is possible for people who are unable to work because they care for children or a sick or disabled person at home to reduce the number of qualifying years required. This is called home responsibilities protection (HRP) and can be given for any tax year since April 1978; the number of years for which HRP is given is deducted from the number of qualifying years needed. From April 2002, HRP may also qualify the recipient for additional State Pension through the State Second Pension.

The amount of Additional Pension paid depends on the amount of earnings a person has, or is treated as having, between the lower and upper earnings limits for each complete tax year between 6 April 1978 (when the scheme started) and the tax year before they reach state pension age. The right to Additional Pension does not depend on the person's right to basic State Pension. The amount of additional State Pension paid also depends on when a person reaches state pension age; changes phased in from 6 April 1999 mean that pensions are calculated differently from that date. Men or women widowed before 6 October 2002 inherit all their late spouse's additional State Pension. From 6 October 2002, the maximum percentage of SERPS that a person can inherit from a late spouse will depend on their late spouse's date of birth:

Maximum % SERPS entitlement for surviving spouse	*d.o.b (men)*	*d.o.b (women)*
100%	5/10/37 or earlier	5/10/42 or earlier
90%	6/10/37 to 5/10/39	6/10/42 to 5/10/44
80%	6/10/39 to 5/10/41	6/10/44 to 5/10/46
70%	6/10/41 to 5/10/43	6/10/46 to 5/10/48
60%	6/10/43 to 5/10/45	6/10/48 to 5/7/50
50%	6/10/45 or later	6/7/50 or later

The maximum State Second Pension a person can inherit from a late spouse is 50 per cent.

There are four categories of State Pension provided under the Social Security Contributions and Benefits Act 1992:

- Category A, a contributory pension made up of a basic State Pension dependent on the number of qualifying years in one's working life and an additional State Pension dependent on earnings since April 1978
- Category B, a contributory pension made up of basic and additional elements, payable to married women, widows and widowers based on their spouse's qualifying years and earnings. From 6 April 2010 both men and women will be able to get a basic State Pension based on their spouse's NICs, if this is better than the pension based on their own NIC record
- Category C, this pension is now obsolete
- Category D, a non-contributory State Pension for those aged 80 and over. Graduated Retirement Benefit is also available to those who paid graduated NICs into the scheme when it existed between April 1961 and April 1975

The Pension Service provides a State Pension forecasting service. T 0845-300 0168

From 1978 to 2002, additional pension was called the State Earnings-Related Pension Scheme (SERPS). SERPS covered all earnings by employees from 6 April 1978 to 5 April 1997 on which standard rate class 1 National Insurance had been paid and earnings between 6 April 1997 and 5 April 2002 if the standard rate class 1 contributions had been contracted-in.

In 2002 The Welfare Reform and Pensions Act 1999 replaced SERPS with State Second Pension, targeted at low and moderate earners and certain carers and people with long-term illness or disability. If earnings on which Class 1 NICs have been paid or can be treated as paid are above the annual National Insurance Lower Earnings Limit (£4,108 for 2004–5) but below the new Low Earnings Threshold (£11,600 for 2004–5), the State Second Pension regards this as earnings of £11,600 and it is treated equivalently. Certain carers and people with long term illness and disability will be considered as at the Low Earnings Threshold for each complete tax year even if they do not work at all, or earn less than the annual Lower Earnings Limit.

CONTRACTED-OUT PENSION SCHEMES

Personal Pension Schemes

Since July 1988, an employee has been able to start a personal pension which, if it meets certain conditions, can be used in place of additional State Pension. These pensions are known as Appropriate Personal Pensions (APPs). That part of an APP derived from the protected rights (rights comprising mainly the NIC rebate and its investment return) is intended to provide benefits broadly equivalent to those given up in the additional State Pension. At retirement, a contracted-out deduction will be made from additional State Pension built up from 6 April 1987 to 5 April 1997. The reduction may be more or less than that part of the pension derived from the protected right. From 6 April 1997 to 5 April 2002, members of an APP scheme will not have built up any entitlement to additional State Pension during the period of their membership. From 6 April 2002, employees contracted-out into a personal pension and earning between the lower earnings limit and the low earnings threshold (£4,108 and £11,600 in 2004–5) will be entitled to a reduced amount of State Second Pension.

Stakeholder Pension Schemes

Introduced in 2001, Stakeholder pensions are available to everyone but are principally for moderate earners who do not have access to a good value company pension scheme. Stakeholder pensions must meet a number of minimum standards to make sure they are flexible and not expensive (the annual management charge is capped). The minimum contribution is £20 per month.

As with personal pensions it is possible to invest up to £3,600 (including tax relief) into stakeholder pensions each year without evidence of earnings. Contributions can be made on someone else's behalf, for example, a non-working partner. Some people who are already members of occupational pension schemes can also contribute to a stakeholder pension scheme. If it meets certain conditions, it can be used to contract out of the State Second Pension (formerly SERPS). When someone contracts out of the State scheme with either an APP or a Stakeholder Pension, both the employee and their employers pay NICs at the full not contracted out rate. At the end of the tax year to which those NICs relate, the Inland Revenue pays an age-related rebate (which increases with age) and tax relief on the employee's share of the rebate directly into to the scheme for investment on behalf of the employee.

OCCUPATIONAL PENSION SCHEMES

Contracted-Out Salary-Related (COSR) Scheme

- this scheme provides a pension related to earnings
- any notional additional pension built up from 6 April 1978 to 5 April 1997 will be reduced by the amount of Guaranteed Minimum Pension (GMP) built up during that period (the contracted-out deduction)
- from 6 April 1997 these schemes no longer provide a GMP. Instead, as a condition of contracting out they have to satisfy a reference scheme test to ensure that the benefits provided are at least as good as a prescribed standard
- when someone contracts out of the additional State Pension through a COSR scheme, both the scheme member and the employer pay a reduced rate of NICs (known as the rebate) to compensate for the State Pension given up

Contracted-Out Money Purchase (COMP) Scheme

- this scheme provides a pension based on the value of the fund at retirement i.e. the money paid in, along with the investment return
- that part of the COMP fund derived from protected rights is intended to provide benefits broadly equivalent to those given up in the additional State Pension
- a contracted-out deduction, which may be more or less than that part of the pension derived from the protected rights will be made from any additional pension built up from 6 April 1988 to 5 April 1997. Between 6 April 1997 and 5 April 2002 members of a COMP scheme will not have built up any entitlement to additional State Pension during the period of their membership
- as with a COSR scheme, when someone contracts out of the additional State Pension through a COMP scheme, both the scheme member and the employer pay a reduced rate of NICs to compensate for the State Pension given up. In addition, at the end of the tax year to which the NICs relate, the Inland Revenue pays an additional age-related rebate direct to the scheme for investment on behalf of the employer

Contracted-Out Mixed Benefit (COMB) Scheme

A mixed benefit scheme has two active sections, one salary related and the other money purchase. Scheme rules set out which section individual employees may join and the circumstances (if any), in which members may move between sections. Each section must satisfy the respective contracting-out conditions for COSR and COMP schemes.

From April 2002, members of contracted-out occupational schemes earning between £4,108 and £26,600 (in 2004–5) may build up entitlement to a reduced amount of State Second Pension as well as that built up in their occupational pension.

COMPLAINTS

The Pensions Advisory Service (OPAS) gives free help and advice to people who have problems with occupational or personal pensions. There are two bodies for pension complaints. The Financial Ombudsman Service deals with complaints which predominantly concern the sale and marketing of occupational, stakeholder and personal pensions. The Pensions Ombudsman deals with complaints which predominantly concern the management (after sale or marketing) of occupational, stakeholder and personal pensions. The Occupational Pensions Regulatory Authority (OPRA) was set up by parliament to help make sure occupational pension schemes are safe and well run, it can impose penalties where there are breaches of the law.

TAX CREDITS

From April 2003 Working Families' Tax Credit, Disabled Person's Tax Credit and the Children's Tax Credit were replaced with Working Tax Credit and Child Tax Credit. Tax Credits are administered by the Inland Revenue and are awarded for up to 12 months, although they can be adjusted during the year to reflect changes of income or circumstances.

WORKING TAX CREDIT

Working Tax Credit is made up of a basic payment with additional payments for couples, lone parents, people working over 30 hours a week, disabled workers and people aged 50 or over returning to work after a period of benefits. The tax credit will be paid with wages to people who are employed and directly to the self-employed. It is available to:

- People with dependant children and/or a disability, working at least 16 hours a week
- People aged 25 or over and working at least 30 hours a week

The aim of the tax credit system is to provide a guaranteed income from full-time work for those aged 25 or over without children or a disability, of £193 a week for couples, and £164 a week for single people.

WORKING TAX CREDIT 2004–5

*Annual Income/status**	*Tax Credit per annum*
£5,000	
Single	–
Couple	–
Single adult with a disability	£3,675
£8,000	
Single	£1,125
Couple	£2,675
Single adult with a disability	£3,230
£10,000	
Single	£385
Couple	£1,935
Single adult with a disability	£2,490
£15,000	
Single	–
Couple	–
Single adult with a disability	£640

* Those with incomes of £5,000 a year are assumed to work part-time (working between 16 and 30 hours a week). In families with an income of £8,000 a year or more, at least one adult is assumed to be working 30 or more hours a week.

CHILD CARE

In families where a lone parent or both partners in a couple work for at least 16 hours a week, or where one partner works and the other is disabled, the family is entitled to child care payments. This payment can contribute up to £135 a week to the cost of child care for one child and up to £200 a week for two or more children. Families can only claim if they use an approved child care provider.

CHILD TAX CREDIT

Child Tax Credit combines all income-related support for children and is paid direct to the main carer. The credit is made up of a main 'family' payment with additional payments for each extra child in the household, for

children with a disability and an extra payment for children who are severely disabled. Child Tax Credit is available to households where:
- There is at least one dependant child under 16 years old
- There is at least one dependant young person under 19 years old and in full-time non-advanced education or registered with the Careers or Connexions Service (does not include Scotland or Northern Ireland)

CHILD TAX CREDIT 2004–5
(£ per year)

	One Child		*Two Children*	
Annual Income	*No Childcare*	*Maximum Childcare*	*No Childcare*	*Maximum Childcare*
0	2,175	2,175	3,800	3,800
5,000	5,295	10,220	6,920	14,225
8,000	4,850	9,775	6,475	13,780
10,000	4,110	9,035	5,735	13,040
15,000	2,260	7,185	3,885	11,190
20,000	545	5,335	2,035	9,340
25,000	545	3,485	545	7,490
30,000	545	1,635	545	5,640
35,000	545	545	545	3,790
40,000	545	545	545	1,940
45,000	545	545	545	545
50,000	545	545	545	545
60,000	–	–	–	–

BENEFITS

Leaflets relating to the various benefits and contribution conditions for different benefits are available from local social security offices; leaflet GL23 *Social Security Benefit Rates* is a general guide to benefit rates and contributions.

CONTRIBUTORY BENEFITS

Entitlement to contributory benefits depends on contribution conditions being satisfied either by the claimant or by some other person (depending on the kind of benefit). The class or classes of contribution which for this purpose are relevant to each benefit are:

Jobseeker's Allowance (contribution-based)	Class 1
Incapacity Benefit	Class 1 or 2
Maternity Allowance	Class 1 or 2
Widow's Benefit and Bereavement Benefit	Class 1, 2 or 3
State Pensions, categories A and B	Class 1, 2 or 3

The system of contribution conditions relates to yearly levels of earnings on which contributions have been paid.

JOBSEEKER'S ALLOWANCE

Jobseeker's allowance (JSA) replaced unemployment benefit and income support for unemployed people under pension age from 7 October 1996. There are two routes of entitlement. Contribution-based JSA is paid as a personal rate (i.e. additional benefit for dependants is not paid) to those who have made sufficient NI contributions in two particular tax years. Savings and partner's earnings are not taken into account and payment can be made for up to six months. Rates of JSA correspond to income support rates.

Claims for this benefit are made through Jobcentre Plus offices and Jobcentres. A person wishing to claim JSA must be unemployed, capable of work and available for any work which they can reasonably be expected to do, usually for at least 40 hours per week. They must agree and sign a 'jobseeker's agreement', which will set out each claimant's plans to find work, and must actively seek work. If they refuse work or training their benefit may be sanctioned for between one and 26 weeks.

A person will be sanctioned from JSA for up to 26 weeks if they have left a job voluntarily without just cause or through misconduct. In these circumstances, it may be possible to receive hardship payments, particularly where the claimant or their family is vulnerable, e.g. if sick or pregnant, or for those with children or caring responsibilities. *See* leaflet JSAL5.

INCAPACITY BENEFIT

Incapacity Benefit is available to those who are incapable of work but cannot get statutory sick pay from their employer. It is not payable to those over State Pension age. However, people who are already in receipt of short-term Incapacity Benefit when they reach State Pension age may continue to receive this benefit for up to 52 weeks. Apart from those people who qualify under the special provisions for people incapacitated in youth, entitlement is based on a person's National Insurance Contribution record. In order to qualify for Incapacity Benefit, two contribution conditions, based on the last three tax years before the year in which benefit is claimed, must be satisfied. The amount of Incapacity Benefit payable may be reduced where a claimant receives more than a specified amount of occupational or personal pension. Severely disabled people aged between 16 and 19 should receive Incapacity Benefit without meeting the national insurance contribution conditions. There are three rates of Incapacity Benefit:
- short-term lower rate for the first 28 weeks of sickness
- short-term higher rate from weeks 29 to 52
- long-term rate from week 53 onwards

The terminally ill and those entitled to the highest rate care component of disability living allowance are paid the long-term rate after 28 weeks. Incapacity benefit is taxable after 28 weeks.

Two rates of age addition are paid with long-term benefit based on the claimant's age when incapacity started. The higher rate is payable where incapacity for work commenced before the age of 35; and the lower rate where incapacity commenced before the age of 45. Increases for dependants are also payable with short and long-term incapacity benefit.

There are two medical tests of incapacity: the 'own occupation' test and the 'personal capability' assessment. Those who worked before becoming incapable of working will be assessed, for the first 28 weeks of incapacity, on their ability to do their own job. After 28 weeks (or from the start of incapacity for those who were not working) claimants are assessed on their ability to carry out a range of work-related activities. *See* leaflets IB1 and IB214. Since October 2001 all new benefit claimants in the 51 Jobcentre Plus areas receive a service combining jobs and benefits advice and support. The government plans to extend this as Jobcentre Plus is rolled out nationally. New Incapacity Benefit claimants will be invited back for work-focused interviews at intervals of not longer than three years. The interviews do not include medical tests, but if the claimant is due for a medical test around the same time, their local office will aim to schedule both together. People who are severely disabled and those who are terminally ill will not be asked to attend these interviews.

BEREAVEMENT BENEFITS

Bereavement benefits replaced widow's benefit on 9 April 2001. Those claiming widow's benefit before this date will continue to receive them under the old scheme for as long as they qualify. The new system provides bereavement benefits for widows and widowers providing that their deceased spouse paid National Insurance contributions. The new system offers benefits in three forms:

Bereavement Payment – may be received by a man or woman who is under the state pension age at the time of their spouse's death, or whose husband or wife was not entitled to a Category A retirement pension when he or she died. It is a single tax-free lump sum of £2,000 payable immediately on becoming a widow or widower

Widowed Parent's Allowance – a taxable benefit payable to the surviving partner if he or she is entitled or treated as entitled to child benefit, or to a widow if she is expecting her husband's baby

Bereavement Allowance – a taxable weekly benefit paid for 52 weeks after the spouse's death. A widow or widower may receive this pension if aged 45 or over at the time of his or her spouse's death or if his or her Widowed Parent's Allowance ends before 52 weeks. If aged 55 or over he or she will receive the full Bereavement Allowance

It is not possible to receive Widowed Parent's Allowance and Bereavement Allowance at the same time. Bereavement benefits and widow's benefit, in any form, cease upon remarriage or are suspended during a period of cohabitation as man and wife without being legally married. *See* leaflet GL14, D49 (D49S for deaths that occur in Scotland).

STATE PENSION: CATEGORIES A AND B

Category A pension is payable for life to men and women who reach State Pension age and who satisfy the contributions conditions. Category B pension is payable for life to married women, widows and widowers and is based on their wife or husband's contributions. It is payable to a married woman only when the wife and husband have claimed their State Pension and they have both reached State Pension age. From April 2010, a married man will be able to qualify for a Category B pension from his wife's contributions providing she was born on or after 6 April 1950. A Category B pension is also payable on widowhood after the State Pension age. This is payable to widows regardless of the age of their husband when he died. At present it is paid to widowers only if their wife had reached State Pension age when she died. Widowers who reach State Pension age on or after 6 April 2010 will be able to get a Category B pension on the same terms as widows. There are special rules for those who are widowed before reaching State Pension age.

Where a person is entitled to both a Category A and Category B pension then only one can be paid. The person can choose which to get. If no choice is made, the most favourable one will be paid.

A person may defer claiming their pension for five years after State Pension age. In doing so they may earn increments which will increase the weekly amount paid when they claim their State Pension. If a married man defers his Category A pension, his wife cannot claim a Category B pension on his contributions but she may earn increments on her State Pension during this time. A woman can defer her Category B pension, and earn increments, even if her husband is claiming his Category A pension.

The basic State Pension is £79.60 per week plus any additional (earnings-related) State Pension the person may be entitled to. An increase of £47.65 is paid for an adult dependant, providing the dependant's earnings do not exceed the rate of Jobseeker's Allowance for a single person (*see* below) and the couple are living together. If the couple are not living together an increase is payable of the dependant's earnings are not above £47.65. Before April 2003 it was also possible to get an increase of Category A and B pensions for a child or children. Since April 2003 provision for children has been made through Child Tax Credits. An age addition of 25p per week is payable with a State Pension if a pensioner is aged 80 or over.

Since 1989 pensioners have been allowed to have unlimited earnings without affecting their State Pension. Income support can be paid where a person's income is below a set level and pensioners may also be entitled to housing and council tax benefits.

GRADUATED RETIREMENT BENEFIT

Graduated NI contributions were first payable from 1961 and were calculated as a percentage of earnings between certain bands. They were discontinued in 1975. Graduated Retirement Benefit is paid in addition to any State Pension. A husband or wife can only get a graduated pension in return for his/her own graduated contributions, but not for his/her spouse's.

Graduated Retirement Benefit is at a weekly rate for each 'unit' of graduated contributions paid by the employee (half a unit or more counts as a whole unit); the rate varies from person to person. A unit of graduated Retirement Benefit can be calculated by adding together all graduated contributions and dividing by 7.5 (men) or 9.0 (women). If a person defers making a claim beyond 65 (60 for a woman), entitlement may be increased by one seventh of a penny per £1 of its weekly rate for each complete week of deferred retirement, as long as the retirement is deferred for a minimum of seven weeks.

In April 2002 the Pension Service, part of the Department for Work and Pensions was set up to provide an improved service for pensioners, through its network of pension centres and local services.

WEEKLY RATES OF BENEFIT *from April 2004*

Jobseeker's Allowance (JSA) (contribution-based)

Person under 18	£33.50
Person aged 18–24	£44.05
Person aged 25 to State Pension age	£55.65

From October 2003 people between 60 and State Pension age can choose to claim Pension Credits instead of JSA.

Short-term Incapacity Benefit

Person under State Pension age – lower rate	£55.90
Person under State Pension age – higher rate	£66.15
Increase for adult dependant	£34.60
Person over State Pension age	£71.15
Person over State Pension age – higher rate	£74.15
Increase for adult dependant	£42.65

Long-term Incapacity Benefit

Person under State Pension age	£74.15
Increase for adult dependant	£44.35
Age addition – lower rate	£7.80
Age addition – higher rate	£15.55

Widow's Benefit (from April 2004)

Widowed mother's allowance	£79.60
Widow's pension, full entitlement (aged 55 and over at time of spouse's death)	£79.60

Amount of widow's pension by age of widow at spouse's death (for deaths occurring before 11 April 1988 refer to the age-points in brackets):

aged 54 (49)	£74.03
aged 53 (48)	£68.46
aged 52 (47)	£62.88
aged 51 (46)	£57.31
aged 50 (45)	£51.74
aged 49 (44)	£46.17
aged 48 (43)	£40.60
aged 47 (42)	£35.02
aged 46 (41)	£29.45
aged 45 (40)	£23.88

Bereavement Benefit (from April 2003)

Bereavement Payment (lump sum)	£2,000.00
Widowed Parent's Allowance	£79.60
Bereavement Allowance, full entitlement (aged 55 and over at time of spouse's death)	£79.60

Amount of Bereavement Allowance by age of widow/widower at spouse's death:

aged 54	£74.03
aged 53	£68.46
aged 52	£62.88
aged 51	£57.31
aged 50	£51.74
aged 49	£46.17
aged 48	£40.60
aged 47	£35.02
aged 46	£29.45
aged 45	£23.88

State Pension: categories A and B

Single person	£79.60
Increase for adult dependant	£47.65

NON-CONTRIBUTORY BENEFITS

These benefits are paid from general taxation and are not dependent on NI contributions. Unless otherwise stated, a benefit is tax-free and is not means tested.

JOBSEEKER'S ALLOWANCE (INCOME-BASED)

Those who do not qualify for contribution-based Jobseeker's Allowance (JSA(c)), those who have exhausted their entitlement to contribution-based JSA or those for whom contribution-based JSA provides insufficient income may qualify for income-based JSA. The amount paid depends on age, number of dependants, amount of income and savings. Income-based JSA comprises of three parts:

- A personal allowance for the jobseeker and his/her partner and an allowance for each child or young person for whom they are responsible (*see* below)
- Premiums for people with special needs
- Premiums for housing costs

The rules of entitlement are the same as for contribution-based JSA.

If one person in a couple was born after 28 October 1957 and neither person in the couple has responsibility for a child or children, then the couple will have to make a joint claim for JSA if they wish to receive income-based JSA.

Since April 2003 claimants have had the option to choose to claim Child Tax Credit instead of an increase of JSA for children.

MATERNITY ALLOWANCE

Maternity Allowance (MA) covers women who are self-employed or otherwise do not qualify for Statutory Maternity Pay (SMP). In order to qualify for payment, a woman must have been employed and/or self-employed for at least 26 weeks in the 66 week period up to and including the week before the baby is due (test period). She must also have average weekly earning of at least £30 (Maternity Allowance Threshold) in any 13 weeks of the test period. Women who are self-employed will be deemed to have earnings at or above the Maternity Allowance Threshold. A woman can choose to start receiving MA from the 11th week before the week in which the baby is due up to the day following the day of birth. This will depend on when the woman stops work to have her baby or if the baby is born before she stops work. However, where the woman is absent from work for pregnancy related illness on or after the Sunday of the 4th week before the baby is due to be born, MA will start the day following the first day of absence from work for a pregnancy related illness. MA is paid up to 26 weeks and is only paid while the woman is not working.

CHILD BENEFIT

Child Benefit is payable for virtually all children aged under 16, and for those aged 16 to 18 who are studying full-time up to and including A-level or equivalent standard. It is also payable for a short period if the child has left school recently and is registered for work or work-based training for young people at a careers office or with the Connexions Service (in Northern Ireland, Training and Employment Agency).

GUARDIAN'S ALLOWANCE

Where the parents of a child are dead, the person who has the child in his/her family may claim a Guardian's Allowance in addition to Child Benefit. In specified circumstances the allowance is payable on the death of only one parent. *See* leaflet NI14.

CARER'S ALLOWANCE

Carer's Allowance (CA) is a benefit payable to people who spend at least 35 hours per week caring for a severely disabled person. To qualify for CA a person must be caring for someone in receipt of one of the following benefits:

- the middle or highest rate of disability living allowance care component
- either rate of attendance allowance
- constant attendance allowance, paid at not less than the normal maximum rate, under the industrial injuries or war pension schemes

See leaflets SD1 and SD4.

SEVERE DISABLEMENT ALLOWANCE

Since April 2001 Severe Disablement Allowance (SDA) has not been available to new claimants. Those claiming SDA before that date will continue to receive it for as long as they qualify. *See* leaflet NI252.

ATTENDANCE ALLOWANCE

This is payable to disabled people who claim after the age of 65 and who need a lot of care or supervision because of physical or mental disability for a period of at least six months. Attendance Allowance has two rates: the lower rate is for day or night care, and the higher rate is for day and night care. People not expected to live for more than six months because of an illness can receive the highest rate of Attendance Allowance straight away. *See* leaflets DS702 and SD1.

DISABILITY LIVING ALLOWANCE
This is payable to disabled people who claim before the age of 65 who have personal care and/or mobility needs because of an illness or disability for a period of at least three months and are likely to have those needs for a further six months or more. The allowance has two components: the care component, which has three rates, and the mobility component, which has two rates. The rates depend on the care and mobility needs of the claimant. People not expected to live for more than six months because of an illness will automatically receive the highest rate of the care component. *See* leaflets DS704 and SD1.

STATE PENSION: CATEGORY D
Category D pension is provided for people aged 80 and over if they are not entitled to another category of pension or are entitled to less than the Category D rate. The person must also normally live in Great Britain and have done so for a continuous period of ten years within any 20-year period since their 60th birthday.

WEEKLY RATES OF BENEFIT *from April 2004*

Jobseeker's Allowance (income-based)	
Person under 18, living with family	£33.50
Person under 18, living away from home	£44.05
Person aged 18–24	£44.05
Person aged 25 to state pension age	£55.65
Couple with one or both under 18	£33.50–£87.30 (depending on circumstances)
Couple aged 18 to state pension age	£87.30
Dependant children and young persons premium up to 16	£42.27
16–19 years	£42.27
Family premium	£15.95
Family premium (lone parent)	£15.95
Maternity Allowance	
Standard rate	£100 or 90% of the women's average weekly earnings if less than £100
Increase for adult dependant	£34.60
Child Benefit	
Eldest child	£16.50
Each subsequent child	£11.05
Guardian's allowance	
Each child	£11.85
Carer's Allowance	£44.35
Increase for dependant adult	£26.50
Severe Disablement Allowance	
*Basic rate	£44.80
Age related addition:	
Under 40	£15.55
40–49	£10.00
50–59	£5.00
Additions may be payable for dependant adults	
Attendance allowance	
Higher rate	£58.80
Lower rate	£39.35
Disability living allowance	
Care component	
Higher rate	£58.80
Middle rate	£39.35
Lowest rate	£15.55
Mobility component	
Higher rate	£41.05
Lower rate	£15.55
State Pension: category D	
Single person	£47.65
Increase for wife/other adult dependant	£28.50
Age addition to State Pension at age 80	£0.25

* The age addition applies to the age when incapacity began

INCOME SUPPORT
Income Support is a benefit for those aged 16 and over whose income is below a certain level. It can be paid to people who are not expected to sign on as unemployed (Income Support for unemployed people was replaced by Jobseeker's Allowance in October 1996) and who are:
– incapable of work due to sickness or disability
– bringing up children alone
– looking after a person who has a disability
– registered blind

Pension Credit replaced Income Support for people aged 60 or over on 6 October 2003. Some people who are not in these categories may also be able to claim income support.

Income Support is also payable to people who work for less than 16 hours a week on average (or 24 hours for a partner). Some people can claim Income Support if they work longer hours.

Income Support is not payable if the claimant, or claimant and partner, have capital or savings in excess of £8,000. For capital and savings in excess of £3,000, a deduction of £1 is made for every £250 or part of £250 held. Different limits apply to people permanently in residential care and nursing homes: the upper limit is £16,000 and deductions apply for capital in excess of £10,000.

Sums payable depend on fixed allowances laid down by law for people in different circumstances. If both partners are entitled to Income Support, either may claim it for the couple. People receiving Income Support may be able to receive Housing Benefit, help with mortgage or home loan interest and help with health care. They may also be eligible for help with exceptional expenses from the Social Fund. Special rates may apply to some people living in residential care or nursing homes. Leaflet IS20 gives a detailed explanation of income support.

In October 1998 the Government's voluntary New Deal for Lone Parents programme became available throughout the UK. All lone parents receiving Income Support are assigned a personal adviser at a Jobcentre who will provide guidance and support with a view to enabling the claimant to find work.

INCOME SUPPORT PREMIUMS
Income Support premiums are additional weekly payments for those with special needs. People qualifying for more than one premium will normally only receive the highest single premium for which they qualify. However,

family premium, disabled child premium, severe disability premium and carer premium are payable in addition to other premiums.

People with children may qualify for:

- the family premium if they have at least one child (a higher rate is paid to lone parents, although from 6 April 1998 it has not been available to new claimants)
- the disabled child premium if they have a child who receives Disability Living Allowance or is registered blind

Carers may qualify for:

- the carer premium if they or their partner are in receipt of Carer's Allowance

Long-term sick or disabled people may qualify for:

- the disability premium if they or their partner are receiving certain benefits because they are disabled or cannot work; are registered blind; or if the claimant has been incapable of work or receiving Statutory Sick Pay for at least 364 days (196 days if the person is terminally ill), including periods of incapacity separated by eight weeks or less
- the severe disability premium if the person lives alone and receives Attendance Allowance or the middle or higher rate of Disability Living Allowance care component and no one receives Carer's Allowance for caring for that person. This premium is also available to couples where both partners meet the above conditions

WEEKLY RATES OF BENEFIT *from April 2004*

Income Support

Single person	
under 18	£33.50
under 18 (higher)	£44.05
aged 18–24	£44.05
aged 25 and over	£55.65
aged under 18 and a single parent (lower)	£33.50
aged under 18 and a single parent (higher)	£44.05
aged 18 and over and a single parent	£55.65
Couples	
Both under 18	£66.50
One or both aged 18 or over	£87.30
For each child in a family from birth to day before 19th birthday	£42.27
Premiums	
Family premium	£15.95
Family (lone parent) premium	£15.95
Disabled child premium	£42.49
Carer premium	£25.55
Disability premium	
Single	£23.70
Couple	£33.85
Enhanced disability premium	
Single	£11.60
Enhanced disabled child premium	£17.08
Severe disability premium	
Lower rate (single person and some couples)	£44.15
Higher rate (couples)	£88.30

PENSION CREDIT

Pension Credit was introduced on 6 October 2003 and replaces Income Support for those aged 60 and over.

There are two elements to Pension Credit:

The Guarantee Credit

The guarantee credit provides a guaranteed minimum income, with additional elements for people who have:

- relevant housing costs
- severe disabilities
- caring responsibilities

Income from State Pension, private pensions, income from capital, earnings and certain benefits are taken into account when calculating the guarantee credit. For savings and capital in excess of £6,000 a deduction of £1 is made for every £500 or part of £500 held.

People receiving the guarantee credit element of Pension Credit may be able to receive Housing Benefit, Council Tax Benefit and help with health care.

The Savings Credit

Single people aged 65 or over (and couples where one member is 65 or over) may be entitled to a Savings Credit which will reward pensioners who have modest income or savings. The Savings Credit is calculated by taking into account any qualifying income above the Savings Credit threshold. For 2004–5 the threshold is £79.60 for single people and £127.25 for couples. The Savings Credit gives pensioners a cash addition calculated at 60p for every pound of qualifying income they have between the Savings Credit threshold and the Guarantee Credit. After this, the maximum reward will be reduced by 40p for every pound of income above the guarantee level. The maximum Savings Credit is £15.51 per week (£20.22 a week for couples).

Income that qualifies towards the Savings Credit includes state pensions, earnings, second pensions and capital above £6,000.

Where only the Savings Credit is in payment, people need to claim standard Housing Benefit or Council Tax Benefit. Although local authorities take any Savings Credit into account in the Housing Benefit/Council Tax Benefit assessment. The Housing Benefit/Council Tax Benefit applicable amount for people aged 65 and over is enhanced to ensure that gains in Pension Credit are not depleted.

WEEKLY RATES OF BENEFIT *from April 2004*

Standard minimum guarantee:	
Single	£105.45
Couple	£160.95
Additional amount for:	
Severe disability	£44.15
Carers	£25.55
Savings Credit threshold	
Single	£79.60
Couple	£127.25

HOUSING BENEFIT

Housing Benefit is designed to help people with rent (including rent for accommodation in guesthouses, lodgings or hostels). It does not cover mortgage payments. The amount of benefit paid depends on:

- the income of the claimant, and partner if there is one, including earned income, unearned income (any other income including some other benefits) and savings
- number of dependants
- certain extra needs of the claimant, partner or any dependants
- number and gross income of people sharing the home who are not dependent on the claimant
- how much rent is paid

Housing Benefit is not payable if the claimant, or claimant and partner, have savings of over £16,000. The amount of benefit is affected if savings held exceed £3,000 (£6,000 for pensioners and £10,000 for people living in care homes). Housing Benefit is not paid for meals, fuel or certain service charges that may be included in the rent. Deductions are also made for most non-dependants who live in the same accommodation as the claimant (and their partner).

The maximum amount of benefit (which is not necessarily the same as the amount of rent paid) may be paid where the claimant is in receipt of Income Support or income-based Jobseeker's Allowance or where the claimant's income is less than the amount allowed for their needs. Any income over that allowed for their needs will mean that their benefit is reduced. *See* leaflets GL16 and RR2.

COUNCIL TAX BENEFIT

Nearly all the rules which apply to Housing Benefit apply to Council Tax Benefit, which helps people on low incomes to pay council tax bills. The amount payable depends on how much council tax is paid and who lives with the claimant. The benefit may be available to those receiving Income Support or income-based Jobseeker's Allowance or to those whose income is less than that allowed for their needs. Any income over that allowed for their needs will mean that their Council Tax Benefit is reduced. Deductions are made for non-dependants.

The maximum amount that is payable for those living in properties in council tax bands A to E is 100 per cent of the claimant's council tax liability. This also applies to those living in properties in bands F to H who were in receipt of the benefit at 31 March 1998 if they have remained in the same property. From 1 April 1998 council tax benefit for new claimants living in property bands F to H (or existing claimants moving into these bands) was restricted to the level payable for band E.

If a person shares a home with one or more adults (not their partner) who are on a low income, it may be possible to claim a second adult rebate. Those who are entitled to both Council Tax Benefit and second adult rebate will be awarded whichever is the greater. Second adult rebate may be claimed by those not in receipt of Council Tax Benefit.

ONE-OFF 70+ PAYMENT

In 2004 the Government made a one-off payment of up to £100 to each household with one occupier aged 70 or over to help them with living expenses, including council tax bills. To be eligible for the payment, the person had to reside in the UK on any day of the week between 20–26 September 2004 and have reached the age of 70 on or before 26 September 2004. The payment was a tax-free lump sum that did not affect any state pensions or benefits received. The One-off 70+ Payment was paid automatically with the Winter Fuel Payment.

THE SOCIAL FUND

REGULATED PAYMENTS

Sure Start Maternity Grant

The Sure Start Maternity Grant (SSMG) is a one-off payment of £500 for parents on low incomes to buy essential items for new babies. To qualify, mothers and expectant mothers must also receive health and welfare advice for themselves and their child from an approved health professional. SSMG can be claimed any time from the 29th week of pregnancy until the child is three months old. Those eligible are mothers or their partners in receipt of Income Support, income-based Jobseeker's Allowance, Child Tax Credit at a rate higher than the family element or Working Tax Credit where a disability or severe disability element is in payment.

Funeral Payments

Payable for the necessary cost of burial or cremation, plus other funeral expenses reasonably incurred up to £700, to people receiving Income Support, income-based Jobseeker's Allowance, Child Tax Credit at a higher rate than the family element, Working Tax Credit where a disability or severe disability element is in payment, Council Tax Benefit or Housing Benefit who have good reason for taking responsibility for the funeral expenses. These payments are recoverable from any estate of the deceased.

Cold Weather Payments

A payment of £8.50 when the average temperature over seven consecutive days is recorded at or forecast to be 0°C or below in the qualifying person's area. Payments are made to people on Income Support or income-based Jobseeker's Allowance and those who have a child under five or whose benefit includes a pensioner or disability premium. Payments do not have to be repaid.

Winter Fuel Payments

An annual payment of £200 per household paid to most people aged 60 or over. The majority of eligible people are paid automatically before Christmas, although a few need to claim. Payments do not have to be repaid.

DISCRETIONARY PAYMENTS

Community Care Grants

These are intended to help people on Income Support or income-based Jobseeker's Allowance or receiving payments on account of such benefits (or those likely to receive these benefits on leaving residential or institutional accommodation) to live as independently as possible in the community; ease exceptional pressures on families; care for a prisoner or young offender released on temporary licence; help people set up home as part of a resettlement programme and/or assist with certain travelling expenses. They do not have to be repaid.

Budgeting Loans

These are interest-free loans to people who have been receiving Income Support or income-based Jobseeker's Allowance, or payments on account of such benefits for at least 26 weeks, for intermittent expenses that may be difficult to budget for.

Crisis Loans

These are interest-free loans to anyone, whether receiving benefits or not, who is without resources in an emergency, where there is no other means of preventing serious damage or serious risk to their health or safety.

SAVINGS

Savings over £500 (£1,000 for people aged 60 or over) are taken into account for Community Care Grants and Budgeting Loans. All savings are taken into account for Crisis Loans. Savings are not taken into account for Sure Start Maternity Grants, Funeral Payments, Cold Weather or Winter Fuel Payments.

INDUSTRIAL INJURIES AND DISABLEMENT BENEFITS

The industrial injuries scheme, administered under the Social Security Contributions and Benefits Act 1992, provides a range of benefits designed to compensate for disablement resulting from an industrial accident (i.e. an accident arising out of and in the course of an employed earner's employment) or from a prescribed disease due to the nature of a person's employment. Those who are self-employed are not covered by this scheme.

INDUSTRIAL INJURIES DISABLEMENT BENEFIT

A person must be at least 14 per cent disabled (except for certain respiratory diseases) in order to qualify for this benefit. The amount paid depends on the degree of disablement:

- those assessed as 14–19 per cent disabled are paid at the 20 per cent rate
- those with disablement of over 20 per cent will have the percentage rounded up or down to the nearest ten per cent, e.g. a disablement of 44 per cent will be paid at the 40 per cent rate while a disablement of 45 per cent will be paid at the 50 per cent rate

Benefit is payable 15 weeks (90 days) after the date of the accident or onset of the disease and may be payable for a limited period or for life. The benefit is payable whether the person works or not and those who are incapable of work are entitled to draw statutory sick pay or incapacity benefit in addition to industrial injuries disablement benefit. It may also be possible to claim the following allowances:

- reduced earnings allowance for those who are unable to return to their regular work or work of the same standard and who had their accident (or whose disease started) before 1 October 1990
- retirement allowance for those who were entitled to reduced earnings allowance who have reached State Pension age
- constant attendance allowance for those with a disablement of 100 per cent who need constant care. There are four rates of allowance depending on how much care the person needs
- exceptionally severe disablement allowance for those who are entitled to constant care attendance allowance at one of the higher rates and who need constant care permanently

See leaflets SD6, SD7 and SD8.

OTHER BENEFITS

People who are disabled because of an accident or disease that was the result of work that they did before 5 July 1948 are not entitled to industrial injuries disablement benefit. They may, however, be entitled to payment under the workmen's compensation scheme or the pneumoconiosis, byssinosis and miscellaneous diseases benefit scheme. *See* leaflet GL23. People who suffer from certain industrial diseases caused by dust, or their dependants, can make a claim for an additional payment under the Pneumoconiosis etc. (Workers' Compensation) Act 1979 if they are unable to get damages from the employer who caused or contributed to the disease.

WEEKLY RATES OF BENEFIT *from April 2004*

*Disablement benefit/pension	
Degree of disablement:	
100 per cent	£120.10
90	£108.09
80	£96.08
70	£84.07
60	£72.06
50	£60.05
40	£48.04
30	£36.03
20	£24.02
Unemployability supplement	£74.15
Addition for adult dependant (subject to earnings rule)	£44.35
Reduced earnings allowance (maximum)	£48.04
Retirement allowance (maximum)	£12.01
Constant attendance allowance (normal maximum rate)	£48.10
Exceptionally severe disablement allowance	£48.10

* There is a weekly benefit for those under 18 with no dependants which is set at a lower rate

CLAIMS AND QUESTIONS

Entitlement to benefit and regulated Social Fund payments is determined by a decision maker on behalf of the Secretary of State for the Department of Work and Pensions. A claimant who is dissatisfied with that decision can ask for an explanation. They can dispute the decision by applying to have it revised or, in particular circumstances, superseded. If they are still dissatisfied they can go to the Appeals Service where it will be heard by an independent tribunal. There is a further right of appeal to a Social Security Commissioner against the tribunal's decision but this is on a point of law only and leave to appeal must first be obtained.

Decisions on claims and applications for Housing Benefit and Council Tax Benefit are made by Local Authority decision makers. The explanation, dispute and appeals process is the same as for other benefits. *See* leaflets GL24 and NI260DMA.

Decisions on applications to the discretionary Social Fund are made by Social Fund Officers. Applicants can ask for a review within 28 days of the date on the decision letter. The Social Fund Review Officer will review the case and there is a further right of review by an independent Social Fund Inspector.

EMPLOYER PAYMENTS

STATUTORY MATERNITY PAY

Employers pay Statutory Maternity Pay (SMP) to pregnant women who have been employed by them full or part-time for at least 26 weeks into the 15th week before the week the baby is due, and whose earnings on average at least equal the lower earnings limit applied to NI contributions (£79 per week from April 2004). All women who meet these conditions receive payment of 90 per cent of their average earnings for the first six weeks, followed by a maximum of 20 weeks at £102.80 or 90 per cent of the woman's average weekly earnings if this is less than £102.80. SMP can be paid, at the earliest, 11 weeks before the week in which the baby is due, up to the day following the birth. Women can decide when they wish their maternity leave to start and can work until the baby is born. However, where the woman is absent from work for a pregnancy related illness on or after the

Sunday of the 4th week before the baby is due to be born, SMP will start the day following the first day of absence from work for the pregnancy related illness. SMP is not payable for any week in which the woman works. Employers are reimbursed for 92 per cent of the SMP they pay. Small employers with annual gross NI payments of £45,000 or less recover 100 per cent of the SMP paid out plus 4.5 per cent in compensation for the secondary National Insurance Contributions paid on SMP. *See* Leaflet NI17A and Inland Revenue guide for employers E15.

STATUTORY PATERNITY PAY

Employers pay Statutory Paternity Pay (SPP) to employees who are taking leave when a child is born or placed for adoption. To qualify the employee must:

- have responsibility for the child's upbringing
- be the biological father of the child (or the child's adopter), or the husband/partner of the mother or adopter
- be taking time off work to care for the child and/or support the mother or adopter
- have been employed by the same employer for at least 26 weeks ending with the 15th week before the baby is due (or the week in which the adopter is notified of having been matched with a child)
- continue working for the employer up to the child's birth (or placement for adoption)
- have earnings on average at least equal to the lower earnings limit applied to NI contributions (£79 per week from April 2004)

Employees who meet these conditions receive payment of £102.80 or 90 per cent of the employee's average weekly earnings if this is less than £102.80. The employee can choose to be paid for one or two consecutive weeks. The earliest the SPP period can begin is the date of the child's birth or placement for adoption. The SPP period must be completed within eight weeks of that date. SSP is not payable for any week in which the employee works. Employers are reimbursed in the same way as for Statutory Maternity Pay. *See* Department of Trade and Industry leaflet PL514 and PL515.

STATUTORY ADOPTION PAY

Employers pay Statutory Adoption Pay (SAP) to employees taking adoption leave from their employers. To qualify for SAP the employee must:

- be newly matched with a child by an adoption agency
- have been employed by the same employer for at least 26 weeks ending the week in which they have been notified of being matched with a child
- have earnings at least equal to the lower earnings limit applied to NI contributions (£79 per week from April 2004)

Employees who meet these conditions receive payment of £102.80 or 90 per cent of their average weekly earnings if this is less than £102.80 for up to 26 weeks. The SAP period can start from the date of the child's placement. SAP is not payable for any week in which the employee works. Where a couple adopt a child only one of them may receive SAP, the other may be able to receive Statutory Paternity Pay (SPP) if they meet the eligibility criteria. Employers are reimbursed in the same way as for Statutory Maternity Pay. *See* Department of Trade and Industry leaflet PL515.

STATUTORY SICK PAY

Employers pay Statutory Sick Pay (SSP) for up to 28 weeks to any employee incapable of work for four or more consecutive days. SSP is payable to employees between the ages of 16 and 65 who have average earnings at or above the point at which earnings become relevant for NI purposes (£79 from April 2004) in a specified period. SSP is paid at £66.15 per week and is subject to PAYE and NI contributions. Employees who cannot obtain SSP may be able to claim Incapacity Benefit. Employers may be able to recover some SSP costs. *See* Inland Revenue Leaflets CA86 *Employees* and CA30 *Employer Manual.*

WAR PENSIONS

The Veteran's Agency (originally known as The War Pensions Agency) became an executive agency of the Ministry of Defence in June 2001. The Agency awards war pensions under the Naval, Military and Air Forces, Etc. (Disablement and Death) Service Pensions Order 1983 to members of the armed forces in respect of disablement or death due to service. There is also a scheme for civilians and civil defence workers in respect of the 1939–45 war, and other schemes for groups such as merchant seamen and Polish armed forces who served under British command during World War II.

PENSIONS

War disablement pension is awarded for the disabling effects of any injury, wound or disease which is the result of, or has been aggravated by, conditions of service in the armed forces. Claims can only be considered once the person has left the armed forces. The amount of pension paid depends on the severity of disablement, which is assessed by comparing the health of the claimant with that of a healthy person of the same age and sex. The person's earning capacity or occupation are not taken into account in this assessment. A pension is awarded if the person has a disablement of 20 per cent or more and a lump sum is usually payable to those with a disablement of less than 20 per cent. No award is made for noise-induced sensorineural hearing loss where the assessment of disablement is less than 20 per cent.

War widow/widower's pension is payable where the spouse's death was due to, or hastened by, service in the armed forces or where the spouse was in receipt of a war disablement pension constant attendance allowance (or would have been if not in hospital) at the time of death. A war widow/widower's pension is also payable if the spouse was getting War Disablement Pension at the 80 per cent rate or higher and was receiving unemployability supplement at the time of death. War widows/widowers receive a standard rank-related rate but a lower weekly rate is payable to war widows/widowers of personnel below the rank of Major who are under the age of 40, without children and capable of maintaining themselves. This is increased to the standard rate at age 40. Allowances are paid for children (in addition to child benefit) and adult dependants. An age allowance is automatically given when the widow/widower reaches 65 and increased at ages 70 and 80.

All war pensions and war widow/widower's pensions are tax-free and pensioners living overseas receive the same amount as those resident in the UK.

SUPPLEMENTARY ALLOWANCES

A number of supplementary allowances may be awarded to a war pensioner which are intended to meet various needs which may result from disablement or death and take account of its particular effect on the pensioner or spouse. The principal supplementary allowances are unemployability supplement, allowance for lowered standard of occupation and constant attendance allowance. Others include exceptionally severe disablement allowance, severe disablement occupational allowance, treatment allowance, mobility supplement, comforts allowance, clothing allowance, age allowance and widow/widower's age allowance. Rent and children's allowances are also available on war widow/widower's pensions.

DEPARTMENT FOR WORK AND PENSIONS BENEFITS

Most benefits are paid in addition to the basic war disablement pension or war widow/widower's pension, but may be affected by supplementary allowances in payment. Any State Pension for which a war widow/ widower qualifies on their own NI contribution record can be paid in addition to war widow/widower's pension.

CLAIMS AND QUESTIONS

To claim a war pension it is necessary to contact the nearest war pensioners' welfare service office, the address of which is available from local social security offices, or to write to the Veteran's Agency, Norcross, Blackpool FY5 3WP. Claims can also be made through authorised agents, usually ex-service organisations such as the RBL, BLESMA etc. General advice on any war pensions matter can be obtained by ringing the War Pensions Freeline (UK only) on 0800-169 2277. If living overseas, call T (+44) (125) 386-6043 E help@veteransagency.mod.uk W www.veteransagency.mod.uk

THE WATER INDUSTRY

ENGLAND AND WALES

The water industry supplies around 18,000 million litres of water every day. In 2002 water companies in England and Wales carried out around 2.9 million tests on drinking water samples of which 99.87 per cent met all British and European standards. In England and Wales the Secretary of State for Environment, Food and Rural Affairs and the National Assembly for Wales have overall responsibility for water policy and oversee environmental standards for the water industry.

THE WATER COMPANIES

Until 1989 nine regional water authorities in England and the Welsh Water Authority in Wales were responsible for water supply and the development of water resources, sewerage and sewage disposal, pollution control, freshwater fisheries, flood protection, water recreation and environmental conservation. The Water Act 1989 provided for the creation of a privatised water industry under public regulation. The functions of the regional water authorities were taken over by ten holding companies and the regulatory bodies and have since been consolidated into the Water Industry Act 1991.

Water UK is the industry association that represents all UK water and wastewater service suppliers at national and European level. Water UK provides a framework for the water industry to engage with government, regulators, stakeholder organisations and the public. Water UK is funded directly by its members who are the service suppliers for England, Scotland, Wales and Northern Ireland; every member has a seat on the Water UK Council.

WATER UK, 1 Queen Anne's Gate, London SW1H 9BT T 020-7344 1844 W www.water.org.uk
Chief Executive, Pamela Taylor

WATER SERVICE COMPANIES

ANGLIAN WATER SERVICES LTD, Anglian House, Ambury Road, Huntingdon, Cambs PE29 3NZ T 01480-323000 W www.anglianwater.co.uk

BOURNEMOUTH & WEST HAMPSHIRE WATER PLC, George Jessel House, Francis Avenue, Bournemouth, Dorset BH11 8NB T 01202-591111 W www.bwhwater.co.uk

BRISTOL WATER PLC, PO Box 218, Bridgwater Road, Bristol BS99 7AU T 0117-966 5881 W www.bristolwater.co.uk

CAMBRIDGE WATER PLC, 41 Rustat Road, Cambridge CB1 3QS T 01223-403000 W www.cambridge-water.co.uk

CHOLDERTON & DISTRICT WATER COMPANY, Estate Office, Cholderton, Salisbury, Wiltshire SP4 0DR T 01980-629203

DEE VALLEY WATER PLC, Packsaddle, Wrexham Road, Rhostyllen, Wrexham LL14 4EH T 01978-846946

DWR CYMRU CYFYNGEDIG (WELSH WATER), Pentwyn Road, Nelson, Treharris, Mid Glamorgan CF46 6LY T 01443-452300 W www.dwrcymru.co.uk

ESSEX & SUFFOLK WATER PLC (subsidiary of Northumbrian Water Ltd), Hall Street, Chelmsford, Essex CM2 0HH T 01245-491234 W www.eswater.co.uk

FOLKSTONE & DOVER WATER SERVICES LTD, Cherry Garden Lane, Folkestone, Kent CT19 4QB T 01303-298800

MID KENT WATER PLC, Snodland, Kent ME6 5AH T 01634-873111 W www.midkentwater.co.uk

NORTHUMBRIAN WATER LTD, Abbey Road, Pity Me, Durham DH1 5FJ T 0191-383 2222 W www.nwl.co.uk

PORTSMOUTH WATER PLC, PO Box 8, West Street, Havant, Hampshire PO9 1LG T 02392-499888 W www.portsmouthwater.co.uk

SEVERN TRENT PLC, 2297 Coventry Road, Birmingham B26 3PU T 0121-722 4000 W www.severn-trent.com

SOUTH EAST WATER PLC, 3 Church Road, Haywards Heath, West Sussex RH16 3NY T 01444-448200 W www.southeastwater.co.uk

SOUTH STAFFORDSHIRE WATER PLC, Green Lane, Walsall, West Midlands WS2 7PD T 01922-638282 W www.south-staffs-water.co.uk

SOUTH WEST WATER LTD, Peninsula House, Rydon Lane, Exeter EX2 7HR T 01392-446688 W www.swwater.co.uk

SOUTHERN WATER, Southern House, Yeoman Road, Worthing, W. Sussex BN13 3NX T 01903-264444 W www.southernwater.co.uk

SUTTON AND EAST SURREY WATER PLC, London Road, Redhill, Surrey RH1 1LY T 01737-772000 W www.waterplc.com

TENDRING HUNDRED WATER SERVICES LTD, Mill Hill, Manningtree, Essex CO11 2AZ T 01206-399200 W www.thws.co.uk

THAMES WATER UTILITIES LTD, 14 Cavendish Place, London W1M 0NU T 020-7636 8686 W www.thameswater.com

THREE VALLEYS WATER PLC, PO Box 48, Bishops Rise, Hatfield, Hertfordshire AL10 9HL T 01707-268111 W www.3valleys.co.uk

UNITED UTILITIES WATER PLC, Dawson House, Liverpool Road, Great Sankey, Warrington WA5 3LW T 01925-234000 W www.unitedutilities.com

WESSEX WATER SERVICES LTD, Claverton Down, Bath BA2 7WW T 01225-526000 W wessexwater.co.uk

YORKSHIRE WATER SERVICES LTD, Western House, Western Way, Halifax Road, Bradford BD6 2LZ T 01274-600111 W www.yorkshirewater.com

ISLAND WATER AUTHORITIES (NOT MEMBERS OF WATER UK)

COUNCIL OF THE ISLES OF SCILLY, Town Hall, St Mary's, Isles of Scilly TR21 0LW T 01720-422902

ISLE OF MAN WATER AUTHORITY, Drill House, Tromode Road, Isle of Man IM2 5PA T 01624-624414

JERSEY NEW WATERWORKS COMPANY LTD, Mulcaster House, Westmount Road, St Helier, Jersey JE1 1DG T 01534-509999

STATES OF GUERNSEY WATER BOARD, PO Box 30, South Esplanade, St Peter Port, Guernsey GY1 3AS T 01481-724552 W www.gov.gg

WATER SUPPLY AND CONSUMPTION 2002–3

	Supply		*Consumption*			
	Supply from Treatment Works (Ml/day)	*Total Leakage (Ml/day)*	*Household (l/head/day) Unmetered*	*Metered*	*Non-household (l/prop/day) Unmetered*	*Metered*
WATER AND SEWERAGE COMPANIES						
Anglian	1,150	192	159	123	254	3,003
Dwr Cymru	883	234	151	140	705	2,409
Northumbrian	736	153	146	128	831	4,355
Severn Trent	1,929	514	129	132	600	2,185
South West	447	84	159	138	1,481	1,614
Southern	595	92	162	148	550	2,631
Thames	2,842	943	165	149	962	3,334
United Utilities	1,952	465	149	128	759	2,642
Wessex	368	75	147	129	2,636	2,393
Yorkshire	1,299	296	146	137	123	2,879
Total	12,201	3,048	—	—	—	—
Average	—	—	150	135	771	2,702
WATER ONLY COMPANIES						
Total	3,203	559	—	—	—	—
Average	—	—	153	137	885	2,701

Source: Office of Water Services

REGULATORY BODIES

The Office of Water Services (Ofwat) was set up under the Water Act 1989 and is the independent economic regulator of the water and sewerage companies in England and Wales. Overall responsibility for water policy and overseeing environmental standards for the water industry lies with the Department for Environment, Food and Rural Affairs and the Welsh Assembly. Ofwat's main duty is to ensure that the companies can finance and carry out their statutory functions and to protect the interests of water customers. Ofwat is a non-ministerial government department headed by the Director-General of Water Services.

Under the Competition Act 1998, from 1 March 2000 the Competition Appeal Tribunal has heard appeals against the regulator's decisions regarding anti-competitive agreements and abuse of a dominant position in the marketplace. The 2003 Water Bill placed a new duty on Ofwat to have regard to sustainable development.

The Environment Agency was set up by the 1995 Environment Act as a non-departmental public body and is sponsored largely by the Department for Environment, Food and Rural Affairs and the Welsh Assembly. The Environment Agency has statutory duties and powers in relation to water resources, pollution control, flood defence, fisheries, recreation, conservation and navigation in England and Wales. They are also responsible for issuing permits, licences, consents and registrations such as industrial licences to abstract water and fishing licences.

The Drinking Water Inspectorate (DWI) is the drinking water quality regulator for England and Wales, responsible for assessing the quality of the drinking water supplied by the water companies and investigating any incidents affecting drinking water quality, initiating prosecution where necessary. The DWI also provides scientific advice on drinking water policy issues to the Department of the Environment, Food and Rural Affairs and the Welsh Assembly.

OFWAT, Centre City Tower, 7 Hill Street, Birmingham, B5 4UA
T 0121-625 1300 E enquiries@ofwat.gsi.gov.uk
W www.ofwat.gov.uk
Director-General: Philip Fletcher

METHODS OF CHARGING

In England and Wales, most domestic customers still pay for domestic water supply and sewerage services through charges based on the old rateable value of their property. It is expected that by March 2005 about 26 per cent of householders will be charged according to consumption, which is recorded by meter. Industrial and most commercial customers are charged according to consumption.

Under the Water Industry Act 1999, water companies can continue basing their charges on the old rateable value of property. Domestic customers can continue paying on an unmeasured basis unless they choose to pay according to consumption. After having a meter installed (which is free of charge), a customer can revert to unmeasured charging within 12 months. Domestic, school and hospital customers cannot be disconnected for non-payment.

Price Limits for the period 2000–5 were set by Ofwat in November 1999. Price limits for the period 2005–10 will be finalised by Ofwat in December 2004.

AVERAGE HOUSEHOLD WATER BILLS 2004–5

	Unmetered (£)	*Metered (£)*
Water	122	101
Sewerage	136	121
Combined	258	222

SCOTLAND

Overall responsibility for national water policy in Scotland rested with the Secretary of State for Scotland until July 1999 when it was devolved to the Scottish Ministers. Until The Local Government (Scotland) Act 1994, water supply and sewerage services were local authority responsibilities. The Central Scotland Water Development Board had the function of developing new sources of water supply for the purpose of providing water in bulk to water authorities whose limits of supply were within the Board's area. Under the Act, three new public water authorities, covering the north, east and west of Scotland respectively, took over the provision of water and sewerage services from April 1996. The Central Scotland Water Development Board was then abolished. The Act also established the Scottish Water and Sewerage Customers Council representing consumer interests. It monitored the performance of the authorities; approved charges schemes; investigated complaints; and advised the Secretary of State. The Water Industry Act 1999, whose Scottish provisions were accepted by the Scottish Executive, abolished the Scottish Water and Sewerage Customers Council and replaced it in November 1999 by a Water Industry Commissioner.

The Water Industry (Scotland) Act 2002 resulted from the Scottish Executive's proposal that a single authority was better placed than three separate authorities to harmonise changes across the Scottish water industry. In 2002 the three existing water authorities, East of Scotland Water, North of Scotland Water and West of Scotland Water merged to form Scottish Water. Scottish Water is a public sector company, structured and managed like a private company, but remains answerable to the Scottish Parliament. Scottish Water is regulated by the Water Industry Commissioner for Scotland, the Scottish Environment Protection Agency (SEPA), and the Drinking Water Quality Regulator for Scotland. The Water Industry Commissioner is responsible for regulating all aspects of economic and customer service performance, including water and sewerage charges and SEPA is responsible for environmental issues, including controlling pollution and promoting the cleanliness of Scotland's rivers, lochs and coastal waters.

SCOTTISH WATER, 26 Castle Drive, Carnegie Campus, Dunfermline KY11 8GG **T** 01383-848200 **W** www.scottishwater.co.uk

SCOTTISH ENVIRONMENT PROTECTION AGENCY, Erskine Court, Castle Business Park, Stirling FK9 4TR **T** 01786-457700 **W** www.sepa.org.uk

WATER INDUSTRY COMMISSIONER FOR SCOTLAND, Ochil House, Springkerse Business Park, Stirling, FK7 7XE **T** 01786-430200 **W** www.watercommissioner.co.uk

METHODS OF CHARGING

Scottish Water sets charges for domestic and non-domestic water and sewerage provision through charges schemes which are regulated by the Water Industries Commissioner for Scotland. In February 2004 the harmonisation of all household charges across the country was completed following the merger of the separate authorities under Scottish Water.

NORTHERN IRELAND

In Northern Ireland ministerial responsibility for water services lies with The Minister of the Department for Regional Development. The Water Service, which is an executive agency of the Department for Regional Development, is responsible for policy and co-ordination with regard to supply, distribution and cleanliness of water, and the provision and maintenance of sewerage services.

The Water Service comprises four Divisions: Eastern, Northern, Western and Southern. The main divisional offices are based in Belfast, Ballymena, Londonderry and Craigavon.

METHODS OF CHARGING

The Water service is currently funded from public funds and direct charges. The department's policy is to meter all properties that are not exclusively domestic. They are, however, granted an allowance of 200 cubic metres per annum to reflect domestic usage – this is known as the domestic usage allowance. Customers are charged only for water used in excess of the domestic usage allowance together with a standing charge, which is intended to cover the costs of meter provision, maintenance, reading and billing. This allowance is not granted if rates are not paid on the property. Traders operating from de-rated, rate exempt or rate rebated premises are required to pay for the treatment and disposal of trade effluent which they discharge into the public sewer.

In December 2002, the Northern Ireland Office announced that water and sewerage services would become self-financed by 2006. Domestic customers would be charged directly for water and sewerage services, currently a proportion of the rates paid on domestic properties. Following a major public consultation on *The Reform of the Water and Sewerage Services In Northern Ireland* the initial conclusions from the Department for Regional Development was that the new domestic charge would included a fixed element and a variable element, the latter determined by property value or consumption.

NORTHERN IRELAND WATER SERVICE, Northland House, 3 Frederick Street, Belfast, BT1 2NR **T** 028-90 244711 **W** www.waterni.gov.uk

ENERGY

The main primary sources of energy in Britain are oil, natural gas, coal, nuclear power and water power. The main secondary sources (e.g. sources derived from the primary sources) are electricity, coke and smokeless fuels and petroleum products. The Department for the Environment, Food and Rural Affairs (DEFRA) is responsible for promoting energy efficiency.

INDIGENOUS PRODUCTION OF PRIMARY FUELS
Million tonnes of oil equivalent

	2003
Coal	19.3
Petroleum	116.2
Natural gas	103.9
Primary electricity	20.9
Nuclear	20.5
Natural flow hydro	0.4
Total	260.4

Source: Department of Trade and Industry

INLAND ENERGY CONSUMPTION BY PRIMARY FUEL
Million tonnes of oil equivalent, seasonally adjusted

	2003
Coal	42.7
Petroleum	74.9
Natural gas	98.0
Primary electricity	21.1
Nuclear	20.5
Natural flow hydro	0.4
Net Imports	0.2
Total	236.7

Source: Department of Trade and Industry

TRADE IN FUELS AND RELATED MATERIALS 2003

	*Quantity**	*Value†*
Imports		
Coal and other solid fuel	22.5	994
Crude petroleum	48.7	5,954
Petroleum products	25.0	3,874
Natural gas	1.0	137
Electricity	0.4	170
Total	97.6	11,129
Total ‡	—	10,318
Exports		
Coal and other solid fuel	0.6	53
Crude petroleum	75.9	9,236
Petroleum products	35.6	5,158
Natural gas	7.3	968
Electricity	0	181
Total	119.4	15,596
Total ‡	—	6,260

* Million tonnes of oil equivalent
† £ million
‡ Adjusted to exclude estimated costs of insurance, freight, etc.
Source: HM Customs & Excise

OIL

Until the 1960s Britain imported almost all its oil supplies. In 1969 oil was discovered in the Arbroath field of the UK Continental Shelf (UKCS). The first oilfield to be brought into production was the Argyll field in 1975, and since the mid-1970s Britain has been a major producer of crude oil.

Licences for exploration and production are granted to companies by the Department of Trade and Industry; the leading British oil companies are BP and Shell. At the end of 2003, 1,155 Seaward Production Licences and 132 onshore Petroleum Exploration and Development Licences had been awarded, and there were a total of 259 offshore oil and gas fields in production. In 2002 there were 9 oil refineries and three smaller refining units processing crude and process oils. There are estimated to be reserves of 1,300 million tonnes of oil remaining in the UKCS. Royalties are payable on fields approved before April 1982 and petroleum revenue tax is levied on fields approved between 1975 and March 1993.

DRILLING ACTIVITY 2003

Number of wells started	*Offshore*	*Onshore*
Exploration and appraisal	45	4
Exploration	26	3
Appraisal	19	1
Development	204	17

VALUE OF UKCS OIL AND GAS PRODUCTION AND INVESTMENT
£ million

	2001	*2002*
Total income	24,074	24,143
Operating costs	4,347	4,596
Gross trading profits*	19,794	19,460
Percentage contribution to GVA	2.3	2.2
Exploration expenditure	420	389
Other Capital investment	3,570	3,598
Percentage contribution to industrial investment	15	16

* Net of stock appreciation
Source: Department of Trade and Industry

INDIGENOUS PRODUCTION AND REFINERY RECEIPTS

	2002	*2003*
Indigenous production (thousand tonnes)	115,944	106,073
Crude oil	107,430	97,835
NGLs*	8,514	8,238
Refinery receipts (thousand tonnes)		
Indigenous	28,556	30,794
Other†	2,333	2,315
Net foreign imports	54,114	52,721

* Natural Gas Liquids: condensates and petroleum gases derived at onshore treatment plants
† Mainly recycled products
Source: Department of Trade and Industry

DELIVERIES OF PETROLEUM PRODUCTS FOR INLAND CONSUMPTION BY ENERGY USE
Thousand tonnes

	2002	2003
Industry	6,126	6,597
Transport	48,803	47,933
Domestic	3,260	3,239
Other	1,684	1,275
Total	59,873	59,044

Source: Department of Trade and Industry

COAL

Coal has been mined in Britain for centuries and the availability of coal was crucial to the industrial revolution of the 18th- and 19th-centuries. Mines were in private ownership until 1947 when they were nationalised and came under the management of the National Coal Board, later the British Coal Corporation. In addition to producing coal at its own deep-mine and opencast sites, of which there were 850 in 1955, British Coal was responsible for licensing private operators.

Under the Coal Industry Act 1994, the Coal Authority was established to take over ownership of coal reserves and to issue licences to private mining companies as part of the privatisation of British Coal. The Coal Authority also deals with the physical legacy of mining, e.g. subsidence damage claims, and is responsible for holding and making available all existing records. The mines were sold as five separate businesses in 1994 and coal production in the UK is now undertaken entirely in the private sector.

The main UK customer for coal is the electricity supply industry. A review of energy policy was undertaken in 1998 and the Government announced measures in its October 1998 Energy White Paper which included a freeze on new applications to build gas-fired power stations in order to increase opportunities for coal-fired power stations. The moratorium on new gas-fired power stations was lifted in 2000 in the light of two measures to improve the competitiveness of coal-fired generation. Firstly, the Government reached an agreement with the European Commission to make available temporary state aid for the coal industry with such aid to end with the termination of the European Coal and Steel Community Treaty in 2002. The second measure was the reform of the electricity wholesale market and the replacement of the Electricity Pool with the New Electricity Trading Arrangement (NETA) which took effect from 27 March 2001. In 2003, the Government launched Coal Investment Aid with a budget of up to £60 million to be allocated between 2003–5 to coal producers for projects that maintain access to coal reserves. An Energy White Paper published on 24 February 2003 stated that coal generation still provides around a third of the UK's power output but recognised that for a low-carbon economy the development of cleaner coal technologies is required. By 2020 coal generation's contribution to the UK's power output is likely to be significantly lower than today.

COAL PRODUCTION AND FOREIGN TRADE
Thousand tonnes

	2002	2003p
Total production	29,991	28,234
Deep-mined	16,391	15,635
Opencast	13,149	12,126
Imports*	28,686	32,141
Exports†	537	543

* Includes an estimate for slurry
† As recorded in the Overseas Trade Statistics of the United Kingdom, although these are based on estimates from extra-EC trade until monthly statistics for intra-EC trade become available from HM Customs and Excise
p provisional
Source: Department of Trade and Industry

INLAND COAL USE
Thousand tonnes

	2002	2003p
Fuel producers		
Collieries	9	5
Electricity generators	47,712	53,252
Heat generation*	712	547
Coke ovens and blast furnaces	6,533	6,614
Other conversion industries†	436	396
Final users		
Industry‡	1,324	543
Domestic	1,803	1,183
Public administration, commerce and agriculture	65	72
Total	58,641	62,615

* Generation of heat for sale under the provision of a contract
† Low temperature carbonisation and patent fuel plants
‡ Includes estimates of imports
p provisional
Source: Department of Trade and Industry

GAS

From the late 18th-century gas in Britain was produced from coal. In the 1960s town gas began to be produced from oil-based feedstocks using imported oil. In 1965 gas was discovered in the North Sea in the West Sole field, which became the first gasfield in production in 1967, and from the late 1960s natural gas began to replace town gas. Britain is now the world's fourth largest producer of gas and in 1998 only 1.5 per cent of gas available for consumption in the UK was imported. From October 1998 Britain was connected to the continental European gas system via a pipeline from Bacton, Norfolk to Zeebrugge, Belgium. There are 275,000km of mains pipeline including 6,400km of high pressure gas pipelines owned and operated in the UK by National Grid Transco.

The gas industry in Britain was nationalised in 1949 and operated as the Gas Council. The Gas Council was replaced by the British Gas Corporation in 1972 and the industry became more centralised. The British Gas Corporation was privatised in 1986 as British Gas plc.

In 1993 the Monopolies and Mergers Commission found that British Gas's integrated business in Great Britain as a gas trader and the owner of the gas transportation system could operate against the public interest. In February 1997, British Gas demerged its trading arm to become two separate companies, BG plc and Centrica plc. BG Group, as the company is now known, is an international natural gas company whose principal business is finding and developing gas reserves and building gas markets. Its core operations are located in the UK, South America, Egypt, Trinidad & Tobago, Kazakhstan and India. Centrica runs the trading and services operations under the British Gas brand name in Great Britain. In October 2000 BG demerged its pipeline business, Transco, which became part of Lattice Group, finally merging with the National

Grid Group in 2002 to become National Grid Transco plc.

Competition was gradually introduced into the industrial gas market from 1986. Supply of gas to the domestic market was opened to companies other than British Gas, starting in April 1996 with a pilot project in the West Country and Wales. From early 1997 competition was progressively introduced throughout the rest of Britain in stages which were completed in May 1998.

BG GROUP PLC, 100 Thames Valley Park Drive, Reading RG6 1PT T 0118-935 3222 W www.bg-group.com
Chairman, Sir Robert Wilson
Chief Executive, Frank Chapman

CENTRICA PLC, Millstream, Maidenhead Road, Windsor, Berkshire, SL4 5GD T 01753-494000 W www.centrica.co.uk
Chief Executive, Sir Roy Gardner

NATIONAL GRID TRANSCO PLC, 1–3 Strand, London, WC2N 5EH T 020-7004 3000 W www.ngtgroup.com
Chairman, Sir John Parker
Chief Executive, Roger Urwin

UK NATURAL GAS PRODUCTION
GWh

	2001	*2002*
Power stations	309,732	326,220
Coal extraction and manufacture of solid fuels	4	—
Coke ovens	—	—
Petroleum Refineries	4,192	3,240
Nuclear fuel production	1,210	402
Production and distribution of other energy	451	709
Total final producers	315,589	330,571

Source: The Stationery Office: *Annual Abstract of Statistics 2004* (Crown copyright)

NATURAL GAS CONSUMPTION
GWh

	2001	*2002*
Iron and steel industry	20,969	19,533
Other industries	16,585	16,433
Domestic	379,163	376,327
Public administration	46,121	43,715
Agriculture	1,623	1,509
Miscellaneous	65,046	56,080
Total final users	529,507	513,597

Source: The Stationery Office: *Annual Abstract of Statistics 2004* (Crown copyright)

ELECTRICITY

The first power station in Britain generating electricity for public supply began operating in 1882. In the 1930s a national transmission grid was developed and it was reconstructed and extended in the 1950s and 1960s. Power stations were operated by the Central Electricity Generating Board.

Under the Electricity Act 1989, 12 regional electricity companies (RECs), which were responsible for the distribution of electricity from the national grid to consumers, were formed from the former area electricity boards in England and Wales. Four companies were formed from the Central Electricity Generating Board: three generating companies (National Power plc, Nuclear Electric plc and PowerGen plc) and the National Grid Company plc, which owned and operated the transmission system. National Power and PowerGen were floated on the stock market in 1991. National Power was demerged in October 2000 to form two separate companies: International Power plc and Innogy plc, which manages the bulk of National Power's UK assets. Nuclear Electric was split into two parts in 1996 British Energy (*see* Nuclear Energy) and Magnox Electric, which owns the magnox nuclear reactors, remained in the public sector and was integrated into British Nuclear Fuels (BNFL) in 1998. The National Grid Company was floated on the stock market in 1995 and formed a new holding company, National Grid Group. National Grid Group completed a merger with Lattice in 2002 to form National Grid Transco, a public limited company.

NATIONAL GRID TRANSCO PLC, 1–3 Strand, London, WC2N 5EH T 020-7004 3000 W www.ngtgroup.com

Generators and suppliers participate in a competitive wholesale trading market known as NETA (New Electricity Trading Arrangements) which began in March 2001, replacing the Electricity Pool. The introduction of competition into the domestic electricity market was completed in May 1999. With the gas market also open, most suppliers now offer their customers both gas and electricity.

In Scotland, three new companies were formed under the Electricity Act 1989: Scottish Power plc and Scottish Hydro-Electric plc, which are responsible for generation, transmission, distribution and supply; and Scottish Nuclear Ltd. Scottish Power and Scottish Hydro-Electric were floated on the stock market in 1991. Scottish Hydro-Electric merged with Southern Electric in 1998 to become Scottish and Southern Energy plc. Scottish Nuclear Ltd. was incorporated into British Energy in 1996.

In Northern Ireland, Northern Ireland Electricity plc was set up in 1993 under a 1991 Order in Council. In 1993 it was floated on the stock market and in 1998 it became part of the Viridian Group and is responsible for distribution and supply.

On 30 September 2003 the Electricity Association, the industry's main trade association, was replaced by three separate trade bodies:

ASSOCIATION OF ELECTRICITY PRODUCERS (AEP), First Floor, 17 Waterloo Place, London, SW1Y 4AR T 020-7930 9390 W www.aepuk.com
Promotes the interests of members who generate electricity

ENERGY NETWORKS ASSOCIATION (ENA), 18 Stanhope Place, London, W2 2HH T 020-7706 5100 W www.energynetworks.org
Represents UK gas and electricity transmission and distribution licence holders

ENERGY RETAIL ASSOCIATION, 2nd Floor, 17 Waterloo Place, London, SW1Y 4AR T 020-7747 2932 W www.energy-retail.org.uk
Represents the main suppliers operating in the UK energy market

ELECTRICITY GENERATION, SUPPLY AND CONSUMPTION
GWh

Electricity generated	*2001*	*2002*
Major power producers: total	352,770	354,208
Conventional thermal and other*	138,626	134,933
Combined cycle gas turbine stations	117,966	123,893
Nuclear stations	89,870	88,043
Hydro-electric stations		
Natural flow	3,215	3,925
Pumped storage	2,356	2,652
Renewables other than hydro	737	762
Other generators: total	31,913	32,934
Electricity used on works: total	17,114	17,360
Major generating companies	15,779	15,960
Other generators	1,335	1,400
Electricity supplied (gross)		
Major power producers: total	336,991	338,248
Conventional thermal and other*	131,885	128,105
Combined cycle gas turbine stations	115,894	121,886
Nuclear stations	82,985	81,090
Hydro-electric stations:		
Natural flow	3,204	3,914
Pumped storage	2,340	2,562
Renewables other than hydro	683	691
Other generators: total	30,578	31,534
Electricity used in pumping		
Major power producers	3,210	3,463
Electricity supplied (net): total	364,359	366,318
Major power producers	333,781	334,785
Other generators	30,578	31,534
Net Imports	10,399	8,414
Electricity available	374,758	374,733
Losses in Transmission	31,980	30,902
Electricity consumption: Total	342,778	343,831
Fuel industries	8,625	9,977
Final users: total	334,153	333,854
Industrial sector	112,867	112,823
Domestic sector	115,336	114,535
Other sectors	105,950	106,496

* Includes electricity supplied by gas turbines, oil engines and plants producing electricity from renewable resources other than hydro.
Source: The Stationery Office – *Annual Abstract of Statistics 2004* (Crown copyright)

GAS AND ELECTRICITY SUPPLIERS

Now that the gas and electricity markets are open, most suppliers now offer their customers both gas and electricity. The majority of gas/electricity companies have become part of larger multi-utility companies, often operating internationally. The following list comprises a selection of some of the suppliers offering gas and electricity. Organisations in italics are subsidiaries of the companies listed in capital letters directly above.

ENGLAND, SCOTLAND AND WALES

CE ELECTRIC UK W www.ce-electricuk.com
Northern Electric Distribution Ltd (NEDL), Manor House, Station Road, New Penshaw, Houghton-le-Spring DH4 7LA T 0845-070 7172
Yorkshire Electricity Distribution (YEDL), 161 Gelderd Road, Leeds LS1 1QZ T 0845-602 4454
CENTRICA PLC, Millstream, Maidenhead Road, Windsor, Berkshire SL4 5GD T 01753-494000 W www.centrica.com
British Gas/Scottish Gas, T 0845-070 9010 W www.house.co.uk
EDF ENERGY, 40 Grosvenor Place, London SW1X 4EN T 020-7242 9050 W www.edfenergy.com
London Energy, 40 Grosvenor Place, London SW1X 4EN T 0800-096 9000 W www.london-energy.com
Seeboard Energy, 40 Grosvenor Place, London SW17 4EN T 0800-096 9696 W www.seeboard-energy.com
SWEB Energy, Osprey Road, Exeter EX2 7HZ T 0800-365000 W www.sweb-energy.com
Virgin Home Energy, Freepost LON14908, Exeter EX2 7BF T 0800-028 8269 W www.virginhome.co.uk
NPOWER, PO Box 93, Tyne House, Birchwood Drive, Peterlee SR8 2XX T 0800-389 2388 W www.npower.com
POWERGEN, PO Box 7750, Nottingham NG1 6WR T 0800-015 2029 W www.powergen.co.uk
SCOTTISH AND SOUTHERN ENERGY PLC, Inveralmond House, 200 Dunkeld Road, Perth PH1 3AQ W www.scottish-southern.co.uk
Scottish Hydro Electric, PO Box 7506, Perth PH1 3QR T 0845-300 2141 W www.hydro.co.uk
Southern Electric, PO Box 7506, Perth PH1 3QR T 0845-744 4555 W www.southern-electric.
SWALEC, PO Box 7506, Perth PH1 3QR T 0800-052 5252 W www.swalec.co.uk
SCOTTISHPOWER, Cathcart House, Cathcart Business Park, Spean Street, Glasgow G44 4BE T 0845-2700 700 W www.scottishpower.co.uk

NORTHERN IRELAND

VIRIDIAN GROUP PLC, 120 Malone Road, Belfast BT9 5HT T 028-9066 8416 W www.viridiangroup.co.uk
Energia, Energia House, 62 Newforge Lane, Belfast BT9 5NF T 028-9068 5900 W www.viridian energia.co.uk
Northern Ireland Electricity, 120 Malone Road, Belfast BT9 5HT T 028-9066 1100 W www.nie.co.uk

REGULATION OF THE GAS AND ELECTRICITY INDUSTRIES

The Office of the Gas and Electricity Markets (Ofgem) supports the Gas and Electricity Markets Authority, the regulator of the gas and electricity industries in Great Britain. Ofgem's aim is to bring choice and value to all gas and electricity customers by promoting competition and regulating monopolies. The Authority's powers are provided for under the Gas Act 1986, the Electricity Act 1989 and the Utilities Act 2000.

OFGEM, 9 Millbank, London SW1P 3GE T 020-7901 7000 W www.ofgem.gov.uk

NUCLEAR POWER

Nuclear reactors began to supply electricity to the national grid in 1956. It is generated at six magnox reactors, seven advanced gas-cooled reactors (AGRs) and one pressurised water reactor (PWR), Sizewell 'B' in Suffolk. In 1989 nuclear stations were withdrawn from privatisation. In 1996 Nuclear Electric Ltd and Scottish

Nuclear Ltd became operating subsidiaries of British Energy and the magnox stations were transferred to Nuclear Electric which became Magnox Electric, later part of British Nuclear Fuels Ltd (BNFL). In September 2002 the Government stepped in to provide a loan facility to British Energy which was facing insolvency and a major financial restructuring package was announced in November 2002. In March 2003 British Energy received formal approvals for loan standstill agreements from its creditors and the Government agreed to extend the loan facility until September 2004.

The UK Atomic Energy Authority (UKAEA) is responsible for the decommissioning of nuclear reactors and other nuclear facilities used in research and development. UKAEA is a non-departmental public body, funded mainly by the Department of Trade and Industry. UK Nirex, which was set up by the nuclear generating companies with the agreement of the Government, is responsible for the disposal of intermediate and some low-level nuclear waste. The Nuclear Safety Directorate of the Health and Safety Executive is the nuclear industry's regulator.

RENEWABLE SOURCES

Renewable sources of energy principally include biofuels, hydro, wind and solar. Renewable sources accounted for 3.2 million tonnes of oil equivalent of primary energy use in 2002; of this, about 2.5 million tonnes was used to generate electricity and 0.7 million tonnes to generate heat.

The Non-Fossil Fuel Obligation (NFFO) Renewables Orders have been the Government's principal mechanism for developing renewable energy sources. NFFO Renewables Orders require the regional electricity companies to buy specified amounts of electricity from specified non-fossil fuel sources.

In January 2000 the government announced a target for renewables to supply 10 per cent of UK electricity by 2010, which would require about 10,000 megawatts of renewables to be installed. A new renewables obligation was introduced in England and Wales in April 2002 to give incentives to generators to supply progressively higher levels of renewable energy over time. These measures included:

- the exemption of renewable electricity sources from the Climate Change Levy
- the creation of a renewables support programme worth £250 million from 2002–5
- the creation of a strategic framework for a major expansion of offshore wind generation
- the formation of a new organisation within the Government (Renewables UK) to help the industry grow and compete internationally

In July 2003 the DTI announced that the world's biggest wind farms will be built in three sites off the English coast (the Thames Estuary, the Wash on the east coast and from Morecambe Bay to north Wales), providing enough power for one in six British homes.

RENEWABLE ENERGY SOURCES 2002

	Percentages
Biofuels and wastes	83.2
Landfill gas	27.9
Sewage gas	5.7
Wood combustion	14.7
Straw combustion	2.2
Waste combustion	22.7
Other biofuels	10.0
Hydro	12.9
Large-scale	12.3
Small-scale	0.6
Wind and wave	3.4
Geothermal and active solar heating	0.5
Total	100

Source: Department of Trade and Industry

TRANSPORT

CIVIL AVIATION

Since the privatisation of British Airways in 1987, UK airlines have been operated entirely by the private sector. In 2003, total capacity of British airlines amounted to 43 billion tonne-km, of which 31 billion tonne-km was on scheduled services. In 2003 British airlines carried 110 million passengers, 76 million on scheduled services and 34 million on charter flights. Overall, passenger traffic grew by six per cent in 2003. In 2003, traffic at the five main London airports grew by 3 per cent over 2002 and regional airlines saw a growth of 11 per cent in 2003, largely due to the expansion of no-frills airlines. The number of passengers is estimated to be growing at 6 per cent each year. Leading British airlines include British Airways, Britannia Airways, BMI British Midland, Air 2000, My Travel, Thomas Cook Airlines, Monarch, Virgin Atlantic and easyJet. Irish airline Ryanair also operates frequent flights from Britain.

There are around 140 licensed civil aerodromes in Britain, with Heathrow and Gatwick handling the highest volume of passengers. BAA PLC owns and operates the seven major airports: Heathrow, Gatwick, Stansted, Southampton, Glasgow, Edinburgh and Aberdeen, which between them handle about 70 per cent of air passengers and a high percentage of air cargo traffic in Britain. Other airports are controlled by local authorities or private companies.

The Civil Aviation Authority (CAA), an independent statutory body, is responsible for the regulation of UK airlines. This includes economic and airspace regulation, air safety, consumer protection and environmental research and consultancy. All commercial airline companies must be granted an Air Operator's Certificate, which is issued by the CAA to operators meeting the required safety standards. The CAA issues airport safety licences, which must be obtained by any airport used for public transport and training flights. All British-registered aircraft must be granted an airworthiness certificate, and the CAA issues professional licences to pilots, flight crew, ground engineers and air traffic controllers. The CAA also manages the Air Travel Organiser's Licence (ATOL), the UK's principal travel protection scheme. The CAA's costs are met entirely from charges on those whom it regulates; there is no direct Government funding of the CAA's work.

The Transport Act, passed by Parliament on 29 November 2000, separated the CAA from its subsidiary, National Air Traffic Services (NATS), which provides air traffic control services to aircraft flying in UK airspace, over the eastern part of the North Atlantic and at 14 of Britain's major airports. In 2003 a total of 2,078,207 flights used UK airspace, an increase of 3.9 per cent on 2002 and 2.8 per cent on 2001. In March 2001, the Airline Group, a consortium of seven UK airlines (British Airways, BMI British Midland, Virgin Atlantic, Britannia, Monarch, easyJet and My Travel), was selected by the government as its strategic partner for NATS. Financial restructuring of NATS was completed in March 2003 with additional equity investment of £65 million each from BAA and the government. The new structure has enabled NATS to begin its £1 billion investment programme to run over the next ten years. NATS is a public private partnership between the Airline Group which holds 42 per cent of the shares, NATS staff who hold 5 per cent, BAA which holds 4 per cent and the government which holds 49 per cent and a golden share.

AIR PASSENGERS 2003*

ALL UK AIRPORTS: TOTAL	199,950,353
LONDON AREA AIRPORTS: TOTAL	118,606,029
Metro London Heliport	0
Heathrow (BAA)	63,208,042
Gatwick (BAA)	29,893,288
Luton	6,785,732
Southend	2,702
Stansted (BAA)	18,716,265
OTHER UK AIRPORTS: TOTAL	81,344,324
Aberdeen (BAA)	2,507,878
Barra (HIAL)†	8,318
Barrow-in-Furness	0
Belfast City	1,974,036
Belfast International	3,954,432
Benbecula (HIAL)†	31,914
Biggin Hill	683
Birmingham	8,923,902
Blackpool	186,604
Bournemouth	460,872
Bristol	3,886,740
Cambridge	2,485
Campbeltown (HIAL)†	8,268
Cardiff	1,899,971
Carlisle	0
City of Derry (Eglinton)	205,505
Coventry	2,429
Dundee	51,734
East Midlands	4,253,684
Edinburgh (BAA)	7,476,357
Exeter	378,010
Glasgow (BAA)	8,115,476
Gloucestershire	0
Hawarden	6,666
Humberside	517,171
Inverness (HIAL)†	434,644
Islay (HIAL)†	21,422
Isle of Man	742,590
Isles of Scilly (St Mary's)	138,466
Isles of Scilly (Tresco)	43,612
Kent International	3,256
Kirkwall (HIAL)†	102,716
Lands End (St Just)	24,751
Leeds Bradford	2,015,320
Lerwick (Tingwall)	2,056
Liverpool	3,175,343
London City	1,470,576
Lydd	4,498
Manchester	19,520,062
Newcastle	3,903,340
Norwich	447,112
Penzance Heliport	130,643
Plymouth	69,928
Prestwick	1,854,484

Scatsta	229,558
Sheffield City	0
Shoreham	263
Southampton (BAA)	1,217,891
Stornoway (HIAL)†	106,233
Sumburgh (HIAL)†	110,482
Teesside	699,838
Tiree (HIAL)†	5,293
Unst	0
Wick (HIAL)†	16,812
CHANNEL ISLANDS AIRPORTS: TOTAL	2,397,339
Alderney	72,075
Guernsey	861,275
Jersey	1,463,989

*Total terminal, transit, scheduled and charter passengers. Passengers carried on air taxi services are excluded
†Highlands and Islands Airports Ltd (HIAL)
Source: Civil Aviation Authority

CAA, CAA House, 45–59 Kingsway, London, WC2B 6TE
T 020-7379 7311 W www.caa.co.uk
BAA PLC, 130 Wilton Road, London, SW1V 1LQ
T 020-7834 9449 W www.baa.co.uk

Heathrow Airport	T 0870-000 0123
Gatwick Airport	T 0870-000 2468
Stansted Airport	T 0870-000 0303
Glasgow Airport	T 0870-040 0008
Edinburgh Airport	T 0870-040 0007
Aberdeen Airport	T 0870-040 0006
Southampton Airport	T 0870-040 0009

BMI BRITISH MIDLAND, Donington Hall, Castle Donington, Derby, DE74 2SB T 01332-854000 W www.flybmi.com
BRITANNIA AIRWAYS, Britannia House, London Luton International Airport, Luton, Bedfordshire, LU2 9ND T 01582-424155 W www.britanniaairways.com
BRITISH AIRWAYS, Waterside, PO Box 365, Harmondsworth, UB7 0G T 0870-850 9850 W www.britishairways.com
EASYJET, London Luton Airport, LU2 9LS T 0871-7500 100 W www.easyjet.com
FIRST CHOICE AIRWAYS (previously known as Air 2000) Commonwealth House, Chicago Avenue, Manchester Airport, M90 3DP T 0870-850 3999 W www.firstchoice.co.uk
MONARCH, Prospect House, Prospect Way, London Luton Airport, LU2 9NU T 01582-400000 W www.monarch-airlines.com
MY TRAVEL, Parkway One, Parkway Business Centre, 300 Princess Road, Manchester, M14 7QU T 0870-238 7777 W www.mytravel.com
THOMAS COOK AIRLINES, Thomas Cook Business Park, Coningsby Road, Peterborough, PE3 8XP T 0870-750 5711 W www.thomascook.cm
VIRGIN ATLANTIC, Manor Royal, Crawley, West Sussex RH10 9NU T 01293-562345 W www.virgin-atlantic.com

RAILWAYS

Britain pioneered railways and a railway network was developed across Britain by private companies in the 19th century. In 1948 the main railway companies were nationalised and were run by a public authority, the British Transport Commission. The Commission was replaced by the British Railways Board in 1963, operating as British Rail. On 1 April 1994, responsibility for managing the track and railway infrastructure passed to a newly-formed company, Railtrack plc. In October 2001 Railtrack was put into administration under the Railways Act 1993 and Ernst and Young was appointed as administrator. In October 2002 Railtrack was taken out of administration and replaced by the not-for-profit company Network Rail. The British Railways Board continued as operator of all train services until 1996–7 when they were sold or franchised to the private sector.

On 15 July 2004 the Government announced a new structure for the rail industry in the white paper, *The Future of Rail*. The Strategic Rail Authority will be abolished (*see* below), the number of rail franchises will be reduced, and devolved governments in Scotland and Wales will have more say in decisions at a local level. The Office of Rail Regulation will also regulate safety, currently the responsibility of the Health and Safety Executive.

OTHER RAIL SYSTEMS

Plans for a public-private partnership (PPP) for London Underground were pushed through by the Government in February 2002 despite opposition from the Mayor of London and a range of transport organisations. Under the PPP, long-term contracts with private companies are estimated to enable around £16 billion to be invested in renewing and upgrading the Underground's infrastructure over 15 years. Responsibility for stations, trains, operations, signalling and safety will remain in the public sector. In 2002–3 there were 942 million passenger journeys on the London Underground, down 1.2 per cent on the previous year.

Britain has seven other light rail systems; Croydon Tramlink, Docklands Light Railway (DLR), Manchester Metrolink, Midland Metro, the Nottingham Express Transit (NET), Sheffield Supertram and Tyne and Wear Metro. Most recently opened was the Nottingham Express Transit in March 2004.

Light rail and metro systems in Great Britain contributed to the growth in public transport, with 136 million passenger journeys in 2002–3, up seven per cent on the previous year. The Government's 10-year Transport Plan target is to double light rail use in England by 2010.

OFFICE OF RAIL REGULATION (ORR)

Under the Railways Act 1993 the Rail Regulator was created with responsibility for the regulation of the monopoly of the railways and the network infrastructure operator, now known as Network Rail (formerly Railtrack). The Transport Act 2000 enabled the Regulator to direct enhancement of a network facility, expand an operator's existing rights and, under the Competition Act 1998, prevent anti-competitive practices. Tom Winsor's five-year appointment as Rail Regulator ended on 4 July 2004 and under the Railways and Transport Safety Bill 2003 he was replaced by a regulatory board. The re-named Office of Rail Regulation consists of a board of nine members headed by a chairman, who is appointed by the Secretary of State for Transport, and a chief executive.

STRATEGIC RAIL AUTHORITY (SRA)

The Strategic Rail Authority (SRA) was created to provide strategic leadership to the rail industry and formally came into being on 1 February 2001 following the passing of the Transport Act 2000. In January 2002 it published its first Strategic Plan, setting out the strategic priorities for Britain's railways over the next ten years. In addition to its coordinating role, the SRA is responsible for allocating Government funding to the railways, awarding and monitoring the franchises for operating rail services, as well as a number of other statutory functions; particularly relating to customer protection. On 15 July 2004 a white paper, *The Future of Rail*, was published which announced that the SRA would be abolished, its strategic functions and financial obligations passing to the Department for Transport. Network Rail will have full responsibility for industry planning and timetables.

For privatisation, domestic passenger services were divided into 25 train operating units, which were franchised to private sector operators via a competitive tendering process overseen by the SRA. The majority of the original franchises were let on a seven-year term, consequently there are now a large number of franchises to be let over the next few years. The SRA has devised a long-term programme to enable a steady state replacement of franchises of approximately three per annum. In November 2002 the SRA issued a franchising policy statement specifying that new franchises should set service levels and quality standards and the private sector should be charged with delivering the standards set. This led to the development of a new standard form of Franchise Agreement, which incorporates rewards and penalties for standards of train and station cleanliness, security and passenger information. It also contains guidelines and incentives for customer services and business priorities such as short and long-term costs. The first franchise to be let under this new agreement was the Greater Anglia franchise (One Railway), incorporating: Anglia; Great Eastern; West Anglia and Stansted Express train services, on 1 April 2004, and operated by the National Express Group plc.

SERVICES

As at March 2004 there were 23 train operating companies (TOCs): Arriva Trains Northern; Arriva Trains Wales; c2c; Central Trains; Chiltern; First Great Western; First Great Western Link; First North Western Trains; Gatwick Express; Great North Eastern Railways; Island Line (Isle of Wight); Midland Mainline; One Railway; ScotRail; Silverlink; South Central; South Eastern Trains; South West Trains; ThamesLink; Virgin Trains (CrossCountry Trains Ltd); Virgin Trains (West Coast Trains Ltd); WAGN and Wessex Trains.

In addition, Eurostar and Merseyrail provide services, but are not subject to the franchise process. The Heathrow Express service is a subsidiary of the airports group BAA.

Network Rail publishes a national timetable which contains details of rail services operated over the network, coastal shipping information and connections with Ireland, the Isle of Man, the Isle of Wight, the Channel Islands and some European destinations.

The national rail enquiries service offers information about train times and fares for any part of the country:

NATIONAL RAIL ENQUIRIES T 08457-484950
W www.nationalrail.co.uk
TRANSPORT FOR LONDON T 020-7941 4500
W www.transportforlondon.gov.uk
EUROSTAR T 08705-186186 W www.eurostar.com

Rail Users' Consultative Committees (RUCCs) were set up under the Railways Act 1993 to protect the interests of users of the services and facilities provided on Britain's rail network. The Transport Act 2000 changed their name to the Rail Passenger Committees (RPCs) and transferred sponsorship from the Rail Regulator to the SRA. There are nine RPCs nationwide, seven for England and one each for Scotland and Wales. They are statutory bodies and have a legal right to make recommendations for changes. The London Transport Users' Committee represents users of buses, the Underground and rail services in and around London, including Eurostar and Heathrow Express, Croydon Tramlink and the Docklands Light Railway. The interests of pedestrians, cyclists and motorists are also represented, as are those of taxi users. Transport for London was established by the Greater London Assembly and the Mayor in 2000.

On privatisation, British Rail's bulk freight haulage companies and Rail Express Systems, which carried Royal Mail traffic, were sold to English, Welsh and Scottish Railways (EWS), which also purchased Railfreight Distribution (international freight) in 1997. At the end of 2003 18.6 billion-tonne-kilometres of freight was transported by EWS and other freight companies. In 2003 Royal Mail announced it would phase out its use of rail for postal distribution by the end of March 2004.

NETWORK RAIL

Network Rail owns and maintains 21,000 miles of track, owns and provides access to 2,500 stations and operates and maintains more than 9,000 level crossings and 40,000 bridges and tunnels. In addition to providing the timetables for the passenger and freight operators Network Rail is also responsible for all the signalling and electrical control equipment needed to operate the rail network.

Network Rail is run as a commercial business but has members instead of shareholders. The members have similar rights to those of shareholders in a public company except they do not receive dividends or share capital and thereby having no financial or economic interest in Network Rail. All of Network Rail's profits are reinvested into maintaining and upgrading the rail infrastructure.

ASSOCIATION OF TRAIN OPERATING COMPANIES (ATOC), 3rd Floor, 40 Bernard Street, London WC1N 1BY T 020-7841 8000 W www.atoc.org

OFFICE OF RAIL REGULATION, 1 Waterhouse Square, 138–142 Holborn, London EC1N 2TQ T 020-7282 2000 W www.rail-reg.gov.uk
Chairman, Chris Bolt

NETWORK RAIL, 40 Melton Street, London NW1 2EE T 020-7557 8000 W www.networkrail.co.uk

RAIL PASSENGERS COUNCIL (RPC), Whittles House, 14 Pentonville Road, London, N1 9HF T 020-7713 2700 W www.railpassengers.org.uk

STRATEGIC RAIL AUTHORITY, 55 Victoria Street, London, SW1H 0EU T 020-7654 6000 W www.sra.gov.uk
Chairman and Chief Executive, Richard Bowker

RAIL SAFETY

The Railways (Safety Case) Regulations 2000 came into force on 31 December 2000 and transferred responsibility for safety cases from Railtrack to HM Railway Inspectorate, part of the Health and Safety Executive (HSE). The regulations demand that rail operators such as Network Rail, London Underground, the station and train operators must prepare a comprehensive safety case and have it accepted by HSE before being allowed to operate their business. The Office of Rail Regulation will not grant a licence to a railway operator without an accepted safety case or an exemption being in place.

Amendments to railway safety case regulations were

announced in March 2003 and came into force on 1 April 2003. The requirement for infrastructure controllers to obtain an independent assessment of safety cases in addition to the Health and Safety Executive's acceptance was removed and the requirement to obtain annual independent health and safety audits of train and station operations was transferred from HSE to individual operators. The Rail Safety and Standards Board (RSSB) was established on 1 April 2003 as a new industry body to provide health and safety leadership for the railway industry.

ACCIDENTS ON RAILWAYS

	2001–2	*2002–3*
Train accidents: total	1,704	1,421
Persons killed: total	5	10
Passengers	0	6
Railway staff	0	1
Others	5	3
Persons injured: total	52	106
Passengers	21	128
Railway staff	23	23
Others	8	15
Other accidents through movement of railway vehicles		
Persons killed	21	32
Persons injured	909	908
Other accidents on railway premises		
Persons killed	6	8
Passengers	3	3
Railway staff	1	4
Others	2	1
Persons injured	3,906	3,983
Trespassers and suicides		
Persons killed	275	256
Persons injured	179	137

Source: Department for Transport

THE CHANNEL TUNNEL

The earliest recorded scheme for a submarine transport connection between Britain and France was in 1802. Tunnelling has begun simultaneously on both sides of the Channel three times: in 1881, in the early 1970s, and on 1 December 1987, when construction workers began to bore the first of the three tunnels which form the Channel Tunnel. They 'holed through' the first tunnel (the service tunnel) on 1 December 1990 and tunnelling was completed in June 1991. The tunnel was officially inaugurated by The Queen and President Mitterrand of France on 6 May 1994.

The submarine link comprises three tunnels. There are two rail tunnels, each carrying trains in one direction, which measure 24.93 ft (7.6 m) in diameter. Between them lies a smaller service tunnel, measuring 15.75 ft (4.8 m) in diameter. The service tunnel is linked to the rail tunnels by 130 cross-passages for maintenance and safety purposes. The tunnels are 31 miles (50 km) long, 24 miles (38 km) of which is under the sea-bed at an average depth of 132 ft (40 m). The rail terminals are situated at Folkestone and Calais, and the tunnels go underground at Shakespeare Cliff, Dover, and Sangatte, west of Calais.

Eurostar is the high speed passenger train connecting London with Paris in three hours and Brussels in two hours 40 minutes, via the Channel Tunnel. Some trains stop en route at Ashford (Kent) and Calais, Disneyland Paris and Lille in France.

RAIL LINKS

The route for the British Channel Tunnel Rail Link will run from Folkestone to a new terminal at St Pancras station, London, with new intermediate stations at Ebbsfleet, Kent, and Stratford, east London; at present services run into a terminal at Waterloo station, London.

Construction of the rail link is being financed by the private sector with a substantial government contribution. A private sector consortium, London and Continental Railways Ltd (LCR), is responsible for the design, construction and ownership of the rail link, and comprises Union Railways and the UK operator of Eurostar. Construction was expected to be completed in 2003, but on 28 January 1998 LCR informed the Government that it was unable to fulfil its obligations. On 3 June 1998 the Government announced a new funding agreement with LCR. The rail link will be constructed in two phases: phase one, from the Channel Tunnel to Fawkham Junction, North Kent began in October 1998 and opened to fare paying passengers on 28 September 2003; phase two, from Southfleet Junction to St Pancras, is due to be completed in 2007. Infrastructure developments in France have been completed and high-speed trains run from Calais to Paris and from Lille to the south of France.

ROADS

HIGHWAY AUTHORITIES

The powers and responsibilities of highway authorities in England and Wales are set out in the Highways Act 1980; for Scotland there is separate legislation.

Responsibility for trunk road motorways and other trunk roads in Great Britain rests in England with the Secretary of State for Transport, in Scotland with the Scottish Executive, and in Wales with the Welsh Assembly. The costs of construction, improvement and maintenance are paid for by central government in England and by the Welsh Assembly in Wales. The highway authority for non-trunk roads in England, Wales and Scotland is, in general, the local authority in whose area the roads lie. With the establishment of the Greater London Authority in July 2000, Transport for London became the highway authority for roads in London.

In Northern Ireland the Department of Regional Development is the statutory road authority responsible for public roads and their maintenance and construction; the Roads Service executive agency carries out these functions on behalf of the Department.

FINANCE

In England all aspects of trunk road and motorway funding are provided directly by the Government to the Highways Agency which operates, maintains and improves around 5,878 miles of motorways and trunk roads on behalf of the Secretary of State. For the financial year 2004–5 the Highways Agency was allocated £1.7 billion, of which £730 million was for maintenance, £508 million for major new roads including private finance payments and £231 million on smaller improvements and traffic management measures.

Government support for local authority capital expenditure on roads and other transport infrastructure is provided through grant and credit approvals as part of the Local Transport Plan (LTP). Local Authorities bid for resources on the basis of a five-year programme built around delivering integrated transport strategies. As well as covering the structural maintenance of local roads and the construction of major new road schemes, LTP funding also includes smaller-scale safety and traffic management measures with associated improvements for public transport, cyclists and pedestrians.

For the financial year 2004–5 local authorities received a total of £1.9 billion in the form of a Local Transport Plan budget. This includes £657 million for small-scale integrated transport measures, £651 million for road maintenance and £459 million for new and existing major projects.

Total expenditure by Welsh Assembly on trunk roads, motorways and transport services (including grants to local authorities and credit approvals) in 2003–4 was £243 million. Forecast expenditure for 2004–5 is £326 million.

Until 1999 the Scottish Office received a block vote from Parliament and the Secretary of State for Scotland determined how much was spent on roads. Since 1 July 1999 all decisions on transport expenditure have been devolved to the Scottish Executive. Total planned expenditure on motorways and trunk road in Scotland during 2003–4 including depreciation and cost of capital charge was £631.2 million. Planned expenditure for 2004–5 is £643.47 million.

In Northern Ireland total expenditure by the Roads Service on trunk roads and motorways for 2003–4 was £84.5 million and £96.5 million has been allocated for expenditure in 2004–5.

The Transport Act 2000 gave English and Welsh local authorities (outside London) powers to introduce road user charging or workplace parking levy schemes. The Act requires that the net revenue raised is used to improve local transport services and facilities for at least ten years. The aim is to reduce congestion and encourage greater use of alternative modes of transport. Schemes developed by local authorities require Government approval. The Government's Ten Year Plan for Transport assumes that eight large road user charging schemes and 12 large workplace parking levy schemes will be developed by 2010. Charging schemes in London are allowed under the 1999 Greater London Authority Act. The Central London Congestion Charge Scheme began on 17 February 2003.

TARGETED PROGRAMME OF IMPROVEMENT

The 1998 Roads Review increased the emphasis given to making better use of the existing road network and improving road maintenance. In addition a carefully targeted programme of major trunk road improvements was announced which initially consisted of 37 schemes. The current programme contains 78 schemes, funded conventionally or through public-private partnerships. A series of 22 studies were announced in March 1999 to look at transport problems across all modes. Based on these studies the Government announced a major national road expansion programme on 10 July 2003.

ROAD LENGTHS (IN KILOMETRES) 2002

	England	*Wales*	*Scotland*	*Great Britain*
Motorways	2,949	141	386	3,477
Dual Carriageway	6,522	543	766	7,831
Single carriageway	25,668	3,634	9,533	38,834
B roads	19,871	2,985	7,336	30,192
C roads	64,720	9,822	10,315	84,857
Unclassified roads	179,436	15,957	31.069	226,462
Total	299,166	33,082	59,405	391,653

MOTORWAYS

ENGLAND AND WALES

M1	London to Yorkshire
M2	London to Faversham
M3	London to Southampton
M4	London to South Wales
M5	Birmingham to Exeter
M6	Catthorpe to Carlisle
M6	Toll Birmingham bypass*
M10	St Albans spur
M11	London to Cambridge
M18	Rotherham to Goole
M20	London to Folkestone
M23	London to Gatwick
M25	London orbital
M26	M20 to M25 spur
M27	Southampton bypass
M32	M4 to Bristol spur
M40	London to Birmingham
M42	South-west of Birmingham to Measham
M45	Dunchurch spur
M48	M4 to South Wales
M49	M4 to M5
M50	Ross spur
M53	Chester to Birkenhead
M54	M6 to Telford
M55	Preston to Blackpool
M56	Manchester to Chester
M57	Liverpool outer ring
M58	Liverpool to Wigan
M60	Manchester ring road
M61	Manchester to Preston
M62	Liverpool to Hull
M65	Calder Valley
M66	Manchester Whitefield to Ramsbottom
M67	Manchester Hyde to Denton
M69	Coventry to Leicester
M180	South Humberside
M181	M180 to Scunthorpe
M271	West of Southampton
M275	M27 to Portsmouth
M602	Eccles to Salford
M606	M62 to Bradford
M621	M1 to M62

SCOTLAND

M8	Edinburgh–Newhouse (Glasgow)
M9	Edinburgh to Dunblane and M9 Spur to A8000
M73	Jn. 4 of M74 to A80 (Mollinsburn)
M74	Glasgow–Gretna
M77	Jn. 22 of M8 to Malletsheugh (Ayr Road)
M80	Jn. 9 of M9 (Stirling) to Jn. 4 of M80/A80 (Haggs) and M80 Stepps Bypass
M90	Forth Bridge Road/Inverkeithing to Perth
M876	Kincardine Bridge to Jn. 5 of M80
M898	Jn. 30 of M8 to Erskine Bridge
A823(M)	Jn. 2 of M90 to A823 (Dunfermline)

* The UK's first toll motorway opened on 9 December 2003

NORTHERN IRELAND

M1	Belfast to Dungannon
M2	Belfast to Antrim
M2	Ballymena bypass
M3	Belfast Cross Harbour Bridge
M5	M2 to Greencastle
M12	M1 to Craigavon
M22	Antrim to Randalstown

ROAD USE

ESTIMATED TRAFFIC ON ALL ROADS (GREAT BRITAIN) 2002

Million vehicle kilometres	
All motor vehicles	485,900
Cars and taxis	392,400
Two-wheeled motor vehicles	5,100
Buses and coaches	5,200
Light vans	55,000
Other goods vehicles	28,300
Pedal cycles	4,400

Source: Department for Transport

ROAD GOODS TRANSPORT (GREAT BRITAIN) 2003
Analysis by mode of working and by gross weight of vehicle

Estimated tonne kilometres (thousand million)	151.7
Own account	37.4
Public haulage	114.3
By gross weight of vehicle (billion tonne kilometres)	
Estimated tonnes lifted (millions)	1,643
Own account	590
Public haulage	1,053
By gross weight of vehicle (million tonnes)	
Not over 25 tonnes	265
Over 25 tonnes	1,378

Source: Department for Transport

BUSES

Nearly all bus and coach services in Great Britain are provided by private sector companies. The Transport Act 2000 outlines a 10-year transport plan intended to promote bus use, through agreements between local authorities and bus operators and to improve the standard and efficiency of services. The 10-year plan sets targets for bus patronage and reliability of services. There are a number of ways in which the Government supports bus services:

- Bus Service Operators Grant (BSOG) is paid directly to bus operators and reimburses 80 per cent of fuel duty and 100 per cent of duty for some 'clean' fuels
- Local authorities outside London have a duty to secure socially necessary bus services not provided commercially. Services are tendered and let to commercial operators in return for payment from the local authority
- Rural Bus Challenge supports innovative and flexible rural transport solutions, such as taxi-bus services and awarded £20 million to 42 projects in 2003
- Rural Bus subsidy grant was £48.5 million in 2003–4 and supported some 21,000 services
- Urban Bus Challenge aims to improve transport in deprived urban areas and awarded £19.6 million to 40 projects in 2003

Since June 2001 it has been a statutory minimum requirement for all local authorities to provide at least half fares and a free bus pass to pensioners and disabled people in the area. Local authorities recompense operators for the reduced fare revenue.

In London, Transport for London (TfL) has overall responsibility for setting routes, service standards and fares for the bus network. Almost all routes are competitively tendered to commercial operators. TfL budget for buses in 2004–5 is £229 million, in addition London also benefits from a share of the funding schemes listed above.

In Northern Ireland, passenger transport services are provided by Ulsterbus Limited and Citybus Limited, two wholly owned subsidiaries of the Northern Ireland Transport Holding Company. Along with Northern Ireland Railways, Ulsterbus and Citybus operate under the brand name of Translink and are publicly owned. Ulsterbus is responsible for virtually all bus services in Northern Ireland except Belfast city services which are operated by Citybus.

BUSES AND COACHES (GREAT BRITAIN) 2001–2

Vehicle kilometres (millions)	4,226
Local bus services passenger journeys (millions)	4,347
Passenger receipts (£ million)	4,625

Source: Department for Transport

TAXIS

A taxi is a public transport vehicle with fewer than nine passenger seats, which is licenced to 'ply for hire'. This distinguishes taxis from private hire vehicles which must be booked in advance through an operator.

In London, taxis and their drivers are licensed by The Public Carriage Office (PCO) which is part of Transport for London (TfL). At the end of December 2001 there were 59,682 licensed taxis in England, of which 20,500 were in London. At the end of 2001, 3,381 taxis were licensed in Wales and 9,343 in Scotland.

AVERAGE TAXI FARE FOR A FOUR-MILE JOURNEY BY REGION 2002

Region	*Fare in £*
London (Transport for London)	9.10
North East	5.64
North West	5.96
Yorkshire & the Humber	5.85
East Midlands	6.09
West Midlands	6.14
East	6.58
South East	6.87
South West	7.14
Wales	6.07

ROAD SAFETY

In March 2000, the Government published a new road safety strategy, *Tomorrow's Roads – Safer for Everyone,* which set new casualty reduction targets for 2010. The new targets include a 40 per cent reduction in the overall number of people killed or seriously injured in road accidents, a 50 per cent reduction in the number of children killed or seriously injured and a 10 per cent reduction in the slight casualty rate, all compared with the average for 1994–8.

There were 290,607 reported casualties on roads in Great Britain in 2003, 4 per cent less than in 2002. Road traffic levels were estimated to be 1 per cent higher than in 2002, consequently the casualty rate per 100 million vehicle kilometres was five per cent lower. Child casualties fell by eight per cent with 171 child fatalities, 4 per cent less than in 2002. Car user casualties decreased by 5 per cent on the 2002 level to 188,342, although fatalities were one per cent higher. Pedestrian casualties were

36,405 in 2003, 6 per cent less than 2002 and pedal cyclist casualties fell marginally to 17,033.

ROAD ACCIDENT CASUALTIES 2003

	Fatal	*Serious*	*Slight*	*All Severities*
England	3,004	29,292	225,603	257,899
Wales	173	1,482	12,381	14,036
Scotland	331	2,933	15,408	18,672
Great Britain	3,508	33,707	253,392	290,607

	Killed	*Injured*
1965	7,952	389,985
1970	7,499	355,869
1975	6,366	318,584
1980	6,010	323,000
1985	5,165	312,359
1990	5,217	335,924
1995	3,621	306,885
1996	3,598	316,704
1997	3,599	323,945
1998	3,421	321,791
1999	3,423	316,887
2000	3,409	316,872
2001	3,450	313,309
2002	3,431	302,605
2003	3,508	290,607

Source: Department for Transport

DRIVING LICENCES

It is necessary to hold a valid full licence in order to drive unaccompanied on public roads in the UK. Learner drivers must obtain a provisional driving licence before starting to learn to drive and must then pass theory and practical tests to obtain a full driving licence.

There are separate tests for driving motor cycles, cars, passenger-carrying vehicles (PCVs) and large goods vehicles (LGVs). Drivers must hold full car entitlement before they can apply for PCV or LGV entitlements.

The Driver and Vehicle Licensing Agency (DVLA) ceased the issue of paper licences in March 2000, however, those currently in circulation will remain valid until they expire or the details on them change. The photocard driving licence was introduced to comply with the second EC directive on driving licences. This requires a photograph of the driver to be included on all UK licences issued from July 2001.

To apply for a first photocard driving licence, individuals are required to complete the forms *Application for a Driving Licence* (D1) and *Application for a Photocard Driving Licence* (D750). Application forms are available from post offices.

The minimum age for driving motor cars, light goods vehicles up to 3.5 tonnes and motor cycles is 17 (moped, 16). Since June 1997, drivers who collect six or more penalty points within two years of qualifying lose their licence and are required to take another test. A leaflet, *What You Need to Know About Driving Licences* (form D100), is available from post offices.

The DVLA is responsible for issuing driving licences, registering and licensing vehicles, and collecting excise duty in Great Britain. In Northern Ireland the Driver and Vehicle Licensing Agency (Northern Ireland) has similar responsibilities.

DRIVING LICENCE FEES *as at 1 April 2004*

First provisional licence	
Car, motorcycle or moped	£38.00
Bus or lorry	Free
Changing a car, motorcycle or moped provisional licence to a full licence	
If first provisional licence issued before 1 March 2004	£9.00
If first provisional licence issued after 1 March 2004	Free
Changing a bus or lorry provisional licence to a full licence	Free
Licence renewal	
At age 70 and over	Free
For medical reasons	Free
Bus or lorry	Free
After disqualification	£50.00
After disqualification for some drink driving offences*	£75.00
After revocation	£38.00
Replacing a lost or stolen licence	£19.00
Adding an entitlement to a full licence	Free
Removing expired endorsements	£19.00
Exchanging	
a paper licence for a photocard licence	£19.00
for a full Northern Ireland car licence	Free
for a full EC/EEA or other foreign licence (including Channel Islands and Isle of Man)	£38.00
Change of name or address (existing licence must be surrendered)	Free

* For an alcohol related offence where the DVLA needed to arrange medical enquiries.

DRIVING TESTS

The Driving Standards Agency is responsible for carrying out driving tests and approving driving instructors in Great Britain. In Northern Ireland the Driver and Vehicle Testing Agency (Northern Ireland) is responsible for testing drivers and vehicles.

DRIVING TESTS TAKEN/PERCENTAGE PASSED
April 2003–March 2004

Type of Test	*Number Taken*	*Percentage Passed*
Practical Tests		
Car	1,399,115	43%
Motorcycle	83,428	64%
Large goods vehicle	61,594	49%
Passenger carrying vehicle	9,373	46%
Theory Tests		
Car	1,297,635	57%
Motorcycle	81,879	77%
Large goods vehicle	44,067	64%
Passenger carrying vehicle	10,542	61%

The theory and practical driving tests can be booked by postal application, online at www.dsa.gov.uk or by telephoning 0870-010 1372.

DRIVING TEST FEES (weekday rate/evening and Saturday rate) *effective from 1 September 2003**

For cars	£39.00/£48.00
For motor cycles	£48.00/£57.00
For lorries, buses	£76.00/£94.00
Extended Test for cars (after disqualification)	£78.00/£96.00
Extended Test for motorcycles (after disqualification)	£96.00/£114.00
Motorcycle Compulsory Basic Training Certificate (CBT)	£8.00
Theory Test for all categories	£20.50

* Correct at the time of going to press – see DSA website for further information: www.dsa.gov.uk

MOTOR VEHICLES

Vehicles must be licensed by the DVLA or the DVLNI before they can be driven on public roads. They must also be approved as roadworthy by the Vehicle Certification Agency. The Vehicle Inspectorate carries out annual testing and inspection of goods vehicles, buses and coaches.

There were 31,207 thousand vehicles licensed at the DVLA at the end of 2003.

VEHICLE LICENCES

Registration and first licensing of vehicles is through local offices of the Driver and Vehicle Licensing Agency in Swansea. Local facilities for relicensing are available at any post office which deals with vehicle licensing. Applicants will need to take their vehicle registration document; if this is not available the applicant must complete form V62 which is held at post offices. Postal applications can be made to the post offices shown in the V100 booklet, available at any post office. This V100 also provides guidance on registering and licensing vehicles.

Details of the present duties chargeable on motor vehicles are available at post offices and Local Offices. The Vehicle Excise and Registration Act 1994 provides *inter alia* that any vehicle kept on a public road but not used on roads is chargeable to excise duty as if it were in use. All non-commercial vehicles constructed before 1 January 1973 are exempt from vehicle excise duty. Any vehicle licensed on or after 31 January 1998, not in use and not kept on public roads must be registered as SORN (Statutory Off Road Notification) to be exempted from vehicle excise duty. From 1 January 2004 the registered keeper of a vehicle remains responsible for licensing a vehicle or making a SORN declaration until that liability is formally transferred to a new keeper.

MOTOR VEHICLES CURRENTLY LICENSED BY BODY TYPE 2003 (GREAT BRITAIN)

Thousands	
All Cars (including exempt)	26,240
All company cars	2,212
Taxis (black cabs only)	39
Motor cycles, Scooters and Mopeds	1,135
Tricycles	19
Light goods vehicles	2,434
Goods vehicles	639
Buses and coaches	175
Other vehicles	526
Total	31,207

Source: Department for Transport: *Vehicle Licensing Statistics 2003*

VEHICLE EXCISE DUTY RATES *from 1 March 2004*

REGISTERED BEFORE 1 MARCH 2001

	Twelve Months £	*Six Months* £
Motor Cars		
Light vans, cars, taxis, etc.		
Under 1549cc	110.00	60.50
Over 1549cc	165.00	90.75
Motor Cycles (with or without sidecar)		
Not over 150 cc	15.00	–
151–400 cc	30.00	–
401–600 cc	45.00	–
All other motorcycles	60.00	33.00
Tricycles		
Not over 150 cc	15.00	–
All Others	60.00	33.00
Buses (excluding driver)*		
Seating 9–16 persons	165.00 (165.00)	90.75 (90.75)
Seating 17–35 persons	220.00 (165.00)	121.00 (90.75)
Seating 36–60 persons	330.00 (165.00)	181.50 (90.75)
Seating over 61 persons	500.00 (165.00)	275.00 (90.75)

* Figures in parentheses refer to reduced pollution vehicles.

REGISTERED ON OR AFTER 1 MARCH 2001

Band	CO^2 *Emissions (g/km)*	Diesel Car *12 month rate £*	*6 month rate £*	Petrol Car *12 month rate £*	*6 month rate £*	Alternative Fuel Car *12 month rate £*	*6 month rate £*
AAA	Up to 100	75.00	41.25	65.00	35.75	55.00	30.25
AA	101–120	85.00	46.75	75.00	41.25	65.00	35.75
A	121–150	115.00	63.25	105.00	57.75	95.00	52.25
B	151–165	135.00	74.25	125.00	68.75	115.00	63.25
C	166–185	155.00	85.25	145.00	79.75	135.00	74.25
D	Over 185	165.00	90.75	160.00	88.00	155.00	85.25

MOT TESTING

Cars, motor cycles, motor caravans, light goods and dual-purpose vehicles more than three years old must be covered by a current MOT test certificate. However, some vehicles i.e. minibuses may require a certificate at one year old. All certificates must be renewed annually. The MOT testing scheme is administered by the Vehicle and Operator Services Agency (VOSA) on behalf of the Secretary of State for Transport.

A fee is payable to MOT testing stations, which must be authorised to carry out tests. The maximum fees, which are prescribed by regulations, are:

For cars and light vans	£40.75	
For solo motor cycles	£15.20	
For motor cycle combinations	£24.85	
For three-wheeled vehicles	£29.00	
Motor caravans	£40.75	
Dual purpose vehicles	£40.75	
Public service vehicles (up to 8 seats)	£40.75	
Ambulances and Taxis	£40.75	
Private passenger vehicles and ambulances		
With 9–12 passenger seats	£42.65	£47.85*
13–16 passenger seats	£45.70	£61.80*
Over 16 passenger seats	£61.95	£95.65*
For light goods vehicles between 3,000 and 3,500 kg	£44.40	

*Including seatbelt installation check

METHOD OF TRAVEL TO WORK, GREAT BRITAIN
(percentage)*

	1997	*2002*
Car, van, minibus, works van	71	70
Bus, coach, private bus	8	8
Train (incl. Underground and light rail)	6	7
Walk	11	11
Other	5	5
All	100	100

* All figures are rounded
Source: DfT/The Stationery Office – *Transport Statistics Great Britain* (Crown copyright)

SHIPPING AND PORTS

Since earliest times sea trade has played a central role in Britain's economy. By the 17th century Britain had built up a substantial merchant fleet and by the early 20th century it dominated the world shipping industry. Until the late 1990s the size and tonnage of the UK-registered trading fleet had been steadily declining. In December 1998 the Government published, *British Shipping: Charting a New Course*, which outlined strategies to promote the long-term interests of British shipping. By the end of 2003 the number of ships in the UK fleet had increased by 55 per cent whilst tonnage more than tripled; and the UK-flagged merchant fleet now constitutes over 1 per cent of the world fleet.

Freight is carried by liner and bulk services, almost all scheduled liner services being containerised. About 95 per cent by weight of Britain's overseas trade is carried by sea; this amounts to 75 per cent of its total value. Passengers and vehicles are carried by roll-on, roll-off ferries, hovercraft, hydrofoils and high-speed catamarans. There were about 51 million ferry passengers a year in 2002, of whom 29 million travelled internationally. The leading British operators of passenger services are P&O Ferries and Stena Line (which has a Swedish parent company).

Lloyd's of London provides the most comprehensive shipping intelligence service in the world. *Lloyd's Shipping Index*, published daily, lists some 25,000 ocean-going vessels and gives the latest known report of each.

PORTS

There are about 100 commercially significant ports in Great Britain, including such ports as London, Dover, Forth, Tees and Hartlepool, Grimsby and Immingham, Sullom Voe, Milford Haven, Southampton, Felixstowe and Liverpool. Belfast is the principal freight port in Northern Ireland.

Broadly speaking, ports are owned and operated by private companies, local authorities or trusts. The largest operator is Associated British Ports which owns 21 ports. Total freight traffic through UK ports in 2002 amounted to 558 million tonnes, a decrease of 1 per cent on the previous year's figure of 566 million tonnes.

MARINE SAFETY

From 1 October 2002 all roll-on, roll-off ferries operating to and from the UK are required to meet the new international safety standards on stability established by the Stockholm Agreement.

The Maritime and Coastguard Agency (MCA) was established on 1 April 1998 by the merger of the Coastguard Agency and the Marine Safety Agency. It is an executive agency of the Department for Transport. The Agency's aims are to reduce accidents and deaths at sea and minimise pollution in UK waters. HM Coastguard co-ordinates all civil maritime Search and Rescue around the UK and over a large part of the eastern Atlantic. There are about 560 full-time Coastguard Officers and a further 3,100 Auxiliary Coastguards. Each year HM Coastguard responds to around 13,000 incidents of which 7,500 are accidents to which search and rescue resources are deployed.

Locations hazardous to shipping in coastal waters are marked by lighthouses and other lights and buoys. The lighthouse authorities are the Corporation of Trinity House (for England, Wales and the Channel Islands), the Northern Lighthouse Board (for Scotland and the Isle of Man), and the Commissioners of Irish Lights (for Northern Ireland and the Republic of Ireland). Trinity House maintains 72 lighthouses, 11 major floating aids to navigation, 412 buoys, 19 beacons and 7 DGPS (Differential Positioning System) beacons*. The Northern Lighthouse Board maintains 198 lighthouses and 131 buoys; and Irish Lights 80 lighthouses and 145 buoys.

Harbour authorities are responsible for pilotage within their harbour areas; and the Ports Act 1991 provides for the transfer of lights and buoys to harbour authorities where these are used for mainly local navigation.

* DGPS is a satellite based navigation system provided under the three Lighthouse Authorities' Marine Navigation Plan and became operational on 1 July 2002

UK OWNED TRADING VESSELS OF 100 GROSS TONS AND OVER *as at end 2002*

Type of vessel	*No.*	*Gross tonnage*
Tankers	140	2,628,000
Bulk carriers	35	1,772,000
Specialised carriers	14	101,000
Fully cellular container	72	2,509,000
Ro-Ro (passenger & cargo)	140	1,432,000
Other general cargo	149	580,000
Passenger	40	730,000
Total	590	9,752,000

Source: Department for Transport

UK INTERNATIONAL PASSENGER MOVEMENTS BY SEA 2002*

All passenger movements†	29,295,000
Irish Republic, European continent and Mediterranean Sea area	28,726,000
Rest of the World	32,000
Pleasure cruises†	537,000

* Passengers are included at both departure and arrival if their journeys begin and end at a UK seaport
† provisional figures
Source: The Stationery Office – *Annual Abstract of Statistics 2004* (Crown copyright)

MARINECALL WEATHER FORECAST SERVICE

Marinecall provides information for coastal, inshore and offshore UK sea areas by telephone. Forecasts include gale and strong wind warnings, the general situation, wind speed and direction, probability and strength of gusts, developing weather conditions, visibility and sea state and can vary in format from current observations to six-hour summaries, to 48-hour and five-day forecasts.

	By Phone *6-hour coastal location and 5-day outlook forecast*	By Fax *6-hour coastal location and 48-hour outlook forecasts*
COASTAL/INSHORE AREA	09014-737 4+	09065-300 2+
National inshore waters (3–5 day outlook only)	60	–
Cape Wrath – Rattray Head	61	51
Rattray Head – Berwick	62	52
Berwick – Whitby	63	53
Whitby – The Wash	64	54
The Wash – North Foreland	65	55
North Foreland – Selsey Bill	66	56
Selsey Bill – Lyme Regis	67	57
Lyme Regis – Hartland Point	68	58
Hartland Point – St David's Head	69	59
St David's Head – Colwyn Bay	70	60
Colwyn Bay – Mull of Galloway	71	61
Mull of Galloway – Mull of Kintrye	72	62
Mull of Kintrye – Ardnamurchan	73	63
Ardnamurchan – Cape Wrath*	74	64
Lough Foyle – Carlingford Lough*	75	65
Channel Islands*	76	66
OFFSHORE AREA		
English Channel	41	70
Southern North Sea	42	71
Irish Sea	43	73
Biscay	44	74
North-west Scotland	45	75
Northern North Sea	46	76

* Localised 6-hour forecasts are unavailable for these areas
Based upon calls from a BT landline. Marinecall by telephone is charged at 60p per minute. Marinecall by fax is charged at £1.50 per minute.

UK SHIPPING FORECAST AREAS

Weather bulletins for shipping are broadcast daily on BBC Radio 4 at the following times: 0048 and 0535 (long wave and FM), 1200 and 1755 (normally long wave only). The bulletins consist of a gale warning summary, general synopsis, sea-area forecasts and coastal station reports. In addition, gale warnings are broadcast at the first available programme break after receipt. If this does not coincide with a news bulletin, the warning is repeated after the next news bulletin.

RELIGION IN THE UK

The 2001 census included a voluntary question on religion for the first time (although the question had been included in previous censuses in Northern Ireland); 92 per cent of people chose to answer the question. In the UK, 71.6 per cent of people in Britain identified themselves as Christian (42.1 million people). After Christianity, the next most prevalent faith was Islam with 2.7 per cent describing their religion as Muslim (1.6 million people). The next largest religious groups were Hindus (559,000), followed by Sikhs (336,000), Jews (267,000), Buddhists (152,000) and people from other religions (179,000). Together, these groups accounted for less than 3 per cent of the total UK population. People in Northern Ireland were most likely to say that they identified with a religion (86 per cent) compared with 77 per cent in England and Wales and 67 per cent in Scotland. About 16 per cent of the UK population stated that they had no religion. This category included those who identified themselves as agnostics, atheists, heathens and Jedi Knights.

CENSUS 2001 RESULTS – RELIGIONS IN THE UK
(thousands)

Christian	42,079	71.6%
Buddhist	152	0.3%
Hindu	559	1.0%
Jewish	267	0.5%
Muslim	1,591	2.7%
Sikh	336	0.6%
Other religion	179	0.3%
All religions	45,163	76.8%
No religion	9,104	15.5%
Not stated	4,289	7.3%
All no religion/not stated	13,626	23.2%
Total	58,789	100%

Source: Census 2001

ADHERENTS TO RELIGIONS IN THE UK
(millions)

	1975	1985	1995	2000
Christian (Trinitarian)	40.2	39.1	38.1	37.5
Non-Trinitarian	0.7	1.0	1.3	1.3
Hindu	0.3	0.4	0.4	0.5
Jew	0.4	0.3	0.3	0.3
Muslim	0.4	0.9	1.2	1.4
Sikh	0.2	0.3	0.6	0.6
Other	0.1	0.3	0.3	0.4
Total	42.3	42.3	42.2	42.0

Source: Christian Research – *UK Christian Handbook Religious Trends No. 3 2002–3*

INTER-CHURCH AND INTER-FAITH CO-OPERATION

The main umbrella body for the Christian churches in the UK is the Churches Together in Britain and Ireland. There are also ecumenical bodies in each of the constituent countries of the UK: Churches Together in England, Action of Churches Together in Scotland, CYTUN (Churches Together in Wales), and the Irish Council of Churches. The Free Churches' Council comprises most of the Free Churches in England and Wales, and the Evangelical Alliance represents evangelical Christians.

The Inter Faith Network for the United Kingdom promotes co-operation between faiths, and the Council of Christians and Jews works to improve relations between the two religions. Churches Together in Britain and Ireland also has a Commission on Inter-Faith Relations.

ACTION OF CHURCHES TOGETHER IN SCOTLAND, Scottish Churches House, Kirk Street, Dunblane, Perthshire FK15 0AJ **T** 01786-823588 **F** 01786-825844 **E** ecumenical@acts-scotland.org **W** www.acts-scotland.org
General Secretary, Revd Dr Kevin Franz

CHURCHES TOGETHER IN BRITAIN AND IRELAND, Bastille Court, 2 Paris Garden, London SE1 8ND **T** 020-7654 7254 **F** 020-7654 7222 **E** info@ctbi.org.uk **W** www.ctbi.org.uk
General Secretary, Dr David Goodbourn

CHURCHES TOGETHER IN ENGLAND, 27 Tavistock Square, London WC1H 9HH **T** 020-7529 8141 **F** 020-7529 8134 **W** www.churches-together.org.uk
General Secretary, Revd Bill Snelson

COUNCIL OF CHRISTIANS AND JEWS, Camelford House, 87–89 Albert Embankment, London, SE1 7TP **T** 020-7820 0090 **F** 020-7820 0504 **E** cjrelations@ccj.org.uk **W** www.ccj.org.uk
Director, Sister Margaret Shepherd

CYTUN (CHURCHES TOGETHER IN WALES), 58 Richmond Road, Cardiff CF24 3UR **T** 029-2046 4204 **F** 029-2045 5427 **E** post@cytun.org.uk **W** www.cytun.org.uk
General Secretary, Revd Gethin Abraham-Williams

EVANGELICAL ALLIANCE, Whitefield House, 186 Kennington Park Road, London SE11 4BT **T** 020-7207 2100 **F** 020-7207 2150 **E** london@eauk.org **W** www.eauk.org
General Director, Revd Joel Edwards

INTER FAITH NETWORK FOR THE UNITED KINGDOM, 8A Lower Grosvenor Place, London SW1W 0EN **T** 020-7931 7766 **F** 020-7931 7722 **E** ifnet@interfaith.org.uk **W** www.interfaith.org.uk
Director, Brian Pearce, OBE

IRISH COUNCIL OF CHURCHES, Inter-Church Centre, 48 Elmwood Avenue, Belfast BT9 6AZ **T** 028-9066 3145 **F** 028-9066 4160 **E** icpep@email.com **W** www.irishchurches.org
General Secretary, Michael Earle

CHRISTIANITY

Christianity is a monotheistic faith based on the person and teachings of Jesus Christ and all Christian denominations claim his authority. Central to its teaching is the concept of God and his son Jesus Christ, who was crucified and resurrected in order to enable mankind to attain salvation. The Jewish scriptures predicted the coming of a *Messiah*, an 'anointed one', who would bring salvation. To Christians, Jesus of Nazareth, a Jewish rabbi (teacher), who was born in Palestine, was the promised Messiah. Jesus' birth, teachings, crucifixion and subsequent resurrection are recorded in the *Gospels*, which, together with other scriptures that summarise Christian belief, form the *New Testament*. This, together with the Hebrew scriptures, entitled the *Old Testament* by Christians, makes up the *Bible*, the sacred texts of Christianity.

BELIEFS
Christians believe that sin distanced mankind from God, and that Jesus was the Son of God, sent to redeem mankind from that sin by his death. In addition, many believe that Jesus will return again at some future date, triumph over evil and establish a kingdom on earth, thus inaugurating a new age. The Gospel assures Christians that those who believe in Jesus and obey his teachings will be forgiven their sins and will be resurrected from the dead.

PRACTICES
Christian practices vary widely between different Christian churches, but prayer is universal to all, as is charity, giving for the maintenance of the church buildings, for the work of the church, and to the poor and needy. In addition, certain days of observance, i.e. the *Sabbath*, *Easter* and *Christmas*, are celebrated by most Christians. The Orthodox, Roman Catholic and Anglican churches celebrate many more days of observance, based on saints and significant events in the life of Jesus. The belief in sacraments, physical signs believed to have been ordained by Jesus Christ to symbolise and convey spiritual gifts, varies greatly between Christian denominations; *Baptism* and the *Eucharist* are practised by most Christians. Baptism, symbolising repentance and faith in Jesus is an act marking entry into the Christian community; the Eucharist, the ritual re-enactment of the Last Supper, Jesus' final meal with his disciples, is also practised by most denominations. Other sacraments, such as anointing the sick, the laying on of hands to symbolise the passing on of the office of priesthood or to heal the sick and speaking in tongues, where it is believed that the person is possessed by the Holy Spirit, the Spirit of God, are less common. In denominations where infant baptism is practised, confirmation is common, where the person repeats the commitments made for him or her at infancy. Matrimony and the ordination of priests are also widely believed to be sacraments. Many Protestants only view baptism and the Eucharist as sacraments; the Quakers and the Salvation Army reject the use of sacraments. Most Christians believe that God actively guides the Church.

THE EARLY CHURCH
The apostles were Jesus' first converts and are recognised by Christians as the founders of the Christian community. The new faith spread rapidly throughout the eastern provinces of the Roman Empire. Early Christianity was subject to great persecution until 313 AD, when Emperor Constantine's Edict of Toleration confirmed its right to exist and it became established as the religion of the Roman Empire in 381 AD.

The Christian faith was slowly formulated in the first millennium of the Christian era. Between AD 325 and 787 there were seven Oecumenical Councils at which bishops from the entire Christian world assembled to resolve various doctrinal disputes. The estrangement between East and West began after Constantine moved the centre of the Roman Empire from Rome to Constantinople, and it grew after the division of the Roman Empire into eastern and western halves. Linguistic and cultural differences between Greek East and Latin West served to encourage separate ecclesiastical developments which became pronounced in the tenth and early 11th centuries.

Administration of the church was divided between five ancient patriarchates: Rome and all the West, Constantinople (the imperial city – the 'New Rome'), Jerusalem and all Palestine, Antioch and all the East, and Alexandria and all Africa. Of these, only Rome was in the Latin West and after the schism in 1054, Rome developed a structure of authority centralised on the Papacy, while the Orthodox East maintained the style of localised administration. Papal authority over the doctrine and jurisdiction of the Church in western Europe was unrivalled after the split with the Eastern Orthodox Church until the Protestant Reformation in the 16th century.

CHRISTIANITY IN BRITAIN
An English Church already existed when Pope Gregory sent Augustine to evangelise the English in AD 596. Conflicts between Church and State during the Middle Ages culminated in the Act of Supremacy in 1534, which repudiated papal supremacy and declared King Henry VIII to be the supreme head of the Church in England. Since 1559 the English monarch has been termed the Supreme Governor of the Church of England. In 1560 the jurisdiction of the Roman Catholic Church in Scotland was abolished and the first assembly of the Church of Scotland ratified the Confession of Faith, drawn up by a committee including John Knox. In 1592 Parliament passed an Act guaranteeing the liberties of the Church and its presbyterian government. King James VI (James I of England) and later Stuart monarchs attempted to reintroduce episcopacy, but a presbyterian church was finally restored in 1690 and secured by the Act of Settlement (1690) and the Act of Union (1707).

PORVOO DECLARATION
The Porvoo Declaration was drawn up by representatives of the British and Irish Anglican churches and the Nordic and Baltic Lutheran churches and was approved by the General Synod of the Church of England in July 1995. Churches that approve the Declaration regard baptised members of each other's churches as members of their own, and allow free interchange of episcopally ordained ministers within the rules of each church.

NON-CHRISTIAN RELIGIONS AND BELIEFS

BAHÁ'Í FAITH

Mirza Husayn-'Ali, known as *Bahá'u'lláh* (Glory of God) was born in Iran in 1817 and became a follower of the *Báb*, a religious reformer and prophet who was imprisoned for his beliefs and executed on the grounds of heresy in 1850. *Bahá'u'lláh* was himself imprisoned in 1852, and in 1853 he had a vision that he was the Promised One foretold by the *Báb*. He was exiled after his release from prison and eventually arrived in Acre, now in Israel, where he continued to compose the Bahá'í sacred scriptures. He died in 1892 and was succeeded by his son, Abdu'l-Bahá, as spiritual leader, under whose guidance the faith spread to Europe and North America. He was followed by Shoghi Effendi, his grandson, who translated many of *Bahá'u'lláh*'s works into English. Upon his death in 1957, a democratic system of leadership was brought into operation. The Bahá'í faith recognises the unity and relativity of religious truth and teaches that there is only one God, whose will has been revealed to mankind by a series of messengers, such as Zoroaster, Abraham, Moses, Buddha, Krishna, Christ, Muhammad, the Báb and Bahá'u'lláh, who were seen as the founders of separate religions, but whose common purpose was to bring God's message to mankind. It teaches that all races and both sexes are equal and deserving of equal opportunities and treatment, that education is a fundamental right and encourages a fair distribution of wealth. In addition, mankind is exhorted to establish a world federal system to promote peace and tolerance.

A Feast is held every 19 days, which consists of prayer and readings of Bahá'í scriptures, consultation on community business, and social activities. Music, food and beverages usually accompany the proceedings. There is no clergy; each local community elects a local assembly, which co-ordinates community activities, enrols new members, counsels and assists members in need, and conducts Bahá'í marriages and funerals. A national assembly is elected annually by locally elected delegates, and every five years the national spiritual assemblies meet together to elect the Universal House of Justice, the supreme international governing body of the Bahá'í Faith. World-wide there are over 13,000 local spiritual assemblies; there are around five million members residing in about 235 countries, of which 182 have national organisations.

THE BAHÁ'Í OFFICE OF PUBLIC INFORMATION, 27 Rutland Gate, London SW7 1PD T 020-7584 2566 F 020-7584 9402 E nsa@bahai.org.uk W www.bahai.org.uk
Secretary of the National UK Spiritual Assembly, The Hon. Barnabus Leith

BUDDHISM

Buddhism originated in northern India, in the teachings of Siddharta Gautama, who was born near Kapilavastu about 560 BC and became the *Buddha* (Enlightened One).

Fundamental to Buddhism is the concept of rebirth. Each life carries with it the consequences of the conduct of earlier lives (known as the law of *karma*). This cycle of death and rebirth is broken only when the state of *nirvana* has been reached. Buddhism steers a middle path between belief in personal immortality and belief in death as the final end.

The Four Noble Truths of Buddhism (*dukkha*, suffering; *tanha*, a thirst or desire for continued existence which causes dukkha; *nirvana*, the final liberation from desire and ignorance; and *ariya*, the path to nirvana) are all held to be universal and to sum up the *dhamma* or true nature of life. Necessary qualities to promote spiritual development are *sila* (morality), *samadhi* (meditation) and *panna* (wisdom).

There are two main schools of Buddhism: *Theravada* Buddhism, the earliest extant school, which is more traditional, and *Mahayana* Buddhism, which began to develop about 500 years after the Buddha's death and is more liberal; it teaches that all people may attain Buddhahood. Important schools that have developed within Mahayana Buddhism are *Zen* Buddhism, *Nichiren* Buddhism and Pure Land Buddhism or *Amidism*. There are also distinctive Tibetan forms of Buddhism. Buddhism began to establish itself in the West in the early 20th century. The scripture of Theravada Buddhism is the *Pali Canon*, which dates from the first century BC. Mahayana Buddhism uses a Sanskrit version of the Pali Canon but also has many other works of scripture.

There is no set time for Buddhist worship, which may take place in a temple or in the home. Worship centres around meditation, acts of devotion centring on the image of the Buddha, and, where possible, offerings to a relic of the Buddha. Buddhist festivals vary according to local traditions and within Theravada and Mahayana Buddhism. For religious purposes Buddhists use solar and lunar calendars, the New Year being celebrated in April. Other festivals mark events in the life of the Buddha.

There is no supreme governing authority in Buddhism. In the United Kingdom communities representing all schools of Buddhism have developed and operate independently. The Buddhist Society was established in 1924; it runs courses and lectures, and publishes books about Buddhism. It represents no one school of Buddhism.

There are estimated to be at least 300 million Buddhists world-wide, and more than 500 groups and centres and up to 20 temples or monasteries in the UK.

THE BUDDHIST SOCIETY, 58 Eccleston Square, London SW1V 1PH T 020-7834 5858 F 020-7976 5238 E info@thebuddhistsociety.org.uk W www.thebuddhistsociety.org.uk

FRIENDS OF THE WESTERN BUDDHIST ORDER, FWBO Communications Office, 59 Roman Road, E2 0QN T 020-8981 8000 W www.lbc.org.uk

THE NETWORK OF BUDDHIST ORGANISATIONS, 6 Tyne Road, Bishopston, Bristol BS7 8EE T 0845-345 8978 E secretary@nbo.org.uk W www.nbo.org.uk

OFFICE OF TIBET, Tibet House, 1 Culworth Street, London NW8 7AF T 020-7722 5378

SOKA GAKKAI UK, Taplow Court, Taplow, Maidenhead, Berkshire SL6 0ER T 01628-773163 W www.sgi-uk.org

HINDUISM

Hinduism has no historical founder but had become highly developed in India by about 1200 BC. Its adherents originally called themselves Aryans; Muslim invaders first called the Aryans 'Hindus' (derived from 'Sindhu', the name of the river Indus) in the eighth century.

Most Hindus hold that *satya* (truthfulness), *ahimsa* (non-violence), honesty, sincerity and devotion to God are essential for good living. They believe in one supreme spirit *(Brahman)*, and in the transmigration of *atman* (the soul). Most Hindus accept the doctrine of *karma* (consequences of actions), the concept of *samsara* (successive lives) and the possibility of all atmans achieving *moksha* (liberation from samsara) through *jnana* (knowledge), *yoga* (meditation), *karma* (work or action) and *bhakti* (devotion).

Most Hindus offer worship to *murtis* (images of deities) representing different incarnations or aspects of Brahman, and follow their *dharma* (religious and social duty) according to the traditions of their *varna* (social class), *ashrama* (stage in life), *jati* (caste) and *kula* (family).

Hinduism's sacred texts are divided into *shruti* ('that which is heard'), including the *Vedas*; or *smriti* ('that which is remembered'), including the *Ramayana*, the *Mahabharata*, the *Puranas* (ancient myths), and the sacred law books. Most Hindus recognise the authority of the *Vedas*, the oldest holy books, and accept the philosophical teachings of the *Upanishads*, the *Vedanta Sutras* and the *Bhagavad-Gita*.

Brahman is omniscient, omnipotent, limitless and all-pervading, and is usually worshipped in His deity form. Brahma, Vishnu and Shiva are the most important gods worshipped by Hindus; their respective consorts are

Saraswati, Lakshmi and Durga or Parvati, also known as Shakti. There are believed to have been ten *avatars* (incarnations) of Vishnu, of whom the most important are Rama and Krishna. Other popular gods are Ganesha, Hanuman and Subrahmanyam. All gods are seen as aspects of the supreme God, not as competing deities.

Orthodox Hindus revere all gods and goddesses equally, but there are many denominations, including the Hare-Krishna movement (ISKCon), the Arya Samaj, the Swami Narayan Hindu mission and the Satya Sai-Baba movement, in which worship is concentrated on one deity. The *guru* (spiritual teacher) is seen as the source of spiritual guidance.

Hinduism does not have a centrally-trained and ordained priesthood. The pronouncements of the *shankaracharyas* (heads of monasteries) of Shringeri, Puri, Dwarka and Badrinath are heeded by the orthodox but may be ignored by the various sects.

The commonest form of worship is a *puja*, in which offerings of water, flowers, food, fruit, incense and light are made to a deity. Puja may be done either in a home shrine or a *mandir* (temple). Many British Hindus celebrate *samskars* (purification rites) to name a baby, the sacred thread (an initiation ceremony), marriage and cremation.

The largest communities of Hindus in Britain are in Leicester, London, Birmingham and Bradford, and developed as a result of immigration from India, eastern Africa and Sri Lanka.

There are an estimated 800 million Hindus worldwide; there are about 500,000 adherents, according to the 2001 UK census, and over 150 temples in the UK.

ARYA PRATINIDHI SABHA (UK) AND ARYA SAMAJ LONDON, 69A Argyle Road, London W13 0LY
T 020-8991 1732

BHARATIYA VIDYA BHAVAN, Institute of Indian Art and Culture, 4A Castletown Road, London W14 9HE
T 020-7381 3086 E info@bhavan.net W www.bhavan.net
Executive Director, Dr M. N. Nandakumara

INTERNATIONAL SOCIETY FOR KRISHNA CONSCIOUSNESS (ISKCON), Bhaktivedanta Manor, Dharam Marg, Hilfield Lane, Aldenham, Watford, Herts WD2 8EZ T 01923-857244 W www.krishnatemple.com
Temple President, Gauri Das

NATIONAL COUNCIL OF HINDU TEMPLES (UK), Bhakrivedanta Manor, Letchmore Heath, Watford WD2 8EP
T 01923-856269
Secretary, Bimal Krishna Das

SWAMINARAYAN HINDU MISSION (SHRI SWAMINARAYAN MANDIR), 105–119 Brentfield Road, London NW10 8LD T 020-8965 2651 F 020 8965 6313
E admin@mandir.org W www.mandir.org

VISHWA HINDU PARISHAD (UK), 48 Wharfedale Gardens, Thornton Heath, Surrey CR7 6LB T 020-8684 9716
General Secretary, Kishor Ruparelia

HUMANISM

Humanism traces its roots back to ancient times, with Indian, Chinese, Greek and Roman philosophers expressing Humanist ideas some 2,500 years ago. Confucius, the Chinese philosopher who lived around 500 BC, believed that religious observances should be replaced with moral values as the basis of social and political order and that 'the true way' is based on reason and humanity. He also stressed the importance of benevolence, respect for others and believed that the individual situation should be considered rather than the global application of traditional rules. Humanists believe that there is no God or other supernatural beings and that humans have only one life within the material universe (Humanists do not believe in an after-life or reincarnation). Humanists believe that humans can live ethical and fulfilling lives without religious beliefs through a moral code derived from the lessons of history, personal experience and thought. Particular emphasis is placed on science as the only reliable source of knowledge of the universe. Humanists have a positive outlook on life believing that the world's problems can be solved through co-operation and mutual respect and that personal inspiration can be gained from life, especially art, culture and the natural world. There are no sacred Humanist texts. Humanists believe in ceremonies to mark important occasions in life and the British Humanist Association has a network of accredited officials and celebrants who are qualified to conduct baby namings, weddings and funerals.

BRITISH HUMANIST ASSOCIATION, 1 Gower Street, London, WC1E 6HD T 020-7079 3580
F 020-7079 3588 E info@humanism.org.uk
W www.humanism.org.uk

ISLAM

Islam (which means 'peace arising from submission to the will of Allah' in Arabic) is a monotheistic religion which was taught in Arabia by the Prophet Muhammad, who was born in Mecca (Al-Makkah) in 570 CE. Islam spread to Egypt, North Africa, Spain and the borders of China in the century following the Prophet's death, and is now the predominant religion in Indonesia, the Near and Middle East, northern and parts of western Africa, Pakistan, Bangladesh, Malaysia and some of the former Soviet republics. There are also large Muslim communities in other countries.

For Muslims (adherents of Islam), there is one God (*Allah*), who holds absolute power. His commands were revealed to mankind through the prophets, who include Abraham, Moses and Jesus, but his message was gradually corrupted until revealed finally and in perfect form to Muhammad through the angel *Jibril* (Gabriel) over a period of 23 years. This last, incorruptible message has been recorded in the *Qur'an* (Koran), which contains 114 divisions called *surahs*, each made up of *ayahs*, and is held to be the essence of all previous scriptures. The *Ahadith* are the records of the Prophet Muhammad's deeds and sayings (the *Sunnah*) as recounted by his immediate followers. A culture and a system of law and theology gradually developed to form a distinctive Islamic civilisation. Islam makes no distinction between sacred and worldly affairs and provides rules for every aspect of human life. The *Shari'ah* is the sacred law of Islam based upon prescriptions derived from the Qur'an and the *Sunnah* of the Prophet.

The 'five pillars of Islam' are *shahadah* (a declaration of faith in the oneness and supremacy of Allah and the messengership of Muhammad); *salat* (formal prayer, to be performed five times a day facing the *Ka'bah* (sacred house in the holy city of Al-Makkah)); *zakat* (welfare due); *sawm* (fasting during the month of Ramadan); and *hajj* (pilgrimage to Al-Makkah); some Muslims would add *jihad* (striving for the cause of good and resistance to evil).

Two main groups developed among Muslims. *Sunni* Muslims accept the legitimacy of Muhammad's first four *caliphs* (successors as head of the Muslim community) and of the authority of the Muslim community as a whole. About 90 per cent of Muslims are Sunni Muslims.

Shi'ites recognise only Muhammad's son-in-law Ali as his rightful successor and the *Imams* (descendants of Ali, not to be confused with *imams* (prayer leaders or religious teachers)) as the principal legitimate religious authority. The largest group within Shi'ism is *Twelver Shi'ism*, which has been the official school of law and theology in Iran since the 16th century; other subsects include the *Ismailis*, the *Druze* and the *Alawis*, the latter two differing considerably from the main body of Muslims. The *Ibadhis* of Oman are neither Sunni nor Shi'a, deriving from the strictly observant *Khariji* (Seceeders). There is no organised priesthood, but learned men such as *ulama*, *imams* and *ayatollahs* are accorded great respect. The *Sufis* are the mystics of Islam. Mosques are centres for worship and teaching and also for social and welfare activities.

Islam was first known in western Europe in the eighth century AD when 800 years of Muslim rule began in Spain. Later, Islam spread to eastern Europe. More recently, Muslims came to Europe from Africa, the Middle East and Asia in the late 19th century. Both the Sunni and Shi'a traditions are represented in Britain, but the majority of Muslims in Britain adhere to Sunni Islam. Efforts to establish a representative central organisation recognised by all Muslims in Britain are beginning to yield results with the emergence of the Muslim Council of Britain. In addition, there are many other Muslim organisations in Britain. There are about 1,000 million Muslims world-wide, with nearly two million adherents and about 1,200 mosques in Britain.

IMAMS AND MOSQUES COUNCIL, 20–22 Creffield Road, London W5 3RP T 020-8992 6636
Chairman of the Council and Principal of the Muslim College, Dr M. A. Z. Badawi

ISLAMIC CULTURAL CENTRE, 146 Park Road, London NW8 7RG T 020-7724 3363 F 020-7724 0493
E islamic200@aol.com W www.islamicculturalcentre.co.uk
Director, Dr A. Al-Dubayan

MUSLIM COUNCIL OF BRITAIN, Suite 5, Boardman House, 64 Broadway, Stratford, London E15 1NT T 020-8432 0585
F 020-8432 0587 E admin@mcb.org.uk
W www.mcb.org.uk
Secretary-General, Iqbal Sacranie

MUSLIM WORLD LEAGUE, 46 Goodge Street, London W1P 1FJ T 020-7636 7568 E mwlgb@btconnect.com
Secretary, Ghulamur Rahman

UNION OF MUSLIM ORGANISATIONS OF THE UK AND EIRE, 109 Campden Hill Road, London W8 7TL
T 020-7229 0538/7221 6608
Secretary-General, Dr Syed A. Pasha

JAINISM

Jainism traces its history to Vardhamana Jnatiputra, known as *Tirthankara Mahavira* (The Great Hero) whose traditional dates were 599–527 BC. He was the last of a series of 24 *Jinas* (those who overcome all passions and desires) or *Tirthankaras* (those who show a way across the ocean of life) stretching back to remote antiquity. Born to a noble family in north-eastern India, he renounced the world for the life of a wandering ascetic and after 12 years of austerity and meditation he attained enlightenment. He then preached his message until, at the age of 72, he passed away and reached *moksha*, total liberation from the cycle of death and rebirth.

Jains deny the authority of the *Vedas*, the Hindu sacred scriptures. They recognise some of the minor deities of the Hindu pantheon, but the supreme objects of worship are the *Tirthankaras*. The pious Jain does not ask favours from the *Tirthankaras*, but seeks to emulate their example in his or her own life.

Jains believe that the universe is eternal and self-subsisting: there is no omnipotent creator God ruling it and the destiny of the individual is in his or her own hands. *Karma*, the fruit of past actions, determines the place of every living being and rebirth may be in the heavens, on earth as a human, an animal or other lower being, or in the hells. The ultimate goal of existence is *moksha* or *nirvana*, a state of perfect knowledge and tranquility for each individual soul, which can be achieved only by gaining enlightenment.

The path to liberation is defined by the Three Jewels, *samyak darsana* (right thought), *samyak jnana* (right knowledge) and *samyak charitra* (right conduct).

There are about 25,000 Jains in Britain, sizeable communities in North America and East Africa and smaller groups in many other countries.

INSTITUTE OF JAINOLOGY, Unit 18, Silicon Business Centre, 28 Wadsworth Road, Greenford, Middx, UB6 7JZ
T 020-8997 2300 W www.jainology.org
Chairman, Ratilal P. Chandaria

JUDAISM

Judaism is the oldest monotheistic faith. The primary authority of Judaism is the Hebrew Bible or *Tanakh*, which records how the descendants of Abraham were led by Moses out of their slavery in Egypt to Mount Sinai where God's law *(Torah)* was revealed to them as the chosen people. The *Talmud*, which consists of commentaries on the *Mishnah* (the first text of rabbinical Judaism), is also held to be authoritative, and may be divided into two main categories: the *halakah* (dealing with legal and ritual matters) and the *Aggadah* (dealing with theological and ethical matters not directly concerned with the regulation of conduct). The *Midrash* comprises rabbinic writings containing biblical interpretations in the spirit of the Aggadah. The *halakah* has become a source of division; Orthodox Jews regard Jewish law as derived from God and therefore unalterable; Reform and Liberal Jews seek to interpret it in the light of contemporary considerations; and Conservative Jews aim to maintain most of the traditional rituals but to allow changes in accordance with tradition. Reconstructionist Judaism, a 20th-century movement, regards Judaism as a culture rather than a theological system and accepts all forms of Jewish practice.

The family is the basic unit of Jewish ritual, with the synagogue playing an important role as the centre for public worship and religious study. A synagogue is led by a group of laymen who are elected to office. The Rabbi is primarily a teacher and spiritual guide. The Sabbath is the central religious observance. Most British Jews are descendants of either the *Ashkenazim* of central and eastern Europe or the *Sephardim* of Spain, Portugal and the Middle East.

The Chief Rabbi of the United Hebrew Congregations of the Commonwealth is appointed by a Chief Rabbinate Conference, and is the rabbinical authority of the mainstream Orthodox sector of the Ashkenazi Jewish community, the largest body of which is the United Synagogue. His formal ecclesiastical authority is not recognised by the Reform Synagogues of Great Britain (the largest progressive group), the Union of Liberal and

Progressive Synagogues, the Sephardi community, or the Assembly of Masorti Synagogues. He is, however, generally recognised both outside the Jewish community and within it as the public religious representative of the totality of British Jewry. The Chief Rabbi is President of the London *Beth Din*. *Beth Din* (Court of Judgement) is a rabbinic court. The *Dayanim* (Assessors) adjudicate in disputes or on matters of Jewish law and tradition; they also oversee dietary law administration.

The Board of Deputies of British Jews, established in 1760, is the representative body of British Jewry. The basis of representation is mainly synagogal, but communal organisations are also represented. It watches over the interests of British Jewry, acts as the central voice of the community and seeks to counter anti-Jewish discrimination and antisemitic activities. In November 1998 a Consultative Committee was established comprising representatives of the Assembly of Masorti Synagogues, Reform Synagogues of Great Britain, Union of Liberal and Progressive Synagogues and the United Synagogue. The Committee holds discussions to further communal harmony and development.

There are over 12.5 million Jews world-wide; in Great Britain and Ireland there are an estimated 285,000 adherents and about 365 synagogues. Of these, 191 congregations and about 175 rabbis and ministers are under the jurisdiction of the Chief Rabbi; 99 orthodox congregations have a more independent status; and 79 congregations are outside the jurisdiction of the Chief Rabbi.

CHIEF RABBINATE, Adler House, 735 High Road, London N12 0US **T** 020-8343 6301 **F** 020-8343 6310 **E** info@chiefrabbi.org **W** www.chiefrabbi.org
Chief Rabbi, Dr Jonathan Sacks
Executive Director, Syma Weinberg

BETH DIN (COURT OF THE CHIEF RABBI), 735 High Road, London N12 0US **T** 020-8343 6270 **F** 020-8343 6257 **E** info@bethdin.org.uk
Registrar, D. Frei; *Dayanim*, Rabbi Chanoch Ehrentreu; Ivan Binstock; Menachem Gelley; Yonason Abraham; I. Berger

BOARD OF DEPUTIES OF BRITISH JEWS, 6 Bloomsbury Square, London WC1A 2LP **T** 020-7543 5400 **F** 020-7543 0010 **E** info@bod.org.uk **W** www.bod.org.uk
President, Henry Grunwald, QC

ASSEMBLY OF MASORTI SYNAGOGUES, 1097 Finchley Road, London NW11 0PU **T** 020-8201 8772 **F** 020-8201 8917 **E** office@masorti.org.uk **W** www.masorti.org.uk
Executive Director, Michael Gluckman

FEDERATION OF SYNAGOGUES, 65 Watford Way, London NW4 3AQ **T** 020-8202 2263 **F** 020-8203 0610
Chief Executive, G. D. Coleman

BETH DIN OF THE FEDERATION OF SYNAGOGUES, 65 Watford Way, London NW4 3AQ **T** 020-8202 2263
Registrar, Rabbi Zalman Unsdorfer; *Dayanim*, Yisroel Lichtenstein; Berel Berkovits; M. D. Elzas

LIBERAL JUDAISM, The Montagu Centre, 21 Maple Street, London W1T 4BE **T** 020-7580 1663 **F** 020-7631 9838 **E** montagu@liberaljudaism.org **W** www.liberaljudaism.org

REFORM SYNAGOGUE OF GREAT BRITAIN, The Sternberg Centre for Judaism, 80 East End Road, London N3 2SY **T** 020-8349 5640 **F** 020-8349 5699 **E** admin@reformjudaism.org.uk **W** www.reformjudaism.org.uk
Chief Executive, Rabbi Tony Bayfield

SPANISH AND PORTUGUESE JEWS' CONGREGATION, 2 Ashworth Road, London W9 1JY **T** 020-7289 2573 **F** 020-7289 2709 **E** howardmiller@spsyn.org.uk **W** www.sandp.org
Chief Executive, Howard Miller

UNION OF ORTHODOX HEBREW CONGREGATIONS, 140 Stamford Hill, London N16 6QT **T** 020-8802 6226
Principal Rabbinical Authority, Rabbi Ephraim Padwa

UNITED SYNAGOGUE HEAD OFFICE, Adler House, 735 High Road, London N12 0US **T** 020-8343 8989 **F** 020-8343 6262 **E** info@unitedsynagogue.org.uk **W** www.unitedsynagogue.org.uk
Chief Executive, Rabbi Saul Zneimer

PAGANISM

Paganism draws on the ideas of the Celtic people of pre-Roman Europe and is closely linked to Druidism. The first historical record of Druidry comes from classical Greek and Roman writers of the 3rd century BC, who noted the existence of Druids among a people called the Keltoi who inhabited central and southern Europe. The word druid may derive from the Indo-European 'dreo-vid', meaning 'one who knows the truth'. In practice it was probably understood to mean something like 'wise-one' or 'philospher-priest'. Pagans place much emphasis on the natural world and the ongoing cycle of life and death is central to Pagan beliefs. Most Pagans are eco-friendly and seek to live in a way that minimises harm to the natural environment. Pagans worship many different forms. The most important and widely recognised of these are the God and Goddess whose annual cycle of procreation, birth and dying defines the Pagan year. Paganism strongly emphasises the equality of the sexes with women playing a prominent role in the modern Pagan movement and Goddess worship featuring in most ceremonies. Paganism is not based on doctrine and many pagans follow the code 'if it harms none, do what you will'.

The Pagan Federation was founded in 1971 to provide information on Paganism and publishes a quarterly journal, *Pagan Dawn*, and other publications. It arranges members-only and public events and maintains personal contact by letter with individual members and the wider Pagan community. An annual conference is held at the end of each November and there are regional gatherings throughout the year. The aims of the Pagan Federation are to provide contact between national and international Pagan organisations.

THE PAGAN FEDERATION, BM Box 7097, London, WC1N 3XX

SIKHISM

The Sikh religion dates from the birth of Guru Nanak in the Punjab in 1469. 'Guru' means teacher but in Sikh tradition has come to represent the divine presence of God giving inner spiritual guidance. Nanak's role as the human vessel of the divine guru was passed on to nine successors, the last of whom (Guru Gobind Singh) died in 1708. The immortal guru is now held to reside in the sacred scripture, *Guru Granth Sahib*, and so to be present in all Sikh gatherings.

Guru Nanak taught that there is one God and that different religions are like different roads leading to the same destination. He condemned religious conflict, ritualism and caste prejudices. The fifth Guru, Guru Arjan Dev, largely compiled the Sikh Holy Book, a collection of hymns *(gurbani)* known as the *Adi Granth*. It includes the writings of the first five Gurus and the ninth Guru, and selected writings of Hindu and Muslim saints whose views are in accord with the Gurus' teachings. Guru Arjan Dev also built the Golden Temple at Amritsar, the centre of Sikhism. The tenth Guru, Guru Gobind Singh, passed on the guruship to the sacred scripture, Guru Granth Sahib. He also founded the *Khalsa*, an order intended to fight against tyranny and injustice. Male initiates to the order added 'Singh' to their given names and women added 'Kaur'. Guru Gobind Singh also made five symbols obligatory: *kaccha* (a special undergarment), *kara* (a steel bangle), *kirpan* (a small sword), *kesh* (long unshorn hair, and consequently the wearing of a turban), and *kangha* (a comb). These practices are still compulsory for those Sikhs who are initiated into the Khalsa (the *Amritdharis*). Those who do not seek initiation are known as *Sehajdharis*.

There are no professional priests in Sikhism; anyone with a reasonable proficiency in the Punjabi language can conduct a service. Worship can be offered individually or communally, and in a private house or a *gurdwara* (temple). Sikhs are forbidden to eat meat prepared by ritual slaughter; they are also asked to abstain from smoking, alcohol and other intoxicants. Such abstention is compulsory for the *Amritdharis*.

There are about 20 million Sikhs world-wide and about 500,000 adherents and 250 gurdwaras in Great Britain. Every gurdwara manages its own affairs and there is no central body in the UK. The Sikh Missionary Society provides an information service.

SIKH MISSIONARY SOCIETY UK, 10 Featherstone Road, Southall, Middx UB2 5AA **T** 020-8574 1902
Hon. General Secretary, M. S. Chahal

WORLD SIKH FOUNDATION (THE SIKH COURIER INTERNATIONAL), 33 Wargrave Road, South Harrow, Middx HA2 8LL **T** 020-8864 9228
Managing Editor, Mrs H. B. Bharara

ZOROASTRIANISM

Zoroastrianism was founded by Zarathushtra (or Zoroaster in its hellenised form) in Persia. Linguistic analysis of the earliest extant Zoroastrian texts suggests that he lived around 1500 BC. Zarathushtra's words are recorded in five poems called the *Gathas*, which, together with other scriptures, forms the *Avesta*.

Zoroastrianism teaches that there is one God, *Ahura Mazda* (the Wise Lord), and that all creation stems ultimately from God; the Gathas teach that human beings have free will, are responsible for their own actions and can choose between good and evil: Choosing *Asha* (truth or righteousness), with the aid of *Vohu Manah* (good mind), leads to happiness for the individual and society, whereas choosing evil leads to unhappiness and conflict. The *Gathas* also encourage hard work, good deeds and charitable acts. Zoroastrians believe that after death, the immortal soul is judged by God, and is then sent to paradise or hell, where it will stay until the end of time. It will be resurrected for the final judgement.

In Zoroastrian places of worship, an urn containing fire is the central feature; the fire symbolises purity, light, and truth and is a visible symbol of the *Fravashi* or *Farohar*, the presence of *Ahura Mazda* in every human being.

Zoroastrians respect nature and much importance is attached to cultivating land and protecting the air, the earth and water. The practice of leaving corpses on mountain tops or towers developed to avoid pollution.

Zoroastrians were persecuted in Iran following the Arab invasion of Persia in the seventh century AD, which also brought Islam and a group migrated to India in the tenth century AD, who are known as Parsis, to avoid harassment and persecution; there are fewer than 150,000 Zoroastrians world-wide, of which 7,000 reside in Britain, mainly in London and the south east.

ZOROASTRIAN TRUST FUNDS OF EUROPE, 88 Compayne Gardens, London NW6 3RU **T** 020-7328 6018 **E** secretary@ztfe.com **W** www.ztfe.com
President, Dorab E. Mistry

CHURCHES

There are two established, i.e. state, churches in the United Kingdom: the Church of England and the Church of Scotland. There are no established churches in Wales or Northern Ireland, though the Church in Wales, the Scottish Episcopal Church and the Church of Ireland are members of the Anglican Communion.

THE CHURCH OF ENGLAND

The Church of England is the established (i.e. national) church in England and seeks to serve the nation through its dioceses and parishes. It traces its life back to the first coming of Christianity to England. Its position is defined by the ancient creeds of the Church and by the 39 Articles of Religion (1571), the Book of Common Prayer (1662) and the Ordinal. The Church of England is thus both catholic and reformed. It is the mother church of the Anglican Communion.

THE ANGLICAN COMMUNION

The Anglican Communion consists of 38 independent provincial or national Christian churches throughout the world, many of which are in Commonwealth countries and originated from missionary activity by the Church of England. Every ten years all the bishops in the Communion meet at the Lambeth Conference, convened by the Archbishop of Canterbury. The Conference has no policy-making authority but is an important forum for discussing and forming consensus around issues common concern. The Anglican Consultative Council was set up in 1968 to liaise between the member churches and provinces of the Anglican Communion. It meets every three years. Meetings of the Anglican primates have taken place every two years since 1979.

There are about 70 million Anglicans organised into 500 dioceses and 64,000 individual congregations world-wide.

STRUCTURE

The Church of England is divided into the two provinces of Canterbury and York, each under an archbishop. The two provinces are subdivided into 44 dioceses.

Legislative provision for the Church of England is made by the General Synod, established in 1970. It also discusses and expresses opinion on any other matter of religious or public interest. The General Synod has 580 members in total, divided between three houses: the House of Bishops, the House of Clergy and the House of Laity. It is presided over jointly by the Archbishops of Canterbury and York and normally meets twice a year. The Synod has the power, delegated by Parliament, to frame statute law (known as a Measure) on any matter concerning the Church of England. A Measure must be laid before both Houses of Parliament, who may accept or reject it but cannot amend it. Once accepted the Measure is submitted for royal assent and then has the full force of law. In addition to the General Synod, there are Synods at diocesan level.

The Archbishops' Council was established in January 1999. Its creation was the result of changes to the Church of England's national structure proposed in 1995 and subsequently approved by the Synod and Parliament. The Council's purpose, set out in the National Institutions Measure 1998, is 'to co-ordinate, promote and further the work and mission of the Church of England'. It reports to the General Synod. The Archbishops' Council comprises the Archbishops of Canterbury and York, *ex officio*, the Prolocutors elected by the Convocations of Canterbury and York, the Chairman and Vice-Chairman of the House of Laity, elected by that House, two bishops, two clergy and two lay persons elected by their respective Houses of the General Synod, and up to six persons appointed jointly by the two Archbishops with the approval of the General Synod.

There are also a number of national Boards, Councils and other bodies working on matters such as social responsibility, mission, Christian unity and education which report to the General Synod through the Archbishops' Council.

GENERAL SYNOD OF THE CHURCH OF ENGLAND, Church House, Great Smith Street, London SW1P 3NZ T 020-7898 1000
Joint Presidents, The Archbishops of Canterbury and York

HOUSE OF BISHOPS: *Chairman,* The Archbishop of Canterbury; *Vice-Chairman,* The Archbishop of York

HOUSE OF CLERGY: *Chairmen (alternating),* Canon Bob Baker; Canon Glyn Webster

HOUSE OF LAITY: *Chairman,* Dr Christina Baxter; *Vice-Chairman,* Brian McHenry

ARCHBISHOPS' COUNCIL, Church House, Great Smith Street, London SW1P 3NZ T 020-7898 1000
Joint Presidents, The Archbishops of Canterbury and York; *Secretary-General,* William Fittall

THE ORDINATION OF WOMEN

The canon making it possible for women to be ordained to the priesthood was promulgated in the General Synod in February 1994 and the first 32 women priests were ordained on 12 March 1994.

MEMBERSHIP

In 2001, 153,000 people were baptised, the Church of England had an electoral roll membership of 1.4 million, and each week about 1.2 million people attended services. As at December 2002 there were over 16,000 churches and places of worship. At December 2002 there were 370 dignitaries (including bishops, archdeacons and cathedral clergy); 8,712 parochial stipendiary clergy; 399 non parochial stipendiary clergy; 1,159 chaplains etc; 35 lay workers and Church Army evangelists; 8,384 licensed readers and 1,900 readers with permission to officiate and active emeriti; and approximately 4,600 active retired ordained clergy.

FULL-TIME DIOCESAN CLERGY AND CHURCH ELECTORAL ROLL 2002

	Clergy		
	Male	*Female*	*Membership*
Bath and Wells	202	31	38,000
Birmingham	160	26	18,200

Blackburn	217	17	34,300
Bradford	103	12	12,300
Bristol	121	25	16,600
Canterbury	143	18	21,000
Carlisle	133	20	20,600
Chelmsford	347	53	48,600
Chester	230	35	45,700
Chichester	321	10	51,800
Coventry	120	23	16,300
Derby	156	18	20,700
Durham	192	27	24,000
Ely	122	26	19,100
Europe	98	1	9,300
Exeter	243	24	30,500
Gloucester	128	19	23,600
Guildford	153	36	29,500
Hereford	83	22	18,100
Leicester	136	28	17,000
Lichfield	293	51	45,000
Lincoln	166	38	27,800
Liverpool	197	34	28,800
London	464	60	59,600
Manchester	244	42	34,500
Newcastle	128	22	16,700
Norwich	181	21	23,900
Oxford	338	72	54,600
Peterborough	132	22	18,000
Portsmouth	100	12	27,500
Ripon and Leeds	112	29	17,600
Rochester	190	29	29,900
St Albans	216	55	39,400
St Edmundsbury and Ipswich	139	23	24,100
Salisbury	193	33	40,500
Sheffield	157	28	18,600
Sodor and Man	19	0	2,400
Southwark	295	63	44,200
Southwell	137	29	18,300
Truro	114	12	16,900
Wakefield	141	28	20,300
Winchester	221	25	38,500
Worcester	125	28	20,300
York	210	35	33,400
Total	7,920	1,262	1,206,000

STIPENDS 2004–5

Archbishop of Canterbury	£62,520
Archbishop of York	£54,770
Bishop of London	£51,080
Other diocesan bishops	£33,930
Suffragan bishops	£27,850
Assistant bishops (full-time)	£26,740
Deans and provosts	£27,850
Archdeacons (recommended)	£27,660
Residentiary canons	£22,690
Incumbents and clergy of similar status	£18,480*

*National Stipends Benchmark

CANTERBURY

104th ARCHBISHOP AND PRIMATE OF ALL ENGLAND
Most Revd and Rt. Hon. Rowan Williams, *cons.* 1992, *apptd* 2002; Lambeth Palace, London SE1 7JU
Signs Rowan Cantuar

BISHOPS SUFFRAGAN
Dover, Rt. Revd Stephen Venner, *cons.* 1994, *apptd* 1999; Upway, St Martin's Hill, Canterbury, Kent CT1 1PR
Maidstone, Rt. Revd Graham Cray, *cons.* 2001, *apptd* 2001, Bishop's House, Pett Lane, Charing, Ashford, Kent TN27 0DL
Ebbsfleet, Rt. Revd Andrew Burnham, *cons.* 2001, *apptd* 2001 (provincial episcopal visitor); Bishop's House, Dry Sandford, Oxon OX13 6JP
Richborough, Rt. Revd Keith Newton, *cons.* 2002, *apptd* 2002 (provincial episcopal visitor); 6 Mellis Gardens, Woodford Green, Essex IG8 0BH

DEAN
Very Revd Robert Willis, *apptd* 2001

CANONS RESIDENTIARY
Edward Condry, *apptd* 2002; Richard Marsh, *apptd* 2001

Organist, D. Flood, FRCO, *apptd* 1988

ARCHDEACONS
Canterbury, Ven. Patrick Evans, *apptd* 2002
Maidstone, Ven. Philip Down, *apptd* 2002

Vicar-General of Province and Diocese, Chancellor Sheila Cameron, QC
Commissary-General, His Hon. Judge Richard Walker
Joint Registrars of the Province, F. E. Robson, OBE; B. J. T. Hanson, CBE
Diocesan Registrar and Legal Adviser, Richard Sturt
Diocesan Secretary, David Kemp, Diocesan House, Lady Wootton's Green, Canterbury CT1 1NQ T 01227-459401

YORK

96th ARCHBISHOP AND PRIMATE OF ENGLAND
Most Revd and Rt. Hon. David M. Hope, KCVO, DPHIL., LLD, *cons.* 1985, *trans.* 1995; Bishopthorpe, York YO23 2GE
Signs David Ebor

BISHOPS SUFFRAGAN
Hull, Rt. Revd Richard M. C. Frith, *cons.* 1998, *apptd* 1998; Hullen House, Woodfield Lane, Hessle, Hull HU13 0ES
Selby, Rt. Revd Martin Wallace, *cons.* 2003, *apptd* 2003; Bishop's House, Barton le Street, Malton, York YO17 6PL
Whitby, Rt. Revd Robert S. Ladds, *cons.* 1999, *apptd* 1999; 60 West Green, Stokesley, Middlesbrough TS9 5BD
Beverley, Rt. Revd Martyn Jarrett, *cons.* 1994, *apptd* 2000 (provincial episcopal visitor); 3 North Lane, Roundhay, Leeds LS8 2QJ

DEAN
Very Revd Keith Jones, *apptd* 2004

CANONS RESIDENTIARY
Edward Norman, PHD, *apptd* 1999; Glyn Webster, *apptd* 1999; Jonathan Draper, *apptd* 2000; Jeremy Fletcher, *apptd* 2002

CANONS LAY
Lindsay Mackinlay, *apptd* 2000; Carol Rymer, *apptd* 2000; Dr Allen Warren, *apptd* 2000; Brig. Peter Lyddon (as Chapter Steward), *apptd* 2000; Peter Collier, QC, *apptd 2001*

Organist, Philip Moore, FRCO, *apptd* 1983

ARCHDEACONS
Cleveland, Ven. Paul Ferguson, *apptd* 2001
East Riding, Ven. Peter Harrison, *apptd* 1998
York, Ven. Richard Seed, *apptd* 1999

Official Principal and Auditor of the Chancery Court, Sir John Owen, QC
Chancellor of the Diocese, His Hon. Judge Coningsby, QC, *apptd* 1977
Vicar-General of the Province and Official Principal of the Consistory Court, His Hon. Judge Coningsby, QC
Registrar and Legal Secretary, Lionel Lennox
Diocesan Secretary, Colin Sheppard, Diocesan House, Aviator Court, Clifton Moor, York YO30 4WJ
T 01904-699500

LONDON *(Province of Canterbury)*

132nd BISHOP
Rt. Revd and Rt. Hon Richard J. C. Chartres, *cons.* 1992, *apptd.* 1995; The Old Deanery, Dean's Court, London EC4V 5AA
Signs Richard Londin

AREA BISHOPS
Edmonton, Rt. Revd Peter W. Wheatley, *cons.* 1999, *apptd* 1999; 27 Thurlow Road, London NW3 5PP
Kensington, Rt. Revd Michael J. Colclough, *cons.* 1996, *apptd* 1996; Dial House, Riverside, Twickenham, Middx TW1 3DT
Stepney, Rt. Revd Canon Stephen J. Oliver, *cons.* 2003, *apptd* 2003; 63 Coborn Road, London E3 2DB
Willesden, Rt. Revd Peter Broadbent, *cons.* 2001, *apptd* 2001; 173 Willesden Lane, London NW6 7YN

BISHOP SUFFRAGAN
Fulham, Rt. Revd John C. Broadhurst, *cons.* 1996, *apptd* 1996; 26 Canonbury Park South, London N1 2FN

DEAN OF ST PAUL'S
Very Revd John H. Moses, PHD, *apptd* 1996

CANONS RESIDENTIARY
Philip Buckler, *apptd* 1999; Peter Chapman, *apptd* 2001; Edmund Newall, *apptd* 2001; Martin Warner, *apptd* 2003; Lucy Winckett, *apptd* 2003

Registrar and Receiver of St Paul's, Maj.-Gen. John Milne

Organist, John Scott, FRCO, *apptd* 1990

ARCHDEACONS
Charing Cross, Ven. Dr William Jacob, *apptd* 1996
Hackney, Ven. Lyle Dennen, *apptd* 1999
Hampstead, Ven. Michael Lawson, *apptd* 1999
London, Ven. Peter Delaney, *apptd* 1999
Middlesex, Ven. Malcolm Colmer, *apptd* 1996
Northolt, Ven. Christopher Chessun, *apptd* 2001

Chancellor, Nigel Seed, QC, *apptd* 2002
Registrar and Legal Secretary, Paul Morris
Diocesan Secretary, Keith Robinson, London Diocesan House, 36 Causton Street, London SW1P 4AU
T 020-7932 1226

DURHAM *(Province of York)*

71st BISHOP
Rt. Revd Dr N. Thomas Wright, *cons.* 2003, *apptd* 2003; Auckland Castle, Bishop Auckland DL14 7NR
Signs Thomas Dunelm

BISHOP SUFFRAGAN
Jarrow, Rt. Revd John Pritchard, *cons.* 2002, *apptd* 2002; Bishop's House, Ivy Lane, Low Fell, Gateshead NE9 6QD

DEAN
Very Revd Michael Sadgrove, *apptd* 2003

CANONS RESIDENTIARY
Prof David Brown, *apptd* 1990; Stephen Conway, *apptd* 2002; David Kennedy, *apptd* 2001; Martin Kitchen, *apptd* 1997

Organist, James Lancelot, FRCO, *apptd* 1985

ARCHDEACONS
Auckland, Ven. Ian Jagger, *apptd* 2001
Durham, Ven. Stephen Conway, *apptd* 2002
Sunderland, Ven. Stuart Bain, *apptd* 2002

Chancellor, Revd Canon Rupert Bursell, QC, *apptd* 1989
Registrar and Legal Secretary, A. N. Fairclough
Diocesan Secretary, Jonathan Cryer, Auckland Castle, Bishop Auckland, Co. Durham DL14 7QJ T 01388-604515

WINCHESTER *(Canterbury)*

96th BISHOP
Rt. Revd Michael C. Scott-Joynt, *cons.* 1987, *trans.* 1995; Wolvesey, Winchester SO23 9ND
Signs Michael Winton

BISHOPS SUFFRAGAN
Basingstoke, Rt. Revd Trevor Willmott, *cons.* 2002, *apptd* 2002; Bishopswood End, Kingswood Rise, Four Marks, Alton, Hants GU34 5BD
Southampton, Rt. Revd Paul Butler, *cons.* 2004, *apptd* 2004; Ham House, The Crescent, Romsey SO51 7NG

DEAN
Very Revd Michael Till, *apptd* 1996

Dean of Jersey (A Peculiar), Very Revd John Seaford, *apptd* 1993
Dean of Guernsey (A Peculiar), Very Revd K. Paul Mellor, *apptd* 2003

CANONS RESIDENTIARY
Keith Anderson, *apptd* 2003; Ven. John Guille, *apptd* 1998; Charles Stewart, *apptd* 1997; Flora Winfield, *apptd* 2002

Organist, Andrew Lumsden, *apptd* 2002

ARCHDEACONS
Bournemouth, Ven. Adrian Harbidge, *apptd* 1998
Winchester, Ven. John Guille, *apptd* 1998

Chancellor, Christopher Clark, *apptd* 1993
Registrar and Legal Secretary, Peter White
Diocesan Secretary, Ray Anderton, Church House, 9 The Close, Winchester, Hants SO23 9LS
T 01962-844644

BATH AND WELLS *(Canterbury)*

78th BISHOP
Rt. Revd Peter Price, *cons.* 1997, *apptd* 2002; The Palace, Wells BA5 2PD
Signs Peter Bath & Wells

BISHOP SUFFRAGAN
Taunton, Rt. Revd Andrew John Radford, *cons.* 1998, *apptd* 1998; The Bishop's Lodge, Monkton Heights, West Monkton, Taunton, Somerset TA2 8LU

DEAN
Very Revd John Clarke *apptd* 2004

CANONS RESIDENTIARY
Russell Bowman-Eadie, *apptd* 2002; Melvyn Matthews, *apptd* 1997; Peter Maurice, *apptd* 2003; Patrick Woodhouse, *apptd* 2000

Organist, Malcolm Archer, *apptd* 1996

ARCHDEACONS
Bath, vacant
Taunton, Ven. John Reed, *apptd* 1999
Wells, Ven. Peter Maurice, *apptd* 2003
Chancellor, Timothy Briden, *apptd* 1993
Registrar and Legal Secretary, Tim Berry
Diocesan Secretary, Nicholas Denison, The Old Deanery, Wells, Somerset BA5 2UG T 01749-670777

BIRMINGHAM *(Canterbury)*
8th BISHOP
Rt. Revd Dr John Sentamu, *cons.* 1996, *apptd* 2002; Bishop's Croft, Harborne, Birmingham B17 0BG
Signs Sentamu Birmingham

BISHOP SUFFRAGAN
Aston, Rt. Revd John Austin, *cons.* 1992, *apptd* 1992; Strensham House, 8 Strensham Hill, Moseley, Birmingham B13 8AG

PROVOST
The Very Revd Gordon Mursell, *apptd* 2000

CANON RESIDENTIARY
Revd Gary O'Neill, *apptd* 1997

Organist, Marcus Huxley, FRCO, *apptd* 1986

ARCHDEACONS
Aston, vacant
Birmingham, Ven. Hayward Osborne, *apptd* 2001

Chancellor, vacant
Vice-Chancellor, David Pittaway
Registrar and Legal Secretary, Hugh Carslake
Diocesan Secretary, Jim Drennan, 175 Harborne Park Road, Harborne, Birmingham B17 0BH T 0121-426 0400

BLACKBURN *(York)*
8th BISHOP
Rt. Revd Nicholas Reade, *apptd* 2003, *cons.* March 2004; Bishop's House, Ribchester Road, Blackburn BB1 9EF
Signs Nicholas Blackburn

BISHOPS SUFFRAGAN
Burnley, Rt. Revd John Goddard, *cons.* 2000, *apptd* 2000; Dean House, 449 Padiham Road, Burnley BB12 6TE
Lancaster, Rt. Revd Stephen Pedley, *cons.* 1998, *apptd* 1998; Shireshead Vicarage, Whinneybrow, Forton, Preston PR3 0AE

DEAN
Very Revd Christopher Armstrong, *apptd* 2001

CANONS RESIDENTIARY
Peter Ballard, *apptd* 1998; Andrew Clitherow, *apptd* 2000; Andrew Hindley, *apptd* 1996

Organist, Richard Tanner, *apptd* 1998

ARCHDEACONS
Blackburn, Ven. John Hawley, *apptd* 2002
Lancaster, Ven. Colin Williams, *apptd* 1999

Chancellor, John Bullimore, *apptd* 1990
Registrar and Legal Secretary, Thomas Hoyle
Diocesan Secretary, Revd Canon Michael Wedgeworth, Diocesan Office, Cathedral Close, Blackburn BB1 5AA T 01254-54421

BRADFORD *(York)*
9th BISHOP
Rt. Revd David James, *apptd* 2002; Bishopscroft, Ashwell Road, Heaton, Bradford BD9 4AU
Signs David Bradford

DEAN
Very Revd Dr Christopher David Hancock, *apptd* 2002

CANON RESIDENTIARY
vacant

Organist, Andrew Teague, FRCO, *apptd* 2003

ARCHDEACONS
Bradford, Ven. David Lee, *apptd* 2004
Craven, Ven. Malcolm Grundy, *apptd* 1994

Chancellor, John de G. Walford, *apptd* 1999
Registrar and Legal Secretary, Peter Foskett
Diocesan Secretary, Malcolm Halliday, Kadugli House, Elmsley Street, Steeton, Keighley BD20 6SE T 01535-650555

BRISTOL *(Canterbury)*
55th BISHOP
Rt. Revd Michael Hill, *cons.* 1998, *apptd* 2003; Wethered House, 11 The Avenue, Clifton, Bristol BS8 3HG
Signs Michael Bristol

BISHOP SUFFRAGAN
Swindon, vacant

DEAN
Very Revd Robert W. Grimley, *apptd* 1997

CANONS RESIDENTIARY
Brendan Clover, *apptd* 1999; Douglas Holt, *apptd* 1998; Peter Johnson, *apptd* 1990

Organist, Mark Lee, *apptd* 1998

ARCHDEACONS
Bristol, Ven. Tim McClure, *apptd* 1999
Malmesbury, Ven. Alan Hawker, *apptd* 1998

Chancellor, Sir David Calcutt, QC, *apptd* 1971
Registrar and Legal Secretary, Tim Berry
Diocesan Secretary, Lesley Farrall, Diocesan Church House, 23 Great George Street, Bristol, Avon BS1 5QZ T 0117-906 0100

CARLISLE *(York)*
66th BISHOP
Rt. Revd Graham Dow, *cons.* 1985, *apptd* 2000; Rose Castle, Dalston, Carlisle CA5 7BZ
Signs Graham Carlisle

BISHOP SUFFRAGAN
Penrith, Rt. Revd James Newcome, *cons.* 2002, *apptd* 2002; Holm Croft, Castle Road, Kendal, Cumbria LA9 7AU

DEAN
Very Revd Mark Boyling, *apptd* 2004

CANONS RESIDENTIARY
David Jenkins, *apptd* 2004; David Weston, *apptd* 1994

Organist, Jeremy Suter, FRCO, *apptd* 1991

ARCHDEACONS
Carlisle, Ven. David Thomson, *apptd* 2002
West Cumberland, Ven. Colin Hill *apptd* 2004
Westmorland and Furness, Ven. George Howe, *apptd* 2000

Chancellor, Geoffrey Tattersall, QC, *apptd* 2003
Registrar and Legal Secretary, Susan Holmes
Diocesan Secretary, vacant, Church House, West Walls, Carlisle CA3 8UE T 01228-522573

CHELMSFORD *(Canterbury)*

9th BISHOP
Rt. Revd John Warren Gladwin, *cons.* 1994, *apptd* 2003, *trans.* 2004; Bishopscourt, Margaretting, Ingatestone CM4 0HD *Signs* John Chelmsford

BISHOPS SUFFRAGAN
Barking, Rt. Revd David Hawkins, *apptd* 2002
Bradwell, Rt. Revd Laurence Green, *cons.* 1993, *apptd* 1993; The Vicarage, Orsett Road, Horndon-on-the-Hill, Stanford-le-Hope, Essex SS17 8NS
Colchester, Rt. Revd Christopher Morgan, 1 Fitzwalter Road, Colchester, Essex CO3 3SS

DEAN
Very Revd Peter S. M. Judd, *apptd* 1997

CANONS RESIDENTIARY
Walter King, *apptd* 2001; Andrew Knowles, *apptd* 1998; Genny Tunbridge, *apptd* 2002

Master of Music, Peter Nardone, *apptd* 2000

ARCHDEACONS
Colchester, Ven. Annette Cooper, *apptd* 2004
Harlow, Ven. Peter Taylor, *apptd* 1996
Southend, Ven. David Lowman, *apptd* 2001
West Ham, Ven. Michael Fox, *apptd* 1996

Chancellor, George Pulman, *apptd* 2001
Registrar and Legal Secretary, Brian Hood
Diocesan Secretary, David Phillips, 53 New Street, Chelmsford, Essex CM1 1AT T 01245-294400

CHESTER *(York)*

40th BISHOP
Rt. Revd Peter R. Forster, PHD, *cons.* 1996, *apptd* 1996; Bishop's House, Chester CH1 2JD *Signs* Peter Cestr

BISHOPS SUFFRAGAN
Birkenhead, Rt. Revd David A. Urquhart, *cons.* 2000, *apptd* 2000; Bishop's Lodge, 67 Bidston Road, Oxton, Birkenhead CH43 6TR
Stockport, Rt. Revd Nigel Stock, *cons.* 2000, *apptd* 2000; Bishop's Lodge, Back Lane, Dunham Town, Altrincham, Cheshire WA14 4SG

DEAN
Very Revd Dr Gordon McPhate

CANONS RESIDENTIARY
Christopher Burkett, *apptd* 2000; Trevor Dennis, *apptd* 1994; Judy Hunt, *apptd* 2002; John Roff, *apptd* 2000

Organist and Director of Music, David Poulter, FRCO, *apptd* 1997

ARCHDEACONS
Chester, Ven. Donald Allister, *apptd* 2002
Macclesfield, Ven. Richard Gillings, *apptd* 1994

Chancellor, David Turner, QC, *apptd* 1998
Registrar and Legal Secretary, Alan McAllester
Diocesan Secretary, Stephen P. A. Marriott, Church House, Lower Lane, Aldford, Chester CH3 6HP T 01244-620444

CHICHESTER *(Canterbury)*

102nd BISHOP
Rt. Revd John Hind, *cons.* 1991, *apptd* 2001; The Palace, Chichester PO19 1PY *Signs* John Cicestr

BISHOPS SUFFRAGAN
Horsham, Rt. Revd Lindsay G. Urwin, *cons.* 1993, *apptd* 1993; Bishop's House, 21 Guildford Road, Horsham, W. Sussex RH12 1LU
Lewes, Rt. Revd Wallace P. Benn, *cons.* 1997, *apptd* 1997; Bishop's Lodge, 16A Prideaux Road, Eastbourne, E. Sussex BN21 2NB

DEAN
Revd Nicholas Frayling, *apptd* 2002

CANONS RESIDENTIARY
Peter Atkinson, *apptd* 1997; John Ford, *apptd* 2000; Peter Kefford, *apptd* 2001

Organist, Alan Thurlow, FRCO, *apptd* 1980

ARCHDEACONS
Chichester, Ven. Douglas McKittrick, *apptd* 2002
Horsham, Ven. Roger Combes, *apptd* 2003
Lewes and Hastings, vacant

Chancellor, Mark Hill
Registrar and Legal Secretary, Tim Gleeson
Diocesan Secretary, Jonathan Prichard, Diocesan Church House, 211 New Church Road, Hove, E. Sussex BN3 4ED T 01273-421021

COVENTRY *(Canterbury)*

8th BISHOP
Rt. Revd Colin J. Bennetts, *cons.* 1994, *apptd* 1997; The Bishop's House, 23 Davenport Road, Coventry CV5 6PW *Signs* Colin Coventry

BISHOP SUFFRAGAN
Warwick, vacant

DEAN
Very Revd John Irvine, *apptd* 2001

CANONS RESIDENTIARY
Stuart Beake, *apptd* 2000; Adrian Daffern, *apptd* 2003; Justin Welby, *apptd* 2002; Andrew White, *apptd* 1998

Director of Music, Rupert Jeffcoat, *apptd* 1997

ARCHDEACONS
Coventry, Ven. Mark Bryant, *apptd* 2001
Warwick, Ven. Michael Paget-Wilkes, *apptd* 1990

Chancellor, Sir William Gage, *apptd* 1980
Registrar and Legal Secretary, David Dumbleton
Diocesan Secretary, Isobel Chapman, Church House, Palmerston Road, Coventry CV5 6FJ T 024-7671 0500

DERBY *(Canterbury)*

6th BISHOP
Rt. Revd Jonathan S. Bailey, *cons.* 1992, *apptd* 1995; Derby Church House, Full Street, Derby DE1 3DR
Signs Jonathan Derby

BISHOP SUFFRAGAN
Repton, Rt. Revd David C. Hawtin, *cons.* 1999, *apptd* 1999; Repton House, Lea, Matlock, Derbys DE4 5JP

DEAN
vacant

CANONS RESIDENTIARY
Andrew Brown, *apptd* 2003; Barrie Gauge, *apptd* 1999; Nicholas Henshall, *apptd* 2002; Elaine Jones, *apptd* 2004

Organist, Peter Gould, *apptd* 1982

ARCHDEACONS
Chesterfield, Ven. David Garnett, *apptd* 1996
Derby, Ven. Ian Gatford, *apptd* 1992

Chancellor, His Hon. Judge John Bullimore, *apptd* 1981
Registrar and Legal Secretary, Mrs Nadine Waldron
Diocesan Secretary, Bob Carey, Derby Church House, Full Street, Derby DE1 3DR T 01332-388650

ELY *(Canterbury)*

68th BISHOP
Rt. Revd Dr Anthony Russell, *cons.* 1988, *apptd* 2000; The Bishop's House, Ely, Cambs CB7 4DW
Signs Anthony Ely

BISHOP SUFFRAGAN
Huntingdon, Rt. Revd Dr John Inge, *cons.* 2003, *apptd* 2003; 14 Lynn Road, Ely, Cambs CB6 1DA

DEAN
Very Revd Dr Michael Chandler, *apptd* 2003

CANONS RESIDENTIARY
Dr Alan Hargrave, *apptd* 2004; Dr Peter Sills, *apptd* 2000

CANON PRECENTOR
Revd David Pritchard, *apptd* 2004

Organist, Paul Trepte, FRCO, *apptd* 1991

ARCHDEACONS
Ely, vacant
Huntingdon Wisbech, Ven. John Beer, *apptd* 1997

Chancellor, William Gage, QC
Registrar, Peter Beesley
Diocesan Secretary, Dr Matthew Lavis, Bishop Woodford House, Barton Road, Ely, Cambs CB7 4DX T 01353-652701

EXETER *(Canterbury)*

70th BISHOP
Rt. Revd Michael L. Langrish, *cons.* 1993, *apptd* 2000; The Palace, Exeter, EX1 1HY
Signs Michael Exon

BISHOPS SUFFRAGAN
Crediton, Rt. Revd Robert Evens, *cons.* 2004, *apptd* 2004; 10 The Close, Exeter EX1 1EZ
Plymouth, Rt. Revd John Garton, *cons.* 1996, *apptd* 1996; 31 Riverside Walk, Tamerton Foliot, Plymouth PL5 4AQ

DEAN
vacant

CANONS RESIDENTIARY
Neil Collings, *apptd* 1999; David Ison, *apptd* 1997; Carl Turner, *apptd* 2001

Director of Music, Andrew Millington, *apptd* 1999

ARCHDEACONS
Barnstaple, Ven. David Gunn-Johnson, *apptd* 2003
Exeter, Ven. Dr Paul Gardner, *apptd* 2003
Plymouth, Ven. Tony Wilds, *apptd* 2001
Totnes, Ven. Richard Gilpin, *apptd* 1996

Chancellor, Sir David Calcutt
Registrar and Legal Secretary, R. Wheeler
Diocesan Secretary, Mark Beedell, Diocesan House, Palace Gate, Exeter, Devon EX1 1HX T 01392-272686

GIBRALTAR IN EUROPE *(Canterbury)*

BISHOP
Rt. Revd Dr Geoffrey Rowell, *cons.* 1994, *apptd* 2001; Bishop's Lodge, Church Road, Worth, Crawley, West Sussex, RH10 7RT

BISHOP SUFFRAGAN
In Europe, Rt. Revd David Hamid, *cons.* 2002, *apptd* 2002; 14 Tufton Street, London SW1P 3QZ
Dean, Cathedral Church of the Holy Trinity, Gibraltar, Very Revd Alan Woods

Chancellor, Pro-Cathedral of St Paul, Valletta, Malta, Canon Thomas Mendel
Chancellor, Pro-Cathedral of the Holy Trinity, Brussels, Belgium, Canon Nigel Walker

ARCHDEACONS
Eastern, Ven. Patrick Curran
North-West Europe, Ven. Geoffrey Allen
France, Ven. Anthony Wells
Gibraltar, Ven. Howell Sasser
Italy, Rt. Revd David Hamid *(Acting)*
Scandinavia and Germany, Ven. David Ratcliff
Switzerland, Ven. John Williams

Chancellor, Sir David Calcutt, QC
Registrar and Legal Secretary, John Underwood
Diocesan Secretary, Adrian Mumford, 14 Tufton Street, London SW1P 3QZ T 020-7898 1155

GLOUCESTER *(Canterbury)*

40th BISHOP
Rt. Revd Michael Perham, *cons.* 2004, *apptd* 2004; Bishopscourt, Pitt Street, Gloucester GL1 2BQ
Signs Michael Gloucestr

BISHOP SUFFRAGAN
Tewkesbury, Rt. Revd John S. Went, *cons.* 1995, *apptd* 1995; Bishop's House, Staverton, Cheltenham GL51 0TW

DEAN
Very Revd Nicholas Bury, *apptd* 1997

CANONS RESIDENTIARY
Guy Bridgewater, *apptd* 2002; Neil Heavisides, *apptd* 1993; David Hoyle, *apptd* 2002; Celia Thomson, *apptd* 2003

Director of Music, Andrew Nethsingha, *apptd* 2002

ARCHDEACONS
Cheltenham, Ven. Hedley Ringrose, *apptd* 1998
Gloucester, Ven. Geoffrey Sidaway, *apptd* 2000

Chancellor and Vicar-General, June Rodgers, *apptd* 1990
Registrar and Legal Secretary, Chris Peak
Diocesan Secretary, Michael Williams, Church House, College Green, Gloucester GL1 2LY T01452-410022

GUILDFORD *(Canterbury)*
9th BISHOP
vacant; Willow Grange, Woking Road, Guildford GU4 7QS

BISHOP SUFFRAGAN
Dorking, Rt. Revd Ian Brackley, *cons.* 1996, *apptd* 1995; Dayspring, 13 Pilgrims Way, Guildford GU4 8AD

DEAN
Very Revd Victor Stock, *apptd* 2002

CANONS RESIDENTIARY
Jonathan Frost, *apptd* 2002; Julian Hubbard, *apptd* 1999; Dr Maureen Palmer, *apptd* 1996; Dr Nicholas Thistlethwaite, *apptd* 1999

Organist, Stephen Farr, FRCO, *apptd* 1999

ARCHDEACONS
Dorking, Ven. Mark Wilson, *apptd* 1996
Surrey, Ven. Robert Reiss, *apptd* 1996

Chancellor, The Worshipful Andrew Jordan
Registrar and Legal Secretary, Peter Beesley
Diocesan Secretary, Stephen Marriott

HEREFORD *(Canterbury)*
105th BISHOP
Rt. Revd Anthony Priddis, *cons.* 2004, *apptd* 2004; The Palace, Hereford HR4 9BN

BISHOP SUFFRAGAN
Ludlow, Ven. Michael Wrenford Hooper, *cons.* 2002, *apptd* 2002; Bishop's House, Halford, Craven Arms, Shropshire SY7 9BT

DEAN
Very Revd Michael Tavinor, *apptd* 2002

CANONS RESIDENTIARY
Val Hamer, *apptd* 2002; Andrew Piper, *apptd* 2002; John Tiller, *apptd* 1984

Organist, Geraint Bowen, FRCO, *apptd* 2001

ARCHDEACONS
Hereford, Ven. John Tiller, *apptd* 2002
Ludlow, Michael Wrenford Hooper, *apptd* 2002

Chancellor, Val Hamer
Joint Registrars and Legal Secretaries, Tom Jordan; Peter Beesley
Diocesan Secretary, John Clark, The Palace, Hereford HR4 9BL T 01432-373300

LEICESTER *(Canterbury)*
6th BISHOP
Rt. Revd Timothy J. Stevens, *cons.* 1995, *apptd* 1999; Bishop's Lodge, 10 Springfield Road, Leicester LE2 3BD *Signs* Timothy Leicester

DEAN
Very Revd Vivienne F. Faull, *apptd* 2000

CANONS RESIDENTIARY
Stephen Foster, *apptd* 2004; Michael Wilson, *apptd* 1988

Master of Music, Jonathan Gregory, *apptd* 1994

ARCHDEACONS
Leicester, Ven. Richard Atkinson, *apptd* 2002
Loughborough, Ven. Ian Stanes, *apptd* 1992

Chancellor, James Behrens
Registrar and Legal Secretary, Trevor Kirkman
Diocesan Secretary, Jane Easton, Church House, 3–5 St Martin's East, Leicester LE1 5FX T 0116-248 7400

LICHFIELD *(Canterbury)*
98th BISHOP
Rt. Revd Jonathan Gledhill, *cons.* 1996, *apptd* 2003; Bishop's House, The Close, Lichfield WS13 7LG

BISHOPS SUFFRAGAN
Shrewsbury, Rt. Revd Alan Smith, *cons.* 2001, *apptd* 2002; 68 London Road, Shrewsbury SY2 6PG
Stafford, Rt. Revd Christopher J. Hill, *cons.* 1996, *apptd* 1996; Ash Garth, Broughton Crescent, Barlaston, Staffs ST12 9DD
Wolverhampton, Rt. Revd Michael G. Bourke, *cons.* 1993, *apptd* 1993; 61 Richmond Road, Wolverhampton WV3 9JH

DEAN
Very Revd Michael Yorke, *apptd* 1999

CANONS RESIDENTIARY
A. Barnard, *apptd* 1977; Ven. Christopher Liley, *apptd* 2001; C. Taylor, *apptd* 1995

Organist, Philip Scriven, *apptd* 2002

ARCHDEACONS
Lichfield, Ven. Christopher Liley, *apptd* 2001
Salop, Ven. John Hall, *apptd* 1998
Stoke-on-Trent, Ven. Godfrey Owen Stone, *apptd* 2002
Walsall, Revd Robert Jackson, *apptd* 2004

Chancellor, His Hon. Judge John Shand
Joint Registrars and Legal Secretaries, J. P. Thorneycroft; N. Blackie
Diocesan Secretary, D. R. Taylor, St Mary's House, The Close, Lichfield, Staffs WS13 7LD T 01543-306030

LINCOLN *(Canterbury)*

71st BISHOP
Rt. Revd Dr John Saxbee, *cons.* 1994, *apptd* 2002; Bishop's House, Eastgate, Lincoln LN2 1QQ *Signs* John Lincoln

BISHOPS SUFFRAGAN
Grantham, Rt. Revd Alastair L. J. Redfern, *cons.* 1997, *apptd* 1997; Fairacre, 234 Barrowby Road, Grantham, Lincs NG31 8NP
Grimsby, Rt. Revd David D. J. Rossdale, *cons.* 2000, *apptd* 2000; Bishop's House, Church Lane, Irby-upon-Humber, Grimsby DN37 7JR

DEAN
Very Revd Alexander Knight, *apptd* 1998

CANONS RESIDENTIARY
Gavin Kirk, *apptd* 2003; Alan Nugent, *apptd* 2003; Michael West, *apptd* 2003

Director of Music, A. Prentice, *apptd* 2003

ARCHDEACONS
Lincoln, Ven. Arthur Hawes, *apptd* 1995
Lindsey and Stow, Ven. Dr Timothy Ellis, *apptd* 2001
Chancellor, Peter N. Collier, QC, *apptd* 1999
Registrar and Legal Secretary, Derek Wellman
Diocesan Secretary, Max Manin, The Old Palace, Lincoln LN2 1PU T 01522-529241

LIVERPOOL *(York)*

7th BISHOP
Rt. Revd James Jones, *cons.* 1994, *apptd* 1998; Bishop's Lodge, Woolton Park, Liverpool L25 6DT *Signs* James Liverpool

BISHOP SUFFRAGAN
Warrington, Rt. Revd David Jennings, *cons.* 2000, *apptd* 2000; 34 Central Avenue, Eccleston Park, Prescot, Merseyside L34 2QP

DEAN
Rt. Revd Dean Dr Rupert W. N. Hoare, *apptd* 2000

CANON RESIDENTIARY
Anthony Hawley, *apptd* 2002

Organist, Prof. Ian Tracey, *apptd* 1980

ARCHDEACONS
Liverpool, Ven Richard Panter, *apptd* 2002
Warrington, Ven. Peter Bradley, *apptd* 2001

Chancellor, Hon. Sir Mark Hedley
Registrar and Legal Secretary, Roger Arden
Diocesan Secretary, Mike Eastwood, Church House, 1 Hanover Street, Liverpool L1 3DW T 0151-709 9722

MANCHESTER *(York)*

11th BISHOP
Rt. Revd Nigel McCulloch, *cons.* 1986, *apptd* 2002, *trans.* 2002; Bishopscourt, Bury New Road, Manchester M7 4LE *Signs* Nigel Manchester

BISHOPS SUFFRAGAN
Bolton, Rt. Revd David K. Gillett, *cons.* 1999, *apptd* 1999; 4 Bishop's Lodge, Bolton Road, Hawkshaw, Bury BL8 4JN
Hulme, Rt. Revd Stephen R. Lowe, *cons.* 1999, *apptd.* 1999; 14 Moorgate Avenue, Withington, Manchester M20 1HE
Middleton, Rt. Revd Michael A. O. Lewis, *cons.* 1999, *apptd* 1999; The Hollies, Manchester Road, Rochdale OL11 3QY

DEAN
Very Revd Kenneth Riley, *apptd* 1993

CANONS RESIDENTIARY
Paul Denby, *apptd* 1995; Robin Gamble, *apptd* 2002; Andrew Shanks, *apptd* 2004

Organist, Christopher Stokes, *apptd* 1992

ARCHDEACONS
Bolton, John Applegate, *apptd* 2002
Manchester, vacant
Rochdale, Ven. Andrew Ballard, *apptd* 2000

Chancellor, G. F. Tattersall
Registrar and Legal Secretary, Michael Darlington
Diocesan Secretary, Nigel Spraggins, 1st Floor, Diocesan Church House, 90 Deansgate, Manchester M3 2GH T 0161-833 9521

NEWCASTLE *(York)*

11th BISHOP
Rt. Revd J. Martin Wharton, *cons.* 1992, *apptd* 1997; Bishop's House, 29 Moor Road South, Gosforth, Newcastle upon Tyne NE3 1PA *Signs* Martin Newcastle

STIPENDIARY ASSISTANT BISHOP
Rt. Revd Paul Richardson, *cons.* 1987, *apptd* 1999

HON. ASSISTANT BISHOP
Rt. Revd K. E. Gill, *cons.* 1972, *apptd* 1998

DEAN
Very Revd Christopher C. Dalliston, *apptd* 2003

CANONS RESIDENTIARY
David Elkington, *apptd* 2002; Ven. Peter Elliott, *apptd* 1993; Geoffrey Miller, *apptd* 1999; Peter Strange, *apptd* 1986

Director of Music, Scott Farrell, *apptd* 2002

ARCHDEACONS
Lindisfarne, Ven. Robert Langley, *apptd* 2001
Northumberland, Ven. Peter Elliott, *apptd* 1993

Chancellor, Prof. David McClean, *apptd* 1998
Registrar and Legal Secretary, Jane Lowdon
Diocesan Secretary, Philip Davies, Church House, St John's Terrace, North Shields, NE29 6HS T 0191-270 4100

NORWICH *(Canterbury)*

71st BISHOP
Rt. Revd Graham R. James, *cons.* 1993, *apptd* 2000; Bishop's House, Norwich NR3 1SB *Signs* Graham Norvic

BISHOPS SUFFRAGAN
Lynn, Rt. Revd James Langstaff, *cons.* 2004, *apptd* 2004; The Old Vicarage, Castle Acre, King's Lynn PE32 2AA
Thetford, Rt. Revd David J. Atkinson, *cons.* 2001, *apptd* 2001; Rectory Meadow, Bramerton, Norwich NR14 7DW

DEAN
Very Revd Graham Smith, *apptd* 2004

CANONS RESIDENTIARY
Michael Kitchener, *apptd* 1999; Richard Hanmer, *apptd* 1994; Jeremy Haselock, *apptd* 1998; Ven. Clifford Offer, *apptd* 1994

Organist, David Dunnett, *apptd* 1996

ARCHDEACONS
Lynn, Ven. Martin Gray, *apptd* 1999
Norfolk, Ven. David Hayden, *apptd* 2002
Norwich, Ven. Clifford Offer, *apptd* 1994

Chancellor, The Hon. Mr Justice Blofeld, *apptd* 1998
Registrar and Legal Secretary, John Herring
Diocesan Secretary, Revd Richard Bowett, Diocesan House, 109 Dereham Road, Easton, Norwich, Norfolk NR9 5ES T 01603-880853

OXFORD *(Canterbury)*
41st BISHOP
Rt. Revd Richard D. Harries, *cons.* 1987, *apptd* 1987; Diocesan Church House, North Hinksey Lane, Oxford OX2 0NB *Signs* Richard Oxon

AREA BISHOPS
Buckingham, Rt. Revd Alan Wilson *cons.* 2003, *apptd* 2003; Sheridan, Grimms Hill, Great Missenden, Bucks HP16 9BD
Dorchester, Rt. Revd Colin Fletcher, *cons.* 2000, *apptd* 2000; Arran House, Sandy Lane, Yarnton, Oxon OX5 1PB
Reading, Rt. Revd Stephen Cottrell, *cons.* 2004, *apptd* 2004; Bishop's House, Tidmarsh Lane, Tidmarsh, Reading RG8 8HA

DEAN OF CHRIST CHURCH
Very Revd Christopher Lewis, *apptd* 2003

CANONS RESIDENTIARY
Marilyn McCord Adams, *apptd* 2004; Nicholas Coulton, *apptd* 2002; Ven. John Morrison, *apptd* 1998; Oliver O'Donovan, *apptd* 1982; Marilyn Parry, *apptd* 2001; George Pattison, *apptd* 2004

Organist, Stephen Darlington, FRCO, *apptd* 1985

ARCHDEACONS
Berkshire, Ven. Norman Russell, *apptd* 1998
Buckingham, Ven. Sheila Watson, *apptd* 2002
Oxford, Ven. John Morrison, *apptd* 1998

Chancellor, Revd Dr Rupert Bursell, *apptd* 2001
Registrars and Legal Secretaries, Dr F. E. Robson and Revd. Canon John Rees
Diocesan Secretary, Rosemary Pearce, Diocesan Church House, North Hinksey, Oxford OX2 0NB T 01865-208202

PETERBOROUGH *(Canterbury)*
37th BISHOP
Rt. Revd Ian P. M. Cundy, *cons.* 1992, *apptd* 1996; Bishop's Lodging, The Palace, Peterborough PE1 1YA *Signs* Ian Petriburg

BISHOP SUFFRAGAN
Brixworth, Rt. Revd Frank White, *cons.* 2002, *apptd* 2002; 4 The Avenue, Dallington, Northampton NN1 4RZ

DEAN
Very Revd Michael Bunker, *apptd* 1992

CANONS RESIDENTIARY
Jonathan Baker, *apptd* 2004; David Painter, *apptd* 2000; Bruce Ruddock, *apptd* 2004
Organist, Andrew Reid, *apptd* 2004

ARCHDEACONS
Northampton, vacant
Oakham, Ven. David Painter, *apptd* 2000

Chancellor, Thomas Coningsby, QC, *apptd* 1989
Registrar and Legal Secretary, Canon Raymond Hemingray
Diocesan Secretary, Richard Pestell, Diocesan Office, The Palace, Peterborough, Cambs PE1 1YB T 01733-887000

PORTSMOUTH *(Canterbury)*
8th BISHOP
Rt. Revd Dr Kenneth Stevenson, *cons.* 1995, *apptd* 1995; Bishopsgrove, 26 Osborn Road, Fareham, Hants PO16 7DQ *Signs* Kenneth Portsmouth

DEAN
Very Revd David Brindley, *apptd* 2002

CANONS RESIDENTIARY
Nicholas Ash, *apptd* 2003; David Isaac, *apptd* 1990; Michael Tristram *apptd* 2003

Organist, David Price, *apptd* 1996

ARCHDEACONS
Isle of Wight, Ven. Trevor Reader, *apptd* 2003
Portsdown, Ven. Christopher Lowson, *apptd* 1999
The Meon, Ven. Peter Hancock, *apptd* 1999

Chancellor, C. Clark, QC
Registrar and Legal Secretary, Hilary Tyler
Diocesan Secretary, Michael Jordan, Cathedral House, St Thomas's Street, Portsmouth, Hants PO1 2HA T 023-9282 5731

RIPON AND LEEDS *(York)*
12th BISHOP
Rt. Revd John R. Packer, *cons.* 1996, *apptd* 2000; Bishop Mount, Ripon HG4 5DP *Signs* John Ripon and Leeds

BISHOP SUFFRAGAN
Knaresborough, Rt. Revd James Bell, *cons.* 2004, *apptd* 2004; Thistledown, Main Street, Exelby, Bedale DL8 2HD

DEAN
Very Revd John Methuen, *apptd* 1995

CANONS RESIDENTIARY
Michael Glanville-Smith, *apptd* 1990; Keith Punshon, *apptd* 1996

Organist, Simon Morley *apptd* 2003

ARCHDEACONS
Leeds, Ven. John Oliver, *apptd* 1992
Richmond, Ven. Kenneth Good, *apptd* 1993

Chancellor, His Hon. Judge Grenfell, *apptd* 1992
Registrars and Legal Secretaries, Christopher Tunnard, Nichola Harding
Diocesan Secretary, Philip Arundel, Diocesan Office, St Mary's Street, Leeds LS9 7DP T 0113-200 0540

ROCHESTER *(Canterbury)*

106th BISHOP
Rt. Revd Dr Michael Nazir-Ali, *cons.* 1984, *apptd* 1994; Bishopscourt, Rochester ME1 1TS *Signs* Michael Roffen

BISHOP SUFFRAGAN
Tonbridge, Rt. Revd Dr Brian C. Castle, *cons.* 2002, *apptd* 2002; Bishop's Lodge, 48 St Botolph's Road, Sevenoaks TN13 3AG

DEAN
Adrian Newman, *apptd* 2004

CANONS RESIDENTIARY
Canon Ralph Godsall, *apptd* 2001; Jonathan Meyrick, *apptd* 1998

Director of Music, Roger Sayer, FRCO, *apptd* 1995

ARCHDEACONS
Bromley, Ven. Paul Wright, *apptd* 2003
Rochester, Ven. Peter Lock, *apptd* 2000
Tonbridge, Ven. Clive Mansell, *apptd* 2002

Chancellor, His Hon. Judge Michael Goodman, *apptd* 1971
Registrar and Legal Secretary, Michael Thatcher
Diocesan Secretary, Mrs Louise Gilbert, St Nicholas Church, Boley Hill, Rochester ME1 1SL T 01634-830333

ST ALBANS *(Canterbury)*

9th BISHOP
Rt. Revd Christopher W. Herbert, *cons.* 1995, *apptd* 1995; Abbey Gate House, St Albans AL3 4HD *Signs* Christopher St Albans

BISHOPS SUFFRAGAN
Bedford, Rt. Revd Richard N. Inwood, *apptd* 2002
Hertford, Rt. Revd Christopher R. J. Foster, *cons.* 2001, *apptd* 2001; Hertford House, Abbey Mill Lane, St Albans AL3 4HE

DEAN
Very Revd Jeffrey John, *apptd* 2004

CANONS RESIDENTIARY
Stephen Lake, *apptd* 2001; Iain Lane, *apptd* 2000; Michael Sansom, *apptd* 1988; Dennis Stamps, *apptd* 2002; Richard Wheeler, *apptd* 2001

Organist, Andrew Lucas, *apptd* 1998

ARCHDEACONS
Bedford, Ven. Paul Hughes, *apptd* 2004
Hertford, Ven. Trevor Jones, *apptd* 1997
St Albans, Ven. Helen Cunliffe, *apptd* 2003

Chancellor, Roger Kaye, *apptd* 2002
Registrar and Legal Secretary, David Cheetham
Diocesan Secretary, Susan Pope, Holywell Lodge, 41 Holywell Hill, St Albans AL1 1HE T 01727-854532

ST EDMUNDSBURY AND IPSWICH *(Canterbury)*

9th BISHOP
Rt. Revd J. H. Richard Lewis, *cons.* 1992, *apptd* 1997; Bishop's House, 4 Park Road, Ipswich IP1 3ST *Signs* Richard St Edmundsbury and Ipswich

BISHOP SUFFRAGAN
Dunwich, Rt. Revd Clive Young, *cons.* 1999, *apptd* 1999; 28 Westerfield Road, Ipswich IP4 2UJ

DEAN
Very Revd James Atwell, *apptd* 1995

CANONS RESIDENTIARY
Peter Barham, *apptd* 2003; Andrew Todd, *apptd* 2001

Organist, James Thomas, *apptd* 1997

ARCHDEACONS
Ipswich, Ven. Terry Gibson, *apptd* 1987
Sudbury, Ven. John Cox, *apptd* 1995
Suffolk, Ven. Geoffrey Arrand, *apptd* 1994

Chancellor, The Hon. Mr Justice Blofeld, *apptd* 1974
Registrar and Legal Secretary, James Hall
Diocesan Secretary, Nicholas Edgell, Churchgates House, Cutler Street, Ipswich IP1 1QU T 01473-298500

SALISBURY *(Canterbury)*

77TH BISHOP
Rt. Revd David S. Stancliffe, *cons.* 1993, *apptd* 1993; South Canonry, The Close, Salisbury SP1 2ER *Signs* David Sarum

BISHOPS SUFFRAGAN
Ramsbury, Rt. Revd Peter F. Hullah, *cons.* 1999, *apptd* 1999
Sherborne, Rt. Revd Timothy M. Thornton, *cons.* 2001, *apptd* 2001

DEAN
Very Revd. June Osborne, *apptd* 2004

CANONS RESIDENTIARY
Mark Bonney, *apptd* 2004; Jeremy Davies, *apptd* 1985; Edward Probert, *apptd* 2004

Organist, Simon Lole, *apptd* 1997

ARCHDEACONS
Dorset, Ven. Alistair Magowan, *apptd* 2000
Sherborne, Ven. Paul Taylor, *apptd* 2004
Wilts, Ven. John Wraw, *apptd* 2004
Sarum, Ven. Alan Jeans, *apptd* 2003

Chancellor, His Hon. Judge Samuel Wiggs, *apptd* 1997
Registrar and Legal Secretary, Andrew Johnson
Diocesan Secretary, Lucinda Herklots, Church House, Crane Street, Salisbury SP1 2QB T 01722-411922

SHEFFIELD *(York)*

6th BISHOP
Rt. Revd John (Jack) Nicholls, *cons.* 1990, *apptd* 1997; Bishopscroft, Snaithing Lane, Sheffield S10 3LG *Signs* Jack Sheffield

BISHOP SUFFRAGAN
Doncaster, Rt. Revd Cyril Guy Ashton, *cons.* 2000, *apptd* 2000; Bishop's House, 3 Farrington Court, Wickersley, Rotherham S66 1JQ

DEAN
Very Revd Peter Bradley, *apptd* 2003

CANONS RESIDENTIARY

Ven. Richard Blackburn, *apptd* 1999; Revd Canon Nick Howe, *apptd* 2003; Revd Canon Paul Shackerley, *apptd* 2002; Revd Canon Howard Such, *apptd* 2003

Master of Music, Neil Taylor, *apptd* 1997

ARCHDEACONS

Doncaster, Ven. Robert Fitzharris, *apptd* 2001
Sheffield, Ven. Richard Blackburn, *apptd* 1999

Chancellor, Prof. David McClean, *apptd* 1992
Registrar and Legal Secretary, Mrs Miranda Myers
Diocesan Secretary, Tony Beck, FCIS, Diocesan Church House, 95–99 Effingham Street, Rotherham S65 1BL T 01709-309100

SODOR AND MAN *(York)*

80th BISHOP

Rt. Revd Graeme Knowles, *cons.* 2003, *apptd* 2003; Bishop's House, The Falls, Tromode Road, Cronkbourne, Douglas, Isle of Man IM4 4PZ
Signs Graeme Sodor and Man

CANONS

Malcolm Convery, *apptd* 1999; Duncan Whitworth, *apptd* 1996

ARCHDEACON

Isle of Man, vacant

Vicar-General and Chancellor, Clare Faulds
Registrar and Legal Secretary, Christopher Callow
Diocesan Secretary, Christine Roberts, Holly Cottage, Ballaughton Meadows, Douglas, Isle of Man IM2 1JG T 01624-626994

SOUTHWARK *(Canterbury)*

9TH BISHOP

Rt. Revd Dr Tom F. Butler, *cons.* 1985, *apptd* 1998; Bishop's House, 38 Tooting Bec Gardens, London SW16 1QZ
Signs Thomas Southwark

AREA BISHOPS

Croydon, Rt. Revd Nicholas Baines, *cons.* 2003, *apptd* 2003
Kingston upon Thames, Rt. Revd Richard Cheetham, *cons.* 2002, *apptd* 2002
Woolwich vacant

DEAN

Very Revd Colin B. Slee, OBE, *apptd* 1994

CANONS RESIDENTIARY

Andrew Nunn, *apptd* 1999; Stephen Roberts, *apptd* 2000; Bruce Saunders, *apptd* 1997

Organist, Peter Wright, FRCO, *apptd* 1989

ARCHDEACONS

Croydon, Ven. Tony Davies, *apptd* 1994
Lambeth, Ven. Christopher Skilton, *apptd* 2004
Lewisham, Ven. Christine Hardman, *apptd* 2001
Reigate, Ven. Daniel Kajumba, *apptd* 2001
Southwark, Revd Dr Michael Ipgrave, *apptd* 2004
Wandsworth, Ven. David Gerrard, *apptd* 1989

Chancellor, Charles George, QC
Registrar and Legal Secretary, Paul Morris
Diocesan Secretary, Simon Parton, Trinity House, 4 Chapel Court, Borough High Street, London SE1 1HW T 020-7939 9400

SOUTHWELL *(York)*

10th BISHOP

Rt. Revd George H. Cassidy, *cons.* 1999, *apptd* 1999; Bishop's Manor, Southwell NG25 0JR *Signs* George Southwell

BISHOP SUFFRAGAN

Sherwood, Rt. Revd Alan W. Morgan, *cons.* 1989, *apptd* 1989; Dunham House, Westgate, Southwell, Notts NG25 0JL

DEAN

Very Revd David Leaning, *apptd* 1991

CANON RESIDENTIARY

Jacqueline Jones, *apptd* 2003

Organist, Paul Hale, *apptd* 1989

ARCHDEACONS

Newark, Ven. Nigel Peyton, *apptd* 1999
Nottingham, Ven. Gordon Ogilvie, *apptd* 1996

Chancellor, John Shand, *apptd* 1981
Registrar and Legal Secretary, Christopher Hodson
Diocesan Secretary, Dunham House, Westgate, Southwell, Notts NG25 0JL T 01636-817204

TRURO *(Canterbury)*

14th BISHOP

Rt. Revd William Ind, *cons.* 1987, *apptd* 1997; Lis Escop, Truro TR3 6QQ *Signs* William Truro

BISHOP SUFFRAGAN

St Germans, Revd Royden Screech, *cons.* 2000, *apptd* 2000

DEAN

Very Revd Michael A. Moxon, LVO, *apptd* 1998

CANONS RESIDENTIARY

Roger Bush, *apptd* 2004; Perran Gay, *apptd* 1994; Peter Walker, *apptd* 2001

Organist, Robert Sharpe, *apptd* 2002

ARCHDEACONS

Cornwall, Ven. Rodney Whiteman, *apptd* 2000
Bodmin, Ven. Clive Cohen, *apptd* 2000

Chancellor, Timothy Briden, *apptd* 1998
Registrar and Legal Secretary, Michael Follett
Diocesan Secretary, Sheri Sturgess, Diocesan House, Kenwyn, Truro TR1 1JQ T 01872-274351

WAKEFIELD *(York)*

12th BISHOP

Rt. Revd Stephen Platten, *cons.* 2003, *apptd* 2003; Bishop's Lodge, Woodthorpe Lane, Wakefield, WF2 6JL
Signs Stephen Wakefield

BISHOP SUFFRAGAN

Pontefract, Rt. Revd Anthony William Robinson, *cons.* 2003, *apptd* 2002; Pontefract House, 181A Manygates Lane, Wakefield WF2 7DR

DEAN

Very Revd George P. Nairn-Briggs, *apptd* 1997

CANONS RESIDENTIARY
Richard Capper, *apptd* 1997; Robert Gage, *apptd* 1997; Ian Gaskell, *apptd* 1998; John Holmes, *apptd* 1998

Organist, Jonathan Bielby, FRCO, *apptd* 1972

ARCHDEACONS
Halifax, Ven. Robert Freeman, *apptd* 2003
Pontefract, Ven. Jonathan Greener, *apptd* 2003

Chancellor, Peter Collier, QC, *apptd* 1992
Registrar and Legal Secretary, Linda Box
Diocesan Secretary, Ashley Ellis, Church House, 1 South Parade, Wakefield WF1 1LP T 01924-371802

WORCESTER *(Canterbury)*

112th BISHOP
Rt. Revd Dr Peter S. M. Selby, *cons.* 1984, *apptd* 1997; The Bishop's House, Hartlebury Castle, Kidderminster DY11 7XX *Signs* Peter Wigorn

SUFFRAGAN BISHOP
Dudley, Rt. Revd Dr David S. Walker, *cons.* 2000, *apptd* 2000; The Bishop's House, Bishop's Walk, Cradley Heath B64 7JF

DEAN
Very Revd Peter J. Marshall, *apptd* 1997

CANONS RESIDENTIARY
Alvyn Pettersen, *apptd* 2002; Ven. Joy Tetley, *apptd* 1999

Organist, Adrian Lucas, *apptd* 1996

ARCHDEACONS
Dudley, Ven. Fred Trethewey, *apptd* 2001
Worcester, Ven. Dr Joy Tetley

Chancellor, Charles Mynors, *apptd* 1999
Registrar and Legal Secretary, Michael Huskinson
Diocesan Secretary, Robert Higham, The Old Palace, Deansway, Worcester WR1 2JE T 01905-20537

ROYAL PECULIARS

WESTMINSTER

The Collegiate Church of St Peter

Dean, Very Revd Dr Wesley Carr, *apptd* 1997
Sub Dean and Archdeacon, David Hutt, *apptd* 1995
Canons of Westminster, David Hutt, *apptd* 1995; Michael Middleton, *apptd* 1997; Nicholas Sagovsky, *apptd* 2004; Robert Wright, *apptd* 1998; Dr Tom Wright, *apptd* 1999
Chapter Clerk and Receiver-General, Maj.-Gen. David Burden, CB, CBE, Chapter Office, 20 Dean's Yard, London SW1P 3PA
Organist, James O'Donnell, *apptd* 1999
Registrar, Stuart Holmes, MVO
Legal Secretary, Christopher Vyse, *apptd* 2000

WINDSOR

The Queen's Free Chapel of St George within Her Castle of Windsor

Dean, Rt. Revd David Conner, *apptd* 1998
Canons Residentiary, Laurence Gunner, *apptd* 1996; John Ovenden, *apptd* 1998; John White, *apptd* 1982
Chapter Clerk, Charlotte Manley, LVO, OBE, *apptd* 2003, Chapter Office, The Cloisters, Windsor Castle, Windsor, Berks SL4 1NJ
Director of Music, Timothy Byram-Wigfield, *apptd* 2004

OTHER ANGLICAN CHURCHES

THE CHURCH IN WALES

The Anglican Church was the established church in Wales from the 16th century until 1920, when the estrangement of the majority of Welsh people from Anglicanism resulted in disestablishment. Since then the Church in Wales has been an autonomous province consisting of six sees. The bishops are elected by an electoral college comprising elected lay and clerical members, who also elect one of the diocesan bishops as Archbishop of Wales.

The legislative body of the Church in Wales is the Governing Body, which has 350 members divided between the three orders of bishops, clergy and laity. Its President is the Archbishop of Wales and it meets twice annually. Its decisions are binding upon all members of the Church. The Church's property and finances are the responsibility of the Representative Body. There are about 84,000 members of the Church in Wales, with 648 stipendiary clergy and 1,020 parishes.

THE GOVERNING BODY OF THE CHURCH IN WALES, 39 Cathedral Road, Cardiff CF1 9XF T 029-2034 8200
Lay Secretary, John Shirley
12th ARCHBISHOP OF WALES, The Most Revd Dr Barry C. Morgan (Bishop of Llandaff), *elected* 2003
Signs Barry Cambrensis

BISHOPS
Bangor (80th), Rt. Revd Anthony Crockett, *b.* 1946, *cons.* 2004, *elected* 2004; Ty'r Esgob, Bangor, Gwynedd LL57 2SS *Signs* Anthony Bangor. *Stipendiary clergy*, 71
Llandaff (102nd), The Most Revd Dr Barry C. Morgan, *b.* 1947, *cons.* 1993, *trans.* 1999; Llys Esgob, The Cathedral Green, Llandaff, Cardiff CF5 2YE
Signs Barry Landav. *Stipendiary clergy*, 146
Monmouth (9th), Rt. Revd Dominic Walker, *b.* 1948, *cons.* 1997, *elected* 2003; Bishopstow, Stow Hill, Newport NP20 4EA
Signs, Dominic Monmouth. *Stipendiary clergy*, 104
St Asaph (74th), Rt. Revd John S. Davies, *b.* 1943, *cons.* 1999, *elected* 1999; Esgobty, St Asaph, Denbighshire LL17 0TW *Signs* John St Asaph. *Stipendiary clergy*, 116
St David's (127th), Rt. Revd Carl N. Cooper, *b.* 1960, *cons.* 2002, *elected* 2002; Llys Esgob, Abergwili, Carmarthen SA31 2JG
Signs Carl St Davids. *Stipendiary clergy*, 126
Swansea and Brecon (8th), Rt. Revd Anthony E. Pierce, *b.* 1941, *cons.* 1999, *elected* 1999; Ely Tower, Brecon, Powys LD3 9DE *Signs* Anthony Swansea & Brecon. *Stipendiary clergy*, 85

The stipend for a diocesan bishop of the Church in Wales is £32,005 a year for 2004–5.

THE SCOTTISH EPISCOPAL CHURCH

The Scottish Episcopal Church was founded after the Act of Settlement (1690) established the presbyterian nature of the Church of Scotland. The Scottish Episcopal Church is a member of the world-wide Anglican Communion. The governing authority is the General Synod, an elected body of approximately 140 members which meets once a year. The diocesan bishop who convenes and presides at meetings of the General Synod is called the Primus and is elected by his fellow bishops.

There are 44,280 members of the Scottish Episcopal Church, of whom 29,251 are communicants. There are seven bishops, approximately 482 serving clergy, and 313 churches and places of worship.

THE GENERAL SYNOD OF THE SCOTTISH EPISCOPAL CHURCH, 21 Grosvenor Crescent, Edinburgh EH12 5EE T 0131-225 6357 W www.scottishepiscopal.com
Secretary-General, J. F. Stuart
PRIMUS OF THE SCOTTISH EPISCOPAL CHURCH, Most Revd A. Bruce Cameron (Bishop of Aberdeen and Orkney), *elected* 2000

BISHOPS
Aberdeen and Orkney, A. Bruce Cameron, *b.* 1941, *cons.* 1992, *elected* 1992. *Clergy*, 54
Argyll and the Isles, Martin Shaw, *b.* 1944, *cons.* 2004, *elected* 2004. *Clergy*, 22
Brechin, Neville Chamberlain, *b.* 1939, *cons.* 1997, *elected* 1997. *Clergy*, 35
Edinburgh, Brian Smith, *b.* 1943, *cons.* 1993, *elected* 2001. *Clergy*, 162
Glasgow and Galloway, Idris Jones, *b.* 1943, *cons.* 1998, *elected* 1998. *Clergy*, 99
Moray, Ross and Caithness, John Crook, *b.* 1940, *cons.* 1999, *elected* 1999. *Clergy*, 31
St Andrews, Dunkeld and Dunblane, vacant. *Clergy*, 86

The minimum stipend of a diocesan bishop of the Scottish Episcopal Church for 2004–5 is £27,540 (i.e. 1.5 times the minimum clergy stipend of £18,360)

THE CHURCH OF IRELAND

The Anglican Church was the established church in Ireland from the 16th century but never secured the allegiance of the majority and was disestablished in 1871. The Church of Ireland is divided into the provinces of Armagh and Dublin, each under an archbishop. The provinces are subdivided into 12 dioceses.

The legislative body is the General Synod, which has 660 members in total, divided between the House of Bishops and the House of Representatives. The Archbishop of Armagh is elected by the House of Bishops; other episcopal elections are made by an electoral college.

There are about 375,000 members of the Church of Ireland, with two archbishops, ten bishops, about 600 clergy and about 1,100 churches and places of worship.

CENTRAL OFFICE, Church of Ireland House, Church Avenue, Rathmines, Dublin 6 T (00 353) (1) 4978422
Chief Officer and Secretary of the Representative Church Body, D. C. Reardon

PROVINCE OF ARMAGH
ARCHBISHOP OF ARMAGH, PRIMATE OF ALL IRELAND AND METROPOLITAN, Most Revd Robert H. A. Eames, PHD, *b.* 1937, *cons.* 1975, *trans.* 1986. *Clergy*, 55

BISHOPS
Clogher, Michael G. Jackson, PHD, DPHIL, *b.* 1956, *cons.* 2002, *apptd* 2002. *Clergy*, 32
Connor, Alan E. T. Harper, OBE, *b.* 1944, *cons.* 2002, *apptd* 2002. *Clergy*, 106
Derry and Raphoe, Kenneth R. Good, *b.* 1952, *cons.* 2002, *apptd* 2002. *Clergy*, 51
Down and Dromore, Harold C. Miller, *b.* 1950, *cons.* 1997, *apptd* 1997. *Clergy*, 116
Kilmore, Elphin and Ardagh, Kenneth H. Clarke, *b.* 1949, *cons.* 2001, *apptd* 2001. *Clergy*, 21
Tuam, Killala and Achonry, Richard C. A. Henderson, DPHIL, *b.* 1957, *cons.* 1998, *apptd* 1998. *Clergy*, 13

PROVINCE OF DUBLIN
ARCHBISHOP OF DUBLIN, BISHOP OF GLENDALOUGH, PRIMATE OF IRELAND AND METROPOLITAN, Most Revd John R. W. Neill, *b.* 1945, *apptd* 2002. *Clergy*, 86

BISHOPS
Cashel and Ossory, Peter F. Barrett, *b.* 1956, *cons.* 2003, *apptd* 2003. *Clergy*, 42
Cork, Cloyne and Ross, W. Paul Colton, *b.* 1960, *cons.* 1999, *apptd* 1999. *Clergy*, 30
Limerick and Killaloe, Michael H. G. Mayes, *b.* 1941, *cons.* 1993, *trans.* 2000. *Clergy*, 19
Meath and Kildare, (Most Revd) Richard L. Clarke, PHD, *b.* 1949, *cons.* 1996, *apptd* 1996. *Clergy*, 26

OVERSEAS

PRIMATES
PRIMATE AND PRESIDING BISHOP OF AOTEAROA, NEW ZEALAND AND POLYNESIA, Most Revd Whakahuihui Vercoe
PRIMATE OF AUSTRALIA, Most Revd Peter Carnley
PRIMATE OF BRAZIL, Most Revd Orlando Santos de Oliveira
ARCHBISHOP OF THE PROVINCE OF BURUNDI, Most Revd Samuel Ndayisenga
ARCHBISHOP AND PRIMATE OF CANADA, Most Revd Andrew Sandford Hutchison
ARCHBISHOP OF THE PROVINCE OF CENTRAL AFRICA, Most Revd Bernard Amos Malango
PRIMATE OF THE CENTRAL REGION OF AMERICA, Most Revd Martin de Jesus Barahona
ARCHBISHOP OF THE PROVINCE OF CONGO, Most Revd Dr Dirokpa Balufuga Fidèle
PRIMATE OF THE PROVINCE OF HONG KONG SHENG KUNG HUI, Most Revd Peter Kwong
ARCHBISHOP OF THE PROVINCE OF THE INDIAN OCEAN, Most Revd Remi Rabenirina
PRESIDENT-BISHOP OF JERUSALEM AND THE MIDDLE EAST, Most Revd George Handford
ARCHBISHOP OF THE PROVINCE OF KENYA, Most Revd Benjamin M. P. Nzimbi
ARCHBISHOP OF THE PROVINCE OF KOREA, Most Revd Dr Matthew Chul Bum Chung
ARCHBISHOP OF THE PROVINCE OF MELANESIA, Most Revd Sir Ellison L. Pogo, KBE
ARCHBISHOP OF MEXICO, Most Revd Carlos Touche-Porter
ARCHBISHOP OF THE PROVINCE OF MYANMAR, Most Revd Samuel Si Htay
ARCHBISHOP OF THE PROVINCE OF NIGERIA, Most Revd Peter Akinola
PRIMATE OF NIPPON SEI KO KAI, Most Revd James Toru Uno
ARCHBISHOP OF PAPUA NEW GUINEA, Most Revd James Ayong
PRIME BISHOP OF THE PHILIPPINES, Most Revd Ignacio C. Soliba
ARCHBISHOP OF THE PROVINCE OF RWANDA, Most Revd Emmanuel Musaba Kolini
PRIMATE OF THE PROVINCE OF SOUTH EAST ASIA, Most Revd Datuk Yong Ping Chung
METROPOLITAN OF THE PROVINCE OF SOUTHERN AFRICA, Most Revd Njongonkulu W. H. Ndungane
PRESIDING BISHOP OF THE SOUTHERN CONE OF AMERICA, Most Revd Gregory James Venables
ARCHBISHOP OF THE PROVINCE OF THE SUDAN, Most Revd Joseph Marona

ARCHBISHOP OF THE PROVINCE OF TANZANIA, Most Revd Donald L. Mtetemela
ARCHBISHOP OF THE PROVINCE OF UGANDA, Most Revd Henry Luke Orombi
PRESIDING BISHOP AND PRIMATE OF THE USA, Most Revd Frank T. Griswold
ARCHBISHOP OF THE PROVINCE OF WEST AFRICA, Most Revd Justice Ofei Akrofi
ARCHBISHOP OF THE PROVINCE OF THE WEST INDIES, Most Revd Drexel Gomez

OTHER CHURCHES AND EXTRA-PROVINCIAL DIOCESES
ANGLICAN CHURCH OF BERMUDA, *extra-provincial to Canterbury*
Bishop of Bermuda, Rt. Revd Ewen Ratteray
CHURCH OF CEYLON, *extra-provincial to Canterbury*
Bishop of Colombo, Rt. Revd Duleep de Chickera
Bishop of Kurunagala, Rt. Revd Kumara Illangasinghe
EPISCOPAL CHURCH OF CUBA, Rt. Revd Jorge Perera Hurtado
LUSITANIAN CHURCH (*Portuguese Episcopal Church*), *extra-provincial to Canterbury*
Bishop of Lustanian Church, Rt. Revd Fernando Soares
SPANISH REFORMED EPISCOPAL CHURCH, Rt. Revd Carlos López-Lozano

MODERATION OF CHURCHES IN FULL COMMUNION WITH THE ANGLICAN COMMUNION
CHURCH OF BANGLADESH, Rt. Revd Michael Baroi
CHURCH OF NORTH INDIA, Most Revd Zechariah J. Terom
CHURCH OF SOUTH INDIA, Most Revd Badda Peter Sugandhar
CHURCH OF PAKISTAN, Rt. Revd Dr Alexander John Malik

THE CHURCH OF SCOTLAND

The Church of Scotland is the established (i.e. national) church of Scotland. The Church is Reformed in doctrine, and presbyterian in constitution, i.e. based on a hierarchy of councils of ministers and elders and, since 1990, of members of a diaconate. At local level the Kirk Session consists of the parish minister and ruling elders. At district level the presbyteries, of which there are 44 in Britain, consist of all the ministers in the district, one ruling elder from each congregation, and those members of the diaconate who qualify for membership. The General Assembly is the supreme authority, and is presided over by a Moderator chosen annually by the Assembly. The Sovereign, if not present in person, is represented by a Lord High Commissioner who is appointed each year by the Crown.

The Church of Scotland has about 550,000 members, 1,100 ministers and 1,500 churches. There are about 100 ministers and other personnel working overseas.

Lord High Commissioner (2004), The Rt. Hon. Lord Steel of Aikwood
Moderator of the General Assembly (2004), Dr Alison J. Elliot
Principal Clerk, Very Revd Dr F. A. J. Macdonald
Depute Principal Clerk, Revd. Dr M. A. MacLean
Procurator, P. S. Hodge
Law Agent and Solicitor of the Church, Mrs J. S. Wilson
Parliamentary Agent, I. McCulloch *(London)*
General Treasurer, D. F. Ross
Secretary, Church and Nation Committee, Revd Dr D. Sinclair
CHURCH OFFICE, 121 George Street, Edinburgh EH2 4YN T 0131-225 5722

PRESBYTERIES AND CLERKS
Edinburgh, Revd W. P. Graham
West Lothian, Revd D. Shaw

Lothian, J. D. McCulloch, DL
Melrose and Peebles, Revd A. J. Morton
Duns, J. Watson
Jedburgh, Revd N. R. Combe

Annandale and Eskdale, Revd C. B. Haston
Dumfries and Kirkcudbright, Revd G. M. A. Savage
Wigtown and Stranraer, Revd D. W. Dutton
Ayr, Revd J. Crichton
Irvine and Kilmarnock, Revd C. G. G. Brockie
Ardrossan, Revd J. Mackay

Lanark, Revd M. Frew
Greenock and Paisley, Revd David Kay
Glasgow, Revd D. W. Lunan
Hamilton, Revd S. Paterson
Dumbarton, Revd D. P. Munro

Argyll, I. MacLagan

Falkirk, Revd I. W. Black
Stirling, Revd M. MacCormick

Dunfermline, Revd W. E. Farquhar
Kirkcaldy, A. Moore
St Andrews, Revd Dr D. Sinclair
Dunkeld and Meigle, Revd J. Russell
Perth, Revd D. G. Lawson
Dundee, Revd J. A. Roy
Angus, Revd M. I. G. Rooney

Aberdeen, Revd I. MacLean
Kincardine and Deeside, Revd J. Holt
Gordon, Revd E. Glen
Buchan, George Barston
Moray, Revd G. M. Wood

Abernethy, Revd J. A. I. MacEwan
Inverness, Revd A. S. Younger
Lochaber, Revd D. M. Anderson

Ross, Revd T. M. McWilliam
Sutherland, Revd J. L. Goskirk
Caithness, Mrs M. Gillies, MBE
Lochcarron-Skye, Revd A. I. MacArthur
Uist, Revd M. Smith
Lewis, Revd T. S. Sinclair

Orkney, Revd T. G. Hunt
Shetland, Revd C. H. M.Greig
England, Revd W. A. Cairns
Europe, Revd J. A. Cowie

The stipends for ministers in the Church of Scotland in 2004 range from £20,090–£24,659, depending on length of service. In addition, congregations can make extra payments.

THE ROMAN CATHOLIC CHURCH

The Roman Catholic Church is one world-wide Christian Church acknowledging as its head the Bishop of Rome, known as the Pope (Father). He leads a communion of followers of Christ, who believe they continue his presence in the world as servants of faith, hope and love to all society. The Pope is held to be the successor of St Peter and thus invested with the power which was entrusted to St Peter by Jesus Christ. A direct line of succession is therefore claimed from the earliest Christian communities. With the fall of the Roman Empire the Pope also became an important political leader. His territory is now limited to the 107 acres of the Vatican City State, created to provide some independence to the Pope from Italy and other nations.

The Pope exercises spiritual authority over the Church with the advice and assistance of the Sacred College of Cardinals, the supreme council of the Church. He is also advised by bishops in communion with him, by a group of officers which form the Roman Curia and by his ambassadors, called Apostolic Nuncios, who liaise with the Bishops' Conference in each country.

Those members of the College of Cardinals who are under the age of 80 elect a successor of the Pope following his death. The assembly of the Cardinals called to the Vatican for the election of a new Pope is known as the Conclave. In complete seclusion the Cardinals vote by a secret ballot; a two-thirds majority is necessary before the vote can be accepted as final. When a Cardinal receives the necessary number of votes, the Dean of the Sacred College formally asks him if he will accept election and the name by which he wishes to be known. On his acceptance of the office of Supreme Pontiff, the Conclave is dissolved and the first Cardinal Deacon announces the election to the assembled crowd in St Peter's Square.

The number of cardinals was fixed at 70 by Pope Sixtus V in 1586 but has been steadily increased since the pontificate of John XXIII and at the end of October 2003 stood at 194, plus two cardinals created 'in pectore' (their names being kept secret by the Pope for fear of persecution; they are thought to be Chinese).

The Pope has full legislative, judicial and administrative power over the whole church. He is aided in his administration by the Curia, which is made up of a number of departments. The Secretariat of State is the central office for carrying out the Pope's instructions and is presided over by the Cardinal Secretary of State. It maintains relations with the departments of the Curia, with the episcopate, with the representatives of the Holy See in various countries, governments and private persons. The congregations and pontifical councils are the Pope's ministries and include departments such as the Congregation for the Doctrine of Faith, whose field of competence concern faith and morals; the Congregation for the Clergy and the Congregation for the Evangelisation of Peoples, the Pontifical Council for the Family and the Pontifical Council for the Promotion of Christian Unity.

The Vatican State does not have diplomatic representatives. The Holy See, composed of the Pope and those who help him in his mission for the Church, is recognised by the Conventions of Vienna as an International Moral Body. The representatives of the Holy See are known as Apostolic Nuncio's. Where representation is only to the local churches and not to the government of a country, the Papal representative is known as an apostolic delegate. The Roman Catholic Church has an estimated 840 million adherents under the care of some 2,500 diocesan bishops world-wide.

SOVEREIGN PONTIFF

His Holiness Pope John Paul II (Karol Wojtyla), *born* Wadowice, Poland, 18 May 1920; *ordained priest* 1946; *appointed Archbishop* of Kraków 1964; *created Cardinal* 1967; *assumed pontificate* 16 October 1978

SECRETARIAT OF STATE

Secretary of State, HE Cardinal Angelo Sodano
First Section (General Affairs), Archbishop Leonardo Sandri (Titular Archbishop of Cittanova)
Second Section (Relations with other states), Most Revd Giovanni Lajolo (Titular Archbishop of Cesariana)

BISHOPS' CONFERENCE

The Roman Catholic Church in England and Wales consists of a total of 22 dioceses and is governed by the Bishops' Conference, membership of which includes the Diocesan Bishops, the Apostolic Exarch of the Ukrainians, the Bishop of the Forces and the Auxiliary Bishops. The Conference is headed by the President *(HE Cardinal Cormac Murphy-O'Connor, Archbishop of Westminster)* and Vice-President *(The Most Revd Patrick Kelly, Archbishop of Liverpool)*. There are five departments, each with an episcopal chairman: the Department for Christian Life and Worship (the Bishop of Menevia), the Department for Mission and Unity (the Bishop of Portsmouth), the Department for Catholic Education and Formation (the Archbishop of Birmingham), the Department for Christian Responsibility and Citizenship (the Archbishop of Cardiff), and the Department for International Affairs (the Bishop of Leeds).

The Bishops' Standing Committee, made up of all the Archbishops and the chairman of each of the above departments, has general responsibility for continuity of policy between the plenary sessions of the Conference. It prepares the Conference agenda and implements its decisions. It is serviced by a General Secretariat. There are also agencies and consultative bodies affiliated to the Conference.

The Bishops' Conference of Scotland is the permanently constituted assembly of the Bishops of Scotland. The Conference is headed by the President *(HE Cardinal Keith Patrick O'Brien, Archbishop of St. Andrews and Edinburgh)*. To promote its work, the Conference establishes various agencies which have an advisory function in relation to the Conference. The more important of these agencies are called Commissions and each one has a Bishop President who, with the other members of the Commissions, are appointed by the Conference.

The Irish Episcopal Conference has as its president Archbishop Brady of Armagh. Its membership comprises all the Archbishops and Bishops of Ireland and it appoints various Commissions to assist it in its work. There are three types of Commissions: (a) those made up of lay and clerical members chosen for their skills and experience, and staffed by full-time expert secretariats; (b) Commissions whose members are selected from existing institutions and whose services are supplied on a part-time basis; and (c) Commissions of Bishops only.

The Roman Catholic Church in the UK has an estimated 1,631,449 members, 6,583 priests and 4,475 churches.

Bishops' Conferences secretariats:

ENGLAND AND WALES, 39 Eccleston Square, London SW1V 1BX **T** 020-7630 8220 **F** 020 7901 4821
E secretariat@cbcew.org.uk **W** www.catholic-ew.org.uk
General Secretary, Mgr Andrew Summersgill

SCOTLAND, 64 Aitken Street, Airdrie, Lanarkshire ML6 6LT
General Secretary, Rt. Revd Mgr Henry Docherty
IRELAND, Columba Centre, Maynooth, County Kildare.
Secretary, The Most Revd William Lee (Bishop of Waterford and Lismore); *Executive Secretary*, Revd Aidan O'Boyle

GREAT BRITAIN

APOSTOLIC NUNCIO TO GREAT BRITAIN
The Most Revd Pablo Puente, 54 Parkside, London SW19 5NE T 020-8944 7189

ENGLAND AND WALES
THE MOST REVD ARCHBISHOPS
Westminster, HE Cardinal Cormac Murphy-O'Connor, *cons.* 1977, *apptd* 2000. *Auxiliaries*, James J. O'Brien, *cons.* 1977; George Stack, *cons.* 2001; Bernard Longley *cons.* 2003; Alan Hopes *cons.* 2003. *Clergy*, 779. *Archbishop's Residence*, Archbishop's House, Ambrosden Avenue, London SW1P 1QJ T 020-7798 9033
Birmingham, Vincent Nichols, *cons.* 1992, *apptd* 2000. *Auxiliaries*, Philip Pargeter, *cons.* 1990. *Clergy*, 443. *Diocesan Curia*, Cathedral House, St Chad's Queensway, Birmingham B4 6EX T 0121-236 5535
Cardiff, Peter Smith, *cons.* 1995, *apptd* 2001. *Clergy*, 126. *Diocesan Curia*, Archbishop's House, 41–43 Cathedral Road, Cardiff CF11 9HD T 029-2022 0411
Liverpool, Patrick Kelly, *cons.* 1984, *apptd* 1996. *Auxiliaries*, Vincent Malone, *cons.* 1989; Thomas Williams, *cons.* 2003. *Clergy*, 486. *Diocesan Curia*, Archdiocese of Liverpool, Centre for Evangelisation, Croxteth Drive, Sefton Park, Liverpool L17 1AA T 0151-522 1000
Southwark, Kevin McDonald, *cons.* 2001, *apptd* 2003. *Auxiliary*, John Hine, *cons.* 2001. *Clergy*, 498. *Diocesan Curia*, Archbishop's House, 150 St George's Road, London SE1 6HX T 020-7928 5592

THE RT. REVD BISHOPS
Arundel and Brighton, Kieran Conry, *cons.* 2001, *apptd* 2001. *Clergy*, 111. *Diocesan Curia*, Bishop's House, The Upper Drive, Hove, E. Sussex BN3 6NE T 01273-506387
Brentwood, Thomas McMahon, *cons.* 1980, *apptd* 1980. *Clergy*, 175. *Bishop's Office*, Cathedral House, Ingrave Road, Brentwood, Essex CM15 8AT T 01277-232266
Clifton, Declan Lang, *cons.* 2001, *apptd* 2001. *Clergy*, 251. *Bishop's House*, St Ambrose, North Road, Leigh Woods, Bristol BS8 3PW T 0117-973 3072
East Anglia, Michael Evans, *cons.* 2003, *apptd* 2003. *Clergy*, 129. *Diocesan Curia*, The White House, 21 Upgate, Poringland, Norwich NR14 7SH T 01508-492202
Hallam, John Rawsthorne, *cons.* 1981, *apptd* 1997. *Clergy*, 75. *Bishop's House*, 75 Norfolk Road, Sheffield S2 2SZ T 0114-278 7988
Hexham and Newcastle, Kevin Dunn, *cons.* 2004, *apptd* 2004. *Clergy*, 214. *Diocesan Curia*, Bishop's House, East Denton Hall, 800 West Road, Newcastle upon Tyne NE5 2BJ T 0191-228 0003
Lancaster, Patrick O'Donoghue, *cons.* 1993, *apptd* 2001. *Clergy*, 248. *Bishop's Residence*, Bishop's Apartment, Cathedral House, Balmoral Road, Lancaster LA1 3BT T 01524-596050
Leeds, Arthur Roche, *cons.* 2001, *apptd* 2004. *Clergy*, 226. *Diocesan Curia*, Hinsley Hall, 62 Headingley Lane, Leeds LS6 2BU T 0113-261 8000
Menevia (Wales), Mark Jabalé, *cons.* 2001, *apptd* 2001. *Clergy*, 60. *Diocesan Curia*, 27 Convent Street, Greenhill, Swansea SA1 2BX T 01792-644017
Middlesbrough, John Crowley, *cons.* 1986, *apptd* 1992. *Clergy*, 113. *Diocesan Curia*, 50a The Avenue, Linthorpe, Middlesbrough, Cleveland TS5 6QT T 01642-850505
Northampton, vacant. *Clergy*, 159. *Diocesan Curia*, Bishop's House, Marriott Street, Northampton NN2 6AW T 01604-715635
Nottingham, Malcolm McMahon, *cons.* 2000, *apptd* 2000. *Clergy*, 214. *Bishop's House*, 27 Cavendish Road East, The Park, Nottingham NG7 1BB T 0115-947 4786
Plymouth, Christopher Budd, *cons.* 1986, *apptd* 1985. *Clergy*, 125. *Diocesan Curia*, Bishop's House, 31 Wyndham Street West, Plymouth PL1 5RZ T 01752-224414
Portsmouth, F. Crispian Hollis, *cons.* 1987, *apptd* 1989. *Clergy*, 282. *Bishop's Residence*, Bishop's House, Edinburgh Road, Portsmouth, Hants PO1 3HG T 023-9282 0894
Salford, Terence J. Brain, *cons.* 1991, *apptd* 1997. *Clergy*, 346. *Diocesan Curia*, 5 Gerald Road, Pendleton, Salford M6 6DL T 0161-736 1421
Shrewsbury, Brian Noble, *cons.* 1995, *apptd* 1995. *Clergy* 180. *Diocesan Curia*, 2 Park Road South, Prenton, Wirral CH43 4UX T 0151-652 9855
Wrexham (Wales), Edwin Regan, *cons.* 1994, *apptd* 1994. *Clergy*, 83. *Diocesan Curia*, Bishop's House, Sontley Road, Wrexham LL13 7EW T 01978-262726

SCOTLAND

THE MOST REVD ARCHBISHOPS
St Andrews and Edinburgh, HE Cardinal Keith Patrick O'Brien, *cons.* 1985, *apptd* 1985, *elevated* 2003. *Clergy*, 160. *Archbishop's House*, 42 Greenhall Gardens, Edinburgh EH10 4BJ T 0131-447 3337
Glasgow, Mario Joseph Conti, *cons.* 1977, *apptd* 2002. *Clergy*, 252. *Diocesan Curia*, 196 Clyde Street, Glasgow G1 4JY T 0141-226 5898

THE RT. REVD BISHOPS
Aberdeen, Peter Moran, *cons.* 2003, *apptd* 2003. *Clergy*, 46. *Diocesan Curia*, Bishop's House, 3 Queen's Cross, Aberdeen AB15 4XU T 01224-319154
Argyll and the Isles, Ian Murray, *cons.* 1999, *apptd* 1999. *Clergy*, 26. *Bishop's House*, Esplanade, Oban, Argyll PA34 5AB T 01631-571395
Dunkeld, Vincent Logan, *cons.* 1981. *Clergy*, 44. *Diocesan Curia*, 24–28 Lawside Road, Dundee DD3 6XY T 01382-225453
Galloway, John Cunningham, *cons.* 2004, *apptd* 2004. *Clergy*, 61. *Diocesan Curia*, 8 Corsehill Road, Ayr KA7 2ST T 01292-266750
Motherwell, Joseph Devine, *cons.* 1977, *apptd* 1983. *Clergy*, 129. *Diocesan Curia*, Coursington Road, Motherwell ML1 1PP T 01698-269114
Paisley, John A. Mone, *cons.* 1984, *apptd* 1988. *Clergy*, 56. *Diocesan Curia*, Diocesan Centre, Cathedral Precincts, Incle Street, Paisley PA1 1HR T 0141-847 6130

BISHOPRIC OF THE FORCES
Rt. Revd Thomas Matthew Burns, *cons.* 2002, *apptd* 2002. *Administration*, Bishopric of the Forces, Middle Hill, Aldershot, Hants GU11 1PP T 01252-349004

IRELAND

There is one hierarchy for the whole of Ireland. Several of the dioceses have territory partly in the Republic of Ireland and partly in Northern Ireland.

APOSTOLIC NUNCIO TO IRELAND

Most Revd Giuseppe Lazzarotto (Titular Archbishop of Numana), 183 Navan Road, Dublin 7 T (00 353) (1) 838 0577 F (00 353) (1) 838 0276

THE MOST REVD ARCHBISHOPS

Armagh, Sean Brady, *cons.* 1995, *apptd* 1996. *Auxiliary*, Gerard Clifford, *cons.* 1991. *Clergy*, 183. *Diocesan Curia*, Ara Coeli, Armagh BT61 7QY T 028-3752 2045

Cashel and Emly, Dermot Clifford, *cons.* 1986, *apptd* 1988. *Clergy*, 128. *Archbishop's Residence*, Archbishop's House, Thurles, Co. Tipperary T (00 353) (504) 21512

Dublin, HE Cardinal Desmond Connell, *cons.* 1988, *apptd* 1988, *elevated* 2001. *Coadjutor Archbishop*, Diarmuid Martin, *apptd* 2003. *Auxiliaries*, Eamonn Walsh, *cons.* 1990; Fiachra O'Ceallaigh, *cons.* 1994; Martin Drennan, *cons.* 1997; Raymond Field, *cons.* 1997. *Clergy*, 994. *Archbishop's Residence*, Archbishop's House, Dublin 9 T (00 353) (1) 836 0723

Tuam, Michael Neary, *cons.* 1992, *apptd* 1995. *Clergy*, 141. *Archbishop's Residence*, Archbishop's House, Tuam, Co. Galway T (00 353) (93) 24166

THE MOST REVD BISHOPS

Achonry, Thomas Flynn, *cons.* 1975, *apptd* 1977. *Clergy*, 62. *Bishop's Residence*, Bishop's House, Ballaghaderreen, Co. Roscommon T (00 353) (9498) 60021

Ardagh and Clonmacnois, Colm O'Reilly, *cons.* 1983, *apptd* 1983. *Clergy*, 64. *Bishop's Residence*, St Michael's, Longford, Co. Longford T (00 353) (43) 46432

Clogher, Joseph Duffy, *cons.* 1979, *apptd* 1979. *Clergy*, 108. *Bishop's Residence*, Bishop's House, Monaghan T (00 353) (47) 81019

Clonfert, John Kirby, *cons.* 1988. *Clergy*, 71. *Bishop's Residence*, St Brendan's, Coorheen, Loughrea, Co. Galway T (0 353) (91) 841560

Cloyne, John Magee, *cons.* 1987, *apptd* 1987. *Clergy*, 153. *Diocesan Centre*, Cobh, Co. Cork T (00 353) (21) 4811430

Cork and Ross, John Buckley, *cons.* 1984, *apptd* 1998. *Clergy*, 153. *Diocesan Office*, Cork and Ross Offices, Redemption Road, Cork T (00 353) (21) 4301717

Derry, Seamus Hegarty, *cons.* 1982, *apptd* 1994. *Clergy*, 138. *Bishop's Residence*, Bishop's House, St Eugene's Cathedral, Derry BT48 9AP T 028-7126 2302. *Auxiliary*, Francis Lagan, *cons.* 1988

Down and Connor, Patrick J. Walsh, *cons.* 1983, *apptd* 1991. *Clergy*, 240. *Bishop's Residence*, Lisbreen, 73 Somerton Road, Belfast, Co. Antrim BT15 4DE T 028-9077 6185. *Auxiliaries*, Anthony Farquhar, *cons.* 1983; Donal McKeown, *cons.* 2001

Dromore, John McAreavey, *cons.* 1999, *apptd* 1999. *Clergy*, 78. *Bishop's Residence*, Bishop's House, 44 Armagh Road, Newry, Co. Down BT35 6PN T 028-3026 2444

Elphin, Christopher Jones, *cons.* 1994, *apptd* 1994. *Clergy*, 70. *Bishop's Residence*, St Mary's, Sligo T (00 353) (71) 9162670

Ferns, Éamonn Walsh, *cons.* 1990, *apptd* 2002. *Clergy*, 138. *Bishop's Residence*, Bishop's House, Summerhill, Wexford T (00 353) (53) 22177

Galway and Kilmacduagh, James McLoughlin, *cons.* 1993, *apptd* 1993. *Clergy*, 87. *Diocesan Office*, The Cathedral, Galway T (00 353) (91) 563566

Kerry, William Murphy, *cons.* 1995, *apptd* 1995. *Clergy*, 126. *Bishop's Residence*, Bishop's House, Killarney, Co. Kerry T (00 353) (64) 31168

Kildare and Leighlin, James Moriarty, *apptd* 2002. *Clergy*, 127. *Bishop's Residence*, Bishop's House, Carlow T (00 353) (59) 917 6725

Killala, John Fleming, *cons.* 2002, *apptd* 2002. *Clergy*, 52. *Bishop's Residence*, Bishop's House, Ballina, Co. Mayo T (00 353) (96) 21518

Killaloe, William Walsh, *cons.* 1994. *Clergy*, 149. *Bishop's Residence*, Westbourne, Ennis, Co. Clare T (00 353) (65) 6828638

Kilmore, Leo O'Reilly, *cons.* 1997, *apptd* 1998. *Clergy*, 98. *Bishop's Residence*, Bishop's House, Cullies, Co. Cavan T (00 353) (49) 4331496

Limerick, Donal Murray, *cons.* 1982, *apptd* 1996. *Clergy*, 110. *Diocesan Offices*, 66 O'Connell Street, Limerick T (00 353) (61) 315856

Meath, Michael Smith, *cons.* 1984, *apptd* 1990. *Clergy*, 141. *Bishop's Residence*, Bishop's House, Dublin Road, Mullingar, Co. Westmeath T (00 353) (44) 48841

Ossory, Laurence Forristal, *cons.* 1980, *apptd* 1981. *Clergy*, 91. *Bishop's Residence*, Sion House, Kilkenny T (00 353) (56) 7762448

Raphoe, Philip Boyce, *cons.* 1995, *apptd* 1995. *Clergy*, 90. *Bishop's Residence*, Ard Adhamhnáin, Letterkenny, Co. Donegal T (00 353) (74) 9121208

Waterford and Lismore, William Lee, *cons.* 1993, *apptd* 1993. *Clergy*, 114. *Bishop's Residence*, John's Hill, Waterford T (00 353) (51) 874463

OTHER CHURCHES IN THE UK

AFRICAN AND AFRO-CARIBBEAN CHURCHES

There are more than 160 Christian churches or groups of African or Afro-Caribbean origin in the UK. These include the Apostolic Faith Church, the Cherubim and Seraphim Church, the New Testament Church Assembly, the New Testament Church of God, the Wesleyan Holiness Church and the Aladura Churches. The Afro-West Indian United Council of Churches and the Council of African and Afro-Caribbean Churches UK (which was initiated as the Council of African and Allied Churches in 1979 to give one voice to the various Christian churches of African origin in the UK) are the media through which the member churches can work jointly to provide services they cannot easily provide individually.

There are about 70,000 adherents of African and Afro-Caribbean churches in the UK, and over 1,000 congregations. The Council of African and Afro-Caribbean Churches UK has about 17,000 members, 250 ministers and 125 congregations.

COUNCIL OF AFRICAN AND AFRO-CARIBBEAN CHURCHES UK , 31 Norton House, Sidney Road, London SW9 0UJ T 020-7274 5589

Chairman, His Grace The Most Revd Father Olu A. Abiola, OBE

ASSOCIATED PRESBYTERIAN CHURCHES OF SCOTLAND

The Associated Presbyterian Churches came into being in 1989 as a result of a division within the Free Presbyterian Church of Scotland. Following two controversial disciplinary cases, the culmination of deepening differences within the Church, a presbytery was formed calling itself the Associated Presbyterian Churches (APC). The Associated Presbyterian Churches has about 900 members, 9 ministers and 16 churches.

Clerk of the Scottish Presbytery, Revd A. N. McPhail, Fernhill, Polvinster Road, Oban PA34 5TN T 01631-567076

THE BAPTIST CHURCH

Baptists trace their origins to John Smyth, who in 1609 in Amsterdam reinstituted the baptism of conscious believers as the basis of the fellowship of a gathered church. Members of Smyth's church established the first Baptist church in England in 1612. They came to be known as 'General' Baptists and their theology was Arminian, whereas a later group of Calvinists who adopted the baptism of believers came to be known as 'Particular' Baptists. The two sections of the Baptists were united into one body, the Baptist Union of Great Britain and Ireland, in 1891. In 1988 the title was changed to the Baptist Union of Great Britain.

Baptists emphasise the complete autonomy of the local church, although individual churches are linked in various kinds of associations. There are international bodies (such as the Baptist World Alliance) and national bodies, but some Baptist churches belong to neither. However, in Great Britain the majority of churches and associations belong to the Baptist Union of Great Britain. There are also Baptist Unions in Wales, Scotland and Ireland which are much smaller than the Baptist Union of Great Britain, and there is some overlap of membership.

There are over 40 million Baptist church members world-wide; in the Baptist Union of Great Britain there are 139,028 members, 1,917 pastors and 2,099 churches. In the Baptist Union of Scotland there are 14,002 members, 120 pastors and 176 churches. In the Baptist Union of Wales (Undeb Bedyddwyr Cymru) there are about 15,073 members, 100 pastors and 443 churches. In the Association of Baptist Churches in Ireland (formerly the Baptist Union of Ireland) there are 8,251 members, 85 pastors and 111 churches.

President of the Baptist Union of Great Britain (2004–5), Revd Peter Manson

General Secretary, Revd David Coffey, Baptist House, PO Box 44, 129 Broadway, Didcot, Oxon OX11 8RT
T 01235-517700 E info@baptist.org.uk
W www.baptist.org.uk

General Director of the Baptist Union of Scotland, Revd William Slack, 14 Aytoun Road, Glasgow G41 5RT
T 0141-423 6169 F 0141-424 1422
E admin@scottishbaptist.org.uk

President of the English Assembly of the Baptist Union of Wales (2004–5), Revd Keith Fantham

President of the Welsh Assembly of the Baptist Union of Wales (2004–5), Revd Idris Hughes

General Secretaries of the Baptist Union of Wales, Revd Peter Thomas and Revd W. O. Meredith Powell, 94 Mansel Street, Swansea SA1 5TZ T 01792-655468

Secretary of the Association of Baptist Churches in Ireland, Revd W. Colville, The Baptist Centre, 19 Hillsborough Road, Moira BT67 0HG T 028-9261 9267
E abc@thebaptistcentre.org

THE CONGREGATIONAL FEDERATION

The Congregational Federation was founded by members of Congregational churches in England and Wales who did not join the United Reformed Church in 1972. There are also churches in Scotland and France affiliated to the Federation. The Federation exists to encourage congregations of believers to worship in free assembly, but it has no authority over them and emphasises their right to independence and self-government.

The Federation has 10,058 members, 59 accredited ministers and 294 churches in England, Wales and Scotland.

President of the Federation (2004–5), Val Price

General Secretary, Revd. M. Heaney, 4 Castle Gate, Nottingham NG1 7AS T 0115-911 1460
E admin@congregational.org.uk

THE FREE CHURCH OF ENGLAND

The Free Church of England is a union of two bodies in the Anglican tradition, the Free Church of England, founded in 1844 as a protest against the Oxford Movement in the established Church, and the Reformed Episcopal Church, founded in America in 1873 but which also had congregations in England. As both Churches sought to maintain the historic faith, tradition and practice of the Anglican Church since the Reformation, they decided to unite as one body in England in 1927. The historic episcopate was conferred on the English Church in 1876 through the line of the American bishops, who had pioneered an open table Communion policy towards members of other denominations.

The Free Church of England has 1,300 members, 45 ministers and 30 churches in England. It also has three house churches and three ministers in New Zealand and one church and one minister in St Petersburg, Russia.

General Secretary, Revd Paul Hunt, 329 Wolverhampton Road West, Willen Hall WV13 2RL T 01902-607335

THE FREE CHURCH OF SCOTLAND

The Free Church of Scotland was formed in 1843 when over 400 ministers withdrew from the Church of Scotland as a result of interference in the internal affairs of the church by the civil authorities. In 1900, all but 26 ministers joined with others to form the United Free Church (most of which rejoined the Church of Scotland in 1929). In 1904 the remaining 26 ministers were recognised by the House of Lords as continuing the Free Church of Scotland.

The Church maintains strict adherence to the Westminster Confession of Faith (1648) and accepts the Bible as the sole rule of faith and conduct. Its General Assembly meets annually. It also has links with Reformed Churches overseas. In January 2000, a division occurred within the church, the larger body retains the name of the Free Church of Scotland with the smaller body known as the Free Church of Scotland (Continuing) and has around 2,000 members. The Free Church of Scotland has about 11,500 members, 82 ministers and 162 churches.

General Treasurer, I. D. Gill, The Mound, Edinburgh EH1 2LS
T 0131-226 5286 E offices@freechurchofscotland.org.uk

THE FREE PRESBYTERIAN CHURCH OF SCOTLAND

The Free Presbyterian Church of Scotland was formed in 1893 by two ministers of the Free Church of Scotland who refused to accept a Declaratory Act passed by the Free Church General Assembly in 1892. The Free Presbyterian Church of Scotland is Calvinistic in doctrine and emphasises observance of the Sabbath. It adheres strictly to the Westminster Confession of Faith of 1648.

The Church has about 3,000 members in Scotland and about 4,000 in overseas congregations. It has 16 ministers and 50 churches in the UK.

Moderator, Revd R. MacLeod, 4 Laurel Park Close, Glasgow G13 1RD

Clerk of Synod, Revd J. MacLeod, 16 Matheson Road, Stornoway, Isle of Lewis HS1 2LA T 01851-702755

THE HOLY APOSTOLIC CATHOLIC ASSYRIAN CHURCH OF THE EAST

The Holy Apostolic Catholic Assyrian Church of the East traces its beginnings to the middle of the first century. It spread from Upper Mesopotamia throughout the territories of the Persian Empire. The Assyrian church of the East became theologically separated from the rest of the Christian community following the Council of Ephesus in 431. The Church is headed by the Catholicos Patriarch and is episcopal in government. The liturgical language is Syriac (Aramaic). The Assyrian Church of the East and the Roman Catholic Church agreed a common Christological declaration in 1994 and a process of dialogue between the Assyrian Church of the East and the Chaldean Catholic Church, which is in communion with Rome but shares the Syriac liturgy, was instituted in 1996.

The Church numbers about 400,000 members in the Middle East, India, Europe, North America and Australasia. There are around 600 members in the UK.

The Church in Great Britain forms part of the diocese of Europe under Mar Odisho Oraham.

Representative in Great Britain, Very Revd Younan Y. Younan, 66 Montague Road, London W7 3PQ T 020-8579 7259

THE INDEPENDENT METHODIST CHURCHES

The Independent Methodist Churches were formed in 1805 and remained independent when the Methodist Church in Great Britain was formed in 1932. They are mainly concentrated in the industrial areas of the north of England.

The churches are Methodist in doctrine but their organisation is congregational. All the churches are members of the Independent Methodist Connexion of Churches. The controlling body of the Connexion is the Annual Meeting, to which churches send delegates. The Connexional President is elected annually. Between annual meetings the affairs of the Connexion are handled by departmental committees. Ministers are appointed by the churches and trained through the Connexion. The ministry is open to both men and women and is unpaid.

There are 2,108 members, 90 ministers and 89 churches in Great Britain.

Connexional President (2003–5), Geoffrey Lomas

General Secretary, W. C. Gabb, 66 Kirkstone Drive, Loughborough LE11 3RW T 01942-223526

THE LUTHERAN CHURCH

Lutheranism is based on the teachings of Martin Luther, the German leader of the Protestant Reformation. The authority of the scriptures is held to be supreme over Church tradition. The teachings of Lutheranism are explained in detail in 16th century confessional writings, particularly the Augsburg Confession. Lutheranism is one of the largest Protestant denominations and it is particularly strong in northern Europe and the USA. Some Lutheran churches are episcopal, while others have a synodal form of organisation; unity is based on doctrine rather than structure. Most Lutheran churches are members of the Lutheran World Federation, based in Geneva.

Lutheran services in Great Britain are held in 18 languages to serve members of different nationalities. Services usually follow ancient liturgies. English-language congregations are members either of the Lutheran Church in Great Britain, or of the Evangelical Lutheran Church of England. The Lutheran Church in Great Britain and other Lutheran churches in Britain are members of the Lutheran Council of Great Britain, which represents them and co-ordinates their common work.

There are over 70 million Lutherans world-wide; in Great Britain there are about 100,000 members, 50 clergy and 100 congregations.

General Secretary of the Lutheran Council of Great Britain, Revd T. Bruch, 30 Thanet Street, London WC1H 9QH T 020-7554 2900 F 020-7383 3081 E enquiries@lutheran.org.uk W www.lutheran.org.uk

THE METHODIST CHURCH

The Methodist movement started in England in 1729 when the Revd John Wesley, an Anglican priest, and his brother Charles met with others in Oxford and resolved to conduct their lives and study by 'rule and method'. In 1739 the Wesleys began evangelistic preaching and the first Methodist chapel was founded in Bristol in the same year. In 1744 the first annual conference was held, at which the Articles of Religion were drawn up. Doctrinal emphases included repentance, faith, the assurance of salvation, social concern and the priesthood of all believers. After John Wesley's death in 1791 the Methodists withdrew from the established Church to form the Methodist Church. Methodists gradually drifted into many groups, but in 1932 the Wesleyan Methodist Church, the United Methodist Church and the Primitive Methodist Church united to form the Methodist Church in Great Britain as it now exists.

The governing body and supreme authority of the Methodist Church is the Conference, but there are also 33 district synods, consisting of all the ministers and selected lay people in each district, and circuit meetings of the ministers and lay people of each circuit. There are over 60 million Methodists world-wide; in Great Britain in 2001 there were 327,724 members, 3,626 ministers, 9,951 lay preachers and 6,378 churches.

President of the Conference in Great Britain (2004–5), Revd W. Morrey

Vice-President of the Conference (2004–5), Deacon M. Poxon

Secretary of the Conference, Revd David G. Deeks, Methodist Church, 25 Marylebone Road, London NW1 5JR T 020-7486 5502 F 020-7467 5226 E generalsecretary@methodistchurch.org.uk W www.methodist.org.uk

THE METHODIST CHURCH IN IRELAND

The Methodist Church in Ireland is autonomous but has close links with British Methodism. It has a community roll of 53,829, 15,800 members, 203 ministers, 287 lay preachers and 223 churches.

President of the Methodist Church in Ireland (2004–5), Revd Dr W. Brian Fletcher, 33a Arderlee Avenue, Belfast BT9 0AA T 028-9045 1521

Secretary of the Methodist Church in Ireland, Revd W. Winston Graham, 1 Fountainville Avenue, Belfast BT9 6AN T 028-9032 4554

THE (EASTERN) ORTHODOX CHURCH

The Eastern (or Byzantine) Orthodox Church is a communion of self-governing Christian churches recognising the honorary primacy of the Oecumenical Patriarch of Constantinople.

The position of Orthodox Christians is that the faith was fully defined during the period of the Oecumenical Councils. In doctrine it is strongly trinitarian, and stresses the mystery and importance of the sacraments. It is episcopal in government. The structure of the Orthodox Christian year differs from that of western Churches.

Orthodox Christians throughout the world are estimated to number about 300 million; there are an estimated 284,298 in the UK.

EASTERN ORTHODOX CHURCHES IN THE UK

THE PATRIARCHATE OF ANTIOCH

There are ten parishes served by 15 clergy. In Great Britain the Patriarchate is represented by the Revd Fr **Samir Gholam**, St George's Cathedral, 1A Redhill Street, London NW1 4BG **T** 020-7383 0403

THE GREEK ORTHODOX CHURCH (PATRIARCHATE OF CONSTANTINOPLE)

The presence of Greek Orthodox Christians in Britain dates back at least to 1677 when Archbishop Joseph Geogirenes of Samos fled from Turkish persecution and came to London. The present Greek cathedral in Moscow Road, Bayswater, was opened for public worship in 1879 and the Diocese of Thyateira and Great Britain was established in 1922. There are now 121 parishes and other communities (including monasteries) in the UK, served by five bishops, 110 clergy, nine cathedrals and about 93 churches.

In Great Britain the Patriarchate of Constantinople is represented by **Archbishop Gregorios of Thyateira and Great Britain**, Thyateira House, 5 Craven Hill, London W2 3EN **T** 020-7723 4787 **F** 020-7224 9301

THE RUSSIAN ORTHODOX CHURCH (PATRIARCHATE OF MOSCOW) AND THE RUSSIAN ORTHODOX CHURCH OUTSIDE RUSSIA

The records of Russian Orthodox Church activities in Britain date from the visit to England of Tsar Peter I in the early 18th century. Clergy were sent from Russia to serve the chapel established to minister to the staff of the Imperial Russian Embassy in London.

In Great Britain the Patriarchate of Moscow is represented by **Bishop Basil of Sergievo**, 94a Banbury Road, Oxford OX2 6JT. He is assisted by one bishop and 30 clergy. There are 30 parishes and smaller communities. The Russian Orthodox Church Outside Russia is represented by Archbishop Mark of Berlin, Germany and Great Britain, c/o *Dean of English-Language Parishes*, **Very Revd Archimandrite Alexis**, Saint Edward Brotherhood, St Cyprian's Avenue, Brookwood, Surrey GU24 0BL **T** 01483-487763 **W** www.rocorbritishisles.org.

There are eight communities, including two monasteries in England and one mission in Northern Ireland.

THE SERBIAN ORTHODOX CHURCH (PATRIARCHATE OF SERBIA)

There are 33 parishes and smaller communities in Great Britain served by 11 clergy. The Patriarchate of Serbia is represented by the Episcopal Vicar, the **Very Revd Milenko Zebic**, 131 Cob Lane, Bournville, Birmingham B30 1QE **T** 0121-458 5273

OTHER NATIONALITIES

Most of the Ukrainian parishes in Britain have joined the Patriarchate of Constantinople, leaving a small number of Ukrainian parishes in Britain under the care of other patriarchates (not all of which are recognised by the other Orthodox Churches). The Latvian, Polish and some Belarusian parishes are also under the care of the Patriarchate of Constantinople. The Patriarchate of Romania has one parish served by two clergy. The Patriarchate of Bulgaria has one parish served by one priest. The Belarusian Autocephalous Orthodox Church has five parishes served by two priests.

THE ORIENTAL ORTHODOX CHURCHES

The term 'Oriental Orthodox Churches' is now generally used to describe a group of six ancient eastern churches which reject the Christological definition of the Council of Chalcedon (AD 451) and use Christological terms in different ways from the Eastern Orthodox Church. There are about 34 million members world-wide of the Oriental Orthodox Churches and about 22,020 in the UK.

ORIENTAL ORTHODOX CHURCHES IN THE UK

THE ARMENIAN ORTHODOX CHURCH (PATRIARCHATE OF ETCHMIADZIN)

The Armenian Orthodox Church is the longest-established Oriental Orthodox community in Great Britain. It is represented by the **Rt. Revd Bishop Nathan Hovhannisian, Armenian Primate of Great Britain**, Armenian Vicarage, Iverna Gardens, London W8 6TP **T** 020-7937 0152 **E** armchurchlondon@aol.com

THE COPTIC ORTHODOX CHURCH

The Coptic Orthodox Church is the largest Oriental Orthodox community in Great Britain.

Coptic Orthodox Church, **Bishop Angaelos**, Coptic Orthodox Church Centre, Shephalbury Manor, Broadhall Way, Stevenage, Herts SG2 8RH **T** 01438-748473 **F** 01438-313879 **E** angaelos@copticcentre.com **W** www.copticcentre.com

The British Orthodox Church, **Metropolitan Seraphim**, 10 Heathwood Gardens, Charlton, London SE7 8EP **T** 020-8854 3090 **E** boc@nildram.co.uk **W** www.britishorthodox.org

THE ERITREAN ORTHODOX CHURCH

In Great Britain the Eritrean Orthodox Church is represented by **Bishop Markos**, 78 Edmund Street, Camberwell, London SE5 7NR

THE MALANKARA ORTHODOX SYRIAN CHURCH

The Malankara Orthodox Syrian Church is part of the Diocese of Europe, UK and Canada under Metropolitan Thomas Mar Makarios. The church in Great Britain can be contacted via **Fr Abraham Thomas**, St Gregorios Indian Orthodox Church, Cranfield Road, Brockley, London SE4 1UF **T** 020-8691 9456

THE SYRIAN ORTHODOX CHURCH

The Syrian Orthodox Church in Great Britain comes under the Patriarchal Vicar, whose representative is **Fr Touma Hazim Dakkama**, Antiochian, 5 Canning Road, Croydon CR0 6QA **T** 020-8654 7531

THE COUNCIL OF ORIENTAL ORTHODOX CHURCHES,

Secretary, **Deacon Aziz M. A. Nour**, 34 Chertsey Road, Church Square, Shepperton, Middlesex TW17 9LF **T** 020-8368 8447 ***President***, Rt. Revd Bishop Nathan Hovhannisian

PENTECOSTAL CHURCHES

Pentecostalism is inspired by the descent of the Holy Spirit upon the apostles at Pentecost. The movement began in Los Angeles, USA, in 1906 and is characterised by baptism with the Holy Spirit, divine healing, speaking in tongues (glossolalia), and a literal interpretation of the scriptures. The Pentecostal movement in Britain dates from 1907. Initially, groups of Pentecostalists were led by laymen and did not organise formally. However, in 1915 the Elim Foursquare Gospel Alliance (more usually called the Elim Pentecostal Church) was founded in Ireland by George Jeffreys and in 1924 about 70 independent assemblies formed a fellowship, the Assemblies of God in Great Britain and Ireland. The Apostolic Church grew out of the 1904–5 revivals in South Wales and was established in 1916, and the New Testament Church of God was established in England in 1953. In recent years many aspects of Pentecostalism have been adopted by the growing charismatic movement within the Roman Catholic, Protestant and Eastern Orthodox churches. There are about 105 million Pentecostalists world-wide, with about 280,260 adherents in Great Britain and Ireland.

THE APOSTOLIC CHURCH, International Administration Offices, PO Box 389, 24–27 St Helens Road, Swansea SA1 1ZH **T** 01792-473992 *National Leader*, Warren Jones
The Apostolic Church has about 106 churches, 4,481 adherents and 77 ministers

THE ASSEMBLIES OF GOD INCORPORATED, PO Box 7634, Nottingham NG11 6ZY **T** 0115-921 7272 **F** 0115-921 7273 **E** info@aog.org.uk *General Superintendent*, P. C. Weaver
The Assemblies of God has 640 churches, about 60,000 adherents (including children) and 1,039 accredited ministers

THE ELIM PENTECOSTAL CHURCH, PO Box 38, Cheltenham, Glos GL50 3HN **T** 01242-519904 **E** info@elimhq.com
General Superintendent, Revd J. J. Glass
The Elim Pentecostal Church has 600 churches, 68,500 adherents and 650 accredited ministers

THE NEW TESTAMENT CHURCH OF GOD, Main House, Overstone Park, Overstone, Northampton NN6 0AD **T** 01604-643311 *National Overseer*, Bishop Eric Arthur Brown
The New Testament Church of God has about 120 organised congregations, about 21,540 members and 280 accredited ministers

PLYMOUTH BRETHREN

The Brethren was founded in Dublin in 1827–28. It rejected denominationalism and clericalism and based itself on the structures and practices of the early Church. Many groups sprang up and that at Plymouth became the best known, which resulted in the designation by others as Plymouth Brethren. Other groups are based in Ireland, USA, Burma and Guyana.

Early worship had a prescribed form but quickly assumed an unstructured, non-liturgical format. There were services devoted to worship, usually involving the breaking of bread, and separate preaching meetings. There was no salaried ministry.

A theological dispute led in 1848 to schism between the Open Brethren and the Closed or Exclusive Brethren, each branch later suffering further divisions.

Open Brethren churches are completely independent, but freely co-operate with each other. Churches are run by appointed elders. Exclusive Brethren churches believe in a universal fellowship between congregations. They do not have elders, but appoint respected members of their congregation to perform certain administrative functions.

The Brethren are established throughout the UK, Ireland, Europe, India, Africa and Australasia. Total membership in the UK is 80,210.

GOSPEL TRACT PUBLICATIONS, 7 Beech Avenue, Dumbreck, Glasgow G41 5BY **T** 0141-427 4661

CHAPTER TWO, Fountain House, Conduit Mews, London SE18 7AP **T** 020-8316 5389

THE PRESBYTERIAN CHURCH IN IRELAND

The Presbyterian Church in Ireland is Calvinistic in doctrine and presbyterian in constitution. Presbyterianism was established in Ireland as a result of the Ulster plantation in the early 17th century, when English and Scottish Protestants settled in the north of Ireland.

There are 21 presbyteries and five regional synods under the chief court known as the General Assembly. The General Assembly meets annually and is presided over by a Moderator who is elected for one year. The ongoing work of the Church is undertaken by 18 boards under which there are a number of specialist committees.

There are about 179,549 Presbyterians in Ireland, mainly in the north, in 460 congregations and with 370 ministers.

Moderator (2004–5), Rt. Revd Ken Newell
Clerk of Assembly and General Secretary, Revd Dr Donald Watts, Church House, Belfast BT1 6DW **T** 028-9032 2284

THE PRESBYTERIAN CHURCH OF WALES

The Presbyterian Church of Wales or Calvinistic Methodist Church of Wales is Calvinistic in doctrine and presbyterian in constitution. It was formed in 1811 when Welsh Calvinists severed the relationship with the established church by ordaining their own ministers. It secured its own confession of faith in 1823 and a Constitutional Deed in 1826, and since 1864 the General Assembly has met annually, presided over by a Moderator elected for a year. The doctrine and constitutional structure of the Presbyterian Church of Wales was confirmed by Act of Parliament in 1931–2.

The Church has about 31,970 members, 93 ministers and 762 churches.

Moderator (2004–5), Revd W. G. Edwards
General Secretary, Revd Ifan Roberts, Tabernacle Chapel, 81 Merthyr Road, Whitchurch, Cardiff CF14 1DD **T** 029-2062 7465

THE RELIGIOUS SOCIETY OF FRIENDS (QUAKERS)

Quakerism is a movement, not a church, which was founded in the 17th century by George Fox and others in an attempt to revive what they saw as 'primitive Christianity'. The movement was based originally in the Midlands, Yorkshire and north-west England, but there are now Quakers in 36 countries around the world. The colony of Pennsylvania, founded by William Penn, was originally Quaker.

Emphasis is placed on the experience of God in daily life rather than on sacraments or religious occasions. There is no church calendar. Worship is largely silent and there are no appointed ministers; the responsibility for conducting a meeting is shared equally among those present. Social reform and religious tolerance have always been important to Quakers, together with a commitment to non-violence in resolving disputes.

There are 213,800 Quakers world-wide, with over 16,000 in Great Britain and Ireland. There are about 500 meetings in Great Britain.

CENTRAL OFFICES: (GREAT BRITAIN) Friends House, 173–177 Euston Road, London NW1 2BJ **T** 020-7663 1000 **F** 020-7663 1001 **W** www.quaker.org.uk

THE SALVATION ARMY

The Salvation Army was founded by a Methodist minister, William Booth, in the east end of London in 1865, and has since become established in 108 countries world-wide. In 1878 it adopted a quasi-military command structure intended to inspire and regulate its endeavours and to reflect its view that the Church was engaged in spiritual warfare. Salvationists emphasise evangelism and the provision of social welfare. World-wide there are about 26,000 active officers (full-time ordained ministers) and 15,500 worship centres and outposts. In Great Britain and Ireland there are 45,000 members, 1,400 active officers and 800 worship centres.

International Leader, Gen. John Larsson
UK Leader, Commissioner Alex Hughes
TERRITORIAL HEADQUARTERS, 101 Newington Causeway, London SE1 6BN T 020-7367 4500
E thq@salvationarmy.org.uk
W www.salvationarmy.org.uk

THE SEVENTH-DAY ADVENTIST CHURCH

The Seventh-day Adventist Church was founded in 1863 in the USA and the first church in the UK was established in 1886. Its members look forward to the second coming of Christ and observe the Sabbath (the seventh day) as a day of rest, worship and ministry. The Church bases its faith and practice wholly on the Bible and has developed 27 core beliefs. The World Church is divided into 13 divisions, each made up of unions of churches. The Seventh-day Adventist Church in the British Isles is known as the British Union Conference of Seventh-day Adventists and is a member of the Trans-European Division. In the British Isles the administrative organisation of the church is arranged in three tiers: the local churches; the regional conferences for south England, north England, Wales, Scotland and Ireland; and the national headquarters. There are over 12 million members and 53,500 churches in 203 countries. In the UK and Ireland there are 22,205 members and 249 churches.

President of the British Union Conference, Cecil Perry
BRITISH ISLES HEADQUARTERS, Stanborough Park, Watford WD25 9JZ T 01923-672251

THE (SWEDENBORGIAN) NEW CHURCH

The New Church is based on the teachings of the 18th century Swedish scientist and theologian Emanuel Swedenborg (1688–1772), who believed that Jesus Christ appeared to him and instructed him to reveal the spiritual meaning of the Bible. He claimed to have visions of the spiritual world, including heaven and hell, and conversations with angels and spirits. He published several theological works, including descriptions of the spiritual world and a Bible commentary.

The Second Coming of Jesus Christ is believed to have already taken place and is still taking place, being not an actual physical reappearance of Christ, but rather His return in spirit. It is also believed that concurrent with our life on earth is life in a parallel spiritual world, of which we are usually unconscious until death. There are around 30,000 Swedenborgians world-wide, with 1,130 members, 27 Churches and 10 ministers in the UK.

THE GENERAL CONFERENCE OF THE NEW CHURCH, Swedenborg House, 20 Bloomsbury Way, London WC1A 2TH T 020-7229 9340

UNDEB YR ANNIBYNWYR CYMRAEG

Undeb Yr Annibynwyr Cyraeg, the Union of Welsh Independents was formed in 1872 and is a voluntary association of Welsh Congregational Churches and personal members. It is mainly Welsh-speaking. Congregationalism in Wales dates back to 1639 when the first Welsh Congregational Church was opened in Gwent. Member churches are Calvinistic in doctrine, although a wide range of interpretations are permitted, and congregationalist in organisation. Each church has complete independence in the government and administration of its affairs.

The Union has 32,500 members, 220 ministers and 500 member churches.

President of the Union (2004–5), Dr Hefin Jones
General Secretary, Revd D. Myrddin Hughes, Ty John Penry, 11 Heol Sant Helen, Swansea SA1 4AL T 01792-652542
F 01792-650647

THE UNITED REFORM CHURCH

The United Reformed Church was first formed by the union of most of the Congregational churches in England and Wales with the Presbyterian Church of England in 1972. Congregationalism dates from the mid 16th century. It is Calvinistic in doctrine, and its followers form independent self-governing congregations bound under God by covenant, a principle laid down in the writings of Robert Browne (1550–1633). From the late 16th century the movement was driven underground by persecution, but the cause was defended at the Westminster Assembly in 1643 and the Savoy Declaration of 1658 laid down its principles. Congregational churches formed county associations for mutual support and in 1832 these associations merged to form the Congregational Union of England and Wales.

Presbyterianism in England also dates from the mid 16th century, and was Calvinistic and evangelical in its doctrine. It was governed by a hierarchy of courts.

In the 1960s there was close co-operation locally and nationally between Congregational and Presbyterian Churches. This led to union negotiations and a Scheme of Union, supported by Act of Parliament in 1972. In 1981 a further unification took place, with the Reformed Association of Churches of Christ becoming part of the URC. In 2000 a third union took place, with the Congregational Union of Scotland. In its basis the United Reformed Church reflects local church initiative and responsibility with a conciliar pattern of oversight. The General Assembly is the central body, and is made up of equal numbers of ministers and lay members.

The United Reformed Church is divided into 13 Synods, each with a Synod Moderator, and 78 Districts. There are 87,732 members, 628 full-time stipendiary ministers, 83 part-time stipendiary ministers, 173 non-stipendiary ministers, 16 active church related community workers and 1,719 local churches.

General Secretary, Revd Dr David C. Cornick, 86 Tavistock Place, London WC1H 9RT T 020-7916 2020 F 7916 2021
E david.cornick@urc.org.uk

THE WESLEYAN REFORM UNION

The Wesleyan Reform Union was founded by Methodists who left or were expelled from Wesleyan Methodism in 1849 following a period of internal conflict. Its doctrine is conservative evangelical and its organisation is congregational, each church having complete independence in the government and administration of its affairs. The Union has 1,947 members, 17 ministers, 131 lay preachers and 108 churches.

President (2004–5), Revd R. Brindley
General Secretary, Revd A. J. Williams, Wesleyan Reform Church House, 123 Queen Street, Sheffield S1 2DU T 0114-272 1938

NON-TRINITARIAN CHURCHES

CHRISTADELPHIANISM

Christadelphians believe that the Bible is the word of God and that it reveals both God's dealing with mankind in the past and his plans for the future. These plans centre on the work of Jesus Christ, who is believed shortly to return to earth to establish God's kingdom. Christadelphians have existed since the 1850s, beginning in the USA through the work of an Englishman, Dr John Thomas.

THE CHRISTADELPHIANISM MAGAZINE AND PUBLISHING ASSOCIATION, 404 Shaftmoor Lane, Birmingham B28 8SZ T 0121-777 6324 F 0121-778 5024

THE CHURCH OF CHRIST, SCIENTIST

The Church of Christ, Scientist was founded by Mary Baker Eddy in the USA in 1879 to 'reinstate primitive Christianity and its lost element of healing'. Christian Science teaches the need for spiritual regeneration and salvation from sin, but is best known for its reliance on prayer alone in the healing of sickness. Adherents believe that such healing is a law, or Science, and is in direct line with that practised by Jesus Christ (revered, not as God, but as the Son of God) and by the early Christian Church.

The denomination consists of The First Church of Christ, Scientist, in Boston, Massachusetts, USA (the Mother Church) and its branch churches in over 80 countries world-wide. The Bible and Mary Baker Eddy's book, *Science and Health with Key to the Scriptures*, are used at services; there are no clergy. Those engaged in full-time healing are called practitioners, of whom there are 3,500 world-wide.

No membership figures are available, since Mary Baker Eddy felt that numbers are no measure of spiritual vitality and ruled that such statistics should not be published. There are over 2,000 branch churches world-wide, including nearly 120 in the UK.

CHRISTIAN SCIENCE COMMITTEE ON PUBLICATION, Claridge House, 29 Barnes High Street, London SW13 9LW T 020-8282 1645 F 020-8487 1566 E londoncs@csps.com
District Manager for the UK and the Republic of Ireland, Tony Lobl

THE CHURCH OF JESUS CHRIST OF LATTER-DAY SAINTS

The Church (often referred to as 'the Mormons') was founded in New York State, USA, in 1830, and came to Britain in 1837. The oldest continuous branch in the world is to be found in Preston, Lancs. Mormons are Christians who claim to belong to the 'Restored Church' of Jesus Christ. They believe that true Christianity died when the last original apostle died, but that it was given back to the world by God and Christ through Joseph Smith, the Church's founder and first president. They accept and use the Bible as scripture, but believe in continuing revelation from God and use additional scriptures, including *The Book of Mormon: Another Testament of Jesus Christ*. The importance of the family is central to the Church's beliefs and practices. Church members set aside Monday evenings as Family Home Evenings when Christian family values are taught. Polygamy was formally discontinued in 1890. The Church has no paid ministry; local congregations are headed by a leader chosen from amongst their number. The world governing body, based in Utah, USA, is the three-man First Presidency, assisted by the Quorum of the Twelve Apostles. There are more than 11 million members world-wide, with about 178,000 adherents in Britain in 371 congregations.

BRITISH HEADQUARTERS, Church Offices, 751 Warwick Road, Solihull, W. Midlands B91 3DQ T 0121-712 1207

JEHOVAH'S WITNESS

The movement now known as Jehovah's Witnesses grew from a Bible study group formed by Charles Taze Russell in 1872 in Pennsylvania, USA. In 1896 it adopted the name of the Watch Tower Bible and Tract Society, and in 1931 its members became known as Jehovah's Witnesses. Jehovah's (God's) Witnesses believe in the Bible as the word of God, and consider it to be inspired and historically accurate. They take the scriptures literally, except where there are obvious indications that they are figurative or symbolic, and reject the doctrine of the Trinity. Witnesses also believe that the earth will remain for ever and that all those approved of by Jehovah will have eternal life on a cleansed and beautified earth; only 144,000 will go to heaven to rule with Christ. They believe that the second coming of Christ began in 1914 and his thousand-year reign on earth is imminent, and that Armageddon (a final battle in which evil will be defeated) will precede Christ's rule of peace. They refuse to take part in military service, and do not accept blood transfusions. The 10-member world governing body is based in New York, USA. There is no paid ministry, but each congregation has elders assigned to look after various duties and every Witness is assigned homes to visit in their congregation. There are over 6 million Jehovah's Witnesses world-wide, with 130,000 Witnesses in the UK organised into over 1,400 congregations.

BRITISH ISLES HEADQUARTERS, Watch Tower House, The Ridgeway, London NW7 1RN T 020-8906 2211 F 020-8371 0051 E pr@wtbts.org.uk W www.watchtower.org

UNITARIAN AND FREE CHRISTIAN CHURCHES

Unitarianism has its historical roots in the Judaeo-Christian tradition but rejects the deity of Christ and the doctrine of the trinity. It allows the individual to embrace insights from all the world's faiths and philosophies, as there is no fixed creed. It is accepted that beliefs may evolve in the light of personal experience.

Unitarian communities first became established in Poland and Transylvania in the 16th century. The first avowedly Unitarian place of worship in the British Isles opened in London in 1774. The General Assembly of Unitarian and Free Christian Churches came into existence in 1928 as the result of the amalgamation of two earlier organisations.

There are about 4,400 Unitarians in Great Britain and Ireland and about 72 Unitarian ministers. Nearly 200 self-governing congregations and fellowship groups, including a small number overseas, are members of the General Assembly.

GENERAL ASSEMBLY OF UNITARIAN AND FREE CHRISTIAN CHURCHES, Essex Hall, 1–6 Essex Street, London WC2R 3HY T 020-7240 2384 F 020-7240 3089 E ga@unitarian.org.uk W www.unitarian.org.uk
President 2004–5, Dawn Buckle

COMMUNICATIONS

POSTAL SERVICES

The Royal Mail Group plc operates Parcelforce, Post Office and Royal Mail, which handles over 82 million items of mail each day. The Postal Services Commission (Postcomm), an independent regulator accountable to parliament, oversees postal operations in the UK and is tasked with the gradual introduction of competition into postal services.

POSTCOMM, 6 Hercules Road, London SE1 7DB
T 020-7593 2100 **W** www.postcomm.gov.uk
POSTWATCH, 28 Grosvenor Gardens, London SW1W 0TT
T 08456-013265 **E** info@postwatch.co.uk

Postwatch is the consumer organisation responsible for postal services and takes up complaints on behalf of consumers against any licensed provider of postal services. Below are details of a number of popular postal services along with prices correct as at July 2004. For further details please contact the relevant service provider, i.e. Royal Mail or Parcelforce.

INLAND POSTAL SERVICES AND REGULATIONS

INLAND LETTER POST RATES

Weight up to	*1st class*	*2nd class†*
60g	£0.28	£0.21
100g	£0.42	£0.35
150g	£0.60	£0.47
200g	£0.75	£0.58
250g	£0.88	£0.71
300g	£1.01	£0.83
350g	£1.15	£0.94
400g	£1.33	£1.14
450g	£1.50	£1.30
500g	£1.68	£1.48
600g	£2.03	£1.75
700g	£2.38	£2.00
750g	£2.55	£2.12
800g	£2.73	(not
900g	£3.10	admissible
1kg	£3.45	over 750 g)

Costs for first class items over 1kg are £3.45 and then £0.89 for each extra 250g or part thereof.

*Postcards travel at the same rates as letter post

† First class letters are normally delivered the following day and second class post within three days

UK PARCEL RATES

Standard Tariff

Weight up to	
1kg	£3.46
1.5kg	£4.45
2kg	£4.78
4kg	£7.20
6kg	£7.86
8kg	£8.96
10kg	£9.62

OVERSEAS POSTAL SERVICES AND REGULATIONS

Royal Mail divides the world into three zones: **Europe** (Albania, Andorra, Armenia, Austria, Azerbaijan, Azores, Balearic Islands, Belarus, Belgium, Bosnia-Hercegovina, Bulgaria, Canary Islands, Corsica, Croatia, Cyprus, Czech Republic, Denmark, Estonia, Faroe Islands, Finland, France, Georgia, Germany, Gibraltar, Greece, Greenland, Hungary, Iceland, Ireland, Italy, Kazakhstan, Kyrgystan, Latvia, Liechtenstein, Lithuania, Luxembourg, Macedonia, Madeira, Malta, Modova, Monaco, Netherlands, Norway, Poland, Portugal, Romania, Russia, San Marino, Serbia and Montenegro, Slovakia, Slovenia, Spain, Spitzbergen, Sweden, Switzerland, Tajikistan, Turkey, Turkmenistan, Ukraine, Uzbekistan, Vatican City State); **Zone 1** (USA, Canada, South America, the Middle East, Africa, parts of Asia and the Indian sub-continent, most of south east Asia and Hong Kong); **Zone 2** (American Samoa, Australia, China, East Timor, Fiji, French Southern and Antarctic Territories, French Polynesia, Guam, Japan, Kiribati, Korea, Marshall Islands, Micronesia, Mongolia, Nauru, New Caledonia, New Zealand & Territories, Norfolk Island, North Mariana Island, Palau, Papua New Guinea, Philippines, Pitcairn Islands, Samoa, Solomon Islands, Taiwan, Tonga, Tuvalu, Vanuatu, Wake Island, Wallis and Futuna Island, Western Samoa).

OVERSEAS SURFACE MAIL RATES (WORLD ZONES 1 & 2)

Letters

Weight not over		*Weight not over*	
20g*	£0.39	450g	£3.52
60g	£0.66	500g	£3.89
100g	£0.93	750g	£5.74
150g	£1.30	1,000g	£7.59
200g	£1.67	1,250g	£9.44
250g	£2.04	1,500g	£11.29
300g	£2.41	1,750g	£13.14
350g	£2.78	2,000g	£14.99
400g	£3.15		

* Including postcards

AIRMAIL LETTER RATES

Europe: Letters

Weight not over		*Weight not over*	
20g	£0.40	280g	£2.54
40g	£0.57	300g	£2.70
60g	£0.74	320g	£2.86
80g	£0.91	340g	£3.02
100g	£1.08	360g	£3.18
120g	£1.25	380g	£3.34
140g	£1.42	400g	£3.50
160g	£1.58	420g	£3.66
180g	£1.74	440g	£3.82
200g	£1.90	460g	£3.98
220g	£2.06	480g	£4.14
240g	£2.22	500g	£4.30
260g	£2.38	1,000g	£8.30
		*2,000g	£16.30

* Max. 2kg

Zones 1 & 2: Letters

Postcards	*Not over 10g*	*Not over 20g*	*Over 20g*
43p	47p	68p	price varies

SPECIAL DELIVERY SERVICES

ROYAL MAIL SPECIAL DELIVERY

A guaranteed next working day delivery service by noon to most UK destinations for first class letters and packets. Prices start at £3.75. There is also a service which guarantees delivery by 9 a.m. Prices start at £6.95. Compensation of up to £2,500 is available for lost or damaged items.

INTERNATIONAL SIGNED FOR AND AIRSURE

Express airmail services. The fee for International Signed For is £3.30 plus airmail postage. The fee for Airsure is £4.00 plus airmail postage.

RECORDED MAIL (SIGNED FOR)

Provides a record of posting and delivery of letters and ensures a signature on delivery. This service is recommended for items of little or no monetary value. All packets must be handed to the post office and a certificate of posting issued. Charges: 65p plus the standard first or second class postage.

OTHER SERVICES

BUSINESS SERVICES

A range of postal services are available to businesses including business collection, freepost, business reply services, business packaging for special deliveries and international mailing options.

COMPENSATION

Compensation for loss or damage to an item sent varies according to the service used to send the item. Royal Mail does not accept responsibility for loss or damage arising from faulty packing.

PASSPORT APPLICATIONS

Around 2,000 post offices process passport applications. To find out your nearest office, and for further information, *see* contact details below.

TRACK AND TRACE

This service enables customers to track the progress of items sent using selected delivery services. *See* below for contact details.

REDIRECTION

A printed form obtainable from the Post Office must be signed by the person to whom the letters are to be addressed. A fee is payable for each different surname on the application form. Charges: 1 month, £6.55 (abroad via airmail, £13.15); 3 months, £14.30 (£28.60); 6 months, £22.00 (£44.05); 12 months, £33.00 (£66.05).

INTERNATIONAL PREPAID PRODUCTS

Prepaid products are a secure way of packaging items that are to be sent overseas. There are a number of different types of prepaid products to choose from, depending on the weight of the article to be sent, ranging in price up to £6.99.

KEEPSAFE

Mail is held for up to two months while the addressee is away and is delivered when the addressee returns. Prices start at £5.25. Perishable items are returned to the sender. Recorded items are held for a week and Special Delivery items are held for three weeks before being returned to the sender.

POST OFFICE BOX

A PO Box provides a short and easy-to-remember alternative address. Mail is held at a local delivery office until the addressee is ready to collect it. Prices start at £43.00.

SMALL PACKETS AND PRINTED PAPERS (INTERNATIONAL)

Weight not over		*Weight not over*	
100g	£0.64	450g	£2.11
150g	£0.85	500g	£2.32
200g	£1.06	750g	£3.37
250g	£1.27	1,000g	£4.42
300g	£1.48	1,500g	£6.52
350g	£1.69	2,000g	£8.62
400g	£1.90		

CONTACT DETAILS

Royal Mail general enquiries: T 08457-740740
Royal Mail business enquiries: T 08457-950950
Postcode enquiry line: T 08457-111222 **or** 0906-302 1222
Online shop: T 08457-641641
Parcelforce Worldwide: T 08708-501150
Post Office enquires: T 08457-223344
Track and Trace: T 08457-001200
W www.royalmail.com

IDD CODES

INTERNATIONAL DIRECT DIALLING (IDD)

International dialling codes are composed of four elements which are dialled in sequence:

(i) the international code
(ii) the country code
(iii) the area code
(iv) the telephone number

Calls to some countries must be made via the international operator.

*Can vary depending on area and/or carrier

Country	*IDD from UK*	*IDD to UK*
Afghanistan	00 93	00 44
Albania	00 355	00 44
Algeria	00 213	00 44
Andorra	00 376	00 44
Angola	00 244	00 44
Anguilla	00 1 264	11 44
Antigua and Barbuda	00 1 268	011 44
Argentina	00 54	00 44
Armenia	00 374	810 44
Aruba	00 297	00 44
Ascension Island	00 247	00 44
Australia	00 61	00 11 44
Austria	00 43	00 44
Azerbaijan	00 994	810 44
Azores	00 351	00 44
Bahamas	00 1 242	11 44
Bahrain	00 973	0 44
Bangladesh	00 880	00 44
Barbados	00 1 246	11 44
Belarus	00 375	810 44
Belgium	00 32	00 44
Belize	00 501	00 44
Benin	00 229	00 44
Bermuda	00 1 441	11 44
Bhutan	00 975	00 44
Bolivia	00 591	00 44
Bosnia-Hercegovina		
Muslim-Croat Federation	00 387	00 44
Republika Srpska	00 381	00 44
Botswana	00 267	00 44
Brazil	00 55	00 44
British Virgin Islands	00 1 284	11 44
Brunei	00 673	00 44
Bulgaria	00 359	00 44
Burkina Faso	00 226	00 44
Burundi	00 257	90 44
Cambodia	00 855	00 44
Cameroon	00 237	00 44
Canada	00 1	011 44
Canary Islands	00 34	00 44
Cape Verde	00 238	0 44
Cayman Islands	00 1 345	11 44
Central African Republic	00 236	19 44
Chad	00 235	15 44
Chile	00 56	00 44
China	00 86	00 44
Hong Kong	00 852	1 44
Macao	00 853	00 44
Colombia	00 57	9 44
Comoros	00 269	00 44
Congo, Dem. Rep. of	00 243	00 44
Congo, Republic of	00 242	00 44
Cook Islands	00 682	00 44
Costa Rica	00 506	00 44
Côte d'Ivoire	00 225	00 44
Croatia	00 385	00 44
Cuba	00 53	119 44
Cyprus	00 357	00 44
Czech Republic	00 420	00 44
Denmark	00 45	00 44
Djibouti	00 253	00 44
Dominica	00 1 767	11 44
Dominican Republic	00 1 809	11 44
East Timor	00 670	00 44
Ecuador	00 593	00 44
Egypt	00 20	00 44
El Salvador	00 503	0 44
Equatorial Guinea	00 240	00 44
Eritrea	00 291	00 44
Estonia	00 372	800 44
Ethiopia	00 251	00 44
Falkland Islands	00 500	0 44
Faroe Islands	00 298	9 44
Fiji	00 679	5 44
Finland	00 358	00 44*
France	00 33	00 44
French Guiana	00 594	00 44
French Polynesia	00 689	00 44
Gabon	00 241	00 44
Gambia	00 220	00 44
Georgia	00 995	810 44
Germany	00 49	00 44
Ghana	00 233	00 44
Gibraltar	00 350	00 44
Greece	00 30	00 44
Greenland	00 299	99 44
Grenada	00 1 473	11 44
Guadeloupe	00 590	00 44
Guam	00 1 671	1 44
Guatemala	00 502	00 44
Guinea	00 224	00 44
Guinea-Bissau	00 245	99 44
Guyana	00 592	1 44
Haiti	00 509	00 44
Honduras	00 504	00 44
Hungary	00 36	00 44
Iceland	00 354	00 44
India	00 91	00 44
Indonesia	00 61	008 44*
Iran	00 98	00 44
Iraq	00 964	00 44
Ireland, Republic of	00 353	00 44
Israel	00 972	00 44*
Italy	00 39	00 44
Jamaica	00 1 876	11 44
Japan	00 81	001 44*
		0041 44*
		0061 44*
Jordan	00 962	00 44*
Kazakhstan	00 7	810 44
Kenya	00 254	00 44
Kiribati	00 686	00 44
Korea, North	00 850	00 44
Korea, South	00 82	001 44*
Kuwait	00 965	00 44
Kyrgyzstan	00 996	00 44

Country	*IDD from UK*	*IDD to UK*
Laos	00 856	00 44
Latvia	00 371	00 44
Lebanon	00 961	00 44
Lesotho	00 266	00 44
Liberia	00 231	00 44
Libya	00 218	00 44
Liechtenstein	00 423	00 44
Lithuania	00 370	810 44
Luxembourg	00 352	00 44
Macedonia	00 389	99 44
Madagascar	00 261	00 44
Madeira	00 351	00 44*
Malawi	00 265	00 44
Malaysia	00 60	00 44
Maldives	00 960	00 44
Mali	00 223	00 44
Malta	00 356	00 44
Mariana Islands, Northern	00 1 670	11 44
Marshall Islands	00 692	11 44
Martinique	00 596	00 44
Mauritania	00 222	00 44
Mauritius	00 230	00 44
Mayotte	00 269	10 44
Mexico	00 52	98 44
Micronesia, Federated States of	00 691	11 44
Moldova	00 373	810 44
Monaco	00 377	00 44
Mongolia	00 976	00 44
Montenegro	00 381	99 44
Montserrat	00 1 664	11 44
Morocco	00 212	00 44
Mozambique	00 258	00 44
Myanmar	00 95	00 44
Namibia	00 264	00 44
Nauru	00 674	00 44
Nepal	00 977	00 44
Netherlands	00 31	00 44
Netherlands Antilles	00 599	00 44
New Caledonia	00 687	00 44
New Zealand	00 64	00 44
Nicaragua	00 505	00 44
Niger	00 227	00 44
Nigeria	00 234	9 44
Niue	00 683	00 44
Norfolk Island	00 672	101 44
Norway	00 47	00 44
Oman	00 968	00 44
Pakistan	00 92	00 44
Palau	00 680	011 44
Panama	00 507	00 44
Papua New Guinea	00 675	5 44
Paraguay	00 595	002 44
Peru	00 51	00 44
Philippines	00 63	00 44
Poland	00 48	00 44
Portugal	00 351	00 44
Puerto Rico	00 1 787	11 44
Qatar	00 974	00 44
Réunion	00 262	00 44
Romania	00 40	00 44
Russia	00 7	810 44
Rwanda	00 250	00 44
St Christopher and Nevis	00 1 869	11 44
St Helena	00 290	00 44
St Lucia	00 1 758	11 44
St Pierre and Miquelon	00 508	00 44
St Vincent and the Grenadines	00 1 784	1 44
Samoa	00 685	0 44
Samoa, American	00 684	00 44
San Marino	00 378	00 44
Sao Tomé and Principe	00 239	00 44
Saudi Arabia	00 966	00 44
Senegal	00 221	00 44
Serbia & Montenegro	00 381	99 44
Seychelles	00 248	00 44
Sierra Leone	00 232	00 44
Singapore	00 65	1 44
Slovakia	00 421	00 44
Slovenia	00 386	00 44
Solomon Islands	00 677	00 44
Somalia	00 252	16 44
South Africa	00 27	09 44
Spain	00 34	00 44
Sri Lanka	00 94	00 44
Sudan	00 249	00 44
Suriname	00 597	00 44
Swaziland	00 268	00 44
Sweden	00 46	00 44
Switzerland	00 41	00 44
Syria	00 963	00 44
Taiwan	00 886	2 44
Tajikistan	00 992	810 44
Tanzania	00 255	00 44
Thailand	00 66	1 44
Tibet	00 86	00 44
Togo	00 228	00 44
Tonga	00 676	00 44
Trinidad and Tobago	00 1 868	11 44
Tunisia	00 216	00 44
Turkey	00 90	00 44
Turkmenistan	00 993	810 44
Turks and Caicos Islands	00 1 649	00 44
Tuvalu	00 688	00 44
Uganda	00 256	00 44
Ukraine	00 380	810 44
United Arab Emirates	00 971	00 44
Uruguay	00 598	00 44
USA	00 1	011 44
Alaska	00 1 907	011 44
Hawaii	00 1 808	011 44
Uzbekistan	00 998	810 44
Vanuatu	00 678	00 44
Vatican City State	00 390 66982	00 44
Venezuela	00 58	00 44
Vietnam	00 84	00 44
Virgin Islands (US)	00 1 340	11 44
Yemen	00 967	00 44
Zambia	00 260	00 44
Zimbabwe	00 263	00 44

MOBILE COMMUNICATIONS

CURRENT NETWORK OPERATOR MARKET SHARES

January 2004	O_2	*Vodafone*	*T-Mobile*	*Orange*	*Hutchison*
Current Subscriber Base	10,897,740	16,773,480	9,190,260	13,358,520	n/a
Total Market Share	21.7%	33.4%	18.3%	26.6%	n/a

5-YEAR SUBSCRIBER GROWTH

Date	*Jan 1999*	*Jan 2000*	*Jan 2001*	*Jan 2002*	*Jan 2003*	*Jan 2004*
Subscriber Base	13,001,000	23,944,000	40,057,300	45,677,600	46,922,000	50,220,000
Penetration Rate	22.3%	41%	67.2%	76.6%	78.8%	84.4%

The UK mobile communications industry is continuing to be dominated by the introduction of new technologies. This has led to an increasing emphasis on expanding the traditional mobile operator services as well as encouraging consumer use of more expensive handset devices. The push towards new technology and enhanced service offerings is due to the near to saturation point of the mobile market and the need to increase revenues through other means. The combination of fewer 'new' customers, heavy licence fees for mobile Network Operators, the government having sold the 3G operating licences at a great profit and the costs associated with technology upgrades have left the Network Operators with financial holes to fill.

INDUSTRY PLAYERS

The mobile communications industry has a number of players: Network Operators who own the infrastructure and provide services; Service Providers and MVNOs who do not own infrastructure but have commercial agreements with the Network Operators; and the Regulator, who is responsible for setting the controls of the mobile market, implementing EU-wide legislation and ensuring that industry players do not behave anti-competitively.

NETWORK OPERATORS

Competition was introduced into the UK's mobile market at an early stage. Until recently there were only four network operators rolling out their mobile networks and actively offering mobile services. A fifth, Hutchison 3G, was launched in March 2003. The licensed Network Operators in the UK are detailed in the table below. Network Operators are responsible for setting tariffs, billing, offering services and maintaining the network infrastructure.

UK MOBILE NETWORK OPERATORS

Operator	*Ownership*	*Licence*	*Launch Date*
O_2	Formerly BT Cellnet	Tacs-900	January 1985
	100% O_2	GSM	January 1994
Vodafone	100% Vodafone	Tacs-900	January 1985
		GSM	July 1992
T-Mobile	Formerly One2One 100% – Deutsche Telekom	GSM 1800	September 1993
Orange	100% – France Telecom	GSM 1800	April 1994
Hutchison 3G	65% – Hutchison Whampoa 20% – DoCoMo 15% – KPN Mobile	UMTS	March 2003

ALTERNATIVE SERVICE PROVIDERS

Service Providers were introduced into the UK market from its inception as a means to stimulate competition. Service Providers buy airtime wholesale from the Network Operators and sell it on to end users. This agreement means that they can set their own tariff structures and have a direct billing relationship with customers. O_2 and Vodafone have an obligation under the terms of their licences to offer wholesale minutes of airtime to Service Providers while Orange and T-Mobile have not been subject to this condition. There are said to be around 50 Service Providers operating in the UK market and in order to maintain a viable business operation many of these have diversified their product offering away from pure mobile services to other telecommunication or Internet based services.

The newest players in the mobile market offering mobile services are MVNOs, Mobile Virtual Network Operators. Whereas a number of the Network Operators are obliged to open their networks to Service Providers, none of the Network Operators are currently obliged to open their networks to MVNOs. That they choose to do so, is purely a commercial agreement between the MVNO and Network Operator.

The main difference between Service Providers and MVNOs is the degree of ownership over the equipment used. A true MVNO has its own mobile network code, issues its own SIM cards (Subscriber Identity Module card – the 'brain' of a handset), operates its own mobile switching centre and has a pricing structure fully independent from the Network Operator. MVNOs include Virgin Mobile and FT Mobile, a joint venture between the Financial Times and the Carphone Warehouse.

TYPES OF MOBILE SERVICE

Network Operators, Service Providers and MVNOs offer two basic types of service, contract and pre-paid (pay-as-you-go). Contracts (generally paid on a monthly basis though fixed to a minimum contract term) mean that the end user pays a fixed subscription fee each month that entitles them to a number of services (for example voicemail, SMS text messaging, downloadable games, access to news and other information updates) and gives them a certain amount of 'free' airtime/access to services each month. Pre-paid subscribers have access to the same services but pay in advance and simply top up their account when it is running low. The introduction of pre-paid services has allowed industry players to target additional consumer segments, in particular the youth market and customers who do not have an acceptable credit rating for a contract service. Pre-paid has proven to be a very popular option as it allows customers to control their spend. For the first half of 2004, the split between pre-paid and contract customers in the UK remained constant at around 68:32.

NETWORK TECHNOLOGY

DEVELOPMENT OF MOBILE INFRASTRUCTURE

The first technology introduced into the UK was an analogue technology called TACS which was adopted in 1985. In 1992 Vodafone launched a new digital GSM network, usually referred to as 2G or second generation. BT Cellnet (now O_2) and two more entrants launched GSM services in the following two years making the UK one of Europe's most competitive markets.

More recently, GSM networks have been modified to enable them to transfer packet-switch data and this technology is known as GPRS (General Packet Radio Service). GPRS is not a completely new network – rather it is an upgrade from the existing GSM infrastructure and is also referred to as 2.5G. The main difference between GSM and GPRS technology is the ability to transmit data as well as voice across the network. This is a result of higher bandwidth and with GPRS.

The industry is still waiting for the fully-fledged delivery of next generation mobile services, 3G or UMTS (Universal Mobile Telecommunications System). The main difference between GPRS and UMTS lies with the capacity of UMTS to offer even faster data transmission speeds, therefore allowing expanded data facilities and access to the internet. Additionally, UMTS has the potential to offer further advantages over GSM/GPRS such as international roaming, whereas at present, despite GSM's widespread presence, other mobile technologies used in other parts of the world are incompatible with GSM handsets, for instance in parts of Asia and in America.

As 3G or UMTS technology is an entirely new network, Network Operators must hold a licence to deploy it. The UK was the third European country to licence 3G operators after Finland and Spain but was the first to auction its licences. Auctions are not new to the European communications industry – many of the second and third entrants to Europe's communications markets had to bid for their licences – but what was spectacular about the UK's 3G auction was the size of the bids. While industry observers had speculated that the auction might reach £4 billion, a total of £22 billion was raised from the sale of the spectrum.

DATA SERVICES

GSM from analogue brought clearer voice quality, while the upgrade from GSM through GPRS to UMTS has brought not only improved voice quality but also new services, primarily data-based services as seen in the table below.

DATA SERVICES MIGRATION PATH

Mobile Infrastructure	*Data Services available*
GSM (2G)	Phone calls
Speed:	Voice mail
10kb/sec	Receipt of simple email messages
GPRS (2.5G)	Phone calls/fax
Speed:	Voice mail
64–144kb/sec	Receipt and transmission of large emails
	Web browsing
	Navigation/maps
UMTS (3G)	Phone calls/fax
Speed:	Global roaming
144kb–2mb/sec	Receipt and transmission of large emails
	High speed web
	Navigation/maps
	Video-conferencing
	TV Streaming
	Electronic agenda meeting reminder

The provision of improved and new services is crucially important for the industry as it reaches saturation point. In order to maintain revenues, Network Operators have had to change focus from customer acquisition strategies to increasing customer service usage levels, as well as encouraging more frequent handset renewal.

2G & 2.5G DATA SERVICES

To date, the most popular and readily available data service has been SMS (Short Messaging Service). SMS or 'text messaging' allows consumers to send and receive text messages up to 160 characters long on their mobile phones. Due to its simplicity and popularity, particularly among young users, the number of SMS messages being sent has increased dramatically. In 2003 approximately 1.75 billion SMS messages were sent per month compared with 271 million per month in 1999. In the last few years, SMS has helped boost revenues for network operators through integrated use with interactive TV – for example, during Channel 4's *Big Brother* in 2003 over 10m text alerts and 5.5m votes were recorded.

WAP, Wireless Application Protocol, is a software language that allows Internet-style data to be downloaded and viewed on a mobile phone. WAP was billed as 'mobile internet' – that consumers could access content from mobile portals which, like traditional Internet portals, aggregate and display mobile Internet content in an accessible manner. WAP has been generally used by consumers to obtain travel information, sports headlines, financial news and emails. Mobile operators such as Vodafone, Orange, T-Mobile, and O_2 all launched pan-European portals which allowed customers to have very similar – if not the same – services around their different countries of operations. However, WAP mobile portals have been characterised by their poor usability and the limited online experience offered to end-users. Many factors have been responsible for this, including unreliable early handsets, limited content, slow connections, and poor portal navigation.

Many of the factors that made WAP so cumbersome have been largely solved by improved handsets, better content and high-speed infrastructure. Portal navigation remains a problem though, with users routinely expected to make perhaps 20–25 'clicks' on their mobile handset in order to locate content, thus greatly limiting accessibility.

With increased consumer familiarity and accessibility of SMS technology, network operators have re-positioned their service offerings from an emphasis on mobile phones being billed as 'mobile internet' to other new services (sending logos, basic pictures and downloading personal ring-tones) that have proved to be very popular. These types of services are referred to as EMS, Enhanced Messaging Services. In late 2002, Vodafone launched its 'Live!' service which offered mobile users access to multimedia services, including the taking, sending and receiving of photos with an integrated camera, Java games, email, polyphonic ring-tones, chat, SMS and mobile phone calls. Vodafone Live! has been popular with over 2 million customers subscribing to the service in its first year.

Consumers are clearly attracted to enhanced data-services as well as the colour screens, improved quality in sound and more intuitive user interfaces that have been introduced in parallel with operator branded initiatives. Both T-Mobile and O_2 have followed suit by launching similar services called T-Zone and Active respectively.

3G DATA SERVICES

The main difference between UMTS and GPRS/GSM from the customer's viewpoint is the extension of data services that are accessible through one's mobile. All operators have launched 3G style services over their GPRS networks though these services will be further enhanced (for example by the introduction of video messaging) once the move to the 3G network has taken place. Hutchison 3G was the first to launch its highly advertised '3' service which offers video calling, content browsing, interactive games and location based services which took place in March 2003. The uptake of '3' to date has been disappointing, with only 361,000 subscribers by March 2004 compared with an initial target of 1 million.) The slowness of up-take and launch of 3G has been exacerbated by delays in handset availability (leading to high handset prices), network teething problems – including many reports of 'lost' calls, and the reticence by the mobile consumer market to upgrade to a new technology.

Vodafone officially launched its 3G service in the UK at the start of April 2004, though at this stage, the 3G service is accessible only with laptop 3G data cards, not handsets. Vodafone's services are aimed mainly at business users. Currently, the service works in the UK, Sweden, Italy, Spain, the Netherlands, Japan and Portugal. Both T-Mobile and Orange have launched similar initiatives. Vodafone has not yet revealed when 3G services will be made available to mobile phone users.

REGULATION

Until July 2003, the industry was regulated by two government bodies; Oftel, a government department independent of ministerial control, headed by the Director General of Telecommunications; and the Radiocommunications Agency, which was the part of the Department of Trade and Industry (DTI). The greater part of regulatory control was assumed by Oftel; it had authority over licensing procedures, tariffing, interconnection issues (where one operator has access to another's infrastructure), and acted as arbitrator in operator disputes. The Radiocommunications Agency was responsible for radio frequency allocation.

In July 2003, the regulation of the mobile industry changed significantly, with the passing of a Communications Bill in the UK and the implementation of new EU framework for the regulation of electronic communications networks and service providers. The aim of the EU framework is to set out a technology-neutral regime for the regulation of communications companies across the EU. This technology neutral regime is based on EU directives that cover interconnections and access, data protection, universal services, authorisation of electronic communications networks and services and a common regulatory framework.

The Communications Bill in the UK took forward four of the Directives and following its enactment has changed the UK's regulatory structure by creating a new regulatory body for the whole communications industry – Ofcom (the Office of Communications). Ofcom has replaced the existing communications and broadcasting regulators, including Oftel and the Radiocommunications Agency and has a different funding structure to Oftel – while Oftel was funded by licence fees, Ofcom levies administration charges. Ofcom is responsible for furthering the interests of the users of television, radio, telecommunications and wireless communications services.

Key features of the 2003 Communications Act are:

– *The abolition of licensing requirements* – With the removal of licensing requirements, Ofcom has drawn up a set of conditions for providers in the areas of universal service, significant market power, access and privileged supplier obligations – these conditions are effectively regulations but are much more flexible than the previous system
– *The provision for spectrum trading* – Previously, when an operator was awarded a mobile licence, the allocated spectrum could only be used by that named company; under the new Bill, licencees are able to transfer the entitlement to use the spectrum to another player
– *New enforcement provisions for dealing with anti-competitive behaviour* – Ofcom has the power to levy a fine of up to 10 per cent of turnover (or suspend a licence in extreme cases) should a mobile operator breach the conditions of its authorisation instead of having to refer cases to the Competition Authority

CONTACTS

DEPARTMENT OF TRADE AND INDUSTRY (DTI)
1 Victoria Street, London SW1H 0ET
T 020-7215 5000 **F** 020-7215 2909
W www.dti.gov.uk

OFCOM
Riverside House, 2A Southwark Bridge Road, London SE1 9HA
T 020-7981 3000 **F** 020-7981 3333 **W** www.ofcom.org.uk

O_2
260 Bath Road, Slough, Berkshire SL1 4DX
T 01753-565000 **F** 01753-565010 **W** www.O2.co.uk

HUTCHISON 3G UK
43 New Bond Street, London W1Y 9HB
T 020-7499 1886 **F** 020-7491 7266
W www.three.co.uk

ORANGE PLC
50 George Street, London W1U 7DZ
T 020-7984 1600 **F** 020-7984 1601
W www.orange.co.uk

T-MOBILE
Imperial Place, Maxwell Road, Borehamwood WD6 1EA
T 020-8214 2121 **F** 020-8214 3601
W www.t-mobile.co.uk

VODAFONE GROUP
The Courtyard, 2–4 London Road, Newbury RG14 1JX
T 01635-33251 **F** 01635-45713
W www.vodafone.co.uk

INFORMATION TECHNOLOGY

ANCESTRY

The ancestors of the modern computer are the Difference Engine and the Analytical Engine devised by mathematician Charles Babbage. Designed in 1820 to automatically compute mathematical tables, Babbage abandoned construction of his mechanical, clockwork-like Difference Engine in the 1840s for personal and financial reasons. In 1834 he began work on his Analytical Engine. Unlike the Difference Engine, the Analytical Engine was designed as a general-purpose tool with a store to hold information.

Babbage's work relied heavily on mechanics and physical machinery. It was not until the twentieth century invention of the electrical vacuum tube, and then the transistor, that computers became a feasible means to solving problems.

FIRST GENERATION

War has been a significant factor in the development of the computer. In 1943, during World War II, the British and Americans developed electro-mechanical computers. Colossus, a British effort, was specifically developed to crack German coding ciphers, whilst an American effort, Harvard Mark I, was developed as a more general-purpose electro-mechanical programmable computer (partly for atom bomb research). Regarded as early first generation computers, these machines primarily comprised wired circuits and vacuum valves. Punched cards and paper tape were largely employed as the input, output and main storage systems. ENIAC (Electronic Numerical Integrator and Computer) was completed in 1946 at the University of Pennsylvania, USA. Capable of carrying out 100,000 calculations a second, it was remarkable for its day despite weighing thirty tons.

SECOND GENERATION

Similar to light bulbs, valves were prone to failure, requiring tedious checks to resolve problems (ENIAC alone contained 18,000 vacuum valves). In 1947, the transistor was invented. Performing the same role as a vacuum valve but less prone to failure, smaller and more efficient, the transistor allowed smaller 'second generation' computers to be developed throughout the 1950s and early 1960s.

THIRD GENERATION

In 1958 Jack St Claire Kilby produced the first integrated circuit 'microchip'. A microchip is comprised of a large number of transistors and other components bonded to a wafer ('chip') of silicon, interconnected by a surface film of conductive material rather than by wires. By reducing distance between components, savings are made in both size and electricity. In 1963 the first 'third generation' computers based on microchip technology appeared.

FOURTH GENERATION

In 1971 Intel produced the first 'microprocessor' heralding a 'fourth generation' of computers. The Intel 4004 (capable of 60,000 instructions per second) grouped much of the processing functions onto a single microchip. Around the same time, Intel invented the RAM (random access memory) chip which grouped significant amounts of memory onto a single chip. Supercomputers and mainframes, utilising scores of microprocessors, had terrific power in the order of 150 million instructions per second. Developments such as multi-layer circuits, and the use of copper instead of gold in microchips, yielded improvements in size and performance through miniaturisation. The size of the transistor was scaled down from thumb size to far smaller than the thickness of a human hair, allowing for greater density and thus exponentially increasing the total power of the computer.

NEXT GENERATION

Most modern computers are still regarded as 'fourth generation' as they use essentially the same technology, albeit highly miniaturised. The future of computer technology is widely thought to be dependent on the physics of light. Already used extensively in the computer industry for high-speed communications, light offers future possibilities for both calculation and storage.

Gordon Moore, co-founder of Intel, observed in 1965 that the number of transistors per square inch had doubled every 12 months since the inception of the integrated circuit. The pace of development has slowed somewhat. The widely recognised current definition of the so-called 'Moore's Law' is that data density doubles every 18 months and is likely to do so for the next few decades.

PROGRAMMING LANGUAGES

Numerous programming languages have been adopted with the common purpose of devising a program of instructions for computers to follow to achieve a task. The languages are categorised by generation:

1GL or first-generation language is the machine language that the processor chips execute in raw binary form (strings of zeros and ones).

2GL or second-generation language. Assembly language is a human-understandable language insofar as it uses names as well as numbers. An assembler program takes assembly language and turns it into a machine code program. Very common in early systems where resources (speed, storage) were at a premium, it is typically only used today as an output from 3GL and higher systems.

3GL or third-generation language is a 'high-level' programming language typically more readable and concise than assembly language.

4GL or fourth generation language is designed to be closer to natural language than a 3GL language.

5GL or fifth-generation programming uses graphical development environments to create source language to be compiled with a 3GL or 4GL language compiler. Often a mix of generations is used, with a high level language (4 or 5GL) used to produce interface elements and a lower level language used to provide the processing power.

OPERATING SYSTEMS

An operating system (OS) is a set of utility programs that acts as the liaison between the computer user, the hardware (processor unit, memory) and its peripherals (disk, mouse, display, printer, network, etc.) and the program that the user is running (e.g. a word processor). The first computers had no operating system, and each program had to directly control the hardware on its own, adding greatly to the burden of programming. Early operating systems were hardware and manufacturer-specific with assembly language or machine code as the programming language. Each computer model or series tended to have its own specific operating system. UNIX was one of the first operating systems that could be ported (converted) to a variety of system hardware. This ability was enabled largely through the use of the 'C' programming language.

PERSONAL COMPUTER OPERATING SYSTEMS

Since the 1990s, the personal computer world has been dominated by Microsoft Corporation. Although not a significant manufacturer of computer equipment, the Microsoft Corporation has built on its market share secured in the 1980s with MS-DOS to become the market leading operating system provider. Microsoft's MS Windows personal computer operating systems are installed on more computers than any other commercial operating system. Microsoft's main personal computer rival is Apple which was established in the 1970s.

THE INTERNET

Prior to the Internet ('the Net' or 'the Web') computers tended to be connected together by hardware and protocols that were specific to each particular connection. Typically, links were point-to-point (a link had to be directly and physically established between the two computers). In 1969 ARPANET was formed by the US Department of Defence to establish a way for the computer capability of the military to be dispersed so that no one centre was critical to the operation of the network as a whole. This was achieved by interconnecting computers both directly and by way of other intermediary computers; thus if one computer was hit by a nuclear bomb, other pathways of communication could be established. The interconnections, when drawn, appeared as a mesh, or net or web. ARPANET was extended to non-military users such as universities early in the 1970s, with initial international links appearing in 1972.

The introduction of domain names (e.g. www.whitakersalmanack.com) in 1984 offered an easier means of using the Web. Prior to domain names one had to remember IP numbers (e.g.192.168.1.100) for accessing destination computers. However, before 1989 the Internet was still primarily limited to government agencies, the military, academic and research organisations and some big businesses.

In 1989, what most people perceive as 'the Net' was born. It was effectively invented at CERN (the European Particle Physics Laboratory) by Tim Berners-Lee as a way for scientists to share information by placing it in a prescribed format on a server. Initially text only, development of computer capability allowed inclusion of images.

By 1993 a whole new industry of ISPs (Internet Service Providers) had begun, allowing computer users to dial up via a modem and access the Internet and to view the Web through a browser (*see* glossary). Developments throughout the late 1990s (such as the widespread introduction of 'broadband') have allowed music, video, games, text, graphics and telephone calls to travel the Internet in much greater quantities and speeds than ever before. The future is likely to see the majority of telephone calls, and probably video, being transmitted over the Internet for at least part of their journey. Expansion of fibre-optic cable networks to homes and businesses will underpin this.

INTERNET STATISTICS

- 19% of households had access to the Internet in 1998 compared with 40% of households in 2001/2 and approximately 48% in 2003
- 32% of UK homes access the Internet via dial-up/narrowband
- 15% of UK homes access the Internet via broadband
- 33% of businesses with between 1 and 250 employees access the Internet via dial-up/narrowband
- 32% of businesses with between 1 and 250 employees access the Internet via broadband

Sources: Oftel 2003; UK 2004 published by TSO; Office for National Statistics Expenditure and Food Survey

COUNTRIES WITH THE HIGHEST NUMBER OF BROADBAND SUBSCRIBERS

Global Ranking	Country	Broadband subscribers as at 31 December 2003
1	China	10,950,000
2	Japan	10,272,052
3	USA	9,119,000
4	South Korea	6,435,955
5	Germany	4,500,000
6	France	3,262,700
7	Taiwan	2,800,000
8	Italy	2,280,000
9	Canada	2,170,243
10	UK	1,820,230

Source: www.dslforum.org

GLOSSARY OF TERMS

The following is a selected list of modern computing terms. It is by no means exhaustive but is intended to cover those that the average computer user might encounter.

3G: Third Generation wireless – a popular term commonly used to describe high bandwidth (2 Mbps) wireless technologies for mobile phones. 3G is still in its infancy but will offer high speed and capacity transmission of sound, vision and data to and from wireless devices and networks.

ADSL: Asymmetric Digital Subscriber Line – high speed Internet connection, four or more times faster than a modem, but using the same standard cables as regular telephone. Faster at downloading than uploading.

BLOG: A blog (short for weblog) is an online personal journal that is frequently updated and intended to be read by the public. Blogs are kept by 'bloggers'.

BLUETOOTH: Standard for short-range (10 metre) wireless connectivity between devices such as laptops, mobile telephones and printers to interact without cables. Bluetooth typically operates at speeds of up to 2Mbps.

BROADBAND: Generic term to describe high speed Internet access technologies such as ADSL, cable etc. as opposed to narrowband connections via modem.

BROWSER: Typically referring to a 'web browser' program that allows a computer user to view web page content on their computer, e.g. Microsoft Explorer, Netscape Navigator, AOL, etc.

BURN: To 'burn' a file or files to a CD-ROM or similar media means to copy the files to the media from hard disk (or other source). Derived from the fact that CD-ROMs are burnt by a laser during the process of writing to the disk.

C: A 3GL programming language developed in the late 1960s in parallel with the UNIX operating system. Primarily limited to UNIX until the mid-1980s when standards such as POSIX emerged, allowing C to be widely adopted on many operating systems. UNIX used C as its core programming language.

CACHING: In order to provide enhanced response times or to reduce the demands on computer resources, a *cache* is often employed to hold copies of recently or frequently accessed content (e.g. web pages). The cache (stored on a user's machine, or on a *proxy server)* is searched for the requested item. If a sufficiently fresh copy is not available it is retrieved from the remote server, a copy stored in the cache and another supplied to the requesting machine. If for example ten users request the same page it is only retrieved from the remote server once if a *caching proxy* is used. If a user requests the same page multiple times it can be downloaded once and retrieved from the cache many times. Hard disk drives and computer memory employ similar caching techniques to optimise performance.

CAT-5: An electrical performance and cable quality standard prescribed to support high-speed Ethernet networks. There are higher category and capability specifications denoted by higher numbers but Cat-5 is the most commonly installed today.

CD: Compact Disc – a digital disk format capable of storing 650 megabytes of information per side. A laser head detects pits etched into the substrate of the spinning disk and interprets them as information. Widely used in an audio format for storing recorded music. The computer format CD-ROM is likely to be superceded by the higher capacity DVD in the next few years. CD-RAM/CD-RW and CD-R are modifiable versions that use lasers to alter the disk substrate to make the pits interpreted later as information. *See also* DVD.

DNS: Domain Name Server – a server that translates domain names into the IP numbers used by programs to directly access computers on the Internet. Each server has an IP number and a name. DNS is analogous to the telephone directory enquiry service, providing a means of looking up and locating a computer connected to the Internet.

DOMAIN: A set of words, numbers and letters separated by dots used to identify an Internet server or group of servers, e.g. www.whitakersalmanack.co.uk, where 'www' denotes a web (http) server, 'whitakersalmanack' denotes the organisation name, 'co' denotes that the organisation is a company and 'uk' denotes United Kingdom (there are alternatives for every country but 'us' is typically omitted for the United States).

DVD: Digital Versatile Disc – DVD-ROM is a high capacity (read only) disk format that has the same form factor as CD-ROM but can store several gigabytes of information on each surface and can have four readable surfaces (through laser focusing technology). DVD-RAM is a modifiable version. Various formats are available, the most common being that used to store high-quality digital video, an alternative to the laser disk or videotape. *See also* CD.

EMAIL: Electronic mail – an email message is a document that is addressed to one or more persons from an individual address. Usually containing a message, it can also include other documents. The advent of the Internet has seen an explosion in the use of email in modern life. Without encryption or digital signature, an Internet email is not secure.

ETHERNET: Utilising simple, standard and relatively cheap cable and connectors, Ethernet has become the standard for local area networks. Ethernet employs a system whereby each computer listens for information addressed to its own unique address. Before transmitting, each computer waits for silence on the line; if multiple computers start transmitting simultaneously, they each detect the 'collision' and each wait a random period of time before trying again, thus allowing communications to proceed politely.

EXTRANET: An extranet is a secure and private subset of the Internet, protected by security protocols and typically used for exchanging information and services between a specific group.

FILE SERVER: A computer on a network that stores computer files that users can access from other computers on the network. Popular modern systems include Microsoft Windows, UNIX, Linux, and MacOS Server.

FIREWALL: Computer or device to protect a network from security risks posed by the Internet. Just as a firewall protects parts of a building from a fire raging on the other side, a network firewall stops risks posed by the Internet from egressing into a private network.

FIREWIRE: Apple Computer's implementation of IEEE 1394. *See also* IEEE 1394.

FTP: File Transfer Protocol – an Internet protocol whereby an FTP client program can exchange files with a remote server.

GBPS: Giga bits per second – denoting 1,000 million bits transmitted per second.

GIF: Graphics Interchange Format – compressed graphic format suitable for logos and non-photographic images. Invented by Unisys to allow images to be sent electronically in an efficient manner.

GPRS: General Packet Radio Services – a service for continuous wireless communication over the Internet from mobile phones and computers. Presently available in data rates of between 56 and 114K Bps, GPRS is normally charged by volume of information transferred rather than by time connected.

HTML: HyperText Mark-up Language – a small programming language used to denote or mark-up how an Internet page should be presented to a user from an HTTP server via a web browser. HTML is an evolving standard that has grown greatly from its first version to accommodate new types of web content and features provided by the different web browsers.

HTTP: HyperText Transfer Protocol – an Internet protocol whereby a web server sends web pages, images and files to a web browser.

IEEE 1394: High-speed serial (400 Mbps) connection standard for hard disks, digital video cameras and other multimedia devices. Popularised as iLink (Sony) and FireWire (Apple).

iLINK: Sony's implementation of IEEE 1394. *See also* IEEE 1394.

IMAP: Internet Mail Access Protocol – an Internet protocol IMAP allows a user to review, manipulate and store email on a central server from one or more workstations without necessitating message removal from the server.

INTERNET: An abstract concept applied to describe the global network of INTER-connected computer NET-works of computers. *See* body of article.

INTRANET: Subset of the Internet, using Internet protocols over a local area network, common today for publishing information and services within an organisation.

iPOD: Market leading high capacity personal MP3 player marketed by Apple Computer.

IRC: Internet Relay Chat – protocol that allows users to 'chat' online with other users using their keyboards. Under IRC a user can log into various chat rooms under their own name or an alias and have a text 'conversation' in real time with other users.

ISDN: Integrated Services Digital Network – widely adopted in the United Kingdom and Europe but not North America, ISDN allows both digital computer data and voice telephony to exist simultaneously on the same cable circuits. Data can be digitally exchanged at 64 Kbps per circuit. Used for file transfer of large documents and on-demand Internet access, it is increasingly being replaced by broadband connections such as ADSL.

JPEG: Joint Photographic Experts Group – compressed graphic format suitable for compression of photographic images, losing some detail in the process.

KBPS: Kilo bits per second – measure of transmission speed, denoting approximately 1,000 bits of information transmitted per second.

LINUX: A UNIX-like operating system first developed as a free or low cost system for personal computers. Linux was first developed by Linus Torvalds but its source code is now in the public domain and there are many distributions (versions) available. It is increasingly popular for business enterprise applications, highly scalable and can be used for anything from running a vehicles engine managementsystem to controlling a supercomputing cluster. *See also* UNIX.

MACOS: Operating system developed by Apple Computer for use on their own Macintosh computers.

MBPS: Mega bits per second – denoting approximately 1 million bits of information transmitted per second.

MODEM: A device that modulates digital signals from a computer into analogue signals for transmission over a standard telephone line and demodulates an incoming analogue signal and converts it to a digital signal for the computer.

MP3: Popular format for compressing audio information for transmission over the Internet for later playback on personal computers, music players and other devices.

MPEG: Motion Picture Encoding Group – popular format standard for compressing video and audio information for transmission over the Internet for later playback on personal computers and other players.

MS-DOS: Microsoft Corporation's Disk Operating System – an early OS commercially developed, but not invented, by Microsoft for use on early Intel-based personal computers. *See also* Operating System.

NNTP: Network News Transfer Protocol – an Internet protocol that implements a bulletin board on a global scale. Using a NNTP browser one can subscribe and contribute to one or more news groups covering a large variety of topics.

OPERATING SYSTEM (OS): Computer software developed to provide computer programs with standard facilities to interact with users and with computer hardware (via drivers). *See also* MS-DOS, UNIX, MacOS.

PNG: An improved royalty-free graphics file replacement for GIF.

POP3: Post Office Protocol 3 – an Internet protocol whereby email can be collected from a personal mailbox on an email server and moved off the server to a user's own computer.

PROXY (SERVER): A computer or device that transparently accepts Internet requests from a users computer and forwards them on to the required destination, providing enhanced performance (through caching) and/or enhanced security (by isolating the user computer from the Internet. *See* CACHING.

PRINT SERVER: A computer or device on a network that manages the sharing of one or more printers between multiple computers over a network. Many modern printers have a print server built in.

ROUTER: Where multiple networks are joined together, a router acts like a fast sorting office, examining the destination address of each information packet and passing or routing it to the appropriate network. Routers can select the most efficient route for packets.

SMTP: Simple Mail Transfer Protocol – an Internet protocol whereby a workstation can send email to a server or whereby two servers can exchange email.

SNMP: Simple Network Management Protocol – widely used protocol for remotely monitoring and managing network device status and function.

SPAM: A term used for unsolicited, generally junk, email. To spam someone is to send them (multiple) junk emails. Spam is becoming a major Internet problem with many estimates indicating that spam is becoming more prevalent than legitimate email. Most spam contains offers of pornography, get-rich schemes, prescription drugs, low cost finance or discount goods or services. Many legislatures around the globe are taking steps to ban or regulate spam.

TAR: Compression – a common mechanism on UNIX and Linux operating systems to compress information in order to save resources.

TCP/IP: Transmission Control Protocol/Internet Protocol – a protocol which is the lifeblood of the Internet, TCP/IP defines how information and requests generated by all other protocols are transmitted over the Internet. Information on the Internet is chopped up into small chunks or packets which are addressed with a destination and origination address. It sometimes happens that a packet gets lost and TCP/IP dictates how such a loss is handled.

UNIX: See body of article. Modern derivative versions include Linux, MacOS X, Solaris, BSD.

USB: Universal Serial Bus – standard for connecting serial devices such as scanners, mice, keyboards, modems and printers to computers. With USB, speeds of up to 10 Mbps are possible. USB2 is a revised, higher performance version of USB provides speeds up to 480 Mbps.

URL: Uniform Resource Locator – address of an Internet file or resource accessible on the Internet, e.g. http://www.whitakersalmanack.co.uk.

VIRUS: A computer program or script written for the express purpose of replicating itself onto as many machines as possible (much like its biological namesake) often with negative side effects to the host computer and computer network. Such effects vary from harmless screen messages to corruption of document integrity, network overload or compromising data security or privacy. Historically transmitted slowly by floppy disk and over networks within offices, the prevalence of Internet access allows viruses to spread globally within minutes.

WAP: Wireless Application Protocol – a set of standards to define how portable devices connected via radio waves (such as mobile telephones) can access Internet services.

WARCHALKING: To 'warchalk' is to mark an open or security-exposed Wi-Fi or other wireless network by writing symbols on or outside the relevant buildings in chalk.

WAR DRIVING: The activity of locating and exploiting security exposed Wi-Fi and other wireless networks to gain access to the network resource or information on or accessible to that network.

WI-FI: Industry brand name for the increasingly popular high frequency wireless local area Ethernet networking technology specification IEEE 802.11. Most prevalent is the 802.11b specification offering speeds of up to 11 Mps.

WLAN: Wireless local area network where information is transferred by radio frequency rather than wires between computers and base stations. As radio waves can pass through objects such as walls, it is becoming increasingly important for WLANs to be secured by encryption against unauthorised access.

XML: Extensible Mark-up Language, similar to HTML but more powerful, XML allows information to be encoded or tagged in a manner that is both human and computer readable.

ZIP: Compression – a popular mechanism on PCs to compress to compress information in order to save resources.

THE ENVIRONMENT

Europe's environment has improved in several respects over the last decade but further progress is needed to manage the environmental impacts of agriculture, transport and energy, according to the European Environment Agency.

Emissions from transport are a growing concern throughout the EU. In the accession and candidate countries, carbon dioxide emissions from transport decreased 19 per cent between 1990 and 1995 but rose afterwards and in 2001 were 4 per cent higher than 1990 levels. In the previously existing member states (EU-15) transport emissions increased by nearly 21 per cent between 1990–2001. Environmental policies are developed at several levels – international conventions and protocols (of which there are over 50), European Directives (of which there are over 300), and national legislation and strategies.

EUROPEAN UNION MEASURES

The European Union is developing an interlinked set of policies – the sixth Environmental Action Programme, the Cardiff process for the integration of environment into other policies and the EU sustainable development strategy – which form the framework for more detailed strategies. The Commission is also diversifying the instruments it uses in particular to include market-based instruments such as environmental taxes, and voluntary measures.

The Environmental Action Programme began in the 1970s. The Sixth Environmental Action Programme, *Environment 2010: Our Future, Our Choice*, was adopted in January 2001 and sets the programme to 2010. It proposes five priority areas: improving the implementation of existing legislation; integrating environmental concerns into other policies; working more closely with the market; empowering private citizens and helping them to change behaviour; and taking account of the environment in land-use planning and management decisions. The programme focuses on four topics: climate change, nature and biodiversity, environment and health, and natural resources and waste.

Much European Union environmental legislation is based around the principle that the polluter pays. The Environmental Liability Directive, agreed in February this year, will be used to hold polluters financially liable for damage they cause. It is due to enter into force in 2007.

ENLARGEMENT

Ten countries (EU-10) joined the EU in May 2004 – Cyprus, the Czech Republic, Estonia, Hungary, Latvia, Lithuania, Malta, Poland, Slovenia and Slovakia. The new member states have been granted transition measures, in particular for investment-heavy sectors such as waste water treatment. These measures vary from country to country and include extensions for meeting the targets and legally binding intermediate targets.

In general, most countries are on track to implement legislation. However, some countries have significant work to do in waste management and industrial pollution. Also, there are some worrying trends, such as a decline in rail transport for freight, and a 73 per cent increase in car ownership.

It is estimated that to achieve full implementation the new member states will have to spend on average 2–3 per cent of GDP on the environment in the coming years. Current expenditure is generally well below this target. Financial assistance was given through a variety of EU programmes in the lead up to accession. Following accession, this will almost treble. Until the end of the EU's budgetary period in 2006, the new states will receive some €8 billion, which equates to more than 10 per cent of the total investment requirements.

SUSTAINABLE DEVELOPMENT

The environmental agenda is increasingly becoming part of a wider move to address sustainability which incorporates social, environmental and economic development. In 2002, the World Summit on Sustainable Development was held in Johannesburg. Governments agreed on a series of commitments in five priority areas – water and sanitation, energy, health, agriculture, and biodiversity. Targets and timetables agreed include halving the number of people who lack access to clean water or proper sanitation by 2015 and reducing biodiversity loss by 2010.

Following the summit, the United Nations Commission on Sustainable Development has agreed its programme for the next 15 years. It will work in two-year cycles, with the first (2004–5) focusing on water, sanitation and human settlements. This will be followed by energy, climate change, atmosphere and industrial development in 2006–7. The EU's sustainable development strategy, adopted in May 2001, sets out long-term objectives, such as limiting major threats to public health and breaking the link between economic growth and transport growth.

In April 2004, a consultation was launched to develop a new UK sustainable development strategy. The three-month consultation asks for views on a wide range of issues from what should be in a UK vision of sustainable development to how to tackle unsustainable consumption patterns. The new framework is to be in place by early 2005. It will provide the background for separate strategies and plans by each administration.

The existing UK strategy *A Better Quality of Life* was published in May 1999. It provides a framework for integrating social, environmental and economic policies to meet four objectives: social progress, protection of the environment, prudent use of natural resources, and to maintain high and stable levels of economic growth and employment. The latest annual progress report highlighted areas of particular concern, such as the levels of waste generated and rising road traffic volumes, although the weakening in the link between road traffic and economic growth is encouraging.

The government has also developed a strategy on sustainable consumption and production. Key proposals include breaking the link between economic growth and environmental pollution, examining the whole life-cycle of products, and improving resource efficiency.

Local authorities also have a role to play in sustainable development. Under Local Agenda 21, which came out of the UN Conference on Environment and Development in Rio, Brazil in 1992, local authorities have an obligation to draw up sustainable development strategies for their areas. Regional Development Agencies take Local Agenda 21 strategies into account in sustainable development frameworks for each English region. At the World

Summit, the UK government committed itself to taking further action towards the implementation of Agenda 21 and achieving the Millennium Development Goals which have grown out of agreements and declarations at UN Conferences.

Many businesses are also working towards sustainable development and some are assessing and reporting their own progress with initiatives, such as the Global Reporting Initiative.

WASTE

Waste policy in the UK follows a number of principles: the hierarchy of reduce, reuse, recycle, dispose; the proximity principle of disposing of waste close to its generation; and national self sufficiency. Directives from Europe are playing an increasingly important role in driving UK policy, particularly regarding commercial and industrial waste. For instance, the Landfill Directive, which was adopted in July 1999, sets stringent targets for reducing the amount of waste sent to landfill and the technical requirements for landfill sites.

The proposed European integrated products policy aims to internalise the environmental costs of products throughout their life-cycle through market forces, by focusing on eco-design and incentives to ensure increased demand for greener products. The policy will culminate in 2007 with the identification of a first set of products with the greatest potential for environmental improvement and the beginning of action to tackle them.

Greater responsibility for end-of-life products is already being addressed by the EU's producer responsibility directives for packaging waste, which came into force in the UK in 1997 and for which the EU has recently set new more stringent targets: the end-of-life-vehicle directive, which entered into force in December 2001; and the directives on waste from electrical and electronic equipment and on the restriction of the use of certain hazardous substances in such equipment which came into effect in February. A new directive concerning the collection and recycling of batteries has also been adopted.

In addition to meeting EU directives, the UK also has its own targets. To meet these the public and local authorities will have to vastly increase their current recycling rates. In 2002–3, 15.6 per cent of household waste was recycled and composted, up from 13.6 per cent in 2001–2. Scotland and Northern Ireland also have national waste strategies.

CLIMATE CHANGE AND AIR POLLUTION

The UK's response to climate change is driven by the international Framework Convention on Climate Change. This is a binding agreement that has been signed and ratified by 189 countries. It was ratified in the UK in December 1993 and came into force in March 1994. It is intended to reduce the risks of global warming by limiting 'greenhouse' gas emissions.

Progress towards the convention's targets are assessed at regular conferences. At Kyoto in 1997, a protocol (the Kyoto Protocol) to the convention was adopted. It covers the six main greenhouse gases – carbon dioxide, methane, nitrous oxide, hydrofluorocarbons (HFCs), perfluorocarbons (PFCs) and sulphur hexafluoride. Under the protocol industrialised countries agreed to legally binding targets for cutting emissions of greenhouse gases by 5.2 per cent below 1990 levels by 2008–12. EU members agreed to an 8 per cent reduction and the UK's target is a 12.5 per cent cut. The ten accession (EU-10) countries have all ratified the Kyoto protocol and have their own targets of between 6 per cent and 8 per cent. The EU's 8 per cent target now only refers to the previous 15 member states (EU-15).

The latest data from the European Environment Agency, published in December 2003, shows that emissions of greenhouse gases from the EU have decreased by 2.3 per cent between 1990 and 2001, just over one quarter of the way towards the target. Ten of the EU-15 member states (Austria, Belgium, Denmark, Finland, Greece, Ireland, Italy, the Netherlands, Portugal and Spain) are not on track to meet their targets. Seven of the ten accession countries are on track to achieve their target under Kyoto, with only Slovenia expecting to miss its target.

The Kyoto Protocol will enter into force 90 days after it has been ratified by 55 governments, including developed countries representing at least 55 per cent of that group's carbon dioxide emissions. It had been expected to enter into force in early 2003. This has not happened as ratification by either the US or Russia is still needed. The US has stated that it will not ratify the treaty. Russia has recently pledged to ratify, having been reluctant to do so because of the perceived negative economic impact of such a move. Despite the Government's positive stance, a number of key Russian organisations are lobbying against the move.

In November 2000, a UK climate change programme was published which sets out how the UK intends to meet its Kyoto target and progress towards its domestic goal of a 20 per cent cut in carbon dioxide emissions by 2010.

The European Commission also set up a European Climate Change Programme in 2000 to identify measures to meet the Kyoto target and will introduce a mandatory emissions trading scheme at company level for carbon dioxide in the European Union beginning in January 2005. The companies covered by the scheme account for almost half of the EU's total carbon dioxide emissions. The EU has also indicated that it is willing to link the scheme to trading schemes in other countries that have ratified the Kyoto Protocol. Under the scheme, member states will set limits on carbon dioxide emissions from energy-intensive companies by issuing allowances according to how much they are allowed to emit. Reductions below these limits will be tradable.

Member states are required to submit national allocation plans setting out how they will issue allowances to companies. The deadline for plans was 31 March for the EU-15 and 1 May for the EU-10. In May, the Commission had received just nine from the EU-15 and three from the EU-10 and infringement proceedings have started against those that have not submitted.

The EU's national emission ceilings directive sets upper limits for each member state for the total emissions in 2010 of the four pollutants responsible for acidification, eutrophication and ground-level ozone pollution (sulphur dioxide, nitrogen oxides, volatile organic compounds and ammonia), but leaves it largely to the member states to decide which measures to take in order to comply. For emissions of ground-level ozone, only the UK, Germany, the Netherlands and Finland are below the target path to meet their obligations under the directive. Emissions of Portugal, Spain, Greece, Ireland and Belgium are significantly above their target paths while of the accession countries, Slovenia, Hungary, Poland and the Czech Republic will need significant reductions to meet their 2010 targets.

At a European level, air pollutant emissions show a general decreasing trend. Between 1990 and 2000, emissions of acidifying pollutants and ozone precursor gases decreased by 40 per cent and 29 per cent respectively. The European Integrated Pollution Prevention and Control (IPPC) Directive regulates emissions to any environmental medium from certain industrial and includes returning sites to a satisfactory state on closure, using energy efficiently and noise and vibration regulation. IPPC has been implemented in the UK through the Pollution Prevention and Control regulations 2000. Also, the UK's National Air Quality Strategy sets air quality objectives for the main pollutants (benzene, 1-3, butadiene, carbon monoxide, lead, nitrogen dioxide, sulphur dioxide, ozone, and particulates) to be met by 2003–8.

WATER

Water quality targets are set at both EU and UK level for drinking water sources, waste water discharges, rivers, coastal water and bathing water. The EU's water framework directive, which entered into force in December 2000, has an objective to achieve 'good water status' throughout the EU by 2015. In response to the requirements of the framework directive, the Commission has proposed a new directive to protect groundwater from pollution. The UK's Water Act was granted royal assent late last year.

The Water Environment and Water Services Bill for Scotland completed its passage through the Scottish parliament in early 2003. It establishes, for the first time, a source-to-sea planning framework for river basin management. Meanwhile, proposals for amending the regulatory framework for water and sewerage services were published for consultation late last year.

The EC Bathing Water Directive sets standards for bathing waters. This applies to 391 coastal and nine inland bathing waters in the UK. This directive is over 25 years old. The commission adopted a proposal for a new directive in October 2002 which would set a much tighter bathing water quality standard than the existing Directive.

The Environment Agency sets river quality objectives for each stretch of river. Water quality is currently protected through licensing abstraction and regulating discharges. Consents to discharge sewage and industrial effluent are regulated under the Water Resources Act 1991 and the IPPC regime. Discharge consents are based on the river quality objectives and relevant EU directives and specify the concentration and quantity permitted.

The European Urban Waste Water Treatment Directive sets minimum standards for sewage treatment before discharge into coastal waters with the levels of treatment needed depending on the sensitivity of the receiving water. In 1999 the government set more stringent UK targets for all significant coastal discharges to have a minimum of secondary treatment by 2005.

ENERGY

In February 2003, the UK government published a White Paper setting out a long-term strategy for UK Energy policy to 2050 combining environmental, security of supply, competitiveness and social goals. It builds on the Performance and Innovation Unit's (now the Prime Minister's Strategy Unit) Energy Review, published a year earlier.

In April 2004, the UK government published its first annual report on implementation of the white paper. A total of 112 milestones had been set as a first step towards achieving the long-term commitments, 56 have been met. An energy bill was also introduced in November 2003.

ENVIRONMENT AND HEALTH

In October 2003, the European Commission put forward a proposal for a new chemicals policy under which industry will have to provide information on the effects of chemicals on human health and the environment as well as on safe ways of handling them. The proposal has been met with stiff opposition and still has a long way to go before it is implemented. The Commission has also launched a strategy that will tackle environmental risks for human health in a broader sense. The strategy on science, children, awareness, legislation and evaluation, known as Scale, was launched in June 2003. Apart from aiming to reduce diseases caused by environmental factors in Europe, it aims to strengthen the EU's capacity for policy making in the area.

The first cycle of the strategy, running from 2004 to 2010, will focus on four health effects – childhood respiratory diseases, asthma and allergies; neuro-development disorders; childhood cancer; and endocrine disrupting effects.

SELECTED UK TARGETS

Global atmosphere

- Reduce greenhouse gas emissions to 12.5 per cent below 1990 levels by 2010
- Reduce carbon dioxide emissions to 20 per cent below 1990 levels by 2010, and by 60 per cent by 2050

Air quality

- Reduce sulphur dioxide emissions by 63 per cent based on 1990 levels by 2010
- Reduce emissions of nitrogen oxides by 41 per cent based on 1990 levels by 2010
- Reduce emissions of volatile organic compounds by 40 per cent based on 1990 levels by 2010

Fresh water and sea

- 97 per cent of bathing waters to meet European directive standards consistently by 2005
- Provide secondary treatment for all significant coastal discharges (over 2,000 population equivalent) by 2005

Waste

- Reduce industrial and commercial waste going to landfill by 85 per cent of 1998 levels by 2005
- Recover 40 per cent of municipal waste by 2005, 45 per cent by 2010 and 67 per cent by 2015
- Recycle or compost 25 per cent of household waste by 2005, 30 per cent by 2010 and 33 per cent by 2015
- Reduce biodegradable municipal waste sent to landfill to 75 per cent of 1995 levels by 2010
- Ensure 65 per cent of UK newspaper feedstock content is waste paper by end of 2003 and 70 per cent by end of 2006
- Proposed re-use and recovery of 85 per cent of the mass of end-of-life vehicles with a minimum of 80 per cent recycling by 2006, 95 per cent and 85 per cent by 2015
- EU target to reduce the amount of waste going to final disposal by 20 per cent by 2010 and 50 per cent by 2050
- Collect 4kg of household waste electrical and electronic equipment per head of population per year by 31 December 2006
- Provide segregated kerbside waste collection to over 90 per cent of households in Scotland by 2020

Land

- Ensure 60 per cent of all new housing is built on re-used sites

Energy

- Provide 10.4 per cent of electricity from renewable sources by 2010 in UK and Scotland

CONSERVATION AND HERITAGE

NATIONAL PARKS

ENGLAND AND WALES

The ten National Parks of England and Wales were set up under the provisions of the National Parks and Access to the Countryside Act 1949 to conserve and protect scenic landscapes from inappropriate development and to provide access to the land for public enjoyment.

The Countryside Agency (established on 1 April 1999 from the merger of the Countryside Commission and the Rural Development Commission) is the statutory body which has the power to designate National Parks in England, and the Countryside Council for Wales is responsible for National Parks in Wales. Designations in England are confirmed by the Secretary of State for Environment, Food and Rural Affairs and those in Wales by the National Assembly for Wales. The designation of a National Park does not affect the ownership of the land or remove the rights of the local community. The majority of the land in the National Parks is owned by private landowners (74 per cent) or by bodies such as the National Trust (7 per cent) and the Forestry Commission (7 per cent). The National Park Authorities own only 2.3 per cent of the land.

The Environment Act 1995 replaced the existing National Park boards and committees with free-standing National Park Authorities (NPAs). NPAs are the sole local planning authorities for their areas and as such influence land use and development, and deal with planning applications. Their duties include conserving and enhancing the natural beauty, wildlife and cultural heritage of the National Parks; promoting opportunities for public understanding and enjoyment of the National Parks; and fostering the economic and social well-being of the communities within National Parks. The NPAs publish management plans as statements of their policies and appoint their own officers and staff.

Membership of the NPAs differs slightly between England and Wales. In England, those local authorities that have land in the Parks appoint one half of the members of the National Parks Authorities plus one other person. Of the remaining members, one half minus one person are parish representatives who are elected through a process of local democracy while the rest are appointed by the Secretary of State to represent the national interest. In Wales two-thirds of NPA members are appointed by the constituent local authorities and one-third by the National Assembly for Wales, advised by the Countryside Council for Wales.

Since April 2004 the Department for Environment, Food and Rural Affairs has provided 100 per cent of the funding for the parks in England through the National Park and Broads Authority Grant; a total of £35.76 million in 2004–5. In Wales, National Parks are funded via a grant from the National Assembly and levies raised from participating local authorities. In addition, all NPAs and the Broads Authority can take advantage of grants from other bodies including lottery and European grants.

The National Parks (with date designation confirmed) are:

BRECON BEACONS (1957), Powys (66 per cent)/ Carmarthenshire/Rhondda, Cynon and Taff/Merthyr Tydfil/Blaenau Gwent/Monmouthshire, 1,349sq. km/519 sq. miles – The park is centred on the Beacons, Pen y Fan, Corn Du and Cribyn, but also includes the valley of the Usk, the Black Mountains to the east and the Black Mountain to the west. There are information centres at Brecon, Craig-y-nos Country Park, Abergavenny and Llandovery, a study centre at Danywenallt and a day visitor centre near Libanus.
Information Office, Plas y Ffynnon, Cambrian Way, Brecon, Powys LD3 7HP T 01874-624437
E enquiries@breconbeacons.org
National Park Officer, Christopher Gledhill

DARTMOOR (1951 and 1994), Devon, 954 sq. km/ 368 sq. miles – The park consists of moorland and rocky granite tors, and is rich in prehistoric remains. There are information centres at Haytor, Newbridge, Princetown and Postbridge.
Information Office, Parke, Bovey Tracey, Devon TQ13 9JQ T 01626-832093 E hq@dartmoor-npa.gov.uk
Chief Executive, Dr Nick Atkinson

EXMOOR (1954), Somerset (71 per cent)/Devon, 693 sq. km/268 sq. miles – Exmoor is a moorland plateau inhabited by wild ponies and red deer. There are many ancient remains and burial mounds. There are information centres at Lynmouth, County Gate, Dulverton and Combe Martin.
Information Office, Exmoor House, Dulverton, Somerset TA21 9HL T 01398-323665
E info@exmoor-nationalpark.gov.uk
National Park Officer, Dr Nigel Stone

LAKE DISTRICT (1951), Cumbria, 2,292 sq. km/885 sq. miles – The Lake District includes England's highest mountains (Scafell Pike, Helvellyn and Skiddaw) but it is most famous for its glaciated lakes. There are information centres at Broughton, Keswick, Waterhead, Hawkshead, Seatoller, Bowness, Grasmere, Coniston, Glenridding and Pooley Bridge and a park centre at Brockhole, Windermere.
Information Office, Murley Moss, Oxenholme Road, Kendal, Cumbria, LA9 7RL T 01539-724555
E hq@lake-district.gov.uk
National Park Officer, Paul Tiplady

NORTH YORK MOORS (1952), North Yorkshire (96 per cent)/Redcar and Cleveland, 1,432 sq. km/554 sq. miles – The park consists of woodland and moorland, and includes the Hambleton Hills and the Cleveland Way. There are information centres at Danby, Sutton Bank and at The Old Coastguard Station in Robin Hood's Bay.
Information Office, The Old Vicarage, Bondgate, Helmsley, York YO6 5BP T 01439-770657
E general@northyorkmoors-npa.gov.uk
National Park Officer, Andrew Wilson

NORTHUMBERLAND (1956), Northumberland, 1,049 sq. km/405 sq. miles – The park is an area of hill country stretching from Hadrian's Wall to the Scottish Border. There are information centres at Ingram, Once Brewed and Rothbury.

Information Office, Eastburn, South Park, Hexham, Northumberland NE46 1BS T 01434-605555
E admin@nnpa.org.uk
National Park Officer, Graham Taylor

PEAK DISTRICT (1951), Derbyshire (64 per cent)/ Staffordshire/South Yorkshire/Cheshire/West Yorkshire/Greater Manchester, 1,438 sq. km/555 sq. miles – The Peak District includes the gritstone moors of the 'Dark Peak' and the limestone dales of the 'White Peak'. There are information centres at Bakewell, Edale, Castleton and Upper Derwent.
Information Office, Aldern House, Baslow Road, Bakewell, Derbyshire DE45 1AE T 01629-816200
E aldern@peakdistrict-npa.gov.uk
National Park Officer, Jim Dixon

PEMBROKESHIRE COAST (1952 and 1995), Pembrokeshire, 620 sq. km/240 sq. miles – The park includes cliffs, moorland and a number of islands, including Skomer. There are information centres at St David's and Newport.
Information Office, Llanion Park, Pembroke Dock, Pembrokeshire SA72 6DF T 0845-345 7275
E pcnp@pembrokeshirecoast.org.uk
National Park Officer, Nic Wheeler

SNOWDONIA/ERYRI (1951), Gwynedd/Conwy, 2,171 sq. km/835 sq. miles – Snowdonia is an area of deep valleys and rugged mountains. There are information centres at Aberdyfi, Beddgelert, Betws y Coed, Blaenau Ffestiniog, Conwy, Dolgellau and Harlech.
Information Office, Penrhyndeudraeth, Gwynedd LL48 6LF
T 01766-770274 E parc@eryri-npa.gov.uk
Chief Executive, Aneurin Phillips

YORKSHIRE DALES (1954), North Yorkshire (88 per cent)/Cumbria, 1,769 sq. km/683 sq. miles – The Yorkshire Dales are composed primarily of limestone overlaid in places by millstone grit. The three peaks of Ingleborough, Whernside and Pen-y-Ghent are within the park. There are information centres at Grassington, Hawes, Aysgarth Falls, Malham, Reeth and Sedbergh.
Information Office, Yorebridge House, Bainbridge, Leyburn, N. Yorks DL8 3EE T 01969-650456
E info@yorkshiredales.org.uk
Chief Executive, David Butterworth

Two other areas considered to have equivalent status to the National Parks are the Broads and the New Forest. The Broads Authority was established in 1989 under separate legislation to develop, conserve and manage the Norfolk and Suffolk Broads. In 1999 the Countryside Agency began the process of designating the New Forest and the South Downs (within the Sussex Downs and East Hampshire 'Areas of Outstanding Natural Beauty') as National Parks. On 28 June 2004 the Government announced that, following the finalisation of the boundary, the New Forest will become a National Park.

THE BROADS (1989), Norfolk, 303 sq. km/117 sq. miles – The Broads are located between Norwich and Great Yarmouth on the flood plains of the five rivers flowing through the area to the sea. The area is one of fens, winding waterways, woodland and marsh. The 40 or so broads are man-made, and are connected to the rivers by dikes, providing over 200 km of navigable waterways. There are information centres at Beccles, Hoveton, North West Tower (Yarmouth), Potter Heigham, Ranworth and Toad Hole.
The Broads Authority, 18 Colegate, Norwich NR3 1BQ
T 01603 610734 E broads@broads-authority.gov.uk
Chief Executive, Dr John Packman

THE NEW FOREST Hampshire, 580 sq. km/224 sq. miles – The forest has been protected since 1079 when it was declared a royal hunting forest. The area consists of forest, ancient woodland and heathland. Much of the Forest is managed by the Forestry Commission, which provides several camp-sites. The main villages are Brockenhurst, Burley and Lyndhurst, which has a visitor centre.
The New Forest Committee, 4 High Street, Lyndhurst, Hants SO43 7BD T 023-8028 4144
E office@newforestcommittee.org.uk
Chairman, Ted Johnson, FRICS, *Committee Officer*, Maddy Jago

THE SOUTH DOWNS, West Sussex/Hampshire,1,637 sq. km/632 sq. miles – The South Downs contains a diversity of natural habitats, including flower-studded chalk grassland, ancient woodland, flood meadow, lowland heath and rare chalk heathland.
Sussex Downs Conservation Board, Victorian Barn, Victorian Business Centre, Ford Lane, Ford, Arundel, West Sussex, BN18 0EF T 01234-558700
E info@southdowns-aonb.gov.uk
Chief Officer, Martin Beaton

SCOTLAND

On 9 August 2000 The National Parks (Scotland) Bill received Royal Assent, providing the Parliament with the ability to create National Parks in Scotland. The first two Scottish National Parks, *Loch Lomond and the Trossachs* and the *Cairngorms*, became operational in 2002 and 2003 respectively. The Act gives Scottish Parks wider powers than in England and Wales, including statutory responsibilities for the economy and rural communities. Membership of the two NPAs in Scotland consists of 20 per cent directly elected members. The remaining 80 per cent are chosen by the Secretary of State, 40 per cent of which are nominated by the constituent Local Authorities. In Scotland, the National Parks are central Government bodies and wholly funded by the Scottish Executive.

CAIRNGORMS (2003), Morayshire, 3,800 sq. km/1,461 sq. miles – The Cairngorms National Park is the largest in the UK. It displays a vast collection of landforms and includes four of Scotland's highest mountains.
Information Office, 14 The Square, Grantown-on-Spey, Morayshire, PH26 3HG T 01479-873535
E mainoffice@cairngorms.co.uk
Chief Executive, Jane Hope

LOCH LOMOND AND THE TROSSACHS (2002), Argyll and Bute/Stirling/West Dunbartonshire, 1,865 sq. km/720 sq. miles – The park boundaries encompass lochs, rivers, forests, 20 mountains above 3,000 ft including Ben Moore and a further 20 mountains between 2,500 ft and 3,000 ft.
Information Office, The Old Station, Balloch Road, Balloch G83 8SS T 01389-722600 E info@lochlomond-trossachs.org
Chief Executive, Bill Dalrymple

NORTHERN IRELAND

There is power to designate National Parks in Northern Ireland under the Amenity Lands Act 1965 and the Nature Conservation and Amenity Lands Order (Northern Ireland) 1985.

AREAS OF OUTSTANDING NATURAL BEAUTY

ENGLAND AND WALES

Under the National Parks and Access to the Countryside Act 1949, provision was made for the designation of Areas of Outstanding Natural Beauty (AONBs) by the Countryside Commission. The Countryside Agency is now responsible for AONBs in England and since April 1991 the Countryside Council for Wales has been responsible for the Welsh AONBs. Designations in England are confirmed by the Secretary of State for Environment, Food and Rural Affairs and those in Wales by the National Assembly for Wales. The Countryside and Rights of Way Act 2000 provided for the creation of conservation boards for individual AONBs and placed greater responsibility on local authorities to protect them.

Although less emphasis is placed upon the provision of open-air enjoyment for the public than in the national parks, AONBs are areas which require the same degree of protection to conserve and enhance the natural beauty of the countryside. This includes protecting flora and fauna, geological and other landscape features. Overall responsibility for AONBs lies with the relevant local authorities, however, most fall within more than one local authority area. To co-ordinate planning and management responsibilities, AONBs are overseen by a Joint Advisory Committee (or similar body) which includes representatives from the local authorities, landowners, farmers, residents and conservation and recreation groups. In addition, an AONB officer is appointed to oversee matters. All AONBs also have to prepare Statements of Intent (or Commitment) and Management Plans. Since April 2002, 75 per cent of core funding for AONBs has been provided by central government through the Countryside Agency and Countryside Council for Wales.

The 41 Areas of Outstanding Natural Beauty (with date designation confirmed) are:

ANGLESEY (1967), Anglesey, 221 sq. km/85 sq. miles
ARNSIDE AND SILVERDALE (1972), Cumbria/Lancashire, 75 sq. km/29 sq. miles
BLACKDOWN HILLS (1991), Devon/Somerset, 370 sq. km/143 sq. miles
CANNOCK CHASE (1958), Staffordshire, 68 sq. km/26 sq. miles
CHICHESTER HARBOUR (1964), Hampshire/West Sussex, 74 sq. km/29 sq. miles
CHILTERNS (1965; extended 1990), Bedfordshire/Buckinghamshire/Herefordshire/Oxfordshire, 833 sq. km/322 sq. miles
CLWYDIAN RANGE (1985), Denbighshire/Flintshire, 157 sq. km/60 sq. miles
CORNWALL (1959; Camel estuary 1983), 958 sq. km/370 sq. miles
COTSWOLDS (1966; extended 1990), Gloucestershire/Oxfordshire/Wiltshire/Warwickshire/Worcestershire, 2,038 sq. km/787 sq. miles
CRANBORNE CHASE AND WEST WILTSHIRE DOWNS (1983), Dorset/Hampshire/Somerset/Wiltshire, 983 sq. km/379 sq. miles
DEDHAM VALE (1970; extended 1978, 1991), Essex/Suffolk, 90 sq. km/35 sq. miles
DORSET (1959), 1,129 sq. km/436 sq. miles
EAST DEVON (1963), 268 sq. km/103 sq. miles
EAST HAMPSHIRE (1962), 383 sq. km/148 sq. miles
FOREST OF BOWLAND (1964), Lancashire/North Yorkshire, 802 sq. km/310 sq. miles
GOWER (1956), Swansea, 188 sq. km/73 sq. miles
HIGH WEALD (1983), Kent/East Sussex/Surrey/West Sussex, 1,460 sq. km/564 sq. miles
HOWARDIAN HILLS (1987), North Yorkshire, 204 sq. km/79 sq. miles
ISLE OF WIGHT (1963), 189 sq. km/73 sq. miles
ISLES OF SCILLY (1976), 16 sq. km/6 sq. miles
KENT DOWNS (1968), 878 sq. km/339 sq. miles
LINCOLNSHIRE WOLDS (1973), 558 sq. km/215 sq. miles
LLEYN (1957), Gwynedd, 161 sq. km/62 sq. miles
MALVERN HILLS (1959), Gloucestershire/Worcestershire, 150 sq. km/58 sq. miles
MENDIP HILLS (1972; extended 1989), Somerset, 198 sq. km/76 sq. miles
NIDDERDALE (1994), North Yorkshire, 603 sq. km/233 sq. miles
NORFOLK COAST (1968), 451 sq. km/174 sq. miles
NORTH DEVON (1960), 171 sq. km/66 sq. miles
NORTH PENNINES (1988), Cumbria/Durham/Northumberland, 1,983 sq. km/766 sq. miles
NORTH WESSEX DOWNS (1972), Hampshire/Oxfordshire/Wiltshire, 1,730 sq. km/668 sq. miles
NORTHUMBERLAND COAST (1958), 135 sq. km/52 sq. miles
QUANTOCK HILLS (1957), Somerset, 99 sq. km/38 sq. miles
SHROPSHIRE HILLS (1959), 804 sq. km/310 sq. miles
SOLWAY COAST (1964), Cumbria, 115 sq. km/44 sq. miles
SOUTH DEVON (1960), 337 sq. km/130 sq. miles
SOUTH HAMPSHIRE COAST (1967), 77 sq. km/30 sq. miles
SUFFOLK COAST AND HEATHS (1970), 403 sq. km/156 sq. miles
SURREY HILLS (1958), 419 sq. km/162 sq. miles
SUSSEX DOWNS (1966), 983 sq. km/379 sq. miles
TAMAR VALLEY (1995), Cornwall/Devon, 195 sq. km/115 sq. miles
WYE VALLEY (1971), Gloucestershire/Herefordshire/Monmouthshire, 326 sq. km/126 sq. miles

NORTHERN IRELAND

The Department of the Environment for Northern Ireland, with advice from the Council for Nature Conservation and the Countryside, designates Areas of Outstanding Natural Beauty in Northern Ireland. At present there are nine and these cover a total area of approximately 284,948 hectares (704,103 acres). Dates given are those of designation.

ANTRIM COAST AND GLENS (1988), Co. Antrim, 70,600 ha/174,452 acres
CAUSEWAY COAST (1989), Co. Antrim, 4,200 ha/10,378 acres
LAGAN VALLEY (1965), Co. Down, 2,072 ha/5,119 acres
LECALE COAST (1967), Co. Down, 3,108 ha/7,679 acres
MOURNE (1986), Co. Down, 57,012 ha/140,876 acres
NORTH DERRY (1966), Co. Londonderry, 12,950 ha/31,999 acres
RING OF GULLION (1991), Co. Armagh, 15,353 ha/37,938 acres
SPERRIN (1968), Co. Tyrone/Co. Londonderry, 101,006 ha/249,585 acres

STRANGFORD LOUGH (1972), Co. Down, 18,647 ha/ 46,077 acres

NATIONAL SCENIC AREAS

In Scotland, National Scenic Areas have a broadly equivalent status to AONBs. Scottish Natural Heritage recognises areas of national scenic significance. At the end of June 2004 there were 40, covering a total area of 1,001,800 hectares (2,475,448 acres).

Development within National Scenic Areas is dealt with by local authorities, who are required to consult Scottish Natural Heritage concerning certain categories of development. Disagreements between Scottish Natural Heritage and local authorities are referred to the Scottish Executive. Land management uses can also be modified in the interest of scenic conservation.

ASSYNT-COIGACH, Highland, 90,200 ha/222,884 acres
BEN NEVIS AND GLEN COE, Highland, 101,600 ha/ 251,053 acres
CAIRNGORM MOUNTAINS, Highland/Aberdeenshire/ Moray, 67,200 ha/166,051 acres
CUILLIN HILLS, Highland, 21,900 ha/54,115 acres
DEESIDE AND LOCHNAGAR, Aberdeenshire, 40,000 ha/ 98,840 acres
DORNOCH FIRTH, Highland, 7,500 ha/18,532 acres
EAST STEWARTRY COAST, Dumfries and Galloway, 4,500 ha/11,119 acres
EILDON AND LEADERFOOT, The Borders, 3,600 ha/ 8,896 acres
FLEET VALLEY, Dumfries and Galloway, 5,300 ha/ 13,096 acres
GLEN AFFRIC, Highland, 19,300 ha/47,690 acres
GLEN STRATHFARRAR, Highland, 3,800 ha/9,390 acres
HOY AND WEST MAINLAND, Orkney Islands, 14,800 ha/36,571 acres
JURA, Argyll and Bute, 21,800 ha/53,868 acres
KINTAIL, Highland, 15,500 ha/38,300 acres
KNAPDALE, Argyll and Bute, 19,800 ha/48,926 acres
KNOYDART, Highland, 39,500 ha/97,604 acres
KYLE OF TONGUE, Highland, 18,500 ha/45,713 acres
KYLES OF BUTE, Argyll and Bute, 4,400 ha/10,872 acres
LOCH NA KEAL, MULL, Argyll and Bute, 12,700 ha/ 31,382 acres
LOCH LOMOND, Argyll and Bute, 27,400 ha/67,705 acres
LOCH RANNOCH AND GLEN LYON, Perthshire and Kinross, 48,400 ha/119,596 acres
LOCH SHIEL, Highland, 13,400 ha/33,111 acres
LOCH TUMMEL, Perthshire and Kinross, 9,200 ha/ 22,733 acres
LYNN OF LORN, Argyll and Bute, 4,800 ha/11,861 acres
MORAR, MOIDART AND ARDNAMURCHAN, Highland, 13,500 ha/33,358 acres
NORTH-WEST SUTHERLAND, Highland, 20,500 ha/ 50,655 acres
NITH ESTUARY, Dumfries and Galloway, 9,300 ha/ 22,980 acres
NORTH ARRAN, North Ayrshire, 23,800 ha/58,810 acres
RIVER EARN, Perthshire and Kinross, 3,000 ha/7,413 acres
RIVER TAY, Perthshire and Kinross, 5,600 ha/13,838 acres
ST KILDA, Western Isles, 900 ha/2,224 acres
SCARBA, LUNGA AND THE GARVELLACHS, Argyll and Bute, 1,900 ha/4,695 acres
SHETLAND, Shetland Isles, 11,600 ha/28,664 acres
SMALL ISLANDS, Highland, 15,500 ha/38,300 acres
SOUTH LEWIS, HARRIS AND NORTH UIST, Western Isles, 109,600 ha/270,822 acres
SOUTH UIST MACHAIR, Western Isles, 6,100 ha/15,073 acres
THE TROSSACHS, Stirling, 4,600 ha/11,367 acres
TROTTERNISH, Highland, 5,000 ha/12,355 acres
UPPER TWEEDDALE, The Borders, 10,500 ha/25,945 acres
WESTER ROSS, Highland, 145,300 ha/359,036 acres

THE NATIONAL FOREST

The National Forest is being planted across 200 square miles of Derbyshire, Leicestershire and Staffordshire. Nearly six million trees, of mixed species but mainly broadleaved, have been planted, with the aim being to eventually cover about one-third of the designated area. The project is funded by the Department for Environment, Food and Rural Affairs. It was developed in 1992–5 by the Countryside Commission and is now run by the National Forest Company, which was established in April 1995. Under the National Forest Tender Scheme, anybody wishing to undertake a woodland creation project can submit a competitive bid to the National Forest Company.

NATIONAL FOREST COMPANY, Enterprise Glade, Bath Lane, Moira, Swadlincote, Derbyshire DE12 6BD
T 01283-551211 W www.nationalforest.org
Chief Executive, Miss S. Bell, OBE

SITES OF SPECIAL SCIENTIFIC INTEREST

Site of Special Scientific Interest (SSSI) is a legal notification applied to land in England, Scotland or Wales which English Nature (EN), Scottish Natural Heritage (SNH) or the Countryside Council for Wales (CCW) identifies as being of special interest because of its flora, fauna, geological or physiographical features. In some cases, SSSIs are managed as nature reserves.

EN, SNH and CCW must notify the designation of an SSSI to the local planning authority, every owner/ occupier of the land, and the Secretary of State for Environment, Food and Rural Affairs, the Scottish Ministers or the National Assembly for Wales. Forestry and agricultural departments and a number of other bodies are also informed of this notification.

Objections to the notification of an SSSI can be made and ultimately considered at a full meeting of the Council of EN or CCW. In Scotland an objection will be dealt with by the appropriate area board or the main board of SNH, depending on the nature of the objection. Unresolved objections on scientific grounds must be referred to the Advisory Committee on SSSI.

The protection of these sites depends on the co-operation of individual landowners and occupiers. Owner/occupiers must consult EN, SNH or CCW and, in England and Wales, gain written consent before they can undertake certain listed activities on the site. In Scotland, owner/occupiers can carry out a listed operation four months after consultation, unless SNH obtains a Nature Conservation Order from Scottish Ministers. Funds are available through management agreements and grants to assist owners and occupiers in conserving sites' interests. As a last resort a site can be purchased.

The number and area of SSSIs in Britain as at May 2004 was:

	No.	Hectares	Acres
England	4,111	1,076,704	2,660,536
Scotland	1,451	1,005,152	2,482,725
Wales*	1,021	264,354	652,954

* Some sites in Wales amalgamated 2002–3

NORTHERN IRELAND
In Northern Ireland 208 Areas of Special Scientific Interest (ASSIs) have been declared by the Department of the Environment for Northern Ireland.

NATIONAL NATURE RESERVES

National Nature Reserves are defined in the National Parks and Access to the Countryside Act 1949 as land designated for the study and preservation of flora and fauna, or of geological or physiographical features.

English Nature (EN), Scottish Natural Heritage (SNH) or the Countryside Council for Wales (CCW) can designate as a National Nature Reserve land which is being managed as a nature reserve under an agreement with one of the statutory nature conservation agencies; land held and managed by EN, SNH or CCW; or land held and managed as a nature reserve by another approved body. EN, SNH or CCW can make by-laws to protect reserves from undesirable activities; these are subject to confirmation by the Secretary of State for Environment, Food and Rural Affairs, the National Assembly for Wales or the Scottish Ministers in Scotland.

The number and area of National Nature Reserves in Britain as at May 2004 was:

	No.	Hectares	Acres
England	215	87,917	217,242
Scotland	66	117,228	289,612
Wales	67	24,123	59,584

NORTHERN IRELAND
National Nature Reserves are established and managed by the Department of the Environment for Northern Ireland, with advice from the Council for Nature Conservation and the Countryside. There are 48 National Nature Reserves covering 4,746.3 hectares (11,723 acres).

LOCAL NATURE RESERVES

Local Nature Reserves are defined in the National Parks and Access to the Countryside Act 1949 as land designated for the study and preservation of flora and fauna, or of geological or physiographical features. The Act gives local authorities in England, Scotland and Wales the power to acquire, declare and manage local nature reserves in consultation with English Nature, Scottish Natural Heritage and the Countryside Council for Wales. Other organisations, including wildlife trusts, may manage local nature reserves, providing that a local authority has a legal interest in the land.

The number and area of designated Local Nature Reserves in Britain as at May 2004 was:

	No.	Hectares	Acres
England	947	31,012	76,631
Scotland	36	9,410	23,252
Wales	54	4,890	12,078

FOREST NATURE RESERVES

In 1999 responsibility for forestry was transferred to Scottish Ministers and the National Assembly for Wales. Westminster retained responsibility for forestry in England and for international issues. In April 2003 Forest Enterprise, an executive agency of the Forestry Commission, ceased to exist as a single agency. Three new bodies for England, Scotland and Wales were created in its place. The Forest Enterprise manages 665,000 hectares in Scotland, 258,500 hectares in England and 130,000 hectares in Wales.

Forest Nature Reserves extend in size from under 50 hectares (124 acres) to over 500 hectares (1,236 acres). The largest include the Black Wood of Rannoch, by Loch Rannoch; Cannop Valley Oakwoods, Forest of Dean; Culbin Forest, near Forres; Glen Affric, near Fort Augustus; Kylerhea, Skye; Pembrey, Carmarthen Bay; Starr Forest, in Galloway Forest Park; and Wyre Forest, near Kidderminster.

NORTHERN IRELAND
There are 34 Forest Nature Reserves in Northern Ireland, covering 1,512 hectares (3,736 acres). They are designated and administered by the Forest Service, an agency of the Department of Agriculture and Rural Development for Northern Ireland. There are also 16 National Nature Reserves on Forest Service-owned property.

MARINE NATURE RESERVES

The Secretary of State for Environment, Food and Rural Affairs, the National Assembly for Wales and the Scottish Executive have the power to designate Marine Nature Reserves. English Nature, Scottish Natural Heritage and the Countryside Council for Wales select and manage these reserves. Marine Nature Reserves may be established in Northern Ireland under a 1985 Order.

Marine Nature Reserves provide protection for marine flora and fauna, and geological and physiographical features on land covered by tidal waters or parts of the sea in or adjacent to the UK. Reserves also provide opportunities for study and research.

The three statutory Marine Nature Reserves are:

LUNDY (1986), Bristol Channel
KOMER (1990), Dyfed
STRANGFORD LOUGH (1995), Northern Ireland

Non-statutory marine reserves have also been set up by conservation groups.

EUROPEAN MARINE SITES
The 1992 EC Habitats Directive and the 1979 Birds Directive allow the UK government to establish Special Areas of Conservation (SACs) or Special Protection Areas (SPAs) for animals and birds on land and at sea. Where the designated area includes sea or seashore it is described as a European marine site. The 1998–2002 UK Marine SACs project formed a demonstration initiative, funded partly by the EU, to establish management schemes for twelve of the marine SACs in the UK. In England, a further 11 management schemes have been published and five are being developed.

WORLD HERITAGE SITES

The Convention Concerning the Protection of the World Cultural and Natural Heritage was adopted by the United Nations Educational, Scientific and Cultural Organisation (UNESCO) in 1972 and ratified by the UK in 1984. As at 1 May 2004 the convention had been ratified by 178 states. The convention provides for the identification, protection and conservation of cultural and natural sites of outstanding universal value.

Cultural sites may be:
- monuments
- groups of buildings
- sites of historic, aesthetic, archaeological, scientific, ethnologic or anthropologic value
- historic areas of towns
- 'cultural landscapes', i.e. sites whose characteristics are marked by significant interactions between human populations and their natural environment

Natural sites may be:
- those with remarkable physical, biological or geological formations
- those with outstanding universal value from the point of view of science, conservation or natural beauty
- the habitat of threatened species and plants

Governments which are party to the convention nominate sites in their country for inclusion in the World Cultural and Natural Heritage List. Nominations are considered by the World Heritage Committee, an inter-governmental committee composed of 21 representatives of the parties to the convention. The committee is advised by the International Council on Monuments and Sites (ICOMOS), the International Centre for the Study of the Preservation and Restoration of Cultural Property (ICCROM) and the World Conservation Union (IUCN). ICOMOS evaluates and reports on proposed cultural sites, ICCROM provides expert advice and training on how to conserve the listed sites and IUCN advises on proposed natural sites. The Department for Culture, Media and Sport represents the UK government in matters relating to the convention.

A prerequisite for inclusion in the World Cultural and Natural Heritage List is the existence of an effective legal protection system in the country in which the site is situated (e.g. listing, conservation areas and planning controls in the United Kingdom) and a detailed management plan to ensure the conservation of the site. Inclusion in the list does not confer any greater degree of protection on the site than that offered by the national protection framework.

If a site is considered to be in serious danger of decay or damage the committee may add it to a complementary list, the World Heritage in Danger List. Sites on this list may benefit from particular attention or emergency measures.

Financial support for the conservation of sites on the World Cultural and Natural Heritage List is provided by the World Heritage Fund. This is administered by the World Heritage Committee, which determines the financial and technical aid to be allocated. The fund's income is derived from contributions of the parties to the convention, voluntary contributions from other States, other United Nations and intergovernmental organisations, public or private bodies and individuals, through interest due on the fund and from events organised for the benefit of the fund.

DESIGNATED SITES

As at 3 July 2004 there were 788 sites in 134 countries on the World Cultural and Natural Heritage List. Of these, 23 are in the United Kingdom and three in British overseas territories; 20 are listed for their cultural significance (†) and six for their natural significance (*). The year in which sites were designated appears in parentheses.

UNITED KINGDOM

†Bath – the city (1987)
†Blaenarvon, Wales (2000)
†Blenheim Palace and Park, Oxfordshire (1987)
†Canterbury Cathedral, St Augustine's Abbey, St Martin's Church, Kent (1988)
†Castle and town walls of King Edward I, north Wales – Beaumaris, Anglesey, Caernarfon Castle, Conwy Castle, Harlech Castle (1986)
†Derwent Valley Mills, Derbyshire (2001)
*Dorset and East Devon Coast (2001)
†Durham Cathedral and Castle (1986)
†Edinburgh Old and New Towns (1995)
*Giant's Causeway and Causeway coast, Co. Antrim (1986)
†Greenwich, London – maritime Greenwich, including the Royal Naval College, Old Royal Observatory, Queen's House, town centre (1997)
†Hadrian's Wall, northern England (1987)
†Heart of Neolithic Orkney (1999)
†Ironbridge Gorge, Shropshire – the world's first iron bridge and other early industrial sites (1986)
†Liverpool – six areas of the Maritime Mercantile City (2004)
†New Lanark, South Lanarkshire, Scotland (2001)
†Royal Botanic Gardens, Kew (2003)
*St Kilda, Western Isles (1986)
†Saltaire, West Yorkshire (2001)
†Stonehenge, Avebury and related megalithic sites, Wiltshire (1986)
†Studley Royal Park, Fountains Abbey, St Mary's Church, N. Yorkshire (1986)
†Tower of London (1988)
†Westminster Abbey, Palace of Westminster, St Margaret's Church, London (1987)

BRITISH OVERSEAS TERRITORIES

*Henderson Island, Pitcairn Islands, South Pacific Ocean (1988)
*Gough Island wildlife reserve (part of Tristan da Cunha), South Atlantic Ocean (1995)
*St George town and related fortifications, Bermuda (2000)

CONTACTS

ARCHITECTURE AND HISTORIC ENVIRONMENT DIVISION, Department for Culture, Media and Sport, Queen's Yard, 179a Tottenham Court Road, London W1T 7PA T 020-7211 2330

WORLD HERITAGE CENTRE, UNESCO, 7 Place de Fontenoy, 75007 Paris, France W www.unesco.org

INTERNATIONAL CENTRE FOR THE STUDY OF THE PRESERVATION AND RESTORATION OF CULTURAL PROPERTY (ICCROM), Via di San Michele 13, I-00153 Rome, Italy T (+ 39) (06) 585 531 W www.iccrom.org

INTERNATIONAL COUNCIL ON MONUMENTS AND SITES (ICOMOS), 70 Cowcross Street, London EC1M 6EJ T 020-7566 0031 W www.icomos.org

WORLD CONSERVATION UNION (IUCN), Rue Mauverney 28, 1196 Gland, Switzerland T (+ 41) (22) 999 0000 W www.iucn.org

CONSERVATION OF WILDLIFE AND HABITATS

The UK is party to a number of international conventions.

RAMSAR CONVENTION

The 1971 Ramsar Convention on Wetlands of International Importance especially as Waterfowl Habitat, entered into force in the UK in May 1976. As at May 2004, 138 countries were party to the convention.

The aim of the convention is the conservation and wise use of wetlands and their flora and fauna. Governments that are party to the convention must designate wetlands and include wetland conservation considerations in their land-use planning. A total of 1,364 wetland sites, totalling 121 million hectares have been designated for inclusion in the List of Wetlands of International Importance. The UK currently has 159* designated sites covering 849,106 hectares. The member countries meet every three years to assess the progress of the convention and the next meeting is scheduled for November 2005.

The UK has set targets under the Ramsar Strategic Plan, 2003–8. Progress towards these is monitored by the UK Ramsar Committee, known as the Joint Working Party. The UK and the Republic of Ireland have established a formal protocol to ensure common monitoring standards for waterbirds in the two countries.

* The UK government consolidated a number of overlapping sites in 2004, resulting in a lower total compared with 2003.

RAMSAR CONVENTION BUREAU, Rue Mauverney 28, CH-1196 Gland, Switzerland **T** (+41) (22) 999 0170 **W** www.ramsar.org

BIODIVERSITY

There is much synergy between the Ramsar Convention and the 1992 Convention on Biological Diversity. In 1996 the Ramsar Secretariat became a lead partner in implementing activities under the Convention on Biological Diversity with joint work plans. The UK ratified the Convention on Biological Diversity in June 1994. As at May 2004 there were 188 parties to the convention.

The objectives are the conservation of biological diversity, the sustainable use of its components and the fair and equitable sharing of the benefits arising out of the use of genetic resources. There are thematic work programmes addressing marine and coastal, forest, inland waters, dry land and sub-humid land. The Conference of the Parties to the Convention on Biological Diversity adopted a supplementary agreement to the Convention known as the *Cartagena Protocol on Biosafety* on 29 January 2000. The protocol seeks to protect biological diversity from potential risks that may be posed by introducing modified living organisms, resulting from modern biotechnology, into the environment. As at May 2004 101 countries were party to the protocol. The UK became party to the protocol on 17 February 2004.

The UK published its own Biodiversity Action Plan in 1994. A report from the UK Biodiversity Steering Group, published in 1995, proposed monitoring a list of 1,252 species to check on biodiversity within the UK.

A report, *Sustaining the Variety of Life: 5 years of the UK Biodiversity Action Plan*, was published in March 2001 and made a number of recommendations including to support actions for the conservation of species and habitats at UK, county and local levels. There are around 391 Species Action Plans, 45 Habitat Action Plans and 162 Local Biodiversity Action Plans. There are four country groups: England Biodiversity Group, Scotland Biodiversity Forum, Northern Ireland Biodiversity Group and Wales Biodiversity Partnership. These are involved in implementing the action plans at national level. In October 2002, the England Biodiversity Group, DEFRA and the Biodiversity Policy Unit jointly launched a *Biodiversity Strategy for England* as part of the UK Biodiversity Action Plan.

BIODIVERSITY POLICY UNIT, Zone 1/10b, Temple Quay House, 2 The Square, Temple Quay, Bristol BS1 6EB **T** 0117-372 6276 **E** admin@ukbap.org.uk **W** www.ukbap.org.uk

CITES

The 1973 Convention on International Trade in Endangered Species of Wild Fauna and Flora (CITES) came into force in the UK in July 1975. Currently 166 countries are members. The countries party to the convention ban commercial international trade in an agreed list of endangered species and regulate and monitor trade in others species that might become endangered. The convention covers approximately 5,000 species of animals and 28,000 species of plants.

The Conference of the Parties to CITES meets every two to three years to review the convention's implementation. The Global Wildlife Division at the Department for Environment, Food and Rural Affairs carries out the government's responsibilities under CITES and the Bonn Convention on the Conservation of Migratory Species of Wild Animals.

CITES SECRETARIAT, International Environment House, Chemin des Anémones, CH-1219 Châtelaine, Geneva, Switzerland **T** (+41) (22) 917 8139/8140 **E** cities@unep.ch **W** www.cites.org

BONN CONVENTION

The 1979 Convention on Conservation of Migratory Species of Wild Animals came into force in the UK in October 1979. As at 1 June 2004, 86 countries were party to the convention.

It requires the protection of listed endangered migratory species and encourages international agreements covering these and other threatened species. International agreements can range from legally binding treaties to less formal memoranda of understanding.

Six agreements have been concluded to date under the convention. They aim to conserve: seals in the Wadden Sea; bat populations in Europe; small cetaceans of the Baltic and North Seas; African-Eurasian migratory waterbirds; cetaceans of the Mediterranean and Black Seas; and albatrosses and petrels. A further seven memorandums of understanding have been agreed for the Siberian Crane, Slender-billed Curlew, marine turtles of the Atlantic coast of Africa, Indian Ocean and South-East Asia, the middle-European population of the Great Bustard, Bukhara Deer and the Aquatic Warbler.

UNEP/CMS SECRETARIAT, Martin-Luther-King-Str. 8, D-53175, Bonn, Germany **T** (+49) (228) 81 2401/2 **E** secretariat@cms.int **W** www.cms.int

BERN CONVENTION

The 1979 Bern Convention on the Conservation of European Wildlife and Natural Habitats came into force in the UK in June 1982. Currently there are 45 Contracting Parties and a number of other states attend meetings as observers.

The aims are to conserve wild flora and fauna and their natural habitats, especially where this requires the co-operation of several countries, and to promote such co-operation. The convention gives particular emphasis to endangered and vulnerable species.

All parties to the convention must promote national conservation policies and take account of the conservation of wild flora and fauna when setting planning and development policies. Reports on contracting parties' conservation policies must be submitted to the Standing Committee every four years.

SECRETARIAT OF THE BERN CONVENTION STANDING COMMITTEE, Council of Europe, 67075 Strasbourg-Cedex, France **T** (+33) (3) 8841 2000 **W** www.coe.int

EUROPEAN WILDLIFE TRADE REGULATION

The Council (EC) Regulation on the Protection of Species of Wild Fauna and Flora by Regulating Trade Therein came into force in the UK on 1 June 1997. It is intended to standardise wildlife trade regulations across Europe and to improve the application of CITES.

UK LEGISLATION

The Wildlife and Countryside Act 1981 gives legal protection to a wide range of wild animals and plants. Subject to parliamentary approval, the Secretary of State for Environment, Food and Rural Affairs may vary the animals and plants given legal protection. The most recent variation of Schedules 5 and 8 came into effect in March and April 1998.

Under Section 9 of the Act it is an offence to kill, injure, take, possess or sell (whether alive or dead) any wild animal included in Schedule 5 of the Act and to disturb its place of shelter and protection or to destroy that place.

Under Section 13 of the Act it is illegal without a licence to pick, uproot, sell or destroy plants listed in Schedule 8. Since January 2001, under the Countryside and Rights of Way Act 2000, persons found guilty of an offence under part 1 of the Wildlife and Countryside Act 1981 face a maximun penalty of up to £5,000 and/or up to six months custodial sentence per specimen.

The Act lays down a close season for wild birds (other than game birds) from 1 February to 31 August inclusive, each year. Exceptions to these dates are made for:

Capercaillie and (except Scotland) Woodcock – 1 February to 30 September
Snipe – 1 February to 11 August
Birds listed on Schedule 2, part 1 (*see* below) (below high water mark) – 21 February to 31 August

Birds listed on Schedule 2, Part 1, which may be killed or taken outside the close season (except on Sundays and on Christmas Day in Scotland, and on Sundays in prescribed areas of England and Wales) are capercaille, coot, certain wild duck (gadwall, goldeneye, mallard, pintail, pochard, shoveler, teal, tufted duck, wigeon), certain wild geese (Canada, greylag, pink-footed, white-fronted (in England and Wales only)), moorhen, golden plover and woodcock.

Section 16 of the 1981 Act allows licences to be issued on either an individual or general basis, to allow the killing, taking and sale of certain birds for specified reasons such as public health and safety. All other British birds are fully protected by law throughout the year.

ANIMALS PROTECTED BY SCHEDULE 5
Adder *(Vipera berus)*
Allis shad *(Alosa alosa)*
Atlantic Stream Crayfish *(Austropotomobius pallipes)*
Anemone, Ivell's Sea *(Edwardsia ivelli)*
Anemone, Starlet Sea *(Nematosella vectensis)*
Apus, Tadpole shrimp *(Triops cancriformis)*
Bat, Horseshoe *(Rhinolophidae*, all species*)*
Bat, Typical *(Vespertilionidae*, all species*)*
Beetle (G*raphoderus zonatus)*
Beetle *(Hypebaeus flavipes)*
Beetle, Lesser Silver Water *(Hydrochara caraboides)*
Beetle, Mire Pill *(Curimopsis nigrita)*
Beetle, Rainbow Leaf *(Chrysolina cerealis)*
Beetle, Stag *(Lucanus cervus)*
Beetle, Violet Click *(Limoniscus violaceus)*
Beetle, Water *(Paracymus aeneus)*
Burbot *(Lota lota)*
Butterfly, Adonis Blue *(Lysandra bellargus)*
Butterfly, Black Hairstreak *(Strymonidia pruni)*
Butterfly, Brown Hairstreak *(Thecla betulae)*
Butterfly, Chalkhill Blue *(Lysandra coridon)*
Butterfly, Chequered Skipper *(Carterocephalus palaemon)*
Butterfly, Duke of Burgundy Fritillary *(Hamearis lucina)*
Butterfly, Glanville Fritillary *(Melitaea cinxia)*
Butterfly, Heath Fritillary *(Mellicta athalia* (or *Melitaea athalia))*
Butterfly, High Brown Fritillary *(Argynnis adippe)*
Butterfly, Large Blue *(Maculinea arion)*
Butterfly, Large Copper *(Lycaena dispar)*
Butterfly, Large Heath *(Coenonympha tullia)*
Butterfly, Large Tortoiseshell *(Nymphalis polychloros)*
Butterfly, Lulworth Skipper *(Thymelicus acteon)*
Butterfly, Marsh Fritillary *(Eurodryas aurinia)*
Butterfly, Mountain Ringlet *(Erebia epiphron)*
Butterfly, Northern Brown Argus *(Aricia artaxerxes)*
Butterfly, Pearl-bordered Fritillary *(Boloria euphrosyne)*
Butterfly, Purple Emperor *(Apatura iris)*
Butterfly, Silver Spotted Skipper *(Hesperia comma)*
Butterfly, Silver-studded Blue *(Plebejus argus)*
Butterfly, Small Blue *(Cupido minimus)*
Butterfly, Swallowtail *(Papilio machaon)*
Butterfly, White Letter Hairstreak *(Stymonida w-album)*
Butterfly, Wood White *(Leptidea sinapis)*
Cat, Wild *(Felis silvestris)*
Cicada, New Forest *(Cicadetta montana)*
Cricket, Field *(Gryllus campestris)*
Cricket, Mole *(Gryllotalpa gryllotalpa)*
Damselfly, Southern *(Coenagrion mercuriale)*
Dolphin *(Cetacea)*
Dormouse *(Muscardinus avellanarius)*
Dragonfly, Norfolk Aeshna *(Aeshna isosceles)*
Frog, Common *(Rana temporaria)*
Goby, Couch's *(Gobius couchii)*
Goby, Giant *(Gobius cobitis)*
Grasshopper, Wart-biter *(Decticus verrucivorus)*
Hatchet Shell, Northern *(Thyasira gouldi)*
Hydroid, Marine *(Clavopsella navis)*
Lagoon Snail *(Paludinella littorina)*
Lagoon Snail, De Folin's *(Caecum armoricum)*
Lagoon Worm, Tentacled *(Alkmaria romijni)*

Leech, Medicinal *(Hirudo medicinalis)*
Lizard, Sand *(Lacerta agilis)*
Lizard, Viviparous *(Lacerta vivipara)*
Marten, Pine *(Martes martes)*
Mat, Trembling Sea *(Victorella pavida)*
Moth, Barberry Carpet *(Pareulype berberata)*
Moth, Black-veined *(Siona lineata* (or *Idaea lineata))*
Moth, Essex Emerald *(Thetidia smaragdaria)*
Moth, Fiery clearwing *(Bembecia chrysidiformis)*
Moth, Fisher's estuarine *(Gortyna borelii)*
Moth, New Forest Burnet *(Zygaena viciae)*
Moth, Reddish Buff *(Acosmetia caliginosa)*
Moth, Sussex Emerald *(Thalera fimbrialis)*
Mussel, Fan *(Atrina fragilis)*
Mussel, Freshwater Pearl *(Margaritifera margaritifera)*
Newt, Great Crested (or Warty) *(Triturus cristatus)*
Newt, Palmate *(Triturus helveticus)*
Newt, Smooth *(Triturus vulgaris)*
Otter, Common *(Lutra lutra)*
Porpoise *(Cetacea)*
Sandworm, Lagoon *(Armandia cirrhosa)*
Sea Fan, Pink *(Eunicella verrucosa)*
Sea Slug, Lagoon *(Tenellia adspersa)*
Shad, Twaite *(alosa fallax)*
Shark, Basking *(Cetorhinus maximus)*
Shrimp, Fairy *(Chirocephalus diaphanus)*
Shrimp, Lagoon Sand *(Gammarus insensibilis)*
Slow-worm *(Anguis fragilis)*
Snail, Glutinous *(Myxas glutinosa)*
Snail, Sandbowl *(Catinella arenaria)*
Snake, Grass *(Natrix natrix (Natrix helvetica))*
Snake, Smooth *(Coronella austriaca)*
Spider, Fen Raft *(Dolomedes plantarius)*
Spider, Ladybird *(Eresus niger)*
Squirrel, Red *(Sciurus vulgaris)*
Sturgeon *(Acipenser sturio)*
Toad, Common *(Bufo bufo)*
Toad, Natterjack *(Bufo calamita)*
Turtle, Marine *(Dermochelyidae* and *Cheloniidae*, all species)
Vendace *(Coregonus albula)*
Vole, Water *(Arvicola terrestris)*
Walrus *(Odobenus rosmarus)*
Whale *(Cetacea)*
Whitefish *(Coregonus lavaretus)*

PLANTS PROTECTED BY SCHEDULE 8

Adder's tongue, Least *(Ophioglossum lusitanicum)*
Alison, Small *(Alyssum alyssoides)*
Anomodon, Long leaved *(Anomodon longifolius)*
Beech-lichen, New Forest *(Enterographa elaborata)*
Blackwort *(Southbya nigrella)*
Bluebell *(Hyacinthoides non-scripta)*
Bolete, Royal *(Boletus regius)*
Broomrape, Bedstraw *(Orobanche caryophyllacea)*
Broomrape, Oxtongue *(Orobanche loricata)*
Broomrape, Thistle *(Orobanche reticulata)*
Cabbage, Lundy *(Rhynchosinapis wrightii)*
Calamint, Wood *(Calamintha sylvatica)*
Caloplaca, Snow *(Caloplaca nivalis)*
Catapyrenium, Tree *(Catapyrenium psoromoides)*
Catchfly, Alpine *(Lychnis alpina)*
Catillaria, Laurer's *(Catellaria laureri)*
Centaury, Slender *(Centaurium tenuiflorum)*
Cinquefoil, Rock *(Potentilla rupestris)*
Cladonia, Convoluted *(Cladonia convoluta)*
Cladonia, Upright Mountain *(Cladonia stricta)*
Clary, Meadow *(Salvia pratensis)*
Club-rush, Triangular *(Scirpus triquetrus)*
Colt's-foot, Purple *(Homogyne alpina)*
Cotoneaster, Wild *(Cotoneaster integerrimus)*
Cottongrass, Slender *(Eriophorum gracile)*
Cow-wheat, Field *(Melampyrum arvense)*
Crocus, Sand *(Romulea columnae)*
Crystalwort, Lizard *(Riccia bifurca)*
Cudweed, Broad-leaved *(Filago pyramidata)*
Cudweed, Jersey *(Gnaphalium luteoalbum)*
Cudweed, Red-tipped *(Filago lutescens)*
Cut-grass *(Leersia oryzoides)*
Deptford Pink (England and Wales only) *(Dianthus armeria)*
Diapensia *(Diapensia lapponica)*
Dock, Shore *(Rumex rupestris)*
Earwort, Marsh *(Jamesoniella undulifolia)*
Eryngo, Field *(Eryngium campestre)*
Feather-moss, Polar *(Hygrohypnum polare)*
Fern, Dickie's bladder *(Cystopteris dickieana)*
Fern, Killarney *(Trichomanes speciosum)*
Flapwort, Norfolk *(Leiocolea rutheana)*
Fleabane, Alpine *(Erigeron borealis)*
Fleabane, Small *(Pulicaria vulgaris)*
Frostwort, Pointed *(Gymnomitrion apiculatum)*
Fungus, Hedgehog *(Hericium erinaceum)*
Galingale, Brown *(Cyperus fuscus)*
Gentian, Alpine *(Gentiana nivalis)*
Gentian, Dune *(Gentianella uliginosa)*
Gentian, Early *(Gentianella anglica)*
Gentian, Fringed *(Gentianella ciliata)*
Gentian, Spring *(Gentiana verna)*
Germander, Cut-leaved *(Teucrium botrys)*
Germander, Water *(Teucrium scordium)*
Gladiolus, Wild *(Gladiolus illyricus)*
Goblin Lights *(Catolechia wahlenbergii)*
Goosefoot, Stinking *(Chenopodium vulvaria)*
Grass-poly *(Lythrum hyssopifolia)*
Grimmia, Blunt-leaved *(Grimmia unicolor)*
Gyalecta, Elm *(Gyalecta ulmi)*
Hare's-ear, Sickle-leaved *(Bupleurum falcatum)*
Hare's-ear, Small *(Bupleurum baldense)*
Hawk's-beard, Stinking *(Crepis foetida)*
Hawkweed, Northroe *(Hieracium northroense)*
Hawkweed, Shetland *(Hieracium zetlandicum)*
Hawkweed, Weak-leaved *(Hieracium attenuatifolium)*
Heath, Blue *(Phyllodoce caerulea)*
Helleborine, Red *(Cephalanthera rubra)*
Helleborine, Young's *(Epipactis youngiana)*
Horsetail, Branched *(Equisetum ramosissimum)*
Hound's-tongue, Green *(Cynoglossum germanicum)*
Knawel, Perennial *(Scleranthus perennis)*
Knotgrass, Sea *(Polygonum maritimum)*
Lady's-slipper *(Cypripedium calceolus)*
Lecanactis, Churchyard *(Lecanactis hemisphaerica)*
Lecanora, Tarn *(Lecanora archariana)*
Lecidea, Copper *(Lecidea inops)*
Leek, Round-headed *(Allium sphaerocephalon)*
Lettuce, Least *(Lactuca saligna)*
Lichen, Arctic kidney *(Nephroma arcticum)*
Lichen, Ciliate strap *(Heterodermia leucomelos)*
Lichen, Coralloid rosette *(Heterodermia propagulifera)*
Lichen, Ear-lobed dog *(Peltigera lepidophora)*
Lichen, Forked hair *(Bryoria furcellata)*
Lichen, Golden hair *(Teloschistes flavicans)*
Lichen, Orange fruited Elm *(Caloplaca luteoalba)*
Lichen, River jelly *(Collema dichotomum)*
Lichen, Scaly breck *(Squamarina lentigera)*
Lichen, Stary breck *(Buellia asterella)*
Lily, Snowdon *(Lloydia serotina)*

Liverwort *(Petallophyllum ralfsi)*
Liverwort, Lindenberg's Leafy *(Adelanthus lindenbergianus)*
Marsh-mallow, Rough *(Althaea hirsuta)*
Marshwort, Creeping *(Apium repens)*
Milk-parsley, Cambridge *(Selinum carvifolia)*
Moss *(Drepanocladius vernicosus)*
Moss, Alpine copper *(Mielichoferia mielichoferi)*
Moss, Baltic bog *(Sphagnum balticum)*
Moss, Blue dew *(Saelania glaucescens)*
Moss, Blunt-leaved bristle *(Orthotrichum obtusifolium)*
Moss, Bright green cave *(Cyclodictyon laetevirens)*
Moss, Cordate beard *(Barbula cordata)*
Moss, Cornish path *(Ditrichum cornubicum)*
Moss, Derbyshire feather *(Thamnobryum angustifolium)*
Moss, Dune thread *(Bryum mamillatum)*
Moss, Flamingo *(Desmatodon cernuus)*
Moss, Glaucous beard *(Barbula glauca)*
Moss, Green shield *(Buxbaumia viridis)*
Moss, Hair silk *(Plagiothecium piliferum)*
Moss, Knothole *(Zygodon forsteri)*
Moss, Large yellow feather *(Scorpidium turgescens)*
Moss, Millimetre *(Micromitrium tenerum)*
Moss, Multifruited river *(Cryphaea lamyana)*
Moss, Nowell's limestone *(Zygodon gracilis)*
Moss, Rigid apple *(Bartramia stricta)*
Moss, Round-leaved feather *(Rhyncostegium rotundifolium)*
Moss, Schleicher's thread *(Bryum schleicheri)*
Moss, Triangular pygmy *(Acaulon triquetrum)*
Moss, Vaucher's feather *(Hypnum vaucheri)*
Mudwort, Welsh *(Limosella austeralis)*
Naiad, Holly-leaved *(Najas marina)*
Naiad, Slender *(Najas flexilis)*
Orache, Stalked *(Halimione pedunculata)*
Orchid, Early spider *(Ophrys sphegodes)*
Orchid, Fen *(Liparis loeselii)*
Orchid, Ghost *(Epipogium aphyllum)*
Orchid, Lapland marsh *(Dactylorhiza lapponica)*
Orchid, Late spider *(Ophrys fuciflora)*
Orchid, Lizard *(Himantoglossum hircinum)*
Orchid, Military *(Orchis militaris)*
Orchid, Monkey *(Orchis simia)*
Pannaria, Caledonia *(Panneria ignobilis)*
Parmelia, New Forest *(Parmelia minarum)*
Parmentaria, Oil stain *(Parmentaria chilensis)*
Pear, Plymouth *(Pyrus cordata)*
Penny-cress, Perfoliate *(Thlaspi perfoliatum)*
Pennyroyal *(Mentha pulegium)*
Pertusaria, Alpine moss *(Pertusaria bryontha)*
Physcia, Southern grey *(Physcia tribacioides)*
Pigmyweed *(Crassula aquatica)*
Pine, Ground *(Ajuga chamaepitys)*
Pink, Cheddar *(Dianthus gratianopolitanus)*
Pink, Childing *(Petroraghia nanteuilii)*
Plantain, Floating water *(Luronium natans)*
Polypore, Oak *(Buglossoporus pulvinus)*
Pseudocyphellaria, Ragged *(Pseudocyphellaria lacerata)*
Psora, Rusty Alpine *(Psora rubiformis)*
Puffball, Sandy Stilt *(Battarraea phalloides)*
Ragwort, Fen *(Senecio paludosus)*
Ramping-fumitory, Martin's *(Fumaria martinii)*
Rampion, Spiked *(Phyteuma spicatum)*
Restharrow, Small *(Ononis reclinata)*
Rock-cress, Alpine *(Arabis alpina)*
Rock-cress, Bristol *(Arabis stricta)*
Rustwort, Western *(Marsupella profunda)*
Sandwort, Norwegian *(Arenaria norvegica)*
Sandwort, Teesdale *(Minuartia stricta)*
Saxifrage, Drooping *(Saxifraga cernua)*
Saxifrage, Marsh *(Saxifrage hirulus)*
Saxifrage, Tufted *(Saxifraga cespitosa)*
Solenopsora, Serpentine *(Solenopsora liparina)*
Solomon's-seal, Whorled *(Polygonatum verticillatum)*
Sow-thistle, Alpine *(Cicerbita alpina)*
Spearwort, Adder's-tongue *(Ranunculus ophioglossifolius)*
Speedwell, Fingered *(Veronica triphyllos)*
Speedwell, Spiked *(Veronica spicata)*
Spike rush, Dwarf *(Eleocharis parvula)*
Stack Fleawort, South *(Tephroseris integrifolia (ssp maritima))*
Star-of-Bethlehem, Early *(Gagea bohemica)*
Starfruit *(Damasonium alisma)*
Stonewort, Bearded *(Chara canescens)*
Stonewort, Foxtail *(Lamprothamnium papulosum)*
Strapwort *(Corrigiola litoralis)*
Sulphur-tresses, Alpine *(Alectoria ochroleuca)*
Threadmoss, Long-leaved *(Bryum neodamense)*
Turpswort *(Geocalyx graveolens)*
Violet, Fen *(Viola persicifolia)*
Viper's-grass *(Scorzonera humilis)*
Water-plantain, Ribbon-leaved *(Alisma gramineum)*
Wood-sedge, Starved *(Carex depauperata)*
Woodsia, Alpine *(Woodsia alpina)*
Woodsia, Oblong *(Woodsia ilvenis)*
Wormwood, Field *(Artemisia campestris)*
Woundwort, Downy *(Stachys germanica)*
Woundwort, Limestone *(Stachys alpina)*
Yellow-rattle, Greater *(Rhinanthus serotinus)*

MOST UNDER THREAT

The animals and birds considered to be most under threat in Great Britain by the Joint Nature Conservation Committee are the high brown fritillary butterfly; violet click beetle; new forest burnet moth; corncrake; aquatic warbler; tree sparrow; wryneck; water vole; red squirrel; allis shad; and twaite shad.

HISTORIC BUILDINGS AND MONUMENTS

Under the Planning (Listed Buildings and Conservation Areas) Act 1990, the Secretary of State for Culture, Media and Sport has a statutory duty to compile lists of buildings or groups of buildings in England which are of special architectural or historic interest. Under the Ancient Monuments and Archaeological Areas Act 1979 as amended by the National Heritage Act 1983, the Secretary of State is also responsible for compiling a schedule of ancient monuments. Decisions are taken on the advice of English Heritage.

Listed buildings are classified into Grade I, Grade II* and Grade II. There are currently about 370,000 individual listed buildings in England, of which about 92 per cent are Grade II listed. Almost all pre-1700 buildings are listed, and most buildings of 1700 to 1840. English Heritage carries out thematic surveys of particular types of buildings with a view to making recommendations for listing, and members of the public may propose a building for consideration. The main purpose of listing is to ensure that care is taken in deciding the future of a building. No changes which affect the architectural or historic character of a listed building can be made without listed building consent (in addition to planning permission where relevant). Applications for listed building consent are normally dealt with by the local planning authority, although English Heritage is always consulted about proposals affecting Grade I and Grade II* properties. It is a criminal offence to demolish a listed building, or alter it in such a way as to affect its character, without consent.

There are currently about 18,300 scheduled monuments in England. English Heritage is carrying out a Monuments Protection Programme assessing archaeological sites with a view to making recommendations for scheduling, and members of the public may propose a monument for consideration. All monuments proposed for scheduling are considered to be of national importance. Where buildings are both scheduled and listed, ancient monuments legislation takes precedence. The main purpose of scheduling a monument is to preserve it for the future and to protect it from damage, destruction or any unnecessary interference. Once a monument has been scheduled, scheduled monument consent is required before any works can be carried out. The scope of the control is more extensive and more detailed than that applied to listed buildings, but certain minor works, as detailed in the Ancient Monuments (Class Consents) Order 1994, may be carried out without consent. It is a criminal offence to carry out unauthorised work to scheduled monuments.

Under the Planning (Listed Buildings and Conservation Areas) Act 1990 and the Ancient Monuments and Archaeological Areas Act 1979, the Secretary of State for Wales is responsible for listing buildings and scheduling monuments in Wales on the advice of CADW, the Historic Buildings Council for Wales and the Royal Commission on the Ancient and Historical Monuments of Wales. The criteria for evaluating buildings are similar to those in England and the same listing system is used. There are approximately 26,400 listed buildings and approximately 3,500 scheduled monuments in Wales.

Under the Planning (Listed Buildings and Conservation Areas) (Scotland) Act 1997 and the Ancient Monuments and Archaeological Areas Act 1979, Scottish Ministers are responsible for listing buildings and scheduling monuments in Scotland on the advice of Historic Scotland, the Historic Buildings Council for Scotland and the Royal Commission on the Ancient and Historical Monuments of Scotland. The criteria for evaluating buildings are similar to those in England but an A, B, C categorisation is used. There are approximately 46,000 listed buildings and 6,500 scheduled monuments in Scotland.

Under the Planning (Northern Ireland) Order 1991 and the Historic Monuments and Archaeological Objects (Northern Ireland) Order 1995, the Department of the Environment of the Northern Ireland Executive is responsible for listing buildings and scheduling monuments in Northern Ireland on the advice of the Historic Buildings Council for Northern Ireland and the Historic Monuments Council for Northern Ireland. The criteria for evaluating buildings are similar to those in England but no statutory grading system is used. There are approximately 8,500 listed buildings and 1,500 scheduled monuments in Northern Ireland.

OPENING TO THE PUBLIC

The following is a selection of the many historic buildings and monuments open to the public. Admission charges and opening hours vary. Many properties are closed in winter (usually November–March) and some are also closed in the mornings. Most properties are closed on Christmas Eve, Christmas Day, Boxing Day and New Year's Day, and many are closed on Good Friday. During the winter season, many English Heritage monuments are closed on Mondays and Tuesdays and monuments in the care of CADW are closed on Sunday mornings. In Northern Ireland many monuments are closed on Mondays except on bank holidays. Information about a specific property should be checked by telephone or online.

ENGLAND

For more information on any of the English Heritage properties listed below, the official website is:
www.english-heritage.org.uk
For more information on any of the National Trust properties listed below, the official website is:
www.nationaltrust.org.uk
EH English Heritage property
NT National Trust property

A LA RONDE (NT), Summer Lane, Exmouth, Devon EX8 5BD
T 01395-265514
Unique 16-sided house completed *c.*1796

ALNWICK CASTLE, Northumberland NE66 1NQ
T 01665-510777 W www.alnwickcastle.com
Seat of the Dukes of Northumberland since 1309; Italian Renaissance-style interior. Gardens with spectacular water features

ALTHORP, Northants NN7 4HQ T 0870-167 9000
W www.althorp.com
Spencer family seat. Diana, Princess of Wales memorabilia

ANGLESEY ABBEY (NT), Cambridge CB5 9EJ
T 01223-810080

House built c.1600. Houses many paintings and a unique clock collection. Gardens and Lode Mill

APSLEY HOUSE, London W1J 7NT T 020-7499 5676 W www.apsleyhouse.org.uk
Built by Robert Adam 1771–8, home of the Dukes of Wellington since 1817 and known as 'No. 1 London'. Collection of fine and decorative arts

ARUNDEL CASTLE, W. Sussex BN18 9AB T 01903-883173 W www.arundelcastle.org
Castle dating from the Norman Conquest. Seat of the Dukes of Norfolk

AVEBURY (NT), Wilts SN8 1RF T 01672-539250
Remains of stone circles constructed 4,000 years ago surrounding the later village of Avebury

BANQUETING HOUSE, Whitehall, London SW1A 2ER T 0870-751 5178 W www.hrp.org.uk
Designed by Inigo Jones; ceiling paintings by Rubens. Site of the execution of Charles I

BASILDON PARK (NT), Reading RG8 9NR T 0118-984 3040
Palladian house built in 1776–83 by John Carr

BATTLE ABBEY (EH), E. Sussex T 01424-773792 Remains of the abbey founded by William the Conqueror on the site of the Battle of Hastings

BEAULIEU, Hants SO42 7ZN T 01590-612345 W www.beaulieu.co.uk
House and gardens, Beaulieu Abbey and exhibition of monastic life, National Motor Museum

BEESTON CASTLE (EH), Cheshire CW6 9TX T 01829-260464. Thirteenth-century inner ward with gatehouse and towers, and remains of outer ward built by Ranulf sixth Earl of Chester

BELTON HOUSE (NT), Leics NG32 2LS T 01476-566116
Fine 17th-century house, formal gardens in landscaped park

BELVOIR CASTLE, Leics NG32 1PD T 01476-871000 W www.belvoircastle.com.
Seat of the Dukes of Rutland; 19th-century Gothic-style castle

BERKELEY CASTLE, Glos GL13 9BQ T 01453-810332
Completed 1153; site of the murder of Edward II (1327)

BLENHEIM PALACE, Woodstock, Oxon OX20 1PX T 0870-060 2080 W www.blenheimpalace.com
Seat of the Dukes of Marlborough and Winston Churchill's birthplace; designed by Vanbrugh

BLICKLING HALL (NT), Norwich NR11 6NF T 01263-738030
Jacobean house with state rooms, temple and 18th-century orangery

BODIAM CASTLE (NT), E. Sussex TN32 5UA T 01580-830436
Well-preserved medieval moated castle, built 1385

BOLSOVER CASTLE (EH), Derbys S44 6PR T 01246-822844
Notable 17th-century buildings

BOSCOBEL HOUSE (EH), Shropshire T 01902-850244
Timber-framed 17th-century hunting lodge, refuge of fugitive Charles II

BOUGHTON HOUSE, Northants NN14 1BJ T 01536-515731 W www.boughtonhouse.org.uk
A 17th-century house with French-style additions. Home of the Dukes of Buccleuch and Queensbury

BOWOOD HOUSE, Wilts SN11 0PQ T 01249-812102 W www.bowood-house.co.uk
An 18th-century house in Capability Brown park, with lake, temple and arboretum

BROADLANDS, Hants SO51 9ZD T 01794-505010 W www.broadlands.net
Palladian mansion in Capability Brown parkland. Mountbatten exhibition

BRONTË PARSONAGE, Haworth, W. Yorks BD22 8DR T 01535-642323 W www.bronte.org,uk
Home of the Brontë sisters; museum and memorabilia

BUCKFAST ABBEY, Devon TQ11 0EE T 01364-642500 W www.buckfast.org.uk
Benedictine monastery on medieval foundations

BUCKINGHAM PALACE, London SW1A 1AA T 020-7839 1377 W www.royal.gov.uk
Purchased by George III in 1762, the Sovereign's official London residence since 1837. Eighteen state rooms, including the Throne Room, and Picture Gallery

BUCKLAND ABBEY (NT), Devon PL20 6EY T 01822-853607
A 13th-century Cistercian monastery. Home of Sir Francis Drake

BURGHLEY HOUSE, Stamford, Lincs T 01780-752451 W www.burghley.co.uk
Late Elizabethan house built by William Cecil, first Lord Burghley

CALKE ABBEY (NT), Derbys DE73 1LE T 01332-863822
Baroque 18th-century mansion

CARISBROOKE CASTLE (EH), Isle of Wight PO30 1XY T 01983-522107 W www.carisbrookecastlemuseum.org.uk
Norman castle; prison of Charles I 1647–8

CARLISLE CASTLE (EH), Cumbria CA3 8UR T 01228-591922
Medieval castle, prison of Mary Queen of Scots

CARLYLE'S HOUSE (NT), Cheyne Row, London SW3 5HL T 020-7352 7087
Home of Thomas Carlyle

CASTLE ACRE PRIORY (EH), Norfolk T 01760-755394
Remains include 12th-century church and prior's lodgings

CASTLE DROGO (NT), Devon EX6 6PB T 01647-433306
Granite castle designed by Lutyens

CASTLE HOWARD, N. Yorks YO60 7DA T 01653-648444 W www.castlehoward.co.uk
Designed by Vanbrugh 1699–1726; mausoleum designed by Hawksmoor

CASTLE RISING (EH), Norfolk T 01553-631330
A 12th-century keep in a massive earthwork with gate-house and bridge

CHARTWELL (NT), Kent TN16 1PS T 01732-868381
Home of Sir Winston Churchill

CHATSWORTH, Derbys DE45 1PP T 01246-582204 W www.chatsworth-house.co.uk
Tudor mansion in magnificent parkland

CHESTERS ROMAN FORT (EH), Northumberland T 01434-681379
Roman cavalry fort

CHYSAUSTER ANCIENT VILLAGE (EH), Cornwall T 07831-757934 Remains of Celtic settlement. Eight stone-walled homesteads

CLIFFORD'S TOWER (EH), York T 01904-646940
A 13th-century tower built on a mound

CLIVEDEN (NT), Maidenhead SL6 0JA T 01628-605069
Former home of the Astors, now a hotel set in garden and woodland

CORBRIDGE ROMAN SITE (EH), Northumberland T 01434-632349
Excavated central area of a Roman town and successive military bases

CORFE CASTLE (NT), Wareham BH20 5EZ T 01929-481294
Ruined former royal castle dating from 11th-century

CROFT CASTLE (NT), Herefordshire HR6 9PW T 01568-780246
Pre-Conquest border castle with Georgian-Gothic interi

DEAL CASTLE (EH), Kent T 01304-372762
Largest of the coastal defence forts built by Henry VIII

DICKENS'S HOUSE, 48 Doughty Street, London WC1N 2LX T 020-7405 2127 W www.dickensmuseum.com
House occupied by Charles Dickens 1837–9; manuscripts, furniture and portraits

DOVE COTTAGE, Grasmere, Cumbria LA22 9SH T 01539-435544 W www.wordsworth.org.uk
Wordsworth's home 1799–1808; museum

DOVER CASTLE (EH), Kent CT16 1HU T 01304-201628
Castle with Roman, Saxon and Norman features; wartime operations rooms

DR JOHNSON'S HOUSE, 17 Gough Square, London EC4A 3DE T 020-7353 3745 W www.drjh.dircon.co.uk
Home of Samuel Johnson

DUNSTANBURGH CASTLE (EH), Northumberland T 01665-576231
A 14th-century castle on a cliff, with a substantial gatehouse-keep

ELTHAM PALACE (EH), Court Yard, Eltham, London SE9 5QE T 020-8294 2548
Combines an Art Deco country house and remains of medieval palace set in moated gardens.

FARLEIGH HUNGERFORD CASTLE (EH), Somerset BA2 7RS T 01225-754026
Late 14th-century castle with two courts; chapel with tomb of Sir Thomas Hungerford

FARNHAM CASTLE KEEP (EH), Surrey GU9 0AG T 01252-713393
Large 12th-century Motte and Bailey

FOUNTAINS ABBEY (NT), nr Ripon, N. Yorks HG4 3DY T 01765-608888 W www.fountainsabbey.org.uk
Deer park, visitor centre and St Church. Ruined Cistercian monastery; 18th-century landscaped gardens of Studley Royal estate

FRAMLINGHAM CASTLE (EH), Suffolk T 01728-724189 W www.framlingham.com
Castle (*c*.1200) with high curtain walls enclosing an almshouse (1639)

FURNESS ABBEY (EH), Cumbria T 01229-823420
Remains of church and conventual buildings founded in 1123

GLASTONBURY ABBEY, Somerset BA6 9EL T 01458-832267 W www.glastonburyabbey.com
Ruins of a 12th-century abbey rebuilt after fire. Site of an early Christian settlement

GOODRICH CASTLE (EH), Herefordshire T 01600-890538
Remains of 13th- and 14th-century castle with 12th-century keep

GREENWICH, London SE10 T 020-8858 6565 W www.rog.nmm.ac.uk
Former Royal Observatory (founded 1675) housing the time ball and zero meridian of longitude. The Queen's House. T 020-8858 4422. Designed for Queen Anne, wife of James I, by Inigo Jones. Painted Hall and Chapel (Royal Naval College)

GRIMES GRAVES (EH), Norfolk T 01842-810656
Neolithic flint mines. One shaft can be descended

GUILDHALL, London EC2P 2EJ T 020-7606 3030
Centre of civic government of the City. Built *c*.1441; facade built 1788–9

HADDON HALL, Derbys DE45 1LA T 01629-812855 W www.haddonhall.co.uk
Well-preserved 12th-century manor house

HAILES ABBEY (EH), Glos GL54 5PB T 01242-602398
Ruins of a 13th-century Cistercian monastery

HAM HOUSE (NT), Richmond, Surrey TW10 7RS T 020-8940 1950
Stuart house with fine interiors

HAMPTON COURT PALACE, East Molesey, Surrey KT8 9AU T 0870-752 7777 W www.hrp.org.uk
A 16th-century palace with additions by Wren. Gardens with maze; Tudor tennis court (summer only)

HARDWICK HALL (NT), Derbys S44 5QJ T 01246-850430
Built 1591–7 for Bess of Hardwick; notable furnishings

HARDY'S COTTAGE (NT), Dorset DT2 8QJ T 01305-262366
Birthplace and home of Thomas Hardy

HAREWOOD HOUSE, W. Yorks LS17 9LQ T 0113-218 1010
An 18th-century house designed by John Carr and Robert Adam; park by Capability Brown

HATFIELD HOUSE, Herts AL9 5NQ T 01707-287000 W www.hatfield-house.co.uk
Jacobean house built by Robert Cecil; surviving wing of Royal Palace of Hatfield (1497)

HELMSLEY CASTLE (EH), N. Yorks YO62 5AB T 01439-770442
A 12th-century keep and curtain wall with 16th-century buildings. Spectacular earthwork defences

HEVER CASTLE, Kent TN8 7NG T 01732-865224 W www.hevercastle.co.uk
A 13th-century double-moated castle, childhood home of Anne Boleyn

HOLKER HALL, Cumbria LA11 7PL T 01539-558328 W www.holker-hall.co.uk
Former home of the Dukes of Devonshire; award-winning gardens

HOLKHAM HALL, Norfolk NR23 1AB T 01328-710227 W www.holkham.co.uk
Fine Palladian mansion

HOUSESTEADS ROMAN FORT (EH), Northumberland. T 01434-344363 W www.hadrians-wall.org
Excavated infantry fort on Hadrian's Wall with extra-mural civilian settlement

HUGHENDEN MANOR (NT), High Wycombe HP14 4LA T 01494-755565
Home of Disraeli; small formal garden

JANE AUSTEN'S HOUSE, Chawton, Hants GU34 1SD T 01420-83262 Jane Austen's home 1809–17

KEDLESTON HALL (NT), Derby DE22 5JH T 01332-842191
A classical Palladian mansion built 1759–65; complete Robert Adam interiors.

KELMSCOTT MANOR, nr Lechlade, Glos GL7 3HJ T 01367-252486 W www.kelmscottmanor.co.uk
Summer home of William Morris, with products of Morris and Co.

KENILWORTH CASTLE (EH), Warks CV8 1NE T 01926-852078 Largest castle ruin in England

KENSINGTON PALACE, London W8 4PX T 0870-751 5170 W www.hrp.org.uk
Built in 1605 and enlarged by Wren; bought by William and Mary in 1689. Birthplace of Queen Victoria. Royal Ceremonial Dress Collection

KENWOOD HOUSE (EH), Hampstead Lane, London NW3 7JR T 020-8348 1286
Adam villa housing the Iveagh bequest of paintings and furniture

KEW, Surrey TW9 3AB T 020-8332 5655 W www.rbgkew.org.uk Queen Charlotte's Cottage

KINGSTON LACY (NT), Dorset BH21 4EA T 01202-882402
A 17th-century house with 19th-century alterations; important art collection

KNEBWORTH HOUSE, Herts SG3 6PY T 01438-812661 W www.knebworthhouse.com
Tudor manor house concealed by 19th-century Gothic decoration; Lutyens gardens

KNOLE (NT), Kent TN15 0RP T 01732-450608
House dating from 1456 set in parkland; fine art treasures

LAMBETH PALACE, London SE1 7JU T 020-7898 1200
W www.archbishopofcanterbury.org. Official residence of the Archbishop of Canterbury. A 19th-century house with parts dating from the 12th-century

LANERCOST PRIORY (EH), Cumbria CA8 2HQ
T 01697-73030
The nave of the Augustinian priory church, c.1166, is still used; remains of other claustral buildings

LANHYDROCK (NT), Cornwall PL30 5AD T 01208-265950
House dating from the 17th-century; 45 rooms, including kitchen and nursery

LEEDS CASTLE, Kent ME17 1PL T 01622-765400
W www.leeds-castle.com
Castle dating from 9th-century, on two islands in lake

LEVENS HALL, Cumbria LA8 0PD T 01539-560321
W www.levenshall.co.uk
Elizabethan house with unique topiary garden (1694). Steam engine collection

LINCOLN CASTLE LN1 3AA T 01522-511068
Built by William the Conqueror in 1068

LINDISFARNE PRIORY (EH), Northumberland.
T 01289-389200
Founded in AD 635; re-established in the 12th-century as a Benedictine priory, now ruined

LITTLE MORETON HALL (NT), Cheshire CW12 4SD
T 01260-272018 Timber-framed moated manor house with knot garden

LONGLEAT HOUSE, Wilts BA12 7NW T 01985-844400
W www.longleat.co.uk
Elizabethan house in Italian Renaissance style

LULLINGSTONE ROMAN VILLA (EH), Kent.
T 01322-863467
Large villa occupied for much of the Roman period; fine mosaics

MANSION HOUSE, London EC4N 8BH T 020-7626 2500
W www.cityoflondon.gov.uk
The official residence of the Lord Mayor of London

MARBLE HILL HOUSE (EH), Twickenham, Middx TW1 2NL
T 020-8892 5115 English Palladian villa with Georgian paintings and furniture

MICHELHAM PRIORY, E. Sussex T 01323-844224
Tudor house built onto an Augustinian priory

MIDDLEHAM CASTLE (EH), N. Yorks DL8 4QR
T 01969-623899
A 12th-century keep within later fortifications. Childhood home of Richard III

MONTACUTE HOUSE (NT), Somerset TA15 6XP
T 01935-823289
Elizabethan house with National Portrait Gallery. Portraits from the period

MOUNT GRACE PRIORY (EH), N. Yorks DL6 3JG
T 01609-883494. Carthusian monastery, with remains of monastic buildings

NETLEY ABBEY (EH), Hants SO31 5GA T 023-9258 1059
Remains of 13th-century Cistercian abbey, used as house in Tudor period

OLD SARUM (EH), Wilts. T 01722-335398
Earthworks enclosing remains of the castle and the 11th-century cathedral

ORFORD CASTLE (EH), Suffolk. T 01394-450472
Circular keep of c.1170 and remains of coastal defence castle built by Henry II

OSBORNE HOUSE (EH), Isle of Wight. T 01983-200022
Queen Victoria's seaside residence

OSTERLEY PARK HOUSE (NT), Isleworth, Middx TW7 4RB
T 020-8232 5050 W www.osterleypark.org.uk
Elizabethan mansion set in parkland

PENDENNIS CASTLE (EH), Cornwall. T 01326-316594
Well-preserved 16th-century coastal defence castle

PENSHURST PLACE, Kent TN11 8DG T 01892-870307
W www.penhurstplace.com
House with medieval Baron's Hall and 14th-century gardens

PETWORTH (NT), W. Sussex GU28 0AE T 01798-343929
Late 17th-century house set in Capability Brown landscaped park

PEVENSEY CASTLE (EH), E. Sussex. T 01323-762604
Walls of a 4th-century Roman fort; remains of an 11th-century castle

PEVERIL CASTLE (EH), Derbys S33 8WQ T 01433-620613
A 12th-century castle defended on two sides by precipitous rocks

POLESDEN LACEY (NT), Surrey RH5 6BD T 01372-458203
Regency villa remodelled in the Edwardian era. Fine paintings and furnishings

PORTCHESTER CASTLE (EH), Hants PO3 5LY
T 023-9237 8291 Walls of a late Roman fort enclosing a Norman keep and an Augustinian priory church

POWDERHAM CASTLE, Devon EX6 8JQ T 01626-890243
W www.powderham.co.uk
Medieval castle with 18th- and 19th-century alterations. Historic home of the Earl of Devon

RABY CASTLE, Co. Durham DL2 3AH T 01833-660202
W www.rabycastle.com
A 14th-century castle with walled gardens

RAGLEY HALL, Warks B49 5NJ T 01789-762090
W www.ragleyhall.com
A 17th-century house with gardens, park and lake

RICHBOROUGH ROMAN FORT (EH), Kent.
T 01304-612013. Landing-site of the Claudian invasion in AD 43

RICHMOND CASTLE (EH), N. Yorks. T 01748-822493
A 12th-century keep with 11th-century curtain wall and domestic buildings

RIEVAULX ABBEY (EH), N. Yorks YO6 5LB T 01439-798228
Remains of a Cistercian abbey founded c.1132

ROCHESTER CASTLE (EH), Kent ME1 1SX T 01634-402276
An 11th-century castle partly on the Roman city wall, with a square keep of c.1130

ROCKINGHAM CASTLE, Leics LE16 8TH T 01536-770240
W www.rockinghamcastle.com
Built by William the Conqueror

ROYAL PAVILION, Brighton BN1 1EE T 01273-290900
Palace of George IV, in Chinese style with Indian exterior and Regency gardens

RUFFORD OLD HALL (NT), Lancs L40 1SG T 01704-821254
A 16th-century hall with unique screen

ST AUGUSTINE'S ABBEY (EH), Kent T 01227-767345
Remains of Benedictine monastery, with Norman church, on site of abbey founded AD 597 by St Augustine

ST MAWES CASTLE (EH), Cornwall TR2 3AA
T 01326-270526. Coastal defence castle built by Henry VIII

ST MICHAEL'S MOUNT (NT), Cornwall TR17 0EF
T 01736-710265
A 12th-century castle with later additions, off the coast at Marazion

SANDRINGHAM, Norfolk PE35 6EN T 01553-772675
W www.sandringhamestate.co.uk
The Queen's private residence; a neo-Jacobean house built in 1870

SCARBOROUGH CASTLE (EH), N. Yorks T 01723-372451
Remains of 12th-century keep and curtain walls

SHERBORNE CASTLE, Dorset DT9 3PY T 01935-813182 W www.sherbornecastle.com. Sixteenth-century castle built by Sir Walter Raleigh set in landscaped gardens

SHUGBOROUGH (NT), Staffs ST17 0XB T 01889-881388 House set in 18th-century park with monuments, temples and pavilions in the Greek Revival style. Seat of the Earls of Lichfield

SKIPTON CASTLE, N. Yorks BD23 1AQ T 01756-792442 W www.skiptoncastle.co.uk D-shaped castle with six round towers and beautiful inner courtyard

SMALLHYTHE PLACE (NT), Kent TN30 7NG T 01580-762334 Half-timbered 16th-century house; home of Ellen Terry 1899–1928. Barn Theatre

STANFORD HALL, Leics LE17 6DH T 01788-860250 W www.stanfordhall.co.uk William and Mary house with Stuart portraits. Motorcycle museum

STONEHENGE (EH), Wilts T 01980-624715 Prehistoric monument consisting of concentric stone circles surrounded by a ditch and bank

STONOR PARK, Oxon RG9 6HF T 01491-638587 W www.stonor.com Medieval house with Georgian facade. Centre of Roman Catholicism after the Reformation

STOURHEAD (NT), Wilts BA12 6QD T 01747-841152 English Palladian mansion with famous gardens

STRATFIELD SAYE HOUSE, Hants RG7 2BT T 01256-882882 W www.stratfield-saye.co.uk House built 1630–40; home of the Dukes of Wellington since 1817

STRATFORD-UPON-AVON, Warks. Shakespeare's Birthplace Trust with Shakespeare Centre; Anne Hathaway's Cottage, home of Shakespeare's wife; Mary Arden's House, home of Shakespeare's mother; Nash's House and New Place, where Shakespeare died; and Hall's Croft, home of Shakespeare's daughter. T 01789-204016 W www.shakespeare.org.uk Also Grammar School attended by Shakespeare, Holy Trinity Church, where Shakespeare is buried, Royal Shakespeare Theatre (burnt down 1926, rebuilt 1932) and Swan Theatre (opened 1986)

SUDELEY CASTLE, Glos GL54 5JD T 01242-602308 W www.sudeleycastle.co.uk Castle built in 1442; restored in the 19th-century

SULGRAVE MANOR, nr Banbury OX17 2SD T 01295-760205 W www.sulgravemanor.org.uk Home of George Washington's family

SYON HOUSE, Brentford, Middx TW8 8JF T 020-8560 0881 W www.syonpark.co.uk Built on the site of a former monastery; Adam interior; Capability Brown parkland

TILBURY FORT (EH), Essex RM18 7NR T 01375-858489 A 17th-century coastal fort

TINTAGEL CASTLE (EH), Cornwall T 01840-770328 A 12th-century cliff-top castle and Dark Age settlement site; linked with Arthurian legend

TOWER OF LONDON, London EC3N 4AB T 0870-756 6060 W www.hrp.org.uk. Royal palace and fortress begun by William the Conqueror in 1078. Houses the Crown Jewels

TRERICE (NT), Cornwall TR8 4PG T 01637-875404 Elizabethan manor house

TYNEMOUTH PRIORY AND CASTLE (EH), Tyne and Wear. T 0191-257 1090. Remains of a Benedictine priory, founded *c.*1090, on Saxon monastic site

UPPARK (NT), W. Sussex GU31 5QR T 01730-825857 Late 17th-century house, completely restored after fire. Fetherstonhaugh art collection

WALMER CASTLE (EH), Kent T 01304-364288 One of Henry VIII's coastal defence castles, now the residence of the Lord Warden of the Cinque Ports

WALTHAM ABBEY (EH), Essex. T 01992-702200 Ruined abbey including the nave of the abbey church, 'Harold's Bridge' and late 14th-century gatehouse. Traditionally the burial place of Harold II (1066)

WARKWORTH CASTLE (EH), Northumberland T 01665-711423 A 15th-century keep amidst earlier ruins, with 14th-century hermitage upstream

WARWICK CASTLE Warks CV34 4QU T 0870-442 200 W www.warwick-castle.co.uk Medieval castle with Madame Tussaud's waxworks, in Capability Brown parkland

WHITBY ABBEY (EH), N. Yorks T 01947-603568 Remains of Norman church on the site of a monastery founded in AD 657

WILTON HOUSE, Wilts SP2 0BJ T 01722-746720 W www.wiltonhouse.co.uk A 17th-century house on the site of a Tudor house and 9th Century nunnery

WINDSOR CASTLE, Berks SL4 1NJ T 020-7321 2233 W www.royal.gov.uk Official residence of The Queen; oldest royal residence still in regular use. Also *St George's Chapel*

WOBURN ABBEY, Beds MK17 9WA T 01525-290666 W www.woburnabbey.co.uk Built on the site of a Cistercian abbey; seat of the Dukes of Bedford. Important art collection; antiques centre

WROXETER ROMAN CITY (EH), Shropshire T 01743-761330 Second-century public baths and part of the forum of the Roman town of Viroconium

WALES

For more information on any of the National Trust properties listed below, the official website is: www.nationaltrust.org.uk

For more information on any of the CADW properties listed below, the official website is: www.cadw.wales.gov.uk

(C) Property of CADW: Welsh Historic Monuments
(NT) National Trust property

BEAUMARIS CASTLE (C), Anglesey T 01248-810361 Concentrically-planned castle, still almost intact

CAERLEON ROMAN BATHS AND AMPHITHEATRE (C), nr Newport T 01633-422518 Rare example of a legionary bath-house and late 1st-century arena surrounded by bank for spectators

CAERNARFON CASTLE (C). T 01286-677617 Important Edwardian castle built, with the town wall, between 1283 and 1330

CAERPHILLY CASTLE (C) CF83 1JD T 029-2088 3143 Concentrically-planned castle (*c.*1270) notable for its scale and use of water defences

CARDIFF CASTLE CF10 3RB T 029-2087 8100 W www.cardiffcastle.com. Castle built on the site of a Roman fort; spectacular towers and rich interior

CASTELL COCH (C), nr Cardiff CF15 7JS T 029-2081 0101 'Fairy Castle' rebuilt 1875–90 on medieval foundations

CHEPSTOW CASTLE (C) NP16 5EY T 01291-624065 Rectangular keep amid extensive fortifications

CONWY CASTLE (C) LL32 8LD T 01492-592358
Built by Edward I, 1283–7
CRICCIETH CASTLE (C) Gwynedd LL52 0DP
T 01766-522227
Native Welsh 13th-century castle, altered by Edward I
DENBIGH CASTLE (C) LL16 3NB T 01745-813385
Remains of the castle (begun 1282), including triple-towered gatehouse
HARLECH CASTLE (C) LL46 2YH T 01766-780552
Well-preserved Edwardian castle, constructed 1283–90, on an outcrop above the former shoreline
PEMBROKE CASTLE SA71 4LA T 01646-681510
W www.pembrokecastle.co.uk
Castle founded in 1093; Great Tower built 1200; birthplace of King Henry VII
PENRHYN CASTLE (NT), Bangor LL57 4HN T 01248-353084
Neo-Norman castle built in the 19th-century. Industrial railway museum
PORTMEIRION, Gwynedd LL48 6ET T 01766-770000
W www.portmeirion-village.com
Village in Italianate style
POWIS CASTLE (NT), Welshpool SY21 8RF T 01938-551944
Medieval castle with interior in variety of styles; 17th-century gardens and Clive of India museum
RAGLAN CASTLE (C) NP15 2BT T 01291-690228
Remains of 15th-century castle with moated hexagonal keep
ST DAVIDS BISHOP'S PALACE (C), St Davids SA62 6PE
T 01437-720517
Remains of residence of Bishops of St Davids built 1328–47
TINTERN ABBEY (C), nr Chepstow T 01291-689251
Remains of 13th-century church and conventual buildings of a Cistercian monastery
TRETOWER COURT AND CASTLE (C), nr Crickhowell NP8 2RF T 01874-730279
Medieval house with remains of 12th-century castle nearby

SCOTLAND

For more information on any of the Historic Scotland properties listed below, the official website is:
www.historic-scotland.gov.uk
For more information on any of the National Trust For Scotland properties listed below, the official website is:
www.nts.org.uk
(HS) Historic Scotland property
(NTS) National Trust for Scotland property

ABBOTSFORD HOUSE, Melrose, Scottish Borders TD6 9BQ
T 01869-752043
Home of Sir Walter Scott
ANTONINE WALL, between the Clyde and the Forth.
Built about AD 142, consists of ditch, turf rampart and road, with forts every two miles
BALMORAL CASTLE, nr Braemar AB35 5TB T 01339-742534
W www.balmoralcastle.com Baronial-style castle built for Victoria and Albert. The Queen's private residence
BLACKHOUSE, ARNOL (HS), Lewis, Western Isles
T 01851-710395
Traditional Lewis thatched house
BLAIR CASTLE, Blair Atholl PH18 5TL T 01796-481207
W www.blair-castle.co.uk
Mid 18th-century mansion with 13th-century tower; seat of the Dukes of Atholl
BONAWE IRON FURNACE (HS), Argyll and Bute PA35 1JQ
T 01866-822432
Charcoal-fuelled ironworks founded in 1753
BOWHILL, Selkirk TD7 5ET T 01750-22204
Seat of the Dukes of Buccleuch and Queensberry; fine collection of paintings, including portrait miniatures
BROUGH OF BIRSAY (HS), Orkney T 01856-841815
Remains of Norse church and village on the tidal island of Birsay.
CAERLAVEROCK CASTLE (HS), nr Dumfries DG1 4RN
T 01387-770244
Fine early classical Renaissance building
CAIRNPAPPLE HILL (HS), West Lothian T 01506-634622
Neolithic and Bronze age burial chambers and henge
CALANAIS STANDING STONES (HS), Lewis, Western Isles
T 01851-621422 Standing stones in a cross-shaped setting, dating from 2900–2600 BC
CATERTHUNS (BROWN AND WHITE) (HS), nr Brechin
Two large Iron Age hill forts
CAWDOR CASTLE, Inverness IV12 5RD T 01667-404401
W www.cawdorcastle.com
A 14th-century keep with 15th- and 17th-century additions
CLAVA CAIRNS (HS), Highlands T 01667-460232
Late Neolithic or early Bronze Age cairns
CRATHES CASTLE (NTS), nr Banchory AB31 5QJ
T 01330-844525
A 16th-century baronial castle in woodland, fields and gardens
CULZEAN CASTLE (NTS), S. Ayrshire KA19 8LE
T 01655-884455
An 18th-century Adam castle with oval staircase and circular saloon
DUNFERMLINE ABBEY AND PALACE (HS), Fife
T 01383-739026 W www.dunfabbey.freeserve.co.uk
Remains of Abbey and Royal Palace
DRYBURGH ABBEY (HS), Scottish Borders T 01835-822381
A 12th-century abbey containing tomb of Sir Walter Scott
DUNVEGAN CASTLE, Skye IV55 8WF T 01470-521206
W www.dunvegancastle.com
A 13th-century castle with later additions; home of the chiefs of the Clan MacLeod; trips to seal colony
EDINBURGH CASTLE (HS) EH1 2NG T 0131-225 9846
Includes the Scottish Crown Jewels, Scottish National War Memorial, Scottish United Services Museum and historic apartments
EDZELL CASTLE (HS), nr Brechin DD9 7UE T 01356-648631
Medieval tower house; unique walled garden
EILEAN DONAN CASTLE, Wester Ross IV40 8DX
T 01599-555202
A 13th-century castle with Jacobite relics
ELGIN CATHEDRAL (HS), Moray T 01343-547171
A 13th-century cathedral with fine chapterhouse
FLOORS CASTLE, Kelso T 01573-223333
W www.floorscastle.com
Largest inhabited castle in Scotland; seat of the Dukes of Roxburghe. Built 1721 by William Adam.
FORT GEORGE (HS), Highlands T 01667-462777
An 18th-century fort
GLAMIS CASTLE, Angus T 01307-840393
W www.strathmore-estates.co.uk
Seat of the Lyon family (later Earls of Strathmore and Kinghorne) since 1372
GLASGOW CATHEDRAL (HS). T 0141-552 6891
Medieval cathedral with elaborately vaulted crypt
GLENELG BROCHS (HS), Highlands T 01667-460232
Two broch towers with well-preserved structural features

HILL HOUSE, Helensburgh G84 9AJ T 01436-673900
House and furnishings designed by Charles Rennie Macintosh
HOPETOUN HOUSE, nr Edinburgh EH30 9SL
T 0131-331 2451 W www.hopetounhouse.com
House designed by Sir William Bruce, enlarged by William Adam
HUNTLY CASTLE (HS) Aberdeenshire T 01466-793191
Ruin of a 16th- and 17th-century house
INVERARAY CASTLE, Argyll T 01499-302203
W www.inveraray-castle.com Gothic-style 18th-century castle; seat of the Dukes of Argyll
IONA ABBEY (HS), Inner Hebrides
Monastery founded by St Columba in AD 563
JARLSHOF (HS), Shetland T 01950-460112 Prehistoric and Norse settlement
JEDBURGH ABBEY (HS), Scottish Borders T 01835-863925
Romanesque and early Gothic church founded *c.*1138
KELSO ABBEY (HS), Scottish Borders.
Remains of great abbey church founded 1128 by David I
KISIMUL CASTLE (HS), Barra, Hebrides T 01871-810313
Historic home of clan MacNeill
LINLITHGOW PALACE (HS) EH49 7AL T 01506-842896
Ruin of royal palace in park setting. Birthplace of Mary, Queen of Scots
MAES HOWE (HS), Orkney T 01856-761606
Neolithic tomb
MEIGLE SCULPTURED STONES (HS), Angus
T 01828-640612
Twenty six Celtic Christian stones
MELROSE ABBEY (HS), Scottish Borders T 01896-822562
Ruin of Cistercian abbey founded *c.*1136 by David I
MOUSA BROCH (HS), Shetland T 01466-793191
Finest surviving Iron Age broch tower
NEW ABBEY CORN MILL (HS), nr Dumfries
T 01387-850260
Water-powered mill
PALACE OF HOLYROODHOUSE, Edinburgh
T 0131-556 5100 W www.royal.gov.uk
The Queen's official Scottish residence. Main part of the palace built 1671–9
RING OF BROGAR (HS), Orkney T 01865-841815
Neolithic circle of upright stones with an enclosing ditch
ROSSLYN CHAPEL, Midlothian EH25 9PU
W www.rosslynchapel.org.uk
Historic church with unique stone carvings
RUTHWELL CROSS (HS), Dumfries and Galloway
T 01387-870249
Seventh-century Anglian cross
ST ANDREWS CASTLE AND CATHEDRAL (HS), Fife KY16 9AR T 01334-477196 (castle); 01334-472563 (cathedral)
Ruins of 13th-century castle and remains of the largest cathedral in Scotland
SCONE PALACE, Perth PH2 6BD T 01738-552300
W www.scone-palace.co.uk
House built 1802–13 on the site of a medieval palace. Home of the Earls of Mansfield
SKARA BRAE (HS), Orkney T 01856-841815
Prehistoric village with adjacent 17th-century house
SMAILHOLM TOWER (HS), Scottish Borders
T 01573-460365
Well-preserved tower-house
STIRLING CASTLE (HS) FK8 1EJ T 01786-450000
Great Hall and gatehouse of James IV, palace of James V, Chapel Royal remodelled by James VI
TANTALLON CASTLE (HS), E. Lothian EH39 5PN
T 01620-892727 Fortification with earthwork defences and a 14th-century curtain wall with towers
THREAVE CASTLE (HS), Dumfries and Galloway
Late 14th-century tower on an island; reached by boat, long walk to castle
URQUHART CASTLE (HS), Loch Ness IV63 6XJ
T 01456-450551 Castle remains with well-preserved tower

NORTHERN IRELAND

For more information on any of the National Trust properties listed below, the official website is:
www.nationaltrust.org.uk
For the Northern Ireland Environment and Heritage Service, the official website is:
www.ehsni.gov.uk
EHS Property in the care of the Northern Ireland Environment and Heritage Service
NT National Trust property

CARRICKFERGUS CASTLE (EHS), Co. Antrim BT38 7BG
T 028-9335 1273 Castle begun in 1180 and garrisoned until 1928
CASTLE COOLE (NT), Co. Fermanagh BT74 6JY
T 028-6632 2690
An 18th-century mansion by James Wyatt in parkland
CASTLE WARD (NT), Co. Down BT30 7LS T 028-4488 1204
An 18th-century house with Classical and Gothic facades
DEVENISH ISLAND (EHS), Co. Fermanagh T 028-6862 1588
Island monastery founded in the 6th century by St Molaise
DOWNHILL CASTLE (NT), Co. Londonderry T 028-7084 8728 Ruins of palatial house in landscaped estate including Mussenden Temple.
DUNLUCE CASTLE (EHS), Co. Antrim T 028-2073 1938
Ruins of 16th-century stronghold of the MacDonnells
FLORENCE COURT (NT), Co. Fermanagh BT92 1DB
T 028-6634 8249
Mid-18th-century house with rococo decoration
GREY ABBEY (EHS), Co. Down T 028-9181 1491
Substantial remains of a Cistercian abbey founded in 1193
HILLSBOROUGH FORT (EHS), Co. Down T 028-9268 3285
Built in 1650
MOUNT STEWART (NT), Co. Down BT22 2AD
T 028-4278 8387
An 18th-century house, childhood home of Lord Castlereagh
NENDRUM MONASTERY (EHS), Mahee Island, Co. Down
T 028-9181 1491
Founded in the 5th century by St Machaoi
TULLY CASTLE (EHS), Co. Fermanagh T 028-6862 1588
Fortified house and bawn built in 1613
WHITE ISLAND (EHS), Co. Fermanagh
Tenth-century monastery and 12th-century church. Access by ferry

MUSEUMS AND GALLERIES

There are over 2,500 museums and galleries in the United Kingdom. Around 1,800 are registered with the Museums, Libraries and Archives Council (MLA), which indicates that they have an appropriate constitution, are soundly financed, have adequate collection management standards and public services, and have access to professional curatorial advice. Museums must achieve full or provisional registration status in order to be eligible for grants from MLA and from Area Museums Councils. Many registered museums are run by a local authority.

The national museums and galleries receive direct government grant-in-aid. These are: British Museum; Imperial War Museum; National Army Museum; National Galleries of Scotland; National Gallery; National Maritime Museum; National Museums and Galleries on Merseyside; National Museum of Wales; National Museums of Scotland; National Portrait Gallery; Natural History Museum; RAF Museum; Royal Armouries; Science Museum; Tate Gallery; Ulster Folk and Transport Museum; Ulster Museum; Victoria and Albert Museum; Wallace Collection. An online art museum (www.24hourmuseum.org.uk) has also been awarded national collection status.

ENGLAND

BARNARD CASTLE, Co. Durham – *The Bowes Museum*, Westwick Road DL12 8NP T 01833-690606 W www.bowesmuseum.org.uk
European art from the late medieval period to the 19th-century; music and costume galleries; English period rooms from Elizabeth I to Victoria; local archaeology

BATH - *American Museum*, Claverton Manor BA2 7BD T 01225-460503 W www.americanmuseum.org
American decorative arts from the 17th- to 19th-century

Museum of Costume, Bennett Street BA1 2QH T 01225-477789 W www.museumofcostume.co.uk
Fashion from the 16th-century to the present day

Roman Baths Museum, Pump Room, Stall Street BA1 1LZ T 01225-477785 W www.romanbaths.co.uk
Museum adjoins the remains of a Roman baths and temple complex

Victoria Art Gallery, Bridge Street BA2 4AT T 01225-477772 W www.victoriagal.org.uk
European Old Masters and British art since the 18th-century

BEAMISH, Co. Durham – *Beamish, The North of England Open Air Museum*, DH9 0RG T 0191-370 4000 W www.beamish.org.uk
Recreated northern town *c.*1900, with rebuilt and furnished local buildings, colliery village, farm, railway station, tramway, Pockerley Manor and horse-yard (set *c.*1800)

BEAULIEU, Hants – *National Motor Museum*, SO42 7ZN T 01590-612345 W www.beaulieu.co.uk
Displays of over 250 vehicles dating from 1895 to the present day

BIRMINGHAM - *Aston Hall*, Trinity Road, B6 6JD T 0121-327 0062 W www.bmag.org.uk/aston_hall
Jacobean House containing paintings, furniture and tapestries from the 17th- to 19th-century

Barber Institute of Fine Arts, off Edgbaston Park Road, B15 2TS T 0121-414 7333 W www.barber.org.uk
Fine arts, including Old Masters

Birmingham Nature Centre, Pershore Road, Edgbaston, B5 7RL T 0121-472 7775
Indoor and outdoor enclosures displaying wildlife, especially British and European

City Museum and Art Gallery, Chamberlain Square B3 3DH T 0121-303 2834 W www.bmag.org.uk/museum_and_art_gallery
Includes notable collection of Pre-Raphaelite art

Museum of the Jewellery Quarter, Vyse Street, Hockley B18 6HA T 0121-554 3598 W www.bmag.org.uk/jewellery_quarter
Built around a real jewellery workshop

Soho House, Soho Avenue B18 5LB T 0121-554 9122 W www.bmag.org.uk/soho_house
Eighteenth-century home of industrialist Matthew Boulton

BOVINGTON CAMP, Dorset – *Tank Museum BH20 6JG* T 01929-405096 W www.tankmuseum.co.uk
Collection of 300 tanks from the earliest days of tank warfare to the present

BRADFORD - *Cartwright Hall Art Gallery*, Lister Park BD9 4NS T 01274-751212
British 19th- and 20th-century fine art

Industrial Museum and Horses at Work, Moorside Road BD2 3HP T 01274-631756
Engineering, textiles, transport and social history exhibits, including recreated back-to-back cottages, shire horses and horse tram-rides

National Museum of Photography, Film and Television, Bradford BD1 1NQ T 0870-701 0200 W www.nmpft.org.uk
Photography, film and television interactive exhibits. Features the UK's first IMAX cinema and the only public Cinerama screen in the world

BRIGHTON - *Booth Museum of Natural History*, Dyke Road BN1 5AA T 01273-292777 W www.booth.virtualmuseum.info
Zoology, botany and geology collections; British birds in recreated habitats

Brighton Museum and Gallery, Royal Pavilion Gardens, BN1 1EE T 01273-290900 W www.brighton.virtualmuseum.info
Includes fine art and design, fashion, non-Western art, Brighton history

BRISTOL - *Arnolfini*, Narrow Quay BS1 4QA T 0117-917 2303 W www.arnolfini.demon.co.uk
Contemporary visual arts, dance, performance, music, talks and workshops

Blaise Castle House Museum, Henbury BS10 7QS T 0117-903 9818 W www.bristol-city.gov.uk/museums
Agricultural and social history collections in an 18th-century mansion

Bristol Industrial Museum, Princes Wharf BS1 4RN T 0117-925 1470 W www.bristol-city.gov.uk/museums
Industrial, maritime and transport collections

British Empire and Commonwealth Museum, Temple Meads BS1 6QH T 0117-925 4980 W www.empiremuseum.co.uk

City Museum and Art Gallery, Queen's Road BS8 1RL T 0117-922 3571 W www.bristol-city.gov.uk
Includes fine and decorative art, oriental art, Egyptology and Bristol ceramics and paintings

CAMBRIDGE - *Duxford Imperial War Museum*, Duxford CB2 4QR T 01223-835000 W www.iwm.org.uk

Displays of military and civil aircraft, tanks, guns and naval exhibits

Fitzwilliam Museum, Trumpington Street CB2 1RB
T 01223-332900 **W** www.fitzmuseum.cam.ac.uk
Antiquities, fine and applied arts, clocks, ceramics, manuscripts, furniture, sculpture, coins and medals, temporary exhibitions

Sedgwick Museum of Earth Sciences, Downing Street, CB2 3EQ
T 01223-333456 **W** www.sedgwickmuseum.org
Extensive geological collection

University Museum of Archaeology and Anthropology, Downing Street CB2 3DZ **T** 01223-333516
Archaeology and anthropology from all parts of the world

University Museum of Zoology, Downing Street CB2 3EJ
T 01223-336650 **W** www.zoo.cam.ac.uk
Extensive zoological collection

Whipple Museum of the History of Science, Free School Lane CB2 3RH **T** 01223-330906 **W** www.hps.cam.ac.uk/whipple
Scientific instruments from 14th-century to the present

CARLISLE - *Tullie House Museum and Art Gallery*, Castle Street CA3 8TP **T** 01228-534781 **W** www.tulliehouse.co.uk
Prehistoric archaeology, Hadrian's Wall, Viking and medieval Cumbria, and the social history of Carlisle; also British 19th- and 20th-century art and English porcelain

CHATHAM – *World Naval Base* ME4 4TZ **T** 01634-823800
W www.chdt.org.uk
Maritime attractions including HMS Cavalier, the UK's last World War II destroyer

Royal Engineers Museum of Military Engineering, Prince Arthur Road ME4 4UG **T** 01634-822839
W www.army.mod.uk/royalengineers
Regimental history, ethnography, decorative art and photography

CHELTENHAM – *Art Gallery and Museum* Clarence Street GL50 3JT **T** 01242-237431
W www.cheltenhammuseum.org.uk
Paintings, arts and crafts

CHESTER - *Grosvenor Museum*, Grosvenor Street CH1 2DD
T 01244-402008
W www.chestercc.gov.uk/heritage/museum/home
Roman collections, natural history, art, Chester silver, local history and costume

CHICHESTER - *Weald and Downland Open Air Museum*, Singleton PO18 0EU **T** 01243-811363
W www.wealddown.co.uk
Rebuilt vernacular buildings from south-east England; includes medieval houses, agricultural and rural craft buildings and a working watermill

COLCHESTER - *Colchester Castle Museum*, Castle Park CO1 1TJ **T** 01206-282939 **W** www.colchestermuseums.org.uk
Largest Norman keep in Europe standing on foundations of Roman Temple of Claudius; tours of the Roman vaults, castle walls and chapel with medieval and prison displays

COVENTRY - *Herbert Art Gallery and Museum*, Jordan Well CV1 5QP **T** 024-7683 2381 **W** www.coventrymuseum.org.uk
Local history, archaeology and industry, and fine and decorative art

Museum of British Road Transport, Hales Street CV1 1PN
T 024-7683 2425 **W** www.mbrt.co.uk
Hundreds of motor vehicles and bicycles

CRICH, nr Matlock, Derbys – *Crich Tramway Museum* DE4 5DP
T 0870-758 7267 **W** www.tramway.co.uk
Open-air working museum with tram rides

DERBY - *Derby Museum and Art Gallery*, The Strand DE1 1BS
T 01332-716659 **W** www.derby.gov.uk/museums
Includes paintings by Joseph Wright of Derby and Derby porcelain

Industrial Museum, off Full Street DE1 3AR **T** 01332-255308
W www.derby.gov.uk/museums
Rolls-Royce aero engine collection and a railway engineering gallery

Pickford's House Museum, Friar Gate DE1 1DA **T** 01332-255363
W www.derby.gov.uk/museums
Georgian Town House by architect Joseph Pickford; reconstructed period rooms and garden

DEVIZES - *Wiltshire Heritage Museum*, Long Street SN10 1NS
T 01380-727369 **W** www.wiltshireheritage.org.uk
Natural and local history, art gallery, archaeological finds from Bronze Age, Iron Age, Roman and Saxon sites

DORCHESTER - *Dorset County Museum*, High West Street, DT1 1XA **T** 01305-262735 **W** www.dorsetcountymuseum.org
Includes a collection of Thomas Hardy's manuscripts, books, notebooks and drawings

DOVER – *Dover Museum*, Market Square CT16 1PB
T 01304-201066 **W** www.dovermuseum.co.uk
Contains Dover Bronze Age Boat Gallery and archaeological finds from Bronze Age, Roman and Saxon sites.

ELLESMERE PORT – *Boat Museum*, South Pier Road CH65 4FW **T** 0151-355 5017 **W** www.boatmuseum.org.uk
Craft and boating history

EXETER – *Royal Albert Memorial Museum and Art Gallery*, Queen Street EX4 3RX **T** 01392-665858
W www.exeter.gov.uk/museums
Natural history, archaeology, worldwide fine and decorative art including Exeter silver

GATESHEAD – *Shipley Art Gallery*, Prince Consort Road NE8 4JB **T** 0191-477 1495
Contemporary crafts

Baltic Centre for Contemporary Art, South Shore Road, Gateshead, NE8 3BA **T** 0191-478 1810 **W** www.balticmill.com
Presents a constantly changing programme of contemporary art exhibitions and events

GAYDON, Warwick – *British Motor Industry Heritage Trust*, Heritage Motor Centre, Banbury Road CV35 0BJ
T 01926-641188 **W** www.heritage.org.uk
History of British motor industry from 1895 to present; classic vehicles; engineering gallery; Corgi and Lucas collections

GLOUCESTER - *National Waterways Museum*, Llanthony Warehouse, Gloucester Docks GL1 2EH **T** 01452-318200
W www.nwm.org.uk
Two-hundred-year history of Britain's canals and inland waterways

GOSPORT, Hants – *Royal Navy Submarine Museum*, Haslar Jetty Road PO12 2AS **T** 023-9252 9217 **W** www.rnsubmus.co.uk
Underwater warfare, including the submarine Alliance; historical and nuclear galleries; and first Royal Navy submarine

GRASMERE, Cumbria – *Dove Cottage* and the *Wordsworth Museum* LA22 9SH **T** 01539-433554
W www.wordsworth.org.uk

HALIFAX - *Eureka! The Museum for Children*, Discovery Road HX1 2NE **T** 01422-330069 **W** www.eureka.org.uk
Hands-on museum designed for children up to age 12

HULL - *Ferens Art Gallery*, Queen Victoria Square HU1 3RA
T 01482-613902 **W** www.hullcc.gov.uk/museums
European art, especially Dutch 17th-century paintings, British portraits from 17th- to 20th-century, and marine paintings

Hull Maritime Museum, Queen Victoria Square HU1 3DX
T 01482-613902 **W** www.hullcc.gov.uk/museums
Whaling, fishing and navigation exhibits

HUNTINGDON - *Cromwell Museum*, Grammar School Walk PE29 3LF **T** 01480-375830
W www.edweb.camcnty.gov.uk/cromwell
Portraits and memorabilia relating to Oliver Cromwell

IPSWICH - *Christchurch Mansion and Wolsey Art Gallery*, Christchurch Park IP4 2BE **T** 01473-433554
Tudor house with paintings by Gainsborough, Constable and other Suffolk artists; furniture and 18th-century ceramics. Art gallery for temporary exhibitions

LEEDS – *City Art Gallery*, The Headrow LS1 3AA **T** 0113-247 8248 **W** www.leeds.gov.uk/artgallery
British and European paintings including English watercolours, modern sculpture, Henry Moore gallery, print room

Leeds Industrial Museum at Armley Mills, Canal Road, Armley LS12 2QF **T** 0113-263 7861 **W** www. leeds.gov.uk/armleymills
Largest woollen mill in world

Lotherton Hall, Aberford LS25 3EB **T** 0113-281 3259
W www.leeds.gov.uk/lothertonhall
Costume and oriental collections in furnished Edwardian house; deer park and bird garden

Royal Armouries Museum, Armouries Drive LS10 1LT
T 0113-220-1916 **W** www.armouries.org.uk
National collection of arms and armour from BC to present; demonstrations of foot combat in museum's five galleries; falconry and mounted combat in the tiltyard

Temple Newsam House LS15 0AE **T** 0113-264 7321
W www.leeds.gov.uk/templenewsam
Old Masters and 17th- and 18th-century decorative art in furnished Jacobean/Tudor house

LEICESTER - *Jewry Wall Museum*, St Nicholas Circle LE1 4LB
T 0116-225 4971 **W** www.leicestermuseums.ac.uk
Archaeology, Roman Jewry Wall and baths, and mosaics

New Walk Museum and Art Gallery, New Walk LE1 7EA
T 0116-255 4900 **W** www.leicestermuseums.ac.uk
Natural history, geology, ancient Egypt gallery, European art and decorative arts

Snibston Discovery Park, Coalville LE67 3LN **T** 01530-278444
Open-air science and industry museum on site of a coal mine; country park with nature trail

LINCOLN - *Museum of Lincolnshire Life*, Burton Road LN1 3LY
T 01522-528448
Social history and agricultural collection

Usher Gallery, Lindum Road LN2 1NN **T** 01522-527980
Watches, miniatures, porcelain, silver; collection of Peter de Wint works; Lincolnshire topography and Royal Lincs Regiment memorabilia

LIVERPOOL - *Lady Lever Art Gallery*, Wirral CH62 5EQ
T 0151-478 4136 **W** www.ladyleverartgallery.org.uk
Paintings, furniture and porcelain

Liverpool Museum, William Brown Street L3 8EN
T 0151-478 4399 **W** www.nmgm.org.uk
Includes Egyptian mummies, weapons and classical sculpture; planetarium, aquarium, vivarium and natural history centre

Merseyside Maritime Museum, Albert Dock L3 4AQ
T 0151-478 4499 **W** www.liverpoolmuseums.org.uk
Floating exhibits, working displays and craft demonstrations; incorporates HM Customs and Excise National Museum

Museum of Liverpool Life, Pier Head, Albert Dock L3 1QA
T 0151-478 4080 **W** www.nmgm.org.uk
The history of Liverpool

Sudley House, Mossley Hill Road L18 8BX
T 0151-724 3245
Late 18th- and 19th-century British paintings in former shipowner's home

Tate Gallery Liverpool, Albert Dock L3 4BB **T** 0151-702 7400
W www.tate.org.uk/liverpool
Twentieth-century painting and sculpture

Walker Art Gallery, William Brown Street L3 8EL **T** 0151-478 4199
W www.nmgm.org.uk
Paintings from the 14th- to 20th-century

LONDON: GALLERIES - *Barbican Art Gallery*, Barbican Centre EC2Y 8DS **T** 020-7638 8891 **W** www.barbican.org.uk
Temporary exhibitions

Courtauld Gallery, Somerset House, Strand, WC2R 0RN
T 020-7848 2526 **W** www.courtauld.ac.uk
The University of London galleries

Dulwich Picture Gallery, Gallery Road, SE21 7AD
T 020-8693 5254
W www.dulwichpicturegallery.org.uk
Built by Sir John Soane to house 17th- and 18th-century paintings

Hayward Gallery, Belvedere Road, SE1 8XZ **T** 020-7921 0830
W www.hayward.org.uk
Temporary exhibitions

National Gallery, Trafalgar Square, WC2N 5DN **T** 020-7747 2885
W www.nationalgallery.org.uk
Western painting from the 13th- to 20th-century; early Renaissance collection in the Sainsbury wing

National Portrait Gallery, St Martin's Place, WC2H 0HE
T 020-7306 0055 **W** www.npg.org.uk
Portraits of eminent people in British history

Percival David Foundation of Chinese Art, Gordon Square, WC1H 0PD **T** 020-7387 3909 **W** www.pdfmuseum.org.uk
Chinese ceramics from 10th- to 18th-century

Photographers' Gallery, Great Newport Street, WC2H 7HY
T 020-7831 1772 **W** www.photonet.org.uk
Temporary exhibitions

The Queen's Gallery, Buckingham Palace, SW1A 1AA
T 020-7766 7301 **W** www.royal.gov.uk
Art from the Royal Collection

Royal Academy of Arts, Piccadilly, W1J 0BD **T** 020-7300 8000
W www.royalacademy.org.uk
British art since 1750 and temporary exhibitions; annual Summer Exhibition

Saatchi Gallery, County Hall, South Bank SE1 7PB
T 020-7928 8195 **W** www.saatchi-gallery.co.uk
Contemporary art including paintings, photographs, sculpture and installations

Serpentine Gallery, Kensington Gardens, W2 3XA
T 020-7402 6075 **W** www.serpentinegallery.org
Temporary exhibitions of British and international contemporary art

Tate Britain, Millbank SW1P 4RG **T** 020-7887 8000
W www.tate.org.uk
British painting and 20th-century painting and sculpture

Tate Modern, Bankside, SE1 9TG **T** 020-7887 8000
W www.tate.org.uk
International modern art from 1900 to the present

Wallace Collection, Manchester Square, W1U 3BN
T 020-7563 9500 **W** www.twallacecollection.org.uk
Paintings and drawings, French 18th-century furniture, armour, porcelain, clocks and sculpture

Whitechapel Art Gallery, Whitechapel High Street, E1 7QX
T 020-7522 7888 **W** www.whitechapel.org
Temporary exhibitions of modern art

LONDON: MUSEUMS - *Bank of England Museum*, Threadneedle Street, EC2R 8AH (entrance from Bartholomew Lane). **T** 020-7601 5491 **W** www.bankofengland.co.uk
History of the Bank since 1694

Bethnal Green Museum of Childhood, Cambridge Heath Road, E2 9PA **T** 020-8983 2415 **W** www.museumofchildhood.org.uk

Toys, games and exhibits relating to the social history of childhood

British Museum, Great Russell Street, WC1B 3DG
T 020-7323 8299 W www.thebritishmuseum.ac.uk
Antiquities, coins, medals, prints and drawings

Cabinet War Rooms, King Charles Street, SW1A 2AQ
T 020-7930 6961 W www.iwm.org.uk/cabinet
Underground rooms used by Churchill and the Government during the Second World War

Cutty Sark, Greenwich, SE10 9HT T 020-8858 3445
W www.cuttysark.org.uk
Restored and re-rigged tea clipper with exhibits on board.

Design Museum, Shad Thames, SE1 2YD T 020-7378 6055
W www.designmuseum.org
The development of design and the mass-production of consumer objects

Estorick Collection, Canonbury Square, N1 2AN
T 020-7704 9522 W www.estorickcollection.com
Stages the main Estorick Collection of modern Italian art together with temporary loan exhibitions

Firepower! The Royal Artillery Museum, Royal Arsenal, Woolwich, SE18 6ST T 020-8855 7755 W www.firepower.org.uk
The history and development of artillery over the last 700 years including the collections of the Royal Regiment of Artillery

Geffrye Museum, Kingsland Road, E2 8EA T 020-7739 9893
W www.geffrye-museum.org.uk
English urban domestic interiors from 1600 to present day; also paintings, furniture, decorative arts, walled herb garden and period garden rooms

Gilbert Collection, Somerset House WC2R 1LA T 020-7420 9400
W www.gilbert-collection.org.uk
The collection comprises some 800 works of art including European silver, gold snuff boxes and Italian mosaics

HMS Belfast, Morgan's Lane, Tooley Street, SE1 2JH
T 020-7940 6300 W www.iwm.org.uk/belfast
Life on a World War II warship

Horniman Museum and Gardens, London Road SE23 3PQ
T 020-8699 1872 W www.horniman.ac.uk
Museum of ethnography, musical instruments, natural history and aquarium; reference library; sunken, water and flower gardens

Imperial War Museum, Lambeth Road SE1 6HZ T 020-7416 5320
W www.iwm.org.uk
All aspects of the two world wars and other military operations involving Britain and the Commonwealth since 1914

Jewish Museum, Camden Town, Albert Street NW1 7NB
T 020-7284 1997 W www.jewishmuseum.org.uk
Jewish life, history and religion

Jewish Museum, Finchley, East End Road N3 2SY
T 020–8349 1143 W www.jewishmuseum.org.uk
Jewish life in London and Holocaust education

London's Transport Museum, Covent Garden WC2E 7BB
T 020-7379 6344 W www.ltmuseum.co.uk
Vehicles, photographs and graphic art relating to the history of transport in London

MCC Museum, Lord's NW8 8QN T 020-7616 8595
W www.mcc.org.uk
Cricket museum. Conducted tours by appointment with Tours Manager

Museum in Docklands, West India Quay, Hertsmere Road E14 4AL
T 0870-444 3856 W www.museumindocklands.org.uk
Explores the story of London's river, port and people over 2,000 years; from Roman times through to the recent regeneration of London's Docklands

Museum of Garden History, Lambeth Palace Road SE1 7LB
T 020-7401 8865
W www.museumgardenhistory.org
Exhibition of aspects of garden history and re-created 17th-century garden

Museum of London, London Wall, EC2Y 5HN T 020-7600 3699
W www.museumoflondon.org.uk
History of London from prehistoric times to present day

National Army Museum, Royal Hospital Road SW3 4HT
T 020-7730 0717 W www.national-army-museum.ac.uk
Five-hundred-year history of the British soldier; exhibits include model of the Battle of Waterloo and Army for Today gallery

Natural History Museum, Cromwell Road SW7 5BD
T 020-7942 5000 W www.nhm.ac.uk
Natural history collections

National Maritime Museum, Greenwich SE10 9NF
T 020-8858 4422 W www.nmm.ac.uk
Comprises the main building, the Royal Observatory and the Queen's House. Maritime history of Britain; collections include globes, clocks, telescopes and paintings

Petrie Museum of Egyptian Archaeology, University College London, Malet Place WC1E 6BT T 020-7679 2884
W www.petrie.ucl.ac.uk
Egyptian archaeology collection

Royal Air Force Museum, Hendon, NW9 5LL T 020-8205 2266
W www.rafmuseum.org
National museum of aviation with over 70 full-size aircraft; aviation from before the Wright brothers to the present-day RAF; flight simulator

Royal Mews, Buckingham Palace SW1A 1AA T 020-7766 7302
W www.royal.gov.uk
Carriages, coaches, stables and horses

Science Museum, Exhibition Road, SW7 2DD T 0870-870 4868
W www.sciencemuseum.org.uk
Science, technology, industry and medicine collections

Shakespeare Globe Theatre and Exhibition, Bankside SE1 9DT
T 020-7902 1500 W www.shakespeares-globe.org
Recreation of Elizabethan theatre using 16th-century techniques

Sherlock Holmes Museum, Baker Street NW1 6XE
T 020-7935 8866 W www.sherlock-holmes.co.uk
Recreated rooms of the fictional detective

Sir John Soane's Museum, Lincoln's Inn Fields WC2A 3BP
T 020-7405 2107 W www.soane.org
Art and antiques

Theatre Museum, Russell Street WC2E 7PR T 020-7943 4700
W www.theatremuseum.org
History of the performing arts

Tower Bridge Experience, SE1 2UP T 020-7403 3761
W www.towerbridge.org.uk
History of the bridge and display of Victorian steam machinery; panoramic views from walkways

Victoria and Albert Museum, Cromwell Road SW7 2RL
T 020-7942 2000 W www.vam.ac.uk
Includes National Art Library and Print Room. Fine and applied art and design, including furniture, glass, textiles, dress collections

Wellington Museum, Apsley House, W1J 7NT T 020-7499 5676
W www.apsleyhouse.org.uk

Wimbledon Lawn Tennis Museum, Church Road SW19 5AE
T 020-8946 6131 W www.wimbledon.org/museum
Tennis trophies, fashion and memorabilia; view of Centre Court

MANCHESTER - *Gallery of Costume*, Rusholme M14 5LL
T 0161-224 5217 W www.manchestergalleries.org
Exhibits from the 16th- to 20th-century

Imperial War Museum North, Trafford Wharf Road, Trafford Park, Manchester, M17 1TZ **T** 0161-836 4000 **W** www.iwm.org.uk/north

Manchester Art Gallery, Mosley Street M2 3JL **T** 0161-235 8888 **W** www.manchestergalleries.org

Manchester Museum, Oxford Road M13 9PL **T** 0161-275 2634 **W** www.museum.man.ac.uk.
Archaeology, archery, botany, Egyptology, entomology, ethnography, geology, natural history, numismatics, oriental and zoology collections

Museum of Science and Industry, Castlefield M3 4FP **T** 0161-832 2244 **W** www.msim.org.uk
On site of world's oldest passenger railway station; galleries relating to space, energy, power, transport, aviation, textiles and social history; interactive science centre

People's History Museum, Pump House, Bridge Street M3 3ER **T** 0161-839 6061 **W** www.peopleshistorymuseum.org.uk
Political and working life history

Whitworth Art Gallery, Oxford Road M15 6ER **T** 0161-275 7450 **W** www.whitworth.man.ac.uk
Watercolours, drawings, prints, textiles, wallpapers and 20th-century British art

MILTON KEYNES - Bletchley Park, Bucks **W** www.bletchleypark.org.uk
Enigma codebreaking and other WW2 collections

MONKWEARMOUTH – *Monkwearmouth Station Museum* North Bridge Street SR5 1AP **T** 0191-567 7075 **W** www.twmuseums.org.uk/monkwearmouth
Victorian train station

NEWCASTLE UPON TYNE - *Hancock Museum*, Barras Bridge NE2 4PT **T** 0191-222 6765 **W** www.twmuseums.org.uk
Natural history. Egyptology

Laing Art Gallery, New Bridge Street NE1 8AG **T** 0191-232 7734 **W** www.twmuseums.org.uk
British and European art, ceramics, glass, silver, textiles and costume; *Art on Tyneside* display

Discovery Museum, Blandford Square NE1 4JA **T** 0191-232 6789 **W** www.twmuseums.org.uk
Science and industry, local history, fashion and Tyneside's maritime history; *Turbinia* (first steam-driven vessel) gallery

NEWMARKET - *National Horseracing Museum*, High Street CB8 8JL **T** 01638-667333 **W** www.nhrm.co.uk
The Essential Horse Millennium Exhibition, horseracing exhibits and tours of local trainers' yards and studs

NORTHAMPTON – *Central Museum and Art Gallery*, Guildhall Road NN1 1DP **T** 01604-238548 **W** www.northampton.gov.uk/museums
Boot and shoe collection

NORTH SHIELDS - *Stephenson Railway Museum*, Middle Engine Lane NE29 8DX **T** 0191-200 7146 **W** www.twmuseums.org.uk/stephenson
Locomotive engines and rolling stock

NOTTINGHAM - *Brewhouse Yard Museum*, Castle Boulevard NG7 1FB **T** 0115-915 3600
Daily life from the 17th- to 20th-century

Castle Museum and Art Gallery NG1 6EL **T** 0115-915 3700
Paintings, ceramics, silver and glass; history of Nottingham

Industrial Museum, Wollaton Park NG8 2AE **T** 0115-915 3900
Lacemaking machinery, steam engines and transport exhibits

Museum of Costume and Textiles, Castle Gate NG1 6AF **T** 0115-915 3500
Costume displays from 1790 to the mid-20th century in period rooms

Natural History Museum, Wollaton Park NG8 2AE **T** 0115-915 3900
Local natural history and wildlife dioramas

OXFORD - *Ashmolean Museum*, Beaumont Street OX1 2PH **T** 01865-278000 **W** www.ashmol.ox.ac.uk
European and Oriental fine and applied arts, archaeology, Egyptology and numismatics

Museum of Modern Art, Pembroke Street OX1 1BP **T** 01865-722733 **W** www.modernartoxford.org.uk
Temporary exhibitions

Museum of the History of Science, Broad Street OX1 3AZ **T** 01865-277280 **W** www.mhs.ox.ac.uk
Displays include early scientific instruments, chemical apparatus, clocks and watches

Oxford University Museum of Natural History, Parks Road OX1 3PW **T** 01865-272950 **W** www.oum.ox.ac.uk
Entomology, geology, mineralogy and zoology

Pitt Rivers Museum, South Parks Road OX1 3PP **T** 01865-270927 **W** www.prm.ox.ac.uk
Ethnographic and archaeological artefacts

PLYMOUTH - *City Museum and Art Gallery*, Drake Circus PL4 8AJ **T** 01752-304774 **W** www.plymouthmuseum.gov.uk
Local and natural history, ceramics, silver, Old Masters, temporary exhibitions

The Dome, The Hoe PL1 2NZ **T** 01752-603300 **W** www.plymouthdome.info
Maritime history museum

PORTSMOUTH - *Charles Dickens Birthplace Museum*, Old Commercial Road PO1 4QL **T** 023-9282 7261 **W** www.charlesdickensbirthplace.co.uk
Dickens memorabilia

D-Day Museum, Clarence Esplanade PO5 3NT **T** 023-9282 7261 **W** www.ddaymuseum.co.uk
Includes the Overlord Embroidery

Flagship Portsmouth, HM Naval Base (**W** www.flagship.org.uk). Incorporates the *Royal Naval Museum* (**T** 023-9272 7562 **W** www.royalnavalmuseum.org), HMS *Victory* (**T** 023-9286 1512 **W** www.hms-victory.com), HMS *Warrior* (**T** 023-9286 1512 **W** www.hmswarrior.org), the *Mary Rose* (**T** 023-9286 1512 **W** www.maryrose.org) and the *Dockyard Museum*.
History of the Royal Navy and of the dockyard and the trades in it

PRESTON - *Harris Museum and Art Gallery*, Market Square PR1 2PP **T** 01772-258248
British art since the 18th-century, ceramics, glass, costume and local history; also contemporary exhibitions

READING – *Rural History Centre*, University of Reading, Whiteknights RG6 6AG **T** 0118-931 8660 **W** www.ruralhistory.org
History of farming and the countryside over the last 200 years

ST ALBANS - *Verulamium Museum*, St Michael's AL3 4SW **T** 01727-751810 **W** www.stalbansmuseums.org.uk
Iron Age and Roman Verulamium, including wall plasters, jewellery, mosaics and room reconstructions

ST IVES, Cornwall – *Tate Gallery St Ives*, Porthmeor Beach TR26 1TG **T** 01736-796226 **W** www.tate.org.uk/stives
Modern art, much by artists associated with St Ives. Includes the Barbara Hepworth Museum and Sculpture Garden

SALISBURY – *Salisbury and South Wiltshire Museum*, The Close SP1 2EN **T** 01722-332151 **W** www.salisburymuseum.org.uk
Archaeology collection

SHEFFIELD - *City Museum and Mappin Art Gallery*, Weston Park S10 2TP **T** 0114-278 2600 **W** www.sheffieldgalleries.org.uk
Includes applied arts, natural history, Bronze Age archaeology and ethnography, 19th- and 20th-century art

Graves Art Gallery, Surrey Street S1 1XZ T 0114-278 2600
20th-century British art, Grice Collection of Chinese ivories
Kelham Island Industrial Museum, Alma Street. T 0114-272 2106
Local industrial and social history
Ruskin Gallery and Ruskin Craft Gallery, Arundle Gate S1 2PP T 0114-278 2600
SOUTHAMPTON – *City Art Gallery*, Commercial Road SO14 7LP T 023-8083 2277 W www.southampton.gov.uk/art
Fine art, especially 20th-century British
Maritime Museum, Town Quay SO14 2AR T 023-8063 5904
Southampton maritime history
Museum of Archaeology, Town Quay SO14 2NY T 023-8063 5904
Roman, Saxon and medieval archaeology
Tudor House Museum and Garden, Bugle Street SO14 2AD T 023-8063 5904
Restored 16th-century garden; social history exhibitions
SOUTH SHIELDS – *Arbeia Roman Fort*, Baring Street NE33 2BB T 0191-456 1369 W www.twmuseums.org.uk/arbeia
Excavated ruins
South Shields Museum and Art Gallery, Ocean Road NE33 2JA T 0191-456 8740 W www.twmuseums.org.uk/southshields
South Tyneside history, including reconstructed street
STOKE-ON-TRENT - *Etruria Industrial Museum*, Etruria ST4 7AF T 01782-233144
Britain's sole surviving steam-powered potter's mill
Gladstone Pottery Museum, Longton ST3 1PQ T 01782-319232
A working Victorian pottery
Potteries Museum and Art Gallery, Hanley ST1 3DE T 01782-232323
Pottery, china and porcelain collections and a Mark XVI Spitfire. Pottery factory tours are available by arrangement, at the following: *Royal Doulton*, Burslem; *Spode*, Stoke; *Wedgwood*, Barlaston; *W. Moorcroft*, Cobridge; H & R Johnson Tiles, Tunstall; *Staffordshire Enamels*, Longton; *Royale Stratford China*, Fenton
STYAL, Cheshire – *Quarry Bank Mill SK9 4LA* T 01625-527468 W www.quarrybankmill.org.uk
Working mill illustrating history of cotton industry; costumed guides at restored Apprentice House
SUNDERLAND – *Sunderland Museum and Winter Gardens*, Sunderland SR1 1PP T 0191-553 2323 W www.twmuseums.org.uk/sunderland
Fine and decorative art, local history and gardens
TELFORD - *Ironbridge Gorge Museums TF8 7DQ* T 01952-884391 W www.ironbridge.org.uk
Includes first iron bridge; Blists Hill (late Victorian working town); Museum of Iron; Jackfield Tile Museum; Coalport China Museum; Tar Tunnel; Broseley Pipeworks
WAKEFIELD - *Yorkshire Sculpture Park*, West Bretton WF4 4LG T 01924-830302 W www.ysp.co.uk
Open-air sculpture gallery including works by Moore, Hepworth, Frink and others in 300 acres of parkland
WASHINGTON – *Washington 'F' Pit Museum* Albany Way, NE37 1BJ
Colliery-related collection
WEYBRIDGE - Brooklands Motorsport and Aviation Museum KT13 0QN T 01932-857381 W www.brooklandsmuseum.com
Birthplace of British Motorsport
WORCESTER - *City Museum and Art Gallery*, Foregate Street WR1 1DT T 01905-25371 W www.worcestercitymuseums.org.uk
Includes a military museum, River Severn Gallery and changing art exhibitions
Museum of Worcester Porcelain and Royal Worcester Visitor Centre, Severn Street WR1 2NE T 01905-746000
WROUGHTON, nr Swindon, Wilts – *Science Museum*, Wroughton Airfield. T 01793-846200 W www.sciencemuseum.org.uk
Aircraft displays and some of the Science Museum's transport and agricultural collection
YEOVIL, Somerset – *Fleet Air Arm Museum*, Royal Naval Air Station, Yeovilton BA22 8HT T 01935-840565 W www.fleetairarm.com
History of naval aviation; historic aircraft, including Concorde 002
YORKSHIRE - *Beningbrough Hall*, Beningbrough YO30 1DD T 01904-470666
Portraits from the National Portrait Gallery
Castle Museum, Eye of York YO1 9RY T 01904-650333 W www.york.castle.museum
Reconstructed streets; costume and military collections
City Art Gallery, Exhibition Square YO1 7EW T 01904-697979 W www.york.art.museum
European and British painting spanning seven centuries; modern pottery
Eden Camp, Malton, North Yorkshire W www.edencamp.co.uk
Restored POW camp and WW2 memorabilia
Jorvik – The Viking City, Coppergate YO1 9WT T 01904-543403 W www.jorvik-viking-centre.co.uk
Reconstruction of Viking York
National Railway Museum, Leeman Road YO26 4XJ T 01904-621261 W www.nrm.org.uk
Includes locomotives, rolling stock and carriages
Yorkshire Museum, Museum Gardens YO1 7FR T 01904-687687 W www.york.yorkshire.museum
Yorkshire life from Roman to medieval times; geology gallery

WALES

BLAENAFON, Torfaen – *Big Pit National Mining Museum* NP4 9XP T 01495-790311 W www.nmgw.ac.uk/bigpit
Colliery with underground tour
BODELWYDDAN, Denbighshire – *Bodelwyddan Castle* LL18 5YA T 01745-584060 W www.bodelwyddan-castle.co.uk
Portraits from the National Portrait Gallery, furniture from the Victoria and Albert Museum and sculptures from the Royal Academy
CAERLEON - *Roman Legionary Museum* NP6 1AE T 01633-423134 W www.nmgw.ac.uk/rlm
Material from the site of the Roman fortress of Isca and its suburbs
CARDIFF - *National Museum and Gallery Cardiff*, Cathays Park CF10 3NP T 029-2039 7951 W www.nmgw.ac.uk/nmgc
Includes natural sciences, archaeology and Impressionist paintings
Museum of Welsh Life, St Fagans CF5 6XB T 029-2057 3500 W www.nmgw.ac.uk/mwl
Open-air museum with re-erected buildings, agricultural equipment and costume
DRE-FACH FELINDRE, nr Llandysul – *Museum of the Welsh Woollen Industry SA44 5UP* T 01559-370929 W www.nmgw.ac.uk/mwwi
Exhibitions, a working woollen mill and craft workshops
LLANBERIS, nr Caernarfon – *Welsh Slate Museum LL55 4TY* T 01286-870630 W www.nmgw.ac.uk/wsm
Former slate quarry with original machinery and plant; slate crafts demonstrations
LLANDRINDOD WELLS – *National Cycle Collection*, Automobile Palace, Temple Street LD1 5DL T 01597-825531 W www.cyclemuseum.org.uk.

Over 200 bicycles on display, from 1818 to the present day

SWANSEA - *Glynn Vivian Art Gallery and Museum*, Alexandra Road SA1 5DZ T 01792-655006
W www.swansea.gov.uk/glynnvivian
Paintings, ceramics, Swansea pottery and porcelain, clocks, glass and Welsh art

Swansea Museum, Victoria Road SA1 1SN
T 01792-653763
W www.swansea.gov.uk
Archaeology, social history, Swansea pottery

SCOTLAND

ABERDEEN – *Aberdeen Art Gallery*, Schoolhill AB10 1FQ
T 01224-523700 W www.aagm.co.uk
Art from the 18th- to 20th-century

Aberdeen Maritime Museum, Shiprow AB11 5BY
T 01224-337700 W www.aagm.co.uk
Maritime history, incl. shipbuilding and North Sea oil

EDINBURGH - *Britannia*, Leith docks EH6 6JJ
T 0131-555 5566 W www.royalyachtbritannia.co.uk
Former royal yacht with royal barge and royal family picture gallery. Tickets must be pre-booked

City Art Centre, Market Street EH1 1DE T 0131-529 3993
W www.cac.org.uk
Late 19th- and 20th-century art and temporary exhibitions

Museum of Childhood, High Street EH1 1TG
T 0131-529 4142
W www.cac.org.uk
Toys, games, clothes and exhibits relating to the social history of childhood

Museum of Edinburgh, Canongate EH8 8DD
T 0131-529 4143
W www.cac.org.uk
Local history, silver, glass and Scottish pottery

Museum of Flight, East Fortune Airfield, East Lothian EH39 5LF
T 01620-880308
Display of aircraft

Museum of Scotland, Chambers Street EH1 1JF
T 0131-247 4422 W www.nms.ac.uk
Scottish history from prehistoric times to the present

Museum of Scottish Country Life, East Kilbride G76 9HR
T 0131-247 4377
W www.nms.ac.uk
History of rural life and work

National Gallery of Scotland, The Mound EH2 2EL
T 0131-624 6200 W www.nationalgalleries.org
Paintings, drawings and prints from the 16th- to 20th- century, and the national collection of Scottish art

National War Museum of Scotland, Edinburgh Castle EH1 2NG
T 0131-225 7534 W www.nms.ac.uk
History of Scottish military and conflicts

The People's Story, Canongate EH8 8BN T 0131-529 4057
W www.cac.org.uk
Edinburgh life since the 18th-century

Royal Museum of Scotland, Chambers Street EH1 1JF
T 0131-247 4219 W www.nms.ac.uk
Scottish and international collections from prehistoric times to the present

Scottish National Gallery of Modern Art, Belford Road EH4 3DR
T 0131-624 6200 W www.nationalgalleries.org
20th-century painting, sculpture and graphic art

Scottish National Portrait Gallery, Queen Street EH2 1JD
T 0131-624 6200 W www.nationalgalleries.org
Portraits of eminent people in Scottish history, and the national collection of photography

The Writers' Museum, Lawnmarket EH1 2PA T 0131-529 4901
W www.cac.org.uk
Robert Louis Stevenson, Walter Scott and Robert Burns exhibits

FORT WILLIAM - *West Highland Museum*, Cameron Square PH33 6AJ T 01397-702169 W www.fort-william.net/museum
Includes tartan collections and exhibits relating to 1745 uprising

GLASGOW - *Burrell Collection*, Pollokshaws Road G43 1AT
T 0141-287 2550 W www.glasgowmuseums.com
Paintings, textiles, furniture, ceramics, stained glass and silver from classical times to the 19th-century

Gallery of Modern Art, Queen Street G1 3AH T 0141-229 1996
W www.glasgowmuseums.com
Collection of contemporary Scottish and world art

Hunterian Art Gallery, Hillhead Street G12 8QQ
T 0141-330 4221
W www.hunterian.gla.ac.uk
Rennie Mackintosh and Whistler collections; Old Masters, Scottish paintings and modern paintings, sculpture and prints

Kelvingrove Art Gallery and Museum G3 8AG
T 0141-287 2699
W www.glasgowmuseums.com
Includes Old Masters, 19th-century French paintings and armour collection. Closed until 2006 for refurbishment

McLellan Galleries, Sauchiehall Street G2 3EH T 0141-331 1854
W www.glasgowmuseums.com
Temporary exhibitions

Museum of Transport, Bunhouse Road G3 8DP
T 0141-287 2720
W www.glasgowmuseums.com
Includes a reproduction of a 1938 Glasgow street, cars since the 1930s, trams and a Glasgow subway station

People's Palace Museum, Glasgow Green G40 1AT
T 0141-554 0223 W www.glasgowmuseums.com
History of Glasgow since 1175

St Mungo Museum of Religious Life and Art, Castle Street G4 0RH
T 0141-553 2557 W www.glasgowmuseums.com
Explores universal themes through objects of all the main world religions

ST ANDREWS - British Golf Museum, Bruce Embankment KY16 9AB T 01334-460046
W www.british golfmuseum.com
History of golf

NORTHERN IRELAND

BELFAST – *Ulster Museum*, Botanic Gardens BT9 5AB
T 028-9038 3000
W www.ulstermuseum.org.uk
Irish antiquities, natural and local history, fine and applied arts

HOLYWOOD, Co. Down – *Ulster Folk and Transport Museum*, Cultra BT18 0EU
Open-air museum with original buildings from Ulster town and rural life *c*.1900; indoor galleries including Irish rail and road transport and *Titanic* exhibitions

LONDONDERRY - *The Tower Museum*, Union Hall Place BT48 6LU T 028-7137 2411
Tells the story of Ireland through the history of Londonderry

OMAGH, Co. Tyrone – *Ulster American Folk Park*, Castletown BT78 5QY T 028-8224 3292 W www.folkpark.com
Open-air museum telling the story of Ulster's emigrants to America; restored or recreated dwellings and workshops; ship and dockside gallery

SIGHTS OF LONDON

For historic buildings, museums and galleries in London, *see* the Historic Buildings and Monuments and Museums and Galleries sections.

BRIDGES

The bridges over the Thames (from east to west) are:

The Queen Elizabeth II Bridge, opened 1991, from Dartford to Thurrock
Tower Bridge, opened 1894
London Bridge, opened after rebuilding by Rennie, 1831; the new London Bridge opened 1973
Alexandra Bridge (railway bridge), built 1863–6
Southwark Bridge (Rennie), built 1814–19; rebuilt 1912–21
Millennium Bridge, opened June 2000; reopened after modification February 2002
Blackfriars Railway Bridge, completed 1864
Blackfriars Bridge, built 1760–9; rebuilt 1860–9; widened 1907–10
Waterloo Bridge (Rennie), opened 1817; rebuilt 1937–42
Hungerford Footbridge, opened 2002
Hungerford Railway Bridge (Brunel), suspension bridge built 1841–5; replaced by present railway and footbridge 1863
Westminster Bridge, opened 1750; rebuilt 1854–62
Lambeth Bridge, built 1862; rebuilt 1929–32
Vauxhall Bridge, built 1811–16; rebuilt 1895–1906
Grosvenor Bridge (railway bridge), built 1859–60; rebuilt 1963–7
Chelsea Bridge, built 1851–8; replaced by suspension bridge 1934; widened 1937
Albert Bridge, opened 1873; restructured (Bazalgette) 1884; strengthened 1971–3
Battersea Bridge (Holland), opened 1772; rebuilt (Bazalgette) 1890
Battersea Railway Bridge, opened 1863
Wandsworth Bridge, opened 1873; rebuilt 1940
Putney Railway Bridge, opened 1889
Putney Bridge, built 1727–9; rebuilt (Bazalgette) 1882–6; starting point of Oxford and Cambridge Boat Race
Hammersmith Bridge, built 1824–7; rebuilt (Bazalgette) 1883–7; closed 1997–9 for safety work
Barnes Railway Bridge (also pedestrian), built 1846–9; restructured 1893
Chiswick Bridge, opened 1933
Kew Railway Bridge, opened 1869
Kew Bridge, built 1758–9; rebuilt and renamed King Edward VII Bridge 1903
Richmond Lock, lock, weir and footbridge opened 1894
Twickenham Bridge, opened 1933
Richmond Railway Bridge, opened 1848; restructured 1906–8
Richmond Bridge, built 1774–7; widened 1937
Teddington Lock, footbridge opened 1889; marks the end of the tidal reach of the Thames
Kingston Bridge, built 1825–8; widened 1914
Hampton Court Bridge, built 1753; replaced by iron bridge 1865; present bridge built 1933

CEMETERIES

Abney Park, Stamford Hill, N16 (35 acres), tomb of General Booth, founder of the Salvation Army, and memorials to many Nonconformist divines. *Brompton*, Old Brompton Road, SW10 (40 acres), graves of Sir Henry Cole, Emmeline Pankhurst, John Wisden. *City of London Cemetery and Crematorium*, Aldersbrook Road, E12 (200 acres). *Golders Green Crematorium*, Hoop Lane, NW11 (12 acres), with Garden of Rest and memorials to many famous men and women. *Hampstead*, Fortune Green Road, NW6 (36 acres), graves of Kate Greenaway, Lord Lister, Marie Lloyd. *Highgate*, Swains Lane, N6 (38 acres), tombs of George Eliot, Faraday and Marx; guided tours only, west side. *Kensal Green*, Harrow Road, W10 (70 acres), tombs of Thackeray, Trollope, Sydney Smith, Wilkie Collins, Tom Hood, George Cruikshank, Leigh Hunt, I. K. Brunel and Charles Kemble. Churchyard of the former *Marylebone Chapel*, Marylebone High Street, W1, Charles Wesley and his son Samuel Wesley buried; chapel demolished in 1949, now Garden of Rest. *Nunhead*, Linden Grove, SE15 (26 acres), closed in 1969, subsequently restored and opened for burials. *St Marylebone Cemetery and Crematorium*, East End Road, N2 (47 acres). *West Norwood Cemetery and Crematorium*, Norwood High Street, SE27 (42 acres), tombs of Sir Henry Bessemer, Mrs Beeton, Sir Henry Tate and Joseph Whitaker *(Whitaker's Almanack)*.

MARKETS

The London markets are mostly administered by the Corporation of London. *Billingsgate* (fish), Thames Street site dating from 1875, a market site for over 1,000 years, moved to the Isle of Dogs in 1982. *Borough*, SE1 (vegetables, fruit, flowers, etc.), established on present site 1756, privately owned and run. *Covent Garden* (vegetables, fruit, flowers, etc.), established in 1661 under a charter of Charles II, moved in 1973 to Nine Elms, SW8. *Leadenhall*, EC3 (meat, poultry, fish, etc.), built 1881, part recently demolished. *London Fruit Exchange*, Brushfield Street, built by Corporation of London 1928–9 as buildings for Spitalfields market; not connected with the market since it moved in 1991. *Petticoat Lane*, Middlesex Street, E1, a market has existed on the site for over 500 years, now a Sunday morning market selling almost anything. *Portobello Road*, W11, originally for herbs and horse-trading from 1870; became famous for antiques after the closure of the Caledonian Market in 1948. *Smithfield, Central Meat, Fish, Fruit, Vegetable and Poultry Markets*, built 1851–66, the site of St Bartholomew's Fair from 12th- to 19th-century, new hall built 1963, market refurbished 1993–4. *Spitalfields*, E1 (vegetables, fruit, etc.), established 1682, modernised 1928, moved to Leyton in 1991. A much smaller market still exists on the original site on Commercial Street, selling arts, crafts, books, clothes and antiques on Sundays.

MONUMENTS

CENOTAPH, Whitehall, London SW1. The word 'cenotaph' means 'empty tomb'. The monument, erected 'To the Glorious Dead', is a memorial to all ranks of the sea, land and air forces who gave their lives in the service of the Empire during the First World War. Designed by Sir Edwin Lutyens and erected as a temporary memorial in 1919, it was replaced by a permanent structure unveiled by George V on Armistice Day

1920. An additional inscription was made after the Second World War to commemorate those who gave their lives in that conflict.

LONDON MONUMENT, (commonly called The Monument), Monument Street, EC3. Built from designs of Wren, 1671–7, to commemorate the Great Fire of London, which broke out in Pudding Lane on 2 September 1666. The fluted Doric column is 120 ft high; the moulded cylinder above the balcony supporting a flaming vase of gilt bronze is an additional 42 ft; and the column is based on a square plinth 40 ft high (with fine carvings on the west face) making a total height of 202 ft. Splendid views of London from gallery at top of column (311 steps).

OTHER MONUMENTS, (sculptor's name in parenthesis). *Albert Memorial* (Durham), Kensington Gore; *Royal Air Force* (Blomfield), Victoria Embankment; *Viscount Alanbrooke,* Whitehall; *Beaconsfield,* Parliament Square; *Beatty* (Macmillan), Trafalgar Square; *Belgian Gratitude* (setting by Blomfield, statue by Rousseau), Victoria Embankment; *Boadicea* (or Boudicca), Queen of the Iceni (Thornycroft), Westminster Bridge; *Brunel* (Marochetti), Victoria Embankment; *Burghers of Calais* (Rodin), Victoria Tower Gardens, Westminster; *Burns* (Steel), Embankment Gardens; *Canada Memorial* (Granche), Green Park; *Carlyle* (Boehm), Chelsea Embankment; *Cavalry* (Jones), Hyde Park; *Edith Cavell* (Frampton), St Martin's Place; *Cenotaph* (Lutyens), Whitehall; *Charles I* (Le Sueur), Trafalgar Square; *Charles II* (Gibbons), South Court, Chelsea Hospital; *Churchill* (Roberts-Jones), Parliament Square; *Cleopatra's Needle,* (38.5 ft high, *c.*1500 BC, erected in 1877–8; the sphinxes are Victorian), Thames Embankment; *Clive* (Tweed), King Charles Street; *Captain Cook* (Brock), The Mall; *Crimean,* Broad Sanctuary; *Oliver Cromwell* (Thornycroft), outside Westminster Hall; *Cunningham* (Belsky), Trafalgar Square; *Gen. Charles de Gaulle,* Carlton Gardens; *Lord Dowding* (Faith Winter), Strand; *Duke of Cambridge* (Jones), Whitehall; *Duke of York* (124 ft), Carlton House Terrace; *Edward VII* (Mackennal), Waterloo Place; *Elizabeth I* (1586, oldest outdoor statue in London; from Ludgate), Fleet Street; *Eros* (Shaftesbury Memorial) (Gilbert), Piccadilly Circus; *Marechal Foch* (Mallisard, copy of one in Cassel, France), Grosvenor Gardens; *Charles James Fox* (Westmacott), Bloomsbury Square; *George III* (Cotes Wyatt), Cockspur Street; *George IV* (Chantrey), Trafalgar Square; *George V* (Reid Dick), Old Palace Yard; *George VI* (Macmillan), Carlton Gardens; *Gladstone* (Thornycroft), Strand; *Guards'* (Crimea) (Bell), Waterloo Place; *(Great War)* (Ledward, figures, Bradshaw, cenotaph), Horse Guards' Parade; *Haig* (Hardiman), Whitehall; *Sir Arthur (Bomber) Harris* (Faith Winter), Strand; *Irving* (Brock), north side of National Portrait Gallery; *James II* (Gibbons and/or pupils), Trafalgar Square; *Jellicoe* (Wheeler), Trafalgar Square; *Samuel Johnson* (Fitzgerald), opposite St Clement Danes; *Kitchener* (Tweed), Horse Guards' Parade; *Abraham Lincoln* (Saint-Gaudens, copy of one in Chicago), Parliament Square; *Milton* (Montford), St Giles, Cripplegate; *Mountbatten,* Foreign Office Green; *Nelson* (170 ft 2 in), Trafalgar Square, with Landseer's lions (cast from guns recovered from the wreck of the *Royal George*); *Florence Nightingale* (Walker), Waterloo Place; *Palmerston* (Woolner), Parliament Square; *Peel* (Noble), Parliament Square; *Pitt* (Chantrey), Hanover Square; *Portal* (Nemon), Embankment Gardens; *Prince Consort* (Bacon), Holborn Circus; *Queen Elizabeth Gate,* Hyde Park Corner; *Raleigh* (Macmillan), Whitehall; *Richard I (Coeur de Lion)* (Marochetti), Old Palace Yard; *Roberts* (Bates), Horse Guards' Parade; *Franklin D. Roosevelt* (Reid Dick), Grosvenor Square; *Royal Artillery* (South Africa) (Colton), The Mall; (Great War), Hyde Park Corner; *Captain Scott* (Lady Scott), Waterloo Place; *Shackleton* (Sarjeant Jagger), Kensington Gore; *Shakespeare* (Fontana, copy of one by Scheemakers in Westminster Abbey), Leicester Square; *Smuts* (Epstein), Parliament Square; *Sullivan* (Goscombe John), Victoria Embankment; *Trenchard* (Macmillan), Victoria Embankment; *Victoria Memorial,* in front of Buckingham Palace; *Raoul Wallenberg* (Phillip Jackson), Great Cumberland Place; *George Washington* (Houdon copy), Trafalgar Square; *Wellington* (Boehm), Hyde Park Corner, (Chantrey), outside Royal Exchange; *John Wesley* (Adams Acton), City Road; *William III* (Bacon), St James's Square; *Wolseley* (Goscombe John), Horse Guards' Parade.

PARKS, GARDENS AND OPEN SPACES

CORPORATION OF LONDON OPEN SPACES

Ashtead Common (500 acres), Surrey

Burnham Beeches and *Fleet Wood* (540 acres), Bucks. Purchased by the Corporation for the benefit of the public in 1880, Fleet Wood (65 acres) being presented in 1921.

Coulsdon Common (133 acres), Surrey

Epping Forest (6,000 acres), Essex. Purchased by the Corporation and opened to the public in 1882. The present forest is 12 miles long by 1 to 2 miles wide, about one-tenth of its original area.

Farthing Downs (121 acres), Surrey

Hampstead Heath (789 acres), NW3. Including: Golders Hill (36 acres) and Parliament Hill (271 acres)

Highgate Wood (70 acres), N6/N10

Kenley Common (138 acres), Surrey

Queen's Park (30 acres), NW6

Riddlesdown (90 acres), Surrey

Spring Park (51 acres), Kent

West Ham Park (77 acres), E15

West Wickham Common (25 acres), Kent

Woodredon and Warlies Park Estate (740 acres), Waltham Abbey.

Also smaller open spaces within the City of London, including *Finsbury Circus Gardens.*

OTHER PARKS AND GARDENS

CHELSEA PHYSIC GARDEN, 66 Royal Hospital Road, SW3 4HS T 020-7352 5646 W www.chelseaphysicgarden.co.uk. A garden of general botanical research and education, maintaining a wide range of rare and unusual plants. The garden was established in 1673 by the Society of Apothecaries.

ROYAL PARKS

W www.royalparks.gov.uk

Bushy Park (1,099 acres), Middx. Adjoining Hampton Court, contains avenue of horse-chestnuts enclosed in a fourfold avenue of limes planted by William III.

Green Park (40 acres), W1. Between Piccadilly and St James's Park, with Constitution Hill leading to Hyde Park Corner.

Greenwich Park (183 acres), SE10

Hyde Park (350 acres), W1/W2. From Park Lane to Kensington Gardens, containing the Serpentine lake. Fine gateway at Hyde Park Corner, with Apsley House, the Achilles Statue, Rotten Row and the Ladies' Mile. To the north-east is the Marble Arch, originally erected by George IV at the entrance to Buckingham Palace and re-erected in the present position in 1851.

Kensington Gardens (275 acres), W2/W8. From the western boundary of Hyde Park to Kensington Palace, containing the Albert Memorial, Serpentine Gallery and Peter Pan statue.

Kew, Royal Botanic Gardens Richmond, Surrey, TW9 3AB T 020-8332 5655 E info@kew.org W www.rbgkew.org.uk. Officially inscribed on the UNESCO list of World Heritage Sites in July 2003.

Regent's Park and *Primrose Hill* (487 acres), NW1. From Marylebone Road to Primrose Hill surrounded by the Outer Circle and divided by the Broad Walk leading to the Zoological Gardens.

Richmond Park (2,500 acres), Middlesex

St James's Park (93 acres), SW1. From Whitehall to Buckingham Palace. Ornamental lake of 12 acres. The original suspension bridge built in 1857 was replaced in 1957. The Mall leads from the Admiralty Arch to Buckingham Palace, Birdcage Walk from Storey's Gate to Buckingham Palace.

Hampton Court Park and Gardens (669 acres), Surrey

PLACES OF HISTORICAL AND CULTURAL INTEREST

ALEXANDRA PALACE, Alexandra Palace Way, Wood Green, N22 7AY T 020-8365 2121 W www.alexandrapalace.com The Victorian palace was severely damaged by fire in 1980 but was restored, and reopened in 1988. Alexandra Palace now provides modern facilities for exhibitions, conferences, banquets and leisure activities. There is an ice rink, a boating lake, the Phoenix Bar and a conservation area.

BARBICAN CENTRE, Silk Street, EC2Y 8DS T 020-7638 4141 W www.barbican.org.uk Owned, funded and managed by the Corporation of London, the Barbican Centre opened in 1982 and houses the Barbican Theatre, a studio theatre called The Pit, the Barbican Hall and is home to the London Symphony Orchestra. There are also three cinemas, six conference rooms, two art galleries, a sculpture court, a lending library, trade and banqueting facilities, a conservatory, shops, restaurants, cafes and bars.

CHARTERHOUSE, Charterhouse Square, EC1M 6AN T 020-7253 9503 A Carthusian monastery from 1371 to 1537, purchased in 1611 by Thomas Sutton, who endowed it as a residence for aged men 'of gentle birth' and a school for poor scholars (removed to Godalming in 1872).

DOWNING STREET, SW1 Number 10 Downing Street is the official town residence of the Prime Minister, No. 11 to the Chancellor of the Exchequer and No. 12 is the office of the Government Whips. The street was named after Sir George Downing, Bt., soldier and diplomat, who was MP for Morpeth from 1660 to 1684.

GEORGE INN, Borough High Street, SE1 1NH The last galleried inn in London, built in 1677. Now run as an ordinary public house.

GREENWICH, SE10. The Royal Naval College, T 020-8269 4747, was until 1873 the Greenwich Hospital. It was built by Charles II, largely from designs by John Webb, and by Queen Mary II and William III, from designs by Wren. It stands on the site of an ancient abbey, a royal house and Greenwich Palace which was constructed by Henry VII. Henry VIII, Mary I and Elizabeth I were born in the royal palace and Edward VI died there. *Greenwich Park* (196.5 acres), T 020-8858 2608, was enclosed by Humphrey, Duke of Gloucester, and laid out by Charles II from the designs of Le Nôtre. On a hill in Greenwich Park is the *Royal Observatory* (founded 1675). Its buildings are now managed by the *National Maritime Museum*, T 020-8858 4422 and the earliest building is named Flamsteed House, after John Flamsteed (1646–1719), the first Astronomer Royal. *The Cutty Sark*, T 020-8858 3445 The last of the famous tea clippers was moved into a specially constructed dry dock in 1954 and opened to the public in 1957. Sir Francis Chichester's round-the-world yacht, *Gipsy Moth IV*, can also be seen.

HORSE GUARDS, Whitehall, SW1 Archway and offices built about 1753. The changing of the guard takes place at 11a.m. (10a.m. on Sundays) and the dismounted inspection at 4p.m. Only those with the Queen's permission may drive through the gates and archway into *Horse Guards' Parade*, where the Colour is 'trooped' on The Queen's official birthday.

HOUSE OF COMMONS, Westminster, London, SW1A 0AA T 020-7219 4272 E hcinfo@parliament.uk

HOUSE OF LORDS, Westminster, London, SW1A 0PW T 020-7219 3107 E hlinfo@parliament.uk

The royal palace of Westminster, originally built by Edward the Confessor, was the normal meeting place of Parliament from about 1340. St Stephen's Chapel was used from about 1550 for the meetings of the House of Commons, which had previously been held in the Chapter House or Refectory of Westminster Abbey. The House of Lords met in an apartment of the royal palace. The fire of 1834 destroyed much of the palace and the present Houses of Parliament were erected on the site from the designs of Sir Charles Barry and Augustus Welby Pugin between 1840 and 1867. The chamber of the House of Commons was destroyed by bombing in 1941 and a new Chamber designed by Sir Giles Gilbert Scott was used for the first time in 1950. *Westminster Hall and the Crypt Chapel* was the only part of the old palace of Westminster to survive the fire of 1834. It was built by William Rufus (1097–9) and altered by Richard II (1394–9). The hammerbeam roof of carved oak dates from 1396–8. The Hall was the scene of the trial of Charles I. *The Victoria Tower* of the House of Lords is about 330 ft high, and when Parliament is sitting the Union flag flies by day from its flagstaff. *The Clock Tower* of the House of Commons is about 320 ft high and contains 'Big Ben', the hour bell said to be named after Sir Benjamin Hall, First Commissioner of Works when the original bell was cast in 1856. This bell, which weighed 16 tons 11 cwt, was found to be cracked in 1857. The present bell (13.5 tons) is a recasting of the original and was first brought into use in 1859. The dials of the clock are 23 ft in diameter, the hands being 9 ft and 14 ft long (including balance piece). A light is displayed from the Clock Tower at night when Parliament is sitting. During session tours of the Houses of Parliament are only available to UK residents who have made advance arrangements through an MP or peer. Overseas visitors are no longer provided with permits to tour the Houses of Parliament during session, although they can tour during the summer opening and attend debates for both houses in the Strangers' Galleries (*see* below). During the summer recess tickets for tours of the Houses of Parliament can be booked by T 0870-906 3773 or bought on site at the ticket office on Abingdon Green opposite Parliament and the Victoria Tower Gardens. The Strangers' Gallery of the House of Commons is open to the public when the house is sitting. To acquire tickets in advance UK residents should write to their local MP and overseas visitors should apply to their Embassy or High Commission in the UK for a permit. If none of these arrangements have been made, visitors should join the public queue outside St Stephen's Entrance, where there is also a queue for entry to the House of Lords Gallery.

INNS OF COURT The Inns of Court are ancient unincorporated bodies of lawyers which for more than five centuries have had the power to call to the Bar those of their members who have qualified for the rank or degree of Barrister-at-Law. There are four Inns of Court as well as many lesser inns.

Lincoln's Inn, Chancery Lane/Lincoln's Inn Fields, WC2 T 020-7405 1393 W www.lincolnsinn.org.uk The most ancient of the inns with records dating back to 1422. The hall and library buildings are of 1845, although the library is first mentioned in 1474; the old hall (late 15th-century) and the chapel were rebuilt *c.* 1619–23.

Inner Temple, King's Bench Walk, EC4 T 020-7797 8208 W www.innertemple.org.uk

Middle Temple, Fleet Street/Victoria Embankment, EC4 T 020-7427 4800 W www.middletemple.org.uk

Records for the Middle and Inner temple date back to the beginning of the 16th century. The site was originally occupied by the Order of Knights Templars *c.*1160–1312. The two inns have separate halls thought to have been formed *c.* 1350. The division between the two societies was formalised in 1732 with Temple Church and the Masters house remaining in common. The Inner Temple Garden is normally open to the public on weekdays between 12.30p.m. and 3p.m.

Temple Church, EC4 T 020-7353 3470 The nave forms one of five remaining round churches in England. *Master of the Temple,* Revd Robin Griffith-Jones.

Gray's Inn, South Square, WC1 T 020-7458 7900 W www.graysinn.org.uk Founded early 14th-century; Hall 1556–8.

No other 'Inns' are active, but there are remains of *Staple Inn,* a gabled front on Holborn (opposite Gray's Inn Road). *Clement's Inn* (near St Clement Danes Church), *Clifford's Inn,* Fleet Street, and *Thavies Inn,* Holborn Circus, are all rebuilt. *Serjeants' Inn,* Fleet Street, and another (demolished 1910) of the same name in Chancery Lane, were composed of Serjeants-at-Law, the last of whom died in 1922.

LLOYD'S, One Lime Street, EC3M 7HA T 020-7327 1000 W www.lloydsoflondon.com International insurance market which evolved during the 17th-century from Lloyd's Coffee House. The present building was opened for business in May 1986, and houses the Lutine Bell. Underwriting is on three floors with a total area of 114,000 sq. ft. The Lloyd's building is not open to the general public.

LONDON EYE, The Thames South Bank, SE1 T 0870-500 0600 W www.londoneye.com Opened in February 2000 as London's millennium landmark, this 450ft observation wheel is the capital's fourth largest structure. The wheel provides a 30 minute ride offering spectacular panoramic views of the capital.

LONDON ZOO, Regent's Park, NW1 T 020-7722 3333 W www.londonzoo.org

MADAME TUSSAUD'S AND THE LONDON PLANETARIUM, Marylebone Road, NW1 5LR T 0870-400 3000 W www.madame-tussauds.co.uk Waxwork exhibition and interactive star show

MARLBOROUGH HOUSE, Pall Mall, SW1A 5HX Built by Wren for the first Duke of Marlborough and completed in 1711, the house reverted to the Crown in 1835. In 1863 it became the London house of the Prince of Wales and was the London home of Queen Mary until her death in 1953. In 1959 Marlborough House was given by The Queen as the headquarters for the Commonwealth Secretariat and it was opened as such in 1965. The Queen's Chapel, Marlborough Gate was begun in 1623 from the designs of Inigo Jones for the Infanta Maria of Spain, and completed for Queen Henrietta Maria.

PORT OF LONDON, Port of London Authority, Bakers' Hall, 7 Harp Lane, EC3R 6LB T 020-7743 7900 W www.portoflondon.co.uk The Port of London covers the tidal section of the River Thames from Teddington to the seaward limit (the outer Tongue buoy and the Sunk light vessel), a distance of 150km. The governing body is the Port of London Authority (PLA). Cargo is handled at privately operated riverside terminals between Fulham and Canvey Island, including the enclosed dock at Tilbury, 40km below London Bridge. Passenger vessels and cruise liners can be handled at moorings at Greenwich, Tower Bridge and Tilbury.

ROMAN REMAINS, The city wall of Roman *Londinium* was largely rebuilt during the medieval period but sections may be seen near the White Tower in the Tower of London; at Tower Hill; at Coopers' Row; at All Hallows, London Wall, its vestry being built on the remains of a semi-circular Roman bastion; at St Alphage, London Wall, showing a succession of building repairs from the Roman until the late medieval period; and at St Giles, Cripplegate. Sections of the great forum and basilica, more than 165m^2, have been encountered during excavations in the area of Leadenhall, Gracechurch Street and Lombard Street. Traces of Roman activity along the river include a massive riverside wall built in the late Roman period, and a succession of Roman timber quays along Lower and Upper Thames Street. Finds from these sites can be seen at the Museum of London.

Other major buildings are the amphitheatre at Guildhall; remains of bath-buildings in Upper and Lower Thames Street; and the temple of Mithras in Walbrook.

ROYAL ALBERT HALL, Kensington Gore, SW7 2AP T 020-7589 8212 W www.royalalberthall.com The elliptical hall, one of the largest in the world, was completed in 1871, and since 1941 has been the venue each summer for the Promenade Concerts founded in 1895 by Sir Henry Wood. Other events include pop and classical music concerts, dance, opera, sporting events, conferences and banquets.

ROYAL HOSPITAL, CHELSEA, Royal Hospital Road, SW3 4SR T 020-7881 5204 W www.chelsea-pensioners.co.uk Founded by Charles II in 1682, and built by Wren; opened in 1692 for old and disabled soldiers. The extensive grounds include the former Ranelagh Gardens and are the venue for the Chelsea Flower Show each May. *Governor,* Gen. Sir Jeremy Mackenzie, GCB, OBE.

ROYAL OPERA HOUSE, Covent Garden, WC2E 9DD T 020-7304 4000 W www.royalopera.org Home of The Royal Ballet (1931) and The Royal Opera (1946). The Royal Opera House is the third theatre to be built on the site, opening 1858; the first was opened in 1732.

ST JAMES'S PALACE, Pall Mall, SW1A 1BP T 020-7930 4832 W www.royal.gov.uk Built by Henry VIII; the Gatehouse and Presence Chamber remain; later alterations were made by Wren and Kent. Representatives of foreign powers are still accredited 'to the Court of St James's'. *Clarence House* (1825), the official London residence of the Prince of Wales and his sons, stands within the St James's Palace environs.

ST PAUL'S CATHEDRAL, St Paul's Churchyard, EC4M 8AD T 020-7236 4128 E chapter@stpaulscathedral.org.uk W www.stpauls.co.uk Built 1675–1710, cost £747,660. The cross on the dome is 365 ft above the ground level, the inner cupola 218 ft above the floor. 'Great Paul' in the south-west tower weighs nearly 17 tons. The organ by Father Smith (enlarged by Willis and rebuilt by Mander) is in a case carved by Grinling Gibbons, who also carved the choir stalls.

SOMERSET HOUSE, Strand and Victoria Embankment, WC2 The river façade (600 ft long) was built in 1776–86 from the designs of Sir William Chambers; the eastern extension, which houses part of King's College, was built by Smirke in 1829. Somerset House was the property of Lord Protector Somerset, at whose attainder in 1552 the palace passed to the Crown, and it was a royal residence until 1692. Somerset House has recently undergone extensive renovation and is home to the Gilbert Collection, Hermitage Rooms and the Courtauld Institute Gallery. Open-air concerts and ice-skating (Nov–Jan) are held in the courtyard

SOUTH BANK, SE1 The arts complex on the south bank of the River Thames which consists of the *Royal Festival Hall* T 020-7921 0600 W www.rfh.org.uk (opened in 1951 for the Festival of Britain), the adjacent 1,056-seat *Queen Elizabeth Hall*, the *Purcell Room*, and the *Voice Box*.

The *National Film Theatre* (Opened 1952) T 020-7928 3232 W www.bfi.org.uk Administered by the British Film Institute, has three auditoria showing over 2,000 films a year. The London Film Festival is held here every November. There is also an IMAX cinema with 500 seats.

The *Royal National Theatre* T 020-7452 3000 W www.nationaltheatre.org.uk Opened in 1976 and stages classical, modern, new and neglected plays in its three auditoria: the Olivier theatre, the Lyttelton theatre and the Cottesloe theatre.

SOUTHWARK CATHEDRAL, London Bridge, SE1 9DA T 020-7367 6700 E cathedral@dswark.org.uk W www.dswark.org Mainly 13th-century, but the nave is largely rebuilt. The tomb of John Gower (1330–1408) is between the Bunyan and Chaucer memorial windows in the north aisle; Shakespeare's effigy, backed by a view of Southwark and the Globe Theatre, is in the south aisle; the tomb of Bishop Andrewes (died 1626) is near the screen. The lady chapel was the scene of the consistory courts of the reign of Mary (Gardiner and Bonner) and is still used as a consistory court. John Harvard, after whom Harvard University is named, was baptised here in 1607, and the chapel by the north choir aisle is his memorial chapel.

THAMES EMBANKMENTS. The *Victoria Embankment*, on the north side from Westminster to Blackfriars, was constructed by Sir Joseph Bazalgette (1819–91) for the Metropolitan Board of Works, 1864–70; the seats, of which the supports of some are a kneeling camel, laden with spicery, and of others a winged sphinx, were presented by the Grocers' Company and by W. H. Smith, MP, in 1874; the *Albert Embankment*, on the south side from Westminster Bridge to Vauxhall, 1866–9; the *Chelsea Embankment*, 1871–4. The total cost exceeded £2,000,000. Bazalgette also inaugurated the London main drainage system, 1858–65. A medallion (*Flumini vincula posuit*) has been placed on a pier of the *Victoria Embankment* to commemorate the engineer.

THAMES FLOOD BARRIER. Officially opened in May 1984, though first used in February 1983, the barrier consists of ten rising sector gates which span 570 yards from bank to bank of the Thames at Woolwich Reach. When not in use the gates lie horizontally, allowing shipping to navigate the river normally; when the barrier is closed, the gates turn through 90 degrees to stand vertically more than 50 feet above the river bed. The barrier took eight years to complete and can be raised within about 30 minutes.

THAMES TUNNELS. The *Rotherhithe Tunnel*, opened 1908, connects Commercial Road, E14, with Lower Road, Rotherhithe SE16; it is 1 mile 332 yards long, of which 525 yards are under the river. The first *Blackwall Tunnel* (northbound vehicles only), opened 1897, connects East India Dock Road, Poplar, with Blackwall Lane, East Greenwich. The height restriction on the northbound tunnel is 13ft 4in. A second tunnel (for southbound vehicles only) opened 1967. The lengths of the tunnels measured from East India Dock Road to the Gate House on the south side are 6,215 ft (old tunnel) and 6,152 ft. *Greenwich Tunnel* (pedestrians only), opened 1902, connects the Isle of Dogs, Poplar, with Greenwich; it is 406 yards long. The *Woolwich Tunnel* (pedestrians only), opened 1912, connects North and South Woolwich below the passenger and vehicular ferry from North Woolwich Station, E6, to High Street, Woolwich, SE18; it is 552 yards long.

WALTHAM CROSS, Herts. One of the crosses (partly restored) erected by Edward I to mark a resting place of the corpse of Queen Eleanor on its way to Westminster Abbey. Ten crosses were erected, but only those at Geddington, Northampton and Waltham survive; 'Charing' Cross originally stood near the spot now occupied by the statue of Charles I at Whitehall.

WESTMINSTER ABBEY, Broad Sanctuary, SW1P 3PA T 0207-7222 5152 E info@westminster-abbey.org W www. westminster-abbey.org
Founded as a Benedictine monastery over 1,000 years ago, the Church was rebuilt by Edward the Confessor in 1065 and again by Henry III in the 13th-century. The Abbey is the resting place for monarchs including Edward I, Henry III, Henry V, Henry VII, Elizabeth I, Mary I and Mary Queen of Scots, and has been the setting of coronations since that of William the Conqueror in 1066. In Poets' Corner there are memorials to many literary figures, and many scientists and musicians are also remembered here. The grave of the Unknown Warrior is to be found in the nave.

WESTMINSTER CATHEDRAL, 42 Francis Street, SW1P 1QW T 020-7798 9055 W www.westminstercathedral.org.uk Roman Catholic cathedral built 1895–1903 from the designs of J. F. Bentley. The campanile is 283 feet high.

THEATRES

ADELPHI THEATRE, Strand, WC2E 7NA
Tube: Charing Cross **T** 020-7344 0055
ALBERY THEATRE, St Martin's Lane, WC2N 4AH
Tube: Leicester Square **T** 020-7369 1740
ALDWYCH THEATRE, Aldwych, WC2B 4DF
Tube: Covent Garden **T** 020-7379 3367
ALMEIDA THEATRE, Almeida Street, N1 1TA
Tube: Highbury & Islington **T** 020-7359 4404
APOLLO THEATRE, Shaftesbury Avenue, W1V 7HD
Tube: Piccadilly Circus **T** 020-7494 5070
APOLLO VICTORIA THEATRE, Wilton Road, SW1V 1LL
Tube: Victoria **T** 0870-400 0650
ARCOLA THEATRE, Arcola Street, E8 2DJ
Tube: Highbury & Islington **T** 020-7503 1645
ARTS THEATRE, Great Newport Street, WC2H 7JB
Tube: Leicester Square **T** 020-7836 3334
BARBICAN THEATRE, Barbican Centre, EC2Y 8BQ
Tube: Barbican **T** 020-7638 8891
BATTERSEA ARTS CENTRE, Lavender Hill, SW11 5TN
Tube: Clapham Common **T** 020-7223 6557
BRIDEWELL THEATRE, Bride Lane EC4Y 8EQ
Tube: Blackfriars **T** 020-7353 0259
CAMBRIDGE THEATRE, Earlham Street, WC2 9HH
Tube: Covent Garden **T** 020-7494 5549
COLISEUM, St. Martin's Lane WC2
Tube: Charing Cross **T** 020-7836 0111
COMEDY THEATRE, Panton Street, SW1Y 4DN
Tube: Leicester Square **T** 020-7369 1731
CRITERION THEATRE, Piccadilly Circus, W1V 9LB
Tube: Piccadilly Circus **T** 020-7413 1437
DOMINION THEATRE, Tottenham Court Road, W1P 0AG
Tube: Tottenham Court Road **T** 020-7413 3546
DONMAR WAREHOUSE, Earlham Street, WC2H 9LX
Tube: Covent Garden **T** 020-7240 4882
DRURY LANE, Theatre Royal, Catherine Street, WC2B 5JF
Tube: Covent Garden **T** 020-7494 5000
DUCHESS THEATRE, Catherine Street, WC2B 5LA
Tube: Covent Garden **T** 020-7494 5075
DUKE OF YORK'S THEATRE, St Martin's Lane, WC2H 4BG
Tube: Leicester Square **T** 020-7369 1791
FORTUNE THEATRE, Russell Street, WC2B 5HH
Tube: Covent Garden **T** 020-7369 1737
GARRICK THEATRE, Charing Cross Road, WC2H 0HH
Tube: Charing Cross **T** 020-7494 5080
GLOBE THEATRE, New Globe Walk, SE1 9DT
Tube: Mansion House **T** 020-7902 1400
GIELGUD THEATRE, Shaftesbury Avenue, W1V 8AR
Tube: Piccadilly Circus **T** 020-7494 5065
HACKNEY EMPIRE, Mare Street, E8 1EJ
Tube: Bethnal Green **T** 020-8510 4500
HAYMARKET THEATRE, Haymarket, SW1Y 4HT
Tube: Piccadilly Circus **T** 020-7930 8800
HER MAJESTY'S THEATRE, Haymarket, SW1Y 4QL
Tube: Piccadilly Circus **T** 020-7494 5400
LONDON PALLADIUM, Argyll Street, W1A 3AB
Tube: Oxford Circus **T** 020-7494 5570
LYCEUM THEATRE, Wellington Street, WC2E 7DA
Tube: Covent Garden **T** 0870-243 9000
LYRIC THEATRE, Shaftesbury Avenue, W1V 7HA
Tube: Piccadilly Circus **T** 020-7494 5045
NATIONAL THEATRE, South Bank, SE1 9PX
Tube: Waterloo **T** 020-7452 3000
NEW AMBASSADORS THEATRE, West Street, WC2H 9ND
Tube: Leicester Square **T** 020-7369 1761
NEW LONDON THEATRE, Drury Lane, WC2B 5PW
Tube: Holborn **T** 0870-890 0141
OLD VIC THEATRE, Waterloo Road, SE1 8NB
Tube: Waterloo **T** 020-7369 1722
OPEN AIR THEATRE, Regent's Park NW1 4NR
Tube: Regent's Park **T** 020-7935 5756
PALACE THEATRE, Shaftesbury Avenue, W1V 8AY
Tube: Leicester Square **T** 020-7434 0909
PHOENIX THEATRE, Charing Cross Road, WC2H 0JP
Tube: Tottenham Court Road **T** 020 7369 1733
PICCADILLY THEATRE, Denman Street, W1V 8DY
Tube: Piccadilly Circus **T** 020-7369 1734
PLAYHOUSE THEATRE, Northumberland Avenue, WC2N 5DE **Tube**: Embankment **T** 020-7839 4401
PRINCE EDWARD THEATRE, Old Compton Street, W1V 6HS **Tube**: Leicester Square/Tottenham Court Road **T** 020-7447 5400
PRINCE OF WALES THEATRE, Coventry Street, W1V 8AS
Tube: Piccadilly Circus **T** 020-7839 5972
QUEENS THEATRE, Shaftesbury Avenue, W1V 8BA
Tube: Piccadilly Circus **T** 020-7494 5040
ROYAL ALBERT HALL, Kensington Gore, SW7 2AP
Tube: South Kensington **T** 020-7589 8212
ROYAL COURT THEATRE, Sloane Square, SW1W 8AS
Tube: Sloane Square **T** 020-7565 5000
ROYAL FESTIVAL HALL, South Bank SE1 8XX
Tube: Waterloo **T** 020-7921 0600
SADLER'S WELLS, Rosebery Avenue, EC1R 4TN
Tube: Angel **T** 020-7863 8198
SAVOY THEATRE, Strand, WC2R 0ET
Tube: Charing Cross **T** 0870-166 7372
SOHO THEATRE, Dean Street, W1D 3NE
Tube: Tottenham Court Road **T** 020-7287 5060
SHAFTESBURY THEATRE, Shaftesbury Avenue, WC2H 8DP
Tube: Holborn **T** 0870-906 3798
ST MARTIN'S THEATRE, West Street, WC2H 9NH
Tube: Leicester Square **T** 020-7836 1443
STRAND THEATRE, Strand, WC2B 5LD
Tube: Charing Cross **T** 0870-060 2335
VAUDEVILLE THEATRE, Strand, WC2R 0NH
Tube: Charing Cross **T** 0870-890 0511
THE VENUE (NOTRE DAME HALL), Leicester Place, WC2H 7BP **Tube**: Leicester Square **T** 0870-899 3335
VICTORIA PALACE THEATRE, Victoria Street, SW1E 5EA
Tube: Victoria **T** 020-7834 1317
WHITEHALL THEATRE, Whitehall, SW1X 2DY
Tube: Charing Cross **T** 0870-060 6632
WYNDHAM'S THEATRE, Charing Cross Road, WC2H 0DA
Tube: Leicester Square **T** 020-7369 1736
YOUNG VIC, The Cut, SE1 8LZ
Tube: Waterloo **T** 020-7928 6363

HALLMARKS

Hallmarks are the symbols stamped on gold, silver or platinum articles to indicate that they have been tested at an official Assay Office and that they conform to one of the legal standards. With certain exceptions, all gold, silver or platinum articles are required by law to be hallmarked before they are offered for sale. Hallmarking was instituted in England in 1300 under a statute of Edward I.

MODERN HALLMARKS

Since 1 January 1999, UK hallmarks have consisted of three compulsory symbols – the sponsor's mark, the fineness (purity) mark and the assay office mark. Traditional marks such as the year date letter, the Britannia for 958 silver, the lion passant for 925 silver (lion rampant in Scotland) and the orb for 950 platinum may be added voluntarily. The distinction between UK and foreign articles has been removed, and more finenesses are now legal, reflecting the more common finenesses elsewhere in Europe.

SPONSOR'S MARK

Instituted in England in 1363, the sponsor's mark was originally a device such as a bird or fleur-de-lis. Now it consists of the initial letters of the name or names of the manufacturer or firm. Where two or more sponsors have the same initials, there is a variation in the surrounding shield or style of letters.

FINENESS (PURITY) MARK

The fineness (purity) mark indicates that the content of the precious metal in the alloy from which the article is made, is not less than the legal standard. The legal standard is the minimum content of precious metal by weight in parts per thousand, and the standards are:

Gold	999	
	990	
	916.6	(22 carat)
	750	(18 carat)
	585	(14 carat)
	375	(9 carat)
Silver	999	
	958.4	(Britannia)
	925	(sterling)
	800	
Platinum	999	
	950	
	900	
	850	

ASSAY OFFICE MARK

This mark identifies the particular assay office at which the article was tested and marked. The British assay offices are:

LONDON, Goldsmiths' Hall, Gutter Lane, London EC2V 8AQ T 020-7606 8971 W www.thegoldsmiths.co.uk

BIRMINGHAM, PO Box 151, Newhall Street, Birmingham B3 1SB T 0121-236 6951 W www.theassayoffice.co.uk

SHEFFIELD, Guardian's Hall, 137 Portobello Street, Sheffield S1 4DS T 0114-275 5111 W www.assayoffice.co.uk

EDINBURGH, Goldsmiths' Hall, 24a Broughton Street, Edinburgh EH1 3RH T 0131-556 1144 W www.assayofficescotland.com

Assay offices formerly existed in other towns, e.g. Chester, Exeter, Glasgow, Newcastle, Norwich and York, each having its own distinguishing mark.

DATE LETTER

The date letter shows the year in which an article was assayed and hallmarked. Each alphabetical cycle has a distinctive style of lettering or shape of shield. The date letters were different at the various assay offices and the particular office must be established from the assay office mark before reference is made to tables of date letters. Date letter marks became voluntary from 1 January 1999.

The table below shows specimen shields and letters used by the London Assay Office on silver articles in each period from 1498. The same letters are found on gold articles but the surrounding shield may differ. Since 1 January 1975, each office has used the same style of date letter and shield for all articles.

OTHER MARKS

FOREIGN GOODS

Foreign goods imported into the UK are required to be hallmarked before sale, unless they already bear a convention mark (*see* below) or a hallmark struck by an independent assay office in the European Economic Area which is deemed to be equivalent to a UK hallmark.

The following are the assay office marks used for gold until the end of 1998. For silver and platinum the symbols remain the same but the shields differ in shape.

 *London*  *Sheffield*

 *Birmingham*  *Edinburgh*

CONVENTION HALLMARKS

Special marks at authorised assay offices of the signatory countries of the International Convention on Hallmarking (Austria, the Czech Republic, Denmark, Finland, Ireland, the Netherlands, Norway, Portugal, Sweden, Switzerland and the UK) are legally recognised in the United Kingdom as approved hallmarks. These consist of a sponsor's mark, a common control mark, a fineness mark (arabic numerals showing the standard in parts per thousand), and an assay office mark. There is no date letter.

The common control marks are:

	*Gold (18 carat)*
	*Silver*
	*Platinum*

COMMEMORATIVE MARKS

There are three other marks to commemorate special events: the silver jubilee of King George V and Queen Mary in 1935, the coronation of Queen Elizabeth II in 1953, and her silver jubilee in 1977. During 1999 and 2000 there was a voluntary additional Millennium Mark. A mark to commemorate the golden jubilee of Queen Elizabeth II was available during 2002.

LONDON (GOLDSMITHS' HALL) DATE

LETTERS FROM 1498

	Black letter, small	1498–9	1517–8
	Lombardic	1518–9	1537–8
	Roman and other capitals	1538–9	1557–8
	Black letter, small	1558–9	1577–8
	Roman letter, capitals	1578–9	1597–8
	Lombardic. external cusps	1598–9	1617–8
	Italic letter, small	1618–9	1637–8
	Court hand	1638–9	1657–8
	Black letter, capitals	1658–9	1677–8
	Black letter, small	1678–9	1696–7
	Court hand	1697	1715–6
	Roman letter, capitals	1716–7	1735–6
	Roman letter, small	1736–7	1738–9
	Roman letter, small	1739–40	1755–6
	Old English, capitals	1756–7	1775–6
	Roman letter, small	1776–7	1795–6
	Roman letter, capitals	1796–7	1815–6
	Roman letter, small	1816–7	1835–6
	Old English, capitals	1836–7	1855–6
	Old English, small	1856–7	1875–6
	Roman letter, capitals [A to M *square* shield N to Z as shown]	1876–7	1895–6
	Roman letter, small	1896–7	1915–6
	Black letter, small	1916–7	1935–6
	Roman letter, small	1936–7	1955–6
	Italic letter, small	1956–7	1974
	Italic letter, capitals	1975	

BRITISH CURRENCY

The unit of currency is the pound sterling (£) of 100 pence. The decimal system was introduced on 15 February 1971.

COIN

Gold Coins
*One hundred pounds £100
*Fifty pounds £50
*Twenty-five pounds £25
*Ten pounds £10
Five pounds £5
Two pounds £2
Sovereign £1
Half-Sovereign 50p

Silver Coins
*(*Britannia coins)*
Two pounds £2
One pound £1
50 pence 50p
Twenty pence 20p

†Maundy Money
Fourpence 4p
Threepence 3p
Twopence 2p
Penny 1p

‡Bi-colour Coins
Two pounds £2

Nickel-Brass Coins
§Two pounds £2 (pre-1997)
One pound £1

Cupro-Nickel Coins
Crown £5 (since 1990)
50 pence 50p
Crown 25p (pre-1990)
20 pence 20p
10 pence 10p
5 pence 5p

Bronze Coins
2 pence 2p
1 penny 1p

¶Copper-plated Steel Coins
2 pence 2p
1 penny 1p

*Britannia coins: gold bullion coins introduced 1987; silver coins introduced 1997
†Gifts of special money distributed by the Sovereign annually on Maundy Thursday to the number of aged poor men and women corresponding to the Sovereign's own age
‡Cupro-nickel centre and nickel-brass outer ring
§Commemorative coins; not intended for general circulation
¶Since September 1992, although in 1998 the 2p was struck in both copper-plated steel and bronze

GOLD COIN
Gold ceased to circulate during the First World War. Since then controls on buying, selling and holding gold coin have been imposed at various times but have subsequently been revoked. Under the Exchange Control (Gold Coins Exemption) Order 1979, gold coins may now be imported and exported without restriction, except gold coins which are more than 50 years old and valued at a sum in excess of £8,000; these cannot be exported without specific authorisation from the Department of Trade and Industry.

Value Added Taxation on the sale of gold coins was revoked in 2000.

SILVER COIN
Prior to 1920 silver coins were struck from sterling silver, an alloy of which 925 parts in 1,000 were silver. In 1920 the proportion of silver was reduced to 500 parts. From 1 January 1947 all 'silver' coins, except Maundy money, have been struck from cupro-nickel, an alloy of copper 75 parts and nickel 25 parts, except for the 20p, composed of copper 84 parts, nickel 16 parts. Maundy coins continue to be struck from sterling silver.

BRONZE COIN
Bronze, introduced in 1860 to replace copper, is an alloy of copper 97 parts, zinc 2.5 parts and tin 0.5 part. These proportions have been subject to slight variations in the past. Bronze was replaced by copper-plated steel in September 1992 with the exception of 1998 when the 2p was made in both copper-plated steel and bronze.

LEGAL TENDER

Gold (dated 1838 onwards, if not below least current weight)	to any amount
£5 (Crown since 1990)	to any amount
£2	to any amount
£1	to any amount
50p	up to £10
25p (Crown pre-1990)	up to £10
20p	up to £10
10p	up to £5
5p	up to £5
2p	up to 20p
1p	up to 20p

The £1 coin was introduced in 1983 to replace the £1 note. The following coins have ceased to be legal tender:

Farthing	31 December 1960
Halfpenny (½ d)	1 July 1969
Half-crown	1 January 1970
Threepence	31 August 1971
Penny (1d)	31 August 1971
Sixpence	30 June 1980
Halfpenny (½ p)	31 December 1984
old 5 pence	31 December 1990
old 10 pence	30 June 1993
old 50 pence	28 February 1998

The Channel Islands and the Isle of Man issue their own coinage, which are legal tender only in the island of issue.

	Metal	*Standard weight (g)*	*Standard diameter (mm)*
Penny	bronze	3.564	20.3
Penny	copper-plated steel	3.564	20.3
2 pence	bronze	7.128	25.9
2 pence	copper-plated steel	7.128	25.9
5p	cupro-nickel	3.25	18.0
10p	cupro-nickel	6.5	24.5
20p	cupro-nickel	5.0	21.4
25p Crown	cupro-nickel	28.28	38.6
50p	cupro-nickel	8.00	27.3
£1	nickel-brass	9.5	22.5
£2	nickel-brass	15.98	28.4
£2	cupro-nickel, nickel-brass	12.00	28.4
£5 Crown	cupro-nickel	28.28	38.6

The 'remedy' is the amount of variation from standard permitted in weight and fineness of coins when first issued from the Mint.

The Trial of the Pyx is the examination by a jury to ascertain that coins made by the Royal Mint, which have been set aside in the pyx (or box), are of the proper weight, diameter and composition required by law. The trial is held annually, presided over by the Queen's Remembrancer (the Senior Master of the Supreme Court), with a jury of freemen of the Company of Goldsmiths.

BANKNOTES

Bank of England notes are currently issued in denominations of £5, £10, £20 and £50 for the amount of the fiduciary note issue, and are legal tender in England and Wales. No £1 notes have been issued since 1984 and in March 1998 the outstanding notes were written off in accordance with the provision of the Currency Act 1983.

The current E series of notes was introduced from June 1990, replacing the D series (*see* below). The historical figures portrayed in this series are:

£5	May 2002–date	Elizabeth Fry
£5	June 1990–2003	George Stephenson*
£10	November 2000–date	Charles Darwin†
£20	June 1991–2001	Michael Faraday‡
£20	June 1999–date	Sir Edward Elgar
£50	April 1994–date	Sir John Houblon

* Ceased to be legal tender on 21 November 2003

†The version of the Bank of England £10 banknote issued in April 1992, bearing a portrait of Charles Dickens, ceased to be legal tender on 31 July 2003

‡ Withdrawn from circulation on 28 February 2001

NOTE CIRCULATION

Note circulation is highest at the two peak spending periods of the year, around Christmas and during the summer holiday period. The total value of notes in circulation at 2 January 2004 was £39,330 million, compared to £32,574 million at 23 December 2000.

The value of notes in circulation at the end of February 2002 and 2003 was:

	2002	2003
£5	£1,044m	£1,051m
£10	£5,928m	£5,932m
£20	£16,335m	£18,131m
£50	£5,203m	£5,446m
Other notes*	£874m	£3,306m
Total	£29,384m	£33,866m

* Includes higher value notes used internally in the Bank of England, e.g. as cover for the note issues of banks in Scotland and Northern Ireland in excess of their permitted issue.

LEGAL TENDER

Banknotes which are no longer legal tender are payable when presented at the head office of the Bank of England in London.

The white notes for £10, £20, £50, £100, £500 and £1,000, which were issued until April 1943, ceased to be legal tender in May 1945, and the white £5 note in March 1946.

The white £5 note issued between October 1945 and September 1956, the £5 notes issued between 1957 and 1963 (bearing a portrait of Britannia) and the first series to bear a portrait of The Queen, issued between 1963 and 1971, ceased to be legal tender in March 1961, June 1967 and September 1973 respectively.

The series of £1 notes issued during the years 1928 to 1960 and the 10 shilling notes issued from 1928 to 1961 (those without the royal portrait) ceased to be legal tender in May and October 1962 respectively. The £1 note first issued in March 1960 (bearing on the back a representation of Britannia) and the £10 note first issued in February 1964 (bearing a lion on the back), both bearing a portrait of The Queen on the front, ceased to be legal tender in June 1979. The £1 note first issued in 1978 ceased to be legal tender on 11 March 1988. The 10 shilling note was replaced by the 50p coin in October 1969, and ceased to be legal tender on 21 November 1970.

The D series of banknotes was introduced from 1970 and ceased to be legal tender from the dates shown below. The predominant identifying feature of each note was the portrayal on the back of a prominent figure from British history:

£1	Feb. 1978–March 1988	Sir Isaac Newton
£5	Nov. 1971–Nov. 1991	The Duke of Wellington
£10	Feb. 1975–May 1994	Florence Nightingale
£20	July 1970–March 1993	William Shakespeare
£50	March 1981–Sept. 1996	Sir Christopher Wren

The £1 coin was introduced on 21 April 1983 to replace the £1 note.

OTHER BANKNOTES

SCOTLAND – Banknotes are issued by three Scottish banks. The Royal Bank of Scotland issues notes for £1, £5, £10, £20 and £100. Bank of Scotland and the Clydesdale Bank issue notes for £5, £10, £20, £50 and £100. Scottish notes are not legal tender in Scotland but they are an authorised currency.

NORTHERN IRELAND – Banknotes are issued by four banks in Northern Ireland. The Bank of Ireland, the Northern Bank and the Ulster Bank issue notes for £5, £10, £20, £50 and £100. The First Trust Bank issues notes for £10, £20, £50 and £100. Northern Ireland notes are not legal tender in Northern Ireland but they circulate widely and enjoy a status comparable to that of Bank of England notes.

CHANNEL ISLANDS – The States of Guernsey issues its own currency notes and coinage. The notes are for £1, £5, £10, £20 and £50, and the coins are for 1p, 2p, 5p, 10p, 20p, 50p, £1, £2 and £5. The States of Jersey issues its own currency notes and coinage. The notes are for £1, £5, £10, £20 and £50, and the coins are for 1p, 2p, 5p, 10p, 20p, 50p, £1 and £2.

THE ISLE OF MAN – The Isle of Man Government issues notes for £1, £5, £10, £20 and £50. Although these notes are only legal tender in the Isle of Man, they are accepted at face value in branches of the clearing banks in the UK. The Isle of Man issues coins for 1p, 2p, 5p, 10p, 20p, 50p, £1, £2 and £5.

Although none of the series of notes specified above is legal tender in the UK, they are generally accepted by banks irrespective of their place of issue. At one time banks made a commission charge for handling Scottish and Irish notes but this was abolished some years ago.

BANKING

The two main types of deposit-taking institutions are banks and building societies, although National Savings and Investments also provides savings products. Banks and building societies are supervised by the Financial Services Authority and National Savings and Investments is accountable to the Treasury. As a result of the conversion of several building societies into banks in the 1990s, the size of the banking sector, which was already substantially greater than the non-bank deposit-taking sector, increased further.

The main institutions within the British banking system are the Bank of England (the central bank), retail banks, investment banks and overseas banks. In its role as the central bank, the Bank of England acts as banker to the Government and as a note-issuing authority; it also oversees the efficient functioning of payment and settlement systems.

Since May 1997, the Bank of England has had operational responsibility for monetary policy. At monthly meetings of its monetary policy committee the Bank sets the interest rate at which it will lend to the money markets.

OFFICIAL INTEREST RATES 2001–4

5 April 2001	5.50%
10 May 2001	5.25%
2 August 2001	5.00%
18 September 2001	4.75%
4 October 2001	4.50%
8 November 2001	4.00%
6 February 2003	3.75%
10 July 2003	3.50%
6 November 2003	3.75%
5 February 2004	4.00%
6 May 2004	4.25%
10 June 2004	4.50%
5 August 2004	4.75%

RETAIL BANKS

Retail banks offer a wide variety of financial services to individuals and companies, including current and deposit accounts, loan and overdraft facilities, automated teller (cash dispenser) machines, cheque guarantee cards, credit and debit cards, investment services, pensions, insurance and mortgages. All banks offer varying degrees of telephone and internet banking facilities in addition to traditional branch services.

The Financial Ombudsman Service provides independent and impartial arbitration in disputes between banks and their customers.

PAYMENT CLEARINGS

The Association for Payment Clearing Services (APACS) was set up in 1985 as a non-statutory association of major banks and building societies and is now an umbrella organisation for money transmission and payment clearings in the UK. It manages three clearing companies:

- BACS Payment Schemes Ltd (Banker's Automated Clearing Services) is responsible for bulk electronic clearing, processing direct debits, direct credits and standing orders
- the Cheque and Credit Clearing Company Ltd operates bulk clearing systems for cheques and paper credit items in Great Britain
- CHAPS Ltd (Clearing House Automated Payment System) provides multi-national same-day clearing for electronic funds transfers in sterling and euro

Membership of APACS is open to any member of a payment scheme which is widely used or significant in the UK. As at May 2004, APACS had 33 members, comprising the major banks, building societies and Royal Mail Group.

ASSOCIATION FOR PAYMENT CLEARING SERVICES (APACS), Mercury House, Triton Court, 14 Finsbury Square, London EC2A 1LQ **T** 020-7711 6200 **F** 020-7256 5527 **W** www.apacs.org.uk

GLOSSARY OF FINANCIAL TERMS

AER (ANNUAL EQUIVALENT RATE) – A notional rate quoted on savings and investment products which demonstrates the return on interest if interest was compounded and paid annually instead of monthly.

APR (ANNUAL PERCENTAGE RATE) – APR calculates the total amount of interest that is payable over the whole term of a loan. Companies offering loans, credit cards, mortgages or overdrafts are required by law to provide the APR rate.

ATM (AUTOMATED TELLER MACHINES) – Commonly referred to as cash machines, they enable users to access their bank accounts using a card and carry out transactions such as withdrawing cash. Some banks and independent ATM deployers charge for transactions.

MAJOR RETAIL BANKS' FINANCIAL RESULTS 2003

Bank Group	*Profit/(loss) before taxation* £m	*Profit/(loss) after taxation* £m	*Total assets* £m	*Number of UK Branches*
Abbey	(686)	(644)	176,775	–
Alliance and Leicester	525	379	48,424	300
Barclays (incorporating Woolwich)	3,845	2,769	443,361	2,070
HBOS (Halifax/Bank of Scotland)	3,766	2,675	408,413	–
HSBC	2,244	1,603	246,104	1602
Lloyds/TSB	4,348	3,323	252,012	2,200+
Northern Rock	387	276	37,160	56
RBS Group (Royal Bank of Scotland including National Westminster)	6,159	4,249	455,275	2,270+

BANKER'S DRAFT – A cheque drawn on a bank against a cash deposit. Banker's drafts are considered to be a secure way of receiving money in instances where a cheque would otherwise 'bounce' or where it is not desirable to receive cash.

BASE RATE – The minimum rate at which banks are prepared to lend money. The base rate acts as a benchmark for other interest rates, e.g. for mortgages or personal loans.

CAPPED RATE MORTGAGES – The interest rate applied to the loan is capped at a certain rate for a set period of time. Even if the base interest rate rises the borrower has the security of knowing that interest payments will not increase above a certain level. If the standard variable mortgage rate is less than the capped rate the borrower is charged at that rate, benefiting from any decrease in the base interest rate.

CASH CARD – Issued by banks and building societies for withdrawing cash from cash machines.

CHARGE CARD – Charge cards, e.g. American Express and Diners Club, can be used in a similar way to credit cards but the debt must be settled in full each month.

CHIP AND PIN CARD – A credit/debit card which incorporates an embedded chip containing unique owner details. When used with a PIN number, such cards offer greater security as they are less prone to fraud.

CREDIT CARD – Normally issued with a credit limit, credit cards can be used for purchases until the limit is reached. There is normally an interest-free period on the outstanding balance of up to 56 days. Charges can be avoided if the balance is paid off in full within the interest-free period. Alternatively part of the balance can be paid and in most cases there is a minimum amount set by the issuer (normally a percentage of the outstanding balance) which must be paid on a monthly basis. Some card issuers charge an annual fee and most issuers belong to a least one major credit card network, e.g. Mastercard or Visa.

CRITICAL ILLNESS COVER – Insurance cover against critical illnesses such as stroke, heart attack or cancer, which is designed to protect mortgage or other loan payments.

DEBIT CARD – Debit cards were introduced on a large scale in the UK in the mid-1980s, replacing cash and cheques for many smaller transactions, and can be used to purchase goods and services in shops and via mail order. They can be used to withdraw cash from ATMs in the UK and abroad and may also function as a cheque guarantee card. Funds are automatically withdrawn from an individual's bank account after making a purchase and no interest is charged.

DISCOUNTED MORTGAGE – Discounted mortgages offer an interest rate set at a margin below the standard variable rate for a set period of time.

ENDOWMENT MORTGAGE – Only the interest on a property loan is paid back to the lender each month as long as an endowment life insurance policy is taken out for an agreed amount of time, typically 25 years. When the policy matures the lender will take repayment of the money owed on the property loan and any surplus goes to the policyholder. If the Endowment policy shows a shortfall on projected returns, the policy holder must make further provision to pay off the mortgage.

EPS (EARNINGS PER SHARE) – EPS is a measure of how many pence a company is earning for every share issued. The EPS is calculated by dividing the company's pre-tax profit dividend by the number of shares in issue.

EQUITY – In housing terms, equity is the difference between the value of a property and the amount outstanding on any loan secured against it. Negative equity occurs when the loan is greater than the market value of the property.

FIXED RATE MORTGAGE – A repayment mortgage where the interest on the loan is fixed at a certain rate for a set amount of time, normally a period of between one and ten years. The interest rate does not vary with changes to the base rate resulting in the monthly mortgage payment remaining the same for the duration of the fixed period.

INTEREST ONLY MORTGAGE – Only interest is payed by the borrower and capital remains constant for the term of the loan. The onus is on the borrower to make provision to repay the capital at the end of the term. This is usually achieved through an investment vehicle such as an endowment policy or pension.

ISA – The Individual Savings Account is a means by which investors can save and invest without paying income or capital gains taxes on the proceeds. Money can be invested across three investment elements: cash, stocks and shares and life insurance products. There are limits to how much can be invested during any given tax year.

LOAN TO VALUE – The Loan to Value is the ratio between the size of a mortgage loan sought and the mortgage lender's valuation. On a loan of £55,000, for example on a property valued at £100,000, the loan to value is 55 per cent meaning that there is sufficient enough equity in the property for the lender to be reassured that if interest/capital repayments were stopped, it could sell property and recoup the money owed.

MIG (MORTGAGE INDEMNITY GUARANTEE) – MIG is an insurance policy designed to protect the lender against loss in the event of the borrower defaulting or ceasing to repay a mortgage.

ONLINE BANKING – Also known as internet or e-banking where everything from paying bills to arranging overdrafts can be carried out online.

PIN (PERSONAL IDENTIFICATION NUMBER) – A PIN is issued alongside a cash card to allow the user to access a bank account via an ATM. PINs are also issued with Smart, Credit and Debit Cards and are often requested in shops and restaurants as a further security measure when making a purchase.

SMART CARDS – Smart Cards are a new generation of cashless payment system. They carry more information than debit cards including mortgage and health details and a fixed number of units of real money. The card is used in conjunction with a PIN and once the money on the card is spent, it must be loaded up again by transferring money to it from a bank account via an ATM or by telephone.

TELEPHONE BANKING – Banking facilities which can be accessed via the telephone.

VARIABLE RATE MORTGAGE – Repayment mortgages where the interest rate set by the lender increases or decreases in relation to the base interest rate occasionally resulting in fluctuations in monthly repayments.

FINANCIAL SERVICES REGULATION

FINANCIAL SERVICES AUTHORITY

The FSA has been the single regulator for financial services in the UK since 1 December 2001, when the Financial Services and Markets Act 2000 (FSMA) came into force. The FSA's aim is to maintain efficient, orderly and clean financial markets and help consumers get a fair deal. The FSA is required to pursue four statutory objectives:

- maintaining market confidence
- raising public awareness
- protecting consumers
- reducing financial crime

The legislation also requires the FSA to carry out its general functions, whilst having regard to:

- using its resources in the most efficient way
- the responsibilities of regulated firms' own management
- being proportionate in imposing burdens or restrictions on the industry
- facilitating innovation
- the international character of financial services and the competitive position of the United Kingdom
- not impeding or distorting competition unnecessarily

ORGANISATION AND STRUCTURE

The FSA is a company limited by guarantee, financed by levies on the industry. It receives no funds from the public purse. It is accountable to Treasury ministers and, through them, to Parliament. The FSA must report annually on the achievement of its statutory objectives to the Treasury, which is required to lay the report before Parliament.

The FSA's governing body is a board appointed by the Treasury and consists of a Chairman, a Chief Executive Officer, three executive directors and 11 non-executive directors (including the Deputy Chairman). The Board sets overall FSA policy. Day-to-day operational decisions and management of the staff are the responsibility of the Executive, which consists of three units: Regulatory Services, Retail Markets and Wholesale and Institutional Markets, each headed by a managing director.

The Budget for the FSA's mainstream regulatory activities for 2004–5 is £201.6 million, 2.2 percent higher than in 2003–4.

FSA REGISTER OF AUTHORISED FIRMS AND PERSONS

The FSA maintains a register of all firms that are authorised to carry out investment business and are authorised deposit takers. The entry for each firm gives its name, address and telephone number; a reference number; its authorisation status (outlining exactly what financial services the firm is authorised to provide), stating which organisation regulates it and whether it can handle client money. In addition the FSA keeps a list of approved persons in the industry who are authorised to carry out functions regulated by the FSA. Each entry includes the list of controlled functions an individual is authorised to perform and for which firms.

From 31 October 2004, mortgage lending, sales and administration and from 14 January 2005, general insurance sales and administration will become regulated activities. As a statutory requirement all companies carrying out these activities will need to be authorised by the FSA.

The Consumer Helpline is available to members of the public seeking information about firms and individuals listed on the register. In addition, the Helpline explains complaints procedures and provides information on what is and is not regulated by the FSA. Firms and individuals can also be checked on the FSA website.

FINANCIAL SERVICES AUTHORITY
25 the North Colonade, Canary Wharf, London E14 5HS
T 020-7066 1000 Helpline 0845-606 1234 F 020-7066 1099
W www.fsa.gov.uk
Chairman, Callum McCarthy
Chief Executive Officer, John Tiner

COMPENSATION

Under the FSMA the Financial Services Compensation Scheme (FSCS) replaced eight previous compensation schemes. It provides compensation if an authorised firm is unable or likely to be unable to pay claims against it. This is usually when a firm stops trading or is insolvent. The FSCS covers deposits, insurance and investments. The FSCS is independent from the FSA, with separate staff and premises. However, the FSA appoints the board of the FSCS and sets its guidelines. The FSCS is funded by levies on authorised firms.

FINANCIAL SERVICES COMPENSATION SCHEME
7th Floor, Lloyds Chambers, 1 Portsoken Street, E1 8BN
T 020-7892 7300 F 020-7892 7301
E enquiries@fscs.org.uk W www.fscs.org.uk
Chairman, Nigel Hamilton
Interim Chief Executive, Ron Devlin

DESIGNATED PROFESSIONAL BODIES

Professional firms are exempt from requiring direct regulation by the FSA if they carry out only certain restricted activities that arise out of, or are complementary to the provision of professional services, such as arranging the sale of shares on the instructions of executors or trustees or providing services to small, private companies. These firms are, however, supervised by Designated Professional Bodies (DPBs). There are a number of safeguards to protect consumers dealing with firms that do not require direct regulation. These arrangements include:

- the FSA's power to ban a specific firm from taking advantage of the exemption and to restrict the regulated activities permitted to the firms
- rules which require professional firms to ensure that their clients are aware that they are not authorised persons
- a requirement for the DPBs to supervise and regulate the firms and inform the FSA on how the professional firms carry on their regulated activities

The DPBs are:

INSTITUTE OF CHARTERED ACCOUNTANTS IN ENGLAND AND WALES, Chartered Accountants' Hall, PO Box 433, Moorgate Place, London EC2P 2BJ T 020-7920 8100 W www.icaew.co.uk

INSTITUTE OF CHARTERED ACCOUNTANTS OF SCOTLAND, CA House, 21 Haymarket Yards, Edinburgh EH12 5BH T 0131-347 0100 W www.icas.org.uk

INSTITUTE OF CHARTERED ACCOUNTANTS IN IRELAND, 11 Donegall Square South, Belfast BT1 5JE T 028-9032 1600 W www.icai.ie

ASSOCIATION OF CHARTERED CERTIFIED ACCOUNTANTS, 29 Lincoln's Inn Fields, London WC2A 3EE T 020-7242 6855 7000 W www.acca.co.uk

INSTITUTE OF ACTUARIES, Staple Inn Hall, High Holborn, London WC1V 7QJ T 020-7632 2100 W www.actuaries.org.uk

THE LAW SOCIETY OF ENGLAND AND WALES, 113 Chancery Lane, London WC2A 1PL T 020-7242 1222 W www.lawsociety.org.uk

LAW SOCIETY OF NORTHERN IRELAND, Law Society House, 98 Victoria Street, Belfast BT1 3JT T 028-9023 1614 W www.lawsoc-ni.org

LAW SOCIETY OF SCOTLAND, 26 Drumsheugh Gardens, Edinburgh EH3 7YR T 0131-226 7411 W www.lawscot.org.uk

RECOGNISED INVESTMENT EXCHANGES

The FSA supervises seven Recognised Investment Exchanges (RIEs). These are organised markets on which member firms can trade investments such as equities and derivatives. Examples are the London Stock Exchange and the London Metal exchange. As a regulator the FSA must also focus on the impact of changes brought about by the continued growth in electronic trading by exchanges and other organisations. Issues such as how these changes affect market quality, reliability and access are important and the FSA works with the exchanges to ensure that new systems meet regulatory requirements. The RIEs are listed with their year of recognition:

INTERNATIONAL PETROLEUM EXCHANGE (IPE) (1988), International House, 1 St Katharine's Way, London E1W 1UY T 020-7481 0643 F 020-7481 8485 W www.theipe.uk.com

LONDON INTERNATIONAL FINANCIAL FUTURES EXCHANGE (LIFFE) (1988), Cannon Bridge House, 1 Cousin Lane, London EC4R 3XX T 020-7623 0444 W www.liffe.com

LONDON METAL EXCHANGE (LME) (1988), 56 Leadenhall Street, London EC3A 2DX T 020-7264 5555 F 020-7680 0505 W www.lme.co.uk

LONDON STOCK EXCHANGE (LSE) (1988), 10 Paternoster Square, London EC4M 7LS T 020-7797 1000 W www.londonstockexchange.com

OM LONDON EXCHANGE LTD (1989), 131 Finsbury Pavement, London EC2A 1NT T 020-7065 8000 F 020-7065 8001 W www.omhex.com

VIRT-X EXCHANGE LTD (2001), 34th Floor, One Canada Square, London E14 5AA T 020-7074 4444 W www.virt-x.com

EUROPEAN DERIVATIVES EXCHANGE LONDON LTD (EDX) (2003), 10 Paternoster Square, London EC4M 7LS T 020-7797 1000 (*see also* London Stock Exchange section)

RECOGNISED CLEARING HOUSES

The FSA is also responsible for recognising and supervising Recognised Clearing Houses. These bodies organise the settlement of transactions on Recognised Investment Exchanges. There are currently two Recognised Clearing Houses.

CREST CO LTD (1996), 33 Cannon Street, London EC4M 5SB T 020-7849 0000 F 020-7849 0130 E info@crestco.co.uk W www.crestco.co.uk

LONDON CLEARING HOUSE CLEARNET GROUP (LCH.CLEARNET) (1988), Aldgate House, 33 Aldgate High Street, London EC3N 1EA T 020-7426 7000 W www.lchclearnet.com

OMBUDSMAN SCHEMES

The Financial Ombudsman Service was set up by the Financial Services and Markets Act to provide consumers with a free, independent service for resolving disputes with financial firms. It brought together eight complaints-handling schemes within the financial sector including the Banking Ombudsman, the Insurance Ombudsman, the Investment Ombudsman and the Personal Investment Authority Ombudsman. It can make binding awards up to £100,000. The Financial Ombudsman Service can help with most financial complaints about:

- Banking services
- Credit cards issued by banks and building societies
- Endowment policies
- Financial and investment advice
- Health and loan protection insurance
- Household and buildings insurance
- Investment portfolio management
- Life assurance
- Mortgages
- Motor insurance
- Personal pension plans
- Private medical insurance
- Saving plans and accounts
- Stocks and shares
- Travel insurance
- Unit trusts and income bonds

Complainants must first complain to the firm involved. They do not have to accept the ombudsman's decision and are free to go to court if they wish.

The Pensions Ombudsman is appointed and operates under the Pension Schemes Act 1993 as amended by the Pensions Act 1995; he is responsible to Parliament. He investigates and decides complaints and disputes concerning occupational and personal pension schemes, primarily alleged maladministration by the persons responsible for managing pension schemes.

FINANCIAL OMBUDSMAN SERVICE, South Quay Plaza, 183 Marsh Wall, London, E14 9SR **T** 0845-080 1800 (helpline); 020-7964 1000 **F** 020-7964 1001
W www.financial-ombudsman.org.uk
E complaint.info@financial-ombudsman.org.uk
Chief Ombudsman: Walter Merricks
Principal Ombudsmen: Tony Boorman; David Thomas; Jane Whittles

PENSIONS OMBUDSMAN, 6th Floor, 11 Belgrave Road, London SW1V 1RB **T** 020-7834 9144
Pensions Ombudsman, D. Laverick

THE TAKEOVER PANEL

The Takeover Panel was set up in 1968 in response to concern about practices unfair to shareholders in take-over bids for public and certain private companies. Its principal objective is to ensure equality of treatment, and fair opportunity for all shareholders to consider on its merits an offer that would result in the change of control of a company. It is a non-statutory body that operates the City code on take-overs and mergers.

The chairman, deputy chairmen and three lay members of the panel are appointed by the Bank of England. The remainder are representatives of the banking, insurance, investment, pension fund and accountancy professional bodies and the CBI.

PANEL ON TAKEOVERS AND MERGERS, 10 Paternoster Square, London EC4M 7DY **T** 020-7382 9026
W www.takeoverpanel.org.uk
Chairman, Peter Scott, QC

NATIONAL SAVINGS AND INVESTMENTS

National Savings and Investments (formerly National Savings) is one of the largest savings organisations in the UK, and is a government department and executive agency of HM Treasury. Savings and investment products are offered to personal savers and investors and the money is used to manage the national debt more effectively. When people invest in National Savings and Investments they are lending money to the government which pays them interest in return.

TAX-FREE PRODUCTS

NATIONAL SAVINGS AND INVESTMENT CERTIFICATES

INDEX-LINKED SAVING CERTIFICATES

Index-linked Saving Certificates are fixed rate investments that pay tax-free returns guaranteed to be above inflation. They are available in three and five-year terms and are sold in issues. The minimum investment for each issue is £100 and the maximum £15,000.

FIXED INTEREST CERTIFICATES

Fixed Interest Certificates are fixed rate investments that pay tax-free returns. They are available in two and five-year terms and are sold in issues for which the minimum investment is £100 and the maximum £15,000. The certificates are repaid in full with all interest gained at the end of the term.

PREMIUM BONDS

Premium Bonds are a government security and were first introduced in 1956. Premium Bonds enable savers to enter a regular draw for tax-free prizes, while retaining the right to get their money back. A sum equivalent to interest on each bond is put into a prize fund and distributed by monthly prize draws. The prizes are drawn by ERNIE (electronic random number indicator equipment) and are free of all UK income tax and capital gains tax. The top prize is £1 million.

Bonds are in units of £1, with a minimum purchase of £100; above this, purchases must be in multiples of £10, up to a maximum holding limit of £30,000 per person. The scheme offers a facility to reinvest prize wins automatically. Upon completion of an automatic prize reinvestment mandate, holders receive new bonds which are immediately eligible for future prize draws. Bonds can only be held in the name of an individual and not by organisations.

Bonds become eligible for prizes once they have been held for one clear calendar month following the month of purchase. Each £1 unit can win only one prize per draw, but it will be awarded the highest for which it is drawn. Bonds remain eligible for prizes until they are repaid. When a holder dies, bonds remain eligible for prizes up to and including the twelfth monthly draw after the month in which the holder dies.

Since the first prize draw in 1957, over 109 million prizes totalling £7 billion have been distributed.

CHILDREN'S BONUS BONDS

Children's Bonus Bonds were introduced in 1991. They can be bought for any child under 16 and will go on growing in value until he or she is 21. The bonds are sold in five-year issues at multiples of £25. For each issue the minimum holding is £25 and the maximum holding is £1,000 per child. Bonds for children under 16 must be held by a parent or guardian. All returns are totally exempt from UK income tax and a bonus is payable if the bond is held for the full five years.

OTHER PRODUCTS

GUARANTEED EQUITY BONDS

Guaranteed Equity Bonds are five year investments where the returns are linked to the performance of the FTSE-100 index with a guarantee that the original capital invested will be returned even if the FTSE-100 index fell over the five years. They are sold in limited issues with a minimum investment of £1,000 and a maximum of £1 million. The returns are subject to income tax on maturity.

SAVINGS AND INVESTMENT ACCOUNTS

The Easy Access Savings Account was launched in January 2004 replacing the Ordinary Account (also known as the Post Office Savings Account) which was closed on 31 July 2004. The Easy Access Savings Account, offers access to savings via Post Office counters, an ATM card, telephone and the internet and can be opened with a minimum balance of £100 and has a maximum limit of £2 million (£4 million jointly). The interest is paid without deduction of tax at source. Holders of the Ordinary Account can no longer undertake transactions except for closing the account or transferring the funds to an Easy Access Savings Account or the Investment Account.

The Investment Account is a passbook account and requires one month notice for withdrawals. Repayments can be made without notice but incur a penalty equivalent to the previous 30 days' interest on the amount withdrawn.

Since April 1999 Individual Savings Accounts (ISAs) have been offered by National Savings and Investments. A cash mini ISA can be opened with £10. Interest is calculated daily and is free of tax. The same regulations apply for ISAs offered by all companies.

INCOME BONDS

National Savings and Investments Income Bonds were introduced in 1982. They are suitable for those who want to receive regular monthly payments of interest while preserving the full cash value of their capital. The bonds are sold in multiples of £500. The minimum holding is £500 and the maximum £1 million (sole or joint holding). Interest is calculated on a day-to-day basis and paid monthly. Interest is taxable but is paid without deduction of tax at source.

PENSIONERS GUARANTEED INCOME BONDS

Pensioners Guaranteed Income Bonds were introduced in January 1994 and are designed for people aged 60 and over who wish to receive regular monthly payments with a rate of interest that is fixed for a period whilst preserving the full cash value of their investment. Five, two and one-year terms are available and are sold in issues. The minimum limit for each issue is £500. The maximum holding is £1,000,000 (sole or joint holding) with the rate of interest fixed and guaranteed for each bond purchased. Interest is taxable but is paid without deduction of tax at source. The original capital investment is repaid in full at the end of the term.

FIXED RATE SAVINGS BOND
Fixed Rate Savings Bonds are investments that earn fixed rates of interest. Five, three and one-year terms are available and are sold in issues. The minimum investment is £500 and the maximum £1 million. Interest, from which basic rate tax is deducted at source, can be paid out or reinvested into the bond monthly, annually or at the end of the term. Holders can also choose where the interest is paid. The original capital investment is repaid in full at the end of the term.

CAPITAL BONDS
National Savings and Investments Capital Bonds were introduced in 1989. Five year Capital Bonds are sold in issues. The interest is taxable each year (for those who pay income tax) but is not deducted at source. For each issue, the minimum investment is £100 and the maximum £1 million. Capital Bonds are repaid in full with all interest gained at the end of five years.

TREASURER'S ACCOUNT
The Treasurer's Account, introduced in September 1996, offers attractive rates and security to non-profit making organisations such as charities, friendly societies, clubs, etc. The minimum holding is £10,000 and the maximum is £2 million.

FURTHER INFORMATION
For the latest information on National Savings and Investments' products and interest rates call T 0845-964 5000 or visit W www.nsandi.com or a Post Office branch. To buy National Savings and Investments' products call T 0500-500 000 or visit www.nsandi.com or a Post Office branch.

THE LONDON STOCK EXCHANGE

The London Stock Exchange serves the needs of industry and investors by providing facilities for raising capital and a central market-place for securities trading. This market-place covers government stocks (called gilts), UK and overseas company shares (called equities and fixed interest stocks), and other instruments such as covered warrants and Exchange Traded Funds (EFTs).

PRIMARY MARKETS

The Exchange enables companies to raise capital for development and growth through the issue of securities. For a company entering the market for the first time there is a choice of Exchange markets, depending upon the size, history and requirements of the company. The first is the Main Market. A company's securities are admitted to the Official List by the UK Listing Authority (UKLA), a division of the Financial Services Authority, and also admitted to trading by the Exchange.

The Alternative Investment Market (AIM) was established in June 1995. It enables small, young and growing companies to raise capital, widen their investor base and have their shares traded on a regulated market without the expense of a full Exchange listing. Many companies use AIM as a stepping-stone to a full listing.

Once admitted to the AIM, all companies are obliged to keep their shareholders informed of their progress, making announcements of a price-sensitive nature through a Primary Information Provider. At 31 December 2003 there were 1,557 UK companies listed on the London Stock Exchange; their equity capital had a total market value of £1,356 billion. In addition, 381 international companies were listed, with a total equity market value of £1,975 billion. By the end of 2003 AIM had attracted 754 companies, with a total capitalisation of £184 billion.

UK equity turnover in 2003 was £1,876,922 million with an average of 182,000 bargains a day. International equity turnover in 2003 totalled £1,759,120 million.

BIG BANG

During 1986 the London Stock Exchange went through the greatest period of change in its 200-year history. In March 1986 it opened its doors for the first time to overseas and corporate membership, allowing banks, insurance companies and overseas securities houses to become members of the Exchange and to buy existing member firms. On 27 October 1986, three major reforms took place and became known as 'Big Bang':

- the abolition of scales of minimum commissions, allowing clients to negotiate freely with their brokers about the charge for their services
- the abolition of the separation of member firms into brokers and jobbers: firms are now broker/dealers, able to act as agents on behalf of clients; to act as principals buying and selling shares for their own account; and to become registered market makers, making continuous buying and selling prices in specific securities
- the introduction of the Stock Exchange Automated Quotations (SEAQ) system

Since the introduction of SEAQ in 1986, dealing in stocks and shares has taken place by telephone in the firms' own dealing rooms, rather than face to face on the floor of the Exchange. The Stock Exchange Electronic Trading Service (SETS), launched in 1997, introduced order-driven trading in which deals are executed electronically on an electronic order book. SETS runs alongside SEAQ and allows remote access to the Exchange. The new systems also provide increased investor protection. All deals taking place via the Exchange systems are recorded on a database which can be used to resolve disputes or to carry out investigations.

Firms Trading on the London Stock Exchange buy and sell shares on behalf of the public, as well as institutions such as pension funds or insurance companies. In return for transacting the deal, the broker will charge a commission, which is usually based upon the value of the transaction. The market makers, or wholesalers, in each security do not charge a commission for their services, but will quote the broker two prices, a price at which they will buy and a price at which they will sell. It is the middle of these two prices which is published in lists of share prices in newspapers.

REGULATION

The Financial Services Authority (FSA) has overall responsibility for regulating the UK's financial industry under the provisions of the Financial Services Act 1986. This Act requires investment businesses to be authorised and regulated by a self-regulating organisation (SRO) and compels business to be conducted through a recognised investment exchange (RIE). The London Stock Exchange is an RIE, regulating three main markets: UK equities, international equities and gilts.

DEVELOPMENTS

On 15 March 2000, the 298 members voted to become shareholders in a demutualised London Stock Exchange, making possible the further commercialisation of the company.

At the end of May 2001 the exchange announced its intention to list on its own main market. The exchange listed on 20 July following an annual general meeting on 19 July 2001. The full listing is intended to enable the Exchange to exploit business opportunities with greater flexibility.

In 2003 the London Stock Exchange created EDX London (European Derivatives Exchange), a new international equity derivatives business, in partnership with the OM Group.

LONDON STOCK EXCHANGE, 10 Paternoster Square, London EC4M 7LS T 020-7797 1000
W www.londonstockexchange.com
Chairman, Chris Gibson-Smith
Chief Executive, Clara Furse

INSURANCE

AUTHORISATION AND REGULATION OF INSURANCE COMPANIES

On 1 December 2001 the Financial Services Authority (FSA) assumed its powers under the Financial Services and Markets Act 2000. This saw the FSA take over responsibility for a wide range of activities including the authorisation of insurance companies operating in the UK, the regulation of investment related insurance products and the preparations for a statutory regulation regime for general insurance products.

FINANCIAL SERVICES AUTHORITY
25 The North Colonnade, London E14 5HS
T 020-7066 1000 W www.fsa.gov.uk

AUTHORISATION

The FSA's role is to ensure that firms to which it grants authorisation satisfy the necessary financial criteria, that the senior managers of the company are 'fit and proper persons' and that unauthorised firms are not permitted to trade. This part of FSA's role was previously undertaken by HM Treasury under the Insurance Companies Act 1982 which was repealed when the Financial Services and Markets Act came fully into force. At the end of 2003 there were over 1,000 insurance companies and friendly societies with authorisation from the FSA to transact one or more classes of insurance business in the UK. However, the single European insurance market, established in 1994, gave insurers authorised in any other EU country automatic UK authorisation without further formality. This means a potential market of over 5,000 insurance companies.

REGULATION

At present, only investment-related life insurance contracts are regulated by statute. This is achieved by the formulation (after consultation) by the FSA of rules and guidance for regulated organisations. The FSA is also responsible for consumer education and the reduction of financial crime, in particular money laundering.

COMPLAINTS

Disputes between policyholders and life or general insurers can be referred to the Financial Ombudsman Service. Policyholders with a complaint against their financial services provider must firstly take the matter to the highest level within that organisation. Thereafter, if it remains unresolved, the problem can be referred, free of charge, to the Ombudsman who examines the facts of the complaint and delivers a decision which is binding on the insurer (but not the policyholder). Small businesses with a turnover of up to £1m can also use the Financial Ombudsman Service which covers not just insurers but banks, building societies and investment firms.

FINANCIAL SERVICES OMBUDSMAN SERVICE
South Quay Plaza, 183 Marsh Wall, London E14 9SR
T 020-7964 1000
W www.financial-ombudsman.org.uk
Ombudsman, Walter Merricks

ASSOCIATION OF BRITISH INSURERS

Over 96 per cent of the world-wide business of UK insurance companies is transacted by the 380 members of the Association of British Insurers (ABI). The ABI is a trade association which protects and promotes the interests of life and general insurers. Only insurers authorised in EU countries are eligible for membership. Brokers, intermediaries and claims handlers may not join the ABI but may have their own trade associations.

ASSOCIATION OF BRITISH INSURERS (ABI)
51 Gresham Street, London EC2V 7HQ
W www.abi.org.uk
Chairman, Richard Harvey
Director-General, Mary Francis

GENERAL INSURANCE STANDARDS COUNCIL

The General Insurance Standards Council (GISC) is a non-statutory regulatory organisation for the general insurance industry. It was initially intended that the GISC would regulate the sales, advisory and service standards of insurers, intermediaries and brokers. However, in December 2001 the Treasury announced that the selling of general insurance would be regulated by the FSA. The transfer of responsibilities to the FSA is expected to take place on 14 January 2005.

GENERAL INSURANCE STANDARDS COUNCIL
110 Cannon Street, London EC4N 6EU

BALANCE OF PAYMENTS

The insurance industry contributes 1.2 per cent to the UK's Gross Domestic Product (GDP). In 2002 insurance companies generated net exports of £6.9bn.

TAKE-OVERS AND MERGERS

Falling stock market returns continued to make insurance companies unattractive take-over targets in 2003. The result was the continuation of a very quiet period for take-overs and mergers.

GENERAL INSURANCE

Liability insurance came under the spotlight in 2003 with the announcement just before Christmas 2002 of two official inquiries into the cost and availability of liability insurance. The first, from the Office of Fair Trading looked at all types of liability insurance. The second enquiry was conducted by the Department of Work and Pensions (DWP) and focused on the future of the compulsory, unlimited employers' liability system in the UK. Both inquiries had reported by June 2003 and concluded that premiums for this type of cover were in fact low by European standards and premium increases reflected the greater risks being faced due to an increasingly litigious society. This did not satisfy employers who continued to press the Government for action on premium levels. Insurers responded with an initiative on loss prevention and workplace risk reduction which the DWP applauded in its second and final report, published in autumn 2003.

Publicity surrounding the cost of commercial insurance lead to suggestions that other types general insurance premiums were rising sharply. However, the AA Premium Index suggested that premium increases for home and motor insurance were at their lowest for around six years.

1 January 2003 saw the ABI statement of principles on flood insurance come into effect. This committed all ABI members (all the major insurers) to continue to cover homes and businesses in areas protected from flood to the Government's minimum standard or where there were plans to reach those standards by 2007. This was followed in March 2003 by an announcement from the Government of a major reform of flood protection spending. As weather damage claims are a very important part of property insurers' calculations, insurers have been determined to ensure that the Government adheres to its promised action on flood defences.

Insurers were alarmed in June 2003 by the announcement that the EU's Employment and Social Affairs Commissioner was considering the introduction of anti-discrimination legislation which would outlaw taking sex into account when setting premiums. Insurers pointed out that consumers often benefited from their ability to rate men and women differently, as in the case of premium discounts for women drivers for motor insurance. The end of 2003 saw the publication of the Draft Directive and the continuation of fierce lobbying by insurers to try to prevent the effects of this proposal which they maintain restricts their ability to underwrite.

During 2003 the FSA published its draft conduct of business rules for regulating general insurance which take effect in January 2005. An unlikely alliance of insurers, brokers and the Consumers' Association united to persuade the Government to reverse the FSA's proposal to exclude travel insurance sold by travel agents from the regulatory scheme.

Claims figures from insurers were, on the whole, good for 2003 with a dry summer causing subsidence to be the only type of property insurance claim recording rises on the previous year.

LONDON INSURANCE MARKET

The London Insurance Market is a unique wholesale marketplace and a distinct, separate sector of the UK insurance and reinsurance industry. It is the world's leading market for internationally traded insurance and reinsurance, its business comprising mainly overseas non-life large and high-exposure risks. The market is centred on the City of London, which provides the required financial, banking, legal and other support infrastructure. Currently 52 per cent of London Market business is transacted at Lloyd's with 45 per cent through insurance companies and 3 per cent through Protection and Indemnity Clubs. In 2002 the market had a written gross premium income of over £24,000 million. Around 140 Lloyd's brokers service the market.

The trade association for the international insurers and reinsurers writing primarily non-marine insurance and all classes of reinsurance business in the London Market is the International Underwriting Association (IUA).

INTERNATIONAL UNDERWRITING ASSOCIATION (IUA)
London Underwriting Centre, 3 Mincing Lane, London EC3R 7DD **W** www.iua.co.uk

LLOYD'S OF LONDON

Lloyd's of London is an international market for almost all types of general insurance. Lloyd's currently has a capacity to accept insurance premiums of around £15,000 million. Much of this business comes from outside Great Britain and makes a valuable contribution to the balance of payments.

A policy is underwritten at Lloyd's by a mixture of private and corporate members, with corporate members having been admitted for the first time in 1992. Specialist underwriters accept insurance risks at Lloyd's on behalf of members (referred to as 'Names') grouped in syndicates. There are currently 66 syndicates of varying sizes, each managed by an underwriting agent approved by the Council of Lloyd's.

Individual members are still in the majority at Lloyd's with a total of 2,048 individuals as opposed to 752 corporate members. In 2003 the market capacity of the corporate sector was £13,092 million while individuals represented £1,869 million of capacity.

Lloyd's is incorporated by an Act of Parliament (Lloyd's Acts 1971 onwards) and is governed by the Council of Lloyd's which has 18 members. The structure immediately below this changed when, in September 2002, Lloyd's Members voted at an Extraordinary General Meeting to implement a new franchise system for the market with the aim of improving profitability. The first move was the introduction of a new governance structure replacing the Lloyd's Market Board and the Lloyd's Regulatory Board with a new Lloyd's Franchise Board comprising 11 members. Four main Committees report to this Board.

The Corporation is a non-profit making body chiefly financed by its members' subscriptions. It provides the premises, administrative staff and services enabling Lloyd's underwriting syndicates to conduct their business. It does not, however, assume corporate liability for the risks accepted by its members. Individual members are responsible to the full extent of their personal means for their underwriting affairs.

At present, Lloyd's syndicates have no direct contact with the public. All business is transacted through insurance brokers accredited by the Corporation of Lloyd's. In addition, non-Lloyd's brokers in the UK, when guaranteed by Lloyd's brokers, are able to deal directly with Lloyd's motor syndicates, a facility which has made the Lloyd's market more accessible to the insuring public.

The FSA has ultimate responsibility for the regulation of the Lloyd's market. However, in situations where Lloyd's internal regulatory and compensation arrangements are more far-reaching, as for example with the Lloyd's Central Fund, which safeguards claim payments to policyholders, the regulatory role is delegated to the Council of Lloyd's.

Lloyd's also provides the most comprehensive shipping intelligence service in the world. The shipping and other information received from Lloyd's agents, shipowners, news agencies and other sources throughout the world is collated and distributed to the media as well as to the maritime and commercial sectors in general. *Lloyd's List* is London's oldest daily newspaper and contains news of general commercial interest as well as shipping information. *Lloyd's Shipping Index*, also published daily, lists some 25,000 ocean-going vessels in alphabetical order and gives the latest known report of each.

DEVELOPMENTS IN 2003

The 2003 result, on a pro-forma annual accounting basis, of £1,900 million profit was little short of remarkable and many of those who maintained their confidence in the Lloyd's market during the heavy losses and unrest of the past decades might be forgiven for having a broad smile at this result. It saw a doubling of the record profit of 2002 and reflected the very 'hard market' currently being experienced. The lack of any substantial catastrophes or natural disasters giving rise to insurance claims also contributed to this record figure.

Naturally, insurers are not naive enough to imagine that this kind of market or results like these will occur indefinitely, but the result has certainly helped the new corporate structure at Lloyd's get off to an excellent start.

The Market was shocked and saddened in 2003 by the premature death of former Chairman Saxon Riley. Mr Riley chaired the committee that masterminded the recent changes to the Lloyd's market structure.

LLOYD'S OF LONDON

One Lime Street, London EC3M 7HA
T 020-7327 1000 W www.lloydsoflondon.co.uk
Chairman, Lord Levene of Portsoken
Chief Executive, Nick Prettejohn

LLOYD'S MEMBERSHIP

	2001	*2002*	*2003*
Individuals	2,848	2,466	2,048
Corporate	895	837	752

TOTAL MARKET CAPACITY

	2001 £m	*2002* £m	*2003* £m
Individual	1,800	1,766	1,869
Corporate	9,258	11,473	13,092
Total	11,058	13,239	14,961

LLOYD'S GLOBAL ACCOUNTS

	2000 and prior years of account £m	*2001 pure year result* £m
Gross premiums written (net of brokerage)	9,693	10,904
Outward reinsurance premiums	3,477	3,961
Net premiums	6,216	6,943
Reinsurance to close premiums received from earlier years of account	5,270	—
Amounts retained to meet all known and unknown outstanding liabilities brought forward	1,868	—
	13,354	6,943
Gross claims paid	9,728	7,439
Reinsurers' share	3,595	3,292
Net claims	6,133	4,147
Reinsurance premiums paid to close the year of account	6,375	2,565
Amounts retained to meet all known and unknown outstanding liabilities carried forward	2,969	1,627
	15,477	8,339
Underwriting result	(2,123)	(1,396)
Profit/(loss) on exchange	(5)	11
Syndicate operating expenses	(590)	(634)
Balance on technical account	(2,718)	(2,270)
Investment income	536	527
Investment expenses and charges	(11)	(17)
Investment gains less losses	72	(38)
Result before personal expenses	(2,121)	(1,798)
Personal expenses	(276)	(295)
Result after personal expenses	(2,397)	(2,093)

BRITISH INSURANCE COMPANIES

The following insurance company figures refer to members and certain non-members of the ABI.

CLAIMS STATISTICS

	1999 £m	*2000* £m	*2001* £m	*2002* £m	*2003* £m
Theft	708	740	728	773	630
Fire	866	855	1,049	1,040	1,016
Weather	861	1,298	932	1,258	610
Domestic Subsidence	364	350	265	183	390
Business Interruption	123	202	97	236	92
Total	2,922	3,445	3,071	3,490	2,738

WORLD-WIDE GENERAL BUSINESS TRADING RESULT

	2001 £m	*2002* £m
Net Written Premiums	39,368	39,259
Underwriting profit (loss) for one year account business	(2,890)	(594)
Marine, Aviation, Transport	(136)	(45)
Other	(408)	(157)
Total Underwriting Result	(3,432)	(796)
Net investment income	4,758	3,696
Overall trading profit	1,326	2,900
Profit as % of premium income	3.4	7.4

WORLD-WIDE GENERAL BUSINESS UNDERWRITING RESULT

	2001 UK	Overseas	Total	*2002* UK	Overseas	Total
Motor						
Premiums: £m	8,886	4,742	13,628	9,500	4,240	13,740
Profit (loss): £m	(123)	(307)	(430)	(74)	(222)	(296)
% of premiums	1.4	6.5	3.2	0.8	5.2	2.2
Non-motor						
Premiums: £m	15,048	7,635	22,568	17,033	6,086	23,119
Profit (loss): £m	(636)	(1,168)	(1,784)	272	(643)	(371)
% of premiums	4.2	15.3	8.0	1.6	10.6	1.6

NET PREMIUM INCOME BY TERRITORY 2002

	UK £m	*Overseas* £m
Motor	9,500	4,240
Non-Motor	17,033	6,086
Marine, Aviation and Transport	596	124
Reinsurance	1,075	300
Total General Business	28,204	10,750
Ordinary long-term	96,084	25,269
Industrial long-term	534	—
Total Long-term Business	96,618	25,269

LLOYD'S PREMIUM INCOME 2002 BY CATEGORY

	MAT £m	*Home Foreign* £m	*Non-marine Treaty* £m	*Accident & Health* £m	*Motor* £m	*Property* £m	*General Liability* £m	*Pecuniary Loss* £m	*Total* £m
Gross Premiums	4,151	5,213	3,379	197	1,337	768	1,080	200	16,325
Net Premiums	2,707	3,616	2,458	146	1,089	511	763	148	11,438

LIFE AND LONG-TERM INSURANCE AND PENSIONS

Life insurance and pensions providers seem to have spent 2003 trying to persuade the public, regulators and politicians that their products are not as bad as the media and others would suggest. Figures published in July 2003 suggest they still have some way to go as sales of stakeholder pensions were down 22 per cent on the same period of the previous year. It was not all bad news, however, as a report published in March 2003 pointed out that the returns on a 10 year with-profit policy were 6.4 per cent compared to 3.7 per cent for an average deposit account and 1.5 per cent for the stock market generally. Politicians did not seem to be impressed though as, in December 2003, the Treasury Select Committee launched an inquiry into the life insurance and savings industry and 'grilled' leading industry and regulatory figures on pension mis-selling and endowments.

In December 2002 the Government published the Pensions Green Paper, which called for more financial education, lighter regulation and simpler products to encourage more people to make better provision for their retirement. Although the Green Paper contained some good ideas some commentators felt it did not go far enough to address the problem of the 'savings gap' which could leave thirteen million future pensioners with inadequate provision. In a move in July 2003 the Government announced a Pension Protection Fund but showed no inclination to offer financial incentives to encourage more saving.

In January 2003 the Treasury turned down a call from the Consumers' Association for a formal review on endowment policies. This reaction may have been based on a report from the Financial Services Authority which suggested that eight out of ten endowment mortgage holders said their mortgage was either on track or they had the savings to make up any shortfall. The survey also stated that two-thirds of those surveyed blamed the economy for their endowment's performance rather than their provider.

The war on Iraq raised some well-worn issues with insurers denying press reports that life insurance policies for service men and women would not pay if the policyholder was killed in action. This is wrong as, assuming it is correctly arranged, a life insurance policy pays out on death – with some conditions relating to suicide – no matter how it is caused.

The move by the EU to outlaw premium differences for men and women outlined in the general insurance section (above) was also causing concerns for life insurers. Annuities and life insurances both take account of the differing life expectancies of men and women – action which could be outlawed under the EU proposals.

In general, 2003 was another difficult year for life insurers with poor investment returns and bad publicity substantially reducing sales of new endowment policies.

WORLD-WIDE LONG-TERM PREMIUM INCOME 1998–2002

	1998	*1999*	*2000*	*2001*	*2002*
UK Life Insurance					
Regular Premium	12,567	13,085	13,041	12,226	12,015
Single Premium	17,452	23,384	25,727	25,340	23,731
Total	30,019	36,469	38,768	37,566	35,747
Individual Pensions					
Regular Premium	7,375	8,042	8,046	7,821	8,547
Single Premium	9,788	10,874	13,442	17,702	19,443
Total	17,163	18,916	21,488	25,523	27,990
Other Pensions					
Regular Premium	4,601	4,604	4,143	3,563	3,744
Single Premium	18,228	26,371	49,798	24,981	26,682
Total	22,829	30,975	53,941	28,544	30,426

Other (e.g. Income protection and Annuities)	1,222	1,208	1,641	1,806	1,922
Total UK Premium Income	71,233	87,568	115,838	93,439	96,085
Overseas Premium Income					
Regular Premium	4,872	5,118	6,583	6,933	7,436
Single Premium	10,113	12,943	13,885	17,038	17,833
Total	14,985	18,061	20,468	23,970	25,269
Total World-wide Premium Income	86,218	105,629	136,306	117,409	121,354

PAYMENTS TO POLICYHOLDERS

	2001 £m	*2002* £m
Payments to UK policyholders	88,977	90,203
Payments to overseas policyholders	12,918	14,719
Total	101,895	104,922

PRIVATE MEDICAL INSURANCE 1998–2002

	1998	*1999*	*2000*	*2001*	*2002*
Number of policyholders (000s)					
Corporate	2,043	2,207	2,325	2,506	2,587
Personal	1,209	1,193	1,145	1,129	1,124
Total	3,252	3,400	3,470	3,635	3,711
Number of people covered (000s)					
Corporate	4,157	4,237	4,517	4,704	4,840
Personal	1,984	1,892	1,949	1,885	1,887
Total	6,141	6,129	6,466	6,589	6,727
Gross Earned Premiums, £m					
Corporate	966	1,027	1,092	1,253	1,363
Personal	1,004	1,039	1,146	1,256	1,369
Total	1,970	2,066	2,238	2,509	2,732
Gross Claims Incurred, £m	1,632	1,708	1,788	1,946	2,152

INVESTMENTS OF INSURANCE COMPANIES 2002

Investment of funds	*Long-term business £m*	*General business £m*
Index-linked British Government securities	24,445	1,100
Non-index-linked British Government securities	99,415	12,246
Other UK public sector debt securities	12,320	1,650
Overseas government, provincial and municipal securities	44,363	10,862
Debentures, loan shares, preference and guaranteed stocks and shares		
UK	114,935	5,917
Overseas	77,937	9,364
Ordinary stocks and shares		
UK	231,515	9,130
Overseas	99,081	2,800
Unit trusts		
Equities	59,254	1,021
Fixed interest	5,949	237
Loans secured on property	15,373	1,136
Real property and ground rents	59,330	3,243
Other invested assets	82,911	30,094
Total invested assets	926,828	88,800
Net investment income	39,221	3,696

NEW BUSINESS 1999–2003

	New Individual Regular Premiums				*New Individual Single Premiums*					*Group Business*	
	Life	Pensions	Collective Investment Schemes	Total Regular	Life	Pensions	Pension Annuities & Income Drawdown	Collective Investment Schemes	Total Single	Regular	Single
1999	1,683	1,474	570	3,728	23,505	6,999	7,569	8,587	46,660	978	4,723
2000	1,334	1,593	626	3,552	25,109	7,329	7,911	8,718	49,067	940	3,539
2001	1,221	2,415	473	4,109	25,129	8,768	8,545	7,582	50,024	1,139	4,349
2002	1,311	2,233	417	3,961	23,886	11,201	9,577	7,314	51,978	1,075	5,146
2003	1,288	1,875	369	3,532	17,635	9,931	9,203	7,757	44,257	1,097	5,248

MUTUAL SOCIETIES

The term 'mutual societies' covers member-based organisations registered under the Building Societies Acts, the Friendly Societies Acts and the Industrial and Provident Societies Acts, many of which are familiar, long-established names.

Until 30 November 2001 the various statutory responsibilities for the supervision and registration of mutual societies rested with the Chief Registrar of Friendly Societies (CR), the Building Societies Commission (BSC) and the Friendly Societies Commission (FSC). The office of the CR and the Registry of Friendly Societies (RFS), from which the BSC and FSC were more recently supported, dated back to 1875. However, the existence in one form or another of an office for the registration of friendly societies dating back to 1829, was seen as bringing regulation and social control over a potentially revolutionary popular movement.

In 1997 the Government announced the creation of a single financial regulatory authority for the UK, the Financial Services Authority (FSA). The FSA initially supported the functions of the CR, BSC and FSC under contract. On the full entry into force of the Financial Services and Markets Act 2000 on 1 December 2001, the responsibilities and powers of the BSC, FSC and CR passed to the FSA. Information on the numbers of mutual societies with additions to and removals from the register in the year to 30 November 2002 are given in the following table:

	On register at beginning of year	*Added during year*	*Removed during year*	*On register at end of year*
Friendly Societies Acts				
Friendly Societies				
Orders	13	–	–	13
Collecting societies	11	–	–	11
Other centralised societies	217	–	9	208
Total	241	–	9	232
Others				
Branches of orders	612	1	7	606
Benevolent societies	55	–	–	55
Working men's clubs	1,842	–	30	1,812
Specially authorised societies	101	–	3	98
Total	2,610	1	40	2,570
Industrial and Provident Societies Acts				
Housing	2,941	44	70	2,915
Social and recreation	3,269	47	34	3,282
Agricultural	807	2	50	759
General service	1,021	92	28	1,085
Retail, wholesale and productive	198	12	7	203
Fishing	68	–	–	68
Credit unions	697	29	39	687
Total	9,001	226	228	8,999
Building Societies Act				
Building Societies	66	–	1	65

More recent, similarly detailed registration statistics have not been published by the FSA despite the intentions set out in its publication *Reporting on Mutual Societies under the Single Regulator* (June 2002). At the time of going to press the information made available gave the number of societies registered with the FSA as at 31 March 2004 in the following terms:

*Industrial and Provident Societies**	*Societies (and branches) registered under the Friendly Societies Acts 1974 and 1992***	*Credit Unions†*	*Building Societies‡*
8,322	2,377	628	63

* Registered under the Industrial and Provident Societies Act 1965

** Includes friendly societies, working men's clubs, benevolent societies and specially authorised societies

† Registered as credit unions under the Industrial and Provident Societies Act 1965

‡ Registered under the Building Societies Act 1986

FRIENDLY SOCIETIES IN BRITAIN

Four different classes of society are registered under the Friendly Societies Act 1974. These are friendly societies, benevolent societies, working men's clubs and specially authorised societies. Friendly societies are voluntary mutual organisations, where the main purposes are assisting members during sickness, unemployment or retirement, and the provision of life assurance. Many of the older traditional societies complement their business activities by social activity and a general care for individual members in ways normally outside the scope of a purely commercial organisation. There are three main categories of friendly societies: societies with separately registered branches, commonly called orders; centralised societies, which conduct business directly with members (having no separately registered branches); and collecting societies which have traditionally conducted home service assurance. Collecting societies benefit from a number of deregulatory measures included in the Financial Services and Markets Act 2000 involving relaxation for the future administration of existing contracts and by the removal of special requirements, in the industrial assurance legislation, concerning the selling of future contracts. Such business is subject to the general conduct of business rules governing the marketing and selling of investment products.

The Friendly Societies Act 1992 created a new legislative framework for friendly societies, enabling them to provide a wider range of services to their members and allowing them to compete on more equal terms with other financial institutions. At the same time it provided for more flexible prudential supervision to safeguard members of societies.

The Act enabled friendly societies to incorporate and establish subsidiaries, to provide various financial and other services to their members and the public. The activities which subsidiaries are able to conduct include those to establish and manage unit trust schemes and personal equity plans; to arrange for the provision of credit, whether as agents or providers; to carry on long-term or general insurance business; to provide insurance intermediary services; to provide fund management services for trustees of pension funds; to administer estates and execute trusts of wills; and to establish and manage sheltered housing, residential homes for the elderly, hospitals and nursing homes.

The Act established a new framework to oversee friendly societies, including a Friendly Societies Commission, now superseded by the FSA, whose principal functions are to regulate the activities of friendly societies, promote their financial stability and protect members' funds. All friendly societies carrying on insurance or non-insurance business require authorisation by the FSA, which has a broad range of prudential powers.

At 31 December 2001 there were 37 'life directive' societies, i.e. those subject to the requirements of EU Life Insurance Directives, and five 'incorporated' societies which were transacting long-term insurance business but not subject to the Directives. These 42 societies accounted for over 95 per cent of the total funds of the movement at 31 December 2001. Of the remaining 194 societies on the register, representing five per cent of the movement, almost 70 per cent were not authorised to accept new business though they continued to have liabilities to meet.

LIFE DIRECTIVE AND INCORPORATED SOCIETIES

	2000	*2001*
No. of Societies	43	42
Membership (000s)	5,512	4,936
Contribution income (000s)	1,219,663	1,285,166
Investment income (000s)	255,772	45,130
Benefits paid (000s)	1,201,628	1,252,807
Management expenses (000s)	327,864	235,895
Total assets	15,019,152	14,285,338

No new friendly societies may now be registered under the 1974 Act. Benevolent societies are established for any charitable or benevolent purpose, to provide the same type of benefits as would be permissible for a friendly society, but in contrast the benefits must be for persons who are not members instead of or in addition to members. Working men's clubs provide social and recreational facilities for members. Specially authorised societies are registered for any purpose authorised by the Treasury as a purpose to which some or all of the provisions of the 1974 Act ought to be extended. Examples are societies for the promotion of science, literature and the arts, or to enable members to pursue an interest in sports and games.

INDUSTRIAL AND PROVIDENT SOCIETIES IN BRITAIN

The Industrial and Provident Societies Act 1965 provides for the registration of societies and lays down the broad framework within which they must operate. Internal relations of societies are governed by their registered rules. Registration under the Act confers upon a society corporate status by its registered name with perpetual succession and a common seal, and limited liability. A society qualifies for registration if it is carrying on an industry, business or trade, and it satisfies the FSA either (a) that it is a bona fide co-operative society, or (b) that in view of the fact that its business is being, or is intended to be, conducted for the benefit of the community, there are special reasons why it should be registered under the Act rather than as a company under the Companies Act.

The Credit Unions Act 1979 added a new class of society registrable under the 1965 Act. It also made provision for the supervision of these savings and loan bodies. Unlike other classes, where the role of the FSA remains solely that of a registration authority, for Credit Unions (CUs) it became also the financial supervisor. On 2 July 2002 a new system of regulation by the FSA for all CUs came into effect. The key features of the new regulatory regime for CUs were: to meet a basic test of solvency (with additional capital requirements for the larger CUs); to maintain a minimum liquidity ratio; to meet the standard in FSA's rules for approved persons; to operate an effective complaints scheme with access to the Financial Ombudsman; to participate in the Financial Services Compensation Scheme providing members with deposit protection for the first time.

New legislation for industrial and provident societies, the Industrial and Provident Societies Act 2002, came into force in September 2002. It introduced two measures. The first brought industrial and provident societies into line with building societies on voting thresholds for conversion to company status. A resolution to convert would need to secure a 75 per cent majority on a minimum vote of 50 per cent of the membership to be successful. The second measure enabled the legislation to be amended more easily to bring it into line with company law.

Comparative figures for 2001 show that the housing sector remained the largest in terms of asset holdings at 30,724 million, followed by the general service sector at 25,409 million. Registration statistics for the year to November 2002 show that the clubs sector remained the largest in terms of numbers of societies with 3,269 clubs on the register at the beginning of the year, increasing to 3,282 by the end. The total number of societies (excluding credit unions) showed a net increase from 8,304 to 8,312 in the year to 30 November 2002.

Total membership in the credit union sector continued to grow with 366,000 members at the end of 2001 compared to 325,000 a year earlier. However, in 2001 there were only 23 new credit unions registered - the lowest number since 1987 - and 18 credit unions closed. In 2002 the total number of credit unions reduced from 698 to 686. By the 31 March 2004 the total was down to 628.

The principal statistics for all classes of society at the end of 2001 are given below. In this case, the figures relate to the end of 2001 except for the agriculture sector which are given as at the end of 2000.

	No. of societies	No. of members 000s	Funds of members £000s	Total assets £000s
Retail	133	4,558	1,904,469	3,233,109
Wholesale productive	65	45	858,925	2,573,656
Agricultural	817	1,101	189,221	539,997
Fishing	68	3	7,422	15,814
Clubs	3,205	1,828	358,202	511,302
General service	1,108	605	2,193,797	25,409,438
Housing	2,865	434	9,078,603	30,724,286
Credit unions	698	366	248,674	263,404

BUILDING SOCIETIES IN THE UK

The Building Societies Act 1997, which received royal assent on 21 March 1997, made substantive amendments to, but did not replace, the Building Societies Act 1986. It liberalised the statutory regime for building societies to enable them to compete on more level terms with other financial institutions without having to forego their mutual status. The Building Societies Act 1986 gave building societies a completely new legal framework for the first time since the initial comprehensive building society legislation in 1874. The 1986 Act set out detailed provisions in relation to: the constitution of building societies; building societies' powers in relation to raising funds, advances, loans, other assets and the provision of services; the powers of control of the Building Societies Commission (now superseded by the FSA); protection of investors, and complaints and disputes and; management of building societies, accounts and audit and mergers and transfers of business.

The 1986 Act was prescriptive in respect of building societies' powers and the way in which they were exercised. However, it gave numerous powers to the Building Societies Commission and/or the Treasury to make statutory instruments which, subject to parliamentary approval, can amend, extend and supplement the provisions of the Act. Since it came into force on 1 January 1987 the Act had been amended and extended considerably, especially in respect of building societies' powers.

The main purposes of the Building Societies Act 1997 are to: remove the prescriptive powers' regime relating to building societies and to replace it with a permissive regime with appropriately revised balance-sheet 'nature limits', thus increasing the commercial freedom of societies and allowing increased competition and wider choice for customers; enhance the powers of control of the Building Societies Commission (now superseded by the FSA) and; introduce a package of measures to enhance the accountability of building societies' boards to their members and to make changes to the provisions relating to the transfer of a building society's business to a company.

The Act came fully into force on 21 October 1997. Under it a building society may pursue any activities set out in its memorandum, subject only to: principal purpose: its purpose or principal purpose must be that of making loans which are secured on residential properties and are funded substantially by its members; lending limit: at least 75 per cent of its business assets must be loans fully secured on residential property; funding limit: at least 50 per cent of its funds must be raised in the form of shares held by individual members; restrictions: subject to certain exceptions, it must not act as a market maker in securities, commodities or currencies; trade in commodities or currencies; enter into transactions involving derivatives, except in relation to hedging; nor create a floating charge over its assets and; prudential: it must comply with the criteria of prudential management.

All authorised building societies, after making the necessary changes to their memoranda and rules, are now operating under the more liberal statutory regime set out in the 1997 Act.

OMBUDSMAN SCHEME

Complaints about the actions of building societies may be resolved through societies' own internal complaints procedures. All authorised building societies are, in addition, members of the Building Societies Ombudsmen scheme which provides an independent service to consider and determine complaints which are within its remit. The Financial Ombudsman Services provides consumers with a free, informal and independent service for resolving disputes with most providers of financial products and services. Complainants may contact the Service at South Quay Plaza, 183 Marsh Wall, London E14 9SR T 020-8964 1000.

Statistics for building society service activity, liabilities and assets for the five years 1999–2003 are set out in the following tables:

BUILDING SOCIETIES 1999–2003
SERVICE ACTIVITY

Year	Societies Authorised	Branches	Estate Agency Offices	Staff Full time	Staff Part time	Shareholders 000s	Depositors 000s	Borrowers 000s	Advances During Year Number 000s	Advances During Year Amount £m
1999	69	2,384	611	32,722	10,379	21,774	722	3,044	519	26,555
2000	67	2,361	607	32,334	10,823	22,237	740	3,107	548	31,514
2001	65	2,126	241	28,200	9,150	20,310	568	2,750	509	31,845
2002	65	2,103	229	28,982	9,257	20,724	511	2,688	558	37,303
2003	63	2,081	556	32,502	11,440	20,897	520	2,679	736	49,628

LIABILITIES (£ m)

	Funding							
Year	*Shares*	*Deposits from individuals*	*Wholesale*	*Taxation and other liabilities*	*Reserves*	*Other*	*Life fund liabilities*	*Total liabilities and capital*
1999	109,137.6	5,055.4	29,523.8	2,259.8	8,733.0	1,529.9	901.0	157,140.5
2000	119,295.5	5,531.0	38,047.5	2,033.6	9,577.0	1,861.7	1,397.8	177,747.1
2001	119,815.2	4,385.1	33,600.1	1,532.0	9,152.2	1,391.7	1,498.7	171,375.0
2002	132,373.0	4,191.2	33,459.6	1,401.1	9,932.8	1,684.8	1,410.3	184,452.8
2003	142,456.9	4,289.9	44,914.5	1,498.8	10,592.8	2,510.3	1,471.7	207,734.9

ASSETS (£ m)

	Loans fully secured on land to:							
Year	*Individuals on residential properties*	*Others*	*Other loans and investments*	*Liquidity*	*Office premises*	*Other assets*	*Life fund assets*	*Total assets*
1999	113,190.2	7,219.3	1,480.7	31,207.9	1,037.7	2,103.7	901.0	157,140.5
2000	125,555.9	8,544.2	1,230.0	37,900.8	1,044.7	2,073.7	1,397.8	177,747.1
2001	119,515.7	8,805.9	1,551.1	37,158.1	1,007.9	1,837.6	1,498.7	171,375.0
2002	129,001.3	9,882.7	1,877.1	39,201.8	1,050.6	2,029.0	1,410.3	184,452.8
2003	145,648.6	10,747.5	2,333.2	44,500.4	1,115.0	1,918.5	1,471.7	207,734.9

BUILDING SOCIETIES AND TOTAL ASSETS *(£m) as at December 2003*

Barnsley T 01226-733999 (£313m)
Bath Investment T 01225-423271 (£134m)
Beverley T 01482-881510 (£82m)
Britannia T 01538-399399 (£20,865m)
Buckinghamshire T 01494-879500 (£116m)
Cambridge T 01223-727727 (£660m)
Catholic T 020-7222 6736 (£36m)
Century (£18m)
Chelsea T 01242-271271 (£7,828m)
Chesham T 01494-782575 (£182m)
Cheshire T 01625-613612 (£4,026m)
Chorley and District T 01257-279373 (£125m)
City of Derry T 028-7137 0037 (£23m)
Coventry T 0845-766 5522 (£8,937m)
Cumberland T 01228-541341 (£935m)
Darlington T 01325-366366 (£544m)
Derbyshire T 01332-841000 (£3,914m)
Dudley T 01334-231414 (£152m)
Dunfermline T 01383-627727 (£1,869m)
Earl Shilton T 01455-844422 (£84m)
Ecology T 01535-650770 (£50m)
Furness T 01229-824560 (£668m)
Hanley Economic T 01782-255000 (£266m)
Harpenden T 01582-765411 (£102m)
Hinckley and Rugby T 01455-251234 (£555m)
Holmesdale T 01737-245716 (£127m)
Ipswich T 01473-211021 (£325m)
Kent Reliance T 01634-848944 (£838m)
Lambeth T 020-7928 1331 (£901m)
Leeds and Holbeck T 0113-225 7777 (£5,362m)
Leek United T 01538-384151 (£590m)
Loughborough T 01509-610707 (£189m)
Manchester T 0161-833 8888 (£407m)
Mansfield T 01623-676300 (£173m)
Market Harborough T 01858-463244 (£336m)
Marsden T 01282-440500 (£319m)
Melton Mowbray T 01664-563937 (£334m)
Mercantile, T 01912-959500 (£229m)
Monmouthshire T 01633-844444 (£364m)
National Counties T 01372-742211 (£758m)
Nationwide T 01793-513513 (£83,284m)
Newbury T 01635-555700 (£429m)
Newcastle T 0191-244 2000 (£3,077m)
Norwich and Peterborough T 01733-372372 (£2,839m)
Nottingham T 0115-948 1444 (£1,911m)
Penrith T 01768-863675 (£70m)
Portman T 01202-292444 (£14,099m)
Principality T 029-2038 2000 (£3,574m)
Progressive T 028-9024 4926 (£1,014m)
Saffron Walden Herts & Essex T 01799-522211 (£468m)
Scarborough T 01723-368155 (£1,287m)
Scottish T 0131-220 1111 (£196m)
Shepshed T 01509-822000 (£65m)
Skipton T 01756-705000 (£7,133m)
Stafford Railway T 01785-223212 (£97m)
Stroud and Swindon T 01453-757011 (£2,076m)
Swansea T 01792-483700 (£72m)
Teachers T 01202-843500 (£212)
Tipton and Coseley T 0121-557 2551 (£232m)
Universal T 0191-232 0973 (£503m)
Vernon T 0161-429 6262 (£180m)
West Bromwich T 0121-525 7070 (£4,282m)
Yorkshire T 01274-740740 (£14,382m)

ECONOMIC STATISTICS

THE BUDGET 2004

GOVERNMENT RECEIPTS

£ billion

	Outturn 2002–3	*Outturn Estimate 2003–4*	*Projection 2004–5*
Inland Revenue			
Income tax (gross of tax credits)	112.6	119.1	127.8
Social security contributions	64.6	72.2	77.7
Corporation tax[1]	29.5	28.7	34.8
Tax credits[2]	–3.4	–4.8	–4.1
Petroleum revenue tax	1.0	1.2	1.0
Capital gains tax	1.6	1.2	1.5
Inheritance tax	2.4	2.5	2.8
Stamp duties	7.5	7.5	9.4
INLAND REVENUE (NET OF TAX CREDITS)	215.8	227.6	251.0
Customs and excise			
Value added tax	63.5	69.7	73.1
Fuel duties	22.1	22.8	24.4
Tobacco duties	8.1	8.1	8.1
Spirits duties	2.3	2.4	2.4
Wine duties	1.9	2.0	2.0
Beer and cider duties	3.1	3.2	3.3
Betting and gaming duties	1.3	1.3	1.3
Air passenger duty	0.8	0.8	0.9
Insurance premium tax	2.1	2.3	2.4
Landfill tax	0.5	0.6	0.6
Climate change levy	0.8	0.8	0.8
Aggregates levy	0.2	0.3	0.3
Customs duties and levies	1.9	1.9	1.9
TOTAL CUSTOMS AND EXCISE	108.7	116.4	121.6
Vehicle excise duties	4.6	4.7	4.9
Oil royalties	0.4	0.0	0.0
Business rates[3]	18.5	18.7	19.1
Council tax	16.7	18.6	19.7
Other taxes and royalties[4]	10.9	12.3	13.2
NET TAXES AND SOCIAL SECURITY CONTRIBUTIONS[5]	375.6	398.2	429.4
Accrual adjustments on taxes	–0.3	3.0	0.8
Less own resources contribution to EC budget	–4.4	–4.5	–3.7
Less PC corporation tax payments	–0.1	–0.1	–0.1
Tax credits adjustment[6]	1.1	0.5	0.6
Interest and dividends	4.5	4.1	4.9
Other receipts[7]	19.8	20.3	22.7
CURRENT RECEIPTS	396.2	421.5	454.7
North Sea revenues[8]	4.9	4.3	3.6

1 National Accounts measure: gross of enhanced and payable tax credits.

2 Includes enhanced company tax credits

3 Includes district council rates in Northern Ireland paid by business.

4 Includes VAT refunds and money paid into the National Lottery Distribution Fund.

5 Includes VAT and 'traditional own resources' contributions to EC budget.

6 Tax credits which are scored as negative tax in the calculation of net taxes and social security contributions but expenditure in the National accounts.

7 Includes gross operating surplus and rent; net of oil royalties and business rate payments by Local Authorities.

8 Consists of North Sea corporation tax, petroleum revenue tax and royalties.

Source: The Stationery Office – *Budget 2004* (Crown Copyright).

GOVERNMENT EXPENDITURE

The Economic and Fiscal Strategy Report in June 1998 introduced changes to the public expenditure control regime. Three-year departmental expenditure limits (DELs) now apply to most government departments. Spending which cannot easily be subject to three-year planning is reviewed annually in the Budget as annually managed expenditure (AME). Current and capital expenditure are treated separately.

DEPARTMENTAL EXPENDITURE LIMITS

RESOURCE AND CAPITAL BUDGETS

£ billion

	Outturn 2002–3	*Estimate 2003–4*	*Plans 2004–5*
Resource Budget			
Education and Skills[1]	21.2	22.9	23.9
Health[1]	55.9	63.1	68.7
(of which NHS)	54.2	61.4	66.5
Transport	6.2	8.0	7.5
Office of the Deputy Prime Minister	3.9	4.7	4.7
Local Government	37.4	41.0	43.4
Home Office	11.1	11.9	12.2
Departments for Consitutional Affairs	3.3	3.3	3.3
Attorney General's Departments	0.5	0.6	0.5
Defence	36.4	32.3	31.6
Foreign and Commonwealth Office	1.5	1.7	1.5
International Development	3.6	3.9	3.8
Trade and Industry	4.0	5.0	5.0
Environment, Food and Rural Affairs	2.3	2.8	3.1
Culture, Media and Sport	1.2	1.4	1.5
Work and Pensions	7.3	8.4	8.1
Scotland[1]	16.6	18.9	19.6
Wales[1]	9.1	10.0	10.4
Northern Ireland Executive[1]	6.6	6.7	6.8
Northern Ireland Office	1.1	1.1	1.1
Chancellor's Departments	4.4	4.7	4.8
Cabinet Office	1.6	1.8	1.9
Invest to Save budget	0.0	0.0	0.0
Reserve	0.0	0.0	0.5

Unallocated special reserve[2]	0.0	0.0	0.3
Allowance for shortfall[3]	0.0	−2.2	0.0
TOTAL RESOURCE BUDGET DEL	235.3	251.9	263.9
Capital Budget			
Education and Skills	2.7	3.4	3.8
Health	2.0	2.7	3.0
of which NHS	1.9	2.6	2.9
Transport	3.1	3.3	3.7
Office of the Deputy Prime Minister	1.5	2.2	2.3
Local Government	0.2	0.2	0.3
Home Office	0.7	1.0	1.0
Departments for Constitutional Affairs	0.1	0.2	0.1
Attorney General's Departments	0.0	0.0	0.0
Defence	6.1	6.4	6.3
Foreign and Commonwealth Office	0.1	0.1	0.1
International Development	0.0	0.0	0.0
Trade and Industry	0.3	0.6	0.2
Environment, Food and Rural Affairs	0.3	0.3	0.3
Culture, Media and Sport	0.0	0.2	0.1
Work and Pensions	0.3	0.2	0.2
Scotland[1]	1.6	1.3	2.0
Wales[1]	0.7	0.7	0.9
Northern Ireland Executive[1]	0.5	0.5	0.4
Northern Ireland Office	0.1	0.1	0.1
Chancellor's departments	0.3	0.3	0.3
Cabinet Office	0.2	0.6	0.2
Invest to Save Budget	0.0	0.0	0.0
Reserve	0.0	0.0	1.0
Allowance for shortfall[3]	0.0	−0.4	0.0
TOTAL CAPITAL BUDGET DEL	20.7	23.9	26.3
Depreciation	−15.5	−10.5	−11.0
TOTAL DEPARTMENTAL EXPENDITURE LIMITS	240.6	265.3	279.3

[1] For Scotland, Wales and Northern Ireland, the split between current and capital budgets is decided by the respective executives

[2] This represents provision for the costs of the military conflict in Iraq and other International obligations

[3] The allowance for shortfall reflect likely underspends in departmental forecasts

Source: The Stationery Office – *Budget 2004* (Crown Copyright).

ANNUALLY MANAGED EXPENDITURE *£ billion*

	Outturn 2002–3	*Estimate 2003–4*	*Projection 2004–5*
Social security benefits[1,2]	109.9	116.7	123.3
Tax credits[1]	10.0	14.0	13.8
Common agricultural policy	2.6	2.5	2.5
Net public service pensions[3]	3.5	0.7	0.4
National Lottery	1.8	2.0	2.0
Non-cash items in AME	30.1	30.0	28.1
Other departmental expenditure	2.3	1.9	2.7
Net payment to EC institutions[4]	2.3	2.4	2.7
Locally financed expenditure	19.7	22.4	24.2
Central government gross debt interest	20.9	22.2	23.9
Public corporations' own-financed capital expenditure	2.0	2.5	2.6
AME margin	0.0	0.0	1.0
Accounting adjustments	−32.2	−26.7	−18.0
Annually managed expenditure	165.5	177.0	191.9

[1] All child allowances in Income Support and Jobseekers' Allowance which, from 2003–4 are part of the Child Tax Credit, have been included in the tax credits line and excluded from the social security benefits line. This is in order to give figures a consistent definition over the forecast period.

[2] Only includes Member States.

Source: The Stationery Office – *Budget 2003* (Crown Copyright).

PUBLIC SECTOR FINANCES *£ billion*

PUBLIC SECTOR CAPITAL EXPENDITURE

	Outturn 2002–3	*Estimate 2003–4*	*Projection 2004–5*
Capital Budget DEL	20.7	23.9	26.3
Locally financed expenditure	0.2	1.1	2.0
National Lottery	0.9	1.0	1.0
Public corporations' own-financed capital expenditure	2.0	2.5	2.6
Other capital spending in AME	1.3	2.5	5.8
AME margin	0.0	0.0	0.1
Public sector gross investment[1]	25.0	31.0	37.9
Less depreciation	14.4	14.8	15.5
Public sector net investment	10.6	16.2	22.4
Proceeds from the sale of fixed assets[2]	6.1	6.0	5.5

[1] This and previous lines are all net of sales of fixed assets.

[2] Projections of total receipts from the sale of fixed assets by public sector.

Source: The Stationery Office – *Budget 2004* (Crown Copyright).

UK GDP

$1.6 trillion (2002)

Source: IMF – *International Financial Statistics Yearbook*

EMPLOYMENT

DISTRIBUTION OF THE UK WORKFORCE
(as at mid-June 2003)

Claimant count	948,000
Workforce jobs	29,695,000
HM Forces	207,000
Self-employment jobs	3,563,000
Employees jobs	25,825,000
Government-supported trainees	101,000

Source: The Stationery Office – *Annual Abstract of Statistics 2004* (Crown copyright)

UK EMPLOYMENT BY AGE AND GENDER 2003

	Thousands	
Age	*Male*	*Female*
16–17	322	337
18–24	1,760	1,602
25–34	3,496	2,898
35–49	5,616	4,911
50–64(m)/59(f)	3,688	2,543
65+(m)/60+(f)	341	598
All aged 16+	15,221	12,889

Source: The Stationery Office – *Annual Abstract of Statistics 2004*

UK UNEMPLOYMENT BY AGE AND GENDER 2003

	Thousands	
Age	*Male*	*Female*
16–17	101	76
18–24	244	160
25–34	188	123
35–49	211	152
50–64(m)/59(f)	149	62
65+(m)/60+(f)	8	10
All aged 16+	900	584

Source: The Stationery Office – *Annual Abstract of Statistics 2004*

DURATION OF UNEMPLOYMENT IN THE UK
(as at Spring 2003, seasonally adjusted)

	Thousands
All Unemployed	1,484
Duration of unemployment	
– Less than 6 months	965
– 6 months–1 year	201
– 1 year +	318
– *1 year +* as percentage of total	21.4

Source: The Stationery Office – *Annual Abstract of Statistics 2004*

AVERAGE GROSS WEEKLY EARNINGS OF FULL-TIME EMPLOYEES ON ADULT RATES 2003 (GREAT BRITAIN)

All adults	£469.30
All men	£496.40
Manual, men	£388.00
Non-manual, men	£615.50
All women	£365.20
Manual, women	£260.50
Non-manual, women	£408.10

Source: The Stationery Office – *Annual Abstract of Statistics 2004*

NUMBER OF INDUSTRIAL STOPPAGES BY DURATION 2002 (UK)

Not more than five days	118,000
5–10 days	16,000
11–20 days	3,000
21–30 days	3,000
31–50 days	1,000
50+ days	5,000
Total number of stoppages	146,000

Source: The Stationery Office – *Annual Abstract of Statistics 2004*

NUMBER OF INDUSTRIAL STOPPAGES BY INDUSTRY 2002 (UK)

Mining, quarrying, electricity, gas and water	2,000
Manufacturing	33,000
Construction	3,000
Transport, storage and communications	51,000
Public administration and defence	20,000
Education	16,000
Health and social work	14,000
Other community, social and personal services	11,000
All other industries and services	12,000

Source: The Stationery Office – *Annual Abstract of Statistics 2004*

NUMBER AND MEMBERSHIP OF TRADE UNIONS (UK)

Year	*No. of unions at end of year*	*Total membership at end of year*
1991	306	9,555
1992	315	9,171
1993	302	8,848
1994	281	8,297
1995	271	8,111
1996	261	7,982
1997	257	7,841
1998	243	7,894
1999	241	7,940
2000	230	7,823
2001	220	7,796

Source: The Stationery Office – *Annual Abstract of Statistics 2004*

UK TRADE

UK TRADE IN GOODS ON A BALANCE OF PAYMENTS BASIS

			£ million
	Exports	*Imports*	
1992	107,863	120,913	–13,050
1993	122,229	135,295	–13,066
1994	135,143	146,269	–11,126
1995	153,577	165,600	–12,023
1996	167,196	180,918	–13,722
1997	171,923	184,265	–12,342
1998	164,056	185,869	–21,813
1999	166,166	195,217	–29,051
2000	187,936	220,912	–32,976
2001	190,050	230,670	–40,620
2002	186,257	232,712	–46,455

Source: The Stationery Office – *Annual Abstract of Statistics 2004*

BALANCE OF PAYMENTS 2002

CURRENT ACCOUNT	*£ million*
Trade in good and services	
Trade in goods	–46,455
Trade in services	15,166
Total trade in goods and services	–31,289
Income	
Compensation of employees	67
Investment income	21,052
Total income	21,119
Current transfers	
Central government	–5,752
Other sectors	–3,043
Total current transfers	–8,795
Total (current balance)	–18,965

Source: The Stationery Office – *Annual Abstract of Statistics 2004*

VALUE OF UK EXPORTS AND IMPORTS BY AREA 2002

	Exports	Imports (£ million)
European Union	109,611	129,858
Other Western Europe	6,535	12,571
North America	32,256	29,602
Other OECD countries	10,767	16,843
Oil exporting countries	6,227	3,759
Rest of the World	20,861	40,079

Source: The Stationery Office – *Annual Abstract of Statistics 2004* (Crown copyright)

HOUSEHOLD INCOME AND EXPENDITURE

AVERAGE INCOME OF UK HOUSEHOLDS BEFORE AND AFTER TAXES AND BENEFITS 2001–2

Number of Households in the UK population	24,888,000
Original annual income	£25,176
Disposable annual income	£22,925
Post-tax annual income	£18,595

Source: The Stationery Office – *Annual Abstract of Statistics 2004* (Crown copyright)

AVERAGE WEEKLY UK HOUSEHOLD EXPENDITURE ON COMMODITIES AND SERVICES 2002–3

	£	*As % of total*
Housing	66.70	16
Fuel and power	11.70	3
Food	64.30	16
Alcoholic drink	14.80	4
Tobacco	5.40	1
Clothing and footwear	22.00	5
Household goods	33.80	8
Household services	23.30	6
Personal goods and services	15.20	4
Motoring expenditure	61.70	15
Fares and other travel costs	9.70	2
Leisure goods	20.50	5
Leisure services	53.60	13
Miscellaneous	2.00	—
Total	404.70	100

Source: The Stationery Office – *Annual Abstract of Statistics 2004* (Crown copyright)

AVERAGE WEEKLY HOUSEHOLD EXPENDITURE ON SELECTED LEISURE ITEMS AND ACTIVITIES BY REGION 2002–3

	England	*Wales*	*Scotland*	*Northern Ireland* (£ per week)
Games, toys and hobbies[1]	3.40	2.90	2.70	3.30
Package holidays	13.00	11.60	11.50	9.00
Holiday accommodation (UK and abroad)	5.20	3.60	4.40	2.10
Restaurant and cafe meals	11.60	8.70	9.90	10.60
Alcoholic drinks (away from home)	9.00	8.20	8.00	8.70

[1] Includes computer software and games

Source: The Stationery Office – *Social Trends 2004* (Crown copyright)

AVERAGE WEEKLY UK HOUSEHOLD INCOME BY SOURCE 2002–3

	£	*As % of total*
Wages and salaries	373.90	68
Self-employment	44.50	8
Investments	18.80	3
Annuities and pensions (other than social security benefits)	39.90	7
Social security benefits	68.50	12
Other sources	6.70	1
Total	552.30	100

Source: The Stationery Office – *Annual Abstract of Statistics 2004* (Crown copyright)

AVAILABILITY IN UK HOUSEHOLDS OF CERTAIN DURABLE GOODS 2002–3

	% of households
Car	74
One	44
Two	25
Three or more	6
Central heating, full or partial	93
Washing machine	94
Fridge/freezer or deep freezer	96
Dishwasher	29
Telephone	94
Home computer	55
Internet Access	45
Video recorder	90

Source: The Stationery Office – *Annual Abstract of Statistics 2004* (Crown copyright)

MONEY SPENT ON GAMBLING 2002–3 (UK)

	£ millions
National Lottery – Total[1]	4,548
Online	3,385
Instants	574
Thunderball	280
Lottery Extra	90
Hot Picks	218
Other Lotteries[2,3]	130
Casinos[2,3]	3,797
Bingo clubs[3]	1,222

[1] Includes Easy Play tickets which are not shown separately
[2] Includes Hotspot lotteries
[3] Great Britain only

Source: The Stationery Office – *Annual Abstract of Statistics 2004* (Crown copyright)

SAVINGS

SAVINGS BY HOUSEHOLD TYPE AND AMOUNT 2001–2 IN GREAT BRITAIN *Percentages*

	No savings	*Less than £1,500*	*£1,500–£10,000*	*£10,000–£20,000*	*£20,000+*
One adult over pensionable age, no children	28	19	27	10	16
Two adults, one or both over pensionable age, no children	17	14	25	14	30
Two adults under pensionable age					
No children	19	22	30	12	17
One or more children	30	26	26	8	9
One adult under pensionable age					
No children	37	22	26	8	8
One or more children	67	23	7	1	2
Other households	21	23	29	12	15
Total Households	28	21	26	10	15

Source: The Stationery Office – *Annual Abstract of Statistics 2004* (Crown copyright)

CREDIT AND DEBIT CARD USAGE

UK DEBIT AND CREDIT CARD SPENDING BY TYPE OF PURCHASE 2002 *£ billions*

	Debit cards[1]	*Credit cards*[2]
Food and drink	30.93	11.94
Motoring	13.92	11.51
Household	9.61	12.95
Clothing	7.07	5.42
Mixed business	6.52	7.04
Travel	5.99	11.70
Entertainment	5.07	6.23
Financial	1.32	0.60
Hotels	1.16	4.23
Other Services	12.84	13.27
Other retail	12.59	16.89
Total	107.00	101.77

[1] Visa and Switch cards only
[2] Mastercard and Visa cards only
Source: The Stationery Office – *Annual Abstract of Statistics 2004* (Crown copyright)

AVERAGE DWELLING PRICES

BY REGION AND TYPE OF ACCOMMODATION 2001

	Bungalow	*Detached house*	*Semi-detached house*	*Terraced house*	*Purpose-built flat/maisonette*	*Other**	*All Dwellings*
United Kingdom	113,419	173,295	99,412	87,470	90,356	121,456	112,835
England	121,577	182,487	104,220	92,193	101,867	130,306	119,563
North East	79,281	116,619	60,170	45,945	52,544	68,483	69,813
North West	95,386	139,939	75,486	54,486	69,710	76,864	82,403
Yorkshire & the Humber	87,588	127,888	65,334	52,775	58,499	71,512	76,368
East Midlands	91,274	134,679	68,850	58,028	52,973	74,093	87,280
West Midlands	111,508	162,802	78,857	65,879	69,063	77,526	97,650
East	118,186	202,021	118,771	96,546	78,346	78,349	127,858
London	196,184	331,324	231,228	187,493	138,939	176,471	182,325
South East	169,281	254,138	146,033	117,133	93,559	94,913	156,964
South West	130,157	185,670	107,483	87,641	81,472	88,955	118,639
Wales	87,675	126,644	66,922	53,079	61,009	55,525	79,628
Scotland	89,983	121,705	66,255	58,190	53,585	69,609	73,570
Northern Ireland	82,441	124,012	76,529	57,302	38,838	50,145	79,885

* Includes converted flats
Source: The Stationery Office – *Annual Abstract of Statistics 2004* (Crown copyright)

COST OF LIVING AND INFLATION RATES

The first cost of living index to be calculated took July 1914 as 100 and was based on the pattern of expenditure of working-class families in 1914. The cost of living index was superseded in 1947 by the general index of retail prices (RPI), although the older term is still popularly applied to it.

The Harmonised Index of Consumer Prices (HICP) was introduced in 1997 to enable comparisons within the European Union using an agreed methodology. On 10 December 2003 the Chancellor of the Exchequer announced that the UK inflation target was to change from one based on the Retail Prices Index excluding mortgage interest payments (RPIX) to one based on the HICP. At this time the National Statistician renamed the HICP as the Consumer Prices Index (CPI) to reflect its role as the main target measure of inflation for macroeconomic purposes. The UK HICP and CPI are one and the same and do not replace the RPI as the most general purpose measure of inflation for UK domestic use. Pensions and benefits and index-linked gilts continue to be calculated with reference to RPI or its derivatives.

GENERAL INDEX OF RETAIL PRICES

The general index of retail prices measures the changes month by month in the average level of prices of goods and services purchased by households in the United Kingdom. The Office for National Statistics reviews the components of the Retail Price Index once every year to reflect changes in consumer preferences and the establishment of new products. The expenditure of high-income households (top 4 per cent) and of households which derive at least three quarters of their total income from state pensions and benefits are excluded.

The index is compiled using a selection of around 650 goods and services, and the prices charged for these items are collected at regular intervals in about 150 locations throughout the country. For the index, the price changes are weighted in accordance with the pattern of consumption of the average family.

INFLATION RATE

The twelve-monthly percentage change in the 'all items' index of the RPI is usually referred to as the rate of inflation. The percentage change in prices between any two months/years can be obtained using the following formula:

$$\frac{\text{Later date RPI} - \text{Earlier date RPI}}{\text{Earlier date RPI}} \times 100$$

e.g. to find the rate of inflation for 1997, using the annual averages for 1996 and 1997:

$$\frac{157.5 - 152.7}{152.7} \times 100$$

PURCHASING POWER OF THE POUND

Changes in the internal purchasing power of the pound may be defined as the 'inverse' of changes in the level of prices: when prices go up, the amount which can be purchased with a given sum of money goes down. To find the purchasing power of the pound in one month or year, given that it was 100p in a previous month or year, the calculation would be:

$$100\text{p} \times \frac{\text{Earlier month/year RPI}}{\text{Later month/year RPI}}$$

Thus, if the purchasing power of the pound is taken to be 100p in 1975, the comparable purchasing power in 2002 would be:

$$100\text{p} \times \frac{34.2}{176.2} = 19.4\text{p}$$

For longer term comparisons, it has been the practice to use an index which has been constructed by linking together the RPI for the period 1962 to date; an index derived from the consumers expenditure deflator for the period from 1938 to 1962; and the prewar 'cost of living' index for the period 1914 to 1938. This long-term index enables the internal purchasing power of the pound to be calculated for any year from 1914 onwards. It should be noted that these figures can only be approximate.

	Annual average RPI (January 1987 = 100)	*Comparable purchasing power of £ in 1998*	*Rate of inflation (annual average)*
1914	2.8	58.18	
1915	3.5	46.54	
1920	7.0	23.27	
1925	5.0	32.58	
1930	4.5	36.20	
1935	4.0	40.72	
1938	4.4	37.02	
There are no official figures for 1939–45			
1946	7.4	22.01	
1950	9.0	18.10	
1955	11.2	14.54	
1960	12.6	12.93	
1965	14.8	11.00	
1970	18.5	8.80	
1975	34.2	4.76	
1980	66.8	2.44	18.0
1985	94.6	1.72	6.1
1990	126.1	1.29	9.5
1995	149.1	1.09	3.5
1996	152.7	1.07	2.4
1997	157.5	1.03	3.1
1998	162.9	1.00	3.4
1999	165.4	0.98	1.5
2000	170.3	0.96	3.0
2001	173.3	0.94	1.8
2002	176.2	0.92	1.7
2003	181.3	0.90	2.9

The RPI figures are published by the Office for National Statistics on either the second or third Tuesday in each month in a Consumer Price Indices bulletin and electronically on the National Statistics website www.statistics.gov.uk. They are also available as a recorded message which can be heard by telephoning 020-7533 5866.

OFFICE FOR NATIONAL STATISTICS, 1 Drummond Gate, London SW1V 2QQ T 0845-601 3034

TAXATION

INCOME TAX

Income tax is charged on the taxable income of individuals for a year of assessment commencing on 6 April and ending on the following 5 April. Many changes have been introduced during recent years which affect both the calculation of income chargeable to tax and the rate or rates at which the amount of tax due must be determined. The following information is confined to the year of assessment 2004–5 ending on 5 April 2005 and has only limited application to earlier years. Changes which are to come into operation at a later date are briefly mentioned where information is available.

An individual's liability to satisfy income tax for 2004–5 is determined by establishing the level of taxable income for the year. This income must then be allocated between three different headings, namely: (a) all income excluding that arising from savings and dividends; (b) income from savings; and (c) company dividends, including distributions.

Once this allocation has been completed the first calculation must be limited to taxable income excluding that arising from both savings and dividends. This income will be reduced by an individual's personal allowance and any other available allowances. The first £2,020 of taxable income remaining is assessed to income tax at the starting rate of 10 per cent. The next £29,380 is taxable at the basic rate of 22 per cent. Should any excess over £31,400 (£2,020 plus £29,380) remain, this will be taxable at the higher rate of 40 per cent.

The second calculation is limited to income from savings, if any. Liability may arise at the starting rate of 10 per cent, the lower rate of 20 per cent or the higher rate of 40 per cent. There is no liability to income tax at the basic rate of 22 per cent. The appropriate rate which must be used is determined by adding income from savings to other taxable income, excluding dividends. To the extent that the addition does not increase taxable income above £2,020, income from savings is taxed at the starting rate of 10 per cent. Should this level be exceeded but total income does not reach £31,400 any excess remains taxable at the lower rate of 20 per cent. Where the addition of income from savings extends total income above £31,400 the excess is taxed at the higher rate of 40 per cent.

Finally, any company dividends are taxed at either the Schedule F ordinary rate of 10 per cent or the Schedule F upper rate of 32.5 per cent. The amount of dividends (with the addition of any tax credit) must be added to taxable income comprising general income together with income from savings. If this addition does not increase total taxable income above £31,400 dividends remain taxable at the ordinary rate of 10 per cent only. However, if or to the extent that the addition discloses dividends exceeding the £31,400 level the excess is taxed at the upper rate of 32.5 per cent.

Trustees administering settled property and personal representatives dealing with the estate of a deceased person are chargeable to income tax at the basic rate of 22 per cent. Where trustees retain discretionary powers or income from settled property is accumulated, liability may be increased to 40 per cent. Lower rates apply where income is received in the form of dividends. It is expected that for 2005–6 and future years the first £500 of trust income will be taxed at the basic rate, in substitution for 40 per cent.

Companies residing in the UK are not liable to income tax but suffer corporation tax on income, profits and gains. Income arising overseas will often incur liability to foreign taxation. If that income is also chargeable to UK income tax, excessive liability could arise. The UK has concluded double taxation agreements with the governments of many overseas territories and these ensure that the same slice of income is not doubly taxed.

HUSBAND AND WIFE

A husband and wife are separately taxed, with each entitled to his or her personal allowance. A married man 'living with' his wife can only obtain a married couple's allowance if one party to the marriage was over the age of 64 years before 6 April 2000. In the absence of any claim, this allowance must be used by the husband but where any balance remains the surplus may be transferred to the wife. It is possible for a married woman to claim half the basic married couple's allowance as of right. The entire basic allowance may be claimed by the wife, if her husband so agrees. Each spouse may obtain other allowances and reliefs where the required conditions are satisfied. Income must be accurately allocated between the couple by reference to the individual beneficially entitled to that income. Where income arises from jointly-held assets, this must be apportioned equally between husband and wife. However, from 6 April 2004 where the assets comprise shares in closely controlled companies, the allocation of dividends and other distributions will be based on the beneficial interests of each spouse. In other cases where the beneficial interests in jointly-held assets are not equal, a special declaration can be made to apportion income by reference to the actual interests in that income.

SELF-ASSESSMENT

Self-assessment for income tax purposes affects individuals, trustees and personal representatives. Central to self-assessment is the requirement to deliver a completed tax return. This must normally be submitted by 31 January following the end of the year of assessment (the previous 5 April) to which the return relates. The taxpayer must also calculate the amount of income tax due. If a taxpayer wishes the Inland Revenue to calculate the tax due, the return must be forwarded to the Inland Revenue not later than the previous 30 September.

It is the responsibility of the taxpayer to submit payments of income tax on time. There are three different dates on which payments may fall due:

(a) an interim payment due on 31 January in the year of assessment itself
(b) a second interim payment due on the following 31 July
(c) a balancing payment, or possibly a repayment, on the following 31 January

The two interim payments will be based on tax payable

for the previous year of assessment but liability may be reduced where income has fallen or avoided entirely where the amounts are not substantial.

The impact of self-assessment is largely restricted to some nine million persons receiving tax returns. These comprise self-employed individuals, those receiving income from the exploitation of land in the UK, company directors, others with investment income liable to higher rate income tax, trustees and personal representatives. Elderly persons receiving small amounts of untaxed income may be excluded from the need to complete a tax return. Others having relatively straightforward affairs may complete a shortened version of the normal return form.

Failure to submit completed tax returns by 31 January or to discharge payments of income tax on time will incur a liability to interest, surcharges and penalties.

INCOME TAXABLE

For many years income tax has been assessed using a range of different schedules, with each applying to determine both the extent of liability and the amount to be included in taxable income. In most instances these schedules require that the actual income arising, or that which is deemed to arise, in a year of assessment will be charged to income tax for that year. However, a different basis must be used for business profits taxable under Case I or Case II of Schedule D. This basis requires taxable profits to be those for the business accounting period ending in the year of assessment, with special adjustments for the opening and closing years of a business.

The use of various schedules is being rapidly eroded. Schedule B no longer applies following the withdrawal of income tax liability on most commercial woodlands in the UK. Schedule C has also been withdrawn as a result of further changes in the tax system. However, as a result of the income tax legislation being re-written Schedule E ceased to apply on 6 April 2003, although this did not affect future liability to income tax on matters previously dealt with under that schedule. It is anticipated that the remaining schedules will be withdrawn on 6 April 2005 but, similarly, the replacement of those schedules with new legislation is unlikely to have any significant impact on income tax commitments.

The contents of those schedules which remain in operation for 2004–5 is outlined below, with a brief reference to the now obsolete Schedule E.

Schedule A

Tax is charged under Schedule A on the annual profits or gains arising from a business carried on for the exploitation of land in the UK. The determination of profits from a Schedule A business adopts principles identical to those used when establishing the profits or gains of a trade, profession or vocation. Rents and other income from the exploitation of land are included in the calculation, and outgoings incurred wholly and exclusively for the purposes of the Schedule A business may be deducted from income.

Schedule A does not extend to profits from farming, market gardening or woodlands, nor does it apply to mineral rents and royalties. Premiums arising on the grant of a lease for a period not exceeding 50 years in duration are treated as rents. However, the amount of the taxable premium may be reduced by 2 per cent for each complete year, after the first 12 months, of the leasing period. Income arising from the provision of certain furnished holiday accommodation attracts a number of tax advantages not otherwise available for most income chargeable under Schedule A. Receipts not exceeding £4,250 annually and accruing to an individual from letting property furnished in his or her own home are usually excluded from liability to income tax.

Schedule D

This Schedule is divided into six Cases:

Cases I and II – profits arising from trades, professions and vocations, including farming and market gardening. Profits must be calculated on an accounting basis which provides 'a true and fair view' of business results. This remains subject to any statutory adjustment which may be required. For example, only sums laid out 'wholly and exclusively' for the purposes of a business may be subtracted from receipts, notwithstanding that those outgoings may reflect a proper accounting charge. Capital expenditure incurred on assets used for business purposes will often produce an entitlement to capital allowances which reduce the profits chargeable. These profits may also be reduced by claims for loss relief and other matters.

Case III – interest on government stocks not taxed at source, interest on National Savings and Investments deposits and discounts. Interest up to £70 on ordinary National Savings and Investments deposits is exempt from income tax. The exemption applies to both husband and wife separately. Interest on National Savings and Investments special investment accounts is not exempt. Interest and other items of savings income incur liability at the starting rate, lower rate or the higher rate depending on the level of the recipient's income.

Cases IV and V – interest from overseas securities, rents, dividends and most other income accruing outside the UK. Assessment is based on the full amount of income arising, whether remitted to the UK or retained overseas, but individuals who are either not domiciled in the UK or who are ordinarily resident overseas may be taxed on a remittance basis. Interest received on most overseas investments is chargeable at the same rates as those which apply to interest from sources within the UK. Overseas dividends are usually taxed at 10 per cent or 32.5 per cent.

Case VI – sundry profits and annual receipts not assessed under any other Case or Schedule. These may include insurance commissions, post-cessation receipts from a discontinued business and numerous other receipts specifically charged under Case VI.

Schedule E

This Schedule ceased to apply after 5 April 2003. Matters previously dealt with under Schedule E have been replaced by the following three headings, none of which involves the use of a Schedule:

(a) employment income
(b) pension income
(c) social security income

This change in approach has not significantly affected the calculation of, and liability to, income tax (see below).

Schedule F

This Schedule is concerned with dividends and distributions received from a UK resident company.

EMPLOYMENT INCOME

Net taxable earnings arising in a year of assessment ending on 5 April are chargeable to income tax as employment income. This charge reflects taxable earnings remaining after subtracting the total of allowable deductions.

Taxable earnings will include all salaries, wages, director's fees and other money sums. In addition, the value of a wide range of benefits must be added. These benefits include the provision of living accommodation on advantageous terms and advantages arising from the use of vouchers.

Further taxable benefits accrue to directors and employees who are not classed as 'lower paid'. These exempt individuals receive annual earnings of no more than £8,500 calculated by including potentially taxable benefits. Such taxable benefits include the reimbursement of expenses, the availability of motor cars for private motoring, the provision of fuel for private motoring, interest free loans and other benefits provided at the employer's expense. The cost of providing a limited range of childcare facilities and a works bus for the transportation of employees may be ignored. Mileage allowances paid to employees who provide their own motor vehicles or cycles for business travel may also be excluded, unless they exceed stated limits.

All taxable earnings received by an individual who is resident, ordinarily resident and domiciled in the UK are chargeable to income tax. However, limitations may apply where there is some foreign element.

A 'receipts basis' applies for determining the year of assessment to which taxable earnings must be allocated. In general, the date of receipt will comprise the earlier of the date of payment or the date entitlement arises. In the case of company directors it is the earlier of these two dates, with the addition of the following three, which establishes the time of receipt: the date earnings are credited in the company's books; where earnings for a period are determined after the end of that period, the date of determination; where earnings for a period are determined in that period, the last day of that period.

In arriving at the amount of net taxable earnings all expenses incurred wholly, exclusively and necessarily in the performance of the duties, together with the cost of business travel, may be deducted. Fees and subscriptions paid to certain professional bodies and learned societies may also be deducted. In addition, fees paid to managers by entertainers, actors and others in respect of taxable earnings may be deducted, up to a maximum of 17.5 per cent.

Compensation for loss of office and other sums received on the termination of an employment are assessable to income tax. However, the first £30,000 may be excluded with only the balance remaining chargeable, unless the compensatory payment is linked with the retirement of the recipient or the performance of their duties.

A range of other matters loosely linked to an employment may also create employment income. Rules similar to those outlined above apply also to the holder of an office.

PENSION INCOME

Pensions received from various sources, including an occupational pension scheme, personal pension scheme, retirement annuity scheme and from other types of arrangement are treated as pension income chargeable to income tax. Liability is based on the amounts received in a year of assessment. However, where the pension is attributable to certain payments made overseas, only 90 per cent is taxable.

SOCIAL SECURITY INCOME

Many social security benefits are not liable to income tax. However, benefits which are taxable as social security income include the state retirement pension, widow's pension, widowed mother's allowance and jobseeker's allowance. Short-term sick pay and maternity pay payable by an employer are also chargeable to tax. Incapacity benefit remains taxable but no liability arises on most short-term benefit.

PAY AS YOU EARN

The Pay as You Earn (PAYE) system is not an independent form of taxation but is designed to collect income tax by deduction from most taxable earnings. When paying taxable earnings to employees an employer is usually required to deduct income tax and to account for that tax to the Inland Revenue. In many cases this deduction procedure will fully exhaust the individual's liability to income tax, unless there is other income. The date of 'receipt' used to establish the time employment income arises also identifies the date of 'payment' when establishing liability to PAYE.

The PAYE system is used to collect tax on certain payments made 'in kind'. The system is also applied when collecting tax on many pensions, jobseeker's benefits, some incapacity benefits and maternity pay.

INCOME FROM SAVINGS

Many payments of interest made by building societies and banks are received after the deduction of income tax at the lower rate of 20 per cent. However, investors not liable to income tax may arrange to receive interest gross with no tax being deducted on payment.

Interest of this nature represents 'income from savings'; an expression which also extends to interest on government securities, interest on a restricted range of National Savings and Investments products and the income element of purchased life annuities. In addition, 'income from savings' may extend to other income of a similar nature arising outside the United Kingdom. Not all forms of investment income are included in the list, notable exceptions comprising income from letting property and company dividends.

A great deal of interest arising from sources in the United Kingdom will be received after deduction of income tax at the lower rate of 20 per cent. Although this interest is not taxable at the basic rate it remains chargeable at the starting rate of 10 per cent, the lower rate of 20 per cent or the higher rate of 40 per cent. Where such interest, when added to other income, excluding dividends, falls within the starting rate band tax will be due at 10 per cent. As tax will have been suffered by deduction at the lower rate of 20 per cent a repayment of the excess may well be obtained from the Inland Revenue. To the extent that interest from savings when added to other income exceeds £2,020 but does not exceed £31,400, liability arises at the lower rate of 20 per cent. In those situations where, or to the extent that, income from savings when added to other income produces a combined total exceeding £31,400, liability arises at the higher rate of 40 per cent. As income tax will usually have been deducted at source at the rate of 20 per cent, higher rate liability arises at a further 20 per cent (40 per cent less 20 per cent).

DIVIDENDS

Dividends and other distributions paid by a UK resident company have a tax credit attached equal to one-ninth of the sum received in 2004–5. Therefore, a recipient shareholder also residing in the UK who receives a cash dividend of £90 will have a tax credit of £10. The gross dividend or distribution (sum received plus tax credit) is regarded as having suffered income tax, equal to the tax credit, at the rate of 10 per cent. Where the shareholder is not liable, or not fully liable, to income tax it is not possible to claim a repayment of the tax credit. However, for 2004–5 dividends are taxed at the Schedule F ordinary rate of 10 per cent or the Schedule F upper rate of 32.5 per cent. Where the total income of an individual is not unduly substantial the amount of the tax credit, namely 10 per cent, will be offset against the Schedule F ordinary rate of income tax, which is also 10 per cent, leaving no further liability. Should the gross amount of dividends or distributions when added to other taxable income exceed £31,400 the excess is chargeable at the Schedule F upper rate of 32.5 per cent. The amount of the tax credit will then reduce tax otherwise payable at the upper rate. Although the rates of 10 per cent and 32.5 per cent apply primarily to dividends and distributions from United Kingdom companies, they also extend to income of a similar nature arising outside the UK.

INCOME NOT TAXABLE

Income which is not taxable in 2004–5 includes interest on National Savings and Investments saving certificates, most scholarship income, bounty payments to members of the armed services and annuities payable to the holders of certain awards. Dividend income arising from qualifying investments in personal equity plans (PEPs) and venture capital trusts is exempt from tax. Tax credits on dividends from such trusts cannot be recovered, nor is it possible for PEP managers to obtain repayment of credits after 5 April 2004. Payments made to an individual for the adoption of a child, together with income received under maintenance agreements and court orders made following separation or divorce will not be liable to tax. Nor will payments made under many deeds of covenant be recognised for tax purposes, unless the recipient is a charity. Interest arising on a tax exempt special savings account (TESSA) opened with a building society or bank will be exempt from tax if the account is maintained throughout a five-year period.

A popular investment, the individual savings account (ISA), is available to United Kingdom residents aged 18 years and over. The ISA may have three components, namely cash, stocks and shares and life assurance. Interest on the cash component, usually comprising bank or building society deposits, is exempt from income tax. Dividends on most quoted holdings in the stocks and shares component are also immune from liability to income tax, with tax credits being repaid only for years up to and including that ending on 5 April 2004. Income and gains accruing to the provider of the life assurance component will be free of all liability to taxation.

A maximum subscription of £7,000 can be made by an individual to an ISA during 2004–5. Of this sum no more than £3,000 can be allocated to the cash component and £1,000 to the life assurance component. Potential investors are provided with the choice of whether to invest in a maxi-ISA or in mini-ISAs. Should a maxi-ISA be selected, the entire £7,000 can be invested in stocks and shares, but the use of a mini-ISA limits such an investment to £3,000 with the balance of £4,000 capable of being used to invest in the cash and life assurance components. The maximum permitted subscription will be reduced after 5 April 2006.

Although new TESSA accounts can no longer be opened, where an existing TESSA matures at the end of a five-year period the capital (but not the income) proceeds can be separately invested in the cash component of an ISA. This is in addition to the normal limits governing investment in an ISA.

FOSTER CARERS

Profits arising to an individual from the provision of foster care are chargeable to income tax. Previously, the calculation of these taxable profits produced a great deal of uncertainty but a new arrangement was introduced for 2003–4 and future years. When determining the application of this arrangement for 2004–5, an individual must calculate two factors, namely:

(a) a fixed amount of £10,000 for a given residence in a year. Where the residence is shared by two or more individuals providing foster care the amount of £10,000 must be apportioned. Should the period of review fall short of a full twelve-month period, £10,000 must be suitably reduced.
(b) an amount per week for each foster child, comprising £200 per week for a child aged under 11 years and £250 per week for a child aged 11 or above.

Should the total receipts of an individual from the provision of foster care fall below the aggregate of (a) and (b) no liability to income tax will arise. However, should the receipts exceed the aggregate of (a) and (b) the individual is provided with a choice, namely:

(i) to calculate profits in the normal way on total receipts less actual expenses and capital allowances, or
(ii) to treat as taxable profits the amount by which total receipts from the provision of foster care exceed the aggregate of (a) and (b), without any separate relief for expenses or capital allowances.

ALLOWANCES

Allowances which can be obtained for 2004–5 are shown below.

Personal allowance

Basic personal allowance	£4,745
Those over 64 on 5 April 2005	£6,830
Those over 74 on 5 April 2005	£6,950

The increased allowance for older individuals is available for those who died during the year of assessment but who would otherwise have achieved the appropriate age not later than 5 April 2005. The amount of the increased personal allowance for older taxpayers will be reduced by one-half of total income in excess of £18,900. This reduction in the allowance will continue until it has been reduced to the basic personal allowance of £4,745. The personal allowance is given as a deduction in calculating taxable income and may therefore produce relief at the rate of 10, 22 or 40 per cent, as appropriate.

Married couple's allowance

A married man who was 'living with' his wife at any time in the year ending on 5 April 2005 will be entitled to a married couple's allowance if at least one party to the marriage reached the age of 65 years before 6 April 2000. The allowance, which therefore applies only to those born before 6 April 1935, cannot be obtained where a husband or wife reaches 65 on some future date.

The allowance is £5,725. It may be increased to

£5,795 where either party to the marriage was 75 or over on 5 April 2005. Where an individual would otherwise have reached the age of 75 by 5 April 2005 but who died earlier in the year, the increased allowance is given. The amount of the married couple's allowance will be reduced where the income of the husband (excluding the income of the wife) exceeds £18,900. In this situation the amount to be deducted from the allowance will comprise:

(a) one-half of the husband's total income in excess of £18,900, less
(b) the amount of any reduction made when calculating the husband's increased personal allowance.

This reduction in the married couple's allowance cannot reduce that allowance below a basic allowance of £2,210.

If a husband and wife were married during 2004–5, the married couple's allowance must be reduced by one-twelfth for each complete month commencing on 6 April 2004 and preceding the date of marriage.

Unlike the personal allowance, the married couple's allowance does not reduce taxable income. Relief is granted by reducing the tax otherwise payable by 10 per cent of the allowance. For example, where the basic allowance of £2,210 is available, the amount of tax payable may be reduced by £221. Should the amount of the reduction exceed tax otherwise payable, no tax will be due, nor will any repayment arise.

In the absence of any further action, the married couple's allowance will be given to the husband. If he is unable to utilise all or any part of that allowance due to an absence of income, the husband may transfer the unused portion to his wife. The decision whether or not to transfer remains at the discretion of the husband. However, a wife may file an election to obtain one-half of the basic married couple's allowance of £2,210 as of right, leaving the husband with the balance of that allowance. Alternatively, the couple may jointly elect that the entire basic allowance should be allocated to the wife only. Should either spouse be unable to utilise his or her share of the total married couple's allowance the unused part may be transferred to the other spouse.

Blind person's allowance

An allowance of £1,560 is available to an individual if at any time during the year ending on 5 April 2005, he or she was registered as blind. If the individual is 'living with' a wife or husband, any unused part of the blind person's allowance can be transferred to the other spouse. The allowance reduces taxable income and may therefore give rise to relief at the taxpayer's highest rate of income tax suffered.

MAINTENANCE PAYMENTS

Relief for maintenance payments made in 2004–5 to a separated spouse or a divorced former spouse is limited to £2,210 or the amount of the payment, whichever is smaller. A further requirement before relief can be obtained is that at least one of the parties to the transaction had reached his/her 65th birthday before 6 April 2000. No relief is available to younger parties. Relief is given at the rate of 10 per cent and subtracted from the amount of tax otherwise due by the payer. The maintenance payment is exempt from liability to income tax in the hands of the recipient.

INTEREST

In some instances, interest paid by a business proprietor may be included when calculating profits chargeable to income tax under Case I or Case II of Schedule D. In addition, relief for interest paid on a loan applied to acquire or develop land and buildings for letting may be obtained by including the outlay in the calculation of income chargeable under Schedule A. However, many private individuals cannot obtain relief in this manner and must satisfy stringent requirements before relief will be forthcoming. In general terms it is a requirement that before interest can qualify for relief it must be paid for a qualifying purpose. Relief will not be available to the extent that interest exceeds a reasonable commercial rate and no relief is forthcoming for interest on an overdraft.

Interest paid in 2004–5 which can be treated as laid out for a qualifying purpose will include the following payments:

(a) Interest on a loan used to acquire an interest in a close company or in a partnership, or to advance money to such a person or body
(b) Interest on a loan to a member of a partnership to acquire machinery or plant for use in the partnership business
(c) Interest on a loan to an employed person to acquire machinery or plant for the purposes of his or her employment
(d) Interest on a loan made for the purpose of contributing capital to an industrial co-operative
(e) Interest on a loan applied for investment in an employee-controlled company
(f) Interest on a loan to personal representatives to provide funds for the payment of inheritance tax
(g) Interest on a loan made to elderly persons for the purchase of an annuity where the loan is secured on land. If the loan exceeds £30,000, relief is limited to interest on this amount. This relief is restricted to income tax at the basic rate of 22 per cent. Whilst the relief remains for some borrowers, it cannot be obtained for interest only loans taken out after 8 March 1999.

Relief under headings (a) to (f) is given by deducting interest from taxable income. This enables the taxpayer to obtain relief at his or her top rate of tax suffered.

CHARITABLE DONATIONS

A number of charitable donations and qualify for tax relief and may involve donations of money or transferable assets. A popular arrangement is the Gift Aid scheme which requires the making of a money payment to a recognised charity. Providing that the donor receives little or no benefit in return, and certain formalities are complied with, the donation is then treated as a net sum paid after deducting income tax at the basic rate of 22 per cent. On the assumption that the donor suffers a sufficient amount of income tax at that rate, no additional income tax will be payable. However, if the donor suffers liability at the higher rate of 40 per cent, he/she may obtain relief for the outlay at the difference between the basic rate of 22 per cent and the higher rate of 40 per cent – 18 per cent – on the grossed up amount of the donation.

OTHER OUTGOINGS

Many employees pay contributions to an approved occupational pension scheme. The amount of their contributions may be deducted when calculating net taxable earnings treated as employment income. Relief should also be available for any additional voluntary contributions paid. Self-employed individuals and those receiving earnings not covered by an occupational pension scheme may contribute under personal pension scheme arrangements or under stakeholder schemes. Individuals may also pay premiums under retirement annuity schemes if the arrangements were concluded before 1 July 1988. Contributions paid under all headings and which do not exceed upper limits may obtain income tax relief by deduction from taxable income. Revised arrangements governing relief for pension contributions and the treatment of pension schemes are to be introduced on 6 April 2006.

Subject to a maximum of £200,000 in 2004–5, the cost of subscribing for shares in an unquoted trading company or companies may qualify for relief under the Enterprise Investment Scheme. Many requirements must be satisfied before this relief can be obtained, but a husband and wife may each take advantage of the £200,000 maximum. Relief is given by reducing tax payable at the rate of 20 per cent of the share subscription cost. Further relief on an outlay up to a maximum of £200,000 annually is given at the increased rate of 40 per cent for a subscription of shares in a venture capital trust company. This increased rate applies only where shares are issued by such trusts after 5 April 2004 and not later than 5 April 2006 although the maximum investment limit continues beyond the latter date.

TAX CREDITS

Child tax credits and working tax credits are payable to qualifying individuals. Although the title of both credits incorporates the word 'tax', neither affects the amount of income tax payable or repayable. Both take the form of social security benefits.

CAPITAL GAINS TAX

An individual is potentially chargeable to capital gains tax on chargeable gains that accrue from disposals made by him/her during a year of assessment. The following information is largely confined to the year of assessment 2004–5, ending on 5 April 2005.

Liability extends to individuals who are either resident or ordinarily resident for the year but special rules apply where a person permanently leaves the UK or comes to this territory for the purpose of acquiring residence. Non-residents are not usually liable to capital gains tax unless they carry on a business in the UK through a branch or agency. However, individuals who left the UK after 16 March 1998 and who have been resident or ordinarily resident in at least four of the seven years preceding departure may remain liable to capital gains tax unless they reside overseas throughout a period of five complete tax years. Exceptions from this may apply where there is a disposal of assets acquired in the period of absence.

Trustees residing in the UK, together with personal representatives administering the estate of the deceased person, are chargeable to capital gains tax at the flat rate of 40 per cent but chargeable gains accruing to companies are assessable to corporation tax.

In earlier years, capital gains tax was chargeable on the net chargeable gains accruing to a person in a year of assessment after subtracting the annual exemption for that year. Net chargeable gains represented capital gains less capital losses arising from disposals carried out during the year. Unused losses brought forward from an earlier year could be offset against current net chargeable gains, but in the case of individuals were not to reduce the net gains below the annual exemption limit. It was possible to utilise trading losses against chargeable gains where those losses had not been offset against income.

TAPER RELIEF

However, the calculation of net gains chargeable to capital gains tax is now governed by the availability of taper relief. The purpose of this relief, which replaced the former indexation allowance, is to require that only a percentage of gains become chargeable to capital gains tax. Taper relief draws a distinction between business assets and non-business assets. The expression 'business asset' broadly identifies an asset used for business purposes in addition to some holdings of shares in both trading and non-trading companies. Where the nature of an asset has changed during the period of ownership from a business asset to a non-business asset, or vice versa, the asset must be effectively broken down into two parts. This may be particularly relevant where the period overlaps 5 April 2000, 5 April 2002 or 5 April 2003 when, on each occasion, some previously non-business assets were re-classified as business assets.

The percentage which must be used to calculate taper relief is governed by the number of complete years of ownership falling after 5 April 1998. Initially an additional 'bonus year' could be added for most assets acquired before 17 March 1998. This 'bonus year' continues to apply to non-business assets but has been withdrawn where the disposal of a business asset takes place after 5 April 2000.

The maximum percentage attributable to business assets was initially achieved after an ownership period extending throughout ten years but this period was reduced to one of four years only where the disposal occurred after 5 April 2000 and before 6 April 2002. Finally, where the disposal of business assets takes place on and after 6 April 2002 the ownership period has been further reduced. Once that period exceeds one year only 50 per cent of the gain will be chargeable, falling to 25 per cent where two whole years are exceeded. No corresponding changes have been made to the ownership period of non-business assets, which has remained unchanged since the introduction of taper relief on 6 April 1998. The percentages of gains remaining chargeable for disposals taking place on and after 6 April 2003 are shown in the following table:

No. of whole years of ownership	*Percentage of gain chargeable* Business assets	Non-business assets
	%	%
1	50	100
2	25	100
3	25	95
4	25	90
5	25	85
6	25	80
7	25	75
8	25	70
9	25	65
10	25	60

If only chargeable gains arise from disposals carried out in 2004–5 the taper relief, if any, must be calculated by reference to each disposal. The aggregate sum of taper relief will then be subtracted from the total chargeable gains to produce the net gains for the year. Where disposals made in 2004–5 give rise to both gains and losses, the losses must be subtracted from the gains and taper relief calculated on the net sum remaining. It is necessary to allocate the losses between the gains where there are two or more disposals producing gains. Losses brought forward from an earlier year must also be subtracted when calculating the net gains qualifying for taper relief. However, the losses brought forward are not to reduce the net gains below the annual exemption limit of £8,200 which applies for 2004–5.

ANNUAL EXEMPTION

The initial slice of net gains arising in a tax year is exempt from liability to capital gains tax. This slice, comprising the annual exemption, is £8,200 for 2004–5. Should any part of the exemption remain unused, this cannot be carried forward to a future year. A smaller exemption limit applies to most trusts.

RATES OF TAX

The net gains remaining, if any, calculated after subtracting the annual exemption, incur liability to capital gains tax for 2004–5. Although income tax rates are used for this purpose, liability arises only at the starting rate of 10 per cent, the lower rate of 20 per cent, the higher rate of 40 per cent, or a combination of the three rates. Unlike some income tax commitments, there is no liability at the basic rate of 22 per cent.

The first step is to calculate the amount of taxable income chargeable to income tax. This will include income from savings, company dividends and all other forms of taxable income. The second step is to add the amount of net chargeable gains to the taxable income chargeable to income tax. To the extent that this does not increase the aggregate total above £2,020, capital gains tax will be charged at the rate of 10 per cent. If the aggregate total exceeds £2,020 but does not exceed £31,400 any balance needed to reach £2,020 is chargeable at 10 per cent and the excess at 20 per cent. If, or to the extent that, any part of the chargeable gains exceed the limit of £31,400 the excess is chargeable at 40 per cent. Although some income tax rates are used, capital gains tax remains an entirely separate tax. Capital gains tax for 2004–5 falls due for payment in full on 31 January 2006. If payment is delayed, interest or surcharges may be imposed.

HUSBAND AND WIFE

Independent taxation requires that a husband and wife 'living together' are separately assessed to capital gains tax. Each spouse must independently calculate his or her gains and losses, with each entitled to the benefit of taper relief, if any, and the annual exemption of £8,200 for 2004–5. No liability to capital gains tax arises from the transfer of assets between husband and wife 'living together'.

DISPOSAL OF ASSETS

Before chargeable gains potentially liable to capital gains tax can arise, a disposal or deemed disposal of an asset must take place. This occurs not only where assets are sold or exchanged but applies on the making of a gift. There is also a disposal of assets where any capital sum is derived from assets, e.g. where compensation is received for loss or damage to an asset. The date on which a disposal must be treated as having taken place will determine the year of assessment into which the chargeable gain or allowable loss falls. In those cases where a disposal is made under an unconditional contract, the time of disposal will be that when the contract was entered into and not the subsequent date of conveyance or transfer. A disposal under a conditional contract or option is treated as taking place when the contract becomes unconditional or the option is exercised. Disposals by way of gift are undertaken when the gift becomes effective.

VALUATION OF ASSETS

The amount received as consideration for the disposal of an asset will be the sum from which very limited outgoings must be deducted for the purpose of establishing the gain or loss. In cases where the consideration does not accurately reflect the value of the asset, a different basis must be used. This applies, in particular, where an asset is transferred by way of gift or otherwise than by a bargain made at arm's length. Such transactions are deemed to take place for a consideration representing market value, which will determine both the disposal proceeds accruing to the transferor and the cost of acquisition to the transferee.

Market value represents the price which an asset might reasonably be expected to fetch on a sale in the open market. In the case of unquoted shares or securities, it is to be assumed that the hypothetical purchaser in the open market would have available all the information which a prudent prospective purchaser of shares or securities might reasonably require if that person were proposing to purchase them from a willing vendor by private treaty and at arm's length. The market value of unquoted shares or securities will often be established following negotiations with the Inland Revenue Shares Valuation Division. The valuation of land and interests in land in the UK will be dealt with by the District Valuer. Special rules apply to determine the market value of shares quoted on the Stock Exchange.

DEDUCTION FOR OUTGOINGS

Once the actual or notional disposal proceeds have been determined, it only remains to subtract eligible outgoings for the purpose of computing the gain or loss. There is the general rule that any outgoings deducted, or which are available to be deducted, when calculating income tax liability must be ignored. Subject to this, deductions will usually be limited to:

(a) the cost of acquiring the asset, together with incidental costs wholly and exclusively incurred in connection with the acquisition
(b) expenditure incurred wholly and exclusively on the asset in enhancing its value, being expenditure reflected in the state or nature of the asset at the time of the disposal, and any other expenditure wholly and exclusively incurred in establishing, preserving or defending title to, or a right over, the asset
(c) the incidental costs of making the disposal

Where the disposal concerns a leasehold interest having less than 50 years to run, any expenditure falling under (a) and (b) must be written off throughout the duration of the lease using a 'curved line' approach.

INDEXATION ALLOWANCE

For many years an indexation allowance could be inserted when calculating a gain on the disposal of an asset. The allowance was based on percentage increases in the retail prices index between the month of March 1982, or the month in which expenditure was incurred if later, and the month of disposal.

Taper relief has largely replaced the indexation allowance for disposals made after 5 April 1998. However, where an asset was acquired before this date, the indexation allowance will be calculated to the month of April 1998 and frozen. The frozen allowance then enters into the calculation of chargeable gain, if any, when the asset is disposed of at some later date. The adjustment for the indexation allowance must be made before calculating taper relief on the net sum remaining.

EXEMPTIONS

There is a general exemption from liability to capital gains tax where the net gains of an individual for 2004–5 do not exceed £8,200. This general exemption applies separately to a husband and wife whether or not the parties are 'living together'. The disposal of many assets will not give rise to chargeable gains or allowable losses and these assets include:

(a) private motor cars
(b) government securities
(c) loan stock and other securities (but not shares)
(d) options and contracts relating to securities within (b) and (c)
(e) National Savings and Investments Savings Certificates, Premium Bonds, Defence Bonds and National Development Bonds
(f) currency of any description acquired for personal expenditure outside the UK
(g) decorations awarded for valour
(h) betting wins and pools, lottery or games prizes
(i) compensation or damages for any wrong or injury suffered by an individual in his or her person, profession or vocation
(j) life assurance and deferred annuity contracts where the person making the disposal is the original beneficial owner
(k) dwelling-houses and land enjoyed with the residence which is an individual's only or main residence
(l) tangible movable property, the consideration for the disposal of which does not exceed £6,000
(m) certain tangible movable property which is a wasting asset having a life not exceeding 50 years
(n) assets transferred to charities and other bodies
(o) works of art, historic buildings and similar assets
(p) assets used to provide maintenance funds for historic buildings
(q) assets transferred to trustees for the benefit of employees
(r) assets held in a Personal Equity Plan or Individual Savings Account

DWELLING-HOUSES

Exemption from capital gains tax will usually be available for any gain which accrues to an individual from the disposal of, or of an interest in, a dwelling-house or part of a dwelling-house which has been his or her only or main residence. The exemption extends to land which has been occupied and enjoyed with the residence as its garden or grounds. Some restriction may be necessary where the land exceeds half a hectare.

The gain will not be chargeable to capital gains tax if the dwelling-house, or part, has been the individual's only or main residence throughout the period of ownership, or throughout the entire period except for all or any part of the final three years. A proportionate part of the gain will be exempt in other cases if the dwelling-house has been the individual's only or main residence for part only of the period of ownership. In the case of property acquired before 31 March 1982, the period of ownership is treated as commencing on this date. Where part of the dwelling-house has been used exclusively for business purposes, that part of the gain attributable to business use will not be exempt. In those cases where part of a qualifying dwelling-house has been used to provide rented residential accommodation, this non-personal use may frequently be ignored when calculating exemption from capital gains tax, unless relatively substantial sums are involved. Dwellings occupied by dependent relatives, separated spouses or divorced former spouses, may also qualify for the exemption, but only where occupation commenced before 6 April 1988.

ROLL-OVER RELIEF

Persons carrying on business will often undertake the disposal of an asset and use the proceeds to finance the acquisition of a replacement asset. Where this situation arises, a claim for roll-over relief may be available. The broad effect of such a claim is that all or part of the gain arising on the disposal of the old asset may be disregarded. The gain or part is then subtracted from the cost of acquiring the replacement asset. As this cost is reduced, any gain arising from the future disposal of the replacement asset will be correspondingly increased, unless a further roll-over situation then develops.

It remains a requirement that both the old and the replacement asset must be used for the purpose of the taxpayer's business or for the purpose of business carried out by a company in which the taxpayer retains an interest. Relief will only be available if the acquisition of the replacement asset takes place within a period commencing twelve months before, and ending three years after, the disposal of the old asset, although the Inland Revenue retains a discretion to extend this period where the circumstances were such that it was impossible for the taxpayer to acquire the replacement asset before the expiration of the normal time limit. Whilst many business assets qualify for roll-over relief there are exceptions.

Roll-over relief may also be available where a gain arises on the disposal of land or buildings to an authority capable of exercising compulsory purchase powers. Similar relief may be forthcoming where shares in a company are transferred to trustees administering an employees' share incentive plan for the benefit of persons employed by that company or group of companies of which the company is a member.

DEFERRAL RELIEF

A form of roll-over relief, known as 'deferral relief' enables gains arising on the disposal of an asset to be matched, in whole or in part, with a subscription for shares in a restricted range of unquoted trading companies, including certain companies whose shares are dealt in on the Alternative Investment Market. Where matching can be achieved any part of the gain arising on disposal, not exceeding the cost of the qualifying share subscription, may become the subject of a claim. Unlike the usual form of roll-over relief, this claim for deferral relief does not eliminate or reduce the chargeable gain. It has the effect of deferring that gain until the time of some future event, which will usually be identified by the disposal of the newly acquired shares or the loss of UK residential status by the shareholder. A similar form of deferral relief was previously available for gains arising on disposals which were matched with a qualifying share investment in a venture capital trust company. To the extent of the gain arising, which could not exceed the amount of the investment qualifying for income tax relief, that gain was deferred until the time of a future event, which would normally comprise the disposal of shares in the venture capital trust company or the loss of UK residential status. However, this form of deferral relief was withdrawn for shares issued by a venture capital trust after 5 April 2004.

HOLD-OVER RELIEF – GIFTS

The gift of an asset is treated as a disposal made for a consideration equal to market value, with a corresponding acquisition by the transferee at an identical value. In the case of gifts made by individuals and a limited range of trustees to a transferee resident in the UK, a form of hold-over relief may be available. Relief, which must be claimed, is limited to the transfer of certain assets, including the following:

(a) assets used for the purposes of a trade or similar activity carried on by the transferor or his/her personal company
(b) shares or securities of a trading company which is not listed on a stock exchange
(c) shares or securities of a trading company which is listed but which is the transferor's personal company
(d) many interests in agricultural property qualifying for agricultural property relief for inheritance tax purposes
(e) assets involved in transactions which are lifetime transfers for inheritance tax purposes, other than potentially exempt transfers

The transfer of shares or securities to a company is now precluded from obtaining relief. Restrictions may also arise where, after 10 December 2003, an individual transfers assets to trustees administering a trust in which the individual retains an interest or the assets transferred comprise a dwelling-house. Subject to these exceptions, the effect of a valid claim for hold-over relief is similar to that following a claim for roll-over relief on the disposal of business assets, but adjustments may be necessary where some consideration is given for the transfer, the asset has not been used for business purposes throughout the period of ownership, or not all assets of a company are used for business purposes.

DEATH

No capital gains tax is chargeable on the value of assets retained by an individual at the time of death. However, the personal representatives administering the deceased's estate are deemed to acquire those assets for a consideration representing market value on death. This ensures that any increase in value occurring before the date of death will not be chargeable to capital gains tax. If a legatee or other person acquires an asset under a will or intestacy no chargeable gain will accrue to the personal representatives, and the person taking the asset will also be treated as having acquired it at the time of death for its then market value.

INHERITANCE TAX

Liability to inheritance tax may arise on a limited range of lifetime gifts and other dispositions and also on the value of assets retained, or deemed to be retained, at the time of death. An individual's domicile at the time of any gift or on death is an important matter. Domicile will generally be determined by applying normal rules, although special considerations may be necessary where an individual was previously domiciled in the UK but subsequently acquired a domicile of choice overseas. In addition, individuals who have been resident in the UK for at least 17 of the previous 20 years at the time of an event are treated as domiciled in the UK for this purpose. Where a person was domiciled, or treated as domiciled, in the UK at the time of a disposition or on death the location of assets is immaterial and full liability to inheritance tax arises. Individuals domiciled outside the UK are, however, chargeable to inheritance tax only on transactions or events affecting assets located in the UK. The assets of husband and wife are not merged for inheritance tax purposes. Each spouse is treated as a separate individual entitled to receive the benefit of his or her exemptions, reliefs and rates of tax. Where husband and wife retain similar assets, e.g. shares in the same family company, special 'related property' provisions may require the merger of those assets for valuation purposes only.

LIFETIME GIFTS AND DISPOSITIONS

Gifts and dispositions made during lifetime fall under four broad headings, namely:

(a) dispositions which are not transfers of value
(b) exempt transfers
(c) potentially exempt transfers
(d) chargeable transfers

Dispositions which are not transfers of value

Several lifetime transactions are not treated as transfers of value and may be entirely disregarded for inheritance tax purposes. These include transactions not intended to confer gratuitous benefit, the provision of family maintenance, the waiver of the right to receive remuneration or dividends, and the grant of agricultural tenancies for full consideration.

Exempt transfers

The main exempt transfers are:

Transfers between spouses – Transfers between husband and wife are usually exempt. However, if the transferor is, but the transferee spouse is not, domiciled in the UK, transfers will be exempt only to the extent that the total does not exceed £55,000. Unlike the requirement used for income tax and capital gains tax purposes, it is immaterial whether husband and wife are living together.

Annual exemption – The first £3,000 of gifts and other dispositions made in a year ending on 5 April is exempt. If the exemption is not used, or not wholly used, in any year the balance may be carried forward to the following year only. The annual exemption will only be available for a potentially exempt transfer if that transfer becomes chargeable by reason of the donor's subsequent death.

Small gifts – Outright gifts of £250 or less to any person in one year ending on 5 April are exempt.

Normal expenditure – A transfer made during lifetime and comprising normal expenditure is exempt. To obtain this exemption it must be shown that:

(a) the transfer was made as part of the normal expenditure of the transferor;
(b) taking one year with another, the transfer was made out of income; and
(c) after allowing for all transfers of value forming part of normal expenditure the transferor was left with sufficient income to maintain his or her usual standard of living

Gifts in consideration of marriage – These are exempt if they satisfy certain requirements. The amount allowed will be governed by the relationship between the donor and a party to the marriage. Allowable amounts:

(a) gifts by a parent, £5,000
(b) gifts by a grandparent, £2,500
(c) gifts by a party to the marriage, £2,500
(d) gifts by other persons, £1,000

Gifts to charities – These are exempt from liability.

Gifts to political parties – Gifts which satisfy certain requirements are generally exempt.

Gifts for national purposes – Gifts made to certain bodies are exempt from liability. These bodies include, among others, the National Gallery, the British Museum, the National Trust, the National Art Collections Fund, the National Heritage Memorial Fund, the Historic Buildings and Monuments Commission for England (English Heritage), any local authority, and any university or university college in the UK.

A number of other gifts made for the public benefit are also exempt.

Potentially exempt transfers

Lifetime gifts and dispositions which are neither to be ignored nor comprise exempt transfers incur possible liability to inheritance tax. However, relief is available for a range of potentially exempt transfers. These comprise gifts made by an individual to:

(a) a second individual
(b) trustees administering an accumulation and maintenance trust
(c) trustees administering a disabled person's trust

The accumulation and maintenance trust mentioned in (b) must provide that on reaching a specified age, not exceeding 25 years, a beneficiary will become absolutely entitled to trust assets or obtain an interest in possession in the income from those assets. Additions to the above list affect settled property administered by trustees where an individual, or individuals, retain an interest in possession. The transfer of assets to, the removal of assets from, or the rearrangement of interests in such property comprise potentially exempt transfers if the person transferring an interest and the person benefiting from the transfer are both individuals.

No immediate liability to inheritance tax will arise on the making of a potentially exempt transfer. Should the donor survive for a period of seven years, immunity from liability will be confirmed. However, the donor's death within the seven-year *inter vivos* period produces liability if the amounts involved are sufficiently substantial (*see* below).

Chargeable transfers

Any remaining lifetime gifts or dispositions which are neither to be ignored nor represent exempt transfers or potentially exempt transfers, incur liability to inheritance tax.

GIFTS WITH RESERVATION

A lifetime gift of assets made at any time after 17 March 1986 may incur additional liability to inheritance tax if the donor retains some interest in the subject matter of the gift. This may arise, for example, where a parent transfers a dwelling-house to a son or daughter and continues to occupy the property or to enjoy some benefit from that property. The retention of a benefit may be ignored where it is enjoyed in return for full consideration, perhaps a commercial rent, or where the benefit arises from changed circumstances which could not have been foreseen at the time of the original gift. The gift with reservation provisions will not usually apply to most exempt transfers.

There are three possibilities which may arise where the donor reserves or enjoys some benefit from the subject matter of a previous gift and subsequently dies, namely:

(a) if no benefit is enjoyed within a period of seven years before death there can be no further liability
(b) if the benefit ceased to be enjoyed within a period of seven years before the date of death, the original donor is deemed to have made a potentially exempt transfer representing the value of the asset at the time of cessation
(c) if the benefit is enjoyed at the time of death, the value of the asset must be included when arriving at the value of the deceased's estate on death

It must be emphasised that the existence of a benefit enjoyed at any time within a period of seven years before death will establish liability to tax on gifts with reservation, notwithstanding that the gift may have been made many years earlier, providing it was undertaken after 17 March 1986.

DEATH

Immediately before the time of death an individual is deemed to make a transfer of value. This transfer will comprise the value of assets forming part of the deceased's estate after subtracting most liabilities. Any exempt transfers may, however, be excluded. These include transfers for the benefit of a surviving spouse, a charity and a qualifying political party, together with bequests to approved bodies and for national purposes.

Death may also trigger three additional liabilities:

(a) A potentially exempt transfer made within the period of seven years ending on death loses its potential status and becomes chargeable to inheritance tax
(b) The value of gifts made with reservation may incur liability if any benefit was enjoyed within a period of seven years preceding death
(c) Additional tax may become payable for chargeable lifetime transfers made within seven years before death

VALUATIONS

The valuation of assets establishes the value transferred for lifetime dispositions and also the value of a person's estate at the time of death. The value of property will represent the price which might reasonably be expected from a sale in the open market.

In some cases it may be necessary to incorporate the value of 'related property'. This will include property comprised in the estate of the transferor's spouse and certain property previously transferred to charities. The purpose of the related property valuation rules is not to add the value of the property to the estate of the transferor. Related property must be merged to establish the aggregate value of the respective interests and this value is then apportioned, usually on a *pro rata* basis, to the separate interests.

The value of shares and securities listed on the Stock Exchange will be determined by extracting figures from the daily list of official prices.

Where quoted shares and securities are sold or the quotation is suspended within a period of 12 months following the date of death, a claim may be made to substitute the proceeds or subsequent value for the value on death. This claim will only be beneficial if the gross proceeds realised are lower or the value has fallen below market value at the time of death. A similar claim may be available for interests in land sold within a period of four years following death.

RELIEF FOR SELECTED ASSETS

Special relief is made available for certain assets as follows:

Woodlands

Where woodlands pass on death the value will usually be included in the deceased's estate. However, an election may be made in respect of land in the UK on which trees or underwood is growing to delete the value of those assets. Relief is confined to the value of trees or underwood and does not extend to the land on which they are growing. Liability to inheritance tax will arise if and when the trees or underwood are subsequently sold.

Agricultural property

Relief is available for the agricultural value of agricultural property. Such property must be occupied and used for agricultural purposes and relief is confined to the agricultural value only.

The value transferred, either on a lifetime gift or on death, must be determined. This value may then be reduced by a percentage. For events taking place after 9 March 1992, a 100 per cent deduction will be available if the transferor retained vacant possession or could have obtained that possession within a period of 12 months following the transfer. In other cases, notably including land let to tenants, a lower deduction of 50 per cent is usually available. However, this lower deduction may be increased to 100 per cent if the letting was made after 31 August 1995.

It remains a requirement that the agricultural property was either occupied by the transferor for the purposes of agriculture throughout a two-year period ending on the date of the transfer, or was owned by him or her throughout a period of seven years ending on that date and also occupied for agricultural purposes.

Business property

Where the value transferred is attributable to relevant business property, that value may be reduced by a percentage. The reduction in value applies to:

(a) property consisting of a business or an interest in a business (i.e. a partnership)
(b) securities of an unquoted company which, together with any unquoted shares in the same company provided the transferor with control
(c) other unquoted shares in a company
(d) shares or securities of a quoted company which provided the transferor with control
(e) any land, building, machinery or plant which, immediately before the transfer, was used wholly or mainly for the purposes of a business carried on by a company of which the transferor had control
(f) any land, building, machinery or plant which, immediately before the transfer, was used wholly or mainly for the purposes of a business carried on by a partnership of which the transferor was a partner
(g) any land, building, machinery or plant which, immediately before the transfer, was used wholly or mainly for the purposes of a business carried on by the transferor and was then settled property in which he/she retained an interest in possession

The percentage deduction has changed from time to time but for events occurring after 5 April 1996, a deduction of 100 per cent is available for assets falling within (a), (b) and (c). A deduction of 50 per cent remains for assets within (d) to (g).

It is a general requirement that the property must have been retained for a period of two years before the transfer or death and restrictions may be necessary if the property has not been used wholly for business purposes. The same property cannot obtain both business property relief and the relief available for agricultural property.

CALCULATION OF TAX PAYABLE

The calculation of inheritance tax payable adopts the use of a cumulative total. Each chargeable lifetime transfer is added to the total with a final addition made on death. The top slice added to the total for the current event determines the rate at which inheritance tax must be paid. However, the cumulative total will only include transfers made within a period of seven years before the current event and those undertaken outside this period must be excluded.

Lifetime chargeable transfers

The value transferred by the limited range of lifetime chargeable transfers must be added to the seven-year cumulative total to calculate whether any inheritance tax is due. Should the nil rate band be exceeded, tax will be imposed on the excess at the rate of 20 per cent. However, if the donor dies within a period of seven years from the date of the chargeable lifetime transfer, additional tax may be due. This is calculated by applying tax at the full rate or 40 per cent in substitution for the rate of 20 per cent previously used. The amount of tax is then reduced to a percentage by applying tapering relief. This percentage is governed by the number of years from the date of the lifetime gift to the date of death, as follows:

Period of years before death	
Not more than 3	100%
More than 3 but not more than 4	80%
More than 4 but not more than 5	60%
More than 5 but not more than 6	40%
More than 6 but not more than 7	20%

Should this exercise produce liability greater than that previously paid at the 20 per cent rate on the lifetime transfer, additional tax, representing the difference, must be discharged. Where the calculation shows an amount falling below tax paid on the lifetime transfer, no additional liability can arise nor will the shortfall become repayable.

Tapering relief will, of course, only be available if the calculation discloses a liability to inheritance tax. There can be no liability to the extent that the lifetime transfer falls within the nil rate band.

Potentially exempt transfers

Where a potentially exempt transfer loses immunity from liability due to the donor's death within the seven-year *inter vivos* period, the value transferred by that transfer enters into the cumulative total. Any liability to inheritance tax will be calculated by applying the full rate of 40 per cent, reduced to the percentage governed by tapering relief if the original transfer occurred more than three years before death. Liability can only arise to the extent, if any, that the nil rate band is exceeded.

Death

The final addition to the seven-year cumulative total will comprise the value of an estate on death. Inheritance tax will be calculated by applying the full rate of 40 per cent to the extent the nil rate band is exceeded. No tapering relief can be obtained.

RATES OF TAX

In earlier times there were several rates of inheritance tax which progressively increased as the value transferred grew in size. However, since 1988 there have been only three rates, namely:

(a) a nil rate
(b) a lifetime rate of 20 per cent
(c) a full rate of 40 per cent

The nil rate band usually changes on an annual basis and for events taking place after 5 April 2004 applies to the first £263,000. Any excess over this level is taxable at 20 per cent or 40 per cent as the case may be.

PAYMENT OF TAX

Inheritance tax usually falls due for payment six months after the end of the month in which the chargeable transaction takes place. Where a transfer other than that made on death occurs after 5 April and before the following 1 October, tax falls due on the following 30 April, although there are some exceptions to this. Inheritance tax attributable to the transfer of certain land, controlling shareholding interests, unquoted shares, businesses and interests in businesses, together with agricultural property, may usually be satisfied by instalments spread over ten years. Except in the case of non-agricultural land, where interest is charged on outstanding instalments, no liability to interest arises where tax is paid on the due date. In all cases, delay in the payment of tax may incur a liability to discharge interest.

SETTLED PROPERTY

Complex rules apply to establish inheritance tax liability on settled property. Where a person is beneficially entitled to an interest in possession, that person is effectively deemed to own the property in which the interest subsists. It follows that where the interest comes to an end during the beneficiary's lifetime and some other person becomes entitled to the property or interest, the beneficiary is treated as having made a transfer of value. However, this will usually comprise a potentially exempt transfer incurring no immediate liability. In addition, no liability will arise where the property vests in the absolute ownership of the beneficiary retaining the interest in possession. The death of a person entitled to an interest in possession will require the value of the underlying property to be added to the value of the deceased's estate.

In the case of other settled property where there is no interest in possession (e.g. discretionary trusts), liability to tax will arise on each ten-year anniversary of the trust. There will also be liability if property ceases to be held on discretionary trusts before the first ten-year anniversary date is reached or between anniversaries. The rate of tax suffered will be governed by several considerations, including previous dispositions made by the settlor of the trust, transactions concluded by the trustees, and the period throughout which property has been held in trust.

Accumulation and maintenance settlements which require assets to be distributed, or interests in income to be created, not later than a beneficiary's 25th birthday may be exempt from any liability to inheritance tax.

CORPORATION TAX

Profits, gains and income accruing to companies resident in the UK incur liability to corporation tax. Non-resident companies are immune from this tax unless they carry on a trade in the UK through a permanent establishment, branch or office. Companies residing outside the UK may be liable to income tax at the basic rate on other income arising in the UK, perhaps from letting property. The following comments are confined to companies resident in the UK. Liability to corporation tax is governed by the profits, gains or income for an accounting period. This is usually the period for which financial accounts are made up, and in the case of companies preparing accounts to the same accounting date annually will comprise successive periods of 12 months.

RATE OF TAX

The amount of profits or income for an accounting period must be determined on normal taxation principles. The special rules which apply to individuals where a source of income is acquired or discontinued are ignored and consideration is confined to the actual profits or income for an accounting period.

The rate of corporation tax is fixed for a financial year ending on 31 March. Where the accounting period of a company overlaps this date and there is a change in the rate of corporation tax, profits and income must be apportioned.

The main rate of corporation tax for each of the seven financial years ending on the 31 March 2000 to 31 March 2006 inclusive is 30 per cent. This may be reduced to a lower level where profits fall within the small companies' rate or companies' starting rate bands. Although the main rate of tax for the year ending on 31 March 2006 is known in advance, the small companies rate and the starting rate for the same year will not be announced until a later date.

SMALL COMPANIES' RATE

Where the profits of a company do not exceed stated limits, corporation tax becomes payable at the small companies' rate. This may be replaced by a lower starting rate where profits are very small, as discussed later. It is the amount of profits and not the size of the company which governs the application of both the small companies' rate and the starting rate.

For each of the three financial years ending on 31 March 2000, 31 March 2001 and 31 March 2002 the small companies' rate remained at 20 per cent. It was then reduced to 19 per cent for each of the three years ending on 31 March 2003, 31 March 2004 and 31 March 2005.

The level of profits which a company may derive without losing the benefit of the small companies' rate is £300,000 for each of the six years. However, if profits exceed £300,000 but fall below £1,500,000, marginal small companies' rate relief applies. The effect of marginal relief is that the average rate of corporation tax imposed on all profits steadily increases from the lower small companies' rate of 19 per cent (or previously 20 per cent) to the main rate of 30 per cent, with tax being imposed on profits in the margin at an increased rate. Where a change in the rate of tax is introduced and the accounting period of a company overlaps 31 March, profits must be apportioned to establish the appropriate rate for each part of those profits.

The lower limit of £300,000 and the upper limit of £1,500,000 apply to a period of 12 months and must be proportionately reduced for shorter periods. Some restriction in the small companies' rate and the marginal rate may be necessary if there are two or more associated companies, namely companies under common control.

The small companies' rate is not available for close investment-holding companies.

COMPANIES' STARTING RATE

A companies' starting rate is available for each of the four financial years ending on 31 March 2001, 2002, 2003 and 2004. This rate applies where profits of a twelve-month period do not exceed £10,000, with marginal relief where profits exceed this figure but are not in excess of £50,000. The starting rate was 10 per cent for each of the financial years ending on 31 March 2001 and 31 March 2002 and zero for the two financial years ending on 31 March 2003 and 31 March 2004. The effect of marginal relief is to increase the average rate of tax suffered until it reaches the small companies' rate for the same financial year. The starting rate also applies for the twelve-month financial year ending on 31 March 2005 but there are two significant distinctions when compared with the previous year. The first requires that where profits do not exceed £10,000, a starting rate of 10 per cent will apply with marginal relief where larger profits are not in excess of £50,000. The second distinction applies where the company pays dividends or other distributions to a person who is not a second company. In this situation the amount of the distributions made in the financial year ending on 31 March 2005 must be established and compared with profits otherwise qualifying for the starting rate. The starting rate will not then apply to the amount of profits treated as distributed will attract corporation tax at the distribution rate of 19 per cent. Only the balance, if any, of profit not treated as distributed will be taxed at the starting rate. Should the distributions exceed the amount of profits, the excess distributions will be carried forward to future accounting periods thereby restricting the starting rate in those periods.

PAYMENT OF TAX

Corporation tax charged on profits for an accounting period usually falls due for payment in a single lump sum nine months after the end of that period. Most companies discharge corporation tax on this basis but other arrangements concern large companies for accounting periods ending on or after 1 July 1999. These companies must discharge their liability by four instalments. The receipt of annual profits amounting to £1,500,000 or more is sufficient to identify a large company. Where a company is a member of a group the profits of the entire group must be merged to establish whether the company is large.

CAPITAL GAINS

Chargeable gains arising to a company are calculated in a manner similar to that used for individuals. However, the withdrawal of the indexation allowance after April 1998, and the introduction of taper relief from the same date, have no application to companies. Nor are companies entitled to the annual exemption of £8,200. However, many gains arising to companies from the disposal of substantial shareholdings after 31 March 2002 are exempt from tax. Companies do not suffer capital gains tax on chargeable gains but incur liability to corporation tax. Tax is due on the full chargeable gain of an accounting period after subtracting relief for losses, if any.

DISTRIBUTIONS

Dividends and other qualifying distributions made by a UK resident company on or after 6 April 1999 are not satisfied after deduction of income tax. Similar outgoings made by a company previously required the payment of advance corporation tax but this obligation no longer applies. The only effect which the payment of a dividend or the making of a distribution now has on a company is that the outlay cannot form an ingredient in the calculation of profits.

INTEREST

On making many payments of interest a company is required to deduct income tax at the lower rate of 20 per cent and account for the tax deducted to the Inland Revenue. The gross amount of interest paid will usually be included in the calculation of profits on which corporation tax becomes payable. The requirement to deduct tax will not usually apply where payments are being made to a second company.

GROUPS OF COMPANIES

Each company within a group is separately charged to corporation tax on profits, gains and income. However, where one group member realises a loss for which special rules apply, other than a capital loss, a claim may be made to offset the deficiency against profits of some other member of the same group.

The transfer of capital assets from one member of a group to a fellow member will usually incur no liability to tax on chargeable gains.

SPORTS CLUBS

Corporation tax is payable by 'companies', an expression which includes unincorporated associations. It follows that most clubs must be treated as companies potentially liable to corporation tax. However, a substantial exemption from liability is available to qualifying registered community amateur sports clubs. From April 2002 registered clubs have been exempt from liability to corporation tax on:

(a) trading profits if turnover does not exceed £15,000 in a twelve-month period
(b) bank and building society interest
(c) income from property where gross rental income does not exceed £10,000 in a twelve-month period and
(d) chargeable gains

The limit in (a) was doubled to £30,000 and that in (c) to £20,000 from 1 April 2004.

Among other advantages available to registered clubs is that donations may be received under the Gift Aid arrangements. Charities are also generally exempt from corporation tax where they operate through a company structure.

COMPLIANCE

For several years a 'pay and file' system affected all companies. A feature of this system required that tax should be payable nine months following the end of the accounting period involved, with accounts and returns being submitted three months later. This system was replaced following the introduction of self-assessment which extends to all companies for accounting periods ending after 30 June 1999.

Self-assessment requires that the corporation tax return should normally be submitted not later than 12 months following the end of the accounting period to which it relates. In addition, a copy of the financial accounts must be included. Failure to file the return within the appropriate time limit will incur a liability to penalties.

VALUE ADDED TAX

Value added tax (VAT) is charged on the value of the supplies made by a registered trader and extends to both the supply of goods and the supply of services. Throughout it has been administered by Customs and Excise which merged with the Inland Revenue on 1 September 2004. Liability to account for VAT also arises on the value of goods imported into the UK from sources outside the European Community. In contrast goods imported by a trader from a second trader in a member state of the European Community attract no VAT on importation. Instead there is an acquisition tax whereby a trader who acquires goods must include the acquisition in his normal VAT return and account for the tax due. A UK trader who exports goods to a member state will not be required to account for VAT on the supply, if that trader observes the requirements laid down by regulations.

REGISTRATION

All traders, including professional persons and companies, making taxable supplies of a value exceeding stated limits are required to register for VAT purposes. Taxable supplies represent the supply of goods and services potentially chargeable with VAT. The limits which govern mandatory registration are amended periodically, and from 1 April 2004 an unregistered trader must register:

(a) at any time, if there are reasonable grounds for believing that the value of taxable supplies in the next 30 days will exceed £58,000
(b) at the end of any month if the value of taxable supplies in the 12 months then ending has exceeded £58,000.

Liability to register under (b) may be avoided if it can be shown that the value of supplies in the period of 12 months then beginning will not exceed £56,000. There may, however, be liability to register immediately where a business is taken over from another trader as a 'going concern'. Other limits apply where goods are acquired from within the European Community.

Where the limits governing mandatory registration have been exceeded, the trader must notify Customs and Excise. In the event of failure to provide prompt notification, the person concerned will be required to account for VAT from the proper registration date. A trader whose taxable supplies do not reach the mandatory registration limits may apply for voluntary registration. This step may be thought advisable to recover input tax or to compete with other registered traders.

A registered trader may submit an application for deregistration if the value of taxable supplies subsequently falls. From 1 April 2004, an application for deregistration can be made if the value of taxable supplies for the year beginning on the application date is not expected to exceed £56,000.

INPUT TAX

A registered trader will both suffer tax (input tax) when obtaining goods or services for the purposes of his business and also become liable to account for tax (output tax) on the value of goods and services which he or she supplies. Relief can usually be obtained for input tax suffered, either by setting that tax against output tax due or by repayment. Most items of input tax can be relieved in this manner. Where a registered trader makes both exempt supplies and taxable supplies to his customers or clients, there may be some restriction in the amount of input tax which can be recovered.

OUTPUT TAX

When making a taxable supply of goods or services, a registered trader must account for output tax, if any, on the value of the supply. Usually the price charged by the registered trader will be increased by adding VAT but failure to make the required addition will not remove liability to account for output tax. The liability to account for output tax, and also relief for input tax, may be affected where a trader is using a special second-hand goods scheme.

EXEMPT SUPPLIES

No VAT is chargeable on the supply of goods or services which are treated as exempt supplies. These include the provision of burial and cremation facilities, insurance, finance and education. The granting of a lease to occupy land or the sale of land will usually comprise an exempt supply, but there are numerous exceptions. In particular, the sale of new non-domestic buildings or certain buildings used by charities cannot be treated as exempt supplies. A taxable person may elect to tax rents and other supplies relating to buildings and agricultural land not used for residential or charitable purposes. Exempt supplies do not enter into the calculation of taxable supplies which governs liability to mandatory registration. Such supplies made by a registered trader may, however, limit the amount of input tax which can be relieved. It is for this reason that the election may be useful.

RATES OF TAX

Two main rates of VAT have applied for many years, namely:

(a) a zero, or nil, rate
(b) a standard rate of 17.5 per cent

In addition, a special reduced rate of 5 per cent applies to a limited range of supplies including domestic fuels, installation of energy saving materials in domestic premises, certain residential conversions and renovations, and children's car seats. From 1 June 2004 the 5 per cent rate was extended to ground source heat pumps.

ZERO-RATING

A large number of supplies are zero-rated. The following list is not exhaustive but indicates the wide range of supplies which may be included under this heading:

(a) the supply of many items of food and drink. This does not include ice creams, chocolates, sweets, potato crisps and alcoholic drinks. Nor does it extend to supplies made in the course of catering or to items supplied for consumption in a restaurant or café. Whilst the supply of cold items, e.g. sandwiches for consumption away from the supplier's premises, is zero-rated, the supply of hot food, e.g. fish and chips, is not
(b) animal feeding stuffs
(c) sewerage and water, unless for industrial purposes
(d) books, brochures, pamphlets, leaflets, newspapers, maps and charts
(e) talking books for the blind and handicapped, and wireless sets for the blind
(f) supplies of services, other than professional services, when constructing a new domestic building or a building to be used by a charity. The supply of materials for such a building is zero-rated, together with the sale or the grant of a long lease. Alterations to some protected buildings are zero-rated
(g) the transportation of persons in a vehicle, ship or aircraft designed to carry not less than 10 persons

(h) supplies of drugs, medicines and other aids for the handicapped
(i) supplies of children's clothing and footwear
(j) supplies of pedal cycle helmets
(k) exports

Although no tax is due on a zero-rated supply, this does comprise a taxable supply which must be included in the calculation governing liability to register.

COLLECTION OF TAX

Registered traders submit VAT returns for accounting periods usually of three months in duration but arrangements can be made to submit returns on a monthly basis. Very large traders must account for tax on a monthly basis but this does not affect the three-monthly return. The return will show both the output tax due for supplies made by the trader in the accounting period and also the input tax for which relief is claimed. If the output tax exceeds input tax the balance must be remitted with the VAT return. Where input tax suffered exceeds the output tax due the registered trader may claim recovery of the excess from Customs and Excise.

This basis for collecting tax explains the structure of VAT. Where supplies are made between registered traders the supplier will account for an amount of tax which will usually be identical to the tax recovered by the person to whom the supply is made. However, where the supply is made to a person who is not a registered trader there can be no recovery of input tax and it is on this person that the final burden of VAT eventually falls.

Where goods are acquired by a UK trader from a supplier within a member state of the European Community, the trader must also account for the tax due on acquisition.

An optional annual accounting scheme is available for registered traders having an annual turnover of taxable supplies not exceeding £660,000. Traders joining the scheme may render returns annually. Nine interim payments of VAT will be made on account with a final balancing payment accompanying submission of the return. The number of interim payments may be reduced if turnover is small. Once a trader has joined the annual accounting scheme membership may continue until the annual taxable turnover reaches £825,000.

A further optional scheme, the flat rate scheme, is available to small businesses having an annual taxable turnover not exceeding £150,000 and whose total turnover including both exempt and other non-taxable income does not exceed £187,500 annually. Businesses able to satisfy these requirements may discharge VAT calculating a flat rate percentage of their total turnover. The rate used is governed by the trade sector into which the business falls. The scheme can no longer be used once turnover exceeds £225,000.

BAD DEBTS

Many retailers operate special retail schemes for calculating the amount of VAT due. These schemes are based on the volume of consideration received in an accounting period. Should a customer fail to pay for goods or services supplied, there will be no consideration on which to calculate VAT.

To avoid the problem of bad debts incurred by traders not operating a special retail scheme, an optional system of cash accounting is available. This scheme, confined to traders with annual taxable supplies not exceeding £660,000, enables returns to be made on a cash basis, in substitution for the normal supply basis. Traders using such a scheme will not include bad debts in the calculation of cash receipts. Use of the scheme will be discontinued once annual taxable turnover reaches £825,000.

Where neither the cash accounting arrangements nor a special retail scheme applies, output tax falls due on the value of the supply and liability is not affected by failure to receive consideration. However, where a debt is more than six months old, relief for bad debts will be forthcoming. The calculation of the six-month period commences from the date on which payment for the supply falls due. In those cases where a supplier obtains relief for a bad debt, the person to whom the supply has been made must refund any input tax relief which may have been granted.

OTHER SPECIAL SCHEMES

In addition to the schemes for retailers, there are several special schemes applied to calculate the amount of VAT due and which also limit the ability to recover input tax.

FARMERS

Farmers may elect to apply a special flat rate scheme. This scheme is available to farmers who are not registered traders.

STAMP DUTY

For the majority of people, contact with stamp duty arises when they purchase a property. Duty is payable by the buyer as a way of raising revenue for the government based on the purchase price of a property, stocks and shares. This section aims to provide a broad overview of stamp duty as it may affect the average person. For comprehensive information, please consult a specialist publication or contact the Inland Revenue.

STAMP DUTY LAND TAX

Stamp Duty Land Tax was introduced on 1 December 2003 and covers the purchase of houses, flats and other land, buildings and certain leases in the UK. The law was changed primarily to reduce tax avoidance in high-value commercial transactions while at the same time reducing the burden on small businesses and modernising the administration of tax for individuals. Under the new system, stamp duty on transactions involving property other than land, shares and interests in partnerships is abolished, removing many transactions from a tax burden. The majority of individuals buying or renting a residential property will see no immediate changes under the new regime, although administrative changes such as the ability to notify liability and pay duty electronically will help speed up the house-buying process in the long term.

Before 1 December 2003, purchasers of property had to submit documents providing all details of their purchase to the Stamp Office for 'stamping'. The purchaser's solicitor or licensed conveyancer would then send the stamped documentation to the appropriate land registry to register ownership of the property. Under Stamp Duty Land Tax, purchasers do not have to send documents for stamping – instead, a land transaction return form (SDLT1), which contains all information regarding the purchase that is relevant to the Inland Revenue, is signed by the purchaser. Buyers of property are responsible for completing the land transaction return and payment of Stamp Duty Land Tax, however, it is generally the case that a solicitor or licensed conveyancer acting for a buyer in a land transaction will complete the relevant paperwork.

Once the Inland Revenue has received the completed land transaction return and the payment of of any Stamp Duty Land Tax due, a certificate will be issued which enables a solicitor or licensed conveyancer to register the property in the new owner's name at the Land Registry.

RATES OF STAMP DUTY LAND TAX

The Stamp Duty Land Tax rates for buying a residential property (freehold or leasehold) are the same as under the pre-1 December 2003 system:

Purchase Price	Rate of Tax (% of purchase price)
£60,000 or less*	0%
£60,001 to £250,000	1%
£250,001 to £500,000	3%
£500,001 or more	4%

*For transactions of non-residential property, the 0 per cent rate applies for purchases of up to £150,000. A 1 per cent rate is payable for transactions of £150,001 – £250,000; thereafter, rates are as per residential property transactions.

When assessing how much Stamp Duty Land Tax is payable, the entire purchase price must be taken into account. For example, on a property purchased for £300,000, 3 per cent, £9,000 is payable.

There are special rates for the rental element of leases. Since 1 December 2003, the charges have followed modern commercial practice in valuing the rent payable over the term of the lease at its net present value (NPV). There is a single rate of tax of 1 per cent of the amount by which the NPV of rental payments exceeds the threshold of £60,000 (residential property) or £150,000 (non-residential property). Where the NPV of a property is less than £60,000 (residential) or £150,000 (non-residential), no Stamp Duty Land Tax is payable on the rental element.

FIXTURES AND CHATTELS

As well as buying a property a purchaser may buy things inside the property. Some things inside a property are, in law, part of the land. These are called 'fixtures'. Examples are fitted kitchen units and bathroom suites. Because these fixtures are part of the land, any price paid for them must be taken into account for Stamp Duty Land Tax purposes. Things inside a property that are not part of the land are called 'chattels'. Examples are free-standing cookers, curtains and fitted carpets. The purchase of chattels is not chargeable to Stamp Duty Land Tax. However, where both a property and chattels are purchased, the amount shown on the Land Transaction Return as the purchase price of the property must be a 'just and reasonable' apportionment of the total amount paid. As with other entries on the form, the purchaser is responsible for the accuracy of this information.

STAMP DUTY RESERVE TAX

The main purpose of Stamp Duty Reserve Tax is to cover paperless share transactions and agreements to transfer 'chargeable securities' for consideration in money or money's worth. Stamp Duty Reserve Tax is collected primarily on share transactions that do not fall within the chargeable realm of Stamp Duty Land Tax. Stamp Duty Reserve Tax now accounts for the majority of taxation collected on share transactions effected through the UK's Exchanges.

LATE RETURNS

The purchaser must send a Land Transaction Return, together with payment of any tax due, to the Inland Revenue within 30 days of the completion of the purchase. Where this is not done the purchaser will be charged a flat-rate penalty of £100 if the return is delivered within three months after the filing date, and £200 in any other case.

HELP AND INFORMATION

Help and information on all aspects of Stamp Duty Land Tax and Stamp Duty Reserve Tax is available from www.inlandrevenue.gov.uk or by contacting 0845-603 0135.

LEGAL NOTES

These notes outline certain aspects of the law as they might affect the average person; they are intended only as a broad guideline and are by no means definitive. The law is constantly changing so expert advice should always be taken. It is always advisable to consult a solicitor without delay; timely advice will set your mind at rest and sitting on your rights can mean that you lose them. Anyone who does not have a solicitor already can contact the following for assistance in finding one: Citizens Advice Bureau (W www.nacab.org.uk), the Community Legal Service (W www.legalservices.gov.uk), the Law Society of England and Wales (T 020-7242 1222 W www.lawsociety.co.uk) or the Law Society of Scotland (T 0131-226 7411 W www.lawscot.org.uk). The community legal service fund and legal aid and assistance schemes exist to make the help of a lawyer available to those who would not otherwise be able to afford one. Entitlement depends on an individual's means.

ABORTION

Under the provisions of the Abortion Act 1967, a legally-induced abortion must be: performed by a registered medical practitioner; carried out in an NHS hospital or other approved premises; and certified by two registered medical practitioners as justified on one or more of the following grounds:

- that the pregnancy has not exceeded its twenty-fourth week and that the continuance of the pregnancy would involve risk, greater than if the pregnancy were terminated, of injury to the physical or mental health of the pregnant woman or any existing children of her family
- that the termination is necessary to prevent grave permanent injury to the physical or mental health of the pregnant woman
- that the continuance of the pregnancy would involve risk to the life of the pregnant woman, greater than if the pregnancy were terminated
- that there is a substantial risk that if the child were born it would suffer from such physical or mental abnormalities as to be seriously handicapped

In determining whether the continuance of a pregnancy would involve risk of injury to health, account may be taken of the pregnant woman's actual or reasonably foreseeable environment. The requirements relating to the opinion of two registered medical practitioners and to the performance of the abortion at an NHS hospital or other approved place cease to apply in circumstances where a registered medical practitioner is of the opinion, formed in good faith, that a termination is immediately necessary to save the life, or to prevent grave permanent injury to the physical or mental health, of the pregnant woman.

Further information and advice can be obtained from:

FAMILY PLANNING ASSOCIATION (UK)
2–12 Pentonville Road, London N1 9FP T 0845-310 1334

FAMILY PLANNING ASSOCIATION (SCOTLAND)
Unit 10, Firhill Business Centre, 76 Firhill Road, Glasgow G20 7BA T 0141-576 5088

BRITISH PREGNANCY ADVISORY SERVICE (BPAS)
T 08457-304030 W www.bpas.org

ADOPTION

The Adoption of Children Act 2002 reforms the framework for domestic and inter-country adoption in England and Wales and some parts extend to Scotland and Northern Ireland. This section deals with the Act which, at the time of writing (1 August 2004), was only partially in force.

ADOPTION ORDERS

A couple (whether married or two people living as partners in an enduring family relationship) may apply for an adoption order where both of them are over 21 or where one is only 18 but is the natural parent and the other is 21. An adoption order may be made for one applicant where that person is 21 and (a) the court is satisfied that person is the partner of a parent of the person to be adopted; (b) they are not married; or (c) they are married but their spouse is either unable to be found, is incapable by reason of ill-health of making an application or is separated from that person, living apart and the separation is likely to be permanent. There are certain qualifying conditions an applicant must meet, e.g. residency in the British Isles.

There are nine steps that may only be taken by an adoption agency (local authorities or adoption societies registered with them) or a person acting in pursuance of an order of the high court. These steps relate to arranging an adoption, receiving a child for adoption or causing another to carry out one of the steps. If a person or an adoption society act contrary to this provision they may commit an offence. There may be a defence to some steps taken where the proposed adopter is a parent (or partner to that parent), relative or guardian of the child.

Once an adoption has been arranged, a court order is necessary to make it legal; this may be obtained from the high court, county court or magistrate's court (including family proceedings court). An adoption order may not be given unless the court is either satisfied that the consent of the child's natural parents (or guardians) has correctly been given or that consent should be dispensed with, e.g. where the parent or guardian cannot be found, is incapable of giving consent or where the welfare of the child so demands.

An adoption order has the effect of extinguishing the parental responsibility that a person other than the adopters (or adopter) has for the child, although where an order is made on the application of the partner of the parent, that parent keeps parental responsibility. This means that once adopted, the child has the same status as a child born to the adoptive parents. In addition the child may lose rights to the estates of those losing their parental responsibility.

All adoption orders made in England and Wales must be added to in the Adopted Children Register that also contains particulars of children adopted under registrable foreign adoptions. The General Register Office keeps this register from which certificates may be obtained in a similar way to birth certificates. The General Register

Office also has equivalents in Scotland and Northern Ireland.

TRACING PARENTS OR ADOPTED CHILDREN

An adult adopted person may apply to the Registrar-General to obtain a certified copy of his/her birth certificate. For those adopted before 12 November 1975 it is obligatory to receive counselling services before this information is given; for those adopted after that date counselling services are optional. There is an Adoption Contact Register, created after the 1989 Children Act, which provides a safe and confidential way for birth parents and other relatives to assure an adopted person that contact would be welcome. Further information can be obtained from:

BRITISH ASSOCIATION FOR ADOPTION AND FOSTERING (BAAF)
Skyline House, 200 Union Street, London SE1 0LX
T 020-7593 2000 W www.baaf.org.uk

SCOTLAND

The relevant legislation is the Adoption (Scotland) Act 1978 (as amended by the Children Act 1995) and the Adoption and Children Act 2002. The provisions are similar to those described above. In Scotland, petitions for adoption are made to the Sheriff Court or the Court of Session. Further information can be obtained from:

BRITISH ASSOCIATION FOR ADOPTION AND FOSTERING (BAAF)
BAAF Scottish Centre, 40 Shandwick Place, Edinburgh EH2 4RT
T 0131-225 9285

SCOTTISH ADOPTION ADVICE SERVICE
16 Sandyford Place, Glasgow G3 7NB T 0141-248 7530

BIRTHS (REGISTRATION)

It is the duty of the parents of a child born in England or Wales to register the birth within 42 days of the date of birth at the register office in the district in which the baby was born. If it is inconvenient to go to the district where the birth took place, the information for the registration may be given to a registrar in another district. Failure to register the birth within 42 days without reasonable cause may leave the parents liable to a penalty. If a birth has not been registered within 12 months of its occurrence it is possible for the late registration of the birth to be authorised by the Registrar-General provided certain requirements can be met.

If the parents of the child were married to each other at the time of the birth (or conception), either the mother or the father may register the birth. If the parents were not married to each other at the time of the child's birth (or conception), the father's particulars may be entered in the register only where he attends the register office with the mother and they sign the birth register together. Where an unmarried parent is unable to attend the register office, either parent may submit to the registrar a statutory declaration acknowledging the father's paternity; alternatively a parental responsibility agreement or appropriate court order may be produced to the registrar.

If the parents do not register the birth of their child the following people may do so: the occupier of the house or hospital where the child was born; a person who was present at the birth; or a person who is responsible for the child. Upon registration of the birth a short certificate is issued.

BIRTHS ABROAD

In certain countries the British Consul or High Commission may register the births and issue certificates which are then sent to the General Register Office. If a birth is registered in this way, the registration would show the person's claim to British citizenship, British Dependent Territories citizenship or British Overseas citizenship.

SCOTLAND

In Scotland the birth of a child must be registered within 21 days at the register office of either the district in which the baby was born or the district in which the mother was resident at the time of the birth. Responsibility for registration is the same as in England and Wales. However, if the father of the child is not married to the mother and has not been married to her since the child's conception, the mother alone is responsible for registration. However, if the parents fail to register the birth, it may be registered by a relative of either parent. Failure to register the birth in the requisite time may lead to a court decree being granted by a Sheriff. If the child is born, either in or out of Scotland, on a ship, aircraft or land vehicle that ends its journey at any place in Scotland, the child, in most cases, will be registered as if born in that place.

BIRTH, DEATH AND MARRIAGE CERTIFICATES

Certificates of births, deaths or marriages that have taken place in England and Wales since 1837 can be obtained from the Office for National Statistics (General Register Office) or the Family Records Centre. Certificates of births, marriages and deaths may be obtained: by a personal visit to the Family Records Centre; by post, telephone, fax or online; or locally from the register office where the event was originally registered. Marriage or death certificates may be obtained from the minister of the church in which the marriage took place. Any register office can advise about the best way to obtain certificates.

The fees for certificates are:

From the Family Records Centre, London by personal application:
Full certificate of birth, marriage or death, £7.00
Full certificate of adoption, £7.00
Short certificate of birth, £7.00
Short certificate of adoption, £5.50

By postal application:
Full certificate of birth, marriage or death, £11.50
Full certificate of birth, marriage or death with GRO index supplied, £8.50
Short abbreviated certificate of birth, £11.50
Short abbreviated certificate of adoption, £9.50
Extra copies of the same birth, marriage or death certificate issued at the same time, £7.00

A priority service is also available with certificates despatched on the working day following receipt of your application. For further information: T 0870-243 7788 W www.statistics.gov.uk

Indexes prepared from the registers are available for searching by the public at the Family Records Centre in London or at a Superintendent Registrar's Office; indexes at the latter relate only to births, deaths and marriages which occurred in that registration district. There is no charge for searching the indexes in the Public Search Room at the Family Records Centre but a general search fee is charged for searches at a Superintendent Registrar's Office. A fee is charged for verifying index references against the records. The Society of Genealogists has many records of baptisms, marriages and deaths prior to 1837.

SCOTLAND

Certificates of births, deaths or marriages that have taken place in Scotland since 1855 can be obtained from the General Register Office for Scotland by personal, postal, telephone or fax application or from the appropriate local registrar. The General Register Office for Scotland also keeps the Register of Divorces (including decrees of declaration of nullity of marriage), and holds parish registers dating from before 1855.

Statutory indexes of births between 1855 to 1903, marriages between 1855 to 1928 and deaths between 1855 to 1953 are available online at www.scotlandspeople.gov.uk. Fees for certificates are:

Certificates (full or abbreviated) of birth, death, marriage or adoption:
Personal application: £11.00
Postal/telephone/fax: £13.00
Internet: £16.00

A priority service for a response within 24 hours is available for an additional fee of £10.00

General search in the indexes to the statutory registers and parochial registers, per day or part thereof:
Full day search (i.e. 9a.m. to 4.30p.m.), £17.00
Afternoon (i.e. 1p.m. to 4.30p.m.) search £10.00
Discounted full day (i.e. 9a.m. to 4.30p.m.) search with payment being made not less than 14 days in advance, £13.00 (only available for the period 1 December 2004 to 31 January 2005, bookings taken from 20 October)
One week search, £65.00
Four week search, £220.00
One quarter search, £500.00
One year search, £1,500.00
For more information, visit: www.scotlandspeople.gov.uk
Further information can be obtained from:

THE GENERAL REGISTER OFFICE
Office for National Statistics, Smedley Hydro, Trafalgar Road, Southport, Merseyside PR8 2HH **T** 0870-243 7788

FAMILY RECORDS CENTRE
1 Myddelton Street, London EC1R 1UW

THE GENERAL REGISTER OFFICE FOR SCOTLAND
New Register House, Edinburgh EH1 3YT **T** 0131-314 4452
W www.gro-scotland.gov.uk

THE SOCIETY OF GENEALOGISTS
14 Charterhouse Buildings, Goswell Road, London EC1M 7BA
T 020-7251 8799

BRITISH CITIZENSHIP

The British Nationality Act 1981, as amended by the Nationality Immigration Act 2002, the British Overseas Territories Act 2002, the Adoption and Children Act 2002 and the Hong Kong (British Nationality) Order 1986 (as amended) which came into force on 1 January 1983 established three types of citizenship to replace the single form of Citizenship of the UK and Colonies created by the British Nationality Act 1948. The three forms of citizenship are: British citizenship; British Dependent Territories citizenship; and British Overseas citizenship. Three residual categories were created: British Subjects; British Protected Persons; and British Nationals (Overseas).

Almost everyone who was a citizen of the UK and colonies and had a right of abode in the UK prior to the 1981 Act became British citizens when the Act came into force. British citizens have the right to live permanently in the UK and are free to leave and re-enter the UK at any time.

A person born on or after 1 January 1983 in the UK is entitled to British citizenship if he/she falls into one of the following categories:

- he/she has a parent who is a British citizen
- he/she has a parent who is settled in the UK
- he/she is a newborn infant found abandoned in the UK
- his/her parents subsequently settle in the UK
- he/she lives in the UK for the first ten years of his/her life and is not absent for more than 90 days in each of those years
- he/she is adopted in the UK and one of the adopters is a British Citizen

A person born outside the UK may acquire British citizenship if he/she falls into one of the following categories:

- he/she has a parent who is a British citizen otherwise than by descent, e.g., a parent who was born in the UK
- he/she has a parent who is a British citizen serving the Crown overseas
- the Home Secretary consents to his/her registration while he/she is a minor
- he/she is a British Dependent Territories citizen, a British Overseas citizen, a British subject or a British protected person and has been lawfully resident in the UK for five years
- he/she is a British Overseas Territories citizen, a British National (Overseas), a British Overseas citizen, a British subject or a British protected person and has been lawfully resident in the UK for five years
- he/she is adopted or naturalised

Where parents are married, the status of either may confer citizenship on their child. Currently if a child is illegitimate, the status of the mother determines the child's citizenship, however, this distinction is removed by the 2002 Act.

Under the 1981 Act, Commonwealth citizens and citizens of the Republic of Ireland were entitled to registration as British citizens before 1 January 1988. In 1985, citizens of the Falkland Islands were granted British citizenship.

Renunciation of British citizenship must be registered with the Home Secretary and will be revoked if no new citizenship or nationality is acquired within six months. If the renunciation was required in order to retain or acquire another citizenship or nationality, the citizenship may be reacquired once. The Secretary of State may deprive a person of a citizenship status if he is satisfied that the person has done anything seriously prejudicial to the vital interests of the United Kingdom, or a British overseas territory, unless making the order would have the effect of rendering a person stateless. A person may also be deprived of a citizenship status which results from his registration or naturalisation if the Secretary of State is satisfied that the registration or naturalisation was obtained by means of fraud, false representation or concealment of a material fact.

BRITISH OVERSEAS TERRITORIES CITIZENSHIP

Under the 1981 Act, British Dependent Territories citizenship was conferred on citizens of the UK and colonies by birth, naturalisation or registration in British Dependent Territories. The Nationality, Immigration and Asylum Act 2002 removes the right of a wife or minor of a British Dependent Territories citizen to register automatically as a British Dependent Territories citizen. By virtue of the British Overseas Territories Act 2002, the British Dependent Territories are now known as British Overseas Territories and the citizens are British Overseas Territories citizens. Further, under that Act, anyone who is a British Overseas Territories Citizen (BOTC) (as renamed) immediately before commencement is to become a British citizen on commencement, although this does not apply to a person who is a BOTC by virtue only of a connection with the Sovereign Base Areas in Cyprus. In future, a BOTC may apply to be registered as a British citizen unless they are a BOTC by virtue only of a connection with the Sovereign Base Areas in Cyprus or have previously renounced British Citizenship.

The British Overseas Territories Act 2002 confers British citizenship and/or BOTC on persons connected by descent with the British Indian Ocean Territory if born between 1969 and 1983 to a mother who was a citizen of the UK and colonies by virtue of her birth in the British Indian Ocean Territory and who was not a British citizen or BOTC before commencement.

On 1 July 1997 citizens of Hong Kong who did not qualify to register as British citizens under the British Nationality (Hong Kong) Act 1990 lost their British Dependent Territories citizenship on the handover of sovereignty to China; they may, however, have applied to register as British Nationals (Overseas).

BRITISH OVERSEAS CITIZENSHIP

Under the 1981 Act, this type of citizenship was conferred on any UK and colonies citizens who did not qualify for British citizenship or citizenship of the British Dependent (now Overseas) Territories. Following the Nationality, Immigration and Asylum Act 2002, the wife and minors of a British Overseas citizen may not automatically register as British Overseas citizens. By virtue of the 2002 Act, British Overseas citizens may be entitled to registration as British Citizens on completion of five years' legal residence in the UK or if they do not have any other nationality or citizenship and have not voluntarily renounced British citizenship after 4 July 2002.

RESIDUAL CATEGORIES

British subjects, British protected persons and British Overseas citizens may be entitled to registration as British citizens if they do not have any other nationality or citizenship and have not voluntarily renounced any citizenship after 4 July 2002. Citizens of the Republic of Ireland who were also British subjects before 1 January 1949 can retain that status if they fulfil certain conditions.

NATURALISATION

Naturalisation is granted at the discretion of the Home Secretary. The basic requirements are five years' residence (three years if the applicant is married to a British citizen), good character, adequate knowledge of the English, Welsh or Scottish Gaelic language, and an intention to reside permanently in the UK. The Nationality, Immigration and Asylum Act 2002 imposes an additional requirement that the applicant must demonstrate sufficient knowledge about life in the UK and should attend a citizenship ceremony.

CONSUMER LAW

SALE OF GOODS

A sale of goods contract is the most common type of contract. It is governed by the Sale of Goods Act 1979 (as amended by the Sale and Supply of Goods Act 1994). The Act provides protection for buyers by implying terms into every sale of goods contract. These terms include:

- an implied term that the seller will pass good title to the buyer (unless the seller agrees to transfer only such title as he has)
- where the seller sells goods by reference to a description, an implied term that the goods will match that description and, where the sale is by sample and description, it will not be sufficient that the bulk of the goods corresponds with the sample if the goods do not also correspond with the description
- where goods are sold by a business seller, an implied term that the goods will be of satisfactory quality if they meet the standard that a reasonable person would regard as satisfactory taking into account any description of the goods, the price, and all other relevant circumstances. The quality of the goods includes their state and condition, relevant aspects being whether they are fit for the purposes for which such goods are commonly supplied, their appearance and finish, freedom from minor defects and their safety and durability. This term will not be implied, however, if a buyer has examined the goods and should have noticed the defect or if the seller specifically drew the buyer's attention to the defect
- where goods are sold by a business seller, an implied term that the goods are reasonably fit for any purpose made known to the seller by the buyer (either expressly or by implication), unless it is shown that the buyer does not rely on the seller's judgement, or it is not reasonable for him/her to do so
- where goods are sold by sample, implied terms that the bulk of the sample will correspond with the sample in quality, and that the goods are free from any defect rendering them unsatisfactory which would have been apparent on a reasonable examination of the sample.

Some of the above terms can be excluded from contracts by the seller. The seller's right to do this is, however, restricted by the Unfair Contract Terms Act 1977. The Act offers more protection to a buyer who 'deals as a consumer', (that is where the seller is selling in the course of a business, the goods are of a type ordinarily bought for private use and the goods are bought by a buyer who is not a business buyer though not allowing any liability for breach of the implied terms described above to be excluded). In a sale by auction or competitive tender, a buyer never deals as consumer. Also, a seller can never exclude the implied term as to title mentioned above.

HIRE-PURCHASE AGREEMENTS

Terms similar to those implied in contracts of sales of goods are implied into contracts of hire purchase, under the Supply of Goods (Implied Terms) Act 1973. The 1977 Act limits the exclusion of these implied terms as before.

SUPPLY OF GOODS AND SERVICES

Under the Supply of Goods and Services Act 1982, similar terms are also implied in other types of contract under which ownership of goods passes, e.g., a contract for 'work and materials' such as supplying new parts while servicing a car, and contracts for the hire of goods (though not hire-purchase agreements). These types of contracts have additional implied terms:

- that the supplier will use reasonable care and skill in carrying out the service
- that the supplier will carry out the service in a reasonable time (unless the time has been agreed)
- that the supplier will make a reasonable charge (unless the charge has already been agreed)

The 1977 Act limits the exclusion of these implied terms in a similar manner as before.

UNFAIR TERMS

The Unfair Terms in Consumer Contracts Regulations 1999 apply to contracts between business sellers (or suppliers of goods and services) and consumers. Where the terms have not been individually negotiated, i.e. when the terms were drafted in advance so that the consumer was unable to influence those terms, there will be an unfair term where a term operates to the detriment of the consumer (i.e. carries a significant imbalance in the parties' rights and obligations arising under the contract). An unfair term does not bind the consumer but the contract will continue to bind the parties if it is capable of existing without the unfair term. The regulations contain a non-exhaustive list of terms which are regarded as unfair. Whether a term is regarded as fair or not will depend on many factors, including the nature of the goods or services, the surrounding circumstances (such as the bargaining strength of both parties) and the other terms in the contract.

TRADE DESCRIPTIONS

It is a criminal offence under the Trade Descriptions Act 1968 for a business seller to apply a false trade description of goods or to supply or offer to supply any goods to which a false description has been applied. A 'trade description' includes descriptions of quality, size, composition, fitness for purpose, performance, method of manufacture, and place and date of manufacture of the goods.

FAIR TRADING

The Fair Trading Act 1973 is designed to protect the consumer. It provides for the appointment of a Director-General of Fair Trading, one of whose duties is to review commercial activities in the UK relating to the supply of goods and services to consumers. An example of a practice which has been prohibited by a reference made under this Act is that of business sellers posing in advertisements as private sellers.

CONSUMER PROTECTION AND CREDIT

Under the Consumer Protection Act 1987, producers of goods are liable for any injury or for any damage exceeding £275 caused by a defect in their product (subject to certain defences).

The Consumer Protection (Cancellation of Contracts Concluded Away from Business Premises) Regulations 1987 allow consumers a seven-day period in which to cancel contracts for the supply of goods and services, where the contracts were made during an unsolicited visit by a trader to the consumer's home or workplace. A contract will not be enforceable at all in this situation unless the trader has written to the consumer to notify them of the right to cancel within 7 days.

Consumers are also afforded protection under the Consumer Protection (Distance Selling) Regulations 2000 in relation to e.g. cancellation periods.

In matters relating to the provision of credit (or the supply of goods on hire or hire-purchase), consumers are also protected by the Consumer Credit Act 1974. Under this Act a licence, issued by the Director-General of Fair Trading, is required to conduct a consumer credit or consumer hire business or an ancillary credit business. Any 'fit' person as defined within the Act may apply to the Director-General of Fair Trading for a licence, which is normally renewable after five years. A licence is not necessary if only exempt agreements are involved. The provisions of the Act only apply to 'regulated' agreements, i.e. those that are with individuals or partnerships, those that are not exempt (certain local authority and building society loans will be exempt), and those where the total credit does not exceed £25,000. Provisions include:

- the terms of the regulated agreement can be altered by the creditor provided the agreement gives him/her the right to do so; in such cases the debtor must be given proper notice of this
- in order for a creditor to enforce a regulated agreement, the agreement must comply with certain formalities and must be properly executed. The debtor must also be given specified information by the creditor or his/her broker or agent during the negotiations which take place before the signing of the agreement. The agreement must state certain information such as the amount of credit, the annual interest rate, the amount and timing of repayments
- if an agreement is signed other than at the creditor's (or credit broker's or negotiator's) place of business and oral representations were made in the debtor's presence during discussions pre-agreement, the debtor has a right to cancel the agreement. Time for cancellation expires five clear days after the debtor receives a second copy of the agreement. The agreement must inform the debtor of his right to cancel and how to cancel
- if the debtor is in arrears (or otherwise in breach of the agreement), the creditor must serve a default notice before taking any action such as repossessing the goods
- if the agreement is a hire-purchase or conditional sale agreement, the creditor cannot repossess the goods without a court order if the debtor has paid one-third of the total price of the goods
- in agreements where the debtor is required to make grossly exorbitant payments or where the agreement grossly contravenes the ordinary principles of fair trading, the debtor may request that the court alter or set aside some of the terms of the agreement. The agreement can also be reopened during enforcement proceedings by the court itself

Where a credit reference agency has been used to check the debtor's financial standing, the creditor must give the agency's name to the debtor, who is entitled to see the agency's file on him. A fee of £1 is payable to the agency.

SCOTLAND

The legislation governing the sale and supply of goods applies to Scotland as follows:

- the Sale of Goods Act 1979 applies with some modifications and it has been amended by the Sale and Supply of Goods Act 1994 and the Sale and Supply of Goods to Consumers Regulations 2002
- the Supply of Goods (Implied Terms) Act 1973 applies
- the Supply of Goods and Services Act 1982 does not extend to Scotland but some of its provisions were introduced by the Sale and Supply of Goods Act 1994
- only Parts II and III of the Unfair Contract Terms Act 1977 apply

- the Trade Descriptions Act 1968 applies with minor modifications
- the Consumer Credit Act 1974 applies
- the Consumer Protection Act 1987 applies
- the General Product Safety Regulations 1994 apply
- the Unfair Terms in Consumer Contracts Regulations 1999 apply
- the Unfair Terms in Consumer Contracts (Amendment) Regulations 2001 apply
- the Consumer Protection (Distance Selling) Regulations 2000 apply
- the Sale and Supply of Goods to Consumers Regulations 2002 apply

DEATHS

If a death (including stillbirth) was expected, the doctor who attended the deceased during their final illness should be contacted. If the death was sudden or unexpected, the family doctor (if known) and police should be contacted. If the cause of death is quite clear the doctor will provide: a medical certificate that shows the cause of death and a formal notice that states that the doctor has signed the medical certificate and that explains how to get the death registered.

If the death was known to be caused by a natural illness but the doctor wishes to know more about the cause of death, he/she may ask the relatives for permission to carry out a post-mortem examination.

In England and Wales a coroner is responsible for investigating deaths occurring in the following circumstances:

- where there is no doctor who can issue a medical certificate of cause of death
- when no doctor has treated the deceased during his or her last illness or when the doctor attending the patient did not see him or her within 14 days before death, or after death
- when the death occurred during an operation or before recovery from the effect of an anaesthetic
- when the death was sudden and unexplained or attended by suspicious circumstances
- when the death might be due to an industrial injury or disease, or to accident, violence, neglect or abortion, attended by suspicious circumstances
- the death occurred in prison or in police custody

The doctor will write on the formal notice that the death has been referred to the coroner; if the post mortem shows that death was due to natural causes, the coroner may issue a notification which gives the cause of death so that the death can be registered. If the cause of death was violent or unnatural, the coroner is obliged to hold an inquest.

In Scotland the office of coroner does not exist. The local procurator fiscal inquires into sudden or suspicious deaths. A fatal accident inquiry will be held before the sheriff where the death has resulted from an accident during the course of the employment of the person who has died, or where the person who has died was in legal custody, or where the Lord Advocate deems it in the public interest that an inquiry be held.

REGISTERING A DEATH

In England and Wales the death must be registered by the registrar of births and deaths for the district in which it occurred; details can be obtained from the doctor or local council, or at a post office or police station. From April 1997, information concerning a death can be given before any registrar of births and deaths in England and Wales. The registrar will pass the relevant details to the registrar for the district where the death occurred, who will then register the death.

In England and Wales the death must normally be registered within five days; in Scotland it must be registered within eight days. If the death has been referred to the coroner/local procurator fiscal it cannot be registered until the registrar has received authority from the coroner/local procurator fiscal to do so. Failure to register a death involves a penalty in England and Wales and may lead to a court decree being granted by a sheriff in Scotland.

If the death occurred at a house or hospital, the death may be registered by:

- any relative of the deceased
- any person present at the death
- the occupier or any inmate of the house or hospital if he/she knew of the occurrence of the death
- any person making the funeral arrangements
- in Scotland, the deceased's executor or legal representative.

For deaths that took place elsewhere, the death may be registered by

- any relative of the deceased
- someone present at the death
- someone who found the body
- a person in charge of the body
- any person making the funeral arrangements

The majority of deaths are registered by a relative of the deceased. The registrar would normally allow one of the other listed persons to register the death only if there were no relatives available.

The person registering the death should take the medical certificate of the cause of death with them; it is also useful, though not essential, to take the deceased's birth and marriage certificates, NHS medical card (if possible), pension documents and life assurance details. The details given to the registrar must be absolutely correct, otherwise it may be difficult to change them later. The person registering the death should check the entry carefully before it is signed. The registrar will issue a certificate for burial or cremation and a certificate of registration of death; both are free of charge. A death certificate is a certified copy of the entry in the death register; these can be provided on payment of a fee and may be required for the following purposes:

- the will
- bank and building society accounts
- savings bank certificates and premium bonds
- insurance policies
- pension claims
- certificate for applicable Social Security Benefits.

If the death occurred abroad or on a foreign ship or aircraft, the death should be registered according to the local regulations of the relevant country and a death certificate should be obtained. The death can also be registered with the British Consul in that country and a record will be kept at the General Register Office. This avoids the expense of bringing the body back. After 12 months (3 months in Scotland) of death or the finding of a dead body, no death can be registered without the consent of the Registrar-General.

BURIAL AND CREMATION

In most circumstances in England and Wales a certificate for burial or cremation must be obtained from the registrar before the burial or cremation can take place. If the death has been referred to the coroner, an order for burial or a certificate for cremation must be obtained. In

Scotland a body may be buried (but not cremated) before the death is registered.

Funeral costs can normally be repaid out of the deceased's estate and will be given priority over any other claims. If the deceased has left a will it may contain directions concerning the funeral; however, these directions need not be followed by the executor.

The deceased's papers should also indicate whether a grave space had already been arranged. This information will be contained in a document known as a 'Deed of Grant'. Most town churchyards and many suburban churchyards are no longer open for burial because they are full. Most cemeteries are non-denominational and may be owned by local authorities or private companies; fees vary.

If the body is to be cremated, an application form, two cremation certificates (for which there is a charge) or a certificate for cremation if the death was referred to the coroner, and a certificate signed by the medical referee must be completed in addition to the certificate for burial or cremation (the form is not required if the coroner has issued a certificate for cremation). All the forms are available from the funeral director or crematorium.

The registrar must be notified of the date, place and means of disposal of the body within 96 hours (England and Wales) or three days (Scotland).

If the death occurred abroad or on a foreign ship or aircraft, a local burial or cremation may be arranged. If the body is to be brought back to England or Wales, a death certificate from the relevant country or an authorisation for the removal of the body from the country of death from the coroner or relevant authority will be required. To arrange a funeral in England or Wales, an authenticated translation of a foreign death certificate or a death certificate issued in Scotland or Northern Ireland which must show the cause of death, is needed, together with a certificate of no liability to register from the registrar in England and Wales in whose sub-district it is intended to bury or cremate the body. If it is intended to cremate the body, a cremation order will be required from the Home Office or a certificate for cremation. Further information can be obtained from:

THE GENERAL REGISTER OFFICE
Office for National Statistics, Smedley Hydro, Trafalgar Road, Southport, Merseyside PR8 2HH **T** 0870-243 7788 or 0151-471 4805

THE GENERAL REGISTER OFFICE FOR SCOTLAND
New Register House, Edinburgh EH1 3YT **T** 0131-314 4452

DIVORCE AND RELATED MATTERS

ENGLAND AND WALES

There are three types of matrimonial suit: those seeking the annulment of marriage, judicial separation and divorce. To obtain an annulment, judicial separation or divorce in England and Wales: if a European Union court (except Denmark) has jurisdiction, and the one commencing the proceedings (the petitioner) and the one defending the proceedings (the respondent) must be habitually resident in England and Wales; or the petitioner and the respondent must have been habitually resident in England and Wales and one of them must continue to reside there; or the respondent must be habitually resident in England and Wales; or the petitioner must have been habitually resident in England and Wales throughout the period of at least one year ending with the start of proceedings; or the petitioner must be domiciled in England and Wales and must have been habitually resident in England and Wales throughout the period of at least six months, ending with the start of the proceedings; or both parties must have been domiciled in England and Wales; or if no European Union court (except Denmark) has jurisdiction, one or both of them must be domiciled in England and Wales. All cases are commenced in a divorce county court or in the Principal Registry in London. If a suit is defended, it may be transferred to the High Court.

NULLITY OF MARRIAGE

Various circumstances will render a marriage invalid including if: there has been wilful non-consummation of the marriage; one partner has a venereal disease at the time of the marriage and the other did not know about it; the female partner was pregnant at the time of the marriage with another person's child and the male partner did not know of the pregnancy; the parties were within prohibited degrees of consanguinity, affinity or adoption; the parties were not male and female; either of the parties was already married; either of the parties was under the age of sixteen; the formalities of the marriage were defective, e.g. the marriage did not take place in an authorised building and both parties knew of the defect.

SEPARATION

A couple may enter into a private agreement to separate by consent but for the agreement to be valid it must be followed by an immediate separation. Judicial separation does not dissolve a marriage and it is not necessary to prove that the marriage has irretrievably broken down. Either party can petition for a judicial separation at any time; the grounds listed below as grounds for divorce are also grounds for judicial separation. To petition for judicial separation, the parties do not have to prove that they have been married for twelve months or more. A financial settlement between spouses in a separation agreement or which accompanies a judicial separation will not necessarily bind the court after instigation of divorce proceedings.

DIVORCE

Neither party can petition for divorce until at least one year after the date of the marriage. The sole ground for divorce is the irretrievable breakdown of the marriage; this must be proved on one or more of the following grounds:

- the respondent has committed adultery and the petitioner finds it intolerable to live with him/her; however, the petitioner cannot rely on an act of adultery by the respondent if they have lived together for more than six months after the discovery of the adultery
- the respondent has behaved in such a way that the petitioner cannot be reasonably be expected to continue living with him/her
- the respondent has deserted the petitioner for two years immediately before the petition
- the petitioner and the respondent have lived separately for two years immediately before the petition and the respondent consents to the divorce
- the petitioner and the respondent have lived separately for five years immediately before the petition

A total period of less than six months during which the parties have resumed living together is disregarded in determining whether the prescribed period of separation or desertion has been continuous (but may not be included as part of the period of separation). The Matrimonial Causes Act 1973 requires the solicitor for the petitioner to certify whether the possibility of a reconciliation has been discussed with the petitioner.

THE DECREE NISI
A decree nisi does not dissolve or annul the marriage, but must be obtained before a divorce or annulment can take place. Where the suit is undefended, the evidence normally takes the form of a sworn written statement made by the petitioner which is considered by a district judge. If the judge is satisfied that the petitioner has proved the contents of the petition, a date will be set for the pronouncement of the decree nisi in open court: neither party need attend. If the judge is not satisfied that the petitioner has proved the contents of the petition or if the suit is defended, the petition will be heard in open court with parties giving oral evidence.

THE DECREE ABSOLUTE
The decree nisi is made absolute on the application of the petitioner after six weeks. If the petitioner does not apply, the respondent must wait for a further three months before application may be made. If the judge thinks it may be necessary to exercise a judge's powers under the Children Act 1989 in exceptional circumstances the granting of the decree absolute may be delayed. The decree absolute dissolves or annuls the marriage. Where the couple were married in accordance with Jewish or other religious usages, the court may require them to produce a declaration that they have taken such steps as are required to dissolve the marriage in accordance with those usages before the decree absolute is issued.

MAINTENANCE
Either party may be liable to pay maintenance to a spouse or former spouse. If there were any children of the marriage, both parties have a legal responsibility to support them financially if they can afford to do so. The courts are responsible for assessing maintenance for a spouse or former spouse, taking into account each parties' income and essential outgoings and other aspects of the case. The court also deals with any maintenance for a child that has been treated by the spouses as a child of the family such as a step-child and any property settlements.

The Child Support Agency (CSA) is responsible for assessing the maintenance that absent parents shall pay for their natural or adopted children (whether or not a marriage has taken place). The CSA accepts applications only when all the people involved are habitually resident in the UK; the courts will continue to deal with cases where one of the individuals lives abroad. The CSA deals with all new cases unless it is agreed by the spouses that the court may grant an Order for child support (but even in agreed jurisdiction cases one parent may give the other fourteen months' notice to have the case dealt with by the CSA).

A formula is used to work out how much child maintenance is payable under CSA jurisdiction. The formula requires the absent parent to pay 15 per cent net of post-tax, national insurance and pension contributions for one child, 20 per cent for two and 25 per cent for more than two. An earnings cap of £104,000 net a year applies. The income of the parent with care is not taken into account. Deductions are applied for staying contact for further children in the absent parent's household. In court jurisdiction cases, the CSA formula is adopted as a guideline only.

Some cases involving unusual circumstances are treated as special cases and the assessment is modified and in some cases the court retains jurisdiction (for educational costs and high income cases, for example). Where there is financial need (e.g. because of disability or continuing education) maintenance may be ordered by the court for children even beyond the age of eighteen. CSA maintenance is reviewed automatically every two years. Either parent can report a change of circumstances and request a review at any time. An independent complaints examiner for the CSA has been appointed. If the absent parent does not pay CSA maintenance, the CSA may make an order for payments to be deducted directly from his/her salary; if all other methods fail, the CSA may take court action to enforce payment.

OTHER FINANCIAL RELIEF
After allowing the claimant's reasonable needs in terms of housing and a fund to provide income for life, the court has to measure a provisional award against the yardstick of equal division. The approach is based on percentage division and reasons being advanced for departure from it. Ongoing spousal maintenance cases can justify a departure. The court has a duty to consider making a once and for all capital award, such as a payment and/or property or pension transfer if this can be afforded. This is known as a clean break. Alternatively the court will make a capital award and an ongoing spousal maintenance award if a clean break cannot be afforded. Maintenance is often payable during joint lives or until the recipient's remarriage, subject to the ability to vary or terminate in the meantime. There is no concept of separate or marital property in England and Wales: all assets however derived are potentially vulnerable on divorce. This includes inherited wealth, gifted wealth and pre-marriage acquired wealth.

The court must consider the following factors when making financial orders, after giving first consideration to the welfare of any minor children of the family: the income, earning capacity, property and other financial resources which each of the parties to the marriage has or is likely to have in the foreseeable future, including in the case of earning capacity, any increase in that capacity which it would, in the opinion of the court, be reasonable to expect a party to the marriage to take steps to acquire; the financial needs, obligations and responsibilities which each of the parties to the marriage has or is likely to have in the foreseeable future; the standard of living enjoyed by the family before the breakdown of the marriage; the age of each party to the marriage and the duration of the marriage; any physical or mental disability of either of the parties to the marriage; the contribution which each of the parties has made or is likely in the foreseeable future to make to the welfare of the family, including any contribution by looking after the home or caring for the family; the conduct of each of the parties, if that conduct is such that it would, in the opinion of the court, be inequitable to disregard it; and in the case of proceedings for divorce or nullity of marriage, the value to each of the parties to the marriage of any benefit (for example a pension) which by reason of the dissolution of the marriage that party will lose the chance of acquiring.

The court has the power to award in addition to maintenance a lump sum order, a property transfer order and a pension sharing order as the main forms of financial relief.

COHABITING COUPLES
Rights of unmarried couples are not the same as for married couples. Agreements, whether express or inferred by conduct, often determine interests in money and property. Reliance upon inferences is problematic. By

virtue of this, it is worth considering entering into a contract which establishes how money and property should be divided in the event of a relationship breakdown. These contracts are commonly known as 'separation deeds' or 'cohabitation contracts'. New legislation is expected for homosexual couples entering into a civil partnership. They will secure similar rights and responsibilities to married couples.

SCOTLAND

Although there is separate legislation for Scotland covering nullity of marriage, judicial separation, divorce and ancillary matters, the provisions are in most respects the same as those for England and Wales. The following is confined to major points on which the law in Scotland differs. An action for 'declarator of nullity' can be brought only in the Court of Session. Where a spouse is capable of sexual intercourse but refuses to consummate the marriage, this is not a ground of nullity in Scots law, though it could be a ground for divorce. The fact that a spouse was suffering from venereal disease at the time of marriage and the other spouse did not know this, is not a ground of nullity in Scots law, neither is the fact that a wife was pregnant by another man at the time of marriage and her husband did not know this. An action for judicial separation or divorce may be raised in the Court of Session; it may also be raised in the Sheriff Court if either party was resident in the sheriffdom for 40 days immediately before the date of the action or for 40 days ending not more than 40 days before the date of the action. The fee for starting a divorce petition in the Sheriff Court is £81.

When adultery is cited as proof that the marriage has broken down irretrievably, it is not necessary in Scotland to prove also that it is intolerable for the pursuer to live with the defender. In the case of desertion, irretrievable breakdown is not established if, after the two year desertion period has expired, the parties resume living together at any time after the end of three months from the date when they first resume living together.

Where a divorce action has been raised, it may be sisted or put on hold for a variety of reasons.

If the parties do cohabit during such postponement, no account is taken of the cohabitation if the action later proceeds.

In actions for divorce and separation, the court has the power to award a residence order in respect of any children of the marriage. The welfare of the children is of paramount importance, and the fact that a spouse has caused the breakdown of the marriage does not in itself preclude him/her from being awarded residence.

A simplified procedure for 'do-it-yourself' divorce was introduced in 1983 for certain divorces. If the action is based on two or five years' separation and will not be opposed, and if there are no children under 16 and no financial claims, and there is no sign that the applicant's spouse is unable to manage his or her affairs through mental illness or handicap, the applicant can write directly to the local sheriff court or to the Court of Session for the appropriate forms to enable him or her to proceed. The fee is £62, unless the applicant receives income support, family credit or legal advice and assistance, in which case there is no fee. An extract decree, which brings the marriage to an end, will be made available 14 days after the divorce has been granted. Further information can be obtained from:

THE PRINCIPAL REGISTRY
First Avenue House, 42–49 High Holborn, London WC2V 6NP

THE COURT OF SESSION
Parliament House, Parliament Square, Edinburgh EH1 1RQ
T 0131-225 2595

THE CHILD SUPPORT AGENCY
National Enquiry Line 08457-133133
Minicom 08457-138924 **W** www.csa.gov.uk

EMPLOYMENT LAW

PAY AND CONDITIONS

The Employment Rights Act 1996 consolidates the statutory provisions relating to employees' rights. Employers must give each employee employed for one month or more a written statement containing the following information: names of employer and employee; date when employment began and the date on which the employee's period of *continuous* employment began (taking into account any employment with a previous employer which counts towards that period); remuneration and intervals at which it will be paid; job title or description of job; hours and place(s) of work; holiday entitlement and holiday pay; provisions concerning incapacity for work due to sickness and injury, including provisions for sick pay; details of pension scheme(s); length of notice period that employer and employee need to give to terminate employment; if the employment is not intended to be permanent, the period for which it is expected to continue or, if it is for a fixed term, the end date of the contract; details of any collective agreement which affects the terms of employment; details of disciplinary and grievance procedures; if the employee is to work outside the UK for more than one month, the period of such work and the currency in which payment is made.

This must be given to the employee within two months of the start of their employment. The Working Time Regulations 1998, the National Minimum Wage Act 1998 and the Employment Relations Act 1999 now supplement the 1996 Act. If the employer does not provide the written statement within two months then the employee can complain to an employment tribunal, which can specify the information that the employer should have given. The Employment Act 2002 is due to bring in a new provision allowing the tribunal to award compensation of between 2 and 4 weeks' pay when, in the context of an employee's successful tribunal claim, the employer is also found to have been in breach of the duty to provide the written statement at the time proceedings were commenced.

FLEXIBLE WORKING

The Employment Act 2002 gives employees the right to apply for a flexible working pattern for the purpose of caring for a child and is intended to cover anyone who has responsibility for the upbringing of a child. If an application under the Act is rejected, it is open to the employee to complain to an employment tribunal.

SICK PAY

Employees absent from work through illness or injury are entitled to receive Statutory Sick Pay (SSP) from the employer for a maximum period of 28 weeks in any three-year period. This applies to all employees, both men and women, up to the age of 65. The rate of SSP, as from 4 April 2004, is £102.80 per week.

MATERNITY AND PARENTAL RIGHTS

Under the Employment Relations Act 1999, the

Employment Act 2002 and the Maternity and Parental Leave (Amendment) Regulations, both men and women are entitled to leave where they become a parent. Women are protected from discrimination, detriment or dismissal by reason of their pregnancy. Men are protected from suffering a detriment or dismissal for taking paternity or parental leave.

Women are entitled to 26 weeks' Ordinary Maternity Leave. There is no qualifying period of employment. Any woman who is absent from work during her Ordinary Maternity Leave period has the right to return to the job in which she was employed before her absence. An employee may take Additional Maternity Leave of up to 26 weeks if she has been continuously employed for not less than 26 weeks at the beginning of the 14th week before the expected week of childbirth. Women who qualify for Additional Maternity Leave will also qualify for Statutory Maternity Pay. Statutory Maternity Pay is payable for 26 weeks and generally starts when the employee stops work. Then first six weeks of SMP are paid at 90 per cent of the employer's average weekly earnings, and the remaining twenty weeks are paid at the rate of £102.80 per week (from 4 April 2004), or 90 per cent of weekly earnings, whichever is lower.

Employees are entitled to paternity leave for the purpose of caring for a child or supporting the child's mother on the birth or adoption of a child. The qualifying period of employment for this right is the same as for Additional Maternity Leave (that is, the employee must have been continuously employed for not less than 26 weeks at the beginning of the 14th week before the expected week of childbirth). The employee may take either one week's leave or two consecutive weeks' leave. This leave may be taken from the date of the child's birth to 56 days later. During their Paternity Leave, most employees will be entitled to Statutory Paternity Pay, which is paid at the same rate as Statutory Maternity Pay.

Employees are entitled to Ordinary Adoption Leave, Additional Adoption Leave and Adoption Pay subject to fulfilment of criteria similar to those in relation to Maternity Leave and Pay. Where a couple is adopting a child, one may take Adoption Leave, and the adopter's spouse or partner may take Paternity Leave.

Any employee with one year's service who has, or expects to have, responsibility for a child may take parental leave. Each parent is entitled to a total of 13 weeks' parental leave for each of their children but this leave must be taken before the child's fifth birthday (or eighteenth birthday if the child is disabled).

SUNDAY TRADING

The Sunday Trading Act 1994 gives shop workers the right not to be dismissed, selected for redundancy or to suffer any detriment (such as the denial of overtime, promotion or training) if they refuse to work on Sundays. This does not apply to those who, under their contracts, are employed to work on Sundays.

TERMINATION OF EMPLOYMENT

An employee may be dismissed without notice if guilty of gross misconduct but in other cases a period of notice must be given by the employer. The minimum periods of notice specified in the Employment Rights Act 1996 are: one week if the employee has been continuously employed for one month or more but for less than two years or two weeks if the employee has been continuously employed for at least two years. A week is added for every complete year of continuous employment up to 12 years up to a maximum of 12 weeks, however, longer periods apply if these are specified in the contract of employment.

If an employee is dismissed with less notice than he/she is entitled to by statute, or under their contract if longer, the employer is generally liable to pay the employee in lieu of notice (or for the period of the contract for those on fixed-term contracts). Generally, no notice needs to be given of the expiry of a fixed-term contract. If the employer does not give the employee pay in lieu of notice then the employer becomes liable to pay the employee damages for wrongful dismissal. This claim for wrongful dismissal can be brought by the employee either in the court system or the employment tribunal, but if brought in the tribunal the maximum amount that can be awarded is £25,000. This claim can also be brought by an employee whose fixed-term contract has been terminated prematurely, and without justification, by the employer.

REDUNDANCY

An employee dismissed because of redundancy may be entitled to redundancy pay. This applies if: the employee has at least two years' continuous service; the employee is actually dismissed by the employer (even in cases of voluntary redundancy); or dismissal is due to redundancy. Redundancy can mean closure of the entire business, closure of a particular site of the business, overmanning (surplus employees) or reduction in work of a particular kind.

An employee may not be entitled to a redundancy payment if offered a suitable alternative job by the same employer. The amount of payment depends on the length of service, the age of the employee, and their earnings, subject to a weekly maximum of (currently) £270. The maximum award that can be made is £8,100. The redundancy payment is guaranteed by the State in cases where the employer becomes insolvent (subject to the conditions above).

UNFAIR DISMISSAL

Complaints of unfair dismissal are dealt with by an employment tribunal. Any employee with one year's continuous service (subject to exceptions) regardless of their hours of work, can make a complaint to the tribunal. At the tribunal, the employee must prove that he or she was dismissed, but it is for the employer to prove that the dismissal was due to one or more of the following acceptable reasons: the employee's capability or qualifications for the job he was employed to do; the employee's conduct; redundancy; a legal restriction preventing the continuation of the employee's contract; or some other substantial reason.

If the employer succeeds in showing this, the tribunal must then decide whether the employer acted reasonably in dismissing the employee for that reason. If the employee is found to have been unfairly dismissed, the tribunal can order that he/she be reinstated or compensated. Any person believing that they may have been unfairly dismissed should contact their local Citizens Advice Bureau or seek legal advice. A claim must be brought within 3 months of the date of termination of employment. The maximum award for unfair dismissal is £55,000 which relates to dismissals occurring on or after 1 February 2004.

DISCRIMINATION

Discrimination in employment on the grounds of sex, sexual orientation, race, colour, nationality, ethnic or national origins, religion or belief, married status or (subject to wide exceptions) disability is unlawful. Discrimination legislation also covers sexual harassment and gender reassignment. Discrimination on the grounds of age will become unlawful when age discrimination legislation comes into force on 1 October 2006. The following legislation applies to those employed in Great Britain but not to employees in Northern Ireland or (subject to EC exceptions) to those who work mainly abroad:

- The Equal Pay Act 1970 (as amended) entitles men and women to equality in matters related to their contracts of employment. Those doing like work for the same employer are entitled to the same pay and conditions regardless of their sex
- The Sex Discrimination Act 1975 (as amended by the Sex Discrimination Act 1986) makes it unlawful to discriminate on grounds of sex or marital status (although, under the Act it is, in fact, only unlawful to discriminate against people because they are married, not because they are single). This covers all aspects of employment, including advertising for recruits, terms offered, opportunities for promotion and training, and dismissal procedures
- The Race Relations Act 1976 gives individuals the right not to be discriminated against on the grounds of race, colour, nationality, or ethnic or national origins. It applies to all aspects of employment
- The Disability Discrimination Act 1995 makes discrimination against a disabled person in all aspects of employment unlawful. An employer may show that the less favourable treatment is justified. The Act also imposes a duty on employers to make 'reasonable adjustments' to the arrangements and physical features of the workplace if these place disabled people at a substantial disadvantage compared with those who are not disabled. Employers with fewer than 15 employees are exempt from the Act's requirements
- The Employment Equality (Religion or Belief) Regulations 2003, which implement an EC Directive, make discrimination against a person on the grounds of religion or belief, in all aspects of employment, unlawful
- The Employment Equality (Sexual Orientation) Regulations 2003, which implement another aspect of the same EC directive, make discrimination against an individual on the grounds of sexual orientation, in all aspects of employment, unlawful

In Northern Ireland similar provisions exist but are contained in separate legislation (although the Disability Discrimination Act does extend to Northern Ireland).

The Employment Relations Act 1999 made a number of important changes to the existing law: a right of accompaniment. A worker attending a serious disciplinary or grievance hearing has the right to be accompanied by a trade union representative or co-worker of their choice; a new scheme of compulsory trade union recognition following a workplace ballot; greater protection from dismissal for striking employees.

The Employment Act 2002 has also made significant changes to the law in this area. It introduced a wide range of provisions covering new rights for working parents, dispute resolution in the workplace, including statutory grievance and disciplinary procedures, improvements to employment tribunal procedures, including the introduction of an equal pay questionnaire, provisions to implement the Fixed Term Work Directive, a new right to time off work for union learning representatives and a new right to request flexible working by parents of young children.

ILLEGITIMACY AND LEGITIMATION

The Children Act 1989 gives the mother parental responsibility for the child. An unmarried father does not automatically acquire parental responsibility but can do so either by agreement with the mother (in prescribed form) or by applying to the court. The Adoption and Children Act 2002 (not yet fully in force) also makes provision for a father who is not married to the child's mother to acquire parental responsibility for the child if he becomes registered as the child's father. If an illegitimate child is to be adopted, the father's consent is required only where he has been awarded parental rights by the court.

Every child born to a married woman during marriage is presumed to be legitimate, unless the couple are separated under court order when the child is conceived, in which case the child is presumed not to be the husband's child. It is possible to challenge the presumption of legitimacy or illegitimacy through civil proceedings.

In Scotland, the relevant legislation is the Children (Scotland) Act 1995, which also gives the mother parental responsibility for her child whether or not she is married to the child's father. The father has automatic parental rights only if married to the mother. An unmarried father has no automatic parental rights but can acquire parental responsibility by applying to the court or by acquiring them under a parental responsibilities and parental rights agreement made with the mother. A child's father will only have automatic rights and responsibilities if he was married to the mother at the time of conception or subsequently marries her. The father of any child, regardless of parental rights, has a duty to aliment that child until he/she is 18 (25 if he/she is still in full-time education).

LEGITIMATION

Under the Legitimacy Act 1976, an illegitimate person automatically becomes legitimate when his/her parents marry. This applies even where one of the parents was married to a third person at the time of the birth. In such cases it is necessary to re-register the birth of the child. In Scotland, the relevant legislation is the Legitimation (Scotland) Act 1968, the Adoption (Scotland) Act 1978 and the Law Reform Parent and Child) Scotland Act 1986 which gives illegitimate and legitimate persons equal status.

JURY SERVICE

ENGLAND AND WALES

The Juries Act 1976, as amended by the Criminal Justice Act 2003 provides that every person registered as a parliamentary or local government elector between the ages of 18 and 70 who has been ordinarily resident in the UK (including, for this purpose, the Channel Islands and the Isle of Man) for any period of at least five years since reaching the age of 13, who is not mentally disordered or disqualified, is qualified to serve on a jury.

Under the amended Juries Act 1974, mentally disordered persons are defined as:

- A person who suffers or has suffered from mental illness, psychopathic disorder, mental handicap or severe mental handicap and on account of that condition either (a) is resident in a hospital or similar institution or (b) regularly attends for treatment by a medical practitioner.
- A person for the time being under guardianship under section 7 of the Mental Health Act 1983.

– A person who, under Part 7 of that Act, has been determined by a judge to be incapable, by reason of mental disorder, of managing and administering his property and affairs.

Disqualified persons are those:

– on bail in criminal proceedings
– who have at any time been sentenced in the United Kingdom, the Channel Islands or the Isle of Man (a) to imprisonment for life, detention for life or custody for life, (b) to detention during her Majesty's pleasure or during the pleasure of the Secretary of State, (c) to imprisonment for public protection or detention for public protection, (d) to an extended sentence under section 227 or 228 of the Criminal Justice Act 2003 or section 210A of the Criminal Procedure (Scotland) Act 1995, or (e) to a term of imprisonment of five years or more or a term of detention of five years or more.
– who at any time in the last ten years have
  (a) in the United Kingdom, the Channel Islands or the Isle of Man
    (i) served any part of a sentence of imprisonment or a sentence of detention, or (ii) had passed on him/her a suspended sentence of imprisonment or had made in respect of him/her a suspended order for detention
  (b) in England and Wales, had made in respect of him/her a community order under section 177 of the Criminal Justice Act 2003, a community rehabilitation order, a community punishment order, a community punishment and rehabilitation order, a drug treatment and testing order or a drug abstinence order, or
  (c) had made in respect of him/her any corresponding order under the law of Scotland, Northern Ireland, the Isle of Man or any of the Channel Islands

There is no longer a right to be excused from jury service, except for those who have served on a jury in the previous two years, but the court does have the discretion to excuse a juror from service, or defer the date of service, if good reason is shown.

If a person serves on a jury knowing himself/herself to be ineligible or disqualified, he/she is liable to be fined up to £5,000 if disqualified and up to £1,000 for all other offences. The defendant can object to any juror if he/she can show cause.

A juror may claim travelling expenses, a subsistence allowance and an allowance for other financial loss (e.g. loss of earnings or benefits, fees paid to carers or child-minders) up to a stated limit, however, following the amendments contained in the Criminal Justice Act 2003, the subsistence allowance may be paid for otherwise than in cash (such as the provision of facilities).

It is an offence for a juror to disclose what happened in the jury room even after the trial is over. A jury's verdict must normally be unanimous, but if no verdict has been reached after two hours' consideration (or such longer period as the court deems to be reasonable) a majority verdict is acceptable if ten jurors agree to it.

SCOTLAND

Qualification criteria for jury service in Scotland are contained in the Law Reform (Miscellaneous Provisions) (Scotland) Act 1980 as amended by the Criminal Justice (Scotland) Act 2003. The maximum age for a juror is 65 and there are wide categories of people ineligible to serve as jurors or who can refuse to do so as of right.

Those ineligible for jury service include:

– the Judiciary, including those who have been classed as such in the last 10 years (including judges, sheriffs, tribunal chairman, magistrates and registrars)
– those who have within the previous 5 years been concerned with the administration of justice (including advocates, solicitors, police and court officials)
– the mentally disordered (including persons receiving medical treatment for mental disorder and either are resident in a hospital or attend on more than one day each week and persons for the time being subject to guardianship under the Adults with Incapacity (Scotland) Act 2000)

Those disqualified from jury service include:

– those who have at any time been sentenced by a court in the UK (including, for this purpose, the Channel Islands and the Isle of Man) to a term of imprisonment or youth custody of 5 years or more
– those who have within the previous 10 years served any part of a sentence of 3 months or more of imprisonment, detention or youth custody or been detained in a borstal institution, and who are not rehabilitated persons for the purposes of the Rehabilitation of Offenders Act 1974
– persons who have been convicted of an offence where one or more of the following orders was made: (i) a probation order; (ii) a drug treatment and testing order; (iii) a community service order; (iv) a restriction of liberty order; (v) a community order under the Powers of Criminal Courts (Sentencing) Act 2000 or the Criminal Justice (Northern Ireland) Order; except where they are rehabilitated persons for the purposes of the Rehabilitation of Offenders Act 1974

Those who may be excused as of right from jury service include:

– members and officers of the Houses of Parliament; the Scottish Parliament and Executive and the European Parliament
– full-time serving members of the armed forces
– registered and practising members of the medical, dental, nursing, veterinary and pharmaceutical professions
– ministers of any religion, vowed members of religious communities and those who are practising members of religious societies or orders whose beliefs are incompatible with jury service
– those who have served on a jury in the previous 5 years

The maximum fine for a person serving on a jury knowing himself/herself to be ineligible is £1,000. The maximum fine for failing to attend without good cause is also £1,000. Further information can be obtained from:

THE COURT SERVICE
Southside, 105 Victoria Street, London SW1E 6QT
T 020-7210 2266

THE CLERK OF JUSTICIARY
High Court of Justiciary, Lawnmarket, Edinburgh EH1 1RF
T 0131-240 6900

LANDLORD AND TENANT

RESIDENTIAL LETTINGS

The provisions outlined here apply only where the tenant lives in a separate dwelling from the landlord and where the dwelling is the tenant's only or main home. It does not apply to licensees such as lodgers, guests or service occupiers. The 1996 Housing Act radically changed certain aspects of the legislation referred to below; in particular, the grant of assured and assured shorthold tenancies under the Housing Act 1988.

ASSURED SHORTHOLD TENANCIES

If a tenancy was granted on or after 15 January 1989 and before 28 February 1997, the tenant might have an assured tenancy giving that tenant greater rights. The tenant could, for example, stay in possession of the dwelling for as long as the tenant observed the terms of the tenancy. The landlord cannot obtain possession from such a tenant unless the landlord can establish a specific ground for possession (set out in the Housing Act 1988) and obtains a court order. The rent payable is that agreed with the landlord unless the rent has been fixed by the rent assessment committee of the local authority. The tenant or the landlord may request that the committee sets the rent in line with open market rents for that type of property. Any rent increases that are to take place should be written into the agreement, but failing that, the landlord must give advance notice of the increase.

Under the Housing Act 1996, most new lettings entered into on or after 28 February 1997 will be assured shorthold tenancies. This means that tenants are given limited rights. The landlord must obtain a court order, however, to obtain possession if the tenant refuses to vacate at the end of the tenancy. If the tenant owes two months' rent or more, the landlord can serve notice proceedings and apply to the courts for an order for possession. If the tenancy is an assured shorthold tenancy, the court must grant the order.

REGULATED AND SECURE TENANCIES

Before the Housing Act 1988 came into force (15 January 1989) there were regulated tenancies; some are still in existence and are protected by the Rent Act 1977. Under this Act it is possible for the landlord or the tenant to apply to the local rent officer to have a 'fair' rent registered. The fair rent is then the maximum rent payable.

Secure tenancies are generally given to tenants of local authorities, housing associations and certain other bodies. This gives the tenant lifelong tenure unless the terms of the agreement are broken by the tenant. In certain circumstances those with secure tenancies may have the right to buy their property. In practice this right is generally only available to council tenants.

AGRICULTURAL PROPERTY

Tenancies in agricultural properties are governed by the Agricultural Holdings Act 1986 and the Rent (Agricultural) Act 1976, which give similar protections to those described above, e.g. security of tenure, right to compensation for disturbance, etc. The Agricultural Holdings (Scotland) Act 1991 applies similar provisions to Scotland.

EVICTION

Under the Protection from Eviction Act 1977 (as amended by the Housing Act 1988), a landlord must give reasonable notice that he/she is to evict the tenant, and in most cases a possession order, granted in court, is necessary. Notice is generally to be at least four weeks and in prescribed statutory form. It is illegal for a landlord to evict a person by putting their belongings onto the street, by changing the locks and so on. It is also illegal for a landlord to harass a tenant in any way in order to persuade him/her to give up the tenancy.

LANDLORD RESPONSIBILITIES

Under the Landlord and Tenant Act 1985, where the term of the lease is less than seven years, the landlord is responsible for maintaining the structure and exterior of the property, for sanitation, for heating and hot water, and all installations for the supply of water, gas and electricity.

LEASEHOLDERS

Legally leaseholders have bought a long lease rather than a property and in certain limited circumstances the landlord can end the tenancy. Under the Leasehold Reform Act 1967 (as amended by the Housing Acts 1969, 1974 and 1980), leaseholders of houses may have the right to buy the freehold or to take an extended lease for a term of 50 years. This applies to leases where the term of the lease is over 21 years and where the leaseholder has occupied the house as his/her main residence for the last three years, or for a total of three years over the last ten.

The Leasehold Reform, Housing and Urban Development Act came into force in 1993 and allows the leaseholders of flats in certain circumstances to buy the freehold of the building in which they live.

Responsibility for maintenance of the structure, exterior and interior of the building should be set out in the lease. Usually the upkeep of the interior of his/her part of the property is the responsibility of the leaseholder, and responsibility for the structure, exterior and common interior areas is shared between the freeholder and the leaseholder(s).

If leaseholders are in any way dissatisfied with treatment from their landlord or with charges made in respect of lease extensions, they are entitled to have their situation evaluated by the Leasehold Valuation Tribunal.

The Commonhold and Leasehold Reform Act 2002 (not in force at the time of writing (1 August 2003)) makes provision for the freehold estate in land to be registered as commonhold land and for the legal interest in the land to be vested in a 'commonhold association' i.e. a private limited company.

BUSINESS LETTINGS

The Landlord and Tenant Acts 1927 and 1954 (as amended) give security of tenure to the tenants of most business premises. The landlord can only evict the tenant on one of the grounds laid down in the 1954 Act, and in some cases where the landlord repossesses the property the tenant may be entitled to compensation.

SCOTLAND

In Scotland assured and short assured tenancies exist for lettings after 2 January 1989 and are similar to assured tenancies in England and Wales. The relevant legislation is the Housing (Scotland) Act 1988.

Most tenancies created before 2 January 1989 were regulated tenancies and the Rent (Scotland) Act 1984 still applies where these exist. The Act defines, among other things, the circumstances in which a landlord can increase the rent when improvements are made to the property. The provisions of the Rent Act do not apply to tenancies where the landlord is the Crown, a local authority, the development corporation of a new town or a housing corporation.

The Housing (Scotland) Act 1987 and its provisions relate to local authority responsibilities for housing, the right to buy, and local authority secured tenancies. The provisions are broadly similar to England and Wales.

In Scotland, business premises are not controlled by statute to the same extent as in England and Wales, although the Tenancy of Shops (Scotland) Act 1949 gives some security to tenants of shops. Tenants of shops can apply to the sheriff, within 21 days of being served a notice to quit, for a renewal of tenancy if threatened with eviction. This application may be dismissed on various grounds including where the landlord has offered to sell the property to the tenant at an agreed price or, in the absence of agreement as to price, at a price fixed by a single arbiter appointed by the parties or the sheriff. The Act extends to properties where the Crown or government departments are the landlords or the tenants. Under the Leases Act 1449 the landlord's successors (either purchasers or creditors) are bound by the agreement made with any tenants so long as the following conditions are met: the lease, if for more than one year, must be in writing; there must be a rent; there must be a term of expiry; the tenant must have entered into possession; the subjects of the lease must be land; and the landlord, if owner, must be infeft – i.e. the title deeds are recorded in the Register of Sasines or the Land Register.

LEGAL AID

The Access to Justice Act 1999 has transformed what used to be known as the Legal Aid system. The Legal Aid Board has been abolished and replaced from 2 April 2000 with the Legal Services Commission (85 Gray's Inn Road, London, WC1X 8TX T 020-7759 0000 W www.legalservices.gov.uk). The Legal Services Commission is responsible for the development and administration of two legal funding schemes in England and Wales, namely the Criminal Defence Service which replaced the old system of criminal legal aid, and the Community Legal Service fund, which replaced the old civil scheme of legal aid. The Community Legal Service is designed to increase access to legal information and advice by involving a much wider network of funders and providers in giving publicly funded legal services. In Scotland, provision of legal aid is governed by the Legal Aid (Scotland) Act 1986 and is administered by the Scottish Legal Aid Board. Information can be obtained from:

THE SCOTTISH LEGAL AID BOARD, 44 Drumsheugh Gardens, Edinburgh EH3 7SW T 0131-226 7961

CIVIL LEGAL AID

From 1 January 2000, only organisations (solicitors or Citizens Advice Bureaux) with a contract with the Legal Services Commission have been able to give initial help in any civil matter. Moreover, from that date decisions about funding were devolved from the Legal Services Commission to contracted organisations in relation to any level of publicly funded service in family and immigration cases. For other types of case, applications for public funding are made through a solicitor (or other contracted legal services providers) in much the same way as the former Legal Aid. On 1 April 2001 the so-called civil contracting scheme was extended to cover all levels of service for all types of cases.

Under the new civil funding scheme there are broadly seven levels of service available: legal help; help at court (the first two types of service are limited to advice and assistance with preparing a case, but do not include representation); proved family help – either general family help or help with mediation (special levels of service for family cases); legal representation – either investigative help or full representation (this covers assistance with representation in court); support funding – either investigative support or litigation support (this is a new type of assistance which allows the costs of a privately funded case to be topped up from public funds. It is only available for personal injury claims (excluding clinical negligence) and some multi-party action only); family mediation; and such other services as are specifically authorised by the Lord Chancellor.

In general, public funding is not available for the following type of cases: personal injury (except for the availability of support funding and clinical negligence claims); allegations of negligent damage to property; conveyancing; boundary disputes; the making of wills; matters of trust law; defamation proceedings; partnership disputes and company law; and other matters arising out of the carrying on of a business.

ELIGIBILITY

Eligibility for funding from the Community Legal Service depends broadly on five factors: the level of service sought; whether the applicant qualifies financially; the merits of the applicant's case; a costs-benefits analysis (if the costs are likely to outweigh any benefit that might be gained from the proceedings, funding may be refused); and whether there is any public interest in the case being litigated (i.e. whether the case has a wider public interest beyond that of the parties involved – for example, a human rights case). The limits on capital and income above which a person is not entitled to public funding vary with the type of service sought.

CONTRIBUTIONS

Some of those who qualify for Community Legal Service funding will have to contribute towards their legal costs. Contributions must be paid by anyone who has a disposable income or disposable capital exceeding a prescribed amount. The rules relating to applicable contributions are complex and detailed information can be obtained from the Legal Services Commission.

STATUTORY CHARGE

A statutory charge is made if a person receives money or property in a case for which they have received legal aid. This means that the amount paid by the Community Legal Service fund on their behalf is deducted from the amount that the person receives. This does not apply if the court has ordered that the costs be paid by the other party (unless the amount paid by the other party does not cover all of the costs) or if the payments are for maintenance

- or to the first £2,500 of any money or property the applicant gains or keeps in divorce cases and most other family proceedings
- where the solicitor is advising the applicant whilst they attend family mediation under a 'help with mediation' certificate
- where advice is given only under the 'legal help' scheme in any matter other than family or personal injury after 1 April 2000.

CONTINGENCY OR CONDITIONAL FEES

Under this system legal representation is offered on a 'no win, no fee' basis. It provides an alternative form of assistance, especially for those cases which are ineligible for funding by the Community Legal Service. The main area for such work is in the field of personal injuries which claims are now largely exempt from public funding (except for clinical negligence claims).

Not all solicitors offer such a scheme and different solicitors may have different terms. The effect of the agreement is that solicitors will not make any charges until the case is concluded successfully. If a case is won then the losing party will usually have to pay towards costs, with the winning party contributing around one-third.

SCOTLAND

Civil legal aid in Scotland is administered by the Scottish Legal Aid Board and is available on a broadly similar basis to that which is available in England and Wales.

Under the Legal Advice and Assistance scheme, solicitors can provide initial legal advice and assistance short of representing clients in court proceedings on any legal matter subject to the prior authorisation of the Scottish Legal Aid Board of any further work. Under the same scheme, solicitors can also provide initial Advice By Way of Representation (ABWOR) to individuals in certain proceedings, again subject to the prior authorisation of the Board of any further representation work.

Under the Civil Legal Aid scheme, solicitors can provide representation to individuals in a wide variety of civil proceedings including family law and personal injury matters. Before Civil Legal Aid will be granted, the Scottish Legal Aid Board must be satisfied that the individual is financially eligible, that the case has merit and that the grant of Civil Legal Aid would be a reasonable expenditure of public funds. Representation can be provided in urgent cases under emergency Civil Legal Aid whilst an application for Civil Legal Aid is considered by the Board.

In order qualify for Legal Advice and Assistance and/or Civil Legal Aid, individuals must be financially eligible according the Scottish Legal Aid Board's criteria, which are similar to those used by under the CLS scheme in England and Wales. As in that jurisdiction, individuals may require to pay a contribution from income and/or capital, and a charge similar to the Statutory Charge (see above) is made against any money or property recovered or preserved on behalf of the individual.

Further information about the eligibility criteria for Legal Advice and Assistance and Civil Legal Aid in Scotland can be obtained from The Scottish Legal Aid Board (see details above) or from Scottish solicitors or Citizens Advice Bureaux.

CRIMINAL LEGAL AID

The courts will grant criminal legal aid for representation if it is desirable in the interests of justice (e.g. if there are important questions of law to be argued or the case is so serious that if found guilty the person may go to prison) and the person needs help to pay their legal costs. Criminal legal aid covers the cost of preparing a case and legal representation (including the cost of a barrister) in criminal proceedings. It is also available for appeals against verdicts or sentences in magistrates' courts, the Crown Court or the Court of Appeal. It is not available for bringing a private prosecution in a criminal court.

If granted criminal legal aid, either the person may choose their own solicitor or the court will assign one. Contributions to the legal costs must be paid by anyone who has a disposable income or disposable capital which exceeds a prescribed amount. The rules relating to applicable contributions are complex and detaile information can be obtained from the Legal Services Commission.

DUTY SOLICITORS

The Legal Aid Act 1988 also provides free advice and assistance to anyone questioned by the police (whether under arrest or helping the police with their enquiries). No means test or contributions are required for this.

SCOTLAND

In Scotland, publicly funded legal advice, assistance and representation, and duty solicitors are available to persons suspected or accused of criminal offences on a similar basis to that in England and Wales. These services are administered by the Scottish Legal Aid Board, and fall into three main categories:

- Advice and Assistance – covers initial help by solicitors for persons who are financially eligible including general advice, correspondence and negotiation
- Advice by Way of Representation (ABWOR) under the Advice and Assistance scheme – covers preparation for and initial representation in certain proceedings including proceedings against financially eligible persons who have failed to obey certain orders of the sheriff court
- Criminal Legal Aid – covers representation of financially eligible persons charged with criminal offences, including dealing with bail, preparing their defence cases and, where appropriate, instructing advocates (the Scottish equivalent of barristers), as well as advice on appeals and preparation of notices of appeal

The instructed solicitor will decide whether an individual is financially eligible for initial Advice and Assistance or ABWOR, based upon their capital and income together with those of their spouse or partner, if they have one, unless they are separated or there is a conflict of interest between them. The individual may require to pay a contribution towards the cost and further work under Advice and Assistance or ABWOR is subject to the prior authorisation of the Scottish Legal Aid Board.

In 'summary' cases in the District or Sheriff Court in which a Justice of the Peace or Sheriff sits alone, applications for Criminal Legal Aid are made to the Scottish Legal Aid Board. In more serious 'solemn' cases in the Sheriff or High Court in which a Sheriff or Judge sits with a jury, applications are made to the court. The Board or court will decide whether it is 'in the interests of justice' to grant representation; for example, where the consequences of conviction could be loss of employment or imprisonment, where there are complex questions of law or where the accused person cannot understand the proceedings because they cannot speak English or are mentally ill. The accused person will not be required to pay a contribution to the cost of the case.

Further information about the eligibility criteria for Legal Advice and Assistance, ABWOR and Criminal Legal Aid in Scotland can be obtained from The Scottish Legal Aid Board (see details above) or from Scottish solicitors or Citizens Advice Bureaux. Further information can be obtained from:

THE SCOTTISH LEGAL AID BOARD
44 Drumsheugh Gardens, Edinburgh EH3 7SW
T 0131-226 7061

MARRIAGE

Any two persons may marry provided that:

- they are at least 16 years old on the day of the marriage (in England and Wales persons under the age of 18 must generally obtain the consent of their parents; if consent is refused an appeal may be made to the High Court, the county court or a court of summary jurisdiction)
- they are not related to one another in a way which would prevent their marrying

- they are unmarried (a person who has already been married must produce documentary evidence that the previous marriage has been ended by death, divorce or annulment)
- they are not of the same sex
- they are capable of understanding the nature of a marriage ceremony and of consenting to marriage
- the marriage may be valid in England and Wales and void by the law of the domicile of both or either of the parties. The parties should check the marriage will be recognised as valid in their home country

DEGREES OF RELATIONSHIP

A marriage between persons within the prohibited degrees of consanguinity, affinity or adoption is void.

A man may not marry his mother, daughter, grandmother, granddaughter, sister, aunt, niece, great-grandmother, great-granddaughter, adoptive mother, former adoptive mother, adopted daughter or former adopted daughter. In some circumstances he may now be allowed to marry his former wife's daughter, former wife's granddaughter, father's former wife or grandfather's former wife.

A woman may not marry her father, son, grandfather, grandson, brother, uncle, nephew, great-grandfather, great-grandson, adoptive father, former adoptive father, adopted son or former adopted son. In some circumstances she may be allowed to marry her former husband's son, former husband's grandson, mother's former husband or grandmother's former husband.

ENGLAND AND WALES

TYPES OF MARRIAGE CEREMONY

It is possible to marry by either religious or civil ceremony. A religious ceremony can take place at a church or chapel of the Church of England or the Church in Wales, or at any other place of worship which has been formally registered by the Registrar General.

A civil ceremony can take place at a register office, a registered building or any other premises approved by the local authority.

An application for an approved premises licence must be made by the owners or trustees of the building concerned; it cannot be made by the prospective marriage couple. Approved premises must be regularly open to the public so that the marriage can be witnessed; the venue must be deemed to be a permanent and immovable structure. Open-air ceremonies are prohibited.

Non-Anglican marriages may also be solemnised following the issue of a Registrar-General's licence in unregistered premises where one of the parties is seriously ill, is not expected to recover, and cannot be moved to registered premises. Detained and housebound persons may be married at their place of residence.

MARRIAGE IN THE CHURCH OF ENGLAND OR THE CHURCH IN WALES

Marriage by banns

The marriage must take place in a parish in which one of the parties lives, or in a church in another parish if it is the usual place of worship of either or both of the parties. The banns must be called in the parish in which the marriage is to take place on three Sundays before the day of the ceremony; if either or both of the parties lives in a different parish the banns must also be called there. After three months the banns are no longer valid. The minister will not perform the marriage unless he or she is satisfied that the banns have been properly called.

Marriage by common licence

The vicar who is to conduct the marriage will arrange for a common licence to be issued by the diocesan bishop; this dispenses with the necessity for banns. One of the parties must have lived in the parish for 15 days immediately before the issuing of the licence or must usually worship at the church. At least one of the parties must be baptised. The licence is valid for three months.

Marriage by special licence

A special licence is granted by the Archbishop of Canterbury in special circumstances for the marriage to take place at any place, with or without previous residence in the parish, or at any time. Application must be made to the registrar of the

FACULTY OFFICE, 1 The Sanctuary, London SW1P 3JT
T 020-7222 5381

Marriage by certificate

The marriage can be conducted on the authority of the superintendent registrar's certificate, provided that the vicar's consent is obtained. One of the parties must live in the parish or must usually worship at the church.

MARRIAGE BY OTHER RELIGIOUS CEREMONY

One of the parties must normally live in the registration district where the marriage is to take place. In addition to giving notice to the superintendent registrar it may also be necessary to book a registrar to be present at the ceremony.

CIVIL MARRIAGE

A marriage may be solemnised at any register office, registered building or approved premises in England and Wales. The superintendent registrar of the district should be contacted, and, if the marriage is to take place at approved premises, the necessary arrangements at the venue must also be made.

NOTICE OF MARRIAGE

A notice of the marriage must be given in person to the superintendent registrar. Notice of marriage may be given in the following ways:

- by certificate. Both parties must have lived in a registration district in England or Wales for at least seven days immediately before giving notice at the local register office. If they live in different registration districts, notice must be given in both districts. The marriage can take place in any register office or other approved premises in England and Wales no sooner than 16 days after notice has been given, when the superintendent registrar issues a certificate
- by licence (often known as 'special licence'). One of the parties must have lived in a registration district in England or Wales for at least 15 days before giving notice at the register office; the other party need only be a resident of, or be physically in, England and Wales on the day notice is given. The marriage can take place one clear day (other than a Sunday, Christmas Day or Good Friday) after notice has been given

A notice of marriage is valid for 12 months, unless it is to take place in the Church of England or Church of Wales, when it will usually only be accepted within three months of publication. It should be possible to make an advance (provisional) booking 12 months before the ceremony. In this case it is still necessary to give formal notice three months before the marriage. When giving notice of the marriage it is necessary to produce official proof that any previous marriage has ended in divorce or death by producing a decree absolute or death certificate; it is also useful, but not necessary, to take birth certificates or passports as proof of age and identity.

SOLEMNISATION OF THE MARRIAGE

On the day of the wedding there must be at least two other people present who are prepared to act as witnesses and sign the marriage register. A registrar of marriages must be present at a marriage in a register office or at approved premises, but an authorised person may act in the capacity of registrar in a registered building.

If the marriage takes place at approved premises, the room must be separate from any other activity on the premises at the time of the ceremony, and no food or drink can be sold or consumed in the room during the ceremony or for one hour beforehand.

The marriage must be solemnised between 8 a.m. and 6 p.m., with open doors. At some time during the ceremony the parties must make a declaration that they know of no legal impediment to the marriage and they must also say the contracting words; the declaratory and contracting words may vary according to the form of service. A civil marriage cannot contain any religious aspects.

CIVIL FEES

Marriage at a Register Office

By superintendent registrar's certificate, £94.00

This includes a fee of £34.00 for the registrar's attendance on the day of the wedding.

Marriage on Approved Premises

By superintendent registrar's certificate, £60.00

An additional fee will also be payable for the superintendent registrar's and registrar's attendance at the marriage. This is set locally by the local authority responsible. A further charge is likely to be made by the owners of the building for the use of the premises. For marriages taking place in a religious building other than the Church of England or Church of Wales, an additional fee of £40.00 is payable for the registrar's attendance at the marriage unless an 'Authorised Person' appointed by the trustees of the building have agreed to register the marriage. Additional fees may be charged by the trustees of the building for the wedding and by the person who performs the ceremony.

ECCLESIASTICAL FEES

(Church of England and Church in Wales*)

Marriage by banns

For publication of banns, £18.00

For certificate of banns issued at time of publication, £9.00

For marriage service, £180.00

Marriage by common licence

Fee for licence, £62.00

Marriage by special licence

Fee for licence, £130.00

* Some of these fees may not apply to the Church in Wales

SCOTLAND

REGULAR MARRIAGES

A regular marriage is one that is celebrated by a minister of religion or authorised registrar or other celebrant. Each of the parties must complete a marriage notice form and return it to the district registrar for the area in which they are to be married, irrespective of where they live, at least 15 days before the ceremony is due to take place. The district registrar must then enter the date of receipt and certain details in a marriage book kept for this purpose, and must also enter the names of the parties and the proposed date of marriage in a list which is displayed in a conspicuous place at the registration office until the date of the marriage has passed. All persons wishing to enter into a regular marriage in Scotland must follow the same preliminary procedure regardless of whether they intend to have a religious or civil ceremony. Before the marriage ceremony takes place any person may submit an objection in writing to the district registrar.

A marriage schedule, which is prepared by the registrar, will be issued to one or both of the parties in person up to seven days before a religious marriage; for a civil marriage the schedule will be available at the ceremony. The schedule must be handed to the celebrant before the ceremony starts; it must be signed immediately after the wedding and the marriage must be registered within three days.

The authority to conduct a religious marriage is deemed to be vested in the authorised celebrant rather than the building in which it takes place; open-air religious ceremonies are therefore permissible in Scotland.

Since 10 June 2002 it has been possible, under the Marriage (Scotland) Act 2002, for venues or couples to apply to the local council for a licence to allow a civil ceremony to take place at a venue other than a registration office. A list of licensed venues is also available on the General Registers of Scotland website at www.gro-scotland.gov.uk.

MARRIAGE BY COHABITATION WITH HABIT AND REPUTE

If two people live together constantly as husband and wife and are generally held to be such by the neighbourhood and among their friends and relations, there may arise a presumption from which marriage can be inferred. Before such a marriage can be registered, however, a decree of declarator of marriage must be obtained from the Court of Session.

CIVIL FEES

The fee for a religious marriage is £48.50, comprising a fee of £20.00 per person for the statutory notice of an intention to marry and an £8.50 fee for a copy of the marriage certificate. The basic fee for marriage in a registration office or under a local authority licence is £93.50, comprising a fee of £20 per person for each person submitting a notice of marriage to the district registrar, £45 for solemnisation of a civil marriage and £8.50 for a copy of the marriage certificate. There can be additional fees charged by the local authority. Further information can be obtained from:

THE GENERAL REGISTER OFFICE
Office for National Statistics, Smedley Hydro, Trafalgar Road, Southport, Merseyside PR8 2HH **T** 0870-243 7788

THE GENERAL REGISTER OFFICE FOR SCOTLAND
New Register House, Edinburgh EH1 3YT **T** 0131-225 4452

TOWN AND COUNTRY PLANNING

The planning system is important in helping to protect the environment, as well as assisting individuals in assessing their land rights. There are a number of Acts governing the development of land and buildings in England and Wales and advice should always be sought from a Citizens Advice Bureau or local planning authority before undertaking building works on any land or to property. If development takes place which requires planning permission without permission being given enforcement action may take place and the situation may need to be rectified.

PLANNING PERMISSION

Planning permission is needed if the work involves:

- making a material change in use, such as dividing off part of the house so that it can be used as a separate home or dividing off part of the house for commercial use, e.g. for a workshop
- going against the terms of the original planning permission, e.g. there may be a restriction on fences in front gardens on an open-plan estate
- building, engineering for mining, except for the permissions below
- new or wider access to a main road
- additions or extensions to flats or maisonettes

Planning permission is not needed to carry out internal alterations or work which does not affect the external appearance of the building, and are not works for making good damage or works begun after 5 December 1968 for the alteration of a building by providing additional space in it underground.

There are certain types of development for which the Secretary of State for the Environment has granted general permissions (permitted development rights). These include: house extensions and additions (including conservatories, loft conversions, garages and dormer windows); buildings such as garden sheds and greenhouses; adding a porch; putting up fences, walls and gates; and laying patios, paths or driveways for domestic use. However, before carrying out any of the above permitted developments you must contact your local authority to find out whether the general permission has been modified in your area.

OTHER RESTRICTIONS

It may be necessary to obtain other types of permissions before carrying out any development. These permissions are separate from planning permission and apply regardless of whether or not planning permission is needed, e.g.:

- building regulations will probably apply if a new building is to be erected, if an existing one is to be altered or extended, or if the work involves building over a drain or sewer. The building control department of the local authority will advise on this
- any alterations to a listed building or the grounds of a listed building must be approved by the local authority. Listing will include not only the main building but everything in the curtilage of the building
- local authority approval is necessary if a building (or, in some circumstances, gates, walls, fences or railings) in a conservation area is to be demolished; each local authority keeps a register of all local buildings that are in conservation areas
- many trees are protected by tree preservation orders and must not be pruned or taken down without local authority consent
- bats and other species are protected and English Nature, the Countryside Council for Wales or Scottish Natural Heritage must be notified before any work is carried out that will affect the habitat of protected species, e.g. timber treatment, renovation or extensions of lofts
- any development in areas designated as a National Park, an Area of Outstanding National Beauty, a National Scenic Area or in the Norfolk or Suffolk Broads is subject to greater restrictions. The local planning authority will advise or refer enquirers to the relevant authority.

If you think you require planning permission, contact your local authority. There may also be restriction on development contained in the title to the property which should be considered when works are planned.

VOTERS' QUALIFICATIONS

Those entitled to vote at parliamentary, European Union and local government elections are those who are:

- on the electoral roll. Local authorities administer the roll and non-registration can lead to a fine of up to £1,000
- over 18 years old
- Commonwealth (which includes British) citizens or citizens of the Republic of Ireland
- In Northern Ireland electors must have been resident in Northern Ireland during the whole of the three month period prior to the relevant date

British citizens resident abroad are entitled to vote, for 15 years after leaving Britain, as overseas electors in parliamentary and EU elections in the constituency in which they were last resident. Members of the armed forces, Crown servants and employees of the British Council who are overseas and their spouses are entitled to vote regardless of how long they have been abroad. British citizens who have never been registered as an elector in the UK are not eligible to register as an overseas voter unless they left the UK before they were 18, providing they left the country no more than 15 years ago.

European Union citizens resident in the UK may vote in EU and local government elections. The main categories of people who are not entitled to vote are: sitting peers in the House of Lords (although members of the House of Lords can vote at elections to local authorities, devolved legislatures and European Parliament); patients detained under mental health legislation who have criminal convictions; those serving prison sentences; and those convicted within the previous five years of corrupt or illegal election practices.

Under the Representation of the Peoples Act 2000, several new groups of people are permitted to vote for the first time. These include: people who live on barges; unconvicted or remand prisoners; people in mental health hospitals (other than those with criminal convictions) and homeless people who have made a 'declaration of local connection'.

REGISTERING TO VOTE

Voters must be entered on an electoral register, which is updated on a monthly basis. The registration officer for each constituency is responsible for preparing and publishing the register. A registration form is sent to all households in the autumn of each year and the householder is required to provide details of all occupants who are eligible to vote, including ones who will reach their 18th birthday in the year covered by the register. Those who fail to give the required information or who give false information are liable to be fined. A draft register is usually published at the end of November. Any person whose name has been omitted may ask to be registered and should contact the registration officer.

Anyone on the register may object to the inclusion of another person's name, in which case he/she should notify the registration officer, who will investigate that person's eligibility. Supplementary electors lists are published throughout the duration of the register.

VOTING
Voting is not compulsory in the UK. Those who wish to vote generally vote in person at an allotted polling station. Postal votes are now available on request. Those who will be away at the time of the election, those who will not be able to attend in person due to physical incapacity or the nature of their occupation, and those who have changed address during the period for which the register is valid, may apply for a postal vote or nominate a proxy to vote for them. Overseas electors who wish to vote must do so by proxy.
Further information can be obtained from the local authority's electoral registration officer in England and Wales or the electoral registration office in Scotland, or the Chief Electoral Officer in Northern Ireland.

WILLS AND INTESTACY

In a will a person leaves instructions as to the disposal of their property after they die. A will is also used to appoint executors (who will administer the estate), give directions as to the disposal of the body, appoint guardians for children and, for larger estates, can operate to reduce the level of inheritance tax. It is best to have a will drawn up by a solicitor but if a solicitor is not employed, the following points must be taken into account:
- if possible the will must not be prepared on behalf of another person by someone who is to benefit from it or who is a close relative of a major beneficiary
- the language used must be clear and unambiguous and it is better to avoid the use of legal terms where the same thing can be expressed in plain language
- it is better to rewrite the whole document if a mistake is made. If necessary, alterations can be made by striking through the words with a pen, and the signature or initials of the testator and the witnesses must be put in the margin opposite the alteration. No alteration of any kind should be made after the will has been executed
- if the person later wishes to change the will or part of it, it is better to write a new will revoking the old. The use of codicils (documents written as supplements or containing modifications to the will) should be left to a solicitor
- the will should be typed or printed, or if handwritten be legible and preferably in ink. Commercial will forms can be obtained from some stationers

LAPSED LEGATEES
If a person who has been left property in a will dies before the person who made the will, the gift fails and will pass to the person entitled to everything not otherwise disposed of (the residuary estate). If the person left the residuary estate dies before the person who made the will, their share will generally pass to the closest relative(s) of the person who made the will (as in intestacy) unless the will names a beneficiary such as a charity who will take as a 'long stop' if this gift is unable to take effect for any reason. It is always better to draw up a new will if a beneficiary predeceases the person who made the will.

EXECUTORS
It is usual to appoint two executors, although one is sufficient. No more than four persons can deal with the estate of the person who has died. The name and address of each executor should be given in full (the addresses are not essential but including them adds clarity to the document). Executors should be 18 years of age or over. An executor may be a beneficiary of the will.

WITNESSES
A person who is a beneficiary of a will, or the spouse of a beneficiary at the time the will is signed, must not act as a witness or else he/she will be unable to take his/her gift. Husband and wife can both act as witnesses provided neither benefits from the will.

It is better that a person does not act as an executor and as a witness, as he/she can take no benefit under a will to which he/she is witness. The identity of the witnesses should be made as explicit as possible.

EXECUTION OF A WILL
The person making the will should sign his/her name at the foot of the document, in the presence of the two witnesses. The witnesses must then sign their names while the person making the will looks on. If this procedure is not adhered to, the will will be considered invalid. There are certain exceptional circumstances where these rules are relaxed, e.g. where the person may be too ill to sign.

CAPACITY TO MAKE A WILL
Anyone aged 18 or over can make a will. However, if there is any suspicion that the person making the will is not, through reasons of infirmity or age, fully in command of his/her faculties, it is advisable to arrange for a medical practitioner to examine the person making the will at the time it is to be executed to verify his/her mental capacity and to record that medical opinion in writing, and to ask the examining practitioner to act as a witness. If a person is not mentally able to make a will, the Court may do this for him/her by virtue of the Mental Health Act 1983.

REVOCATION
A will may be revoked or cancelled in a number of ways: a later will revokes an earlier one if it says so; otherwise the earlier will is impliedly revoked by the later one to the extent that it contradicts or repeats the earlier one; a will is also revoked if the physical document on which it is written is destroyed by the person whose will it is. There must be an intention to revoke the will. It may not be sufficient to obliterate the will with a pen; a will is revoked when the person marries, unless it is clear from the will that the person intended the will to stand after the marriage; and where a marriage ends in divorce or is annulled or declared void, gifts to the spouse and the appointment of the spouse as executor fail unless the will says that this is not to happen. A former spouse is treated as having predeceased the testator. A separation does not change the effect of a married person's will.

PROBATE AND LETTERS OF ADMINISTRATION
Probate is granted to the executors named in a will and once granted, the executors are obliged to carry out the instructions of the will. Letters of administration are granted where no executor is named in a will or is willing or able to act or where there is no will or no valid will; this gives a person, often the next of kin, similar powers and duties to those of an executor.

Applications for probate or for letters of administration can be made to the Principal Registry of the Family Division, to a district probate registry or to a probate sub-registry. Applicants will need the following documents: the original will (if any); a certificate of death; oath for executors or administrators; particulars of all property and assets left by the deceased; a list of debts and funeral expenses. Certain property, up to the value of £5,000, may be disposed of without a grant of probate or letters of administration.

WHERE TO FIND A PROVED WILL

Since 1858 wills which have been proved, that is wills on which probate or letters of administration have been granted, must have been proved at the Principal Registry of the Family Division or at a district probate registry. The Lord Chancellor has power to direct where the original documents are kept but most are filed where they were proved and may be inspected there and a copy obtained. The Principal Registry also holds copies of all wills proved at district probate registries and these may be inspected at First Avenue House, High Holborn. An index of all grants, both of probate and of letters of administration, is compiled by the Principal Registry and may be seen either at the Principal Registry or at a district probate registry.

It is also possible to discover when a grant of probate or letters of administration is issued by requesting a standing search. In response to a request and for a small fee, a district probate registry will supply the names and addresses of executors or administrators and the registry in which the grant was made, of any grant in the estate of a specified person made in the previous 12 months or following six months. This is useful for applicants who may be beneficiaries to a will but who have lost contact with the deceased and for creditors of the deceased.

SCOTLAND

In Scotland any person over 12 and of sound mind can make a will. The person making the will can only freely dispose of the heritage and what is known as the 'dead's part' of the estate because: the spouse has the right to inherit one-third of the moveable estate if there are children or other descendants, and one-half of it if there are not; and children are entitled to one-third of the moveable estate if there is a surviving spouse, and one-half of it if there is not. The remaining portion is the dead's part, and legacies and bequests are payable from this. Debts are payable out of the whole estate before any division.

Since August 1995, wills no longer need to be 'holographed' and it is now only necessary to have one witness. The person making the will still needs to sign each page. It is better that the will is not witnessed by a beneficiary although the attestation would still be sound and the beneficiary would not have to relinquish the gift.

Subsequent marriage does not revoke a will but the birth of a child who is not provided for may do so. A will may be revoked by a subsequent will, either expressly or by implication, but in so far as the two can be read together both have effect. If a subsequent will is revoked, the earlier will is revived.

Wills may be registered in the sheriff court Books of the Sheriffdom in which the deceased lived or in the Books of Council and Session at the Registers of Scotland.

CONFIRMATION

Confirmation (the Scottish equivalent of probate) is obtained in the sheriff court of the sheriffdom in which the deceased was resident at the time of death. Executives are either 'nominate' (named by the deceased in the will) or 'dative' (appointed by the court in cases where no executor is named in a will or in cases of intestacy). Applicants for confirmation must first provide an inventory of the deceased's estate and a schedule of debts, with an affidavit. In estates under £25,000 gross, confirmation can be obtained under a simplified procedure at reduced fees, with no need for a solicitor. The local sheriff clerk's office can provide assistance.

Further information can be obtained from:

SHERIFF CLERK'S OFFICE
Commissary Section, Sheriff Court House, Chambers Street, Edinburgh, EH1 1LB T 0131-225 2525

PRINCIPAL REGISTRY
Family Division, First Avenue House, 42–49 High Holborn, London WC2V 6NP T 020 7947 6980

REGISTERS OF SCOTLAND
Meadowbank House, 153 London Road, Edinburgh, EH8 7AU
T 0131-659 6111

INTESTACY

Intestacy occurs when someone dies without leaving a will or leaves a will which is invalid or which does not take effect for some reason. Intestacy can be partial, for instance, if there is a will which disposes of some but not all of the testator's property. In such cases the person's estate (property, possessions, other assets following the payment of debts) passes to certain members of the family. The relevant legislation is the Administration of Estates Act 1925, as amended by various legislation including the Intestates Estates Act 1952, the Law Reform (Succession) Act 1995, and the Trusts of Land and Appointment of Trustees Act 1996 and Orders made there under. Some of the provisions of this legislation are described below. If a will has been written that disposes of only part of a person's property, these rules apply to the part which is undisposed of. If the person (intestate) leaves a spouse who survives for 28 days and children (legitimate, illegitimate and adopted children and other descendants), the estate is divided as follows:

- the spouse takes the 'personal chattels' (household articles, including cars, but nothing used for business purposes), £125,000 free of tax (with interest payable at 6 per cent from the time of the death until payment) and a life interest in half of the rest of the estate (which can be capitalised by the spouse if he/she wishes)
- the rest of the estate goes to the children*.

If the person leaves a spouse who survives for 28 days but no children:

- the spouse takes the personal chattels, £200,000 free of tax (interest payable as before) and full ownership of half of the rest of the estate
- the other half of the rest of the estate goes to the parents (equally, if both alive) or, if none, to the brothers and sisters of the whole blood*
- if there are no parents or brothers or sisters of the whole blood or their children, the spouse takes the whole estate.

If there is no surviving spouse, the estate is distributed among those who survive the intestate as follows:

- to surviving children*, but if none to
- parents (equally, if both alive), but if none to
- brothers and sisters of the whole blood* (including issues of deceased ones), but if none to
- brothers and sisters of the half blood* (including issues of deceased ones), but if none to

– grandparents (equally, if more than one), but if none to
– aunts and uncles of the whole blood*, but if none to
– aunts and uncles of the half blood*, but if none to
– the Crown, Duchy of Lancaster or the Duke of Cornwall *(bona vacantia)*

* To inherit, a member of these groups must survive the intestate and attain 18, or marry under that age. If they die under 18 (unless married under that age), their share goes to others, if any, in the same group. If any member of these groups predeceases the intestate leaving children, their share is divided equally among their children.

In England and Wales the provisions of the Inheritance (Provision for Family and Dependants) Act 1975 may allow other people to claim provision from the deceased's assets. This Act also applies to cases where a will has been made and allows a person to apply to the Court if they feel that the will or rules of intestacy or both do not make adequate provision for them. The Court can order payment from the deceased's assets or the transfer of property from them if the applicant's claim is accepted. The application must be made within six months of the grant of probate or letters of administration and the following people can make an application:
– the spouse
– a former spouse who has not remarried
– a child of the deceased
– someone treated as a child of the deceased's family
– someone maintained by the deceased
– someone who has cohabited for two years before the death in the same household as the deceased and as the husband or wife of the deceased

SCOTLAND

The rules of distribution are contained in the Succession (Scotland) Act 1964. A surviving spouse is entitled to 'prior rights'. This means that the spouse has the right to inherit:
– the matrimonial home up to a value of £130,000, or one matrimonial home if there is more than one, or, in certain circumstances, the value of the matrimonial home
– the furnishings and contents of that home, up to the value of £22,000
– a cash sum of £35,000 if the deceased left children or other descendants, or £58,000 if not.

These figures are increased from time to time by regulations.

Once prior rights have been satisfied jus relicti(ae) and legitim are settled. Legal rights are:

Jus relicti(ae) – the right of a surviving spouse to one half of the net moveable estate, after satisfaction of prior rights, if there are no surviving children; if there are surviving children, the spouse is entitled to one-third of the net moveable estate

Legitim – the right of surviving children to one-half of the net moveable estate if there is no surviving spouse; if there is a surviving spouse, the children are entitled to one-third of the net moveable estate after the satisfaction of prior rights

Where there are no surviving spouse or children, half of the estate is taken by the parents and half by the brothers and sisters. Failing that, the lines of succession, in general, are:
– to descendants
– if no descendants, then to collaterals (i.e. brothers and sisters) and parents
– surviving spouse
– if no collaterals or parents or spouse, then to ascendants collaterals (i.e. aunts and uncles), and so on in an ascending scale
– if all lines of succession fail, the estate passes to the Crown

Relatives of the whole blood are preferred to relatives of the half blood. The right of representation, i.e. the right of the issue of a person who would have succeeded if he/she had survived the intestate, also applies.

CRIME STATISTICS

RECORDED CRIME STATISTICS
England and Wales (000s)

Offence	*1998*	*2000*	*2002*
Violence against the person	502.8	600.9	835.1
Sexual offences	36.2	37.3	48.7
Burglary	953.2	836.0	889.0
Robbery	66.8	95.2	108.0
Theft and handling stolen goods	2,191.4	2,145.4	2,365.5
Fraud and forgery	279.5	319.3	330.1
Criminal damage	879.6	960.1	1,109.4
Drug offences	135.9	113.5	141.1
Other offences	63.6	65.7	72.6

OFFENDERS FOUND GUILTY BY OFFENCE GROUP
Magistrates' Courts and the Crown Court
England and Wales (000s)

Offence	*1992*	*1996*	*2000*	*2002*
Murder	0.2	0.3	0.3	0.3
Manslaughter	0.3	0.3	0.3	0.3
Sexual offences	5.0	4.4	3.9	4.4
Burglary	44.3	32.3	26.2	26.7
Robbery	5.1	5.9	6.0	7.7
Theft and handling stolen goods	127.9	114.5	128.0	127.3
Criminal damage	9.8	9.8	10.2	11.0
Drugs offences	22.7	34.1	44.6	49.0
Motoring offences	10.7	9.9	7.6	8.2

CRIMES AND OFFENCES RECORDED BY THE POLICE
Scotland (000s)

Offence	*1998*	*2000*	*2002*
Serious assault	6.6	7.0	7.6
Robbery	5.0	4.4	4.9
Rape and Attempted Rape	0.8	0.7	0.9
Housebreaking	56.6	48.7	43.8

RECORDED CRIME STATISTICS
Northern Ireland (000s)

Offence	*1998/9*	*2000/1*	*2002/3*
Violence against the person	18.5	21.4	28.5
Sexual offences	1.6	1.2	1.5
Burglary	15.5	15.8	18.7
Robbery	1.4	1.8	2.5
Theft	35.4	36.9	41.9
Fraud and forgery	6.8	8.0	8.8
Criminal damage	27.7	32.3	36.6
Offences against the state	0.6	0.8	1.8
Other notifiable offences (incl. drugs)	1.4	1.5	1.9

Source: The Stationary Office – *Annual Abstract of Statistics 2004* (Crown copyright)

INTELLECTUAL PROPERTY

COPYRIGHT

Copyright protects all original literary, dramatic, musical and artistic works (including photographs, maps and plans), published editions of works, computer programs, sound recordings, films (including video and DVD) and broadcasts (including cable, radio and satellite broadcasts, but excluding most transmissions on the internet). Under copyright the creators of these works can control the various ways in which their material may be exploited, the rights broadly covering copying, adapting, issuing (including renting and lending) copies to the public, performing in public, and broadcasting the material. The transfer of copyright works to formats accessible to visually impaired persons without infringement of copyright was enacted in 2002.

Copyright protection in the United Kingdom is automatic and there is no official registration system. Steps can be taken by the work's creator to provide evidence that he/she had the work at a particular time (e.g. by depositing a copy with a bank or solicitor). The main legislation is the Copyright, Designs and Patents Act 1988, which has been amended by other Acts and by Statutory Instrument to take account of EU Directives. As a result of an EU Directive effective from January 1996, the term of copyright protection for literary, dramatic, musical and artistic works lasts for 70 years after the death of the author, and for film lasts for 70 years after the death of the last to survive of the director, authors of the screenplay and dialogue, or the composer of any music specially created for the film. Sound recordings are protected for 50 years after their publication, and broadcasts for 50 years from the end of the year in which the first broadcast/transmission is made. Published editions remain under copyright protection for 25 years from the end of the year in which the edition was published.

The main international treaties protecting copyright are the Bern Convention for the Protection of Literary and Artistic Works (administered by the World Intellectual Property Organisation (WIPO)), the Rome Convention for the Protection of Performers, Producers of Phonograms and Broadcasting Organisations (administered jointly by UNESCO and the International Labour Organisation), and the Universal Copyright Convention (UNESCO); the UK is a signatory to these conventions. Copyright material created by UK nationals or residents is protected in each country which is a member of the conventions by the national law of that country. A list of participating countries may be obtained from the Patent Office.

Two treaties which strengthen and update international standards of protection, particularly in relation to new technologies, were agreed in December 1996: the WIPO Copyright Treaty, and the WIPO Performance and Phonograms Treaty. In May 2001 the European Union passed a new Directive, which in 2003 became law in the UK, aimed at harmonising copyright law throughout the EU to take account of the internet and other technologies. Further information can be found at

www.intellectual-property.gov.uk.

LICENSING

Use of copyright material without seeking permission in each instance may be permitted under 'blanket' licences available from copyright licensing agencies. The International Federation of Reproduction Rights Organisations facilitates agreements between its member licensing agencies and on behalf of its members with organisations such as the WIPO, UNESCO, the European Union and the Council of Europe.

PATENTS

A patent is a document issued by the Patent Office relating to an invention and giving the proprietor the right for a limited period to stop others from making, using or selling the invention without the inventor's permission. In return the patentee pays a fee to cover the costs of processing the patent and publicly discloses details of the invention.

To qualify for a patent an invention must be new, must exhibit an inventive step, and must be capable of industrial application. The patent is valid for a maximum of 20 years from the date on which the application was filed, subject to payment of annual fees from the end of the fourth year. The Patent Office, established in 1852, is responsible for ensuring that all stages of an application comply with the Patents Act 1977, and that the invention meets the criteria for a patent.

The WIPO is responsible for administering many of the international conventions on intellectual property. The Patent Co-operation Treaty allows inventors to file a single application for patent rights in some or all of the contracting states. This application is searched by an International Searching Authority and published by the International Bureau of WIPO. It may also be the subject of an (optional) international preliminary examination. Applicants must then deal directly with the patent offices in the countries where they are seeking patent rights. The European Patent Convention allows inventors to obtain patent rights in all the contracting states by filing a single application with the European Patent Office.

TRADE MARKS

Trade marks are a means of identification, whether a word or device or a combination of both, a logo, or the shape of goods or their packaging, which enable traders to make their goods or services readily distinguishable from those supplied by other traders. Registration prevents other traders using the same or similar trade marks for similar products or services for which the mark is registered. In the UK trade marks are registered at the Trade Marks Registry in the Patent Office. In order to qualify for registration a mark must be capable of distinguishing its proprietor's goods or services from those of other undertakings; it should be non-deceptive, should not be contrary to law or morality and should not be similar or identical to any earlier marks for the same or similar goods or services. The relevant current legislation is the Trade Marks Act 1994.

It is possible to obtain an international trade mark registration, effective in 76 countries, under the Madrid Agreement or the Madrid Protocol, to which the UK is party. British companies can obtain international trade mark registration through a single application to the WIPO in those countries party to the protocol.

The EC trade mark regulation is now in force and is administered by the Office for Harmonisation in the Internal Market (Trade Marks and Designs). The office registers EC trade marks, which are valid throughout the European Union. The national registration of trade marks in member states continues in parallel with EC trade mark registration.

DOMAIN NAMES
A domain name is a name by which a company or organisation is known on the internet and is a short-hand way of identifying a company's website. A domain name has to be registered separately from a trade mark. Although there are many registrars prepared to register domain names, each country has a central registry to store unique names and addresses used on the internet. A list of accredited registrars can be found on www.icann.org.

DESIGN PROTECTION

Design protection covers the outward appearance of an article and takes two forms in the UK, registered design and design right, which are not mutually exclusive. Registered design protects the aesthetic appearance of an article, including shape, configuration, pattern or ornament, although artistic works such as sculptures are excluded, being generally protected by copyright. In order to qualify for protection, a design must be new and materially different from earlier UK published designs. The owner of the design must apply to the Designs Registry at the Patent Office. Initial registration lasts for five years and can be extended in five-year increments to a maximum of 25 years. The current legislation is the Registered Designs Act 1949 (as amended).

UK applicants wishing to protect their designs in the EU can do so by applying for a Registered Community Design with the Office of Harmonisation in the Internal Market. Outside the EU separate applications must be made in each country in which protection is sought.

Design right is an automatic right which applies to the shape or configuration of articles and does not require registration. Unlike registered design, two-dimensional designs do not qualify for protection but designs of semiconductor chips (topographies) are protected by design right. Designs must be original and non-commonplace. The term of design right is ten years from first marketing of the design and the right is effective only in the UK. The current legislation is Part 3 of the Copyright, Designs and Patents Act 1988, amended on 9 December 2001 to incorporate the European Designs Directive.

LEGAL DEPOSIT

Publishers are legally obliged to send one copy of every new printed publication distributed in the United Kingdom or Republic of Ireland to each of the legal deposit libraries within one month of publication. This is based on the Copyright Act of 1911 and the Irish Copyright Act 1963, replaced by similar provisions in the Copyright and Related Rights Act 2000. All printed publications come within the scope of legal deposit. A code of practice exists in the UK for the deposit of non-printed publications, however, the Legal Deposit Libraries Act 2003, which is not yet in force, extends legal deposit legislation to automatically include non-print publications. The aim of legal deposit is to keep a complete national archive of published works as a current reference and information source. The legal deposit libraries are the British Library, the Bodleian Library in Oxford, Cambridge University Library, the National Library of Scotland, the National Library of Wales, and Trinity College Library in Dublin.

INTELLECTUAL PROPERTY ORGANISATIONS

COPYRIGHT LIBRARIES AGENCY, 100 Euston Street, London NW1 2HQ **T** 020-7388 5061

CHARTERED INSTITUTE OF PATENT AGENTS, 97 Chancery Lane, London WC2A 1DT **T** 020-7405 9450 **W** www.cipa.org.uk

DESIGNS REGISTRY, The Patent Office, Cardiff Road, Newport NP10 8QQ **T** 0845-950 0505

EUROPEAN PATENT OFFICE, Headquarters, Erhardtstrasse 27, D-8000, Munich 2, Germany **T** (+49) 892 3990 **W** www.european-patent-office.org

INTERNATIONAL FEDERATION OF REPRODUCTION RIGHTS ORGANISATIONS (IFRRO), rue du Prince Royal 87, B-1050 Brussels, Belgium **T** (+32) 551 0899 **W** www.ifrro.org

LEGAL DEPOSIT OFFICE, The British Library, Boston Spa, Wetherby, W. Yorks LS23 7BY **T** 01937-546267 **E** legal-deposit-serials@bl.uk

NEWSPAPER LEGAL DEPOSIT OFFICE, The British Library, Newspaper Library, Colindale Avenue, London NW9 5LF **T** 020-7412 7382

OFFICE FOR HARMONISATION IN THE INTERNAL MARKET (TRADE MARKS AND DESIGNS), Avenida de Europa 4, E-03080 Alicante, Spain **T** (+34) 965 139100 **W** http://oami.eu.int/en

THE PATENT OFFICE, Cardiff Road, Newport NP10 8QQ **T** 0845-950 0505 **W** www.patent.gov.uk

STATIONERS' HALL REGISTRY LTD, The Registrar, Stationers' Hall, Ave Maria Lane, London EC4M 7DD **T** 020-7248 2934

TRADE MARKS REGISTRY, The Patent Office, Cardiff Road, Newport NP10 8QQ **T** 0845-950 0505

WORLD INTELLECTUAL PROPERTY ORGANISATION (WIPO), 34 chemin des Colombettes, CH-1211 Geneva 20, Switzerland **T** (+41) 22 338 9111 **W** www.wipo.int

COPYRIGHT LICENSING/COLLECTING AGENCIES

AUTHORS' LICENSING AND COLLECTING SOCIETY, Marlborough Court, 14–18 Holborn, London EC1N 2LE **T** 020-7395 0600 **W** www.alcs.co.uk

COPYRIGHT LICENSING AGENCY LTD, 90 Tottenham Court Road, London W1T 0LP **T** 020-7631 5555 **W** www.cla.co.uk

DESIGN AND ARTISTS COPYRIGHT SOCIETY, Parchment House, 13 Northburgh Street, London EC1V 0JP **T** 020-7336 8811 **W** www.dacs.org.uk

EDUCATIONAL RECORDING AGENCY LTD, New Premier House, 150 Southampton Row, London WC1B 5AL **T** 020-7837 3222 **W** www.era.org.uk

INTERNATIONAL FEDERATION OF THE PHONOGRAPHIC INDUSTRIES, 54 Regent Street, London W1B 5RE **T** 020-7878 7900 **W** www.ifpi.org

MCPS-PRS ALLIANCE, Copyright House, 29–33 Berners Street, London W1T 3AB **T** 020-7580 5544 **W** www.mcps-prs-alliance.co.uk

NEWSPAPER LICENSING AGENCY, 7–9 Church Road, Wellington Gate, Tunbridge Wells, Kent TN1 1NL **T** 01892-525273 **W** www.nla.co.uk

PHONOGRAPHIC PERFORMANCE LTD, 1 Upper James Street, London W1F 9DE **T** 020-7534 1000 **W** www.ppluk.com

PUBLISHERS LICENSING SOCIETY, 37–41 Gower Street, London WC1E 6HH **T** 020-7299 7730 **W** www.pls.org.uk

VIDEO PERFORMANCE LTD, 1 Upper James Street, London W1F 9DE **T** 020-7534 1400

THE MEDIA

OFFICE OF COMMUNICATIONS

The Office of Communications (OFCOM) is the regulator for the communication industries in the UK and has responsibility for television, radio, telecommunications and wireless communications services. It replaces the Broadcasting Standards Commission, the Independent Television Commission, the Radio Authority, the Radio Communications Agency and OFTEL. OFCOM is required to report annually to parliament and exists to further the interests of consumers by: balancing choice and competition with the duty to foster plurality, protect viewers and listeners and promote cultural diversity in the media; and ensuring full and fair competition between communications providers.

OFFICE OF COMMUNICATIONS (OFCOM)
Riverside House, 2A Southwark Bridge Road, London SE1 9HA
T 020-7981 3000
E enq@ofcom.org.uk
W www.ofcom.org.uk
Chief Executive, Stephen Carter

CROSS-MEDIA OWNERSHIP

The Communications Act 2003, which received Royal Assent on 17 July 2003, has overhauled the rules surrounding cross-media ownership. Some of them have been simplified and relaxed to encourage dispersion of ownership and new market entry while preventing the most influential media in any community being controlled by too narrow a range of interests. However, transfers and mergers will not be solely subject to examination on competition grounds by the competition authorities. The Secretary of State has a wide discretion to intervene and decide if a transaction is permissible on public interest grounds (relating both to newspapers and cross-media criteria, if broadcasting interests are also involved). OFCOM has an advisory role. Government and Parliamentary assurances were given that any intervention into local newspaper transfers would be rare and exceptional.

Cross-media regulation has been reduced to three core rules:

- No-one controlling more than 20 per cent of the national newspaper market may hold any licence for ITV or hold a stake in any of its services. A company may not own more than a 20 per cent share in such a service if more than 20 per cent of its stock is in turn owned by a national newspaper proprietor with more than 20 per cent of the market
- No-one owning a regional ITV licence may own more than 20 per cent of the local/regional newspaper market in the same region
- There should be at least three local commercial radio operators, and at least three local or regional commercial media voices (in TV, radio and newspapers) in most local communities.

As a consequence, some new forms of cross-holding have been introduced:

- Joint-ownership of national TV and national radio licences
- Joint ownership of a regional Channel 3 licence and a local radio licence in the same area (as long as there are two or more other radio stations that reach more than 50 per cent of the adult population in the radio station's area)
- Ownership of more than 20 per cent of the national newspaper market and national and/or local radio licences

BROADCASTING

The public service television broadcasters in the UK are: the British Broadcasting Corporation (BBC), a public corporation, funded mainly by the television licence fee; Channel 4, a public corporation self-funded by advertising revenues; S4C, a public corporation broadcasting the fourth channel in Wales and funded by grant-in-aid from the Government and advertising revenue; and Channel 3 (ITV), Channel 5 (Five) and Teletext, commercial television companies, funded by advertising revenues. The Government sets the licence fee and awards grants to support the BBC and S4C.

On 1 May 1996 a royal charter came into force, establishing the framework for the BBC's activities until 2006. Within the framework provided by the charter, the BBC Governors are responsible for ensuring that the BBC meets all its statutory obligations. However, the Secretary of State for the Department of Culture, Media and Sport has the power to approve and review the operation of new licence fee funded public sevices. The BBC's regulator is the Office of Communications (OFCOM), although the Governors have some exclusive responsibilities, such as ensuring the editorial independence of the BBC. The S4C Authority regulates S4C, subject to the regulatory powers vested in OFCOM by the Communications Act 2003. OFCOM also monitors and licences Channel 3, Channel 4 and Channel 5. All three commercial stations have to fulfil programming obligations.

COMPLAINTS

Under the Communications Act 2003 licensees are obliged to adhere to the provisions of OFCOM codes (including advertising, programme standards, fairness, privacy and sponsorship). OFCOM also inherited the Broadcasting Standards Comission's Standards Code and is transitionally applying it in respect of BBC/S4C programmes. Complainants should contact the broadcaster in the first instance (details can be found on OFCOM's website), however, if the complainant wishes the complaint to be considered by OFCOM, it will do so. Complaints should be made within a reasonable time as broadcasters are only required to keep recordings for the following periods of time: radio – 42 days, television – 90 days, and cable and satellite – 60 days.

TELEVISION

All terrestrial channels are broadcast in colour on 625 lines UHF from a network of transmitting stations.

Transmissions are available to 99.4 per cent of the population. Signals of acceptable quality cannot be obtained where the line of sight path between transmitters and consumers is obstructed by hills, buildings or even local atmospheric conditions. The Department for Culture Media and Sport is responsible for the policy on the allocation of frequencies for television and radio broadcasting together with reception matters, liaising with OFCOM, which has overall control for the management of frequencies.

The Broadcasting Act 1990 made the BBC responsible for licence administration, and TV Licensing is the trading name used by the agents who collect the licence fee on behalf of the BBC. The total number of television licences in force in the UK at the end of 2004 was around 23 million of which over 99 per cent were for colour televisions. Annual television licence fees from 1 April 2004 are black and white £40.50; colour £121.00.

DIGITAL TELEVISION

Digital broadcasting has dramatically increased the number and reception quality of television channels. Sound and pictures are converted into a digital format and compressed, using as few bits as possible to convey the information on a digital signal. This technique enables several television channels to be carried in the space used by the current analogue signals to carry one channel. Digital signals can be received by standard aerials, satellite dishes or via cable but have to be decoded and turned back into sound and pictures by using a separate set-top box, or a decoder built into the television set (an integrated digital TV set/ iDTV). A basic package of channels is available for free and services are also offered by cable and satellite companies.

The Broadcasting Act 1996 provided for the licensing of 20 or more digital terrestrial television channels (on six frequency channels or 'multiplexes'). The first digital services went on air in autumn 1998. Analogue broadcasting will eventually be discontinued, with the frequencies sold to mobile telephone companies.

In June 2002, following the collapse of the ITV Digital terrestrial service, a consortium made up of the BBC, BSkyB and Crown Castle, the transmitter company, was awarded the DTT (Digital Terrestrial Television) licence by the Independent Television Commission. Freeview, a digital network, was launched on 30 October 2002. By 31 March 2004 digital penetration had reached over 53 per cent of UK households.

ESTIMATED AUDIENCE SHARE 2002–3

	*Percentage**
ITV companies	24.0
BBC ONE	26.3
BBC TWO	11.3
Channel 4	9.6
Five	6.4
S4C Wales	0.3
Cable, satellite and digital channels	18.6

Source: Independent Television Commission (replaced by Ofcom)

*Rounded to one decimal point and only channels achieving a share of more than 0.1 per cent are included

THE BRITISH BROADCASTING CORPORATION

BBC TELEVISION
Television Centre, Wood Lane, London W12 7RJ
T 020-8743 8000 W www.bbc.co.uk/info

The BBC's experiments in television broadcasting started in 1929 and in 1936 it began the world's first public service of high-definition television from Alexandra Palace. The BBC broadcasts two UK-wide terrestrial television services, BBC One and BBC Two; outside England these services are designated BBC Scotland on One, BBC Scotland on Two, BBC One Northern Ireland, BBC Two Northern Ireland, BBC Wales on One and BBC Wales on Two. The BBC's digital services include BBC One, BBC Two, BBC Three, BBC Four, BBC Knowledge, BBC News 24 and BBC Parliament. The services are funded by the licence fee.

BBC WORLDWIDE LTD
Woodlands, 80 Wood Lane, London W12 0TT
T 020-8433 2000 W www.bbcworldwide.com

BBC Worldwide Limited is the commercial arm, and a wholly owned subsidiary, of the British Broadcasting Corporation. The company was formed in 1994 and exists in order to maximise the value of the BBC's programme and publishing assets for the benefit of the licence payer, re-investing profit in public service programming. BBC Worldwide's businesses include international programming distribution, television channels, magazines, books, videos, spoken word, music, DVDs, licensed products, CD-ROMs, English language teaching, videos for education and training, interactive telephony, co-production, library footage sales, exhibitions, live events, film and media monitoring.

INDEPENDENT TELEVISION NETWORK

The ITV network comprises 15 independent regional television licensees and one licensee providing the national breakfast-time service. Their licences were awarded by competitive tender for a minimum of ten years and commenced in January 1993. In addition to the terrestrial channel ITV1, ITV has launched the following digital channels: ITV2, ITV News and CiTV. Channel 4 and S4C (the fourth channel in Wales) were set up to provide programmes with a distinctive character and which appeal to interests not catered for by ITV and are also funded through advertising. Channel 5 began broadcasting in 1997 and now reaches about 80 per cent of the population.

ITV NETWORK CENTRE/ITV ASSOCIATION
200 Gray's Inn Road, London WC1X 8HF
T 020-7843 8000 W www.itv.com

The ITV Network Centre is wholly owned by the ITV companies and undertakes commissioning and scheduling of programmes shown across the ITV network and, as with the BBC, 25 per cent of programmes must come from independent producers. There are over 1,500 independent production companies in the UK which generate over £1 billion of programming.
Chairman, Sir Peter Burt

INDEPENDENT TELEVISION NETWORK REGIONS

ANGLIA *(east of England)*, Anglia House, Norwich NR1 3JG T 01603-615151 W www.angliatv.com

BORDER *(Borders and the Isle of Man)*, The Television Centre, Carlisle CA1 3NT T 01228-525101 W www.border-tv.com

CENTRAL *(east, west and south Midlands)*, Carlton Television, Lenton Lane, Nottingham NG7 2NA T 01159-863322 W www2.itv.com/central

CHANNEL *(Channel Islands)*, The Television Centre, St Helier, Jersey JE1 3ZD T 01534-816816 W www.channeltv.co.uk

GRAMPIAN *(north of Scotland)*, Craigshaw Business Park, Aberdeen AB12 3QH W www.grampiantv.co.uk

GRANADA *(north-west England)*, Quay Street, Manchester M60 9EA T 0161-832 7211 W www.granadatv.com

LONDON *(London)*, The London Television Centre, Upper Ground, London SE1 9LT T 020-7620 1620 W www.lwt.co.uk

MERIDIAN *(south and south-east England)*, The Television Centre, Southampton SO14 0PZ T 023-8022 2555 W www.meridiantv.com

SCOTTISH *(central Scotland)*, 200 Renfield Street, Glasgow G2 3PR T 0141-300 3000 W www.scottishtv.co.uk

TYNE TEES *(north-east England)*, The Television Centre, City Road, Newcastle-upon-Tyne NE1 2AL T 0191-261 0181 W www.tynetees.tv

ULSTER *(Northern Ireland)*, Havelock House, Ormeau Road, Belfast BT7 1EB T 028-9032 8122 W www.u.tv

WALES *(Wales)*, The Television Centre, Culverhouse Cross, Cardiff CF5 6XJ T 029-2059 0590

WEST *(west of England)*, The Television Centre, Bath Road, Bristol BS4 3HG T 0117-972 2722

WESTCOUNTRY *(south-west England)*, Langage Science Park, Plymouth PL7 5BQ T 01752-333444 W www2.itv.com/westcountry

YORKSHIRE *(Yorkshire)*, The Television Centre, Kirkstall Road, Leeds LS3 1JS T 0113-243 8283 W www.yorkshiretv.com

OTHER TELEVISION COMPANIES

CHANNEL FOUR TELEVISION CORPORATION, 124 Horseferry Road, London SW1P 2TX T 020-7396 4444 W www.channel4.com Provides a service to the UK except Wales and its remit is to cater for interests under-represented by the ITV network companies. Channel 4 sells its own advertising.

FIVE BROADCASTING LTD, 22 Long Acre, London WC2E 9LY T 020-7550 5555 W www.five.tv

GMTV *(breakfast television)*, The London Television Centre, Upper Ground, London SE1 9TT T 0870-243 4333 W www.gmtv.co.uk

INDEPENDENT TELEVISION NEWS LTD, 200 Gray's Inn Road, London WC1X 8XZ T 020-7833 3000 W www.itn.co.uk

TELETEXT LTD, Building 10, Chiswick Park, 566 Chiswick High Road London W4 5TS T 0870-731 3000 W www.teletext.com. Provides teletext services for the ITV companies and Channel 4

WELSH FOURTH CHANNEL AUTHORITY (Sianel Pedwar Cymru), Parc Ty Glas, Llanishen, Cardiff CF4 5DU T 029-2074 7444. S4C schedules Welsh language and most Channel 4 programmes.

DIRECT BROADCASTING BY SATELLITE TELEVISION

BRITISH SKY BROADCASTING LTD
6 Centaurs Business Park, Grant Way, Isleworth, Middx TW7 5QD
T 020-7705 3000 W www.sky.com

British Sky Broadcasting is a direct broadcast satellite service operating in the UK and Ireland. Launched in February 1989, it was originally a four channel service, broadcast on a satellite owned by a Luxembourg-based consortium. The failure of rival company British Satellite Broadcasting lead to a merger in 1990 and the formation of British Sky Broadcasting.

Sky Digital, launched on 1 October 1998, offers over 300 channels, pay-per-view services and interactive entertainment, including email, on-screen shopping and voting. BSkyB has 16 million viewers in 6.7 million households. BSkyB's own channels such as Sky News, Sky One and Sky Sports are available in a further 5.3 million homes receiving cable services in the UK and Ireland. BSkyB is listed on the London and New York Stock Exchanges.

RADIO

UK domestic radio services are broadcast across three wavebands: FM (or VHF), medium wave and long wave (used by BBC Radio 4). In the UK the FM waveband extends in frequency from 87.5 MHz to 108 MHz and the medium wave band extends from 531 kHz to 1602 kHz. Older radios are calibrated in wavelengths rather than frequency. To convert frequency to wavelength, divide 300,000 by the frequency in kHz. A number of radio stations are now being broadcast in both analogue and digital as well as a growing number in digital alone.

DIGITAL RADIO

DAB (Digital Audio Broadcasting) digital radio allows more services to be broadcast to a higher technical quality and provides the data facility for text and pictures. It improves the robustness of high fidelity radio services, especially compared with current FM and AM radio transmissions. It was developed in a collaborative research project under the pan-European EUREKA initiative and has been adopted as a world standard for new digital radio systems. The frequencies allocated for terrestrial digital radio in the UK are 217.5 to 230 MHz. Plans are underway for developing a framework for frequencies in the 1.5 GHz (or L-Band) range.

The Broadcasting Act 1996 provided for the licensing of digital radio services (on 'multiplexes', where a number of stations share one frequency to transmit their services). The BBC has been allocated a multiplex capable of broadcasting six to eight national stereo services; BBC digital broadcasts began in the London area in September 1995. A national digital multiplex has also been made available to the three independent national radio stations, and local and regional services (BBC and commercial) will use the remaining five multiplexes. OFCOM is responsible for awarding licences for capacity on the non-BBC multiplexes. The first national independent radio digital licence was awarded to Digital One, which began broadcasting in November 1999. The first local multiplex licence was awarded in May 1999 (to CE Digital, for Birmingham) and commenced broadcasting in May 2000.

It is necessary to possess a digital radio set in order to receive digital radio broadcasts. Several types of sets are available including portable radios, hi-fi stacks, car radios and PC cards. The latter bring digital radio to the desktop and associated data to the computer screen. The latest DAB radios include new functionality such as rewind, pause and record.

ESTIMATED AUDIENCE SHARE *as at end June 2004*

	Percentage
BBC Radio 1	8.3
BBC Radio 2	16.2
BBC Radio 3	1.1
BBC Radio 4	11.0
BBC Radio 5 Live	4.5
BBC Local/Regional	10.9
BBC World Service	0.6
All BBC	53.1
All commercial	45.0
All national commercial	10.1
All local commercial	34.9
Other	1.9

Source: RAJAR/RSL

BBC RADIO AND WORLD SERVICE

BBC RADIO

Broadcasting House, Portland Place, London W1A 1AA
T 020-7580 4468

BBC Radio broadcasts network services to the UK, Isle of Man and the Channel Islands. There is also a tier of national services in Wales, Scotland and Northern Ireland and 40 local radio stations in England and the Channel Islands. In Wales and Scotland there are also dedicated language services in Welsh and Gaelic respectively. The frequency allocated for digital BBC broadcasts is 225.648 MHz.

BBC NETWORK RADIO SERVICES

RADIO 1 (Contemporary pop music and entertainment news) – 24 hours a day. *Frequencies:* 97.6–99.8 FM, coverage 99%

RADIO 2 (Popular music, entertainment, comedy and the arts) – 24 hours a day. *Frequencies:* 88–90.2 FM, coverage 99%

RADIO 3 (Classical music, classic drama, documentaries and features) – 24 hours a day. *Frequencies:* 90.2–92.4 FM, coverage 99%

RADIO 4 (News, documentaries, drama, entertainment, and cricket on long wave in season) – 5.55 a.m.–1.00 a.m. daily, with BBC World Service overnight. *Frequencies:* 92.4–94.6 FM and 198 LW, coverage 99%

RADIO 5 LIVE (News and sport) – 24 hours a day. *Frequencies:* 693 and 909 MW

RADIO 6 (Digital only) (Contemporary and classic pop and rock music) – 24 hours a day.

RADIO 7 (Digital only) (Comedy and drama) – 7 a.m. to 1 a.m.

BRITISH ASIAN RADIO (Digital only) (news, music and sport for British Asians)

1XTRA (Digital only) (new black music) – 24 hours a day.

BBC NATIONAL RADIO SERVICES

RADIO CYMRU (Welsh-language) *Frequencies:* 92.4–94.6 FM, 95.7 FM (Llanfyllin), 96.1 FM (Llandinam), 96.8 FM and 103.5–105 FM, coverage 97%

RADIO FOYLE, *Frequencies:* 792 AM; 93.1 MW

RADIO NAN GAIDHEAL (Gaelic service) *Frequencies:* 103.5–105 FM, 990 MW in Aberdeen, coverage 90%.

RADIO SCOTLAND Frequencies: 810 MW plus two local fillers; 92.4–94.7 FM, coverage 99%. Local programmes on FM as above: Highlands; North-East; Borders; South-West (also 585 MW); Orkney; Shetland

RADIO ULSTER *Frequencies:* 1341 MW (873 MW Enniskillen), plus two local fillers; 92.4–95.4 FM, coverage 96%. Local programmes on RADIO FOYLE

RADIO WALES *Frequencies:* 882 MW plus two local fillers; 95.1 FM, 95.9 FM (Gwent), 103.9 FM (Cardiff), 95.4 FM (Wrexham), coverage 97%

BBC LOCAL RADIO STATIONS

There are 40 local stations serving England and the Channel Islands:

BERKSHIRE, PO Box 1044, Reading RG94 8FH
T 0645 311444 *Frequencies*: 94.6, 95.4, 104.1, 104.4 FM

BRISTOL, PO Box 194, Bristol BS99 7QT T 0117-974 1111
Frequencies: 94.9, 95.5, 104.6, 1548 MW

CAMBRIDGESHIRE, PO Box 96, Hills Road, Cambridge CB2 1LD T 01223-259696
Frequencies: 95.7/96.0 FM, 1026/1449 MW

CLEVELAND, PO Box 95FM, Newport Road, Middlesbrough TS1 5DG T 01642-225211
Frequencies: 95.0/95.8 FM

CORNWALL, Phoenix Wharf, Truro, Cornwall TR1 1UA
T 01872-275421 *Frequencies:* 95.2/96.0/103.9 FM, 630/657 MW

CUMBRIA, Annetwell Street, Carlisle CA3 8BB
T 01228-592444 *Frequencies:* 95.2/95.6/96.1/104.1 FM, 756/837/1458 MW

DERBY, PO Box 269, Derby DE1 3HL T 01332-361111
Frequencies: 94.2/95.3/104.5 FM, 1116 MW

DEVON, PO Box 5, Plymouth PL1 1XT
T 01752-260323 *Frequencies:* 103.4/96.0/95.8/94.8 FM, 801, 855, 990, 1458 MW

ESSEX, 198 New London Road, Chelmsford CM2 9XB
T 01245-616000 *Frequencies:* 95.3/103.3 FM, 729/765/1530 MW

GLOUCESTERSHIRE, London Road, Gloucester GL1 1SW
T 01452-308585 *Frequencies:* 95/95.8/104.7 FM

GMR (GREATER MANCHESTER RADIO), PO Box 951, Oxford Road, Manchester M60 1SD
T 0161-200 2000 *Frequencies:* 95.1/104.6 FM

GUERNSEY, Commerce House, Les Banques, St Peter Port, Guernsey GY1 2HS T 01481-728977
Frequencies: 1116 AM, 93.2 FM

HEREFORD AND WORCESTER, Hylton Road, Worcester WR2 5WW T 01905-748485
Frequencies: 94.7/104.0/104.6 FM, 818/738 MW

HUMBERSIDE, 9 Chapel Street, Hull HU1 3NU
T 01482-323232 *Frequencies:* 95.9 FM, 1485 MW

JERSEY, 18 Parade Road, St Helier, Jersey JE2 3PL
T 01534-870000 *Frequencies:* 1026 AM, 88.8 FM

KENT, Sun Pier, Chatham, Kent ME4 4EZ
T 01634-830505 *Frequencies:* 96.7/97.6/104.2 FM, 774/1602 MW

LANCASHIRE, 26 Darwen Street, Blackburn BB2 2EA
T 01254-262411 *Frequencies:* 95.5/103.9/104.5 FM, 855/1557 MW

LEEDS, Broadcasting House, Woodhouse Lane, Leeds LS2 9PN
T 0113-244 2131 *Frequencies:* 774 AM, 92.4/95.3/103.9 FM, 774 MW

LEICESTER/ASIAN NETWORK, Epic House, Charles Street, Leicester LE1 3SH T 0116-251 6688
Frequency: 104.9 FM

LINCOLNSHIRE, PO Box 219, Newport, Lincoln LN1 3XY
T 01522-511411 *Frequencies:* 94.9 FM, 1368 MW

LONDON, BBC London Live, 35C Marylebone High Street, London W1A 4LG
T 020-7224 2424 *Frequency:* 94.9 FM

MERSEYSIDE, 55 Paradise Street, Liverpool L1 3BP
T 0151-708 5500 *Frequency:* 95.8 FM, 1485 MW
NEWCASTLE, Broadcasting Centre, Barrack Road, Newcastle upon Tyne NE99 1RN T 0191-232 4141
Frequencies: 95.4/96.0/103.7/104.4 FM, 206 MW
NORFOLK, Norfolk Tower, Surrey Street, Norwich NR1 3PA
T 01603-617411 *Frequencies:* 95.1/104.4 FM, 855/873 MW
NORTHAMPTON, Broadcasting House, Abington Street, Northampton NN1 2BH
T 01604-239100 *Frequencies:* 103.6/104.2 FM, 1107 MW
NOTTINGHAM, York House, Mansfield Road, Nottingham NG1 3JB T 0115-955 0500
Frequencies: 95.5/103.8 FM, 1584 MW
OXFORD, BBC Radio Oxford, 269 Banbury Road, Oxford OX2 7DW T 01865-311444
Frequency: 95.2 FM
SHEFFIELD, Ashdell Grove, 60 Westbourne Road, Sheffield S10 2QU T 0114-268 6185
Frequencies: 88.6/94.7/104.1 FM
SHROPSHIRE, 2–4 Boscobel Drive, Shrewsbury SY1 3TT
T 01743-248484
Frequencies: 95.0/96.0 FM, 1584 MW
SOLENT, Broadcasting House, Havelock Road, Southampton SO14 7PW T 023-8063 1311.
Frequencies: 96.1/ FM, 999 MW
SOMERSET SOUND, Broadcasting House, Park Street, Taunton, Somerset TA1 4DA T 01823-348920
Frequency: 1566 AM
SOUTHERN COUNTIES, Broadcasting Centre, Guildford GU2 5AP T 01483-306306
Frequencies: 95–95.3/104–104.8 FM
STOKE, Cheapside, Hanley, Stoke-on-Trent ST1 1JJ
T 01782-208080 *Frequencies:* 94.6/104.1 FM, 1503 MW
SUFFOLK, Broadcasting House, St Matthew's Street, Ipswich IP1 3EP T 01473-250000
Frequencies: 95.5/103.9/104.6 FM
SWINDON, PO Box 1234, Trowbridge, Swindon & Salisbury.
T 01793-513626 *Frequencies:* 103.6 FM
THREE COUNTIES RADIO, PO Box 3CR, Luton, Beds LU1 5XL T 01582-637400
Frequencies: 95.5/103.8/104.5 FM, 630/1161 MW
WILTSHIRE SOUND, Broadcasting House, Prospect Place, Swindon SN1 3RW T 01793-513626.
Frequencies: 103.5/103.6/104.3/104.9 FM, 1332/1368
WM (COVENTRY AND WARWICKSHIRE), Holt Court, 1 Greyfriars Road, Coventry CV1 2WR
T 024-7623 1231 *Frequencies:* 94.8/103.7/104.0 FM
WM (WEST MIDLANDS), Pebble Mill Road, Birmingham B5 7SD T 0121-432 8484
Frequency: 95.6 FM.
YORK, 20 Bootham Row, York YO3 7BR
T 01904-641351 *Frequencies:* 95.5/103.7/104.3 FM, 666/1260 MW

BBC WORLD SERVICE
Bush House, Strand, London WC2B 4PH
T 020-7240 3456

The BBC World Service broadcasts over 1,280 hours of programmes a week in 43 languages including English. It has a weekly audience of 150 million globally, of whom 42 million listen to English language services. Many services are also available by satellite and on the Internet. *UK frequencies:* 648 MW in southern England and on BBC Radio 4 at night.

The World Service is organised into five world regions, each responsible for programmes in English as well as regional languages.

AFRICA AND THE MIDDLE EAST, Arabic, French, Hausa, Kinyarwanda/Kirundi, Portuguese, Somali and Swahili; English programmes including *Network Africa* and *Focus on Africa*
ASIA AND THE PACIFIC, Bengali, Burmese, Cantonese, Hindi, Indonesian, Mandarin, Nepali, Sinhala, Tamil, Thai, Urdu and Vietnamese; English programmes including *East Asia Today*
EUROPE, Albanian, Bulgarian, Croatian, Czech, Greek, Hungarian, Macedonian, Polish, Romanian, Serbian, Slovak and Slovene; English programmes including *The World Today*
FORMER SOVIET UNION AND SOUTH-WEST ASIA, Azeri, Kazakh, Kyrgyz, Pashto, Persian, Russian, Turkish, Ukrainian and Uzbek
THE AMERICAS, Portuguese for Brazil, Spanish; English programmes including *The World* (a global news magazine for American listeners), *Caribbean Report* and *Calling the Falklands*
BBC ENGLISH teaches English world-wide through radio, television and a wide range of published and online courses
BBC AUDIENCE AND MARKET RESEARCH carries out audience research and sells printed publications and data
BBC MONITORING supplies news and information from the output of overseas radio and television stations and news agency sources
BBC WORLD SERVICE TRAINING runs journalism, management and skills training courses for overseas broadcasters
BBC WORLD SERVICE TRUST is a registered charity established in 1999 by BBC World Service. It promotes development through the innovative use of the media in the developing world. The trust presently works in 23 countries worldwide, tackling health, education and good governance.

INDEPENDENT RADIO

The Radio Authority (RA) began advertising new licences for the development of independent radio in January 1991. It awarded national and local radio licences (including regional licences), satellite and cable services licences, and long-term restricted service licences for stations serving non-commercial establishments such as hospitals and universities. The first national commercial digital multiplex licence was awarded in October 1998, a number of local digital multiplex licences followed. OFCOM is now responsible for licensing administration. As at August 2004, the impact of the changes in the regulation of commercial radio remained to be felt, however, OFCOM plans to take a different approach from the RA and there have been encouraging signs that a cost effective, transparent methodology will soon be implemented.

The Commercial Radio Companies Association is the trade body for commercial radio companies in the United Kingdom. It is a voluntary, non profit making body, funded by the subscriptions of its member radio companies, who share the cost of CRCA in proportion to their shares of the industry's broadcasting revenue, and was formed by the first radio companies when Independent Radio began in 1973.

COMMERCIAL RADIO COMPANIES ASSOCIATION
77 Shaftesbury Avenue, London W1D 5DU T 020-7306 2603
E info@crca.co.uk W www.crca.co.uk
Chief Executive, P. Brown

INDEPENDENT NATIONAL RADIO STATIONS

CLASSIC FM, 7 Swallow Place, London W1B 2AG T 020-7343 9000 *Frequencies:* 99.9/101.9 FM

TALK SPORT, 18 Hatfields, London SE1 8DJ T 020-7959 7800 24 hours a day. *Frequencies:* 1053/1089 AM

VIRGIN 1215, 1 Golden Square, London W1F 9DJ T 020-7434 1215 *Frequencies:* 1215/1197/1233/1242/1260 AM

INDEPENDENT LOCAL RADIO STATIONS

England

2-TEN FM, PO Box 2020, Reading RG31 7FG T 0118-945 4400 *Frequencies:* 97.0/102.9/103.4 FM

2BR, Imex Lomeshaye Business Village, Nelson, Lancs BB9 7DR T 01282-690000 *Frequency:* 99.8 FM

2CR FM, 5–7 Southcote Road, Bournemouth BH1 3LR T 01202-259259 *Frequency:* 102.3 FM

95.8 CAPITAL FM, 30 Leicester Square, London WC2H 7LA T 020-7766 6000 *Frequency:* 95.8 FM

96 TRENT FM, 29–31 Castle Gate, Nottingham NG1 7AP T 0115-952 7000 *Frequencies:* 96.2/96.5 FM

96.3 RADIO AIRE, 51 Burley Road, Leeds LS3 1LR T 0113-283 5500 *Frequency:* 96.3 FM

96.4 FM BRMB, Nine Brindleyplace, 4 Oozells Square, Birmingham B1 2DJ T 0121-245 5000 *Frequency:* 96.4 FM

96.4 THE EAGLE, Dolphin House, North Street, Guildford, Surrey GU1 4AA T 01483-300964 *Frequency:* 96.4 FM

96.9 CHILTERN FM, 55 Goldington Road, Bedford MK40 3LT T 01234-325137 *Frequency:* 96.9 FM

96.9 VIKING FM, The Boathouse, Commercial Road, Hull, East Yorkshire HU1 2SG T 01482-325141 *Frequency:* 96.9 FM

97.2 STRAY FM, The Hamlet, Hornbeam Park Avenue, Harrogate HG2 8RE T 01423-522972 *Frequency:* 97.2 FM

97.4 ROCK FM, PO Box 974, St. Paul's Square, Preston, Lancashire PR1 1YE T 01772-477700 *Frequency:* 97.4 FM

97.4 VALE FM, Longmead Studios, Shaftesbury, Dorset SP7 8QQ T 01747-855711 *Frequency:* 97.4 FM

100–102 CENTURY FM, Century House, PO Box 100, Gateshead NE8 2YY T 0191-477 6666 *Frequencies:* 96.2/96.4/100.7/101.8 FM

100.7 HEART FM, 1 The Square, 11 Broad Street, Birmingham B15 1AS T 0121-695 0000 *Frequency:* 100.7 FM

102.4 WISH FM, Orrell Lodge, Orrell Road, Orrell, Wigan WN5 8HJ T 01942-761024 *Frequency:* 102.4 FM

102.7 HEREWARD FM, PO Box 225, Queensgate Centre, Peterborough PE1 1XJ T 01733-460600 *Frequency:* 102.7 FM

103.2 POWER FM, Radio House, Whittle Avenue, Segensworth West, Fareham, Hants PO15 5SH T 01489-589911 *Frequency:* 103.2 FM

106.9 SILK FM, Radio House, Bridge Street, Macclesfield, Cheshire SK11 6DJ T 01625-268000 *Frequency:* 106.9 FM

107 OAK FM, 7 Waldron Court, Prince William Road, Loughborough, Leics LE11 5GD T 01509-211711 *Frequency:* 107.0 FM

107.2 WIRE FM, Warrington Business Park, Long Lane, Warrington WA2 8TX T 01925-445545 *Frequency:* 107.2 FM

107.4 THE QUAY, Flagship Studios, PO Box 1074, Portsmouth PO2 8YG T 023 9236 4141 *Frequency:* 107.4 FM

107.4 TELFORD FM, c/o The Shropshire Star, Waterloo Road, Ketley TF1 5HU T 01952-280011 *Frequency:* 107.4 FM

107.5 3TR FM, Riverside Studios, Boreham Mill, Bishopstrow, Warminster, Wiltshire BA12 9HQ T 01985-211111 *Frequency:* 107.5

107.2 WIN FM, PO Box 1072, The Brooks, Winchester, Hampshire SO23 8FT T 01962-841071 *Frequency:* 107.2 FM

107.6 KESTREL FM, 2nd Floor, Paddington House, Festival Place, Basingstoke, Hampshire RG21 7LJ T 01256-694 000 *Frequency:* 107.6 FM

107.8 ARROW FM, Priory Meadow Centre, Hastings, E. Sussex TN34 1PJ T 01424-461177 *Frequency:* 107.8 FM

ALPHA 103.2, Radio House, 11 Woodland Road, Darlington DL3 7BJ T 01325-255552 *Frequency:* 103.2 FM

ASIAN SOUND RADIO, Globe House, Southall Street, Manchester M3 1LG T 0161-288 1000 *Frequencies:* 1377/963 AM

BATH FM, Station House, Ashley Avenue, Lower Weston, Bath BA1 3DS T 01225-471571 *Frequency:* 107.9 FM

THE BAY, PO Box 969, St George's Quay, Lancaster LA1 3LD T 01524-848747 *Frequencies:* 96.9/102.3/103.2 FM

BEACON FM, 267 Tettenhall Road, Wolverhampton WV6 0DE T 01902-461300 *Frequencies:* 97.2 FM (Wolverhampton and Black Country); 103.1 FM (Shrewsbury and Telford)

THE BEACH, PO Box 103.4, Lowestoft, Suffolk NR32 2TL T 0845-345 1035 *Frequency:* 103.4 FM

THE BEAR 102 FM, The Guard House Studios Banbury Road, Stratford upon Avon, Warwickshire CV37 7HX T 01789-262636 *Frequency:* 102 FM

BRIDGWATER'S 107.4 BCR FM, Royal Clarence House, York Buildings, High Street, Bridgwater, Somerset TA6 3AT T 01278-727701 *Frequency:* 107.4 FM

BRIGHT 106.4, 11A The Market Place Shopping Centre, Burgess Hill, West Sussex RH15 9NP T 01444-248127 *Frequency:* 106.4 FM

BROADLAND 102, St George's Plain, 47–49 Colegate, Norwich NR3 1DB T 01603-630621 *Frequency:* 102.4 FM

CAPITAL GOLD (1152), Nine Brindleyplace, 4 Oozells Square, Birmingham B1 2DJ T 0121-245 5000 *Frequency:* 1152 AM

CAPITAL GOLD (1170 and 1557), Radio House, Whittle Avenue, Segensworth West, Farnham, Hants PO15 5SH T 01489-589911 *Frequencies:* 1170/1557 AM

CAPITAL GOLD (1242 and 603), Radio House, John Wilson Business Park, Whitstable, Kent CT5 3QX T 01227-772004 *Frequencies:* 603 AM (East Kent); 1242 AM (Maidstone and Medway)

CAPITAL GOLD (1323 and 945), Radio House, PO Box 2000, Brighton BN41 2SS T 01273-430111 *Frequencies:* 945/1323 AM

CAPITAL 1458 AM, Laser House, Waterfront Quays, Manchester M5 2XW T 0161-400 0105 *Frequency:* 1458 AM

CAPITAL GOLD (1548), 30 Leicester Square, London WC2H 7LA T 020-7766 6000 *Frequency:* 1548 AM

CENTRE FM, 5–6 Aldergate, Tamworth, Staffs B79 7DJ T 01827-318000 *Frequencies:* 101.6/102.4 FM

CENTURY (106), City Link, Nottingham NG2 4NG T 0115-910 6100 *Frequency:* 106 FM

CFM, PO Box 964, Carlisle, Cumbria CA1 3NG T 01228-818964 *Frequencies:* 96.4 FM (Penrith); 102.5 FM (Carlisle); 102.2 FM (Workington); 103.4 FM (Whitehaven)

CHANNEL 103 FM, 6 Tunnell Street, St Helier, Jersey JE2 4LU T 01534-888103 *Frequency:* 103.7 FM

CHILTERN FM (97.6), Chiltern Road, Dunstable, Beds LU6 1HQ T 01582-676200 *Frequency:* 97.6 FM

CHOICE FM, 291–299 Borough High Street, London SE1 1JG T 020-7378 3969 *Frequency:* 96.9 FM

CHOICE (107.1), 291–299 Borough High Street, London SE1 1JG T 020-7378 3969 *Frequency:* 107.1 FM

CLASSIC GOLD 666/954, Hawthorn House, Exeter Business Park, Exeter EX1 3QS T 01392-444444 *Frequencies:* 666/954 AM

CLASSIC GOLD 774, Bridge Studios, Eastgate Centre, Gloucester GL1 1SS T 01452-313200 *Frequency:* 774 AM

CLASSIC GOLD 792/828, Chiltern Road, Dunstable, Beds LU6 1HQ T 01582-676200 *Frequencies:* 792 AM (Bedford); 828 AM (Luton)

CLASSIC GOLD 828, 5–7 Southcote Road, Bournemouth, Dorset BH1 3LR T 01202-259259 *Frequency:* 828 AM

CLASSIC GOLD 936/1161 AM, Lime Kiln Studio, Wootton Bassett, Swindon SN4 7EX T 01793-842600 *Frequencies:* 936 AM (West Wilts); 1161 AM (Swindon)

CLASSIC GOLD 1152 AM, Earl's Acre, Plymouth PL3 4HX T 01752 275600 *Frequency:* 1152 AM

CLASSIC GOLD 1260, PO Box 2000, One Passage Street, Bristol BS99 7SN T 0117-984 3200 *Frequency:* 1260 AM

CLASSIC GOLD 1332 AM, PO Box 225, Queensgate Centre, Peterborough PE1 1XJ T 01733-460460 *Frequency:* 1332 AM

CLASSIC GOLD 1359, Hertford Place, Coventry CV1 3TT T 024-7686 8200 *Frequency:* 1359 AM

CLASSIC GOLD 1431/1485, The Chase, Calcot, Reading, Berks RG3 7FG T 0118-945 4400 *Frequencies:* 1431/1485 AM

CLASSIC GOLD 1521, 9 The Stanley Centre, Kelvin Way, Crawley, West Sussex RH10 9SE T 01293-519161 *Frequency:* 1521 AM

CLASSIC GOLD 1557, 19–21 St Edmunds Road, Northampton NN1 5DY T 01604-795600 *Frequency:* 1557 AM

CLASSIC GOLD AMBER (NORFOLK), Colegate, Norwich NR3 1DB T 01603-630621 *Frequency:* 1152 AM

CLASSIC GOLD AMBER (SUFFOLK), Alpha Business Park, 6–12 White House Road, Ipswich IP1 5LT T 01473-461000 *Frequency:* 1170 AM (Ipswich); 1251 AM (Bury St Edmunds)

CLASSIC GOLD GEM, 29–31 Castle Gate, Nottingham NG1 7AP T 0115-952 7000 *Frequencies:* 945/999 AM

CLASSIC GOLD BREEZE, Radio House, Clifftown Road, Southend-on-Sea Essex SS1 1SX T 01702-333711 *Frequencies:* 1359/1431 AM

CLASSIC GOLD WABC, 267 Tettenhall Road, Wolverhampton WV6 0DQ T 01902-461300 *Frequencies:* 990 AM (Wolverhampton); 1017 AM (Shrewsbury and Telford)

CLASSIC HITS 954/1530, PO Box 262, Worcester, WR6 5ZE, T 01905- 740600 *Frequencies:* 954 AM (Hereford); 1530 AM (Worcester)

CLUB ASIA, Asia House, 227–247 Gascoigne Road, Barking, Essex IG11 7LN T 020 8594 6662 *Frequencies:* 936/972 AM

COMPASS FM, 26 Wellowgate, Grimsby DN32 0RA T 01472-346666 *Frequency:* 96.4 FM

CONNECT FM, Unit 1, Centre 2000, Kettering, Northants, NN16 8PU T 01536-412413 *Frequency:* 97.2 FM/107.4 FM

COUNTY SOUND RADIO 1566 MW, Dolphin House, North Street, Guildford GU1 4AA T 01483-300964 *Frequency:* 1566 MW

DEARNE FM, Unit 7, Networkcentre, Zenith Park, Whaley Road, Barnsley S75 1HT T 01226-321733 *Frequency:* to be confirmed

DEE 106.3, 2 Chantry Court, Chester CH1 4QN T 01244-391000 *Frequency:* 106.3

DELTA FM 97.1, 65 Weyhill, Haslemere, Surrey GU27 1HN T 01428-651971 *Frequency:* 97.1/101.6/102 FM

DERBY'S RAM FM, 35–36 Irongate, Derby DE1 3GA T 01332 205599 *Frequency:* 102.8 FM

DREAM FM, Northgate House, St Peter's Street, Colchester, CO1 1HT T 01206-764466 *Frequency:* 100.2 FM

DREAM 107.7, Cater House, High Street, Chelmsford CM1 1AL T 01245-259400 *Frequency:* 107.7 FM

DUNE FM, The Power Station, Victoria Way, Southport PR8 1RR T 01704-502500 *Frequency:* 107.9 FM

EASY RADIO LONDON (1035), 43–51 Wembley Hill Road, Wembley, Middlesex HA9 8AU T 020-8795 1035 *Frequency:* 1035 AM

ENERGY FM, 100 Market Street, Douglas, Isle of Man IM1 2PH T 01624-611936 *Frequencies:* 91.2 (Laxey)/93.4 (North Isle of Man)/98.4 (Ramsey)/98.6 Douglas & South/ 105.2 (North East Coast)

ESSEX FM, Radio House, Clifftown Road, Southend-on-Sea, Essex SS1 1SX T 01702-323206 *Frequencies:* 96.3 FM (Southend); 97.5 FM (Southend Centre); 102.6 FM (Chelmsford)

FM 102 – THE BEAR, The Guard House Studios, Banbury Road, Stratford-upon-Avon, Warks CV37 7HX T 01789-262636 *Frequency:* 102.0 FM

FM 103 HORIZON, The Broadcast Centre, 14 Vincent Avenue, Crownhill, Milton Keynes MK8 0AB T 01908-269111 *Frequency:* 103.3 FM

FM 107.6 THE FIRE, Quadrant Studios, Old Christchurch Road, Bournemouth BH1 2AD T 01202-318100 *Frequency:* 107.6 FM

FEN RADIO 107.55 Church Mews, Wisbech, Cambridgeshire PE13 1HL T 01945-467107 *Frequencies:* 107.1/107.5 FM

FOSSEWAY RADIO, Suite 1, 1 Castle Street, Hinckley, Leics LE10 1DA T 01455-614151 *Frequency:* 107.9 FM

FOX FM, Brush House, Pony Road, Oxford OX4 2XR T 01865-871000 *Frequencies:* 102.6/97.4 FM

FRESH RADIO, Firth Mill, Skipton, NorthYorkshire, BD23 2PT T 01756-799991 *Frequencies:* 936 MW (Hawes); 1413 MW (Skipton)

FUSION 107.3 FM, Astra House, Arklow Road, London SE14 6EB T 020-8691 9202 *Frequency:* 107.3 FM

GALAXY 102, 5th Floor, The Triangle, Hanging Ditch, Manchester M4 3TR T 0161-279 0300 *Frequency:* 102.0 FM

GALAXY 102.2, 1 The Square, 111 Broad Street, Birmingham B15 1AS T 0121-695 0000 *Frequency:* 102.2 FM

GALAXY 105, Joseph's Well, Westgate, Leeds LS3 1AB T 0113-213 0105 *Frequencies:* 105.1 FM (Leeds); 105.6 FM (Bradford and Sheffield); 105.8 FM (Hull)

GALAXY 105–106, Kingfisher Way, Silverlink Business Park, Tyne and Wear NE28 9NX T 0191-206 8000 *Frequencies:* 105.3/105.6/106.4 FM

GEMINI FM, Hawthorn House, Exeter Business Park, Exeter EX1 3QS T 01392-444444 *Frequencies:* 96.4/97.0/103.0 FM

GWR FM (BRISTOL AND BATH), PO Box 2000, One Passage Street, Bristol BS99 7SN T 0117-984 3200 *Frequencies:* 96.3 FM (Bristol); 103.0 FM (Bath)

GWR FM (SWINDON AND WEST WILTSHIRE), PO Box 2000, Swindon SN4 7EX T 01793-842600 *Frequencies:* 97.2 FM (Swindon); 102.2 FM (West Wilts); 96.5 FM (Marlborough)

HALLAM FM, Radio House, 900 Herries Road, Sheffield S6 1RH T 0114-209 1000 *Frequencies:* 97.4 FM (Sheffield); 102.9 FM (Barnsley); 103.4 FM (Doncaster)

HEART 106.2, The Chrysalis Building, Bramley Road, London W10 6SP T 020-7468 1062 *Frequency:* 106.2 FM

HEART FM, *see* 100.7 Heart FM

HERTBEAT 106.9 FM, The Pump House, Knebworth Park, Hertfordshire SG3 6HQ T 01438-810900 *Frequencies:* 106.7/106.9 FM

HIGH PEAK RADIO, The Studios, Smithbrook Close, Chapel-en-le-Frith, High Park, Derbyshire SK23 0QD T 01298-813144 *Frequencies:* 106.4/103.3

HOME 107.9, The Old Stableblock, Lockwood Park, Huddersfield HD1 3UR T 01484-321107 *Frequency:* 107.9 FM

IMAGINE FM, Regent House, Heaton Lane, Stockport

SK4 1BX T 0161-609 1400
Frequencies: 96.4 FM (Cheshire); 104.9 FM (Stockport)

INVICTA FM, Radio House, John Wilson Business Park, Whitstable, Kent CT5 3QX T 01227-772004
Frequencies: 103.1 FM (Maidstone and Medway); 102.8 FM (Canterbury); 95.9 FM (Thanet); 97.0 FM (Dover); 96.1 FM (Ashford)

ISLAND FM, 12 Westerbrook, St Sampsons, Guernsey GY2 4QQ T 01481-242000 *Frequencies:* 93.7 FM (Alderney); 104.7 FM (Guernsey)

ISLE OF WIGHT RADIO, Dodnor Park, Newport, Isle of Wight PO30 5XE T 01983-822557
Frequencies: 102.0/107.0 FM

IVEL FM, The Studios, Middle Street, Yeovil, Somerset BA20 1DJ T 01935-848488
Frequency: to be confirmed

JAZZ FM 102.2, 26–27 Castlereagh Street, London W1H 5DL T 020-7706 4100 *Frequency:* 102.2 FM

JUICE 107.2, 170 North Street, Brighton BN1 1EA T 01273-386107 *Frequency:* 107.2 FM

JUICE 107.6, 27 Fleet Street, Liverpool L1 4AR T 0151-707 3107 *Frequency:* 107.6 FM

KCR 106.7, The Studios, Cables Retail Park, Prescot, Merseyside L34 5SW T 0151-290 1501
Frequency: 106.7 FM

KL.FM 96.7, 18 Blackfriars Street, King's Lynn, Norfolk PE30 1NN T 01553-772777 *Frequency:* 96.7 FM

KEY 103, Castle Quay, Castlefield, Manchester M15 4PR T 0161-288 5000 *Frequency:* 103 FM

KICK FM, The Studios, 42 Bone Lane, Newbury, Berks RG14 5SD T 01635-841600 *Frequencies:* 105.6/107.4 FM

KISS 100, Mappin House, 4 Winsley Street, London W1W 8HF T 020-79758100 *Frequency:* 100.0 FM

KIX 96, Watch Close, Spon Street, Coventry CV1 3LN T 024-7652 5656 *Frequency:* 96.2 FM

KM-FM FOR CANTERBURY, 9 St. Georges Place, Canterbury, Kent CT1 1UU T 01227-475950
Frequency: 106 FM

KM-FM FOR FOLKSTONE & DOVER, 93–95 Sandgate Road, Folkstone, Kent CT20 2BQ T 01303-220303
Frequencies: 96.4/106.8 FM

KM-FM MEDWAY, Medway House, Ginsbury Close, Sir Thomas Longley Road, Medway City Estate, Strood, Rochester, Kent ME2 4DU T 01634-711079
Frequencies: 107.9/100.4

KM-FM THANET, Imperial House, 2–14 High Street, Margate, Kent CT9 1DH T 01843-220222 *Frequency:* 107.2

KM-FM WEST KENT, 1 East Street, Tonbridge, Kent, TN9 1AR T 01732-369200 *Frequencies:* 96.2/101.6 FM

LAKELAND RADIO, Lakeland Food Park, Plumgarths, Crook Road, Kendal, Cumbria LA8 8QJ T 01539-737380
Frequencies: 100.1/100.8

LANTERN FM, 2b Lauder Lane, Roundswell Business Park, Barnstaple EX31 3TA T 01271-340340
Frequency: 96.2 FM

LBC 97.3 FM, The Chrysalis Building,13 Bramley Road, London W10 6SP T 020-7314 7300 *Frequency:* 97.3 FM

LBC NEWS 1152 AM, The Chrysalis Building,13 Bramley Road, London W10 6SP T 020-7221 2213 *Frequency:* 1152 AM

LEICESTER SOUND, 6 Dominus Way, Meridian Business Park, Leicester LE19 1RP T 0116-256 1300
Frequency: 105.4 FM

LINCS FM, Witham Park, Waterside South, Lincoln LN5 7JN T 01522-549900 *Frequencies:* 102.2/96.7 FM (Grantham Relay)/97.6 FM (Scunthorpe Relay)

LITE FM, 2nd Floor, 5 Church Street, Peterborough PE1 1XB T 01733-898106 *Frequency:* 106.8 FM

LONDON GREEK RADIO, LGR House, 437 High Road, London N12 0AP T 020-8349 6950 *Frequency:* 103.3 FM

LONDON TURKISH RADIO, 185B High Road, Wood Green, London N22 6BA T 020-8881 0606 *Frequency:* 1584 AM

MAGIC 105.4 FM, Mappin House, 4 Winsley Street, London W1W 8HF T 020-7955 1054 *Frequency:* 105.4 FM

MAGIC 828, 51 Burley Road, Leeds LS3 1LR T 0113-283 5500
Frequency: 828 AM

MAGIC 999, St Paul's Square, Preston, Lancs, PR1 1YE T 01772-477700 *Frequency:* 999 AM

MAGIC 1152 AM, Newcastle upon Tyne NE99 1BB T 0191-420 3040 *Frequency:* 1152 AM

MAGIC 1161 AM, Commercial Road, Hull HU1 2SG T 01482-325141 *Frequency:* 1161 AM

MAGIC 1170, Radio House, Yales Crescent, Thornaby, Stockton-on-Tees, Cleveland TS17 6AA T 01642-888222
Frequency: 1170 AM

MAGIC 1548, St John's Beacon, 1 Houghton Street, Liverpool L1 1RL T 0151-472 6800 *Frequency:* 1548 AM

MAGIC AM, Radio House, 900 Herries Road, Sheffield S6 1RH T 0114-209 1000 *Frequencies:* 990/1305/1548 AM

MANCHESTER'S MAGIC (1152), Castle Quay, Castlefield, Manchester M1 4AW T 0161-288 5000
Frequency: 1152 AM

MANSFIELD 103.2, The Media Suite, Brunts Business Centre, Samuel Brunts Way, Mansfield, Notts NG18 2AH T 01623-646666 *Frequency:* 103.2 FM

MANX RADIO, PO Box 1368, Broadcasting House, Douglas, Isle of Man, IM 99 1SW T 01624-682600
Frequencies: 103.7/89.0/97.2 FM, 1368 AM

MERCIA FM, Hertford Place, Coventry CV1 3TT T 024-7686 8200 *Frequencies:* 97.0/102.9 FM

MERCURY FM, The Stanley Centre, Kelvin Way, Crawley, W. Sussex RH10 9SE T 01293-519161
Frequencies: 97.5/102.7 FM

METRO RADIO, Newcastle upon Tyne NE99 1BB T 0191-420 0971 *Frequencies:* 97.1 FM (Northumberland, Tyne and Wear, Durham); 103.0 FM (Tyne Valley); 102.6 FM (Alnwick); 103.2 FM (Hexham)

MINSTER FM, PO Box 123, Dunnington, York YO19 5ZX T 01904-488888
Frequencies: 104.7 FM (York); 102.3 FM (Thirsk)

MIX 96, Friars Square Studios, 11 Bourbon Street, Aylesbury, Bucks HP20 2PZ T 01296-399396 *Frequency:* 96.2 FM

MIX 107, 11 Duke Street, High Wycombe, Buckinghamshire HP13 6EE T 01494-446611 *Frequencies:* 107.4/107.7 FM

NORTHANTS 96, 19–21 St Edmunds Road, Northampton NN1 5DY T 01604-795600 *Frequency:* 96.6 FM

NORTH NORFOLK RADIO, The Studio, Breck Farm, Stody, Norfolk NR24 2ER T 011263 860808
Frequency: to be confirmed

OCEAN FM, Radio House, Whittle Avenue, Segensworth West, Fareham, Hants PO15 5SH T 01489-589911
Frequencies: 96.7/97.5 FM

ORCHARD FM, Haygrove House, Taunton, Somerset TA3 7BT T 01823-338448 *Frequencies:* 96.5 FM (Taunton); 97.1 FM (Yeovil); 102.6 FM (Somerset)

PASSION FM 107.9, 270 Woodstock Road, Oxford OX2 7NW T 01865-351980 *Frequency:* 107.9

PEAK 107 FM, Radio House, Foxwood Road, Chesterfield, Derbys S41 9RF T 01246-269107 *Frequencies:* 107.4 FM (Chesterfield and NE Derbyshire); 102.0 FM (Matlock and Bakewell)

PIRATE FM 102, Carn Brea Studios, Wilson Way, Redruth, Cornwall TR15 3XX T 01209-314400 *Frequencies:* 102.2 FM (East Cornwall and West Devon); 102.8 FM (West Cornwall and Isles of Scilly)

FM PLYMOUTH SOUND, Earl's Acre, Plymouth PL3 4HX T 01752-275600 *Frequencies:* 96.6/97.0 FM

PREMIER CHRISTIAN RADIO, 22 Chapter Street, London SW1P 4NP T 020-7316 1300 *Frequencies:* 1305/1332/1413 AM

THE PULSE, Pennine House, Forster Square, Bradford BD1 5NE T 01274-203040 *Frequencies:* 97.5 FM (Bradford); 102.5 FM (Huddersfield and Halifax)

PULSE CLASSIC GOLD (1278 & 1530 AM), Forster Square, Bradford, West Yorkshire BD1 5NE T 01274-203040 *Frequencies:* 1278 & 1530 AM

Q103 FM, Enterprise House, The Vision Park, Chivers Way, Histon, Cambridge CB4 9WW T 01223-235255 *Frequencies:* 103.0 FM (Cambridge); 97.4 FM (Newmarket)

QUAY WEST RADIO, Harbour Studios, The Esplanade, Watchet, Somerset TA23 0AJ T 01984-634900 *Frequency:* 102.4 FM

RADIO CITY 96.7, St John's Beacon, 1 Houghton Street, Liverpool L1 1RL T 0151-472 6800 *Frequency:* 96.7 FM

READING 107 FM, Radio House, Madejski Stadium, Reading, Berkshire RG2 0FN T 0118-986 2555 *Frequency:* 107 FM

REVOLUTION, Sarah Moor Studios, Henshaw Street, Oldham OL1 1JF T 0161-621 6500 *Frequency:* 96.2 FM

RIDINGS FM, 2 Thornes Office Park, Monckton Road, Wakefield WF2 7AN T 01924-367177 *Frequency:* 106.8 FM

RUGBY FM, Dunsmore Business Centre, Spring Street, Rugby, Warwickshire CV21 3HH T 01788-541100 *Frequency:* 107.1 FM

RUTLAND RADIO, 40 Melton Road, Oakham, Rutland LE15 6AY T 01572-757868 *Frequencies:* 107.2 FM (Rutland); 97.4 FM (Stamford)

SABRAS RADIO, Radio House, 63 Melton Road, Leicester LE4 6PN T 0116-261 0666 *Frequency:* 1260 AM

SAGA 105.7 FM, 3rd floor, Crown House, Beaufort Court, 123 Hagley Road, Edgbaston, Birmingham B16 8LD T 0121-452 1057 *Frequency:* 105.7 FM

SAGA 106.6 FM, Saga Radio House, Unit 2, Alder Court, Rennie Hogg Road, Riverside Retail Park, Nottingham NG2 1RX T 0115-986 1066 *Frequency:* 106.6 FM

THE SAINT, Saints Radio Ltd., The Friends Provident, St. Mary's Stadium, Britannia Road, Southampton SO14 5FP T 023-8033 0300 *Frequency:* 107.8 FM

SEVERN SOUND FM, Bridge Studios, Eastgate Centre, Gloucester GL1 1SS T 01452-313200 *Frequencies:* 103.0/102.4 FM

SGR COLCHESTER, Abbeygate Two, 9 Whitewell Road, Colchester CO2 7DE T 01206-575859 *Frequency:* 96.1 FM

SGR-FM, Radio House, Alpha Business Park, 6–12 White House Road, Ipswich IP1 5LT T 01473-461000 *Frequencies:* 97.1 FM (Ipswich); 96.4 FM (Bury St Edmunds)

SIGNAL 1, Stoke Road, Stoke-on-Trent ST4 2SR T 01782-441300 *Frequencies:* 96.9/102.6 FM

SIGNAL 2, Stoke Road, Stoke-on-Trent ST4 2SR T 01782-441300 *Frequency:* 1170 AM

SMOOTH FM 100.48 Exchange Quay, Manchester M5 3EJ T 0845-050 1004 *Frequency:* 100.4 FM

SOUTH CITY FM, City Studios, Marsh Lane, Southampton, SO14 3ST T 023-8022 0020 *Frequency:* 107.8 FM

SOUTHERN FM, Radio House, PO Box 2000, Brighton BN41 2SS T 01273-430111 *Frequencies:* 102.0 FM (Hastings); 102.4 FM (Eastbourne); 96.9 FM (Newhaven); 103.5 FM (Brighton)

SOUTH HAMS RADIO, Unit 1G, South Hams Business Park, Churchstow, Knightsbridge, Devon TQ7 3QH T 01548-854595 *Frequency:* 100.5 FM (Totnes); 100.8 FM (Dartmouth); 101.2 FM (South Hams); 101.9 FM (Ivybridge)

SOVEREIGN RADIO, 14 St Mary's Walk, Hailsham, E. Sussex BN27 1AF T 01323-442700 *Frequency:* 107.5 FM

SPECTRUM RADIO, 4 Ingate Place, Battersea, London SW8 3NS T 020-7627 4433 *Frequency:* 558 AM

SPIRE FM, City Hall Studios, Malthouse Lane, Salisbury, Wilts SP2 7QQ T 01722-416644 *Frequency:* 102.0 FM

SPIRIT FM, Dukes Court, Bognor Road, Chichester, W. Sussex PO19 8FX T 01243-773600 *Frequencies:* 96.6/102.3 FM

SPLASH FM, Guildbourne Centre, Worthing, West Sussex BN11 1LZ T 01903-233005 *Frequency:* 107.7 FM

STAR 106.6, The Observatory Shopping Centre, Slough, Berks SL1 1LH T 01753-551066 *Frequency:* 106.6 FM

STAR 107, Brunel Mall, London Road, Stroud, Gloucestershire, GL5 2BP T 01453-767369 *Frequency:* 107.2/9

STAR 107.2, Bristol Evening Post Building, Temple Way, Bristol BS99 7HD T 0117-910 6600 *Frequency:* 107.2 FM

STAR 107.5, Cheltenham Film Studios, 1st Floor, West Suite Arle Court, Hatherley Lane, Cheltenham Gloucester GL51 6PN T 01242-699555 *Frequency:* 107.5 FM

STAR 107.7 FM, 11 Beaconsfield Road, Weston-Super-Mare BS23 1YE T 01934-624455 *Frequency:* 107.7 FM

STAR 107.9, Radio House, Sturton Street, Cambridge CB1 2QF T 01223-722300 *Frequency:* 107.9 FM

SUN FM, PO Box 1034, Sunderland SR5 2YL T 0191-548 1034 *Frequency:* 103.4 FM

SUNRISE FM, Sunrise House, 30 Chapel Street, Little Germany, Bradford BD1 5DN T 01274-735043 *Frequency:* 103.2 FM

SUNRISE RADIO, Sunrise House, Sunrise Road, Southall, Middx UB2 4AU T 020-8574 6666 *Frequency:* 1458 AM

SUNSHINE 855, Unit 11, Burway Trading Estate, Ludlow, Shropshire SY8 1EN T 01584-873795 *Frequency:* 855 AM

SWAN FM, PO Box 1170, High Wycombe, Bucks HP13 6WQ T 01494-446611 *Frequency:* 1170 FM

TEN 17, Latton Bush Centre, Southern Way, Harlow, Essex CM18 7BB T 01279-431017 *Frequency:* 101.7 FM

TFM, Radio House, Yale Crescent, Thornaby, Stockton-on-Tees TS17 6AA T 01642-888222 *Frequency:* 96.6 FM

THAMES 107.8, The Old Post Office, 110–112 Tolworth, Broadway, Surbiton, Surrey KT6 7JD T 020-8288 1300 *Frequency:* 107.8 FM

TIME FM (106.8 & 107.3), 2–6 Basildon Road, Abbey Wood, London SE2 0EW T 020-8311 3112 *Frequency:* 106.8 & 107.3 FM

TIME 107.5, Lambourne House, 7 Western Road, Romford, Essex RM1 3LP T 01708-731643 *Frequency:* 107.5 FM

TOWER FM, The Mill, Brownlow Way, Bolton BL1 2RA T 01204-387000 *Frequency:* 107.4 FM

TRAX FM BASSETLAW, White Hart Yard, Bridge Street, Worksop, Nottinghamshire S80 1HR T 01909-500611 *Frequency:* 107.9 FM

TRAX FM DONCASTER, 5 Sidings Court, White Rose Way, Doncaster DN4 5SE T 01302-341166
Frequency: 107.1 FM

VIBE FM, Alpha Business Park, 6–12 White House Road Ipswich, Suffolk IP31 5LT T 01473-467500 *Frequencies:* 105.6 FM (Cambridge); 106.1 FM (Norwich); 106.4 FM (Ipswich); 107.7 FM (Peterborough)

VICTORY 107.4, Media House, Tipner Wharf, Twyford Avenue, Portsmouth PO2 8PE T 023-9263 9922 *Frequency:* 107.4 FM

VIRGIN 105.8, 1 Golden Square, London W1F 9DJ T 020-7434 1215 *Frequency:* 105.8 FM

WATERFORD'S MERCURY 96.6, Unit 5, The Metro Centre, Dwight Road, Watford WD18 9UP T 01923-205470 *Frequency:* 96.6 FM

WAVE 96.5, 965 Mowbray Drive, Blackpool FY3 7JR T 01253-304965 *Frequency:* 96.5 FM

WAVE 105 FM, 5 Manor Court, Barnes Wallis Road, Segensworth East, Fareham, Hampshire PO15 5TH T 01489-481050 ***Frequencies:*** 105.2 FM (Solent); 105.8 FM (Poole)

WESSEX FM, Radio House, Trinity Street, Dorchester DT1 1DJ T 01305-250333 ***Frequencies:*** 97.2/96.0 FM

WIRRAL'S BUZZ 97.1, Media House, Claughton Road Birkenhead CH41 6EY T 0151-6501700 ***Frequency:*** 97.1 FM

THE WOLF 107.7, 10th Floor, Mander House, Wolverhampton WV1 3NB T 01902-571070 ***Frequency:*** 107.7 FM

WYVERN FM, 5–6 Barbourne Terrace, Worcester WR1 3JZ T 01905-612212 ***Frequencies:*** 97.6 FM (Hereford); 102.8 FM (Worcester); 96.7 FM (Kidderminster)

XFM, 30 Leicester Square, London WC2H 7LA T 020-7766 6600 ***Frequency:*** 104.9 FM

YORKSHIRE COAST RADIO (SCARBOROUGH), Unit 2B, Newchase Business Centre, Hopper Hill Road, Scarborough, YO11 3YS ***Frequencies:*** 96.2/103.1 FM

YORKSHIRE COAST RADIO (BRIDLINGTON), Old Harbour Master's Office, Harbour Road, Bridlington, E. Yorks YO15 2NR T 01262-404400 ***Frequency:*** 102.4 FM

Wales

96.4 FM THE WAVE, PO Box 964, Victoria Road, Gowerton, Swansea SA4 3AB T 01792-511964 ***Frequency:*** 96.4 FM

106.3 BRIDGE FM, PO Box 1063, Bridgend CF31 1WF T 01656-647777 ***Frequency:*** 106.3 FM

CAPITAL GOLD (1359 & 1305), Atlantic Wharf, Cardiff CF10 4DJ T 029-2066 2066 ***Frequencies:*** 1359 AM (Cardiff); 1305 AM (Newport)

97.1 CARMARTHENSHIRE, Unit 14, The Old School Estate, Station Road, Narbarth, Pembrokeshire SA67 7DU T 01834- 869384 ***Frequency:*** 97.1/97.5 FM

CHAMPION FM, Llys y Dderwen, Parc Menai, Bangor LL55 4BN T 01248-671888 ***Frequency:*** 103.0 FM

CLASSIC GOLD MARCHER 1260 AM, The Studios, Mold Road, Wrexham LL11 4AF T 01978-752202 ***Frequency:*** 101.2

COAST FM, PO Box 963, Bangor LL57 4ZR T 01428-673272 ***Frequency:*** 96.3 FM

M FM 103.4, The Studios, Mold Road, Gwersyllt, Wrexham LL11 4AF T 01978-752202 ***Frequency:*** 103.4 FM

RADIO CEREDIGION, Yr Hen Ysgol Gymraeg, Ffordd Alexandra, Aberystwyth SY23 1LF T 01970-627999 ***Frequencies:*** 96.6/97.4/103.3/FM

RADIO MALDWYN, The Studios, The Park, Newtown, Powys SY16 2NZ T 01686-623555 ***Frequency:*** 756 AM

REAL RADIO, Unit 1, Ty-Nant Court, Ty-Nant Road, Morganstown, Cardiff CF15 8LW T 029-2031 5100 ***Frequencies:*** 105/106 FM

RED DRAGON FM, Atlantic Wharf, Cardiff CF10 4DJ T 029-2066 2066 ***Frequencies:*** 103.2 FM (Cardiff); 97.4 FM (Newport)

SWANSEA SOUND, PO Box 1170, Victoria Road, Gowerton, Swansea SA4 3AB T 01792-511170 ***Frequency:*** 1170 AM

VALLEYS RADIO, PO Box 1116 Ebbw Vale, Gwent NP23 8XW T 01495-301116 ***Frequencies:*** 999/1116 AM

Scotland

96.3 QFM, 65 Sussex Street, Glasgow G41 1XD T 0141-429 9430 ***Frequency:*** 96.3 FM

107 THE EDGE, Radio House, Rowantree Avenue, Newhouse Industrial Estate, Newhouse ML1 5RX T 01689-733107 ***Frequency:*** 107.5/107.9 FM

ARGYLL FM, 27–29 Longrow, Campbeltown, Argyll PA28 8ER T 01586-551800 ***Frequencies:*** 107.1/107.7/106.5 FM

BEAT 106, Four Winds Pavilion, Pacific Quay, Glasgow G51 1EB T 0141-566 6106 ***Frequencies:*** 105.7/106.1 FM

CASTLE ROCK FM, Pioneer Park Studios, Unit 3, 80 Castlegreen Street, Dumbarton G82 1JB T 01389-734422 ***Frequency:*** 103 FM

CENTRAL FM, 201–203 High Street, Falkirk FK1 1DU T 01324-611164 ***Frequency:*** 103.1 FM

CLYDE 1 (FM) AND 2 (AM), Clydebank Business Park, Clydebank, Glasgow G81 2RX T 0141-565 2200 ***Frequencies:*** 102.5 FM; 103.3 FM (Firth of Clyde); 97.0 FM (Vale of Leven); 1152 AM

CLYDE 2, Clydebank Business Park, Glasgow G81 2RX T 0141 565 2200 ***Frequency:*** 1152 AM

CULLIN FM, Tigh Lisigarry, Bridge Road, Portee, Isle of Skye IV51 9ER T 01478-612921 ***Frequency:*** to be confirmed

FORTH ONE, Forth House, Forth Street, Edinburgh EH1 3LE T 0131-556 9255 ***Frequencies:*** 1548 AM, 97.3/97.6/102.2

FORTH 2, Forth House, Forth Street, Edinburgh EH1 3LE T 0131-556 9255 ***Frequencies:*** 1548 AM

HEARTLAND FM, Atholl Curling Rink, Lower Oakfield, Pitlochry, Perthshire PH16 5HQ T 01796-474040 ***Frequency:*** 97.5 FM

ISLES FM, PO Box 333, Stornoway, Isle of Lewis HS1 2RE T 01851-703333 ***Frequency:*** 103.0 FM

KINGDOM FM, Haig House, Haig Business Park, Markinch, Fife KY7 6AQ T 01592-753753 ***Frequencies:*** 95.2/96.1 FM

LOCHBROOM FM, Radio House, Mill Street, Ullapool, Ross-shire IV26 2UN T 01854-613131 ***Frequency:*** 102.2 FM

MORAY FIRTH RADIO, Scorguie Place, Inverness IV3 8UJ T 01463-224433 ***Frequencies:*** 97.4 FM, 1107 AM; ***local opt-outs:*** MFR Speysound 96.6 FM, MFR Keith Community Radio 102.8 FM; MFR Kinnaird Radio 96.7 FM; MFR Caithness 102.5 FM

NECR (NORTH-EAST COMMUNITY RADIO), The Shed, School Road, Kintore, Aberdeenshire, AB51 0US T 01467-632909 ***Frequencies:*** 97.1 FM (Braemar); 102.1 FM (Meldrum and Inverurie); 102.6 FM (Kildrummy); 103.2 FM (Colpy)

NEVIS RADIO, Ben Nevis Estate, Claggan, Fort William PH33 6PR T 01397-700007 ***Frequencies:*** 96.6 FM (Fort William); 97.0 FM (Glencoe); 102.3 FM (Skye); 102.4 FM (Loch Leven)

NORTHSOUND ONE (FM) and TWO (FM), Abbotswell Road, West Tullos, Aberdeen AB12 3AJ T 01224-337000 ***Frequencies:*** 1035 AM, 96.9/97.6/103.0 FM

OBAN FM, 132 George Street, Oban, Argyll PA34 5NT T 01631-570057 ***Frequency:*** 103.3 FM

RADIO BORDERS, Tweedside Park, Galashiels TD1 3TD T 01896-759444 ***Frequencies:*** 96.8/97.5/103.1/103.4 FM

RADIO TAY AM and TAY FM, 6 North Isla Street, Dundee DD3 7JQ T 01382-200800 ***Frequencies:*** 1161 AM, 102.8 FM (Dundee); 1584 AM, 96.4 FM (Perth)

REAL RADIO SCOTLAND, Parkway Court, Glasgow Business Park, Glasgow G69 6GA T 0141-781 1011 ***Frequencies:*** 100–101 FM

RIVER FM, Stadium House, Alderstone Road, Livingston EH54 7DN T 0141-781 1011 ***Frequency:*** to be confirmed

RNA FM, Radio North Angus Ltd., Rosemount Road, Arbroath, Angus DD11 2AT T 01241-879660 ***Frequency:*** 96.6 FM

SIBC, Market Street, Lerwick, Shetland ZE1 0JN T 01595-695299 ***Frequencies:*** 96.2/102.2 FM

SOUTH WEST SOUND, Unit 40, The Loreburne Centre, High St, Dumfries DG1 4DA T 01387-250999 ***Frequencies:*** 96.5/97.0/103.0 FM

TWO LOCHS RADIO, Gairloch, Ross-Shire IV21 2LR T 0870-741 4657 ***Frequency:*** to be confirmed

WAVE 102, 8 South Tay Street, Dundee DD1 1PA T 01382-901000 ***Frequency:*** 102 FM

WAVES RADIO PETERHEAD, 7 Blackhouse Circle, Blackhouse Industrial Estate, Peterhead, Aberdeenshire AB42 1BW T 01779-491012 ***Frequency:*** 101.2 FM

WEST FM, Radio House, 54a Holmston Road, Ayr KA7 3BE T 01292 283662 ***Frequency:*** 97.5 FM

WEST SOUND AM AND WEST FM, Radio House, 54A Holmston Road, Ayr KA7 3BE T 01292-283662 ***Frequencies:*** 1035 AM, 96.7 FM (Ayr); 97.5 FM (Girvan)

Northern Ireland

CITY BEAT 96.7, Lamont Buildings, Stranmillis Embankment, Belfast BT9 5FN T 028-9020 5967 ***Frequency:*** 96.7 FM

COOL FM, PO Box 974, Belfast BT1 1RT T 028-9181 7181 ***Frequency:*** 97.4 FM

DOWNTOWN RADIO, Newtownards, Co. Down BT23 4ES T 028-9181 5555 ***Frequencies:*** 1026 AM (Belfast); 96.4 FM (Limavady); 96.6 FM (Enniskillen); 97.1 FM (Larne); 102.3 FM (Ballymena); 102.4 FM (Londonderry); 103.1 FM (Newry); 103.4 FM (Newcastle); 102.6 AM (Belfast)

MID 106, 2c Park Avenue, Burn Road, Cookstown BT80 5AH T 02886-758696 ***Frequency:*** 106 FM

Q97.2 FM, 24 Cloyfin Road, Coleraine BT52 2NU T 028-7035 9100 ***Frequency:*** 97.2 FM

Q101.2 FM, 42A Market Street, Omagh, Co. Tyrone BT78 1EH 1A Belmore Mews, Enniskillen, BT74 6AA T 028-8224 5777 ***Frequency:*** 101.2

Q102.9 FM, The Riverview Suite, 87 Rossdowney Road, Waterside, Londonderry BT47 5SU T 028-7134 4449 ***Frequency:*** 102.9 FM

Channel Islands

104.7 ISLAND FM, 12 Westerbrook, St Sampsons, Guernsey GY2 4QQ T 01481-242000 ***Frequencies:*** 104.7 FM (Guernsey); 93.7 FM (Alderney)

CHANNEL 103 FM, 6 Tunnell Street, St Helier, Jersey JE2 4LU T 01534-888103 ***Frequency:*** 103.7 FM

DIGITAL MULTIPLEXES

The information contained in this section is correct at the time of writing (August 2004), however, it is advisable to check with the multiplex operator for accurate listings.

CAPITAL RADIO DIGITAL, 30 Leicester Square, London WC2H 7LA T 020-7766 6000
Cardiff & Newport Programme services: Red Dragon FM; Capital Gold; Centry; Xfm; BBC Radio Wales; BBC Radio Cymru. ***Frequency:*** 11C
Kent Programme services: Invicta FM; Capital Gold; Kent Digital Extra; Saga Radio; Xfm; Kiss; Swale Sound; Totally Radio; BBC Radio Kent. ***Frequency:*** 11C
South Hampshire Programme services: Ocean FM; 103.2 Power FM; Capital Gold; Wave 105.2; Saga Radio; Capital Disney; The Saint; Xfm; Southampton Hospital Radio; BBC Radio Solent. ***Frequency:*** 11C
Sussex coast Programme services: Southern FM; Capital Gold; Juice 107.2; Xfm; Saga; Kiss; Gaydar Radio; Spirit FM; Totally Radio; BBC Southern Counties Radio. ***Frequency:*** 11B

CE DIGITAL LTD, 30 Leicester Square, London WC2H 7LA T 020-7766 6000
Birmingham, Programme services: BRMB; Capital Gold; Xfm; Magic; Radio XL; Kiss; Sunrise; Century; Beat 106; BBC Radio WM. ***Frequency***: 11C
London, Programme services: Capital FM; Capital Gold; Capital Disney; Kiss; Xfm, Magic; Sunrise Radio; LBC97.3 & 1152; Smash! Hits, Century London. ***Frequency***: 12C
Manchester, Programme services: Key 103; Magic 1152; Kiss; Capital Gold; Xfm; Asian Sound Radio; Smash! Hits; BBC GMR. ***Frequency***: 11C

DIGITAL ONE, 7 Swallow Place, London W1B 2AG T 020-7288 4600 Programme services: Classic FM; Virgin Radio; TalkSport; Planet Rock; Core; Life; Oneword; PrimeTime Radio. ***Frequencies***: 11D (England and Wales); 12A (Scotland)

THE DIGITAL RADIO GROUP, 7 Swallow Place; London W1R 7AA T 020-7911 7300 Programme services: The Arrow; AbracaDABra; Choice; Liquid; Passion for the Planet; Gaydar Radio; Easy Radio; The Storm; Breeze; SBN; Panjab Radio; Heat; The Mix. ***Frequency:*** 11B

EMAP DIGITAL RADIO LTD, Mappin House, 4 Winsley Street, London W1W 8HF T 020-7436 1515
Central Lancashire, Emap Performance, Mappin House, 4 Winsley Street, London W1W 8HF T 020-7436 1515 Programme services: 97.4 Rock FM; Kiss; Magic 999; Classic Gold; Xfm; 3C; Smash! Hits; BBC Radio Lancashire; The Hits; Heat. ***Frequency***: 12A
Humberside, Programme services: Viking FM; Magic 1161; Lincs FM; Classic Gold; Xfm; Smash! Hits; Kiss; BBC Radio Humberside; The Hits; Heat. ***Frequency***: 11B
Leeds, Programme services: 96.3 Aire FM; Classic Gold; Kiss; Magic 828; Ridings FM; Xfm; Smash! Hits; BBC Radio Leeds; The Hits; Heat. ***Frequency***: 12D
Liverpool, Programme services: Radio City 96.7; Magic 1548; Kiss; Classic Gold; Xfm; 3C; Smash! Hits; BBC Radio Merseyside; The Hits; Heat. ***Frequency***: 12D
South Yorkshire, Programme services: Hallam FM; Magic; Kiss; Trax FM; Classic Gold; Xfm; Smash! Hits; BBC Radio Sheffield; The Hits; Heat. ***Frequency***: 11C
Teesside, Programme services: Classic Gold; Kiss; Magic 1170; 96.6 TFM; Xfm; 3C; Smash! Hits; BBC Radio Cleveland; The Hits; Heat. ***Frequency***: 11B
Tyne and Wear, Programme services: Metro FM; Magic 1152; Kiss; 3C; Classic Gold; Xfm; Smash! Hits; BBC Radio Newcastle; The Hits; Heat. ***Frequency***: 11C

MXR, The Chrysalis Building, 13 Bramley Road, London W10 6SP T 020-7470 2213
North East England, Programme services: Heart; The Arrow; Smooth; Digital News Network; Jazz FM; Galaxy; Century FM; Urban Choice; Capital Disney. ***Frequency***: 12C
North West England, Programme services: Urban Choice; Heart; The Arrow; Smooth; Digital News Network; Galaxy; Jazz FM; Century FM; Capital Disney; Real Radio. ***Frequency***: 12C
South Wales/Severn Estuary, Programme services: Urban Choice; Heart; The Arrow; Smooth; Digital News Network; Vibe 101; Jazz FM; Real Radio; Century; Capital Disney. ***Frequency***: 12C
West Midlands, Programme services: Urban Choice; Galaxy 102.2; 100.7 Heart; Saga 105.7; Capital Disney; Jazz FM; The Arrow; Smooth; Digital News Network; Kerrang! ***Frequency***: 12A
Yorkshire, Programme services: Capital Disney, Urban Choice, Heart; Jazz FM, The Arrow, Smooth, Digital New Network, Galaxy, Real Radio. ***Frequency:*** 12A

NOW DIGITAL LTD, PO Box 2000, Bristol BS99 7SN T 020-7911 7300 W www.now-digital.com

Bournemouth, Programme services: 2CR FM, Classic Gold; Kiss; Wave 105; Saga; Passion for the Planet; The Storm; SBN; BBC Radio Solent. *Frequency:* 11B

Bristol/Bath, Programme services: GWR FM; Classic Gold; The Storm; Xfm; Kiss; Saga; Passion for the Planet; SBN; BBC Radio Bristol. *Frequency*: 11B

Coventry, Programme services: Mercia FM; Classic Gold 1359; Kix 96; The Storm; Sunrise radio; SBN; Kiss; Yarr; BBC Radio Coventry and Warwickshire. *Frequency*: 12B

Exeter & Torbay, Programme services: Gemini FM; Classic Gold; Kiss; The Storm; Passion for the Planet; SBN; BBC Radio Devon. *Frequency:* 11C

Leicester, Programme services: Leicester Sound; Classic Gold GEM; Galaxy; Capital Disney; The Storm; Sabras Radio; A Plus; Century 106; BBC Radio Leicester. *Frequency:* 11B

Norwich, Programme services: Broadland 102; Classic Gold Amber; Vibe; 103.4 The Beach; The Storm; Passion for the Planet; 3C; SBN; Smash! Hits; Zeta Digital; BBC Radio Norfolk. *Frequency:* 11B

Nottingham, Programme services: 96 Trent FM; Classic Gold GEM; 106 Century FM; Galaxy; Capital Disney; The Storm; A Plus; BBC Radio Nottingham. *Frequency* 12C

Peterborough, Programme services: Hereward FM; Classic Gold; Vibe; 3C; Passion for the Planet; SBN; Smash! Hits; BBC Radio Cambridge. *Frequency:* 12D

Southend and Chelmsford, Programme services: Essex FM; Classic Gold; Saga; The Storm; Passion for the Planet; TBC; Kiss; SBN; BBC Radio Essex. *Frequency*: 12D

Swindon and West Wiltshire, Programme services: Kiss; Capital Disney; The Storm; Passion for the Planet; Classic Gold; SBN; GWR FM Bath; GWR FM Wilts; Saga; Swindon FM; BBC Radio Swindon; BBC Radio Wiltshire.

Wolverhampton, Shrewsbury and Telford, Programme services: Beacon FM; Classic Gold WABC; The Storm; Yarr; Kiss; SBN; Xfm; Sunrise radio; BBC Radio WM; BBC Radio Shropshire. *Frequency*: 11B

SCORE DIGITAL, 3 South Avenue, Clydebank Business Park, Glasgow G81 2RX T 0141-565 2347 W www.scoredigital.co.uk

Ayr, Programme services: West FM, West Sound; 3C; UCA Radio; The Storm; Smash! Hits; BBC Radio Scotland; BBC Radio Gaidheal. *Frequency:* 11B

Dundee & Perth, Programme services: Tay FM; Tay AM; 3C; The Access Channel; The Storm; Smash! Hits; BBC Scotland; BBC Nan Gaidheal. *Frequency:* 11B

Edinburgh, Programme services: Forth One; Forth 2; 3C; Sunrise Radio; Xfm; Kiss; Saga Radio; BBC Radio Scotland. *Frequency:* 12D

Glasgow, Clyde 1; Clyde 2; 3C; Sunrise Radio; 96.3 QFM; Xfm; Kiss; Saga Radio; BBC Radio Scotland. *Frequency:* 11C

Inverness, Programme services: MFR; 3C; MFR 1107; BBC Radio Scotland; BBC Nan Gaidheal. *Frequency:* 11B

Northern Ireland, Programme services: Downtown; Cool FM; City Beat; Q102.9; Classic FM; PrimeTime; 3C; Kiss; BBC Radio Ulster. *Frequency*: 12D

SWITCHDIGITAL LTD, 18 Hatfields, London SE1 8DJ T 020-7959 7800 W www.switchdigital.com

Aberdeen, Programme services: Kiss; Smash! Hits; Waves Radio; NECR; Northsound One; Northsound Two; Kerrang!, BBC Radio Scotland; BBC Nan Gaidheal. *Frequency*: 11C

Central Scotland, Programme services: Galaxy Jazz FM; Beat 106; Real Radio; The Arrow; Heart; Smash! Hits; The Hits; BBC Radio Nan Galdheal. *Frequency*: 11D

Greater London, Programme services: Hits; Galaxy; Yarr; The Groove; Travel Now; Heart 106.2 FM; Kerrang!, Jazz FM; Saga Radio, Spectrum Radio 558AM; BBC London Live. *Frequency*: 12A

TWG–EMAP (B & H) LTD, 18 Hatfields, London SE1 8DJ T 0207959 7800

Bradford & Huddersfield, Programme services: The Pulse; Classic Gold; Sunrise Radio; Smash! Hits; Kiss; Panjab Radio, Yarr. *Frequency:* 11B

Stoke-on Trent, Programme services: Signal 1; Signal 2; Kiss; Smash! Hits; BBC Radio Stoke. *Frequency:* 12D

Swansea, Programme services: The Wave; Swansea Sound; Kiss; Smash! Hits; BBC Radio Cymru; BBC Radio Wales. *Frequency* 12A

THE PRESS

The newspaper and periodical press in the UK is large and diverse, catering for a wide variety of views and interests. There is no state control or censorship of the press, though it is subject to the laws on publication and the Press Complaints Commission was set up by the industry as a means of self-regulation.

The press is not state-subsidised and receives few tax concessions. The income of most newspapers and periodicals is derived largely from sales and from advertising; the press is the largest advertising medium in Britain.

SELF-REGULATION

The Press Complaints Commission was founded by the newspaper and magazine industry in January 1991 to replace the Press Council (established in 1953). It is a voluntary, non-statutory body set up to operate the press's self-regulation system following the Calcutt report in 1990 on privacy and related matters, when the industry feared that failure to regulate itself might lead to statutory regulation of the press. The performance of the Press Complaints Commission was reviewed after 18 months of operation (the *Calcutt Review of Press Self-Regulation*, presented to Parliament in January 1993) to determine whether statutory measures were required. No proposals for replacing the self-regulation system have been made to date. The Commission is funded by the industry through the Press Standards Board of Finance.

COMPLAINTS

The Press Complaints Commission's aims are to consider, adjudicate, conciliate, and resolve complaints of unfair treatment by the press; and to ensure that the press maintains the highest professional standards with respect for generally recognised freedoms, including freedom of expression, the public's right to know, and the right of the press to operate free from improper pressure. The Commission judges newspaper and magazine conduct by a code of practice drafted by editors, agreed by the industry and ratified by the Commission.

Six of the Commission's members are editors of national, regional and local newspapers and magazines, and nine, including the chairman, are drawn from other fields. One member has been appointed Privacy Commissioner with special powers to investigate complaints about invasion of privacy. The PCC received 3,649 complaints in 2003.

PRESS COMPLAINTS COMMISSION, 1 Salisbury Square, London EC4Y 8JB
T 020-7353 1248 F 020-7353 8355
E complaints@pcc.org.uk
W www.pcc.org.uk
Chairman, Sir Christopher Meyer, KCMG

NEWSPAPERS

Newspapers are mostly financially independent of any political party, though most adopt a political stance in their editorial comments, usually reflecting proprietorial influence. Ownership of the national and regional daily newspapers is concentrated in the hands of large corporations whose interests cover publishing and communications. The rules on cross-media ownership, as amended by the Broadcasting Act 1996, which limited the extent to which newspaper organisations may become involved in broadcasting, have been relaxed by the Communications Act 2003. Newspapers with over 20 per cent share of national circulation may own national and/ or local radio licences.

There are about 13 daily and 13 Sunday national papers and several hundred local papers that are published weekly or twice-weekly. Scotland, Wales and Northern Ireland all have at least one daily and one Sunday national paper.

Newspapers are usually published in either broadsheet or tabloid format. The 'quality' daily papers, e.g. those providing detailed coverage of a wide range of public matters, have a broadsheet format. The tabloid papers take a more popular approach and are more illustrated.

CIRCULATION *(Net average for July 2004)*

National Daily Newspapers	
Daily Express	939,384
Daily Mail	2,418,743
Daily Mirror	1,816,908
Daily Record	485,802
Daily Star	919,103
Daily Telegraph	904,981
Financial Times	421,179
The Guardian	371,129
The Independent	262,086
Racing Post	83,121
The Scotsman	65,069
The Sun	3,378,306
The Times	650,448

National Sunday Newspapers	
The Business	211,805
Independent on Sunday	209,003
Mail on Sunday	2,412,785
News of the World	3,706,972
The Observer	441,193
The People	1,022,243
Sunday Express	985,457
Scotland on Sunday	75,667
Sunday Mail	579,579
Sunday Mirror	1,569,781
Sunday Sport	159,198
Sunday Telegraph	692,021
Sunday Times	1,304,600

Source: Audit Bureau of Circulations Ltd, September 2004. For further information please see www.abc.org.uk

NATIONAL DAILY NEWSPAPERS

DAILY EXPRESS
Ludgate House, 245 Blackfriars Road, London SE1 9UX
T 0161-228 0789 *Editor*, Peter Hill

DAILY MAIL
Northcliffe House, 2 Derry Street, London W8 5TT
T 020-7938 6000 *Editor*, Paul Dacre

DAILY MIRROR
1 Canada Square, Canary Wharf, London E14 5AP
T 020-7293 3000 *Editor,* Richard Wallace

DAILY RECORD
1 Central Quay, Glasgow G3 8DA
T 0141-309 3000
W www.record-mail.co.uk/rm *Editor,* Bruce Waddell

DAILY SPORT
19 Great Ancoats Street, Manchester M60 4BT
T 0161-236 4466 *Editor,* David Beevers; *Editor-in-Chief,* Tony Livesey

DAILY STAR
Ludgate House, 245 Blackfriars Road, London SE1 9UX
T 020-79288000 *Editor,* Dawn Neesom

THE DAILY TELEGRAPH
1 Canada Square, Canary Wharf, London E14 5DT
T 020-7538 5000
W www.telegraph.co.uk *Editor,* Martin Newland

FINANCIAL TIMES
1 Southwark Bridge, London SE1 9HL
T 020-7873 3000
W www.ft.com *Editor,* Andrew Gowers

THE GUARDIAN
119 Farringdon Road, London EC1R 3ER
T 020-7278 2332
W www.guardian.co.uk *Editor,* Alan Rusbridger

THE HERALD
Scottish Media Newspapers Ltd, 200 Renfield Street, Glasgow G2 3PR
T 0141-302 7000
W www.theherald.co.uk *Editor,* Mark Douglas-Home

THE INDEPENDENT
Independent House, 191 Marsh Wall, London E14 9RS
T 020-7005 2000 *Editor-in-Chief,* Simon Kelner

MORNING STAR
People's Press Printing Society Ltd, William Rust House, 52 Beachy Road, London E3 2NS
T 020-8510 0815 *Editor,* John Haylett

THE SCOTSMAN
Barclay House, 108 Holyrood Road, Edinburgh EH8 8AS
T 0131-620 8620 *Editor,* Iain Martin

THE SUN
News Group Newspapers Ltd, Virginia Street, London E1 9XP
T 020-7782 4000 *Editor,* Rebekah Wade

THE TIMES
1 Pennington Street, London E98 1TT
T 020-7782 5000
W www.the-times.co.uk *Editor,* Robert Thomson

WEEKLY NEWSPAPERS

THE BUSINESS
292 Vauxhall Bridge Road, London SW1V 1DE
T 020-7961 0000

DAILY STAR SUNDAY
Ludgate House, 245 Blackfriars Road, London SE1 9UX
T 020-7928 8000 *Editor,* Peter Hill

INDEPENDENT ON SUNDAY
Independent House, 191 Marsh Wall, London E14 9RS
T 020-7005 2000 *Editor,* Tristan Davies; *Editor-at-Large* Janet Street-Porter

MAIL ON SUNDAY
Northcliffe House, 2 Derry Street, London W8 5TS
T 020-7938 6000 *Editor,* Peter Wright

NEWS OF THE WORLD
1 Virginia Street, London E98 1NW
T 020-7782 1000 *Editor,* Andy Coulson

THE OBSERVER
119 Farringdon Road, London EC1R 3ER
T 020-7278 2332 *Editor,* Roger Alton

THE PEOPLE
1 Canada Square, Canary Wharf, London E14 5AP
T 020-7293 3000
W www.people.co.uk *Editor,* Mark Thomas

SCOTLAND ON SUNDAY
108 Holyrood Road, Edinburgh EH8 8AS
T 0131-620 8620

SUNDAY EXPRESS
Ludgate House, 245 Blackfriars Road, London SE1 9UX
T 020-7928 8000 *Editor,* Martin Townsend

SUNDAY HERALD
200 Renfield Street, Glasgow G2 3QB
T 0141-302 7800
W www.sundayherald.com *Editor,* Andrew Jaspan

SUNDAY MAIL
1 Central Quay, Glasgow G3 8DA
T 0141-309 3000
W www.record-mail.co.uk/rm *Editor,* Allan Rennie

SUNDAY MIRROR
1 Canada Square, Canary Wharf, London E14 5AP
T 020-7293 3000
W www.sundaymirror.co.uk *Editor,* Tina Weaver

SUNDAY POST
D.C. Thomson & Co. Ltd, 144 Port Dundas Road, Glasgow G4 0HZ
T 0141-332 9933 *Editor,* David Pollington

SUNDAY SPORT
19 Great Ancoats Street, Manchester M60 4BT
T 0161-236 4466 *Editor,* Paul Carter

SUNDAY TELEGRAPH
1 Canada Square, Canary Wharf, London E14 5DT
T 020-7538 5000 *Editor,* Dominic Lawson

THE SUNDAY TIMES
1 Pennington Street, London E98 1ST
T 020-7782 5000
W www.sunday-times.co.uk *Editor,* John Witherow

THE SUNDAY TIMES SCOTLAND
Times Newspapers Ltd, 124 Portman Street, Kinning Park, Glasgow G41 1EJ
T 0141-420 5100 *Editor,* Les Snowdon

WALES ON SUNDAY
Thomson House, Havelock Street, Cardiff CF10 1XR
T 029-2058 3583 *Editor,* Tim Gordon

REGIONAL DAILY NEWSPAPERS

EAST ANGLIA

CAMBRIDGE EVENING NEWS
Winship Road, Milton, Cambs. CB4 6PP
T 01223-434434 *Editor,* Colin Grant

EAST ANGLIAN DAILY TIMES
30 Lower Brook Street, Ipswich, Suffolk IP4 1AN
T 01473-230023 *Editor,* Terry Hunt

EASTERN DAILY PRESS
Prospect House, Rouen Road, Norwich NR1 1RE
T 01603-628311
W www.edp24.co.uk *Editor,* Peter Franzen

EVENING NEWS
Prospect House, Rouen Road, Norwich NR1 1RE
T 01603-628311 *Editor,* David Bourn

EAST MIDLANDS

BURTON MAIL
Burton Daily Mail Ltd, 65–68 High Street, Burton on Trent DE14 1LE
T 01283-512345 *Editor,* Paul Hazeldine

CHRONICLE & ECHO, NORTHAMPTON
Northamptonshire Newspapers Ltd, Upper Mounts, Northampton NN1 3HR
T 01604-467000 *Editor,* Mark Edwards

DERBY EVENING TELEGRAPH
Northcliffe House, Meadow Road, Derby DE1 2DW
T 01332-291111
W www.thisisderbyshire.co.uk *Editor,* Mike Norton

THE LEICESTER MERCURY
St George Street, Leicester LE1 9FQ
T 0116-251 2512 *Editor,* Nick Carter

NOTTINGHAM EVENING POST
Castle Wharf House, Nottingham NG1 7EU
T 0115-948 2000
W www.thisisnottingham.co.uk *Editor,* Graham Glen

LONDON

EVENING STANDARD
Northcliffe House, 2 Derry Street, London W8 5EE
T 020-7938 6000
W www.thisislondon.com *Editor,* Veronica Wadley

NORTH

EVENING CHRONICLE
Newcastle Chronicle and Journal Ltd, Groat Market, Newcastle upon Tyne NE1 1ED
T 0191-232 7500 *Editor,* Paul Robertson

EVENING GAZETTE
Gazette Media Company Ltd, Borough Road, Middlesbrough TS1 3AZ
T 01642-245401 *Editor,* Steve Dyson

HARTLEPOOL MAIL
Northeast Press Ltd, New Clarence House, Wesley Square, Hartlepool TS24 8BX
T 01429-239333 *Editor,* Paul Napier

THE JOURNAL
Groat Market, Newcastle upon Tyne NE1 1ED
T 0191-232 7500 *Editor,* Brian Aitken

THE NORTHERN ECHO
Priestgate, Darlington, Co. Durham DL1 1NF
T 01325-381313 *Editor,* Peter Barron

NORTH-WEST EVENING MAIL
Newspaper House, Abbey Road, Barrow-in-Furness, Cumbria LA14 5QS
T 01229-840150 *Editor,* Steve Brauner

THE SUNDAY SUN
Groat Market, Newcastle upon Tyne NE1 1ED
T 0191-201 6158 *Editor,* Peter Montellier

SUNDERLAND ECHO
Echo House, Pennywell, Sunderland, Tyne & Wear SR4 9ER
T 0191-501 5800
W www.sunderlandtoday.co.uk *Editor,* Rob Lawson

NORTH WEST

THE BLACKPOOL GAZETTE
Avroe House, Avroe Crescent, Blackpool Business Park, Squires Gate, Blackpool FY4 2DP
T 01253-400888
W www.blackpoolgazette.co.uk *Editor,* David Helliwell

BOLTON EVENING NEWS
Newspaper House, Churchgate, Bolton, Lancs. BL1 1DE
T 01204-522345
W www.thisisbolton.co.uk

DAILY POST
PO Box 48, Old Hall Street, Liverpool L69 3EB
T 0151-227 2000 *Editor,* Jane Wolstenholme

LANCASHIRE EVENING POST
Oliver's Place, Fulwood, Preston PR2 9ZA
T 01772-254841 *Editor,* Simon Reynolds

LANCASHIRE & WIGAN EVENING TELEGRAPH
Newspaper House, High Street, Blackburn, Lancs. BB1 1HT
T 01254-678678
W www.thisislancashire.co.uk *Editor,* Simon Reynolds

LIVERPOOL ECHO
PO Box 48, Old Hall Street, Liverpool L69 3EB
T 0151-227 2000
W www.liverpool.com *Editor,* Mark Dickinson

MANCHESTER EVENING NEWS
164 Deansgate, Manchester M60 2RD
T 0161-832 7200
W www.manchesteronline.co.uk *Editor,* Paul Horrocks

OLDHAM CHRONICLE
PO Box 47, Union Street, Oldham, Lancs. OL1 1EQ
T 0161-633 2121
W www.oldham-chronicle.co.uk *Editor,* Jim Williams

SOUTH EAST

THE ARGUS
Argus House, Crowhurst Road, Hollingbury, Brighton SN1 8AR
T 01273-544544
W www.newsquest.co.uk *Editor,* Simon Bradshaw

EVENING ECHO
Newspaper House, Chester Hall Lane, Basildon, Essex SS14 3BL
T 01268-522792 *Editor,* Martin McNeill

MEDWAY MESSENGER
Medway House, Ginsbury Close, Sir Thomas Longley Road, Medway City Estate, Strood, Kent ME2 2DU
T 01634-227800

THE NEWS, PORTSMOUTH
The News Centre, Hilsea, Portsmouth PO2 9SX
T 023-9266 4488
W www.thenews.co.uk *Editor,* Mike Gilson

OXFORD MAIL
Newspaper House, Osney Mead, Oxford OX2 0EJ
T 01765-425262
W www.newsquest.co.uk *Editor,* Jim McClure

READING EVENING POST
8 Tessa Road, Reading, Berks. RG1 8NS
T 0118-918 3000 *Editor,* Andy Murrill

THE SOUTHERN DAILY ECHO
Newspaper House, Test Lane, Redbridge, Southampton SO16 9JX
T 023-8042 4777 *Editor,* Ian Murray

SWINDON EVENING ADVERTISER
100 Victoria Road, Old Town, Swindon SN1 3BE
T 01793-528144
W www.thisiswiltshire.co.uk *Editor,* Simon O'Neill

SOUTH WEST

THE BATH CHRONICLE
Bath Newspapers, Windsor House, Windsor Bridge, Bath BA2 3AU
T 01225-322322 *Editor,* David Gledhill

BRISTOL EVENING POST
Temple Way, Bristol BS99 7HD
T 0117-934 3000 *Editor,* Mike Lowe

DAILY ECHO
Richmond Hill, Bournemouth BH2 6HH
T 01202-554601
W www.thisisdorset.co.uk *Editor,* Neal Butterworth

DORSET ECHO
Newscom, Fleet House, Hampshire Road, Weymouth, Dorset DT4 9XD
T 01305-830930 *Editor,* David Murdock

EVENING HERALD
17 Brest Road, Derriford Business Park, Plymouth, Devon PL6 5AA
T 01752-765529
W www.thisisplymouth.co.uk *Editor,* Alan Qualtrough

EXPRESS & ECHO
Express & Echo Publications Ltd, Heron Road, Sowton, Exeter, Devon EX2 7NF
T 01392-442211 *Editor,* Steve Hall

THE GLOUCESTER CITIZEN
Gloucestershire Newspapers Ltd, St John's Lane, Gloucester GL1 2AY
T 01452-424442 *Editor,* Ian Mean

GLOUCESTERSHIRE ECHO
Cheltenham Newspaper Co. Ltd, 1 Clarence Parade, Cheltenham, Glos. GL50 3NY
T 01242-271900
W www.thisisgloucestershire.co.uk *Editor,* Anita Syvret

HERALD EXPRESS
Harmsworth House, Barton Hill Road, Torquay, Devon TQ2 8JN
T 01803-676000
W www.thisissouthdevon.co.uk *Editor,* Brendon Hanrahan

SUNDAY INDEPENDENT
Southern Newspapers plc, Burrington Way, Plymouth PL5 3LN
T 01752-206600 *Editor,* Nikki Rowlands

WESTERN DAILY PRESS
Bristol Evening Post and Press Ltd, Temple Way, Bristol BS99 7HD
T 0117-934 3000
W www.westpress.co.uk *Editor,* Terry Manners

THE WESTERN MORNING NEWS
Brest Road, Derriford, Plymouth PL6 5AA
T 01752-765500 *Editor,* Barrie Williams

WEST MIDLANDS

BIRMINGHAM EVENING MAIL
PO Box 78, Weaman Street, Birmingham B4 6AY
T 0121-236 3366 *Editor,* Roger Borrell

THE BIRMINGHAM POST
Weaman Street, Birmingham B4 6AT
T 0121-236 3366 *Editor,* Fiona Alexander

COVENTRY EVENING TELEGRAPH
Corporation Street, Coventry CV1 1FP
T 024-7663 3633 *Editor,* Alan Kirby

EXPRESS & STAR
Queen Street, Wolverhampton WV1 1ES
T 01902-313131
W www.westmidlands.com

THE SENTINEL
Staffordshire Sentinel Newspapers Ltd, Sentinel House, Etruria, Stoke-on-Trent ST1 5SS
T 01782-602525
W www.thisisstaffordshire.co.uk *Editor,* Sean Dooley

SHROPSHIRE STAR
Ketley, Telford TF1 5HU
T 01952-242424 *Editor,* Sarah Jane Smith

SUNDAY MERCURY
Colmore Circus, Birmingham B4 6AZ
T 0121-234 5567 *Editor,* David Brookes

WORCESTER EVENING NEWS
Berrows House, Hylton Road, Worcester WR2 5JX
T 01905-742277
W www.thisisworcester.co.uk *Editor,* Stewart Gilbert

YORKSHIRE/HUMBERSIDE

EVENING COURIER
PO Box 19, King Cross Street, Halifax HX1 2SF
T 01422-260200
W www.halifaxcourier.co.uk *Editor,* John Furbisher

EVENING NEWS
17–23 Aberdeen Walk, Scarborough, North Yorkshire YO11 1BB
T 01723-363636
W www.scarborougheveningnews.co.uk
Editor, Ed Asquith

EVENING PRESS
York and County Press, PO Box 29, 76–86 Walmgate, York YO1 9YN
T 01904-653051
W www.thisisyork.co.uk *Editor,* Kevin Booth

GRIMSBY EVENING TELEGRAPH
80 Cleethorpe Road, Grimsby, North East Lincolnshire DN31 3EH
T 01472-360360
W www.thisisgrimsby.co.uk *Editor,* Michelle Lalor

THE HUDDERSFIELD DAILY EXAMINER
Examiner News & Information Services Ltd, PO Box A26, Queen Street South, Huddersfield HD1 2TD
T 01484-430000
W www.examiner.co.uk *Editor,* Roy Wright

HULL DAILY MAIL
Blundell Corner, Beverley Road, Hull HU3 1XS
T 01482-327111
W www.hulldailymail.co.uk *Editor,* John Meehan

THE STAR
York Street, Sheffield S1 1PU
T 0114-276 7676
W www.sheffweb.co.uk *Editor,* Peter Charlton

TELEGRAPH & ARGUS
Hall Ings, Bradford, West Yorkshire BD1 1JR
T 01274-729511
W www.thisisbradford.co.uk *Editor,* Perry Austin-Clarke

YORKSHIRE EVENING POST
PO Box 168, Wellington Street, Leeds LS1 1RF
T 0113-2432701 *Editor,* N. R. Hodgkinson

YORKSHIRE POST
Wellington Street, Leeds LS1 1RF
T 0113-243 2701
W www.yorkshireposttoday.co.uk *Editor,* Rachel Campey

SCOTLAND

THE COURIER AND ADVERTISER
D.C. Thomson & Co. Ltd, 80 Kingsway East, Dundee DD4 8SL
T 01382-223131
W www.thecourier.co.uk

DUNDEE EVENING TELEGRAPH AND POST
D.C. Thomson & Co. Ltd, 80 Kingsway East, Dundee DD4 8SL
T 01382-223131
W www.eveningtelegraph.co.uk

EVENING NEWS (EDINBURGH)
108 Holyrood Road, Edinburgh EH8 8AS
T 0131-620 8620 *Editor,* Ian Stewart

EVENING EXPRESS (ABERDEEN)
Aberdeen Journals Ltd, PO Box 43, Lang Stracht, Mastrick, Aberdeen AB15 6DF
T 01224-690222 *Editor,* Donald Martin

GLASGOW EVENING TIMES
200 Renfield Street, Glasgow G2 3PR
T 0141-302 7000
W www.eveningtimes.co.uk *Editor,* Charles McGhee

INVERNESS COURIER
PO Box 13, 9–11 Bank Lane, Inverness IV1 1QW
T 01463-233059 *Editor,* Jim Love

PAISLEY DAILY EXPRESS
Scottish and Universal Newspapers Ltd, 14 New Street, Paisley, Renfrewshire PA1 1YA
T 0141-887 7911
W www.insidescotland.co.uk *Editor,* Jonathan Russell

THE PRESS AND JOURNAL
Lang Stracht, Aberdeen AB15 6DF
T 01224-690222
W www.thisisnorthscotland.co.uk *Editor,* Derek Tucker

THE SUN
News International Newspapers, Scotland, 124 Portman Street, Kinning Park, Glasgow G41 1EJ
T 0141-420 5200 *Editor,* Rob Dalton

WALES

SOUTH WALES ARGUS
South Wales Argus Ltd, Cardiff Road, Maesglas, Newport, Gwent NP20 3QN
T 01633-777219 *Editor,* Gerry Keighley

SOUTH WALES ECHO
Thomson House, Havelock Street, Cardiff CF10 1XR
T 029-2058 3622 *Editor,* Alastair Milburn

SOUTH WALES EVENING POST
PO Box 14, Adelaide Street, Swansea SA1 1QT
T 01792-51000
W www.swep.co.uk *Editor,* Spencer Feeney

THE WESTERN MAIL
Thomson House, Havelock Street, Cardiff CF10 1XR
T 029-2058 3583 *Editor,* Alan Edmunds

NORTHERN IRELAND

BELFAST TELEGRAPH
124–144 Royal Avenue, Belfast BT1 1EB
T 028-9026 4000
W www.belfasttelegraph.co.uk *Editor,* Edmund Curran

IRISH NEWS
113–117 Donegall Street, Belfast BT1 2GE
T 028-9032 2226
W www.irishnews.com *Editor,* Noel Doran

NEWS LETTER
46–56 Boucher Crescent, Boucher Road, Belfast BT12 6QY
T 028-9068 0000
W www.newsletter.co.uk *Editor,* Austin Hunter

THE PEOPLE
415 Holywood Road, Belfast BT4 2GU
T 028-9056 8000 *Editor,* Greg Harkin

SUNDAY LIFE
124 Royal Avenue, Belfast BT1 1EB
T 028-9026 4300 *Editor,* Martin Lindsay

CHANNEL ISLANDS

GUERNSEY PRESS AND STAR
Braye Road, Vale, Guernsey GY1 3BW
T 01481-240240 *Editor,* Richard Digard

JERSEY EVENING POST
PO Box 582, Five Oaks, St Saviour, Jersey JE4 8XQ
T 01534-611611 *Editor,* Chris Bright

PERIODICALS

ACCOUNTANCY
40 Bernard Street, London WC1N 1LD
T 020-7833 3291 W www.accountancymagazine.com
Editor, Chris Quick

ACCOUNTANCY AGE
VNU Business Publications, VNU House, 32–34 Broadwick Street, London W1A 2HG
T 020-7316 9236 W www.accountancyage.com
Editor, Damian Wild

ACCOUNTING & BUSINESS
Association of Chartered Certified Accountants, 10–11 Lincolns Inn Fields, London WC2A 3BP
T 020-7396 5966 W www.accaglobal.com
Editor, John Prosser

ACE TENNIS MAGAZINE
Tennis GB, 9–11 North End Road, London W14 8ST
T 020-7605 8000 *Editor,* Nigel Billen

ACTIVE LIFE
Computer Publishing, 221–223 High Street, Berkhamstead, Herts HP4 1AD
T 01442-289600 *Editor,* Paul Jacques

ACUMEN
6 The Mount, Higher Furzeham, Brixham, South Devon TQ5 8QY
T 01803-851098 *Editor,* Patricia Oxley

AEROPLANE MONTHLY
IPC Magazines Ltd, King's Reach Tower, Stamford Street, London SE1 9LS
T 020-7261 5849 W www.aeroplanemonthly.com
Editors, John Carroll, Martin Smith

AFRICA CONFIDENTIAL
Blackwell Publishers Ltd, 73 Farringdon Road, London EC1M 3JQ
T 020-7831 3511 W www.africa-confidential.com
Editor, Patrick Smith

AFRICAN BUSINESS
IC Publications Ltd, 7 Coldbath Square, London EC1R 4LQ
T 020-7713 7711 *Editor,* Anver Versi

AIR INTERNATIONAL
Key Publishing Ltd, PO Box 100, Stamford, Lincs. PE9 1XQ
T 01780-755131 *Editor,* Malcolm English

AMATEUR GARDENING
IPC Media Ltd, Westover House, West Quay Road, Poole, Dorset BH15 1JG
T 01202-440840 *Editor,* Tim Rumball

AMATEUR PHOTOGRAPHER
IPC Magazines Ltd, King's Reach Tower, Stamford Street, London SE1 9LS
T 020-7261 5100 *Editor,* Garry Coward-Williams

AMATEUR STAGE
Platform Publications Ltd, Hampden House, 2 Weymouth Street, London W1W 5BT
T 020-7636 4343
W www.amdram.org.uk/amstagel.htm
Editor, Charles Vance

AMBIT
17 Priory Gardens, London N6 5QY
T 020-8340 3566
W ambitmagazine.co.uk *Editor,* Martin Bax

ANGLING TIMES
EMAP Active, Bushfield House, Orton Centre, Peterborough PE2 5UW
T 01733-232600 *Editor,* Richard Lee

AN MAGAZINE
AN: The Artists Information Company, 1st Floor, 7–15 Pink Lane, Newcastle upon Tyne NE1 5DW
T 0191-241 8000
W www.a-n.co.uk

ANTIQUES & ART INDEPENDENT
PO Box 1945, Comely Bank, Edinburgh EH4 1AB
T 07000-268478
W www.antiquesnews.co.uk
Publisher/Editor, Tony Keniston

ANTIQUES AND COLLECTABLES
Merricks Media Ltd, Charlotte House, 12 Charlotte Street, Bath BA1 2NE
T 01225-786800
W www.antiques-collectables.co.uk
Editor, Diana Cambridge

APOLLO
20 Theobalds Road, London WC1X 8PF
Editor, Michael Hall

THE ARCHITECTS' JOURNAL
EMAP Business Communications, 151 Rosebery Avenue, London EC1R 4GB
T 020-7505 6700 *Editor,* Isabel Allen

ARCHITECTURAL DESIGN
John Wiley & Sons Ltd, 4th Floor, International House, Ealing Broadway Centre, London W5 5DB
T 020-8326 3800
W www.wiley.co.uk/ad/ *Editor,* Helen Castle

THE ARCHITECTURAL REVIEW
EMAP Construct, 151 Rosebery Avenue, London EC1R 4GB
T 020-7505 6725
W www.arplus.com/ *Editor,* Peter Davey

ARCHITECTURE TODAY
161 Rosebery Avenue, London EC1R 4QX
T 020-7837 0143 *Editors,* Ian Latham, Mark Swenarton

ARENA
EMAP East, Endeavour House, 189 Shaftesbury Avenue, London WC2H 8JG
T 020-7437 9011 *Editor,* Anthony Noguera

ART BUSINESS TODAY
The Fine Art Trade Guild, 16–18 Empress Place, London SW6 1TT
T 020-7381 6616
W www.abtonline.co.uk *Editor,* Mike Sims

ART MONTHLY
4th Floor, 28 Charing Cross Road, London WC2H 0DB
T 020-7240 0389
W www.artmonthly.co.uk *Editor,* Patricia Bickers

THE ART NEWSPAPER
70 South Lambeth Road, London SW8 1RL
T 020-7735 3331
W www.theartnewspaper.com *Editor,* Christina Ruiz

ART REVIEW
Art Review Ltd, Hereford House, 23–24 Smithfield Street, London EC1A 9LB
T 020-7236 4880
W www.art-review.com

ASIAN TIMES
Ethnic Media Group, Unit 2.01, Technology Centre, 65 Whitechapel Road, London E1 1DU
T 020-7650 2000 *Editor,* Isaac Ham

ASTRONOMY NOW
Pole Star Publications, PO Box 175, Tonbridge, Kent TN10 4ZY
T 01903-266165
W www.astronomynow.com
Managing Editor, Steven Young

ATHLETICS WEEKLY
Descartes Publishing Ltd, 83 Park Road, Peterborough PE1 2TN
T 01733-898440 *Editor,* Jason Henderson

THE AUTHOR
84 Drayton Gardens, London SW10 9SB
T 020-7373 6642 *Editor,* Fanny Blake

AUTOCAR
Haymarket Publishing Ltd, 60 Waldegrave Road, Teddington, Middlesex TW11 8LG
T 020-8267 5630 *Editor,* Steve Sutcliffe

AUTO EXPRESS
Dennis Publishing Ltd, 30 Cleveland Street, London W1T 4JD
T 020-7907 6200
W www.autoexpress.co.uk *Editor,* David Johns

B
Attic Futura UK-Ltd, 16–17 Berners Street, London W1T 3LN
T 020-7664 6470 *Editor,* Fran Sheen

THE BANKER
Tabernacle Court, 16–28 Tabernacle Court, London EC2 4DD
T 020-7382 8000 *Editor-in-Chief,* Stephen Timewell

BAPTIST TIMES
PO Box 54, 129 Broadway, Didcot, Oxon OX11 8XB
T 01235-517670 *Editor,* Hazel Southam

THE BEANO
D. C. Thomson & Co. Ltd, Albert Square, Dundee DD1 9QJ
T 01382-223131

BELLA
H. Bauer Publishing, Academic House, 24–28 Oval Road, London NW1 7DT
T 020-7241 8000
Editor, Jayne Marsden; *Features Editor,* Clare Swatman

BEST
The National Magazine Company, 33 Broadwick Street, London W1F 0DQ
T 020-7439 5000 *Editor,* Louise Court

THE BIG ISSUE
1–5 Wandsworth Road, London SW8 2LN
T 020-7526 3200 *Editor,* Matt Ford

BIKE
EMAP Automotive Ltd, Media House, Lynchwood, Peterborough PE2 6EA
T 01733-468000 *Editor,* Tim Thompson

BIRDING WORLD
Sea Lawn, Coast Road, Cley next the Sea, Holt, Norfolk NR25 7RZ
T 01263-740913
W www.birdingworld.co.uk *Editor,* Steve Gantlett

BIRDWATCH
Solo Publishing Ltd, 3rd Floor, Leroy House, 436 Essex Road, London N1 3QP
T 020-7704 9495
W www.birdwatch.co.uk *Editor,* Dominic Mitchell

BIRD WATCHING
EMAP Active Ltd, Bretton Court, Bretton, Peterborough PE3 8DZ
T 01733-264666 *Editor,* David Cromack

BIZARRE
Dennis Publishing, Cleveland Street, London W1T 4JD
T 020-7687 7000
W www.bizarremag.com *Editor,* Alex Godfrey

BLISS
EMAP Media, Endeavour House, 189 Shaftesbury Avenue, London WC2H 8JG
T 020-7437 9011
W www.blissmag.co.uk *Editor,* Charlotte Crisp

BLUEPRINT
ETP Ltd, Rosebery House, 41 Springfield Road, Chelmsford CM2 6JJ
T 01245-491717 *Editor,* Vicky Richardson

BMA NEWS
British Medical Association, BMA House, Tavistock Square, London WC1H 9JP
T 020-7383 6122
Joint Editors, Julia Bell, Caroline Winter-Jones

BOARDS
Yachting Press Ltd, 196 Eastern Esplanade, Southend-on-Sea, Essex SS1 3AB
T 01702-582245
W www.boards.co.uk *Editor,* Bill Dawes

THE BOOK COLLECTOR
The Collector Ltd, PO Box 12426, London W11 3GW
T 020-7792 3492

BOOK AND MAGAZINE COLLECTOR
Diamond Publishing Ltd, 45 St Mary's Road, London W5 5RQ
T 020-8579 1082 *Editor,* Jono Scott

THE BOOKSELLER
VNU Entertainment Media Ltd, 5th Floor, Endeavour House, 189 Shaftesbury Avenue, London WC2H 8TJ
T 020-7420 6006
W www.thebookseller.com *Editor,* Nicholas Clee

BRITISH JOURNALISM REVIEW
BJR Publishing Ltd, c/o Sage Publications, 6 Bonhill Street, London EC2A 4PU
T 020-7374 0645 *Editor,* Bill Hagerty

THE BRITISH JOURNAL OF PHOTOGRAPHY
Incisive Photographics Ltd, Incisive Media, Haymarket House, 28–29 Haymarket, London SW1Y
T 020-7484 9700
W www.bjp-online.com *Editor,* Simon Bainbridge

BRITISH MEDICAL JOURNAL
BMA House, Tavistock Square, London WC1H 9JR
T 020-7387 4499
W www.bmj.com *Editor,* Richard Smith

BROADCAST
EMAP Media, 33–39 Bowling Green Lane, London EC1R 0DA
T 020-7505 8014 *Editor,* Conor Dignam

BUILDING
The Builder Group plc, 7th Floor, Anchorage House, 2 Clove Crescent, London E14 2BE
T 020-7560 4000 *Editor,* Adrian Barrick

BUILDING DESIGN
CMP Information Ltd, Ludgate House, 245 Blackfriars Road, London SE1 9UY
T 020-7861 6467 *Editor,* Robert Booth

THE BURLINGTON MAGAZINE
14–16 Duke's Road, London WC1H 9SZ
T 020-7388 1228 *Editor,* Richard Shone

BUSINESS LIFE
Pegasus House, 37–43 Sackville Street, London W15 3EH
T 020-7925 2544
W www.cedarcom.co.uk *Editor,* Alex Finer

BUSINESS SCOTLAND
Peebles Media Group, Bergius House, Clifton Street, Glasgow G3 7LA
T 0141-567 6000 *Editor,* Graham Lironi

BUSINESS TRAVELLER
Perry Publications Ltd, Nestor House, Playhouse Yard, London EC4V 5EX
T 020-7778 0000
W www.btonline.co.uk *Editor,* Julia Brookes

CAMPAIGN
Haymarket Business Publications Ltd, 174 Hammersmith Road, London W6 7JP
T 020-8943 5000
W www.brandrepublic.com *Editor,* Caroline Marshall

CAR
EMAP Automotive Ltd, 3rd Floor, Media House, Lynchwood, Peterborough PE2 6EA
T 01733-468000 *Editor,* Greg Fountain

THE CATHOLIC HERALD
Herald House, Lambs Passage, Bunhill Row, London EC1Y 8TQ
T 020-7588 3101
W www.catholicherald.co.uk *Editor,* Luke Coppen

CATHOLIC TIMES
1st Floor, St James's Buildings, Oxford Street, Manchester M1 6FP
T 0161-236 8856 *Editor,* Kevin Flaherty

CHARTERED SECRETARY
16 Park Crescent, London W1B 1AH
T 020-7612 7045
W www.charteredsecretary.net *Editor,* Will Booth

CHILD EDUCATION
Scholastic Ltd, Villiers House, Clarendon Avenue, Leamington Spa, Warks. CV32 5PR
T 01926-887799
W www.scholastic.co.uk *Acting Editor,* Michael Ward

THE CHINA QUARTERLY
School of Oriental and African Studies, Thornhaugh Street, Russell Square, London WC1H 0XG
T 020-7898 4063 *Editor,* Dr Julia Strauss

CHOICE
1st Floor, 2 King Street, Peterborough PE1 1LT
T 01733-555123 *Editor,* Norman Wright

CHRISTIAN HERALD
Christian Media Centre, Garcia Estate, Canterbury Road, Worthing, West Sussex BN13 1EH
T 01903-821082
W www.christianherald.org.uk

CHURCH OF ENGLAND NEWSPAPER
20–26 Brunswick Place, London N1 6DZ
T 020-7417 5800
W www.churchnewspaper.com

CHURCH TIMES
33 Upper Street, London N1 0PN
T 020-7359 4570
W www.churchtimes.co.uk *Editor,* Paul Handley

CLASSICAL MUSIC
Rhinegold Publishing Ltd, 241 Shaftesbury Avenue, London WC2H 8TF
T 020-7333 1742
W www.rhinegold.co.uk *Editor,* Keith Clarke

CLASSIC & SPORTS CAR
Haymarket Specialist Motoring Publications Ltd, Somerset House, Somerset Road, Teddington, Middlesex W11 8RT
T 020-8267 5399 *Editor,* James Elliott

CLASSIC CARS
EMAP Automotive Ltd, Media House, Lynchwood, Peterborough Business Park, Peterborough PE2 6EA
T 01733-468219
W www.classiccarsmagazine.co.uk *Editor,* Martyn Moore

COMPANY
National Magazine House, 72 Broadwick Street, London W1V 2BP
T 020-7439 5000 *Editor,* Victoria White

COMPUTER WEEKLY
Reed Business Information Ltd, Quadrant House, The Quadrant, Sutton, Surrey SM2 5AS
T 020-8652 3122
W www.computerweekly.com *Editor,* Hooman Bassirian

COMPUTING
VNU Business Publications, VNU House, 32–34 Broadwick Street, London W1A 2HG
T 020-7316 9158
W www.computing-media.co.uk *Editor,* Colin Barker

CONTEMPORARY
Suite K101, Tower Bridge Business Complex, 100 Clements Road, London SE16 4DG
T 020-7740 1704
W www.contemporary-magazine.com
Editors, Roger Tatley, Mark Rappolt

CONTEMPORARY REVIEW
Contemporary Review Co. Ltd, PO Box 1242, Oxford OX1 4FJ
T 01865-201529 *Editor,* Dr Richard Mullen

COSMOPOLITAN
National Magazine House, 72 Broadwick Street, London W1V 2BP
T 020-7439 5000 *Editor-in-Chief,* Lorraine Candy

COUNTRY HOMES AND INTERIORS
IPC Magazines Ltd, King's Reach Tower, Stamford Street, London SE1 9LS
T 020-7261 6451 *Editor,* Deborah Barker

COUNTRY LIFE
IPC Media Ltd, King's Reach Tower, Stamford Street, London SE1 9LS
T 020-7261 7058 *Editor,* Clive Aslet

COUNTRY LIVING
National Magazine House, 72 Broadwick Street, London W1F 9EP
T 020-7439 5000
W www.countryliving.co.uk *Editor,* Susy Smith

CRAFTS
44a Pentonville Road, London N1 9BY
T 020-7278 7700
W www.craftscouncil.org.uk *Editor,* Geraldine Rudge

CYCLING WEEKLY
IPC Music and Sport Ltd, 5th Floor, Focus House, 9 Dingwall Avenue, Croydon CR9 2TA
T 020-8774 0811 *Editor,* Robert Garbutt

DAIRY FARMER
CMP Information Ltd, Sovereign House, Sovereign Way, Tonbridge, Kent TN9 1RW
T 01732-377273 *Editor,* Peter Hollinshead

DANCING TIMES
The Dancing Times Ltd, 45–47 Clerkenwell Green, London EC1R 0EB
T 020-7250 3006
W www.dancing-times.co.uk *Editor,* Mary Clarke

THE DANDY
D.C. Thomson & Co. Ltd, Albert Square, Dundee DD1 9QJ
T 01382-223131

DECANTER
IPC Country & Leisure Media Ltd, 1st Floor, Broadway House, 2–6 Fulham Broadway, London SW6 1AA
T 020-7610 3929
W www.decanter.com *Editor,* Amy Wislocki

DISABILITY NOW
6 Market Road, London N7 9PW
T 020-7619 7323
W www.disabilitynow.org.uk *Editor,* Mary Wilkinson

DRAPERS
EMAP Communications, 33–39 Bowling Green Lane, London EC1R 0DA
T 020-7812 3700
W www.drapersrecord.com *Editor-in-Chief,* Eric Musgrave

EARLY MUSIC
Oxford University Press, 70 Baker Street, London W1M 7DN
T 020-7616 5902
W www.em.oupjournals.org *Editor,* Tess Knighton

EASTERN ART REPORT
Eastern Art Publishing Group, PO Box 13666, 27 Wallorton Gardens, London SW14 8WF
T 020-8392 1122 *Managing Editor,* Sajid Rizvi

THE ECOLOGIST
Unit 18, Chelsea Wharf, 15 Lots Road, London SW10 0QJ
T 020-7351 3578 *Editors,* Zac Goldsmith

ECONOMICA
STICERD, London School of Economics, Houghton Street, London WC2A 2AE
T 020-7955 7855 *Editors,* Prof F. A. Cowell, Prof Alan Manning, Prof Tore Ellingsen

THE ECONOMIST
25 St James's Street, London SW1A 1HG
T 020-7830 7000
W www.economist.com *Editor,* Bill Emmott

THE EDGE
65 Guinness Buildings, London W6 8BD
T 020-8563 1310
W www.theedge.abelgratis.co.uk *Editor,* David Clark

EDINBURGH REVIEW
220A Buccleuch Place, Edinburgh EH8 9LN
T 0131-651 1415 *Editor,* Ronald Turnbull

EDUCATION JOURNAL
17 Park Road, Hampton Hill, Middlesex TW12 1HE
T 020-8979 9473 *Editor,* George Low

ELLE UK
Hachette Filipacchi UK, 16–18 Berners Street, London W1T 3LN
T 020-7150 7000 *Acting Editor,* Laurel Ives

EMPIRE
Mappin House, 4 Winsley Street, London W1W 8HF
T 020-7436 1515
W www.empireonline.co.uk *Editor,* Colin Kennedy

THE ENGINEER
Centaur Communications Ltd, St Giles House, 50 Poland Street, London W1F 7AX
T 020-7970 4106
W www.e4engineering.com *Editor,* Sean Brierley

THE EROTIC REVIEW
30 Cleveland Street, London W1T 4JD
T 020-7907 6404
W www.theeroticreview.co.uk *Editor,* Rowan Pelling

ESQUIRE
National Magazine House, 72 Broadwick Street, London W1F 9EP
T 020-7439 5000 *Editor,* Simon Tiffin

ESSENTIALS
IPC Media, King's Reach Tower, Stamford Street, London SE1 9LS
T 020-7261 6970 *Editor,* Karen Livermore

FARMERS WEEKLY
Reed Business Information, Quadrant House, The Quadrant, Sutton, Surrey SM2 5AS
T 020-8652 4911
W www.fwi.co.uk *Editor,* Stephen Howe

FHM (FOR HIM MAGAZINE)
EMAP Élan Network, Mappin House, 4 Winsley Street, London W1W 8HF
T 020-7436 1515
W www.fhm.com *Editor,* David Davies

THE FIELD
IPC Media Ltd, King's Reach Tower, Stamford Street, London SE1 9LS
T 020-7261 5198
W www.thefield.co.uk

FILM REVIEW
Visual Imagination Ltd, 9 Blades Court, Deodar Road, London SW15 2NU
T 020-8875 1520 *Editor,* Neil Corry

FLIGHT INTERNATIONAL
Reed Business Information Ltd, Quadrant House, The Quadrant, Sutton, Surrey SM2 5AS
T 020-8652 3842
W www.flightinternational.com *Editor,* Murdo Morrison

FORTEAN TIMES
Box 2409, London NW5 4NP
T 020-7907 6235
W www.forteantimes.com/ *Editor,* David Sutton

GARDEN NEWS
EMAP Active Ltd, Bretton Court, Bretton Centre, Peterborough PE3 8DZ
T 01733-264666 *Editor,* Sarah Page

GAY TIMES
Spectrum House, 32–34 Gordon House Road, London NW5 1LP
T 020-7424 7400
W www.gaytimes.co.uk *Editor,* Vicky Powell

GEOGRAPHICAL
Campion Interactive Publishing Ltd, Unit 11, Pall Mall Deposit, 124–8 Barlby Road, London W10 6BL
T 020-8960 6400
W www.geographical.co.uk

GEOLOGICAL MAGAZINE
Cambridge University Press, The Edinburgh Building, Shaftesbury Road, Cambridge CB2 2RU
T 01223-312393 *Editors,* Prof I. N. McCave, Dr M. B. Allen, Dr D. M. Pyle, Dr G. E. Budd

GLAMOUR
Condé Nast Publications, Vogue House, Hanover Square, London W1S 1JU
T 020-7499 9080
W www.glamour.com *Editor,* Jo Elvin

GOOD HOUSEKEEPING
National Magazine House, 72 Broadwick Street, London W1F 9EP
T 020-7439 5000
W www.natmags.co.uk
Editor-in-Chief, Lindsay Nicholson

GQ
Condé Nast Publications, Vogue House, Hanover Square, London W1S 1JU
T 020-7499 9080
W www.gq/magazine.co.uk *Editor,* Dylan Jones

GRANTA
2–3 Hanover Yard, Noel Road, London N1 8BE
T 020-7704 9776
W www.granta.com *Editor,* Ian Jack

THE GROCER
William Reed Publishing Ltd, Broadfield Park, Crawley, West Sussex RH11 9RT
T 01293-613400
W www.foodanddrink.co.uk *Editor,* Julian Hunt

HARPERS & QUEEN
National Magazine House, 72 Broadwick Street, London W1F 9EP
T 020-7439 5000 *Editor,* Lucy Yeomans

HEAT
Emap plc, Endeavour House, 189 Shaftesbury Avenue, London WC2H 8JG
T 020-7437 9011

HELLO!
Wellington House, 69–71 Upper Ground, London SE1 9PQ
T 020-7667 8700 *Editor,* Ronnie Whelan

HISTORY TODAY
20 Old Compton Street, London W1D 4TW
T 020-7534 8000
W admin@historytoday.com *Editor,* Peter Furtado

HOMES AND GARDENS
IPC Magazines Ltd, King's Reach Tower, Stamford Street, London SE1 9LS
T 020-7261 5000

HORSE & HOUND
IPC Media Ltd, King's Reach Tower, Stamford Street, London SE1 9LS
T 020-7261 6315
W www.horseandhound.co.uk *Editor,* Lucy Higginson

HOUSE & GARDEN
Vogue House, Hanover Square, London W1S 1JU
T 020-7499 9080 *Editor,* Susan Crewe

I-D MAGAZINE
124 Tabernacle Street, London EC2A 4SA
T 020-7490 9710 *Editor,* Avril Mair

INDEX ON CENSORSHIP
Lancaster House, 33 Islington High Street, London N1 9LH
T 020-7278 2313
W www.indexoncensorship.org
Editor-in-Chief, Ursula Owen

INSTYLE
Time Life International Inc., 5th Floor, Brettenham House, Lancaster Place, London WC2E 7TL
T 020-7322 1510 *Editor,* Dee Nolan

INTERMEDIA
International Institute of Communications, 35 Portland Place, London W1B 1AE
T 020-7323 9622 *Editor,* Martin Sims

INTERNATIONAL AFFAIRS
Royal Institute of International Affairs, Chatham House, 10 St James's Square, London SW1Y 4LE
T 020-7957 5700
W www.riia.org *Editor,* Caroline Soper

INVESTORS CHRONICLE
Tabernacle Court, 16–28 Tabernacle Street, London EC2A 4DD
Editor, Matthew Vincent

JANE'S DEFENCE WEEKLY
Sentinel House, 163 Brighton Road, Coulsdon, Surrey CR5 2YH
T 020-8700 3700
W jdw.janes.com *Editor,* Clifford Beal

THE JEWISH QUARTERLY
92 Dartmouth Road, London NW2 4HA
T 020-8830 5367 *Editor,* Matthew Reisz

JEWISH TELEGRAPH
Telegraph House, 11 Park Hill, Bury Old Road, Prestwich, Manchester M25 0HH
T 0161-740 9321
W www.jewishtelegraph.com

KERRANG!
EMAP Performance 2001, PO Box 2930, London W1A 6DZ
T 020-7436 1515 *Editor,* Ashley Bird

LANCET
32 Jamestown Road, London NW1 7BY
T 020-7424 4910
W www.thelancet.com *Editor,* Dr Richard Horton

LAND & LIBERTY
Suite 427, The London Fruit Exchange, Brushfield Street, London E1 6EL
T 020-7377 8885
W www.landandliberty.org.uk *Editor,* Peter Gibb

THE LAWYER
Centaur Communications Group, 50 Poland Street, London W1V 4AX
T 020-7970 4614
W www.thelawyer.com *Editor,* Catrin Griffiths

LEGAL WEEK
Global Professional Media Ltd, 99 Charterhouse Street, London EC1M 6HR
T 020-7566 5600
W www.legalweek.net *Editor,* John Malpas

LGC (LOCAL GOVERNMENT CHRONICLE)
Greater London House, Hampstead Road, London NW1 7EJ
T 020-7347 1800
W www.lgcnet.com

THE LINGUIST
The Institute of Linguists, Saxon House, 48 Southwark Street, London SE1 1UN
T 020-7226 2822
W www.linguistonline.co.uk *Editor,* Pat Treasure

THE LITERARY REVIEW
44 Lexington Street, London W1F 0LW
T 020-7437 9392 *Editor,* Nancy Sladek

LOADED
PC Media Ltd, King's Reach Tower, Stamford Street, London SE1 9LS
T 020-7261 5000
W www.uploaded.com *Editor,* Martin Daubney

LONDON REVIEW OF BOOKS
28 Little Russell Street, London WC1A 2HN
T 020-7209 1101 *Editor,* Mary-Kay Wilmers

MARIE CLAIRE
European Magazines Ltd, 13th Floor, King's Reach Tower, Stamford Street, London SE1 9LS
T 020-7261 5240 *Editor,* Marie O'Riordan

MARKETING WEEK
St Giles House, 50 Poland Street, London W1F 7AX
T 020-7970 4000
W www.marketing-week.co.uk *Editor,* Stuart Smith

MAXIM
Dennis Publishing Ltd, 30 Cleveland Street, London W1T 4JD
T 020-7907 6410
W www.maxim-magazine.co.uk *Editor,* Tom Loxley

MEDIA WEEK
Quantum Business Media Ltd, Quantum House, 19 Scarbrook Road, Croydon CR9 1LX
T 020-8565 4317 *Editor,* Tim Burrowes

MIXMAG
EMAP plc, Mappin House, 4 Winsley Street, London W1N 8HF
T 020-7436 1515
W www.mixmag.net *Editor,* Viv Crask

MODERN PAINTERS
3rd Floor, 52 Bermondsey Street, London SE1 3UD
T 020-7407 9246
W www.modernpainters.co.uk *Editor,* Karen Wright

MOJO
EMAP Metro, Mappin House, 4 Winsley Street, London W1W 8HF
T 020-7436 1515
W www.mojo4music.com *Editor,* Paul Trynka

MONEYWISE
RD Publications Ltd, 11 Westferry Circus, Canary Wharf, London E14 4HE
T 020-7715 8465
W www.moneywise.co.uk *Editor,* Ben Livesey

MORE
EMAP Élan, Endeavour House, 189 Shaftesbury Avenue, London WC2H 8JG
T 020-7208 3165 *Editor,* Alison Hall

MOTHER & BABY
EMAP Esprit, Greater London House, Hampstead Road, London NW1 7EJ
T 020-7347 1869
W www.motherandbaby.co.uk *Editor,* Dani Zur

MUSICAL TIMES
22 Gibson Square, London N1 0RD *Editor,* Antony Bye

MUSIC WEEK
CMP, 7th Floor, Ludgate House, 245 Blackfriars Road, London SE1 9UR
T 020-7921 8348 *Executive Editor,* Martin Talbot

THE NATIONAL TRUST MAGAZINE
The National Trust, 36 Queen Anne's Gate, London SW1H 9AS
T 020-7222 9251
W www.nationaltrust.org.uk *Editor,* Gaynor Aaltonen

NATURE
Macmillan Magazines Ltd, The Macmillan Building, 4 Crinan Street, London N1 9XW
T 020-7833 4000
W www.nature.com/nature *Editor,* Philip Campbell

NEW HUMANIST
1 Gower Street, London WC1E 6HD
T 020-7436 1151
W www.newhumanist.org.uk *Editor,* Frank Jordans

NEW INTERNATIONALIST
55 Rectory Road, Oxford OX4 1BW
T 01865-728181
W www.newint.org *Editors,* Vanessa Baird, Katharine Ainger, David Ransom

NEW MUSICAL EXPRESS (NME)
IPC Magazines Ltd, 25th Floor, King's Reach Tower, Stamford Street, London SE1 9LS
T 020-7261 5000 *Editor,* Conor McNicholas

NEW SCIENTIST
RBI Ltd, 151 Wardour Street, London W1F 8WE
T 020-8652 3500
W www.newscientist.com *Editor,* Jeremy Webb

NEW STATESMAN
3rd Floor, 52 Grosvenor Gardens, London SW1W 0AU
T 020-7700 3444 *Editor,* Peter Wilby

NOW
IPC Media Ltd, King's Reach Tower, Stamford Street, London SE1 9LS
T 020-7261 7366 *Editor,* Jane Ennis

NURSING TIMES
EMAP Healthcare, Greater London House, Hampstead Road, London NW1 7EJ
T 020-7874 0500 *Editor,* Rachel Downey

OK!
Northern & Shell plc, Ludgate House, 245 Blackfriars Road, London SE1 9UX
T 020-7928 8000 *Editor,* Nic McCarthy

THE OLDIE
65 Newman Street, London W1T 3EG
T 020-7436 8801
W www.theoldie.co.uk *Editor,* Richard Ingrams

OPERA NOW
241 Shaftesbury Avenue, London WC2H 8TF
T 020-7333 1740
W www.rhinegold.co.uk *Editor,* Ashutosh Khandekar

PENSIONS WORLD
LexisNexis UK, Tolley House, 2 Addiscombe Road, Croydon CR9 5AF
T 020-8686 9141
W www.pensionsworld.co.uk
Editor, Stephanie Hawthorne

PERSONAL FINANCE
Charterhouse Communications, Arnold House, 36–41 Holywell Lane, London EC2A 3SF
T 020-7827 5454 *Editor,* Martin Fagan

THE PHOTOGRAPHER
The British Institute of Professional Photography, Fox Talbot House, 2 Amwell End, Ware, Herts. SG12 9HN
T 01920-487268
W www.bipp.com

THE PINK PAPER
2nd Floor, Medius House, 63–69 New Oxford Street, London WC1A 1DN
T 020-7845 4300
W www.pinkpaper.com *Editor,* Tris Reid-Smith

POETRY REVIEW
22 Betterton Street, London WC2H 9BX
T 020-7420 9880
W www.poetrysociety.org.uk
Editors, Robert Potts, David Herd

POLICE REVIEW
Jane's Information Group, Sentinel House, 163 Brighton Road, Coulsdon CR5 2YH
T 020-8276 4701 *Editor,* Catriona Marchant

THE POLITICAL QUARTERLY
Blackwell Publishing, 9600 Garsington Road, Oxford OX4 2DQ
T 01865-776868
W www.blackwellpublishing.com
Editors, Tony Wright MP, Prof. Andrew Gamble

THE PRACTITIONER
CMP Information Ltd, City Reach, 5 Greenwich View Place, Millharbour, London E14 9NN
T 020-7861 6478 *Editor,* Gavin Atkin

PRIMA
National Magazine Company, 72 Broadwick Street, London W1F 9EP
T 020-7439 5000

PRIVATE EYE
6 Carlisle Street, London W1V 5RG
T 020-7437 4017
W www.private-eye.co.uk *Editor,* Ian Hislop

PROSPECT
Prospect Publishing Ltd, 2 Bloomsbury Place, London WC1A 2QA
T 020-7255 1281
W www.prospect-magazine.co.uk *Editor,* David Goodhart

PR WEEK
Haymarket Marketing Publications, 174 Hammersmith Road, London W6 7JP
T 020-8267 4520 *Editor,* Kate Nicholas

PUBLISHING NEWS
39 Store Street, London WC1E 7DS
T 020-7692 2900
W www.publishingnews.co.uk *Editor,* Liz Thomson

PULSE
CMP Information Ltd, Ludgate House, 245 Blackfriars Road, London SE1 9UY
T 020-7921 8102 *Editor,* Phil Johnson

Q MAGAZINE
EMAP Performance, Mappin House, 4 Winsley Street, London W1W 8HF
T 020-7436 1515
W www.q4music.com *Editor,* Paul Rees

RACING POST
Trinity Mirror, Floor 23, One Canada Square, Canary Wharf, London E14 5AP
T 020-7293 3291
W www.racingpost.co.uk *Editor,* Chris Smith

RADIO TIMES
BBC Worldwide Ltd, 80 Wood Lane, London W12 0TT
T 020-8433 3400
W www.radiotimes.com *Editor,* Gill Hudson

RA MAGAZINE
Royal Academy of Arts, Burlington House, Piccadilly, London W1J 0BD
T 020-7300 5820
W www.royalacademy.org.uk *Editor,* Sarah Greenberg

READER'S DIGEST
The Reader's Digest Association Ltd, 11 Westferry Circus, Canary Wharf, London E14 4HE
T 020-7715 8000
W www.readersdigest.co.uk
Editor-in-Chief, Katherine Walker

RECORD COLLECTOR
Unit 101, Wales Farm Road, London W3 6UG
T 0870-732 8080
W www.recordcollectormag.com *Editor,* Alan Lewis

RED
Hachette Filipacchi UK Ltd, 64 North Row, London W1K 7LL
T 020-7150 7000 *Editor,* Trish Halpin

RETAIL WEEK
EMAP Retail, 33–39 Bowling Green Lane, London EC1R 0DA
T 020-7520 1500 *Editor,* Neill Denny

ROYAL NATIONAL INSTITUTE OF THE BLIND
PO Box 173, Peterborough, Cambs. PE2 6WS
T 0845-7023153
W www.rnib.org.uk/wesupply/magazine/welcome.htm

RUSI JOURNAL
Whitehall, London SW1A 2ET
T 020-7930 5854
W www.rusi.org *Editor,* Dr Terence McNamee

SAGA MAGAZINE
Saga Publishing Ltd, The Saga Building, Enbrook Park, Folkestone, Kent CT20 3SE
T 01303-771523 *Editor,* Emma Soames

THE SCHOOL LIBRARIAN
The School Library Association, Unit 2, Lotmead Business Village, Lotmead Farm, Wanborough, Swindon SN4 0UY
T 01793-791787
W www.sla.org.uk *Editor,* Ray Lonsdale

SCIENCE PROGRESS
Science Reviews, PO Box 314, St Albans, Herts. AL1 4ZG
T 01727-847323
Editors, Prof. David Phillips, Prof. Robin Rowbury

SCREEN INTERNATIONAL
EMAP Media, 33–39 Bowling Green Lane, London EC1R 0DA
T 020-7505 8080
W www.screendaily.com

SHE
National Magazine House, 72 Broadwick Street, London W1F 9EP
T 020-7439 5000 *Editor,* Terry Tavner

SIGHT AND SOUND
British Film Institute, 21 Stephen Street, London W1T 1LN
T 020-7255 1444 *Editor,* Nick James

SLIMMING MAGAZINE
EMAP Esprit, Greater London House, Hampstead Road, London NW1 7EJ
T 020-7347 1854 *Editor,* Rashmi Madan

SMASH HITS
EMAP Performance, Mappin House, 4 Winsley Street, London W1W 8HF
T 020-7312 8718 *Editor,* Lisa Smosarski

SOLICITORS JOURNAL
Wilmington Business Information Ltd, Paulton House, 8 Shepherdess Walk, London N1 7LB
T 020-7490 0049

SONGWRITING AND COMPOSING
Sovereign House, 12 Trewartha Road, Praa Sands, Penzance, Cornwall TR20 9ST
T 01736-762826
W www.songwriters-guild.co.uk
General Secretary, Carole Jones

THE SPECTATOR
56 Doughty Street, London WC1N 2LL
T 020-7405 1706 *Editor,* Boris Johnson

SPORT FIRST
20–26 Brunswick Place, London N1 6DZ
T 020-7490 7575
W www.sportfirst.com

THE STAGE
Stage House, 47 Bermondsey Street, London SE1 3XT
T 020-7403 1818 W www.thestage.co.uk
Editor, Brian Attwood

STAMP MAGAZINE
IPC Media Ltd, Focus Network, 9 Dingwall Avenue, Croydon CR9 2TA
T 020-8774 0772 *Editor,* Steve Fairclough

THE STRAD
Orpheus Publications, Newsquest Magazines, 330 High Holborn, London WC1V 7QT
T 020-7203 6731
W www.thestrad.com

SUGAR
Hachette Filipacchi, 64 North Row, London W1K 7LL
T 020-7150 7000 *Acting Editor,* Nick Chalmers

THE TABLET
1 King Street Cloisters, Clifton Walk, London W6 0QZ
T 020-8748 8484
W www.thetablet.co.uk

TAKE A BREAK
H. Bauer Publishing Ltd, Academic House, 24–28 Oval Road, London NW1 7DT
T 020-7241 8000
W www.bauer.com

TATE
Condé Nast Publications Ltd, Vogue House, Hanover Square, London W1S 1JU
T 020-7499 9080 *Editor,* Robert Violette

TATLER
Condé Nast Publications Ltd, Vogue House, Hanover Square, London W1S 1JU
T 020-7499 9080 W www.tatler.co.uk
Editor, Geordie Greig

TAXATION
2 Addiscombe Road, Croydon, Surrey CR9 5AF
T 020-8686 9141
W www.taxation.co.uk

THE TEACHER
National Union of Teachers, Hamilton House, Mabledon Place, London WC1H 9BD
T 020-7380 4708 *Editor,* Mitch Howard

TEMPO
Cambridge University Press, The Edinburgh Building, Shaftesbury Road, Cambridge CB2 2RU
Editor, Calum MacDonald

TIME OUT
Time Out Group Ltd, Universal House, 251 Tottenham Court Road, London W1T 7AB
T 020-7813 3000
W www.timeout.com *Editor,* Laura Lee Davies

THE TIMES EDUCATIONAL SUPPLEMENT
Admiral House, 66–68 East Smithfield, London E1W 1BX
T 020-7782 3000
W www.tes.co.uk *Editor,* Bob Doe

TIMES HIGHER EDUCATION SUPPLEMENT
Admiral House, 66–68 East Smithfield, London E1W 1BX
T 020-7782 3000 *Editor,* John O'Leary

THE TIMES LITERARY SUPPLEMENT
Admiral House, 66–68 East Smithfield, London E1W 1BX
T 020-7782 3000 *Editor,* Peter Stothard

TOTAL FILM
99 Baker Street, London W1U 6FP
T 020-7317 2600 *Editor,* Matt Mueller

TRIBUNE
9 Arkwright Road, London NW3 6AN
T 020-7433 6410 *Editor,* Mark Seddon

TV TIMES MAGAZINE
IPC Media Ltd, 10th Floor, King's Reach Tower, Stamford Street, London SE1 9LS
T 020-7261 7000 *Editor,* Mike Hollingsworth

VANITY FAIR
Condé Nast Publications Ltd, Vogue House, Hanover Square, London W1S 1JU
T 020-7499 9080
W www.condenast.co.uk *London Editor,* Graydon Carter

VENUE
Venue Publishing, 64–65 North Road, Bristol BS6 5AQ
T 0117-942 8491
W www.venue.co.uk *Editor,* Dave Higgitt

VETERINARY REVIEW
John C. Alborough Ltd, Lion Lane, Needham Market, Suffolk IP6 8NT
T 01449-723800 *Editor,* David Watson

VIZ
Dennis Publishing, Cleveland Street, London W1T 4JD
T 020-7687 7000
W www.viz.co.uk

VOGUE
Condé Nast Publications Ltd, Vogue House, Hanover Square, London W1S 1JU
T 020-7499 9080
W www.vogue.co.uk *Editor,* Alexandra Shulman

THE VOICE
Blue Star House, 8th Floor, 234–244 Stockwell Road, London SW9 9UG
T 020-7737 7377
W www.voice-online.co.uk *Group Editor,* Deidre Forbes

WALK
The Ramblers' Association, 2nd Floor, Camelford House, 87–90 Albert Embankment, London SE1 7TW
T 020-7339 8500
W www.ramblers.org.uk *Editor,* Christopher Sparrow

WALLPAPER
IPC Media, Brettenham House, Lancaster Place, London WC2E 7TL
T 020-7322 1177
W www.wallpaper.com *Editor-in-Chief,* Jeremy Langmead

THE WAR CRY
The Salvation Army, 101 Newington Causeway, London SE1 6BN
T 020-7367 4900
W www.salvationarmy.org/warcry
Editor, Maj. Nigel Bovey

THE WEEKLY NEWS
D.C. Thomson & Co. Ltd, Albert Square, Dundee DD1 9QJ
T 01382-223131

WINE
Quest Magazines Ltd, Wilmington Publishing, 6–8 Underwood Street, London N1 7JQ
T 020-7549 2571 *Editor,* Catharine Lowe

THE WISDEN CRICKETER
The New Boathouse, 136–142 Bramley Road, London W10 6SR
T 020-7565 3080 *Editor,* John Stern

WOMAN'S OWN
IPC Connect Ltd, King's Reach Tower, Stamford Street, London SE1 9LS
T 020-7261 5000 *Editor,* Elsa McAlonan

WOMAN'S WEEKLY
IPC Media Ltd, King's Reach Tower, Stamford Street, London SE1 9LS
T 0870-4445000 *Editor,* Gilly Sinclair

WOMEN'S HEALTH
Highbury Lifestyle, 1–3 Highbury Station Road, London N1 1SE
T 020-7226 2222 *Editor,* Tracey Smith

THE WOODWORKER
Highbury Leisure, Berwick House, 8–10 Knoll Rise, Orpington, Kent BR6 0PS
T 01689-899207 *Editor,* Mark Ramuz

THE WORLD OF INTERIORS
The Condé Nast Publications Ltd, Vogue House, Hanover Square, London W1S 1JU
T 020-7499 9080
W www.worldofinteriors.co.uk *Editor,* Rupert Thomas

THE WORLD TODAY
The Royal Institute of International Affairs, Chatham House, 10 St James's Square, London SW1Y 4LE
T 020-7957 5712
W www.theworldtoday.org *Editor,* Graham Walker

WRITERS' FORUM
Writers' International Ltd, PO Box 3229, Bournemouth BH1 1ZS
W www.writers-forum.com *Publisher,* John Jenkins

WRITERS' NEWS
1st Floor, Victoria House, 143–145 The Headrow, Leeds LS1 5RL
T 0113-200 2929
W www.writersnews.co.uk *Editor,* Derek Hudson

WRITING MAGAZINE
1st Floor, Victoria House, 143–145 The Headrow, Leeds LS1 5RL
T 0113-200 2929
W www.writersnews.co.uk *Editor,* Derek Hudson

YACHTING MONTHLY
IPC Media Ltd, Room 2215, King's Reach Tower, Stamford Street, London SE1 9LS
T 020-7261 6040 *Editor,* Paul Gelder

ZEST
National Magazine House, 72 Broadwick Street, London W1F 9EP
T 020-7439 5000 *Editor,* Alison Pylkkanen

BOOK PUBLISHERS

There are over 50,000 active publishers in the UK, but many of these are subsidiaries of larger publishing houses. The following list comprises a selection of publishers, their contact details and a letter code indicating the type of books published.

A	Fiction
B	Education
C	Religious
D	Technical and Scientific
E	Legal and Parliamentary
F	Medical
G	Commercial and Professional
H	Naval and Military
I	Dictionaries
J	Reference Books
K	Maps and Atlases
L	Directories and Guides
M	Music and Dance
N	Poetry, Film and Drama
O	Illustrated
P	Art and Architecture
Q	History, Archaeology, Biography
R	Politics, Sociology, Political Economy
S	Philosophy
T	Other Academic
U	Children's Books
V	Sports, Hobbies and Interests
W	Foreign language
X	General Literature, e.g. Travel, Essays, Humour

AA PUBLISHING
Automobile Association and Business Services, Fanum House, Basingstoke, Hants RG21 4EA **T** 01256-491538 **W** www.theaa.com K, L, O

ABSOLUTE PRESS
Scarborough House, 29 James Street West, Bath BA1 2BT **T** 01225-316013 **E** sales@absolutepress.co.uk **W** www.absolutepress.co.uk V

IAN ALLAN PUBLISHING LTD
Riverdene Business Park, Molesey Road, Hersham, Surrey KT12 4RG **T** 01932-266600 **E** info@ianallanpub.co.uk **W** www.ianallanpublishing.com H, J, V

J. A. ALLEN
Clerkenwell House, 45–47 Clerkenwell Green, London EC1R 0HT **T** 020-7251 2661 **E** allen@halebooks.com V

ANDERSEN PRESS LTD
20 Vauxhall Bridge Road, London SW1V 2SA **T** 020-7840 8703 **E** andersenpress@randomhouse.co.uk **W** www.andersenpress.co.uk U

ANTIQUE COLLECTORS' CLUB LTD
Sandy Lane, Old Martlesham, Woodbridge, Suffolk IP12 4SD **T** 01394-389950 **E** sales@antique-acc.com **W** www.antique-acc.com P, V

ANVIL PRESS POETRY
Neptune House, 70 Royal Hill, London SE10 8RF **T** 020-8469 3033 **E** anvil@anvilpresspoetry.com **W** www.anvilpresspoetry.com N

ARCADIA BOOKS LTD
15–16 Nassau Street, London W1W 7AB **T** 020-7436 9898 **E** info@arcadiabooks.co.uk **W** www.arcadiabooks.co.uk A

AUTUMN PUBLISHING
Appledram Barns, Birdham Road, Chichester, West Sussex **T** 01243-531660 **E** autumn@autumnpublishing.co.uk **W** www.autumnpublishing.co.uk U

DUNCAN BAIRD PUBLISHERS
6th Floor, Castle House, 75–76 Wells Street, London W1T 3QH **T** 020-7323 2229 J, O

BAREFOOT BOOKS LTD
124 Walcot Street, Bath BA1 5BG **T** 01225-322400 **E** info@barefootbooks.co.uk **W** www.barefootbooks.co.uk U

BFI PUBLISHING
British Film Institute, 21 Stephen Street, London W1P 2LN **T** 020-7255 1444 **W** www.bfi.org.uk N

A & C BLACK PUBLISHERS LTD
37 Soho Square, London W1D 3QZ **T** 020-7758 0200 **E** enquiries@acblack.com **W** www.acblack.com B, I, J, L, M, N, O, P, U, V

BLACK ACE BOOKS
PO Box 6557, Forfar DD8 2YS **T** 01307-465096 **W** www.blackacebooks.com A, Q, S

BLACK & WHITE PUBLISHING LTD
99 Giles Street, Edinburgh EH6 6BZ **T** 0131-625 4500 **E** mail@blackandwhitepublishing.com **W** www.blackandwhitepublishing.com A, V, X

BLACKSTAFF PRESS LTD
4C Heron Wharf, Sydenham Business Park, Belfast BT3 9LE **T** 028-9045 5006 **E** info@blackstaffpress.com **W** www.blackstaffpress.com A, B, N, Q, V, X

BLACKWELL PUBLISHING LTD
9600 Garsington Road, Oxford OX4 2DQ **T** 01865-776868 **W** www.blackwellpublishing.com D, F, Q, R, T

BLAKE PUBLISHING
3 Bramber Court, 2 Bramber Road, London W14 9PB **T** 020-7381 0666 **E** words@blake.co.uk Q

BLOODAXE BOOKS LTD
Highgreen, Tarset, Northumberland NE48 1RP **T** 01434-240500 **E** editor@bloodaxebooks.demon.co.uk **W** www.bloodaxebooks.com N, T

BLOOMSBURY PUBLISHING PLC
38 Soho Square, London W1D 3HB **T** 020-7494 2111 **W** www.bloomsbury.com A, J, O, Q, U, V

BOOTH-CLIBBORN EDITIONS
12 Percy Street, London W1T 1DW **T** 020-7637 4255 **E** info@booth-clibborn.com **W** www.booth-clibborn.com P

BOWKER
3rd Floor, Farringdon House, Wood Street, East Grinstead, West Sussex RH19 IU2 **T** 01342-310450 **E** vales@bowker.co.uk **W** www.bowker.co.uk L

MARION BOYARS PUBLISHERS LTD
24 Lacy Road, London SW15 1NL **T** 020-8788 9522 **E** catheryn@marionboyars.com **W** www.marionboyars.co.uk A, M, N, V

BRITISH LIBRARY PUBLICATIONS
Publishing Office, The British Library, 96 Euston Road, London NW1 2DB **T** 020-7412 7704 **E** blpublications@bl.uk **W** www.bl.uk K, L, M, Q

CADOGAN GUIDES
Network House, 1 Ariel Way, London W12 7SL **T** 020-8740 2050 **E** info@cadoganguides.co.uk **W** www.cadoganguides.com L, X

CALDER PUBLICATIONS LTD
51 The Cut, London SE1 8LF T 020-7633 0599
E info@calderpublications.com
W www.calderpublications.com A, P, Q, R, T

CAMBRIDGE UNIVERSITY PRESS
The Edinburgh Building, Shaftesbury Road, Cambridge CB2 2RU T 01223-325892 E information@cambridge.org
W www.cambridge.org
B, C, D, F, G, I, N, P, R, S, T

CAMERON & HOLLIS
PO Box 1, Moffat, Dumfriesshire DG10 9SU T 01683-220808
E editorial@cameronbooks.co.uk
W www.cameronbooks.co.uk P

CANONGATE BOOKS LTD
14 High Street, Edinburgh EH1 1TE T 0131-557 5111
E info@canongate.co.uk W www.canongate.net A, Q, X

CARCANET PRESS LTD
4th Floor, Alliance House, 28–34 Cross Street, Manchester M2 7AQ T 0161-834 8730 E pnr@carcanet.u-net.com
W www.carcanet.co.uk N

CHAMBERS HARRAP PUBLISHERS LTD
7 Hopetoun Crescent, Edinburgh EH7 4AY T 0131-556 5929
E admin@chambersharrap.co.uk I, J

CONSTABLE & ROBINSON LTD
3 The Lanchesters, 162 Fulham Palace Road, London W6 9ER
T 020-8741 3663 E enquiries@constablerobinson.com
W www.constablerobinson.com A, H, Q, U, X

CRESCENT MOON PUBLISHING
PO Box 393, Maidstone, Kent ME14 5XU T 01622-729593
E cresmopub@yahoo.co.uk W www.crescentmoon.org.uk
N, T, X

DAVID & CHARLES LTD
Brunel House, Newton Abbot, Devon TQ12 4PU
T 01626-323200 H, V

DEDALUS LTD
24 St Judith's Lane, Sawtry, Cambs PE28 5XE
T 01487-832382 E info@dedalusbooks.com
W www.dedalusbooks.com A

DORLING KINDERSLEY
80 Strand, London WC2R 0RL T 020-7010 3000
W www.penguin.co.uk J, U, V

GERALD DUCKWORTH & CO. LTD
First Floor, 90–93 Cowcross Street, London EC1M 6BF
T 020-7434 4242 E info@duckworth-publishers.co.uk
W www.ducknet.co.uk H, Q, T

EDINBURGH UNIVERSITY PRESS
22 George Square, Edinburgh EH8 9LF T 0131-650 4218
W www.eup.ed.ac.uk E, Q, R, S, X

EGMONT BOOKS
239 Kensington High Street, London W8 6SA
T 020-7761 3500 E firstname.surname@ecb.egmont.com
W www.egmont.co.uk U

ELSEVIER LTD
The Boulevard, Langford Lane, Kidlington, Oxford OX5 1GB
T 01865-843000 W www.elsevier.com D, F

ENCYCLOPAEDIA BRITANNICA UK LTD
2nd Floor, Unity Wharf, Mill Street, London SE1 2BH
T 020-7500 7800 E enquiries@britannica.co.uk
W www.britannica.co.uk J

EUROPA PUBLICATIONS LTD
Haynes House, 21 John Street, London WC1N 2BP
T 020-7583 9855 E sales@europapublications.co.uk J, L

EVANS BROTHERS LTD
2A Portman Mansions, Chiltern Street, London W1V 6NR
T 020-7487 0920 E sales@evansbooks.co.uk
W www.evansbooks.co.uk B

EVERYMAN'S LIBRARY
Northburgh House, 10 Northburgh Street, London EC1V 0AT
T 020-7566 6350 K, N, U, V, X

EXLEY PUBLICATIONS LTD
16 Chalk Hill, Watford, Herts WD19 4BG T 01923-250505 O

FABER & FABER LTD
3 Queen Square, London WC1N 3AU T 020-7465 0045
W www.faber.co.uk A, M, N, U

C. J. FALLON
Lucan Road, Palmerstown, Dublin 20, Republic of Ireland
T 01-6166400 E editorial@cjfallon.ie B

FOLENS PUBLISHERS
Apex Business Centre, Boscombe Road, Dunstable LU5 4RL
T 0870-609 1237 E folens@folens.com W www.folens.com
B

W. FOULSHAM & CO. LTD
The Publishing House, Bennetts Close, Slough, Berks SL1 5AP
T 01753-526769 V

SAMUEL FRENCH LTD
52 Fitzroy Street, London W1T 5JR T 020-7387 9373
E theatre@samuelfrench-london.co.uk
W www.samuelfrench-london.co.uk N

DAVID FULTON PUBLISHERS LTD
Chiswick Centre, 414 Chiswick High Road, London W4 5TF
T 020-8996 3610 E mail@fultonpublishers.co.uk
W www.fultonpublishers.co.uk B

GARNET PUBLISHING LTD
8 Southern Court, South Street, Reading RG1 4QS
T 0118-959 7847 E enquiries@garnetpublishing.co.uk
A, C, P, X

GAY MEN'S PRESS
PO Box 3220, Brighton BN2 5AU T 01273-672823
E peterburton@easicom.com X

STANLEY GIBBONS PUBLICATIONS
5 Parkside, Christchurch Road, Ringwood, Hants BH24 3SH
T 01425-472363 E info@stangib.demon.co.uk
W www.stanleygibbons.com V

GOMER PRESS
Llandysul, Ceredigion SA44 4QL T 01559-362371
E gwasg@gomer.co.uk W www.gomer.co.uk X

GRANTA PUBLICATIONS
2–3 Hanover Yard, Noel Road, London N1 8BE
T 020-7704 9776 W www.granta.com A, Q, R, X

GUINNESS WORLD RECORDS
338 Euston Road, London NW1 3BD T 020-7891 4567 J

HARCOURT EDUCATION LTD
Halley Court, Jordan Hill, Oxford OX2 8EJ T 01865-310533
E uk.schools@harcourteducation.co.uk
W www.harcourteducation.co.uk B

HARLEQUIN MILLS & BOON LTD
Eton House, 18–24 Paradise Road, Richmond, Surrey TW9 1SR T 020-8288 2800 A

HARPERCOLLINS PUBLISHERS
77–85 Fulham Palace Road, London W6 8JB
T 020-8741 7070 E firstname.surname@harpercollins.co.uk
W www.harpercollins.co.uk
A, I, J, K, L, Q, R, U, V, X

HAYNES PUBLISHING
Sparkford, Yeovil, Somerset BA22 7JJ T 01963-440635
W www.haynes.co.uk D, J, L, V

HODDER HEADLINE LTD
338 Euston Road, London NW1 3BH T 020-7873 6000
A, B, C, Q, U, V, X

HOLLIS PUBLISHING LTD
Harlequin House, 7 High Street, Teddington, Middlesex TW11 8EL T 020-8977 7711
W www.hollis-pr.co.uk L

JOHN HUNT PUBLISHING LTD
46A West Street, New Alresford, Hants SO24 9AU
T 01962-736880 E john@johnhunt-publishing.com
C, U

ICON BOOKS LTD
Grange Road, Duxford, Cambridge CB2 4QF
T 01763-208008 E info@iconbooks.co.uk
W www.iconbooks.co.uk C, D, M, N, Q, R, X

INDEPENDENT MUSIC PRESS/IMP FICTION
PO Box 14691, London SE1 2ZA T 01440-788561
E info@impbooks.com W www.impbooks.com M

INSIGHT GUIDES/BERLITZ PUBLISHING
58 Borough High Street, London SE1 1XF
T 020-7403 0284 W www.insightguides.com I, L, V

INTER-VARSITY PRESS
38 De Montfort Street, Leicester LE1 7GP T 0116-255 1754
E ivp@uccf.org.uk W www.ivpbooks.com C

IVY PRESS LTD
The Old Candlemakers, West Street, Lewes, East Sussex BN7 2NZ T 01273-487440 E surname@ivypress.com
W www.ivypress.com P, V

JANE'S INFORMATION GROUP
163 Brighton Road, Coulsdon, Surrey CR5 2YH T 020-8700 3700 W www.janes.com H

JARROLD PUBLISHING
Whitefriars, Norwich NR3 1JR T 01603-763300 L

JORDAN PUBLISHING LTD
21 St Thomas Street, Bristol BS1 6JS T 0117-923 0600
W www.jordanpublishing.co.uk E

KENILWORTH PRESS LTD
Addington, Buckingham MK18 2JR T 0129 671-5101
E mail@kenilworthpress.co.uk
W www.kenilworthpress.co.uk V

KINGFISHER PUBLICATIONS PLC
New Penderel House, 283–288 High Holborn, London WC1V 7HZ T 020-7903 9999 E sales@kingfisherpub.co.uk
W www.kingfisher.com J, U

LAURENCE KING PUBLISHING LTD
71 Great Russell Street, London WC1B 3BP T 020-7430 8850
E enquiries@laurenceking.co.uk W www.laurenceking.co.uk
N, P

JESSICA KINGSLEY PUBLISHERS
116 Pentonville Road, London N1 9JB T 020-7833 2307
E post@jkp.com W www.jkp.com B, C, E, F, R

KLUWER ACADEMIC/PLENUM PUBLISHERS
Suite 52, Alpha House, 100 Borough High Street, London SE1 1LB T 020-7863 3318 W www.wkap.nl D, F, R

KOGAN PAGE LTD
120 Pentonville Road, London N1 9JN T 020-7278 0433
W www.kogan.page.co.uk G, D

LAWRENCE & WISHART LTD
99A Wallis Road, London E9 5LN T 020-8533 2506
E lw@lwbooks.demon.co.uk W www.lwbooks.co.uk
R, S

LETTS EDUCATIONAL
Chiswick Centre, 414 Chiswick High Road, London W4 5TF
T 020-8996 3333 E mail@lettsed.co.uk
W www.lettsed.co.uk B, D, G

LEXISNEXIS UK
Halsbury House, 35 Chancery Lane, London WC2A 1EL
T 020-7400 2500 E customer.services@lexisnexis.co.uk
W www.lexisnexis.co.uk E, G

FRANCES LINCOLN LTD
4 Torriano Mews, Torriano Avenue, London NW5 2RZ
T 020-7284 4009 E reception@frances-lincoln.com
W www.frances-lincoln.com O, U, V

LION HUDSON PLC
Mayfield House, 256 Banbury Road, Oxford OX2 7DH
T 01865-302750 E enquiries@lionhudson.com
W www.lionhudson.com C, U
W www.lion-publishing.co.uk

LIVERPOOL UNIVERSITY PRESS
4 Cambridge Street, Liverpool L69 7ZU T 0151-794 2233
E robblo@liv.ac.uk W www.liverpool-unipress.co.uk Q, R, X

LONELY PLANET PUBLICATIONS
72–82 Rosebery Avenue, London EC1R 4RW
T 020-7841 9000 E go@lonelyplanet.co.uk
W www.lonelyplanet.com L, V

MCGRAW-HILL EDUCATION
McGraw-Hill House, Shoppenhangers Road, Maidenhead, Berks SL6 2QL T 01628-502500
E emea_queries@mcgraw-hill.com
W www.mcgraw-hill.co.uk B, D, F, G, J, Q, R

MACMILLAN PUBLISHERS LTD
The Macmillan Building, 4 Crinan Street, London N1 9XW
T 020-7833 4000 W www.macmillan.co.uk
A, B, G, H, J, N, Q, S, U, V

MANCHESTER UNIVERSITY PRESS
Oxford Road, Manchester M13 9NR T 0161-275 2310
E mup@man.ac.uk W www.manchesteruniversitypress.co.uk
B, E, P, Q, R, W, X

MERRELL PUBLISHERS LTD
42 Southwark Street, London SE1 1UN T 020-7403 2047
E mail@merrellpublishers.com
W www.merrellpublishers.com O, P

METHUEN PUBLISHING LTD
215 Vauxhall Bridge Road, London SW1V 1EJ
T 020-7798 1600 A, Q, N, X

MICHELIN TRAVEL PUBLICATIONS
Hannay House, 39 Clarendon Road, Watford, Herts WD17 1JA T 01923-205240 W www.viamichelin.com K, L

JOHN MURRAY PUBLISHERS LTD
338 Euston Road, London NW1 3BH T 020-7873 6000
F 020-7873 6446 A, Q, X

NATIONAL ASSOCIATION FOR THE TEACHING OF ENGLISH (NATE)
50 Broadfield Road, Sheffield S8 0XJ T 0114-255 5419
E natehq@btconnect.com W www.nate.org.uk B

NELSON THORNES LTD
Delta Place, 27 Bath Road, Cheltenham, Glos GL53 7TH
T 01242-267100 E name@nelsonthornes.com
W www.nelsonthornes.com B

NEW CAVENDISH BOOKS
3 Denbigh Road, London W11 2SJ T 020-7229 6765
E sales@cavbooks.demon.co.uk
W www.newcavendishbooks.co.uk L, P

NEW HOLLAND PUBLISHERS UK LTD
Garfield House, 86 Edgware Road, London W2 2EA
T 020-7724 7773 E postmaster@nhpub.co.uk
W www.newhollandpublishers.com V

JANE NISSEN BOOKS
Swan House, Chiswick Mall, London W4 2PS
T 020-8994 8203 E niss@easynet.co.uk U

W. W. NORTON & COMPANY
Castle House, 75–76 Wells Street, London W1T 3QT
T 020-7323 1579 A, D, M, X

OBERON BOOKS
521 Caledonian Road, London N7 9RH T 020-7607 3637
E oberon.books@btinternet.com W www.oberonbooks.com
N

OCTAGON PRESS LTD
PO Box 227, London N6 4EW T 020-8348 9392
E octagon@schredds.demon.co.uk
W www.octagonpress.com C, D, S

OCTOPUS PUBLISHING GROUP
2–4 Heron Quays, London E14 4JP T 020-7531 8400
E firstname.lastname@octopus-publishing.co.uk
W www.octopus-publishing.co.uk K, V

MICHAEL O'MARA BOOKS LTD
9 Lion Yard, Tremadoc Road, London SW4 7NQ
T 020-7720 8643 W www.mombooks.com Q, U, X

ONEWORLD PUBLICATIONS
185 Banbury Road, Oxford OX2 7AR T 01865-310597
E info@oneworld-publications.com
W www.oneworld-publications.com C, Q, S

ONLYWOMEN PRESS LTD
40 St Lawrence Terrace, London W10 5ST T 020-8354 0796
E onlywomenpress@aol.com W www.onlywomenpress.com
A, N, X

ORION PUBLISHING GROUP LTD
Orion House, 5 Upper St Martin's Lane, London WC2H 9EA
T 020-7240 3444 W www.orionbooks.co.uk
A, J, U

OSPREY PUBLISHING LTD
Elms Court, Chapel Way, Botley, Oxford OX2 9LP
T 01865-727022 E info@ospreypublishing.com
W www.ospreypublishing.com H

PETER OWEN LTD
73 Kenway Road, London SW5 0RE
T 020-7373 5628/370 6093 E admin@peterowen.com
W www.peterowen.com A, N, Q, X

OXFORD UNIVERSITY PRESS
Great Clarendon Street, Oxford OX2 6DP T 01865-556767
E enquiry@oup.com W www.oup.com
B, C, D, E, F, H, I, J, K, M, P, Q, R, S, U

PAVILION PUBLISHING BRIGHTON LTD
The Ironworks, Cheapside, Brighton BN1 4GD
T 01273-623222 E info@pavpub.com W www.pavpub.com
G

PEARSON EDUCATION
Edinburgh Gate, Harlow, Essex CM20 2JE T 01279-623623
E firstname.lastname@pearsoned-ema.com
W www.pearsoned.co.uk
B

PEN & SWORD BOOKS LTD
47 Church Street, Barnsley, South Yorkshire S70 2AS
T 01226-734222 E charles@pen-and-sword.co.uk
W www.pen-and-sword.co.uk H, Q

PENGUIN GROUP (UK)
80 Strand, London WC2R 0RL T 020-7010 3000
W www.penguin.co.uk A, I, J, N, R, U, V, X

PETERLOO POETS
The Old Chapel, Sand Lane, Calstock, Cornwall PL18 9QX
T 01822-833473 E poets@peterloo.fsnet.co.uk
W www.peterloopoets.co.uk N

PHAIDON PRESS LTD
Regent's Wharf, All Saints Street, London N1 9PA
T 020-7843 1000 W www.phaidon.com M, N, P

PIATKUS BOOKS
5 Windmill Street, London W1T 2JA T 020-7631 0710
E info@piatkus.co.uk W www.piatkus.co.uk A, J, Q, V

PLUTO PRESS
345 Archway Road, London N6 5AA T 020-8348 2724
E pluto@plutobooks.com W www.plutobooks.com Q, R, T

POLITY PRESS
65 Bridge Street, Cambridge CB2 1UR T 01223-324315
W www.polity.co.uk Q, R, S

QUADRILLE PUBLISHING
5th Floor, Alhambra House, 27–31 Charing Cross Road,
London WC2H 0LS T 020-7839 7117 V

QUARTET BOOKS LTD
27 Goodge Street, London W1T 2LD T 020-7636 3992
E quartetbooks@easynet.co.uk A, M, Q

QUEEN ANNE PRESS
Windmill Cottage, Mackerye End, Harpenden, Herts AL5 5DR
T 01582-715866 E stephenson@lennardqap.co.uk V

RAGGED BEARS PUBLISHING LTD
Unit 14A, Bennett's Field Trading Estate, Southgate Road,
Wincanton, Somerset BA9 9DT T 01963-824184
E info@raggedbears.co.uk W www.raggedbears.co.uk U

RANDOM HOUSE GROUP LTD
20 Vauxhall Bridge Road, London SW1V 2SA
T 020-7840 8400 W www.randomhouse.co.uk
A, G, J, M, N, Q, R, S, U, V

READER'S DIGEST ASSOCIATION LTD
11 Westferry Circus, Canary Wharf, London E14 4HE
T 020-7715 8000 A, I, J, K, L, M, V

REAKTION BOOKS
77–79 Farringdon Road, London EC1M 3JU T 020-7404 9930
E info@reaktionbooks.co.uk W www.reaktionbooks.co.uk
N, P, Q

SCHOFIELD & SIMS LTD
Dogley Mill, Fenay Bridge, Huddersfield HD8 0NQ
T 01484-607080 E sales@schofieldandsims.co.uk B, U

SCHOLASTIC LTD
Villiers House, Clarendon Avenue, Leamington Spa, Warks
CV32 5PR T 01926-887799 W www.scholastic.co.uk
B, U

SIMON & SCHUSTER
Africa House, 64–78 Kingsway, London WC2B 6AH
T 020-7316 1900 W www.simonsays.co.uk A, Q, U, X

SWEET & MAXWELL
100 Avenue Road, London NW3 3PF T 020-7393 7000 E

I. B. TAURIS & CO. LTD
6 Salem Road, London W2 4BU T 020-7243 1225
E mail@ibtauris.com W www.ibtauris.com
N, P, Q, R, L, X

TAYLOR AND FRANCIS BOOKS LTD
4 Park Road, Milton Park, Abingdon, Oxon OX14 4RN
T 01235-828600 E info@tandf.co.uk W www.tandf.co.uk
D, F, G, H, J, P, Q, E,

THAMES & HUDSON LTD
181A High Holborn, London WC1V 7QX T 020-7845 5000
E sales@thameshudson.co.uk
W www.thamesandhudson.com P

TITAN BOOKS
144 Southwark Street, London SE1 0UP T 020-7620 0200
E editorial@titanemail.com W www.titanbooks.com A

TRANSWORLD PUBLISHERS
61–63 Uxbridge Road, London W5 5SA T 020-8579 2652
E info@transworld-publishers.co.uk
W www.booksattransworld.co.uk H, Q, M, U, V, X

TSO (THE STATIONERY OFFICE)
St Crispins, Duke Street, Norwich NR3 1PD
T 0870-6005522 W www.tso.co.uk B, F, J, L,

USBORNE PUBLISHING LTD
Usborne House, 83–85 Saffron Hill, London EC1N 8RT
T 020-7430 2800 E mail@usborne.co.uk
W www.usborne.com U, V

VERSO LTD
6 Meard Street, London W1F 0EG T 020-7437 3546
E verso@verso.co.uk Q, R, S

VIRGIN BOOKS LTD
Thames Wharf Studios, Rainville Road, London W6 9HA
T 020-7386 3300 W www.virgin.com/books
A, M, N, V, X

WALKER BOOKS LTD
87 Vauxhall Walk, London SE11 5HJ **T** 020-7793 0909
E mail@walker.co.uk **W** www.walkerbooks.co.uk **U**

WARD LOCK EDUCATIONAL CO. LTD
BIC Ling Kee House, 1 Christopher Road, East Grinstead, West Sussex RH19 3BT **T** 01342-318980 **E** wle@lingkee.com
W www.wardlockeducational.com **B**

WATTS PUBLISHING GROUP LTD
96 Leonard Street, London EC2A 4XD **T** 020-7739 2929
E gm@wattspub.co.uk **W** www.wattspublishing.co.uk **U**

WEBSTERS INTERNATIONAL PUBLISHERS LTD
2nd Floor, Axe & Bottle Court, 70 Newcomen Street, London SE1 1YT **T** 020-7940 4700 **W** www.websters.co.uk **V**

WEIDENFELD & NICOLSON
Orion House, 5 Upper St Martin's Lane, London WC2H 9EA
T 020-7240 3444 **A, H, I, J, O, Q, V**

JOSEF WEINBERGER PLAYS LTD
12–14 Mortimer Street, London W1T 3JJ **T** 020-7580 2827
E general.info@jwmail.co.uk **W** www.josef-weinberger.com
N

WELSH ACADEMIC PRESS
PO Box 733, Cardiff CF14 2YX **T** 029-2056 0343
E post@welsh-academic-press.com
W www.welsh-academic-press.com **Q, R**

WHICH? LTD
2 Marylebone Road, London NW1 4DF **T** 020-7770 7000
E books@which.net **L, V**

WILEY EUROPE LTD
The Atrium, Southern Gate, Chichester, West Sussex PO19 8SQ **T** 01243-779777 **E** europe@wiley.co.uk
W www.wileyeurope.com **D, F, G, J, L, P**

WINDRUSH PRESS
Windrush House, Adlestrop, Moreton-in-Marsh, Glos GL56 0YN **T** 01608-658758
E victoriama.huxley@btinternet.com
W www.windrushpress.com **Q, X**

WOMEN'S PRESS
Top Floor, 27 Goodge Street, London W1P 2LD
T 020-7580 7806 **W** www.the-womens-press.com
A, Q, R

EMPLOYERS' AND TRADE ASSOCIATIONS

Most national employers' associations are members of the Confederation of British Industry (CBI).

CBI

Centre Point, 103 New Oxford Street, London WC1A 1DU
T 020-7379 7400

The CBI was founded in 1965 and is an independent non-party political body financed by industry and commerce. It exists primarily to ensure that the Government understands the intentions, needs and problems of British business. It is the recognised spokesman for the business viewpoint and is consulted as such by the Government.

The CBI has a direct corporate membership employing over 4 million, and a trade association membership over 6 million of the workforce.

The governing body of the CBI is the Council, which meets four times a year in London under the chairmanship of the President. It is assisted by 17 expert standing committees which advise on the main aspects of policy. There are 12 regional councils and offices, covering the administrative regions of England, Wales, Scotland and Northern Ireland. There is also an office in Brussels and one in Washington.

President, Sir John Egan
Director-General, Digby Jones

WALES: 2 Caspian Point, Caspian Way, Cardiff Bay, Cardiff, CF10 4DQ T 029-2045 3710
Regional Director, David Rosser

SCOTLAND: 16 Robertson Street, Glasgow G2 8DS T 0141-222 2184
Regional Director, Ian McMillan

NORTHERN IRELAND: Scottish Amicable Building, 11 Donegall Square, Belfast BT1 5SE T 028-9032 6658
Regional Director, Nigel Smyth

ASSOCIATIONS

ADVERTISING ASSOCIATION, Abford House, 15 Wilton Road, London SW1V 1NJ T 020-7828 2771 E aa@adassoc.org.uk W www.adassoc.org.uk
Director-General, Andrew Brown

ASSOCIATION OF BRITISH INSURERS, 51 Gresham Street, London EC2V 7HQ T 020-7600 3333 E info@abi.org.uk W www.abi.org.uk
Director-General, M. Francis

ASSOCIATION OF PRIVATE MARKET OPERATORS, 4 Worrygoose Lane, Rotherham S60 4AD T 01709-700072 E marketsman@lineone.net W www.apmomarkets.co.uk
General Secretary, David J. Glasby

BLC LEATHER TECHNOLOGY CENTRE LTD, Leather Trade House, Kings Park Road, Moulton Park, Northampton NN3 6JD T 01604-679999 E info@blcleathertech.com W www.blcleathertech.com
Managing Director, M. W. Parsons

BOSS FEDERATION, 12 Corporation Street, High Wycombe HP13 6TQ T 0845-450 1565 E info@bossfederation.co.uk W www.bossfederation.co.uk
Chief Executive, K. Davies

BRITISH APPAREL AND TEXTILE CONFEDERATION, 5 Portland Place, London W1B 1PW T 020-7636 7788 E batc@dial.pipex.com W www.batc.co.uk
Director-General, J. R. Wilson, OBE

BRITISH BANKERS' ASSOCIATION, Pinners Hall, 105–108 Old Broad Street, London EC2N 1EX T 020-7216 8800 W www.bba.org.uk *Chief Executive*, Ian Mullen

BRITISH BEER AND PUB ASSOCIATION, Market Towers, 1 Nine Elms Lane, London SW8 5NQ T 020-7627 9191 E enquiries@beerandpub.com W www.beerandpub.com
Chief Executive Officer, R. Hayward, OBE

BRITISH CLOTHING INDUSTRY ASSOCIATION LTD, 5 Portland Place, London W1B 1PW T 020-7636 7788 E bcia@dial.pipex.com *Director*, J. R. Wilson, OBE

BRITISH MARINE FEDERATION, Marine House, Thorpe Lea Road, Egham TW20 8BF T 01784-473377 E info@britishmarine.co.uk W www.britishmarine.co.uk
Chief Executive, John Clarke, CBE, LVO, MBE

BRITISH PLASTICS FEDERATION, 6 Bath Place, Rivington Street, London EC2A 3JE T 020-7457 5000 E bpf@bpf.co.uk
Director-General, P. Davis, OBE

BRITISH PORTS ASSOCIATION, Africa House, 64–78 Kingsway, London WC2B 6AH T 020-7242 1200 E info@britishports.org.uk W www.britishports.org.uk
Director, D. Whitehead

BRITISH PRINTING INDUSTRIES FEDERATION, Farringdon Point, 29–35 Farringdon Road, London EC1M 3JF T 0870-240 4085 E info@bpif.org.uk
Chief Executive, Michael Johnson

BRITISH PROPERTY FEDERATION, 7th Floor, 1 Warwick Row, London SW1E 5ER T 020-7828 0111 E info@bpf.org.uk W www.bpf.org.uk
Chief Executive, Mrs L. Peace

BRITISH RETAIL CONSORTIUM, 2nd Floor, 21 Dartmouth Street, London SW1H 9BP T 020-7854 8900 E info@brc.org.uk W www.brc.org.uk
Director-General, W. Moyes

BRITISH RUBBER MANUFACTURERS' ASSOCIATION LTD, 6 Bath Place, Rivington Street, London EC2A 3JE T 020-7457 5040 E mail@brma.co.uk W www.brma.co.uk
Director, A. J. Dorken

CHAMBER OF SHIPPING LTD, Carthusian Court, 12 Carthusian Street, London EC1M 6EZ T 020-7417 2800 E postmaster@british-shipping.org
Director-General, Mr M. Brownrigg

CHEMICAL INDUSTRIES ASSOCIATION LTD, Kings Buildings, Smith Square, London SW1P 3JJ T 020-7834 3399 E enquiries@cia.org.uk
Director-General, Mrs Judith Hackitt

COMMERCIAL RADIO COMPANIES ASSOCIATION (CRCA), The Radiocentre, 77 Shaftesbury Avenue, London W1D 5DU T 020-7306 2603 E info@crca.co.uk W www.crca.co.uk
Chief Executive, P. Brown, CBE

CONFEDERATION OF PAPER INDUSTRIES, Rivenhall Road, Swindon SN5 7BD T 01793-889600 E fedn@paper.org.uk W www.paper.org.uk
Director-General, Dr Martin Oldman

CONFEDERATION OF PASSENGER TRANSPORT UK, Imperial House, 15–19 Kingsway, London WC2B 6UN T 020-7240 3131 E cpt@cpt-uk.org W www.cpt-uk.org/cpt
Director-General, Brian Nimick, OBE

CONSTRUCTION CONFEDERATION, Construction House, 56–64 Leonard Street, London EC2A 4JX T 020-7608 5000 E enquiries@constructionconfederation.co.uk W www.constructionconfederation.co.uk
Chief Executive, S. Ratcliffe

CONSTRUCTION PRODUCTS ASSOCIATION, 26 Store Street, London WC1E 7BT T 020-7323 3770 E enquiries@constprod.org.uk W www.constprod.org.uk
Chief Executive, M. G. Ankers, FRSA

DAIRY INDUSTRY ASSOCIATION LTD, 93 Baker Street, London W1U 6RL T 020-7486 7244 E info@dia-ltd.org.uk
Director-General, J. Begg

ENGINEERING EMPLOYERS' FEDERATION (EEF), Broadway House, Tothill Street, London SW1H 9NQ T 020-7222 7777 E enquiries@eef-fed.org.uk W www.eef.org.uk
Director-General, M. J. Temple

FEDERATION OF BAKERS, 6 Catherine Street, London WC2B 5JW T 020-7420 7190 E info@bakersfederation.org.uk W www.bakersfederation.org.uk
Director, J. S. White

FEDERATION OF BRITISH ELECTROTECHNICAL AND ALLIED MANUFACTURERS' ASSOCIATIONS (BEAMA), Westminster Tower, 3 Albert Embankment, London SE1 7SL T 020-7793 3000 E info@beama.org.uk W www.beama.org.uk
Director-General, David Dossett

FEDERATION OF MASTER BUILDERS, Gordon Fisher House, 14–15 Great James Street, London WC1N 3DP T 020-7242 7583 E central@fmb.org.uk W www.fmb.org.uk
Director-General, I. Davis

FINANCE AND LEASING ASSOCIATION, 2nd Floor, Imperial House, 15–19 Kingsway, London WC2B 6UN T 020-7836 6511 E info@fla.org.uk W www.fla.org.uk
Director-General, M. A. Hall, MVO

FOOD AND DRINK FEDERATION, 6 Catherine Street, London WC2B 5JJ T 020-7836 2460 E generalenquiries@fdf.org.uk W www.fdf.org.uk
Director-General, Sylvia Jay

FREIGHT TRANSPORT ASSOCIATION LTD, Hermes House, St John's Road, Tunbridge Wells TN4 9UZ T 01892-526171 E enquiries@fta.org.uk W www.fta.org.uk
Chief Executive, Richard Turner

INSTITUTE OF CHARTERED FORESTERS, 7A St Colme Street, Edinburgh EH3 6AA T 0131-225 2705 E icf@charteredforesters.org W www.charteredforesters.org
Executive Director, Mrs M. W. Dick, FRSA, OBE

KNITTING INDUSTRIES' FEDERATION LTD, 53 Oxford Street, Leicester LE1 5XY T 0116-254 1608 E directorate@knitfed.co.uk
Director, Anne Carvell

LEATHER PRODUCERS' ASSOCIATION, 8 Queensberry Road, Kettering NN15 7HL T 01536-483668
National Secretary, J. Purvis

MANAGEMENT CONSULTANCIES ASSOCIATION, 49 Whitehall, London SW1A 2BX T 020-7321 3990 W www.mca.org.uk
Executive Director, B. Petter

NATIONAL FARMERS' UNION (NFU), Agriculture House, 164 Shaftesbury Avenue, London WC2H 8HL T 020-7331 7200 E nfu@nfuonline.com W www.nfu.org.uk
Director-General, R. Macdonald

NATIONAL FEDERATION OF RETAIL NEWSAGENTS, Suite A, Manhattan House, 140 High Street, Crowthorne RG45 7AY T 0845-601 5818 E info@nfrn.org.uk
Regional Manager, Paul Howell

NATIONAL MARKET TRADERS' FEDERATION, Hampton House, Hawshaw Lane, Hoyland, Barnsley S74 0HA T 01226-749021 W www.nmtf.co.uk E enquiries@nmtf.co.uk
General Secretary, D. E. Feeny

NEWSPAPER PUBLISHERS ASSOCIATION LTD, 34 Southwark Bridge Road, London SE1 9EU T 020-7207 2200
Director, S. Oram

NEWSPAPER SOCIETY, Bloomsbury House, 74–77 Great Russell Street, London WC1B 3DA T 020-7636 7014 E directorate@newspapersoc.org.uk W www.newspapersoc.org.uk
Director, D. Newell

PUBLISHERS ASSOCIATION, 29B Montague Street, London WC1B 5BW T 020-7691 9191 E mail@publishers.org.uk W www.publishers.org.uk
Chief Executive, A. R. Williams, OBE

ROAD HAULAGE ASSOCIATION LTD, Roadway House, 35 Monument Hill, Weybridge KT13 8RN T 01932-841515 E weybridge@rha.net W www.rha.net
Chief Executive, R. King

SOCIETY OF BRITISH AEROSPACE COMPANIES LTD, Duxbury House, 60 Petty France, London SW1H 9EU T 020-7227 1000 W www.sbac.co.uk E post@sbac.co.uk

SOCIETY OF MOTOR MANUFACTURERS AND TRADERS LTD, Forbes House, Halkin Street, London SW1X 7DS T 020-7235 7000 W www.smmt.co.uk E membership@smmt.co.uk
Chief Executive, C. Macgowan

SPORT INDUSTRIES FEDERATION, Federation House, National Agricultural Centre, Stoneleigh Park, Kenilworth CV8 2RF T 024-7641 4999 W www.sports-life.com E admin@sportslife.org.uk
Managing Director, David Gent

TIMBER TRADE FEDERATION, Clareville House, 26–27 Oxendon Street, London SW1Y 4EL T 020-7839 1891 W www.ttf.co.uk E ttf@ttf.co.uk
Director-General, P. C. Martin

UK OFFSHORE OPERATORS ASSOCIATION LTD, Second Floor, 232–242 Vauxhall Bridge Road, London SW1V 1AY T 020-7802 2400 E info@ukooa.co.uk
Chief Executive, Malcolm Webb

UK PETROLEUM INDUSTRY ASSOCIATION LTD, 9 Kingsway, London WC2B 6XF T 020-7240 0289 E info@ukpia.com W www.ukpia.com
Director-General, Chris Hunt

ULSTER FARMERS' UNION, 475 Antrim Road, Belfast BT15 3DA T 028-9037 0222 W www.ufuni.org E info@ufuhq.com
Director-General, C. Black

TRADE UNIONS

Nearly 80 per cent of trade union members belong to unions affiliated to the TUC.

The Central Arbitration Committee arbitrates on trade disputes, adjudicates on disclosure of information complaints, determines claims for statutory recognition under the Employment Relations Act 1999 and certain issues relating to the implementation of the European Works Council Directive.

CENTRAL ARBITRATION COMMITTEE

Discovery House, 28–42 Banner Street, London EC1Y 8QE
T 020-7251 9747 **F** 020-7251 3114 **W** www.cac.gov.uk
Chairman, Sir Michael Burton
Secretary and Chief Executive, Graeme Charles

TRADES UNION CONGRESS (TUC)

Congress House, 23–28 Great Russell Street, London WC1B 3LS
T 020-7636 4030 **F** 020-7636 0632
W www.tuc.org.uk

The Trades Union Congress, founded in 1868, is an independent association of trade unions. The TUC promotes the rights and welfare of those in work and helps the unemployed. It helps its member unions promote membership in new areas and industries, and campaigns for rights at work for all employees, including part-time and temporary workers, whether union members or not. TUC representatives sit on many public bodies at national and international level. It makes representations to government, political parties, employers and international bodies such as the European Union.

The governing body of the TUC is the annual Congress. Between Congresses, business is conducted by a General Council, which meets five times a year, and an Executive Committee, which meets monthly. The full-time staff is headed by the General Secretary who is elected by Congress and is a permanent member of the General Council.

There are some 71 affiliated unions with a membership of nearly 7,000,000.
President (2004–5), Jeannie Drake
General Secretary, B. Barber, elected 2002

SCOTTISH TRADES UNION CONGRESS

333 Woodlands Road, Glasgow G3 6NG **T** 0141-337 8100
F 0141-337 8101 **E** info@stuc.org.uk

The Congress was formed in 1897 and acts as a national centre for the trade union movement in Scotland. The STUC promotes the rights to welfare of those in work and helps the unemployed. It helps its member unions to promote membership in new areas and industries, and campaigns for rights at work for all employees, including part-time temporary workers, whether union members or not. It makes representations to government and employers. In June 2004 it consisted of 46 unions with a total membership of over 630,000.

The Annual Congress in April elects a 39-member General Council on the basis of six industrial sections.
Chairperson, Sandy Boyle
General Secretary, Bill Speirs

AFFILIATED UNIONS

As at April 2004

ABBEY NATIONAL GROUP UNION (ANGU), 2nd Floor, 16–17 High Street, Tring HP23 5AH **T** 01442-891122 **E** info@angu.org.uk **W** www.angu.org.uk
General Secretary, Linda Rolph *Membership:* 9,000

ACCORD, Simmons House, 46 Old Bath Road, Charvil RG10 9QR **T** 0118-934 1808 **E** info@accordhq.org **W** www.accord-myunion.org
General Secretary, Ged Nichols *Membership:* 23,772

ALLIANCE AND LEICESTER GROUP UNION OF STAFF (ALGUS), 22 Upper King Street Leicester LE1 6XE **T** 0116-285 6585 **E** terrialgus@aol.com **W** www.algus.org.uk
General Secretary, Clare Clark *Membership:* 2,838

AMICUS (FORMERLY AEEU AND MSF), 33 King Street, London WC2E 8JG **T** 020-7420 8900 **W** www.amicustheunion.org
Joint General Secretaries, Derek Simpson/Roger Lyons *Membership:* 1,061,199

ASSOCIATED SOCIETY OF LOCOMOTIVE ENGINEERS AND FIREMEN (ASLEF), 9 Arkwright Road, London NW3 6AB **T** 020-7317 8600 **E** info@aslef.org.uk **W** www.aslef.org.uk
General Secretary, Shaun Brady *Membership:* 16,172

ASSOCIATION FOR COLLEGE MANAGEMENT (ACM), 10 De Montfort Street, Leicester LE1 7GG **T** 0116-275 5076 **E** admin@acm.uk.com **W** www.acm.uk.com
General Secretary, Peter Pendle *Membership:* 3,481

ASSOCIATION OF EDUCATIONAL PSYCHOLOGISTS (AEP), 26 The Avenue, Durham DH1 4ED **T** 0191-384 9512 **E** sao@aep.org.uk **W** www.aep.org.uk
General Secretary, B. Harrison-Jennings *Membership:* 2,741

ASSOCIATION OF FIRST DIVISION CIVIL SERVANTS (FDA), 2 Caxton Street, London SW1H 0QH **T** 020-7343 1111 **E** head-office@fda.org.uk **W** www.fda.org.uk
General Secretary, Jonathan Baume *Membership:* 10,883

ASSOCIATION OF FLIGHT ATTENDANTS (AFA), United Airlines Cargo Centre, AFA Council 07, Shoreham Road East, Heathrow Airport TW6 3UA **T** 020-8276 6723 **E** afa@afalhr.org.uk **W** www.afalhr.org.uk
President, Kevin Creighan *Membership:* 750

ASSOCIATION OF MAGISTERIAL OFFICERS (AMO), 1 Fellmongers Path, 176 Tower Bridge Road, London SE1 3LY **T** 020-7403 2244 **E** hq@amo.org.uk **W** www.amo-online.org.uk
General Secretary, Rosie Eagleson *Membership:* 6,813

ASSOCIATION OF TEACHERS AND LECTURERS (ATL), 7 Northumberland Street, London WC2N 5RD **T** 020-7930 6441 **E** info@atl.org.uk **W** www.askatl.org.uk
General Secretary, Dr Mary Boustead *Membership:* 160,000

ASSOCIATION OF UNIVERSITY TEACHERS (AUT), Egmont House, 25–31 Tavistock Place, London WC1H 9UT **T** 020-7670 9700 **E** hq@aut.org.uk **W** www.aut.org.uk
General Secretary, Sally Hunt *Membership:* 46,223

BAKERS, FOOD AND ALLIED WORKERS' UNION (BFAWU), Stanborough House, Great North Road, Stanborough, Welwyn Garden City AL8 7TA **T** 01707-260150 **E** bfawuho@aol.com **W** www.bfawu.org
General Secretary, Joe Marino *Membership:* 28,168

BRITANNIA STAFF UNION (BSU), Court Lodge, Leonard Street, Leek ST13 5JP T 01538-399627 E bsu@themail.co.uk W www.britanniasu.org.uk
General Secretary, David O'Dowd
Membership: 2,352

BRITISH AIR LINE PILOTS ASSOCIATION (BALPA), 81 New Road, Harlington, Hayes UB3 5BG T 020-8476 4000 E balpa@balpa.org W www.balpa.org
General Secretary, Jim McAuslan
Membership: 7,985

BRITISH AND IRISH ORTHOPTIC SOCIETY, Tavistock House North, Tavistock Square, London WC1H 9HX T 020-7387 7992 E bos@orthoptics.org.uk W www.orthoptics.org.uk
Hon. Secretary, Rosie Auld *Membership:* 1,400

BRITISH ASSOCIATION OF COLLIERY MANAGEMENT – TECHNICAL, ENERGY AND ADMINISTRATIVE MANAGEMENT (BACM-TEAM), 17 South Parade, Doncaster DN1 2DR T 01302-815551 E enquiries@bacmteam.org.uk W www.bacmteam.org.uk
General Secretary, Pat Carragher *Membership:* 5,000

BRITISH DIETETIC ASSOCIATION (BDA), 5th Floor, Charles House, 148–149 Great Charles Street, Queensway, Birmingham B3 3HT T 0121-200 8010 E info@bda.uk.com W www.bda.uk.com
General Secretary, Fiona Scott *Membership:* 5,000

BROADCASTING, ENTERTAINMENT, CINEMATOGRAPH AND THEATRE UNION (BECTU), 373–377 Clapham Road, London SW9 9BT T 020-7346 0900 E info@bectu.org.uk W www.bectu.org.uk
General Secretary, Roger Bolton *Membership:* 25,000

CARD SETTING MACHINE TENTERS' SOCIETY (CSMTS), 48 Scar End Lane, Staincliffe, Dewsbury WF13 4NY T 01924-400206
Secretary, Anthony John Moorhouse *Membership:* 88

CERAMIC AND ALLIED TRADES UNION (CATU), Hillcrest House, Garth Street, Hanley, Stoke-on-Trent ST1 2AB T 01782-272755 W www.catu.org.uk
General Secretary, G. Bagnall *Membership:* 12,497

CHARTERED SOCIETY OF PHYSIOTHERAPY (CSP), 14 Bedford Row, London WC1R 4ED T 020-7306 6666 W www.csp.org.uk
Director of Employment Relations, Richard Griffin
Membership: 34,857

COMMUNICATION WORKERS UNION (CWU), 150 The Broadway, Wimbledon, London SW19 1RX T 020-8971 7200 E info@cwu.org W www.cwu.org
General Secretary, B. Hayes *Membership:* 266,067

COMMUNITY AND DISTRICT NURSING ASSOCIATION (CDNA), Walpole House, 18–22 Bond Street, Ealing, London W5 5AA T 020-8231 0180 E cdna@tvu.ac.uk W www.cdna.tvu.ac.uk
Director, Anne Duffy *Membership:* 5,500

COMMUNITY AND YOUTH WORKERS UNION (CYWU), Unit 302, The Argent Centre, 60 Frederick Street, Birmingham B1 3HS T 0121-244 3344 E kerry@cywu.org.uk W www.cywu.org.uk
General Secretary, D. Nicholls *Membership:* 4,800

CONNECT, THE UNION FOR PROFESSIONALS IN COMMUNICATIONS, 30 St George's Road, London SW19 4BD T 020-8971 6000 E union@connectuk.org W www.connectuk.org
General Secretary, A. Askew *Membership:* 19,363

DERBYSHIRE BUILDING SOCIETY STAFF ASSOCIATION, The Mews, Duffield Hall, DE56 1AG T 01332-844396 E dsmith@dbssa.co.uk
Chairman, Deidre Smith *Membership:* 464

DIAGEO STAFF ASSOCIATION (DSA), Sun Works Cottage, Park Royal Brewery, London NW10 7RR T 020-8978 6069 E diageo.staff.association@diageo.com
Executive Chairman, D. Orton *Membership:* 605

EDUCATIONAL INSTITUTE OF SCOTLAND (EIS), 46 Moray Place, Edinburgh EH3 6BH T 0131-225 6244 E enquiries@eis.org.uk W www.eis.org.uk
General Secretary, Ronald A. Smith *Membership:* 53,424

EQUITY, Guild House, Upper St Martin's Lane, London WC2H 9EG T 020-7379 6000 E info@equity.org.uk W www.equity.org.uk
General Secretary, Ian McGarry *Membership:* 35,410

FIRE BRIGADES UNION, THE (FBU), Bradley House, 68 Coombe Road, Kingston upon Thames KT2 7AE T 020-8541 1765 E office@fbu.org.uk W www.fbu.org.uk
General Secretary, Andy Gilchrist *Membership:* 52,500

GENERAL UNION OF LOOM OVERLOOKERS (GULO), 9 Wellington Street, St John's, Blackburn BB1 8AF T 01254-51760
General Secretary, Don Rishton *Membership:* 265

GMB, 22–24 Worple Road, London SW19 4DD T 020-8947 3131 E kevincurran@gmb.org.uk W www.gmb.org.uk
General Secretary, Kevin Curran *Membership:* 700,000

GRAPHICAL, PAPER AND MEDIA UNION (GPMU), Keys House, 63–67 Bromham Road, Bedford MK40 2AG T 01234-351521 E general@gpmu.org.uk W www.gpmu.org.uk
General Secretary, A. D. Dubbins *Membership:* 170,279

HOSPITAL CONSULTANTS AND SPECIALISTS ASSOCIATION (HCSA), 1 Kingsclere Road, Overton, Basingstoke RG25 3JA T 01256-771777 E conspec@hcsa.com W www.hcsa.com
Chief Executive, Stephen Campion *Membership:* 2,850

ISTC – THE COMMUNITY UNION, Swinton House, 324 Gray's Inn Road, London WC1X 8DD T 020-7239 1200 E istc@istc-tu.org W www.istc-tu.org
General Secretary, Michael Leahy *Membership:* 29,000

MUSICIANS' UNION (MU), 60–62 Clapham Road, London SW9 0JJ T 020-7582 5566 E info@musiciansunion.org.uk W www.musiciansunion.org.uk
General Secretary, John Smith *Membership:* 31,312

NASUWT (NATIONAL ASSOCIATION OF SCHOOLMASTERS/UNION OF WOMEN TEACHERS), 5 King Street, London WC2E 8SD T 020-7420 9670 E nasuwt@mail.nasuwt.org.uk W www.teachersunion.org.uk
General Secretary, Eamonn O'Kane *Membership:* 211,779

NATFHE (THE UNIVERSITY AND COLLEGE LECTURERS' UNION), 27 Britannia Street, London WC1X 9JP T 020-7837 3636 E hq@natfhe.org.uk W www.natfhe.org.uk
General Secretary, P. Mackney *Membership:* 66,319

NATIONAL ASSOCIATION OF COLLIERY OVERMEN, DEPUTIES AND SHOTFIRERS (NACODS), Wadsworth House, 130–132 Doncaster Road, Barnsley S70 1TP T 01226-203743 E natnacods@aol.com W www.nacods.co.uk
General Secretary, Ian Parker *Membership:* 700

NATIONAL ASSOCIATION OF CO-OPERATIVE OFFICIALS (NACO), 6A Clarendon Place, Hyde, Cheshire, SK14 2QZ T 0161-351 7900 E lwe@nacoco-op.org
General Secretary, L. W. Ewing *Membership:* 2,750

NATIONAL ASSOCIATION OF EDUCATIONAL INSPECTORS, ADVISERS AND CONSULTANTS, Woolley Hall, Woolley WF4 2JR T 01226-383428 E naeiac@gensoft.co.uk W www.naeiac.org
General Secretary, J. Chowcat *Membership:* 3,401

NATIONAL UNION OF DOMESTIC APPLIANCES AND GENERAL OPERATIVES (NUDAGO), 1st Floor, 7–8 Imperial Buildings, Corporation Street, Rotherham S60 1PB **T** 01709-382820 **E** nudago@btclick.com
General Secretary, A. McCarthy *Membership:* 2,011

NATIONAL UNION OF JOURNALISTS (NUJ), Headland House, 308–312 Gray's Inn Road, London WC1X 8DP **T** 020-7278 7916 **E** info@nuj.org.uk **W** www.nuj.org.uk
General Secretary, Jeremy Dear *Membership:* 23,342

NATIONAL UNION OF KNITWEAR, FOOTWEAR AND APPAREL TRADES (KFAT), 55 New Walk, Leicester LE1 7EA **T** 0116-255 6703 **E** head-office@kfat.org.uk **W** www.kfat.org.uk
General Secretary, P. Gates *Membership:* 12,471

NATIONAL UNION OF LOCK AND METAL WORKERS (NULMW), Bellamy House, Wilkes Street, Willenhall WV13 2BS **T** 01902-366651 **E** nulmw@zoom.co.uk
General Secretary, R. Ward *Membership:* 3,708

NATIONAL UNION OF MARINE, AVIATION AND SHIPPING TRANSPORT OFFICERS (NUMAST), Oceanair House, 750–760 High Road, London E11 3BB **T** 020-8989 6677 **E** info@numast.org **W** www.numast.org
General Secretary, Brian Orrell *Membership:* 19,133

NATIONAL UNION OF MINEWORKERS (NUM), Miners' Offices, 2 Huddersfield Road, Barnsley S70 2LS **T** 01226-215555
National Secretary, S. Kemp *Membership:* 5,000

NATIONAL UNION OF RAIL, MARITIME AND TRANSPORT WORKERS (RMT), Unity House, 39 Chalton Street, London NW1 1JD **T** 020-7387 4771 **E** info@rmt.org.uk **W** www.rmt.org.uk
General Secretary, Bob Crow *Membership:* 63,084

NATIONAL UNION OF TEACHERS (NUT), Hamilton House, Mabledon Place, London WC1H 9BD **T** 020-7388 6191 **W** www.teachers.org.uk
General Secretary, Doug McAvoy *Membership:* 247,252

NATIONWIDE GROUP STAFF UNION (NGSU), Middleton Farmhouse, 37 Main Road, Middleton Cheney, Banbury OX17 2QT **T** 01295-710767 **E** ngsu@ngsu.org.uk **W** www.ngsu.org.uk
General Secretary, Tim Poil *Membership:* 12,000

PRISON OFFICERS' ASSOCIATION (POA), Cronin House, 245 Church Street, London N9 9HW **T** 020-8803 0255 **W** www.poauk.org.uk
General Secretary, B. Caton *Membership:* 33,500

PROFESSIONAL FOOTBALLERS' ASSOCIATION (PFA), 20 Oxford Court, Bishopsgate, Manchester M2 3WQ **T** 0161-236 0575 **E** info@thepfa.co.uk **W** www.thepfa.co.uk
Chief Executive, Gordon Taylor *Membership:* 3,848

PROSPECT, Prospect House, 75–79 York Road, London SE1 7AQ **T** 020-7902 6600 **E** enquiries@prospect.org.uk **W** www.prospect.org.uk
General Secretary, P. Noon *Membership:* 105,480

PUBLIC AND COMMERCIAL SERVICES UNION (PCS), 160 Falcon Road, London SW11 2LN **T** 020-7924 2727 **E** ben@pcs.org.uk **W** www.pcs.org.uk
General Secretary, Mark Serwotka
Membership: 281,923

SHEFFIELD WOOL SHEAR WORKERS' UNION (SWSWU), 17 Galsworthy Road, Sheffield S5 8QX **T** 07718-559 439
Secretary, B. Whomersley *Membership:* 15

SOCIETY OF CHIROPODISTS AND PODIATRISTS (SCP), 1 Fellmonger's Path, Tower Bridge Road, London SE1 3LY **T** 020-7234 8620 **E** enq@scpod.org **W** www.feetforlife.org
Acting Chief Executive, Joanna Brown
Membership: 7,592

SOCIETY OF RADIOGRAPHERS (SOR), 207 Providence Square, Mill Street, London SE1 2EW **T** 020-7740 7200 **E** info@sor.org **W** www.sor.org
Chief Executive, Richard Evans
Membership: 21,570

TRADE UNION AND PROFESSIONAL ASSOCIATION FOR FAMILY COURT AND PROBATION STAFF (NAPO), 4 Chivalry Road, London SW11 1HT **T** 020-7223 4887 **E** info@napo.org.uk **W** www.napo.org.uk
General Secretary, Judy McKnight *Membership:* 7,500

TRANSPORT AND GENERAL WORKERS' UNION (T&G), Transport House, 128 Theobalds Road, London WC1X 8TN **T** 020-7611 2500 **E** tgwu@tgwu.org.uk **W** www.tgwu.org.uk
General Secretary, Tony Woodley *Membership:* 835,351

TRANSPORT SALARIED STAFFS' ASSOCIATION (TSSA), Walkden House, 10 Melton Street, London NW1 2EJ **T** 020-7387 2101 **E** enquiries@tssa.org.uk **W** www.tssa.org.uk
General Secretary, Gerry Doherty
Membership: 32,345

UBAC (UNION FOR BRADFORD AND BINGLEY STAFF AND STAFF IN ASSOCIATED COMPANIES), 18D Market Place, Malton YO17 7LX **T** 01653-697634 **E** ubac@btconnect.com
General Secretary, D. Matthews *Membership:* 2,796

UNDEB CENEDLAETHOL ATHRAWON CYMRU (NATIONAL UNION OF THE TEACHERS OF WALES), Pen Roc, Rhodfa'r Môr, Aberystwyth SY23 2AZ **T** 01970-639950 **E** ucac@athrawon.com **W** www.athrawon.com
General Secretary, Moelwen Gwyndaf
Membership: 4,099

UNIFI, Sheffield House, 1B Amity Grove, London SW20 0LG **T** 020-8946 9151 **E** info@unifi.org.uk **W** www.unifi.org.uk
General Secretary, E. Sweeney *Membership:* 147,607

UNION OF CONSTRUCTION, ALLIED TRADES AND TECHNICIANS (UCATT), UCATT House, 177 Abbeville Road, London SW4 9RL **T** 020-7622 2442 **E** info@ucatt.org.uk **W** www.ucatt.org.uk
General Secretary, G. Brumwell *Membership:* 115,007

UNION OF SHOP, DISTRIBUTIVE AND ALLIED WORKERS (USDAW), 188 Wilmslow Road, Manchester M14 6LJ **T** 0161-224 2804 **E** enquiries@usdaw.org.uk **W** www.usdaw.org.uk
General Secretary, Sir Bill Connor *Membership:* 330,000

UNISON, 1 Mabledon Place, London WC1H 9AJ **T** 0845-355 0845 **W** www.unison.org.uk
General Secretary, Dave Prentis *Membership:* 1,300,500

WRITERS' GUILD OF GREAT BRITAIN (WGGB), 15 Britannia Street, London WC1X 9JN **T** 020-7833 0777 **E** admin@writersguild.org.uk **W** www.writersguild.org.uk
General Secretary, Bernie Corbett *Membership:* 2,000

YORKSHIRE INDEPENDENT STAFF ASSOCIATION (YISA), c/o Yorkshire Building Society, 3/5 Saturday Market, Beverley HU17 8BB **T** 01274-472 453 **E** kmwatson@ybs.co.uk
Chairperson, Karen Watson *Membership:* 1,436

NON-AFFILIATED UNIONS

As at April 2004

BRITISH DENTAL ASSOCIATION, 64 Wimpole Street, London W1G 8YS **T** 020-7935 0875 **E** enquiries@bda.org **W** www.bda.org.uk
Chair of the Executive Board, John Renshaw

CHARTERED INSTITUTE OF JOURNALISTS, 2 Dock Offices, Surrey Quays Road, London SE16 2XU **T** 020-7252 1187 **E** memberservices@ioj.co.uk **W** www.ioj.co.uk
General Secretary, Dominic Cooper

NATIONAL ASSOCIATION OF HEAD TEACHERS (NAHT), 1 Heath Square, Boltro Road, Haywards Heath RH16 1BL **T** 01444-472472 **E** info@naht.org.uk **W** www.naht.org.uk
General Secretary, David Hart, OBE

NATIONAL SOCIETY FOR EDUCATION IN ART AND DESIGN, The Gatehouse, Corsham Court, Corsham SN13 0BZ **T** 01249-714825 **E** bookshop@nsead.org **W** www.nsead.org
General Secretary, Dr J. M. Steers

PRISON GOVERNORS ASSOCIATION, Room 405, Horseferry House, Dean Ryle Street, London SW1P 2AW **T** 020-7217 8591 **W** www.prisongovernors.org.uk
General Secretary, C. Bushell

RETAIL BOOK, STATIONERY AND ALLIED TRADES EMPLOYEES' ASSOCIATION, 8–9 Commercial Road, Swindon SN1 5NF **T** 01793-615811 **E** office@the-rba.org
President, D. Pickles

ROYAL COLLEGE OF MIDWIVES, 15 Mansfield Street, London W1G 9NH **T** 020-7312 3535 **E** info@rcm.org.uk **W** www.rcm.org.uk
General Secretary, Dame Karlene Davis, DBE

SCOTTISH SECONDARY TEACHERS' ASSOCIATION (SSTA), 15 Dundas Street, Edinburgh EH3 6QG **T** 0131-556 5919 **E** info@ssta.org.uk **W** www.ssta.org.uk
General Secretary, David Eaglesham

SECONDARY HEADS ASSOCIATION, 130 Regent Road, Leicester LE1 7PG **T** 0116-299 1122 **E** info@sha.org.uk **W** www.sha.org.uk
General Secretary, Dr J. E. Dunford, OBE

SOCIETY OF AUTHORS, 84 Drayton Gardens, London SW10 9SB **T** 020-7373 6642 **E** info@societyofauthors.org **W** www.societyofauthors.org
General Secretary, M. Le Fanu, OBE

UNITED ROAD TRANSPORT UNION, 76 High Lane, Chorlton-cum-Hardy, Manchester M21 9EF **T** 0800-526639 **E** info@urtu.com **W** www.urtu.com
General Secretary, Robert Monks

SPORTS BODIES

SPORTS COUNCILS

CENTRAL COUNCIL OF PHYSICAL RECREATION, Francis House, Francis Street, London SW1P 1DE **T** 020-7854 8500 **E** info@ccpr.org.uk **W** www.ccpr.org.uk
General Secretary, Margaret Talbot, FRSA, OBE

SPORT ENGLAND, 3rd Floor, Victoria House, Bloomsbury Square, London WC1B 4SE **T** 020-7273 1500 **E** info@sportengland.org **W** www.sportengland.org
Chief Executive, Roger Draper

SPORT SCOTLAND, Caledonia House, South Gyle, Edinburgh EH12 9BQ **T** 0131-317 7200 **E** library@sportscotland.org.uk **W** www.sportscotland.org.uk
Chief Executive, I. Robson

SPORTS COUNCIL FOR NORTHERN IRELAND, House of Sport, Upper Malone Road, Belfast BT9 5LA **T** 028-9038 1222 **E** info@sportni.net **W** www.sportni.net
Chief Executive, E. McCartan

SPORTS COUNCIL FOR WALES, Sophia Gardens, Cardiff CF11 9SW **T** 029-2030 0500 **E** scw@scw.co.uk **W** www.sports-council-wales.co.uk
Chief Executive, Dr H. Jones

UK SPORT, 40 Bernard Street, London WC1N 1ST **T** 020-7211 5100 **E** info@uksport.gov.uk **W** www.uksport.gov.uk
Chief Executive, Liz Nicholl

ANGLING

NATIONAL FEDERATION OF ANGLERS, Halliday House Egginton Junction DE65 6GU **T** 01283-734735 **E** office@nfahq.freeserve.co.uk **W** www.nfadirect.com
Administration Manager, Mrs J. A. Price

ARCHERY

GRAND NATIONAL ARCHERY SOCIETY, Lilleshall National Sports Centre, Newport TF10 9AT **T** 01952-677888 **E** enquiries@gnas.org **W** www.gnas.org
Chief Executive, D. Sherratt

ASSOCIATION FOOTBALL

FOOTBALL ASSOCIATION, 25 Soho Square, London W1D 4FA **T** 020-7745 4545 **W** www.the-fa.org
Chief Executive, Mark Palios

FOOTBALL ASSOCIATION OF WALES, Plymouth Chambers, 3 Westgate Street, Cardiff CF10 1DP **T** 029-2037 2325 **E** info@faw.org.uk **W** www.faw.org.uk
Secretary-General, D. G. Collins

FOOTBALL LEAGUE LTD, 11 Connaught Place London W2 2ET **T** 0870-4420 1888 **E** fl@football-league.co.uk **W** www.football-league.co.uk
Director of Operations, Andy Willliamson

IRISH FOOTBALL ASSOCIATION, 20 Windsor Avenue, Belfast BT9 6EE **T** 028-9066 9458 **E** enquiries@irishfa.com **W** www.irishfa.com
General Secretary, D. I. Bowen

IRISH FOOTBALL LEAGUE, 96 University Street, Belfast BT7 1HE **T** 028-9024 2888 **E** mail@irish-league.co.uk **W** www.irish-league.co.uk
Secretary, H. Wallace

SCOTTISH FOOTBALL ASSOCIATION, Hampden Park, Glasgow G42 9AY **T** 0141-616 6000 **E** info@scottishfa.co.uk **W** www.scottishfa.co.uk
Chief Executive, D. Taylor

SCOTTISH FOOTBALL LEAGUE, The National Stadium, Hampden Park, Glasgow G42 9EB **T** 0141-620 4160 **E** info@scottishfootballleague.com **W** www.scottishfootballleague.com
Secretary, Peter Donald

ATHLETICS

ATHLETICS ASSOCIATION OF WALES, The Manor, Coldra Woods, Newport NP18 1WA **T** 01633-416633 **E** info@welshathletics.org **W** www.welshathletics.org
President, Gwilym Evans

NORTHERN IRELAND ATHLETIC FEDERATION, Athletics House, Old Coach Road, Belfast BT9 5PR **T** 028-9060 2707 **E** info@niathletics.org **W** www.niathletics.org
Secretary, J. Allen

SCOTTISH ATHLETICS, 9a South Gyle Crescent, Edinburgh EH12 9EB **T** 0131-539 7320 **E** admin@scottishathletics.org.uk **W** www.scottishathletics.org.uk
Senior Administrator, Mary Anderson

UK ATHLETICS, Athletics House, 10 Harborne Road, Edgbaston, Birmingham B15 3AA **T** 0870-998 6800 **E** information@ukathletics.org.uk **W** www.ukathletics.net
Chief Executive, D. Moorcroft, OBE

BADMINTON

BADMINTON ASSOCIATION OF ENGLAND LTD, National Badminton Centre, Bradwell Road, Loughton Lodge, Milton Keynes MK8 9LA **T** 01908-268400 **E** enquiries@baofe.co.uk **W** www.baofe.co.uk
Chief Executive, S. Baddeley

SCOTTISH BADMINTON UNION, Cockburn Centre, 40 Bogmoor Place, Glasgow G51 4QT **T** 0141-445 1218 **E** name@badmintonscotland.org.uk **W** www.badmintonscotland.org.uk
Chief Executive, Miss A. Smillie

WELSH BADMINTON UNION, 4th Floor, Plymouth Chambers, 3 Westgate Street, Cardiff CF10 1DP **T** 029-2022 2082 **E** wbu@welshbadminton.net **W** www.welshbadminton.net
Executive Director, L. Williams

BASKETBALL

BASKETBALL SCOTLAND, Caledonia House, South Gyle, Edinburgh EH12 9DQ **T** 0131-317 7260 **E** enquiries@basketball-scotland.com **W** www.basketball-scotland.com
Chief Executive, Fiona Justin

ENGLISH BASKETBALL ASSOCIATION, EIS Sheffield, Coleridge Road, Sheffield S9 5DA **T** 0870-7744225 **E** info@englandbasketball.co.uk **W** www.englandbasketball.co.uk
Chief Executive, Keith Mair

BILLIARDS AND SNOOKER

WORLD LADIES BILLIARDS AND SNOOKER ASSOCIATION, PO Box 16, 231 Ramnoth Road, Wisbech, PE13 2SX **T** 01945-588598
Chairwoman, Mandy Fisher

WORLD PROFESSIONAL BILLIARDS AND SNOOKER ASSOCIATION, Ground Floor, Albert House, 111–117 Victoria Street, Bristol BS1 6AX T 0117-317 8200 E enq@worldsnooker.com W www.worldsnooker.com

BOBSLEIGH

BRITISH BOBSLEIGH ASSOCIATION, Department of Sports Development and Recreation, University of Bath, Claverton Down, Bath BA2 7AY T 01225-826802 E bba@dial.pipex.com W www.british-bobsleigh.com
Chairman, R. B. B. Ropner

BOWLS

BRITISH ISLES BOWLS COUNCIL, 23 Leysland Avenue, Countesthorpe, LE8 5XX T 0116-277 3234
Hon. Secretary, Mr M. Swatland

BRITISH ISLES WOMEN'S BOWLING COUNCIL, EWBA Office, Victoria Park, Archery Road, Leamington Spa EX12 2AP T 01296-430686
Hon. Secretary, Mrs N. Colling, MBE

BRITISH ISLES WOMEN'S INDOOR BOWLS COUNCIL, 101 Skyline Drive, Lambeg BT27 4HW
Secretary, Mrs Doreen Miskelly

ENGLISH BOWLING ASSOCIATION, Lyndhurst Road, Worthing BN11 2AZ T 01903-820222 E ebaqueries@bowlsengland.com W www.bowlsengland.com
Chief Executive, A. Allcock, MBE

ENGLISH INDOOR BOWLING ASSOCIATION, David Cornwell House, Bowling Green, Leicester Road, Melton Mowbray LE13 0FA T 01664-481900 E info@eiba.co.uk W www.eiba.co.uk
Secretary, S. A. Rodwell

ENGLISH WOMEN'S BOWLING ASSOCIATION, EWBA Office, Victoria Park, Archery Road, Royal Leamington Spa CV31 3PT T 01926-430686 E ewba.victoriapark@virgin.net
Chief Executive, Mrs P. A. Biddlecombe

ENGLISH WOMEN'S INDOOR BOWLING ASSOCIATION, 3 Moulton Business Park, Scirocco Close, Northampton NN3 6AP T 01604-494163 E ewiba@btinternet.com W www.ewiba.com
Secretary, Mrs T. Thomas

BOXING

AMATEUR BOXING ASSOCIATION OF ENGLAND LTD, Crystal Palace National Sports Centre London SE19 2BB T 020-8778 0251 E hq@abae.org.uk
Chairman, Jim Smart

BRITISH AMATEUR BOXING ASSOCIATION, 96 High Street, Lochee, Dundee DD2 3AY T 01382-611412/508261 E frankhendry@accnet.zzn.com
Chief Executive, F. Hendry

BRITISH BOXING BOARD OF CONTROL LTD, The Old Library, Trinity Street, Cardiff CF10 1BH T 02920-367000 W www.bbbofc.com E info@bbbc.com
General Secretary, S. J. Block

CANOEING

BRITISH CANOE UNION, John Dudderidge House, Adbolton Lane, West Bridgford, Nottingham NG2 5AS T 0115-982 1100 E info@bcu.org.uk W www.bcu.org.uk
Chief Executive, P. Owen

CHESS

BRITISH CHESS FEDERATION, The Watch Oak, Chain Lane, Battle TN33 0YD T 01424-775222 E office@bcf.org.uk W www.bcf.ndirect.co.uk
President, Gerry Walsh

CRICKET

ENGLAND AND WALES CRICKET BOARD, Lord's Cricket Ground London NW8 8QN T 020-7432 1200 W www.ecb.co.uk
Chief Executive, T. Lamb

MCC, Lord's Cricket Ground London NW8 8QN T 020-7616 8500 W www.lords.org E communications@mcc.org.uk
Secretary and Chief Executive, R. D. V. Knight

CROQUET

CROQUET ASSOCIATION, c/o Cheltenham Croquet Club, Old Bath Road, Cheltenham GL53 7DF T 01242-242318 E caoffice@croquet.org.uk W www.croquet.org.uk
Secretary, N. R. Graves

CYCLING

BRITISH CYCLING FEDERATION, National Cycling Centre, Stuart Street, Manchester M11 4DQ T 0870-871 2000 E info@britishcycling.org.uk W www.britishcycling.org.uk
Chief Executive, P. King

CYCLING TIME TRIALS, 77 Arlington Drive, Pennington, Leigh WN7 3QP T 01942-603976 E nationalsecretary@rttchq.freeserve.co.uk W www.ctt.org.uk
National Secretary, P. Heaton

DARTS

BRITISH DARTS ORGANISATION, 2 Pages Lane, Muswell Hill, London N10 1PS T 020-8883 5544 E britishdartsorg@btconnect.com W www.bdodarts.com
Chairman, Sam Hawkins

EQUESTRIANISM

BRITISH EQUESTRIAN FEDERATION, National Agricultural Centre, Stoneleigh Park, Kenilworth CV8 2RH T 024-7669 8871 E info@bef.co.uk W www.bef.co.uk
Chief Executive, A. Finding

BRITISH EVENTING, National Agricultural Centre, Stoneleigh Park, Kenilworth CV8 2RN T 024-7669 8856 E info@britisheventing.com W www.britisheventing.com
Chief Executive, P. Durrant

ETON FIVES

ETON FIVES ASSOCIATION, 3 Bourchier Close, Sevenoaks TN13 1PD T 01732-458775 E efa@etonfives.co.uk W www.etonfives.co.uk
Secretary, M. R. Fenn

GLIDING

BRITISH GLIDING ASSOCIATION, Kimberley House, Vaughan Way, Leicester LE1 4SE T 0116-253 1051 E bga@gliding.co.uk W www.gliding.co.uk
Chairman, David Roberts

GOLF

LADIES' GOLF UNION, The Scores, St Andrews KY16 9AT T 01334-475811 E info@lgu.org W www.lgu.org
Secretary/CEO, Andy Salmon

ROYAL AND ANCIENT GOLF CLUB OF ST ANDREWS, Golf Place, St Andrews KY16 9JD T 01334-460000 E thesecretary@randagc.org W www.randa.org
Secretary, P. Dawson

GREYHOUND RACING

NATIONAL GREYHOUND RACING CLUB LTD, Twyman House, 16 Bonny Street, London NW1 9QD T 020-7267 9256 E mail@ngrc.org.uk W www.ngrc.org.uk
Chief Executive, F. Melville

GYMNASTICS

BRITISH GYMNASTICS, Ford Hall, Lilleshall National Sports Centre, Newport TF10 9NB T 0845-129 7129 E information@british-gymnastics.org W www.british-gymnastics.org
Chief Executive, Alan Sommerville

HOCKEY

ENGLAND HOCKEY, The National Hockey Stadium, Silbury Boulevard, Milton Keynes MK9 1HA T 01908-544644 E info@englishhockey.org W www.hockeyonline.co.uk
Executive Chairman, Philip Kimberley

SCOTTISH HOCKEY UNION, 589 Lanark Road, Edinburgh EH14 5DA T 0131-453 9070 E info@scottish-hockey.org.uk W www.scottish-hockey.org.uk
Chairman, G. Ralph

WELSH HOCKEY UNION, 80 Woodville Road, Cathays, Cardiff CF24 4ED T 029-2023 3257 E info@welsh-hockey.co.uk W www.welsh-hockey.co.uk
Chairman, A. J. Rookes

HORSE RACING

BRITISH HORSERACING BOARD, PO Box 4013, London W1A 6NG T 08700-721724 E info@bhb.co.uk W www.bhb.co.uk
Chairman, P. Savill

JOCKEY CLUB, 42 Portman Square, London W1H 6EN T 020-7486 4921 E info@thejockeyclub.co.uk W www.thejockeyclub.co.uk
Senior Steward, J. Richmond-Watson

ICE HOCKEY

ICE HOCKEY UK, 47 Westminster Buildings, Theatre Square, Nottingham, NG1 6LG T 0115-924 1441 E hockey@icehockeyuk.co.uk W www.icehockeyuk.co.uk
Chairman, Stuart Robertson

ICE SKATING

NATIONAL ICE SKATING ASSOCIATION OF THE UK LTD, National Ice Centre, Lower Parliament Street, Nottingham NG1 1LA T 0870-758 0278 E nisa@iceskating.org.uk W www.iceskating.org.uk
Chairman, Haig Oundjian

JUDO

BRITISH JUDO ASSOCIATION, Suite B, Loughborough Technology Centre, Epinal Way, Loughborough LE11 3GE T 01509-631670 E bja@britishjudo.org.uk W www.britishjudo.org.uk
Chairman, Densign White

LAWN TENNIS

LAWN TENNIS ASSOCIATION, The Queen's Club, Palliser Road, London W14 9EG T 020-7381 5965 W www.lta.org.uk
Secretary, J. C. U. James

MARTIAL ARTS

MARTIAL ARTS DEVELOPMENT COMMISSION, PO Box 416, Wembley, HA0 3WD T 0870-770 0461 E office@madec.org W www.madec.org
Administration Manager, Dawn Howe

MOTOR SPORTS

BRITISH SUPERBIKES RACE ORGANISATION, MCRCB, PO Box 6450, Woodford Halse, Daventry NN11 3ZD T 01327-264010 E dougbarnfield@mcrcb.jslife.co.uk
Manager, D. R. Barnfield

MOTORCYCLE GREAT BRITAIN, Auto-Cycle Union, ACU House, Wood Street, Rugby CV21 2YX T 01788-566400 E admin@acu.org.uk W www.motorcyclinggb.com
General Secretary, Gary Thompson, MBE, BEM

MOTOR SPORTS ASSOCIATION, Motor Sports House, Riverside Park, Colnbrook, SL3 0HG T 01753-765000 W www.msauk.org
Chief Executive, Colin Hilton

SCOTTISH AUTO CYCLE UNION LTD, 28 West Main Street, Uphall EH52 5DW T 01506-858354 E office@sacu.co.uk W www.sacu.co.uk
Office Manager, Eric Jones

MOUNTAINEERING

BRITISH MOUNTAINEERING COUNCIL, 177–179 Burton Road, West Didsbury, Manchester M20 2BB T 0870-010 4878 E office@thebmc.co.uk W www.thebmc.co.uk
Chief Officer, D. Turnbull

MULTI-SPORTS BODIES

BRITISH OLYMPIC ASSOCIATION, 1 Wandsworth Plain, London SW18 1EH T 020-8871 2677 E firstname.surname@boa.org.uk W www.olympics.org.uk
Chief Executive, S. Clegg

BRITISH UNIVERSITIES SPORTS ASSOCIATION, 8 Union Street, London SE1 1SZ T 020-7357 8555 W www.busa.org.uk
Chief Executive, G. Gregory-Jones

COMMONWEALTH GAMES COUNCIL FOR ENGLAND, Tavistock House South, Tavistock Square, London WC1H 9JZ T 020-7388 6643 E info@cgce.co.uk W www.cgce.co.uk
Chief Executive, Miss A. Hogbin

COMMONWEALTH GAMES FEDERATION, 4th Floor, 26 Upper Brook Street, London W1K 7QE T 020-7491 8801 E office@thecgf.com W www.thecgf.com
Chief Executive Officer, Michael Hooper

NETBALL

ALL ENGLAND NETBALL ASSOCIATION LTD, Netball House, 9 Paynes Park, Hitchin SG5 1EH T 01462-442344 E info@aena.co.uk W www.england-netball.co.uk
Chief Executive, Mrs P. Harrison

NETBALL NORTHERN IRELAND, House of Sport, Upper Malone Road, Belfast BT9 5LA T 028-9038 1222 E netballni@houseofsport.ni.net
Secretary, Mrs P. Williams

NETBALL SCOTLAND, Suite 196, 2nd Floor, Central Chambers, 93 Hope Street, Glasgow G2 4LD T 0141-572 0114 E tellus@netballscotland.com W www.netballscotland.com
Administrator, vacant

WELSH NETBALL ASSOCIATION, 2nd Floor, 33–35 Cathedral Rd, Cardiff CF11 9HB T 029-2023 7048 E welshnetball@welshnetball.com W www.welshnetball.co.uk
Chief Executive Officer, Mrs S. J. Holvey

ORIENTEERING

BRITISH ORIENTEERING FEDERATION, Riversdale, Dale Road North, Darley Dale, Matlock DE4 2HX T 01629-734042 E bof@britishorienteering.org.uk W www.britishorienteering.org.uk
Chief Executive, Robin Field

POLO

HURLINGHAM POLO ASSOCIATION, Manor Farm, Little Coxwell, Faringdon SN7 7LW T 01367-242828
E enquiries@hpa-polo.co.uk W www.hpa-polo.co.uk
Chief Executive, D. J. B. Woodd

RACKETS AND REAL TENNIS

TENNIS AND RACKETS ASSOCIATION, c/o The Queen's Club, Palliser Road, London W14 9EQ T 020-7386 3447/8
E ceo@tennis-rackets.net W www.rackets.co.uk
Chief Executive and Secretary, James D. Wyatt

RIFLE SHOOTING

NATIONAL RIFLE ASSOCIATION, Bisley Camp, Brookwood, Woking GU24 0PB T 01483-797777 E info@nra.org.uk
W www.nra.org.uk
Secretary-General, R. J. Fishwick

NATIONAL SMALL-BORE RIFLE ASSOCIATION, Lord Roberts House, Bisley Camp, Brookwood, Woking GU24 0NP
T 0845-130 6772 E info@nsra.co.uk W www.nsra.co.uk
Secretary, Lt.-Col. J. D. Hoare

ROWING

AMATEUR ROWING ASSOCIATION LTD, The Priory, 6 Lower Mall, London W6 9DJ T 020-8237 6700
E info@ara-rowing.org W www.ara-rowing.org
National Manager, Mrs R. Napp

HENLEY ROYAL REGATTA, Regatta Headquarters Henley-on-Thames RG9 2LY T 01491-572153 W www.hrr.co.uk
Secretary, R. S. Goddard

RUGBY FIVES

RUGBY FIVES ASSOCIATION, 32 Ashbourne Grove, East Dulwich, London SE22 8RL T 0208-693 0488
W www.rfa.org.uk
General Secretary, Ian Fuller

RUGBY LEAGUE

BRITISH AMATEUR RUGBY LEAGUE ASSOCIATION, West Yorkshire House, 4 New North Parade, Huddersfield HD1 5JP
T 01484-544131 E info@barla.org.uk
W www.barla.org.uk
Chief Executive, I. Cooper

RUGBY FOOTBALL LEAGUE, Red Hall, Red Hall Lane, Leeds LS17 8NB T 0113-232 9111 E rfl@rfl.uk.com
W www.rfl.uk.com
Executive Chairman, Richard Lewis

RUGBY UNION

IRISH RUGBY FOOTBALL UNION, 62 Lansdowne Road, Ballsbridge, Dublin 4 T 00 353-1-647 3800
E manager@irishrugby.ie W www.irishrugby.ie
Chief Executive, P. R. Browne

RUGBY FOOTBALL UNION, Rugby House, Rugby Road, Twickenham TW1 1DS T 020-8892 2000 W www.rfu.com
Chief Executive, F. Baron

RUGBY FOOTBALL UNION FOR WOMEN, Rugby House, Rugby Road, Twickenham TW1 1DS T 020-8831 7996
W www.rfu-women.co.uk E rfuwo@therfu.com
Chairman, Sue Eakers

SCOTTISH RUGBY UNION, Murrayfield, Roseburn Street, Edinburgh EH12 5PJ T 0131-346 5000
E feedback@sru.org.uk W www.sru.org.uk
Chief Executive, David Mackay *(Acting)*

SCOTTISH WOMEN'S RUGBY UNION, Scottish Rugby Union, Roseburn Terrace, Murrayfield, Edinburgh EH12 5PJ
T 0131-346 5163 E barbara.wilson@sru.org.uk
W www.scottishrugby.org
Chairwoman, Sandra Kinnear

WELSH RUGBY UNION LTD, 1st Floor, Golate House, 101 St Mary Street, Cardiff CF10 1GE T 029-20934000
E info@wru.co.uk W www.wru.co.uk
Group Chief Executive, D. Moffett

SHOOTING

CLAY PIGEON SHOOTING ASSOCIATION LTD, Edmonton House, Bisley Camp, Brookwood, Woking GU24 0NP
T 01483-485400 E info@cpsa.co.uk W www.cpsa.co.uk
Director, Mr P. J. Boakes

SKIING AND SNOWBOARDING

SNOWSPORT GB, Hillend, Biggar Road, Midlothian EH10 7EF
T 0131-445 7676 E info@snowsportgb.com
W www.snowsportgb.com
Operations Director, Mrs F. McNeilly

SNOWSPORT SCOTLAND, Hillend, Biggar Road, Midlothian, EH10 7EF T 0131-445 4151 E info@snowsportscotland.org
W www.snowsportscotland.org

SPEEDWAY

SPEEDWAY CONTROL BOARD, ACU Headquarters, Wood Street, Rugby CV21 2YX T 01788-565603
E office.scb@lineone.net

SQUASH RACKETS

ENGLAND SQUASH, National Squash Centre, Rowsley Street, Manchester M11 3FF T 0161-438 4312
E enquires@englandsquash.com
W www.englandsquash.com
Chief Executive, Nick Rider

SCOTTISH SQUASH, Caledonia House, South Gyle, Edinburgh EH12 9DQ T 0131-317 7343 E scottishsquash@aol.com
W www.scottishsquash.org
Administration Manager, Derek Welch

SQUASH WALES, St Mellons Country Club, St Mellons, Cardiff CF3 2XR T 01633-682108 E enquiries@squashwales.co.uk
W www.squashwales.co.uk
Administrator, Mrs D. Selley

SUB-AQUA

BRITISH SUB-AQUA CLUB, Telfords Quay, South Pier Road, Ellesmere Port CH65 4FL T 0151-350 6200
E postmaster@bsac.com W www.bsac.com
Chairman, P. Harrison

SWIMMING

AMATEUR SWIMMING ASSOCIATION, Harold Fern House, Derby Square, Loughborough LE11 5AL T 01509-618700
E customerservices@swimming.org
W www.britishswimming.org
Chief Executive, D. Sparkes

SCOTTISH SWIMMING, National Swimming Academy, University of Stirling, Stirling, FK9 4LA T 01786-466520
E info@scottishswimming.com
W www.scottishswimming.com
Chief Executive, Ashley Howard

WELSH AMATEUR SWIMMING ASSOCIATION, Wales National Pool, Sketty Lane, Swansea SA2 8QG
T 01792-513636 E secretary@welshasa.co.uk
W www.welshasa.co.uk
Director of Swimming Development, B. Williams

TABLE TENNIS

ENGLISH TABLE TENNIS ASSOCIATION, Queensbury House, Havelock Road, Hastings TN34 IHF T 01424-722525
E admin@ettahq.freeserve.co.uk W www.etta.co.uk
Chief Executive, R. Yule

VOLLEYBALL

ENGLISH VOLLEYBALL ASSOCIATION, Suite B, Loughborough Technology Centre, Epinal Way, Loughborough LE11 3GE **T** 01509-631699
E general@england-volleyball.demon.co.uk
W www.volleyballengland.org
Hon. President, Don Anthony

SCOTTISH VOLLEYBALL ASSOCIATION, 48 The Pleasance, Edinburgh EH8 9TJ **T** 0131-556 4633
E info@scottishvolleyball.org **W** www.scottishvolleyball.org
Chief Executive, Kenny Barton

WALKING

RACE WALKING ASSOCIATION, Hufflers, Heard's Lane, Shenfield, Brentwood CM15 0SF **T** 01277-220687
E racewalkingassociation@btinternet.com
W www.racewalkingassociation.btinternet.co.uk
Hon. General Secretary, P. J. Cassidy

WATER SKIING

BRITISH WATER SKI FEDERATION, The Tower, Thorpe Road, Chertsey, KT16 8PH **T** 01932-570885
E info@bwsf.co.uk **W** www.bwsf.co.uk
Executive Officer, Ms G. Hill

WEIGHTLIFTING

BRITISH WEIGHTLIFTERS ASSOCIATION (BWLA), Lilleshall National Sports Centre, Newport TF10 9AT
T 01952-604201 **E** jane@bawla.com **W** www.bawla.com
Chief Executive, S. Cannon

WRESTLING

BRITISH WRESTLING ASSOCIATION, 12 Westwood Lane, Brimington, Chesterfield S43 1PA **T** 01246-236443
E admin@britishwrestling.org **W** www.britishwrestling.org
Chairman, M. Morley

YACHTING

ROYAL YACHTING ASSOCIATION, RYA House, Ensign Way, Hamble, Southampton SO31 4YA **T** 0845-3450400
E info@rya.org.uk **W** www.rya.org.uk
Chief Executive, R. P. Carr

CLUBS

LONDON CLUBS

ALPINE CLUB (1857), 55 Charlotte Road, London EC2A 3QF T 020-7613 0755 E admin@alpine-club.org.uk W www.alpine-club.org.uk
Hon. Secretary, R. M. Scott

AMERICAN WOMEN'S CLUB (1899), 68 Old Brompton Road, London SW7 3LQ T 020-7589 8292 E awc@awclondon.org W www.awclondon.org
President, J. Kocher (Women only)

ANGLO-BELGIAN CLUB (1955), 60 Knightsbridge, London SW1X 7LF T 020-7235 2121 E secretary@ra-bc.com
Chairman, Alistair Voaden, FRICS

ARMY AND NAVY CLUB (1837), 36 Pall Mall, London SW1Y 5JN T 020-7930 9721 E secretary@therag.co.uk W www.armynavyclub.co.uk
Chief Executive and Secretary, Cdr. J. A. Holt, MBE, RN

ARTS CLUB (1863), 40 Dover Street, London W1S 4NP T 020-7499 8581 E secretary@artclub.fsnet.co.uk W www.theartsclub.co.uk *Secretary,* Tony Derrett

ATHENAEUM (1824), 107 Pall Mall, London SW1Y 5ER T 020-7930 4843 E library@hellenist.org.uk
Secretary, J. H. Ford

AUTHORS' CLUB (1892), 40 Dover Street, London W1S 4NP T 020-7499 8581 W www.theartsclub.fsnet.co.uk
Club Secretary, Mrs A. de La Grange

BEEFSTEAK CLUB (1876), 9 Irving Street, London WC2H 7AH T 020-7930 5722
Secretary, Sir John Lucas-Tooth, Bt. (Men only)

BOODLE'S (1762), 28 St James's Street, London SW1A 1HJ T 020-7930 7166 *Secretary,* Andrew Phillips

BROOKS'S (1764), St James's Street, London SW1A 1LN T 020-7493 4411 E secretary@brooksclub.org
Secretary, G. Snell (Men only)

BUCK'S CLUB (1919), 18 Clifford Street, London W1X 1RG T 020-7734 2337 E secretary@bucksclub.co.uk
Secretary, Mrs G. Thompson (Men only)

CALEDONIAN CLUB (1891), 9 Halkin Street, London SW1X 7DR T 020-7235 5162 E pjv@caledonian-club.org.uk W www.caledonian-club.org.uk
Secretary, P. J. Varney

CANNING CLUB (1910), 4 St James's Square, London SW1Y 4JU T 020-7827 5757 E canningclub@compuserve.com
Secretary, T. M. Harrington

CARLTON CLUB (1832), 69 St James's Street, London SW1A 1PJ T 020-7493 1164 E secretary@carltonclub.co.uk W www.carltonclub.co.uk
Secretary, A. E. Telfer

CAVALRY AND GUARDS CLUB (1893), 127 Piccadilly, London W1J 7PX T 020-7499 1261 E secretary@cavgds.co.uk W www.cavgds.co.uk
Secretary, Cdr. I. R. Wellesley-Harding, RN

CHELSEA ARTS CLUB (1891), 143 Old Church Street, London SW3 6EB T 020-7376 3311 E secretary@chelseaartsclub.com W chelseaartsclub.com
Secretary, D. Winterbottom

CITY LIVERY CLUB (1914), 38 St. Mary Avenue, London EC3A 8EX T 020-7369 1672 E postbox@cityliveryclub.com W www.cityliveryclub.com
Hon. Secretary, P. Herbage

CITY OF LONDON CLUB (1832), 19 Old Broad Street, London EC2N 1DS T 020-7588 7991 E secretary@cityoflondonclub.com W www.cityclub.uk.com
Club Secretary, Ian Faul (Men only)

CITY UNIVERSITY CLUB (1895), 50 Cornhill, London EC3V 3PD T 020-7626 8571 E secretary@cityuniversityclub.co.uk W www.cityuniversityclub.co.uk
Secretary, Miss R. C. Graham

DEN NORSKE KLUB LTD (1887), In & Out, 4 St James's Square, London SW1Y 4JU T 020-7839 6242 W www.dennorskeklub.co.uk
Secretary, Bjørg Tangen

EAST INDIA CLUB (1849), 16 St James's Square, London SW1A 2EL T 020-7930 3577 E eastindi@globalnet.co.uk
Secretary, M. Howell (Men only)

FARMERS CLUB (1842), 3 Whitehall Court, London SW1A 2EL T 020-7930 3751 W www.thefarmersclub.com
Secretary, Gp Capt. G. P. Carson

FLYFISHERS' CLUB (1884), 69 Brook Street, London W1K 4ER T 020-7629 5958
Secretary, Cdr. T. H. Boycott, OBE, RN (Men only)

GARRICK CLUB (1831), 15 Garrick Street, London WC2E 9AY T 020-7379 6478 W www.garrickclub.co.uk
Secretary, M. J. Harvey (Men only)

GROUCHO CLUB (1985), 45 Dean Street, London W1V 5AF T 020-7439 4685
Chief Executive, Joel Cadbury

HURLINGHAM CLUB (1869), Ranelagh Gardens, London SW6 3PR T 020-736 8411 E membership@hurlinghamclub.org.uk
Secretary, Lucie Salmon

KENNEL CLUB (1873), 1–5 Clarges Street, London W1J 8AB T 0870-606 6750 E info@the-kennel-club.org.uk W www.the-kennel-club.org.uk
Chief Executive, Rosemary Smart

LANSDOWNE CLUB (1934), 9 Fitzmaurice Place, London W1J 5JD T 020-7629 7200 E info@lansdowneclub.com W www.lansdowneclub.com
Chief Executive and Secretary, M. Anderson

LONDON ROWING CLUB (1856), Embankment, Putney, London SW15 1LB T 020-8788 1400 W www.londonrc.org.uk
Hon. Secretary, J. R. R. Ebsworth

MCC (MARYLEBONE CRICKET CLUB) (1787), Lord's Cricket Ground London NW8 8QN T 020-7289 1611 W www.lords.org
Secretary & Chief Executive, R. D. V. Knight

NATIONAL CLUB (1845), c/o Carlton Club, 69 St James's Street, London SW1A 1PJ T 020-8579 0874 E ivorsowton@tiscali.co.uk
Hon. Secretary, I. A. Sowton (Men only)

NATIONAL LIBERAL CLUB (1882), Whitehall Place, London SW1A 2HE T 020-7930 9871 E secretary@nlc.org.uk W www.nlc.org.uk
Secretary, S. J. Roberts

NAVAL AND MILITARY CLUB (1862), 4 St James's Square, London SW1Y 4JU T 020-7827 5757 E club@navalandmilitaryclub.co.uk W www.navalandmilitaryclub.co.uk
Club Secretary, Lt.-Col. K. F. Robbin, MBE

NAVAL CLUB (1946), 38 Hill Street, London W1J 5NS T 020-7493 7672 E reservations@navalclub.co.uk W www.navalclub.co.uk
Chief Executive, Cdr. J. L. L. Prichard

NEW CAVENDISH CLUB (1920), 44 Great Cumberland Place, London W1H 7BS T 020-7723 0391 E jeanpaulncc@aol.com
General Manager, J. P. Dauvergne

ORIENTAL CLUB (1824), Stratford House, Stratford Place, London W1C 1ES T 020-7629 5126 E sec@orientalclub.org.uk
Secretary, S. C. Doble

OXFORD AND CAMBRIDGE CLUB (1972), 71 Pall Mall, London SW1Y 5HD T 020-7930 5151 E club@oandc.uk.com W www.oxfordandcambridgeclub.co.uk
Secretary, G. R. Buchanan

PORTLAND CLUB (1816), 69 Brook Street, London W1Y 4ER T 020-7499 1523
Secretary, J. Burns, CBE

PRATT'S CLUB (1841), 14 Park Place, London SW1A 1LP T 020-7493 0397 E secretary@prattsclub.org
Secretary, G. Snell (Men only)

QUEEN'S CLUB (1886), Palliser Road, London W14 9EQ T 020-7385 3421 E admin@queensclub.co.uk W www.queensclub.co.uk
Secretary, P. D. Elviss

REFORM CLUB (1836), 104–105 Pall Mall, London SW1Y 5EW T 020-7930 9374 E reform_club@msn.com W www.reformclub.com
Secretary, R. A. M. Forrest

ROEHAMPTON CLUB (1901), Roehampton Lane, London SW15 5LR T 020 -8480 4205 E admin@roehamptonclub.co.uk W www.roehamptonclub.co.uk
Chief Executive, Mark Wilson

ROYAL AIR FORCE CLUB (1918), 128 Piccadilly, London W1J 7PY T 020-7399 1000 E admin@rafclub.org.uk W www.rafclub.org.uk *Secretary,* P. N. Owen

ROYAL AUTOMOBILE CLUB (1897), Pall Mall Clubhouse, 89 Pall Mall, London SW1Y 5HS T 020-7930 2345 E secretary@royalautomobileclub.co.uk W www.royalautomobileclub.co.uk
Secretary, A. I. G. Kennedy

ROYAL OCEAN RACING CLUB (1925), 20 St James's Place, London SW1A 1NN T 020-7493 2248 E info@rorc.org W www.rorc.org
General Manager, P. C. Wykeham-Martin

ROYAL OVER-SEAS LEAGUE (1910), Over-Seas House, Park Place, St James's Street, London SW1A 1LR T 020-7408 0214 E info@rosl.org.uk W www.rosl.org.uk
Director-General, R. F. Newell, LVO

SAVAGE CLUB (1857), 1 Whitehall Place, London SW1A 2HD T 020-7930 8118 E info@savageclub.com W www.savageclub.com
Hon. Secretary, The Ven. B. H. Lucas, CB (Men only)

SAVILE CLUB (1868), 69 Brook Street, London W1K 4ER T 020-7629 5462 E secretariat@savileclub.co.uk W www.savileclub.co.uk
Secretary, J. Malone-Lee (Men only)

SKI CLUB OF GREAT BRITAIN (1903), The White House, 57–63 Church Road, Wimbledon SW19 5DQ T 020-8410 2000 E skiers@skiclub.co.uk W www.skiclub.co.uk
Managing Director, Ms C. Stuart-Taylor

ST STEPHEN'S CLUB (1870), 34 Queen Anne's Gate, London SW1H 9AB T 020-7222 1382 E info@ststephensclub.co.uk W www.ststephensclub.co.uk
Chief Executive, James M. Wilson

THAMES ROWING CLUB (1860), Putney Embankment, London SW15 1LB T 020-8788 0798 E secretary@thamesrc.co.uk W www.thamesrc.demon.co.uk
Hon. Secretaries, Jess Wright and Alison Pressley

TRAVELLERS CLUB (1819), 106 Pall Mall, London SW1Y 5EP T 020-7930 8688 E secretary@thetravellersclub.org.uk W www.csma.org.uk
Secretary, M. S. Allcock (Men only)

TURF CLUB (1868), 5 Carlton House Terrace, London SW1Y 5AQ T 020-7930 8555 E mail@turfclub.co.uk
Secretary, Lt.-Col. O. R. StJ. Breakwell, MBE

UNIVERSITY WOMEN'S CLUB (1886), 2 Audley Square, London W1K 1DB T 020-7499 2268 E uwc@uwc-london.com W www.universitywomensclub.com
Club Secretary, Miss Lynne Paterson (Women only)

VICTORY SERVICES CLUB (1907), 63–79 Seymour Street, London W2 2HF T 020-7723 4474 E res@vsc.co.uk W www.vsc.co.uk
Chief Executive, Brig. R. N. Lennox, CBE

WHITE'S (1693), 37–38 St James's Street, London SW1A 1JG T 020-7493 6671
Secretary, D. A. Anderson (Men only)

WIG AND PEN CLUB (1908), 229–230 Strand, London WC2R 1BA T 020-7583 7255
Chairman, E. Ertan

CLUBS OUTSIDE LONDON AND YACHT CLUBS

BATH AND COUNTY CLUB (1858), Queen's Parade, Bath BA1 2NJ T 01225-423732 E secretary@bathandcountyclub.com W www.bathandcountyclub.com
President, Sir Alec Morris, KBE, CB

BEMBRIDGE SAILING CLUB (1886), Embankment Road, Bembridge PO35 5NR T 01983-872237 E bsc@clara.net W www.bembridgesailingclub.org
Secretary, Lt.-Col. M. J. Samuelson, RM

BRISTOL CHANNEL YACHT CLUB (1875), 744 Mumbles Road, Mumbles, Swansea SA3 4EL T 01792-366000
Hon. Secretary, R. L. Morgan

CARDIFF AND COUNTY CLUB (1866), Westgate Street, Cardiff CF10 1DA T 029-2022 0846 E mail@countyclub.org W www.countyclub.org
Hon. Secretary, Cdr. J. E. Payn, RD (Men only)

CASTLE CLUB (1865), 3 The Esplanade, Rochester ME1 1QE T 01634-843168
Hon Secretary, R. C. Abel (Men only)

CHICHESTER YACHT CLUB (1967), Chichester Marina, Birdham, Chichester PO20 7EJ T 01243-512918 E secretary@cyc.co.uk W www.cyc.co.uk
Secretary, I. M. Clarke

CLIFTON CLUB (1882), 22 The Mall, Clifton, Bristol BS8 4DS T 0117-974 5039 E thesecretary@cliftonclub.co.uk
Secretary, R. B. Annesley (Men only)

COUNTY CLUB, 158 High Street, Guildford GU1 3HJ T 01483-575370 E cp@thecountyclub.co.uk W www.countyclubguildford.co.uk
Hon. Secretary, R. H. Middlehurst

CRUISING ASSOCIATION (1908), CA House, 1 Northey Street, Limehouse Basin, London E14 8BT T 020-7537 2828 E office@cruising.org.uk W www.cruising.org.uk
General Secretary, Mrs L. Hammett

DISTRICT AND UNION CLUB (1849), Northwood, 1 West Park Road, Blackburn BB2 6DE T 01254-51474
Hon. Secretary, A. Breckell (Men only)

DURHAM COUNTY CLUB (1890), 52 Old Elvet, Durham DH1 3HJ T 0191-384 8156 *Secretary,* S. Smith

EAST DORSET SAILING CLUB (1875), 352 Sandbanks Road, Poole BH14 8HY T 01202-706111
Hon. Secretary, Mrs T. Neely

ESSEX YACHT CLUB (1890), HQS Bembridge, Foreshore, Leigh-on-Sea SS9 1BD T 01702-478404 E leighsailing.club@btinternet.com W www.sailinginleigh.com
Hon. Secretary, Mrs K. Hanman

FREWEN CLUB (1869), 98 St Aldate's, Oxford OX1 1BT T 01865-243816
Hon. Secretary, B. R. Boyt (Men only)

HOVE CLUB (1882), 28 Fourth Avenue, Hove BN3 2PJ T 01273-730872
Secretary, R. L. Silverthorne (Men only)

JOCKEY CLUB (1752), 101 High Street, Newmarket CB8 8JL T 01638 664151 E enquires@jockey-club-estates.co.uk W www.jockey-club-estates.co.uk
Director, George Paul

KENT AND CANTERBURY CLUB (1873), The Elms, 17 Old Dover Road, Canterbury CT1 3JB T 01227-462181 E sec@kentcanterbury.org W www.kentcanterbury.org
Secretary, J. H. Davies

KINGSWAY CLUB (1868), Lightfoot Institute, Kingsway, Bishop Auckland DL14 7JN T 01388-603219
President, P. E. Cooke (Men only)

LEAMINGTON TENNIS COURT CLUB (1846), 50 Bedford Street, Leamington Spa CV32 5DT T 01926-424977
Chairman, O. D. R. Dixon (Men only)

LEANDER CLUB (1818), Henley-on-Thames RG9 2LP T 01491-575782 E info@leander.co.uk W www.leander.co.uk
Hon. Secretary, I. Codrington

LEEDS CLUB (1849), 3 Albion Place, Leeds LS1 6JL T 0113-242 1591 E nick@leedsclub.org.uk W www.leedsclub.org.uk
General Manager, Nicholas Fawcett

NEW CLUB (1874), 2 Atherstone Lawn, Montpellier Parade, Cheltenham GL50 1UD T 01242-541121 E secretary@newclub.org.uk W www.newclub.org.uk
Hon. Secretary, Neville Whitfield

NORFOLK CLUB (1770), 17 Upper King Street, Norwich NR3 1RB T 01603-626767 *Secretary,* G. G. Hardaker

NORTH BAILEY CLUB Durham Union Society, Palace Green, Durham T 0191-384 3724 W www.dus.org.uk

NORTHERN CONSTITUTIONAL CLUB (1882), 37 Pilgrim Street, Newcastle upon Tyne NE1 6QE T 0191-232 0884
Hon. Secretary, D. Blake

NOTTINGHAM CLUB (1920), Newdigate House, Castle Gate, Nottingham NG1 6AF T 0115-912 6220
Chairman, A. Trease

OLD BOYS' AND PARK GREEN CLUB (1771), 7 Churchside, Macclesfield SK10 1HG T 01625-423292
Hon. Secretary, C. J. Q. Brooks (Men only)

PAIGNTON CLUB (1882), The Esplanade, Paignton TQ4 6ED T 01803-559682 E pgrafton@eurobell.co.uk
Hon. Secretary, P. Grafton

PARKSTONE YACHT CLUB (1895), Pearce Avenue, Poole BH14 8EH T 01202-738824 E office@parkstoneyc.co.uk W www.parkstoneyc.co.uk
General Manager, M. Simms

PENARTH YACHT CLUB (1880), The Esplanade, Penarth CF64 3AU T 029-2070 8196 W www.penarthyachtclub.com
Hon. Secretary, R. S. McGregor

PHYLLIS COURT CLUB (1906), Marlow Road, Henley-on-Thames RG9 2HT T 01491-570500 E enquiries@phylliscourt.co.uk W www.phylliscourt.co.uk
General Manager, L. Petas

POOLE HARBOUR YACHT CLUB (1949), 40 Salterns Way, Lilliput, Poole BH14 8JR T 01202-709971 E marina@salterns.co.uk W www.salterns.co.uk
Managing Director, J. N. J. Smith

POOLE YACHT CLUB (1865), New Harbour Road West, Hamworthy, Poole BH15 4AQ T 01202-672687 E secretary@pooleyc.co.uk W www.pooleyc.co.uk
Hon. Treasurer, R. Cooper

ROYAL AIR FORCE YACHT CLUB (1932), Riverside House, Rope Walk, Hamble, Southampton SO31 4HD T 023-8045 2208 E office@rafyc.co.uk W www.rafyc.co.uk
Hon. Secretary, J. Chitson

ROYAL ANGLESEY YACHT CLUB (1802), 6–7 Green Edge, Beaumaris LL58 8BY T 01248-810295 E info@royalangleseyyc.org.uk W www.royalangleseyyc.org.uk
Hon. Secretary, Jilly Dobinson

ROYAL CANOE CLUB (1866), The Clubhouse, Trowlock Way, Teddington TW11 9QZ T 020-8977 5269 E info@royalcanoeclub.com W www.royalcanoeclub.com
Hon. Secretary, Mrs J. S. Evans

ROYAL CHANNEL ISLANDS YACHT CLUB (1862), Le Mont du Boulevard St Brelade, Jersey JE3 8AD T 01534-745783 E rciyc@localdial.com
Hon. Secretary, B. Murray

ROYAL CINQUE PORTS YACHT CLUB (1872), 5 Waterloo Crescent, Dover CT16 1LA T 01304-206262
Hon. Secretary, David Upton

ROYAL CORINTHIAN YACHT CLUB (1872), The Quay, Burnham-on-Crouch CM0 8AX T 01621-782105 E info@royalcorinthian.co.uk W www.royalcorinthian.co.uk
Hon. Secretary, J. Hill

ROYAL DART YACHT CLUB (1866), Priory Street, Kingswear, Dartmouth TQ6 0AB T 01803-752496 E office@royaldart.co.uk W www.royaldart.co.uk
Hon. Secretary, C. Beckett

ROYAL DORSET YACHT CLUB (1875), 11 Custom House Quay, Weymouth DT4 8BG T 01305-786258 E rdyc@weymouthharbour.fsnet.co.uk W www.rdyc.freeuk.com *Secretary,* Mrs M. Tye

ROYAL FOWEY YACHT CLUB (1881), Whitford Yard, Fowey PL23 1BH T 01726-833573 E honsec@rfyc-fowey.org.uk W www.rfyc.fowey.org.uk
Commodore, G. R. Coombs

ROYAL HARWICH YACHT CLUB (1843), Woolverstone, Ipswich IP9 1AT T 01473-780319 E secretary@rhyc.demon.co.uk W www.rhyc.demon.co.uk
Secretary, Colin Burrows

ROYAL LYMINGTON YACHT CLUB (1922), Bath Road, Lymington SO41 3SE T 01590-672677 E sail@rlymyc.org.uk W www.rlymyc.org.uk
Secretary, I. Gawn

ROYAL MERSEY YACHT CLUB (1844), Bedford Road East, Rock Ferry, Birkenhead CH42 1LS T 0151-645 3204 W www.royalmersey.co.uk
Hon. Secretary, P. A. Bastow

ROYAL NAVAL CLUB AND ROYAL ALBERT YACHT CLUB (1867), 17 Pembroke Road, Portsmouth PO1 2NT
T 023-9282 5924 E rncrayc@aol.com W www.mc-rayc.co.uk
Secretary, Cdr. P. Bolas, RN

ROYAL NORFOLK AND SUFFOLK YACHT CLUB (1859), Royal Plain, Lowestoft NR33 0AQ T 01502-566726
E rnsyc@ctc-net.co.uk W www.rnsyc.co.uk
Commodore, Dr D. J. Turner

ROYAL PLYMOUTH CORINTHIAN YACHT CLUB (1877), Madeira Road, Plymouth PL1 2NY T 01752-664327
E admin@rpcyc.com W www.rpcyc.com
Hon. Secretary, A. L. Cooper

ROYAL SOLENT YACHT CLUB (1878), The Square, Yarmouth PO41 0NS T 01983-760256
E royal_solentyc@compuserve.com
W www.royalsolentyc.org.uk
Secretary, Mrs S. Tribe

ROYAL SOUTHAMPTON YACHT CLUB (1875), 1 Channel Way, Ocean Village, Southampton SO14 3QF
T 023-8022 3352 E rsyc@rsyc.org.uk W www.rsyc.org.uk
Secretary, A. M. Paterson

ROYAL SOUTHERN YACHT CLUB (1837), Rope Walk, Hamble, Southampton SO31 4HB T 023-8045 0300
E sailing@royal-southern.co.uk
W www.royal-southern.co.uk
Secretary, G. H. Robinson

ROYAL TEMPLE YACHT CLUB (1857), 6 Westcliff Mansions, Ramsgate CT11 9HY T 01843-591766
E info@rtyc.com W www.rtyc.com
Hon. Secretary, R. Green

ROYAL THAMES YACHT CLUB (1775), 60 Knightsbridge, London SW1X 7LF T 020-7235 2121
E club@royalthames.com W www.royalthames.com
Secretary, Capt. D. Goldson, RN

ROYAL TORBAY YACHT CLUB (1863), 12 Beacon Terrace, Torquay TQ1 2BH T 01803-292006
E admin@royaltorbayyc.org.uk
W www.royaltorbayyc.org.uk
Secretary, R. M. Porteous

ROYAL WELSH YACHT CLUB (1847), Porth-Yr-Aur, Caernarfon LL55 1SN T 01286-672599
W www.rwyc.org.uk
Hon. Secretary, Dylan I. R. Kalis

ROYAL WESTERN YACHT CLUB OF ENGLAND (1827), Queen Anne's Battery, Plymouth PL4 0TW T 01752-660077
E admin@rwyc.org W www.rwyc.org
General Manager/Club Secretary, Mel Bryant

ROYAL WINDERMERE YACHT CLUB (1860), Fallbarrow Road, Bowness-on-Windermere, Windermere LA23 3DJ
T 01539-443106 E rwindermere@rya-online.net
Hon. Secretary, Mrs M. A. Kirk

ROYAL YACHT SQUADRON (1815), The Castle, Cowes PO31 7QT T 01983-292191 E mail@royalyachtsquadron.org
W www.rys.org.uk
Secretary, Mrs P. Lewington

ROYAL YORKSHIRE YACHT CLUB (1847), 1 Windsor Crescent, Bridlington YO15 3HX T 01262-672041
E sec@ryyc.org.uk W www.ryyc.org.uk
Secretary, Anita L. Ingham

SCOTTISH ARTS CLUB (1872), 24 Rutland Square, Edinburgh EH1 2BW T 0131-229 8157
E info@scottishartsclub.co.uk W www.scottishartsclub.o.uk

STOURBRIDGE OLD EDWARDIAN CLUB (1898), Drury Lane, Stourbridge DY8 1BL T 01384-395635
Hon. Secretary, C. M. Bowen-Davies (Men only)

ULSTER REFORM CLUB (1885), 4 Royal Avenue, Belfast BT1 1DA T 028-9032 3411 E info@ulsterreformclub.com
W www.ulsterreformclub.com
General Manager, A. W. Graham

VICTORIA CLUB (1853), Beresford Street, St Helier, Jersey JE2 4WN T 01534-723381 E victoriaclub@jerseymail.co.uk
Secretary, C. J. Blackstone

SOCIETIES AND INSTITUTIONS

ABBEYFIELD SOCIETY (1956), Abbeyfield House, 53 Victoria Street, St Albans AL1 3UW **T** 01727-857536 **E** post@abbeyfield.com **W** www.abbeyfield.com
Chief Executive, B. House

ACE STUDY TOURS (1958), Babraham, Cambridge CB2 4AP **T** 01223-835055 **E** ace@study-tours.org **W** www.study-tours.org
General Secretary, Paul Barnes

ACTION FOR BLIND PEOPLE (1857), 14–16 Verney Road, London SE16 3DZ **T** 020-7635 4800 **E** info@afbp.org **W** www.afbp.org
Chief Executive, S. Remington

ACTION MEDICAL RESEARCH (1952), Vincent House, Horsham RH12 2DP **T** 01403-210406 **E** info@action.org.uk **W** www.action.org.uk
Chief Executive, Simon Moore

ACTORS' BENEVOLENT FUND (1882), 6 Adam Street, London WC2N 6AD **T** 020-7836 6378 **E** office@abf.org.uk **W** www.actorsbenevolentfund.co.uk
General Secretary, W. Bicket

ACTORS' CHARITABLE TRUST (1896), 255–256 Africa House, 64–78 Kingsway, London WC2B 6BD **T** 020-7242 0111 **E** robert@tactactors.org **W** www.tactactors.org
General Secretary, R. Ashby

ADAM SMITH INSTITUTE (1977), 23 Great Smith Street, London SW1P 3BL **T** 020-7222 4995 **E** info@adamsmith.org.uk **W** www.adamsmith.org.uk
President, Dr M. Pirie

ADVERTISING STANDARDS AUTHORITY (1962), 2 Torrington Place, London WC1E 7HW **T** 020-7580 5555 **E** inquiries@asa.org.uk **W** www.asa.org.uk
Director-General, Christopher Graham

AGE CONCERN CYMRU, 4th Floor, 1 Cathedral Road, Cardiff CF11 9SD **T** 029-2037 1566 **E** enquiries@accymru.org.uk **W** www.accymru.org.uk
Director, R. W. Taylor

AGE CONCERN ENGLAND (1940), Astral House, 1268 London Road, London SW16 4ER **T** 020-8765 7200; **Helpline** 0800-009966 **E** ace@ace.org.uk **W** www.ageconcern.org.uk
Director-General, G. Lishman, OBE

AGE CONCERN SCOTLAND (1943), 113 Rose Street, Edinburgh EH2 3DT **T** 0131-220 3345 **E** enquiries@acscot.org.uk **W** www.ageconcernscotland.org.uk
Director, Ms M. O'Neill

AGRICULTURAL ENGINEERS ASSOCIATION (1875), Samuelson House, Paxton Road, Orton Centre, Peterborough PE2 5LT **T** 01733-362925 **E** dg@aea.uk.com **W** www.aea.uk.com
Director-General, J. Vowles

ALCOHOLICS ANONYMOUS (1947), PO Box 1, Stonebow House, Stonebow, York YO1 2NJ **T** 01904-644026. **National Helpline** 0845-769 7555 **W** www.alcoholics-anonymous.org.uk
General-Secretary, A. Napier

ALEXANDRA ROSE DAY (1912), 5 Mead Lane, Farnham, Surrey GU9 7DY **T** 0870-770 0275
National Director, Alan Leng

ALZHEIMER'S SOCIETY (1979), Gordon House, 10 Greencoat Place, London SW1P 1PH **T** 020-7306 0606. **Helpline** 0845-300 0336 **E** info@alzheimers.org.uk **W** www.alzheimers.org.uk
Chief Executive, N. Hunt

AMNESTY INTERNATIONAL UNITED KINGDOM (1961), 99–119 Rosebery Avenue, London EC1R 4RE **T** 020-7814 6200 **E** info@amnesty.org.uk **W** www.amnesty.org.uk
Campaigns Director, Stephen Bowen

ANCIENT MONUMENTS SOCIETY (1924), St Ann's Vestry Hall, 2 Church Entry, London EC4V 5HB **T** 020-7236 3934 **E** office@ancientmonumentssociety.org.uk **W** www.ancientmonumentssociety.org.uk
Secretary, M. J. Saunders, MBE

ANGLO-BELGIAN SOCIETY (1982), 5 Hartley Close, Bickley BR1 2TP **T** 020-8467 8442
Hon. Secretary, P. R. Bresnan

ANGLO-BRAZILIAN SOCIETY (1943), 32 Green Street, London W1K 7AU **T** 020-7493 8493 **E** info@anglobraziliansociety.org **W** www.anglobraziliansociety.org
Secretary, E. Dell'Aglio

ANGLO-DANISH SOCIETY (1924), Danewood, 4 Daleside, Gerrards Cross SL9 7JF **T** 01753-883510
Chairman, Mr P. J. Willoughby

ANGLO-NORSE SOCIETY (1918), 25 Belgrave Square, London SW1X 8QD **T** 020-7235 9529 **E** anglonorse@yahoo.co.uk
Chairman, Sir Richard Dales, KCMG

ANIMAL CONCERN (1876), PO Box 5178, Dumbarton G82 5YJ **T** 01389-841639 **E** animals@jfrobins.force9.co.uk **W** www.animalconcern.com

ANIMAL HEALTH TRUST (1942), Lanwades Park, Kentford, Newmarket CB8 7UU **T** 08700-502424 **E** info@aht.org.uk **W** www.aht.org.uk
Executive Chairman, E. A. Chandler

ANTI-SLAVERY INTERNATIONAL (1839), Thomas Clarkson House, The Stableyard, Broomgrove Road, London SW9 9TL **T** 020-7501 8920 **E** antislavery@antislavery.org **W** www.antislavery.org
Director, M. Cunneen

ARCHITECTS BENEVOLENT SOCIETY (1850), 43 Portland Place, London W1B 1QH **T** 020-7580 2823 **E** help@absnet.org.uk **W** www.absnet.org.uk
Secretary, K. Robinson

ARCHITECTURAL HERITAGE FUND (1976), Clareville House, 26–27 Oxendon Street, London SW1Y 4EL **T** 020-7925 0199 **E** ahf@ahfund.org.uk **W** www.ahfund.org.uk
Director, I. Lush

ARLIS/UK AND IRELAND (1969), 17–21 Fountainhall Road, Edinburgh EH9 2LN **T** 0131-529 5537 **E** margaret.young@edinburgh.gov.uk **W** www.arlis.org.uk
Chair, Mrs M. Young

ARMY CADET FORCE ASSOCIATION (1930), Holderness House, 51–61 Clifton Street, London EC2A 4DW **T** 020-7426 8377 **E** acfa@armycadets.com **W** www.armycadets.com
General Secretary, Brig. I. D. T. McGill, CBE

ART FUND (1903), Millais House, 7 Cromwell Place, London SW7 2JN **T** 020-7225 4800 **E** info@artfund.org **W** www.artfund.org
Director, D. Barrie

ARTHRITIS CARE (1949), 18 Stephenson Way, London NW1 2HD **T** 020-7380 6500 **W** www.arthritiscare.org.uk
Chief Executive, William Butler

ASIAN FAMILY COUNSELLING SERVICE (1985), Suite 51, The Lodge, Windmill Place, 2–4 Windmill Lane, Southall UB2 4NJ **T** 020-8571 3933 **E** afcs99@hotmail.com
Director, R. Atma

ASSOCIATION OF ACCOUNTING TECHNICIANS (1980), 154 Clerkenwell Road, London EC1R 5AD **T** 020-7837 8600 **E** aat@aat.org.uk **W** www.aat.org.uk
Chief Executive, Ms J. Scott Paul

ASSOCIATION OF BRITISH CORRESPONDENCE COLLEGES (1955), PO Box 17926, London SW19 3WB **T** 020-8544 9559 **E** info@homestudy.org.uk **W** www.homestudy.org.uk
Secretary, Mrs H. Owen

ASSOCIATION OF BRITISH DISPENSING OPTICIANS (1925), 199 Gloucester Terrace, London W2 6LD **T** 020-7298 5100 **E** general@abdo.org.uk **W** www.abdo.org.uk
General Secretary, Sir Anthony Garrett, CBE

ASSOCIATION OF BRITISH INSURERS (1985), 51 Gresham Street, London EC2V 7HQ **T** 020-7600 3333 **E** info@abi.org.uk **W** www.abi.org.uk
Director-General, Mrs M. Francis

ASSOCIATION OF BRITISH TRAVEL AGENTS (1950), 68–71 Newman Street, London W1T 3AH **T** 020-7637 2444 **E** abta@abta.co.uk **W** www.abta.com
Chief Executive, I. Reynolds

ASSOCIATION OF BUILDING ENGINEERS (1925), Lutyens House, Billing Brook Road, Weston Favell, Northampton NN3 8NW **T** 01604-404121 **E** building.engineers@abe.org.uk **W** www.abe.org.uk
Chief Executive, D. Gibson

ASSOCIATION OF BUSINESS RECOVERY PROFESSIONALS (1990), 8th Floor, 120 Aldersgate Street, London EC1A 4JQ **T** 020-7566 4200 **E** association@r3.org.uk **W** www.r3.org.uk
Chief Operating Officer, R. M. Stancombe

ASSOCIATION OF CHARTERED CERTIFIED ACCOUNTANTS (1904), 29 Lincoln's Inn Fields, London WC2A 3EE **T** 020-7396 7000 **E** info@accaglobal.com **W** www.accaglobal.com
Chief Executive, Mr Allen Blewitt

ASSOCIATION OF CONSULTING SCIENTISTS (1958), PO Box 4040, Thorpe-le-Soken, Clacton-on-Sea CO16 0EL **T** 01255-862526 **E** secretary@consultingscientists.co.uk **W** www.consultingscientists.co.uk
Secretary, Dr D. Simpson

ASSOCIATION OF CONVENIENCE STORES LTD (1995), Federation House, 17 Farnborough Street, Farnborough GU14 8AG **T** 01252-515001 **E** acs@acs.org.uk **W** www.thelocalshop.com
Chief Executive, David Rae

ASSOCIATION OF CORPORATE TREASURERS (1979), Ocean House, 10–12 Little Trinity Lane, London EC4V 2DJ **T** 020-7213 9728 **E** enquiries@treasurers.co.uk **W** www.treasurers.org
Chief Executive, Richard Raeburn

ASSOCIATION OF COUNTY CHIEF EXECUTIVES (1974), Office of the Chief Executive, County Hall, Trowbridge, BA14 8JF **T** 01225-713101 **E** jeanpotter@wiltshire.gov.uk
Hon. Secretary, K. Robinson

ASSOCIATION OF DRAINAGE AUTHORITIES (1937), The Mews, 3 Royal Oak Passage, High Street, Huntingdon PE29 3EA **T** 01480-411123 **E** admin@ada.org.uk **W** www.ada.org.uk
Chief Executive, D. Noble

ASSOCIATION OF FRIENDLY SOCIETIES (1995), 10–13 Lovat Lane, London EC3R 8DT **T** 020-7397 9550 **E** info@afs.org.uk **W** www.afs.org.uk
Secretary, D. Thow

ASSOCIATION OF GENEALOGISTS AND RESEARCHERS IN ARCHIVES (1968), 29 Badgers Close, Horsham RH12 5RU **E** agra@agra.org.uk **W** www.agra.org.uk
Company Secretary, David R. Young

ASSOCIATION OF HIGH SHERIFFS OF ENGLAND & WALES (1971), PO Box 198, Letchworth SG6 3ZQ **T** 01462-620356 **E** michael.mccartney2@ntlworld.com **W** www.highsheriffs.com
Hon. Secretary, Michael McCartney

ASSOCIATION OF INTERNATIONAL ACCOUNTANTS (1928), South Bank Building, Kingsway, Team Valley, Newcastle upon Tyne NE11 0JS **T** 0191-482 4409 **E** aia@aia.org.uk **W** www.aia.org.uk
Chief Executive, Philip J. J. Turnbull

ASSOCIATION OF ROYAL NAVY OFFICERS (1920), 70 Porchester Terrace, London W2 3TP **T** 020-7402 5231 **E** arno@eurosurf.com **W** www.eurosurf.com/arno
Secretary, Lt.-Cdr. A. Littleboy

ASSOCIATION OF SPEAKERS CLUBS (1971), Beanlands Chase, 20 Rivermead Drive, Garstang, Preston PR3 1JJ **T** 01995-602560 **E** natsecasc@lineone.net **W** www.the-asc.org.uk
National President, Colin Dove

ASSOCIATION OF TEACHERS OF MATHEMATICS (1952), Unit 7, Prime Industrial Park, Shaftesbury Street, Derby DE23 8YB **T** 01332-346599 **E** admin@atm.org.uk **W** www.atm.org.uk
Hon. Secretary, Cheryl Periton

AUTOMOBILE ASSOCIATION (1905), Southwood East, Apollo Rise, Farnborough GU14 0JW **T** 08705-500600 **E** customer.services@theaa.com **W** www.theaa.com
Managing Director, Roger Wood

BALTIC AIR CHARTER ASSOCIATION (1949), The Baltic Exchange, St Mary Axe, London EC3A 8BH **T** 020-7623 5501 **W** www.baca.org.uk
Chairman, Mrs Geraldine Malempre

BALTIC EXCHANGE (1744), St Mary Axe, London EC3A 8BH **T** 020-7623 5501 **E** enquiries@balticexchange.com **W** www.balticexchange.com
Chief Executive, J. Penn

BAR ASSOCIATION FOR LOCAL GOVERNMENT AND THE PUBLIC SERVICE (1945), c/o Birmingham City Council, Ingleby House, 11–14 Cannon Street, Birmingham B2 5EN **T** 0121-303 9991 **E** chairman@balgps.org.uk **W** www.balgps.org.uk
Chairman, M. F. N. Ahmad

BARNARDO'S (1866), Tanners Lane, Barkingside, Ilford IG6 1QG **T** 020-8550 8822 **E** information@barnardos.org.uk **W** www.barnardos.org.uk
Chief Executive, R. Singleton

BARRISTERS' BENEVOLENT ASSOCIATION (1873), 14 Gray's Inn Square, London WC1R 5JP **T** 020-7242 4761 **E** linda@the-bba.com **W** www.the-bba.com
Secretary, Mrs L. C. Carlier

BCCB (1965), One Westminster Palace Gardens, 1–7 Artillery Row, London SW1P 1RJ **T** 020-7222 3651 **E** mail@bccb.org.uk **W** www.bccb.org.uk
Chief Executive Officer, G. Hand, CBE

BESO (BRITISH EXECUTIVE SERVICE OVERSEAS) (1972), 164 Vauxhall Bridge Road, London SW1V 2RB **T** 020-7630 0644 **E** team@beso.org **W** www.beso.org
Chief Executive, G. Ramsey, CBE

BEVIN BOYS ASSOCIATION (1989), School Cottage, 49a Hogshill Street, Beaminster, DT8 3AG **T** 01308-861488
Vice-President and Public Relations, W. H. Taylor, MBE

BIBLIOGRAPHICAL SOCIETY (1892), c/o Institute of English Studies, Room 304, Senate House, Malet Street, London WC1E 7HU **T** 020-7862 8679 **E** secretary@bibsoc.org.uk **W** www.bibsoc.org.uk
Hon. Secretary, M. L. Ford

BIRMINGHAM AND WARWICKSHIRE ARCHAEOLOGICAL SOCIETY (1870), c/o Birmingham and Midland Institute, Margaret Street, Birmingham B3 3BS **W** www.bwas.org.uk
Hon. Secretary, Miss S. Middleton

BLUE CROSS (1897), Shilton Road, Burford OX18 4PF **T** 01993-822651 **E** info@bluecross.org.uk **W** www.bluecross.org.uk
Chief Executive, John Rutter

BOOK AID INTERNATIONAL (1954), 39–41 Coldharbour Lane, London SE5 9NR **T** 020-7733 3577 **E** info@bookaid.org **W** www.bookaid.org
Director, Mrs S. Harrity, MBE

BOOKSELLERS ASSOCIATION OF THE UK & IRELAND LTD (1895), Minster House, 272 Vauxhall Bridge Road, London SW1V 1BA **T** 020-7802 0802 **E** mail@booksellers.org.uk **W** www.booksellers.org.uk
Chief Executive, T. E. Godfray

BOOKTRUST (1926), Book House, 45 East Hill, London SW18 2QZ **T** 020-8516 2977 **E** info@booktrust.org.uk **W** www.booktrust.org.uk
Executive Director, C. Meade

BOTANICAL SOCIETY OF SCOTLAND (1836), c/o Royal Botanic Garden, Inverleith Row, Edinburgh EH3 5LR **T** 0131-552 7171
Hon. General Secretary, Dr P. Cochrane

BOTANICAL SOCIETY OF THE BRITISH ISLES (1836), c/o Department of Botany, The Natural History Museum, Cromwell Road, London SW7 5BD **T** 020-7942 5002 **E** dpearman4@aol.com **W** www.bsbi.org.uk
Acting Hon. General Secretary, D. Pearman

BRISTOL AND GLOUCESTERSHIRE ARCHAEOLOGICAL SOCIETY (1876), 22 Beaumont Road, Gloucester GL2 0EJ T 01452-302610
W www.bgas.org.uk
Hon. Secretary, D. J. H. Smith, FSA

BRITAIN-NEPAL SOCIETY (1960), 95B Eaton Place, London SW1X 8LZ T 020-8993 0173
Hon. Secretary, Mrs Pat Mellor

BRITISH ACADEMY, 10 Carlton House Terrace, London SW1Y 5AH T 020-7969 5200 E secretary@britac.ac.uk
W www.britac.ac.uk

BRITISH ACADEMY OF FORENSIC SCIENCES, Anaesthetic Unit, The Royal London Hospital, Whitechapel, London E1 1BB T 020-7377 9201
Secretary-General, Dr P. J. Flynn

BRITISH AND FOREIGN BIBLE SOCIETY (1804), Stonehill Green, Westlea, Swindon SN5 7DG
T 01793-418100 E contactus@biblesociety.org.uk
W www.biblesociety.org.uk
Chief Executive, James Catford

BRITISH ANTIQUE DEALERS' ASSOCIATION (1918), 20 Rutland Gate, London SW7 1BD
T 020-7589 4128 E info@bada.org W www.bada.org
Secretary-General, Mrs E. J. Dean

BRITISH ASSOCIATION FOR EARLY CHILDHOOD EDUCATION (1923), 136 Cavell Street, London E1 2JA
T 020-7539 5400 E office@early-education.org.uk
W www.early-education.org.uk

BRITISH ASSOCIATION FOR LOCAL HISTORY (1952), PO Box 6549, Somersal Herbert DE6 5WH
T 01283-585947 W www.balh.co.uk
Business Manager, A. Jones

BRITISH ASSOCIATION FOR SEXUAL HEALTH AND HIV (BASHH) (2003), 1 Wimpole Street, London W1G 0AE T 020-7290 2968 E bashh@rsm.ac.uk
W www.bashh.org
General Secretary, Dr Keith Radcliffe

BRITISH ASSOCIATION FOR THE ADVANCEMENT OF SCIENCE (1831), Wellcome Wolfson Building, 165 Queen's Gate, London SW7 5HE T 0870-770 7101
E info@the-ba.net W www.the-ba.net
Chief Executive, Dr R. Jackson

BRITISH ASSOCIATION OF COMMUNICATORS IN BUSINESS (1949), Suite A, First Floor, The Auriga Building, Davy Avenue, Knowlhill, Milton Keynes MK5 8ND
T 0870-121 7606 E enquiries@cib.uk.com
W www.cib.uk.com
Secretary-General, Mrs K. Jones

BRITISH ASSOCIATION OF SOCIAL WORKERS (1970), 16 Kent Street, Birmingham B5 6RD
T 0121-622 3911 W www.basw.co.uk
Director, I. Johnston

BRITISH ASTRONOMICAL ASSOCIATION (1890), Burlington House, Piccadilly, London W1J 0DU
T 020-7734 4145 E office@britastro.com
W www.britastro.org
President, Tom Boles

BRITISH BEE-KEEPERS' ASSOCIATION (1874), National Beekeeping Centre, Stoneleigh Park, Kenilworth CV8 2LG T 0247-669 6679
E information@bbka.demon.co.uk
W www.bbka.demon.co.uk
General Secretary, C. Waring

BRITISH BOARD OF FILM CLASSIFICATION (1912), 3 Soho Square, London W1D 3HD T 020-7440 1570
E webmaster@bbfc.co.uk W www.bbfc.co.uk
Director, R. Duval

BRITISH CATTLE BREEDERS' CLUB LTD (1950), Lake Villa, Bradworthy, Holsworthy, Devon EX22 7SQ
T 01409-241579 E lesley.lewin@cattlebreeders.org.uk
Secretary, Mrs L. Lewin

BRITISH CHAMBERS OF COMMERCE, 1st Floor, 65 Petty France, St James Park, London SW1H 9EU
T 020-7654 5800 E info@britishchambers.org.uk
W www.chamberonline.co.uk
Director-General, David Frost

BRITISH CHESS FEDERATION (1904), The Watch Oak, Chain Lane, Battle TN33 0YD T 01424-775222
E office@bcf.org.uk W www.bcf.org.uk
President, Gerry Walsh

BRITISH COMPUTER SOCIETY (1957), 1 Sanford Street, Swindon SN1 1HJ T 01793-417417
E bcshq@hq.bcs.org.uk W www.bcs.org.uk
Chief Executive, David Clarke

BRITISH COPYRIGHT COUNCIL (1965), 29–33 Berners Street, London W1T 3AB T 01986-788122
E copyright@bcc2.demon.co.uk
Secretary, Ms J. Ibbotson

BRITISH DEAF ASSOCIATION (1890), 1–3 Worship Street, London EC2A 2AB T 020-7588 3529
E helpline@bda.org.uk W www.bda.org.uk
Chief Executive, J. McWhinney

BRITISH DENTAL ASSOCIATION (1880), 64 Wimpole Street, London W1G 8YS T 020-7935 0875
E enquiries@bda.org W www.bda.org
Chief Executive, Ian Wylie

BRITISH DRIVING SOCIETY LTD (1957), 27 Dugard Place, Barford CV35 8DX T 01926-624420
E email@britishdrivingsociety.co.uk
W www.britishdrivingsociety.co.uk
Secretary, Mrs J. M. Dillon

BRITISH ECOLOGICAL SOCIETY, 26 Blades Court, Deodar Road, London SW15 2NU T 020-8871 9797 E info@britishecologicalsociety.org W www.britishecologicalsociety.org

BRITISH FALSE MEMORY SOCIETY (1993), Bradford on Avon BA15 1NF T 01225-868682 E bfms@bfms.org.uk W www.bfms.org.uk
Director, M. Greenhalgh

BRITISH FEDERATION OF WOMEN GRADUATES (1907), 4 Mandeville Courtyard, 142 Battersea Park Road, London SW11 4NB T 020-7498 8037 E bfwg@bfwg.demon.co.uk W www.bfwg.org.uk
Secretary, Mrs A. B. Stein

BRITISH GLIDING ASSOCIATION (1929), Kimberley House, Vaughan Way, Leicester LE1 4SE T 0116-253 1051 E bga@gliding.co.uk W www.gliding.co.uk
Secretary, P. Stratten

BRITISH HEALTH CARE ASSOCIATION (1930), 24A Main Street, Garforth, Leeds LS25 1AA T 0113-232 0903 E cbell@bhca.org.uk W www.bhca.org.uk
Chief Executive, Mrs C. Bell

BRITISH HEART FOUNDATION (1961), 14 Fitzhardinge Street, London W1H 6DH T 020-7935 0185 E directorate@bhf.org.uk W www.bhf.org.uk
Director-General, P. Hollins

BRITISH HEDGEHOG PRESERVATION SOCIETY (1982), Hedgehog House, Dhustone, Ludlow SY8 3PL T 01584-890801 E bhps@dhustone.fsbusiness.co.uk W www.software-technics.com/bhps
Chief Executive, Fay Vass

BRITISH HERPETOLOGICAL SOCIETY (1947), c/o Zoological Society of London, Regent's Park, London NW1 4RY T 020-8452 9578
Secretary, Mrs M. Green

BRITISH HORSE SOCIETY (1947), Stoneleigh Deer Park, Kenilworth CV8 2XZ T 08701-202244 E enquiry@bhs.org.uk W www.bhs.org.uk
Chief Executive, Mrs Kay Driver

BRITISH HOSPITALITY ASSOCIATION (1907), Queens House, 55–56 Lincoln's Inn Fields, London WC2A 3BH T 020-7404 7744 E bha@bha.org.uk W www.bha-online.org.uk
Chief Executive, Bob Cotton, OBE

BRITISH HUMANIST ASSOCIATION (1896), 1 Gower Street, London WC1E 6HD T 020-7079 3580 E info@humanism.org.uk W www.humanism.org.uk
Executive Director, Hanne Stinson

BRITISH INSTITUTE IN EASTERN AFRICA (1959), 10 Carlton House Terrace, London SW1Y 5AH T 020-7969 5201 E biea@britac.ac.uk W www.britac.ac.uk/institutes/eafrica
London Secretary, Mrs J. Moyo

BRITISH INSTITUTE OF GRAPHOLOGY, PO Box 3060, Gerrards Cross, SL9 9XP T 01753-891241 E contact@britishgraphology.org W www.britishgraphology.org
Chairman, Elaine Quigley

BRITISH INSTITUTE OF PROFESSIONAL PHOTOGRAPHY (1901), Fox Talbot House, Amwell End, Ware SG12 9HN T 01920-464011 E info@bipp.com W www.bipp.com
Executive Officer, M. Berry

BRITISH INSURANCE BROKERS' ASSOCIATION (1978), BIBA House, 14 Bevis Marks, London EC3A 7NT T 020-7623 9043 E enquiries@biba.org.uk W www.biba.org.uk
Chief Executive, R. M. Williams

BRITISH INTERPLANETARY SOCIETY (1933), 27–29 South Lambeth Road, London SW8 1SZ T 020-7735 3160 E mail@bis-spaceflight.com W www.bis-spaceflight.com
Executive Secretary, Suszann Parry

BRITISH ISRAEL WORLD FEDERATION (1919), 121 Low Etherley, Bishop Auckland, Co Durham DL14 0HA T 01388-834395 E admin@britishisrael.co.uk W www.britishisrael.co.uk
Hon. Secretary, M. A. Clark

BRITISH LUNG FOUNDATION (1985), 73–75 Goswell Road, London EC1V 7ER T 020-7688 5555 E enquiries@blf-uk.org W www.lunguk.org
Chief Executive, Dame Helena Shovelton

BRITISH MEDICAL ASSOCIATION (1832), BMA House, Tavistock Square, London WC1H 9JP T 020-7387 4499 E info.web@bma.org.uk W www.bma.org.uk
Secretary, J. Strachan

BRITISH MENSA LTD (1946), St John's House, St Johns Square, Wolverhampton WV2 4AH T 01902-772771 E enquiries@mensa.org.uk W www.mensa.org.uk
Chief Executive and Company Secretary, John Stevenage

BRITISH MUSIC HALL SOCIETY, 82 Fernlea Road, London SW12 9RW T 020-8673 2175 W www.music-hall-society.com
Hon. Secretary, Daphne Masterton

BRITISH NATIONAL TEMPERANCE LEAGUE (1834), Westbrook Court, 2 Sharrow Vale Road, Sheffield S11 8YZ T 0114-267 9976 E info@bntl.org W www.bntl.org
Manager, Mrs B. Briggs

BRITISH NATURALISTS' ASSOCIATION (1905), 1 Bracken Mews, London E4 7UT W www.bna-naturalists.org
Hon. Membership Secretary, Mrs Y. H. Griffiths

BRITISH NUCLEAR ENERGY SOCIETY, 1–7 Great George Street, London SW1P 3AA T 020-7665 2241 E ian.andrews@ice.org.uk W www.bnes.org.uk
Secretary, I. M. Andrews, FRSA

BRITISH NUTRITION FOUNDATION (1967), High Holborn House, 52–54 High Holborn, London WC1V 6RQ
T 020-7404 6504 E postbox@nutrition.org.uk
W www.nutrition.org.uk
Director-General, Prof. R. S. Pickard, PHD, CBIOL

BRITISH PHARMACOLOGICAL SOCIETY (1931), 16 Angel Gate, City Road, London EC1V 2SG T 020-7239 0170
E yn@bps.ac.uk W www.bps.ac.uk
President, Prof. J. C. Buckingham

BRITISH PIG ASSOCIATION (1884), Trumpington Mews, 40b High Street, Cambridge CB2 2LS
T 01233-845100 E bpa@britishpigs.org
W www.britishpigs.org
Chief Executive, M. Bates

BRITISH PSYCHOLOGICAL SOCIETY (1901), St Andrews House, 48 Princess Road East, Leicester LE1 7DR
T 0116-254 9568 E mail@bps.org.uk W www.bps.org.uk
Chief Executive, B. A. Brooking

BRITISH RED CROSS (1870), 9 Grosvenor Crescent, London SW1X 7EJ T 020-7235 5454
E information@redcross.org.uk
W www.redcross.org.uk and www.redcrossdonations.org.uk
Chief Executive, Sir Nicholas Young

BRITISH REFUGEE COUNCIL (1992), 240–250 Ferndale Road, London SW9 8BB T 020-7346 6700
W www.refugeecouncil.org.uk
Chair, Naaz Coker

BRITISH SOCIETY OF DOWSERS (1933), Sycamore Barn, Hastingleigh, Ashford TN25 5HW T 01684-576969
E secretary@britishdowsers.org W www.britishdowsers.org
Administrator, I. Clements

BRITISH TRUST FOR ORNITHOLOGY, The Nunnery, Thetford IP24 2PU T 01842-750050 E general@bto.org
W www.bto.org
Director, Dr J. J. D. Greenwood

BRITISH UNION FOR THE ABOLITION OF VIVISECTION (1898), 16A Crane Grove, London N7 8NN T 020-7700 4888 E info@buav.org
W www.buav.org

BRITISH VETERINARY ASSOCIATION (1883), 7 Mansfield Street, London W1G 9NQ T 020-7636 6541
E bvahq@bva.co.uk W www.bva.co.uk
Chairman of the Board, B. D. Hoskins

BRITISH WOOD PRESERVING AND DAMP-PROOFING ASSOCIATION (1930), 1 Gleneagles House, Vernon Gate, Derby DE1 1UP T 01332-225100
E info@bwpda.co.uk W www.bwpda.co.uk
Director, Dr C. R. Coggins

BTBS THE BOOK TRADE CHARITY (1837), The Foyle Centre, The Retreat, Kings Langley WD4 8LT
T 01923-263128 E btbs@booktradecharity.demon.co.uk
W www.booktradecharity.demon.co.uk
Chief Executive, David Hicks

BUCKINGHAMSHIRE ARCHAEOLOGICAL SOCIETY (1847), County Museum, Church Street, Aylesbury HP20 2QP T 01296-678114
Hon. Secretary, Mrs M. E. A. Brown

BUDGERIGAR SOCIETY (1925), Spring Gardens, Northampton NN1 1DR T 01604-624549
W www.budgerigarsociety.com
General Secretary, D. Whittaker

BUILDING SOCIETIES ASSOCIATION (1869), 3 Savile Row, London W1S 3PB T 020-7437 0655
W www.bsa.org.uk
Director-General, A. Coles

CAFOD (CATHOLIC FUND FOR OVERSEAS DEVELOPMENT) (1962), Romero Close, Stockwell Road, London SW9 9TY T 020-7733 7900
E hq@cafod.org.uk W www.cafod.org.uk
Director, C. Bain

CALOUSTE GULBENKIAN FOUNDATION (1956), 98 Portland Place, London W1B 1ET T 020-7636 5313
E info@gulbenkian.org.uk W www.gulbenkian.org.uk
Director, Ms P. Ridley

CAMBRIDGE ANTIQUARIAN SOCIETY (1840), 21 High Street, West Wickham, Cambridge CB1 6RY
E jmmorris@jmmorris.plus.com W www.camantsoc.org
Hon. Secretary, Mrs J. Morris

CAMBRIDGE PRESERVATION SOCIETY (1928), Wandlebury Ring, Gog Magog Hills, Babraham, Cambridge CB2 4AE T 01223-243830 E admin@cpswandlebury.org.uk
W www.cpswandlebury.org
Director, J. Cornish

CAMERON FUND (1970), Tavistock House North, Tavistock Square, London WC1H 9HR T 020-7388 0796
E secretary@cameronfund.org.uk
W www.cameronfund.org.uk
Secretary, Mrs L. Dluska-Miziura

CAMPAIGN FOR FREEDOM OF INFORMATION (1984), Suite 102, 16 Baldwin Gardens, London EC1N 7RJ
T 020-7831 7477 E admin@cfoi.demon.co.uk
W www.cfoi.org.uk
Director, M. Frankel

CAMPAIGN FOR NUCLEAR DISARMAMENT (CND) (1958), 162 Holloway Road, London N7 8DQ
T 020-7700 2393 E enquiries@cnduk.org
W www.cnduk.org
Chair, Kate Hudson

CAMPAIGN FOR THE PROTECTION OF RURAL WALES (1928), Ty Gwyn, 31 High Street, Welshpool SY21 7YD T 01938-552525 E info@cprw.org.uk
W www.cprw.org.uk
Director, P. Ogden

CANADA-UNITED KINGDOM CHAMBER OF COMMERCE (1921), 38 Grosvenor Street, London W1K 4DP T 020-7258 6576 E info@canada-uk.org
W www.canada-uk.org
Services Director, R. Wormell

CANCER RESEARCH UK (2002), PO Box 123, London WC2A 3PX **T** 020-7242 0200 **W** www.cancerresearchuk.org
Chief Executive, Prof Alex Markham

CARERS UK (1988), Ruth Pitter House, 20–25 Glasshouse Yard, London EC1A 4JT **T** 020-7490 8818 **E** info@ukcarers.org **W** www.carersonline.org.uk
Chief Executive, Ms I. Redmond

CARNEGIE HERO FUND TRUST (1908), Abbey Park House, Abbey Park Place, Dunfermline KY12 7PB **T** 01383-723638
Chief Executive, B. A. Anderson

CARNEGIE UNITED KINGDOM TRUST (1913), Comely Park House, Dunfermline KY12 7EJ **T** 01383-721445 **W** www.carnegieuktrust.org.uk
Chief Executive, C. McConnell, OBE

CATHEDRALS FABRIC COMMISSION FOR ENGLAND (1991), Church House, Great Smith Street, London SW1P 3NZ **T** 020-7898 1863 **E** enquiries@cfce.c-of-e.org.uk
Secretary, Ms Paula Griffiths

CATHOLIC TRUTH SOCIETY (1868), 40–46 Harleyford Road, London SE11 5AY **T** 020-7640 0042 **E** info@cts-online.org.uk **W** www.cts-online.org.uk
General Secretary, F. Martin

CATHOLIC UNION OF GREAT BRITAIN (1872), St Maxmilian Kolbe House, 63 Jeddo Road, London W12 9EE **T** 020-8749 1321 **E** phiggs@cathunion.fsnet.co.uk **W** www.catholicunion.org
Secretary, P. H. Higgs

CENTRAL AND CECIL HOUSING TRUST (1926), 266 Waterloo Road, London, Richmond SE1 8RQ **T** 020-7922 5300 **E** enquiries@ccht.org.uk **W** www.ccht.org.uk
Chief Executive, Dorry McLaughlin

CENTRAL COUNCIL OF CHURCH BELL RINGERS (1891), The Cottage, School Hill, Warnham, Horsham RH12 3QN **T** 01403-269743 **W** www.cccbr.org.uk
Secretary, Mr I. H. Oram

CENTREPOINT (1969), Neil House, 7 Whitechapel Road, London E1 1DU **T** 020-7426 5300 **W** www.centrepoint.org.uk
Chief Executive, Anthony Lawton

CEREDIGION HISTORICAL SOCIETY, Henllys, Lôn Tyllwyd, Llanfarian SY23 4UH **T** 01970-625818
Hon. Secretary, M. Humphreys

CHARITIES AID FOUNDATION (1924), Kings Hill, West Malling ME19 4TA **T** 01732-520000 **E** enquiries@cafonline.org **W** www.cafonline.org
Chief Executive, Stephen Ainger

CHARTERED INSTITUTE OF ENVIRONMENTAL HEALTH (1883), Chadwick Court, 15 Hatfields, London SE1 8DJ **T** 020-7928 6006 **E** information@cieh.org **W** www.cieh.org.uk
Chief Executive, G. Jukes

CHARTERED INSTITUTE OF LIBRARY AND INFORMATION PROFESSIONALS (2002), 7 Ridgmount Street, London WC1E 7AE **T** 020-7255 0500; **Textphone** 020-7255 0505 **E** info@cilip.org.uk **W** www.cilip.org.uk
Chief Executive, Dr R. A. McKee, FRSA, MCLIP

CHARTERED INSTITUTE OF PURCHASING AND SUPPLY (1932), Easton House, Easton on the Hill, Stamford PE9 3NZ **T** 01780-756777 **E** info@cips.org **W** www.cips.org
Chief Executive, K. James

CHARTERED INSTITUTE OF TAXATION (1930), 12 Upper Belgrave Street, London SW1X 8BB **T** 020-7235 9381 **E** post@ciot.org.uk **W** www.tax.org.uk
Secretary-General, R. A. Dommett

CHARTERED INSTITUTION OF BUILDING SERVICES ENGINEERS (1898), Delta House, 222 Balham High Road, London SW12 9BS **T** 020-8675 5211 **E** enquiries@cibse.org **W** www.cibse.org
Chief Executive, J. Amey

CHARTERED INSTITUTION OF WASTES MANAGEMENT (1898), 9 Saxon Court, St Peter's Gardens, Northampton NN1 1SX **T** 01604-620426 **E** technical@ciwm.co.uk **W** www.ciwm.co.uk
Chief Executive, S. Lee

CHARTERED INSTITUTION OF WATER AND ENVIRONMENTAL MANAGEMENT (CIWEM) (1895), 15 John Street, London WC1N 2EB **T** 020-7831 3110 **E** admin@ciwem.org.uk **W** www.ciwem.org.uk
Executive Director, Nick Reeves

CHARTERED INSURANCE INSTITUTE (1897), 20 Aldermanbury, London EC2V 7HY **T** 020-7417 4401 **W** www.cii.co.uk
Director-General, Dr A. Scott

CHARTERED MANAGEMENT INSTITUTE (1947), Management House, Cottingham Road, Corby NN17 1TT **T** 01536-204222 **E** enquiries@managers.org.uk **W** www.managers.org.uk
Chief Executive, Ms M. Chapman

CHESTER ARCHAEOLOGICAL SOCIETY (1849), Ochr Cottage, Porch Lane, Hope Mountain, Caergwrle LL12 9HG **T** 01978-760834 **E** djpmason@dircon.co.uk **W** www.chesterarchaeolsoc.org.uk
Secretary, Dr D. J. P. Mason, FSA

CHILDREN 1ST (1884), 83 Whitehouse Loan, Edinburgh EH9 1AT **T** 0131-446 2300 **E** info@children1st.org.uk **W** www.children1st.org.uk
Chief Executive, Margaret McKay

CHILDREN'S SOCIETY (1881), Edward Rudolf House, Margery Street, London WC1X 0JL **T** 020-7841 4000 **E** supporteraction@childrenssociety.org.uk **W** www.childrenssociety.org.uk
Chief Executive, Bob Reitermeier

CHRISTIAN AID SCOTLAND, 41 George IV Bridge, Edinburgh EH1 1EL **T** 0131-220 1254
E edinburgh@christian-aid.org **W** www.christian-aid.org.uk
National Secretary, Revd J. Wylie

CHURCHILL SOCIETY - LONDON (1990), c/o 18 Grove Lane, Ipswich IP4 1NR **T** 01473-413533
E secretary@churchill-society-london.org.uk
W www.churchill-society-london.org.uk/index.htm
General Secretary, N. H. Rogers

CHURCH LADS' AND CHURCH GIRLS' BRIGADE (1891), 2 Barnsley Road, Wath upon Dearne, Rotherham S63 6PY **T** 01709-876535 **E** generalsecretary@clcgb.org.uk
W www.clcgb.org.uk
General Secretary, A. J. Reed Screen

CHURCH MISSION SOCIETY, Partnership House, 157 Waterloo Road, London SE1 8UU **T** 020-7928 8681
E info@cms-uk.org **W** www.cms-uk.org
General Secretary, Revd Canon T. Dakin

CHURCH MONUMENTS SOCIETY (1979), 34 Bridge Street, Shepshed, LE12 9AD **T** 01509-569035
E churchmonuments@aol.com
W www.churchmonumentssociety.org
Hon. Secretary, Dr Sophie Oosterwijk

CHURCH UNION (1859), Faith House, 7 Tufton Street, London SW1P 3QN **T** 020-7222 6952
E churchunion@care4free.net
W www.churchunion.care4free.net
Chairman, D. Morgan

CITIZENS ADVICE (1939), Myddelton House, 115–123 Pentonville Road, London N1 9LZ **T** 020-7833 2181
W www.citizensadvice.org.uk
Chief Executive, D. Harker

CITY OF COVENTRY FREEMEN'S GUILD (1946), 47 Brownshill Green Road, Coventry CV6 2AP
T 024-7627 4321 **W** www.coventryfreemensguild.co.uk
Hon. Clerk, K. Talbot

CITY OF STOKE-ON-TRENT MUSEUM ARCHAEOLOGICAL SOCIETY (1959), The Potteries Museum and Art Gallery, Hanley, Stoke-on-Trent ST1 3DW
T 01782-232323 **W** www.stoke.gov.uk/museums/pmag/archaeology/archsoc.htm
Chairman, E. E. Royle, MBE

CITY PAROCHIAL FOUNDATION (1891), 6 Middle Street, London EC1A 7PH **T** 020-7606 6145
E info@cityparochial.org.uk **W** www.cityparochial.org.uk
Clerk, B. Mehta, OBE

CIVIC TRUST (1957), 17 Carlton House Terrace, London SW1Y 5AW **T** 020-7170 4299 **E** info@civictrust.org.uk
W www.civictrust.org.uk
Chairman, N. Burton

CLASSICAL ASSOCIATION (1903), Senate House, Malet Street, London WC1E 7HU **T** 020-7862 8706
E croberts@sas.ac.uk **W** www.sas.ac.uk/icls/classass
Secretary, C. L. Roberts

COLLEGE OF OPTOMETRISTS (1980), 42 Craven Street, London WC2N 5NG **T** 020-7839 6000
E optometry@college-optometrists.org
W www.college-optometrists.org
Chief Executive, Mrs Bryony Pawinska

COLLEGE OF TEACHERS (1849), Institute of Education, 57 Gordon Square, London WC1H 0NU **T** 020-7947 9536
E enquiries@cot.ac.uk **W** www.collegeofteachers.ac.uk
Chief Executive Officer, R. Page

CO-OPERATIVE GROUP (CWS) LTD. (1863), PO Box 53, New Century House, Manchester M60 4ES
T 0161-834 1212 **W** www.co-op.co.uk
Chief Executive, M. D. Beaumont

CORAM FAMILY (1739), 49 Mecklenburgh Square, London WC1N 2QA **T** 020-7520 0300
E reception@coram.org.uk **W** www.coram.org.uk
Chief Executive, Dr G. Pugh, OBE

CORONER'S SOCIETY OF ENGLAND AND WALES (1846), The Court House, Bewdley Road, Stourport on Severn, Worcestershire DY13 8XE **T** 01562-887795
E honsec.corsoc@btinternet.com
Hon. Secretary, V. Round

CORPORATION OF CHURCH HOUSE (1888), Church House, Dean's Yard, London SW1P 3NZ **T** 020-7898 1000
Secretary, C. D. L. Menzies

COUNCIL FOR BRITISH ARCHAEOLOGY (1944), Bowes Morrell House, 111 Walmgate, York YO1 9WA
T 01904-671417 **E** info@britarch.ac.uk
W www.britarch.ac.uk
Director, G. Lambrick

COUNCIL FOR WORLD MISSION (1977), Ipalo House, 32–34 Great Peter Street, London SW1P 2DB
T 020-7222 4214 **E** council@cwmission.org.uk
W www.cwmission.org.uk
General Secretary, Revd Dr D. van der Water

COUNSEL AND CARE (1954), Twyman House, 16 Bonny Street, London NW1 9PG **T** 020-7241 8555
E advice@counselandcare.org.uk
W www.counselandcare.org.uk
Chief Executive, M. Green

CRISIS UK (1967), 64 Commercial Street, London E1 6LT
T 0870-011 3335 **E** enquiries@crisis.org.uk
W www.crisis.org.uk
Chief Executive, S. Ghosh

CRUSE BEREAVEMENT CARE (1959), 126 Sheen Road, Richmond TW9 1UR
T 020-8939 9530. **Helpline** 0870-167 1677
E info@crusebereavementcare.org.uk
W www.crusebereavementcare.org.uk
Chief Executive, Anne Viney

CTC (THE UK'S NATIONAL CYCLISTS' ORGANISATION) (1878), 69 Meadrow, Godalming GU7 3HS T 0870-873 0060 E cycling@ctc.org.uk W www.ctc.org.uk
Director, K. Mayne

CUMBERLAND AND WESTMORLAND ANTIQUARIAN AND ARCHAEOLOGICAL SOCIETY (1866), 2 High Tenterfell, Kendal LA9 4PG T 01539-445276 E info@cwaas.org.uk W www.cwaas.org.uk
Hon. Secretary, E. A. Jones

CYSTIC FIBROSIS TRUST (1964), 11 London Road, Bromley BR1 1BY T 020-8464 7211 E enquiries@cftrust.org.uk W www.cftrust.org.uk
Chief Executive, Mrs R. Barnes

DATA (DESIGN AND TECHNOLOGY ASSOCIATION) (1989), 16 Wellesbourne House, Walton Road, Wellesbourne CV35 9JB T 01789-470007 E data@data.org.uk W www.data.org.uk
Chairman, Dr R.V. Peacock, OBE

DEVON ARCHAEOLOGICAL SOCIETY (1929), Royal Albert Memorial Museum, Queen Street, Exeter EX4 3RX
Hon. Secretary, Lorinda Legge

DIABETES UK (1934), 10 Parkway, London NW1 7AA T 020-7424 1000 E info@diabetes.org.uk W www.diabetes.org.uk
Chief Executive, Benet Middleton

DIRECTORY & DATABASE PUBLISHERS ASSOCIATION (1970), PO Box 23034, London W6 0RJ T 020-8846 9707 E rosemary.pettit@onetel.net.uk W www.directory-publisher.co.uk
Secretary, Ms R. Pettit

DOWN'S SYNDROME ASSOCIATION (1970), The Langdon Down Centre, 2a Langdon Park, Teddington TW11 9PS T 0845-230 0372 E info@downs-syndrome.org.uk W www.downs-syndrome.org.uk
Chief Executive Officer, Ms C. Boys

DUKE OF EDINBURGH'S AWARD, Gulliver House, Madeira Walk, Windsor SL4 1EU T 01753-727400 E info@theaward.org W www.theaward.org
Director, Vice-Adm. M. P. Gretton, CB

DYSLEXIA INSTITUTE (1972), Park House, Wick Road, Egham TW20 0HH T 01784-222300 E info@dyslexia-inst.org.uk W www.dyslexia-inst.org.uk
Chief Executive, Shirley Cramer

EATING DISORDERS ASSOCIATION, First Floor, Wensum House, 103 Prince of Wales Road, Norwich NR1 1DW T 0845-634 1414. Youthline 0845-634 7650 E info@edauk.com W www.edauk.com
Chief Executive, Mrs S. Ringwood

EDINBURGH CHAMBER OF COMMERCE (1786), 27 Melville Street, Edinburgh EH3 7JF T 0131-477 7000 E information@ecce.org W www.ecce.org
Chief Executive, W. Furness

EGYPT EXPLORATION SOCIETY (1882), 3 Doughty Mews, London WC1N 2PG T 020-7242 1880 E enquiries@ees.ac.uk W www.ees.ac.uk
Secretary-General, Dr P. A. Spencer

ELGAR FOUNDATION (1935), The Elgar Birthplace Museum, Lower Broadheath, Worcester WR2 6RH T 01905-333224 E birthplace@elgarmuseum.org W www.elgarmuseum.org
Museum Director, Catherine Sloan

ELGAR SOCIETY (1951), c/o 29 Van Diemens Close, Chinnor OX39 4QE T 01844-354096 E elgar@music.com W www.elgar.org
Hon. Secretary, Ms W. Hillary

ENABLE (1954), 7 Buchanan Street, Glasgow G1 3HL T 0141-226 4541 E enable@enable.org.uk W www.enable.org.uk
Director, N. Dunning

ENERGY INSTITUTE (2003), 61 New Cavendish Street, London W1G 7AR T 020-7467 7100 E info@energyinst.org.uk W www.energyinst.org.uk
Chief Executive, Mrs L. Kingham

ENERGYWATCH (2000), 4th Floor, Artillery House, Artillery Row, London SW1P 1RT T 020-7799 8340 W www.energywatch.org.uk
Chief Executive, A. Asher

ENGINEERING COUNCIL (UK) (2002), 10 Maltravers Street, London WC2R 3ER T 020-7240 7891 E info@engc.org.uk W www.engc.org.uk
Executive Director, Andrew Ramsay

ENGLISH ASSOCIATION (1906), University of Leicester, University Road, Leicester LE1 7RH T 0116-252 3982 E engassoc@le.ac.uk W www.le.ac.uk/engassoc/
Chief Executive, Ms H. Lucas

ENGLISH FOLK DANCE AND SONG SOCIETY (1932), Cecil Sharp House, 2 Regent's Park Road, London NW1 7AY T 020-7485 2206 W www.efdss.org.com
Chief Executive, H. Miller

ENGLISH-SPEAKING UNION OF THE COMMONWEALTH (1918), Dartmouth House, 37 Charles Street, London W1J 5ED T 020-7529 1550 E esu@esu.org W www.esu.org
Director-General, Mrs V. Mitchell, OBE

ENVIRONMENT COUNCIL (1970), 212 High Holborn, London WC1V 7BF T 020-7836 2626 E info@envcouncil.org.uk W www.the-environment-council.org.uk
Chief Executive, M. King

EPILEPSY ACTION (1950), New Anstey House, Gate Way Drive, Yeadon, Leeds LS19 7XY
T 0113-210 8800 **Helpline** 0808-800 5050
E epilepsy@epilepsy.org.uk **W** www.epilepsy.org.uk
Chief Executive, P. Lee

ESPERANTO ASSOCIATION OF BRITAIN, Esperanto House, Barlaston, Stoke-on-Trent ST12 9DG
T 01782-372141 **E** eab@esperanto-gb.org
W www.esperanto-gb.org
President, Prof. J. Wells

EVANGELICAL LIBRARY, 78A Chiltern Street, London W1U 5HB **T** 020-7935 6997 **E** stlibrary@aol.com
W www.elib.org.uk
Librarian, S. J. Taylor

EX-SERVICES MENTAL WELFARE SOCIETY (1919), Hollybush House, Hollybush, nr Ayr KA6 7EA
T 01292-560214 **E** contactus@combatstress.org.uk
W www.combatstress.com
Clinical Manager, Mrs F. Robertson

FABIAN SOCIETY (1884), 11 Dartmouth Street, London SW1H 9BN **T** 020-7227 4900 **E** info@fabian-society.org.uk
W www.fabian-society.org.uk
General Secretary, Mrs Katwala

FACULTY OF ROYAL DESIGNERS FOR INDUSTRY, RSA, 8 John Adam Street, London WC2N 6EZ
T 020-7451 6892 **E** rdi@rsa.org.uk **W** www.rsa.org.uk

FAIR ISLE BIRD OBSERVATORY TRUST (1948), Fair Isle Bird Observatory, Fair Isle ZE2 9JU **T** 01595-760258
E fairisle.birdobs@zetnet.co.uk **W** www.fairislebirdobs.co.uk
Administrator, H. Shaw

FAITH AND THOUGHT (1865), 41 Marne Avenue, Welling, DA16 2EY **T** 020-8303 0465
W www.faithandthought.org.uk
Chairman of Council, T. C. Mitchell

FAMILY WELFARE ASSOCIATION (1869), 501–505 Kingsland Road, London E8 4AU **T** 020-7254 6251
E fwa.headoffice@fwa.org.uk **W** www.fwa.org.uk
Chief Executive, Ms H. Dent

FAUNA AND FLORA INTERNATIONAL (1903), Great Eastern House, Tenison Road, Cambridge CB1 2TT
T 01223-571000 **E** info@fauna-flora.org
W www.fauna-flora.org
Chief Executive Officer, M. Rose

FEDERATION OF BRITISH ARTISTS (1961), 17 Carlton House Terrace, London SW1Y 5BD
T 020-7930 6844 **E** headoffice@field-studies-council.org
W www.mallgalleries.org.uk
Chairman, J. R. S. Boas

FEDERATION OF FAMILY HISTORY SOCIETIES (1974), PO Box 2425, Coventry, CV5 6YX **T** 07041-492032
E info@ffhs.org.uk **W** www.ffhs.org.uk
Administrator, Maggie Loughran

FIELD STUDIES COUNCIL (1943), Preston Montford, Montford Bridge, Shrewsbury SY4 1HW **T** 01743-852100
E headoffice@field-studies-council.org
W www.field-studies-council.org
Chief Executive, A. D. Thomas

FIRE SERVICES NATIONAL BENEVOLENT FUND (1943), Fund Headquarters, Marine Court, Fitzalan Road, Littlehampton BN17 5NF **T** 01903-736063
W www.fsnbf.org.uk
Chief Executive, R. Lawrenson

FLEET AIR ARM OFFICERS' ASSOCIATION (1957), 4 St James's Square, London SW1Y 4JU **T** 020-7930 7722
E faaoa@fleetairarmoa.org **W** www.fleetairarmoa.org
Administration Director, Cdr J. D. O. Macdonald, RN

FOREIGN PRESS ASSOCIATION IN LONDON (1888), 11 Carlton House Terrace, London SW1Y 5AJ
T 020-7930 0445 **E** secretariat@foreign-press.org.uk
W www.foreign-press.org.uk
General Manager, B. Jenner

FOUNDATION FOR SPORT AND THE ARTS (1991), PO Box 20, Liverpool L13 1HB **T** 0151-259 5505
Secretary, R. Boardley, OBE

FPA (1930), 2–12 Pentonville Road, London N1 9FP
T 020-7837 5432 **W** www.fpa.org.uk
Chief Executive, Ms A. Weyman

FRANCO-BRITISH SOCIETY (1904), Room 227, Linen Hall, 162–168 Regent Street, London W1R 5TB
T 020-7734 0815 **E** execsec@francobritishsociety.org.uk
W www.francobritishsociety.org.uk
Executive Secretary, Mrs K. Brayn

FRIENDS OF CATHEDRAL MUSIC (1956), Aeron House, Llangeitho, Tregaron, Ceredigion SY25 6SU
E info@fcm.org.uk **W** www.fcm.org.uk
Secretary, M. J. Cooke

FRIENDS OF FRIENDLESS CHURCHES (1957), St Ann's Vestry Hall, 2 Church Entry, London EC4V 5HB
T 020-7236 3934
E office@friendsoffriendlesschurches.org.uk
W www.friendsoffrriendlesschurches.org.uk
Hon. Director, M. Saunders, MBE

FRIENDS OF THE BODLEIAN (1925), Bodleian Library, Oxford OX1 3BG **T** 01865-277022/277234
E fob@bodley.ox.ac.uk **W** www.bodley.ox.ac.uk/friends
Secretary, G. Groom

FRIENDS OF THE EARTH SCOTLAND (1978), Lamb's House, Burgess Street, Edinburgh EH6 6RD
T 0131-554 9977 **E** info@foe-scotland.org.uk
W www.foe-scotland.org.uk
Chief Executive, Duncan McLaren, OBE

FURNITURE HISTORY SOCIETY (1964), 1 Mercedes Cottages, St John's Road, Haywards Heath RH16 4EH
T 01444-413845 **E** furniturehistorysociety@hotmail.com
Membership Secretary, Dr B. Austen

GALLIPOLI ASSOCIATION (1969), Earleydene Orchard, Earleydene, Ascot SL5 9JY **T** 01344-626523
E webmaster@gallipoli-association.org
W www.gallipoli-association.org
Hon. Secretary, J. C. Watson Smith

GARDEN HISTORY SOCIETY (1965), 70 Cowcross Street, London EC1M 6EJ **T** 020-7608 2409
E enquiries@gardenhistorysociety.org
Director, D. Cole

GEMMOLOGICAL ASSOCIATION AND GEM TESTING LABORATORY OF GREAT BRITAIN (1931), 27 Greville Street, (Saffron Hill entrance), London EC1N 8TN **T** 020-7404 3334 **E** gagtl@btinternet.com
W www.gem-a.info
Director, Terry Davidson

GENERAL DENTAL COUNCIL (1956), 37 Wimpole Street, London W1G 8DQ **T** 020-7887 3800
E information@gdc-uk.org **W** www.gdc-uk.org
Chief Executive & Registrar, Antony Townsend

GENERAL MEDICAL COUNCIL (1858), 178 Great Portland Street, London W1W 5JE **T** 020-7580 7642
E gmc@gmc-uk.org **W** www.gmc-uk.org
President, Sir Graeme Catto

GENERAL OPTICAL COUNCIL (1959), 41 Harley Street, London W1G 8DJ **T** 020-7580 3898 **E** goc@optical.org
W www.optical.org
Chief Executive and Registrar, P. C. Coe

GENERAL OSTEOPATHIC COUNCIL (1993), Osteopathy House, 176 Tower Bridge Road, London SE1 3LU
T 020-7357 6655 **E** info@osteopathy.org.uk
W www.osteopathy.org.uk
Chief Executive & Registrar, Miss M. J. Craggs

GEOGRAPHICAL ASSOCIATION (1893), 160 Solly Street, Sheffield S1 4BF **T** 0114-296 0088
E ga@geography.org.uk **W** www.geography.org.uk
Chief Executive, David Lambert

GEOLOGISTS' ASSOCIATION (1858), Burlington House, Piccadilly, London W1V 9AG **T** 020-7434 9298
E geol.assoc@btinternet.com
W www.geologist.demon.co.uk
Executive Secretary, Mrs S. Stafford

GILBERT AND SULLIVAN SOCIETY (1924), 7/20 Hampden Gurney Street, London W1H 5AX
Hon. Secretary, Miss V. C. Colin-Russ

GINGERBREAD (1970), 7 Sovereign Close, London E1W 3HW **T** 020-7488 9300 Helpline: 0800-018 4318
E office@gingerbread.org.uk **W** www.gingerbread.org.uk
Chief Executive, Ms Gwen Vaughan

GIRLGUIDING UK (1910), 17–19 Buckingham Palace Road, London SW1W 0PT **T** 020-7834 6242
E chq@girlguiding.org.uk **W** www.girlguiding.org.uk
Chief Guide, Mrs Jenny Leach

GIRLS' BRIGADE ENGLAND AND WALES, PO Box 196, 129 The Broadway, Didcot OX11 8XN **T** 01235-510425
E admin@girlsbrigadeew.org.uk
W www.girlsbrigadeew.org.uk
National Director, Ruth Gilson

GIRLS' VENTURE CORPS AIR CADETS (1964), Phoenix House, 3 Handley Square, Finningley Airport, Doncaster DH9 3GH **E** gvcachql@btopenworld.com
W www.gvcac.org.uk
Chair, Mrs Y. McCarthy

GLASGOW CHAMBER OF COMMERCE AND MANUFACTURES (1783), 30 George Square, Glasgow G2 1EQ **T** 0141-204 2121 **E** chamber@glasgowchamber.org
W www.glasgowchamber.org
Chief Executive, Dr Lesley Sawers

GRAND LODGE OF MARK MASTER MASONS (1856), Mark Masons' Hall, 86 St James's Street, London SW1A 1PL **T** 020-7839 5274
E grandsecretary@markmasonshall.org.uk
Grand Secretary, T. J. Lewis

GREEK INSTITUTE (1969), 34 Bush Hill Road, London N21 2DS **T** 020-8360 7968 **E** info@greekinstitute.co.uk
W www.greekinstitute.co.uk
Director, Dr K. Tofallis

GREENPEACE UK, Canonbury Villas, London N1 2PN
T 020-7865 8100 **E** info@uk.greenpeace.org
W www.greenpeace.org.uk
Executive Director, Stephen Tindale

GUIDE DOGS FOR THE BLIND ASSOCIATION (1934), Hillfields, Burghfield Common, Reading RG7 3YG
T 0870-600 2323 **E** guidedogs@guidedogs.org.uk
W www.gdba.org.uk
Chief Executive, Mrs G. Peacock

GUILD OF AID FOR GENTLEPEOPLE (1904), 10 St Christopher's Place, London W1U 1HZ **T** 020-7935 0641
Secretary, Miss N. E. Inkson

GUILD OF FREEMEN OF THE CITY OF LONDON (1908), 4 Dowgate Hill, London EC4R 2SH
T 020-8541 1435 **E** clerk@guild-freemen-london.co.uk
Clerk, Brigadier M. I. Keun

GUILD OF GLASS ENGRAVERS (1975), 87 Nether Street, Finchley, London N12 7NP **T** 020-8446 4050
E enquiries@gge.org.uk **W** www.gge.org.uk
Secretary, Ms C. Reyland

HAEMOPHILIA SOCIETY (1950), Chesterfield House, 385 Euston Road, London NW1 3AU **T** 020-7380 0600
E info@haemophilia.org.uk **W** www.haemophilia.org.uk
Chief Executive, G. Whitehead

HAIG HOMES (1929), Alban Dobson House, Green Lane, Morden SM4 5NS **T** 020-8685 5777
E haig@haighomes.org.uk **W** www.haighomes.org.uk
Major-General, P. V. R. Besgrove

HAKLUYT SOCIETY (1846), c/o Map Library, The British Library, 96 Euston Road, London NW1 2DB
T 01428-641850 E office@hakluyt.com
W www.hakluyt.com
President, Prof. R. C. Bridges

HALIFAX ANTIQUARIAN SOCIETY (1900), 66 Drub Lane, Gomersal, Cleckheaton BD19 4BU T 01274-865418
W www.halifaxhistory.org.uk
Hon. Secretary, J. H. Patchett

HANSARD SOCIETY FOR PARLIAMENTARY GOVERNMENT (1944), St Philips Building North, Sheffield Street, London WC2A 2EX T 020-7395 4000
E hansard@hansard.lse.ac.uk W www.hansardsociety.org.uk
Director, Clare Ettinghausen

HARVEIAN SOCIETY OF LONDON (1831), Lettsom House, 11 Chandos Street, London W19 9EB
T 020-7580 1043
Executive Secretary, Col. R. Kinsella-Bevan

HAWICK ARCHAEOLOGICAL SOCIETY (1856), Orrock House, Stirches Road, Hawick TD9 7HF
T 01450-375546
Hon. Secretary, I. W. Landles

HEALTH PROFESSIONS WALES (2002), 2nd Floor, Golate House, 101 St Mary Street, Cardiff CF10 1DX
T 029-2026 1400 E info@hpw.org.uk W www.hpw.org.uk
Acting Chief Executive, Mrs Barbara Bale

HEARING CONCERN (1947), 4th Floor, 275–281 King Street, Hammersmith, London W6 9LZ
T 020-8233 2929 Helpline 0845-0744600
E info@hearingconcern.org.uk
W www.hearingconcern.org.uk
Director, Fiona Robertson

HELP THE AGED (1961), 207–221 Pentonville Road, London N1 9UZ T 020-7278 1114
E info@helptheaged.org.uk W www.helptheaged.org.uk
Director-General, C. M. Lake, CBE

HISTORICAL ASSOCIATION (1906), 59A Kennington Park Road, London SE11 4JH T 020-7735 3901
E enquiry@history.org.uk W www.history.org.uk
Chief Executive, Mrs M. Stiles

HISTORIC HOUSES ASSOCIATION (1973), 2 Chester Street, London SW1X 7BB T 020-7259 5688
E info@hha.org.uk W www.hha.org.uk
Director-General, R. C. Wilkin, LVO, MBE

HONOURABLE SOCIETY OF CYMMRODORION (1751), 30 Eastcastle Street, London W1W 8DJ
T 020-7631 0502 E aelodau1751we@yahoo.co.uk
W www.cymmrodorion1751.org.uk
Hon. Secretary, J. Samuel

HOSPITAL SAVING ASSOCIATION (1922), Hambleden House, Andover SP10 1LQ T 01264-353211
W www.hsa.co.uk
Chief Executive, Des Benjamin

HOSTELLING INTERNATIONAL NORTHERN IRELAND, 22–32 Donegall Road, Belfast BT12 5JN
T 028-9032 4733 E info@hini.org.uk W www.hini.org.uk
Hon. Secretary, D. Forsythe

HOUSING JUSTICE (1956), 209 Old Marylebone Road, London NW1 5QT T 020-7723 7273
E info@housingjustice.org.uk W www.housingjustice.org.uk
Chief Executive, Ms R. Rafferty

HOWARD LEAGUE FOR PENAL REFORM (1866), 1 Ardleigh Road, London N1 4HS T 020-7249 7373
E info@howardleague.org W www.howardleague.org
Director, Ms F. Crook

HR SOCIETY LTD (1970), Bridge House, Church Road, Burnham-on-Crouch CM0 8BZ T 01621-781035
W www.hrsociety.co.uk
President, Dr Clive Purkis

HUGUENOT SOCIETY OF GREAT BRITAIN AND IRELAND (1885), The Huguenot Library, University College, Gower Street, London WC1E 6BT T 020-7679 5199
E ucyldon@ucl.ac.uk W www.huguenotsociety.org.uk
Hon. Secretary, Mrs M. Bayliss

HUMANE RESEARCH TRUST (1962), Brook House, 29 Bramhall Lane South, Bramhall, Stockport SK7 2DN
T 0161-439 8041 E info@humaneresearch.org.uk
W www.humaneresearch.org.uk
Chairman, K. Cholerton

HYDROGRAPHIC SOCIETY (1972), PO Box 103, Plymouth PL4 7YP T 01752-223512
E helen@hydrographicsociety.org
W www.hydrographicsociety.org
Hon. Secretary, P. J. H. Warden

I CAN (1888), 4 Dyers Buildings, Holborn, London EC1N 2QP
T 0845-225 4071 E info@ican.org.uk
W www.ican.org.uk
Chief Executive, Ms G. Edelman

IMMIGRATION ADVISORY SERVICE (1970), 3rd Floor, County House, 190 Great Dover Street, London SE1 4YB
T 020-7967 1200 E advice@iasuk.org W www.iasuk.org
Chief Executive, Keith Best

INCORPORATED COUNCIL OF LAW REPORTING FOR ENGLAND AND WALES (1865), Megarry House, 119 Chancery Lane, London WC2A 1PP T 020-7242 6471
E postmaster@iclr.co.uk W www.lawreports.co.uk
Secretary, J. Cobbett

INCORPORATED SOCIETY OF MUSICIANS (1882), 10 Stratford Place, London W1C 1AA T 020-7629 4413
E membership@ism.org W www.ism.org
Chief Executive, N. Hoyle

INDEPENDENT SCHOOLS COUNCIL (1986), Grosvenor Gardens House, 35–37 Grosvenor Gardens, London SW1W 0BS T 020-7798 1500 E info@iscis.uk.net
W www.iscis.uk.net
General Secretary, Jonathan Shephard, OBE

INSTITUTE FOR PUBLIC POLICY RESEARCH (1988), 30–32 Southampton Street, London WC2E 7RA T 020-7470 6100 E info@ippr.org W www.ippr.org.uk
Chairman, Chris Powell

INSTITUTE OF ACOUSTICS (1974), 77A St Peter's Street, St Albans AL1 3BN T 01727-848195 E ioa@ioa.org.uk W www.ioa.org.uk
Chief Executive, Roy D. Bratby

INSTITUTE OF ACTUARIES (1848), Staple Inn Hall, High Holborn, London WC1V 7QJ T 020-7632 2100 E institute@actuaries.org.uk W www.actuaries.org.uk
President, Michael Alan Pomery

INSTITUTE OF BIOLOGY (1950), 20–22 Queensberry Place, London SW7 2DZ T 020-7581 8333 E info@iob.org W www.iob.org
Chief Executive, Prof. A. D. B. Malcolm

INSTITUTE OF CANCER RESEARCH: ROYAL CANCER HOSPITAL (1909), 123 Old Brompton Road, London SW7 3RP T 020-7352 8133 W www.icr.ac.uk
Chief Executive, Prof. P. W. J. Rigby

INSTITUTE OF CAST METAL ENGINEERS (1904), National Metalforming Centre, 47 Birmingham Road, West Bromwich B70 6PY T 0121-601 6979 E info@icme.org.uk W www.icme.org.uk
Operations Manager, Mrs M. Holland

INSTITUTE OF CHARTERED ACCOUNTANTS IN ENGLAND AND WALES (1880), Chartered Accountants' Hall, PO Box 433, Moorgate Place, London EC2P 2BJ T 020-7920 8100 W www.icaew.co.uk
Chief Executive, Eric Anstee

INSTITUTE OF CHARTERED SECRETARIES AND ADMINISTRATORS (1891), 16 Park Crescent, London W1B 1AH T 020-7580 4741 E info@icsa.co.uk W www.icsa.org.uk
Chief Executive, M. J. Ainsworth

INSTITUTE OF CHARTERED SHIPBROKERS (1911), 3 St Helen's Place, London EC3A 6EJ T 020-7623 1111 E info@ics.org.uk W www.ics.org.uk
Director-General, D. A. Phillips

INSTITUTE OF DIRECTORS (1903), 116 Pall Mall, London SW1Y 5ED T 020-7839 1233 E enquiries@iod.com W www.iod.com
Chief Operating Officer, A. Main Wilson

INSTITUTE OF ECONOMIC AFFAIRS (1955), 2 Lord North Street, Westminster, London SW1P 3LB T 020-7799 8900 E inquiries@iea.org.uk W www.iea.org.uk
Director-General, J. Blundell

INSTITUTE OF FINANCIAL ACCOUNTANTS (1916), Burford House, 44 London Road, Sevenoaks TN13 1AS T 01732-458080 E mail@ifa.org.uk W www.ifa.org.uk
Chief Executive, J. M. Dean

INSTITUTE OF FOOD SCIENCE AND TECHNOLOGY (1964), 5 Cambridge Court, 210 Shepherd's Bush Road, London W6 7NJ T 020-7603 6316 E info@ifst.org W www.ifst.org
President, Peter Belton

INSTITUTE OF HEALTHCARE MANAGEMENT, PO Box 33239, London SW1W 0WN T 020-7881 9235 E enquiries@ihm.org.uk W www.ihm.org.uk
Chief Executive, Maurice Cheng

INSTITUTE OF HEALTH PROMOTION AND EDUCATION, Department of Oral Health and Development, University Dental Hospital, Higher Cambridge Street, Manchester M15 6FH T 0161-275 6610 W www.ihpe.org.uk
Hon. Secretary, Prof. A. S. Blinkhorn

INSTITUTE OF HERALDIC AND GENEALOGICAL STUDIES (1961), 79–82 Northgate, Canterbury CT1 1BA T 01227-768664 E ihgs@ihgs.ac.uk W www.ihgs.ac.uk
Registrar, J. Palmer

INSTITUTE OF LEGAL EXECUTIVES (1963), Kempston Manor, Kempston MK42 7AB T 01234-841000 E info@ilex.org.uk W www.ilex.org.uk
Secretary-General, Mrs D. Burleigh

INSTITUTE OF LINGUISTS (1910), Saxon House, 48 Southwark Street, London SE1 1UN T 020-7940 3100 E info@iol.org.uk W www.iol.org.uk
Director and Chief Executive, H. Pavlovich

INSTITUTE OF LOGISTICS AND TRANSPORT (1926), 11/12 Buckingham Gate, London SW1E 6LB T 01536-740100 E enquiry@iolt.org.uk W www.iolt.org.uk
Chief Executive, Graham Ewer

INSTITUTE OF MARINE ENGINEERING, SCIENCE AND TECHNOLOGY (1889), 80 Coleman Street, London EC2R 5BJ T 020-7382 2600 E info@imarest.org W www.imarest.org
Director-General, K. F. Read, CBE

INSTITUTE OF MASTERS OF WINE (1953), Five Kings House, 1 Queen Street Place, London EC4R 1QS T 020-7236 4427 E enquiries@masters-of-wine.org W www.masters-of-wine.org
Executive Director, Siobhan Turner

INSTITUTE OF MATERIALS, MINERALS AND MINING (2002), 1 Carlton House Terrace, London SW1Y 5DB T 020-7451 7300 E admin@iom3.org W www.iom3.org
Chief Executive, Dr Bernie Rickinson

INSTITUTE OF MATHEMATICS AND ITS APPLICATIONS (1964), Catherine Richards House, 16 Nelson Street, Southend-on-Sea SS1 1EF T 01702-354020 E post@ima.org.uk W www.ima.org.uk
Executive Director, David Youdan

INSTITUTE OF MEASUREMENT AND CONTROL (1944), 87 Gower Street, London WC1E 6AF
T 020-7387 4949 **E** m.yates@instmc.org.uk
W www.instmc.org.uk
Secretary, M. J. Yates

INSTITUTE OF PATENTEES AND INVENTORS (1919), Suite 505A, Triumph House, 189 Regent Street, London W1B 4 JY **T** 020-8541 4197 **E** ipi@invent.org.uk
W www.invent.org.uk
Chairman, D. Wardell

INSTITUTE OF PHYSICS AND ENGINEERING IN MEDICINE, Fairmount House, 230 Tadcaster Road, York YO24 1ES **T** 01904-610821 **E** office@ipem.org.uk
W www.ipem.org.uk
General Secretary, R. W. Neilson

INSTITUTE OF QUARRYING (1917), 7 Regent Street, Nottingham NG1 5BS **T** 0115-945 3880 **E** iq@qmj.co.uk
W www.quarrying.org
Secretary, Mrs L. Bryden

INSTITUTE OF SPORTS MEDICINE (1965), Department of Surgery, Royal Free and University College Medical School, 67/73 Riding House Street, London W1W 7EJ **T** 020-7813 2832 **E** johnlloydparry@aol.com
Company Secretary, D. Meynell

INSTITUTE OF THE MOTOR INDUSTRY (IMI) (1920), Fanshaws, Brickendon, Hertford SG13 8PQ
T 01992-511521 **E** imi@motor.org.uk **W** www.motor.org.uk
Chief Executive, Sarah Sillars

INSTITUTE OF TRANSLATION AND INTERPRETING (1986), Fortuna House, South Fifth Street, Milton Keynes, MK9 2EU **T** 01908-325250
E info@iti.org.uk **W** www.iti.org.uk
Chief Executive, A. Wheatley

INSTITUTION OF BRITISH ENGINEERS (1928), Clifford Hill Court, Clifford Chambers, Stratford-upon-Avon, CV37 8AA **T** 01789-298739 **E** info@britishengineers.com
W www.britishengineers.com
President, Dr John Fenton

INSTITUTION OF CIVIL ENGINEERS (1818), 1 Great George Street, London SW1P 3AA **T** 020-7222 7722
W www.ice.org.uk
Director-General, Tom Foulkes

INSTITUTION OF FIRE ENGINEERS, 148 New Walk, Leicester LE1 7QB **T** 0116-255 3654 **E** info@ife.org.uk
W www.ife.org.uk
Chief Executive Officer, Ellen Jessett

INSTITUTION OF GAS ENGINEERS & MANAGERS (1863), Charnwood Wing, Holywell Park, Ashby Road, Loughborough LE11 3GR **T** 01509-282728
E general@igem.org.uk **W** www.igem.org.uk
Chief Executive, G. Davies

INSTITUTION OF OCCUPATIONAL SAFETY AND HEALTH (IOSH) (1945), The Grange, Highfield Drive, Wigston LE18 1NN **T** 0116-257 3100 **E** techinfo@iosh.co.uk
W www.iosh.co.uk
Chief Executive, R. W. H. Strange

INSTITUTION OF ROYAL ENGINEERS (1875), Brompton Barracks, Chatham ME4 4UG **T** 01634-842669
E corps.secretary@inst-royal-engrs.co.uk
Secretary, Lt. Col. D. N. Hamilton, MBE

INTERCONTINENTAL CHURCH SOCIETY (1823), 1 Athena Drive, Tachbrook Park CV34 6NL **T** 01926-430347
E enquiries@ics-uk.org **W** www.ics-uk.org
Chief Executive, The Revd Canon Ian Watson

INTERNATIONAL AFRICAN INSTITUTE (1926), SOAS, Thornhaugh Street, Russell Square, London WC1H 0XG **T** 020-7898 4420 **E** iai@soas.ac.uk
W www.iaionthe.net
Hon. Director, Prof. P. Spencer

INTERNATIONAL CHURCHILL SOCIETY (1968), PO Box 1257, Melksham, Wilts SN12 6GQ **T** 01380-828609
W www.winstonchurchill.org
Chairman, N. B. Knocker

INTERNATIONAL FRIENDSHIP LEAGUE (1931), 3 Creswick Road, Acton, London W3 9HE
T 020-8752 0055 **E** bookings@ifl-peacehaven.co.uk
W www.itl-peacehaven.co.uk
Chairman, M. Hewett

INTERNATIONAL HOSPITAL FEDERATION (1947), 13 Chemin du Levant, Immeuble JB SAY, Ferney Voltaire, France F-01210 **T** (+33) 0450-426003 **E** info@ihf-fih.org
W www.hospitalmanagement.net and www.ihf.co.uk
Director-General, Prof. Per-Gunnar Svensson

INTERNATIONAL INSTITUTE FOR CONSERVATION OF HISTORIC AND ARTISTIC WORKS (1950), 6 Buckingham Street, London WC2N 6BA **T** 020-7839 5975 **E** iicon@compuserve.com
W www.iiconservation.org
Secretary-General, J. Ashley-Smith

INTERNATIONAL PEN (1921), 9–10 Charterhouse Buildings, Goswell Road, London EC1M 7AT
T 020-7253 4308 **E** intpen@dircon.co.uk
W www.internationalpen.org.uk
International Secretary, T. Carlbom

INTERNATIONAL POLICE ASSOCIATION (BRITISH SECTION) (1950), 1 Fox Road, West Bridgford, Nottingham NG2 6AJ **T** 0115-981 3638 **E** mail@ipa-uk.org
W www.ipa-uk.org
Executive Officer, Mrs E. Jones

INTERNATIONAL TREE FOUNDATION (1924), Sandy Lane, Crawley Down RH10 4HS **T** 0870-774 4269
E info@internationaltreefoundation.org
W www.internationaltreefoundation.org
Office Manager, Lynne Witheyman

INTERSERVE (1852), 325 Kennington Road, London SE11 4QH **T** 020-7735 8227 **E** enquiries@isewi.org **W** www.interserveonline.org.uk
National Director, R. Clark

IRAN SOCIETY (1935), 2 Belgrave Square, London SW1X 8PJ **T** 020-7235 5122 **E** iransoc@rsaa.org.uk **W** www.iransoc.dircon.co.uk
Chairman, M. Noël-Clarke

ISLE OF WIGHT NATURAL HISTORY AND ARCHAEOLOGICAL SOCIETY (1919), Salisbury Gardens, Dudley Road, Ventnor, PO38 1EJ **T** 01983-855385
Hon. Secretary, Dr M. Jackson

JACQUELINE DU PRÉ MUSIC BUILDING LTD (1995), St Hilda's College, Oxford OX4 1DY **T** 01865-276821 **E** jdp@st-hildas.ox.ac.uk **W** www.sthildas.ox.ac.uk/jdp
Manager, Ms M. A. Frappat

JAPAN SOCIETY (1891), Swire House, 59 Buckingham Gate, London SW1E 6AJ **T** 020-7828 6330 **E** info@japansociety.org.uk **W** www.japansociety.org.uk
Executive Director, Capt. Robert Guy

JERUSALEM AND THE MIDDLE EAST CHURCH ASSOCIATION, 1 Hart House, The Hart, Farnham GU9 7HJ **T** 01252-726994 **E** jmeca@lineone.net **W** www.jmeca.org.uk
Secretary, Mrs V. Wells

JUSTICE (1957), 59 Carter Lane, London EC4V 5AQ **T** 020-7329 5100 **E** admin@justice.org.uk **W** www.justice.org.uk
Director, Roger Smith

JUSTICES' CLERKS' SOCIETY, 2nd Floor, Port of Liverpool Building, Pier Head, Liverpool L3 1BY **T** 0151-255 0790 **E** secretariat@jc-society.co.uk **W** www.jc-society.co.uk
Chief Executive, Sid Brighton

KENT ARCHAEOLOGICAL SOCIETY (1857), Three Elms, Woodlands Lane, Shorne, Gravesend DA12 3HH **T** 01474-822280 **E** secretary@kentarchaeology.org.uk **W** www.kentarchaeology.org.uk
Hon. General Secretary, A. I. Moffat

KING'S FUND (1897), 11–13 Cavendish Square, London W1G 0AN **T** 020-7307 2400 **W** www.kingsfund.org.uk
Chief Executive, Niall Dickson

KIPLING SOCIETY (1927), 6 Clifton Road, London W9 1SS **T** 020-7286 0194 **E** jane@keskar.fsworld.co.uk **W** www.kipling.org.uk
Hon. Secretary, Jane Keskar

LCIA (LONDON COURT OF INTERNATIONAL ARBITRATION) (1892), 70 Fleet Street, London EC4Y 1EU **T** 020-7936 7007 **E** lcia@lcia-arbitration.com **W** www.lcia-arbitration.com
Director-General and Registrar, Adrian Winstanley

LEAGUE OF THE HELPING HAND (1908), Little Finches, Wheatsheaf Road, Henfield, TW10 7AL **T** 01273-493551 **E** secretary@lhh.org.uk **W** www.lhh.org.uk
Secretary, Mrs Moira Parrot

LEPROSY MISSION (ENGLAND AND WALES) (1874), Goldhay Way, Orton Goldhay, Peterborough PE2 5GZ **T** 01733-370505 **E** post@tlmew.org.uk **W** www.leprosymission.org.uk
National Director, Warren Lancaster

LEUKAEMIA RESEARCH FUND (1960), 43 Great Ormond Street, London WC1N 3JJ **T** 020-7405 0101 **E** info@lrf.org.uk **W** www.lrf.org.uk
Chief Executive, D. L. Osborne

LIBERAL PARTY (1877), 323 Hurcott Road, Kidderminster DY10 2RQ **T** 01562-68361 **E** libparty@libparty.demon.co.uk **W** www.liberal.org.uk
Membership Secretary, Paul Harrison

LIBERTY (NATIONAL COUNCIL FOR CIVIL LIBERTIES) (1934), 21 Tabard Street, London SE1 4LA **T** 020-7403 3888 **E** info@liberty-human-rights.org.uk **W** www.liberty-human-rights.org.uk
Director, Shami Chakrabarti

LIONS CLUBS INTERNATIONAL (BRITISH ISLES AND IRELAND) (1950), 257 Alcester Road South, Kings Heath, Birmingham B14 6DT **T** 0121-441 4544
Office Manager, Mrs J. Davis

LISTENING BOOKS, 12 Lant Street, London SE1 1QH **T** 020-7407 9417 **E** info@listening-books.org.uk **W** www.listening-books.org.uk
Director, Bill Dee

LLOYD'S OF LONDON, One Lime Street, London EC3M 7HA **T** 020-7327 6930 **E** maureen.clarke@lloyds.com **W** www.lloyds.com
Chief Executive Officer, N. E. T. Prettejohn

LOCAL GOVERNMENT ASSOCIATION (1997), Local Government House, Smith Square, London SW1P 3HZ **T** 020-7664 3131 **E** info@lga.gov.uk **W** www.lga.gov.uk
Chief Executive, Sir Brian Briscoe

LONDON AND MIDDLESEX ARCHAEOLOGICAL SOCIETY (1855), c/o Museum of London, 150 London Wall, London EC2Y 5HN **W** www.lamas.org.uk
Hon. Secretary, Nikola Burdon

LONDON CATALYST (1873), 45 Westminster Bridge Road, London SE1 7JB **T** 020-7021 4204 **E** ruth@peabody.org.uk **W** www.londoncatalyst.org.uk
Director, Ruth Scott

LONDON COLLEGE OF OSTEOPATHIC MEDICINE, 8–10 Boston Place, London NW1 6QH **T** 020-7262 1128
Clinic Manager, Mrs A. Dalby

LONDON DISTRICT SURVEYORS ASSOCIATION (1845), PO Box 37, Civic Centre, Harrow, HA1 2UY
W www.londonbuildingcontrol.org.uk
President, Robert Weaver

LONDON LIBRARY (1841), 14 St James's Square, London SW1Y 4LG **T** 020-7930 7705
E membership@londonlibrary.co.uk
W www.londonlibrary.co.uk
Librarian, Inez T. P. A. Lynn

LONDON MAGISTRATES' CLERKS' ASSOCIATION (1889), c/o Marylebone Magistrates' Court, 181 Marylebone Road, London NW1 5QJ **T** 020-7506 3704
Hon. Chairman, J. Mulreany

LONDON PLAYING FIELDS SOCIETY (1890), Fraser House, 21/22 Grosvenor Street, London W1K 4QJ
T 020-7491 4992 **E** enquiries@lpfs.org.uk
W www.lpfs.org.uk
Chief Executive, Dr C. Goodson-Wickes, DL

LONDON SOCIETY (1912), Mortimer Wheeler House, 46 Eagle Wharf Road, London N1 7ED **T** 020-7253 9400
E info@londonsociety.org.uk **W** www.londonsociety.org.uk
Hon. Secretary, John D. Hill

LORD'S DAY OBSERVANCE SOCIETY (1831), 3 Epsom Business Park, Kiln Lane, Epsom KT17 1JF **T** 01568-613740
E info@lordsday.co.uk **W** www.lordsday.co.uk
General Secretary, J. G. Roberts

LOTTERIES COUNCIL (1979), 2 Regan Road, Moira, Ashby-de-la Zouch DE12 6DS **T** 01283-229811
W www.lotteriescouncil.org.uk
Chairman, Mr A. Austin

MACMILLAN CANCER RELIEF (1911), 89 Albert Embankment, London SE1 7UQ **T** 020-7840 7840
E cancerline@macmillan.org.uk **W** www.macmillan.org.uk
Chief Executive, Peter Cardy

MAGISTRATES' ASSOCIATION (1920), 28 Fitzroy Square, London W1T 6DD **T** 020-7387 2353
E secretariat@magistrates-association.org.uk
W www.magistrates-association.org.uk
Chief Executive and Secretary, Ms S. Dickinson

MAKING MUSIC, THE NATIONAL FEDERATION OF MUSIC SOCIETIES (1935), 7–15 Rosebery Avenue, London EC1R 4SP **T** 0870-903 3780
E info@makingmusic.org.uk **W** www.makingmusic.org.uk
Chief Executive, R. Osterley

MANIC DEPRESSION FELLOWSHIP (1983), Castle Works, 21 St George's Road, London SE1 6ES
T 020-7793 2600 **E** mdf@mdf.org.uk **W** www.mdf.org.uk
Chief Executive, Michelle Rowett

MANORIAL SOCIETY OF GREAT BRITAIN (1906), 104 Kennington Road, London SE11 6RE **T** 020-7735 6633
E manorial@msgb.co.uk **W** www.msgb.co.uk
Hon. Chairman, R. A. Smith

MARIE CURIE CANCER CARE (1948), 89 Albert Embankment, London SE1 7TP **T** 020-7599 7777
E info@mariecurie.org.uk **W** www.mariecurie.org.uk
Chief Executive, Thomas Hughes-Hallett

MARINE BIOLOGICAL ASSOCIATION OF THE UK (1884), Citadel Hill, Plymouth PL1 2PB **T** 01752-633207
E sec@mba.ac.uk **W** www.mba.ac.uk
Director, Prof. S. J. Hawkins

MARINE SOCIETY (1756), 202 Lambeth Road, London SE1 7JW **T** 020-7261 9535 **E** enq@marine-society.org
W www.marine-society.org
Director, Capt. J. J. Howard

MARRIAGE CARE (1946), Clitherow House, 1 Blythe Mews, Blythe Road, London W14 0NW **T** 020-7371 1341
W www.marriagecare.org.uk
Chief Executive, Terry Prendergast

MATHEMATICAL ASSOCIATION (1871), 259 London Road, Leicester LE2 3BE **T** 0116-221 0013
E office@m-a.org.uk **W** www.m-a.org.uk
Senior Administrator, Ms M. Murray

ME ASSOCIATION, 4 Top Angel, Buckingham Industrial Pk., Buckingham MK18 1TH **T** 0870-444 8233
E meconnect@meassociation.org.uk
W www.meassociation.org.uk
Operations Manager, G. Briody

MEDICAL SOCIETY OF LONDON (1773), Lettsom House, 11 Chandos Street, London W1G 9EB
T 020-7580 1043
Registrar, Col. R. Kinsella-Bevan

MEDICAL WOMEN'S FEDERATION (1917), Tavistock House North, Tavistock Square, London WC1H 9HX
T 020-7387 7765 **E** mwf@btconnect.com
W www.medicalwomensfederation.co.uk
President, Dr S. Gray

MENCAP (ROYAL MENCAP SOCIETY) (1946), 123 Golden Lane, London EC1Y 0RT **T** 020-7454 0454
E information@mencap.org.uk **W** www.mencap.org.uk
Chief Executive, Jo Williams

MENTAL HEALTH FOUNDATION, 7th Floor, 83 Victoria Street, London SW1H 0HW **T** 020-7802 0300
E mhf@mhf.org.uk **W** www.mentalhealth.org.uk
Chief Executive, Andrew McCulloch

MERCHANT NAVY WELFARE BOARD (1948), 30 Palmerston Road, Southampton SO14 1LL **T** 023-8033 7799
E enquiries@mnwb.org.uk **W** www.mnwb.org
General Secretary, Capt. D. A. Parsons

MIDDLE EAST ASSOCIATION (1961), Bury House, 33 Bury Street. London SW1Y 6AX **T** 020-7839 2137
E mail@the-mea.co.uk **W** www.the-mea.co.uk
Director-General, James Lawday

MIGRAINE ACTION ASSOCIATION (1958), Unit 6, Oakley Hay Lodge Business Park, Great Oakley, NN18 9AS T 01536-461333 E info@migraine.org.uk W www.migraine.org.uk
Director, Mrs A. Turner

MIND (NATIONAL ASSOCIATION FOR MENTAL HEALTH) (1946), Granta House, 15–19 Broadway, London E15 4BQ T 020-8519 2122 E contact@mind.org.uk W www.mind.org.uk
Chief Executive, Richard Brook

MINERALOGICAL SOCIETY (1876), 41 Queen's Gate, London SW7 5HR T 020-7584 7516 E info@minersoc.org W www.minersoc.org
General Secretary, Dr F. Wall

MULTIPLE SCLEROSIS SOCIETY (1953), MS National Centre, 372 Edgware Road, Staples Corner, London NW2 6ND T 020-8438 0700 W www.mssociety.org.uk
Chairperson, Sarah Phillips

MUSEUMS ASSOCIATION, 24 Calvin Street, London E1 6NW T 020-7426 6970 E info@museumassociation.org W www.museumsassociation.org
Director, Mark Taylor

MUSICIANS BENEVOLENT FUND (1921), 16 Ogle Street, London W1W 6JA T 020-7636 4481 E info@mbf.org.uk W www.mbf.org.uk
Chief Executive, Ms H. Faulkner

NABS, 32 Wigmore Street, London W1U 2RP T 020-7292 7330 E nabs@nabs.org.uk W www.nabs.org.uk
Chief Executive, Miss K. Harris

NATIONAL AIDS TRUST (1987), New City Cloisters, 196 Old Street, London EC1V 9FR T 020-7814 6767 E info@nat.org.uk W www.nat.org.uk
Chief Executive, Deborah Jack

NATIONAL ASSOCIATION FOR COLITIS AND CROHN'S DISEASE (1979), 4 Beaumont House, Sutton Road, St Albans AL1 5HH T 01727-830038 E nacc@nacc.org.uk W www.nacc.org.uk
Director, R. Driscoll

NATIONAL ASSOCIATION OF BRITISH MARKET AUTHORITIES (1919), 13 Moor Road, Orrell Post, Wigan WN5 8ND T 01942-203797 E nabma@nabma.com W www.nabma.com
General Secretary, J. Edwards

NATIONAL ASSOCIATION OF ESTATE AGENTS (1962), Arbon House, 21 Jury Street, Warwick CV34 4EH T 01926-496800 E info@naea.co.uk W www.naea.co.uk
President, Richard Hair

NATIONAL ASTHMA CAMPAIGN (1990), Providence House, Providence Place, London N1 0NT T 020-7226 2260 W www.asthma.org.uk

NATIONAL BLOOD SERVICE, Oak House, Reeds Crescent, Watford WD24 4QN T 020-8258 2700 W www.blood.co.uk
Chairman, M. Fogden, CB

NATIONAL CAMPAIGN FOR THE ARTS LTD (1985), Pegasus House, 37–43 Sackville Street, London W1S 3EH T 020-7333 0375 E nca@artscampaign.org.uk W www.artscampaign.org.uk
Director, Ms V. Todd

NATIONAL CATTLE ASSOCIATION (DAIRY) (1998), Brick House, Risbury, Leominster, HR6 0NQ T 01568-760632
Executive Secretary, Tim Brigstocke

NATIONAL CHILDBIRTH TRUST (1956), Alexandra House, Oldham Terrace, Acton, London W3 6NH T 0870-770 3236; Enquiries 0870 444 8707 E enquiries@national-childbirth-trust.co.uk W www.nctms.co.uk
Chief Executive, Ms B. Phipps

NATIONAL COUNCIL OF WOMEN OF GREAT BRITAIN, 36 Danbury Street, London N1 8JU T 020-7354 2395 E ncwgb@danburystreet.freeserve.co.uk W www.ncwgb.org
President, Amy Gibbs

NATIONAL FAMILY MEDIATION (1981), Alexander House, Telephone Avenue, Bristol BS1 4BS T 0117-904 2825 E mediation@nfm.org.uk W www.nfm.u-net.com
Chief Executive, Jane Robey

NATIONAL FEDERATION OF RETIREMENT PENSIONS ASSOCIATIONS (1940), Thwaites House, Railway Road, Blackburn BB1 5AX T 01254-52606
General Secretary, R. Stansfield

NATIONAL FEDERATION OF WOMEN'S INSTITUTES (1915), 104 New Kings Road, London SW6 4LY T 020-7371 9300 E cs@nfwi.org.uk W www.womens-insitute.org.uk
General Secretary, Mrs J. Osborne

NATIONAL FOUNDATION FOR EDUCATIONAL RESEARCH IN ENGLAND AND WALES (1946), The Mere, Upton Park, Slough SL1 2DQ T 01753-574123 E enquiries@nfer.ac.uk W www.nfer.ac.uk
Director, Dr S. Hegarty

NATIONAL GARDENS SCHEME CHARITABLE TRUST (1927), Hatchlands Park, East Clandon, Guildford GU4 7RT T 01483-211535 E ngs@ngs.org.uk W www.ngs.org.uk
Chief Executive, Beryl Evans

NATIONAL LIBRARY FOR THE BLIND (1828), Far Cromwell Road, Bredbury, Stockport SK6 2SG T 0161-355 2000 E enquiries@nlbuk.org W www.nlb-online.org
Chief Executive, Helen Brazier

NATIONAL MISSING PERSONS HELPLINE (1992), Roebuck House, 284–286 Upper Richmond Road West, London SW14 7JE **T** 020-8392 4590; **Helpline** 0500-700700 **E** admin@missingpersons.org **W** www.missingpersons.org
Co-Founders, Mrs M. Asprey, OBE; Mrs J. Newman, OBE

NATIONAL OSTEOPOROSIS SOCIETY (1986), Camerton, Bath BA2 0PJ **T** 01761-471771 **E** info@nos.org.uk **W** www.nos.org.uk
Communications Manager, Trevor Reid

NATIONAL SECULAR SOCIETY (1866), 25 Red Lion Square, London WC1R 4RL **T** 020-7404 3126 **E** enquiries@secularism.org.uk **W** www.secularism.org.uk
Executive Director, K. P. Wood

NATIONAL SOCIETY (1811), Church House, Great Smith Street, London SW1P 3NZ **T** 020-7898 1518 **E** info@natsoc.c-of-e.org.uk **W** www.natsoc.org.uk
General Secretary, Canon J. Hall

NATIONAL SOCIETY FOR CLEAN AIR AND ENVIRONMENTAL PROTECTION (1898), 44 Grand Parade, Brighton BN2 9QA **T** 01273-878770 **E** admin@nsca.org.uk **W** www.nsca.org.uk
Secretary-General, R. Mills

NATIONAL SOCIETY FOR EPILEPSY (1892), Chesham Lane, Chalfont St Peter, SL9 0RJ **T** 01494-601300 **W** www.epilepsynse.org.uk
Chief Executive, Graham Faulkner

NATIONAL TRUST (1895), 36 Queen Anne's Gate, London SW1H 9AS **T** 0870-609 5380 **E** enquiries@thenationaltrust.org.uk **W** www.nationaltrust.org.uk
Director-General, Fiona Reynolds

NATIONAL UNION OF STUDENTS (1922), Nelson Mandela House, 461 Holloway Road, London N7 6LJ **T** 020-7272 8900 **E** nusuk@nus.org.uk **W** www.nusonline.co.uk

NATIONAL WOMEN'S REGISTER, 3A Vulcan House, Vulcan Road North, Norwich NR6 6AQ **T** 01603-406767 **E** office@nwr.org **W** www.nwr.org
Marketing and Membership Co-ordinators, Mrs M. Dodkins; Mrs E. Thorn

NAVY RECORDS SOCIETY (1893), c/o Department of War Studies, King's College, The Strand, London WC2R 2LS **W** www.navyrecordssociety.com
Hon. Secretary, Prof A. D. Lambert

NEWSPAPER PRESS FUND (1864), Dickens House, 35 Wathen Road, Dorking RH4 1JY **T** 01306-887511 **E** enquiries@pressfund.org.uk
Director, D. Ilott

NOISE ABATEMENT SOCIETY, 44 Grand Parade, Brighton, BN2 9QA **T** Helpline: 01273-878782 **E** nas@noiseabatementsociety.fsnet.co.uk **W** www.noiseabatementsociety.com
Chairman, Gloria Elliott

NORFOLK AND NORWICH ARCHAEOLOGICAL SOCIETY (1846), 30 Brettingham Avenue, Norwich NR4 6XG **T** 01603-455913
Secretary, R. Bellinger

NORTHERN IRELAND TOURIST BOARD, St Anne's Court, 59 North Street, Belfast BT1 1NB **T** 028-9023 1221 **E** info@nitb.com **W** www.nitb.com
Chief Executive, A. Clarke

NORTH OF ENGLAND ZOOLOGICAL SOCIETY (1934), Chester Zoo, Upton, Chester CH2 1LH **T** 01244-380280 **E** reception@chesterzoo.co.uk **W** www.chesterzoo.co.uk
Zoo Director, Prof. G. McGregor Reid

NOTARIES SOCIETY (1882), 23 New Street, Woodbridge IP12 1DN **T** 01394-384134 **E** notariessociety@compuserve.com **W** www.thenotariessociety.org.uk
Secretary, A. G. Dunford

NSPCC (NATIONAL SOCIETY FOR THE PREVENTION OF CRUELTY TO CHILDREN) (1884), Weston House, 42 Curtain Road, London EC2A 3NH **T** 020-7825 2500 **W** www.nspcc.org.uk
Chief Executive, Mary Marsh

NUFFIELD TRUST (1940), 59 New Cavendish Street, London W1G 7LP **T** 020-7631 8450 **E** mail@nuffieldtrust.org.uk **W** www.nuffieldtrust.org.uk
Secretary, J. Wyn Owen, CB

NURSE AID (1919), Flints, Petersfield Road, Winchester SO23 0JD **T** 01962-860900 **E** natnurses.fund@virgin.net
Administrator, Mrs A. Rich

NURSING AND MIDWIFERY COUNCIL (2002), 23 Portland Place, London W1B 1PZ **T** 020-7637 7181 **W** www.nmc-uk.org
Chief Executive, Sarah Thewlis

OFFICERS' ASSOCIATION (1920), 48 Pall Mall, London SW1Y 5JY **T** 020-7930 0125 **E** postmaster@oaed.org.uk **W** www.officersassociation.org.uk
General Secretary, Maj.-Gen. J. C. B. Sutherell, CBE

OMBUDSMAN FOR ESTATE AGENTS (1998), Beckett House, 4 Bridge Street, Salisbury SP1 2LX **T** 01722-333306 **E** admin@oea.co.uk **W** www.oea.co.uk
Ombudsman, S. R. Carr-Smith

OPAS (THE PENSIONS ADVISORY SERVICE) (1983), 11 Belgrave Road, London SW1V 1RB **T** 0845-601 2923 **W** www.opas.org.uk
Chief Executive, M. McLean, OBE

OPEN-AIR MISSION (1853), 19 John Street, London WC1N 2DL **T** 01582-841141 **E** oamission@btinternet.com **W** www.oamission.com
Secretary, A. N. Banton

OPEN SPACES SOCIETY (1865), 25A Bell Street, Henley-on-Thames RG9 2BA **T** 01491-573535 **E** hq@oss.org.uk **W** www.oss.org.uk
General Secretary, Miss K. Ashbrook

OPSIS (1992), c/o Queen Alexandra College, Court Oak Road, Birmingham B17 9TG **T** 0121-428 5037 **E** opsis@dircon.co.uk **W** www.opsis.org.uk
Chief Executive, Mike Brace

ORDERS AND MEDALS RESEARCH SOCIETY (1942), PO Box 1904, Southam CV47 2ZX **T** 01295-690009 **W** www.omrs.org.uk
General Secretary, P. M. R. Helmore

OUTWARD BOUND SCOTLAND (1941), Loch Eil Centre, Achdalieu, Corpach, Fort William PH33 7NN **T** 01397-772866 **W** www.outwardbound-uk.org
Director, Sir Michael Hobbs, KCVO, CBE

OVERSEAS DEVELOPMENT INSTITUTE, 111 Westminster Bridge Road, London SE1 7JD **T** 020-7922 0300 **E** odi@odi.org.uk **W** www.odi.org.uk
Director, S. Maxwell

OVERSEAS SERVICE PENSIONERS' ASSOCIATION (1960), 138 High Street, Tonbridge TN9 1AX **T** 01732-363836 **E** mail@ospa.org.uk **W** www.ospa.org.uk
Secretary, D. F. B. Le Breton, CBE

OXFAM GREAT BRITAIN (1942), Oxfam House, 274 Banbury Road, Oxford OX2 7DZ **T** 01865-311311 **E** oxfam@oxfam.org.uk **W** www.oxfam.org.uk
Director, B. Stocking, CBE

OXFORD PRESERVATION TRUST (1927), 10 Turn Again Lane, St Ebbes, Oxford OX1 1QL **T** 01865-242918 **E** info@oxfordpreservation.org.uk **W** www.oxfordpreservation.org.uk
Director, Mrs D. Dance

OXFORDSHIRE ARCHITECTURAL AND HISTORICAL SOCIETY (1839), 53 Radley Road, Abingdon OX14 3PN **T** 01235-525960 **E** tony@oahs.org.uk **W** www.oahs.org.uk
Hon. Secretary, Dr A. J. Dodd

OXFORD UNIVERSITY SOCIETY, Oxenford House, Magdalen Street, Oxford OX1 3AB **T** 01865-288088 **E** enquiries@ousoc.ox.ac.uk **W** www.alumni.ox.ac.uk
Secretary, Lady Nancy Kenny

PALAEONTOLOGICAL ASSOCIATION (1957), c/o Department of Geological Sciences, The University, South Road, Durham DH1 3LE **T** 0121-414 4173 **E** h.a.armstrong@durham.ac.uk **W** www.palass.org
Secretary, Dr H. A. Armstrong

PARLIAMENTARY AND SCIENTIFIC COMMITTEE (1939), 3 Birdcage Walk, Westminster, London SW1H 9JJ **T** 020-7222 7085 **W** www.pandsctte.demon.co.uk
Administrative Secretary, Peter Simpson

PATIENTS ASSOCIATION (1963), PO Box 935, Harrow HA1 3YJ **T** 020-8423 9111. **Helpline** 0845-608 4455 **E** mailbox@patients-association.com **W** www.patients-association.com
Chairman, Michael Summers

PHYSIOLOGICAL SOCIETY (1876), PO Box 11319, London WC1X 8WQ **T** 020-7269 5710 **E** admin@physoc.org **W** www.physoc.org
Executive Secretary, David Sewell

PILGRIMS OF GREAT BRITAIN (1902), Allington Castle, Maidstone ME16 0NB **T** 01622-606404 **E** sec@pilgrimsociety.org
Chairman, R. M. Worcester

PILGRIM TRUST (1930), Cowley House, 9 Little College Street, London SW1P 3SH **T** 020-7222 4723 **W** www.thepilgrimtrust.org.uk
Director, Miss G. Nayler

PLAIN ENGLISH CAMPAIGN (1979), PO Box 3, New Mills, High Peak SK22 4QP **T** 01663-744409 **E** info@plainenglish.co.uk **W** www.plainenglish.co.uk
Director, Ms C. Maher

POETRY SOCIETY (1909), 22 Betterton Street, London WC2H 9BX **T** 020-7420 9880 **E** info@poetrysociety.org.uk **W** www.poetrysociety.org.uk
Director, Jules Mann

POLICE REHABILITATION AND RETRAINING TRUST (1999), Maryfield Complex, 100 Belfast Road, Holywood, Co. Down, Northern Ireland BT18 9QY **T** 028-9042 7788 **E** info@prrt.org **W** www.prrt.org

POLITE SOCIETY AND CAMPAIGN FOR COURTESY (1986), 16 Grice Road, Hartshill, Stoke-on-Trent ST4 7PJ **T** 01782-614407
Secretary, The Revd Ian Gregory

POSTWATCH (2001), 28–30 Grosvenor Gardens, London SW1W 0TT **T** 08456-013265 **E** info@postwatch.co.uk **W** www.postwatch.co.uk
Chairman, Peter Carr

POWYSLAND CLUB (1867), Llgyad y Dyffryn, Llanidloes SY18 6JD **T** 01686-412277 **W** www.powyslandclub.co.uk
Hon. Secretary, Miss P. M. Davies

PRINCESS ROYAL TRUST FOR CARERS (1991), 142 Minories, London EC3N 1LB **T** 020-7480 7788 **E** info@carers.org **W** www.carers.org
Chief Executive, Ms A. Ryan

PRINCE'S TRUST (1976), 18 Park Square East, London NW1 4LH **T** 0800-842842 **E** info@princes-trust.org.uk **W** www.princes-trust.org.uk
Chief Executive, M. Milburn

PRINTERS' CHARITABLE CORPORATION (1827), 7 Cantelupe Mews, Cantelupe Road, East Grinstead RH19 3BG **T** 01342-318882 **E** sandra@pccorp.fsnet.co.uk **W** www.printerscharitablecorporation.co.uk
Director, S. Gilbert

PRIVATE LIBRARIES ASSOCIATION (1956), Ravelston, South View Road, Pinner HA5 3YD **E** dchambers@aol.com **W** www.the-old-school.demon.co.uk/pla.htm
Hon. Secretary, James Brown

PROFESSIONAL CLASSES AID COUNCIL (1921), 10 St Christopher's Place, London W1U 1HZ **T** 020-7935 0641 **E** admin@pcac.org.uk
Secretary, Miss N. E. Inkson

PROTESTANT ALLIANCE (1845), 77 Ampthill Road, Flitwick, Bedford MK45 1BD **T** 01525-712348
General Secretary, Dr S. J. Scott-Pearson

PSORIASIS ASSOCIATION (1968), 7 Milton Street, Northampton NN2 7JG **T** 01604-711129 **E** mail@psoriasis.demon.co.uk **W** www.psoriasis-association.org.uk
Chief Executive, Gladys Edwards

QUEEN'S ENGLISH SOCIETY (1973), 20 Jessica Road, London SW18 2QN **T** 020-8874 2200 **W** www.queens-english-society.com
Hon. Secretary, Miss P. Raper

QUEEN'S NURSING INSTITUTE (1887), 3 Albemarle Way, London EC1V 4RQ **T** 020-7490 4227 **E** mail@qni.org.uk **W** www.qni.org.uk
Director, Mrs J. Hesketh

QUEEN VICTORIA CLERGY FUND (1897), Church House, Dean's Yard, London SW1P 3NZ **T** 020-7898 1000
Secretary, C. D. L. Menzies

QUEEN VICTORIA SCHOOL (1908), Dunblane FK15 0JY **T** 01786-822288 **E** enquiries@qvs.org.uk **W** www.qvs.org.uk
Headmaster, B. Raine

RADAR (ROYAL ASSOCIATION FOR DISABILITY AND REHABILITATION) (1977), 12 City Forum, 250 City Road, London EC1V 8AF **T** 020-7250 3222 **E** radar@radar.org.uk **W** www.radar.org.uk
Director, Kate Nash

RAILWAY AND CANAL HISTORICAL SOCIETY (1954), 3 West Court, West Street, Oxford OX2 0NP **T** 01865-240514 **E** ms@bodley.ox.ac.uk **W** www.bodley.ox.ac.uk/external/rchs/index.html
Hon. Secretary, M. Searle

RAILWAY BENEVOLENT INSTITUTION (1858), Electra Way, Crewe Business Park, Crewe CW1 6HS **T** 01270-251316
Director, B. R. Whitnall

RAMBLERS' ASSOCIATION (1935), 2nd Floor, Camelford House, 87–90 Albert Embankment, London SE1 7TW **T** 020-7339 8500 **E** ramblers@london.ramblers.org.uk **W** www.ramblers.org.uk
Chief Executive, Nick Barrett

RARE BREEDS SURVIVAL TRUST (1973), National Agricultural Centre, Stoneleigh Park, Kenilworth CV8 2LG **T** 024-7669 6551 **E** enquiries@rbst.org.uk **W** www.rbst.org.uk
Secretary, R. Terry

REGIONAL STUDIES ASSOCIATION (1965), PO Box 2058, Seaford BN25 4QU **T** 01323-899698 **E** rsa@mailbox.ulcc.ac.uk **W** www.regional-studies-assoc.ac.uk
Chief Executive, Mrs S. Hardy

RELATE (1938), Herbert Gray College, Little Church Street, Rugby CV21 3AP **T** 01788-753241 **E** enquiries@relate.org.uk **W** www.relate.org.uk
Chief Executive, Ms A. Sibson

RESEARCH DEFENCE SOCIETY (RDS) (1908), 25 Shaftesbury Avenue, London W1D 7EG **T** 020-7287 2818 **E** info@rds-online.org.uk **W** www.rds-online.org.uk
Executive Director, Dr M. Matfield

RESERVE FORCES' AND CADETS' ASSOCIATIONS (1972), Holderness House, 51–61 Clifton Street, London EC2A 4EY **T** 020-7426 8350 **E** info@rfcacouncil.org.uk
Secretary-General, Air Vice-Marshal A. J. Stables, CBE

RETHINK (1972), 30 Tabernacle Street, EC2A 4DD **T** 0845-456 0455 **E** info@rethink.org **W** www.rethink.org
Chief Executive, Cliff Prior

RETIRED NURSES' NATIONAL HOME (1934), Riverside Avenue, Bournemouth BH7 7EE **T** 01202-396418 **E** anything@rnnh.co.uk **W** www.rnnh.co.uk
Chairman, Mrs J. Kelleway

RICHARD III SOCIETY (1924), 4 Oakley Street, London SW3 5NN **E** neil_trump@rich ardiii.net **W** www.richardiii.net
Secretary, Miss E. M. Nokes

RNIB (ROYAL NATIONAL INSTITUTE OF THE BLIND) (1868), 105 Judd Street, London WC1H 9NE **T** 0845-669999 **E** helpline@rnib.org.uk **W** www.rnib.org.uk
Director-General, Lesley Anne Alexander

ROADS AND ROAD TRANSPORT HISTORY ASSOCIATION (1992), Copper Beeches, 134 Wood End Road, Erdington, Birmingham B24 8BN **T** 0121-382 5036 **E** jabhibbs2@hotmail.com
Chairman, Prof John Hibbs, OBE

ROTARY INTERNATIONAL IN GREAT BRITAIN AND IRELAND (1905), Kinwarton Road, Alcester B49 6BP **T** 01789-765411 **E** secretary@ribi.org **W** www.rotary-ribi.org
Secretary, R. Freeman

ROYAL AERONAUTICAL SOCIETY (1866), 4 Hamilton Place, London W1J 7BQ **T** 020-7670 4302 **W** www.aerosociety.com
Chief Executive, K. Mans

ROYAL AGRICULTURAL BENEVOLENT INSTITUTION (1860), Shaw House, 27 West Way, Oxford OX2 0QH T 01865-724931 E info@rabi.org.uk W www.rabi.org.uk
Chief Executive, W. A. McMahon, CVO, AFC

ROYAL AGRICULTURAL SOCIETY OF ENGLAND (1840), National Agricultural Centre, Stoneleigh Park, CV8 2LZ T 024-7669 6969
Chief Executive, M. Calvert

ROYAL AGRICULTURAL SOCIETY OF THE COMMONWEALTH (1957), 2 Grosvenor Gardens, London SW1W 0DH T 020-7259 9678 E rasc@commagshow.org W www.commagshow.org
Hon. Secretary, C. Runge, FRAGS

ROYAL AIR FORCE BENEVOLENT FUND (1919), 67 Portland Place, London W1B 1AR T 020-7580 8343 E info@rafbf.org.uk W www.rafbf.org.uk
Controller, Air Chief Marshal Sir David Cousins, KCB, AFC, BA

ROYAL AIR FORCES ASSOCIATION, 117 Loughborough Road, Leicester LE4 5ND T 0116-266 5224 W www.rafa.org.uk
Secretary-General, E. Jarron

ROYAL ASSOCIATION FOR DEAF PEOPLE, Centre for Deaf People, Walsingham Road, Colchester CO2 7BP T 01206-509509 Text: 01206 711260 E info@royaldeaf.org.uk W www.royaldeaf.org.uk
Chief Executive, Tom Fenton

ROYAL ASSOCIATION OF BRITISH DAIRY FARMERS (1879), Dairy House, 60 Kenilworth Road, Leamington Spa CV32 6JX T 01926-887477 E office@rabdf.co.uk
Chief Executive, N. Everington

ROYAL BIRMINGHAM SOCIETY OF ARTISTS (1814), 4 Brook Street, Birmingham B3 1SA T 0121-236 4353 E secretary@rbsa.org.uk W www.rbsa.org.uk
Gallery Director, Marie Considine

ROYAL BRITISH LEGION (1921), 48 Pall Mall, London SW1Y 5JY T 0845-772 5725 E info@britishlegion.org.uk W www.britishlegion.org.uk
Secretary-General, Brig. I. G. Townsend

ROYAL BRITISH LEGION SCOTLAND (1921), New Haig House, Logie Green Road, Edinburgh EH7 4HR E admin@rblscotland.org W www.rblscotland.org
General Secretary, Wing Cdr R. J. Woodroffe, MBE

ROYAL CAMBRIAN ACADEMY (1882), Crown Lane, Conwy LL32 8AN T 01492-593413 E rca@rcaconwy.co.uk W www.rcaconwy.co.uk
President, Sir Kyffin Williams

ROYAL CELTIC SOCIETY (1820), 23 Rutland Street, Edinburgh EH1 2RN T 0131-228 6449 E gcameron@stuartandstuart.co.uk
Secretary, J. G. Cameron, WS

ROYAL COLLEGE OF ART (1837), Kensington Gore, London, SW7 2EU T 020-7590 4444 E admissions@rca.ac.uk W www.rca.ac.uk

ROYAL COLLEGE OF GENERAL PRACTITIONERS (1952), 14 Princes Gate, London SW7 1PU T 020-7581 3232 E info@rcgp.org.uk W www.rcgp.org.uk
Chairman of Council, David Haslam

ROYAL COLLEGE OF MIDWIVES, 15 Mansfield Street, London W1G 9NH T 020-7312 3535 E info@rcm.org.uk W www.rcm.org.uk
Director, Anne Jackson-Baker

ROYAL COLLEGE OF NURSING (1916), 20 Cavendish Square, London W1G 0RN T 020-7409 3333 E corpaffairs.dept@rcn.org.uk W www.rcn.org.uk
General Secretary, Dr Beverly Malone

ROYAL COLLEGE OF OBSTETRICIANS AND GYNAECOLOGISTS (1929), 27 Sussex Place, Regent's Park, London NW1 4RG T 020-7772 6200 E coll.sec@rcog.org.uk W www.rcog.org.uk
President, Prof William Dunlop

ROYAL COLLEGE OF PAEDIATRICS AND CHILD HEALTH, 50 Hallam Street, London W1W 6DE T 020-7307 5600 W www.rcpch.ac.uk
President, Prof. Alan Craft

ROYAL COLLEGE OF PATHOLOGISTS, 2 Carlton House Terrace, London SW1Y 5AF T 020-7451 6700 E info@rcpath.org W www.rcpath.org
President, Prof. James Underwood

ROYAL COLLEGE OF PHYSICIANS (1518), 11 St Andrews Place, Regent's Park, London NW1 4LE T 020-7935 1174 E info@rcplondon.ac.uk W www.rcplondon.ac.uk
Chief Executive, A. P. Masterton-Smith

ROYAL COLLEGE OF PSYCHIATRISTS (1841), 17 Belgrave Square, London SW1X 8PG T 020-7235 2351 E rcpsych@rcpsych.ac.uk W www.rcpsych.ac.uk
Chief Executive, Dr M. Shooter

ROYAL COLLEGE OF RADIOLOGISTS (1975), 38 Portland Place, London W1N 4JQ T 020-7636 4432 E enquiries@rcr.ac.uk W www.rcr.ac.uk
Chief Executive, A. Hall

ROYAL COLLEGE OF SURGEONS OF ENGLAND (1800), 35–43 Lincoln's Inn Fields, London WC2A 3PE T 020-7405 3474 W www.rcseng.ac.uk
Chief Executive, Craig Duncan

ROYAL COLLEGE OF VETERINARY SURGEONS (1844), Belgravia House, 62–64 Horseferry Road, London SW1P 2AF T 020-7222 2001 E admin@rcvs.org.uk W www.rcvs.org.uk
Registrar, Miss J. C. Hern

ROYAL FORESTRY SOCIETY OF ENGLAND, WALES AND NORTHERN IRELAND (1882), 102 High Street, Tring HP23 4AF **T** 01442-822028 **E** rfshq@rfs.org.uk **W** www.rfs.org.uk
Director, Dr J. E. Jackson

ROYAL GEOGRAPHICAL SOCIETY (WITH THE INSTITUTE OF BRITISH GEOGRAPHERS) (1830), 1 Kensington Gore, London SW7 2AR **T** 020-7591 3000 **E** info@rgs.org **W** www.rgs.org
Director, Dr R. Gardner, CBE

ROYAL HIGHLAND AND AGRICULTURAL SOCIETY OF SCOTLAND (1784), Royal Highland Centre, Ingliston, Edinburgh EH28 8NF **T** 0131-335 6200 **E** info@rhass.org.uk **W** www.rhass.org.uk
Chief Executive, R. Jones

ROYAL HISTORICAL SOCIETY (1868), University College London, Gower Street, London WC1E 6BT **T** 020-7387 7532 **E** royalhistsoc@ucl.ac.uk **W** www.rhs.ac.uk
Executive Secretary, Mrs J. N. McCarthy

ROYAL HORTICULTURAL SOCIETY (1804), 80 Vincent Square, London SW1P 2PE **T** 020-7834 4333 **E** info@rhs.org.uk **W** www.rhs.org.uk
Director-General, Dr A. Colquhoun

ROYAL HOSPITAL FOR NEURO-DISABILITY (1854), West Hill, Putney, London SW15 3SW **T** 020-8780 4500 **E** info@rhn.org.uk **W** www.rhn.org.uk
Chief Executive, Peter Franklyn

ROYAL HUMANE SOCIETY (1774), Brettenham House, Lancaster Place, London WC2E 7EP **T** 020-7836 8155 **E** rhs@supanet.co.uk **W** www.royalhumane.org
Secretary, Maj.-Gen. C. Tyler, CB

ROYAL INCORPORATION OF ARCHITECTS IN SCOTLAND (1916), 15 Rutland Square, Edinburgh EH1 2BE **T** 0131-229 7545 **E** stombs@rias.org.uk **W** www.rias.org.uk
Secretary and Treasurer, S. Tombs

ROYAL INSTITUTE OF BRITISH ARCHITECTS (1837), 66 Portland Place, London W1B 1AD **T** 020-7580 5533. **Information** 0906-302 0400 **E** info@inst.riba.org **W** www.architecture.org
Chief Executive, Richard Hastilow, CBE

ROYAL INSTITUTE OF NAVIGATION (1947), 1 Kensington Gore, London SW7 2AT **T** 020-7591 3130 **E** info@rin.org.uk **W** www.rin.org.uk
Director, Gp Capt. D. W. Broughton, MBE

ROYAL INSTITUTE OF OIL PAINTERS (1882), 17 Carlton House Terrace, London SW1Y 5BD **T** 020-7930 6844 **E** info@mallgalleries.com **W** www.mallgalleries.org.uk
President, Dennis Syrett

ROYAL INSTITUTE OF PAINTERS IN WATER COLOURS (1831), 17 Carlton House Terrace, London SW1Y 5BD **T** 020-7930 6844 **E** info@mallgalleries.com **W** www.mallgalleries.org.uk
President, Ronald Maddox

ROYAL INSTITUTE OF PHILOSOPHY (1925), 14 Gordon Square, London WC1H 0AG **T** 020-7387 4130 **E** secretary@royalinstitutephilosophy.org **W** www.royalinstitutephilosophy.org
President, The Lord Quinton

ROYAL INSTITUTION OF CHARTERED SURVEYORS (1868), 12 Great George Street, Parliament Square, London SW1P 3AD **T** 020-7222 7000 **E** contactrics@rics.org **W** www.rics.org
Chief Executive, J. H. A. J. Armstrong

ROYAL INSTITUTION OF GREAT BRITAIN (1799), 21 Albemarle Street, London W1S 4BS **T** 020-7409 2900 **E** ri@ri.ac.uk **W** www.rigb.org
Director, Baroness Greenfield, CBE

ROYAL INSTITUTION OF NAVAL ARCHITECTS (1860), 10 Upper Belgrave Street, London SW1X 8BQ **T** 020-7235 4622 **E** hq@rina.org.uk **W** www.rina.org.uk
Chief Executive, T. Blakeley

ROYAL MASONIC TRUST FOR GIRLS AND BOYS (1982), 31 Great Queen Street, London WC2B 5AG **T** 020-7405 2644 **W** www.rmtgb.org
Secretary, Lt.-Col. J. C. Chambers

ROYAL MEDICAL BENEVOLENT FUND (1836), 24 Kings Road, London SW19 8QN **T** 020-8540 9194 **E** info@rmbf.org **W** www.rmbf.co.uk
Chief Executive, M. Baber

ROYAL MICROSCOPICAL SOCIETY (1839), 37–38 St Clements, Oxford OX4 1AJ **T** 01865-248768 **E** info@rms.org.uk **W** www.rms.org.uk
Administrator, P. B. Hirst

ROYAL NATIONAL COLLEGE FOR THE BLIND (1872), College Road, Hereford HR1 1EB **T** 01432-265725 **E** info@rncb.ac.uk **W** www.rncb.ac.uk
Principal, Mrs R. Burge

ROYAL NATIONAL LIFEBOAT INSTITUTION (1824), West Quay Road, Poole BT15 1HZ **T** 01202-663000 **E** info@rnli.org.uk **W** www.rnli.org.uk
Chief Executive, A. Freemantle, MBE

ROYAL NAVAL ASSOCIATION, 82 Chelsea Manor Street, London SW3 5QJ **T** 020-7352 6764 **E** rna@netcomuk.co.uk **W** www.royal-naval-association.co.uk
President, Vice-Adm. John McAnally, CB, LVO

ROYAL NAVAL BENEVOLENT TRUST (1922), Castaway House, 311 Twyford Avenue, Portsmouth PO2 8RN **T** 023-9269 0112/9266 0296 **E** rnbt@rnbt.org.uk **W** www.rnbt.org.uk
Chief Executive, Cdr. J. Owens, RN

ROYAL PATRIOTIC FUND CORPORATION (1854), 40 Queen Anne's Gate, London SW1H 9AP
T 020-7233 1894 E rpat@fish.co.uk
Secretary, Col. R. J. Sandy

ROYAL PHARMACEUTICAL SOCIETY OF GREAT BRITAIN (1841), 1 Lambeth High Street, London SE1 7JN
T 020-7735 9141 E enquiries@rpsgb.org W www.rpsgb.org
Secretary and Registrar, Ms A. M. Lewis, OBE

ROYAL PHILATELIC SOCIETY LONDON (1869), 41 Devonshire Place, London W1G 6JY T 020-7486 1044
E secretary@rpsl.org.uk W www.rpsl.org.uk
Hon. Secretary, K. B. Fitton

ROYAL PHILHARMONIC SOCIETY (1813), 10 Stratford Place, London W1C 1BA T 020-7491 8110
E admin@rps-uk.demon.co.uk
W www.royalphilharmonicsociety.org.uk
Chairman, Tony Fell

ROYAL PHOTOGRAPHIC SOCIETY (1853), The Octagon, Milsom Street, Bath BA1 1DN T 01225-462841
E rps@rps.org W www.rps.org
President, R. Reynolds

ROYAL SCHOOL OF CHURCH MUSIC (1927), Cleveland Lodge, Westhumble, Dorking RH5 6BW
T 01306-872800 E enquiries@rscm.com W www.rscm.com
Director-General, Prof. J. Harper

ROYAL SCHOOL OF NEEDLEWORK (1872), Apartment 12A, Hampton Court Palace, KT8 9AU
T 020-8943 1432 E enquiries@royal-needlework.co.uk
W www.royal-needlework.co.uk
Principal, Mrs E. Elvin

ROYAL SOCIETY, 6–9 Carlton House Terrace, London SW1Y 5AG T 020-7451 2000 E info@royalsoc.ac.uk
W www.royalsoc.ac.uk

ROYAL SOCIETY FOR ASIAN AFFAIRS (1901), 2 Belgrave Square, London SW1X 8PJ T 020-7235 5122
E sec@rsaa.org.uk W www.rsaa.org.uk
Chairman, Sir Harold Walker, KCMG

ROYAL SOCIETY FOR THE ENCOURAGEMENT OF ARTS, MANUFACTURES AND COMMERCE (RSA) (1754), 8 John Adam Street, London WC2N 6EZ
T 020-7930 5115 E general@rsa.org.uk W www.thersa.org
Executive Director, Penny Egan

ROYAL SOCIETY FOR THE PREVENTION OF ACCIDENTS (1917), ROSPA House, Edgbaston Park, 353 Bristol Road, Birmingham B5 7ST T 0121-248 2000
E help@rospa.com W www.rospa.com
Chief Executive, John Howard, OBE

ROYAL SOCIETY FOR THE PREVENTION OF CRUELTY TO ANIMALS (1824), Wilberforce Way, Horsham RH13 9RS T 0870-010 1181 W www.rspca.org.uk
Director-General, Jackie Ballard

ROYAL SOCIETY FOR THE PROMOTION OF HEALTH (1876), 38A St George's Drive, London SW1V 4BH T 020-7630 0121 E rshealth@rshealth.org.uk
W www.rsph.org
Chief Executive, S. Royston

ROYAL SOCIETY FOR THE PROTECTION OF BIRDS (RSPB) (1889), The Lodge, Sandy SG19 2DL
T 01767-680551 W www.rspb.org.uk
Chief Executive, G. R. Wynne

ROYAL SOCIETY OF MARINE ARTISTS (1945), 17 Carlton House Terrace, London SW1Y 5BD
T 020-7930 6844 E info@mallgalleries.com
W www.mallgalleries.org.uk
Secretary, G. Hunt

ROYAL SOCIETY OF MEDICINE (1805), 1 Wimpole Street, London W1G 0AE T 020-7290 2900
E membership@rsm.ac.uk W www.rsm.ac.uk
Executive Director, Dr A. Grocock

ROYAL SOCIETY OF MINIATURE PAINTERS, SCULPTORS AND GRAVERS (1895), 1 Knapp Cottages, Wyke, Gillingham SP8 4NQ T 01747-825718
E hendersons@dial.pipex.com
W www.royal-miniature-society.org.uk
Executive Secretary, Pam Henderson

ROYAL SOCIETY OF MUSICIANS OF GREAT BRITAIN (1738), 10 Stratford Place, London W1C 1BA
T 020-7629 6137
Secretary, Mrs M. Gibb

ROYAL SOCIETY OF PORTRAIT PAINTERS (1891), 17 Carlton House Terrace, London SW1Y 5BD
T 020-7930 6844 E info@mallgalleries.com
W www.mallgalleries.org.uk
President, Andrew Festing

ROYAL SOCIETY OF ST GEORGE (1894), 127 Sandgate Road, Folkstone CT20 2BH T 01303-241795
E info@rssg.u-net.com W www.royalsocietyofstgeorge.com
Chairman, J. C. Clemence, QPM

ROYAL STAR AND GARTER HOME FOR DISABLED EX-SERVICE MEN AND WOMEN (1916), Richmond Hill, Richmond TW10 6RR T 020-8940 3314
E generalenquiries@starandgarter.org
W www.starandgarter.org
Chief Executive, Lynn McDougall

ROYAL THEATRICAL FUND (1839), 11 Garrick Street, London WC2E 9AR T 020-7836 3322 E admin@trtf.com
W www.trtf.com
Secretary, Mrs R. M. Foster

ROYAL ULSTER AGRICULTURAL SOCIETY (1896), The King's Hall, Balmoral, Belfast BT9 6GW
T 028-9066 5225 E general@kingshall.co.uk
W www.balmoralshow.co.uk
Chief Executive, Michael Guest

ROYAL UNITED KINGDOM BENEFICENT ASSOCIATION (1863), 6 Avonmore Road, London W14 8RL T 020-7605 4200 E charity@rukba.org.uk W www.rukba.org.uk
Chief Executive, Jonathan Powell

ROYAL UNITED SERVICES INSTITUTE FOR DEFENCE STUDIES (1831), Whitehall, London SW1A 2ET T 020-7930 5854 E defence@rusi.org W www.rusi.org
Director, Rear-Adm. R. Cobbold, CB

RURAL SCOTLAND (1926), 3rd Floor, Gladstone's Land, 483 Lawnmarket, Edinburgh EH1 2NT T 0131-225 7012/3 E aprs@aprs.org.uk W www.aprs.org.uk
Director, C. A. Strang

SALTIRE SOCIETY (1936), 9 Fountain Close, 22 High Street, Edinburgh EH1 1TF T 0131-556 1836 E saltire@saltiresociety.org.uk W www.saltiresociety.org.uk
Administrator, Mrs K. Munro, MBE

SAMARITANS (1953), The Upper Mill, Kingston Road, Ewell KT17 2AF T 020-8394 8300 E admin@samaritans.org W www.samaritans.org
Chief Executive, David King

SANE (1986), 1st Floor, Cityside House, 40 Adler Street, London E1 1EE T 020-7375 1002. Helpline: 0845-767 8000 E info@sane.org.uk W www.sane.org.uk
Chief Executive, Ms M. Wallace, MBE

SAVE BRITAIN'S HERITAGE (1975), 70 Cowcross Street, London EC1M 6EJ T 020-7253 3500 E save@btinternet.com W www.savebritainsheritage.org
Secretary, A. Wilkinson

SAVE THE CHILDREN UK (1919), 1 St. John's Lane, London EC1M 4AR T 020-7012 6400 E enquiries@scfuk.org.uk W www.savethechildren.org.uk
Director-General, M. Aaronson

SCHOOL LIBRARY ASSOCIATION (1937), Unit 2, Lotmead Business Village, Lotmead Farm, Wanborough, nr Swindon SN4 0UY T 01793-791787 E info@sla.org.uk W www.sla.org.uk
Chief Executive, Ms K. Lemaire

SCHOOLMISTRESSES AND GOVERNESSES BENEVOLENT INSTITUTION (1848), Queen Mary House, Manor Park Road, Chislehurst BR7 5PY T 020-8468 7997
Director, L. I. Baggott

SCHOOL OF PUBLIC POLICY (1996), University College London, 29 Tavistock Square, London WC1H 9QU T 020-7679 4999 E spp@ucl.ac.uk W www.ucl.ac.uk/spp/
Director, Professor Helen Margetts

SCOPE (1952), 6 Market Road, London N7 9PW T 0808-800 3333 E cphelpline@scope.org.uk W www.scope.org.uk
Chief Executive, Gerald McCarthy

SCOTTISH CHAMBERS OF COMMERCE (1948), 30 George Square, Glasgow G2 1EQ T 0141-204 8316 E admin@scottishchambers.org.uk W www.scottishchambers.org.uk
Director, Robert Leitch

SCOTTISH COUNCIL FOR VOLUNTARY ORGANISATIONS, Mansfield Traquair Centre, 15 Mansfield Place, Edinburgh EH3 6BB T 0131-556 3882 E enquiries@scvo.org.uk W www.scvo.org.uk
Chief Executive, M. Sime

SCOTTISH GENEALOGY SOCIETY (1953), Library and Family History Centre, 15 Victoria Terrace, Edinburgh EH1 2JL T 0131-220 3677 E info@scotsgenealogy.com W www.scotsgenealogy.com
Hon. Secretary, K. A. M Nisbet

SCOTTISH NATIONAL WAR MEMORIAL, The Castle, Edinburgh EH1 2YT T 0131-226 7393 W www.snwm.org
Secretary to the Trustees, Lt.-Col. I. Shepherd

SCOTTISH NATURAL HISTORY LIBRARY (1970), Foremount House, Kilbarchan, PA10 2EZ T 01505-702419
Director, Dr J. A. Gibson

SCOTTISH RURAL PROPERTY AND BUSINESS ASSOCIATION (SRPBA), Stuart House, Eskmills Business Park, Musselburgh EH21 7PB T 0131-653 5400 E info@srpba.com W www.srpba.com
Chief Executive, Dr M. S. Hankey

SCOTTISH SOCIETY FOR THE PREVENTION OF CRUELTY TO ANIMALS (1839), Braehead Mains, 603 Queensferry Road, Edinburgh EH4 6EA T 0131-339 0222 E enquiries@scottishspca.org W www.scottishspca.org
Chief Executive, Mrs K. Driver

SCOTTISH SOCIETY FOR THE PROTECTION OF WILD BIRDS (1927), Foremount House, Kilbarchan PA10 2EZ T 01505-702419
Secretary, Dr J. A. Gibson

SCOTTISH WILDLIFE TRUST (1964), Cramond House, Cramond Glebe Road, Edinburgh EH4 6NS T 0131-312 7765 E enquiries@swt.org.uk W www.swt.org.uk
Chief Executive, S. Sankey

SCOTTISH YOUTH HOSTELS ASSOCIATION (1931), 7 Glebe Crescent, Stirling FK8 2JA T 01786-891400 E syha@syha.org.uk W www.syha.org.uk
Chairman, John Dickson

SCOUT ASSOCIATION (1907), Gilwell Park, Chingford, London E4 7QW T 020-8443 7100 E info.centre@scout.org.uk W www.scoutbase.org.uk/
Chief Executive, D. M. Twine

SEEABILITY (1799), seeAbility House, Hook Road, Epsom, KT19 8SQ T 01372-755000 E reception@seeability.org
Chief Executive, D. Scott-Ralphs

SELDEN SOCIETY (1887), Faculty of Laws, Queen Mary and Westfield College, Mile End Road, London E1 4NS
T 020-7882 5136 E selden-society@qmw.ac.uk
W www.selden-society.qmw.ac.uk
Secretary, V. Tunkel

SENSE (THE NATIONAL DEAFBLIND AND RUBELLA ASSOCIATION), 11–13 Clifton Terrace, London N4 3SR
T 020-7272 7774 E enquiries@sense.org.uk
W www.sense.org.uk
Chief Executive, A. Best

SHAFTESBURY HOMES AND ARETHUSA (1843), The Chapel, Royal Victoria Patriotic Building, Trinity Road, London SW18 3SX T 020-8875 1555
E info@shaftesbury.org.uk
Chief Executive, Ms A. Chesney

SHAFTESBURY SOCIETY (1844), 16 Kingston Road, London SW19 1JZ T 020-8239 5555
E info@shaftesburysoc.org.uk
W www.shaftesburysociety.org
Chief Executive, Mrs Mary Bishop

SHELLFISH ASSOCIATION OF GREAT BRITAIN (1903), Fishmongers' Hall, London Bridge, London EC4R 9EL T 020-7283 8305 E sagb@shellfish.org.uk
W www.shellfish.org.uk
Director, Dr P. Hunt

SHERLOCK HOLMES SOCIETY OF LONDON (1951), 13 Crofton Avenue, Orpington BR6 8DU
T 01689-811314
W www.sherlock-holmes.org.uk
Membership Secretary, R. J. Ellis

SHROPSHIRE ARCHAEOLOGICAL AND HISTORICAL SOCIETY (1877), Westcott Farm, Pontesbury SY5 0SQ T 01743-790531 E jlwestcott@aol.com
Chairman, J. B. Lawson

SIGHT SAVERS INTERNATIONAL (ROYAL COMMONWEALTH SOCIETY FOR THE BLIND) (1950), Grosvenor Hall, Bolnore Road, Haywards Heath RH16 4BX T 01444-446600
E generalinformation@sightsavers.org
W www.sightsavers.org.uk
Executive Director, R. Porter

SIR OSWALD STOLL FOUNDATION (1916), 446 Fulham Road, London SW6 1DT T 020-7385 2110
E info@oswaldstoll.org.uk W www.oswaldstoll.org.uk
Chief Executive, R. C. Brunwin

SOCIALIST PARTY (1904), 52 Clapham High Street, London SW4 7UN T 020-7622 3811
E spgb@worldsocialism.org W www.worldsocialism.org

SOCIÉTÉ JERSIAISE, ARCHAEOLOGICAL SECTION (1873), 7 Pier Road, St Helier, JE2 4XW T 01534-758314
E societe@societe-jersiaise.org W www.societe-jersiaise.org
Chairperson, Mrs P. Syuret

SOCIETY FOR PROMOTING CHRISTIAN KNOWLEDGE (SPCK) (1698), Holy Trinity Church, Marylebone Road, London NW1 4DU T 020-7643 0382
E spck@spck.org.uk W www.spck.org.uk
General Secretary, G. C. King

SOCIETY FOR PROMOTING THE TRAINING OF WOMEN (1859), Deep Carrs Farm Cottage, Golf Course Drive, Worksop S81 8BQ T 01909-475891
President, The Baroness Park of Monmouth, OBE, CMG

SOCIETY FOR PSYCHICAL RESEARCH (1882), 49 Marloes Road, London W8 6LA T 020-7937 8984
W www.spr.ac.uk

SOCIETY FOR THEATRE RESEARCH (1948), c/o The Theatre Museum, 1E Tavistock Street, London WC2E 7PR
E e.cottis@btinternet.com W www.str.org.uk
Hon. Secretary, Ms E. Cottis

SOCIETY FOR THE PROMOTION OF ROMAN STUDIES (1910), Senate House, Malet Street, London WC1E 7HU T 020-7862 8727 E romansoc@sas.ac.uk
W www.sas.ac.uk/icls/roman/
Secretary, Dr H. M. Cockle

SOCIETY FOR THE PROTECTION OF ANCIENT BUILDINGS (1877), 37 Spital Square, London E1 6DY
T 020-7377 1644 E info@spab.org.uk W www.spab.org.uk
Secretary, P. Venning, OBE, FSA

SOCIETY OF ANTIQUARIES OF NEWCASTLE UPON TYNE (1813), Black Gate, Castle Garth, Newcastle upon Tyne NE1 1RQ T 0191-261 5390
E admin@newcastle-antiquaries.org.uk
W www.newcastle-antiquaries.org.uk
Secretary, N. Hodgson

SOCIETY OF ANTIQUARIES OF SCOTLAND (1780), Royal Museum, Chambers Street, Edinburgh EH1 1JF
T 0131-247 4115/4133 E director@socanscot.org
W www.socantscot.org
Director, A. Smith

SOCIETY OF APOTHECARIES OF LONDON (1617), Black Friars Lane, London EC4V 6EJ T 020-7236 1189
E clerk@apothecaries.org W www.apothecaries.org
Clerk, A. M. Wallington-Smith

SOCIETY OF ARCHIVISTS (1947), Prioryfield House, 20 Canon Street, Taunton TA1 1SW T 01823-327030
E societyofarchivists@archives.org.uk
W www.archives.org.uk
Executive Secretary, P. S. Cleary

SOCIETY OF AUTHORS (1884), 84 Drayton Gardens, London SW10 9SB T 020-7373 6642
E info@societyofauthors.org W www.societyofauthors.org
General Secretary, M. Le Fanu, OBE

SOCIETY OF BOTANICAL ARTS (1985), 1 Knapp Cottages, Wyke, Gillingham SP8 4NQ T 01747-825718
E pam@soc-botanical-artists.org
W www.soc-botanical-artists.org
Executive Secretary, Pam Henderson

SOCIETY OF CHIROPODISTS AND PODIATRISTS (1912), 1 Fellmongers Path, Tower Bridge Road, London SE1 3LY T 0845-450 3720 E enq@scpod.org W www.feetforlife.org
Acting Chief Executive, Joanna Brown

SOCIETY OF EDITORS (1999), University Centre, Granta Place, Cambridge CB2 1RU T 01223-304080 E info@societyofeditors.org W www.societyofeditors.org
Executive Director, R. Satchwell

SOCIETY OF ENGINEERS (1854), Guinea Wiggs, Nayland, Colchester CO6 7NF T 01206-263332 E chiefexecutive@society-of-engineers.org.uk W www.society-of-engineers.org.uk
Chief Executive, Iain A. C. Wright

SOCIETY OF GLASS TECHNOLOGY (1916), Don Valley House, Savile Street East, Sheffield S4 7UQ T 0114-263 4455 E info@sgt.org W www.sgt.org
Managing Editor, D. Moore

SOCIETY OF INDEXERS (1957), Blades Enterprise Centre, John Street, Sheffield S2 4SU T 0114-292 2350 E admin@indexers.org.uk W www.indexers.org.uk
Secretary, Mrs Ann Kingdom

SOCIETY OF LEGAL SCHOLARS (1908), School of Law, Southampton University, Southampton SO17 1BJ T 023-8059 3416 E njw@soton.ac.uk W www.legalscholars.ac.uk
Hon. Secretary, Prof. N. J. Wikeley

SOCIETY OF LOCAL AUTHORITY CHIEF EXECUTIVES AND SENIOR MANAGERS (1972), Hope House, 45 Great Peter Street, London SW1P 3LT T 0845-601 0649 E enquiries@solace.org.uk W www.solace.org.uk
Director-General, David Clark

SOCIETY OF NAUTICAL RESEARCH (1910), c/o National Maritime Museum, Greenwich, London SE10 9NF T 020-8312 6712 E lxveri@nmm.ac.uk W www.snr.org.uk
Hon. Secretary, Liza Verity

SOCIETY OF OPERATIONS ENGINEERS (2000), 22 Greencoat Place, London SW1P 1PR T 020-7630 1111 E soe@soe.org.uk W www.soe.org.uk
Chief Executive, T. Shelley, MBA, IENG

SOCIETY OF SCRIBES AND ILLUMINATORS (1921), 6 Queen Square, London WC1N 3AT T 01524-251534 E scribe@calligraphyonline.org W www.calligraphyonline.org
Chairman, Tony Curtis

SOCIETY OF SOLICITORS IN THE SUPREME COURT OF SCOTLAND (1784), SSC Library, Parliament House, 11 Parliament Square, Edinburgh EH1 1RF T 0131-225 6268 E enquiries@ssclibrary.co.uk W www.ssclibrary.co.uk
Secretary, I. L. S. Balfour

SOCIETY OF WOMEN ARTISTS (1855), 1 Knapp Cottages, Wyke, Gillingham SP8 4NQ T 01747-825718 E hendersons@dial.pipex.com W www.society-women-artists.org.uk
Executive Secretary, Mrs P. Henderson

SOIL ASSOCIATION (1946), Bristol House, 40–56 Victoria Street, Bristol BS1 6BY T 0117-929 0661 E info@soilassociation.org W www.soilassociation.org
Director, P. Holden

SOMERSET ARCHAEOLOGICAL AND NATURAL HISTORY SOCIETY (1849), Taunton Castle, Taunton TA1 4AA T 01823-272429 E secretary@sanhs.freeserve.co.uk W www.sanhs.org
Hon. Secretary, Alex Maxwell-Findlater

SOUTH WALES INSTITUTE OF ENGINEERS (1857), 2nd Floor, Empire House, Mount Stuart Square, Cardiff CF10 5FN T 029-2048 1726 E swie@celtic.co.uk W www.swie.org.uk
Hon. Secretary, D. M. Morgan

SSAFA FORCES HELP (1885), 19 Queen Elizabeth Street, London SE1 2LP T 020-7403 8783 E info@ssafa.org.uk W www.ssafa.org.uk
Controller, Andrew Cumming, CBE

ST ALBANS AND HERTFORDSHIRE ARCHITECTURAL AND ARCHAEOLOGICAL SOCIETY (1845), 24 Rose Walk, St Albans AL4 9AF T 01727-853204
Hon. Secretary, B. E. Moody

STANDING COUNCIL OF SCOTTISH CHIEFS, Hope Chambers, 52 Leith Walk, Edinburgh EH6 5HW T 0131-553 2232 E bevkel@btinternet.com
General Secretary, Romilly Squire of Rubislaw

STANDING COUNCIL OF THE BARONETAGE (1903), 3 Eastcroft Road, West Ewell, Epsom KT19 9TX T 020-8393 6620 E secretary@baronetage.org W www.baronetage.org
Chairman, Sir Geoffrey Errington, BT, OBE

ST DEINIOL'S RESIDENTIAL LIBRARY (1894), Hawarden, Deeside CH5 3DF T 01244-532350 E deiniol.visitors@btconnect.com W www.st-deiniols.org
Warden and Chief Librarian, Revd P. B. Francis

ST DUNSTAN'S (1915), 12–14 Harcourt Street, London W1H 4HD T 020-7723 5021 E enquiries@st-dunstans.org.uk W www.st-dunstans.org.uk
Chief Executive, Robert Leader

STEWART SOCIETY (1899), 53 George Street, Edinburgh EH2 2HT T 0131-220 4512 E info@stewartsociety.org W www.stewartsociety.org
Secretary, Mrs M. V. A. Stark

ST JOHN AMBULANCE, 27 St John's Lane, London EC1M 4BU T 020-7324 4000 E pr@nhq.sja.org.uk W www.sja.org.uk
Chief Executive, Roger Holmes

STRATEGIC PLANNING SOCIETY (1967), Weston Street, London SE1 3ER T 020-7091 1310
E enquiries@sps.org.uk W www.sps.org.uk
Chairman, Jon Vyse

SUFFOLK HORSE SOCIETY (1877), The Market Hill, Woodbridge IP12 4LU T 01394-380643
E sec@suffolkhorsesociety.org.uk
W www.suffolkhorsesociety.org.uk
Secretary, Mrs A. V. Hillier

SUNDERLAND ANTIQUARIAN SOCIETY (1900), c/o Southwark Community School, Ryhope Road, Sunderland SR2 7TF T 0191-522 0517
President, D. W. Smith

SURVIVAL INTERNATIONAL (1969), 6 Charterhouse Buildings, London EC1M 7ET T 020-7687 8700
E info@survival-international.org
W www.survival-international.org
Director, S. Corry

SUSSEX ARCHAEOLOGICAL SOCIETY (1846), Bull House, 92 High Street, Lewes BN7 1XH T 01273-486260
E admin@sussexpast.co.uk W www.sussexpast.co.uk
Chief Executive, J. Manley

SUZY LAMPLUGH TRUST (1986), 14 East Sheen Avenue, London SW14 8AS T 020-8876 0305
E info@suzylamplugh.org W www.suzylamplugh.org
Chief Executive, Julie Bentley, OBE

SWEDENBORG SOCIETY (1810), 20/21 Bloomsbury Way, London WC1A 2TH T 020-7405 7986
E swed.soc@netmatters.co.uk W www.swedenborg.org.uk
Secretary, Richard Lines

TAVISTOCK INSTITUTE (1947), 30 Tabernacle Street, London EC2A 4UE T 020-7417 0407
W www.tavistockinstitute.org
Principal, John Kelleher

TERRENCE HIGGINS TRUST (1982), 52–54 Grays Inn Road, London WC1X 8JU T 020-7831 0330
E info@tht.org.uk W www.tht.org.uk
Chief Executive, Nick Partridge

THEATRES TRUST (1976), 22 Charing Cross Road, London WC2H 0QL T 020-7836 8591
E info@theatrestrust.org.uk W www.theatrestrust.org.uk
Director, P. Longman

THEOSOPHICAL SOCIETY IN ENGLAND (1875), 50 Gloucester Place, London W1U 8EA T 020-7935 9261
E info@theosophical.society.org.uk
W www.theosophical-society.org.uk
National President, C. Price

THE ROYAL LIFE SAVING SOCIETY UK (1891), River House, High Street, Broom B50 4HN T 01789-773994
E lifesavers@rlss.org.uk W www.lifesavers.org.uk
Chief Executive, D. Standley

THORESBY SOCIETY (1889), Claremont, 23 Clarendon Road, Leeds LS2 9NZ T 0113-245 7910
W www.thoresby.org.uk
President, Mr P. S. Morrish

TOC H (1915), 1 Forest Close, Wendover, Aylesbury HP22 6BT T 01296-642020 E info@toch.org.uk
W www.toch.org.uk
Chief Executive Officer, Revd G. Smith

TOWNSWOMEN'S GUILDS, Chamber of Commerce House, 75 Harborne Road, Birmingham B15 3DA
T 0121-456 3435 E tghq@townswomen.org.uk
W www.townswomen.org.uk
National Secretary, Mrs D. Calvert

TREE COUNCIL (1974), 51 Catherine Place, London SW1E 6DY T 020-7407 9992 E info@treecouncil.org.uk
W www.treecouncil.org.uk
Director-General, Pauline Buchanan Black

TURNER SOCIETY (1975), BCM Box Turner, London WC1N 3XX E turner@equinox.demon.co.uk
W www.turnersociety.org.uk
Chairman, Eric Shanes

UFAW (1926), The Old School, Brewhouse Hill, Wheathampstead AL4 8AN T 01582-831818
E www.ufaw.org.uk W www.ufaw3.org.uk
Scientific Director, Dr J. K. Kirkwood

UK YOUTH (1911), 2nd Floor, Kirby House, 20–24 Kirby Street, London EC1N 8TS T 020-7242 4045
E info@ukyouth.org.uk W www.ukyouth.org.uk
Chief Executive, J. Bateman, OBE

UNITED GRAND LODGE OF ENGLAND (1717), Freemasons' Hall, Great Queen Street, London WC2B 5AZ
T 020-7831 9811 E ugle@ugle.org.uk W www.ugle.org.uk
Grand Master, HRH The Duke of Kent, KG, GCMG, GCVO

UNITED REFORMED CHURCH HISTORY SOCIETY (1972), Westminster College, Madingley Road, Cambridge CB3 0AA T 01223-741300 E mt212@cam.ac.uk
Hon. Secretary, Revd E. J. Brown

UNIVERSITIES UK, Woburn House, 20 Tavistock Square, London WC1H 9HQ T 020-7419 4111
E info@universitiesuk.ac.uk W www.universitiesuk.ac.uk
Chief Executive, Baroness Warwick

VEGAN SOCIETY (1944), Donald Watson House, 7 Battle Road, St Leonards-on-Sea TN37 7AA T 0845-458 8244
E info@vegansociety.com W www.vegansociety.com
Chief Executive, Rick Savage

VEGETARIAN SOCIETY OF THE UNITED KINGDOM LTD (1847), Parkdale, Dunham Road, Altrincham, Cheshire WA14 4QG T 0161-925 2000
E info@vegsoc.org W www.vegsoc.org
Chief Executive, Ms T. Fox

VERNACULAR ARCHITECTURE GROUP (1952), 'Ashley', Willows Green, Chelmsford CM3 1QD
T 01245-361408 W www.vag.org.uk
Hon. Secretary, Mrs B. A. Watkin

VICTIM SUPPORT SCOTLAND (1985), 15–23 Hardwell Close, Edinburgh EH8 9RX T 0131-668 4486
E info@victimsupportsco.demon.co.uk
W www.victimsupportsco.org
Chief Executive, D. McKenna

VICTORIA CROSS AND GEORGE CROSS ASSOCIATION (1956), Horse Guards, Whitehall, London SW1A 2AX T 020-7930 3506
Secretary, Mrs D. Grahame, MVO

VICTORIAN SOCIETY (1958), 1 Priory Gardens, Bedford Park, London W4 1TT T 020-8994 1019
E admin@victorian-society.org
W www.victorian-society.org.uk
Director, Dr Ian Dungavell

VIKING SOCIETY FOR NORTHERN RESEARCH (1892), Department of Scandinavian Studies, University College, Gower Street, London WC1E 6BT T 020-7679 7176
E vsnr@ucl.ac.uk
Hon. Secretaries, Prof. M. P. Barnes; Prof. J. Jesh

VISITSCOTLAND (1969), 23 Ravelston Terrace, Edinburgh EH4 3TP T 0131-332 2433
E firstname.lastname@visitscotland.com
W www.visitscotland.com
Chief Executive, Philip Riddle

VSO (VOLUNTARY SERVICE OVERSEAS) (1958), 317 Putney Bridge Road, London SW15 2PN T 020-8780 7200
E enquiry@vso.org.uk W www.vso.org.uk
Chief Executive, Mark Goldring

WALES TOURIST BOARD (1969), Brunel House, 2 Fitzalan Road, Cardiff CF24 0UY T 029-2049 9909
W www.visitwales.com and www.wtbonline.gov.uk
Chief Executive, Jonathan Jones

WELLBEING - HEALTH RESEARCH CHARITY FOR WOMEN AND BABIES (1965), 27 Sussex Place, Regent's Park, London NW1 4SP T 020-7772 6400
E wellbeing@rcog.org.uk W www.wellbeing.org.uk
Director, Ms S. Farmer

WESLEY HISTORICAL SOCIETY (1893), 34 Spiceland Road, Northfield, Birmingham B31 1NJ T 0121-475 4914
E edgraham@tesco.net
General Secretary, Dr E. D. Graham

WEST LONDON MISSION (1893), 19 Thayer Street, London W1U 2QJ T 020-7935 6179 E office@wlm.org.uk
W www.wlm.org.uk
Superintendent, Revd Geoff Cornell

WESTMINSTER FOUNDATION FOR DEMOCRACY (1992), 2nd Floor, 125 Pall Mall, London SW1Y 5EA
T 020-7930 0408 E wfd@wfd.org W www.wfd.org
Chief Executive, David French

WILDFOWL AND WETLANDS TRUST (1946), Slimbridge GL2 7BT T 01453-891900
E enquiries@wwt.org.uk W www.wwt.org.uk
Managing Director, M. Spray

WILLIAM MORRIS SOCIETY AND KELMSCOTT FELLOWSHIP (1955), Kelmscott House, 26 Upper Mall, London W6 9TA T 020-8741 3735
E williammorris@care4free.net W www.morrissociety.org
Hon. Secretary, P. Faulkner

WILTSHIRE ARCHAEOLOGICAL AND NATURAL HISTORY SOCIETY (1853), Wiltshire Heritage Museum, 41 Long Street, Devizes SN10 1NS
T 01380-727369 E wanhs@wiltshireheritage.org.uk
W www.wiltshireheritage.org.uk
Curator, Dr P. H. Robinson

WOMEN'S ENGINEERING SOCIETY (1919), 22 Old Queen Street, London SW1H 9HW T 020-7233 1974
E info@wes.org.uk W www.wes.org.uk
Secretary, Mrs C. MacGillivray

WOMEN'S ROYAL NAVAL SERVICE BENEVOLENT TRUST (1941), 311 Twyford Avenue, Portsmouth PO2 8RN T 023-9265 5301 E wrnsbt@care4free.net
General Secretary, Mrs S. Tarabella

WOODLAND TRUST (1972), Autumn Park, Dysart Road, Grantham NG31 6LL T 01476-581111
E enquiries@woodland-trust.org.uk
W www.woodland-trust.org.uk
Chief Executive, Mike Townsend

WORCESTERSHIRE ARCHAEOLOGICAL SOCIETY (1854), 26 Albert Park Road, Malvern WR14 1HN
T 01299-250416 E museum@worcestershire.gov.uk
W www.worcestershire.gov.uk/museum
Hon. Secretary, Dr J. W. Dunleavey

WORK FOUNDATION, Peter Runge House, 3 Carlton House Terrace, London SW1Y 5DG T 0870-165 6700
E contactcentre@theworkfoundation.com
W www.theworkfoundation.com
Chief Executive, Will Hutton

WORKING FAMILIES (2003), 1–3 Berry Street, London EC1V 0AA T 020-7253 7243
E office@workingfamilies.org.uk
W www.workingfamilies.org.uk
Chief Executive, Ms S. Jackson

WRVS (1938), Garden House, Milton Hill, Abingdon OX13 6AD T 01235-442900 E enquiries@wrvs.org.uk
W www.wrvs.org.uk
Chairman, Ms T. Tietjen

YORKSHIRE AGRICULTURAL SOCIETY (1837), Great Yorkshire Showground, Harrogate HG2 8PW
T 01423-541000 E info@yas.co.uk W www.yas.co.uk
Chief Executive, Nigel Pulling

YORKSHIRE SOCIETY (1812), 35 Waldorf Heights, Camberley **T** 01276-516484
Secretary, G. G. Prince, FCIS, TD

YOUNG MEN'S CHRISTIAN ASSOCIATION (YMCA), National Council of YMCAs, 640 Forest Road, London E17 3DZ **T** 020-8520 5599
E national.secretary@england.ymca.org.uk
W www.ymca.org.uk
National Secretary, K. Williams

YOUTH HOSTELS ASSOCIATION (ENGLAND & WALES) (1930), Trevelyan House, Dimple Road, Matlock, DE4 3YH **T** 01629-592600 **E** customerservices@yha.org.uk
W www.yha.org.uk
National Secretary, Terry Rollinson

YWCA ENGLAND & WALES (1855), Clarendon House, 52 Cornmarket Street, Oxford OX1 3EJ **T** 01865-304200
E info@ywca-gb.org.uk **W** www.ywca-gb.org.uk
Chief Executive, Ms G. Tishler

ZOOLOGICAL SOCIETY OF LONDON (1826), Regent's Park, London NW1 4RY **T** 020-7722 3333
W www.zsl.org
President, Prof. Sir Patrick Bateson

THE WORLD

WORLD GEOGRAPHICAL STATISTICS

THE EARTH

The shape of the Earth is that of an oblate spheroid or solid of revolution whose meridian sections are ellipses, whilst the sections at right angles are circles.

DIMENSIONS

Equatorial diameter = 12,756.27 km (7,926.38 miles)
Polar diameter = 12,713.50 km (7,899.80 miles)
Equatorial circumference = 40,075.01 km (24,901.46 miles)
Polar circumference = 40,007.86 km (24,859.73 miles)
Mass = 5,974,000,000,000,000,000,000 tonnes (5.879×10^{21} tons)

The equatorial circumference is divided into 360 degrees of longitude, which is measured in degrees, minutes and seconds east or west of the Greenwich meridian (0°) to 180°, the meridian 180° E. coinciding with 180° W. This dateline was internationally ratified on 13 October 1884.

Distance north and south of the Equator is measured in degrees, minutes and seconds of latitude. The Equator is 0°, the North Pole is 90° N. and the South Pole is 90° S. The Tropics lie at 23° 27′ N. (Tropic of Cancer) and 23° 27′ S. (Tropic of Capricorn). The Arctic Circle lies at 66° 33′ N. and the Antarctic Circle at 66° 33′ S. (NB The Tropics and the Arctic and Antarctic circles are affected by the slow decrease in obliquity of the ecliptic, of about 0.47 arcseconds per year. The effect of this is that the Arctic and Antarctic circles are currently moving towards their respective poles by about 14 metres per annum, while the Tropics move towards the Equator by the same amount.

AREA, ETC.

The surface area of the Earth is 510,069,120 km² (196,938,800 miles²), of which the water area is 70.92 per cent and the land area is 29.08 per cent.

The radial velocity on the Earth's surface at the Equator is 1,669.79 km per hour (1,037.56 m.p.h.). The Earth's mean velocity in its orbit around the Sun is 107,229 km per hour (66,629 m.p.h.). The Earth's mean distance from the Sun is 149,597,870 km (92,955,807 miles).

OCEANS

AREA

	km²	miles²
Pacific	155,557,000	59,270,000
Atlantic	76,762,000	29,638,000
Indian	68,556,000	26,467,000
Southern	20,327,000	7,848,300
Arctic	14,056,000	5,427,000

The Equator divides the Pacific into the North and South Pacific and the Atlantic into the North and South Atlantic. In 2000 the International Hydrographic Organisation approved the description of the 20,327,000 km² (7,848,300 miles²) of circum-Antarctic waters up to 60° S. as the Southern Ocean – a seventh ocean.

GREATEST OCEAN DEPTHS

Greatest depth	*Location*	*metres*	*feet*
Mariana Trench*	Pacific	10,924	35,840
Puerto Rico Trench	Atlantic	8,605	28,232
South Sandwich Trench	Southern	7,235	23,737
Java (Sunda) Trench	Indian	7,125	23,376
Molloy Deep	Arctic	5,680	18,400

* A depth here of 11,034 metres/36,200 feet by the Soviet Vityaz is not internationally accepted.

SEAS

AREAS

	km²	miles²
South China	2,974,600	1,148,500
Caribbean	2,515,900	971,400
Mediterranean	2,509,900	969,100
Bering	2,261,000	873,000
Gulf of Mexico	1,507,600	582,100
Okhotsk	1,392,000	537,500
Japan	1,012,900	391,100
Hudson Bay	730,100	281,900
East China	664,600	256,600
Andaman	564,880	218,100
Black Sea	507,900	196,100
Red Sea	453,000	174,900
North Sea	427,100	164,900
Baltic Sea	382,000	147,500
Yellow Sea	294,000	113,500
Persian/Arabian Gulf	230,000	88,800

GREATEST DEPTHS OF SEAS LISTED ABOVE

	Maximum depth metres	feet
Caribbean	8,605	28,232
East China (Ryu Kyu Trench)	7,507	24,629
South China	7,258	23,812
Mediterranean (Ionian Basin)	5,150	16,896
Andaman	4,267	14,000
Bering	3,936	12,913
Gulf of Mexico	3,504	11,496
Okhotsk	3,365	11,040
Japan	3,053	10,016
Red Sea	2,266	7,434
Black Sea	2,212	7,257
North Sea	439	1,440
Hudson Bay	111	364
Baltic Sea	90	295
Persian Gulf	73	240
Yellow Sea	58	190

THE CONTINENTS

There are six geographic continents, although America is often divided politically into North and Central America, and South America, so making seven.

AFRICA is surrounded by sea except for the narrow isthmus of Suez in the north-east, through which was cut the Suez Canal (1869). Its extreme longitudes are 17° 20′

W. at Cape Verde, Senegal, and 51° 24′ E. at Raas Xaafunn, Somalia. The extreme latitudes are 37° 20′ N. at Cape Blanc, Tunisia, and 34° 50′ S. at Cape Agulhas, South Africa, about 4,400 miles apart. The Equator passes through the middle of the continent.

NORTH AMERICA, including Mexico, is surrounded by ocean except in the south, where the isthmian states of CENTRAL AMERICA link North America with South America. Its extreme longitudes are 168° 5′ W. at Cape Prince of Wales, Alaska, and 55° 40′ W. at Cape Charles, Newfoundland. The extreme continental latitudes are the tip of the Boothia peninsula, NW Territories, Canada (71° 51′ N.) and 14° 22′ N. in southern Mexico near La Victoria, Guatemala.

SOUTH AMERICA lies mostly in the southern hemisphere; the Equator passing through the north of the continent. It is surrounded by ocean except where it is joined to Central America in the north by the narrow isthmus through which was cut the Panama Canal (1914). Its extreme longitudes are 34° 47′ W. at Cape Branco in Brazil and 81° 20′ W. at Punta Pariña, Peru. The extreme continental latitudes are 12° 25′ N. at Punta Gallinas, Colombia, and 53° 54′ S. at the southernmost tip of Peninsula de Brunswick, Chile. Cape Horn, on Cape Island, Chile, lies in 55° 59′ S.

ANTARCTICA lies almost entirely within the Antarctic Circle (66° 33′ S.) and is the largest of the world's glaciated areas. Ninety-eight per cent of the continent is permanently ice-covered. The ice amounts to some 7.2 million cubic miles (30 million km^3) and represents more than 70 per cent of the world's fresh water. The environment is too hostile for unsupported human habitation.

ASIA is the largest continent and occupies 29.6 per cent of the world's land surface. The extreme longitudes are 26° 05′ E. at Baba Buran, Turkey and 169° 40′ W. at Mys Dezhneva (East Cape), Russia, a distance of about 6,000 miles. Its extreme northern latitude is 77° 45′ N. at Mys Chelyuskin, Russia, and it extends over 5,000 miles south to Tanjong Piai, Malaysia.

AUSTRALIA is the smallest of the continents and lies in the southern hemisphere. It is entirely surrounded by ocean. Its extreme longitudes are 113° 11′ E. at Steep Point and 153° 11′ E. at Cape Byron. The extreme latitudes are 10° 42′ S. at Cape York and 39° S. at South East Point, Tasmania. Australia, together with New Zealand (Australasia), Papua New Guinea and the Pacific Islands, comprises Oceania.

EUROPE, including European Russia, is the smallest continent in the northern hemisphere. Its extreme latitudes are 71° 11′ N. at Nord Kapp in Norway, and 36° 23′ N. at Ákra Tainaron (Matapás) in southern Greece, a distance of about 2,400 miles. Its breadth from Cabo Carvoeiro in Portugal (9° 34′ W.) in the west to the Kara River, north of the Urals (66° 30′ E.) in the east is about 3,300 miles. The division between Europe and Asia is generally regarded as the watershed of the Ural Mountains; down the Ural river to Guryev, Kazakhstan; across the Caspian Sea to Apsheronskiy Poluostrov, near Baku; along the watershed of the Caucasus Mountains to Anapa and thence across the Black Sea to the Bosporus in Turkey; across the Sea of Marmara to Çanakkale Bogazi (Dardanelles).

	Area km^2	miles^2
Asia	43,998,000	16,988,000
* America	41,918,000	16,185,000
Africa	29,800,000	11,506,000
Antarctica	13,209,000	5,100,000
†Europe	9,699,000	3,745,000
Australia	7,618,493	2,941,526

* North and Central America has an area of 24,255,000 km^2 (9,365,000 miles^2)

†Includes 5,571,000 km^2; (2,151,000 miles^2) of former USSR territory, including the Baltic states, Belarus, Moldova, Ukraine and the part of Russia west of the Ural Mountains and Kazakhstan west of the Ural river. European Turkey (24,378 km^2/9,412 miles^2) comprises territory to the west and north of the Bosporus and the Dardanelles

GLACIATED AREAS

It is estimated that 15,915,000 km^2 (6,145,000 miles^2) or 10.73 per cent of the world's land surface is permanently covered with ice. The largest glacier is the 515 km/320 mile-long Lambert-Fisher Ice Passage, Mac Robertson Land, Eastern Antarctica.

	Area km^2	miles^2
South Polar regions	13,830,000	5,340,000
North Polar regions (incl. Greenland or Kalaallit Nunaat)	1,965,000	758,500
Alaska-Canada	58,800	22,700
Asia	37,800	14,600
South America	11,900	4,600
Europe	10,700	4,128
New Zealand	1,015	391
Africa	238	92

PENINSULAS

	Area km^2	miles^2
Arabian	3,250,000	1,250,000
Southern Indian	2,072,000	800,000
Alaskan	1,500,000	580,000
Labradorian	1,300,000	500,000
Scandinavian	800,300	309,000
Iberian	584,000	225,500

LARGEST ISLANDS

Island and Ocean	*Area* km^2	miles^2
Greenland (Kalaallit Nunaat), Arctic	2,175,500	840,000
New Guinea, Pacific	792,500	306,000
Borneo, Pacific	725,450	280,100
Madagascar, Indian	587,041	226,674
Baffin Island, Arctic	507,451	195,928
Sumatra, Indian	427,350	165,000
Honshu, Pacific	227,413	87,805
* Great Britain, Atlantic	218,077	84,200
Victoria Island, Arctic	217,292	83,897
Ellesmere Island, Arctic	196,236	75,767
Sulawesi (Celebes), Indian	189,036	72,987
South Island, NZ, Pacific	151,213	58,384

Java (Jawa), Indian	126,650	48,900
North Island, NZ, Pacific	114,487	44,204
Cuba, Atlantic	110,862	42,804
Newfoundland, Atlantic	108,855	42,030
Luzon, Pacific	105,360	40,680
Iceland, Atlantic	102,820	39,700
Mindanao, Pacific	95,247	36,775
Ireland, Atlantic	82,462	31,839

* Mainland only

LARGEST DESERTS

	Area (approx) km²	miles²
The Sahara, N. Africa	9,000,000	3,500,000
The Gobi, Mongolia/China	1,300,000	500,000
Australian Desert (Great Sandy, Gibson, Simpson and Great Victoria)	1,120,000	460,000
Arabian Desert	1,000,000	385,000
Kalahari Desert, Botswana/Namibia/S. Africa	570,000	220,000
Taklimakan Shamo, Mongolia/China	320,000	125,000
* Kara Kum, Turkmenistan	310,000	120,000
Thar Desert, India/Pakistan	260,000	100,000
Somali Desert, Somalia	260,000	100,000
Atacama Desert, Chile	180,000	70,000
Sonoran Desert, USA/Mexico	180,000	70,000
Namib Namibia	135,000	52,000
Dasht-e Lut, Iran	52,000	20,000
Mojave Desert, USA	38,850	15,000

* Together with the Kyzyl Kum (100,000 miles²) known as the Turkestan Desert

Antarctica is described as a Polar Desert since precipitation is less than 5cm per annum.

DEEPEST DEPRESSIONS

	Maximum depth below sea level metres	feet
Dead Sea, Jordan/Israel	408	1,338
Lake Assal, Djibouti	156	511
Turfan Depression, Sinkiang, China	153	505
Qattara Depression, Egypt	132	436
Mangyshlak peninsula, Kazakhstan	131	433
Danakil Depression, Ethiopia	116	383
Death Valley, California, USA	86	282
Salton Sink, California, USA	71	235
W. of Ustyurt plateau, Kazakhstan	70	230
Prikaspiyskaya Nizmennost', Russia/Kazakhstan	67	220
Lake Sarykamysh, Uzbekistan/Turkmenistan	45	148
El Faiyûm, Egypt	44	147
Península Valdés, Chubut, Argentina	40	131
Lake Eyre, South Australia	16	52

The world's largest exposed depression is the Prikaspiyskaya Nizmennost' covering the hinterland of the northern third of the Caspian Sea, which is itself 28 m (92 ft) below sea level.

Western Antarctica and Central Greenland largely comprise crypto-depressions under ice burdens. The Antarctic Bentley subglacial trench has a bedrock 2,538 m (8,326 ft) below sea-level. In Greenland (lat. 73° N., long. 39° W.) the bedrock is 365 m (1,197 ft) below sea-level.

Nearly one quarter of the area of The Netherlands lies marginally below sea-level, an area of more than 10,000 km²/3,860 miles².

LONGEST MOUNTAIN RANGES

Range, and location	*Length* km	miles
Cordillera de Los Andes, W. South America	7,200	4,500
Rocky Mountains, W. North America	4,800	3,000
Himalaya-Karakoram-Hindu Kush, S. Central Asia	3,850	2,400
Great Dividing Range, E. Australia	3,620	2,250
Trans-Antarctic Mts, Antarctica	3,540	2,200
Atlantic Coast Range, E. Brazil	3,050	1,900
West Sumatran-Javan Range, Indonesia	2,900	1,800
Aleutian Range, Alaska and NW Pacific	2,650	1,650
Tien Shan, S. Central Asia	2,250	1,400
Central New Guinea Range, Irian Jaya/Papua New Guinea	2,010	1,250

HIGHEST MOUNTAINS

The world's twelve 8,000-metre (26,246 ft) mountains *(with five subsidiary peaks)* are all in the Himalaya-Karakoram-Hindu Kush ranges.

Mountain	*Height* metres	feet
Mt Everest* (Qomolangma)	8,850	29,035
K2 (Qogir)†	8,611	28,251
Kangchenjunga	8,597	28,208
Lhotse I	*8,510*	*27,923*
Makalu I	8,480	27,824
Lhotse Shar (II)	*8,400*	*27,560*
Dhaulagiri I	8,171	26,810
Manaslu I (Kutang I)	8,156	26,760
Cho Oyu	8,153	26,750
Nanga Parbat (Diamir)	8,125	26,660
Annapurna I	8,078	26,504
Gasherbrum I (Hidden Peak)	8,068	26,470
Broad Peak I	8,046	26,400
Shisham Pangma (Gosainthan)	8,012	26,287
Gasherbrum II	*8,034*	*26,360*
Makalu South-East	*8,010*	*26,280*
Broad Peak Central	*8,000*	*26,246*

* Named after Sir George Everest (1790–1866), Surveyor-General of India 1830–43, in 1863. He pronounced his name Eve-rest

† Formerly named after Col. H. H. Godwin-Austen (1834–1923)

The culminating summits in the other major mountain ranges are:

Mountain, by range or country	*Height* metres	feet
Pik Pobedy, Tien Shan	7,439	24,406
Cerro Aconcagua, Cordillera de Los Andes	6,960	22,834
Mt McKinley (*S. Peak*), Alaska Range	6,194	20,320
Kilimanjaro (Kibo), Tanzania	5,894	19,340
Hkakabo Razi, Myanmar	5,881	19,296
El'brus, (*W. Peak*), Caucasus	5,642	18,510
Citlaltépetl (Orizaba), Sierra Madre Oriental, Mexico	5,655	18,555
Vinson Massif, E. Antarctica	4,897	16,066
Puncak Jaya, Central New Guinea Range	4,884	16,023
Mt Blanc, Alps	4,807	15,771
Klyuchevskaya Sopka, Kamchatka peninsula, Russia	4,750	15,584
Ras Dashan, Ethiopian Highlands	4,620	15,158
Zard Kuh, Zagros Mts, Iran	4,547	14,921
Mt Kirkpatrick, Trans Antarctic	4,527	14,855
Mt Belukha, Altai Mts, Russia/ Kazakhstan	4,505	14,783
Mt Elbert, Rocky Mountains	4,400	14,433
Mt Rainier, Cascade Range, N. America	4,392	14,410
Nevado de Colima, Sierra Madre Occidental, Mexico	4,268	14,003
Jebel Toubkal, Atlas Mts, N. Africa	4,165	13,665
Kinabalu, Crocker Range, Borneo	4,101	13,455
Kerinci, West Sumatran-Javan Range, Indonesia	3,800	12,467
Jabal an Nabi Shu'ayb, N. Tihamat, Yemen	3,760	12,336
Mt Cook (Aorangi), Southern Alps, New Zealand	3,754	12,315
Teotepec, Sierra Madre del Sur, Mexico	3,703	12,149
Thaban Ntlenyana, Drakensberg, South Africa	3,482	11,425
Pico de Bandeira, Atlantic Coast Range	2,890	9,482
Shishaldin, Aleutian Range	2,861	9,387
Kosciusko, Great Dividing Range, Australia	2,228	7,310

HIGHEST ACTIVE VOLCANOES

Volcano and location	*Height* metres	feet
Ojos del Salado, Andes, Argentina/Chile	6,880	22,572
Volcán Llullaillaco, Andes, Argentina/Chile	6,723	22,057
Volcán Guallatiri, Andes, Chile	6,069	19,882
Cotopaxi, Andes, Ecuador	5,897	19,347
Tupungatito, Andes, Chile	5,640	18,504
Láscar, Andes, Chile	5,591	18,346
Popocatépetl, Mexico	5,465	17,930
Nevado del Ruiz, Colombia	5,321	17,457
Sangay, Andes, Ecuador	5,188	17,021
Irruputuncu, Chile	5,163	16,939
Klyuchevskaya Sopka, Kamchatka peninsula, Russia	4,835	15,863
Guagua Pichincha, Andes, Ecuador	4,784	15,696
Puracé, Colombia	4,756	15,601
Wrangell, Alaska, USA	4,316	14,163
Shasta, California, USA	4,316	14,163
Galeras, Colombia	4,275	14,028
Mauna Loa, Hawaii Is.	4,170	13,680
Cameroon, Cameroon	4,095	13,435

OTHER NOTABLE VOLCANOES

	Height metres	feet
Erebus, Ross Island, Antarctica	3,794	12,448
Fuji, Honshu, Japan	3,775	12,388
Santa Maria, Guatemala	3,772	12,375
Semeru, Java, Indonesia	3,675	12,060
Nyiragongo, Dem Rep. of Congo	3,474	11,400
Mt Etna, Sicily, Italy	3,368	11,053
Raung, Java, Indonesia	3,322	10,932
Sheveluch, Kamchatka, Russia	3,283	10,771
Llaima, Chile	3,125	10,253
Mt St Helens, Washington State, USA	2,549	8,363
Beerenberg, Jan Mayen Island	2,277	7,470
Pinatubo, Luzon, Philippines	1,598	5,249
Hekla, Iceland	1,491	4,892
Mt Unzen, Kyushu, Japan	1,360	4,462
Vesuvius, Italy	1,281	4,203
Kilauea, Hawaii, USA	1,249	4,009
Soufrière, St Vincent	1,178	3,865
Soufrière Hills, Montserrat	914	3,001
Stromboli, Lipari Is., Italy	926	3,038
Krakatau, Sunda Strait, Indonesia	813	2,667
Santoríni (Thíra), Aegean Sea, Greece	564	1,850
Tristan da Cunha, South Atlantic	243	800
Surtsey, off Iceland	173	568

LARGEST LAKES

The areas of some of the lakes listed are subject to seasonal variation.

	Area km²	miles²	*Length* km	miles
Caspian Sea, Iran/ Azerbaijan/Russia/ Turkmenistan/ Kazakhstan	371,000	143,000	1,171	728
* Michigan–Huron, USA/ Canada	117,610	45,300	1,010	627
Superior, Canada/USA	82,100	31,700	563	350
Victoria, Uganda/ Tanzania/Kenya	69,500	26,828	362	225
Tanganyika, Dem. Rep. of Congo/ Tanzania/Zambia/ Burundi	32,900	12,665	725	450
Great Bear, Canada	31,328	12,096	309	192
‡Aral Sea,Kazakhstan/ Uzbekistan	30,700	11,850	320	200
†Baykal (*Baikal*), Russia	30,500	11,776	620	385
Malawi (Nyasa),Tanzania/ Malawi/Mozambique	28,900	11,150	580	360
Great Slave, Canada	28,570	11,031	480	298
Erie, Canada/USA	25,670	9,910	388	241
Winnipeg, Canada	24,390	9,417	428	266

Ontario, Canada/USA	19,010	7,340	310	193
Balkhash, Kazakhstan	18,427	7,115	605	376
Ladozhskoye (*Ladoga*), Russia	17,700	6,835	193	120

* Lakes Michigan and Huron may be regarded as lobes of the same lake. The Michigan lobe has an area of $57,750^2$ (22,300 miles^2) and the Huron lobe an area of 59,570 km^2 (23,000 miles^2)

†World's deepest lake (1,940 m/6,365 ft)

‡Northern part (Little Aral Sea) dammed off in 1997

The most voluminous lakes are the Caspian Sea (saline) with 78,700 km^3 (18,880 miles^3) and Baikal (fresh water) with 23,000 km^3 (5,518 miles^3).

UNITED KINGDOM, BY COUNTRY

Lough Neagh, Northern Ireland	381.73	147.39	28.90	18.00
Loch Lomond, Scotland	71.12	27.46	36.44	22.64
Windermere, England	14.74	5.69	16.90	10.50
Lake Vyrnwy, Wales (artificial)	4.53	1.75	7.56	4.70
Llyn Tegid *(Bala)*, Wales (natural)	4.38	1.69	5.80	3.65

LONGEST RIVERS

River, source and outflow	*Length* km	miles
Nile *(Bahr-el-Nil)*, R. Luvironza, Burundi–E. Mediterranean Sea	6,725	4,180
Amazon *(Amazonas)*, Lago Villafro, Peru–S. Atlantic Ocean	6,448	4,007
Yangtze-Kiang (*Chang Jiang*), Kunlun Mts, W. China–Yellow Sea	6,380	3,964
Mississippi-Missouri-Red Rock, Montana–Gulf of Mexico	5,970	3,710
Yenisey-Angara, W. Mongolia–Kara Sea	5,536	3,440
Huang He *(Yellow River)*, Bayan Har Shan range, Central China–Yellow Sea	5,463	3,395
Ob'-Irtysh, W. Mongolia–Kara Sea	5,410	3,362
Zaïre *(Congo)*, R. Lualaba, Dem. Rep. of Congo-Zambia–S. Atlantic Ocean	4,665	2,900
Amur-Argun, R. Argun, Khingan Mts, N. China–Sea of Okhotsk	4,416	2,744
Lena-Kirenga, R. Kirenga, W. of Lake Baykal–Laptev Sea, Arctic Ocean	4,400	2,734
Mekong, Lants'ang, Tibet–South China Sea	4,345	2,700
Mackenzie-Peace, Tatlatui Lake, British Columbia–Beaufort Sea	4,240	2,635
Paraná-Río de la Plata, R. Paranáiba, central Brazil–S. Atlantic Ocean	4,240	2,635
Niger, Loma Mts, Guinea–Gulf of Guinea, E. Atlantic Ocean	4,170	2,590
Murray-Darling, SE Queensland–Lake Alexandrina, S. Australia	3,717	2,310
Volga, Valdai plateau–Caspian Sea	3,685	2,290

OTHER NOTABLE RIVERS

Río Grande, USA–Mexican border	3,057	1,900
Ganges-Brahmaputra, R. Matsang, SW Tibet–Bay of Bengal	2,900	1,800
Indus, R. Sengge, SW Tibet–N. Arabian Sea	2,897	1,799
Danube *(Donau)*, Black Forest, SW Germany–Black Sea	2,856	1,775
Tigris-Euphrates, R. Murat, E. Turkey–Persian Gulf	2,800	1,740
Zambezi, NW Zambia–S. Indian Ocean	2,735	1,700
Irrawaddy, R. Mali Hka, Myanmar–Andaman Sea	2,151	1,337
Don, SE of Novomoskovsk–Sea of Azov	1,969	1,224

BRITISH ISLES

Shannon, Co. Cavan, Rep. of Ireland–Atlantic Ocean	386	240
Severn, Powys, Wales–Bristol Channel	354	220
Thames, Gloucestershire, England–North Sea	346	215
Tay, Perthshire, Scotland–North Sea	188	117
Clyde, Lanarkshire, Scotland–Firth of Clyde	158	98.5
Tweed, Peeblesshire, Scotland–North Sea	155	96.5
Bann (Upper and Lower), Co. Down, N. Ireland–Atlantic Ocean	122	76

GREATEST WATERFALLS – BY HEIGHT

Waterfall, river and location	*Total drop* metres	feet	*Greatest single leap* metres	feet
Saltó Angel, Carrao Auyán Tepuí, Venezuela	979	3,212	807	2,648
Tugela, Tugela, Natal, S. Africa (5 leaps)	948	3,110	410	1,350
Utigård, Jostedal Glacier, Norway	800	2,625	600	1,970
Mongefossen, Monge, Norway	774	2,540	—	—
Yosemite, Yosemite Creek, USA	739	2,425	435	1,430
*Østre Mardøla Foss, Mardals, Norway	655	2,149	296	974
*Tyssestrengene, Tysso, Norway	646	2,120	289	948
Cuquenán, Arabopó, Venezuela	610	2,000	—	—
Sutherland, Arthur, NZ	580	1,904	248	815

* Volume much affected by hydroelectric harnessing

BRITISH ISLES, BY COUNTRY

Waterfall, river and location	*Total drop* metres	feet	
Eas a' Chuàl Aluinn, Glas Bheinn, Sutherland, Scotland	200	658	
Powerscourt Falls, Dargle, Co. Wicklow, Rep. of Ireland	106	350	
Pistyll-y-Llyn, Powys/ Dyfed border, Wales	*c.*72	*c.*235	(cascades)
Pistyll Rhyadr, Clwyd/ Powys border, Wales	71.5	235	(single leap)
Caldron Snout, R. Tees, Cumbria/ Durham, England	61	200	(cascades)

GREATEST WATERFALLS – BY VOLUME

Waterfall, river and location	*Mean annual flow* m^3/sec	galls/sec
Inga (Congo dam site), Livingstone Falls, Dem. Rep. of Congo	43,000	9,460,000
Khône, Mekong, Laos	41,000	9,000,000
Boyoma (Stanley), R. Lualaba, Dem. Rep. of Congo	*c.*17,000	*c.*3,750,000
Guaíra (Sete Quedas), Pavaná, Brazil (submerged by Itaipu hydroelectric dams, 1982)	13,000	2,860,000
Niagara (Horseshoe), R. Niagara/ Lake Erie–Lake Ontario	6,000	1,320,000
Paulo Afonso, R. São Francisco, Brazil	2,830	622,500
Urubupunga, Alto Parañá, Brazil	2,745	604,000
Cataratas del Iguazú, R. Iguaçu, Brazil/Argentina	1,750	380,000
Patos-Maribando, Rio Grande, Brazil	1,500	330,000
Churchill, R. Churchill, Canada	1,132	249,000
Victoria *(Mosi-oa-tunya)*, R. Zambezi, Zambia/ Zimbabwe	1,000	222,000

TALLEST DAMS

	metres	feet
*Rogun, R. Vakhsh, Tajikistan	335	1,098
Nurek, R. Vakhsh, Tajikistan	300	984
Grande Dixence, Switzerland	285	935
*Longtan, R. Hangshui, China	285	935
Inguri, Georgia	272	892
Borucu, Costa Rica	267	876
Vaiont, Italy	262	859
Manuel M. Torres, Chicoasén, Mexico	261	856
Tehri, R. Bhagivathi, India	261	856

*Construction ceased

The world's most massive dam is the Syncrude Tailings dam in Alberta, Canada, which will have a volume of 540 million cubic metres/706 million cubic yards. The Three Gorges Chang Jiang (Yangtze) Dam, China, with a crest length of 1,983 m/6,505 ft, is due for completion in 2009 (stage 3).

The Yacyretá-Apipe dam across the River Paraná, Argentina-Paraguay, is being completed to a length of 69,600 m/43.24 miles

TALLEST INHABITED BUILDINGS

Building and city	*Height* metres	feet
Taipei 101, Taipei, Taiwan (2003) (101 storeys)	509	1,671
Petronas Towers I and II, Kuala Lumpur, Malaysia (1998) (88 storeys)	451.9	1,482
Sears Tower, Chicago (1974), (110 storeys)	443	1,454
Jin Mao, Shanghai, China (1998) (86 storeys)	420	1,378
International Finance Centre, Hong Kong (2003)	412	1,352
CITIC Plaza, Guangzhou, China (1996)	391	1,283
Shun Hing Square, Shenzhen, China (1996)	384	1,260
Empire State Building, New York[2] (1931)	381	1,250
Central Plaza, Hong Kong (1992)	373	1,227
Bank of China Tower, Hong Kong (1989)	368	1,209
Emirates Tower One, Dubai (2000)	355	1,165
The Centre, Hong Kong (1998)	350	1,148
Tuntex & Chein-Tai Tower, Taiwan (1998)	347	1,140
Aon Centre, Chicago (1973)	346	1,136
Kingdom Centre, Riadh, Saudi Arabia (2001)	345	1,132
John Hancock Centre, Chicago (1969)	343	1,127
Baurj al Arab Hotel, Dubai (1999)	321	1,053
Chrysler Building, New York (1930)	318	1,046

1. With TV antennae, 520 m/1,707 ft
2. With TV tower (added 1950–1), 430.9 m/1,414 ft

Note: The Two World Trade Centre towers, One/North (1972) 110 storeys, 415 m 1,368 ft or 521m 1,716 ft with TV antennae; and Two/South (1973) 110 storeys, 415m 1,362 ft, were destroyed by two terrorist hijacked aircraft on 11 September 2001.

TALLEST STRUCTURES

Structure and location	*Height* metres	feet
*Warszawa Radio Mast, Konstantynow, Poland (1974)	646	2,120
KVLY (formerly KTHI)-TV Mast, Blanchard, North Dakota (guyed) (1963)	629	2,063
Indosat Telkom Tower, Jakarta, Indonesia	558	1,831
CN Tower, Metro Centre, Toronto, Canada (1975)	555	1,822
Ostankino Tower, Moscow (1967)	540	1,772

*Collapsed during renovation, August 1991. New structure planned on site at Solkajawski. The USA has 8 other guyed TV towers above 555m (1,822 ft).

LONGEST BRIDGES – BY SPAN

Bridge and location	*Length* metres	feet
SUSPENSION SPANS		
Akashi-Kaikyo, Shikoku, Japan (1998)	1,990	6,529
Storebaelt East Bridge, Denmark (1998)	1,624	5,328
Humber Estuary, Humberside, England (1981)	1,410	4,626
Jiangyin (Yangtze), China (1999)	1,385	4,544
Tsing Ma, Hong Kong, China (1997)	1,377	4,518
Verrazano Narrows, Brooklyn–Staten I, USA (1964)	1,298	4,260
Golden Gate, San Francisco Bay, USA (1937)	1,280	4,200
Höga Kusten, Sweden (1997)	1,210	3,970
Chesapeake Bay No.2, Virginia, USA (1999)	1,158	3,800
Mackinac Straits, Michigan, USA (1957)	1,158	3,800
Minami Bisan-Seto, Japan (1988)	1,100	3,609
Bosporus II Fatih Sultan Mehmet, Istanbul, Turkey (1992)	1,090	3,576
Bosporus I, Istanbul, Turkey (1973)	1,074	3,524
George Washington, Hudson River, New York City, USA (1931)	1,067	3,500
Kurushima III, Japan (1999)	1,030	3,379
Kurushima II, Japan (1999)	1,020	3,346
Ponte 25 de Abril (Tagus), Lisbon, Portugal (1966) (road and rail)	1,013	3,323
Firth of Forth (road), nr Edinburgh, Scotland (1964)	1,006	3,300
Kita Bisan-Seto, Japan (1988)	990	3,248
*Severn River, Severn Estuary, England (1966)	988	3,240

*The main span of the 5.15 km/3.2 mile long Second Severn bridging, opened in 1996, is 456 m/1,496 ft.

CANTILEVER SPANS		
Pont de Québec (rail-road), St Lawrence, Canada (1917)	548.6	1,800
Ravenswood, W. Virginia, USA	525.1	1,723
Firth of Forth (rail), nr Edinburgh, Scotland (two spans of 1,710 ft each) (1890)	521.2	1,710
Minato (Nanko), Osaka, Japan (1974)	510.0	1,673
Commodore Barry, Chester, Pennsylvania, USA (1975)	494.3	1,622
Greater New Orleans, Louisiana, USA (I 1958, II 1988)	480.0	1,575
Howrah (rail-road), Calcutta, India (1936–43)	457.2	1,500
STEEL ARCH SPANS		
Lupu, Shanghai, China (2003)	550.0	1,804
New River Gorge, Fayetteville, W. Virginia, USA (1977)	518.0	1,700
Bayonne (Kill van Kull), Bayonne, NJ–Staten I., USA (1931)	510.5	1,675
Sydney Harbour, Sydney, Australia (1932)	502.9	1,650

The 'floating' bridging at Evergreen Point, Seattle, Washington State, USA (1963), is 3,839 m/12,596 ft long, of which 2,310 m/7,578 ft floats.

The longest stretch of bridgings of any kind is that carrying the Interstate 55 and Interstate 10 highways at Manchac, Louisiana (1979), on twin concrete trestles over 55.21 km/34.31 miles.

LONGEST VEHICULAR TUNNELS

Tunnel and location	*Length* km	miles
*Seikan (rail), Tsugaru Channel, Japan (1988)	53.85	33.46
*Channel Tunnel, (rail) Cheriton, Kent–Sangatte, Calais (1994)	50.45	31.35
Moscow metro, Belyaevo–Bittsevsky, Moscow, Russia (1979)	37.90	23.50
Northern Line tube, East Finchley–Morden, London (1939)	27.84	17.30
Iwate (rail), Japan (2002)	25.81	16.03
Laerdal–Aurland Road Link (2000)	24.51	15.22
*Oshimizu (rail), Honshu, Japan (1982)	22.17	13.78
Simplon II (rail), Brigue, Switzerland–Iselle, Italy (1922)	19.82	12.31
Simplon I (rail), Brigue, Switzerland–Iselle, Italy (1906)	19.80	12.30
Vereina, Switzerland (1999)	19.06	11.84
*Shin-Kanmon (rail), Kanmon Strait, Japan (1975)	18.68	11.61
Appennino (rail), Vernio, Italy (1934)	18.50	11.50
St Gotthard (road), Göschenen–Airolo, Switzerland (1980, re-opened 2001)	16.91	10.51

*Sub-aqueous

The longest non-vehicular tunnelling in the world is the Delaware Aqueduct in New York, constructed in 1937–44 to a length of 168.9 km/105 miles.

The St. Gotthard (rail) tunnel (2010) will be 57.07 km/35.46 miles.

BRITISH RAIL TUNNELS

	miles	yards
Severn, Bristol–Newport (1873–86)	4	484
Totley, Manchester–Sheffield	3	950
Standedge, Manchester–Huddersfield	3	66
Sodbury, Swindon–Bristol	2	924
Strood, Medway, Kent	2	426
Disley, Stockport–Sheffield	2	346
Ffestiniog, Llandudno–Blaenau Ffestiniog	2	338
Bramhope, Leeds–Harrogate	2	241
Cowburn, Manchester–Sheffield	2	182

The longest road tunnel in Britain is the Mersey Queensway Tunnel (1934) 3.42 km/2 miles 228 yards long. The longest canal tunnel, at Standedge, W. Yorks, is 5.12 km/3 miles 417 yards long. It was opened in 1811, closed in 1944 and reopened in 2001.

LONGEST SHIP CANALS

Canal (opening date)	*Length* km	miles	*Min. depth* metres	feet
White Sea-Baltic (formerly Stalin) (1933), of which Canalised river 51.5 km/32 miles	235	146.02	5.0	16.5
* Suez (1869) Links Red and Mediterranean Seas	162	100.60	12.9	42.3
V. I. Lenin Volga-Don (1952) Links Black and Caspian Seas	100	62.20	n/a	n/a
Kiel (or North Sea) (1895) Links North and Baltic Seas	98	60.90	13.7	45.0
* Houston (1940) Links inland city with sea	91	56.70	10.4	34.0
Alphonse XIII (1926) Gives Seville access to sea	85	53.00	7.6	25.0
Panama (1914) Links Pacific Ocean and Caribbean Sea; lake chain, 78.9 km/49 miles dug	82	50.71	12.5	41.0
Manchester Ship (1894) Links city with Irish Channel	64	39.70	8.5	28.0
Welland (1932) Circumvents Niagara Falls and Rapids	43.5	27.00	8.8	29.0
Brussels (Rupel Sea) (1922) Renders Brussels an inland port	32	19.80	6.4	21.0

* Has no locks

The first section of China's Grand Canal, running 1,782 km/1,107 miles from Beijing to Hangzhou, was opened AD 610 and completed in 1283. Today it is limited to 2,000 tonne vessels.

The St Lawrence Seaway comprises the Beauharnois, Welland and Welland Bypass and Seaway 54–59 canals, and allows access to Duluth, Minnesota, USA via the Great Lakes from the Atlantic end of Canada's Gulf of St Lawrence, a distance of 3,769 km/2,342 miles. The St Lawrence Canal, completed in 1959, is 293 km/182 miles long.

DISTANCES FROM LONDON BY AIR

This list details the distances in miles from London, Heathrow, to various cities (airports) abroad.

To	*Miles*
Abidjan	3,197
Abu Dhabi (International)	3,425
Addis Ababa	3,675
Adelaide (International)	10,111
Aden	3,670
Algiers	1,035
'Amman (Queen Alia)	2,287
Amsterdam (Schiphol)	230
Ankara (Esenboga)	1,770
Athens	1,500
Atlanta	4,198
Auckland	11,404
Baghdad (International)	2,551
Bahrain	3,163
Baku	2,485
Bangkok	5,928
Barbados (Grantley Adams)	4,193
Barcelona (Muntadas)	712
Basel-Mulhouse	447
Beijing (Capital)	5,063
Beirut	2,161
Belfast (Aldergrove)	325
Belgrade	1,056
Berlin (Tegel)	588
Bermuda	3,428
Bern	476
Bogotá	5,262
Bombay (Mumbai)	4,478
Boston	3,255
Brasília	5,452
Bratislava	817
Brisbane (Eagle Farm)	10,273
Brussels	217
Bucharest (Otopeni)	1,307
Budapest (Ferihegy)	923
Buenos Aires	6,915
Cairo (International)	2,194
Calcutta	4,958
Calgary	4,357
Canberra	10,563
Cape Town	6,011
Caracas	4,639
Casablanca (Mohamed V)	1,300
Chicago (O'Hare)	3,941
Cologne	331
Colombo (Katunayake)	5,411
Copenhagen	608
Dakar	2,706
Dallas (Fort Worth)	4,736
Dallas (Lovefield)	4,732
Damascus (International)	2,223
Dar-es-Salaam	4,662
Darwin	8,613
Delhi	4,180
Denver	4,655
Detroit (Metropolitan)	3,754
Dhahran	3,143
Dhaka	4,976
Doha	3,253
Dubai	3,414
Dublin	279
Durban	5,937
Düsseldorf	310
Entebbe	4,033
Frankfurt (Main)	406
Freetown	3,046
Geneva	468
Gibraltar	1,084
Gothenburg (Landvetter)	664
Hamburg (Fuhlsbüttel)	463
Harare	5,156
Havana	4,647
Helsinki (Vantaa)	1,148
Hobart	10,826
Ho Chi Minh City	6,345
Hong Kong	5,990
Honolulu	7,220
Houston (Intercontinental)	4,821
Houston (William P. Hobby)	4,837
Islamabad	3,767
Istanbul (Atatürk)	1,560
Jakarta (Halim Perdanakusuma)	7,295
Jeddah	2,947
Johannesburg	5,634
Kabul	3,558
Karachi	3,935
Kathmandu	4,570
Khartoum	3,071
Kiev (Borispol)	1,357
Kiev (Julyany)	1,337
Kingston, Jamaica	4,668
Kuala Lumpur (Subang)	6,557
Kuwait	2,903
Lagos	3,107
Larnaca	2,036
Lima (Callao)	6,303
Lisbon	972
Lomé	3,129
Los Angeles (International)	5,439
Madras	5,113
Madrid (Barajas)	773
Malta	1,305
Manila (Ninoy Aquino)	6,685
Marseille (Provence)	614
Mauritius	6,075
Melbourne (Essendon)	10,504
Melbourne (Tullamarine)	10,499
Mexico City	5,529
Miami	4,414
Milan (Linate)	609
Minsk	1,176
Montego Bay	4,687
Montevideo	6,841
Montreal (Dorval)	3,241
Moscow (Sheremetyevo)	1,557
Munich (Franz Josef Strauss)	584
Muscat	3,621
Nairobi (Jomo Kenyatta)	4,248
Naples	1,011
Nassau	4,333
New York (J. F. Kennedy)	3,440
Nice (Côte d'Azur)	645
Oporto	806
Oslo (Gardermoen)	722
Ottawa	3,321
Palma, Majorca (Son San Juan)	836
Paris (Charles de Gaulle)	215
Paris (Le Bourget)	215
Paris (Orly)	227
Perth, Australia	9,008
Port of Spain	4,404
Prague (Ruzine)	649
Pretoria	5,602
Reykjavík (Domestic)	1,167
Reykjavík (Keflavík)	1,177
Rhodes	1,743
Rio de Janeiro (Galeão)	5,745
Riyadh (King Khaled) International	3,067
Rome (Leonardo da Vinci)	895
St John's, Newfoundland	2,308
St Petersburg	1,314
Salzburg (Mozart)	651
San Francisco	5,351
São Paulo (Guarulhos)	5,892
Sarajevo	1,017
Seoul (Kimpo)	5,507
Shanghai	5,725
Shannon	369
Singapore (Changi)	6,756
Sofia	1,266
Stockholm (Arlanda)	908
Suva	10,119
Sydney (Kingsford Smith)	10,568
Tangier	1,120
Tehran	2,741
Tel Aviv	2,227
Tokyo (Narita)	5,956
Toronto	3,544
Tripoli (International)	1,468
Tunis	1,137
Turin (Caselle)	570
Ulaanbaatar	4,340
Valencia	826
Vancouver	4,707
Venice (Marco Polo)	715
Vienna (Schwechat)	790
Vladivostok	5,298
Warsaw	912
Washington (Dulles)	3,665
Wellington	11,692
Yangon/Rangoon	5,582
Yokohama (Aomori)	5,647
Zagreb	848
Zürich	490

TIME ZONES

Standard time differences from the Greenwich meridian

- \+ hours ahead of GMT
- – hours behind GMT
- * may vary from standard time at some part of the year (Summer Time or Daylight Saving Time)
- ‡ some areas may keep another time zone
- *h* hours
- *m* minutes

	h	*m*
Afghanistan	+ 4	30
*Albania	+ 1	
Algeria	+ 1	
*Andorra	+ 1	
Angola	+ 1	
Anguilla	– 4	
Antigua and Barbuda	– 4	
Argentina	– 3	
*Armenia	+ 4	
Aruba	– 4	
Ascension Island	0	
*Australia		
ACT, NSW (except Broken Hill area) Qld, Tas., Vic, Whitsunday Islands	+10	
*Broken Hill area (NSW)	+ 9	30
*Lord Howe Island	+10	30
Northern Territory	+ 9	30
*South Australia	+ 9	30
Western Australia	+ 8	
*Austria	+ 1	
*Azerbaijan	+ 4	
*Bahamas	– 5	
Bahrain	+ 3	
Bangladesh	+ 6	
Barbados	– 4	
*Belarus	+ 2	
*Belgium	+ 1	
Belize	– 6	
Benin	+ 1	
*Bermuda	– 4	
Bhutan	+ 6	
Bolivia	– 4	
*Bosnia-Hercegovina	+ 1	
Botswana	+ 2	
Brazil		
western states	– 5	
central states	– 4	
N. and NE coastal states	– 3	
*S. and E. coastal states, including Brasilia	– 3	
Fernando de Noronha Island	– 2	
British Antarctic Territory	– 3	
British Indian Ocean Territory	+ 5	
Diego Garcia	+ 6	
British Virgin Islands	– 4	
Brunei	+ 8	
*Bulgaria	+ 2	
Burkina Faso	0	
Burundi	+ 2	
Cambodia	+ 7	
Cameroon	+ 1	
Canada		
*Alberta	– 7	
*‡British Columbia	– 8	
*‡Labrador	– 4	
*Manitoba	– 6	
*New Brunswick	– 4	
*Newfoundland	– 3	30
*Northwest Territories		
east of 85° W.	– 5	
85° W. – 102° W.	– 6	
*Nunavut	– 7	
*Nova Scotia	– 4	
Ontario		
*east of 90° W.	– 5	
west of 90° W.	– 5	
*Prince Edward Island	– 4	
Québec		
east of 63° W.	– 4	
*west of 63° W.	– 5	
‡Saskatchewan	– 6	
*Yukon	– 8	
Cape Verde	– 1	
Cayman Islands	– 5	
Central African Republic	+ 1	
Chad	+ 1	
*Chatham Islands	+12	45
*Chile	– 4	
China (inc. Hong Kong and Macao)	+ 8	
Christmas Island (Indian Ocean)	+ 7	
Cocos (Keeling) Islands	+ 6	30
Colombia	– 5	
Comoros	+ 3	
Congo (Dem. Rep.)		
Haut-Zaïre, Kasai, Kivu, Shaba	+ 2	
Kinshasa, Mbandaka	+ 1	
Congo-Brazzaville	+ 1	
Costa Rica	– 6	
Côte d'Ivoire	0	
*Croatia	+ 1	
*Cuba	– 5	
*Cyprus	+ 2	
*Czech Republic	+ 1	
*Denmark	+ 1	
*Færøe Islands	0	
*Greenland	– 3	
Danmarkshavn, Mesters Vig	0	
*Scoresby Sound	– 1	
*Thule area	– 4	
Djibouti	+ 3	
Dominica	– 4	
Dominican Republic	– 5	
East Timor	+ 9	
Ecuador	– 5	
Galápagos Islands	– 6	
*Egypt	+ 2	
El Salvador	– 6	
Equatorial Guinea	+ 1	
Eritrea	+ 3	
Estonia	+ 2	
Ethiopia	+ 3	
*Falkland Islands	– 4	
Fiji	+12	
*Finland	+ 2	
*France	+ 1	
French Guiana	– 3	
French Polynesia	–10	
Guadeloupe	– 4	
Martinique	– 4	
Réunion	+ 4	
Marquesas Islands	– 9	30
Gabon	+ 1	
Gambia	0	
*Georgia	+ 3	
*Germany	+ 1	
Ghana	0	
*Gibraltar	+ 1	
*Greece	+ 2	
Grenada	– 4	
Guam	+10	
Guatemala	– 6	
Guinea	0	
Guinea-Bissau	0	
Guyana	– 4	
Haîti	– 5	
Honduras	– 6	
*Hungary	+ 1	
Iceland	0	
India	+ 5	30
Indonesia		
Java, Kalimantan (west and central), Madura, Sumatra	+ 7	
Bali, Flores, Kalimantan (south and east), Lombok, Sulawesi, Sumbawa, West Timor	+ 8	
Irian Jaya, Maluku,	+ 9	
*Iran	+ 3	30
*Iraq	+ 3	
*Ireland, Republic of	0	
*Israel	+ 2	
*Italy	+ 1	
Jamaica	– 5	
Japan	+ 9	
*Jordan	+ 2	
*Kazakhstan		
western	+ 4	
central	+ 5	
eastern	+ 6	
Kenya	+ 3	
Kiribati	+12	
Line Islands	+14	
Phoenix Islands	+13	

	h	*m*
Korea, North	+ 9	
Korea, South	+ 9	
Kuwait	+ 3	
*Kyrgyzstan	+ 5	
Laos	+ 7	
Latvia	+ 2	
*Lebanon	+ 2	
Lesotho	+ 2	
Liberia	0	
Libya	+ 2	
*Liechtenstein	+ 1	
Line Islands not part of Kiribati	−10	
Lithuania	+ 2	
*Luxembourg	+ 1	
*Macedonia	+ 1	
Madagascar	+ 3	
Malawi	+ 2	
Malaysia	+ 8	
Maldives	+ 5	
Mali	0	
*Malta	+ 1	
Marshall Islands	+12	
Ebon Atoll	−12	
Mauritania	0	
Mauritius	+ 4	
*Mexico	− 6	
*Nayarit, Sinaloa, S. Baja California	− 7	
Sonora	− 7	
N. Baja California	− 8	
Micronesia		
Caroline Islands	+10	
Kosrae, Pingelap, Pohnpei	+11	
*Moldova	+ 2	
*Monaco	+ 1	
Mongolia	+ 8	
Montserrat	− 4	
Morocco	0	
Mozambique	+ 2	
Myanmar	+ 6	30
*Namibia	+ 1	
Nauru	+12	
Nepal	+ 5	45
*Netherlands	+ 1	
Netherlands Antilles	− 4	
New Caledonia	+11	
*New Zealand	+12	
*Cook Islands	−10	
Nicaragua	− 6	
Niger	+ 1	
Nigeria	+ 1	
Niue	−11	
Norfolk Island	+11	30
Northern Mariana Islands	+10	
*Norway	+ 1	
Oman	+ 4	
Pakistan	+ 5	
Palau	+ 9	
Panama	− 5	
Papua New Guinea	+10	
*Paraguay	− 4	
Peru	− 5	
Philippines	+ 8	
*Poland	+ 1	
*Portugal	0	
*Azores	− 1	
*Madeira	0	
Puerto Rico	− 4	
Qatar	+ 3	
Réunion	+ 4	
*Romania	+ 2	
*Russia		
Zone 1	+ 2	
Zone 2	+ 3	
Zone 3	+ 4	
Zone 4	+ 5	
Zone 5	+ 6	
Zone 6	+ 7	
Zone 7	+ 8	
Zone 8	+ 9	
Zone 9	+10	
Zone 10	+11	
Zone 11	+12	
Rwanda	+ 2	
St Helena	0	
St Christopher and Nevis	− 4	
St Lucia	− 4	
*St Pierre and Miquelon	− 3	
St Vincent and the Grenadines	− 4	
Samoa	−11	
Samoa, American	−11	
*San Marino	+ 1	
São Tomé and Princípe	0	
Saudi Arabia	+ 3	
Senegal	0	
Serbia & Montenegro	+ 1	
Seychelles	+ 4	
Sierra Leone	0	
Singapore	+ 8	
*Slovakia	+ 1	
*Slovenia	+ 1	
Solomon Islands	+11	
Somalia	+ 3	
South Africa	+ 2	
South Georgia	− 2	
*Spain	+ 1	
*Canary Islands	0	
Sri Lanka	+ 6	
Sudan	+ 3	
Suriname	− 3	
Swaziland	+ 2	
*Sweden	+ 1	
*Switzerland	+ 1	
*Syria	+ 2	
Taiwan	+ 8	
Tajikistan	+ 5	
Tanzania	+ 3	
Thailand	+ 7	
Togo	0	
*Tonga	+13	
Trinidad and Tobago	− 4	
Tristan da Cunha	0	
Tunisia	+ 1	
*Turkey	+ 2	
Turkmenistan	+ 5	
*Turks and Caicos Islands	− 5	
Tuvalu	+12	
Uganda	+ 3	
*Ukraine	+ 2	
United Arab Emirates	+ 4	
*United Kingdom	0	
*United States of America		
Alaska	− 9	
Aleutian Islands, east of 169° 30′ W.	− 9	
Aleutian Islands, west of 169° 30′ W.	−10	
eastern time	− 5	
central time	− 6	
Hawaii	−10	
mountain time	− 7	
Pacific time	− 8	
Uruguay	− 3	
Uzbekistan	+ 5	
Vanuatu	+11	
*Vatican City State	+ 1	
Venezuela	− 4	
Vietnam	+ 7	
Virgin Islands (US)	− 4	
Yemen	+ 3	
Zambia	+ 2	
Zimbabwe	+ 2	

CURRENCIES AND EXCHANGE RATES

AGAINST £ STERLING

COUNTRY/TERRITORY	MONETARY UNIT	AVERAGE RATE TO £1 *29 August 2003*	AVERAGE RATE TO £1 *27 August 2004*
Afghanistan	Afghani (Af) of 100 puls	Af 67.87	Af 77.16
Albania	Lek (Lk) of 100 qindraka	Lk 196.37	Lk 186.10
Algeria	Algerian dinar (DA) of 100 centimes	DA 121.55	DA 129.69
American Samoa	Currency is that of the USA	US$1.58	US$1.79
Andorra	Euro (€) of 100 cents	€1.45	€1.48
Angola	Readjusted kwanza (Krzl) of 100 lwei	Kzrl 125.89	Kzrl 145.95
Anguilla	East Caribbean dollar (EC$) of 100 cents	EC$4.21	EC$4.84
Antigua and Barbuda	East Caribbean dollar (EC$) of 100 cents	EC$4.21	EC$4.84
Argentina	Peso of 10,000 australes	Pesos 4.70	Pesos 5.37
Armenia	Dram of 100 louma	Dram 880.91	Dram 926.93
Aruba	Aruban florin	Florins 2.83	Florins 3.21
Ascension Island	Currency is that of St Helena	at parity with £ sterling	
Australia	Australian dollar ($A) of 100 cents	$A2.47	$A2.55
Norfolk Island	Currency is that of Australia	$A2.47	$A2.55
Austria	Euro (€) of 100 cents	€1.45	€1.48
Azerbaijan	Manat of 100 gopik	Manat 7757.35	Manat 8813.53
The Bahamas	Bahamian dollar (B$) of 100 cents	B$1.58	B$1.79
Bahrain	Bahraini dinar (BD) of 1,000 fils	BD 0.60	BD 0.67
Bangladesh	Taka (Tk) of 100 poisha	Tk 92.20	Tk 106.486
Barbados	Barbados dollar (BD$) of 100 cents	BD$3.14	BD$3.58
Belarus	Belarusian rouble of 100 kopeks	BYR 3311.27	BYR 3883.62
Belgium	Euro (€) of 100 cents	€1.45	€1.48
Belize	Belize dollar (BZ$) of 100 cents	BZ$3.11	BZ$3.55
Benin	Franc FCA	Francs 949.21	Francs 973.63
Bermuda	Bermuda dollar of 100 cents	$1.58	$1.79
Bhutan	Ngultrum of 100 chetrum (Indian currency is also legal tender)	Ngultrum 72.39	Ngultrum 83.09
Bolivia	Boliviano ($b) of 100 centavos	$b12.20	$b14.27
Bosnia-Hercegovina	Convertible marka	Marka 2.83	Marka 2.83
Botswana	Pula (P) of 100 thebe	P 7.69	P 8.64
Brazil	Real of 100 centavos	Real 4.67	Real 5.29
Brunei	Brunei dollar (B$) of 100 sen (fully interchangeable with Singapore currency)	B$2.77	B$3.07
Bulgaria	Lev of 100 stotinki	Leva 2.82	Leva 2.90
Burkina Faso	Franc CFA	Francs 949.21	Francs 973.63
Burundi	Burundi franc of 100 centimes	Francs 1696.67	Francs 1902.34
Cambodia	Riel of 100 sen	Riel 6052.78	Riel 6900.43
Cameroon	Franc CFA	Francs 949.21	Francs 973.63
Canada	Canadian dollar (C$) 100 cents	C$2.20	C$2.35
Cape Verde	Escudo Caboverdiano of 100 centavos	Esc 171.96	Esc 164.56
Cayman Islands	Cayman Islands dollar (CI$) of 100 cents	CI$1.29	CI$1.48
Central African Republic	Franc CFA	Francs 949.21	Francs 973.63
Chad	Franc CFA	Francs 949.21	Francs 973.63
Chile	Chilean peso of 100 centavos	Pesos 1104.57	Pesos 1126.95
China	Renminbi Yuan of 10 jiao or 100 fen	Yuan 13.06	Yuan 14.85
Hong Kong	Hong Kong (HK$) of 100 cents	HK$12.31	HK$13.99
Macao	Pataca of 100 avos	Pataca 12.68	Pataca 14.41
Colombia	Colombian peso of 100 centavos	Pesos 4493.58	Pesos 4611.76
Comoros	Comorian franc (KMF) of 100 centimes	Francs 717.06	Francs 730.221
Congo, Rep. of	Franc CFA	Francs 949.21	Francs 973.63
Congo, Dem. Rep. of	Congolese franc	CFr 681.83	CFr 698.5
Costa Rica	Costa Rican colón (₡) of 100 céntimos	₡639.56	₡797.05
Cote d'Ivoire	Franc CFA	Francs 949.21	Francs 973.63
Croatia	Kuna of 100 lipa	Kuna 10.81	Kuna 10.97

Cuba	Cuban peso of 100 centavos	Pesos 33.14	Pesos 37.56
Cyprus	Cyprus pound (C£) of 100 cents	C£0.85	C£0.85
Czech Republic	Koruna (Kčs) of 100 haléřu	Kčs 46.96	Kčs 47.35
Denmark	Danish krone of 100 øre	Kroner 10.75	Kroner 11.03
Faroe Islands	Currency is that of Denmark	Kroner 10.75	Kroner 11.03
Dijbouti	Dijbouti franc of 100 centimes	Francs 276.20	Francs 305.53
Dominica	East Caribbean dollar (EC$) of 100 cents	EC$4.21	EC$4.84
Dominican Republic	Dominican Republic peso (RD$) of 100 centavos	RD$52.24	RD$69.09
East Timor	Currency is that of the USA	US$1.58	US$1.79
Ecuador	Currency is that of the USA (formerly sucre of 100 centavos)	US$1.58	US$1.79
Egypt	Egyptian pound (£E) of 100 piastres or 1,000 millièmes	£E9.71	£E11.12
El Salvador	Currency is that of the USA	US$1.58	US$1.79
Equatorial Guinea	Franc CFA	Francs 949.21	Francs 973.63
Eritrea	Nakfa	—	Nafka 24.22
Estonia	Kroon of 100 sents	Kroons 22.64	Kroons 23.22
Ethiopia	Ethiopian birr (EB) of 100 cents	EB 13.49	EB 15.43
Falkland Islands	Falkland pound of 100 pence	at parity with £ sterling	
Fiji	Fiji dollar (F$) of 100 cents	F$3.03	F$ 3.19
Finland	Euro (€) of 100 cents	€1.45	€1.48
France	Euro (€) of 100 cents	€1.45	€1.48
French Guiana	Euro (€) of 100 cents	€1.45	€1.48
French Polynesia	Franc CFP	Francs 167.95	Francs 177.00
Gabon	Franc CFA	Francs 949.21	Francs 973.63
Gambia	Dalasi (D) of 100 butut	D 46.56	D 52.04
Georgia	Laria of 100 tetri	Laria 3.33	Laria 3.91
Germany	Euro (€) of 100 cents	€1.45	€1.48
Ghana	Cedi of 100 pesewas	Cedi 13739.1	Cedi 16196.7
Gibraltar	Gibraltar pound of 100 pence	at parity with £ sterling	
Greece	Euro (€) of 100 cents	€1.45	€1.48
Greenland	Currency is that of Denmark	Kroner 10.75	Kroner 11.30
Grenada	East Caribbean dollar (EC$) of 100 cents	EC$4.21	EC$4.84
Guadeloupe	Euro (€) of 100 cents	€1.45	€1.48
Guam	Currency is that of the USA	US$1.58	US$1.79
Guatemala	Quetzal (Q) of 100 centavos	Q 12.54	Q 14.18
Guinea	Guinea franc of 100 centimes	Francs 3156.60	Francs 4585.33
Guinea-Bissau	Franc CFA	Francs 949.21	Francs 973.63
Guyana	Guyana dollar (G$) of 100 cents	G$ 282.52	G$321.24
Haiti	Gourde of 100 centimes	Gourdes 60.92	Gourdes 61.1
Honduras	Lempira of 100 centavos	Lempiras 27.45	Lempiras 32.94
Hungary	Forint of 100 fillér	Forints 371.98	Forints 370.58
Iceland	Icelandic króna (Kr) of 100 aurar	Kr 126.40	Kr 129.215
India	Indian rupee (Rs) of 100 paisa	Rs 72.39	Rs 83.09
Indonesia	Rupiah (Rp) of 100 sen	Rp 13439.2	Rp 16699.2
Iran	Rial	Rials 13123.6	Rials 15663.7
Iraq	New Iraqi dinar (NID)	—	NID 2624.67
Ireland, Republic of	Euro (€) of 100 cents	€1.45	€1.48
Israel	Shekel of 100 agora	Shekels 7.03	Shekels 8.15
Italy	Euro (€) of 100 cents	€1.45	€1.48
Jamaica	Jamaican dollar (J$) of 100 cents	J$92.33	J$109.72
Japan	Yen	Yen 185.36	Yen 196.64
Jordan	Jordanian dinar (JD) of 1,000 fils	JD 1.12	JD 1.27
Kazakhstan	Tenge	Tenge 232.43	Tenge 245.13
Kenya	Kenya shilling (Ksh) of 100 cents	Ksh 121.14	Ksh 145.54
Kiribati	Australian dollar ($A) of 100 cents	$A2.47	$A2.55
Korea, Dem. People's Rep. Of	Won of 100 chon	—	Won 1615.18
Korea, Republic of	Won	Won 1860.03	Won 2070.13
Kuwait	Kuwaiti dinar (KD) of 1,000 fils	KD 0.47	KD 0.52
Kyrgyzstan	Som	Som 67.23	Som 75.67
Laos	Kip (K) of 100 at	K 11995.1	K 14071.8
Latvia	Lats of 100 santims	Lats 0.91	Lats 0.97
Lebanon	Lebanese pound (L£) of of 100 piastres	L£2389.74	L£2718.00
Lesotho	Loti (M) of 100 lisente	M 11.60	M 11.84

Liberia	Liberian dollar (L$) of 100 cents	L$1.58	L$1.50
Libya	Libyan dinar (LD) of 1,000 dirhams	LD 2.19	LD 2.35
Liechtenstein	Swiss franc of 100 rappen (or centimes)	Francs 2.23	Francs 2.28
Lithuania	Litas of 100 centas	Litas 4.99	Litas 5.12
Luxembourg	Euro (€) of 100 cents	€1.45	€1.48
Macedonia	Denar of 100 deni	Den 89.23	Den 90.28
Madagascar	Franc malgache (FMG) of 100 centimes	FMG 9390.89	FMG 18260.6
Malawi	Kwacha (K) of 100 tambala	MK 166.51	MK 195.25
Malaysia	Malaysian dollar (ringgit) (M$) of 100 sen	M$5.99	M$6.81
Maldives	Rufiyaa of 100 laaris	Rufiyaa 20.20	Rufiyaa 22.97
Mali	Franc CFA	Francs 949.21	Francs 973.63
Malta	Maltese lira (LM) of 100 cents of 1,000 mils	LM 0.61	LM 0.63
Marshall Islands	Currency is that of the USA	US$1.58	US$1.79
Martinique	Currency is that of France	€1.45	€1.48
Mauritania	Ouguiya (UM) of 5 khoums	UM 420.22	UM 477.37
Mauritius	Mauritius rupee of 100 cents	Rs 45.69	Rs 50.96
Mayotte	Euro (€) of 100 cents	€1.45	€1.48
Mexico	Peso of 100 centavos	Pesos 17.35	Pesos 20.40
Micronesia, Federated States of	Currency is that of the USA	US$1.58	US$1.79
Moldova	Moldovan leu of 100 bani	MDL 21.94	MDL 21.57
Monaco	Euro (€) of 100 cents	€1.45	€1.48
Mongolia	Tugrik of 100 möngö	Tugriks 1777.17	Tugriks 2141.2
Montserrat	East Caribbean dollar (EC$) of 100 cents	EC$4.21	EC$4.84
Morocco	Dirham (DH) of 100 centimes	DH 15.54	DH 16.28
Mozambique	Metical (MT) of 100 centavos	MT 36814.6	MT 39502.8
Myanmar	Kyat (K) of 100 pyas	K 9.79	K 11.52
Namibia	Namibian dollar of 100 cents	at parity with SA Rand	
Nauru	Australian dollar ($A) of 100 cents	$A2.47	$A2.55
Nepal	Nepalese rupee of 100 paisa	Rs 117.74	Rs 132.94
The Netherlands	Euro (€) of 100 cents	€1.45	€1.48
Netherlands Antilles	Netherlands Antilles guilder of 100 cents	Guilders 2.81	Guilders 3.21
New Caledonia	Franc CFP	Francs 167.95	Francs 191.04
New Zealand	New Zealand dollar (NZ$) of 100 cents	NZ$2.77	NZ$2.75
Cook Islands	Currency is that of New Zealand	NZ$2.77	NZ$2.75
Niue	Currency is that of New Zealand	NZ$2.77	NZ$2.75
Tokelau	Currency is that of New Zealand	NZ$2.77	NZ$2.75
Nicaragua	Córdoba (C$) of 100 centavos	C$23.94	C$28.60
Niger	Franc CFA	Francs 949.21	Francs 973.63
Nigeria	Naira (N) of 100 kobo	N 207.23	N 239.22
Northern Mariana Islands	Currency is that of the USA	US$1.58	US$1.79
Norway	Krone of 100 øre	Kroner 11.99	Kroner 12.37
Oman	Rial Omani (OR) of 1,000 baisas	OR 0.61	OR 0.69
Pakistan	Pakistan rupee of 100 paisa	Rs 91.08	Rs 105.301
Palau	Currency is that of the USA	US$1.58	US$1.79
Panama	Balboa of 100 centésimos (US notes are also in circulation)	Balboa 1.58	Balboa 1.79
Papua New Guinea	Kina (K) of 100 toea	K 5.35	K 5.48
Paraguay	Guarani (Gs) of 100 céntimos	Gs 9903.83	Gs 10615.4
Peru	New Sol of 100 cénts	New Sol 5.49	New Sol 6.05
The Philippines	Philippine peso (P) of 100 centavos	P 86.65	P 100.55
Pitcairn Islands	Currency is that of New Zealand	NZ$2.77	NZ$2.75
Poland	Zloty of 100 groszy	Zlotych 6.30	Zlotych 6.66
Portugal	Euro (€) of 100 cents	€1.45	€1.48
Puerto Rico	Currency is that of the USA	US$1.58	US$1.79
Qatar	Qatar riyal of 100 dirhams	Riyals 5.75	Riyals 6.53
Réunion	Euro (€) of 100 cents	€1.45	€1.48
Romania	Leu of 100 bani	Lei 53574.6	Lei 60900.3
Russia	Rouble of 100 kopeks	Rbl 48.13	Rbl 52.43
Rwanda	Rwanda franc of 100 centimes	Francs 845.65	Francs 1012.00
St Christopher and Nevis	East Caribbean dollar (EC$) of 100 cents	EC$4.21	EC$4.84
St Helena	St Helena pound (£) of 100 pence	at parity with £ sterling	

St Lucia	East Caribbean dollar (EC$) of 100 cents	EC$4.21	EC$4.84
St Pierre and Miquelon	Euro (€) of 100 cents	€1.45	€1.48
St Vincent and the Grenadines	East Caribbean dollar (EC$) of 100 cents	EC$4.21	EC$4.84
Samoa	Tala (S$) of 100 sene	S$4.66	S$5.07
San Marino	Euro (€) of 100 cents	€1.45	€1.48
São Tomé and Princípe	Dobra of 100 centavos	Dobra 13731.2	Dobra 15818.0
Saudi Arabia	Saudi riyal (SR) of 20 qursh or 100 halala	SR 5.92	SR 6.73
Senegal	Franc CFA	Francs 949.21	Francs 973.63
Serbia and Montenegro	New dinar of 100 paras	New Dinars 94.88	New Dinars 99.00
Seychelles	Seychelles rupee of 100 cents	Rs 8.80	Rs 9.90
Sierra Leone	Leone (Le) of 100 cents	Le 3712.95	Le 4405.89
Singapore	Singapore dollar (S$) of 100 cents	S$2.77	S$3.07
Slovakia	Koruna (Sk) of 100 halierov	Kčs 60.77	Kčs 59.75
Slovenia	Tolar (SIT) of 100 stotin	Tolars 340.22	Tolars 356.19
Solomon Islands	Solomon Islands dollar (SI$) of 100 cents	SI$11.89	SI$13.34
Somalia	Somali shilling of 100 cents	Shillings 4135.15	Shillings 4886.83
South Africa	Rand (R) of 100 cents	R 11.60	R 11.84
Spain	Euro (€) of 100 cents	€1.45	€1.48
Sri Lanka	Sri Lankan rupee of 100 cents	Rs 152.57	Rs 184.84
Sudan	Sudanese dinar (SD) of 100 piastres	SD 412.41	SD 464.85
Suriname	Surinamese guilder of 100 cents	Guilders 3969.43	Guilders 4476.29
Swaziland	Lilangeni (E) of 100 cents (South African currency is also in circulation)	at parity with SA Rand	
Sweden	Swedish krona of 100 öre	Kronor 13.35	Kronor 13.55
Switzerland	Swiss franc of 100 rappen (or centimes)	Francs 2.23	Francs 2.28
Syria	Syrian pound (S£) of 100 piastres	S£72.60	S£92.71
Taiwan	New Taiwan dollar (NT$) of 100 cents	NT$53.98	NT$60.88
Tajikistan	Somoni (TJS) of 100 dirams	—	—
Tanzania	Tanzanian shilling of 100 cents	Shillings 1650.11	Shillings 1948.99
Thailand	Baht of 100 satang	Baht 64.95	Baht 74.75
Togo	Franc CFA	Francs 949.21	Francs 973.63
Tonga	Pa'anga (T$) of 100 seniti	T$2.47	T$3.57
Trinidad and Tobago	Trinidad and Tobago dollar (TT$) of 100 cents	TT$9.70	TT$11.17
Tristan da Cunha	Currency is that of the UK	—	—
Tunisia	Tunisian dinar of 1,000 millimes	Dinars 2.08	Dinars 2.27
Turkey	Turkish lira (TL) of 100 kurus	TL 2214355	TL 2711717
Turkmenistan	Manat of 100 tenge	—	—
Turks and Caicos Islands	US dollar (US$)	US$1.58	US$1.79
Tuvalu	Australian dollar ($A) of 100 cents	$A2.47	$A2.55
Uganda	Uganda shilling of 100 cents	Shillings 3154.23	Shillings 3073.34
Ukraine	Hryvna of 100 kopiykas	UAH 8.42	UAH 9.55
United Arab Emirates	UAE dirham (Dh) of 100 fils	Dirham 5.80	Dirham 6.59
United States of America	US dollar (US$) of 100 cents	US$1.58	US$1.79
Uruguay	Uruguayan peso of 100 centésimos	Pesos 43.99	Pesos 52.10
Uzbekistan	Sum of 100 tiyin	Sum 1536.46	Sum 1849.53
Vanatu	Vatu of 100 centimes	Vatu 194.54	Vatu 206.04
Vatican City State	Euro (€) of 100 cents y	€1.45	€1.48
Venezuela	Bolívar (Bs) of 100 céntimos	Bs 2522.12	Bs 4711.75
Vietnam	Dông of 10 hào or 100 xu	Dông 24501.5	Dông 28309.7
Virgin Islands, British	US dollar (US$) (£ sterling and EC$ also circulate)	US$1.58	US$1.79
Virgin Islands, US	Currency is that of the USA	US$1.58	US$1.79
Wallis and Futuna Islands	Franc CFP	Francs 167.95	Francs 191.04
Yemen	Riyal of 100 fils	Riyals 280.95	Riyals 331.68
Zambia	Kwacha (K) of 100 ngwee	K 7346.99	K 8524.60
Zimbabwe	Zimbabwe dollar (Z$) of 100 cents	Z$1300.52	Z$10068.8

†The euro is also legal tender in Kosovo and Serbia and Montenegro

THE WORLD IN FIGURES

The total population of the world in mid-2003 was estimated at 6,301 million, compared with 5,292 million in 1990 and 3,019 million in 1960.

Continent, etc.	Area Sq. miles 000s	Sq. km 000s	Estimated population mid-2003
Africa	11,704	30,313	850,558,000
North America[1]	8,311	21,525	325,698,000
Latin America[2]	7,933	20,547	543,246,000
Asia[3]	10,637*	27,549*	3,823,390,000
Europe[4]	1,915†	4,961†	726,338,000
Oceania[5]	3,286	8,510	32,234,000
Former USSR	8,649	22,402	–
Total	52,435	135,807	6,301,463,000

[1] Includes Greenland and Hawaii
[2] Mexico, the Caribbean and the remainder of the Americas south of the USA
[3] Includes European Turkey
[4] Excludes European Turkey
[5] Includes Australia, New Zealand and the islands inhabited by Micronesian, Melanesian and Polynesian peoples
* Figure includes some former USSR countries
† Figure excludes some former USSR countries
Source: UN Population Division; Department of Economic and Social Affairs (2003)

The population forecast for the years 2025 and 2050 is:

Estimated population (million)

Continent	*2025*	*2050*
Africa	1,292,085	1,803,298
North America[1]	394,312	447,931
Latin America[2]	686,857	767,685
Asia	4,742,232	5,222,058
Europe	696,036	631,938
Oceania	39,933	45,815
Total	7,851,455	8,918,725

[1] Includes Bermuda, Greenland, and St Pierre and Miquelon
[2] Mexico, the Caribbean and the remainder of the Americas south of the USA

GLOBAL STATISTICS

The following tables are intended to provide a 'snapshot' of world-wide socio-economic and environmental trends.

WORLD COMPETITIVENESS SCOREBOARD 2001*

Rank	*Country*	*Score*
1	United States	100.00
2	Singapore	87.66
3	Finland	83.38
4	Luxembourg	82.81
5	Netherlands	81.46
6	Hong Kong	79.55
7	Ireland	79.20
8	Sweden	77.86
9	Canada	76.94
10	Switzerland	76.81
11	Australia	75.87
12	Germany	74.04
13	Iceland	73.75
14	Austria	72.54
15	Denmark	71.79
16	Israel	67.92
17	Belgium	66.03
18	Taiwan	64.84
19	United Kingdom	64.78
20	Norway	63.10
21	New Zealand	61.73
22	Estonia	60.20
23	Spain	60.14
24	Chile	59.84
25	France	59.56
26	Japan	57.52
27	Hungary	55.64
28	South Korea	51.08
29	Malaysia	50.03
30	Greece	49.96
31	Brazil	49.66
32	Italy	49.58
33	China	49.53
34	Portugal	48.36
35	Czech Republic	46.68
36	Mexico	43.67
37	Slovakia	43.59
38	Thailand	42.67
39	Slovenia	42.48
40	Philippines	40.60
41	India	40.41
42	South Africa	38.61
43	Argentina	37.51
44	Turkey	35.44
45	Russia	34.57
46	Colombia	32.84
47	Poland	32.01
48	Venezuela	30.66
49	Indonesia	28.26

Source: The Business, Bloomsbury Publishing plc

* Calculated using four basic categories: economic performance, Government efficiency, business efficiency and infrastructure

CREDIT CARD TRANSACTIONS*

Country	*Credit card transactions (US$ million) 2000*
United States	1,233,500
United Kingdom	267,950
France	169,700
China	156,270
South Korea	127,270
Japan	114,340
Canada	87,940
Brazil	69,630
Spain	67,380
Australia	50,390
Mexico	44,840
Argentina	33,160
Sweden	30,450
Germany	27,140
Turkey	26,810
Taiwan	23,890
Norway	22,400
Italy	22,340
Portugal	18,780
Hong Kong	18,310
Israel	17,270
Saudi Arabia	11,990
Denmark	10,650
Switzerland	10,560
Poland	9,810
South Africa	9,670
Finland	6,780
Kuwait	6,560
Netherlands	6,540
Colombia	6,380
Belgium	5,950
New Zealand	5,050
Singapore	4,740
Ireland	4,720
Peru	4,620
Thailand	4,500
United Arab Emirates	4,390
Malaysia	4,340
Chile	4,120
Venezuela	4,010
Iceland	3,990
Hungary	3,960
Czech Republic	3,490
Austria	3,250
Greece	2,840
Puerto Rico	2,290
Costa Rica	1,740
Russia	1,670
Dominican Republic	1,560
Luxembourg	1,530

Source: The Business, Bloomsbury Publishing plc

* Visa and Mastercard

COUNTRIES WITH THE MOST BILLIONAIRES 2001

Country	*No. of billionaires*
United States	265
Germany	57
France	31
Japan	29
United Kingdom	29
Italy	19
Switzerland	19
Canada	16
Hong Kong	14
Mexico	13
World total	620

Source: The Business, Bloomsbury Publishing plc

HUMAN DEVELOPMENT INDEX (HDI) (2003)*

Ten highest ranking countries

Country
Norway
Iceland
Sweden
Australia
Netherlands
Belgium
United States
Canada
Japan
Switzerland

Ten lowest ranking countries

Country
Sierra Leone
Niger
Burkina Faso
Mali
Burundi
Mozambique
Ethiopia
Central African Republic
Democratic Republic of Congo
Guinea-Bissau

* The HDI is an index that measures a country's average achievements in three basic aspects of human development: longevity (life expectancy), knowledge (adult literacy rate) and standard of living (GDP per capita).

CANCER PREVALENCE AND CARDIOVASCULAR DEATHS*

Country	*Cancer deaths (per 100,000) 2000*	*Cardiovascular deaths (per 100,000) 1994–98*
Hungary	420	1,725
Czech Republic	350	1,392
Croatia	335	–
Denmark	329	1,150
Slovakia	327	1,464
Uruguay	324	–
Slovenia	319	–
Poland	317	1,442
Russia	312	1,961
Belgium	312	1,001
Estonia	306	–
Kazakhstan	304	–
Netherlands	302	979
Luxembourg	300	–
France	300	831
Latvia	299	–
United Kingdom	299	958
New Zealand	298	–
Ireland	298	1,109
Germany	294	987

Source: The Business, Bloomsbury Publishing plc

HIGHEST PER CAPITA CARBON EMISSIONS

Country	*CO_2 emissions per capita (tonnes) 1999*	*Growth in CO_2 emissions (%) 1990–99*
Australia	28.0	6
Canada	23.1	30
United States	21.5	21
Ireland	17.6	25
Belgium	14.7	7
New Zealand	14.0	3
Czech Republic	13.9	–25
Netherlands	13.6	3
Russia	13.5	–35
Luxembourg	13.0	–57
Denmark	12.7	–1
Greece	12.6	26
Finland	12.0	16
Germany	11.9	–18
United Kingdom	11.0	–13
Iceland	10.0	0
Japan	10.0	10
Italy	9.2	7
Austria	8.9	6
Bulgaria	8.9	–53

Source: The Business, Bloomsbury Publishing plc

HIGHEST DENSITY OF PCs 2001

Country	*PCs (per 100 people)*
United States	62.5
Sweden	56.1
Australia	51.6
Luxembourg	51.5
Norway	50.8
Singapore	50.8
Switzerland	50.0
Bermuda	49.5
Denmark	43.2
Netherlands	42.8

Source: The Business, Bloomsbury Publishing plc

GREATEST ACCESS TO TV

Country	*TV sets (per 100 people) 1999*
United States	84.4
Latvia	74.1
Japan	71.9
Canada	71.5
Australia	70.6
United Kingdom	65.2
Norway	64.8
Finland	64.3
France	62.3
Denmark	62.1

Source: The Business, Bloomsbury Publishing plc

GREATEST ACCESS TO MAINLINE TELEPHONES 2001

Country	*Main telephone lines (per 100 people)*	*Mobile subscrib (per 100 peop*
Bermuda	87.2	20
Luxembourg	78.3	96
Sweden	73.9	79
Denmark	72.3	73
Norway	72.0	82
Switzerland	71.8	72
United States	66.5	45
Iceland	66.4	82
Canada	65.5	36
Cyprus	64.3	45

Source: The Business, Bloomsbury Publishing plc

TRAVEL OVERSEAS

PASSPORT REGULATIONS

Application forms for United Kingdom passports can be obtained from the UK Passport Service's general telephone enquiry line or website, regional passport offices, or from main post offices and WorldChoice travel agents.
T 0870-521 0410
F 0901-4700 120
W www.ukpa.gov.uk

DURHAM
Passport Office, Millburngate House, Durham DH97 1PA

LONDON
Passport Office, Globe House, 89 Eccleston Square, London SW1V 9PN

LIVERPOOL
Passport Office, 5th Floor, India Buildings, Water Street, Liverpool L2 0QZ

NEWPORT
Passport Office, Olympia House, Upper Dock Street, Newport, Gwent NP20 1XA

PETERBOROUGH
Passport Office, Aragon Court, Northminster Road, Peterborough PE1 1QG

GLASGOW
Passport Office, 3 Northgate, 96 Milton Street, Cowcaddens, Glasgow G4 0BT

BELFAST
Passport Office, Hampton House, 47–53 High Street, Belfast BT1 2QS

The passport offices are open Monday–Saturday on an appointment-only basis (appointments should be arranged by calling the central telephone number listed above).

Standard postal applications are processed within three weeks. The completed application form should be posted, with the appropriate supporting documents and fee, to the regional passport office indicated on the addressed envelope which is provided with each application form. Accompanying cheques and postal orders should be crossed and made payable to 'The Passport Office'.

Applications can also be submitted through selected main post offices and WorldChoice travel agents ('partners'), who, in exchange for a small handling charge, will forward the application form to the relevant regional passport office after having checked that it has been completed correctly and has the appropriate documents attached. Applications through partners take a minimum of two weeks.

A passport cannot be issued or extended on behalf of a person already abroad; such persons should apply to the nearest British High Commission or Consulate.

UK passports are granted to:

(i) British citizens
(ii) British Dependent Territories citizens
(iii) British Nationals (Overseas)
(iv) British Overseas citizens
(v) British Subjects
(vi) British Protected Persons

UK passports are generally available for travel to all countries. The possession of a passport does not, however, exempt the holder from compliance with any immigration regulations in force in British or foreign countries, or from the necessity of obtaining a visa where required.

ADULTS

A passport granted to a person over 16 will normally be valid for ten years and will not be renewable. Thereafter, or if at any time the passport contains no further space for visas, a new passport must be obtained.

The issue of passports including details of the holder's spouse has been discontinued, but existing family passports may be used until expiry. A spouse who is included in a family passport cannot travel on the passport without the holder.

CHILDREN

Since 5 October 1998 all children under the age of 16 are required to have their own passport. This is primarily to help prevent child abductions. The passports are normally valid for five years, after which point a new passport application must be made. This replaced the system whereby children under the age of 16 could either have their own passport or be added to their parents' passports.

A passport granted to a child prior to this date was still valid for five years. On expiry, a new application must be made. Children included in their parents' passports when the new regulations came into force are not affected and can continue to travel on them until they reach the age of 16 or the passport expires or is amended.

COUNTERSIGNATURES

The completed passport application form should be countersigned by an MP, justice of the peace, minister of religion, a professionally qualified person (e.g. doctor, engineer, lawyer, teacher), bank officer, military officer, established civil servant, police officer or a person of similar standing who has known the applicant for at least two years, and who is either a British citizen, British Dependent Territories citizen, British National (Overseas), British Overseas citizen, British Subject or a citizen of a Commonwealth country. A relative must not countersign the application.

If the application is for a child under the age of 16, the countersignature should be by someone of relevant standing who has known the parent or person with parental responsibility who signs the declaration of consent, rather than the child.

PHOTOGRAPHS
Two identical unmounted recent photographs of the applicant must be sent. These photographs should be printed on normal thin photographic paper and should be taken full face against a white background. The person who countersigns the application form should certify one photograph as a true likeness of the applicant.

DOCUMENTATION
The applicant's birth certificate or previous British passport, and other documents in support of the statements made in the application must be produced at the time of applying. Details of which documents are required are set out in the notes accompanying the application form.

If the applicant for a passport is a British national by naturalisation or registration, the certificate proving this must be produced with the application, unless the applicant holds a previous UK passport issued after registration or naturalisation.

48-PAGE PASSPORTS
The 48-page passport is intended to meet the needs of frequent travellers who fill standard passports well before the validity has expired. It is valid for ten years but is not available for children.

PASSPORT FEES*
from September 2004

New adult passport	£42
New child passport	£25
Renewal or amendment of passport	£42
Renewal or amendment of child passport	£25
48-page passport	£54.50

* Standard postal applications only. A £6 charge is added for applications made in person at a partner office in the UK.

HEALTH ADVICE

Health Advice for Travellers (booklet T6), published by the Department of Health, contains information on health precautions, reciprocal health agreements with other countries, and immunisation. It is available from some travel agents, local post offices or the Department of Health, Richmond House, 79 Whitehall, London SW1.
T 020-7210 4850 Minicom 020-7210 5025
E dhmail@doh.gsi.gov.uk (single copy orders).

IMMUNISATION
In very general terms immunisation against typhoid, polio and hepatitis A should be considered for all countries where standards of hygiene and sanitation may be less than ideal. Protection against malaria, in the form of tablets, as well as measures to avoid mosquito bites, is advised for visits to malarious areas.

Immunisation against yellow fever is compulsory for entry into some countries, either for all travellers or for those arriving from a yellow fever-infected area, and is recommended for all travellers to infected areas.

A doctor should be consulted, preferably at least eight weeks before departure, and will advise travellers and arrange vaccinations. Most doctors will charge a fee for a course of vaccinations. If children will be travelling outside Europe, North America, Australia and New Zealand, the doctor should be informed, especially if they have not completed their full course of childhood immunisation. As a precaution, it is also recommended that all travellers be up to date with their polio and tetanus inoculations.

Country-by-country guidance is set out in *Health Advice for Travellers*. Health care professionals can obtain up-to-date information about immunisation recommendations from the Department of Health publication *Health Information for Overseas Travel* or from:

ENGLAND
Health Protection Agency, Floor 11, The Adelphi Building, John Adam Street, London WC2N 6HT
T 020-7339 1300
F 020-7339 1302
W www.hpa.org.uk

WALES
T 01222-825111

SCOTLAND
Scottish Executive Health Department, St Andrew's House, Edinburgh EH1 3DG T 0131-556 8400
The Scottish Centre for Infection and Environmental Health, Clifton House, Clifton Place, Glasgow G3 7LN
T 0141-300 1100

NORTHERN IRELAND
DHSSPS, Castle Buildings, Stormont, Belfast BT4 3SJ
T 028-9052 0500
W www.dhsspsni.gov.uk

MEDICAL TREATMENT ABROAD
Details of free or reduced cost emergency medical treatment when visiting European countries, and countries with which the UK has reciprocal health arrangements, are set out in *Health Advice for Travellers*. It also contains Form E111, the certificate that entitles people to urgent medical treatment in the European Economic Area (EEA), as well as guidance on its completion.

For countries where the UK has no health care agreements, including Canada, the USA, India, the Far East, and the whole of Africa and Latin America, it is advisable to take out medical insurance. A certain amount of insurance is also needed in countries with which the UK has health care agreements.

ANTARCTIC

The Antarctic is generally defined as the area lying within the Antarctic Convergence, the zone where cold northward-flowing Antarctic sea water sinks below warmer southward-flowing water. This zone is at about latitude 50° S. in the Atlantic Ocean and latitude 55°–62° S. in the Pacific Ocean. The continent itself lies almost entirely within the Antarctic Circle, an area of about 13.66 million sq. km (5.3 million sq. miles), 99.67 per cent of which is permanently ice-covered. The average thickness of the ice is 2,450 m (7,100 ft) but in places exceeds 4,500 m (14,500 ft). Some mountains protrude, the highest being Vinson Massif, 4,897 m (16,067 ft). The lowest point has been recorded as the Bentley Subglacial Trench at −2,540 metres. The ice amounts to some 30 million cubic km (7.2 million cubic miles) and represents more than 70 per cent of the world's fresh water and 90 per cent of the world's ice. Much of the sea freezes in winter, forming fast ice which breaks up in summer and drifts north as pack ice.

The most conspicuous physical features of the continent are its high inland plateau (much of it over 3,000 m (10,000 ft)), the Transantarctic Mountains and the mountainous Antarctic Peninula and off-lying islands which extend northwards towards South America.

CLIMATE

On land, summer temperatures range from just above freezing around the coast to −34° C (about −30° F) on the plateau, and in winter from −20° C (about −4° F) on the coast to −65° C (about −85° F) inland. Over a large area the maxima do not exceed −15° C (+5° F).

Precipitation is scant over the plateau but amounts to 25–76 cm (10–30 in) (water equivalent) along the coast and some scientific stations are permanently buried by snow. Some rain falls over the more northerly areas in summer. Gravity winds on the plateau slopes and cyclonic storms further north can both exceed 160 km/h (100 mph).

FLORA AND FAUNA

Although a small number of flowering plants, ferns and clubmosses occur on the sub-Antarctic islands, only two (a grass and a pearlwort) extend south of 60° S. Antarctic vegetation is dominated by lichens and mosses, with a few liverworts, algae and fungi.

The only land animals are tiny insects and mites with nematodes, rotifers and tardigrades in the mosses, but large numbers of seals, penguins and other sea-birds go ashore to breed in the summer. The emperor penguin is the only species that breeds ashore throughout the winter. By contrast, the Antarctic seas abound with life, a wide variety of invertebrates (including krill) and fish providing food for the seals, penguins and other birds, and a residual population of whales.

POTENTIAL RESOURCES

Minerals may be present in great variety but not in commercially exploitable concentrations in accessible localities. There are indications that off-shore hydrocarbons may be present but mostly below great depths of stormy, ice-filled seas.

Currently, the chief interest is in marine protein, including the shrimp-like krill already fished commercially by Japan and Poland. It is estimated that these could sustain a yield equal to the present total annual world fish catch.

THE ANTARCTIC TREATY

The co-operative 12 nations (Argentina, Australia, Belgium, Chile, France, Japan, New Zealand, Norway, South Africa, the Soviet Union, the UK and the USA) pledged themselves to promote scientific and technical co-operation unhampered by politics, and the Antarctic Treaty was signed by the 12 states in 1959. The signatories agreed to establish free use of the Antarctic continent for peaceful scientific purposes; to freeze all territorial claims and disputes in the Antarctic; to ban all military activities in the area; and to prohibit nuclear explosions and the disposal of radioactive waste. Since then additional agreements have been reached to promote conservation and regulate tourism, waste disposal and pollution.

The Antarctic Treaty was defined as covering areas south of latitude 60° S., excluding the high seas but including the ice shelves, and came into force in 1961. It has since been signed by a further 31 states, 14 of which are active in the Antarctic and have therefore been accorded consultative status, bringing the number of consultative parties to 26. In 1998 an extension to the treaty came into effect, placing a 50-year ban on mining, oil exploration and mineral extraction in Antarctica. Furthermore, all tourists, explorers and expeditions will now need permission to enter the Antarctic.

TERRITORIAL CLAIMS

Under the provisions of the Antarctic Treaty all territorial claims and disputes were frozen. The US and Soviet governments also made it clear that although they had not made any specific territorial claims, they did not relinquish the right to make such claims.

Seven states have made claims in the Antarctic: Argentina claims the part of Antarctica between 74° W. and 25° W.; Chile that part between 90° W. and 53° W.; Britain claims the British Antarctic Territory, an area of 1,709,340 sq. km (660,000 sq. miles) between 20° and 80° W. longitude; France claims Terre Adélie, 432,000 sq. km (166,800 sq. miles) between 136° and 142° E.; Australia claims the Australian Antarctic Territory, 6,120,000 sq. km (2,320,000 sq. miles) between 160° and 45° E. longitude excluding Terre Adélie; Norway claims Queen Maud Land between 20° W. and 45° E.; and New Zealand claims the Ross Dependency, 450,000 sq. km (175,000 sq. miles) between 160° E. and 150° W. longitude. The Argentinian, British and Chilean claims overlap; the part of the continent between 90° W. and 150° W. is unclaimed by any state.

SCIENTIFIC RESEARCH

There are some 26 nations with permanent research stations in Antarctica: Argentina (14), Australia (7), Brazil (1), Bulgaria (1), Chile (9), China (2), Ecuador (1), Finland (1), France (5), Germany (3), India (1), Italy (2), Japan (4), New Zealand (1), Norway (2), Peru (1), Poland (1), Republic of Korea (1), Russia (8), South Africa (4), Spain (2), Sweden (1), UK (5), Ukraine (1), Uruguay (1), USA (3).

While there are no indigenous inhabitants, during the summer (January) the population reaches around 3,500 people, mostly comprising of tourists, scientists and seasonal research workers.

THE EUROPEAN UNION

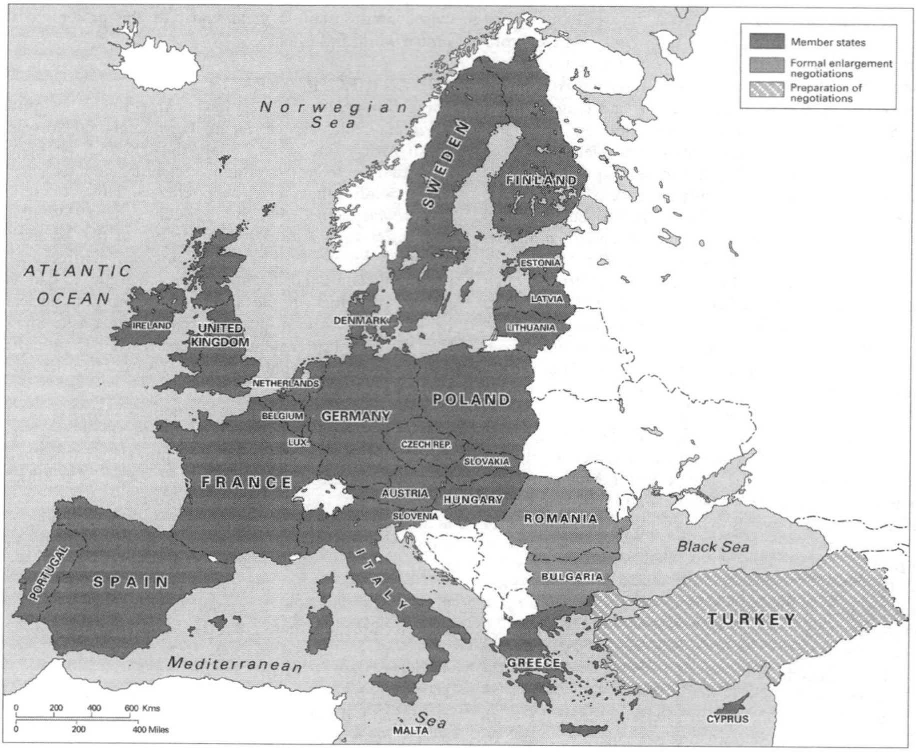

MEMBER STATE	ACCESSION DATE	POPULATION (approx) (2003)	COUNCIL VOTES	EP SEATS
Austria	1 January 1995	8,100,000	10	18
Belgium	1 January 1958	10,400,000	12	24
Cyprus	1 May 2004	800,000	4	6
Czech Republic	1 May 2004	10,400,000	12	24
Denmark	1 January 1973	5,400,000	7	14
Estonia	1 May 2004	1,360,000	4	6
Finland	1 January 1995	5,200,000	7	14
France	1 January 1958	59,600,000	29	78
Germany	1 January 1958	82,500,000	29	99
Greece	1 January 1981	11,000,000	12	24
Hungary	1 May 2004	10,100,000	12	24
Ireland	1 January 1973	4,000,000	7	13
Italy	1 January 1958	57,300,000	29	78
Latvia	1 May 2004	2,400,000	4	9
Lithuania	1 May 2004	3,700,000	7	13
Luxembourg	1 January 1958	400,000	4	6
Malta	1 May 2004	390,000	3	5
Netherlands	1 January 1958	16,200,000	13	27
Poland	1 May 2004	38,600,000	27	54
Portugal	1 January 1986	10,400,000	12	24
Slovakia	1 May 2004	5,400,000	7	14
Slovenia	1 May 2004	2,000,000	4	7
Spain	1 January 1986	40,700,000	27	54
Sweden	1 January 1995	8,900,000	10	19
UK	1 January 1973	59,300,000	29	78

DEVELOPMENT

1950 Robert Schuman (French foreign minister) proposes that France and West Germany pool their coal and steel industries under a supranational authority (Schuman Plan)
1951 Paris Treaty signed by France, West Germany, Belgium, Italy, Luxembourg and the Netherlands, establishes the European Coal and Steel Community (ECSC)
1952 ECSC Treaty enters into force
1957 25 March: Treaty of Rome signed by the six ECSC member countries, establishes the European Economic Community (EEC) and the European Atomic Energy Authority (EURATOM). Treaty aims to create a customs union; remove obstacles to free movement of capital, goods, people and services; establish common external trade policy and common agricultural and fisheries policies; co-ordinate economic policies; harmonise social policies; promote co-operation in nuclear research
1958 1 January: EEC and EURATOM begin operation. Joint Parliament and Court of Justice established for all three communities, and the Commission, Council of Ministers, Economic and Social Committee and Investment Bank for the EEC established
1962 Common Agricultural Policy (CAP) agreed
1967 EEC, ECSC and EURATOM merge to form the European Communities (EC), with a single Council of Ministers and Commission
1968 EEC customs union completed
Implementation of CAP completed
1974 Regular heads of governments summits begin
1975 'Own resources' funding of EC budget introduced
UK renegotiates its terms of accession
European Regional Development Fund created
1979 European Monetary System (EMS) comes into operation
First direct elections to European Parliament (June)
1984 Fontainebleau summit settles UK annual budget rebate and agrees first major CAP reform
1986 Single European Act (SEA) signed
European Political Co-operation (EPC) established
1988 Second major CAP reform
1991 Maastricht Treaty agreed
1992 31 December: Single internal market programme completed
1993 September: the exchange rate mechanism (ERM) of the EMS effectively suspended
1 November: The Maastricht Treaty enters into force, establishing the European Union (EU)
1994 1 January: European Economic Area (EEA) agreement comes into operation
Norway rejects EU membership in referendum
1997 Amsterdam Treaty agreed
1998 11 states chosen to enter first round of European Monetary Union (EMU)
European Central Bank replaces European Monetary Institute
1999 1 January: Euro launched March: 'Agenda 2000' financial and policy reform agreed
1 May: The Amsterdam Treaty enters into force
2000 9 December: Treaty of Nice agreed
2001 7 June: Ireland rejects Treaty of Nice in referendum
2002 1 January: Euro coins and banknotes enter circulation
23 July: ECSC Treaty expires following transfer of coal and steel sectors to the Treaty of Rome
2004 1 May: Cyprus, Czech Republic, Estonia, Hungary, Latvia, Lithuania, Malta, Poland, Slovakia and Slovenia become members of the European Union
May: A draft EU constitution is discussed by the European Foreign ministers following the breakdown of discussion on the topic at the European Council summit in December 2003.
18 June: The European Constitution is finalised at the Brussels summit and it is agreed that the new constitution will be signed on 20 November 2004 in the Campidoglio Palace in Rome. It is scheduled to come into force in 2006.

ENLARGEMENT AND EXTERNAL RELATIONS

The procedure for accession to the EU is laid down in the Treaty of Rome; states must be stable European democracies governed by the rule of law with free market economies. A membership application is studied by the Commission, which produces an Opinion. If the Opinion is positive, negotiations may be opened leading to an Accession Treaty which must be approved by all member state governments and parliaments, the European Parliament, and the applicant state's government and parliament.

Recent applicants: Morocco (applied 1987/rejected 1987), Turkey (applied 1987/negative Opinion 1989/offered accession partnership 1999), Cyprus (applied 1990/negotiations begun 1998), Malta (applied 1990/reapplied following a change of government 1998/negotiations begun 2000), Switzerland (applied 1992/application put on hold 1994), Hungary (applied 1994/negotiations begun 1998), Poland (applied 1994/negotiations begun 1998), Bulgaria (applied 1995/offered partnership 1998/negotiations begun 2000), Estonia (applied 1995/negotiations begun 1998), Latvia (applied 1995/offered partnership 1998/negotiations begun 2000), Lithuania (applied 1995/offered partnership 1998/negotiations begun 2000), Romania (applied 1995/offered partnership 1998/negotiations begun 2000), Slovakia (applied 1995/offered partnership 1998/negotiations begun 2000), the Czech Republic (applied 1996/negotiations begun 1998), Slovenia (applied 1996/negotiations begun 1998), Croatia (applied 2003).

Apart from the EEA Agreement, the EU has three types of agreements with other European and CIS states. 'Europe' agreements commit the EU and signatory states to long-term political and economic integration, a free trade zone (apart from agriculture and labour movement) and eventual EU membership. Government representatives from the signatory states are entitled to attend one summit and two finance and foreign council meetings a year. Agreements have been signed with Bulgaria (1993) and Romania (1993). Association agreements include a commitment to EU financial aid and to eventual membership; an agreement has been signed with Turkey (1963). Partnership and co-operation agreements (PCAs) are legal frameworks, based on the respect of democratic principles and human rights, setting out the political, economic and trade relationship between the EU and its partner countries. Each PCA is a ten-year bilateral treaty signed and ratified by the EU and the individual state. Agreements have been implemented with Russia (1997), Ukraine (1998) and Armenia, Azerbaijan, Georgia, Kazakhstan, Kyrgyzstan, Moldova and Uzbekistan (1999). Agreements have been signed with Belarus (1995) and Turkmenistan (1998) but are not yet in force. At the PCA Council's St Petersburg summit in May 2003, it was decided to strengthen the existing co-operation council between Russia and the EU, to a Permanent Partnership Council (PPC). At the Council's first meeting on 27 April 2004 a protocol to the Partnership and Co-operation Agreement between the EU and the Russian Federation was signed, extending the agreement to the ten new Member States of the EU.

Agenda 2000, a document issued by the Commission in 1997, addressed both the challenges posed by further enlargement of the Union, the institutional reforms that would be required to enable the Union to function effectively with additional members, and also evaluated each applicant in relation to the accession criteria, establishing a new financial framework for the period 2000–6.

In March 1998, formal accession negotiations were begun with Hungary, Poland, Estonia, the Czech Republic, Slovenia and Cyprus; they were begun with Bulgaria, Romania, Latvia, Lithuania, Malta and Slovakia in 2000, following the Helsinki summit in December 1999, when it was also agreed that an accession partnership should be offered to Turkey.

The Göteborg summit in June 2001 agreed on a timetable for accession for the first group of countries to complete negotiations. At the Copenhagen summit in December 2002, Cyprus, the Czech Republic, Estonia, Hungary, Latvia, Lithuania, Malta, Poland, Slovakia and Slovenia were invited to join the EU. The ten countries signed the Treaty of Accession in Athens on 16 April 2003 and became full members of the EU on 1 May 2004.

Following the findings of the European Commission's 2002 Regular Reports, accession plans for Bulgaria and Romania, which set 2007 as the target date for accession, were proposed. These plans were endorsed by the Copenhagen European Council in December 2002. In order for accession to take place in 2007, it was agreed by the Council that following the Commission's final recommendation on the readiness of the two countries for accession, a common Accession Treaty for Bulgaria and Romania should be signed by the end of 2005.

At the European Council meeting in Copenhagen in December 2002, the decision was made to recall the offer of an accession partnership to Turkey, following the Commission's conclusion that Turkey did not yet fully meet the required political criteria. The Commission was due to issue a report and recommendation by October 2004, on whether Turkey has fulfilled the Copenhagen political criteria. This is expected to influence the decision of the European Council, at its December 2004 meeting, on the possible opening of accession negotiations with Turkey.

THE LEGISLATIVE PROCESS

The core of the EU policymaking process is a dialogue between the Commission, which initiates and implements policy, and the Council of Ministers, which takes policy decisions. An increasing degree of democratic control is exercised by the European Parliament.

The original legislative process is known as the consultative procedure. The Commission drafts a proposal which it submits to the Council and to the Parliament. The Council then consults the Economic and Social Committee (ESC), the Parliament and the Committee of the Regions; the Parliament may request that amendments are made. With or without these amendments, the proposal is then adopted by the Council and becomes law.

Under the Single European Act (SEA), the role of the Parliament was strengthened by the introduction of the co-operation procedure. The Parliament now has a second reading of proposals in some fields, and after the second reading its rejection of a proposal can only be overturned by a unanimous decision of the Council. The Maastricht Treaty extended the scope of the co-operation procedure, which was applied to Single Market laws and harmonisation, trans-European networks, development policy, the social fund, and some aspects of transport, environment, research, social policy and competition policy.

The SEA introduced the assent procedure, whereby an absolute majority of the Parliament must vote to approve laws in certain fields before they are passed. Issues covered by the assent procedure include foreign treaties, accession treaties, international agreements with budgetary implications, citizenship, residence rights, the CAP, and regional and structural funds.

The Maastricht Treaty introduced the co-decision procedure; if, after the Parliament's second reading of a proposal, the Council and Parliament fail to agree, a conciliation committee of the two will reach a compromise. If a compromise is not reached, the Parliament can reject the legislation by the vote of an absolute majority of its members. The Amsterdam Treaty extended the co-decision procedure to all areas covered by qualified majority voting, with the exception of measures related to European Monetary Union (EMU).

The Council issues the following legislation:

- Regulations, which are binding in their entirety and directly applicable to all member states; they do not need to be incorporated into national law to come into effect
- Directives, which are less specific, binding as to the result to be achieved but leaving the method of implementation open to member states; a directive thus has no force until it is incorporated into national law
- Decisions, which are also binding but are addressed solely to one or more member states or individuals in a member state
- Recommendations
- Opinions, which are merely persuasive

The Council also has certain budgetary powers, including the power to reject the budget as a whole and to increase expenditure or redistribute money within sectors. However, the final decision on whether the budget should be adopted or rejected lies with the Parliament.

The Council may delegate legislative powers to the Commission. These consist of implementing powers and technical updating of existing legislation.

The European Central Bank has legislative powers within its field of competence. The Commission also has limited legislative powers, where it has been delegated the power to implement or revise legislation by the Council.

THE COMMUNITY BUDGET

The principles of funding the European Community budget were established by the Treaty of Rome and remain with modifications to this day. There is a legally binding limit on the overall level of resources (known as 'own resources') that the Community can raise from its member states; this limit is defined as a percentage of gross national product (GNP). Budget revenue and expenditure must balance and there is therefore no deficit financing. The 'own resources' decision, which came into effect in 1975 and has been regularly updated, states that there are four sources of Community funding under which each member state makes contributions: levies charged on agricultural imports into the Community from non-member states; customs duties on imports from non-member states; contributions based on member states' shares of a notional Community harmonised VAT base; and contributions based on member states' shares of Community GNP. The latter is the budget-balancing item and covers the difference between total expenditure and the revenue from the other three sources. Since 1984 the UK has had an annual rebate equivalent to 66 per cent of the difference between what the UK contributes to the budget and what it receives. This was introduced to compensate the UK for disproportionate contributions caused by its high proportion of agricultural and non-agricultural imports from non-member states and its relatively small receipts from the Common Agricultural Policy, the most important portion of Community expenditure.

BUDGET 2004

	Million euro*
Agriculture	46.8
Structural Operations	41.0
External Action	5.2
Pre-accession Strategy	1.7
Internal policies	8.7
Administration	6.0
Compensation	1.4
Reserves	0.4
TOTAL	111.2

Source: General Budget of the European Union for the Financial Year 2004

* 1 euro = £0.656 as at 17 June 2004

Under the Edinburgh summit agreement (December 1992) the EC budget rose to a maximum of 1.27 per cent of the EU's GNP in 1999. The agreed budget for 2000–6 will keep the 1.27 per cent ceiling, but resources devoted to the existing member states will fall to 0.98 per cent, with the remaining resources devoted to enlargement.

THE COMMON AGRICULTURAL POLICY

The Common Agricultural Policy (CAP) was established to increase agricultural production, provide a fair standard of living for farmers and ensure the availability of food at reasonable prices. This aim was achieved by a number of mechanisms:

– import levies
– intervention purchase
– export subsidies

These measures stimulated production but also placed increasing demands on the EC budget which were exacerbated by the increase in EC members and yields enlarged by technological innovation; CAP now accounts for over 40 per cent of EC expenditure. To surmount these problems reforms were agreed in 1984, 1988, 1992, 1997, 1999 and 2003.

REFORMS

The 1984 reforms created the system of co-responsibility levies: farm payments to the EC by volume of product sold. This system was supplemented by national quotas for particular products, such as milk. The 1988 reforms emphasised 'set-aside', whereby farmers are given direct grants to take land out of production as a means of reducing surpluses. The set-aside reforms were extended in 1993 for another five years and to every farm in the EC. The 1999 reforms will further reduce surpluses of cereals, beef and milk by cutting the intervention prices by up to 20 per cent and compensating producers by making area payments. Under the reforms, CAP rules will also be simplified, eliminating inconsistencies between policies.

Under the Uruguay round agreement of GATT concluded in 1993, the EU was required, over a six-year period from 1 January 1995, to reduce its import levies by 36 per cent, reduce its domestic subsidies by 20 per cent, reduce its export subsidies by 36 per cent in value, and reduce its subsidised exports by 21 per cent in volume. Agenda 2000, the programme to overhaul the policies of the EU and prepare it for the accession of new member states, will temporarily increase the cost of the CAP by €1,000 million a year in compensation payments, but leave it broadly stable by the end of the current planning period in 2006.

On 26 June 2003, EU farm ministers adopted a fundamental reform of the CAP, which include the following provisions:

– a single farm payment for EU farmers, independent from production
– payment to be linked to the respect of environmental, food safety, animal and plant health and animal welfare standards, and the requirement to keep all farmland in good condition
– a strengthened rural development policy with more EU money to help farmers meet EU production standards starting in 2005
– a reduction in direct payments for bigger farms
– a mechanism for financial discipline to ensure that the farm budget fixed until 2013 is not exceeded

The single farm payment will enter into force in 2005, however, if a member state needs a transitional period due to its specific agricultural conditions, it may apply the single farm payment from 2007 at the latest. The 10 new EU members were also given access to a special €5.8 billion three-year funding package.

THE SINGLE MARKET

Even after the removal of tariffs and quotas between member states in the 1970s and 1980s, the EC was still separated into a number of national markets by a series of non-tariff barriers. It was to overcome these internal barriers to trade that the concept of the Single Market was developed. The measures to be undertaken were codified in the Commission's 1985 White Paper on completing the internal market.

The White Paper included articles removing obstacles that distorted the internal market: the elimination of frontier controls; the mutual recognition of professional qualifications; the harmonisation of product specifications, largely by the mutual recognition of national standards; open tendering for public procurement contracts; the free movement of capital; the harmonisation of VAT and excise duties; and the reduction of state aid to particular industries. The target date for the completion of this process was 31 December 1992. The Single European Act aided the completion of the Single Market by changing the legislative process within the EC, particularly with the introduction of qualified majority voting in the Council of Ministers for some policy areas, and the introduction of the assent procedure in the European Parliament. The SEA also extends EC competence into the fields of technology, the environment, regional policy, monetary policy and external policy. The Single Market came into effect on 1 January 1993. The full implementation of the elimination of frontier controls and the harmonisation of taxes have, however, been repeatedly delayed.

THE EUROPEAN ECONOMIC AREA

The EC Single Market programme spurred European non-member states to open negotiations with the EC on preferential access for their goods, services, labour and capital to the Single Market. Principal among these states were European Free Trade Association (EFTA) members who opened negotiations on extending the Single Market to EFTA by the formation of the European Economic Area (EEA) encompassing all 19 EC and EFTA states. Agreement was reached in May 1992 but the operation of the EEA was delayed by its rejection in a Swiss referendum, necessitating an additional protocol agreed by the remaining 18 states. The EEA came into effect on 1 January 1994 after ratification by 17 member states (Liechtenstein joined on 1 May 1995 after adapting its customs union with Switzerland).

Austria, Finland and Sweden joined the EU itself on 1 January 1995, leaving only Norway, Iceland and Liechtenstein as the non-EU EEA members. Under the EEA agreement, the three states are to adopt the EU's *acquis communautaire*, apart from in the fields of agriculture, fisheries, and coal and steel.

The EEA is controlled by regular ministerial meetings and by a joint EU-EFTA committee which extends relevant EU legislation to EEA states. Apart from single market measures, there is co-operation in education, research and development, consumer policy and tourism. An EFTA Court of Justice has been established in Luxembourg and an EFTA Surveillance Authority in Brussels to supervise the implementation of the EEA Agreement.

THE EUROPEAN MONETARY SYSTEM AND THE SINGLE CURRENCY

The European monetary system (EMS) began operation in March 1979 with three main purposes. The first was to establish monetary stability in Europe, initially in exchange rates between EC member state currencies through the exchange rate mechanism (ERM), and in the longer term to be part of a wider stabilisation process, overcoming inflation and budget and trade deficits. The second purpose was to overcome the constraints resulting from the interdependence of EC economies, and the third was to aid the long-term process of European monetary integration.

The Maastricht Treaty set in motion timetables for achieving economic and monetary union (EMU) and a single currency (the euro). At the Brussels summit in May 1998, 11 member states were judged to fulfil or be close to fulfilling the necessary convergence criteria for participation in the first stage of EMU: Austria, Belgium, Finland, France, Germany, Ireland, Italy, Luxembourg, the Netherlands, Portugal and Spain.

The criteria were that:

- the budget deficit should be 3 per cent or less of gross domestic product (GDP)
- total national debt must not exceed 60 per cent of GDP
- inflation should be no more than 1.5 per cent above the average rate of the three best performing economies in the EU
- long-term interest rates should be no more than 2 per cent above the average of the three best performing economies in the EU in the previous 12 months
- applicants must have been members of the ERM for two years without having realigned or devalued their currency

Under the terms of a stability and growth pact agreed in Dublin in December 1996, penalties may be imposed on EMU members with high budget deficits. Governments with deficits exceeding 3 per cent of GDP will receive a warning and will be obliged to pay up to 0.5 per cent of their GDP into a fund after ten months. This will become a fine if the budget deficit is not rectified within two years. A member state with negative growth will be allowed to apply for an exemption from the fine in 'exceptional circumstances', e.g. a recession whereby GDP had fallen by 0.75 per cent or more during one year.

On 1 January 1999, the qualifying member states adopted the euro at irrevocably fixed exchange rates, the European Central Bank (ECB) took charge of the single monetary policy, and the euro replaced the ECU on a one-for-one basis.

On 19 June 2000, Greece was judged to have fulfilled the criteria for participation and adopted the euro on 1 January 2001. A referendum on the adoption of the euro was held in Denmark on 28 September 2000, but participation was rejected by the electorate.

The euro is now the legal currency in the participating states. Euro notes and coins were introduced on 1 January 2002 and circulated alongside national currencies for a period of up to two months, after which time national notes and coins ceased to be legal tender. The Swedish government held a referendum on adoption of the euro on 14 September 2003, in which 56 per cent voted against adopting the euro. On 10 June 2003 Britain announced that the euro would not be adopted at present on the grounds that the country was not economically ready to join the single currency. A future joining of the euro-zone was not ruled out. The 10 new EU member states are expected to adopt the euro when the necessary economic conditions have been met.

The ECB meets every two weeks to set interest rates for the countries participating in the euro. Its governing council has 17 members, being the six members of the ECB's executive board and the 12 governors of the national central banks of the participating states.

With the advent of EMU, the ERM was revised and Denmark became a member of ERM II, which requires it to maintain its currencies within set margins of the euro. Membership of ERM II is voluntary, although all member states outside the euro zone are encouraged to take part. Sweden and the UK are currently not members.

THE MAASTRICHT TREATY

The Treaty on European Union was agreed at a meeting of the European Council in Maastricht, the Netherlands, in

December 1991. It came into effect in November 1993 following ratification by the member states.

Three 'pillars' formed the basis of the new treaty:
- the European Community with its established institutions and decision-making processes
- a Common Foreign and Security Policy (*see* below) with the Western European Union as the potential defence component of the EU
- co-operation in justice and home affairs, with the Council of Ministers to co-ordinate policies on asylum, immigration, conditions of entry, cross-border crime, drug trafficking and terrorism

The Treaty established a common European citizenship for nationals of all member states and introduced the principle of subsidiarity whereby decisions are taken at the most appropriate level: national, regional or local. It extended EC competency into the areas of environmental and industrial policies, consumer affairs, health, and education and training, and extended qualified majority voting in the Council of Ministers to some areas which had previously required a unanimous vote. The powers of the European Parliament over the budget and over the Commission were also enhanced and a co-decision procedure enabled the Parliament to override decisions made by the Council of Ministers in certain policy areas. A separate protocol to the Maastricht Treaty on social policy was agreed by 11 states and was incorporated into the Amsterdam Treaty in 1997 following adoption by the UK.

COMMON FOREIGN AND SECURITY POLICY

The Common Foreign and Security Policy (CFSP) was created as a pillar of the EU by the Maastricht Treaty (*see* above). It adopted the machinery of the European Political Co-operation (EPC) framework which it replaced and was charged with providing a forum for member states and EU institutions to consult on foreign affairs.

The CFSP system is headed by the Council of the European Union, which provides general lines of policy. Specific policy decisions are taken by the Council of Foreign Ministers, which meets at least four times a year to determine areas for joint action. The High Representative of the CFSP initiates action, manages the CFSP and represents it abroad. The Council of Ministers is supported by the Political Committee which meets monthly, or within 48 hours if there is a crisis, to prepare for ministerial discussions. A group of correspondents, designated diplomats in each member's foreign ministry, provides day-to-day contact.

The Amsterdam Treaty introduced qualified majority voting for foreign affairs and created a high representative on CFSP to act as a spokesperson. It also established a new policy planning and early warning unit to monitor international developments. The unit is to consist of specialists from the member states, the Council and the Commission, as well as from the Western European Union (WEU).

The member states agreed at the Helsinki summit in December 1999 to establish a capability for military crisis-management operations, known as the rapid reaction force, which would be able to undertake peacemaking missions independently of NATO. The force was declared operational at the Laeken summit on 14–15 December 2001.

THE AMSTERDAM TREATY

The treaties of Rome and Maastricht were again amended through the Treaty of Amsterdam, which was signed in October 1997 and which came into effect on 1 May 1999. It extends the scope of qualified majority voting and the powers of the European Parliament. It also includes a formal commitment to fundamental human rights, gives additional powers to the European Court of Justice and provides for the appointment of a High Representative for EU Common Foreign and Security Policy.

THE SCHENGEN AGREEMENT

The Schengen Agreement was signed by France, Germany, Belgium, Luxembourg and the Netherlands in 1985. The Agreement committed the five states to abolishing internal border controls, erecting external frontiers against illegal immigrants, drug traffickers, terrorists and organised crime, and implementing the Schengen Information System to enable police stations and consular agents from Schengen member states to access data on specific individuals or vehicles and objects which are lost or stolen.

Subsequently signed by Spain and Portugal, the Agreement was ratified by the seven signatory states and entered into force in March 1995 with the removal of internal frontier, passport, customs and immigration controls. Italy and Austria became full members in April 1998 and Greece achieved full membership on 1 January 2000. Provisional agreement was reached in June 1995 between the signatory states and the Nordic Union on a merger of the two frontier-free zones – Denmark, Finland and Sweden joined in December 1996 and in March 2001 it was decided that the Schengen arrangements would also apply to Iceland and Norway. The ten member states who became members of the EU on 1 May 2004, do not yet form part of the Schengen zone but are timetabled to become full members of the zone by 2006. The UK and the Republic of Ireland have not signed the Agreement, but have expressed their intention to join in some aspects of its work.

The Schengen Agreement originated as an intergovernmental agreement but became part of the EU following the signing of the Amsterdam Treaty. A second generation Schengen Information System (SIS II) is planned for development.

THE TREATY OF NICE

The Treaty of Nice aims to enable the EU to accommodate up to 13 new member states. It extends qualified majority voting to 30 further articles of the treaties that previously required unanimity. The weighting of votes in the EU Council is to be altered from 1 January 2005 in preparation for the new member states, whose numbers of votes have been set. To obtain a qualified majority, a decision will require a specified number of votes (to be reviewed following each accession); the decision will have to be approved by a majority of member states and represent at least 62 per cent of the total population of the EU. The Treaty also sets the number of MEPs that both existing and new member states will have following enlargement.

The Treaty of Maastricht established the right of groups of member states to work together without requiring the participation of all members (enhanced co-operation); the Treaty of Nice removes the right of individual member states to veto the launch of enhanced co-operation and establishes a minimum number of eight member states for enhanced co-operation in the field of common foreign and security policy (CFSP).

The European Commission will be limited to one member per member state from 2005, with a maximum of 27 commissioners; a rotation system is to be introduced once EU membership exceeds 27 states.

The Treaty also adds to the powers of the President of the Commission and amends the rules of the operation of the Court of Justice.

The Treaty was rejected by 54 per cent of voters in a referendum in Ireland, the only country to put the issue to its electorate.

THE LAEKEN SUMMIT

At the European Council held in Laeken, Belgium on 14–15 December 2001, a declaration was agreed which established a convention to prepare for treaty reforms at the intergovernmental conference which was held on 17–18 July 2004. The convention, composed of representatives from national governments (15 members), national parliaments (30), the European Parliament (16), the European Commission (2) and the applicant states (39), started work on 28 February 2002, under the chairmanship of former French president Valérie Giscard d'Estaing.

At the Intergovernmental Conference in July 2004, the Council produced a provisional consolidated version of the draft treaty establishing a Constitution for Europe. The treaty will replace the existing EU and EC treaties. It was expected to be signed by the Heads of State in October/November 2004. The European Constitution will only enter into force once it has been ratified by all the Member States.

The Laeken European Council also agreed a common definition of terrorism, decided to institute an EU-wide arrest warrant, creating a single security area and thereby making it no longer necessary to extradite those accused of serious crimes, and established Eurojust to co-ordinate cross-border co-operation in crime investigation.

THE COUNCIL OF THE EUROPEAN UNION

Wetstraat 175, B-1048 Brussels, Belgium

The Council of the European Union (Council of Ministers) formally comprises the foreign ministers of the member states but in practice the ministers attending depend on the subject under discussion. Council decisions are taken by qualified majority vote (in which members' votes are weighted), by a simple majority, or by unanimity. The Council is assisted by a General Secretariat, whose head has since 1999 been the High Representative for the Common Foreign and Security Policy.

Unanimity votes are taken on sensitive issues such as taxation and constitutional matters; in preparation for an expanded Union, the Amsterdam Treaty extended areas where qualified majority votes may be taken, to areas such as Single Market laws and harmonisation, environment policy, health and safety, transport policy, overseas aid, research and development, culture, consumer protection, education and training, the development of a single currency and some aspects of social policy. Member states have weighted votes in the Council loosely proportional to their relative population sizes (*see* introductory table), with a total of 321 votes. The acts of the Council can take the form of regulations, directives, decisions, common actions or common positions, recommendations or opinions. The Council can also adopt conclusions, declarations or resolutions. The number of votes each member state can cast is set by Treaties. The Treaties also define cases in which a simple majority, qualified majority or unanimity are required. From 1 November 2004, a qualified majority will be reached if the following two conditions are met:

- if a majority of member states approve (in some cases a two-thirds majority)
- a minimum of 232 votes is cast in favour of the proposal, i.e. 72.3 per cent of the total (roughly the same share as under the previous system)

In addition, a member state may ask for confirmation that the votes in favour represent at least 62 per cent of the total population of the Union. If this is found not to be the case, the decision will not be adopted.

The Treaty of Nice, which was agreed on 7–9 December 2000 and signed on 26 February 2001, agreed amendments to the treaties in relation to the size and composition of the European Commission, the weighting of votes and the extension of qualified majority voting in the Council of Ministers and other issues relating to the Treaty of Amsterdam. The extension of qualified majority voting to external border controls, the EU budget, the composition of the European Courts and certain committees, visa rules and, by 2007, structural funds, was also agreed.

The European Council, comprising the heads of state or government of the member states and the President of the European Commission, meets twice a year to provide overall policy direction. The presidency of the EC is held in rotation for six-month periods, setting the agenda for and chairing all Council meetings. The European Council holds a summit in the country holding the presidency at the end of its period in office. The holders of the presidency for the years 2004–5 are:

2004 Ireland, Netherlands
2005 Luxembourg, UK

GENERAL SECRETARIAT OF THE COUNCIL OF THE EUROPEAN UNION
Wetstraat 175, B-1048 Brussels, Belgium
E public.info@consilium.eu.int
Secretary-General of the Council of the European Union and High Representative for the Common Foreign and Security Policy, Javier Solana Madariaga (Spain)

OFFICE OF THE UNITED KINGDOM PERMANENT REPRESENTATIVE TO THE EUROPEAN UNION
Ave Diauderghem 10, B-1040 Brussels, Belgium
Ambassador and UK Permanent Representative, John Grant, CMG, *apptd* 2000

THE EUROPEAN COMMISSION

Wetstraat 200, B-1049 Brussels, Belgium

Until 1 January 2005 the Commission consists of 25 Commissioners, two each from France, Germany, Italy, Spain and the UK, and one each from the remaining member states. As of 1 January 2005, and until the EU has 27 members, there will be one Commissioner per country. The members of the Commission are appointed for five-year renewable terms by the agreement of the member states; the terms run concurrently with the terms of the

European Parliament. The President and the other Commissioners are nominated by the governments of the member states, and, under the terms of the Nice Treaty, the appointments are approved by the European Parliament. The Commissioners pledge sole allegiance to the EC. The Commission initiates and implements EC legislation and is the guardian of the EC treaties. It is the exponent of Community-wide interests rather than the national preoccupations of the Council. Each Commissioner is supported by advisers and oversees whichever of the departments, known as Directorates-General (DGs), is assigned to him. Each Directorate-General is headed by a Director-General.

President José Durão Barroso was nominated by the governments of the member states on 28 June 2004 and the European Parliament confirmed his appointment with a secret ballot vote on 22 July 2004. He announced his new commission in August and officially took up the post in November 2004.

The Commission has a total staff of around 16,000 permanent civil servants.

COMMISSIONERS *as at August 2004*
President, José Manuel Barroso (Portugal)
Vice-President, Enterprise and Industry, Günter Verheugen (Germany)
Vice-President, Institutional Relations and Communication Strategy, Margot Wallström (Sweden)
Vice-President, Justice, Freedom and Security, Rocco Buttiglione (Italy)
Vice-President, Transport, Jacques Barrot (France)
Administrative Affairs, Audit and Anti-Fraud, Siim Kallas (Estonia)
Agriculture and Rural Development, Marian Fischer Boel (Denmark)
Competition, Neelie Kroes-Smit (Netherlands)
Development and Humanitarian Aid, Louis Michel (Belgium)
Economic and Monetary Affairs, Joaquin Almunia (Spain)
Education, Training, Culture and Multilingualism, Ján Figel (Slovakia)
Employment, Social Affairs and Equal Opportunities, Vladimir Spidla (Czech Republic)
Energy, László Kovács (Hungary)
Enlargement, Olli Rehn (Finland)
Environment, Stavros Dimas (Greece)
External Relations and European Neighbourhood Policy, Benita Ferrero-Waldner (Austria)
Financial Programming and Budget, Dalia Grybauskaite (Lithuania)
Fisheries and Maritime Affairs, Joe Borg (Malta)
Health and Consumers Protection, Markos Kyprianou (Cyprus)
Information Society and Media, Viviane Reding (Luxembourg)
Internal Market and Services, Charlie McCreevy (Ireland)
Regional Policy, Danuta Hübner (Poland)
Science and Research, Janez Potocnik (Slovenia)
Taxation and Customs Union, Ingrida Udre (Latvia)
Trade, Peter Mandelson (UK)

THE EUROPEAN PARLIAMENT

E civis@europarl.eu.int W www.europarl.eu.int

The European Parliament (EP) originated as the Common Assembly of the ECSC; it acquired its present name in 1962. Members (MEPs) were initially appointed from the membership of national parliaments; direct elections to the Parliament were first held in 1979 and take place at five-year intervals. Elections to the Parliament are held on differing bases throughout the EC; in June 1999, British MEPs were elected for the first time by a 'regional list' system of proportional representation. The Parliament comprises 732 seats. The most recent elections were held in June 2004 and the next elections are to be held in June 2009. MEPs serve on committees which scrutinise draft EC legislation and the activities of the Commission. A minimum of 12 plenary sessions a year are held in Strasbourg and six additional shorter plenary sessions a year are held in Brussels, committees meet in Brussels, and the Secretariat's headquarters is in Luxembourg.

The EP has gradually expanded its influence within the EU through the Single European Act, which introduced the co-operation procedure, the Maastricht Treaty, which extended the co-operation procedure and introduced the co-decision procedure (*see* Legislative Process), and the Amsterdam Treaty, which effectively extended co-decision to all areas except economic and monetary union. It has general powers of supervision over the Commission, and consultation and co-decision with the Council; it votes to approve a newly appointed Commission and can dismiss it at any time by a two-thirds majority (as it threatened to do in January 1999). Under the Maastricht Treaty it has the right to be consulted on the appointment of the new Commission and can veto its appointment. It can reject the EU budget as a whole, alter non-compulsory expenditure not specified in the EU primary legislation, and can question the Commission's management of the budget and call in the Court of Auditors. Although the EP cannot directly initiate legislation, its reports can spur the Commission into action. In accordance with the Maastricht Treaty the EP appointed an ombudsman in October 1995, to provide citizens with redress against maladministration by EU institutions.

The Parliament's organisation is deliberately biased in favour of multinational political groupings, recognition of a political grouping in the parliament entitling it to offices, funding, representation on committees and influence in debates and legislation. A political grouping must comprise members from more than one member state; a grouping with members from two countries needs 23 members for recognition, a grouping with members from three countries needs 18 members, and a grouping with members from four or more countries needs only 14 members.

PARLIAMENT, Palais de l'Europe, Allée du Printemps, BP 1024/F, F-67070 Strasbourg Cedex, France.
T (+33) (3) 8817 4001 F (+33) (3) 8825 6501
Wiertzstraat, Postbus 1047, B-1047 Brussels, Belgium.
T (+32) (2) 284 2111 F (+32) (2) 284 6974
SECRETARIAT, Centre Européen, Plateau du Kirchberg, BP 1601, L-2929 Luxembourg. T (+352) 43001
F (+352) 4300 29393/29292
President, Patrick Cox (Ireland)
OMBUDSMAN, Nikiforos Diamandouros (Greece),
1 avenue du Président Robert Schuman, BP 403, F-67001, Strasbourg Cedex, France.
E euro-ombudsman@europarl.eu.int
W www.euro-ombudsman.eu.int

THE COMMITTEE OF THE REGIONS

Rue Montoyer 92–102, B-1000 Brussels, Belgium
E info@cor.eu.int W www.cor.eu.int

The Committee of the Regions (CoR) is the political assembly which provides local and regional authorities with a voice within the European Union. The EU Treaties oblige the European Commission and Council of Ministers to consult the Committee of the Regions whenever new proposals are made in areas which have repercussions at regional or local level. The CoR issues opinions on proposals for EU laws, which directly affect local and regional authorities. It can also draw up opinions on its own initiative, which enables it to put issues on the EU agenda.

The Committee has 317 full members and the same number of alternate members. They are proposed by the Member States to the Council of Ministers, which appoints them for a four-year renewable term of office. Members must hold a regional or local authority electoral mandate or be politically accountable to an elected assembly. They participate in the work of six specialist commissions which are responsible for drafting the CoR's opinions, for example on economic and social cohesion, trans-European infrastructure networks, social policy, the environment and vocational training.
President, Peter Straub
Secretary-General, Gerhard Stahl

COURT OF FIRST INSTANCE

Palais de la Cour de justice, Boulevard Konrad Adenauer, Kirchberg, L-2925 Luxembourg

Established under powers conferred by the Single European Act, the Court of First Instance has jurisdiction to hear and determine all actions brought by natural or legal persons. It is composed of 25 judges, appointed for renewable six-year terms by the governments of the member states. During 2003, 466 new cases were lodged at the court and 339 cases were concluded.
President, B. Vesterdorf

COURT OF JUSTICE OF THE EUROPEAN COMMUNITIES

Palais de la Cour de justice, Boulevard Konrad Adenauer, Kirchberg, L-2925 Luxembourg
E info@curia.eu.int W www.curia.eu.int

The Court of Justice is common to the two European Communities. It exists to safeguard the law in the interpretation and application of the Community treaties, to decide on the legality of decisions of the Council of Ministers or the Commission, and to determine infringements of the treaties. Cases may be brought to it by the member states, the Community institutions, firms or individuals. Its decisions are directly binding in the member countries, and the Maastricht Treaty enhanced the Court's powers by permitting it to impose fines on member states. The 25 judges and eight advocates general of the Court are appointed for renewable six-year terms by the member governments in concert. During 2003, 561 new cases were lodged at the court and 494 cases were concluded.
President, V. Skouris
First Advocate-General, A. Tizzano

THE EUROPEAN CENTRAL BANK

29 Kaiserstrasse, D-60311 Frankfurt-am-Main, Germany
E info@ecb.int W www.ecb.int

The European Central Bank (ECB), which superseded the European Monetary Institute, was established on 1 July 1998. Its governing bodies are the Executive Board, the Governing Council and the General Council. The Executive Board consists of the President, the Vice-President and four other members, who are appointed by the governments of the states participating in the single currency, at the level of Heads of State and Government. The Governing Council comprises the six members of the Executive Board and the governors of the national central banks of the participating states; the General Council comprises the President and Vice-President and the 25 governors of the national central banks, the other members of the Executive Board being entitled to participate but not to vote. The ECB is independent of national governments and of all other EU institutions. It became fully operational on 1 January 1999, and defines and implements the single monetary policy necessary for EMU. It operates as part of the European System of Central Banks (ESCB), which consists of the ECB and the national central banks of the EU member states.
President, Jean-Claude Trichet (France)
Vice-President, Lucas Papademos (Greece)

THE EUROPEAN COURT OF AUDITORS

12 rue Alcide De Gasperi, L-1615 Luxembourg
E euraud@eca.eu.int W www.eca.eu.int

The European Court of Auditors, established in 1977, examines the accounts of all revenue and expenditure of the European Communities and Community bodies and evaluates whether all revenue has been received and all expenditure incurred in a lawful and regular manner and in accordance with the principles of sound financial management. The Court issues an annual report and a statement of assurance as to the reliability of the accounts and the legality and regularity of the underlying transactions. It also publishes special reports on specific topics and delivers opinions on financial matters. The Court has one member from each member state appointed for a six-year term by the Council of Ministers following consultation with the European Parliament.
President, Juan Manuel Fabra Vallés (Spain)

THE EUROPEAN ECONOMIC AND SOCIAL COMMITTEE

Rue Belliard 97/113, B-1000 Brussels, Belgium
W www.esc.eu.int

The European Economic and Social Committee (EESC) is an advisory and consultative body. As of June 2004, it has 317 members appointed by the governments of 25 member states, and is divided into three groups: employers, workers, and other interest groups such as consumers, farmers and the self-employed. It issues opinions on draft EC legislation and can bring matters to the attention of the Commission, Council and Parliament. The EESC's competencies have increased as a result of revisions to the Treaty of Rome, and the Treaty Nice formally recognised the importance of the opinions of the EU's economic and social partners.
President, Roger Briesch (France)

THE EUROPEAN ENVIRONMENT AGENCY

Kongens Nytorv 6, DK-1050 Copenhagen K, Denmark
T (+45) 3336 7100 F (+45) 3336 7199
E eea@eea.eu.int W org.eea.eu.int

The European Environment Agency (EEA) aims to support sustainable development and to help achieve significant and measurable improvement in Europe's environment, through the provision of information to policy-making agents and the public. The EEA has been operational since 1994. It is a European Union body but is open to non-EU countries that share its objectives. Following the accession of the 10 new European member states in June 2004, it has 31 members.
Executive Director, Ms Jacqueline McGlade

THE EUROPEAN INVESTMENT BANK

100 boulevard Konrad Adenauer, L-2950 Luxembourg
E info@eib.org W www.eib.org

The European Investment Bank (EIB) was set up in 1958 under the terms of the Treaty of Rome to finance capital investment projects promoting the balanced development of the European Community by providing loans for capital investment projects furthering EU policy objectives, in fields such as regional development, transport and communications, security of energy supplies, the environment, international competitiveness, support for small and medium-sized enterprises, health and education investment, and investment to encourage a knowledge-based economy.

Outside the EU, the EIB participates in the implementation of the EU's development policy, through long-term loans from its own resources or subordinated loans and risk capital from EU or member states' budgetary funds, in some 150 non-EU countries: in pre-accession countries and, under the terms of different association or co-operation agreements, with countries in the Mediterranean region, in the Balkans, in Latin America, Asia and South Africa, in Africa, the Caribbean and the Pacific.

The Bank's total financing operations in 2003 amounted to €42.3 billion, of which €34.2 billion was for investment within the EU.

In June 2000, the EIB launched the Innovation 2000 Initiative (i2i). At end 2003, the EIB Group had fully achieved its i2i objectives: in the period 2000–3, the EIB Group signed over 350 operations totalling €19.5 billion (€17 billion EIB plus €2.5 billion EIF). By the end of 2003 the i2i programme had completed the three-year term initially fixed by the Bank's Board of Directors, and the objective set under the 'Lisbon Strategy' was reaffirmed by various European Councils, resulting in a prolongation of the i2i programme until 2010.

The shareholders of the EIB are the 25 member states of the EU, who have all subscribed to the Bank's capital of €163.7 billion. The bulk of the funds required by the Bank to carry out its tasks are borrowed on the capital markets of the EU and non-member countries, and on the international market.

As it operates on a non-profit-making basis, the interest rates charged by the EIB reflect the cost of the Bank's borrowings and closely follow conditions in world capital markets.

The Board of Governors of the EIB consists of one government minister nominated by each of the member countries, usually the finance, economic affairs or treasury minister, who lay down general directives on the credit policy of the Bank and appoint members to the Board of Directors (24 nominated by the member states, one by the European Commission), which takes decisions on the granting and raising of loans and the fixing of interest rates. A Management Committee, composed of the Bank's President and seven Vice-Presidents, also appointed by the Board of Governors, is responsible for the day-to-day operations of the Bank. The President and Vice-Presidents also preside as Chairmen and Vice-Chairmen at meetings of the Board of Directors.
President, Philippe Maystadt (Belgium)

THE EUROPEAN POLICE OFFICE

PO Box 90850, NL-2509 LW The Hague, The Netherlands
E info@europol.eu.int W www.europol.eu.int

The European Police Office (Europol) came into being on 1 October 1998 and assumed its full powers on 1 July 1999. It superseded the Europol Drugs Unit and exists to improve police co-operation between member states and to combat terrorism, illicit traffic in drugs and other serious forms of international crime. It is ultimately responsible to the Council. Each member state has set up a national unit to liaise with Europol, and the units send at least one liaison officer to represent its interests at Europol headquarters. Europol maintains a computerised information system, designed to facilitate the exchange of information between member states; the system is maintained by the national units and may be consulted by Europol agents. The computerised database may contain both personal and non-personal data; individuals are entitled to request access to data concerning themselves. Europol has a Management Board comprising one senior police representative from each member state. All Europol activities are monitored by an independent joint supervisory body to ensure the rights of the individual are upheld.
Director, Jürgen Storbeck (Germany)

EUROPEAN COMMUNITY INFORMATION

EUROPEAN COMMISSION REPRESENTATION OFFICES

ENGLAND, 8 Storey's Gate, London SW1P 3AT T 020-7973 1992
WALES, 2 Caspian Point, Caspian Way, Cardiff CF10 4QQ T 029-208 95020
SCOTLAND, 9 Alva Street, Edinburgh EH2 4PH T 0131-225 2058
NORTHERN IRELAND, Windsor House, 9–15 Bedford Street, Belfast BT2 7EG T 028-9024 0708
REPUBLIC OF IRELAND, 18 Dawson Street, Dublin 2

EUROPEAN COMMISSION DELEGATIONS

AUSTRALIA, 18 Arkana Street, Yarralumla, ACT 2600 (and a number of other cities)
CANADA, Inn of the Provinces, Office Tower (Suite 1110), 350 Sparks Street, Ottawa, Ontario K1R 7SA
USA, 2300 M Street NW (Suite 707), Washington DC 20037; 1 Dag Hammarskjöld Plaza, 254 East 47th Street, New York, NY 10017
UK OFFICE OF THE EUROPEAN PARLIAMENT 2 Queen Anne's Gate, London SW1H 9AA T 020-7227 4300

EUROPEAN PARLIAMENT

POLITICAL GROUPINGS *as at June 2004*

	EPP-ED	PES	ELDR	EUL/NGL	Green/EFA	UEN	EDD	Others	Total
Austria	6	7	–	–	2	–	–	3	18
Belgium	7	7	5	–	2	–	–	3	24
Cyprus	2	–	1	2	–	–	–	1	6
Czech Republic	11	2	–	6	–	–	–	5	24
Denmark	1	5	4	2	–	1	1	–	14
Estonia	1	3	2	–	–	–	–	–	6
Finland	4	3	5	1	1	–	–	–	14
France	28	31	–	3	6	–	–	10	78
Germany	49	23	7	7	13	–	–	–	99
Greece	11	8	–	4	–	–	–	1	24
Hungary	13	9	2	–	–	–	–	–	24
Ireland	5	1	–	–	–	4	–	3	13
Italy	28	15	9	7	2	9	–	8	78
Latvia	3	–	1	–	1	4	–	–	9
Lithuania	3	2	3	–	–	–	–	5	13
Luxembourg	3	1	1	–	1	–	–	–	6
Malta	2	3	–	–	–	–	–	–	5
Netherlands	7	7	5	2	2	–	2	2	27
Poland	19	8	4	–	–	7	–	16	54
Portugal	7	12	–	2	–	2	–	1	24
Slovakia	8	3	–	–	–	–	–	3	14
Slovenia	4	1	2	–	–	–	–	–	7
Spain	23	24	1	1	5	–	–	–	54
Sweden	5	5	3	2	1	–	–	3	19
UK	28	19	12	–	5	–	12	2	78
Total	278	199	67	39	41	27	15	66	732

PES — Party of European Socialists (including the British, Irish and Dutch Labour Parties, Northern Ireland Social Democratic and Labour Party, Austrian, Danish, Finnish, German, Italian and Swedish Social Democrats, Belgian, French, Greek, Portuguese, and Spanish Socialists, Italian Democratic Left Party, Luxembourg Socialist Workers' Party, Cyprus KISOS Party, Czech Social Democrats (CSSD), Malta's Partit Laburista Party, Estonian, Latvian, Lithuanian, Polish, Slovakian, Slovenian and Hungarian Social Democrat Parties), Socialist, Social Democratic and Labour parties

EPP-ED — European People's Party and European Democrats (including British and Danish Conservative Parties, Spanish Popular Party, French Nouvelle UDF, RPR and DL, Irish Fine Gael, Swedish Moderate Party, Finnish National Coalition Party, Austrian People's Party, Greek New Democracy, Belgian Christian Socialists, Czech, Cypriot, Estonian, Hungarian, Italian , Latvian, Polish, Slovak and Slovenian Christian Democrats, Pensioners' Party and People's Party, Luxembourg Christian Socialists, Portuguese Social Democrats), Christian Democrats, Christian Socialists and Conservatives

UEN — Union for a Europe of Nations (including French, Italian, Irish, Portuguese, Danish, Polish, Estonian, Latvian and Slovak national parties

ELDR — European Liberal, Democrat and Reform Party (including British Liberal Democrats, Danish Left and Radical Left Parties, Dutch Democrats '66 and People's Party for Freedom and Democracy, Belgian Liberals, Italian and Luxembourg Democrats, Swedish Liberal People's Party, Finnish Swedish People's Party and Centre Party, Estonian Reform Party, Latvia's Way Party, Lithuanian Liberal Centre Union, Polish Liberal Party, Hungarian Alliance of Free Democrats, the Czech Democratic Alliance, Slovenian Liberals, and United Democrats Cyprus), centre and liberal parties

GUE/NGL — Confederal Group of the European United Left/ Nordic Green Left (French, Greek, Italian, Czech, Slovak and Portuguese Communist Parties, Italian Refounded Communist Party, Cypriot Progressive Party of Working People, Danish, Dutch, Swedish, Finnish, Greek, Latvian and Spanish Socialist/Left parties)

Green/EFA — Greens/European Free Alliance Group (Austrian, British, Cypriot, Czech, Danish, Estonian, Finnish, French, German, Greek, Hungarian, Irish, Italian, Latvian, Luxembourgish, Maltese, Portuguese, Slovak, Spanish and Swedish Green Parties, Dutch Green Left Party, Belgian Ecological Parties, Plaid Cymru and Scottish National Parties), green and nationalist parties

EDD — Group for a Europe of Democracies and Diversities (French Hunting, Fishing, Nature and Traditions, Dutch Calvinists and Christians, UK Independence Party, Danish June Movement and Movement Against the EU), anti-EU, anti-federalist and religious parties

Others — (Austrian Freedom Party, Belgian Flemish Block, French National Front, Italian National Alliance, Northern Ireland Democratic Unionist Party, Polish Self-Defence Party)

INTERNATIONAL ORGANISATIONS

ANDEAN COMMUNITY

General Secretariat, Paseo de la Republica 3895, esq. Aramburs, San Isidro, Lima 27, Peru
T (+51) (1) 411 1400 F (+51) (1) 221 3329
E contacto@comunidadandina.org
W www.comunidadandina.org

The Andean Community came into being on 1 August 1997. It comprises five member states (Bolivia, Colombia, Ecuador, Peru and Venezuela) as well as the bodies of the Andean Integrated System (AIS). The Andean Community facilitates the development of the member countries through economic and social integration and co-operation, acceleration of the economic growth of the Andean countries, the promotion of job creation, furthering the aim of creating a Latin American common market, strengthening the position of the member states in the international economic context, and reducing the differences in development that exist between the member states.

It aims to achieve its objectives by a programme of complete trade liberalisation, a common external tariff, the reduction of border controls, the progressive harmonisation of economic and social policies, the co-ordination of national legislation in relevant fields, promoting industrialisation and agricultural development, and supporting technological development programmes.

The General Secretariat of the Andean Community is the executive body, which is responsible for administration, ensuring that member states comply with their obligations and resolving disputes. The General Secretariat operates under the direction of the Secretary-General, who is elected by the Andean Council of Foreign Ministers (ACFM). The General Secretariat can propose decisions or suggestions to the ACFM and to the Commission. It also manages the integration process, ensures that Community commitments are fulfilled, and maintains relations with the member countries and the executive bodies of other international organisations.

The Andean Presidential Council is the highest-level body of the AIS and comprises the presidents of the member states; it meets at least once a year and decides on new policies, evaluates the integration process and makes decisions on reports and suggestions from other bodies. The chairmanship is rotated among the members of the council on a calendar year basis. The ACFM co-ordinates the positions of the member states in international issues, signs international agreements on behalf of its member states and can issue decisions that are legally binding in the member states. The Commission of the Andean Community is composed of a plenipotentiary representative from each member state and makes, implements and evaluates policies in the field of trade and investment in the region. The Court of Justice of the Andean Community comprises one judge from each member state. It ensures the uniform implementation of decisions and settles disputes. The Andean Development Corporation aims to support the sustainable development of the member states by promoting trade and investment. The Andean Parliament became directly elected in 2003.
Secretary-General, Allan Wagner Tizon

ARAB MAGHREB UNION

14 Rue Zalagh, Agdal, Rabat, Morocco
T (+212) (376) 71274 F (+212) (376) 71253
E sg.uma@maghrebarabe.org
W www.maghrebarabe.org

The treaty establishing the Arab Maghreb Union (AMU) was signed on 17 February 1989 by the heads of state of the five member states, Algeria, Libya, Mauritania, Morocco and Tunisia. The AMU aims to strengthen ties between the member states, who share strong historical, cultural and linguistic affinities, by developing agriculture and commerce, introducing the free circulation of goods and services, and establishing joint projects and economic co-operation programmes.

Decisions are made by the Council of Heads of State, which meets annually, and must be unanimous. A Council of Foreign Affairs Ministers meets regularly to prepare for the sessions of the Council of Heads of State. The Secretariat is based in Rabat and there is a Consultative Assembly, which consists of 30 representatives from each member state, based in Algiers, and a Court of Justice, with two judges from each country, based in Nouakchott, Mauritania.
Secretary-General, Habib Boulares (Tunisia)

ARCTIC COUNCIL

Ministry for Foreign Affairs of Iceland, Raudararstigur 25, 15-150 Reykjavik, Iceland
T (+354) 545 9900 F (+354) 562 2373
W www.arctic-council.org

The Arctic Council was founded in 1996 in Ottawa, Canada and is a regional forum for socio-economic development and scientific research within the Arctic region. An inter-governmental forum, the Arctic Council comprises eight states including Canada, the USA, Denmark (including Greenland and The Faroe Islands), Finland, Norway, Sweden, Iceland and Russia. A further six organisations representing indigenous peoples are granted permanent participatory status and include the Saami Council, Inuit Circumpolar Conference and the Arctic Athabaskan Council.

Decisions within the Arctic Council are taken at biennial ministerial meetings attended by Foreign Ministers or designates of the member states. The chairmanship of the Council and Secretariat rotates among member states, also on a biennial basis. Between these meetings, the operation of the Council is administered by the Committee of Senior Arctic Officials.

The main scientific work of the Arctic Council is carried out in five working groups, each focusing on specific issues such as monitoring, assessment and prevention of pollution, climate change, biodiversity and public health.
Executive-Secretary, Bryndis Kjartandottir (Iceland)

ASIAN DEVELOPMENT BANK

PO Box 789, 0980 Manila, Philippines
T (+63) (632) 632 4444 F (+63 (632) 636 2444
E information@adb.org
W www.adb.org

The Asian Development Bank (ADB) was founded in 1966 and is a multilateral financial institution dedicated to reducing poverty in Asia and the Pacific. The ADB extends loans, equity investments and technical assistance to governments and public and private enterprises in its developing member countries, promotes the investment of public and private capital for development and assists in the co-ordination of development policies and plans in the developing member countries. The bank's projects and programmes prioritise economic growth, human development, gender and development, good governance, environmental protection, private sector development and regional co-operation.

The ADB raises funds through members' contributions and bond issues on the world's capital markets. In 2002, the ADB provided loans totalling US$5,600 million and technical assistance costing US$179 million. There are 63 member countries in the Asian and Pacific region and in Western Europe and North America. The ADB's headquarters is in the Philippines and there are 24 offices around the world.

President, Tadao Chino (Japan)

ASIA-PACIFIC ECONOMIC CO-OPERATION

35 Heng Mui Keng Terrace, Singapore 119616
T (+65) 6775 6012 F (+65) 6775 6013
E info@mail.apecsec.org.sg
W www.apecsec.org.sg

Asia-Pacific Economic Co-operation (APEC) was founded in 1989 in response to the growing interdependence among Asia-Pacific economies. The 1994 Declaration of Common Resolve envisaged a free trade zone, to be established by 2010 in industrialised countries and by 2020 in developing member states. There are three pillars of APEC activities: trade and investment liberalisation, business facilitation, and economic and technical co-operation. Members define and fund work programmes for APEC's four committees, 11 working groups and other APEC fora.

The members are: Australia, Brunei, Canada, Chile, China (People's Republic), China (Hong Kong), Indonesia, Japan, Republic of Korea, Malaysia, Mexico, New Zealand, Papua New Guinea, Peru, the Philippines, Russia, Singapore, Chinese Taipei, Thailand, the USA and Vietnam.

The APEC chairman is responsible for hosting the annual ministerial meeting of foreign and economic ministers. The chairmanship rotates annually among member states. Senior officials of the organisation make recommendations to the ministers and carry out their decisions. They oversee and co-ordinate budgets and work programmes. In addition, there are many advisory groups.

There is a permanent secretariat based in Singapore.

Executive-Director, HE Mario Artaza

ASSOCIATION OF SOUTH EAST ASIAN NATIONS

70A Jalan Sisingamangaraja, Jakarta 12110, Indonesia
T (+62) (21) 726 2991 F (+62) (21) 739 8234
E public@asean.or.id
W www.asean.or.id

The Association of South East Asian Nations (ASEAN) was formed in 1967 with the aims of accelerating economic growth, social progress and cultural development, and ensuring regional stability. The founding members are Indonesia, Malaysia, the Philippines, Singapore and Thailand. Brunei and Vietnam joined in 1984 and 1995 respectively. Laos and Myanmar were admitted in July 1997. Cambodia was admitted on 30 April 1999.

The ASEAN Summit, a meeting of the heads of government, which convenes every three years, is ASEAN's highest authority, but informal summits are held annually. The ASEAN Ministerial Meeting (AMM) is an annual meeting of ASEAN foreign ministers and is responsible for the formulation of policy guidelines and the co-ordination of activities, although other relevant ministers are included in the AMM depending on the subject under discussion. The ASEAN Economic Ministers (AEM) meet annually to co-ordinate economic policy. The AMM and AEM usually hold a joint ministerial meeting before an ASEAN summit.

The 1992 Summit agreed to set up the ASEAN Free Trade Area (AFTA), which was fully implemented in 2003. A common preferential tariff was introduced in 1993. At the annual summit in 1995, a South East Asia nuclear weapon-free zone was declared.

The Secretary-General of ASEAN is appointed on merit by the heads of government and can initiate, advise, co-ordinate and implement ASEAN activities. In addition to the ASEAN Secretariat based in Jakarta, each member state has a national secretariat in its foreign ministry which organises and implements activities at national level.

Secretary-General, Ong Keng Yong (Singapore)

ASEAN COMMITTEE IN THE UK
Singapore High Commission, 9 Wilton Road, London SW1X 9SA
T 020-7235 8315 F 020-7235 5874
Chairman, HE Prof. Pang Eng Fong

BALTIC ASSEMBLY

Tornu 4, Kazarmas III, Section C, Room 301, Riga, LV1050, Latvia
T (+371) 7225 178 F (+371) 7225 366
E baltasam@parks.lv W www.baltasam.org

Established in November 1991, the Baltic Assembly (BA) is an international organisation for co-operation between the parliaments of Estonia, Latvia and Lithuania. The legislature of each member state appoints 20 parliamentarians to the Assembly, including a head and deputy head of the national delegation. The Assembly holds two sessions per year in each of the member states in rotation. In addition, there are permanent and ad-hoc committees.

The Baltic Assembly meets once a year with the Baltic Council of Ministers, which comprises the heads of government and ministers of the Baltic states and promotes intergovernmental and regional co-operation between the Baltic States; the joint sessions are known as the Baltic Council.

President, Janis Reivs (Latvia)

BANK FOR INTERNATIONAL SETTLEMENTS

Centralbahnplatz 2 & Aeschenplatz 1, CH-4002 Basel, Switzerland
T (+41) (61) 280 8080 F (+41) (61) 280 9100/8100
E email@bis.org
W www.bis.org

The Bank for International Settlements (BIS), which was founded in 1930, fosters international monetary and financial co-operation by acting as a forum to promote discussion and facilitate decision-making processes among central banks and within the international financial community. It also acts as a centre for economic and monetary research and an agent in connection with international financial operations.

The statutory organs of the BIS are the General Meeting and the Board of Directors. There are 50 member central banks. At present, around 130 central banks and international financial institutions place deposits with the BIS. Total currency deposits placed with the BIS amounted to approximately US$122.5 billion at the end of March 2003, representing 6.5 per cent of world foreign exchange reserves. Administrative control is vested in the Board of Directors which comprises 17 members, including the Governor of the Bank of England.

Chairman of the Board of Directors and President of the Bank for International Settlements, Nout Wellink (Netherlands)

CAB INTERNATIONAL

Wallingford, Oxon OX10 8DE
T 01491-832111 F 01491-833508
E cabi@cabi.org W www.cabi.org

CAB International (CABI) (formerly the Commonwealth Agricultural Bureau) was founded in 1929. It generates, disseminates and applies scientific knowledge in support of sustainable development, with an emphasis on agriculture, forestry and natural resources and the needs of developing countries. The organisation is owned and governed by its 40 member governments, each represented on an Executive Council. A Governing Board provides guidance on policy issues.

CABI has two divisions: bioscience and publishing. These undertake research and consultancy aimed at raising agricultural productivity, conserving biological resources, protecting the environment and controlling disease. The organisation publishes books, journals and newsletters and produces bibliographic databases on agriculture, health and allied disciplines. It also undertakes contracted scientific research and provides consultancy services and information support to developing countries. Any country is eligible to apply for membership. Applications are by invitation from existing members and are authorised by a head of state or delegated authority.

Director-General, Dr Denis Blight

CARIBBEAN COMMUNITY AND COMMON MARKET

PO Box 10827, Georgetown, Guyana
T (+592) 226 9281/9 F (+592) 226 7816
E carisec3@caricom.org
W www.caricom.org

The Caribbean Community and Common Market (CARICOM) was established in 1973 with the signing of the Treaty of Chaguaramas, which was revised in 2001. The objectives of CARICOM are to improve working and living standards, to aim for full employment, to promote economic development and convergence, to expand economic relations with third states, to enhance economic competitiveness and productivity, to co-ordinate member states' foreign and economic policies and enhance functional co-operation in the delivery of common services, including the promotion of activities in the fields of health, education, transport and telecommunications.

The supreme organ is the Conference of Heads of Government, which determines policy, takes strategic decisions and is responsible for resolving conflicts and all matters relating to the founding treaty. The Community Council of Ministers consists of ministers of government responsible for CARICOM affairs and any other ministers designated by member states, and is responsible for strategic planning in the areas of economic integration, functional co-operation and external relations. The principal administrative arm is the Secretariat, based in Guyana. The Bureau of the Conference of Heads of Government is the executive body. It comprises the Chairman of the Conference, the outgoing Chairman and the Secretary-General, who are authorised to initiate proposals and to secure the implementation of CARICOM decisions. In addition, there are four ministerial councils dealing with trade and economic development, foreign and community relations, human and social development, and finance and planning.

The 15 member states are Antigua and Barbuda, the Bahamas (which is not a member of the Common Market), Barbados, Belize, Dominica, Grenada, Guyana, Haiti, Jamaica, Montserrat, St Christopher and Nevis, St Lucia, St Vincent and the Grenadines, Suriname and Trinidad and Tobago. Anguilla, the British Virgin Islands and the Turks and Caicos Islands are associate members. Aruba, Bermuda, the Cayman Islands, Colombia, the Dominican Republic, Mexico, the Netherlands' Antilles, Puerto Rico and Venezuela have observer status.

Secretary-General, Edwin W. Carrington

COMMISSION OF THE AFRICAN UNION

PO Box 3243, Addis Ababa, Ethiopia
T (+251) (1) 517700 F (+251) (1) 517844

The Organisation of African Unity (OAU) was established in 1963 and has 53 members; Morocco suspended its participation in 1985 in protest at the Polisario-proclaimed Saharan Arab Democratic Republic (SADR), representing Western Sahara, being admitted as a member. The OAU aims to further African unity and solidarity, to co-ordinate political, economic, social and defence policies, and to eliminate colonialism in Africa.

The chief organs are the Assembly of heads of state or government, which is the supreme organ of the OAU and meets once a year to consider matters of common African concern and to co-ordinate the Organisation's policies; the Council of foreign ministers, which is the Organisation's executive body responsible for the implementation of the Assembly's policies, and which meets twice a year; and the Commission of Mediation, Conciliation and Arbitration which promotes the peaceful settlement of disputes between member countries. The main administrative body is the General Secretariat, based in Addis Ababa, headed by a Secretary-General who is elected by the Assembly for a four-year term.

Substantial budgetary arrears due to delays in the payment of national contributions has meant that the OAU continually faces difficulties in furthering its aims. In June 1991 the Assembly adopted an African Economic

Community Treaty which envisages establishment of the Economic Community after ratification by two-thirds of the OAU's membership. In June 1993 a mechanism was created for conflict prevention, management and resolution, and a peace fund was established.

Following an initiative put forward by Libyan leader Col. Muammar al-Gadhafi in September 1999, it was agreed at the 36th summit of the OAU in July 2000 in Lomé, Togo, to establish an African Union.

The creation of the African Union was declared at a summit meeting in Sirte on 1–2 March 2001, and it legally began operations on 26 May 2001. The first Assembly of the African Union took place in 2002.
Secretary-General, Amara Essy (Cote d'Ivoire)

THE COMMONWEALTH

The Commonwealth is a voluntary association of 54 sovereign independent states together with their associated states and dependencies. All of the states were formerly parts of the British Empire or League of Nations (later the UN) mandated territories, except for Mozambique which was admitted as a unique case because of its history of co-operation with neighbouring Commonwealth nations.

The status and relationship of member nations were first defined by the Inter-Imperial Relations Committee of the 1926 Imperial Conference, when the six existing dominions (Australia, Canada, the Irish Free State, Newfoundland, New Zealand and South Africa) were described as 'autonomous Communities within the British Empire, equal in status, in no way subordinate one to another in any aspect of their domestic or external affairs, though united by a common allegiance to the Crown and freely associated as Members of the British Commonwealth of Nations'. This formula was given legal substance by the Statute of Westminster 1931.

This concept of a group of countries owing allegiance to a single Crown changed in 1949 when India decided to become a republic. Her continued membership of the Commonwealth was agreed by the other members on the basis of her 'acceptance of the monarch as the symbol of the free association of its independent member nations and as such the Head of the Commonwealth'. This paved the way for other republics to join the association in due course. Member nations agreed at the time of the accession of Queen Elizabeth II to recognise Her Majesty as the new Head of the Commonwealth. However, the position is not vested in the British Crown.

THE MODERN COMMONWEALTH

As the UK's former colonies joined, initially with India and Pakistan in 1947, the Commonwealth was transformed from a grouping of all-white dominions into a multiracial association of equal, sovereign nations. It increasingly focused on promoting development and racial equality. South Africa withdrew in 1961 when it became clear that its reapplication for membership on becoming a republic would be rejected over its policy of apartheid.

The new goals of advocating democracy, the rule of law, good government and social justice were enshrined in the Harare Commonwealth Declaration (1991), which formed the basis of new membership guidelines agreed in Cyprus in 1993. Following the adoption of measures at the New Zealand summit in 1995 against serious or persistent violations of these principles, Nigeria was suspended in 1995 and Sierra Leone was suspended in 1997 for anti-democratic behaviour. Sierra Leone's suspension was revoked in March 1998 when the legitimate government was returned to power. Similarly, Nigeria's suspension was lifted on 29 May 1999, the day a newly elected civilian president took office. The heads of government meeting in Edinburgh in 1997 established a set of economic principles for the Commonwealth, promoting economic growth whilst protecting smaller member states from the negative effects of globalisation.

MEMBERSHIP

Membership of the Commonwealth involves acceptance of the association's basic principles and is subject to the approval of existing members. There are 54 members at present. (The date of joining the Commonwealth is shown in parenthesis.)

*Antigua and Barbuda (1981)
*Australia (1931)
*The Bahamas (1973)
Bangladesh (1972)
*Barbados (1966)
*Belize (1981)
Botswana (1966)
Brunei (1984)
Cameroon (1995)
*Canada (1931)
Cyprus (1961)
Dominica (1978)
Fiji (1970, 1997, 2001)
The Gambia (1965)
Ghana (1957)
*Grenada (1974)
Guyana (1966)
India (1947)
*Jamaica (1962)
Kenya (1963)
Kiribati (1979)
Lesotho (1966)
Malawi (1964)
Malaysia (1957)
The Maldives (1982)
Malta (1964)
Mauritius (1968)
Mozambique (1995)
Namibia (1990)
Nauru (1968)
*New Zealand (1931)
Nigeria (1960)
†Pakistan (1947)
*Papua New Guinea (1975)
*St Christopher and Nevis (1983)
*St Lucia (1979)
*St Vincent and the Grenadines (1979)
Samoa (1970)
Seychelles (1976)
Sierra Leone (1961)
Singapore (1965)
*Solomon Islands (1978)
South Africa (1931)
Sri Lanka (1948)
Swaziland (1968)
Tanzania (1961)
Tonga (1970)
Trinidad and Tobago (1962)
*§Tuvalu (1978)
Uganda (1962)
*United Kingdom
Vanuatu (1980)
Zambia (1964)
‡Zimbabwe (1980)

* Realms of Queen Elizabeth II
† Suspended 18 October 1999
‡ Suspended 20 March 2002
§ Originally a Special Member due to its small size, small economy and limited involvement in international affairs, Tuvalu became a full member on 1 September 2000.

COUNTRIES WHICH HAVE LEFT THE COMMONWEALTH

Fiji (1987, rejoined 1997, suspended 2000, readmitted 21 December 2001)
Republic of Ireland (1949)
Pakistan (1972, rejoined 1989, suspended 1999)
South Africa (1961, rejoined 1994)

Of the 54 member states, 16 have Queen Elizabeth II as head of state, 33 are republics, and five have national monarchies.

In each of the realms where Queen Elizabeth II is head of state (except for the UK), she is personally represented by a Governor-General, who holds in all essential respects the same position in relation to the administration of public affairs in the realm as is held by Her Majesty in Britain. The Governor-General is appointed by The Queen on the advice of the government of the state concerned.

INTERGOVERNMENTAL AND OTHER LINKS
The main forum for consultation is the Commonwealth heads of government meetings held biennially to discuss international developments and to consider co-operation among members. Decisions are reached by consensus, and the views of the meeting are set out in a communiqué. There are also annual meetings of finance ministers and frequent meetings of ministers and officials in other fields, such as education, health, women's affairs, agriculture and science. Intergovernmental links are complemented by the activities of some 300 Commonwealth non-governmental organisations linking professionals, sportsmen and sportswomen, and interest groups, forming a 'people's Commonwealth'. The Commonwealth Games take place every four years.

Assistance to other Commonwealth countries normally has priority in the bilateral aid programmes of the association's developed members (Australia, Britain, Canada and New Zealand), who direct about 30 per cent of their aid to other member countries. Developing Commonwealth nations also assist their poorer partners, and many Commonwealth voluntary organisations promote development.

COMMONWEALTH SECRETARIAT
The Commonwealth has a secretariat, established in 1965 in London, which is funded by all member governments. This is the main agency for multilateral communication between member governments on issues relating to the Commonwealth as a whole. It promotes consultation and co-operation, disseminates information on matters of common concern, organises meetings including the biennial summits, co-ordinates Commonwealth activities, and provides technical assistance for economic and social development through the Commonwealth Fund for Technical Co-operation.

The Commonwealth Foundation was established by Commonwealth governments in 1966 as an autonomous body with a board of governors representing Commonwealth governments that fund the Foundation. It promotes and funds exchanges and other activities aimed at strengthening the skills and effectiveness of professionals and non-governmental organisations. It also promotes culture, rural development, social welfare and the role of women.

COMMONWEALTH SECRETARIAT, Marlborough House, Pall Mall, London SW1Y 5HX T 020-7747 6500
F 020-7930 0827 E info@commonwealth.int
W www.thecommonwealth.org
Secretary-General, Rt. Hon. Don McKinnon (New Zealand)

COMMONWEALTH FOUNDATION, Marlborough House, Pall Mall, London SW1Y 5HY T 020-7930 3783
Director, Colin Ball (UK)

COMMONWEALTH INSTITUTE, Kensington High Street, London W8 6NQ T 020-7603 4535
Director-General, David French

COMMONWEALTH OF INDEPENDENT STATES

Ul. Kirova 17, Minsk, Belarus
T (+375) (17) 222 3517 F (+375) (17) 227 2339
E webmaster@www.cis.minsk.by
W www.cis.minsk.by

The Commonwealth of Independent States (CIS) is a multilateral grouping of 12 sovereign states that were formerly constituent republics of the USSR (Armenia, Azerbaijan, Belarus, Georgia, Kazakhstan, Kyrgyzstan, Moldova, Russia, Tajikistan, Turkmenistan, Ukraine and Uzbekistan). It was formed in 1991. Georgia joined in 1993. The CIS charter, signed in 1993 by seven states (Armenia, Belarus, Kazakhstan, Kyrgyzstan, Russia, Tajikistan, Uzbekistan) and open for signing by the other states, formally established the functions of the organisation and the obligations of its member states.

The CIS acts as a co-ordinating mechanism for foreign, defence and economic policies and is a forum for addressing problems which have arisen from the break-up of the USSR. These matters are addressed in more than 70 inter-state, intergovernmental co-ordinating and consultative statutory bodies. However, member states have criticised the CIS for operating ineffectively and for failing to carry through decisions made by CIS organs.

STRUCTURE
The two supreme CIS bodies are the Council of Heads of State and the Council of Heads of Government. The Council of Heads of State is the highest organ of the CIS and there are various ministerial, parliamentary, banking, economic and security councils. The Executive Committee, based in Minsk and Moscow, provides administrative support.

DEFENCE CO-OPERATION
On becoming members of the CIS, the member states agreed to recognise their existing borders, respect one another's territorial integrity and reject the use of military force or other forms of coercion to settle disputes between them.

A Treaty on Collective Security was signed in 1992 by six states and a joint peacemaking force, to intervene in CIS conflicts, was agreed upon by nine states. Russia concluded bilateral and multilateral agreements with other CIS states under the supervision of the Council of Heads of Collective Security (established 1993). These were gradually upgraded into CIS agreements under the umbrella of the Treaty on Collective Security, enabling Russia to station troops in eight of the other 11 CIS states (not Moldova, Turkmenistan or Ukraine), and giving Russian forces *de facto* control of virtually all of the former USSR's external borders. Only Ukraine and Moldova remained outside the defence co-operation framework and did not sign the Treaty on Collective Security, from which Azerbaijan, Georgia and Uzbekistan withdrew in 1999, forming a new defensive grouping with Moldova and Ukraine. Russian border guards were also withdrawn from Georgia, Kyrgyzstan and Turkmenistan in 1999.

ECONOMIC CO-OPERATION
In 1991, 11 republics signed a treaty forming an economic community. The principles of the treaty were embodied within the CIS and formed the basis of its economic co-operation. Members agreed to refrain from economic actions that would damage each other and to co-ordinate economic and monetary policies. A Co-ordinating Consultative Committee, an economic arbitration court and an inter-state bank were established. A single monetary unit, the rouble, was originally agreed upon by all member states, and the members recognised that the basis of recovery for their economies was private ownership, free enterprise and competition.

The 11 CIS members who signed the Treaty on the Establishment of an Economic Union in September 1993 (Ukraine is an associate member of the economic union)

committed themselves to a common economic space with free movement of goods, services, capital and labour. Belarus, Kazakhstan, Kyrgyzstan and Russia signed the Treaty on the Establishment of a Customs Union in March 1996; the treaty was later signed by Tajikistan and on 10 October 2000, the presidents of the five countries approved a treaty establishing the Eurasian Economic Community. In 2003, Russia, Ukraine, Belarus and Kazakhstan proposed the formation of a united economic zone.
Executive Secretary, Yuri Yarov

CO-OPERATION COUNCIL FOR THE ARAB STATES OF THE GULF

PO Box 7153, Riyadh 11-462, Saudi Arabia
T (+966) (01) 482 7777 F (+966) (01) 482 9109
W www.gcc-sg.org

The Co-operation Council for the Arab States of the Gulf, or Gulf Co-operation Council (GCC), as it is informally known, was established on 25 May 1981 with the objectives of increasing co-ordination and integration between its member states, harmonising economic, commercial, educational and social policies and promoting scientific and technical innovation in key economic areas. The GCC has six members: Bahrain, Kuwait, Oman, Qatar, Saudi Arabia and the United Arab Emirates.

The highest authority of the GCC is the Supreme Council, whose presidency rotates among members' heads of states based on the (Arabic) alphabetical order of their names. It holds one regular session every year, but extraordinary sessions may be convened if necessary. The meeting of the Supreme Council is considered valid if attended by two-thirds of the member states.

The Ministerial Council, which ordinarily meets every three months, consists of the Foreign Ministers of the member states or other delegated ministers. The presidency of the Ministerial Council is held by the state which last presided over the Supreme Council or, if necessary, the state which is next to preside over the Supreme Council.
Secretary-General, Abdul-Rhaman bin Hamad Al-Attiyah (Qatar)

COUNCIL OF THE BALTIC SEA STATES

Secretariat, Stromsberg, PO Box 2010, S-103 11 Stockholm, Sweden
T (+46) (8) 440 1920 F (+46) (8) 440 1944
E cbss@cbss.st
W www.cbss.st

The Council of the Baltic Sea States (CBSS) was founded in March 1992 with the aim of creating a regional forum to increase co-operation and co-ordination among the states which border on the Baltic Sea in assisting new democratic institutions, economic and technical development, humanitarian aid and health, energy and environmental issues, cultural programmes, education, tourism, transportation and communication.

There are 12 members: Denmark, Estonia, Finland, Germany, Iceland, Latvia, Lithuania, Norway, Poland, Russia, Sweden and the European Commission.

The Council consists of the foreign ministers of each member state and a member of the European Commission. Chairmanship of the Council rotates on an annual basis, and the annual session is held in the country currently in the chair. The foreign minister of the presiding country is responsible for co-ordinating activities between the sessions.
Chairmanship, 2004–5, Poland

COUNCIL OF EUROPE

F-67075 Strasbourg, France
T (+33) (3) 8841 2033 F (+33) (3) 8841 2745
E infopoint@coe.int
W www.coe.int

The Council of Europe was founded in 1949. Its aim is to achieve greater unity between its members, to safeguard their European heritage and to facilitate their progress in economic, social, cultural, educational, scientific, legal and administrative matters, and in the furtherance of pluralist democracy, human rights and fundamental freedoms.

There are 45 members. The organs are the Committee of Ministers, consisting of the foreign ministers of member countries, who meet twice yearly, and the Parliamentary Assembly of 313 members (and 313 substitutes), elected or chosen by the national parliaments of member countries in proportion to the relative strength of political parties. There is also a Joint Committee of Ministers and Representatives of the Parliamentary Assembly.

The Committee of Ministers is the executive organ. The majority of its conclusions take the form of international agreements (known as European Conventions) or recommendations to governments. Decisions of the Ministers may also be embodied in partial agreements to which a limited number of member governments are party. Member governments accredit Permanent Representatives to the Council in Strasbourg, who are also the Ministers' Deputies. The Committee of Deputies meets every month to transact business and to take decisions on behalf of Ministers.

The Parliamentary Assembly holds three week-long sessions a year. Its 13 permanent committees meet once or twice between each public plenary session of the Assembly. The Congress of Local and Regional Authorities of Europe each year brings together mayors and municipal councillors in the same numbers as the members of the Parliamentary Assembly.

One of the principal achievements of the Council of Europe is the European Convention on Human Rights (1950) under which was established the European Commission and the European Court of Human Rights, which were merged in 1993. The reorganised European Court of Human Rights sits in chambers of seven judges or exceptionally as a grand chamber of 17 judges. Litigants must exhaust legal processes in their own country before bringing cases before the court.

Among other conventions and agreements are the European Social Charter, the European Cultural Convention, the European Code of Social Security, the European Convention on the Protection of National Minorities, and conventions on extradition, the legal status of migrant workers, torture prevention, conservation and the transfer of sentenced prisoners. Most recently, the specialised bodies of the Venice Commission and Demosthenes have been set up to assist in developing legislative, administrative and constitutional reforms in central and eastern Europe.

Non-member states take part in certain Council of Europe activities on a regular or *ad hoc* basis; thus the Holy See participates in all the educational, cultural and sports activities. The European Youth Centre is an educational residential centre for young people. The European Youth Foundation provides youth organisations with funds for their international activities. The Council's ordinary budget for 2004 totalled €180,500,000.
Secretary-General, Walter Schwimmer (Austria)

Permanent UK Representative, HE Stephen Howarth, *apptd* 2003

ECONOMIC COMMUNITY OF WEST AFRICAN STATES

Secretariat Building, 60 Yakubu Gowon Crescent, PMB 401, Abuja, Nigeria
T (+234) (9) 314 7647 9 F (+234) (9) 314 3005/6
E info@ecowasmail.net
W www.ecowas.int

The Economic Community of West African States (ECOWAS) was founded in 1975 and came into operation in 1977. It aims to promote the cultural, economic and social development of West Africa through mutual co-operation. A revised ECOWAS Treaty was signed in 1993 and came into effect in July 1995. It makes the prevention and control of regional conflicts an aim of ECOWAS and provides for the imposition of a community tax and for the establishment of a regional parliament, an economic and social council and a court of justice.

The supreme authority of ECOWAS is vested in the annual summit of heads of government of all 15 member states. A Council of Ministers, two from each member state, meets biannually to monitor the organisation and make recommendations to the summit. ECOWAS operates through a Secretariat, headed by the Executive Secretary. In addition there are four Deputy Executive Secretaries. The ECOWAS Parliament was inaugurated in November 2000 and justices for the Court of Justice were sworn in January 2001.

The Fund for Co-operation, Compensation and Development, situated at Lomé, Togo, has been restructured into three funds: the ECOWAS Regional Development Fund, the ECOWAS Bank for Investment and Development and the ECOWAS Regional Investment Bank. The funds finance development projects and provide compensation to member states that have suffered losses as a result of ECOWAS's policies, particularly trade liberalisation.

The members of ECOWAS are: Benin, Burkina Faso, Cape Verde, Cote d'Ivoire, Gambia, Ghana, Guinea, Guinea-Bissau, Liberia, Mali, Niger, Nigeria, Senegal, Sierra Leone and Togo.

An ECOWAS Monitoring Group (ECOMOG) peacekeeping force has been involved in attempts to restore peace in Liberia (1990–6), in Guinea-Bissau (1998–9) and in Sierra Leone (1997–9).

Executive Secretary, Dr Mohammed Ibn Chambas (Ghana)

EUROPEAN BANK FOR RECONSTRUCTION AND DEVELOPMENT

One Exchange Square, London EC2A 2JN
T 020-7338 6000 F 020-7338 6100
W www.ebrd.com

The European Bank for Reconstruction and Development (EBRD), established in 1991, is an international institution with 62 members (60 countries, the European Community and the European Investment Bank).

The aim of the EBRD is to build market economies and democracies in 27 countries in central and eastern Europe and central Asia.

The EBRD finances projects in both the private and public sectors, providing direct funding for financial institutions, infrastructure and other key sectors. The main forms of the EBRD financing are loans, equity investments and guarantees. No more than 40 per cent of the EBRD's investment can be made in state-owned concerns. The EBRD is the largest foreign investor in the region's private sector and in addition to its own lending, facilitates significant foreign direct investment. The EBRD pays particular attention to strengthening the financial sector and to promoting small and medium-sized enterprises. It works in co-operation with national governments, private companies, and international organisations such as the OECD, the IMF, the World Bank and the UN specialised agencies.

The EBRD has a subscribed capital of €20 billion. The EBRD is also able to borrow on world capital markets. Its major subscribers are the USA, 10 per cent; Britain, France, Germany, Italy and Japan, 8.5 per cent each. As at the end of 2003, the EBRD had committed €3,700 million to 119 new projects. Net profit in 2003 reached €378,200 million.

The highest authority is the Board of Governors; each member appoints one Governor and one Alternate. The Governors delegate most powers to a 23-member Board of Directors; the Directors are responsible for the EBRD's operations and budget, and are elected by the Governors for three-year terms. The Governors also elect the President of the Board of Directors, who acts as the Bank's president for a four-year term.

President of the Board of Directors, Jean Lemierre (France)

EUROPEAN FREE TRADE ASSOCIATION

Headquarters: 9–11 rue de Varembé, CH-1211 Geneva 20, Switzerland
T (+41)(22) 749 1111
W www.efta.int
EEA matters: Trierstraat 74, B-1040 Brussels, Belgium
T (+32) (2) 286 1711 F (+32) (2) 286 1750
E mail.bx1@efta.int

The European Free Trade Association (EFTA) was established in 1960 by Austria, Denmark, Norway, Portugal, Sweden, Switzerland and the UK, and was subsequently joined by Finland (associate member 1961, full member 1986), Iceland (1970) and Liechtenstein (1991). Six members have left to join the European Union: Denmark and the UK (1972), Portugal (1985), Austria, Finland and Sweden (1995). The existing members are Iceland, Liechtenstein, Norway and Switzerland.

The first objective of EFTA was to establish free trade in industrial products between members; this was achieved in 1966. Its second objective was the creation of a single market in western Europe and in 1972 EFTA signed free trade agreements with the EC covering trade in industrial goods; the remaining tariffs on industrial products were abolished in 1977 and the Luxembourg Declaration on broader co-operation between EFTA and the European Community was signed in 1984.

An agreement on the creation of the European Economic Area (EEA), an extension of the EC single market to the EFTA states, was signed in 1992 and entered into force on 1 January 1994. Switzerland rejected EEA membership in a referendum in 1992 and Liechtenstein joined on 1 May 1995 after adapting its customs union with Switzerland. The implementation of the agreement is supervised by the EEA Council, composed of EFTA and EU ministers, and the EFTA Surveillance Authority. The three EFTA EEA members also participate in a wide range of other EC programmes including research and development, environmental matters, and education and training.

In June 2002, a free trade agreement between the EFTA states and Singapore was signed in Egilsstagir (Iceland). In March 2003, EFTA initialled a free trade agreement with Chile in Geneva (Switzerland). The agreement with Chile is the second free trade agreement that the EFTA states have concluded with a country in the Americas, after the agreement concluded with Mexico in 2000. In March 2004, an initial Free Trade Agreement was reached with Lebanon. With these agreements the EFTA states will have concluded free trade agreements with 21 states and territories, representing a population of 344 million, in addition to the free trade relations with the European Union, comprising a population of 375 million. Negotiations on free trade agreements with South Africa, Tunisia and Egypt continued during 2004.

The EFTA Council is the principal organ of the Association. It meets regularly at the level of ambassadors to the EFTA Secretariat in Geneva.

Secretary-General, William Rossier (Switzerland)
Deputy Secretary-General (Geneva), Pétur G. Thorsteinsson (Iceland)
Deputy Secretary-General (Brussels), Oystein Hovdkinn (Norway)

EUROPEAN ORGANISATION FOR NUCLEAR RESEARCH (CERN)

CH-1211 Geneva 23, Switzerland
T (+41) (22) 767 6111 F (+41) (22) 767 6555
W www.cern.ch

The Convention establishing the European Organisation for Nuclear Research (CERN) came into force in 1954. CERN promotes European collaboration in high energy physics of a scientific, rather than a military nature.

The member countries are Austria, Belgium, Bulgaria, the Czech Republic, Denmark, Finland, France, Germany, Greece, Hungary, Italy, the Netherlands, Norway, Poland, Portugal, Slovakia, Spain, Sweden, Switzerland and the UK. India, Israel, Japan, Russia, Turkey, the USA, the EU Commission and UNESCO have observer status.

The Council, which is the highest policy-making body, comprises two delegates from each member state and is chaired by the President who is elected by the Council in Session. The Council also elects the Director-General, who is responsible for the internal organisation of CERN. The Director-General heads a workforce of approximately 2,500, including physicists, craftsmen, technicians and administrative staff. At present over 6,500 physicists use CERN's facilities.

The member countries contribute to the budget in proportion to their net national revenue. The 2004 budget was SFr 1,325 million.

President of the Council, Enzo Iarocci (Italy)
Director-General (2004–8), Dr Robert Aymar (France)

EUROPEAN SPACE AGENCY

8–10 rue Mario Nikis, F-75738 Paris Cedex 15, France
T (+33) (1) 5369 7654 F (+33) (1) 5369 7560
W www.esa.int

The European Space Agency (ESA) was created in 1975 by the merger of the European Space Research Organisation (ESRO) and the European Launcher Development Organisation (ELDO). Its aims include the advancement of space research and technology and the implementation of a long-term European space policy.

The member countries are Austria, Belgium, Denmark, Finland, France, Germany, Ireland, Italy, the Netherlands, Norway, Portugal, Spain, Sweden, Switzerland and the UK. Greece and Luxembourg were due to officially join in 2004. Canada and Hungary are co-operating states. ESA's mandatory activities are funded by contributions from all the member states, calculated in accordance with each country's gross national income (GNI). In 2003, ESA's budget was €2,700 million.

The agency is directed by a Council composed of the representatives of the member states; its chief officer is the Director-General who is elected by the Council every four years.

Director-General, Jean-Jacques Dordain, *apptd* 2003

FOOD AND AGRICULTURE ORGANISATION OF THE UNITED NATIONS

Viale delle Terme di Caracalla, I-00100 Rome, Italy
T (+39) (06) 57051 F (+39) (06) 5705 3152
E fao-hq@fao.org
W www.fao.org

The Food and Agriculture Organisation (FAO) is a specialised UN agency, established in 1945. It assists rural populations by raising levels of nutrition and living standards, and by encouraging greater efficiency in food production and distribution. It analyses and disseminates information on agriculture and natural resources. The FAO also advises governments on national agricultural policy and planning; its Investment Centre, together with the World Bank and other financial institutions, helps to prepare development projects. The FAO's field programme covers a range of activities, including strengthening crop production, rural and livestock development, and conservation.

The FAO's top priorities are sustainable agriculture, rural development and food security. The Organisation attempts to ensure the availability of adequate food supplies, stability in the flow of supplies and the securing of access to food by the poor. The FAO monitors potential famine areas. The Emergency Operations and Rehabilitation Division channels emergency aid from governments and other agencies, and assists in rehabilitation. The Technical Co-operation Programme responds to urgent or unforeseen requests for technical assistance.

The FAO has 188 members (187 states plus the EU). It is governed by a biennial conference of its members which sets a programme and budget. The budget for 2004–5 was US$749.1 million, funded by member countries in proportion to their gross national products. The FAO is also funded by the UN Development Programme, donor governments and other institutions.

The Conference elects a Director-General and a 49-member Council which governs between conferences. The Regular and Field Programmes are administered by a Secretariat, headed by the Director-General. Five regional, five sub-regional and over 78 national offices help administer the Field Programme.

Director-General, Jacques Diouf (Senegal)

GUUAM

Office 105 Institute of International Relations,
36/1 Melnykova Street, Kyiv, Ukraine
T (+380) 213-7457 F (+380) 211-4428
W www.guuam.org

GUUAM (Georgia, Ukraine, Uzbekistan, Azerbaijan and Moldova) was founded as a political, economic and strategic alliance designed to strengthen the independence and sovereignty of its members.

GUUAM seeks to promote trade, economic growth, and co-operation between its members primarily through the establishment of a Eurasian-Transcaucasian transportation corridor (TRACECA). GUUAM is also a forum for the discussion of security problems, promoting conflict resolution and a common position in international organisations.

Following growing co-operation between their countries, on 10 October 1997, the presidents of Azerbaijan, Georgia, Moldova and Ukraine declared their mutual interest in promoting co-operation, security, political and economic contacts. Uzbekistan joined the group in April 1999.

It was decided in September 2000 to convene summits of the Heads of State at least once a year, and meetings at the level of Ministers for Foreign Affairs at least twice a year. A Committee of National Co-ordinators meets quarterly.

INTERNATIONAL ATOMIC ENERGY AGENCY

Vienna International Centre, Wagramerstrasse 5, PO Box 100, A-1400 Vienna, Austria
T (+43) (1) 26000 F (+43) (1) 26007
E official.mail@iaea.org
W www.iaea.org

The International Atomic Energy Agency (IAEA) was established in 1957. It is an intergovernmental organisation that reports to, but is not a specialised agency of, the UN.

The IAEA aims to enhance the contribution of atomic energy to peace, health and prosperity and to ensure that any assistance that it provides is not used for military purposes. It establishes atomic energy safety standards and offers services to its member states for the safe operation of their nuclear facilities and for radiation protection. It is the focal point for international conventions on the early notification of a nuclear accident, assistance in the case of such an accident, civil liability for nuclear damage, physical protection of nuclear material, nuclear safety and the safety of spent fuel and radioactive waste management. The IAEA also encourages research and training in nuclear power. It is additionally charged with drawing up safeguards and verifying their use in accordance with the Nuclear Non-Proliferation Treaty (NPT) 1968, the Treaty for the Prohibition of Nuclear Weapons in Latin America (Tlatelolco Treaty) 1968, the Treaty on a South Pacific Nuclear Free Zone (Rarotonga Treaty), the South East Asia Nuclear Weapon-Free Zone Treaty (Bangkok Treaty) and the African Nuclear Weapon-Free Zone Treaty (Pelindaba Treaty) 1996. Together with the Food and Agriculture Organisation and the World Health Organisation, the IAEA established an International Consultative Group on Food Irradiation in 1983.

The IAEA currently had 137 members as at June 2004. A General Conference of all its members meets annually to decide policy, a programme and a budget (2004, US$268 million), as well as electing a Director-General and a 35-member Board of Governors. The Board meets four times a year to formulate policy which is implemented by the Secretariat under a Director-General.

Director-General, Mohamed El Baradei (Egypt)

INTERNATIONAL CIVIL AVIATION ORGANISATION

999 University Street, Montréal, Québec, Canada H3C 5H7
T (+1) (514) 954 8219 F (+1) (514) 954 6077
E icaohq@icao.int
W www.icao.int

The International Civil Aviation Organisation (ICAO) was founded with the signing of the Chicago Convention on International Civil Aviation in 1944 and became a specialised agency of the United Nations in 1947. It sets international technical standards and recommends practices for all areas of civil aviation, including airworthiness, air navigation, air traffic control and pilot licensing. It encourages uniformity and simplicity in ground regulations and operations at international airports, including immigration and customs control. The ICAO also promotes regional air navigation, plans for ground facilities and collects and distributes air transport statistics world-wide. It is dedicated to improving safety and to the orderly development of civil aviation throughout the world.

The ICAO has 188 members and is governed by an assembly which meets at least once every three years. A Council of 52 members is elected, which represents leading air transport nations as well as less developed countries. The Council elects the President, appoints the Secretary-General and supervises the organisation through subsidiary committees, serviced by a Secretariat.

President of the Council, Dr Assad Kotaite (Lebanon)
Secretary-General, Dr Taieb Cherif (Algeria)
UK Representative, N. J. Denton

INTERNATIONAL CONFEDERATION OF FREE TRADE UNIONS

Koning Albert II laan 5, Bus 1, B-1210 Brussels, Belgium
T (+32) (2) 224 0211 F (+32) (2) 201 5815
E press@icftu.org
W www.icftu.org

The International Confederation of Free Trade Unions (ICFTU) was created in 1949. It aims to establish, maintain and promote free trade unions, and to promote peace with economic security and social justice.

Affiliated to the ICFTU are 233 individual unions and representative bodies in 152 countries and territories. There are 150 million members.

The Congress, the supreme authority of the ICFTU, convenes at least every four years. It is composed of delegates from the affiliated trade union organisations. The Congress elects an Executive Board of 53 members, including five nominated by the Women's Committee and one representing young workers, which meets not less than once a year. The Board establishes the budget and receives suggestions and proposals from affiliates as well as acting on behalf of the Confederation. The Congress also elects the General Secretary.

General Secretary, Guy Ryder (UK)
UK Affiliate, TUC, Congress House, 23–28 Great Russell Street, London WC1B 3LS T 020-7636 4030

INTERNATIONAL CRIMINAL POLICE (INTERPOL)

200 Quai Charles de Gaulle, F-69006 Lyon, France
T (+33) (4) 7244 7000 F (+33) (4) 7244 7163
E compr@interpol.int
W www.interpol.int

Interpol was set up in 1923 to establish an international criminal records office and to harmonise extradition procedures. As at May, the organisation comprised 181 member states.

Interpol's aims are to promote co-operation between criminal police authorities, and to support government agencies concerned with combating crime, whilst respecting national sovereignty. It is financed by annual contributions from the governments of member states.

Interpol's policy is decided by the General Assembly which meets annually; it is composed of delegates appointed by the member states. The 13-member Executive Committee is elected by the General Assembly from among the member states' delegates, and is chaired by the President, who has a four-year term of office. The permanent administrative organ is the General Secretariat, headed by the Secretary-General, who is appointed by the General Assembly.

Secretary-General, Ronald Noble (USA)

INTERNATIONAL ENERGY AGENCY

9 rue de la Fédération, F-75739 Paris Cedex 15, France
T (+33) (1) 4057 6551 F (+33) (1) 4057 6559
E info@iea.org
W www.iea.org

The International Energy Agency (IEA), founded in 1974, is an autonomous agency within the framework of the Organisation for Economic Co-operation and Development (OECD).

The IEA's objectives include improvement of energy co-operation world-wide, increased efficiency, development of alternative energy sources and the promotion of relations between oil producing and oil consuming countries. The IEA also maintains an emergency system to alleviate the effects of severe oil supply disruptions.

The main decision-making body is the Governing Board, composed of senior energy officials from member countries. Various standing groups and special committees exist to facilitate the work of the Board. The IEA Secretariat, with a staff of energy experts, carries out the work of the Governing Board and its subordinate bodies. The Executive Director is appointed by the Board. The IEA has 26 member states.

Executive Director, Claude Mandil (France)

INTERNATIONAL FRANCOPHONE ORGANISATION

Cabinet du Secretaire General, 28 rue de Bourgogne, F-75007 Paris, France
T (+33) (1) 441112 50 F (+33) (1) 441112 76
E oif@francophonie.org
W www.francophonie.org

The International Francophone Organisation (known as La Francophonie) is an intergovernmental organisation founded in 1970 by 21 French-speaking countries. It aims to prevent conflict and promote development and co-operation between the Francophone countries, to represent its member states internationally and to promote French culture and the use of the French language.

The Conference of Heads of State and Heads of Government of Countries using French as a Common Language, also known as the Francophone Summit, takes place biennially. Other institutions include the Ministerial Conference of La Francophonie, the Permanent Council of La Francophonie and the Secretariat.

The Ministerial Conference of La Francophonie, which consists of the foreign minister or the minister responsible for Francophone affairs of each member state, implements decisions made at the summits and makes preparations for the following summit. It also puts forward prospective new members.

The Permanent Council of La Francophonie, which is chaired by the Secretary-General and consists of representatives of the member states, oversees the execution of decisions made by the Ministerial Conference, allocates funds, and reviews and approves projects.

La Francophonie has a current membership of 51 member states and 5 observers.

Secretary-General, Abdou Diouf

INTERNATIONAL FUND FOR AGRICULTURAL DEVELOPMENT

107 Via del Serafico, I-00142 Rome, Italy
T (+39) (6) 54591 F (+39) (6) 5459 2143
E ifad@ifad.org
W www.ifad.org

The establishment of the International Fund for Agricultural Development (IFAD) was proposed by the 1974 World Food Conference and IFAD began operations as a UN specialised agency in 1977. Its purpose is to mobilise additional funds for agricultural and rural development projects in developing countries, provide employment and additional income for poor farmers, reduce malnutrition and improve food security systems.

IFAD has 163 members and membership is divided into three lists: List A (OECD countries), List B (OPEC countries), and List C (developing countries) which is subdivided into C1 (Africa), C2 (Europe, Asia and the Pacific) and C3 (Latin America and the Caribbean). All powers are vested in a Governing Council of all member countries. It elects an 18-member Executive Board (with 18 alternate members) responsible for IFAD's operations. The Council meets annually and elects a President who is also chairman of the Board. The President serves a four-year term that is renewable once and is assisted by a Vice-President and three Assistant Presidents.

Since its establishment, IFAD has committed a total of US$8,100 million in loans and US$35,400 million in grants for 653 approved projects in 115 countries and territories. IFAD's current annual commitment level is approximately $450 million.

President, Lennart Båge (Sweden), *apptd* 2001

INTERNATIONAL HYDROGRAPHIC ORGANISATION

International Hydrographic Bureau, 4 Quai Antoine 1ev, B.P. 445, MC98011, Monaco Cedex
T (+377) 9310 8100 F (+377) 9310 8140
E info@ihb.mc W www.iho.shom.fr

The International Hydrographic Organisation (IHO) was established in 1970 with its permanent Secretariat based in Monaco. An intergovernmental organisation that works in a purely consultative role, the IHO aims to support safety in international navigation and set policy for marine conservation. The IHO has a membership of 74

states that meet at five-yearly conferences to set policy, approve budget, review progress and adopt programmes of work to be pursued in the ensuing five-year period. Each member is represented at these conferences by their most senior hydrographer, usually the head of the hydrographic office for each particular country. All member states have an opportunity to initiate new proposals for IHO consideration and, during this time, a Directing Committee of three senior Hydrographers is also elected. Outside of its membership, the IHO acts to promote hydrography and facilitate the exchange of technology with developing countries as well as working towards a standardisation of nautical products, services and survey practices.
President, Vice-Admiral Alexandros Maratos (Greece)

INTERNATIONAL LABOUR ORGANISATION

4 route des Morillons, CH-1211 Geneva 22, Switzerland
T (+41) (22) 799 6111 F (+41) (22) 798 8685
W www.ilo.org

The International Labour Organisation (ILO) was established in 1919 as an autonomous body of the League of Nations and became the UN's first specialised agency in 1946. The ILO aims to increase employment, improve working conditions, raise living standards and encourage democratic development. It sets minimum international labour standards through the drafting of international conventions. Member countries are obliged to submit these to their domestic authorities for ratification, and thus undertake to bring their domestic legislation in line with the conventions. Members must report to the ILO periodically on how these regulations are being implemented. The ILO plays a major role in helping developing countries achieve economic stability and job expansion through its wide-ranging programme of technical co-operation. The ILO is also the world's principal resource centre for information, analysis and guidance on labour and employment. The organisation aims to improve working and living conditions throughout the world and to support the transition to democracy and market economies under way in many states.

The ILO had 176 members as at June 2004. It is composed of the International Labour Conference, the Governing Body and the International Labour Office. The Conference of members meets annually, and is attended by national delegations comprising two government delegates, one worker delegate and one employer delegate. It formulates international labour conventions and recommendations, provides a forum for discussion of world employment and social issues, and approves the ILO's programme and budget. The programme and budget set out four strategic objectives for the ILO: the promotion of fundamental principles and rights at work; the creation of greater employment and earning opportunities; the enhancement of social protection; and the strengthening of social dialogue.

The 56-member Governing Body, composed of 28 government, 14 worker and 14 employer members, acts as the ILO's executive council. Ten governments, including the UK, hold permanent seats on the Governing Body because of their industrial importance. There are also various regional conferences and advisory committees. The International Labour Office acts as a secretariat and as a centre for operations, publishing and research.
Director-General, Juan Somavia (Chile)
UK OFFICE, Millbank Tower, 21–24 Millbank, London SW1P 4QP T 020-7828 6401 F 020-7233-5925
E ipu@ilo-london.org.uk

INTERNATIONAL MARITIME ORGANISATION

4 Albert Embankment, London SE1 7SR
T 020-7735 7611 F 020-7587 3210
E media@imo.org
W www.imo.org

The International Maritime Organisation (IMO) was established as a UN specialised agency in 1948. Owing to delays in treaty ratification it did not commence operations until 1958. Originally it was called the Inter-Governmental Maritime Consultative Organisation (IMCO) but changed its name in 1982.

The IMO fosters intergovernmental co-operation in technical matters relating to international shipping, especially with regard to safety at sea, efficiency in navigation and protecting the marine environment by preventing and controlling marine pollution caused by shipping. The IMO is responsible for convening maritime conferences and drafting marine conventions. It also provides technical aid to countries wishing to develop their activities at sea.

The IMO had 163 members and three associate members as at March 2004. It is governed by an Assembly comprising delegates of all its members. It meets biennially to formulate policy, set a budget (2004–5, £46.2 million), vote on specific recommendations on pollution and maritime safety and elect the Council. The Council, which meets twice a year, fulfils the functions of the Assembly between sessions and appoints the Secretary-General. It consists of 40 members: ten from the world's largest shipping nations, ten from the nations most dependent on seaborne trade, and 20 other members to ensure a fair geographical representation. The Maritime Safety, Marine Environment Protection, Legal, Technical Co-operation and Facilitation Committees make reports and recommendations to the Council and the Assembly. There are a number of other specialist subsidiary committees. The IMO acts as the secretariat for the London Convention (1972) which regulates the disposal of land-generated waste at sea.
Secretary-General, Efthimios E. Mitropoulos (Greece)

INTERNATIONAL MONETARY FUND

700 19th Street NW, Washington DC 20431, USA
T (+1) (202) 623 7300 F (+1) (202) 623 6278
E publicaffairs@imf.org
W www.imf.org

The International Monetary Fund (IMF) was established in 1944, at the UN Monetary and Financial Conference held at Bretton Woods, New Hampshire. Its Articles of Agreement entered into force in 1945 and it began operations in 1947.

The IMF exists to promote international monetary co-operation, the expansion of world trade, and exchange stability. It advises members on their economic and financial policies; promotes policy co-ordination among the major industrial countries; and gives technical assistance in central banking, balance of payments accounting, taxation, and other financial matters. The IMF serves as a forum for members to discuss important financial and monetary issues and seeks the balanced growth of international trade and, through this, high levels of employment, income and productive capacity. As at June 2004 the IMF had 184 members.

Upon joining the IMF, a member is assigned a 'quota', based on the member's relative standing in the world economy and its balance of payments position, that determines its capital subscription to the Fund, its access to IMF resources, its voting power, and its share in the allocation of Special Drawing Rights (SDRs). Quotas are reviewed every five years and adjusted accordingly. The SDR, an international reserve asset issued by the IMF, is calculated daily on a basket of usable currencies and is the IMF's unit of account; on 30 May 2004, 1 SDR equalled US$1.45412. SDRs are allocated at intervals to supplement members' reserves and thereby improve international financial liquidity.

IMF financial resources derive primarily from members' capital subscriptions, which are equivalent to their quotas. In addition, the IMF is authorised to borrow from official lenders. It may also draw on a line of credit of SDR 18.5 billion from various countries under the so-called General Arrangements to Borrow (GAB). Periodic charges are also levied on financial assistance. At the end of January 2003, total outstanding IMF credits amounted to SDR 107 billion.

The IMF is not a bank and does not lend money; it provides temporary financial assistance by selling a member's SDRs or other members' currencies in exchange for the member's own currency. The member can then use the purchased currency to alleviate its balance of payments difficulties. The IMF's credit under its regular facilities is made available to members in tranches or segments of 25 per cent of quota. For first credit tranche purchases, members are required to demonstrate reasonable efforts to overcome their balance of payments difficulties. There are no performance criteria. Upper credit tranche purchases are normally associated with stand-by arrangements and are aimed at overcoming balance of payment difficulties and are required to meet certain performance criteria. Repurchases are made in three and a quarter to five years.

The IMF supports long-term efforts at economic reform and transformation as well as medium-term programmes under the extended Fund facility, which runs for three to four years and is aimed at overcoming balance of payments difficulties stemming from macroeconomic and structural problems. Members experiencing a temporary balance of payments shortfall have access to the compensatory and contingency financing facility.

The IMF is headed by a Board of Governors, comprising representatives of all members, which meets annually. The Governors delegate powers to 24 Executive Directors, who are appointed or elected by member countries. The Executive Directors operate the Fund on a daily basis under a Managing Director, whom they elect.

Managing Director, Rodrigo Rato (Spain)

UK Executive Director, Tom Scholar, Room 11-120, IMF, 700 19th Street NW, Washington DC 20431, USA

INTERNATIONAL ORGANISATION FOR MIGRATION

17, Route des Morillons, CH-1211 Geneva 19, Switzerland
T (+41) 22717 9111 **F** (+41) 22798 6150
E info@iom.int **W** www.iom.int

The International Organisation for Migration (IOM) was founded in 1951 as an organisation to resettle European displaced persons and refugees. During the 1960s and 1970s the IOM developed links with the United Nations High Commissioner for Refugees (UNHCR) and began a programme of assistance and reintegration outside of the European region. There are currently 102 member states and 29 observers (including governmental and non-governmental organisations). Internally, the IOM is led by a Director-General who is elected for a five-year term. The Director-General's Office has the constitutional authority to manage the organisation, carry out the activities within its mandate and develop current policies, procedures and strategies. The Office of the Inspector-General (OIG) incorporates the functions of evaluation, internal audit and assessment of projects for oversight purposes. The OIG is also involved in investigations within the formal complaints procedure.

The role of the IOM has recently expanded to cover migration health services, counter-trafficking measures, emergency and post-crises management and assisted voluntary returns.

Director-General, Brunson McKinley (USA)

INTERNATIONAL RED CROSS AND RED CRESCENT MOVEMENT

19 avenue de la Paix, CH-1202 Geneva, Switzerland
T (+41) 22734-6001 **W** www.icrc.org

The International Red Cross and Red Crescent Movement is composed of three elements — the International Committee of the Red Cross, the International Federation of Red Cross and Red Crescent Societies and the national Red Cross and Red Crescent societies.

The International Committee of the Red Cross (ICRC), the organisation's founding body, was formed in 1863. It aims to negotiate between warring factions and to protect and assist victims of armed conflict. It also seeks to ensure the application of the Geneva Conventions with regard to prisoners of war and detainees.

The International Federation of Red Cross and Red Crescent Societies was founded in 1919 to contribute to the development of the humanitarian activities of national societies, to co-ordinate their relief operations for victims of natural disasters, and to care for refugees outside areas of conflict. There are Red Cross and Red Crescent societies in 175 countries, with a total membership of 250 million.

The International Conference of the Red Cross and Red Crescent meets every four years, bringing together delegates of the ICRC, the International Federation and the national societies, as well as representatives of nations bound by the Geneva Conventions.

President of the ICRC, Jakob Kellenberger

BRITISH RED CROSS, 9 Grosvenor Crescent, London SW1X 7EJ **T** 020-7235 5454 **F** 020-7245 6315 **E** information@redcross.org.uk **W** www.redcross.org.uk

Chief Executive, Sir Nicholas Young

INTERNATIONAL TELECOMMUNICATION UNION

Place des Nations, CH-1211 Geneva 20, Switzerland
T (+41) (22) 730 5111 **F** (+41) (22) 733 7256
E itumail@itu.int
W www.itu.int

The International Telecommunication Union (ITU) was founded in Paris in 1865 as the International Telegraph Union and became a UN specialised agency in 1947.

ITU is an intergovernmental organisation for the development of telecommunications and the harmonisation of national telecommunication policies. ITU comprises 189 member states and some 700 members who represent public and private organisations involved in telecommunications. ITU's mission is to promote the development of telecommunications and information and communication technologies; to promote and offer technical assistance to developing countries; and to promote at international level the adoption of a broader approach to the issues of telecommunications.

ITU fulfils its mission through initiatives aimed at promoting the growth and expansion of electronic commerce; a programme of strategic workshops; the adoption of international regulations and treaties governing uses of the frequency spectrum; the adoption of technical standards that foster global interconnectivity and interoperability and the provision of policy advice and technical assistance to developing countries.

ITU also organises world-wide and regional exhibitions and forums to exchange ideas, knowledge and technology.

Secretary-General, Yoshio Utsumi (Japan)

LEAGUE OF ARAB STATES

Maidane Al-Tahrir, Cairo, Egypt
T (+20) (2) 575 0511 **F** (+20) (2) 574 0331

The purpose of the League of Arab States, founded in 1945, is to ensure co-operation among member states and protect their independence and sovereignty, to supervise the affairs and interests of Arab countries, to control the execution of agreements concluded among the member states, and to promote the process of integration among them. The League considers itself a regional organisation and has observer status at the United Nations.

Member states are Algeria, Bahrain, the Comoros, Djibouti, Egypt, Iraq, Jordan, Kuwait, Lebanon, Libya, Mauritania, Morocco, Oman, Palestine, Qatar, Saudi Arabia, Somalia, Sudan, Syria, Tunisia, the UAE and Yemen.

Member states participate in various specialised agencies of the League whose role is to develop specific areas of co-operation between Arab states. These include: the Arab Organisation for Mineral Resources; the Arab Monetary Fund; the Arab Satellite Communications Organisation; the Arab Academy of Maritime Transport; the Arab Bank for Economic Development in Africa; the Arab League Educational, Cultural and Scientific Organisation and the Council of Arab Economic Unity.

Secretary-General, Amre Moussa (Egypt)

UK OFFICE, 52 Green Street, London W1Y 3RH
T 020-7629 0044 **F** 020-7493 7943

MERCOSUR

Luis Piera 1992, piso 1, 11200-Montevideo, Uruguay
T (+598) (2) 402 9024 **F** (+598) (2) 400 0958
E secretaria@mercosur.org.uk
W www.mercosur.org.uy

Brazil and Argentina signed a Treaty for Integration, Co-operation and Development in 1988 which aimed to create a common market between the two countries within ten years, with the elimination of all tariff barriers and harmonisation of macroeconomic policies; the agreement was to be open to other Latin American countries. Paraguay and Uruguay expressed their interest and MERCOSUR (the Southern Common Market) was created by the Treaty of Asunción, which was signed by the four countries on 26 March 1991. Chile became an associate member in 1996 and Bolivia in 1997.

The Common Market Council (CMC) is the highest-level agency of MERCOSUR, with authority to conduct its policy, and responsibility for compliance with the objects and time frames set forth in the Asunción Treaty. It comprises the ministers of foreign affairs and the economy of the member states. Each country presides over the council for a period of six months, in rotating alphabetical order. The CMC meets at least once a year. The presidents of the member states can take part whenever possible.

The Common Market Group (CMG) is the executive body of MERCOSUR and is co-ordinated by the foreign ministries of the member states. Its function is to ensure compliance with the Asunción Treaty and to implement decisions made by the CMC, and where necessary, to help resolve disputes. It can establish subgroups to work on particular issues. It is composed of four permanent members and four substitutes from each country. It normally meets at least four times a year.

Other bodies include a Joint Parliamentary Committee, a Trade Commission and a Socio-economic Advisory Forum.

NON-ALIGNED MOVEMENT

Permanent Representative to the UN, New York 10016, USA
T (+1) (212) 213 5583 **F** (+1) (212) 592 2498
W www.nam.gov.za

The Non-Aligned Movement (NAM) was created following a conference of non-aligned states held in Belgrade, Yugoslavia in September 1961. Members must be committed to the coexistence of states with different political and social systems, they must not be members of multinational military alliances allied to the great powers, and they should support national liberation movements.

NAM was set up to campaign for an end to colonialism, neo-colonialism, racism and occupation, the dissolution of military blocs, national self-determination for all countries and non-interference in internal affairs, north-south dialogue and political-economic co-operation in the third world (south-south relations) and a new world economic mechanism involving military disarmament and the use of the thereby freed means for development projects.

There are 117 members and 14 observers and about 28 further countries have guest status.

The chairmanship of NAM is held by the head of state of the country due to hold the following summit. The chairman is responsible for the promotion of the principles and activities of the movement and the country's ambassador to the UN represents the organisation at UN level.

NORDIC COUNCIL

The Nordic Council was established in March 1952 as an advisory body on economic and social co-operation, comprising parliamentary delegates from Denmark, Iceland, Norway and Sweden. It was subsequently joined by Finland (1956), and representatives from the Faroes (1970), the Åland Islands (1970), and Greenland (1984).

Co-operation is regulated by the Treaty of Helsinki signed in 1962. This was amended in 1971 to create the Nordic Council of Ministers, which discusses all matters except defence and foreign affairs. Matters are given preparatory consideration by a Committee of Co-operation Ministers' Deputies and joint committees of officials. Decisions of the Council of Ministers, which are taken by consensus, are binding, although if ratification by member parliaments is required, decisions only become effective following parliamentary approval. The Council of Ministers is advised by the Nordic Council, to which it reports annually. There are Ministers for Nordic Co-operation in every member government.

The Nordic Council, comprising 87 voting delegates nominated from member parliaments and about 80 non-voting government representatives, meets at least once a year in plenary sessions. The full Council chooses a 13-member Praesidium, which conducts business between sessions. A Secretariat, headed by a Secretary-General, liaises with the Council of Ministers and provides administrative support. The Council of Ministers has a separate Secretariat.

SECRETARIAT OF THE NORDIC COUNCIL, PO Box 3043, DK-1021 Copenhagen K, Denmark T (+45) 3396 0400
F (+45) 3311 1870 E nordisk-rad@norden.org
W www.norden.org
Secretary-General, Frida Nokken (Norway)

SECRETARIAT OF THE NORDIC COUNCIL OF MINISTERS, Store Strandstræde 18, DK-1255 Copenhagen K, Denmark T (+45) 3396 0200
F (+45) 3396 0202 W www.norden.org
Secretary-General, Per Unckel (Sweden)

NORTH AMERICAN FREE TRADE AGREEMENT

NAFTA Secretariat, Canadian Section, 90 Sparks Street, Suite 705, Ottawa, Ontario K1P 5B4, Canada
T (+1) (613) 992 9388 F (+1) (613) 992 9392
E canada@nafta-sec-alena.org
NAFTA Secretariat, Mexican Section, Blvd. Adolfo López Mateos 3025, 2° Piso, Col. Héroes de Padierna, C.P. 10700, Mexico, D.F.
T (+52) (5) 629 9630 F (+52) (5) 629 9637
E mexico@nafta-sec-alena.org
NAFTA Secretariat, US Section, 14th Street and Constitution Avenue, NW, Room 2061, Washington DC, 20230, USA
T (+1) (202) 482 5438 F (+1) (202) 482 0148
E usa@nafta-sec-alena.org
W www.nafta-sec-alena.org

The leaders of Canada, Mexico and the USA signed the North American Free Trade Agreement (NAFTA) on 17 December 1992 in their respective capitals; it came into force on 1 January 1994 after being ratified by the legislatures of the three member states.

NAFTA aims to eliminate barriers to trade in goods and services, promote fair competition within the free trade area, protect and enforce intellectual property rights and create a framework for further co-operation. To achieve these aims, import tariffs and quotas are being removed, with the aim of achieving a free trade zone by 2008 at the latest.

The NAFTA Secretariat is composed of Canadian, Mexican and US sections. It is responsible for the administration of the dispute settlement provisions of the agreement, provides assistance to the Free Trade Commission and support for various committees and working groups, and facilitates the operation of the agreement.

NORTH ATLANTIC TREATY ORGANISATION

Leopold III laan, Brussels B-1110, Belgium
T (+32) (2) 707 4111 F (+32) (2) 707 4579
E natodoc@hq.nato.int
W www.nato.int

The North Atlantic Treaty (Treaty of Washington) was signed in 1949 by Belgium, Canada, Denmark, France, Iceland, Italy, Luxembourg, the Netherlands, Norway, Portugal, the UK and the USA. Greece and Turkey acceded to the Treaty in 1952, the Federal Republic of Germany in 1955 (the reunited Germany acceded in October 1990), Spain in 1982, and the Czech Republic, Hungary and Poland in 1999. Bulgaria, Estonia, Latvia, Lithuania, Romania, Slovakia and Slovenia signed membership accords on 26 March 2003 and officially joined The North Atlantic Treaty Organisation (NATO) on 29 March 2004.

NATO is the structural framework for a political and military alliance designed to provide common security for its members through co-operation and consultation in political, military and economic as well as scientific and other non-military fields.

STRUCTURE

The North Atlantic Council (NAC), chaired by the Secretary-General, is the highest authority of the Alliance and is composed of permanent representatives of the 26 member countries. It meets at ministerial level (foreign and/or defence ministers) at least twice a year. The permanent representatives (ambassadors) head national delegations of advisers and experts. The Defence Planning Committee (DPC) and the Nuclear Planning Group (NPG) are composed of representatives of all member countries except France (which does not participate in the integrated military structure). Both the DPC and the NPG also meet at ministerial level (defence ministers) at least twice a year. The NATO Secretary-General chairs the Council, the DPC and the NPG.

The senior military authority in NATO, under the Council and DPC, is the Military Committee composed of the Chief of Defence Staffs of each member country except Iceland, which has no military and is represented by a civilian. The Military Committee, which is assisted by an integrated international military staff, also meets in permanent session with permanent military representatives and is responsible for making recommendations to the Council and DPC on measures considered necessary for the common defence of the NATO area and for supplying guidance on military matters to the major NATO commanders. The Chairman of the Military Committee, elected for a period of two to three years, represents the committee on the Council.

The strategic area covered by the North Atlantic Treaty is divided between two major NATO commands (MNCs), European and Atlantic; and three major subordinate commands (MSCs) within Allied Command Europe, South, Central and North-West. There is also a Regional Planning Group (Canada and the United States).

The major NATO commanders are responsible for the development of defence plans for their respective areas, for the determination of force requirements and for the deployment and exercise of the forces under their command. The major NATO commanders report to the Military Committee. The 2002 Prague summit agreed to the reorganisation of NATO's command structure into two strategic commands, the (operational) Allied Command Operations (Europe) and the (functional) Allied Command Transformation (United States).

POST COLD-WAR DEVELOPMENTS

The Euro-Atlantic Partnership Council (EAPC) was established in 1997 to develop closer security links with eastern European and former Soviet states. It focuses on defence planning, defence industry conversion, defence management and force structuring, and the democratic concepts of civilian-military relations. Its membership comprises the 26 NATO members and Albania, Armenia,

Austria, Azerbaijan, Belarus, Croatia, Finland, Georgia, Ireland, Kazakhstan, Kyrgyzstan, Macedonia, Moldova, Russia, Sweden, Switzerland, Tajikistan, Turkmenistan, Ukraine and Uzbekistan. Partnership for Peace (PfP) is the basis for practical security co-operation between NATO and individual partner countries in the fields of defence planning and budgeting, military exercises and civil emergency operations.

In 1997 NATO and Ukraine signed a charter establishing a programme of co-operation and consultation between them. NATO and Russia committed themselves to help build a stable, secure and undivided continent on the basis of partnership and mutual interest, when they signed the 1997 Founding Act on Mutual Relations, Co-operation and Security, which provided for the creation of a Permanent Joint Council, which meets at foreign minister level at least twice a year. In May 2002 agreement was reached on the establishment of the NATO-Russia Council in which Russia and the NATO member countries have an equal role in decision-making on policy to counter terrorism and other security threats. The Council meets every month with four ministerial-level meetings each year. The Mediterranean Dialogue, launched in 1994, aims to promote security and stability in the Mediterranean region and involves the NATO members plus Algeria, Egypt, Israel, Jordan, Mauritania, Morocco and Tunisia.

The development of a European Security and Defence Identity (ESDI), which would strengthen NATO's European pillar, was agreed at the 1999 Washington summit.

At the Washington summit a Defence Capabilities Initiative (DCI) was launched, which aims to improve defence capabilities and interoperability among Alliance forces to ensure the effectiveness of future multinational operations. A temporary High Level Steering Group (HLSG) was established to oversee the implementation of the DCI.

At the 2002 Prague summit a military concept for defence against terrorism was agreed, initiatives in the area of nuclear, biological and chemical weapons defence were endorsed and decisions were taken to strengthen NATO's defence against cyber attacks and to initiate a missile defence feasibility study.

NATO AND THE FORMER YUGOSLAVIA

In March 1999, NATO began air operations against military and industrial targets in Yugoslavia following the repression and ethnic cleansing of ethnic Albanians in Kosovo. Yugoslavia accepted a peace plan drawn up by NATO and Russia on 3 June 1999 and the withdrawal of Yugoslav forces from Kosovo took place between 10–20 June. On 12 June 1999, the NATO-led security force (KFOR) entered Kosovo to oversee the demilitarisation of the Kosovo Liberation Army (KLA), facilitate the return of over 850,000 refugees and provide humanitarian support. Demilitarisation of the KLA was completed on 20 September. KFOR remains in Kosovo providing assistance to the UN Mission in Kosovo (UNMIK) in creating a secure environment.

Following the brokering of a cease-fire to end fighting between ethnic Albanians and the Macedonian armed forces, NATO launched 'Operation Essential Harvest' on 22 August 2001 at the request of the Macedonian government. On 16 December 2002 'Operation Amber Fox/Task Force Fox' was replaced by 'Operation Allied Harmony', to provide support for international monitors and to assist the Macedonian government in taking ownership of security throughout the country. 'Operation Allied Harmony' was terminated on 31 March 2003 and peacekeeping operations were handed over to the European Union.

11 SEPTEMBER 2001

Following the terrorist attacks on the USA on 11 September 2001, the NATO members immediately declared their solidarity with the USA and on 12 September formally invoked Article 5 of the Washington Treaty (which stipulates that an armed attack against one or more NATO members is to be considered an attack against all), declaring that the terrorist attack on the USA was an attack on the NATO alliance.

IRAQ WAR

On 19 February 2003, following a request by Turkey for defensive assistance in the event of a US-led war with Iraq, NATO's Defence and Planning Committee authorised deployment of surveillance aircraft and missile defences to help protect the country in the event of an attack on its territory or population. The deployment began on 20 February and was concluded on 16 April; the last elements of NATO forces deployed to Turkey left the country on 3 May 2003.

Secretary-General and Chairman of the North Atlantic Council, of the DPC and of the NPG, Japp de hoop Schetto (Netherlands)

UK Permanent Representative on the North Atlantic Council, Sir Peter Ricketts

Chairman of the Military Committee, Gen. Harald Kujat (Germany)

ORGANISATION FOR ECONOMIC CO-OPERATION AND DEVELOPMENT

2 rue André-Pascal, F-75775 Paris
T (+33) (1) 4524 8200 F (+33) (1) 4524 8500
E webmaster@oecd.org
W www.oecd.org

The Organisation for Economic Co-operation and Development (OECD) was formed in 1961 to replace the Organisation for European Economic Co-operation. It is the instrument for international co-operation among industrialised member countries on economic and social policies. Its objectives are to assist its member governments in the formulation and co-ordination of policies designed to achieve high, sustained economic growth while maintaining financial stability, to contribute to world trade on a multilateral basis and to stimulate members' aid to developing countries.

The members are Australia, Austria, Belgium, Canada, Czech Republic, Denmark, Finland, France, Germany, Greece, Hungary, Iceland, Republic of Ireland, Italy, Japan, Republic of Korea, Luxembourg, Mexico, the Netherlands, New Zealand, Norway, Poland, Portugal, Slovakia, Spain, Sweden, Switzerland, Turkey, the UK and the USA.

The Council is the supreme body of the organisation. It is composed of one representative for each member country and meets at permanent representative level under the chairmanship of the Secretary-General, and at ministerial level (usually once a year) under the chairmanship of a minister elected annually. Decisions and recommendations are adopted by the unanimous agreement of all members. Most of the OECD's work is undertaken in over 150 specialised committees and working parties. Five autonomous or semi-autonomous bodies are associated in varying degrees to the Organisation: the Nuclear Energy Agency, the International Energy Agency, the Development Centre, the Centre for Educational Research and Innovation, and the European Conference of Ministers of Transport. These bodies, the committees and the Council are serviced by an international Secretariat headed by the Secretary-General.

Secretary-General, Donald J. Johnston (Canada)
UK Permanent Representative, David Lyscom

ORGANISATION FOR SECURITY AND CO-OPERATION IN EUROPE

Kärntner Ring 5–7, A-1010 Vienna, Austria
T (+43) (1) 514 36 180 F (+43) (1) 514 36 105
E info@osce.org
W www.osce.org

The Organisation for Security and Co-operation in Europe (OSCE) was launched in 1975 (as the Conference on Security and Co-operation in Europe (CSCE) under the Helsinki Final Act. This established agreements between NATO members, Warsaw Pact members, and neutral and non-aligned European countries covering security, co-operation and human rights.

The Charter of Paris for a New Europe, signed on 21 November 1990, committed members to support multiparty democracy, free-market economics, the rule of law, and human rights. The signatories also agreed to regular meetings of heads of government, ministers and officials. The first institutionalised heads of state and government summit was held in Helsinki in December 1992, at which the Helsinki Document was adopted. This declared the CSCE to be a regional organisation and defined the structures of the organisation. The summit also appointed a High Commissioner on National Minorities. At its December 1994 summit the CSCE was renamed the Organisation for Security and Co-operation in Europe.

Three structures have been established: the Ministerial Council, which comprises the foreign ministers of participating states and is the central decision-making and governing body, and which meets at least once a year; the Senior Council, which prepares work for the Ministerial Council, carries out its decisions and is responsible for the overview, management and co-ordination of OSCE activities and meets at least three times a year; and the Permanent Council, which is responsible for the day-to-day operational tasks of the OSCE and is the regular body for political consultation, meeting weekly. The chairmanship of the Ministerial Council, Senior Council and Permanent Council rotates among participating states with the Senior Council meeting in Prague and the Permanent Council in Vienna.

The OSCE is also underpinned by four permanent institutions: a Secretariat (Vienna); an Office for Democratic Institutions and Human Rights (Warsaw), which is charged with furthering human rights, democracy and the rule of law; an office of the High Commissioner on National Minorities (The Hague), which identifies ethnic tensions that might endanger peace and promotes their resolution; and a Representative on Freedom of the Media (Vienna), which is responsible for assisting governments in the furthering of free, independent and pluralistic media. There is also a documentation and conference centre in Prague, an OSCE Parliamentary Assembly with a secretariat based in Copenhagen, and a Court of Conciliation and Arbitration in Geneva.

The OSCE has monitoring missions in 16 OSCE countries. The OSCE supervised all elections in Bosnia-Hercegovina between 1996 and 2000 and in Kosovo since 2000. A Joint Consultative Group of the OSCE promotes the objectives and implementation of the Conventional Armed Forces in Europe (CFE) Treaty (1990) which limits conventional ground and air forces. In November 1999, the Charter on European Security committed the OSCE to co-operate with other organisations and institutions concerned with the promotion of security within the OSCE area. The OSCE has 55 participating states.

Chair of the OSCE, Bulgaria (2004); Slovenia (2005)
Chairman-in-Office, Dr. Solomon Passy (Bulgaria)

ORGANISATION OF AMERICAN STATES

17th Street and Constitution Avenue NW, Washington DC 20006, USA
T (+1) (202) 458 3000 F (+1) (202) 458 6421
E pi@oas.org
W www.oas.org

Originally founded in 1890 for largely commercial purposes, the Organisation of American States (OAS) adopted its present name and charter in 1948. The charter entered into force in 1951 and was amended in 1967, 1985 and 1996; the 1992 Protocol of Washington, which gives the OAS the right to suspend a member state whose democratically elected government is overturned by force, was ratified in 1997.

The OAS aims to strengthen the peace and security of the continent; to promote and consolidate representative democracy with due respect for the principle of non-intervention; to prevent possible causes of difficulties and to ensure the peaceful resolution of disputes arising among its member states; to provide for common action on the part of those states in the event of aggression; to seek the resolution of political, judicial and economic problems that may arise among them; to promote, by co-operative action, their economic, social and cultural development; and to achieve an effective limitation of conventional weapons so that resources can be devoted to economic and social development.

The Declaration of Principles and the Plan of Action resulting from the 1994 Miami summit and signed by all the members except Cuba, envisage the establishment of a free trade area, in which barriers to trade and investment will be progressively eliminated.

Policy is determined by the annual General Assembly, which is the supreme authority and elects the Secretary-General for a five-year term. The Meeting of Consultation of ministers of foreign affairs considers urgent problems on an *ad hoc* basis. The Permanent Council, comprising one representative from each member state, promotes friendly inter-state relations, acts as an intermediary in case of disputes arising between states and oversees the General Secretariat, the main administrative body. The Inter-American Council for Integral Development was created in 1996 by the ratification of the Protocol of Managua to promote sustainable development.

The 35 member states are Antigua and Barbuda, Argentina, the Bahamas, Barbados, Belize, Bolivia, Brazil, Canada, Chile, Colombia, Costa Rica, Cuba, Dominica, Dominican Republic, Ecuador, El Salvador, Grenada, Guatemala, Guyana, Haiti, Honduras, Jamaica, Mexico, Nicaragua, Panama, Paraguay, Peru, St Christopher and Nevis, St Lucia, St Vincent and the Grenadines, Suriname, Trinidad and Tobago, Uruguay, the USA and Venezuela.

The European Union and 58 non-American states have permanent observer status.
Secretary-General, Dr César Gaviria Trujillo (Colombia)

ORGANISATION OF ARAB PETROLEUM EXPORTING COUNTRIES

PO Box 20501, Safat 13066, Kuwait
T (+965) 484 4500 F (+965) 481 5747
E oapec@qualitynet.net
W www.oapecorg.org

The Organisation of Arab Petroleum Exporting Countries (OAPEC) was founded in 1968. Its objectives are to promote co-operation in economic activities, to safeguard members' interests, to unite efforts to ensure the flow of oil to consumer markets, and to create a favourable climate for the investment of capital and expertise.

The Ministerial Council is composed of oil ministers from the member countries and meets twice a year to determine policy and to approve the budgets and accounts of the General Secretariat and the Judicial Tribunal. The Judicial Tribunal is composed of seven part-time judges who rule on disputes between member countries and disputes between countries and oil companies. The executive organ of OAPEC is the General Secretariat.

The members are Algeria, Bahrain, Egypt, Iraq, Kuwait, Libya, Qatar, Saudi Arabia, Syria and the United Arab Emirates. Tunisia's membership has been inactive since 1987.
Secretary-General, Abdel-Aziz A. Al-Turki

ORGANISATION OF THE BLACK SEA ECONOMIC CO-OPERATION

Permanent International Secretariat, Istinye Caddesi, Müsir Fuad Pasa Yalisi, Eski Tersane, 34460 Istinye-Istanbul, Turkey
T (+90) (212) 229 6330/6335 F (+90) (212) 229 6336
E bsec@turk.net
W www.bsec-organization.org

The Black Sea Economic Co-operation (BSEC) resulted from the Istanbul Summit Declaration and the adoption of the Bosporus Statement on 25 June 1992. BSEC acquired a permanent secretariat in 1994. Following the Yalta Summit of the Heads of State or Government in June 1998, a charter was drawn up to found the Organisation of the Black Sea Economic Co-operation, which was inaugurated on 1 May 1999.

The organisation aims to promote closer political and economic co-operation in the context of the European integration process between the countries in the Black Sea region and to foster security, regional initiatives, social justice, economic liberty and respect for human rights.

The Council of the Ministers of Foreign Affairs, the highest decision-making authority, meets twice yearly. The meetings rotate among the member states and the chairman is the foreign minister of the state in which the meeting is held. There is also a Committee of Senior Officials and 15 working groups, which deal with specific areas of co-operation.

There are 11 member states: Albania, Armenia, Azerbaijan, Bulgaria, Georgia, Greece, Moldova, Romania, Russia, Turkey and Ukraine.
Secretary-General, Valeri Chechelashvili (Georgia)

ORGANISATION OF THE ISLAMIC CONFERENCE

PO Box 178, Jeddah 21411, Saudi Arabia
T (+966) (2) 680 0800 F (+966) (2) 687 3568
E oiccabinet@oic-un.org
W www.oic-oci.org

The Organisation of the Islamic Conference (OIC) was established in 1969 with the purpose of promoting solidarity and co-operation between Islamic countries. It also has the specific aims of co-ordinating efforts to safeguard the Muslim holy places, supporting the formation of a Palestinian state, assisting member states to maintain their independence, co-ordinating the views of member states in international forums such as the UN, and improving co-operation in the economic, cultural and scientific fields.

The OIC has three central organs, supreme among them the Conference of the Heads of State which meets once every three years to discuss issues of importance to Islamic states. The Conference of Foreign Ministers meets annually to prepare reports for the Conference of Heads of State. The General Secretariat carries out administrative tasks. It is headed by a Secretary-General who is elected by the Conference of Foreign Ministers for a non-renewable four-year term.

In addition to this structure, the OIC has several subsidiary bodies, specialised institutions, affiliated bodies and standing committees. These include the Islamic Solidarity Fund, to aid Islamic institutions in member countries, the Islamic Development Bank, to finance development projects in poorer member states and the Islamic Educational, Scientific and Cultural Organisation. The OIC runs various offices to organise the economic boycott of Israel.

The achievement of the OIC's aims has often been prevented by political rivalry and conflicts between member states, such as the Iran-Iraq war and the Iraqi invasion of Kuwait. Egypt's membership was suspended from 1979 to 1984 because of its peace treaty with Israel. Saudi Arabia, the main source of funding, exercises great influence within the OIC. Since 1991 the OIC has become more united and has spoken out against violence against Muslims in India, the Occupied Territories and Bosnia-Hercegovina. From 1993 to 1995 the OIC co-ordinated the offering of troops to the UN by Muslim states to protect Muslim areas of Bosnia-Hercegovina.

The Organisation has 56 members (55 sovereign Muslim states in Africa, the Middle East, central and south-east Asia and Europe, plus the Palestine Liberation Organisation) and three observers, the Central African Republic, Turkish Northern Cyprus and Cote d'Ivoire. It has an annual budget of US$11 million.
Secretary-General, Dr Abdelouahed Belkeziz (Morocco)

ORGANISATION OF THE PETROLEUM EXPORTING COUNTRIES

Obere Donaustrasse 93, A-1020 Vienna, Austria
T (+43) (1) 21112 279 F (+43) (1) 214 9827
E prid@opec.org
W www.opec.org

The Organisation of the Petroleum Exporting Countries (OPEC) was created in 1960 as a permanent intergovernmental organisation with the principal aims of unifying and co-ordinating the petroleum policies of its members, determining ways of protecting their interests individually and collectively, and ensuring the stabilisation of prices in international oil markets with a view to eliminating unnecessary fluctuations. Since 1982 OPEC has attempted (only partially successfully) to impose overall production limits and production quotas in an attempt to maintain stable oil prices.

The supreme authority is the Conference of Ministers of oil, mines and energy of member countries, which meets at least twice a year to formulate policy. The Board of Governors, nominated by member countries, directs the management of OPEC and implements conference resolutions. The Secretariat carries out executive functions under the direction of the Board of Governors.

The member states are Algeria, Indonesia, Iran, Iraq, Kuwait, Libya, Nigeria, Qatar, Saudi Arabia, the UAE and Venezuela. Ecuador withdrew in 1992 and Gabon in 1995.

OPEC member countries account for about 40 per cent of global crude oil production and 48 per cent of internationally traded crude oil, and have 80 per cent of the world's proven oil reserves. The value of OPEC oil exports in 2003 was US$258 billion.

Secretary-General, HE Dr Purnomo Yusgiantoro (Indonesia)

PACIFIC ISLANDS FORUM

Secretariat, Private Mail Bag, Suva, Fiji
T (+679) 331 2600 **F** (+679) 330 5573
E info@forumsec.org.fj
W www.forumsec.org.fj

The Pacific Islands Forum (PIF) was established in 1971 and represents heads of governments of all the independent and self-governing Pacific Island countries. It aims to foster co-operation between its governments and to represent the interests of the region in international organisations. The PIF meets annually, following which a dialogue is conducted at ministerial level with the Forum dialogue partners (Canada, China, the European Union, France, India, Indonesia, Japan, Korea, Malaysia, the Philippines, the UK and the USA).

The members of the PIF are Australia, the Cook Islands, Micronesia, Fiji, Kiribati, Nauru, New Zealand, Niue, Palau, Papua New Guinea, the Marshall Islands, Samoa, the Solomon Islands, Tonga, Tuvalu and Vanuatu.

The PIF Secretariat comprises divisions dealing with development and economic policy, trade and investment, political and international affairs, and corporate services.

Secretary-General, Gregory Lawrence Urwin (Australia)

SECRETARIAT OF THE PACIFIC COMMUNITY

BP D5, 98848 Nouméa Cedex, New Caledonia
T (+687) 262000 **F** (+687) 263818
E spc@spc.int
W www.spc.int

The Secretariat of the Pacific Community (formerly the South Pacific Commission) was established in 1947 by Australia, France, the Netherlands, New Zealand, the UK and the USA with the aim of promoting the economic and social stability of the islands in the region. The Community now numbers 27 member states and territories: the five remaining founder states (the Netherlands has withdrawn), in which no programmes are run, and the other 22 states and territories of Melanesia, Micronesia and Polynesia.

The Secretariat of the Pacific Community (SPC) is a technical assistance agency with programmes in marine resources (coastal and oceanic fisheries; maritime programme), land resources (agriculture, animal health and plant protection; forestry) and social resources (community health; socio-economic and statistical services; community education services). The governing body is the Conference of the Pacific Community, which meets every two years.

Director-General, Lourdes Pangelinan (Guam)

SOUTH ASIAN ASSOCIATION FOR REGIONAL CO-OPERATION

PO Box 4222, Kathmandu, Nepal
T (+977) (1) 4221794/4221785 **F** (+977) (1) 4227033/4223991
E saarc@saarc-sec.org
W www.saarc-sec.org

The South Asian Association for Regional Co-operation (SAARC) was established in 1985 by Bangladesh, Bhutan, India, the Maldives, Nepal, Pakistan and Sri Lanka. Its primary objective is the acceleration of the process of economic and social development in member states through collective action in agreed areas of co-operation. These include agriculture and rural development, human resource development, environment, meteorology and forestry, science and technology, transport and communications, energy, and social development.

A SAARC Preferential Trading Arrangement (SAPTA), which is designed to reduce tariffs on trade between SAARC member states, was signed in 1993 and entered into force in December 1995. A committee of experts was established in 1998 to draft a comprehensive treaty to create a South Asian Free Trade Area (SAFTA). Agreement was reached in January 2002 to work towards the establishment of a South Asian economic union.

The highest authority rests with the heads of state or government of each member state. The Council of Ministers, which meets twice a year, is made up of the foreign ministers of the member states; it is responsible for formulating policy and considering new projects. The Standing Committee is composed of the foreign secretaries of the member states and monitors and co-ordinates SAARC programmes; it meets twice a year. Technical committees are responsible for individual areas of SAARC's activities. The Secretariat co-ordinates, monitors, facilitates and promotes SAARC's activities and serves as a channel of communication between the association and other regional and intergovernmental institutions.

Secretary-General, Q. A. M. A. Rahim (Bangladesh)

SOUTHERN AFRICAN DEVELOPMENT COMMUNITY

Private Bag 0095, Gaborone, Botswana
T (+267) 351 863 **F** (+267) 372 848
E sadcsec@sadc.int
W www.sadc.int

The Southern African Development Community (SADC) was formed in August 1992 by the members of its predecessor, the Southern African Development Co-ordination Conference, founded in 1980 to harmonise economic development among the countries in Southern Africa and reduce their dependence on South Africa. The SADC now comprises 14 countries, including South Africa, and works on a regional basis to increase economic integration and regional security.

It aims to evolve common political values, systems and

institutions, to promote development and economic growth, regional security, self-sustaining development and the interdependence of member states, and to maximise production and strengthen and consolidate the historical, social and cultural links among the peoples of the region.

The headquarters of the SADC is in Gaborone, Botswana, but member states each have a responsibility for an area of economic activity.

Executive Secretary, Dr Prega Ramsamy
Chairman, José Eduardo dos Santos (Angola)

UNITED NATIONS

UN Plaza, New York, NY 10017, USA
T (+1) (212) 963 1234
W www.un.org

The United Nations (UN) is an intergovernmental organisation of member states, dedicated through signature of the UN Charter to the maintenance of international peace and security and the solution of economic, social and political problems through international co-operation.

The UN was founded as a successor to the League of Nations and inherited many of its procedures and institutions. The name 'United Nations' was first used in the Washington Declaration 1942 to describe the 26 states that had allied to fight the Axis powers. The UN Charter developed from discussions at the Moscow Conference of the foreign ministers of China, the UK, the USA and the Soviet Union in 1943. Further progress was made at Dumbarton Oaks, Washington, in 1944 during talks involving the same states. The role of the Security Council was formulated at the Yalta Conference in 1945. The Charter was formally drawn up by 50 allied nations at the San Francisco Conference between April and 26 June 1945, when it was signed. Following ratification the UN came into effect on 24 October 1945, which is celebrated annually as United Nations Day. The UN flag is light blue with the UN emblem centred in white.

The principal organs of the UN are the General Assembly, the Security Council, the Economic and Social Council, the Trusteeship Council, the Secretariat and the International Court of Justice. The Economic and Social Council and the Trusteeship Council are auxiliaries, charged with assisting and advising the General Assembly and Security Council. The official languages used are Arabic, Chinese, English, French, Russian and Spanish. Deliberations at the International Court of Justice are in English and French only.

A Millennium summit was held in New York on 6–8 September 2000 at which the reform of the UN was debated and an attempt was made to redefine its role.

MEMBERSHIP

Membership is open to all countries which accept the Charter and its principle of peaceful co-existence. New members are admitted by the General Assembly on the recommendation of the Security Council. The original membership of 51 states has grown to 191.

Afghanistan; Albania; Algeria; Andorra; Angola; Antigua and Barbuda; Argentina*; Armenia; Australia*; Austria; Azerbaijan; Bahamas; Bahrain; Bangladesh; Barbados; Belarus*; Belgium*; Belize; Benin; Bhutan; Bolivia*; Bosnia-Hercegovina; Botswana; Brazil*; Brunei Darussalam; Bulgaria; Burkina Faso; Burundi; Cambodia; Cameroon; Canada*; Cape Verde; Central African Republic; Chad; Chile*; China*; Colombia*; Comoros; Congo; Costa Rica*; Côte d'Ivoire; Croatia; Cuba*; Cyprus; Czech Republic; Democratic People's Republic of Korea; Democratic Republic of the Congo; Denmark*; Djibouti; Dominica; Dominican Republic*; Ecuador*; Egypt*; El Salvador*; Equatorial Guinea; Eritrea; Estonia; Ethiopia*; Fiji; Finland; France*; Gabon; Gambia; Georgia; Germany; Ghana; Greece*; Grenada; Guatemala*; Guinea; Guinea-Bissau; Guyana; Haiti*; Honduras*; Hungary; Iceland; India*; Indonesia; Iran*; Iraq*; Ireland; Israel; Italy; Jamaica; Japan; Jordan; Kazakhstan; Kenya; Kiribati; Korea, Democratic People's Republic of; Korea, Republic of; Kuwait; Kyrgyzstan; Laos; Latvia; Lebanon*; Lesotho; Liberia*; Libya; Liechtenstein; Lithuania; Luxembourg*; Macedonia; Madagascar; Malawi; Malaysia; Maldives; Mali; Malta; Marshall Islands; Mauritania; Mauritius; Mexico*; Micronesia (Federated States of); Moldova; Monaco; Mongolia; Morocco; Mozambique; Myanmar; Namibia; Nauru; Nepal; Netherlands*; New Zealand*; Nicaragua*; Niger; Nigeria; Norway*; Oman; Pakistan; Palau; Panama*; Papua New Guinea; Paraguay*; Peru*; Philippines*; Poland*; Portugal; Qatar; Romania; Russia*; Rwanda; St Christopher and Nevis; St Lucia; St Vincent and the Grenadines; Samoa; San Marino; São Tomé and Princípe; Saudi Arabia*; Senegal; Serbia and Montenegro; Seychelles; Sierra Leone; Singapore; Slovakia; Slovenia; Solomon Islands; Somalia; South Africa*; Spain; Sri Lanka; Sudan; Suriname; Swaziland; Sweden; Syrian Arab Republic*;Tajikistan; Tanzania; Thailand; Togo; Tonga; Trinidad and Tobago; Tunisia; Turkey*; Turkmenistan; Tuvalu; Uganda; Ukraine*; United Arab Emirates; United Kingdom*; United States of America*; Uruguay*; Uzbekistan; Vanuatu; Venezuela*; Vietnam; Yemen; Zambia; Zimbabwe.

*Original member (i.e. from 1945). Czechoslovakia, Yugoslavia and the USSR were all original members until their dissolution.

OBSERVERS

Permanent observer status is held by the Holy See. The Palestine Liberation Organisation has special observer status.

THE GENERAL ASSEMBLY

UN Plaza, New York, NY 10017, USA

The General Assembly is the main deliberative organ of the UN. It consists of all members, each entitled to five representatives but having only one vote. The annual session begins on the third Tuesday of September, when the President is elected, and usually continues until mid-December. Special sessions are held on specific issues and emergency special sessions can be called within 24 hours.

The Assembly is empowered to discuss any matter within the scope of the Charter, except when it is under consideration by the Security Council, and to make recommendations. Under the 'uniting for peace' resolution, adopted in 1950, the Assembly may also take action to maintain international peace and security when the Security Council fails to do so because of a lack of unanimity of its permanent members. Important decisions, such as those on peace and security, the election of officers, the budget, etc., need a two-thirds majority. Others need a simple majority. The Assembly has effective power only over the internal operations of the UN itself; external recommendations are not legally binding.

The work of the General Assembly is divided among six main committees, on each of which every member has the right to be represented: disarmament and international security; economic and financial; social, humanitarian and cultural; special political issues and decolonisation (including non-self governing territories); administrative and budgetary; and legal. In addition, the General Assembly appoints *ad hoc* committees to consider special issues, such as human rights, peacekeeping, disarmament and international law. All committees consider items referred to them by the Assembly and recommend draft resolutions to its plenary meeting.

The Assembly is assisted by a number of functional committees. The General Committee co-ordinates its proceedings and operations, while the Credentials Committee verifies the credentials of representatives. There are also two standing committees, the Advisory Committee on Administration and Budgetary Questions and the Committee on Contributions, which suggests the scale of members' payments to the UN.

President of the General Assembly (2004–5), Julian R. Hunte

The Assembly has created a large number of specialised bodies over the years, which are supervised jointly with the Economic and Social Council. They are supported by UN and voluntary contributions from governments, non-governmental organisations and individuals. These organisations include:

CONFERENCE ON DISARMAMENT
Palais des Nations, CH-1211 Geneva 10, Switzerland

Established by the UN as the Committee on Disarmament in 1962, the CD is the single multilateral disarmament negotiating forum. The present title of the organisation was adopted in 1984. There are 66 members.

A Chemical Weapons Convention was agreed in Paris in 1993 and came into force in April 1997 after being ratified by 87 countries. It bans the use, production, stockpiling and transfer of all chemical weapons. All US and Russian weapons must be destroyed within 15 years of the Convention entering into force and all other states' weapons must be destroyed within ten years.

THE UNITED NATIONS CHILDREN'S FUND (UNICEF)
3 UN Plaza, New York, NY 10017, USA

Established in 1947 to assist children and mothers in the immediate post-war period, UNICEF now concentrates on developing countries. It provides primary healthcare and health education. In particular, it conducts programmes in oral hydration, immunisation against leading diseases, child growth monitoring and the encouragement of breast-feeding. Its operations are often conducted in co-operation with the World Health Organisation (WHO).

THE UNITED NATIONS DEVELOPMENT PROGRAMME (UNDP)
1 UN Plaza, New York, NY 10017, USA

Established in 1966 from the merger of the UN Expanded Programme of Technical Assistance and the UN Special Fund, UNDP is the central funding agency for economic and social development projects around the world. Much of its annual expenditure is channelled through UN specialised agencies, governments and non-governmental organisations.

THE UNITED NATIONS HIGH COMMISSIONER FOR REFUGEES (UNHCR)
94 rue Montbrillant, PO Box 2500, CH-1211 Geneva 2, Switzerland

Established in 1951 to protect the rights and interests of refugees, UNHCR organises emergency relief and longer-term solutions, such as voluntary repatriation, local integration or resettlement.

THE UN RELIEF AND WORKS AGENCY FOR PALESTINE REFUGEES IN THE NEAR EAST (UNRWA)
Vienna International Centre, Wagramerstrasse 5, PO Box 700, A-1400 Vienna, Austria

Established in 1949 to bring relief to the Palestinians displaced by the Arab-Israeli conflict.

THE UNITED NATIONS HIGH COMMISSIONER FOR HUMAN RIGHTS
Established in 1993 to secure respect for, and prevent violations of human rights by engaging in dialogue with governments and international organisations. Responsible for the co-ordination of all UN human rights activities.

THE SECURITY COUNCIL
UN Plaza, New York, NY 10017, USA

The Security Council is the senior arm of the UN and has the primary responsibility for maintaining world peace and security. It consists of 15 members, each with one representative and one vote. There are five permanent members, China, France, Russia, the UK and the USA, and ten non-permanent members. Each of the non-permanent members is elected for a two-year term by a two-thirds majority of the General Assembly and is ineligible for immediate re-election. Five of the elective seats are allocated to Africa and Asia, one to eastern Europe, two to Latin America and two to western Europe and remaining countries. Procedural questions are determined by a majority vote. Other matters require a majority inclusive of the votes of the permanent members; they thus have a right of veto. The abstention of a permanent member does not constitute a veto. The presidency rotates each month by state in (English) alphabetical order. Parties to a dispute, other non-members and individuals can be invited to participate in Security Council debates but are not permitted to vote.

The Security Council is empowered to settle or adjudicate in disputes or situations which threaten international peace and security. It can adopt political, economic and military measures to achieve this end. Any matter considered to be a threat to or breach of the peace or an act of aggression can be brought to the Security Council's attention by any member state or by the Secretary-General. The Charter envisaged members placing at the disposal of the Security Council armed forces and other facilities which would be co-ordinated by the Military Staff Committee, composed of military representatives of the five permanent members. The Security Council is also supported by a Committee of Experts, to advise on procedural and technical matters, and a Committee on Admission of New Members.

Owing to superpower disunity, the Security Council rarely played the decisive role set out in the Charter; the Military Staff Committee was effectively suspended from 1948 until 1990, when a meeting was convened during the Gulf Crisis on the formation and control of

UN-supervised armed forces. However, at an extraordinary meeting of the Security Council in January 1992, heads of government laid plans to transform the UN in light of the changed post-Cold War world. The Secretary-General was asked to draw up a report on enhancing the UN's preventive diplomacy, peacemaking and peacekeeping ability. The report, *An Agenda for Peace,* was produced in June 1992 and centred on the establishment of a UN army composed of national contingents on permanent standby, as envisaged at the time of the UN's formation.

PEACEKEEPING FORCES

The Security Council has established a number of peacekeeping forces since its foundation, comprising contingents provided mainly by neutral and non-aligned UN members. Current operations include: the UN Truce Supervision Organisation (UNTSO), Israel, 1948; the UN Military Observer Group in India and Pakistan (UNMOGIP), 1949; the UN Peacekeeping Force in Cyprus (UNFICYP), 1964; the UN Disengagement Observer Force (UNDOF), Golan Heights, Syria, 1974; the UN Interim Force in Lebanon (UNIFIL), 1978; the UN Mission for the Referendum in Western Sahara (MINURSO), 1991; the UN Observer Mission in Georgia (UNOMIG), 1993; the United Nations Interim Administration Mission in Kosovo (UNMIK), 1999; the United Nations Mission in Sierra Leone (UNAMISIL), 1999; the United Nations Organisation Mission in the Democratic Republic of the Congo (MONUC), 1999; the United Nations Mission in Ethiopia and Eritrea (UNMEE), 2000; the United Nations Mission of Support in East Timor (UNMISET), 2002; the United Nations Mission in Cote d'Ivoire (MINUCI), 2003 (replaced by the United Nations Operations in Cote d'Ivoire (UNOCI) in April 2004).

THE ECONOMIC AND SOCIAL COUNCIL

UN Plaza, New York, NY 10017, USA

The Economic and Social Council is responsible under the General Assembly for the economic and social work of the UN and for the co-ordination of the activities of the 15 specialised agencies and other UN bodies. It makes reports and recommendations on economic, social, cultural, educational, health and related matters, often in consultation with non-governmental organisations, passing the reports to the General Assembly and other UN bodies. It also drafts conventions for submission to the Assembly and calls conferences on matters within its remit.

The Council consists of 54 members, 18 of whom are elected annually by the General Assembly for a three-year term. Each has one vote and can be immediately re-elected on retirement. A President is elected annually and is also eligible for re-election. One substantive session is held annually and decisions are reached by simple majority vote of those present.

The Council has established a number of standing committees on particular issues and several commissions. Commissions include: Statistical, Human Rights, Social Development, Sustainable Development, Status of Women, Crime Prevention and Criminal Justice, Narcotic Drugs, Science and Technology for Development and Population; and Regional Economic Commissions for Europe, Asia and the Pacific, Western Asia, Latin America and Africa.

THE TRUSTEESHIP COUNCIL

UN Plaza, New York, NY10017, USA

With the independence of the Republic of Palau in October 1994, all eleven trusteeships have now progressed to independence or merged with neighbouring states and the Trusteeship Council suspended its operations on 1 November 1994.

THE SECRETARIAT

UN Plaza, New York, NY 10017, USA

The Secretariat services the other UN organs and is headed by a Secretary-General elected by a majority vote of the General Assembly on the recommendation of the Security Council. He is assisted by an international staff, chosen to represent the international character of the organisation. The Secretary-General is charged with bringing to the attention of the Security Council any matter which he considers poses a threat to international peace and security. He may also bring other matters to the attention of the General Assembly and other UN bodies and may be entrusted by them with additional duties. As chief administrator to the UN, the Secretary-General is present in person or via representatives at all meetings of the other five main organs of the UN. He may also act as an impartial mediator in disputes between member states.

The power and influence of the Secretary-General has been determined largely by the character of the office-holder and by the state of relations between the superpowers. The thaw in these relations since the mid-1980s has increased the effectiveness of the UN, particularly in its attempts to intervene in international disputes. It helped to end the Iran-Iraq war and sponsored peace in Central America. Following Iraq's invasion of Kuwait in 1990 the UN took its first collective security action since the Korean War. Conflicts in Cyprus, East Timor, Libya, Nigeria and Western Sahara have been successfully prevented from escalating or spreading during Kofi Annan's time in office. In addition to maintenance of international security, ending poverty and inequality, improving education, reducing HIV/AIDS and safeguarding the environment were some of the issues outlined in the UN Millennium Report.

Secretary-General, Kofi Annan, apptd 1996 (Ghana)
Deputy Secretary-General, Louise Frechette

FORMER SECRETARIES-GENERAL

1946–53	Trygve Lie (Norway)
1953–61	Dag Hammarskjöld (Sweden)
1961–71	U Thant (Burma)
1971–81	Kurt Waldheim (Austria)
1981–91	Javier Pérez de Cuéllar (Peru)
1991–96	Boutros Boutros-Ghali (Egypt)

INTERNATIONAL COURT OF JUSTICE

The Peace Palace, NL-2517 KJ The Hague, The Netherlands

The International Court of Justice is the principal judicial organ of the UN. The Statute of the Court is an integral part of the Charter and all members of the UN are ipso facto parties to it. The Court is composed of 15 judges, elected by both the General Assembly and the Security Council for nine-year terms which are renewable. Judges may deliberate over cases in which their country is involved. If no judge on the bench is from a country which is a party to a dispute under consideration, that party may designate a judge to participate ad hoc in that

particular deliberation. If any party to a case fails to adhere to the judgement of the Court, the other party may have recourse to the Security Council.
President, Shi Jiuyong (China)
Vice-President, Raymond Ranjeva (Madagascar)
Judges, Rosalyn Higgins (UK); Pieter H. Kooijmans (Netherlands); Abdul G. Koroma (Sierra Leone); Gonzalo Parra-Aranguren (Venezuela); José Francisco Rezek (Brazil); Vladlen S. Vereshchetin (Russia); Awn Shawkat Al-Khasawneh (Jordan); Thomas Buergenthal (USA); Gilbert Guillaume (France); Nabil Elaraby (Egypt); Hisashi Owada (Japan); Bruno Simma (Germany); Peter Tomka (Slovakia)

INTERNATIONAL CRIMINAL TRIBUNAL FOR THE FORMER YUGOSLAVIA

Churchill Plein 1, PO Box 13888, NL-2501 EW The Hague, The Netherlands

In February 1993, the Security Council voted to establish a war crimes tribunal for the former Yugoslavia to hear cases covering grave breaches of the Geneva Conventions and crimes against humanity. The Court was inaugurated in November 1993 in The Hague with 11 judges elected by the UN General Assembly from 11 states, divided into two trial chambers of three judges each and an appeal chamber of five judges. The court is unable to force suspects to stand trial but is empowered to pass verdicts in the absence of suspects and can put suspects under an 'act of accusation' which prevents them from leaving their own country.

In October 1995, the tribunal formally charged the Bosnian Serb leaders Radovan Karadzić and Gen. Ratko Mladić, the Croatian Serb President Milan Martić and 21 others with genocide and crimes against humanity. By January 1997 only one of the 75 suspected war criminals to be indicted had been imprisoned. In May 1999, the tribunal formally charged the Yugoslav president Slobodan Milošević, the Serbian president Milan Milutinović, two other Serb politicians and the Yugoslav armed forces chief of staff Dragoljub Ojdanić.

For up-to-date information regarding indictments and judgements of the Tribunal, visit www.un.org/icty
President, Theodor Meron (United States)

INTERNATIONAL CRIMINAL TRIBUNAL FOR RWANDA

Following serious violations of humanitarian law in Rwanda, the United Nations Security Council created the International Criminal Tribunal for Rwanda (ICTR) on 8 November 1994. The purpose of this measure was to contribute to the process of national reconciliation in Rwanda and to the maintenance of peace in the region. The tribunal was established for the prosecution of persons responsible for genocide and other serious violations of international humanitarian law committed in the territory of Rwanda between 1 January 1994 and 31 December 1994. It may also deal with the prosecution of Rwandan citizens responsible for genocide and other such violations of international law committed in the territory of neighbouring states during the same period.
President, Judge Erik Mose (Norway)

UNITED NATIONS MONITORING, VERIFICATION AND INSPECTION COMMISSION

Room S-3120, New York, NY 10017, USA
T (+1) (212) 963 3018 **F** (+1) (212) 963 3922
W www.unmovic.org

The United Nations Monitoring, Verification and Inspection Commission (UNMOVIC), was created by UN Security Council Resolution 1284, adopted in December 1999.

UNMOVIC is mandated to verify Iraq's compliance with its obligation not to possess or acquire weapons of mass destruction (biological or chemical weapons of mass destruction, together with ballistic missiles with a target distance of more than 150 km), to destroy all research, development and production facilities and to desist from the future development or acquisition of such weapons and operate a monitoring and verification programme to ensure that prohibited items and programmes are not reactivated.

In January 2003, three months after UN weapons inspectors were re-admitted, Dr Blix stated that Iraq had failed to disarm, greatly strengthening the American and British case for war. He insisted, however, that the weapons inspectors be given more time. US president George Bush presented the deadline of 17 March 2003 for Iraq to disarm and the UN removed all their staff from the region. A second UN resolution was not granted and on 19 March 2003 airstrikes led by the USA began against Baghdad without UN backing. In the thirteenth quarterly report of UNMOVIC, covering March to May 2003, Hans Blix stated that the Commission had at no point during the inspections in Iraq found evidence of the continuation or resumption of programmes of weapons of mass destruction or significant quantity of proscribed items – whether pre-1991 or after. He stressed that this did not mean that such items could not exist as there remained long lists of unaccounted items.

In resolution 1483 (May 2003) lifting Iraqi economic sanctions, the Security Council declared its intention to revisit the mandate of UNMOVIC, which remains ready to resume its work in Iraq. In July 2003 Kofi Annan announced the appointment of a new Executive Chairman to replace Hans Blix.
Executive Chairman, Demetrius Perricos (Greece)

UK MISSION TO THE UN

1 Dag Hammarskjöld Plaza, 885 Second Avenue, New York, NY 10017, USA
T (+1) (212) 745 9250 **F** (+1) (212) 745 9316
E uk@un.int **W** www.ukun.org
Permanent Representative to the United Nations and Representative on the Security Council, Sir Emyr Jones Parry, KCMG, *apptd* 2003
Deputy Permanent Representative, Adam Thomson

UK MISSION TO THE OFFICE OF THE UN AND OTHER INTERNATIONAL ORGANISATIONS IN GENEVA

37–39 rue de Vermont, CH-1211 Geneva 20, Switzerland
T (+41) (22) 918 2300 **F** (+41) (22) 918 2333
E mission.uk@ties.itu.int
Permanent UK Representative, Nicholas Thorne, CMG, *apptd* 2003
Deputy Permanent Representative, N. M. McMillan, CMG

UK MISSION TO THE UN IN VIENNA

Jaurčsgasse 12, A-1030 Vienna, Austria
UK Permanent Representative, P. R Jenkins, *apptd* 2001
Deputy Permanent Representative, T. J. Andrews

REGIONAL UN INFORMATION CENTRE
Block C, Level 5, Residence Palace, 155 Rue de la Loi, Wetstraat 155, Brussels 1040, Belgium
T (+32) 2287-4019 F (+32) 2502-4061
E info@runic-europe.org W www.runic-europe.org

UNITED NATIONS EDUCATION, SCIENTIFIC AND CULTURAL ORGANISATION

7 place de Fontenoy, F-75352 Paris 07 SP, France
T (+33) (1) 4568 1000 F (+33) (1) 4567 1690
E spokesperson@unesco.org
W www.unesco.org

The United Nations Educational, Scientific and Cultural Organisation (UNESCO) was established in 1946. It promotes collaboration among its member states in education, science, culture and communication. It aims to further a universal respect for human rights, justice and the rule of law, without distinction of race, sex, language or religion, in accordance with the UN Charter.

UNESCO runs a number of programmes to improve education and extend access to it. It provides assistance to ensure the free flow of information and its wider and better balanced dissemination without any obstacle to freedom of expression, and to maintain cultural heritage in the face of development. It fosters research and study in all areas of the social and environmental sciences.

UNESCO had 190 member states as at June 2004. The General Conference, consisting of representatives of all the members, meets biennially to decide the programme and the budget. It elects the 58-member Executive Board, which supervises operations, and appoints a Director-General who heads a Secretariat responsible for carrying out the organisation's programmes. In most member states national commissions liaise with UNESCO to execute its programme. The UK withdrew from UNESCO in 1985; it rejoined on 1 July 1997.

Director-General, Koichiro Matsuura (Japan)

UNITED NATIONS INDUSTRIAL DEVELOPMENT ORGANISATION

Vienna International Centre, Wagramerstrasse 5, PO Box 300, A-1400 Vienna, Austria
T (+43) (1) 260 260 F (+43) (1) 269 2669
E unido@unido.org W www.unido.org

The United Nations Industrial Development Organisation (UNIDO) was established in 1966 by the UN General Assembly to act as the central co-ordinating body for industrial activities within the UN. It became a UN specialised agency in 1985. UNIDO aims to help developing countries and those with economies in transition to develop sustainable industrialisation by concentrating on economic competitiveness, environmental awareness and employment issues both in the public and private sectors. UNIDO designs and implements programmes to support industrial development in individual member states and offers specialised support for programme development.

UNIDO had 171 members as at June 2004. It is funded by regular and operational budgets, together with contributions for technical co-operation activities. The regular budget is derived from member states' contributions. Technical co-operation is funded mainly through voluntary contributions from donor countries and institutions and by intergovernmental and non-governmental organisations. A General Conference of all the members meets biennially to discuss strategy and policy, approve the budget (2004–5, regular budget €144 million) and elect the Director-General. The Industrial Development Board is composed of members from 53 member states and reviews the work programme and the budget, which is prepared by the Programme and Budget Committee.

Director-General, Carlos Magarinos (Argentina)
Permanent UK Representative, Peter Jenkins, British Embassy, Vienna

UNIVERSAL POSTAL UNION

Weltpoststrasse 4, CH-3000 Bern 15, Switzerland
T (+41) (31) 350 3111 F (+41) (31) 350 3110
E info@upu.int
W www.upu.int

The Universal Postal Union (UPU) was established by the Treaty of Bern 1874, taking effect from 1875, and became a UN specialised agency in 1948. The UPU is an intergovernmental organisation that exists to form and regulate a single postal territory of all member countries for the reciprocal exchange of correspondence without discrimination. With a total of 190 members, it also assists and advises on the improvement of postal services.

A Universal Postal Congress is the UPU's supreme authority and meets every five years. A Council of Administration composed of 41 members meets annually to ensure continuity between congresses, study regulatory developments and broad policies, approve the budget and examine proposed Treaty changes. A Postal Operations Council, composed of 40 members elected by the Congress, meets annually to deal with specific technical and operational issues. The three UPU bodies are served by the International Bureau, a secretariat headed by a Director-General.

Funding is provided by members according to a scale of contributions drawn up by the Congress. The Council of Administration sets the budget which amounts to approximately SFr 35,000,000 per year.

Director-General, Thomas E. Leavey (USA)

UNREPRESENTED NATIONS AND PEOPLES ORGANISATION

PO Box 85878, 2508 CN The Hague, The Netherlands
T (+31) (70) 364 6504 F (+31) (70) 364 6608
E unpo@unpo.org
W www.unpo.org

The Unrepresented Nations and Peoples Organisation (UNPO) was founded in 1991 to offer an international forum for occupied nations, indigenous peoples and national minorities who are not represented in other international organisations.

UNPO does not aim to represent these nations and peoples, but rather to assist and empower them to represent themselves more effectively, and provides professional services and facilities as well as education and training in the fields of diplomacy, international and human rights law, democratic processes, institution building, conflict management and resolution, and environmental protection.

Participation is open to all nations and peoples who are inadequately represented at the United Nations and who declare allegiance to five principles relating to the right of self-determination of all peoples, human rights, democracy, non-violence and the rejection of terrorism, and protection of the natural environment. Applicants must show that they constitute a 'nation or people' and that the organisation applying for membership is representative of that nation or people.

As at June 2004, there were 55 full members and five former members, who have achieved full independence.

Director-General, Marino Busdachin (Croatia)

WESTERN EUROPEAN UNION

Rue de l'Association 15, B-1000 Brussels, Belgium
T (+32) (2) 500 4412 F (+32) (2) 500 4470
E ueo.secretariatgeneral@skynet.be
W www.weu.int

The Western European Union (WEU) originated as the Brussels Treaty Organisation (BTO) established under the Treaty of Brussels, signed in 1948 by Belgium, France, Luxembourg, the Netherlands and the UK, to provide collective self-defence and economic and social collaboration amongst its signatories. The BTO was modified to become the WEU in 1954 with the admission of West Germany and Italy.

From the late 1970s onwards efforts were made to add a security dimension to the EC's European Political Co-operation. Opposition to these efforts from Denmark, Greece and Ireland led the remaining EC countries, all WEU members, to decide to reactivate the Union in 1984. Members committed themselves to harmonising their views on defence and security and developing a European security identity, while bearing in mind the importance of transatlantic relations. Portugal and Spain joined the WEU in 1988, and Greece became a full member in 1995.

In 1991, the EU Maastricht Treaty committed the European Community to the establishment of a Common Foreign and Security Policy (CFSP). The WEU was designated as the future defence component of the European Union and member states of the EU who were not already members of the WEU were invited to join or become observers. In November 1992 the WEU's role as the common security dimension of the EU was enhanced when WEU ministers signed a declaration with remaining European NATO members to give them various forms of WEU membership. Iceland, Norway and Turkey became associate members; the Republic of Ireland, Denmark, Austria, Finland and Sweden became observers. In 1994 the WEU reached agreements with Estonia, Latvia, Lithuania, Poland, the Czech Republic, Slovakia, Hungary, Romania and Bulgaria, under which they all became associate partners; Slovenia became an associate partner in 1996. The Czech Republic, Hungary and Poland, who had been associate partners, became associate members in 1999, following their accession to NATO.

The WEU has worked in close co-operation with the Atlantic Alliance, and relations between the WEU and NATO were developed on the basis of transparency and complementarity. The 1993 Luxembourg Declaration states that the WEU is ready to participate in the future work of the NATO Alliance as its European pillar, and at the Atlantic Alliance summit in January 1994, NATO expressed its readiness to make Alliance assets and capabilities available for WEU operations. In June 1996, NATO foreign and defence ministers approved the Combined Joint Task Force (CJTF) concept and the elaboration of multinational European command arrangements for WEU-led operations.

A Council of Ministers (foreign and defence) has met biannually in the capital of the presiding country; the presidency rotates biannually, and from 1999 the sequence of WEU presidencies has been harmonised with those of the EU Council of Ministers. A Permanent Council of the member states' permanent representatives meets in Brussels. The Permanent Council is chaired by the Secretary-General and serviced by the Secretariat.

In 1999, NATO and the EU decided to establish a direct relationship; the EU committed itself to ensuring that it was able to take decisions on conflict prevention and crisis management and NATO agreed to give the EU access to its collective assets and capabilities for operations in which NATO as a whole was not engaged. The WEU's crisis management functions were transferred to the EU in July 2001. The necessary WEU functions and structures remain in place to enable member states to fulfil commitments arising from the modified Brussels Treaty including those relating to collective defence and institutional relationship with the WEU.

The Assembly of the WEU is composed of 115 parliamentarians of member states and meets twice annually in Paris to debate matters within the scope of the revised Brussels Treaty.

Presidency (2004) Spain, Netherlands;
(2005) Luxembourg, United Kingdom
Secretary-General, Javier Solana Madariaga (Spain)
UK Representative on the Permanent Council, Peter Gooderham
ASSEMBLY, 43 avenue du Président Wilson, F-75775 Paris Cedex 16, France

WORLD BANK GROUP

1818 H Street NW, Washington DC 20433, USA
T (+1) (202) 473 1000 F (+1) (202) 477 6391
E feedback@worldbank.org
W www.worldbank.org

The World Bank Group was founded in 1944 and is one of the world's largest sources of development assistance. The Bank has 183 members. Originally directed towards post-war reconstruction in Europe, the Bank subsequently turned towards assisting less-developed countries and is currently working in more than 100 developing countries. The Bank, works with government agencies, non-governmental organisations and the private sector to formulate assistance strategies. Its local offices implement the Bank's programme in each country. It has offices in more than 100 countries.

The Bank is owned by the governments of member countries and its capital is subscribed by its members. It finances its lending primarily from borrowing in world capital markets, and derives a substantial contribution to its resources from its retained earnings and the repayment of loans. The interest rate on its loans is calculated in relation to its cost of borrowing. Loans generally have a grace period of five years and are repayable within 20 years.

The World Bank Group consists of five institutions. The International Bank for Reconstruction and Development (IBRD) provides loans and development assistance to middle-income countries and creditworthy poorer countries. The International Finance Corporation (IFC) promotes private sector investment in developing member countries by mobilising domestic and foreign capital. The International Development Association (IDA) performs the same function as the World Bank but primarily to less-developed countries and on terms that bear less heavily on their balance of payments than IBRD loans. The Multilateral Investment Guarantee Agency (MIGA) promotes foreign direct investment in developing states by providing guarantees to potential investors and advisory services to developing member countries. MIGA has a membership of 163 countries. The International Centre for Settlement of Investment Disputes (ICSID) provides facilities for the settlement by conciliation or arbitration of investment disputes between foreign investors and their host countries. ICSID has a membership of 154 countries.

The IBRD and its affiliates are financially and legally distinct but share headquarters. The IBRD is headed by a Board of Governors, consisting of one Governor and one alternate Governor appointed by each member country. Twenty-four Executive Directors exercise all powers of the Bank except those reserved to the Board of Governors. The President, elected by the Executive Directors, conducts the business of the Bank, assisted by an international staff. Membership in both the IFC and the IDA is open to all IBRD countries. The IDA is administered by the same staff as the Bank; the IFC has its own personnel but draws on the IBRD for administrative and other support. All share the same President.

President, James D. Wolfensohn (USA)

UK OFFICE, New Zealand House, 15th Floor, Haymarket, London SW1Y 4TQ **T** 020-7930 8511 **F** 020-7930 8515

WORLD CUSTOMS ORGANISATION

30 Rue du Marche, B-1210, Brussels, Belgium
T (+32) 2209 9211 **F** (+32) 2209 9292
E information@wcoomd.org **W** www.wcoomd.org

The World Customs Organisation (WCO) is an independent body that works to enhance the effectiveness and efficiency of customs administrations worldwide. By developing the Harmonised Commodity Description and Coding System, the WCO introduced a universal goods classification and revenue collection method. The WCO also administers the World Trade Organisation Valuation Agreement.

With 159 member governments that process more than 95 per cent of international trade, the WCO is organised into a forum where each member has one representative and one vote. The WCO is directed by a Council and Policy Commission with financial advice from a Committee. Locally recruited staff are used to provide secretarial, translation, interpretation and general support services.

Secretary-General, Michel Danet (France)

WORLD HEALTH ORGANISATION

20 avenue Appia, CH-1211 Geneva 27, Switzerland
T (+41) (22) 791 2111 **F** (+41) (22) 791 0746
E info@who.intch
W www.who.ch

The UN International Health Conference, held in 1946, established the World Health Organisation (WHO) as a UN specialised agency, with effect from 1948. It is dedicated to attaining the highest possible level of health for all. It collaborates with member governments, UN agencies and other bodies to improve health standards, control communicable diseases and promote all aspects of family and environmental health. It seeks to raise the standards of health teaching and training, and promotes research through collaborating research centres world-wide.

WHO has 192 members and is governed by the annual World Health Assembly of members which meets to set policy, approve the budget, appoint a Director-General, and adopt health conventions and regulations. It also elects 32 members who designate one expert to serve on the Executive Board. The Board effects the programme, suggests initiatives and is empowered to deal with emergencies. A Secretariat, headed by the Director-General, supervises the activities of six regional offices.

Director-General, Dr Jong-Wook Lee (Republic of Korea)

WORLD INTELLECTUAL PROPERTY ORGANISATION

34 Chemin des Colombettes, CH-1211 Geneva 20, Switzerland
T (+41) (22) 338 9111 **F** (+41) (22) 733 5428
E wipo@wipo.int
W www.wipo.int

The World Intellectual Property Organisation (WIPO) was established in 1967 by the Stockholm Convention, which entered into force in 1970. In addition to that Convention, WIPO administers 23 treaties, the principal ones being the Paris Convention for the Protection of Industrial Property and the Bern Convention for the Protection of Literary and Artistic Works. WIPO became a UN specialised agency in 1974.

WIPO promotes the protection of intellectual property throughout the world through co-operation among states, and the administration of various 'Unions', each founded on a multilateral treaty and dealing with the legal and administrative aspects of intellectual property.

Intellectual property comprises two main branches: industrial property (inventions, trademarks, industrial designs and appellations of origin); and copyright (literary, musical, photographic, audiovisual and artistic works, etc.). WIPO also assists creative intellectual activity and facilitates technology transfer, particularly to developing countries.

WIPO had 180 members as at June 2004. The biennial session of all its governing bodies sets policy, a programme and a budget (2004–5, SFr 639 million). A separate International Union for the Protection of New Varieties of Plants (UPOV), established by convention in 1961, is linked to WIPO. It has 45 members.

Director-General, Dr Kamil Idris (Sudan)

WORLD METEOROLOGICAL ORGANISATION

7 bis, avenue de la Paix, PO Box 2300, CH-1211 Geneva 2, Switzerland
T (+41) (22) 730 8111 **F** (+41) (22) 730 8181
E wmo@gateway.wmo.ch
W www.wmo.int

The World Meteorological Organisation (WMO) was established in 1950 and became a UN specialised agency in 1951, succeeding the International Meteorological Organisation founded in 1873. It facilitates co-operation in the establishment of networks for making meteorological, climatological, hydrological and geophysical observations, as well as their exchange, processing and standardisation, and assists technology transfer, training and research. It also fosters collaboration between meteorological and hydrological services, and furthers the application of meteorology to aviation, shipping, environment, water problems, agriculture and the mitigation of natural disasters.

The WMO had 181 member states and six member territories as at March 2004. Six regional associations are responsible for the co-ordination of activities within their own regions, There are also eight technical commissions, which study meteorological and hydrological problems, establish methodology and procedures, and make recommendations to the Executive Council and the Congress. The supreme authority is the World Meteorological Congress of member states and member territories, which meets every four years to determine general policy, make recommendations and set a budget (SFr 253.8 million for 2004–7). It also elects 27 members of the 37-member Executive Council, the other members being the President and three Vice-Presidents of the WMO, and the Presidents of the six regional associations, who are ex-officio members. The Council supervises the implementation of Congress decisions, initiates studies and makes recommendations on matters needing international action. The Secretariat is headed by a Secretary-General, appointed by the Congress.

Secretary-General, M. Jarraud (France)

WORLD TOURISM ORGANISATION

Capitan Haya 42, 28020 Madrid, Spain
T (+34) 91567 8100 F (+34) 91571 3733
E omt@world-tourism.org W www.world-tourism.org

Originally formed in 1925 as the International Congress of Official Tour Associations, the World Tourism Organisation (WTO) was officially launched in 1975 as an intergovernmental body that acts as an executing agency of the United Nations Development Programme (UNDP). Primarily concerned with developing public and private sector partnerships, the WTO also promotes the Global Code of Ethics for Tourism, a framework of policy aimed at tour operators, governments, labour organisations and travellers.

The General Assembly is the principal gathering of the WTO and meets every two years in order to approve policy and budget. Every four years the Assembly will elect a Secretary-General. The Executive Council is WTO's governing board and meets twice a year to ensure the Organisation adheres to policy and budget. It is composed of 27 members of the General Assembly in a ratio of one to five full members. As host country of WTO's headquarters, Spain has a permanent seat on the Executive Council.

Secretary-General, Francesco Frangialli (France)

WORLD TRADE ORGANISATION

Centre William Rappard, 154 rue de Lausanne,
CH-1211 Geneva 21, Switzerland
T (+41) 22 739 5111 F (+41) 22 731 4206
E enquiries@wto.org
W www.wto.org

The World Trade Organisation was established on 1 January 1995 as the successor to the General Agreement on Tariffs and Trade (GATT). GATT was established in 1948 as an interim agreement until the charter of a new international trade organisation could be drafted by a committee of the UN Economic and Social Council and ratified by member states. The charter was never ratified and GATT became the only regime for the regulation of world trade, evolving its own rules and procedures.

GATT was dedicated to the expansion of non-discriminatory international trade and progressively extended free trade via 'rounds' of multilateral negotiations. Eight rounds were concluded: Geneva (1947), Annecy (1948), Torquay (1950), Geneva (1956), Dillon (1960–1), Kennedy (1964–7), Tokyo (1973–9) and Uruguay (1986–94). The Final Act of the Uruguay Round was signed by trade ministers from the 128 GATT negotiating states and the EU in Marrakesh, Morocco, on 15 April 1994. It established the World Trade Organisation (WTO) to supersede GATT and implement the Uruguay Round agreements. The implementation of the Uruguay Round measures in 2002 resulted in a reduction on duties on manufactured goods from 40 per cent in the 1940s to 3 per cent. New talks on agriculture and services began in 2000 and were incorporated into a broader agenda launched at the 2001 Ministerial Conference in Doha, Qatar. The current round of negotiations is scheduled to be concluded by 2005.

The WTO is the legal and institutional foundation of the multilateral trading system. It provides the contractual obligations determining how governments frame and implement trade policy and provides the forum for the debate, negotiation and adjudication of trade problems. The WTO's principal aims are to liberalise world trade and place it on a secure basis, and it seeks to achieve this partly by an agreed set of trade rules and market access agreements and partly through further trade liberalisation negotiations. The WTO also administers and implements a further 29 multilateral agreements in fields such as agriculture, textiles and clothing, services, government procurement, rules of origin and intellectual property.

The highest authority of the WTO is the Ministerial Conference composed of all members, which meets at least once every two years. The General Council meets as required and acts on behalf of the Ministerial Conference in regard to the regular working of the WTO. Composed of all members, the General Council also convenes in two particular forms: as the Dispute Settlement Body, dealing with disputes between members arising from the Uruguay Round Final Act; and as the Trade Policy Review Body, conducting regular reviews of the trade policies of members. A secretariat of 500 staff headed by a Director-General services WTO bodies and provides trade performance and trade policy analysis.

As at June 2004 there were 147 WTO members. The WTO budget for 2004 was US$125 million, with members' contributions calculated on the basis of their share of the total trade conducted by WTO members. The official languages of the WTO are English, French and Spanish.

Director-General, Dr Supachai Panitchpakdi

Permanent UK Representative, Simon Fuller, 37–39 rue de Vermont, CH-1211 Geneva 20

COUNTRIES OF THE WORLD A–Z

AFGHANISTAN

Afğānistān (Pushtu)/
Afqânestân (Dari)
The Islamic Transitional State of Afghanistan

AREA – 652,090 sq. km. Neighbours: Iran (west), Pakistan (east and south), Tajikistan, Uzbekistan and Turkmenistan (north), China (north-east)
POPULATION – 22,132,000: Pushtuns (44 per cent) predominate in the south and west; Tajiks (25 per cent); Hazaras (10 per cent) in the centre; Uzbeks (8 per cent) in the north; Aimaqs (4 per cent); Baluchis (0.5 per cent). The principal languages are Dari (a form of Persian) and Pushtu
CAPITAL – Kabul (population, 1,781,012, 1999)
MAJOR CITIES – Herat; Jalalabad; Qandahar; Mazar-e-Sharif
CURRENCY – Afghani (Af) of 100 puls
NATIONAL ANTHEM – Sorud-e-Melli
NATIONAL DAY – 19 August
NATIONAL FLAG – Three vertical stripes of black, red and green with the royal arms and Arabic device 'There is no God but Allah and Muhammad is His Messenger' in the centre
MORTALITY RATE (per 1,000 population) – 17.15 (2003)
HIV / AIDS ADULT PREVALENCE – 0.01 (2001)
DEATH PENALTY – Yes
POPULATION GROWTH RATE – 2.7 per cent
POPULATION DENSITY – 34 per sq. km (1999)

CLIMATE AND TERRAIN

Mountains, chief among which are the Hindu Kush, cover three-quarters of the country, with plains in the north and south-west. Elevation extremes range from 7,485 m at the highest point (Amu Darya) to 258 m at the lowest (Nowshak). There are three great river basins, the Oxus, Helmand, and Kabul. Natural hazards are flooding, drought and earthquakes. The climate is arid to semi-arid, with extreme temperatures. Summers are hot and dry and the winters cold with heavy snowfalls, particularly in the northern mountains. Annual rainfall varies between 101 mm and 406 mm per year. The temperatures in Kabul range between −22°C in January to 39°C in June.

HISTORY AND POLITICS

In December 1979 Soviet troops invaded Afghanistan and installed a pro-Soviet government. Armed Islamic resistance groups, the mujahidin, fought against Soviet and Afghan forces until the government collapsed in April 1992. Mujahidin forces overran Kabul and declared an Islamic state.

Between 1994–98, divided mujahidin forces suffered heavy defeats at the hands of the Taliban (armed Islamic students), which extended its power across more than 90 per cent of the country. The forces of the former government were driven northwards. The United Islamic Front for the Salvation of Afghanistan (UIFSA) or Northern Alliance was formed by the four main mujahidin factions. The Taliban, thought to be backed by Pakistan and Saudi Arabia, imposed strict Shari'ah law.

Following the 11 September 2001 terrorist attacks on the USA, which had been carried out by Osama bin Laden's al-Qa'eda (the base) organisation, and Afghanistan's subsequent refusal to surrender bin Laden and the al-Qa'eda leadership to the US authorities, US and UK forces began military operations against al-Qa'eda and Taliban targets in Afghanistan on 7 October 2001. Intensive US air bombardment conducted from bases in Uzbekistan, Tajikistan and Pakistan, together with material and intelligence assistance by US and UK ground troops to Northern Alliance forces, swiftly caused the Taliban regime to collapse.

Moves to form an alternative government from among the anti-Taliban factions began in 2001 and leaders met near Bonn, Germany, where a multi-ethnic interim government was named. However, attempts to locate and capture Osama bin Laden and Mullah Omar, the Taliban leader, were unsuccessful and pockets of al-Qa'eda and Taliban forces remained at large in the country. Tensions stayed high throughout 2002 and 2003 and a 5,000-strong UN-mandated peacekeeping force, the International Security Assistance Force (ISAF), and 8,000 US troops remain in the country.

POLITICAL SYSTEM

Following the collapse of Taliban rule in December 2001, an interim government was agreed, which was to hold office for six months pending the holding of a *Loya Jirga* (tribal council), which would appoint a transitional government. In June 2002, the *Loya Jirga* selected Hamid Karzai as transitional president of the country and the new government was sworn in, tasked with preparing for nationwide elections in October 2004. A new constitution was adopted in January 2004 establishing Afghanistan as an Islamic republic.

HEAD OF STATE
Transitional President, Hamid Karzai, *elected* 13 June 2002
Transitional Vice-Presidents, Marshal Mohammad Qasim Fahim Khan *(Defence)*; Marshal Mohd Qassim Fahim; Karim Khalili; Ustad Niematullah Shahrani

SELECTED GOVERNMENT MEMBERS *as at July 2004*
Foreign Affairs, Abdullah Abdullah
Finance, Ashraf Ghani Ahmadzai
Interior, Ali Ahmad Jalali

EMBASSY OF THE TRANSITIONAL ISLAMIC GOVERNMENT OF AFGHANISTAN
31 Princes Gate, London SW7 1QQ
T 020-7589 8891
E info@afghanembassy.co.uk
Ambassador Extraordinary and Plenipotentiary, HE Ahmad Wali Masud

BRITISH EMBASSY
15th Street Roundabout Wazir Akbar Khan
PO Box 334, Kabul
T (+93) (0) (70) 102250
E kabulconsular@fco.gov.uk

Ambassador Extraordinary and Plenipotentiary, HE Dr Rosalind M Marsden, CMG

ECONOMY AND TRADE

The economy has been devastated by the political upheavals of the last 20 years. During this period, up to one-third of the population fled the country, with Pakistan and Iraq sheltering a combined peak of 4–6 million refugees. Afghanistan's problems were compounded by three successive years of drought, and by the end of 2000 one million people were thought to be close to starvation. However, by October 2002 1.7 million refugees had returned to the country.

While the traditional industries of agriculture, sheep rearing and the manufacture of silk, woollen hair cloths and carpets have diminished, the narcotics trade has grown. Opium production, banned under the Taliban, rose from 185 tonnes in 2001 to 2,700 tonnes in 2002. It is currently estimated that 80–90 per cent of heroin consumed in Europe comes from Afghan opium. Salt, silver, copper, coal, iron, lead, rubies, lapis lazuli, gold, chrome, barite, uranium and talc can be found in the region.

International efforts to rebuild Afghanistan were addressed at the Tokyo Donors Conference for Afghan Reconstruction in January 2002, when US$4,500 million was pledged. Further World Bank and other aid was given in 2003. The eradication of the illegal opium trade and the search for oil and gas resources in the northern region are two major long-term objectives.

In the past, exports have been Persian lambskins (Karakul), dried fruits, nuts, cotton, raw wool, carpets, spice and natural gas, while the imports are chiefly oil, cotton yarn and piece goods, tea, sugar, machinery and transport equipment.

GDP – US$19,000 million (2002); US$700 per capita (2002)
ANNUAL AVERAGE GROWTH OF GDP – 6.0 per cent (1998)
INFLATION RATE – 56.7 per cent (1991); estimated to be 400 per cent in 1996
IMPORTS – US$1,300 million (2001)
EXPORTS – US$1,200 million (2001)

Trade with UK	*2002*	*2003*
Imports from UK	£2,918,000	£9,871,000
Exports to UK	249,000	467,000

COMMUNICATIONS

Main roads run from Kabul to Qandahar, Herat, Meymaneh via Mazar-e-Sharif and Feyzabad. Roads cross the border with Pakistan at Chaman and via the Khyber Pass, and there are roads from Herat to the borders of Turkmenistan and Iran. Much of the country's road system has been damaged during the fighting, although reconstruction work began in 2002. There are two international airports at Kabul and Qandahar and about 1,200 km of inland waterways.

EDUCATION

Education is free and nominally compulsory, elementary schools having been established in most centres; there are secondary schools in large urban areas and four universities, in Kabul, Jalalabad, Balkh and Herat. In March 2002, schools reopened to 1.5 million children, many of whom had not received schooling for six years under the Taliban.

ILLITERACY RATE – (m) 48.1 per cent; (f) 78.1 per cent (2000)
ENROLMENT (percentage of age group) – primary 29 per cent (1993); secondary 14 per cent (1993); tertiary 1.8 per cent (1990)

MEDIA

Afghanistan's media were seriously restricted under Taliban rule. However, in late 2001 Radio Afghanistan returned to the air in Kabul after the Taliban deserted the capital, and within days Kabul TV also began broadcasting. Relays of foreign radio stations are available in Kabul, including the BBC, Radio France Internationale, the German-run Voice of Freedom, US-funded broadcasts from Radio Free Afghanistan and the Voice of America, and Radio Azadi run by the International Security Assistance Force (ISAF). Local radio stations include Radio Afghanistan, Erat Radio Khilid Kabul (RKK) and Arman FM. Television services are mainly provided by the state-run TV Afghanistan, but ownership of television sets is very limited (100,000 in 1999). Afghanistan's press now enjoys considerable freedom of expression, although print runs are small. Titles include *Hewad*, *Anis* and the Northern Alliance organ *Payam-e Mojahed*.

CULTURE

Afghanistan has been at the crossroads of civilisations stretching back at least 3,000 years. Its strategic importance – located as it once was at the meeting point of Chinese, Indian and European civilisations along the ancient Silk Route – means that it has long been fought over, despite its forbidding terrain.

Due to prolonged armed conflicts, much of the outstanding cultural heritage has been destroyed. During the civil war the Kabul Museum was looted, and treasures such as the Kunduz Hoard (silver Greek-style coins) were stolen. This was followed during the Taliban regime by systematic ideological destruction. Most notably the giant Bamiyan Buddhas, carved by Buddhist monks in the fourth to sixth centuries, were demolished in March 2001, and Kabul's remaining collections of statues destroyed, including many stored within the Ministry of Information and Culture.

ALBANIA

Republika e Shqipërisë – Republic of Albania

AREA – 28,748 sq. km. Neighbours: Serbia and Montenegro (north), Kosovo and Macedonia (east), Greece (south)
POPULATION – 3,731,000. Muslim (70 per cent), Greek Orthodox (20 per cent), Roman Catholic (10 per cent). The language is Albanian
CAPITAL – Tirana (population, 353, 400, 2003)
CURRENCY – Lek (Lk) of 100 qindarka
NATIONAL ANTHEM – Rreth Flamurit Të Për Bashkuar (The Flag That United Us In The Struggle)
NATIONAL DAY – 28 November
NATIONAL FLAG – Black two-headed eagle on a red field

MORTALITY RATE (per 1,000 population) – 6.48 (2003)
HIV / AIDS ADULT PREVALENCE – 0.1 per cent (2001)
DEATH PENALTY – Yes*
POPULATION BELOW POVERTY LINE – 30 per cent (2001)
POPULATION GROWTH RATE – 3.7 per cent
POPULATION DENSITY – 108 per sq. km (1999)
ILLITERACY RATE – (m) 7.6 per cent; (f) 20.5 per cent (2003)
ENROLMENT (percentage of age group) – primary 100 per cent (1997); tertiary 12 per cent (1997)

CLIMATE AND TERRAIN

Much of the country is mountainous, with the highest point at 2,753 m (Maja e Korabit), and nearly half is covered by forest. The lowest point of elevation is 0 m (Adriatic Sea). The climate is Mediterranean with frequent thunderstorms. The average daily temperature ranges from 8°C in January to 25°C in July.

HISTORY AND POLITICS

Albania was under Turkish suzerainty from 1468 until 1912, when independence was declared. After a period of unrest, a republic was declared in 1925 and in 1928 a monarchy. The King went into exile in 1939 when the country was occupied by the Italians; Albania was liberated in November 1944. Elections in 1945 resulted in a Communist-controlled Assembly; the King was deposed *in absentia* and a republic declared in January 1946.

From 1946 to 1990 Albania was a one-party, Communist state. In 1990 the ban on religious worship was lifted and between 1990 and 1992 democratic elections took place. Rioting broke out in 1997 following the collapse of several pyramid investment schemes. Anti-government protests, taking the form of armed rebellion, spread throughout the country.

In 1999, Yugoslavia expelled thousands of Kosovar Albanians and over 400,000 fled to Albania. In April, Albania granted NATO unrestricted access to Albania's airspace, ports and military infrastructure and over 10,000 NATO troops were stationed there. By the end of 1999, nearly all of the refugees had left Albania and the number of NATO troops currently stationed in the country has fallen to 1,000.

The general election of 2001 resulted in the Socialist Party of Albania (SP) winning 70 seats and the Democratic Alliance (DAP) winning 36 seats in the 140-member People's Assembly. Albania's next election is scheduled for June 2005.

HEAD OF STATE
President, Gen. Alfred Moisiu, (ret'd), *elected by the People's Assembly* 24 June 2002, *took office* 24 July 2002

SELECTED GOVERNMENT MEMBERS *as at July 2004*
Prime Minister, Fatos Nano
Deputy Prime Minister, Namik Dokle
Foreign Affairs, Kastriot Islami
Defence, Pandeli Majko
Economy, Anastas Angjeli
Finance, Arben Malaj

EMBASSY OF THE REPUBLIC OF ALBANIA
2nd Floor, 24 Buckingham Gate, London SW1E 6LB
T 020-7828 8897
Ambassador Extraordinary and Plenipotentiary, HE Kastriot Robo, apptd 2002

BRITISH EMBASSY
Rruga Skenderbeg 12, Tirana
T (+ 355) (42) 34973/4/5
Ambassador Extraordinary and Plenipotentiary, HE Richard Jones

BRITISH COUNCIL DIRECTOR, Joan Barry
Rr. 'Ded Gjo Luli' 3/1, Tirana T (+355) (4) 240856/7
E info@britishcouncil.org.al

DEFENCE

The Army has 373 main battle tanks and 86 armoured personnel carriers. The Navy has 20 patrol and coastal combatant vessels at two bases. The Air Force has 26 combat aircraft.
MILITARY EXPENDITURE – 2.5 per cent of GDP (2002)
MILITARY PERSONNEL – 22,000: Army 16,000, Navy 2,500, Air Force 3,500

ECONOMY AND TRADE

Albania is one of the poorest countries in Europe – a legacy of Communist rule and a sign of Albania's uneasy relationship with the post-Communist free-market economy.

Agriculture accounts for 40 per cent of economic output although only 20 per cent of this is exported. The main crops are wheat, maize, sugar beet, potatoes and fruit. Production is frequently restricted due to droughts and the use of outdated equipment. The principal industries are agricultural product processing, textiles, oil products and cement.

Since April 1992, the government has imposed austerity measures in an attempt to reduce the budget deficit and to cut inflation. Albania receives annual remittances from overseas workers (mainly in Greece and Turkey), of US$400–600 million.

Exports include crude oil, minerals (bitumen, chrome, nickel, copper), tobacco, fruit and vegetables. Large chromium deposits are found in the region.
GNI – US$4,833 million (2002); US$1,380 per capita (2002)
GDP – US$4,114 million (2001); US$1,197 per capita (2000)
ANNUAL AVERAGE GROWTH OF GDP – 6.0 per cent (2002)
INFLATION RATE – 6 per cent (2002)
TOTAL EXTERNAL DEBT – US$800 million (2002)
IMPORTS – US$1,504 million (2002)
EXPORTS – US$330 million (2002)

BALANCE OF PAYMENTS
Trade – US$1,155 million deficit (2002)
Current account – US$408 million deficit (2002)

Trade with UK	*2002*	*2003*
Imports from UK	£18,905,000	£9,884,000
Exports to UK	2,873,000	3,927,000

MEDIA

The public broadcaster is Albanian Radio and TV (RTSh). There are around 75 private television channels and approximately 30 private radio stations. Political parties, trade unions, religious groups and state bodies are prohibited from owning private television and radio stations but can own newspapers.

CULTURE

Albanian culture is influenced by its geographical location (midway between Rome and Istanbul), its recent Russian-dominated political past, and its religions (Sunni Muslim, Roman Catholic and Albanian Orthodox). These influences can be discerned in the work of Albanian writers, who have gained prominence since 1909, when written Albanian was standardised. One of the country's most famous writers and literary critics is Fan Noli (1882–1965). Albania's most prominent contemporary writer is Ismail Kadare (b.1936).

ALGERIA

Al-Jumhūriyya al-Jazā'iriyya ad-Dimuqratiyya ash-Sha'biyya – People's Democratic Republic of Algeria

AREA – 2,381,700 sq. km Neighbours: Morocco and Western Sahara (west), Mauritania and Mali (south-west), Niger (south-east), Libya and Tunisia (east)
POPULATION – 30,841,000 (2001). Arabic and Berber are the official languages although French is also spoken. The state religion is Sunni Islam
CAPITAL – ΨAlgiers (El Djazair, Al-Jaza'ir) (population, 1,507,241, 1987). It is one of the principal ports of the Mediterranean
MAJOR CITIES – ΨAnnaba; ΨBejaia; Blida (El Boulaida); Constantine (Qacentina); ΨMostaganem; ΨOran (Wahran); Setif; Sidi-Bel-Abbes; ΨSkikda; Tizi Ouzou; Tlemcen
CURRENCY – Algerian dinar (DA) of 100 centimes
NATIONAL ANTHEM – Qassaman Bin Nazilat Il-Mahiqat (We Swear By The Lightning That Destroys)
NATIONAL DAY – 1 November
NATIONAL FLAG – Divided vertically green and white with a red crescent and star over all in the centre
LIFE EXPECTANCY (years) – 70 (2001)
MORTALITY RATE (per 1,000 population) – 5.09 (2003)
INFANT MORTALITY (per 1,000 live births) – 39 (2001)
HIV / AIDS ADULT PREVALENCE – 0.1 per cent (2003)
DEATH PENALTY – Yes
POPULATION BELOW POVERTY LINE – 23 per cent (1999)
POPULATION GROWTH RATE – 2 per cent (1990–2001)
POPULATION DENSITY – 13 per sq. km (2001)
ILLITERACY RATE – (m) 21.8 per cent; (f) 42.9 per cent (2000)
ENROLMENT (percentage of age group) – primary 100 per cent (1997); secondary 63 per cent (1997); tertiary 12 per cent (1997)

CLIMATE AND TERRAIN

Algeria, the second largest country in Africa after Sudan, has mild, wet winters and hot, dry summers. The climate is drier along the coastline and the high plateaus support cold winters.

Algeria is dominated by the Sahara Desert, which covers 80 per cent of its territory, and the majority of the population live on the northern coast. The mountains are subject to earthquakes, flooding and mudslides during the rainy season (November to March). The highest point of elevation is 3,003 m (Tahat) and the lowest is -40 m (Chott Melrhir).

HISTORY AND POLITICS

Algeria was annexed to France from 1830 until gaining its independence in 1962 following an eight-year armed liberation struggle by the socialist Front de Libration Nationale (FLN). Ben Bella was elected president in 1963, but was deposed in 1965 by Col. Houari Boumedine, who was formally elected president in 1976. Boumedine died in 1978 and was succeeded by Chadli Bendjedid.

A new constitution agreed by referendum in 1988 moved Algeria towards pluralism. However, the 1991 legislative elections were abandoned in anticipation of the success of the opposition Islamic Salvation Front (FIS), which had campaigned on a radical Islamist platform. President Bendjedid resigned and a Higher Committee of State (HCS), headed by former FLN veteran Mohammed Boudiaf, took power. Gen. Liamine Zeroual was elected president for a five-year term in November 1995, but announced his intention to stand down from office in September 1998. Abdelaziz Bouteflika was elected president in 1999. The other candidates decided to boycott the election some days before it took place, alleging that the military had intervened to rig the vote.

The FLN won the majority of the vote in the legislative elections of May 2002 (winning 199 of the 388 seats) and also achieved control in the municipal elections of October 2002. The most recent presidential elections took place in April 2004 and a second term was won by Abdelaziz Bouteflika (with 85 per cent of the vote). The FIS was banned in 1991 triggering civil unrest and an armed campaign between Islamic groups (the FIS-backed Islamic Salvation Army and the more extreme Armed Islamic Group) and the military. This conflict has claimed an estimated 100,000 lives since 1992.

Rioting broke out in the Berber-populated Kabyle region in 2001 resulting in about 80 deaths. A session of the National People's Assembly backed reform to give the Berber language, Tamazight, equal status with Arabic. The reform bill was approved by 482 votes with two abstentions and no opposition. During 2003 there was a resurgence of Islamist violence.

POLITICAL SYSTEM
The legislature is bicameral. The National People's Assembly (the lower chamber) has 389 members, directly elected for a five-year term. The *Majlis al-Umma* (Council of the Nation) is the upper chamber, with a third of its 144 members appointed by the President; two-thirds are indirectly elected for six-year terms, of which half are re-elected every three years.

HEAD OF STATE
President, Defence, Abdelaziz Bouteflika, re-*elected* April 2004

SELECTED GOVERMENT MEMBERS *as at July 2004*
Prime Minister, Ahmed Ouyahia
Finance, Abdelatif Benachenhou
Ministers of State, Abdelaziz Belkhadem *(Foreign Affairs)*; Noureddine Yazid Zerhouni *(Interior and Local Authorities)*

ALGERIAN EMBASSY
54 Holland Park, London W11 3RS
T 020-7221 7800
Ambassador Extraordinary and Plenipotentiary, HE Ahmed Attaf, apptd 2001

BRITISH EMBASSY
7th floor, Hotel Hilton International Algiers, Pins Maritimes, Palais des Expositions, El Mohammadia, Algiers
T (+1) (213) (21) 230068
Ambassador Extraordinary and Plenipotentiary, HE Brian Stewart, apptd 2004

BRITISH COUNCIL, c/o The British Embassy
E rachida.benyahia@fco.gov.uk

DEFENCE

The Army has 1,000 main battle tanks and 730 armoured personnel carriers. The Navy has two submarines, three frigates and 25 patrol and coastal vessels. The Air Force has 175 combat aircraft and 93 armed helicopters.
MILITARY EXPENDITURE – 5.9 per cent of GDP (2002)
MILITARY PERSONNEL – 127,500: Army 110,000, Navy 7,500, Air Force 10,000; Paramilitaries 181,200
CONSCRIPTION DURATION – 18 months

ECONOMY AND TRADE

The main industry is hydrocarbons which accounted for 60 per cent of budget revenues and 30 per cent of GDP in 2003. Services provided 32 per cent of GDP and agriculture 8 per cent of GDP in 2003. Oil and natural gas are pumped from the Sahara to terminals on the coast before being exported; the gas is first liquefied at liquefaction plants at Skikda and Arzew, although pipelines serve Libya and Italy direct. In November 1996 a 1,200-km gas pipeline to Spain was opened, enabling Algeria to double its gas exports to Morocco, Spain, Germany and France.

Other major industries include a steel industry, motor vehicles, building materials, paper making, chemical products and metal manufactures. Most major industrial enterprises are still under state control.

Prior to 1989 the economy was centrally planned and state-controlled in most sectors. In 1994 the government accepted full economic reform and liberalisation under a programme agreed with the IMF. The government reduced the budget deficit, devalued the currency and freed price controls. Algeria's foreign debt fell from 71.9 per cent of GDP in 1996 to 40.7 per cent in 2001. An extensive privatisation programme began in 1997. During 2000–3 the country's finances improved due to increased trade surpluses, record foreign exchange reserves and continued reductions to foreign debt.

Export earnings come mainly from crude oil and liquefied natural gas sales (97 per cent in 2003). Algeria's main trading partners are Italy, France, Spain, the USA and Brazil. Dates and wine are among the main food imports.
GNI – US$51,000 million (2001); US$1,650 per capita (2001)
ANNUAL AVERAGE GROWTH OF GDP – 6.0 per cent (2002)
INFLATION RATE – 5.3 per cent (2002)
UNEMPLOYMENT – 29.8 per cent (2000)
TOTAL EXTERNAL DEBT – US$25,002 million (2000)
IMPORTS – US$10,791 million (2002)
EXPORTS – US$18,635 million (2002)
FOREIGN DIRECT INVESTMENT - US$29 million (1997–2000)

Trade with UK	*2002*	*2003*
Imports from UK	£131,522,000	£190,142,000
Exports to UK	341,690,000	261,837,000

MEDIA

The state controls the television (Enterprise Nationale de Television) and radio stations (Radio-Television Algerienne) but domestic satellite dishes are used by the general population to receive French and European channels, some of which actively target Algerian viewers. There are five main daily newspapers, all of them published in French.

ANDORRA

Principat d'Andorra – Principality of Andorra

AREA – 464 sq. km. Neighbours: Spain and France
POPULATION – 90,000 (2001); less than one-quarter of the population is Andorran. The official language is Catalan, but French and Spanish (Castilian) are also spoken. The established religion is Roman Catholicism
CAPITAL – Andorra la Vella (population, 20,724, 2002)
CURRENCY – Euro (€) of 100 cents
NATIONAL ANTHEM – El Gran Carlemany, Mon Pare (Great Charlemagne, My Father)
NATIONAL DAY – 8 September
NATIONAL FLAG – Three vertical bands, blue, yellow, red; Andorran coat of arms frequently imposed on central (yellow) band but not essential
LIFE EXPECTANCY (years) – 83 (2001)
MORTALITY RATE (per 1,000 population) – 5.74 (2003)
INFANT MORTALITY (per 1,000 births) – 6 (2001)
DEATH PENALTY – No (abolished 1993)
POPULATION GROWTH RATE – 4.8 per cent (1990–2001)
POPULATION DENSITY – 194 per sq. km (2001)

CLIMATE AND TERRAIN

Located between the French and Spanish borders, Andorra is a country of dramatic mountains intersected with narrow valleys. A third of the country is classified as forest. The highest point of elevation is 2,946 m (Coma Pedrosa) while the lowest is 840 m (Riu Runer). The climate is alpine, with heavy snowfall in winter and warm summers. The average annual temperature ranges from 2°C in January to 19°C in July.

HISTORY AND POLITICS

Andorra is a small, neutral principality formed by a treaty in 1278. The first elections under the new constitution were held in 1993, and on 20 January 1994 the first sovereign government of Andorra took office. The Liberal Party of Andorra won the legislative elections of 2001, gaining 16 of the 28 seats in the General Council.

POLITICAL SYSTEM

Under a new constitution promulgated in May 1993, Andorra became an independent, democratic parliamentary co-principality, with sovereignty vested in the people rather than in the two co-princes, as had previously been the case. The constitution enables Andorra to establish an independent judiciary and to carry out its own foreign policy, whilst its people may now join trade unions and political parties. The two co-princes, the President of the French Republic and the Spanish Bishop of Urgel, remain heads of state but now only have the power to veto treaties with France and Spain which affect the state's borders and security. The co-princes are represented by Permanent Delegates of whom one is the French Prefect of the Pyrénées Orientales department at Perpignan and the other is the Spanish Vicar-General of the diocese of Urgel.

Andorra has a unicameral legislature of 28 members known as the *Consell General de las Valls d'Andorra* (Valleys of Andorra General Council), elected for a four-year term. Fourteen members are elected on a national list basis and 14 in seven dual-member constituencies based on Andorra's seven parishes. The Council appoints the head of the executive government, who designates government members.

Permanent French Delegate, Philippe Massoni
Permanent Episcopal Delegate, Nemesi Marqués Oste

SELECTED GOVERNMENT MEMBERS *as at July 2004*
President of the Executive Council, Marc Forné Molné
Finance, Mireia Maestre Cortadella
Foreign Affairs, Juli Minoves Triquell
Justice and Interior, Jordi Visent Guitart

ANDORRAN EMBASSY, 63 Westover Road, London SW18 2RF T 020-8874 4806
Ambassador Extraordinary and Plenipotentiary, HE Albert Pintat, apptd 2002

BRITISH AMBASSADOR – HE Stephen Wright, resident at Madrid, apptd 2003

ECONOMY AND TRADE

The economy is largely based on tourism (80 per cent of GDP, with nine million visitors annually), banking and commerce (due in part to the principality's tax-free status), tobacco, construction and forestry. Andorra has negotiated a customs union with the European Union which came into force in 1991.

GNI – US$18,000 per capita (2001)
ANNUAL AVERAGE GROWTH OF GDP – 4.0 per cent (1998)

Trade with UK	*2002*	*2003*
Imports from UK	£7,355,000	£9,333,000
Exports to UK	169,000	314,000

TRANSPORT INFRASTRUCTURE

There are a total of 269 km of roads but no railways, airports, waterways or harbours. A road into Andorra from Spain is open all year round, and that from France is closed only occasionally in winter.

MEDIA

The Andorran media is heavily influenced by French and Spanish culture. There are two radio stations in Andorra, one privately owned and Radio Andorra, operated by the government, as well as a state owned television station and one major daily newspaper *(Diari d'Andorra El Periodic).*

CULTURE

The capital, Andorra la Vella, is over 1,100 years old and retains some of its ancient architecture and atmosphere in the Old Quarter (Barri Antic). The photographer Valenti Claverol (1902–2004) is particularly noted for his documentation of day-to-day life in Andorra and his work is considered a major example of vernacular photography.

ANGOLA

República de Angola – Republic of Angola

AREA – 1,246,700 sq. km. Neighbours: Democratic Republic of Congo (north and east), Zambia (east), Namibia (south). The enclave of Cabinda is separated from the rest of Angola by the Democratic Republic of Congo and also borders on the Republic of Congo
POPULATION – 13,527,000. Main ethnic groups are Ovimbundu (37 per cent); Kimbundu (25 per cent); Bakongo (13 per cent). The official language is Portuguese
CAPITAL – ΨLuanda (population, 1,822,407, 1993)
CURRENCY – Readjusted kwanza (Kzrl) of 100 lwei
NATIONAL ANTHEM – Angola Avante (Advance Angola)
NATIONAL DAY – 11 November (Independence Day)
NATIONAL FLAG – Red and black with a yellow star, machete and cog-wheel
LIFE EXPECTANCY (years) – 45 (2001)
MORTALITY RATE (per 1,000 population) – 25.83 (2003)
INFANT MORTALITY (per 1,000 births) – 154 (2001)
HIV / AIDS ADULT PREVALENCE – 5.5 per cent (2001)
DEATH PENALTY – No (abolished 1992)
POPULATION GROWTH RATE – 3.1 per cent (1990–2001)
POPULATION DENSITY – 11 per sq. km (2001)
ILLITERACY RATE – (m) 44 per cent; (f) 72 per cent (1998)
ENROLMENT (percentage of age group) – tertiary 0.7 per cent (1991)

CLIMATE AND TERRAIN

Angola's climate is tropical in the north (with a cool, dry season from May to October and a hot, rainy season from November to April) and sub-tropical in the south and along the coast to Luanda. Angola's land rises from a narrow coastal plain to a large interior plateau that is prone to periodic flooding. The highest point of elevation is 2,620 m (Morro de Moco) and the lowest is 0 m (Atlantic Ocean).

HISTORY AND POLITICS

After a Portuguese presence of five centuries, and an anti-colonial war since 1961, Angola became independent on 11 November 1975 in the midst of civil war. The Popular Movement for the Liberation of Angola (MPLA) took control early in 1976, but remained under pressure from the National Union for the Total Independence of Angola (UNITA). A peace agreement was signed between the government and UNITA in 1991 and multiparty legislative and presidential elections took place in 1992, which were won by the MPLA and its leader, José Eduardo dos Santos. UNITA refused to accept the results and the civil war resumed in 1993. In 1994 the UN sent in peacekeeping forces.

UNITA and the MPLA government signed a peace agreement (the Lusaka Protocol) in 1994. A government of national reconciliation was formed in April 1997 and 70 UNITA legislators took up their seats in parliament, although UNITA's leader, Dr Jonas Savimbi, rejected an offer of the vice-presidency. UNITA also refused to allow central state administration to be restored in key areas and fighting resumed in May 1997.

In October 1997 the UN Security Council ordered sanctions against UNITA for failing to meet its obligations under the Lusaka Protocol. UNITA returned much of its territory to government control in December, and in March 1998 UNITA became a legitimate political party. Three of its representatives were appointed governors of provinces of Angola.

Fighting continued and the UN Security Council adopted a resolution in September 1998 which urged the rejection of military force by all parties and named UNITA as 'the primary cause of the crisis in Angola'. In February 1999 the UN Security Council voted to withdraw the UN Observer Mission in Angola, the UN Secretary-General Kofi Annan having declared that the country was on the verge of a catastrophic breakdown and that there was no more peace to keep. The UN Security Council adopted a further resolution in April 2000, which called for an investigation into allegations that several countries had violated sanctions imposed on UNITA. Government forces succeeded in capturing large tracts of UNITA-controlled territory in late 2000. Following the death of Dr Jonas Savimbi in February 2002, UNITA and the government signed a formal cease-fire agreement in Luanda on 4 April 2002 and pledged to adhere to the 1994 peace agreement. In addition, provision was made for the demobilisation of around 100,000 UNITA fighters, to be monitored by the UN, and the provision of state aid for some 300,000 family members of these soldiers. In December 2002 the UN Security Council lifted all remaining economic and financial sanctions imposed on UNITA. Isaias Samakuva was elected leader of UNITA on 27 June 2003.

SECESSION

In the northern enclave of Cabinda, the Front for the Liberation of the Cabinda Enclave (FLEC) fought a 20-year war of independence until the signing of a cease-fire with the government in September 1995, which was followed by the initialling of a peace agreement in April 1996.

POLITICAL SYSTEM

The MPLA, formerly a Marxist-Leninist party, was the sole legal party until early 1991 when a multiparty system was adopted. The constitution declares Angola to be a democratic state and provides for a President, who appoints a Council of Ministers to assist him, and a 220-member National Assembly. In November 1996 the National Assembly adopted a constitutional amendment extending its mandate for between two and four years. The mandate was extended by the National Assembly on 17 October 2000 with no end date set.

HEAD OF STATE
President, José Eduardo dos Santos, *re-elected* 30 September 1992

SELECTED GOVERNMENT MEMBERS *as at July 2004*
Prime Minister, Interior, Fernando da Piedade Dias dos Santos 'Nando'
Deputy Prime Minister, Aguinaldo Jaime
Defence, Kundi Paihama
Finance, José Pedro de Morais
Foreign Affairs, João Bernardo de Miranda
Interior, Osvaldo de Jesus Serra Van-Dúnem

EMBASSY OF THE REPUBLIC OF ANGOLA
22 Dorset Street, London W1U 3QY
T 020-7299 9850
Ambassador Extraordinary and Plenipotentiary, HE António DaCosta Fernandes, apptd 1993

BRITISH EMBASSY
Rua Diogo Cao 4 (Caixa Postal 1244), Luanda
T (+244) (2) 334582
Ambassador Extraordinary and Plenipotentiary, HE John Thompson, MBE, apptd 2002

DEFENCE

The Army has 400 main battle tanks and 170 armoured personnel carriers. The Navy has seven patrol vessels. The Air Force has 105 combat aircraft and 16 armed helicopters.
MILITARY EXPENDITURE – 9.8 per cent of GDP (2002)
MILITARY PERSONNEL – 129,000: Army 120,000, Navy 3,000, Air Force 6,000; Paramilitaries 10,000

ECONOMY AND TRADE

Angola is Africa's second-largest exporter of oil (after Nigeria) and in 2002 oil accounted for 45 per cent of GDP and 90 per cent of foreign exchange earnings and government revenue. The government plans to double oil production by 2010. Angola is also rich in diamond deposits but much of the trade in these gems is unregulated. Principal agricultural crops are cassava, maize, bananas, coffee, palm oil and kernels, cotton and sisal. Coffee, sisal, maize and palm oil are exported; exports also include mahogany and other hardwoods from the tropical rain forests in the north of the country.

The government is attempting to restructure the socialist economy by free market reforms but is making little progress, with high inflation and a fragile economy.

The government raised fuel prices by 1,600 per cent in February 2000 in response to IMF demands to remove state subsidies on petroleum products.
GNI – US$6,700 million (2001); US$500 per capita (2001)

ANNUAL AVERAGE GROWTH OF GDP – 17.1 per cent (2002)
INFLATION RATE – 95.0 per cent (2002)
TOTAL EXTERNAL DEBT – US$9,900 million (2002)
FOREIGN DIRECT INVESTMENT – US$ 4,879 million (1997–2000)

Trade with UK	*2002*	*2003*
Imports from UK	£66,917,000	£103,728,000
Exports to UK	26,461,000	9,751,000

TRANSPORT INFRASTRUCTURE

There are 51,429 km of roads, 46,080 km of which are unsurfaced. The majority of roads are in very poor condition and most travel is by convoy. There are many uncleared landmines in Angola, especially on roads in remote areas. There are 2,761 km of railway. Most internal travel takes place by air between the country's 244 airports (32 of which have surfaced runways).

MEDIA

Angola's only news agency, Angop, the country's biggest broadcaster, Televisao Popular de Angola (TPA), and the country's only daily newspaper, *Jornal de Angolais,* are all government owned. There are several commercial radio stations, one private television station, and some subscription services (operated by Multichoice Angola) that include Brazilian and Portuguese channels.

CULTURE

Up until relatively recently Angolan art was strictly controlled by the Ministry of Culture but since it released control in the late 1980s, art has become a significant industry. This liberalisation of the arts has affected many aspects of Angola's cultural life, creating, for example, a thriving traditional and contemporary music scene.

ANTIGUA AND BARBUDA

State of Antigua and Barbuda

AREA – 443 sq. km; Antigua 279 sq. km; Barbuda 160 sq. km; Redonda 1.2 sq. km
POPULATION – 65,000 (2001); the official language is English
CAPITAL – ΨSt John's (population, 24,226, 2000)
MAJOR TOWNS – Barbuda's main town is Codrington
CURRENCY – East Caribbean dollar (EC$) of 100 cents
NATIONAL ANTHEM – Fair Antigua and Barbuda
NATIONAL DAY – 1 November (Independence Day)
NATIONAL FLAG – Red with an inverted triangle divided black over blue over white, with a rising gold sun on the white band
LIFE EXPECTANCY (years) – 71 (2001)
MORTALITY RATE (per 1,000 population) – 5.64 (2003)
INFANT MORTALITY (per 1,000 births) – 12 (2001)
DEATH PENALTY – Yes
POPULATION GROWTH RATE – 0.3 per cent (1990–2001)
POPULATION DENSITY – 147 per sq. km (2001)
URBAN POPULATION – 37 per cent (2001)
ILLITERACY RATE – (m) 5 per cent; (f) 5 per cent (2001)
MILITARY EXPENDITURE – 0.6 per cent of GDP (2001)
MILITARY PERSONNEL – 170: Army 125, Navy 45

CLIMATE AND TERRAIN

The subtropical island of Antigua is part of the Leeward Islands in the eastern Caribbean. The elevation extremes range from 402 m at the highest point (Boggy Peak) to 0 m sea level (Caribbean Sea). It is distinguished from the rest of the Leeward Islands by its absence of high hills and forest, and has a drier climate than most of the West Indies.

Barbuda is 48 km away from Antigua. It is a very flat coral island with a large lagoon. Both of the islands lie within the hurricane belt and are subject to tropical storms and hurricanes between June and November.

HISTORY AND POLITICS

Antigua was first settled by the English in 1632, and was granted to Lord Willoughby by Charles II. It became internally self-governing in 1967 and fully independent on 1 November 1981.

The United Progressive Party won the elections of March 2004 with a landslide victory (4 of 12 seats to the Antigua Labour Party's (ALP) with one tied) that removed the ALP from power for the first time in three decades.

POLITICAL SYSTEM

Antigua and Barbuda is a constitutional monarchy with Queen Elizabeth II as Head of State, represented by the Governor-General. There is a Senate of 17 appointed members and a House of Representatives of 19 members, 17 of whom are elected every five years. The Attorney-General may be appointed.
Governor-General, HE Sir James Carlisle, GCMG

SELECTED GOVERNMENT MEMBERS *as at July 2004*
Prime Minister, Baldwin Spencer
Minister of Finance, Economic Development and Planning, Errol Cort
Attorney General, Minister of Legal Affairs, Justin Simon
Minister of Foreign Affairs, Tourism, International Travel, Trade, Harold Lovell

HIGH COMMISSION FOR ANTIGUA AND BARBUDA
15 Thayer Street, London W1M 5LD
T 020-7486 7073
High Commissioner, (*vacant*)

BRITISH HIGH COMMISSION
PO Box 483, 11 Old Parham Road, St John's
T (+1 268) 462 0008/9
High Commissioner, HE John White, apptd 2001, resident at Bridgetown, Barbados

ECONOMY AND TRADE

Antigua is now one of the Caribbean's most prosperous nations. The economy is largely based on tourism and related services (75 per cent of the workforce are employed in these areas), and offshore financial services. Agricultural production includes livestock, sea island cotton, mixed market gardening and fishing.

GNI – US$630 million (2001); US$9,150 per capita (2001)
ANNUAL AVERAGE GROWTH OF GDP – 0.2 per cent (2001)
INFLATION RATE – 1.0 per cent (2002)
IMPORTS – US$414 million (1999)
EXPORTS – US$38 million (1999)

BALANCE OF PAYMENTS
Trade – US$283 million deficit (2001)
Current Account – US$47 million deficit (2001)

Trade with UK	*2002*	*2003*
Imports from UK	£17,144,000	£17,698,000
Exports to UK	1,853,000	9,657,000

MEDIA
Many of Antigua and Barbuda's television and radio stations are owned or controlled by the Antigua Labour Party. Antigua's first independent radio station began broadcasting in 2001.

CULTURE
Most of the inhabitants of Antigua and Barbuda are descendants of African slaves brought to the islands to work on sugar plantations by the British in the late 17th century. The islands are rich in British naval history (Lord Nelson built Nelson's Dockyard on Antigua in 1784) and perfectly preserved colonial architecture (in English Harbourtown) but support a vibrant and colourful Afro-Caribbean culture.

ARGENTINA

República Argentina – Argentine Republic

AREA – 2,736,700 sq. km. Neighbours: Bolivia (north), Paraguay, Brazil and Uruguay (north-east), Chile (west) from which it is separated by the Cordillera de los Andes
POPULATION – 37,488,000 (2001). The language is Spanish
CAPITAL – ΨBuenos Aires (population, 11,453,725, 2001; metropolitan area 2,768,772)
MAJOR CITIES – Córdoba; ΨLa Plata; ΨMar del Plata; Mendoza; ΨRosario; San Miguel de Tucumán
CURRENCY – Peso of 10,000 australes
NATIONAL ANTHEM – Oid Mortales! (Hear, Oh Mortals!)
NATIONAL DAY – 25 May
NATIONAL FLAG – Horizontal bands of blue, white, blue; gold sun in centre of white band
LIFE EXPECTANCY (years) – 74 (2001)
MORTALITY RATE (per 1,000 population) – 7.58 (2003)
INFANT MORTALITY (per 1,000 births) – 16 (2001)
HIV / AIDS ADULT PREVALENCE – 0.7 per cent (2001)
DEATH PENALTY – Yes*
POPULATION BELOW POVERTY LINE – 37 per cent (2001)
POPULATION GROWTH RATE – 1.3 per cent (1990–2001)
POPULATION DENSITY – 14 per sq. km (2001)
URBAN POPULATION – 88 per cent (2001)

CLIMATE AND TERRAIN
The Andes mountain range runs the full length of Argentina, a dramatic spine to the country's western border with Chile. Parts of the Andes are prone to earthquakes. Subtropical plains can be found in the north-east, arid, desert-like terrain in Patagonia (south), and rich, grassy Pampas in the east. Temperatures range from subtropical to subantarctic with an average annual temperature of 16°C. The highest point of elevation is 6,960 m (Cerro Aconcagua) and the lowest is −105 m (Laguna del Carbon).

HISTORY AND POLITICS
The estuary of La Plata was discovered in 1515 by Juan Díaz de Solís and the region was subsequently colonised by the Spanish. Spain ruled the territory from the 16th century until 1810. In 1816, after a long campaign of liberation conducted by General José de San Martín, independence was declared by the Congress of Tucumán. The country's constitution was adopted in 1853 followed by a period of national organisation.

President Juan Domingo Perón was overthrown in 1955 and there followed 18 years of instability until 1973 when he was recalled from exile. Perón died within a year and was succeeded by his widow, Vice-President Mara Estela Martínez de Perón. A coup led to the establishment of a military junta in 1976. Following the invasion, and subsequent defeat, of the Falkland Islands/ Malvinas in 1982, the President, Gen. Galtieri, resigned and the Army appointed Gen. Bignone. A civilian president was elected in 1983.

In 2000 Vice-President Carlos Alvárez resigned in protest at the President's decision not to dismiss two senior officials involved in a bribery allegation. President Fernando de la Rúa resigned in 2001 in the face of serious unrest caused by the collapsing economy. Following a series of interim presidents, Eduardo Alberto Duhalde was appointed President by Congress on 1 January 2002, to serve for the rest of de la Rúa's term. He resigned before the first round of presidential elections, held in April 2003, in which former President Carlos Menem gained 24.4 per cent of the vote and Néstor Kirchner 22 per cent. Menem withdrew from the second round and Néstor Kirchner became President-elect by default and was sworn in as President on 25 May.

POLITICAL SYSTEM
The 1853 constitution was amended in 1994. Power is vested in the President who appoints the Cabinet and is directly elected for a once-renewable four-year term. A presidential candidate must win at least 45 per cent of the vote, or 40 per cent with a 10 per cent lead over the nearest challenger, to gain victory in the first round of voting; if no candidate meets these criteria, a second round must be held. The legislature consists of a 72-member (three for each province and three for Buenos Aires) Senate and a 257-member Chamber of Deputies. Half of the Chamber of Deputies is elected every two years. Deputies serve for a four-year term. Senators have served for a nine-year term, with a third being elected every three years, but the terms of all sitting senators ended in December 2001. In October 2001 the Senate was directly elected by the provinces for a six-year term, with one-third renewable every two years.

FEDERAL STRUCTURE
The republic is divided into 23 provinces, each with an elected Governor and legislature, and one federal district

(Buenos Aires), with an elected mayor and autonomous government.

HEAD OF STATE
President, Néstor Kirchner, sworn in 25 May 2003
Vice-President, Daniel Scioli

SELECTED GOVERNMENT MEMBERS *as at July 2004*
Cabinet Chief, Alberto Fernández
Defence, José Pampuro
Economy, Roberto Lavagna
Foreign Relations, International Trade and Worship, Rafael Bielsa
Interior, Anbal Fernández

EMBASSY OF THE ARGENTINE REPUBLIC
65 Brook Street, London W1K 4AH
T 020-7318 1300
Ambassador Extraordinary and Plenipotentiary, HE Frederico Mirré

BRITISH EMBASSY
Dr Luis Agote 2412, 1425 Buenos Aires
T (+54) (11) 4808 2200
Ambassador Extraordinary and Plenipotentiary, HE Sir Robin Christopher, KBE, CMG, apptd 2000

BRITISH COUNCIL DIRECTOR, Paul Dick
Marcelo T. de Alvear 590, C1058AAF Buenos Aires
T (+54) (11) 4311/9814/7519
E info@britishcouncil.org.ar

DEFENCE

The Army has 200 main battle tanks, 105 armoured infantry fighting vehicles and 422 armoured personnel carriers. The Navy has three submarines, five destroyers, eight frigates, 14 patrol and coastal vessels, 25 combat aircraft and 21 armed helicopters. The Air Force has 128 combat aircraft and 28 armed helicopters.
MILITARY EXPENDITURE – 1.4 per cent of GDP (2002)
MILITARY PERSONNEL – 71,400: Army 41,400, Navy 17,500, Air Force 12,500; Paramilitaries 31,240

ECONOMY AND TRADE

Since late 1998 Argentina has been in a recession. In 2001, measures to reassure international investors that the country would not default on its debt repayments were introduced. In November 2001, the President announced several economy-boosting measures but in December 2001 the government defaulted on part of its large public debt. A wave of protests took place across the country in the wake of continued economic instability. In 2003 the IMF made available an eight-month standby credit of approximately US$1,580 million to cover Argentina's payment obligations to the IMF. It was also agreed that US$2,000 million in repayments to the IMF would be postponed by one year, enabling Argentina to clear its arrears with the World Bank and the Inter-American Development Bank.

The main crops are wheat, maize, oats, barley, rye, linseed, sunflower seed, alfalfa, sugar, fruit and cotton. Argentina is pre-eminent in the production of beef, mutton and wool. There is an oil refinery in San Lorenzo (Santa Fé province). Natural gas is also produced. Coal, lead, zinc, tungsten, iron ore, sulphur, mica and salt are the other chief minerals being exploited. There are small worked deposits of beryllium, manganese, bismuth, uranium, antimony, copper, kaolin, arsenate, gold, silver and tin. Coal is produced at the Río Turbio mine in the province of Santa Cruz.

Meat-packing is one of the principal industries; flour-milling, sugar-refining, and the wine industry are also important. In recent years progress has been made by the textile, plastic and machine tool industries and engineering, especially in the production of motor vehicles and steel manufactures. Argentina's main trading partners are Brazil and the USA.
GNI – US$260,300 million (2001); US$6,940 per capita (2001)
ANNUAL AVERAGE GROWTH OF GDP – 1.4 per cent (2002)
INFLATION RATE – 0.9 per cent (2000)
UNEMPLOYMENT – 15.0 per cent (2000)
TOTAL EXTERNAL DEBT – US$146,172 million (2000)
IMPORTS – US$8,990 million (2002)
EXPORTS – US$25,709 million (2002)
FOREIGN DIRECT INVESTMENT – US$48,389 million (1997–2000)

BALANCE OF PAYMENTS
Trade – US$7,451 million surplus (2001)
Current Account – US$4,554 million deficit (2001)

Trade with UK	*2002*	*2003*
Imports from UK	£127,923,000	£135,968,000
Exports to UK	246,502,000	257,579,000

TRANSPORT INFRASTRUCTURE

The 34,463 km of railway is state owned. The combined national and provincial road network totals approximately 215,471 km of which 63,348 km are surfaced. Investments of US$20,000 million for new roads and an upgrade of existing infrastructure for road, rail and air transport are taking place (2000–5). There are two large ports at Ensenada (La Plata) and Buenos Aires.

EDUCATION

Education is compulsory and free from the age of six to 15. The total number of universities is over 50 with 24 national, 25 private and a small number of provincial universities.
ILLITERACY RATE – (m) 2.9 per cent; (f) 2.9 per cent (2003)
ENROLMENT (percentage of age group) – primary 100 per cent (1997); secondary 73 per cent (1997); tertiary 36 per cent (1997)

MEDIA

Argentina's media is well developed with over 150 daily newspapers (published in both English and Spanish), including seven major dailies published in Buenos Aires. There are more than a thousand commercial radio stations (many unlicensed), over 40 television stations and widespread access to cable television.

CULTURE

Culturally, Argentina enjoys an exciting blend of pre-colonial and European influences. The arts and literature of Spain still form the bedrock of Argentinean education, while the character of the 'gaucho' (cowboy) remains a powerful and archetypal presence within the cultural landscape.

Despite these often disparate influences, Argentina has produced some of the 20th century's most important writers including Jorge Luis Borges (1899–1986) and Julio Cortazar (1914–1984). Dance, architecture, sport and cinema are all central to cultural life in Argentina.

ARMENIA

Hayastani Hanrapetut'yun – Republic of Armenia

AREA – 29,800 sq. km. Neighbours: Azerbaijan (east and south-west), Georgia (north), Iran (south), Turkey (west)
POPULATION – 3,800,000 (2002 estimate). Armenians 93.8 per cent, Kurds 1.7 per cent and Russians 1.6 per cent. Azeris formed 2.6 per cent of the population, but most fled or were expelled after the outbreak of war with Azerbaijan. There are also Ukrainians, Greeks and Assyrians. The Armenian diaspora numbers some 5,300,000. Armenian is the official language, though Russian is widely spoken and understood. The main religion is Armenian Orthodox Christian (Armenian Church centred in Etchmiadzin). Armenia adopted Christianity as its official religion in AD 301, the first state in the world to do so
CAPITAL – Yerevan (population, 1,254,400, 1996 estimate)
CURRENCY – Dram of 100 louma
NATIONAL ANTHEM – Mer Hayrenik Azat, Ankakh (Land Of Our Fathers)
NATIONAL DAY – 21 September (Independence Day)
NATIONAL FLAG – Three horizontal stripes of red, blue and orange
MORTALITY RATE (per 1,000 population) – 10.16 (2003)
HIV / AIDS ADULT PREVALENCE – 0.2 per cent (2001)
DEATH PENALTY – Yes*
POPULATION BELOW POVERTY LINE – 50 per cent (2002)
POPULATION GROWTH RATE – 0.2 per cent (1991–2001)
POPULATION DENSITY – 127 per sq. km (1999)

CLIMATE AND TERRAIN

Armenia lies between the Black and Caspian Seas, occupying the south-western part of the Caucasus region of the former Soviet Union. It is very mountainous, consisting of several vast tablelands surrounded by ridges. The elevation extremes range from 4,090 m at the highest point (Aragats Lerrnagagat) to 400 m at the lowest (Debed River). The climate is continental, dry and cold, but the Ararat valley has a long, hot and dry summer. Armenia is in an active seismic zone and the north of the country suffered an earthquake in 1988 that left an estimated 50,000 people dead.

HISTORY AND POLITICS

Armenia was first unified in 95 BC but was divided between the Persian and Byzantine empires in AD 387 and then conquered in the 11th century by the Seljuk Turks and the Mongols. In the 16th century most of Armenia was incorporated into the Ottoman Empire. In 1639 the country was divided again, the most easterly areas, now the Republic of Armenia, becoming part of the Persian Empire. In 1828 eastern Armenia became part of the Russian Empire while western Armenia remained under Ottoman rule. The Ottomans launched pogroms against the Armenians from 1894 onwards, and in 1915 to 1918 massacred 1,500,000 Armenians.

Armenia declared its independence on 28 May 1918, but was crushed and divided between Turkish and Soviet forces in 1920, with the area under Soviet control proclaimed a Soviet Socialist Republic in November 1920. The Soviet government was overthrown by a nationalist revolt in 1921 but reinstated by the Red Army a few months later. In early 1922 Armenia acceded to the USSR.

An Armenian nationalist movement gained power in national elections in mid-1990. In a referendum in 1991, 99 per cent of the electorate voted for independence, which was declared on 21 September 1991. Prime Minister Vazgen Sarkissian and six other politicians were shot dead in the National Assembly during an attempted coup on 27 October 1999.

Presidential elections took place in February 2003. Robert Kocharian was re-elected president following the second round of voting in which he gained over 65 per cent of the vote. In the general election held in May 2004 the Republican Party of Armenia (HHK) became the dominant political party.

FOREIGN RELATIONS

The dispute between the (ethnic Armenian) Nagorno-Karabakh forces supported by Armenia and the Azeri government over Nagorny-Karabakh erupted into all-out war in May 1992, when Nagorno-Karabakh forces breached Azerbaijan's defences to form a land bridge to Armenia. By the end of summer 1992 all of Nagorny-Karabakh was under Armenian control, and by the end of 1993 all Azeri territory that separated Nagorny-Karabakh from Armenia and all mountainous Azeri territory around Nagorny-Karabakh was under the control of Nagorno-Karabakh Armenians. Armenia claims this territory as historically Armenian land arbitrarily given to Azerbaijan by Stalin in 1921–2. A cease-fire agreement between Armenia, Azerbaijan and Nagorny-Karabakh was reached in May 1994, and talks mediated by the Organisation for Security and Co-operation in Europe (OSCE) continue to seek a peaceful resolution to the dispute.

In August 1997 Armenia and Russia renewed a Treaty of Friendship, Co-operation and Mutual Assistance in effect since 1991.

POLITICAL SYSTEM

There is a 131-member unicameral National Assembly *(Azgayin Joghov)*, directly elected every four years. A new constitution was approved by a referendum in July 1995.

HEAD OF STATE
President, Robert Kocharian, *elected* 30 March 1998, *re-elected* 5 March 2003

SELECTED GOVERNMENT MEMBERS *as at July 2004*
Prime Minister, Andranik Markarian
Defence, Serge Sarkissian
Finance and Economy, Vardan Khachaturian
Foreign Affairs, Vardan Oskanian

EMBASSY OF THE REPUBLIC OF ARMENIA
25a Cheniston Gardens, London W8 6TG
T 020-7938 5435
Ambassador Extraordinary and Plenipotentiary, HE Dr Vahe Gabrielian, apptd 2003

BRITISH EMBASSY
28 Charents Street, Yerevan 375010
T (+374) (1) 264 301
Ambassador Extraordinary and Plenipotentiary, HE Thorda Abbott-Watt

BRITISH COUNCIL DIRECTOR, Roger Budd, c/o The British Embassy
T (+374) (56) 99 23/24
E info@britishcouncil.am

DEFENCE

The Army has 110 main battle tanks, 110 armoured infantry fighting vehicles and 36 armoured personnel carriers. The Air Force has eight combat aircraft and 10 armed helicopters.

Russia maintains 3,500 army personnel in Armenia. An agreement on military co-operation with Russia was signed in 1996 which paved the way for joint military exercises. A protocol was also signed on the establishment of coalition troops in Transcaucasia and the planned use of Russian and Armenian armed forces as part of coalition troops in cases of mutual interest. On 19 December 2001, Russian President Vladimir Putin signed a federal law relating to an agreement between the Russian Federation and the Republic of Armenia on the joint planning of the use of troops (forces) in the interests of joint security provision. This stipulates measures to prevent the use by third countries of the territory of Armenia for purposes that may inflict damage on Russian national interests.

MILITARY EXPENDITURE – 6.4 per cent of GDP (2002)
MILITARY PERSONNEL – 44,660: Army 41,500, Air Force 3,160; Paramilitaries 1,000
CONSCRIPTION DURATION – Two years

ECONOMY AND TRADE

The Armenian economy has been badly affected by the Azeri and Turkish economic embargoes which have been in place since 1988. Armenia has a strong agricultural sector in low-lying areas, where industrial and fruit crops are grown. Grain is produced in the hills and the country is also noted for its wine and brandy. There are large mineral deposits including copper ore and molybdenum. Armenia has developed chemicals, industrial vehicles and textiles industries.

The government introduced a programme of economic reforms in November 1994 with IMF support, including the liberalisation of prices, stabilisation of the currency and privatisation.

In December 2002, the general council of the World Trade Organisation (WTO) voted to approve Armenia's application for membership.

In 2003, Russia assumed the management of Armenia's only nuclear power station and main electricity producer in exchange for US$40 million in fuel debts.

GNI – US$1,213 million (2002); US$706 per capita (2002)
ANNUAL AVERAGE GROWTH OF GDP – 12.0 per cent (2002)
INFLATION RATE – 3.0 per cent (2002)
UNEMPLOYMENT – 9.3 per cent (1998)
TOTAL EXTERNAL DEBT – US$898 million (2000)
IMPORTS – US$991 million (2002)
EXPORTS – US$507 million (2002)

BALANCE OF PAYMENTS
Trade – US$420 million deficit (2001)
Current Account – US$201 million deficit (2001)

Trade with UK	*2002*	*2003*
Imports from UK	£5,155,000	£5,575,000
Exports to UK	332,000	64,069,000

EDUCATION

State education is free and compulsory for all children aged seven to 14. Children attend primary school for three years, until the age of nine, then progress on to secondary school for five years, until the age of 14. At the end of intermediate school a Certificate of Basic Education is awarded. Senior secondary school may be attended for two years from the ages of 14 to 16. There are 25 institutions of higher education in Armenia (including seven colleges).

ILLITERACY RATE – (m) 0.6 per cent; (f) 2 per cent
ENROLMENT (percentage of age group) – tertiary 12.0 per cent (1996)

MEDIA

Television and radio in Armenia are controlled by the state. All print and broadcast media is obliged to register with the Ministry of Justice.

CULTURE

Armenia is Middle Eastern in character and atmosphere but with Christianity, not Islam, as the dominant religion – there are more than 40,000 churches and monuments throughout the country.

Major cultural figures include the poets Nahapet Kuchak (16th century) and Sayat-Nova (18th century), the composer Aram Khachaturian (1903–78), and the film director Sergo Parajanov (1924–90).

AUSTRALIA

The Commonwealth of Australia

AREA – 7,682,300 sq. km
POPULATION – 19,941,000 (2003): 458,520 of Aboriginal and Torres Strait Islander origin (2001 estimate). The language is English
CAPITAL – Canberra, in the Australian Capital Territory (population, 322,500, 2003 estimate). It has been the seat of government since 1927
MAJOR CITIES – ΨAdelaide; ΨBrisbane; ΨHobart; ΨMelbourne; ΨPerth, including Fremantle; ΨSydney
CURRENCY – Australian dollar ($A) of 100 cents
NATIONAL ANTHEM – Advance Australia Fair
NATIONAL DAY – 26 January (Australia Day)
NATIONAL FLAG – The British Blue Ensign with five stars of the Southern Cross in the fly and the white Commonwealth Star of seven points beneath the Union Flag
LIFE EXPECTANCY (years) – 79 (2001)
MORTALITY RATE (per 1,000 population) – 6.7 (2002)
INFANT MORTALITY (per 1,000 live births) – 6 (2001)

HIV / AIDS ADULT PREVALENCE – 0.1 per cent
DEATH PENALTY – No (abolished 1985)
POPULATION GROWTH RATE – 1.2 per cent (1998–2003)
POPULATION DENSITY – 3 per sq. km (2003)
URBAN POPULATION – 87 per cent (2001)

CLIMATE AND TERRAIN

Australia is a continent, the world's sixth-largest country and home to a wide variety of landscapes and weather conditions. The interior is dominated by hot deserts and is only thinly populated. The eastern and south-eastern coastlines are the most densely populated areas and feature mountains, flat golden beaches and primary rain forests. The highest point of elevation is 2,229 m (Mount Kosciuszko) and the lowest is −15 m (Lake Eyre). The summer begins in December, the winter in June, the spring in September and the autumn in March. Average annual temperatures range from zero to 34°C.

HISTORY AND POLITICS

Australia was discovered by Europeans in the 17th century. Its eastern coast was claimed by Capt. James Cook on behalf of Britain in 1770 and became a penal colony; Tasmania, Western Australia, South Australia, Victoria and Queensland were established as colonies between 1825 and 1859. The colonies were federated as the Commonwealth of Australia on 1 January 1901, at which time Australia gained dominion status within the British Empire. Australia became independent within the British Commonwealth by the 1931 Statute of Westminster. Following a referendum in 1967, the Aboriginal population was granted full political rights. In 1986, the Australia Act was passed, which abolished the remaining legislative, executive and judicial links to the UK, while retaining the British monarch as head of state.

In 1998, the Constitutional Convention voted by 89 votes to 52 to sever constitutional links with the United Kingdom monarchy. A national referendum was held on the issue in 1999; the proposition to make Australia a republic was defeated, with 45.3 per cent voting in favour and 54.7 per cent against.

The general election of 2001 was won by the ruling Liberal Party-National Party Coalition. A general election was scheduled for 9 October 2004.

POLITICAL SYSTEM

The government is a federal commonwealth within the Commonwealth, the executive power being vested in the Sovereign (through the Governor-General) assisted by a federal government. Under the constitution the powers of the federal government are defined, and residuary legislative power remains with the states. The right of a state to legislate on any matter is not abrogated except in connection with matters exclusively under federal control, but where a state law is inconsistent with a law of the Commonwealth the latter prevails to the extent of the inconsistency.

Parliament consists of Queen Elizabeth II, the Senate and the House of Representatives. The constitution provides that the number of members of the House of Representatives shall be, as nearly as practicable, twice the number of senators. Members of the Senate are elected for six years by universal suffrage, half the members retiring every third year, except in the Australian Capital Territory

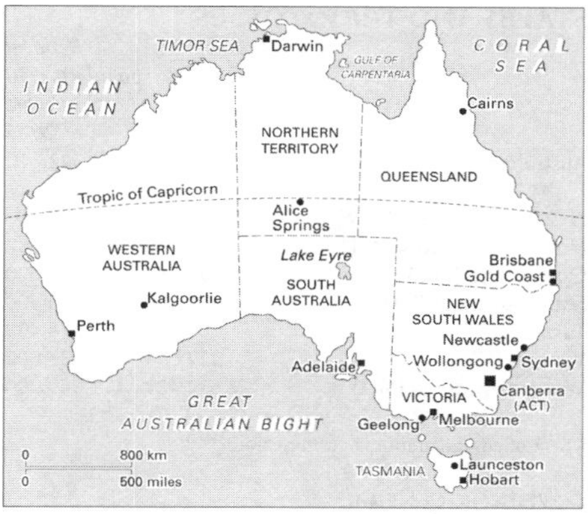

and the Northern Territory, where members are elected for a three-year term. Each of the six states returns 12 senators, and the Australian Capital Territory and the Northern Territory two each. The House of Representatives, similarly elected for a maximum of three years, contains members proportionate to the population, with a minimum of five members for each state. There are now 150 members in the House of Representatives, including two members for the Northern Territory and two for the Australian Capital Territory.

The High Court exercises jurisdiction over all matters arising under the constitution, all matters arising between the states and between residents of different states, matters to which the Commonwealth of Australia is a party, matters arising under any treaty, and matters affecting foreign representatives in Australia. The High Court also hears appeals from the Federal Court and from the Supreme Courts of states and territories.

The Federal Court of Australia has jurisdiction over important industrial and trade practices, intellectual property, administrative law, admiralty law and bankruptcy matters. It also acts as a court of appeal for decisions from the Australian Capital Territory Supreme Court and certain decisions of state Supreme Courts exercising federal jurisdiction. Each state has its own judicature of supreme, superior and minor courts for criminal and civil cases.

FEDERAL STRUCTURE

In the states, executive authority is vested in a Governor (appointed by the Crown), assisted by a Council of Ministers or Executive Council. Each state has a legislature comprising a Legislative Council and a Legislative Assembly or House of Assembly which are elected for four-year terms, except Queensland, which has a Legislative Assembly only.

The Northern Territory and Australian Capital Territory have a Legislative Assembly only.

STATES AND TERRITORIES

	Area (sq. km)	Resident population 30 September 2003	Capital	Governor 2004
Australian Capital Territory (ACT)	2,349	322,600	Canberra	–
New South Wales (NSW)	801,349	6,699,300	Sydney	HE Prof. Marie Bashir, AC
Northern Territory (NT)	1,352,158	198,600	Darwin*	John Anictomatis, OAM†
Queensland (Qld)	1,734,157	3,817,000	Brisbane	HE Quentin Bryce, AC
South Australia (SA)	985,335	1,529,400	Adelaide	Marjorie Jackson-Nelson, AC, MBE
Tasmania (Tas.)	67,914	478,400	Hobart	HE Richard W. Butler, AC
Victoria (Vic.)	227,594	4,933,600	Melbourne	HE John Landy, AC, MBE
Western Australia (WA)	2,534,483	1,959,700	Perth	HE Lt.-Gen. John M. Sanderson, AC

* Seat of administration † Administrator

GOVERNOR-GENERAL
Governor-General, Maj.-Gen. Michael Jeffery AC, CVO, MC, assumed office 11 August 2003

SELECTED GOVERNMENT MEMBERS *as at July 2004*
Prime Minister, John Howard
Deputy Prime Minister, Transport and Regional Services, John Anderson
Defence, Robert Hill
Foreign Affairs, Alexander Downer
Treasurer, Peter Costello

AUSTRALIAN HIGH COMMISSION
Australia House, Strand, London WC2B 4LA
T 020-7379 4334
High Commissioner, HE Michael L'Estrange, apptd 2000

NEW SOUTH WALES GOVERNMENT OFFICE, The Australia Centre, Strand, London WC2B 4LG T 020-7887 5871 *Director*, Leanne Grogan
AGENT-GENERAL FOR QUEENSLAND, 392 Strand, London WC2R 0LZ T 020-7836 1333 *Agent-General*, John Dawson
AGENT-GENERAL FOR SOUTH AUSTRALIA, Australia Centre, Strand, London WC2B 4LG T 020-7836 3455 *Agent-General*, Maurice de Rohan
AGENT-GENERAL FOR VICTORIA, Australia Centre, Strand, London WC2B 4LG T 020-7836 2656 *Agent-General*, David Buckingham
AGENT-GENERAL FOR WESTERN AUSTRALIA, Australia Centre, Strand, London WC2B 4LG T 020-7240 2881 *Agent-General*, Robert Fisher

BRITISH HIGH COMMISSION
Commonwealth Avenue, Yarralumla, Canberra, ACT 2600
T (+61) (2) 6270 6666
High Commissioner, HE Sir Alastair Goodlad, KCMG, apptd 1999
E bhc.canberra@mail.uk.emb.gov.au
Consuls-General, D. H. Cairns *(Brisbane)*; A. D. Sprake *(Melbourne)*; H. Dunnachie *(Perth)*; P. Beckingham *(Sydney)*

BRITISH COUNCIL DIRECTOR, Simon Gammell
PO BOX 88, Edgecliff, Sydney, NSW 2027
T (+61) (2) 9326 2022
E enquiries@britishcouncil.org.au

DEFENCE

The Army has 71 main battle tanks, 364 armoured personnel carriers, 255 light armoured vehicles, six aircraft and 104 armed helicopters. The Navy has six submarines, 11 frigates, 15 patrol and coastal vessels and 16 armed helicopters. There are bases at Sydney, Stirling, Cairns, Darwin, Flinders, Jervis Bay and Noura. The Air Force has 161 combat aircraft.
MILITARY EXPENDITURE – 2.0 per cent of GDP (2002)
MILITARY PERSONNEL – 53,650: Army 26,600, Navy 12,850, Air Force 14,200

ECONOMY AND TRADE

The wide range of climatic and soil conditions has resulted in a diversity of crops. Generally, cereal crops (excluding rice and sorghum) are widely grown, while other crops are confined to specific locations in a few states. However, scant or erratic rainfall, limited potential for irrigation and unsuitable soils or topography have restricted intensive agriculture.

Cattle and sheep ranching is widespread and produces significant agricultural products including meat, meat derivatives, wool and dairy products.

Significant mineral resources include bauxite, coal, copper, crude petroleum, gems, gold, ilmenite, iron ore, lead, limestone, manganese, nickel, rutile, salt, silver, tin, tungsten, uranium, zinc and zircon. In 2001–2 338,000,000 tonnes of coal, 36,100,000 tonnes of crude oil, 36,000,000 cubic metres of natural gas, 185,000,000 tonnes of iron ore, 1,020,000 tonnes of lead, and 264 tonnes of gold were produced.

In 2002–3 the main exports were coal, not agglomerated (10.3 per cent); petroleum and related products (5.1 per cent); gold (4.8 per cent); iron ore and concentrates (4.6 per cent); aluminium (3.5 per cent). The major imports were motor vehicles, excluding public transport (7.7 per cent); petroleum and related products (5.9 per cent); aircraft and associated equipment (4.1 per cent); computer technology (3.7 per cent); medicaments (3.2 per cent); and telecommunications equipment (3.2 per cent)

Australia's main trading partners are Japan, the USA, New Zealand, China, Korea, Germany, Taiwan, Indonesia and the UK.
GNI – US$385,900 million (2001); US$19,900 per capita (2001)
ANNUAL AVERAGE GROWTH OF GDP – 4.0 per cent (2001)
INFLATION RATE – 2.4 per cent (2003)
UNEMPLOYMENT – 5.8 per cent (2004)
FOREIGN DIRECT INVESTMENT – US$32,493 million (1997–2000)
IMPORTS – US$72,690 billion (2002)
EXPORTS – US$65,092 billion (2002)

BALANCE OF PAYMENTS
Trade – US$5,428 million deficit (2002)
Current Account - US$17,879 million deficit (2002)

Trade with UK	*2002*	*2003*
Imports from UK	£2,123,928,000	£2,300,935,000
Exports to UK	1,774,387,000	1,825,400,000

TRANSPORT INFRASTRUCTURE

There are six government-owned railway systems, operated by the State Rail Authority of NSW, VicRail, Queensland Government Railways, Western Australian Government Railways, the State Transport Authority of Southern Australia, and the National Rail Corporation (NRC). The NRC incorporates the former Commonwealth Railways system, and the Tasmanian and non-metropolitan South Australian railways (urban rail services in Southern Australia remain the responsibility of the State Transport Authority). In 2002 there was a total of 41,286 km of railway track.

The Northern Territory has three main ports: Darwin, and the private mining ports of Gove and Groote Eylandt. Most freight in the Territory is moved by road trains. These are massive trucks hauling two or three trailers, having a net capacity of about 100 tonnes and measuring up to 45 metres in length. There are a total of 811,603 km of highways.

EDUCATION

Education is administered by the state governments and is compulsory between the ages of six and 15 (16 in Tasmania). It is available at government schools controlled by the state education department and at private or independent schools, some of which are denominational. Tertiary education is available through universities and technical and further education colleges. There are 41 universities in Australia; the Australian Capital Territory has three universities, New South Wales 13, Queensland nine, Northern Territory one, South Australia three, Tasmania one, Victoria nine and Western Australia five.

ENROLMENT (percentage of age group) – primary 100 per cent (1997); secondary 100 per cent (1997); tertiary 80 per cent (1997)

MEDIA

Australia's leading newspapers are *The Sydney Morning Herald*, the *Herald Sun*, *The Australian*, *The Daily Telegraph*, *The Age*, *The West Australian*, *The Australian Financial Review*, and *The Advertiser*. There is an established tradition of public service broadcasting (via the Australian Broadcasting Corporation and the Special Broadcasting Service) and of commercial television (Seven Network, Nine Network, Ten Network). Australian media tycoon Rupert Murdoch owns News Corporation and a considerable subscription-based television empire.

The Australian film industry is small but highly-regarded and well funded. In 2004 there were 5.2 million internet users.

CULTURE

The roots of Australian Aboriginal art date back 30,000 years and modern Aboriginal artists use traditional forms in contemporary ways. Australian theatre excels in established formats but is also known for its experimental edge. The Australian literary scene is internationally acclaimed with authors such as Patrick White (1912–90) winning the Nobel Prize in 1973 and Peter Carey (b.1943) and Thomas Keneally (b.1935) winning the Booker Prize. Australian actors such as Russell Crowe (b.1964), Nicole Kidman (b.1967) and Mel Gibson (b.1956) enjoy success in Hollywood.

EXTERNAL TERRITORIES

ASHMORE AND CARTIER ISLANDS

Ashmore Islands (known as Middle, East and West Islands) and Cartier Island are situated in the Indian Ocean 850 km and 790 km west of Darwin respectively. The islands are uninhabited. The territory has been administered by the Australian Government since 1933.

THE AUSTRALIAN ANTARCTIC TERRITORY

The Australian Antarctic Territory was established in 1933 and comprises all the islands and territories, other than Adélie Land, which are situated south of latitude 60° S. and lying between 160° E. longitude and 45° E. longitude. The territory is administered by the Antarctic Division of the Department of the Environment and Heritage.

CHRISTMAS ISLAND

AREA – 135 sq. km
POPULATION – 1,928 (2001)

Christmas Island is situated in the Indian Ocean about 1,408 km north-west of North West Cape in Western Australia. The island became an Australian territory in 1958 and is managed by the Department of Transport and Regional Services. The Shire of Christmas Island (SOCI) has nine elected members. SOCI is responsible for municipal functions and services on the island.

COCOS (KEELING) ISLANDS

AREA – 14 sq. km
POPULATION – 600 (2001)

The Cocos (Keeling) Islands are two separate atolls (North Keeling Island and, 24 km to the south, the main atoll) comprising some 27 small coral islands, situated in the Indian Ocean. The main islands of the southern atoll are West Island (about 9 km in length); Home Island, where the Cocos Malay community lives; Direction Island, Horsburgh and South Island.

The islands were declared a British possession in 1857. All land in the islands was granted to George Clunies-Ross and his heirs by Queen Victoria in 1886. In 1978 the Australian Government purchased all Clunies-Ross land and property interests except for the family home and grounds; the last of the remaining grounds were purchased in 1993. Between 1979 and 1984 most of the land was transferred to trusts with the Cocos (Keeling) Islands Council as trustee, the local government body established in 1979 which was replaced by the Shire of the Cocos (Keeling) Islands in July 1992.

In April 1984 the Cocos community, in a UN-supervised Act of Self-Determination, chose to integrate with Australia. The islands are managed by the Australian Government through the Department of Transport and Regional Services.

CORAL SEA ISLANDS TERRITORY

The Coral Sea Islands Territory lies east of Queensland between the Great Barrier Reef and longitude 156° 06′ E., and between latitudes 12° and 24° S. It comprises scattered islands, spread over a sea area of 780,000 sq. km. The islands are formed mainly of coral and sand, and most are extremely small. There is a manned meteorological station in the Willis Group but the remaining islands are uninhabited.

The territory is managed by the Department of Transport and Regional Services.

HEARD ISLAND AND MCDONALD ISLANDS

The Territory of the Heard and McDonald Islands, about 4,100 km south-west of Perth, comprises all the islands and rocks lying between 52° 30′ and 53° 30′ S. latitude and 72° and 74° 30′ E. longitude. The islands are administered by the Antarctic Division of the Department of the Environment and Heritage.

NORFOLK ISLAND

AREA – 34.5 sq. km
POPULATION – 2,037 (2001)
SEAT OF GOVERNMENT – Kingston

Norfolk Island is situated in the South Pacific Ocean. It is about 8 km long by 5 km wide. The climate is mild and subtropical.

The island, discovered by Captain Cook in 1774, served as a penal colony from 1788 to 1814 and from 1825 to 1855. In 1856, 194 descendants of the *Bounty* mutineers accepted an invitation to leave Pitcairn and settle on Norfolk Island.

In 1979 Norfolk Island gained a substantial degree of self-government. Wide powers are exercised by a nine-member Legislative Assembly that is elected every three years. The Administrator is responsible to the Australian Minister for Regional Services, Territories and Local Government.

AUSTRIA

Republik Österreich – Republic of Austria

AREA – 82,700 sq. km. Neighbours: the Czech Republic and Slovakia (north), Italy and Slovenia (south), Hungary (east), Germany (north-west), Switzerland and Liechtenstein (west)
POPULATION – 8,075,000 (2001). The language is German, but the rights of the Slovene, Croat, Hungarian, Czech, Slovak, Roma and Sinti minorities are protected. The predominant religion is Roman Catholicism
CAPITAL – Vienna, on the Danube (population, 1,550,123, 2001 census)
MAJOR CITIES – Graz; Innsbruck; Klagenfurt; Linz; Salzburg
CURRENCY – Euro (€) of 100 cents
NATIONAL ANTHEM – Land Der Berge, Land Am Strome (Land Of Mountains, Land On The River)
NATIONAL DAY – 26 October
NATIONAL FLAG – Three equal horizontal stripes of red, white, red
LIFE EXPECTANCY (years) – 78 (2001)
MORTALITY RATE (per 1,000 population) – 9.69 (2003)
HIV / AIDS ADULT PREVALENCE – 0.2 per cent (2001)
DEATH PENALTY – No (abolished 1968)
INFANT MORTALITY (per 1,000 births) – 5 (2001)
POPULATION GROWTH RATE – 0.4 per cent (1990–2001)
POPULATION DENSITY – 98 per sq. km (2001)

CLIMATE AND TERRAIN

The Austrian Alps (in the west and south of the country) are famous as a winter sports destination. The north and east of the country feature rolling hills and there is a temperate climate which averages from 2°C in January to 20°C in July. The highest point of elevation is 3,798 m (Grossglockner) and the lowest is 115 m (Neusiedler See).

HISTORY AND POLITICS

The Austrian state dates back to the eighth century AD when Emperor Charlemagne conquered the territory and founded the *Ostmark*, the eastern march of the Holy Roman Empire, which had been settled from the sixth century onwards by Bavarian Germans. The Habsburg dynasty established an empire which united much of central Europe, including present-day Austria and Hungary. The Republic of Austria was established in 1918 on the break-up of the Austro-Hungarian Empire. In March 1938 Austria was incorporated into Nazi Germany under the name *Ostmark*. After the liberation of Vienna in 1945, the Republic of Austria was reconstituted within the 1937 frontiers and a freely-elected government took office in December 1945. The country was divided into four zones occupied respectively by the UK, USA, USSR and France, while Vienna was jointly occupied by the four powers. In 1955 the Austrian State Treaty was signed by the foreign ministers of the four powers and of Austria. This treaty recognised the re-establishment of Austria as a sovereign, independent and democratic state, having the same frontiers as on 1 January 1938. Austria acceded to the European Union on 1 January 1995.

After the Social Democrats and the Austrian People's Party (ÖVP) failed to form a coalition following the general election of 1999, a coalition government comprising the ÖVP and the far-right Austrian Freedom Party (FPÖ) (led by Jörg Haider, who had expressed support for some aspects of the wartime Nazi regime) was sworn in on 5 February 2000 after both parties signed a document expressing their commitment to the European Union and aversion to discrimination and intolerance. International opposition to the inclusion of the FP in the government resulted in the suspension of bilateral relations between the governments of the other EU members and Austria. In May, Jörg Haider resigned as leader of the FPÖ in an attempt to calm the situation. The suspension of relations between the EU members and Austria was lifted in September 2000 following an investigation into the Austrian government which cleared it of any wrongdoing. The ÖVP won the legislative elections of November 2002 with 42.3 per cent of the vote. But the Party did not gain enough votes to form a government of its own. After coalition talks with the Social Democrats and Greens failed, ÖVP leader Walter Schüssel announced in February 2003 that he had reformed his previous coalition with the FPÖ and a new Cabinet was appointed.

POLITICAL SYSTEM

There is a bicameral national assembly; the lower house *(Nationalrat)* has 183 directly-elected members and the upper house *(Bundesrat)* has 64 representatives of the nine provinces (dependent on population). There is a four per cent qualification for parliamentary representation.

FEDERAL STRUCTURE
There are nine provinces (population figures for 2001): Burgenland (277,569); Carinthia (559,404); Lower Austria (1,545,804); Salzburg (515,327); Styria (1,183,303); Tirol (673,504); Upper Austria (1,376,797); Vienna (1,550,123); Vorarlberg (351,095).

HEAD OF STATE
President of the Republic of Austria, Heinz Fischer, *took office* 8 July 2004

SELECTED GOVERNMENT MEMBERS *as at July 2004*
Chancellor, Wolfgang Schüssel
Vice-Chancellor, Minister for Infrastructure, Hubert Gorbach
Defence, Günther Platter
Finance, Karl-Heinz Grasser
Foreign Affairs, Benita Ferrero-Waldner
Interior, Ernst Strasser

AUSTRIAN EMBASSY
18 Belgrave Mews West, London SW1 8HU
T 020-7235 3731
Ambassador Extraordinary and Plenipotentiary, HE Alexander Christiani, apptd 2000

BRITISH EMBASSY
Jaurèsgasse 12, 1030 Vienna
T (+43) (1) 716130
Ambassador Extraordinary and Plenipotentiary, HE John MacGregor, CVO, apptd 2003

BRITISH COUNCIL DIRECTOR, Dr Simon Cole
Schenkenstrasse 4, A-1010 Vienna
T (+43) (1) 533 2616
E bc.vienna@britishcouncil.at

DEFENCE
The Army has 274 main battle tanks and 493 armoured personnel carriers. The Air Force has 52 combat aircraft and 11 armed helicopters.
MILITARY EXPENDITURE – 0.8 per cent of GDP (2001)
MILITARY PERSONNEL – Army 34,600, of which Air Force 6,850
CONSCRIPTION DURATION – Eight months, or seven months plus refresher training

ECONOMY AND TRADE
Major industries include iron and steel production, chemicals, electrical goods, mechanical engineering, textiles and paper production. Agricultural products include wheat, rye, barley, oats, maize, potatoes, sugar beet and turnips. Timber forms a valuable source of Austria's indigenous wealth with approximately 47 per cent of the total land area consisting of forest areas. However, strict regulations have preserved Austria's environment from over-production. Foreign exchange receipts from tourism are a major contribution to the balance of payments. Austria suffered low economic growth in 2001 and 2002.

Main exports are processed goods (iron and steel, other metal goods, textiles, paper and cardboard products), machinery and transport equipment, other finished goods (including clothing), raw materials, chemical products and foodstuffs. Main imports are machinery and transport equipment, processed goods, chemical products, foodstuffs, fuel and energy. Austria's main trading partners are Germany, Italy, France and Switzerland.
GNI – US$194,700 million (2001); US$23,940 per capita (2001)
ANNUAL AVERAGE GROWTH OF GDP – 3.3 per cent (2000)
INFLATION RATE – 2.4 per cent (2000)
UNEMPLOYMENT – 3.6 per cent (2000)
FOREIGN DIRECT INVESTMENT – US$20,400 (1997–2000)
IMPORTS – US$71,841 million (2002)
EXPORTS – US$72,708 million (2002)

BALANCE OF PAYMENTS
Trade – US$3,572 million surplus (2002)
Current Account – US$838 million surplus (2002)

Trade with UK	*2002*	*2003*
Imports from UK	£1,204,200,000	£924,572,000
Exports to UK	2,177,800,000	1,869,438,000

TRANSPORT INFRASTRUCTURE
There are 200,000 km of roads and a network of 1,613 km of *Autobahn* between major cities that also link up with German and Italian networks. The railways are state-owned and comprised 6,123 km of track in 2002, which includes 3,523 km of electrified track. Of the 425 km of waterways, 351 km are navigable and there is considerable trade through the Danube ports by both local and foreign shipping. There are six commercial airports.

EDUCATION
Education is free and compulsory between the ages of six and 15 and there are good facilities for secondary, technical and professional education. There are 14 public, six private and six art universities.
ENROLMENT (percentage of age group) – primary 100 per cent (1997); secondary 100 per cent (1997); tertiary 48 per cent (1997)

MEDIA
The public broadcaster Oesterreichischer Rundfunk (ORF) dominated Austrian television and radio for many years but there are now an increasing number of private broadcasters. By contrast, Austria's print media is largely privately owned. There are approximately six main daily titles including *Der Standard* and *Neve Vorarlberger*. In 2004 there were approximately 3.7 million internet users.

CULTURE
During the 18th, 19th and 20th centuries Vienna was one of Europe's most culturally important cities, attracting musicians (Wolfgang Amadeus Mozart (1756–91), Johann Strauss Jr. (1825–99), Arnold Schoenberg (1874–1951), and Alban Berg (1885–1935)), philosophers (Ludwig Wittgenstein (1889-1951)), artists (Gustav Klimt (1862–1918)), physicists (Ludwig Boltzman (1844–1906) and Erwin Schrödinger (1887–1961)) and alternative thinkers (psychoanalyst Sigmund Freud (1865–1939)).

AZERBAIJAN

Azerbaycan Respublıkası – Republic of Azerbaijan

AREA – 86,600 sq. km. Neighbours: Iran (south), Armenia (west), Georgia and Russia (north)
POPULATION – 8,100,000 (2002 estimate): 83 per cent Azeri, 6 per cent Russian and 6 per cent Armenian. There are also Kurds, Jews, Georgians and Turks. There are more Azeris in Iran than in Azerbaijan. The population is predominantly Shia Muslim although it was heavily secularised during the Soviet era. The language is Azeri
CAPITAL – ΨBaki (Baku), population, 1,817,900, 2001 estimate
MAJOR CITIES – Gäncä; Sumqayit
CURRENCY – Manat of 100 gopik
NATIONAL ANTHEM – Azerbaijan! Azerbaijan!
NATIONAL DAY – 28 May (Independence Day)
NATIONAL FLAG – Three horizontal stripes of blue, red and green with a white crescent and eight-pointed star in the centre
MORTALITY RATE (per 1,000 population) – 9.68 (2002)
HIV / AIDS ADULT PREVALENCE – 0.1 per cent (2001)
DEATH PENALTY – No (abolished 1998)
POPULATION BELOW POVERTY LINE – 49 per cent (2002)
POPULATION GROWTH RATE –1 per cent (1991–2001)
POPULATION DENSITY – 92 per sq. km (1999)

CLIMATE AND TERRAIN

Azerbaijan occupies the eastern part of the Caucasus region of the former Soviet Union, on the shore of the Caspian Sea. The highest point of elevation is 4,485 m (Bazarduzu Dagi) while the lowest is –28 m (Caspian Sea). The north-eastern part of the republic is taken up by the south-eastern end of the main Caucasus ridge, its south-western part by the smaller Caucasus hills and its south-eastern corner by the spurs of the Talysh Ridge. Central Azerbaijan is formed by a depression irrigated by the River Kura and the lower reaches of its tributary the Araks. Azerbaijan has a continental climate.

HISTORY AND POLITICS

The Turkic Azeri people formed an independent state in the first century BC. By the seventh century, this precarious civilisation was invaded by Muslim Arabs who introduced Islam and secured the region as a province of the Muslim Caliphate. Azerbaijan was again invaded by Persia in the 16th century. The country was divided during the Russo-Persian wars of the early 19th century, the northern portion (present-day Azerbaijan) becoming part of the Russian Empire and the southern portion remaining Persian and subsequently Iranian.

In 1918 the Azerbaijan Democratic Republic was established. It was overthrown by Communists in 1918 and Azerbaijan acceded to the USSR in 1922.

In January 1990, the Azeri Popular Front took power from the local Communist Party and declared independence from the Soviet Union. Soviet troops overthrew the Popular Front and restored the Communist regime, which declared Azerbaijan's independence in August 1991.

Incumbent President Heydar Aliyev won the presidential elections of 1998, with 76.1 per cent of the vote. However, the elections were criticised by the Organisation for Security and Co-operation in Europe (OSCE) and other international monitoring groups. A general election was held in 2000. The New Azerbaijan party, founded by Aliyev, won 62.5 per cent of the vote (78 seats). The election was boycotted by several parties, who alleged that electoral fraud had been committed; their claims were supported by OSCE observers. Repeat elections were held in January 2001 in 11 districts and Aliyev again took the vote. In October 2003 Aliyev withdrew from the presidential race due to health problems (he died in December 2003) and endorsed the campaign of his son, Ilham, who was elected.

SECESSION

In 1988 fighting broke out in the predominantly Armenian-populated region of Nagorny-Karabakh between Soviet Azeri forces and ethnic Armenians demanding unification with Armenia. In late 1993 Nagorno-Karabakh forces captured all of the region, together with all Azeri territory separating the region from Armenia (20 per cent of Azeri territory). Azeri forces pushed back the Nagorno-Karabakh forces in early 1994 before a cease-fire agreement was signed in May 1994. The fighting briefly flared up again along the Azeri-Armenian border in April and May 1997. Peace talks, held under the auspices of the OSCE, have yet to yield any significant results, although both sides reaffirmed their commitment to finding a peaceful solution at a meeting in October 1997, in which both sides rejected the idea of full independence for Nagorny-Karabakh as 'unrealistic'. President Aliyev held talks with President Kocharian of Armenia in 2001, but the leaders failed to reach an agreement.

POLITICAL SYSTEM

A new constitution was approved by a referendum in November 1995, which created a presidential republic with executive power to be exercised by the President and with legislative power vested in the unicameral *Milli Majlis* (National Assembly). The *Milli Majlis* has 125 seats, of which 100 are directly elected and 25 are allocated by proportional representation. The President appoints the Prime Minister and the Cabinet. Both the President and the National Assembly are directly elected for five-year terms.

HEAD OF STATE
President, Ilham Aliyev, *assumed office* 31 October 2003

SELECTED GOVERNMENT MEMBERS *as at July 2004*
Prime Minister, Artur Rasizade
First Deputy Prime Ministers, Yagub Abdulla Eyyubov; Abbas Abbasov
Deputy Prime Ministers, Abid Sarifov; Ali Gasanov *(Chair of State Refugee Committee)*; Elehin Efendiyev
Defence, Lt.-Gen. Safar Abiyev
Finance, Avaz Alakbarov
Foreign Affairs, Elmar Mamedyarov
Interior, Lt.-Gen. Ramil Usubov

EMBASSY OF THE REPUBLIC OF AZERBAIJAN
4 Kensington Court, London W8 5DL
T 020-7938 5482
Ambassador Extraordinary and Plenipotentiary, HE Rafael Ibrahimov, apptd 2001

BRITISH EMBASSY
45 Khagani Street, Baku AZ1010
T (+994) (12) 975188/89/90
E office@britemb.baku.az

Ambassador Extraordinary and Plenipotentiary, HE Dr Laurie Bristow

BRITISH COUNCIL DIRECTOR, Margaret Jack
1 Vali Mammadov Street, Icheri Sheher, Baku AZ1000
T (+994) (12) 972013, 971593, 972390, 972280, 972290
E enquiries@britishcouncil.az

DEFENCE

The Army has 220 main battle tanks, 135 armoured infantry fighting vehicles and 381 armoured personnel carriers. The Navy is based at Baku, with a share of the former Soviet Caspian Fleet Flotilla, comprising six patrol and coastal vessels. The Air Force has 48 combat aircraft and 15 attack helicopters.

MILITARY EXPENDITURE – 3.3 per cent of GDP (2002)
MILITARY PERSONNEL – 66,490: Army 56,840, Navy 1,750, Air Force 7,900; Paramilitaries 15,000
CONSCRIPTION DURATION – 17 months

ECONOMY AND TRADE

Industry is dominated by oil and natural gas extraction and related industries centred in Baku and Sumgait and the large oil deposits in the Caspian Sea, estimated at more than 6,000 million barrels. Natural gas reserves are estimated to be more than 1,200,000 million cubic metres.

The republic is also rich in mineral resources, with iron, copper, aluminium, lead and zinc, and is important as cotton-growing and silkworm-breeding areas.

Around 90 per cent of agricultural land has been privatised. Grapes, cereals (primarily wheat, barley, maize and rice), cotton, vegetables and fruit are the major agricultural products.

GNI – US$4,851 million (2000); US$600 per capita (2000)
GDP – US$5,692 million (2001); US$655 per capita (2000)
ANNUAL AVERAGE GROWTH OF GDP – 11.0 per cent (1998)
INFLATION RATE – 1.8 per cent (2000)
UNEMPLOYMENT – 1.2 per cent (1999)
TOTAL EXTERNAL DEBT – US$1,184 million (2000)
IMPORTS – US$1,036 million (1999)
EXPORTS – US$929 million (1999)

BALANCE OF PAYMENTS
Trade – US$482 million surplus (2002)
Current Account – US$768 million deficit (2002)

Trade with UK	*2002*	*2003*
Imports from UK	£56,260,000	£139,681,000
Exports to UK	11,070,000	16,385,000

TRANSPORT INFRASTRUCTURE

There are 2,200 km of railway track, much of it electrified, and over 25,000 km of roads. There are ferry links to Turkmenistan. Oil pipelines (1,631 km) link the Azeri oilfields to the Russian Black Sea port of Novorossiysk and the Georgian port of Supsa. Moscow has agreed to grant US$300 million for the construction of the Azeri part of the north-south transport highway linking northern and central Europe with the Gulf countries across Azerbaijan. There are 72 airports.

EDUCATION

Education up to university level is free. There are several universities and colleges of higher education.

ILLITERACY RATE – (m) 1 per cent; (f) 4 per cent (1989)

MEDIA

The state runs press, television and radio in Azerbaijan but there is an increasingly successful private sector, boosted by the issue of five new regional television licences in 2002.

CULTURE

Azerbaijan reflects both European (mainly Turkish and Russian) and Islamic cultures and has ancient and distinguished literary and musical traditions. The country is famous for its textiles – colourfully embroidered carpets, veils, towels and shawls featuring geometric patterns, sometimes worked with real gold or silver.

Azerbaijan was the birthplace of the prophet Zoroaster, who founded one of the first monotheistic religions in the world (sixth century BC).

THE BAHAMAS

The Commonwealth of The Bahamas

AREA – 13,939 sq. km
POPULATION – 308,000 (2001). The language is English
CAPITAL – ΨNassau (population, 172,196, 1996 estimate)
CURRENCY – Bahamian dollar (B$) of 100 cents
NATIONAL ANTHEM – March On, Bahamaland
NATIONAL DAY – 10 July (Independence Day)
NATIONAL FLAG – Horizontal stripes of aquamarine, gold and aquamarine, with a black equilateral triangle on the hoist
LIFE EXPECTANCY (years) – 69 (2001)
MORTALITY RATES (per 1,000 population) – 8.68 (2003)
INFANT MORTALITY (per 1,000 births) – 13 (2001)
HIV / AIDS ADULT PREVALENCE – 3.5 per cent (2001)
DEATH PENALTY – Yes
POPULATION GROWTH RATE – 1.7 per cent (1990-2001)
POPULATION DENSITY – 22 per sq. km (2001)

CLIMATE AND TERRAIN

The Bahamas extend from the coast of Florida on the north-west almost to Hispaniola on the south-east. The group consists of more than 700 islands, and 2,400 cays. The extremes of elevation range from 63 m at the highest point (Mount Alvernia, Cat Island) to 0 m at the lowest (Atlantic Ocean). The 14 major islands are inhabited, as are a few of the smaller islands. The principal islands include: Abaco, Acklins, Andros, Berry Islands, Bimini, Cat Island, Crooked Island, Eleuthera, Exuma, Grand Bahama, Harbour Island, Inagua, Long Island, Mayaguana, New Providence (on which the capital, Nassau, is located), Ragged Island, Rum Cay, San Salvador and Spanish Wells. The climate is semitropical. The hurricane season is June to November.

HISTORY AND POLITICS

The Bahamas were settled by the British and became a Crown colony in 1717. Taken over in 1782 by the Spanish, the Treaty of Versailles in 1783 restored them to the British. The Bahamas gained independence on 10 July 1973.

A general election held in 2002 was won by the Progressive Liberal Party (PLP) which defeated the Free National Movement Party (FNM). The PLP holds 28 seats in the House of Assembly, the FNM eight seats and Independents four seats.

POLITICAL SYSTEM

The head of state is Queen Elizabeth II who is represented in the islands by a Governor-General. There is an appointed Senate of 16 members and a House of Assembly of 40 members elected by universal suffrage.
Governor-General, Dame Ivy Dumont, DCMG

SELECTED GOVERNMENT MEMBERS *as at July 2004*
Prime Minister, Finance, Perry Christie
Deputy Prime Minister, National Security, Cynthia Pratt
Minister of State for Finance, James Smith
Foreign Affairs, Public Service, Fred Mitchell

BAHAMAS HIGH COMMISSION
10 Chesterfield Street, London W1J 5JL
T 020-7408 4488
High Commissioner, HE Basil O'Brien, CMG, apptd 1999

BRITISH HIGH COMMISSION
Ansbacher House (3rd Floor), East Street
PO Box N-7516, Nassau
T (+1 242) 325 7471
High Commissioner, HE Roderick Gemmell, OBE apptd 2003

DEFENCE

The Navy has seven patrol and coastal vessels, three harbour patrol units and four light aircraft.
MILITARY EXPENDITURE – 0.5 per cent of GDP (2002)
MILITARY PERSONNEL – Navy 860

ECONOMY AND TRADE

The Bahamas enjoy low inflation and have enjoyed sustained economic growth – making it the third wealthiest independent nation in the Americas.

Tourism (90 per cent of which originates from North America) employs about 40 per cent of the labour force and provides about half of the country's GDP. International banking and finance are also important, accounting for about 15 per cent of GDP. The absence of direct taxation coupled with internal stability have enabled the country to become one of the world's leading offshore financial centres. A securities exchange was opened in May 2000.

Manufacturing and agriculture account for less than 10 per cent of GDP. The most established industries are seafood, rum and salt. Agricultural production is mainly of fresh vegetables, fruit, meat and eggs. Reserves of aragonite and limestone are commercially exploited. Freeport is the country's leading industrial centre, with a pharmaceutical and chemicals plant, an oil trans-shipment and storage terminal, and port and bunkering facilities. There are also a brewery and a rum distillery on New Providence.

The imports are chiefly vehicles, manufactured articles, chemicals and petroleum. The chief exports are machinery and transport equipment, foodstuffs and livestock, raw materials, chemicals, manufactured goods, and beverages and tobacco.
GNI – US$20,100 per capita (2001)
ANNUAL AVERAGE GROWTH OF GDP – 2.2 per cent (1998)
INFLATION RATE – 1.3 per cent (2004)
UNEMPLOYMENT – 7.7 per cent (1998)
IMPORTS – US$1,614 billion (2002)
EXPORTS – US$649 million (2002)

BALANCE OF PAYMENTS
Trade – US$1,151 million deficit (2001)
Current Account – US$348 million deficit (2001)

Trade with UK	*2002*	*2003*
Imports from UK	£36,257,000	£27,561,000
Exports to UK	20,676,000	5,210,000

TRANSPORT INFRASTRUCTURE

The main ports are Nassau (New Providence), Freeport (Grand Bahama) and Matthew Town (Inagua). International air services are operated from Abaco, Bimini, Eleuthera, Exuma, Grand Bahama and New Providence. More than 60 smaller airports and landing strips facilitate services between the islands, the services being mainly provided by Bahamasair, the national carrier. The Bahamas has some 2,693 km of roads, 1,546 km of which are paved. There are no railways.

EDUCATION

Education is compulsory between the ages of five and 16. More than 66,000 students are enrolled in Ministry of Education and independent schools in New Providence and the Family Islands.
ILLITERACY RATE – (m) 5.0 per cent; (f) 3.6 per cent (2000)

CULTURE

The urban centres of the Bahamas, such as Nassau and Freeport, are heavily influenced by North American culture but many islands have retained a unique atmosphere. English is the dominant language but it is sprinkled with a colourful *patois*. There are strong musical traditions in the islands, 'rake 'n' scrape' bands comprising guitar, accordion and shakers, being particularly popular.

BAHRAIN

Dawlat al-Bahrayn – The Kingdom of Bahrain

AREA – 694 sq. km
POPULATION – 652,000 (2001); about 70 per cent are Bahraini; about 40 per cent of the Bahrainis are Sunni Muslims, the remaining 60 per cent being Shias; the ruling family and many of the most prominent merchants are Sunnis. The official language is Arabic; English is often used for business, and Farsi, Hindi and Urdu are also spoken
CAPITAL – ΨManama (Al-Manamah) (population, 140,401, 1991 census)
CURRENCY – Bahraini dinar (BD) of 1,000 fils

NATIONAL ANTHEM – Bahrayn Ona, Baladolaman (Our Bahrain, Secure)
NATIONAL DAY – 16 December
NATIONAL FLAG – Red, with vertical serrated white bar next to staff
LIFE EXPECTANCY (years) – 74 (2001)
MORTALITY RATE (per 1,000 population) – 3.99 (2003)
HIV / AIDS ADULT PREVALENCE – 0.3 per cent (2001)
INFANT MORTALITY (per 1,000 births) – 13 (2001)
DEATH PENALTY – Yes
POPULATION GROWTH RATE – 2.6 per cent (1990–2001)
POPULATION DENSITY – 939 per sq. km (2001)
ILLITERACY RATE – (m) 9.0 per cent; (f) 17.4 per cent (2000)

CLIMATE AND TERRAIN

Bahrain consists of a group of 33 low-lying islands situated approximately half-way down The Gulf, some 32 km off the east coast of Saudi Arabia. The largest of these, Bahrain Island, is about 48 km long and 16 km wide at its broadest, with the capital, Manama, situated on the north shore. The elevation extremes range from 122 m at the highest point (Jabal ad Dukhan) to 0 m at the lowest (Persian Gulf). The climate is hot and humid (with average annual temperatures ranging from 20°C to 40°C) with little rainfall.

HISTORY AND POLITICS

Bahrain is a constitutional monarchy and has been fully independent since 1971, when British protectorate status was ended. The 1973 constitution provided for a National Assembly but this was dissolved in 1975. A 40-member Consultative Council, the *Majlis al-Shura*, was appointed in September 1996 but this is an advisory body with no legislative powers. A new constitution providing for Bahrain to become a constitutional monarchy with a partially elected parliament was approved in December 2000, endorsed by a referendum, in which women were able to vote for the first time.

The first legislative elections since 1973 were held on 24 October 2002 when 174 candidates, including eight women, stood for 37 seats in the newly created House of Representatives. Moderate Sunni Islamists and Independents won 21 of the 40 seats. However, the country's main Shia opposition groups boycotted the poll, citing a proposed legislative right of veto by the Shura Council.

INSURGENCIES

Since 1994 Shi'ite protestors demanding the re-establishment of the National Assembly have regularly clashed with security forces and Shi'ite leaders have been detained. Opponents of the government have engaged in a sustained bombing campaign.

HEAD OF STATE

HH The Amir of Bahrain, C.-in -C., Bahrain Defence Force, Shaikh Hamad bin Isa al-Khalifa, KCMG *succeeded* 6 March 1999, *proclaimed king* 14 Feburary 2002
Crown Prince, Chair of the National Economic Development Council, Shaikh Salman bin Hamad al-Khalifa

SELECTED GOVERNMENT MEMBERS *as at July 2004*
Prime Minister, HH Shaikh Khalifa bin Sulman al-Khalifa
Deputy Prime Minister, Foreign Affairs, Shaikh Mohammed bin Mubarak al-Khalifa
Deputy Prime Minister, Islamic Affairs, Shaikh Abdullah bin Khalid al-Khalifa
Defence, Maj.-Gen. Shaikh Khalifa bin Ahmed al-Khalifa
Finance and National Economy, Abdullah Hassan Seif
Interior, Maj.-Gen. Shaikh Rashid bin Abdulla bin Ahmed al-Khalifa

EMBASSY OF THE KINGDOM OF BAHRAIN
Belgrave Square, London SW1X 8QB
T 020-7201 9170
Ambassador Extraordinary and Plenipotentiary, HE Shaikh Khalid bin Ahmed al Khalifa, apptd 2001

BRITISH EMBASSY
21 Government Avenue, Manama 306, PO Box 114
T (+973) 17574100
Ambassador Extraordinary and Plenipotentiary, HE Robin Lamb, apptd 2003

BRITISH COUNCIL DIRECTOR, Amanda Burrell
146 Shaikh Salman Highway, Manama 356, PO Box 452
T (+973) 17261555
E bc.enquiries@britishcouncil.org.bh

DEFENCE

The Army has 140 main battle tanks and 235 armoured personnel carriers. The Navy, based at Mina Salman, has one frigate and 10 patrol and coastal vessels. The Air Force has 34 combat aircraft and 40 armed helicopters.
MILITARY EXPENDITURE – 4.0 per cent of GDP (2002)
MILITARY PERSONNEL – 11,200: Army 8,500, Navy 1,200, Air Force 1,500; Paramilitaries 10,160

ECONOMY AND TRADE

The largest sources of revenue are oil production and refining. The Bahrain field, discovered in 1932, is wholly owned by the Bahrain National Oil Co. The Sitra refinery derives about 70 per cent of its crude oil by submarine pipeline from Saudi Arabia. Bahrain also has a half share with Saudi Arabia in the profits of the offshore Abu Sa'afa field. A reservoir of natural gas has recently been developed on Bahrain Island. Petroleum accounted for 60 per cent of total export value in 2002. There is some heavy industry on the islands that includes a ship-repairing industry and a number of small to medium-sized industrial units. Bahrain has continued to develop as a financial centre and as a tourist destination. Apart from several commercial banks, many international banks have been licensed as offshore units; there are also money brokers and merchant banks. Services accounted for 64 per cent of GDP in 2002.
GNI – US$7,250 million (2001); US$11,130 per capita (2001)
ANNUAL AVERAGE GROWTH OF GDP – 4.9 per cent (2003)
INFLATION RATE – –0.2 per cent (2003)
IMPORTS – US$4,985 billion (2002)
EXPORTS – US$5,369 billion (2002)

BALANCE OF PAYMENTS
Trade – US$1,536 million surplus (2001)
Current Account – US$157 million surplus (2001)

Trade with UK	*2002*	*2003*
Imports from UK	£132,414,000	£154,770,000
Exports to UK	77,724,000	80,552,000

TRANSPORT INFRASTRUCTURE

Bahrain International airport is one of the main air traffic centres of the Gulf; it is the headquarters of Gulf Air, and a stopping point on routes between Europe and Australia and the Far East for other airlines. A 25-km causeway links Bahrain to Saudi Arabia. Of the 3,261 km of road, over three quarters (2,531 km) is paved. There are no railways.

MEDIA

Domestic television and radio is state run by the Bahrain Radio and Television Corporation (BRTC). Bahrain has a free press but self-censorship is widely practised. There are four main daily newspapers, two of which are published in English. In 2002 there were 140,000 internet users.

CULTURE

Bahrain is one of the most liberal Gulf States. The capital, Manama, is typically modern but a slower, more traditional pace and way of life can still be found in the surrounding villages and islands.

BANGLADESH

Gaṇ Prajātantrī Bamlādeś – People's Republic of Bangladesh

AREA –130,200 sq. km. Neighbours: India (west, north and east), Myanmar (east)
POPULATION – 140,369,000 (2001). The state language is Bengali. Use of Bengali is compulsory in all government departments. English is understood and is used widely as an unofficial second language. The faith of 88 per cent of the population is Islam and 10.5 per cent Hinduism. Islam has been declared the state religion
CAPITAL – Dhaka (population, 9,912,908, 2001 census)
CURRENCY – Taka (Tk) of 100 paisa
NATIONAL ANTHEM – Amar Sonar Bangla (My Golden Bengal)
NATIONAL DAY – 26 March (Independence Day)
NATIONAL FLAG – Red circle on a bottle-green ground
LIFE EXPECTANCY (years) – 60 (2001)
MORTALITY RATE (per 1,000 population) – 8.63 (2003)
HIV / AIDS ADULT PREVALENCE – 0.1 per cent (2001)
INFANT MORTALITY (per 1,000 births) – 51 (2001)
DEATH PENALTY – Yes
POPULATION LIVING BELOW POVERTY LINE – 33.7 per cent (2000)
POPULATION GROWTH RATE – 2.2 per cent (1990–2001)
POPULATION DENSITY – 1,078 per sq. km (2001)
URBAN POPULATION – 26 per cent (2001)

CLIMATE AND TERRAIN

The climate is tropical: hot, wet and extremely humid during the summer, and mild and dry during the winter.

The country is crossed by a network of rivers, including the eastern arms of the Ganges (Padma), the Jamuna (Brahmaputra) and the Meghna, flowing into the Bay of Bengal. About a third of the country floods every year during the monsoon season (June to September). Heavy flooding during the summer of 1998 left 23 million people homeless and killed 1,500.

The elevation extremes range from the highest point at 1,230 m (Keokradong) to the lowest at 0 m (Indian Ocean). Bangladesh is located in a high-risk earthquake zone.

HISTORY AND POLITICS

Prior to becoming the eastern province of Pakistan, Bangladesh had been the region of East Bengal and the Sylhet district of Assam of British India. The territory acceded to Pakistan in August 1947, then became a republic on 23 March 1956. Bangladesh achieved its independence from Pakistan on 16 December 1971, following a civil war. Pakistan and Bangladesh accorded one another mutual recognition in 1974.

In 1975 a one-party presidential system was introduced by the ruling Awami League, but this was replaced by a multiparty presidential system of government in 1978 by President Zia Rahman. After President Zia's assassination in 1981, Justice Abdus Sattar became President and was overthrown in a coup led by Army Chief Gen. Ershad in 1982. Following parliamentary elections in 1986, Gen. Ershad was elected president. Popular unrest forced his resignation in December 1990; the Bangladesh Nationalist Party (BNP) won the subsequent parliamentary elections. In August 1991 a constitutional amendment returned Bangladesh to parliamentary rule.

In December 1994, the opposition parties resigned from parliament, demanding fresh elections. Public disorder persisted despite a general election in 1996 which was won by the BNP, although turnout was a mere five per cent. In March 1996, Prime Minister Zia agreed to new elections; these elections in June 1996 produced a majority for the Awami League under Prime Minister Sheikh Hasina Wajed. In 1997 the BNP walked out of parliament, accusing the government of repression. They returned the following year after signing a memorandum of understanding with the government.

Border clashes occurred between Bangladeshi and Indian troops on the northern border in 2001.

In the elections of 2001, held under a caretaker government, the BNP-led four party alliance won more than two-thirds of the seats in Parliament. In October, Khaleda Zia was sworn in as prime minister for a fourth time. President Badruddoza Chowdhury resigned in June 2002 and Jamiruddin Sircar was appointed acting president. Iajuddin Ahmed was elected president in September 2002.

POLITICAL SYSTEM

There is a unicameral parliament *(Jatiya Sangsad)* of 300 directly elected members who can amend the constitution by a two-thirds majority.

HEAD OF STATE

President, Iajuddin Ahmed, *elected by Parliament* 5 September 2002

SELECTED GOVERNMENT MEMBERS *as at July 2004*
Prime Minister, Armed Forces Division, Cabinet Division, Defence, Establishment, Energy and Minerals, Hill Tracts Affairs, Primary and Mass Education, Khaleda Zia
Finance and Planning, Saifur Rahman
Foreign Affairs, Morshed Khan
Minister of Law, Justice and Parliamentary Affairs, Moudad Ahmed

BANGLADESH HIGH COMMISSION
28 Queen's Gate, London SW7 5JA
T 020-7584 0081
High Commissioner, HE A. H. Mofazzal Karim

BRITISH HIGH COMMISSION
United Nations Road, Baridhara,
PO Box 6079, Dhaka-1212
T (+880) (2) 882 2705
High Commissioner, HE Anwar Chowdry

BRITISH COUNCIL DIRECTOR, Dr June Rollinson
5 Fuller Road, PO Box 161, Dhaka 1000
T (+880) (2) 861 8905/7
E dhaka.enquiries@bd.britishcouncil.org

DEFENCE

The army has 180 main battle tanks and 130 armoured personnel carriers. The Navy has five frigates and 33 patrol and coastal vessels. The Air Force has 83 combat aircraft.
MILITARY EXPENDITURE – 1.4 per cent of GDP (2002)
MILITARY PERSONNEL – 125,500: Army 110,000, Navy 9,000, Air Force 6,500; Paramilitaries 63,200

ECONOMY AND TRADE

Bangladesh remains reliant on food production through agriculture, a primary occupation of over 70 per cent of the population. Products include rice, wheat, tobacco, tea, oil seeds, pulses and sugar cane. The chief industries are jute, cotton, tea, leather, pharmaceuticals, fertiliser, sugar, prawn fishing and natural gas. Garment manufacturing is the main export providing 73 per cent of export earnings (2003). Remittances sent home by Bangladeshis abroad are of considerable significance to the economy.

International financial institutions agreed in 2000 to provide around US$2,000 million in additional aid over a 20-year period dependent on the introduction of free-market reforms.
GNI – US$48,600 million (2001); US$360 per capita (2001)
ANNUAL AVERAGE GROWTH OF GDP – 5.3 per cent (2001)
INFLATION RATE – 2.3 per cent (2000)
TOTAL EXTERNAL DEBT – US$16,500 million (2002)
FOREIGN DIRECT INVESTMENT – US$902 million (1997–2000)
IMPORTS – US$7,914million (2002)
EXPORTS – US$4,566 million (2002)

BALANCE OF PAYMENTS
Current Account – US$535 million deficit (2001)
Trade – US$2,049 million deficit (2001)

Trade with UK	*2002*	*2003*
Imports from UK	£66,185,000	£56,001,000
Exports to UK	481,836,000	570,802,000

TRANSPORT INFRASTRUCTURE

Principal seaports are Chittagong and Mongla. The Bangladesh Shipping Corporation was set up by the government to operate the Bangladesh merchant fleet. The principal airports are Dhaka (Zia International) and Chittagong. The international airline, Bangladesh Biman, serves Europe, the Middle East, South and South-East Asia, and an internal network. There are 2,706 km of railways, including a railway line linking the Bangladeshi town of Benapol with Petrapol in India. The country's 207,486-km road network has only 19,773 km of paved roads.

EDUCATION

Primary education is compulsory and free. There are 16 public universities, 29 private universities and more than 600 colleges.
ILLITERACY RATE – (m) 46.1 per cent; (f) 68.2 per cent (2003)
ENROLMENT (percentage of age group) – primary 96.6 per cent (2000); secondary 42.8 per cent (2000); tertiary 4.4 per cent (1990)

MEDIA

The main broadcast media (Bangladesh Television, (BTV)) is subject to censorship and is state owned. The main commercial stations are ATN Bangla TV and Channel i. The four main newspapers are *The Daily Star, The Dhaka Courier, The Independent* and *The New Nation.*

CULTURE

Bangladesh has a rich and ancient culture. Religious, theatre and folk traditions have Buddhist, Hindu and Muslim roots. Literature is dominated by the reputation of the great Bengali poet Rabindranath Tagore (1861–1941).

BARBADOS

AREA – 431 sq. km
POPULATION – 277,264 (2003). The official language is English
CAPITAL – ΨBridgetown in the parish of St Michael (population, 108,000, 1990)
MAJOR TOWNS – Holetown in St James, Oistins in Christ Church and Speightstown in St Peter
CURRENCY – Barbados dollar (BD$) of 100 cents
NATIONAL ANTHEM – In Plenty And In Time Of Need
NATIONAL DAY– 30 November (Independence Day)
NATIONAL FLAG – Three vertical stripes, aquamarine, gold and aquamarine, with a trident head on gold stripe
LIFE EXPECTANCY (years) – 77 (2001)
MORTALITY RATE (per 1,000 population) – 9.02
INFANT MORTALITY (per 1,000 births) – 12 (2001)
HIV / AIDS ADULT PREVALENCE RATE – 1.2 per cent
DEATH PENALTY – Yes
POPULATION GROWTH RATE – 0.4 per cent (1990–2001)
POPULATION DENSITY – 622 per sq. km (2001)
URBAN POPULATION – 51 per cent (2001)
MILITARY EXPENDITURE – 0.5 per cent of GDP (2001)
MILITARY PERSONNEL – 610: Army 500, Navy 110

CLIMATE AND TERRAIN

Barbados is the most easterly of the Caribbean islands. The climate is tropical (the wet season is June to October) and the island is subject to occasional hurricanes. The land rises in a series of terraced tablelands and elevation extremes range from 336 m (Mt Hillaby) at the highest point to 0 m (Atlantic Ocean) at the lowest.

HISTORY AND POLITICS

The first inhabitants of Barbados were Arawak Indians but the island was uninhabited when settled by the British in 1627. It was a Crown Colony from 1652 during which time sugar, rum and molasses were its chief products. Barbados became an independent state within the Commonwealth on 30 November 1966.

In the general election of 2003 the governing Barbados Labour Party (BLP) won 23 seats in the 30-seat House of Assembly with the Democratic Labour Party (DLP) gaining seven seats.

POLITICAL SYSTEM

The head of state is the British sovereign whose local representative is the Governor-General. The legislature consists of a Senate and a House of Assembly. The Senate comprises 21 Senators appointed by the Governor-General for a five-year term, of whom 12 are appointed on the advice of the Prime Minister, two on the advice of the Leader of the Opposition and seven by the Governor-General at his/her discretion to represent religious, economic or social interests. The House of Assembly comprises 30 members elected every five years by adult suffrage.

There are 11 administrative areas (parishes): St Michael, Christ Church, St Andrew, St George, St James, St John, St Joseph, St Lucy, St Peter, St Philip and St Thomas.

Governor-General, HE Sir Clifford Husbands, GCMG, KA, apptd June 1996

SELECTED GOVERNMENT MEMBERS *as at July 2004*
Prime Minister, Defence and Security, Finance and Economic Affairs, Owen Arthur
Deputy Prime Minister, Attorney-General, Home Affairs, Mia Mottley
Commerce, Consumer Affairs and Business Development, Lynette Eastmond
Foreign Affairs, Foreign Trade, Billie Miller
Minister of State, Foreign Affairs and Foreign Trade, Kerrie Symmonds

BARBADOS HIGH COMMISSION
1 Great Russell Street, London WC1B 3ND
T 020-7631 4975
High Commissioner, HE Edwin Pollard

BRITISH HIGH COMMISSION
Lower Collymore Rock, PO Box 676, Bridgetown
T (+1 246) 430 7800
E britishhc@sunbeach.net
High Commissioner, HE C. John White, apptd 2001

ECONOMY AND TRADE

The economy has suffered as a result of the downturn in tourism in recent years, but offshore finance and information services remain a valuable source of foreign exchange earnings. Chief exports are sugar, chemicals, electronic components and clothing.

GNI – US$2,610 million (2001); US$9,750 per capita (2001)
ANNUAL AVERAGE GROWTH OF GDP – 2.5 per cent (1999)
INFLATION RATE – 2.4 per cent (2000)
UNEMPLOYMENT – 10.5 per cent (1999)
TOTAL EXTERNAL DEBT – US$589 million (1999)
IMPORTS – US$1,039 million (2002)
EXPORTS – US$206 million (2002)

BALANCE OF PAYMENTS
Trade – US$681 million deficit (2001)
Current Account – US$94 million deficit (2001)

Trade with UK	*2002*	*2003*
Imports from UK	£39,600,000	£52,347,000
Exports to UK	25,008,000	20,921,000

TRANSPORT INFRASTRUCTURE

Barbados has some 1,793 km of roads, of which only 74 km are not surfaced. The Grantley Adams International airport is situated at Seawell, 19 km from Bridgetown. Bridgetown, the only port of entry, has a deep-water harbour with berths for eight ships; oil is pumped ashore at Spring Garden and at an Esso installation on the west coast.

EDUCATION

Education is free in government schools at primary (ages four to 11) and secondary (ages 11 to 18) levels. There are 74 government primary schools, 30 private primary schools, 23 government secondary schools and ten private secondary schools. Tertiary education is provided by a teachers college, a polytechnic, a community college and one of the three campuses of the University of the West Indies (the other two are on Trinidad and Jamaica).

ILLITERACY RATE – (m) 2 per cent; (f) 3.2 per cent (2003)

BELARUS

Respublika Belarus – Republic of Belarus

AREA – 207,500 sq. km. Neighbours: Latvia and Lithuania (north), Russia (east), Ukraine (south), Poland (west)
POPULATION – 10,147,000 (2001): 78 per cent Belarusian, 13 per cent Russian, 4 per cent Polish and 3 per cent Ukrainian, with smaller numbers of Jews and Lithuanians. Belarusian and Russian have equal official language status. Most of the population are Belarusian Orthodox with a minority of Roman Catholics
CAPITAL – Minsk (population, 1,725,100); the administrative centre of the CIS
MAJOR CITIES – Brest; Homyel; Hrodna; Mahilyow; Vitsyebsk
CURRENCY – Belarusian rouble
NATIONAL ANTHEM – The former Soviet national anthem but with the words omitted
NATIONAL DAY – 3 July (Independence Day)
NATIONAL FLAG – Red with a green strip along the lower edge, and in the hoist a vertical red and white ornamental pattern
LIFE EXPECTANCY (years) – 69 (2001)
MORTALITY RATE (per 1,000 population) – 14.05 (2003)
HIV / AIDS ADULT PREVALENCE – 0.3 per cent (2001)
DEATH PENALTY – Yes
INFANT MORTALITY (per 1,000 births) – 17 (2001)
POPULATION BELOW POVERTY LINE – 22 per cent (1995)
POPULATION GROWTH RATE – 0.1 per cent (1990–2001)
POPULATION DENSITY – 49 per sq. km (2001)
URBAN POPULATION – 70 per cent (2001)

CLIMATE AND TERRAIN

Belarus is a landlocked country situated in the western part of the European area of the former USSR. The main rivers are the upper reaches of the Dnieper, of the Niemen and of the Western Dvina. Much of the land is a plain, with many lakes, forests, swamps and marshy areas. The climate is continental with mild, humid winters and relatively cool and rainy summers. Elevation extremes range from 346 m (Dzyarzhynskaya Hara) at the highest point to 90 m (Nyoman River) at the lowest.

HISTORY AND POLITICS

After being absorbed into Lithuania in the 13th century, Belarus flourished as a culturally significant medieval state. A period of Polish rule followed, but was superseded in the 18th century by a steadily expanding Russian Empire.

Belarus was devastated by German invasion in the Second World War; 25 per cent of the population was killed and thousands deported.

Belarus issued a Declaration of State Sovereignty on 27 July 1990 and declared its independence from the Soviet Union after the failed coup in Moscow in August 1991. Stanislav Shuskevich became Belarusian leader at the head of a coalition of communists and democrats, but he was forced to resign in January 1994 and was replaced by Gen. Mecheslav Grib who pursued closer political, economic and trade relations with Russia. The presidential election in June 1994 was won by Alexander Lukashenko.

The legislative election held in October 2000 was condemned as neither free nor fair by opposition groups and international observers from the Organisation for Security and Co-operation in Europe (OSCE), the European Parliament and the Council of Europe. Most opposition parties boycotted the election and many opposition candidates were prevented from standing or intimidated into withdrawing by the authorities. Repeat elections were held in 13 of the 110 constituencies of the House of Representatives in March and April 2001. In the presidential elections held in September 2001 Lukashenko was re-elected with more than 75 per cent of the vote. Observers from the Commonwealth of Independent States (CIS) stated that the election was legitimate but observers from the OSCE announced that the election did not comply with OSCE standards. During 2002 the Belarusian authorities refused to renew the visas of OSCE staff but in December 2002 an agreement to open a new office in Minsk was reached and OSCE staff were readmitted to the country. This led to the lifting in April 2003 of travel bans imposed by the EU and the USA on President Lukashenko and seven other senior Belarusian officials because of the country's poor human rights record.

FOREIGN RELATIONS

An agreement was signed with Russia in April 1996 to form a Commonwealth of Independent States (CIS). In April 1997 a treaty of union was signed with Russia. On 8 December 1999, the presidents of Belarus and Russia signed the Treaty on the Creation of a Union State, which committed the two countries to eventually becoming a confederal state.

POLITICAL SYSTEM

The President's term of office is five years. The President has the authority to appoint half the members of the constitutional court and the electoral commission. The legislature is the bicameral National Assembly, comprising a 110-member House of Representatives (lower chamber) and a 64-member Council of the Republic (upper chamber). Eight members of the upper chamber are appointed by the President, the rest are indirectly elected by members of the local soviets (councils) in each region. Legislative elections were due to take place in October 2004.

HEAD OF STATE

President, Alexander Lukashenko, *elected* 10 July 1994, *re-elected* 9 September 2001

SELECTED GOVERNMENT MEMBERS *as at July 2004*

Prime Minister, Sergei Sidorsky
First Deputy Prime Minister, Vladimir I. Semashko
Deputy Prime Ministers, Roman Vnuchko *(Agroindustrial Complex)*; Andrei Kobyakov *(Economics, Trade and International Co-operation)*; Anatoly Tsutsunov; Vladimir Drazhin *(Labour and Social Security, Social Affairs, Science)*
Defence, Col.-Gen. Leonid Maltsev
Finance, Nikolai Korbut
Foreign Affairs, Sergei Martynov
Internal Affairs, Maj.-Gen. Vladimir Naumov

EMBASSY OF THE REPUBLIC OF BELARUS

6 Kensington Court, London W8 5DL
T 020-7937 3288
Ambassador Extraordinary and Plenipotentiary, HE Dr Alyaksei Mazhukhou, apptd 2002

BRITISH EMBASSY
37 Karl Marx Street, 220030 Minsk
T (+375) (172) 105920
E pia@bepost.belpak.minsk.by
Ambassador Extraordinary and Plenipotentiary, HE Brian Bennett, apptd 2002

DEFENCE

The Army has 1,586 main battle tanks, 1,588 armoured infantry fighting vehicles and 916 armoured personnel carriers. The Air Force has 210 combat aircraft and 50 armed helicopters.

MILITARY EXPENDITURE – 2.5 per cent of GDP (2001)
MILITARY PERSONNEL – 72,940: Army 29,600, Central Units 25,170, Air Force and Air Defence Forces 18,170; Paramilitaries 110,000
CONSCRIPTION DURATION – Nine to 12 months

ECONOMY AND TRADE

In May 1995 a customs union agreement with Russia took effect. A treaty was signed with Kazakhstan, Kyrgyzstan and Russia in March 1996 aimed at the establishment of a single customs territory. In 2000 the National Bank of Belarus (NBB) took action to liberalise the exchange market but it continues to struggle to maintain a stable exchange rate.

Industrial output increased 2.5 per cent in 2002. The principal industries are transport vehicles, machine-building, electronics, defence, chemicals and civil engineering.

GNI – US$12,900 million (2001); US$1,290 per capita (2001)
AVERAGE ANNUAL GROWTH OF GDP – 4.7 per cent (2002)
INFLATION RATE – 168.6 per cent (2000)
UNEMPLOYMENT – 2.1 per cent (2000)
TOTAL EXTERNAL DEBT – US$851 million (2000)
FOREIGN DIRECT INVESTMENT – US$664 million (1997–2000)
IMPORTS – US$8,980 million (2002)
EXPORTS – US$8,098 million (2002)

BALANCE OF PAYMENTS
Trade – US$779 million deficit (2001)
Current Account – US$270 million deficit (2001)

Trade with UK	*2002*	*2003*
Imports from UK	£34,432,000	£39,182,000
Exports to UK	33,838,000	22,672,000

TRANSPORT INFRASTRUCTURE

Belarus has 5,523 km of railways and an extensive canal and river system. Of the 74,385 km of roads only 8,182 km are unsurfaced but many are in bad repair. Of the 124 airports, 28 have paved runways.

EDUCATION

The national education system comprises pre-school, general secondary, out-of-school, vocational training and trade schools, secondary specialised and higher education. General secondary education begins at the age of six.

ILLITERACY RATE – (m) 0.2 per cent; (f) 0.5 per cent (2003)
ENROLMENT (percentage of age group) – primary 98 per cent (1997); tertiary 44.0 per cent (1997)

MEDIA

A Soviet-era attitude to press freedom remains as government controls media content and the appointment of senior editors in the print and broadcast media. State run newspapers and television channels receive large subsidies and support government policies. The most popular privately owned newspaper is *Belorusskaya Delovaya Gazeta*. The Belarusian National State Teleradio Company operates domestic radio and TV channels. Radio Baltic Waves (Baltijos Bangos) is a private broadcaster that targets Belarusian audiences but operates from Vilnius in Lithuania. In 2002 there were 808,700 internet users.

CULTURE

Belarus has a strong musical tradition – in the form of Orthodox hymns and sermons as well as secular folk music – both ancient and modern. The literature of Belarus is very distinguished with the 17th-century poet Symeon of Polatsk being most influential in introducing the Baroque style to Russia. The country's most famous 20th-century writer is Natalia Arseneva, author of *Beneath the Blue Sky*.

BELGIUM

Koninkrijk België / Royaume de Belgique / Königreich Belgien – Kingdom of Belgium

AREA – 30,200 sq. km. Neighbours: the Netherlands (north), France (south), Germany and Luxembourg (east)
POPULATION – 10,309,725 (2002). Greater Brussels 978,384; Flanders 5,972,781; Wallonia 3,358,560. Roman Catholicism is the religion of 86 per cent of the population. The official languages are Flemish, French and German
CAPITAL – Brussels (population, 978,384, 2002)
MAJOR CITIES – ΨAntwerp, the chief port; Bruges; Charleroi; ΨGhent; Liège; Leuven; Mons; Namur
CURRENCY – Euro (€) of 100 cents
NATIONAL ANTHEM – O Vaderland, O Edel Land Der Belgen (Oh Fatherland, Oh Noble Land Of The Belgians)
NATIONAL DAY – 21 July (Accession of King Leopold I, 1831)
NATIONAL FLAG – Three vertical bands, black, yellow, red
LIFE EXPECTANCY (years) – 79 (2001)
MORTALITY RATE (per 1,000 population) – 10.7 (2003)
HIV / AIDS ADULT PREVALENCE RATE – 0.2 per cent (2001)
INFANT MORTALITY (per 1,000 births) – 5 (2001)
DEATH PENALTY – No (abolished 1996)
POPULATION GROWTH RATE – 0.3 per cent (1990–2001)
POPULATION DENSITY – 340 per sq. km (2001)
URBAN POPULATION – 97 per cent (2001)

CLIMATE AND TERRAIN

Belgium is divided into two distinct and contrasting regions. The west of the country is generally low-lying and fertile, while the eastern region, the tableland of the Ardennes, is more rugged with poorer soil. Elevation extremes range from 0 m sea level (North Sea) to 694 m at the highest point (Signal de Botrange). The polders near the coast, which are protected by dykes against floods, cover an area of 499 sq. km. The principal rivers are the Schelde and the Maas. Average temperatures range from 2°C in January to 18°C in July.

HISTORY AND POLITICS

The kingdom formed part of the Low Countries (Netherlands) from 1815 until 14 October 1830, when a National Congress proclaimed its independence. Belgium was invaded by Germany in 1914 and Eupen and Malmédy were ceded to Belgium by Germany under the Versailles Treaty of 1919. The kingdom was again invaded by Germany in 1940 and was occupied by Nazi troops until liberated by the Allies in September 1944.

A general election was held in 2003 and a coalition government of Liberals and Socialists was sworn in on 12 July with Guy Verhofstadt of the Liberals and Democrats (VLD) as prime minister.

POLITICAL SYSTEM

Belgium is a constitutional representative and hereditary monarchy with a bicameral legislature, consisting of the King, the Senate and the Chamber of Deputies. The parliamentary term is four years. Amendments to the constitution since 1968 have devolved power to the regions. The national government retains competence only in foreign and defence policies, the national budget and monetary policy, social security, and the judicial, legal and penal systems. The Senate has 71 seats, of which 40 are directly elected, 21 indirectly elected and ten co-opted by the Flemish and Francophone Communities. The Chamber of Deputies has 150 seats.

FEDERAL STRUCTURE

There are three communities: Flemish, Francophone, Germanophone. Each community has its own assembly, which elects the community government. At this level, Flanders is covered by the Flemish Community Assembly; most of Wallonia is covered by the Francophone Community Assembly, and the areas of Wallonia in the German-speaking communities of Eupen and Malmédy are covered by the Germanophone Community Assembly; Brussels is covered by a Joint Community Commission of the Flemish and Francophone Community Assemblies.

At regional level, Belgium is divided into the three regions of Wallonia, Brussels and Flanders. Each region has its own assembly and government.

The ten provinces of Belgium are (with 2002 population): Antwerp (1,652,450); East Flanders (1,366,652); Flemish Brabant (1,022,821); Limburg (798,583); West Flanders (1,132,275); Hainaut (1,281,042); Liege (1,024,130); Luxembourg (250,406); Namur (447,775); Walloon Brabant (355,207). In addition, Belgium has 589 communes as the lowest level of local government.

Minister-President of the Flemish Community and Flemish Region, Patrick Dewael
Minister-President of the Walloon Region, Jean-Claude Van Cauwenberghe
Minister-President of the French Community, Hervé Hasquin
Minister-President of the German-Speaking Community, Karl-Heinz Lambertz
Minister-President of the Brussels Capital Government, Jacques Simonet

HEAD OF STATE
HM The King of the Belgians, King Albert II, *born* 6 June 1934; *succeeded* 9 August 1993; *Heir,* HRH Prince Philippe Léopold Louis Marie, *born* 15 April 1960

SELECTED GOVERNMENT MEMBERS *as at July 2004*
Prime Minister, Guy Verhofstadt
Deputy Prime Minister and Minister for Budget and Private Enterprise, Johan Vande Lanotte
Deputy Prime Minister and Minister for Foreign Affairs, Louis Michel
Deputy Prime Minister for Interior, Patrick Dewael
Deputy Prime Minister and Minister of Justice, Laurette Onkelinx
Minister for Defence, André Flahaut
Minister of Finance, Didier Reynders

BELGIAN EMBASSY
103 Eaton Square, London SW1W 9AB
T 020-7470 3700
Ambassador Extraordinary and Plenipotentiary, HE Thierry de Grüben, apptd 2002

BRITISH EMBASSY
Rue d'Arlon 85 Aarlenstraat, B-1040 Brussels
T (+32) (2) 287 6211
Ambassador Extraordinary and Plenipotentiary, HE Richard Kinchen

BRITISH COUNCIL DIRECTOR FOR BELGIUM AND LUXEMBOURG – Dr Ray Thomas
Leopold Plaza, Rue de Trône 108 Troonstraat, B-1050 Brussels
T (+32) (2) 227 0840
E enquiries@britishcouncil.be

DEFENCE

The Army has 143 main battle tanks, 332 armoured personnel carriers, 236 armoured infantry fighting vehicles and 74 helicopters. The Navy is based at Ostend and Zeebrugge and has three frigates. The Air Force has 90 combat aircraft.

The headquarters of NATO, SHAPE and the Western European Union Military Planning Cell are in Belgium; 1,400 US personnel are stationed in the country.

MILITARY EXPENDITURE – 1.3 per cent of GDP (2002)
MILITARY PERSONNEL – 37,500: Army 24,800, Navy 2,450, Air Force 10,250

ECONOMY AND TRADE

The establishment of the European Commission and other EU institutions in Belgium in the 1950s brought multinational companies to the country and promoted the service sector which accounts for over two-thirds of Belgium's GDP. With no natural resources except coal, production of which has now ceased, industry is based largely on the processing of imported raw materials for export. Principal industries are steel and metal products, chemicals and petrochemicals, textiles, glass, and foodstuffs. Industry accounts for 24.4 per cent of GDP and services for 74.3 per cent (2001) – significantly lower than in previous years. In 2002 public debt was 100 per cent of GDP.

Belgium adopted the euro as its unit of currency on 1 January 2001.

External trade figures relate to Luxembourg as well as Belgium since the two countries formed an economic union in 1921. The main trading partners are Germany, France, the Netherlands and the UK. Around 75 per cent of Belgium's trade is with other European Union countries.

GNI – US$245,300 million (2001); US$23,850 per capita (2001)
ANNUAL AVERAGE GROWTH OF GDP – 4.0 per cent (2000)
INFLATION RATE – 2.5 per cent (2000)
UNEMPLOYMENT – 7.0 per cent (2000)
IMPORTS – US$195,940 million (2002)
EXPORTS – US$213 481 million (2002)

BALANCE OF PAYMENTS
Trade – US$5,955 million surplus (Belgium and Luxembourg) (2002)
Current Account – US$11,515 million surplus (2002)

Trade with UK	*2002*	*2003*
Imports from UK	£9,733,000,000	£8,091,023,000
Exports to UK	11,317,000,000	8,841,482,000

TRANSPORT INFRASTRUCTURE

The rail system is run by Belgian National Railways and at 3,471 km the network is one of the densest in the world. Major ports include Antwerp (the third largest port in Europe), Zeebrugge, Ghent and Ostend. There are 1,570 km of inland waterways; ship canals link Ghent with Terneuzen in the Netherlands, Willebroek Rupel with Brussels, Zeebrugge with Bruges, Liège with Antwerp and Charleroi with Brussels. The rivers Maas, Sambre and Schelde form an integral part of the network. There are nearly 148,216 km of roads, including 1,727 km of motorways.

EDUCATION

Nursery schools provide free education for children from two-and-a-half to six years. There are over 4,000 primary schools (six to 12 years), more than 1,000 secondary schools offering a general academic education, slightly over half of which are free institutions (predominantly Roman Catholic and subsidised by the state) and the remainder official institutions. The official school-leaving age is 18.

ENROLMENT (percentage of age group) – primary 100 per cent (1997); secondary 100 per cent (1997); tertiary 100 per cent (1997)

MEDIA

The Belgian media reflects the multi-lingual population. There are two broadcasting authorities with programming priorities in radio, TV and external broadcasting. RTBF is the French-language broadcaster. VRT is the Flemish broadcaster. There are also French and Flemish commercial television channels and Belgischer Rundfunk (BRF), a German-language radio broadcaster. Cable television is very popular with 95 per cent of the population subscribing to domestic and foreign channels. A small number of media groups own and run the main news publications. In 2002 there were 3.76 million internet users.

CULTURE

Brussels is a powerful European capital due to its status as the headquarters of the European Union and the North Atlantic Treaty Organisation (NATO).

Bruges, Belgium's top tourist destination, is a beautifully-preserved 13th-century town and is home to several excellent art collections.

Belgium is defined by language. The country is divided between those who speak Dutch (the Flemings) and those who speak French (the Walloons). Dutch is recognised as the official language in the northern areas and French in the southern (Walloon) area. Brussels is officially bilingual. There is a small German-speaking area (Eupen and Malmédy) along the German border, east of Liège. Famous Belgian writers include Georges Simenon (1903–89) and Jean Ray (1887–1954).

BELIZE

AREA – 22,800 sq. km. Neighbours: Mexico (north and north-west), Guatemala (west and south)
POPULATION – 231,000 (2001): 44 per cent Mestizo (Maya-Spanish); 26 per cent Creole; 11 per cent Maya; plus a number of East Indian and Spanish descent. The races are now inter-mixed. The majority of the population is Christian, about 58 per cent Catholic and 34 per cent Protestant. The official language and language of instruction is English. Spanish is also widely spoken and English Creole is the vernacular. There are also Garifuna and Maya speakers
CAPITAL – Belmopan (population, 8,130, 2000 census)
MAJOR CITIES – ΨBelize City, the former capital; Corozal; Dangriga; Orange Walk; San Ignacio
CURRENCY – Belize dollar (BZ$) of 100 cents. The Belize dollar is tied to the US dollar
NATIONAL ANTHEM – Land Of The Free
NATIONAL DAY – 21 September (Independence Day)
NATIONAL FLAG – Blue ground with red band along top and bottom edges, and in the centre a white disc containing the coat of arms surrounded by a green garland
LIFE EXPECTANCY (years) – 74 (2001)
MORTALITY RATE (per 1,000 population) – 6.05 (2001)
INFANT MORTALITY (per 1,000 births) – 34 (2001)
HIV / AIDS ADULT PREVALENCE RATE – 2 per cent (2001)
DEATH PENALTY – Yes
POPULATION BELOW POVERTY LINE – 33 per cent (1999)
POPULATION GROWTH RATE – 2 per cent (1990–2001)
POPULATION DENSITY – 10 per sq. km (2001)
URBAN POPULATION – 48 per cent (2001)
MILITARY EXPENDITURE – 2.3 per cent of GDP (2002)
MILITARY PERSONNEL – Army 1,050

CLIMATE AND TERRAIN

Belize comprises a large coastal plain, swamps (in the north), fertile land (in the south) and the Maya Mountains. The highest point of elevation is 1,160 m (Victoria Peak), the lowest is at 0 m (Caribbean Sea). The climate is subtropical but is cooled by trade winds. There are frequent hurricanes (the hurricane season is June to November). Belize's inner coastal waters are protected by the world's second-largest barrier reef.

HISTORY AND POLITICS

Numerous ruins in the area indicate that Belize was heavily populated by the Maya Indians. The first British settlement was established in 1638 but was subject to repeated attacks by the Spanish, who claimed sovereignty until defeated by the British Royal Navy and settlers in 1798. In 1871 the area was recognised by Britain as a colony and called British Honduras. The colony became self-governing in 1964, with the UK retaining control of foreign policy, internal security and defence. In 1973 the colony was renamed Belize, and was granted independence on 21 September 1981.

The general election held in 2003 was won by the ruling People's United Party who took 22 of the 29 seats in the House of Representatives.

FOREIGN RELATIONS

There has been a longstanding territorial dispute with Guatemala which claims half of the territory of Belize. In September 2002 Belize and Guatemala agreed on a draft settlement to the dispute but by August 2003 Guatemala had informed the Organisation of American States (OAS), the brokers of the agreement, that it could not accept the terms of the settlement. The OAS continues to work with Guatemala and Belize to resolve the dispute.

POLITICAL SYSTEM

Queen Elizabeth II is head of state, represented in Belize by a Governor-General. There is a bicameral National Assembly, comprising a House of Representatives (29 members directly elected for five years) and a Senate (13 members appointed by the Governor-General, including seven on the advice of the Prime Minister, three on the advice of the opposition leader, and one each from the National Trade Union Congress of Civil Society, the Belize Council of Churches and the Belize Chamber of Commerce). Executive power is vested in the Cabinet, which is responsible to the National Assembly.

Governor-General, HE Sir Colville Norbert Young, GCMG, apptd 17 November 1993

SELECTED GOVERNMENT MEMBERS *as at July 2004*

Prime Minister, Education and Public Service, Said Musa
Deputy Prime Minister, Natural Resources, Environment, Commerce and Industry, John Briceo
Foreign Affairs, Defence and National Emergency Management, Godfrey Smith
Home Affairs, Finance and Investment, Ralph Fonseca

BELIZE HIGH COMMISSION
22 Harcourt House, 19 Cavendish Square, London W1G 0PL
T 020-7499 9728
High Commissioner, HE Alexis Rosado, apptd 2002

BRITISH HIGH COMMISSION
PO Box 91, Belmopan
T (+501) (8222146
E brithicom@btl.net
High Commissioner, HE Philip Priestley, CBE, apptd 2001

ECONOMY AND TRADE

About 27 per cent of the population is engaged in agriculture, which along with fishing accounted for more than 60 per cent of export revenue in 2002. The country is more or less self-sufficient in fresh beef, pork and poultry, but processed meat and dairy products are imported. About 25 per cent of timber production (mostly mahogany) is exported and there is a large US market for lobster, conch and scale fish. The main export items are sugar, citrus fruits and juice, bananas and marine products. The UK and the USA account for over 90 per cent of export revenue. Tourism is the second largest foreign exchange earner after agriculture, providing over 20 per cent of GDP in 2001.

GNI – US$730 million (2001); US$2,940 per capita (2001)
ANNUAL AVERAGE GROWTH OF GDP – 8.9 per cent (2000)
INFLATION RATE – 0.6 per cent (2000)
TOTAL EXTERNAL DEBT – US$499 million (2000)
IMPORTS – US$409 million (2001)
EXPORTS – US$166 million (2001)

BALANCE OF PAYMENTS
Trade – US$191 million deficit (2000)
Current Account – US$139 million deficit (2000)

Trade with UK	*2002*	*2003*
Imports from UK	£13,710,000	£17,405,000
Exports to UK	31,559,000	42,000,000

TRANSPORT INFRASTRUCTURE

The principal airport is at Belize City and various airlines operate international flights to the USA and other Central American states. The main port is also Belize City, which has deep water quays. Several inland waterways are navigable. There are 2,984 km of roads, including four main highways, but there is no railway system.

EDUCATION

Education is free and compulsory from six to 14 years of age. There are 280 government and government-aided primary schools, 30 secondary schools and 11 tertiary institutions. The government maintains some schools but most are run by churches. The government administers and funds a school for mentally handicapped children and another for children with physical disabilities. Belize's first university, University College of Belize, opened in 1986.

ILLITERACY RATE – (m) 6.7 per cent; (f) 6.8 per cent (2000)

MEDIA

The government-operated radio service was privatised in 1998 and there are now a variety of commercial radio stations. There are no daily newspapers but there is a number of privately owned weekly news publications. There are three main television stations (Channels 5, 7 and 9), all of which are commercial. An automatic telephone service, operated by Belize Telecommunications Ltd, covers the whole country.

BENIN

République du Benin – Republic of Benin

AREA – 112,622 sq. km. Neighbours: Togo (west), Burkina Faso and Niger (north), Nigeria (east)
POPULATION – 5,828,000. The official language is French
CAPITAL – ΨPorto Novo (population, 232,756, 2000)
MAJOR TOWNS – ΨCotonou is the principal commercial town and port

CURRENCY – Franc CFA of 100 centimes
NATIONAL ANTHEM – L'aube nouvelle (The New Dawn)
NATIONAL DAY – 30 November
NATIONAL FLAG – Two horizontal stripes of yellow over red with a vertical green band in the hoist
MORTALITY RATE (per 1,000 population) – 13.65 (2003)
HIV / AIDS ADULT PREVALENCE – 3.6 per cent (2001)
DEATH PENALTY – Yes
POPULATION BELOW POVERTY LINE – 37 per cent (2001)
POPULATION GROWTH RATE – 2.8 per cent (1990–2001)
POPULATION DENSITY – 54 per sq. km (1999)
MILITARY EXPENDITURE – 1.8 per cent of GDP (2002)
MILITARY PERSONNEL – 4,550: Army 4,300, Navy 100, Air Force 150; Paramilitaries 2,500
CONSCRIPTION DURATION – 18 months (selective)
ILLITERACY RATE – (m) 43.1 per cent; (f) 75.3 per cent (2000)
ENROLMENT (percentage of age group) – primary 79 per cent (1997); tertiary 3 per cent (1997)

CLIMATE AND TERRAIN

Benin (formerly known as Dahomey) has a short coastline of 124 km on the Gulf of Guinea but extends northwards inland for 699 km. The coast is a sandbar backed by lagoons that are fed by rivers. Elevation extremes range from 658 m (Mont Sokbara) at the highest point to 0 m (Atlantic Ocean) at the lowest. Benin has a tropical climate.

HISTORY AND POLITICS

Very little is known of Benin's pre-colonial origins. Dahomey, on the site of modern-day Benin, was a West African kingdom founded in the 11th and 12th centuries that rose to prominence during the 15th and 16th centuries.

The first Europeans to visit the country were the Portuguese in 1472. Slavery became the region's primary commodity (hence its historical name of the Slave Coast).

Benin was placed under French administration in 1892 after the defeat of the Dahomey king and became an independent republic within the French Community in 1958; full independence outside the Community was proclaimed on 1 August 1960. Between 1963 and 1972 successive governments were overthrown by the military until a coup d'état in 1972 brought to power a Marxist-Leninist military government headed by Lt.-Col. Mathieu Kérékou.

A pluralistic constitution was adopted in December 1990 and legislative and presidential elections were held in 1991. Nicéphore Soglo was sworn in as president and appointed a Benin Renaissance Party (PRB)-dominated provisional government. He was defeated by Gen. Kérékou (by then a civilian politician) in the presidential election of 1996. In legislative elections held in 2003, the Presidential Movement won an overall parliamentary majority, winning 52 of the 83 seats in the National Assembly.

POLITICAL SYSTEM

The President is head of government as well as head of state, and is directly elected for a five-year term. The President appoints and presides over the Council of Ministers. The National Assembly has 83 members, directly elected for a maximum of four years and by proportional representation.

HEAD OF STATE

President and Head of the Armed Forces, HE Gen. Mathieu Kérékou, *elected* 1996, *re-elected* 22 March 2001, *sworn in* 3 April 2001

SELECTED GOVERNMENT MEMBERS *as at July 2004*

Finance and Economy, Grégoire Laourou
Foreign Affairs and African Integration, Rogatien Biaou
Interior, Security and Territorial Administration, Daniel Tawéma
Minister of State for National Defence, Pierre Osho

EMBASSY OF THE REPUBLIC OF BENIN

87 Avenue Victor Hugo, F-75116 Paris, France
T (+33) (1) 4500 9882
Ambassador Extraordinary and Plenipotentiary, HE Edgar-Yves Monnou
Chargé d'Affaires, Antoine Afouda

BRITISH AMBASSADOR, HE Philip Thomas, CMG, resident at Abuja, Nigeria

HONORARY CONSULATE OF BENIN

Dolphin House, 16 The Broadway, Stanmore, Middlesex HA7 4DW
T 020-8954 8800
Honorary Consul, Lawrence Landau

ECONOMY AND TRADE

The principal exports are cotton (accounting for 80 per cent of official exports and 40 per cent of GDP), palm products, groundnuts, shea-nuts, and coffee. Agriculture employs an estimated 55 per cent of the workforce. Small deposits of gold, iron and chrome have been found. Oil production started in 1983. Industries have been steadily privatised since 2001.

In 2000 the IMF and the International Development Association agreed to a US$460 million debt reduction package for Benin. In March 2003 the IMF announced that Benin had taken the necessary steps to reach its completion point under the enhanced Heavily Indebted Poor Countries (HIPC) initiative.

GNI – US$2,398 million (2000); US$380 per capita (2001)
ANNUAL AVERAGE GROWTH OF GDP – 5.0 per cent (2000)
INFLATION RATE – 4.2 per cent (2000)
TOTAL EXTERNAL DEBT – US$1,599 million (2000)
IMPORTS – US$613 million (2000)
EXPORTS – US$392 million (2000)

BALANCE OF PAYMENTS

Trade – US$214 million deficit (2000)
Current Account – US$111 million deficit (2000)

Trade with UK	*2002*	*2003*
Imports from UK	£43,387,000	£46,563,000
Exports to UK	6,886,000	2,989,000

CULTURE

Benin's population is ethnically varied but the main cultural divide is between the northern and southern regions. Benin's largest group, the Fon, live in the south, as do the Yoruba. The largest group in the north is the Bariba.

Pre-colonial Benin encouraged diverse artistic traditions some of which (such as the bronze heads of the Ife) have now disappeared and others, such as the appliqué tapestries, now form the basis of an internationally important contemporary arts scene. Benin's most famous contemporary musician is Angelique Kidjo (b. 1960), who sings in Fon, Yuroba, English, French and Mina.

BHUTAN

Druk Gyal Khab – Kingdom of Bhutan

AREA – 47,000 sq. km. Neighbours: Tibet (north), India (west, south and east)
POPULATION – 2,139,549 (2003): about 80 per cent are Buddhists, the remainder (mostly the Nepali Bhutanese) are Hindu. The official language, for administrative and religious purposes, is Dzongkha, a variant of Tibetan, which functions as a lingua franca amongst a variety of languages and dialects. Nepali remains a recognised language and English remains the medium of instruction and the working language of the administration
CAPITAL – Thimphu (population, 30,340, 1993 estimate)
CURRENCY – Ngultrum of 100 chetrum (Indian currency is also legal tender)
NATIONAL ANTHEM – Druk Tsendhen Koipi Gyelknap Na (In The Thunder Dragon Kingdom)
NATIONAL DAY – 17 December
NATIONAL FLAG – Saffron yellow and orange-red divided diagonally, with dragon device in centre
MORTALITY RATE (per 1,000 population) – 13.47 (2003)
HIV / AIDS ADULT PREVALENCE – 0.1 per cent (2001)
DEATH PENALTY – NO (abolished 2004)
POPULATION GROWTH RATE – 2.8 per cent
POPULATION DENSITY – 44 per sq. km (1999)
MILITARY EXPENDITURE – 3.3 per cent of GDP (2001)
ILLITERACY RATE – (m) 38.9 per cent; (f) 66.4 per cent (2000)

CLIMATE AND TERRAIN

Bhutan is a landlocked country between China and India. There is a mountainous northern region which is infertile and sparsely populated, a central zone of upland valleys, where most of the population and cultivated land is found, and in the south the densely forested foothills of the Himalayas, which are mainly inhabited by Nepalese settlers and indigenous tribespeople. Extremes of elevation range from 7,553 m (Kula Kangri) at the highest point to 97 m (Drangme Chhu) at the lowest. The climate is dependent on altitude and average temperatures range from 4°C in January to 17°C in July. There is heavy annual rainfall of around 1,000 mm in the central valleys and 5,000 mm in the south.

HISTORY AND POLITICS

In 1865 Britain and Bhutan signed the Treaty of Sinchulu in which Britain agreed to pay Bhutan an annual sum of money in return for some border territory. Under a 1949 treaty, Bhutan was guided by the advice of India in regard to its external relations. It retained its own diplomatic representatives and became a member of the UN. Bhutan receives an annual payment of Rs500,000 from India as compensation for portions of its territory annexed by the British Government in India in 1864.

Since the 1950s Bhutan has been moving towards the establishment of more formal political institutions. In January 1989 the King introduced a code of national etiquette designed to protect the national culture and language from Nepali encroachment. These measures, together with the granting of citizenship only to Nepalis settled in Bhutan before 1958, led to an exodus of ethnic Nepalis to Nepal. In March 2001 Bhutan and Nepal began an agreed process of assessing which refugees were entitled to return to Bhutan. However, a number of Nepalese refugees went on hunger strike in early 2003 in protest against their conditions and the slow progress of the verification and repatriation process. The most recent legislative election was in June 2003 and all six cabinet ministers were re-elected.

POLITICAL SYSTEM

Bhutan has a 150-member unicameral *Tshogdu Chhenmo* (National Assembly). The National Assembly meets twice a year. The ten-member Royal Advisory Council, nominated by the King and the National Assembly, acts as a consultative body when the National Assembly is not in session. The King is also assisted by the *Lhengyal Shungtshog* (Cabinet) which is led by an annually rotating chairman. Ministers are elected for a five-year term after which time they must face a vote of confidence. There are no political parties.

In July 1998 the King introduced reforms giving the legislature the right to dismiss the King (dependent on a two-thirds majority) and to nominate the members of the Cabinet, although the King retains the right to assign their portfolios. In November 2001 a draft constitution was initiated.

HEAD OF STATE

HM The King of Bhutan, Jigme Singye Wangchuck, *born* 11 November 1955; *succeeded his father* July 1972; *crowned* 2 June 1974
Heir, Crown Prince Jigme Gesar Namgyal Wangchuck, *designated* 31 October 1988

SELECTED GOVERNMENT MEMBERS *as at July 2004*

Chairman of the Cabinet, Home and Cultural Affairs, Jigme Thinley
Finance, Wangdi Norbu
Foreign Affairs, Khandu Wangchuk

ECONOMY

The economy is based on industry, which in 2002 accounted for 37 per cent of GDP, and agriculture (34 per cent of GDP). Agriculture and animal husbandry engage around 85 per cent of the workforce in what is largely a self-sufficient rural society. Services accounted for 29 per cent of GDP in 2002. The principal food crops are rice, wheat, maize and barley. Vegetables and fruit are also produced. Bhutan is the world's largest producer of cardamom, which forms its principal export to countries other than India. Agriculture is, however, limited by the country's mountainous topography and 60 per cent forest cover.

The mountains contain rich deposits of limestone, gypsum, dolomite and graphite and small amounts of coal, which are exported to India. There are a distillery and cement, chemicals and food-processing plants; a forestry industries complex is being expanded. Tourism and postage stamps are increasingly important sources of foreign exchange.

Principal exports are electricity, calcium carbide and timber; main imports are rice, machinery and diesel oil.

GNI – US$479 million (2000); US$640 per capita (2001)
ANNUAL AVERAGE GROWTH OF GDP – 7.0 per cent (2001)
INFLATION RATE – 6.8 per cent (1999)
TOTAL EXTERNAL DEBT – US$198 million (2000)
IMPORTS – US$182 million (1999)
EXPORTS – US$116 million (1999)

Trade with UK	*2002*	*2003*
Imports from UK	£1,279,000	£2,060,000
Exports to UK	640,000	347,000

BOLIVIA

República de Bolivia – Republic of Bolivia

AREA – 1,084,400 sq. km. Neighbours: Brazil (north and east), Paraguay and Argentina (south), Chile and Peru (west)
POPULATION – 8,516,000 (2001): 12 per cent is of white European descent, 30 per cent Mestizo (mixed European-Indian), 25 per cent Quechua Indian and 17 per cent Aymará Indian. The official language is Spanish; Quechua and Aymará are also spoken. Roman Catholicism was the state religion until disestablishment in 1961
CAPITAL – La Paz, the seat of government (population, 739,453, 1998 estimate)
MAJOR CITIES – Cochabamba; El Alto; Oruro; Potosí; Santa Cruz; Sucre, the legal capital and seat of the judiciary
CURRENCY – Boliviano ($b) of 100 centavos
NATIONAL ANTHEM – Bolivianos, El Hado Propicio (Oh Bolivia, Our Long-Felt Desires)
NATIONAL DAY – 6 August (Independence Day)
NATIONAL FLAG – Three horizontal bands, red, yellow, green
LIFE EXPECTANCY (years) – 63 (2001)
MORTALITY RATE (per 1,000 population) – 7.91 (2003)
INFANT MORTALITY (per 1,000 births) – 60 (2001)
HIV / AIDS ADULT PREVALENCE RATE – 0.1 per cent (2001)
DEATH PENALTY – Yes*
POPULATION BELOW POVERTY LINE – 70 per cent (1999)
POPULATION GROWTH RATE – 2.4 per cent (1990–2001)
POPULATION DENSITY – 8 per sq. km (2001)
URBAN POPULATION – 63 per cent (2001)

CLIMATE AND TERRAIN

Bolivia's chief topographical feature is its great central plateau. Over 800 km in length, at an average altitude of 3,750 m above sea level, this plateau lies between the two great chains of the Andes, which traverse the country from south to north. Elevation extremes range from 6,542 m (Nevado Sajama) at the highest point to 90 m (Rio Paraguay) at the lowest. The total length of the navigable rivers is about 19,200 km, the principal rivers being the Itenez, Beni, Mamore and Madre de Dios. Bolivia is landlocked. The wet season is November to March. There is an average temperature of 26°C in most of the country but the south is prone to droughts and temperatures become subpolar at an altitude of 500 m.

HISTORY AND POLITICS

The area of present-day Bolivia was assimilated into the Inca Empire in 1450. The Inca Empire was conquered by the Spanish in 1525. Bolivia won its independence from Spain in 1825 after a war of liberation led by Simón Bolívar (1783–1830), from whom the country derives its name. From 1964 to 1982 Bolivia was ruled by military juntas until civilian rule was restored.

A wave of protests and strikes took place in 2000 over economic hardship, but ended after the government made concessions to public sector workers and promised investment in areas where coca was produced. In April 2001 the protestors claimed that the government had failed to deliver the promised concessions and recommenced the campaign of demonstrations and strikes. Presidential and legislative elections were held in June 2002, but were inconclusive. Gonzalo Sánchez de Lozada was elected President in a vote by Congress on 4 August but resigned in October following extensive civil unrest. Vice-President Carlos D. Mesa Gisbert was sworn in as President on 17 October 2003.

POLITICAL SYSTEM

The constitution provides for a directly elected Executive President who appoints the Cabinet. The legislature (Congress) consists of a 27-member Senate and a 130-member Chamber of Deputies. Both chambers and the President are elected for five-year terms.

HEAD OF STATE
President, Carlos D. Mesa Gisbert, *sworn in* 17 October 2003

SELECTED GOVERNMENT MEMBERS *as at July 2004*
Defence, Gonzalo Arredondo
Finance, Javier Gonzalo Cuevas
Foreign Affairs and Worship, Juan Ignacio Siles
Interior, Alfonso Ferrufino

BOLIVIAN EMBASSY
106 Eaton Square, London SW1W 9AD
T 020-7235 4248
Ambassador Extraordinary and Plenipotentiary, HE Gonzalo Montenegro

BRITISH EMBASSY
Avenida Arce No. 2732, Casilla (PO Box) 694 La Paz
T (+591) (2) 2433424
E ppa@megalink.com
Ambassador Extraordinary and Plenipotentiary, HE William Sinton, OBE, apptd 2001

BRITISH COUNCIL DIRECTOR, Eric Lawrie
Avenida Arce 2708 (esq. Campos), Casilla 15047, La Paz
T (+591) (2) 2431240
E information@britishcouncil.org.bo

DEFENCE

The Army has 77 armoured personnel carriers. The Navy has 78 patrol vessels. The Air Force has 37 combat aircraft and 16 armed helicopters.

MILITARY EXPENDITURE – 1.6 per cent of GDP (2002)
MILITARY PERSONNEL – 31,500: Army 25,000, Navy 3,500, Air Force 3,000; Paramilitaries 37,100
CONSCRIPTION DURATION – 12 months (selective)

ECONOMY AND TRADE

Mining, natural gas, petroleum and agriculture are the principal industries. The ancient silver mines of Potosí are now worked chiefly for tin, but gold is obtained on the Eastern Cordillera of the Andes. Following a decline in the price of tin, many workers have taken to growing coca, which has become a significant export. Small quantities of oil are produced for internal consumption and gas (currently providing about a quarter of export income) is piped to Argentina; in December 1997 the World Bank approved financing for the 3,150-km Bolivia-Brazil gas pipeline, which is now in operation. Bolivia's natural gas output is an estimated 4,100 million cubic metres per year.

In 1996 the government signed an agreement with the South American Common Market (Mercosur) to create a free trade zone within 18 years.

Bolivia's principal exports are natural gas, tin, zinc, silver, gold, coffee and soya beans. The USA and UK are Bolivia's largest export trading partners. The country's low level of industrialisation requires Bolivia to be highly dependent on imports, mainly wheat and flour, iron and steel products, machinery, vehicles and textiles.

In 2004 President Mesa Gisbert announced an economic plan designed to revive the economy and bring debt under control.

GNI – US$8,100 million (2001); US$950 per capita (2001)
ANNUAL AVERAGE GROWTH OF GDP – 4.7 per cent (1998)
INFLATION RATE – 4.6 per cent (2000)
UNEMPLOYMENT – 7.4 per cent (2000)
TOTAL EXTERNAL DEBT – US$5,762 million (2000)
FOREIGN DIRECT INVESTMENT – US$3,222 million (1997–2000)
IMPORTS – US$1,770 million (2002)
EXPORTS – US$1,310 million (2002)

BALANCE OF PAYMENTS
Trade – US$222 million deficit (2002)
Current Account – US$335 million deficit (2002)

Trade with UK	*2002*	*2003*
Imports from UK	£8,111,000	£6,386,000
Exports to UK	11,593,000	10,540,000

TRANSPORT INFRASTRUCTURE

There are 3,519 km of railways in operation, but they are in a state of decay. There are about 53,790 km of roads, of which about 5 per cent are paved. Bolivia has 1,081 airports but only 12 have surfaced runways. In 1993 Bolivia and Peru signed an agreement granting Bolivia a concession of 162 hectares at the southern Peruvian port of Ilo for 98 years to construct a free trade zone.

EDUCATION

Elementary education is compulsory and free from the ages of six to 11. There are secondary schools in urban centres but only about a third of children of secondary school age attend. There are 22 universities, four of which are private.

ILLITERACY RATE – (m) 6.9 per cent; (f) 18.4 per cent (2002)

MEDIA

Radio is the most important news media in Bolivia due to low literacy levels (particularly in rural areas). The media is largely privately owned and run. Journalists practise self-censorship. There are six daily newspapers. Television is mostly commercial with only one government run channel.

CULTURE

Bolivia's folk culture of weaving, dancing and music stretch back 3,000 years and have distinct regional characteristics. Religion is a mixture of Roman Catholicism and traditional Aymaran beliefs. Bolivia has the largest proportion of indigenous people (approximately two-thirds of the population) of any Latin American country and their lifestyles contrast sharply with the mostly Spanish-descended urban population.

BOSNIA-HERCEGOVINA

Republika Bosna i Hercegovina – Republic of Bosnia and Hercegovina

AREA – 51,197 sq. km. Neighbours: Serbia and Montenegro (east), Croatia (north and west)
POPULATION – 3,784,000; 4.4 million (2001 census): 44 per cent Bosniac, 33 per cent Serbs and 17 per cent Croats. The languages are Bosnian (spoken by Bosniacs and written in the Latin script), Serbian (spoken by Serbs and written in the Cyrillic alphabet) and Croatian (spoken by Croats and written in the Latin script)
CAPITAL – Sarajevo (population, 529,021, 2001 estimate)
MAJOR CITIES – Banja Luka; Mostar; Tuzla; Zenica
CURRENCY – Convertible marka
NATIONAL ANTHEM – Jedna Si Jedina (You Are Unique)
NATIONAL DAY – 1 March (anniversary of 1992 declaration of independence)
NATIONAL FLAG – Blue, bearing a yellow triangle above a line of white stars
MORTALITY RATE (per 1,000 population) – 8.21 (2003)
HIV / AIDS ADULT PREVALENCE RATE – 0.1 per cent (2001)
DEATH PENALTY – No (abolished 2001)
POPULATION GROWTH RATE – 2.1 per cent (1999)
POPULATION DENSITY – 75 per sq. km (1999)
MILITARY EXPENDITURE – 2.4 per cent of GDP (2002)
MILITARY PERSONNEL – Bosniac Army (VF-B): 9,200; Croat Defence Council (VF-H): 4,000; Bosnian Serb Army (VRS): 6,600

CLIMATE AND TERRAIN

Bosnia-Hercegovina is a mountainous country on the Balkan Peninsula. The highest point of elevation is 2,386 m (Maglic), the lowest point is 0 m (Adriatic Sea).

HISTORY AND POLITICS

The country was settled by Slavs in the seventh century and conquered by the Ottoman Turks in 1463. Ruled by the Turks for over 400 years, the country came under Austro-Hungarian control in 1878. The assassination of the heir to the Austro-Hungarian throne in Sarajevo by an ethnic Serb precipitated the First World War, after which Bosnia-Hercegovina became part of the 'Kingdom of Serbs, Croats and Slovenes' (renamed Yugoslavia in 1929). It was occupied by German and Axis forces between 1941 and 1945. At the end of the war Bosnia-Hercegovina became part of the Socialist Federal Republic of Yugoslavia, which eventually collapsed with the secession of Slovenia and Croatia in 1991.

The Bosnia-Hercegovina government issued a declaration of sovereignty in October 1991 against the wishes of the ethnic Serb Democratic Party. Independence was declared on 1 March 1992 following a referendum which was boycotted by the Bosnian Serbs. Bosnia-Hercegovina was recognised as an independent state by the EU and USA in April 1992 and was admitted to UN membership in May 1992.

THE WAR

Fighting broke out in March 1992 between the pro-independence Muslims and Bosnian Serbs who wanted to merge with the Serbian republic to form a Greater Serbia. The Bosnian Serbs, assisted by the Federal Yugoslav Army (JNA), gained control of 70 per cent of Bosnia and in August 1992 declared their own 'Republika Srpska' with its capital at Pale.

The Bosnian government (Muslim) forces formed an alliance with Bosnian Croat and Croat forces in early 1992 which collapsed in 1993. The Muslims then came under fire from both Bosnian Serb and Bosnian Croat forces.

In August 1993 the Bosnian Croats declared a 'Republic of Herceg-Bosna', with its capital in Mostar, and following a cease-fire in February 1994 joined the government forces in a Muslim-Croat Federation.

NATO galvanised the USA, Britain, France, Germany and Russia to form the Contact Group (CG) to co-ordinate peace efforts. The CG brought about a cease-fire in June 1994 and presented a peace plan, which was rejected by the Bosnian Serbs.

Fighting intensified in 1995, climaxing in a land-grab during the final months of the war. Bosnian Serb forces overran the UN safe areas of Zepa and Srebrenica in July, allegedly massacring thousands of fleeing Muslims, and then laid siege to the Bihać 'safe area' together with Croatian Serbs and rebel Muslims. Bosnian government and Croatian forces lifted the siege of Bihać in August, enabling a joint attack on Serb-held central Bosnia.

The foreign ministers of Bosnia, Croatia and Serbia (rump Yugoslavia) met in Geneva in September 1995 and agreed to a US-sponsored peace accord. A cease-fire agreement was signed on 5 October and observed from 22 October, delayed by a Federation advance in the west and north-west, and Bosnian Serbs overrunning Tuzla. In November 2002, Bosnian Serb Mitar Vasiljevic was sentenced by the International Criminal Tribunal for the Former Yugoslavia in The Hague to 20 years imprisonment for war crimes. Biljana Plavsic, the former President of the Republika Srpska, was sentenced in February 2003, to 11 years' imprisonment for crimes against humanity. Former Serbian President Milan Milutinovic; former Yugoslav President Slobodan Milosevic; Dragoljub Ojdanic, Yugoslav Chief of Staff; Nikola Sainovic, Deputy Prime Minister of Serbia and Vlajako Stojiljkovic, Minister of Internal Affairs of Serbia, are all currently on trial.

THE PEACE AGREEMENT

The Dayton Peace Accord was signed in Paris on 14 December 1995. It was agreed to preserve Bosnia as a single state with a 51:49 division of territory between the Bosnian and Croat Federation and the Republika Srpska (Bosnian Serbs). A republican (national) government, presidency and democratically elected institutions, based in Federation-controlled Sarajevo, were provided for.

The Dayton agreement provided for the deployment of a NATO-led Peace Implementation Force (IFOR) which took over from UNPROFOR on 20 December 1995 and was mandated until December 1996. IFOR (60,000 troops) was replaced by a NATO-led Stabilisation Force (SFOR) (12,000 troops, reduced to 7,000 troops in May 2004).

POLITICAL SYSTEM

Under the Dayton Peace Accord, the Bosnian republican (national) government was made responsible for foreign affairs, currency, citizenship and immigration. Executive authority was vested in a democratically elected rotating presidential triumvirate comprising a representative from each community, but in March 2001 the Assembly of Bosnia-Hercegovina nominated two members of a multi-ethnic party.

Legislative authority is vested in a bicameral parliament, the Assembly of Bosnia-Hercegovina, comprising a House of Peoples and a House of Representatives. Both houses have two-year terms. The House of Peoples has 15 members, ten from the Bosniac-Croat Federation and five from the Republika Srpska, who are selected by the House of Representatives. The House of Representatives has 42 members who are directly elected to the two constituent chambers, the Chamber of Deputies of the Federation, which has 28 members, and the Chamber of Deputies of the Republika Srpska, which has 14 members. Within the Bosniac-Croat Federation there is a 140-member House of Representatives and ten cantonal assemblies; in the Republika Srpska there is an 83-member People's Assembly.

Legislative elections and elections for the collective presidency and the presidency of the Republika Srpska were held in 2002. The winning parties were: the Bosniac Party of Democratic Action (SDA); the Serb Democratic Party (SDS) and the Croatian Democratic Community (HDZ). Dragan Čavić was elected President of the Republika Srpska and sworn in on 28 November. In January 2003, the all-Bosnian legislature approved the coalition government of Adnan Terzic of the SDA. Mirko Sarović, who was inaugurated as the first chair of the collective presidency in October 2002, resigned in April 2003. Borislav Paravac was elected to replace him and took office on 10 April. The chair of the Presidency rotates among its three members every eight months.

HEADS OF STATE (FOR ALL BOSNIA-HERCEGOVINA)

Presidency Members, Sulejman Tihic, Borislav Paravac, Dragan Ćović

HEAD OF THE FEDERATION
President, Niko Lozancić
Vice-Presidents, Sahbaz Dzikanovic; Desnica Radivojevic

HEAD OF REPUBLIKA SRPSKA
President, Dragan Čavić
Vice-Presidents, Adil Osmanović; Ivan Tomljenovic

SELECTED GOVERNMENT MEMBERS (for all Bosnia-Hercegovina) *as at July 2004*
Prime Minister, European Integration, Adnan Terzić
Finance and Treasury, Ljerka Marić
Foreign Affairs, Mladen Ivanić

SELECTED GOVERNMENT MEMBERS OF FEDERATION CABINET *as at July 2004*
Prime Minister, Ahmet Hadžipašić
Deputy Prime Minister, Culture and Sport, Gavrilo Grahovac
Deputy Prime Minister, Finance, Dragan Vrankić
Defence, Miroslav Nikolić
Interior, Mevludin Halilović

SELECTED GOVERNMENT MEMBERS OF REPUBLIKA SRPSKA *as at July 2004*
Prime Minister, Finance (acting), Dragan Mikerević
Defence, Milovan Stanković
Finance, Branko Krsmanović
Interior, Zoran Djerić

EMBASSY OF BOSNIA HERCEGOVINA
5–7 Lexham Gardens, London W8 5JJ
T 020-7373 0867
Ambassador Extraordinary and Plenipotentiary, HE Elvira Begovic, apptd 2001

BRITISH EMBASSY
8 Tina Ujevica, Sarajevo
T (+387) (33) 444429
E britemb@bih.net.ba
Ambassador Extraordinary and Plenipotentiary, HE Ian Cliff, OBE, apptd 2001

BRITISH COUNCIL DIRECTOR, Chris Rawlings
Ljubljanska 9, 71000 Sarajevo
T (+387) (33) 250220
E british.council@britishcouncil.ba

ECONOMY AND TRADE

Wheat, maize, potatoes and cabbage are among the major crops; crude steel and lignite are among the principal mineral products.

GNI – US$4,899 million (2000); US$1,230 per capita (2000)
GDP – US$4,769 million (2001); US$1,074 per capita (2000)
ANNUAL AVERAGE GROWTH OF GDP – 20 per cent (1998)
TOTAL EXTERNAL DEBT – US$2,828 million (2000)

Trade with UK	*2002*	*2003*
Imports from UK	£16,007,000	£12,531,000
Exports to UK	3,765,000	4,048,000

TRANSPORT INFRASTRUCTURE

There are 1,021 km of railways and 21,846 km of roads, 11,424 km of which are paved. Many waterways are still blocked by destroyed bridges, debris and silt. There are five heliports and 27 airports, eight of which are surfaced.

MEDIA

During the war all branches of the media were used by political factions to further their own propaganda aims. Since the 1995 Dayton Peace Accord, efforts have been made to reintroduce a more balanced press that crosses ethnic divides. These efforts have not been entirely successful and there is only limited press freedom. The Office of the High Representative is overseeing the development of a national broadcasting service. There are more than 200 commercial television and radio stations.

CULTURE

Modern-day Bosnia-Hercegovina is still dealing with the wounds left by three years of inter-ethnic war and people now divide geographically along religious lines – the Serb Republic is almost totally Christian and the Federation is mostly Muslim.

The country's most famous novelist is Ivo Andric (1892–1974), winner of the Nobel Prize for literature in 1961.

BOTSWANA

The Republic of Botswana

AREA – 600,300 sq. km. Neighbours: South Africa (south and east), Zimbabwe (north and north-east), Namibia (west), Zambia (north)
POPULATION – 1,554,000 (2001): Batswana (95 per cent); the remainder are Bakalanga, Basarwa, Bakgalagadi, Basubya, Baherero, Bayei, Bambukushu and Europeans. The national language is Setswana and the official language is English
CAPITAL – Gaborone (population, 186,007, 2001 census)
MAJOR CITIES – Francistown; Molepolole; Selebi-Phikwe
CURRENCY – Pula (P) of 100 thebe
NATIONAL ANTHEM – Fatshe La Rona (Blessed Be This Noble Land)
NATIONAL DAY – 30 September
NATIONAL FLAG – Light blue with a horizontal black stripe fimbriated in white across the centre
LIFE EXPECTANCY (years) – 39 (2001)
MORTALITY RATE (per 1,000 population) – 31
INFANT MORTALITY (per 1,000 births) – 80 (2001)
HIV / AIDS ADULT PREVALENCE – 38.8 per cent (2001)
DEATH PENALTY – Yes
POPULATION BELOW POVERTY LINE – 47 per cent (2001)
POPULATION GROWTH RATE – 2.1 per cent (1990–2001)
POPULATION DENSITY – 3 per sq. km (2001)
URBAN POPULATION – 49 per cent (2001)

CLIMATE AND TERRAIN

A plateau at a height of about 1,200 m divides Botswana into two main topographical regions. To the east of the plateau, streams run into the Marico, Notwani and Limpopo rivers; to the west lies a flat region comprising the Bakgalagadi Desert, the Okavango Swamps and the Northern State Lands area. Elevation extremes range from 1,489 m (Tsodilo Hills) at the highest point to 513 m (junction of the Limpopo and Shashe Rivers) at the lowest. The climate is subtropical in the north (Okavango Delta, including the Central Kalahari Game Reserve) at the lowest, arid in the south and west (Kalahari Desert), and temperate in the east (arable farming land). Average annual temperatures range from 26°C in January to 13°C in July.

HISTORY AND POLITICS

The Tswana people were dominant in the area now known as Botswana from the 17th century. In 1885, at the request of indigenous chiefs fearing invasion by the Boers, Britain formally took control of Bechuanaland, and the northern part of the territory was declared a British protectorate, while land to the south of the Molopo river became British Bechuanaland, which was later incorporated into the Cape Colony. On 30 September 1966 the British Protectorate of Bechuanaland became a republic within the Commonwealth under the name Botswana.

The last general election (1999) was won by the Botswana Democratic Party with 33 seats to the Botswana National Front's seven seats. A general election was due to take place in October 2004.

POLITICAL SYSTEM

The President is head of state and is elected by an absolute majority in the National Assembly. He appoints as Vice-President a member of the National Assembly who is leader of government business in the National Assembly. The Assembly consists of the President, 40 members elected on a basis of universal adult suffrage, four co-opted members, and the Attorney-General (non-voting). Presidential and legislative elections are held every five years. There is also a 15-member House of Chiefs which considers legislation affecting the constitution and chieftaincy matters. In August 1997 the minimum voting age was lowered from 21 to 18. In 2002 the cabinet was increased in size from 16 to 20 members with the creation of four new ministerial posts.

HEAD OF STATE
President, C.-in-C. of the Armed Forces, HE Festus Mogae, *sworn in* 2 April 1998
Vice-President, Lt.-Gen. Ian Khama

SELECTED GOVERNMENT MEMBERS *as at July 2004*
Finance and Development Planning, Baledzi Gaolathe
Foreign Affairs, Lt.-Gen. Mompati Merafhe

BOTSWANA HIGH COMMISSION
6 Stratford Place, London W1C 1AY
T 020-7499 0031
High Commissioner, HE Roy Blackbeard, apptd 1998

BRITISH HIGH COMMISSION
Private Bag 0023, Gaborone
T (+ 267) 3952841
E bhc@botsnet.bw
High Commissioner, HE David Merry, CMG, apptd 2001

BRITISH COUNCIL DIRECTOR, David Knox
British High Commission Building, Queen's Road, The Mall, PO Box 439, Gaborone
T (+267) 3953602
E general.enquiries@british council.org.bw

DEFENCE

The Army has 34 armoured personnel carriers. The Air Wing has 30 combat aircraft.

MILITARY EXPENDITURE – 4.5 per cent of GDP (2002)
MILITARY PERSONNEL – 9,000: Army 8,500, Air Wing 500; Paramilitaries 1,500

ECONOMY AND TRADE

Botswana is one of Africa's oldest continuous multiparty democracies and is commonly regarded as the continent's most stable and least corrupt country. Agriculture is predominantly pastoral and accounts for around 3 per cent of GDP. Cattle rearing accounts for about 85 per cent of agricultural output.

Mineral extraction and processing is now the major source of income following the opening of large mines for diamonds, copper and nickel. Botswana is the world's largest producer of diamonds (20 million carats a year), with diamonds accounting for 50 per cent of foreign exchange earnings and 33 per cent of GDP. Large deposits of coal have been discovered and are now being mined.

Service industries account for nearly half of GDP. Tourism is the third largest industry, generating about 7 per cent of GDP. Main imports are motor vehicles, machinery and electrical equipment and foodstuffs; main exports are diamonds, motor vehicles, cupro-nickel and beef.

Botswana is one of the few countries in Africa that invests in, rather than borrows from, the World Bank.

GNI – US$5,300 million (2001); US$3,100 per capita (2001)
ANNUAL AVERAGE GROWTH OF GDP – 4.2 per cent (2002)
INFLATION RATE – 8.6 per cent (2000)
TOTAL EXTERNAL DEBT – US$360 million (2002)
FOREIGN DIRECT INVESTMENT – US$262 million (2001)
IMPORTS – US$1,809 million (2001)
EXPORTS – US$1,948 million (1998)

BALANCE OF PAYMENTS
Trade – US$675 million surplus (1999)
Current Account – US$517 million surplus (1999)

Trade with UK	*2002*	*2003*
Imports from UK	£16,837,000	£13,194,000
Exports to UK	£1,036,914,000	£1,106,814,000

TRANSPORT INFRASTRUCTURE

The railway from Cape Town to Zimbabwe passes through eastern Botswana. The major road is the 595 km Trans-Kalahari Highway, completed in 1998, which connects the capital of Namibia with Gaborone. There are a total of 10,217 km of roads.

EDUCATION

Botswana does not have a compulsory education policy. Many children undergo ten years of education but the government announced in June 2004 that efforts would be made to increase this to 12 years (seven years of primary education, three years of junior secondary, and two years of senior secondary). There are 800 primary schools, 206 community junior secondary schools, 23 government and government-aided senior secondary schools and one university.

ILLITERACY RATE – (m) 23.1 per cent; (f) 17.6 per cent (2003)

ENROLMENT (percentage of age group) – primary 100 per cent (1997); secondary 65 per cent (1997); tertiary 6 per cent (1997)

MEDIA

Newspapers are mostly found in cities and towns. In rural areas radio is the most important news medium (there are state run and private commercial stations and programmes are broadcast in both English and Setswana). State run television (Botswana Television) was established in 2000.

BRAZIL

República Federativa do Brasil – Federative Republic of Brazil

AREA – 8,456,500 sq. km. Neighbours: Guyana, Suriname, French Guiana, Colombia and Venezuela (north), Peru, Bolivia, Paraguay and Argentina (west), Uruguay (south)

POPULATION – 172,559,000 (2001). Portuguese is the national language. Spanish and English are widely spoken

CAPITAL – Brasília (population, 1,737,813, 2000 census)

MAJOR CITIES – Belo Horizonte; ΨFortaleza; ΨPorto Alegre; ΨRecife; ΨRio de Janeiro, the former capital; ΨSalvador; São Paulo

CURRENCY – Real of 100 centavos

NATIONAL ANTHEM – Ouviram Do Ipiranga Às Margens Plácidas (From Peaceful Ypiranga's Banks)

NATIONAL DAY – 7 September (Independence Day)

NATIONAL FLAG – Green with a yellow lozenge containing a blue sphere studded with white stars, and crossed by a white band with the motto *Ordem e Progresso*

LIFE EXPECTANCY (years) – 68 (2001)

MORTALITY RATE (per 1,000 population) – 6.13 (2003)

INFANT MORTALITY (per 1,000 births) – 31 (2001)

HIV / AIDS ADULT PREVALENCE – 0.7 per cent (2001)

DEATH PENALTY – Yes*

POPULATION BELOW POVERTY LINE – 22 per cent (1998)

POPULATION GROWTH RATE – 1.4 per cent (1990–2001)

POPULATION DENSITY – 20 per sq. km (2001)

URBAN POPULATION – 82 per cent (2001)

CLIMATE AND TERRAIN

Brazil is South America's biggest country, taking up almost half of the continent. There are five distinct topographical areas: the Amazon Basin (north and west, taking up nearly a third of the country), the River Plate Basin (south), the Guyanan Highlands (north of the Amazon), the Brazilian Highlands (south of the Amazon), and the coastal strip. Brazil is mostly tropical with the equator passing through the north and the Tropic of Capricorn through the south-east. It is home to the world's biggest rain forest. The Amazon Basin sees annual rainfall of up to 2,000 mm a year and there is no dry season (average temperature 17°C). The north-east is the driest area of the country and can experience long periods of drought (average temperature 40°C). The southern states have a seasonal temperate climate (the average temperature is between 17°C and 19°C). Elevation extremes range from 3,014 m (Pico da Neblina) at the highest point to 0 m (Atlantic Ocean) at the lowest.

HISTORY AND POLITICS

Brazil was claimed by the Portuguese navigator Pedro lvares Cabral in 1500 and colonised by Portugal in the early 16th century. In 1822 it became independent under Dom Pedro I, son of King João VI of Portugal, who had been forced to flee to Brazil during the Napoleonic Wars. In 1889, Dom Pedro II was dethroned and a republic was proclaimed. In 1985 Brazil returned to democratic rule after two decades of military government.

In the first round of presidential elections held in 2002 Luis Inácio 'Lula' da Silva of the Workers' Party (PT) gained 46.4 per cent of the vote. In the second round of the elections da Silva was elected President with 61.3 per cent of the vote. In the legislative elections of the same year the Workers' Party became the largest party in the Chamber of Deputies, winning 91 of the 513 seats. The PT then formed a coalition government with 11 other parties giving it control of 381 seats in the Chamber of Deputies and 53 seats out of 81 in the Senate.

POLITICAL SYSTEM

Under the 1988 constitution the President, who heads the executive, is directly elected for a four-year term; in June 1997 the constitution was amended to allow the President to stand for a second term. The Congress consists of an 81-member Senate (three senators per state elected for an eight-year term) and a 513-member Chamber of Deputies which is elected every four years; the number of deputies per state depends upon the state's population. Each state has a Governor, and a Legislative Assembly with a four-year term.

FEDERAL STRUCTURE

The Federative Republic of Brazil is composed of the federal district and 26 states (population 2000 census): Distrito Federal (2,043,169); Goiás (4,996,439); Mato Grosso (2,502,260); Mato Grosso do Sul (2,074,877); Acre (557,226); Amapá (423,581); Amazonas (2,813,085); Pará (6,189,550); Rondônia (1,337,792); Roraima (324,152); Tocantins (1,155,913); Alagoas (2,819,172); Bahia (13,066,910); Ceará (7,418,476); Maranhão (5,642,960); Paraíba (3,439,344); Pernambuco (7,911,937); Piauí (2,841,202); Rio Grande de Norte (2,771,538); Sergipe (1,781,714); Paraná (9,558,454); Rio Grande de Sul (10,181,749); Santa Catarina (5,349,580); Espírito Santo (3,094,390); Minas Gerais (17,866,402); Rio de Janeiro (14,367,083); São Paulo (39,969,476).

HEAD OF STATE

President, Luis Inácio 'Lula' da Silva, *sworn in* 1 January 2003

Vice-President, José Alencar Gomes da Silva

SELECTED GOVERNMENT MEMBERS *as at July 2004*
Chief Minister of the Cabinet, José Dirceu
Defence, José Viegas Filho
External Relations, Celso Amorim
Finance, Antonio Palocci

BRAZILIAN EMBASSY
32 Green Street, London W1K 7AT
T 020-7040 8900
Ambassador Extraordinary and Plenipotentiary, HE José Maurício Bustani, apptd 2003

BRITISH EMBASSY
Setor de Embaixadas Sul, Quadra 801, Conjunto K, 70408-900, Brasília DF
T (+55) (61) 225 2710
E britemb@zaz.com.br
Ambassador Extraordinary and Plenipotentiary, HE Sir Roger Bone, KCMG, apptd 1999

BRITISH COUNCIL DIRECTOR, Dr David Cooke
Edificio Centro Empresarial Varig, SCN Quadra 04, Bloco B, Torre Oeste Conjunto 202, 70710-926 Brasília DF
T (+ 55) (61) 21067500
E brasilia@britishcouncil.org.br

DEFENCE

The Army has 178 main battle tanks, 803 armoured personnel carriers and 78 helicopters. The Navy has bases at Rio de Janeiro, Salvador, Recife, Belém, Florianópolis and Ladario. It is equipped with four submarines, one aircraft carrier, 14 frigates and 50 patrol and coastal vessels. Naval aviation has 24 combat aircraft and 54 armed helicopters; the Marines have 33 armoured personnel carriers. The Air Force has 254 combat aircraft.
MILITARY EXPENDITURE – 2.3 per cent of GDP (2002)
MILITARY PERSONNEL – 287,600: Army 189,000, Navy 48,600, Air Force 50,000; Paramilitaries 385,600
CONSCRIPTION DURATION – 12 months (can be extended to 18)

ECONOMY AND TRADE

There are large mineral deposits including iron ore (hematite), manganese, bauxite, beryllium, chrome, nickel, tungsten, cassiterite, lead, gold, monazite (containing rare earths and thorium) and zirconium. Diamonds and precious and semi-precious stones are also found. Brazil is the world's largest producer of coffee; the other main agricultural products are cassava, maize, soya, rice, wheat, sugar, potatoes, cotton, cocoa, tobacco and peanuts. Tourism is a growing industry; Brazil attracted 5.1 million visitors in 2000. Services generated 72.9 per cent of GDP in 2002.

A new currency, the real, was introduced in 1994 to help control inflation, however, inflation rose to 12.5 per cent in 2002, the highest level for eight years.

Principal imports are machinery, fuel and lubricants, mineral products, transport equipment and chemicals. Principal exports are industrial goods, coffee, sugar cane, iron ore, tobacco and soya.
GNI – US$528,900 million (2001); US$3,070 per capita (2001)
ANNUAL AVERAGE GROWTH OF GDP – 1.5 per cent (2001)
INFLATION RATE – 10.2 per cent (2002)
UNEMPLOYMENT – 9.6 per cent (1999)
TOTAL EXTERNAL DEBT – US$237,953 million (2000)
FOREIGN DIRECT INVESTMENT – US$117,003 million (1997–2000)
IMPORTS – US$49,580 million (2002)
EXPORTS – US$60,362 million (2002)

BALANCE OF PAYMENTS
Trade – US$13,143 million surplus (2002)
Current Account – US$7,696 million deficit (2002)

Trade with UK	*2002*	*2003*
Imports from UK	£887,614,000	£828,586,000
Exports to UK	1,414,884,000	1,512,283,000

TRANSPORT INFRASTRUCTURE

There are 1,670,148 km of roads, of which 161,503 km are paved, and the route-length of railways is 30,129 km, of which 2,150 km are electrified. There are ten international airports and internal air services are highly developed. There are 43,000 km of navigable inland waterways. Rio de Janeiro and Santos are the two leading ports but there are also another 14 fully equipped harbours. A 3,415-km gas pipeline running from Santa Cruz, Bolivia, to São Paolo, was opened in 2000.

EDUCATION

The education system includes both public and private institutions. Public education is free at all levels. Brazil has 42 million students (2002) and 30.5 million of these are enrolled in primary education.
ILLITERACY RATE – (m) 14.9 per cent; (f) 14.6 per cent (2000)
ENROLMENT (percentage of age group) – primary 96.5 per cent (2001); secondary 71.6 per cent (2001); tertiary 11 per cent (2002)

MEDIA

Brazilian television is South America's biggest media industry with Brazilian-made soap operas, game shows and dramas exported all over the world. There are many Brazilian radio stations and television channels. Globo, Brazil's most successful broadcasting conglomerate, dominates the market and owns television and radio networks, newspapers and subscription television stations. In 2002 there were 14.3 million internet users.

CULTURE

Brazil is a melting pot of races (European, African, Asian, Arab and indigenous communities are all well established), cultures, religious traditions, music and dance (the samba, bossa nova and lambada are world-famous). Luis de Camoes (1525–80) is widely regarded as Brazil's national poet. Like many other Latin American countries, one of Brazil's biggest cultural exports is football. The national team has won the World Cup a record five times.

BRUNEI

Negara Brunei Darussalam – State of Brunei Darussalam

AREA – 5,300 sq. km. Neighbour: Malaysia
POPULATION – 335,000 (2001): 66.9 per cent Malay, 15.2 per cent Chinese, 5.9 per cent indigenous races and 12 per cent European, Indian and other races. The majority are Sunni Muslims. The official language is Malay; English and dialects of Chinese are also spoken
CAPITAL – Bandar Seri Begawan (population, 46,000, 2001 estimate)
CURRENCY – Brunei dollar (B$) of 100 sen (fully interchangeable with Singapore currency)
NATIONAL ANTHEM – Allah Peliharakan Sultan (God Bless His Majesty)
NATIONAL DAY – 23 February
NATIONAL FLAG – Yellow with diagonal stripes of white over black and the arms in red all over the centre
LIFE EXPECTANCY (years) – 76 (2001)
MORTALITY RATE (per 1,000 population) – 3.39 (2003)
INFANT MORTALITY (per 1,000 births) – 6 (2001)
HIV / AIDS ADULT PREVALENCE – 0.2 per cent (2001)
DEATH PENALTY – No (abolished 1957)
POPULATION GROWTH RATE – 2.4 per cent (1990–2001)
POPULATION DENSITY – 63 per sq. km (2001)

CLIMATE AND TERRAIN

Brunei is a tropical country with high levels of humidity and an average daily temperature of between 24°C and 30°C. The country is mostly rain forest (75 per cent), with extensive mangrove swamps along the coastal plain. There are mountains on the border with Sarawak (Malaysia). Elevation extremes range from 1,850 m (Bukit Pagon) at the highest point to 0 m (South China Sea) at the lowest.

HISTORY AND POLITICS

Formerly a powerful Muslim sultanate that controlled Borneo and parts of the Philippines, Brunei was reduced to its present size by the mid-19th century and became a British Protectorate in 1888. In 1959 the Sultan promulgated the first written constitution and on 1 January 1984 Brunei resumed full independence from Britain.

POLITICAL SYSTEM

Supreme executive authority rests with the Sultan, who presides over and is advised by the Privy Council, the Religious Council and the Council of Ministers. The Sultan effectively rules by decree as a state of emergency has been in effect since a revolt in 1962; there are no political parties and no elections.

HEAD OF STATE

HM The Sultan of Brunei, HM Sultan Haji Hassanal Bolkiah Mu'izzaddin Waddaullah, Sultan and Yang Di-Pertuan, GCB, *acceded* 1967, *crowned* 1 August 1968

SELECTED GOVERNMENT MEMBERS *as at July 2004*
Prime Minister, Defence, Finance, HM The Sultan
Deputy Ministers, Haji ibnu Basith Apong *(Defence)*; Dato Paduka Haji Yakub bin abu Bakar and Pehin Dato Haji Awang Ahmad *(Finance)*; Pehin Dato Haji Ali bin Haji Awang *(Foreign Affairs)*
Foreign Affairs, Prince Mohamed Bolkiah
Home Affairs, Special Adviser in the Prime Minister's Office, Pehin Dato Haji Isa Utama

BRUNEI DARUSSALAM HIGH COMMISSION
19–20 Belgrave Square, London SW1X 8PG
T 020-7581 0521
High Commissioner, HE Pengiran Haji Yunus, apptd 2001

BRITISH HIGH COMMISSION
PO Box 2197, Bandar Seri Begawan 8674
E brithc@brunet.bn
T (+673) (2) 222231
High Commissioner, Andrew Caie, apptd 2002

BRITISH COUNCIL DIRECTOR, Amanda Griffiths
Level 2, Block D, Yayasan Sultan Hj Hassanal Bolkiah, Jl Pretty, Bandar Seri Begawan B58711 T (+673) (2) 237742
E all.enquiries@bn.britishcouncil.org

DEFENCE

The Army has 39 armoured personnel carriers. The Navy, based in Muara, has six patrol and coastal vessels. The Air Force has five armed helicopters. On 9 January 2003 it was agreed by the Sultan and Tony Blair, that a battalion of the British Brigade of Gurkhas would continue to be stationed in Brunei for a further five years from 29 September 2003.
MILITARY EXPENDITURE – 5.2 per cent of GDP (2002)
MILITARY PERSONNEL – 7,000: Army 4,900, Navy 1,000, Air Force 1,100; Paramilitaries 3,750

ECONOMY AND TRADE

Brunei is the fourth largest world producer of natural gas and in 1999 this was the country's top export. The economy is based on the production of this gas along with oil and also on income from overseas investments (which now exceed oil revenues). Royalties and taxes from these operations form the bulk of government revenue and have enabled the construction of free health, education and welfare services.

In 2001 agriculture accounted for 5 per cent of GDP, industry accounted for 45 per cent and services for 50 per cent. Imports cover 80 per cent of domestic food requirements.
GNI – US$24,630 (2001)
ANNUAL AVERAGE GROWTH OF GDP – 1.0 per cent (1998)

Trade with UK	*2001*	*2002*
Imports from UK	£59,666,000	£61,263,000
Exports to UK	34,090,000	36,442,000

TRANSPORT INFRASTRUCTURE

There are five ports, at Muara, Bandar Seri Begawan, Seria, Tutong and Kuala Belait, and an international airport at Bandar Seri Begawan. There are three heliports and 209 km of waterways. There are 13 km of privately owned railway. There is a road network of 2,525 km.

EDUCATION

All levels of education are free. Children undertake seven years of primary education, three of lower secondary and two years of upper secondary which can be in a secondary school, a vocational school or technical college. There are 169 primary schools, 38 secondary schools, six technical and vocational colleges and two universities.
ILLITERACY RATE – (m) 1 per cent; (f) 1 per cent (2003)

MEDIA

The media is privately owned. The main publications are the *Borneo Bulletin* (English-language daily), *Brunei Direct* (online news service) and *Media Permata* (Malay-language daily). The only broadcast media organisation, radio Television Brunei (RTB), is state owned and controlled. It broadcasts television in Malay and English and radio in Malay, English, Mandarin Chinese and Gurkhali.

CULTURE

Brunei is famous for its traditional crafts of silverwork and weaving. The capital, Bandar Seri Begawan, is the only large town and is a mix of old (Kampung Ayer, an ancient area of 28 water villages built on stilts in the Brunei River) and new (ultra-modern public and government buildings set back from wide streets). Brunei is a Muslim country and Shari'ah law prevails in some areas.

BULGARIA

Republika Bălgarija – Republic of Bulgaria

AREA – 110,600 sq. km. Neighbours: Romania (north), Serbia and the Former Yugoslav Republic of Macedonia (west), Greece and Turkey (south)
POPULATION – 7,867,000 (2001): 85.7 per cent Bulgarian, 9.4 per cent Turkish, 3.7 per cent Roma, 1.2 per cent others. The language is Bulgarian, a Southern Slavonic tongue closely allied to Serbo-Croat and Russian with local admixtures of modern Greek, Albanian and Turkish words. The alphabet is Cyrillic. The predominant religion is the Bulgarian Orthodox Church (85.7 per cent of the population); Islam is the second largest religion (13.1 per cent).
CAPITAL – Sofia (population, 1,096,389, 2001 census)
MAJOR CITIES – ΨBurgas; Plovdiv; ΨVarna
CURRENCY – Lev of 100 stotinki
NATIONAL ANTHEM – Gorda Stara Planina (Proud And Ancient Mountains)
NATIONAL DAY – 3 March
NATIONAL FLAG – Three horizontal bands, white, green, red
LIFE EXPECTANCY (years) – 71 (2001)
MORTALITY RATE (per 1,000 population) – 14.34 (2003)
INFANT MORTALITY (per 1,000 births) – 14 (2001)
HIV / AIDS ADULT PREVALENCE – 0.1 per cent (2001)
DEATH PENALTY – No (abolished 1998)
POPULATION BELOW POVERTY LINE – 12.6 per cent (2001)
POPULATION GROWTH RATE – 0.9 per cent (1990–2001)
POPULATION DENSITY – 71 per sq. km (2001)
URBAN POPULATION – 68 per cent (2001)

CLIMATE AND TERRAIN

The Bulgarian landscape is dominated by mountains: the Balkan Mountains cross the country from west to east averaging 2,000 m in height; the Rhodope Mountains are found in the south-west, climbing to almost 3,000 m. Elevation extremes range from 2,925 m (Musala) at the highest point to 0 m (Black Sea) at the lowest. Major rivers include the Danube, the Iskur and the Maritsa.

HISTORY AND POLITICS

Bulgarians are descended from Slavs who came to the area of modern-day Bulgaria in the fifth century AD. The Bulgarian state can trace its foundation back to 680 AD. Bulgaria was part of the Ottoman Empire from 1390 until 1877 when this period of rule was brought to an end with the aid of Russia.

A principality of Bulgaria was created by the Treaty of Berlin in 1878, and in 1908 the country was declared an independent kingdom. A coup d'état in September 1944 gave power to the Fatherland Front, a coalition of Communists, Agrarians and Social Democrats. In August 1945, the main body of Agrarians and Social Democrats left the government. A referendum in September 1946 led to the abolition of the monarchy and the establishment of a republic.

The Communist Party (BCP) dominated the post-war period. Bulgaria became a multiparty democracy in 1990.

In November 2001 the Bulgarian Socialist Party's (BSP) candidate, Georgi Parvanov, became president. The general election held in June was won by the National Movement for Simeon II (NDSV), a movement founded in April (2001) by the former king, which won 43.74 per cent of the vote and 120 of the 240 seats in the legislature. Simeon Saxecoburggotski, the former King, took office as prime minister on 24 July heading a cabinet dominated by the NDSV.

POLITICAL SYSTEM

A new constitution was adopted in 1991. It provides for a directly-elected President who serves for no more than two five-year terms. The chief executive is the Prime Minister, who is appointed by the President, and is usually the leader of the largest party in the legislature. There is a unicameral National Assembly of 240 members who are directly elected by proportional representation for four-year terms. Parliamentary elections are due in 2005 and Presidential elections in 2006.

HEAD OF STATE

President, Georgi Parvanov (BSP), *elected* 18 November 2001, *took office* 19 January 2002
Vice-President, Angel Marin (BSP)

SELECTED GOVERNMENT MEMBERS *as at July 2004*

Prime Minister, Simeon Saxecoburggotski
First Deputy Prime Minister, European Affairs Co-ordinator, Plamen Panayton
Deputy Prime Minister, Economy, Lydia Santova Shouleva
Deputy Prime Minister, Labour and Social Policy, Nikolay Vassilev Vassilev
Defence, Nikolay Avramov Svinarov
Finance, Milen Emilov Velchev
Foreign Affairs, Solomon Isak Passy
Internal Affairs, Georgi Petrov Petkanov

EMBASSY OF THE REPUBLIC OF BULGARIA

186–188 Queen's Gate, London SW7 5HL
T 020-7584 9400/9433
E info@bulgarianembassy.org.uk

Ambassador Extraordinary and Plenipotentiary, HE Valentin Dobrev, apptd 1998

BRITISH EMBASSY
9 Moskovska Street, Sofia
T (+359) (2) 980 1220
E britembinf@mail.orbitel.bg
Ambassador Extraordinary and Plenipotentiary, HE Jeremy Hill

BRITISH COUNCIL DIRECTOR, Ian Stewart
7 Krakra Street, BG-1504 Sofia
T (+359) (2) 942 4344
E bc.sofia@britishcouncil.bg

DEFENCE

The Army has 1,474 main battle tanks, 214 armoured infantry fighting vehicles and 1,643 armoured personnel carriers. The Navy has one submarine, one frigate, 23 patrol and coastal vessels, and nine armed helicopters. The Air Force has 232 combat aircraft and 43 armed helicopters. Bulgaria became a member of NATO in March 2004.

MILITARY EXPENDITURE – 2.5 per cent of GDP (2002)
MILITARY PERSONNEL – 42,470: Army 25,000, Navy 4,370, Air Force 13,100; Paramilitaries 34,000
CONSCRIPTION DURATION – Nine months

ECONOMY AND TRADE

The principal crops are wheat, maize, beet, tomatoes, tobacco, oleaginous seeds, fruit, vegetables and cotton. Around 24 per cent of the population is engaged in agriculture, which accounted for 12.5 per cent of GDP in 2002. Cadmium, coal, copper, pig iron, kaolin, lead, silver and zinc are produced. Industry accounted for about 28 per cent of GDP in 2002.

The government adopted a radical reform package in 1997, including pegging the lev to the Deutsche mark to stimulate the economy. A US$300 million agreement was negotiated with the IMF at the end of 2001 to promote economic growth.

Bulgaria is highly dependent on trade and has been a member of the World Trade Organisation since 1996. The principal exports are textiles and clothing, iron and steel products, foodstuffs, beverages, industrial equipment, telecommunications and sound recording equipment, oil derivatives and non-ferrous metals.

Bulgaria is scheduled to join the European Union in 2007.

GNI – US$13,200 million (2001); US$1,650 per capita (2001)
ANNUAL AVERAGE GROWTH OF GDP – 3.5 per cent (1998)
INFLATION RATE – 10.3 per cent (2000)
UNEMPLOYMENT – 16.4 per cent (2000)
TOTAL EXTERNAL DEBT – US$10,026 million (2000)
FOREIGN DIRECT INVESTMENT – US$2,707 million (1997–2000)
IMPORTS – US$7,981 million (2002)
EXPORTS – US$5,745 million (2002)

BALANCE OF PAYMENTS
Trade – US$1,593 million deficit (2002)
Current Account – US$677 million deficit (2002)

Trade with UK	*2002*	*2003*
Imports from UK	£133,712,000	£153,709,000
Exports to UK	119,026,000	125,978,000

EDUCATION

Education is free and compulsory for children from six to 16 years inclusive. There are three universities (at Sofia, Plovdiv and Veliko Turnovo), an American University and 21 higher education establishments.

ILLITERACY RATE – (m) 0.9 per cent; (f) 1.8 per cent (2003)
ENROLMENT (percentage of age group) – primary 92 per cent (1996); secondary 74 per cent (1996); tertiary 41.2 per cent (1996)

TRANSPORT INFRASTRUCTURE

Bulgaria has a total of 4,294 km of railways, 37,286 km of roads and 470 km of waterways. There are six harbours (Burgas, Lom, Nesebur, Ruse, Varna and Vidin), 216 airports, 128 of which are surfaced, and one heliport.

MEDIA

In 1996 Bulgaria gave national radio and television the status of public services and granted them independence. In 2003 BTV, the country's first national commercial channel (part of the Rupert Murdoch News Corporation) was launched. In 2003 Nova TV became the second national commercial channel.

CULTURE

Bulgaria is still a country in transition from Communism. Some rural areas are virtually unchanged since the Communist era while urban centres are now radically Western in character and outlook. Bulgaria's Roman and Byzantine ruins are culturally significant, as are its churches and monasteries. Famous Bulgarian writers include Stoyan Mikhaylovski (1856–1927) and Iordan Iovkov (1884–1938).

BURKINA FASO

République Démocratique du Burkina Faso – Democratic Republic of Burkina Faso

AREA – 274,000 sq. km. Neighbours: Mali (west), Niger and Benin (east), Togo, Ghana and Côte d'Ivoire (south)
POPULATION – 11,087,000. The official language is French. Mossi, More, Dioula and Gourmantché are indigenous languages
CAPITAL – Ouagadougou (population, 1,000,000, 2000 estimate)
MAJOR CITIES – Bobo-Dioulasso; Koudougou
CURRENCY – Franc CFA of 100 centimes
NATIONAL ANTHEM – Ditanyé (Hymn of Victory)
NATIONAL DAY – 11 December
NATIONAL FLAG – Equal bands of red over green, with a yellow star in centre
MORTALITY RATE (per 1,000 population) – 18.76 (2003)
HIV / AIDS ADULT PREVALENCE – 6.5 per cent (2001)
DEATH PENALTY – No (abolished 1988)
POPULATION BELOW POVERTY LINE – 45 per cent (2001)
POPULATION GROWTH RATE – 3 per cent

POPULATION DENSITY – 42 per sq. km (1999)
MILITARY EXPENDITURE – 1.5 per cent of GDP (2002)
MILITARY PERSONNEL – 10,800: Army 6,400, Air Force 200, Paramilitaries 4,200
ILLITERACY RATE – (m) 66.1 per cent; (f) 85.9 per cent (2000)
ENROLMENT (percentage of age group) – primary 40 per cent (1997); tertiary 1 per cent (1997)

CLIMATE AND TERRAIN

Burkina Faso is a landlocked state in West Africa. There are wooded savannahs in the south and the north is semi-desert with elevation extremes ranging from 749 m (Tena Kourou) at the highest point to 200 m (Mouhoun River) at the lowest. The wet season runs from June to October and the dry season from December to May (there are recurring droughts). Average annual temperatures range from 24°C in January to 28°C in July.

HISTORY AND POLITICS

Burkina Faso (formerly Upper Volta) was part of the Mossi Empire during the 18th and 19th centuries. It was annexed by France in 1896 and between 1932 and 1947 was administered as part of the Colony of the Ivory Coast. It decided on 11 December 1958 to remain an autonomous republic within the French Community; full independence outside the Community was proclaimed on 5 August 1960. The name Burkina Faso ('land of upright men') was given to the country after independence (1983).

Following a number of military coups, Capt. Blaise Compaoré seized power from Thomas Sankara (who had also taken power by coup) in 1987. A new constitution was adopted in 1991. A general election was held in May 2002 and won by the Congress for Democracy and Progress (CDP). Presidential elections were held in November 1998 and won by Compaoré, the CDP candidate, in the face of a boycott by the opposition parties.

POLITICAL SYSTEM

The parliament has two chambers: the Assemblée Nationale (111 deputies elected for five years) and the Chambre des Representants (178 members elected for three-year terms). The President is elected on a seven-year mandate although there is a proposal to change this to five years from 2005.

HEAD OF STATE

President, Capt. Blaise Compaoré, *assumed office* October 1987, *elected* December 1991, *re-elected* November 1998

SELECTED GOVERNMENT MEMBERS *as at July 2004*
Prime Minister, Paramanga Ernest Yonli
Defence, Yero Boli
Finance and Budget, Jean-Baptiste Compaoré
Minister of State, Youssouf Ouédraogo

EMBASSY OF THE REPUBLIC OF BURKINA FASO
16 Place Guy d'Arezzo, 1180 Brussels, Belgium
T (+32) (2) 345 9912
Ambassador Extraordinary and Plenipotentiary, HE Kadré Désiré Ouédraogo, apptd 2001

BRITISH AMBASSADOR, HE Franois Gordon, CMG, resident at Abidjan, Côte d'Ivoire

ECONOMY AND TRADE

The principal industry is cattle and sheep rearing. Agriculture employs over 90 per cent of the workforce and contributes 33 per cent of GDP. The chief exports are cotton, livestock and animal feed, and gold. The chief imports are capital goods, foodstuffs and fuel oils.

The economy is fragile due to the high cost of services such as electricity, water and telephones, restricted access to healthcare and the limited nature of the export market. In June 2003 the IMF granted Burkina Faso a new three-year Poverty Reduction and Growth Facility worth around US$17 million. The majority of this money will be used for macroeconomic restructuring.

GNI – US$2,422 million (2000); US$210 per capita (2000)
ANNUAL AVERAGE GROWTH OF GDP – 2.2 per cent (2000)
INFLATION RATE – 0.3 per cent (2000)
TOTAL EXTERNAL DEBT – US$1,332 million (2000)
IMPORTS – US$656 million (2001)
EXPORTS – US$175 million (2001)

Trade with UK	*2002*	*2003*
Imports from UK	£2,553,000	£3,730,000
Exports to UK	238,000	153,000

TRANSPORT INFRASTRUCTURE

There are 12,506 km of roads, of which 2,001 km are surfaced. An estimated 60 per cent of the country's villages are further than 3 km from a main road and paths are impassable during the wet season. There are 622 km of railway track in operation and two main airports.

MEDIA

The Ministry of Communication and Culture regulates the media. There are several private radio stations and a private television channel.

CULTURE

The largest tribe is the Mossi (48 per cent) whose king, the Moro Naba, still wields moral influence. There are over 60 other ethnic groups including Gurunsi, Sénufo, Lobi, Bobo, Mande and Fulani, Despite its poverty Burkina Faso is admired for its music, dance, theatre and film. The art of the Mossi, Bobo and Lobi is famous (Burkina Faso has Africa's largest crafts market). Burkina Faso also plays host to the Pan-African Film Festival every two years.

BURUNDI

République du Burundi – Republic of Burundi

AREA – 27,834 sq. km. Neighbours: Rwanda (north), Tanzania (east and south), Democratic Republic of Congo (west)
POPULATION – 6,194,000: 83 per cent Hutu, 15 per cent Tutsi. The official languages are Kirundi, a Bantu language, and French. Kiswahili is also used
CAPITAL – Bujumbura (formerly Usumbura) (population, 235,440, 1990)
MAJOR CITIES – Kitega
CURRENCY – Burundi franc of 100 centimes
NATIONAL DAY – 1 July
NATIONAL FLAG – Divided diagonally by a white saltire into red and green triangles; on a white disc in the centre three red six-pointed stars edged in green
NATIONAL ANTHEM – Burundi Bwacu (Dear Burundi)
MORTALITY RATE (per 1,000 population) – 17.8 (2003)
HIV / AIDS ADULT PREVALENCE – 8.3 per cent (2001)
DEATH PENALTY – Yes
POPULATION BELOW POVERTY LINE – 70 per cent (2002)
POPULATION GROWTH RATE – 2 per cent (1990–2001)
POPULATION DENSITY – 233 per sq. km (1999)
MILITARY EXPENDITURE – 5.9 per cent of GDP (2002)
MILITARY PERSONNEL – 50,500: Army 45,000, Paramilitaries 5,500
ILLITERACY RATE – (m) 43.4 per cent; (f) 59.3 per cent (2000)
ENROLMENT (percentage of age group) – primary 51 per cent (1997); secondary 7 per cent (1997)

CLIMATE AND TERRAIN

This Central African state lies across the Nile-Congo watershed. An interior plateau rises 1,500 m to the country's highest point at 2,685 m (Mt Karonje). The River Ruzizi forms part of the north-west frontier with Zaire and Lake Kiki, in Rwanda, with Lake Tanganyika (at 780 m the lowest elevation in the country) in the south and east. The climate is equatorial. The dry season runs from June to September while the average daily temperature is 23°C.

HISTORY AND POLITICS

Ruled by the Tutsi kingdom during the 16th century and then occupied by Germany in 1890, Burundi became independent as a constitutional monarchy on 1 July 1962. However, the monarchy was overthrown in 1966 and the country became a republic.

Although most of the population is Hutu, political and military power has traditionally rested with the Tutsi minority. Since the 1960s, Hutu attempts to overthrow Tutsi rule have resulted in ethnic massacres. The Tutsi-dominated army attempted a coup in 1993 in which President Melchior Ndadaye was killed. The government regained control in December but two months of inter-racial fighting left more than 30,000 dead and 500,000 as refugees.

The Front for Democracy in Burundi (FRODEBU) and the National Unity and Progress Party (UPRONA) agreed to form a coalition government in 1994 with a Tutsi prime minister and President Ntaryamira, a Hutu. On 6 April 1994 Ntaryamira was killed when the aircraft he was travelling in with President Habyarimana of Rwanda was shot down near Kigali, Rwanda's capital. The government was unable to halt attacks by the Tutsi-dominated army and Hutu militias on each other's communities. The fighting claimed 200,000 lives in 1993–5.

In July 1996 the army again seized power and installed Maj. Buyoya as president. Political parties were banned and the National Assembly was suspended until October 1996 when fewer than half its deputies attended. A multi-ethnic government of national unity was formed in August 1996.

A transitional constitution, designed to provide for a political partnership between Hutus and Tutsis, came into being in June 1998 and a 117-member Transitional National Assembly was inaugurated in July 1998. An additional 53 members of the National Assembly were elected on 1 January 2002, in accordance with the Arusha peace deal.

In July 2001, Burundi's 19 political parties agreed a peace accord at talks hosted by former South African president, Nelson Mandela. Under the agreement, provision was made for a three-year transitional government to be headed by President Buyoya, a Tutsi, with a Hutu as vice-president – the two switching roles midway through the three-year term. In December 2002 the government signed a cease-fire agreement with the main Hutu rebel group, the National Council for the Defence of Democracy Forces for the Defence of Democracy (CNDD FDD). It was due to become effective on 30 December, but implementation of the cease-fire was delayed indefinitely. As part of the power-sharing agreement President Buyoya handed over the presidency to his Hutu vice-president, Domitien Ndayizeye, who was sworn into office on 30 April 2003 for an initial term of 18 months after which presidential elections would be held.

HEAD OF STATE
President, Domitien Ndayizeye, *sworn in* 30 April 2003
Vice-President, Alphonse Marie Kadege

SELECTED GOVERNMENT MEMBERS *as at July 2004*
Defence, Maj.-Gen. Vincent Niyungeko
External Relations and Co operation, Therence Sinunguraza
Finance, Athanase Gahungu
Interior, Simon Nyandwi

EMBASSY OF THE REPUBLIC OF BURUNDI
46 Sq. Marie Louise, 1000 Brussels, Belgium
T (+32) (2) 2304535
Ambassador Extraordinary and Plenipotentiary, HE Ferdinand Nyabenda, apptd 2003

BRITISH AMBASSADOR, HE Susan Hogwood, OBE, apptd 2001, resident at Kigali, Rwanda

ECONOMY AND TRADE

The chief crop is coffee, accounting for around 50 per cent of export earnings in 2002. Tea, mineral, hide and skin exports are also important. Agriculture accounted for 41 per cent of GDP and employed over 90 per cent of the workforce in 2002. On 9 October 2002 the IMF approved a credit of US$7.3 million in emergency post-conflict assistance to support the country's reconstruction and economic recovery programme.
GNI – US$732 million (2000); US$110 per capita (2000)
ANNUAL AVERAGE GROWTH OF GDP – 4.5 per cent (1998)
INFLATION RATE – 24.3 per cent (2000)
TOTAL EXTERNAL DEBT – US$1,100 million (2000)

IMPORTS – US$139 million (2001)
EXPORTS – US$39 million (2001)

BALANCE OF PAYMENTS
Trade – US$59 million deficit (2000)
Current Account – US$49 million deficit (2000)

Trade with UK	*2002*	*2003*
Imports from UK	£1,712,000	£1,940,000
Exports to UK	434,000	617,000

TRANSPORT INFRASTRUCTURE

There are no railways in Burundi. There are 14,480 km of roads, but only 1,014 km of these are paved. There is one port, Bujumbura, and seven airports (one has a surfaced runway).

MEDIA

La Radiodiffusion et Television Nationale de Burundi (RTNB) is the main TV station and it is government controlled. Low literacy levels mean that the dominant news media is radio. Radio Burundi (RTNB) broadcasts in Kirundi, Swahili, French and English and is state controlled. There are several newspapers but they are published sporadically due to government influence.

CAMBODIA

Preăh Réachéanachâkr Kâmpuchéa –
The Kingdom of Cambodia

AREA – 181,035 sq. km. Neighbours: Laos (north), Thailand (north and west), Vietnam (east)
POPULATION – 13,000,000 (2003 census). The official language is Khmer. Chinese, Vietnamese and French are also spoken
CAPITAL – ΨPhnom Penh (population, 1,200,000, 2003 census)
CURRENCY – Riel of 100 sen
NATIONAL ANTHEM – Nokoreach
NATIONAL DAY – 9 November (Independence Day)
NATIONAL FLAG – Three horizontal stripes of blue, red, blue, with the blue of double width and containing a representation of the temple of Angkor in white
LIFE EXPECTANCY (years) – 57 (2001)
HIV / AIDS ADULT PREVALENCE – 2.7 per cent (2001)
DEATH PENALTY – No (abolished 1997)
POPULATION GROWTH RATE – 2.7 per cent (1990–2001)
POPULATION DENSITY – 60 per sq. km (1999)
ENROLMENT (percentage of age group) – primary 100 per cent (1997); tertiary 24 per cent (1997)

CLIMATE AND TERRAIN

Cambodia is a mostly flat county (with the exception of the Cardamom Mountains in the south-west and the uplands of the north-east). Dominated by the Mekong River, Cambodia is also home to Tonle Sap, the largest lake in south-east Asia. The monsoon season is from May to November. The highest point of elevation is at 1,810 m (Phnum Aoral) while the lowest is 0 m (Gulf of Thailand).

HISTORY AND POLITICS

Although the Khmer people have inhabited the region for almost 2,000 years, the Khmer kingdom was at its strongest during the 11th century, with lands reaching to modern-day Laos, Thailand and Vietnam. The kingdom lost power and territory from 1432 onwards.

Cambodia became a French protectorate in 1863 and was granted independence within the French Union as an Associate State in 1949. Although full independence was proclaimed in 1953 and Prince Norodom Sihanouk became head of state, by 1970 Sihanouk was deposed and a Khmer Republic was declared.

In 1975, Phnom Penh fell to the North Vietnamese-backed Khmer Rouge. During Khmer Rouge rule hundreds of thousands of Cambodians fled into exile and an estimated two million were killed.

In 1978, Vietnamese troops invaded Cambodia and the state was renamed the People's Republic of Kampuchea (PRK); in 1989 it became the State of Cambodia (SOC). Following the Vietnamese withdrawal in 1989, the resistance forces regained ground.

In September 1990, the government and the resistance forces established a Supreme National Council and peace agreements were signed in October 1991. In March 1992 the United Nations Transitional Authority for Cambodia (UNTAC) assumed authority from the government in the run-up to the multiparty elections, which were held in May 1993. In September 1993 a new constitution was adopted under which Cambodia became a pluralist liberal democracy with a constitutional monarchy. Prince Sihanouk was elected king and he appointed a new government.

In 1998 a coalition government was formed with Hun Sen as Prime Minister and Prince Ranariddh as chairman of the National Assembly. Elections to the National Assembly were held on 27 July 2003. Prime Minister Hun Sen and his Cambodian People's Party (CPP) won 73 of the 123 parliamentary seats.

INSURGENCIES

The Khmer Rouge was outlawed in 1994 and its leader Pol Pot was captured by a group of defectors in June 1997 and died in captivity in April 1998. The remaining 4,332 Khmer Rouge soldiers surrendered in February 1999.

In 1997 negotiations began between the Royal Government and the UN to set up an international tribunal to prosecute former leaders of the Khmer Rouge regime for atrocities committed during its rule. In 2001 the Royal Government approved legislation for the creation of the tribunal but in 2002 the UN broke off negotiations claiming that the planned court did not comply with international standards of justice. Negotiations resumed in November 2002 and in 2003 an agreement was signed by Cambodia and the UN allowing the majority of tribunal judges to be Cambodian but with a requirement for at least one foreign judge to support a tribunal ruling.

POLITICAL SYSTEM

Legislative power is vested in the National Assembly, which has 123 members elected for five-year terms, and the Senate, which has 61 appointed members and was formed on 25 March 1999, following an amendment to the constitution by the National Assembly. Executive power rests with the Royal Government, with the King having the power only to make appointments and declare a state of emergency, in consultation with the government.

HEAD OF STATE
HM The King of Cambodia, Norodom Sihanouk, *elected by the Council of the Throne* 24 September 1993
Chair of the National Assembly, Prince Norodom Ranariddh

SELECTED GOVERNMENT MEMBERS *as at July 2004*
Prime Minister, Hun Sen
Deputy Prime Minister, Co-Minister of Interior, Sar Kheng
Deputy Prime Minister, Education, Youth and Sports, Tol Loah
Co-Minister of National Defence, Prince Sisowath Sereiroat
Commerce, Cham Prasit
Senior Minister, Co-Minister of Interior, Yu Hokkri
Senior Minister, Co-Minister of National Defence, Gen. Tea Banh
Senior Minister, Economy and Finance, Keat Chhon

ROYAL EMBASSY OF CAMBODIA
4 rue Adolph Yvon, F-75116 Paris, France
T (+33) (1) 45 03 4720
Ambassador Extraordinary and Plenipotentiary, HE Uch Kiman, apptd 2003

BRITISH EMBASSY
27–29 Street 75, Phnom Penh
T (+855) (23) 427124
Ambassador Extraordinary and Plenipotentiary, HE Stephen Bridges, apptd 2001

DEFENCE

The Army has 150 main battle tanks and 190 armoured personnel carriers. The Navy has 4 patrol and coastal vessels. The Air Force has 24 combat aircraft.
MILITARY EXPENDITURE – 2.5 per cent of GDP (2002)
MILITARY PERSONNEL – 125,000: Army 75,000, Navy 3,000, Air Force 2,000, Provincial Forces 45,000; Paramilitaries 67,000

ECONOMY AND TRADE

The economy is largely based on agriculture, fishing and forestry. Agriculture employs over 75 per cent of the workforce and produced 30 per cent of GDP in 2003. In addition to rice, which is the staple crop, the major products are rubber, livestock, maize, timber, pepper, palm sugar, fresh and dried fish, kapok, beans, soya and tobacco. Textiles, leather goods, furnishings, timber and rubber are the main exports; the main imports are cigarettes, gold, diesel and oil. Tourism is the fastest-growing sector of the economy.

Extreme drought and flooding in 2002 ruined some US$30 million worth of rice crops. Cambodia's debt to China was written off in November 2002.
GNI – US$3,150 million (2000); US$260 per capita (2000)
ANNUAL AVERAGE GROWTH OF GDP – 4.5 per cent (2003)
INFLATION RATE – 3.5 per cent (2002)
TOTAL EXTERNAL DEBT – US$2,357 million (2000)
IMPORTS – US$1,456million (2001)
EXPORTS – US$1,296 million (2001)
BALANCE OF PAYMENTS
Trade – US$348 million deficit (2001)
Current Account – US$105 million deficit (2001)

Trade with UK	*2002*	*2003*
Imports from UK	£3,871,000	£3,572,000
Exports to UK	88,871,000	100,887,000

TRANSPORT INFRASTRUCTURE

The country has about 34,100 km of roads, although most are now in a state of disrepair. There are two railways, one from Phnom Penh to the Thai border, the other from Phnom Penh to Kampot and Sihanoukville (Kompong Som). Phnom Penh is on a river capable of receiving ships of up to 2,500 tons all the year round. The deep-water port at Sihanoukville (Kompong Som) on the Gulf of Thailand can receive ships of up to 10,000 tons. The port is linked to Phnom Penh by a modern highway.

MEDIA

Much of the Cambodian media is owned by political parties but the Prime Minister, Hun Sen, has been active in encouraging press freedom. The state broadcaster is National Television of Cambodia (TVK) and there are five other major commercial and privately owned channels. There are no restrictions on the ownership and use of private satellite dishes and foreign radio is also easily received and widely accessed.

CULTURE

Cambodia's Khmer culture can still be seen in the capital's many museums and temples. There are also vestiges of French colonial influence, most notably in the architecture and cuisine. The abandoned temples of Angkor Wat (9–13th centuries), a religious and administrative centre built by Khmer kings, are the country's most popular tourist destination.

CAMEROON

République du Cameroun – Republic of Cameroon

AREA – 465,400 sq. km. Neighbours: Nigeria (north and west), Chad and Central African Republic (east), Republic of Congo, Gabon and Equatorial Guinea (south)
POPULATION – 15,203,000 (2001). French and English are both official languages and enjoy equal status
CAPITAL – Yaoundé (population, 653,670, 1986 estimate)
MAJOR CITIES – ΨDouala is the commercial centre
CURRENCY – Franc CFA of 100 centimes
NATIONAL ANTHEM – O Cameroun, Berceau De Nos Ancêtres (O Cameroon, Thou Cradle Of Our Forefathers)
NATIONAL DAY – 20 May

NATIONAL FLAG – Vertical stripes of green, red and yellow with single five-pointed yellow star in centre of red stripe
LIFE EXPECTANCY (years) – 50 (2001)
MORTALITY RATE (per 1,000 population) – 15.3 (2003)
INFANT MORTALITY (per 1,000 births) – 96 (2001)
HIV / AIDS ADULT PREVALENCE – 11.8 per cent (2001)
DEATH PENALTY – Yes
POPULATION BELOW POVERTY LINE – 48 per cent (2000)
POPULATION GROWTH RATE – 2.4 per cent (1990–2001)
POPULATION DENSITY – 33 per sq. km (2001)
MILITARY EXPENDITURE – 1.2 per cent of GDP (2002)
MILITARY PERSONNEL – 23,100: Army 12,500, Navy 1,300, Air Force 300, Paramilitaries 9,000
ILLITERACY RATE – (m) 17.9 per cent; (f) 30.0 per cent (2000)
ENROLMENT (percentage of age group) – secondary 85 per cent (1997)

CLIMATE AND TERRAIN

There are three main geographic zones: desert plains in the north (Lake Chad), mountains in the central region, and tropical rain forests in the south and east. The wet season runs from June to September in the north and from May to November in the south. Elevation extremes range from 4,095 m (Fako, on Mt Cameroon) at the highest point to 0 m (Atlantic Ocean) at the lowest.

HISTORY AND POLITICS

The Bakas (Pygmies) and Bantu speakers of the Cameroonian highlands were probably the country's earliest peoples. Cameroon was controlled by the Dutch in the 17th century who established trade with Spain, Britain, France, Germany and the USA. The Fulani people of the western Sahel conquered northern Cameroon from the 1770s to the early 1800s.

The German colony of Kamerun, established in 1884, was captured by British and French forces in 1916 and divided into the League of Nations-mandated territories (later UN trusteeships) of East (French) and West (British) Cameroon. On 1 January 1960 East Cameroon became independent as the Republic of Cameroon. This was joined on 1 October 1961 by the southern part of West Cameroon after a plebiscite held under the auspices of the United Nations; the northern part joined Nigeria. Cameroon became a federal republic with separate East and West Cameroon state governments. After a plebiscite held in 1972, Cameroon became a unitary republic and a one-party state.

A coalition government was formed after the multiparty elections of 1992, following extensive unrest.

The Cameroon People's Democratic Movement (RDCP) retained its overall majority in the National Assembly in the legislative election of 2002. Opposition groups alleged widespread fraud in the conduct of the elections. A presidential election was scheduled for October 2004.

INTERNATIONAL RELATIONS

There have been armed clashes with Nigeria over the disputed Bakassi peninsula which is rich in oil. In October 2002 Cameroon was given possession of the peninsula in a ruling by the International Court of Justice. Nigeria was awarded a series of other strategically significant territories near the land border. It was agreed on 15 November 2002 that a UN-led commission, the Cameroon-Nigeria Mixed Commission (CNMC), would be established to defuse tension in the long-running dispute. Negotiations are ongoing.

POLITICAL SYSTEM

The President is directly elected for a seven-year term, and appoints the Prime Minister and Cabinet. The National Assembly comprises 180 members, directly elected for a five-year term. The 1995 constitutional amendments provided for the establishment of a senate (100 seats, ten per province with 70 members indirectly elected and 30 appointed by the President) however, this has yet to come into force.

HEAD OF STATE
President and Commander-in-Chief of the Armed Forces, Paul Biya, *acceded* 6 November 1982, *elected* 14 January 1984, *re-elected* 24 April 1988, 10 October 1992, 12 October 1997

SELECTED GOVERNMENT MEMBERS *as at July 2004*
Prime Minister, Peter Mafany Musonge
Defence, Laurent Esso
Finance, Michel Meva'a M'Eboutou
Foreign Affairs, Franois-Xavier N'Goubeyou
Interior, Marafa Hamidou Yaya

HIGH COMMISSION FOR THE REPUBLIC OF CAMEROON
84 Holland Park, London W11 3SB
T 020-7727 0771
Ambassador Extraordinary and Plenipotentiary, HE Samuel Libock-Mbei, apptd 1995

BRITISH HIGH COMMISSION
Avenue Winston Churchill, BP 547 Yaoundé
T (+237) (2) 220545
High Commissioner, HE Richard Wildash, LVO, apptd 2002

BRITISH COUNCIL DIRECTOR, Tom Hinton
Avenue Charles de Gaulle, BP 818, Yaoundé
T (+237) (2) 211696/203172
E bc-yaounde@britishcouncil.cm

ECONOMY AND TRADE

Principal products are cocoa, coffee, bananas, cotton, timber, groundnuts, aluminium, rubber and palm products. Crude petroleum is also one of Cameroon's principal products. Agriculture accounts for 46 per cent of GDP and employs 70 per cent of the workforce, services 33 per cent, and industry 21 per cent.

In July 2003 a new oil pipeline originating in Chad and passing through Cameroon opened. It is estimated that this could bring US$500 million into Cameroon over the next 25 years. France, Italy, Spain, Belgium, the UK and Nigeria are Cameroon's main trading partners.

GNI – US$8,700 million (2001); US$580 per capita (2001)
ANNUAL AVERAGE GROWTH OF GDP – 5.3 per cent (2001)
INFLATION RATE – 5.3 per cent (1999)
TOTAL EXTERNAL DEBT – US$8,600 million (2002)
FOREIGN DIRECT INVESTMENT – US$166 million (1997–2000)

IMPORTS – US$1,318 million (1999)
EXPORTS – US$1,601 million (1999)

BALANCE OF PAYMENTS
Trade – US$627 million surplus (1995)
Current Account – US$90 million surplus (1995)

Trade with UK	*2002*	*2003*
Imports from UK	£35,739,000	£33,121,000
Exports to UK	64,673,000	97,610,000

MEDIA

The government controls the media in Cameroon via the state run Cameroon Radio-Television Corporation (CRTV) which operates national television and radio networks as well as provincial stations. Newspapers are also subject to government controls. There are two private television stations and numerous private radio stations.

CULTURE

Cameroon is characterised by an extraordinary geographical, cultural and linguistic diversity that is reflected in the work of Mongo Beti (1932–2001) and Ferdinand Oyono (b. 1929), two of Cameroon's most celebrated writers.

CANADA

AREA – 9,221,000 sq. km. Neighbours: USA (south), Alaska (USA) (west)
POPULATION – 31,015,000 (2001). The languages are English and French
CAPITAL – Ottawa (population, 1,063,664, 2001 census).
MAJOR CITIES – Calgary; Edmonton; Hamilton; ΨMontréal; Québec; Toronto; ΨVancouver; Winnipeg
CURRENCY – Canadian dollar (C$) of 100 cents
NATIONAL ANTHEM – O Canada
NATIONAL DAY – 1 July (Canada Day)
NATIONAL FLAG – Red maple leaf with 11 points on white square, flanked by vertical red bars one-half the width of the square
LIFE EXPECTANCY (years) – 79 (2001)
MORTALITY RATE (per 1,000 population) – 7.61 (2003)
INFANT MORTALITY (per 1,000 births) – 5 (2001)
HIV / AIDS ADULT PREVALENCE – 0.3 per cent (2001)
DEATH PENALTY – No (abolished 1998)
POPULATION GROWTH RATE – 1 per cent (1990–2001)
POPULATION DENSITY – 3 per sq. km (2001)
URBAN POPULATION – 79 per cent (2001)

CLIMATE AND TERRAIN

Canada occupies the whole of the northern part of the North American continent, with the exception of Alaska. In eastern Canada, the most southerly point is Middle Island in Lake Erie. The six main physiographic divisions are: the Appalachian-Acadian region, the Canadian shield, which comprises more than half the country, the St Lawrence-Great Lakes lowland, the interior plains, the Cordilleran region and the Arctic archipelago.

The climate of the eastern and central portions presents greater extremes than in corresponding latitudes in Europe, but in the south-western portion of the prairie region and the southern portions of the Pacific slope, the climate is milder. The tornado season is May to September, peaking in June and early July in southern Ontario, Alberta, south-eastern Quebec and southern Saskatchewan and Manitoba through to Thunder Bay. The interior of British Columbia and western New Brunswick are also tornado zones. Elevation extremes range from 5,959 m (Mt Logan) at the highest point to 0 m (Atlantic Ocean) at the lowest.

HISTORY AND POLITICS

Canada was discovered by Sebastian Cabot (1474–1557) in 1497 and the French took possession of the country in 1534. The first permanent settlement at Port Royal (now Annapolis), Nova Scotia, was founded in 1605, and Québec was founded in 1608. In 1759 Québec was captured by British forces under General Wolfe and in 1763 the whole territory of Canada became a possession of Great Britain by the Treaty of Paris (1763). Nova Scotia was ceded in 1713 by the Treaty of Utrecht, the provinces of New Brunswick and Prince Edward Island being subsequently formed out of it. British Columbia was formed into a Crown colony in 1858, having previously been a part of the Hudson Bay Territory, and was united to Vancouver Island in 1866.

The constitution of Canada has its source in the British North America Act of 1867 which formed a Dominion, under the name of Canada, of the four provinces of Ontario, Québec, New Brunswick and Nova Scotia. To this federation the other provinces and territories have subsequently been admitted: Manitoba and Northwest Territories (1870), British Columbia (1871), Prince Edward Island (1873), Yukon (1898), Alberta and Saskatchewan (1905) and Newfoundland (1949). In 1982, the constitution was patriated (severed from the British parliament) with the approval of all provinces except Québec. In 1985, the federal Prime Minister and the provincial premiers concluded the Meech Lake Accord which provided for Québec to be recognised as a distinct society within Canada. However, two provincial legislatures withheld approval and the accord did not come into force. In Québec, a referendum calling for sovereignty and a new political and economic partnership was defeated in October 1995. In September 1997 Québec was recognised as having a 'unique character' by leaders of the other provinces and territories. A new territory, Nunavut, which means 'our land' in the Inuit language of Inuktitut, was created on 1 April 1999 by partitioning the Northwest Territories.

In the federal election of 28 June 2004 the Liberal Party won a fourth consecutive term of office. The state of parties in the House of Commons following the election was Liberals 135, Conservative Party of Canada 99, Bloc Québécois 54 and New Democratic Party 19.

POLITICAL SYSTEM

Executive power is vested in a Governor-General appointed by the Sovereign on the advice of the Prime Minister.

Parliament consists of a Senate and a House of Commons. The Senate consists of 104 members, nominated by the Governor-General on the advice of the Prime Minister, the seats being distributed between the various provinces. Senate members serve until the age of 75. The House of Commons has 301 members directly elected for a five-year term. Representation is proportional to the population of each province.

The judicature is administered by judges following the civil law in Québec province and common law in other provinces. Each province has a Court of Appeal. All superior, county and district court judges are appointed by the Governor-General, the others by the Lieutenant-Governors of the provinces.

The highest federal court is the Supreme Court of Canada, which exercises general appellate jurisdiction throughout Canada in civil and criminal cases. There is one other federally constituted court, the Federal Court of Canada, which has jurisdiction on appeals from its trial division, from federal tribunals and reviews of decisions and references by federal boards and commissions.

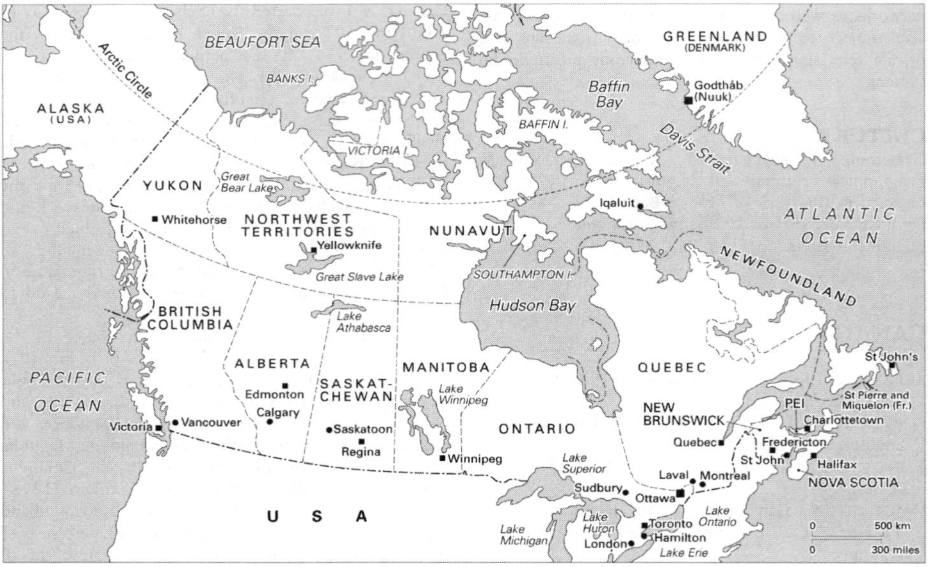

FEDERAL STRUCTURE

Provinces or Territories (with official contractions)	*Population, 1 January 2001*	*Capital*	*Lieutenant-Governor*	*Premier*
Alberta (AB)	3,022,861	Edmonton	Lois Hole	Ralph Klein
British Columbia (BC)	4,077,369	Victoria	Iona Campagnolo	Gordon Campbell
Manitoba (MB)	1,149,220	Winnipeg	Peter Liba	Gary Doer
New Brunswick (NB)	757,267	Fredericton	Hermenegilde Chiasson	Bernard Lord
Newfoundland and Labrador (NF)	537,797	St John's	Arthur House	Danny Williams
Northwest Territories (NT)	42,105	Yellowknife	†Glenna Hansen	Joe Handley
Nova Scotia (NS)	942,322	Halifax	Myra Freeman	John Hamm
Nunavut (NT)§	27,978	Iqaluit	†Peter Irniq	Paul Okalik
Ontario (ON)	11,741,793	Toronto	James Bartleman	Dalton McGinley
Prince Edward Island (PE)	139,078	Charlottetown	J. Léonce Bernard	Patrick Binns
Québec (QC)	7,383,300	Québec	Lise Thibeault	Jean Charest
Saskatchewan (SK)	1,020,650	Regina	Lynda Haverstock	Lorne Calvert
Yukon Territory (YT)	30,194	Whitehorse	†Jack Cable	Dennis Fentie

Area figures include land and water area

† Commissioner

§ Nunavut was created in 1999 from the Northwest Territories

GOVERNOR-GENERAL
Governor-General and Commander-in-Chief, HE Adrienne Clarkson

SELECTED GOVERNMENT MEMBERS *as at July 2004*
Prime Minister, Paul Martin
Deputy Prime Minister, Public Safety and Emergency Preparedness, Anne McLellan
Finance, Ralph Goodale
Foreign Affairs, William Graham
National Defence, David Pratt

CANADIAN HIGH COMMISSION
Macdonald House, 1 Grosvenor Square, London W1K 4AB
T 020-7258 6600
High Commissioner, HE Mel Cappe, apptd 2002

BRITISH HIGH COMMISSION
80 Elgin Street, Ottawa K1P 5K7
T (+1) (613) 237 1530
High Commissioner, HE David Reddaway, apptd 2003

CONSULATES-GENERAL – Montréal, Toronto, Vancouver
CONSULATES – Halifax/Dartmouth, Québec City, St John's, Winnipeg

BRITISH COUNCIL DIRECTOR, Peter Chenery
T (+1) (613) 237 1530
E ottawa.enquiries@ca.britishcouncil.org

BRITISH COUNCIL DIRECTOR IN QUÉBEC
Sarah Dawbarn, 1000 Ouest rue de La Gauchetière, Bureau 4200, Montréal, Québec H3B 4W5
T (+1) (514) 866 5863
E montreal.enquiries@ca.britishcouncil.org

DEFENCE

The Canadian armed forces are unified and organised into three functional commands: Land Force Command; Maritime Command; Air Command.

The Army (Land Forces) has 114 main battle tanks and 1,218 armoured personnel carriers. The Navy (Maritime Forces) has two submarines, four destroyers, 12 frigates and 14 patrol and coastal vessels. The Air Force has 140 combat aircraft.

MILITARY EXPENDITURE – 1.1 per cent of GDP (2002)
MILITARY PERSONNEL – 41,800: Army 19,300, Navy 9,000, Air Force 13,500; Paramilitaries 9,350

ECONOMY AND TRADE

About 68 million hectares of land is farmed, around 7.3 per cent of the total land area. Over 60 per cent of this is under cultivation, the remainder being predominantly classified as unimproved pasture. More than 80 per cent of the cultivated land is in the prairie region of western Canada. The country is one of the world's leading food producers and in 2002 agriculture accounted for 2.1 per cent of GDP and employs about 3.7 per cent of the labour force.

Almost half of Canada's land area is forest, making it the world's largest exporter of timber, pulp and newsprint. The fishing industry employs 120,000 Canadians and contributes C$5,000 million a year to the economy, but Atlantic fish stocks are under restriction orders.

Canada is one of the world's largest exporters of minerals, including potash, nickel, asbestos, cadmium, zinc, elemental sulphur and uranium (Canada is the world's largest single producer of uranium, meeting 28 per cent of world demand). The country is also rich in gold, copper, lead, molybdenum, platinum group metals, gypsum, cobalt, titanium concentrates, and aluminium. The total value of mineral production in 2003 was C$20,200 million.

Canada's second diamond mine opened in the Northwest Territories in 2003, bringing total production value to C$1,700 million. Canada ranks third in the world in terms of diamond production value.

The services sector contributed to 68.2 per cent of GDP in 2001 with finance and real estate generating the most revenue at 16.1 per cent.

There were 20 million foreign visitors in 2002 and four out of five tourists were from the USA.

Canada had relatively high growth in GDP during 2002 at 3.3 per cent and this allowed for an increase of 11.5 per cent in federal expenditure for 2003–4.

The main exports are automotive products, including cars, trucks and parts, machinery and equipment, industrial products and raw materials, forestry products, including wood, wood pulp and paper products, agricultural products (chiefly wheat and meat products), fishery products, and energy products, including crude petroleum and natural gas.

Trade with the USA accounts for about 88 per cent of Canada's exports and 62 per cent of its imports.

GNI – US$681,600 million (2001); US$21,930 per capita (2001)
ANNUAL AVERAGE GROWTH OF GDP – 3.3 per cent (2002)
INFLATION RATE – 2.7 per cent (2000)
UNEMPLOYMENT – 6.8 per cent (2000)
FOREIGN DIRECT INVESTMENT – US$111,533 million (1997–2000)
IMPORTS – US$227,499 million (2002)
EXPORTS – US$252,394 million (2002)

BALANCE OF PAYMENTS
Trade – US$36,838 million surplus (2002)
Current Account – US$14,909 million surplus (2002)

Trade with UK	*2002*	*2003*
Imports from UK	£3,152,213,000	£3,282,649,000
Exports to UK	3,688,378,000	3,795,671,000

TRANSPORT INFRASTRUCTURE

In 2002 there were 1,408 million km of roads, of which 497,306 km were paved, including 16,900 km of national highways. The 7,300 km Trans-Canadian Highway links all ten provinces. There are about 50,000 km of railway track in operation.

The bulk of the 3,000 km of canal shipping in Canada is handled through the two sections of the St Lawrence Seaway, which provide access to the Great Lakes for ocean-going ships. There are 1,390 airports in Canada, 507 of which have surfaced runways.

EDUCATION

Education is under the control of the provincial governments, the cost of the publicly controlled schools being met by local taxation and aided by provincial grants. Education is compulsory between the ages of 6 and 15 or 7 and 16. There are 100 universities and 200 technical institutes and community colleges.

ENROLMENT (percentage of age group) – primary 100 per cent (2002); secondary 100 per cent (2002); tertiary 88 per cent (1997)

MEDIA

The public broadcaster, the Canadian Broadcasting Corporation (CBC), was established in the 1930s and transmits programmes in English and French. Societe Radio Canada is the French-language public broadcast service. There are several commercial TV channels. The CBC also operates four radio networks, and television channels and radio services for indigenous peoples in the north of the country. There are 2,000 licensed radio stations in Canada. The broadcasting regulator enforces quotas of Canadian material (30–35 per cent) on Canadian radio and television.

CULTURE

Canada is a multicultural society with British (28 per cent of people claim British descent), French (23 per cent claim French descent), aboriginal (2 per cent), Asian, German, Ukranian, Dutch, Greek, Polish and Italian influences most dominant. Ninety per cent of the population lives within 200 km of the southern border with the USA.

Notable Canadians include the Nobel laureate Saul Bellow (b. 1915), the poet and novelist Margaret Atwood (b. 1939), the novelist Michael Ondaatje (b. 1943), the classical pianist Glenn Gould (1932–82) and the composer Howard Shore (b. 1946).

CAPE VERDE

República de Cabo Verde – Republic of Cape Verde

AREA – 4,033 sq. km. Comprising the Windward Islands (Santo Antão, São Vicente, Santa Luzia, São Nicolau, Bõa Vista and Sal) and Leeward Islands (Maio, São Tiago, Fogo and Brava)
POPULATION – 406,000, the majority of whom are Roman Catholic. The official language is Portuguese; a creole is spoken by most of the population
CAPITAL – ΨPraia (population, 61,644, 1995 estimate)
CURRENCY – Escudo Caboverdiano of 100 centavos
NATIONAL ANTHEM – É Patria Amada (This Is Our Beloved Country)
NATIONAL DAY – 5 July (Independence Day)
NATIONAL FLAG – Blue with three horizontal stripes of white, red, white near the bottom; over all on these near the hoist a ring of ten yellow stars
MORTALITY RATE (per 1,000 population) – 6.86 (2003)
HIV / AIDS ADULT PREVALENCE RATE – 0.04 per cent (2001)
DEATH PENALTY – No (abolished 1981)
POPULATION LIVING BELOW POVERTY LINE – 30 per cent (2000)
POPULATION GROWTH RATE – 2 per cent (1990–2001)
POPULATION DENSITY – 104 per sq. km (1999)
MILITARY EXPENDITURE – 3.2 per cent of GDP (2002)
MILITARY PERSONNEL – 1,200: Army 1,000, Air Force 100, Coast Guard 100
CONSCRIPTION DURATION – Selective conscription
ILLITERACY RATE – (m) 14.2 per cent; (f) 30.8 per cent (2003)
ENROLMENT (percentage of age group) – primary 100 per cent (1989); secondary 48 per cent (1997)

CLIMATE AND TERRAIN

Cape Verde comprises ten main islands of volcanic origin lying 600 km off the West African coast. The climate is hot and dry. Elevation extremes range from 2,829 m (Mt Fogo) at the highest point to 0 m (Atlantic Ocean) at the lowest.

HISTORY AND POLITICS

The islands were uninhabited when they were first discovered and colonised *c.*1460 by Portugal. Cape Verde achieved independence from Portugal on 5 July 1975 under the Partido Africano da Independência da Guiné e Cabo Verde (PAIGC), a unified party with Guinea-Bissau. A federation of the islands with Guinea Bissau was planned but this was dropped following the 1980 coup in Guinea Bissau.

The republic was a one-party state under President Aristides Pereira and his African Party for the Independence of Cape Verde (PAICV). until the constitution was amended in 1990. Multiparty elections, held in 1991, were won by the opposition Movement for Democracy (MPD). A new constitution was introduced in 1992 which reduced the power of the President and increased the powers of parliament. The MPD, was re-elected in the legislative elections of December 1995 with a landslide victory. President António Mascarenhas Monteiro of the MPD was elected in 1991 and re-elected, unopposed, in 1996. The general election of 2001 returned the PAICV to power with 40 of the 72 seats in the National Assembly. The MPD won 30 seats and the Democratic Alliance for Change won two seats. Pedro Pires of the PAICV narrowly won the second round of the presidential election. The MPD candidate, Carlos Veiga, appealed to the Supreme Court, citing irregularities in the conduct of the elections; the court upheld some of the appeals, which reduced Pires's winning margin to just 12 votes.

POLITICAL SYSTEM

Power is vested in a unicameral National Assembly (Assembleia Nacional) of 72 seats. Members are elected by popular vote to serve five-year terms. The Council of Ministers (Cabinet) is appointed by the President on the recommendation of the Prime Minister. The Prime Minister is nominated by the National Assembly and appointed by the President.

HEAD OF STATE
President, Pedro Pires, *elected* 25 February 2001, *assumed office* 22 March 2001

SELECTED GOVERNMENT MEMBERS *as at July 2004*
Prime Minister, José Maria Neves
Deputy Minister for Culture and Sports, Jorge Tolentino
Economy, Growth and Competitiveness, Avelino Bonifacio
Finance and Planning, Joao Serra
Foreign Affairs and Communities, Victor Borges
Interior Administration, Julio Correia
Parliamentary Affairs and Defence, Armindo Cipriano Mauricio

EMBASSY OF THE REPUBLIC OF CAPE VERDE
Burgemeester Patijnlaan 1930,
2585 CB, The Hague
T (+355) (36) 51/78
Ambassador Extraordinary and Plenipotentiary, vacant

BRITISH AMBASSADOR, HE Alan Burner, resident at Dakar, Senegal

ECONOMY AND TRADE

The islands have little rain and agriculture is mostly confined to irrigated inland valleys. The chief products are bananas and coffee (for export), maize, sugar cane and nuts. Fish and shellfish are important exports. Salt is obtained on Sal, Bõa Vista and Maio; volcanic rock is also mined for export.

The economy is heavily dependent on services, with tourism, commerce and public services accounting for 70 per cent of GDP.

Around 700,000 Cape Verdeans live outside the islands, particularly in the USA and Portugal. The remittances sent home provide an important source of revenue and investment in the economy. Cape Verde has been a member of the Economic Community of West African States (ECOWAS) since 1977. The country is also a member of the Community of Portuguese-speaking Countries (CPLP).

GNI – US$587 million (2000); US$1,340 per capita (2001)
ANNUAL AVERAGE GROWTH OF GDP – 3.3 per cent (2001)
INFLATION RATE – 4.4 per cent (1998)
TOTAL EXTERNAL DEBT – US$325 million (2002)
IMPORTS – US$233 million (2002)
EXPORTS – US$10 million (2001)

BALANCE OF PAYMENTS
Trade – US$236 million deficit (2001)
Current Account – US$71 million deficit (2002)

Trade with UK	*2002*	*2003*
Imports from UK	£5,854,000	£5,918,000
Exports to UK	4,069,000	3,356,000

TRANSPORT INFRASTRUCTURE

The main ports are Praia, Mindelo and Tarrafal, and there is an international airport on Sal. There is a network of internal flights between the islands with daily flights between Praia, Mindelo and Sal. Within the islands there are no railways or waterways. There are 1,100 km of road, 242 km of which are unpaved.

CULTURE

Cape Verdeans have more in common with Portuguese culture than with African culture. The islands are famed for their rich traditions of literature (in both Portuguese and Crioulo) and distinctive musical styles such as the *funana*, dance music and *morna*, a slow, atmospheric song style, accompanied by clarinet, accordion, violin and caraquinho, a Portuguese stringed instrument.

CENTRAL AFRICAN REPUBLIC

République Centrafricaine/Ködrö tî Bê-Afrîka – Central African Republic

AREA – 622,984 sq. km. Neighbours: Chad (north), Sudan (east), Democratic Republic of Congo and Congo-Brazzaville (south), Cameroon (west)
POPULATION – 3,245,000. French is the official language; the national language is Sangho.
CAPITAL – Bangui (population, 560,000, 1994 estimate)
CURRENCY – Franc CFA of 100 centimes
NATIONAL ANTHEM – La Renaissance (The Revival)
NATIONAL DAY – 1 December
NATIONAL FLAG – Four horizontal stripes, blue, white, green, yellow, crossed by central vertical red stripe with a yellow five-pointed star in top left-hand corner
MORTALITY RATE (per 1,000 population) – 6.86 (2003)
HIV / AIDS ADULT PREVALENCE – 0.04 per cent (2001)
DEATH PENALTY – No (abolished 1981)
POPULATION GROWTH RATE – 1.9 per cent (1990–2001)
POPULATION DENSITY – 6 per sq. km (1999)
MILITARY EXPENDITURE – 2.1 per cent of GDP (2002)
MILITARY PERSONNEL – 2,550: Army 1,400, Air Force 150, Paramilitaries 1,000
CONSCRIPTION DURATION – Two years (selective)
ILLITERACY RATE – (m) 40.2 per cent; (f) 65.1 per cent (2000)
ENROLMENT (percentage of age group) – primary 53 per cent (1990); tertiary 1.4 per cent (1991)

CLIMATE AND TERRAIN

This central African state is a plateau between the Chad and Congo river basins. The main river is the Oubangui and at 335 m it is the lowest point of elevation. The climate is tropical with a wet season in the north from June to September and from May to October in the south. The north can reach a temperature of 40°C between February and May and the humidity can be extreme. The south has a more equatorial climate. The highest point of elevation is 1,420 m (Mount Ngaoui).

HISTORY AND POLITICS

In December 1958 the French colony of Ubanghi Shari elected to remain within the French Community and adopted the title of the Central African Republic. It became fully independent on 17 August 1960. The first President, David Dacko, was overthrown in 1966 by the then Col. Bokassa, who in 1976 proclaimed himself Emperor and renamed the country the Central African Empire. In 1979 Bokassa was deposed by Dacko in a bloodless coup and the country reverted to a republic. President Dacko surrendered power in 1981 to Gen. André Kolingba, who instituted military rule until 1985, when a civilian-dominated Cabinet was appointed. In November 1986 a referendum was held which approved a new constitution and the establishment of a one-party state.

President Kolingba formed a coalition government in February 1993. Ange-Félix Patassé of the Central African People's Liberation Party (MLPC) won the presidential elections of 1993 and 1999. A multiparty coalition government was formed after the legislative elections of 1998.

A coup took place in March 2003, in which Franois Bozizé took power, declared himself President, suspended the constitution and dismissed the Cabinet. A broad-based transitional government was formed on 31 March.

POLITICAL SYSTEM

Constitutional reforms were passed in a national referendum in December 1994 which created a constitutional court, introduced elected local assemblies, extended the presidential mandate to a maximum of two six-year terms and subordinated the government to the President. Following the March 2003 coup, President François Bozizé established a 63-member National Transitional Council to assist the President with legislation, draft a new constitution and prepare for elections which were scheduled to take place in December 2004/January 2005.

HEAD OF STATE

President, Minister of Defence, Gen. François Bozizé, *took power* 15 March 2003
Vice-President, Abel Goumba

SELECTED GOVERNMENT MEMBERS *as at July 2004*
Prime Minister, Celestin le Roi Gaoumbalet
Minister for Economy, Finance, Budget, Planning and International Co-operation, Jean-Pierre Lebouder
Foreign Affairs, Regional Integration and Francophone Affairs, Charles Herve Ouenezoui
Interior and Territorial Administration, Marcel Malonga

EMBASSY OF THE CENTRAL AFRICAN REPUBLIC
30 rue des Perchamps, F-75016, Paris
T (+33) (1) 4224 4256
Ambassador Extraordinary and Plenipotentiary, vacant

BRITISH AMBASSADOR, HE Richard Wildash, LVO, resident at Yaoundé, Cameroon

ECONOMY AND TRADE

The Central African Republic is a largely undeveloped country. The majority of the population is engaged in subsistence farming and bananas, cassava, maize and yams are the main crops.

Cotton, diamonds, coffee and timber are the major exports. Industrial goods, machinery and transport equipment, foodstuffs and fuels are the main imports. Major trading partners are Benelux, France, Cameroon, Spain and China.

GNI – US$1,053 million (2000); US$260 per capita (2001)
ANNUAL AVERAGE GROWTH OF GDP – 5.5 per cent (1998)
INFLATION RATE – 1.5 per cent (1999)
TOTAL EXTERNAL DEBT – US$872 million (2000)
IMPORTS – US$107 million (2001)
EXPORTS – US$142 million (2001)

Trade with UK	*2002*	*2003*
Imports from UK	£1,903,000	£902,000
Exports to UK	200,000	1,224,000

TRANSPORT INFRASTRUCTURE

There are no railways. Most travel takes place on the 23,810 km of roads, of which only 643 km are paved. There are 50 airports.

MEDIA

The most balanced media output is from the UN-sponsored radio broadcaster Radio Ndeke Luka. Central African Republic's other radio and television stations are operated by the state via Television Centrafricaine, (TVCA). There are a number of privately owned newspapers but low literacy levels mean that they have little influence.

CULTURE

Central African Republic has a vibrant and sophisticated musical tradition that encompasses the African music of the Congo regions and also reflects the influence of jazz, Latin and the Caribbean.

CHAD

République du Tchad – Republic of Chad

AREA – 1,284,000 sq. km. Neighbours: Niger, Nigeria and Cameroon (west), Libya (north), Sudan (east), Central African Republic (south)
POPULATION – 8,600,000 (2003 estimate); French and Arabic are the official languages; there are more than 50 indigenous languages, of which the most widely spoken is Sara
CAPITAL – N'Djaména (population, 530,100, 1993 census)
CURRENCY – Franc CFA of 100 centimes
NATIONAL ANTHEM – Peuple Tchadien, Debout Et À L'ouvrage (People Of Chad, Arise And To Work)
NATIONAL DAY – 1 December
NATIONAL FLAG – Vertical stripes, blue, yellow and red
MORTALITY RATE (per 1,000 population) – 16.38 (2003)
INFANT MORTALITY RATE (per 1,000 live births) – 117
DEATH PENALTY – Yes
POPULATION LIVING BELOW POVERTY LINE – 80 per cent (2001)
POPULATION GROWTH RATE – 2.7 per cent
POPULATION DENSITY – 6 per sq. km (1999)
MILITARY EXPENDITURE – 0.8 per cent of GDP (2002)
MILITARY PERSONNEL – 30,350: Army 25,000, Air Force 350, Republican Guard 5,000; Paramilitaries 4,500
ILLITERACY RATE – (m) 48.4 per cent; (f) 66.0 per cent (2000)
ENROLMENT (percentage of age group) – primary 58 per cent (1997); secondary 10 per cent (1997); tertiary 1 per cent (1997)

CLIMATE AND TERRAIN

The population of Chad is concentrated in the fertile lowlands of the south, away from the arid central and northern desert areas. The highest point of elevation is 3,415 m (Emi Koussi) and the lowest is at 160 m (the Djourab Depression). The north is almost rainless, the south is tropical and the central plain is hot and dry with a wet season from June to September.

HISTORY AND POLITICS

Chad became a member state of the French Community in 1958, and was proclaimed fully independent on 11 August 1960. The constitution was suspended in 1975 when President Tombalbaye was killed in a coup by Gen. Félix Malloum; following a succession of further coups, Idriss Déby came to power in 1990 and announced the adoption of a multiparty system, allowing the legalisation of political parties in 1991 and 1992. A Higher Transitional Council (CST) was elected in 1993 to serve as the transitional legislature and appointed a transitional government in conjunction with President Déby. The CST has twice extended the transitional period by one year to allow sufficient time to organise elections. A new constitution, establishing a unified, democratic state, was confirmed by a referendum held in March 1996. Déby won the first multiparty presidential elections in 1996 and was re-elected in the presidential elections held in 2001. Elections to the 154-member National Assembly in 2002 were won by the pro-Déby Patriotic Salvation Movement (MPS).

POLITICAL SYSTEM

The constitution makes provision for a bicameral system, consisting of a National Assembly of 155 members elected by popular vote to serve four-year terms, and a Senate. The Senate serves a six-year term of office with one-third of membership renewable every two years. At June 2004 the Senate had not yet been established.

INSURGENCIES

Three rebel movements, the Movement for Unity and the Republic (MUR), the Movement for Democracy and Justice in Chad (MDJT), and the Democratic Revolutionary Council (DRC), announced that they had formed an alliance in February 2000.

In January 2002 the government signed a peace accord with the MDJT and on 9 January 2003 an agreement was signed between the government and rebels of the National Resistance Army (ANR), which provided for an immediate cease-fire and a general amnesty. However, the agreement was rejected by at least one of the eight different movements within the ANR.

HEAD OF STATE

President, Idriss Déby, *took power* December 1990, *elected* 3 July 1996, *re-elected* 20 May 2001

SELECTED GOVERNMENT MEMBERS *as at July 2004*

Prime Minister, Moussa Faki
Finance and Economy, Ahmat Awat Sakine
Foreign Affairs and African Integration, Nagoum Yamassoum
National Defence, Veterans and Victims of War, General Allafouza Koni

EMBASSY OF THE REPUBLIC OF CHAD

52 Boulevard Lambermont 1030, Brussels, Belgium
T (+ 32) (2) 215 1975
Ambassador Extraordinary and Plenipotentiary, HE Abderahim Yacoub Ndiaye, apptd 2000

BRITISH AMBASSADOR, HE Richard Wildash, LVO, resident at Yaoundé, Cameroon

ECONOMY AND TRADE

About 90 per cent of the workforce is occupied in agriculture, fishing and forestry. Salt is mined around Lake Chad, but the most important activities are cotton growing and animal husbandry. Raw cotton (accounting for 40 per cent of total exports in 1999), meat and groundnuts are the main exports. Chad's main trading partners are France, Portugal, Germany, Thailand, Costa Rica, South Africa, Nigeria and Cameroon.

In July 2003 Chad began piping oil from the Doba basin in the south of the country. This oil is piped into Cameroon and onwards to international markets. It is estimated that this new industry could bring US$2,000 million into Chad over the next 25 years. The pipeline is expected to increase government revenues by 45–50 per cent during 2004–5.

In January 2000 the IMF approved a loan facility of around US$49.9 million to support the government's 1999–2002 economic programme. In October 2002 Chad's request for an extension of the commitment period under the Poverty Reduction and Growth Facility (PRGF) arrangement was approved by the IMF.

GNI – US$1,504 million (2000); US$230 per capita (2001)
ANNUAL AVERAGE GROWTH OF GDP – 6.0 per cent (1998)
INFLATION RATE – 3.8 per cent (2000)
TOTAL EXTERNAL DEBT – US$1,116 million (2000)
IMPORTS – US$997 million (2002)
EXPORTS – US$189 million (2002)

BALANCE OF PAYMENTS

Trade – US$77 million deficit (1994)
Current Account – US$38 million deficit (1994)

Trade with UK	*2002*	*2003*
Imports from UK	£4,438,000	£3,383,000
Exports to UK	119,000	1,144,000

TRANSPORT INFRASTRUCTURE

There are no railways in Chad. There are 33,400 km of roads, 267 km of which are paved. There are 2,000 km of waterways and 50 airports, seven of which have surfaced runways.

MEDIA

Low levels of literacy make radio the most important news media. Radiodiffusion Nationale Tchadienne is the state controlled radio station. There are private radio stations but they are closely monitored by the government. There is only one television station, Teletchad, and it is state owned and controlled. Privately owned newspapers circulate in the capital.

CULTURE

Chad is made up of 200 ethnic groups, three major religious groupings (Islam, Christianity and traditional faiths), three different climatic zones and many differing lifestyles (from the urban to rural). For some peoples (the Maba) pre-Islamic social structures are still in place, while others (the Toubou) are nomadic, their territory defined by wells and oases.

CHILE

República de Chile – Republic of Chile

AREA – 748,800 sq. km. Neighbours: Peru (north), Bolivia and Argentina (east)
POPULATION – 15,402,000 (2001). The main groups are: indigenous Araucanian Indians, Fuegians, Rapanui and Changos; Spanish settlers and their descendants; mixed Spanish Indians; and European immigrants. Because of extensive intermarriage only a few indigenous Indians are racially separate. The language is Spanish, with admixtures of local words of Indian origin. The main religion is Roman Catholicism
CAPITAL – Santiago (population, 4,690,684, 1998 UN estimate)
MAJOR CITIES – ΨAntofagasta; Concepción; Puente Alto; ΨValparaíso; ΨPunta Arenas, on the Straits of Magellan, is the southernmost city in the world
CURRENCY – Chilean peso of 100 centavos
NATIONAL ANTHEM – Canción Nacional De Chile (National Anthem Of Chile)
NATIONAL DAY – 18 September (National Anniversary)
NATIONAL FLAG – Two horizontal bands, white, red; in top sixth a white star on blue square, next staff
LIFE EXPECTANCY (years) – 75 (2001)
MORTALITY RATE (per 1,000 population) – 5.63 (2003)
INFANT MORTALITY (per 1,000 births) – 10 (2001)
HIV / AIDS ADULT PREVALENCE RATE – 0.3 per cent (2001)
DEATH PENALTY – Yes*
POPULATION LIVING BELOW POVERTY LINE – 17 per cent (2001)
POPULATION GROWTH RATE – 1.5 per cent (1990–2001)
POPULATION DENSITY – 21 per sq. km (2001)
URBAN POPULATION – 86 per cent (2001)

CLIMATE AND TERRAIN

Chile lies between the Andes (1,524 m to 4,572 m above sea level) and the shores of the South Pacific, extending from the arid north around Arica to Cape Horn. The length of the country is about 4,480 km, with an average breadth, north of 41°, of 160 km. Elevation extremes range from 6,880 m (Nevado Ojos del Salado) at the highest point to 0 m sea level (Pacific Ocean) at the lowest.

HISTORY AND POLITICS

Chile was discovered by Spanish adventurers in the 16th century and remained under Spanish rule until 1810, when the first autonomous government was established. Full independence was consolidated in 1818 after a revolutionary war.

A Marxist, Salvador Allende, was elected President in 1970 as the candidate of the Popular Front alliance, but was overthrown and killed in a military coup in 1973.

Gen. Pinochet, who led the coup, assumed the presidency until presidential and congressional elections were held in 1989, beginning the transition to full democracy.

Gen. Augusto Pinochet was arrested in London in October 1998 following a request by the Spanish government for his extradition, but extradition proceedings were dropped on the grounds of poor health in March 2000, and Pinochet was freed and allowed to return to Chile. The Chilean Supreme Court lifted his immunity from prosecution in August 2000 and in December he was put under house arrest pending trial on charges relating to the kidnapping and murder of more than 70 political opponents. The charges were dismissed by the Court of Appeal, but formally reinstated in January 2001 after it had been determined that Gen. Pinochet was fit to stand trial. In March the charges were reduced to conspiracy to conceal the actions of military death squads. In May 2004 a Chilean appeal court stripped Gen. Pinochet of his immunity leading to speculation that he may soon stand trial for human rights atrocities committed during his time in office.

Ricardo Lagos Escobar of the Party for Democracy (PPD) won the presidential election of January 2000. In the legislative elections held in December 2001, the Coalition of Parties for Democracy (CPD) remained the largest group in the Chamber of Deputies but lost its majority in elections to the Senate.

POLITICAL SYSTEM

Executive power is held by the President who is advised by a cabinet of unelected Ministers. Legislative power is exercised by a Congress which comprises a Senate of 48 senators (38 elected and ten appointed) and a Chamber of Deputies of 118 elected members. Senators serve eight-year terms and deputies serve four-year terms. The presidential term is six years with no possibility of re-election.

HEAD OF STATE

President of the Republic, Ricardo Lagos Escobar, *elected* 16 January 2000, *sworn in* 11 March 2000

SELECTED GOVERNMENT MEMBERS *as at July 2004*
Defence, Michelle Bachelet
Economy and Energy, Jorge Rodríguez Grossi
Finance, Nicolás Eyzaguirre
Foreign Affairs, María Soledad Alvear
Interior, José Miguel Insulza

EMBASSY OF CHILE
12 Devonshire Street, London W1G 7DS
T 020-7580 6392
E embachile@embachile.co.uk
Ambassador Extraordinary and Plenipotentiary, HE Mariano Fernández, apptd 2002

BRITISH EMBASSY
Avenida El Bosque 0125, Casilla 72-D, Santiago
T (+56) (2) 370 4100
E chancery@santiago.mail.fsc.gov.uk
Ambassador Extraordinary and Plenipotentiary, HE Richard Wilkinson, apptd 2003

BRITISH COUNCIL DIRECTOR, John Knagg, OBE
Eliodoro Yáñez 832, Providencia, Santiago
T (+56) (2) 410 6900
E info@britishcouncil.cl

DEFENCE

The Army has 260 main battle tanks, 20 armoured infantry fighting vehicles and 908 armoured personnel carriers. The Navy has three submarines, three destroyers, three frigates, 27 patrol and coastal vessels, 10 combat aircraft and 11 armed helicopters. The Air Force has 79 combat aircraft.

MILITARY EXPENDITURE – 4.1 per cent of GDP (2002)
MILITARY PERSONNEL – 77,300: Army 47,700, Navy 19,000, Air Force 10,600; Paramilitaries 36,800
CONSCRIPTION DURATION – One to 22 months (voluntary from 2005)

ECONOMY AND TRADE

Economic reforms during the late 1970s and the 1980s, with large-scale privatisation and deregulation, have made Chile one of the most successful economies in Latin America. Cereals, vegetables, fruit, tobacco, hemp and vines are grown extensively and livestock accounts for nearly 40 per cent of agricultural production. Sheep farming predominates in the extreme south. Agriculture employs about 12 per cent of the workforce. There are large timber tracts in the central and southern zones which produce timber, cellulose and wood for export. Fishing is also a major industry.

Chile is rich in copper-ore (around 20 per cent of global reserves), iron-ore and nitrates, and is the only commercial producer of nitrate of soda (Chile saltpetre) from natural resources in the world. There are large deposits of high-grade sulphur. Oil and natural gas are produced in the Magallanes area, but domestic production is now declining.

The principal exports are minerals, timber and metal products, fish products and vegetables. The principal imports are food products, industrial raw materials, machinery, and equipment and spares. The main trade partners are Japan, the USA, Argentina, the UK and Brazil; in 1996 Chile joined the Mercosur Free Trade Zone, and in March 1998 signed an extension to a free trade agreement with Mexico. In January 2004, a free trade agreement was signed between the United States and Chile.

GNI – US$70,600 million (2001); US$4,590 per capita (2001)
ANNUAL AVERAGE GROWTH OF GDP – 5.4 per cent (2000)
INFLATION RATE – 1.1 per cent (2003)
UNEMPLOYMENT – 11.6 per cent (2002)
TOTAL EXTERNAL DEBT – US$40,956 million (2002)
FOREIGN DIRECT INVESTMENT US$22,951 million (1997–2000)
IMPORTS – US$18,340 million (2002)
EXPORTS – US$17,093 million (2002)

BALANCE OF PAYMENTS
Trade – US$2,094 million surplus (2001)
Current Account – US$1,241 million deficit (2001)

Trade with UK	*2002*	*2003*
Imports from UK	£116,614,000	£122,238,000
Exports to UK	477,977,000	425,170,000

TRANSPORT INFRASTRUCTURE

With the improvement of the roads an increasing share of internal transportation is moving by road and rail, although shipping is still important. The road system is about 80,000 km in length, of which 15,484 km is paved.

There are 6,585 km of railway track. A railway line runs from Valparaíso through La Calera and Santiago to Puerto Montt. With the completion of a section of 696 km from Corumba, Brazil, to Santa Cruz, Bolivia, the Trans-Continental Line will link the Chilean Pacific port of Arica with Rio de Janeiro on the Atlantic. A line runs from Antofagasta to Salta (Argentina).

Domestic air traffic is carried by Línea Aérea Nacional (LAN) and LADECO, which also operate internationally, and smaller regional carriers.

EDUCATION

Elementary education is free and compulsory. There are 25 state universities and 45 private universities.

ILLITERACY RATE – (m) 4.1 per cent; (f) 4.5 per cent (2000)
ENROLMENT (percentage of age group) – primary 100 per cent (1997); secondary 75 per cent (1997); tertiary 32 per cent (1997)

MEDIA

Television is a combination of national and local, private and state run, cable and terrestrial channels. Radio is the country's most important news medium with 800 stations country-wide. In 2004 there were 3.5 million internet users.

CULTURE

Chile is the most 'European' of the Latin American countries with a vibrant arts culture. Chilean Nobel Prize winners for Literature include the writers Gabriela Mistral (1889–1957), who won in 1945, and Pablo Neruda (1904–74), who won in 1971. There are numerous art galleries, museums and theatres and Chilean art, architecture and music have considerable international influence.

Island possessions include the Juan Fernández group (three islands) about 576 km from Valparaíso; one of these islands is the reputed scene of Alexander Selkirk's (of *Robinson Crusoe* fame) shipwreck. Easter Island, about 3,200 km away in the South Pacific Ocean, contains stone platforms and hundreds of mysterious stone figures.

CHINA

Zhonghua Renmin Gongheguo – The People's Republic of China

AREA – 9,327,400 sq. km. Neighbours: Russia and Mongolia (north), North Korea (east), Vietnam, Laos, Myanmar, India, Bhutan and Nepal (south), India, Pakistan, Afghanistan, Tajikistan, Kyrgyzstan and Kazakhstan (west)
POPULATION – 1,284,972,000 (2001). Han Chinese make up 91.9 per cent of the population and the remainder of the population belongs to around 55 ethnic minorities. Among the largest are the Zhuang of Guangxi, the Hui of Ningxia, the Miao of southern China, the Manchu of Heilongjiang, the Uygurs and Kazakhs of Xinjiang, the Tibetans and the Mongols. The indigenous religions are Confucianism, Taoism and Buddhism. There are also Muslims (officially estimated at about 12 million) and Christians (unofficially estimated at about 50 million). The official language is Mandarin Chinese; of the many local dialects the largest are Cantonese, Fukienese, Xiamenhua and Hakka. The autonomous regions of Mongolia, Tibet and Xinjiang have their own languages

CAPITAL – Beijing (population, 7,362,426, 1990 estimate)
MAJOR CITIES – Chengdu; Chongqing; Dalian; Guangzhou (Canton); Harbin; Qingdo; ΨShanghai; Shenyang; Tianjin; Wuhan; Wuxi; Yantai; Zaozhuang
CURRENCY – Renminbi Yuan of 10 jiao or 100 fen
NATIONAL ANTHEM – Yiyongjun Jinxingqu (March Of The Volunteers)
NATIONAL DAY – 1 October (Founding of People's Republic)
NATIONAL FLAG – Red, with large gold five-point star and four small gold stars in crescent, all in upper quarter next staff
LIFE EXPECTANCY (years) – 71 (2001)
MORTALITY RATE (per 1,000 population) – 6.74 (2003)
INFANT MORTALITY (per 1,000 live births) – 31 (2001)
HIV / AIDS ADULT PREVALENCE – 0.1 per cent (2001)
DEATH PENALTY – Yes
POPULATION LIVING BELOW POVERTY LINE – 10 per cent (2001)
POPULATION GROWTH RATE – 1 per cent (1990–2001)
POPULATION DENSITY – 138 per sq. km (2001)
URBAN POPULATION – 37 per cent (2001)

CLIMATE AND TERRAIN

China is twice the size of Western Europe and represents a vast range of landscapes and climates within its borders. Two-thirds of the country is hilly or mountainous. The highest mountains are on the Tibetan plateau, in the west of the country, where the highest elevation is 8,850 m (Mount Everest) and the lowest is −154 m (Turpan Pendi). The southern plains and east coast have the most fertile land and are the most heavily populated. There are seven climate zones. The north-east has cold winters, fierce winds, hot and humid summers and erratic rainfall. The south-west has mild winters and warm summers. Inner Mongolia has cold winters and hot summers. Central China has hot and humid summers with the occasional tropical cyclone. South China is partly tropical with heavy rainfall. Xizang is a high plateau surrounded by mountains that is subject to harsh winters. Xinjiang and the west have a desert climate, cold winters and year-round rain.

HISTORY AND POLITICS

China was ruled by imperial dynasties for over 20 centuries until revolutionaries led by Sun Yat-sen forced the Emperor to abdicate on 12 February 1912. Neither the new Nationalist Party (Kuomintang (KMT)) government nor the emergent Chinese Communist Party (CCP) were able to unify China, or to agree on the basis for further reform. Warlord infighting rendered China weak, enabling Japan to occupy Manchuria and all the important northern and coastal areas of China by 1939. Japan's occupation was ended by its defeat by the allies in 1945.

The Communists established control over large areas of China in the early 1940s, seizing the territory abandoned by Japan in 1945. Civil war lasted until 1949 when the CCP, led by Mao Zedong (Mao Tse-tung), inaugurated the People's Republic of China (PRC), and the KMT under Chiang Kai-shek went into exile in Taiwan. The USA continued to recognise the Chiang Kai-shek regime as the rightful government of China until 1971, when the PRC took over China's membership of the United Nations from Taiwan.

Under Mao Zedong China was ruled on the basis of four 'cardinal principles': Marxist-Leninist-Maoist thought, the Socialist Road, the dictatorship of the proletariat, and the leadership of the CCP. Mao's 'Great Leap Forward" (1958–61) was an attempt to industrialise rural areas which resulted in a famine in which 30–40 million people died. China was plunged into chaos during the Cultural Revolution (1966–70) when the Red Guards were used to rid the country of 'rightist elements'.

Following the death of Mao Zedong in 1976, the disgraced Deng Xiaoping was recalled. In 1977 he was elected Vice-Chairman of the CCP, becoming the dominant force within the party by eliminating leftist influence, rehabilitating fallen leaders and promoting an 'open door' policy of economic liberalisation. The Congresses of 1982 and 1987 reaffirmed Deng's policies, and in 1987 most of the revolutionary generation was replaced in the top posts by younger, more liberal supporters of reform.

Student-led pro-democracy demonstrations in April and May 1989, centred on Tiananmen Square in Beijing, ended on 3–4 June when the army took control of Beijing, killing thousands of protesters. This strengthened the position of hardliners within the leadership, who readopted policies of centralisation based on Marxist ideology. Deng retired from his last official post in November 1989 but retained effective control until late 1994.

At Deng's instigation during 1992 the emphasis switched back to economic reform and the power of the hardliners waned. The 14th Party Congress in 1992 endorsed Deng's calls for faster, bolder economic reforms and his 'socialist market economy'. Deng died on 19 February 1997 and Jiang Zemin assumed the mantle of leader. Jiang continued the economic reforms and also sought to improve China's standing in the international community.

At the 16th Party Congress in 2002 vice-president Hu Jintao was elected general secretary of the CCP. On 15 March 2003 Hu Jintao was elected by the National People's Congress as the new state president replacing Jiang Zemin who retained his position as head of the Central Military Commission.

INSURGENCIES

Separatists from the Uygur Muslim minority group in Xinjiang Autonomous Region have demonstrated against Han rule. They have claimed responsibility for bomb attacks in the provincial capital, Ürümqi, and in Beijing. Two Muslim separatists were executed in 1999 as part of an effort to tighten control of the region and in 2001, the death sentence was passed on the founder of an underground Islamic party.

The government banned the Falun gong cult in 1999, which had claimed to have 70 million followers, after it was revealed that a large number of Chinese Communist Party officials and senior officers in the People's Liberation Army had joined the cult. Tens of thousands of Falun gong members have been arrested since the ban.

POLITICAL SYSTEM

Under the 1982 constitution, the National People's Congress is the highest organ of state power. It is elected for a term of five years, has 2,979 members and is supposed to hold one session a year. It is empowered to amend the constitution, make laws, select the President and Vice-President and other leading officials of the state, approve the national economic plan, the state budget and the final state accounts, and to decide on questions of war and peace. The State Council is the highest organ of the state administration. It is composed of the Premier, the Vice-Premiers, the State Councillors, heads of Ministries and Commissions, the Auditor-General and the Secretary-General. Command over the armed forces is vested in the Central Military Commission.

Deputies to Congresses at the primary level are 'directly elected' by the voters 'through a secret ballot after democratic consultation'. This is now extended to county level. These Congresses elect the deputies to the Congress at the next higher level. Deputies to the National People's Congress are elected by the People's Congresses of the provinces, autonomous regions and municipalities directly under the central government, and by the armed forces.

Local government is conducted through People's Governments at provincial, municipal and county levels. Autonomous regions, prefectures and counties exist for national minorities and are described as self-governing.

HEAD OF STATE
President of the People's Republic of China, Hu Jintao, elected 15 March 2003
Vice-President, Zeng Qinghong

STATE COUNCIL *as at July 2004*
Premier, Wen Jiabao
Vice-Premiers, Huang Ju; Wu Yi *(Minister of Health)*; Zeng Peiyan; Hui Liangyu
State Councillors, Zhou Yongkang; Cao Gangchuan *(Minister for National Defence)*; Tang Jiaxuan; Hua Jianmin *(Secretary-General of the State Council)*; Chen Zhili

SELECTED GOVERNMENT MEMBERS *as at July 2004*
Civil Affairs, Li Xueju
Finance, Jin Renqing
Foreign Affairs, Li Zhaoxing
State Security, Xu Yongyue

EMBASSY OF THE PEOPLE'S REPUBLIC OF CHINA
49–51 Portland Place, London W1 1JL
T 020-7299 4049
Ambassador Extraordinary and Plenipotentiary, HE Zha Peixin, apptd 2002

BRITISH EMBASSY
11 Guang Hua Lu, Jian Guo Men Wai, Beijing 100600
T (+86) (10) 6532 1961
E beinfo@public.bta.net.cn
Ambassador, HE Christopher Hum, CMG, apptd 2002

BRITISH CONSULATES-GENERAL – Chongqing, Shanghai and Guangzhou,

BRITISH COUNCIL DIRECTOR, Michael O'Sullivan
Cultural and Education Section, British Embassy,
4th Floor Landmark Building Tower 1, 8 North Dongsanhuan Beilu, Beijing 100004
T (+86) (10) 6590 6903 E enquiry@britishcouncil.org.cn

DEFENCE

All three military arms are parts of the People's Liberation Army (PLA). China has at least 30 intercontinental and 110 intermediate range land-based, and 13 submarine-launched nuclear ballistic missiles. The Army has some

7,180 main battle tanks and over 4,500 armoured personnel carriers and armoured infantry fighting vehicles.

The Navy has 69 submarines, 21 destroyers, 42 frigates, 368 patrol and coastal vessels, 700 shore-based combat aircraft and 45 armed helicopters. The Air Force has more than 1,900 combat aircraft and some armed helicopters.

MILITARY EXPENDITURE – 4.1 per cent of GDP (2002)
MILITARY PERSONNEL – 2,450,000: Army 1,700,000, Navy 250,000, Air Force 400,000, Strategic Missile Forces 100,000; Paramilitaries 1,500,000
CONSCRIPTION DURATION – Two years (selective)

ECONOMY AND TRADE

Economic liberalisation in the early 1980s reduced central planning and broadened the role of the market, which led to an increase in manufacturing, concentrated in China's coastal regions. Foreign direct investment, especially from Hong Kong and Taiwan, enabled the construction of a significant industrial base and transport infrastructure. In the coastal regions the economy has become a free market in all but name, with several stock markets and Shanghai's emergence as a financial centre. Since 1980, special economic zones have been established in Guangdong, Fujian and Hainan provinces. In addition, there are free trade and development zones throughout the country, designed to stimulate both foreign trade and internal economic development. The reforms have enabled the economy to grow more than five-fold since 1980. China has become the third-largest beneficiary of foreign investment in the world, primarily into its export industries.

Agriculture remains of great importance, employing half the working population and accounting for about 15 per cent of GDP in 2002. Cereals, with peas and beans, are grown in the northern provinces, and rice, tea and sugar in the south. Cotton (mostly in valleys of the Yangtze and Yellow rivers), tea (in the west and south), with hemp, jute and flax, are the most important crops. Livestock is raised in large numbers. Sericulture is one of the oldest industries. Cottons, woollens and silks are manufactured in large quantities.

Coal, iron ore, tin, antimony, wolfram, bismuth and molybdenum are abundant. Oil is produced in several northern provinces, particularly in Heilongjiang and Shandong but China desperately needs access to greater supplies of oil if economic expansion is to continue at the present rate (China has now overtaken Japan as the word's second-largest importer of oil after the United States). Plans for a 2,400-km oil pipeline from Russia's east Siberian reserves to Daqing in China were first announced in 2001 and in May 2003 a co-operation pact was signed between Russia and China. The agreement has since run into difficulties as the Japanese government has offered Russia large financial incentives to construct an alternative pipeline that would bypass China and directly supply Japan. Economic analysts predict that this need for oil will lead to tensions within the region in the coming years and may have an effect on annual growth rates.

In June 2003 the sluice gates on the Three Gorges dam above the Yangtse river in central China were closed to allow the reservoir to fill up and the first generator went into operation in July. The world's largest hydroelectric power project, costing US$25,000 million, will supply electricity to power grids in central and eastern China. More than one million people have been displaced since construction began in 1993. The dam is due to be completed in 2009.

Overcapacity in some of the traditional industries is being tackled, with the closure of 26,000 coal mines and 2,500 steel smelters. There are long-term plans to privatise all corporations except those in sectors considered essential to national security.

Tourism has become a major industry, with over 91 million foreign visitors in 2003. An outbreak of the Severe Acute Respiratory Syndrome (SARS) virus between November 2002 and June 2003 resulted in a decline in overseas visitors in early 2003.

Foreign trade and external economic relations have grown enormously since 1978. In 1995, import tariffs were cut to an average 23 per cent in line with China's attempts to join the World Trade Organisation to which China was formally admitted as a member in November 2001. The principal exports are clothing, electronics, machine plant, yarns and fabrics, chemicals, footwear, travel goods, and iron and steel. The principal imports are machinery, electronics, raw materials, yarns and fabrics, plastics and motor vehicles. The main trading partners are Japan, the USA, Hong Kong, South Korea, Taiwan and Germany.

GNI – US$1,131,200 million (2001); US$890 per capita (2001)
ANNUAL AVERAGE GROWTH OF GDP – 8.0 per cent (2000)
INFLATION RATE – 1.4 per cent (2001)
UNEMPLOYMENT – 3.1 per cent (2000)
TOTAL EXTERNAL DEBT – US$149,800 million (2000)
FOREIGN DIRECT INVESTMENT – US$165,139 million (1997–2000)
IMPORTS – US$295,171 million (2002)
EXPORTS – US$325,591 (2002)

BALANCE OF PAYMENTS
Trade – US$44,167 million surplus (2002)
Current Account – US$35,422 million surplus (2002)

Trade with UK	*2002*	*2003*
Imports from UK	£1,505,238,000	£1,933,271,000
Exports to UK	6,972,976,000	8,554,222,000

TRANSPORT INFRASTRUCTURE

There are 70,058 km of railway lines, of which 18,668 km are electrified, and approximately 1,402,698 km of roads, 314,204 km of which are paved and 16,314 km are motorways. In addition, internal civil aviation has been developed, with routes totalling more than 1,506,000 km. Thirty new airports were due for completion by 2005.

In the past the principal means of communication east to west was by the rivers, the most important of which are the Yangtze (Jinsha Jiang) (5,440 km), the Yellow River (Huang He) (4,160 km) and the West River (Xi Jiang) (2,640 km). These, together with the network of canals connecting them, are still much used but their overall importance has declined. Coastal port facilities are being improved and the merchant fleet expanded.

EDUCATION

Primary education lasts six years and secondary education lasts six years (three years in junior middle school and three years in senior middle school). In 1998 there were 1,022 universities and colleges.

ILLITERACY RATE – (m) 8.3 per cent; (f) 23.7 per cent (2000)
ENROLMENT (percentage of age group) – primary 100 per cent (1997); tertiary 6 per cent (1997)

MEDIA

China's media industry is huge – it has 25,000 newspapers and magazines, 750,000 journalists and 12,000 radio and television stations. In 2002 Communist Party officials stated that China has a domestic television audience of 1,100 million. subscription services are expected to have a market of 128 million by the year 2010. The Communist Party has always maintained a firm grip on the nation's news reporting but with the installation of a new president, Hu Jintao, a more liberal approach seems to have been adopted. Market reforms are also being introduced into the media with the closure in 2004 of hundreds of state-funded publications that relied on government departments for their readership. Despite these reforms journalists still exercise a significant degree of self-censorship and the Communist Party still attempts to restrict access to foreign news media by blocking news websites and radio broadcasts and limiting the distribution of overseas newspapers. It is estimated that there were 68 million internet users in China as at mid-2003, the second highest in the world after the USA.

CULTURE

The Chinese language has many dialects, notably Cantonese, Hakka, Amoy, Foochow, Changsha, Nanchang, Wu (Shanghai) and the northern dialect. The Common Speech or *putonghua* (often referred to as Mandarin) is based on the northern dialect. The Communists have promoted it as the national language and it is taught throughout the country. As *putonghua* encourages the use of the spoken language in writing, the old literary style and ideographic form of writing has fallen into disuse. Since 1956 simplified characters have been introduced to make reading and writing easier. In 1958 the National People's Congress adopted a system of romanisation known as pinyin.

Chinese literature is one of the oldest in the world. Paper has been employed for writing and printing for nearly 2,000 years. The Confucian classics, which formed the basis of traditional Chinese culture, date from the Warring States period (fourth to third centuries BC), as do the earliest texts of Taoism. Histories, philosophical and scientific works, poetry, literary and art criticism, novels and romances survive from most periods.

TIBET

AREA – 1,199,164 sq. km
POPULATION – 2,610,000 (2001 estimate)
CAPITAL – Lhasa

Tibet is a plateau seldom lower than 3,000 m, which forms the northern frontier of India (boundary imperfectly demarcated), from Kashmir to Myanmar, but is separated therefrom by the Himalayas.

From 1911 to 1950, Tibet was virtually an independent country though its status was never officially so recognised. In 1950 Chinese Communist forces invaded eastern Tibet. In 1951 an agreement was reached whereby the Chinese army was allowed entry into Tibet, and a Communist military and administrative headquarters was set up. A series of revolts against Chinese rule culminated in 1959 in a rising in Lhasa, the capital. Fighting continued for several days before the rebellion was crushed and military rule was imposed. The Dalai Lama fled to India where he and his followers were granted political asylum and established a government in exile.

In 1964 the Dalai Lama and the Panchen Lama were dismissed, marking the end of co-operation between the Chinese government and the traditional religious authorities. Tibet became an Autonomous Region of China in 1965. Martial law was declared in Tibet in 1989 and sporadic outbursts of unrest continue.

The Panchen Lama died in 1989. China rejected the Dalai Lama's choice of successor, who is believed to have been executed, and enthroned its own candidate.

In December 1997, the International Commission of Jurists issued a report declaring that Tibet was 'under alien subjugation' and called for a UN-managed referendum to decide its future status. China contested that the report failed to acknowledge its historical claims to the region.

The 17th Karmapa Lama, the first reincarnation of a living Buddha to be recognised by both China and the Dalai Lama, defected from Tibet in late December 1999 and fled to India, where he appealed for political asylum. On 16 January 2000, the seventh Reting Lama was ordained in Tibet; the Dalai Lama had refused to recognise him as the reincarnation of the previous Reting Lama. Representatives of the Dalai Lama visited China in September 2002, in an attempt to improve the situation, but relations remain tense.

In May 2001 the government published details of a modernisation programme for Tibet which aimed to improve the low standard of living by promoting market reforms and extensive public construction projects.

SPECIAL ADMINISTRATIVE REGIONS

HONG KONG

AREA – 1,092 sq. km
POPULATION – 6,725,000 (2001)
CURRENCY – Hong Kong dollar (HK$) of 100 cents
FLAG – Red, with a white bauhinia flower of five petals each containing a red star
LIFE EXPECTANCY (years) – 81 (2001)
MORTALITY RATE (per 1,000 population) – 6.19 (2003)
INFANT MORTALITY (per 1,000 births) – 6 (2001)
HIV / AIDS ADULT PREVALENCE – 0.1 per cent (2001)
POPULATION GROWTH RATE – 0.9 per cent
POPULATION DENSITY – 6,158 per sq. km (2001)
URBAN POPULATION – 93.1 per cent (2000 estimate)

CLIMATE AND TERRAIN

Hong Kong, consisting of more than 230 islands and of a portion of the mainland (Kowloon and the New Territories) on the south-east coast of China, is situated at the eastern side of the mouth of the Pearl River. Hong Kong Island is about 18 km long and from three to eight km broad. It is separated from the mainland by a narrow strait. Elevation extremes range from 958 m (Tai Mo Shan) at the highest point to 0 m (South China Sea) at the lowest.

The climate is subtropical, tending towards the temperate for nearly half the year. The mean monthly temperature ranges from 16°C to 29°C. The average annual rainfall is 2,214 mm, of which nearly 80 per cent falls between May and September. Tropical cyclones occur between May and November, causing high winds and heavy rain.

HISTORY AND POLITICS

Hong Kong Island was first occupied by Great Britain in 1841 and formally ceded by the Treaty of Nanking in 1842. Kowloon was acquired by the Beijing Convention of 1860 and the New Territories, consisting of a peninsula in the southern part of the Guangdong province together with adjacent islands, by a 99-year lease signed on 9 June 1898.

On 19 December 1984 the UK and China signed a Joint Declaration in which it was agreed that China would resume sovereignty over Hong Kong on 1 July 1997. In the run-up to the 1997 handover, the Chinese government's insistence on a greater say in the running of the colony and Governor Patten's plan for an extension of democracy prompted acrimonious disputes. The Chinese government refused to accept the reforms and replaced the Legislative Council.

On 1 July 1997, Hong Kong became a Special Administrative Region (SAR) of the People's Republic of China.

The Joint Declaration, which took effect in May 1985, guarantees: the free movement of goods and capital; the retention of Hong Kong's free port status, separate customs territory and freely convertible currency; the protection of property rights and foreign investment; the right of free movement to and from Hong Kong; Hong Kong's autonomy in the conduct of its external commercial relations and its own monetary and financial policies; and judicial independence. Hong Kong's constitution is the Basic Law, which was passed by China's National People's Congress in 1990 and guarantees that the SAR's social and economic systems will remain unchanged for 50 years.

A Legislative Council election was held in 2000. The Democratic Party, a pro-democracy opposition party, remained the largest party in the legislature with 12 seats and the pro-China Democratic Alliance for the Betterment of Hong Kong won 11 seats; 20 seats were won by independent candidates.

Following mass pro-democracy demonstrations in July 2003 against a proposed anti-subversion law, the government announced that public consultation on the controversial bill would re-open in September. The bill has since been shelved indefinitely. Protestors also demanded direct elections for Hong Kong's leader and all members of the Legislative Council.

POLITICAL SYSTEM

Hong Kong is administered by the Hong Kong SAR Government, headed by the Chief Executive, who is appointed by a 400-strong selection committee and aided by an Executive Council and a Legislative Council. The Executive Council consists of 15 Principal Officials and five non-officials. The Chief Executive serves a five-year term.

The Legislative Council consists of 60 members, of whom 20 are directly elected. Thirty members are elected by functional constituencies composed of professional and business groups and ten are elected by an election committee composed of 800 representatives of the community.

Chief Executive, Tung Chee-hwa, *sworn in* 1 July 1997

EXECUTIVE COUNCIL *as at July 2004*
Non-official Members, Leung Chun-ying; Jasper Tsang; Yok-sing Cheng Yiu-tong; Andrew Liao Cheung-sing
Ex-officio Members, Tung Chee-hwa (plus heads of government departments)

SELECTED GOVERNMENT MEMBERS *as at July 2004*
Chief Secretary for Administration, Donald Tsang Yam-kuen
Financial Services and the Treasury, Frederick Ma Si-hang
Home Affairs, Patrick Ho Chi-ping
Security, vacant

CONSUL-GENERAL, Stephen Bradley
1 Supreme Court Road, Central (PO Box 528), Hong Kong
T (+852) 2901 3000
E consular@britishconsulate.org.hk

BRITISH COUNCIL DIRECTOR, Ruth Gee
3 Supreme Court Road, Admiralty, Hong Kong
T (+852) 2913 5100
E info@britishcouncil.org.hk

HONG KONG ECONOMIC AND TRADE OFFICE,
6 Grafton Street, London W1S 4EQ
T 020-7499 9821.
Director-General, Andrew K. P. Leung, JP, apptd 2001

ECONOMY AND TRADE

The main economic sector is the services industry, especially financial services, insurance and real estate. It employed 19.5 per cent of the workforce and contributed 85 per cent of GDP in 2002. Principal exports are clothing, electrical machinery and apparatus, and textiles.

Diversification in terms of products and markets continues to be the main feature of recent industrial development, as are industrial partnerships with overseas companies. The economy is based on export rather than the domestic market. Tourism is very important to the economy; 15.54 million people visited Hong Kong in 2003. The spread of the SARS virus to Hong Kong in March 2003 had a detrimental effect on the economy, especially the tourism industry, with a 70 per cent reduction in the number of visitors in April 2003 compared with the previous year. The World Health Organisation removed Hong Kong from its list of SARS-infected areas in June 2003.

In 2003 imports totalled US$230,300 million and exports US$225,900 million. Hong Kong's principal customers for its domestic products, in order of value of trade, were China, USA and Japan. China was Hong Kong's principal supplier.

GNI – US$170,300 million (2001); US$25,330 per capita (2001)
ANNUAL AVERAGE GROWTH OF GDP – 10.5 per cent (2000)
INFLATION RATE – 3.7 per cent (2000)

Trade with UK	*2002*	*2003*
Imports from UK	£2,430,799,000	£2,500,875,000
Exports to UK	5,766,795,000	5,640,490,000

TRANSPORT INFRASTRUCTURE

Hong Kong has one of the world's finest natural harbours, and it is the busiest container port in the world, with eight terminals, as well as large modern cargo and liner terminals. Dockyard facilities include eight floating drydocks, the largest being capable of docking vessels up to 150,000 tonnes deadweight. An international airport built on reclaimed land at Chek Lap Kok opened in July 1998.

EDUCATION

Education is free of charge and compulsory for children up to the age of 15. Post-secondary education is provided by six universities and one college. The Open Learning Institute of Hong Kong provides university education. There are also seven technical institutes and the Hong Kong Institute of Education.

ILLITERACY RATE – (m) 3.5 per cent; (f) 9.8 per cent (2000)

ENROLMENT (percentage of age group) – primary 98.7 per cent (2001); secondary 91 per cent (2001); tertiary 31.8 per cent (2001)

MACAO (AOMEN)

AREA – 24 sq. km

POPULATION – 460,000 (2001)

CURRENCY – Pataca of 100 avos

FLAG – Green, with a white lotus flower above a white stylised bridge and water, under a large gold five-point star and four gold stars in crescent

CLIMATE AND TERRAIN

Macao, situated at the mouth of the Pearl River, comprises a peninsula and the islands of Coloane and Taipa and is 64 km from Hong Kong. The climate is subtropical. Elevation extremes range from 172.4 m (Coloane Alto) at the highest point to 0 m (South China Sea) at the lowest.

HISTORY AND POLITICS

The first Portuguese ship arrived at Macao in 1513 and trade with China commenced in 1553. Macao became a Portuguese colony in 1557; in a Sino-Portuguese treaty of 1887 China recognised Portugal's sovereignty over Macao. An agreement to transfer the administration of Macao to the Chinese authorities was signed on 13 April 1987. Macao became the Macao Special Administrative Region (MSAR) of China when power was transferred by the outgoing Portuguese governor Vasco Rocha Vieira to the new chief executive on 19 December 1999. The final session of the Macao SAR Basic Law Drafting Committee was held in Beijing in January 1993 and approved the Basic Law that has served as Macao's constitution since 1999.

In April 1999 a 200-member committee of Macao residents was established to determine the composition of the first government of the Macao SAR. They elected Edmund Ho Hao Wah to be its first chief executive. The chief executive serves a five-year term of office. The chief executive announced in September 1999 that he had appointed the ten members of his Executive Council, a body intended to assist the chief executive in policy-making. In addition, he appointed seven legislators to the 23-member MSAR First Legislative Council, which included 15 members of the previous 16-member Legislative Assembly; a replacement was chosen for the member who had not wished to continue.

Edmund Ho Hao Wah was to finish his first term of office on 19 December 2004. The election of the next chief executive must take place no more than 60 days before the current office-holder's five-year term expires.

Chief Executive, Edmund Ho Hao Wah

SELECTED GOVERNMENT MEMBERS *as at July 2004*
Economy and Finance, Francis Tam Pak Yuen
Security, Cheong Kuoc Va
Social Affairs and Culture, Fernando Chui Sai On

CONSUL-GENERAL, Stephen Bradley, resident at Hong Kong

ECONOMY AND TRADE

The service industries comprise the greatest part of the economy, providing 87 per cent of GDP in 2002. In 2003, gambling provided 40 per cent of GNP and there were 6.9 million foreign visitors. Gaming taxes accounted for about 70 per cent of government revenues in 2002. In 2002 imports totalled US$2,356 million and exports US$2,530 million.

The main trading partners are the EU, the USA, China, Hong Kong and Japan.

Trade with UK	*2002*	*2003*
Imports from UK	£12,621,000	£14,332,000
Exports to UK	31,365,000	42,343,000

COLOMBIA

República de Colombia – Republic of Colombia

AREA – 1,038,700 sq. km. Neighbours: Venezuela (north and east), Brazil (south-east), Peru (south), Ecuador (south-west), Panama (north-west)

POPULATION – 42,803,000 (2001): 58 per cent mestizo, 20 per cent white, 14 per cent mulatto, 4 per cent black, 3 per cent mixed black-Amerindian, 1 per cent Amerindian. The language is Spanish. Roman Catholicism is the established religion

CAPITAL – Bogotá (population, 6,712,247, 2002 estimate)

MAJOR CITIES – ΨBarranquilla, the major port on the Caribbean; Bucaramanga; ΨBuenaventura, the major port on the Pacific; Cali; ΨCartagena; Medellín

CURRENCY – Colombian peso of 100 centavos

NATIONAL ANTHEM – Oh Gloria Inmarcesible (Oh Glory Unfading!)

NATIONAL DAY – 20 July (National Independence Day)

NATIONAL FLAG – Broad yellow band in upper half, surmounting equal bands of blue and red

LIFE EXPECTANCY (years) – 71 (2001)

MORTALITY RATE (per 1,000 population) – 5.63 (2003)

HIV / AIDS ADULT PREVALENCE RATE – 0.4 per cent

INFANT MORTALITY (per 1,000 births) – 19 (2001)

DEATH PENALTY – No (abolished 1910)

POPULATION BELOW POVERTY LINE – 55 per cent (2001)

POPULATION GROWTH RATE – 1.8 per cent (1990–2001)

POPULATION DENSITY – 41 per sq. km (2001)

URBAN POPULATION – 76 per cent (2001)

CLIMATE AND TERRAIN

Colombia lies in the extreme north-west of South America, having a coastline on both the Caribbean Sea and Pacific Ocean. Elevation extremes range from 5,775 m (Pico Cristobal Colon) at the highest point to 0 m (Pacific Ocean) at the lowest.

The country is divided by the Cordillera de los Andes into a coastal region in the north and west and extensive plains in the east. The eastern range of the Colombian Andes is a series of vast tablelands. This temperate region is the most densely peopled portion of the country. The principal rivers are the Magdalena, Guaviare, Cauca, Atrato, Caquetá, Putumayo and Patia. The climate is predominantly tropical but the Caribbean coastline is typically drier than the rest of the country.

HISTORY AND POLITICS

The Colombian coast was visited in 1502 by Columbus, and in 1536 a Spanish expedition penetrated the interior and established a government. The country remained under Spanish rule until 1819 when Simón Bolivar established the Republic of Colombia, consisting of the territories now known as Colombia, Panama, Venezuela and Ecuador. In 1829–30 Venezuela and Ecuador withdrew, and in 1831 the remaining territories formed the Republic of New Granada. The name was changed to the Granadine Confederation in 1858, to the United States of Colombia in 1861 and to the Republic of Colombia in 1866. Panama seceded in 1903.

From 1957 to 1974 the country was governed under the 'National Front' agreement with an alternating presidency and equal numbers of ministerial posts. The alternation of the presidency ended in 1974 and parity in appointments in 1978.

Elections to the legislature took place in 2002. In the House of Representatives the Liberal Party (PL) secured 54 seats, while the Social Conservative Party (PSC) won 21, leaving the balance of power in the hands of minor parties. In the Senate, the Liberal Party won 28 seats while some 38 minor parties collectively secured 49 seats. The 2002 presidential election was held in May and was won by Álvaro Uribe Vélez.

INSURGENCIES

Colombia is dogged by insurgency from left-wing guerrillas. The main active guerrilla factions are the Revolutionary Armed Forces of Colombia (FARC) and the National Liberation Army (ELN). Formal peace talks began in November 1998, but fighting continued. The peace process was terminated in 2002 by President Pastrana Arango after the ELN and FARC carried out joint actions against the right-wing paramilitary United Self-Defence Forces of Colombia (AUC), who had attacked civilians in towns and villages thought to be pro-FARC in December 2000.

FARC explosions in August 2002 prompted a state of emergency, which was extended for a further 90 days in November. An indefinite cease-fire was declared by the AUC in December 2002. There were further FARC bomb attacks in early 2003. In April 2003 Colombia signed agreements with Panama and Venezuela to enhance border security and place tighter controls on drug trafficking. In June 2003 President Uribe unveiled a government security plan to end the civil war and combat the drugs trade. The plan aimed to establish police forces in all parts of the country and to eradicate all drugs crops. In July the government and the AUC agreed to start formal talks aimed at disarming all the paramilitary group's 10,000 gunmen by the end of 2005.

POLITICAL SYSTEM

The Congress is a bicameral legislature. The lower house (the House of Representatives) has 165 members directly elected for a four-year term. The upper house (the Senate) has 102 members, directly elected for four years; two seats are reserved for representatives of indigenous people. The President, who appoints the Cabinet, is directly elected for a single four-year term.

HEAD OF STATE

President, Álvaro Uribe Vélez, *elected* 26 May 2002, *sworn in* 7 August 2003
Vice-President, Francisco Santos

SELECTED GOVERNMENT MEMBERS *as at July 2004*

Defence, Jorge Alberto Uribe Echavarria
Finance and Public Credit, Alberto Carrasquilla Barrera
Foreign Affairs, Carolina Barco
Interior and Justice, Sabas Pretelt de la Vega

EMBASSY OF COLOMBIA

Flat 3A, 3 Hans Crescent, London SW1X 0LN
T 020-7589 9177/5037
E mail@colombianembassy.co.uk
Ambassador Extraordinary and Plenipotentiary, HE Alfonso Lopez-Caballero, apptd 2002

BRITISH EMBASSY

Edificio ING Barings, Carrera 9, No 76–49, Piso 9, Bogotá
T (+57) (1) 317 6690/6310/6321
E britain@cable.net.co
Ambassador Extraordinary and Plenipotentiary, HE Tom Duggin, apptd 2001

BRITISH COUNCIL DIRECTOR, Joe Docherty

Calle 87 No. 12–79, Bogotá
T (+57) (1) 618 7680
E info@britishcouncil.org.co

DEFENCE

The Army has 12 light tanks and 204 armoured personnel carriers. The Navy has four submarines, four corvettes, 27 patrol and coastal vessels, eight aircraft and four helicopters at nine bases. The Air Force has 57 combat aircraft and 23 armed helicopters.
MILITARY EXPENDITURE – 3.7 per cent of GDP (2002)
MILITARY PERSONNEL – 200,000: Army 178,000, Navy 15,000, Air Force 7,000; Paramilitaries 121,000
CONSCRIPTION DURATION – 12–18 months

ECONOMY AND TRADE

Coal, natural gas and hydroelectricity resources remain largely unexploited, although development of coal is now being given priority. The hydrocarbon sector accounts for over half of the mining output, precious metals (gold, platinum and silver) and iron ore accounting for the remainder. Other mineral deposits include nickel, bauxite, copper, gypsum, limestone, phosphates, sulphur and uranium. Colombia is also the world's largest producer of emeralds. Mining generates five per cent of GDP.

Major cash crops are coffee, sugar, bananas, cut flowers and cotton. Cattle are raised in large numbers, and meat and cured skins and hides are also exported.

The government has encouraged diversification to reduce dependence on coffee as the major export and this has led to the growth of new export-orientated industries, particularly textiles, paper products and leather goods. Services account for around 56 per cent of GDP, industry

30 per cent and agriculture 14 per cent (2002). The IMF approved a two-year standby facility of US$2,100 million in January 2003 to underpin government policies designed to reduce the fiscal deficit. Colombia also received a loan of US$3,300 million over three years from the World Bank for economic reform.

In 1996 and 1997 Colombia was blacklisted by the USA for failing to sufficiently curb levels of drug production. These sanctions were ended in 1998. Under US$7,500 million 'Plan Colombia', the USA pledged military aid to train Colombian armed forces to control the rebel-dominated coca-growing regions which supply the bulk of the cocaine used in the USA.

Principal trading partners are the USA, the EU and Latin America.

GNI – US$81,600 million (2001); US$1,890 per capita (2001)
ANNUAL AVERAGE GROWTH OF GDP – 2.8 per cent (2000)
INFLATION RATE – 9.5 per cent (2000)
UNEMPLOYMENT – 20.5 per cent (2000)
TOTAL EXTERNAL DEBT – US$34,081 million (2000)
DIRECT FOREIGN INVESTMENT – US$12,505 million (1997–2000)
IMPORTS – US$12,738 million (2002)
EXPORTS – US$12,001 million (2002)

BALANCE OF PAYMENTS
Trade – US$228 million surplus (2002)
Current Account – US$1,578 million deficit (2002)

Trade with UK	*2002*	*2003*
Imports from UK	£84,112,000	£106,436,000
Exports to UK	218,734,000	227,945,000

TRANSPORT INFRASTRUCTURE

There are 1,052 airports, 96 of which are surfaced. There are daily air services between Bogotá and all the principal towns, as well as frequent services to other countries. The road network consists of more than 110,000 km of roads, of which around 26,000 km are surfaced. There are 3,304 km of railways and 18,140 km of waterways.

EDUCATION

Elementary education is free of charge and compulsory for five years. Most primary schools are run by the Roman Catholic church and courses in Roman Catholicism are compulsory. There are some Protestant church schools (mainly in the capital). The government finances secondary and university level education. There are 235 institutions of higher education in Colombia.

ILLITERACY RATE – (m) 8.2 per cent; (f) 8.2 per cent (2000)
ENROLMENT (percentage of age group) – primary 100 per cent (1997); secondary 67 per cent (1997); tertiary 17 per cent (1997)

MEDIA

There are state owned television (Inravision) and radio stations (Radiodifusora Nacional de Colombia) as well as private commercial networks. There are five main daily newspapers including *El Espacio, La Republica* and *El Tiempo.*

CULTURE

Colombia's culture reflects its indigenous Indian, Spanish and African backgrounds. Pre-Colonial art, primarily stone sculpture, pottery and gold, has influenced Western art and contemporary Indian art fuses these roots with modern techniques. Colombian music is also international and widely exported. Gabriel García Márquez (b. 1928) is Colombia's most famous writer (winner of the Nobel Prize for Literature in 1982).

THE COMOROS

L'Union des Comores – Union of the Comoros

AREA – 2,235 sq. km. The Comoro archipelago includes the islands of Njazidja (formerly Grande Comore), Anjouan (also known as Nzwani), Mayotte and Moheli (also known as Mwali) and certain islets in the Indian Ocean
POPULATION – 651,000, mostly Muslim. French and Arabic are the official languages; the majority of the population speak Comoran, a blend of Arabic and Swahili
CAPITAL – Moroni (population, 30,365, 1991 census), on Ngazidja
CURRENCY – Comorian franc (KMF) of 100 centimes. The Franc CFA of 100 centimes is also used
NATIONAL ANTHEM – Udzima Wa Ya Masiwa (The Union Of The Islands)
NATIONAL DAY – 6 July (Independence Day)
NATIONAL FLAG – Four horizontal stripes – gold, white, red, blue; a green triangle based on the hoist containing a white crescent and four white stars, horns towards the fly
MORTALITY RATE (per 1,000 population) – 5.63 (2003)
HIV / AIDS ADULT PREVALENCE RATE – 0.12 per cent (2001)
DEATH PENALTY – Yes
POPULATION BELOW POVERTY LINE – 60 per cent (2002)
POPULATION DENSITY – 302 per sq. km (1999)
ILLITERACY RATE – (m) 33.5 per cent; (f) 47.2 per cent (2000)
ENROLMENT (percentage of age group) – primary 52 per cent (1993); tertiary 0.6 per cent (1995)

CLIMATE AND TERRAIN

The Comoros are a group of islands located in the Mozambique Channel between Africa and Madagascar. Njazidja, Anjouan and Moheli are volcanic. Njazidja has an active volcano, Karthala, which last erupted in August 2003. Elevation extremes range from 2,360 m (Karthala) at the highest point to 0 m (Indian Ocean) at the lowest. There is a tropical climate with a dry season from May to October and a hot season from November to April. The average temperatures range from 20°C to 28°C. Regular cyclones afflict the islands between January and April.

HISTORY AND POLITICS

The islanders voted for independence from France in December 1974 and three islands became independent on 6 July 1975. The island of Mayotte opposed independence and has remained under French administration.

An election in 1993 brought President Djohar's National Rally for Development party (RND) to power. Djohar was temporarily ousted in a coup in 1995 that was thwarted by French troops. While Djohar was abroad for medical attention, Prime Minister Caabi el-Yachroutou declared himself interim President and refused to acknowledge Djohar's authority, resulting in the formation of a rival government. Djohar returned to the Comoros in January 1996 but was prohibited from contesting the March 1996 presidential election, which was won by Mohammad Taki Abdoulkarim of the National Union for Democracy in the Comoros. Taki dissolved the National Assembly and legislative elections were held in December 1996 although they were boycotted by the opposition Forum for National Recovery party (FRN).

President Taki died in office on 6 November 1998 and Tajiddine Ben Said Massonde took over as interim President. His government was deposed in a coup on 30 April 1999 by Col. Assoumani Azali, who was sworn in as President on 6 May. On 2 September 1999, an unsuccessful coup was launched while Col. Azali was overseas. He announced that he would retain power until a presidential election was held, which was due to take place by April 2000. The election did not take place and Col. Azali declared that he would not restore civilian rule due to the issue of Anjouan separatism. However, in March 2001, he announced that the country would be restored to civilian rule in 2002 and that he would not contest the presidential election. However, he resigned as President on 21 January 2002 in order to stand in the April presidential election. The presidential elections were held in March, April and May 2002. Elections to the Union parliament were postponed indefinitely in March 2003.

INSURGENCIES

In August 1997 separatists on the islands of Anjouan and Moheli demanded independence from the Comoros and a return to French rule. Following a failed attempt to resolve the situation by force, President Taki assumed absolute power and established a State Transition Commission to function as a Cabinet. In a referendum in October 1997, the inhabitants of Anjouan voted overwhelmingly for independence. Talks mediated by the Organisation of African Unity (OAU) began in December 1997 and an agreement drawn up with OAU support, which would have given each island considerable autonomy, was signed by Njazidja and Moheli, but was rejected by Anjouan. Anjouan citizens voted by a large majority against re-incorporation into the Comoros in a referendum held on 23 January 2000.

In 1998, Anjouan's self-proclaimed President Abdallah Ibrahim appointed a prime minister and cabinet, though their legitimacy has not been recognised internationally. Fighting broke out between President Ibrahim's forces and those of a previous Anjouan prime minister, Chamassi Said Omar, in December of that year. On 1 August 1999, President Ibrahim resigned and transferred most of his powers to Col. Said Abeid. A general election was held in Anjouan in August 1999.

President Azali and the leader of Anjouan, Lt.-Col. Abderemane, signed an agreement on national reconciliation on 17 February 2001, which would have given Anjouan considerable autonomy. The Anjouan government withdrew from the reconciliation process in April, alleging that the conditions of the agreement had not been met. In February 2003, security officials confirmed they had foiled a coup aimed at removing the Union government of Col. Assoumani Azali.

POLITICAL SYSTEM

A new constitution which would create a federal structure for Njazidja, Anjouan and Moheli and give greater autonomy for the islands was approved, in outline, by referendum on 23 December 2001. The final version was accepted by referendum in March 2002 on Moheli and Anjouan but was not accepted by the voters of Njazidja until a second vote in April. Under the new constitutional arrangements each island has its own President, constitution and legislative assembly. Island Presidents rotate the role of President of the Union with Njazidja taking the first turn. Each island President can appoint eight Ministers to deal with local issues while foreign affairs, finance, defence, judicial and religious matters are to be dealt with by the Union authorities. There are still areas of dispute, principally over security, budget control and customs revenue. Legislative elections for a new Parliament to define the powers of the various authorities are yet to be held.

HEAD OF STATE

President of the Union, Col. Assoumani Azali, *elected* 14 April 2002, *sworn in* 31 May 2002

SELECTED GOVERNMENT MEMBERS *as at July 2004*

Vice-President, Finance, Budget, Economy, External Trade, Investment and Privatisation, Caabi el-Yachroutu

Vice-President, Justice, Information, Religious Affairs, Human Rights, and Relations with the Houses of Parliament, Rachid Ben Massoundi

EMBASSY OF THE FEDERAL ISLAMIC REPUBLIC OF THE COMOROS

20 rue Marbeau, F-75016 Paris, France

T (+33) (1) 4067 9054

BRITISH AMBASSADOR, HE Brian Donaldson, resident at Antananarivo, Madagascar

ECONOMY AND TRADE

The principal exports are vanilla, copra, cloves and essential oils; cacao, sisal and coffee are also cultivated. Njazidja is well forested and produces some timber. Agriculture accounts for 40 per cent of GDP, service industries 56 per cent and the manufacturing industry 4 per cent. The Comoros are heavily dependent on foreign aid. The islands are a potential haven for tourists but political instability undermines the tourist industry.

GNI – US$213 million (2000); US$1,610 per capita (2001)

ANNUAL AVERAGE GROWTH OF GDP – 1.1 per cent (1998)

TOTAL EXTERNAL DEBT – US$177 million (2001)

Trade with UK	*2002*	*2003*
Imports from UK	£743,000	£402,000
Exports to UK	211,000	35,000

DEMOCRATIC REPUBLIC OF CONGO

République Démocratique du Congo – Democratic Republic of Congo

AREA – 2,344,858 sq. km. Neighbours: Central African Republic (north), Sudan (north-east), Uganda, Rwanda, Burundi and Tanzania (east), Zambia (south), Angola (south-west), Republic of Congo (north-west)
POPULATION – 48,040,000 (1997 UN estimate). The population was 34,671,607 at the 1985 census, composed of Bantu, Hamitic, Nilotic, Sudanese and Pygmoid groups, divided into more than 200 semi-autonomous tribes. More than 400 languages are spoken. Swahili, a Bantu language with an admixture of Arabic, is the nearest approach to a common language in the east and south, while Lingala is the language of a large area along the river and in the north, and Kikongo of the region between Kinshasa and the sea. French is the language of administration. Roman Catholicism is the predominant religion; there are also Protestants, Muslims and Kimbanguists
CAPITAL – Kinshasa (population, 4,655,313, 1994 estimate)
MAJOR CITIES – Kananga; Kisangani; Likasi; Lubumbashi; ΨMatadi; Mbandaka
CURRENCY – Congolese franc
NATIONAL ANTHEM – Debout Congolais (Stand Up, Congolese)
NATIONAL DAY – 30 June (Independence Day)
NATIONAL FLAG – Blue with a large yellow five-pointed star in the centre and five small yellow five-pointed stars in a vertical line down the hoist
MORTALITY RATE (per 1,000 population) – 14.87 (2003)
HIV / AIDS ADULT PREVALENCE – 4.9 per cent (2001)
DEATH PENALTY – Yes
POPULATION GROWTH RATE – 2.6 per cent
POPULATION DENSITY – 21 per sq. km (1999)
MILITARY EXPENDITURE – 21.7 per cent of GDP (2002)
MILITARY PERSONNEL – 81,400: Army 79,000, Navy 900, Air Force 1,500
ILLITERACY RATE – (m) 26.9 per cent; (f) 49.8 per cent (2000)
ENROLMENT (percentage of age group) – primary 72 per cent (1997); secondary 26 per cent (1997); tertiary 2 per cent (1997)

CLIMATE AND TERRAIN

The Democratic Republic of Congo is Africa's third largest state. Elevation extremes range from 5,110 m (Mount Ngaliema, also known as Mount Stanley) at the highest point to 0 m (Atlantic Ocean) at the lowest. The central region has an equatorial climate with high humidity and an average temperature of 26°C. The northern and southern regions have different climatic cycles with the dry season in the north taking place from December to February and the dry season in the south taking place from May to September.

HISTORY AND POLITICS

The state of the Congo, founded in 1885, became a Belgian colony in 1908 and gained its independence in 1960. Mobutu Sésé Seko came to power in a coup in 1965 and was elected president in 1970. Legislative power was vested in a unicameral National Legislative Council, with candidates proposed by the sole legal political party, Mouvement Populaire de la Révolution (MPR).

The government began moves towards a multiparty system from the end of the 1980s onwards but progress was hindered by army revolts and political disagreements.

In October 1996 fighting broke out between Zaïrean Tutsis *(Banyamulenge)* and the Zaïrean army in North and South Kivu provinces which had received an influx of Hutu refugees from Rwanda. The pro-Hutu army attempted to expel the Tutsis from the region but found themselves outgunned by the rebels, under the leadership of Laurent Kabila, who were backed by the Rwandan and Ugandan governments. Kabila's Alliance of Democratic Forces for the Liberation of Congo-Zaïre (AFDL) captured Kinshasa in May 1997 and President Mobutu fled. Zaïre was renamed the Democratic Republic of Congo.

A rebellion against the government of Laurent Kabila began in Kivu in August 1998 and by the end of the month the rebels had seized large areas in the east and west of the country. Angola, Chad, Kenya, Namibia and Zimbabwe promised President Kabila military support. The Angolan army quickly recaptured several towns in the south-west, but the rebels maintained their grip on the eastern regions. The rebel movement, the Congolese Democratic Rally (RCD), was supported by Uganda and Rwanda. On 17 May 1999, Ernest Wamba dia Wamba, the RCD leader, was ousted, splitting the movement into two distinct factions, that led by Wamba dia Wamba being called the Congolese Democratic Rally-Liberation Movement (RCD-LM). A cease-fire signed on 31 August 1999 between the government and the two rebel groups has remained largely intact, although localised clashes have been frequent. The main rebel groups, the RCD, the RCD-LM and the Congolese Liberation Movement (MLC) reached agreement on 20 December 1999 to form an umbrella organisation to defeat the government. A new rebel group, the Congolese Democratic Rally-National (RCD-N), was founded in October 2000 and in January 2001, the RCD and the RCD-LM were reunited as the Congolese Liberation Front (FLC).

By December 2000, an agreement between the government and the rebel groups was signed to withdraw troops from the front line. All parties to the civil war had withdrawn their troops 15 km from their frontline positions by 26 March 2001.

President Laurent Désiré Kabila died on 18 January 2001, having been shot by his bodyguard. His son, Maj.-Gen. Joseph Kabila, was sworn in as President on 26 January. No elections have been held since.

UN-sponsored peace talks began in South Africa in February 2002 and on 16 December the government and the main rebel groups signed a power-sharing agreement. A transitional government including the political opposition as well as representatives of the RCD and FLC was to hold power for two years, after which elections would be held. On 16 March 2003 a draft constitution was agreed whereby incumbent President Joseph Kabila would be supported during the two-year transition period by four vice-presidents. On 7 April Joseph Kabila was sworn in as President of the transitional government and in July he named the transitional government cabinet. The four vice-presidents and most of the cabinet members were sworn in in July. However the ministers representing the RCD and the FLC refused to take the oath of allegiance to President Kabila as head of the transitional government. The last Ugandan troops left eastern Congo in May 2003 but clashes between rival militias led to the deployment of French peacekeepers in Bunia as part of a UN rapid reaction force in June. By July 2004, there remained in the region over 10,000 UN troops from over 50 countries.

POLITICAL SYSTEM

A 300-member Transitional Constituent Assembly was established in August 2000. The members of the Assembly were appointed by former President Laurent Kabila.

There are 11 regions, each under a Governor and provincial administration: Bas-Zaïre (provincial capital, Matadi); Bandundu (Bandundu); Equateur (Mbandaka); Haut-Zaïre (Kisangani); Kinshasa (Kinshasa); Maniema (Kindu); North Kivu (Goma); South Kivu (Bukavu); Shaba (Katanga) (Lubumbashi); East Kasai (Mbuji-Mayi); West Kasai (Kananga).

HEAD OF STATE

President, Maj.-Gen. Joseph Kabila, *sworn in* 26 January 2001, *sworn in as President of the transitional government* 7 April 2003

Vice-Presidents, Abdoulaye Yerodia *(government)*; Z'Ahidi Ngoma *(civilian opposition)*; Jean-Pierre Bemba (FLC); Azarias Ruberwa Manywa (RCD)

SELECTED GOVERNMENT MEMBERS *as at July 2004*

Defence, Jean-Pierre Ondekane *(RCD)*
Economy, Célestin Vunabandi *(RCD)*
Finance, Pierre Futa *(Government)*
Foreign Affairs, Antoine Ghonda Mangalibi *(FLC)*
Interior, Théophile Mbemba Fundu *(Government)*

EMBASSY OF THE DEMOCRATIC REPUBLIC OF CONGO
218 Gray's Inn Road, London WC1X 8QF
T 020-87278 9825
Ambassador Extraordinary and Plenipotentiary, Henri N'Swana, apptd July 2003

BRITISH EMBASSY
83 Avenue du Roi Baudouin, Kinshasa
T (+243) 98 169 100/111/200
Ambassador Extraordinary and Plenipotentiary, HE Jim Atkinson, apptd 2000

ECONOMY AND TRADE

Coffee, rubber, cocoa and timber are the most important agricultural exports but the production of cotton, pyrethrum and copal is steadily increasing. Copper is widely exploited, and industrial diamonds and cobalt are also produced. Oil deposits are exploited off the Zaïre estuary and reef-gold is mined in the north-east of the country.

The main industrial products are foodstuffs, beverages, tobacco, textiles, leather, wood products, cement and building materials, metallurgy, small river craft and bicycles. There are reserves of hydroelectric power and the Inga dam on the river Zaïre supplies electricity to Matadi, Kinshasa and Shaba.

Whilst the country has many natural resources, civil war has led to the collapse of the economy, with total debt amounting to more than twice the GNI.

In July 2003 the IMF announced that US$10,000 million of debt relief would be granted to the Democratic Republic of Congo under the Heavily Indebted Poor Countries (HIPC) initiative. In addition, the World Bank approved a US$120 million loan to boost investment and support public enterprises in key economic sectors.

GNI – US$5,024 million (1998); US$110 per capita (1998)
GDP – US$5,187 million (2001); US$129 per capita (2000)
ANNUAL AVERAGE GROWTH OF GDP – 4.5 per cent (2001)
INFLATION RATE – 175.5 per cent (1997)
TOTAL EXTERNAL DEBT – US$11,645 million (2000)

Trade with UK	*2002*	*2003*
Imports from UK	£5,591,000	£8,092,000
Exports to UK	942,000	1,409,000

TRANSPORT INFRASTRUCTURE

There are approximately 157,000 km of roads, including 30 km of expressway. The expressway is surfaced and 20,500 km of roads are unsurfaced. There are 6,000 km of railways. The country has four international and 40 principal airports.

MEDIA

The state controlled media (Radio-Television Nationale Congolaise (RTNC) and La Voix du Congo) has the greatest influence and broadcast reach. There are some eight other private and commercial television stations and ten radio stations (some run by the Catholic church, some by the UN). Around 15 newspapers are published regularly in Kinshasa.

REPUBLIC OF CONGO

République du Congo – Republic of Congo

AREA – 342,000 sq. km. Neighbours: Gabon (west), Cameroon and Central African Republic (north), Angola (Cabinda) (south-west), the Democratic Republic of Congo (east and south)
POPULATION – 2,745,000. The official language is French; Lingala, Monokutuba and Kikongo are widely spoken
CAPITAL – Brazzaville (population, 937,579, 1992 estimate)
MAJOR CITIES – ΨPointe Noire, the main commercial centre
CURRENCY – Franc CFA of 100 centimes
NATIONAL ANTHEM – La Congolaise
NATIONAL DAY – 15 August
NATIONAL FLAG – Divided diagonally into green, yellow and red bands
MORTALITY RATE (per 1,000 population) – 14.2 (2003)
HIV / AIDS ADULT PREVALENCE – 7.2 per cent (2001)

POPULATION GROWTH RATE – 2.8 per cent
POPULATION DENSITY – 8 per sq. km (1999)
MILITARY EXPENDITURE – 3.1 per cent of GDP (2002)
MILITARY PERSONNEL – 10,000: Army 8,000, Navy 800, Air Force 1,200; Paramilitaries 2,000
ILLITERACY RATE – (m) 10.4 per cent; (f) 21.6 per cent (2003)
ENROLMENT (percentage of age group) – primary 100 per cent (1997); tertiary 7 per cent (1997)

CLIMATE AND TERRAIN

The Republic of Congo is covered by grassland, mangrove and dense rainforest. Elevation extremes range from 903 m (Mount Berongou) at the highest point to 0 m (Atlantic Ocean) at the lowest. The main rivers are the Sangha and Alima in the north. The climate is equatorial. The annual daily temperature in Brazzaville is between 28°C and 33°C. The dry season is June to September. The country is prone to flooding during the wet season (March to June).

HISTORY AND POLITICS

The French colony of Middle Congo, now the Republic of Congo, became a member state of the French Community on 28 November 1958 and fully independent on 17 August 1960.

In 1968, a National Council of army officers took power and created the Parti Congolais du Travail (PCT) and the People's Republic of the Congo. After popular pressure, the PCT abandoned its monopoly of power and renounced Marxism in 1990. In 1992 the country adopted a new multi-party constitution with a directly elected president and a bicameral parliament.

The lack of a parliamentary majority forced President Lissouba to call fresh elections in 1993. These were won by the Pan-African Union for Social Democracy (UPADS) but the results were disputed by opposition groups and violence broke out between rival parties. A new UPADS-dominated government was appointed in January 1995. In June 1997, fighting broke out between forces of President Lissouba and followers of former President Sassou-Nguesso, who was re-installed as President in October 1997. Elections scheduled for July 1997 were called off and a National Forum for Unity and Democracy was set up to schedule legislative elections. It declared a three-year transition period after which democratic elections would be held. A constitutional committee was inaugurated in November 1998, charged with drafting a constitution to be approved by referendum in 1999.

In April 1999, supporters of former Prime Minister Bernard Kolelas formed themselves into a political party, the Patriotic Union of Ninja Forces. Following a period of intense fighting, negotiations between the government and the rebels began in November 1999; an accord was reached in which the two sides agreed to an unconditional end to hostilities and the demilitarisation of political parties.

A 'non-exclusive national dialogue' was held between 17 March and 14 April 2001. Rebel leaders and the government adopted a draft constitution, which aimed to establish a directly elected executive presidency and bicameral legislature. The new constitution was approved in a referendum in January 2002. A presidential election held in March 2002 was won by Denis Sassou-Nguesso who secured nearly 90 per cent of the vote. The Congolese Labour Party (PCT) won an overall majority in elections to the National Assembly held in May and June 2002. There was heavy fighting throughout 2002 but two agreements were signed between the government and the Ninja fighters in March 2003 to end hostilities and restore free movement and the rule of law.

HEAD OF STATE
President, Defence, Denis Sassou-Nguesso, *sworn in* 25 October 1997, *elected* 10 March 2002

SELECTED GOVERNMENT MEMBERS *as at July 2004*
Economy, Finance and Budget, Roger Rigobert Andely
Foreign Affairs, Co-operation and Francophone Affairs, Rodolphe Adada
Minister in the President's Office in charge of State Control, Simon Mfoutou
Minister-Delegate, Brig.-Gen. Jacques Yvon Ndolou *(National Defence)*

EMBASSY OF THE REPUBLIC OF CONGO BRAZZAVILLE
37 bis Rue Paul Valéry, 75116 Paris, France
T (+33) (1) 4500 6057
Ambassador Extraordinary and Plenipotentiary, HE Henri Marie Joseph Lopes, apptd 1999

BRITISH AMBASSADOR, HE Jim Atkinson, resident at Kinshasa, Democratic Republic of Congo

ECONOMY AND TRADE

The Republic of Congo has its own oil deposits, producing about nine million tonnes annually. These deposits make up over half of The Congo's economy. It also produces lead, zinc and gold. The principal agricultural products are timber, cassava and yams. Imports are mainly of machinery. Agriculture accounts for about 10 per cent of GDP.

In 2000 the government, the World Bank and the IMF agreed a Post-Conflict Assistance Programme which provided US$14 million for post-war reconstruction and economic development.

37 per cent of imports come from France, making it the Republic's biggest trading partner.

GNI – US$1,847 million (2000); US$580 per capita (2001)
ANNUAL AVERAGE GROWTH OF GDP – 1.3 per cent (1998)
INFLATION RATE – 0.9 per cent (2000)
TOTAL EXTERNAL DEBT – US$4,887 million (2000)
IMPORTS – US$655 million (2000)
EXPORTS – US$3,101 million (2000)

Trade with UK	*2002*	*2003*
Imports from UK	£16,771,000	£12,621,000
Exports to UK	5,844,000	7,604,000

TRANSPORT INFRASTRUCTURE

Pointe Noire is the main port and is the centre of the offshore oil industry. It is linked to Brazzaville by rail and road. There are 894 km of railways and 12,800 km of roads, 1,242 km of which are surfaced. Four of the 31 airports have surfaced runways. There are 1,120 km of commercially navigable waterways on the Congo and Ubango rivers.

MEDIA

Brazzaville is at the centre of the print media industry with five privately owned newspapers regularly published there. TV Congo is the only television station and it is state owned and controlled by Radiodiffusion Television Congolaise. Radio Congo is also state controlled.

COSTA RICA

República de Costa Rica – Republic of Costa Rica

AREA – 51,100 sq. km. Neighbours: Nicaragua, Panama
POPULATION – 4,112,000 (2001), mainly of European origin. The language is Spanish
CAPITAL – San José (population, 1,982,339, 2000 census)
MAJOR CITIES – Alajuela; Cartago
CURRENCY – Costa Rican colón of 100 céntimos
NATIONAL ANTHEM – Noble Patria, Tu Hermosa Bandera (Noble Fatherland, Your Beautiful Flag)
NATIONAL DAY – 15 September
NATIONAL FLAG – Five horizontal bands, blue, white, red, white, blue (the red band twice the width of the others with emblem near staff)
LIFE EXPECTANCY (years) – 77 (2001)
MORTALITY RATE (per 1,000 population) – 4.31 (2003)
INFANT MORTALITY (per 1,000 births) – 9 (2001)
HIV / AIDS ADULT PREVALENCE RATE – 0.6 per cent (2001)
DEATH PENALTY – No (abolished 1877)
POPULATION BELOW POVERTY LINE – 20.6 per cent (1999)
POPULATION GROWTH RATE – 2.7 per cent (1990–2001)
POPULATION DENSITY – 80 per sq. km (2001)
URBAN POPULATION – 60 per cent (2001)
MILITARY EXPENDITURE – 0.6 per cent of GDP (2002)
MILITARY PERSONNEL – 8,400 Paramilitaries
ILLITERACY RATE – (m) 4.1 per cent; (f) 3.3 per cent (2003)
ENROLMENT (percentage of age group) – primary 100 per cent (1997); secondary 48 per cent (1997); tertiary 48 per cent (1997)

CLIMATE AND TERRAIN

Cordillera de Guanacaste, (north-west) Cordillera Central, and Cordillera de Talamanca form the series of volcanic mountain ranges that split the country from north to south. Elevation extremes range from 3,180 m (Chirripó Grande) to 0 m (Pacific Ocean) at the lowest. The climate is tropical with an average annual temperature of 26°C to 28°C. The wet season runs from May to November. The area is subject to occasional earthquakes, hurricanes, flooding and landslides.

HISTORY AND POLITICS

For nearly three centuries (1530–1821) Costa Rica was under Spanish rule. In 1821 the country obtained its independence, although from 1824 to 1839 it was one of the United States of Central America.

The main political parties are the Social Christian Unity Party (PUSC) and the National Liberation Party (PLN). In the legislative elections held in 2002 none of the main parties won the required 40 per cent of the vote. In a second round of elections in April the PUSC won against the PLN by a margin of 58 per cent to 42 per cent. The presidential election of the same period was won by the PUSC candidate Abel Pacheco.

POLITICAL SYSTEM

Executive power is vested in the President, who is head of state and government, with legislative power vested in the 57-member Legislative Assembly (Asamblea Legislativa). Under the constitution both the President and the members of the Legislative Assembly are elected for a single four-year term and may not be re-elected.

HEAD OF STATE

President, Abel Pacheco, *elected* 7 April 2002
First Vice-President, Co-ordinator of Social Policy, Planning, Lineth Saborio Chaverri
Second Vice-President (suspended), Luis Fishman

SELECTED GOVERNMENT MEMBERS *as at July 2004*

Finance, Alberto Dent
Foreign Affairs and Religion, Roberto Tovar Faja
Interior, Police and Public Security, Rogelio Ramos Martinez

COSTA RICAN EMBASSY

Flat 1, 14 Lancaster Gate, London W2 3LH
T 020-7706 8844
Ambassador Extraordinary and Plenipotentiary, HE Rodolfo Gutiérrez Carranza, apptd 1998

BRITISH EMBASSY

Apartado 815–1007, Edificio Centro Colón (Eleventh Floor), San José
T (+506) 258 2025
E britemb@racsa.co.cr
Ambassador Extraordinary and Plenipotentiary and Consul-General, Georgina Butler, apptd 2002

ECONOMY AND TRADE

Tourism is the largest single industry, and with one third of the country as national parkland or nature reserve, 'ecotourism' is on the increase. Abundant flora and fauna, such as macaws, toucans and over 1,000 species of orchid, attract large numbers of visitors. In 2002, there were 1,113,359 tourists. The manufacturing industry accounts for around 30 per cent of GDP, the principal products being computer components, foodstuffs, textiles, plastic goods and pharmaceuticals. The principal agricultural products are coffee, bananas, sugar and cattle (for meat).

The chief exports are manufactured goods, bananas, coffee, fish and shellfish, machinery and tropical fruits. The chief imports are raw materials for industry, consumer goods, capital equipment, and fuel and mineral oils. The USA is Costa Rica's largest trading partner and accounts for around 36.7 per cent of imports and 31.5 per cent of exports. Other major trading partners are Japan, the UK, Mexico and the Netherlands.

GNI – US$15,700 million (2001); US$4,060 per capita (2001)

ANNUAL AVERAGE GROWTH OF GDP – 1.7 per cent (2000)
INFLATION RATE – 11.0 per cent (2000)
UNEMPLOYMENT – 5.2 per cent (2000)
TOTAL EXTERNAL DEBT – US$4,800 million (2002)
FOREIGN DIRECT INVESTMENT – US$1,694 million (1997–2000)
IMPORTS – US$7,175 million (2002)
EXPORTS – US$5,258 million (2002)

Trade with UK	*2002*	*2003*
Imports from UK	£51,024,000	£40,466,000
Exports to UK	317,299,000	437,198,000

TRANSPORT INFRASTRUCTURE

The chief ports are Limón on the Atlantic coast, through which passes most of the coffee exported, and Caldera on the Pacific coast. LACSA is the national airline, operating flights throughout Central and South America, the Caribbean and the USA, besides internal flights to over 100 local airports. There are 950 km of railways and 35,892 km of roads, 7,896 of which are surfaced. There are 151 airports, 30 of which have surfaced runways.

MEDIA AND CULTURE

Costa Rica has nine major newspapers, at least 18 television stations and over 35 radio stations. It is one of the most peaceful and prosperous countries in Central America. The city of Escazú is home to several contemporary artists including Dinorah Bolandi (b. 1968) and Mirta Castro (b. 1967). Costa Rican music is diverse, reflecting its African, Pre-Colombian and Spanish roots.

CÔTE D'IVOIRE

République de la Côte d'Ivoire – Republic of Côte d'Ivoire

AREA – 318,000 sq. km. Neighbours: Guinea and Liberia (west), Mali and Burkina Faso (north), Ghana (east)
POPULATION – 16,349,000 (2001): 39 per cent Muslim, 28 per cent Christian (mainly Roman Catholic) and 17 per cent maintain traditional beliefs. The official language is French, but Agni, Baoulé, Dioula, Senoufo and Yacouba are spoken
CAPITAL – Yamoussoukro (population, 126,191, 1988), the political and administrative capital since 1983
MAJOR CITIES – ΨAbidjan, the economic and financial centre
CURRENCY – Franc CFA of 100 centimes
NATIONAL ANTHEM – L'Abidjanaise
NATIONAL DAY – 7 August
NATIONAL FLAG – Three vertical stripes, orange, white and green
LIFE EXPECTANCY (years) – 48 (2001)
MORTALITY RATE (per 1,000 population) – 18.41 (2003)
INFANT MORTALITY (per 1,000 births) – 102 (2001)
HIV / AIDS ADULT PREVALENCE – 9.7 per cent (2001)
DEATH PENALTY – No (abolished 2000)
POPULATION GROWTH RATE – 2.4 per cent (1990–2001)
POPULATION DENSITY – 51 per sq. km (2001)
MILITARY EXPENDITURE – 1.4 per cent of GDP (2002)
MILITARY PERSONNEL – 17,050: Army 6,500, Navy 900, Air Force 700, Paramilitaries 8,950
CONSCRIPTION DURATION – 18 months (selective)
ILLITERACY RATE – (m) 45.1 per cent; (f) 61.2 per cent (2000)
ENROLMENT (percentage of age group) – primary 71 per cent (1997); tertiary 6 per cent (1997)

CLIMATE AND TERRAIN

The climate is equatorial in the southern and western forest areas; tropical in the central and eastern savannah regions and dry and tropical in the north. Elevation extremes range from 1,752 m (Mount Nimba) at the highest point to 0 m (Gulf of Guinea) at the lowest. Average annual temperatures range from 24°C in August to 27°C in March.

HISTORY AND POLITICS

Although French contact was made in the first half of the 19th century, Côte d'Ivoire became a colony only in 1893 and was finally pacified in 1912. It decided in 1958 to remain an autonomous republic within the French Community; full independence outside the Community was proclaimed on 7 August 1960.

After having been President since independence in 1960, President Houphouët-Boigny died in 1993 and was replaced by the parliamentary speaker Henri Konan-Bédié. The President was deposed by Gen. Robert Guëi in a military coup on 24–25 December 1999 and a transitional government was announced in January 2000.

A referendum on a new constitution was held in July 2000, which was approved by 86.58 per cent of those who voted.

In October 2000 a presidential election was held. President Guëi dissolved the electoral commission following early results which indicated that Laurent Gbagbo of the Ivorian Popular Front (FPI) was leading, and it was announced that Guëi had won. Demonstrations and mounting violence led to Guëi fleeing the country on 26 October and Gbagbo was inaugurated as President.

In elections to the National Assembly held in December 2000 and January 2001, the FPI won 96 seats and the Democratic Party of Côte d'Ivoire (PDCI) won 94 seats. The election was boycotted by the Rally of Republicans (RDR), the strongest party in the north of the country.

Fighting broke out between government forces and rebel forces in September 2002 during which Guëi was killed. A short-lived cease-fire in October gave way to further clashes. France deployed hundreds of troops in December after many civilians had been killed. In March 2003 the government agreed to include nine members from rebel ranks. A cease-fire was signed between the armed forces and rebel groups in May but sporadic outbreaks of violence continued until December.

POLITICAL SYSTEM

The Côte d'Ivoire has a presidential system of government and a single-chamber National Assembly of 225 members, directly elected for a five-year term. It has been a multiparty system since 1990. The President's term of office is five years, renewable once only.

It was proposed that a Senate should be created in the next general election which is due to take place in 2005.

HEAD OF STATE
President, Laurent Gbagbo, *elected* 22 October 2000, *sworn in* 26 October 2000

SELECTED GOVERNMENT MEMBERS *as at July 2004*
Prime Minister, Planning and Development, Seydou Diarra
Minister of Defence, Rene Amani
Ministers of State, Bouabre Bohoun *(Finance and Economy)*; Bamba Mamadou *(Foreign Affairs and Ivorians Abroad)*

EMBASSY OF THE REPUBLIC OF CÔTE D'IVOIRE
2 Upper Belgrave Street, London SW1X 8BJ
T 020-7235 6991
Ambassador Extraordinary and Plenipotentiary, HE Youssoufou Bamba, apptd 2001

BRITISH EMBASSY
Immeuble Bank of Africa (3rd and 4th Floors), Angle Ave., Terrasson de Fougeres et Rue Gourgas Abidjan-Plateau, BP 2581
T (+225) (20) 300800
E britemb.a@aviso.ci
Ambassador Extraordinary and Plenipotentiary, HE Franois Gordon, CMG, apptd 2001

ECONOMY AND TRADE

In the late 1980s the economy contracted considerably. Exports began to lose value as the currencies of neighbouring states deteriorated. The situation worsened as the franc CFA remained pegged to the value of the French Franc. An economic reform and stabilisation programme began in 1989 under IMF auspices and has brought down inflation, increased investment and led to GDP growth. The devaluation of the CFA franc in January 1994 increased exports considerably and restored a trade surplus. In February 1998 a further economic reform programme began. Agriculture accounts for 29 per cent of GDP, the manufacturing industry for 22 per cent and the service industries for 49 per cent. Côte d'Ivoire's main trading partner is France. Agriculture employs around 68 per cent of the workforce.

The principal exports are coffee, cocoa (Côte d'Ivoire is the world's largest producer, supplying 40 per cent of global demand), timber, palm oil, sugar, rubber, pineapples, bananas, and cotton. There are some deposits of diamonds and minerals including manganese and iron. Oil and gas deposits have been exploited since 1995.

GNI – US$10,300 million (2001); US$630 per capita (2001)
ANNUAL AVERAGE GROWTH OF GDP – 0.9 per cent (2001)
INFLATION RATE – 2.5 per cent (2000)
TOTAL EXTERNAL DEBT – US$12,138 million (2000)
DIRECT FOREIGN INVESTMENT – US$1,218 million (1997–2000)
IMPORTS – US$3,783 million (2002)
EXPORTS – US$5,167 million (2002)

BALANCE OF PAYMENTS
Trade – US$2,735 million surplus (2002)
Current Account – US$767 million surplus (2002)

Trade	*2002*	*2003*
Imports from UK	£40,481,000	£43,745,000
Exports to UK	92,981,000	108,618,000

TRANSPORT INFRASTRUCTURE

Côte d'Ivoire has 660 km of railways and 50,400 km of roads, 4,889 km of which are surfaced. There are 980 km of navigable rivers and canals and the main ports are Abidjan, Aboisso, Dabou and San-Pedro. There are 36 airports, seven of which have surfaced runways.

MEDIA

The state broadcaster is Radiodiffusion Television Ivoirienne (RTI). RTI operates two national radio stations (La Chaine Nationale and Frequence 2) and two television channels (La Premiere and TV2). There are no private terrestrial television stations although subscription services are available. Radio is the most popular medium for news with around 30 non-commercial community radio stations located throughout the country. The print media is represented by two government-owned daily newspapers and around 20 privately owned newspapers.

CULTURE

The wooden mask carvings of the Baulé, the Dan (Yacouba) and the Senoufo are highly accomplished and the art of these ethnic groups is internationally acclaimed. The people of Côte d'Ivoire are also famous for their music (village entertainers, *griot*, create music with instruments made from local materials such as gourds and skins).

CROATIA

Republika Hrvatska – Republic of Croatia

AREA – 55,900 sq. km. Neighbours: Slovenia, Hungary (north), Serbia and Montenegro (east), Bosnia-Hercegovina (south, and east of Adriatic coastal strip)
POPULATION – 4,655,000 (2001): 78 per cent Croat, 12 per cent Serb, 2 per cent Yugoslav; also Hungarians, Italians, Albanians, Czechs, Ukrainians and Jews. Roman Catholic 76.5 per cent, Eastern Orthodox 11.1 per cent, Protestant 1.4 per cent, Muslim 1.2 per cent. The language is Croatian in the Latin script
CAPITAL – Zagreb (population, 867,717, 2001 census)
MAJOR CITIES – Osijek; Rijeka; Split
CURRENCY – Kuna of 100 lipa
NATIONAL ANTHEM – Lijepa Naša Domovina (Our Beautiful Homeland)
NATIONAL DAY – 30 May (Statehood Day)
NATIONAL FLAG – Three horizontal stripes of red, white, blue, with the national arms in the centre
LIFE EXPECTANCY (years) – 74 (2001)
MORTALITY RATE (per 1,000 population) – 11.25 (2003)
INFANT MORTALITY (per 1,000 births) – 7 (2001)
HIV / AIDS ADULT PREVALENCE – 0.1 per cent (2001)
DEATH PENALTY – No (abolished 1990)
POPULATION GROWTH RATE – 0.3 per cent (1990–2001)
POPULATION DENSITY – 83 per sq. km (2001)
ILLITERACY RATE – (m) 0.7 per cent; (f) 2.7 per cent (2000)

ENROLMENT (percentage of age group) – primary 87 per cent (1997); secondary 82 per cent (1997); tertiary 28 per cent (1997)

CLIMATE AND TERRAIN

Croatia is divided into three major geographic areas: the Pannonian region in the north, the central mountain belt, and the Adriatic coast region of Istria and Dalmatia which has 1,185 islands and islets and 1,778 km of coastline. Elevation extremes range from 1,830 m (Dinara) at the highest point to 0 m (Adriatic Sea) at the lowest. The climate is continental on the Pannonian Basin with average temperatures ranging from −1°C to 19°C. The climate is Mediterranean on the Adriatic coast with average temperatures from 6°C (January) to 24°C (July).

HISTORY AND POLITICS

Croatia was part of the Austro-Hungarian Empire from 1526 to 1918. On 29 October 1918 the Croatian parliament declared Croatia independent and soon after Croatia joined with Slovenia, Bosnia-Hercegovina, Serbia and Montenegro to form the 'Kingdom of Serbs, Croats and Slovenes' (renamed Yugoslavia in 1929). From 1941 to 1945 Yugoslavia was occupied by the Axis powers, with Italy and Hungary annexing parts of Croatia and a pro-Nazi Croat puppet state being established in the remainder of Croatia and Bosnia-Hercegovina. The armed extremists of this state (Ustaše) engaged in fierce fighting with Serbian royalists, Communist partisans and pro-Allied Croat partisans.

At the end of the war Yugoslavia was re-established as a federal republic under Communist rule but gradually disintegrated following the death of the wartime partisan leader Josep Tito (b. 1892) in 1980.

In April and May 1990 Croatia's first free, democratic elections were won by the Croatian Democratic Union (HDZ) of Dr Franjo Tudjman. War broke out in September 1991 between Croatia and Serbia after the ethnic Serb minority in Croatia rejected Croatia's independence from Yugoslavia, which had been declared on 30 May. The war in Croatia continued until January 1992 when a cease-fire was declared. The Federal Yugoslav Army (JNA) and Serb forces had secured control of virtually all ethnic Serb areas in Croatia.

Despite the cease-fire sporadic violence continued. Croatian troops recaptured the Straits of Maslenica in January 1993. In May 1995 operation Flash, a sudden military offensive, was launched by Croatian forces and resulted in the recapture of Western Slavonia. In August of the same year operation Storm regained control of the Krajina, leaving Eastern Slavonia as the only Serb-controlled area within Croatia's territory.

The Parliamentary elections of October 1995 maintained the HDZ's power. In December 1995 President Tudjman signed the Dayton Accord. President Tudjman was re-elected in 1997, but was temporarily replaced by Vlatko Pavletić on 26 November 1999 after he fell ill; he died on 10 December. In the general election held in January 2000, the opposition coalition of the Social Democratic Party of Croatia (SPH) and the Croatian Social Liberal Party (HSLS) scored a decisive victory, winning a total of 68 seats. Stjepan Mesic was elected in presidential elections held in February 2000.

Croatia submitted an application for EU membership in February 2003 which is currently under consideration.

SECESSION

Croatia's ethnic Serbs voted to establish a Republic of Serbian Krajina (RSK) in 1993.

The Croatian government seized Western Slavonia in May 1995 and the whole of Krajina in August 1995 prompting the withdrawal of 10,000 UNCRO peacekeepers and the flight of 150,000 Serbs. The last Croatian Serb-held area of Eastern Slavonia agreed in November 1995 to its eventual re-integration into Croatia, which took place on 15 January 1998.

FOREIGN RELATIONS

Croatia was sworn in as a member of the Council of Europe in November 1996. There has been a dispute with Yugoslavia spanning around ten years, over the Prevlaka peninsula, which lies within Croatian territory, yet controls access to Kotor Bay, Yugoslavia's most important deep water port. A temporary protocol was signed between the two governments in December 2002 which gave Croatia full sovereignty, although the area must remain demilitarised and have joint maritime police patrols.

POLITICAL SYSTEM

Executive power is vested in a President and Government. The President is directly elected for a five-year term. Legislative power is vested in the 153-member Chamber of Representatives, whose members are directly elected for a four-year term.

The constitution was amended in November 2000 to reduce the powers of the presidency. A further amendment was agreed in March 2001, when the Chamber of Representatives voted to abolish the Chamber of Counties, the upper house of the legislature.

HEAD OF STATE

President, Stjepan Mesic, *elected* 7 February 2000

SELECTED GOVERNMENT MEMBERS *as at July 2004*

Prime Minister, Ivo Sanader
Deputy Prime Minister, Jadranker Kosor
Deputy Prime Minister, Andrija Hebranj
Defence, Berislav Roncevic
Finance, Ivan Suker
Foreign Affairs, Miomir Zuzul
Interior, Marijan Mlinaric

EMBASSY OF THE REPUBLIC OF CROATIA

21 Conway Street, London W1T 6BN
T 020-7387 2022
Ambassador Extraordinary and Plenipotentiary, HE Josip Paro, apptd 2002

BRITISH EMBASSY

Ivana Lucica 4, Zagreb
T (+385) (1) 6009 100
E british.embassyzagreb@fco.gov.uk
Ambassador Extraordinary and Plenipotentiary, HE Nicholas Jarrold, apptd 2000

BRITISH COUNCIL DIRECTOR, Roy Cross

Illica 12, PO Box 55, 10001 Zagreb
T (+385) (1) 4899 500
E zagreb.info@britishcouncil.hr

DEFENCE

The Army has 287 main battle tanks, 28 armoured personnel carriers and 104 armoured infantry fighting vehicles. The Air Force has 24 combat aircraft and 10 armed helicopters. The Navy has one submarine and seven patrol and coastal combatants at five bases.

MILITARY EXPENDITURE – 2.4 per cent of GDP (2002)
MILITARY PERSONNEL – 18,850: Army 14,050, Navy 2,500, Air Force 2,300; Paramilitaries 10,000
CONSCRIPTION DURATION – Six months

ECONOMY AND TRADE

Industrial production was severely hampered during the conflict in 1991–5; damage to the infrastructure was estimated by the government to be US$27,000 million, with the loss of over 13,000 lives. Large areas of farmland were destroyed and the tourist industry, which provided one third of total foreign exchange earnings in 1990, was decimated. However, Croatia has seen a rise in tourism since 2000.

The manufacturing industry accounts for 33 per cent of GDP. Shipbuilding and fishing are major industries on the Adriatic coast. Inland there is a light manufacturing sector, food-processing industries, bauxite deposits, thermal mineral springs, hydroelectric potential, and agriculture (nine per cent of GDP) based on grain, horticulture, livestock and tobacco. The textile industry is one of the most important, employing more than 17 per cent of the population. The service industries account for 58 per cent of GDP. In February 2003 the IMF approved a 14-month standby credit of around US$145.5 million to support Croatia's economic and financial programme.

GNI – US$19,900 million (2001); US$4,550 per capita (2001)
ANNUAL AVERAGE GROWTH OF GDP – 2.7 per cent (1998)
INFLATION RATE – 5.4 per cent (2000)
UNEMPLOYMENT – 16.1 per cent (2000)
TOTAL EXTERNAL DEBT – US$12,120 million (2000)
FOREIGN DIRECT INVESTMENT – US$3,595 million (1997–2000)
IMPORTS – US$10,713 million (2002)
EXPORTS – US$4,899 million (2002)

BALANCE OF PAYMENTS
Trade – US$5,279 million deficit (2002)
Current Account – US$1,547 million deficit (2002)

Trade with UK	*2002*	*2003*
Imports from UK	£94,486,000	£139,903,000
Exports to UK	70,277,000	50,088,000

TRANSPORT INFRASTRUCTURE

There are 2,296 km of railways and 28,123 km of roads, 23,792 of which are surfaced. There are 59 airports, 16 of which are surfaced, and one heliport.

MEDIA

Croatia's constitution guarantees freedom of the press. Croatian Radio-Television (HRT) is the national state owned broadcaster and is the main source of news. Nove TV is the country's first national private network. There are four main news publications: *Vecernji List* (daily), *Feral Tribune* (weekly), *Vjesnik* (daily), *Nacional* (weekly).

CULTURE

Before the conflicts of recent years Croatia was one of Europe's most popular tourist destinations (ten million visitors a year visited the Adriatic shoreline prior to 1991).

Twentieth-century cultural figures include sculptor Ivan Mestrovic (1883–1962), whose work can be seen in public squares all over Croatia, and the novelist Miroslav-Krleza (1893–1981).

CUBA

República de Cuba – Republic of Cuba

AREA – 109,800 sq. km
POPULATION – 11,237,000 (2001). The language is Spanish
CAPITAL – ΨHavana (population, 2,184,990, 1996 UN estimate)
MAJOR CITIES – Camagüey; Guantánamo; Holguín; Santa Clara; ΨSantiago
CURRENCY – Cuban peso of 100 centavos
NATIONAL ANTHEM – Al Combate, Corred Bayameses (To Battle, Men Of Bayamo)
NATIONAL DAY – 1 January (Day of Liberation)
NATIONAL FLAG – Five horizontal bands, blue and white (blue at top and bottom) with red triangle, close to staff, charged with five-point star
LIFE EXPECTANCY (years) – 76 (2001)
MORTALITY RATE (per 1,000 population) – 7.38 (2003)
INFANT MORTALITY (per 1,000 births) – 7 (2001)
HIV / AIDS ADULT PREVALENCE – 0.1 per cent (2001)
DEATH PENALTY – Yes
POPULATION GROWTH RATE – 0.5 per cent (1990–2001)
POPULATION DENSITY – 102 per sq. km (2001)
URBAN POPULATION – 75 per cent (2001)

CLIMATE AND TERRAIN

Cuba, the largest island in the Caribbean, is part of an archipelago which also includes Isla de la Juventud and 1,600 other islets and cays. The island of Cuba itself has three mountainous ranges running from east to west (the Oriental, Central and Occidental ranges). Cuba has a subtropical climate with an average annual temperature of 25°C. Elevation extremes range from 2,005 m (Pico Turquino) at the highest point to 0 m (Caribbean Sea) at the lowest.

HISTORY AND POLITICS

The island was visited by Columbus in 1492. Early in the 16th century the island was conquered by the Spanish, and for almost four centuries remained under Spanish rule. Separatist agitation in the closing years of the 19th century culminated in open warfare. In 1898 the USA intervened and demanded the evacuation of Cuba by Spanish forces. The Spanish-American war led to the abandonment of the island, which came under American military rule from 1899 until 1902, when an autonomous government was inaugurated with an elected president, and bicameral legislature.

A revolution led by Dr Fidel Castro overthrew the government of Gen. Batista in 1959. In 1965 the Communist Party of Cuba (PCC) was formed to succeed the United Party of the Socialist Revolution; it is the only authorised political party. A new Socialist constitution came into force in 1976 and indirect elections to the National Assembly of People's Power were subsequently held. The first direct elections to the National Assembly were held in 1993; all candidates were officially approved by the Communist Party and ran for election unopposed. The 14 provincial assemblies were elected in the same manner. At the election of deputies to the National Assembly held in 2003, all 609 unopposed PCC candidates received the required 50 per cent of the vote, and on 6 March the National Assembly confirmed Dr Castro as President for a further five-year term.

In June 2003, the European Union imposed restrictions in its political and cultural contacts with Cuba over its poor human rights record.

HEAD OF STATE
President of Council of State and Council of Ministers, Dr Fidel Castro Ruz, since 1959, *appointed* 2 November 1976, *re-elected* 15 March 1993, 24 February 1998, 6 March 2003

COUNCIL OF STATE *as at March 2004*
President, Dr Fidel Castro Ruz
First Vice-President, Gen. Raúl Castro Ruz

SELECTED GOVERNMENT MEMBERS *as at July 2004*
President, Dr Fidel Castro Ruz
First Vice-President, Revolutionary Armed Forces, Gen. Raúl Castro Ruz
Ministers, Georgina Barreiro Fajardo *(Finance and Prices)*; Felipe Pérez Roque *(Foreign Relations)*; Gen. Abelardo Colomé Ibarra *(Interior)*

EMBASSY OF THE REPUBLIC OF CUBA
167 High Holborn, London WC1 6PA
T 020-7240 2488
Ambassador Extraordinary and Plenipotentiary, HE Dr José Fernández de Cossío, apptd 2000

BRITISH EMBASSY
Calle 34 No. 702/4, entre 7ma Avenida y 17, Miramar, Havana
T (+53) (7) 204 1771
Ambassador Extraordinary and Plenipotentiary, HE Paul Hare, LVO, apptd 2001

BRITISH COUNCIL DIRECTOR, William Edmundson
7ma Avenida, e, Calle 34 y 36, Miramar, Havana
T (+53) (7) 204 1771/2
E information@cu.britishcouncil.org

DEFENCE

The Army has about 900 main battle tanks and 700 armoured personnel carriers. The Navy has five patrol and coastal vessels at seven bases. The Air Force has 130 combat aircraft (of which only some 25 are operational) and 45 armed helicopters.

The last former Soviet combat personnel left Cuba in 1993, but 810 Russian military advisers remain to operate military intelligence facilities. In January 2002 Lourdes, Russia's last military base, closed down. The United States has 2,039 personnel at Guantánamo Bay Naval Base, which has been leased since before the 1959 revolution. Suspected al-Qa'eda prisoners taken in the 2001 war in Afghanistan were flown to Guantánamo Bay for interrogation in early 2002.

MILITARY EXPENDITURE – 3.9 per cent of GDP (2002)
MILITARY PERSONNEL – 46,000: Army 35,000, Navy 3,000, Air Force 8,000; Paramilitaries 26,500
CONSCRIPTION DURATION – Two years

ECONOMY AND TRADE

After the revolution virtually all land and industrial and commercial enterprises were nationalised. Following the curtailing of Cuba's privileged trading relationships with the Soviet bloc in 1989, the economy deteriorated sharply and it became necessary to introduce rationing of energy, food and consumer goods. GDP fell by 75 per cent between 1989 and 1994, and the government was forced to introduce reforms. Since 1993, the government has legalised the holding of US dollars by private individuals, permitted private enterprise, cut subsidies to loss-making state industries, allowed prices for some goods and services to rise, and introduced income tax. State farms have been transformed into co-operatives run by private individuals and permitted to sell 20 per cent of produce on the open market, but remain relatively unproductive. In 1995, foreign investors were permitted to buy property and own Cuban-based companies, with British and Canadian firms becoming involved in the oil and mining industries.

Sugar is still one of the mainstays of the economy but is subject to fluctuating world prices. Sugar exports generated US$441 million in 2002 and the industry employs 327,000 workers. In June 2002 the government announced that it would be closing 70 of its 156 sugar cane mills and switching 14 of the remaining mills to the production of honey and/or turning them into tourist attractions. Nickel production fell in 2002 but the world price rose to bring the economy an estimated US$512 million in revenue. Lack of external finance has been a major obstacle to economic recovery, as has the long-standing trade and economic embargo imposed by the USA, which has been criticised repeatedly by the UN and was condemned by the European Parliament in November 1998. In November 2002 the UN General Assembly voted in favour of a non-binding resolution calling for an end to the US trade embargo.

In 2003 1.9 million tourists visited Cuba.

Trade between Cuba and the former socialist economies of Europe has declined since 1989, although Russia is Cuba's second largest export partner (after the Netherlands at 18.5 per cent), taking 17.5 per cent of exports in 2002. The US trade embargo was relaxed in March 1998 to allow food and medicine into the country. Principal exports are sugar, nickel, seafood, citrus fruits, tobacco and rum.

GDP – US$23,901 million (1998); US$2,384 per capita (2000)
ANNUAL AVERAGE GROWTH OF GDP – 1.2 per cent (1999)

Trade with UK	*2002*	*2003*
Imports from UK	£11,333,000	£17,372,000
Exports to UK	8,088,000	9,074,000

TRANSPORT INFRASTRUCTURE

There are 3,442 km of railways, with an additional 7,742 km of track used exclusively by the sugar plantations. There are 60,858 km of roads, 29,820 km of which is surfaced and 638 km of which is expressway. In March 1998 the ban on direct flights between Cuba and the USA was lifted, although the only air connection with the USA is a weekly charter service between Miami and Havana.

EDUCATION

Education is free of charge and compulsory at all levels. In some rural areas children attend boarding schools where agricultural tasks are compulsory in addition to schoolwork. After basic education students can choose to go to a pre-collegiate school or a technical school. The pre-collegiate school is free to graduates.

ILLITERACY RATE – (m) 2.8 per cent; (f) 3.1 per cent (2003)

ENROLMENT (percentage of age group) – primary 100 per cent (1997); secondary 81 per cent (1997); tertiary 12 per cent (1997)

MEDIA

Private ownership of electronic media is prohibited. The official Communist Party newspaper is *Granma.* The main television stations are Cubavision, Tele-Rebelde and CHTV, a subsidiary of Tele-Rebelde. The main radio stations are Radio Rebelde and Radio Reloj. Radio-TV Marti is a US government backed station that targets Cuban listeners from its transmitting base in Florida.

CULTURE

Cubans are perhaps most famous for their music – a vibrant mix of Spanish traditional guitar melodies and African rhythms. Rumba, mambo, bolero, salsa and cha-cha-cha all evolved from *son,* a type of Cuban music that originated in the hills of Oriente at the turn of the 20th century.

Cuba has produced writers of international standing such as José Martí (1853–95), Cirilo Villverde y de la Paz (1812–94), Alejo Carpentier (1904–80), Nicolás Guillén (1902–89) and Guillermo Cabrera Infante (b. 1929).

CYPRUS

Kypriaki Dimokratía/Kıbrıs Çumhuriyeti – Republic of Cyprus

AREA – 9,200 sq. km

POPULATION – 790,000 (2001): 85 per cent Greek, 12 per cent Turkish. Greek and Turkish are the official languages

CAPITAL – Nicosia, (195,300, 2000 estimate)

MAJOR CITIES – ΨFamagusta; ΨLarnaca; ΨLimassol; Paphos

CURRENCY – Cyprus pound (C£) of 100 cents

NATIONAL ANTHEM – Ymnos Eis Tin Eleftherian (Ode To Freedom)

NATIONAL DAY – 1 October (Independence Day)

NATIONAL FLAG – White with a gold map of Cyprus above crossed olive branches

LIFE EXPECTANCY (years) – 78 (2001)

MORTALITY RATE (per 1,000 population)

INFANT MORTALITY (per 1,000 births) – 5 (2001)

HIV / AIDS ADULT PREVALENCE – 0.3 per cent (2001)

DEATH PENALTY – No (abolished 1962)

POPULATION GROWTH RATE – 1.3 per cent (1990–2001)

POPULATION DENSITY – 86 per sq. km (2001)

URBAN POPULATION – 70 per cent (2001)

ILLITERACY RATE – (m) 1.3 per cent; (f) 4.5 per cent (2000)

ENROLMENT (percentage of age group) – primary 96 per cent (1995); secondary 93 per cent (1995); tertiary 23 per cent (1996)

CLIMATE AND TERRAIN

Cyprus is the third largest island in the Mediterranean. It has two mountain ranges, the Pentadaktylos range along the north coast, and the Troodos range (which includes Mount Olympus) in the central and western areas of the island. Elevation extremes range from 1,952 m (Mount Olympus) at the highest point to 0 m (Mediterranean Sea) at the lowest. The climate is Mediterranean.

HISTORY AND POLITICS

Cyprus came under British administration from 1878, and was formally annexed to Britain in 1914 on the outbreak of war with Turkey. From 1925 to 1960 it was a Crown Colony. Following the launch in 1955 of an armed campaign by the National Organisation of Cypriot Fighters (EOKA) in support of union with Greece and against British rule, a state of emergency was declared which lasted for four years. An agreement was signed on 19 February 1959 between the United Kingdom, Greece, Turkey, and the Greek and Turkish Cypriots which stipulated that Cyprus would become an independent republic.

The island became independent on 16 August 1960. The constitution provided for a Greek Cypriot president and a Turkish Cypriot vice-president but this system proved unworkable and led to intercommunal trouble. The UN Peacekeeping Force in Cyprus (UNFICYP) was set up in 1964.

The Progressive Party of the Working People (AKEL) became the largest party in the House of Representatives following the election of 2001, winning 20 seats with the Democratic Coalition (DISI). Tassos Papadopoulos of the Democratic Party (DIKO) won the presidential election of 2003 with 15.5 per cent of the vote.

A peace plan to re-unify the island was presented to Cyprus by the UN in November 2002 stipulating a federation with two constituent parts (one Greek, one Turkish) with a loose central government and a rotating presidency. Following four years of accession talks, in December 2002 Cyprus was invited to joint the EU providing the two communities agreed to the UN plan by March 2003. The deadline passed without agreement and the EU stated that without re-unification only Greek Cyprus would be granted membership. On 30 April the Greek Cypriot Government announced confidence-building measures designed to end the isolation of Turkish Cypriots.

On 24 April 2004 a referendum was held on the UN plan for repatriation. The plan was rejected by 75.8 per cent of Greek Cypriots but accepted by a 64.9 per cent majority by Turkish Cypriots.

The Greek sector of Cyprus joined the European Union on 1 May 2004.

HEAD OF STATE

President, Tassos Papadopoulos, *elected* 16 February 2003, *sworn in* 1 March 2003

Deputy President, Khristodhoulos Pasiardhis

SELECTED GOVERNMENT MEMBERS *as at July 2004*

Defence, Kiriakos Mavronikolas

Finance, Iakovos Keravnos

Foreign Affairs, Georgios Iakovou

Interior, Andreas Christou

CYPRUS HIGH COMMISSION
93 Park Street, London W1K 7ET
T 020-7499 8272
High Commissioner, HE Myrna Kleopas, apptd 2000

BRITISH HIGH COMMISSION
Alexander Pallis Street (PO Box 21978), 1587 Nicosia
T (+357) (22) 861100
High Commissioner, HE Lyn Parker, apptd 2001

BRITISH COUNCIL DIRECTOR, Peter Skelton
3 Museum Street (PO Box 25654), 1097 Nicosia
T (+357) 22585000
E enquiries@cy.britishcouncil.org

BRITISH SOVEREIGN BASE AREAS
The UK retained full sovereignty and jurisdiction over two areas of 253 sq. km in all: Ayios Nicolaos and Dhekelia. The British Administrator of these areas is appointed by The Queen and is responsible to the Secretary of State for Defence. The combined total of army and RAF personnel stationed in the areas is 3,500.
Administrator of the British Sovereign Base Areas, Air Vice-Marshal T. W. Rimmer, OBE

DEFENCE
The National Guard has 145 main battle tanks, 43 armoured infantry fighting vehicles and 310 armoured personnel carriers. Turkey has about 36,000 troops in northern Cyprus.

In January 1998, a military airfield in Paphos was completed. It is intended to provide a base for Greek military aircraft, as Cyprus does not possess its own air force.

MILITARY EXPENDITURE – 2.4 per cent of GDP (2002)
MILITARY PERSONNEL – National Guard 10,000, Paramilitaries 750; Northern Cyprus Army 5,000, Paramilitaries 150
CONSCRIPTION DURATION – 26 months

ECONOMY AND TRADE
In Greek Cyprus, the service industries accounted for 75.5 per cent of GDP in 2000; the manufacturing industry 13.1 per cent, construction 6.9 per cent and agriculture 4.5 per cent. In Turkish Cyprus, services accounted for about 74 per cent of GDP in 1998. Main products are citrus fruits, grapes and other vine products, meat, milk, potatoes and other vegetables. Manufacturing, construction, distribution and other service industries are additional major employers. Tourism is the main growth industry with around 2.5 million visitors every year. Tourism earns more than US$2,000 million annually and represents 20 per cent of GDP. Twenty per cent of the world's ships are Cypriot registered. The accession of Greek Cyprus to the EU in 2004 is expected to have a detrimental effect upon the economic future of the Turkish community.

The UK was the main export market for Cyprus in 2003 with 28.2 per cent of all exports going to Britain. Russia was the main import partner and provided 17.9 per cent of imported commodities.

GNI – US$9,370 million (2001); US$12,320 per capita (2001)
ANNUAL AVERAGE GROWTH OF GDP – 4.0 per cent (2001)
INFLATION RATE – 4.1 per cent (2000)
UNEMPLOYMENT – 4.9 per cent (2000)
IMPORTS – US$4,084 million (2002)
EXPORTS – US$843 million (2002)

Trade with UK	*2002*	*2003*
Imports from UK	£272,094,000	£315,909,000
Exports to UK	251,678,000	255,707,000

CULTURE
European and Middle Eastern cultures have been converging in Cyprus for over 9,000 years. Cyprus is a country of ancient castles (built during the crusades), Greek temples, monasteries (still inhabited by the Greek Orthodox monks of the south) and elaborate mosaics (left by the Romans). Osman Turkay (1927–2001), a Turkish Cypriot poet, was nominated for the Nobel Prize in Literature in 1988.

TURKISH REPUBLIC OF NORTHERN CYPRUS
In 1974, mainland Greek officers under instructions from the military junta in Athens launched a coup and installed a former EOKA member, Nikos Sampson, as president. Turkey invaded northern Cyprus and occupied over a third of the island. In 1975 a 'Turkish Federated State of Cyprus' under Rauf Denktaş was declared in this area and in 1983 a 'Declaration of Statehood' was issued which purported to establish the 'Turkish Republic of Northern Cyprus'. The declaration was condemned by the UN Security Council and only Turkey has recognised the new 'state'. In 1985, Denktaş was elected president and a general election was held. Denktaş was re-elected in 1990, 1995 and on 15 April 2000. A UN plan for the re-unification of the island was formally rejected by him on 31 August 1998. On 6 December 1998, elections to the 50-seat Republican Assembly resulted in a coalition government between the National Unity Party, who gained 24 seats, and the Democrat Party, who gained 13 seats. UN-sponsored proximity talks were held on 3–14 December 1999 between representatives of the Greek and Turkish communities, but no agreement was reached. In March 2003 President Dentkaş rejected a UN re-unification plan. Recent confidence-building measures instituted by both governments have improved relations between the two communities.

DE FACTO HEAD OF STATE
President, Rauf Denktaš, *elected* 1985, *re-elected* 1990, 1995; 15 April 2000
Prime Minister, Mehmet Ali Talat

CZECH REPUBLIC

Česká Republika – Czech Republic

AREA – 77,300 sq. km. Neighbours: Poland (north-east), Germany (west and north-west), Austria (south), Slovakia (east)
POPULATION – 10,260,000 (2001), 10,302,000 (1991 census): 95 per cent Czech, 3 per cent Slovak. Czech is the official language. The majority of the population is Roman Catholic, with a small Protestant minority
CAPITAL – Prague (Praha) on the Vltava (Moldau) (population, 1,178,576, 2001)

MAJOR CITIES – Brno (Brünn) (379,185); Ostrava (319,293); Plzen (Pilsen); (166,274), 2001
CURRENCY – Koruna (Kcs) of 100 haléřů
NATIONAL ANTHEM – Kde Domov Můj (Where Is My Motherland)
NATIONAL DAY – 28 October
NATIONAL FLAG – White over red horizontally with a blue triangle extending from the hoist to the centre of the flag
LIFE EXPECTANCY (years) – 75 (2001)
MORTALITY RATE (per 1,000 population) – 10.74 (2003)
INFANT MORTALITY (per 1,000 births) – 4 (2001)
HIV / AIDS ADULT PREVALENCE – 0.1 per cent (2001)
DEATH PENALTY – No (abolished 1990)
POPULATION DENSITY – 133 per sq. km (2001)
URBAN POPULATION – 75 per cent (2001)

CLIMATE AND TERRAIN

The Czech Republic is composed of Bohemia and Moravia. Bohemia is surrounded by mountain ranges while Moravian land stretches to the Danubian basin. Roughly a third of the country is covered by forest. Elevation extremes range from 1,602 m (Snezka) at the highest point to 115 m (Elbe River) at the lowest. The climate is continental with warm, humid summers and cold, dry winters. The average temperature in Prague ranges from 2°C in January to 19°C in July.

HISTORY AND POLITICS

The area came under the rule of the Habsburg dynasty in 1526 and remained part of the Austro-Hungarian Empire until 1918. The rise of Czech nationalism in the late 19th century led to Czechoslovakia's independence on 28 October 1918 following an amalgamation of Bohemia, Moravia, Slovakia and Ruthenia and was confirmed by the Versailles Peace Conference in 1919.

Czechoslovakia was forced to cede the ethnic German Sudetenland to Nazi Germany in 1938 after the Munich Agreement. German forces invaded the Czech Republic in 1939 and incorporated it into Germany while Slovakia became a puppet state. The Czech Republic was liberated by Soviet and American forces in 1945. The pre-war democratic Czechoslovak state was re-established in 1945, having ceded Ruthenia to the Soviet Union. The Communists took power in a coup in 1948 and remained in power until 1989.

In 1968 the Communist Party under Alexander Dubček embarked on a political and economic reform programme (known as the Prague Spring). The reforms were suppressed following an invasion by Warsaw Pact troops on the night of 20 August 1968, and were abandoned when Gustáv Husák became leader of the Communist Party in 1969.

Mass protests in November 1989 led to the resignation of the Communist Party Central Committee. The Party was forced to concede its monopoly of power and on 10 December a new government was appointed in which only half the ministers were Communists. Husák resigned as president and was replaced by the dissident writer Václav Havel. Free elections were held in June 1990 in which the Communist Party was defeated.

In late 1992 the leaders of the Czech and Slovak republics agreed to dissolve the federation and form two sovereign states, this took effect on 1 January 1993.

The general election of June 2002 produced no outright winner. Vladimír Špidla, leader of the Czech Social Democratic Party (ČSSD) formed a coalition government on 15 July. The ČSSD lost its majority in the Senate following elections held in October and November 2002. President Havel left office in February 2003 but parliament failed to elect a successor and Prime Minister Vladimír Špidla became acting president. On 28 February, Václav Klaus of the Civic Democrat Party (ODS) was elected president and took office in March.

The Czech Republic became a full member of the EU on 1 May 2004.

POLITICAL SYSTEM

The constitution vests legislative power in the bicameral parliament, comprising a 200-member Chamber of Deputies elected for a four-year term and an 81-member Senate elected for a six-year term, one-third being renewed every two years. The President is elected by Parliament for a five-year term. Executive power is held by the Prime Minister and Council of Ministers. The Council of Ministers is appointed by the President on the recommendation of the Prime Minister. The Prime Minister is appointed by the President. A two-thirds majority in parliament is necessary to amend the constitution, and federal laws remain in place unless superseded by Czech ones. A Constitutional Court has been established comprising 15 judges nominated by the President for ten-year terms with Senate approval.

HEAD OF STATE
President, Václav Klaus, *elected by parliament* 28 February 2003, *sworn in* 7 March 2003

SELECTED GOVERNMENT MEMBERS *as at July 2004*
Prime Minister (acting), Interior, Stanislav Gross
Vice-Premier, Foreign Affairs and Security Policy, Cyril Svoboda
Vice-Premier, Science, Research and Human Resources, Petr Mareš
Vice-Premier, Finance, Bohuslav Sobotka
Defence, Miroslav Kostelka

EMBASSY OF THE CZECH REPUBLIC
26 Kensington Palace Gardens, London W8 4QY
T 020-7243 1115
Ambassador Extraordinary and Plenipotentiary, HE Štefan Füle, apptd 2003

BRITISH EMBASSY
Thunovská 14, CZ-118 00 Prague 1
T (+ 420) 25740 2111
E info@britain.cz
Ambassador Extraordinary and Plenipotentiary, HE Anne Pringle, apptd 2001

BRITISH COUNCIL DIRECTOR /CULTURAL COUNSELLOR, Mandy Johnson
Bredovsky dvur, Politickych veznu 13ý
110 00 Prague 1
T (+420) 221 991 162
F (+420) 224 933 847
E info.praha@britishcouncil.cz

DEFENCE

The army has 541 main battle tanks, 879 armoured infantry fighting vehicles and 355 armoured personnel carriers. The Air Force has 54 combat aircraft and 34 attack helicopters. The Czech Republic became a member of NATO on 12 March 1999.
MILITARY EXPENDITURE – 2.1 per cent of GDP (2002)

MILITARY PERSONNEL – 52,950: Army 39,850, Air Force 13,100; Paramilitaries 5,600
CONSCRIPTION DURATION – 12 months

ECONOMY AND TRADE

Under Communist rule industry and most agricultural land was state-owned. An economic reform programme began in 1990 to produce a free-market economy. This has necessitated a restrictive monetary policy to stem inflation and a restructuring of industry to be competitive, and these were major reasons for the break with Slovakia. As a result, foreign investment (about US$8,500 million in 2002) and private enterprises have grown, over 90 per cent of the economy has been privatised, and reliance on trade with the former Soviet bloc countries has ended.

A customs union between the Czech and Slovak Republics is in place but separate currencies were introduced in February 1993 following speculation. The Koruna was made fully convertible in October 1995.

Principal agricultural products are sugar beet, potatoes and cereal crops; the timber industry is also very important. Having been the major industrial area of the Austro-Hungarian Empire, the country has long been industrialised, and machinery, industrial consumer goods and raw materials are major exports. Industry accounts for 41 per cent of GDP compared to 3.8 per cent for agriculture. Services account for 55.2 per cent of GDP. The country's principal trading partner is Germany, which accounts for 40.2 per cent of exports and 39.1 per cent of imports.

GNI – US$54,300 million (2001); US$5,310 per capita (2001)
ANNUAL AVERAGE GROWTH OF GDP – 2.0 per cent (2002)
INFLATION RATE – 4.1 per cent (2001)
UNEMPLOYMENT – 9.2 per cent (2002)
TOTAL EXTERNAL DEBT – US$21,299 million (2000)
FOREIGN DIRECT INVESTMENT – US$13,516 million (1997–2000)
IMPORTS – US$42,793 million (2002)
EXPORTS – US$38,358 million (2002)

BALANCE OF PAYMENTS
Trade – US$3,078 million deficit (2002)
Current Account – US$2,624 million deficit (2001)

Trade with UK	*2002*	*2003*
Imports from UK	£1,030,500,000	£999,393,000
Exports to UK	1,273,427,000	1,434,385,000

EDUCATION

Education is free of charge and compulsory for all children from the age of six to 15. Primary education lasts for nine years, divided into two stages of five and four years respectively. Secondary education comprises three main types of school: general schools, technical schools and vocational schools. There are nine universities of which the oldest and most famous is Charles University in Prague (founded 1348).

ENROLMENT (percentage of age group) – primary 100 per cent (1997); secondary 99 per cent (1997); tertiary 24 per cent (1997)

MEDIA

The public broadcaster is Česk Televize (CT) and it runs two channels. There are several private television stations. Czech public radio, Český Rozhlas (CRo), operates three national networks and local services alongside over 70 private radio stations throughout the country.

CULTURE

Prague is famous for its Art Nouveau architecture, cobbled streets and squares and a thriving cultural life (particularly its contemporary jazz scene). Some of the most famous Czech composers are Antonin Dvorak (1841–1904), Bedrich Smetana (1824–84) and Leos Janacek (1854–1928). Important writers include Franz Kafka (1883–1924), Milan Kundera (b. 1929), Ivan Klima (b. 1931) and Václav Havel (b. 1936).

DENMARK

Kongeriget Danmark/Kingdom of Denmark

AREA – 42,400 sq. km. Neighbour: Germany (south)
POPULATION – 5,333,000 (2001). The majority of the population is Lutheran. The language is Danish
CAPITAL – ΨCopenhagen (population, 1,081,673, 2001)
MAJOR CITIES – ΨÅlborg; ΨÅrhus; ΨOdense
CURRENCY – Danish krone of 100 øre
NATIONAL ANTHEMS – Kong Kristian stod ved højen mast (King Christian Stood By The Lofty Mast); Det er et yndigt land (There Is A Lovely Land)
NATIONAL DAY – 5 June (Constitution Day)
NATIONAL FLAG – Red, with white cross
LIFE EXPECTANCY (years) – 76 (2001)
MORTALITY RATE (per 1,000 population) –10.72 (2003)
INFANT MORTALITY (per 1,000 births) – 4 (2001)
HIV / AIDS ADULT PREVALENCE – 0.2 per cent (2001)
DEATH PENALTY – No (abolished 1978)
POPULATION GROWTH RATE – 0.3 per cent (1990–2001)
POPULATION DENSITY – 126 per sq. km (2001)

CLIMATE AND TERRAIN

Denmark is a low-lying country indented by lagoons and fjords along its shoreline (which consists of the bulk of the Jutland peninsula). Denmark also comprises 406 islands, many of them in the Baltic Sea and some of the North Frisian Islands in the North Sea. There are cold winters and warm summers. Temperatures range from 0.5°C in January to 17°C in July. Elevation extremes range from 173 m (Yding Skovhoej) at the highest point to –7 m (Lammefjord) at the lowest.

HISTORY AND POLITICS

The Danes were at the forefront of Viking expansionism and briefly united England and Scandinavia under Cnut (Canute) (995–1035).

The Union of Kalmar (1397) brought Norway and Sweden (including Finland) under Danish rule. Danish power waned during the 16th century, however, enabling Sweden to re-establish its independence in 1523. In the 19th century Norway was ceded to Sweden under the Treaty of Kiel (1814) and both Schleswig and Holstein, which had been subsumed in 1460, were surrendered to Germany.

Denmark remained neutral during the First World War, and in a plebiscite held in accordance with the Versailles Treaty (1919), northern Schleswig voted to return to Danish sovereignty. In 1939 Denmark signed a non-aggression pact with Germany but was invaded in 1940 and coerced into contributing to the German war effort. Iceland declared its independence from Denmark in 1944 and the Faroe Islands were granted home rule in 1948. Greenland, which had had the status of a colony, was integrated into Denmark in 1953 and granted home rule in 1979. Social Democrat-led coalitions dominated the post-war era until 1982 when a right-wing government was elected. Denmark joined the European Community in 1973.

A referendum was held on 28 September 2000 on membership of the European single currency. Membership was rejected by 53.1 per cent of those who voted.

The most recent legislative elections were in 2001 and the Liberal Party became the largest party in Parliament. A coalition government was formed by Anders Fogh Rasmussen between the Liberal Party and the Danish People's Party (DPP).

POLITICAL SYSTEM

The legislature consists of one chamber, the *Folketing*, of 179 members, including two for the Faroes and two for Greenland, which is elected for a four-year term. The voting age is 18 with an electoral system based on proportional representation and a 2 per cent threshold for parliamentary representation.

HEAD OF STATE
HM The Queen of Denmark, Queen Margrethe II, KG, *born* 16 April 1940, *succeeded* 14 January 1972
Heir, HRH Crown Prince Frederik, *born* 26 May 1968

SELECTED GOVERNMENT MEMBERS *as at July 2004*
Prime Minister, Anders Fogh Rasmussen
Defence, Søren Gade
Finance, Thor Pedersen
Foreign Affairs, Per Stig Moeller
Interior and Health, Lars Loekke Rasmussen

ROYAL DANISH EMBASSY
55 Sloane Street, London SW1X 9SR
T 020-7333 0200
Ambassador Extraordinary and Plenipotentiary, HE Tom Risdahl Jensen, apptd 2001

BRITISH EMBASSY
36–40 Kastelsvej, DK-2100 Copenhagen Ø
T (+45) 3544 5200
E info@britishembassy.dk
Ambassador Extraordinary and Plenipotentiary, HE Sir Nicholas Browne, apptd 2003

BRITISH COUNCIL DIRECTOR, Dr Michael Sørensen-Jones, Gammel Mønt 12.3, DK-1117 Copenhagen K
T (+45) (33) 369 400
E british.council@britishcouncil.dk

DEFENCE

The Army has 238 main battle tanks, 300 armoured personnel carriers and 12 attack helicopters. The Navy has four submarines, three offshore patrol frigates and 27 patrol and coastal vessels at three bases. The Air Force has 68 combat aircraft.
MILITARY EXPENDITURE – 1.6 per cent of GDP (2002)
MILITARY PERSONNEL – 22,200: Army 14,700, Navy 4,000, Air Force 3,500
CONSCRIPTION DURATION – Four to 12 months

ECONOMY AND TRADE

The largest sectors of employment are professional services and administration (71 per cent of GDP); manufacturing (26 per cent of GDP) and agriculture (3 per cent of GDP). The chief agricultural products are fish, pigs, dairy products, poultry and eggs, seeds and cereals; in the main imported raw materials supply the manfacturing industry but there are also considerable imports of finished goods. Denmark is self-sufficient in oil and natural gas and in 2000 became a net energy exporter through exports of natural gas to Sweden.

The principal imports are industrial raw materials, consumer goods, construction inputs, machinery, raw materials, vehicles and textile products. The chief exports are manufactured articles, windmills, chemicals, fish, ships and agricultural and dairy products. Germany and Sweden are Denmark's main trading partners.
GNI – US$164,000 million (2001); US$30,600 per capita (2001)
ANNUAL AVERAGE GROWTH OF GDP – 2.9 per cent (2000)
INFLATION RATE – 2.4 per cent (2001)
UNEMPLOYMENT – 4.7 per cent (2001)
DIRECT FOREIGN INVESTMENT – US$51,839 million (1997–2000)
IMPORTS – US$47,704 million (2002)
EXPORTS – US$55,758 million (2002)

BALANCE OF PAYMENTS
Trade – US$8,360 million surplus (2002)
Current Account – US$4,918 million surplus (2002)

Trade with UK	*2002*	*2003*
Imports from UK	£2,607,000,000	£1,641,042,000
Exports to UK	2,584,000,000	2,113,971,000

TRANSPORT INFRASTRUCTURE

In 2002, the Danish mercantile fleet numbered 282 ships of more than 100 gross tonnage. There are 3,164 km of railway, of which 595 km are electrified. An additional network of 526 km is operated by private companies. A rail tunnel and bridge linking the islands of Sjælland and Fyn were opened in 1997, and a road and rail tunnel and bridge across the Øresund, linking Copenhagen with the Swedish city of Malmö, were opened on 1 July 2000. There are 71,591 km of roads, including 880 km of expressways.

EDUCATION

Education is free of charge and compulsory. Specialist schools are numerous, with commercial, technical and agricultural predominating. There are universities at Copenhagen (founded in 1479), Århus (1928), Odense (1966), Roskilde (1972) and Ålborg (1974).
ENROLMENT (percentage of age group) – primary 100 per cent (1997); secondary 100 per cent (1997); tertiary 48 per cent (1997)

MEDIA

The public broadcaster is Danmarks Radio (DR). DR operates two television networks and national and regional radio stations. Private television stations can be obtained via satellite and cable. There are some 250 local commercial and community radio stations in operation. Some 38 newspapers are published in Denmark; eight daily papers are published in Copenhagen.

CULTURE

Denmark is a small country but has made significant contributions to the world of science. Nobel laureates include atomic physicist Niels Bohr (1885–1962) and medical researcher Niels Finsen (1860–1904). Notable contributions have been made in music: Carl Nielsen (1865–1931); design: Arne Jacobsen (1902–71), Georg Jensen (1866–1935); and literature: Hans Christian Anderson (1805–75), Karen Blixen (1885–1962) and Peter Høeg (b. 1957).

THE FAROE ISLANDS

AREA – 1,399 sq. km
POPULATION – 47,000 (2001)
CAPITAL – Tórshavn (population, 16,511, 2001)

Since 1948 the Faroe or Sheep Islands (18 in total) have had a degree of home rule. The islands are governed by a *Løgting* of between 27 and 32 members (elected for a four-year term) and a *Landsstri* of three to six members which deals with special Faroes affairs, sending two representatives to the *Folketing* at Copenhagen. The Faroes are not part of the EU. In elections to the *Løgting* held on 30 April 2002, Prime Minister Anfinn Kallsberg's coalition won 16 of the 32 seats, losing his overall majority. The next elections must take place no later than April 2006.

Prime Minister, Anfinn Kallsberg

Trade with UK	*2001*	*2002*
Imports from UK	£27,935,000	£6,715,000
Exports to UK	108,873,000	100,816,000

GREENLAND

AREA – 2,175,600 sq. km of which about 16 per cent is ice-free
POPULATION – 56,000 (2002)
CAPITAL – Godthåb (Nuuk) (population, 13,889, 2002)

Greenland attained a status of internal autonomy in May 1979 and a government *(Landsstyret)* was established. It has a *Landsting* (parliament) of 31 members (elected for a four-year term) and sends two representatives to the *Folketing* at Copenhagen. In parliamentary elections held on 3 December 2002 the Forward (Siumut) party won ten seats. Hans Enoksen of the Forward party became prime minister and formed a coalition government with the Feeling of Community (Atássut) party. Greenland negotiated its withdrawal from the EU, without discontinuing relations with Denmark, and left on 1 February 1985. The USA has acquired certain rights to maintain air bases in Greenland.

Prime Minister, Hans Enoksen

Trade with UK	*2002*	*2003*
Imports from UK	£343,000	£658,000
Exports to UK	137,000	153,000

DJIBOUTI

Jumhūriyya Jībūtī/République Djibouti – Republic of Djibouti

AREA – 23,200 sq. km. Neighbours: Eritrea (north), Ethiopia (west and south), Somalia (south-east)
POPULATION – 634,000, mostly Afar or Issas. The official languages are Arabic and French; Afar and Somali are also spoken
CAPITAL – ΨDjibouti (population, 62,000, 1991)
CURRENCY – Djibouti franc of 100 centimes
NATIONAL ANTHEM – Hinjinne u sara kaca (Arise With Strength)
NATIONAL DAY – 27 June (Independence Day)
NATIONAL FLAG – Blue over green with white triangle in the hoist containing a red star
MORTALITY RATE (per 1,000 population) – 19.45 (2003)
HIV / AIDS ADULT PREVALENCE – 50 per cent (2001)
DEATH PENALTY – No (abolished 1995)
POPULATION BELOW POVERTY LINE – 50 per cent (2001)
POPULATION GROWTH RATE – 1.2 per cent
POPULATION DENSITY – 27 per sq. km (1999)
MILITARY EXPENDITURE – 3.9 per cent of GDP (2001)
MILITARY PERSONNEL – 9,850: Army 8,000, Navy 200, Air Force 250, Gendarmerie 1,400; Paramilitaries 2,500
GNI – US$553 million (2000); US$880 per capita (2000)
GDP – US$576 million (2001); US$847 per capita (2000)
ANNUAL AVERAGE GROWTH OF GDP – 2.1 per cent (1998)
TOTAL EXTERNAL DEBT – US$262 million (2000)
ILLITERACY RATE – (m) 24.4 per cent; (f) 45.6 per cent (2000)
ENROLMENT (percentage of age group) – primary 32 per cent (1996); secondary 12 per cent (1996); tertiary 0.3 per cent (1996)

CLIMATE AND TERRAIN

Djibouti is situated on the east coast of Africa, at the point where the Gulf of Arden and The Red Sea meet. Elevation extremes range from 2,028 m (Moussa Ali) at the highest point to 155 m (Lake Assal) at the lowest. The country is prone to flash floods as well as cyclones, droughts and earthquakes. The climate is semi-arid with a hot season between May and September.

HISTORY AND POLITICS

Formerly French Somaliland (from 1888), Djibouti became the French Territory of the Afars and the Issas, named after the two main ethnic groups in the country. The Republic of Djibouti became independent on 27 June 1977. Hassan Gouled Aptidon (an Issa) of the Rassemblement Populaire pour le Progres (RPP) party was the Republic's first president. He was confirmed in office in 1981 and was re-elected in 1987.

In November 1991 Afar rebel groups attacked government troops in the north of Djibouti (Afar areas). The attacks escalated and the rebels formed an alliance, the Front pour la Restauration de L'Unite et de la Democratie (FRUD), and gained control of two-thirds of the country (but not the capital or the south). In 1993 government troops regained much of the territory lost to the rebels. The civil war ended with the signing of a peace accord in 1996.

A multiparty constitution was adopted by referendum in 1992 and subsequent multiparty elections held in December 1992 were won by the RPP. President Aptidon was re-elected for a fourth six-year term in 1993. In December 1997, in the first elections since the 1996 peace accord, the RPP and FRUD formed an alliance and won all 65 seats in the National Assembly. In April 1999, President Ismael Omar Guelleh (nephew of President Aptidon) was elected, gaining approximately three-quarters of the votes cast; about 60 per cent of the electorate were estimated to have voted. In May 2001, the government signed a peace agreement with a breakaway faction of the FRUD, which had continued its armed opposition to the government after the 1996 peace accord.

In December 2000, an attempted coup by a group of police officers was quickly put down by the armed forces.

In legislative elections held in 2003, the first elections since independence where the number of parties allowed to contest an election was not limited, the Union for Presidential Majority (UMP), an alliance of four parties supporting President Guelleh, won all 65 seats in the National Assembly. Presidential elections are scheduled for April 2005.

HEAD OF STATE
President, Ismael Omar Guelleh, *elected* 9 April 1999

SELECTED GOVERNMENT MEMBERS *as at July 2004*
Prime Minister, National and Regional Development, Dilleita Mohamed Dilleita
Defence, Ougoure Kifle Ahmed
Economy, Finance and Privatisation, Yacin Elmi Bouh
Foreign Affairs and International Co-operation, Relations with Parliament, Ali Abdi Farah

EMBASSY OF THE REPUBLIC OF DJIBOUTI
26 Rue Emile Ménier, F-75116 Paris, France
T (+33) (1) 4727 4922
Ambassador Extraordinary and Plenipotentiary, HE Mohamed Gomaneh Guirreh, apptd 2002

BRITISH AMBASSADOR, HE Myles Wickstead, apptd 2000, resident at Addis Ababa, Ethiopia

ECONOMY AND TRADE

The economy depends mainly on the operation of the free port, which accounts for 80 per cent of Djibouti's GDP. Agriculture accounts for less than 4 per cent of GDP, but employs three-quarters of the workforce. Industry accounts for 15 per cent of GDP. The main imports are foodstuffs, machinery, clothing, oil and oil derivatives. The main exports are agricultural produce. Djibouti's primary trading partners are Ethiopia, Somalia, Yemen and France.

Trade with UK	*2002*	*2003*
Imports from UK	£12,995,000	£22,152,000
Exports to UK	96,000	797,000

TRANSPORT INFRASTRUCTURE

There is 100 km of railway (the Djibouti section of the Addis Ababa–Djibouti railway, controlled by both Djibouti and Ethiopia) and 2,890 km of roads, 364 km of which are surfaced. The Port of Djibouti is important both to trade and to the French and US military who are stationed there. Three of the 13 airports have surfaced runways.

MEDIA

The government owns *La Nation*, the main newspaper in Djibouti, as well as Radiodiffusion-Television de Djibouti (RTD), the company which operates national radio and television stations. There are a number of privately owned newspapers including *Al Qarn*, *La Republique*, and *Le Renouveau*. Independent newspapers are generally allowed to circulate freely, but journalists exercise self-censorship.

CULTURE

The people of Djibouti are either Issas, with roots in Somalia, or Afars, with links to Eritrea and Ethiopia. There is French-influenced cuisine as well as traditional North African fare. Djibouti has very close cultural ties with France – something the present government is keen to maintain and further promote. French colonial architecture is mixed with that of modern Arabic culture and Islam.

DOMINICA

The Commonwealth of Dominica

AREA – 750 sq. km
POPULATION – 71,000 (2001). English is the official language although Creole French is more commonly used
CAPITAL – ΨRoseau (population, 16,243, 1991)
CURRENCY – East Caribbean dollar (EC$) of 100 cents
NATIONAL ANTHEM – Isle Of Beauty
NATIONAL DAY – 3 November (Independence Day)
NATIONAL FLAG – Green ground with a cross overall of yellow, black and white stripes, and in the centre a red disc charged with a Sisserou parrot in natural colours within a ring of ten green stars
LIFE EXPECTANCY – 74 (2001)
MORTALITY RATE (per 1,000 population) – 6.99 (2003)
INFANT MORTALITY (per 1,000 births) –14 (2001)
DEATH PENALTY – Yes
POPULATION BELOW POVERTY LINE – 30 per cent (2002)
POPULATION DENSITY – 95 per sq. km (2001)
ILLITERACY RATE – (m) 6 per cent; (f) 6 per cent (2000)

CLIMATE AND TERRAIN

Dominica, in the Lesser Antilles, lies in the Windward Islands group 95 miles south of Antigua. It is about 46 km long and 25 km wide. Elevation extremes range from 1,447 m (Morne Diablotin) at the highest point to 0 m (Caribbean Sea) at the lowest. The climate is tropical with average daily temperatures ranging from 25°C to 32°C. The island is prone to hurricanes.

HISTORY AND POLITICS

Dominica was discovered by Columbus in 1493, when it was a stronghold of the Caribs, the sole inhabitants of the island until the French introduced settlements in the 18th century. It was captured by the British in 1759 but passed back and forth between France and Britain until 1805, after which British possession was not challenged. From 1871 to 1939 Dominica was part of the Leeward Islands colony, then from 1940 the island was a unit of the Windward Islands group. Internal self government from

1967 was followed on 3 November 1978 by independence as a republic.

The general election of 2000 was won by the Dominica Labour Party (DLP), which gained ten seats in the House of Assembly, with nine seats going to the United Workers' Party (UWP) and two seats to the Dominica Freedom Party (DFP).

Roosevelt Skerrit was appointed Prime Minister in January 2004 after the sudden death of Pierre Charles.

POLITICAL SYSTEM

Executive authority is vested in the President, who is elected by the House of Assembly for not more than two terms of five years. Parliament consists of the President and the House of Assembly (21 representatives elected by universal adult suffrage for a five-year term) and nine Senators, five of whom are appointed on the advice of the Prime Minister and the other four on the advice of the Leader of the Opposition.

HEAD OF STATE

President, Dr Nicholas Liverpool, *elected* 2 October 2003, *took office* 6 October 2003

SELECTED GOVERNMENT MEMBERS *as at July 2004*

Prime Minister, Finance and Planning, Caribbean Affairs, Roosevelt Skerrit

Foreign Affairs, Trade and Marketing, Osborne Riviere

HIGH COMMISSION FOR THE COMMONWEALTH OF DOMINICA

1 Collingham Gardens, London SW5 0HW

T 020-7370 5194/5

High Commissioner, vacant

BRITISH HIGH COMMISSIONER, HE C John White, resident at Bridgetown, Barbados

BRITISH CONSULATE

PO Box 2269, Roseau

T (+1) (767) 448 7655

Honorary Consul, Simon Maynard

ECONOMY AND TRADE

Agriculture is the principal occupation, with tropical and citrus fruits being the main crops. Products for export are bananas, fruit juices, lime oil, bay oil, copra and rum. Forestry, fisheries and agro-processing are being encouraged. The only commercially exploitable mineral is pumice, used chiefly for building purposes. Manufacturing consists largely of the processing of agricultural products although there have been attempts to diversify into light industry.

GNI – US$230 million (2001); US$3,200 per capita (2001)

ANNUAL AVERAGE GROWTH OF GDP – 2.6 per cent (1998)

INFLATION RATE – 0.8 per cent (2000)

TOTAL EXTERNAL DEBT – US$108 million (2000)

IMPORTS – US$115 million (2002)

EXPORTS – US$42 million (2002)

BALANCE OF PAYMENTS

Trade – US$71 million deficit (2002)

Current Account – US$49 million deficit (2002)

Trade with UK	*2002*	*2003*
Imports from UK	£9,365,000	£6,293,000
Exports to UK	16,112,000	8,850,000

MEDIA

While there is no national television service, a private cable network covers part of the island. There are no daily newspapers but there are weekly publications. Private and public radio stations are in operation throughout the country.

CULTURE

While the island has taken its political structure and love of football and cricket from the British, African, West Indian and French influences have combined to produce an unmistakable Creole culture with food, the local patois, customs and art all reflecting these multiple origins. The island's most famous writer is Jean Rhys (1894–1979), author of *Wide Sargasso Sea*.

DOMINICAN REPUBLIC

República Dominicana – Dominican Republic

AREA – 48,400 sq. km. Neighbour: Haiti (west)

POPULATION – 8,507,000 (2001). The language is Spanish

CAPITAL – ΨSanto Domingo (population, 2,134,779, 1993)

MAJOR CITIES – Duarte; La Vega; Puerto Plata; San Cristóbal; San Juan; Santiago de los Caballeros

CURRENCY – Dominican Republic peso (RD$) of 100 centavos

NATIONAL FLAG – Divided into blue and red quarters by a white cross

NATIONAL ANTHEM – Quisqueyanos Valientes, Alcemos (Brave Men Of Quisqueya, Let's Raise Our Song)

NATIONAL DAY – 27 February (Independence Day 1844)

LIFE EXPECTANCY (years) – 67 (2001)

MORTALITY RATE (per 1,000 population) – 6.88 (2003)

INFANT MORTALITY (per 1,000 births) – 41 (2001)

HIV / AIDS ADULT PREVALENCE – 2.5 per cent (2001)

DEATH PENALTY – No (abolished 1966)

POPULATION BELOW POVERTY LINE – 25 per cent (2002)

POPULATION GROWTH RATE – 1.7 per cent (1990–2001)

POPULATION DENSITY – 176 per sq. km (2001)

URBAN POPULATION – 66 per cent (2001)

MILITARY EXPENDITURE – 0.7 per cent of GDP (2002)

MILITARY PERSONNEL – 24,500: Army 15,000, Navy 4,000, Air Force 5,500; Paramilitaries 15,000

ILLITERACY RATE – (m) 16.4 per cent; (f) 16.4 per cent (2000)

ENROLMENT (percentage of age group) – primary 94 per cent (1997); secondary 54 per cent (1997); tertiary 54 per cent (1997)

CLIMATE AND TERRAIN

The Dominican Republic forms the eastern two-thirds of the island of Hispaniola (the remainder is Haiti). The Republic is crossed from the north-west to the south-east by the Cordillera Central mountain range. Many of the mountains are over 3,000 m. Elevation extremes range from 3,175 m (Pico Duarte) at the highest point to –46 m (Lake Enriquillo) at the lowest. The climate is maritime tropical with average temperatures of between 23°C and 27°C.

HISTORY AND POLITICS

Santo Domingo was discovered by Columbus in 1492, and was a Spanish colony until 1797, when it passed to France. It was restored to Spanish rule in 1809. Independence was declared in 1821, but in 1822 it was subjugated by the neighbouring Haitians who remained in control until 1844, when the Dominican Republic was proclaimed. The country was occupied by American marines from 1916 until 1924, and ruled by Gen. Rafael Trujillo from 1930 until 1961.

The general election of May 2002 resulted in the Dominican Revolutionary Party (PRD) winning 73 seats in the Chamber of Deputies and 29 seats in the Senate. The most recent presidential election was in May 2004 and was won by Leonel Fernandez of the Dominican Liberation Party with 57.1 per cent of the vote.

POLITICAL SYSTEM

Executive power is vested in the President, who is directly elected for a four-year term, renewable once only, and appoints the Cabinet. Legislative power is exercised by the Congress, which has a term of four years. The Congress comprises the Senate of 30 Senators, one for each province and one for Santo Domingo, and the 120-member Chamber of Deputies.

HEAD OF STATE

President, Leonel Fernandez, *elected* May 2004, *sworn in* August 2004

Vice-President, Secretary of State for Education, Arts and Public Worship, Milagros Ortiz Bosch

SELECTED GOVERNMENT MEMBERS *as at July 2004*

Secretary of State for Foreign Affairs, Hugo Tolentino Dipp

Secretary of State for Defence, José Miguel Soto Jiménez

Secretary of State for Finance, José Malkum

Secretary of State for the Interior and Police, Pedro Franco Badia

EMBASSY OF THE DOMINICAN REPUBLIC

139 Inverness Terrace, London, W2 6JF

T 020-7727 6285

Ambassador Extraordinary and Plenipotentiary, HE Rafael Ludovino Fernández, apptd 2000

BRITISH EMBASSY

Edificio Corominas Pepín, Ave 27 de Febrero No 233, Santo Domingo

T (+1 809) 472 7111

E brit.emb.sadom@codetel.net.do

Ambassador Extraordinary and Plenipotentiary, HE Andrew Ashcroft, apptd 2002

ECONOMY AND TRADE

Tourism is an important part of the economy, with three million foreign visitors to the Dominican Republic in 2000, generating US$2,900 million. Services account for 55 per cent of GDP. Sugar, cocoa, coffee, bananas, rice and tobacco are the main crops. Other products are maize, molasses, beans, tomatoes, cement, ferro-nickel, gold, silver and cattle. Agriculture accounts for 11 per cent of GDP. Light industry producing beer, tinned foodstuffs, glass products, textiles, soap, cigarettes, construction materials, plastic articles, paint, rum, matches and peanut oil accounts for 34 per cent of GDP.

The chief imports are fuel oils, foodstuffs, motor vehicles, pharmaceuticals and machinery components. The chief exports are minerals, sugar and sugar by-products, coffee and cocoa. The USA is the main trading partner with 85 per cent of exports going to the US market.

Remittances from Dominicans living in the United States are estimated to be US$1,500 million a year. Floods in June 2004 caused widespread damage to over 7,000 hectares of cultivated land in the Jimani region.

GNI – US$19,000 million (2001); US$2,230 per capita (2001)

ANNUAL AVERAGE GROWTH OF GDP – 6.5 per cent (2000)

INFLATION RATE – 6.5 per cent (1999)

TOTAL EXTERNAL DEBT – US$4,598 million (2000)

FOREIGN DIRECT INVESTMENT – US$3,387 (1997–2000)

IMPORTS – US$7,379 million (2000)

EXPORTS – US$834 million (2002)

BALANCE OF PAYMENTS

Trade – US$3,699 million deficit (2002)

Current Account – US$875 million deficit (2002)

Trade with UK	*2002*	*2003*
Imports from UK	£50,912,000	£40,429,000
Exports to UK	53,447,000	48,876,000

TRANSPORT INFRASTRUCTURE

There are over 12,600 km of roads, 6,224 km of which are surfaced, and a direct road from Santo Domingo to Port-au-Prince, the capital of Haiti, but that part of it in the border area has fallen into disuse. The frontier has been closed since 1967, except for a section that links the two capitals. The construction of a railway between the port of Haina and Santiago was expected to be completed by mid-2004. There are 30 airports, 13 of which have surfaced runways.

MEDIA

There are several terrestrial commercial broadcasting stations and 30 multi-channel cable TV operators. The government owned channel is Radio Television Dominicana (Canal 4). There are more than 200 commercial radio stations as well as two government stations.

CULTURE

Rafael Trujillo founded the Escueld Nacional de Bellas Artes in 1942, instituting the country's fine painting tradition. Architecture is another important element of Dominican culture, from the well preserved colonial Spanish buildings of Santo Domingo, to the brightly coloured farmhouses of the countryside.

Plena, African-derived work songs, have fused with *decima,* a ten-line, 17th-century Spanish verse form of song, to create a sophisticated Dominican tradition. The dance most associated with this fusion is the *merengue.*

EAST TIMOR

República Democrática de Timor-Leste/Republik Demokratis Timor Leste/Repúblika Demokrátika Timór-Leste – Democratic Republic of East Timor (Timor-Lorosae)

AREA – 14,874 sq. km. Neighbour: Indonesia (west). The enclave of Oekussi is separated from the rest of East Timor by the Indonesian province of West Timor

POPULATION – 952,618 (2002 estimate): 78 per cent Timorese, 20 per cent Indonesian, 2 per cent Chinese. Tetum is the national language and is spoken by about 60 per cent of the population, although Mambai, Tokodede, Kemak, Galoli, Idate, Waima'a, Naueti, Bunak, Makasae and Fatuluku are also spoken. Portuguese and Bahasa Indonesian are widely understood. The population is predominantly Roman Catholic

CAPITAL – ΨDili (population, 56,000, 2001 estimate)

MAJOR CITY – Lautem

CURRENCY – Currency is that of the USA

NATIONAL ANTHEM – Pátria, Pátria (Fatherland, Fatherland)

NATIONAL FLAG – Red with a yellow triangle based on the hoist and surmounted by a black triangle containing a white star

MORTALITY RATE (per 1,000 population) – 6.41 (2003)

DEATH PENALTY – No (abolished 1999)

POPULATION BELOW POVERTY LINE – 42 per cent (2002)

POPULATION GROWTH RATE – 2.1 per cent (2004)

POPULATION DENSITY – 59 per sq. km (1999)

CLIMATE AND TERRAIN

Timor is an island about 296 km long and 72 km wide at the eastern end of the Indonesian archipelago. The climate is tropical. The interior is covered in forests and mountains. Elevation extremes range from 2,963 m (Mt Tatamailau) at the highest point to 0 m (Timor Sea) at the lowest.

HISTORY AND POLITICS

East Timor was a Portuguese colony from 1702 until control collapsed following the 1974 coup in Portugal. Local elections were held in early 1975, in which the left-wing, pro-independence Revolutionary Front for an Independent East Timor (FRETLIN) emerged as the strongest party. Indonesia had supported the Popular Democratic Association of Timor (APODETI), which urged the integration of the territory into Indonesia. Following its failure to gain a substantial proportion of the vote, Indonesia encouraged the pro-autonomy Democratic Union of Timor (UDT) to attempt a coup in August 1975, but this was suppressed by the better equipped and disciplined FRETLIN. The Portuguese administration withdrew without formally handing over power. Indonesia began to infiltrate the border and attack villages in the frontier regions to create the illusion that the civil war was still continuing in order to justify an invasion. FRETLIN proclaimed the Democratic Republic of East Timor on 28 November 1975, which was recognised by Portugal. The following day the leaders of APODETI and UDT, who had fled to Indonesia following the failed coup, were coerced into signing a request for Indonesian assistance to restore order in East Timor. Indonesian forces began to invade East Timor on 7 December 1975 and declared East Timor Indonesia's 27th province on 17 July 1976 following their establishment of a provisional East Timorese government consisting of APODETI ministers, which signed a petition requesting integration with Indonesia. FRETLIN forces resisted strongly, but by 1979 most of East Timor was under Indonesian control. Resistance, atrocities committed by Indonesian troops and famine, left at least 200,000 East Timorese dead, mostly civilians. About 150,000 Muslims were settled in East Timor alongside the predominantly Roman Catholic population (80 per cent in 1975). The UN did not recognise the annexation.

Following the resignation of President Suharto of Indonesia, President B. J. Habibie agreed to a plebiscite which would offer East Timor autonomy within Indonesia. The plebiscite was held on 30 August 1999, and resulted in a turnout of 98.5 per cent of the electorate, with 78.5 per cent voting against autonomy for East Timor within Indonesia – thereby asserting an implied wish for full independence.

With the agreement of the Indonesian government, the UN sent in peacekeeping troops in September 1999 after civilians were forcibly evacuated from their homes and suffered extensive violence and intimidation at the hands of pro-Indonesian militias and Indonesian troops. Indonesian troops began to withdraw and in October, the Indonesian Consultative Assembly unanimously ratified the result of the referendum on the independence of East Timor. By early October, the UN-established International Force for East Timor (INTERFET) had managed to install its forces on the border with West Timor with the aim of preventing cross-border attacks by pro-Indonesia militias. INTERFET also managed to land troops in the East Timorese enclave of Oekussi. The commander of Indonesian forces in West Timor signed an agreement with INTERFET on the repatriation of refugees in November 1999.

The UN Security Council voted unanimously on 25 October 1999 to replace INTERFET with a UN force of up to 8,950 troops and 1,600 police to support the establishment of a UN Transitional Administration in East Timor (UNTAET). In November, the pro-independence activist José Xanana Gusmão visited Jakarta to establish relations with the Indonesian government. The East Timor National Council (ETNC), which was established to make policy recommendations to UNTAET, held its first meeting in December.

Two reports, published in January 2000, concluded that the Indonesian authorities had co-operated with the pro-Indonesian militias in wide-ranging human rights abuses and called for the establishment of an international war crimes tribunal. UN prosecutors began issuing indictments in December 2000.

Indonesia's President Wahid signed a memorandum of understanding with UNTAET in February, to allow the resumption of cross-border trade and transport between East Timor and Indonesia.

José Xanana Gusmão resigned as President of the ETNC on 28 March 2001 and was replaced by Manuel Carrascalão.

East Timor's first presidential elections were held on 14 April 2002 and were won by José Xanana Gusmão with 82.7 per cent of the vote.

Independence was achieved on 20 May 2002 and UNTAET was succeeded by the UN Mission of Support in East Timor (UNMISET). On 27 September 2002, East Timor became a member of the UN.

In November 2002 former pro-Jakarta militia leader Eurico Guterres received a UN indictment for crimes against humanity for his role in the 1999 massacre and a further seven senior Indonesian military officers were indicted in February 2003. Indonesia's former military chief in East Timor, Brigadier-General Noer Muis, was sentenced to five years' imprisonment in March 2003 for crimes against humanity.

Serious civil unrest including the looting and burning of shops, offices and the prime minister's home in late 2002 and early 2003, led to the UN Security Council's approval of the strengthening of the 651-member police component of UNMISET in April 2003. UNMISET's mandate has since been extended to May 2005.

POLITICAL SYSTEM

An 88-member (one from each of the 13 districts elected by a first-past-the-post system and 75 nationally elected by proportional representation) Constituent Assembly was voted in on 30 August 2001 and inaugurated in September. Members are elected for a five-year term.

HEAD OF STATE

President, José Xanana Gusmão, *elected* 14 April 2002, *took office* 20 May 2002

SELECTED GOVERNMENT MEMBERS *as at July 2004*

Prime Minister, Environment and Development, Mari bin Hamud Alkatiri
Interior, Rogerio Lobato
Minister of State for Foreign Affairs, José Ramos-Horta
National Defence, Roque Felix de Jesus Rodrigues

BRITISH EMBASSY

Pantai Kelapa (Avenida de Portugal), PO Box 194, Dili
T (+670) 331 2652
E herminia.freitas@fco.gov.uk
Ambassador Extraordinary and Plenipotentiary, HE Tina Redshaw, apptd 2004

ECONOMY AND TRADE

East Timor's economy has suffered as a result of the Indonesian withdrawal. One in three households live below the poverty line (on an average of less than US$0.55 a day).

The main commercially grown crops include timber, coffee, coconuts, cloves and cocoa. There are oil and gas reserves beneath the sea to the south of the island (Timor Sea oil) and under a deal with Australia negotiated by the UN administration, East Timor is set to receive its largest ever proportion of revenue in 2007–8 when gas will be shipped to Japan.

Trade with UK	*2002*	*2003*
Imports from UK	£1,586,000	£1,880,000
Exports to UK	532,000	563,000

TRANSPORT INFRASTRUCTURE

There are no railways, waterways, ports or harbours. There is one major road, which links the main townships along the northern coast to the east of Dili. There are 3,800 km of roads in total, 428 km of which are surfaced. There are eight airports, three of which are surfaced, and one heliport.

MEDIA

East Timor's national public radio and television services began broadcasting in May 2002 but television broadcasts do not extend far beyond Dili.

CULTURE

Dili is distinctly Portuguese in character with a garrison built in 1627 and colonial villas scattered along the beachfronts. The predominately Catholic nature of the country is evident in the number of churches in the capital and rural areas.

ECUADOR

República del Ecuador – Republic of Ecuador

AREA – 276,800 sq. km. Neighbours: Colombia (north), Peru (east and south)
POPULATION – 12,880,000 (2001), descendants of the Spanish, Amerindians, and mestizos. Spanish is the principal language but Quechua is also a recognised language and is spoken by most Indians
CAPITAL – Quito (population, 1,399,814, 2001 census)
MAJOR CITIES – Cuenca; ΨGuayaquil, the chief port
CURRENCY – Currency is that of the USA
NATIONAL ANTHEM – Salve, Oh Patria, Mil Veces, Oh Patria (Hail, Oh Fatherland, A Thousand Times, Oh Fatherland)
NATIONAL DAY – 10 August (Independence Day)
NATIONAL FLAG – Three horizontal bands, yellow, blue and red (the yellow band twice the width of the others); emblem in centre
LIFE EXPECTANCY (years) – 70 (2001)
MORTALITY RATE (per 1,000 population) – 5.29 (2003)
INFANT MORTALITY (per 1,000 births) – 24 (2001)
HIV / AIDS ADULT PREVALENCE RATE – 0.3 per cent (2001)
DEATH PENALTY – No (abolished 1906)
POPULATION BELOW POVERTY LINE – 70 per cent (2001)
POPULATION GROWTH RATE – 2.1 per cent (1990–2001)
POPULATION DENSITY – 47 per sq. km (2001)
URBAN POPULATION – 63 per cent (2001)
MILITARY EXPENDITURE – 3.0 per cent of GDP (2002)
MILITARY PERSONNEL – 59,500: Army 50,000, Navy 5,500, Air Force 4,000; Paramilitaries 270
CONSCRIPTION DURATION – 12 months (selective)

CLIMATE AND TERRAIN

Ecuador is an equatorial state in the north-west of South America. It has five different climatic zones and is one of the most bio-diverse nations on earth. It extends across the Western Andes, some of the highest peaks being Cotopaxi (5,896 m) and Cayambe (5,790 m) in the Eastern Cordillera. Ecuador is located in an earthquake zone and has two active volcanoes (Pichincha, only 12 km away from the capital, and Tungurahua). The average annual temperature in Quito is 15°C. Elevation extremes range from 6,310 m (Chimborazo) at the highest point to 0 m (Pacific Ocean) at the lowest.

HISTORY AND POLITICS

The former kingdom of Quito was conquered by the Incas of Peru in the 15th century. In 1534 Francisco Pizarro's (1475–1541) conquests led to the inclusion of the present territory of Ecuador in the Spanish viceroyalty of Quito. Independence was achieved in a revolutionary war that culminated in the battle of Mount Pichincha (1822).

After seven years of military rule, Ecuador returned to democracy in 1979. In the 1996 elections the ruling Social Christian Party (PSC) won a majority of seats but was replaced as the largest party in the National Congress by the Popular Democracy Party (DP) in the 1998 elections. Abdala Bucaram was elected President in July 1996, and appointed a coalition government. Bucaram was ousted by the legislature on the grounds of insanity and replaced firstly by Vice-President Arteaga and then by the Speaker of the National Congress, Fabián Alarcón.

A series of strikes and protests caused disruption throughout July 1999 and led to mass demonstrations calling for the removal of the President. Proposed tax increases led to another wave of protest in November, which again called for the removal of the President. On 18 January 2000, Quito and most provincial capitals were occupied by thousands of Indians. President Mahaud was deposed in a coup by a military junta on 21 January 2000, which was dissolved by the military just five hours after taking office and Vice-President Noboa was elevated to the presidency.

A tax reform bill to reduce the budget deficit, which would have increased value added tax and fuel costs, provoked widespread demonstrations and strikes by an alliance of indigenous farmers, public sector workers and students in January 2001. The government and the protestors reached a compromise agreement in February, but on 8 May the National Congress refused to pass the bill. Further protests took place in February 2002 with the indigenous people's demand that more of the country's oil revenue be invested in their communities.

In legislative elections held in October 2002 the Social Christian Party (PSC) became the largest party in the National Congress, with 24 seats. Col. Lucio Gutiérrez, the joint candidate of the Popular Socialist Party (SPS) and the New Country – Pachakutik United Movement (MUPP) was elected President in the second round of voting held in November. Col. Gutiérrez took office in January 2003 and appointed a new Cabinet. The SPS alliance with the MUPP was formally dissolved in January 2004.

FOREIGN RELATIONS

The border with Peru was demarcated by a 1942 treaty that was partly revoked by Ecuador in 1960 in relation to a disputed 80 km stretch. An inconclusive four-week border war was fought with Peru in February 1995 until a cease-fire was signed on 1 March 1995. An 86 km demilitarised zone was agreed in July 1995. An agreement was signed on 26 October 1998 by the Presidents of the two countries formally ending the territorial dispute after mediation by Argentina, Brazil, Chile and the USA.

POLITICAL SYSTEM

The 1998 constitution provides for an elected President and Vice-President who serve for a single four-year term. There is a unicameral National Congress which meets for two months a year and has 100 members, elected on a national basis for four-year terms. Voting is compulsory for all literate citizens and voluntary for all illiterate citizens over the age of 18. The republic is divided into 22 provinces.

HEAD OF STATE

President, Col. Lucio Gutiérrez, *elected* 24 November 2002, *took office* 15 January 2003

Vice-President, Alfredo Palacio

SELECTED GOVERNMENT MEMBERS *as at July 2004*

Finance and Economy, Mauricio Yepez

Foreign Relations, Patricio Zuquilanda

National Defence, Nelson Herrera

EMBASSY OF ECUADOR

Flat 3B, 3 Hans Crescent, London SW1X 0LS

T 020-7584 1367/2648/8084

Ambassador Extraordinary and Plenipotentiary, HE Eduardo Cabezas, apptd 2003

Chargé d'Affaires Ricardo Falconi-Puig

BRITISH EMBASSY

Citiplaza Building, Av. Naciones Unidas and República de El Salvador, 14th Floor, PO Box 17-17-830, Quito

T (+593) (2) 2970 800/1

E britembq@interactive.net.ec

Ambassador Extraordinary and Plenipotentiary, HE Richard Lewington, LVO, apptd 2003

ECONOMY AND TRADE

Agriculture is the most important sector of the economy. The main products for export are fish (shrimp), bananas, which provide a third of agricultural exports, cocoa and coffee. Other important crops are sugar, soya, rice, cotton, African palm, vegetables, fruit and timber. The main imports are manufactured goods and machinery.

The economy was transformed by the discovery in 1972 of major oil fields in the Oriente area, and oil is now a principal export, accounting for approximately 50 per cent of public sector revenue and export earnings.

The US dollar was adopted in 1999 in order to stabilise the economy and lower inflation.

GNI – US$14,000 million (2001); US$1,080 per capita (2001)

ANNUAL AVERAGE GROWTH OF GDP – 2.3 per cent (2000)

INFLATION RATE – 96.1 per cent (2000)

UNEMPLOYMENT – 11.5 per cent (1998)

TOTAL EXTERNAL DEBT – US$13,281 million (2000)

FOREIGN DIRECT INVESTMENT – US$2,808 million (1997–2000)

IMPORTS – US$6,431million (2002)

EXPORTS – US$5,030 million (2002)

BALANCE OF PAYMENTS

Trade – US$3,699 million deficit (2002)

Current Account – US$1,222 million deficit (2002)

Trade with UK	*2002*	*2003*
Imports from UK	£44,312,000	£31,875,000
Exports to UK	36,400,000	31,742,000

TRANSPORT INFRASTRUCTURE

There are 43,197 km of permanent roads, 8,164 of which are surfaced. There are 966 km of railways. Ten commercial airlines operate international flights and there are internal services between all major towns.

EDUCATION

Elementary education is free of charge and compulsory. There are ten universities (three at Quito, three at Guayaquil, and one each at Cuenca, Machala, Loja and Portoviejo), polytechnic schools at Quito and Guayaquil and eight technical colleges in other provincial capitals.

ILLITERACY RATE – (m) 6.9 per cent; (f) 10.5 per cent (2000)

ENROLMENT (percentage of age group) – primary 100 per cent (1997); tertiary 20.0 per cent (1990)

MEDIA

Ecuadorian newspapers include *El Mercurio, El Universo* and *Dairio Hoy.* There are four commercial television stations including Ecuavision, Teleamazon, ETV Telerama and TC Television. Radio Nacional del Ecuador is the government owned radio station.

CULTURE

Quito has been a World Heritage Site since 1978 and the old town's colonial and traditional architecture and ancient churches have been preserved. South America's most famous market, which pre-dates Inca times, can be found in the small town of Otavalo. Ecuador's most celebrated author is Jorge Icaza Coronel (1906–78).

GALÁPAGOS ISLANDS

The Galápagos (Giant Tortoise) Islands, forming the province of the Archipelago de Colón, were annexed by Ecuador in 1832. The archipelago lies in the Pacific, about 800 km from the mainland. There are 12 large and several hundred smaller islands with a total area of about 7,769 sq. km and an estimated population of 18,640. The capital is Puerto Barquerizo Moreno, on San Cristóbal Island. Although the archipelago lies on the equator, the temperature of the surrounding water is well below equatorial average owing to the Humboldt current. The province consists for the most part of National Park territory, where unique marine birds, iguanas, and the giant tortoises are conserved. There is some local subsistence farming; the main industry, apart from tourism, is tuna and lobster fishing.

EGYPT

Al-Jumhūriyya al-Miṣriyya al-'Arabiyya – Arab Republic of Egypt

AREA – 995,500 sq. km. Neighbours: Sudan (south), Libya (west), Gaza Strip and Israel (east)

POPULATION – 69,080,000 (2001). The largest, or 'Egyptian' element, is a Hamito-Semite race. A second element is the *Bedouin,* or nomadic Arabs of the Western and Eastern deserts, who are now mainly semi-sedentary tent-dwellers. The third element is the *Nubian* of the Nile Valley of mixed Arab and Negro blood. Over 90 per cent of the population are Muslims of the Sunni denomination, and most of the rest are Coptic Christians. Arabic is the official language

CAPITAL – Cairo (population, 7,200,000, 1998 estimate) stands on the Nile about 14 miles from the head of the delta

MAJOR CITIES – ΨAlexandria, founded 332 BC by Alexander the Great, was the capital for over 1,000 years; Asyut; Faiyum; Ismailia; ΨPort Said; ΨSuez

CURRENCY – Egyptian pound (£E) of 100 piastres or 1,000 millièmes

NATIONAL ANTHEM – Biladi (My Homeland)

NATIONAL DAY – 23 July (Anniversary of Revolution in 1952)

NATIONAL FLAG – Horizontal bands of red, white and black, with an eagle in the centre of the white band

LIFE EXPECTANCY (years) – 68 (2001)

MORTALITY RATE (per 1,000 population) – 5.35 (2003)

INFANT MORTALITY (per 1,000 births) – 35 (2001)

HIV / AIDS ADULT PREVALENCE – 0.1 per cent (2001)

DEATH PENALTY – Yes

POPULATION BELOW POVERTY LINE – 22.9 per cent (2002)

POPULATION GROWTH RATE – 1.9 per cent (1990–2001)

POPULATION DENSITY – 69 per sq. km (2001)

URBAN POPULATION – 43 per cent (2001)

ILLITERACY RATE – (m) 33.3 per cent; (f) 56.1 per cent (2000)

ENROLMENT (percentage of age group) – primary 100 per cent (1997); secondary 78 per cent (1997); tertiary 20 per cent (1997)

CLIMATE AND TERRAIN

The country is mainly flat but there are mountainous areas in the south-west, along the Red Sea coast and in the south of the Sinai peninsula. Elevation extremes range from 2,629 m (Mount Catherina) at the highest point to −133 m (Qattara Depression) at the lowest. Most of the land is desert and the Nile valley and delta were the only fertile areas until the opening of the Aswan Dam allowed areas of desert to be reclaimed. West of the Nile Valley is the Western Desert, containing some depressions whose springs irrigate oases. The Eastern Desert between the Nile and the mountains along the Red Sea coast is mostly plateaux dissected by wadis (dry watercourses). The average daily temperature ranges from 18°C to 30°C.

HISTORY AND POLITICS

The unification of the kingdoms of Lower and Upper Egypt under the Pharaohs *c.*3100 BC marked the establishment of the Egyptian state, with Memphis as its capital. Egypt was ruled for nearly 2,800 years by a succession of 31 Pharaonic dynasties which built the pyramids at Gizeh. A period of Hellenic rule began in 332 BC, followed by a period of rule by Rome (30 BC to AD 324) and then by the Byzantine Empire. In AD 640 Egypt was subjugated by Arab Muslim invaders. In 1517 the country was incorporated into the Ottoman Empire, under which it remained until the early 19th century. A British Protectorate over Egypt lasted from 1914 to 1922, when Sultan Ahmed Fuad was proclaimed King of Egypt. In 1953 the monarchy was deposed and Egypt became a republic.

In 1956 President Nasser seized the assets of the Suez Canal Company. Egyptian occupation of the Canal Zone was used as a pretext for military action by Britain and

France in support of their Suez Canal Company interests. A cease-fire and Anglo-French withdrawal were negotiated by the UN.

The Israeli invasion of 1956 overran the Sinai peninsula but six months later Israel withdrew. However, mounting tension culminated in a second invasion of Sinai (the Six Day War in June 1967) and occupation of the peninsula by Israel. Sinai was returned to Egypt in 1982 under the treaty of 1979 which resulted from the Camp David talks and formally terminated a 31-year-old state of war between the two countries.

President Mubarak was nominated by the legislature to run unopposed for a fourth six-year term in June 1999, and was endorsed by a national referendum held in September.

A general election was held in three rounds between October and November 2000. The ruling National Democratic Party (NDP) won 388 of the 444 elective seats, which included some 210 independent candidates who joined the party immediately after the election.

INSURGENCY

Militant Islamist fundamentalists re-emerged in 1992, carrying out attacks on tourists, Coptic Christians, government ministers, civil servants and the security forces. On 27 March 1999, the largest fundamentalist organisation, Gamaat-i-Islamiya, announced that it had given up its violent campaign to overthrow the government. In November 2002, 43 members of the fundamentalist Islamic group Islamic Jihad were arrested for allegedly planning to carry out terrorist attacks against government officials and a foreign establishment.

POLITICAL SYSTEM

The constitution of 1971 provides for an Executive President who appoints the Council of Ministers and determines government policy. The President is elected by the legislature every six years. The legislature is the People's Assembly which has 454 members, 444 of whom are elected for a five-year term, the remaining ten nominated by the President. The *Majlis al-Shura* Council or Advisory Council (264 members, 176 of whom are elected, the remainder are Presidential appointees) has an advisory role. A state of emergency, which was first introduced following the assassination of President Sadat in 1981, remains in force.

HEAD OF STATE

President, Mohammed Hosni Mubarak, *elected* 1981, *re-elected* 1987, 1993, 2 June 1999, *confirmed by national referendum* 26 September 1999

SELECTED GOVERNMENT MEMBERS *as at July 2004*

Prime Minister, Economy, Atef Mohammad Obeid
Deputy PM, Agriculture and Land Reclamation, Yousef Amin Wali
Defence and Military Production, Field Marshal Mohammad Hussein Tantawi
Finance, Mohammed Midhat Hasanayn
Foreign Affairs, Ahmed Maher
Interior, Maj.-Gen. Habib al-Adli

EMBASSY OF THE ARAB REPUBLIC OF EGYPT
26 South Street, London W1K 1DW
T 020-7499 2401/3304
Ambassador Extraordinary and Plenipotentiary, HE Adel El-Gazzar, apptd 1997

BRITISH EMBASSY
7 Ahmed Ragheb Street, Garden City, Cairo
T (+20) (2) 794 0850/2/8
E info@britishembassy.org.eg
Ambassador Extraordinary and Plenipotentiary, HE Sir Derek Plumbly, apptd 2003

BRITISH COUNCIL DIRECTOR, Dr John Grote, OBE (Cultural Counsellor), 192 El Nil Street, Agouza, Cairo
T (+20) (2) 303 1514
E british.council@britishcouncil.org.eg

DEFENCE

The Army has 3,860 main battle tanks, 670 armoured infantry fighting vehicles and 4,267 armoured personnel carriers. The Navy has one destroyer, ten frigates, four submarines, 47 patrol and coastal vessels and 24 armed helicopters at eight bases. The Air Force has 608 combat aircraft and 128 armed helicopters.

MILITARY EXPENDITURE – 3.9 per cent of GDP (2002)
MILITARY PERSONNEL – 450,000: Army 320,000, Navy 20,000, Air Force 30,000, Air Defence Command 80,000; Paramilitaries 330,000
CONSCRIPTION DURATION – 12 months to three years (selective)

ECONOMY AND TRADE

Despite increasing industrialisation, agriculture remains the most important economic activity, employing 29 per cent of the labour force and producing 17 per cent of GDP in 2002–3. Egypt is still a net importer of foodstuffs, especially grain, and a food security programme has been set up with the aim of achieving self-sufficiency. The main cash crop is cotton, of which Egypt is one of the world's main producers. Other important crops are maize, rice, sugar cane, wheat and potatoes. Other fruits and vegetables are also grown.

With its considerable reserves of petroleum and natural gas, and the hydroelectric power produced by the Aswan and High Dams, Egypt is self-sufficient in energy. In 2003 5.6 million foreign tourists visited Egypt.

The government transferred control over exchange rates to the central bank in January 2001. In January 2003 the government allowed the Egyptian pound to free-float against the US dollar in an attempt to pre-empt the detrimental effect the imminent war with Iraq would be likely to have upon the economy.

The main imports are wheat, maize, chemicals and motor vehicles and parts. The main exports are crude petroleum, cotton, cotton yarn, oranges, rice and cotton textiles.

GNI – US$99,600 million (2001); US$1,530 per capita (2001)
ANNUAL AVERAGE GROWTH OF GDP – 6.4 per cent (2000)
INFLATION RATE – 2.7 per cent (2000)
UNEMPLOYMENT – 8.1 per cent (1999)
TOTAL EXTERNAL DEBT – US$30,500 million (2002)
FOREIGN DIRECT INVESTMENT US$4,267 million (1997–2000)
IMPORTS – US$12,552 million (2002)
EXPORTS – US$4,708 million (2002)

BALANCE OF PAYMENTS
Trade – US$5,741 million deficit (2002)
Current Account – US$470 million surplus (2002)

Trade with UK	*2002*	*2003*
Imports from UK	£464,587,000	£462,052,000
Exports to UK	432,298,000	442,035,000

COMMUNICATIONS

Egypt has 5,105 km of railways and 64,000 km of roads, 49,984 km of which are surfaced. There are international airports at Cairo and Luxor. Road and rail networks link the Nile Valley and delta with the main development areas east and west of the river. Egypt has 3,500 km of waterways, of which half are canals. The Suez Canal was re-opened in 1975 and a two-stage development project begun to widen and deepen the canal to allow the passage of larger shipping and to permit two-way traffic. Port Said and Suez have been reconstructed and the port of Alexandria is being improved.

MEDIA

Egyptian media takes a central role in the Arab world and its newspapers are some of the most widely read and influential in the region. There are two state run national television channels and six regional channels. Egypt has an important satellite television industry (Egypt was the first Arab country to have its own satellite, Nilesat 101) that is watched all over the Arab-speaking world. In 2001 Dream 1, Dream 2 and Al-Mihwar TV, the country's first private television stations, came on air. The state has a monopoly on all radio broadcasting. The government has actively encouraged foreign media to base itself in Egypt by setting up a Free Media Zone in 2000 that offers economic incentives and access to its media infrastructure.

CULTURE

Egypt lies at the heart of the Arab world even though it is located on the African continent. It is most famous for the Pyramids of Giza and the art and architecture of its ancient civilisations (beginning in the fourth millennium BC and waning around 341 BC) but the modern-day Egyptian state is also of great cultural, political and economic importance to the region.

The Egyptian author Naguib Mahfouz (b. 1911) won the Nobel Prize for Literature in 1988.

EL SALVADOR

República de El Salvador – Republic of El Salvador

AREA – 20,700 sq. km. Neighbours: Guatemala (north-west), Honduras (north-east and east)
POPULATION – 6,400,000 (2001): 90 per cent mestizo, 1 per cent Amerindian, 9 per cent European. The language is Spanish
CAPITAL – San Salvador (population, 1,985,294, 2000 estimate)
MAJOR CITIES – San Miguel; Santa Ana
CURRENCY – US dollar (US$) of 100 cents
NATIONAL ANTHEM – Saludemos La Patria Orgullosos (Let Us Proudly Hail The Fatherland)
NATIONAL DAY – 15 September
NATIONAL FLAG – Three horizontal bands, sky blue, white, sky blue; coat of arms on white band
LIFE EXPECTANCY (years) – 70 (2001)
MORTALITY RATE (per 1,000 population) – 6.01 (2003)
INFANT MORTALITY (per 1,000 births) – 33 (2001)
HIV / AIDS ADULT PREVALENCE – 0.6 per cent (2001)
DEATH PENALTY – Yes*
POPULATION BELOW POVERTY LINE – 48 per cent (1999)
POPULATION GROWTH RATE – 2 per cent (1990–2001)
POPULATION DENSITY – 309 per sq. km (2001)
URBAN POPULATION – 61 per cent (2001)
MILITARY EXPENDITURE – 1.2 per cent of GDP (2002)
MILITARY PERSONNEL – 15,500: Army 13,850, Navy 700, Air Force 950; Paramilitaries 12,000
CONSCRIPTION DURATION – 12 months (selective)

CLIMATE AND TERRAIN

El Salvador extends along the Pacific coast of Central America for 307 km. The country is very mountainous (much of the interior has an average altitude of 600 m) and many of its peaks are extinct volcanoes. There are also numerous volcanic lakes. Elevation extremes range from 2,730 m (Cerro El Pital) at the highest point to 0 m (Pacific Ocean) at the lowest. Average temperatures vary with altitude but coastal areas tend to be much hotter. The average annual temperature in San Salvador is 23°C. Earthquakes are common.

HISTORY AND POLITICS

El Salvador was conquered in 1524 by Pedro de Alvarado, and formed part of the Spanish viceroyalty of Guatemala until 1821. It is divided into 14 Departments.

Decades of military rule ended in October 1979; a Legislative Assembly was elected in 1982. Subsequent presidential and parliamentary elections were boycotted by the Farabundo Martí National Liberation Front (FMLN) guerrilla movement. Conflict between the guerrillas and the government continued throughout the 1980s in a bitter civil war until negotiations culminated in a peace plan signed in January 1992. In December 1992 the FMLN disarmed and became a political party.

In legislative elections held in March 2003 the FMLN remained the largest party in the Legislative Assembly winning 31 of the 84 seats; the National Republican Alliance (ARENA) won 27 seats and the National Conciliation Party (PCN) won 16 seats. In March 2004 Elias Antonio Saca of the ARENA party won the presidential elections with 57 per cent of the vote.

POLITICAL SYSTEM

The 84 members of the Legislative Assembly serve for a three-year term. The President is elected by universal suffrage and serves a five-year term.

HEAD OF STATE

President, Elias Antonio Saca, *elected* 21 March 2004, *took office* 1 June 2004
Vice-President, Ana Vilma Albanez de Escobar

SELECTED GOVERNMENT MEMBERS *as at July 2004*

Defence, Gen. Otto Romero
Economy, Yolanda Mayora de Garida
Foreign Affairs, Francisco Lainez
Justice, Public Security and Interior, Rene Figueroa

EMBASSY OF EL SALVADOR
Mayfair House, 39 Great Portland Street, London W1W 7JZ
T 020-7436 8282
E elsalvadorembassy@rree.gob.sv
Ambassador Extraordinary and Plenipotentiary, HE Eduardo Ernesto Vilanova, apptd 2002

BRITISH AMBASSADOR, HE Richard Lavers, apptd 2003, resident at Guatemala City

ECONOMY AND TRADE

The principal agricultural products are coffee, cotton, sugar cane, maize, shrimps and balsam. In the lower altitudes towards the east, sisal is produced and used in the manufacture of coffee and cereal bags.

The US dollar was adopted on 1 January 2001; the colón remained in use for a transitional period, but has been gradually phased out.

Chief exports are coffee, cotton, sugar, shrimps, sisal, balsam, meat, cotton, hides and skins. The chief imports are chemicals, petroleum, manufactured goods, industrial and electronic machinery, pharmaceutical goods, vehicles and consumer goods. The USA is El Salvador's main trading partner.

GNI – US$13,000 million (2001); US$2,040 per capita (2001)
ANNUAL AVERAGE GROWTH OF GDP – 2.0 per cent (2000)
INFLATION RATE – 2.3 per cent (2000)
UNEMPLOYMENT – 7.0 per cent (1999)
TOTAL EXTERNAL DEBT – US$5,600 million (2001)
FOREIGN DIRECT INVESTMENT – US$439 million (1997–2000)
IMPORTS – US$3,907 million (2002)
EXPORTS – US$1,234 million (2002)

BALANCE OF PAYMENTS
Trade – US$1,913 million deficit (2002)
Current Account – US$177 million deficit (2001)

Trade with UK	*2002*	*2003*
Imports from UK	£13,045,000	£17,395,000
Exports to UK	7,500,000	49,411,000

TRANSPORT INFRASTRUCTURE

The principal ports are Cutuco, La Unión and Acajutla but ports in Honduras and Guatemala are also used. There are 10,029 km of roads of which 1,986 km are surfaced; there are 283 km of railways. The Pan-American Highway from the Guatemalan frontier passes through San Salvador and Santa Ana, and continues to the Honduran frontier. Comalapa international airport has daily flights to other Central American capitals, Mexico and the USA.

EDUCATION

Primary education is run by the state and is free of charge and compulsory. Children are supposed to attend five years of primary school, but a large number do not. It is estimated that up to 40 per cent of primary-age children enrol but do not finish primary education. There are 2,400 primary schools and 240 secondary schools. There are 23 vocational and technical schools and three universities.

ILLITERACY RATE – (m) 18.3 per cent; (f) 23.8 per cent (2000)
ENROLMENT (percentage of age group) – primary 97 per cent (1997); secondary 37 per cent (1997); tertiary 18 per cent (1997)

MEDIA

There are three major commercial television channels operating in El Salvador: Teledos, Canal Seis and TV Doce. There are hundreds of private radio stations (70 operate in San Salvador alone).

EQUATORIAL GUINEA

República de Guinea Ecuatorial – Republic of Equatorial Guinea

AREA – 28,051 sq. km. Neighbours: Cameroon (north), Gabon (east and south)
POPULATION – 486,060 (2001 estimate). The official languages are Spanish and French; Bubi, Fang, Ibo and pidgin English are also spoken
CAPITAL – ΨMalabo on Bioko Island (population, 30,418, 1983 estimate)
MAJOR TOWN – ΨBata is the principal town and port of Rio Muni
CURRENCY – Franc CFA of 100 centimes
NATIONAL ANTHEM – Caminemos Pisando La Senda De Nuestra Inmensa Felicidad (Let's Walk Down The Path Of Our Immense Happiness)
NATIONAL DAY – 12 October
NATIONAL FLAG – Three horizontal bands, green over white over red; blue triangle next staff; coat of arms in centre of white band
MORTALITY RATE (per 1,000 population) – 12.54 (2002)
HIV / AIDS ADULT PREVALENCE – 3.4 per cent
DEATH PENALTY – Yes
POPULATION GROWTH RATE – 2.5 per cent
POPULATION DENSITY – 16 per sq. km (1999)
MILITARY EXPENDITURE – 0.2 per cent of GDP (2002)
MILITARY PERSONNEL – 1,320: Army 1,100, Navy 120, Air Force 100
ILLITERACY RATE – (m) 7.5 per cent; (f) 25.6 per cent (2000)

CLIMATE AND TERRAIN

There are two provinces: Bioko Island (40 km off the coast of Cameroon) and the mainland, where 80 per cent of the population live. Equatorial Guinea is covered in dense vegetation and is mountainous inland. The climate is tropical with a rainy season from July to January on Bioko and from April to May and October to December on the mainland. Elevation extremes range from 3,008 m (Pico Basile) at the highest point to 0 m (Atlantic Ocean) at the lowest.

HISTORY AND POLITICS

Formerly colonies of Spain, the territories now forming Equatorial Guinea were constituted as two provinces of Metropolitan Spain in 1959 and became autonomous in 1963 and fully independent in 1968. Francisco Macias Nguema won the first multi-party elections. In 1970 President Nguema merged all the political parties into one, the Partido Unico Nacional de los Trabajadores (PUNT). In 1972 he declared himself President for Life.

In August 1979 President Nguema was deposed, tried and executed by a revolutionary military council headed by Col. Obiang Nguema (the former president's nephew). Constitutional amendments in 1982 provided for legislative elections, which were held in 1983 and 1988, but all candidates were chosen by the new president.

A multiparty political system under a new constitution was approved by a referendum in 1991 and ten opposition parties have been legalised, operating alongside the ruling Equatorial Guinea Democratic Party (PDGE). A National Pact was agreed and signed in March 1993 but legislative elections in November, which were won by the PDGE, were boycotted by most of the electorate and opposition parties. In the February 1996 election, the president claimed to have won more than 99 per cent of the vote. Most opposition parties boycotted the ballot. In June 1997 the Progress Party (PPGE), the largest opposition party, was banned by the government, and in February 1998 opposition party coalitions were deemed illegal. The PDGE won 75 of the 80 seats in the National Assembly elections of 1999 amid allegations of electoral malpractice.

Prime Minister Angel Serafín Seriche Dougan resigned in February 2001 due to his growing unpopularity. He was replaced by Cándido Muatetema Rivas. Incumbent President Teodoro Obiang Nguema Mbasogo won the presidential elections of 15 December 2002. Opposition candidates withdrew after voting commenced due to alleged irregularities. In March 2004 another alleged coup was suppressed and 15 people arrested in Malabo and 70 in Harare, Zimbabwe. Municipal and legislative elections were held in April 2004. The PDGE took 98 out of 100 seats in parliament and 237 out of 244 councillor seats.

HEAD OF STATE
President of the Supreme Military Council and Minister of Defence, Brig.-Gen. Teodoro Obiang Nguema Mbasogo, *took office* August 1979, *re-elected* June 1989, 25 February 1996, 15 December 2002

SELECTED GOVERNMENT MEMBERS *as at July 2004*
Prime Minister, Miguel Abia Biteo Borico
Deputy PM, Marcelino Oyono Ntutumu
Deputy PM, Ricardo Mangue Oboma Nfube
Economy and Trade, Jaime Ela Ndong
Foreign Affairs, International Co-operation and Francophone Affairs, Pastor Micha Ondo Bile
Interior and Local Corporations, Clemente Engonga Nguema Onguene

EMBASSY OF THE REPUBLIC OF EQUATORIAL GUINEA
29 Boulevard de Courcelles, 75008 Paris, France
T (+33) 15688 5454
Ambassador Extraordinary and Plenipotentiary, Eduardo Ndong Elo Nzang, apptd 2004

BRITISH AMBASSADOR, HE Richard Wildash, LVO, apptd 2002, resident at Yaoundé, Cameroon

ECONOMY AND TRADE

During the 1980s the chief products were cocoa, coffee and wood. Production has declined and except for cocoa there is now little commercial agriculture. The discovery of large oil and gas deposits off Bioko in the 1990s has led to an economic boom. A growth rate of 65 per cent was achieved in 2001, making Equatorial Guinea the fastest growing economy in Africa. Over 90 per cent of exports come from the oil industry. However, the economy is still heavily dependent on outside aid, principally from Spain and the IMF. Oil reserves are expected to run out in the next ten years. Equatorial Guinea entered the 'franc zone' in 1985.

GNI – US$327 million (2001); US$700 per capita (2001)
ANNUAL AVERAGE GROWTH OF GDP – 1.3 per cent (2001)
TOTAL EXTERNAL DEBT – US$248 million (2000)
IMPORTS – US$451 million (2000)
EXPORTS – US$1,097 million (2000)

BALANCE OF PAYMENTS
Trade – US$117 million deficit (1996)
Current Account – US$344 million deficit (1996)

Trade with UK	*2002*	*2003*
Imports from UK	£36,502,000	£108,842,000
Exports to UK	6,737,000	7,973,000

MEDIA

Television and radio broadcasts are state controlled and the government owns Equatorial Guinea's only television station, Television Nacional, and radio station, Radio Nacional de Guinea Ecuatorial. There is a second radio station, Radio Asonga, which is owned by the President's son. The main newspaper, *Ebano*, is state owned. A few privately owned publications appear sporadically.

CULTURE

Equatorial Guinea has retained its strong traditional religions, dance forms and music. The Fang people are dominant on the mainland and their spiritual leaders remain central to the community.

ERITREA

Hagere Eretra / al-Dawla al-Iritra – State of Eritrea

AREA – 117,600 sq. km. Neighbours: Sudan (north and north-west), Ethiopia (south and south-west), Djibouti (south-east)
POPULATION – 4,298,269 (2001 estimate), roughly half Coptic Christian (mainly highlanders) and half Muslim (mainly lowlanders). Arabic, Tigrinya and English are the main working languages. Italian is also widely spoken. There are nine indigenous language groups: Afar; Bilen; Hadareb; Kunama; Nara; Rashida; Saho; Tigre; Tigrinya
CAPITAL – Asmara (population, 450,000, 2001 estimate)
MAJOR TOWNS – ΨAssab; ΨMassawa
CURRENCY – Nakfa
NATIONAL DAY – 24 May (Independence Day)
NATIONAL FLAG – Divided into three triangles; the one based on the hoist is red and bears a gold olive wreath; the upper triangle is green and the lower one light blue
MORTALITY RATE (per 1,000 population) – 13.23 (2003)
HIV / AIDS ADULT PREVALENCE – 2.8 per cent (2001)
DEATH PENALTY – Yes
POPULATION BELOW POVERTY LINE – 53 per cent (1994)
POPULATION GROWTH RATE – 2.5 per cent (2001)

POPULATION DENSITY – 32 per sq. km (1999)
ILLITERACY RATE – (m) 32.7 per cent; (f) 55.5 per cent (2000)
ENROLMENT (percentage of age group) – primary 53 per cent (1997); secondary 20 per cent (1997); tertiary 1 per cent (1997)

CLIMATE AND TERRAIN

The climate changes with the country's varying altitudes (from 16°C in the mountains of the central highlands to 30°C on the coastal desert plain). Elevation extremes range from 3,018 m (Soira) at the highest point to –75 m (Denakil Depression) at the lowest.

HISTORY AND POLITICS

Eritrea was colonised by Italy in the late 19th century and was the base for the 1936 Italian invasion of Abyssinia (now Ethiopia). After the Italian defeat in East Africa in 1941 by British and Commonwealth forces, Eritrea became a British protectorate. This lasted until 15 September 1952 when Eritrea was federated with Ethiopia. The Ethiopian Emperor Haile Selassie incorporated Eritrea as a province of Ethiopia in 1962. An armed campaign for independence began in 1961, first against Emperor Haile Selassie's forces and from 1974 against the communist Mengistu regime.

In 1991 the Mengistu government was overthrown by the Eritrean People's Liberation Front (EPLF) and the People's Front for Democracy and Justice (PFDJ). The new PFDJ-led government in Ethiopia agreed to an Eritrean referendum on independence which was held in April 1993 and recorded a 99.89 per cent vote in favour. Independence was declared on 24 May 1993.

In February 2002, the European Parliament adopted a resolution that expressed concern at increasing authoritarian tendencies in the country. Legislative elections scheduled for December 2001 did not take place, and no new date has been announced.

FOREIGN RELATIONS

Eritrea had claimed the Hanish and Mohabaka Islands in the Red Sea, which it seized from Yemen in December 1995; however, in October 1998, the International Court of Justice ruled that the Hanish Islands belonged to Yemen and Eritrea formally handed them back on 1 November 1998. The land border with Djibouti is also disputed.

In May 1998 sporadic fighting with Ethiopia flared up, with both countries accusing the other of sending troops across the border. Proposals for a resolution of the conflict drawn up by the Organisation for African Unity (OAU) which called on Eritrea to hand back the disputed town of Badme pending adjudication, were rejected. Full scale fighting broke out in February 1999 and Ethiopia had captured the town by 28 February. Eritrea accepted the OAU's proposals in March, but fighting continued. A further proposal to end the fighting was brokered by the OAU in July 1999, which envisaged a return to the original borders and was provisionally accepted by both sides, but Ethiopia later rejected some of the provisions. Fighting resumed in February 2000 and in May, Ethiopia launched a full-scale invasion, which ended in early June after Ethiopian forces had captured much of Eritrea's western lowlands. An interim peace plan was signed by both countries on 18 June.

UN observers began to deploy on 15 September 2000. Direct talks between Eritrea and Ethiopia opened in October and in December a comprehensive peace agreement was signed in Algeria; UN peacekeeping troops moved into the buffer zone in April 2001 and on 21 May Eritrea and Ethiopia agreed to set up regional military commissions to solve local security issues. In April 2002 the independent Eritrea-Ethiopia Boundary Commission (EEBC), set up to establish a legal international border, defined the border between the two countries but its ruling failed to indicate clearly whether the town of Badme was Eritrean or Ethiopian. On 28 March 2003 the EEBC announced that Badme was on the Eritrean side of the border. On 4 April the Ethiopian government declared its opposition to the boundary ruling and relations between the two countries remain strained. The UN continues to patrol the boundary area.

POLITICAL SYSTEM

Under the 1997 constitution, the head of state is the President, elected for a five-year term by the National Assembly, of which he is chair. The 150-member unicameral legislature (the *Hagerawi Baito*) is directly elected for four years. The President is head of Government and presides over a State Council.

HEAD OF STATE
President, Chairman of the National Assembly, Isaias Afewerki, *elected by the National Assembly* 22 May 1993

SELECTED GOVERNMENT MEMBERS *as at July 2004*
Defence, Gen. Sebhat Ephrem
Finance and Development, Berhane Abrehe
Foreign Affairs, Ali Said Abdellah

EMBASSY OF THE STATE OF ERITREA
96 White Lion Street, London N1 9PF
T 020-7713 0096.
Ambassador Extraordinary and Plenipotentiary, HE Negassi Sengal Ghebrezghi, apptd 2003

BRITISH EMBASSY
66–68 Mariam Ghimbi Street, PO Box 5584, Asmara
T (+291) (1) 120145
E asmara.enquiries@fco.gov.uk
Ambassador Extraordinary and Plenipotentiary, HE Michael Murray, apptd 2002

BRITISH COUNCIL DIRECTOR, Dr Negusse Araya
Street 175–11, No 23, PO Box 997, Asmara
T (+291) (1) 123415/120529
E information@britishcouncil.org.er

DEFENCE

The Army has 150 main battle tanks and 40 armoured infantry fighting vehicles and armoured personnel carriers. The Navy has eight patrol and coastal combatants. The Air Force has 17 combat aircraft.
MILITARY EXPENDITURE – 16.0 per cent of GDP (2002)
MILITARY PERSONNEL – 202,200: Army 200,000, Navy 1,400, Air Force 800
CONSCRIPTION DURATION – 16 months

ECONOMY AND TRADE

The government hopes to base the rebuilding of the economy on the return of well-educated exiles, international aid and investment, the development of tourism along the coast, and the diversification of the economy away from subsistence agriculture which involves around 80 per cent of the population.

Mineral reserves include zinc, potash, gold, platinum, and oil, but they are not fully exploited. Industries include cement, construction, salt, paper, leather goods, textiles, clothing and chemicals. Exports are skins, meat, live animals and gum arabic. The major imports are food, machinery, transportation equipment and manufactured goods.

Eritrea's largest source of foreign exchange is remittances from overseas Eritreans, estimated to be around US$250 million annually.

GNI – US$699 million (2000); US$170 per capita (2001)
ANNUAL AVERAGE GROWTH OF GDP – 9.7 per cent (2001)
TOTAL EXTERNAL DEBT – US$311 million (2000)

Trade with UK	*2002*	*2003*
Imports from UK	£3,599,000	£7,521,000
Exports to UK	101,000	165,000

TRANSPORT INFRASTRUCTURE

Since 1991 the government has attempted to rebuild a transport infrastructure that was devastated by the war of independence. The rebuilding programme has focused on the ports of Massawa and Assab, the roads from the ports to Ethiopia, and the railway from Massawa to Sudan via Asmara. There are 306 km of railways and 4,010 km of roads of which 874 km are surfaced.

MEDIA

All privately owned news media organisations were closed down by the government in 2001. Eri TV is the state run television station. There are no private networks or radio stations.

ESTONIA

Eesti Vabariik – Republic of Estonia

AREA – 42,300 sq. km. Neighbours: Russia (east), Latvia (south)
POPULATION – 1,377,000 (2001): 65.3 per cent Estonian, 28.1 per cent Russian, 1.5 per cent Ukrainian, 0.9 per cent Belarusian, 0.9 per cent Finnish. The majority religion is Lutheran, with Russian Orthodox and Baptist minorities. Estonian is the first language of 64.2 per cent and Russian of 28.7 per cent
CAPITAL – Tallinn (population, 404,000, 2000 census)
MAJOR TOWNS AND CITIES – Kohtla-Järve (65,566); Narva (73,295); Pärnu (46,700); Tartu (100,100)
CURRENCY – Kroon of 100 sents
NATIONAL ANTHEM – Mu Isamaa, Ja Rõõm (My Native Land, My Joy, Delight)
NATIONAL DAY – 24 February (Independence Day)
NATIONAL FLAG – Three horizontal stripes of blue, black, white
LIFE EXPECTANCY (years) – 71 (2001)
MORTALITY RATE (per 1,000 population) – 13.42 (2003)
INFANT MORTALITY (per 1,000 births) – 11 (2001)
HIV / AIDS ADULT PREVALENCE – 1 per cent (2001)
DEATH PENALTY – No (abolished 1998)
POPULATION GROWTH RATE – 1.2 per cent (1990–2001)
POPULATION DENSITY – 33 per sq. km (2001)
URBAN POPULATION – 69 per cent (2001)
MILITARY EXPENDITURE – 1.6 per cent of GDP (2002)
MILITARY PERSONNEL – 5,510: Army 2,550, Navy 440, Air Force 220; Paramilitaries 2,600
CONSCRIPTION DURATION – Eight to 11 months

CLIMATE AND TERRAIN

Estonia is a mostly flat country. Elevation extremes range from 318 m (a hill, Suur Munamagi) at the highest point to 0 m (Baltic Sea) at the lowest. The climate is mild with average temperatures ranging from −6°C in January to 17°C in July.

HISTORY AND POLITICS

Estonia, a former province of the Russian Empire, declared its independence on 24 February 1918. A war of independence was fought against the German army until November 1918, and then against Soviet forces until the peace treaty of Tartu was signed in 1920. By this treaty the Soviet Union recognised Estonia's independence.

The Soviet Union annexed Estonia in 1940 under the terms of the Molotov-Ribbentrop pact with Germany (1939). Estonia was occupied when Germany invaded the Soviet Union during the Second World War. In 1944 the Soviet Union recaptured the country from Germany and confirmed its annexation.

The Estonian Supreme Soviet in November 1989 declared the republic to be sovereign and its 1940 annexation by the Soviet Union to be illegal. In February 1990 the leading role of the Communist Party was abolished, and following multiparty elections in March 1990 a period of transition to independence was inaugurated. Independence was declared on 20 August 1991.

Presidential elections held in August and September 2001 were won by Arnold Rüütel. In legislative elections held in March 2003 the left-wing Centrist Party (KP) and the right-wing Union for the Republic-Res Publica (RP) each won 28 seats in the parliament. Juhan Parts of the RP was then invited to form a government and a centre-right coalition cabinet comprising the RP, the Reform Party (RE) and the Estonian People's Union (RL), he took office on 10 April.

Estonia joined NATO in April 2004 and the EU in May 2004.

POLITICAL SYSTEM

Legislative power is exercised by the unicameral *Riigikogu* of 101 members elected by proportional representation every four years. The President is elected for a five-year term by the *Riigikogu* by a two-thirds majority or, if no candidate receives this majority after three rounds of voting, by an electoral assembly composed of *Riigikogu* members and local government officials. Executive authority is vested in a Prime Minister who is nominated by the President and who forms a Government. Members of the Government need not be members of the *Riigikogu*.

HEAD OF STATE

President, Arnold Rüütel, *elected by electoral assembly* 21 September 2001, *sworn in* 8 October 2001

SELECTED GOVERNMENT MEMBERS *as at July 2004*
Prime Minister, Juhan Parts
Defence, Margus Hanson
Finance, Taavi Veskimagi
Foreign Affairs, Kristiina Ojuland
Interior, Margus Leivo

EMBASSY OF THE REPUBLIC OF ESTONIA
16 Hyde Park Gate, London SW7 5DG
T 020-7589 3428
E embassy.london@estonia.gov.uk
Ambassador Extraordinary and Plenipotentiary, HE Kaja Tael, apptd 2001

BRITISH EMBASSY
Wismari 6, Tallinn 10136
T (+372) 667 4700
E information@britishembassy.ee
Ambassador Extraordinary and Plenipotentiary, HE Nigel Haywood, apptd 2003

BRITISH COUNCIL DIRECTOR, Kyllike Tohver
Vana Posti 7, Tallinn 10146
T (+372) 625 7788
E british.council@britishcouncil.ee

ECONOMY AND TRADE

Since 1992 the government has introduced free-market reforms, privatisation and restructuring. Estonia is still dependent on Russian natural gas supplies.

Eleven per cent of the workforce is engaged in agriculture, which accounts for six per cent of GDP, the main products being rye, oats, barley, flax, potatoes, meat, milk, butter and eggs. Industry accounts for 20 per cent of employment and 28.6 per cent of GDP, concentrating on textiles, clothing and footwear, forestry, wood and paper products, and food and fish processing. Some heavy industry exists, mostly in the manufacture of chemicals and power equipment.

Estonia's main trading partners are Finland, Sweden, Germany, Japan and Latvia. The main imports are machinery and equipment, chemicals, clothing and footwear, foodstuffs and vehicles. Exports consist mainly of machinery and equipment, timber and wood products, textiles and clothing, foodstuffs, metals and furniture.

GNI – US$5,300 million (2001); US$3,870 per capita (2001)
ANNUAL AVERAGE GROWTH OF GDP – 6.4 per cent (2000)
INFLATION RATE – 4.0 per cent (2000)
UNEMPLOYMENT – 13.7 per cent (2000)
TOTAL EXTERNAL DEBT – US$3,300 million (2001)
FOREIGN DIRECT INVESTMENT – US$1,539 million (1997–2001)
IMPORTS – US$4,810 million (2002)
EXPORTS – US$3,444 million (2002)

BALANCE OF PAYMENTS
Trade – US$787 million deficit (2001)
Current Account – US$339 million deficit (2001)

Trade with UK	*2002*	*2003*
Imports from UK	£98,922,000	£92,067,000
Exports to UK	334,768,000	268,149,000

EDUCATION

Estonia has a three-tier education system, consisting of primary level (four years), secondary level (six years) and university level (four to six years). Primary and secondary level education is compulsory from the age of seven to 17. There are ten universities: six public and four private. The country's most famous university is Tartu, founded in 1632.

ENROLMENT (percentage of age group) – primary 94 per cent (1997); secondary 100 per cent (1997); tertiary 42 per cent (1997)

MEDIA

Freedom of the press is guaranteed in the constitution, and the state monopoly on television and radio ended soon after independence. All newspapers have been privatised and broadcasting channels are in the process of being privatised (only one state owned channel remains). Russian-language news and programmes are provided on Estonian Television.

CULTURE

The old town area of Tallinn is home to the country's parliament and national cathedral and is a UNESCO world heritage site.

Estonia's cultural heritage is rich in traditional folk songs and poetry both of which have influenced much contemporary writing, art and music. Estonia is particularly distinguished in the field of classical music and has produced many world-famous conductors, such as Neeme Järvi (b. 1937) and Tõnu Kaljuste (b. 1953), and composers Arvo Pärt (b. 1935), Veljo Tormis (b. 1930) and Erkki-Sven Tüür (b. 1959).

ETHIOPIA

Ya'Ityopya Federalawi Dimokrasyawi Repeblik – Federal Democratic Republic of Ethiopia

AREA – 1,127,130 sq. km. Neighbours: Sudan (west), Kenya (south), Djibouti and Somalia (east), Eritrea (north)
POPULATION – 64,459,000 (2001). About one-third are of Semitic origin (Amharas and Tigreans) and the remainder mainly Oromos (40 per cent), Somalis (6 per cent) and Afar (4 per cent). Amharas, Tigreans and many Oromos are Ethiopian Orthodox Christians. The Afar people in the north and the Somalis in the south-east, as well as some Oromos, are Muslim. Amharic is the most widely used of the 70 indigenous languages
CAPITAL – Addis Ababa (population, 2,495,000, 2000 estimate)
MAJOR CITY – Dire Dawa
CURRENCY – Ethiopian birr (EB) of 100 cents
NATIONAL ANTHEM – Yezeginet Kibir
NATIONAL DAY – 28 May
NATIONAL FLAG – Three horizontal bands: green, yellow, red; in the centre a blue disc, containing a yellow pentagram
LIFE EXPECTANCY (years) – 44 (2001)
MORTALITY RATE (per 1,000 population) – 20.17 (2003)

INFANT MORTALITY (per 1,000 births) – 116 (2001)
HIV / AIDS ADULT PREVALENCE – 6.4 per cent (2001)
DEATH PENALTY – Yes
POPULATION BELOW POVERTY LINE – 45 per cent (2002)
POPULATION GROWTH RATE – 2.8 per cent (1990–2001)
POPULATION DENSITY – 57 per sq. km (2001)
URBAN POPULATION – 16 per cent (2001)

CLIMATE AND TERRAIN

Ethiopia is a landlocked country dominated by a central plateau that has an average height of 2,400 m. This plateau is divided by the Great Rift Valley. Elevation extremes range from 4,620 m (Ras Dejen) at the highest point to −125 m (Denakil Depression) at the lowest. There is a tropical monsoon climate that varies according to altitude. The wet season is April to September.

HISTORY AND POLITICS

The Hamitic culture was heavily influenced by Semitic immigration from Arabia at about the time of Christ and Christianity was introduced in the fourth century. The empire attained its zenith in the sixth century under the Axum rulers but was checked by Islamic expansion from the east. Modern Ethiopia dates from 1855 when Theodros established supremacy over the various tribes. The last emperor was Haile Selassie who reigned from 1930 until 1974, when he was deposed by the armed forces. After ten years of military rule, a Workers' Party based on the Soviet model was formed with Lt.-Col. Mengistu Haile Mariam as general secretary. The People's Democratic Republic of Ethiopia was established under a new constitution in 1987 with Lt.-Col. Mengistu as president. Armed insurgencies by the Eritrean People's Liberation Front (EPLF) and the Ethiopian People's Revolutionary Democratic Front (EPRDF), originating in Tigre, brought down Mengistu's government in May 1991.

A transitional administration comprising the EPRDF and other opposition groups formed a Council of Representatives which governed until 1995 under President Meles Zenawi. In 1994, the Council agreed on a draft federal constitution, which was adopted by an elected constituent assembly on 8 December 1994. Multiparty elections in May and June 1995 were won by the EPRDF. The Federal Democratic Republic of Ethiopia was proclaimed on 22 August 1995.

In the general election held in 2000, the EPRDF won 472 seats. The presidential elections of 2001 were won by Lt. Girma Wolde Giorgis.

FOREIGN RELATIONS

Eritrea, which since 1962 had been a province of Ethiopia, seceded and became independent on 24 May 1993. Relations between the two countries had been good until fighting broke out in June 1998 with each side accusing the other of sending troops across the border. Ethiopia launched an attack on Eritrea in May 2000, capturing much of the west of the country. An interim peace plan was signed in June, and a comprehensive peace agreement was signed in December. A new common border was proposed to both countries in April 2002; however both sides lay claim to the town of Badme although an independent boundary commission in April 2003 ruled that it lay in Eritrea. On 4 April 2003 the Ethiopian government declared its opposition to the boundary ruling and relations between the two countries remain strained. The UN continues to patrol the boundary area.

POLITICAL SYSTEM

The constitution provides for a federal government responsible for foreign affairs, defence and economic policy. The President is elected by both houses of the legislature for a six-year term. The House of People's Representatives *(Yehizb Tewokayoch Mekir Bet)* has 548 directly elected members who serve a five-year term. The House of Federation *(Yefederesbn Mekir Bet)* has 108 members, indirectly elected for a five-year term by regional administrations, who have considerable autonomy and the right to secede. The next legislative elections should be held before May 2005.

HEAD OF STATE
President, Lt Girma Wolde Giorgis, *elected by parliament* 8 October 2001

SELECTED GOVERNMENT MEMBERS *as at July 2004*
Prime Minister, C.-in-C. of the National Armed Forces, Meles Zenawi
Deputy Prime Minister, Rural Development, Addisu Legesse
Finance and Economic Development, Sofian Ahmed
Foreign Affairs, Seyoum Mesfin
National Defence, Abbadula Gemeda

EMBASSY OF THE FEDERAL DEMOCRATIC REPUBLIC OF ETHIOPIA
17 Princes Gate, London SW7 1PZ
T 020-7589 7212
E info@ethioembassy.org.uk
Ambassador Extraordinary and Plenipotentiary, HE Fisseha Adugna, apptd 2002

BRITISH EMBASSY
Fikre Mariam Abatechan Street (PO Box 858), Addis Ababa
T (+251) (1) 612354
E britishembassy.addisababa@fco.gov.uk
Ambassador Extraordinary and Plenipotentiary, HE Robert Dewar, apptd 2004

BRITISH COUNCIL DIRECTOR, Michael Moore MBE,
PO Box 1043, Artistic Building, Adwa Avenue, Addis Ababa
T (+251) (1) 550 022
E bc.addisababa@et.britishcouncil.org

DEFENCE

The Army has 270 main battle tanks and 400 armoured infantry fighting vehicles and armoured personnel carriers. The Air Force has 50 combat aircraft and 25 armed helicopters.
MILITARY EXPENDITURE – 8.0 per cent of GDP (2002)
MILITARY PERSONNEL – 162,500: Army 160,000, Air Force 2,500

ECONOMY AND TRADE

The post-Mengistu government implemented a programme of free-market economic reform that reduced government spending and inflation.

Agriculture, hunting, forestry and fishing accounts for approximately 50 per cent of GDP and around 85 per cent of the people are dependent upon the land for a living. The major food crops are teff, maize, barley, sorghum, wheat, pulses and oil seeds. Recurring droughts led to famine conditions in 1984–5, 1992, 1997, 2000 and 2002. The economy deteriorated sharply in 1999 and 2000 as a result of drought, a worsening balance of trade, and war with Eritrea. Ethiopia's largely unexploited, natural resources include gold, platinum, copper and potash. Traces of oil and natural gas have been found.

The chief imports by value are machinery and transport equipment, manufactured goods and chemicals; the principal exports by value are coffee (which normally provides about 60 per cent of Ethiopia's foreign exchange earnings), oil seeds, hides and skins, and pulses. The country's main markets for exports are the UK, Djibouti, Germany, Italy, Japan, Saudi Arabia and the USA.

GNI – US$6,700 million (2001); US$710 per capita (2001)
ANNUAL AVERAGE GROWTH OF GDP – 0.5 per cent (1998)
INFLATION RATE – 5.9 per cent (1999)
TOTAL EXTERNAL DEBT – US$5,481 million (2000)
FOREIGN DIRECT INVESTMENT – $149 million (1997–2000)
IMPORTS – US$1,317 million (1999)
EXPORTS – US$561 million (1999)

BALANCE OF PAYMENTS
Trade – US$645 million deficit (2000)
Current Account – US$16 million surplus (2000)

Trade with UK	*2002*	*2003*
Imports from UK	£40,794,000	£44,743,000
Exports to UK	70,405,000	15,375,000

TRANSPORT INFRASTRUCTURE

A network of roads in rural areas links the major cities with each other, with the Sudanese and Kenyan borders and through Eritrea to the Red Sea coast. There are 31,571 km of roads, 3,789 km of which are surfaced.

There is a railway link from Addis Ababa to Djibouti (the Ethiopian section is 681 km in length). Ethiopian Airlines maintains regular services throughout Africa and to Europe.

EDUCATION

Elementary and secondary education are provided by government schools in the main centres of population; there are also mission schools. The National University (founded 1961) co-ordinates the institutions of higher education. There are also universities at Alemaya (agricultural), Debub, Mekele, Bashir Dar and Jimma.
ILLITERACY RATE – (m) 56.4 per cent; (f) 66.8 per cent (2000)
ENROLMENT (percentage of age group) – primary 43 per cent (1997); tertiary 1 per cent (1997)

MEDIA

There are over 50 privately owned newspapers in addition to the state owned daily *Addis Zemen*. There is only one television station, the state owned Ethiopian Television (ETV). Radio Ethiopia is state owned but several private stations were given licences at the end of 2004.

CULTURE

Ethiopia is Africa's oldest independent country (for over 2,000 years) and (apart from five years of occupation by Italy) was never colonised. Addis Ababa is home to the United Nations Economic Commission for Africa and the National Museum which holds the remains of 'Lucy', an *Australopithecus afarensis* skeleton found in Ethiopia in 1974. The city's market is the largest in Africa.

FIJI

Matanitu ko Viti – Republic of the Fiji Islands

AREA – 18,274 sq. km
POPULATION – 844,330 (2001 estimate), 44 per cent Indians, 51 per cent Fijians, and 5 per cent other races. Since the 1987 coup many ethnic Indians have left and by 1994 Melanesian Fijians formed the largest population group. The main languages are Fijian and Hindi
CAPITAL – ΨSuva (population, 77,366, 1996), on Viti Levu Island
CURRENCY – Fiji dollar (F$) of 100 cents
NATIONAL ANTHEM – God Bless Fiji
NATIONAL DAY – 10 October (Fiji Day)
NATIONAL FLAG – Light blue ground with Union flag in top left quarter and the shield of Fiji in the fly
MORTALITY RATE (per 1,000 population) – 5.7 (2003)
HIV / AIDS ADULT PREVALENCE – 0.1 per cent (2001)
DEATH PENALTY – Yes*
POPULATION BELOW POVERTY LINE – 25.5 per cent (1991)
POPULATION GROWTH RATE – 0.3 per cent
POPULATION DENSITY – 44 per sq. km (1999)
MILITARY EXPENDITURE – 1.6 per cent of GDP (2002)
MILITARY PERSONNEL – 3,500: Army 3,200, Navy 300
ILLITERACY RATE – (m) 5.1 per cent; (f) 9.2 per cent (2000)

CLIMATE AND TERRAIN

Fiji is composed of roughly 332 islands (about 100 permanently inhabited) and over 500 islets in the South Pacific, about 1,760 km north of New Zealand. The group extends 480 km from east to west and 480 km north to south. The International Date Line has been diverted to the east of the island group. The largest islands are Viti Levu and Vanua Levu. Elevation extremes range from 1,324 m (Tomaniivi) at the highest point to 0 m (Pacific Ocean) at the lowest. Fiji has a tropical oceanic climate with high humidity and an average annual temperature of 27°C.

HISTORY AND POLITICS

Fiji was a British colony from 1874 until 10 October 1970 when it became an independent state and a member of the Commonwealth. In 1987, following a general election won by an Indian-dominated coalition, Lt.-Col.

Sitveni Rabuka led two military coups and declared Fiji a republic. Rabuka was appointed prime minister in 1992 after the introduction of a new constitution in 1990. The new constitution guaranteed indigenous Fijians the most senior positions in government, however, the constitution was revised in 1997 (implemented 1998) to include greater racial integration and equality in government.

In the general election of May 1999, the Fijian Political Party was swept from power by a coalition of parties led by the Fiji Labour Party (FLP). Its leader, Mahendra Chaudhry, became Fiji's first ethnic Indian prime minister.

In May 2000 a group of indigenous Fijian rebels stormed parliament and took the prime minister and most of the cabinet hostage. The army revoked the constitutional revisions of 1997 and declared martial law on 29 May following the resignation of President Ratu Sir Kamisese Mara. An interim administration was set up in June following unsuccessful negotiations between the military government and the rebels. The military named an all-indigenous government to replace the multiracial coalition of the deposed premier. The interim government was to rule for two years and prepare for fresh elections. Following the release of the last hostages in July, the Great Council of Chiefs announced the appointment of Ratu Josefa Iloilo as president.

The Fijian High Court ruled on 15 November 2000 that the 1997 constitution remained in force. Following an appeal by the interim government, the Court of Appeal ruled on 1 March 2001 that the 1997 constitution was still in force, that the parliament had been suspended rather than dissolved, and that the interim government was not legitimate, but accepted that the then Vice-President Iloilo had the right to exercise presidential powers after the resignation of President Ratu Sir Kamisese Mara. On 7 March the interim government led by Laisenia Qarase offered its collective resignation and Mahendra Chaudhry was reappointed as prime minister. On 8th March the Great Council of Chiefs rejected the judgement of the Court of Appeal and reaffirmed its support for the interim government and again nominated Iloilo as president. Mahendra Chaudhry was dismissed by President Iloilo on 14 March. Qarase was reappointed as interim prime minister the following day.

Fiji's membership of the Commonwealth was suspended following the coup but the suspension was revoked in December 2001.

Following legislative elections held in August and September 2001, the United Fiji Party (SDL) became the largest party in the house of representatives with 31 seats. The FLP won 27 seats.

HEAD OF STATE

President, Ratu Josefa Iloilo, *appointed* 13 July 2000, *reappointed* 13 March 2001, *sworn in* 15 March 2001

Vice-President, Ratu Jope Naucabalavu Seniloii

SELECTED GOVERNMENT MEMBERS *as at July 2004*

Prime Minister, Minister for Fijian Affairs, Culture and Heritage, National Reconciliation and Unity, Laisenia Qarase

Finance and National Planning, Communications, Ratu Jone Kubuabola

Foreign Affairs and *External Trade*, Kaliopate Tavola

Home Affairs and Immigration, Joketani Cokanasiga

HIGH COMMISSION OF THE REPUBLIC OF FIJI

34 Hyde Park Gate, London SW7 5DN

T 020-7584 3661

E fijirepuk@compuserve.com

High Commissioner, Emitai Lausiki Boladuadua, apptd 2002

BRITISH HIGH COMMISSION

Victoria House, 47 Gladstone Road, PO Box 1355, Suva

T (+679) 322 9100

E consularsuva@fco.gov.uk

High Commissioner, HE Charles Mochan, apptd 2002

ECONOMY AND TRADE

Agriculture accounts for 18 per cent of GDP and employed approximately 70 per cent of the workforce in 2001. The principal cash crop is sugar cane, which is the main export, followed by coconuts, ginger, fish, lumber, molasses and copra. A variety of other fruit, vegetables and root crops are also grown, and self-sufficiency in rice is a major aim. Forestry, fishing and beef production are being encouraged in order to diversify the economy. The processing of agricultural, marine and timber products are the main manufacturing industries, along with gold mining and textiles.

The chief imports are foodstuffs, machinery, mineral fuels, chemicals, beverages, tobacco and manufactured articles. Tourism is a major source of foreign exchange with over 300,000 annually visitors.

A cyclone hit Fiji's northern island of Vanua Levu in January 2003. The total estimated cost of the damage was F$60 million.

GNI – US$1,480 million (2000); US$2,150 per capita (2001)

ANNUAL AVERAGE GROWTH OF GDP – 1.8 per cent (1997)

INFLATION RATE – 1.1 per cent (2000)

UNEMPLOYMENT – 5.4 per cent (1995)

TOTAL EXTERNAL DEBT – US$136 million (2000)

IMPORTS – US$721 million (1998)

EXPORTS – US$510 million (1998)

BALANCE OF PAYMENTS

Trade – US$116 million deficit (1999)

Current Account – US$13 million surplus (1999)

Trade with UK	*2002*	*2003*
Imports from UK	£3,110,000	£5,016,000
Exports to UK	48,008,000	64,581,000

TRANSPORT INFRASTRUCTURE

Fiji is one of the main aerial crossroads in the Pacific, providing services to New Zealand, Australia, Tonga, Samoa, Vanuatu, the Solomon Islands, Kiribati, Tuvalu, New Caledonia and American Samoa. Fiji has three ports of entry, at Suva, Lautoka and Levuka. There are 3,440 km of roads, 1,692 km of which are surfaced. There are 597 km of railways.

MEDIA

Fiji's privately owned press is published in English, Fijian and Hindi. Government owned newspapers are also multi-lingual. Radio (both public and private) is the most important source of news, particularly on the more remote islands. There are two main television networks: Fiji 1, a national channel operated by Fiji Television Ltd, and Sky Fiji, a subscription channel, also operated by Fiji Television.

CULTURE
Native Fijian and ethnic Indian communities are protective of their own cultural identities and customs. Traditional Fijian dance, architectural styles, cloth-making, wood-carving, pottery and music are of significant cultural value and influence much of contemporary life.

FINLAND

Suomen Tasavalta/Republiken Finland – Republic of Finland

AREA – 304,600 sq. km. Neighbours: Norway (north-west and north), Russia (east), Sweden (west)
POPULATION – 5,178,000 (2001). Finnish and Swedish are both official languages, 93 per cent speaking Finnish as their first language and 5.6 per cent Swedish. Sami is spoken by 1,700 of the 6,500-strong Sami population who live in the far north. The population is predominantly Lutheran
CAPITAL – ΨHelsinki (Helsingfors) (population, 1,163,000, 2000 estimate)
MAJOR CITIES – Espoo (Esbo); ΨOulu (Uleåborg); Tampere (Tammerfors); ΨTurku (bo); Vantaa (Vanda)
CURRENCY – Euro (€) of 100 cents
NATIONAL ANTHEM – Maamme/Vårt Land (Our Land)
NATIONAL DAY – 6 December (Independence Day)
NATIONAL FLAG – White with blue cross
LIFE EXPECTANCY (years) – 78 (2001)
MORTALITY RATE (per 1,000 population) – 10 (2002)
INFANT MORTALITY (per 1,000 births) – 4 (2001)
HIV / AIDS ADULT PREVALENCE – 0.1 per cent (2002)
DEATH PENALTY – No (abolished 1972)
POPULATION GROWTH RATE – 0.3 per cent (1990–2001)
POPULATION DENSITY – 17 per sq. km (2001)
URBAN POPULATION – 59 per cent (2001)

CLIMATE AND TERRAIN
Finland is a low, glaciated plateau and in the south-east there are over 60,000 lakes. A third of the country is north of the Arctic Circle and over 65 per cent is covered by forest. In the south-west the Archipelago of Saaristomeri comprises more than 17,000 islands. Elevation extremes range from 1,328 m (Haltaitunturi) at the highest point to 0 m (Baltic Sea) at the lowest. Temperatures in the Arctic Circle range from –20°C in January to 10°C in July. Temperatures in Helsinki range from –6°C in January to 17°C in July.

HISTORY AND POLITICS
Finland was part of the Swedish Empire from the Middle Ages until it was ceded to Russia in 1809 and became an autonomous grand duchy of the Russian Empire. Finland became independent after the Russian revolution of 1917, but was forced to cede around one-tenth of its land to the Soviet Union and to resettle 10 per cent of its population under the Treaty of Paris (1947). A Soviet-Finnish Co-operation Treaty forced Finland to demilitarise its Soviet border, to enter into a barter trade agreement and to adopt a stance of neutrality. These terms lasted until the demise of the Soviet Union in 1991.

Finland joined the European Union on 1 January 1995 following a referendum in October 1994.

Presidential elections held in 2000 were won by Tarja Halonen of the Finnish Social Democratic Party (SDP). Legislative elections held in March 2003 were narrowly won by the Centre Party (KESK) with 55 seats in parliament. A centre-left coalition comprising KESK, the SDP and the Swedish People's Party (SFP) took office on 17 April. In June Parliament elected Matti Vanhanen of KESK as prime minister.

POLITICAL SYSTEM
Under the constitution there is a unicameral legislature, the *Eduskunta*, composed of 200 members elected by universal suffrage for a four-year term. The highest executive power is held by the President who is directly elected for a period of six years. The first direct elections for the presidency were held in 1994.

HEAD OF STATE
President, Tarja Kaarina Halonen, *elected* 6 February 2000, *inaugurated* 1 March 2000

SELECTED GOVERNMENT MEMBERS *as at July 2004*
Prime Minister, Matti Vanhanen
Defence, Seppo Kääriäinen
Finance, Antti Kalliomäki
Foreign Affairs, Erkki Tuomioja
Interior, Kari Rajamäki

EMBASSY OF FINLAND
38 Chesham Place, London SW1X 8HW
T 020-7838 6200
Ambassador Extraordinary and Plenipotentiary, HE Pertti Salolainen, apptd 1996

BRITISH EMBASSY
Itäinen Puistotie 17, FIN-00140 Helsinki
T (+358) (9) 2286 5100
E info@britishembassy.fi
Ambassador Extraordinary and Plenipotentiary, HE Matthew Kirk, apptd 2002

BRITISH COUNCIL DIRECTOR, Tuija Talvitie
Hakaniemenkatu 2, FIN-00530 Helsinki
T (+358) (9) 7743 330
E office@britishcouncil.fi

DEFENCE
The Army has 235 main battle tanks, 278 armoured infantry fighting vehicles and 1,101 armoured personnel carriers. The Navy has nine patrol and coastal vessels. The Air Force has 63 combat aircraft.
MILITARY EXPENDITURE – 1.4 per cent of GDP (2002)
MILITARY PERSONNEL – 27,000: Army 19,200, Navy 5,000, Air Force 2,800; Paramilitaries 3,100
CONSCRIPTION DURATION – Six to 12 months

ECONOMY AND TRADE
Important industries are the manufacture of mobile phones, rubber, plastics, chemicals, timber and pharmaceuticals, glass, ceramics, furniture, footwear, foodstuffs and shipbuilding. The principal imports are raw materials, machinery and manufactured goods. The main exports are electronic and electrical goods, paper and wood pulp, machinery, and metal products. Trade with EU countries accounts for more than half of Finland's total trade.

The euro replaced the Finnish markka in January 2002, Finland being the only Nordic country to adopt the euro.

At the start of 2004 the World Economic Forum rated Finland at the top of its league for business competitiveness.

GNI – US$123,400 million (2001); US$23,780 per capita (2001)
ANNUAL AVERAGE GROWTH OF GDP – 5.9 per cent (2000)
INFLATION RATE – 3.4 per cent (2000)
UNEMPLOYMENT – 9.7 per cent (2000)
DIRECT FOREIGN INVESTMENT – US$28,036 million (1997–2000)
IMPORTS – US$32,108 million (2001)
EXPORTS – US$42,794 million (2001)

BALANCE OF PAYMENTS
Trade – US$13,146 million surplus (2002)
Current Account – US$9,890 million surplus (2002)

Trade with UK	*2002*	*2003*
Imports from UK	£2,668,000,000	£1,291,666,000
Exports to UK	1,377,000,000	1,950,476,000

TRANSPORT INFRASTRUCTURE

There are 5,850 km of railroad, railway connections with Russia, and passenger boat connections with Sweden, Germany and Estonia. There are also passenger and cargo services between Finland and Britain. There are 77,943 km of roads, 50,305 km of which are surfaced.

EDUCATION

Primary education (co-educational comprehensive school) is free of charge and compulsory for children from seven to 16 years. There are 4,300 schools ranging in size from ten pupils to 900. There are 20 institutes of higher education; ten universities, three technical colleges, three schools of economics and business administration and four art colleges.

ENROLMENT (percentage of age group) – primary 99 per cent (1997); secondary 100 per cent (1997); tertiary 74 per cent (1997)

MEDIA

Newspapers are privately owned and offer a wide spectrum of political views. Broadcasting in Finland is both commercial and state owned (the state broadcaster is Yleisradio Oy (YLE)).

CULTURE

Newspapers, books, plays and films appear in both Finnish and Swedish. Finland's most famous composer is Jean Sibelius (1865–1957) and musicians include Esa-Pekka Salonen (b. 1958). Its most famous author is Tove Jansson (1914–2001), author of the Moomintroll books for children which were originally published in the 1940s and have been translated into over 30 languages.

FRANCE

La République Française – The French Republic

AREA – 550,100 sq. km. Neighbours: Belgium and Luxembourg (north-east), Germany, Switzerland and Italy (east), Monaco (south), Spain and Andorra (south-west)
POPULATION – 59,453,000 (2001); 57,218,000 (Metropolitan France), and 58,745,000 including overseas departments (1992 official estimate): 72 per cent Catholic, 8 per cent Muslim, 2 per cent Jewish. The language is French; there are several regional languages including Basque, Breton, Catalan, Corsican, Dutch, German and Occitan
CAPITAL – Paris (population, 9,644,507, 1999 census)
MAJOR CITIES – ΨBordeaux; Grenoble; Lille; Lyon; ΨMarseille; Nantes; Nice; Strasbourg; Toulon; Toulouse. The chief towns of Corsica are ΨAjaccio and ΨBastia
CURRENCY – Euro (€) of 100 cents
NATIONAL ANTHEM – La Marseillaise
NATIONAL DAY – 14 July (Bastille Day 1789)
NATIONAL FLAG – The tricolour, three vertical bands, blue, white, red (blue next to flagstaff)
LIFE EXPECTANCY (years) – 79 (2001)
MORTALITY RATE (per 1,000 population) – 9.05 (2003)
INFANT MORTALITY (per 1,000 births) – 4 (2001)
DEATH PENALTY – No (abolished 1981)
POPULATION GROWTH RATE – 0.4 per cent (1990–2001)
POPULATION DENSITY – 108 per sq. km (2001)

CLIMATE AND TERRAIN

The French Alps lie in the east of the country and the Pyrenees lie in the south. The north and west of the country comprises either flat plains or hilly terrain. Elevation extremes range from 4,807 m (Mont Blanc) at the highest point to −2 m (Rhone River delta) at the lowest. The south of France has a Mediterranean climate with warm winters (average temperature 3°C) and hot, arid summers (average temperature 18°C). The east of France has a continental climate.

HISTORY AND POLITICS

Gaul, the area that is now France, was conquered by Julius Caesar in the first century BC and remained a part of the Roman Empire until the Frankish invasions of the fifth and sixth centuries. The Treaty of Verdun (AD 843) divided the Frankish Empire into three parts, of which the western part, *Francia Occidentalis*, became the basis for modern France.

As a result of the French Revolution (1789), a republic was declared in 1792 and the king, Louis XVI, was executed. The republic was overthrown by Napoléon Bonaparte, who established the first French Empire, which ended in 1815. The ensuing Congress of Vienna restored the monarchy, but in 1848 the Second Republic was declared, which lasted only until 1852, when the Second Empire was proclaimed under Napoléon III. He was forced to abdicate after the defeat of France in the Franco-Prussian war (1870–71) and the Third Republic was established.

In 1940, Germany invaded France, occupying most of the country and establishing a pro-German government in the south. France was liberated in 1944, a provisional government was established under Gen. Charles de Gaulle, and the Fourth Republic was declared in 1946. In 1958, the threat of a military coup following a rebellion in Algeria, resulted in the assembly inviting Gen. de Gaulle to return as premier; a new constitution which strengthened the powers of the president was adopted, the Fifth Republic was proclaimed, and Gen. De Gaulle

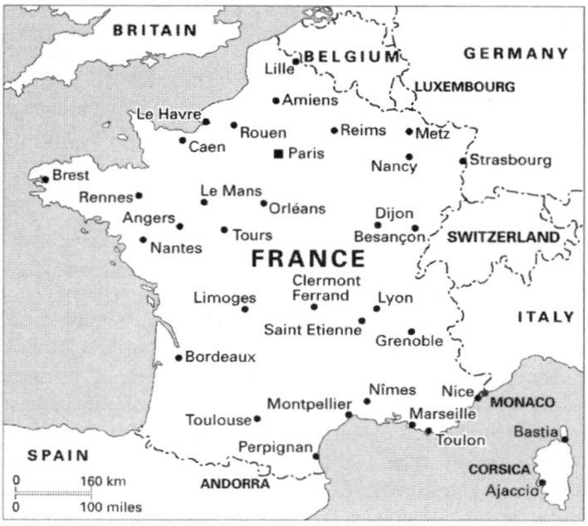

was elected president. France granted its colonies independence between 1954 and 1962.

President Jacques Chirac, the candidate of the Rally for the Republic (RPR), was elected in May 1995.

In the first round of the presidential elections in April 2002, Jacques Chirac won the most votes and National Front leader Jean-Marie Le Pen gained just under 200,000 more votes than Prime Minister Lionel Jospin of the Socialist Party. Jacques Chirac won the second round run-off with Le Pen in May with 82.2 per cent of the vote.

In the elections to the national assembly held in June 2002 the Union for a Presidential Majority (UMP), an election coalition of the RPR and Liberal Democracy (DL), won an overall majority and a coalition comprising UMP and the Union for French Democracy (UDF) took office in June. In September 2002 the RPR, DL and parts of the UDF merged to form the Union for a Popular Movement (UMP).

A governmental plan for a major decentralisation of power from Paris was launched in October 2002. In March 2003 parliament approved constitutional amendments paving the way for the devolution to regions and departments of powers over economic development, transport, tourism, culture and further education.

INSURGENCIES

A desire for greater autonomy and recognition of Corsica's distinctive culture and language led to a campaign of separatist bombings and shootings that began in the mid-1970s. In November 1999, Prime Minister Jospin invited all political groups on the island to engage in dialogue with the French government on the constitutional future of the island. Following discussions, Jospin presented proposals to combine the island's two departments, and give the regional parliament powers over cultural, educational, structural and planning affairs and limited legislative autonomy by 2004 in return for a permanent end to terrorism. The proposals, which were accepted by the Corsican regional parliament in July 2000 and narrowly passed by the national assembly in December 2001, suffered a setback in January 2002 when the Constitutional Council rejected the legislation as unconstitutional, but allowed provisions permitting the Corsican language to become part of the primary school curriculum. A referendum held in July 2003 narrowly voted against the establishment of a new unified assembly for Corsica with limited powers to raise and spend taxes.

POLITICAL SYSTEM

The head of state is a directly elected President, whose term of office is five years. The legislature consists of the National Assembly and the Senate. The National Assembly has 577 deputies (555 for metropolitan France and 22 for the overseas departments and territories). Members are elected by popular vote for five years. The Senate currently has 321 Senators (296 for metropolitan France, 13 for the overseas departments and territories and 12 for French citizens abroad). Members are elected by an electoral college to serve nine-year terms, elected by thirds every three years. By 2010, 25 new seats will be added to the Senate to make a total of 346 senators (326 for metropolitan France and the overseas departments, two for New Caledonia, two for Mayotte, one for St-Pierre and Miquelon, three for overseas territories and 12 for French nationals living abroad). By 2010 members will be elected by an electoral college to serve six-year terms, with one half of the seats being renewed every three years.

The Prime Minister is nominated by the National Assembly and appointed by the President, as is the Council of Ministers. They are responsible to the legislature, but as the executive is constitutionally separate from the legislature, ministers may not sit in the legislature and must hand over their seats to a substitute.

HEAD OF STATE

President of the French Republic, Jacques René Chirac, *elected* 7 May 1995, *re-elected* 5 May 2002

SELECTED GOVERNMENT MEMBERS *as at July 2004*

Prime Minister, Jean-Pierre Raffarin
Defence, War Veterans, Michèle Alliot-Marie
Economy, Finance and Industry, Nicolas Sarkozy
Foreign Affairs Co-operation and Francophonie, Michel Barnier
Interior, Internal Security and Local Freedoms, Dominique de Villepin

FRENCH EMBASSY

58 Knightsbridge, London SW1X 7JT
T 020-7073 1000
E consulat.londres-amba@diplomatie.fr
Ambassador Extraordinary and Plenipotentiary, HE Gérard Errera, apptd 2002

BRITISH EMBASSY

35 rue du Faubourg St Honoré, 75383 Paris Cedex 08
T (+33) (1) 4451 3100
Ambassador Extraordinary and Plenipotentiary, HE Sir John Eaton Holmes KBE, CVO, CMG, apptd 2001

BRITISH COUNCIL DIRECTOR, John Tod, OBE

9 rue de Constantine, 75340 Paris Cédex 07
T (+33) (1) 4955 7300
E information@britishcouncil.fr

DEFENCE

The Army has 614 main battle tanks, 3,700 armoured personnel carriers, 384 armoured infantry fighting vehicles and 418 helicopters.

The Navy has ten submarines, one aircraft carrier, one cruiser, 12 destroyers, 20 frigates and 35 patrol and coastal vessels, 58 combat aircraft and 30 armed helicopters. The Navy has four domestic and five overseas bases. The Air Force has 478 combat aircraft. There are currently two military satellites in service.

France deploys 34,981 armed forces personnel abroad; 3,200 in Germany (including members of Eurocorps); 15,900 in French Overseas Departments and Territories; 9,400 in former French colonies in Africa and 6,200 on UN and peacekeeping duties. Compulsory military service was abolished in June 2001.

MILITARY EXPENDITURE – 2.5 per cent of GDP (2002)
MILITARY PERSONNEL – 250,050: Army 137,000, Strategic Nuclear Forces 4,800, Navy 44,250, Air Force 64,000; Paramilitaries (Gendarmerie) 101,399

ECONOMY AND TRADE

Viniculture is extensive, regions famous for their wines include Bordeaux, Burgundy and Champagne. Production of wine in 2003 was 47.1 million hectolitres. Cognac, liqueurs and cider are also produced. Other important agricultural products include sugar beet, dairy products, cereals and oil seeds. Nearly 55 per cent of the land area of metropolitan France is utilised for agricultural production and a further quarter is accounted for by forests.

Oil is produced from fields in the Landes area, but France is a net importer of crude oil, for processing by its important oil-refining industry. Natural gas is produced in the foothills of the Pyrenees.

Heavy industries include the production of iron, steel and aluminium. In 2002 production of pig iron was 14 million tonnes and steel 20.3 million tonnes. Other important industries are in the construction and civil engineering sectors, chemicals, rubber and plastics, pharmaceutical industries, and vehicle production and telecommunications services.

The principal imports are raw materials for the heavy and manufacturing industries (e.g. oil, minerals, chemicals), machinery and precision instruments, agricultural products, chemicals and vehicles. Agricultural products, chemicals, pharmaceuticals and vehicles are also the principal exports. Most of France's trade is done with other EU countries. There are around 45 million hectares of farmland.

The Banque de France was made independent of the government in 1994 with the formation of a nine-member monetary policy council to define and implement monetary policy. France has participated in the European Single Currency since January 1999 and in January 2002 the euro replaced the franc.

Government moves towards privatisation sparked a public sector strike in November 2002 and a series of national strikes took place in May and June 2003 over planned pension reforms.

GNI – US$1,380,700 million (2001); US$22,730 per capita (2001)
ANNUAL AVERAGE GROWTH OF GDP – 3.3 per cent (2000)
INFLATION RATE – 1.7 per cent (2000)
UNEMPLOYMENT – 10.0 per cent (2000)
FOREIGN DIRECT INVESTMENT – US$133,044 (1997–2000)
IMPORTS – US$306,527 million (2002)
EXPORTS – US$308,798 million (2002)

BALANCE OF PAYMENTS
Trade – US$8,992 million surplus (2002)
Current Account – US$25,744 million surplus (2002)

Trade with UK	*2002*	*2003*
Imports from UK	£17,844,000,000	£16,423,925,000
Exports to UK	17,982,000,000	14,227,880,000

TRANSPORT INFRASTRUCTURE

There are approximately 11,500 km of motorways and around 900,000 km of other roads. There are 14,932 km of navigable waterways. The railroad system is extensive. The length of the rail network in 2002 was around 32,682 km. The French mercantile marine consisted in 2003 of 150 ships of 1,000 gross tonnage or over, 118 of which are registered overseas.

EDUCATION

Education is compulsory, free of charge and secular from six to 16. Schools may be single-sex or co-educational. Primary education is given in nursery schools, primary schools and *collèges d'enseignement général* (four-year secondary modern course); secondary education in *collèges d'enseignement technique, collèges d'enseignement secondaire* and *lycées* (a seven-year course leading to one of the five *baccalauréats*). Specialist schools are numerous.

There are many *grandes écoles* in France which award diplomas in many subjects not taught at university, especially applied science and engineering. Most of these are state institutions but have a competitive system of entry, unlike universities. There are universities in 24 towns including 13 in Paris.

ENROLMENT (percentage of age group) – primary 100 per cent (1997); secondary 100 per cent (1997); tertiary 51 per cent (1997)

MEDIA

There are over 100 daily newspapers in France. The main publications are: *Le Monde, Le Matin, Les Echos, Le Figaro, Liberation, La Tribune,* and *Le Parisien.* The press is mostly privately owned. French state radio caters for both domestic (Radio France) and overseas (Radio France Internationale) audiences. Channel TV5 is an international French-language television channel co-financed by Belgium, Canada, France and Switzerland. The main domestic channel, TF1, was privatised in 1987. There are two digital satellite TV companies. In 2004 there were 23 million internet users.

CULTURE

From Nouveau Cuisine to post-structural semiotics, France has enjoyed a steady influence on world culture. French culture has consistently produced the finest artists, philosophers, poets, film-makers, architects and politicians. Notable figures include the writers Jean-Paul Sartre (1905–80) and Simone de Beauvoir (1908–86), the artists Claude Monet (1840–1926) and Edgar Degas (1834–1917), the composers Claude-Achille Debussy (1862–1918) and Camille Saint-Saëns (1835–1921) and the psychoanalyst Jacques Lacan (1901–81).

OVERSEAS DEPARTMENTS

Greater powers of self-government were granted to French Guiana, Guadeloupe, Martinique and Réunion in 1982. These former colonies had enjoyed departmental status since 1946. Their directly elected Assemblies operate in parallel with the existing, indirectly constituted Regional Councils. The French government is represented by a Prefect in each.

FRENCH GUIANA
AREA – 83,534 sq. km
POPULATION – 185,000 (2001)
CAPITAL – ΨCayenne (50,675, 1999 census)

Situated on the north-eastern coast of South America, French Guiana is flanked by Surinam on the west and by Brazil on the south and east. Under the administration of French Guiana is a group of islands (St Joseph, le Royal and le du Diable), known as les du Salut.
Prefect, Ange Mancini

GUADELOUPE
AREA – 1,780 sq. km
POPULATION – 436,000 (2001)
CAPITAL – ΨBasse-Terre (12,410, 1999 census) on Guadeloupe

A number of islands in the Leeward Islands group of the West Indies, consisting of the two main islands of Guadeloupe (or Basse-Terre) and Grande-Terre, with the adjacent islands of Marie-Galante, La Désirade and les des Saintes, and islands of St-Barthélemy and the part of St-Martin under French administration, which lie over 240 km to the north-west. The main towns are ΨLes Abymes; ΨSt-Martin; ΨPointe-à-Pitre in Grande-Terre and ΨGrand Bourg in Marie-Galante.
Prefect, Dominique Vian

MARTINIQUE
AREA – 1,128 sq. km
POPULATION – 390,000 (2001)
CAPITAL – ΨFort-de-France (94,778, 1999 census)

Martinique is an island situated in the Windward Islands group of the West Indies, between Dominica in the north and St Lucia in the south. The main towns are ΨLe Marin, Fort-de-France and ΨSchoelcher.
Prefect, Yves Dassonville

RÉUNION
AREA – 2,547 sq. km
POPULATION – 745,000 (2001)
CAPITAL – St-Denis (158,139, 1999)

Réunion, which became a French possession in 1638, lies in the Indian Ocean, about 911 km east of Madagascar and 110 miles south-west of Mauritius. Other towns are Saint-Paul and Saint-Pierre. The smaller, uninhabited islands of Bassas da India, Europa, les Glorieuses, Juan de Nova and Tromelin are administered from Réunion.
Prefect, Gonthier Friederici

TERRITORIAL COLLECTIVITIES

MAYOTTE
AREA – 372 sq. km
POPULATION – 170,879 (2002 estimate)
CAPITAL – Mamoudzou (32,733, 1997 census)

Part of the Comoros Islands group, Mayotte remained a French dependency when the other three islands became independent as the Comoros Republic in 1975. Since 1976 the island has been a *collectivité territoriale,* an intermediate status between Overseas Department and Overseas Territory.
Prefect, Jean-Jacques Brot

Trade with UK	*2001*	*2002*
Imports from UK	£968,000	£217,000
Exports to UK	536,000	300,000

ST PIERRE AND MIQUELON
AREA – 242 sq. km
POPULATION – 6,954 (2002 estimate)
CAPITAL – ΨSt-Pierre (5,618, 1999)

These two small groups of islands off the coast of Newfoundland became a *collectivité territoriale* in 1985.
Prefect, Claude Valleix

Trade with UK	*2001*	*2002*
Imports from UK	£2,578,000	£454,000
Exports to UK	75,000	—

OVERSEAS TERRITORIES

FRENCH POLYNESIA
AREA – 3,887 sq. km
POPULATION – 248,000 (2001)
CAPITAL – ΨPapeete (26,181), in Tahiti

Five archipelagos in the south Pacific, comprising the Society Islands (Windward Islands group includes Tahiti, Moorea, Makatea, Mehetia, Tetiaroa, Tubuai Manu; Leeward Islands group includes Huahine, Raiatea, Tahaa, Bora-Bora, Maupiti), the Tuamotu Islands (Rangiroa, Hao, Turéia, etc.), the Gambier Islands (Mangareva, etc.), the Tubuai Islands (Rimatara, Rurutu, Tubuai, Raivavae, Rapa, etc.) and the Marquesas Islands (Nuku-Hiva, Hiva-Oa, Fatu-Hiva, Tahuata, Ua Huka, etc.).
High Commissioner, Michel Mathieu

Trade with UK	2001	2002
Imports from UK	£5,928,000	£7,532,000
Exports to UK	365,000	556,000

NEW CALEDONIA
AREA – 18,736 sq. km
POPULATION – 219,000 (2001)
CAPITAL – ΨNouméa (97,581)

New Caledonia is a large island in the western Pacific, 1,120 km east of Queensland. Dependencies are the Isles of Pines, the Loyalty Islands (Mahé, Lifou, Urea, etc.), the Bélep Archipelago, the Chesterfield Islands, the Huon Islands and Walpole.

New Caledonia was discovered in 1774 and annexed by France in 1853; from 1871 to 1896 it was a convict settlement. In 1995, the territory was divided into three provinces, each with a provincial assembly which combined to form the Territorial Assembly. In elections in 1995, Kanaks won majorities in North province and the Loyalty Islands, whereas pro-French settlers won a majority in the South province.

A referendum in 1987 on the question of independence was boycotted by the indigenous Kanaks, and New Caledonia therefore voted to remain French. In April 1998 an agreement was reached between the pro-independence Kanak Socialist National Liberation Front, the anti-independence Rally for Caledonia in the Republic and the French government, to hold a referendum on independence in 2014 and for greater autonomy for the indigenous people in the intervening period. A referendum on the agreement, the Nouméa Accord, was held on 8 November 1998. It was supported by 71.9 per cent of voters; more than 74 per cent of registered voters took part.
High Commissioner, Daniel Constantin

Trade with UK	*2001*	*2002*
Imports from UK	£9,231,000	£8,700,000
Exports to UK	136,000	153,000

SOUTHERN AND ANTARCTIC TERRITORIES
Created in 1955 from former Réunion dependencies, the territory comprises the islands of Amsterdam (64 sq. km) and St Paul (7 sq. km), the Kerguelen Islands (6,992 sq. km) and Crozet Islands (300 sq. km) archipelagos and Adélie Land (302,500 sq. km) in the Antarctic continent. The population consists only of members of staff of the scientific stations.
Administrator, François Garde

WALLIS AND FUTUNA ISLANDS
AREA – 200 sq. km
POPULATION – 15, 585 (2002 estimate)
CAPITAL – ΨMata-Utu on Uvea, the main island of the Wallis group

Two groups of islands (the Wallis Archipelago and the Îles de Horne) in the central Pacific, north-east of Fiji.
Administrator, Christian Job

Trade with UK	*2001*	*2002*
Imports from UK	£1,000	£1,000
Exports to UK	47,000	—

THE FRENCH COMMUNITY
The constitution of the Fifth French Republic, promulgated in 1958, envisaged the establishment of a French Community of States. A number of the former French states in Africa have seceded from the Community but for all practical purposes continue to enjoy the same close links with France as those that remain formally members. Most former French African colonies are closely linked to France by financial, technical and economic agreements.

GABON

République Gabonaise – Gabonese Republic

AREA – 257,700 sq. km. Neighbours: Equatorial Guinea and Cameroon (north), Republic of Congo (east and south)
POPULATION – 1,262,000 (2001). The official language is French; Fang is widely spoken
CAPITAL – ΨLibreville (population, 362,400, 1993)
CURRENCY – Franc CFA of 100 centimes
NATIONAL ANTHEM – La Concorde
NATIONAL DAY – 17 August
NATIONAL FLAG – Horizontal bands, green, yellow and blue
LIFE EXPECTANCY (years) – 53 (2001)
MORTALITY RATE (per 1,000 population) – 11.17 (2003)
INFANT MORTALITY (per 1,000 births) – 60 (2001)
HIV / AIDS ADULT PREVALENCE – 9 per cent (2001)
DEATH PENALTY – Yes
POPULATION GROWTH RATE – 2.7 per cent (1990–2001)
POPULATION DENSITY – 5 per sq. km (2001)
MILITARY EXPENDITURE – 1.7 per cent of GDP (2002)
MILITARY PERSONNEL – 4,700: Army 3,200, Navy 500, Air Force 1,000; Paramilitaries 2,000
ILLITERACY RATE – (m) 20.2 per cent; (f) 37.8 per cent (2000)

CLIMATE AND TERRAIN
Gabon is equatorial and approximately 85 per cent of the land is rain forest. Elevation extremes range from 1,575 m (Mount Iboundji) at the highest point to 0 m (Atlantic Ocean) at the lowest. The climate is hot and humid with an average temperature of 27°C. There are two wet seasons, the first is from February to May, the second is from October to December.

HISTORY AND POLITICS
The first Europeans to visit the region were the Portuguese in the 15th century and Dutch, French and English traders arrived soon after. Sovereignty was signed over to the French in 1839 by a local Mpongwe ruler. In 1849 a slave ship was captured by the French, and the freed slaves formed a settlement which they called Libreville, the current capital.

Gabon elected in 1958 to remain an autonomous republic within the French Community and gained full independence on 17 August 1960.

Multiparty elections held in autumn 1990 were won by the ruling Parti Démocratique Gabonais (PDG), amid allegations of fraud. The PDG formed a coalition government, although the other parties left the government in 1991 in protest at PDG domination. In September 1994, the government and opposition parties signed the Paris Agreement, which provided for a new coalition government and parliamentary elections. The elections, held in December 1996, returned the PDG to power. President Bongo of the PDG, who first took office in 1967, was re-elected for a fifth term of office in December 1998. The next presidential elections are scheduled to be held in 2005. The last elections to the National Assembly took place in December 2001. The government is dominated by the PDG but includes opposition party members.

POLITICAL SYSTEM
The constitution provides for an Executive President, directly elected for a seven-year term, who appoints the Prime Minister. The Prime Minister then appoints the Council of Ministers in consultation with the President. There is a 120-member National Assembly, directly elected for a five-year term, and a 91-member Senate, elected by municipal and regional councillors for a six-year term.

HEAD OF STATE
President, El Hadj Omar Bongo, *assumed office* December 1967, *re-elected* 1973, 1979, 1986, 1993 and 6 December 1998
Vice-President, Didjob Divungi-di-Ndinge

SELECTED GOVERNMENT MEMBERS *as at July 2004*
Prime Minister, Jean-François Ntoutoume-Emane
Deputy Prime Minister, Human Rights, Agriculture, Livestock and Rural Development, Paul Mba Abessole
Deputy Prime Minister, Town and Country Planning, Emmanuel Ondo Methogo
Deputy Prime Minister, Urban Affairs, Antoine de Padoue Mboumbou Miyakou
Defence, Ali Ben Bongo
Finance, Economy, Budget and Privatisation, Paul Toungui
Foreign Affairs, Co-operation and Francophone Affairs, Jean Ping

Interior, Public Security, Decentralisation, Gen. Idriss Ngari

EMBASSY OF THE REPUBLIC OF GABON
27 Elvaston Place, London SW7 5NL
T 020-7823 9986
Ambassador Extraordinary and Plenipotentiary, HE Alain Mensah-Zaguelet, apptd 2003

BRITISH AMBASSADOR, HE Richard Wildash, LVO, resident at Yaoundé, Cameroon

ECONOMY AND TRADE

One of the most economically stable countries in Africa, Gabon has the highest income per capita in the region. The economy is heavily dependent on oil, which contributes 50 per cent of GDP and is the leading export, and, to a lesser extent, on other mineral resources, including manganese and uranium. Gabon has considerable timber reserves with 85 per cent of the country still forested, although production has stagnated in recent years.

The government has begun investment in agriculture in order to ease the country's dependence on oil revenue. Agricultural products include cocoa, coffee, rubber, sugar and pineapples.

GNI – US$4,000 million (2001); US$3,160 per capita (2001)
ANNUAL AVERAGE GROWTH OF GDP – 2.5 per cent (2001)
INFLATION RATE – 1.5 per cent (2000)
TOTAL EXTERNAL DEBT – US$3,800 million (2002)
FOREIGN DIRECT INVESTMENT – US$200 million (1997–2000)
IMPORTS – US$994 million (2000)
EXPORTS – US$3,024 million (1997)

Trade with UK	*2002*	*2003*
Imports from UK	£24,625,000	£33,289,000
Exports to UK	5,795,000	23,644,000

MEDIA

The biggest broadcaster, Radiodiffusion-Television Gabonaise, is state controlled and operates two stations. There are two other main channels: TeleAfrica, which is privately owned; and TV Sat, a subscription operator. There are several privately owned newspapers that usually publish on a weekly basis. The only daily newspaper, *L'Union*, is government run. Radio is an important news medium because of rural illiteracy rates. Africa No1 is a pan-African broadcaster based in Gabon which is partly French owned.

CULTURE

Due in part to the influx of oil money, the cities of Gabon are some of the most modern in Africa. The Gabonese are mainly of Bantu descent and subdivide into about ten main ethnic groups, the largest of which is the Fang. Historically, Gabon has been admired for its woodcarving and Fang masks are the most famous of all the Gabonese woodcarving traditions.

THE GAMBIA

The Republic of the Gambia

AREA – 11,295 sq. km. Neighbour: Senegal, which surrounds the Gambia except at the coast
POPULATION – 1,501,050 (2003 estimate), mainly Wollof, Mandinka and Fula peoples who originally migrated from the north and east. The official language is English; Fula, Jola, Mandinka, Serahule and Wollof are indigenous languages
CAPITAL – ΨBanjul (population, 42,407, 1993 census)
CURRENCY – Dalasi (D) of 100 butut
NATIONAL ANTHEM – For The Gambia, Our Homeland
NATIONAL DAY – 18 February (Independence Day)
NATIONAL FLAG – Horizontal stripes of red, blue and green, separated by narrow white stripes
MORTALITY RATE (per 1,000 population) – 12.35 (2003)
HIV / AIDS ADULT PREVALENCE – 1.6 per cent (2001)
DEATH PENALTY – No (abolished 1981)
POPULATION GROWTH RATE – 3.3 per cent
POPULATION DENSITY – 112 per sq. km (1999)
MILITARY EXPENDITURE – 1.0 per cent of GDP (2002)
MILITARY PERSONNEL – Army 800

CLIMATE AND TERRAIN

The Gambia is a flat, low-lying country where elevation extremes range from 53 m at the highest point to 0 m (Atlantic Ocean) at the lowest. The Gambia River runs the entire length of the country making the Gambia itself mostly a flood plain with some low hills. The climate is tropical with an average temperature of between 23°C and 40°C. The wet season runs from June to September.

HISTORY AND POLITICS

The Gambia River basin was part of a region dominated in the 10th to 16th centuries by the Songhai and Mali kingdoms. The Portuguese reached the Gambia River in 1447; English merchants began to trade along the river from 1588. Merchants from France, Courland (now Latvia) and the Netherlands also established trading posts there. In 1816 the British stationed a garrison on an island at the river mouth that became the capital of a small British-administered colony. In 1889 France agreed that the British rights along the upper river should extend to 10 km from the river on either bank. The Gambia became independent within the Commonwealth on 18 February 1965, and a republic on 24 April 1970.

In July 1994, junior army officers launched a coup which ousted the president and the government, and a military council was formed. The coup leader, Lt. (later Capt.) Jammeh, assumed the presidency, the constitution was suspended and a civilian-military government was formed to rule in conjunction with the Ruling Military Council. A referendum approved a new constitution in August 1996, Jammeh was elected president the following month and the Ruling Military Council was dissolved. The latest presidential elections were held in October 2001 when Jammeh secured his presidency with 56 per cent of the vote. Legislative elections held in 2002 were won by President Jammeh's party, The Alliance for Patriotic Reorientation and Construction (APRC). The election was boycotted by opposition parties.

POLITICAL SYSTEM

The constitution gives enhanced powers to the President who is elected for an indefinite term. The National

Assembly has 53 members, of whom 48 are directly elected, and five appointed by the President, for a five-year term.

HEAD OF STATE
President, Defence, Capt. Yahya A. J. J. Jammeh, *took power* 23 July 1994, *elected* 26 September 1996 *re-elected* 18 October 2001
Vice-President, Women and Social Affairs, Isatou Njie-Saidy

SELECTED GOVERNMENT MEMBERS *as at July 2004*
External Affairs, Baboucarr Blaise Jagne
Finance and Economic Affairs, Bala Musa Gaye
Interior, Sulayman Masaneh Ceesay

GAMBIA HIGH COMMISSION
57 Kensington Court, London W8 5DG
T 020-7937 6316/7/8
High Commissioner, HE Gibril Sumen Joof, apptd 2000

BRITISH HIGH COMMISSION
48 Atlantic Road, Fajara (PO Box 507), Banjul
T (+220) 449 5133
E bhcbanjul@gamtel.gm
High Commissioner, HE Eric Jenkinson, apptd 2003

ECONOMY AND TRADE

Agriculture accounts for 75 per cent of employment and contributes 33 per cent of GDP. The chief product, groundnuts, forms over 80 per cent of exports. Other crops are cotton, rice, millet, sorghum, sesame, palm kernels, corn, cassava and maize. Manufacturing is limited to groundnut processing, minor metal fabrications, paints, furniture, soap and bottling. Trade through the Gambia re-exporting imported goods to neighbouring countries was an important element in the economy which was damaged in 1999 when the government imposed preshipment inspection plans. The main exports are groundnuts, cotton, fish and fish products. The main imports are foodstuffs and live animals, industrial goods, machinery and transport equipment, and fuels.

In February 2004 President Jammeh announced that large oil deposits had been discovered off the coast of the Gambia.

GNI – US$422 million (2000); US$320 per capita (2001)
ANNUAL AVERAGE GROWTH OF GDP – 5.4 per cent (1997)
INFLATION RATE – 0.8 per cent (2000)
TOTAL EXTERNAL DEBT – US$471 million (2000)
IMPORTS – US$92 million (1999)
EXPORTS – US$7 million (1999)

BALANCE OF PAYMENTS
Trade – US$87 million deficit (1997)
Current Account – US$24 million deficit (1997)

Trade with UK	2002	2003
Imports from UK	£16,402,000	£18,958,000
Exports to UK	4,805,000	2,766,000

EDUCATION

There are four types of school in the Gambia: primary school (ages four to 10); junior school (ages 11–14); secondary school (ages 14–15), and Islamic school. There are 15 secondary schools. Two high schools provide A-level education. The Gambia College provides post-secondary courses in education, agriculture, public health and nursing. There are seven vocational training institutions. There is one university, based in Serrekunda.

ILLITERACY RATE – (m) 56.0 per cent; (f) 70.6 per cent (2000)
ENROLMENT (percentage of age group) – primary 77 per cent (1997); secondary 25 per cent (1997); tertiary 2 per cent (1997)

MEDIA

Since 2002 private newspapers and radio stations have been regulated by a government run commission that has the power to suspend publication or transmission licences and imprison journalists. The state operates the only national television station, Gambia Television. There is one private satellite channel, Premium TV Network. State run Radio Gambia produces tightly controlled news broadcasts, which are relayed by private radio stations.

CULTURE

The Gambia has a rich musical and literary tradition that plays an important part in everyday life. *Griots*, or 'praise-singers', preserve and pass on the stories of families and clans. There is also a vibrant modern literary tradition. Contemporary Gambian authors include Ebou Dibba (1943–2000), Lenrie Peters (b.1932) and William Conton (1925–2003).

GEORGIA

Sak'art'velos Respublikis – Georgia

AREA – 69,700 sq. km. Neighbours: Russia (north), Azerbaijan (south-east), Armenia (south), Turkey (south-west)
POPULATION – 5,239,000 (2001): 70 per cent Georgian, 8 per cent Armenian, 6 per cent Russian, 6 per cent Azerbaijani, 3 per cent Ossetian and 2 per cent Abkhazian, with smaller groups of Greeks, Ukrainians, Jews and Kurds. Georgian is the sole official language, except in Abkhazia where Abkhazian is also officially recognised. Russian and Armenian are commonly spoken. About 65 per cent of the population are adherents of the Georgian Orthodox Church, 11 per cent are Muslims, 10 per cent are Russian Orthodox and 8 per cent are Armenian Orthodox
CAPITAL – Tbilisi (population, 1,253,100, 1997 estimate)
MAJOR CITIES – Batumi; Kutaisi; Rustavi; Sukhumi (capital of Abkhazia)
CURRENCY – Lari of 100 tetri
NATIONAL ANTHEM – Dideba Zetsit Kurtheuls (Praise Be To The Heavenly Bestower Of Blessings)
NATIONAL DAY – 26 May (Independence Day)
NATIONAL FLAG – Cherry red with a canton in the upper hoist divided black over white
LIFE EXPECTANCY (years) – 73 (2001)
MORTALITY RATE (per 1,000 population) – 14.71 (2003)
INFANT MORTALITY (per 1,000 births) – 24 (2001)
HIV / AIDS ADULT PREVALENCE – 0.1 per cent (2001)
DEATH PENALTY – No (abolished 1997)
POPULATION BELOW POVERTY LINE – 54 per cent (2001)

POPULATION GROWTH RATE – 0.4 per cent (1990–2001)
POPULATION DENSITY – 75 per sq. km (2001)
URBAN POPULATION – 56 per cent (2001)
MILITARY EXPENDITURE – 1.7 per cent of GDP (2002)
MILITARY PERSONNEL – 11,700: Army 8,620, Navy 1,830, Air Force 1,250; Paramilitaries 11,700
CONSCRIPTION DURATION – 18 months
ENROLMENT (percentage of age group) – primary 88 per cent (1997); secondary 77 per cent (1997); tertiary 42 per cent (1997)

CLIMATE AND TERRAIN

Georgia occupies the north-western part of the Caucasus region of the former Soviet Union. It contains the two autonomous republics of Abkhazia and Adjaria and the disputed region of South Ossetia (Tskhinvali). Georgia is a mountainous country with the Great Caucasus mountains in the north and the Lesser Caucasus mountains in the south. Elevation extremes range from 5,201 m (Mt'a Shkhara) at the highest point to 0 m (Black Sea) at the lowest.

HISTORY AND POLITICS

The Georgians formed two states, Colchis and Iberia, on the edge of the Black Sea around 1000 BC. After centuries of invasions by Arabs, Turks and Khazars, Georgia entered its 'Golden Age' in the 12th century AD when trade, irrigation and communications were developed. Invasions by the Khazars and Mongols led to the division of Georgia into several states. These precarious states struggled against the Turkish and the Persian empires from the 16th to the 18th centuries, gradually turning to the Russian empire for protection and support. Eastern Georgia signed a treaty of alliance with Russia which recognised Russian supremacy in 1783 and joined the Russian empire in 1801, followed soon after by Western Georgia.

In the late 19th century, nationalist and Marxist movements competed for limited political influence under autocratic Russian rule. One of the most prominent Marxist activists was Iosif Dzhugashvili (Josef Stalin). After the Russian Revolution of 1917, a nationalist government came to power in Georgia supported by allied intervention forces. In 1921 Soviet forces occupied Tbilisi, and in 1922 Georgia joined the Soviet Union as part of the Transcaucasian Soviet Socialist Republic.

In March 1990 the Georgian Supreme Soviet declared illegal the treaties of 1921–2 by which Georgia had joined the Soviet Union. The Communist Party's monopoly on power was abolished and in multiparty elections held in October and November 1990 the nationalist leader Zviad Gamsakhurdia was elected president. Georgia declared its independence from the Soviet Union in May 1991 and was admitted to UN membership in 1992.

Gamsakhurdia's government faced armed opposition from 1991 onwards. Defeat in the ensuing civil war in Tbilisi led to Gamsakhurdia's overthrow in January 1992, and in March a state council was appointed with the former Soviet foreign minister Eduard Shevardnadze as chairman. Fighting continued throughout 1992 and 1993. In October 1992 Shevardnadze was elected head of state and chairman of the parliament, and a loose alliance of pro-Shevardnadze parties formed a government.

Gamsakhurdia returned to western Georgia in September 1993. President Shevardnadze failed to prevent the advance of Gamsakhurdia's rebels as most government forces were engaged in Abkhazia. Shevardnadze was forced to accept Russian armaments and troops to defeat the rebellion and in return agreed to join the Commonwealth of Independent States (CIS). Georgia rescinded its participation in the CIS Collective Security treaty in February 1999 and Russian troops, who had been guarding Georgia's frontier with Turkey, began to withdraw. The legislative election held in October and November 1999 was won by the Union of the Citizens of Georgia (Shevardnadze's party) which gained 130 of the 235 seats in the parliament. In the presidential election of 2000, President Shevardnadze was re-elected, gaining 79.8 per cent of the vote. Shevardnadze resigned in November 2003 after public demonstrations against alleged electoral fraud in parliamentary elections. Mikhail Saakashvili, leader of the National Movement, was elected president in a landslide victory in January 2004. Parliamentary elections were held in May 2004 and the National Movement Democrats won 67 per cent of the vote.

SECESSION

In late 1990 the South Ossetians took up arms against Georgian rule in an attempt to join North Ossetia, itself part of Russia. The South Ossetian provincial parliament voted in November 1992 to secede from Georgia and join Russia. Fighting ceased in June 1992 and a joint Russian-Georgian-Ossetian peacekeeping force was dispatched. Representatives of the South Ossetian and Georgian governments met in April 1996 to agree security and confidence-building measures.

The presidential elections of December 2001 were won by Eduard Kokoiti, a Russian citizen. Parliamentary elections were held in May 2004 but were unrecognised by Tbilisi.

In July 1992 the parliament of the Autonomous Republic of Abkhazia declared Abkhazia independent. Fighting broke out between Georgian forces and Abkhazian separatists supported by Russia; Georgian forces were defeated and were forced to withdraw in September 1993. Negotiations under Russian auspices led to an Abkhaz-Georgian cease fire and a separation of forces agreement being signed in May 1994 and the deployment of UN peacekeepers on the Abkhaz-Georgian border (along the Inguri River). In November 1994 the Abkhaz Supreme Soviet declared Abkhazia's independence again and elected Vladislav Ardzinba as president. Abkhazia was given autonomous republic status under the 1995 constitution; this was rejected by the republican parliament. Elections to the self-declared Abkhaz People's Assembly were held in 1996. Following a guarantee of security from President Ardzinba, ethnic Georgians who had fled Abkhazia during the fighting began returning in 1999. A referendum held in Abkhazia in October 1999 approved a new constitution which held Abkhazia to be a sovereign state. In July 2000, Georgia and Abkhazia signed a UN-sponsored protocol on stabilisation measures, agreeing to refrain from the use of force and to establish groups to combat cross-border crime. On 7 March 2003 Russia and Georgia agreed that the CIS collective peacekeeping forces would remain in Abkhazia indefinitely.

Ajaria is a semi-autonomous region of Georgia on the country's Black Sea coast bordering Turkey. After the 2004 presidential elections, relations between Ajaria and Georgia rapidly deteriorated. Aslan Abashidze, Ajaria's leader since 1991, disputed a claim by Georgia that Ajaria owed large sums of money in unpaid taxes and customs duties and in May 2004 Abashidze accused Saakashvili of having plans to invade Ajaria and subsequently ordered the destruction of bridges between Ajaria and Georgia. Public demonstrations against Abashidze followed and he was forced to resign. Abashidze's post has now been abolished by Georgia and an interim government (administered by Georgia) remained in control until parliamentary elections in June 2004. Georgian President Saakashvili won 77 per cent of the vote with his party Saakashvili-Victorious Ajaria (SUA).

FOREIGN RELATIONS

Georgia has signed a Partnership and Co-operation Agreement with the European Union (1996). In May 2002, US military instructors arrived in Tbilisi to train up to 2,000 troops in military strategy and tactics to counter militant activity. A written commitment was issued promising that the troops would not be used against Abkhazia.

Tension grew between Georgia and Russia in September 2002 over Russian accusations that Georgia was harbouring Chechen militants in the Pankisi Gorge in north-east Georgia. Russian President Vladimir Putin warned of military action if Georgia failed to deal with them. Relations improved when a successful two-month anti-terrorist operation was completed.

POLITICAL SYSTEM

The 1995 Constitution provides for a federal republic with a unicameral legislature, to become bicameral 'following the creation of appropriate conditions'; and a popularly elected President who serves a maximum of two five-year terms. The present Parliament has 235 members, directly elected for a four-year term.

HEAD OF STATE

President, Mikhail Saakashvili, *elected* 4 January 2004, *sworn in* 25 January 2004

SELECTED GOVERNMENT MEMBERS *as at July 2004*

Prime Minister, Zurab Zhvania
Deputy Prime Minister, Security, Vano Merabishvili
Defence, Giorgi Baramidze
Finance and Tax Revenue, Zurab Noghaideli
Interior, Irakli Okruashvili

EMBASSY OF GEORGIA

4 Russell Gardens, London W14 8EZ
T 020-7603 7799
E geoemb@dircon.co.uk
Ambassador Extraordinary and Plenipotentiary, HE Amiran Kavadze, apptd 2004

BRITISH EMBASSY

Sheraton Metechi Palace Hotel, GE-380003 Tbilisi
T (+995) (32) 955497
E british.embassy@caucasus.net
Ambassador Extraordinary and Plenipotentiary, HE The MacLaren of MacLaren, apptd 2004

BRITISH COUNCIL DIRECTOR, Jo Bakowski

34 Rustaveli Avenue, Tbilisi, 380008 Tbilisi
T (+995) (32) 250407/ 988014
E office.bc@britishcouncil.org.ge

ECONOMY AND TRADE

The economy was brought to the brink of collapse by civil and secessionist wars and the ending of former Soviet trading relationships. Although Georgia has deposits of coal, they have not been exploited and it is desperately short of energy supplies. In May 2003 work began on the Georgian section of an oil pipeline from Baku, Azerbaijan through Georgia to Ceyhan, Turkey. The only productive sector of the economy is agriculture, which employs 30 per cent of the workforce and generates 21 per cent of GDP, with a concentration on viniculture, tea and tobacco-growing and citrus fruits. The main exports are iron alloys, wine, nuts, chemical fertilisers, and oil and oil products. The main imports are oil and oil products, gas, automobiles, pharmaceuticals and wheat. In January 2001 the IMF approved a three-year loan to Georgia, amounting to some US$152 million but this programme was halted in 2003 because the Georgian authorities failed to comply with the requirements set by the fund.

GNI – US$3,100 million (2001); US$590 per capita (2001)
ANNUAL AVERAGE GROWTH OF GDP – 11.3 per cent (1997)
INFLATION RATE – 19.1 per cent (1999)
UNEMPLOYMENT – 10.8 per cent (2000)
TOTAL EXTERNAL DEBT – US$1,633 million (2000)
FOREIGN DIRECT INVESTMENT US$313 million (1997–2000)
IMPORTS – US$887 million (1998)
EXPORTS – US$192 million (1998)

Trade with UK	*2002*	*2003*
Imports from UK	£17,165,000	£25,469,000
Exports to UK	2,647,000	5,406,000

MEDIA

Georgia has a press of over 200 privately owned newspapers. *Sakartvelos Respublika* is the main state owned newspaper. Georgian State TV is the state owned broadcaster.

GERMANY

Bundesrepublik Deutschland – Federal Republic of Germany

AREA – 356,700 sq. km. Neighbours: Denmark (north), Poland (east), Czech Republic (east and south-east), Austria (south-east and south), Switzerland (south), France, Luxembourg, Belgium and the Netherlands (west)
POPULATION – 82,007,000 (2001). Approximately 80 per cent of the population live in former West Germany. 34 per cent of the population are Protestant, 34 per cent Roman Catholic, 28 per cent unaffiliated or of other religions and 4 per cent Muslim. The language is German; there are Danish- and Frisian-speaking minorities in Schleswig-Holstein and a Sorbian-speaking minority in Saxony

CAPITAL – Berlin (population, 3,388,434, 2001 estimate). The seat of government and parliament was transferred from Bonn to Berlin in 2000
MAJOR CITIES – Bremen; Cologne; Dortmund; Dresden; Duisburg; Düsseldorf; Essen; Frankfurt am Main; Hamburg; Hannover; Leipzig; Munich; Nuremberg; Stuttgart
CURRENCY – Euro (€) of 100 cents
NATIONAL ANTHEM – Einigkeit Und Recht Und Freiheit (Unity And Right And Freedom)
NATIONAL DAY – 3 October (Anniversary of 1990 Unification)
NATIONAL FLAG – Horizontal bars of black, red and gold
LIFE EXPECTANCY (years) – 78 (2001)
MORTALITY RATE (per 1,000 population) – 10.34 (2003)
INFANT MORTALITY (per 1,000 births) – 4 (2001)
HIV / AIDS ADULT PREVALENCE – 0.1 per cent (2001)
DEATH PENALTY – No (abolished 1949 in FRG and 1987 in GDR)
POPULATION GROWTH RATE – 0.3 per cent (1990–2001)
POPULATION DENSITY – 230 per sq. km (2001)
URBAN POPULATION – 88 per cent (2001)

CLIMATE AND TERRAIN

The north of the country is low-lying, rising in the central region to uplands, alpine foothills and then to the Bavarian Alps in the south. The Rhine crosses the country from south to north. More than a third of the country is covered by forest. Elevation extremes range from 2,963 m (the Bavarian peak of Zugspitze) at the highest point to −3.54 m (Neuendorf bei Wilster) at the lowest. Germany has a temperate climate with average annual temperatures ranging from −5°C in January to 19°C in July.

HISTORY AND POLITICS

The first German realm was the Holy Roman Empire, established in AD 962 when Otto I of Saxony was crowned emperor. The empire endured until 1806, but the achievement of a national state was prevented by fragmentation into small principalities and dukedoms.

The Empire was replaced by a loose association of sovereign states known as the German confederation, which was dissolved in 1866 and replaced by the Prussian-dominated North German Federation. The south German principalities united with the northern federation to form a second German empire in 1871 and the King of Prussia was proclaimed emperor.

Defeat in the First World War led to the abdication of the emperor, and the country became a republic. The Treaty of Versailles (1919) ceded Alsace-Lorraine to France, and large areas in the east were lost to Poland. The world economic crisis of 1929 contributed to the collapse of the Weimar Republic and the subsequent rise to power of the National Socialist movement of Adolf Hitler, who became chancellor in 1933.

After concluding a Treaty of Non-Aggression with the Soviet Union in August 1939, Germany invaded Poland (1 September 1939), precipitating the Second World War, which lasted until 1945. Hitler committed suicide on 30 April 1945. On 8 May 1945, Germany unconditionally surrendered.

THE POST-WAR PERIOD

Germany was divided into American, French, British and Soviet zones of occupation. The territories to the east of the Oder and Neisse rivers were placed under Polish and Russian administration and some 7.75 million Germans were deported.

The Federal Republic of Germany (FRG) was created out of the three western zones in 1949. A Communist government was established in the Soviet zone (henceforth the German Democratic Republic (GDR)). In 1961 the Soviet zone of Berlin was sealed off, and the Berlin Wall was built along the zonal boundary, partitioning the western sectors of the city from the eastern.

Soviet-initiated reform in eastern Europe during the late 1980s led to unrest in the GDR, culminating in the opening of the Berlin Wall in November 1989 and the collapse of the Communist government. The 'Treaty on the Final Settlement with Respect to Germany' concluded between the FRG, GDR and the four former occupying powers in September 1990, unified Germany with effect from 3 October 1990 as a fully sovereign state. Economic and monetary union preceded formal union on 1 July 1990. Unification is constitutionally the accession of Berlin and the five reformed *Länder* (states) of the GDR to the FRG, which remains in being. Berlin was declared to be the capital of the unified Germany and parliament and government departments were transferred from Bonn.

The distribution of seats following the last election for the Bundestag in September 2002 was: Social Democratic Party (SPD) 250; Christian Democratic Union (CDU)/Christian Social Union (CSU) 248; Greens 55; Free Democratic Party (FDP) 47; Party of Democratic Socialism (PDS) 2. Gerhard Schröder of the SPD was re-elected as federal chancellor and formed a coalition government of the SPD and the Greens. Chancellor Schröder resigned as chairman of the SPD in February 2004 to concentrate on German reform processes. Franz Muenterfering succeeded him as the leader of the Social Democrats. Presidential elections were held in May 2004 and Johannes Rau was replaced by Professor Horst Koehler, a former director of the IMF.

POLITICAL SYSTEM

The Basic Law (Constitution) provides for a President, elected by a Federal Convention (electoral college) for a five-year term; a lower house *(Bundestag)* of 603 members elected by direct universal suffrage for a four-year term of office; and an upper house *(Bundesrat)* composed of 69 members appointed by the Governments of the State *(Länder)* in proportion to *Länder* populations, without a fixed term of office. German elections are governed by a system of proportional representation.

Judicial authority is exercised by the Federal Constitutional Court *(Bundesverfassungsgericht)*, the Federal Courts provided for in the Basic Law and the courts of the *Länder*.

FEDERAL STRUCTURE

Germany is a federal republic composed of 16 States *(Länder)* (ten from the former West, five from the former East, and Berlin). Each *Land* has its own directly elected legislature and government led by Minister-Presidents (Prime Ministers) or equivalents. The 1949 Basic Law vests executive power in the *Länder* governments except in those areas reserved for the Federal Government.

State	Capital	Population (2001)
Baden-Württemberg	Stuttgart	10.6m
Bavaria	Munich	12.3m
Berlin	—	3.4m
Brandenberg	Potsdam	2.6m
Bremen	—	0.7m
Hamburg	—	1.7m
Hesse	Wiesbaden	6.1m
Lower Saxony	Hannover	8.0m
Mecklenburg-Western Pomerania	Schwerin	1.8m
North Rhine-Westphalia	Düsseldorf	18.0m
Rhineland-Palatinate	Mainz	4.0m
Saarland	Saarbrücken	1.1m
Saxony	Dresden	4.4m
Saxony-Anhalt	Magdeburg	2.6m
Schleswig-Holstein	Kiel	2.8m
Thuringia	Erfurt	2.4m

HEAD OF STATE
Federal President, Horst Koehler, *elected* 23 May, *sworn in* 1 July 2004

SELECTED GOVERNMENT MEMBERS *as at July 2004*
Federal Chancellor, Gerhard Schröder
Federal Vice-Chancellor, *Foreign Affairs*, Joschka Fischer
Defence, Peter Struck
Interior, Otto Schily

EMBASSY OF THE FEDERAL REPUBLIC OF GERMANY
23 Belgrave Square/Chesham Place, London SW1X 8PZ
T 020-7824 1300
E mail@german-embassy.org.uk
Ambassador Extraordinary and Plenipotentiary, HE Thomas Matussek, apptd 2002

BRITISH EMBASSY
Wilhelmstrasse 70, D-10117 Berlin
T (+49) (30) 204570
Ambassador Extraordinary and Plenipotentiary, HE Sir Peter Torry, KCMG, apptd 2003

BRITISH COUNCIL DIRECTOR, Kathryn Board,
Hackescher Markt 1, D-10178 Berlin
T (+49) (30) 311 0990
E bc.berlin@britishcouncil.de

DEFENCE

The Army has 2,398 main battle tanks, 3,130 armoured personnel carriers, 2,255 armoured infantry fighting vehicles, and 199 attack helicopters. The Navy has 12 submarines, one destroyer, 12 frigates, 25 patrol and coastal vessels, 65 combat aircraft and 22 armed helicopters. The Air Force has 376 combat aircraft. There remain 100,700 NATO personnel in Germany (USA 73,500; UK 22,000; Belgium 2,000; France 3,200; Netherlands (2,600). Major cuts were made in military procurement in late 2002.
MILITARY EXPENDITURE – 1.5 per cent of GDP (2002)
MILITARY PERSONNEL – 284,500: Army 191,350, Navy 25,650, Air Force 67,500.
CONSCRIPTION DURATION – Nine months

ECONOMY AND TRADE

Germany has the world's fifth largest economy but recent years have seen stagnation with unemployment, slow growth, and a budget deficit in excess of the 3 per cent required by Eurozone rules.

The government announced in June 2000 that it was to abolish all 19 of Germany's nuclear power stations over a 32-year period, which supplied over 30 per cent of the energy generated in the country.

After a mini-boom generated by new East German demand in 1990 and 1991, Germany entered its most severe recession since the Second World War induced by the costs of reunification. In 1993 a 'Solidarity Pact' was agreed, which lays down the basis of future funding transfers to the East based on a 5.5 per cent rise in income taxes, wage restraint in the West, more private investment in the East, and the distribution of the funding burden between the federal and *Länder* governments.

The rate of economic growth increased in 1999 and 2000, aided by the weakness of the euro, but began to slow in the first quarter of 2001 and achieved less than one per cent growth between 2001 and 2003. The euro replaced the Deutsche mark in January 2002.

Unemployment rose in 2002 and continued to rise in early 2003. In 2003 Chancellor Schröder set out a major reform package of tax cuts and labour and welfare reforms designed to reduce unemployment and revive the country's economy.

Principal industries are coal mining, iron and steel production, machine construction, the domestic electrical industry, the manufacture of steel and metal products, chemicals, automobile production, electronics, textiles and the processing of foodstuffs.
GNI – US$1,939,600 million (2001); US$23,560 per capita (2001)
ANNUAL AVERAGE GROWTH OF GDP – 3.1 per cent (2000)
INFLATION RATE – 1.9 per cent (2000)
UNEMPLOYMENT – 7.8 per cent (2001)
FOREIGN DIRECT INVESTMENT – $259,778 million (1997–2000)
IMPORTS – US$493,350 million (2002)
EXPORTS – US$612,598 million (2001)

BALANCE OF PAYMENTS
Trade – US$122,182 million surplus (2002)
Current Account – US$46,586 million surplus (2002)

Trade with UK	*2002*	*2003*
Imports from UK	£21,022,600,000	£15,057,073,000
Exports to UK	29,381,000,000	24,070,953,000

TRANSPORT INFRASTRUCTURE

There was a total road network of around 230,735 km in 2000, comprising 11,515 km of expressways. There are 45,514 km of railways. Around 20 per cent of domestic freight is carried on the 7,500 km of inland waterways.

EDUCATION

Education is free of charge and compulsory between the ages of six and 18 and comprises nine years of full-time education at primary and main schools and three years of vocational education on a part-time basis. The secondary school leaving examination *(Abitur)* entitles the holder to a place at a university or another institution of higher education.

Children below the age of 18 who are not attending a general secondary or a full-time vocational school have compulsory day-release at a vocational school.

There are over 300 higher education institutes and the largest universities are in Munich, Berlin, Hamburg, Bonn, Frankfurt and Cologne. Germany's oldest university is Heidelberg, founded in 1386.

ENROLMENT (percentage of age group) – primary 100 per cent (1997); secondary 100 per cent (1997); tertiary 47 per cent (1997)

MEDIA

Each of the country's 16 federal states operates its own television stations, both private and public. Germany is implementing digital radio and television and will cease analogue services in 2010. Over 90 per cent of German households recieve cable or satellite television. Germany also has a considerable press industry and is home to many international media companies.

CULTURE

Modern German language has steadily developed from the time of the Reformation to the present day. Differences in dialect can be found in Austria, Alsace, Luxembourg, Liechtenstein and the German-speaking cantons of Switzerland. Great figures emerge from all areas of the cultural landscape, from literature (Goethe 1749–1832) and philosophy (Kant 1724–1804), to classical music (Beethoven 1770–1827) and physics (Einstein 1879–1955).

GHANA

The Republic of Ghana

AREA – 227,500 sq. km. Neighbours: Burkina Faso (north), Côte d'Ivoire (west), Togo (east)

POPULATION – 19,734,000 (2001); most are black Sudanese, although Hamitic strains are common in the north. The official language is English. The principal indigenous language group is Akan, of which Twi and Fanti are the most commonly used. Ga, Ewe and languages of the Mole-Dagbani group are common in certain regions. Most Ghanaians are Christians, although there is a substantial Muslim minority in the north

CAPITAL – ΨAccra (population, 1,445,515, 1998), Greater Accra Region (including Tema) 2,909,643 (2000 census)

MAJOR CITIES – Koforidua; Kumasi; ΨTakoradi; Tamale

CURRENCY – Cedi of 100 pesewas

NATIONAL FLAG – Equal horizontal bands of red over gold over green; five-point black star on gold stripe

NATIONAL ANTHEM – God Bless Our Homeland Ghana

NATIONAL DAY – 6 March (Independence Day)

LIFE EXPECTANCY (years) – 57 (2001)

MORTALITY RATE (per 1,000 population) – 10.53 (2003)

INFANT MORTALITY (per 1,000 births) – 57 (2001)

HIV / AIDS ADULT PREVALENCE – 3 per cent (2001)

DEATH PENALTY – Yes

POPULATION BELOW POVERTY LINE – 31.4 per cent (1992)

POPULATION GROWTH RATE – 2.4 per cent (1990–2001)

POPULATION DENSITY – 87 per sq. km (2001)

MILITARY EXPENDITURE – 0.5 per cent of GDP (2002)

MILITARY PERSONNEL – 7,000: Army 5,000, Navy 1,000, Air Force 1,000

CLIMATE AND TERRAIN

Ghana has inland plains that lead to the Ashanti plateau in the west and the river Volta basin in the east. Elevation extremes range from 880 m (Mount Afadjato) at the highest point to 0 m (Atlantic Ocean) at the lowest. The climate is tropical but there is also a warm and dry coastal area in the south-east. The average temperature in Accra is 30°C.

HISTORY AND POLITICS

First reached by Europeans in the 15th century, the constituent parts of Ghana came under British administration at various times, the original Gold Coast colony being constituted in 1874, and Ashanti and the Northern Territories Protectorate in 1901. Trans-Volta-Togoland, part of the former German colony of Togo, was mandated to Britain by the League of Nations after the First World War and was integrated with the Gold Coast colony in 1956 following a plebiscite. The former Gold Coast colony and associated territories became the independent state of Ghana on 6 March 1957 and became a republic in 1960.

Since 1966, Ghana has experienced long periods of military rule interspersed with short-lived civilian governments. A coup in 1979 led to the formation of an Armed Forces Revolutionary Council chaired by Flt. Lt. Jerry Rawlings. Civilian rule was restored in 1979 but another coup in December 1981 brought Rawlings back to power.

A referendum in 1992 approved a new multiparty constitution and the legalisation of political parties. The National Democratic Congress (NDC) was established as a political party from the ruling Provisional National Defence Council. The presidential and parliamentary elections in late 1992 were won by Rawlings and the NDC.

The NDC lost power in the general election of 2000, which was won by the New Patriotic Party (NPP), with 101 seats; the NDC won 92 seats. The presidential election was won by John Kufuor of the NPP.

A state of emergency was declared in the Dagbon region of north Ghana after ethnic violence erupted in March 2002.

In May 2002 President Kufuor inaugurated a reconciliation commission to investigate human rights violations during military rule and the commission began hearing testimonies in January 2003. In July 2004, the commission began work on a final report (due in October) that will include findings and recommendations.

POLITICAL SYSTEM

The head of state is an Executive President elected for a four-year term, renewable only once. The President nominates members of the Council of Ministers subject to approval by Parliament. The unicameral legislature, the Parliament, has 200 members directly elected for a four-year term.

HEAD OF STATE
President, John Kufuor, *elected* 28 December 2000, *sworn in* 7 January 2001
Vice-President, Aliu Mahama

SELECTED GOVERNMENT MEMBERS *as at July 2004*
Defence, Kwame Addo-Kufuor
Finance and Economic Planning, Yaw Osafo Maado
Foreign Affairs, Nana Akufo Addo
Interior, Hackman Owusu-Agyemang

OFFICE OF THE HIGH COMMISSION OF GHANA
13 Belgrave Square, London SW1X 8PN
T 020-7235 4142
High Commissioner, HE Isaac Osei, apptd 2001

BRITISH HIGH COMMISSION
Osu Link, off Gamel Abdul Nasser Avenue, PO Box 296, Accra
T (+233) (21) 221665/7010650
E high.commission.accra@fco.gov.uk
High Commissioner, Gordon Wetherell

BRITISH COUNCIL DIRECTOR, Terence Humphreys
Liberia Road, PO Box GP 771, Accra
T (+233) (21) 683068
E infoaccra@gh.britishcouncil.org

ECONOMY AND TRADE

Agriculture is the basis of the economy, generating 35 per cent of GDP. Crops include cocoa, rice, cassava, plantains, oranges and pineapples, groundnuts, corn, millet, oil palms, yams, maize and vegetables. Livestock is raised in uncultivated areas. Fishing is important in coastal areas and in the Volta lake and river system. Around 60 per cent of the workforce are employed in farming, forestry and fishing.

Manganese production ranks among the world's largest, with an average of 280,000 tonnes of ore being produced annually. Ghana is Africa's second largest gold producer after South Africa and gold is the main export, providing over 25 per cent of export revenue. Diamonds and bauxite are also produced. Other exports include pineapples, tuna, cocoa (which provides the largest single source of revenue, 25 per cent of export earnings), electricity, timber and prepared fish.

Principal imports are capital goods, semi-manufactures, consumables and petroleum.

Since 1966 the Volta Dams at Akosombo and Kpong have generated hydroelectric power for the processing of bauxite and fed a power transmission network for most of Ghana, Togo and Benin. There is considerable foreign investment in Ghana, and its economy has grown consistently.

GNI – US$5,700 million (2001); US$290 per capita (2001)
ANNUAL AVERAGE GROWTH OF GDP – 3.8 per cent (1998)
INFLATION RATE – 25.2 per cent (2000)
TOTAL EXTERNAL DEBT – US$7,200 million (2002)
FOREIGN DIRECT INVESTMENT – $US313 million (1997–2000)
IMPORTS – US$2,973 million (2000)
EXPORTS – US$1,795 million (1998)

BALANCE OF PAYMENTS
Trade – US$843 million deficit (2000)
Current Account – US$413 million deficit (2000)

Trade with UK	*2002*	*2003*
Imports from UK	£139,416,000	£152,219,000
Exports to UK	121,834,000	143,323,000

EDUCATION

The government of Ghana invests heavily in education in order to provide compulsory, free basic education for all children. Investment in 2003 constituted 25 per cent of all government spending. Ghana has one of Africa's oldest universities, at Legon in Accra.

ILLITERACY RATE – (m) 19.7 per cent; (f) 37.1 per cent (2000)
ENROLMENT (percentage of age group) – primary 79 per cent (1997)

MEDIA

The Ghana Broadcasting Corporation (GBC) is the state owned broadcaster. GBC operates a television network and various radio stations that transmit in English and Ghanaian dialects. TV3 is a private television channel, Multichoice is a cable television operator and Metro TV is jointly owned by the government and private backers. Ghana's private press and broadcasters operate without major restrictions.

CULTURE

The largest tribe in Ghana is the Ashanti. The Ashanti are famous for their skill as craftsmen, particularly in the areas of hand-carved stools, fertility dolls, and *kente* cloth, a cloth woven in thin strips of bright colour for ceremonial occasions. The Ewe tribe is also well-known for its *kente* cloth, which features geometric patterns.

GREECE

Elliniki Dimokratia – Hellenic Republic

AREA – 128,900 sq. km. Neighbours: Albania, Bulgaria and Macedonia (north), Turkey (east)
POPULATION – 10,623,000 (2001): 98 per cent Greek Orthodox, 1 per cent Catholic, 1 per cent Muslim. The language is Greek
CAPITAL – Athens (population 3,072,922, 1991); including ΨPiraeus and suburbs, 3,096,775 (1991 census)
MAJOR CITIES – ΨIráklion (Heraklion); Lárisa; ΨPátrai (Patras); ΨThessaloníki (Salonika); ΨVólos
CURRENCY – Euro (€) of 100 cents
NATIONAL ANTHEM – Imnos Eis Tin Eleftherian (Hymn To Freedom)
NATIONAL DAY – 25 March (Independence Day)
NATIONAL FLAG – Blue and white stripes with a white cross on a blue field in the canton
LIFE EXPECTANCY (years) – 78 (2001)
MORTALITY RATE (per 1,000 population) – 9
INFANT MORTALITY (per 1,000 births) – 5 (2001)
HIV / AIDS ADULT PREVALENCE – 0.2 per cent (2001)
DEATH PENALTY – Yes*
POPULATION GROWTH RATE – 0.4 per cent (1990–2001)
POPULATION DENSITY – 272 per sq. km (2001)

CLIMATE AND TERRAIN

The main areas are: Macedonia, Thrace, Epirus, Thessaly, Continental Greece, Crete and the Peloponnese. The main island groups are the Sporades, the Dodecanese or Southern Sporades, the Cyclades, the Ionian islands, and the Aegean islands (Chios, Lesbos, Limnos and Samos). Elevation extremes range from 2,917 m (Mount Olympus) at the highest point to 0 m (Mediterranean Sea) at the lowest. The coastline and islands have a Mediterranean climate with hot, dry summers and mild, wet winters. The average annual temperature in Athens ranges from 9°C in January to 28°C in July.

HISTORY AND POLITICS

Greece was under Turkish rule from the mid-15th century until a war of independence (1821–7) led to the establishment of a Greek kingdom in the Peloponnese in 1829. The remainder of Greece gradually became independent until the Dodecanese were returned by Italy in 1947. After the German Nazi occupation of 1941–4, a civil war between monarchist and Communist groups lasted from 1946 to 1949, and tension between right-wing and radical groups continued after 1949. In 1967 right-wing elements in the army seized power and established a military regime (the 'Greek Colonels'). The King went into voluntary exile in 1967. Unrest in Athens in 1973–4 intensified after the government was involved in the overthrow of President Makarios of Cyprus in July 1974, and led the Colonels to surrender power. Konstantinos Karamanlis (prime minister 1955–63) returned from exile to form a provisional government, and the first elections for ten years were held in 1974. The restoration of the monarchy was rejected by referendum on 8 December 1974 and Greece became a republic.

In 1975 a new constitution was introduced to mark the transition to a parliamentary democracy. The constitution was revised in 1986. From 1974 onwards Greek politics was dominated by Constantine Karamanlis, who founded the conservative New Democracy Party (ND), and Andreas Papandreou, who founded the left-wing Panhellenic Socialist Party (PASOK). The ND were elected with a total of 165 seats in the most recent general elections of March 2004, ousting PASOK (with 117 seats), which had been in power since 1994.

POLITICAL SYSTEM

In 1986 most executive power was transferred from the President to the Government. The unicameral 300-member Parliament *(Vouli)* is elected for a four-year term by universal adult suffrage under a system of proportional representation, with a 3 per cent threshold for parliamentary representation. The head of state is a President, elected by Parliament for a five-year term, renewable once only.

HEAD OF STATE

President of the Hellenic Republic, Konstandinos Stephanopoulos, *elected by parliament* 1995, *re-elected* 8 February 2000, *re-elected* 7 March 2004

SELECTED GOVERNMENT MEMBERS *as at July 2004*

Prime Minister, Minister for Culture, Costas Karamanlis
Foreign Minister, Petros Molyviatis
Foreign Affairs, Tasos Giannitsis
Interior, Public Administration and Decentralisation, Prokopis Pavlopoulos
National Defence, Spilios Spiliotopoulos
National Economy and Finance, Georgios Alogoskoufis

EMBASSY OF GREECE

1A Holland Park, London W11 3TP
T 020-7229 3850
E consulategeneral@greekembassy.org.uk
Ambassador Extraordinary and Plenipotentiary, HE Anastase Scopelitis, apptd 2003

BRITISH EMBASSY

1 Ploutarchou Street, GR-106 75 Athens
T (+30) (210) 727 2600
E information.athens@fco.gov.uk
Ambassador Extraordinary and Plenipotentiary, HE Sir David C. A. Madden, KCMG, apptd 1999

BRITISH COUNCIL DIRECTOR, Chris Hickey
17 Kolonaki Square, GR 106 73, Athens
T (+30) (210)369 2333
E general.enquiries@britishcouncil.gr

DEFENCE

The Army has 1,723 main battle tanks, 1,440 armoured personnel carriers and 501 armoured infantry fighting vehicles. The Navy has eight submarines, two destroyers, 12 frigates, 40 patrol and coastal vessels and 18 armed helicopters. The Air Force has a total of 418 combat aircraft.

Greece maintains 1,250 army personnel in Cyprus. There are 310 US military personnel stationed in Greece.

MILITARY EXPENDITURE – 4.4 per cent of GDP (2002)
MILITARY PERSONNEL – 166,600: Army 114,000, Navy 19,000, Air Force 33,000; Paramilitaries 4,000
CONSCRIPTION DURATION – Up to 19 months

ECONOMY AND TRADE

The principal minerals are nickel, bauxite, iron ore, iron pyrites, manganese magnesite, chrome, lead, zinc and emery. The chief industries are textiles (cotton, wool and synthetics), chemicals, cement, glass, metallurgy, shipbuilding, domestic electrical equipment and footwear, the production of aluminium, nickel, iron and steel products, tyres, chemicals, fertilisers and sugar (from locally-grown beet). Food processing and ancillary industries are also expanding.

In March 2002 Greece and Turkey signed an agreement to build a gas pipeline which will supply Greece with gas from Turkey.

Tourism is a major industry, accounting for an estimated 15 per cent of annual GDP and contributing more than US$8,000 million every year in foreign exchange earnings.

Though there has been substantial industrialisation, agriculture still employs a fifth of the working population and contributes 8.1 per cent of GDP. The most important agricultural products are tobacco, wheat, cotton, sugar, rice, fruit (olives, peaches, vines, oranges, lemons, figs, almonds and currant-vines). Exports of fresh fruit, currants and vegetables are an important contributor to the economy.

In March 1998 the drachma was admitted to the ERM; Greece became a member of EMU on 1 January 2001 since when it has participated in the European Single Currency. The euro replaced the drachma in January 2002.

GNI – US$121,000 million (2001); US$11,430 per capita (2001)
ANNUAL AVERAGE GROWTH OF GDP – 4.1 per cent (2000)
INFLATION RATE – 3.2 per cent (2000)
UNEMPLOYMENT – 11.1 per cent (2000)
FOREIGN DIRECT INVESTMENT – US$3,051 million (1997–2000)
IMPORTS – US$31,164 million (2002)
EXPORTS – US$10,315 million (2002)

BALANCE OF PAYMENTS
Trade – US$21,452 million deficit (2002)
Current Account – US$10,405 million deficit (2002)

Trade with UK	*2002*	*2003*
Imports from UK	£1,140,800,000	£885,063,000
Exports to UK	546,400,000	463,517,000

TRANSPORT INFRASTRUCTURE
Railways are state owned, with the exception of the Athens–Piraeus Electric Railway. There are 9,255 km of motorways and 29,350 km of provincial roads. There is an extensive ferry system that operates between the islands and the mainland.

EDUCATION
Education is free of charge and compulsory from the age of six to 15 and is maintained by state grants. There are eighteen universities and several other institutes of higher education.

ILLITERACY RATE – (m) 1.5 per cent; (f) 4.0 per cent (2000)
ENROLMENT (percentage of age group) – primary 93 per cent (1997); secondary 95 per cent (1997); tertiary 47 per cent (1997)

MEDIA
Although the Greek media is considerably free from regulation, editors and publishers risk prosecution should their material be deemed offensive to religious beliefs or the President. A sizeable proportion of the country's 1,700 private radio and television stations are unlicensed. In 2004 there were an estimated 1.7 million internet users.

CULTURE
Greek civilisation emerged *c.*1300 BC and the poems of Homer, which were probably current *c.*800 BC, record the struggle between the Achaeans of Greece and the Phrygians of Troy (1194 to 1184 BC).

The spoken language of modern Greece is descended from the Common Greek of Alexander the Great's empire. *Katharevousa*, a conservative literary dialect evolved by Adamantios Korais (Diamant Coray, 1748–1833) and used for official and technical matters, has been phased out. Novels and poetry are mostly in *Dimotiki*, a progressive literary dialect which owes much to John Psycharis (1854–1929). The poets Dionysios Solomos (1798–1857), Constantine P. Cavafy (1863–1933) and Angelos Sikelianos (1884–1951) have won a European reputation. George Seferis (1900–71) and Odysseus Elytis (1911–96) have both won the Nobel Prize for Literature in 1963 and 1979 respectively.

GRENADA

The State of Grenada

AREA – 345 sq. km
POPULATION – 94,000 (2001), of which about 75 per cent are of African descent; there are minorities of Europeans and Indians. The language is English
CAPITAL – ΨSt George's (population, 4,788, 1981)
CURRENCY – East Caribbean dollar (EC$) of 100 cents
NATIONAL ANTHEM – Hail Grenada, Land Of Ours
NATIONAL DAY – 7 February (Independence Day)
NATIONAL FLAG – Divided diagonally into yellow and green triangles within a red border containing six yellow stars, a yellow star on a red disc in the centre and a nutmeg on the green triangle in the hoist
LIFE EXPECTANCY (years) – 65 (2001)
MORTALITY RATE (per 1,000 population) – 7.46 (2003)
INFANT MORTALITY (per 1,000 births) – 20 (2001)
DEATH PENALTY – No
POPULATION BELOW POVERTY LINE – 32 per cent (2000)
POPULATION GROWTH RATE – 0.3 per cent (1990–2001)
POPULATION DENSITY – 272 per sq. km (2001)

CLIMATE AND TERRAIN
The most southerly of the Windward Islands. Grenada comprises three islands – Grenada (the largest at 18 km in length and 34 km in width), Carriacou and Petite Martinique. Elevation extremes range from 840 m (Mount Saint Catherine) at the highest point to 0 m (Caribbean Sea) at the lowest. The climate is subtropical with a wet season running from June to December. Grenada is within a hurricane zone.

HISTORY AND POLITICS
Discovered by Columbus in 1498, and named Concepción, Grenada was originally colonised by France and was ceded to Great Britain in 1763. It became a Crown colony in 1877, an Associated State in 1967 and

an independent nation within the Commonwealth on 7 February 1974.

The government was overthrown in 1979 by the New Jewel Movement led by Maurice Bishop and a People's Revolutionary Government (PRG) was set up. In October 1983 disagreements within the PRG led to the death of Prime Minister Bishop, whose government was replaced by a Revolutionary Military Council. These events prompted the intervention of Caribbean and US forces. The Governor-General installed an advisory council to act as an interim government until a general election was held in December 1984. A phased withdrawal of US forces was completed by June 1985.

In the general election of November 2003 Dr Keith Mitchell, leader of the New National Party (NNP), was elected to his third successive term of office when his party won eight of a possible 15 seats.

POLITICAL SYSTEM
Queen Elizabeth II is head of state and is represented by a Governor-General. Legislative power is vested in a bicameral Parliament consisting of an elected 15-member House of Representatives and a 13-member Senate appointed by the Governor-General.
Governor-General, HE Sir Daniel Williams, GCMG, QC, apptd 1996

SELECTED GOVERNMENT MEMBERS *as at July 2004*
Prime Minister, National Security and Information, Keith Mitchell
Finance, Trade, Industry and Planning, Anthony Boatswain
Foreign Affairs and International Trade, Legal Affairs, Carriacou and Petit Martinique Affairs, Elvin Nimrod

HIGH COMMISSION FOR GRENADA
5 Chandos Street, London W1G 9DG
T 020-7631 4277
E grenada@high-commission.demon.co.uk
High Commissioner, HE Ruth Elizabeth Rouse, apptd 1999

BRITISH HIGH COMMISSION
Netherlands Building, Grand Anse, St George's
T (+1 473) 440 3536/ 3222
E bhcgrenada@caribsurf.com
High Commissioner, C. John White, resident at Bridgetown, Barbados

ECONOMY AND TRADE
The service industries account for 62 per cent of employment and 68.4 per cent of GDP. The economy was principally agrarian, but agriculture now employs only 24 per cent of the workforce and produces seven per cent of GDP. Manufacturing consists of processing agricultural products and the production of textiles, concrete, aluminium and handicrafts. Tourism is the main foreign exchange earner. In 2001 123,351 tourists visited Grenada.

The most important exports are nutmeg and cocoa. Grenada is the world's second-largest producer of nutmeg, accounting for about a third of the world's annual supply. Imports include machinery and transport equipment, livestock, foodstuffs and beverages, manufactured goods, and fuels. The main trading partners are the USA, Germany, Bangladesh, the Netherlands, France, the UK and Trinidad and Tobago.

GNI – US$360 million (2001); US$3,610 per capita (2001)
ANNUAL AVERAGE GROWTH OF GDP – 3.6 per cent (1998)
INFLATION RATE – 2.2 per cent (2000)
UNEMPLOYMENT – 11.0 per cent (2000)
TOTAL EXTERNAL DEBT – US$207 million (2000)
IMPORTS – US$200 million (1998)
EXPORTS – US$27 million (1998)

BALANCE OF PAYMENTS
Trade – US$136 million deficit (2000)
Current Account – US$79 million deficit (2000)

Trade with UK	*2002*	*2003*
Imports from UK	£5,496,000	£7,485,000
Exports to UK	1,307,000	1,735,000

MEDIA
There are no daily newspapers but several weekly publications. There are two television stations: GBN TV, which is operated by the public broadcaster Grenada Broadcasting Network, and MTV which is owned by the US company Viacom. There are several radio stations jointly owned by the public and private sector.

GUATEMALA

República de Guatemala – Republic of Guatemala

AREA – 108,400 sq. km. Neighbours: Mexico (north and west), El Salvador, Honduras and Belize (east)
POPULATION – 11,687,000 (2001): 56 per cent mestizo, 44 per cent Amerindian. The language is Spanish, but 40 per cent of the population speak an Indian language
CAPITAL – Guatemala City (population, 1,675,589, 1990 estimate)
MAJOR CITIES – Mazatenango; ΨPuerto Barrios; Quetzaltenango; Cobán; Escuintla
CURRENCY – Quetzal (Q) of 100 centavos
NATIONAL ANTHEM – Guatemala Feliz (Guatemala Be Praised)
NATIONAL DAY – 15 September
NATIONAL FLAG – Three vertical bands, blue, white, blue; coat of arms on white stripe
LIFE EXPECTANCY (years) – 65 (2001)
MORTALITY RATE (per 1,000 population) – 6.78 (2003)
INFANT MORTALITY (per 1,000 births) – 43 (2001)
HIV / AIDS ADULT PREVALENCE RATE – 1 per cent (2001)
DEATH PENALTY – Yes
POPULATION BELOW POVERTY LINE – 75 per cent (2002)
POPULATION GROWTH RATE – 2.6 per cent (1990–2001)
POPULATION DENSITY – 108 per sq. km (2001)
URBAN POPULATION – 40 per cent (2001)
MILITARY EXPENDITURE – 0.8 per cent of GDP (2002)
MILITARY PERSONNEL – 31,400: Army 29,200, Navy 1,500, Air Force 700; Paramilitaries 19,000
CONSCRIPTION DURATION – 30 months (selective)

ILLITERACY RATE – (m) 23.8 per cent; (f) 38.7 per cent (2000)
ENROLMENT (percentage of age group) – primary 88 per cent (1997); secondary 26 per cent (1997); tertiary 9 per cent (1997)

CLIMATE AND TERRAIN

Guatemala is a mountainous country and has 33 volcanoes. Elevation extremes range from 4,211 m (Volcan Tajumulco) at the highest point to 0 m (Pacific Ocean) at the lowest. The climate is tropical but is cooler in the highlands. The wet season runs from May to October and mudslides and hurricanes can occur during this period. There are also frequent minor earth tremors and some earthquakes.

HISTORY AND POLITICS

Guatemala was under Spanish rule from 1523 until gaining independence in 1821. It formed part of the Confederation of Central America from 1823 to 1835.

After a series of military coups, civilian rule was restored with the election of a Constituent Assembly in 1984 and the promulgation of a new constitution in 1985. In May 1993 President Serrano partially suspended the constitution and attempted to rule by decree but was effectively ousted by the army on 1 June. Ramiro de León Carpio was elected president by congress to serve out Serrano's term to January 1996.

The legislative elections of 2003 were won by Gran Alianza Nacional (GANA) with 49 seats. The presidential elections were won by Oscar Berger of GANA with 54 per cent of the vote.

INSURGENCY

Since 1960 the armed forces had been fighting insurgency by the left-wing, mainly Mayan Indian, guerrillas of the Guatemalan Revolutionary National Unity Movement (URNG). Some 200,000 were killed in the fighting. Government–URNG negotiations began in 1991, leading to a reduction in fighting and agreements in 1993. In March 1994 a human rights accord was reached under which a 300-strong UN Observer Mission (MINUGUA) was established in November 1994 to supervise the implementation of government–URNG accords. An accord recognising the rights of the indigenous population was signed in March 1995, but in a referendum held on 16 May 1999, constitutional reforms which would have amended the constitution to allow for the implementation of peace accords were rejected. Representatives of the four rebel groups comprising the URNG signed a peace treaty with the government in December 1996; an independent commission into the 36-year civil war, set up under the 1996 peace treaty, published a report on 25 February 1999 which concluded that the army had committed 93 per cent of the acts of genocide against the indigenous Mayan population. In August 2000 President Portillo admitted the state's responsibility for atrocities committed during the civil war and vowed that those responsible would be prosecuted. Three per cent of those military personnel found to be responsible for atrocities have been prosecuted.

POLITICAL SYSTEM

Executive power is vested in the President, who is directly elected for a single four-year term. He appoints the Cabinet. Legislative authority is vested in the National Congress, whose 158 members (increased from 113 in the 2003 Legislative elections) are directly elected for a four-year term.

HEAD OF STATE
President, Oscar Berger, *elected* December 2003, *sworn in* 14 January 2004
Vice-President, Eduardo Stein Barillas

SELECTED GOVERNMENT MEMBERS *as at July 2004*
Defence, Gen. Cesar Augusto Mendez
Economy, Marcio Cuevas
Foreign Affairs, Jorge Briz Abularach
Interior, Manuel Arturo Soto Aguirre

EMBASSY OF GUATEMALA
13 Fawcett Street, London SW10 9HN
T 020-7351 3042
Ambassador Extraordinary and Plenipotentiary, HE Alberto Sandoval, apptd 2003

BRITISH EMBASSY
Edificio Torre Internacional, Nivel 11, 16 Calle 0-55, Zona 10, Guatemala City
T (+502) 367 5425/6/7/8/9
E embassy@intelnett.com
Ambassador Extraordinary and Plenipotentiary, Richard D. Lavers, apptd 2001

ECONOMY AND TRADE

Agriculture provides 22.5 per cent of GDP and employs half of the workforce. The principal export is coffee (approximately a third of exports), with other exports including manufactured goods, sugar, bananas (15 per cent of exports) and cardamom. The chief imports are raw materials and semi-manufactures, capital goods, consumer goods, and fuel oils. Guatemala has a free-trade agreement with El Salvador, Honduras and Mexico; the USA is also one of the country's main trading partners.

On 5 April 2002, the IMF announced that a one-year standby credit of US$67 million had been approved in order to underpin the government's economic policies and the implementation of the 1996 peace accords. In June 2003 a further US$84 million of credit was made available until 2004.

GNI – US$19,600 million (2001); US$1,680 per capita (2001)
ANNUAL AVERAGE GROWTH OF GDP – 3.3 per cent (2000)
INFLATION RATE – 6.0 per cent (2000)
TOTAL EXTERNAL DEBT – US$4,622 million (2000)
FOREIGN DIRECT INVESTMENT – US$1,148 million (1997–2000)
IMPORTS – US$6,078 million (2002)
EXPORTS – US$2,232 million (2002)

BALANCE OF PAYMENTS
Trade – US$2,950 million deficit (2002)
Current Account – US$1,193 million deficit (2002)

Trade with UK	*2002*	*2003*
Imports from UK	£33,752,000	£25,739,000
Exports to UK	13,756,000	15,452,000

CULTURE

The ruins of Guatemala's ancient Mayan civilisation (at its height between AD 600 and AD 900) dot the country. Influences of African culture can be seen along the Caribbean coast. Guatemala has been home to many distinguished writers including Miguel Angel Asturias (1899–1974), who won the Nobel Prize for Literature in 1967.

GUINEA

République de Guinée – Republic of Guinea

AREA – 245,857 sq. km. Neighbours: Guinea-Bissau (west), Senegal and Mali (north), Côte d'Ivoire (east), Sierra Leone and Liberia (south)
POPULATION – 7,613,870 (2001 estimate); the official language is French; Fullah, Malinké and Soussou are the indigenous languages
CAPITAL – ΨConakry (population, 763,000)
MAJOR CITIES – Kankan; Kindia; Labé; Mamou; N'Zérékoré; Siguiri
CURRENCY – Guinea franc of 100 centimes
NATIONAL ANTHEM – Liberté
NATIONAL DAY – 2 October (Anniversary of the Proclamation of Independence)
NATIONAL FLAG – Three vertical stripes of red, yellow and green
MORTALITY RATE (per 1,000 population) – 15.7 (2003)
HIV / AIDS ADULT PREVALENCE RATE – 1.54 per cent (2001)
DEATH PENALTY – Yes
POPULATION BELOW POVERTY LINE – 40 per cent (2001)
POPULATION DENSITY – 30 per sq. km (1999)
MILITARY EXPENDITURE – 1.8 per cent of GDP (2002)
MILITARY PERSONNEL – 9,700: Army 8,500, Navy 400, Air Force 800; Paramilitaries 2,600
CONSCRIPTION DURATION – Two years
ILLITERACY RATE – (m) 44.9 per cent; (f) 73.0 per cent (2000)
ENROLMENT (percentage of age group) – primary 54 per cent (1997); secondary 14 per cent (1997); tertiary 1 per cent (1997)

CLIMATE AND TERRAIN

Guinea has a flat coastal plain that rises to a mountainous interior. Elevation extremes range from 1,752 m (Mont Nimba) at the highest point to 0 m at the lowest (Atlantic Ocean). There is a wet season from June to November and the average daily temperature is 27°C.

HISTORY AND POLITICS

Guinea was separated from Senegal in 1891 and administered by France as a separate colony. On 2 October 1958 Guinea became an independent republic. French President Charles de Gaulle offered France's West African colonies a choice between autonomy and immediate independence in 1958. Ahmed Sekou Touré, who was elected president in 1961, chose full independence. The ensuing flight of French nationals from the country resulted in the destruction of much of Guinea's infrastructure. Four decades of economic stagnation followed as Sekou Touré first attempted to ally Guinea to the Soviet Union, then, when the relationship with the USSR soured, he imposed a series of socialist reforms. Touré died in 1984, shortly after making limited free-market reforms. A military coup soon followed, led by Lansana Conté.

A presidential election held on 14 December 1998 was won by the incumbent President Lansana Conté with 54 per cent of the vote. Legislative elections took place on 30 June 2002 and were won by President Conté's Party of Unity and Progress (PUP), which gained 85 of the 114 National Assembly seats. Presidential elections in 2003 returned Conté to power with a majority vote of 95 per cent, although several of the main opposition parties did not take part. In May 2004 Prime Minister Francois Fall resigned and went into exile after just two months in the job, protesting that President Conté was blocking his attempts at political and economic reform.

HEAD OF STATE
President, Maj.-Gen. Lansana Conté, *took power* 3 April 1984, *elected* 19 December 1993, *re-elected* 14 December 1998 and 21 December 2003

SELECTED GOVERNMENT MEMBERS *as at July 2004*
Prime Minister, vacant
Minister of Security, Moussa Sampil
Economic Affairs, Finance, Mady Kaba Kamara
Foreign Affairs, Mamady Conde

EMBASSY OF THE REPUBLIC OF GUINEA
51 rue de la Faisanderie, F-75016 Paris, France
T (+33) (1) 4704 8148
Ambassador Extraordinary and Plenipotentiary, Ibrahima Chérif Haidara, apptd 2003

BRITISH CONSULATE GENERAL
BP 834 Conakry, Guinea
T (+224) 455 807/456 020/452 959
British Ambassador, HE Helen Horn, resident at Freetown, Sierra Leone

ECONOMY AND TRADE

Guinea is the world's second largest exporter of bauxite, and holds over 30 per cent of global bauxite resources. Guinea also exports alumina (a by-product of bauxite), gold, diamonds, coffee, fish and agricultural products. Rice, coffee, pineapples, sweet potatoes and cassava all form part of Guinea's agricultural produce.
GNI – US$3,345 million (2000); US$410 per capita (2001)
ANNUAL AVERAGE GROWTH OF GDP – 5.0 per cent (1998)
TOTAL EXTERNAL DEBT – US$3,388 million (2000)

BALANCE OF PAYMENTS
Trade – US$94 million surplus (1999)
Current Account – US$152 million deficit (1999)

Trade with UK	*2002*	*2003*
Imports from UK	£26,625,000	£26,180,000
Exports to UK	2,934,000	1,393,000

TRANSPORT INFRASTRUCTURE

Guinea has over 1,000 km of railway, 30,000 km of roads and 1,295 km of navigable waterways. There are three major ports: Boke, Conakry and Kamsar. Guinea has 15 airports including five with surfaced runways.

MEDIA AND CULTURE

There are five national newspapers and a single state run television broadcaster. The varied musical tradition of Guinea remains strong through the verse of the *griots*, a social caste of professional musicians.

GUINEA-BISSAU

Repûblica da Guiné-Bissau – Republic of Guinea-Bissau

AREA – 36,125 sq. km. Neighbours: Senegal (north), Guinea (east and south)
POPULATION – 1,315,822 (2001 estimate). The main ethnic groups are the Balante, Malinké, Fulani, Mandjako and Pepel. The official language is Portuguese; most of the population speak Guinean Creole
CAPITAL – ΨBissau (population, 195,400, 1991)
CURRENCY – Franc CFA
NATIONAL ANTHEM – É Patria Amada (This Is Our Beloved Country)
NATIONAL DAY – 24 September (Independence Day)
NATIONAL FLAG – Horizontal bands of yellow over green with vertical red band in the hoist charged with a black star
MORTALITY RATE (per 1,000 population) – 16.62 (2003)
HIV / AIDS ADULT PREVALENCE – 2.8 per cent (2001)
DEATH PENALTY – No (abolished 1993)
POPULATION GROWTH RATE – 2.2 per cent (1990–2001)
POPULATION DENSITY – 33 per sq. km (1999)
MILITARY EXPENDITURE – 1.6 per cent of GDP (2002)
MILITARY PERSONNEL – 9,250: Army 6,800, Navy 350, Air Force 100, Paramilitaries 2,000
CONSCRIPTION DURATION – Selective conscription
ILLITERACY RATE – (m) 40.3 per cent; (f) 81.0 per cent (2000)
ENROLMENT (percentage of age group) – primary 62 per cent (1997)

CLIMATE AND TERRAIN

Elevation extremes range from 300 m (unnamed location) at the highest point to 0 m (Atlantic Ocean) at the lowest. Guinea-Bissau has a low coastal plain that rises to savannah in the east. Average yearly temperatures range from 24°C in January to 27°C in October with a wet season from June to November.

HISTORY AND POLITICS

A part of the ancient African empire of Mali, Guinea-Bissau was once the kingdom of Gabú. In 1446 Portuguese traders reached the coast and Guinea-Bissau became a centre of the Portuguese slave trade. Though a Portuguese colony, Guinea-Bissau remained in a state of under-development throughout the colonial period. Since its independence in 1974, Guinea-Bissau has suffered severe political instability. Until 1994 the country was governed by the one-party socialist regime of the PAIGC (African Party for the Independence of Guinea and Cape Verde) and military rule.

An army revolt against General Joao Bernardo 'Nino' Vieira in 1998 led to fighting around the capital, Bissau, and was only quelled by troops from ECOMOG, the military force of the Economic Community of West African States (ECOWAS). Withdrawal of ECOMOG troops in 1999 saw a return to conflict which ended with the exile of General Vieira.

The presidential elections of 1999 saw Kumba Yala returned to office with 72 per cent of the vote. Relations between Yala and the military, however, were fraught, and in September 2003 the president was deposed in a bloodless coup. ECOWAS intervened and the military was persuaded to accept a form of constitutional government that included a large civilian element. A transitional government was set up including an interim president and prime minister. In the legislative elections of March 2004, the African Independance Party of Guinea and Cape Verde (AIPGCV) won 45 seats in the National People's Assembly with 34 per cent of the vote, while the Party for Social Renewal (PSR) won 35 seats and 24.8 per cent of the vote. The third major party, the United Social Democratic Party (USDP), won 27 seats and 16.1 per cent of the overall vote. Presidential elections are due in 2005.

POLITICAL SYSTEM

A new Constitution, which limited the tenure of the Presidency to two terms, was adopted in July 1999. Under the constitution, the President is the head of government and appoints the Council of Ministers. There is a unicameral legislature, the Assembleia Nacional Popular (National People's Assembly), composed of 102 members elected by universal suffrage for a four-year term.

HEAD OF STATE

Interim President, Henrique Rosa, *took office* 28 September 2003
President of the National Transitional Council, Gen. Verissimo Correia Seabra

SELECTED GOVERNMENT MEMBERS *as at July 2004*

Prime Minister, Carlos Gomez
Economy and Finance, Joao al Hadji Amadu Fadia
Foreign Affairs, Soares Sambu
Internal Administration, Lassana Siedi
National Defence, Daniel Gomes

EMBASSY OF THE REPUBLIC OF GUINEA-BISSAU

94 rue St Lazare, Paris F-75009, France
T (+33) (1) 4526 1851
Ambassador Extraordinary and Plenipotentiary, vacant
Chargé d'Affaires, Fali Embalo

BRITISH CONSULATE

Mavegro Int., CP100, Bissau
T (+245) 201 224/201 216
British Ambassador, HE Alan Burner, resident at Dakar, Senegal

ECONOMY AND TRADE

The economy of Guinea-Bissau is almost exclusively based on agriculture and fishing. Guinea-Bissau exports fish, seafood, peanuts, palm kernels and timber. Although there is the possibility of offshore oil reserves, Guinea-Bissau has very few natural resources.

GNI – US$221 million (2000); US$160 per capita (2001)
ANNUAL AVERAGE GROWTH OF GDP – 2.4 per cent (1998)
INFLATION RATE – 8.6 per cent (2000)
TOTAL EXTERNAL DEBT – US$942 million (2000)

IMPORTS – US$62 million (2000)
EXPORTS – US$62 million (2000)

BALANCE OF PAYMENTS
Trade – US$14 million deficit (1997)
Current Account – US$30 million deficit (1997)

Trade with UK	*2002*	*2003*
Imports from UK	£1,105,000	£804,000
Exports to UK	1,000	215,000

TRANSPORT INFRASTRUCTURE

Guinea-Bissau has 4,400 km of roads, of which only 453 km are surfaced. There are 28 airports, three have surfaced runways. There are no railways.

MEDIA AND CULTURE

Of the four national newspapers, three are privately owned. Guinea-Bissau's single television station, Radio Televisao de Guinea-Bissau (RTGB), is state run. RTP Africa is a television broadcaster set up by Portugal in each of its former colonies. Radio consists of the national broadcaster, Radio Nacional, and two commercial stations, Radio Mavegro and Radio Pindjiguiti.

Guinea-Bissau retains much of the musical tradition of the empire of Mali. The country has many *griots*, a social caste of professional musicians. This musical tradition of the Mandinga people consists of epics and songs often accompanied by the 21-string *kora*.

GUYANA

The Co-operative Republic of Guyana

AREA – 214,969 sq. km. Neighbours: Venezuela (west), Brazil (west and south), Suriname (east)
POPULATION – 697,181 (2001 estimate): 51 per cent East Indian (mainly rural), 30 per cent African (mainly urban), Amerindians, Europeans, Chinese and people of mixed descent; 50 per cent Christian, 35 per cent Hindu, less than 10 per cent Muslim. Guyana is the only English-speaking country in South America
CAPITAL – ΨGeorgetown (population, 250,000)
MAJOR TOWNS – Corriverton; Linden; ΨNew Amsterdam
CURRENCY – Guyana dollar (G$) of 100 cents
NATIONAL ANTHEM – Dear Land Of Guyana
NATIONAL DAYS – 26 May (Independence Day); 23 February (Republic Day)
NATIONAL FLAG – Green with a yellow, white-bordered triangle based on the hoist and surmounted by a red, black-bordered triangle
MORTALITY RATE (per 1,000 population) – 9.27 (2003)
HIV / AIDS ADULT PREVALENCE RATE – 2.7 per cent (2001)
DEATH PENALTY – Yes
POPULATION GROWTH RATE – 0.8 per cent (1990–2001)
POPULATION DENSITY – 4 per sq. km (1999)
URBAN POPULATION – 38 per cent (2001)
MILITARY EXPENDITURE – 0.7 per cent of GDP (2002)
MILITARY PERSONNEL – 1,600: Army 1,400, Navy 100, Air Force 100; Paramilitaries 1,500

CLIMATE AND TERRAIN

The interior of the country is covered in forest, with elevation extremes ranging from 2,835 m (Mount Roraima) at the highest point to 0 m (Atlantic Ocean) at the lowest. Guyana's average daily temperature is 28°C.

HISTORY AND POLITICS

Carib and Arawak Indians inhabited the coastal region of Guyana and began trading with Dutch merchants who founded the first European settlement in 1615. Guyana became an important producer of sugar produced on plantations worked by African slaves. Britain became rulers of Guyana in 1796 and, with the addition of several new territories by 1831, created British Guiana.

Guyana (formerly British Guiana) became independent on 26 May 1966, with a Governor-General appointed by Queen Elizabeth II. It became a republic on 23 February 1970. Guyana was ruled by Forbes Burnham from 1970 to 1985. Burnham, who had co-founded Guyana's first political party, the People's Progressive Party (PPP), has been widely criticised for his autocratic style of government. As a result Guyanese politics has been characterised by suspicious elections, a deterioration in respect for civil liberties and human rights, and two major political assassinations. Bharrat Jagdeo was elected president in 2001 with the PPP winning 34 seats, securing its third consecutive term of office; the PNC won 27 seats. Jagdeo's premiership has seen attempts to encourage joint action between the government and the private sector and soon after the elections he called for reconciliation between the PPP and Guyana's other political parties in order to prevent further political violence.

POLITICAL SYSTEM
The 1980 Constitution provides for an executive President who serves a five-year term, and a National Assembly of 65 members, of which 53 are elected nationally by proportional representation and 12 are regional representatives.

HEAD OF STATE
President, Bharrat Jagdeo, *succeeded* 11 August 1999, *elected* 19 March 2001

SELECTED GOVERNMENT MEMBERS *as at July 2004*
Prime Minister, Public Works, Samuel Hinds
Finance, Saisnaraine Kowlessar
Foreign Affairs, Samuel Rudy Insanally
Home Affairs, Ronald Gajraj

HIGH COMMISSION FOR GUYANA
3 Palace Court, Bayswater Road, London W2 4LP
T 020-7229 7684
E ghc.1@ic24.net
High Commissioner, HE Laleshwar Singh, apptd 1993

BRITISH HIGH COMMISSION
44 Main Street (PO Box 10849), Georgetown
T (+592) (22) 65881/2/3/4
High Commissioner, HE Stephen Hiscock, apptd 2002

ECONOMY AND TRADE

The IMF classes Guyana as a Highly Indebted Poor Country. The sugar industry, which accounts for ten per cent of the GDP, is Guyana's most important industry. In 1998 Guyana suffered negative growth of −1.8 per cent after six consecutive years of growth of at least five per cent. Donor agencies and the World Bank play a major role in funding development projects. Agriculture is the principal economic activity, accounting for 39 per cent of GDP and employing 19 per cent of the workforce. Main export items include sugar, gold, rice and bauxite. Diamonds are also mined. There is some cattle ranching, and oil deposits have been recently discovered. Emphasis is now being placed on eco-tourism.

GNP – US$652 million (2000); US$860 per capita (2000)

ANNUAL AVERAGE GROWTH OF GDP – 3.0 per cent (1998)

INFLATION RATE – 6.1 per cent (2000)

TOTAL EXTERNAL DEBT – US$1,455 million (2000)

IMPORTS – US$563 million (2002)

EXPORTS – US$493 million (2001)

Trade with UK	*2002*	*2003*
Imports from UK	£18,545,000	£23,026,000
Exports to UK	51,451,000	51,434,000

TRANSPORT INFRASTRUCTURE

Guyana has five main ports. There are a total of 49 airports, though only eight have surfaced runways. There is a very limited railway system of only 187 km. Roads and navigable waterways form the main arteries of communication in the country, though only 590 km of roads, out of a total of 7,970 km are surfaced.

EDUCATION

Education is compulsory between the ages of six and 14. Nursery, primary and secondary education is free of charge but fees are payable for study at the University of Guyana. There are several technical and vocational institutions, as well as some 30 adult education schools. There are also a number of technical and vocational institutions not under the aegis of the Ministry of Education.

ILLITERACY RATE – (m) 1.1 per cent; (f) 1.9 per cent (2000)

ENROLMENT (percentage of age group) – primary 87 per cent (1995); secondary 66 per cent (1995); tertiary 11 per cent (1996)

MEDIA AND CULTURE

Guyana has six radio stations and three television stations. One television station is state run and the remaining two are privately owned.

Traditions in the visual arts and music are particularly strong in a country distinguished by a large number of distinct cultures. The novelist E. R. Braithwaite (b. 1920) is Guyana's most famous writer.

HAITI

République d'Haïti – Republic of Haiti

AREA – 27,750 sq. km. Neighbour: Dominican Republic (east)

POPULATION – 6,964,549 (2001 estimate) of which 90 per cent are black and 10 per cent mulatto (mixed race). Some 80 per cent of the population are Roman Catholic and 16 per cent Protestant; around half the population also practices Voodoo which was recognised as an official religion in April 2003. Both French and Creole are regarded as official languages. French is the language of government and the press but it is only spoken by the educated mulatto minority. The usual language is Creole

CAPITAL – ΨPort-au-Prince (population, 884,472, 1996 estimate)

MAJOR CITIES – ΨCap Haïtien; Carrefour; Delmas

CURRENCY – Gourde of 100 centimes

NATIONAL ANTHEM – La Dessalinienne

NATIONAL DAY – 1 January

NATIONAL FLAG – Horizontally blue over red

MORTALITY RATE (per 1,000 population) – 13.36 (2003)

HIV / AIDS ADULT PREVALENCE – 6.1 per cent (2001)

DEATH PENALTY – No (abolished 1987)

POPULATION BELOW POVERTY LINE – 80 per cent (2002)

POPULATION GROWTH RATE – 2.1 per cent (1990–2001)

POPULATION DENSITY – 281 per sq. km (1999)

URBAN POPULATION – 35.7 per cent (2000)

MILITARY EXPENDITURE – 1.0 per cent of GDP (2002)

CLIMATE AND TERRAIN

Elevation extremes range from 2,680 m (Chaine de la Selle) at the highest point to 0 m (Caribbean Sea) at the lowest.

HISTORY AND POLITICS

Haiti, the western third of the island of Hispaniola, was ceded to France by Spain in 1697. It was named Saint Domingue and was popularly known as the 'pearl of the Antilles' as it became the richest colony in the French empire. This wealth was generated by African slaves working in the sugar and coffee plantations. In 1791 Toussaint L'Ouverture, Jean-Jacques Dessalines and Henri Christophe led a slave rebellion which expelled the French from the northern part of the colony and instigated a long war between freed slaves and colonists. By 1804 the Republic of Haiti was founded, marking the inception of the world's first black republic and, after the USA, the oldest republic in the western hemisphere.

Haiti, however, has enjoyed very little stability since. The country endured 22 changes of government between 1843 and 1915. The resulting upheaval led the USA to intervene in 1915. This marked the beginning of 19 years of US occupation and Haiti was restored to sovereign rule in 1934.

In 1957 the Duvalier family gained control of the country and began a dictatorial rule which was to last 29 years. A series of transitional governments followed before Jean-Bertrand Aristide won 67 per cent of the vote in the presidential election of 1990. Aristide was deposed in a coup the following year which instigated a period of military rule. The severity of the military's repression prompted the UN to authorise US-led intervention in 1994. Though re-elected in 2000, Aristide's administration became the focus of mounting accusations of corruption. In 2004 an anti-Aristide rebel movement seized a number of towns and cities. Aristide went into exile, accusing the USA of forcing him from the country. US and French troops have remained in Haiti as a another interim government attempts to disarm the remaining rebels.

POLITICAL SYSTEM
The head of state is the President, directly elected for a five-year term that may not be renewed immediately. The National Assembly is the bicameral legislature; the lower house, the Chamber of Deputies, has 83 members directly elected for four years. The upper house or Senate has 27 members elected for six years; one-third of the Senators are elected every two years. The President appoints the Prime Minister, who must be approved by the National Assembly.

HEAD OF STATE
Interim President, Boniface Alexandre, *sworn in* 8 March 2004

SELECTED GOVERNMENT MEMBERS *as at 2004*
Prime Minister, Gerard Latourte
Foreign and Religious Affairs, Yvon Simeon
Finance and Economy, Henri Bazin
Interior, Herard Abraham

BRITISH AMBASSADOR, HE Andrew Ashcroft, apptd 2002, resident at Santo Domingo, Dominican Republic

BRITISH CONSULATE, Hotel Montana (PO Box 1302), Port-au-Prince
T (+509) 257 3969

ECONOMY AND TRADE
Around 70 per cent of the population depend on agriculture, predominantly small-scale subsistence farming. Massive inflation has only partly been alleviated by aid following the departure of former president Jean-Bertrand Aristide. Remittances from the estimated one in six Haitians living abroad, principally in the USA, are of importance. Leather goods, textiles, electronic components and sports equipment are manufactured, using imported raw materials, for re-export. Principal imports are foodstuffs, machinery and transport equipment and fuels. In July 2002 Haiti was accepted as the 15th member of the Caribbean Community (Caricom) trade bloc.
GNI – US$4,034 million (2000); US$480 per capita (2001)
ANNUAL AVERAGE GROWTH OF GDP – 1.1 per cent (2000)
INFLATION RATE – 13.7 per cent (2000)
TOTAL EXTERNAL DEBT – US$1,169 million (2000)
IMPORTS – US$1,130 million (2002)
EXPORTS – US$280 million (2002)

BALANCE OF PAYMENTS
Trade – US$341 million deficit (1998)
Current Account – US$38 million deficit (1998)

Trade with UK	*2002*	*2003*
Imports from UK	£11,983,000	£15,480,000
Exports to UK	1,008,000	381,000

TRANSPORT INFRASTRUCTURE
Haiti has approximately 40 km of railway. Nearly a quarter of the country's 4,160 km of highways are surfaced, and less than 100 km of waterways are navigable. Haiti has 12 airports of which only three have surfaced runways. Haitian and Port au Prince are the largest ports in Haiti.

EDUCATION
Private and religious organisations provide 75 per cent of schooling.
ILLITERACY RATE – (m) 48.0 per cent; (f) 52.1 per cent (2000)
ENROLMENT (percentage of age group) – primary 22 per cent (1990)

MEDIA
There are more than 250 radio stations broadcasting in French and Creole. A single state broadcaster, Television Nationale d'Haiti, provides four television channels and these have been joined by two privately owned French-language stations.

HONDURAS

República de Honduras – Republic of Honduras

AREA – 112,088 sq. km. Neighbours: Guatemala (north-west), El Salvador (south-west), Nicaragua (south)
POPULATION – 6,406,052 (2001 estimate) of mixed Spanish and Indian blood. The Garifunas in the north are of West Indian origin. The language is Spanish, although English is spoken on the Bay Islands
CAPITAL – Tegucigalpa (population, 850,445, 2001 census)
MAJOR CITIES – Choluteca; ΨLa Ceiba; ΨPuerto Cortés; San Pedro Sula; ΨTela (2001 census)
CURRENCY – Lempira of 100 centavos
NATIONAL ANTHEM – Tu Bandera Es Un Lampo De Cielo (Your Flag Is A Heavenly Light)
NATIONAL DAY – 15 September
NATIONAL FLAG – Three horizontal bands, blue, white, blue (with five blue stars on the white band)
MORTALITY RATE (per 1,000 population) – 6.44 (2003)
HIV / AIDS ADULT PREVALENCE – 1.6 per cent (2001)
DEATH PENALTY – No (abolished 1956)
POPULATION BELOW POVERTY LINE – 53 per cent (1993)
POPULATION GROWTH RATE – 3.3 per cent (1990–2001)
POPULATION DENSITY – 57 per sq. km (1999)
MILITARY EXPENDITURE – 1.7 per cent of GDP (2002)
MILITARY PERSONNEL – 12,000: Army 8,300, Navy 1,400, Air Force 2,300; Paramilitaries 8,000

CLIMATE AND TERRAIN
Honduras is the second largest country in central America. Elevation extremes range from 2,870 m (Cerro Las Minas) at the highest point to 0 m (Caribbean Sea) at the lowest. Average annual temperatures range from 19°C in January to 23°C in June.

HISTORY AND POLITICS
Honduras hosted an arm of the Mayan civilisation between the fifth and ninth centuries AD. Christopher Columbus first set foot on the American mainland at Trujillo in Honduras in 1502, but it was 20 years before Spanish conquistadors reached the country. The economic

importance of Honduras declined in the 18th century. In 1824 Honduras joined all its neighbouring Central American provinces in declaring independence from Spain.

The Sandinista revolution in neighbouring Nicaragua in 1979 made Honduras a centre for US endeavours to back the anti-Sandinista Nicaraguan Contras. Honduras returned to civilian rule in 1981 with an executive presidency, a 128-seat unicameral congress, and a multiparty system. In October 1997, congress approved a constitutional amendment reducing the legislature to 80 members. The ending of the civil wars in Nicaragua and El Salvador meant a reduction in the number of US troops in Honduras and a decline in the power of the army.

Legislative elections held on 25 November 2001 were won by the National Party (PNH) who gained 61 seats, with the Liberal Party (PLH) gaining 55 seats. The presidential election held on the same day was won by Ricardo Maduro of the PNH.

HEAD OF STATE
President of the Republic, C-in-C of the Armed Forces, Ricardo Maduro, *elected* 25 November 2001, took office 27 January 2002
Vice-Presidents, Vicente Williams; Armida De Lopez; Alberto Diaz

SELECTED GOVERNMENT MEMBERS *as at July 2004*
Defence, Federico Breve
Finance, Arturo Alvarado
Foreign Relations, Guillermo Pérez Cadalso
Interior and Justice, Jorge Ramón Hernández Alcerro

EMBASSY OF HONDURAS
115 Gloucester Place, London W1U 6JT
T 020-7486 4880
Ambassador Extraordinary and Plenipotentiary, HE Hernán Antonio Bermúdez, apptd 1999

BRITISH EMBASSY
Ambassador Extraordinary and Plenipotentiary, HE Richard Lavers, apptd 2003

ECONOMY AND TRADE

Economic reliance in Honduras is on banana and coffee exports but the markets for both of these crops have been in steady decline over recent years. Other chief exports include frozen meat, shrimps, lobsters and timber, the most important being pine, mahogany and cedar. The main imports are machinery and electrical equipment, industrial chemicals and lubricants.

A foreign debt of around 80 per cent of total GDP and the devastation to the country's infrastructure caused by Hurricane Mitch in 1998, have caused considerable economic problems for Honduras. In 2003 President Ricardo Maduro joined the heads of Central American states to push for a Central American Free Trade Agreement with the USA. In 2004 Honduras signed agreements with the IMF which, if targets are met, will allow Honduras to be granted debt relief under the Heavily Indebted Poor Countries (HIPC) initiative.

GNP – US$5,517 million (2000); US$860 per capita (2000)
ANNUAL AVERAGE GROWTH OF GDP – 4.8 per cent (2000)
INFLATION RATE – 11.1 per cent (2000)
UNEMPLOYMENT – 3.7 per cent (1999)
TOTAL EXTERNAL DEBT – US$5,487 million (2000)
IMPORTS – US$2,979 million (2002)
EXPORTS – US$1,284 million (2002)

BALANCE OF PAYMENTS
Trade – US$877 million deficit (2001)
Current Account – US$670 million deficit (2001)

Trade with UK	*2002*	*2003*
Imports from UK	£9,757,000	£14,666,000
Exports to UK	19,116,000	23,890,000

TRANSPORT INFRASTRUCTURE

Honduras has a number of ports and 465 km of waterways are navigable by small craft. There are 699 km of railway and 13,603 km of roads. The mountainous terrain has led to the development of a large number of airports, though only 12 of the 115 have surfaced runways.

EDUCATION

Primary and secondary education is free of charge, primary education is compulsory from the age of seven to 12, and the government has launched a campaign to eradicate illiteracy.

ILLITERACY RATE – (m) 25.6 per cent; (f) 25.2 per cent (2000)
ENROLMENT (percentage of age group) – primary 100 per cent (1997); secondary 21 per cent (1991); tertiary 10.0 per cent (1997)

MEDIA AND CULTURE

Honduras has a state owned radio station as well as several privately run broadcasters and newspapers. Televicentro operates several television channels.

The most historically important Mayan site in Honduras is located at Copán, and is famous for its stone carvings and temple complexes. The town of Santa Rosa de Copán is renowned for its fine colonial architecture. The poet and playwright José Reyes (1797–1855) founded the National University of Honduras.

HUNGARY

Magyar Köztársaság – Republic of Hungary

AREA – 92,300 sq. km. Neighbours: Slovakia (north), Ukraine and Romania (east), Serbia and Montenegro and Croatia (south), Slovenia and Austria (west)
POPULATION – 9,917,000 (2001). There are minorities of Romanies (4 per cent), ethnic Germans (3 per cent), Serbs (2 per cent), Romanians (1 per cent) and Slovaks (1 per cent). About two-thirds of the population are Roman Catholic and the remainder mostly Calvinist. The language is Hungarian (Magyar)
CAPITAL – Budapest, (population, 1,775,203, 2001 census)
MAJOR CITIES – Debrecen; Miskolc; Pécs; Szeged
CURRENCY – Forint of 100 fillér
NATIONAL ANTHEM – Isten Aldd Meg A Magyart (God Bless The Hungarians)
NATIONAL DAYS – 15 March, 20 August, 23 October
NATIONAL FLAG – Red, white, green (horizontally)
LIFE EXPECTANCY (years) – 72 (2001)
MORTALITY RATE (per 1,000 population) – 13 (2003)
INFANT MORTALITY (per 1,000 births) – 8 (2001)
HIV / AIDS ADULT PREVALENCE – 0.1 per cent (2001)
DEATH PENALTY – No (abolished 1990)

POPULATION BELOW POVERTY LINE – 8.6 per cent (1993)
POPULATION GROWTH RATE – 0.4 per cent (1990–2001)
POPULATION DENSITY – 107 per sq. km (2001)
URBAN POPULATION – 65 per cent (2001)

CLIMATE AND TERRAIN

A landlocked state in central Europe, Hungary is mostly low-lying with a mountainous region in the north. Elevation extremes range from 1,014 m (Kekes) at the highest point to 78 m (Tisza River) at the lowest. Average annual temperatures range from −1°C in January to 21°C in July.

HISTORY AND POLITICS

Hungary became a Christian kingdom in the year AD 1,000, but had been settled by Magyar tribes (the ancestors of modern Hungarians) since 896. Between 1699 and 1867, Hungary was precariously ruled as a province of the Austrian Habsburg empire. Following years of Hungarian agitation, a Dual Monarchy was created giving Hungary control of internal affairs in return for the continued union of the Austrian and Hungarian crowns. The Austro-Hungarian empire is remembered as a time of great cultural achievement and economic success. Nevertheless, the union took the country into the First World War on the side of Germany resulting in defeat for the Hungarians and the destruction of the Habsburgs. An unstable republic after the war, Hungary suffered invasion from Romania and was reduced in size following the Treaty of Trianon. Hungary looked to the fascist regimes in Germany and Italy for aid in re-establishing its historic size, and so entered the Second World War on the side of the Axis powers. Hungary suffered massive military defeat at the hands of the Soviets and the destruction of its Jewish community at the hands of the Nazis.

The elections of 1947, which brought the communists to power, set the tone for subsequent communist rule. The communist leader János Kádár's attempts at national reconciliation led to reforms which developed Hungary's most wealthy and liberal regime.

The collapse of communist rule saw Hungary become the Republic of Hungary in 1989. Free and fair elections were not matched by economic success and the early 1990s saw Hungary suffer a host of economic problems. In the legislative elections in April 2002, no one party won an overall majority. The Federation of Young Democrats-Hungarian Civic Party (Fidesz-MPP) won the largest number of seats but Péter Medgyessy of the Hungarian Socialist Party (MSzP), formed a coalition government with the Alliance of Free Democrats (SzDSz). The composition of the national assembly as at July 2004 was: Fidesz-MPP 188, MSzP 178, SzDSz 20.

POLITICAL SYSTEM

The unicameral 386-seat National Assembly is elected on a mixed first-past-the-post and proportional representation basis. The President, elected by the National Assembly, has a largely ceremonial role, but his powers include appointing the Prime Minister, who in turn selects the Cabinet ministers and has the exclusive right to dismiss them.

HEAD OF STATE

President, Ferenc Mádl, *elected* 6 June 2000, *sworn in* 4 August 2000

SELECTED GOVERNMENT MEMBERS *as at July 2004*
Prime Minister, Péter Medgyessy
Defence, Ferenc Juhász
Finance, Tibor Draskovics
Foreign Affairs, László Kovács
Interior, Mónika Lamperth

EMBASSY OF THE REPUBLIC OF HUNGARY
35 Eaton Place, London SW1X 8BY
T 020-7235 5218
Ambassador Extraordinary and Plenipotentiary, HE Béla Szombati, apptd 2002

BRITISH EMBASSY
Harmincad Utca 6, H-1051 Budapest
T (+36) (1) 266 2888 E info@britemb.hu
Ambassador Extraordinary and Plenipotentiary, HE John Nichols, apptd 2003

BRITISH COUNCIL DIRECTOR, Jim McGrath
Benczúr Utca 26, H-1068 Budapest
T (+36) (1) 478 4700
E information@britishcouncil.hu

DEFENCE

The Army has 743 main battle tanks, 680 armoured infantry fighting vehicles and 798 armoured personnel carriers. The Air Force has 37 combat aircraft and 49 attack helicopters. Hungary became a member of NATO in March 1999.
MILITARY EXPENDITURE – 1.8 per cent of GDP (2002)
MILITARY PERSONNEL – 33,400: Army 23,600, Army Maritime Wing 270, Air Force 7,700; Paramilitaries 14,000
CONSCRIPTION DURATION – Six months

ECONOMY AND TRADE

Hungary is one of the largest economies of the ten countries to enter the European Union in 2004. The private sector accounts for around 80 per cent of GDP and Hungary has attracted large amounts of foreign investment since the end of communist rule in 1989. Industry includes mining, metallurgy, construction materials, processed foods, textiles, chemicals (especially pharmaceuticals) and motor vehicles. Targets for 2004 include a reduction in the public sector deficit and a cap on rises in wage levels. Germany remains Hungary's largest trading partner.
GNI – US$49,200 million (2001); US$4,830 per capita (2001)
ANNUAL AVERAGE GROWTH OF GDP – 3.5 per cent (2003)
INFLATION RATE – 4.7 per cent (2004)
UNEMPLOYMENT – 5.5 per cent (2003)
TOTAL EXTERNAL DEBT – US$29,415 million (2000)
FOREIGN DIRECT INVESTMENT – US$7,657 million (1997–2000)
IMPORTS – US$37,787 million (2002)
EXPORTS – US$34,512 million (2002)

BALANCE OF PAYMENTS
Trade – US$2,119 million deficit (2002)
Current Account – US$2,644 million deficit (2002)

Trade with UK	*2002*	*2003*
Imports from UK	£748,681,000	£851,910,000
Exports to UK	863,120,000	1,136,610,000

TRANSPORT INFRASTRUCTURE

Hungary has 188,203 km of highways, 7,875 km of railways (including a cross-border line to Austria, jointly managed by the two countries) and 1,373 km of permanently navigable waterways. Hungary maintains several major ports and harbours on the Danube River including the capital Budapest.

EDUCATION

Hungarians have 10 years of compulsory education, though a further two years at secondary level is optional.

ILLITERACY RATE – (m) 0.5 per cent; (f) 0.8 per cent (2000)

ENROLMENT (percentage of age group) – primary 100 per cent (1997); secondary 98 per cent (1997); tertiary 24 per cent (1997)

MEDIA AND CULTURE

Hungary's state run broadcaster (Magyar Televizo) competes with privately owned television and radio stations. Hungary has a wide range of weekly and daily newspapers, some of which are owned by foreign investors.

Hungary has an exceptional folk culture which has influenced a powerful musical tradition including the composers Franz Liszt (1811–86), Béla Bartók (1881–1945), Zoltan Kordaly (1882–1967) and Gyorgy Ligeti (b. 1923). Janos Arandy (1817–82) and Endre Ady (1887–1919) are two of Hungary's finest poets. Hungary's most famous author is Imre Kertesz (b. 1929) who won the Nobel Prize for Literature in 2002.

ICELAND

Lýđveldiđ Ísland – Republic of Iceland

AREA – 103,000 sq. km

POPULATION – 291,000 (2004). Some 86.5 per cent of the population are members of the (Lutheran) Church of Iceland. The language is Icelandic

CAPITAL – ΨReykjavík (population, 113,387, 2004)

MAJOR CITIES – Akranes; ΨAkureyri; Egilsstađir; ΨHafnarfjörđur; ΨIsafjörđur; Kópavogur; Reykjanesbær; ΨSiglufjörđur

CURRENCY – Icelandic króna (Kr) of 100 aurar

NATIONAL ANTHEM – O Gud Vors Lamds (God Of Our Country)

NATIONAL DAY – 17 June

NATIONAL FLAG – Blue, with white-bordered red cross

LIFE EXPECTANCY (years) – 79 (2001)

MORTALITY RATE (per 1,000 population) – 6.95 (2003)

INFANT MORTALITY (per 1,000 births) – 3 (2001)

HIV / AIDS ADULT PREVALENCE – 0.2 per cent (2001)

DEATH PENALTY – No (abolished 1928)

POPULATION GROWTH RATE – 0.9 per cent (1990–2001)

POPULATION DENSITY – 3 per sq. km (2001)

URBAN POPULATION – 93 per cent (2001)

ENROLMENT (percentage of age group) – primary 98 per cent (1996); secondary 87 per cent (1995); tertiary 37 per cent (1996)

MILITARY PERSONNEL – Paramilitaries: 130

CLIMATE AND TERRAIN

Iceland is located in the North Atlantic Ocean, to the east of Greenland and to the west of Norway. Sitting on the cusp of the Arctic Circle, Iceland's average annual temperatures range from –3°C in January to 11°C in July. Although mostly flat, there are mountainous areas in the north with elevation extremes ranging from 2,119 m (Hvannadalshnukur) at the highest point, to 0 m (North Atlantic Ocean) at the lowest. Seventy-nine per cent of Iceland's land area is covered with glaciers, lakes and lava fields. It is estimated that over the past 500 years, Iceland has emitted a third of the earth's total lava flow.

HISTORY AND POLITICS

The first major settlements occurred from about 870 onwards as turmoil in Scandinavia drove migrants to seek new homelands. Iceland hosted a flourishing Viking culture in the 9th and 10th centuries but became a fully Christian country in 999. Throughout the middle ages Iceland came under Danish and then Norwegian rule but in 1874 a constitution was drafted giving Iceland control over domestic affairs. Though it became an independent state within the Kingdom of Denmark in 1918, Copenhagen still controlled foreign policy and defence. It was only with the German occupation of Denmark in 1940 that Iceland requested full independence, which it finally gained in 1944.

In the parliamentary *(Althingi)* elections of 10 May 2003, the Conservative Independence Party (SSF) retained 22 seats. Incumbent prime minister David Oddsson of the SSF was sworn into office for a further term on 23 May 2003. In the presidential elections of June 2004, the incumbent president, Ólafur Grímsson, received 85.6 per cent of the vote and was sworn into office for a third consecutive term.

HEAD OF STATE

President, Ólafur Ragnar Grímsson, *elected* 29 June 1996, *re-installed* 1 August 2000

SELECTED GOVERNMENT MEMBERS *as at July 2004*

Prime Minister, Statistical Bureau of Iceland, David Oddsson

Finance, Geir Haarde

Foreign Affairs, Halldór Ásgrímsson

Social Affairs, Arni Magnusson

EMBASSY OF ICELAND

2A Hans Street, London SW1X 0JE

T 020-7259 3999

Ambassador Extraordinary and Plenipotentiary, HE Sverrir Haukur Gunnlaugsson, apptd 2003

BRITISH EMBASSY

Laufásvegur 31, IS-101 Reykjavík

T (+354) 550 5100 E britemb@centrum.is

Ambassador Extraordinary and Plenipotentiary and Consul-General, HE Alp Mehmet, MVO, apptd 2004

ECONOMY AND TRADE

The Icelandic economy is heavily reliant on the fishing industry and 70 per cent of Iceland's exports are marine products. Careful management of the industry, including the banning of direct foreign investment, has allowed stocks to recover from the over-fishing of the 1980s. Although only five per cent of land in Iceland is suitable for farming, the country is self sufficient in meat and dairy products. Attempts to reduce the country's dependence on fishing have included the introduction of aluminium smelters, which can be run on Iceland's plentiful supply of clean geothermal fuel. Tourism is encouraged and is becoming increasingly popular with over 40,000 tourists coming from the UK in 2000. Iceland's main export markets are the UK, Germany, the USA, The Netherlands, Spain, Norway, Denmark, Japan and Switzerland.

GNI – US$8,150 million (2001); US$28,910 per capita (2001)

ANNUAL AVERAGE GROWTH OF GDP – 4.0 per cent (2003 estimate)

INFLATION RATE – 4.6 per cent (2002)

UNEMPLOYMENT – 2.1 per cent (2002)

IMPORTS – US$2,639 million (2002)

EXPORTS – US$2,598 million (2002)

BALANCE OF PAYMENTS

Trade – US$77 million deficit (2001)

Current Account – US$333 million deficit (2001)

Trade with UK	*2002*	*2003*
Imports from UK	£141,621,000	£146,296,000
Exports to UK	310,812,000	309,900,000

TRANSPORT INFRASTRUCTURE

Iceland has no railways and no navigable waterways. Although the country has almost 13,000 km of roads, the majority remain unsurfaced and due to the extreme climate in winter, are often blocked by snow. Iceland has 100 airports. There are nine major ports and the capital, Reykjavík, operates shipping services to the USA and several European countries, including the UK.

MEDIA AND CULTURE

The state provides a public service broadcaster for television and radio, the Icelandic National Broadcasting Service (RUV), which is joined by several commercial stations.

The *Icelandic Sagas* are regarded as among the most important works of European medieval literature. Written anonymously between the 12th and 13th centuries, the Sagas relate the battles and triumphs of the original Icelanders who settled from Norway and Denmark. One of Iceland's most famous contemporary writers is Halldor Laxness (1902–98) who won the Nobel Prize for Literature in 1958.

INDIA

The Republic of India/Bhāratīya Ganarājya

AREA – 2,973,200 sq. km. Neighbours: Pakistan (north-west), China, Tibet, Nepal and Bhutan (north), Myanmar (east), Bangladesh

POPULATION – 1,025,096,000 (2001): Hindu (81 per cent), the rest being Muslim (12 per cent), Christian (2.3 per cent), Sikh (1.9 per cent), Buddhist (0.8 per cent) and Jain (0.4 per cent). The official languages are Hindi in the Devanagari script and English, though 17 regional languages are also recognised for adoption as official state languages

CAPITAL – New Delhi (population, 9,817,439 including Delhi/Dilli, 2001)

MAJOR CITIES – Ahmedabad; Bangalore; ΨBombay/Mumbai; ΨCalcutta/Kolkata; Hyderabad; Kanpur; Lucknow; ΨMadras/Chennai; Pune

CURRENCY – Indian rupee (Rs) of 100 paise

NATIONAL ANTHEM – Jana-Gana-Mana (Thou Art The Ruler Of The Minds Of All People)

NATIONAL DAY – 26 January (Republic Day)

NATIONAL FLAG – A horizontal tricolour with bands of deep saffron, white and dark green in equal proportions. In the centre of the white band appears an Asoka wheel in navy blue

LIFE EXPECTANCY (years) – 64 (2001)

MORTALITY RATE (per 1,000 population) – 8.49 (2003)

INFANT MORTALITY (per 1,000 births) – 67 (2001)

HIV / AIDS ADULT PREVALENCE – 0.8 per cent (2001)

DEATH PENALTY – Yes

POPULATION BELOW POVERTY LINE – 25 per cent (2002)

POPULATION GROWTH RATE – 1.8 per cent (1990–2001)

POPULATION DENSITY – 345 per sq. km (2001)

URBAN POPULATION – 28 per cent (2001)

ILLITERACY RATE – (m) 31.6 per cent; (f) 54.6 per cent (2000)

ENROLMENT (percentage of age group) – tertiary 7 per cent (1997)

CLIMATE AND TERRAIN

India has three well-defined regions: the mountain range of the Himalayas, the Indo-Gangetic plain, and the southern peninsula. The main mountain ranges are the Himalayas and the Western and Eastern Ghats. Elevation extremes range from 8,598 m (Kanchenjunga) at the highest point to 0 m (Indian Ocean) at the lowest. The average annual temperature in New Delhi ranges from 14°C in January to 34°C in June.

HISTORY AND POLITICS

The beginnings of Hinduism were developed in the Indus River valley region from *c.* 2500 BC. Between 1500 and 200 BC Aryan tribes from central Asia made repeated invasions of the sub-continent. Buddhism emerged in India from *c.* 500 BC and was embraced by the Emperor Ashoka. However, a Hindu revival from AD 40 onwards pushed Buddhism into decline.

The first Muslim advances into India occurred in the 10th and 11th centuries. Incursions swept across the north of the country where large Muslim communities were established. India was thus established as a country with two great religious traditions: a Muslim dominated north, and a largely Hindu south. Europeans arrived in India in the 16th century, though it was not until 1803, when the British East India Company consolidated its influence, that a single power came to dominate the entire subcontinent. In 1857 rule passed to the British government. Opposition to British rule, led by the Indian National Congress (INC) under the leadership of Mahatma Gandhi, became a concerted nationwide movement, and India achieved its independence in 1947. Against a backdrop of violence India's predominantly Muslim regions were partitioned and became East and West Pakistan. The latter eventually seceding from Pakistan to become Bangladesh.

Partition produced a bitter stand-off between India and Pakistan over the largely Muslim state of Kashmir. The state, split between the two countries, was claimed in its entirety by both. Outbreaks of war in 1965, 1971 and 1999 have blighted Kashmir since partition.

The murder of Mahatma Gandhi in 1948 was the first act in a series of political assassinations in independent India. The election of Jawaharlal Nehru began the rise of India's great political dynasty – the Gandhi family, which came to dominate the INC. Indira Gandhi, Nehru's daughter, was elected in 1966 but was assassinated by her Sikh bodyguards in 1984.

The long dominance of the INC over Indian politics appeared to be over in the early 1990s when the Hindu nationalist Bharatiya Janata Party (BJP), on a Hindu nationalist platform, began to beat the INC at the polls and formed a series of coalition governments. The Gandhi dynasty returned to popularity when the INC won a surprise victory in the parliamentary elections of May 2004 with 34.6 per cent of the vote and 217 seats in the *Lok Sabha* (House of the People). Italian-born Sonia Gandhi was elected, but almost immediately declared she was standing down, claiming she never intended to become prime minister. She was replaced by Manmohan Singh, who became prime minister and led a coalition government called the United Progressive Alliance. The appointment of Singh marked the arrival of India's first Sikh prime minister.

COMMUNALISM

Tensions between India's Hindu majority and large Muslim minority have never been fully resolved. Violence between the two at the time of partition in 1947 is thought to have cost the lives of up to one million people. The rise of Hindu nationalism in the 1990s accompanied a rise in communal clashes. In 1992 a mosque in the town of Ayodhya was destroyed by Hindus who claimed it was built on the site of the Hindu god Rama's birth. Anti-Muslim mobs rampaged through many parts of India and the army was called upon to restore order.

FOREIGN RELATIONS

In addition to the territory it won as a result of the Sino-Indian war in 1962, China claims Arunachal Pradesh and does not recognise Indian sovereignty over Sikkim. Talks between India and China in June 2003 resulted in India's formal recognition of the Tibetan Autonomous Region as a part of China and a cross-border trade agreement on Sikkim. India and Pakistan have fought three major wars since independence, in 1947–8, 1965 and 1971. Since 1985 they have continued a low-level war at altitude for control of the Siachen glacier in Kashmir.

In May 1998, India confirmed its nuclear status with five underground nuclear tests and within three weeks, Pakistan had followed suit. Both countries' tests sparked international condemnation. In May 1999 India launched air attacks on Muslim insurgents who had occupied mountainous areas within Indian-controlled Kashmir. Small-scale incidents between the Indian and Pakistani troops stationed along the line of control dividing Kashmir continue to occur on a regular basis. The presidents of India and Pakistan held a summit in Agra in July 2001, but failed to agree a joint declaration. A terrorist attack on the federal parliament in New Delhi on 13 December left 14 people dead. India held the Islamic separatist organisations Jaish-e-Mohammed (JeM) and Lashkar-e-Tayyeba (LeT) responsible. The Kashmir crisis continued into 2002 and tensions increased in early 2003 with frequent exchanges of fire and shelling between the Indian and Pakistani armies. However, in New Delhi in June 2004, the first diplomatic talks for three years were held between the Indian and Pakistani foreign ministers. The two ministers agreed to re-open the consulates in Karachi and Bombay that have been closed since 1994.

POLITICAL SYSTEM

Executive power is vested in the President, elected for a five-year term by an electoral college consisting of the elected members of the Union and State legislatures. The President appoints the Prime Minister. The Council of Ministers is collectively responsible to the *Lok Sabha* (House of the People). The Vice-President is *ex-officio* chairman of the *Rajya Sabha* (House of the States). Legislative power rests with the President, the *Rajya Sabha* (245 members serving six-year terms) and the *Lok Sabha* (545 members). Twelve members of the *Rajya Sabha* are Presidential nominees, the rest are indirectly elected representatives of the State and Union Territories. The 543 members of the *Lok Sabha* representing the States and Union Territories are directly elected by universal adult suffrage for a five-year term, and the two representatives of the Anglo-Indian community are nominated by the President.

FEDERAL STRUCTURE

There are 28 States and seven Union Territories. Each state is headed by a Governor, who is appointed by the President and holds office for five years, and by a Council of Ministers. All states have a Legislative Assembly, and some also have a Legislative Council, elected directly by adult suffrage for a maximum period of five years. The Union Territories are administered, except where otherwise provided by Parliament, by the President acting through an Administrator or Lieutenant-Governor, or other authority appointed by him.

HEAD OF STATE

President of the Republic of India, A. P. J. Abdul Kalam, *elected* 15 July 2002, *took office* 25 July 2002
Vice-President, Bhairon Singh Shekhawat

SELECTED GOVERNMENT MEMBERS *as at July 2004*

Prime Minister, Atomic Energy, Planning, Space, Statistics and Programme Implementation, Manmohan Singh
Defence, Pranab Mukherjee
Foreign Affairs, K. Natwar Singh
Finance, Palaniappan Chidambaram

INDIAN HIGH COMMISSION

India House, Aldwych, London WC2B 4NA
T 020-7836 8484
High Commissioner, HE Satyabrata Pal, apptd 2004

BRITISH HIGH COMMISSION

Chanakyapuri, New Delhi 110021
T (+91) (11) 687 2161
High Commissioner, HE Sir Michael Arthur, apptd 2003

BRITISH COUNCIL MINISTER – Edmund Marsden

17 Kasturba Gandhi Marg, New Delhi 110 001
T (+91) (11) 2371 1401
E delhi.enquiry@inbritishcouncil.org

DEFENCE

The Army has 3,898 main battle tanks, 1,600 armoured infantry fighting vehicles and 317 armoured personnel carriers. The Navy has 19 submarines, one aircraft carrier, eight destroyers, 11 frigates, 39 patrol and coastal vessels, 35 combat aircraft and 50 armed helicopters. It has nine bases including one under construction. The Air Force has 744 combat aircraft and 40 armed helicopters.

India exploded its first nuclear weapon in 1974 and is since believed to have acquired a stockpile of nuclear arms. It conducted further nuclear tests in May 1998. In 1993–4 India successfully test-fired its intermediate-range 'Agni' and 'Prithvi' ballistic missiles, and the latter went into production in September 1997.

MILITARY EXPENDITURE – 2.7 per cent of GDP (2002)

MILITARY PERSONNEL – 1,325,000: Army 1,100,000, Navy 55,000, Air Force 170,000; Paramilitaries 1,089,700

ECONOMY AND TRADE

India remains largely agrarian with agriculture, forestry and fishing supporting approximately 75 per cent of the population and contributing 30 per cent of GDP. Food crops occupy three-quarters of the total cultivated area. The main food crops are rice, cereals (principally wheat) and pulses. The major cash crops include sugarcane, jute, cotton and tea. Other products include oil seeds, spices, groundnuts, soya beans, tobacco, rubber and coffee. Livestock is raised, principally for dairy purposes or for the hides.

Large numbers of graduates have driven the growth of knowledge-based sectors such as information, communications and technology. Other industries, such as pharmaceuticals, are also experiencing growth. The economy has experienced an average growth rate of six per cent since 1990. Large-scale problems remain with a public-sector budget deficit of ten per cent of GDP.

India exports textile goods, gems and jewellery, engineering goods, chemicals and leather goods. Tourism has become a major industry for the country. Agricultural development has been hampered by serious environmental issues. Deforestation, soil erosion, overgrazing and desertification threaten India's agriculture and forests. Air pollution is particularly severe in the cities.

GNI – US$477,400 million (2001); US$460 per capita (2001)

ANNUAL AVERAGE GROWTH OF GDP – 7.2 per cent (1999)

INFLATION RATE – 4.0 per cent (2000)

TOTAL EXTERNAL DEBT – US$100,600 million (2001)

IMPORTS – US$49,618 million (2001)

EXPORTS – US$43,611 million (2001)

FOREIGN DIRECT INVESTMENT – US$7,657 million (1997–2000)

BALANCE OF PAYMENTS

Trade – US$12,193 million deficit (2000)

Current Account – US$4,198 million deficit (2000)

Trade with UK	*2002*	*2003*
Imports from UK	£1,768,288,000	£2,293,037,000
Exports to UK	1,870,245,000	2,147,328,000

TRANSPORT INFRASTRUCTURE

India has over 63,518 km of railway, 3,319,644 km of roads and 3,631 km of navigable waterways. There are 333 airports. The chief seaports are Bombay/Mumbai, Jawahar Lal Nehru, Calcutta/Kolkata, Haldia, Madras/Chennai, Mormugao, Cochin, Visakhapatnam, Kandla, Paradip, Mangalore, Ennore and Tuticorin.

EDUCATION

Education is free of charge and compulsory up to the age of 14. There are 226 universities in India and education spending reached over four per cent of GDP in 2001–2.

ILLITERACY RATE – (m) 31.6 per cent; (f) 54.6 per cent (2000)

ENROLMENT (percentage of age group) – tertiary 7 per cent (1997)

MEDIA AND CULTURE

The state's monopoly of television broadcasting ended in 1992, and India has seen an increase in the number of channels available. English language newspapers include *Times of India, Indian Express* and *Hindustan Times*, while popular Hindi titles are *Aman Ujala, Dainak Jagran* and the *NavBharat Times*.

Successive empires and invaders have left distinctive traces on Indian art. The Hindu Mauryans, from the third century BC and the Muslim Mughals from the 16th century both instigated what are considered to be the 'Golden Ages' of Indian culture.

There is a fertile literary scene in India which includes the writers Vikram Seth (b. 1952), Salman Rushdie (b. 1947), Arundhati Roy (b. 1967) and Shashi Deshpande (b. 1938). The Indian film industry is perhaps the most successful in the world. Known as 'Bollywood', there are an estimated 800 films made every year.

INDONESIA

Republik Indonesia – Republic of Indonesia

AREA – 1,811,600 sq. km. Indonesia shares borders with Malaysia (on Borneo) and Papua New Guinea (on New Guinea) and Timor Leste

POPULATION – 214,840,000 (2001): 87 per cent Muslim, with Christian, Buddhist, Hindu and Animist minorities. Bahasa Indonesian, a variant of Malay, is the national language, although more than 250 dialects are spoken

CAPITAL – ΨJakarta (population, 8,347,083, 2000 estimate)

MAJOR CITIES – (Java) Bandung, ΨSemarang, ΨSurabaya; (Kalimantan) Banjarmasin, ΨPontianak; (Maluku) Ambon; (Sulawesi) ΨUjung Pandang; (Sumatra) Medan, Palembang

CURRENCY – Rupiah (Rp) of 100 sen

NATIONAL ANTHEM – Indonesia Raya (Great Indonesia)

NATIONAL DAY – 17 August (Anniversary of Proclamation of Independence)

NATIONAL FLAG – Equal bands of red over white

LIFE EXPECTANCY (years) – 67 (2001)

MORTALITY RATE (per 1,000 population) – 6.26 (2003)

INFANT MORTALITY (per 1,000 births) – 33 (2001)

HIV / AIDS ADULT PREVALENCE – 0.1 per cent (2001)

DEATH PENALTY – Yes

POPULATION GROWTH RATE – 1.5 per cent (1990–2001)

POPULATION DENSITY – 119 per sq. km (2001)

URBAN POPULATION – 42 per cent (2001)

ILLITERACY RATE – (m) 8.1 per cent; (f) 17.9 per cent (2000)

ENROLMENT (percentage of age group) – primary 100 per cent (1997); secondary 56 per cent (1997); tertiary 56 per cent (1997)

CLIMATE AND TERRAIN

Indonesia comprises the islands of Java, Madura, Sumatra, the Riouw-Lingga archipelago, Bangka and Billiton, part of the island of Borneo (Kalimantan), Sulawesi (formerly Celebes), Maluku (formerly Moluccas), the islands of Bali, Lombok, Sumbawa, Sumba, Flores and others comprising the provinces of East and West Nusa Tenggara and the western half of the islands of New Guinea (Irian Jaya) and Timor. Elevation extremes range from 5,030 m (Puncak Jaya) at the highest point to 0 m (Indian Ocean) at the lowest. Average annual temperatures in Jakarta range from 23°C in January to 32°C in August.

HISTORY AND POLITICS

The first great Islamic empire was centred at Melaka (Malacca) but did not survive the Portuguese invasion of 1511. The Portuguese themselves were displaced by the Dutch East India Company which, lured by the rich spice trade, came to dominate the whole of Indonesia by the early 20th century. Japanese occupation of Indonesia during the Second World War strengthened nationalism and Achmed Soekarno, the foremost proponent of self-rule since the 1920s, became president when full sovereignty was transferred to the new Indonesian republic in 1949. In 1966, Soekarno was deposed in a military coup. The new president, General Soeharto, remained in power until 1998 when, amidst economic and social upheaval, he was succeeded by his deputy B. J. Habibie. Habibie failed to implement the social and economic reforms necessary and many Indonesians continued to demand autonomy or full independence.

On 30 August 1999 East Timor voted for independence but the province quickly descended into civil unrest. An intervention by the Australian military ended the troubles and East Timor gained independence after 25 years of Indonesian occupation.

Abdurrahman Wahid was elected president in October 1999 but was impeached for alleged financial corruption in 2001 and was replaced by Megawati Soekarnoputri (daughter of Soekarno, Indonesia's first president) in July 2001. On 10 August 2002, the House of Representatives voted in favour of amendments to the constitution introducing direct elections for the president and vice-president who had been formerly elected by the People's Consultative Assembly.

On 12 October 2002 a terrorist attack in Bali killed at least 184 people and injured more than 300. On 7 August 2003 Amrozi bin Nurhasyim was found guilty of carrying out the bombings and sentenced to death.

The first round of presidential elections took place in July 2004 and was won by Susilo Yudhoyono. The second round took place on 20 September but the final result was not known at the time of going to press.

HEAD OF STATE *as at August 2004*
President, Megawati Soekarnoputri, *sworn in* 23 July 2001
Vice-President, Hamzah Haz

SELECTED GOVERNMENT MEMBERS *as at July 2004*
Defence, Mathori Abdul Djalil
Finance, Budiono
Foreign Affairs, Hasan Wirayuda
Home Affairs, Hari Sabarno

INDONESIAN EMBASSY
38 Grosvenor Square, London W1K 2HW
T 020-7499 7661
Ambassador Extraordinary and Plenipotentiary, HE Juwono Sudarsono, apptd 2003

BRITISH EMBASSY
Jalan M. H. Thamrin 75, Jakarta 10310
T (+62) (21) 315 6264
Ambassador Extraordinary and Plenipotentiary, HE Charles Humfrey

BRITISH COUNCIL DIRECTOR, Dr Patrick Brazier,
S. Widjojo Centre, Jalan Jenderal Sudirman Kav 71, Jakarta 12190
T (+62) (21) 252 4115
E information@britishcouncil.or.id

DEFENCE

The Army has 481 armoured personnel carriers, 11 armoured infantry fighting vehicles and 11 aircraft. The Navy has two submarines, 17 frigates, 36 patrol and coastal vessels and 17 armed helicopters. There are five principal naval bases. The Air Force has 90 combat aircraft (of which 45 per cent are operational).
MILITARY EXPENDITURE – 3.7 per cent of GDP (2002)
MILITARY PERSONNEL – 302,000: Army 230,000, Navy 45,000, Air Force 27,000; Paramilitaries 195,000
CONSCRIPTION DURATION – Two years (selective)

ECONOMY AND TRADE

Indonesia has a wide range of natural resources including petroleum, tin, natural gas, nickel, timber, bauxite, copper, fertile soils, coal, gold and silver. The country has a large agricultural sector with 45 per cent of the labour force engaged in agriculture.

Indonesian industries include the production of petroleum and natural gas. It is also the world's biggest producer of tin. Timber is Indonesia's second largest foreign exchange earner after oil while textiles, mining and chemicals are also important to the economy. Tourism has begun to slowly recover after the Bali bombing of 2002. In 2003 Indonesia graduated from IMF support. Inflation and interest rates have both declined and the budget deficit has been reduced to 1.8 per cent of GDP and debt has fallen to 65 per cent of GDP.
GNI – US$144,700 million (2001); US$690 per capita (2001)
ANNUAL AVERAGE GROWTH OF GDP – 4.8 per cent (2000)
INFLATION RATE – 3.7 per cent (2000)
UNEMPLOYMENT – 5.5 per cent (1998)
TOTAL EXTERNAL DEBT – US$141,803 million (2000)
FOREIGN DIRECT INVESTMENT – US$2,974 million (1997–2000)
IMPORTS – US$25,388 million (2002)
EXPORTS – US$38,354 million (2002)

BALANCE OF PAYMENTS
Trade – US$23,212 million surplus (2002)
Current Account – US$7,451 million surplus (2002)

Trade with UK	*2002*	*2003*
Imports from UK	£327,163,000	£452,316,000
Exports to UK	1,076,944,000	958,693,000

TRANSPORT INFRASTRUCTURE

Indonesia has 342,700 km of highways and 6,458 km of railways. An extensive network of ferry services links the islands. There are 661 airports and 21,579 km of navigable waterways.

MEDIA AND CULTURE

A state-run television broadcaster, Televisi Republik Indonesia (TVRI), competes with several commercial stations. There are several nationwide newspapers and many radio stations. In 2003 more than 2,000 unlicensed radio and television stations were given the chance to apply for licences.

Indonesian Islam is, in places, strongly influenced by the country's Hindu and Buddhist traditions. Much of Indonesian society is influenced by *adat,* a code of behaviour covering social and religious duty. In Java, puppetry has evolved into a complex theatrical form that narrates the story of the *Mahabharata,* one of the world's longest literary epics and a key Hindu text that explores religion, philosophy and mythology.

IRAN

Jomhûri-ye-Eslâmi-ye-Îrân – Islamic Republic of Iran

AREA – 1,622,000 sq. km. Neighbours: Armenia, Azerbaijan, Turkmenistan (north), Afghanistan (north-east), Pakistan (south-east), Iraq (south-west), Turkey (north-west)
POPULATION – 71,369,000 (2001): 99 per cent Muslims (Shia 89 per cent and Sunni 10 per cent) with small minorities of Zoroastrians, Jews, and Armenian and Assyrian Christians. The official language is Persian (Farsi). Minority languages are Turkic (26 per cent), Kurdish (9 per cent), Luri (2 per cent), Arabic, Baluchi and Turkish (1 per cent each)
CAPITAL – Tehran (population 6,758,845, 1996 census)
MAJOR CITIES – Ahwaz; Esfahan; Mashhad; Qom; Shiraz; Tabriz
CURRENCY – Rial
NATIONAL ANTHEM – Sorûd-E Jomhûri-Ye Eslâmi (Anthem Of The Islamic Republic Of Iran)
NATIONAL DAY – 11 February
NATIONAL FLAG – Three horizontal stripes of green, white, red, with the slogan *Allahu Akbar* repeated 22 times along the edges of the green and red stripes, and the national emblem in the centre
LIFE EXPECTANCY (years) – 69 (2001)
MORTALITY RATE (per 1,000 population) – 5.54 (2003)
INFANT MORTALITY (per 1,000 births) – 35 (2001)
HIV / AIDS ADULT PREVALENCE – 0.1 per cent (2001)
DEATH PENALTY – Yes
POPULATION BELOW POVERTY LINE – 40 per cent (2002)
POPULATION GROWTH RATE – 1.8 per cent (1990–2001)
POPULATION DENSITY – 44 per sq. km (2001)
URBAN POPULATION – 65 per cent (2001)

CLIMATE AND TERRAIN

Elevation extremes range from 5,671 m (Qolleh-ye Damavand) at the highest point to 0 m (Persian Gulf) at the lowest. Average annual temperatures in Tehran are 3°C in January and 30°C in July.

HISTORY AND POLITICS

Iran is a part of the Middle East's 'fertile crescent', an area associated with the development of sophisticated agriculture. In the sixth century BC the Achaemenian king, Cyrus the Great, developed his control over the area. His dynasty founded the Persian empire under the Zoroastrian religion. In the fourth century BC Persia was conquered by Alexander the Great. Alexander's death led to a period of economic turbulence, civil conflict and foreign invasion for Iran. In AD 637 Arab conquerors re-united the country and introduced Islam, converting the majority of the population and creating a cultural revolution.

The Safavid Dynasty which ruled Iran between the 16th and 18th centuries is recognised as the progenitor of one of Iran's periods of great cultural production.

Reza Khan, on becoming prime minister in 1923, firmly established the *Majlis,* a legislative assembly appointed by election. In the light of increasing economic strain Khan, who had assumed the title of *Shah,* became an increasingly isolated figure. Popular discontent followed and, in 1979, Khan was exiled. He was replaced by Ayatollah Khomeini, who established Iran as an Islamic Republic in April 1979.

In 1980, Iraqi President Saddam Hussein invaded Iran and a bitter eight-year war ensued.

Ayatollah Khomeini died in 1989 and was replaced by Seyyed Ali Khamenei. In 1997 a moderate cleric, Mohammad Khatami was elected President. Since Khatami's election Iran has been split between reforming and conservative aspirations. The presidential elections of 8 June 2001 resulted in the re-election of Mohammad Khatami, who obtained over 76 per cent of the vote.

Parliamentary elections were held in February 2004 but as at July, no results have been released.

POLITICAL SYSTEM

The leader of the Republic is elected by the Council of Experts whose 83 members are popularly elected every eight years. The President, who is the Chief Executive, is directly elected for a four-year term, renewable once. Ministers are nominated by the President and must obtain a vote of confidence in the *Majlis.* The *Majlis* comprises 290 representatives who are directly elected for a four-year term. Laws passed by the *Majlis* must be approved by the 12-member Guardian Council. In November 1997, President Khatami announced the establishment of the Committee for the Implementation and Supervision of the Constitution, a five-member body to ensure the Constitution was abided by and that people's rights were respected.

In the legislative elections of 2000, the Reformist Party held 189 seats in the *Majlis,* while the Radical Islamists won 54. Independent candidates secured 42 seats.

Spiritual Leader of the Islamic Republic and C.-in-C. of Armed Forces, Ayatollah Seyed Ali Khamenei, *appointed* June 1989
President, Seyed Mohammad Khatami, *elected* 23 May 1997, *re-elected* 8 June 2001
First Vice-President, Mohammad Reza Aref

SELECTED GOVERNMENT MEMBERS *as at July 2004*
Defence and Logistics, Adm. Ali Shamkhani
Economic Affairs and Finance, Safdar Hoseyni
Foreign Affairs, Kamal Kharrazi

Interior, Chair of State Security Council, Abdulvahed Moussavi-Lari

EMBASSY OF THE ISLAMIC REPUBLIC OF IRAN
16 Prince's Gate, London SW7 1PT
T 020-7225 3000
Ambassador Extraordinary and Plenipotentiary, HE Morteza Sarmadi, apptd 2000

BRITISH EMBASSY
143 Ferdowsi Avenue, PO Box 11365–4474, Tehran 11344
T (+98) (21) 670 5011
Ambassador Extraordinary and Plenipotentiary, HE Richard Dalton, CMG, apptd 2002

DEFENCE

The Army has around 1,565 main battle tanks, 670 armoured personnel carriers, 750 armoured infantry fighting vehicles and 50 attack helicopters. The Navy has three submarines, three frigates, 56 patrol and coastal vessels, five combat aircraft and 19 armed helicopters. There are seven naval bases. The Air Force has some 306 combat aircraft, of which about 60–80 per cent are serviceable.

MILITARY EXPENDITURE – 4.6 per cent of GDP (2002)
MILITARY PERSONNEL – 540,000: Army 350,000, Revolutionary Guard Corps 120,000, Navy 18,000, Air Force 52,000; Paramilitaries 40,000
CONSCRIPTION DURATION – 21 months

ECONOMY AND TRADE

Iran's economy is heavily reliant on its state run oil industry and has benefited from relatively high oil prices in recent years, enabling it to amass some US$15,000 million in foreign exchange reserves. Petroleum also accounts for 85 per cent of Iran's export commodities. Apart from petroleum and petrochemicals, Iran produces textiles, construction materials and armaments. Agricultural production includes wheat, rice, other grains, sugar beets, fruits, nuts, cotton, dairy products, wool and caviar.

It was announced in April 2000 that reserves of gas had been found in the Gavband region with an estimated value of US$16,500 million.

GNI – US$108,700 million (2001); US$1,680 per capita (2001)
ANNUAL AVERAGE GROWTH OF GDP – 2.1 per cent (1998)
INFLATION RATE – 14.5 per cent (2000)
TOTAL EXTERNAL DEBT – US$7,953 million (2000)
FOREIGN DIRECT INVESTMENT – US$198 million (1997–2000)
IMPORTS – US$22,190 million (2002)
EXPORTS – US$24,440 million (2002)

BALANCE OF PAYMENTS
Trade – US$13,138 million surplus (2000)
Current Account – US$12,645 million surplus (2000)

Trade with UK	*2002*	*2003*
Imports from UK	£401,728,000	£476,882,000
Exports to UK	35,918,000	30,608,000

TRANSPORT INFRASTRUCTURE

Iran has a number of ports on the Persian Gulf though Abadan was largely destroyed during the war with Iraq. Iran has 904 km of waterways in total, the most important being the Shatt al Arab, which is navigable for 130 km. There are a total of 167,157 km of roads of which 94,109 km are surfaced and 7,201 km of railways.

EDUCATION

Since 1943 primary education has been compulsory and free of charge. Iran has 48 universities.

ILLITERACY RATE – (m) 16.5 per cent; (f) 30.1 per cent (2000)
ENROLMENT (percentage of age group) – primary 98 per cent (1997); secondary 77 per cent (1997); tertiary 18 per cent (1997)

MEDIA AND CULTURE

President Khatami's reformist government has pushed for greater freedom in the Iranian media. Restrictions on satellite television have also been relaxed. The Islamic Republic of Iran Broadcasting (IRIB) is a state run national television broadcaster which is supplemented by regional channels.

Iran is exceptionally rich in both Islamic and pre-Islamic architecture. Persepolis, the seat of the Achaemenian empire, constructed by Darius in the sixth century BC, lies at the foot of Kuh-i-Rahmat, in the plain of Marv Dasht 400 miles south of the present capital city of Tehran.

Iranian cinema has recently emerged as one of the world's most respected film industries and in 1997 the director Abbas Kiarostami (b. 1940) won the coveted Palme d'Or at the Cannes film festival for *Taste of Cherry*.

IRAQ

Al-Jumhūriyya al-`Īraqiyya – Republic of Iraq

AREA – 437,400 sq. km. Neighbours: Iran (east), Saudi Arabia, Kuwait (south), Jordan (west), Syria (north-west), Turkey (north)
POPULATION – 23,584,000 (2001), 16,278,316 (1987 census). The official language is Arabic. Minority languages include Kurdish (about 15 per cent), Turkic and Aramaic
CAPITAL – Baghdad (population, 3,841,268, 1987)
MAJOR CITIES – ΨAl-Basra; Kirkuk; Al-Mawsil
CURRENCY – Iraqi dinar (ID) of 1,000 fils
NATIONAL ANTHEM – Land Of Two Rivers
NATIONAL DAY – 9 April (Overthrow of Ba'ath regime of Saddam Hussein)
NATIONAL FLAG – Pale blue crescent on a white background, with a yellow strip between two blue lines at the bottom
LIFE EXPECTANCY (years) – 63 (2001)
MORTALITY RATE (per 1,000 population) – 5.84 (2003)
INFANT MORTALITY (per 1,000 births) – 107 (2001)
HIV / AIDS ADULT PREVALENCE – 0.1 per cent (2001)
POPULATION GROWTH RATE – 2.8 per cent (1990–2001)
POPULATION DENSITY – 54 per sq. km (2001)
URBAN POPULATION – 68 per cent (2001)
ILLITERACY RATE – (m) 34.4 per cent; (f) 54.1 per cent (2000)

ENROLMENT (percentage of age group) – primary 85 per cent (1997); secondary 42 per cent (1997); tertiary 11.2 per cent (1995)

CLIMATE AND TERRAIN

Iraq is mostly desert with mountainous areas in the north. Elevation extremes range from 3,600 m (Haji Ibrahim) at the highest point to 0 m (Persian Gulf) at the lowest. Average temperatures in Baghdad range from 9°C in January to 35°C in July.

HISTORY AND POLITICS

The Sumerians were the first people to populate the areas around the Tigris and Euphrates rivers. They began to build city states from around 3,000 BC of which Ur, Lagash and Eridu are the earliest examples. In AD 637 Iraq was conquered by Arab Muslims. The Battle of Karbala in AD 680 marked one of the decisive moments in Islamic history: a split between Sunnis and Shias was created when the Shiite leader Hussein was killed attempting to claim the Caliphate. In 1533 Iraq came under the control of the Ottoman empire until 1916 when the Ottomans, weakened by the First World War ceded control to the British. A provisional government was set up in 1920, and in 1921 the Emir Faisal was elected King of Iraq. King Faisal II was assassinated in July 1958, and Iraq came under the control of the Ba'ath Socialist Party.

In 1979 Saddam Hussein deposed President Bakr, and installed himself as president. Following the invasion of Iraq by coalition forces in March 2003, the UN Security Council approved a resolution recognising the US-led Coalition Provisional Authority (CPA), headed by Paul Bremner, as the occupying authority in Iraq and economic sanctions were lifted. Twenty-five ministers were named to the transitional government on 1 September 2003. Izzadine Saleem, became president of the Iraqi Interim Governing Council (IGC) in May 2004, but was assassinated on 17 May. He was replaced immediately by Ghazi Mashal Ajil al-Yawer, who had already been chosen to succeed him in June.

The CPA formally handed over sovereignty to the Iraqi interim government on 28 June 2004.

FOREIGN RELATIONS

In 1980 Saddam Hussein pressed territorial claims for the whole of the Shatt al-Arab, a waterway that divides Iraq from Iran, and invaded Iran. The end of the war in 1988 left the borders in much the same position as they had been in 1980. Iraqi Kurds, who had demanded an autonomous homeland, were punished for their support of Iran with a brutal military campaign. Thousands were killed with poison gas. Saddam Hussein invaded Kuwait in 1990, abolished its sovereignty, and declared it a province of Iraq. The UN Security Council declared the annexation void and in January 1991, an alliance of NATO and Middle East countries launched an offensive and liberated Kuwait in February 1991.

The UN created a United Nations Special Committee (UNSCOM), charged with ensuring that Iraq cease production and destroy all stocks of chemical, biological and nuclear weapons. The committee was often hampered in its activities by Iraqi security forces. A new weapons inspection body was created in December 1999. The UN Monitoring Verification and Inspection Committee (UNMOVIC) had the power to suspend sanctions, which the UN had imposed on Iraq, if the country was found to be in compliance with UN resolutions on disarmament. In spite of its efforts, it remained impossible to verify the end of Iraq's weapons programmes.

In November 2002 the UN resumed inspections following a unanimous resolution in the Security Council. The US threatened to attack if Iraq did not comply. The US and UK began the invasion of Iraq on 20 March 2003. The war was started without the support of the UN with several prominent member states – such as Germany, France and Russia – registering objections. On 14 April 2004 US forces took control of Tikrit, the last bastion of the old regime. Saddam Hussein was captured on 14 December 2003. US-led attempts to stabilise the country and hand power over to an Iraqi government have been severely disrupted by the actions of Iraqi insurgents.

POLITICAL SYSTEM

The new constitution provides for a *Majlis Watani* (National Assembly), to be elected no later than January 2005. The assembly will elect the President who along with two deputies will form a Presidency Council to represent the sovereignty of Iraq and oversee the higher affairs of the country. The Presidency Council appoints the Prime Minister of Iraq and the Government, all of whom must be approved by the Assembly.

HEAD OF STATE IN INTERIM GOVERNMENT
President, Ghazi Mashal Ajil al-Yawer, *sworn in* 18 May 2004
Vice-President, Ibrahim al-Jaafari
Vice-President, Rowsch Shaways

SELECTED GOVERNMENT MEMBERS *as at July 2004*
Prime Minister, Iyad Allawi
Deputy Prime Minister National Security, Barham Saleh
Foreign Affairs, Hoshyar Zebari
Finance, Adil Abdel-Mahdi
Defence, Hazem Shalan al-Khuzaei
Interior, Falah Hassan al-Nagib

BRITISH DIPLOMATIC REPRESENTATION
c/o Iraq Policy Unit, King Charles Street, London, SW1A 2AH
T 020 7008-1500
Ambassador Extraordinary and Plenipotentiary, HE Edward Chaplin, CMG, OBE, apptd 2004 (resident in Baghdad)

ECONOMY AND TRADE

Iraq's major industry is oil production which was nationalised in 1972. However, years of dictatorship, warfare and UN sanctions have seriously damaged production. Since the end of Saddam Hussein's regime, the reconstruction of the oil industry, the electricity supply and other essential infrastructure has proceeded but has been hampered by continuing violence and instability. The UN and World Bank estimated the cost of reconstruction at $55 billion. In October 2003, US$33 billion of aid was pledged by international donors. Petroleum has traditionally accounted for about 95 per cent of Iraq's foreign exchange earnings. Industries include the production of textiles, chemicals and construction materials. Free trade agreements have been signed with Egypt, Syria and Tunisia, which were to be put into effect when UN sanctions were lifted.

GDP – US$73,848 million (1998); US$3,352 per capita (2000)
ANNUAL AVERAGE GROWTH OF GDP – 15.0 per cent (1998)

Trade with UK	*2002*	*2003*
Imports from UK	£47,078,000	£129,593,000
Exports to UK	95,000	145,000

TRANSPORT INFRASTRUCTURE

Iraq's transport infrastructure was severely damaged during the war in 2003. Iraq has 1,963 km of railways and 45,550 km of highways. The Shatt al-Arab, Iraq's main waterway, is navigable for 130 km. The Tigris and Euphrates rivers have navigable sections for shallow draft boats.

EDUCATION

When the CPA took responsibility for the control of Iraq after the fall of Saddam Hussein's regime, it reviewed the country's education system. Over 2,500 schools have been refurbished and more than 70 million textbooks have been reprinted.

ILLITERACY RATE – (m) 34.4 per cent; (f) 54.1 per cent (2000)

ENROLMENT (percentage of age group) – primary 85 per cent (1997); secondary 42 per cent (1997); tertiary 11.2 per cent (1995)

MEDIA AND CULTURE

Once strictly controlled under Saddam Hussein, the media has begun to flourish since the end of Ba'ath rule. There are more than 200 newspapers and periodicals, many with an ethnic or religious affiliation, and private radio and television has also begun to thrive. The Coalition Provisional Authority (CPA) operates the Iraqi Media Network (IMN), which reaches two-thirds of Iraqi homes. The CPA prints *Al-Sabah* and this is joined by *Al-Zaman*, a daily newspaper based in London but printed in Baghdad and Basra.

Much of the rich cultural history of Iraq has been destroyed or irreparably damaged through years of war and state control. However, since the end of the 2003 war, many former dissident writers and artists have returned to the country. Significant figures include the poet Fawzi Karim (b. 1945), the filmmaker Saad Salman (b. 1950) and the artist Ismaayl Fattah (1936–2004) who is best known for creating the *Martyr* sculpture in Baghdad.

IRELAND

Éire/Ireland

AREA – 68,900 sq. km. Neighbour: Northern Ireland (north)

POPULATION – 3,841,000 (2001). In 2000 religious adherence as a percentage of the population was: Roman Catholic 87.2 per cent, Protestant 0.9 per cent, Anglican 3.7 per cent. Irish is the first official language; English is recognised as a second official language, but is more commonly used

CAPITAL – ΨDublin *(Baile Átha Cliath)* (population, 1.122,600, 2002 census)

MAJOR CITIES – ΨCork *(Corcaigh)*; ΨGalway *(Gaillimh)*; ΨLimerick *(Luimheach)*; ΨWaterford *(Port Láirge)*

CURRENCY – Euro (€) of 100 cents

NATIONAL ANTHEM – Amhrán na bhFiann (The Soldier's Song)

NATIONAL DAY – 17 March (St Patrick's Day)

NATIONAL FLAG – Equal vertical stripes of green, white and orange

LIFE EXPECTANCY (years) – 77 (2001)

MORTALITY RATE (per 1,000 population) – 7.94 (2003)

INFANT MORTALITY (per 1,000 births) – 6 (2001)

HIV / AIDS ADULT PREVALENCE – 0.1 per cent (2001)

DEATH PENALTY – No (abolished 1990)

POPULATION GROWTH RATE – 0.8 per cent (1990–2001)

POPULATION DENSITY – 56 per sq. km (2001)

URBAN POPULATION – 59 per cent (2001)

MILITARY EXPENDITURE – 0.6 per cent of GDP (2002)

MILITARY PERSONNEL – 10,460: Army 8,500, Navy 1,100, Air Force 860

CLIMATE AND TERRAIN

The greatest length of the island, from north-east to south-west (Torr Head to Mizen Head), is 486 km, and the greatest breadth, from east to west (Dundrum Bay to Annagh Head), is 280 km. On the north coast of Achill Island (Co. Mayo) are the highest cliffs in the British Isles, 609 m above sea level. Elevation extremes range from 1,040 m (Carrantuohill) at the highest point to 0 m (Irish Sea) at the lowest. The principal river is the Shannon (386 km), which drains the central plain. The Slaney flows into Wexford Harbour, the Liffey to Dublin Bay, the Boyne to Drogheda, the Lee to Cork Harbour, the Blackwater to Youghal Harbour, and the Suir, Barrow and Nore to Waterford Harbour.

The principal hydrographic feature is the loughs; the Shannon chain of Allen, Boderg, Forbes, Ree and Derg, and the Erne chain of Gowna, Oughter, Lower Erne and Erne; Melvin, Gill, Gara and Conn in the north-west; and Corrib and Mask (joined by a hidden channel) in the west.

HISTORY AND POLITICS

Settled by the Celts around 300 BC, Ireland developed a flourishing and distinct culture that remained largely intact until Christianity was introduced in the fifth century AD. The spread of Christianity is attributed in large part to St Patrick. By the 12h century Ireland experienced the first incursions by Anglo-Norman invaders, marking the beginning of a long and fraught history between Ireland and Britain.

As English power became consolidated throughout Ireland, and the north-eastern kingdom of Ulster emerged as the final stronghold of Celtic power at the beginning of the 17th century, England began a programme of sending Protestant Scottish settlers to the area. This policy produced a long-standing rivalry, sometimes erupting into hostility, between the north's Protestant and Catholic populations.

In the mid-17th century there was widespread support in Ireland for the Royalist side in the English Civil War (largely because of the marriage of Charles I to a Roman Catholic). This prompted bloody reprisals from Oliver Cromwell, who invaded Ireland after the Parliamentarian victory and ordered the execution of Charles I. Popular discontent in the late 18th century led to the Protestant gentry appealing to England for assistance, and in 1800, the Act of Union united Britain and Ireland. Simultaneously, Catholic opposition to foreign rule became increasingly organised with the formation of the Catholic Association under the leadership of Daniel O'Connell.

By 1916 demands for independence from Britain had reached the point of full-scale rebellion. Violence broke out in Dublin. Known as the Easter Uprising, it was eventually repressed by the British but inspired Irish nationalists to contest the 1918 elections and, on gaining a majority of the Irish seats, to declare Irish Independence under the leadership of Eamon de Valera. The British response was an attempt at violent suppression of the nationalists. The ensuing Anglo-Irish War lasted from 1919 to 1921 when the two sides, each unable to produce a victory, negotiated the creation of the Irish Free State under the Anglo Irish Treaty. Ireland became independent, but remained part of the Commonwealth, and Britain retained some privileges, such as the presence of naval bases. The six majority Protestant counties in the north remained part of the UK.

Ireland incrementally loosened what remaining ties it had with Britain over the following years. Irish neutrality during the Second World War was followed by the declaration of a republic in 1948. The status of Northern Ireland remained divisive. The Catholic minority began a civil rights movement in the 1960s in response to what they claimed was discrimination. Sectarian rioting ensued and British troops were deployed to restore order. The relationship between the British military and Irish Catholics swiftly deteriorated and Northern Ireland entered a period known as 'The Troubles', characterised by conflict fought between the British security forces and Irish republicans, notably the Irish Republican Army (IRA). A cease-fire in 1994 was not universally observed, but did pave the way for an eventual peace process.

Following the Good Friday Agreement of 10 April 1998, a referendum was held, in which 94 per cent of voters in the Irish Republic and 71 per cent of voters in Northern Ireland approved the agreement. The agreement recognises that Northern Ireland remains part of the UK and shall not cease to be so without the consent of a majority of the people of Northern Ireland. Additionally, it was established that a North–South Ministerial Council, comprising officials from both countries, would meet to regulate areas of common interest.

The presidential election in October 1997 was won by Mary McAleese with almost 59 per cent of second-round votes. In the elections to the House of Representatives *(Dáil Eireann)* held on 17 May 2002, Fianna Fáil (FF) remained the largest party but without an overall majority. The coalition government, led by Bertie Ahern of the FF, includes members of the Progressive Democrats (PD). The composition of the *Dáil Eireann* as at July 2004 was: FF 81; Fine Gael 31; Labour 21; PD 8; Green Party 6; Sinn Fein 5; Socialist Party 1; Independents 13.

POLITICAL SYSTEM

The President *(Uachtarán na Éireann)* is directly elected for a term of seven years, and is eligible for a second term. The President is aided and advised by a Council of State. The National Parliament *(Oireachtas)* consists of the President, House of Representatives *(Dáil Éireann)* and Senate *(Seanad Éireann)*. *Dáil Éireann* is composed of 166 members elected for a five-year term on a basis of proportional representation by means of the single transferable vote. *Seanad Éireann* is composed of 60 members, of whom 11 are nominated by the Prime Minister *(Taoiseach)* and 49 are elected, six by institutions of higher education and 43 from panels of candidates established on a vocational basis.

Executive power is vested in the Government subject to the constitution. The government is responsible to the *Dáil Éireann*. The *Taoiseach* is appointed by the President on the nomination of the *Dáil Éireann* while other members of the government are appointed by the President on the nomination of the *Taoiseach* with the previous approval of the *Dáil Éireann*. The *Taoiseach* appoints a member of the government to be deputy (the *Tánaiste*).

The judicial system comprises courts of first instance and a court of final appeal called the Supreme Court *(Cúirt Uachtarach)*. The courts of first instance include a High Court *(Ard-Chúirt)* and courts of local and limited jurisdiction, with a right of appeal as determined by law. The High Court alone has original jurisdiction to consider the question of the validity of any law having regard to the provisions of the constitution. The Supreme Court has appellate jurisdiction from decisions of the High Court.

HEAD OF STATE

President, Mary McAleese, *elected* 30 October 1997, *sworn in* 11 November 1997

SELECTED GOVERNMENT MEMBERS *as at July 2004*

Taoiseach (Prime Minister), Bertie Ahern

Tánaiste (Deputy PM), Enterprise, Trade and Employment, Mary Harney

Defence, Michael Smith

Finance, Charlie McCreevy

Foreign Affairs, Brian Cowen

IRISH EMBASSY

17 Grosvenor Place, London SW1X 7HR

T 020-7235 2171

Ambassador Extraordinary and Plenipotentiary, HE Dáithí O'Ceallaigh, apptd 2001

BRITISH EMBASSY

29 Merrion Road, Ballsbridge, IE-Dublin 4

T (+353) (1) 205 3700

E bembassy@internet-ireland.ie

Ambassador Extraordinary and Plenipotentiary, HE Stewart Eldon, CMG, OBE, apptd 2003

BRITISH COUNCIL DIRECTOR, Tony Reilly, MBE

Newmount House, 22/24 Lower Mount Street, IE-Dublin 2

T (+353) (1) 676 4088

E helen.jones@ie.britishcouncil.org

ECONOMY AND TRADE

Ireland's economy boomed during the 1990s, largely thanks to investment from the EU. Ireland's major industries are computer software, information technology, food and drink production, pharmaceuticals and tourism which have helped transform Ireland from a mainly rural economy. Agriculture has been entirely overtaken by light industry and the service industries, and now accounts for only five per cent of the economy. Growth between 1995 and 2002 was eight per cent, however, this slowed to 2.1 per cent in 2003 attributed to the global slowdown in the information technology sector.

The Kinsale gas field off the south coast provided 28 per cent of Ireland's gas needs in 2000, with 72 per cent coming via an undersea pipeline from Moffat, Scotland. There are five government funded power stations. Hydroelectric power from the Shannon barrage and other schemes are also important but Ireland still imports 47 per cent of oil and coal for power generation. Metal content of ores raised in 2000 included: lead (86,896 tonnes) and zinc, (431,426 tonnes).

Per capita GDP is 10 per cent above that of the four biggest west European economies.

GNI – US$87,700 million (2001); US$22,850 per capita (2001)
ANNUAL AVERAGE GROWTH OF GDP – 8.9 per cent (1998)
INFLATION RATE – 5.6 per cent (2000)
UNEMPLOYMENT – 3.8 per cent (2001)
FOREIGN DIRECT INVESTMENT – US$47,516 million (1997–2000)
IMPORTS – US$51,470 million (2002)
EXPORTS – US$87,442 million (2002)

BALANCE OF PAYMENTS
Trade – US$34,898 million surplus (2002)
Current Account – US$925 million deficit (2002)

Trade with UK	*2002*	*2003*
Imports from UK	£14,701,800,000	£14,277,800,000
Exports to UK	8,998,600,000	8,953,187,000

TRANSPORT INFRASTRUCTURE

Ireland has 92,500 km of highways and 3,312 km of railways. There are 700 km of waterways, though these have limited uses for commercial traffic. Ireland's major ports are Arklow, Cork, Drogheda, Dublin, Foynes, Galway, Limerick, New Ross and Waterford.

EDUCATION

Primary education is directed by the state, with the exception of 37 private primary schools. In 1998–9 there were 3,181 state primary schools, 432 recognised secondary schools under private management (mainly religious orders), and 245 vocational schools. There were 16 state comprehensive schools and 66 community schools. Third-level education is catered for by seven university colleges, 13 institutes of technology, seven teacher training colleges and a number of other tertiary institutions.

ENROLMENT (percentage of age group) – primary 100 per cent (1997); secondary 100 per cent (1997); tertiary 41 per cent (1997)

MEDIA AND CULTURE

Irish broadcasting is regulated by a commission appointed by the Department of Communications. The main Irish broadcaster is the state run Radio Telefis Eireann (RTE). The British satellite broadcaster, BskyB, is widely available throughout Ireland. There are three national newspapers: the *Irish Times*, *Irish Independent* and *Irish Examiner*.

Notable literary figures include George Bernard Shaw ((1856–1950) winner of the Nobel Prize for Literature in 1925), W. B. Yeats ((1865–1939) winner of the Nobel Prize for Literature in 1923), James Joyce (1882–1942), Samuel Beckett ((1909–89) Nobel Prize for Literature, 1969) and Roddy Doyle (b. 1958). Other famous cultural figures include the artist Francis Bacon (1909–92), the musician Sir James Galway (b. 1939), the physicist Ernest Walton ((1903–95) joint winner of the Nobel Prize for Physics in 1951) and the scientist Sir Francis Beaufort (1774–1857), famous for the introduction of the Beaufort Wind Force Scale.

ISRAEL

Medinat Yisra'el/Dawlat Isrā'īl – State of Israel

AREA – 20,600 sq. km. Neighbours: Lebanon (north), Syria (north-east), Jordan and the West Bank (east), the Gaza Strip and the Egyptian province of Sinai (south-west)
POPULATION – 6,172,000 (2001): roughly 82 per cent Jewish, 14 per cent Arab Muslims, 2.5 per cent Christians of which 90 per cent are Arab, and 2 per cent Druze. Since independence Israel has had a policy of granting an immigration visa to every Jew who expresses a desire to settle in Israel. Between 1948 and 1992, 2.3 million immigrants had entered Israel from over 100 different countries. Hebrew and Arabic are the official languages. Arabs are entitled to transact all official business with government departments in Arabic
CAPITAL – Most of the government departments are in Jerusalem, population 758,000 (2001 estimate). A resolution proclaiming Jerusalem as the capital of Israel was adopted by the *Knesset* in 1950. It is not, however, recognised as the capital by the UN because East Jerusalem is part of the Occupied Territories captured in 1967. The UN and international law continues to reject the Israeli annexation of East Jerusalem and considers the pre-1950 capital Tel Aviv (population, 1,919,700) to be the capital.
MAJOR CITIES – Beersheba; ΨHaifa; Rishon Le'Zion
CURRENCY – Shekel of 100 agora
NATIONAL ANTHEM – Hatikvah (The Hope)
NATIONAL FLAG – White, with two horizontal blue stripes, the Shield of David in the centre
LIFE EXPECTANCY (years) – 79 (2001)
MORTALITY RATE (per 1,000 population) – 6.2 (2003)
INFANT MORTALITY (per 1,000 births) – 6 (2001)
HIV / AIDS ADULT PREVALENCE – 0.1 per cent (2001)
DEATH PENALTY – Yes*
POPULATION BELOW POVERTY LINE – 18 per cent (2001)
POPULATION GROWTH RATE – 2.8 per cent (1990–2001)
POPULATION DENSITY – 300 per sq. km (2001)
URBAN POPULATION – 92 per cent (2001)

CLIMATE AND TERRAIN

Elevation extremes range from 2,000 m (Mt Hermon) at the highest point, to –408 m (Dead Sea) at the lowest, which is the Earth's deepest depression. Israel comprises the hill country of Galilee and parts of Judea and Samaria, the coastal plain from the Gaza strip to north of Acre, including the plain of Esdraelon running from Haifa Bay to the south-east which divides the hill region; the Negev, a semi-desert triangular-shaped region, extending from a base south of Beersheba to an apex at the head of the Gulf of Aqaba, and parts of the Jordan valley, including the Hula region, Tiberias and the south-western extremity of the Dead Sea. Average temperatures in Tel Aviv range from 14°C in January to 27°C in August.

HISTORY AND POLITICS

In 1917 Palestine was captured from the Ottoman Empire by the British. In the same year the British government made the Balfour Declaration, which pledged a homeland for Jewish people in the same country. Jewish immigration from Europe was encouraged but resulted in tension with the Arab population of Palestine who had also been promised recognition for an Arab state from the British.

As increasing numbers of Jewish refugees from Europe arrived after the Second World War, the British mandate became increasingly untenable and in 1947 the British withdrew. This prompted the first of a series of conflicts between Arabs and Israelis. The creation of the state of Israel on 14 May 1948 created a large number of Palestinian refugees. A further war in 1967, in which Israel pre-emptively attacked the Arab countries, saw Israel extend its territory. The Palestine Liberation Organisation (PLO) under Yasser Arafat began a long struggle against the Israelis. Yet another war in 1973 saw Egypt sign a mutual recognition pact with Israel. However, the 1981 invasion of Lebanon led to an Israeli withdrawal in 1985. The southern area of Lebanon bordering Israel remained an Israeli occupied zone until 2000.

A popular Palestinian uprising, the first *Intifada*, begun in 1987, aimed at ending the Israeli occupation of the Palestinian areas captured in 1967.

Some progress appeared to have been made with the Oslo Peace Accord in 1993, which culminated in an historic handshake between Yasser Arafat and Israeli Prime Minister Yitzhak Rabin. Rabin was assassinated in 1995, and the accord failed.

In 2000 Ariel Sharon, leader of Israel's Likud party well known for taking a hardline approach towards Palestinians, made a visit to the al-Aqsa Mosque/Temple Mount in Jerusalem. This visit to the most hotly disputed religious site in the area, deeply important to both Muslims and Jews, sparked the second Intifada.

On 24 June 2002, US President George Bush laid out a 'road map' for peace which envisioned a two-state solution to the conflict. However, its implementation has faced serious problems. Prime Minister Sharon has proposed the removal of some settlers from the disputed Gaza Strip, but has faced strong opposition from within his own party.

President Ezer Weizman announced that he would resign from office on 10 July 2000 following allegations of fraud. On 31 July, Moshe Katsav was elected president. Ehud Barak resigned as Prime Minister on 9 December 2000 and called a prime ministerial election, which was held on 6 February 2001; it was won by Likud leader Ariel Sharon, who formed a broad-based eight-party coalition which commanded the support of 72 of the 120 members of the *Knesset*. Saleh Tarif became the first Israeli Arab to be appointed to the cabinet. On 19 August 2001 the Centre Party agreed to join the coalition, bringing its support in the *Knesset* to 83 members. The Likud-led National Unity government collapsed on 30 October 2002 after the Labour Party withdrew from the coalition in a dispute over the 2003 budget. A general election on 28 January 2003 resulted in a victory for Likud with 37 seats in the *Knesset* but without an overall majority. A Likud-dominated coalition government was appointed on 27 February 2003 which also included the National Union (NU), the Change-Centre Party (Shinui) and the National Religious Party (NRP). The coalition controls 68 of the 120 seats in the *Knesset*.

In 2003, Israel began the construction of a large barrier separating Israel from the Occupied Territories. Designed to prevent suicide bombers reaching Israel from the Territories, the wall has been widely criticised for enclosing Palestinian land. In 2004, the International Court of Justice ruled that the barrier was illegal and should be dismantled.

POLITICAL SYSTEM

Israel is a Sovereign Democratic Republic with executive power vested in a Prime Minister and Cabinet, and legislative power in a unicameral legislature *(Knesset)* of 120 members elected by proportional representation for a maximum term of four years. In March 2001 the *Knesset* passed an amendment to the Basic Law on Government ending the system of separate Prime Ministerial elections and reverting to the former position where the Prime Minister is responsible to Parliament and formally appointed by the President. The President is head of state and is elected by the *Knesset*. Previous presidents had been elected for a maximum of two five-year terms, but under a bill approved by the *Knesset* in December 1998, the President is now elected for a seven-year non-renewable term.

HEAD OF STATE

President of Israel, Moshe Katsav, *elected* 31 July 2000, *sworn in* 1 August 2000

SELECTED GOVERNMENT MEMBERS *as at August 2004*

Prime Minister, Communications and Religious Affairs, Ariel Sharon
Deputy Prime Minister, Foreign Affairs, Sylvan Shalom
Deputy Prime Minister, Justice, Yosef Tommy Lapid
Deputy Prime Minister, Trade and Industry, Ehud Olmert
Defence, Gen. Shaul Mofaz
Finance, Binyamin Netanyahu
Interior and Communications, Avraham Poraz

EMBASSY OF ISRAEL

2 Palace Green, Kensington, London W8 4QB
T 020-7957 9500

BRITISH EMBASSY

192 Hayarkon Street, Tel Aviv 63405
T (+972) (3) 725 1222
Ambassador Extraordinary and Plenipotentiary, HE Simon McDonald, CMG, LVO, apptd 2003

BRITISH COUNCIL DIRECTOR, Kevin Lewis

Crystal House, 12 Hahilazon Street, Ramat Gan 52136 Tel Aviv
T (+972) (3) 611 3600
E bcta@britishcouncil.org.il

DEFENCE

Israel is believed to have a nuclear capacity of around 200 warheads which could be delivered by aircraft or Jericho I and II missiles. The Army has 3,950 main battle tanks and around 12,700 armoured personnel carriers. The Navy has three submarines and 48 patrol and coastal vessels at three bases. The Air Force has 438 combat aircraft and 100 armed helicopters.

MILITARY EXPENDITURE – 9.7 per cent of GDP (2002)
MILITARY PERSONNEL – 167,600: Army 125,000, Navy 7,600, Air Force 35,000; Paramilitaries 8,050
CONSCRIPTION DURATION – 24–48 months (Jews and Druze only)

ECONOMY AND TRADE

Israel exports diamonds, chemicals and agricultural products and has developed a respected technology sector, central to which are the electronics, biotechnology and software industries. As well as a strong technology sector, Israel is an important producer of citrus fruits, vegetables, cotton, beef, poultry and dairy products.

Other important manufacturing industries include plastics, rubber, cement, glass, paper and oil refining. Industry accounted for 27 per cent and the service industries for 47 per cent of GDP in 2000.

In 2001 the country entered recession. Conflict with Palestine and a downturn in the technology sector produced the country's longest recession since the 1960s. A recovery package was approved by the *Knesset* in 2003. Israeli trade unions forced some reforms on the measures, which included cuts in public spending. In 2004 interest rates were reduced to eight per cent, and there were signs of rising business and consumer confidence as well as increased demand for exports.

Around half of Israel's debt is owed to the USA, which is Israel's main source of economic and military aid. The USA is also Israel's main trading partner, accounting for 40.3 per cent of exports in 2002.

GNI – US$106,600 million (2001); US$16,750 per capita (2001)
ANNUAL AVERAGE GROWTH OF GDP – 5.7 per cent (2000)
INFLATION RATE – 1.1 per cent (2000)
UNEMPLOYMENT – 8.8 per cent (2000)
FOREIGN DIRECT INVESTMENT – US$11,311 million (1997–2000)
IMPORTS – US$35,517 million (2002)
EXPORTS – US$29,513 million (2002)

BALANCE OF PAYMENTS
Trade – US$3,757 million deficit (2002)
Current Account – US$2,135 million deficit (2002)

Trade with UK	*2002*	*2003*
Imports from UK	£1,440,191,000	£1,377,010,000
Exports to UK	910,853,000	881,639,000

TRANSPORT INFRASTRUCTURE

Israel State Railways serves Haifa, Tel Aviv, Jerusalem, Lod, Nahariya, Beersheba, Dimona, Ashdod and intermediate stations with a network of 647 km. There were 15,965 km of surfaced roads in 2000. A major road building programme has been under way in the West Bank since 1992. The chief ports are Haifa and Ashdod on the Mediterranean, and Eilat on the Red Sea; Acre has an anchorage for small vessels. The chief international airport is Ben Gurion between Tel Aviv and Jerusalem.

EDUCATION

Education from five to 16 years is free of charge and compulsory. Youths aged 16–18, who are in work but have not completed their education, can be given time off to complete their studies. There are seven universities including two engineering and technological institutes.

ILLITERACY RATE – (m) 2.1 per cent; (f) 5.8 per cent (2000)
ENROLMENT (percentage of age group) – tertiary 41.1 per cent (1997)

MEDIA

The Israeli Broadcasting Authority (IBA) is a public broadcaster operating television and radio services funded largely by a licence fee. This competes with two main terrestrial commercial channels and a number of satellite and cable stations. The radio sector features a number of commercial stations, but there are also a large number of unlicensed radio stations. The press includes five national dailies including *Haaretz*, *Jerusalem Post*, *Maariv* and *The Jerusalem Report*.

CULTURE

The Israel Museum in Jerusalem houses the Dead Sea Scrolls along with an extensive collection of Jewish religious and folk art. Jerusalem has a vast number of historic sites, including the Church of the Holy Sepulchre, sacred to Christians, and the al-Aqsa Mosque, which stands on the remains of Temple Mount.

Israel has absorbed large numbers of Jewish refugees from Europe and so has strong traditions in European classical music. Shmuel Yosef Agno (1880–1970) was the first Hebrew writer to win the Nobel Prize for Literature in 1966.

PALESTINIAN AUTONOMOUS AREAS

AREA – The total area is 6,231 sq. km. The area which is fully autonomous is 412 sq. km, of which the Gaza Strip is 352 sq. km and the Jericho enclave 60 sq. km. The partially autonomous area is the remainder of the West Bank, some 5,819 sq. km. The UN and the international community also recognise East Jerusalem as part of the Occupied Territories
POPULATION – 3,634,585 (2003 estimate), of whom 394,105 live in East Jerusalem. In addition there are 176,000 Jewish settlers in the West Bank and 6,900 in the Gaza Strip (2000 estimate) who remain under Israeli administration and jurisdiction. Some 90 per cent of Palestinians are Muslim (the vast majority Sunni) and 10 per cent are Christians
CAPITAL – Although Palestinians claim East Jerusalem as their capital, the administrative capital has been established in Gaza City (population 460,899)
MAJOR TOWNS – Khan Yunis, Rafah in the Gaza Strip; Nablus, Hebron, Jericho, Ramallah and Bethlehem on the West Bank
FLAG – Three horizontal stripes of black, white, green with a red triangle based on the hoist (the PLO flag)
NATIONAL ANTHEM – Fidai, Fidai (Freedom Fighter, Freedom Fighter)

HISTORY AND POLITICS

From 1967 to 1994, the West Bank and Gaza Strip were administered by the Israeli Ministry of Defence. Frustration at continued Israeli occupation led to the start of the *Intifada*, a campaign of sustained unrest, in 1987. When the 1991 Madrid peace process stalled, Israeli and Palistinian Liberation Organisation (PLO) officials engaged in secret negotiations in Norway which led to signing the 'Declaration of Principles on Interim Self-Government Arrangements' on 13 September 1993. The Declaration of Principles established a timetable for progress towards a final settlement.

The 'Oslo B' or Taba Accord was signed on 28 September 1995 and provided for Israeli withdrawal from six towns and 85 per cent of Hebron; the extension of self-rule to most of the West Bank by 1998; the release of 5,300 Palestinian prisoners; and the striking out of the demand for Israel's destruction from the PLO's charter. On 29 December 1995 an agreement was reached on the transfer of 17 areas of civilian power to the PNA in Hebron.

Israeli troops left Ramallah, the last of the six West Bank towns, on 27 December 1995 and the inaugural Palestinian National Council meeting on 23 April 1996 voted to amend the PLO charter. The final element of the Declaration of Principles, the 'final status talks', opened in Taba, Egypt, on 5 May 1996 to decide the final status of the West Bank, Gaza and Jerusalem. The election of a Likud-led government opposed to the establishment of a Palestinian state resulted in a deadlock in negotiations in 1997 and delays in the withdrawal of Israeli troops from Hebron.

A new round of peace talks began on 14 December and a US draft accord was discussed, which envisaged a Palestinian state on 95 per cent of the West Bank and the entire Gaza Strip. Agreement could not be reached and the talks broke down on 27 January 2001. Relations remained volatile throughout 2002 with Palestinian suicide bombings and Israeli retaliation amid cease-fires and intense diplomatic intervention. Renewed violent conflict took place in late 2002–3 and Yasser Arafat was subjected to a ten-day siege by Israeli security forces in September 2002 following a fatal suicide bombing in Tel Aviv on 19 September. The siege was lifted on 29 September after a UN Security Council resolution demanded the withdrawal of Israeli forces.

The Palestinian cabinet resigned on 11 September 2002 after the Palestine Legislative Council (PLC) threatened to pass a vote of no confidence in it. Arafat named Mahmoud Abbas as prime minister on 19 March. Abbas's appointment and his cabinet were approved by the PLC on 29 April after extensive negotiations.

The 'road map' peace plan, set out by the EU, Russia, the UN and the USA was launched on 30 April 2003 and endorsed by the Palestinian and Israeli prime ministers at a summit with US President George Bush on 5 June. The plan was intended to be a phase-by-phase route to ending the violence in the region leading to the establishment of an autonomous Palestinian state by 2005. Although Hamas rejected the 'road map' peace plan, the group, along with Islamic *Jihad* and *Fatah*, announced on 30 June 2003 that they would observe a three-month truce with Israel. In July of the same year, Israeli forces withdrew from some key areas in the West Bank and the Gaza Strip. However, Mahmoud Abbas, reportedly frustrated at the road map's lack of progress, resigned as prime minister on 6 September 2003. His replacement, Ahmed Qurei was named by Arafat on 7 September 2003, but he resigned his post in June 2004, citing a lack of control over security issues. However, after crisis talks with President Arafat, he retracted the resignation. Presidential and legislative elections were scheduled for late 2004.

POLITICAL SYSTEM

Executive authority is vested in the Palestinian National Authority which is headed by a popularly elected leader *(Rais)*. Legislative authority is vested in the 88-member Palestinian Legislative Council which is directly elected by means of a first past the post system, and itself elects the four-fifths of the PNA not appointed by the leader.

SELECTED GOVERNMENT MEMBERS *as at July 2004*
President, Yasser Arafat
Prime Minister, Information, Ahmed Qurei
Economy, Trade and Industry, Mahir al-Masri
Foreign Affairs, Nabil Sha'ath
Interior, Hakam Balaawi

PALESTINIAN GENERAL DELEGATION
5 Galena Road, London W6 0LT
T 020-8563 0008
General Delegate, Afif Safieh

BRITISH CONSULATE-GENERAL
19 Nashashibi Street, PO Box 19690, East Jerusalem 97200
T (+972) (2) 541 4100
Consul-General, John Jenkins, CMG, LVO, apptd 2003

BRITISH COUNCIL DIRECTOR, Sarah Ewans, OBE
31 Nablus Road, PO Box 19136, East Jerusalem
T (+972) (2) 628 2545
E british.council@ej.britishcouncil.org

ECONOMY AND TRADE

The major industries are construction materials, textiles and metal goods, mainly run by small family businesses. The main export is citrus fruits, and the main trading partners are Israel and Jordan.

GNI – US$3,000 million (2002); US$930 per capita (2002)
ANNUAL AVERAGE GROWTH OF GDP – 19.1 per cent (2002)
INFLATION RATE – 23.6 per cent (2002)
POPULATION BELOW POVERTY LINE – 59 per cent (2002)

Trade with UK	*2002*	*2003*
Imports from UK	£111,000	£691,000
Exports to UK	241,000	442,000

ITALY

Repubblica Italiana – Italian Republic

AREA – 294,100 sq. km. Neighbours: Switzerland and Austria (north), Slovenia (east), France (west)
POPULATION – 57,503,000 (2001): 83 per cent Catholic. The language is Italian, a Romance language derived from Latin. There are several regional languages including Sardinian and Catalan in Sardinia, Friulian in Friuli, German and Ladin in the South Tyrol, French in the Valle d'Aosta, and Slovene in parts of Gorizia
CAPITAL – Rome (population, 2,459,776, 2001 census). The Eternal City was founded, according to legend, by Romulus in 753 BC. It was the centre of Latin civilisation and capital of the Roman Republic and Roman Empire
MAJOR CITIES – Bologna; Florence; ΨGenoa; Milan; ΨNaples; Turin; Sicily, ΨPalermo; Sardinia, ΨCagliari
CURRENCY – Euro (€) of 100 cents
NATIONAL ANTHEM – Inno Di Mameli (Hymn Of Mameli)
NATIONAL DAY – 2 June
NATIONAL FLAG – Vertical stripes of green, white and red
LIFE EXPECTANCY (years) – 79 (2001)
MORTALITY RATE (per 1,000 population) – 10.12 (2003)
INFANT MORTALITY (per 1,000 births) – 4 (2001)
HIV / AIDS ADULT PREVALENCE – 0.4 per cent (2001)
DEATH PENALTY – No (abolished 1994)
POPULATION GROWTH RATE – 0.1 per cent (1990–2001)
POPULATION DENSITY – 196 per sq. km (2001)
URBAN POPULATION – 67 per cent (2001)

CLIMATE AND TERRAIN

Italy consists of a peninsula, the islands of Sicily, Sardinia, Elba and about 70 other small islands. The peninsula is for the most part mountainous, but between the Apennines, which form its spine, and the eastern coastline are two large fertile plains: Emilia-Romagna in the north and Apulia in the south. The Alps divide Italy from France, Switzerland, Austria and Slovenia. Elevation extremes range from 4,061 m (Gran Paradiso) at the highest point to 0 m (Mediterranean Sea) at the lowest. The chief rivers are the Po (651 km) which flows through Piedmont, Lombardy and the Veneto; the Adige (Trentino and Veneto); the Arno (Florentine plain); and the Tiber (flowing through Rome to Ostia).

HISTORY AND POLITICS

The Etruscans were the first people to control the Italian peninsula. Their empire flourished between the 12th and eighth centuries BC, but was eventually overtaken by the Romans. At the height of its power, the Roman Empire spread from Italy across Europe, Asia Minor and North Africa. Conquered and settled by a variety of invaders throughout the 'Dark Ages', Italy began to develop into a number of competing city states. These, with their powerful and wealthy merchant classes, became the locations (and provided the capital) for the Renaissance. Italian nationalists began to agitate for a unified Italy throughout the 19th century, culminating in the declaration of the Kingdom of Italy in 1861. The major figures in Italian unification were Mazzini (1805–72), Garibaldi (1807–82) and Cavour (1810–61).

In 1923 the fascist leader Benito Mussolini, promising a firm rule to end the disruption, seized power. Mussolini tied Italy into an alliance with Adolf Hitler's Germany, and thus led Italy into the Second World War on the Axis side. The Allies invaded Sicily in 1943, which led to a coup to depose Mussolini, who was eventually captured and killed by partisans on 28 April 1945. Italy became a republic after the war, with the king abdicating shortly after the country's new constitution came into force, abolishing the monarchy. A post-war boom lasted until the late 1970s when inflation and unemployment ensued. This was a time of serious civil unrest, with unions opposed to often corrupt governments and extreme right- and left-wing groups conducting violent campaigns.

In the early 1990s Italy experienced a drive to reform its political establishment. Links between the government and organised crime were exposed and many politicians were arrested. However, this exposed new divisions within Italian society, chiefly a secessionist movement called the Northern League, which claimed to be dedicated to independence for the northern territories of Italy from the poorer south.

Ulivo (Olive Tree) was a coalition of left-wing parties led by Romano Prodi that won the general election in 1996. Though unstable (the coalition had three different prime ministers in five years), it successfully prepared Italy to enter as one of the founding members of the single European currency on 1 January 2002.

The general election held on 13 May 2001 was won by the centre-right House of Freedom alliance, which obtained 368 seats. The alliance was led by Forza Italia and also comprised the Christian Democratic Centre, the Christian Democratic Union, the National Alliance, the New Italian Socialist Party and the Northern League. Silvio Berlusconi was sworn in as prime minister on 11 June. However, in 2003 he appeared in court on corruption charges relating to the alleged bribery of judges during a business take-over in 1985. Berlusconi denied the charges and in January 2003 stated he would retain his position even if found guilty. The trial was halted in June after parliament passed law-granting immunity from prosecution to five holders of key state posts, including the prime minister.

POLITICAL SYSTEM

The constitution provides for the election of the President for a seven-year term by an electoral college which consists of the two houses of the Parliament (the Chamber of Deputies and the Senate) sitting in joint session, together with three delegates from each region (one in the case of the Valle d'Aosta). The President, who must be over 50 years of age, has the right to dissolve one or both houses after consultation with the Speakers. Members of both houses were elected wholly by proportional representation until 1993. Now 75 per cent (232) of the 315 elected seats in the Senate are elected on a first past the post basis and the remaining elected seats are filled by proportional representation. There is a variable number of life senators, who are past Presidents and senators appointed by incumbent Presidents. In the Chamber of Deputies 75 per cent (472) of seats are elected on a first past the post basis, and 25 per cent (158) by proportional representation, with a four per cent threshold for parliamentary representation. A referendum on 18 April 1999 on abolishing the seats elected by proportional representation foundered when less than the required 50 per cent of the electorate participated.

HEAD OF STATE

President, Carlo Azeglio Ciampi, *elected* 13 May 1999, *took office* 18 May 1999

SELECTED GOVERNMENT MEMBERS *as at July 2004*

Prime Minister, Silvio Berlusconi
Deputy Prime Minister, Gianfranco Fini
Defence, Antonio Martino
Economy and Finance, Domenico Siniscalco
Foreign Affairs, Franco Frattini
Interior, Giuseppe Pisanu

ITALIAN EMBASSY

14 Three Kings Yard, Davies Street, London W1K 4EH
T 020-7312 2200
Ambassador Extraordinary and Plenipotentiary, HE Giancarlo Aragona, apptd 2004

BRITISH EMBASSY

Via XX Settembre 80A, I-00187 Rome
T (+39) (6) 4220 0001
Ambassador Extraordinary and Plenipotentiary, HE Sir Ivor Roberts, KCMG, apptd 2003

BRITISH COUNCIL DIRECTOR, Paul Docherty

Via Quattro Fontane 20, I-00184 Rome
E studyandcultureuk@britishcouncil.it

DEFENCE

The Army has 1,183 main battle tanks and 2,136 armoured personnel carriers. The Navy has six submarines, one aircraft carrier, one cruiser, four destroyers, 14 frigates, 16 patrol and coastal vessels, 18 combat aircraft and 80 armed helicopters. There are four

naval bases. The Air Force has 263 combat aircraft and six armed helicopters.
MILITARY EXPENDITURE – 1.9 per cent of GDP (2002)
MILITARY PERSONNEL – 200,000: Army 116,000, Navy 36,000, Air Force 48,000; Paramilitaries 254,300
CONSCRIPTION DURATION – Ten months

ECONOMY AND TRADE

Italy is the world's fifth-largest industrial economy, and it has achieved this with few natural resources. Italy remains divided between a prosperous and industrially developed north and a largely agricultural south that has suffered high unemployment. Agricultural produce includes fruits, vegetables, grapes, potatoes, sugar beets, soy beans, grain, olives; beef, dairy products and fish.

Small- and medium-sized family industries provide a large amount of economic output. Many of these are centred around manufactured goods. Major industries include motor vehicles, chemicals, pharmaceuticals, electrical goods, textiles, fashion, clothing and footwear. 54.4 per cent of trade takes place within the European Union, with Germany being Italy's main trading partner.
GNI – US$1,123,800 million (2001); US$19,390 per capita (2001)
ANNUAL AVERAGE GROWTH OF GDP – 2.9 per cent (2000)
INFLATION RATE – 2.7 per cent (2003)
UNEMPLOYMENT – 8.7 per cent (2004)
FOREIGN DIRECT INVESTMENT – US$26,293 million (1997–2000)
IMPORTS – US$244,178 million (2002)
EXPORTS – US$253,228 million (2002)

BALANCE OF PAYMENTS
Trade – US$16,533 million surplus (2002)
Current Account – US$6,741 million deficit (2002)

Trade with UK	*2002*	*2003*
Imports from UK	£8,079,900,000	£6,279,175,000
Exports to UK	9,951,500,000	8,387,810,000

TRANSPORT INFRASTRUCTURE

The main railway system is state run by the *Ferrovia dello Stato*. There are 19,466 km of railways. A 9,500 km network of motorways *(autostrade)* covers the country but there are 305,881 km of roads in total. Alitalia is the principal international and domestic airline. In January 2001, the Italian and French presidents agreed plans to build a 52 km rail tunnel through the Alps as part of a high-speed rail link between Turin and Lyons. Commissioning of the project is scheduled for 2012.

EDUCATION

Education is free of charge and compulsory between the ages of six and 16. Pupils who obtain a middle school certificate may seek admission to any 'senior secondary school', which may be a lyceum with a classical or scientific or artistic bias, or an institute directed at technology, trade or industry, or teacher-training. Courses at the lyceums and technical institutes usually last five years and success in the final examination qualifies for admission to university. There are 42 state and six private universities, three technical universities and 12 university institutes. The universities at Bologna, Modena, Parma and Padua are of ancient foundation and were started in the 12th century.

ILLITERACY RATE – (m) 1.1 per cent; (f) 2.0 per cent (2000)
ENROLMENT (percentage of age group) – primary 100 per cent (1997); tertiary 47 per cent (1997)

MEDIA

Rai is Italy's public broadcaster and competes with a number of private broadcasters including Mediaset. The Italian press contains many regional publications, as well as five national dailies. Italy has one of Europe's highest levels of internet use with 28.61 million users in 2004.

CULTURE

Florence, the capital of Tuscany, was one of the greatest cities in Europe from the 11th to the 16th centuries, and the cradle of the Renaissance. Under the Medici family in the 15th century flourished many of the greatest names in Italian art, including Filippo Lippi, Botticelli, Donatello and Brunelleschi and, in the 16th century, Michelangelo and Leonardo da Vinci.

Dante Alighieri (1265–1321) and Boccaccio (1313–75) were two of the earliest writers to compose works in vernacular languages. Notable contemporary Italian writers include Umberto Eco (b. 1932), Dario Fo ((b. 1926) winner of the Nobel Prize for Literature in 1997) and Eugenio Montale ((1896–1981) winner of the Nobel Prize for Literature in 1975).

In the 20th century, Italian cinema was distinguished as a powerful force by directors such as Luchino Visconti (1906–76) and Roberto Rossellini (1906–77).

ISLANDS

Capri, in the Bay of Naples; Eolian Islands, including Lipari; Flegrean Islands, including Ischia; Pantelleria Island (part of Trapani Province) in the Sicilian Narrows; The Pelagian Islands (Lampedusa, Linosa and Lampione) are part of the province of Agrigento; Pontine Archipelago, including Ponza; Tremiti Islands; The Tuscan Archipelago (including Elba).

JAMAICA

AREA – 10,800 sq. km
POPULATION – 2,598,000 (2001). The official language is English; a local patois is also spoken
CAPITAL – ΨKingston (population, 524,638, 1991)
MAJOR CITIES – Mandeville; May Pen; ΨMontego Bay; Ocho Rios; Spanish Town
CURRENCY – Jamaican dollar (J$) of 100 cents
NATIONAL ANTHEM – Jamaica, Land We Love
NATIONAL DAY – 6 August (Independence Day)
NATIONAL FLAG – Gold diagonal cross forming triangles of green at top and bottom, triangles of black at hoist and in fly
LIFE EXPECTANCY (years) – 75 (2001)
MORTALITY RATE (per 1,000 population) – 5.42 (2003)
INFANT MORTALITY (per 1,000 births) – 17 (2001)
HIV / AIDS ADULT PREVALENCE – 1.2 per cent (2001)
DEATH PENALTY – Yes
POPULATION BELOW POVERTY LINE – 34.2 per cent (2002)
POPULATION GROWTH RATE – 0.8 per cent (1990–2001)
POPULATION DENSITY – 241 per sq. km (2001)
URBAN POPULATION – 57 per cent (2001)
MILITARY EXPENDITURE – 0.5 per cent of GDP (2002)
MILITARY PERSONNEL – 2,830: Army 2,500, Coast Guard 190, Air Wing 140

ILLITERACY RATE – (m) 17.1 per cent; (f) 9.3 per cent (2000)
ENROLMENT (percentage of age group) – primary 100 per cent (1999); secondary 69 per cent (1999); tertiary 13 per cent (1999)

CLIMATE AND TERRAIN

Jamaica is located in the Caribbean Sea, with Cuba to the north and the Dominican Republic and Haiti to the east. Elevation extremes range from 2,256 m (Blue Mountain Peak) at the highest point to 0 m (Caribbean Sea) at the lowest. Jamaica has a temperate, humid climate with average temperatures ranging from 25°C in January to 29°C in July.

HISTORY AND POLITICS

Jamaica was settled by the Spanish from 1510, and taken over by the British in 1654. Slavery was abolished in 1834, autonomy from Britain came in 1947 followed by independence in 1962.

Post-independence Jamaican politics has been dominated by the Jamaican Labour Party (JLP) and People's National Party (PNP). Relations between the two parties have been fraught, and Jamaican elections and political life have often been marred by violence. The People's National Party (PNP) has been in power since 1989. At the general election of 16 October 2002, the PNP retained an overall majority with 34 out of a total of 60 seats, securing a fourth term for the party and a third term for Prime Minister Percival Patterson, who was sworn in on 23 October.

POLITICAL SYSTEM
Queen Elizabeth II is the Head of State, represented by the Governor-General. The legislature consists of a Senate of 21 nominated members and a House of Representatives consisting of 60 members elected by universal adult suffrage for a five-year term. The Prime Minister is the leader of the majority party in the House.
Governor-General, HE Sir Howard Felix Hanlon Cooke, GCMG, GCVO, apptd 1991

SELECTED GOVERNMENT MEMBERS *as at July 2004*
Prime Minister, Defence, Percival J. Patterson, QC
Finance and Planning, Omar Davies
Foreign Affairs and Foreign Trade, Keith Desmond Knight

JAMAICAN HIGH COMMISSION
1–2 Prince Consort Road, London SW7 2BZ
T 020-7823 9911
High Commissioner, HE Maxine Roberts, CD, apptd 2002

BRITISH HIGH COMMISSION
PO Box 575, Trafalgar Road, Kingston 10
T (+1 876) 510 0700
E bhckingston@cwjamaica.com
High Commissioner, HE Peter Mathers, LVO, apptd 2002

BRITISH COUNCIL MANAGER, Nicola Johnson
28 Trafalgar Road, Kingston 10
T (+1 876) 929 7090
E bcjamaica@britishcouncil.org.jm

ECONOMY AND TRADE

Sugarcane and bananas continue to play a major part in the Jamaican economy but it is now far more reliant on the service industries, including tourism, which makes up 70 per cent of GDP; industry accounted for 24 per cent, and agriculture for 6 per cent in 2003.

Natural resources include alumina and bauxite, which comprise the majority of Jamaican exports. Remittances from Jamaicans living abroad are also of economic significance.

Tight fiscal and monetary policies have slowed inflation but Jamaica has been affected by high interest rates, increased foreign competition, unemployment and a growing internal debt. However, in 2003 the economy benefited from an exceptionally good tourist season.
GNI – US$7,300 million (2001); US$2,800 per capita (2001)
ANNUAL AVERAGE GROWTH OF GDP – 0.8 per cent (2000)
INFLATION RATE – 8.2 per cent (2000)
UNEMPLOYMENT – 15.8 per cent (1999)
TOTAL EXTERNAL DEBT – US$4,287 million (2000)
FOREIGN DIRECT INVESTMENT – US$1,486 million (1997–2000)
IMPORTS – US$3,533 million (2002)
EXPORTS – US$1,114 million (2002)

BALANCE OF PAYMENTS
Trade – US$1,618 million deficit (2001)
Current Account – US$788 million deficit (2001)

Trade with UK	*2002*	*2003*
Imports from UK	£81,792,000	£60,488,000
Exports to UK	106,512,000	119,652,000

TRANSPORT INFRASTRUCTURE

There are several harbours, Kingston being the principal port. The island has 2,944 miles of main roads and 7,264 miles of subsidiary roads.

MEDIA

The state broadcaster was privatised in 1997, and now operates Television Jamaica Limited (TVJ). It competes with a commercial and a religious broadcaster.

CULTURE

Jamaica's diverse cultural heritage includes a vibrant contemporary music scene (Kingston is widely regarded as the birthplace and spiritual home of reggae), as well as a strong literary tradition. Significant cultural figures include the poet Linton Kwasi-Johnson (b. 1952), the musician Bob Marley (1945–81) and the politician and activist Marcus Garvey (1887–1940).

JAPAN

Nihon-koku – State of Japan

AREA – 364,500 sq. km
POPULATION – 129,619,000 (2003). The principal religions are Mahayana Buddhism and Shinto. About 1 per cent of Japanese are Christians. The language is Japanese
CAPITAL – Tokyo (population, 12,310,000, 2003 census)
MAJOR CITIES – ΨFukuoka; ΨKobe; Kyoto, the ancient capital; ΨNagoya; ΨOsaka; Sapporo; ΨYokohama
CURRENCY – Yen
NATIONAL ANTHEM – Kimigayo (His Majesty's Reign)
NATIONAL FLAG – White, charged with sun (red)
LIFE EXPECTANCY (years) – 81 (2001)

INFANT MORTALITY (per 1,000 births) – 3 (2001)
DEATH PENALTY – Yes
POPULATION GROWTH RATE – 0.14 per cent (2002–2003)
POPULATION DENSITY – 349 per sq. km (2001)
URBAN POPULATION – 79 per cent (2001)

CLIMATE AND TERRAIN

Japan consists of four large islands: *Honshu* (or Mainland) 230,448 sq. km, *Shikoku*, 18,757 sq. km, *Kyushu*, 42,079 sq. km, *Hokkaido*, 78,508 sq. km, and many small islands (including Okinawa). The interior is very mountainous, and crossing the mainland from the Sea of Japan to the Pacific is a group of volcanoes, mainly extinct or dormant. Elevation extremes range from 3,776 m (Mount Fuji) at the highest point to –4 m (Hachiro gata) at the lowest. Average temperatures in Tokyo range from 3°C in January to 27°C in August.

HISTORY AND POLITICS

By the ninth century AD, a single empire had been established across what is now modern Japan. In the 12th century, the country was plunged into a centuries-long period of rivalry and aggression between different *samurai* (Japan's feudal warrior class) families. Imperial domination was re-established in 1868 after long periods of civil warfare.

In the 19th century, A US naval officer, Commodore Perry, was among the first to persuade the Japanese to receive foreign trade, and an agreement was signed between the US and Japan on 31 March 1834. Industrialisation followed and Japan adopted a western-style constitution in 1889.

Emperor Hirohito ascended the throne in 1926, ushering in a period of intense nationalism, which was simultaneously accompanied by a rise in militarism that led the country into an invasion of China in 1931 and a pact with the European fascist powers of Germany and Italy in 1940.

Japan's defeat in the Second World War was followed by a period of extraordinary economic growth but in the 1990s Japan suffered an economic slowdown and a massive earthquake at Kobe, which killed more than 5,000 people.

Following the legislative elections of 2003, the Liberal Democrat Party (LDP) won 237 seats in the *Shugi-in* (house of representatives), making it the majority party with 37.4 per cent of the total number of seats. Prime Minister Koizumi was re-elected for another term of office. The July 2004 elections to the *Sangi-in* (house of councillors) saw the LDP retain 114 of 247 seats.

POLITICAL SYSTEM

Legislative authority rests with the bicameral Diet *(Kokkai)*, which comprises a 480-member House of Representatives, and a 247-member House of Councillors. The House of Representatives chooses the prime minister from among its ranks, ratifies treaties and passes budget bills. Since January 2000, 180 of its members are elected by proportional representation in 11 regional blocks and 300 in single-member, first past the post constituencies. All members serve four-year terms. The House of Councillors elects half its members every three years for six-year terms. Unlike the lower house it cannot be dissolved by the Prime Minister. Executive authority is vested in the Cabinet which is responsible to the legislature.

HEAD OF STATE
His Imperial Majesty The Emperor of Japan, Emperor Akihito, *born* 23 December 1933; *succeeded* 8 January 1989; *enthroned* 12 November 1990
Heir, HRH Crown Prince Naruhito Hironomiya, *born* 23 February 1960

SELECTED GOVERNMENT MEMBERS *as at September 2004*
Prime Minister, Junichiro Koizumi
Finance, Sadakazu Tanigaki
Foreign Affairs, Nobutaka Machimura
Internal Affairs and Communications, Taro Aso

EMBASSY OF JAPAN
101–104 Piccadilly, London W1J 7JT
T 020-7465 6500
Ambassador Extraordinary and Plenipotentiary, HE Masaki Orita, apptd 2001

BRITISH EMBASSY
No. 1 Ichiban-cho, Chiyoda-ku, Tokyo 102–8381
T (+81) (3) 5211–1100
E embassytokyo@fco.gov.uk
Ambassador Extraordinary and Plenipotentiary, HE Sir Stephen Gomersall, KCMG, apptd 1999

BRITISH COUNCIL DIRECTOR, Alan Currey
1–2 Kagurazaka, Shinjuku-ku, Tokyo 162–0825
T (+81) (3) 3235 8031
E enquires@britishcouncil.or.jp

DEFENCE

The constitution prohibits the maintenance of armed forces, although internal security forces were created in the 1950s and their mission was extended in 1954 to include the defence of Japan against aggression. In the 1990s legislation was passed permitting the armed forces limited participation in UN peacekeeping missions and allowing them to enter foreign conflicts in order to rescue Japanese nationals. A revision to the USA–Japan defence co-operation guidelines agreed in 1997 permits Japan to play a supporting role in US military operations in areas surrounding Japan. In July 2003 the Japanese parliament passed legislation approving the deployment of Japanese troops in Iraq to assist with post-war reconstruction.

The Ground Self-Defence Force (GSDF) has some 1,040 main battle tanks, around 830 armoured personnel carriers, 60 infantry fighting vehicles, ten aircraft and 90 attack helicopters. The Maritime Self-Defence Force (MSDF) has 16 submarines, 45 destroyers, ten frigates, five patrol and coastal vessels, 80 combat aircraft and 102 armed helicopters at five bases. The Air Self-Defence Force (ASDF) has 270 combat aircraft.
MILITARY EXPENDITURE – 1.0 per cent of GDP (2002)
MILITARY PERSONNEL – 239,900: Army 148,200, Navy 44,400, Air Force 45,600; Paramilitaries 12,250

ECONOMY AND TRADE

Japan is the third-largest economy in the world after the USA and China. Over-investment in the late 1980s slowed the economy in the 1990s, but between 2003 and 2004 the growth rate has averaged four per cent. A package of economic reforms was announced on 5 April 2001, which focused on the structural reform of the financial industry.

Owing to the mountainous nature of the country less than 20 per cent of its area can be cultivated and only 14 per cent is used for agriculture; 67 per cent is wooded. The soil is only moderately fertile but intensive cultivation secures good crops. Tobacco, tea, potatoes, rice, maize, wheat and other cereals are all cultivated. Rice is the staple foodstuff.

Major Japanese industries include the production of motor vehicles, electronic equipment, machine tools, steel and non-ferrous metals, ships, chemicals, textiles and processed foods. Motor vehicles, semiconductors, office machinery and chemicals make up Japan's major export commodities. The service industries contribute 67.7 per cent of Japanese GDP and industry 30.9 per cent, agriculture makes up 1.9 per cent of GDP. The USA is by far the largest trading partner and takes 28.8 per cent of exports. China is of increasing importance and takes 9.6 per cent.

GNI – US$4,523,300 million (2001); US$35,610 per capita (2001)
ANNUAL AVERAGE GROWTH OF GDP – 0.5 per cent (2000)
INFLATION RATE – 0.1 per cent (2001)
UNEMPLOYMENT – 5.0 per cent (2004)
FOREIGN DIRECT INVESTMENT – US$27,003 million (1997–2000)
IMPORTS – US$337,194 million (2002)
EXPORTS – US$416,726 million (2002)

BALANCE OF PAYMENTS
Trade – US$93,829 million surplus (2002)
Current Account – US$112,447 million surplus (2002)

Trade with UK	*2002*	*2003*
Imports from UK	£3,593,405,000	£3,739,070,000
Exports to UK	8,489,641,000	8,247,215,000

TRANSPORT INFRASTRUCTURE
There are 23,654 km of railway track and 1,152,207 km of roads. *Shinkansen* (bullet train) tracks are currently being expanded. The Seikan rail tunnel and the Seto Ohashi rail bridge link the four major islands. There are six international airports.

EDUCATION
Elementary education is free of charge and compulsory at elementary level (six-year course) and lower secondary (three-year course). The upper secondary schools (three-year course) are attended by 96.7 per cent of the relevant age group. There are two- or three-year colleges and four-year universities. In 1999 there were 622 universities and colleges, most of which are privately maintained.
ENROLMENT (percentage of age group) – primary 100 per cent (1997); secondary 100 per cent (1997); tertiary 41 per cent (1997)

MEDIA
A public broadcaster, NHK, competes with four national terrestrial television companies. NHK also runs national radio networks. Satellite and cable television is widespread and digital broadcasting is increasingly significant. Newspaper readership is high, with 80 per cent of the population reading one of the five main national dailies.

CULTURE
Japanese is said to be one of the Ural-Altaic group of languages and remained a spoken language until the fifth to seventh centuries AD, when Chinese characters came into use. Modern Japanese is written in a mixture of Chinese characters (about 1,800) and also the syllabary characters called Kana. Traditional arts include woodblock printing and the production of intricate silk hangings. Notable writers include Kawabata Yasunari ((1899–1972) winner of the Nobel Prize for Literature in 1968) and Kazuo Ishiguro (b. 1954).

JORDAN

Al-Mamlaka al-Urdunniyya al-Hashimiyya – Hashemite Kingdom of Jordan

AREA – 88,900 sq. km. Neighbours: Syria (north), Israel and the West Bank (west), Saudi Arabia (south and east), Iraq (east)
POPULATION – 5,051,000 (2001). The majority are Sunni Muslims and Islam is the religion of the state; however, freedom of belief is guaranteed by the constitution
CAPITAL – Amman (population, 1,270,000, 1997 estimate)
MAJOR CITIES – Irbid; Az-Zarqa
CURRENCY – Jordanian dinar (JD) of 1,000 fils
NATIONAL ANTHEM – Asha Al Malik (Long Live The King)
NATIONAL DAY – 25 May (Independence Day)
NATIONAL FLAG – Three horizontal stripes of black, white, green and a red triangle based on the hoist, containing a seven-pointed white star
LIFE EXPECTANCY (years) – 71 (2001)
MORTALITY RATE (per 1,000 population) – 2.62 (2003)
INFANT MORTALITY (per 1,000 births) – 27 (2001)
HIV / AIDS ADULT PREVALENCE – 0.1 per cent (2001)
DEATH PENALTY – Yes
POPULATION BELOW POVERTY LINE – 30 per cent (2002)
POPULATION GROWTH RATE – 4 per cent (1990–2001)
POPULATION DENSITY – 57 per sq. km (2001)
ILLITERACY RATE – (m) 5.2 per cent; (f) 15.7 per cent (2000)
ENROLMENT (percentage of age group) – primary 71 per cent (1997); secondary 57 per cent (1997); tertiary 18 per cent (1997)

CLIMATE AND TERRAIN
Elevation extremes range from 1,734 m (Jabal Ram) at the highest point to –408 m (Dead Sea) at the lowest. The Great Rift Valley is an important topographical feature that separates the east and west banks of the River Jordan. Average temperatures in Amman range from 7°C in January to 26°C in August, although temperatures in the Jordan Valley have been known to reach 49°C.

HISTORY AND POLITICS
The end of the Ottoman Empire in 1918 saw the British create the state of Transjordan which, during the first Arab–Israeli War of 1948, seized the West Bank and part of Jerusalem. The Six Day War of 1967 resulted in the recapture of these areas by Israel, and an influx of Palestinian refugees into Transjordan.

In 1988 Jordan announced that it would hand over the representation of the Palestinian people in the Occupied Territories to the Palestine Liberation Organisation

(PLO). Shortly before King Hussein's death in 1999, Jordan renounced sovereignty over the West Bank and East Jerusalem.

Jordan's economy declined in the 1980s and internal stability became increasingly precarious. Riots in 1989 forced the government to adopt a process of economic liberalisation. The first free elections under universal suffrage in the country's history took place in December 1989. Real power, however, still rested with the King, with parliament amending or approving legislation originating with the monarch.

Islamist parties made inroads in further elections in 1993 but remained a minority under a system that favoured people's tribal loyalties over their religious affiliation.

Legislative elections were held on 17 June 2003 and independent candidates loyal to King Abdullah won 62 out of 110 seats in the House of Deputies. Candidates for the Islamic Action Front party were also elected to the house. A quota for women resulted, for the first time in Jordan's history, in the election of six female candidates.

POLITICAL SYSTEM

The Constitution provides for a Senate of 40 members (all appointed by the King for a four-year term) and an elected House of Deputies which has 110 members, directly elected for a four-year term. The King appoints the members of the Council of Ministers. In 1991 a new National Charter was formulated which lifted the ban on political parties, imposed in 1957.

HEAD OF STATE

His Majesty The King of the Jordan, Abdullah II, *born* 30 January 1962, *succeeded* 7 February 1999

Crown Prince, Hamzeh ibn al-Hussein, *born* 29 March 1982

SELECTED GOVERNMENT MEMBERS *as at July 2004*

Prime Minister, Defence, Faisal al-Fayez

Deputy Prime Minister; Minister of Trade and Culture, Mohammad Halaika

Finance, Mohammad Abu Hammour

Foreign Affairs, Marwan al-Mu'ashir

Interior, Samir Habashneh

EMBASSY OF THE HASHEMITE KINGDOM OF JORDAN

6 Upper Phillimore Gardens, London W8 7HA

T 020-7937 3685

Ambassador Extraordinary and Plenipotentiary, HE Timoor Daghistani, GCVO, apptd 1999

BRITISH EMBASSY

Abdoun (PO Box 87), Amman

T (+962) (6) 592 3100

Ambassador Extraordinary and Plenipotentiary, HE Christopher Prentice, apptd 2002

BRITISH COUNCIL DIRECTOR, Tim Gore

Rainbow Street, PO Box 634, Amman 11118

T (+962) (6) 463 6147

E bcamman@britishcouncil.org.jo

DEFENCE

The Army has 1,018 main battle tanks, 1,200 armoured personnel carriers and 226 armoured infantry fighting vehicles. The Navy has three patrol and coastal vessels at its base at Aqaba. The Air Force has 101 combat aircraft and 22 armed helicopters.

MILITARY EXPENDITURE – 9.3 per cent of GDP (2002)

MILITARY PERSONNEL – 100,500: Army 85,000, Navy 500, Air Force 15,000; Paramilitaries 10,000

ECONOMY AND TRADE

The Jordanian economy is affected by several external factors and not least by the conflict between Israel and Palestine which has restricted Jordan's trading capacity. Iraq, which would normally represent a significant market for Jordanian goods, has been affected by war, UN sanctions and extreme political instability.

King Abdullah has embarked on economic reforms including a shrinking of the public sector, privatisation and a commitment to trade liberalisation. The country has recently been rewarded with debt rescheduling and increased exports to the USA and EU.

Jordan relies on Iraqi oil, and the invasion of Iraq in 2003 cut off supplies. Several Gulf states agreed to temporarily extend aid to Jordan in order to compensate for the loss. The Trans-Arabian oil pipeline (Tapline) runs through north Jordan from Saudi Arabia to the Lebanese port of Sidon. A branch pipeline, together with oil brought by road from Iraq, feeds a refinery at Zerqa, which meets most of Jordan's requirements for refined petroleum products. Sufficient reserves of natural gas have been discovered in the north-east to produce electricity for the national grid since 1989.

Of the Jordanian labour force, 12.5 per cent are engaged in industry that include phosphate mining, pharmaceuticals, petroleum refining, cement, potash and light manufacturing. Of the remainder of the labour force, 82.5 per cent are engaged in the service industries and only five per cent in agriculture. Jordan's agricultural products include wheat, barley, citrus, tomatoes, melons, olives; sheep, goats and poultry.

GNI – US$8,800 million (2001); US$1,750 per capita (2001)

ANNUAL AVERAGE GROWTH OF GDP – 4.2 per cent (2001)

INFLATION RATE – 3.3 per cent (2002)

TOTAL EXTERNAL DEBT – US$8,226 million (2000)

FOREIGN DIRECT INVESTMENT – US$1,048 million (1997–2000)

IMPORTS – US$4,844 million (2001)

EXPORTS – US$2,293 million (2001)

BALANCE OF PAYMENTS

Trade – US$2,007 million deficit (2001)

Current Account – US$4 million deficit (2001)

Trade with UK	*2002*	*2003*
Imports from UK	£180,150,000	£175,155,000
Exports to UK	31,627,000	17,761,000

TRANSPORT INFRASTRUCTURE

Amman is linked to Aqaba, Damascus, Baghdad and Jiddah by roads which are of considerable importance in the overland trade of the Middle East. The former Hejaz Railway runs from Syria through Jordan, and is used mainly for freight between Amman and Damascus. The Aqaba railway carries phosphate rock from the mines of al-Hasa and al-Abiad to Aqaba. Jordan has 7,245 km of highways, but no waterways. Jordan's main port is al-'Aqabah.

MEDIA

Jordan practices strict media censorship. Laws were tightened in 2001, and long prison sentences were introduced for anyone criticising the king or harming the country's reputation. Jordan Radio and Television is a state run broadcaster. It operates three terrestrial channels and a satellite channel. These broadcast a mixture of sport, films and general programming. There are radio services in Arabic, English and French. Radio Fann is an entertainment station run by the armed forces.

CULTURE

Jordan has a large Bedouin population and this ancient nomadic culture is reflected in Jordanian music and cuisine. Jordan is also home to one of the best-known works of Arab literature, *Alf Layla wa Layla (A Thousand and One Nights)*.

KAZAKHSTAN

Qazaqstan Respublikasy – Republic of Kazakhstan

AREA – 2,699,700 sq. km. Neighbours: Russia (north and west), Turkmenistan, Uzbekistan and Kyrgyzstan (south), China (east)

POPULATION – 16,095,000 (2001): Kazakhs (53 per cent), Russians (30 per cent), Ukrainians (4 per cent) and ethnic Germans (2 per cent), with smaller numbers of Tatars, Uzbeks, Koreans and Belarusians. The Russian population is concentrated in the north of the country, where it forms a significant majority, and in Almaty. The majority of ethnic Kazakhs are Sunni Muslims, and this is the main religion of the republic. Kazakh (one of the Turkic languages) became the official language in 1993; a law passed in July 1997 decreed Kazakh as the language of state administration; Russian has a special status as the 'social language between peoples'. Otherwise each ethnic group uses its own language

CAPITAL – Astana (population, 320,000, 2000 estimate, known as Akmola until May 1998). The capital was moved from Alma-Ata (Almaty) in December 1997

MAJOR CITIES – Almaty; Pavlodar; Karagandy; Shymkent

CURRENCY – Tenge

NATIONAL DAY – 25 October (Republic Day)

NATIONAL FLAG – Dark blue with a sun and a soaring eagle in the centre all in gold, and a red vertical ornamentation stripe near the hoist

LIFE EXPECTANCY (years) – 65 (2001)

MORTALITY RATE (per 1,000 population) – 10.78 (2003)

INFANT MORTALITY (per 1,000 births) – 61 (2001)

HIV / AIDS ADULT PREVALENCE – 0.1 per cent (2001)

POPULATION BELOW POVERTY LINE – 26 per cent (2001)

POPULATION GROWTH RATE – –0.4 per cent (1990–2001)

POPULATION DENSITY – 6 per sq. km (2001)

URBAN POPULATION – 56 per cent (2001)

ENROLMENT (percentage of age group) – tertiary 33 per cent (1997)

CLIMATE AND TERRAIN

Kazakhstan occupies the northern part of what was Soviet Central Asia. It stretches from the Volga and the Caspian Sea in the west to the Altai and Tien Shan mountains in the east. The terrain consists of arid steppes and semi-deserts, flat in the west, hilly in the east and mountainous in the south-east (Southern Altai and Tien Shan mountains). Elevation extremes range from 6,995 m (Khan Tangiri Shyngy) at the highest point to –132 m (Vpadina Kaundy) at the lowest. Average yearly temperatures in the capital Astana range from –16°C in January to 24°C in July.

HISTORY AND POLITICS

Kazakhstan was inhabited by nomadic tribes before being invaded by Ghenghis Khan and incorporated into his empire in 1218. After his empire disintegrated, feudal towns emerged based on large oases. These towns affiliated and established a Kazakh state in the late 15th century which engaged in almost continuous warfare with the marauding Khanates on its southern border. After appealing to Russia for aid and protection, in 1731 Kazakhstan acceded to the Russian Empire under a voluntary act of accession.

The Bolshevik Revolution in Russia in 1917 reached Central Asia over the following years and Kazakhstan became an autonomous republic within the Russian Federation in August 1920.

Kazakhstan suffered bitterly under Stalin's twin policies of collectivisation and 'sedentarisation', where nomadic tribes were forced to become farmers. The country lost around two million people, or half its population, to famine and disease. Later Soviet rule saw the country used as a testing ground for nuclear weapons. Kazakhstan declared independence in 1991, the same year it became part of the Commonwealth of Independent States (CIS), a confederation of 11 former Soviet states.

President Nazarbayev was elected with 98 per cent of the vote on 1 December 1991. He secured a further massive victory in 1999, though this was achieved with the banning of several opposition parties.

The 1999 elections were monitored by an Organisation for Security and Co-operation in Europe (OSCE) Election Observation Mission. Standards of accountability and transparency were not high, according to the mission, though legislation in 2004 addressed some of these concerns. Elections to the *Majlis* took place on 19 September 2004; *see* Stop Press for final results.

POLITICAL SYSTEM

Executive power is vested in the President and Government. The President must be a Kazakh speaker and has the power to appoint the Prime Minister, other senior ministers and all ambassadors. A constitution approved by referendum on 30 August 1995 granted the President the power to dissolve the legislature and to rule by decree. It also nominated Kazakh as the sole official language; prohibited dual citizenship; and created a new bicameral legislature composed of a 39-member Senate, of whom 32 are indirectly elected and seven appointed, and a 77-member directly elected *Majlis* (lower house of legislature). The Constitutional Court, which opposed the new Constitution, was replaced by a Constitutional Council which was made subject to Presidential veto.

HEAD OF STATE

President, Commander-in-Chief of the Armed Forces, Nursultan Nazarbayev, *elected* 1 December 1991, *confirmed in office by referendum* 29 April 1995, *re-elected* 10 January 1999

SELECTED GOVERNMENT MEMBERS *as at July 2004*
Prime Minister, Daniyal Akhmetov
First Deputy Prime Minister, Akhmetzhan Yessimov
Deputy Prime Ministers, Sauat Mynbayev; Bryganym Aitmova
Defence, Gen. Mukhtar Altynbayev
Finance and State Revenues, Arman Dunaev
Foreign Affairs, Kasymzhomart Tokayev
Interior, Zautbek Turisbekov

EMBASSY OF THE REPUBLIC OF KAZAKHSTAN
33 Thurloe Square, London SW7 2SD
T 020-7581 4646
Ambassador Extraordinary and Plenipotentiary, Yerlan Idrissov, apptd 2002

BRITISH EMBASSY
ul Furmanova 173, Almaty
T (+ 7) (3272) 506191/2
E british-embassy@kaznet.kz
Ambassador Extraordinary and Plenipotentiary, HE James Sharp, apptd 2002

BRITISH COUNCIL DIRECTOR, James Kennedy
Republic Square 13, KZ-480013 Almaty
T (+ 7) (3272) 633339
E general@kz.britishcouncil.org

DEFENCE

An agreement signed with Russia in January 1995 provides for eventual re-unification of the two states' armed forces. The CIS mutual defence treaty of 1993, to which Kazakhstan is a signatory, retains a common air defence force, while Kazakh forces also take part in the CIS peacekeeping force along the Tajikistan–Afghanistan border. By 1996, all nuclear warheads had been returned to Russia although Kazakhstan retained 48 SS-18 intercontinental ballistic missiles. Kazakhstan participates in the NATO Partnership for Peace programme. The Army has 650 main battle tanks and 1,750 armoured combat vehicles. The Caspian Sea Flotilla, which Kazakhstan shares with Russia and Turkmenistan, operates under Russian command. The Air Force has 164 combat aircraft.

MILITARY EXPENDITURE – 2.0 per cent of GDP (2002)
MILITARY PERSONNEL – 65,800: Army 46,800, Air Force 19,000; Paramilitaries 34,500
CONSCRIPTION DURATION – 31 months

ECONOMY AND TRADE

As part of the Soviet Union, the Kazakh economy was dominated by the production of raw materials such as phosphorus, chrome, lead, zinc and silver. The post-Soviet economy still relies on these resources as well as oil and natural gas supplies. Russia takes 30 per cent of Kazakh exports and agriculture accounts for 11 per cent of GDP. Kazakhstan exports oil and oil products, ferrous metals, chemicals, machinery, grain, wool, meat and coal.

Agriculture, including stock-raising, is highly developed, particularly in the central and south-west of the republic. Grain is grown in the north and north-east, and cotton and wool produced in the south and south-east. In 1999 12.5 million tonnes of wheat and 3.5 million tonnes of barley were grown.

The opening of the Caspian Consortium pipeline in 2001, from western Kazakhstan's Tengiz oilfield to the Black Sea, has significantly boosted Kazakhstan's energy industry. However, the country has also attempted to reduce its dependency on oil by diversifying the economy with light industry.

The labour force is divided by 30 per cent engaged in industry, 20 per cent in agriculture and 50 per cent in services. The tenge was floated on 5 April 1999 in a bid to reduce the trade deficit.

GNI – US$20,100 million (2001); US$1,350 per capita (2001)
ANNUAL AVERAGE GROWTH OF GDP – 13.2 per cent (2001)
INFLATION RATE – 6 per cent (2002)
UNEMPLOYMENT – 13.7 per cent (1998)
TOTAL EXTERNAL DEBT – US$6,664 million (2000)
FOREIGN DIRECT INVESTMENT US$5,316 million (1997–2000)
IMPORTS – US$6,491 million (2002)
EXPORTS – US$9,709 million (2002)

BALANCE OF PAYMENTS
Trade – US$2,420 million surplus (2002)
Current Account – US$596 million deficit (2002)

Trade with UK	*2002*	*2003*
Imports from UK	£91,512,000	£103,419,000
Exports to UK	34,333,000	51,851,000

TRANSPORT INFRASTRUCTURE

Kazakhstan has several important ports on the Caspian and Aral seas. Kazakhstan's size makes internal air travel essential, and the country has 392 airports. There are 13,601 km of railways, and 81,331 km of highways. The Syr Darya and Irtysh rivers constitute 3,900 km of waterways.

MEDIA

There are several public television broadcasters operating in Kazakhstan including Kazakh Television and Khabar TV (which is broadcast in Russian). Popular newspapers include *Ak Zhayik*, *Akmolinskaya Pravda* and the English language title *Almaty Herald*. Although freedom of the press is protected by the constitution, opposition and privately owned media are subject to censorship.

CULTURE

In the 19th century Abai Kunanbaev (1845–1904) translated Russian works into Kazakh, and so founded Kazakhstan's literary culture, which until then had been chiefly oral. The capital city Almaty is home to the celebrated Abai Kazak Academic Opera and Ballet Theatre while the Kazakh Film Studio, founded in 1944, is noted for its contribution to world cinema.

KENYA

Jamhuri ya Kenya – Republic of Kenya

AREA – 569,100 sq. km. Neighbours: Somalia (east), Ethiopia (north), Sudan (north-west), Uganda (west), Tanzania (south)

POPULATION – 31,293,000 (2001). The main tribal groups are the Kikuyu, Luhya, Luo, Kalenjin, Kamba and Masai. The official languages are Swahili, which is generally understood throughout Kenya, and English; numerous indigenous languages are also spoken
CAPITAL – Nairobi (population, 2,143,254, 1999)
MAJOR CITIES – ΨKisumu; ΨMombasa; Nakuru
CURRENCY – Kenya shilling (Ksh) of 100 cents
NATIONAL ANTHEM – Ee Mungu Nguvu Yetu (Oh God Of All Creation)
NATIONAL DAY – 12 December (Independence Day)
NATIONAL FLAG – Horizontally black, red and green with the red fimbriated in white, and with a shield and crossed spears in the centre
LIFE EXPECTANCY (years) – 50 (2001)
MORTALITY RATE (per 1,000 population) – 16.01 (2003)
HIV / AIDS ADULT PREVALENCE – 15 per cent (2001)
INFANT MORTALITY (per 1,000 births) – 78 (2001)
DEATH PENALTY – Yes
POPULATION BELOW POVERTY LINE – 50 per cent (2001)
POPULATION GROWTH RATE – 2.6 per cent (1990–2001)
POPULATION DENSITY – 55 per sq. km (2001)
MILITARY EXPENDITURE – 3.2 per cent of GDP (2002)
MILITARY PERSONNEL – 24,120: Army 20,000, Navy 1,620, Air Force 2,500; Paramilitaries 5,000
ILLITERACY RATE – (m) 11.1 per cent; (f) 24.0 per cent (2000)
ENROLMENT (percentage of age group) – primary 85 per cent (1997)

CLIMATE AND TERRAIN

Elevation extremes range from 5,199 m (Mount Kenya) at the highest point to 0 m (Indian Ocean) at the lowest. The interior of the country is mostly arid desert but a fertile plateau can be found in the west. As an equatorial country, the climate of Kenya is humid with average temperatures reaching 27°C in February and 22°C in June.

HISTORY AND POLITICS

Arabs and Persians settled on the Kenyan coast from the eighth century AD. By 1895, Kenya had become a British protectorate. Opposition to colonial rule, both armed and political, grew throughout the 20th century, and in 1944 Jomo Kenyatta formed the Kenya African Union (KAU). This nationalist organisation demanded reform which would give land to Africans. The Mau Mau rebellion of 1952–6 brought about a state of emergency which was not lifted until 1960. Elections in 1962 gave the Kenya African National Union party (KANU) a large majority. Kenya became a republic, with Kenyatta as president, in 1964.

Kenya was a one-party state between 1972 and 1992 (with KANU as the single party). In the legislative elections of 27 December 2002 KANU lost power to the National Rainbow Coalition (NARC) who gained 125 out of 210 seats. Mwai Kibaki of NARC won the simultaneous presidential election with 62.2 per cent of the vote. He took office on 30 December 2002 and the new cabinet was sworn in on 6 January 2003.

POLITICAL SYSTEM

The head of state is the President, directly elected for a five-year term, who is head of Government and appoints the Cabinet. The unicameral legislature, the *Bunge* (National Assembly), has 224 members, of whom 210 are directly elected for a five-year term, 12 appointed by the President, and two *ex-officio* members, the Attorney-General and the Speaker. In November 1999, an amendment to the Constitution was passed which limited the powers of the President over the National Assembly and affirmed the *Bunge*'s supremacy.

HEAD OF STATE
President and C.-in-C. Armed Forces, Mwai Kibaki (NARC), *elected* 27 December 2002, *took office* 30 December 2002
Vice-President, Minister for Home Affairs and National Heritage, Moody Awori

SELECTED GOVERNMENT MEMBERS *as at July 2004*
Finance, David Mwiraria
Foreign Affairs and International Co-operation, Chirau Ali Mwakwere
Minister of State in the Vice-President's Office for Home Affairs, Linah Jebii Kilimo

KENYA HIGH COMMISSION
45 Portland Place, London W1B 1AS
T 020-7636 2371
High Commissioner, HE Joseph Kirugumi Muchemi

BRITISH HIGH COMMISSION
Upper Hill Road, PO Box 30465 Nairobi
T (+254) (2) 714699
E consular@nairobi.mail.fco.gov.uk
High Commissioner, HE Edward Clay, CMG, apptd 2001

BRITISH COUNCIL DIRECTOR, Peter Elborn
ICEA Building, Kenyatta Avenue, PO Box 40751, Nairobi.
T (+254) (2) 334 855/6
E information@britishcouncil.or.ke

ECONOMY AND TRADE

Kenya's wealth of fertile land makes it an overwhelmingly agricultural country with up to 80 per cent of the population engaged in agricultural and horticultural production. The world's fourth largest producer of tea, it also grows coffee, maize, sugarcane and wheat.

In 2003 the IMF approved a three year Poverty Reduction and Growth Facility.

There has been considerable industrial development over the last 15 years. New industries are the production of steel, textiles, tyres and processing of dehydrated vegetables. Smaller schemes have added to the country's manufacturing base in consumer goods. There is an oil refinery in Mombasa supplying both Kenya and Uganda, and a fuel pipeline connects Mombasa and Nairobi.

Tourism generates some US$400 million per year but the industry was adversely affected during 2002 and 2003 by fears of terrorist attacks.

Principal exports are coffee and tea, which account for roughly one-third of total export earnings. Also exported are fruit, vegetables and agricultural products. Industrial machinery is the largest single import; other imports are transport equipment, petroleum and petroleum products, metals, pharmaceuticals and chemicals.

Kenya's natural resources include gold, limestone, soda ash, salt, rubies, garnets, wildlife and hydropower.
GNI – US$10,700 million (2001); US$350 per capita (2001)

ANNUAL AVERAGE GROWTH OF GDP – 1.1 per cent (2001)
INFLATION RATE – 5.9 per cent (2000)
TOTAL EXTERNAL DEBT – US$5,700 million (2002)
FOREIGN DIRECT INVESTMENT – US$156 million (1997–2000)
IMPORTS – US$3,192 million (2001)
EXPORTS – US$1,944 million (2001)

BALANCE OF PAYMENTS
Trade – US$1,282 million deficit (2001)
Current Account – US$318 million deficit (2001)

Trade with UK	*2002*	*2003*
Imports from UK	£158,864,000	£171,992,000
Exports to UK	216,461,000	217,126,000

TRANSPORT INFRASTRUCTURE
The Kenya Railways Corporation has 2,778 km of railways. There are also 67,000 km of road, of which 8,900 km are surfaced. The principal port is Mombasa, operated by the Kenya Ports Authority. International air services operate from airports at Nairobi and Mombasa.

MEDIA AND CULTURE
There are a number of television channels, including the state administered Kenya Broadcasting Corporation (KBC). Radio is a popular medium outside urban areas. There are six national newspapers that report a range of political views including *The Daily Nation, The East African Standard* and *The East African.*

Benga is a type of dance music derived from the Luo people from the west of the country. Nugigi wa Thiong'o (b. 1958) is one of Kenya's most celebrated authors and was the first East African to be published in English.

KIRIBATI

Ribaberikin Kiribati – Republic of Kiribati

AREA – 726 sq. km
POPULATION – 94,149 (2001 estimate): predominantly Christian. The languages are I-Kiribati and English
CAPITAL – Tarawa (population, 36,717, 2000)
CURRENCY – Australian dollar ($A) of 100 cents
NATIONAL ANTHEM – Teirake Kain Kiribati (Stand Kiribati)
NATIONAL DAY – 12 July (Independence Day)
NATIONAL FLAG – Red, with blue and white wavy lines in base, and in the centre a gold rising sun and a flying frigate bird
MORTALITY RATE (per 1,000 population) – 8.63 (2003)
DEATH PENALTY – No (abolished 1979)
POPULATION GROWTH RATE – 1.4 per cent (1990–2001)
POPULATION DENSITY – 113 per sq. km (1999)

CLIMATE AND TERRAIN
Kiribati (pronounced Kiribas) comprises 36 islands: the Gilberts Group (17) including Banaba (formerly Ocean Island), the Phoenix Islands (8), and the Line Islands (11), which are situated in the south-west Central Pacific around the point at which the International Date Line cuts the Equator. Few of the atolls are more than 800 m in width or more than 3 m high.

HISTORY AND POLITICS
Known as the Gilbert and Ellice Islands, Kiribati was proclaimed a British protectorate in 1892. After the Second World War the islanders began to agitate for independence. This was postponed as Kiritimati (Christmas) Island became the site of British nuclear weapons tests in the 1950s and 1960s. Full independence came in 1979, and in 1999 Kiribati became a member of the United Nations.

Teburoro Tito won the presidential election of 1998 and was re-elected in elections held in January and February 2003. However, he was defeated in parliament after a vote of no confidence and resigned in March. Legislative elections were held on 9 and 16 May 2003 with the Maneaban Te Mauri (Protect the Maneaba) gaining 24 seats and Boutokaan Te Koaua (BTK, Pillars of Truth) winning 16 seats in the House of Assembly. Presidential elections took place on 4 July 2003 in which Anote Tong of the BTK defeated his brother, Harry Tong, with 47.4 per cent of the vote.

POLITICAL SYSTEM
The President is head of state as well as head of Government and is directly elected. There is a House of Assembly of 41 members (39 elected members, the Attorney-General and a representative of the Banaban community from Rabi Island). Executive authority is vested in the Cabinet.

HEAD OF STATE
President, Foreign Affairs, Anote Tong, *elected* 4 July 2003, *sworn in* 6 July 2003
Vice-President, Minister for Education, Youth and Sport Development, Teima Onorio

SELECTED GOVERNMENT MEMBERS *as at July 2004*
Internal Affairs and Social Development, Amberoti Nikora
Finance and Economic Development, Nabuti Mwemwenikarawa

KIRIBATI HIGH COMMISSION
c/o Office of the President, PO Box 68, Bairiki, Tarawa
Acting High Commissioner, Tam Biribo

BRITISH HIGH COMMISSIONER, HE Charles Mochan, apptd 2002, resident at Suva, Fiji

ECONOMY AND TRADE
Once rich in phosphates, Kiribati's natural resources were all but exhausted at the time of independence from the UK in 1979. Fishing and tourism are of great importance to the islands, and remittances from islanders working abroad account for over $5 million a year. The principal imports are foodstuffs, consumer goods, machinery and transport equipment. The principal exports are copra and fish. In May 2000, Japanese-funded improved port facilities at Betio were opened.
GNP – US$86 million (2000); US$950 per capita (2000)
ANNUAL AVERAGE GROWTH OF GDP – 2.0 per cent (1998)

Trade with UK	*2002*	*2003*
Imports from UK	£170,000	£32,000
Exports to UK	165,000	1,000

TRANSPORT INFRASTRUCTURE
Air communication exists between most of the islands and is operated by Air Kiribati, a statutory corporation. Air Marshall Islands operates a weekly service between Majuro, Tarawa, Funafuti and Nadi, and Air Nauru between Tarawa, Nauru and Nadi. Inter-island shipping is operated by a statutory corporation, the Shipping Corporation of Kiribati.

MEDIA AND CULTURE
Kiribati has no domestic television, so radio forms the islands' main source of communication. There is one government run and one private weekly newspaper. Handicrafts and *Tabiteuea*, an indigenous martial art, are fundamental aspects of Kiribatian culture.

KOREA

Korea's southern and western coasts are fringed with innumerable islands, of which the largest, forming a province of its own, is Cheju. The Korean language is of the Ural-Altaic Group. Its script, Hangul, was invented in the 15th century; prior to this Chinese characters alone were used. Despite the great cultural influence of the Chinese, Koreans have developed and preserved their own cultural heritage.

HISTORY AND POLITICS
United and independent since AD 668, Korea developed a civilisation distinct from Chinese and Japanese influences. Contact with outside cultures was discouraged by successive internal Korean empires until 1876, when Japan 'opened' the country. Subsequently, Japan, China and Russia competed for influence, with Japan emerging as the dominant state and annexing Korea in 1910. Japanese rule ended with its defeat in 1945, though Korea was divided along the 38th parallel: US troops occupying the south and Soviet troops occupying the north. The Republic of Korea was founded in the south on 15 August 1948, and the Democratic People's Republic of Korea (DPRK) in the north on 9 September the same year.

A general election was held on 10 May 1948, and the first National Assembly met in Seoul on 31 May. The Assembly passed a constitution on 12 July and on 15 August 1948 the republic was formally inaugurated and American military government came to an end. Meanwhile, in the Soviet-occupied zone north of the 38th parallel the Democratic People's Republic had been established with its capital at Pyongyang. A Supreme People's Soviet was elected in September 1948, and a Soviet-style constitution adopted.

THE KOREAN WAR
Kim Il-sung, Stalin's choice for leader in North Korea, began to build a separate government in defiance of United Nations plans for nationwide elections which would eventually unify the country. Elections took place in the south in 1950, prompting a declaration of southern independence, and an invasion from the north.

A United Nations Command (UNC), a multi-national force with a large-scale US contingent, was established to assist the Republic of Korea. The force enjoyed some initial success, and pushed the DPRK forces back almost to the Chinese border. The entire peninsula was devastated by the war. Over one million people died from each side and North Korea was devastated by aerial bombardment.

An armistice was signed on 27 July 1953, with Korea divided along the 38th parallel and with neither side having gained territory. Talks between North and South Korea on the re-unification of the country have taken place intermittently. A non-aggression accord was signed between North and South Korea in 1991 and an agreement on the denuclearisation of the Korean peninsula was reached in 1992. A summit meeting between the presidents of North and South Korea took place on 13–15 June 2000 at which a communiqué was signed agreeing to promote economic co-operation, achieve reconciliation and eventually re-unify the two countries.

DEMOCRATIC PEOPLE'S REPUBLIC OF KOREA

Chosun Minchu-chui Inmin Kongwa-guk – Democratic People's Republic of Korea

AREA – 120,400 sq. km. Neighbours: China, Russia (north), Republic of Korea (south)
POPULATION – 22,428,000 (2001). The language is Korean
CAPITAL – Pyongyang (2,741,260)
CURRENCY – Won of 100 chon
NATIONAL ANTHEM – Aegug-ga (Patriotic Hymn)
NATIONAL DAY – 16 February (Kim Jong-il's birthday)
NATIONAL FLAG – Red with white fimbriations and blue borders at top and bottom; a large red star on a white disc near the hoist
LIFE EXPECTANCY (years) – 65 (2001)
MORTALITY RATE (per 1,000 population) – 6.93 (2003)
INFANT MORTALITY (per 1,000 births) – 42 (2001)
DEATH PENALTY – Yes
POPULATION GROWTH RATE – 1.1 per cent (1990–2001)
POPULATION DENSITY – 186 per sq. km (2001)
URBAN POPULATION – 61 per cent (2001)

CLIMATE AND TERRAIN
The Democratic People's Republic of Korea occupies the northern half of the Korean Peninsula. Elevation extremes range from 2,744 m (Paektu-san) at the highest point to 0 m (Sea of Japan) at the lowest.

HISTORY AND POLITICS
At the end of the Korean war in 1953, Kim Il-sung began a process of Soviet-style reform in North Korea. Il-sung also developed *Juche* (self-reliance) an ideology which demanded North Korea's total economic independence.

Kim Il-sung died in 1994 and was pronounced 'Eternal President'. His son, Kim Jong-il became Chairman of the National Defence Commission, the second highest post in North Korea.

Kim Dae-jung who became president in South Korea in 1998, instituted a policy of engagement with the North designed to reduce tensions. Meetings between the two sides became increasingly frequent after a Joint Declaration was signed on 15 June 2000. This declaration obliged the two sides to work independently for national unification and to recognise the common elements in the two sides' proposals for federation-confederation.

In March 2001 North Korea withdrew contacts from South Korea because of what it perceived as US hostility. Contacts eventually resumed and ministerial co-operation and reunions between Northern and Southern families became more frequent. But in October 2002 it became apparent that North Korea was continuing with its nuclear weapons programme, in breach of the Treaty on the Non-Proliferation of Nuclear Weapons (NPT) and a number of other international agreements. Talks between the USA and North Korea, hosted and mediated by China and designed to resolve the nuclear issue, occurred in 2003 and February 2004. These talks agreed a Working Group to facilitate progress towards a peaceful resolution. As at August 2004, negotiations continued.

POLITICAL SYSTEM
The Constitution of the Democratic People's Republic of Korea provides for a Supreme People's Assembly, presently consisting of 687 deputies, which is elected from a single list of candidates every five years by universal suffrage. The Assembly elects a President for a five-year term, and the Central People's Committee. In turn, the Central People's Committee directs the Administrative Council which implements the policy formulated by the Committee.

The Administrative Council (36 members), the Government of North Korea, includes the Prime Minister and various ministers. In practice, however, the country is ruled by the Korean Workers' Party which elects a Central Committee; this in turn appoints a Politburo. The senior ministers of the Administrative Council are all members of the Communist Party Central Committee and the majority are also members of the Politburo.

Elections to the Supreme People's Assembly were held on 3 August 2003 in which only candidates from the Democratic Front for the Reunification of the Fatherland were allowed to participate.

HEAD OF STATE
Eternal President, Kim Il-sung (deceased)
Chair of the National Defence Commission, Kim Jong-il
Chair of the Presidium of the Supreme People's Assembly, Kim Yong-nam

SELECTED GOVERNMENT MEMBERS *as at July 2004*
Premier, Pak Pong-chu
Deputy Premier, Kwak Pon-ki,
Deputy Premier, Ro Tu-chol
Deputy Premier, Chon Sung-hun
Finance, Mun Il-bong
Foreign Affairs, Paek Nam-sun
People's Armed Forces, Vice-Marshall Kim Il-chol

DEFENCE
The Army has about 3,500 main battle tanks and 2,500 armoured personnel carriers. The Navy has 26 submarines, three frigates and about 310 patrol and coastal vessels at 15 bases. The Air Force has 605 combat aircraft and 24 armed helicopters.
MILITARY EXPENDITURE – 20.5 per cent of GDP (2002)
MILITARY PERSONNEL – 1,082,000: Army 950,000, Navy 46,000, Air Force 86,000; Paramilitaries 189,000
CONSCRIPTION DURATION – Three to ten years

ECONOMY AND TRADE
North Korea is rich in natural resources such as coal, iron ore, magnesite, graphite, copper, zinc, lead, and precious metals. Japan developed heavy industry during its years of occupation at the beginning of the 20th century, however, low export levels, increasing debt and internal mismanagement sent the economy into a long decline that was compounded by the collapse of communism in the 1990s.

A series of disastrous harvests in the 1990s brought famine, and the centrally planned economy has not been able to pull North Korea out of its desperate condition. Industrial output is centred on coal, steel, chemicals and machine tools, but antiquated machinery and fuel shortages have meant capacity is at a fraction of pre-1989 levels.

A lack of arable land, collective farming, weather-related problems, and chronic shortages of fertilizer and fuel have reduced food production. There has been some relaxation of restrictions on farmers markets since 2003, meaning that some groups have been able to purchase extra food, but large sections of the population continue to suffer shortages.

The USA increased food aid to North Korea in May 1999 but political tension in 2002–3 over North Korea's nuclear programme has led to a reduction in international food and fuel aid.
GNI – US$1,000 per capita (2001)
ANNUAL AVERAGE GROWTH OF GDP – 1.1 per cent (1998)
IMPORTS – US$431 million (2002)
EXPORTS – US$298 million (2002)

BALANCE OF PAYMENTS
Trade – US$217 million deficit (2002)
Current Account – US$82 million deficit (2002)

Trade with UK	*2002*	*2003*
Imports from UK	£16,683,000	£8,715,000
Exports to UK	997,000	1,205,000

TRANSPORT INFRASTRUCTURE
North Korea has 5,214 km of railways and 31,200 km of highways. There are some 2,253 km of navigable waterways.

MEDIA AND CULTURE
There is no independent media in North Korea. All televisions and radios are pre-tuned to government stations which broadcast state propaganda. There are five national papers in circulation that include the titles *Nodung simmum* (Workers' Daily) and *Minju Chosn* (Democratic Korea). Traditional Korean arts and culture have been strongly promoted since the reign of Kim Il-sung.

REPUBLIC OF KOREA

Taehan Min'guk – Republic of Korea

AREA – 98,700 sq. km. Neighbour: Democratic People's Republic of Korea (north)
POPULATION – 47,925,000 (2003). The largest religions are Buddhism (10.3 million) and Christianity (8.8 million Protestants, 2.9 million Roman Catholics). The language is Korean
CAPITAL – Seoul (population, 10,321,000, 1999 estimate)
MAJOR CITIES – ΨInchon; ΨPusan; Taegu
CURRENCY – Won
NATIONAL ANTHEM – Aegug-ga (Patriotic Hymn)
NATIONAL DAY – 15 August (Liberation Day)
NATIONAL FLAG – White with a red and blue yin-yang symbol in the centre, surrounded by four black trigrams
LIFE EXPECTANCY (years) – 75 (2001)
MORTALITY RATE (per 1,000 births) – 6.03 (2003)
INFANT MORTALITY (per 1,000 births) – 5 (2001)
DEATH PENALTY – Yes
POPULATION GROWTH RATE – 0.6 per cent (1990–2001)
POPULATION DENSITY – 477 per sq. km (2001)
URBAN POPULATION – 82 per cent (2001)

CLIMATE AND TERRAIN

Highland and mountainous areas account for around 70 per cent of the country's land area with elevation extremes ranging from 1,950 m (Halla-san) at the highest point to 0 m (Sea of Japan) at the lowest. Average temperatures in Seoul range from −4°C in January to 29°C in August.

HISTORY

On 12 March 2004 the South Korean National Assembly passed a motion to impeach President Roh Moo-hyun. The president had been accused of breaking a law which required public officials to be politically neutral. During the process Prime Minister Goh Kun became acting president, but immediately stepped down when the courts rejected Roh Moo-hyun's impeachment in May. Goh Kun himself resigned in May 2004, and was succeeded by Lee Hai-chan, who was appointed on 29 June.

POLITICAL SYSTEM

A new Constitution was adopted in 1988 following a year of political unrest. The President, who is Head of State, Chief of the Executive and Commander-in-Chief of the armed forces, is directly elected for a single five-year term. He appoints the Prime Minister with the consent of the National Assembly, and members of the State Council (Cabinet) on the recommendation of the Prime Minister. The President is also empowered to take wide-ranging measures in an emergency, including the declaration of martial law, but must obtain the agreement of the National Assembly. The National Assembly of 273 members is directly elected for a four-year term.

HEAD OF STATE
President, Roh Moo-hyun, *elected* 19 December 2002, *sworn in* 25 February 2003

SELECTED GOVERNMENT MEMBERS *as at July 2004*
Prime Minister, Lee Hae-chan
Deputy Prime Minister, Education and Human Resources, Ahn Byung-young
Deputy Prime Minister, Finance and Economy, Lee Hun-jai
Defence, Cho Young-kil
Foreign Affairs and Trade, Ban Ki-moon
Government Administration and Home Affairs, Huh Sung-kwan

EMBASSY OF THE REPUBLIC OF KOREA
60 Buckingham Gate, London SW1E 6AJ
T 020-7227 5500/2
Ambassador Extraordinary and Plenipotentiary, HE Lee Tae-sik, apptd 2003

BRITISH EMBASSY
No. 4, Chung-dong, Chung-Ku, Seoul 100–120
T (+ 82) (2) 3210 5500 E bembassy@britain.or.kr
Ambassador Extraordinary and Plenipotentiary, HE Warwick Morris, apptd 2003

BRITISH COUNCIL DIRECTOR, Shoba Ponnappa
Joongwhoo Building, 61–21 Taepyungro1-Ka, Choong-ku, Seoul 100–101
E info@britishcouncil.or.kr

DEFENCE

The Army has 2,350 main battle tanks, 2,480 armoured personnel carriers and 117 armed helicopters. The Navy has 20 submarines, six destroyers, nine frigates, 84 patrol and coastal vessels, 16 combat aircraft, 43 armed helicopters and 60 main battle tanks. There are eight naval bases. The Air Force has 538 combat aircraft.

The USA maintains 38,500 personnel in the country.
MILITARY EXPENDITURE – 2.8 per cent of GDP (2002)
MILITARY PERSONNEL – 686,000: Army 560,000, Navy 63,000, Air Force 63,000; Paramilitaries 4,500
CONSCRIPTION DURATION – 26–30 months

ECONOMY AND TRADE

The Republic of Korea became the world's eleventh largest economy in 1997 and transformed itself from a predominantly agrarian country into one of the Asian 'miracle' economies with an annual GDP growth rate of eight per cent.

The effects of the Asian financial crisis began to be felt in the country in 1997 when Hanbo Steel, one of Korea's flagship companies, collapsed. The situation deteriorated further and the country was forced to appeal to the IMF for assistance. Per capita GDP fell and unemployment rose but strict financial policy by President Kim Dae-jung saw the country return to growth in 2000. Major manufacturing industries include steel, automobiles, shipbuilding, electronics, textiles, clothing and leather goods and chemicals. Tourism is a growing industry, with 5,320,000 foreign visitors in 2000.

Electronic products, machinery, metal goods, passenger vehicles, chemical products and fabric and clothing are the main exports. Electronic products, petroleum, machinery and chemical products are the main imports. The USA, Japan, the EU and China are the main trading partners.
GNI – US$447,600 million (2001); US$9,460 per capita (2001)
ANNUAL AVERAGE GROWTH OF GDP – 8.8 per cent (2000)
INFLATION RATE – 3.5 per cent (2003)
UNEMPLOYMENT – 3.4 per cent (2003)
TOTAL EXTERNAL DEBT – US$159,800 million (2003)
IMPORTS – US$152,126 million (2002)
EXPORTS – US$162,471 million (2002)

BALANCE OF PAYMENTS
Trade – US$14,180 million surplus (2002)
Current Account – US$6,092 million surplus (2002)

Trade with UK	*2002*	*2003*
Imports from UK	£1,464,328,000	£1,461,871,000
Exports to UK	2,869,107,000	2,616,393,000

TRANSPORT INFRASTRUCTURE

In 2000, there were 3,124 km of railway in commercial operation, of which 661 km were electrified. A high-speed railway line is being constructed between Seoul and Pusan and there are plans to build high-speed rail links between Seoul and Mokp'o and Seoul and Kangnŭng. There were 88,775 km of roads, of which 2,131 km are motorways. There are international airports in Seoul (Kimpo), Kimhae (near Pusan), Taegu and Cheju city. An international airport was opened at Inch'ŏn in March 2001. Pusan and Inch'ŏn are the major ports with Pusan serving the industrial areas of the south-east. The port of Inch'ŏn, 28 miles from Seoul, serves the capital, but development and operation at Inch'ŏn are hampered by tidal variations of 9–10 m.

EDUCATION

Primary education is free of charge and compulsory for six years from the age of six. Secondary and higher education is extensive with the option of middle school to age 15 and high school to age 18.

ILLITERACY RATE – (m) 0.9 per cent; (f) 3.6 per cent (2000)

ENROLMENT (percentage of age group) – primary 94 per cent (1997); secondary 100 per cent (1997); tertiary 68 per cent (1997)

MEDIA

Korea has a number of public broadcasters such as Korea Broadcasting System (KBS), Munhwa Broadcasting Corporation (MBC) and Education Broadcasting System (EBS). RTV is South Korea's first public-access television station and is run by the Citizen's Broadcast Foundation. Newspapers currently in circulation include *Hangyore simmun*, *Tonga ilbo* and the English language title *Korea Central Daily*.

KUWAIT

Dawlat al-Kuwayt – State of Kuwait

AREA – 17,800 sq. km. Neighbours: Iraq (north and west); Saudi Arabia (south and south-west)

POPULATION – 1,971,000 (2001): 41.6 per cent are Kuwaiti citizens, the remainder being other Arabs, Iranians, Indians, Pakistanis and Westerners. Islam is the official religion, though religious freedom is constitutionally guaranteed. The official language is Arabic, and English is widely spoken as a second language

CAPITAL – ΨKuwait City (Al-Kuwayt) (population, 388,663, 1998)

CURRENCY – Kuwaiti dinar (KD) of 1,000 fils

NATIONAL ANTHEM – Al-Nashid Al-Watani (National Anthem)

NATIONAL DAY – 25 February

NATIONAL FLAG – Three horizontal stripes of green, white and red, with black trapezoid next to staff

LIFE EXPECTANCY (years) – 76 (2001)

MORTALITY RATE (per 1,000 population) – 2 (2003)

INFANT MORTALITY (per 1,000 births) – 9 (2001)

HIV / AIDS ADULT PREVALENCE – 0.12 per cent (2001)

DEATH PENALTY – Yes

POPULATION GROWTH RATE – 0.8 per cent (1990–2001)

POPULATION DENSITY – 111 per sq. km (2001)

CLIMATE AND TERRAIN

Kuwait is an almost entirely flat and arid country with average temperatures ranging from 10°C in January to 37°C in July. Elevation extremes range from 306 m (unnamed location) at the highest point to 0 m (Persian Gulf) at the lowest.

HISTORY AND POLITICS

Kuwait entered into 'The Special Treaty of Friendship' with Great Britain in 1899, in order to protect itself from Ottoman or Saudi domination. The borders between Kuwait, Saudi Arabia and Iraq were drawn up in the 1920s and 30s and Kuwait became a sovereign country in 1961 when the Treaty ended. Britain retained a military presence in the country until 1971. Kuwait gained a written constitution in 1962 and the first elections to a National Assembly were held in 1963.

In 1990 Saddam Hussein invaded Kuwait, abolished Kuwaiti sovereignty and proclaimed the country a province of Iraq. An international coalition force mounted a military campaign, Operation Desert Storm, which expelled Iraqi forces in 1991.

Rebuilding the country after the war was a priority throughout the 1990s. In 2003 the National Assembly rejected a proposal to give Kuwaiti women the right to vote. Shaikh Sabah, who became prime minister in July 2003, has expressed an intention to force the Assembly to return to this issue.

Elections to the National Assembly were held on 5 July 2003 in which Islamists won 21 of the 50 seats, government supporters won 14, Liberals won 3 and Independents won 12. On 13 July the Amir of Kuwait appointed Shaikh Sabah al-Ahmad al-Jaber al-Sabah as prime minister, thus separating the post from the role of heir to the throne for the first time since independence.

POLITICAL SYSTEM

Under the constitution legislative power is vested in the Amir and the 50-member National Assembly, and executive power in the Amir and the Cabinet. The electorate consists of all Kuwaiti male nationals over 21 whose families have lived in the Emirate since before 1921. There are no political parties. There are six Governorates: Capital, Hawalli, Ahmadi, Al-Jahrah, Al-Farwaniya and Al-Asimah

HEAD OF STATE
HH The Amir of Kuwait, Shaikh Jabir al-Ahmad al-Jabir al-Sabah, *born* 1928, *acceded* 31 December 1977
Crown Prince, HH Shaikh Saad al-Abdullah al-Salim al-Sabah

SELECTED GOVERNMENT MEMBERS *as at July 2004*
Prime Minister, Shaikh Sabah al-Ahmad al-Jaber al-Sabah

Deputy Prime Minister, Cabinet and National Assembly Affairs, Mohammed Dhaifallah Sharar
Deputy Prime Minister, Defence, Shaikh Jaber Mubarak al-Hamad al-Sabah
Deputy Prime Minister, Interior, Shaikh Nawaf al-Ahmad al-Jaber al-Sabah
Finance, Mohammed Abd al-Khalik al-Nuri
Foreign Affairs, Shaikh Muhammad Sabah al-Salem al-Sabah

EMBASSY OF THE STATE OF KUWAIT
2 Albert Gate, London SW1X 7JU
T 020-7590 3400
Ambassador Extraordinary and Plenipotentiary, HE Khaled al-Duwaisan, GCVO, apptd 1993

BRITISH EMBASSY
PO Box 2, Safat, 13001 Kuwait
T (+965) 240 3334/5/6
Ambassador Extraordinary and Plenipotentiary, HE Christopher Wilton, apptd 2002

BRITISH COUNCIL DIRECTOR, John Pare (acting)
2 Al Arabi Street, Block 2, PO Box 345, 13004 Safat, Mansouriya, Kuwait City
T (+965) 252 0067
E bc.kuwait@kw.britishcouncil.org

DEFENCE

The Army has 368 main battle tanks, 321 armoured personnel carriers and 450 armoured infantry fighting vehicles. The Navy has ten patrol and coastal vessels, based at Ras al-Qalaya. The Air Force has 81 combat aircraft and 20 armed helicopters.
MILITARY EXPENDITURE – 10.7 per cent of GDP (2002)
MILITARY PERSONNEL – 15,500: Army 11,000, Navy 2,000, Air Force 2,500; Paramilitaries 6,600

ECONOMY AND TRADE

Kuwait has around nine per cent of the world's oil reserves and proven reserves of around 98 billion barrels. In the financial year 2002–2003, Kuwait earned US$10 billion from oil revenues. Income from foreign reserves and investment is also high. Petroleum accounts for 95 per cent of export revenues and 80 per cent of government income.

The country has a very large immigrant labour force. About 80 per cent of workers are non-Kuwaiti and are mainly comprised of Pakistanis, Indians, Iranians and a significant number of North Americans and Europeans.

Non-oil exports, mainly to Asian countries and the Indian sub-continent, have included chemical fertilisers, ammonia and other chemicals and metal pipes and building materials. Re-exports to neighbouring states traditionally accounted for a major proportion of non-oil exports but were brought to a halt by the Iraqi invasion. Major trading partners are Japan, the USA, the UAE, Saudi Arabia and Western Europe.
GNI – US$37,400 million (2001); US$18,270 per capita (2001)
ANNUAL AVERAGE GROWTH OF GDP – 13.0 per cent (1998)
INFLATION RATE – 1.8 per cent (2000)
FOREIGN DIRECT INVESTMENT – US$163 million (1997–2000)
IMPORTS – US$8,950 million (2002)
EXPORTS – US$15,410 million (2002)

BALANCE OF PAYMENTS
Trade – US$9,241 million surplus (2001)
Current Account – US$8,566 million surplus (2001)

Trade with UK	*2002*	*2003*
Imports from UK	£310,390,000	£381,128,000
Exports to UK	288,275,000	341,679,000

TRANSPORT INFRASTRUCTURE

Kuwait has 4,450 km of highways but no waterways or railways. The main ports are Ash Shu'aybah, Ash Shuwaykh, Kuwait, Mina' 'Abd Allah, Mina' al Ahmadi and Mina' Su'ud.

EDUCATION

Education is free of charge and compulsory from six to 14 years. In 1999 there were 969 schools (608 government run, 322 private and 39 vocational) and one university.
ILLITERACY RATE – (m) 15.4 per cent; (f) 19.7 per cent (2000)
ENROLMENT (percentage of age group) – primary 77 per cent (1997); secondary 65 per cent (1997); tertiary 19 per cent (1997)

MEDIA AND CULTURE

Kuwaiti newspapers are far more outspoken in their coverage of politics than newspapers in neighbouring Arab nations. KUNA (Kuwaiti News Agency) is the official media agency, *Kuwait Times* the English language daily newspaper and Radio Kuwait is the state radio broadcaster.

Kuwait is strongly influenced by Bedouin artistic traditions that include the *Samri*, *Khamari* and *Tanboura*; all traditional dances central to family and social occasions. The *Dar al-Athar al-Islamiyah* (Museum of Islamic Art) in Kuwait City houses a collection of over 20,000 rare Islamic artefacts.

KYRGYZSTAN

Kyrgyz Respublikasy – Kyrgyz Republic

AREA – 199,900 sq. km. Neighbours: Kazakhstan (north), China (east), Tajikistan (south and south-west), Uzbekistan (west)
POPULATION – 5,000,000 (2002 estimate): 64.9 per cent Kyrgyz (Turkic origin), 12.5 per cent Russian and 13.8 per cent Uzbek, with smaller numbers of Ukrainians, Germans, Tatars and Kazakhs. Islam is the main religion. Kyrgyz, the official language since independence, is a Turkic language, written in the Roman alphabet since 1992. Russian is also an official language having equal rights with Kyrgyz
CAPITAL – Bishkek (population, 589,400, 1997 estimate)
CURRENCY – Som of 100 tyin (introduced on 10 May 1993 at rate of 1:200 against the rouble)
NATIONAL ANTHEM – Mamlekettik Gimni (National Anthem)
NATIONAL DAY – 31 August (Independence Day)
NATIONAL FLAG – Red with a rayed sun containing a representation of a yurt, all in gold
LIFE EXPECTANCY (years) – 72 (2001)

MORTALITY RATE (per 1,000 population) – 9.1 (2003)
INFANT MORTALITY RATE (per 1,000 births) – 9.7
HIV / AIDS ADULT PREVALENCE – 0.1 per cent (2001)
DEATH PENALTY – Yes
POPULATION BELOW POVERTY LINE – 55 per cent (2001)
POPULATION GROWTH RATE – 1.5 per cent (1990–2001)
POPULATION DENSITY – 24 per sq. km (1999)
URBAN POPULATION – 33.3 per cent (2000)
MILITARY EXPENDITURE – 1.9 per cent of GDP (2002)
MILITARY PERSONNEL – 10,900: Army 8,500, Air Force 2,400; Paramilitaries 5,000
CONSCRIPTION DURATION – 18 months
ILLITERACY RATE (m) – 1 per cent; (f) – 4 per cent
ENROLMENT (percentage of age group) – primary 100 per cent (1997); tertiary 12 per cent (1997).

CLIMATE AND TERRAIN

Kyrgyzstan (formerly Kyrgyzia) lies between the Tien Shan mountain range in the north-east and the Pamir-Alai mountains to the south-west. Elevation extremes range from 7,439 m (Jengish Chokusu) at the highest point to 132 m (Kara-Darya) at the lowest. The principal rivers are the Naryn and the Chu.

HISTORY AND POLITICS

After a long period under Mongol, Chinese and Persian rule, the Kyrgyz became part of the Russian Empire in the 1860s and 1870s.

Kyrgyzstan became a constituent part of the Soviet Union in 1924, and became a full republic of the Soviet Union in 1936. Reform in the Soviet Union in the 1980s provoked an upsurge in nationalism in Kyrgyzstan, and agitation for independence. The Uzbek minority around the city of Osh, began to demand autonomy in 1989, and suggested that nearby Uzbekistan annex the region. This led to serious rioting in June 1990 between ethnic Uzbeks and Kyrgyz, in the city of Osh.

The demise of the Soviet Union was followed by the election of President Akayev in 1990, the only post-communist Central Asian leader who had not previously been head of the local communist party. Presidential elections held in 2000 were deemed to have failed to comply with democratic standards by the Organisation for Security and Co-operation in Europe (OSCE) which monitored them. There have been persistent rumours of manipulation by President Akayev.

Following anti-government demonstrations in March 2003 in which five people were killed, Prime Minister Kurmanbek Bakiyev and his government resigned on 22 May. Nikolay Tanayev was confirmed as the new prime minister by parliament on 30 May and his cabinet was approved on 13 June 2003.

POLITICAL SYSTEM

The head of state is the President directly elected for a five-year term renewable once only. There is a bicameral legislature composed of a 60-member Legislative Assembly and a 45-member People's Assembly, both of which serve for five-year terms. In February 2003, amendments to the constitution gave President Akayev a right of veto over many acts of legislation. The President appoints the Prime Minister and the other members of the Government. The Assembly of the People of Kyrgyzstan, which comprises the leaders of the Republic's ethnic communities, was designated a consultative body in January 1997.

HEAD OF STATE

President, Askar Akayev, *elected* 12 October 1990, *re-elected* 24 December 1995, 29 October 2000

SELECTED GOVERNMENT MEMBERS *as at July 2004*

Prime Minister, Nikolay Tanayev
First Deputy Prime Minister in charge of Transport and Communications, Kubanychbek Zhumaliyev
Deputy Prime Minister for Social Mobilisation, Ularbek Mateyev
Deputy Prime Minister, Joomart Otorbayev
Defence, Lt.-Gen. Esen Topoyev
Finance, Bolot Abildayev
Foreign Affairs, Askar Aitmatov
Interior, Bakirdin Subanbekov

EMBASSY OF THE KYRGYZ REPUBLIC

Ascot House, 119 Crawford Street, London W1U 1BJ
T 020-7935 1462
Ambassador Extraordinary and Plenipotentiary, Urkaly Isaev, apptd 2004

BRITISH AMBASSADOR, HE James Sharp, apptd 2002, resident at Almaty, Kazakhstan

BRITISH COUNCIL DIRECTOR, James Kennedy
Republic Square 13, 480013 Almaty Kazakhstan
T (+7) 3272 633339
E general@kz.britishcouncil.org

ECONOMY AND TRADE

Co-operating closely with the World Bank and the IMF since 1994, Kyrgyzstan has brought inflation down from 772 per cent in 1993 to 25.6 per cent in 1997. A privatisation programme suspended in 1997 because of fears that assets were being sold too cheaply, was re-instated in 1998. The Russian financial crisis pushed GDP growth down to 6 per cent per annum between 1996 and 1998.

Kyrgyzstan has a highly agrarian economy: agriculture represents 40 per cent of GDP. Though the country does not enjoy vast amounts of natural resources, there are deposits of gold, iron ore and mercury. However, debt remains large: 40 per cent of GDP in 1999 was spent on debt repayments.

GNI – US$1,330 million (2000); US$280 per capita (2001)
ANNUAL AVERAGE GROWTH OF GDP – 5.1 per cent (2003)
INFLATION RATE – 2.4 per cent (2003)
TOTAL EXTERNAL DEBT – US$1,500 million (2002)
IMPORTS – US$468 million (2001)
EXPORTS – US$476 million (2001)

BALANCE OF PAYMENTS

Trade – US$39 million surplus (2001)
Current Account – US$53 million deficit (2001)

Trade with UK	*2002*	*2003*
Imports from UK	£1,854,000	£1,880,000
Exports to UK	206,000	131,000

TRANSPORT INFRASTRUCTURE

Kyrgyzstan has 18,500 km of highways and 420 km of railways. There are 600 km of waterways and 61 airports.

MEDIA AND CULTURE

There are a large number of newspapers currently in circulation, several of which have affiliations to particular political parties. There are also a number of private and independent television and radio broadcasters. However, there have been attempts by the government in recent years to control the press and broadcasters. Any publications by Islamist fundamentalists are banned in Kyrgystan.

Until the 1930s the Kyrgyz language had an oral tradition of literature which included the epic poem *Manas*, which tells the history of the Kyrgyz people. One of the country's best-known writers is Chingiz Aitmatov (b. 1928).

LAOS

Satharanarath Pasathipatai Pasason Lao – Lao People's Democratic Republic

AREA – 236,800 sq. km. Neighbours: China (north), Vietnam (north-east and east), Cambodia (south), Thailand (west), Myanmar (north-west)
POPULATION – 5,635,967 (2001 estimate): 68 per cent Lao Loum (lowland Lao), 22 per cent Lao Theung (upland Lao), 9 per cent Lao Soung (highland Lao, including Hmong and Yau). Lao is the official language; French and English are spoken
CAPITAL – Vientiane (population, 555,100, 1997 estimate)
CURRENCY – Kip (K) of 100 at
NATIONAL ANTHEM – Pheng Xat Lao (Hymn Of The Lao People)
NATIONAL DAY – 2 December
NATIONAL FLAG – Blue background with a central white circle, framed by two horizontal red stripes
MORTALITY RATE (per 1,000 population) – 12.39 (2003)
INFANT MORTALITY RATE (per 1,000 births) – 27.9 (2000)
HIV / AIDS ADULT PREVALENCE – 0.1 per cent (2001)
DEATH PENALTY – Yes
POPULATION Below Poverty Line – 40 per cent (2002)
POPULATION GROWTH RATE – 2.6 per cent (1990–2001)
POPULATION DENSITY – 22 per sq. km (1999)
MILITARY EXPENDITURE – 0.8 per cent of GDP (2002)
MILITARY PERSONNEL – 29,100: Army 25,600, of which Navy 600, Air Force 3,500; Paramilitaries 100,000
CONSCRIPTION DURATION – 18 months minimum
ILLITERACY RATE – (m) 35.9 per cent; (f) 66.8 per cent (2000)
ENROLMENT (percentage of age group) – primary 100 per cent (1997); secondary 29 per cent (1997); tertiary 3 per cent (1997)

CLIMATE AND TERRAIN

Elevation extremes range from 2,817 m (Phon Bia) at the highest point to 70 m (Mekong River) at the lowest. A wet season runs from May to November with average annual temperatures in Vientiane from 14°C in January to 34°C in July.

HISTORY AND POLITICS

The kingdom of Lane Xang 'the Land of a Million Elephants' was founded in the 14th century but broke up at the beginning of the 16th century into the separate kingdoms of Luang Prabang and Vientiane and the principality of Champassac, which came under French protection in 1893.

Japanese occupation during the Second World War spurred a Lao nationalist movement which proclaimed independence in 1945, though the French regained control of the country the following year. Full independence came in 1953. In 1964 the US began bombing Vietnamese forces using the Ho Chi Minh Trail in eastern Laos. This was supplemented by conflict between royalists and communists within Laos that was only resolved by a cease-fire in 1973.

In December 2000 the Lao People's Revolutionary Party (LPRP) celebrated 25 years in power. A general election to the enlarged 109-member National Assembly was held on 24 February 2002; all the candidates were approved by the LPRP, which won 108 seats with the remaining seat being won by an approved non-partisan candidate. The President, Prime Minister and Council of Ministers were confirmed in their posts by the National Assembly on 9 March 2002.

In 2003 Laos suffered some serious civil disturbances, including bombings and armed attacks on buses. Insurgents from the Hmong people have been blamed.

HEAD OF STATE
President, Gen. Khamtay Siphandone, *elected by the National Assembly* 24 February 1998, *re-elected* 9 April 2002
Vice-President, Choummaly Sayasone

SELECTED GOVERNMENT MEMBERS *as at July 2004*
Prime Minister, Bounnyang Vorachit
Deputy Prime Ministers, Somsavat Lengsavad *(Foreign Affairs)*; Thongloun Sisoulit *(State Planning Committee)*; Maj-Gen. Asang Laoly
Finance, Chansy Phosikham
Interior, Maj.-Gen. Soutchay Thammasith
National Defence, Maj.-Gen. Douangchay Phichit

EMBASSY OF THE LAO PEOPLE'S DEMOCRATIC REPUBLIC
74 Avenue Raymond-Poincaré F-75116 Paris
T (+ 33) (1) 4553 0298
Ambassador Extraordinary and Plenipotentiary, HE Soutsakhone Pathammavong, apptd 2003

BRITISH EMBASSY
PO Box 6626, Vientiane
T (+ 856) (21) 413606
Ambassador Extraordinary and Plenipotentiary, HE David Fall, apptd 2003, resident at Bangkok, Thailand

ECONOMY

The government of Laos is officially communist but has been forced to introduce some market reforms. Since 1986 a measure of private enterprise has been encouraged. The economy, however, was damaged during the Asian financial crisis which began in 1997.

Laos is still heavily dependent on subsistence agriculture which accounts for half of GDP and 80 per cent of employment. The seventh congress of the LPRP held in March 2001 defined the principal economic goal to be agricultural development. There is potential for increased hydroelectric power exports to Thailand and there are deposits of coal, tin, iron ore, gold, bauxite and lignite. Foreign investment in infrastructure began with the 1994 opening of the Friendship Bridge over the Mekong River border with Thailand which links road routes from Singapore to China.

GNI – US$1,493 million (2000); US$300 per capita (2001)
ANNUAL AVERAGE GROWTH OF GDP – 5.7 per cent (2000)
INFLATION RATE – 25.1 per cent (2000)
TOTAL EXTERNAL DEBT – US$2,499 million (2000)
IMPORTS – US$431 million (2002)
EXPORTS – US$298 million (2002)

BALANCE OF PAYMENTS
Trade – US$217 million deficit (2001)
Current Account – US$82 million deficit (2001)

Trade with UK	*2002*	*2003*
Imports from UK	£1,574,000	£3,391,000
Exports to UK	10,060,000	9,446,000

TRANSPORT INFRASTRUCTURE

There are no railways in Laos and only a limited road network (21,916 km). There are around 4,587 km of waterways.

MEDIA

There are three state run newspapers, although circulation is low and all media is strictly government controlled. There are also state run television and radio broadcasters.

LATVIA

Latvijas Republika – Republic of Latvia

AREA – 62,100 sq. km. Neighbours: Estonia (north), Lithuania and Belarus (south), the Russian Federation (east)
POPULATION – 2,406,000 (2001): 57.7 per cent Latvian, 29.6 per cent Russian, 4.1 per cent Belarusian, with small Ukrainian and Polish minorities. The main religions are Lutheran, Roman Catholic and Russian Orthodox. The official language is Latvian; Russian is also spoken. Education is in Latvian and Russian. Public sector employees must pass language tests in Latvian to a level commensurate with the nature of their employment. The right of minorities to use their mother tongue has been acknowledged
CAPITAL – Ψ Riga (population, 747,157, 2002 estimate)
MAJOR CITIES – Daugavpils; Jelgava; Jurmala; Ψ Liepaja; Ψ Ventspils
CURRENCY – Lats of 100 santims
NATIONAL ANTHEM – Dievs, Sveti Latviju (God Bless Latvia)
NATIONAL DAY – 18 November (Independence Day 1918)
NATIONAL FLAG – Crimson, with a white horizontal stripe across the centre
LIFE EXPECTANCY (years) – 71 (2001)
INFANT MORTALITY (per 1,000 births) – 17 (2001)
MORTALITY RATE (per 1,000 population) – 14.7 (2003)
HIV / AIDS ADULT PREVALENCE – 0.4 per cent (2001)
POPULATION GROWTH RATE – 0.9 per cent (1990–2001)
POPULATION DENSITY – 39 per sq. km (2001)
URBAN POPULATION – 96 per cent (2001)

CLIMATE AND TERRAIN

Latvia is a flat, low-lying country that has its coast on the eastern shores of the Baltic Sea. Elevation extremes range from 312 m (Gaizinkalns) at the highest point to 0 m (Baltic Sea) at the lowest. Average annual temperatures in the capital city Riga range from –4°C in January to 18°C in July.

HISTORY AND POLITICS

Latvia came under Swedish occupation in the 16th century, and German control during the First World War. Independence was declared in 1918 but fighting continued to flare between the Bolsheviks and nationalists. The non-aggression pact between Germany and the Soviet Union saw Latvia come under Soviet control in the 1930s. This ended in 1941 when Germany invaded the Soviet Union and occupied Latvia.

Latvia suffered huge civilian losses during the Second World War, including the destruction of its large Jewish community. Many more Latvians died after the war in purges and deportations ordered by Stalin.

Latvian nationalist groups became increasingly powerful as communism began to crumble in the Soviet Union in the 1980s. A coup in the Soviet Union failed in 1991 but gave Latvians the chance to proclaim independence.

Elections were held in 1993, and throughout the 1990s Latvia was ruled by a number of brief coalition governments.

The New Era party (JL) became the largest party in the unicameral parliament *(Saeima)* in the general election held on 5 October 2002, winning 26 of the 100 seats. JL leader Einars Repse, was nominated prime minister and formed a coalition government led by the JL and including the Greens and Farmers Union (ZZS), For Fatherland and Freedom (TB-LNNK) and the First Party of Latvia (LPP). The prime minister and cabinet were approved by the *Saeima* by 21 November.

The LPP withdrew from the coalition on 28 January 2004, after the dismissal of LPP deputy prime minister Ainars Slesers. The government lost its parliamentary majority, and resigned on 5 February. Indulis Emsis of the ZZS was nominated prime minister on 20 February. His coalition cabinet, comprising members of the ZZS, LPP and the People's Party (TP), was approved by parliament on 9 March 2004.

Latvia joined the European Union in May 2004.

POLITICAL SYSTEM

Executive authority is vested in a Prime Minister and Cabinet of Ministers. Legislative power is exercised by the unicameral parliament *(Saeima)*, which comprises 100 deputies each elected for four-year terms by proportional representation, with a five per cent threshold for parliamentary representation. The deputies elect a President of State, serving for a four-year term, who in turn appoints the Prime Minister. The Prime Minister appoints, and the *Saeima* approves, the Cabinet of Ministers.

HEAD OF STATE
President, Vaira Vīķe-Freiberga, *elected* 17 June 1999, *re-elected* 20 June 2003, *sworn in* 8 July 2003

SELECTED GOVERNMENT MEMBERS *as at July 2004*
Prime Minister, Indulis Emsis
Deputy Prime Minister, Ainars Slesers
Defence, Atis Slakteris
Finance, Valdis Dombrovskis
Foreign Affairs, Artis Pabriks
Interior, Eriks Jekabsons

EMBASSY OF THE REPUBLIC OF LATVIA
45 Nottingham Place, London W1U 5LR
T 020-7312 0040
Ambassador Extraordinary and Plenipotentiary, HE Janis Dripe, apptd 2002

BRITISH EMBASSY
5, J. Alunana iela, Riga LV-1010
T (+ 371) 777 4700
E british.embassy@apollo.lv
Ambassador Extraordinary and Plenipotentiary, HE Andrew Tesoriere, apptd 2002

BRITISH COUNCIL DIRECTOR, Agita Kalvnia
5a Blaumana iela, Riga LV-1011
T (+ 371) 728 1730
E mail@britishcouncil.lv

DEFENCE

The Army has three main battle tanks and 13 armoured personnel carriers, the Navy has one patrol and coastal vessel and eight defence patrol craft at three bases and the Air Force has 19 aircraft and five helicopters. Latvia joined NATO in April 2004.
MILITARY EXPENDITURE – 1.2 per cent of GDP (2001)
MILITARY PERSONNEL – 4,870: Army 4,000, Navy 620, Air Force 250; Paramilitaries 3,200
CONSCRIPTION DURATION – 12 months

ECONOMY AND TRADE

Western economic markets take approximately 60 per cent of Latvian goods. The largest trading partners are Germany, Sweden and the UK. Most of Latvia's timber products go to the UK.

Latvia plans to join the European Monetary Union in 2005 and to adopt the euro in 2008, however, progress may be hampered by its GDP per capita, which is the lowest of the countries that joined the EU in 2004.

Important Latvian industries include the manufacture of buses, vans, cars, synthetic fibres, agricultural machinery, fertilisers, washing machines, radios, electronics, pharmaceuticals, processed foods and textiles.

Latvia is an agricultural exporter, specialising in cattle and pig breeding, dairy farming and crops, including sugar beet, flax, cereals and potatoes. In 2001, 13.5 per cent of the population was employed in agriculture, which accounted for 4.1 per cent of GDP. Natural resources include limestone, gypsum, peat and timber. Transit, services and banking are also large sectors with services contributing 70.6 per cent of GDP in 2001.

GNI – US$7,600 million (2001); US$3,230 per capita (2001)
ANNUAL AVERAGE GROWTH OF GDP – 6.6 per cent (2000)
INFLATION RATE – 2.7 per cent (2000)
UNEMPLOYMENT – 14.6 per cent (2000)
TOTAL EXTERNAL DEBT – US$3,379 million (2000)
FOREIGN DIRECT INVESTMENT – US$1,633 million (1997–2000)
IMPORTS – US$4,503 million (2002)
EXPORTS – US$2,284 million (2002)

BALANCE OF PAYMENTS
Trade – US$1,444 million deficit (2002)
Current Account – US$659 million deficit (2002)

Trade with UK	*2002*	*2003*
Imports from UK	£76,002,000	£113,448,000
Exports to UK	469,648,000	508,193,000

TRANSPORT INFRASTRUCTURE

Latvia has 2,413 km of railway track and some 20,400 km of roads. There are several warm-water ports, of which three, Riga, Ventspils and Liepaja, are developed for commercial transport

EDUCATION

There are 27 higher education institutions, of which five are universities.
ILLITERACY RATE – (m) 0.2 per cent; (f) 0.2 per cent (2000)
ENROLMENT (percentage of age group) – primary 96 per cent (1997); secondary 84 per cent (1997); tertiary 33 per cent (1997)

MEDIA AND CULTURE

There are around 140 newspapers in circulation including 24 national dailies. The most popular include *Diena Panorama, Latvii* and *Neatkariga RA*. Latvian Television is a public service broadcaster that has two channels while Latvijas Neatkariga Televizija is the biggest private broadcaster.

Latvia has an extensive history of folk songs and poetry that has been composed over the centuries in the traditional Latvian language.

Important Latvian figures include the photographer Philippe Halsman (1906–79) and the poet Juris Kunnoss (1948–98).

LEBANON

Al-Jumhūriyya al-Lubnāniyya – Republic of Lebanon

AREA – 10,200 sq. km. Neighbours: Syria (north and east), Israel (south)
POPULATION – 3,556,000 (2001): 32 per cent Shi'ite Muslim; 21 per cent Sunni Muslim, 40 per cent Christian, 7 per cent Druze. Arabic is the official language, and French and English are also widely used
CAPITAL – ΨBeirut (Bayrut) (population, 1,100,000, 1994)
MAJOR CITIES – ΨSayda (Sidon); ΨTarabulus (Tripoli); ΨSur (Tyre)
CURRENCY – Lebanese pound (L£) of 100 piastres
NATIONAL ANTHEM – Kulluna Lil Watan Lil 'Ula Lil'alam (We All Belong To The Homeland)
NATIONAL DAY – 22 November
NATIONAL FLAG – Horizontal bands of red, white and red with a green cedar of Lebanon in the centre of the white band
LIFE EXPECTANCY (years) – 73 (2001)

MORTALITY RATE (per 1,000 population) – 6.32 (2003)
INFANT MORTALITY (per 1,000 births) – 28 (2001)
HIV / AIDS ADULT PREVALENCE – 0.9 per cent (2001)
DEATH PENALTY – Yes
POPULATION BELOW POVERTY LINE – 28 per cent (1999)
POPULATION GROWTH RATE – 2.5 per cent (1990–2001)
POPULATION DENSITY – 349 per sq. km (2001)
URBAN POPULATION – 90 per cent (2001)

CLIMATE AND TERRAIN

Lebanon forms part of the 'fertile crescent' – a region of well-irrigated land that connects Egypt to Iraq. Elevation extremes range from 3,088 m (Qurnat as Sawda') at the highest point to 0 m (Mediterranean Sea) at the lowest. Lebanon has a Mediterranean climate and average annual temperatures of 13°C in January and 29°C in August.

HISTORY AND POLITICS

Lebanon came under the influence of the Ottoman empire in the 16th century, who were the first to unite the area into what is now modern Lebanon. Following the collapse of the Ottoman empire at the end of the First World War, Lebanon came under French rule, and independence came during the Second World War.

The 1943 National Pact gave Lebanon a complicated system of government designed to give a measure of power to all religions. By 1975 tensions between Christians and Muslims pushed Lebanon into civil war. The first war lasted from between 1975 to 1976 and pitted a coalition of Christian groups against Druze and Muslim militias, as well as the Palestine Liberation Organisation (PLO) which had been expelled from neighbouring Jordan.

Fighting continued despite the presence of Syrian troops in the country, until 1982 when Israel, in an attempt to destroy the PLO, invaded.

Fighting continued throughout the 1980s. The kings of Morocco and Saudi Arabia and the President of Algeria met in 1989 to attempt to resolve the crisis. A seven-point peace plan was agreed and a cease-fire followed. Syria's withdrawal from Lebanon was negotiated, as was a plan to rid the Lebanese political system of religious influence but warfare resumed after the assassination of Rene Moawad, who had been elected president by a meeting of Lebanese deputies.

A fragile peace finally arrived in 1991, after 16 years of civil war. Elections in 1992 were peaceful but were boycotted by some communities. Further elections took place in 1996, and in 1998 the Lebanese Parliament voted General Emile Lahoud as president. The general election held on 27 August and 3 September 2000 was won by supporters of Rafik Hariri, who had been prime minister from 1992 to 1998. Hariri was appointed prime minister by President Lahoud on 23 October 2000 and named his cabinet, composed equally of Christians and Muslims, on 26 October. Hariri resigned with his entire cabinet on 15 April 2003, although he remained as 'caretaker' prime minister at the request of President Lahoud and was re-appointed on 17 April. A new cabinet headed by Hariri was approved on 30 April. Lahoud's presidency was due to end in November 2004.

SOUTH LEBANON

Israel invaded Lebanon and besieged Beirut in 1982. The Israeli army withdrew in 1985, but continued to occupy parts of south Lebanon with the Israeli Defence Force and a proxy army, the South Lebanon Army (SLA). Israel's intention was to create a buffer zone to stop attacks from the group Hezbollah which is financed, armed and trained by Syria and Iran. Israel withdrew from south Lebanon in May 2000 and the UN established a 'Blue Line' demarcating the border between Israel and Lebanon. While there have been continual breaches of the border, and the area remains tense, the two sides have not returned to all-out fighting.

POLITICAL SYSTEM

The National Covenant (1943) is characterised by the division of power between the religious communities. The Executive comprises the President, Prime Minister and Cabinet. The President is elected by the National Assembly for a non-renewable six-year term and must be a Maronite Christian. The Prime Minister is appointed following consultation between the President and National Assembly and must be a Sunni Muslim. The 128-member unicameral National Assembly comprises equal numbers of Christians and Muslims although the speaker must be a Shia Muslim. Political parties are banned.

The constitution was amended on 15 October 1998 to allow the election of Gen. Lahoud as President. Serving State officials had previously been prohibited from standing for the presidency.

HEAD OF STATE

President of the Republic of Lebanon, Gen. Émile Lahoud, *elected* 15 October 1998, *sworn in* 24 November 1998

SELECTED GOVERNMENT MEMBERS *as at July 2004*

Prime Minister, Rafiq Hariri
Deputy Prime Minister, Issam Fares
Finance, Fouad Siniora
Foreign Affairs and Emigrants, Jean Obeid
Interior and Municipal Affairs, Elias Murr
National Defence, Mahmoud Hammud

LEBANESE EMBASSY

15–21 Palace Gardens Mews, London W8 4QN
T 020-7229 7265/7727 6696
Ambassador Extraordinary and Plenipotentiary, HE Jihad Mortada, apptd 1999

BRITISH EMBASSY

Embassies Complex, Army Street, Zkak al-Blat, Serail Hill PO Box 11–471, Beirut
T (+ 961) (1) 990 400
E britemb@cyberia.net.lb
Ambassador Extraordinary and Plenipotentiary, HE James Watt, apptd 2003

BRITISH COUNCIL DIRECTOR, Dr Ken Churchill, OBE
Sidani Street, Azar Building, Ras Beirut
T (+ 961) (1) 740 123
E general.enquiries@lb.britishcouncil.org

DEFENCE

The Army has 310 main battle tanks and 1,338 armoured personnel carriers. The Navy has seven patrol and coastal vessels at two bases. There is a 2,029-strong UN peacekeeping force, 16,000 Syrian troops and 150 Iranian Revolutionary Guards operating in Lebanon.
MILITARY EXPENDITURE – 3.2 per cent of GDP (2002)
MILITARY PERSONNEL – 72,100: Army 70,000, Navy 1,100, Air Force 1,000; Paramilitaries 13,000
CONSCRIPTION DURATION – 12 months

ECONOMY AND TRADE

In the aftermath of the war foreign exchange was provided by remittances from Lebanese working abroad, banking services, manufacturing and farm exports, and international aid. In 1993 the Lebanese government launched 'Horizon 2000', a US$20 billion reconstruction programme. The initiative raised GDP by eight per cent in the following year, though this slowed to three per cent by 2003. The plan was also successful in reducing inflation. The government borrowed heavily to fund reconstruction, and debt is now a serious problem. Receipts from donor nations stabilised government finances throughout 2002 and 2003. Agriculture is an important part of the Lebanese economy and provides much of the country's exports. Principal exports include foodstuffs, chemical products, jewellery, machinery and electrical goods, textiles, metals and metal products, paper and paper products, and vehicles.

Principal imports are foodstuffs, machinery and electrical equipment, vehicles, chemical products, mineral ores, and metals and metal products. There is a free-trade agreement with Syria.

GNI – US$17,600 million (2001); US$4,010 per capita (2001)
ANNUAL AVERAGE GROWTH OF GDP – 5.0 per cent (1998)
INFLATION RATE – 6.8 per cent (1994)
TOTAL EXTERNAL DEBT – US$10,311 million (2000)
FOREIGN DIRECT INVESTMENT – US$898 million (1997–2000)
IMPORTS – US$6,447 million (2002)
EXPORTS – US$1,046 million (2002)

Trade with UK	*2002*	*2003*
Imports from UK	£158,529,000	£210,283,000
Exports to UK	20,084,000	16,625,000

TRANSPORT INFRASTRUCTURE

There are 7,370 km of roads, of which 6,265 km are surfaced; there is 222 km of railway track. There is an international airport at Beirut and an internal service operates from Beirut to Tripoli.

EDUCATION

There is a good provision throughout the country of primary and secondary schools, among which are a great number of private schools. There are 16 universities and colleges of higher education in Lebanon, among them American and French universities, and the Lebanese National University, the Beirut University College, the Kaslik Saint Esprit University and the Arab University in Beirut, with the University of Balamand situated near Tripoli.

ILLITERACY RATE – (m) 7.9 per cent; (f) 19.6 per cent (2000)
ENROLMENT (percentage of age group) – primary 100 per cent (1997); tertiary 27 per cent (1997)

MEDIA AND CULTURE

There are a number of daily newspapers in circulation, including French and English language publications. Tele-Liban is the state run broadcaster that competes with several commercial stations, including the pro-Hezbollah al-Manar TV.

Lebanese literature is dominated by the 19-century mystical poet Khalil Gibran (1833–1931). The country has also produced a number of respected contemporary writers such as Amin Maalouf (b. 1949) and Hanan al-Shaykh (b. 1945).

LESOTHO

Mmuso wa Lesotho – Kingdom of Lesotho

AREA – 30,355 sq. km. Neighbour: South Africa, which completely surrounds Lesotho
POPULATION – 2,177,062 (2001 estimate). The languages are Sesotho and English
CAPITAL – Maseru (population, 367,000, 1992 estimate)
CURRENCY – Loti (M) of 100 lisente. The South African rand is also legal tender
NATIONAL ANTHEM – Pina Ea Sechaba
NATIONAL DAY – 4 October (Independence Day)
NATIONAL FLAG – Diagonally white over blue over green with the white of double width, and an assegai and knobkerrie on a Basotho shield in brown in the upper hoist
MORTALITY RATE (per 1,000 population) – 24.58 (2003)
HIV / AIDS ADULT PREVALENCE – 31 per cent (2001)
DEATH PENALTY – Yes
POPULATION BELOW POVERTY LINE – 49 per cent (1999)
POPULATION GROWTH RATE – 2.3 per cent (1990–2001)
POPULATION DENSITY – 69 per sq. km (1999)
MILITARY EXPENDITURE – 2.9 per cent of GDP (2002)
MILITARY PERSONNEL – Army 2,000

CLIMATE AND TERRAIN

Lethoso mainly comprises a highland plateau region with some hilly and mountainous areas. Elevation extremes range from 3,482 m (Thabana Ntlenyana) at the highest point to 1,400 m (the junction of the Orange and Makhaleng rivers) at the lowest.

HISTORY AND POLITICS

The area was organised into a single territory by Moshoeshoe the Great around 1820. Later in the 19th century the Sotho people came under pressure from both the expanding Zulu nation and Europeans (the Boers) to give up land. In 1868, after fighting two wars with the Europeans, pressure from the Boers forced the Sotho to seek protection from the British government.

Basotholand, as it was known under British rule, gained independence in 1966, and was renamed Lesotho. Chief Jonathan was the first prime minister, but when he faced the country's first elections in 1970 and feared that his Basotho National Party might be defeated, he declared a state of emergency and suspended the constitution.

Lesotho was thereafter ruled by a Military Council until 1993. The Basotho Congress Party (BCP), who had contested the earlier, aborted elections, won a landslide victory. Serious civil disturbances following the ousting of the former military rulers led to another suspension of the constitution and dissolution of parliament. Mediation from the presidents of South Africa, Zimbabwe and Botswana restored democratic rule in 1994, and in 1995 the monarch, King Moshoeshoe II returned from the exile imposed on him by the Military Council in 1990.

Lesotho continued to be troubled by civil violence, and

in 1998, following particularly severe disturbances, the Government established an Interim Political Authority to review the constitution. Elections in May 2002 returned the Lesotho Congress for Democracy to power.

POLITICAL SYSTEM
In September 1999 it was announced that the first past the post electoral system would be replaced by a new system incorporating a degree of proportional representation and that the number of seats in the National Assembly would be increased by 40 to 120.

HEAD OF STATE
HM The King of Lesotho, King Letsie III, *acceded* February 1996, *crowned* 31 October 1997

SELECTED GOVERNMENT MEMBERS *as at July 2004*
Prime Minister, Defence, Public Service, Bethuel Pakalitha Mosisili
Finance and Development Planning, Timothy Thahane
Foreign Affairs, Mohlabi Kenneth Tsekoa
Home Affairs, Motsoahae Thomas Thabane

HIGH COMMISSION FOR THE KINGDOM OF LESOTHO
7 Chesham Place, London SW1X 8HN
T 020-7235 5686
E lhclesotholondon.org.uk
High Commissioner, HE Lebohang Ramohlanka, apptd 2000

BRITISH HIGH COMMISSION
PO Box Ms 521, Maseru 100
T (+ 266) 2231 3961
E hcmaseru@lesoff.co.za
High Commissioner, HE Frank Martin, apptd 2002

ECONOMY AND TRADE
Lesotho's economy is closely linked to South Africa, to which it exports its primary natural resource – water. Lesotho is self-sufficient in power from hydroelectricity facilities, however, Lesotho's economy is also reliant on remittances from miners working in South Africa. Tourism is being developed, especially in the Highlands.

The USA's African Growth and Opportunity Act (AGOA) has gone some way to ameliorate rising unemployment by creating 45,000 jobs in the garment industry, and making Lesotho the second largest exporter in sub-Saharan Africa of garments to the USA. Subsistence agriculture continues to be the largest sector of Lesotho's economy engaging 86 per cent of the resident population. Around 35 per cent of the male labour force is employed in South Africa.

GNP – US$1,181 million (2000); US$580 per capita (2000)
ANNUAL AVERAGE GROWTH OF GDP – 5.5 per cent (1998)
INFLATION RATE – 6.1 per cent (2000)
TOTAL EXTERNAL DEBT – US$735 million (2002)
IMPORTS – US$779 million (2002)
EXPORTS – US$194 million (1998)

BALANCE OF PAYMENTS
Trade – US$516 million deficit (2000)
Current Account – US$95 million deficit (2001)

Trade with UK	*2002*	*2003*
Imports from UK	£1,048,000	£202,000
Exports to UK	1,116,000	516,000

TRANSPORT INFRASTRUCTURE
A surfaced road links Maseru to several of the main lowland towns. The mountainous areas are linked by surfaced, gravelled and rough earth roads and tracks. Other roads link border towns in South Africa with the main towns in Lesotho. Maseru is also connected by rail with the main Bloemfontein-Natal line managed by South African Railways. There are a number of scheduled international air services in operation.

EDUCATION
There are over 1,200 primary and over 180 secondary schools, with emphasis being laid on agricultural and vocational education. The National University of Lesotho at Roma was established in 1975.

ILLITERACY RATE – (m) 27.6 per cent; (f) 6.4 per cent (2000)
ENROLMENT (percentage of age group) – primary 100 per cent (1997); secondary 31 per cent (1997); tertiary 2 per cent (1997)

MEDIA
Lesotho has a mixture of state run and private media. Radio is the most important medium and reforms established in 1998 prompted the growth of a number of commercial stations. State run Radio Lesotho is the only national station. Lesotho's press publishes a range of weekly papers in both Sesotho and English.

LIBERIA

Republic of Liberia

AREA – 111,369 sq. km. Neighbours: Guinea (north), Côte d'Ivoire (east), Sierra Leone (north-west)
POPULATION – 3,225,837 (2001 estimate). The official language is English. The main African languages are Bassa, Kpelle and Kru, though some 16 ethnic languages are spoken
CAPITAL – ΨMonrovia (population, 421,000, 2000 estimate)
MAJOR CITIES – ΨBuchanan (Grand Bassa); ΨGreenville (Sinoe); ΨHarper (Cape Palmas)
CURRENCY – Liberian dollar (L$) of 100 cents
NATIONAL ANTHEM – All Hail, Liberia, Hail
NATIONAL DAY – 26 July
NATIONAL FLAG – Alternate horizontal stripes (five white, six red), with a five-pointed white star on a blue field in the upper corner next to the flagstaff
LIFE EXPECTANCY (years) – 53.9
MORTALITY RATE (per 1,000 population) – 17.84
INFANT MORTALITY RATE (per 1,000 births) – 27.9
HIV / AIDS ADULT PREVALENCE – 9 per cent (1999)
DEATH PENALTY – Yes
POPULATION BELOW POVERTY LINE – 38.6 per cent (2000)
POPULATION GROWTH RATE – 1.5 per cent (1990–2001)
POPULATION DENSITY – 26 per sq. km (1999)
URBAN POPULATION – 44.9 per cent (2000)
MILITARY EXPENDITURE – 4.5 per cent of GDP (2002)
MILITARY PERSONNEL – 15,000 (including militias supporting government forces)

ILLITERACY RATE – (m) 29.9 per cent; (f) 62.3 per cent (2000)

CLIMATE AND TERRAIN

Liberia sits just north of the equator, on the west African coast. There are low mountains in the north-east and rolling coastal plains in the west. Elevation extremes range from 1,380 m (Mount Wuteve) at the highest point to 0 m (Atlantic Sea) at the lowest. Average annual temperatures are an almost constant 28°C.

HISTORY AND POLITICS

The establishment of an independent state for freed slaves by the USA in 1847 began the history of the only west African country not to be colonised.

Throughout the 1980s Liberia's human rights record was poor; arbitrary rule and economic collapse led rebels from Charles Taylor's National Patriotic Forces of Liberia (NPFL) to revolt against the incumbent president Samuel Doe, a revolution ensued, which swiftly descended into civil war. In 1989 Taylor's troops overran the country, captured Doe and executed him. The fighting, however, took on an ethnic character with the Krahn and Mandingo peoples of the Armed Forces of Liberia (AFL) battling the Gio and Mano dominated NPFL.

The Economic Community of West African States (ECOWAS) sent a peace-keeping force, ECOMOG, into the country in 1990 (ECOMOG forces, though drawn from across ECOWAS members, were dominated by Nigerian soldiers). ECOMOG forces fought alongside Liberian dissident forces in an attempt to oust Taylor. Sierra Leone allowed these forces to mount attacks on Liberia from its territory.

A UN arms embargo was imposed in 1992 but, despite a number of peace initiatives and cease-fires between 1991 and 1996, Liberia continued to suffer war, almost continuous political and economic instability, and human rights abuses.

A peace agreement in 1996 was signed in Abuja, Nigeria. The agreement was brought about by pressure from ECOWAS, and resulted in elections in 1997. Liberians, fearing that Charles Taylor would simply restart the civil war if he lost, gave Taylor 80 per cent of the vote.

This result did not address the causes of fighting in Liberia, and rebel groups continued to destabilise the country. Liberians United for Reconciliation and Democracy (LURD) were operating in the north of the country and were supported by Guinea. LURD were joined in the east of the country by Movement of Democracy for Liberia (MODEL). Both militia groups aimed to depose Taylor. By June 2003 MODEL controlled much of the east of the country and LURD were closing in on the capital, Monrovia. ECOWAS again sponsored peace talks, and these coincided with Sierra Leone's attempts to indict Charles Taylor for war crimes and crimes against humanity for his part in the Sierra Leonian civil war.

UN Security Council Resolution 1497 gave Nigerian forces a mandate to enter the country. Charles Taylor went into exile in Nigeria, and his vice president Moses Blah formed an interim government.

The International Contact Group on Liberia, launched in New York in September 2002, brought together a number of African and European countries, as well as the USA, to mediate between Liberia's different factions.

In September 2003 all factions in the Liberian conflict signed the Comprehensive Peace Agreement which created the National Transitional Government of Liberia (NTGL). Gyude Bryant, a former businessman leads the government which is made up of LURD, MODEL, Charles Taylor's forces and Liberian civil society. All these factions agreed to work towards elections in 2005. The UN Security Council passed resolution 1509 in September 2003 which established a peacekeeping force, UNMIL, of 15,000 soldiers to be deployed in Liberia.

POLITICAL SYSTEM

The Head of State is the Executive President, directly elected for a six-year term, who appoints the Cabinet. There is a bicameral legislature consisting of a 64-member lower chamber, the House of Representatives, which is directly elected for a six-year term, and a 26-member Senate, elected for a nine-year term. Under the Comprehensive Peace Agreement a 76-member National Transitional Legislative Assembly (NTLA) was inaugurated on 14 October 2003.

HEAD OF STATE

Chair of the National Transitional Government, Gyude Bryant, *sworn in* 14 October 2003
Vice-Chair, Wesley Momo Johnson

SELECTED GOVERNMENT MEMBERS *as at August 2004*
Defence, Daniel Chea
Finance, Lusinee Kamara
Foreign Affairs, Thomas Yaya Nimely
Internal Affairs, Horatio Dan Morias

EMBASSY OF THE REPUBLIC OF LIBERIA
2 Pembridge Place, London W2 4XB
T 020-7221 1036
Ambassador Extraordinary and Plenipotentiary, vacant

BRITISH AMBASSADOR, HE Jean Gordon, CMG, apptd 2001, resident at Abidjan, Côte d'Ivoire

ECONOMY AND TRADE

The civil war of 1980–2002, has devastated Liberia's economy. Liberia is rich in timber, gold, diamonds and rubber, though the UN has imposed sanctions on the export of timber and diamonds. Agriculture centres around timber, rubber, coffee, cocoa, rice, cassava (tapioca), palm oil, sugarcane, bananas; sheep and goats. Much of the population has no mains electricity or running water. Since the signing of the Comprehensive Peace Agreement, foreign aid has greatly increased.

GDP – US$759 million (1998); US$248 per capita (2000)
ANNUAL AVERAGE GROWTH OF GDP – 2.7 per cent (1998)
TOTAL EXTERNAL DEBT – US$2,032 million (2000)

Trade with UK	*2002*	*2003*
Imports from UK	£6,331,000	£4,966,000
Exports to UK	3,119,000	14,803,000

TRANSPORT INFRASTRUCTURE

The artificial harbour and free port of Monrovia opened in 1948. There are 10,300 km of roads, of which 628 km are surfaced, and 490 km of railway track. There are nine ports of entry, including three river ports. Robertsfield International Airport and Spriggs Payne airfield are currently being used for flights to other West African countries.

MEDIA AND CULTURE

Radio is the main medium for news in Liberia. Many stations were shut down under former President Charles

Taylor's rule, however, there is now a growing number of stations. Liberia has no television service.

A department of Indiana University in the USA has recently begun work on the 'Liberian Collections Project', an archive of official documents, taped recordings of traditional dance music and various artistic and cultural objects including carved masks and clothing.

LIBYA

Al-Jamāhīriyya Al-'Arabiyya Al-Lībiyya Ash-Sha'biyya Al-Ishtirākiyya – Great Socialist People's Libyan Arab Jamahiriya

AREA – 1,759,500 sq. km. Neighbours: Egypt and Sudan (east), Chad and Niger (south), Algeria and Tunisia (west)
POPULATION – 5,408,000 (2001). The people of Libya are principally Arab with some Berbers in the west and some Tuareg tribesmen in the Fezzan. Islam is the official religion. The official language is Arabic
CAPITAL – ΨTripoli (Tarabulus) (population, 1,000,000, 1991 estimate)
MAJOR CITIES – ΨBangazi; ΨMisratah; Sirte
CURRENCY – Libyan dinar (LD) of 1,000 dirhams
NATIONAL ANTHEM – Allahu Akbar (God Is Great)
NATIONAL DAY – 1 September
NATIONAL FLAG – Libya uses a plain emerald green flag
LIFE EXPECTANCY (years) – 71 (2001)
MORTALITY RATE (per 1,000 population) – 3.49 (2003)
INFANT MORTALITY (per 1,000 births) – 16 (2001)
HIV / AIDS ADULT PREVALENCE – 0.2 per cent (2001)
DEATH PENALTY – Yes
POPULATION GROWTH RATE – 2.1 per cent (1990–2001)
POPULATION DENSITY – 3 per sq. km (2001)

CLIMATE AND TERRAIN

Libya's terrain is low-lying and arid, much of which is desert. There are some mountainous regions in the south and north-east of the country. Elevation extremes range from 2,267 m (Bikku Bitti) at the highest point to –47 m (Sabkhat Guzayyil) at the lowest. Average temperatures in Tripoli can range from 13°C in January to 31°C in August.

HISTORY AND POLITICS

Libya has a long history of being conquered – Phoenicians, Carthaginians, Greeks, Romans, Vandals, and Byzantines periodically invaded, occupied and settled in Libya. It came under Arab influence in the seventh century AD. Between the sixteenth century and 1911, when the country was conquered by Italy, Libya was part of the Ottoman Empire. The Italians, after fierce resistance, made Libya a colony.

King Idris I declared independence on 24 December 1951, and Libya became the first country to achieve independence through a UN resolution.

The discovery of oil in Libya made the country wealthy but did not bring stability, and Idris was deposed in a military coup in 1 September 1969. The Revolutionary Command Council (RCC) abolished the monarchy and proclaimed the country the Libyan Arab Republic. Colonel Muammar al-Gaddafi eventually became leader of the RCC and Head of State.

FOREIGN RELATIONS

Colonel Gaddafi embarked on a programme for a brand of Islamic socialism and sought to export his revolutionary theories abroad. This brought him into increasing enmity with Western governments. In 1986 US war planes bombed targets around Tripoli and Benghazi in retaliation for a terrorist attack on a Berlin nightclub in which two American soldiers died.

A bomb on a Pan Am flight over Lockerbie, Scotland in 1988 was widely believed to be the responsibility of Libya, and the country's isolation deepened. Sanctions imposed by the UN were only relaxed when Gaddafi agreed to give up the suspects in the Lockerbie case to the International Court of Justice in 1998. In 2000 the trial of the two accused Libyans, Abdelbaset al-Megrahi and Khalifa Fhimah, began. In January 2001 al-Megrahi was found guilty of the bombing and sentenced to a minimum of 27 years in a Scottish prison. Fhimah was found not guilty and released. In August 2003, an initial compensation payment of US$27,000 million was agreed by the Libyan authorities. However, conditions were applied to the payment including the lifting of UN sanctions.

Since the 2003 General People's Congress, Gaddafi has made further moves to end Libya's isolation, such as economic reform to open Libya to international markets. In March 2004 UK Prime Minister Tony Blair met with Colonel Gaddafi following the Libyan leader's promise to allow UN nuclear weapons inspectors into the country.

POLITICAL SYSTEM

At a local level authority is vested in about 1,500 Basic and 14 Municipal People's Congresses which appoint Popular Committees to execute policy. Officials of these congresses and committees, together with representatives from unions and other organisations, form the 750-member General People's Congress, which normally meets twice each year. In addition, a number of extraordinary sessions are held throughout the year. This is the highest policy-making body in the country. The General People's Congress appoints its own General Secretariat and the General People's Committee, whose members head the Government departments which execute policy at national level. The Secretary of the General People's Committee has functions similar to those of a Prime Minister.

Leader of the Revolution and Supreme Commander of the Armed Forces, Col. Muammar al-Gaddafi

SELECTED GOVERNMENT MEMBERS *as at July 2004*
Secretary-General (Prime Minister), Shukri Muhammad Ghanim
Assistant Secretary-General (Deputy Prime Minister), Al-Baghdadi Ali al-Mahmudi
Secretary, Economy and Trade, Abd-al-Qadir Umar Bilkhayr
Secretary, Finance, Mohamed Ali al-Houeiz
Secretary, Foreign Liaison and International Co-operation, Abdel Rahman Muhammad Shalgam

LIBYAN PEOPLE'S BUREAU
61–62 Ennismore Gardens, London SW7 1NH
T 020-7589 6120

Ambassador Extraordinary and Plenipotentiary, HE Muhammad Abu-al-Qasim al-Zawi, apptd 2001

BRITISH EMBASSY
Sharia Uahran 1, PO Box 4206, Tripoli
T (+ 218) (21) 340 3644/5
Ambassador Extraordinary and Plenipotentiary, HE Anthony Layden, apptd 2002

BRITISH COUNCIL DIRECTOR, Carl Reuter
British Embassy, 24th Floor, Burj al Fatah, PO Box 4206, Tripoli
E info.libya@britishcouncil-ly.org

DEFENCE

The Army has about 800 main battle tanks, 1,000 armoured infantry fighting vehicles and 945 armoured personnel carriers. The Navy has one submarine, one frigate, nine patrol and coastal vessels, and seven armed helicopters at seven bases. The Air Force has 400 combat aircraft and 41 armed helicopters.

MILITARY EXPENDITURE – 3.8 per cent of GDP (2002)
MILITARY PERSONNEL – 76,000: Army 45,000, Navy 8,000, Air Force 23,000
CONSCRIPTION DURATION – One to two years (selective)

ECONOMY AND TRADE

The economy is heavily dependent on the oil industry which remains in state control. Oil accounts for 95 per cent of total exports, 30 per cent of GDP and 75 per cent of revenue. Libya has a small population, and this gives the country a comparatively high per capita GNI. UN sanctions were lifted in 2003 and Libya has applied for WTO membership. In March 2004, the Royal Dutch/ Shell Group announced that a preliminary agreement had been signed in Libya to develop the country's gas resources. There have also been moves to diversify the economy away from such large-scale reliance on oil. The manufacturing and construction sectors, which account for 20 per cent of GDP, have been expanded to include the production of petrochemicals, iron, steel and aluminium. Environmental conditions mean Libya does not have a large agricultural sector and imports 75 per cent of its food.

Principal exports are wool, cattle, sheep and horses, olive oil, and hides and skins. Principal imports are machinery and transport equipment, foodstuffs, livestock, and most construction materials and consumer goods.

Italy is Libya's main trading partner, other trading partners include the UK, France and Germany.

GNI – US$6,700 per capita (2001)
ANNUAL AVERAGE GROWTH OF GDP – 0.6 per cent (1998)
IMPORTS – US$4,397 (2001)
EXPORTS – US$8,915 (2001)

BALANCE OF PAYMENTS
Trade – US$2,974 million surplus (1999)
Current Account – US$2,136 million surplus (1999)

Trade with UK	*2002*	*2003*
Imports from UK	£215,705,000	£241,056,000
Exports to UK	167,037,000	202,093,000

TRANSPORT INFRASTRUCTURE

There are about 19,300 km of roads; the coastal road running from the Tunisian frontier through Tripoli to Benghazi, Tubruq and the Egyptian border, serves the main population centres. Main roads also link the provincial centres, and the oil-producing areas of the south with the coastal towns. Libya has had no railways in operation since 1965, though there are plans to reconstruct some systems.

EDUCATION

There are nine years of compulsory education. The Libyan education system allows for six years each at primary and secondary level.

ILLITERACY RATE – (m) 9.2 per cent; (f) 31.7 per cent (2000)
ENROLMENT (percentage of age group) – primary 49.2 per cent (1997); tertiary 49.9 per cent (1997)

MEDIA AND CULTURE

The state maintains strict control over the media. Great Jamahiriya TV is the state run television broadcaster.

Berber and Tuareg folk culture has a strong influence on Libya. The rock paintings at Tadrart Acacus are believed to be at least 14,000 years old and in 1985 this area was designated a UNESCO World Heritage Site.

LIECHTENSTEIN

Fürstentum Liechtenstein – Principality of Liechtenstein

AREA – 160 sq. km. Neighbours: Austria, Switzerland
POPULATION – 33,863 (2002). The language of the principality is Standard German. An Alemannic dialect is in general use. About 65.8 per cent of the population are Liechtensteiners, the remainder being mainly Swiss, Austrians and Germans. Roman Catholicism is the religion of 80.4 per cent of the population; there is a Protestant minority
CAPITAL – Vaduz (population, 5,038, 2002)
CURRENCY – Swiss franc of 100 rappen (or centimes)
NATIONAL ANTHEM – Oben Am Jungen Rhein (Up On The Young Rhine)
NATIONAL DAY – 15 August
NATIONAL FLAG – Equal horizontal bands of blue over red; gold crown on blue band near staff
LIFE EXPECTANCY (years) – 79 (2001)
MORTALITY RATE (per 1,000 population) – 6.85 (2003)
INFANT MORTALITY (per 1,000 births) – 10 (2001)
DEATH PENALTY – No (abolished 1987)
POPULATION GROWTH RATE – 1.2 per cent (1990–2001)
POPULATION DENSITY – 212 per sq. km (2001)

CLIMATE AND TERRAIN

Elevation extremes in Liechtenstein range from 2,599 m (Garauspitz) at the highest point to 466 m (Ruggeller Riet) at the lowest. There is heavy snowfall in winter and average annual temperatures range from 0°C in January to 21°C in July.

HISTORY AND POLITICS

Liechtenstein became an independent principality of the Holy Roman Empire in 1719 under the Emperor Charles VI, although there had been a state within the present boundaries since 1434. The French emperor Napoleon occupied the country but left in 1815, and the country declared permanent neutrality in 1868. Economic decline in the years following the First World War forced Liechtenstein into a customs and monetary union with Switzerland in 1921. Neither of the World Wars saw Liechtenstein's neutrality violated and the country became extremely prosperous as an international finance sector after the Second World War. Liechtenstein's monarchy has resisted attempts at modernisation. Prince Hans Adam II, who ascended the throne in 1989, threatened to remove himself as head of state when the government suggested a reduction in his powers in 1995.

The Patriotic Union (VU) and the Progressive Citizens' Party (FBP) governed the country in coalition from 1938 until the VU gained power in a general election of 1997. In the general election of 11 February 2001 the FBP won 13 seats and this new government took office on 5 April.

POLITICAL SYSTEM

Liechtenstein is a constitutional monarchy. The Cabinet is appointed by the Prince on the advice of Parliament and consists of a head of Government and four ministers. The 25-member *(Landtag)*, unicameral Parliament, serves for a four-year term. There is a threshold of eight per cent for parties to gain representation. The 19 March 2003 referendum approved constitutional reforms which would give the Monarch increased power, including authority to dismiss the Government and appoint an interim Prime Minister. The Monarch would also not be subject to the authority of the Constitutional Court.

HEAD OF STATE
HSH The Prince of Liechtenstein, Hans Adam II, *born* 14 February 1945; *succeeded* 13 November 1989
Heir, HSH Prince Alois, *born* 11 June 1968

SELECTED GOVERNMENT MEMBERS *as at July 2004*
Head of Government, Construction, Family Affairs and Equal Rights, Finance, General Government Affairs, Otmar Hasler
Deputy Head of Government, Education, Justice, Transport, Rita Kieber-Beck
Economy, Health, Social Matters, Hansjörg Frick
Foreign Affairs, Ernst Walch
Interior, Culture and Sports, Environment, Alois Ospelt

BRITISH AMBASSADOR, Basil Eastwood, CMG, resident at Bern, Switzerland

ECONOMY AND TRADE

Liechtenstein has a highly diversified economy with a light industrial base.

In 1991 Liechtenstein became a member of the European Free Trade Association, and joined the European Economic Area on 1 May 1995.

GNI – US$40,000 per capita (2001)
ANNUAL AVERAGE GROWTH OF GDP – 2.1 per cent (1998)

Trade with UK	*2002*	*2003*
Imports from UK	£4,731,000	£4,705,000
Exports to UK	23,799,000	27,580,000

TRANSPORT INFRASTRUCTURE

Liechtenstein has 250 km of highways, 18.5 km of railways, but no airports.

MEDIA AND CULTURE

Liechtenstein relies on foreign broadcasters for television. Circulation for its two newspapers, *Liechtenstein News* and *Liechtensteiner Vaterland*, is under 10,000. Due in part to its small size, Liechtenstein's cultural identity has been profoundly influenced by its surrounding neighbours. Joseph Rheinburger (1839–1901) is perhaps the country's most famous composer.

LITHUANIA

Lietuvos Respublika – Republic of Lithuania

AREA – 64,800 sq. km. Neighbours: Latvia (north), Belarus (east and south), Poland and the Kaliningrad region of the Russian Federation (south-west)
POPULATION – 3,689,000 (2001): 80.6 per cent Lithuanian, 8.7 per cent Russian, 7 per cent Polish, 1.6 per cent Belarusian, 2.1 per cent other minority ethnic groups. The majority are Roman Catholic (79 per cent), with Russian Orthodox (4.1 per cent) and Lutheran minorities. Lithuanian is the state language
CAPITAL – Vilnius (population, 542,287, 2001 estimate)
MAJOR CITIES – Kaunas; Klaipeda
CURRENCY – Litas of 100 centas, pegged to the euro, €1 = 3.45 litas
NATIONAL ANTHEM – Tautiska Giesme (The National Song)
NATIONAL DAY – 16 February (Independence Day)
NATIONAL FLAG – Three horizontal stripes of yellow, green and red
LIFE EXPECTANCY (years) – 72 (2001)
MORTALITY RATE (per 1,000 population) – 12.89 (2003)
INFANT MORTALITY (per 1,000 births) – 8 (2001)
HIV / AIDS ADULT PREVALENCE – 0.1 per cent (2001)
DEATH PENALTY – No (abolished 1998)
POPULATION GROWTH RATE – 0.1 per cent (1990–2001)
POPULATION DENSITY – 57 per sq. km (2001)
URBAN POPULATION – 69 per cent (2001)

CLIMATE AND TERRAIN

Lithuania contains over 2,800 lakes, many of which lie in the east of the country. Elevation extremes range from 292 m (Kalnas) at the highest point to 0 m (Baltic Sea) at the lowest. The climate is mainly continental and average annual temperatures range from −3°C in January to 17°C in July.

HISTORY AND POLITICS

Lithuania kept its pagan traditions for far longer than any other European country and only became fully Christian in the 15th century, when the Samogitians and the Aukstaitiai, the two main ethnic groups in the region, were converted.

In the 17th century much of Lithuania came under Russian rule. The country joined with Poland in rebelling against Russian domination twice in the 19th century, and it wasn't until 1861 that Lithuanians were emancipated.

During the First World War Lithuania was occupied by Germany, and Lithuanians took the end of the war as an opportunity to declare independence. This was short-lived, however, as a newly independent Poland occupied the country in 1919.

Lithuania was invaded and occupied when Germany invaded the Soviet Union during the Second World War. In 1944, the Soviet Union recaptured the country and confirmed its annexation.

Sajudis (The Movement) was Lithuania's pro-democracy group which formed as the Soviet Union began to collapse in the late 1980s, and the country declared independence, this time from the USSR, on 11 March 1990.

The government formed after the October 2000 general election was a minority-centre right coalition led by Rolandas Paksas. The coalition collapsed in June 2001 and Algirdas Brazauskas of the Social Democratic Party (SD), who had been Lithuania's last communist-era ruler and subsequently its president, formed a coalition government with the New Union (Social Liberals) (NS(SL)), whose withdrawal from the previous government had caused it to collapse. The new government was appointed on 5 July 2001.

Rolandas Paksas was elected president on 5 January 2003 but was later embroiled in allegations of corruption. Paksas was impeached on 6 April 2004. Valdus Adamkus was elected president in June 2004.

POLITICAL SYSTEM

Under the 1992 Constitution, the Head of State composed of a directly elected President, whose five-year term of office is renewable once only. Executive authority is vested in the Government, consisting of the Prime Minister, who is appointed by the President with the approval of the unicameral parliament *(Seimas)*, and ministers appointed upon the recommendation of the Prime Minister.

Legislative power is exercised by the *Seimas*, composed of 141 members directly elected for four-year terms. Seventy-one members are elected in first past the post constituencies and 70 by proportional representation, with a five per cent threshold for representation. The constitution bans an alignment of Lithuania with any post-Soviet eastern alliance.

HEAD OF STATE
President, Valdas Adamkus, *sworn in* 12 July 2004

SELECTED GOVERNMENT MEMBERS *as at July 2004*
Prime Minister, Algirdas Brazauskas
Defence, Linas Linkevicius
Finance, Algidas Butkevicius
Foreign Affairs, Antanas Valionis
Interior, Virgilijus Bulovas

EMBASSY OF THE REPUBLIC OF LITHUANIA
84 Gloucester Place, London W1U 6AU
T 020-7486 6401/2
E chancery@lithuanianembassy.co.uk
Ambassador Extraordinary and Plenipotentiary, HE Aurimas Taurantas, apptd 2002

BRITISH EMBASSY
2 Antakalnio, LT-2055 Vilnius
T (+370) (2) 222 070/1
Ambassador Extraordinary and Plenipotentiary, HE Colin Roberts, apptd 2004

BRITISH COUNCIL DIRECTOR, Lina Balenaite
Business Centre 2000, Jogailos 4, LT 2001 Vilnius
T (+370) 5 264 4890/1
E lina.balenaite@britishcouncil.lt

DEFENCE

The Army has 177 armoured personnel carriers; the Navy has two frigates and five patrol and coastal vessels based at Klaipeda; the Air Force has eight helicopters. The last Russian troops withdrew in 1993. In April 2004 Lithuania officially joined NATO.
MILITARY EXPENDITURE – 1.8 per cent of GDP (2002)
MILITARY PERSONNEL – 9,750: Army 7,950, Navy 650, Air Force 1,150; Paramilitaries 14,600
CONSCRIPTION DURATION – 12 months

ECONOMY AND TRADE

Attempts to transform Lithuania into a free-market economy directly after the fall of communism pushed the country into deep recession. Recovery in the mid-1990s was hampered by the Russian financial crisis of 1998 when Lithuania lost 20 per cent of its export market. Recovery has come courtesy of exports to the European Union, though unemployment remains high.

The EU now takes 50 per cent of Lithuania's exports and large-scale privatisation has led to Lithuania being confirmed as a functioning market economy by the European Commission. Lithuania joined the World Trade Organisation in 2001.

Lithuania has a diverse economy and industries include the mining and cutting of amber, metal-cutting machine tools, electric motors, television sets, refrigerators and freezers, petroleum refining, shipbuilding, furniture making, textiles, food processing, fertilizers, agricultural machinery, optical equipment, electronic components and computers.
GNI – US$11,700 million (2001); US$3,350 per capita (2001)
ANNUAL AVERAGE GROWTH OF GDP – 5.9 per cent (2001)
INFLATION RATE – 1.3 per cent (2001)
UNEMPLOYMENT – 15.4 per cent (2000)
TOTAL EXTERNAL DEBT – US$4,855 million (2000)
FOREIGN DIRECT INVESTMENT – US$2,417 million (1997–2000)
IMPORTS – US$7,838 million (2002)
EXPORTS – US$5,564 million (2002)

BALANCE OF PAYMENTS
Trade – US$1,315 million deficit (2002)
Current Account – US$721 million deficit (2002)

Trade with UK	*2002*	*2003*
Imports from UK	£149,696,000	£188,440,000
Exports to UK	272,102,000	290,168,000

TRANSPORT INFRASTRUCTURE

There were 71,375 km of roads in 2000; there is a relatively well-developed railway system of 2,898 km running east to west and north to south and linking the major towns with Vilnius and Klaipeda, the main international port. Vilnius has an international airport.

EDUCATION

Lithuania re-established a national education system in 1990. Education is free of charge and compulsory from seven to 16 years, with the system comprising elementary schools (four years), nine-year schools (five years), and secondary schools (three years). The language of instruction is predominantly Lithuanian, but there are also Russian and Polish schools. There are 105 vocational schools and 65 colleges. Lithuania has eight universities and seven other institutes of higher education. Vilnius University, founded in 1579, is one of the oldest universities in eastern Europe.

ILLITERACY RATE – (m) 0.3 per cent; (f) 0.5 per cent (2000)

ENROLMENT (percentage of age group) – secondary 98 per cent (1997); tertiary 31 per cent (1997)

MEDIA AND CULTURE

The largest selling daily newspapers are *Lietuvos Rytas* and *Lietuvos Aidas*. There is a mix of public and private television broadcasters operating in Lithuania. BTV is the larget commercial company while LTV is the publicly run station.

Lithuanian language is divided into Low Lithuanian, common in the west, and High Lithuanian, common throughout the rest of the country. Famous Lithuanians include the feminist writer and activist Emma Goldman (1869–1940) and the artist Mikalojus Ciurlionis (1875–1911) whose work can be seen in the Ciurlionis Museum in the city of Kaunas.

LUXEMBOURG

Groussherzogtom Lëtzebuerg / Grand-Duché de Luxembourg / Großherzogtum Luxembourg – Grand Duchy of Luxembourg

AREA – 2,586 sq. km. Neighbours: Germany (east), Belgium (west and north), France (south)

POPULATION – 448,300 (2001), nearly all Roman Catholic. The officially designated 'national language' is Lëtzebuergesch (Luxembourgish), a mainly spoken language. French and German are the official languages for written purposes, and French is the language of administration

CAPITAL – Luxembourg (population, 77,400, 1996)

CURRENCY – Euro (€) of 100 cents

NATIONAL ANTHEM – Ons Hémécht (Our Homeland)

NATIONAL DAY – 23 June

NATIONAL FLAG – Three horizontal bands, red, white and blue

LIFE EXPECTANCY (years) – 78 (2001)

MORTALITY RATE (per 1,000 population) – 8.78 (2003)

INFANT MORTALITY (per 1,000 births) – 5 (2001)

HIV / AIDS ADULT PREVALENCE – 0.2 per cent (2001)

DEATH PENALTY – No (abolished 1979)

POPULATION GROWTH RATE – 1.3 per cent (1990–2001)

POPULATION DENSITY – 171 per sq. km (2001)

ENROLMENT (percentage of age group) – primary 81 per cent (1985); secondary 64 per cent (1994); tertiary 10 per cent (1996)

CLIMATE AND TERRAIN

The Ardennes, in the north of the country, form part of the Natural Germano-Luxembourg Park, which extends east into Germany. The south of the country is mainly fertile farmland and in the east is the wine-growing region of the Moselle Valley. Elevation extremes range from 559 m (Buurgplaatz) at the highest point to 133 m (Moselle River) at the lowest. The climate is mild and average temperatures range from 1°C in January to 22°C in July.

HISTORY AND POLITICS

Count Sigefroid of Ardennes built a castle in Luxembourg in AD 963 and so established the Duchy of Luxembourg. Contested throughout the Middle Ages, and occupied by Napoleon until 1814, Luxembourg became autonomous under the Treaty of London in 1867 and declared itself neutral in international affairs.

German occupation during the Second World War prompted Luxembourg to give up its neutrality and join NATO and the United Nations to become one of the members of the Benelux group of countries. Luxembourg was a founder member of the European Economic Community in 1957.

Claude Juncker's Christian Social Party (CSV) won the legislative elections of 13 June 2004 with 36.1 per cent of the vote. Of the other two main parties, the Luxembourg Socialist Workers' Party (LSWP) won 23.4 per cent of the vote while the Democratic Party (DP) won 16.1 per cent of the vote.

POLITICAL SYSTEM

There is a Chamber of 60 Deputies, elected by universal suffrage for five years. Legislation is submitted to the Council of State.

HEAD OF STATE

HRH The Grand Duke of Luxembourg, HRH Grand Duke Henri, *born* 16 April 1955; *succeeded* 7 October 2000

Heir, HRH Prince Guillaume, *born* 11 November 1981

SELECTED GOVERNMENT MEMBERS *as at July 2004*

Prime Minister, Finance, Jean-Claude Juncker

Deputy Prime Minister, Foreign Affairs and Foreign Trade, Civil Service and Administrative Reform, Lydie Polfer

Development Aid and Defence, Environment, Charles Goerens

Economy, Transport, Henri Grethen

Home Affairs, Michel Wolter

Treasury and Budget, Justice, Luc Frieden

EMBASSY OF LUXEMBOURG

27 Wilton Crescent, London SW1X 8SD

T 020-7235 6961

Ambassador Extraordinary and Plenipotentiary, HE Jean-Louis Wolzfeld, apptd 2002

BRITISH EMBASSY

14 Boulevard Roosevelt, L-2450 Luxembourg

T (+352) 229864/5/6

Ambassador Extraordinary and Plenipotentiary, HE Gordon Wetherell, apptd 2000

DEFENCE

For legal reasons, NATO's squadron of E-3A Sentry airborne early warning aircraft is registered in Luxembourg.

MILITARY EXPENDITURE – 0.9 per cent of GDP (2002)

MILITARY PERSONNEL – Army 900; Paramilitaries 612

ECONOMY AND TRADE

Luxembourg's economy is dominated by steel production and this continues to comprise a quarter of the country's exports. Luxembourg has diversified its industrial sector to include rubber and chemicals. The financial sector now comprises 22 per cent of the GDP. Strong growth, low inflation and low unemployment mean that Luxembourg enjoys an exceptionally high standard of living. The small agricultural sector consists mainly of family owned farms.

GNI – US$17,570 million (2001); US$39,840 per capita (2001)
ANNUAL AVERAGE GROWTH OF GDP – 3.5 per cent (2001)
INFLATION RATE – 2.7 per cent (2001)
UNEMPLOYMENT – 2.6 per cent (2001)
IMPORTS – US$11,612 (2002)
EXPORTS – US$8,570 (2002)

BALANCE OF PAYMENTS
Trade – US$2,163 million deficit (2002)
Current Account – US$1,636 million surplus (2002)

Trade with UK	*2002*	*2003*
Imports from UK	£346,200,000	£208,047,000
Exports to UK	483,500,000	422,203,000

TRANSPORT INFRASTRUCTURE

Luxembourg has 38,200 aircraft departures from its two airports each year. There are 5,189 km of highways (including 114 km of motorways), and 274 km of railways.

MEDIA AND CULTURE

Media group RTL broadcasts to audiences in France, Germany and the UK as well as serving the domestic market. Luxembourg also hosts the Societe Europeenne des Satellites (SES), which operates the Astra satellite fleet, Europe's largest satellite operation. The two best-selling daily newspapers in Luxembourg are *Luxembuger Wort* and *Tageblatt*.

Luxembourg's cultural identity has been heavily influenced by France and Germany. Celebrated artists include the writer Nico Helminger (b. 1953) and the painter Joseph Kutter (1894–1941).

MACEDONIA

Republika Makedonija – Republic of Macedonia

AREA – 25,713 sq. km. Neighbours: Serbia and Montenegro (north), Bulgaria (east), Greece (south), Albania (west)
POPULATION – 2,046,209 (2001 estimate); 1,936,877 (1994 census): 66.5 per cent Macedonian, 22.9 per cent Albanian, 4.0 per cent ethnic Turks, 2.3 per cent Romanies, 2.0 per cent Serbs and 0.4 per cent Vlachs. The census results are disputed by the ethnic Albanians and Serbs. Macedonian Orthodox Christianity is the majority religion, with a Muslim minority. The main language is Macedonian (a south Slavic language), which is written in the Cyrillic script
CAPITAL – Skopje (population, 429,964, 1994)
MAJOR CITIES – Bitola; Kumanovo; Prilep
CURRENCY – Denar of 100 deni
NATIONAL ANTHEM – Denes Nad Makedonija Se Radja Novo Sonce Na Slobodata (Today A New Sun Of Liberty Appears Over Macedonia)
NATIONAL FLAG – Red with an eight-rayed sun displayed over the whole field
LIFE EXPECTANCY (years) – 73 (2001)
MORTALITY RATE (per 1,000 population) – 7.78 (2003)
INFANT MORTALITY RATE (per 1,000 births) – 3.7 (2001)
HIV / AIDS ADULT PREVALENCE – 0.1 per cent (2001)
DEATH PENALTY – No (abolished 1991)
POPULATION BELOW POVERTY LINE – 24 per cent (2001)
POPULATION GROWTH RATE – 0.6 per cent (1999)
POPULATION DENSITY – 78 per sq. km (1999)
URBAN POPULATION – 62 per cent (2000)
MILITARY EXPENDITURE – 2.7 per cent of GDP (2002)
MILITARY PERSONNEL – Army 11,650; Paramilitaries 7,600
CONSCRIPTION DURATION – Nine months
ENROLMENT (percentage of age group) – primary 99 per cent (1997); secondary 63 per cent (1997); tertiary 20 per cent (1997)

CLIMATE AND TERRAIN

The terrain is mountainous and elevation extremes range from 2,753 m (Golem Korab) at the highest point to 50 m (Vardar River) at the lowest. Average temperatures range from 1°C in January to 23°C in July.

HISTORY AND POLITICS

Macedonia was ruled from Constantinople as part of the eastern Roman Empire from the fourth century AD. Slav peoples settled the area in the seventh century and it was absorbed into Bulgaria in the ninth century. Contested by Serbs, Bulgarians and Byzantines, Macedonia came under Ottoman rule after the defeat of the Serbs in 1389.

The Treaty of San Stefano in 1878, brought about by the Russian defeat of Turkey, saw Macedonia pass, once more, to Bulgaria. Western European powers, unhappy at the prospect of a powerful Bulgarian ally of Russia, forced the country to be handed back to Turkey. Such events prompted the creation of a Macedonian nationalist movement: the Internal Macedonian Revolutionary Organisation (IMRO).

Macedonia continued to be traded between the regional powers during the Balkan wars of 1912 and 1913, and the country was split between Serbia and Greece and remained so until German invasion in the Second World War. The majority of the IMRO fought a guerrilla campaign against the occupying German Army, and Macedonia was rewarded after the war with full republic status within Yugoslavia.

The collapse of communism prompted Macedonians to vote in a referendum for full independence on 8 September 1991. Inter-ethnic rivalry grew during the 1990s. Macedonia's ethnic Albanian population complained of deprivation of full civil rights, especially in recognition of cultural and educational equality.

Instability in neighbouring Kosovo spilt over into Macedonia in 2001. Ethnic Albanian insurgents of the National Liberation Army (NLA) mounted a series of attacks on government forces and on 9 April 2001 the opposing sides signed the Stabilisation and Association Agreement (SAA), which aimed to promote dialogue between Macedonia's different ethnic populations. The situation deteriorated, however, and led to the creation of a large number of refugees and internally displaced persons from all ethnicities.

NATO negotiated a cease-fire in June 2001. Peace talks facilitated by the European Union, NATO, the USA and the Organisation for Security and Co-operation in Europe

(OSCE) produced an agreement that aimed to disarm the NLA while securing it an amnesty and facilitating a way to address Albanian grievances. Under the terms of the agreement 3,000 NATO troops were deployed in August.

The process met with a high level of success. Much of the NLA was disarmed, and a large number of displaced persons returned to their homes. On 31 March 2003 NATO forces handed over peace-keeping duties to an EU force: Operation Concordia.

The Macedonian Parliament passed a law on 8 March 2002 which secured amnesty for those involved in the conflict. The Ohrid Framework Agreement, which followed the peace talks, has resulted in the pledge of €307 million in aid to Macedonia.

Elections to the National Assembly *(Sobranīe)* were held on 15 September 2002. The largest group in the Assembly was Together for Macedonia (ZMZ), a coalition of the Social Democratic Alliance of Macedonia (SDSM) and the Liberal Democratic Party (LDP), with 59 of the 120 seats. The Internal Macedonian Revolutionary Organisation – Democratic Party for Macedonian National Unity (VMRO-DMPNE) won 34 seats. A multi-ethnic coalition government, including members of the SDSM, the LDP and the ethnic Albanian Democratic Union for Integration (BDI), was named on 31 October 2002 and took office the following day.

President Trajkovski died in an aircraft accident in February 2004 which prompted an election in April. Prime Minister Branko Crvenkovski was voted President with 42.5 per cent of the vote in round one (14 April) and 60.6 per cent of the vote in round two (28 April). Hari Kostov was elected Prime Minister.

HEAD OF STATE
President, Branko Crvenkovski, *elected,* 28 April 2004, *sworn in,* 12 May 2004

SELECTED GOVERNMENT MEMBERS *as at July 2004*
Prime Minister, Hari Kostov
Deputy Prime Ministers, Nikola Popovski
Deputy Prime Ministers, Without Portfolio, Musa Xharferi, Radmila Secerinska
Defence, Vlado Buckovski
Economy, Stevco Jakimovski
Foreign Affairs, Ilinka Mitreva
Interior, Silijan Avramovksi

EMBASSY OF THE REPUBLIC OF MACEDONIA
5th Floor, 25 James Street, London W1U 1DU
T 020 7935 2823
Ambassador Extraordinary and Plenipotentiary, HE Gjorgji Spasov, apptd, 2003

BRITISH EMBASSY
Dimitrija Chupovski 4/26, Skopje 1000
T (+389) (2) 3299 299
Ambassador Extraordinary and Plenipotentiary, HE George Edgar, apptd 2001

BRITISH COUNCIL DIRECTOR, Andrew Hadley
Bulevar Goce Delcev 6, PO Box 562, MK-1000 Skopje
T (+389) (2) 135 035
E info@britishcouncil.org.mk

ECONOMY

Macedonia has attempted to transform its economy into a market-orientated one and introduced privatisation; by 1997, 45 per cent of the economy was in private hands. In April 2000, the government sold 65 per cent of Macedonia's largest bank, the Stopanska Bank, and parliament voted to return property expropriated during the period under communist rule. An economic co-operation agreement was signed by Macedonia and Albania in July 1999, covering energy, mining and trade. In 2000 63 per cent of GDP was produced by the service industries, 25 per cent by industry, and 12 per cent by agriculture.

The main exports are textiles, tobacco, wine, zinc, iron ore and iron products. The main imports are oil, energy, telecommunications equipment, metal goods, foodstuffs and pharmaceuticals.

GNI – US$3,481 million (2000); US$1,690 per capita (2001)
ANNUAL AVERAGE GROWTH OF GDP – 2.9 per cent (1998)
INFLATION RATE – 1.1 per cent (2002)
TOTAL EXTERNAL DEBT – US$1,465 million (2000)
IMPORTS – US$1,921 million (2002)
EXPORTS – US$1,112 million (2002)

BALANCE OF PAYMENTS
Trade – US$421 million deficit (2001)
Current Account – US$324 million deficit (2000)

Trade with UK	*2002*	*2003*
Imports from UK	£20,540,000	£18,590,000
Exports to UK	17,074,000	24,496,000

TRANSPORT INFRASTRUCTURE

Macedonia has 8,216 km of roads, of which 4,900 km are surfaced. There are 18 airports and 699 km of railways, of which 233 km are electrified. A 53 km railway line from Beljakovci to the Bulgarian border was scheduled for completion in early 2005.

MEDIA AND CULTURE

The three channels of the state run television broadcaster competes with a growing number of commercial stations. There are 11 major daily and weekly press publications, reflecting a range of views. *Nova Makedonija* is the leading newspaper and is partially government owned.

Celebrated Macedonian writers include the poets Blaze Koneski (1921–93) and Aco Soper (b. 1923), and the acclaimed playwright Goran Stefanovski (b. 1952).

MADAGASCAR

Repoblikan'i Madagasikara/République de Madagascar – Republic of Madagascar

AREA – 587,041 sq. km
POPULATION – 15,982,563 (2001 estimate). The people are of mixed Malayo-Polynesian, Arab and African origin. There are sizeable French, Chinese and Indian communities. The official languages are Malagasy and French
CAPITAL – Antananarivo (population, 2,000,000, 1998 estimate)
MAJOR CITIES – ΨAntsiranana; Fianarantsoa; ΨMahajanga; ΨToamasina, the chief port
CURRENCY – Franc malgache (FMG) of 100 centimes
NATIONAL ANTHEM – Ry Tanindrazanay Malala O (O, Our Beloved Country)
NATIONAL DAY – 26 June (Independence Day)
NATIONAL FLAG – Equal horizontal bands of red (above) and green, with vertical white band by staff
LIFE EXPECTANCY (years) – 53 (2001)

MORTALITY RATE (per 1,000 population) – 11.88 (2003)
HIV / AIDS ADULT PREVALENCE – 0.3 per cent (2001)
DEATH PENALTY – No (abolished 1958)
POPULATION BELOW POVERTY LINE – 71 per cent (1999)
POPULATION GROWTH RATE – 3 per cent (1990–2001)
POPULATION DENSITY– 26 per sq. km (1999)
MILITARY EXPENDITURE – 1.0 per cent of GDP (2002)
MILITARY PERSONNEL – 13,500: Army 12,500, Navy 500, Air Force 500; Paramilitaries 8,100
CONSCRIPTION DURATION – 18 months

CLIMATE AND TERRAIN

Madagascar lies 240 miles off the east coast of Africa. The climate is mainly tropical along the coastline and average temperatures range from 9°C in July to 29°C in January. Central Madagascar is mountainous and elevation extremes range from 2,876 m (Maromokotro) at the highest point to 0 m (Indian Ocean) at the lowest.

HISTORY AND POLITICS

The Second World War brought an invasion from the British as they attempted to prevent Japan from using the island as an Indian Ocean base. Madagascar was returned to the French at the end of the war. A post-war nationalist movement attempted to break away from France in 1947. The revolt was brutally crushed, but nationalist agitation continued throughout the 1950s and resulted in independence in 1960.

The military took control in 1972 following civil disturbances and, though Admiral Didier Ratsiraka attempted to civilianise the government in 1975, he pushed the country into close alliance with the communist world, and a genuine democracy movement only started in the 1980s. In 1992 Madagascar adopted the Third Republic constitution and the island became a parliamentary democracy.

Professor Albert Zafy was voted President in the election of 1992–3. His government was ineffective and marked by power struggles with the National Assembly. Prime Minister Norbert Ratsirahonana introduced some important monetary reforms in 1996, which came at the same time as the National Assembly's removal of Zafy.

Subsequently elected as President, Ratsiraka consolidated his power in a referendum in 1998.

Presidential elections in December 2001 were marked by allegations from both sides of vote-rigging. The situation declined into civil unrest and near civil war. The UN, African Union and President of Senegal all tried to mediate for peace, but by May 2001 Marc Ravalomanana had consolidated his position ahead of Ratsiraka. On 17 April 2002, Madagascar's High Constitutional Court annulled the December election results and ordered a re-count. The re-count showed that Ravalomanana was the clear winner with 51.5 per cent of the vote. Ravalomanana was sworn into office on 6 May 2002.

POLITICAL SYSTEM

The President is directly elected and serves a five-year term. The legislature is bicameral. The National Assembly is directly elected and comprises 150 members. The Senate comprises 90 members, of whom two-thirds are elected by an electoral college and one-third are nominated by the President.

HEAD OF STATE

President Marc Ravalomanana, *elected* 29 April 2002, *sworn in* 6 May 2002, *accepted* 5 July 2002.

SELECTED GOVERNMENT MEMBERS *as at July 2004*
Prime Minister, Jacques Sylla
Deputy Prime Minister, Economic Affairs, Local Government, Public Works and Transport, Zaza Manitranja Ramandimbiarison
Defence, Maj.-Gen. Petera Behajaina
Foreign Affairs, Gen. Marcel Ranjeva
Finance and Economy, Benjamin Andriamparany Radavidson

EMBASSY OF THE REPUBLIC OF MADAGASCAR
4 avenue Raphael, F- 75016 Paris, France
T (+ 33) (1) 4504 6211
Ambassador Plenipotentiary and Extraordinary, vacant

BRITISH EMBASSY
Lot II, 164 Ter Alarobia Ambonilioa,
BP 167, Antananarivo 101
T (+ 261) (20) 2249378/9
Ambassador Extraordinary and Plenipotentiary, HE Brian Donaldson, apptd 2002

ECONOMY AND TRADE

Agriculture accounts for 33 per cent of GDP. Crops produced for export include coffee, vanilla, cloves, pepper, fish and prawns. The industrial sector makes up 13 per cent of GDP and includes textiles, wood, cement, paper and soap. Madagascar has extensive natural resources including sapphires, emeralds and mineral resources. Research is under way into potential oil and gas supplies.
GNI – US$3,959 million (2000); US$260 per capita (2000)
ANNUAL AVERAGE GROWTH OF GDP – 4.8 per cent (2000)
INFLATION RATE – 7.4 per cent (2001)
TOTAL EXTERNAL DEBT – US$4,701 million (2000)
IMPORTS – US$378 million (1999)
EXPORTS – US$330 million (1999)

BALANCE OF PAYMENTS
Trade – US$3 million deficit (2001)
Current Account – US$20 million deficit (2001)

Trade with UK	*2002*	*2003*
Imports from UK	£3,033,000	£6,038,000
Exports to UK	17,943,000	16,588,000

TRANSPORT INFRASTRUCTURE

Madagascar has five main ports, 49,827 km of highways and 732 km of railways. There are 116 airports.

EDUCATION

Education is free of charge and compulsory for eight years; primary education (five years) followed by a possible seven years of secondary education. The University of Madagascar was established in 1955.
ILLITERACY RATE – (m) 26.4 per cent; (f) 40.3 per cent (2000)
ENROLMENT (percentage of age group) – primary 92 per cent (1997); tertiary 2 per cent (1997)

MEDIA AND CULTURE

An increasing number of private radio stations is challenging the monopoly of state run broadcasting. A wide range of press publications print a more diverse range of opinions.

Kabary is Madagascar's oratorical tradition that is highly regarded world-wide. Traditional musical instruments include the *kabosy* (a type of five-stringed guitar) and the *sodina* (a type of flute).

MALAWI

Mfuko la Malawi/Republic of Malawi

AREA – 118,484 sq. km. Neighbours: Tanzania (north-east), Zambia (west), Mozambique (south)
POPULATION – 10,548,250 (2001 estimate). The official languages are Chichewa and English
CAPITAL – Lilongwe (population, 505,200, 2000 estimate)
MAJOR CITIES – Blantyre, incorporating Blantyre and Limbe, the major commercial and industrial centre; Mzuzu; Zomba, the former capital
CURRENCY – Kwacha (K) of 100 tambala
NATIONAL ANTHEM – O God Bless Our Land Of Malawi
NATIONAL DAY – 6 July (Independence Day)
NATIONAL FLAG – Horizontal stripes of black, red and green, with a rising sun in the centre of the black stripe
LIFE EXPECTANCY (years) – 38.5 (2001)
MORTALITY RATE (per 1,000 population) – 22.64 (2003)
HIV / AIDS ADULT PREVALENCE – 15 per cent (2001)
DEATH PENALTY – Yes
POPULATION BELOW POVERTY LINE – 65.3 per cent (2000)
POPULATION GROWTH RATE – 1.5 per cent (1997–2001)
POPULATION DENSITY – 90 per sq. km (1999)
MILITARY EXPENDITURE – 0.7 per cent of GDP (2002)
MILITARY PERSONNEL – Army 5,300; Paramilitaries 1,500

CLIMATE AND TERRAIN

Malawi lies in south-eastern Africa and much of its eastern border is formed by Lake Malawi. The northern and central regions are plateaux, and the south is mainly highlands. Elevation extremes range from 3,002 m (Sapitwa) at the highest point to 37 m (Shire River) at the lowest. There is a wet season from November to May and average temperatures range from 9°C in June to 30°C in January.

HISTORY AND POLITICS

Between independence in 1964 and May 1994, Malawi (formerly Nyasaland), was governed by Dr Hastings Banda of the Malawi Congress Party (MCP) as a one-party state. Banda's rule was distinguished by corruption, human rights abuses and economic mismanagement. Banda declared himself 'President for life' in 1971. In the 1990s democratic movements began agitating for reform and, aided by pressure from abroad, Banda was forced to transfer to multi-party democracy following a referendum.

Bakili Muluzi was elected president in 1994 and committed himself to a programme of poverty alleviation and a campaign against corruption. Muluzi was re-elected as president in 1999 and in 2002 he attempted to redefine the constitution and award himself the 'Presidency for life'. The legislative elections of 20 May 2004 saw the MCP win 60 seats in the national assembly while the United Democratic Front (UDF) secured 49. A presidential election was held the same day and Bingu wa Mutharika of the UDF won 35.9 per cent of the vote. The cabinet was dissolved on 21 May 2004 and a cabinet reshuffle, dominated by the UDF, was named on 13 June, and took office on 16 June.

POLITICAL SYSTEM

There is a Cabinet consisting of the President and Ministers. The unicameral National Assembly, which usually meets three times a year, consists of 193 members elected by universal suffrage for a five-year term.

HEAD OF STATE

President, Commander-in-Chief of the Armed Forces, Defence, Bingu wa Mutharika, *elected* 20 May 2004
Vice-President, Privatisation, Cassim Chilumpha

SELECTED GOVERNMENT MEMBERS *as at July 2004*
Finance, Goodall Gondwe
Foreign Affairs and International Co-operation, George Chaponda
Home Affairs and Internal Security, Uladi Mussa

MALAWI HIGH COMMISSION
33 Grosvenor Street, London W1K 4OT
T 020-7491 4172
High Commissioner, HE Ibrahim Laston Bwanausi Milazi

BRITISH HIGH COMMISSION
PO Box 30042, Lilongwe 3
T (+ 265) (1) 772 400
E bhclilongwe@fco.gov.uk
High Commissioner, Norman Ling, apptd 2001

BRITISH COUNCIL DIRECTOR, Richard Weyers
Plot No. 13/20 City Centre, PO Box 30222, Lilongwe 3
T (+ 265) 773 244
E info@britishcouncil.org.mw

ECONOMY

Malawi is a largely agricultural country but the land is threatened by over-population, deforestation and poor farming methods. Rising levels of silt threaten fish stocks in Lake Nyasa. Some 85 per cent of the workforce are engaged in agriculture and 90 per cent of these are subsistence farmers. Tobacco is a major industry and is supplemented by tea, sugar, sawmill products, cement and consumer goods. A number of light manufacturing industries have been established, mainly in agricultural processing, clothing/textiles and building materials. A prolonged drought caused famine throughout 2002–3.

GNI – US$1,884 million (2000); US$160 per capita (2001)
ANNUAL AVERAGE GROWTH OF GDP – 2.3 per cent (2000)
INFLATION RATE – 29.5 per cent (2000)
TOTAL EXTERNAL DEBT – US$2,716 million (2000)
IMPORTS – US$669 million (2001)
EXPORTS – US$447 million (2002)

Trade with UK	*2002*	*2003*
Imports from UK	£13,506,000	£10,181,000
Exports to UK	12,769,000	11,729,000

TRANSPORT INFRASTRUCTURE

A single-track railway runs from Mchinji on the Zambian border, through Lilongwe and Salima on Lake Malawi, through to Blantyre. The route south to the Mozambique port of Beira was severed by the Mozambican civil war, but the route to Nacala in Mozambique re-opened in September 2002, allowing access to the Indian Ocean coast; there are 797 km of railways. There are 16,451 km of roads in Malawi of which 3,126 km are surfaced.

EDUCATION

The State is responsible for primary and secondary schools, technical education and primary teacher training. The University of Malawi was opened in 1965; there are also four colleges and one polytechnic.

ILLITERACY RATE – (m) 25.5 per cent; (f) 53.5 per cent (2000)

ENROLMENT (percentage of age group) – primary 100 per cent (1997); secondary 17 per cent (1997); tertiary 1 per cent (1997)

MEDIA AND CULTURE

There are four national newspapers and Television Malawi is state run. The Malawi Broadcasting Corporation is a state run radio network that competes with a number of private channels.

Malawians are predominantly Bantu peoples and these are split into a number of groups. Jack Mapanje (b. 1944) is an internationally acclaimed Malawi poet who has been published widely in the United Kingdom.

MALAYSIA

AREA – 328,600 sq. km. Thailand borders the Malay peninsula to the north. On Borneo, Malaysia (Sarawak and Sabah) borders Indonesia to the south, and surrounds Brunei to the north

POPULATION – 22,633,000 (2001); Malays (58 per cent), Chinese (27 per cent), and those of Indian and Sri Lankan origin, as well as the indigenous races of Sarawak and Sabah. Bahasa Malaysia (Malay) is the official language, but English, various dialects of Chinese, and Tamil are also widely spoken. There are a few indigenous languages widely spoken in Sabah and Sarawak. Islam is the official religion of Malaysia, each ruler being the head of religion in his state (except in Sabah and Sarawak). The Yang di-Pertuan Agong is the head of religion in Melaka and Penang. The constitution guarantees religious freedom

CAPITAL – Kuala Lumpur (population, 1,297,526, 2000 census); Putrajaya (Administrative Capital)

MAJOR CITIES – Ipoh; Johore Bharu; Petaling Jaya

CURRENCY – Malaysian dollar (M$) (ringgit) of 100 sen

NATIONAL ANTHEM – Negara-Ku (My Country)

NATIONAL DAY – 31 August *(Hari Kebangsaan)*

NATIONAL FLAG – Equal horizontal stripes of red (seven) and white (seven); a 14-point yellow star and crescent in blue canton

LIFE EXPECTANCY (years) – 73 (2001)

MORTALITY RATE (per 1,000 population) – 5.12 (2003)

INFANT MORTALITY (per 1,000 births) – 8 (2001)

HIV / AIDS ADULT PREVALENCE – 0.4 per cent (2001)

DEATH PENALTY – Yes

POPULATION BELOW POVERTY LINE – 8 per cent (1998)

POPULATION GROWTH RATE – 2.2 per cent (1990–2001)

POPULATION DENSITY – 69 per sq. km (2001)

URBAN POPULATION – 58 per cent (2001)

ILLITERACY RATE – (m) 8.6 per cent; (f) 16.5 per cent (2000)

ENROLMENT (percentage of age group) – primary 98 per cent (2000); tertiary 70 per cent (2000)

CLIMATE AND TERRAIN

Malaysia comprises the 11 states of peninsular Malaya plus Sabah and Sarawak. It occupies two distinct regions: the Malay peninsula, which extends from the isthmus of Kra to the Singapore Strait, and the north-western coastal area of the island of Borneo. Each is separated from the other by the South China Sea. Elevation extremes range from 4,100 m (Gunung Kinabalu) at the highest point to 0 m (Indian Ocean) at the lowest. There are monsoon seasons in the south-west of the country from April to October and from October to February in the north-east. Average temperatures in Kuala Lumpur range from 22°C in January to 31°C in September.

HISTORY AND POLITICS

An armed struggle for independence, which began in 1948, succeeded in 1957. The British colonies of Singapore, Sarawak, and Sabah (called North Borneo) joined a federation, thereby forming Malaysia in 1963. Singapore withdrew from the confederation in 1965, and Indonesia, which had opposed the formation of Malaysia, pressed its territorial claims in the east of the country. In 1963, Indonesian troops crossed into Malaysian territory. The confrontation was eventually resolved by the Association of South-East Asian Nations (ASEAN).

Legislative elections on 21 March 2004 returned the Barisan Nasional party to power with 198 seats in the House of Representatives.

POLITICAL SYSTEM

The Constitution provides for a federal Government and a degree of autonomy for the state Governments. It created a constitutional Supreme Head of the Federation (HM the *Yang di-Pertuan Agong*) and a Deputy Supreme Head (HRH *Timbalan Yang di-Pertuan Agong*) to be elected for a five-year term by the rulers from among their number. The Malay rulers are either chosen or succeed to their position in accordance with the custom of the particular state. In other states of Malaysia, choice of the head of state is at the discretion of the Yang di-Pertuan Agong after consultation with the Chief Minister of the state.

The Federal Parliament consists of two houses; the Senate and the House of Representatives. The Senate *(Dewan Negara)* consists of 69 members who serve a six-year term, 26 being elected by the Legislative Assemblies of the states (two from each) and 43 appointed by the Yang di-Pertuan Agong. The House of Representatives (*Dewan Rakyat*) consists of 193 members elected for a five-year term by universal adult suffrage.

FEDERAL STRUCTURE

According to the Constitution, each state shall have its own Constitution not inconsistent with the Federal Constitution, with the Ruler or Governor acting on the advice of an Executive Council appointed on the advice of the Chief Minister and a single-chamber Legislative

Assembly. The Legislative Assemblies are fully elected on the same basis as the Federal Parliament.

HEAD OF STATE
Supreme Head of State, HM Tuanku Syed Sirajuddin Putra Jamalullail (the Yang di-Pertuan Agong of Perlis), *sworn in* 13 December 2001

SELECTED GOVERNMENT MEMBERS *as at July 2004*
Prime Minister, Finance, Home Affairs, Abdullah Ahmed Badawi
Deputy Prime Minister, Defence, Najib Tun Razak
Foreign Affairs, Hamid bin Jaafer Albar

MALAYSIAN HIGH COMMISSION
45 Belgrave Square, London SW1X 8QT
T 020-7235 8033
E mwlondon@btinternet.com
High Commissioner, HE Abd Aziz bin Mohammed

BRITISH HIGH COMMISSION
185 Jalan Ampang 50450 Kuala Lumpur *or* PO Box 11030, 50732 Kuala Lumpur
T (+ 60) (3) 2170 2200
High Commissioner, HE Bruce Cleghorn, CMG, apptd 2001

BRITISH COUNCIL DIRECTOR, Gerry Liston
Ground Floor, West Block, Wisma Selangor Dredging 142 C Jalan Ampang 50450 Kuala Lumpur T (+ 60) (3) 2723 7900
E kualalumpur@britishcouncil.org.my

DEFENCE
The Army has 1,016 armoured personnel carriers. The Royal Malaysian Navy has four frigates, 41 patrol and coastal vessels and six armed helicopters at four bases. The Royal Malaysian Air Force has 95 combat aircraft.
MILITARY EXPENDITURE – 3.6 per cent of GDP (2002)
MILITARY PERSONNEL – 104,000: Army 80,000, Navy 14,000, Air Force 10,000; Paramilitaries 20,100

ECONOMY AND TRADE
Malaysian industry is split into three main bases: Peninsular Malaysia concentrates on rubber and palm oil processing and manufacturing, the light manufacturing industry, electronics, tin mining and smelting, logging and timber processing; Sabah engages in logging and the production of petroleum, while Sarawak features agricultural processing, petroleum production and refining, and logging.
GNI – US$79,300 million (2001); US$3,330 per capita (2001)
ANNUAL AVERAGE GROWTH OF GDP – 8.5 per cent (2000)
INFLATION RATE – 1.5 per cent (2000)
UNEMPLOYMENT – 3.1 per cent (2000)
TOTAL EXTERNAL DEBT – US$41,797 million (2000)
FOREIGN DIRECT INVESTMENT – US$13,319 million (1997–2000)
IMPORTS – US$79,869 million (2002)
EXPORTS – US$93,265 million (2002)

BALANCE OF PAYMENTS
Trade – US$18,383 million surplus (2001)
Current Account – US$7,287 million surplus (2001)

Trade with UK	*2002*	*2003*
Imports from UK	£882,248,000	£1,040,389,000
Exports to UK	1,796,310,000	1,915,245,000

TRANSPORT INFRASTRUCTURE
Malaysia has six main ports, 7,296 km of waterways and 65,877 km of highways. The country's 114 airports handle 175,500 departures per year.

MEDIA AND CULTURE
Malaysia operates extremely strict censorship of its media. There are three main national daily newspapers. Radio Television Malaysia is the state run broadcaster which competes with two main commercial broadcasters.

Shahnon Ahmed (b. 1933) is one of Malaysia's most famous writers.

MALDIVES

Divehi Rājjē ge Jumhūriyyā – Republic of the Maldives

AREA – 298 sq. km
POPULATION – 310,764 (2001 estimate). The people are Sunni Muslims and the Maldivian (Dhivehi) language is akin to Elu or old Sinhalese
CAPITAL – ΨMalé (population, 74,069, 2000)
CURRENCY – Rufiyaa of 100 laaris
NATIONAL ANTHEM – Gavmi Mi Ekuverikan Mati Tibegen Kurime Salam (In National Unity We Salute Our Nation)
NATIONAL DAY – 26 July
NATIONAL FLAG – Green field bearing a white crescent, with wide red border
LIFE EXPECTANCY (years) – 66.8 (2001)
MORTALITY RATE (per 1,000 population) – 7.65 (2003)
HIV / AIDS ADULT PREVALENCE – 0.1 per cent
DEATH PENALTY – No (abolished 1952)
POPULATION GROWTH RATE – 1.9 per cent (2002)
POPULATION DENSITY – 931 per sq. km (1999)
MILITARY EXPENDITURE – 6.2 per cent of GDP (2002)
ILLITERACY RATE – (m) 3.7 per cent; (f) 3.6 per cent (2000)

CLIMATE AND TERRAIN
The Maldives are a chain of coral atolls in the Indian Ocean, 643 km to the south-west of Sri Lanka. There are about 19 coral atolls comprising over 1,200 islands, 198 of which are inhabited. No point in the entire chain of islands is more than eight feet above sea-level. There is a tropical climate and daily temperatures rarely drop below 28°C.

HISTORY AND POLITICS
The Maldives converted to Islam in 1153 and Abu al-Barakat became the first of 84 sultans to rule the islands. An agreement was signed in 1887 which turned the Maldives into a British protectorate.

In 1932 the Maldives' first constitution was drawn up and in 1953 the sultanate was completely abolished and a republic was proclaimed. Within a year the new president was overthrown and the sultan returned to power. True independence was achieved in 1968 and the Maldives became a full member of the commonwealth in 1985. In the presidential elections of 2003, Maumoom Abdul Gayoom won 90.3 per cent of the vote. Legislative elections were due to take place in November 2004.

HEAD OF STATE
President, Commander-in-Chief of the Armed Forces, Defence, National Security, Finance and Treasury, HE Maumoon Abdul Gayoom, *elected* 1978, *re-elected* 1983, 1989, 1993, 1998, 14 May 2003

SELECTED GOVERNMENT MEMBERS *as at July 2004*
Foreign Affairs, Fathullah Jameel
Home Affairs, Housing and Environment, Ismail Shafeeu
Ministers of State, Maj.-Gen. Anbaree Abdul Sattar (*Defence and National Security*); Mohamed Jaleel (*Finance and Treasury*)

HIGH COMMISSION OF THE REPUBLIC OF MALDIVES
22 Nottingham Place, London W1U 5NJ
T 020-7224 2135
High Commissioner, Adam Hassan, apptd 2004

BRITISH HIGH COMMISSIONER, HE Stephen Evans, OBE, apptd 2002, resident at Colombo, Sri Lanka

ECONOMY AND TRADE
Tourism accounts for one-third of GDP. Over 90 per cent of government tax revenue comes from import duties and tourism-related taxes. Fishing accounts for six per cent of GDP. Agriculture and manufacturing have declined because of a dearth of labour and cultivatable land, and this means that most food must be imported. Industry concentrates on the manufacture of clothes, boat-building and handicrafts.
GNI – US$403 million (2000); US$4,520 per capita (2001)
ANNUAL AVERAGE GROWTH OF GDP – 4.8 per cent (2000)
INFLATION RATE – 1.1 per cent (2000)
TOTAL EXTERNAL DEBT – US$281 million (2002)
IMPORTS – US$392 million (2002)
EXPORTS – US$90 million (2002)

BALANCE OF PAYMENTS
Trade – US$238 million deficit (2001)
Current Account – US$61 million deficit (2001)

Trade with UK	*2002*	*2003*
Imports from UK	£3,046,000	£5,930,000
Exports to UK	7,216,000	6,808,000

TRANSPORT INFRASTRUCTURE AND MEDIA
There are no railways, waterways and only a negligible number of highways. The country's five airports handle 6,000 departures a year. There are three daily newspapers.

EDUCATION
The education system in the Maldives is based on state, private and community schools. There is a large population of expatriate teachers, making up 30 per cent of the country's total.

MALI

République du Mali – Republic of Mali

AREA – 1,240,192 sq. km. Neighbours: Senegal (west), Mauritania (north-west), Algeria (north-east), Niger (east), Burkina Faso and Côte d'Ivoire (south), Guinea (south-west)
POPULATION – 11,008,518 (2001 estimate): 50 per cent Mande (Bambara, Malinke, Sarakole), 17 per cent Peul, 12 per cent Voltaic, 6 per cent Songhai, 10 per cent Tuareg and Moor. The official language is French; Bambara is the largest local language
CAPITAL – Bamako (population, 809,552, 1996 UN estimate)
MAJOR CITIES – Gao; Kayes; Mopti; Ségou; Sikasso; Timbuktu
CURRENCY – Franc CFA of 100 centimes
NATIONAL ANTHEM – A Ton Appel, Mali (At Your Call, Mali)
NATIONAL DAY – 22 September
NATIONAL FLAG – Vertical stripes of green (by staff), yellow and red
MORTALITY RATE (per 1,000 population) – 19.21 (2003)
HIV / AIDS ADULT PREVALENCE – 1.7 per cent (2001)
DEATH PENALTY – No (abolished 1980)
POPULATION BELOW POVERTY LINE – 64 per cent (2001)
POPULATION GROWTH RATE – 2.4 per cent (1997–2001)
POPULATION DENSITY – 9 per sq. km (1999)
MILITARY EXPENDITURE – 2.3 per cent of GDP (2002)
MILITARY PERSONNEL – Army 7,350; Paramilitaries 4,800
CONSCRIPTION DURATION – Two years (selective)
ILLITERACY RATE – (m) 51.1 per cent; (f) 65.6 per cent (2000)
ENROLMENT (percentage of age group) – primary 49 per cent (1997); secondary 13 per cent (1997); tertiary 1 per cent (1997)

CLIMATE AND TERRAIN
The terrain is mainly arid desert with some hills in the north-east. Elevation extremes range from 1,155 m (Hombori Tondo) at the highest point to 23 m (Sengal River) at the lowest. Average annual temperatures range from 17°C in January to 31°C in September.

HISTORY AND POLITICS
In 1883 Mali became a French colony but remained undeveloped throughout the colonial period. It gained independence in 1960 and President Mobido Keita declared a single-party state. Keita was overthrown by a military coup in 1968. The army governed until 1991 when General Moussa Traore oversaw a transition to civilian Government. Alpha Oumar Konare was elected as president in 1992, however, he and his government were toppled by popular protests and rioting in the following year. Further elections in 1997 were suspected by opposition parties of being rigged, and the opposition refused to recognise the results.

Former military leader and independent candidate Amadou Toumani Touré won the presidential election held on 12 May 2002. In the legislative elections of 13 July 2002 the Alliance For Democracy in Mali (ADEMA) was initially thought to have retained the majority of seats in the Assembly after a low turnout with many void votes;

this result was overturned on 10 August by the constitutional court which declared that the Spirit 2002 coalition had won the largest number of seats.

HEAD OF STATE
President, Amadou Toumani Touré, *elected* 12 May 2002; *took office* 8 June 2002

SELECTED GOVERNMENT MEMBERS *as at June 2004*
Prime Minister, African Integration, Ousmane Issoufi Maiga
Defence and Veterans, Mamadou Clazie Cissouma
Economy and Finance, Abor-Bacar Traore
Foreign Affairs and International Co-operation, Bien Moctar Ovane

EMBASSY OF THE REPUBLIC OF MALI
Avenue Molière 487, B-1060 Brussels, Belgium
T (+ 32) (2) 345 7432
Ambassador Extraordinary and Plenipotentiary, Ibrahim Bocar Ba

BRITISH EMBASSY
The British Embassy closed on 31 May 2003
Ambassador Extraordinary and Plenipotentiary, HE Alan Burner. *All British Embassy staff reside at Dakar*

ECONOMY AND TRADE

The economy is based primarily on subsistence farming and animal husbandry, although gold and phosphate mining and cotton farming, processing and manufacture are also important. Mali remains one of the world's poorest countries but saw some positive signs in 2003 when a good harvest pushed up cotton production by 48 per cent and cereals by 34 per cent; furthermore a rise in the price of gold significantly increased revenue. However, conflict in Côte d'Ivoire cut Mali off from an important source of imports. In 2003 Mali was eligible for debt relief under the Heavily Indebted Poor Countries Initiative.
GNI – US$2,568 million (2000); US$810 per capita (2001)
ANNUAL AVERAGE GROWTH OF GDP – 5.7 per cent (1998)
INFLATION RATE – 0.7 per cent (2000)
TOTAL EXTERNAL DEBT – US$2,956 million (2000)

Trade with UK	*2002*	*2003*
Imports from UK	£18,946,000	£14,781,000
Exports to UK	3,519,000	8,479,000

TRANSPORT INFRASTRUCTURE

Mali has 15,100 km of highways and 729 km of railways. The main port is Koulikoro on the Niger river.

MEDIA AND CULTURE

State run media compete with more than 50 privately run newspapers and 40 private broadcasters.

Traditional ways of life still flourish in Mali. The Dogon tribe are farmers whose homeland, Pays Dogon, has been designated a World Heritage Site.

MALTA

Repubblika ta' Malta / Republic of Malta

AREA – 316 sq. km
POPULATION – 392,000 (2001). The Maltese are mainly Roman Catholic. The Maltese language is of Semitic origin and held by some to be derived from the Carthaginian and Phoenician tongues. Maltese and English are the official languages
CAPITAL – ΨValletta (population, 7,048, 2000)
CURRENCY – Maltese lira (LM) of 100 cents or 1,000 mils
NATIONAL ANTHEM – L-Innu Malti (Hymn of Malta)
NATIONAL DAYS – 31 March (Freedom Day); 7 June (Sette Giugno Riots); 8 September (Our Lady of Victories); 21 September (Independence Day); 13 December (Republic Day)
NATIONAL FLAG – Two equal vertical stripes, white at the hoist and red at the fly. A representation of the George Cross is carried, edged with red in the canton of the white stripe
LIFE EXPECTANCY (years) – 78 (2001)
MORTALITY RATE (per 1,000 population) – 7.8 (2003)
INFANT MORTALITY (per 1,000 births) – 5 (2001)
HIV / AIDS ADULT PREVALENCE – 0.1 per cent (2001)
DEATH PENALTY – No (abolished 2000)
POPULATION GROWTH RATE – 0.8 per cent (1990–2001)
POPULATION DENSITY – 1,241 per sq. km (2001)
MILITARY EXPENDITURE – 0.7 per cent of GDP (2002)
MILITARY PERSONNEL – 2,140

CLIMATE AND TERRAIN

Malta is an archipelago of six islands located in the Mediterranean sea; Malta, Gozo and Comino are the largest. Elevation extremes range from 253 m (Ta'Dmejrek) at the highest point to 0 m (Mediterranean Sea) at the lowest. The climate is warm and temperate with average summer temperatures reaching 30°C.

HISTORY AND POLITICS

The Sovereign Military Order of Malta (known as the Knights of St John) ruled the Maltese Islands from 1530 until 1798. During this time, the fortified city of Valletta was built. Occupied by Napoleon then liberated by Britain, the island became a British colony in 1814, and Malta developed into a substantial naval base.

Malta became extremely strategically important in the Second World War. An attempt by Germany and Italy to capture the island saw it blockaded for five months and subjected to aerial bombardment. The entire population of the island was awarded the George Cross, the UK's highest award for civilian bravery, in 1942.

Malta gained independence in 1964 and voted in favour of joining the EU by referendum on 8 March 2003, by a narrow margin of 3.6 per cent or 19,500 votes.

Elections to the unicameral parliament of 65 members are held every five years by a system of proportional representation; to ensure that a party receiving more than 50 per cent of the votes obtains a parliamentary majority, extra seats may be allocated to that party.

Elections held on 12 April 2003 were again won by the Nationalist Party (PN) with 35 seats; the Labour Party, which opposed EU accession, gained 30 seats. The victory confirmed the pro-EU referendum result; Edward Fenech Adami was sworn into office as prime minister on 15

April 2003. In March 2004, Adami resigned his post to stand for the presidency. He was elected on 29 March 2004.

HEAD OF STATE
President, Edward Fenech Adami, *took office*, 15 April 2004

SELECTED GOVERNMENT MEMBERS *as at July 2004*
Prime Minister, Finance, Lawrence Gonzi
Deputy Prime Minister, Social Policy, Justice and Home Affairs, Tonio Borg
Foreign Affairs, Michael Frendo

MALTA HIGH COMMISSION
Malta House, 36–38 Piccadilly, London W1J 0LE
T 020-7292 4800
High Commissioner, HE George Bonello Dupuis, apptd 1999

BRITISH HIGH COMMISSION
Whitehall Mansions, Ta'Xbiex Seafront, Ta'Xbiex MSD 11, Malta GC
T (+ 356) 2323 0000
E bhccomm@vol.net.mt
High Commissioner, HE Vincent Fean, apptd 2002

BRITISH COUNCIL DIRECTOR, Ronnie Micallef, c/o British High Commission
E veronica.attard@britcouncil.org.mt

ECONOMY AND TRADE

Malta has low unemployment, low inflation and consistent growth rates. The public sector accounts for a large proportion of revenue – 49 per cent of GDP. The country only produces 20 per cent of its own food, has limited access to fresh water (there is an increasing reliance on desalination) and has no domestic sources of energy. However, tourism is a successful part of the economy with over one million tourists visiting Malta in 2001. There is also a significant ship-building and ship-repair industry. The chief exports are processed food, electronics, textiles, and other manufactures. The principal imports are foodstuffs, fodder, beverages and tobacco, fuels, chemicals, textiles and machinery.

GNI – US$3,640 million (2001); US$9,210 per capita (2001)
ANNUAL AVERAGE GROWTH OF GDP – 4.7 per cent (2000)
INFLATION RATE – 2.4 per cent (2000)
UNEMPLOYMENT – 5.3 per cent (1999)
TOTAL EXTERNAL DEBT – US$10,600 million (1999)
IMPORTS – US$2,592 million (2001)
EXPORTS – US$1,917 million (2001)

BALANCE OF PAYMENTS
Trade – US$511 million deficit (2002)
Current Account – US$180 million deficit (2002)

Trade with UK	*2002*	*2003*
Imports from UK	£227,041,000	£258,750,000
Exports to UK	171,705,000	186,994,000

TRANSPORT INFRASTRUCTURE

The main ports are Marsaxlokk and Valletta. There are 2,254 km of highways, no internal waterways or railways, and one airport.

EDUCATION

Education is free of charge at all levels and compulsory between the ages of five and 16. There are ten junior lyceums, 18 secondary schools and five centres catering for low achievers. The Junior college prepares students specifically for a university course. Tertiary education is available at the University of Malta. The Malta College of Arts, Science and Technology provides technical and vocational courses at post-secondary level.

ILLITERACY RATE – (m) 8.6 per cent; (f) 7.2 per cent (2000)
ENROLMENT (percentage of age group) – primary 100 per cent (1999); secondary 100 per cent (1999); tertiary 21 per cent (1999)

MEDIA AND CULTURE

There are seven major daily and weekly news publications.

Nicholas S. Cammillier (1798–1856) is perhaps Malta's most famous artist.

MARSHALL ISLANDS

Republic of the Marshall Islands

AREA – 181 sq. km
POPULATION – 70,822 (2001 estimate): 99 per cent are Micronesian. Almost half the population is under 15. About 60 per cent of the population is concentrated on the two atolls of Majuro and Kwajalein. The population is Christian, primarily Protestant, but with a substantial Catholic minority. Marshallese and English are the official languages
CAPITAL – Dalap-Uliga-Darrit, on Majuro Atoll (population, 20,000)
MAJOR TOWN – Ebeye
CURRENCY – Currency is that of the USA
NATIONAL ANTHEM – Forever Marshall Islands
NATIONAL DAY – 1 May (Independence Day)
NATIONAL FLAG – Blue with a diagonal ray divided white over orange running from the lower hoist to the upper fly; in the canton a white sun
MORTALITY RATE (per 1,000 population) – 5.03 (2003)
DEATH PENALTY – No (abolished 1986)
POPULATION GROWTH RATE – 2.3 per cent (2004)
POPULATION DENSITY – 343 per sq. km (1999)

CLIMATE AND TERRAIN

The Marshall Islands consist of 29 atolls and five islands in the Pacific Ocean. There is a wet season from May to November and average temperatures range from 25°C in January to 31°C in August.

HISTORY AND POLITICS

The Marshall Islands were claimed by Spain in 1592 but were left undisturbed by the Spanish empire for 300 years. In 1886 the Marshall Islands formally became a German protectorate. In 1914 Japan took control of the islands on behalf of the allied powers. During the Second World War US armed forces seized the islands from the Japanese after intense fighting. In 1947 the USA entered into agreement with the UN Security Council to administer the Micronesia area, of which the Marshall Islands are a part, as the UN Trust Territory of the Pacific Islands.

The islands became internally self-governing in 1979, and the US-UN trusteeship administration came to an end on 21 October 1986, when a Compact of Free

Association between the USA and the Republic of the Marshall Islands came into effect. By this agreement the USA recognised the Republic of the Marshall Islands as a fully sovereign and independent state. The UN Security Council terminated the UN Trust Territory of the Pacific in relation to the Marshall Islands and recognised its independence in December 1990. A new Compact of Free Association was negotiated in 2003.

FOREIGN RELATIONS

The Compact of Free Association places full responsibility for defence of the Marshall Islands on the USA. The US Department of Defense retains control of islands within Kwajalein Atoll where it has a missile test range. In 2000 the government of the Marshall Islands petitioned the US for US$2.7 billion to fund medical care for victims of radiation from US nuclear tests in the islands in the 1940s and 1950s and to rectify environmental damage.

POLITICAL SYSTEM

The Republic is a democracy based on a parliamentary system of government. The Executive is headed by the President, who is elected by the *Nitijela* from among its members. The President serves for a four-year term. The legislature has one chamber, the *Nitijela* of 33 members, and the Council of Chiefs *(Iroij)* of 12 members, which has an advisory role.

The United Democratic Party (UDP) won the parliamentary elections in November 1999 and in November 2003. A presidential election in January 2004 saw Kessai Note return to office.

HEAD OF STATE

President, Kessai Note, *elected* 3 January 2000, *re-elected* 14 January 2004

SELECTED GOVERNMENT MEMBERS *as at July 2004*

Finance, Brendan Wase

Foreign Affairs, Gerald Zackios

Internal Affairs and Welfare, Rien Morris

BRITISH AMBASSADOR, HE Ian Powell, resident at Suva, Fiji

ECONOMY AND TRADE

The economy is largely dependent on aid from the USA. An agreement was signed in 1986 which granted the Marshall Islands and the Federated States of Micronesia US$3.5 billion over 20 years. It is thought that the Marshall Islands has great potential in marine resources and seabed mineral deposits.

GNP – US$102 million (2000); US$1,950 per capita (1999)

GDP – US$96 million (2001); US$1,925 per capita (2000)

ANNUAL AVERAGE GROWTH OF GDP – 2.8 per cent (1998)

Trade with UK	*2002*	*2003*
Imports from UK	£5,076,000	£5,242,000
Exports to UK	824,000	1,145,000

TRANSPORT INFRASTRUCTURE

Air Marshall Islands provides air services within the islands and to Hawaii. Continental Air Micronesia serves Majuro and Kwajalein with flights to Hawaii and Guam. Majuro also has shipping links to Hawaii, Australia, Japan and throughout the Pacific.

MEDIA

The *Marshall Islands Journal* is a private weekly newspaper and the *Marshall Islands Gazette* is a government monthly newspaper.

MAURITANIA

Al-Jumhūriyya al-Islāmiyya al-Mawrītāniyya – Islamic Republic of Mauritania

AREA – 1,025,520 sq. km. Neighbours: Senegal (south-west), Mali (east and south), Algeria and Western Sahara (north)

POPULATION – 2,747,312 (2001 estimate). The official language is Arabic. Pulaar, Soninke, Wolof and French are also spoken

CAPITAL – ΨNouakchott (population, 850,000)

CURRENCY – Ouguiya (UM) of 5 khoums

NATIONAL DAY – 28 November

NATIONAL FLAG – Yellow star and crescent on green ground

LIFE EXPECTANCY (years) – 51.9 (2001)

MORTALITY RATE (per 1,000 population) – 13.04 (2003)

HIV / AIDS ADULT PREVALENCE – 1.8 per cent (2001)

DEATH PENALTY – Yes

POPULATION BELOW POVERTY LINE – 50 per cent (2001)

POPULATION GROWTH RATE – 3.2 per cent (1990–2001)

POPULATION DENSITY – 3 per sq. km (1999)

MILITARY EXPENDITURE – 1.7 per cent of GDP (2002)

MILITARY PERSONNEL – 15,750: Army 15,000, Navy 500, Air Force 250; Paramilitaries 5,000

CONSCRIPTION DURATION – Two years

ILLITERACY RATE – (m) 47.2 per cent; (f) 67.9 per cent (2000)

ENROLMENT (percentage of age group) – primary 79 per cent (1997); tertiary 4 per cent (1997)

CLIMATE AND TERRAIN

Mauritania's terrain is arid and flat, with some hilly regions in the centre of the country. Temperatures range from 16°C in January to 41°C in July.

HISTORY AND POLITICS

Mauritania became part of France's west African protectorate in 1903 and became a French colony in 1920. The country became the Islamic Republic of Mauritania on 28 November 1960 and joined the Arab League in 1973.

Throughout the 1970s Mauritania was troubled by unrest in Western Sahara. The Polisario Front, an organisation dedicated to independence for the region, launched attacks against Mauritanian troops and in 1978 Mauritania renounced all claims to Western Sahara.

By 2003 several years of drought had left thousands of Mauritanians facing food shortages. This led to serious civil disturbance and an attempted coup.

The National Assembly election held in October 2001 was won by the Republican Democratic and Social Party (PRDS) which gained 64 of the 81 seats. The presidential election of November 2003 saw Col. Maaouya ould sid Ahmed Toya re-elected for a fourth term of office with 67 per cent of the vote.

HEAD OF STATE
President, Col. Maaouya ould Sid Ahmed Taya (PRDS), *took power* 12 December 1984, *elected* 17 January 1992, *re-elected* 12 December 1997, 4 November 2003

SELECTED GOVERNMENT MEMBERS *as at July 2004*
Prime Minister, Seghaier ould Mbarek
Defence, Baba ould Sidi
Finance, Mohamed Sidya ould Mohamed Khaled
Foreign Affairs and Co-operation, Mohamed Vall ould Bellal
Interior, Post and Telecommunications, Mohamed Ghaly ould Cherif Ahmed

EMBASSY OF THE ISLAMIC REPUBLIC OF MAURITANIA
8 Carlos Place, London W1K 3AS
T 020-7478 9323
Ambassador Extraordinary and Plenipotentiary, HE Dr Youssouf Diagana, apptd 1999
BRITISH AMBASSADOR, HE Haydon Warren-Gash, apptd 2002, resident at Rabat, Morocco

ECONOMY AND TRADE

Mauritania has a diverse range of natural resources ranging from mineral deposits to rich fishing waters off the coast, but both these resources are threatened by over-exploitation. Mauritania has recently been discovered to have reserves of oil and is now one of four oil-refining countries in west Africa.

In 2002, Mauritania had $188 million of debt wiped out because of its status in the Highly Indebted Poor Countries (HIPC) initiative.

GNP – US$978 million (2000); US$370 per capita (2000)
GDP – US$1,030 million (2001); US$296 per capita (2000)
ANNUAL AVERAGE GROWTH OF GDP – 3.0 per cent (1998)
INFLATION RATE – 3.3 per cent (2000)
TOTAL EXTERNAL DEBT – US$2,500 million (2000)

BALANCE OF PAYMENTS
Trade – US$40 million surplus (1998)
Current Account – US$77 million surplus (1998)

Trade with UK	*2002*	*2003*
Imports from UK	£14,290,000	£22,277,000
Exports to UK	1,636,000	2,406,000

TRANSPORT INFRASTUCTURE

Mauritania's main ports are Bogue, Kaedi, Nouadhibou, Nouakchott and Rosso. There are 717km of railways and 7,720 km of highways. Mauritania operates ferry services on the Senegal River.

MEDIA AND CULTURE

Television and radio services in Mauritania are state owned. There are seven main national press publications.

Traditional Mauritanian culture is centred on the nomadic tribes and their jewellery making and goldsmithing skills.

MAURITIUS

Republic of Mauritius

AREA – 1,864 sq. km
POPULATION – 1,171,000 (2001): Asiatic races (Hindus 51.8 per cent, Muslims 16.5 per cent, Chinese 2.8 per cent), and persons of European (mainly French) extraction, mixed and African descent (28.6 per cent). English is the official language but French may be used in the National Assembly and lower law courts. Creole is the most commonly used language and several Asian languages are also used
CAPITAL – ΨPort Louis (population, 146,499, 2000 estimate)
MAJOR TOWNS – Beau Bassin-Rose Hill; Curepipe; Quatre Bornes; Vacoas-Phoenix
CURRENCY – Mauritius rupee of 100 cents
NATIONAL ANTHEM – Glory To Thee, Motherland
NATIONAL DAY – 12 March
NATIONAL FLAG – Red, blue, yellow and green horizontal stripes
LIFE EXPECTANCY (years) – 72 (2001)
INFANT MORTALITY (per 1,000 births) – 17 (2001)
MORTALITY RATE (per 1,000 population) – 6.81 (2003)
HIV / AIDS ADULT PREVALENCE – 0.1 per cent (2001)
DEATH PENALTY – No (abolished 1995)
POPULATION BELOW POVERTY LINE – 10 per cent (2001)
POPULATION GROWTH RATE – 1.0 per cent (2001)
POPULATION DENSITY – 596 per sq. km (2003)
URBAN POPULATION – 42.6 per cent (2001)
MILITARY EXPENDITURE – 0.1 per cent of GDP (2002)
MILITARY PERSONNEL – Paramilitaries 2,000

CLIMATE AND TERRAIN

Mauritius is an island group lying in the Indian Ocean approximately 885 km east of Madagascar. The island is mainly low-lying and elevation extremes range from 828 m (Mont Piton) at the highest point to 0 m (Indian Ocean) at the lowest. There is a tropical climate, modified by south-east trade winds, and average temperatures range from 25°C in July to 31°C in January.

HISTORY AND POLITICS

The French began to colonise the island in the 18th century, but in 1810 they were deposed by a British invasion. The British abolished slavery in 1835, but started to import thousands of indentured labourers from India to work on the sugar plantations.

Mauritius became independent on 12 March 1968. The Labour Party/Mouvement Militant Mauricien coalition (LP/MMM) won a landlside victory in 1995 and Dr Navinchandra Ramgoolam, became prime minister. The general election held on 11 September 2000 was won by the coalition of the Mauritian Socialist Movement and the Mauritian Militant Movement, who won 54 of the 62 directly elected seats. On 15 February 2002 President Cassam Uteem resigned after refusing to sign a controversial anti-terrorism bill. His successor Angidi Chettiar, also refused to sign the bill and resigned on 18 February. On 19 February the bill was signed into law by interim President Arianga Pillay, and a presidential election held on 25 February was won by Karl Offman.

Offman resigned on 1 October 2003 and was replaced by Sir Anerood Jugnauth on 7 October 2003.

POLITICAL SYSTEM

The President is head of state and is elected by the National Assembly. The Prime Minister, appointed by the President, is chosen for being the member of the National Assembly who appears best able to command the support of the majority of members of the Assembly. Other ministers are appointed by the President acting on the advice of the Prime Minister.

The National Assembly serves a five-year term and consists of 62 elected members (the island of Mauritius is divided into 20 three-member constituencies and the Island of Rodrigues returns two members), and eight specially elected members. Of the latter, four seats go to the 'best loser' of whichever communities on the island are under-represented in the Assembly after the general election, while the four remaining seats are allocated on the basis of both party and community. In November 2001 the National Assembly approved amendments to the constitution giving a considerable degree of autonomy to Rodrigues, including the establishment of an 18-member regional Assembly.

HEAD OF STATE

President, Sir Anerood Jugnauth, *took office* 7 October 2003

SELECTED GOVERNMENT MEMBERS *as at July 2004*

Prime Minister, Defence and Home Affairs, Paul Berenger

Deputy Prime Minister, Finance and the Economy, Pravid Jugnauth

Financial Services and Corporate Affairs, Sushil Kushiram

Foreign Affairs, Anil Gayan

MAURITIUS HIGH COMMISSION

32–33 Elvaston Place, London SW7 5NW

T 020-7581 0294/5

High Commissioner, HE Mohunlall Goburdhun, apptd 2001

BRITISH HIGH COMMISSION

Les Cascades Building, Edith Cavell Street, Port Louis (PO Box 1063)

T (+ 230) 202 9400

E bhc@intnet.mu

High Commissioner, HE David Snoxell, apptd 2000

BRITISH COUNCIL DIRECTOR, Rosalind Burford

Royal Road, PO Box 111, Rose Hill

E general.enquiries@mu.britishcouncil.org

ECONOMY AND TRADE

Since independence Mauritius has diversified its economy from a predominantly agricultural base into one concentrating on the industrial, financial and tourism sectors. Agriculture continues to play a part and the island exports sugarcane, tea, corn, potatoes, bananas, pulses, and fish. Sugarcane, which was the main reason for the island to be developed by colonialists from the 17th century onwards, is grown on 90 per cent of cultivated land and produces 25 per cent of the island's export earnings. The Government is attempting to establish a free port and an expansion of offshore banking services. Information technology is also being given high priority.

Most foodstuffs and raw materials have to be imported while most of the sugar produced is exported, mainly to Britain.

GNI – US$4,600 million (2001); US$3,830 per capita (2001)

ANNUAL AVERAGE GROWTH OF GDP – 7.2 per cent (2001)

INFLATION RATE – 3.9 per cent (2003)

TOTAL EXTERNAL DEBT – US$2,374 million (2000)

FOREIGN DIRECT INVESTMENT – US$380 million (1997–2000)

IMPORTS – US$1,993 million (2002)

EXPORTS – US$1,615 million (2002)

BALANCE OF PAYMENTS

Trade – US$256 million deficit (2001)

Current Account – US$247 million surplus (2001)

Trade with UK	*2002*	*2003*
Imports from UK	£56,418,000	£46,880,000
Exports to UK	337,425,000	325,006,000

TRANSPORT INFRASTRUCTURE

Port Louis, on the north-west coast, handles the bulk of the island's external trade. The international airport is located at Plaisance.

EDUCATION

Primary education is free of charge and compulsory. There are a number of facilities offering vocational training. The Institute of Education is responsible for training primary and secondary school teachers and for curriculum development.

ILLITERACY RATE – (m) 12.1 per cent; (f) 18.6 per cent (2000)

ENROLMENT (percentage of age group) – primary 100 per cent (1997); tertiary 6 per cent (1997)

MEDIA AND CULTURE

Freedom of expression is guaranteed in the constitution and four daily newspapers and eight weekly publications offer a range of political viewpoints. The Mauritius Broadcasting Corporation is state owned and runs television and radio services. Satellite television is available and private radio stations began broadcasting in 2002. Créole culture exerts an exceptionally strong influence on the island.

RODRIGUES AND DEPENDENCIES

The Island of Rodrigues, formerly a dependency but now part of Mauritius, is about 350 miles east of Mauritius, with an area of 40 square miles. The population is 35,776 (2000). The islands of Agalega and St. Brandon are dependencies of Mauritius. Total population 289 (2002).

MEXICO

Estados Unidos Mexicanos – United Mexican States

AREA – 1,908,700 sq. km. Neighbours: USA (north), Guatemala and Belize (south-east)

POPULATION – 100,368,000 (2001). Spanish is the official language and is spoken by about 95 per cent of the population. There are five main groups of Indian languages (Náhuatl, Maya, Zapotec, Otomí, Mixtec) and 59 dialects derived from them

CAPITAL – Mexico City (population, 8,591,309, 2000 census)

MAJOR CITIES – Ciudad Juárez; Ecatepec de Morelos;

Guadalajara; León; Monterrey; Nezahualcóyotl; Puebla; Tijuana; Toluca; Torreón
CURRENCY – Peso of 100 centavos
NATIONAL ANTHEM – Mexicanos, Al Grito De Guerra (Mexicans, To The War Cry)
NATIONAL DAY – 16 September (Proclamation of Independence)
NATIONAL FLAG – Three vertical bands in green, white and red, with the Mexican emblem (an eagle on a cactus devouring a snake) in the centre
LIFE EXPECTANCY (years) – 73 (2001)
MORTALITY RATE (per 1,000 population) – 4.97 (2003)
INFANT MORTALITY (per 1,000 births) – 24 (2001)
HIV / AIDS ADULT PREVALENCE RATE – 0.3 per cent (2001)
DEATH PENALTY – Yes*
POPULATION BELOW POVERTY LINE – 40 per cent (2001)
POPULATION GROWTH RATE – 1.7 per cent (1990–2001)
POPULATION DENSITY – 53 per sq. km (2001)
URBAN POPULATION – 75 per cent (2001)

CLIMATE AND TERRAIN

Mexico's terrain varies from low coastal plains to high mountains. Elevation extremes range from 5,700 m (Volcan Pico de Orizaba) at the highest point to −10 m (Laguna Salada) at the lowest. Average temperatures in Mexico City range from 23°C in October to 30°C in July.

HISTORY AND POLITICS

Between 1200 and 600 BC the Olmecs appeared in the lowlands of southern Veracruz and Tabasco. The Zapotecs of Oaxaca developed their civilisation in 300 BC and in 250 BC the Maya began to build the massive stepped pyramids in the Yucatan peninsula. The Aztecs, who came to the region in the 14th century, formed Mexico's final great indigenous empire.

Hernán Cortés, landed at modern Veracruz on 21 April 1519. The effect of the Spanish arrival on Mexican civilisation was devastating. It is now estimated that around 24 million people of the indigenous population died between the conquest and the early 17th century.

Miguel Hidalgo y Costilla instigated an independence movement on 16 September 1810 and independence came in 1821. Mexico suffered extreme instability, civil war and invasion throughout much of the 19th century. War with the USA in 1845 led to the loss of vast areas of land under the Treaty of Guadeloupe Hidalgo; Britain, France and Spain sent military forces to reclaim massive debts in 1862 and in 1864 the French installed the Archduke Maximilian as emperor. Porfirio Díaz ruled as a dictator between 1878 and 1911. He can be credited with beginning the industrialisation of Mexico, but his tenure was also marked by terrible repression that led to an attempted Marxist revolution in 1910.

After the Second World War, Mexico continued to be troubled by unrest, but the country also underwent development, partly due to the exploitation of oil reserves. President Carlos Salinas de Gortari introduced market reforms in the 1990s and tied Mexico into the North American Free Trade Agreement (NAFTA) in 1994. These reforms led to a degree of social upheaval and, fearing for the status of the already marginalised indigenous peoples, the Zapatista movement began an insurgency in the south of the country.

In the presidential and legislative elections of July 2000, Vicente Fox, the Partido de Accion Nacional (PAN) candidate, was elected as president and the PAN-led alliance gained 224 of the 500 Chamber of Deputies seats. However, in the 2003 legislative elections the political landscape altered with PAN losing its majority to the Partido Revolucionario Institucional (PRI). PAN won 153 seats while the PRI secured 241.

POLITICAL SYSTEM
The Congress of the Union consists of a Senate of 128 members, elected for a six-year term, and of a Chamber of Deputies *(Cámara de Diputados)*, at present numbering 500, elected for a three-year term. The head of Government is the President, who is elected for a six-year term and may not be re-elected.

FEDERAL STRUCTURE
The Republic is a Federal one of 31 states and the federal capital. The states are administered by a Governor and their own Chamber of Deputies.

HEAD OF STATE
President, Vicente Fox, *elected* 2 July 2000, *sworn in* 1 December 2000

SELECTED GOVERNMENT MEMBERS *as at July 2004*
Defence, Gen. Gerardo Clemente Ricardo Vega
Economy, Fernando Canales Clariond
Foreign Affairs, Luis Ernesto Derbez
Interior, Santiago Creel Miranda

MEXICAN EMBASSY
42 Hertford Street, London W1J 7JR
T 020-7499 8586
Ambassador Extraordinary and Plenipotentiary, HE Juan-José Bremer de Martino, *apptd* 2004

BRITISH EMBASSY
Calle Río Lerma 71, Colonia Cuauhtémoc, 06500 Mexico City
T (+ 52) (55) 5242 8500
E consular.mexico@fco.gov.uk
Ambassador Extraordinary and Plenipotentiary, HE Denise Holt, CMG, apptd 2002

BRITISH COUNCIL DIRECTOR, Clive Bruton
Lope de Vega 316, Col. Chapultepec Morales, 11570 Mexico DF
T (+ 52) (55) 5263 1900
E bcmexico@britishcouncil.org.mx

DEFENCE

The Army has 862 armoured personnel carriers. The Navy has three destroyers, eight frigates, 109 patrol and coastal vessels, and eight combat aircraft. There are 20 naval bases. The Air Force has 107 combat aircraft and 71 armed helicopters.
MILITARY EXPENDITURE – 0.9 per cent of GDP (2002)
MILITARY PERSONNEL – 192,770: Army 144,000, Navy 37,000, Air Force 11,770; Paramilitaries 11,000
CONSCRIPTION DURATION – 12 months (four hours per week) by lottery

ECONOMY AND TRADE

One of the major effects of NAFTA membership, which tripled Mexico's trade with Canada and the USA, was to establish a number of large factories in northern Mexico, devoted to the assembly of goods for the US market. It is hoped that trade agreements made with the EU in 2000 and Japan in 2004, may further increase trade.

Tobacco, chemicals, iron and steel, petroleum, mining, textiles, clothing, motor vehicles, and tourism are all major industries in Mexico. Mexico's wealth of cultivatable land means agriculture is diverse and productive; major products include corn, wheat, soy beans, rice, beans, cotton, coffee, fruit, tomatoes, beef, poultry, and dairy products. Agriculture accounts for four per cent of GDP and 18 per cent of the labour force. Principal exports include oil, cars, auto engines, fruits and vegetables, shrimps, coffee, computers, cattle, glass, iron and steel pipes, and copper. Major imports include computers, auto assembly material, electrical parts, car and truck parts, powdered milk, corn and sorghum, vehicles, sound-recording and power-generating equipment, chemicals, industrial machinery, pharmaceuticals and specialised appliances.

GNI – US$550,200 million (2001); US$5,530 per capita (2001)
ANNUAL AVERAGE GROWTH OF GDP – 6.9 per cent (2000)
INFLATION RATE – 3.8 per cent (2003)
UNEMPLOYMENT – 3.3 per cent (2003)
TOTAL EXTERNAL DEBT – US$159,400 million (2003)
FOREIGN DIRECT INVESTMENT – US$47,787 million (1997–2000)
IMPORTS – US$176,607 million (2002)
EXPORTS – US$160,682 million (2002)

BALANCE OF PAYMENTS
Trade – US$7,995 million deficit (2002)
Current Account – US$14,069 million deficit (2002)

Trade with UK	*2002*	*2003*
Imports from UK	£708,461,000	£693,248,000
Exports to UK	523,329,000	509,161,000

TRANSPORT INFRASTRUCTURE

Veracruz, Tampico and Coatzacoalcos are the chief ports on the Atlantic coast, and Guaymas, Mazatlán, Puerto Lázaro Cárdenas and Salina Cruz on the Pacific. Work is proceeding on the reorganisation of the railway network. There are 329,532 km of roads of which 108,087 km are surfaced.

EDUCATION

Although Mexico allows for 10 years of free and compulsory education, on average Mexican adults have only completed 7.2 years. The country's largest university is the National Autonomous University of Mexico, situated in Mexico City.

ILLITERACY RATE – (m) 6.7 per cent; (f) 10.6 per cent (2000)
ENROLMENT (percentage of age group) – primary 100 per cent (1997); secondary 64 per cent (1997); tertiary 16 per cent (1997)

MEDIA AND CULTURE

Televisa used to control all Mexican broadcasting but now competes with other channels. There are six national newspapers, including *Chapas, Baja California* and *Diario de Chihuahua*, and many independent radio stations.

Pre-Columbian civilisation has significantly influenced contemporary Mexican culture. Important cultural figures include the mural painters Diego Rivera (1886–1957) and José Clemente Orozco (1883–1949), as well as writers Octavio Paz (1914–98) and Carlos Fuentes (b. 1928).

FEDERATED STATES OF MICRONESIA

AREA – 702 sq. km
POPULATION – 134,597 (2001 estimate). The population is Micronesian and predominantly Christian. English (official) and eight other languages are used in different parts of the Federated States: Yapese, Ulithian, Woleaian, Pohnpeian, Nukuoran, Kapingamarangi, Chuukese and Kosraean
FEDERAL CAPITAL – Palikir, on ΨKolonia (Pohnpei)
CURRENCY – Currency is the US$
NATIONAL ANTHEM – Patriots of Micronesia
NATIONAL FLAG – United Nations blue with four white stars in the centre
LIFE EXPECTANCY (years) – male 64.4; female 68.8 (2001)
MORTALITY RATE (per 1,000 population) – 5.1 (2003)
DEATH PENALTY – No (abolished 1986)
POPULATION BELOW POVERTY LINE – 26.7 per cent (2001)
POPULATION GROWTH RATE – 0.2 per cent (2004)
POPULATION DENSITY – 165 per sq. km (1999)

CLIMATE AND TERRAIN

The Federated States of Micronesia comprise more than 600 islands extending 2,900 km across the archipelago of the Caroline Islands in the western Pacific Ocean. Elevation extremes range from 791 m (Totolom) at the highest point to 0 m (Pacific Ocean) at the lowest. The climate of Micronesia is tropical with an almost constant 30°C temperature.

HISTORY AND POLITICS

Inhabited since around 4,000 BC by migrants from the Philippines and Indonesia, Micronesia came into contact with Europeans in 1521. The islands were purchased by Germany from Spain in 1899 but were surrendered to Japan during the First World War. The Japanese received a mandate from the League of Nations to govern the islands in 1920.

During the Second World War the USA dislodged the Japanese from the islands and they became a Trust Territory of the Pacific Islands administered by the United Nations. A constitution was adopted in 1979 and full independence came in 1986 under a Compact of Free Association with the USA.

Joseph J. Urusemal was elected by congress as President in May 2003.

POLITICAL SYSTEM

The Constitution separates the executive, legislative and judicial branches. There is a Bill of Rights and provision for traditional rights. The executive comprises a federal President and Vice-President, both of whom must be chosen from amongst the four nationally elected Senators. There is a single-chamber Congress of 14 members, four members elected on a state-wide basis, and ten members elected from Congressional districts apportioned by population.

The judiciary is headed by the Supreme Court, which is divided into trial and appellate divisions. Below this, each state has its own judicial system.

The Compact of Free Association (CFA) places full responsibility for the defence of the Federated States of Micronesia on the USA.

The Federated States of Micronesia is a federal republic of four constituent states: Chuuk, Kosrae, Pohnpei and Yap. Each of the constituent states has its own Government and legislative system.

HEAD OF STATE
President, Joseph J. Urusemal, *elected* 10 May 2003
Vice-President, Redley Killion

SELECTED GOVERNMENT MEMBERS *as at July 2004*
Economic Affairs, Patrick Mackenzie
Finance and Administration, Nick L. Andon
Foreign Affairs, Sebastion L. Anefal

BRITISH AMBASSADOR, HE Ian Powell, resident at Suva, Fiji

ECONOMY AND TRADE

Micronesia is highly dependent on aid from the USA. The islands have few mineral resources apart from deposits of phosphate. Subsistence farming and fishing are the primary economic activities (though climate change and over-fishing threaten both these activities). The islands' extreme isolation hampers the development of tourism. The CFA with the US in 1986, provided for US$1.3 billion in financial assistance over 15 years until 2001. Since then assistance from the US has been gradually reduced. In 2002 aid to Micronesia was US$100 million.

Exports include fish, black pepper, tropical fruits and vegetables, coconuts, tapioca, betel nuts and sweet potatoes.

GNI – US$250 million (2000); US$2,110 per capita (2000)

Trade with UK	*2002*	*2003*
Imports from UK	£10,000	£7,000
Exports to UK	–	1,000

TRANSPORT INFRASTRUCTURE

The main ports are Colonia (Yap), Kolonia (Pohnpei), Lele and Moen. There are 240 km of highways and no railways.

MEDIA

There are four weekly news publications. One Government television channel competes with two commercial channels. There are several radio stations.

MOLDOVA

Republica Moldova – Republic of Moldova

AREA – 33,851 sq. km. Neighbours: Ukraine (north, east and south-east), Romania (west)
POPULATION – 4,335,000 (2001 estimate): 65 per cent are Moldovan, 14.2 per cent Ukrainian and 13 per cent Russian, together with smaller numbers of Gagauz (ethnic Turks), Jews and Bulgarians. Most of the population are adherents of the Moldovan Orthodox Church. Moldovan was made the official language (written in the Latin script) in 1989 but the use of Russian in official business is permitted
CAPITAL – Chişinău (population, 655,940, 1997 estimate)
CURRENCY – Moldovan leu of 100 bani (plural lei)
NATIONAL ANTHEM – Lîmbă Noastră (Our Language)
NATIONAL DAY – 27 August (Independence Day)
NATIONAL FLAG – Vertical stripes of blue, yellow and red, with the national arms in the centre
MORTALITY RATE (per 1,000 population) – 12.7 (2003)
HIV / AIDS ADULT PREVALENCE – 0.2 per cent (2001)
DEATH PENALTY – No (abolished 1995)
POPULATION BELOW POVERTY LINE – 80 per cent (2001)
POPULATION GROWTH RATE – 0.4 per cent (2002)
POPULATION DENSITY – 129 per sq. km (1999)
MILITARY EXPENDITURE – 1.7 per cent of GDP (2002)
MILITARY PERSONNEL – 6,910: Army 5,560, Air Force 1,100; Paramilitaries 3,400
CONSCRIPTION DURATION – 12 months
ILLITERACY RATE – (m) 0.5 per cent; (f) 1.7 per cent (2000)
ENROLMENT (percentage of age group) – tertiary 27 per cent (1997)

CLIMATE AND TERRAIN

Elevation extremes range from 430 m (Dealul Bulanesti) at the highest point to 2 m (Nistru River) at the lowest. Average temperatures range from −4°C in January to 20°C in August.

HISTORY AND POLITICS

Following the fall of the Roman empire and centuries of occupation by numerous invaders, Moldova developed as a coherent state within Romania during the Middle Ages. By the 18th century Moldova was at the centre of a power struggle between Russia, Turkey, Romania and Austria. By 1812, following the Treaty of Bucharest, Moldova had been divided between Russia and Romania, the latter naming its share Bessarabia.

The territory was annexed by the Soviet Union in 1940. After 1947 it was known as the Moldavian Soviet Socialist Republic (MSSR). Strong nationalist sentiment reappeared as President Gorbachev introduced reform in the Soviet Union in the 1980s. The territory declared independence in 1991 but was unable to prevent the country being divided along ethnic lines. Russians, Ukrainians and Gagauz began to work towards a separate state in the Transdnistria region. Armed clashes between Transdnistrian separatists and Moldovan government forces followed in 1992. Several hundred people died and thousands fled to the Ukraine. A fragile peace settlement guaranteed Moldovan territorial integrity but failed to reach a final status solution for Transdnistria.

Negotiations resumed in 1997 and a high degree of Transdnistrian autonomy within a Moldovan state became a possible solution. However, no final agreement was reached. Another round of negotiations in the summer of 2002 were overseen by the Organisation for Security and Co-operation in Europe (OSCE) and mediator states, Russia and Ukraine. By February 2003 a proposal which made provision for a new Moldovan constitution and guaranteed Transdnistria federal status within Moldova was drafted. The question of the exact degree of autonomy that Transdnistria would enjoy remains the major barrier to a final agreement.

European Union involvement in the dispute accelerated in 2003 when the EU announced a visa ban on Transdnistrian officials opposed to settling the dispute. The EU has further threatened restrictive measures against any Transdnistrians thought to be intent on delaying political progress.

The general election of February 2001 was won by the Communist Party of Moldova (PCM), who obtained 71 seats. The new parliament elected the PCM leader, Vladimir Voronin, as President on 4 April 2001 and approved a new government, led by Vasile Tarlev, an independent member of parliament.

POLITICAL SYSTEM
In July 1994 the Moldovan Parliament adopted a new Constitution which established a presidential parliamentary republic and provided for autonomous status for the Gagauz region, which was given its own elected National Assembly. The unicameral Parliament is directly elected for a four-year term. It has 101 members. The President is elected by Parliament and must obtain the support of at least 61 Deputies. If no candidate achieves this, Parliament must be dissolved and a general election held.

HEAD OF STATE
President, Vladimir Voronin, *elected by parliament* 4 April 2001

SELECTED GOVERNMENT MEMBERS *as at July 2004*
Prime Minister, Vasile Tarlev
First Deputy Prime Minister, Vasile Iovv
Deputy Prime Ministers, Dmitrii Todoroglo *(Agriculture and Food Industry)*; Marian Lupu *(Economy and Trade)*; Valerian Cristea (*Without Portfolio)*
Defence, Victor Gaiciuc
Finance, Zinaida Greceanii
Foreign Affairs, Andrei Stratan
Interior, Col. Gheorghe Papuc

EMBASSY OF THE REPUBLIC OF MOLDOVA
Rue Tenbosch 54, Brussels 1050, Belgium
T (+ 32) (2) 732 9659
Ambassador Extraordinary and Plenipotentiary, Mihai Popov

BRITISH AMBASSADOR, HE Bernard Whiteside, CVO, CMG

ECONOMY AND TRADE

The agricultural sector accounts for 23 per cent of GDP. Principal crops include: wheat, corn, barley, tobacco and sugar beet.

Moldova is heavily dependent on the precarious Russian economy. Borrowing from the World Bank and IMF was often interrupted throughout the 1990s by Moldova's failure to meet the conditions of its loans. This process was repeated in 2003 when the IMF announced it would not be continuing with an aid package because Moldova had not met the agreed requirements.

Thirty per cent of the workforce has sought employment in other countries.

GNI – US$1,413 million (2000); US$400 per capita (2001)
ANNUAL AVERAGE GROWTH OF GDP – 6.1 per cent (2002)
INFLATION RATE – 31.3 per cent (2000)
UNEMPLOYMENT – 8.5 per cent (2000)
TOTAL EXTERNAL DEBT – US$1,233 million (2000)
IMPORTS – US$897 million (2001)
EXPORTS – US$570 million (2001)

BALANCE OF PAYMENTS
Trade – US$378 million deficit (2002)
Current Account – US$109 million deficit (2002)

Trade with UK	*2002*	*2003*
Imports from UK	£5,111,000	£6,052,000
Exports to UK	2,978,000	2,921,000

TRANSPORT INFRASTRUCTURE

Moldova has 12,657 km of highways and 1,300 km of railways. Its 36 airports handle 3,900 departures per year.

MEDIA AND CULTURE

Freedom of media expression is guaranteed by the constitution. There are five main newspapers and state run Moldovan television and radio stations (of which there are one each) which compete with a single commercial channel.

Historically, Moldovan culture has been heavily influenced by Romanian folk culture which is highly important to the population; the ancient ballad *Miorita* is central to this tradition.

MONACO

Principauté de Monaco – Principality of Monaco

AREA – 2 sq. km. Neighbour: France
POPULATION – 34,000 (2001). Only 7,175 residents have full Monégasque citizenship and thus the right to vote. The official language is French. Monégasque, a mixture of Provenal and Ligurian, is also spoken
CAPITAL – Monaco
CURRENCY – Euro (€) of 100 cents
NATIONAL ANTHEM – Hymne Monégasque (Monegasque Anthem)
NATIONAL DAY – 19 November
NATIONAL FLAG – Two equal horizontal stripes, red over white
LIFE EXPECTANCY (years) – 79 (2001)
MORTALITY RATE (per 1,000 population) – 12.82 (2003)
INFANT MORTALITY (per 1,000 births) – 4 (2001)
DEATH PENALTY – No (abolished 1962)
POPULATION GROWTH RATE – 1.1 per cent (1990–2001)
POPULATION DENSITY – 17,282 per sq. km (2001)

CLIMATE AND TERRAIN

Elevation extremes range from 140 m (Mount Agel) at the highest point to 0 m (Mediterranean Sea) at the lowest. Monaco has a Mediterranean climate with average temperatures that range from 10°C in January to 23°C in July.

HISTORY AND POLITICS

Monaco has been ruled by the Grimaldi family since the 13th century. Monarchical France recognised Monaco's independence in the 15th century, but Revolutionary France annexed it in the 18th century. Monaco did not regain its independence until 1861 and the principality remains under French protection.

Prince Rainier III ascended the throne in 1949. He decreased the extent to which the Monégasque economy is dependent on gambling and guided Monaco to full membership of the UN in 1993. In 1962 a new constitution was proclaimed. Capital punishment was abolished, female suffrage was introduced and a supreme court was established.

Legislative power is held jointly by the Prince and a unicameral, 24-member National Council elected by universal suffrage. Executive power is exercised by the Prince and a four-member Council of Government, headed by a Minister of State, who is nominated by the Prince from a list of three French diplomats submitted by the French Government. The judicial code is based on that of France. In the legislative elections of 9 February 2003 the Union for Monaco (UPM) won 21 seats, defeating the National and Democratic Union, which had been in power for most of the previous 40 years.

HEAD OF STATE
HSH The Prince of Monaco, Prince Rainier III Louis-Henri-Maxence Bertrand, *born* 31 May 1923, *succeeded* 9 May 1949
Heir, HRH Prince Albert Alexandre Louis Pierre, *born* 14 March 1958

SELECTED GOVERNMENT MEMBERS *as at July 2004*
President of the Crown Council, Charles Ballerio
President of the National Council, Stephane Valeri
Minister of State, Patrick Leclercq
Finance and Economy, Franck Biancheri
Interior, Philippe Deslandes

CONSULATE-GENERAL OF MONACO
4 Cromwell Place, London SW7 2JE
T 020-7225 2679
Consul-General, Ivan Bozidar Ivanovic

BRITISH CONSULATE-GENERAL
33 Boulevard Princesse Charlotte, BP 265, MC 98005 Monaco Cedex
T (+ 377) 93 50 99 66
Consul-General, I. Davies *(resides at Marseille)*

ECONOMY AND TRADE

Monaco's economy benefits from real estate revenue, financial services, some light industry and tourism. A major construction project was undertaken in 2001 to extend the harbour facilities to accommodate cruise ships. Since the state collects no taxes from individuals or businesses it has become a tax haven for the wealthy, and non-Monégasques make up 84 per cent of the population. The Grimaldi family retains monopolies in a number of sectors, including tobacco, the telephone network, and the postal service.
GNI – US$25,000 per capita (2001)
ANNUAL AVERAGE GROWTH OF GDP – 3.3 per cent (1998)

MEDIA

Radio Monte-Carlo started broadcasting across France in the 1960s and Italy in the 1970s. Monaco does not have an indigenous daily press (French newspapers are widely available) but does publish two weekly journals.

MONGOLIA

Mongol Uls – Mongol State

AREA – 1,566,500 sq. km. Neighbours: Russia (north), China (south)
POPULATION – 2,654,999 (2001 estimate). Mongolians also live in China and in the neighbouring regions of Russia, especially the Mongolian Buryat Autonomous Region. The official language is Khalkha Mongolian
CAPITAL – Ulaanbaatar (population, 515,100, 1998 estimate)
CURRENCY – Tugrik of 100 möngö
NATIONAL ANTHEM – Mongol Ulsiin Teriin Duulal (Mongol National Anthem)
NATIONAL DAY – 11 July
NATIONAL FLAG – Vertical tricolour red, blue, red and in the hoist the traditional Soyombo symbol in gold
LIFE EXPECTANCY (years) – 63 (2001)
MORTALITY RATE (per 1,000 population) – 7.18 (2003)
HIV / AIDS ADULT PREVALENCE – 0.1 per cent (2001)
DEATH PENALTY – Yes
POPULATION BELOW POVERTY LINE – 36 per cent (2001)
POPULATION GROWTH RATE – 3.3 per cent (1997–2002)
POPULATION DENSITY – 2 per sq. km (1999)
MILITARY EXPENDITURE – 2.2 per cent of GDP (2002)
MILITARY PERSONNEL – 9,100: Army 7,500, Air Defence 800; Paramilitaries 7,200
CONSCRIPTION DURATION – 12 months
ILLITERACY RATE – (m) 0.8 per cent; (f) 0.7 per cent (2000)
ENROLMENT (percentage of age group) – primary 88 per cent (1997); secondary 56 per cent (1997); tertiary 17.0 per cent (1997)

CLIMATE AND TERRAIN

Mongolia, most of which is at least 1,000 m above sea level, forms part of the central Asiatic plateau and rises towards the west in the mountains of the Mongolian Altai and Hangai ranges. The Gobi region covers much of the southern half of the country and contains sand deserts interspersed with semi-desert. Elevation extremes range from 4,374 m (Nayramadlin Orgil) at the highest point to 518 m (Hoh Nuur) at the lowest. The winter climate in northern Mongolia is extreme and average temperatures in the capital city, Ulaanbaatar, range from −27°C in January to 19°C in July.

HISTORY AND POLITICS

Mongolian tribes, comprised of Turks and Uighurs, led a fiercely independent existence until the 12th century when they were united by Tamburlaine who combined the dispersed tribes and led them on an expedition of conquest which extended the Mongol empire from Beijing to the Caspian Sea. Recognising Tamburlaine's role in Mongolian unification, his subjects named him Genghis Khan. Kublai Khan, Ghenghis's grandson, is credited with establishing Mongolia's 'Golden Age', through the consolidation of the empire that, by his reign in the 13th century, stretched from Hungary to China and as far south as Vietnam.

The empire declined after Kublai's death in 1294, and Mongolia entered a period of great instability and eventual domination by the Chinese Manchu dynasty in 1691. Independence from China did not come until 1911 when the Manchu dynasty collapsed. Mongolian revolutionaries, with Soviet help and encouragement, established the Mongolian People's Republic (MPP) in 1924. This was swiftly absorbed by Stalinist tendencies and Mongolia did not emerge from Soviet domination until 1990.

The Mongolian People's Revolutionary Party (MPRP) dominated the country's politics after the fall of communism until 1996 when an alliance of nationalists

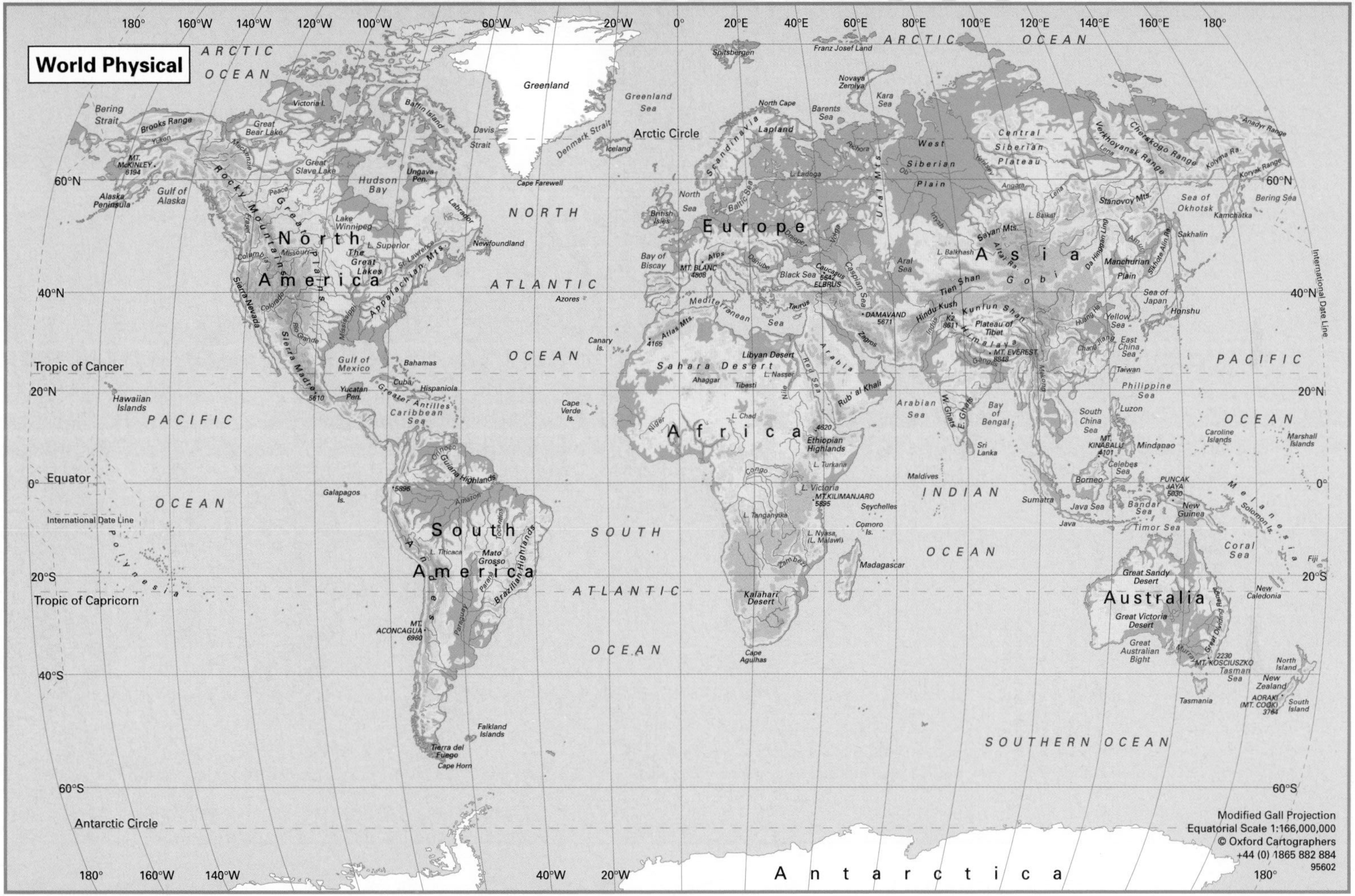
World Physical
ARCTIC OCEAN
NORTH ATLANTIC OCEAN
SOUTH ATLANTIC OCEAN
PACIFIC OCEAN
INDIAN OCEAN
SOUTHERN OCEAN
North America
South America
Europe
Africa
Asia
Australia
Antarctica
Greenland
Arctic Circle
Tropic of Cancer
Equator
Tropic of Capricorn
Antarctic Circle
International Date Line
Rocky Mountains
Great Plains
Appalachian Mts.
Sierra Nevada
Sierra Madre
Hudson Bay
Gulf of Mexico
Caribbean Sea
Andes
Amazon
Brazilian Highlands
Guiana Highlands
Sahara Desert
Libyan Desert
Kalahari Desert
Ethiopian Highlands
Mediterranean Sea
Black Sea
Caspian Sea
Red Sea
Ural Mts.
West Siberian Plain
Central Siberian Plateau
Himalaya
Plateau of Tibet
Gobi
MT. EVEREST 8848
Great Victoria Desert
Great Sandy Desert
Modified Gall Projection
Equatorial Scale 1:166,000,000
© Oxford Cartographers
+44 (0) 1865 882 884
95602

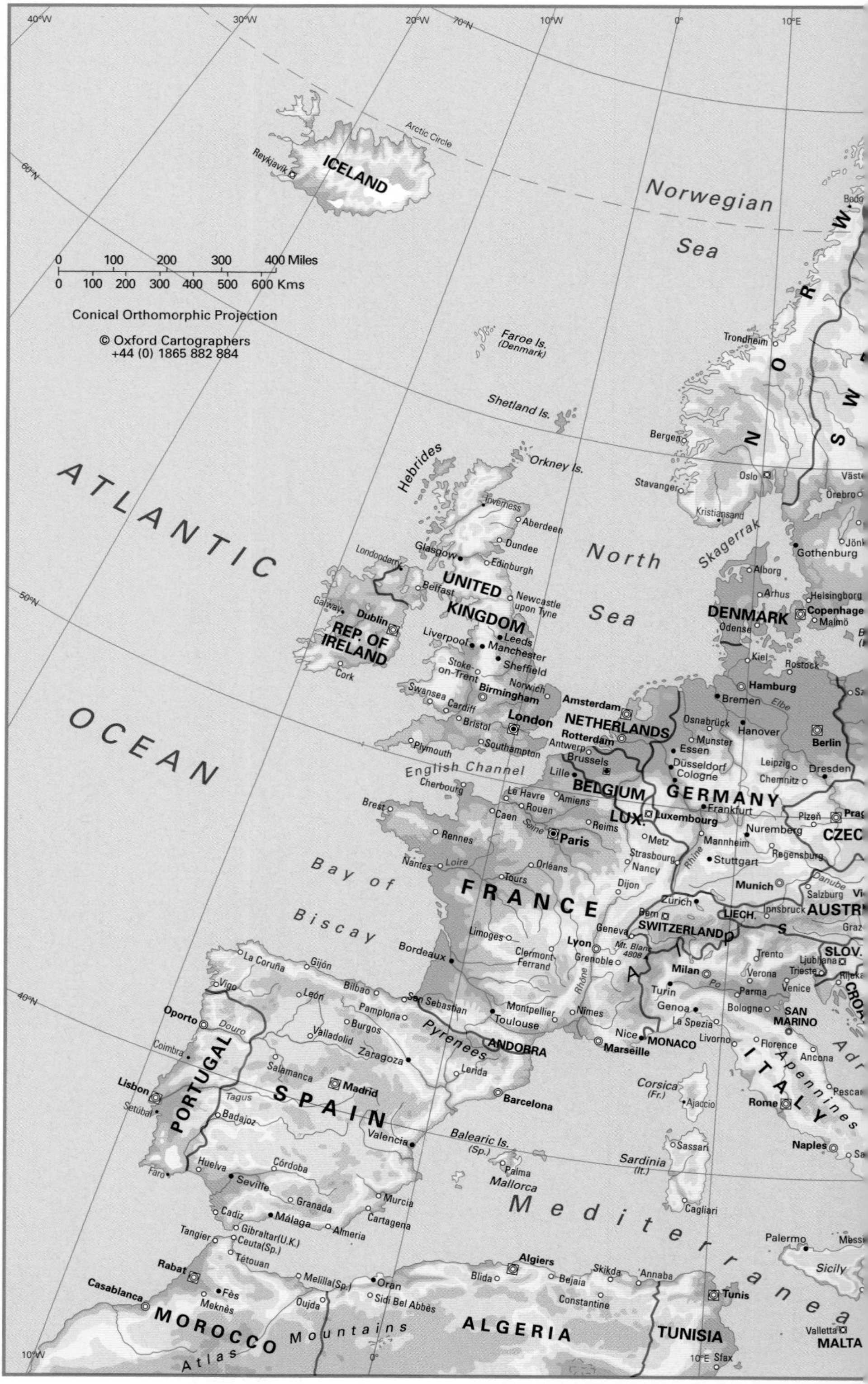

40°W
30°W
20°W
70°N
10°W
0°
10°E
Arctic Circle
Reykjavik
ICELAND
60°N
Norwegian
Sea
0 100 200 300 400 Miles
0 100 200 300 400 500 600 Kms
Conical Orthomorphic Projection
© Oxford Cartographers
+44 (0) 1865 882 884
Faroe Is.
(Denmark)
Shetland Is.
Trondheim
Bergen
Oslo
Stavanger
Kristiansand
Skagerrak
NORW
SW
Bodø
Väst
Örebro
Jönk
Gothenburg
Orkney Is.
Hebrides
Inverness
Aberdeen
Dundee
Glasgow
Edinburgh
North
Sea
ATLANTIC
OCEAN
Londonderry
Belfast
UNITED
KINGDOM
Newcastle
upon Tyne
50°N
Galway
Dublin
REP. OF
IRELAND
Cork
Liverpool
Leeds
Manchester
Sheffield
Stoke-
on-Trent
Norwich
Birmingham
Swansea
Cardiff
Bristol
London
Plymouth
Southampton
Alborg
Århus
Helsingborg
DENMARK
Copenhagen
Malmö
Odense
Kiel
Rostock
Hamburg
Bremen
Elbe
Amsterdam
NETHERLANDS
Rotterdam
Osnabrück
Hanover
Berlin
Münster
Essen
Antwerp
Brussels
Düsseldorf
Cologne
Leipzig
Dresden
Chemnitz
English Channel
Cherbourg
Lille
BELGIUM
GERMANY
Le Havre
Amiens
Rouen
Frankfurt
Brest
Caen
LUX.
Luxembourg
Plzeň
Prag
Seine
Paris
Reims
Metz
Nuremberg
CZEC
Mannheim
Rennes
Strasbourg
Rhine
Stuttgart
Regensburg
Nancy
Nantes
Loire
Orléans
Danube
Bay of
Biscay
Tours
Dijon
Munich
Salzburg
FRANCE
Zurich
Innsbruck
AUSTR
LIECH.
Bern
SWITZERLAND
Limoges
Geneva
Graz
Bordeaux
Clermont-
Ferrand
Lyon
Mt. Blanc
4808
ALP
SLOV.
Grenoble
Trento
Ljubljana
Rijeka
Milan
Po
Verona
Trieste
Venice
La Coruña
Gijón
Rhône
Turin
Parma
CRO
Vigo
Bilbao
San Sebastian
Montpellier
Nîmes
Genoa
Bologne
SAN
MARINO
40°N
León
Pamplona
Toulouse
La Spezia
Oporto
Douro
Burgos
Pyrenees
Nice
MONACO
Livorno
Florence
Ancona
Valladolid
ANDORRA
Marseille
Adr
Coimbra
Zaragoza
Lerida
Apennines
PORTUGAL
Salamanca
Corsica
(Fr.)
ITALY
Pescar
Lisbon
Madrid
Barcelona
Ajaccio
Rome
Setúbal
Tagus
SPAIN
Badajoz
Valencia
Balearic Is.
(Sp.)
Sassari
Naples
Sa
Huelva
Córdoba
Sardinia
(It.)
Faro
Seville
Palma
Mallorca
Granada
Murcia
Mediterranean
Cadiz
Málaga
Cartagena
Cagliari
Almeria
Gibraltar(U.K.)
Tangier
Ceuta(Sp.)
Palermo
Messi
Tétouan
Algiers
Rabat
Melilla(Sp.)
Oran
Blida
Bejaia
Skikda
'Annaba
Sicily
Casablanca
Fès
Sidi Bel Abbès
Constantine
Tunis
Meknès
Oujda
MOROCCO
Mountains
ALGERIA
TUNISIA
Valletta
MALTA
Atlas
10°W
0°
10°E
Sfax

30°E
40°E
70°N
50°E
60°E
70°E
Vadsø
Murmansk
Kola Peninsula
Ural Mountains
60°N
White Sea
Arkhangel'sk
Syktyvkar
Oulu
N. Dvina
Kotlas
Yekaterinburg
Perm
FINLAND
Kuopio
Petrozavodsk
L. Onega
Sukhona
Chelyabinsk
Mikkeli
Kirov
Izevsk
Pori
Tampere
Lake Ladoga
Vologda
RUSSIA
Naberezhnyye Chelny
Ufa
Turku
Helsinki
St. Petersburg
Cherepovets
Magnitogorsk
Gulf of Finland
Tallinn
Kostroma
Cheboksari
Kazan'
ESTONIA
Novgorod
Yaroslavl'
Nizhniy Novgorod
Volga
Tartu
Pskov
Saransk
Ul'yanovsk
Orenburg
Samara
Tver'
Riga
Velikiye-Luki
Moscow
Ryazan'
Penza
50°N
Liepaja
LATVIA
Volga Heights
Ural'sk
Daugavpils
Smolensk
Tula
Saratov
Ural
Klaipėda
Vitsyebsk
LITHUANIA
Kaunas
Vilnius
Tambov
KAZAKHSTAN
RUSSIA
Kaliningrad
Minsk
Mahilyow
Bryansk
Orel
BELARUS
Olsztyn
Grodno
Kursk
Voronezh
Białystok
Bobruysk
Atyrau
Baranovich
Homyel'
Caspian Lowlands
Volgograd
Brest
Pinsk
Mazyr
Don
Chernihiv
Vistula
Volga
Łodz
Radom
Kharkiv
Kiev
Luhansk
Lublin
Rivne
Poltava
Astrakhan
Zhytomyr
UKRAINE
Dniprodzerzhinsk
Częstochawa
Katowice
Rzeszów
Cherkasy
Dniepropetrovsk
Donetsk
Elista
L'viv
Dnieper
Kraków
Vinnytsia
Kirovograd
Zaporozhye
Rostov
Khmel'nitskiy
Kryvyi Rih
Mariupol
Caspian Sea
Carpathians
Bel'tsy
Melitopol'
Stavropol'
Kosice
MOLDOVA
Mykolaiv
Grozny
Miskolc
Chişinău
Sea of Azov
Tiraspol
Kherson
Krasnodar
Maykop
Vladikavkaz
Makhachkala
Budapest
Debrecen
Suceava
Iaşi
Odesa
Elbrus 5642
Oradea
Kerch
Bacau
Caucasus Mountains
Szeged
Cluj-Napoca
Braşov
Simferopol'
Novorossiysk
GEORGIA
AZERBAIJAN
Baku
Timişoara
Sevastopol'
Tbilisi
40°N
Galaţi
Black Sea
Novi Sad
ROMANIA
Ploieşti
Batumi
ARMENIA
Belgrade
Constanţa
Yerevan
Bucharest
SERBIA
Craiova
Ruse
AZER.
Trabzon
&
Danube
Samsun
Niš
Pleven
Varna
Tabriz
MONTENEGRO
BULGARIA
Burgas
Erzurum
Van
Priština
Sofia
Zonguldak
L. Van
Stara Zagora
Sivas
L. Urmia
IRAN
Skopje
Plovdiv
Edirne
Istanbul
F.Y.R. MACEDONIA
Kocaeli
Ankara
Malatya
Diyarbakir
ALBANIA
Bitola
Kirikkale
TURKEY
Al-Mawşil
Arbil
Thessaloníki
Bursa
Eskisehir
Kayseri
Kahramanmaraş
Canakkale
Kirkūk
Balikesir
Gaziantep
Aegean Sea
Tigris
Manisa
Konya
Adana
Osmaniye
Corfu
Lárissa
Izmir
Denizli
Isparta
Halab
Raqqah
Euphrates
GREECE
Aydin
İçel
SYRIA
Al-Kazimiyah
Baghdād
Patras
Piraeus
Athens
Antalya
Al-Lādhiqīyah
IRAQ
Hamah
Hims
Kalamata
Nicosia
Tripoli
Rhodes
CYPRUS
Beirut
Damascus
Iráklion
LEBANON
Syrian Desert
Sea
30°N
Crete
20°E
30°E
40°E
Ammān
JORDAN

ATLANTIC OCEAN
Mediterranean Sea
Red Sea
Gulf of Aden
Gulf of Guinea
Caspian Sea
The Gulf
Sahara Desert
Libyan Desert
Nubian Desert
Eastern Desert
Rub' al Khali
Nafud
Hijaz
Asir
Atlas Mts.
Saharan Atlas
Great Western Erg
Great Eastern Erg
Tanezrouft
Ahaggar
Tibesti
Aïr
Soda Mts.
Marra Mts.
Massif Ennedi
Bodele Depression
Qattara Depression
Libyan Plateau
Ethiopian Highlands
East Rift Valley
Ogaden
Sudd
El Djouf
PORTUGAL
SPAIN
ITALY
MALTA
ALBANIA
F.Y.R. MAC
GREECE
BULGARIA
TURKEY
CYPRUS
SYRIA
LEBANON
ISRAEL
GAZA
JORDAN
IRAQ
IRAN
GEORGIA
ARMENIA
AZERBAIJAN
TURKMENISTAN
KUWAIT
BAHRAIN
QATAR
UNITED ARAB EMIRATES
OMAN
SAUDI ARABIA
YEMEN
MOROCCO
WESTERN SAHARA
ALGERIA
TUNISIA
LIBYA
EGYPT
MAURITANIA
MALI
NIGER
CHAD
SUDAN
ERITREA
DJIBOUTI
ETHIOPIA
SOMALIA
KENYA
UGANDA
SENEGAL
THE GAMBIA
GUINEA-BISSAU
GUINEA
SIERRA LEONE
LIBERIA
CÔTE D'IVOIRE
BURKINA FASO
GHANA
TOGO
BENIN
NIGERIA
CAMEROON
CENTRAL AFRICAN REPUBLIC
EQUATORIAL GUINEA
Lisbon
Oporto
Madrid
Zaragoza
Barcelona
Valencia
Seville
Malaga
Gibraltar(U.K.)
Rome
Naples
Palermo
Tirana
Sofia
Thessaloníki
Athens
Istanbul
Bursa
Izmir
Ankara
Konya
Kayseri
Samsun
Antalya
Adana
Diyarbakir
Urfa
Yerevan
Tabriz
Halab
Hims
Damascus
Nicosia
Beirut
Tel Aviv
Jerusalem
Ammān
Al-Mawsil
Arbil
Baghdad
Bakhtaran (Kermanshah)
Tehrān
Qom
Rasht
Mashhad
Ashgabat
Esfahan
Ahvaz
Abadan
Shiraz
Kuwait
Riyadh
Doha
Al-Madina
Jiddah
Makkah
Sana'a'
Aden
Djibouti
Berbera
Mogadishu
Asmara
Gonder
Ras Dashen 4620
Addis Ababa
Tangier
Tétouan
Rabat
Casablanca
Fès
Meknès
Oujda
Marrakesh
Agadir
Jebel Toubkal 4165
Oran
Sidi-Bel-Abbès
Algiers
Constantine
Tunis
Sfax
G. of Gabès
Tripoli
Gulf of Sirte
Benghazi
Al Bayda
Tobruk
Alexandria
El Giza
Cairo
El Faiyum
Asyut
Luxor
Aswan
Aswan Dam
L. Nasser
Wadi Halfa
Port Said
Suez
Suez Canal
Sinai
G. of Suez
Dakhla Oasis
Kufra Oases
Sabha Oases
Edjeleh
Mt. Tahat 2918
Tamanrasset
Emi Koussi 3415
Canary Islands (Sp.)
Madeira (Portugal)
Tenerife
Gran Canaria
Las Palmas
Lanzarote
Fuerteventura
El-Aaiún
C. Boujdour
Dakhla
Nouadhibou
Nouakchott
Tombouctou
Agadez
Niamey
Bamako
Ouagadougou
Dakar
Banjul
Bissau
Conakry
Freetown
Monrovia
Yamoussoukro
Bouaké
Abidjan
Sekondi Takoradi
Accra
Kumasi
Tamale
Lomé
Cotonou
Porto Novo
Ibadan
Ogbomosho
Lagos
Benin City
Onitsha
Enugu
Port Harcourt
Abuja
Kaduna
Kano
Sokoto
Maiduguri
N'Djamena
Abéché
Sarh
Garoua
Douala
Yaoundé
Mt. Cameroun 4100
Malabo
Bioko
Bangui
Berberati
Bangassou
Khartoum
Umm Durmān
Atbara
Port Sudan
Al-Ubayyid
Sennar
Malakal
Wau
Juba
Kampala
Isiro
Margherita Peak 5110
Libreville
São Tomé
Príncipe
Bight of Benin
C. Palmas
Cape Caseyr
Nile
Blue Nile
White Nile
Niger
Benue
Senegal
Chari
Sobat
Atbara
Bahr el Ghazal
Euphrates
Tigris
Shebele
Jubba
Ubangui
Uele
Aruwimi
Congo
L. Chad
L. Volta
L. Tana
L. Turkana
L. Albert
L. Kyoga
Kainji Res.
Balearic Is. (Sp.)
Mallorca
Sardinia (Italy)
Corsica (Fr.)
Sicily
Crete
Tropic of Cancer
Equator
30°N
20°N
10°N
20°W
10°W
0°
10°E
20°E
30°E
40°E
50°E
60°E

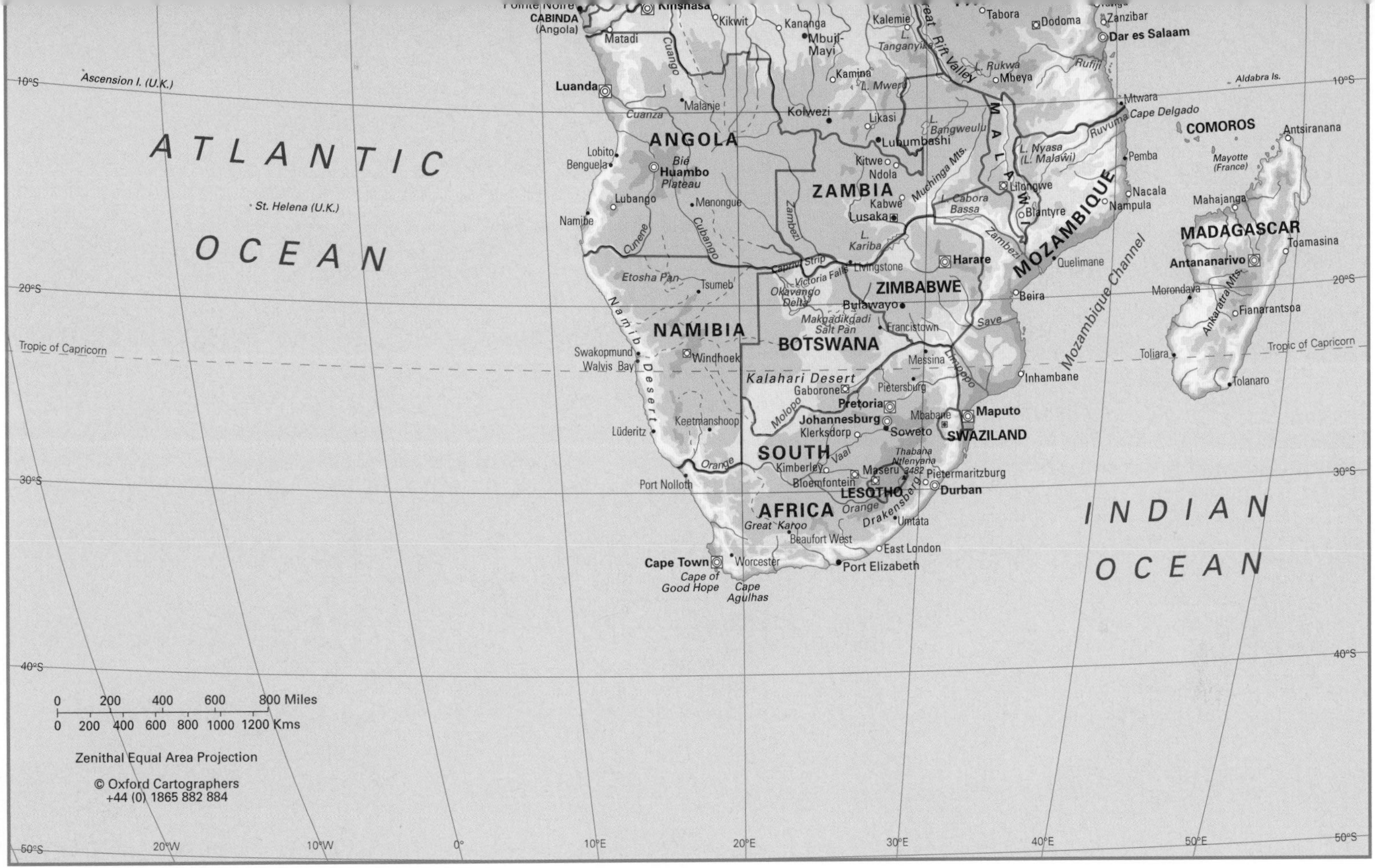
ATLANTIC OCEAN
INDIAN OCEAN
Ascension I. (U.K.)
St. Helena (U.K.)
CABINDA (Angola)
Kinshasa
Kikwit
Kananga
Mbuji-Mayi
Kalemie
L. Tanganyika
Great Rift Valley
Tabora
Dodoma
Zanzibar
Dar es Salaam
Rufiji
L. Rukwa
Mbeya
Aldabra Is.
Matadi
Cuango
Luanda
Malanje
Cuanza
Kamina
L. Mweru
Kolwezi
Likasi
Lubumbashi
L. Bangweulu
Mtwara
Cape Delgado
COMOROS
Antsiranana
ANGOLA
Lobito
Benguela
Bié
Huambo
Plateau
Lubango
Menongue
Namibe
Cunene
Cubango
ZAMBIA
Kitwe
Ndola
Kabwe
Lusaka
Muchinga Mts.
Zambezi
L. Kariba
MALAWI
L. Nyasa (L. Malawi)
Ruvuma
Pemba
Mayotte (France)
Lilongwe
Blantyre
L. Cabora Bassa
Nacala
Nampula
Mahajanga
MOZAMBIQUE
MADAGASCAR
Toamasina
Antananarivo
Quelimane
Harare
Livingstone
Caprivi Strip
Victoria Falls
Okavango Delta
ZIMBABWE
Bulawayo
Etosha Pan
Tsumeb
Beira
Mozambique Channel
Morondava
Ankaratra Mts.
Fianarantsoa
NAMIBIA
Namib Desert
Makgadikgadi Salt Pan
Francistown
Save
BOTSWANA
Tropic of Capricorn
Swakopmund
Walvis Bay
Windhoek
Messina
Limpopo
Inhambane
Toliara
Tolanaro
Kalahari Desert
Gaborone
Pietersburg
Molopo
Pretoria
Mbabane
Maputo
Johannesburg
Klerksdorp
Soweto
SWAZILAND
Lüderitz
Keetmanshoop
SOUTH AFRICA
Vaal
Kimberley
Thabana Ntlenyana 3482
Maseru
Pietermaritzburg
Orange
Bloemfontein
LESOTHO
Durban
Port Nolloth
Drakensberg
Umtata
Great Karoo
Beaufort West
East London
Cape Town
Worcester
Port Elizabeth
Cape of Good Hope
Cape Agulhas
10°S
20°S
30°S
40°S
50°S
20°W
10°W
0°
10°E
20°E
30°E
40°E
50°E
0 200 400 600 800 Miles
0 200 400 600 800 1000 1200 Kms
Zenithal Equal Area Projection
© Oxford Cartographers
+44 (0) 1865 882 884

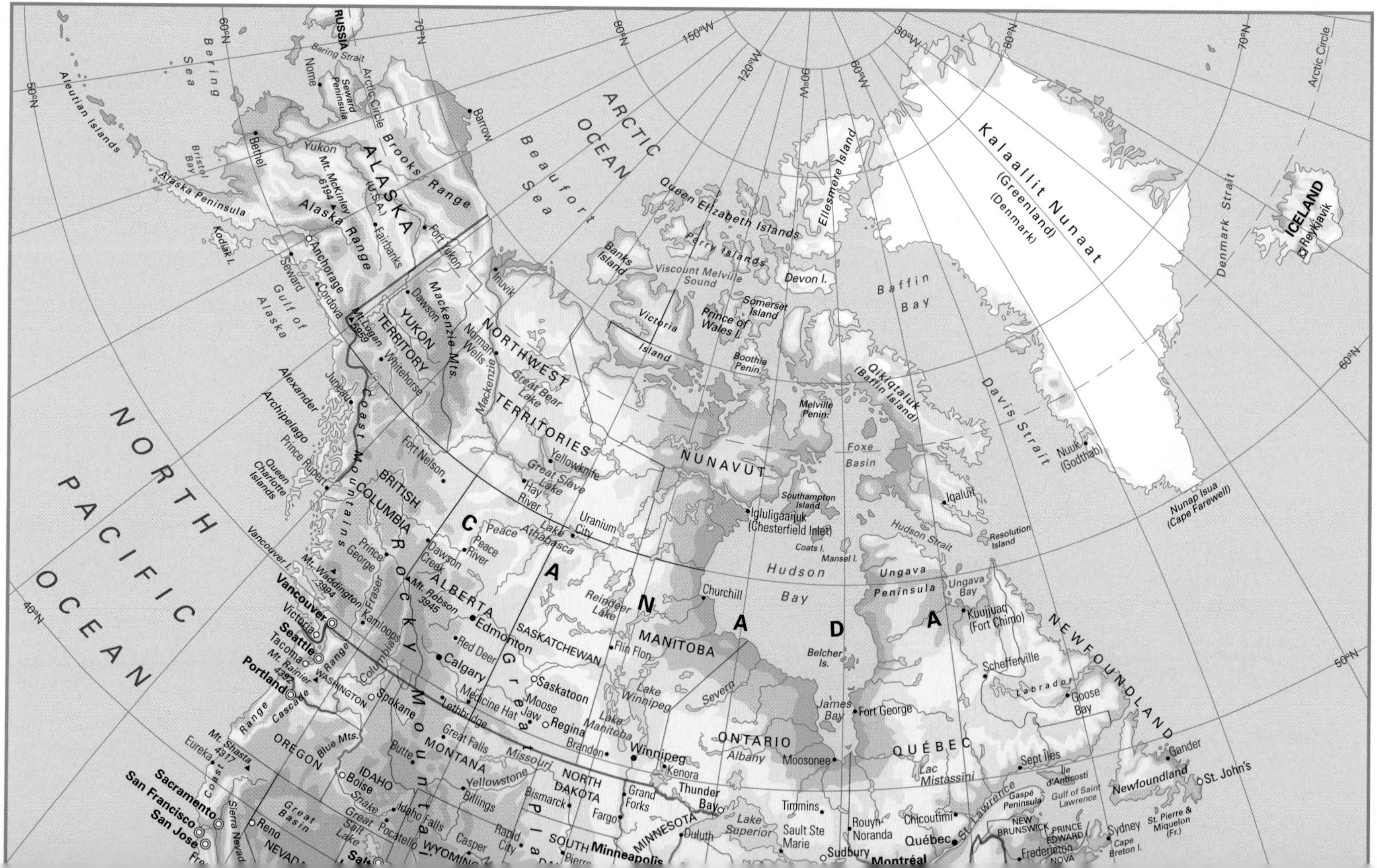
ARCTIC OCEAN
NORTH PACIFIC OCEAN
Kalaallit Nunaat
(Greenland)
(Denmark)
ICELAND
Reykjavik
Arctic Circle
Denmark Strait
Nunap Isua
(Cape Farewell)
Nuuk
(Godthåb)
Davis Strait
Baffin Bay
Qikiqtaluk
(Baffin Island)
Iqaluit
Resolution Island
Hudson Strait
Foxe Basin
Ellesmere Island
Devon I.
Queen Elizabeth Islands
Parry Islands
Viscount Melville Sound
Somerset Island
Prince of Wales I.
Boothia Penin.
Melville Penin.
Southampton Island
Coats I.
Mansel I.
Igluligaarjuk
(Chesterfield Inlet)
Banks Island
Victoria Island
Beaufort Sea
NUNAVUT
NORTHWEST TERRITORIES
Inuvik
Norman Wells
Mackenzie
Great Bear Lake
Yellowknife
Great Slave Lake
Hay River
Uranium City
Lake Athabasca
Peace
Peace River
Dawson Creek
Fort Nelson
Mackenzie Mts.
YUKON TERRITORY
Dawson
Whitehorse
Mt. Logan
5959
Coast Mountains
BRITISH COLUMBIA
Prince George
Fraser
Kamloops
Mt. Waddington
3994
Vancouver I.
Vancouver
Victoria
Prince Rupert
Queen Charlotte Islands
Alexander Archipelago
Juneau
Gulf of Alaska
ALASKA
(U.S.A.)
Barrow
Brooks Range
Fort Yukon
Fairbanks
Alaska Range
Mt. McKinley
6194
Anchorage
Cordova
Seward
Yukon
Seward Peninsula
Nome
Bering Strait
RUSSIA
Bethel
Bristol Bay
Alaska Peninsula
Kodiak I.
Bering Sea
Aleutian Islands
C A N A D A
Hudson Bay
Churchill
Ungava Peninsula
Ungava Bay
Kuujjuaq
(Fort Chimo)
Schefferville
Labrador
Goose Bay
NEWFOUNDLAND
Gander
Newfoundland
St. John's
St. Pierre & Miquelon
(Fr.)
Sydney
Cape Breton I.
Gulf of Saint Lawrence
Île d'Anticosti
Sept Îles
Gaspé Peninsula
NEW BRUNSWICK
PRINCE EDWARD I.
Fredericton
NOVA
St. Lawrence
QUÉBEC
Lac Mistassini
Chicoutimi
Québec
Montréal
Fort George
James Bay
Belcher Is.
Rouyn-Noranda
Sudbury
Moosonee
Timmins
Sault Ste Marie
ONTARIO
Albany
Severn
Lake Superior
Thunder Bay
Duluth
Kenora
MANITOBA
Lake Winnipeg
Lake Manitoba
Winnipeg
Flin Flon
Reindeer Lake
Brandon
SASKATCHEWAN
Saskatoon
Regina
Moose Jaw
Medicine Hat
ALBERTA
Edmonton
Red Deer
Calgary
Lethbridge
Mt. Robson
3945
Rocky Mountains
Great Plains
Columbia
Spokane
WASHINGTON
Seattle
Tacoma
Mt. Rainier
4392
Cascade Range
Portland
OREGON
Blue Mts.
IDAHO
Boise
Snake
Idaho Falls
Pocatello
Great Salt Lake
MONTANA
Great Falls
Butte
Missouri
Yellowstone
Billings
WYOMING
Casper
Rapid City
NORTH DAKOTA
Bismarck
Grand Forks
Fargo
MINNESOTA
Minneapolis
SOUTH
Great Basin
Reno
Sierra Nevada
Mt. Shasta
4317
Eureka
Coast Ranges
Sacramento
San Francisco
San Jose
30°W
60°W
90°W
120°W
150°W
80°N
70°N
60°N
50°N
40°N

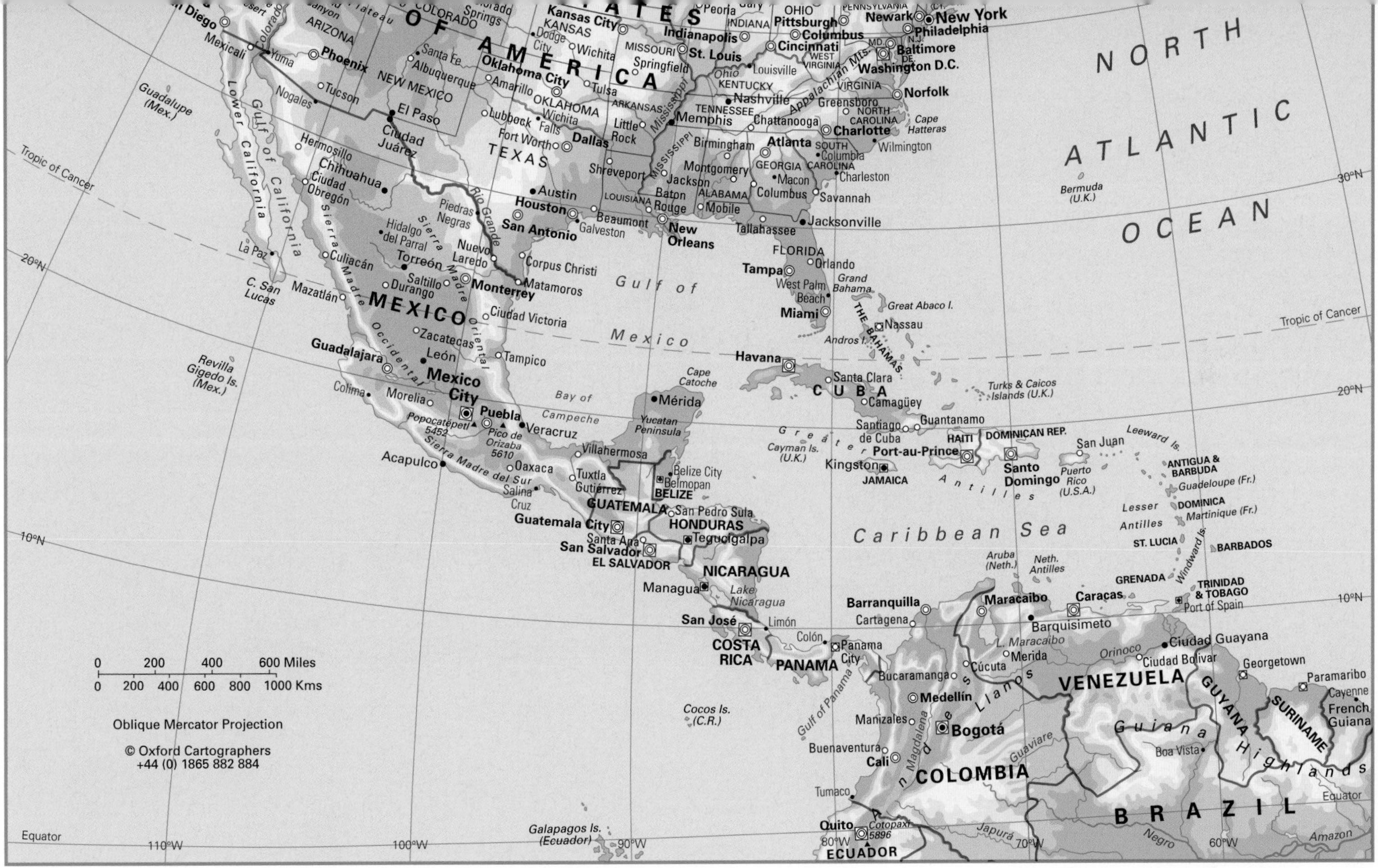
NORTH ATLANTIC OCEAN
UNITED STATES OF AMERICA
MEXICO
Gulf of Mexico
Caribbean Sea
CUBA
THE BAHAMAS
JAMAICA
HAITI
DOMINICAN REP.
BELIZE
GUATEMALA
HONDURAS
EL SALVADOR
NICARAGUA
COSTA RICA
PANAMA
COLOMBIA
VENEZUELA
GUYANA
SURINAME
French Guiana
BRAZIL
ECUADOR
New York
Philadelphia
Baltimore
Washington D.C.
Norfolk
Charlotte
Atlanta
Jacksonville
Tampa
Miami
Houston
San Antonio
Dallas
New Orleans
Memphis
Nashville
St. Louis
Indianapolis
Kansas City
Oklahoma City
Phoenix
El Paso
Havana
Nassau
Port-au-Prince
Santo Domingo
Kingston
San Juan
Mexico City
Guadalajara
Monterrey
Puebla
Veracruz
Acapulco
Mérida
Guatemala City
San Salvador
Tegucigalpa
Managua
San José
Panama City
Barranquilla
Maracaibo
Caracas
Bogotá
Medellín
Cali
Quito
Georgetown
Paramaribo
Cayenne
Tropic of Cancer
Equator
30°N
20°N
10°N
110°W
100°W
90°W
80°W
70°W
60°W
0 200 400 600 Miles
0 200 400 600 800 1000 Kms
Oblique Mercator Projection
© Oxford Cartographers
+44 (0) 1865 882 884

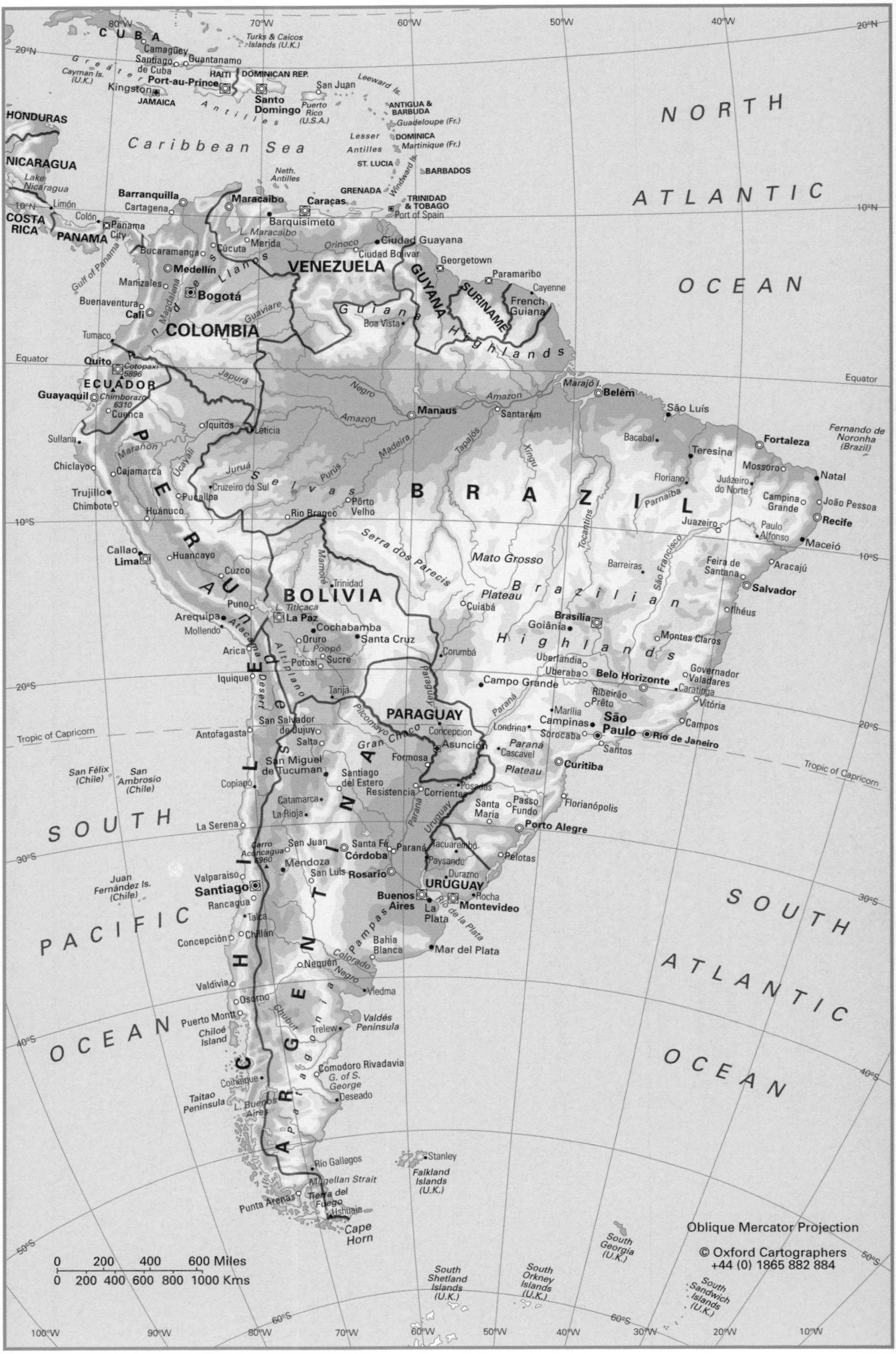
CUBA
Camagüey
Santiago de Cuba
Guantanamo
Turks & Caicos Islands (U.K.)
Cayman Is. (U.K.)
Greater Antilles
HAITI
DOMINICAN REP.
Port-au-Prince
Kingston
JAMAICA
Santo Domingo
San Juan
Puerto Rico (U.S.A.)
Leeward Is.
ANTIGUA & BARBUDA
Guadeloupe (Fr.)
DOMINICA
Martinique (Fr.)
Lesser Antilles
ST. LUCIA
Windward Is.
BARBADOS
GRENADA
TRINIDAD & TOBAGO
Port of Spain
HONDURAS
NICARAGUA
Lake Nicaragua
Caribbean Sea
Neth. Antilles
COSTA RICA
Limón
Colón
PANAMA
Panama City
Gulf of Panama
Barranquilla
Cartagena
Maracaibo
L. Maracaibo
Caracas
Barquisimeto
Cúcuta
Merida
Bucaramanga
Medellín
Manizales
Bogotá
Buenaventura
Cali
Llanos
Magdalena
Orinoco
Ciudad Guayana
Ciudad Bolivar
VENEZUELA
GUYANA
Georgetown
SURINAME
Paramaribo
Cayenne
French Guiana
Guiana Highlands
Boa Vista
Guaviare
COLOMBIA
Tumaco
Equator
Quito
Cotopaxi 5896
ECUADOR
Guayaquil
Chimborazo 6310
Cuenca
Japurá
Negro
Amazon
Manaus
Santarém
Marajó I.
Belém
São Luís
Iquitos
Leticia
Sullana
Marañón
Ucayali
Chiclayo
Cajamarca
Trujillo
Chimbote
Huánuco
Pucallpa
Cruzeiro do Sul
Juruá
Purus
Selvas
Madeira
Tapajós
Xingu
Porto Velho
Rio Branco
BRAZIL
Bacabal
Teresina
Fortaleza
Fernando de Noronha (Brazil)
Mossoró
Natal
Floriano
Parnaíba
Juázeiro do Norte
Campina Grande
João Pessoa
Juazeiro
Recife
Paulo Alfonso
Maceió
Aracajú
Feira de Santana
Salvador
Ilhéus
Tocantins
Barreiras
São Francisco
Serra dos Parecis
Mato Grosso Plateau
Brazilian Highlands
Callao
Lima
Huancayo
Cuzco
PERU
Mamoré
Trinidad
BOLIVIA
Puno
L. Titicaca
La Paz
Arequipa
Mollendo
Cochabamba
Oruro
L. Poopó
Santa Cruz
Potosí
Sucre
Altiplano
Arica
Atacama Desert
Iquique
Cuiabá
Corumbá
Brasília
Goiânia
Montes Claros
Uberlândia
Uberaba
Belo Horizonte
Governador Valadares
Caratinga
Vitória
Campo Grande
Paraguay
Paraná
Ribeirão Prêto
Marília
Campinas
São Paulo
Londrina
Sorocaba
Santos
Rio de Janeiro
Campos
Tarija
PARAGUAY
Pilcomayo
Gran Chaco
Concepcion
Asunción
Formosa
Paraná Plateau
Cascavel
Curitiba
Tropic of Capricorn
Antofagasta
San Salvador de Jujuy
Salta
San Miguel de Tucuman
Santiago del Estero
Resistencia
Corrientes
Posadas
Uruguay
Santa Maria
Passo Fundo
Florianópolis
Porto Alegre
San Félix (Chile)
San Ambrosio (Chile)
Copiapó
Catamarca
La Rioja
La Serena
SOUTH PACIFIC OCEAN
Cerro Aconcagua 6960
San Juan
Mendoza
San Luis
Santa Fé
Córdoba
Paraná
Rosario
Tacuarembó
Paysandu
Durazno
URUGUAY
Pelotas
Juan Fernández Is. (Chile)
Valparaiso
Santiago
Rancagua
Talca
Buenos Aires
La Plata
Rio de la Plata
Montevideo
Rocha
Concepción
Chillán
Pampas
Bahia Blanca
Mar del Plata
CHILE
ARGENTINA
Colorado
Neuquén
Negro
Valdivia
Osorno
Viedma
Puerto Montt
Chiloé Island
Chubut
Valdés Peninsula
Trelew
Patagonia
Comodoro Rivadavia
G. of S. George
Coihaique
Taitao Peninsula
Buenos Aires
Deseado
SOUTH ATLANTIC OCEAN
NORTH ATLANTIC OCEAN
Río Gallegos
Stanley
Falkland Islands (U.K.)
Magellan Strait
Punta Arenas
Tierra del Fuego
Ushuaia
Cape Horn
South Georgia (U.K.)
South Shetland Islands (U.K.)
South Orkney Islands (U.K.)
South Sandwich Islands (U.K.)
Oblique Mercator Projection
© Oxford Cartographers
+44 (0) 1865 882 884
0 200 400 600 Miles
0 200 400 600 800 1000 Kms
100°W
90°W
80°W
70°W
60°W
50°W
40°W
30°W
20°W
10°W
20°N
10°N
10°S
20°S
30°S
40°S
50°S
60°S

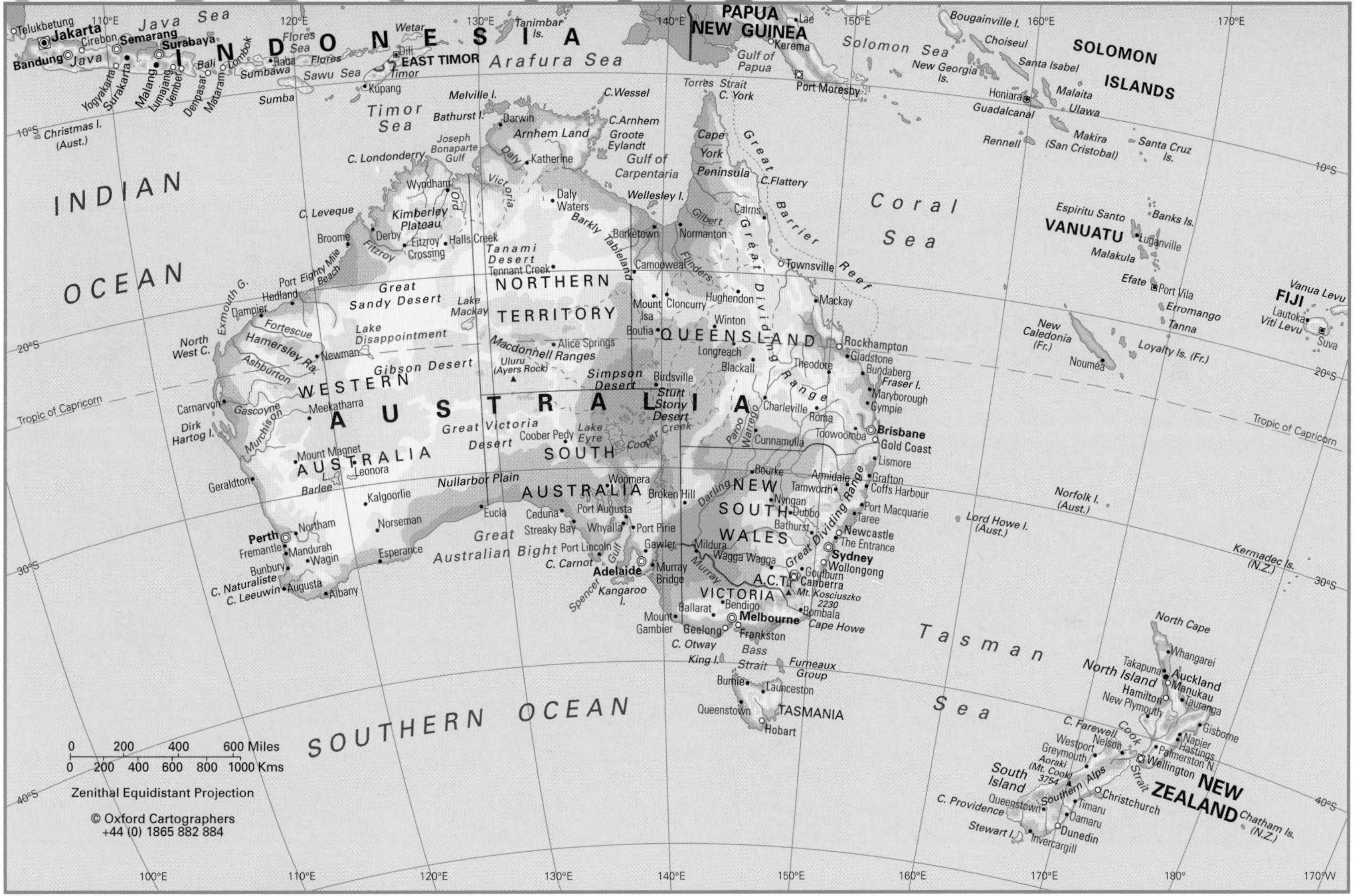
INDONESIA
PAPUA NEW GUINEA
SOLOMON ISLANDS
VANUATU
FIJI
EAST TIMOR
AUSTRALIA
WESTERN AUSTRALIA
NORTHERN TERRITORY
QUEENSLAND
SOUTH AUSTRALIA
NEW SOUTH WALES
VICTORIA
A.C.T.
TASMANIA
NEW ZEALAND
North Island
South Island
INDIAN OCEAN
SOUTHERN OCEAN
Java Sea
Arafura Sea
Timor Sea
Sawu Sea
Flores Sea
Solomon Sea
Coral Sea
Tasman Sea
Gulf of Papua
Gulf of Carpentaria
Joseph Bonaparte Gulf
Great Australian Bight
Spencer Gulf
Exmouth G.
Torres Strait
Bass Strait
Cook Strait
Great Barrier Reef
Great Dividing Range
Southern Alps
Tropic of Capricorn
Jakarta
Bandung
Telukbetung
Cirebon
Semarang
Surabaya
Yogyakarta
Surakarta
Malang
Lumajang
Jember
Denpasar
Mataram
Bali
Lombok
Sumbawa
Raba
Flores
Sumba
Dili
Timor
Kupang
Wetar
Tanimbar Is.
Christmas I. (Aust.)
Lae
Kerema
Port Moresby
Bougainville I.
Choiseul
Santa Isabel
New Georgia Is.
Honiara
Guadalcanal
Malaita
Ulawa
Makira (San Cristobal)
Rennell
Santa Cruz Is.
Espiritu Santo
Banks Is.
Luganville
Malakula
Efate
Port Vila
Erromango
Tanna
New Caledonia (Fr.)
Nouméa
Loyalty Is. (Fr.)
Vanua Levu
Lautoka
Viti Levu
Suva
Melville I.
Bathurst I.
Darwin
Arnhem Land
C.Wessel
C.Arnhem
Groote Eylandt
Daly
Katherine
C. Londonderry
Wyndham
Ord
Victoria
Daly Waters
Kimberley Plateau
C. Leveque
Derby
Broome
Fitzroy
Fitzroy Crossing
Halls Creek
Eighty Mile Beach
Port Hedland
Dampier
Fortescue
Hamersley Ra.
Ashburton
Newman
North West C.
Carnarvon
Gascoyne
Meekatharra
Murchison
Dirk Hartog I.
Mount Magnet
Leonora
L. Barlee
Geraldton
Kalgoorlie
Norseman
Esperance
Perth
Fremantle
Mandurah
Northam
Wagin
Bunbury
C. Naturaliste
C. Leeuwin
Augusta
Albany
Great Sandy Desert
Lake Disappointment
Gibson Desert
Lake Mackay
Tanami Desert
Tennant Creek
Barkly Tableland
Alice Springs
Macdonnell Ranges
Uluru (Ayers Rock)
Simpson Desert
Great Victoria Desert
Nullarbor Plain
Eucla
Coober Pedy
Lake Eyre
Cooper Creek
Sturt Stony Desert
Birdsville
Woomera
Port Augusta
Ceduna
Streaky Bay
Whyalla
Port Pirie
Port Lincoln
C. Carnot
Gawler
Adelaide
Murray Bridge
Kangaroo I.
Mount Gambier
Broken Hill
Wellesley I.
Burketown
Camooweal
Gilbert
Normanton
Flinders
Mount Isa
Cloncurry
Hughenden
Winton
Boulia
Longreach
Blackall
Cape York Peninsula
C. York
C.Flattery
Cairns
Townsville
Mackay
Rockhampton
Gladstone
Theodore
Bundaberg
Fraser I.
Maryborough
Gympie
Charleville
Roma
Toowoomba
Brisbane
Gold Coast
Paroo
Warrego
Cunnamulla
Bourke
Darling
Lismore
Grafton
Armidale
Coffs Harbour
Tamworth
Nyngan
Dubbo
Port Macquarie
Taree
Bathurst
Newcastle
The Entrance
Sydney
Wollongong
Mildura
Wagga Wagga
Murray
Goulburn
Canberra
Mt. Kosciuszko 2230
Bombala
Cape Howe
Ballarat
Bendigo
Melbourne
Geelong
Frankston
C. Otway
King I.
Furneaux Group
Burnie
Launceston
Queenstown
Hobart
Norfolk I. (Aust.)
Lord Howe I. (Aust.)
Kermadec Is. (N.Z.)
North Cape
Whangarei
Takapuna
Auckland
Manukau
Tauranga
Hamilton
New Plymouth
Gisborne
Napier
Hastings
Palmerston N.
Wellington
C. Farewell
Nelson
Westport
Greymouth
Aoraki (Mt. Cook) 3754
Christchurch
Timaru
Oamaru
Dunedin
Queenstown
C. Providence
Stewart I.
Invercargill
Chatham Is. (N.Z.)
10°S
20°S
30°S
40°S
100°E
110°E
120°E
130°E
140°E
150°E
160°E
170°E
180°
170°W
0 200 400 600 Miles
0 200 400 600 800 1000 Kms
Zenithal Equidistant Projection
© Oxford Cartographers
+44 (0) 1865 882 884

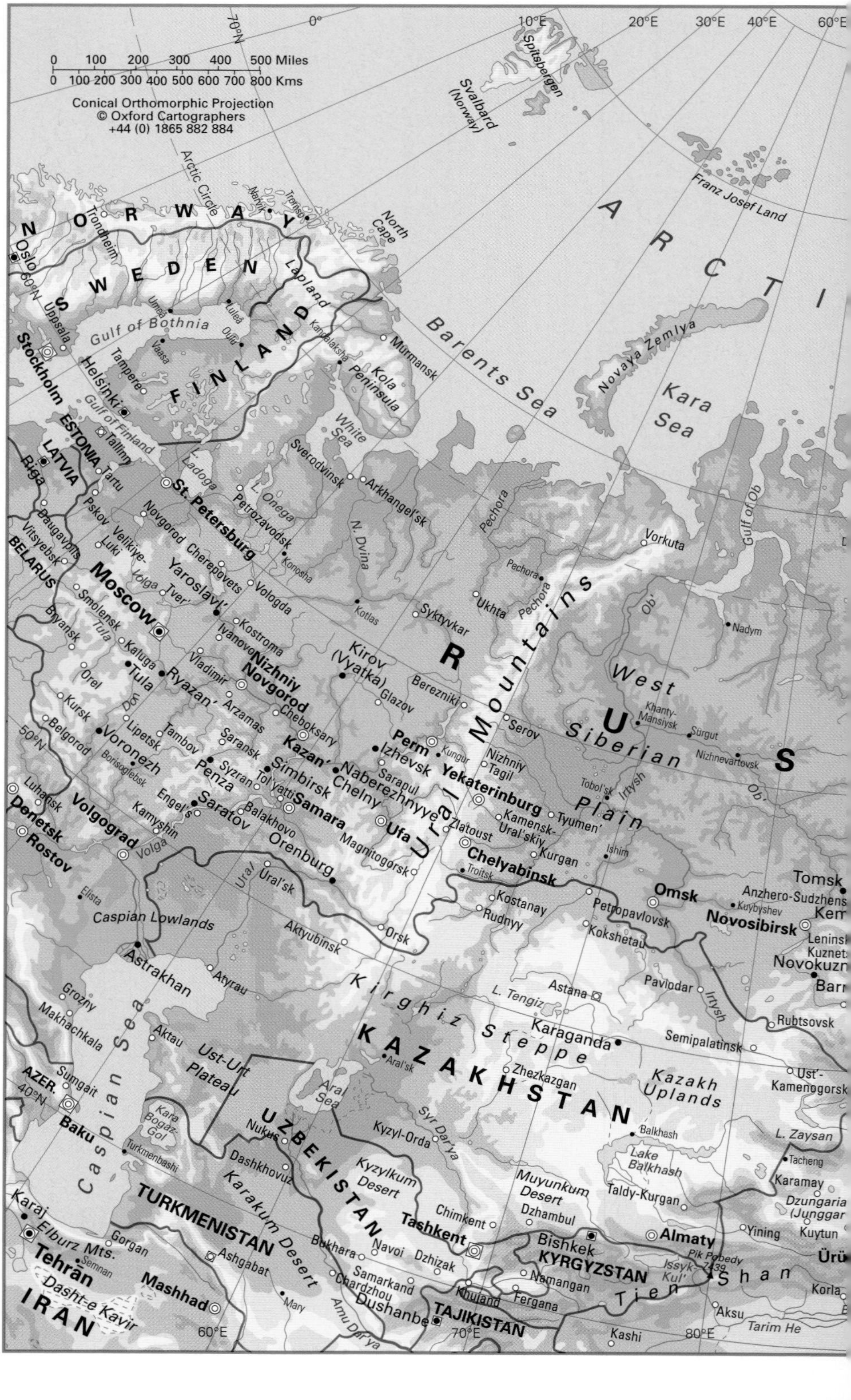
0 100 200 300 400 500 Miles
0 100 200 300 400 500 600 700 800 Kms
Conical Orthomorphic Projection
© Oxford Cartographers
+44 (0) 1865 882 884
70°N
0°
10°E
20°E
30°E
40°E
60°E
Spitsbergen
Svalbard (Norway)
Franz Josef Land
A R C T I
Arctic Circle
Narvik
Tromsø
North Cape
N O R W A Y
Trondheim
Oslo
60°N
S W E D E N
Lapland
Umeå
Luleå
Oulu
Uppsala
Gulf of Bothnia
Stockholm
Vaasa
Kandalaksha
Murmansk
Barents Sea
Novaya Zemlya
Kara Sea
Tampere
Helsinki
F I N L A N D
Kola Peninsula
Gulf of Finland
ESTONIA
Tallinn
White Sea
LATVIA
Riga
Tartu
Ladoga
St. Petersburg
Sverodvinsk
Arkhangel'sk
L. Onega
Petrozavodsk
Pskov
Daugavpils
Vitsyebsk
BELARUS
Velikiye-Luki
Novgorod
Cherepovets
Konosha
N. Dvina
Pechora
Vorkuta
Gulf of Ob
Moscow
Yaroslavl'
Volga
Tver'
Vologda
Kotlas
Syktyvkar
Ukhta
Pechora
Ob'
Nadym
Smolensk
Bryansk
Tula
Kostroma
Ivanovo
Kirov (Vyatka)
Ural Mountains
R
Kaluga
Tula
Vladimir
Nizhniy Novgorod
Glazov
Berezniki
West
Orel
Kursk
Ryazan'
Arzamas
Cheboksary
Serov
Khanty-Mansiysk
Surgut
U
Don
Lipetsk
Saransk
Perm
Kungur
Nizhniy Tagil
Siberian
Nizhnevartovsk
S
50°N
Belgorod
Voronezh
Tambov
Kazan'
Izhevsk
Borisoglebsk
Penza
Syzran
Simbirsk
Tol'yatti
Naberezhnyye Chelny
Sarapul
Yekaterinburg
Tobol'sk
Irtysh
Ob
Luhansk
Donetsk
Volgograd
Engel's
Saratov
Samara
Ufa
Zlatoust
Kamensk-Ural'skiy
Tyumen'
Plain
Rostov
Kamyshin
Balakhovo
Orenburg
Magnitogorsk
Chelyabinsk
Kurgan
Ishim
Volga
Ural
Ural'sk
Troitsk
Tomsk
Elista
Kostanay
Rudnyy
Petropavlovsk
Omsk
Anzhero-Sudzhensk
Kuybyshev
Caspian Lowlands
Novosibirsk
Kem
Aktyubinsk
Orsk
Kokshetau
Leninsk-Kuznetsk
Novokuzn
Astrakhan
Atyrau
Kirghiz Steppe
L. Tengiz
Astana
Pavlodar
Irtysh
Barn
Grozny
Makhachkala
Aktau
Karaganda
Rubtsovsk
Semipalatinsk
K A Z A K H S T A N
Caspian Sea
Ust-Urt Plateau
Aral'sk
Zhezkazgan
Kazakh Uplands
Ust'-Kamenogorsk
AZER.
40°N
Sumgait
Aral Sea
Baku
Kara Bogaz-Gol
Nukus
U Z B E K I S T A N
Kyzyl-Orda
Syr Darya
Balkhash
L. Zaysan
Lake Balkhash
Tacheng
Turkmenbashi
Dashkhovuz
Kyzylkum Desert
Muyunkum Desert
Karamay
Karakum Desert
Taldy-Kurgan
Dzungaria (Junggar
TURKMENISTAN
Chimkent
Dzhambul
Karaj
Tashkent
Elburz Mts.
Gorgan
Almaty
Yining
Kuytun
Semnan
Ashgabat
Bukhara
Navoi
Dzhizak
Bishkek
Pik Pobedy 7439
Ürü
Tehrān
KYRGYZSTAN
Issyk-Kul'
Tien Shan
Samarkand
Namangan
Mashhad
Chardzhou
Khujand
Fergana
Korla
Dasht-e Kavir
Mary
Amu Dar'ya
Dushanbe
TAJIKISTAN
Aksu
Tarim He
IRAN
60°E
70°E
Kashi
80°E

120°E
140°E
150°E
160°E
170°E
180°
70°N
60°N
50°N
40°N
100°E
110°E
120°E
Wrangel I.
Pevek
Anadyr Range
Anadyr
Koryak Range
East Siberian Sea
New Siberia Is.
Lyakhov Is.
Severnaya Zemlya
O C E A N
Laptev Sea
Taymyr Pen.
L. Taymyr
Tiksi
Indigirka
Kolyma
Kolyma Mts.
Yana
Cherskogo Range
Olenek
Verkhoyansk Range
Magadan
Okhotsk
Sea of Okhotsk
Dzhugdzhur Range
Central Siberian Plateau
Lena
Vilyuy
Yakutsk
Aldan
Sakhalin
Tunguska
Olekminsk
Lensk
A
S
I
Neryungri
Stanovoy Mts.
Tynda
Skovorodino
Komsomol'sk na-Amure
Amur
Khabarovsk
Angara
Ust' Ilimsk
Ust'-Kut
Severobaikal'sk
Yablonovyy Mts.
Skovorodino
Belogorsk
Blagoveshchensk
Birobidzhan
Kansk
Tayshek
Bratsk
Achinsk
Krasnoyarsk
Tulun
Lake Baikal
Chita
Sretensk
Yichun
Hegang
Bei'an
Shuangyashan
Qitaihe
Jixi
Jiamusi
Mudanjiang
Sayan Mts.
Abakan
Usol'ye-Sibirskoye
Angarsk
Irkutsk
Ulan-Ude
Hailar
Da Hinggan Ling
Qiqihar
Daqing
Harbin
Ussuriysk
Manzhouli
Kyzyl
Hövsgöl Nuur
Darhan
Ulanhot
Baicheng
Jilin
Yanji
Vladivostok
Chongjin
Uvs Nuur
Ulaanbaatar
Ondorhaan
Changchun
Liaoyuan
Tongliao
Siping
Fushun
DEM. PEOPLE'S REP. OF KOREA
Hangayan Mts.
Hovd
Altay
Altai Range
MONGOLIA
Saynshand
INNER MONGOLIA
Chifeng
Shenyang
Fuxin
Jinzhou
Anshan
Pyongyang
Gobi Desert
Chengde
Korea Bay
Seoul
Inchon
Zhangjiakou
Beijing (Peking)
Tangshan
Tianjin
Dalian
REP. OF KOREA
Jining
Baotou
Hohhot
Datong
Bo Hai
Yantai
Weihai
Hami Depression
Linhe
Huang He (Yellow)
Baoding
Cangzhou
Shijiazhuang
Zibo
Weifang
Dezhou
Qingdao
CHINA
Wuhai
Taiyuan
Yuci
Jinan
Yellow Sea
Lop Nur
Shizuishan
Handan

25°E
30°E
35°E
40°E
45°E
50°E
55°E
60°E
45°N
40°N
35°N
30°N
25°N
20°N
15°N
10°N
5°N
Aktyubinsk
Odesa
UKRAINE
Mariupol
Kherson
Rostov
Volgograd
ROMANIA
Constanţa
Sea of Azov
Kerch
Simferopol'
Sevastopol
RUSSIA
Caspian Lowlands
Emba
KA
Dobrich
Varna
BULGARIA
Burgas
Sudak
Krasnodar
Armavir
Elista
Atyrau
Kir
Aral'sk
Black Sea
Novorossiysk
Tuapse
Stravropol'
Maykop
Astrakhan
Edirne
Bosporus
Bakirkoy
Istanbul
Sochi
Cherkessk
Caucasus Mts.
Aral Sea
Eregli
Zonguldak
Kocaeli
Sakarya
Karabuk
Sinop
Sukhumi
Elbrus 5642
Grozny
Vladikavkaz
Aktau
Ust-Urt Pateau
Caspian Sea
Bursa
Makhachkala
Samsun
Batumi
GEORGIA
Eskisehir
Ankara
Corum
Ordu
Trabzon
Tbilisi
Derbent
UZBEKIS
Kirikkale
Pontine Mountains
Nukus
Yozgat
Aydin
TURKEY
Usak
Sivas
Euphrates
ARMENIA
AZERBAIJAN
Kara-Bogaz-Gol
Dashkhovuz
Khodzheyli
Urgench
Denizli
Isparta
Konya
Kayseri
Erzurum
Mt. Ararat 5123
Yerevan
Sumgait
Baku
Elazig
AZER.
Antalya
Taurus Mts.
Adana
Osmaniye
Malatya
L. Van
Tatvan
Araks
Turkmenbashi
TURKMENISTAN
Kahramanmaras
Diyarbakir
Van
Khvoy
Nebitdag
Içel
Hatay
Gaziantep
Sanliurfa
Batman
Marand
Tabriz
Ardabil
Karakum Desert
Chardzho
35°N
Nicosia
CYPRUS
Halab
Al Qamishli
Orumiyeh
L. Urmia
Raqqah
Al-Mawsil
Maragheh
Mahabad
Rasht
Ashgabat
Limassol
Al-Lādhiqīyah
Arbil
Zanjan
Gonbad
Bojnurd
Mediterranean Sea
Hamah
Tripoli
LEBANON
SYRIA
Hims
Dayr az Zawr
As Sulaymaniyah
Kirkuk
Qazvin
Elburz Mts.
Damavand 5671
Gorgan
Mary
Beirut
Zahlé
Tigris
Sanandaj
Bakhtaran (Kermanshah)
Karaj
Tehran
Sabzevar
Emamrud
Mashhad
Neyshabur
Haifa
ISRAEL
Damascus
Hamadan
Semnan
Tel Aviv
Irbid
Al-Kazimiyah
Qom
Paropa
Jerusalem
Dumyat
GAZA
Zarqa
Ammān
Syrian Desert
Baghdād
Borujerd
Arak
Kashan
Dasht-e Kavir
Cairo
Port Said
Suez Canal
Ismailiya
Dead Sea
Karbala
Al Hillah
Ilam
Khorramabad
Hera
IRAQ
Zagros Mts.
Suez
JORDAN
An Najaf
Dezful
Esfahan
Birjand
EGYPT
Sinai
Elat
Al Amarah
Euphrates
AF
Aqaba
Ahvaz
Yazd
Farah
G. of Suez
Eastern Desert
An Nasiriyah
Nafud
Dasht-e Lut
IRAN
Tabuk
Basra
Abadan
Sharm el Sheikh
Zabol
Nile
Qena
Hurghada
KUWAIT
Jahra
Kuwait
Rafsanjan
Kerman
Helm
Shiraz
Borazjan
Bushehr
Ha'il
The Gulf
Sirjan
Zahedan
Al Wajh
Bam
Luxor
Nok K
Buraydah
Jahrom
Kom Ombo
SAUDI ARABIA
Hajiabad
Aswan
Hijaz
Najd
Ad Dammam
Az-Zahran
BAHRAIN
Al Manamah
Bandar 'Abbas
Lake Nasser
Red Sea
Yanbu
Al-Madīnah
Al-Hufūf
Al Khasab
Ras al Khaimah
Sharjah
OMAN
Riyadh
QATAR
Doha
Dubai
Tropic of Cancer
Makran
Halaib
Hasa
Gulf of Oman
Harad
Abu Dhabi
Chabahar
Gwadar
Al Ain
Sohar
Nubian Desert
UNITED ARAB EMIRATES
Jiddah
Makkah
Muscat
Ar Rustaq
At Taif
Sumail
SUDAN
Port Sudan
Nizwa
Ibra
Sur
Asir
Rub' al Khali
OMAN
Atbara
Abha
Masirah
ERITREA
Farasan Is.
Najran
Kassala
Agordat
Asmara
Jizan
Sa'dah
Dhufar
Ar
Dahlak Arch.
Massawa
Hajjar
Gedaref
Sana'a'
Salalah
Halaaniyat Is.
Hadhramaut
Ras Dashen 4620
Hodeida
Dhamar
YEMEN
Gonder
Ibb
Mukalla
L. Tana
Bahir Dar
Ta'izz
Assab
Aden
Gulf of Aden
Blue Nile
DJIBOUTI
Socotra (Yemen)
ETHIOPIA
Dikhil
Djibouti
Addis Ababa
Boosaaso
Cape Caseyr
Berbera
Dire Dawa
Nazret
Harer
Burao
Jima
Ethiopian Highlands
Hargeisa
SOMALIA
Garoowe
Awasa
Ogaden
Shebele
KENYA
Jubba
INDI

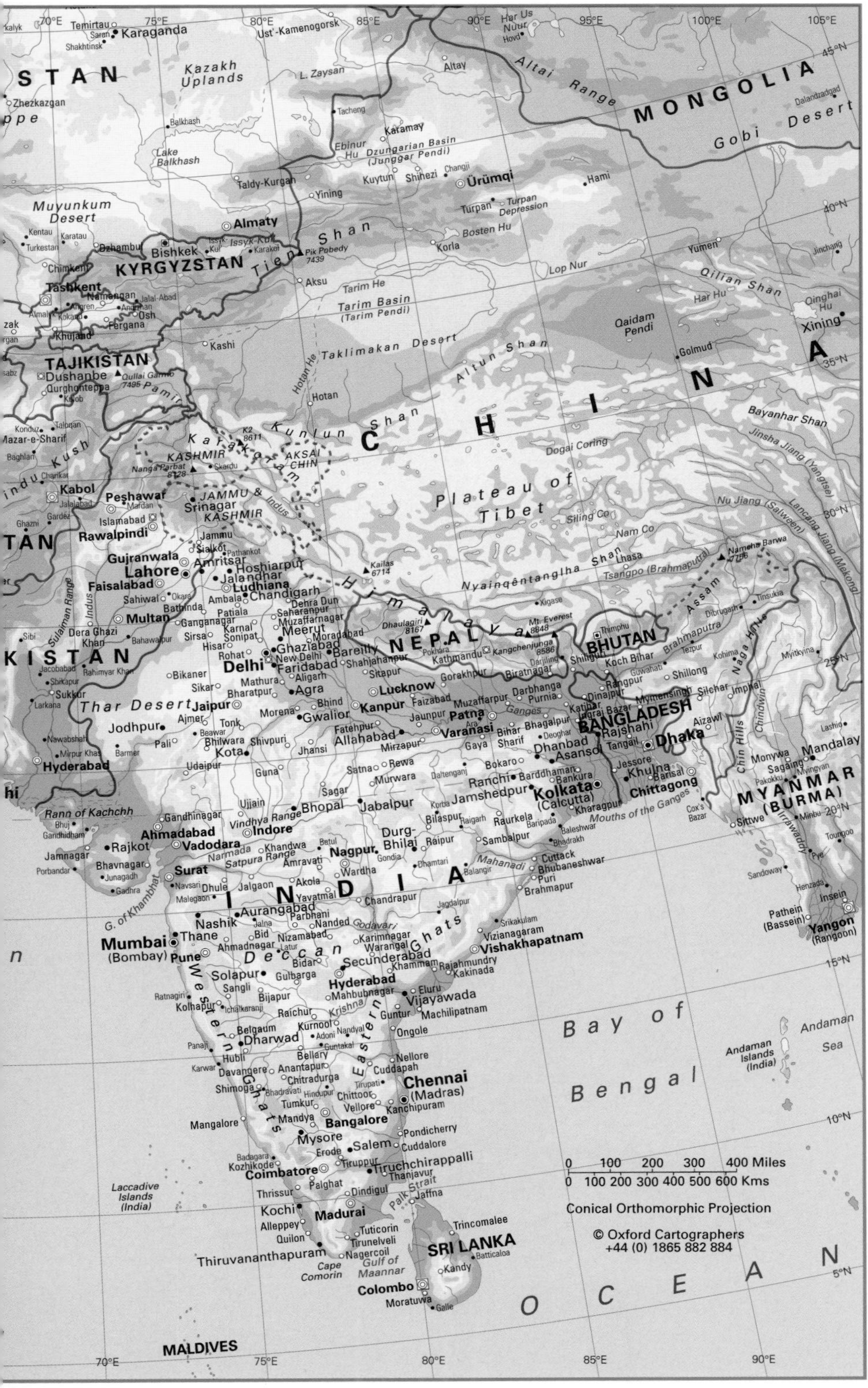

70°E
75°E
80°E
85°E
90°E
95°E
100°E
105°E
45°N
40°N
35°N
30°N
25°N
20°N
15°N
10°N
5°N
Temirtau
Saran
Karaganda
Shakhtinsk
Ust'-Kamenogorsk
Har Us Nuur
Hovd
STAN
Kazakh Uplands
L. Zaysan
Altay
Altai Range
MONGOLIA
Dalandzadgad
Gobi Desert
Zhezkazgan
Balkhash
Tacheng
Karamay
Ebinur Hu
Dzungarian Basin (Junggar Pendi)
Lake Balkhash
Kuytun
Shihezi
Changji
Ürümqi
Hami
Taldy-Kurgan
Yining
Muyunkum Desert
Turpan
Turpan Depression
Almaty
Bosten Hu
Kentau
Karatau
Turkestan
Dzhambul
Bishkek
Issyk-Kul
Karakol
Tien Shan
Pik Pobedy 7439
Korla
Yumen
Jinchang
Chimkent
KYRGYZSTAN
Lop Nur
Qilian Shan
Tashkent
Namangan
Jalal-Abad
Aksu
Tarim He
Har Hu
Qinghai Hu
Almalyk
Angren
Andijan
Osh
Kokand
Fergana
Tarim Basin (Tarim Pendi)
Qaidam Pendi
Xining
Khujand
Kashi
Taklimakan Desert
Golmud
TAJIKISTAN
Dushanbe
Qullai Garmo 7495
Pamir
Kurgan-Teppa
Kulob
Altun Shan
Hotan He
Hotan
CHINA
Bayanhar Shan
Taloqan
Kunduz
Mazar-e-Sharif
Baghlan
K2 8611
Karakoram
Kunlun Shan
Jinsha Jiang (Yangtse)
Dogai Coring
KASHMIR
AKSAI CHIN
Nanga Parbat 8126
Skardu
Hindu Kush
Charikar
Kabol
Jalalabad
Gardez
Ghazni
Peshawar
Mardan
Islamabad
Rawalpindi
JAMMU & KASHMIR
Srinagar
Indus
Plateau of Tibet
Nu Jiang (Salween)
Lancang Jiang (Mekong)
Siling Co
Nam Co
Jammu
Sialkot
Pathankot
Gujranwala
Amritsar
Hoshiarpur
Lahore
Jalandhar
Ludhiana
Chandigarh
Faisalabad
Kailas 6714
Namcha Barwa 7756
Lhasa
Tsangpo (Brahmaputra)
Nyainqêntanglha Shan
Sahiwal
Okara
Ambala
Patiala
Bathinda
Multan
Ganganagar
Dehra Dun
Saharanpur
Muzaffarnagar
Meerut
Moradabad
Himalaya
Xigaze
Assam
Tinsukia
Dibrugarh
Sulaiman Range
Dera Ghazi Khan
Sibi
Bahawalpur
Sirsa
Karnal
Sonipat
Hisar
Rohtak
Ghaziabad
New Delhi
Delhi
Faridabad
Bareilly
Dhaulagiri 8167
NEPAL
Pokhara
Kathmandu
Mt. Everest 8848
Kangchenjunga 8586
Thimphu
BHUTAN
Brahmaputra
Naga Hills
Myitkyina
KISTAN
Jacobabad
Rahimyar Khan
Shikarpur
Sukkur
Larkana
Bikaner
Sikar
Mathura
Aligarh
Agra
Shahjahanpur
Sitapur
Lucknow
Gorakhpur
Biratnagar
Darjiling
Shiliguri
Koch Bihar
Guwahati
Shillong
Tezpur
Kohima
Imphal
Thar Desert
Jaipur
Ajmer
Tonk
Morena
Bhind
Gwalior
Kanpur
Faizabad
Jaunpur
Muzaffarpur
Darbhanga
Purnia
Patna
Ganges
Rangpur
Dinajpur
Mymensingh
Silchar
BANGLADESH
Aizawl
Chindwin
Jodhpur
Beawar
Bhilwara
Shivpuri
Fatehpur
Allahabad
Varanasi
Ara
Bihar Sharif
Bhagalpur
Deoghar
Rajshahi
Tangail
Dhaka
Lashio
Nawabshah
Pali
Kota
Jhansi
Mirzapur
Gaya
Dhanbad
Asansol
Mandalay
Mirpur Khas
Barmer
Hyderabad
Udaipur
Guna
Satna
Rewa
Bokaro
Jessore
Khulna
Monywa
Sagaing
Pakokku
Myingyan
Chin Hills
MYANMAR (BURMA)
Sagar
Murwara
Daltenganj
Ranchi
Barddhaman
Bankura
Kolkata (Calcutta)
Chittagong
Ujjain
Bhopal
Jabalpur
Jamshedpur
Rann of Kachchh
Gandhinagar
Bhuj
Gandhidham
Vindhya Range
Korba
Bilaspur
Raigarh
Raurkela
Baripada
Kharagpur
Mouths of the Ganges
Cox's Bazar
Sittwe
Irrawaddy
Minbu
Ahmadabad
Indore
Vadodara
Rajkot
Khandwa
Betul
Nagpur
Durg-Bhilai
Raipur
Sambalpur
Baleshwar
Bhadrakh
Toungoo
Jamnagar
Narmada
Satpura Range
Amravati
Gondia
Porbandar
Bhavnagar
Junagadh
Surat
Wardha
Dhamtari
Mahanadi
Balangir
Cuttack
Bhubaneshwar
Puri
Pye
Sandoway
Gadhra
G. of Khambhat
Navsari
Malegaon
Dhule
Jalgaon
Akola
Yavatmal
INDIA
Brahmapur
Henzada
Insein
Chandrapur
Jagdalpur
Aurangabad
Nashik
Jalna
Parbhani
Nanded
Srikakulam
Vizianagaram
Vishakhapatnam
Pathein (Bassein)
Yangon (Rangoon)
Mumbai (Bombay)
Thane
Bid
Ahmadnagar
Latur
Nizamabad
Karimnagar
Warangal
Godavari
Pune
Deccan
Bidar
Secunderabad
Khammam
Rajahmundry
Kakinada
Solapur
Gulbarga
Hyderabad
Sangli
Ratnagiri
Kolhapur
Ichalkaranji
Bijapur
Mahbubnagar
Eluru
Vijayawada
Machilipatnam
Krishna
Raichur
Guntur
Western Ghats
Eastern Ghats
Bay of Bengal
Andaman Sea
Andaman Islands (India)
Belgaum
Kurnool
Dharwad
Adoni
Nandyal
Ongole
Panaji
Guntakal
Bellary
Hubli
Nellore
Karwar
Davangere
Anantapur
Cuddapah
Chitradurga
Tirupati
Chennai (Madras)
Shimoga
Bhadravati
Hindupur
Chittoor
Tumkur
Vellore
Kanchipuram
Mangalore
Mandya
Bangalore
Mysore
Pondicherry
Salem
Erode
Cuddalore
Badagara
Kozhikode
Tiruppur
Tiruchchirappalli
Coimbatore
Thanjavur
Laccadive Islands (India)
Thrissur
Palghat
Dindigul
Palk Strait
Jaffna
Kochi
Madurai
Alleppey
Quilon
Tuticorin
Tirunelveli
Trincomalee
SRI LANKA
Batticaloa
Thiruvananthapuram
Nagercoil
Gulf of Maannar
Cape Comorin
Kandy
Colombo
Moratuwa
Galle
OCEAN
MALDIVES
0 100 200 300 400 Miles
0 100 200 300 400 500 600 Kms
Conical Orthomorphic Projection
© Oxford Cartographers
+44 (0) 1865 882 884

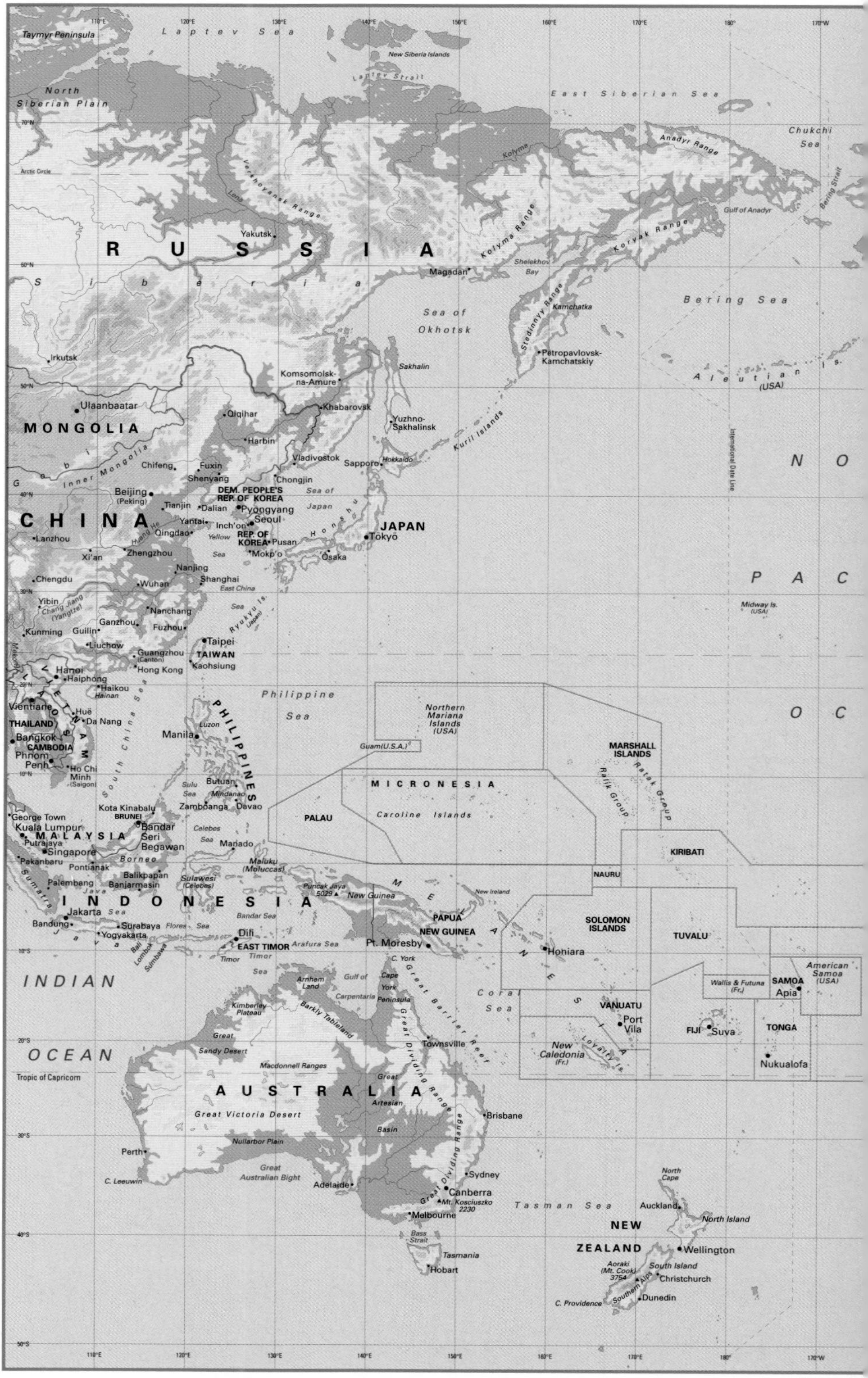
Taymyr Peninsula
Laptev Sea
New Siberia Islands
Laptev Strait
North Siberian Plain
East Siberian Sea
Chukchi Sea
Anadyr Range
Kolyma
Arctic Circle
Verkhoyansk Range
Lena
Bering Strait
Gulf of Anadyr
Koryak Range
Kolyma Range
Yakutsk
RUSSIA
Shelekhov Bay
Magadan
Siberia
Bering Sea
Sea of Okhotsk
Kamchatka
Sredinnyy Range
Petropavlovsk-Kamchatskiy
Irkutsk
Komsomolsk-na-Amure
Sakhalin
Aleutian Is. (USA)
Ulaanbaatar
Qiqihar
Khabarovsk
Yuzhno-Sakhalinsk
MONGOLIA
Harbin
Kuril Islands
International Date Line
Gobi
Inner Mongolia
Chifeng
Fuxin
Vladivostok
Sapporo
Hokkaido
Shenyang
Chongjin
Beijing (Peking)
DEM. PEOPLE'S REP. OF KOREA
Sea of Japan
Tianjin
Dalian
Pyongyang
Honshu
CHINA
Huang He
Yantai
Seoul
Inch'on
JAPAN
Lanzhou
Qingdao
Yellow Sea
REP. OF KOREA
Pusan
Tokyo
Xi'an
Zhengzhou
Mokp'o
Osaka
Nanjing
Chengdu
Shanghai
East China Sea
Wuhan
PACIFIC OCEAN
Yibin
Chang Jiang (Yangtze)
Nanchang
Ryukyu Is. (Japan)
Midway Is. (USA)
Ganzhou
Fuzhou
Kunming
Guilin
Taipei
Liuchow
Guangzhou (Canton)
TAIWAN
Mekong
Hanoi
Hong Kong
Kaohsiung
Haiphong
Haikou
Hainan
VIETNAM
LAOS
Philippine Sea
Vientiane
Hue
Northern Mariana Islands (USA)
Da Nang
PHILIPPINES
THAILAND
Luzon
Bangkok
Manila
Guam (U.S.A.)
MARSHALL ISLANDS
CAMBODIA
Phnom Penh
Ralik Group
Ratak Group
Ho Chi Minh (Saigon)
South China Sea
Sulu Sea
Butuan
MICRONESIA
Mindanao
George Town
Kota Kinabalu
Zamboanga
Davao
PALAU
Caroline Islands
BRUNEI
Kuala Lumpur
Bandar Seri Begawan
Celebes Sea
Putrajaya
MALAYSIA
KIRIBATI
Singapore
Manado
Pekanbaru
Borneo
Pontianak
Maluku (Moluccas)
NAURU
Sumatra
Balikpapan
Palembang
Banjarmasin
Sulawesi (Celebes)
Puncak Jaya 5029
New Guinea
New Ireland
Java Sea
MELANESIA
INDONESIA
SOLOMON ISLANDS
Jakarta
Bandar Sea
PAPUA NEW GUINEA
Bandung
Surabaya
Flores Sea
Dili
TUVALU
Yogyakarta
EAST TIMOR
Arafura Sea
Pt. Moresby
Honiara
Java
Bali
Lombok
Sumbawa
Timor
Timor Sea
C. York
American Samoa (USA)
INDIAN OCEAN
Arnhem Land
Gulf of Carpentaria
Cape York Peninsula
Wallis & Futuna (Fr.)
SAMOA
Apia
Coral Sea
Kimberley Plateau
Barkly Tableland
Great Barrier Reef
VANUATU
Port Vila
Great Dividing Range
FIJI
Suva
TONGA
Great Sandy Desert
Townsville
New Caledonia (Fr.)
Loyalty Is.
Nukualofa
Tropic of Capricorn
Macdonnell Ranges
AUSTRALIA
Great Artesian Basin
Great Victoria Desert
Brisbane
Nullarbor Plain
Perth
Great Australian Bight
Sydney
North Cape
C. Leeuwin
Adelaide
Canberra
Mt. Kosciuszko 2230
Tasman Sea
Auckland
Melbourne
North Island
NEW ZEALAND
Bass Strait
Wellington
Tasmania
Aoraki (Mt. Cook) 3754
South Island
Hobart
Christchurch
Southern Alps
C. Providence
Dunedin
110°E
120°E
130°E
140°E
150°E
160°E
170°E
180°
170°W
70°N
60°N
50°N
40°N
30°N
20°N
10°N
10°S
20°S
30°S
40°S
50°S

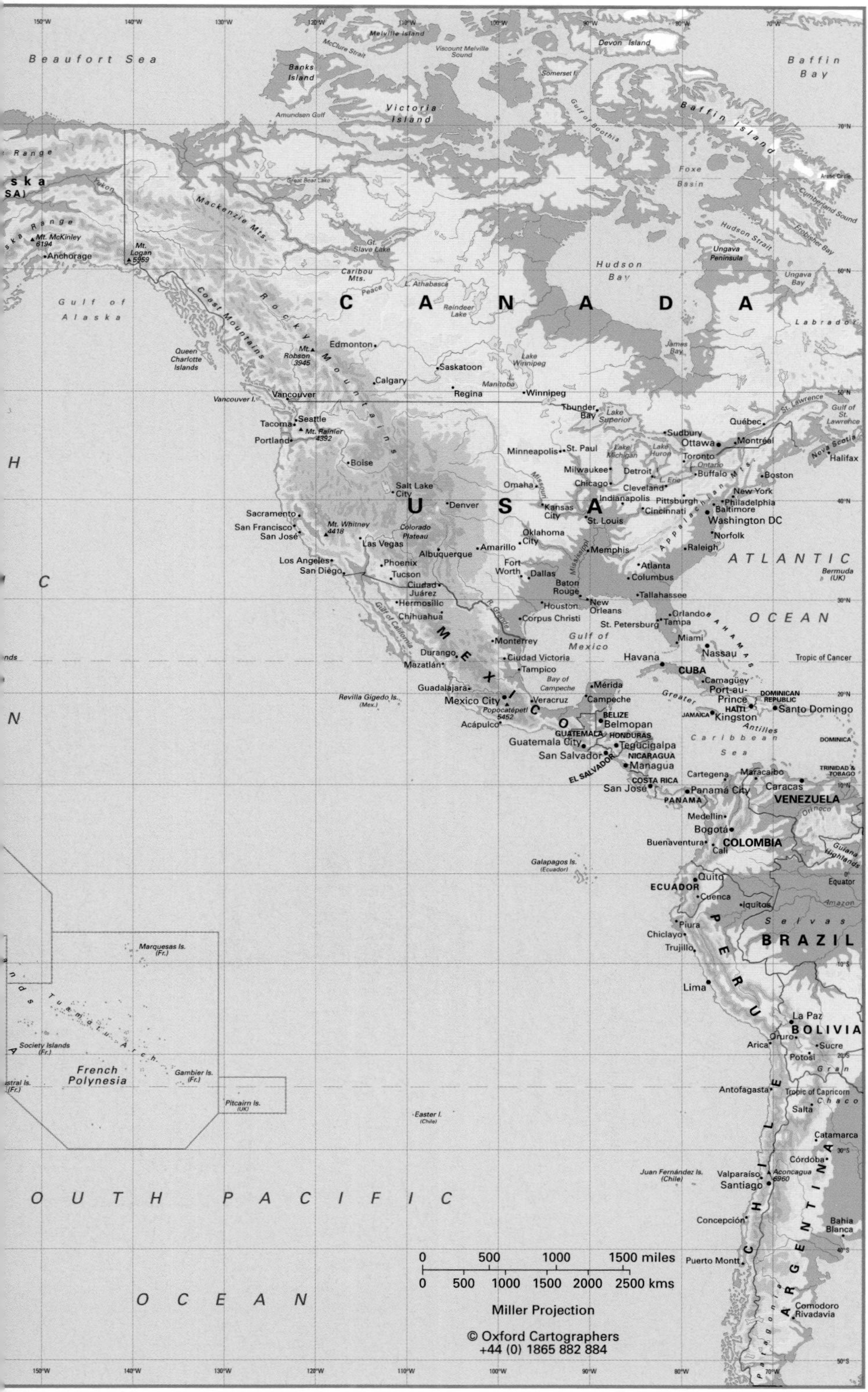
150°W
140°W
130°W
120°W
110°W
100°W
90°W
80°W
70°W
Beaufort Sea
Melville Island
McClure Strait
Viscount Melville Sound
Devon Island
Banks Island
Somerset I.
Baffin Bay
Victoria Island
Amundsen Gulf
Gulf of Boothia
Baffin Island
70°N
Range
ska
SA)
Yukon
Great Bear Lake
Foxe Basin
Arctic Circle
Cumberland Sound
Mackenzie Mts.
Hudson Strait
Frobisher Bay
Mt. McKinley 6194
Anchorage
Mt. Logan 5959
Gt. Slave Lake
Ungava Peninsula
Hudson Bay
Ungava Bay
Caribou Mts.
60°N
L. Athabasca
Peace
Gulf of Alaska
C A N A D A
Reindeer Lake
Coast Mountains
Rocky Mountains
Labrador
Queen Charlotte Islands
Mt. Robson 3945
Edmonton
Lake Winnipeg
James Bay
Saskatoon
Calgary
Manitoba
Regina
Winnipeg
50°N
Vancouver I.
Vancouver
St. Lawrence
Gulf of St. Lawrence
Thunder Bay
Lake Superior
Seattle
Québec
Tacoma
Mt. Rainier 4392
Sudbury
Montréal
Nova Scotia
Portland
Ottawa
Minneapolis
St. Paul
Lake Michigan
Lake Huron
Halifax
H
Toronto
Boise
Lake Ontario
Milwaukee
Detroit
Buffalo
Boston
Chicago
L. Erie
Omaha
Salt Lake City
Cleveland
New York
Missouri
Indianapolis
Pittsburgh
Philadelphia
U S A
Denver
Kansas City
Baltimore
40°N
Sacramento
Cincinnati
Washington DC
St. Louis
San Francisco
San José
Mt. Whitney 4418
Colorado Plateau
Oklahoma City
Appalachian Mts.
Norfolk
Las Vegas
Amarillo
Memphis
Raleigh
Albuquerque
Mississippi
Los Angeles
Phoenix
Fort Worth
Atlanta
ATLANTIC
San Diego
Tucson
Dallas
Columbus
Bermuda (UK)
C
Ciudad Juárez
Baton Rouge
Tallahassee
Hermosillo
New Orleans
30°N
Houston
Gulf of California
Chihuahua
R. Grande
Corpus Christi
Orlando
St. Petersburg
Tampa
OCEAN
BAHAMAS
Gulf of Mexico
MEXICO
Miami
Monterrey
Nassau
Durango
Ciudad Victoria
Havana
Tropic of Cancer
nds
Mazatlán
Tampico
CUBA
Bay of Campeche
Camagüey
Guadalajara
Mérida
Revilla Gigedo Is. (Mex.)
Greater Antilles
Port-au-Prince
DOMINICAN REPUBLIC
20°N
Mexico City
Veracruz
Campeche
HAITI
Santo Domingo
N
Popocatépetl 5452
JAMAICA
Kingston
Acápulco
BELIZE
Belmopan
GUATEMALA
HONDURAS
Caribbean Sea
DOMINICA
Guatemala City
Tegucigalpa
San Salvador
NICARAGUA
Managua
EL SALVADOR
Cartegena
Maracaibo
TRINIDAD & TOBAGO
COSTA RICA
Caracas
San José
Panamá City
10°N
PANAMA
VENEZUELA
Orinoco
Medellín
Bogotá
Buenaventura
COLOMBIA
Cali
Guiana Highlands
Galapagos Is. (Ecuador)
Quito
0°
Equator
ECUADOR
Cuenca
Amazon
Iquitos
Piura
Selvas
Chiclayo
BRAZIL
Trujillo
PERU
10°S
Marquesas Is. (Fr.)
Lima
Tuamotu Arch.
La Paz
BOLIVIA
Oruro
Arica
Sucre
Society Islands (Fr.)
Potosi
20°S
French Polynesia
Gambier Is. (Fr.)
Gran Chaco
stral Is. (Fr.)
Antofagasta
Tropic of Capricorn
Pitcairn Is. (UK)
Easter I. (Chile)
Salta
Catamarca
30°S
Córdoba
Juan Fernández Is. (Chile)
Valparaíso
Aconcagua 6960
Santiago
SOUTH PACIFIC
CHILE
ARGENTINA
Concepción
Bahia Blanca
0 500 1000 1500 miles
0 500 1000 1500 2000 2500 kms
40°S
Puerto Montt
OCEAN
Miller Projection
Patagonia
Comodoro Rivadavia
© Oxford Cartographers
+44 (0) 1865 882 884
50°S

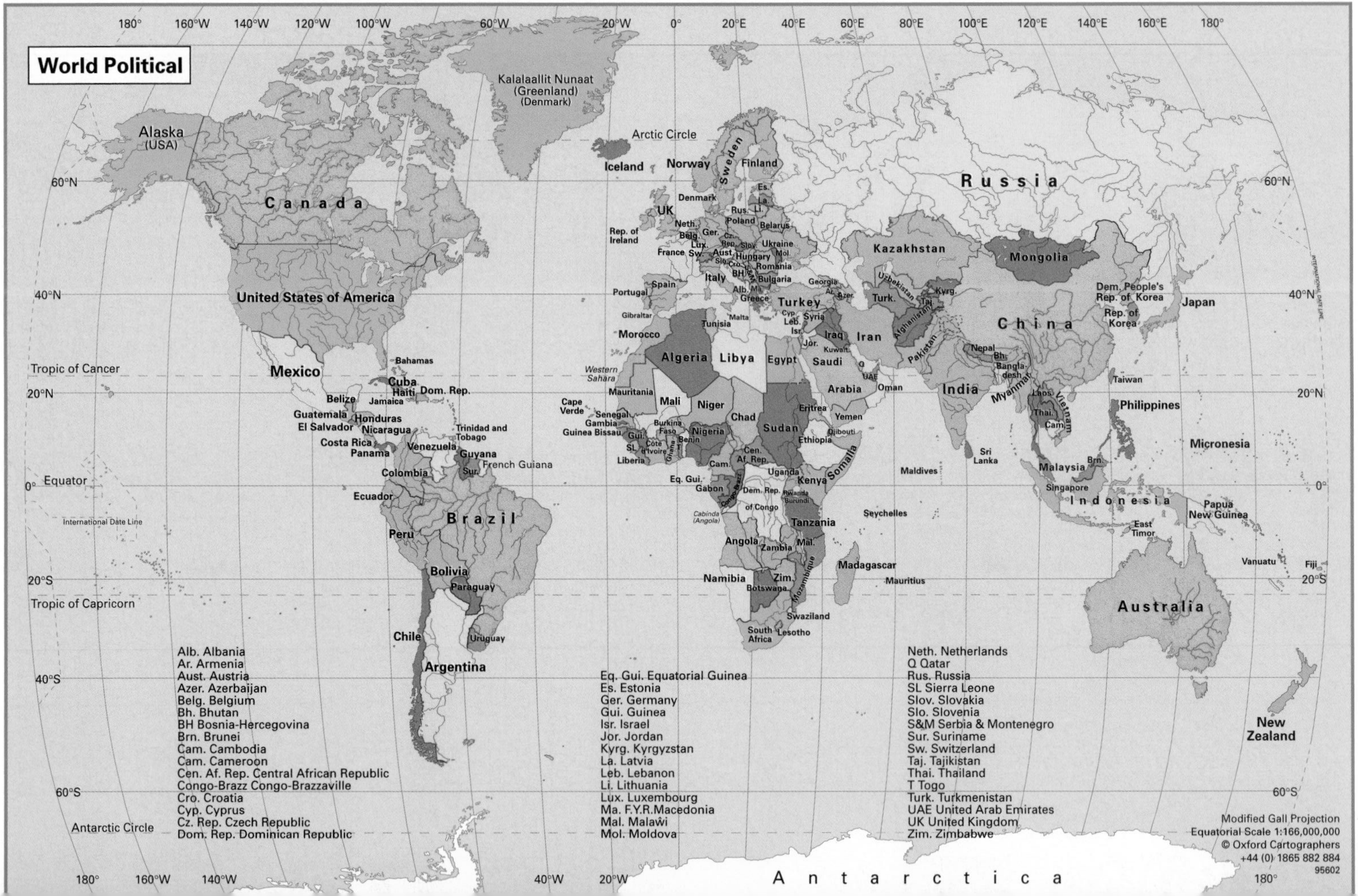
World Political
Kalaallit Nunaat (Greenland) (Denmark)
Alaska (USA)
Arctic Circle
Iceland
Norway
Sweden
Finland
Russia
Canada
United States of America
Mexico
Tropic of Cancer
Equator
Tropic of Capricorn
Antarctic Circle
International Date Line
Kazakhstan
Mongolia
China
Japan
India
Iran
Turkey
Algeria
Libya
Egypt
Sudan
Brazil
Argentina
Australia
New Zealand
Antarctica
Alb. Albania
Ar. Armenia
Aust. Austria
Azer. Azerbaijan
Belg. Belgium
Bh. Bhutan
BH Bosnia-Hercegovina
Brn. Brunei
Cam. Cambodia
Cam. Cameroon
Cen. Af. Rep. Central African Republic
Congo-Brazz Congo-Brazzaville
Cro. Croatia
Cyp. Cyprus
Cz. Rep. Czech Republic
Dom. Rep. Dominican Republic
Eq. Gui. Equatorial Guinea
Es. Estonia
Ger. Germany
Gui. Guinea
Isr. Israel
Jor. Jordan
Kyrg. Kyrgyzstan
La. Latvia
Leb. Lebanon
Li. Lithuania
Lux. Luxembourg
Ma. F.Y.R.Macedonia
Mal. Malawi
Mol. Moldova
Neth. Netherlands
Q Qatar
Rus. Russia
SL Sierra Leone
Slov. Slovakia
Slo. Slovenia
S&M Serbia & Montenegro
Sur. Suriname
Sw. Switzerland
Taj. Tajikistan
Thai. Thailand
T Togo
Turk. Turkmenistan
UAE United Arab Emirates
UK United Kingdom
Zim. Zimbabwe
Modified Gall Projection
Equatorial Scale 1:166,000,000
© Oxford Cartographers
+44 (0) 1865 882 884
95602

and social democrats displaced them. This Democratic Alliance (DA) proposed a swift transition to a market economy, the elimination of corruption and a reduction in social inequalities, but the DA itself became the focus of corruption scandals and a transition to a free market caused large-scale social disruption.

Natasagiyn Bagabandi was re-elected as president in May 2001 with 58.13 per cent of the total vote. Legislative elections held in June 2004 saw the Revolutionary People's Party of Mongolia (RPPM) win 36 out of the 76 seats in the State of Great Assembly. The Motherland Democracy Party secured 34 seats.

POLITICAL SYSTEM
A new Constitution was approved in January 1992 and established a democratic parliamentary system of Government. The President is directly elected for a term of four years. The unicameral legislature is the State Great Hural *(Ulsyn Ikh Khural)*, which has 76 members elected for a four-year term by a simple majority amounting to at least 25 per cent of the votes cast. In July 2000 a constitutional amendment came into force which gives the President the right to dissolve the Great State Hural if it is unable to reach agreement on appointing a Prime Minister.

HEAD OF STATE
President, Natasagiyn Bagabandi, *elected* 18 May 1997, *re-elected* 20 May 2001

SELECTED GOVERNMENT MEMBERS *as at July 2004*
Prime Minister, Nambariyn Enkhbayar
Defence, Jugderdemidyn Gurragchaa
Finance and Economy, Chultemiyn Ulaan
Foreign Affairs, Luvsangyn Erdenechuluun
Justice and Internal Affairs, Tsendyn Nyamdorj

EMBASSY OF MONGOLIA
7 Kensington Court, London W8 5DL
T 020-7937 0150
Ambassador Extraordinary and Plenipotentiary, HE Davaasambuu Dalrain, apptd 2001

BRITISH EMBASSY
30 Enkh Taivny Gudamzh (PO Box 703), Ulaanbaatar 13.
T (+ 976) (11) 458133
E britemb@magicnet.mn
Ambassador Extraordinary and Plenipotentiary, HE Philip Rouse, MBE, apptd 2001

ECONOMY AND TRADE

In recent years the economy has shown signs of growth. A 12.4 per cent increase in the price of copper (which, along with cashmere, is Mongolia's main export commodity) in 2003 delivered an increase in exports. Ample mineral deposits of gold, copper, tin, coal, uranium and tungsten are being exploited and gold mining has increased steadily since 1990. In 2002 11 tons of gold were extracted from mines. Mining, however, has played a part in environmental degradation in the country and other environmental problems such as desertification (caused in part by the rapid conversion of virgin land to agriculture, so accelerating soil erosion), over-grazing and deforestation are increasing. This poses a threat to Mongolia's agrarian sector which makes up 20.6 per cent of GDP. The semi-desert areas of the Gobi region provide pasture for sheep, goats, camels, horses and some cattle. In the steppe areas to the north of the Gobi pasturage is better and livestock more abundant.

Mongolia joined the World Trade Organisation in 1997 and two years later the international donor community pledged over $300 million per year at the Consultative Group Meeting held in Ulaanbaatar. Mongolia has been successful in attracting foreign investors and since 1990, 2,400 foreign companies have invested more than US$800 million into mining, agriculture processing and infrastructure.

GNI – US$947 million (2000); US$390 per capita (2000)
ANNUAL AVERAGE GROWTH OF GDP – 1.4 per cent (2001)
INFLATION RATE – 7.6 per cent (1999)
UNEMPLOYMENT – 5.7 per cent (1998)
TOTAL EXTERNAL DEBT – US$859 million (2000)
IMPORTS – US$630 million (2001)
EXPORTS – US$448 million (2001)

BALANCE OF PAYMENTS
Trade – US$89 million deficit (2001)
Current Account – US$151 million deficit (2001)

Trade with UK	*2002*	*2003*
Imports from UK	£2,436,000	£2,641,000
Exports to UK	3,556,000	1,840,000

TRANSPORT INFRASTRUCTURE

Mongolia has 1,815 km of railways and 49,250 km of highways of which many of the rural roads are unsurfaced.

MEDIA AND CULTURE

There are five daily newspapers including *Onoodor*, with the biggest circulation, and *Unen* the organ of the Mongolian People's Revolutionary Party, and the country's oldest publication. Television is a mixture of state and privately owned broadcasters.

Tibetan Buddhism and nomadism both influence Mongolian society. Each year many devout Mongolians leave their homes *(gers)* in order to make the pilgrimage to Lhasa in Tibet.

MOROCCO

Al-Mamlaka Al-Maghribiyya – Kingdom of Morocco

AREA – 446,300 sq. km. Neighbours: Algeria (east and south-east), Western Sahara (south-west)
POPULATION – 30,430,000 (2001). Standard Arabic is the official language. Maghrebi Arabic and various Berber languages (Tachelhit, Tamazight and Tarafit) are the vernacular. French and Spanish are also spoken, mainly in the towns. Islam is the state religion
CAPITAL – ΨRabat (population, 1,385,872, 1994 census)
MAJOR CITIES – ΨAgadir; ΨCasablanca (Ad-Dar-el-Beida); Fez; Marrakesh; Meknès; Oujda
CURRENCY – Dirham (DH) of 100 centimes
NATIONAL ANTHEM – Hymne Cherifien
NATIONAL DAY – 30 July (Anniversary of the Throne)
NATIONAL FLAG – Red, with a green pentagram
LIFE EXPECTANCY (years) – 68 (2001)
INFANT MORTALITY (per 1,000 births) – 39 (2001)

MORTALITY RATE (per 1,000 population) – 5.78 (2003)
HIV / AIDS ADULT PREVALENCE – 0.1 per cent (2001)
DEATH PENALTY – Yes
POPULATION BELOW POVERTY LINE – 19 per cent (1999)
POPULATION GROWTH RATE – 1.9 per cent (1990–2001)
POPULATION DENSITY – 68 per sq. km (2001)
URBAN POPULATION – 33 per cent (2001)

CLIMATE AND TERRAIN

Elevation extremes range from 4,165 m (Jbel Toubkal) at the highest point to –55 m (Sebkha Tah) at the lowest. Average temperatures in Rabat range from 7°C in January to 29°C in July, although summer temperatures in the desert interior can reach 41°C.

HISTORY AND POLITICS

The end of Spainish rule in 1492 caused economic and social decline in Morocco. It was not until the 17th century that the country regained its pre-eminence in the area when the Alawite family founded a dynasty which survives to the present day.

By 1912 France occupied the entire country. European rule saw tens of thousands of French citizens move into Morocco. A Berber rebellion was crushed in 1926, and Morocco was instrumental as a base for the allies to attack and drive the Germans from North Africa during the Second World War.

Morocco became independent of France in 1956 (though the coastal towns of Ceuta and Melilla remained under Spanish control) under Sultan Mohammed V who became King the following year. Mohammed V was succeeded by his son Hassan II, who annexed the mineral-rich Western Sahara region in 1975.

King Hassan was succeeded by his son, Crown Prince Sidi Mohammed, in 1999. Morocco has since been attempting to move away from the absolute monarchy of King Hassan's era. The Parliamentary elections in 2002 were held to be the most democratic the country had ever witnessed. The Union Socialiste des Forces Populaires (USFP) and the Independence Party remained the two largest parties. Driss Jetou was appointed prime minister on 9 October and a coalition government was named on 8 November 2002.

POLITICAL SYSTEM

The King nominates the Prime Minister and, on the latter's recommendation, appoints the members of the Council of Ministers. The Government is responsible both to Parliament and to the King. There is a bicameral legislature. The House of Representatives *(Majlis al-Nuwab)* has 325 members elected for a five-year term by universal suffrage using a first past the post system. The Chamber of Councillors *(Majlis al-Mustashareen)* has 270 members, 60 per cent of whom are elected by local councils, 20 per cent by employers' associations and 20 per cent by trade unions. One-third of its members are elected every three years.

HEAD OF STATE
HM The King of Morocco, King Mohammed VI (Sidi Mohammed Ben Hassan), *born* 21 August 1963, *acceded* 23 July 1999

SELECTED GOVERNMENT MEMBERS *as at July 2004*
Prime Minister, Driss Jetou
Finance and Privatisation, Fathallah Oualaou
Foreign Affairs and Co-operation, Mohamed Benaissa
Interior Affairs, Al Mustapha Sahel

EMBASSY OF THE KINGDOM OF MOROCCO
49 Queen's Gate Gardens, London SW7 5NE
T 020-7581 5001/4
Ambassador Extraordinary and Plenipotentiary, HE Mohammed Belmahi, apptd 1999

BRITISH EMBASSY
17 Boulevard de la Tour Hassan (BP 45), Rabat
T (+ 212) (0) 37 238600
E consular.rabat@fco.gov.uk
Ambassador Extraordinary and Plenipotentiary, HE Haydon Warren-Gash, apptd 2002

BRITISH COUNCIL DIRECTOR, Steve McNulty
BP 427, 36 rue de Tanger, Rabat
E bc.morocco@britishcouncil.org.ma

DEFENCE

The Army has 744 main battle tanks, 115 armoured infantry fighting vehicles, and 740 armoured personnel carriers. The Navy has two frigates and 27 patrol and coastal combatant vessels at five bases. The Air Force has 95 combat aircraft and 24 armed helicopters.
MILITARY EXPENDITURE – 3.6 per cent of GDP (2002)
MILITARY PERSONNEL – 196,300: Army 175,000, Navy 7,800, Air Force 13,500; Paramilitaries 50,000
CONSCRIPTION DURATION – 18 months

ECONOMY AND TRADE

Morocco has a large agrarian sector and 50 per cent of the labour force is engaged in agricultural production, representing 20 per cent of GDP. There are a number of environmental issues connected with agriculture such as desertification and soil erosion from farming. Raw sewage has contaminated some water supplies. Cereal production is of high importance and the country produces 107,000 metric tonnes per year.

Morocco has some mineral reserves, mainly phosphate rock. Other industries include food processing, textiles and leather goods while tourism is becoming increasingly important. The main imports are petroleum products, machinery, chemical products, iron and steel and grain and textiles. The EU, with which an association agreement was signed in 1995, is Morocco's largest trading partner and in 1998 awarded Morocco grants totalling US$98 million.

Similar to many countries in North Africa, Morocco has a significant population of emigrant workers. Large numbers of Moroccans have left to work in the EU and provide remittances.
GNI – US$34,700 million (2001); US$1,190 per capita (2001)
ANNUAL AVERAGE GROWTH OF GDP – 0.9 per cent (2000)
INFLATION RATE – 1.9 per cent (2000)
UNEMPLOYMENT – 22.0 per cent (1999)
TOTAL EXTERNAL DEBT – US$17,944 million (2000)
FOREIGN DIRECT INVESTMENT – US$1,535 million (1997–2001)
IMPORTS – US$11,647 million (2002)
EXPORTS – US$7,772 million (2002)

BALANCE OF PAYMENTS
Trade – US$3,063 million deficit (2002)

Current Account – US$1,488 million surplus (2002)

Trade with UK	*2002*	*2003*
Imports from UK	£351,019,000	£357,160,000
Exports to UK	470,869,000	456,294,000

TRANSPORT INFRASTRUCTURE

There are 1,907 m of railways linking the major towns. There are 60,449 km of roads; an extensive network of 30,374 km of surfaced roads covers all the main towns. Royal Air Maroc is the national airline.

EDUCATION

Education is compulsory between the ages of seven and 16. There are government primary, secondary and technical schools. At Fez there is a theological university of great repute in the Muslim world. There is a secular university at Rabat. Schools for special denominations, Jewish and Catholic, are permitted and may receive government grants. American schools operate in Rabat and Casablanca. There is an English language university in Ifrane.

ILLITERACY RATE – (m) 38.1 per cent; (f) 63.9 per cent (2000)

ENROLMENT (percentage of age group) – primary 86 per cent (1997); secondary 39 per cent (1997); tertiary 11 per cent (1997)

MEDIA AND CULTURE

There are three daily newspapers, one of which is state owned. State owned television and radio compete with a private broadcaster. *Rai* is a form of music which developed in Algeria but has become popular in Morocco.

WESTERN SAHARA

Al-Jumhūriyya al-'Arabiyya as-Şahrāwiyya ad-Dimuqrāţiyya – Sahrawi Arab Democratic Republic

AREA – 252,120 sq. km. Neighbours: Morocco (north), Algeria (north-east), Mauritania (east and south)

POPULATION – 244,943 (2000 estimate). Arabic is the official language. Hassaniya and Moroccan Arabic are the main spoken languages; Spanish is widely spoken in the towns. Almost all the population is Sunni Muslim

CAPITAL – El-Aaiũn (population, 139,000, 1990 estimate)

NATIONAL FLAG – Three horizontal stripes of black, white and green with a red crescent and a five-pointed star in the centre and a red triangle based on the hoist

POPULATION GROWTH RATE – 3.4 per cent (1999)

POPULATION DENSITY – 1 per sq. km (1999)

Following Spanish withdrawal from Western Sahara in 1975, the territory was divided between Morocco and Mauritania. Mauritania withdrew in 1979 leaving Morocco in sole possession. This, however, was contested by Polisario, an armed group dedicated to the independence of Western Sahara.

Fighting has carried on at differing levels of intensity ever since. Around 180,000 Sahrawi's have been driven into exile; some to Algeria, some to Mauritania. A cease-fire agreed in 1988 and brokered by the UN finally came into force in 1991. Plans for a referendum on the area could not overcome the differences between the Moroccan government and Polisario, and the situation has been deadlocked ever since.

Talks between the Moroccan government and Polisario in 2000 were centred on the question of autonomy for Western Sahara within Morocco. A draft agreement that was proposed by the Moroccan government was rejected by Polisario.

In 2002 Morocco reiterated its support for autonomy for Western Sahara but insisted that it remain part of Morocco. Speaking on the 25th anniversary of the Green March, the movement that saw 350,000 volunteers cross into the territory and claim it for Morocco, King Hassan dismissed the UN plan for a settlement as 'obsolete' and 'inapplicable'.

Former US Secretary of State James Baker, prior to his resignation in 2004 as the UN Secretary-General's Personal Envoy, had proposed a period of autonomy followed by a referendum. This was accepted by Polisario, but not by Morocco.

As at August 2004, the status of Western Sahara has not been determined by the UN and although the cease-fire remains intact, it is estimated that over 100,000 landmines and items of unexploded ordnance remain in the region.

MOZAMBIQUE

República de Moçambique – Republic of Mozambique

AREA – 784,100 sq. km. Neighbours: Swaziland (south), South Africa (south and west), Zimbabwe (west), Zambia and Malawi (north-west), Tanzania (north)

POPULATION – 18,644,000 (2001). The official language is Portuguese but 16 other ethnic languages are spoken

CAPITAL – ΨMaputo (population, 1,039,700, 1998 census)

MAJOR CITIES – ΨBeira; ΨMatola; Nampula

CURRENCY – Metical (MT) of 100 centavos

NATIONAL ANTHEM – Hino Nacional (National Anthem)

NATIONAL DAY – 25 June (Independence Day)

NATIONAL FLAG – Horizontal green, black, yellow with white fimbriations; a red triangle based on the hoist containing the national emblem

LIFE EXPECTANCY (years) – 39 (2001)

MORTALITY RATE (per 1,000 population) – 30 (2003)

INFANT MORTALITY (per 1,000 births) – 125 (2001)

HIV / AIDS ADULT PREVALENCE – 0.1 per cent (2001)

DEATH PENALTY – No (abolished 1990)

POPULATION BELOW POVERTY LINE – 70 per cent (2001)

POPULATION GROWTH RATE – 2.8 per cent (1990–2001)

POPULATION DENSITY – 24 per sq. km (2001)

MILITARY EXPENDITURE – 2.0 per cent of GDP (2002)

MILITARY PERSONNEL – 8,200: Army 7,000, Navy 200, Air Force 1,000

CONSCRIPTION DURATION – Two years

ILLITERACY RATE – (m) 39.9 per cent; (f) 71.3 per cent (2000)

ENROLMENT (percentage of age group) – primary 60 per cent (1997); secondary 7 per cent (1997); tertiary 1 per cent (1997)

CLIMATE AND TERRAIN

There are high plateaux in the north-west of Mozambique and mountains in the west. Elevation extremes range from

2,436 m (Monte Binga) at the highest point to 0 m (Indian Ocean) at the lowest. The climate is tropical with average temperatures in the capital Maputo ranging from 26°C in July to 30°C in January.

HISTORY AND POLITICS

Between the 10th and 14th centuries Mozambique was a stronghold of Bantu civilisation. Trade with India and the Arabian peninsula grew and migrants from both these regions settled in the area.

The Portuguese explorer Vasco de Gama arrived in 1498, and, over the next three centuries the Portuguese exploited Mozambique for gold, ivory, spices and slavery. Though Portugal developed the country into a colony in the 16th century, it did not completely dominate it until 1914. Proximity to the South African gold mines led to the development of Mozambique as an important trading post.

The Salazar dictatorship in Portugal, which ruled between 1932 and 1968, outlawed the private company concessions which had operated as *de facto* rulers over much of Mozambique. Full independence from Portugal came in 1975 but fighting between faction groups ensued. The Frente de Libertaão de Moambique (Frelimo) and the Resistência Nacional de Moambique (Renamo) led the country into a bloody civil war that lasted from the early 1980s until 1992, when the two sides signed the Rome Peace Accord.

Presidential and legislative elections were held on 3–5 December 1999. The incumbent, Joaquim Chissano (Frelimo), won the presidential election with 52.3 per cent of the vote. Frelimo also won the legislative election, gaining 133 seats to Renamo's 117, amid allegations by Renamo of vote-rigging. No other parties were able to secure the five per cent of the total vote necessary to obtain representation. Presidential and legislative elections were scheduled for early 2005.

POLITICAL SYSTEM

The President is directly elected and serves for a five-year term, which is renewable only twice consecutively. The unicameral legislature, the Assembly of the Republic *(Assembleia Da Republica)*, is directly elected for a five-year term and comprises 250 members.

HEAD OF STATE

President, Joaquim Alberto Chissano, *sworn in* November 1986, *elected* 29 October 1994, *re-elected* 5 December 1999

SELECTED GOVERNMENT MEMBERS *as at July 2004*

Prime Minister, Minister of Planning and Finance, Luisa Diogo

Minister in the President's Office, Almirinho da Cruz Manhenje *(Defence, Security Affairs and Interior)*

Foreign Affairs and Co-operation, Leonardo Simão

Industry and Commerce, Carlos Morgado

National Defence, Tobias Dai

HIGH COMMISSION FOR THE REPUBLIC OF MOZAMBIQUE

21 Fitzroy Square, London W1T 6EL

T 020-7383 3800

High Commissioner, HE Antonio Gumende, apptd 2002

BRITISH HIGH COMMISSION

Av. Vladimir I Lenine 310, Box 55, Maputo

T (+ 258) (1) 320111/2/5/6/7

E bhc@virconn.com

High Commissioner, HE Robert Dewar, apptd 2000

BRITISH COUNCIL DIRECTOR, Simon Ingram-Hill

Rua John Issa 226, PO Box 4178, Maputo

T (+ 258) (1) 310 921

E general.enquiries@britishcouncil.org.mz

ECONOMY AND TRADE

Agriculture accounts for 26 per cent of GDP and employs 83 per cent of the labour force. Shellfish, cotton, cashew nuts, sugar and coconuts make up important agricultural exports, and there are considerable oil, gas, mineral and hydro-electric resources. However, large-scale economic problems remain. The reconstruction of infrastructure and the country's industrial base following the civil war has been hampered by floods. The agricultural sector has also been affected by drought in 2002 and 2003.

GNI – US$3,800 million (2001); US$210 per capita (2001)

ANNUAL AVERAGE GROWTH OF GDP– 13.9 per cent (2001)

INFLATION RATE – 15.2 per cent (2002)

TOTAL EXTERNAL DEBT – US$7,135 million (2000)

FOREIGN DIRECT INVESTMENT – US$771 million (1997–2000)

IMPORTS – US$1,158 million (2000)

EXPORTS – US$364 million (2000)

BALANCE OF PAYMENTS

Trade – US$271 million deficit (2001)

Current Account – US$657 million deficit (2001)

Trade with UK	*2002*	*2003*
Imports from UK	£13,671,000	£15,996,000
Exports to UK	3,896,000	8,478,000

TRANSPORT INFRASTRUCTURE

There are a total of 3,123 km of railways, 30,400 km of highways and 3,750 km of navigable waterways. Mozambique has 158 airports although only 22 of these have surfaced runways. A railway has been commissioned to link Mozambique to South Africa and there are plans to develop a similar corridor, linked by rail and road between Malawi and Zambia.

MEDIA AND CULTURE

Freedom of speech is guaranteed in the constitution and there are two daily newspapers and three weekly publications plus two television broadcasters. Radio remains the main media outlet for the majority of the population with UNESCO and the Government funding around 40 stations.

Mia Couto (b. 1955) is one of Mozambique's most famous poets.

MYANMAR

Pyidaungsu Myanmar Naingngandaw – Union of Myanmar

AREA – 676,578 sq. km. Neighbours: Bangladesh (west), India (north-west), China (north-east), Laos and Thailand (east)

POPULATION – 41,994,678 (2001 estimate). The indigenous inhabitants are of similar racial types and speak languages of the Tibeto-Burman, Mon-Khmer and Thai groups. The three significant non-indigenous peoples are Indians, Chinese and Bangladeshis. Burmese is the official language, but minority languages include Bamar, Chin, Kachin, Kayah, Kayin (Karen), Mon, Rakhine and Shan. English is spoken in educated circles. Buddhism is the religion of 89.3 per cent of the people, with 5.6 per cent Christians, 3.8 per cent Muslims, 0.2 per cent Animists and 0.5 per cent Hindus

CAPITAL – ΨRangoon (population, 2,513,023, 1983)

MAJOR CITIES – Mandalay; ΨMawlamyine (Moulmein); ΨPathein (Bassein)

CURRENCY – Kyat (K) of 100 pyas

NATIONAL ANTHEM – Gba Majay Myanmar (We Shall Love Myanmar For Ever)

NATIONAL DAY – 4 January

NATIONAL FLAG – Red, with a canton of dark blue, inside which are a cogwheel and two rice ears surrounded by 14 white stars

LIFE EXPECTANCY (years) – 53 (2001)

MORTALITY RATE (per 1,000 population) – 40 (2001)

DEATH PENALTY – Yes

POPULATION GROWTH RATE – 1.2 per cent (1990–2001)

POPULATION DENSITY – 67 per sq. km (1999)

CLIMATE AND TERRAIN

Elevation extremes range from 5,881 m (Hkakabo Razi) at the highest point to 0 m (Andaman Sea) at the lowest. Myanmar has a tropical climate with a wet season from May until October. Average temperatures range from 16°C in January to 36°C in July, although summer temperatures in the centre of the country can reach up to 43°C.

HISTORY AND POLITICS

Myanmar (previously known as Burma) had a fraught relationship with the British empire in India at the beginning of the 19th century. Throughout the first half of the century border disputes often spiralled into border clashes and eventually invasions. This led to the annexation of Myanmar as part of British India in 1885 following the third Anglo-Burmese War.

The British separated Myanmar from India in 1937 and independence came in 1948, though this was followed by serious civil disturbances.

An army revolt in 1962 installed General Ne Win. Ne Win was replaced in 1989 by General Saw Maung, head of the State Law and Order Council (SLORC). Pro-democracy forces, notably the national League for Democracy (NLD) under Aung San Suu Kyi, continued to oppose military rule, and in 1990 Aung San Suu Kyi won elections despite being under house arrest. The military ignored the election results, repressed the NLD and continued to rule Myanmar by diktat. Aung San Suu Kyi was released from house arrest in 1995, but her movements continued to be restricted by the government.

The State Peace and Development Council (SPDC) detained several hundred NLD members in September 1998 to thwart the NLD's plan to convene a 'People's Parliament' representing the assembly, which would have resulted from the 1990 general election. Instead, the NLD set up an interim representation committee to act on behalf of the 'People's Parliament'. UN-brokered talks between Aung San Suu Kyi and the government began in 2000 and since then about 400 dissidents have been released from prison and Aung San Suu Kyi was released from house arrest in May 2002. However, the reconciliation talks have stalled and in May 2003 Aung San Suu Kyi was taken into 'protective custody' following clashes between her supporters and those of the government.

POLITICAL SYSTEM

The Constitution was effectively abrogated in 1988 when the executive and legislature were abolished and replaced by the SLORC. There are no permitted political parties.

INSURGENCIES

Since independence in 1948 the government has fought various armed insurgent groups, the largest of which were derived from the Kachin, Kayin (Karen), Karenni, and Wa ethnic groups but the Shan, Mon, Arakan and Chin ethnic minorities have also formed armed groups.

Since 1992, as a result of government offensives, 15 ethnic groups have signed cease-fire agreements with the government. In November 1999, the government launched a military offensive against Kayin (Karen) National Union (KNU) guerrillas and their allies in Karen state.

The UK government and non-governmental organisations maintain that human rights abuses against Myanmar's ethnic minorities continue. The United Nations Commission for Human Rights (UNHCR) passed a resolution on 21 April 2004, under co-sponsorship with the EU, to express concern over these alleged abuses.

STATE PEACE AND DEVELOPMENT COUNCIL *as at July 2004*
Chairman, Senior Gen. Than Shwe
Vice-Chairman, Gen. Maung Aye

SELECTED GOVERNMENT MEMBERS *as at July 2004*
Prime Minister, Defence, Senior Gen. Than Shwe
Finance and Revenue, Maj.-Gen. Hla Tun
Foreign Affairs, U Win Aung
Home Affairs, Col. Tin Hlaing

EMBASSY OF THE UNION OF MYANMAR
19A Charles Street, Berkeley Square, London W1J 5DX
T 020-7499 8841
Ambassador Extraordinary and Plenipotentiary, HE Dr Kyaw Win, apptd 1999

BRITISH EMBASSY
80 Strand Road (Box No. 638), Rangoon
T (+ 95) (1) 256918
Ambassador Extraordinary and Plenipotentiary, HE Victoria Bowman, apptd 2002

BRITISH COUNCIL DIRECTOR, Graham Millington *(Cultural Attaché)*, 78 Kanna Road, PO Box 638, Rangoon
E enquiries@britishcouncil.org.mm

DEFENCE

The Army has some 100 main battle tanks and 270 armoured personnel carriers. The Navy has 73 patrol and coastal vessels at six bases. The Air Force has 113 combat aircraft and 29 armed helicopters.

MILITARY EXPENDITURE – 5.0 per cent of GDP (2002)

MILITARY PERSONNEL – 350,000: Army 325,000, Navy 16,000, Air Force 15,000; Paramilitaries 107,250

ECONOMY AND TRADE

Myanmar is extremely rich in natural resources such as timber (it is the world's largest exporter of teak), jade pearls, rubies and sapphires. Fertile soil makes it an excellent environment for agriculture and it enjoys oil and gas deposits. However, the military junta controls all the major industries and the economy is characterised by corruption, mismanagement and massive human rights abuses such as the alleged use of forced labour. The principal imports are capital goods, chiefly transport equipment, machinery and plant, consumer goods and semi-manufactures.

In July 1997, Myanmar became a member of ASEAN. In 1997 the EU stripped Myanmar of trading privileges and the USA imposed economic sanctions; in July 2003 the USA imposed further sanctions on the government.

GDP – US$12,557 million (1998); US$1,816 per capita (2000)

ANNUAL AVERAGE GROWTH OF GDP – 6.2 per cent (2000)

INFLATION RATE – 0.1 per cent (2000)

TOTAL EXTERNAL DEBT – US$6,046 million (2000)

IMPORTS – US$2,348 million (2002)

EXPORTS – US$3,046 million (2002

BALANCE OF PAYMENTS

Trade – US$268 million deficit (2002)

Current Account – US$306 million deficit (2002)

Trade with UK	*2002*	*2003*
Imports from UK	£7,345,000	£5,001,000
Exports to UK	64,337,000	62,251,000

TRANSPORT INFRASTRUCTURE

The Irrawaddy river and its chief tributary, the Chindwin, are important waterways, the main stream being navigable 900 miles from its mouth and carrying much traffic. The chief seaports are Rangoon, Mawlamyine (Moulmein), Akyab (Sittwe) and Pathein (Bassein).

The railway network covers 3,955 km, extending to Myitkyina on the Upper Irrawaddy. There are 2,452 miles of highways and 14,318 miles of other main roads. The airport at Mingaladon, about 13 miles north of Rangoon, handles limited international air traffic.

EDUCATION

Most children attend primary school, and nearly five million are currently enrolled; in middle and high schools, enrolment is over two million. There are 16 universities, nine degree-awarding colleges and 87 other higher education institutions.

Vocational training is provided at 17 teacher training institutes and schools, 11 technical institutes, 17 technical high schools, 17 agricultural institutes and schools, and 41 vocational schools.

ILLITERACY RATE – (m) 11.0 per cent; (f) 19.4 per cent (2000)

ENROLMENT (percentage of age group) – tertiary 5 per cent (1997)

MEDIA

Nearly all the media outlets in Myanmar are controlled by the government. Four national publications and two television stations are all owned and controlled by the state. Democratic Voice of Myanmar is an opposition radio station broadcasting on short-wave from Norway.

NAMIBIA

The Republic of Namibia

AREA – 823,300 sq. km. Neighbours: Angola (north), South Africa (south), Botswana (east), Zambia and Zimbabwe (north-east)

POPULATION – 1,788,000 (2001). The main population groups include: Ovambo (587,000), Kavango (110,000), Damara (89,000), Herero (89,000), whites (78,000), Nama (57,000), mixed race (48,000), Caprivians (44,000), Rehoboth Baster (29,000), Tswana (7,000). English is the official language, with Afrikaans, German and local languages also in use

CAPITAL – Windhoek (population, 147,056, 1995)

MAJOR TOWNS – Ondangwa; Oshakati; Rehoboth; Swakopmund; ΨWalvis Bay

CURRENCY – Namibian dollar of 100 cents, at parity to South African rand

NATIONAL ANTHEM – Namibia, Land Of The Brave

NATIONAL DAY – 21 March (Independence Day)

NATIONAL FLAG – Divided diagonally blue, red and green with the red fimbriated in white; there is a gold twelve-rayed sun in the upper hoist

LIFE EXPECTANCY (years) – 45 (2001)

MORTALITY RATE (per 1,000 population) – 19.17 (2003)

HIV / AIDS ADULT PREVALENCE – 22.5 per cent (2001)

INFANT MORTALITY (per 1,000 births) – 55 (2001)

DEATH PENALTY – No (abolished 1990)

POPULATION BELOW POVERTY LINE – 50 (2002)

POPULATION GROWTH RATE – 2.4 per cent (1990–2001)

POPULATION DENSITY – 2 per sq. km (2001)

MILITARY EXPENDITURE – 2.8 per cent of GDP (2002)

MILITARY PERSONNEL – 9,200: Army 9,000, Coast Guard 200; Paramilitaries 6,000

ILLITERACY RATE – (m) 17.2 per cent; (f) 18.8 per cent (2000)

ENROLMENT (percentage of age group) – primary 100 per cent (1997); secondary 62 per cent (1997); tertiary 8 per cent (1997)

CLIMATE AND TERRAIN

The Kalahari desert covers a large area of eastern Namibia and the terrain is almost completely arid and dry. Elevation extremes range from 2,606 m (Konigstein) at the highest point to 0 m (Atlantic Ocean) at the lowest. Average temperatures range from 21°C in July to 36°C in January.

HISTORY AND POLITICS

Namibia was annexed by Germany in the 19th century but passed into the control of South Africa at the end of the First World War. With the creation of the apartheid system in 1949, South Africa extended parliamentary representation to the white population of Namibia only. Throughout the 1950s the plight of Black Africans in Namibia lead to agitation for independence and the South West Africa People's Organisation (SWAPO) began an armed struggle against South African dominance in 1966.

In 1978 UN Security Council Resolution 435 issued proposals for Namibian independence but full independence was not achieved until 21 March 1990.

The presidential elections of 1999 were won by the incumbent President, Sam Nujoma, and by the South West Africa People's Organisation of Namibia (SWAPO) respectively. In the 72-seat National Assembly SWAPO has 55 seats, the Congress of Democrats and the Democratic Turnhalle Alliance seven seats each, and other parties three seats. In August 2002, Prime Minister Hage Geingob was replaced by Theo-Ben Gurirab. Parliamentary and presidential elections were due to take place in mid-November 2004.

POLITICAL SYSTEM

Namibia has an Executive President as Head of State who exercises the functions of Government with the assistance of a Cabinet headed by a Prime Minister. The President is directly elected for a maximum of two five-year terms; in November 1998, Parliament approved an amendment to the Constitution allowing President Nujoma to stand for a third term of office in the 1999 elections. There is a bicameral legislature consisting of the 72-member National Assembly, elected for a five-year term, and the National Council, whose 26 members are indirectly elected by the regional councils from among their own members. The National Council is elected for a six-year term, and its main function is to review and consider legislation from the National Assembly. The constitution can only be changed by a two-thirds majority in the National Assembly.

HEAD OF STATE

President, Dr Sam Nujoma, *elected* 16 February 1990, *re-elected* 8 December 1994, 1 December 1999

SELECTED GOVERNMENT MEMBERS *as at August 2004*

Prime Minister, Theo-Ben Gurirab
Deputy Prime Minister, Revd Hendrik Witbooi
Defence, Erikki Nghimtina
Finance, Saarah Kuugongelwa-Amathila
Foreign Affairs, Hidipo Hamutenya
Home Affairs, Jerry Ekandjo

HIGH COMMISSION OF THE REPUBLIC OF NAMIBIA

6 Chandos Street, London W1G 9LU
T 020-7636 6244
E namibia-highcomm@btconnect.com
High Commissioner, HE Monica Ndiliawike Nashandi, apptd 1999

BRITISH HIGH COMMISSION

116 Robert Mugabe Avenue, PO Box 22202, Windhoek
T (+ 264) (61) 274800
E bhc@mweb.com.na
High Commissioner, HE Alasdair MacDermott, apptd 2002
British Council Officer, Patience Mahlalela, 1–5 Fidel Castro Street, Windhoek
T (+ 264) (61) 226 776
E general.enquiries@britishcouncil.org.na

ECONOMY AND TRADE

Diamonds and uranium account for 34 per cent and 10 per cent of exports respectively. In total, minerals account for 54 per cent of exports. Agriculture and fisheries are also important. Some 55 per cent of Namibians are subsistence farmers. Tourism is being developed as a way of diversifying the economy. The principal imports are machinery and transport equipment, foodstuffs, beverages, tobacco and mineral fuels.

GNI – US$3,500 million (2001); US$1,960 per capita (2001)
ANNUAL AVERAGE GROWTH OF GDP – 2.7 per cent (2001)
INFLATION RATE – 8 per cent (2001)
FOREIGN DIRECT INVESTMENT – US$187 million (1997–2000)

BALANCE OF PAYMENTS

Trade – US$173 million deficit (1998)
Current Account – US$162 million surplus (1998)

Trade with UK	*2002*	*2003*
Imports from UK	£8,366,000	£10,070,000
Exports to UK	183,888,000	103,947,000

TRANSPORT INFRASTRUCTURE

Namibia has 2,382 km of railways, 66,467 km of highways and 136 airports. The two main ports are Luderitz and Walvis Bay.

MEDIA

There are six national newspapers. The state administered Namibian Broadcasting Corporation runs alongside Desert TV, a private network.

NAURU

The Republic of Nauru/Naoero

AREA – 21 sq. km
POPULATION – 12,088 (2001). About 43 per cent of Nauruans are adherents of the Nauruan Protestant Church and there is a Roman Catholic mission on the island. The main languages are English and Nauruan
CAPITAL – ΨNauru
CURRENCY – Australian dollar ($A) of 100 cents
NATIONAL ANTHEM – Nauru Bwiema (Nauru, Our Homeland)
NATIONAL DAY – 31 January (Independence Day)
NATIONAL FLAG – Twelve-point star (representing the 12 original Nauruan tribes) below a gold bar (representing the Equator), all on a blue background
MORTALITY RATE (per 1,000 population) – 7 (2003)
DEATH PENALTY – No (abolished 1968)
POPULATION GROWTH RATE – 1.8 per cent (2004)
POPULATION DENSITY – 524 per sq. km (1999)

CLIMATE AND TERRAIN

Nauru is one of three low-lying phosphate rock islands in the Pacific Ocean. The climate is tropical, with average daily temperatures an almost consistent 29°C.

HISTORY AND POLITICS

From 1888 until the First World War Nauru was administered by Germany. In 1920 it became a British Empire-mandated territory under the League of Nations, administered by Australia. A trusteeship superseding the mandate was approved in 1947 by the UN and Nauru continued to be administered by Australia until it became independent on 31 January 1968.

President Rene Harris was defeated in a parliamentary vote on 8 January 2003 and was replaced by Bernard Dowiyogo who died on 9 March 2003. Derog Gioura was elected to succeed him on 20 March, but following the legislative elections of 3 May 2003, Ludvig Scotty was elected as president. In 2004, Scotty was dismissed in a vote of no confidence. Rene Harris was named as the new president and he appointed a new government on 22 June 2004.

POLITICAL SYSTEM
Parliament has 18 members including the Cabinet and Speaker. Voting is compulsory for all Nauruans aged over 20, except in certain specified instances. Elections are held every three years. The Cabinet is chosen by the President, who is elected by the Parliament from amongst its own members, and comprises not fewer than five nor more than six members including the president.

HEAD OF STATE
President, Foreign Affairs, Public Service, Nauru Phosphate Royalty Trust and Health, Rene Harris, *elected,* 21 June 2004

HONORARY CONSULATE, Romshed Courtyard, Underriver, nr. Sevenoaks, Kent TN15 0SD
T 01732-746061 E nauru@weald.co.uk
Honorary Consul, Martin Weston

BRITISH HIGH COMMISSIONER, HE Charles Mochan, resident at Suva, Fiji

ECONOMY AND TRADE
Phosphate extraction dominates Nauru's economy. The country is heavily dependent on the import of goods and services which has meant the development of close economic ties with Australia. The Nauru Phosphate Royalties Trust is a fund set up by the island's government using the profits from mining in order to provide an income for Nauru once phosphate reserves have run out. Small-scale Tourism and the fishing and farming industries are also present on Nauru.

GDP – US$32 million (1998); US$2,533 per capita (2000)
ANNUAL AVERAGE GROWTH OF GDP – 1.9 per cent (1998)

Trade with UK	*2002*	*2003*
Imports from UK	£461,000	£402,000
Exports to UK	80,000	211,000

EDUCATION
Education is free of charge and compulsory between the ages of six and 17. There are 10 infant and primary, and two secondary schools on the island with a total enrolment of about 2,707 pupils.

MEDIA
Nauru has no daily press but three weekly or fortnightly publications. A domestic radio service is supplemented by Nauru Television (NTV) which broadcasts programmes from New Zealand.

NEPAL

Nepāl Adhirājya/Kingdom of Nepal

AREA – 147,181 sq. km. Neighbours: China (north), India (south, west and east)
POPULATION – 25,284,463 (2001 estimate). The inhabitants are of mixed stock, with Tibetan characteristics prevailing in the north and Indian in the south. The official religion is Hinduism; 87 per cent of the population are Hindus, 8 per cent Buddhist and 3 per cent Muslim. The official language is Nepali
CAPITAL – Kathmandu (population, 535,000, 1993)
MAJOR CITIES – Lalitpur; Biratnagar; Bhaktapur
CURRENCY – Nepalese rupee of 100 paisa
NATIONAL ANTHEM – Sri Man Gumbhira Nepali Prachanda Pratapi Bhupati (May Glory Crown Our Illustrious Sovereign, The Gallant Nepalese)
NATIONAL DAYS – 18 February (National Democracy Day); 28 December (The King's Birthday)
NATIONAL FLAG – Double pennant of crimson with blue border on peaks; white moon with rays in centre of top peak; white quarter sun, recumbent in centre of bottom peak
LIFE EXPECTANCY (years) – 59 (2001)
MORTALITY RATE (per 1,000 population) – 9.84 (2003)
HIV / AIDS ADULT PREVALENCE – 0.5 per cent (2001)
DEATH PENALTY – No (abolished 1997)
POPULATION BELOW POVERTY LINE – 42 per cent (1996)
POPULATION GROWTH RATE – 2.4 per cent (1990–2001)
POPULATION DENSITY – 152 per sq. km (1999)
MILITARY EXPENDITURE – 1.9 per cent of GDP (2002)
MILITARY PERSONNEL – Army 63,000; Paramilitaries 40,000
ILLITERACY RATE – (m) 40.8 per cent; (f) 76.1 per cent (2000)
ENROLMENT (percentage of age group) – tertiary 5 per cent (1997)

CLIMATE AND TERRAIN
The southern region of Nepal, the Terai, forms approximately 23 per cent of the total land area. The central belt is hilly, but with many fertile valleys, leading up to the snowline at about 4,880 m. Elevation extremes range from 8,850 m (Mt Everest) at the highest point to 70 m (Kanchan Kalan) at the lowest. Average temperatures in Khatmandu range from 2°C in January to 28°C in July.

HISTORY AND POLITICS
Nepal emerged as a nation in the middle of the 18th century when it was unified by the warrior Raja of Gorkha, Prithvi Naryan Shah, who founded the present Nepalese dynasty. Power was seized by Jung Bahdur in 1846. He assumed the title Rana and his dynasty ruled the country until after the Second World War. During this time, the role of the Nepalese monarchy was purely ceremonial. In 1950–1 a revolutionary movement broke the hereditary power of the Ranas and restored the monarchy to its former position. King Mehndra proscribed all political parties and assumed direct powers in 1960. In 1962 he introduced a new constitution embodying a tiered, partyless system of *panchyat* (council) democracy.

Agitation for political reform led to the abolition of the *panchyat* system in April 1990. A new constitution was drawn up in November 1990 and established a multiparty, parliamentary system of government and a constitutional monarchy.

Between 1991 and 2001, politics was extremely factionalised and the country witnessed frequent changes of government. Nepal suffered great social instability and violence when the Communist Party of Nepal (Maoist) began an insurgency in 1996. Beginning in the remote west of the country the Maoists concentrated on disrupting elections and intimidating officials. The troubles spread throughout the country and prompted a brutal backlash from the authorities. Both the communist insurgents and Nepalese police have been implicated in human rights abuses and atrocities. After the deaths of up to 7,000 people a cease-fire was unilaterally adopted by the government and almost immediately reciprocated by the insurgents in July 2001. Fighting not only resumed but intensified in November 2001, when a state of emergency was declared and the Nepalese army became fully engaged. A second cease-fire was negotiated in 2003 but quickly broke down and clashes between the insurgents and security forces have been ongoing.

In June 2001 the royal family was devastated by the murder of King Birendra and several family members by Crown Prince Dipendra, who subsequently killed himself. Prince Gyanendra was pronounced King on 4 June.

Prime Minister Girija Prasad Koirala resigned in July 2001 and was replaced by former Prime Minister Sher Bahadur Deuba. In May 2002 Deuba asked the King to dissolve parliament and call early elections, but in October 2002, Deuba asked the King to delay elections owing to increased Maoist violence. The King dismissed Deuba on 7 October and dissolved parliament, and Lokendra Bahadur Chand was appointed to head the government on 12 October. Chand resigned in May 2003 after a failed attempt by politicians to reopen parliament, which had remained dissolved since October 2002, and in June 2003, the King appointed Surya Badahur Thapa as Prime Minister. Sher Bahadar Deuba was appointed Prime Minister on 2 June 2004. He formed a coalition cabinet that was appointed on 5 July 2004.

POLITICAL SYSTEM

The King retains joint executive power with the Council of Ministers. The bicameral legislature consists of a 205-member House of Representatives, directly elected for a five-year term, and a 60-member National Council comprising 50 who are indirectly elected for a six-year term and ten royal nominees.

HEAD OF STATE

HM The King of Nepal, King Gyanendra Bir Bikram Shah Dev, *acceded* 4 June 2001

Heir, Crown Prince Paras Bir Bikram Shah Dev

SELECTED GOVERNMENT MEMBERS *as at July 2004*

Prime Minister, Defence and Home Affairs, Foreign Affairs, Sher Bahadur Deuba

Finance, Bharat Mohan Adhikari

Home Affairs, Purna Bahadur Khadka

ROYAL NEPALESE EMBASSY

12A Kensington Palace Gardens, London W8 4QU

T 020-7229 1594/6231

E rnelondon@btconnect.com

Ambassador Extraordinary and Plenipotentiary, Prabal Shumsher Jung Bahadur Rana

BRITISH EMBASSY

Lainchaur Kathmandu, PO Box 106

T (+977) (1) 4410583

E britemb@wlink.com.np

Ambassador Extraordinary and Plenipotentiary, HE Keith Bloomfield, apptd 2002

BRITISH COUNCIL DIRECTOR, Barbara Hewitt

PO Box 640, Lainchaur, Kathmandu

T (+977) (1) 410 798

E general.enquiry@britishcouncil.org.np

ECONOMY AND TRADE

About 90 per cent of Nepalese are employed in agricultural production which centres around rice, corn, wheat, sugarcane and root crops. Manufacturing accounts for 9 per cent of GDP with construction and the financial sector contributing 10 per cent each. Nepal suffers from a number of environmental problems such as deforestation and contamination of the water supply.

GNI – US$5,584 million (2000); US$250 per capita (2001)

ANNUAL AVERAGE GROWTH OF GDP – 6.0 per cent (2000)

INFLATION RATE – 1.5 per cent (2000)

TOTAL EXTERNAL DEBT – US$2,823 million (2000)

IMPORTS – US$1,419 million (2002)

EXPORTS – US$568 million (2002)

BALANCE OF PAYMENTS

Trade – US$765 million deficit (2001)

Current Account – US$339 million deficit (2001)

Trade with UK	*2002*	*2003*
Imports from UK	£6,894,000	£6,944,000
Exports to UK	8,800,000	10,179,000

TRANSPORT INFRASTRUCTURE

There is a total of 13,223 km of roads, of which 4,073 km are surfaced. Kathmandu is connected by road with India and Tibet. Internally, the road network links Kathmandu to Kodari and Pokhara, and Pokhara to Sunauli. There are 155 km of railways.

MEDIA

The two most widely circulated newspapers are the *Kathmandu Post* and *Rising Nepal*. The Government run Radio Nepal is the most influential media outlet in the country.

THE NETHERLANDS

Koninkrijk der Nederlanden – Kingdom of the Netherlands

AREA – 33,900 sq. km Neighbours: Belgium (south), Germany (east)

POPULATION – 15,930,000 (2001): 36 per cent Catholic, 27 per cent Reformed Church, 8 per cent Muslim. The language is Dutch, a West Germanic language of Low Franconian origin closely akin to Old English and Low German. It is spoken in the Netherlands and the northern part of Belgium (Flanders). Frisian is spoken in Friesland. Dutch is the

official language in the Netherlands Antilles and Aruba; Papiamento, a mixture of Dutch and Spanish, is the vernacular
CAPITAL – ΨAmsterdam (population, 736,538, 2001)
SEAT OF GOVERNMENT – The Hague (Den Haag or, in full, 's-Gravenhage), population 443,745, (2001)
MAJOR CITIES – Eindhoven; Groningen; Haarlem; ΨRotterdam; Tilburg; Utrecht
CURRENCY – Euro (€) of 100 cents
NATIONAL ANTHEM – Wilhelmus van Nassouwe (William of Nassau)
NATIONAL FLAG – Three horizontal bands of red, white and blue
LIFE EXPECTANCY (years) – 78 (2001)
MORTALITY RATE (per 1,000 population) – 8.66 (2003)
INFANT MORTALITY (per 1,000 births) – 5 (2001)
HIV / AIDS ADULT PREVALENCE – 0.2 per cent (2001)
DEATH PENALTY – No (abolished 1982)
POPULATION GROWTH RATE – 0.6 per cent (1990–2001)
POPULATION DENSITY – 470 per sq. km (2001)
URBAN POPULATION – 90 per cent (2001)

CLIMATE AND TERRAIN

A low-lying country, the terrain of the Netherlands is characterised by its many canals and coastal dikes. The climate is temperate with average temperatures ranging from 0°C in January to 23°C in July.

HISTORY AND POLITICS

Following a revolt against Spanish rule under the leadership of William of Orange, the northern provinces were united by the Union of Utrecht (1579) and in 1581 independence was declared. Dutch economic and military power flourished in the 17th and 18th centuries, however, the Netherlands were overrun by France in the late 18th century, becoming part of the French Empire until 1814 when the southern and northern regions were united into one kingdom. In 1830, the southern provinces seceded to form Belgium and the Duchy of Luxembourg was made an independent state in 1867.

The Netherlands was neutral during the First World War, but during the Second World War the country was invaded by Germany and occupied for five years.

The post-war period was marked by economic expansion, membership of the EU and the construction of a liberal welfare state. The Netherlands was one of the first countries to adopt the euro as its currency.

The general election of 22 January 2003 resulted in a marginal win for the Christian Democratic Appeal (CDA) with 23 out of the 75 seats; the Partij van de Arbeid (PvdA) gained 19 seats. After four months of talks a new coalition, comprised of members of the CDA, the Volkspartij voor Vrijheid en Democratie (VVD) and the Democrats 66, led by Balkenende, was sworn into office on 27 May 2003.

POLITICAL SYSTEM

The States-General consists of the *Eerste Kamer* (First Chamber) of 75 members, elected for four years by the Provincial Councillors; and the *Tweede Kamer* (Second Chamber) of 150 members, elected for four years by voters of 18 years and upwards.

HEAD OF STATE
HM The Queen of the Netherlands, Queen Beatrix Wilhelmina Armgard, KG, GCVO, *born* 31 January 1938; *succeeded* 30 April 1980
Heir, HRH Prince Willem Alexander, *born* 27 April 1967

SELECTED GOVERNMENT MEMBERS *as at August 2004*
Prime Minister, General Affairs, Jan Peter Balkenende
Deputy Prime Ministers, Gerrit Zalm, Thom de Graf
Defence, Henk Kamp
Economic Affairs, Laurens Jan Brinkhorst
Foreign Affairs, Bernard Bot
Interior, Johan Remkes

ROYAL NETHERLANDS EMBASSY
38 Hyde Park Gate, London SW7 5DP
T 020-7590 3200
Ambassador Extraordinary and Plenipotentiary, HE Count Jan Mark Vladimir Anton de Marchant et d'Ansembourg, apptd 2003

BRITISH EMBASSY
Lange Voorhout 10, The Hague, NL-2514 ED
T (+31) (0) 70 4270 427
Ambassador Extraordinary and Plenipotentiary, HE Sir Colin Budd, KCMG, apptd 2001

BRITISH COUNCIL DIRECTOR, David Alderdice
Weteringschans 85A, NL-1017 RZ Amsterdam
T (+31) (0) 20 550 6060
E david.alderdice@britcoun.nl

DEFENCE

The Army has 283 main battle tanks, 345 armoured infantry fighting vehicles and 316 armoured personnel carriers. The Navy has four submarines, six destroyers, nine frigates, ten combat aircraft and 21 armed helicopters. The Air Force has 137 combat aircraft and 30 armed helicopters.
MILITARY EXPENDITURE – 1.6 per cent of GDP (2002)
MILITARY PERSONNEL – 53,130: Army 23,150, Navy 12,130, Air Force 11,050; Paramilitaries 6,800

ECONOMY AND TRADE

Despite employing a mere four per cent of the labour force, agricultural exports such as fruit, flower bulbs and cut flowers form a major part of Dutch economic activity and the country is ranked third in the world for the scale of its agricultural industries. Produce includes wheat, rye, barley, sugarcane, cattle, poultry, pig farming and dairy products. There is also an important fishing industry.

The Dutch have adopted and developed the 'polder model' of industrial relations. This is characterised by policy making by consensus and has ensured good industrial relations in the country. The industrial sector involves the manufacture of electrical machinery and equipment, metal and engineering products, chemicals and petroleum, construction and micro-electronics. The service industries represent 70 per cent of the Dutch economy and 80 per cent of Dutch trade takes place with other EU countries.
GNI – US$390,300 million (2001); US$24,330 per capita (2001)
ANNUAL AVERAGE GROWTH OF GDP – 3.8 per cent (2000)
INFLATION RATE – 2.5 per cent (2000)
UNEMPLOYMENT – 3.3 per cent (2000)
FOREIGN DIRECT INVESTMENT – US$130,363 million (1997–2000)

IMPORTS – US$193,579 million (2002)
EXPORTS – US$222,291 million (2002)

BALANCE OF PAYMENTS
Trade – US$25,754 million surplus (2002)
Current Account – US$9,866 million surplus (2002)

Trade with UK	*2002*	*2003*
Imports from UK	£13,313,600,000	£10,076,160,000
Exports to UK	14,538,400,000	11,066,270,000

TRANSPORT INFRASTRUCTURE

There are 58,133 km of inter-urban roads, of which 2,207 km are motorways. The total extent of navigable rivers including canals is 5,046 km. The total length of the railway system is 2,808 km, of which 2,061 km are electrified.

EDUCATION

Primary and secondary education is given in both denominational and state schools and is compulsory. The principal universities are at Leiden, Utrecht, Groningen, Amsterdam (two), Nijmegen, Maastricht and Rotterdam, and there are technical universities at Delft, Eindhoven, Enschede and Wageningen (agriculture).
ENROLMENT (percentage of age group) – primary 100 per cent (1997); secondary 100 per cent (1997); tertiary 47 per cent (1997)

MEDIA AND CULTURE

There are five national daily papers and a competitive television sector that includes NOS, which oversees the country's three public networks and a large number of commercial stations.

The Netherlands has a long and consistent history of excellence in painting. Notable figures include Rembrandt (1606–69), Jan Vermeer (1632–75) and Vincent van Gogh (1853–90).

OVERSEAS TERRITORIES

ARUBA

AREA – 193 sq. km
POPULATION – 70,007 (2001 estimate)
CAPITAL – ΨOranjestad (population 25,000); and Sint Nicolaas (17,000)
CURRENCY – Aruban florin

The island of Aruba was from 1828 part of the Dutch West Indies and from 1845 part of the Netherlands Antilles. On 1 January 1986 it became a separate territory within the Kingdom of the Netherlands. In 1994 it was decided that Aruba will retain separate status within the Kingdom of the Netherlands and not granted full independence.
Governor, Olindo Koolman
Prime Minister, Nelson O. Oduber

NETHERLANDS ANTILLES

AREA – 800 sq. km
POPULATION – 255,000 (2001), Curaçao 143,387, Bonaire 13,724, St Maarten 41,718, St Eustatius 2,249, Saba 1,704
CAPITAL – ΨWillemstad (on Curaçao) (pop. 50,000)
CURRENCY – Netherlands Antilles guilder of 100 cents

The Netherlands Antilles comprise the islands of Curaçao, Bonaire, part of St Maarten, St Eustatius, and Saba in the West Indies. The Netherlands Antilles, which has a 22-member federal parliament, is largely self-governing under the terms of the Realm Statute which took effect in 1954.
Governor, Frits Goedgedrag
Prime Minister, Etienne Ys

NEW ZEALAND

AREA – 268,000 sq. km
POPULATION – 3,808,000 (2001): 79 per cent European stock, 13 per cent Maori, 5 per cent other Pacific islanders. The main religion is Christianity. In 1991 the principal denominations were Anglican 22.1 per cent, Presbyterian 16.3 per cent, Roman Catholic 15 per cent, Methodist 4.2 per cent, Baptist 2.1 per cent. The official languages are English and Maori
CAPITAL – ΨWellington (population, 340,719, 2001 census)
MAJOR CITIES – ΨAuckland; ΨChristchurch; ΨDunedin; Hamilton; ΨNapier-Hastings
CURRENCY – New Zealand dollar (NZ$) of 100 cents
NATIONAL ANTHEM – God Save The Queen/God Defend New Zealand
NATIONAL DAY – 6 February (Waitangi Day)
NATIONAL FLAG – Blue ground, with Union Flag in top left quarter, four five-pointed red stars with white borders on the fly
LIFE EXPECTANCY (years) – 78 (2001)
MORTALITY RATE (per 1,000 population) – 7.54 (2003)
INFANT MORTALITY (per 1,000 births) – 6 (2001)
HIV / AIDS ADULT PREVALENCE – 0.1 per cent (2001)
DEATH PENALTY – No (abolished 1989)
POPULATION GROWTH RATE – 1.1 per cent (1990–2001)
POPULATION DENSITY – 14 per sq. km (2001)
URBAN POPULATION – 86 per cent (2001)

CLIMATE AND TERRAIN

New Zealand consists of a number of islands in the South Pacific Ocean, and also has administrative responsibility for the Ross Dependency in Antarctica. The two larger islands, North Island and South Island, are separated by a relatively narrow strait. The remaining islands are much smaller and widely dispersed.

Much of the North and South Islands is mountainous. The principal range is the Southern Alps, extending the entire length of the South Island. The North Island mountains include several volcanoes, two of which are active. Elevation extremes range from 3,764 m (Mt Cook) at the highest point to 0 m (Pacific Ocean) at the lowest. Average temperatures in Christchurch range from 1°C in July to 24°C in January.

HISTORY AND POLITICS

Settled by Polynesian tribes since the ninth century, the Dutch navigator, Abel Tasman, sighted the coast of New Zealand in 1642 but did not land. The British explorer James Cook circumnavigated New Zealand and landed in 1769, the year in which the islands were claimed by the British. In 1840 the Treaty of Waitangi established British sovereignty with Maoris retaining some territorial rights. In 1941 New Zealand was created a separate colony distinct from New South Wales and in 1907 the designation was changed to 'The Dominion of New Zealand'.

Following the general election of 27 July 2002, the state of the parties in the House of Representatives was:

Labour Party (LP) 52 seats, National Party 27, New Zealand First 13, ACT New Zealand 9; Green Party 9; United Future 8; Jim Anderton's Progressive Coalition (PC) 2. The Labour Party and the Progressive Coalition formed a minority administration.

POLITICAL SYSTEM
The head of state is the British sovereign, represented by the Governor-General appointed on the advice of the New Zealand Government. The Prime Minister and the Cabinet are appointed by the Governor-General on the advice of the unicameral legislature, the House of Representatives. The House of Representatives has 120 members, elected for a three-year term. A non-binding referendum, held simultaneously with the general election in November 1999, approved a reduction in the number of members to 100 in future parliaments. There is no written constitution. The judicial system comprises a High Court, a Court of Appeal and district courts having both civil and criminal jurisdiction.

GOVERNOR-GENERAL
Governor-General and Commander-in-Chief, HE Dame Silvia Cartwright, *sworn in* April 2001

SELECTED GOVERNMENT MEMBERS *as at August 2004*
Prime Minister, Arts, Culture and Heritage, Helen Clark
Deputy Prime Minister, Finance and Revenue, Dr Michael Cullen
Defence, State-owned Enterprises, Tourism, Mark Burton
Economic Development, Industry and Regional Development, Jim Anderton
Foreign Affairs and Trade, Justice, Pacific Island Affairs, Phil Goff

NEW ZEALAND HIGH COMMISSION
New Zealand House, 80 The Haymarket, London SW1Y 4TQ
T 020-7930 8422
High Commissioner, HE Russell Marshall, apptd 2002

BRITISH HIGH COMMISSION
44 Hill Street (PO Box 1812), Wellington 1
T (+64) (4) 924 2888
E ppa.mailbox@fco.gov.uk
High Commissioner, HE Richard Fell, CVO, apptd 2001

BRITISH COUNCIL DIRECTOR, Paul Atkins
44 Hill Street (PO Box 1812) Wellington 1
T (+64) (4) 495 0987
E enquiries@britishcouncil.org.nz

DEFENCE
The Army has 41 armoured personnel carriers. The Navy has three frigates, four patrol and coastal vessels and three armed helicopters. The Air Force has 6 combat aircraft.
MILITARY EXPENDITURE – 1.2 per cent of GDP (2002)
MILITARY PERSONNEL – 8,610: Army 4,430, Navy 1,980, Air Force 2,200

ECONOMY AND TRADE
New Zealand's economy is diverse and enjoys strong manufacturing and service industries as well as a successful agricultural sector. Historically, New Zealand has traded primarily with Britain, but since the UK joined the EU New Zealand has developed much stronger export links with Asia, especially Japan. Australia and the USA are also trading partners. The major industries are food processing, wood and paper products, wool, textiles, dairy products, iron and steel. Some 32 per cent of New Zealand's total output is from the export of goods and services. Between 70 and 80 per cent of exports are agricultural products, mainly wheat, barley, fruits, vegetables, dairy products and meat.

Non-metallic minerals such as coal, clay, limestone and dolomite are more important than metallic ones. Of the metals, the most important are gold and ironsand. Natural gas deposits in the offshore Taranaki Maui field and onshore fields are increasingly exploited and used for electricity generation.
GNI – US$51,000 million (2001); US$13,250 per capita (2001)
ANNUAL AVERAGE GROWTH OF GDP – 2.0 per cent (2000)
INFLATION RATE – 2.6 per cent (2000)
UNEMPLOYMENT – 6.0 per cent (1999)
FOREIGN DIRECT INVESTMENT – US$4,887 million (1997–2000)
IMPORTS – US$15,077 million (2002)
EXPORTS – US$14,364 million (2002)

BALANCE OF PAYMENTS
Trade – US$503 million surplus (2002)
Current Account – US$1,948 million deficit (2002)

Trade with UK	*2002**	*2003**
Imports from UK	£311,626,000	£413,777,000
Exports to UK	548,625,000	565,109,000

*Includes Niue, Tokelau and Cook Islands

TRANSPORT INFRASTRUCTURE
The national railway system is owned and operated by Tranz Rail Ltd. There are 4,439 km of railway track. There are international airports at Auckland, Christchurch and Wellington.

EDUCATION
Schools are free of charge and compulsory between the ages of six and 15. There are 2,226 state and 56 private primary schools and 320 state and 23 private secondary schools. There are seven universities and 25 polytechnics.
ENROLMENT (percentage of age group) – primary 100 per cent (1997); secondary 100 per cent (1997); tertiary 63 per cent (1997)

MEDIA AND CULTURE
The broadcasting sector was deregulated in 1988. Two public networks, Television New Zealand and Maori TV, compete with four main private networks. There are three main national daily papers and a large number of radio stations, including Ruai Mai, a Moari owned and operated broadcaster.

New Zealand's cultural history is long and complex, stretching back to the first Maori settlers who brought the art form '*Whakapapa*', a type of oral genealogy, to the island. Notable cultural figures include the writers Katherine Mansfield (1888–1923) and Hone Tuwhare (b. 1922), the poet Sam Hunt (b. 1946) and the filmmakers Jane Campion (b. 1954) and Peter Jackson (b. 1961).

TERRITORIES

TOKELAU (OR UNION ISLANDS)
Tokelau is a group of atolls, Fakaofo, Nukunonu and Atafu. It was proclaimed part of New Zealand as of 1 January 1949. The Council of Faipule, composed of one

elected representative from each atoll, was established in 1992 to govern Tokelau when the General Fono was not in session. The position of *Ulu-o-Tokelau* (leader) is rotated among the three Faipule members annually. The General Fono has 48 seats and its numbers are chosen by each atoll's Council of Elders *(Taupulega)* to serve a three-year term. The Tokelau Amendment Act, passed by the New Zealand Parliament in 1996, conferred legislative power on the General Fono.
Administrator, Neil Walter, apptd 2002

THE ROSS DEPENDENCY
The Ross Dependency is defined as all the Antarctic islands and territories between 160° E. and 150° W. longitude which are situated south of the 60° S. parallel, including Edward VII Land and portions of Victoria Land.

ASSOCIATED STATES

COOK ISLANDS
Included in the realm of New Zealand since 1901, the Cook Islands group consists of the islands of Rarotonga, Aitutaki, Mangaia, Atiu, Mauke, Mitiaro, Manuae, Takutea, Palmerston, Penrhyn or Tongareva, Manihiki, Rakahanga, Suwarrow, Pukapuka or Danger, and Nassau. Queen Elizabeth II has a representative on the islands, and there is a New Zealand High Commissioner. Since 1965 the islands have been in free association with New Zealand and enjoyed complete internal self-government, executive power being in the hands of a Cabinet consisting of a Prime Minister and five other ministers. There is a 25-member Legislative Assembly.
Prime Minister, Dr Robert Woonton

NIUE
A New Zealand High Commissioner is stationed at Niue, which since 1974 has been self-governing in free association with New Zealand. Executive power is in the hands of a premier and a Cabinet of three drawn from the Assembly of 20 members. The Assembly is the supreme legislative body.
New Zealand High Commissioner, Sandra Lee

NICARAGUA

República de Nicaragua – Republic of Nicaragua

AREA – 130,000 sq. km. Neighbours: Honduras (north), Costa Rica (south)
POPULATION – 4,918,393 (2001 estimate): three-quarters are of mixed stock, another 15 per cent are white, mostly of pure Spanish descent, and the remaining 10 per cent are West Indians or Indians. The latter group includes the Misquitos, who live on the Atlantic coast. The official language is Spanish and the majority are Roman Catholic, although the English language and the Moravian Church are widespread on the Atlantic coast
CAPITAL – Managua (population, 864,201, 1995 estimate)
MAJOR CITIES – Chinandega; Granada; León; Masaya
CURRENCY – Córdoba (C$) of 100 centavos
NATIONAL ANTHEM – Salve A Tí Nicaragua (Hail, Nicaragua)
NATIONAL DAY – 15 September
NATIONAL FLAG – Horizontal stripes of blue, white and blue, with the Nicaraguan coat of arms in the centre of the white stripe
LIFE EXPECTANCY (years) – 69 (2001)
MORTALITY RATE (per 1,000 population) – 4.69 (2003)
HIV / AIDS ADULT PREVALENCE – 0.2 per cent (2001)
DEATH PENALTY – No (abolished 1979)
POPULATION GROWTH RATE – 2.7 per cent (1990–2001)
POPULATION DENSITY – 38 per sq. km (1999)
ILLITERACY RATE – (m) 33.1 per cent; (f) 29.8 per cent (2000)
ENROLMENT (percentage of age group) – primary 100 per cent (1997); secondary 55 per cent (1997); tertiary 12 per cent (1997)

CLIMATE AND TERRAIN
Nicaragua has extensive coastal plains that rise to central interior mountains. Elevation extremes range from 2,438 m (Mogoton) at the highest point to 0 m (Pacific Ocean) at the lowest. The climate is generally tropical near the coast with average temperatures in Managua ranging from 20°C in January to 34°C in August.

HISTORY AND POLITICS
Spanish colonisation of Nicaragua began in 1523 but independence from Spain was granted in 1821.

The assassination of liberal politician Augusto C. Sandino followed by rigged elections saw dictator General Somoza installed in 1934. The Somoza dynasty ruled Nicaragua until 1979 when a popular revolt against the regime led by the Frente Sandinista de Liberacíon Nacional (FSLN), popularly known as the Sandinistas, was successful in seizing control. However, after ten years in power and a civil war against US-backed anti-communist guerrillas, the Sandinistas lost their parliamentary majority in elections held in 1990. A coalition of former opposition parties, the Unión Nacional de Opositora (UNO), formed a Government and the civil war came to an end.

In presidential and legislative elections held on 4 November 2001, Enrique Bolaños Geyer of the Liberal Constitutionalist Party (PLC) was elected President and the PLC gained 47 seats in the National Assembly, with the FSLN winning 43 seats. The Government is formed by a coalition led by the PLC.

POLITICAL SYSTEM
The head of Government is the President, elected for a five-year term, not immediately renewable. The President appoints the Cabinet. There is a unicameral legislature, the National Assembly, with 90 members directly elected for a five-year term.

HEAD OF STATE
President, Enrique Bolaños Geyer, *elected* 4 November 2001, *sworn in* 10 January 2002
Vice-President, José Rizo Castellon

SELECTED GOVERNMENT MEMBERS *as at July 2004*
Defence, José Adán Guerra
Finance and Public Credit, Eduardo Montealegre Rivas
Foreign Affairs, Norman Caldera Cardinal
Interior, Eduardo Urcuyo Llanes

EMBASSY OF NICARAGUA
Suite 31, Vicarage House, 58–60 Kensington Church Street, London W8 4DP
T 020-7938 2373
Ambassador Extraordinary and Plenipotentiary, HE Juan B. Sacasa, apptd 2001

BRITISH EMBASSY
Apartado A-169, Plaza Churchill, Reparto 'Los Robles', Managua
T (+505) (2) 780014/780887/674050
Ambassador and Consul-General, HE Timothy Brownbill, apptd 2002

DEFENCE

The Army has 127 main battle tanks and 166 armoured personnel carriers. The Navy has five patrol and coastal vessels at three bases. The Air Force has 15 armed helicopters. Full military relations with the USA were restored in 2000 after 21 years.

MILITARY EXPENDITURE – 1.3 per cent of GDP (2002)
MILITARY PERSONNEL – 14,000: Army 12,000, Navy 800, Air Force 1,200
CONSCRIPTION DURATION – 18–36 months

ECONOMY AND TRADE

Nicaragua was devastated by Hurricane Mitch in 1998. Reconstruction spurred economic recovery but a drop in demand for agricultural products meant that growth could not be sustained. The agriculture sector is threatened by deforestation, soil erosion and water pollution.

The agricultural and food processing industries include coffee, sugar, bananas and sesame; cattle rearing and seafood fishing. Light industrial goods are also produced. Considerable quantities of foodstuffs are imported as well as cotton goods, jute, iron and steel, machinery and petroleum products.

GNI – US$2,053 million (2000); US$400 per capita (2000)
ANNUAL AVERAGE GROWTH OF GDP – 5.0 per cent (1999)
INFLATION RATE – 3.7 per cent (2002)
UNEMPLOYMENT – 9.8 per cent (2000)
TOTAL EXTERNAL DEBT – US$7,019 million (2000)
IMPORTS – US$1,795 million (2002)
EXPORTS – US$596 million (2002)

BALANCE OF PAYMENTS
Trade – US$1,031 million deficit (2003)
Current Account – US$888 million deficit (2002)

Trade with UK	*2002*	*2003*
Imports from UK	£4,631,000	£3,680,000
Exports to UK	6,071,000	5,241,000

TRANSPORT INFRASTRUCTURE

The inter-American Highway runs between the Honduras and the Costa Rican borders; the inter-Oceanic highway runs from Corinto on the Pacific coast via Managua to Rama, where there is a natural waterway to Bluefields on the Atlantic; there are 15,478 km of roads and 252 miles of railway. The main airport is at Managua. The chief port is Corinto in the Pacific.

MEDIA AND CULTURE

There are three daily newspapers including *El Nuevo Diario*, a pro-Sandinista publication. Canal 6, the state owned broadcaster, competes with three commercial networks to provide television services. There are a large number of radio stations.

Nicaraguan culture blends Caribbean and Latin American influences and is widely regarded as a forerunner of Central America's literary production. Celebrated writers include Rubén Darío (1867–1916), Joaquín Pasos (1914–47) and Pablo Cuadra (1912–2002).

NIGER

République du Niger – Republic of Niger

AREA – 1,267,000 sq. km. Neighbours: Algeria and Libya (north), Chad (east), Nigeria and Benin (south), Mali and Burkina Faso (west). Apart from a small area along the Niger Valley in the south-west near the capital, the country is entirely savannah or desert
POPULATION – 10,355,156 (2001 estimate): Hausa (54 per cent) in the south, Songhai and Djerma in the south-west, Fulani, Beriberi-Manga, and nomadic Tuareg in the north. The main religion is Islam (95 per cent), with Christian and Animist minorities. The official language is French. Hausa, Djerma and Fulani are also spoken
CAPITAL – Niamey (population, 627,400, 1999 estimate)
CURRENCY – Franc CFA of 100 centimes
NATIONAL ANTHEM – Auprès Du Grand Niger Puissant (By The Banks Of The Mighty Great Niger)
NATIONAL DAY – 18 December
NATIONAL FLAG – Three horizontal stripes, orange, white and green with an orange disc in the middle of the white stripe
LIFE EXPECTANCY (years) – 45 (2001)
MORTALITY RATE (per 1,000 population) – 21.71 (2003)
HIV / AIDS ADULT PREVALENCE – 4 per cent (2001)
DEATH PENALTY – No (abolished 1976)
POPULATION BELOW POVERTY LINE – 63 per cent (1993)
POPULATION GROWTH RATE – 3.2 per cent (2001)
POPULATION DENSITY – 8 per sq. km (1999)
MILITARY EXPENDITURE – 1.6 per cent of GDP (2002)
MILITARY PERSONNEL – 5,300: Army 5,200, Air Force 100; Paramilitaries 5,400
CONSCRIPTION DURATION – Two years (selective)
ILLITERACY RATE – (m) 76.2 per cent; (f) 91.6 per cent (2000)
ENROLMENT (percentage of age group) – primary 29 per cent (1997); secondary 7 per cent (1997); tertiary 0.7 per cent (1991)

CLIMATE AND TERRAIN

Elevation extremes range from 1,944 m (Mt Greboun) at the highest point to 200 m (Niger River) at the lowest. Average temperatures range from 24°C in January to 34°C in May.

HISTORY AND POLITICS

French imperial expansion into west Africa resulted in Niger coming under French control in 1898. The post-imperial era, which began when the country achieved full independence in 1960, did not bring stability. A coup in 1974 ushered in a period of military dictatorship, and it was not until 1990 that the constitution was amended to allow for multi-party democracy. Elections did not take place until 1993. By 1995 the relationship between the President, Mahamane Ousmane, and Prime Minister,

Hama Amadou, had deteriorated to the point that the military used the political deadlock to mount a coup.

Brigadier Ibrahim Barre Mainassara seized power in January 1996, and though he allowed opposition parties to contest elections his victory in July 1996 was condemned as fraudulent by the international community. Mainassara's rule was unpopular and resulted in a rebellion by the Tuareg people which was only resolved through a peace process mediated in Algiers.

Peace in Niger has been interrupted by violent ethnic clashes and popular agitation calling for the removal of Brigadier Mainassara who was eventually killed in a further coup in 1999. A presidential election was held in November 1999 and won by Mamadou Tandja of the National Movement for Society in Development (MNSD). In the simultaneous legislative elections the MNSD won an overall majority in the National Assembly. Presidential elections were due to take place in October 2004 with legislative elections due in late November 2004.

HEAD OF STATE
President, Mamadou Tandja, *elected* 24 November 1999, *sworn in* 22 December 1999

SELECTED GOVERNMENT MEMBERS *as at July 2004*
Prime Minister, Hama Amadou
Finance and Economy, Ali Lamine Zené
Foreign Affairs, Co-operation and African Integration, Aissatou Mindaoudou
Interior and De-centralisation, Albade Abouba
National Defence, Souley Hassane 'Bonto'

EMBASSY OF THE REPUBLIC OF NIGER
154 rue de Longchamp, F-75116, Paris
T (+33) (1) 4504 8060
Ambassador Extraordinary and Plenipotentiary, HE Adamou Seydou

BRITISH AMBASSADOR, HE J. François Gordon, CMG, resident at Abidjan, Côte d'Ivoire

ECONOMY AND TRADE

The cultivation of groundnuts and the production of livestock are the main industries and provide two of the main exports. Other agricultural products include millet, cassava and sugarcane. Agriculture accounts for 90 per cent of the labour force; most of this is at subsistence level. There are large uranium deposits at Arlit and Akouta. Gold deposits exist north-west of Niamey.

Civil unrest in neighbouring Côte d'Ivoire has deprived Niger of access to vital ports and made the export of the country's commodities more expensive and difficult.

Environmental problems facing Niger include overgrazing, deforestation, desertification and the destruction of wildlife through poaching. The country qualified for debt relief in 2000.

GNI – US$1,939 million (2000); US$180 per capita (2000)
ANNUAL AVERAGE GROWTH OF GDP – 3.4 per cent (1998)
INFLATION RATE – 2.9 per cent (2000)
TOTAL EXTERNAL DEBT – US$1,638 million (2000)
IMPORTS – US$400 million (2002)
EXPORTS – US$280 million (2002)

Trade with UK	*2002*	*2003*
Imports from UK	£6,184,000	£6,150,000
Exports to UK	518,000	2,844,000

TRANSPORT INFRASTRUCTURE

There are no ports, harbours or railways. There are 10,100 km of highways, though less than 1,000 km of these are surfaced. The Niger River is navigable from the capital, Niamey, to the Benin frontier between December and March.

MEDIA AND CULTURE

Radio, the most important form of communication in the country, is a growing sector and the state owned broadcaster competes with a number of private stations. A single state owned daily newspaper competes with a proliferating number of private publications.

Niger is the hub of Tuareg culture. One of Niger's most celebrated writers is Oum Ramatou (b. 1970).

NIGERIA

Federal Republic of Nigeria

AREA – 910,800 sq. km. Neighbours: Benin (west), Niger (north), Chad (north-east), Cameroon (east)
POPULATION – 116,929,000 (2001). The main ethnic groups are Hausa/Fulani, Yoruba and Ibo, and the principal languages are English, Hausa, Yoruba and Ibo. There are some 373 ethnic groups, who speak over 500 different languages. The main religions are Christianity (49 per cent, mainly in the south) and Islam (45 per cent, mainly in the north and west), the remainder being Animists
CAPITAL – Abuja (population, 378,671), declared the federal capital in 1991
MAJOR CITIES – Ibadan; Kaduna; Kano; Lagos, the former capital; Ogbomosho; ΨPort Harcourt
CURRENCY – Naira (N) of 100 kobo
NATIONAL ANTHEM – Arise, O Compatriots
NATIONAL DAY – 1 October (Independence Day)
NATIONAL FLAG – Three equal vertical bands, green, white and green
LIFE EXPECTANCY (years) – 52 (2001)
MORTALITY RATE (per 1,000 population) – 13.76 (2003)
INFANT MORTALITY (per 1,000 births) – 110 (2001)
HIV / AIDS ADULT PREVALENCE – 5.8 per cent (2001)
DEATH PENALTY – Yes
POPULATION BELOW POVERTY LINE – 60 per cent (2000)
POPULATION GROWTH RATE – 2.8 per cent (1990–2001)
POPULATION DENSITY – 128 per sq. km (2001)
ILLITERACY RATE – (m) 27.6 per cent; (f) 44.2 per cent (2000)
ENROLMENT (percentage of age group) – tertiary 4.1 per cent (1993)

CULTURE AND TERRAIN

Nigeria's terrain varies from coastal swamps in the south to an arid semi-desert in the north. Elevation extremes range from 2,419 m (Chappal Waddis) at the highest point to 0 m (Atlantic Ocean) at the lowest. Average temperatures in Lagos range from 22°C in July to 32°C in January.

HISTORY AND POLITICS

The Sokoto Caliphate, a powerful Muslim empire, dominated the region from the late 18th century.

The abolition of slavery by the British in 1807 led to several other powers attempting to exploit Nigeria's slave trade. This, in turn, led to British annexation of Lagos in 1861. British power in Nigeria established the Oil Rivers Protectorate in 1885 and the Niger Coast Protectorate in 1894. By 1914 British military expeditions had united the whole of modern Nigeria into a single political and administrative body under the control of the British Empire.

Full independence in 1960 released considerable ethnic tensions. The Igbo people began to agitate for secession following fierce anti-Igbo riots. These were sparked by an attempted coup by several Igbo army officers that resulted in the deaths of a number of government officials. The situation deteriorated into civil war when the Igbo proclaimed the Republic of Biafra in 1967. Biafra surrendered and returned to Nigeria in 1970.

Political stability proved impossible to implant in Nigeria and the 1970s and 1980s were tormented by coups and periods of semi-military rule. In 1993, General Sani Abacha seized power.

The death of Abacha in 1998 allowed the beginnings of a return to civilian rule. His successor, General Abdulsalami Abubakar, instituted a number of democratic reforms that led to the election of Olusegun Obasanjo of the People's Democratic Party (PDP) in 1999.

In legislative elections on 12 April 2003 the PDP retained its majority in both houses of parliament, and on 19 April 2003 Gen. Olusegun Obasanjo was returned to office for a second term with 61.9 per cent of the vote.

The debate on *Shari'ah* law has exacerbated divisions between Muslims and Christians and there have been sporadic clashes in which hundreds of civilians have been killed.

POLITICAL SYSTEM

The country is a federal democratic republic. The President is directly elected for a four-year term, renewable only once. As head of the Government, the President appoints the Federal Executive Council, which must be approved by the Senate. The National Assembly is bicameral; the House of Representatives has 360 members and the Senate has 109 members, both elected for a four-year term.

Several predominantly Muslim northern states introduced the Islamic *Shari'ah* legal system during 2000, which President Obasanjo had declared unconstitutional on 1 November 1999. Bauchi adopted *Shari'ah* law in June 2001.

FEDERAL STATES

Originally comprising three regions, the Federation is now divided into 36 states and the Federal Capital Territory: Sokoto, Zamfara, Kebbi, Niger, Kwara, Kogi, Benue, Plateau, Nassarawa, Taraba, Adamawa, Borno, Yobe, Bauchi, Gombe, Jigawa, Kano, Katsina, Kaduna, Federal Capital Territory, Oyo, Osun, Ogun, Lagos, Ekiti, Edo, Delta, Rivers, Bayelsa, Abia, Imo, Ebonyi, Anambra, Enugu, Cross River and Akwa Ibom.

HEAD OF STATE

President, Olusegun Obasanjo, elected 27 February 1999, *re-elected* 19 April 2003
Vice-President, Atiku Abubakar

SELECTED GOVERNMENT MEMBERS *as at July 2004*

Defence, Rabiu Kwankaso
Finance, Ngozi Okono-Iweala
Foreign Affairs, Oluyemi Adeniji
Internal Affairs, Iyorcha Ayu

NIGERIA HIGH COMMISSION

Nigeria House, 9 Northumberland Avenue, London WC2N 5BX
T 020-7839 1244
High Commissioner, HE Dr Christopher Kolade, apptd 2002

BRITISH HIGH COMMISSION

Shehu Shagari Way (North), Maitama, Abuja
T (+234) (9) 413 2010/2011/2796/2880
E consular.abuja@fco.gov.uk
High Commissioner, HE Richard Gozney apptd 2004

BRITISH COUNCIL DIRECTOR, Cathy Stephens

Plot 2935, IBB Way, Maitama, PMB 550, Garki, Abuja
T (+234) (9) 413 7870-7
E maureen.ideozu@ng.britishcouncil.org

DEFENCE

The Army has 250 main battle tanks and 417 armoured personnel carriers. The Navy has one frigate, five patrol and coastal vessels and four helicopters at three bases. The Air Force has 84 combat aircraft and 15 armed helicopters.

MILITARY EXPENDITURE – 1.2 per cent of GDP (2002)
MILITARY PERSONNEL – 78,500: Army 62,000, Navy 7,000, Air Force 9,500; Paramilitaries 82,000

ECONOMY AND TRADE

Nigeria is the leading sub-Saharan oil producer, accounting for 2.3 million barrels per day. Oil accounts for 20 per cent of GDP, 65 per cent of budgetary revenues and 95 per cent of foreign exchange earnings. Debt relief was suspended in 2002 after Nigeria found it could not meet the imposed spending and exchange rate targets imposed by the IMF.

Agricultural crops include cocoa, peanuts, palm oil, corn, rice, sorghum, millet, cassava (tapioca) and yams. Apart from crude oil, Nigeria has reserves of coal, tin and columbite.

Environmental problems include soil degradation, deforestation, urban air and water pollution and the loss of arable land due to oil spills. There is large-scale migration from rural to urban areas, further threatening the agrarian sector.

GNI – US$37,100 million (2001); US$290 per capita (2001)
ANNUAL AVERAGE GROWTH OF GDP – 2.4 per cent (1998)
INFLATION RATE – 14.2 per cent (2002)
TOTAL EXTERNAL DEBT – US$34,134 million (2000)
FOREIGN DIRECT INVESTMENT – US$4,677 million (1997–2000)
IMPORTS – US$7,547 million (2002)
EXPORTS – US$15,107 million (2002)

BALANCE OF PAYMENTS

Trade – US$4,288 million surplus (1999)
Current Account – US$506 million surplus (1999)

Trade with UK	*2002*	*2003*
Imports from UK	£716,377,000	£750,839,000
Exports to UK	96,807,000	88,559,000

TRANSPORT INFRASTRUCTURE

There are 194,394 km of roads. The Nigerian railway network, which is controlled by the Nigerian Railway Corporation, has 3,557 km of track. The principal international airlines operate from Lagos, Kano and Port Harcourt.

MEDIA AND CULTURE

There are nine main daily newspapers, supplemented by weekly publications. The Nigerian Television Authority (NTA) is a state run broadcaster operating alongside a large number of private and commercial networks. Radio provides Nigerians with their main access to the media.

Nigeria has a strong literary heritage. Wole Soyinka (b. 1934) is the country's best known poet and was winner of the Nobel Prize for Literature in 1986. Novelist Chinua Achebe (b. 1930) developed the African novel into a form which documented the impact of colonialism on African societies. Nigeria's most famous muscian is Fela Kuti (1938–97).

NORWAY

Kongeriket Norge – Kingdom of Norway

AREA – 306,800 sq. km of which Svalbard and Jan Mayen have a combined area of 63,080 sq. km. Neighbours: Sweden, Finland, Russia (east)
POPULATION – 4,488,000 (2001). The language is Norwegian and has two forms: Bokmål and Nynorsk. Sami is spoken in the north of the country. The state religion is Evangelical Lutheran
CAPITAL – ΨOslo (population, 508,726, 2001)
MAJOR CITIES – ΨBergen; ΨKristiansand; ΨStavanger; ΨTrondheim
CURRENCY – Krone of 100 øre
NATIONAL ANTHEM – Ja, Vi Elsker Dette Landet (Yes, We Love This Country)
NATIONAL DAY – 17 May (Constitution Day)
NATIONAL FLAG – Red, with a white-bordered blue cross
LIFE EXPECTANCY (years) – 79 (2001)
MORTALITY RATE (per 1,000 population) – 9.72 (2003)
INFANT MORTALITY (per 1,000 births) – 4 (2001)
HIV / AIDS ADULT PREVALENCE – 0.1 per cent (2001)
DEATH PENALTY – No (abolished 1979)
POPULATION GROWTH RATE – 0.5 per cent (1990–2001)
POPULATION DENSITY – 15 per sq. km (2001)

CLIMATE AND TERRAIN

The Norwegian coastline is deeply indented with numerous fjords and fringed with rocky islands. The surface is mountainous, consisting of elevated and barren tablelands separated by deep and narrow valleys. Elevation extremes range from 2,469 m (Galdhopiggen) at the highest point to 0 m (Norwegian Sea) at the lowest. At the North Cape the sun does not appear to set from about 14 May to 29 July, causing the phenomenon known as the Midnight Sun; conversely, there is no apparent sunrise from about 18 November to 24 January. Average temperatures in Oslo range between −7°C in February to 22°C in August, however, winter temperatures in the north can drop to −15°C.

HISTORY AND POLITICS

Norway became a unified country under rule of King Harald Fairhair in AD 900. The accession of Magnus VI (1319) unified the Norwegian and Swedish crowns until his son became King Haakon VI of Norway in 1343. The monarchies of Norway and Denmark were united in 1380. In 1814 Norway was ceded to Sweden until Norway became fully independent in 1905.

Neutral throughout the First World War, Norway was invaded by Germany in 1940. The Norwegian monarchy and government fled into exile in London and did not return until 7 June 1945.

King Haakon VII, a popular monarch who had reigned throughout the war years, died and was succeeded by his son, Crown Prince Olav. His death in 1991 brought King Harald V to the throne.

Norway joined NATO in 1949 and was a founder member of the European Free Trade Association in 1960. The Labour Party governed from 1945 to 1965 during which time an extensive welfare state was established.

A general election was held on 10 September 2001, in which no party won an outright majority. The Labour Party (DNA) has the largest number of seats (43) but three parties, the Conservative Party (H), the Christian Democratic Party (KrF) and the Liberal Party (V), agreed to form a coalition government, and on 19 October Kjell Magne Bondevik of the KrF was appointed Prime Minister.

FOREIGN RELATIONS

Although a referendum in 1972 rejected membership of the EC, and the ruling centre-right coalition collapsed in 1990 over the question of EC membership the Storting voted in 1992 to apply to join the EC. Negotiations with the EU concluded on 1 March 1994 with a proposed accession date of 1 January 1995, however, in a national referendum on 28 November 1994 the electorate voted against joining the EU by 52.4 per cent to 47.6 per cent.

POLITICAL SYSTEM

Under the 1814 constitution, the 165-member unicameral legislature, the *Storting*, is directly elected for four years. The Storting elects one-quarter of its members to constitute the *Lagting* (Upper Chamber), the other three-quarters forming the *Odelsting* (Lower Chamber), dividing when legislative matters are under discussion.

HEAD OF STATE
HM The King of Norway, King Harald V, KG, GCVO, *born* 21 February 1937; *succeeded* 17 January 1991
Heir, HRH Crown Prince Håkon Magnus, *born* 20 July 1973

SELECTED GOVERNMENT MEMBERS *as at July 2004*
Prime Minister, Kjell Magne Bondevik
Defence, Kristin Krohn Devold
Finance, Per-Kristian Foss
Foreign Affairs, Jan Petersen

ROYAL NORWEGIAN EMBASSY
25 Belgrave Square, London SW1X 8QD
T 020-7591 5500
Ambassador Extraordinary and Plenipotentiary, HE Tarald Osnes Brautaset, apptd 2000

BRITISH EMBASSY
Thomas Heftyesgate 8, N-0244 Oslo
T (+47) 2313 2700
Ambassador Extraordinary and Plenipotentiary, HE Mariot Leslie, apptd 2002

BRITISH COUNCIL DIRECTOR, Sarah Prosser
Fridtjof Nansens Plass 5, N-0160 Oslo
T (+47) (22) 396 190
E british.council@britishcouncil.no

DEFENCE

Norway is a member of NATO. The Army has 170 main battle tanks, 157 armoured infantry fighting vehicles and 189 armoured personnel carriers. The Navy has six submarines, three frigates and 15 patrol and coastal vessels at three bases. The Air Force has 61 combat aircraft.

MILITARY EXPENDITURE – 1.9 per cent of GDP (2002)
MILITARY PERSONNEL – 26,600: Army 14,700, Navy 6,100, Air Force 5,000
CONSCRIPTION DURATION – 12 months plus refresher training

ECONOMY AND TRADE

The Norwegian economy relies primarily upon its oil and gas sectors and fisheries. The third largest oil exporter after Saudi Arabia and Russia, Norway's net exports of oil and petroleum products reached 3.1 million barrels per day in 2002. In 2001 oil and gas accounted for 36 per cent of all exports. The chief imports are motor vehicles, ships and machinery, clothing, foods and textiles.

Shipping freight services are also significant with Norwegian companies controlling 10 per cent of the world's shipping fleet. The export of timber and aluminium is also important.

As a safeguard against the decline of oil and gas stocks, Norway has invested its budget surpluses into the Government Petroleum Fund, now worth about US$ 43,000 million.

GNI – US$160,800 million (2001); US$35,630 per capita (2001)
ANNUAL AVERAGE GROWTH OF GDP – 2.7 per cent (2000)
INFLATION RATE – 1.3 per cent (2001)
UNEMPLOYMENT – 3.4 per cent (2000)
FOREIGN DIRECT INVESTMENT – US$16,621 million (1997–2000)
IMPORTS – US$34,892 million (2002)
EXPORTS – US$59,696 million (2002)

BALANCE OF PAYMENTS
Trade – US$24,371 million surplus (2002)
Current Account – US$25,148 million surplus (2002)

Trade with UK	*2002*	*2003*
Imports from UK	£1,815,245,000	£1,948,815,000
Exports to UK	5,568,449,000	6,591,022,000

TRANSPORT INFRASTRUCTURE

The total length of the rail network open at the end of 1999 was 4,021 km, excluding private lines. There are 90,880 km of public roads in Norway.

EDUCATION

Education from six to 16 is free of charge and compulsory in the 'basic schools', and free from 16 to 19 years. The majority of pupils receive post-compulsory schooling at 'upper secondary' schools, regional colleges, and 11 universities and specialist colleges.

ENROLMENT (percentage of age group) – primary 100 per cent (1997); secondary 100 per cent (1997); tertiary 62 per cent (1997)

MEDIA AND CULTURE

Norwegian broadcasting was deregulated in 1981. There are a number of commercial channels, and satellite networks are becoming increasingly popular. There are five national daily newspapers and a single national weekly newspaper.

Influential cultural figures include the artist Edvard Munch (1863–1944), the writers Knut Hamsun (1859–1952) and Henrik Ibsen (1828–1906), the composer Edvard Grieg (1843–1907) and the ecological philosopher Arne Naess (b. 1912).

TERRITORIES

SVALBARD, area 62,923 sq. km; population 2,332 (2001 estimate). The Svalbard archipelago consists of the main island, Spitsbergen, North East Land, the Wiche Islands, Barents and Edge Islands, Prince Charles Foreland, Hope Island and Bear Island.
JAN MAYEN ISLAND was joined to Norway in 1930

NORWEGIAN ANTARCTIC TERRITORIES

BOUVET ISLAND (since 1930)
PETER THE FIRST ISLAND (since 1931)
PRINCESS RAGNHILD LAND (since 1931)
QUEEN MAUD LAND (since 1939)

OMAN

Saltanat 'Umān – Sultanate of Oman

AREA – 212,500 sq. km. Neighbours: Yemen, Saudi Arabia and the UAE (west)
POPULATION – 2,622,000 (2001). The official language is Arabic. Islam is the official religion. The majority of the population are Ibadhi Muslims; there is a large Sunni and a small Shia minority. Other religions are tolerated
CAPITAL – ΨMuscat (Masqat) (population, 540,000 2001 estimate)
MAJOR CITIES – ΨBarka; ΨMutrah and Ruwi (the commercial centres); ΨSalalah (the main town of Dhofar); ΨSuhar; ΨSur
CURRENCY – Rial Omani (OR) of 1,000 baisas
NATIONAL ANTHEM – Ya Rabbana Ifadh Lana Jalalat Al Sultan (O Lord, Protect For Us His Majesty The Sultan)
NATIONAL DAY – 18 November
NATIONAL FLAG – Red with a white panel in the upper fly and a green one in the lower fly; in the canton the national emblem in white
LIFE EXPECTANCY (years) – 71 (2001)
MORTALITY RATE (per 1,000 population) – 3.97 (2003)
INFANT MORTALITY (per 1,000 births) – 12 (2001)
HIV / AIDS ADULT PREVALENCE – 0.1 per cent (2001)
DEATH PENALTY – Yes
POPULATION GROWTH RATE – 3.5 per cent (1990–2001)
POPULATION DENSITY – 12 per sq. km (2001)

CLIMATE AND TERRAIN

Oman lies at the eastern corner of the Arabian peninsula. The north and the south of the country are divided by nearly 643 km of desert. The Hajjar mountain range runs from north-west to south-east, and elevation extremes range from 2,980 m (Jabal Shams) at the highest point to 0 m (Arabian Sea) at the lowest. Average temperatures range from 12°C in January to 44°C in July.

HISTORY AND POLITICS

Oman began to build an empire in the Middle East from the eighth century AD and remained unchallenged until the arrival of the Portuguese in the 16th century. A century long period of Portuguese occupation was brought to a close in 1650. A second Omani empire flourished, and by the 19th century had reached the African coast and Central Asia where Omanis controlled Baluchistan in modern Pakistan.

As the empire declined in power, Oman was subject to internal disputes. Sultan Qaboos bin Said came to power in 1970 and began to modernise the country.

Basic Law was adopted in 1996 and established a succession mechanism, codified the system of Government and developed political and legal systems. On 4 October 2003 elections for the Consultative Council were held. This poll marked the first time all Omanis over the age of 21 (including women) had been allowed to vote. Two women were elected to the Council.

POLITICAL SYSTEM

In 1996 the Sultan issued the Basic Statute of the State which decreed Oman to be a Hereditary Absolute Monarchy. Effective political power remains with the Sultan, who rules by decree and is advised by the Cabinet of Ministers, which he appoints. The Sultan is advised by the Council of State *(Majlis al-Dawlah)*, whose 41 members are appointed by him. The 83-member Consultative Council *(Majlis ash-Shura)* has been directly elected since September 2000. The Council has the right to review Legislation, question Ministers and make policy proposals.

HEAD OF STATE

HM The Sultan of Oman, Sultan Qaboos bin Said al-Said, *succeeded on deposition of* Sultan Said bin Taimur, 23 July 1970

SELECTED GOVERNMENT MEMBERS *as at July 2004*

Prime Minister, Defence, Finance, Foreign Affairs, The Sultan

Deputy Prime Minister, Fahd bin Mamud al-Said

Defence, Badr bin Saud bin Hareb al-Busaidi

Foreign Affairs, Yusuf bin Alawi bin Abdullah

Interior, Saud bin Ibrahim al-Busaidi

National Economy, Ahmed bin Abdulnabi Makki

EMBASSY OF THE SULTANATE OF OMAN

167 Queen's Gate, London SW7 5HE

T 020-7225 0001

Ambassador Extraordinary and Plenipotentiary, HE Hussain Ali Abdullatif, apptd 1995

BRITISH EMBASSY

PO Box 185, Mina Al Fahal, Muscat, Postal Code 116

T (+968) 609 000

E becomu@omantel.net.om

Ambassador Extraordinary and Plenipotentiary, HE Stuart Laing, apptd 2002

BRITISH COUNCIL DIRECTOR, Jim Scarth

Road One, Madinat al Sultan, Qaboos West, PO Box 73, Muscat

T (+968) 600 548

E bc.muscat@om.britishcouncil.org

DEFENCE

The Army has 117 main battle tanks and 204 armoured personnel carriers. The Navy has 13 patrol and coastal vessels at six bases. The Air Force has 40 combat aircraft.

MILITARY EXPENDITURE – 13.4 per cent of GDP (2001)

MILITARY PERSONNEL – 39,700: Army 25,000, Navy 4,200, Air Force 4,100, Royal Household 6,400; Paramilitaries 4,400

ECONOMY AND TRADE

The economy of Oman is primarily dependent on the export of oil and gas although the agriculture and fishing sectors are also important. Oil production began in 1967 and accounts for 80 per cent of Government revenue. The natural gas industry is being developed, as is tourism and communication technology.

Agriculture is limited, accounting for just 2.1 per cent of GDP, and produces dates, limes, bananas, alfalfa and vegetables.

Oman joined the World Trade Organisation (WTO) in November 2000 and has since embarked on a process of privatising its utilities.

GDP – US$14,162 million (1998); US$7,811 per capita (2000)

ANNUAL AVERAGE GROWTH OF GDP – 5.2 per cent (2000)

INFLATION RATE – 1.1 per cent (2000)

TOTAL EXTERNAL DEBT – US$6,267 million (2000)

FOREIGN DIRECT INVESTMENT – US$279 million (1997–2000)

IMPORTS – US$6,005 million (2002)

EXPORTS – US$5,508 million (1998)

BALANCE OF PAYMENTS

Trade – US$5,763 million surplus (2001)

Current Account – US$2,315 surplus (2001)

Trade with UK	*2002*	*2003*
Imports from UK	£254,951,000	£265,068,000
Exports to UK	86,348,000	87,893,000

TRANSPORT INFRASTRUCTURE

Port Qaboos at Mutrah has eight deep-water berths which have been constructed as part of the harbour facilities. There are some 34,000 km of roads, of which 9,000 km are surfaced. There are airports at Seeb, Salalah, Sur, Masirah, Khasab and Diba.

EDUCATION

In 2000 there were 1,008 state schools. There is one state university and several private universities.

ILLITERACY RATE – (m) 19.8 per cent; (f) 38.4 per cent (2000)

ENROLMENT (percentage of age group) – primary 76 per cent (1997); secondary 67 per cent (1997); tertiary 8 per cent (1997

MEDIA AND CULTURE

The only television broadcaster is the state controlled Oman TV. Satellite television is popular. There are, however, a large number of newspapers including four national dailies.

PAKISTAN

Islāmī Jamhūriya-e-Pākistān – Islamic Republic of Pakistan

AREA – 770,900 sq. km. Neighbours: Iran (west), Afghanistan (north and north-west), China (north-east), the disputed territory of Kashmir, India (east)
POPULATION – 144,971,000 (2001); 95 per cent Muslim, 3.5 per cent Christian, about 1 per cent Hindu, and 0.5 per cent Buddhist. Urdu is the national language, but is only spoken by a small minority of the population. The most widely used language is Punjabi, followed by Sindi and Pushto. English is widely used in business, government and higher education
CAPITAL – Islamabad (population, 350,000, 1998 census)
MAJOR CITIES – Faisalabad; ΨKarachi; Lahore; Rawalpindi
CURRENCY – Pakistan rupee of 100 paisa
NATIONAL ANTHEM – Pak Sarzmin Shad Bad (Blessed Be The Sacred Land)
NATIONAL DAYS – 23 March (Pakistan Day), 14 August (Independence Day)
NATIONAL FLAG – Green with a white crescent and star, and a white vertical strip in the hoist
LIFE EXPECTANCY (years) – 60 (2001)
MORTALITY RATE (per 1,000 population) – 8.79 (2003)
INFANT MORTALITY (per 1,000 births) – 84 (2001)
HIV / AIDS ADULT PREVALENCE – 0.1 per cent (2001)
DEATH PENALTY – Yes
POPULATION BELOW POVERTY LINE – 35 per cent (2001)
POPULATION GROWTH RATE – 2.5 per cent (1990–2001)
POPULATION DENSITY – 188 per sq. km (2001)
URBAN POPULATION – 34 per cent (2001)

CLIMATE AND TERRAIN

There are mountainous regions in the north of the country that include the Karakoram and Himalayan ranges. Elevation extremes range from 8,611 m (K2) at the highest point to 0 m (Indian Ocean) at the lowest. The climate of Pakistan varies greatly. Average temperatures in Islamabad range from 2°C in January to 40°C in June.

HISTORY AND POLITICS

Mughal rule during the 16th and 17th centuries eventually gave way to British domination and Kashmir, Ladakh, the Punjab and Sind all came under British control by 1857.

A constitution was adopted in 1956. It established the country as two territories, West and East Pakistan (East Pakistan being made up of the majority Muslim state of Bengal), which, since they were divided by India, had no land contact. President Mirza initiated the country's first military coup in 1958. A second war with India was lost in 1965 and, in 1971, East Pakistan became Bangladesh. Pakistan and Bangladesh accorded one another mutual recognition in 1974.

Pakistan subsequently experienced further conflict with India, military rule and greater economic decline until the death of General Zia ul-Haq in 1988. He was succeeded in an election by Benazir Bhutto, the first woman to become an elected prime minister of a Muslim country. She was succeeded by Nawaz Sharif in 1997.

In 20 June 2001, Gen. Musharraf dismissed the elected president and assumed the presidency himself. The extension of Musharraf's presidency for a further five years was approved by referendum in April 2002. In August 2002 President Musharraf granted himself new powers, including the right to dissolve parliament and dismiss the Government.

In the elections to the National Assembly on 10 October 2002, 77 of the 342 seats were won by the Pakistan Muslim League (Qaid-i-Azam-PML-Q), making it the largest single party, and it also gained a majority in the senate elections in February. Mir Zafarullah Khan Jamali was elected prime minister on 21 November 2002 and both he and the new cabinet were sworn in on 23 November. Since the 2002 elections, the National Assembly has been unable to function fully because of procedural disruption by members opposed to the president. On 21 August 2003 the North-West Frontier Province voted to introduce *Shari'ah* law. On 26 June 2004, Zafarullah Khan Jamali resigned as prime minster. He was replaced by Chaudhry Shujaat Hussain.

INSURGENCY

Since early 1994 there has been civil disorder in the Sind province, especially in Karachi, in two conflicts: armed militants of the Mohajir Qaumi Movement (MQM), which represents Urdu-speaking Indian Muslims who fled India at partition and their descendants, who are fighting for an autonomous Karachi province; and the armed conflict between Shia and Sunni fundamentalists. During 2002 there were attacks against Christians and Westerners, which were thought to be the work of Islamic militants opposed to Pakistan's support for the US-led war on Afghanistan.

FOREIGN RELATIONS

The conflict with India over Kashmir flared up in May 1999 when India launched air attacks on Muslim insurgents who had occupied mountainous regions inside India-controlled Kashmir. Small-scale conflicts continued but in December 2001, India and Pakistan assembled troops along the common border and during May and June 2002 there was concern that the conflict could spiral into a nuclear exchange. Following intense international diplomatic activity, the threat of war receded and, by the beginning of 2004, relations between the two countries improved when the Indian Prime Minister Atal Behari Vajpayee visited Pakistan for further peace talks.

POLITICAL SYSTEM

The legislature is bicameral, but was suspended following the coup in October 1999. Under the Constitution, the *Majlis as-Shoora* (National Assembly) serves a five-year term and comprises 342 members, of whom 272 are directly elected, 10 represent religious minorities and 60 are co-opted women. The Senate has 100 members. The four provinces each have a provincial assembly and are represented in both legislative chambers.

FEDERAL STRUCTURE

There are six provinces in Pakistan (population census 1998): Baluchistan (6,511,000), Federal Capital Territory Islamabad (805,000), Federally Administered Tribal Areas (3,138,000), North-West Frontier Province (17,555,000), Punjab (72,585,000) and Sind (29,991,000).

HEAD OF STATE
President, Chief of Army Staff, Gen. Pervez Musharraf, *assumed office* 20 June 2001, *confirmed in office by referendum* 30 April 2002

SELECTED GOVERNMENT MEMBERS *as at July 2004*
Prime Minister, Chaudhry Shujaat Hussain
Senior Federal Minister, Defence, Rao Sikandar Iqbal
Finance, Revenue, Economic Affairs, Planning, Development and Statistics, Shaukat Aziz
Foreign Affairs, Law, Justice and Human Rights, Mian Khursheed Mehmood Kasuri
Interior and Narcotics Control, Makhdoom Syed Faisal Saleh Hayat

HIGH COMMISSION FOR THE ISLAMIC REPUBLIC OF PAKISTAN
35–36 Lowndes Square, London SW1X 9JN
T 020-7664 9200
High Commissioner, HE Maleeha Lodhi

BRITISH HIGH COMMISSION
Diplomatic Enclave, Ramna 5, PO Box 1122, Islamabad
T (+92) (51) 2206071/5
E bhctrade@isb.comsats.net.pk
High Commissioner, HE Mark Lyall Grant, CMG, apptd 2003

BRITISH COUNCIL DIRECTOR, Dr Tome Craig-Cameron
PO Box 1135, Islamabad
T (+92) (51) 111 424 424
E bc.islamabad@britishcouncil.org.pk

DEFENCE
The Army has some 2,427 main battle tanks, 1,251 armoured personnel carriers and 19 attack helicopters. The Navy has ten submarines, eight frigates, nine patrol and coastal vessels, six combat aircraft and nine armed helicopters based at Karachi. The Air Force has 374 combat aircraft.
MILITARY EXPENDITURE – 3.9 per cent of GDP (2001)
MILITARY PERSONNEL – 620,000: Army 550,000, Navy 25,000, Air Force 45,000; Paramilitaries 294,000

ECONOMY AND TRADE
Agriculture accounts for 44 per cent of the labour force producing cotton, wheat, rice, sugarcane, fruits, vegetables, milk, beef and mutton. Significant manufacturing industries include cotton yarn, thread, and fabrics. Food processing, pharmaceuticals and construction materials are also important. Principal exports are cotton yarn and cloth, carpets, rice, petroleum products, textiles, leather and fish. Pakistan's massive military expenditure has restricted growth in the economy. Principal imports are petroleum products, machinery, fertilisers, transport equipment, edible oils, chemicals and ferrous metals.

The country has seen large-scale emigration of its labour force to the Middle East (these workers provide important remittances) and this has produced a growth in the use of child labour within Pakistan.
GNI – US$60,000 million (2001); US$420 per capita (2001)
ANNUAL AVERAGE GROWTH OF GDP – 5.6 per cent (2000)
INFLATION RATE – 4.4 per cent (2000)
UNEMPLOYMENT – 5.9 per cent (1998)
TOTAL EXTERNAL DEBT – US$32,091 million (2000)
FOREIGN DIRECT INVESTMENT – US$2,051 million (1997–2000)
IMPORTS – US$11,233 million (2002)
EXPORTS – US$9,913 million (2002)

BALANCE OF PAYMENTS
Trade – US$608 million deficit (2001)
Current Account – US$1,880 million surplus (2001)

Trade with UK	*2002*	*2003*
Imports from UK	£243,643,000	£293,989,000
Exports to UK	488,618,000	532,456,000

TRANSPORT INFRASTRUCTURE
There are 86,597 km of roads and 7,344 km of railways. There are major seaports at Karachi and Port Qasim. The main airports are at Karachi, Islamabad, Lahore, Peshawar and Quetta. Pakistan International Airlines operates domestic air services between the principal cities as well as international services.

EDUCATION
Education is free of charge to upper secondary level. The system consists of five years of primary education (five to nine years), three years of middle or lower secondary (general or vocational), two years of upper secondary, two years of higher secondary (intermediate) and two to five years of higher education in colleges and universities.
ILLITERACY RATE – (m) 40.1 per cent; (f) 68.9 per cent (2000)
ENROLMENT (percentage of age group) – tertiary 3.0 per cent (1991)

MEDIA AND CULTURE
There are eight national newspapers, and the state owned broadcaster, Pakistan Television Corporation Ltd., competes with several private networks. In 2004, the government had granted licences for a number of satellite television and radio stations.

Pakistan is rich in the remains of the earliest Buddhist and Hindu civilisations, as well as the distinct architecture of the Mughal period.

Important Pakistani writers include the poet Allama Muhammad (1877–1938) and the Urdu novelist Altaf Fatima (b. 1929).

PALAU

Belu'u era Belau-Republic of Palau

AREA – 458 sq. km
POPULATION – 20,000 (2001); 13,900 live on Koror and Babelthaup. The population is Micronesian, and predominantly Roman Catholic with a Protestant minority. Palauan and English are the official languages
CAPITAL – Koror (population, 13,303, 2000)
CURRENCY – Currency is that of the USA
NATIONAL FLAG – Light blue with a yellow disc set near the hoist
LIFE EXPECTANCY (years) – 69 (2001)
MORTALITY RATE (per 1,000 population) – 7 (2003)

INFANT MORTALITY (per 1,000 births) – 24 (2001)
DEATH PENALTY – No (abolished 1994)
POPULATION GROWTH RATE – 2.6 per cent (1990–2001)
POPULATION DENSITY – 44 per sq. km (2001)

CLIMATE AND TERRAIN

The Republic of Palau consists of 340 islands and islets in the western Pacific Ocean, of which only eight are inhabited. Elevation extremes range from 242 m (Mt Ngerchelchauus) at the highest point to 0 m (Pacific Ocean) at the lowest. The islands are mainly low-lying and have a tropical climate with a wet season from May to November. Average daily temperatures are an almost constant 27°C.

HISTORY AND POLITICS

Britain became Palau's main trading partner in the 18th century, but did not colonise the islands. Control of the islands passed to Germany in 1889, who exploited the country for its labour force and coconut plantations. Japanese occupation in 1914 eroded much of Palau's indigenous culture.

The USA liberated Palau from Japan during the Second World War and administered the island thereafter. The island became a Trust Territory in 1947 and entered into a Compact of Free Association with the USA in 1982. This entailed the USA recognising the Republic of Palau but retaining some rights to parts of the island for 50 years and assuming responsibility for defence.

Palau eventually adopted its own constitution in 1980 and full independence in 1994. Tommy Remengesau became president in 2000.

POLITICAL SYSTEM

Executive power is vested in the President and Vice-President, who are directly elected for a four-year term; the President appoints the Cabinet. There is a bicameral legislature *(Olbiil era Kelulau)* composed of the 16-member House of Delegates (one member elected from each of the 16 constituent states) and the 14-member Senate. There is also a Council of Chiefs to advise the President on matters concerning traditional law and customs. Each of the 16 component states have their own elected governors and legislatures.

HEAD OF STATE

President, Tommy Remengesau, *elected* 7 November 2000, *took office* 19 January 2001
Vice-President, Health, Sandra Pierantozzi

SELECTED GOVERNMENT MEMBERS *as at July 2004*
Commerce and Trade, Otoichi Besebes
Justice, Michael Rosenthal
Minister of State, Temmy Shmull

BRITISH AMBASSADOR, HE Ian Powell, resident at Suva, Fiji

ECONOMY AND TRADE

Agriculture is largely on the subsistence level and fishing plays a large part in the economy. Agricultural production is centred on crops such as coconuts, copra, cassava and sweet potatoes. Palau's economy is greatly dependent on the tourism industry, which caters for around 50,000 tourists a year. Many other industries are influenced by tourism, such as the production of arts and crafts. The island also derives an income from the sale of licences to fishing fleets.

GNI – US$130 million (2001); US$6,780 per capita (2001)
ANNUAL AVERAGE GROWTH OF GDP – 1.0 per cent (2001)

Trade with UK	*2002*	*2003*
Imports from UK	£51,000	£16,000
Exports to UK	–	–

TRANSPORT INFRASTRUCTURE

There are 61 km of roads in total and no railways or waterways. There are three airports on Koror, Peleliu and Angaur which have daily flights from Guam operated by Continental Micronesia.

MEDIA

Most Palauans rely on satellite and cable services from the US. T8AA Eco Paradise is the government run radio station. There are a further two commercial stations. Palau has three weekly news publications.

PANAMA

República de Panamá – Republic of Panama

AREA – 74,400 sq. km. Neighbours: Colombia (east), Costa Rica (west)
POPULATION – 2,899,000 (2001): 70 per cent mestizo, 14 per cent mixed Amerindian and Black, 10 per cent European, 6 per cent Amerindian. Spanish is the official language
CAPITAL – ΨPanama City (population, 464,928, 2000 census)
CURRENCY – Balboa of 100 centésimos (the US dollar is also in circulation)
NATIONAL ANTHEM – Alcanzamos Por Fin La Victoria (Victory Is Ours At Last)
NATIONAL DAY – 3 November
NATIONAL FLAG – Four quarters; white with blue star (top, next staff), red (in fly), blue (below, next staff) and white with red star
LIFE EXPECTANCY (years) – 74 (2001)
MORTALITY RATE (per 1,000 population) – 6.25 (2003)
INFANT MORTALITY (per 1,000 births) – 19 (2001)
HIV / AIDS ADULT PREVALENCE – 1.5 per cent (2001)
DEATH PENALTY – No (abolished 1903)
POPULATION BELOW POVERTY LINE – 37 per cent (1999)
POPULATION GROWTH RATE – 1.7 per cent (1990–2001)
POPULATION DENSITY – 39 per sq. km (2001)
URBAN POPULATION – 57 per cent (2001)
MILITARY EXPENDITURE – 1.3 per cent of GDP (2002)
MILITARY PERSONNEL – Paramilitaries 11,800
ILLITERACY RATE – (m) 7.5 per cent; (f) 8.7 per cent (2000)
ENROLMENT (percentage of age group) – primary 100 per cent (1997); secondary 69 per cent (1997); tertiary 32 per cent (1997)

CLIMATE AND TERRAIN

Elevation extremes range from 3,475 m (Volcan de Chiriqui) at the highest point to 0 m (Pacific Ocean) at the lowest. The climate is tropical with a prolonged wet season from May to January. Average temperatures range from 20°C in January to 31°C in June.

HISTORY AND POLITICS

Panama gained its independence from Spain in 1821 and joined the confederacy of Gran Colombia (comprising Colombia, Venezuela, Ecuador, Peru, and Bolivia). Towards the end of the 19th century France attempted to construct a canal linking the Atlantic and Pacific oceans across Panama. The attempt failed and cost the lives of an estimated 20,000 workers. The US government eventually intervened and the canal was completed in 1914. Panama had gained its independence from Colombia in 1903 but did not attain full control over the canal until 1999.

General Noriega seized control of Panama in 1984 and instigated a period of military rule but was deposed in a US-led invasion in 1986. Noriega was captured in 1990 and sentenced to 40 years imprisonment in 1992 on money laundering and drug-trafficking charges.

The presidential elections of May 2004 were won by Martín Torrijos Espino of the Partido Revolucionario Democrática (PRD), who gained 47.4 per cent of the vote. In the legislative elections of the same year the PRD won 41 of the 71 seats in the Legislative Assembly.

POLITICAL SYSTEM
Legislative power is vested in a unicameral Legislative Assembly of 71 members; executive power is held by the President, assisted by two elected Vice-Presidents and an appointed Cabinet. Elections are held every five years under a system of universal and compulsory adult suffrage.

HEAD OF STATE
President, Martín Torrijos Espino, *elected* 2 May 2004, *sworn in*, 14 September 2004

EMBASSY OF THE REPUBLIC OF PANAMA
40 Hertford Street, London W1J 7SH
T 020-7493 4646
Ambassador Extraordinary and Plenipotentiary, HE Ariadne Singares Robinson, apptd 2000

BRITISH EMBASSY
Swiss Tower, Calle 53 (Apartado 889) Zona 1, Panama City
T (+507) 269 0866
E britemb@cwpanama.net
Ambassador Extraordinary and Plenipotentiary, HE Jim Malcolm, OBE, apptd 2002

ECONOMY AND TRADE

The service industries form 76 per cent of GDP. Other important industries include petroleum refining, the manufacture of construction materials and sugar refining. Agriculture, which employs 20.8 per cent of the labour force and accounts for seven per cent of GDP, is centred on bananas, rice, coffee, corn and sugarcane.

GNI – US$9,500 million (2001); US$3,260 per capita (2001)
ANNUAL AVERAGE GROWTH OF GDP – 2.7 per cent (2000)
INFLATION RATE – 1.4 per cent (2000)
UNEMPLOYMENT – 11.8 per cent (1999)
TOTAL EXTERNAL DEBT – US$7,000 million (2002)
FOREIGN DIRECT INVESTMENT – US$2,861 million (1997–2000)
IMPORTS – US$2,982 million (2002)
EXPORTS – US$846 million (2002)

BALANCE OF PAYMENTS
Trade – US$1,176 million deficit (2002)
Current Account – US$154 million deficit (2002)

Trade with UK	*2002*	*2003*
Imports from UK	£73,951,000	£86,515,000
Exports to UK	11,008,000	5,900,000

TRANSPORT INFRASTRUCTURE

Apart from the 82 km of the canal, there are 822 km of navigable waterways. These are supplemented by 355 km of railways and 11,400 km of highways. In 2000 the total number of transits by ocean-going commercial traffic was 12,303; canal net tons totalled 229,459,659; cargo tons totalled 193,714,277.

MEDIA

Five television networks and five radio networks – all commercial – join six daily newspapers to constitute the news media.

PAPUA NEW GUINEA

Gau Hedinarai ai Papua-Matamata Guinea – Independent State of Papua New Guinea

AREA – 452,900 sq. km. Neighbour: Indonesia (west, on New Guinea)
POPULATION – 4,920,000 (2001). English is the official language; Hiri Motu and Neo-Melanesian are widely spoken
CAPITAL – ΨPort Moresby (population, 173,500, 2000 estimate)
MAJOR CITIES – Goroka; Lae; Madang; Mount Hagen; Rabaul; Wewak
CURRENCY – Kina (K) of 100 toea
NATIONAL ANTHEM – Arise All You Sons
NATIONAL DAY – 16 September (Independence Day)
NATIONAL FLAG – Divided diagonally red (fly) and black (hoist); on the red is a soaring Bird of Paradise in yellow and on the black five white stars of the Southern Cross
LIFE EXPECTANCY (years) – 57 (2001)
MORTALITY RATE (per 1,000 population) – 7.63 (2003)
INFANT MORTALITY (per 1,000 births) – 70 (2001)
HIV / AIDS ADULT PREVALENCE – 0.7 per cent (2001)
DEATH PENALTY – No (abolished 1950)
POPULATION BELOW POVERTY LINE – 37 per cent (2002)
POPULATION GROWTH RATE – 2.4 per cent (1990–2001)
POPULATION DENSITY – 11 per sq. km (2001)
MILITARY EXPENDITURE – 0.5 per cent of GDP (2002)
MILITARY PERSONNEL – 3,100: Army 2,500, Navy 400, Air Force 200
ILLITERACY RATE – (m) 29.4 per cent; (f) 43.2 per cent (2000)
ENROLMENT (percentage of age group) – tertiary 3 per cent (1997)

CLIMATE AND TERRAIN

Papua New Guinea consists of the eastern half of the island of New Guinea, plus several more outlying islands. Elevation extremes range from 4,509 m (Mt Wilhelm) at the highest point to 0 m (Pacific Ocean) at the lowest.

Average temperatures range from 28°C in August to 31°C in January.

HISTORY AND POLITICS

In 1884 a British protectorate, British New Guinea, was proclaimed over the southern coast of New Guinea (Papua) and the adjacent islands, which were annexed outright in 1888. In 1906 the territory was placed under the authority of Australia. The northern areas were under German administration between 1884 and 1914, when they were occupied by Australian troops and in 1921 became a League of Nations mandate administered by Australia. The territories were occupied by Japan between 1942 and 1945.

In 1989 a civil conflict between the Bougainville Revolutionary Army and the Papuan central authorities began and lasted for nine years. A final resolution was reached in 2001, and the last Papuan government forces left in 2003.

Following elections in June 2002, the National Alliance Party (NAP) was the largest party in Parliament, and on 5 August 2002, the NAP leader Sir Michael Somare was elected prime minister for the third time and formed a coalition cabinet.

POLITICAL SYSTEM

Elections are held every five years. The National Parliament comprises 109 elected members, 20 from regional electorates, the remainder from open electorates. The head of state is the British sovereign, represented by the Governor-General, who is appointed by Parliament for a six-year term. Provincial Governments were abolished in 1995, and replaced with Councils combining local and national politicians and headed by an appointed Governor.

Governor-General, Sir Paulias Matane, *sworn in* 29 June 2004

SELECTED GOVERNMENT MEMBERS *as at August 2004*
Prime Minister, Minster of Housing, Sir Michael Somare
Defence, Matthew Gubag
Finance and Treasury, Bart Philemon
Foreign Affairs and Immigration, Sir Rabbie Namaliu

PAPUA NEW GUINEA HIGH COMMISSION
3rd Floor, 14 Waterloo Place, London SW1R 4AR
T 020-7930 0922/7
High Commissioner, HE Jean L. Kekedo, OBE, apptd 2002

BRITISH HIGH COMMISSION
PO Box 212, Waigani NCD, Port Moresby
T (+ 675) 325 1677
E bhcpng@datec.net.pg
High Commissioner, HE David Gordon-Macleod, apptd 2003

ECONOMY AND TRADE

Papua New Guinea's economy is divided between modern industries such as gold and copper mining and petroleum, and traditional industries like farming and fishing. Corruption, political instability and unresolved land compensation has discouraged foreign investment.

Subsistence farming employs 85 per cent of the population. Over the last decade public services have deteriorated and the advances made in public health in the years following independence have not been sustained.

There are extensive mineral deposits throughout Papua New Guinea, including copper, gold, silver, nickel, bauxite and commercial deposits of oil and natural gas, but exploitation is hampered by the terrain and poor infrastructure.

GNI – US$3,000 million (2001); US$580 per capita (2001)
ANNUAL AVERAGE GROWTH OF GDP – 3.9 per cent (1999)
INFLATION RATE – 9.8 per cent (2002)
TOTAL EXTERNAL DEBT – US$2,604 million (2000)
FOREIGN DIRECT INVESTMENT – US$737 million (1997–2000)
IMPORTS – US$1,100 million (2002)
EXPORTS – US$1,550 million (2002)

BALANCE OF PAYMENTS
Trade – US$881 million surplus (2001)
Current Account – US$282 million surplus (2001)

Trade with UK	*2002*	*2003*
Imports from UK	£12,150,000	£7,979,000
Exports to UK	49,470,000	60,541,000

TRANSPORT INFRASTRUCTURE

There are 21,433 km of roads, the most important road being that linking Lae with the populous highlands. Air Niugini operates regular services to other countries in the region, as well as internal air services. Several shipping companies operate cargo services to Australia, Europe, the Far East and USA. There are very limited cargo and passenger services between the main ports, outports, plantations and missions.

Papua New Guinea has communication links with Australia, Guam, Hong Kong, the Far East and the USA via submarine cables.

MEDIA

EMTV is the country's sole television broadcaster. Radio is of vital importance due to Papua New Guinea's widely scattered population and low levels of literacy. The state run National Broadcasting Corporation runs a radio network which competes with the commercial NAU FM. There are two daily newspapers and a number of weekly publications.

PARAGUAY

República del Paraguay – Republic of Paraguay

AREA – 397,300 sq. km. Neighbours: Bolivia (north-west), Brazil (north-east and east), Argentina (south)
POPULATION – 5,636,000 (2001): 95 per cent mestizo. Spanish is the official language of the country but outside the larger towns Guaraní, the language of the largest single group of Amerindian inhabitants, is widely spoken, and is also an official language
CAPITAL – Asunción (population, 550,060 1997)
MAJOR CITIES – Ciudad del Este; San Lorenzo
CURRENCY – Guaraní (Gs) of 100 céntimos
NATIONAL ANTHEM – Paraguayos, República O Muerte (Paraguayans, Republic Or Death)
NATIONAL DAY – 15 May
NATIONAL FLAG – Three horizontal bands, red, white

and blue with the National seal on the obverse white band and the Treasury seal on the reverse white band
LIFE EXPECTANCY (years) – 70 (2001)
MORTALITY RATE (per 1,000 population) – 4.64 (2003)
INFANT MORTALITY (per 1,000 births) – 26 (2001)
HIV / AIDS ADULT PREVALENCE – 0.11 per cent (2001)
DEATH PENALTY – No (abolished 1992)
POPULATION BELOW POVERTY LINE – 36 per cent (2001)
POPULATION GROWTH RATE – 2.6 per cent (1990–2001)
POPULATION DENSITY – 14 per sq. km (2001)
MILITARY EXPENDITURE – 1.0 per cent of GDP (2002)
MILITARY PERSONNEL – 18,600: Army 14,900, Navy 2,000, Air Force 1,700; Paramilitaries 14,800
CONSCRIPTION DURATION – One to two years

CLIMATE AND TERRAIN

Elevation extremes range from 875 m (Cerro Pero) at the highest point to 46 m (the junction of Rio Paraguay and Rio Parana) at the lowest. Average temperatures in the capital Asunción range from 23°C in June to 34°C in January.

HISTORY AND POLITICS

Spanish colonisation of Paraguay began in the early 16th century and the capital city Asunción was founded on 15 August 1537. Paraguay became independent from Spain in 1811 with José Gaspar Rodriguez de Francia ruling until his death in 1840. His successor instigated a period of reform and modernisation which ended in 1865 with the catastrophic War of the Triple Alliance. This war against Brazil, Uruguay and Argentina not only resulted in the loss of tens of thousands of square miles of Paraguayan territory, but it also resulted in many deaths. Paraguay did not recover for the rest of the 19th century, and the years leading up to the Second World War were marked by social instability.

General Alfredo Stroessner took power in 1954 but his rule was marked by corruption and human rights abuses. His own ousting in a coup in 1989 paved the way for eventual democratic rule and the first elections took place in 1993.

Though Paraguay has continued to be troubled by attempted coups and large-scale corruption, it conducted further elections in 1998. In the presidential and legislative elections on 27 April 2003, the National Republican Association-Colorado Party (ANR-PC) remained the largest party in Congress, winning 16 out of the 45 seats; its candidate, Nicanor Duarte Frutos, won the presidential election with 37.1 per cent of the vote.

POLITICAL SYSTEM

The Constitution provides for a two-chamber legislature consisting of a 45-member Senate and an 80-member Chamber of Deputies, both directly elected for a five-year term. Deputies are elected on a regional basis, the number of seats allocated to each regional department being directly proportional to the department's population. Voting is compulsory for all citizens over 18. The President is elected for a five-year term and may not be re-elected. The Vice-President may only contest the presidency if he resigns his post six months before the election. The President appoints the Council of Ministers, which exercises all the functions of Government.

HEAD OF STATE

President, Nicanor Duarte Frutos, *elected* 27 April 2002, *sworn in* 15 August 2003
Vice-President, Luis Alberto Castiglioni Soria

SELECTED GOVERNMENT MEMBERS *as at July 2004*

Defence, Carlos Romero Pereira
Finance and Economy, Dioniso Borda
Foreign Affairs, Leila Rachid de Cowles
Interior, Orlando Fiorotto

EMBASSY OF PARAGUAY

344 High Street Kensington, 3rd Floor, London W14 8NS
T 020-7610 4180
Ambassador Extraordinary and Plenipotentiary, vacant

BRITISH EMBASSY

Avda Boggiani 5848, C/R I6 Boquerón, Asunción
T (+595) (21) 612611
E brembasu@rieder.net.py
Ambassador Extraordinary and Plenipotentiary, HE Anthony Cantor, apptd 2001

ECONOMY AND TRADE

Paraguay has a large agricultural sector, much of it on a subsistence level, accounting for 27 per cent of GDP. Agricultural production is centred on cassava, seed cotton, sugarcane, corn, wheat, root crops such as sweet potatoes, and fruits such as bananas and oranges. Livestock – cattle, horses, pigs and sheep – is an important aspect of the farming industry. The country has few mineral resources and the main industries are sugar refining, cement production and textiles. The country faces problems such as the lack of infrastructure and national debt and environmental challenges include deforestation and water pollution. In 2004, Congress began to draft a new economic plan that would increase value added tax and strengthen the country's tax and administration infrastructure.

GNI – US$7,600 million (2001); US$1,350 per capita (2001)
ANNUAL AVERAGE GROWTH OF GDP – 0.4 per cent (2000)
INFLATION RATE – 9.0 per cent (2000)
TOTAL EXTERNAL DEBT – US$3,091 million (2000)
FOREIGN DIRECT INVESTMENT – US$660 million (1997–2000)
IMPORTS – US$1,989 million (2001)
EXPORTS – US$990 million (2001)

BALANCE OF PAYMENTS

Trade – US$72 million deficit (2002)
Current Account – US$294 million surplus (2002)

Trade with UK	*2002*	*2003*
Imports from UK	£13,169,000	£14,802,000
Exports to UK	2,117,000	1,325,000

TRANSPORT INFRASTRUCTURE

There are 28,900 km of roads in Paraguay, connecting Asunción with São Paulo via the Bridge of Friendship and Foz de Yguazú, and with Buenos Aires via Puerto Pilcomayo. Many roads are impassable in wet weather. There are 971 km of railways. There are direct shipping services from Asunción to Europe and the USA, and river steamer services for internal transport.

EDUCATION

Education is free of charge and compulsory. There are 11 universities and one institute of education.

ILLITERACY RATE – (m) 5.6 per cent; (f) 7.8 per cent (2000)

ENROLMENT (percentage of age group) – primary 100 per cent (1997); secondary 47 per cent (1997); tertiary 10 per cent (1997)

MEDIA AND CULTURE

Paraguay has three daily newspapers, three commercial television channels and a range of radio broadcasters.

The Guaraní, the original inhabitants of Paraguay, retain large amounts of their traditional culture, with songs, dances and myths constituting a rich body of folklore.

PERU

República del Perú – Republic of Peru

AREA – 1,280,000 sq. km. Neighbours: Ecuador and Colombia (north), Brazil and Bolivia (east), Chile (south)

POPULATION – 27,148,000 (2003 estimate): 50 per cent Amerindian, 40 per cent mestizo, 7 per cent European, also Africans, Chinese and Japanese. The official languages are Spanish and Quechua. Aymara is also widely spoken

CAPITAL – Lima (including ΨCallao, population, 6,723,130, 2000 estimate)

MAJOR CITIES – Arequipa; Chiclayo; Chimbote; Trujillo

CURRENCY – New Sol of 100 cénts

NATIONAL ANTHEM – Somos Libres, Seámoslo Siempre (We Are Free, Let Us Remain So Forever)

NATIONAL DAY – 28 July (Anniversary of Independence)

NATIONAL FLAG – Three vertical stripes of red, white and red

LIFE EXPECTANCY (years) – 69 (2001)

MORTALITY RATE (per 1,000 population) – 5.69 (2003)

INFANT MORTALITY (per 1,000 births) – 30 (2001)

POPULATION BELOW POVERTY LINE – 50 per cent (2001)

POPULATION GROWTH RATE – 1.47 per cent (2003)

POPULATION DENSITY – 20 per sq. km (2001)

MILITARY EXPENDITURE – 1.6 per cent of GDP (2002)

MILITARY PERSONNEL – 100,000: Army 60,000, Navy 25,000, Air Force 15,000; Paramilitaries 77,000

CONSCRIPTION DURATION – Two years (selective)

CLIMATE AND TERRAIN

Peru is traversed by the Andes, running parallel to the Pacific coast. There are three main regions, the Costa, west of the Andes; the Sierra or mountain ranges of the Andes, which include the Punas or mountainous wastes below the region of perpetual snow, and the Montaña or Selva, which is the vast area of jungle stretching from the eastern foothills of the Andes to the eastern frontiers of Peru. Elevation extremes range from 6,768 m (Nevado Huascaran) at the highest point to 0 m (Pacific Ocean) at the lowest. Average temperatures in Lima range from 16°C in July 26°C in January.

HISTORY AND POLITICS

The Incas came to pre-eminence in Peru in the 15th century and the country was conquered by the Spanish in the early 16th century.

Nationalist aspirations grew throughout the 18th century and the Spanish Empire was deposed. The revolutionaries Jose de San Martin, Simon Bolivar and General Antonio Jose de Sucre fought a long campaign of liberation. San Martin declared Peruvian independence on 28 July 1821 but it was not until 1824 that the Spanish forces were finally defeated at Ayacucho. Spain, however, did not recognise Peru's independence until 1879.

Throughout the remainder of the 19th century and a large part of the 20th, Peru suffered periods of oppressive military rule and was troubled by border disputes with its neighbours. The last general to rule the country was General Francisco Morales Bermundez who guided the country to democracy in 1980 and won an election in May of that year. Civilian rule, however, did not bring stability. Two left wing insurgent groups, Sendero Luminoso (Shining Path) and Movimento Revolucionario Tupac Amaru (MRTA), began to challenge the State in the 1980s. Both organisations were finally defeated in 1998, although only after many thousands had been killed by both the government and insurgent sides. Hyperinflation due to economic mismanagement and political instability followed, and in 1990 an unknown college lecturer, Alberto Fujimori, was elected president on a promise of economic reform.

A general election was held on 8 April 2001 in which the Peru Possible (PP) party won 43 seats and the Peruvian Aprista Party (APRA) won 28 seats. The presidential election was held in two rounds on 8 April and 3 June and was won by the PP candidate, Alejandro Toledo, who was sworn in as president on 28 July, becoming the first Amerindian to hold the position. However, Toledo's period in office has been dogged by frequent cabinet reshuffles. A sixth cabinet was appointed in 2004.

FOREIGN RELATIONS

A 78 km stretch of the border with Ecuador has been in dispute since 1960. In 1995 an inconclusive border war was fought between the two countries, and in July 1995 a demilitarised zone was established around the disputed area. Four guarantor countries (Argentina, Brazil, Chile and the USA) adjudicated the claims of both countries and produced an agreement which was signed on 26 October 1998 by the presidents of Ecuador and Peru, formally ending the dispute. In 1999 Peru and Chile finally implemented accords first agreed in 1929 to end a border dispute.

POLITICAL SYSTEM

The Constitution, promulgated in December 1993, provides for the President to be able to serve two terms; a constitutional panel approved a Bill in August 1996 allowing President Fujimori to stand for a third term in office. The unicameral legislature, the Congress of the Republic, has 120 members, directly elected for a five-year term.

HEAD OF STATE

President of the Republic, Alejandro Toledo Manrique, *elected* 3 June 2001, *sworn in* 28 July 2001

First Vice-President, Foreign Trade, Tourism, (vacant)

Second Vice-President, David Waisman

SELECTED GOVERNMENT MEMBERS *as at August 2004*
Defence, Gen. Roberto Chiabra Leon
Economy and Finance, Pedro Pablo Kuczynski
Foreign Affairs, Manuel Rodriguez Cuadros
Interior, Javier Reategui

EMBASSY OF PERU
52 Sloane Street, London SW1X 9SP
T 020-7235 1917/2545/8302
Ambassador Extraordinary and Plenipotentiary, Gustavo Meza-Cuadra (*Cd'A*)

BRITISH EMBASSY
Torre Parque Mar (Piso 22), Avenida José Larco 1301, Miraflores, Lima
T (+51) (1) 617 3000
E consvisa.lima@fco.gov.uk
Ambassador Extraordinary and Plenipotentiary, HE Richard Ralph, CMG, CVO, apptd 2003

BRITISH COUNCIL DIRECTOR, Frank Fitzpatrick
c/o British Embassy, Lima
T (+51) (1) 617 3060
E bc.lima@britishcouncil.org.pe

ECONOMY AND TRADE

Peru has significant mineral wealth (including gold, though much of this has been exhausted). In addition to this, important industries include petroleum, shipbuilding, textiles, food processing and metal fabrication. Agriculture is centred on coffee, cotton, sugarcane, rice, wheat, potatoes, corn, plantains and coca.

Since 1990 the government has launched a radical free-market restructuring programme which has rebuilt the foreign exchange reserves, reduced inflation, cut subsidies and import tariffs, freed interest rates and privatised most state firms. Foreign investment has been encouraged and has grown dramatically.

Peru faces a range of environmental challenges such as deforestation, soil erosion and desertification, all of which are on the increase and may affect the economy. Peru's substantial coastal fishing resources are threatened by pollution from mining wastes.

GNI – US$52,200 million (2001); US$1,980 per capita (2001)
ANNUAL AVERAGE GROWTH OF GDP – 4.2 per cent (2003)
INFLATION RATE – 3.8 per cent (2000)
UNEMPLOYMENT – 7.4 per cent (2000)
TOTAL EXTERNAL DEBT – US$28,560 million (2000)
FOREIGN DIRECT INVESTMENT – US$6,609 (1997–2000)
IMPORTS – US$8,797 million (2000)
EXPORTS – US$7,669 million (2002)

BALANCE OF PAYMENTS
Trade – US$92 million deficit (2001)
Current Account – US$1,098 million deficit (2001)

Trade with UK	*2002*	*2003*
Imports from UK	£43,890,000	£45,159,000
Exports to UK	157,588,000	126,943,000

TRANSPORT INFRASTRUCTURE

There are 73,766 km of roads, of which 16,876 km are surfaced. The Andean Highway forms a link between the Pacific, the Amazon and the Atlantic. The Pan-American Highway runs along the Peruvian coast connecting it with Ecuador and Chile.

The state controlled railway has 1,992 km of track. There is also steam navigation on the Ucayali and Huallaga and, in the south, on Lake Titicaca. Air services are maintained throughout Peru, and there is an international airport at Lima.

EDUCATION

Education is free of charge and compulsory between seven and 16. There are 51 universities.
ILLITERACY RATE – (m) 5.3 per cent; (f) 14.6 per cent (2000)
ENROLMENT (percentage of age group) – primary 100 per cent (1997); secondary 73 per cent (1997); tertiary 26 per cent (1997)

MEDIA AND CULTURE

Media freedom has greatly improved since the end of the Alberto Fujimori administration. Commercial television and radio receives a higher market share than the state networks. There are six national daily newspapers and a host of commercial radio broadcasters. The state owned Television Nacional de Peru competes with three commercial broadcasters including America TV and Panamericana.

Mestizo architecture and Cuzco painting are a fusion of Spanish and indigenous styles that have greatly influenced European art. José Maria Arguedes (1911–69) is one of Peru's most celebrated novelists.

THE PHILIPPINES

Repúblika ng Pilipinas – Republic of the Philippines

AREA – 298,200 sq. km
POPULATION – 77,131,000 (2001). The inhabitants are of Malay stock, with admixtures of Spanish and Chinese blood in many localities. The Chinese minority is estimated at 500,000, with smaller numbers of Spanish, American and Indian. About 90 per cent are Christian, predominantly Roman Catholics. Most of the remainder are Muslims or indigenous animists. The official languages are Filipino and English. Filipino is based on Tagalog, one of the Malay-Polynesian languages. English, the language of government, is spoken by at least 44 per cent of the population. Spanish is now spoken by a very small minority
CAPITAL – ΨManila (population, 9,906,048, 2000 census)
MAJOR CITIES – Quezon; ΨCebu; ΨDavao; ΨIloilo; ΨZamboanga
CURRENCY – Philippine peso (P) of 100 centavos
NATIONAL ANTHEM – Lupang Hinirang (Beloved Land)
NATIONAL DAY – 12 June (Independence Day 1898)
NATIONAL FLAG – Equal horizontal bands of blue (above) and red; a gold sun with three stars on a white triangle next staff
LIFE EXPECTANCY (years) – 70 (2001)
MORTALITY RATE (per 1,000 population) – 5.6 (2003)
INFANT MORTALITY (per 1,000 births) – 29 (2001)
HIV / AIDS ADULT PREVALENCE – 0.1 per cent (2001)

DEATH PENALTY – Yes
POPULATION GROWTH RATE – 2.1 per cent (1990–2001)
POPULATION DENSITY – 259 per sq. km (2001)
URBAN POPULATION – 59 per cent (2001)

CLIMATE AND TERRAIN

The principal islands of the Philippines (area in sq. km) are: Luzon (104,688); Mindanao (94,630); Samar (13,080); Negros (12,710); Palawan (11,785); Panay (11,515); Mindoro (9,735); Leyte (7,214); Cebu (4,422); Bohol (3,865) and Masbate (3,269). Other groups are the Sulu islands (capital, Jolo), Babuyanes and Batanes; the Calamian islands; and Kalayaan Islands. Elevation extremes range from 2,954 (Mt Apo) at the highest point to 0 m (Philippine Sea) at the lowest. The climate is tropical with average temperatures ranging from 23°C in January to 31°C in June.

HISTORY AND POLITICS

The Philippines were conquered by Spain in 1565 and colonial rule lasted until 1898 when US troops captured Manila in the American-Spanish war. The country remained under US control until 1946 when the Republic of the Philippines came into existence.

Similar to many countries emerging from colonialism, the Philippines suffered a period of post-imperial instability. In 1965 Ferdinand Marcos seized power, and declared martial law seven years later. Communist and Islamic insurgencies broke out in several parts of the Philippines, and by 1983 the country was suffering a full political crisis. Rigged elections in 1986 led to the People's Power Revolution, which brought Corazon Aquino to office. A fresh constitution adopted in 1987 planted democratic politics in the Philippines.

Fidel Ramos, who was elected president in 1992, built on the work of his predecessor by instigating peace talks with both the communist and Islamic rebels. Ramos was succeeded by Joseph Estrada in 1998. It was under Estrada's premiership that the peace process with the communist insurgents and the main Islamist insurgent group, the Moro Islamic Liberation Front (MILF), began to stall. The situation was complicated by the emergence of Abu Sayyaf, another Islamist group that began a spate of violent kidnappings. Muslim unrest at Government repression of these groups, as well as general dissatisfaction with Estrada led to his removal in a second People's Revolution.

Gloria Macapagal Arroyo became president in January 2001. She quickly moved to re-establish peace talks with the MILF, and the National Democratic Front (NDF), a front organisation for the communist insurgents. The talks with the MILF, though often interrupted by violence, eventually achieved a cease-fire in 2003.

Progress with the NDF has proved more problematic. The insurgents and government forces continued to clash and it was only in February 2004 that peace talks resumed.

Presidential elections were held on 10 May 2004. However, the process of collecting and collating the votes was severely delayed and as at August 2004, results were unavailable.

POLITICAL SYSTEM

Legislative authority is vested in a bicameral Congress. The House of Representatives has 250 members, of whom 204 are directly elected and 46 appointed by the President for a three-year term. The Senate has 24 members, of whom 12 are re-elected every three years.

The Autonomous Region of Mindanao consists of four provinces: Sulu, Tawi-Tawi, Lanao del Sur and Maguinadanao. There is a 24-member Regional Assembly and a Governor.

HEAD OF STATE
President, Defence, Gloria Macapagal Arroyo, *assumed office* 20 January 2001
Vice-President, Noli de Castro

SELECTED GOVERNMENT MEMBERS *as at August 2004*
Finance, Juanita Amatong
Foreign Affairs, Delia Domingo-Albert
Interior and Local Government, Angelo Reyes

EMBASSY OF THE REPUBLIC OF THE PHILIPPINES
9A Palace Green, London W8 4QE
T 020-7937 1600
Ambassador Extraordinary and Plenipotentiary, HE Edgardo Espiritu, apptd 2003

BRITISH EMBASSY
Floors 15–17, LV Locsin Building, 6752 Ayala Avenue, Corner of Makati Avenue, 1226 Makati, Manila (PO Box 2927 MCPO)
T (+63) (2) 816 7116
E uk@info.com.ph
Ambassador Extraordinary and Plenipotentiary, HE Paul Dimond, apptd 2002

BRITISH COUNCIL DIRECTOR, Gill Westaway
10th Floor, Taipan Place, Emerald Avenue, Ortigas Centre, Pasig City 1605
T (+63) (2) 914 1011
E britishcouncil@britishcouncil.org.ph

DEFENCE

The Army has 85 armoured infantry fighting vehicles and 370 armoured personnel carriers. The Navy has one frigate and 58 patrol and coastal vessels at three bases. The Air Force has 44 combat aircraft and 87 armed helicopters.
MILITARY EXPENDITURE – 2.1 per cent of GDP (2002)
MILITARY PERSONNEL – 106,000: Army 66,000, Navy 24,000, Air Force 16,000; Paramilitaries 44,000

ECONOMY AND TRADE

Major industries in the Philippines include food processing and fishing, electronics assembly, textile manufacture, pharmaceuticals, chemical production and petroleum refining. The country still has a large agricultural sector with 45 per cent of the labour force employed, producing rice, coconuts, corn, sugarcane, bananas and pineapples.

The Philippines experienced GDP growth of 4.5 per cent in 2003 and 6.4 per cent in the first quarter of 2004. This was boosted by growth in agricultural exports and the service industries. Remittances from Filipinos working abroad are also vital to the economy. There are high levels of debt and a large budget deficit. The government is attempting to introduce market reforms but investor confidence has suffered from recent political turmoil and insurgency.

Agriculture and fishing industries face a number of environmental challenges. The country suffers soil erosion, deforestation and air and water pollution on a large scale. There is also pollution of coastal mangrove swamps which are important fish breeding grounds.

GNI – US$80,800 million (2001); US$1,030 per capita (2001)
ANNUAL AVERAGE GROWTH OF GDP – 4.0 per cent (2000)
INFLATION RATE – 4.4 per cent (2000)
UNEMPLOYMENT – 10.1 per cent (2000)
TOTAL EXTERNAL DEBT – US$50,063 million (2000)
FOREIGN DIRECT INVESTMENT – US$5,537 million (1997–2000)
IMPORTS – US$31,358 million (2001)
EXPORTS – US$32,664 million (2001)

BALANCE OF PAYMENTS
Trade – US$2,763 million surplus (2001)
Current Account – US$4,150 million surplus (2001)

Trade with UK	*2002*	*2003*
Imports from UK	£353,931,000	£384,757,000
Exports to UK	979,295,000	730,553,000

TRANSPORT INFRASTRUCTURE

The road system covers about 187,000 km. The Philippine National Railway operates 429 km of railways, and there are 415 ports. There are 82 national airports and 137 privately operated airports. Philippine Airlines has regular flights throughout the Far East, to the USA and Europe, in addition to inter-island services.

EDUCATION

Secondary and higher education is extensive and there are 21 public and 53 private universities recognised by the government, including the Dominican University of Santo Tomás (founded in 1611). There are also 530 other institutions of higher education.
ILLITERACY RATE – (m) 4.5 per cent; (f) 4.8 per cent (2000)
ENROLMENT (percentage of age group) – primary 100 per cent (1997); secondary 78 per cent (1997); tertiary 29 per cent (1997)

MEDIA AND CULTURE

The government owned IBC television network competes with two commercial broadcasters. There is a large number of radio stations and four main national press publications.

Filipino culture is a vibrant mix of traditional dance (*Pandanggo sa Ilaw* is the most famous), folk music and art. Juan Luna (1857–99) and Felix Hidalgo (1855–1913) are two of the country's most celebrated painters.

POLAND

Rzeczpospolita Polska – Republic of Poland

AREA – 304,400 sq. km. Neighbours: the Russian Federation (Kaliningrad) (north), Germany (west), the Czech Republic and Slovakia (south), Belarus, Ukraine and Lithuania (east)
POPULATION – 38,577,000 (2001). Roman Catholicism is the religion of 95 per cent of the inhabitants. The language is Polish; there are German, Ukrainian and Belarusian minorities
CAPITAL – Warsaw (population, 1,609,780, 2001 estimate), on the Vistula
MAJOR CITIES – Bydgoszcz; ΨGdansk (Danzig); Katowice; Krakow; Lodz; Poznan; ΨSzczecin (Stettin); ΨWroclaw (Breslau)
CURRENCY – Zloty of 100 groszy
NATIONAL ANTHEM – Jeszcze Polska Nie Zginela (Poland Has Not Yet Perished)
NATIONAL DAY – 3 May
NATIONAL FLAG – Equal horizontal stripes of white (above) and red
LIFE EXPECTANCY (years) – 74 (2001)
MORTALITY RATE (per 1,000 population) – 9.96 (2003)
INFANT MORTALITY (per 1,000 births) – 8 (2001)
HIV / AIDS ADULT PREVALENCE – 0.1 per cent (2001)
DEATH PENALTY – No (abolished 1997)
POPULATION BELOW POVERTY LINE – 18.4 per cent (2000)
POPULATION GROWTH RATE – 0.1 per cent (1990–2001)
POPULATION DENSITY – 127 per sq. km (2001)
URBAN POPULATION – 63 per cent (2001)

CLIMATE AND TERRAIN

Poland's terrain is mostly flat plain, with mountains along the southern border. Elevation extremes range from 2,499 m (Rysy) at the highest point to –2 m (Raczki Elblaskie) at the lowest. The climate is continental and average temperatures in Warsaw range from –5°C in January to 24° C in July.

HISTORY AND POLITICS

The Polish-Lithuanian Commonwealth ended with its partition by Russia, Prussia and Austria in 1795. This lasted until 1918 when independence was granted with the signing of the Treaty of Versailles.

German forces invaded Poland on 1 September 1939; on 17 September, Russian forces invaded eastern Poland, and on 21 September 1939 Poland was declared by Germany and Russia to have ceased to exist. At the end of the war, its frontiers were redrawn; eastern Poland was ceded to the Soviet Union in return for the German territory east of the rivers Oder and Neisse. A coalition government was formed in which the Polish Workers' Party (PWP) played a large part. In December 1948, the PWP and the Polish Socialist Party merged to form the Polish United Workers' Party (PUWP). A new constitution modelled on the Soviet constitution was adopted in 1952, and was modified in 1976.

As hopes for prosperity dwindled, labour organisation increased, backed by a committed intelligentsia, with workers' delegations convening under the Solidarity trade union banner, led by Lech Walesa. In 1981, the demoralised Communist government declared martial law and interned Walesa and other leaders, driving Solidarity underground. However continuing strikes eventually resulted in talks between Walesa and the PUWP early in 1989. Multiparty parliamentary elections were held later that year, in which Walesa was elected as president and the PUWP ceased to be the ruling party. The post-communist governments introduced a free-market economy but economic difficulties and a fragmented parliament led to a succession of short-lived governments, and Walesa was toppled from the presidency in 1995 by former Communists Aleksander Kwasniewski and Wlodzimierz Cimoszewicz.

Kwasniewski, running for the Democratic Left Alliance (SLD), subsequently took political control and was then re-elected for a second presidential term in October 2000. Elections held on 23 September 2001 were won by an electoral alliance of the SLD and the Labour Union (UP), which won 216 seats in the Diet *(Sejm)* and 75 in the senate. A coalition government comprising the SLD, UP and the Polish Peasant Party (PSL) took office on 19 October. The PSL left the ruling coalition in March 2003 over its opposition to government on tax measures.

FOREIGN RELATIONS
Poland became a member of NATO in March 1999, and joined the EU in May 2004. The country's international profile was raised following its support for the US-led military campaign in Iraq in 2003, when it took command of one of three peacekeeping sectors.

POLITICAL SYSTEM
A new constitution came into effect on 16 October 1997. The President, directly elected for a maximum of two five-year terms, appoints the Prime Minister and has the right to be consulted over the appointment of the foreign, defence and interior ministers. The National Assembly is the bicameral legislature, comprising a 460-member *Sejm* and a Senate of 100 members. Both houses serve a four-year term. The Senate is elected on a provincial basis.

HEAD OF STATE
President, Aleksander Kwasniewski, *elected* 19 November 1995, *sworn in* 23 December 1995, *re-elected* 8 October 2000

SELECTED GOVERNMENT MEMBERS *as at July 2004*
Prime Minister, Marek Belka
Deputy Prime Minister, Economy, Labour and Social Policy, Jerzy Hausner
Deputy Prime Minister, Infrastructure, Marek Pol
Deputy Prime Minister, Internal Affairs and Administration, Jozef Olesky
Defence, Jerzy Szmajdzinski
Foreign Affairs, Wlodzimierz Cimoszewicz
Treasury, Zbigniew Kaniewski

EMBASSY OF THE REPUBLIC OF POLAND
47 Portland Place, London W1B 6JH
T 0870-774 2700
Ambassador Extraordinary and Plenipotentiary, vacant

BRITISH EMBASSY
Aleje Róz No. 1, PL00-556 Warsaw
T (+48) (22) 628 1001/5
E britemb@it.com.pl
Ambassador Extraordinary and Plenipotentiary, HE Charles Crawford

BRITISH COUNCIL DIRECTOR, Susan Maingay, OBE
Al. Jerozolimskie 59, PL-00-697 Warsaw
E bc.warsaw@britishcouncil.pl

DEFENCE
The Army has 947 main battle tanks, 1,281 armoured infantry fighting vehicles and 33 armoured personnel carriers. The Navy has four submarines, one destroyer, three frigates, 23 patrol and coastal vessels, 26 combat aircraft and 12 armed helicopters at five bases. The Air Force has 224 combat aircraft.
MILITARY EXPENDITURE – 1.9 per cent of GDP (2002)
MILITARY PERSONNEL – 163,000: Army 104,050, Navy 14,300, Air Force 36,450; Paramilitaries 21,400
CONSCRIPTION DURATION – 12 months

ECONOMY AND TRADE
Poland has vast mineral resources; there are large reserves of brown coal in central and south-western Poland and hard coal in Upper Silesia, the Walbrzych and Lublin regions; sulphur, copper, zinc, lead, silver, natural gas and salt are also produced.

Poland's major exports include machinery and vehicles, leather and textiles, metal goods, livestock, foodstuffs, luxury goods and chemical products. Its major imports are machinery and vehicles, chemical products, leather and textiles, livestock, foodstuffs, luxury goods and metal products. Germany is Poland's main trading partner.

In 1990, the government embarked upon a series of measures designed to introduce a free-market economy. The transition caused unemployment to double between 1990 and 1995 and it remains high. Industrial output has improved and the growth rate of GDP has increased although inflation remains high.

A programme has taken place to modernise the large agricultural sector and adapt it to the EU's common agricultural policy but the sector remains inefficient and future EU subsidy levels have been a major area of controversy, with corruption being one of the main concerns.

GNI – US$163,600 million (2001); US$4,230 per capita (2001)
ANNUAL AVERAGE GROWTH OF GDP – 4.1 per cent (2000)
INFLATION RATE – 1.9 per cent (2002)
UNEMPLOYMENT – 16.1 per cent (2000)
TOTAL EXTERNAL DEBT – US$63,561 million (2000)
FOREIGN DIRECT INVESTMENT – US$5,537 million (1997–2000)
IMPORTS – US$55,113 million (2002)
EXPORTS – US$41,010 million (2002)

BALANCE OF PAYMENTS
Trade – US$7,660 million deficit (2001)
Current Account – US$5,357 million deficit (2001)

Trade with UK	*2002*	*2003*
Imports from UK	£1,316,718,000	£1,453,498,000
Exports to UK	1,287,746,000	1,568,109,000

TRANSPORT INFRASTRUCTURE
The country has a total of 23,420 km of railways; 364,656 km of roads, and 3,812 km of navigable rivers and canals. Around 122 airports are in use, and principal ports and harbours include Gdansk, Gdynia, Gliwice, Kolobrzeg, Szczecin, Swinoujscie, Ustka, Warsaw and Wroclaw.

EDUCATION
Elementary education (ages seven to 15) is free of charge and compulsory. Secondary education is also free, but optional. There are 179 institutions of higher education, including universities at Krakow, Warsaw, Poznan, Lodz, Wroclaw, Lublin and Torun.
ILLITERACY RATE – (m) 0.3 per cent; (f) 0.3 per cent (2000)

ENROLMENT (percentage of age group) – primary 98 per cent (2000); secondary 91 per cent (2000); tertiary 25 per cent (1997)

MEDIA

Poland's broadcasting network is the largest in eastern and central Europe, and there is freedom and diversity of information in the media, although laws against criticism of the political system are still in force. State owned TV (TVP) still has the largest share of the audience for its two national channels. State owned Polish radio reaches just over half the population and there are more than 200 other commercial local and regional stations on air. Poland has over 300 newspapers, most of them local or regional.

CULTURE

Major writers include Henryk Sienkiewicz (1846–1916), Nobel Prize winner for Literature in 1905; Boleslaw Prus (1847–1912); Stanislaw Reymont (1867–1925), Nobel Prize winner for Literature in 1924; Czeslaw Milosz (b. 1911), Nobel Prize winner for Literature in 1980; and Wislawa Szymborska (b. 1923), Nobel Prize winner for Literature in 1996.

PORTUGAL

República Portuguesa – Portuguese Republic

AREA – 91,500 sq. km. Neighbour: Spain (north and east)
POPULATION – 10,033,000 (2001); 9,833,014 (excluding the Azores and Madeira, 1995). 94 per cent of the population are Catholic. The language is Portuguese
CAPITAL – ΨLisbon (population, 1,878,006, 2000)
MAJOR CITIES – ΨOporto
CURRENCY – Euro (€) of 100 cents
NATIONAL ANTHEM – A Portuguesa
NATIONAL DAY – 10 June
NATIONAL FLAG – Divided vertically into unequal parts of green and red with the national emblem over all on the line of division
LIFE EXPECTANCY (years) – 76 (2001)
MORTALITY RATE (per 1,000 population) – 10.21
INFANT MORTALITY (per 1,000 births) – 5 (2001)
HIV / AIDS ADULT PREVALENCE – 0.5 per cent (2001)
DEATH PENALTY – No (abolished 1976)
POPULATION GROWTH RATE – 0.1 per cent (1990–2001)
POPULATION DENSITY – 110 per sq. km (2001)
URBAN POPULATION – 66 per cent (2001)

CLIMATE AND TERRAIN

The terrain is mountainous north of the Tagus river, with rolling plains in the south. Elevation extremes range from 2,351 m (Ponta do Pico) at the highest point to 0 m (Atlantic Ocean) at the lowest. Portugal's climate is mild, with average temperatures in Lisbon ranging from 8°C in January to 28°C in July.

HISTORY AND POLITICS

Portugal's recent history has been much influenced by its maritime past, when during the 15th and 16th centuries its empire covered Brazil and parts of China as well as vast areas of Africa.

The country was a monarchy from the 12th century until 1910, when an armed uprising in Lisbon drove King Manuel II into exile and a republic was imposed. A period of political instability ensued until the military intervened and abolished political parties in 1926. The constitution of 1933 gave formal expression to the corporative 'Estado Novo' (New State) which was personified by Dr Antonio Salazar, prime minister 1932–68. Dr Caetano succeeded Salazar in 1968 but his failure to liberalise the regime or to conclude the wars in the African colonies resulted in his government's overthrow by a military coup in April 1974. Great political turmoil followed until July 1976, a period in which most of the colonies gained their independence, but with the failure of an attempted coup by the extreme left in November 1975 the situation stabilised. Full civilian government was restored in 1982.

Macao, which had been a Portuguese colony since 1557, was transferred to Chinese sovereignty on 19 December 1999.

In the presidential election held in January 2001, Jorge Sampaio of the Socialist Party was re-elected, gaining 55.8 per cent of the total vote. The subsequent general election, held on 17 March 2002, saw the Social Democratic Party (PSD) become the largest party in the Assembly winning 102 seats. José Manuel Durão Barroso of the PSD was sworn in as prime minister on 6 April, leading a coalition government of the PSD and the People's Party (PP). Mr Barroso resigned in July 2004. His immediate successor was Pedro Santa Lopes who announced a new government, a coalition of the PSD and PP, on 17 July 2004.

POLITICAL SYSTEM

Under the 1976 Constitution, amended in 1982 and 1989, the President is elected for a five-year term by universal adult suffrage. The Prime Minister is designated by the largest party in the legislature. Legislative authority is vested in the 230-member Assembly of the Republic, elected by a system of proportional representation every four years. The President retains certain limited powers to dismiss the Government, dissolve the Assembly or veto laws.

HEAD OF STATE

President of the Republic, Jorge Sampaio, *elected* 14 January 1996, *inaugurated* 9 March 1996, *re-elected* 14 January 2001

SELECTED GOVERNMENT MEMBERS *as at July 2004*

Prime Minister, Pedro Santa Lopes
Foreign Affairs and Portuguese Communities Abroad, António Monteiro
Internal Administration, Daniel Sanches
Minister of State for Finance, António Joséde Castro Bagão Félix
Minister of State for National Defence, Paulo Sacadura Cabral Portas

PORTUGUESE EMBASSY

11 Belgrave Square, London SW1X 8PP
T 020-7235 5331

Ambassador Extraordinary and Plenipotentiary, HE Fernando Andresen Guimaraes, apptd 2003

BRITISH EMBASSY
Rua de São Bernardo 33, P-1249-082 Lisbon
T (+351) (21) 392 4000
E consular@lisbon.mail.fco.gov.uk
Ambassador Extraordinary and Plenipotentiary, HE Dame Glynne Evans, CMG, DBE, apptd 2001

BRITISH COUNCIL DIRECTOR, Rosemary Hilhorst OBE
Rua Luís Fernandes, 1–3, P-1249-062 Lisbon.
T (+351) (21) 321 4500)
E lisbon.enquiries@pt.britishcouncil.org

DEFENCE

The Army has 187 main battle tanks and 353 armoured personnel carriers. The Navy has two submarines, six frigates and 28 patrol and coastal vessels at four bases. The Air Force has 50 combat aircraft.

Lisbon is the base of the NATO Iberian Atlantic Command and the USA maintains 1,120 personnel in mainland Portugal and on the Azores.

MILITARY EXPENDITURE – 2.3 per cent of GDP (2002)
MILITARY PERSONNEL – 44,900: Army 26,700, Navy 10,950, Air Force 7,250; Paramilitaries 47,700
CONSCRIPTION DURATION – Four to 12 months

ECONOMY AND TRADE

Portugal has experienced rapid economic growth since joining the EU in 1986. It was one of 11 states to adopt the European single currency on 1 January 1999, and the euro replaced the escudo on 1 January 2002.

The chief agricultural products are wine, dairy products, potatoes, tomatoes, maize, meat, fruit, olives, wheat, fish and rice. There are extensive forests of pine, cork, eucalyptus and chestnut covering about 38 per cent of the country. Around 13 per cent of the workforce are engaged in agriculture, the highest percentage in the EU. The principal mineral products are limestone, granite, marble, copper, coal, kaolin and wolframite.

The country is moderately industrialised. The principal manufactures are motor vehicle components, clothing and footwear, textiles, machinery, pulp and paper, pharmaceuticals, foodstuffs, chemicals, fertilisers, wood, cork, furniture, cement, glassware and pottery. There are a modern steelworks and large shipbuilding and repair yards at Lisbon and Setúbal, working mainly for foreign shipowners. There are several hydroelectric power stations and two thermal power stations.

The main exports are textiles, clothing and shoes, machinery, automobile parts, wood, pulp, paper and cork, and minerals. Principal imports include machinery, vehicles, textiles, agricultural products, chemicals, oil and base metals.

GNI – US$109,300 million (2001); US$10,900 per capita (2001)
ANNUAL AVERAGE GROWTH OF GDP – 3.3 per cent (2000)
INFLATION RATE – 2.9 per cent (2000)
UNEMPLOYMENT – 4.0 per cent (2000)
FOREIGN DIRECT INVESTMENT – US$10,835 million (1997–2000)
IMPORTS – US$38,309 million (2002)
EXPORTS – US$25,523 million (2002)

BALANCE OF PAYMENTS
Trade – US$12,411 million deficit (2002)
Current Account – US$9,120 million deficit (2002)

Trade with UK	*2002*	*2003*
Imports from UK	£1,444,000,000	£2,158,673,000
Exports to UK	1,596,000,000	1,399,300,000

TRANSPORT INFRASTRUCTURE

There are 2,850 km of railways, of which 623 km are electrified. There is a total of 68,732 km of roads, international airports at Lisbon, Oporto, Faro and Santa Maria, Lages (Azores) and Funchal (Madeira).

EDUCATION

Education is free of charge and compulsory for nine years from the age of six. Secondary education is mainly conducted in state general unified schools, lyceums, technical and professional schools and private schools. There are also military, naval, polytechnic and other specialist schools. There are 17 universities including those at Coimbra (founded in 1290), Oporto, Lisbon, Braga, Aveiro, Vila Real, Faro, Evora and in the Azores.

ILLITERACY RATE – (m) 5.2 per cent; (f) 10.0 per cent (2000)
ENROLMENT (percentage of age group) – primary 100 per cent (1997); secondary 100 per cent (1997); tertiary 39 per cent (1997)

MEDIA

Portugal's public broadcaster RTP enjoyed a monopoly until commercial TV was launched in 1992. Public radio networks are operated by RTP, while the Catholic church owns Radio Renascenca. There are some 300 other local and regional commercial radio stations.

Principal national newspapers include the dailies *Diario de Noticias*, *Publico*, *Correio da Manha* and *Jornal de Noticias*, the weekly *Expresso*, and the English-language *The Portugal News*.

CULTURE

Portuguese culture dates back to prehistoric times, as well as retaining traces of Roman and Arab influences. A rich archaeological legacy includes the prehistoric cave paintings at Escoral, the Roman township of Conimbriga, the Temple of Diana in Évora and the typical Arab-inspired architecture of such southern towns as Olhão and Tavira. Portugal's culture also benefited from other foreign influences, including Flemish, French and Italian. Celebrated Portuguese writers include José Cardosa Pires (1925–98), Fernando Pessoa (1888–1935) and José Saramango (b. 1922), winner of the 1998 Nobel Prize for Literature.

AUTONOMOUS REGIONS

Madeira and The Azores are two administratively autonomous regions of Portugal, having locally elected assemblies and governments.

MADEIRA is a group of islands in the Atlantic Ocean about 520 miles south-west of Lisbon, and consists of Madeira, Porto, Santo and three uninhabited islands (Desertas). Total area is 779 sq. km; population, 253,482 (2001). ΨFunchal in Madeira, the largest island, is the capital (population 103,961)

THE AZORES are a group of nine islands (Flores, Corvo, Terceira, São Jorge, Pico, Faial, Graciosa, São Miguel and Santa Maria) in the Atlantic Ocean; area 2,330 sq. km; population, 243,895 (2001). ΨPonta Delgada, on São Miguel, is the capital (population, 137,700). Other ports are ΨAngra, in Terceira (55,900) and ΨHorta (16,300)

QATAR

Dawlat Qatar – State of Qatar

AREA – 11,000 sq. km. Neighbours: United Arab Emirates (south), Saudi Arabia (south-west)
POPULATION – 575,000 (2001). Most of the population is concentrated in the urban district of Doha. Arabic is the official language. Islam is the religion of 95 per cent of the population
CAPITAL – ΨDoha (Ad-Dawhah) (population, 285,000 2001 estimate)
MAJOR CITIES – Ar-Rayyan; Dukhan; ΨMusay'id; Al-Wakrah
CURRENCY – Qatar riyal of 100 dirhams
NATIONAL DAY – 3 September
NATIONAL FLAG – White and maroon, white portion nearer the mast; vertical indented line comprising 17 angles divides the colours
LIFE EXPECTANCY (years) – 70 (2001)
MORTALITY RATE (per 1,000 population) – 4.43 (2003)
INFANT MORTALITY (per 1,000 births) – 11 (2001)
HIV / AIDS ADULT PREVALENCE – 0.09 per cent (2001)
DEATH PENALTY – Yes
POPULATION GROWTH RATE – 2.2 per cent (1990–2001)
POPULATION DENSITY – 52 per sq. km (2001)
MILITARY EXPENDITURE – 10.6 per cent of GDP (2002)
MILITARY PERSONNEL – 12,400: Army 8,500, Navy 1,800, Air Force 2,100
ILLITERACY RATE – (m) 19.6 per cent; (f) 16.9 per cent (2000)
ENROLMENT (percentage of age group) – primary 80 per cent (1993); secondary 69 per cent (1993); tertiary 27 per cent (1996)

CLIMATE AND TERRAIN

The terrain is mostly flat and barren with elevation extremes ranging from 103 m (Qurayn Abu al Bawl) at the highest point to 0 m (Persian Gulf) at the lowest. The country has a desert climate and average temperatures range from 23°C in January to 35°C in July. Humidity along the coast often reaches 90 per cent during the summer and average annual rainfall is below 75 mm.

HISTORY AND POLITICS

Qatar was one of nine independent emirates in the Gulf in special treaty relations with the UK until 1971. On 2 April 1970, a provisional constitution for Qatar was proclaimed, providing for the establishment of a Council of Ministers and for the formation of a Consultative Council to assist the Council of Ministers in running the affairs of the state. There are no political parties or legislature; ministers are chosen by the Amir.

The Amir, who had ruled since 22 February 1972, was overthrown on 27 June 1995 by his son and heir, who assumed power as Amir the same day. An attempted coup in 1996 failed.

Municipal elections were held on 8 March 1999, the first in which women were allowed to vote and contest seats. In a referendum held on 29 April 2003, voters approved a new constitution, providing for a 45-member (Consultative) Council *(Shura)* of which 30 members will be directly elected and 15 appointed by the Amir. The first elections to the council are due to be held in 2005.

On 5 August 2003 the Amir named his younger son, Prince Tamim, as the crown prince to replace Prince Jassim, who had expressed a desire to give up the post.

HEAD OF STATE
HH Amir of Qatar, Minister of Defence and Commander-in-Chief of Armed Forces, Shaikh Hamad bin Khalifa al-Thani, KCMG, *assumed power* 27 June 1995
Crown Prince, HH Shaikh Tamim bin Hamad al-Thani

SELECTED GOVERNMENT MEMBERS *as at July 2004*
Prime Minister, HH Shaikh Abdulla bin Khalifa al-Thani
First Deputy Prime Minister, Foreign Affairs, Shaikh Hamad bin Jassem bin Jabr al-Thani
Internal Affairs, Shaikh Abdulla bin Khalid al-Thani
Finance, Economy and Trade, Shaikh Hamad bin Faysal al-Thani

EMBASSY OF THE STATE OF QATAR
1 South Audley Street, London W1K 1NB
T 020-7493 2200
Ambassador Extraordinary and Plenipotentiary, HE Nasser bin Hamid M. Al-Khalifa, apptd 2000

BRITISH EMBASSY
PO Box 3, Doha
T (+974) 4421991
E bembcomm@qatar.net.qa
Ambassador Extraordinary and Plenipotentiary, HE David MacLennan, apptd 2002

BRITISH COUNCIL DIRECTOR, Tony Jones,
93 Al Sadd Street, PO Box 2992, Doha
T (+974) 442 6193/4

ECONOMY AND TRADE

The economy is based largely on oil, gas and petrochemicals, which account for more than 55 per cent of GDP, roughly 85 per cent of export earnings, and 70 per cent of government revenues. The state-owned Qatar General Petroleum Corporation controls the industry, and is responsible for oil production onshore and offshore. The large reserves of natural gas in the North Field came into production in September 1991.

Other industries include a steel mill, a fertiliser plant, a cement factory, a petrochemical complex and two natural gas liquids plants. With the exception of the cement works at Umm Bāb, all these industries are at Musay'īd, about 30 miles south of Doha. Qatar is also expanding its infrastructure, including electrical generation and water distillation, roads, houses, and government buildings. The chief imports are machinery and equipment, manufactures, foodstuffs, livestock and chemicals.

GNI – US$17,100 per capita (2001)
ANNUAL AVERAGE GROWTH OF GDP – 4.0 per cent (1998)
INFLATION RATE – 1.9 per cent (2002)
IMPORTS – US$2,500 million (1999)
EXPORTS – US$7,061 million (1999)

Trade with UK	*2002*	*2003*
Imports from UK	£202,999,000	£316,552,000
Exports to UK	28,667,000	54,931,000

TRANSPORT INFRASTRUCTURE

There are 1,210 km of roads, of which 1,089 km are surfaced. Regular air services provided by Gulf Air and Qatar Airways connect Qatar with the other Gulf states, the Middle East, the Indian sub-continent, Africa and Europe.

MEDIA AND CULTURE

Qatar officially lifted its censorship of the media in 1995 and since then the press has been essentially free from government interference. Qatari satellite television – Al Jazeera, launched in 1997 – has become one of the most important broadcasters in the Middle East. Radio is state run by the Qatar Broadcasting Service (QBS), and the BBC World Service is available in Doha. The most popular newspapers are *Al-Watan* and the English-language *Gulf Times*.

Qatar is primarily a Bedouin culture, and the tribal ethos and a strong oral tradition still survives. Traditional Qatari dress is characterised by gold or silver embroidery, known as *al-zari* or *al-qasab*.

ROMANIA

România – Romania

AREA – 230,300 sq. km. Neighbours: Ukraine (north and east), Moldova (east), Bulgaria (south), Serbia and Montenegro (south-west), Hungary (north-west)
POPULATION – 22,388,000 (2001): 89.4 per cent Romanian, 7.1 per cent Hungarian, 1.7 per cent Roma, 0.5 per cent German, 0.3 per cent Ukrainian, 0.04 per cent Jews and other minorities. Religious affiliation: Orthodox 86.8 per cent, Roman Catholic 5 per cent, Reformed 3.5 per cent, Greek Catholic 1 per cent. Romanian is a Romance language with many archaic forms and admixtures from Slavonic, Turkish, Magyar and French
CAPITAL – Bucharest (population, 2,066,723, 2001 estimate)
MAJOR CITIES – ΨBraşov; Constanţa; Cluj-Napoca; Craiova; ΨGalaţi; Iaşi; Oradea; Ploieşti; Timişoara
CURRENCY – Leu (Lei) of 100 bani
NATIONAL ANTHEM – Desteaptă-te, Române, Din Somnul Cel De Moarte (Awake Ye, Romanians, From Your Deadly Slumber)
NATIONAL DAY – 1 December
NATIONAL FLAG – Three vertical bands, blue, yellow and red
LIFE EXPECTANCY (years) – 70 (2001)
MORTALITY RATE (per 1,000 population) – 12.25 (2003)
INFANT MORTALITY (per 1,000 births) – 19 (2001)
HIV / AIDS ADULT PREVALENCE – 0.1 per cent (2001)
DEATH PENALTY – No (abolished 1989)
POPULATION BELOW POVERTY LINE – 44.56 per cent (2000)
POPULATION GROWTH RATE – 0.3 per cent (1990–2001)
POPULATION DENSITY – 97 per sq. km (2001)
URBAN POPULATION – 55 per cent (2001)

CLIMATE AND TERRAIN

The terrain varies, from the plains of the Moldavian region to the thick forests of the Carpathian Mountains. Elevation extremes range from 2,544 m (Moldoveanu) at the highest point to 0 m (Black Sea) at the lowest. Romania has a continental climate and average temperatures in Bucharest range from −2°C in January to 22°C in July.

HISTORY AND POLITICS

Romania was incorporated into the Roman Empire in the early part of the second century AD but abandoned 200 years later when the imperial power of Rome fell into decline. After centuries of rule by invading and often disparate tribal forces, Romania was incorporated into the Ottoman Empire during the 15th century. Unification under a single native ruler came in 1859 and full independence was ratified under the Treaty of Berlin in 1878.

In 1947 Romania became 'The Romanian People's Republic' under the leadership of the Romanian Communist Party. A revolution that began on 17 December 1989 led to the overthrow and execution of Nicolae Ceauşescu, president since 1965. A provisional government abolished the leading role of the Communist Party and held free elections in May 1990.

In the elections held on 26 November 2000 the Social Democratic Party of Romania (PDSR) gained 155 seats in the chamber of deputies and 65 seats in the senate, becoming the largest party in both houses. The PDSR presidential candidate, Ion Iliescu, then won the presidential election held on 10 December, obtaining 66.83 per cent of the vote. On 27 December, the PDSR reached an agreement with other centre-right parties to enable it to form a workable minority government. Presidential and legislative elections were scheduled for mid-November 2004.

Romania became a NATO member in April 2004.

POLITICAL SYSTEM

The Constitution of 1991 formally makes Romania a multiparty democracy that endorses human rights and a market economy. The Parliament comprises the Chamber of Deputies with 345 seats, of which 18 are reserved for ethnic minorities, and the Senate with 140 seats. Both houses are elected for a four-year term.

HEAD OF STATE

President of the Republic, Ion Iliescu, *elected* 10 December 2000

SELECTED GOVERNMENT MEMBERS *as at August 2004*

Prime Minister, Adrian Năstase
Defence, Ioan Mircea Paşcu
Economy and Commerce, Ioan-Dan Popescu
Foreign Affairs, Mircea Geoană
Interior, Marian Saniuta

EMBASSY OF ROMANIA

Arundel House, 4 Palace Green, London W8 4QD
T 020-7937 9666
Ambassador Extraordinary and Plenipotentiary, HE Dan Ghibernea, apptd 2002

BRITISH EMBASSY

24 Strada Jules Michelet, RO-70154 Bucharest
T (+40) (21) 201 7200
Ambassador Extraordinary and Plenipotentiary, HE Quinton Quayle, apptd 2002

BRITISH COUNCIL DIRECTOR, Stephan Roman
Calea Dorobantilor 14, RO-71132 Bucharest
T (+40) (21) 307 9600
E bc.romania@britishcouncil.ro

DEFENCE

The Army has 1,258 main battle tanks, 1,583 armoured personnel carriers and 177 armoured infantry fighting vehicles. The Navy has one frigate, 38 patrol and coastal vessels, and seven helicopters at four bases. The Air Force has 106 combat aircraft.

MILITARY EXPENDITURE – 2.3 per cent of GDP (2002)
MILITARY PERSONNEL – 97,200: Army 66,000, Navy 7,200, Air Force 14,000; Paramilitaries 79,900
CONSCRIPTION DURATION – 12 months

ECONOMY AND TRADE

Following the transition from communism in 1989, Romania's economy, which was characterised by state-owned and co-operative ownership, has been slowly reformed. Since 1996 the pace of privatisation and restructuring has quickened, subsidies have been reduced and prices liberalised. However, the country still suffers from widespread poverty, and corruption and red tape hinder foreign investment.

Agriculture employed 40.8 per cent of the workforce in 2000 and contributed 12.8 per cent of GDP. The principal crops are cereals, vegetables, flax and hemp. Vines and fruits are also grown, and extensive forests in the mountainous regions support an important timber industry.

There are plentiful supplies of natural gas, together with mineral deposits including coal, iron ore, bauxite, chromium and uranium.

Principal exports include textiles, metallurgical products, machinery components, minerals, chemicals, shoes and transport equipment. Italy, Germany, Russia, France and the UK are Romania's most important trading partners. The main imports are machines and equipment, minerals, textiles, chemicals and metallurgical products.

GNI – US$38,600 million (2001); US$1,720 per capita (2001)
ANNUAL AVERAGE GROWTH OF GDP – 5.3 per cent (2001)
INFLATION RATE – 22.5 per cent (2002)
UNEMPLOYMENT – 7.1 per cent (2000)
TOTAL EXTERNAL DEBT – US$10,224 million (2000)
FOREIGN DIRECT INVESTMENT – US$5,312 million (1997–2000)
IMPORTS – US$17,862 million (2002)
EXPORTS – US$13,876 million (2002)

BALANCE OF PAYMENTS
Trade – US$2,613 million deficit (2002)
Current Account – US$1,573 million deficit (2002)

Trade with UK	*2002*	*2003*
Imports from UK	£430,623,000	£507,927,000
Exports to UK	531,728,000	689,850,000

TRANSPORT INFRASTRUCTURE

There are 11,376 km of railways, over one-third of which are electrified. There are 153,358 km of roads of which 78,213 km are surfaced; there are 113 km of motorway. The principal ports are Constanţa and Mangalia (on the Black Sea), Sulina (on the Danube Estuary), Galati, Braila, Giurgiu and Drobeta-Turnu Severin. The Danube and the Black Sea are linked by a canal.

EDUCATION

Primary and secondary education is free of charge and compulsory. There are state universities in seven cities, 66 private universities, six polytechnics, two commercial academies, and five agricultural colleges.

ILLITERACY RATE – (m) 1.0 per cent; (f) 2.8 per cent (2000)
ENROLMENT (percentage of age group) – primary 100 per cent (1997); secondary 78 per cent (1997); tertiary 22.5 per cent (1997)

MEDIA

Romania has a dynamic media network with television audiences predominantly shared between the state owned Romania 1 and the private commercial stations Pro TV and Antena 1. Most households in Bucharest have cable TV. There are more than 100 private radio stations. State run Radio Romania operates four national networks and regional and local stations.

There are four main daily newspapers – *Adevarul, Libertatea, Evenimentul Zillei* and *Romania Libera.*

CULTURE

Romania has a rich folkloric heritage that survives in glass painting, folk music, traditional dance and epic oral literature. Celebrated figures include the philosopher Emil Cioran (1911–95), the composer George Enescu (1881–1955), the playwright Eugéne Ionescu (1909–94) and the sculptor Constantin Brancusi (1876–1957).

RUSSIA

Rossiiskaya Federatsiya – Russian Federation

AREA – 16,888,500 sq. km. Neighbours: Norway, Finland, Estonia, Latvia, Belarus and Ukraine (west), Georgia, Azerbaijan, Kazakhstan, China, Mongolia and North Korea (south). The Kaliningrad enclave borders Lithuania and Poland
POPULATION – 144,664,000 (2001): 87.5 per cent Russian, 3.5 per cent Tatar, 2.7 per cent Ukrainian, 1.3 per cent ethnic German, 1.1 per cent Chuvash, 0.9 per cent Bashkir, 0.7 per cent Belarusian and 0.7 per cent Mordovian. There are another six minorities with populations of over half a million and more than 130 nationalities in total. The Russian Orthodox Church is the predominant religion, though the Tatars and many in the north Caucasus are Muslims and there are Jewish communities in Moscow and St Petersburg. The language is Russian
CAPITAL – Moscow (population, 10,101,500, 2002 estimate), founded about 1147, became the centre of the rising Moscow principality and in the 15th century the capital of the whole of Russia (Muscovy). In 1325 it became the seat of the Metropolitan of Russia. In 1703 Peter the Great transferred the capital to St Petersburg, but on 14 March 1918 Moscow was again designated as the capital
MAJOR CITIES– ΨSt Petersburg, from 1914 to 1924 Petrograd and from 1924 to 1991 Leningrad. Other cities: Chelyabinsk; Kazan; Nizhny-Novgorod/Gorky; Novosibirsk/Novonikolayevsk; Omsk; Perm/Molotov; Rostov-on-Don; Samara/Kuibyshev; Ufa; Yekaterinburg/Sverdlovsk
CURRENCY – Rouble of 100 kopeks
NATIONAL ANTHEM – Russia, Sacred Our Empire (the former Soviet national anthem, with new lyrics)

NATIONAL DAY – 12 June (Independence Day)
NATIONAL FLAG – Three horizontal stripes of white, blue and red
LIFE EXPECTANCY (years) – 66 (2001)
MORTALITY RATE (per 1,000 population) – 13.99 (2003)
INFANT MORTALITY (per 1,000 births) – 18 (2001)
HIV / AIDS ADULT PREVALENCE – 0.9 per cent (2001)
DEATH PENALTY – No (abolished 1997)
POPULATION GROWTH RATE – 0.2 per cent (1990–2001)
POPULATION DENSITY – 9 per sq. km (2001)
URBAN POPULATION – 73 per cent

Russia occupies three-quarters of the land area of the former Soviet Union.

The Russian Federation comprises 89 members: 49 regions *(oblast)* – Amur, Arkhangelsk, Astrakhan, Belgorod, Bryansk, Chelyabinsk, Chita, Irkutsk, Ivanovo, Kaliningrad, Kaluga, Kamchatka, Kemerovo, Kirov, Kostroma, Kurgan, Kursk, Leningrad, Lipetsk, Magadan, Moscow, Murmansk, Nizhny-Novgorod, Novgorod, Novosibirsk, Omsk, Orel, Orenburg, Penza, Perm, Pskov, Rostov, Ryazan, Sakhalin, Samara, Saratov, Smolensk, Sverdlovsk, Tambov, Tomsk, Tula, Tver, Tyumen, Ulyanovsk, Vladimir, Volgograd, Vologda, Voronezh, Yaroslavl; six autonomous territories *(krai)* – Altai, Khabarovsk, Krasnodar, Krasnoyarsk, Primorye, Stavropol; 21 republics – Adygeia, Altai, Bashkortostan, Buryatia, Chechnya, Chuvash, Daghestan, Ingush, Kabardino-Balkar, Kalmykia, Karachai-Cherkessia, Karelia, Khakassia, Komi, Mari-El, Mordovia, North Ossetia (Alania), Sakha, Tatarstan, Tyva, Udmurt; ten autonomous areas – Aga-Buryat, Chuckchi, Evenki, Khanty-Mansi, Komi-Permyak, Koryak, Nenets, Taimyr, Ust-Orda-Buryat, Yamal-Nenets; two cities of federal status – Moscow, St Petersburg; and one autonomous Jewish region, Birobijan.

CLIMATE AND TERRAIN

There are three principal geographic areas: a low-lying flat western area stretching eastwards up to the Yenisei and divided in two by the Ural ridge; the eastern area between the Yenisei and the Pacific, consisting of a number of tablelands and ridges; and a southern mountainous area. Elevation extremes range from 5,633 m (Gora El'brus) at the highest point to –28 m (Caspian Sea) at the lowest. Russia has a very long coastline, including the longest Arctic coastline in the world (over 27,000 km).

The most important rivers are the Volga, the Northern Dvina and the Pechora, the Neva, the Don and the Kuban in the European part, and in the Asiatic part, the Ob, the Irtysh, the Yenisei, the Lena and the Amur, and, further north, Khatanga, Olenek, Yana, Indigirka, Kolyma and Anadyr. Lake Baikal in eastern Siberia is the deepest lake in the world.

Russia's climate varies dramatically, from the frozen tundra of the north Siberian plain, to the temperate regions of the far east. Throughout Russia, winters are cold while summers are hot in the south and relatively warm elsewhere. Rainfall is highest in the westerly mountain regions which have an average annual precipitation of up to 2,000 mm. Average temperatures in Moscow range from –16°C in January to 23°C in July.

HISTORY AND POLITICS

Russia was formally created from the principality of Muscovy and its territories by Tsar Peter I (The Great) (1682–1725), who initiated its territorial expansion, introduced Western ideas of government and founded St Petersburg.

Discontent caused by autocratic rule, the poor conduct of the military in the First World War and wartime privation led to a revolution which broke out in March 1917. A power struggle ensued between the provisional government and the Bolshevik Party. This led to a second revolution in November 1917 in which the Bolsheviks, led by Lenin, seized power.

Civil war between 'red' Bolshevik forces and 'white' monarchist and anti-communist forces lasted until the end of 1922. During the civil war, Russia had been declared a Soviet Republic and other Soviet republics had been formed in Ukraine, Belorussia and Transcaucasia. These four republics merged to form the Union of Soviet Socialist Republics (USSR) on 30 December 1922.

During the 1930s Joseph Stalin introduced a policy of rapid industrialisation under a series of five-year plans, brought all sectors of industry under government control, abolished private ownership and enforced the collectivisation of agriculture. Many ethnic minority groups suffered under Stalin's regime and it is estimated that up to 1.5 million people were deported to the *Gulags* of Siberia and the central Asian republics.

Mikhail Gorbachev became Soviet leader in March 1985 and introduced the policies of *perestroika* (complete restructuring) and *glasnost* (openness) in order to revamp the economy, which had stagnated since the 1970s, to root out corruption and inefficiency, and to end the Cold War. The retreat from total control by the Communist Party unleashed ethnic and nationalist tensions.

Following the defeat of an attempted coup by hardline communists in August 1991, effective political power was in the hands of the republican leaders, especially Russian President Yeltsin, and the Soviet Union began to break up as the constituent republics declared their independence. Gorbachev resigned as Soviet president on 25 December 1991 and the following day the USSR formally ceased to exist.

Russia was recognised as an independent state by the EC and USA in January 1992; it took over the Soviet Union's seat at the UN in December 1991.

A new Russian Federal Treaty was signed on 13 March 1992 between the central government and the autonomous republics. Tatarstan and Bashkortostan signed the treaty in 1994 after securing considerable legislative and economic autonomy.

In the presidential election held on 26 March 2000, Vladimir Putin won 52.94 per cent of the vote, and was formally inaugurated on 7 May 2000. Putin was re-elected to a second term as president by a landslide in March 2004, with 71.2 per cent of the vote.

In February 2004, President Putin dismissed Prime Minister Mikhail Kasyanov and his council of ministers. Putin named Mikhail Fradkov as prime minister on 1 March 2004.

POLITICAL SYSTEM

The 1993 Constitution enshrines the right to private ownership and the freedoms of press, speech, association, worship and travel, and states that Russia is a multiparty democracy. The President is directly elected for a maximum of two four-year terms. The Prime Minister takes over from the President in the event that he is unable to fulfil his duties. Legislative power is vested in the Federal Assembly, comprising the Federation Council (upper house) of 178 members, two elected by each of the 89 members of the Russian Federation; and the State *Duma* (lower house) of 450 members, of which 225 are elected by constituencies on a first past the post basis and 225 by proportional representation, with a five per cent threshold for representation.

The judicial system consists of a Constitutional Court of 19 members appointed for a 12-year term which protects and interprets the Constitution and decides if laws are compatible with it. The Supreme Court adjudicates in criminal and civil law cases. The Arbitration Court deals with commercial disputes between companies.

INSURGENCIES

The Chechen republic declared its independence in November 1991 after a nationalist coup in the republic and refused to sign the Russian Federal Treaty in March 1992. Civil war began in early 1994 between the Chechen government and armed opposition forces tacitly supported by the Russian government. The Russian military launched an invasion of Chechnya in December 1994 and captured Grozny, in February 1995.

Russian troops were withdrawn in January 1997 when presidential and legislative elections were also held in Chechnya. A treaty renouncing the use of force to resolve Chechnya's status was signed between Presidents Maskhadov and Yeltsin in May 1997.

Following an incursion by Islamic militants into Daghestan in August 1999, Russian forces launched air strikes and ground troops entered the territory, capturing Grozny and other Chechen-held towns in February 2000. Nevertheless, Chechen guerrilla attacks on Russian targets continued, and on 8 June 2000, President Putin imposed temporary direct presidential rule on Chechnya.

On 23 October 2002 Chechen separatists seized a Moscow theatre and held some 800 people hostage, a siege which only ended after Russian special forces stormed the building, killing most of the rebels and 119 hostages. Sporadic suicide bombings by Chechen rebels against Russian interests continue.

A referendum took place in Chechnya on 23 March 2003 in which the majority voted in favour of a new constitution promising autonomy for the republic but also stating that Chechnya was an integral part of the territory of the Russian Federation. Although progress towards peace continues, the situation in Chechnya remains delicate, and has been hampered by further acts of terrorism including the assassination of the Moscow-backed President Akhmat Kadyrov in May 2004. In September 2004, over 300 civilians were killed after terrorists took control of a school in Beslan.

HEAD OF STATE
President, Vladimir Putin, *elected* 26 March 2000, *inaugurated* 7 May 2000, *re-elected*, 14 March 2004

SELECTED GOVERNMENT MEMBERS *as at July 2004*
Chair, Mikhail Fradkov
Defence, Sergey Ivanov
Deputy Chair, Finance, Economic Development and Trade, Alexei Kudrin
Foreign Affairs, Sergei Lavrov
Interior, Rashid Nurgaliyev

EMBASSY OF THE RUSSIAN FEDERATION
13 Kensington Palace Gardens, London W8 4QX
T 020-7229 2666/3628/6412
Ambassador Extraordinary and Plenipotentiary, HE Grigory B. Karasin, apptd 2000

BRITISH EMBASSY
Smolenskaya Naberezhnaya 10, 121099 Moscow
T (+7) (095) 956 7200
E moscow@britishembassy.ru
Ambassador Extraordinary and Plenipotentiary, HE Sir Roderic Lyne, KBE, CMG, apptd 2000

BRITISH COUNCIL DIRECTOR, Adrian Greer
Ulitsa Nikoloyamskaya 1, RUS-109189 Moscow
T (+7) (095) 782 0200
E bc.moscow@britishcouncil.ru

DEFENCE

Since the demise of the Soviet Union the Russian armed forces have been considerably reduced. In November 2000 it was announced that the armed forces would be reduced to 850,000 personnel by 2005. Major army reform is planned for the period 2004–10, including the transition from conscription to voluntary service.

A joint CIS air defence system covers Russia, Armenia, Belarus, Kazakhstan, Kyrgyzstan and Uzbekistan.

The Strategic Nuclear Forces have 13 nuclear-powered ballistic missile submarines with 216 missiles, 735 intercontinental ballistic missiles and 100 anti-ballistic missiles.

The Army has about 21,870 main battle tanks, 25,975 armoured personnel carriers and armoured infantry fighting vehicles, and 1,700 helicopters. The Navy has 53 submarines, one aircraft carrier, seven cruisers, 14 destroyers, ten frigates, 88 patrol and coastal vessels, 217 combat aircraft and 102 armed helicopters. The Air Force has 1,736 combat aircraft.

Russia deploys forces in Armenia (3,500), Georgia (3,000), Moldova (1,000) and Tajikistan (7,800). Russia is the world's third largest contributor to peacekeeping operations. An agreement with Ukraine on the division on the Black Sea Fleet was signed in May 1997.

MILITARY EXPENDITURE – 4.8 per cent of GDP (2002)
MILITARY PERSONNEL – 809,600: Strategic Nuclear Forces 149,000, Army 321,000, Navy 155,000, Air Force 184,600; Paramilitaries 409,100
CONSCRIPTION DURATION – 18–24 months

ECONOMY AND TRADE

Under the Soviet regime, an essentially agrarian economy in 1917 was transformed by the early 1960s into the second strongest industrial power in the world. However, by the early 1970s the concentration of resources on the military-industrial complex was causing the civilian economy to stagnate. Free market reforms were introduced by President Gorbachev, including the legalisation of small private businesses, the reduction of state control over the economy, and denationalisation and privatisation. The first stage of mass privatisation of state industries began in October 1992 and the central distribution system was abolished with effect from 1 January 1993. By February 1996, 80 per cent of the economy had been privatised.

From 1994 to 1996, the economy began to stabilise with economic reforms judged to have become irreversible.

The devaluation of the rouble in 1998 caused the return of growth in the Russian economy in 1999. The country ended 2003 with its fifth consecutive year of growth, averaging 6.5 per cent annually, and having improved its international position dramatically: foreign debt now stands at around 28 per cent of GDP, down from 90 per cent. Nevertheless, considerable problems remain to be overcome. The country's manufacturing base is dilapidated, its banking system weak, and widespread corruption has led to a lack of trust in banking institutions.

Russia has some of the richest mineral deposits in the world. Coal is mined in the Kuznetsk area, in the Urals, south of Moscow, in the Donets basin and in the Pechora area in the north. Oil is produced in the northern Caucasus, between the Volga and the Urals, and in western Siberia, which also has large deposits of natural gas. A pipeline to bring Caspian oil into Russia via Daghestan and North Ossetia is under construction. Oil production in 2000 was 323.3 million tonnes. Coal and gas deposits in Siberia and the far east (especially Yakutia) are being developed. The Ural mountains contain many precious natural resources including high-quality iron ore, manganese, copper, aluminium, platinum, precious stones, salt, asbestos, pyrites, coal and oil. Iron ore is also mined near Kursk, Tula, Lipetsk, in several areas in Siberia and in the Kola Peninsula. Non-ferrous metals are found in the Altai, eastern Siberia, the northern Caucasus, the Kuznetsk basin, the far east and the far north. Some 190 tonnes of gold were produced in 2003.

The vast area and the great variety in climatic conditions are reflected in the structure of agriculture. In the far north reindeer breeding, hunting and fishing are predominant. Further south, the timber industry is combined with grain growing. In the southern half of the forest zone and in the adjacent forest-steppe zone, the acreage under grain crops is larger and the structure of agriculture more complex. Between the Volga and the Urals cericulture is predominant (particularly summer wheat), followed by cattle breeding. Beyond the Urals is another important grain-growing and stock-breeding area in the southern part of the western Siberian plain. In 2001 85 million tonnes of grain was harvested, an increase of 20 million tonnes on 2000. In the extreme south cotton is cultivated. Vine, tobacco and other southern crops are grown on the Black Sea shore of the Caucasus.

Moscow and St Petersburg are still the two largest industrial centres in the country, but new industrial areas have been developed in the Urals, the Kuznetsk basin, Siberia and the far east.

Russia's main trading partners are Germany, the USA, Italy, China and the former Soviet states.

GNI – US$253,400 million (2001); US$1,750 per capita (2001)
ANNUAL AVERAGE GROWTH OF GDP – 4.6 per cent (1998)
INFLATION RATE – 20.8 per cent (2000)
UNEMPLOYMENT – 13.4 per cent (1999)
TOTAL EXTERNAL DEBT – US$160,300 million (2000)
FOREIGN DIRECT INVESTMENT – US$15,028 million (1997–2000)
IMPORTS – US$58,992 million (2001)
EXPORTS – US$103,139 million (2001)

BALANCE OF PAYMENTS
Trade – US$46,281 million surplus (2002)
Current Account – US$31,091 million surplus (2002)

Trade with UK	*2002*	*2003*
Imports from UK	£989,683,000	£1,416,739,000
Exports to UK	1,995,701,000	2,481,230,000

TRANSPORT INFRASTRUCTURE

The European area of Russia is well served by railways, but there are still large areas, notably in the far north and Siberia, with few or no railways. In 2001 there were 149,000 km of railways, of which 86,000 km were used for passenger transport.

The most important ports (Taganrog, Rostov and Novorossiisk) lie around the Black Sea and the Sea of Azov. The northern ports (St Petersburg, Murmansk and Arkhangelsk) are, with the exception of Murmansk, icebound during winter. Several ports have been built along the Arctic Sea route between Murmansk and Vladivostok and are in regular use every summer. The far eastern port of Vladivostok, the Pacific naval base of Russia, is kept open by icebreakers all the year round.

There are 95,900 km of waterways. The great rivers of European Russia flow outwards from the centre, linking all parts of the plain with the chief ports. They are supplemented by a system of canals which provide a through route between the White, Baltic, Black and

Caspian Seas. The most notable are the White Sea–Baltic Canal, the Moscow–Volga Canal and the Volga–Don Canal linking the Baltic and the White Seas in the north to the Caspian Sea, the Black Sea and the Sea of Azov in the south.

MEDIA

The country's main national TV networks – Channel One, Radio Broadcasting company (RTR) and NTV are state-run. Many newspapers are privately owned while Russia's principal radio network is run by Russian State Television and RTR, alongside numerous regional and external services.

CULTURE

Russian is a branch of the Slavonic family of languages and is written in the Cyrillic script.

Before the westernisation of Russia under Peter the Great (1682–1725), Russian literature consisted mainly of folk ballads *(byliny)*, epic songs, chronicles and works of moral theology. The 18th and 19th centuries saw the development of poetry and fiction. Poetry reached its zenith with Alexander Pushkin (1799–1837), Mikhail Lermontov (1814–41), Alexander Blok (1880–1921), the 1958 Nobel Prize winner Boris Pasternak (1890–1960), Vladimir Mayakovsky (1893–1930) and Anna Akhmatova (1888–1966). Celebrated figures in philosophy and literary theory include Mikhail Bakhtin (1895–1975) and Viktor Shklovsky (1893–1984). Fiction is associated with the names of Nikolai Gogol (1809–52), Ivan Turgenev (1818–83), Fyodor Dostoevsky (1821–81), Leo Tolstoy (1828–1910), Anton Chekhov (1860–1904), Maxim Gorky (1868–1936), Ivan Bunin (1870–1953), Mikhail Bulgakov (1891–1940), Mikhail Sholokhov (1905–84) and Alexander Solzhenitsyn (*b.* 1918).

Great names in music include Glinka (1804–57), Borodin (1833–87), Mussorgsky (1839–81), Rimsky-Korsakov (1844–1908), Rubinstein (1829–94), Tchaikovsky (1840–93), Rachmaninov (1873–1943), Skriabin (1872–1915), Prokofiev (1891–1953), Stravinsky (1882–1971), Shostakovich (1906–75), Gubaidulina (b. 1931) and Schnittke (1934–98).

RWANDA

Republika y'u Rwanda/République Rwandaise – Republic of Rwanda

AREA – 26,338 sq. km. Neighbours: Burundi (south), Democratic Republic of Congo (west), Uganda (north), Tanzania (east)
POPULATION – 8,162,715 (2002 census): Hutus 90 per cent, Tutsis 9 per cent, Twa (pygmy) 1 per cent. Kinyarwanda, French and English are the official languages. Swahili is also spoken
CAPITAL – Kigali (population, 608,141, 2002 census)
CURRENCY – Rwanda franc of 100 centimes
NATIONAL ANTHEM – Rwanda Rwacu, Rwanda Gihugu Cyambyage (My Rwanda, Rwanda Who Gave Me Birth)
NATIONAL DAY – 1 July
NATIONAL FLAG – Broad blue band in upper half, with a sun next the fly surmounting equal bands of yellow and green
LIFE EXPECTANCY (years) – 38 (2001)
MORTALITY RATE (per 1,000 population) – 21.72 (2003)
INFANT MORTALITY RATE (per 1,000 births) – 96 (2001)
HIV / AIDS ADULT PREVALENCE – 8.9 per cent (2001)
DEATH PENALTY – Yes
POPULATION GROWTH RATE – 1.9 per cent (2001)
POPULATION DENSITY – 275 per sq. km (1999)
MILITARY EXPENDITURE – 4.1 per cent of GDP (2002)
MILITARY PERSONNEL – 41,000: Army 40,000, Air Force 1,000; Paramilitaries 5,000
ILLITERACY RATE – (m) 26.4 per cent; (f) 39.8 per cent (2000)
ENROLMENT (percentage of age group) – primary 75 per cent (1991); secondary 8 per cent (1991); tertiary 0.5 per cent (1990)

CLIMATE AND TERRAIN

The terrain is mostly mountainous and includes the volcanic Virunga range in the north-west. Elevation extremes range from 4,519 m (Volcan Karisimbi) at the highest point to 950 m (Rusizi River) at the lowest. Rwanda has a tropical climate and there are two wet seasons from February to April and November to January. Average daily temperatures range from 15°C in January to 35°C in July.

HISTORY AND POLITICS

Rwanda's history has been dominated by conflict between its two main ethnic groups, the Hutus and the Tutsis. In 1959, three years before independence from Belgian colonial rule, the Hutu population rebelled against Tutsi feudal domination, leading to the massacre of thousands of Tutsis. Some 150,000 fled into exile in Uganda and other neighbouring countries. Rwanda became an independent republic in July 1962.

Armed Tutsi exiles repeatedly attempted to invade Rwanda in the 1960s and 70s but were defeated by the predominantly Hutu army. Continued conflict left thousands dead over a period of 30 years. The exiles eventually formed the Rwandan Patriotic Front (RPF) and, in October 1990, they again invaded the country, forcing the government to introduce a multiparty constitution in 1991. After the government reneged on a 1992 peace agreement, the RPF advanced on Kigali and forced it to restart negotiations, which led to the August 1993 Arusha peace accord.

In 1994, President Habyarimana, who had retained the interim presidency, died in a plane crash widely believed to have been caused by extremist sections of the Hutu army. The army and militia *(interahamwe)* then carried out acts of genocide against the Tutsi minority and moderate Hutus; 800,000 people were massacred in three months. Nevertheless, the RPF gradually re-established its control over the country, forcing the defeated government forces and two million Hutu refugees into exile. In July 1994 the RPF established a broad-based government of national unity in which moderate Hutus were given the presidency and premiership and the RPF took eight of the 22 seats.

A government report issued in 2002 revealed that 1,074,017 people, more than 93 per cent of them Tutsis, were killed between 1990 and 1994. Since then, work has been ongoing to deal with the aftermath of genocide, a task complicated by ongoing attacks by extremist Hutu insurgents and Rwandan involvement in civil war in the neighbouring Democratic Republic of the Congo, which broke out in 1996.

However, repatriation of refugees and political reforms are under way. Rwanda held its first local elections in 1999, and its first presidential elections in August 2003, in which the RPF leader Paul Kagame received 95.1 per cent of the vote. A new constitution was approved in the same year, designed to achieve democracy while preventing another genocide, and not allowing any one ethnic group to dominate the government. An International Criminal Tribunal for Rwanda, based in Tanzania, has also been established and is working to bring those directly responsible for the 1994 genocide to trial.

POLITICAL SYSTEM

Under the 2003 Constitution the President is head of state and is directly elected for a seven-year term, renewable once only. The legislature is bicameral consisting of a National Assembly of 80 members elected by universal suffrage for a five-year term and a 26-member Senate.

HEAD OF STATE

President, Maj-Gen. Paul Kagame, *appointed* 17 April 2000, *sworn in* 22 April 2000, *elected* 25 August 2003

SELECTED GOVERNMENT MEMBERS *as at August 2004*

Prime Minister, Bernard Makusa
Defence and National Security, Maj.-Gen. Marcel Gatsinzi
Finance and Economic Planning, Donald Kaberuka
Foreign Affairs and Regional Co-operation, Charles Murigande
Internal Affairs, Jean de Dieu Ntiruhungwa

EMBASSY OF THE REPUBLIC OF RWANDA

Uganda House, 58–59 Trafalgar Square, London WC2N 5DX
T 020-7930 2570
Ambassador Extraordinary and Plenipotentiary, HE Rosemary K. Museminali, apptd 2000

BRITISH EMBASSY

Parcelle No. 1131, Blvd de l'Umuganda, Kacyira-Sud, BP 576 Kigali
T (+ 250) 84098/85771/85773
Ambassador Extraordinary and Plenipotentiary, HE Susan Elizabeth Hogwood, MBE, apptd 2001

ECONOMY AND TRADE

Rwanda is the most densely populated country in Africa, with few natural resources and minimal industry. Around 90 per cent of the population is engaged in subsistence agriculture. Primary foreign exchange earners are coffee and tea, tin, hides, quinine and pyrethrum are also exported, although the lack of adequate transport infrastructure is a handicap. Rwanda was given IMF-World Bank Heavily Indebted Poor Country (HIPC) status debt relief in late 2000.

GNP – US$1,889 million (2001); US$220 per capita (2001)
GDP – US$1,703 million (2001); US$187 per capita (2000)
ANNUAL AVERAGE GROWTH OF GDP – 6.0 per cent (2000)
INFLATION RATE – 4.3 per cent (2000)
TOTAL EXTERNAL DEBT – US$1,271 million (2000)
IMPORTS – US$203 million (2002)
EXPORTS – US$56 million (2002)

BALANCE OF TRADE

Trade – US$166 million deficit (2002)
Current Account – US$126 million deficit (2002)

Trade with UK	*2002*	*2003*
Imports from UK	£3,394,000	£3,199,000
Exports to UK	1,177,000	248,000

TRANSPORT INFRASTRUCTURE

Rwanda has 12,000 km of roads, of which around 996 km are surfaced. The roads from Kigali to the major towns are good, but landslides do occur during the wet season.

MEDIA

Rwanda's network media is mainly government controlled. A privately run radio station began broadcasting in 2004. The BBC World Service, Voice of America and Deutsche Welle all broadcast in Kigali. There are a growing number of newspapers but they face government restrictions and generally exercise self censorship.

ST CHRISTOPHER AND NEVIS

The Federation of St Christopher and Nevis

AREA – 262 sq. km
POPULATION – 38,000 (2001). The language is English
CAPITAL – ΨBasseterre (population, 12,200, 1994 estimate)
MAJOR TOWNS – ΨCharlestown, the chief town of Nevis
CURRENCY – East Caribbean dollar (EC$) of 100 cents
NATIONAL ANTHEM – Oh Land Of Beauty
NATIONAL DAY – 19 September (Independence Day)
NATIONAL FLAG – Three diagonal bands, green, black and red; each colour separated by a stripe of yellow. Two white stars on the black band
LIFE EXPECTANCY (years) – 71 (2001)
INFANT MORTALITY (per 1,000 births) – 20 (2001)
POPULATION GROWTH RATE – 0.9 per cent (1990–2001)
POPULATION DENSITY – 145 per sq. km (2001)

CLIMATE AND TERRAIN

The State of St Christopher and Nevis is located at the northern end of the eastern Caribbean. It comprises the islands of St Christopher (St Kitts) (109.5 sq. km) and Nevis (58 sq. km). The central area of St Christopher is forest-clad and mountainous, rising to the 1,158 m (Mount Liamuiga) at the highest point. Nevis is separated from the southern tip of St Christopher by a strait two miles wide which is dominated by Nevis Peak, 985 m. The climate is tropical, influenced by north-east trade winds and average annual rainfall – principally during May to September – is 1,375 mm, with average daily temperatures of 24°C.

HISTORY AND POLITICS

St Christopher was the first island in the British West Indies to be colonised (1623). The Territory of St Christopher and Nevis became a State in Association with Britain in 1967, and subsequently an independent nation in September 1983.

On 10 August 1998 a referendum was held in Nevis on the question of independence from St Christopher; although 61.8 per cent voted in favour of secession, it fell short of the two-thirds majority needed for independence.

In the legislative election held on 6 March 2000, the Labour Party won all eight of the seats on St Christopher. On Nevis, the Concerned Citizens' Movement won two seats and the Nevis Reformation Party one seat.

POLITICAL SYSTEM

Under the constitution, Queen Elizabeth II is Head of State, represented in the islands by the Governor-General. There is a central government with a ministerial system, the head of which is the Prime Minister of St Christopher and Nevis, and a National Assembly located on St Christopher. The National Assembly is composed of the Speaker, three Senators (nominated by the Prime Minister and the Leader of the Opposition) and 11 directly elected representatives, who serve for a five-year term. On Nevis there is a Nevis Island Administration, the head being styled Premier of Nevis, and a Nevis Island Assembly of five elected and three nominated members.

Governor-General, HE Sir Cuthbert Montraville Sebastian, GCMG, OBE, apptd 1996

SELECTED GOVERNMENT MEMBERS *as at August 2004*

Prime Minister, Finance, National Security, Planning, Development, Denzil Douglas

Deputy Prime Minister, Labour, Social Security, International Trade and Caricom Affairs, Telecommunications and Technology, Sam Condor

Foreign Affairs, Education, Timothy Harris

HIGH COMMISSION FOR ST CHRISTOPHER AND NEVIS

2nd Floor, 10 Kensington Court, London W8 5DL

T 020-7460 6500

High Commissioner for St Christopher and Nevis, HE James Ernest Williams, apptd 2001

BRITISH HIGH COMMISSIONER, HE C. John White, resident at Bridgetown, Barbados

ECONOMY AND TRADE

The economy of the islands has been based on sugar for over three centuries. Tourism (the chief source of foreign exchange), offshore banking and light industry, concentrating on distilling, food processing, clothing and electronics, are now being developed. The economy of Nevis relies on farming, but a sea-island cotton industry is being developed for export.

The main exports are sugar, lobsters, beverages and electrical equipment. Foodstuffs, energy, machinery and transport equipment are the main imports.

GNI – US$300 million (2001); US$6,630 per capita (2001)

ANNUAL AVERAGE GROWTH OF GDP – 2.8 per cent (1999)

INFLATION RATE – 3.9 per cent (1999)

TOTAL EXTERNAL DEBT – US$140 million (2000)

IMPORTS – US$149 million (1999)

EXPORTS – US$22 million (1999)

Trade with UK	*2002*	*2003*
Imports from UK	£5,714,000	£8,282,000
Exports to UK	3,955,000	5,819,000

TRANSPORT INFRASTRUCTURE

The islands have a total of 320 km of roads, of which 136 km are surfaced, and 50 km of narrow-gauge railways on St Christopher that serve the sugarcane plantations. Basseterre is a port of registry and has deep-water harbour facilities. Robert Bradshaw international airport, on St Christopher, can take most large jet aircraft; Vance Amory international airport on Nevis can take small aircraft and has night-time night-landing facilities. The sea ferry route from Basseterre to Charlestown is 11 miles.

MEDIA AND CULTURE

The government operates national television and radio stations; there are several private radio stations, and multi-channel cable TV offers a range of local and international TV stations.

The islands draw upon a mix of European, African and West Indian traditions. Architecture is predominantly colonial British and cricket is the national sport, but music and dance are very much West Indian and African.

ST LUCIA

AREA – 616 sq. km

POPULATION – 149,000 (2001). The official language is English. French creole is spoken by most of the population

CAPITAL – ΨCastries (population, 62,967, 2000 estimate)

CURRENCY – East Caribbean dollar (EC$) of 100 cents

NATIONAL ANTHEM – Sons And Daughters Of Saint Lucia

NATIONAL DAY – 22 February (Independence Day)

NATIONAL FLAG – Blue, bearing in the centre a device of yellow over black over white triangles having a common base

LIFE EXPECTANCY (years) – 74 (2001)

MORTALITY RATE (per 1,000 population) – 5.24 (2003)

INFANT MORTALITY (per 1,000 births) – 17 (2001)

DEATH PENALTY – Yes

POPULATION GROWTH RATE – 1.2 per cent (1990–2001)

POPULATION DENSITY – 242 per sq. km (2001)

CLIMATE AND TERRAIN

St Lucia, the second largest of the Windward group, is 43.5 km in length, with an extreme breadth of 22.5 km. The terrain is mountainous, with elevation extremes that range from 958 m (Mt Gimie) at the highest point to 0 m (Caribbean Sea) at the lowest. The climate is tropical and there is a wet season from June to September. The average daily temperature is 25°C.

HISTORY AND POLITICS

Originally settled by Arawak and then Carib Indians from AD 800, the Island of St. Lucia saw Dutch forces arrive in 1600 and begin building the fortified base of Vieux. Possession of St Lucia was fiercely disputed and it constantly changed hands between the British and the French until 1814 when it was ceded to Britain by the Treaty of Paris. It became independent within the Commonwealth on 22 February 1979.

The St Lucia Labour Party maintained its majority in the House of Assembly in a general election on 3 December 2001, winning 14 seats.

POLITICAL SYSTEM

The Head of State is Queen Elizabeth II, represented on the island by a St Lucian Governor-General, and there is a bicameral legislature. The Senate has 11 members, six appointed by the ruling party, three by the Opposition and two by the Governor-General. The House of Assembly, which serves for a five-year term, has 17 elected members and a Speaker, who may be appointed from outside the House.

Governor-General, HE Dame Pearlette Louisy, apptd 1997

SELECTED GOVERNMENT MEMBERS *as at August 2004*

Prime Minister, Finance, Economic Affairs, Information, International Financial Services, Kenny Anthony

Foreign Affairs, International Trade and Civil Aviation, Julian Hunte

Home Affairs and Internal Security, Calixte George

HIGH COMMISSION FOR ST LUCIA

1 Collingham Gardens, London SW5 0HW

T 020-7370 7123

High Commissioner for St Lucia, HE Emmanuel Cotter, MBE, apptd 1998

OFFICE OF THE BRITISH HIGH COMMISSION

Francis Compton Building, 2nd Floor (PO Box 227), Waterfront, Castries

T (+1 758) 452 2484/5

E britishhc@candw.lc

High Commissioner, HE C. John White, resident at Bridgetown, Barbados

ECONOMY AND TRADE

The economy is mainly agrarian, with the manufacturing industry based on agricultural and food processing. The principal crops are bananas, coconuts, cocoa, mangoes, breadfruit, yam and citrus fruit. Attempts are being made to increase industrialisation and explore economic diversification, particularly in the offshore banking and tourism sectors.

The principal exports are bananas, coconut products (copra, edible oils, soap), cardboard boxes, beer, and textiles. The chief imports are flour, meat, machinery, building materials, motor vehicles, manufactured goods, petroleum and fertilisers.

GNI – US$620 million (2001); US$3,950 per capita (2001)

ANNUAL AVERAGE GROWTH OF GDP – 2.8 per cent (1998)

INFLATION RATE – 1.7 per cent (2001)

TOTAL EXTERNAL DEBT – US$237 million (2000)

IMPORTS – US$267 million (2002)

EXPORTS – US$44 million (2001)

BALANCE OF PAYMENTS

Trade – US$207 million deficit (2001)

Current Account – US$38 million deficit (2001)

Trade with UK	*2002*	*2003*
Imports from UK	£11,654,000	£15,153,000
Exports to UK	23,588,000	15,940,000

TRANSPORT INFRASTRUCTURE

St Lucia contains around 1,210 km of roads, of which 63 km are surfaced. The island has two airports: Hewanorra international airport in Vieux Fort, at the remote southern tip of the island, and Vigie airport in Castries, near the main tourist area. Castries also has a deep-water harbour.

MEDIA AND CULTURE

St Lucia's TV and radio outlets are mainly privately owned. The government operates a radio network, which broadcasts in English and Creole. There are no daily newspapers; the island's main newspaper is published three times a week.

The writer and poet Derek Walcott (b. 1930) is St Lucia's most celebrated cultural figure. Winner of the Nobel Prize for Literature in 1997, Walcott's plays and poetry are a distinct blend of English, Caribbean and African literary traditions.

ST VINCENT AND THE GRENADINES

AREA – 388 sq. km

POPULATION – 109,022 (2002 estimate). The language is English

CAPITAL – ΨKingstown (population, 13,857, 2000)

CURRENCY – East Caribbean dollar (EC$) of 100 cents

NATIONAL ANTHEM – St Vincent, Land So Beautiful

NATIONAL DAY – 27 October (Independence Day)

NATIONAL FLAG – Three vertical bands, of blue, yellow and green, with three green diamonds in the shape of a 'V' mounted on the yellow band

MORTALITY RATE (per 1,000 population) – 6.08 (2003)

DEATH PENALTY – Yes

POPULATION GROWTH RATE – 0.7 per cent (2001)

POPULATION DENSITY – 289 per sq. km (1999)

CLIMATE AND TERRAIN

The territory of St Vincent includes certain of the Grenadines, a chain of small islands stretching 40 miles across the Caribbean Sea between Grenada and St Vincent, some of the larger of which are Bequia, Canouan, Mayreau, Mustique, Union Island, Petit St Vincent and Prune Island. Elevation extremes range from 1,234 m (La Soufriére) at the highest point to 0 m (Caribbean Sea) at the lowest. The climate is tropical with an average daily temperature of 28°C.

HISTORY AND POLITICS

St Vincent was discovered by Christopher Columbus in 1498. It was granted by Charles I to the Earl of Carlisle in 1627 and after subsequent grants and a series of occupations alternately by the French and English, it was finally restored to Britain in 1783. St Vincent achieved

full independence within the Commonwealth as St Vincent and the Grenadines on 27 October 1979.

After elections in 1998 the New Democratic Party (NDP), which had been in power since 1984, retained the majority of seats. However, following its approval of increased benefits for members of the legislature, it was forced by the opposition United Labour Party (ULP) to hold an early general election. This took place in March 2001 and was decisively won by the ULP, which obtained 12 seats. The NDP won the remaining three seats.

POLITICAL SYSTEM

Queen Elizabeth II is Head of State, represented by a Governor-General. The House of Assembly consists of 15 elected Members and four Senators appointed by the government and two by the Opposition. It is presided over by a Speaker elected by the House from within or without it.

Governor-General, Sir Frederic Ballantyne, GCMG, apptd 2002

SELECTED GOVERNMENT MEMBERS *as at July 2004*

Prime Minister, Finance, Planning, Economic Development, Labour, Information, Grenadine Affairs, Legal Affairs, Ralph Gonsalves

Deputy Prime Minister, Foreign Affairs and International Trade, Louis Straker

National Security, Public Service, Airport Development, Vincent Beache

HIGH COMMISSION FOR ST VINCENT AND THE GRENADINES

10 Kensington Court, London W8 5DL

T 020-7565 2874

E svghighcom@clara.co.uk

High Commissioner for St Vincent and the Grenadines, HE Cenio E. Lewis, apptd 2001

BRITISH HIGH COMMISSION

Granby Street (PO Box 132), Kingstown

T (+1 784) 457 1701

E bhcsvg@caribsurf.com

High Commissioner, HE C. John White, resident at Bridgetown, Barbados

ECONOMY AND TRADE

The economy is based mainly on agriculture but the tourism and manufacturing industries have been expanding. The main products are bananas, arrowroot, coconuts, cocoa, spices and various other kinds of food crops, although these have suffered severely in some years from tropical storms. In common with other Windward Islands, St Vincent and the Grenadines are attempting to reduce their reliance on banana crops, following the EU decision in 1999 to phase out preferential treatment to former colonies over competitors from Latin America. Bananas accounted for 39 per cent of exports in 2002. The main imports are foodstuffs, textiles, lumber, chemicals, motor vehicles and fuel.

GNI – US$317 million (2001); US$2,740 per capita (2001)

ANNUAL AVERAGE GROWTH OF GDP – 5.2 per cent (1998)

INFLATION RATE – 0.2 per cent (2000)

TOTAL EXTERNAL DEBT – US$192 million (2000)

IMPORTS – US$174 million (2002)

EXPORTS – US$38 million (2002)

BALANCE OF PAYMENTS

Trade – US$106 million deficit (2001)

Current Account – US$38 million deficit (2001)

Trade with UK	*2002*	*2003*
Imports from UK	£6,618,000	£9,142,000
Exports to UK	14,902,000	9,679,000

TRANSPORT INFRASTRUCTURE

The islands have around 1,040 km of roads, of which 320 km are surfaced. The main harbour is at Kingstown, and there are six airports, although none can accommodate international traffic.

MEDIA

The press is privately owned, and its freedom to criticise the government is guaranteed by the constitution. Most newspapers are published weekly. There are several private radio stations and a national radio service which is partly government funded. Television broadcasting is operated by the St Vincent and the Grenadines Broadcasting Corporation.

SAMOA

Ole Malo Tutoatasi o Samoa / Independent State of Samoa

AREA – 2,831 sq. km
POPULATION – 179,058 (2001 estimate), the largest numbers being on Upolu (114,980) and ΨSavai'i (43,150). The Samoans are a Polynesian people, though the population also includes other Pacific Islanders, Euronesians, Chinese and Europeans. The main languages are Samoan and English. The islanders are Christians of different denominations
CAPITAL – ΨApia (population, 38,836, 2001), on Upolu.
CURRENCY – Tala (S$) of 100 sene
NATIONAL ANTHEM – The Banner Of Freedom
NATIONAL DAY – 1 June (Independence Day)
NATIONAL FLAG – Red with a blue canton bearing five white stars of the Southern Cross
POPULATION GROWTH RATE – 1.3 per cent (2001)
POPULATION DENSITY – 60 per sq. km (1999)
LIFE EXPECTANCY – 76 years (2001)
MORTALITY RATE (per 1,000 population) – 6.41 (2003)
INFANT MORTALITY (per 1,000 births) – 10 (2001)
DEATH PENALTY – No (abolished 2004)
ILLITERACY RATE – (m) 18.8 per cent; (f) 21.0 per cent (2000)
ENROLMENT (percentage of age group) – primary 96 per cent (1996); secondary 45 per cent (1995)

CLIMATE AND TERRAIN

Samoa consists of the islands of Savai'i, Upolu, Apolima, Manono, Fanuatapu, Namua, Nuutele, Nuulua and Nuusafee. All the islands are mountainous and volcanic, with elevation extremes ranging from 1,857 m (Mauga Silisili) at the highest point to 0 m (Pacific Ocean) at the lowest. The climate is tropical with a wet season from November to April. Average temperatures range between 22 and 30°C all year round.

HISTORY AND POLITICS

Formerly administered by New Zealand (latterly with internal self-government), Western Samoa became fully independent on 1 June 1962. The state was treated as a member country of the Commonwealth until its formal admission in August 1970. A constitutional amendment came into effect on 4 July 1997 changing the state's name to the Independent State of Samoa.

Suffrage was made universal following a referendum held in 1990. In the general election held on 4 March 2001, the Human Rights Protection Party won 23 seats, the Samoan National Development Party won 13 seats and 13 seats were won by independents.

POLITICAL SYSTEM

The 1962 Constitution provides for a head of state to be elected by the 49-member Legislative Assembly *(Fono)* for a five-year term. Initially two of the four Paramount chiefs jointly held the office of head of state for life. When one of the chiefs died in April 1963, Susuga Malietoa Tanumafili II became head of state for life. The head of state's functions are analogous to those of a constitutional monarch. Executive Government is carried out by a Cabinet of Ministers.

HEAD OF STATE
Head of State for Life, HH Susuga Malietoa Tanumafili II, GCMG, CBE, *since* 15 April 1963

SELECTED GOVERNMENT MEMBERS *as at July 2004*
Prime Minister, Foreign Affairs, Attorney-General, Police and Prisons, Immigration, Public Service Commission, Tuilaepa Sailele Malielegaoi
Deputy Prime Minister, Finance, Misa Telefoni Retzlaff

HIGH COMMISSION FOR THE INDEPENDENT STATE OF SAMOA
123 Avenue Franklin D. Roosevelt Bte 14, 1050 Brussels
T (+32) (2) 660 8454
High Commissioner for the Independent State of Samoa, HE Tau'ili'ili'U'ili Meredith, apptd 1998

BRITISH HIGH COMMISSIONER, HE Richard Fell, CVO, apptd 2002, resident at Wellington, New Zealand

ECONOMY AND TRADE

Agriculture is the basis of the economy, employing about two-thirds of the labour force and supplying about 40 per cent of GDP and 90 per cent of exports. The principal cash crops (and exports) are coconuts (copra, oil and cream), cocoa and bananas. Efforts are being made to develop fishing on a commercial scale. Manufacturing is very small in scope and concerned largely with processing agricultural products, but is being encouraged by the government.

The tourism industry is an expanding sector, accounting for 25 per cent of GDP; about 88,000 tourists visited the islands in 2001.

GNI – US$1,490 per capita (2001)
ANNUAL AVERAGE GROWTH OF GDP – 1.1 per cent (1998)
INFLATION RATE – 1.0 per cent (2000)
TOTAL EXTERNAL DEBT – US$197 million (2000)
IMPORTS – US$130 million (2000)
EXPORTS – US$16 million (2000)

BALANCE OF PAYMENTS
Trade – US$98 million deficit (1999)
Current Account – US$19 million deficit (1999)

Trade with UK	*2002*	*2003*
Imports from UK	£1,303,000	£431,000
Exports to UK	81,000	347,000

TRANSPORT INFRASTRUCTURE

There are 790 km of roads, of which 332 km are surfaced. Upolu contains the harbours of Apia and Mulifanua, and

Savai'i the harbour of Salelologa. Most international flights land at Faleolo Airport, 35 km west of Apia on Upolu.

MEDIA AND CULTURE

There are two daily papers, one weekly and one fortnightly. The government operates the sole TV service, Televise Samoa, and there are three FM radio stations and one state run commercial radio service.

Traditional dancing *(siva)*, and longboat racing *(fautasi)* play a major part in Samoan culture. *Kirikiti*, the Samoan version of cricket, is a popular sport.

SAN MARINO

Repubblica di San Marino – Republic of San Marino

AREA – 61 sq. km. Neighbour: Italy
POPULATION – 27,336 (2001 estimate). The official language is Italian and the religion is Roman Catholic
CAPITAL – San Marino (population, 4,357, 1994), on the slope of Monte Titano
CURRENCY – Euro (€) of 100 cents
NATIONAL ANTHEM – Inno Nazionale (National Anthem)
NATIONAL DAY – 3 September
NATIONAL FLAG – Two horizontal bands, white and blue (with the coat of arms of the republic in centre)
MORTALITY RATE (per 1,000 population) – 7.86 (2003)
DEATH PENALTY – No (abolished 1865)
POPULATION GROWTH RATE – 3 per cent (2004)
POPULATION DENSITY – 426 per sq. km (1999)
URBAN POPULATION – 87 per cent (2001)

CLIMATE AND TERRAIN

Elevation extremes range from 755 m (Monte Titano) at the highest point to 55 m (Torrente Aussa) at the lowest. The climate is Mediterranean, characterised by cool winters and warm summers, with moderate rainfall throughout the year. Average annual precipitation is 762 mm while average temperatures range between −6°C in January to 25°C in June.

HISTORY AND POLITICS

San Marino is a small republic in the hills near Rimini, on the Adriatic, founded, it is said, by a pious stonecutter of Dalmatia in the fourth century. The republic resisted papal claims and those of neighbouring dukedoms during the 15th to 18th centuries, and its integrity and sovereignty is recognised and respected by Italy. San Marino became a member of the UN in 1992.

Following a general election in 2001, the number of seats held in the Grand and General Council was as follows: Christian Democratic Party (PDCS) 25, the Socialist Party (PSS) 15, the Progressive Democratic Party (PPDS) 12, others 8.

The PDCS and the PSS formed a coalition government, later joined by the Party of Democrats (PD), which collapsed in June 2002. The PSS, the PD and the Popular Democratic Alliance (APDS) formed a new coalition, which collapsed in December 2002, following which another coalition was formed, which comprises the PSS and the PDCS.

POLITICAL SYSTEM
Executive power is vested in the Congress of State composed of ten ministries under the presidency of the two heads of state, who are elected at six-monthly intervals (every April and October). Legislative power is exercised by the 60-member Great and General Council which is elected for a five-year term. A Council of Twelve forms in certain cases a Supreme Court of Justice.

HEADS OF STATE
Captain – Regent, Paolo Bollini
Captain – Regent, Marino Riccardi

SELECTED GOVERNMENT MEMBERS *as at July 2004*
Finance, Budget, Post and Telecommunications, Relations with the Philatelic and Numismatic State Corporations, Pier Marino Mularoni (PDCS)
Foreign and Political Affairs, Fabio Berardi (PSS)
Internal Affairs, Civil Protection, Loris Francini (PDCS)

EMBASSY OF THE REPUBLIC OF SAN MARINO
c/o Consulate of the Republic of San Marino,
Flat 51, 162 Sloane Street, London SW1X 9BS
T 020-7823 4762
Ambassador Extraordinary and Plenipotentiary, HE Countess Marina Meneghetti de Camillo, apptd 2002, resident at Rome, Italy

BRITISH AMBASSADOR, HE Sir Ivor Roberts, KCMG, apptd 2003, resident at Rome, Italy

BRITISH CONSULATE-GENERAL FOR SAN MARINO
Lungarno Corsini 2, I-50123 Florence, Italy
T (+39) (55) 284133
Consul-General, Moira Macfarlane

ECONOMY AND TRADE

The principal argricultural products are wine, cereals and fruits, and the main manufacturing industries produce metal, machinery, textiles and foodstuffs. Tourism contributes over 50 per cent of GDP. More than three million tourists visited in 2000. The island is in a customs union with the EU.

ANNUAL AVERAGE GROWTH OF GDP – 1.3 per cent (1998)
UNEMPLOYMENT – 3.0 per cent (1999)

Trade with UK	*2002*	*2003*
Imports from UK	£7,668,000	£4,978,000
Exports to UK	5,675,000	5,239,000

MEDIA

San Marino has one state run radio and television station, and one private radio station. Two daily newspapers are published.

SÃO TOMÉ AND PRÍNCIPE

República Democrática de São Tomé e Príncipe – Democratic Republic of São Tomé and Príncipe

AREA – 964 sq. km
POPULATION – 165,034 (2001 estimate). The official language is Portuguese
CAPITAL – ΨSão Tomé (population, 43,420, 1995 estimate)
CURRENCY – Dobra of 100 centavos

NATIONAL ANTHEM – Independência Total (Total Independence)
NATIONAL DAY – 12 July (Independence Day)
NATIONAL FLAG – Horizontal stripes of green, yellow and green, the yellow of double width and bearing two black stars; a red triangle in the hoist
MORTALITY RATE (per 1,000 population) – 7.11 (2003)
DEATH PENALTY – No (abolished 1990)
POPULATION GROWTH RATE – 2 per cent (2001)
POPULATION DENSITY – 149 per sq. km (1999)

CLIMATE AND TERRAIN

The islands of São Tomé and Príncipe are situated in the Gulf of Guinea, off the west coast of Africa. Elevation extremes range from 2,024 m (Pico de São Tomé) at the highest point to 0 m (Atlantic Ocean) at the lowest. The climate is tropical with a wet season from October to May. Average daily temperatures are an almost constant 30°C.

HISTORY AND POLITICS

The islands were first settled by the Portuguese in 1493 and became important suppliers of sugarcane, cocoa and coffee in the 18th and 19th centuries. The islands gained independence from Portugal in July 1975; democratic reforms were instituted in the late 1980s, and the first multiparty elections were held in 1991.

In the presidential election which took place on 29 July 2001, Fradique de Menezes of the Independent Democratic Alliance was elected with 56.31 per cent of the vote. Legislative elections were held on 3 March 2002, in which the Movement for the Liberation of São Tomé and Príncipe (MLSTP-PSD) won 24 of the 55 seats in the National Assembly. The Force for Change Democratic Movement-Democratic Convergence Party (MDFM-PCD) won 23 seats and the Ue Kedadji coalition (UK) won 8 seats. Gabriel Costa of the MLSTP-PSD was appointed prime minister on 26 March and a government of national unity, comprising members of all three parties and independents, was sworn in on 8 April. The president dismissed Costa and the entire government on 26 September 2002. A new government was named on 7 October, led by Maria das Neves de Sousa.

On 16 July 2003 the government was toppled during a week-long military coup which took place while the president was visiting Nigeria. De Menezes returned to São Tomé after a democratic rule was reached with the coup leaders; a general amnesty was given to the perpetrators.

POLITICAL SYSTEM

A multiparty constitution was approved by referendum in August 1990 under which the President, who is directly elected, serves a five-year term and may stand for a second term. The 55-seat unicameral National Assembly *(Assembleia Nacional)* is elected for a four-year term.

HEAD OF STATE

President and Commander-in-Chief of the Armed Forces, Fradique de Menezes, *elected* 29 July 2001, *sworn in* 3 September 2001

SELECTED GOVERNMENT MEMBERS *as at July 2004*
Prime Minister, Maria das Neves de Sousa
Defence and Interior, Oscar Aguiar Sacramento Sousa
Foreign Affairs and Co-operation, Communities, Ovidio Manuel Barbosa Pequeno
Health, Claudina Augusto Cruz
Planning and Finance, Eugenio Soares

EMBASSY OF THE DEMOCRATIC REPUBLIC OF SÃO TOMÉ AND PRÍNCIPE
Square Montgomery, 175 Avenue de Tervuren, B-1150 Brussels
T (+32) (2) 734 8966
Chargé d'Affaires, Antonio de Lima Viegas

BRITISH CONSULATE
Residencial Avenida, Av. Da Independencia CP 257, São Tomé
T (+239) (12) 21026/7
British Ambassador, HE John Thompson, MBE

ECONOMY AND TRADE

Agriculture accounts for nearly a quarter of GDP and employs nearly 40 per cent of the workforce, with cocoa accounting for 86 per cent of exports in 1997. Drought and mismanagement have led to declining cocoa production, which has resulted in balance of payments deficits, although strengthening prices helped to boost export earnings in 2003.

In April 2000, the IMF approved a three-year credit of US$8.7 million to support the government's 2000–2 economic programme. A further debt-reduction package worth about US$200 million was agreed by the IMF and World Bank in December 2000. Principal trading partners are Portugal, Spain, Netherlands and the UK.

In 2001, São Tomé and Nigeria reached an agreement on the exploration of oil reserves in the Gulf of Guinea.

GNI – US$43 million (2000); US$280 per capita (2001)
ANNUAL AVERAGE GROWTH OF GDP – 2.6 per cent (1998)
TOTAL EXTERNAL DEBT – US$316 million (2000)
IMPORTS – US$16 million (1997)
EXPORTS – US$5 million (1997)

Trade with UK	*2002*	*2003*
Imports from UK	£2,772,000	£459,000
Exports to UK	65,000	314,000

TRANSPORT INFRASTRUCTURE

São Tomé and Príncipe has a total of 320 km of roads, only 12 km of which are on Príncipe. The majority are surfaced, though mostly in poor condition. There are ports at Santo Antonio and São Tomé and two international airports.

MEDIA

Freedom of expression is guaranteed by the constitution. The islands' only radio and television stations are state run. There are three privately owned newspapers and one which is published by the government.

SAUDI ARABIA

Al-Mamlaka al-'Arabiyya as-Sa'ūdiyya – Kingdom of Saudi Arabia

AREA – 2,149,700 sq. km. Neighbours: UAE and Qatar (east), Jordan, Iraq and Kuwait (north), Yemen and Oman (south)
POPULATION – 21,028,000 (2001). Islam is the only permitted religion. The language is Arabic
CAPITAL – Riyadh (Ar-Riyad) (population, 4,761,000, 2001)
MAJOR CITIES – ΨJiddah (1.5 million); Buraydah;

ΨAd-Dammam; Al-Hofuf; Al-Makkah (Mecca); Al-Madiinah; Tabuk
CURRENCY – Saudi riyal (SR) of 20 qursh or 100 halala
NATIONAL ANTHEM – Ash Al-Malik (Long Live Our Beloved King)
NATIONAL DAY – 23 September (proclamation and unification of the Kingdom, 1932)
NATIONAL FLAG – Green oblong, white Arabic device in centre: 'There is no God but God and Muhammad is the Prophet of God', and a white scimitar beneath the lettering
LIFE EXPECTANCY (years) – 72 (2001)
MORTALITY RATE (per 1,000 population) – 5.79 (2003)
INFANT MORTALITY (per 1,000 births) – 23 (2001)
DEATH PENALTY – Yes
POPULATION GROWTH RATE – 2.8 per cent (1990–2001)
POPULATION DENSITY – 10 per sq. km (2001)

CLIMATE AND TERRAIN

Saudi Arabia comprises most of the Arabian peninsula. The Nejd ('plateau') extends over the centre of the peninsula, including the Nafud and Dahna deserts. The Hejaz ('the boundary') extends along the Red Sea coast to Asir and contains the holy towns of Mecca (Al-Makkah) and Medina (Al-Madīnah). Asir (meaning inaccessible) is so named for its mountainous terrain, and, with the coastal plain of the Tihama, lies along the southern Red Sea coast from the Hejaz to the border with Yemen. Elevation extremes range from 3,133 m (Jabal Sawda) at the highest point to 0 m (Persian Gulf) at the lowest. Yemen is the only region to enjoy substantial rainfall. The east and south-east of the country are low-lying and largely desert. The climate is hot and dry with average temperatures in Riyadh ranging from 21°C in January to 42°C in July.

HISTORY AND POLITICS

Modern-day Saudi Arabia was formed in 1932 when the head of the Saud dynasty, Abdul Aziz al-Saud, united the disparate regions of the Arabian Peninsula. Britain recognised al-Saud as an independent ruler, King of the Hejaz and of Nejd and its Dependencies, in 1927. On 23 September 1932 al-Saud was proclaimed as king and the country became known as the Kingdom of Saudi Arabia.

Following Iraq's invasion of Kuwait in 1990, Saudi Arabia accepted the Kuwaiti royal family and some 400,000 refugees while allowing Western and Arab troops to deploy on its soil for the liberation of Kuwait the following year. The continuing presence of foreign troops after Operation Desert Storm remained a source of tension between the royal family and the public until the US military withdrawal to neighbouring Qatar in 2003.

In May 2003, suicide bombers suspected of having links with al-Qa'eda killed 35 people – including a number of foreigners – in Riyadh, and further attacks have taken place in 2004.

POLITICAL SYSTEM

Saudi Arabia is a hereditary monarchy, ruled by the sons and grandsons of Abdul Aziz al-Saud, in accordance with Islamic Shari'ah Law. The line of succession passes from brother to brother according to age, although several sons of al-Saud renounced their right to the throne. All sons and grandsons of al-Saud must be consulted before a new king accedes to the throne.

In 1992 King Fahd announced a new Basic Law for the system of government based on Shari'ah Law and including rules to protect personal freedoms. The Constitution is defined as the Holy Koran *(Qur'an)* and the *Sunnah* (the teachings and sayings of the Prophet Muhammad). The King and the Council of Ministers (established in 1953) retain executive power. A Consultative Council *(Majlis-ash-Shura)* of a Chairman and 120 members appointed by the King was set up to share power with, and question, the Government and to make recommendations to the King. The *Majlis-ash-Shura* debates Government policy in the areas of budget, defence, foreign and social affairs. Members of the ruling al-Saud family are excluded from membership of the Council, which serves a four-year term and takes decisions by majority vote. Cabinet ministers serve for four years, with the possibility of a two-year extension.

In 1993 the country was reorganised into 13 provinces: Riyadh; Makkah; Al-Madinah; Al Qasim; Eastern; Asir; Tabuk; Ha'il; Northern Border; Jizan; Najran; Baha; Al-Jawf. Each province has a Governor appointed by the King and a council of prominent local citizens to advise the Governor on local government, budgetary and planning issues.

HEAD OF STATE
Custodian of the Two Holy Mosques and HM The King of Saudi Arabia, King Fahd ibn Abdul Aziz al-Saud, *born* 1923, *ascended the throne* 1 June 1982
HRH Crown Prince, Prince Abdullah ibn Abdul Aziz al-Saud

SELECTED GOVERNMENT MEMBERS *as at July 2004*
Prime Minister, HM The King
First Deputy Prime Minister, Commander of the National Guard, HRH The Crown Prince
Second Deputy Prime Minister, Defence and Civil Aviation, HRH Prince Sultan ibn Abdul Aziz al-Saud
Finance, Ibrahim ibn Abdel Aziz al-Assaf
Foreign Affairs, HRH Prince Saud al-Faisal ibn Abdul Aziz al-Saud
Interior, HRH Prince Nayef ibn Abdul Aziz al-Saud

ROYAL EMBASSY OF SAUDI ARABIA
30 Charles Street, London W1X 7PM
T 020-7917 3000
Ambassador Extraordinary and Plenipotentiary, HRH Prince Turki Al-Faisal, apptd 2003

BRITISH EMBASSY
PO Box 94351, Riyadh 11693
T (+966) (1) 488 0077
Ambassador Extraordinary and Plenipotentiary, HE Sherard Cowper-Cole, apptd 2003

CONSULATE-GENERAL – PO Box 393, Jiddah 21411
T (+966) (2) 622 5550
Consul-General, A. Henderson

BRITISH COUNCIL DIRECTOR, Alan Smart
Tower B, 2nd Floor, Al-Mousa Centre, Olaya Street, PO Box 58012, Riyadh 11594
E enquiry.riyadh@sa.britishcouncil.org

DEFENCE

The Army has 1,055 main battle tanks, 3,150 armoured personnel carriers, 970 armoured infantry fighting vehicles and 12 attack helicopters. The Navy has seven frigates, 26 patrol and coastal vessels and 21 armed helicopters at six bases. The Air Force has 294 combat aircraft.

Saudi Arabia is base to the Gulf Co-operational Council Peninsula Shield Force of 10,000 troops. In April 2003 the US announced that almost all its troops except some training personnel, would be pulled out of Saudi Arabia. Leaders of both countries stressed that co-operation would continue and they would remain allies.

MILITARY EXPENDITURE – 12.0 per cent of GDP (2002)

MILITARY PERSONNEL – 124,500: Army 75,000, Navy 15,500, Air Force 18,000, Air Defence Force 16,000; National Guard 75,000; Paramilitaries 15,500

ECONOMY AND TRADE

The productivity of traditional dryland farming is supplemented by extensive irrigation, desalination and use of aquifers. Agriculture accounted for seven per cent of GDP in 1998.

The principal industry is oil extraction and processing. Oil was first found in commercial quantities in 1938. Proven oil reserves of 259 billion barrels account for more than one-quarter of the world's reserves. The oil and gas industry contributes around 35–40 per cent of GDP depending on world prices. The country is also the world's largest oil exporter, with recoverable gas reserves estimated at over 220 trillion cubic feet. Mineral exploitation of gold, silver, copper and other minerals is also beginning, with gold production of 5.1 tonnes in 1998.

The government, in a series of five-year development plans begun in 1970, has actively encouraged the establishment of a manufacturing industry. So far industries have been developed in the manufacture of construction materials, metal fabrication, simple machinery, electrical equipment and textiles, and in the processing of foodstuffs and beverages and chemicals and plastics.

The seventh development plan, covering 2000–5, was approved in September 2000. It aimed to eliminate the budget and current account deficits, promote economic growth and diversity, encourage the private sector (responsible for around 40 per cent of GDP) and introduce legislation to increase the proportion of Saudi Arabian citizens in the workforce.

The leading suppliers of imports are the USA, the UK, Germany and Japan. The chief export markets are in Japan, the USA, South Korea and Singapore. There is a total ban on the importation of alcohol, pork products, firearms, and items regarded as non-Islamic or pornographic.

GNI – US$181,100 million (2001); US$8,460 per capita (2001)

ANNUAL AVERAGE GROWTH OF GDP – 4.5 per cent (2000)

INFLATION RATE – 0.8 per cent (2000)

IMPORTS – US$32,312 million (2002)

EXPORTS – US$68,064 million (2002)

BALANCE OF PAYMENTS

Trade – US$42,037 million surplus (2002)

Current Account – US$11,696 million surplus (2002)

Trade with UK	*2002*	*2003*
Imports from UK	£1,390,713,000	£1,841,629,000
Exports to UK	725,222,000	780,591,000

TRANSPORT INFRASTRUCTURE

There is one railway service from Ad-Dammam to Riyadh, which was opened in 1951 and is operated by the Saudi Government Railway Organisation. The service is being extended to the port of Al-Jubayl on the Gulf. In 1999 the road network totalled 151,470 km (of which 45,592 km were surfaced), including an expressway system, connecting all the cities and main towns. Jiddah is the main cargo sea port followed by Ad-Dammam. The main oil port (the world's largest) is Ras Tanura. The 25 km- long King Fahd Causeway completed in 1986 connects the Eastern Province to the State of Bahrain and is the world's second longest causeway. There are three international airports at Al-Makkah, Riyadh and Az-Zahran and 22 other commercial airports.

EDUCATION

With the exception of a few schools for expatriate children, all schools are supervised by the government and are segregated. There are universities in Jiddah, Al-Makkah, Riyadh (branches in Abha and Qassim), Ad-Dammam (branch at Al-Hufuf) and Az-Zahran, and there are Islamic universities in Al-Madinah and Riyadh together with 83 tertiary colleges. There is great emphasis on vocational training, provided at literacy and artisan skill training centres and more advanced industrial, commercial and agricultural education institutes.

ILLITERACY RATE – (m) 15.9 per cent; (f) 32.8 per cent (2000)

ENROLMENT (percentage of age group) – primary 61 per cent (1996); secondary 42 per cent (1996); tertiary 16.3 per cent (1996)

MEDIA

Saudi Arabia has one of the most tightly controlled media environments in the Middle East. Criticism of the government and royal family and the questioning of religious tenets are not tolerated.

The state run Broadcasting Service of the Kingdom of Saudi Arabia (BSKSA) is responsible for all broadcasting, operating four TV networks, including the news channel al-Ikhbariyya. Private radio and TV stations cannot operate from Saudi soil, but the country is a key market for pan-Arab satellite and subscription-based broadcasters. Saudi newspapers are created by royal decree. There are 10 dailies and many magazines. Pan-Arab newspapers, subject to censorship, are also available.

CULTURE

Saudi culture revolves almost entirely around Islam – two of Islam's holiest sites are in the country, and it considers itself the birthplace of the religion. Mecca is the birthplace of the Prophet Muhammad, and contains the Great Mosque, within which is the Kaaba *(Ka'abah)* or sacred shrine of the Muslim religion. This is the focus of the annual *Hajj* (pilgrimage). Medina Al-Munawwarah (The City of Light), some 300 km north of Mecca, is celebrated as the first city to embrace Islam and as the burial place of the Prophet Muhammad.

SENEGAL

République du Sénégal – Republic of Senegal

AREA – 196,722 sq. km. Neighbours: Mauritania (north), Mali (east), Guinea-Bissau and Guinea (south), the Gambia
POPULATION – 10,284,929 (2001 estimate), 94 per cent Muslim, 4 per cent Christian, 1 per cent Animist. The official language is French; the principal local language is Wolof. Fulani, Serer, Mandinka, Jola and Sarakole are also spoken
CAPITAL – ΨDakar (population, 1,641,358, 1998 UN estimate)
MAJOR CITIES – Rufisque; Thiés; ΨZiguinchor
CURRENCY – Franc CFA of 100 centimes
NATIONAL ANTHEM – Pincez Tous Vos Koras, Frappez Les Balafons (All Pluck Your Koras, Strike The Balafons)
NATIONAL DAY – 4 April
NATIONAL FLAG – Three vertical bands, green, yellow and red; a green star on the yellow band
MORTALITY RATE (per 1,000 population) – 10.88 (2003)
HIV / AIDS ADULT PREVALENCE – 0.5 per cent (2001)
DEATH PENALTY – No (abolished 1967)
POPULATION BELOW POVERTY LINE – 54 per cent (2001)
POPULATION GROWTH RATE – 2.6 per cent (2004)
POPULATION DENSITY – 47 per sq. km (1999)
MILITARY EXPENDITURE – 1.3 per cent of GDP (2002)
MILITARY PERSONNEL – 13,620: Army 11,900, Navy 950, Air Force 770; Paramilitaries 5,000
CONSCRIPTION DURATION – Two years (selective)
ILLITERACY RATE – (m) 52.7 per cent; (f) 72.3 per cent (2000)
ENROLMENT (percentage of age group) – primary 60 per cent (1997)

CLIMATE AND TERRAIN

The terrain is generally low and rolling, with plains rising to foothills in the southeast. Elevation extremes range from 581 m (Nepen Diakha) at the highest point to 0 m (Atlantic Ocean) at the lowest. Senegal has a tropical climate with a wet season from June to September. Average temperatures in Dakar range from 18°C in January to 32°C in July.

HISTORY AND POLITICS

Formerly a French colony, in 1958 Senegal elected to remain within the French Community as an autonomous republic. It became independent as part of the Federation of Mali in June 1960 and seceded to form the Republic of Senegal in September 1960.

Forty years of domination by the country's Socialist Party (PS) came to an end in March 2000 with the election of Abdoulaye Wade, leader of the Senegalese Democratic Party (PDS). The subsequent legislative election, held in April 2001, was won by an alliance of 40 parties, the *Sopi* (Change) coalition, led by the PDS. The PS retained only ten seats. Abdoulaye Wade dismissed the entire government in November 2002 and appointed Idrissa Seck as Prime Minister, along with a new Council of Ministers. Seck was dismissed by President Wade on 21 April 2004. The interior minister, Macky Sall, was immediately appointed as his successor.

Senegal has a long history of participating in international peacekeeping, and its troops have been deployed in the Democratic Republic of Congo, Liberia and Kosovo.

INSURGENCIES

A separatist civil war has been fought in the southern Casamance region, for the past 17 years. Hundreds of people have been killed and thousands have fled to Guinea-Bissau. Following a cease-fire in December 1999, a meeting between the government and the Movement of Democratic Forces of Casamance (MFDC) in January 2000 agreed to establish a joint body to monitor progress, to withdraw army and rebel forces from occupied villages, and to co-operate on mine clearance and the refugee situation. The two sides signed a peace agreement on 16 March 2001, but violence in the region increased during the election campaign in April 2001 and as at August 2004, the situation remained unresolved.

POLITICAL SYSTEM

A new Constitution was approved by referendum in January 2001. The Constitution dissolved the Senate, reduced the number of Members of Parliament in the National Assembly from 140 to 120, shortened the presidential term of office to five years, renewable only once, and guaranteed the right to form political parties. A general election for the National Assembly is held every five years.

HEAD OF STATE

President, Abdoulaye Wade, *elected* 19 March 2000, *sworn in* 1 April 2000

SELECTED GOVERNMENT MEMBERS *as at July 2004*
Prime Minister, Macky Sall
Defence, Becaye Diop
Finance and Economy, Abdoulaye Diop
Interior, Chiekh Sadibou Fall
Minister of State for Foreign Affairs, Cheikh Tidiane Gadio

EMBASSY OF THE REPUBLIC OF SENEGAL
39 Marloes Road, London W8 6LA
T 020-7938 4048/7937 7237
Chargé d'Affaires, Mamadou Kasse

BRITISH EMBASSY
20 rue du Docteur Guillet (BP 6025), Dakar
T (+221) 823 7392/9971
E britemb@telecomplus.sn
Ambassador Extraordinary and Plenipotentiary, HE E. Alan Burner, apptd 1997

BRITISH COUNCIL DIRECTOR, Andrew McNab
34–36 Blvd de la République, BP 6232, Dakar
T (+221) 822 2015/822 2048
E postmaster@britishcouncil.sn

ECONOMY AND TRADE

Around 60 per cent of the workforce are employed in the agricultural industry. Senegal's principal exports are fish, groundnuts (raw and processed) and phosphates. Senegal also exports fish, furniture, oilseeds and fruit, rubber, fertilisers and animal fodder to the UK. Tourism is also of growing importance as a source of revenue; in 1999 there were some 400,000 overseas visitors. Principal imports are foodstuffs, machinery, fuel oils and transport equipment; other imports, principally from the UK include foodstuffs, cigarettes, chemicals, machinery and transport equipment, vegetable fats and oils, and manufactured goods. Economic reforms have been ongoing since January 1994, with the support of the International Donor Community, and the GDP has seen growth averaging five per cent annually as a result.

GNI – US$4,726 million (2000); US$490 per capita (2001)
ANNUAL AVERAGE GROWTH OF GDP – 5.6 per cent (1998)
INFLATION RATE – 0.7 per cent (2000)
TOTAL EXTERNAL DEBT – US$3,372 million (2000)
IMPORTS – US$1,521 million (2000)
EXPORTS – US$920 million (2000)

BALANCE OF PAYMENTS
Trade – US$346 million deficit (1999)
Current Account – US$320 miillion deficit (1999)

Trade with UK	*2002*	*2003*
Imports from UK	£37,326,000	£52,829,000
Exports to UK	10,490,000	7,906,000

TRANSPORT INFRASTRUCTURE

Senegal has a road network of some 14,576 km, of which 4,271 km are surfaced. There are also 906 km of railways, and 897 km of navigable waterways on the Senegal and Saloum rivers.

MEDIA AND CULTURE

Senegal's constitution guarantees freedom of the news media and there are three private television channels, many private radio stations, and subscription-based television is readily available. Publications must be registered as a formality, but foreign media circulate freely. There are at least five daily newspapers, of which one is state owned.

The country is renowned for its musicians, who base their sounds on traditional *mbalax* rhythms. Catherine N'Diaye (b. 1952) and Nafissatou Niang Diallo (1941–82) are two of Senegal's most celebrated writers.

SERBIA AND MONTENEGRO

Srbija I Crna Gora

AREA – 102,100 sq. km. Neighbours: Hungary (north), Romania and Bulgaria (east), the Former Yugoslav Republic of Macedonia and Albania (south), Bosnia-Hercegovina and Croatia (west)
POPULATION – 10,538,000 (2001): 67.6 per cent Serb and Montenegrin, 16.5 per cent Albanian, 3.2 per cent Muslim Slavs, 3.3 per cent Hungarian, with smaller numbers of Romanies, Croats, Slovaks and Bulgarians. The majority religion is Serbian Orthodox, with significant Muslim and small Roman Catholic minorities. The main language is Serbian (74 per cent), with Albanian and Hungarian minorities. Serbian is a South Slav language usually written in the Cyrillic script
CAPITAL – ΨBelgrade (population, 1,574,050, 2002 census)
MAJOR CITIES – Kragujevac; Niš; ΨNovi Sad; Podgorica, the capital of Montenegro; Priština; Subotica
CURRENCY – New dinar of 100 paras
NATIONAL ANTHEM – Hej, Sloveni, Jošte ivi Reč Naših Dedova (Oh! Slavs, Our Ancestors' Words Still Live)
NATIONAL DAY – 27 April
NATIONAL FLAG – Three horizontal stripes of blue, white and red
LIFE EXPECTANCY (years) – 73 (2001)
MORTALITY RATE (per 1,000 population) – 10.62 (2003)
INFANT MORTALITY (per 1,000 births) – 17 (2001)
HIV / AIDS ADULT PREVALENCE – 0.2 per cent (2001)
DEATH PENALTY – No (abolished 2002)
POPULATION BELOW POVERTY LINE – 30 per cent (2001)
POPULATION GROWTH RATE – 0.3 per cent (1990–2001)
POPULATION DENSITY – 103 per sq. km (2001)
MILITARY EXPENDITURE – 5.3 per cent of GDP (2002)
MILITARY PERSONNEL – 74,200: Army 62,400, Navy 3,800, Air Force 8,000; Paramilitaries 45,100
CONSCRIPTION DURATION – 12–15 months

CLIMATE AND TERRAIN

Montenegro and southern Serbia are extremely mountainous, while the north is dominated by the low-lying plains of the Danube. Elevation extremes range from 2,656 m (Daravica) at the highest point to 0 m (Adriatic Sea) at the lowest. The major rivers are the Danube, the Sava, the Drina and the Morava. The climate inland is moderate and continental, while along the coast a Mediterranean-Adriatic climate prevails. Average temperatures in Belgrade range from 2°C in January to 18°C in July.

HISTORY AND POLITICS

Serbia emerged from the rule of the Byzantine Empire in the 13th century to form a large and prosperous state in the Balkans. Defeat by the Turks in 1389 led to almost 500 years of Turkish rule. After gaining autonomy within the Ottoman Empire in 1815, Serbia became fully independent in 1878 and a kingdom in 1881. Montenegro was part of the Serbian state before it was conquered by the Turks in the 15th century; it became independent in 1878. At the end of the First World War Serbia and Montenegro joined with the former Austro-Hungarian provinces of Slovenia, Croatia and Bosnia-Hercegovina to form the 'Kingdom of Serbs, Croats and Slovenes', which was renamed Yugoslavia in 1929. Yugoslavia was occupied by Axis forces in 1941 and reformed as a Communist federal republic under the presidency of partisan leader Josip Tito in 1945.

Tito died in 1980 and was succeeded by a rotating federal presidency which was unable to contain the growing nationalist movements. Efforts by the six republican presidents to negotiate a new federal or confederal structure for the country failed in 1991. On 25 June 1991 Slovenia and Croatia declared their independence from Yugoslavia.

In Croatia the ethnic Serb minority refused to accept Croatia's independence and fighting began in July 1991 between Croat Defence Forces and Serbian guerrillas, backed by the Yugoslav National Army (JNA). By September 1991 this had escalated into war between Croatia and Yugoslavia. The war in Croatia continued until January 1992 when the EU and the UN were able to bring about a cease-fire (*see* Croatia).

Macedonia declared its independence on 18 September 1991.

Bosnia-Hercegovina declared its independence on 1 March 1992. Independence was supported by the Bosniacs (Muslims) and Croats but rejected by the ethnic Serbs and fighting between Bosniacs and Serbs broke out in March 1992. The JNA intervened against the Bosniacs, but in May 1992 withdrew to Serbia and Montenegro (*see* Bosnia-Hercegovina). On 27 April 1992 the two remaining republics of the former Socialist Federal Republic of Yugoslavia, Serbia and Montenegro, announced the formation of a new 'Federal Republic of Yugoslavia' (FRY) under President Slobodan Milošević, who continued to lead various military intervention efforts to unite ethnic Serbs in neighbouring republics into a 'Greater Serbia'. All these efforts were ultimately unsuccessful.

Presidential and legislative elections for the federation were held on 24 September 2000, but were largely boycotted in Montenegro on the advice of its government. The Democratic Opposition of Serbia (DOS) became the largest party in both chambers of parliament. In the presidential election, the Federal Election Commission announced that Vojislav Koštunica of the Democratic Party of Serbia (DPS), had won 48.22 per cent, just short of the 50 per cent necessary to win without a second round, although an independent monitoring organisation had given him a clear majority. High tensions ensued, but on 7 October Koštunica was finally sworn in, replacing Milošević as President. The DOS and the SPS agreed to dissolve parliament and form a transitional government until a fresh election could be held for the Serbian Parliament. This took place on 23 December 2000 and the DOS won an overwhelming victory, obtaining 176 of the 250 seats.

Former President Milošević was arrested in April 2001 and handed over to the UN International Criminal Tribunal for the Former Yugoslavia, which in May 2001 had indicted him on charges of crimes against humanity, genocide and ethnic cleansing. The trial opened in The Hague in the Netherlands in February 2002.

In March 2002 the leaders of Serbia, Montenegro and the Federal Republic of Yugoslavia signed an agreement to maintain a joint state, and Yugoslavia was re-named Serbia and Montenegro. The constitutional charter for the new union was agreed in December that year, and Svetozvar Marovic was elected President of Serbia and Montenegro the following March by the union parliament.

INSURGENCIES

The province of Kosovo in the south of Serbia is more than 90 per cent ethnically Albanian. In 1998, Slobodan Milošević, then leader of the League of Communists of Serbia, revoked Kosovo's autonomous status, resulting in the progressive exclusion of the Albanian majority from public life. Following clashes between ethnic Albanians and Serbian police in February and March 1998, the Serbian military attacked civilians in the province on the pretext of eliminating support for the Kosovo Liberation Army (KLA), an ethnic Albanian organisation fighting for independence for the province. The international community condemned the brutality of the Serbian forces and a UN arms embargo was imposed on Yugoslavia, but the situation deteriorated. Tens of thousands of Kosovar Albanians fled when Yugoslav forces began to attack Kosovar villages. Following warnings to the Yugoslav authorities, NATO commenced air strikes against military targets in Yugoslavia on 24 March 1999. Over 800,000 people fled or were forced to leave their homes and sought refuge in Albania, Macedonia or Montenegro, which, although part of the Yugoslav Federation, had refused to become involved in the fighting; more than 500,000 people were displaced within Kosovo.

On 3 June President Milošević accepted a peace plan agreed by NATO and Russia, and the Yugoslav army withdrew to be replaced by NATO forces. Since the Yugoslav withdrawal, Kosovo has been under the administration of the UN's Interim Administration Mission in Kosovo (UNMIK), which has established the Kosovo Transitional Council, composed of four UN and four Kosovar representatives. The NATO-led Kosovo Force (KFOR) has established five command sectors, administered by UK, US, French, German and Italian troops respectively, with additional assistance from Russian troops. KFOR has facilitated the disarming of the KLA and the return of over 850,000 Kosovar Albanian refugees, but at least 200,000 Kosovar Serbs have fled, fearing reprisal attacks, which have frequently occurred.

In May 2001, UNMIK announced that a legislative assembly for Kosovo would be established having powers over health, education, environment and the economy, but with UNMIK retaining final authority. Elections to the assembly were held on 17 November 2001 and won by the Democratic League of Kosovo (LDK) who gained 47 of the 120 seats. A power-sharing government was agreed on 28 February 2002 with Bajram Rexhepi of the Democratic Party of Kosovo (PDK) as its head. Ibrahim Rugova of the LDK was elected unopposed as president on 4 March.

Armed fighters belonging to the ethnic Albanian Liberation Army of Preševo, Medvedja and Bujanovac (UCPMB) launched attacks on Serbs in Albanian-populated areas of southern Serbia in November 2000. The rebels wanted to annex these areas into Kosovo. A cease-fire was signed on 12 March 2001 after NATO agreed to permit Yugoslav forces to enter the demilitarised buffer zone which had been established on the Serbian side of the border with Kosovo in 1999.

POLITICAL SYSTEM

The federal legislature, the Assembly of Serbia and Montenegro *(Skupstina Srbije i Crne Gore)*, has 126 members elected by the Republican Assemblies, 91 from Serbia and 35 from Montenegro, for a two-year term. The Union Government consists of a Council of three Serb and two Montenegrin Ministers with the President as *ex officio* chair. The Republics each have their own governments, each led by a Prime Minister. The President of Serbia and Montenegro is elected by the Serbia-Montenegro Union Parliament.

HEAD OF STATE

President, Chair of the Council of Ministers, Svetozar Marovic, *elected* 3 March 2003

SELECTED GOVERNMENT MEMBERS *as at July 2004*

Defence, Prvoslav Davinic (Serbia)

Foreign Affairs, Vuk Draskovic (Serbia) (DOS)

MONTENEGRO

AREA – 13,182 sq. km

POPULATION – 615,000: 62 per cent Montenegrin, 14.5 per cent Bosniac, 6.5 per cent Albanian and 3 per cent Serb

On 20 October 2002 elections to the Montenegrin Republican Assembly took place, in which the Democratic Party of Socialists (DPS) was re-elected. Filip Vujanovic was nominated to form a new government to present to the new assembly in early November. Milo Djukanović, in office since May 1998, resigned as president of Montenegro on 25 November 2002 to become prime minister. Vujanovic, having resigned as prime minister, was elected chair of the parliament and became acting president. On 11 May 2003 Filip Vujanovic was elected Montenegrin president after a third round of elections.

SELECTED GOVERNMENT MEMBERS *as at July 2004*
President, Filip Vujanovic
Prime Minister, Milo Djukanović
Deputy Prime Ministers, Jusuf Kalamperovic; Dragan Djurovic *(Political System, Minister of the Interior)*; Branimir Gvozdenovic *(Economic Policy)*
Finance, Igor Luksic
Foreign Affairs, Miodraq Vlahovic

SERBIA

AREA – 88,538 sq. km
POPULATION – 9,300,000, of whom 66 per cent are Serbs

Serbia includes the provinces of Kosovo (population 1.6 million), of great historic importance to Serbs, and Vojvodina (population 2 million): the autonomy of both was ended in September 1990. Vojvodina, with its capital at Novi Sad, has a large Hungarian minority (21 per cent). Kosovo, with its capital at Priština, is predominantly Albanian (90 per cent).

The Serbian presidential elections of October and December 2002 were invalidated owing to the low turnout of voters. Natasa Micic became acting president in December. The Serbian Prime Minister, Zoran Djindjic was assassinated on 12 March 2003 and Zoran Zikovic was elected prime minister by parliament on 18 March. On 26 February 2004 the parliament voted to abolish the 50 per cent turnout needed to elect a president, and in June 2004 Boris Tadic was elected president with 53 per cent of the vote.

SELECTED GOVERNMENT MEMBERS *as at July 2004*
President, Boris Tadic, *took office 11 July 2004*
Prime Minister, Vojslav Kostunica
Deputy Prime Minister, Miroljub Labus

EMBASSY OF THE SERBIA AND MONTENEGRO
28 Belgrave Square, London SW1X 8QB
T 020-7235 9049
Ambassador Extraordinary and Plenipotentiary, HE Dr Vladeta Jankovic, apptd 2001

BRITISH EMBASSY
Resavska 46, YU-11000 Belgrade
T (+381) (11) 645055
Ambassador Extraordinary and Plenipotentiary, HE David Gowan, apptd 2003

BRITISH COUNCIL DIRECTOR, Chris Gibson,
Terazije 8/1, POB 248, YU-11001 Belgrade
T (+381) (11) 3023 800
E info@britcoun.org.yu

ECONOMY AND TRADE

Since 1991 the economy has been devastated by the wars in Croatia and Bosnia-Hercegovina, by the UN economic sanctions and trade embargo, and because of the lack of free-market reforms. NATO bombing in 1999 further damaged the already fragile situation. However, after the ousting of former President Milošević in October 2000, the Democratic Opposition of Serbia (DOS) coalition government implemented aggressive remedial measures and began to reintegrate into the international community, renewing its membership in the IMF and rejoining the World Bank and the European Bank for Reconstruction and Development. Since then the country has received donor finance for economic restructuring and rescheduled a large proportion of its debts.

Progress, however, remains slow, and only the country's agricultural self-sufficiency has kept it afloat. Industrial production remains extremely low and there is high unemployment, estimated to be around 34.5 per cent in 2003. GDP in 2000 was roughly 40 per cent of 1989 levels.

GNI – US$9,900 million (2001); US$930 per capita (2001)
ANNUAL AVERAGE GROWTH OF GDP – 5.5 per cent (2001)
INFLATION RATE – 19 per cent (2002)
TOTAL EXTERNAL DEBT – US$11,960 million (2000)

Trade with UK	*2002*	*2003*
Imports from UK	£61,628,000	£65,613,000
Exports to UK	31,402,000	34,410,000

TRANSPORT INFRASTRUCTURE

Serbia and Montenegro has some 49,805 km of roads, around 31,029 km of which are surfaced (including 560 km of expressways). There are also 4,059 km of railways, linking Belgrade directly to Athens, Bucharest, Budapest, Istanbul, Ljubljana, Munich, Skopje, Sofia, Thessaloniki, Vienna, and Zagreb. Principal ports and harbours include Bar, Belgrade, Kotor, Novi Sad, Pancevo, Tivat and Zelenika, and the main international airport – currently under renovation – is in Belgrade.

MEDIA

The end of the Milošević era saw a huge proliferation of media outlets. There are many privately owned television stations and around 1,000 radio stations were thought to be operating by late 2003. The state run national broadcaster, RTS, aims to develop into a public service, and private operators anticipate the formulation of regulatory and licensing procedures. Newspapers include *Danas* daily and a weekly publication *Vreme* and *NIN*.

In Kosovo, a Temporary Media Commission (TMC), set up by the UN, has set out a code of conduct for journalists which aims to prevent incitement to hatred in the media.

CULTURE

Serbia and Montenegro has a rich architectural and archaeological heritage that includes ornate orthodox churches, mosques, monasteries and palaces dating from the Ottoman Empire. Notable cultural figures include the writer Ivo Andric (1892–1975) winner of the Nobel Prize for Literature in 1961, the playwright Marin Držic (1508–67), the film producer Branko Lustig (b. 1932), the sculptor Ivan Mestrovic (1833–1962) and composers Jakov Gotovac (1895–1982) and Josip Štolcer-Slavenski (1896–1955).

SEYCHELLES

The Republic of Seychelles / République des Seychelles / Repiblik Sesel

AREA – 455 sq. km
POPULATION – 81,000 (2001). The languages are English, French and Créole
CAPITAL – ΨVictoria (population, 71,000, 1998 estimate), on Mahé
CURRENCY – Seychelles rupee of 100 cents
NATIONAL ANTHEM – Koste Seselwa (Seychellois Unite)
NATIONAL DAY – 18 June
NATIONAL FLAG – Five rays extending from the lower hoist over the whole field, coloured blue, yellow, green, white and red
LIFE EXPECTANCY (years) – 71 (2001)
MORTALITY RATE (per 1,000 population) – 6.49 (2003)
INFANT MORTALITY (per 1,000 births) – 13 (2001)
DEATH PENALTY – No (abolished 1993)
POPULATION GROWTH RATE – 1.3 per cent (1990–2001)
POPULATION DENSITY – 178 per sq. km (2001)
MILITARY EXPENDITURE – 1.7 per cent of GDP (2002)
MILITARY PERSONNEL – Army 200, Paramilitaries 250

CLIMATE AND TERRAIN

The Seychelles consists of 115 islands spread over 643,737 sq. km of ocean. There is a relatively compact granitic group, 32 islands in all, with high hills and mountains, of which Mahé is the largest and most populated (90 per cent of the population live on Mahé); and the outlying coralline group, for the most part only a little above sea-level. Elevation extremes range from 905 m (Morne Seychellois) at the highest point to 0 m (Indian Ocean) at the lowest. The climate is tropical with an average temperature of 26°C.

HISTORY AND POLITICS

Proclaimed French territory in 1756, the Mahé group was settled as a dependency of Mauritius from 1770, but was finally captured and assigned to Great Britain in 1814. In 1903 these islands, together with the coralline group, were formed into a separate colony. On 29 June 1976, the islands became an independent republic within the Commonwealth. A coup d'état took place in 1977. Seychelles was a one-party state from 1979 until 1993, when a multiparty democratic system was established by President France-Albert René.

In presidential elections held in 2001, President René was re-elected with 54 per cent of the vote and in legislative elections held in December 2002, the Seychelles People's Progressive Front retained its overall majority with 23 out of the 34 seats in the National Assembly. Mr René stepped down in April 2004, to be succeeded by the former Vice-President James Michel.

POLITICAL SYSTEM

Under the Constitution adopted in 1993, multiparty politics was institutionalised, a National Assembly of up to 34 members (23 elected by constituencies, up to 11 by proportional representation) was established and the presidential mandate was set at a five-year term, renewable three times.

HEAD OF STATE

President, Head of Government, Defence, Interior and Legal Affairs, James Michel, *assumed office*, 14 April 2004
Vice-President, Finance, Economic Planning, Information Technology and Communications, Joseph Belmont

SELECTED GOVERNMENT MEMBERS *as at July 2004*
Employment and Social Affairs, Vincent Meriton
Foreign Affairs, Jérémie Bonnelame
Industry and International Business, Jacquelin Dugasse

SEYCHELLES HIGH COMMISSION
51 Avenue Mozart, Paris F-75016
T (+331) 42305747

BRITISH HIGH COMMISSION
Oliaji Trade Centre, PO Box 161, Victoria, Mahé
T (+248) 283666
E bhcsey@seychelles.net
High Commissioner, HE Fraser Wilson, MBE, apptd 2002

ECONOMY AND TRADE

The economy is based on the tourist, fishing, small-scale agricultural and manufacturing industries, and the re-export of fuel for aircraft and ships. Deep-sea tuna fishing by foreign fleets under licence, improved port facilities at Victoria and exports from a tuna-canning factory attract growing revenues. The government is attempting to reduce the reliance on the tourist industry, which generates the majority of foreign exchange earnings, by promoting the country as an offshore haven for financial services. There were 129,800 foreign visitors in 2001. Principal exports are tuna, frozen prawns, fish and cinnamon bark. The principal imports are machinery and transport equipment, manufactures, foodstuffs, tobacco, fuel oils and chemicals.
GNI – US$540 million (2001); US$6,530 per capita (2001)
ANNUAL AVERAGE GROWTH OF GDP – 2.9 per cent (1999)
INFLATION RATE – 6.3 per cent (2000)
TOTAL EXTERNAL DEBT – US$163 million (2000)
IMPORTS – US$523 million (2001)
EXPORTS – US$216 million (2001)

BALANCE OF PAYMENTS
Trade – US$172 million deficit (2001)
Current Account – US$100 million deficit (2001)

Trade with UK	*2002*	*2003*
Imports from UK	£13,263,000	£13,207,000
Exports to UK	62,151,000	53,802,000

TRANSPORT INFRASTRUCTURE

The Seychelles has around 373 km of roads, the majority of which are surfaced. The main port is Victoria, and ferries run regularly between Mahé, Praslin and la Digue. Some 15 airports, eight with surfaced runways, serve the islands.

MEDIA

The government controls much of the islands' media, and operates the only radio and TV stations and the sole daily newspaper. Freedom of speech has improved since one-party rule was abolished in 1993, although the opposition weekly newspaper, *Regar*, has regularly been sued for libel by the government, and steep licensing fees have discouraged the development of privately owned broadcast media. The BBC World Service and Radio France Internationale broadcast in the area.

CULTURE

There is no indigenous culture in the Seychelles, but aspects of African origin have survived, and the government-formed National School of Music, and the National Cultural Troupe foster a Créole identity and tradition. The *sombre moutia* is the typical dance of the Seychelles, with strong African and Malagasy rhythms, the music for which is a blend of Indian, European, Chinese and Arabic.

SIERRA LEONE

The Republic of Sierra Leone

AREA – 71,740 sq. km. Neighbours: Guinea (north, north-east), Liberia (south-east)
POPULATION – 5,426,618 (2001 estimate). The south is inhabited by peoples whose languages fall into the Mende group; the north by the Temne and smaller groups such as the Limba, Loko, Koranko and Susu
CAPITAL – ΨFreetown (population, 469,776, 1985)
CURRENCY – Leone (Le) of 100 cents
NATIONAL ANTHEM – High We Exalt Thee, Realm of the Free
NATIONAL DAY – 27 April (Independence Day)
NATIONAL FLAG – Three horizontal stripes of leaf-green, white and cobalt blue
LIFE EXPECTANCY (years) – 34.5 (2001)
MORTALITY RATE (per 1,000 population) – 20.66 (2003)
HIV / AIDS ADULT PREVALENCE – 7 per cent (2001)
DEATH PENALTY – Yes
POPULATION BELOW POVERTY LINE – 68 per cent (2001)
POPULATION GROWTH RATE – 2.3 per cent (2004)
POPULATION DENSITY – 66 per sq. km (1999)
MILITARY EXPENDITURE – 2.2 per cent of GDP (2002)
MILITARY PERSONNEL – Army 14,000: Navy 200

CLIMATE AND TERRAIN

The terrain consists of coastal mangrove swamps, wooded hill country, upland plateau, and mountains in the east. Elevation extremes range from 1,948 m (Bintimani) at the highest point to 0 m (Atlantic Ocean) at the lowest. Sierra Leone has a tropical climate with a wet season from May to October. Average daily temperatures in Freetown are 30°C all year round.

HISTORY AND POLITICS

In the late 18th century a project was begun to settle destitute Africans from England on the Freetown peninsula. In 1808 the settlement was declared a Crown colony and became the main base in West Africa for enforcing the 1807 Act outlawing the slave trade. Africans from North America and the West Indies, and Africans rescued from slave ships, also settled there. In 1896 a protectorate was declared over the hinterland.

In 1951 the colony of Freetown and the protectorate were united and on 27 April 1961 Sierra Leone became a fully independent state within the Commonwealth. The country became a republic in 1971 and a one-party state in 1978, but in September 1991 a new multiparty constitution was adopted and an interim government formed, which was overthrown by a military coup on 29 April 1992. Four years later, the military government surrendered power to a civilian government, headed by Ahmad Tejan Kabbah, of the Sierra Leone People's Party (SLPP).

However, in May 1997 army officers led by Major Johnny Koroma seized power. President Kabbah fled and a 20-member Armed Forces Revolutionary Council was set up with Koroma as chairman and Revolutionary United Front (RUF) leader Foday Sankoh as vice-chairman. In July 1997, a Nigerian-led ECOMOG force was sent to oust Koroma and restore the legitimate government. A peace agreement was reached in October, which provided for Kabbah to return to power and granted immunity from prosecution to Koroma. President Kabbah returned to Freetown on 10 March 1998.

In the presidential elections held on 14 May 2002, President Kabbah was re-elected with 70 per cent of the vote and the SLPP won 83 of the 112 seats in the parliament in the simultaneous legislative election. A new cabinet, composed of members of the SLPP and independents, was appointed.

INSURGENCIES

Since May 1991 government forces have been fighting the RUF, whose aim is to force all foreigners out of the country and to nationalise the mining sector. Attacks by the RUF intensified in December 1998 and on 6 January 1999 the RUF attacked Freetown. ECOMOG troops launched a counter-attack on 9–10 January, recapturing the city.

President Kabbah and Foday Sankoh signed a cease-fire agreement on 18 May 1999 and it was agreed in July 1999 that Sankoh would be appointed vice-president and head the Mineral Resources Commission and that the RUF would be given four cabinet posts. A government of national unity was announced on 2 November 1999. Violence continued, despite the efforts of the UN Mission to Sierra Leone (UNAMSIL), which officially took over from ECOMOG on 29 April 2000. The cease-fire agreement collapsed when the RUF abducted 500 UNAMSIL peacekeepers between 30 April–6 May, and used captured UNAMSIL weaponry to launch an advance on Freetown. UNAMSIL troops, along with Sierra Leonean Army (SLA) and Nigerian Army troops, went on the offensive and drove the RUF back, eventually arresting Foday Sankoh, the RUF leader, on 17 May 2000.

A cease-fire was signed by the government and the RUF on 11 November 2000, but was never fully implemented; another agreement to end hostilities was then signed in May 2001. The state of emergency imposed in 1998 was lifted in March 2002.

In September 2002 the UN decided to extend its military mission within the country for a further eight months and again on 30 March 2003 for a further six months. There are currently around 12,000 UNAMSIL personnel in Sierra Leone.

HEAD OF STATE

President, Defence, Ahmad Tejan Kabbah, *elected* 15 March 1996, *re-elected* 14 May 2002
Vice-President, Solomon Berewa

SELECTED GOVERNMENT MEMBERS *as at July 2004*

Finance, Joseph Bandaba Dauda
Foreign Affairs and International Co-operation, Momodu Koroma

Political and Parliamentary Affairs, Internal Affairs (acting), George Banda Thomas

SIERRA LEONE HIGH COMMISSION
1st and 3rd Floors, Oxford Circus House, 245 Oxford Street, London W1D 2LX
T 020-7287 9884
High Commissioner, HE Sulaiman Tejan-Jalloh, apptd 2000

BRITISH HIGH COMMISSION
Spur Road, Freetown
T (+232) (22) 232961/362/563/565
E bhc@sierratel.sl
High Commissioner, HE John Mitchiner, apptd 2003

BRITISH COUNCIL DIRECTOR, Rajive Bendre
PO Box 124, Tower Hill, Freetown
T (+232) (22) 222 223
E info.enquiry@sl.britishcouncil.org

ECONOMY AND TRADE

On the Freetown peninsula, farming is largely confined to the production of cassava and crops such as maize and vegetables for local consumption. In the hinterland the principal agricultural product is rice, which is the staple food of the country, and cash crops such as cocoa, coffee, palm kernels and ginger. Cattle production is also important.

The economy depends largely on mineral exports, mainly diamonds, gold and bauxite, although mineral production has been disrupted by recent insurgencies. In December 2002 the UN approved a resolution banning the trade in rough diamonds in areas not controlled by the government. Between 60 and 70 per cent of government expenditure is financed by donor support.

GNI – US$693 million (2000); US$140 per capita (2000)
GDP – US$749 million (2001); US$142 per capita (2000)
ANNUAL AVERAGE GROWTH OF GDP – 3.8 per cent (2000)
INFLATION RATE – 0.8 per cent (2000)
TOTAL EXTERNAL DEBT – US$1,273 million (2000)
IMPORTS – US$182 million (2001)
EXPORTS – US$28 million (2001)

Trade with UK	*2002*	*2003*
Imports from UK	£32,084,000	£32,352,000
Exports to UK	2,656,000	4,206,000

TRANSPORT INFRASTRUCTURE

Since the phasing out of the railway system in 1974 the road network has been developed considerably; and there are now 11,200 km (7,000 miles) of roads in the country. A bridge has been constructed over the Mano River linking Sierra Leone and Liberia.

The Freetown international airport is situated at Lungi. The main port is Freetown, which has one of the largest natural harbours in the world. There are smaller ports at Pepel, Bonthe and Niti.

EDUCATION

Technical education is provided in the two government technical institutes, situated in Freetown and Kenema, in two trade centres and in the technical training establishments of the mining companies. Teacher training is carried out at the University of Sierra Leone, six colleges in the provinces and in the Milton Margai Training College near Freetown.

ILLITERACY RATE – (m) 49.3 per cent; (f) 77.4 per cent (2000)
ENROLMENT (percentage of age group) – tertiary 1.3 per cent (1990)

MEDIA

The UN Mission in Sierra Leone (UNMASIL) operates a number of radio services, broadcasting news of UN activities and human rights information, as well as music and news. BBC World Service and Radio France Internationale are broadcast from Freetown. Dozens of privately run newspapers are published in Freetown, despite low literacy levels.

SINGAPORE

Repablik Singapura / Xinjiapo Gongheguo / Singapur Kuṭiyaraśu / Republic of Singapore

AREA – 648 sq. km
POPULATION – 4,108,000 (2001): Chinese 76.8 per cent, Malays 13.9 per cent, Indians (including those of Pakistani, Bangladeshi and Sri Lankan origin) 7.9 per cent and 1.4 per cent from other ethnic groups. Malay, Mandarin, Tamil and English are the official languages. At least eight Chinese dialects are used. Malay is the national language and English is the language of administration. The religions are Buddhism 42.5 per cent, Islam 14.9 per cent, Christianity 14.6 per cent, Taoism 8.5 per cent, Hinduism 4.0 per cent
CURRENCY – Singapore dollar (S$) of 100 cents
NATIONAL ANTHEM – Majullah Singapura (May Singapore Progress)
NATIONAL DAY – 9 August
NATIONAL FLAG – Horizontal bands of red over white; crescent with five five-point stars on red band near staff
LIFE EXPECTANCY (years) – 78 (2001)
MORTALITY RATE (per 1,000 population) – 4.31 (2003)
INFANT MORTALITY (per 1,000 births) – 3 (2001)
HIV / AIDS ADULT PREVALENCE – 0.2 per cent (2001)
DEATH PENALTY – Yes
POPULATION GROWTH RATE – 2.8 per cent (1990–2001)
POPULATION DENSITY – 6,340 per sq. km (2001)
MILITARY EXPENDITURE – 5.2 per cent of GDP (2002)
MILITARY PERSONNEL – 72,500: Army 50,000, Navy 9,000, Air Force 13,500; Paramilitaries 96,300
CONSCRIPTION DURATION – 24–30 months
ILLITERACY RATE – (m) 3.7 per cent; (f) 11.6 per cent (2000)
ENROLMENT (percentage of age group) – primary 93 per cent (1995); tertiary 38.5 per cent (1996)

CLIMATE AND TERRAIN

Singapore consists of the island of Singapore and 63 islets. Singapore island is 42 km long and 22.5 km wide and is situated just north of the Equator off the southern extremity of the Malay peninsula, from which it is separated by the Straits of Johore. A causeway crosses the

1.21 km to the mainland. The average temperature is 29°C all year round. Elevation extremes range from 166 m (Bukit Timah) at the highest point to 0 m (Singapore Strait) at the lowest. Average annual precipitation is 2,410 mm, and floods and violent wind squalls called Sumatras are common.

HISTORY AND POLITICS

Singapore, a major trading site since the 16th century, was incorporated with Penang and Malacca to form the Straits Settlements in 1826. Singapore fell to Japanese forces during the Second World War and civil government was not restored until 1946, when it became a separate colony. Internal self-government was introduced to Singapore in 1959 and it became a state of Malaysia in September 1963, only to become an independent sovereign state within the Commonwealth on 9 August 1965.

Sellapan Rama Nathan became President of Singapore on 1 September 1999; no election was held as he was the sole candidate. After the general election of 3 November 2001 the People's Action Party (PAP) had 82 seats in Parliament. Goh Chok Tong, Prime Minister since 1990, resigned on 12 August 2004. His successor, Lee Hsien Loong, was sworn into office the same day.

POLITICAL SYSTEM

The President is directly elected for a six-year term, and can veto Government decisions relating to internal security, the budget, financial reserves and the appointment of senior civil servants. The President appoints the Prime Minister and, on his advice, the members of the Cabinet. There is a Parliament of 84 directly elected members, with up to six further non-constituency members from opposition parties (NCMPs), directly elected for a five-year term. Up to nine members can also be nominated by the Government for a two-year term (NMPs). In the present Parliament, there are two NCMPs and six NMPs.

HEAD OF STATE
President, Sellapan Rama Nathan, *took office* 1 September 1999

SELECTED GOVERNMENT MEMBERS *as at July 2004*
Prime Minister, Lee Hsien Loong
Senior Minister, Prime Minister's Office, Goh Chok Tong
Senior Minister, Prime Minister's Office, Lee Kuan Yew
Deputy Prime Minister, Defence, Tony Tan Kheng Yam
Foreign Affairs and Law, George Yong Boon Yeo
Home Affairs, Wong Kan Seng

HIGH COMMISSION FOR THE REPUBLIC OF SINGAPORE
9 Wilton Crescent, London SW1X 8SP
T 020-7235 8315
High Commissioner, HE Michael Eng Cheng Teo, apptd 2002

BRITISH HIGH COMMISSION
100 Tanglin Road, Singapore 247919
T (+65) 424 4200
E commercial.singapore@fco.gov.uk
High Commissioner, HE Alan Collins, CMG, apptd 2003

BRITISH COUNCIL DIRECTOR, Les Dangerfield
30 Napier Road, Singapore 258509
T (+65) 6473 111
E english@britishcouncil.org.sg

ECONOMY AND TRADE

Historically Singapore's economy was based on the sale and distribution of raw materials from surrounding countries and on entrepôt trade in finished products. An industrialisation programme launched in 1968 established a wide range of manufacturing industries, including shipbuilding, iron and steel, micro-electronics, electrical goods, telecommunications equipment, office machinery, scientific instruments and pharmaceuticals. Singapore has also become an important financial services centre with significant insurance and foreign exchange markets, a stock exchange, 149 commercial banks and 79 merchant banks and an oil-refining centre. In February 1998 the government announced substantial liberalising reforms of the financial sector, aimed at allowing the country to compete more competitively with other financial sectors in the region. Singapore has not been as badly affected as its neighbours by the economic crisis in south-east Asia, due in part to currency reserves estimated at US$118 billion.

Singapore's major trading partners are the USA, Malaysia, the EU, Hong Kong and Japan.

GNI – US$88,800 million (2001); US$21,500 per capita (2001)
ANNUAL AVERAGE GROWTH OF GDP – 9.9 per cent (2000)
INFLATION RATE – 1.4 per cent (2000)
UNEMPLOYMENT – 4.4 per cent (2000)
FOREIGN DIRECT INVESTMENT – US$29,223 million (1997–2000)
IMPORTS – US$116,441 million (2002)
EXPORTS – US$125,177 million (2002)

BALANCE OF PAYMENTS
Trade – US$12,872 million surplus (2001)
Current Account – US$17,884 million surplus (2001)

Trade with UK	*2002*	*2003*
Imports from UK	£1,458,706,000	£1,588,585,000
Exports to UK	2,030,952,000	2,738,956,000

TRANSPORT INFRASTRUCTURE

There are 25.8 km of railway connected to the Malaysian rail system by the causeway across the Straits of Johore, and 3,122 km of roads. Singapore is one of the largest and busiest seaports in the world, with six terminals, deep-water wharves and ship repairing facilities. In 2000, the total volume of cargo handled was 325,591,100 tonnes. There were 145,383 ship arrivals in 2000. The international airport is at Changi, in the east of the island, with 64 airlines operating flights to 50 countries and 28,618,200 passengers using the airport in 2000.

MEDIA

There are 19 radio and four television channels operated by the Singapore Broadcasting Corporation, and three private broadcasting stations. Singapore Press Holdings, which has close links to the ruling party, has a virtual monopoly of the newspaper industry, and publish 15 newspapers and six periodicals.

CULTURE

Performing arts are central to the cultural life in Singapore and include the spectacular acrobatic Chinese Lion Dance, along with Malay and Indian dances, while Chinese opera is also popular.

SLOVAKIA

Slovenská Republika – Slovak Republic

AREA – 48,100 sq. km. Neighbours: Poland (north), Ukraine (east), Hungary (south), Austria (west), the Czech Republic (north-west)
POPULATION – 5,403,000 (2001): 87.7 per cent are ethnic Slovaks, 10.6 per cent ethnic Hungarians, 1.4 per cent Romany, 1 per cent Czech, with smaller numbers of Ruthenians, Ukrainians and Germans. The population is mainly Christian, some 60 per cent Roman Catholic and 8 per cent Protestant. Slovak is the official language, while Hungarian and Czech are also spoken
CAPITAL – ΨBratislava (population, 428,672, 2001 census), on the Danube
MAJOR CITIES – Košice (236,093), 2001 census
CURRENCY – Koruna (Sk) of 100 halierov
NATIONAL ANTHEM – Nad Tatrou Sa Blýska (Storm Over The Tatras)
NATIONAL DAYS – 1 January (Establishment of Slovak Republic); 5 July (Day of the Slav Missionaries); 29 August (Slovak National Uprising); 1 September (Constitution Day)
NATIONAL FLAG – Three horizontal stripes of white, blue and red with the arms all over near the hoist
LIFE EXPECTANCY (years) – 73 (2001)
MORTALITY RATE (per 1,000 population) – 9 (2003)
INFANT MORTALITY (per 1,000 births) – 8 (2001)
HIV / AIDS ADULT PREVALENCE – 0.1 per cent (2001)
DEATH PENALTY – No (abolished 1990)
POPULATION GROWTH RATE – 0.3 per cent (1990–2001)
POPULATION DENSITY – 112 per sq. km (2001)
URBAN POPULATION – 58 per cent (2001)
ENROLMENT (percentage of age group) – tertiary 22.1 per cent (1996)

CLIMATE AND TERRAIN

Elevation extremes range from 2,655 m (Gerlachorsky Stit) at the highest point to 94 m (Bodrock River) at the lowest. The climate of Slovakia is continental, with warm humid summers and cold dry winters. Average temperatures range from 1°C in January to 21°C in July.

HISTORY AND POLITICS

At the end of the 11th century Slovakia became part of the Hungarian state, under the control of the Magyars. Following the dissolution of the Austro-Hungarian Empire, Slovakia was amalgamated into Czechoslovakia on 28 October 1918, but became an independent state when Germany invaded Czechoslovakia in 1939. Slovakia was liberated by Soviet forces in 1945 and returned to Czechoslovakia. The formation of a federal republic between the Czech lands and Slovakia was the only Prague Spring Reform to survive the Soviet invasion of 1968. Following the collapse of Communist rule in 1989, the Czech and Slovak republics began to negotiate the dissolution of the federation into two sovereign states in 1992. Dissolution took effect on 1 January 1993.

A coalition government led by the Movement for a Democratic Slovakia (HZDS) was sworn in on 12 January 1993 but was brought down by a no-confidence vote in March 1994. Legislative elections later that year returned the HZDS to power at the head of a three-party coalition which took office in December. Led by the authoritarian Prime Minister, Vladimir Meciar, the HZDS dominated a string of coalition governments, pursuing nationalist and populist policies until October 1998, when it was ousted by an alliance of liberals, centrists, left-wingers and ethnic Hungarians, which formed a new coalition under Mikulas Dzurinda of the Slovak Democratic and Christian Union (SDKU). The presidential election, held in May 1999, was won by Rudolf Schuster of the Party of Civil Understanding (SOP).

Under Dzurinda, who won a second term in September 2002, Slovakia forged ahead with reforms in its bid for EU and Nato membership. Slovaks voted in favour of joining the EU in a referendum in May 2003, and the country became a full member of Nato and of the EU in March and May 2004 respectively.

Presidential elections in April 2004 were won by Ivan Gasporovic with 59.9 per cent of the vote.

POLITICAL SYSTEM

The Constitution vests legislative power in the National Council of 150 members directly elected for a four-year term by proportional representation with a five per cent threshold for parliamentary representation. Since a change to the constitution in 1998, the President is directly elected for a five-year term, renewable only once, by direct election; executive power is held by the Prime Minister and Cabinet.

HEAD OF STATE
President, Ivan Gasporovic, *elected* 17 April 2004, *sworn in* 15 June 2004

SELECTED GOVERNMENT MEMBERS *as at July 2004*
Prime Minister, Mikulas Dzurinda
Deputy Prime Ministers, Pal Csaky; Pavol Rusko *(Economy)* Ivan Miklos *(Finance)*; Daniel Lipsic *(Justice)*
Defence, Juraj Liska
Foreign Affairs, Eduard Kukan
Interior, Vladimir Palko

EMBASSY OF THE SLOVAK REPUBLIC
25 Kensington Palace Gardens, London W8 4QY
T 020-7313 6470
Ambassador Extraordinary and Plenipotentiary, HE Frantisek Dlhopolcek, apptd 2000

BRITISH EMBASSY
Panska 16, SK-811 01 Bratislava
T (+421) (2) 5998 2000
E bebra@internet.sk
Ambassador Extraordinary and Plenipotentiary, HE Roderic Todd, apptd 2002

BRITISH COUNCIL DIRECTOR, Huw Jones
PO Box 68, Panska 17, SK-814 99 Bratislava
T (+421) (2) 5443 1074 / 5443 1185
E information.centre@britishcouncil.sk

DEFENCE

The Army has 271 main battle tanks, 120 armoured personnel carriers and 404 armoured infantry fighting vehicles. The Air Force has 71 combat aircraft and 19 attack helicopters.

MILITARY EXPENDITURE – 2.0 per cent of GDP (2002)
MILITARY PERSONNEL – 20,700: Army 13,700, Air Force 7,000; Paramilitaries 4,700
CONSCRIPTION DURATION – Six months

ECONOMY AND TRADE

From independence until mid-1994 Slovakia faced widespread economic difficulties that were caused, partially, by the structure of its centrally planned and inefficiently managed economy. However, there has recently been good progress in macroeconomic stabilisation and structural reform and privatisation, as well as foreign investment have increased.

Major industries include foodstuffs, metal production, gas and oil, textiles, transport vehicles and rubber. Natural resources include brown coal, natural gas, iron ore, antimony, lead and zinc. Major trading partners include Germany, Austria, the Czech Republic and Italy.

GNI – US$20,300 million (2001); US$3,760 per capita (2001)
ANNUAL AVERAGE GROWTH OF GDP – 2.2 per cent (2000)
INFLATION RATE – 12 per cent (2000)
UNEMPLOYMENT – 20 per cent (2003)
TOTAL EXTERNAL DEBT – US$9,462 million (2000)
FOREIGN DIRECT INVESTMENT – US$3,133 million (1997–2000)
IMPORTS – US$13,423 million (2000)
EXPORTS – US$11,889 million (2000)

BALANCE OF PAYMENTS
Trade – US$895 million deficit (2000)
Current Account – US$694 million deficit (2000)

Trade with UK	*2002*	*2003*
Imports from UK	£200,521,000	£236,419,000
Exports to UK	214,996,000	261,664,000

TRANSPORT INFRASTRUCTURE

Slovakia has a total of 42,717 km of roads, of which 37,036 km are surfaced (including 296 km of expressways). There are 3,668 km of railways, and 172 km of navigable waterway on the Danube. The main ports are at Bratislava and Komarno.

MEDIA AND CULTURE

The two main television providers are Slovak TV (public) and TV Markiza (private). All three major daily newspapers are privately owned and there are more than 20 private radio stations, in addition to the public broadcaster Slovak Radio, which operates five national networks and an external service.

Key figures in Slovakian culture include L'udovít Stúr (1815–56), a nationalist who successfully revived the Slovakian literary language, the writer Jan Botto (1829–81) and the poet Andrej Sladkovic (1820–72).

SLOVENIA

Republika Slovenija – Republic of Slovenia

AREA – 20,100 sq. km. Neighbours: Austria (north), Hungary (north-east), Croatia (east and south), Italy (west)
POPULATION – 1,985,000 (2001). The population is mostly Slovenian. There are small Hungarian (0.5 per cent) and Italian (0.1 per cent) minorities, together with a Romany population. The main religion is Roman Catholicism. Slovene is the official language, together with Hungarian and Italian in ethnically mixed regions
CAPITAL – Ljubljana (population, 257,338, 2002 census)
MAJOR CITIES – Maribor
CURRENCY – Tolar (SIT) of 100 stotin
NATIONAL ANTHEM – Zdravljica (A Toast)
NATIONAL DAY – 25 June (Statehood Day)
NATIONAL FLAG – Three horizontal stripes of white, blue and red, with the arms in the upper hoist
LIFE EXPECTANCY (years) – 76 (2001)
MORTALITY RATE (per 1,000 population) – 10.15 (2003)
INFANT MORTALITY (per 1,000 births) – 4 (2001)
HIV / AIDS ADULT PREVALENCE – 0.1 per cent (2001)
DEATH PENALTY – No (abolished 1989)
POPULATION GROWTH RATE – 0.3 per cent (1990–2001)
POPULATION DENSITY – 99 per sq. km (2001)
URBAN POPULATION – 49 per cent (2001)
MILITARY EXPENDITURE – 1.5 per cent of GDP (2002)
MILITARY PERSONNEL – Army 6,500; Paramilitaries 4,500
CONSCRIPTION DURATION – Seven months

CLIMATE AND TERRAIN

The terrain is mountainous and elevation extremes range from 2,864 m (Triglav) at the highest point to 0 m (Adriatic Sea) at the lowest. Average temperatures in Ljubljana range from 0°C in January to 22°C in July.

HISTORY AND POLITICS

The area that is now Slovenia came under the control of the Habsburg Empire in the 13th and 14th centuries and remained so until the defeat of the Austro-Hungarian Empire in 1918, when it came under the control of Yugoslavia. German forces invaded Yugoslavia in 1941 and Slovenia was divided between Germany, Italy and Hungary. Slovenia was reformed as a constituent Republic of the Federal Yugoslav State in May 1945. After a dispute with Italy and nine years of international administration, the Adriatic coast and hinterland were returned to Slovenia in 1954 and Italy retained Trieste.

Slovenian fears of Serbian dominance led the Slovene Assembly in 1989 to amend the republican constitution and to lay the basis of a sovereign state. The first democratic elections, held in April 1990, were won by the pro-independence 'Demos' coalition. In a referendum in December 1990, 88 per cent of the electorate voted for independence, which was declared on 25 June 1991. A ten-day war with the Yugoslav National Army followed before the Army called off hostilities and withdrew under the mediation of the EU.

A coalition led by Liberal Democracy of Slovenia (LDS) formed a government following the 1996 legislative election. President Kučan was re-elected on 23 November 1997.

In the October 2000 general election, the third since

gaining independence, the LDS was returned to power and formed a coalition government with the United List of Social Democrats (ZLSD), and the Democratic Party of Pensioners (DeSUS). Janez Drnovsek was elected president with 56.5 per cent of the vote on 1 December 2002.

In a March 2003 referendum on EU and NATO membership, Slovenes voted 90 per cent in favour of joining the EU and 66 per cent in favour of joining NATO; the country joined NATO in April 2004 and the EU in May 2004. Legislative elections were scheduled for October 2004.

POLITICAL SYSTEM
The Head of State is the President, elected for a five-year term. Executive power is vested in the Prime Minister and Cabinet. The lower house of the legislature, the National Assembly, has 90 members directly elected for a four-year term. The upper house, the 40-member National Council, has an advisory role. The National Assembly is elected on a proportional representation basis, with one seat each reserved for the Italian and Hungarian minorities.

HEAD OF STATE
President, Janez Drnovsek, *elected* 1 December 2002

SELECTED GOVERNMENT MEMBERS *as at July 2004*
President of the Executive Council (Prime Minister), Anton Rop
Defence, Anton Grizold
Finance, Dusan Mramor
Foreign Affairs, Ivo Vajgl
Internal Affairs, Rado Bohinc

EMBASSY OF THE REPUBLIC OF SLOVENIA
10 Little College Street, London SW1P 3SH
T 020-7222 5400
Ambassador Extraordinary and Plenipotentiary, HE Dr Marjan Senjur, *apptd* 2002

BRITISH EMBASSY
4th Floor, Trg Republike 3, SI-1000 Ljubljana
T (+386) (1) 200 3910
E info@british-embassy.si
Ambassador Extraordinary and Plenipotentiary, HE Hugh Mortimer, LVO, apptd 2001

BRITISH COUNCIL DIRECTOR, Steve Green
Cankarjevo nabrezje 27, SI-1000 Ljubljana
T (+386) (1) 200 0130
E info@britishcouncil.si

ECONOMY AND TRADE

Slovenia's economy has emerged as the most stable of the former Yugoslav economies. It has successfully re-orientated its exports towards Western markets, its main trading partners being Germany, Italy, France, Austria and Croatia. The privatisation process was completed in 1998. In 2002 agriculture contributed 3.1 per cent to the total GDP, the manufacturing industry 32.7 per cent and the service industries 64.2 per cent. The main agricultural products are potatoes, wheat, corn, sugarcane and grapes. The major manufacturing sectors are metalworking, electronics, textiles, automobiles and automotive parts, chemicals, glass products and food-processing. The tourist industry is a major earner, with 1,957,000 visitors in 2000.

GNI – US$19,400 million (2001); US$9,760 per capita (2001)
ANNUAL AVERAGE GROWTH OF GDP – 4.8 per cent (2000)
INFLATION RATE – 7.4 per cent (2002)
UNEMPLOYMENT – 7.4 per cent (1999)
TOTAL EXTERNAL DEBT – US$4,762 million (1997); US$5,491 million (1999 estimate)
FOREIGN DIRECT INVESTMENT – US$843 million (1997–2000)
IMPORTS – US$10,937 million (2002)
EXPORTS – US$9,471 million (2002)

BALANCE OF PAYMENTS
Trade – US$241 million deficit (2002)
Current Account – US$375 million deficit (2002)

Trade with UK	*2002*	*2003*
Imports from UK	£180,859,000	£158,931,000
Exports to UK	174,683,000	171,807,000

TRANSPORT INFRASTRUCTURE

There are 20,128 km of roads and 1,201 km of railways, of which 499 km are electrified. Important road and rail communications cross the country from west to east (Milan–Ljubljana–Budapest), and north to south (Munich–Ljubljana–Zagreb–Belgrade–Athens). There are international airports at Ljubljana, Maribor and Portoroz (Adriatic Coast). Koper is a port for receiving shipments from Austria, Hungary, the Czech Republic and Slovakia.

EDUCATION

Education is free of charge and compulsory between the ages of six and 14. There are 44 colleges and two universities (Ljubljana and Maribor).
ILLITERACY RATE – (m) 0.3 per cent; (f) 0.4 per cent (2000)
ENROLMENT (percentage of age group) – primary 95 per cent (1996); tertiary 36.4 per cent (1996)

MEDIA AND CULTURE

The main newspapers are privately owned, and the broadcasting sector is a mix of public and private ownership. The television market is mainly shared between the public service RTV Slovenia and the private stations Pop TV and Kanal A, and about two-thirds of households are connected to cable or satellite.

Important cultural figures include the poet France Prešeren (1800–49) and the architect Jože Plečnik (1872–1957).

SOLOMON ISLANDS

AREA – 28,896 sq. km
POPULATION – 480,442 (2001 estimate). English is the official language; there are over 80 local languages
CAPITAL – ΨHoniara (population, 49,107)
CURRENCY – Solomon Islands dollar (SI$) of 100 cents
NATIONAL ANTHEM – God Bless Our Solomon Islands
NATIONAL DAY – 7 July (Independence Day)
NATIONAL FLAG – Blue over green divided by a diagonal yellow band, with five white stars in the top left quarter
MORTALITY RATE (per 1,000 population) – 4.12 (2003)
DEATH PENALTY – No (abolished 1966)
POPULATION GROWTH RATE – 2.7 per cent (2004)
POPULATION DENSITY – 15 per sq. km (1999)

CLIMATE AND TERRAIN

Forming a scattered archipelago of mountainous islands and low-lying coral atolls, the Solomon Islands stretches about 1,448 km in a south-easterly direction from the Shortland Islands to the Santa Cruz islands. The six biggest islands are Choiseul, New Georgia, Santa Isabel, Guadalcanal, Malaita and Makira. They are characterised by thickly forested mountain ranges intersected by deep, narrow valleys. Elevation extremes range from 2,447 m (Mt Makarakomburu) at the highest point to 0 m (Pacific Ocean) at the lowest. The climate is tropical and the average temperature in Honiara is 27°C. The islands are occasionaly prone to earthquakes, tsunamis and volcanic activity.

HISTORY AND POLITICS

European interest in the islands began in the mid-16th century and continued intermittently for about 300 years, following the inauguration of sugar plantations in Queensland and Fiji (which created a need for labour), and the arrival of missionaries and traders. Britain declared a protectorate in 1893 over the southern Solomons, adding the Santa Cruz group in 1898 and 1899. The islands of the Shortland groups were transferred from Germany to Britain by treaty in 1900. The Solomon Islands achieved internal self-government in 1976, and became independent in July 1978.

In November 2000, a conference of provincial governmental heads called for the introduction of a federal system of government; some of the islands had earlier threatened secession. Legislative elections were held on 5 December 2001 in which the People's Alliance Party gained 20 of the 50 seats in the National Parliament. The party's parliamentary leader, Sir Allan Kemakeza was elected Prime Minister on 17 December and the new cabinet was sworn in on 19 December.

INSURGENCIES

Following tensions between indigenous inhabitants and settlers from other parts of the country, on 28 June 1999, a peace agreement was signed by representatives of the national and provincial governments and the Isatabu Freedom Fighters (IFF), a local militant group, following mediation by the Commonwealth special envoy Sitiveni Rabuka.

Following further tension, the government banned the IFF and their rivals the Malaita Eagles Force (MEF) in February 2000, but lifted the ban in May to facilitate peace talks. MEF guerrillas took Prime Minister Ulufa'alu hostage on 5 June 2000 and took over the capital. Ulufa'alu was freed five days later and the MEF and the IFF agreed to a two-week truce to allow mediation by a Commonwealth delegation. A peace deal was signed by the IFF and the MEF on 15 October 2000.

However, violence escalated during 2002–3 which led to the deployment of the Regional Assistance Mission to the Solomon Islands (RAMSI) in July 2003. Order was quickly restored and RAMSI began a programme of re-construction.

POLITICAL SYSTEM

The Solomon Islands is a constitutional monarchy. Queen Elizabeth II is represented locally by the governor-general. Executive authority is exercised by the Cabinet. Legislative power is vested in a unicameral National Parliament of 50 members, elected for a four-year term.
Governor-General, Nathaniel Waena, apptd 2004

SELECTED GOVERNMENT MEMBERS *as at July 2004*
Prime Minister, Sir Allan Kemakesa
Deputy Prime Minister, Finance, Snyder Rini
Foreign Affairs, and Trade Relations, Laurie Hok Si Chan
Home Affairs, Nelson Kile

HIGH COMMISSION OF THE SOLOMON ISLANDS
Avenue Edourd Lacomble 17, B-1040 Brussels.
T (+32) (2) 2732 7085
E siembassy@compuserve.com
High Commissioner, HE Robert Sisilo, apptd 1996

BRITISH HIGH COMMISSION
Telekom House, Mendana Avenue, Honiara.
T (+677) 21705/6
E bhc@solomon.com.sb
High Commissioner, HE Brian Baldwin, apptd 2001

ECONOMY AND TRADE

The economy remains in severe disarray following the ethnic disturbances, and the Solomon Islands are heavily dependent on foreign aid, principally from Australia. Principal exports are timber, fish, palm oil, copra and cocoa. The main imports are foodstuffs, consumer goods, machinery and transport materials.

GNI – US$253 million (2000); US$590 per capita (2001)
ANNUAL AVERAGE GROWTH OF GDP – 2.2 per cent (1998)
INFLATION RATE – 1.8 per cent (2001)
TOTAL EXTERNAL DEBT – US$137 million (2001)
IMPORTS – US$151 million (1996)
EXPORTS – US$162 million (1996)

BALANCE OF PAYMENTS
Trade – US$55 million surplus (1999)
Current Account – US$21 million surplus (1999)

Trade with UK	*2002*	*2003*
Imports from UK	£393,000	£94,000
Exports to UK	20,000	42,000

TRANSPORT INFRASTRUCTURE

There are 1,360 km of roads, of which only 34 km are surfaced. Solomon Airlines operates international services to other Pacific states and Australia. Air Niugini flies from Port Moresby to Honiara.

MEDIA AND CULTURE

The Solomon Islands Broadcasting Corporation (SIBC) operates a public radio service but there are no television services based on the islands.

Cultural life in the Solomon Islands reflects a rich diversity of Polynesian, Melanesian and Asian influences. *Kastom* is still widely practised throughout the islands and refers to land ownership, traditional beliefs and animism.

SOMALIA

Jamhuuriyadda Dimoqraadiya Soomaaliya – Somali Democratic Republic

AREA – 637,657 sq. km. Neighbours: Djibouti, Ethiopia and Kenya (west)
POPULATION – 7,488,773 (2001 estimate). Somali and Arabic are the official languages. English and Italian are also spoken
CAPITAL – ΨMogadishu (population, 525,000, 1995 estimate)
MAJOR CITIES – ΨBerbera; Boroma; Burao; Hargeysa; ΨKisimaayo
CURRENCY – Somali shilling of 100 cents
NATIONAL FLAG – Five-pointed white star on a blue ground
LIFE EXPECTANCY (years) – 47 (2001)
MORTALITY RATE (per 1,000 population) – 17.64 (2003)
HIV / AIDS ADULT PREVALENCE – 1 per cent (2001)
DEATH PENALTY – Yes
POPULATION GROWTH RATE – 3.3 per cent (2001)
POPULATION DENSITY – 15 per sq. km (1999)

CLIMATE AND TERRAIN

The terrain is mostly flat or undulating plateau, rising to hills in the north. Elevation extremes range from 2,416 m (Shimbiris) at the highest point to 0 m (Indian Ocean) at the lowest. Somalia has an arid and tropical climate influenced by the north-east and south-west monsoons. There are two wet seasons from March to May and October to November, and average temperatures in Mogadishu are an almost constant 33°C.

HISTORY AND POLITICS

Somalia, an Arab sultanate since the 17th century, was conquered by Zanzibar in 1896. In 1950, the country became a UN Trust Territory administered by Italy. The British protectorate of Somaliland and Somalia were joined and became fully independent on 1 July 1960.

In 1969, the armed forces seized power and established a ruling Revolutionary Council under Siad Barre's leadership. Siad Barre was overthrown by rebels in January 1991, sparking civil war between rival clan-based movements. The United Somali Congress (USC) seized control in Mogadishu, while the Somali National Movement (SNM) formed a rival administration in the north. Fighting between the USC and supporters of the Somali National Alliance (SNA) of Gen. Mohammed Aideed devastated Mogadishu and large parts of the south, exacerbating famine conditions. The UN operation in Somalia proved ineffective in securing aid distribution routes and was replaced in December 1992 by a UN-approved, US-led, United Task Force (UNITAF).

The UN withdrew its troops in March 1995, and in June Gen. Aideed was ousted as SNA leader by a joint USC-SNA congress which nominated Osman Ali Ato as its leader. Gen. Aideed responded by declaring himself president on 15 June 1995, but was shot dead in July 1996 and was replaced as president by his son, Hussein Aideed.

A peace plan proposed by Djibouti was overwhelmingly supported in November 1999 by representatives of civil society and the armed factions at a forum in Nairobi. A Somali National Reconciliation Conference in Djibouti opened on 2 May 2000, which aimed to lay the foundations of the transitional institutions of the Somali state, but was opposed by the Rahawein Resistance Army, the Somali Patriotic Movement and the leaders of Puntland. The National Reconciliation Conference appointed a transitional national assembly on 13 August, which on 26 August appointed Abdulkiassim Salat Hassan as president. President Hassan appointed Ali Khalif Galayadh as Prime Minister shortly afterwards.

Fighting between pro- and anti-government militias broke out in the south of the country in July 2001. Prime Minister Galayadh resigned in October following a vote of no confidence and was replaced by Hassan Abshir Farah; a reshuffled cabinet was announced on 16 February 2002.

In October 2002 internationally backed peace talks began in Kenya and a cease-fire agreement was signed by 21 warring factions and the transitional national government, under which hostilities would end for the duration of the talks. The second phase of the peace talks began in Nairobi in February 2003 but was plagued by boycotts and disputes. In 2004, an agreement was signed to establish a federal government and to form a transitional parliament of 351 members which would appoint the federal president. However, President Hassan refused to stand down until a new government had been formed.

INSURGENCIES

With the downfall of Siad Barre, the SNM took control of the north-west (the former British Somaliland protectorate) and in May 1991 declared unilateral independence as the 'Somaliland Republic'. A government and legislature was formed which elected Mohammed Ibrahim Egal as president in May 1993; he was re-elected in February 1997. A referendum on a new constitution, which confirmed the independence of Somaliland, was held on 31 May 2001 and was approved by 97.09 per cent of the vote. Egal died on 3 May 2002 and was succeeded by Vice-President Dahir Riyale Kahin, who was elected president on 14 April 2003.

An autonomous administration was also proclaimed in north-eastern Somalia on 23 July 1998. Col. Ahmed Abdullahi Yusuf was named as president of the region, calling itself Puntland; a cabinet was appointed, and a 69-member parliament inaugurated. On 30 June 2001 Abdullahi was replaced by Yusuf Haji Nur as interim president pending elections held on 14 November in which Jama Ali Jama was elected president. Abdullahi refused to relinquish his claim to the presidency and by May 2002 his supporters had taken control of the whole of the territory.

HEAD OF STATE

Interim President, Abdulkiassim Salat Hassan, *sworn in* 27 August 2000

SELECTED GOVERNMENT MEMBERS *as at July 2004*
Prime Minister, Muhammad Abdi Yusuf
Defence, Adan Ahmed Abdi
Foreign Affairs, Yusuf Hassan Ibrahim Aden
Internal Affairs, Ahmed Gacal Ali Arabow

ECONOMY AND TRADE

Livestock raising is the main occupation and there is a modest export trade in livestock, skins and hides. Italy, the Gulf States and Saudi Arabia import the bulk of the banana crop, the biggest export, which accounts for approximately 40 per cent of exports. The principal imports are machinery and transport equipment, industrial goods and foodstuffs.

GDP – US$1,631 million (1998); US$216 per capita (2000)

ANNUAL AVERAGE GROWTH OF GDP – 2.5 per cent (1998)

TOTAL EXTERNAL DEBT – US$2,562 million (2000)

Trade with UK	*2002*	*2003*
Imports from UK	£9,119,000	£3,597,000
Exports to UK	33,000	76,000

TRANSPORT INFRASTRUCTURE

Somalia has a total of 22,100 km of roads, of which 2,608 km are surfaced. Ports and harbours include Boosaaso, Berbera, Kismaayo, Merca and Mogadishu, and the country has six airports with surfaced runways.

MEDIA

Many new print and broadcast outlets emerged after Siad Barre was ousted in 1991, but most were tied to one or another of the country's warring factions. Even though recent years have seen the emergence of stronger regional media, broadcasters and journalists operate in a dangerous environment, limiting their ability to report freely and objectively. Many Somalis rely on foreign broadcasts for their news: CNN and Al-Jazeera are available in some parts of the country.

SOUTH AFRICA

Republic of South Africa

AREA – 1,221,000 sq. km. Neighbours: Namibia (north-west), Botswana and Zimbabwe (north), Mozambique and Swaziland (north-east), Lesotho, which is completely surrounded by South Africa

POPULATION – 45,454,211 (2002); 78 per cent African, 10.1 per cent white, 8.6 per cent mixed race, 2.5 per cent Indian/Asian. The constitution designates 11 official languages: Afrikaans (spoken by 14.4 per cent as a first language); English (8.6 per cent); IsiNdebele (1.5 per cent); IsiXosa (17.9 per cent), IsiZulu (22.9 per cent); Sepedi (9.2 per cent); Sosetho (7.7 per cent); SiSwati (2.5 per cent); Setswana (8.2 per cent); Tshivenda (2.2 per cent); Xitsonga (4.4 per cent). Afrikaans and English are to remain the languages of administration although any citizen may correspond official business in his own language. The majority (75 per cent) of the population is Christian. There are also Hindus (1.4 per cent), Muslims (1.4 per cent) and Jews (0.2 per cent), as well as native religions (21 per cent)

CAPITAL – The seat of the government is Pretoria (population 1,800,000, 1999 estimate); the seat of the legislature is Cape Town (population, 3,088,028, 1999 estimate); the seat of the judiciary is Bloemfontein (467,400, 1999 estimate)

MAJOR CITIES – ΨDurban; ΨEast London; Johannesburg; Pietermaritzburg; ΨPort Elizabeth

CURRENCY – Rand (R) of 100 cents

NATIONAL ANTHEMS – Nkosi Sikelel' iAfrika (God Bless Africa); Die Stem Van Suid-Afrika (The Call Of South Africa)

NATIONAL DAY – 27 April (Freedom Day)

NATIONAL FLAG – Divided red over blue by a horizontal white-fimbriated green Y; in the hoist is a black triangle fimbriated in yellow

LIFE EXPECTANCY (years) – 50 (2001)

MORTALITY RATE (per 1,000 population) – 18.42 (2003)

INFANT MORTALITY (per 1,000 births) – 56 (2001)

HIV / AIDS ADULT PREVALENCE – 20.1 per cent (2001)

DEATH PENALTY – No (abolished 1997)

POPULATION BELOW POVERTY LINE – 50 per cent (2000)

POPULATION GROWTH RATE – 1.7 per cent (1990–2001)

POPULATION DENSITY – 36 per sq. km (2001)

URBAN POPULATION – 52.6 per cent (2002)

CLIMATE AND TERRAIN

South Africa occupies the southernmost part of the African continent from the courses of the Limpopo, Marico, Molopo, Nosop and Orange rivers to the Cape of Good Hope, with the exception of Lesotho, Swaziland and the extreme south of Mozambique. To the west, east and south lie the south Atlantic and southern Indian Oceans. Some 1,920 km to the south-east of Cape Town lie Prince Edward and Marion Islands, part of South Africa since 1947. Elevation extremes range from 3,408 m (Njesuthi) at the highest point to 0 m (Atlantic Ocean) at the lowest. The climate is temperate and is influenced by the warm Agulhas current from Mozambique. Average temperatures in Pretoria range from 3°C in June to 29°C in January.

HISTORY AND POLITICS

Hunter-gatherers, the San (Bushmen) and Khoikhoi (Hottentots) inhabited southern Africa from *c.* 8,000 BC. By the eighth century AD, Bantu-speaking peoples had settled the north of the country.

The Portuguese navigator Bartolomeu Días charted the coast in 1488 and the Dutch founded the colony of the Cape of Good Hope in 1652, which was taken by Britain in 1806. The Orange Free State and Transvaal republics were founded by the Boers (the descendants of Dutch settlers) and were recognised by Britain in 1853–4. Natal was annexed to Cape Colony by the British in 1844 and then formed as a separate colony in 1856, to which Zululand was added in 1897 after the British victory in the Zulu wars. Transvaal and the Orange Free State became British colonies after the Boer defeat in the Second Boer War 1899–1902. The self-governing colonies became united in 1910 under the name of the Union of South Africa. Independence within the Commonwealth was gained in 1931 under the Statute of Westminster.

From 1948, when the Afrikaner National Party came to power, South Africa's social and political structure was based on apartheid, a policy of racial segregation. Opposition protests culminated in the Sharpeville massacre in 1960, following which the African National Congress (ANC) and other opposition groups were banned. South Africa left the Commonwealth and became a republic on 31 May 1961, largely as a result of international condemnation. South Africa re-joined the Commonwealth following the 1994 general elections.

MOVES TO DEMOCRACY

The first moves to reform apartheid came in 1984, when a new constitution extended the franchise to the mixed race and Indian populations. In 1989, F. W. de Klerk became President of South Africa and lifted the ban on the ANC and restrictions on other anti-apartheid groups and freed Nelson Mandela, the main ANC political detainee. In 1991 the laws implementing apartheid were effectively abolished. In 1992 a referendum amongst the white electorate on continued political reform and a new constitution reached by negotiation was approved.

In 1991 the government, ANC, Inkatha Freedom Party and other civic groups reached agreement on the establishment of an inter-racial administration and the formation of a five-year coalition government following a multiracial election.

In the country's first multiracial general election held on 26–29 April 1994 the ANC gained 252 seats in the 400-seat National Assembly and 60 seats in the 90-seat Senate. Nelson Mandela was elected president.

The parliament has passed two significant pieces of legislation to settle the legacy of the apartheid era. The first, in November 1994, restored the rights of those dispossessed of their land, and the second, in June 1995, established the Truth Commission whose remit is to assess confessions, grant amnesties for political crimes and set compensation for victims.

Following legislative and provincial elections held on 2 June 1999, the ANC gained 266 seats in the National Assembly and, being one seat short of the two-thirds majority required to amend the constitution, entered into a coalition with the Minority Front, which held just one seat in the National Assembly.

On 14 June 1999 the National Assembly met to select a new president. Thabo Mbeki was elected unopposed and was formally sworn in on 16 June 1999. Mbeki was subsequently elected to a second five-year term on 24 April 2004, following the landslide general election victory of his ruling ANC party who gained 70 per cent of the vote and 279 seats in the National Assembly.

POLITICAL SYSTEM

The final constitution came into effect in 1997. Executive power is vested in a President and Cabinet, with the President elected by the National Assembly. Legislative power is vested in a bicameral Parliament, a directly elected 400-member National Assembly elected by proportional representation for a five-year term, and an indirectly elected 90-member National Council of Provinces composed of ten members elected by each of the nine regional legislatures for a five-year term.

South Africa is divided into nine regions (Western Cape, Northern Cape, Eastern Cape, Free State, North-West, KwaZulu/Natal, Gauteng, Limpopo, Mpumalanga). Each region has its own Premier, a legislature of between 30 and 100 seats elected by proportional representation, and its own constitution.

HEAD OF STATE

President, Commander-in-Chief of the Armed Forces, Thabo Mbeki, *elected by parliament* 14 June 1999, *sworn in* 16 June 1999, *re-elected* 24 April 2004

Executive Deputy President, Jacob Zuma

SELECTED GOVERNMENT MEMBERS *as at July 2004*

Defence, Mosiua Lekota

Finance, Trevor Manuel

Foreign Affairs, Nkosazana Dlamini-Zuma

Home Affairs, Nosiriwe Mapisa-Ngakula

HIGH COMMISSION FOR THE REPUBLIC OF SOUTH AFRICA

South Africa House, Trafalgar Square, London WC2N 5DP.

T 020-7451 7299

High Commissioner, HE Dr Lindiwe Mabuza, apptd 2001

BRITISH HIGH COMMISSION

255 Hill Street, Arcadia 0002 Pretoria

T (+27) (12) 421 7800

91 Parliament Street, Cape Town, 8001

T (+27) (21) 405 2400

E britain@icon.co.za

High Commissioner (Cape Town), HE Ann Grant, apptd 2001

BRITISH COUNCIL DIRECTOR, Rosemary Arnott

Ground Floor, Forum 1, Braampark, 33 Hoofd Street, Braamfontein, Johannesburg 2001

T (+27) (11) 718 4300

E information@british council.org.za

DEFENCE

The new South African National Defence Force (SANDF) was created from the merger of the South African Defence Forces (SADF), the Umkhonto we Sizwe (MK) armed wing of the ANC, the Azanian People's Liberation Army (APLA) of the Pan Africanist Congress of Azania, and the defence forces of the four former independent homelands.

The Army has 168 main battle tanks, 929 armoured personnel carriers and 1,200 armoured infantry fighting vehicles. The Navy has two submarines and eight patrol and coastal vessels at two bases. The Air Force has 84 combat aircraft and 12 armed helicopters.

MILITARY EXPENDITURE – 1.7 per cent of GDP (2002)

MILITARY PERSONNEL – 55,750: Army 36,000, Navy 4,500, Air Force 9,250

ECONOMY AND TRADE

Mining is of great importance, employing more than 400,000 people in 2000 and providing the largest source of foreign exchange. The principal minerals produced are gold, coal, diamonds, copper, iron ore, manganese, lime and limestone, uranium, platinum, fluorspar, andalusite, zinc, zirconium, vanadium, titanium and chrome. South Africa is the world's largest producer of gold, platinum, diamonds, manganese, chrome and vanadium, and has the world's largest reserves of chrome ore, manganese, vanadium and andalusite. In 2000, 420 tonnes of gold were produced.

Agriculture, forestry and fishing accounted for 3.2 per cent of GDP in 2000. Over 70 per cent of land is pasture so livestock farming is widespread. Principal crops are maize, sugarcane, fruits and vegetables, wheat, sorghum, sunflower seeds and groundnuts. Cotton is widely grown, and viticulture is also widespread.

The manufacturing industries, concentrated most heavily around Johannesburg, Pretoria and the major ports, process foodstuffs, metals and non-metallic mineral products, produce oil from coal, and also produce beverages and tobacco, motor vehicles, chemicals and chemical products, machinery, textiles and clothing, and paper and paper products. Industry contributed 30.9 per cent of GDP in 2000.

Energy production is based upon coal and natural gas and the production of synthetic liquid fuel from coal. One nuclear power station is in operation and others are planned. South Africa exports electricity through its electricity grid connections to all states in southern Africa.

The tourism industry accounts for 3.4 per cent of GDP. In 2000, 5.9 million foreign tourists visited South Africa.

Principal exports are gold, base metals and metal products, coal, diamonds, food (especially fruit) and wool. Principal imports are machinery, chemicals, motor vehicles, metals and metal products, food, inedible raw materials and textiles. South Africa's main trading partners are Germany, the USA, the UK, Italy and Japan.

GNI – US$156,511 million (2003); US$1,859 per capita (2003)
ANNUAL AVERAGE GROWTH OF GDP – 1.9 per cent (2003)
INFLATION RATE – 5.8 per cent (2003)
UNEMPLOYMENT – 31.2 per cent (2003)
TOTAL EXTERNAL DEBT – US$36,097 million (2003)
FOREIGN DIRECT INVESTMENT – US$4,612 million (1997–2000)
IMPORTS – US$29,267 million (2002)
EXPORTS – US$29,723 million (2002)

BALANCE OF PAYMENTS
Trade – US$4,372 million surplus (2002)
Current Account – US$290 million surplus (2002)

Trade with UK	*2002*	*2003*
Imports from UK	£1,609,067,000	£1,757,340,000
Exports to UK	2,784,786,000	3,026,357,701

TRANSPORT INFRASTRUCTURE

The country has 22,298 km of railways and 362,099 km of roads, of which 73,506 km are surfaced (including 2,032 km of expressways). There are international airports at Johannesburg, Durban and Cape Town. South African Airways operates international services to Europe, South America, the Far East, Africa, Australia and the USA, and it is the principal operator of domestic flights. Durban is the largest seaport. Other major ports are Cape Town, Port Elizabeth, East London, Saldanha Mossel Bay and Richards Bay.

EDUCATION

Higher education is provided at 21 universities and 15 other tertiary-level colleges.

ILLITERACY RATE – (m) 14.0 per cent; (f) 15.4 per cent (2000)
ENROLMENT (percentage of age group) – primary 94 per cent (1996); secondary 51 per cent (1996); tertiary 19 per cent (1995)

MEDIA

The South African Broadcasting Corporation (SABC) is a major state-owned television and radio broadcaster while Channel Africa (owned by SABC) is an external radio service that reaches the entire continent. *The Star* is Johannesburg's oldest daily newspaper, while the *Sunday Times* is the longest running weekly title. *Beeld* is a popular Afrikaan daily title.

CULTURE

South Africa is home to a great diversity of cultures, and traditional black cultures – such as Zulu, Xhosa and Ndebele – are reviving after suppression during the apartheid years. Celebrated figures include the writers J. M. Coetzee (b. 1940), winner of the Nobel Prize for Literature in 2003 and Nadine Gordima (b. 1923), winner of the Nobel Prize for Literature in 1991. Desmond Tutu (b. 1931) was the winner of the Nobel Peace Prize in 1984. South African music, such as that created by groups like Ladysmith Black Mambazo, is gaining wider international recognition.

SPAIN

Reino de España – Kingdom of Spain

AREA – 499,400 sq. km. Neighbours: Portugal (west), France (north)
POPULATION – 39,921,000 (2001): 96 per cent Catholic, 1 per cent Muslim. Castilian Spanish is the official language, although Basque, Catalan, Galician and Valencian, a dialect of Catalan, are spoken and have official status in the autonomous regions where they are spoken
CAPITAL – Madrid (population, 5,086,635, 2001)
MAJOR CITIES – ΨBarcelona; ΨValencia; ΨMálaga; Sevilla; Zaragoza
CURRENCY – Euro (€) of 100 cents
NATIONAL ANTHEM – Marcha Real Española (Spanish Royal March)
NATIONAL DAY – 12 October
NATIONAL FLAG – Three horizontal stripes of red, yellow and red, with the yellow of double width
LIFE EXPECTANCY (years) – 79 (2001)
MORTALITY RATE (per 1,000 population) – 9.48 (2003)
INFANT MORTALITY (per 1,000 births) – 4 (2001)
HIV / AIDS ADULT PREVALENCE – 0.5 per cent (2001)
DEATH PENALTY – No (abolished 1995)
POPULATION GROWTH RATE – 0.1 per cent (1990–2001)
POPULATION DENSITY – 80 per sq. km (2001)
URBAN POPULATION – 78 per cent (2001)

CLIMATE AND TERRAIN

The interior of the Iberian peninsula consists of an elevated tableland surrounded and traversed by mountain ranges: the Pyrenees, the Cantabrian Mountains, the Sierra de Guadarrama, Sierra Morena, Sierra Nevada and the Montes de Toledo. The principal rivers are the Duero, the Tajo, the Guadiana, the Guadalquivir, the Ebro and the Miño. Elevation extremes range from 3,718 m (Pico de Teide) at the highest point to 0 m (Mediterranean Sea) at the lowest. The climate is Mediterranean in the southern and eastern coastal areas, and temperate further inland. Average temperatures in Madrid range from 1°C in January to 31°C in July.

HISTORY AND POLITICS

Modern-day Spain has its roots in the unification of two powerful kingdoms: Castile and Aragón in 1479. By the 16th century, Spain was one of the richest and most powerful nations in Europe with an empire that covered most of central and southern America. However, a succession of costly wars and revolts in the 17th and 18th centuries saw this empire go into steady decline.

Spain was proclaimed a republic in 1931 and in February 1936 the Popular Front (PF), a left-wing coalition, was elected. In July 1936 a counter-revolution broke out in military garrisons in Spanish Morocco and spread throughout Spain. Civil war ensued until March 1939, when the PF governments in Madrid and Barcelona surrendered to the Nationalists (as General Franco's followers were then named). General Franco became president and ruled the country until his death in 1975, when, according to his wishes, he was succeeded as head of state by Prince Juan Carlos of Bourbon (grandson of Alfonso XIII) and Spain again became a monarchy. The first free election was held on 15 June 1977.

The legislative election of March 2004 saw the Socialist Workers' Party (SWP) win 42.6 per cent of the vote and secure 164 seats in the congress of deputies and 81 in the Senate. José Luis Rodríguez Zapatero was named as prime minister.

Polling was overshadowed by a series of explosions on commuter trains in Madrid on 24 March 2004, which killed over 200 people. Responsibility for the attack was attributed to the Islamic militant group al-Qa'eda in retaliation for Spain's support of the USA and Britain's position regarding the war in Iraq. Following his election victory, Zapatero withdrew Spain's 1,300 troops from Iraq at the end of May 2004.

INSURGENCIES

The Basque separatist organisation ETA (*Euzkadi ta Azkatasuna* – Basque Nation and Liberty) has since its formation in 1959 carried out a terrorist campaign of bombings, shootings and kidnappings against the Spanish state in an attempt to gain independence for the Basque country. ETA rejected regional autonomy for the Basque country in 1979 as insufficient and continued its campaign, but was greatly weakened in the early 1990s by increased co-operation between French and Spanish security forces. Following a car bomb explosion in January 2000, over a million people demonstrated in Madrid against ETA terrorist attacks, and in August 2002, Spanish MPs voted to suspend the Basque political party, Batasuna, because of its links with ETA. On 17 March 2003 the supreme court approved a government request for a permanent ban on Batasuna.

POLITICAL SYSTEM

Under the 1978 Constitution there is a bicameral General Assembly *(Cortes Generales)* comprising a 350-member Congress of Deputies *(Congreso de los Diputados)* elected for a maximum term of four years, which elects the Prime Minister; and a Senate *(Senado)* consisting of 208 directly elected representatives and 51 representatives appointed by the assemblies of the autonomous regions. Since the promulgation of the 1978 Constitution, 19 autonomous regions have been established, with their own parliaments and governments. These are Andalucía, Aragón, Asturias, Balearics, the Basque country, Canary Islands, Cantabria, Castilla-La Mancha, Castilla y León, Catalunya, Ceuta, Extremadura, Galicia, Madrid, Melilla, Murcia, Navarra, La Rioja and Valencia.

HEAD OF STATE

HM The King of Spain, King Juan Carlos I de Borbón, KG, GCVO, *born* 5 January 1938, *acceded to the throne* 22 November 1975 Victoria Antonia, *born* 13 June 1965

Heir, HRH The Prince of the Asturias (Príncipe Felipe Juan Pablo Alfonso y Todos los Santos), *born* 30 January 1968

SELECTED GOVERNMENT MEMBERS *as at July 2004*

Prime Minister, José Luis Rodríguez Zapatero

First Deputy Prime Minister, Cabinet Office, Government Spokesperson, Maria Teresa Fernandez de la Vega

Second Deputy Prime Minister, Economy, Pedro Solbes

Foreign Affairs, Miguel Ángel Moratinos

Interior, José Antonio Alonso

SPANISH EMBASSY

39 Chesham Place, London SW1X 8SB

T 020-7235 5555

Ambassador Extraordinary and Plenipotentiary, Chargé d'Affaires, José Argüelles

BRITISH EMBASSY

Calle de Fernando el Santo 16, E-28010 Madrid

T (+34) (91) 700 8200

Ambassador Extraordinary and Plenipotentiary, HE Stephen Wright, CMG, apptd 2003

BRITISH COUNCIL DIRECTOR, Christine Melia *(acting),*

Paseo del General Martínez, Campos 31, E-28010 Madrid

T (+34) (91) 337 3500 E madrid@britishcouncil.es

DEFENCE

The Army has 552 main battle tanks, 2,023 armoured personnel carriers and 28 attack helicopters. The Navy has six submarines, one aircraft carrier, 16 frigates, 37 patrol and coastal vessels, 17 combat aircraft and 37 armed helicopters at seven bases. The Air Force has 186 combat aircraft. The USA maintains 2,030 naval and 360 air force personnel in Spain.

MILITARY EXPENDITURE – 1.2 per cent of GDP (2002)

MILITARY PERSONNEL – 150,700: Army 95,600, Navy 22,900, Air Force 22,750; Paramilitaries 73,360

ECONOMY AND TRADE

The country is generally fertile and olives, oranges, lemons, almonds, pomegranates, bananas, apricots, tomatoes, peppers, cucumbers and grapes are cultivated. Other agricultural products include wheat, barley, oats, rice, hemp and flax. The vine is cultivated widely; in the south-west, around Jerez, sherry and wine are produced. Spain has one of Europe's largest fishing industries.

Spain's mineral resources of coal, iron, wolfram, copper, zinc, lead and iron ores are exploited. The principal industrial goods are cars, steel, ships, manufactured goods, textiles, chemical products, footwear and other leather goods. Tourism is a major industry generating nine per cent of GDP and employing 11 per cent of the population; some 48 million tourists visit per year.

Spain successfully met the criteria laid down for EU economic and monetary union and joined the European single currency in 1999. The centre-right government subsequently withdrew subsidies from uncompetitive industries, privatised the steel industry and reduced income tax.

The principal exports include manufactures, military hardware, vehicles, semi-manufactures, foodstuffs, consumer goods and energy. The principal imports are manufactures, military hardware, semi-manufactures, vehicles, consumer goods, foodstuffs and energy.

GNI – US$588,000 million (2001); US$14,300 per capita (2001)

ANNUAL AVERAGE GROWTH OF GDP – 4.9 per cent (2000)

INFLATION RATE – 3.4 per cent (2000)

UNEMPLOYMENT – 14.1 per cent (2000)

FOREIGN DIRECT INVESTMENT – US$62,292 million (1997–2000)

IMPORTS – US$163,501 million (2002)

EXPORTS – US$123,507 million (2002)

BALANCE OF PAYMENTS

Trade – US$33,098 million deficit (2002)

Current Account – US$15,942 million deficit (2002)

Trade with UK	*2002*	*2003*
Imports from UK	£8,119,300,000	£7,524,060,000
Exports to UK	7,842,300,000	6,388,691,000

TRANSPORT INFRASTRUCTURE

Spain has a total of 663,795 km of roads, of which 657,157 km are surfaced (including 10,317 km of expressways). Railways total 14,189 km, and there are 1,045 km of navigable waterways.

Important ports and harbours include Aviles, Barcelona, Bilbao, Cadiz, Cartagena, Castellon de la Plana, Ceuta, Huelva, A Coruna, Malaga, Melilla, Pasajes, Gijon, Santander, Tarragona, Valencia and Vigo, and there are 94 airports in total, all of which have surfaced runways.

EDUCATION

Education is free of charge from age six to 18, and compulsory up to the age of 16. Private schools (30 per cent of primary and 60 per cent of secondary schools) have to fulfil certain criteria to receive government maintenance grants. There are 73 universities, the oldest of which, Salamanca, was founded in 1218. Other ancient foundations are Valladolid (1346), Barcelona (1430), Zaragoza (1474), Santiago (1495), Valencia (1500), Seville (1505), Madrid (1508), Granada (1531), and Oviedo (1604). Private universities are Deusto in Bilbao, Navarra in Pamplona, Carlos III in Madrid and one in Salamanca.

ILLITERACY RATE – (m) 1.4 per cent; (f) 3.2 per cent (2000)

ENROLMENT (percentage of age group) – primary 100 per cent (1995); secondary 94 per cent (1994); tertiary 51 per cent (1996)

MEDIA

Broadcasting in Spain has expanded in recent years and digital services are becoming increasingly popular. Public radio and TV services are run by RadioTelevision Espanola (RTVE), which is funded by advertising and state subsidies. Many private radio and TV stations operate alongside, on both a national and regional level. There are four Madrid-based daily newspapers, and another two based in Barcelona. Popular titles include *El Mundo, ABC, La Razon* and *El Periodico de Catalunya.*

CULTURE

The literature of Spain is one of the oldest and richest in the world, the *Poem of the Cid*, the earliest of the heroic songs of Spain, having been written about 1140. The outstanding writings of Spain's 'Golden Age' are those of Miguel de Cervantes Saavedra (1547–1616), Lope Felix de Vega Carpio (1562–1635) and Pedro Calderón de la Barca (1600–81). The Nobel Prize for Literature has been awarded to Spanish authors five times: J. Echegaray (1833–1916), J. Benavente (1866–1954), Juan Ramón Jiménez (1881–1938), Vicente Aleixandre (1898–1984) and Camilo José Cela (1916–2002).

Spain has a long and proud tradition in fine art; important artists include Velazquez (1599–1660), Goya (1746–1828), and Picasso (1881–1973).

ISLANDS AND ENCLAVES

THE BALEARIC ISLES form an archipelago off the east coast of Spain. There are four large islands (Majorca, Minorca, Ibiza and Formentera), and seven smaller (Aire, Aucanada, Botafoch, Cabrera, Dragonera, Pinto and El Rey). Area 5,011 sq. km; population 841,669. The archipelago forms a province of Spain, the capital is ΨPalma in Majorca, population 432,113

THE CANARY ISLANDS are an archipelago in the Atlantic, off the African coast, consisting of seven islands and six islets. Area 7,270 sq. km; population 1,694,477. The Canary Islands form two provinces of Spain: Las Palmas, comprising Gran Canaria, Lanzarote (38,500), Fuerteventura (19,500) and the islets of Alegranza, Roque del Este, Roque del Oeste, Graciosa, Montaña Clara and Lobos, with the seat of administration at ΨLas Palmas (587,641) in Gran Canaria; and Santa Cruz de Tenerife, comprising Tenerife, La Palma (76,000), Gomera (31,829), and Hierro (10,000), with the seat of administration at ΨSanta Cruz in Tenerife, population estimate 399,104

ISLA DE FAISANES is an uninhabited Franco-Spanish condominium, at the mouth of the Bidassoa in La Higuera bay

ΨCEUTA is a fortified post on the Moroccan coast, opposite Gibraltar. Area 13 sq. km; population 71,505

ΨMELILLA is a town on a rocky promontory of the Rif coast, connected with the mainland by a narrow isthmus. Population 66,411. Ceuta and Melilla are autonomous regions of Spain

OVERSEAS TERRITORIES

The following territories are Spanish settlements on the Moroccan seaboard.

PEÑÓN DE ALHUCEMAS is a bay including six islands; population 366

PEÑÓN DE LA GOMERA (or Peñón de Velez) is a fortified rocky islet; population 450

THE CHAFFARINAS (or Zaffarines) is a group of three islands near the Algerian frontier; population 610

SRI LANKA

Şrī Lańkā Prajātāntrika Samājavādi Janarajaya/Ilańkaiś Śanañayaka Şośališak Kuţiyaraśa – Democratic Socialist Republic of Sri Lanka

AREA – 64,600 sq. km

POPULATION – 19,104,000 (2001): 74 per cent Sinhalese, 12.6 per cent Sri Lankan Tamils, 5.6 per cent Indian Tamils, 7.1 per cent Sri Lankan Moors, 0.7 per cent Burghers, Malays and others. The religion of the majority is Buddhism (69.3 per cent), then Hinduism (15.5 per cent), Islam (7.6 per cent), and Christianity (7.5 per cent). The national languages are Sinhala and Tamil

CAPITAL – ΨColombo (population, 642,163, 2000)

MAJOR CITIES – ΨGalle; ΨJaffna; Kandy; ΨTrincomalee

CURRENCY – Sri Lankan rupee of 100 cents

NATIONAL ANTHEM – Namo Namo Matha (We All Stand Together)

NATIONAL DAY – 4 February (Independence Day)

NATIONAL FLAG – On a dark red field, within a golden border, a golden lion passant holding a sword in its right paw, and a representation of a *bo*-leaf, issuing from each corner; and to its right, two vertical stripes of saffron and green also placed within a golden border

LIFE EXPECTANCY (years) – 72 (2001)

MORTALITY RATE (per 1,000 population) – 6.46 (2003)

INFANT MORTALITY (per 1,000 births) – 17 (2001)

HIV / AIDS ADULT PREVALENCE – 0.1 per cent (2001)

DEATH PENALTY – No (abolished 1976)

POPULATION GROWTH RATE – 1 per cent (1990–2001)

POPULATION DENSITY – 296 per sq. km (2001)

ILLITERACY RATE – (m) 5.6 per cent; (f) 11.0 per cent (2000)

CLIMATE AND TERRAIN

Sri Lanka (formerly Ceylon) is an island in the Indian Ocean, off the southern tip of India and separated from it by the narrow Palk Strait. Forests, jungle and scrub cover the greater part of the island. In areas over 600 m above sea level grasslands *(patanas* or *talawas)* are found. Elevation extremes range from 2,524 m (Pidurutalagala) at the highest point to 0 m (Indian Ocean) at the lowest. The climate is tropical with little seasonal variation in conditions and humidity, which is frequently around 90 per cent. The island experiences the south-west monsoon in May and the north-east monsoon in November. Average annual temperatures in Colombo are 29°C all year round.

HISTORY AND POLITICS

Modern Sri Lanka is a product of its long history of occupation, which began with the arrival of the Sinhalese late in the sixth century BC and continued with the establishment of the Tamils in the 14th century. The Portuguese landed in the early 16th century and founded settlements, before the Dutch East India Company took control of the country, then known as Ceylon, from 1658 until 1796. The maritime provinces of Ceylon were ceded by the Dutch to the British in 1798, becoming a British Crown Colony in 1802. With the annexation of the Kingdom of Kandy in 1815, all Ceylon came under British rule. Ceylon became a self-governing state and a member of the British Commonwealth on 4 February 1948. A republican constitution was adopted in 1972 and the country was renamed Sri Lanka (meaning 'Resplendent Island').

Eight provincial councils were set up in 1988 under the Indo-Sri Lankan peace accord in an attempt to diffuse ethnic tension. Since then, except for the temporarily merged North-East province, all provinces have had elected provincial councils.

In the presidential election held on 21 December 1999, President Kumaratunga was elected for a second term, gaining 51.37 per cent of the vote.

In the general election of 4 April 2004, the United People's Freedom Alliance won 105 seats in the National Assembly, the United National Party won 82 and the Sri Lanka Tamil Government Party secured 22. Mahinda Rajapakse was named as prime minister on 5 April.

INSURGENCIES

The Liberation Tigers of Tamil Eelam (LTTE) guerrilla group has been fighting Sri Lankan forces for control of the Tamil majority areas in the north and east of the country since 1983. The LTTE was banned in January 1998 following a truck bomb attack against a Buddhist holy shrine. A state of war was imposed by President Kumaratunga on 3 May 2000 after LTTE forces captured the Elephant Pass, the only land link to the Jaffna peninsula.

Between December 2000 and March 2001 the LTTE declared a series of cease-fires, to facilitate peace talks. However, the government refused to reciprocate, and launched a series of attacks on the Jaffna peninsula. Tensions continued and violence broke out between Hindu and Muslim Tamils in June 2002. The ban on the LTTE was lifted ahead of peace talks – the first formal negotiations in seven years – which began in Thailand on 16 September 2002. The talks continued in December, in Norway, during which a power-sharing agreement was reached over a federal system of government with substantial regional autonomy for LTTE-held areas in the north and east of the country. Since April 2003, the peace process has stalled and tensions rose following a car-bomb attack in Colombo.

POLITICAL SYSTEM

The 1978 Constitution introduced a system of proportional representation. Legislative power is vested in the Parliament, whose 225 members are directly elected for a six-year term. Executive power is exercised by the President, elected for a six-year term, and the Cabinet.

HEAD OF STATE

President, Defence, Media, Welfare, Chandrika Bandaranaike Kumaratunga, *elected* 9 November 1994, *re-elected* 21 December 1999, *sworn in* 22 December 1999

SELECTED GOVERNMENT MEMBERS *as at July 2004*

Prime Minister, Policy Development, Implementation and Poverty Alleviation, Mahinda Rajapakse
Finance, Sarath Amunugama
Foreign Affairs, Lakshman Kadirgamar
Home Affairs and Local Government, Alik Aluvihare

HIGH COMMISSION FOR THE DEMOCRATIC SOCIALIST REPUBLIC OF SRI LANKA
13 Hyde Park Gardens, London W2 2LU **T** 020-7262 1841/6
E mail@slhc.globalnet.co.uk
High Commissioner, HE Faisz Musthapha, apptd 2002

BRITISH HIGH COMMISSION
190 Galle Road, Kollupitiya, PO Box 1433, Colombo 3
T (+94) (1) 437336/43 **E** bhc@eureka.lk
High Commissioner, HE Stephen Evans, OBE, apptd 2002

BRITISH COUNCIL DIRECTOR, Tony O'Brien
49 Alfred House Gardens, PO Box 753, Colombo 3
E enquiries@britishcouncil.lk

DEFENCE

The Army has 62 main battle tanks, 217 armoured personnel carriers and 62 armoured infantry fighting vehicles. The Navy has 61 patrol and coastal vessels at five bases. The Air Force has 22 combat aircraft and 24 armed helicopters.

MILITARY EXPENDITURE – 3.2 per cent of GDP (2002)
MILITARY PERSONNEL – 152,300: Army 118,000, Navy 15,000, Air Force 19,300; Paramilitaries 88,600

ECONOMY AND TRADE

The main agricultural crops are tea, rubber, copra and spices; gems are also mined. There is increasing emphasis on local production of food, especially rice, and plans for the large-scale production of sugarcane, cotton and citrus fruits.

The prinicipal exports are industrial goods, agricultural products (especially tea), and oil derivatives. Principal imports are manufactures, textiles and clothing, capital goods, consumer goods and oil. The tourist industry is an important source of revenue, with 400,414 foreign visitors in 2000.

GNI – US$16,400 million (2001); US$880 per capita (2001)
ANNUAL AVERAGE GROWTH OF GDP – 6.0 per cent (2000)
INFLATION RATE – 6.2 per cent (2000)
UNEMPLOYMENT – 8.0 per cent (2000)

TOTAL EXTERNAL DEBT – US$9,066 million (2000)
FOREIGN DIRECT INVESTMENT – US$973 million (1997–2000)
IMPORTS – US$6,105 million (2002)
EXPORTS – US$4,699 million (2002)

BALANCE OF PAYMENTS
Trade – US$553 million deficit (2001)
Current Account – US$265 million deficit (2001)

Trade with UK	*2002*	*2003*
Imports from UK	£126,314,000	£122,155,000
Exports to UK	421,567,000	409,488,000

TRANSPORT INFRASTRUCTURE
There are 96,695 km of roads, of which 91,860 km are surfaced. The rail network is government run and there are 1,459 km of railway. The principal airport is at Katunayake, north of Colombo.

MEDIA
Many of Sri Lanka's main media outlets are government controlled, including two major TV stations and radio networks operated by the Sri Lanka Broadcasting Corporation (SLBC). There are also privately owned broadcast media and newspapers. As part of the ongoing peace process, in 2002 the government permitted Tamil Tiger rebels to broadcast their Voice of Tigers radio station in the north of the island.

CULTURE
Sri Lanka's classical architecture, sculpture and painting is predominantly Buddhist. One of the highest peaks in the central massif is Adam's Peak (2,243 m), a place of pilgrimage for Buddhists, Hindus and Muslims. Most notable are several enormous Buddha sculptures, particularly at Aukana and Buduruvagala. Anuradhapura and Polonnaruwa have the most impressive archaelogical legacy, but Kandy is the most thriving cultural centre today. Acrobatic Sinhalese dancing and masked drama are widespread, and woodcarving, weaving, pottery and metalwork are all highly developed crafts.

SUDAN

Al-Jumhūriyya as-Sūdān – Republic of the Sudan

AREA – 2,376,000 sq. km. Neighbours: Egypt (north), Eritrea and Ethiopia (east), Kenya, Uganda and the Democratic Republic of Congo (south), Central African Republic, Chad and Libya (west)
POPULATION – 31,809,000 (2001). Arab and Nubian peoples populate the north and centre, Nilotic and black African peoples the south. Arabic is the official language and Islam the state religion, although the Nilotics of the Bahr el-Ghazal and Upper Nile valleys are generally Animists or Christians
CAPITAL – Khartoum (Al-Khartum) (population, 947,483, 1993 census). The combined population of Khartoum, Khartoum North and Umm Durman (excluding refugees and displaced people) is estimated at 3,000,000
MAJOR CITIES – Al-Ubayyid; Nyala; ΨPort Sudan (Bur Sudan)
CURRENCY – Sudanese dinar (SD) of 100 piastres
NATIONAL ANTHEM – Nahnu Djundullah (We Are The Army Of God)
NATIONAL DAY – 1 January (Independence Day)
NATIONAL FLAG – Three horizontal stripes of red, white and black with a green triangle next to the hoist
LIFE EXPECTANCY (years) – 56 (2001)
MORTALITY RATE (per 1,000 population) – 9.59 (2003)
INFANT MORTALITY (per 1,000 births) – 65 (2001)
HIV / AIDS ADULT PREVALENCE – 2.6 per cent (2001)
DEATH PENALTY – Yes
POPULATION GROWTH RATE – 2.3 per cent (1990–2001)
POPULATION DENSITY – 13 per sq. km (2001)
URBAN POPULATION – 37 per cent (2001)
MILITARY EXPENDITURE – 4.9 per cent of GDP (2002)
MILITARY PERSONNEL – 104,500: Army 100,000, Navy 1,500, Air Force 3,000; Paramilitaries 10,000
CONSCRIPTION DURATION – Two years

CLIMATE AND TERRAIN
Sudan is the largest country in Africa and is dominated by the River Nile and its tributaries. The terrain is generally low-lying with mountains in the east and west of the countries. Elevation extremes range from 3,187 m (Kinyeti) at the highest point to 0 m (Red Sea) at the lowest. The climate ranges from tropical to continental, while most of the northern half of the country is desert. There is a wet season from April to October with average temperatures in Khartoum ranging from 15°C in January to 38°C in July.

HISTORY AND POLITICS
Present-day Sudan formed part of the Egyptian Empire from 1900 BC. From the eighth century BC onwards, northern Sudan was conquered and occupied by several Arab nations and caliphates. The southern Nubian states however remained independent.

The Anglo-Egyptian condominium over Sudan was established in 1899 and ended when the Sudan House of Representatives, on 19 December 1955, declared Sudan a fully independent sovereign state. A republic was proclaimed on 1 January 1956, and was recognised by Great Britain and Egypt. Sudan was under sporadic military rule from 1958 until presidential and legislative elections were held in March 1996, when President al-Bashir was elected, having faced no serious contender. The founding of political parties was legalised on 1 January 1999. The following December, President al-Bashir suspended the National Assembly and declared a three-month state of emergency, shortly before a vote on constitutional changes, which included the reduction of the powers of the president, was due to be debated. The state of emergency has been repeatedly extended and in December 2001 was extended indefinitely.

Presidential and legislative elections were held in December 2000, but were boycotted by most opposition parties. President al-Bashir was re-elected, winning 86.5 per cent of votes cast, and the National Congress won 355 of the 360 seats up for election. The civil war prevented balloting in three provinces. On 19 August 2002 President Bashir announced a cabinet reshuffle which brought members of opposition groups into the

Cabinet for the first time. Legislative elections were scheduled for December 2004.

INSURGENCIES

Nearly 17 years of insurrection in the southern provinces ended in 1972 with the signing of an agreement recognising southern regional autonomy within the Sudanese state. However, insurrection resumed in 1983 and since then there has been civil war in the south of the country between mainly Muslim government forces and the Christian and Animist majority in the area, organised into the Sudan People's Liberation Army (SPLA). A peace process begun in September 2000 continued through 2001 and a cease-fire was agreed in January 2002. However in March 2002 the SPLA warned that its attacks on oil installations would continue. The warfare has left an estimated 1.4 million people dead, including 300,000 who died in the war-induced famine in 1988 and thousands in a similar situation in 1994. Some three million refugees have fled the fighting, either to the north, to neighbouring states, or to the far south near the Ugandan border. The fighting has left large areas of the south desolate and uninhabitable. In July 2002 the government and SPLA signed a framework deal aimed at ending the civil war which agreed that southern Sudan will be able to hold an independence referendum after a six-year power-sharing transition period. Several rounds of peace talks took place in Kenya during 2003.

A separate, ongoing conflict in the western Darfur region during 2004 has forced around one million people to flee to other parts of the country and across the border into Chad. In July 2004, the UN passed a resolution urging the Sudanese government to do more to stop indiscriminate attacks by militias on the civilian population.

FOREIGN RELATIONS

In 1995 Sudan's relations with its neighbours, notably Egypt, Eritrea and Uganda, deteriorated as they considered that Sudan was arming Islamic and insurgent groups in their states. On 2 May 1999 a peace agreement was signed with Eritrea. Sudan and the UK agreed to resume full diplomatic representation in June 1999. On 8 December 1999, Sudan and Uganda signed an agreement under which they agreed to cease supporting rebel groups in each other's countries, to disarm and disband such groups, and to re-establish full diplomatic links. On 24 December, Sudan and Egypt agreed to normalise their relations and seek a solution to their dispute over the Hala'ib region.

HEAD OF STATE

President, Prime Minister, Lt.-Gen. Omar Hassan Ahmad al-Bashir, *appointed* 16 October 1993, *elected* 17 March 1996, *re-elected* 20 December 2000.
First Vice-President, Maj.-Gen. Ali Osman Mohamad Taha
Vice-President, Moses Machar Kashol

SELECTED GOVERNMENT MEMBERS *as at July 2004*
Defence, Maj.-Gen. Bakri Hassan Salih
Finance and National Economy, Al Zubayr Ahmad Hasan
Foreign Affairs, Mustapha Osman Ismail
Interior, Maj.-Gen. Abd al-Rahim Muhammad Husayn

EMBASSY OF THE REPUBLIC OF THE SUDAN
3 Cleveland Row, London SW1A 1DD
T 020-7839 8080
Ambassador Extraordinary and Plenipotentiary, HE Dr Hasan Abdin, apptd 2000

BRITISH EMBASSY
PO Box 801, Khartoum East
T (+ 249) (183) 777105
E information.khartoum@fco.gov.uk
Ambassador Extraordinary and Plenipotentiary, HE William Patey, apptd 2002

BRITISH COUNCIL DIRECTOR, Paul Doubleday
14 Abu Sin Street (PO Box 1253), Khartoum
E british.council@sd.britishcouncil.org

ECONOMY AND TRADE

Agriculture provides employment for around 80 per cent of the labour force and contributes nearly half of GDP. The industry is based on large and medium-sized public sector irrigation projects; mechanised and traditional agriculture is practised in areas with sufficient rainfall. The principal grain crops are *dura* (great millet) and wheat, the staple food of the population. Sesame and groundnuts are other important crops, which also yield an exportable surplus, and a promising start has been made with castor seed.

Since 1997 Sudan has been implementing IMF economic reforms which, despite the country's chronic instability and vulnerability to drought, have stabilised the economy to a considerable degree. In 1999 Sudan began exporting crude oil, which has since been expanded and contributed 6.1 per cent to GDP growth in 2003.

GNI – US$10,700 million (2001); US$340 per capita (2001)
ANNUAL AVERAGE GROWTH OF GDP – 6.0 per cent (1998)
INFLATION RATE – 9.2 per cent (2002)
TOTAL EXTERNAL DEBT – US$15,741 million (2000)
FOREIGN DIRECT INVESTMENT – US$1,134 million (1997–2000)
IMPORTS – US$1,586 million (2001)
EXPORTS – US$1,699 million (2001)

BALANCE OF PAYMENTS
Trade – US$204 million deficit (2002)
Current Account – US$960 million deficit (2002)

Trade with UK	*2002*	*2003*
Imports from UK	£70,807,000	£88,774,000
Exports to UK	7,770,000	6,257,000

TRANSPORT INFRASTRUCTURE

The railway network, adversely affected by the civil war, is about 5,516 km in length. There are 11,610 km of roads, of which 4,203 km are surfaced. Nile River services between Khartoum and Juba have been interrupted by the southern insurrection. Port Sudan is the country's main seaport. Sudan Airways flies services from Khartoum to other parts of Sudan and to other African states, Europe and the Middle East.

EDUCATION

Education is free of charge for most children but not compulsory. Six years of primary education, is followed by three years of secondary education; there are three types of secondary school: general, academic and vocational. The language of instruction is Arabic. English has not been taught in schools since new Arabisation legislation came into effect in 1991.

In addition to 20 universities there are various technical tertiary institutes as well as professional and vocational training establishments.

ILLITERACY RATE – (m) 30.2 per cent; (f) 53.7 per cent (2000)

MEDIA

Radio and television are controlled by the government, and a permanent military censor ensures that the news reflects official views. There are no privately owned TV broadcasters, and private radio stations are not permitted. Satellite dishes are becoming common in affluent areas and pan-Arab TV stations are popular among viewers, as are foreign radio stations such as the BBC World Service and Paris-based Radio Monte Carlo, which broadcast in Khartoum. There are several privately owned newspapers.

SURINAME

Republiek Suriname – Republic of Suriname

AREA – 163,265 sq. km. Neighbours: French Guiana (east), Brazil (south), Guyana (west)
POPULATION – 433,998 (2001 estimate): 37 per cent Hindustani, 31 per cent Creole, 15 per cent Javanese, 10 per cent African and small numbers of Amerindian, Chinese and Europeans. The official language is Dutch, the native language is Sranang Tongo, and other widely used languages are Hindustani and Javanese
CAPITAL – ΨParamaribo (population, 213,836, 2000)
CURRENCY – Suriname guilder of 100 cents
NATIONAL ANTHEM – God Zij Met Ons Suriname (God Be With Our Suriname)
NATIONAL DAY – 25 November
NATIONAL FLAG – Horizontal stripes of green, white, red, white and green, with a five-pointed yellow star in the centre
MORTALITY RATE (per 1,000 population) – 6.83 (2003)
HIV / AIDS ADULT PREVALENCE – 1.2 per cent (2001)
DEATH PENALTY – No (abolished 1982)
POPULATION BELOW POVERTY LINE – 70 per cent (2002)
POPULATION GROWTH RATE– 0.3 per cent (2004)
POPULATION DENSITY – 3 per sq. km (1999)
MILITARY EXPENDITURE – 5.0 per cent of GDP (2002)
MILITARY PERSONNEL – 1,840: Army 1,400, Navy 240, Air Force 200
ILLITERACY RATE – (m) 4.1 per cent; (f) 7.4 per cent (2000)

CLIMATE AND TERRAIN

Elevation extremes range from 1,230 m (Juliana Top) at the highest point to −2 m (unnamed location) at the lowest. Suriname has a tropical climate characterised by high rainfall, high humidity and hot temperatures which are modified by the north-east trade winds. There are two wet seasons from April to August and November to February. Average annual precipitation in Paramaribo is 2,200 mm and average temperatures are an almost constant 27°C.

HISTORY AND POLITICS

Formerly known as Dutch Guiana, Suriname remained part of the Netherlands West Indies until 25 November 1975, when it achieved complete independence. The civilian government was ousted in 1980 by the military, who appointed a predominantly civilian government in 1982.

The New Front for Democracy, a four-party bloc consisting of the National Party of Suriname (NPS), The Progressive Reform Party, Pertjajah Luhur and the Suriname Labour Party, won 32 of the 51 seats in the elections to the National Assembly on 25 May 2000 and appointed Ronald Venetiaan of the NPS as president on 4 August 2000.

Suriname has a long-running dispute with its neighbour, Guyana, over the ownership of a potentially oil-rich offshore area. A UN tribunal has been set up to try to settle the issue.

POLITICAL SYSTEM

The unicameral legislature, the National Assembly, has 51 members, directly elected for a five-year term. The President is elected by a two-thirds majority in the National Assembly, or if the required majority cannot be achieved, by a specially convened United Peoples' Conference, including district and local council representatives, for a five-year term.

HEAD OF STATE

President, Ronald Venetiaan, *inaugurated* 4 August 2000
Vice-President, Prime Minister, Jules Ajodhia

SELECTED GOVERNMENT MEMBERS *as at July 2004*

Defence, Ronald Assen
Finance, Humphrey Hildenberg
Foreign Affairs, Marie Levens
Internal Affairs, Trade and Industry, Urmila Joella-Sewnundum

EMBASSY OF THE REPUBLIC OF SURINAME

Alexander Gogelweg 2, NL-2517 JH The Hague, The Netherlands
T (+31) (070) 361 7445
Ambassador Extraordinary and Plenipotentiary, vacant
Chargé d'Affaires, Nell Stadwijk Kappel

BRITISH AMBASSADOR, HE Stephen Hiscock, apptd 2002, resident at Georgetown, Guyana

ECONOMY AND TRADE

Suriname has large timber resources. Rice and sugarcane are the main crops. Bauxite is mined and is the principal export, although reserves are declining. Principal trading partners are the Netherlands, the USA and Norway.

GNI – US$761 million (2000); US$1,810 per capita (2001)
ANNUAL AVERAGE GROWTH OF GDP – 5.9 per cent (2001)
INFLATION RATE – 64.3 per cent (2000)
IMPORTS – US$246 million (2000)
EXPORTS – US$399 million (2000)

BALANCE OF PAYMENTS

Trade – US$140 million surplus (2001)
Current Account – US$84 million deficit (2001)

Trade with UK	*2002*	*2003*
Imports from UK	£9,133,000	£10,113,000
Exports to UK	3,707,000	325,000

TRANSPORT INFRASTRUCTURE

There are 4,492 km of roads in total, of which approximately one-quarter is surfaced. The 1,200 km of waterways provide the most effective means of transport. Important ports and harbours include Albina, Moengo, New Nickerie, Paramaribo, Paranam and Wageningen.

MEDIA

State broadcast media offer a range of views, and are on the air alongside commercial radio and TV stations. The country's two daily newspapers are privately owned.

SWAZILAND

Umbuso we Swatini/Kingdom of Swaziland

AREA – 17,364 sq. km. Neighbours: South Africa (north, west and south), Mozambique (east)
POPULATION – 1,104,343 (2001 estimate). The languages are English and Swazi
CAPITAL – Mbabane (population, 67,200, 2002 estimate)
MAJOR TOWNS – Manzini (73,000); Hlatikulu; Mhlume; Nhlangano; Pigg's Peak; Siteki
CURRENCY – Lilangeni (E) of 100 cents (South African currency is also in circulation). Swaziland is a member of the Common Monetary Area and its unit of currency *Emalangeni* (singular *Lilangeni*) has a par value with the South African rand
NATIONAL ANTHEM – Ingoma Yesive
NATIONAL DAY – 6 September (Independence Day)
NATIONAL FLAG – Blue with a wide crimson horizontal band bordered in yellow across the centre, bearing a shield and two spears horizontally
LIFE EXPECTANCY (years) – 38 (2001)
MORTALITY RATE (per 1,000 population) – 21.08 (2003)
HIV / AIDS ADULT PREVALENCE – 33.4 per cent (2001)
DEATH PENALTY – Yes
POPULATION BELOW POVERTY LINE – 40 per cent (1995)
POPULATION GROWTH RATE – 0.5 per cent (2004)
POPULATION DENSITY – 56 per sq. km (1999)
ILLITERACY RATE – (m) 19.3 per cent; (f) 21.4 per cent (2000)
ENROLMENT(percentage of age group) – primary 91 per cent (1996); secondary 37 per cent (1996); tertiary 6 per cent (1996)

CLIMATE AND TERRAIN

The broken mountainous Highveld along the western border, with an average altitude of 1,219 m, is densely forested, mainly with conifers and eucalyptus; the Middleveld, averaging about 609 m, is a mixed farming area; and the Lowveld in the east was mainly scrubland until the introduction of large sugarcane plantations. Four rivers, the Komati, Usutu, Mbuluzi and Ngwavuma, flow from west to east. Elevation extremes range from 1,862 m (Emlembe) at the highest point to 21 m (Great Usutu River) at the lowest.

The climate varies from region to region. The Highveld is humid and temperate, the Middleveld and Lebombo Range are subtropical and the Lowveld is tropical and semi-arid. Average annual temperatures in Mbabane range from 6°C in June to 25°C in January.

HISTORY AND POLITICS

The Kingdom of Swaziland came into being on 25 April 1967 under a self-governing constitution. It became an independent kingdom, headed by HM Sobhuza II, and a member of the Commonwealth on 6 September 1968. King Sobhuza scrapped the constitution in 1973 and banned political parties. He was succeeded by his son, King Mswati III, in 1986.

An illegal general strike was held in November 2000 to support a petition that demanded the legalisation of political parties, the revocation of restrictive labour laws, and the abolition of the right of traditional chiefs to force people to work without pay. The petition had been drawn up by the Swaziland Federation of Trade Unions and a group of illegal political parties. Several trade union and opposition leaders were arrested shortly before the strike took place and during the demonstrations. The findings of a Constitutional Review Commission that was published in August 2001 and which demonstrated that a majority of the population wanted to extend the already wide powers of the King, were opposed by pro-democracy groups. Legislative elections held on 31 October 2003 resulted in the election of Absalom Themba Dlamini as Prime Minister.

POLITICAL SYSTEM

The King, assisted by his appointed Cabinet, holds considerable executive, legislative and judicial authority. There is a bicameral legislative body comprising a Senate and a House of Assembly. Each of the 55 administrative districts *(Tinkhundla)* directly elects one member to the House of Assembly. The King appoints ten members to the House of Assembly, making 65 in all, who then elect ten members of their own number to the Senate. To these are added 20 senators appointed by the King, bringing the full membership of the Senate to 30. In addition, the King appoints Commissions, who assess public opinion. There are also public gatherings, where any citizen can express an opinion. All political parties are banned.

The draft of a new Constitution, which retained the non-party system but increased the protection of human rights, was published on 31 May 2003.

HEAD OF STATE

King of Swaziland, HM King Mswati III, *inaugurated* 25 April 1986

SELECTED GOVERNMENT MEMBERS *as at July 2004*

Prime Minister, Absalom Themba Dlamini
Deputy Prime Minister, Albert Shabangu
Finance, Majozi Sithole
Foreign Affairs and Trade, Mabili Dlamini
Home Affairs, Prince Gabheni Dlamini

KINGDOM OF SWAZILAND HIGH COMMISSION

20 Buckingham Gate, London SW1E 6LB
T 020-7630 6611
High Commissioner, Clement Mabuza (*acting*)

BRITISH HIGH COMMISSION

2nd Floor, Lilunga House, Gilfillan Street, Mbabane
T (+268) 404 2581/2/3/4
E enquiries.mbabane@fco.gov.uk
High Commissioner, HE David Reader, apptd 2001

ECONOMY AND TRADE

Manufacturing has replaced agriculture as the dominant sector, with timber, textiles and footwear the main products. Agricultural products include sugarcane and fruit. GDP growth rates declined in the 1990s, partly as a result of lower growth rates in South Africa, on which the Swazi economy is strongly dependent. South Africa accounts for around 60 per cent of exports from Swaziland and about 85 per cent of imports.

GNI – US$1,388 million (2001); US$1,300 per capita (2001)
ANNUAL AVERAGE GROWTH OF GDP – 3.5 per cent (1999)
INFLATION RATE – 11.8 per cent (2002)
TOTAL EXTERNAL DEBT – US$262 million (2000)
IMPORTS – US$983 million (2002)
EXPORTS – US$937 million (2002)

BALANCE OF PAYMENTS
Trade – US$73 million deficit (2001)
Current Account – US$53 million deficit (2001)

Trade with UK	*2002*	*2003*
Imports from UK	£2,841,000	£1,951,000
Exports to UK	34,576,000	32,320,000

TRANSPORT INFRASTRUCTURE

Swaziland's railway network is 297 km long and connects with the Mozambique port of Maputo and the South African railway to Richards Bay. A rail line to the north-west border provides a link to Komatipoort. There are 3,800 km of roads, of which 1,064 km are surfaced. There is an international airport at Manzini. Royal Swazi National Airways provides scheduled air services to southern and eastern Africa.

MEDIA AND CULTURE

State control of the media is strong: all radio and TV stations, with the exception of a Christian radio station, are under government control, and the country's only private daily newspaper is strictly monitored. Criticism of the monarchy is banned.

Although indigenous religions are not widely practised, traditional Swazi culture remains strong, and important ceremonies, such as the *Incwala* and *Umhlanga* have religious overtones.

SWEDEN

Konungariket Sverige – Kingdom of Sweden

AREA – 411,600 sq. km. Neighbours: Norway (west), Finland (east)
POPULATION – 8,833,000 (2001). The state religion is Lutheran Protestant, to which over 95 per cent officially adhere. The language is Swedish; in the north there are both Finnish- and Lapp-speaking communities
CAPITAL – ΨStockholm (population, 1,684,420, 2002 estimate)
MAJOR CITIES – ΨGothenburg (Göteborg); ΨMalmö; Uppsala
CURRENCY – Swedish krona of 100 öre
NATIONAL ANTHEM – Du Gamla, Du Fria (Thou Ancient, Thou Freeborn)
NATIONAL DAY – 6 June (Day of the Swedish Flag)
NATIONAL FLAG – Yellow cross on a blue ground
LIFE EXPECTANCY (years) – 80 (2001)
MORTALITY RATE (per 1,000 population) – 10.58 (2003)
INFANT MORTALITY (per 1,000 births) – 3 (2001)
HIV / AIDS ADULT PREVALENCE – 0.1 per cent (2001)
DEATH PENALTY – No (abolished 1972)
POPULATION GROWTH RATE – 0.3 per cent (1990–2001)
POPULATION DENSITY – 21 per sq. km (2001)

CLIMATE AND TERRAIN

Sweden's terrain is mostly flat or rolling lowlands, with mountains in the west. Elevation extremes range from 2,111 m (Kebnekaise) at the highest point to 0 m (Baltic Sea) at the lowest. The climate is continental with average temperatures in Stockholm ranging from −5°C in January to 22°C in July.

HISTORY AND POLITICS

Sweden takes its name from the Svear people who inhabited the region during the seventh century AD. The Swedes participated in the Viking expansion during the ninth to 11th centuries and established sovereignty over Finland in the 13th century. The Union of Kalmar (1397) brought Sweden and Norway under Danish rule. Northern Sweden regained its independence following a rebellion by noblemen in 1521 which resulted in the election of Gustav I (of the House of Vasa) to the Swedish throne.

Sweden's power reached its zenith in the 17th century under Gustavus II. The Danes were driven out of southern Sweden, the Baltic coast of Russia was seized, and the Swedish army pushed into Germany after vanquishing the Catholic League. Swedish power waned in the late 17th and 18th centuries. Finland was lost to Russia in 1809; Norway was ceded to Sweden under the Congress of Vienna (1814–15) but seceded in 1905.

Sweden remained neutral during both World Wars. Post-war party politics was dominated by Social Democrat-led coalitions which established a mixed economy and a generous welfare state. Right-wing and centrist parties held power from 1976–82 and 1991–4. Sweden applied for EU membership in July 1991 and joined to the EU on 1 January 1995.

After the general election of 15 September 2002 the Swedish Social Democratic Labour Party (SAP) remained the largest party in the legislature with 144 seats. Prime Minister Goran Persson was unable to conclude an agreement on a coalition government, which again led a minority SAP Cabinet. Foreign Minister Anna Lindh was murdered on 10 September 2003 and her replacement, Laila Freivalds, was named on 10 October 2003.

POLITICAL SYSTEM

Sweden is a constitutional monarchy, with the monarch retaining purely ceremonial functions as head of state. Under the Act of Succession 1810 the throne is hereditary in the House of Bernadotte. The Constitution is based upon the Instrument of Government 1974, which amended the 1810 Act and removed from the monarch the roles of appointing the Prime Minister and signing parliamentary bills into law. A 1979 amendment vested the succession in the monarch's eldest child irrespective of sex.

Executive power is vested in the Prime Minister and Council of Ministers. There is a unicameral legislature *(Riksdag)* of 349 members elected by universal suffrage on a proportional representation basis (with a four per cent threshold for representation) for a four-year term. The Council of Ministers *(Statsråd)* is responsible to the *Riksdag*. Sweden is divided into 24 counties *(län)* and 288 municipalities *(kommun)*.

HEAD OF STATE
HM The King of Sweden, Carl XVI Gustaf, KG, *born* 30 April 1946, *succeeded* 15 September 1973
Heir, HRH Crown Princess Victoria Ingrid Alice Désirée, Duchess of Västergötland, *born* 14 July 1977

SELECTED GOVERNMENT MEMBERS *as at July 2004*
Prime Minister, Göran Persson
Defence, Leni Björklund
Finance, Bosse Ringholm
Foreign Affairs, Laila Freivalds

EMBASSY OF SWEDEN
11 Montagu Place, London W1H 2AL
T 020-7917 6400
Ambassador Extraordinary and Plenipotentiary, HE Mats Bergquist, CMG, apptd 1997

BRITISH EMBASSY
Skarpögatan 6–8, Box 27819, S-115 93 Stockholm
T (+46) (8) 671 3000
Ambassador Extraordinary and Plenipotentiary, HE Anthony Cary

BRITISH COUNCIL DIRECTOR, Jim Potts OBE
PO Box 27819, S-115 93 Stockholm
T (+46) (8) 671 3110
E info@britishcouncil.se

DEFENCE

The Army has 280 main battle tanks, 433 armoured personnel carriers and 1,531 armoured infantry fighting vehicles. The Navy has seven submarines and 36 patrol and coastal vessels at four bases. The Air Force has 207 combat aircraft.

Sweden has a policy of non-alignment in peace and neutrality in war and has declined to become a member of NATO. It maintains a 'total defence' which includes peacetime organisations for civil, economic and psychological defence.

MILITARY EXPENDITURE – 1.7 per cent of GDP (2002)
MILITARY PERSONNEL – 27,600: Army 13,800, Navy 7,900, Air Force 5,900; Paramilitaries 600
CONSCRIPTION DURATION – Seven to 15 months

ECONOMY AND TRADE

Less than ten per cent of the land area is farmland and less than three per cent of the labour force is employed in farming, although Sweden is more than 80 per cent self-sufficient in food.

Industrial prosperity is based on natural resources: forests, mineral deposits and water power. The forests cover about half the total land surface and sustain the timber, finished wood products, pulp and paper milling industries. The mineral resources include iron ore, lead, zinc, sulphur, granite, marble, precious and heavy metals (the latter not exploited) and extensive deposits of low-grade uranium ore. Industries based on mining are important but it is the general engineering industry that provides 80 per cent of Sweden's exports, especially specialised machinery and systems, motor vehicles, aircraft, electrical and electronic equipment, pharmaceuticals, plastics and chemical industries.

Hydroelectricity supplies 15 per cent of energy needs. Sweden has no significant indigenous resources of conventional hydrocarbon fuels and relies for 50 per cent of its energy needs upon imported oil and coal.

Sweden experienced a deep recession between 1992 and 1994. The centre-right government, elected in 1991, introduced austerity measures and free-market economic reforms. In October 1997 Sweden decided not to join European economic and monetary union (EMU) at the first stage; a referendum on EMU membership was held on 14 September 2003, but was rejected by a clear majority.

About 45 per cent of industrial output is exported, mainly in the form of cars, trucks, machinery, and electrical and communications equipment. Sweden conducts 70 per cent of its trade with EFTA and the rest of the EU.

GNI – US$225,900 million (2001); US$25,400 per capita (2001)
ANNUAL AVERAGE GROWTH OF GDP – 4.6 per cent (2000)
INFLATION RATE – 1 per cent (2000)
UNEMPLOYMENT – 4.7 per cent (2000)
FOREIGN DIRECT INVESTMENT – US$110,791 million (1997–2000)
IMPORTS – US$66,106 million (2002)
EXPORTS – US$81,120 million (2002)

BALANCE OF PAYMENTS
Trade – US$13,832 million surplus (2001)
Current Account – US$6,696 million surplus (2001)

Trade with UK	*2002*	*2003*
Imports from UK	£3,642,700,000	£3,443,633,000
Exports to UK	4,102,900,000	3,316,388,000

TRANSPORT INFRASTRUCTURE

The total length of the railway network is 12,821 km. There are approximately 210,000 km of roads, of which 166,500 km are surfaced (including 1,499 km of expressways). There are also 2,052 km of waterways, navigable to small steamers and barges. Ports and harbours include Gavle, Gothenburg, Halmstad, Helsingborg, Hudiksvall, Kalmar, Karlshamn, Luleå, Malmo, Solvesborg, Stockholm and Sundsvall. Regular domestic air traffic is maintained by the Scandinavian Airlines System and by Malmö Aviation. Regular European and intercontinental air traffic is maintained by the Scandinavian Airlines System. The Øresund Bridge connects Sweden to Denmark.

EDUCATION

The state education system provides nine years' free and compulsory schooling from the age of seven to 16 in the comprehensive elementary schools. Around 95 per cent continue into further education of two to four years' duration in the upper secondary schools and a unified higher education system administered in six regional areas containing one of the universities: Uppsala (founded 1477); Lund (1668); Stockholm (1878); Gothenburg (1887); Umeå (1963) and Linköping (1967). There are

40 institutions of higher education including three technical universities in Stockholm, Gothenburg and Luleå.

ENROLMENT (percentage of age group) – primary 100 per cent (1996); secondary 99 per cent (1996); tertiary 50 per cent (1996)

MEDIA

Public television is run by Sveriges Television (SVT). There are a number of commercial stations and around 66 per cent of households have cable or satellite television. Commercial radio began in 1993, and some of the main stations now have near-national networks, in competition with public broadcaster Sveriges Radio. The country is among the top consumers of newspapers in the world, and the government provides subsidies to newspapers regardless of their political affiliation. There are four Stockholm-based daily newspapers and one based in Gothenburg. Titles include *Aftonbladet*, *Expressen* and *Gotenborgs Posten.*

CULTURE

Swedish belongs, with Danish and Norwegian, to the North Germanic language group. Swedish literature dates back to King Magnus Eriksson, who codified the old Swedish provincial laws in 1350. With his translation of the Bible, Olaus Petri (1493–1552) formed the basis for the modern Swedish language. Literature flourished during the reign of Gustavus III, who founded the Swedish Academy in 1786.

Notable Swedish writers include Almquist (1795–1866), Strindberg (1849–1912) and Lagerlöf (1858–1940), winner of the Nobel Prize for Literature in 1909. Contemporary authors include Lagerquist (1891–1974), Nobel Laureate in 1951, Martinson (1904–78) and Johnson (1900–76), joint winners of the Nobel Prize for Literature in 1974. The Swedish scientist Alfred Nobel (1833–96) founded the Nobel Prizes for Literature, Science and Peace.

SWITZERLAND

Schweizerische Eidgenossenschaft/Confédération Suisse/ Confederazione Svizzera/Confederaziun Svizra – Swiss Confederation

AREA – 39,600 sq. km. Neighbours: France (west and north-west), Germany (north), Austria and Liechtenstein (east), Italy (south)

POPULATION – 7,170,000 (2001): 46.1 per cent Roman Catholic, 40 per cent Protestant, 5 per cent other religions and 8.9 per cent without religion. The official languages are German (the first language of 63.7 per cent), French (19.2 per cent), Italian (7.6 per cent) and Romansch (0.6 per cent). German is the dominant language in 19 of the 26 cantons; French in Fribourg, Jura, Geneva, Neuchatel, Valais and Vaud; Italian in Ticino; and Romansch in parts of Graubünden

CAPITAL – Bern (population, 317,367, 2001 estimate)

MAJOR CITIES – Basel; Geneva; Lausanne; Lucerne; Winterthur; Zurich

CURRENCY – Swiss franc of 100 rappen (or centimes)

NATIONAL ANTHEM – Schweizerpsalm (Swiss Psalm)

NATIONAL DAY – 1 August

NATIONAL FLAG – Square and red, bearing a couped white cross

LIFE EXPECTANCY (years) – 79 (2001)

MORTALITY RATE (per 1,000 population) – 8.82 (2003)

INFANT MORTALITY (per 1,000 births) – 5 (2001)

HIV / AIDS ADULT PREVALENCE – 0.5 per cent (2001)

DEATH PENALTY – No (abolished 1992)

POPULATION GROWTH RATE – 0.4 per cent (1990–2001)

POPULATION DENSITY – 181 per sq. km (2001)

URBAN POPULATION – 67 per cent (2001)

CLIMATE AND TERRAIN

Switzerland is the most mountainous country in Europe. The Alps, ranging in height from 1,700 m to 4,634 m, occupy its southern and eastern frontiers and form the chief part of its interior. The highest peaks include Finsteraarhorn (4,274 m), Aletschhorn (4,195 m) and Jungfrau (4,158 m). The climate is temperate with conditions that vary with altitude. Average temperatures in Zurich range from −3°C in January to 24°C in July.

HISTORY AND POLITICS

The Swiss confederation was formed as an alliance of three cantons in 1291 and achieved full independence under the Peace of Westphalia (1648), having been a province of the Holy Roman Empire since 1033. French revolutionary forces seized Switzerland in 1789 and named it the Helvetic Republic. Independence was not restored until the Congress of Vienna (1815), which also joined Geneva, Neuchatel and Valais to the confederation and instituted perpetual neutrality in foreign affairs. In 1847 a war broke out between the Protestant and Roman Catholic cantons, the latter being defeated. A new constitution was adopted in 1848 which enhanced the powers of the central government.

Proportional representation was introduced in 1919 and ensured coalition governments throughout the 20th century. Women were given the vote in 1971.

On 19 October 2003 the conservative Swiss People's Party (SPP) became the largest overall party in the National Council with 55 seats. Since 1959 the confederation has been governed by a coalition of four parties that include the SPP, the Social Democratic Party, the Christian Democratic People's Party and the Radical Democratic Party. Joseph Deiss was elected president on 10 December 2003.

FOREIGN RELATIONS

The Federal Council voted in 1992 to apply for European Community membership. The European Economic Area (EEA) Treaty, which extends the provisions of the EC single internal market to EFTA states, was rejected in a national referendum on 6 December 1992. Switzerland is consequently the only EFTA state outside the EEA. On 21 May 2000, a referendum on seven bilateral agreements with the EU, which would progressively reduce trade barriers and allow the free movement of people between Switzerland and the EU, was passed, with 67.2 per cent of voters in favour. The Swiss administration has continued a policy of long term integration into the EU, but the country has consistently declined EU membership. The latest referendum was voted down in 2001.

Following a referendum held on 3 March 2002 Switzerland formally became a full member of the UN on 10 September 2002.

POLITICAL SYSTEM

The federal government consists of the Federal Assembly of two chambers, a National Council *(Nationalrat)* of 200 members, and a States Council *(Ständerat)* of 46 members (two from each canton and one from each demi-canton). Members of the National Council are elected for four years, elections taking place in October. The executive power is in the hands of a Federal Council (*Bundesrat*) of seven members, elected for four years by the Federal Assembly and presided over by the President of the Confederation. Each year the Federal Assembly elects from the Federal Council the President and the Vice-President. Not more than one person from the same canton may be elected a member of the Federal Council; however, there is a tradition that Italian- and French-speaking areas should between them be represented on the Federal Council by at least two members.

Uniquely, important policy decisions often rest on the results of national referenda. A referendum can be initiated by any citizen able to muster 100,000 voters' signatures in support of holding one on a given issue.

CONFEDERAL STRUCTURE

There are 23 cantons, three of which are subdivided, making 26 in all. Each canton has its own government. The main language in 19 of the cantons is German; in the others it is French (*) or Italian (†).

(Population 2001 census): Aargau (549,500), Appenzell-Ausserrhoden (53,200), Appenzell-Innerrhoden (15,100), Basel-Country (262,300), Basel-Town (187,600), Bern (946,100), *Fribourg (239,200), *Geneva (413,800), Glarus (38,500), Graubünden/ Grischun (187,500), *Jura (68,900), Lucerne (349,600), *Neuchatel (166,600), Nidwalden (38,400), Obwalden (32,700), St Gallen (452,200), Schaffhausen (73,200), Schwyz (133,000), Solothurn (245,100), Thurgau (227,700), †Ticino (312,200), Uri (35,000), *Valais (277,600), *Vaud (625,000), Zug (101,000), Zurich (1,227,900)

SELECTED GOVERNMENT MEMBERS *as at July 2004*

President of the Swiss Confederation, Public Economy (2004), Joseph Deiss

Vice-President, Defence, Civil Protection and Sport (2004), Samuel Schmid

Federal Chancellor, Annemarie Huber-Hotz

Finance, Hans-Rudolf Merz

Foreign Affairs, Micheline Calmy-Rey

EMBASSY OF SWITZERLAND

16–18 Montagu Place, London W1H 2BQ

T 020-7616 6000

Ambassador Extraordinary and Plenipotentiary, HE Bruno Max Spinner, apptd 2000

BRITISH EMBASSY

Thunstrasse 50, CH-3005 Bern

T (+41) (31) 359 7700

E info@britain-in-switzerland.ch

Ambassador Extraordinary and Plenipotentiary, HE Simon Featherstone, apptd 2003

BRITISH COUNCIL DIRECTOR, Caroline Morrissey

Sennweg 2, PO Box 532, CH-3000 Bern 9

T(+31) 301 1473

E britishcouncil@britishcouncil.ch

DEFENCE

The Army has 556 main battle tanks, 1,322 armoured personnel carriers and 435 armoured infantry fighting vehicles. The Air Force has 123 combat aircraft.

MILITARY EXPENDITURE – 1.1 per cent of GDP (2002)

MILITARY PERSONNEL – 3,300 active (351,000 to be mobilised: Army 320,400, Air Force 30,600); Paramilitaries 280,000

CONSCRIPTION DURATION – 15 weeks, then ten refresher courses

ECONOMY AND TRADE

Switzerland has a prosperous and stable modern market economy with low unemployment and a highly skilled labour force. Agriculture is followed chiefly in the valleys and the central plateau, where cereals, flax, hemp, wine and tobacco are produced, and fruits and vegetables are grown. Dairy farming and stock-raising are the principal industries; there are 293,949 hectares of open arable land, 115,933 hectares of cultivated grassland and 626,799 hectares of natural grassland and pasture. The forests cover about 30 per cent of the whole surface. The chief manufacturing industries comprise engineering and electrical engineering, metalworking, chemicals and pharmaceuticals, textiles, watchmaking, woodworking, foodstuffs and footwear. Banking, insurance and tourism are also major industries.

The principal imports are machinery, chemicals, vehicles, metals, textiles, precision instruments, watches and jewellery. The principal exports are machinery, chemicals, precision instruments, watches and jewellery, and metals.

GNI – US$277,200 million (2001); US$38,330 per capita (2001)

ANNUAL AVERAGE GROWTH OF GDP – 3.4 per cent (2000)

INFLATION RATE – 1.6 per cent (2000)

UNEMPLOYMENT – 2.7 per cent (2000)

FOREIGN DIRECT INVESTMENT – US$33,334 million (1997–2000)

IMPORTS – US$79,119 million (2002)

EXPORTS – US$83,912 million (2002)

BALANCE OF PAYMENTS

Trade – US$1,564 million surplus (2001)

Current Account – US$22,624 million surplus (2001)

Trade with UK	*2002*	*2003*
Imports from UK	£3,303,852,000	£2,904,499,000
Exports to UK	4,935,485,000	3,924,072,000

TRANSPORT INFRASTRUCTURE

There are 71,086 km of roads, all of which are surfaced, including 1,613 km of national highways; a further 200 km of motorway construction is expected to be completed by 2010. Railway track comprises 4,511 km, almost all of which is electrified. The Rhine carries heavy shipping traffic on the Basel-Rheinfelden and Schaffhausen-Bodensee stretches, and there are 12 navigable lakes.

EDUCATION

Education is controlled by cantonal and communal authorities and is free and compulsory from age seven to 16. Special schools make a feature of commercial and technical instruction. Universities are Basel (founded 1460), Bern (1834), Fribourg (1889), Geneva (1873), Lausanne (1890), Zurich (1832), and Neuchatel (1909), the technical universities of Lausanne and Zurich and the economics university of St Gall.

ENROLMENT (percentage of age group) – primary 97 per cent (1997); secondary 100 per cent (1997); tertiary 33 per cent (1997)

MEDIA

Switzerland's broadcasting market is dominated by the public-service Swiss Broadcasting Corporation (SRG/SSR) which operates seven TV networks and 18 radio stations, mainly funded through licence fees. There are regional private radio and TV stations operate at a regional level, and television stations from France, Germany and Italy are widely available through multi-channel cable and satellite television. The country's press operates mainly along regional lines which reflects linguistic divisions: there are two German-language dailies based in Zurich, two French-language dailies in Geneva, and an Italian-language daily in Lugano.

CULTURE

Important cultural figures include the writer and philosopher Jean-Jacques Rousseau (1712–78), the psychoanalyst Carl Gustav Jung (1875–1961), the poet Carl Spitteler (1845–1924) who won the Nobel Prize for Literature in 1919, and the writer and founder of modern structural linguistics Ferdinand de Saussure (1857–1913).

SYRIA

Al-Jumhūriyya Al-'Arabiyya as-Sūriyya – Syrian Arab Republic

AREA – 183,800 sq. km. Neighbours: Lebanon (west), Israel and Jordan (south-west), Iraq (east), Turkey (north)
POPULATION – 16,610,000 (2001): mostly Muslim. Arabic is the principal language, but Kurdish, Turkish and Armenian are spoken among significant minorities and a few villages still speak Aramaic, the language spoken by Christ and the Apostles. English has taken over from French as the main foreign language
CAPITAL – Damascus (Dimashq) (population, 1,549,000, 1994)
MAJOR CITIES – Halab (Aleppo); Hamah; Hims; ΨAl-Ladhiqiyah, the principal port
CURRENCY – Syrian pound (S$) of 100 piastres
NATIONAL ANTHEM – Humata Al-Diyari Alaykum Salaam (Defenders Of The Realm On You Be Peace)
NATIONAL DAY – 17 April
NATIONAL FLAG – Red over white over black horizontal bands, with two green stars on central white band
LIFE EXPECTANCY (years) – 71 (2001)
MORTALITY RATES (per 1,000 population) – 5 (2003)
INFANT MORTALITY (per 1,000 births) – 23 (2001)
HIV / AIDS ADULT PREVALENCE – 0.01 per cent (2001)
DEATH PENALTY – Yes
POPULATION GROWTH RATE – 2.7 per cent (1990–2001)
POPULATION DENSITY – 90 per sq. km (2001)
URBAN POPULATION – 52 per cent (2001)

CLIMATE AND TERRAIN

Syria has a Mediterranean climate on the coast characterised by hot dry summers and mild wet winters. The mountainous regions have moderate summers, although the interior plateaux have very hot summers and cold winters while the Hamad region has a desert climate. Average temperatures in Damascus range from 0°C in January to 37°C in August.

Important rivers include the Orontes, which flows northwards from the Lebanon range across the northern boundary to Antakya (Antioch, Turkey) and the Euphrates, which crosses the northern boundary near Jerablus and flows through north-eastern Syria to the boundary of Iraq. The terrain is primarily semi-arid and desert plateau, with a narrow coastal plain and mountains in the west. Elevation extremes range from 2,814 m (Mount Hermon) at the highest point to −200 m (Lake Tiberias) at the lowest.

HISTORY AND POLITICS

Once part of the Ottoman Empire, Syria came under French mandate after the First World War, before becoming an independent republic during the Second World War. The first independently elected parliament met in August 1943, but foreign troops were in occupation until April 1946. Syria remained an independent republic until 1958 when, along with Egypt, it became part of the United Arab Republic, from which seceded September 1961. In 1967 Syria lost the Golan Heights region to Israel.

Elections to the 250-seat People's Council in November 1998 resulted in the National Progressive Front retaining all of its 167 seats unchallenged. This seven-party bloc is dominated by the Ba'ath Party, its allies being the Arab Socialist Union, Socialist Unionist Party, Arab Socialist Movement, Syrian Communist Party and Socialist Unionist Democratic Party.

President Hafez al-Assad, who had seized power in a military coup in 1970 and been elected president in 1971 and re-elected in 1978, 1985, 1992 and 1999, died on 10 June 2000. On 18 June, his son, Bashar al-Assad, was unanimously elected as leader by the Ba'ath Party, and on 10 July he was elected president, gaining 97.29 per cent of the votes cast. Legislative elections took place on 5 March 2003, in which the Ba'ath Party and its allies retained its 167 seats and Independents won 83 seats.

POLITICAL SYSTEM

The Constitution promulgated in 1973 declares that Syria is a democratic, popular socialist state, and that the Arab Socialist Renaissance (Ba'ath) Party, which has been the ruling party since 1963, is the leading party in the state and society. The President is head of state and is elected by parliament for a seven-year term. The legislature, the *Majlis al-Chaab* (People's Council) has 250 members directly elected for a four-year term. The only candidates permitted for elections are from parties allied with the Ba'ath Party or Independents.

HEAD OF STATE
President, Bashar al-Assad, *elected by parliament* 27 June 2000, *approved by referendum* 10 July 2000
Vice-Presidents, Abdel Halim Khaddam; Muhammed Zuheir Mashariqa

SELECTED GOVERNMENT MEMBERS *as at August 2004*
Prime Minister, Mohammed Naji al-Otari
Deputy Prime Minister, Foreign Affairs, Farouk al-Shara
Defence, Lt.-Gen. Hassan Turkmani
Interior, Maj.-Gen. Ali Hammud
Finance, Mohammad al-Husayn
Commerce, Economy and Foreign Trade, Ghassan al-Rifa'i

EMBASSY OF THE SYRIAN ARAB REPUBLIC
8 Belgrave Square, London SW1X 8PH
T 020-7245 9012
Ambassador Extraordinary and Plenipotentiary, Mouafak Nassar, apptd 2002

BRITISH EMBASSY
Kotob Building, 11 Mohammad Kurd Ali Street, Malki, Damascus (PO Box 37)
T (+963) (11) 373 9241/2/3/7
Ambassador Extraordinary and Plenipotentiary, HE Peter Ford, apptd 2003

BRITISH COUNCIL DIRECTOR, Paul Doubleday
Maysaloun Street, Shalaan, PO Box 33105, Damascus
T (+963) (11) 331 0631
E general.enquiries@sy.britishcouncil.org

DEFENCE

The Army has 4,500 main battle tanks, 1,600 armoured personnel carriers and 2,200 armoured infantry fighting vehicles. The Navy has two frigates, 18 patrol and coastal vessels and 16 armed helicopters at three bases. The Air Force has 548 combat aircraft and 71 armed helicopters. Syria maintains a force of some 16,000 men in Lebanon; 1,037 UN troops are deployed on the Golan Heights.

MILITARY EXPENDITURE – 10.3 per cent of GDP (2002)
MILITARY PERSONNEL – 319,000: Army 215,000, Navy 4,000, Air Force 40,000, Air Defence Command 60,000; Paramilitaries 108,000
CONSCRIPTION DURATION – 30 months

ECONOMY AND TRADE

Syria is steadily developing its industrialisation programme which includes leather goods, wool and silk, textiles, vegetable oil, soap, sugar, plastics and metal utensils. Oil production is proceeding in the region of Deir ez Zor and a pipeline has been built to the Mediterranean port of Banias, via Hims. Two oil refineries are in production at Hims and Banias. Oil production in 2002 was 28,600,000 tonnes. Syria also has gas reserves, deposits of phosphate and rock salt, and produces asphalt.

The principal imports are manufactures, metals and metal goods, machinery, foodstuffs and transport equipment. Principal exports include oil and oil derivatives, agricultural products (chiefly fruit and vegetables, cotton and wheat) and textiles.

GNI – US$17,300 million (2001); US$1,040 per capita (2001)
ANNUAL AVERAGE GROWTH OF GDP – 2.8 per cent (2001)
INFLATION RATE – 0.4 per cent (2000)
TOTAL EXTERNAL DEBT – US$21,657 million (2000)
FOREIGN DIRECT INVESTMENT – US$362 million (1997–2000)
IMPORTS – US$19,599 million (2001)
EXPORTS – US$21,648 million (2001)

BALANCE OF PAYMENTS
Trade – US$1,423 million surplus (2000)
Current Account – US$1,062 million surplus (2000)

Trade with UK	*2002*	*2003*
Imports from UK	£83,946,000	£81,963,000
Exports to UK	117,525,000	58,005,000

TRANSPORT INFRASTRUCTURE

A railway track has been opened connecting Hims with Damascus and a track links Hims, Hamah, Halab, Deir ez Zor and Qamishliye to the Iraqi frontier. There are 2,743 km of railways. The country also has 43,381 km of roads, 10,021 km of which are surfaced. All the principal towns are connected by roads which vary from modern dual carriageways to narrow country lanes. An internal air service operates between all major towns, and the main international airport is at Damascus.

EDUCATION

Education is under state control. Elementary education is free at state schools and is compulsory from the age of seven. Secondary education is not compulsory and is free only at the state schools. There are universities at Damascus, Halab, Tishrin, Al-Ladhiqiyah and the Ba'ath University at Hims.

ILLITERACY RATE – (m) 11.7 per cent; (f) 39.5 per cent (2000)
ENROLMENT (percentage of age group) – primary 100 per cent (1997); secondary 43 per cent (1997); tertiary 16 per cent (1997)

MEDIA

In spite of a brief period of press freedom when Bashar al-Assad became president in 2000 and instigated the first licensing of private publications in almost 40 years, most of Syria's print and broadcast media are owned by the government and the Ba'ath Party. There are three state-run television networks, but satellite receivers are permitted and many viewers consequently have access to foreign television broadcasts. Conditions were set out in 2002 for the licensing of private and commercial radio stations.

CULTURE

The region is rich in historical remains. Damascus is said to be the oldest continuously inhabited city in the world, having existed as a city for over 4,000 years. It contains the Omayed Mosque and the Tomb of Saladin, while to the north-east is the Roman outpost of Dmeir and further east is Palmyra. On the Mediterranean coast at Amrit are ruins of the Phoenician town of Marath, and of Crusaders' fortresses at Markab, Sahyoun, and Krak des Chevaliers. One of the oldest alphabets in the world has been discovered at Ugarit (Ras Shamra), a Phoenician village near Al-Lathqiyah. Hittite cities dating from 2000 to 1500 BC, have been explored on the west bank of the Euphrates at Jerablus and Kadesh.

TAIWAN

Chung-hua Min-kuo – Republic of China

AREA – 36,175 sq. km
POPULATION – 22,350,000 (2001). Mandarin Chinese has been the official language since 1949. Now Taiwanese, spoken by 85 per cent of the population, is growing in importance
CAPITAL – ΨTaipei (population, 2,646,474, 2001 estimate)
MAJOR CITIES – ΨKaohsiung; ΨKeelung; Taichung; Tainan
CURRENCY – New Taiwan dollar (NT$) of 100 cents

NATIONAL ANTHEM – San Min Chu I (Our Aim Shall Be To Found A Free Land)
NATIONAL DAY – 10 October
NATIONAL FLAG – Red, with blue quarter at top next staff, bearing a 12-point white sun
LIFE EXPECTANCY (years) – 77 (2001)
MORTALITY RATE (per 1,000 population) – 6.2 (2003)
INFANT MORTALITY (per 1,000 births) – 7 (2001)
DEATH PENALTY – Yes
POPULATION DENSITY – 618 per sq. km (2001)

CLIMATE AND TERRAIN

An island in the China Sea, Taiwan, formerly Formosa, lies 90 miles east of the Chinese mainland. The eastern part of the main island is mountainous and forested. Mt Morrison (Yu Shan) and Mt Sylvia (Tz'ukaoshan) are the highest peaks, and elevation extremes range from 3,952 m (Yu Shan) at the highest point to 0 m (South China Sea) at the lowest.

Territories include the Pescadores Islands (80.47 sq. km), some 56 km west of Taiwan, as well as Kinmen (Quemoy) (109 sq. km) and Matsu (7 sq. km) which are only a few kilometres from mainland China. The climate is tropical, influenced by the monsoons. Typhoons from the South China Sea bring heavy rains between July and September and average temperatures in Taipei range from 12°C in January to 34°C in July.

HISTORY AND POLITICS

Settled for centuries by the Chinese, the island was ceded by China to Japan in 1895 and remained part of the Japanese empire until Japan's defeat in the Second World War. Nationalist Kuomintang (KMT) leader Gen. Chiang Kai-shek withdrew to Taiwan in 1949, towards the end of the war against the Communist regime in mainland China, after which the territory remained under his presidency until his death in 1975. He was succeeded as president by his son Gen. Chiang Ching-kuo who ruled until his death in 1988, when Vice-President Lee Teng-hui was appointed president. Martial law was lifted in 1987 after 38 years.

In 1991, President Lee announced that the 'period of Communist rebellion' on the Chinese mainland was over, recognising *de facto* the People's Republic of China. The announcement also ended emergency measures which had frozen political life on Taiwan since 1949. In 1991–2 power shifted away from mainlanders to native Taiwanese with the forcible retirement of the 'Senior Parliamentarians' who had retained their seats since being elected on the mainland in 1948. The new parliament, the Legislative Yuan, gained control of the budget, of law-making and of the appointment of the prime minister.

President Chen Shui-bian of the Democratic Progressive Party (DPP), in office since May 2000, was re-elected on 20 March 2004 with 51.1 per cent of the vote. In the general election to the Legislative Yuan on 1 December 2001, the DPP won 87 of the 225 seats; the KMT won 68 seats; the People First Party won 46 seats; the Taiwan Solidarity Union won 13 seats; independents and minor parties won 11 seats. President Chen Shui-bian named Yu Shyi Kun as prime minister and he took office on 1 February 2002. Efforts to create a coalition government were rebuffed by the KMT and the Executive Yuan comprises members of the DPP and independents.

FOREIGN RELATIONS

Legally, most nations acknowledge the position of the Chinese government that Taiwan is a province of the People's Republic of China, and as a result Taiwan has formal diplomatic relations with only 26 countries and no seat at the UN.

Direct tourism, trade and communications links between mainland China and the Taiwanese islands of Kinmen and Matsu were inaugurated on 2 January 2001, the first direct links between Taiwan and China since 1949.

POLITICAL SYSTEM

The legislature is bicameral. The Legislative Yuan has 225 members, 176 elected and 49 appointed proportionately by party, and serves a three-year term. Constitutional reforms passed by the Legislative Yuan in 1994 provide for the President and Vice-President to be directly elected for four-year terms (previously the president was elected by parliament). The National Assembly, which had previously been an elected upper chamber, voted on 24 April 2000 to transform itself into a largely ceremonial body, to be convened when necessary to consider constitutional amendments, the impeachment of a President, or territorial changes. Members are appointed proportionally by the parties in the Legislative Yuan.

HEAD OF STATE
President, Chen Shui-bian, *elected* 18 March 2000, *re-elected* 20 March 2004
Vice-President, Annette Lu

SELECTED GOVERNMENT MEMBERS *as at July 2004*
Prime Minister, Yu Shyi-kun
Finance, Lin Chuan
Foreign Affairs, Tan Sun Chen
Interior, Su Jia-chyuan
National Defence, Lee Jye

BRITISH COUNCIL DIRECTOR, Gordon Slaven
7-F-1, British Trade and Cultural Office, Education and Cultural Section, 99 Jen Ai Road, Section 2, Taipei 100
T (+886) (2) 2192 7000
E inquiries@britishcouncil.org.tw

DEFENCE

The Army has 926 main battle tanks, 950 armoured personnel carriers, 225 armoured infantry fighting vehicles and 20 aircraft. The Navy has four submarines, 11 destroyers, 21 frigates, 59 patrol and coastal vessels, 32 combat aircraft and 20 armed helicopters at four bases. The Air Force has 479 combat aircraft.
MILITARY EXPENDITURE– 2.7 per cent of GDP (2002)
MILITARY PERSONNEL – 290,000: Army 200,000, Navy 45,000, Air Force 45,000; Paramilitaries 26,650
CONSCRIPTION DURATION – 22 months

ECONOMY AND TRADE

Taiwan has transformed itself from a mainly agricultural country to a highly developed industrial economy. The industrial base has expanded to include steel, shipbuilding, chemicals, cement, machinery, electrical equipment and textiles, and the island is now one of the world's top producers of computer technology. In 2002 agriculture contributed 2 per cent of GDP, industry 31 per cent and services 67 per cent.

The soil is very fertile, producing sugar, rice, sweet potatoes, tea, fruit and tobacco. Livestock provided a third of the value of Taiwan's agricultural produce in 1996. Taiwan produces one-tenth of its coal needs and some natural gas.

The principal exports are electronic goods, machinery, metal goods, textiles, plastic products, and toys and games. The main imports are oil, chemicals, machinery and natural resources. The main trading partners are China, the USA, Japan, Hong Kong, Germany, and the Republic of Korea.

GNI – US$14,188 million per capita (2001)
IMPORTS – US$112,758 million (2002)
EXPORTS – US$130,457 million (2002)

Trade with UK	*2002*	*2003*
Imports from UK	£853,718,000	£903,977,000
Exports to UK	2,474,824,000	2,254,791,000

TRANSPORT INFRASTRUCTURE

Taiwan has 1,108 km of railways and a total road network of 35,931 km, 31,583 km of which is surfaced (including 608 km of expressways). Major ports and harbours include Keelung, Hua-lien, Kaohsiung, Su-ao and Taichung, and there are international airports at Taoyuan (near Taipei) and Kaohsiung. There are internal flights between all the major cities.

MEDIA AND CULTURE

The media is among the most liberal in Asia. There are some 350 newspapers, all privately owned and reflecting a wide range of views. There are two main Chinese-language dailies, and three published in English.

Traditional Taiwanese culture, based on Buddhism, is very similar to that of China. There is a large number of ornate Buddhist temples and statues, most famously in Tainan on the south-west coast, and religious parades and festivals are common. Chinese opera is an integral part of the culture.

TAJIKISTAN

Çumhurii Toçikiston – Republic of Tajikistan

AREA – 143,100 sq. km. Neighbours: Uzbekistan (north-west), Kyrgyzstan (north-east), China (east), Afghanistan (south)
POPULATION – 6,578,681 (2001 estimate): 62 per cent Tajik, 23 per cent Uzbek and 8 per cent Russian, with smaller numbers of Tatars, Kyrgyz, Germans and Ukrainians. The people are predominantly Sunni Muslim. The main languages are Tajik, Uzbek and Russian. Tajik is close to the Farsi spoken in Iran
CAPITAL – Dushanbe (population, 509,300 1998 estimate)
CURRENCY – Somoni of 100 dirams
NATIONAL DAY – 9 September (Independence Day)
NATIONAL FLAG – Three horizontal stripes of red, white and green with the white of double width and charged with a crown and seven stars, all in gold
MORTALITY RATE (per 1,000 population) – 8.46 (2003)
HIV / AIDS ADULT PREVALENCE – 0.1 per cent (2001)
DEATH PENALTY – Yes
POPULATION GROWTH RATE – 2.1 per cent (2004)
POPULATION DENSITY – 44 per sq. km (1999)
MILITARY EXPENDITURE – 1.7 per cent of GDP (2002)
MILITARY PERSONNEL – Army 6,000; Paramilitaries 1,200
CONSCRIPTION DURATION – Two years
ILLITERACY RATE – (m) 0.4 per cent; (f) 1.2 per cent (2000)
ENROLMENT (percentage of age group) – tertiary 20 per cent (1997)

CLIMATE AND TERRAIN

The country is mountainous with the Pamir highlands in the east and the high ridges of the Pamir-Altai system in the centre. Plains are formed by wide stretches of the Syr-Darya valley in the north and of the Amu-Darya in the south. Elevation extremes range from 7,495 m (Pik Imeni Ismail Samani) at the highest point to 300 m (Syrdariya) at the lowest. The climate is continental with average temperatures ranging from –4°C in January to 18°C in July.

The republic includes the Gorno-Badakhstan Autonomous Province and the Kulyab, Kurgan-Tyubinsk and Khujand Provinces.

HISTORY AND POLITICS

The area that is now Tajikistan was conquered by Alexander the Great in the fourth century BC and remained under Greek and Greco-Persian rule for 200 years, until the Kingdom of Kusha was established, based on Bacharia (Bukhara). Tajikistan was invaded by both the Arabs and the Samanid Persians between the seventh and ninth centuries AD. The cities of Bukhara and Samarkand were two of the most important cultural and educational centres in the Islamic world. The Tajiks lived under the control of various feudal emirates until the area was subsumed within the Russian Empire in 1868. At the time of the Russian revolution in 1917 the central Asian emirates attempted to re-establish their independence. Soviet power was re-established in northern Tajikistan by 1 April 1918, when the Turkestan Soviet Socialist Republic was formed, and the Bukhara emirate was overthrown by Soviet forces in 1920. In 1924 the Tajikistan Autonomous Soviet Socialist Republic was formed as part of the Uzbek Republic, before Tajikistan was given full republican status within the Soviet Union in 1929.

Tajikistan declared independence from the Soviet Union on 9 September 1991. The Islamic-Democratic Alliance formed a government in September 1992 but civil war broke out as forces loyal to the former Communist regime rebelled against the new government. By early November, pro-Communist forces controlled virtually all of the country and the Supreme Soviet installed Emomaly Rakhmonov as its Speaker and head of state.

A cease-fire in October 1994 allowed presidential and parliamentary elections to be held, which were won by Rakhmonov and the ruling (former Communist) People's Democratic Party of Tajikistan (HDKT), although the elections were boycotted by most opposition groups. Fighting restarted in early 1995. A peace agreement was signed in December 1996 which provided for the formation of a National Reconciliation Commission (NRC), a general amnesty and an exchange of prisoners. The agreement has held, although there have been sporadic outbreaks of violence since it was signed.

Presidential elections which took place on 6 November 1999 resulted in a landslide victory for the incumbent President Rakhmonov, who gained over 96 per cent of the vote in a poll which the Organisation for Security and

Co-operation in Europe had refused to monitor due to restrictions imposed on candidates and political parties. Akil Akilov was named as prime minister on 20 December. Following an election to the Assembly of Representatives in February and March 2000, the HDKT won 30 of the 63 seats, the Communist Party won 13 seats, the Islamic Renaissance Party won 2 and independent candidates won 15, with three seats remaining vacant.

POLITICAL SYSTEM
Under new constitutional arrangements agreed in late 1999, the President serves a single seven-year term. However, amendments made in early 2003 permit the current incumbent to stand for two further terms after his current term finishes in 2006. The bicameral legislature consists of a 63-seat *Majlisi Mamoyandogan* (Assembly of Representatives), which is directly elected and serves a five-year term, and the *Majlisi Milli* (National Assembly), which has 33 members, 25 of which are elected for a five-year term by five regional assemblies and eight are appointed by the President. Administratively Tajikistan is divided into two regions and one autonomous region.

HEAD OF STATE
President, Emomaly Sharifovich Rakhmonov, *elected by Supreme Soviet* 19 November 1992, *elected* 6 November 1994, *re-elected* 6 November 1999

SELECTED GOVERNMENT MEMBERS *as at July 2004*
Prime Minister, Akil Akilov
First Deputy Prime Minister, Relations with CIS States, Haji Akbar Turajonzoda
Deputy Prime Ministers, Kozidavlat Koimdodov; Khairinisso Mavlonova; Zokir Vazirov; Maj.-Gen. Saidamir Zuhurov; Asadullo Ghulomov *(Energy)*
Defence, Col.-Gen. Sherali Khayrulloyev
Finance, Safarali Najmiddinov
Foreign Affairs, Talbak Nazarov
Interior, Khumdin Sharipov

BRITISH EMBASSY
43 Lufti Street, Dushanbe 734017
T (+992) (91) 901 5079
Ambassador Extraordinary and Plenipotentiary, HE Michael Smith, apptd 2001

ECONOMY AND TRADE
In spite of steady progress since the end of the civil war, Tajikistan's economy is fragile. A debt restructuring agreement was reached with Russia in December 2002, and the country has received more than $60 million in aid from the USA. Although only around five per cent of the land is arable, agriculture is the major sector of the economy, concentrating on cotton-growing and cattle-breeding. Tajikistan also has rich mineral deposits of mercury, lead, zinc, oil, gold and uranium. Industry specialises in the production of clothing and textiles.
GNI – US$1,102 million (2000); US$180 per capita (2001)
ANNUAL AVERAGE GROWTH OF GDP – 8.3 per cent (2000)
INFLATION RATE – 12 per cent (2001)
TOTAL EXTERNAL DEBT – US$1,000 million (2002)

Trade with UK	*2002*	*2003*
Imports from UK	£707,000	£2,320,000
Exports to UK	1,581,000	1,417,000

TRANSPORT INFRASTRUCTURE
The country has 482 km of railways, and a total of 27,767 km of roads. However, many roads, including the main highway from Dushanbe to Khujand, are only open in the summer months.

MEDIA AND CULTURE
Broadcasting is dominated by state-run radio and television, alongside more than 30 local and regional private television stations and a few private radio stations. Tajikistan also has more than 200 registered newspapers, some government owned and others linked to political parties and movements.

Tajikistan has an ancient heritage and figures from its Persian past are still venerated. Cultural figures include the philosopher Abu Ali ibn Sina (980–1037) and Firdausi (*c.* 934–1032), a poet and composer of the *Shahnameh* (Book of Kings).

TANZANIA

Jamhuri ya Muungano wa Tanzania/United Republic of Tanzania

AREA – 883,600 sq. km. Neighbours: Kenya and Uganda (north), Mozambique (south), Malawi and Zambia (south-west), Rwanda, Burundi and the Democratic Republic of Congo (west)
POPULATION – 35,965,000 (2001). Africans form a large majority, with European, Asian, and other non-African minorities. The African population consists mostly of tribes of mixed Bantu race. The official languages are Swahili and English
CAPITAL – Dodoma (population, 1,502,344, 1995)
MAJOR CITIES – ΨDar es Salaam, the economic and administrative centre; Mbeya; Mwanza; ΨTanga
CURRENCY – Tanzanian shilling of 100 cents
NATIONAL ANTHEM – Mungu Ibariki Afrika (God Bless Africa)
NATIONAL DAY – 26 April (Union Day)
NATIONAL FLAG – Green (above) and blue; divided by diagonal black stripe bordered by gold, running from bottom (next staff) to top (in fly)
LIFE EXPECTANCY (years) – 51 (2001)
MORTALITY RATE (per 1,000 population) – 17.38 (2003)
INFANT MORTALITY (per 1,000 births) – 104 (2001)
HIV / AIDS ADULT PREVALENCE – 7.8 per cent (2001)
DEATH PENALTY – Yes
POPULATION BELOW POVERTY LINE – 30 per cent (2002)
POPULATION GROWTH RATE – 2.9 per cent (1990–2001)
POPULATION DENSITY – 41 per sq. km (2001)
MILITARY EXPENDITURE – 1.5 per cent of GDP (2002)

MILITARY PERSONNEL – 27,000: Army 23,000, Navy 1,000, Air Force 3,000; Paramilitaries 1,400
CONSCRIPTION DURATION – Two years

CLIMATE AND TERRAIN

Tanzania comprises the former Tanganyika, on the mainland of east Africa, and the island of Zanzibar. The greater part of the country is occupied by the central African plateau from which rise, among others, Mount Kilimanjaro (5,894 m), the highest point on the continent of Africa, and Mount Meru (4,564 m). The Serengeti National Park covers an area of 9,656 sq. km in the Arusha, Mwanza and Mara Regions. The climate is tropical equatorial, modified by altitude. The north has two distinct wet seasons with the longest from March to May and the shortest from November to December while the rest of the country has one wet season from November to May. The average temperature in Dar es Salaam is 29°C all year round.

HISTORY AND POLITICS

Tanganyika became an independent state and a member of the British Commonwealth on 9 December 1961, and a republic within the Commonwealth on 9 December 1962. Zanzibar, comprising the islands of Zanzibar, Pemba and Mafia, was formerly ruled by the Sultan of Zanzibar and was a British Protectorate until 10 December 1963 when it became an independent state within the Commonwealth. On 26 April 1964 Tanganyika united with Zanzibar to form the United Republic of Tanzania.

The sole legal political party from 1977 to 1992 was the Chama Cha Mapinduzi, the Revolutionary Party of Tanzania (CCM). The constitution was amended in 1992 to allow multiparty politics, with the stipulation that all parties must be active in both the mainland and in Zanzibar and that parties must not be formed on regional, religious, tribal or racial grounds.

The first multiparty presidential and parliamentary elections were held in October and November 1995 and were won by the CCM.

Presidential and general elections were last held on 29 October 2000. President Mkapa was re-elected, winning 71.7 per cent of the vote, and the CCM won an overwhelming majority in the National Assembly.

The November 2000 presidential and legislative elections in Zanzibar, saw Amani Abeid Karume, the CCM candidate, elected as president and the CCM win a majority in the National Assembly. However, the results of the legislative elections were annulled in 16 of the 50 constituencies by the National Electoral Commission because of irregularities. A re-run was held in the 16 constituencies on 5 November, and all 16 seats were won by the CCM.

POLITICAL SYSTEM

The President is directly elected and may serve two five-year terms. The National Assembly contains up to 296 members, of whom 280 are directly elected, five are chosen by the Zanzibar House of Representatives, up to ten members are appointed by the President and one seat is reserved for the Attorney-General. Constituency members are elected at a general election held at a maximum of five-yearly intervals. The Assembly enacts laws that apply to the entire United Republic of Tanzania, and those that apply only to the mainland; laws that apply specifically to Zanzibar are enacted by the island's own President, Government and 50-member House of Representatives. The President of Zanzibar is also a member of the National Assembly.

HEAD OF STATE
President of the United Republic, Benjamin Mkapa, *elected* 29 October 1995, *re-elected* 5 November 2000
Vice-President, Ali Mohamed Sheni
President of Zanzibar, Amani Abeid Karume

SELECTED GOVERNMENT MEMBERS *as at July 2004*
Prime Minister, Frederick Sumaye
Defence, Philemon Sarungi
Finance, Basil Mramba
Foreign Affairs and International Co-operation, Jakaya Kikwete
Home Affairs, Mohammed Seif Khatib

HIGH COMMISSION FOR THE UNITED REPUBLIC OF TANZANIA
43 Hertford Street, London W1Y 8DB
T 020-7499 8951/4
High Commissioner, HE Hassan Omar Gumbo Kibelloh, apptd 2002

BRITISH HIGH COMMISSION
Umoja House, Garden Avenue (PO Box 9200), Dar es Salaam
T (+255) (22) 211 0101
High Commissioner, HE Andrew Pocock, apptd 2003

BRITISH COUNCIL DIRECTOR, Tom Cowin
Samora Avenue/Ohio Street, PO Box 9100, Dar es Salaam
T (+255) (22) 211 6574
E info@britishcouncil.or.tz

ECONOMY AND TRADE

Progress is being made in updating Tanzania's economic infrastructure in conjunction with the World Bank and International Monetary Fund; there has been a substantial increase in output of minerals (chiefly gold), and banking reforms have helped increase private sector growth and investment.

The islands of Zanzibar and Pemba produce a large part of the world's supply of cloves and clove oil; coconuts, coconut oil and copra are also produced. Tanzania's chief exports are coffee, cotton and cashew nuts. The chief imports are capital equipment, oil and oil derivatives, and consumer goods. Industry, which accounts for 16 per cent of GDP, is largely concerned with the processing of raw material for export or local consumption.

GNI – US$9,400 million (2001); US$270 per capita (2001)
ANNUAL AVERAGE GROWTH OF GDP – 3.8 per cent (1998)
INFLATION RATE – 5.9 per cent (2000)
TOTAL EXTERNAL DEBT – US$7,445 million (2000)
FOREIGN DIRECT INVESTMENT – US$706 million (1997–2000)
IMPORTS – US$1,712 million (2000)
EXPORTS – US$776 million (2000)

BALANCE OF PAYMENTS
Trade – US$674 million deficit (2000)
Current Account – US$480 million deficit (2000)

Trade with UK	*2002*	*2003*
Imports from UK	£61,343,000	£56,514,000
Exports to UK	38,967,000	34,087,000

TRANSPORT INFRASTRUCTURE

Tanzania has a total of 88,200 km of roads, only 3,704 km of which are surfaced. The main ports are Dar es Salaam, Tanga, Mtwara, Zanzibar, Mkoani and Wete, in addition to Mwanza, Musoma and Bukoba on Lake Victoria and Kigoma on Lake Tanganyika. Coastal shipping services connect the mainland to Zanzibar, and lake services are operated on Lake Tanganyika and Lake Malawi with neighbouring countries. The principal international airports are Dar es Salaam, Kilimanjaro and Zanzibar, and two airlines – Air Tanzania and Precision Air – operate domestic flights. There are two railway systems; one connecting Dar es Salaam to Zambia, and the second having two main lines running from Dar es Salaam, one to northern Tanzania and Kenya and the other to Lakes Tanganyika and Victoria.

EDUCATION

The school system is administered in Swahili but the government is making efforts to improve English standards for the purposes of secondary and higher education. There are three institutes of higher education.

ILLITERACY RATE – (m) 15.3 per cent; (f) 32.9 per cent (2000)

ENROLMENT (percentage of age group) – primary 67 per cent (1997); tertiary 1 per cent (1997)

MEDIA AND CULTURE

There are many state-owned and private newspapers available in Tanzania and popular titles include *Daily News, The Express* and *Uhuru*. Radio is prevalent in urban areas and channels include Radio Free Africa and Radio Tanzania Dar es Salaam. State television was officially launched in 2001, several years after the first private television station opened in 1994, but does not yet have national coverage. Zanzibar has a different, less liberal, media policy and there are no private broadcasters or newspapers on the island, although locals can access mainland media.

Culturally, Tanzanian music and dance dominates much of East Africa and there is a thriving dance-band scene while Zanzibar is at the heart of the distinctive *taraab*, or sung poetry, tradition. Penina Muhando (b. 1948) is one of Tanzania's most prominent writers.

THAILAND

Prathes Thai – Kingdom of Thailand

AREA – 510,900 sq. km. Neighbours: Malaysia (south), Myanmar (west), Laos and Cambodia (east)

POPULATION – 63,584,000 (2001). The principal language is Thai, a monosyllabic, tonal language of the Indo-Chinese linguistic family, with a vocabulary strongly influenced by Sanskrit and Pali. It is written in an alphabetic script derived from ancient Indian scripts. Significant minorities speak Chinese (in urban areas), Lao (in the north-east), Khmer (in the east) and Malay (in the far south). The principal religion is Buddhism (94.37 per cent), with Muslim and Christian minorities

CAPITAL – ΨBangkok (population, 5,882,000, 1998 estimate)

MAJOR CITIES – Chiang Mai; Chon Buri; Nakhon Ratchasima; Nanthanburi; Songkhla

CURRENCY – Baht of 100 satang

NATIONAL ANTHEM – Pleng Chart (National Anthem)

NATIONAL DAY – 5 December (The King's Birthday)

NATIONAL FLAG – Five horizontal bands, red, white, dark blue, white, red (the blue band twice the width of the others)

LIFE EXPECTANCY (years) – 70 (2001)

MORTALITY RATE (per 1,000 population) – 6.86 (2003)

INFANT MORTALITY (per 1,000 births) – 24 (2001)

HIV / AIDS ADULT PREVALENCE – 1.8 per cent (2001)

DEATH PENALTY – Yes

POPULATION BELOW POVERTY LINE – 12.5 per cent (2001)

POPULATION GROWTH RATE – 1.4 per cent (1990–2001)

POPULATION DENSITY – 124 per sq. km (2001)

CLIMATE AND TERRAIN

Thailand, formerly known as Siam, is divided geographically into four regions: the centre is a plain; to the north-east there is a plateau area and to the north-west mountains. The south of Thailand consists of a narrow mountainous peninsula. The principal rivers are the Chao Phraya in the central plains, and the Mekong on the northern and north-eastern borders. Extremes of elevation range from 2,576 m (Doi Inthanon) at the highest point to 0 m (Gulf of Thailand) at the lowest. The climate is tropical and average temperatures in Bangkok range from 20°C in January to 35°C in July.

HISTORY AND POLITICS

The Thai nation was founded in the 13th century and although it was occupied by Burma in the 18th century, Thailand remained the only country in the region not to have been colonised by a European power.

Following a revolution in 1932, Thailand became a constitutional monarchy. After a military coup in February 1991, a new constitution was approved under which the military would have significant political power. Parties aligned with the military won the general election in March 1992, but mass demonstrations held in Bangkok, with the help of the King, forced the government from power. Military power was curbed, the 1978 constitution was restored and the interim government sacked military chiefs.

Parliamentary elections in September 1992 resulted in a majority for those parties not allied with the military. The first election to the Senate was held on 4 March 2000. A re–run was held in 78 seats on 29 April following evidence of fraud. Further re-runs were necessary for some seats.

A general election took place on 6 January 2001. The Thai Rak Thai (TRT) party won 248 seats, and its leader – Thaksin Shinawatra – became president. The TRT formed a coalition government with the Chart Thai party and the New Aspiration party.

FOREIGN RELATIONS

Laos occupied two Thai islands in the Mekong river on 19 August 2000 and evicted the inhabitants, claiming that it had jurisdiction over all the islands in the Mekong under a 1926 treaty.

In January 2003 serious diplomatic unrest with Cambodia followed accusations by a Thai actress that Cambodia's Angkor Wat temple complex was stolen from Thailand. The Thai embassy was attacked by angry crowds and more than 500 Thai nationals were evacuated using military planes.

POLITICAL SYSTEM
The Constitution provides for a National Assembly consisting of a 200-member Senate, directly elected on a non-party basis for a six-year term, and a 500-member House of Representatives elected by universal adult suffrage, 400 elected in single-member constituencies and 100 from party lists, for a term of four years.

HEAD OF STATE
HM The King of Thailand, King Bhumibol Adulyadej, *born* 5 December 1927; *succeeded* 9 June 1946
Heir, HRH Crown Prince Maha Vajiralongkorn, *born* 28 July 1952

SELECTED GOVERNMENT MEMBERS *as at July 2004*
Prime Minister, Thaksin Shinawatra
Defence, Chetta Thanajaro
Finance, Somkid Jatusripitak
Foreign Affairs, Surakiet Sathirathai
Interior, Bhokin Bhalakula

ROYAL THAI EMBASSY
29–30 Queen's Gate, London SW7 5JB
T 020-7589 2944
Ambassador Extraordinary and Plenipotentiary, HE Vikrom Koompirochana, apptd 2003

BRITISH EMBASSY
1031 Wireless Road, Lumpini, Pathumwan, Bangkok 10330
T (+662) 305 8333
Ambassador Extraordinary and Plenipotentiary, HE David Fall, apptd 2003

BRITISH COUNCIL DIRECTOR, Peter Upton
254 Chulalongkorn Soi 64, Siam Square, Phayathai Road, Pathumwan, Bangkok 10330 T (+662) 652 5480
E info@britishcouncil.or.tz

DEFENCE
The Army has 333 main battle tanks, 946 armoured personnel carriers and three attack helicopters. The Navy has one aircraft carrier, 12 frigates, 115 patrol and coastal vessels, 44 combat aircraft and eight armed helicopters at five bases. The Air Force has 194 combat aircraft.
MILITARY EXPENDITURE – 1.5 per cent of GDP (2002)
MILITARY PERSONNEL – 314,200: Army 190,000, Navy 79,200, Air Force 45,000; Paramilitaries 113,000

ECONOMY AND TRADE
Thailand was one of the countries worst affected by the economic crisis in south-east Asia in 1997. The stock market fell to an eight-year low and the currency was devalued by 20 per cent, triggering a currency crisis throughout south-east Asia. An IMF loan of US$16.7 billion was announced in return for emergency financial reforms, but the economy continued to contract for another couple of years. However, following a change in government and implementation of remedial measures, the country recovered; it was one of East Asia's best performers in 2002, and GDP grew to 6.3 per cent in 2003.

The agricultural sector employs around half of the labour force. Rice remains the most important crop; other main crops are sugar, maize, sorghum, cassava, rubber, tobacco, kenaf and jute. In recent years fishing and livestock production have gained importance. There are reserves of oil, natural gas and lignite; mineral resources include tin, tungsten, lead and iron.

Important industrial sectors include textiles, transportation vehicles and equipment, construction materials, brewing, petroleum refining, electrical appliances, plastics, computers and parts, and integrated circuits. In 2002, industry contributed 42 per cent of GDP. Since 1982 tourism has been the main foreign exchange earner. In 1998, there were 7.8 million foreign visitors.

Thailand's main exports are computers and parts, cars, integrated circuit boards, precious stones, rice, maize, canned seafood, fabrics, sugar and tin. Main imports are crude oil, chemicals, electrical goods, industrial machinery, iron, steel and transport equipment.
GNI – US$118,500 million (2001); US$1,940 per capita (2001)
ANNUAL AVERAGE GROWTH OF GDP – 4.4 per cent (2000)
INFLATION RATE – 1.5 per cent (2000)
UNEMPLOYMENT – 2.4 per cent (2000)
TOTAL EXTERNAL DEBT– US$79,675 million (2000)
FOREIGN DIRECT INVESTMENT – US$20,265 million (1997–2000)
IMPORTS – US$64,720 million (2002)
EXPORTS – US$68,853 million (2002)

BALANCE OF PAYMENTS
Trade – US$9,775 million surplus (2002)
Current Account – US$7,650 million surplus (2002)

Trade with UK	*2002*	*2003*
Imports from UK	£532,348,000	£572,692,000
Exports to UK	1,608,303,000	1,687,385,000

TRANSPORT INFRASTRUCTURE
Thailand has a total of 64,600 km of roads, almost all of which are surfaced, and around 4,071 km of railways. Bangkok is the international airport, though airports at Chiang Mai, Phuket and Hat Yai also receive international flights. There are two important ports in the country, Bangkok and Sattahip, and 3,999 km of principal waterways, some 3,701 km of which are navigable.

EDUCATION
Primary education is compulsory and free, and secondary education in government schools is free. Private universities and colleges are playing an increasing role in higher education. There are 62 higher institutes of learning.
ILLITERACY RATE – (m) 2.8 per cent; (f) 6.1 per cent (2000)
ENROLMENT (percentage of age group) – tertiary 22 per cent (1997)

MEDIA
The government and military control nearly all the national terrestrial television networks and operate many of the country's radio networks. However, media reforms are currently in progress, aimed at reducing military interest and opening up more opportunities to the private sector. The radio market, particularly in Bangkok, is already fiercely competitive, with more than 60 stations in and around the capital. Newspapers are largely privately-run, with popular titles including *Bangkok Post* and *Thairata.*

CULTURE

Thailand's countryside is rich with Buddhist temples and archaeological remains. Most notable is Ayuthaya, 85 km north of Bangkok, the capital of the Siamese dynasties from 1350, whose scattered temples and ruins have been declared a World Heritage Site. Nakhon Pathom is the country's oldest city, and is home to the sixth century Phra Pathom Chedi, which at 127 m high is the tallest Buddhist monument in the world.

TOGO

République Togolaise – Togolese Republic

AREA – 56,785 sq. km. Neighbours: Ghana (west), Burkina Faso (north), Benin (east)
POPULATION – 5,153,088 (2001 estimate). The official language is French; Ewe, Watchi and Kabiyé are the main indigenous languages
CAPITAL – ΨLomé (population, 700,000, 1997 estimate)
CURRENCY – Franc CFA of 100 centimes
NATIONAL ANTHEM – Écartons Tous Mauvais Esprit Qui Gêne L'unité Nationale (Let Us Discard All Ill Feelings Which Harm National Unity)
NATIONAL DAY – 27 April
NATIONAL FLAG – Five alternating green and yellow horizontal stripes; a quarter in red at top next staff bearing a white star
MORTALITY RATE (per 1,000 population) – 11.51 (2003)
HIV / AIDS ADULT PREVALENCE – 6 per cent (2001)
DEATH PENALTY – Yes
POPULATION GROWTH RATE – 2.6 per cent (1990–2001)
POPULATION DENSITY – 79 per sq. km (1999)
MILITARY EXPENDITURE – 1.8 per cent of GDP (2002)
MILITARY PERSONNEL – 8,550: Army 8,100, Navy 200, Air Force 250; Paramilitaries 750
CONSCRIPTION DURATION– Two years (selective)
ILLITERACY RATE – (m) 25.5 per cent; (f) 59.2 per cent (2000)
ENROLMENT (percentage of age group) – primary 100 per cent (1997); secondary 27 per cent (1997); tertiary 4 per cent (1997)

CLIMATE AND TERRAIN

Togo's climate is tropical with two wet seasons (March to July and September to November). The average temperature in Lome is 27°C all year round. From hills in the centre of the country, the terrain flattens out to savannah in the north and a plateau leading to a marshy coastal plain in the south. Elevation extremes range from 986 m (Mount Agou) at the highest point to 0 m (Atlantic Ocean) at the lowest.

HISTORY AND POLITICS

The first president of Togo, Sylvanus Olympio, was assassinated in 1963. In 1967, there was an army coup d'état and the army commander Lt.-Col. (later Gen.) Eyadéma named himself president. In April 1990, following increasing popular pressure, the government was forced to concede a political amnesty, the introduction of a multiparty constitution and a national conference. In August 1991 the national conference stripped President Eyadéma of all powers, banned the *Rassemblement du peuple togolais* (RPT), which had been the sole legal party, and elected Kokou Koffigoh as prime minister of an interim government. Troops loyal to President Eyadéma attempted to overthrow Koffigoh three times (in October, November and December 1991) but were frustrated by pro-democracy supporters. A new multiparty constitution was approved by referendum in September 1992. In November, Eyadéma, who had regained the position of head of state in August 1992, ordered the Army to crush civil unrest and a general strike against his rule. In February 1993, as violence continued, Koffigoh and Eyadéma agreed on the formation of a crisis government, which the national conference and the Collective Democratic Opposition-2 (COD-2) declared illegal.

The 1998 presidential election was won by Gen. Eyadéma. Legislative elections were announced unexpectedly in September 2002 following repeat postponing and re-scheduling between 2000–2; the election took place on 27 October. The RPT won an overall majority in the National Assembly winning 72 of the 81 seats. In the 2003 presidential election Eyadéma was re-elected with 57.2 per cent of the vote. The government resigned on 24 June 2003 after the president's re-inauguration and Eyadéma stated he intended to appoint a new government of national unity under Prime Minister Koffi Sama, who was re-appointed on 1 July 2003.

HEAD OF STATE
President, Gen. Gnassingbé Eyadéma, *assumed office* 14 April 1967 *re-elected* 1986, 1993, 21 June 1998, 1 June 2003

SELECTED GOVERNMENT MEMBERS *as at July 2004*
Prime Minister, Koffi Sama
Economic Affairs, Finance and Privatisation, Débaba Bale
Interior, Security and Decentralisation, Mj. Akila Esso Boko
Foreign Affairs and Co-operation, Kokou Tozoun
National Defence and Veterans, Brig.-Gen. Assani Tidjani

EMBASSY OF THE REPUBLIC OF TOGO
8 rue Alfred-Roll, F-75017 Paris, France
T (+33) (1) 4380 1213
Ambassador Extraordinary and Plenipotentiary, HE Sotou Bere, apptd 2003

BRITISH AMBASSADOR, HE Rod Pullen, resident at Accra, Ghana

ECONOMY AND TRADE

Although the economy remains largely agricultural, exports of phosphates have superseded agricultural products as the main source of export earnings. Other exports include palm kernels, copra and manioc.

In December 1998 the EU announced that it would not resume developmental aid to Togo following irregularities in the country's election process.
GNI – US$1,279 million (2001); US$270 per capita (2001)
ANNUAL AVERAGE GROWTH OF GDP – 2.7 per cent (2001)
INFLATION RATE – 1.9 per cent (2000)

TOTAL EXTERNAL DEBT – US$1,435 million (2000)
IMPORTS – US$591 million (2002)
EXPORTS – US$250 million (2002)

BALANCE OF PAYMENTS
Trade – US$123 million deficit (2000)
Current Account – US$140 million deficit (2000)

Trade with UK	*2002*	*2003*
Imports from UK	£25,845,000	£38,055,000
Exports to UK	1,547,000	981,000

TRANSPORT INFRASTRUCTURE

Togo has about 7,500 km of roads, of which approximately one third is surfaced; there are also about 500 km of railways. The chief waterway is the Mono river, and the main ports are Lome and Kpeme.

MEDIA

Television Togolaise is the sole national television station, and is government owned. The government owns the national radio station, Radiodiffusion Togolaise, and, in association with the RPT, some of the private stations. Togo's only daily newspaper, the *Togo-Presse*, is also government owned.

TONGA

Pule'anga Tonga/Kingdom of Tonga

AREA – 650 sq. km
POPULATION – 104,227 (2001 estimate). The languages are Tongan and English
CAPITAL – ΨNuku'alofa (population, 34,000, 1990), on Tongatapu
CURRENCY – Pa'anga (T$) of 100 seniti
NATIONAL ANTHEM – E, 'Otua Mafimafi (Oh, Almighty God Above)
NATIONAL DAY – 4 June (Emancipation Day)
NATIONAL FLAG – Red with a white canton containing a couped red cross
MORTALITY RATE (per 1,000 population) – 5.54 (2003)
DEATH PENALTY – No (abolished 1982)
POPULATION GROWTH RATE – 1.9 per cent (2004)
POPULATION DENSITY – 151 per sq. km (1999)

CLIMATE AND TERRAIN

Tonga comprises a group of islands situated in the southern Pacific some 724 km east-south-east of Fiji. Most of the islands are of coral formation, but some are volcanic (Tofua, Kao and Niuafoou or 'Tin Can' Island) and elevation extremes range from 1,033 m (unnamed location on Kao island) at the highest point to 0 m (Pacific Ocean) at the lowest. The climate is subtropical, influenced by prevailing south-west trade winds with average temperatures 26°C all year round.

HISTORY AND POLITICS

The Kingdom of Tonga is an independent constitutional monarchy within the Commonwealth. Prior to 4 June 1970 it had been a British-protected state for 70 years. The constitution provides for a government consisting of the Sovereign, an appointed privy council which functions as a cabinet, a legislative assembly and a judiciary. The 30-member legislative assembly comprises the King, the 11-member privy council, nine hereditary nobles elected by their peers, and nine popularly elected representatives who hold office for three years. The most recent election took place on 7 March 2002 when the Human Rights and Democracy Movement won seven of the popularly elected seats in the Legislative Assembly. In October 2003 constitutional changes gave greater power to the King, that included extended influence over the Legislative Assembly (*Fale Alea*).

HEAD OF STATE
King of Tonga, HM King Taufa'ahau Tupou IV, GCMG, GCVO, KBE, *born* 4 July 1918, *acceded* 16 December 1965
Heir, HRH Crown Prince Tupouto'a

SELECTED GOVERNMENT MEMBERS *as at July 2004*
Prime Minister, Agriculture and Fisheries, Civil Aviation and Communications, Foreign Affairs and Defence, HRH Prince 'Ulukalala Lavaka Ata
Deputy Prime Minister, Works, Marines and Ports and Environment, Cecil Cocker
Finance, Siosiua 'Utoikamanu
Governor of Ha'apai, Malupo
Governor of Vava'u, Akau'ola

TONGA HIGH COMMISSION
36 Molyneux Street, London W1H 5BQ
T 020-7724 5828
High Commissioner, HE Col. Fetu'utolu Tupou, apptd 2000

BRITISH HIGH COMMISSION
PO Box 56, Nuku'alofa
T (+676) 24285/24395
E britcomt@kalianet.to
High Commissioner, HE Paul Nessling, apptd 2002

ECONOMY AND TRADE

The economy is primarily agricultural; the main crops are coconuts, vanilla, yams, taro, cassava, groundnuts, squash pumpkins and other fruit. Fish is an important staple food, though recent shortfalls have led to canned fish being imported. Industry is based on the processing of agricultural produce, and the manufacture of foodstuffs, clothing and sports equipment. Tourism is also important.

The principal exports are fish and vanilla. The principal imports are manufactures, foodstuffs, machinery and transport equipment and combustible fuels.

GNI – US$154 million (2000); US$1,530 per capita (2000)
ANNUAL AVERAGE GROWTH OF GDP – 0.3 per cent (1998)
INFLATION RATE – 5.9 per cent (2000)
TOTAL EXTERNAL DEBT– US$58 million (2000)
IMPORTS – US$73 million (2001)
EXPORTS – US$7 million (2001)

Trade with UK	*2002*	*2003*
Imports from UK	£810,000	£1,059,000
Exports to UK	29,000	57,000

TRANSPORT INFRASTRUCTURE AND MEDIA

There are 680 km of roads in Tonga, 180 km of which are surfaced. Its principal ports are Neiafu, Nuku'alofa, and Pangai.

The government-run broadcasters are Television Tonga

and A3Z Radio Tonga. The weekly newspaper is *Tonga Chronicle*, which is also owned by the state.

TRINIDAD AND TOBAGO

The Republic of Trinidad and Tobago

AREA – 5,100 sq. km
POPULATION – 1,300,000 (2001). The language is English. The main religions are Roman Catholicism (29.4 per cent of the population), Hinduism (23.8 per cent); Anglicanism (10.9 per cent); Islam (5.8 per cent) and Presbyterianism (3.4 per cent)
CAPITAL – ΨPort of Spain (population, 49,031, 2000 census)
MAJOR CITIES – San Fernando; ΨScarborough, the main town of Tobago
CURRENCY – Trinidad and Tobago dollar (TT$) of 100 cents
NATIONAL ANTHEM – Forged From The Love Of Liberty
NATIONAL DAY – 31 August (Independence Day)
NATIONAL FLAG – Black diagonal stripe bordered with white stripes, running from top by staff, all on a red field
LIFE EXPECTANCY (years) – 75 (2001)
MORTALITY RATE (per 1,000 population) – 8.71 (2003)
INFANT MORTALITY (per 1,000 births) – 17 (2001)
HIV / AIDS ADULT PREVALENCE – 2.5 per cent (2001)
DEATH PENALTY – Yes
POPULATION GROWTH RATE – 0.6 per cent (1990–2001)
POPULATION DENSITY – 255 per sq. km (2001)
MILITARY EXPENDITURE – 0.7 per cent of GDP (2002)
MILITARY PERSONNEL – 2,700: Army 2,000, Coast Guard 700

CLIMATE AND TERRAIN

Trinidad, the most southerly of the West Indian islands, lies seven miles off the north coast of Venezuela. The island is approximately 80 km in length by 59 km in width. Two mountain systems, the Northern and Southern Ranges, stretch across almost its entire width and a third, the Central Range, lies diagonally across its middle portion; otherwise the island is mostly flat. Elevation extremes range from 940 m (El Cerro del Aripol) at the highest point to 0 m (Caribbean Sea) at the lowest. Tobago lies 30 km north-east of Trinidad. The island is 51 km long at its widest point, and 17 km wide. Corozal Point and Icacos Point, the north-west and south-west extremities of Trinidad, enclose the Gulf of Paria. West of Corozal Point lie several islands, of which Chacachacare, Huevos, Monos and Gaspar Grande are the most important. There is a wet season from June to December and the average temperature in the coastal regions is 27°C all year round.

HISTORY AND POLITICS

Trinidad is assumed to be the oldest site of human habitation in the Caribbean Archipelago, with excavated human remains dating back some 7,200 years. For much of its history, the islands were home to the Nepuyo, Yaio and QuaQua peoples.

Trinidad was discovered by Columbus in 1498, was colonised in 1532 by Spain, capitulated to the British in 1797, and finally ceded to Britain under the Treaty of Amiens (1802). Tobago was also discovered by Columbus in 1498. Dutch colonists arrived in 1632; Tobago subsequently changed hands numerous times until it was ceded to Britain by France in 1814 and amalgamated with Trinidad in 1888. The Territory of Trinidad and Tobago became an independent state and a member of the British Commonwealth on 31 August 1962, and a republic in 1976.

In the general election of 2001 the ruling United National Congress (UNC) and the opposition People's National Movement (PNM) each won 18 of the 36 seats in the House of Representatives. President Robinson chose Patrick Manning, leader of PNM, as prime minister. The UNC condemned the president's choice and called for fresh elections, but a new cabinet was sworn into office. In 2002 President Robinson suspended parliament because no speaker had been elected. Fresh elections took place later that year, in which the PNM won 20 seats, thereby resolving the political deadlock. Patrick Manning was again sworn in as prime minister. George Maxwell Richards was elected president in 2003.

POLITICAL SYSTEM
The President is elected for five years by all members of the Senate and the House of Representatives. The House of Representatives has 36 members, directly elected for a five-year term, and the Senate has 31, of whom 16 are appointed on the advice of the Prime Minister, six on the advice of the Leader of the Opposition and nine at the discretion of the President. Legislation was passed in 1980 that afforded Tobago a degree of self-administration through the 15-member Tobago House of Assembly, of whom 12 are directly elected and three chosen by the House for a four-year term.

HEAD OF STATE
President, George Maxwell Richards, *elected* 14 February 2003

SELECTED GOVERNMENT MEMBERS *as at July 2004*
Prime Minister, Finance, Patrick Manning
Foreign Affairs, Knowlson Gift
National Security, Martin Joseph

HIGH COMMISSION OF THE REPUBLIC OF TRINIDAD AND TOBAGO
42 Belgrave Square, London SW1X 8NT
T 020-7245 9351
High Commissioner, Glenda Patricia Morean, apptd 2003

BRITISH HIGH COMMISSION
19 St Clair Ave, St Clair, Port of Spain
T (+1 868) 622 2748/8960
E csbhc@opus.co.tt
High Commissioner, HE Peter Harborne, apptd 1999

ECONOMY AND TRADE

Trinidad and Tobago's main source of revenue is oil. Trinidad has large reserves of natural gas, and in March 2000 an agreement was signed to expand significantly the production of liquefied natural gas. In May 2000, it was announced that an additional natural gas deposit of some 56,600 million cubic metres had been discovered and the discovery of a further deposit of some three trillion cubic feet was announced in September. Fertilisers, tyres, clothing, soap, furniture and foodstuffs are manufactured locally while motor vehicles, radios, TV sets, and electro-domestic equipment are assembled from parts, mainly from Japan. The main agricultural products are sugar, cocoa, coffee, horticultural products and teak.

GNI – US$7,800 million (2001); US$5,960 per capita (2001)
ANNUAL AVERAGE GROWTH OF GDP – 5.0 per cent (2001)
INFLATION RATE – 3.6 per cent (2000)
UNEMPLOYMENT – 13.1 per cent (1999)
TOTAL EXTERNAL DEBT– US$2,467 million (2000)
FOREIGN DIRECT INVESTMENT – US$2,353 million (1997–2000)
IMPORTS – US$3,308 million (2000)
EXPORTS – US$4,655 million (2000)

BALANCE OF PAYMENTS
Trade – US$741 million deficit (1998)
Current Account – US$64 million deficit (1998)

Trade with UK	*2002*	*2003*
Imports from UK	£81,380,000	£104,062,000
Exports to UK	56,963,000	75,048,000

TRANSPORT INFRASTRUCTURE

The two islands have about 8,300 km of roads, of which about half are surfaced. There is no passenger–carrying railway service. The three main ports are Scarborough (Tobago), Port of Spain and Point Lisas where new industries powered by local natural gas are located. The international airport, Piarco, is at Port of Spain.

EDUCATION

Education is free at all state owned and government-assisted denominational schools and certain faculties at the University of the West Indies. Attendance is compulsory for children aged six to 12 years, after which attendance at free secondary schools is determined by success in the secondary school entrance examination at 11 years.

ILLITERACY RATE – (m) 1.1 per cent; (f) 2.4 per cent (2000)
ENROLMENT (percentage of age group) – primary 99 per cent (1997); secondary 74 per cent (1997); tertiary 8 per cent (1997)

MEDIA

There are both private and state-run media organisations. Private television and radio stations predominate and the freedom of the press is constitutionally protected.

TUNISIA

Al-Jumhūriyya at-Tūnisiyya – Republic of Tunisia

AREA – 155,400 sq. km. Neighbours: Algeria (west), Libya (south)
POPULATION – 9,562,000 (2001). Arabic is the official language
CAPITAL – ΨTunis (population, 929,500 2001 estimate)
MAJOR CITIES – ΨBizerte; ΨSfax; ΨSousse
CURRENCY – Tunisian dinar of 1,000 millimes
NATIONAL ANTHEM – Himat Al Hima (Defenders Of The Homeland)
NATIONAL DAY – 20 March
NATIONAL FLAG – Red with a white disc containing a red crescent and star
LIFE EXPECTANCY (years) – 70 (2001)
MORTALITY RATE (per 1,000 population) – 5 (2003)
INFANT MORTALITY (per 1,000 births) – 21 (2001)
HIV / AIDS ADULT PREVALENCE – 0.4 per cent (2001)
DEATH PENALTY – Yes
POPULATION BELOW POVERTY LINE – 6 per cent (2000)
POPULATION GROWTH RATE – 1.4 per cent (1990–2001)
POPULATION DENSITY – 62 per sq. km (2001)
URBAN POPULATION – 66 per cent (2001)
MILITARY EXPENDITURE – 1.8 per cent of GDP (2002)
MILITARY PERSONNEL – 35,000: Army 27,000, Navy 4,500, Air Force 3,500; Paramilitaries 12,000
CONSCRIPTION DURATION – 12 months (selective)

CLIMATE AND TERRAIN

The northern part of Tunisia is mountainous with a central plateau that gives way to the semi-arid plains of the south. Elevation extremes range from 1,544 m (Jebel ech Chambi) at the highest point to −17 m (Shatt al Gharsah) at the lowest. The climate varies considerably from north to south, but average temperatures in Tunis range from 11°C in January to 34°C in June.

HISTORY AND POLITICS

A French protectorate from 1881 to 1956, Tunisia became an independent sovereign state on in 1956. In 1957 the Constituent Assembly abolished the monarchy and elected M. Bourguiba president of the republic. In 1975 the National Assembly proclaimed M. Bourguiba president for life. However, he was deposed in 1987 and succeeded by President Zine el-Abidine Ben Ali, who was subsequently elected in 1989 and re-elected in 1994.

President Ben Ali was elected for a third term of office in 1999, gaining 99.4 per cent of the vote; there were two other candidates. A parallel legislative election was won by the Democratic Constitutional Rally (RCD), which gained 148 of the 182 seats in the National Assembly *(Majlis al-Nuwaab)*. The other parties represented were the Movement of Social Democrats (MDS), the Unionist Democratic Union (UDU), the Party of People's Unity (PUP), the Movement for Renewal (MR) and the Social-Liberal Party. Presidential and legislative elections were scheduled for late October 2004.

POLITICAL SYSTEM
The 1959 constitution was amended in 2002 to allow the president to seek a fourth term and to allow the formation of a second parliamentary assembly.

HEAD OF STATE
President, Gen. Zine el-Abidine Ben Ali, *took office* 7 November 1987, *elected* 2 April 1989, *re-elected* 20 March 1994, 24 October 1999

SELECTED GOVERNMENT MEMBERS *as at July 2004*
Prime Minister, Mohammed Ghannouchi
Finance, Mohamed Rachid Kechiche
Foreign Affairs, Habib Ben Yahia
Interior, Hedi M'henni
National Defence, Dali Jazi

TUNISIAN EMBASSY
29 Prince's Gate, London SW7 1QG
T 020-7584 8117

Ambassador Extraordinary and Plenipotentiary, HE Khémaies Jhinaoui, apptd 1999

BRITISH EMBASSY
5 Place de la Victoire, Tunis 1000
T (+216) (7) 341444
E british.emb@planet.tn
Ambassador Extraordinary and Plenipotentiary, HE Robin Kealy, CMG, apptd 2002

ECONOMY AND TRADE

Agriculture and fisheries employed 22 per cent of the workforce in 1999 and accounted for 12 per cent of GDP in 2003. The valleys of the northern region support large amounts of livestock and contain rich agricultural areas in which cereal crops, citrus fruits, dates, melons, potatoes, peppers and tomatoes are grown. Vines and olives are extensively cultivated. Crude oil production in 2002 was 3.6 million tonnes. Gas has also been discovered off the east coast but is only exploited in small quantities. Tourism is the main foreign exchange earner and there were 5.6 million visitors in 2001.

The chief exports are manufactures, textiles and leather goods, phosphates, mechanical and electronic products, agricultural products and energy. The chief imports are manufactures, raw materials and semi-manufactures, consumer goods, capital goods, and foodstuffs. France remains the main trading partner. Tunisia became an associate of the EC in 1969. In July 1995 a new EU-Tunisian partnership agreement was signed which aims to modernise Tunisia's economy and improve its competitiveness with a view to creating a free trade zone with the EU by 2008.

GNI – US$20,000 million (2001); US$2,070 per capita (2001)
ANNUAL AVERAGE GROWTH OF GDP – 5.0 per cent (2000)
INFLATION RATE – 2.9 per cent (2000)
UNEMPLOYMENT – 15.6 per cent (2000)
TOTAL EXTERNAL DEBT– US$10,610 million (2000)
FOREIGN DIRECT INVESTMENT – US$2,068 million (1997–2000)
IMPORTS – US$9,526 million (2002)
EXPORTS – US$6,874 million (2002)

BALANCE OF PAYMENTS
Trade – US$2,123 million deficit (2002)
Current Account – US$746 million deficit (2002)

Trade with UK	*2002*	*2003*
Imports from UK	£135,170,000	£146,523,000
Exports to UK	114,406,000	141,428,000

TRANSPORT INFRASTRUCTURE

Tunisia has 19,000 km of roads, over 12,000 km of which are surfaced. There are 2,100 km of railways. There are major ports at Bizerte, Gabes, La Goulette, Sfax, Sousse, Tunis and Zarzis.

EDUCATION

There are 141 centres of higher education, of which eight are universities.

ILLITERACY RATE – (m) 18.6 per cent; (f) 39.4 per cent (2000)
ENROLMENT (percentage of age group) – primary 100 per cent (1997); secondary 64 per cent (1997); tertiary 14 per cent (1997)

MEDIA AND CULTURE

Alongside the state-run radio and television stations, many satellite television channels are available. In addition, a private radio station has recently been founded, ending the state monopoly on radio broadcasting. An independent press exists in Tunisia but its coverage of local political issues is monitored by the government. Popular titles include *La Presse*, *Assabah* and *Le Quotiden*.

The country's archaeology is one of its biggest attractions and includes the famous Roman ruins of Carthage and El-Jem and the ancient hot springs at Hamman Mellegue. Malouf is the traditional Arab-style music of Tunisia.

TURKEY

Türkiye çumhuriyeti – Republic of Turkey

AREA – 769,600 sq. km. Neighbours: Greece (west), Bulgaria (north), Georgia, Armenia, Azerbaijan and Iran (east), Syria and Iraq (south)
POPULATION – 67,632,000 (2001); Islam ceased to be the state religion in 1928 but 98.99 per cent of the population are Muslim. The main religious minorities, which are concentrated in Istanbul and on the Syrian frontier, are Greek Orthodox, Armenian, Syrian Christian, and Jewish. The language is Turkish; Kurdish is widely spoken in the south-east of the country
CAPITAL – Ankara (Angora), in Asia (population, 3,203,362, 2000 census). Ankara (or Ancyra) was the capital of the Roman Province of *Galatia Prima*, and a marble temple (now in ruins), dedicated to Augustus, contains the *Monumentum (Marmor) Ancyranum*, inscribed with a record of the reign of Augustus Caesar
MAJOR CITIES – Adana; Bursa; Gaziantep; ΨIstanbul; ΨIzmir; Konya Istanbul, in Europe, is the former capital.
CURRENCY – Turkish lira (TL) of 100 kurus
NATIONAL ANTHEM – Istiklal Marşi (The Independence March)
NATIONAL DAY – 29 October (Republic Day)
NATIONAL FLAG – Red, with white crescent and star
LIFE EXPECTANCY (years) – 70 (2001)
MORTALITY RATE (per 1,000 population) – 5.95 (2003)
INFANT MORTALITY (per 1,000 births) – 36 (2001)
HIV / AIDS ADULT PREVALENCE – 0.1 per cent (2001)
DEATH PENALTY – No (abolished 2004)
POPULATION GROWTH RATE – 1.7 per cent (1990–2001)
POPULATION DENSITY – 88 per sq. km (2001)
URBAN POPULATION – 66 per cent (2001)

CLIMATE AND TERRAIN

Turkey in Europe consists of Eastern Thrace, including the cities of Istanbul and Edirne, and is separated from Asia by the Bosporus at Istanbul and by the Dardanelles (about 64 km in length with a width varying from 1.6 km to 6.4 km). Turkey in Asia comprises the whole of Asia Minor or Anatolia. Turkey has several mountain ranges, and narrow coastal plains and elevation extremes range from 5,166 m (Mount Ararat) at the highest point to 0 m

(Mediterranean Sea) at the lowest. Climate varies greatly from region to region. The coastal areas and the mountains (except in the east) have fairly hot summers and wet, mild winters. Average temperatures in Ankara range from –4°C in January to 31°C in June.

HISTORY AND POLITICS

Once the centre of the Ottoman Empire, Turkey was proclaimed a republic on 29 October 1923 and Gazi Mustafa Kemal (later known as Kemal Atatürk) was elected as president. In 1945 a multiparty system was introduced but in 1960 the government was overthrown by the armed forces. A new constitution was adopted in 1961 and a civilian government took office. Civilian governments remained in power until September 1980 when mounting problems with the economy and terrorism incited a military take-over. After the 1983 general election the military leadership handed power to a civilian government.

Following elections in 2002, the Islamic Justice and Development Party (AKP), led by Recep Tayyip Erdoğan, won an overall majority with 363 of the 550 seats in the parliament. However Erdoğan had been prevented from standing for parliament owing to a past conviction, and the deputy leader of the AKP, Abdullah Gül, was therefore appointed as prime minister. The National Assembly then overruled the president's veto and voted to amend the law to permit Erdoğan to stand for election to parliament. He won a by-election in March 2003 and Prime Minister Gül resigned with his entire government. On 14 March Erdoğan was appointed prime minister and named his new government.

In June and July 2003 the parliament passed a package of laws easing restrictions on freedom of speech, on Kurdish language rights and on reducing the political role of the military, as part of a programme that aims to meet EU preconditions to the commencement of accession negotiations. Turkey abolished the death penalty in 2004.

INSURGENCIES

Since 1984 Turkey has been fighting armed guerrillas of the Marxist Leninist Kurdistan Workers' Party (PKK) in the south-east of the country where Kurds are the majority population. The leader of the PKK, Abdullah Öcalan, was captured by Turkish authorities in 1999 in Kenya and returned to Turkey to stand trial, where he was found guilty of treason and sentenced to death. The Turkish government announced in 2000 that it would suspend the execution, pending an appeal and in 2004 Öcalan was granted a reprieve. The PKK then declared that it had renounced violence and removed the word 'Kurdistan', which is illegal in Turkey, from its title. The situation remained fragile in 2004, however, with Kurdish secessionists continuing to threaten to end their cease-fire if insufficient progress is made on granting political and cultural rights to the Kurdish community.

POLITICAL SYSTEM

A new constitution, extending the powers of the president, was approved in 1982. It provided for the separation of powers between the legislature, executive and judiciary, and the holding of free elections to the unicameral Grand National Assembly, which now has 550 members elected every five years.

HEAD OF STATE

President, Ahmet Necdet Sezer, *elected by parliament for a seven-year term* 5 May 2000, *took office* 16 May 2000

SELECTED GOVERNMENT MEMBERS *as at July 2004*

Prime Minister, Recep Tayyip Erdoğan
Deputy Prime Minister, Minister of State and Minister of Foreign Affairs, Abdullah Gül
Deputy Prime Minister, Minister of State, Abdullatif Şener
Deputy Prime Minister, Minister of State, Mehmet Ali Şahin
Finance, Kemal Unakitan
Interior, Abdulkadir Aksu
National Defence, Vecdi Gonul

TURKISH EMBASSY

43 Belgrave Square, London SW1X 8PA
T 020-7393 0202
Ambassador Extraordinary and Plenipotentiary, HE Akin Alptuna, apptd 2000

BRITISH EMBASSY

Şehit Ersan Caddesi 46/A, Çankaya, Ankara
T (+90) (312) 455 3344
E britembinf@turk.net
Ambassador Extraordinary and Plenipotentiary, HE Sir Peter Westmacott, CMG, LVO apptd 2002

BRITISH COUNCIL DIRECTOR, Chris Brown

Esat Caddesi No: 41, Kucukesat, TR-06660 Ankara
T (+90) (312) 424 1644
E bc.ankara@britishcouncil.org.tr

DEFENCE

The Army has 4,205 main battle tanks, 3,643 armoured personnel carriers, 650 armoured infantry fighting vehicles and 37 attack helicopters. The Navy has 13 submarines, 19 frigates, 49 patrol and coastal vessels and 16 armed helicopters at twelve bases. The Air Force has 483 combat aircraft. Between 150,000 and 200,000 troops are stationed in the south-east of the country to prevent Kurdish insurgency. Since its invasion of Cyprus in 1974, Turkey has maintained forces in the north of the island and at present has about 36,000 personnel stationed there.

As a member of NATO, Turkey is host to the Headquarters Joint Command South East and the Sixth Allied Tactical Air Force Headquarters. US (1,742 personnel) air force detachments are based at Incirlik air base in southern Turkey. In March 2003 the parliament rejected a deal which would have allowed deployment of US forces in preparation for the war in Iraq but it allowed US forces the use of Turkish airspace. The deployment of Turkish forces into Kurdish areas of northern Iraq was also authorised.

MILITARY EXPENDITURE – 5.1 per cent of GDP (2002)
MILITARY PERSONNEL – 514,850: Army 402,000, Navy 52,750, Air Force 60,100; Paramilitaries 152,200
CONSCRIPTION DURATION – 18 months

ECONOMY AND TRADE

Agricultural production accounted for 13.8 per cent of GDP in 2002. About 40 per cent of the working population is employed in agriculture. The principal crops are wheat, barley, rice, tobacco, sugar beet, tea, olives, grapes, figs and hazelnuts. Tobacco, sultana and fig cultivation is centred around Izmir, where substantial quantities of cotton are also grown. The main cotton area is in the Cukurova plain around Adana.

The main export minerals are chromate and boron. Tourism is a major industry, with over 7.5 million visitors in 1999.

The bulk of the country's requirements in sugar, cotton,

woollen and silk textiles, and cement, is produced locally. Other industries include vehicle assembly, paper, glass and glassware, iron and steel, leather and leather goods, sulphur refining, canning and rubber goods, soaps and cosmetics, pharmaceutical products, and prepared foodstuffs.

Turkey was accepted as a candidate for EU membership in December 1999 and following an EU summit in December 2002, the end of 2004 was set as the earliest possible date for the commencement of accession negotiations, provided reforms continue. After years of economic difficulty, a controversial economic recovery programme was agreed with the IMF in 2002. The government's main priorities are to make progress with tax reforms and privatisation and to reduce employment in the public sector.

The main imports are machinery, crude oil and petroleum products, iron and steel, vehicles, medicines, chemicals and electrical appliances. Agricultural commodities represented 13.9 per cent of total exports in 2000. Other exports are minerals, textiles, glass and cement. Germany, the USA and Italy are the main trading partners.

GNI – US$167,300 million (2001); US$2,530 per capita (2001)
ANNUAL AVERAGE GROWTH OF GDP – 5.0 per cent (2003)
INFLATION RATE – 18.4 per cent (2003)
UNEMPLOYMENT – 10.3 per cent (2003)
TOTAL EXTERNAL DEBT– US$142,037 million (2003)
FOREIGN DIRECT INVESTMENT – US$3,510 million (1997–2000)
IMPORTS – US$49,663 million (2002)
EXPORTS – US$34,561 million (2002)

BALANCE OF PAYMENTS
Trade – US$8,635 million deficit (2002)
Current Account – US$1,789 deficit (2002)

Trade with UK	*2002*	*2003*
Imports from UK	£1,378,933,000	£1,704,635,000
Exports to UK	2,314,734,000	2,731,967,000

TRANSPORT INFRASTRUCTURE

Turkey has nearly 400,000 km of roads, of which just over a third is surfaced. There are over 8,500 km of railways, and 1,200 km of waterways. The principal ports and harbours are at Gemlik, Hopa, Iskenderun, Istanbul, Izmir, Kocaeli (Izmit), Icel (Mersin), Samsun and Trabzon.

EDUCATION

Education is free and secular, and since August 1997, compulsory from the ages of six to 14. There are elementary, secondary and vocational schools.

ILLITERACY RATE – (m) 6.5 per cent; (f) 23.4 per cent (2000)
ENROLMENT (percentage of age group) – primary 107 per cent (1997); secondary 58 per cent (1997); tertiary 21 per cent (1997)

MEDIA

Turkey has one state television and radio station, TRT, over 300 private television channels and more than 1,000 private radio stations. The authorities monitor and censor broadcasts that cover sensitive political subjects. TRT has begun to broadcast Kurdish-language programmes, to conform with the EU criteria on minority rights. As with the broadcast media, the Turkish press is subject to some censorship. There are several daily newspapers, including the titles *Hurriyet*, *Milliyet* and *Cumhuriyet*. There is an English-language title *Turkish Daily News*.

CULTURE

Turkey is rich archaeological remains, including Ephesus – the cultural centre of the Greek Empire, which features in the Bible; Troy, the Homeric city of Ilium, and a wealth of sites from Byzantine, Ottoman, Roman and other periods.

The Roman city of Byzantium was selected by Constantine the Great as the capital of the Roman Empire in AD 328 and renamed Constantinople. Istanbul contains the celebrated church of St Sophia, which, after becoming a mosque, was made a museum in 1934. It also contains Topkapı, former palace of the Ottoman Sultans, which is also a museum.

A tradition of folk music exists today in Turkey and its various strands are known collectively as *halk* music.

TURKMENISTAN

Turkmenostan Respublikasy – Republic of Turkmenistan

AREA – 488,100 sq. km. Neighbours: Iran and Afghanistan (south), Uzbekistan (east and north), Kazakhstan (north-west)
POPULATION – 5,500,000 (2002 estimate); 4,483,000 (1996 census): 77 per cent Turkmen, 9.2 per cent Uzbek, 6.7 per cent Russian, together with smaller numbers of Kazakhs, Tatars, Ukrainians and Armenians. Most of the population are Sunni Muslims. The main languages are Turkmen (72 per cent), Russian (9 per cent), Uzbek (9 per cent). Turkmen is one of the Turkic languages
CAPITAL – Ashgabat (population, 604,700, 1995)
MAJOR CITIES – Charjou; Tashauz
CURRENCY – Manat of 100 tenge
NATIONAL ANTHEM – Garashciiz Bitarap Turkmenistaniin Devlet Gimni (Independent Neutral Turkmenistan State Anthem)
NATIONAL DAY – 27–28 October (Independence Day)
NATIONAL FLAG – Green with a vertical carpet pattern near the hoist in black, white, green and wine-red; and in the lower part of the carpet design two laurel branches; in the upper hoist a crescent and five stars, all in white
MORTALITY RATE (per 1,000 population) – 8.87 (2003)
HIV / AIDS ADULT PREVALENCE – 0.1 per cent (2001)
DEATH PENALTY – No (abolished 1999)
POPULATION BELOW POVERTY LINE – 34.4 per cent (2001)
POPULATION GROWTH RATE – 2.1 per cent (2004)
POPULATION DENSITY – 9 per sq. km (1999)
MILITARY EXPENDITURE – 0.8 per cent of GDP (2002)
MILITARY PERSONNEL – 29,000: Army 25,000, Navy 1,000, Air Force 3,000
CONSCRIPTION DURATION – Two years

CLIMATE AND TERRAIN

The republic comprises five regions: Ashgabat, Charjou, Krasnovodsk, Mary, and Tashauz. Ninety per cent of the country is taken up by the Kara Kum (Black Sands) desert. Elevation extremes range from 3,139 m (Gora Ayribaba) at the highest point to −81 m (Vpandina Akchanaya) at the lowest. Average temperatures in Ashgabat range from 0°C in January to 29°C in June.

HISTORY AND POLITICS

Turkmenistan has a long history of conquest and has been invaded and occupied by many empires including the Persian, Greek (under Alexander the Great), Parthian and Mongol. From the early 19th century until 1886 Turkmenistan was gradually incorporated into the Russian Empire. Soviet control over Turkmenistan was established on 30 April 1918 when it became an Autonomous Soviet Socialist Republic. Turkmenistan became a full republic of the Soviet Union in 1925. Turkmenistan declared its independence from the Soviet Union on 27 October 1991 and gained UN membership in 1992.

The autocratic government of President Niyazov has, through harassment and authoritarianism, prevented any effective political opposition or free press. The leadership has rejected political pluralism and instead a cult of personality has developed around President Niyazov. The Supreme Soviet voted in 1993 to extend his term of office to 2002 and this was confirmed by a 99.99 per cent vote in a referendum. In 1999, the legislature removed the limit on his term of office, effectively making him life president. The Communist Party, renamed the Democratic Party (DP), remains in power. Legislative elections to the *Khalk Maslakhaty* held in 1998 were won by the Democratic Party. General elections were held on 1999, in which all seats in the *Majlis* were won by candidates of the DP, the sole legal party.

FOREIGN RELATIONS

Agreement on dual citizenship for ethnic Russians in Turkmenistan was reached in 1993. In the same year Turkmenistan signed the CIS charter to become a full CIS member and in 1994 became a member of the CIS economic union. In 2003 the dual citizenship deal was cancelled by President Niyazov and those holding dual citizenship were given two months in which to decide which passport to retain. A diplomatic row with Russia consequently followed as Turkmenistan rejected Russian allegations that the move would force tens of thousands of ethnic Russians with dual citizenship to leave the country, thereby jeopardising their rights.

POLITICAL SYSTEM

The 1992 constitution declares the President head of state and government. The legislature is the 50-member *Majlis* (formerly the Supreme Soviet). The *Khalk Maslakhaty* (People's Council) is a supervisory body with no legislative powers.

HEAD OF STATE

President, Head of Government, Chair of the Council of Ministers, Saparmurad Niyazov, *elected* 27 October 1990, *re-elected* 21 June 1992, *appointed head of government* 18 May 1992, *elected by referendum for an eight-year term* 15 January 1994, *term extended indefinitely* 28 December 1999

SELECTED GOVERNMENT MEMBERS *as at July 2004*

Prime Minister, The President
Deputy Chairs, Yolly Gurbanmuradov; Gurbansoltan Handurdyyeva *(Minister of Foreign Affairs)*; Rashid Meredov
Defence, Secretary of the State Security Council, Col.-Gen. Agageldy Mamedgeldiyev
Economy and Finance, Yazguly Kakalyyev
Interior, Ashir Atayev

EMBASSY OF TURKMENISTAN

2nd Floor South, St George's House, 14/17 Wells Street, London W1P 3FP
T 020-7255 1071
Ambassador Extraordinary and Plenipotentiary, HE Yazmurad Seryaev, apptd 2003
Counsellor, Nurmurat Redjebov

BRITISH EMBASSY

301–308, Office Building, Four Points Ak Altin Hotel, Ashgabat
T (+993) (12) 363462/363463/363464
Ambassador Extraordinary and Plenipotentiary, HE Paul Brummel, apptd 2002

ECONOMY AND TRADE

Revenues from natural gas reserves make the country economically viable and have enabled the government to maintain low stable prices for basic commodities and utilities. The principal industries are cotton cultivation, stock-raising and mineral extraction, together with natural gas production and the silk industry. Arable land is irrigated by the Niyazov (formerly Kara Kum) canal, which cuts through the Kara Kum desert. There are estimated reserves of some 700 million tonnes of oil and 8,000,000 million cubic metres of natural gas. Natural gas is exported by pipeline to Ukraine and western Europe. An agreement to build further pipelines under the Caspian Sea, through Azerbaijan and Georgia, to supply gas to Turkey was reached in November 1999. In April 2003 agreement was reached under which Russia would buy 60 billion cubic metres of gas from Turkmenistan annually, beginning in 2004.

GNI – US$5,143 million (2001); US$950 per capita (2001)
ANNUAL AVERAGE GROWTH OF GDP – 5.0 per cent (1998)
TOTAL EXTERNAL DEBT – US$2,259 million (2000)

BALANCE OF PAYMENTS

Trade – US$231 million deficit (1997)
Current – US580 million deficit (1997)

Trade with UK	*2002*	*2003*
Imports from UK	£6,909,000	£7,241,000
Exports to UK	4,651,000	2,097,000

TRANSPORT INFRASTRUCTURE

Turkmenistan has 24,000 km of roads, nearly 20,000 km of which are paved and there are 2,440 km of railways. There are two important waterways, the Niyazov (Kara Kum) canal and the Amu Darya.

MEDIA AND CULTURE

The government's control of the media, both broadcast and print, is total. Newspapers are produced on government owned presses; programmes from broadcasters other than the state channels are censored before airing in Turkmenistan, and internet access is controlled by the country's communication authorities. Newspapers include *Galkynys, Turkmen Dunyasi* and *Adalet.*

Carpet-weaving is considered an art form. Each tribe in Turkmenistan has distinctive carpet designs, and traditional dress is still used to show allegiance to a tribe. The Turkmen literary tradition is dominated by one figure, the poet and thinker Makhtumkuli (1770–1840).

TUVALU

Fakavae Aliki-Moloi Tuvalu/Constitutional Monarchy of Tuvalu

AREA – 26 sq. km
POPULATION – 10,991 (2001). About 1,500 Tuvaluans work overseas, mostly in Nauru, or as seamen. The people are almost entirely Polynesian. The principal languages are Tuvaluan and English. A large majority of the population is Christian, predominantly Protestant
CAPITAL – ΨFunafuti (population, 3,856)
CURRENCY – The Australian dollar ($A) of 100 cents is legal tender. In addition there are Tuvalu dollar and cent coins in circulation
NATIONAL ANTHEM – Tuvalu Mo Te Atua (Tuvalu For The Almighty)
NATIONAL DAY – 1 October (Independence Day)
NATIONAL FLAG – Light blue ground with Union flag in top left quarter and nine five-pointed gold stars in the fly
MORTALITY RATE (per 1,000 population) – 7.34 (2003)
DEATH PENALTY – No (abolished 1978)
POPULATION GROWTH RATE – 1.4 per cent (2004)
POPULATION DENSITY – 423 per sq. km (1999)

CLIMATE AND TERRAIN

Tuvalu comprises nine narrow coral atolls situated in the south-west Pacific around the point at which the International Date Line cuts the Equator. The climate is tropical, and the average temperature is 26°C all year round.

HISTORY AND POLITICS

Tuvalu, formerly the Ellice Islands, formed part of the Gilbert and Ellice Islands Colony until 1975, when separate constitutions came into force. Separation from the Gilbert Islands was implemented the following year. On 1 October 1978 Tuvalu became a fully independent state within the Commonwealth.

Following the death of Prime Minister Ionatana Ionatana in 2000, Faimalaga Luka was chosen to replace him in February 2001. Luka's government lost a vote of no confidence later that year and Koloa Talake was elected prime minister in December. In parliamentary elections held in July 2002 Prime Minister Talake lost his seat, and Saufatu Sopanga was elected prime minister by parliament.

Tuvalu became a full member of the UN on 17 February 2000.

POLITICAL SYSTEM

The constitution provides for a Prime Minister and four other Ministers, who must be members of the 15-member Parliament, all of whom are directly elected. The Prime Minister presides at meetings of the Cabinet, which consists of the five Ministers and is attended by the Attorney-General. Local government services are provided by elected Island Councils.
Governor-General, Faimalaga Luka

SELECTED GOVERNMENT MEMBERS *as at July 2004*
Prime Minister, Foreign Affairs, Labour, Saufatu Sopoanga
Deputy Prime Minister, Works, Communications and Transport, Maatia Toafa
Finance and Economic Planning, Industry, Bikenibeu Paeniu
Home Affairs and Rural Development, Leti Pelesale

HONORARY CONSULATE OF TUVALU
Tuvalu House, 230 Worple Road, London SW20 8RH
T 020-8879 0985
Honorary Consul, Iftikhar Ayaz

BRITISH HIGH COMMISSIONER, HE Charles Mochan, apptd 2002, resident at Suva, Fiji

ECONOMY AND TRADE

The main imports are foodstuffs, semi-manufactures, machinery and transport equipment and fuels. The main exports are copra and fish, though philatelic sales provide a major source of revenue and handicraft sales are increasing.

Tuvalu has been for many years almost entirely dependent on foreign aid, but in 2000 it sold its internet country suffix, '.tv', for licensing to media companies. This sale, plus the similar leasing of its '900' phone code, now generates several million dollars of revenue annually.
GDP – US$14 million (1998); US$1,491 per capita (2000)
ANNUAL AVERAGE GROWTH OF GDP – 2.0 per cent (1998)

Trade with UK	*2002*	*2003*
Imports from UK	£34,000	£21,000
Exports to UK	511,000	499,000

TRANSPORT INFRASTRUCTURE AND MEDIA

Funafuti has an airfield from which a service operates regularly to Fiji and Kiribati, and is also the main port. There are only 8 km of roads, all unpaved.

Tuvalu has one radio station, operated by the government, but no television channels. *Sikuleo o Tuvalu* is the government owned newspaper.

UGANDA

Republic of Uganda

AREA – 197,100 sq. km. Neighbours: Democratic Republic of Congo (west), Sudan (north), Kenya (east), Tanzania and Rwanda (south)
POPULATION – 24,023,000 (2001): 17 per cent Baganda, 12 per cent Karamojong; many other ethnic groups including Basoga, Iteso, Langi, Banyarwanda, Bagisu, Acholi, Lugbara, Banyoro and Batoro. The official language is English. The main local vernaculars are of Bantu, Nilotic and Hamitic origins. Ki-Swahili is generally understood

CAPITAL – Kampala (population, 774,241, 1991)
MAJOR CITIES – Jinja; Masaka; Mbale (53,987)
CURRENCY – Uganda shilling of 100 cents
NATIONAL ANTHEM – Oh Uganda
NATIONAL DAY – 9 October (Independence Day)
NATIONAL FLAG – Six horizontal stripes of black, yellow, red, with a white disc in the centre containing the badge of a crested crane
LIFE EXPECTANCY (years) – 45 (2001)
MORTALITY RATE (per 1,000 population) – 16.95 (2003)
INFANT MORTALITY (per 1,000 births) – 79 (2001)
HIV / AIDS ADULT PREVALENCE – 5 per cent (2001)
DEATH PENALTY – Yes
POPULATION BELOW POVERTY LINE – 35 per cent (2001)
POPULATION GROWTH RATE – 3 per cent (1990–2001)
POPULATION DENSITY – 122 per sq. km (2001)
URBAN POPULATION – 15 per cent (2001)
MILITARY EXPENDITURE – 2.7 per cent of GDP (2002)
MILITARY PERSONNEL – Ugandan People's Defence Force 60,000; Paramilitaries 1,800

CLIMATE AND TERRAIN

Large parts of Lakes Victoria, Edward and Albert (Mobuto) are within Uganda's boundaries, as are Lakes Kyoga, Kwania, George and Bisina (formerly Salisbury) and the course of the River Nile from its outlet from Lake Victoria to the Sudan border at Nimule. Uganda is mainly a high plateau and elevation extremes range from 5,110 m (Mount Stanley) at the highest point to 621 m (Lake Albert) at the lowest. There is a wet season from December to February and the average temperature in Kampala are an almost constant 24°C.

HISTORY AND POLITICS

Uganda became an independent state within the Commonwealth on 9 October 1962, after some 70 years of British rule. A republic was instituted in 1967. In 1971 an army coup took place and Maj.-Gen. Idi Amin, the army commander, proclaimed himself head of state, and ruled as dictator until his overthrow in 1979. Dr Milton Obote became president in 1980 but was ousted by a military coup in 1985. A military council was installed but the National Resistance Movement led by Yoweri Museveni captured Kampala in January 1986, securing control of the rest of the country in the following few months. Museveni was sworn in as president in January 1986, and won the first direct presidential election in May 1996. Supporters of the president won a majority of seats in the subsequent legislative elections. The suspension of political party activity, introduced by President Museveni in 1986, was endorsed in a referendum held in 2000, in which 90.7 per cent of those voting backed the continuation of the no party 'Movement' system, in which political parties were allowed to exist, but not to contest elections.

President Museveni was re-elected in March 2001, and a general election was held in which most seats were won by supporters of the no party 'Movement' system.

In 2003 both the courts and the president made moves towards allowing political parties to become active once again.

The former President Idi Amin died in 2003. Many of the Ugandan Asians expelled by Amin are returning to Uganda, following an invitation from President Museveni.

INSURGENCIES

When Idi Amin was overthrown in 1979, thousands of his troops fled across the border into Sudan where some joined a rebel group, the Uganda National Rescue Front (UNRF). Over 1,000 rebels made peace after President Museveni came to power in 1986, and the remainder, known as UNRF 2, signed a peace deal in 2002, ending more than five years of negotiations between the government and rebels.

In 2004, civil unrest continued in north-eastern Uganda because of clashes between tribes, and rebel insurgency, particularly by the Lord's Resistance Army.

POLITICAL SYSTEM

A new constitution, promulgated in October 1995, endorsed the existing non-party political system. The President, who is head of government, is directly elected for a five-year term. The legislature, the 276-seat National Assembly, is also directly elected for a five-year term; 214 members are elected by constituencies and 62 are elected indirectly to represent particular groups.

HEAD OF STATE
President, Commander-in-Chief, Yoweri Museveni, *sworn in* 29 January 1986, *elected* 9 May 1996, *re-elected* 12 March 2001
Vice-President, Gilbert Balibaseka Bukenya

SELECTED GOVERNMENT MEMBERS *as at July 2004*
Prime Minister, Apollo Nsibambi
First Deputy Prime Minister, Disaster Preparedness, Brig. Moses Ali
Defence, Amama Mbabazi
Finance, Planning and Economic Development, Gerald Ssendaula
Internal Affairs, Ruhakana Rugunda

UGANDA HIGH COMMISSION
Uganda House, 58–59 Trafalgar Square, London WC2N 5DX
T 020-7839 5783
High Commissioner, HE Tomasi Sisye Kiryapawo, apptd 2003

BRITISH HIGH COMMISSION
10–12 Parliament Avenue, PO Box 7070, Kampala
T (+256) (78) 312000
High Commissioner, HE Adam Wood, apptd 2002

BRITISH COUNCIL DIRECTOR, Philip Goodwin
Rwenzori Courts, Plot 2 and 4A, Nakasero Road, PO Box 7070, Kampala
T (+256) (78) 234 725/730
E info@britishcouncil.or.ug

ECONOMY AND TRADE

On 8 February 2000, the IMF pledged US$139 million in debt relief, and the International Development Association (IDA) announced that it would give assistance of US$629 million over 20 years. In March, donor countries pledged at least US$2,000 million over three years to support economic development. The principal export earners are coffee, tobacco, cotton and tea. Hydroelectricity is produced from the Owen Falls power station, some of which is exported to Kenya, Tanzania and Rwanda. The principal food crops are plantains, sugar cane, cassava, maize and sorghum.

GNI – US$5,900 million (2001); US$260 per capita (2001)
ANNUAL AVERAGE GROWTH OF GDP – 1.4 per cent (1998)
INFLATION RATE – 2.8 per cent (2000)
TOTAL EXTERNAL DEBT – US$3,409 million (2000)
FOREIGN DIRECT INVESTMENT – US$822 million (1997–2000)
IMPORTS – US$1,111 million (2002)
EXPORTS – US$443 million (2002)

BALANCE OF PAYMENTS
Trade – US$575 million deficit (2001)
Current Account – US$802 million deficit (2001)

Trade with UK	*2001*	*2003*
Imports from UK	£33,666,000	£36,765,000
Exports to UK	10,672,000	9,448,000

TRANSPORT INFRASTRUCTURE

There is an international airport at Entebbe, and eight other airfields around the country. Having no coast, Uganda is dependent upon rail and road links to Mombasa in Kenya and Dar es Salaam in Tanzania for its trade. There is over 1,200 km of rail track in Uganda, and 27,000 km of roads, almost all of which are unpaved (only 1,800 km are surfaced).

EDUCATION

Education is a joint undertaking by the government, local authorities and voluntary agencies. In 1996, the Universal Primary Programme was launched, under which four children per family are entitled to receive free primary education.
ILLITERACY RATE – (m) 22.4 per cent; (f) 43.1 per cent (2000)
ENROLMENT (percentage of age group) – tertiary 2 per cent (1997)

MEDIA AND CULTURE

Alongside the one state owned television, and one radio station, there are now more than a hundred private radio and television stations, following the government's relinquishing its control of the media in 1993. There are two main newspapers in Uganda: *New Vision* and *The Monitor*.

Music is central to Ugandan culture as each tribe has a distinctive musical heritage. Popular instruments include the Ugandan lyre, harp, xylophone and the 'thumb piano' or *mbira*. Okot p'Bitek (1931–82) is one of Uganda's best-known writers.

UKRAINE

Ukraïna – Ukraine

AREA – 579,400 sq. km. Neighbours: Belarus (north), Russia (north and east), Romania and Moldova (south-west), Hungary, Slovakia and Poland (west)
POPULATION – 49,112,000 (2001); 51,471,000 (1989 census): 73 per cent Ukrainian, 22 per cent Russian, with smaller numbers of Jews, Belarusians, Moldovans, Tatars, Poles, Hungarians and Greeks. The majority religion is Orthodox Christianity. There are also large numbers of Uniates and Reformed Protestants in the Transcarpathian region and a sizeable Jewish community in Kiev. The official language is Ukrainian. Russian, Romanian, Hungarian and Polish are also used.
CAPITAL – Kiev (Kyiv) (population, 2,602,000, 2001 census)
MAJOR CITIES – Dnipropetrovsk; Donetsk; Kharkiv; Lviv; ΨOdesa; Zaporizhzhya
CURRENCY – Hryvna of 100 kopiykas
NATIONAL ANTHEM – Shche Ne Vmerla, Ukraïna (Thou Hast Not Perished, Ukraine)
NATIONAL DAY – 24 August (Independence Day)
NATIONAL FLAG – Two horizontal stripes of blue over yellow
LIFE EXPECTANCY (years) – 68 (2001)
MORTALITY RATE (per 1,000 population) – 16.39 (2003)
INFANT MORTALITY (per 1,000 births) – 17 (2001)
HIV / AIDS ADULT PREVALENCE – 1 per cent (2001)
DEATH PENALTY – No (abolished 1999)
POPULATION BELOW POVERTY LINE – 29 per cent (2001)
POPULATION GROWTH RATE – 0.5 per cent (1990–2001)
POPULATION DENSITY – 85 per sq. km (2001)
URBAN POPULATION – 68 per cent (2001)
ILLITERACY RATE – (m) 0.3 per cent; (f) 0.5 per cent (2000)
ENROLMENT (percentage of age group) – tertiary 42 per cent (1997)

CLIMATE AND TERRAIN

Ukraine consists of 24 regions and the Autonomous Republic of Crimea. The Carpathian mountains lie in the south-western part of the republic and terrain in the rest of the country is typified by the characteristic steppes and plateaux. Elevation extremes range from 2,061 m (Hora Hoverla) at the highest point to 0 m (Black Sea) at the lowest. The main rivers are the Dnieper with its tributaries, the Southern Bug and the Northern Donets (a tributary of the Don). Average annual temperatures in Kiev range from –8°C in January to 28°C in June.

HISTORY AND POLITICS

The earliest Slavic state was formed in the middle reaches of the Dnieper River with its capital at Kyiv in the ninth century AD. The state lasted until Kyiv fell to the Tatar-Mongols in 1240. For the next four centuries Ukraine was invaded and ruled by Poles and Lithuanians. Kyiv was liberated from the Poles in 1648 and in 1654 Ukraine became a protectorate of Russia.

Ukraine declared its independence in 1918, but was invaded by Poland in 1919 before becoming a constituent republic of the USSR in 1922.

In 1986 Ukraine was the scene of the world's worst nuclear disaster, when a reactor at the Chernobyl nuclear plant exploded. At least 10,000 people have died from radiation poisoning, and the long-term health of millions more has been affected.

Ukraine declared itself independent of the Soviet Union on 24 August 1991. Independence was confirmed by a referendum in December 1991 and Leonid Kravchuk was elected to the presidency. In the 1994 presidential election Leonid Kuchma defeated President Kravchuk and won a further term of office in a presidential election on 14 November 1999, receiving 56.25 per cent of the vote.

In January 2000, the Supreme Council split into two factions, following a failed attempt by the pro-government faction to remove the Speaker, Oleksandr Tkachenko, from office. The minority left-wing faction remained in control of the Supreme Council building until the pro-government majority took it by force.

In legislative elections held in 2002, the Our Ukraine bloc became the largest party in the parliament, ahead of the For United Ukraine bloc and the Communist Party of Ukraine. Following lengthy discussions during the summer of 2002, a coalition comprising supporters of President Kuchma and a number of independents was agreed in late October. The incumbent Prime Minister, Anatoliy Kinakh, was dismissed by the president on 16 November 2002 and Viktor Yanukovych, his replacement, was approved by parliament on 21 November.

INSURGENCIES

A pro-Russian majority in the Crimean parliament voted to make Crimea an autonomous republic in September 1991, a vote that was accepted by Ukraine, but it then voted for independence, which was not accepted, and the declaration of independence was rescinded in May 1992. Elections to the Crimean parliament in 1995 saw a dramatic drop in support for pro-Russian parties. Arkady Demydenko was appointed Prime Minister of Crimea in 1996. A new constitution, which gave Crimea property and budget rights, came into effect in January 1999.

A referendum in 1994 in the Donbass region of eastern Ukraine, in favour of closer economic ties with Russia and making Russian an official language, was overwhelmingly passed, as was one in the Crimea in favour of dual Russian-Ukrainian citizenship.

FOREIGN RELATIONS

In May 1997, a treaty of friendship and co-operation was signed with Russia. Agreement was also reached over the division of the former Soviet Black Sea Fleet. In the following year, a treaty on economic co-operation was signed between Ukraine and Russia which aimed to strengthen industrial and commercial links and move towards the introduction of the free movement of goods, services, capital and labour.

Ukraine signed a partnership and co-operation agreement with the EU in June 1994 and in July 1997, the NATO-Ukraine Charter to enhance co-operation on peacekeeping was signed.

POLITICAL SYSTEM

The unicameral Supreme Council has 450 members, who serve a four-year term. Half of the seats in the Supreme Council are elected from single-seat constituencies by a simple majority, and the other 225 are to be filled by proportional representation from party lists, with a 4 per cent threshold for representation. A member may only be elected if the turnout in the electoral district is above 50 per cent.

HEAD OF STATE

President, Leonid Kuchma, *elected* 10 July 1994, *sworn in* 19 July 1994, *re-elected* 14 November 1999

SELECTED GOVERNMENT MEMBERS *as at July 2004*

Prime Minister, Viktor Yanukovych
First Deputy Prime Minister, Finance, Mykola Azarov
Deputy Prime Ministers, Ivan Kirilenko *(Agriculture)*; Andriy Klyuyev *(Energy)*; Dmitro Tabachnik *(Humanitarian Affairs)*
Defence, Yevhen Marchuk
Economy and European Integration, Mykola Derkach
Foreign Affairs, Konstyantyn Gryshchenko
Interior, Mykola Bilokon

UKRAINIAN EMBASSY
60 Holland Park, London W11 3SJ
T 020-7727 6312
Ambassador Extraordinary and Plenipotentiary, Ihor Mityukov, apptd 2002

BRITISH EMBASSY
UA-01025 Kyiv, Desyatinna 9
T (+380) (44) 462 0011/2/3/4
Ambassador Extraordinary and Plenipotentiary, HE Robert Brinkley, apptd 2002

BRITISH COUNCIL DIRECTOR, Liliana Biglou
4/12 Vul. Hryhoriya Skovorody, UA-04070 Kyiv
T (+380) (44) 490 5600
E enquiry@britishcouncil.org.ua

DEFENCE

The Constitution bans the stationing of foreign troops on Ukrainian soil, but permits Russia to retain naval bases. The Army has 3,784 main battle tanks, 1, 702 armoured personnel carriers, 3,043 armoured infantry fighting vehicles and 205 attack helicopters. The Navy has one submarine, three principal surface combat vessels and nine patrol and coastal vessels at six bases. The Air Force has 499 combat aircraft.

MILITARY EXPENDITURE – 2.2 per cent of GDP (2002)
MILITARY PERSONNEL – 210,600: Army 148,000, Navy 13,500, Air Force 49,100; Paramilitaries 112,500
CONSCRIPTION DURATION – 18 months to two years

ECONOMY AND TRADE

The Communist-led government of 1991–4 was characterised by economic mismanagement and opposition to economic reforms. Successive governments were unable to gain consensus for a reform programme, which delayed economic restructuring. Ukraine joined the CIS economic union as an associate member in 1993.

Since his election in 1999, President Kuchma has introduced a wide-ranging reform programme. Continuing economic difficulties led to the devaluation of the hryvna in February 1999. In March 2000, the IMF issued an interim statement about the alleged misuse of foreign currency reserves and subsequently suspended its loan programme to Ukraine. However, GDP in 2000 showed strong export-based growth of 6 per cent and industrial production grew by 12.9 per cent.

Metal processing, the manufacture of machinery, and the chemical and petrochemical industries are major contributors to Ukraine's GDP; mining and metallurgy account for more than 40 per cent of exports. The southern part of the country contains a coal-mining and iron and steel industrial area. Ukraine also contains engineering and chemical industries and ship building yards on the Black Sea coast. Ukrainian agricultural production is good with large areas under cultivation with wheat, cotton, flax and sugar beet; stock-raising is also important. There are large deposits of coal and salt, iron ore and manganese.

Russia is the main trading partner, accounting for 24 per cent of exports and 41.7 per cent of imports in 2000. Trade negotiations between Ukraine and Russia in April 2002 included agreements on gas transits and oil pipelines. Turkey, Germany, the USA and Turkmenistan are also major trading partners.

GNI – US$35,200 million (2001); US$720 per capita (2001)
ANNUAL AVERAGE GROWTH OF GDP – 6 per cent (2000)
INFLATION RATE – 22.7 per cent (1999)
UNEMPLOYMENT – 11.7 per cent (2000)
TOTAL EXTERNAL DEBT – US$12,166 million (2000)
FOREIGN DIRECT INVESTMENT – US$2,457 million (1997–2000)
IMPORTS – US$11,846 million (1999)
EXPORTS – US$11,582 million (1999)

BALANCE OF PAYMENTS
Trade – US$710 million surplus (2002)
Current Account – US$3,174 million surplus (2002)

Trade with UK	*2002*	*2003*
Imports from UK	£182,436,000	£245,680,000
Exports to UK	148,201,000	96,087,000

TRANSPORT INFRASTRUCTURE

Ukraine has a total of 170,000 km of roads, 164,000 km of which are surfaced. It has 22,500 km of railways, and 4,500 km of waterways. Its ports are at Berdyansk, Feodosiya, Illichivsk, Izmayil, Kerch, Kherson, Kyiv, Kiliya, Mariupol, Mykolayiv, Odesa, Reni, Sevastopol, Yalta and Yuzhnyy.

MEDIA AND CULTURE

There are several private and state owned television and radio networks in operation. Ukraine has seven daily newspapers, many of which are mass-circulation publications and titles include *Silski Visti* and *Segodnya.*

The folk music of Ukraine has an ancestry that can be traced back to the 16th century. The most popular instrument in modern Ukraine is the *bandura,* a large stringed instrument. In the 20th century, Ukrainian literature – which dates back as far as the 12th century – became politically significant, as authors became openly critical of the Soviet occupation. Celebrated cultural figures include Schmuel Yosef Agnon (1888–1970) who won the Nobel Prize for Literature in 1966, the poet Taras Shevchenko (1814–61) and the novelist Olha Kobylianska (1863–1942). Mykola Lysenko (1842–1912) and Dimitri Klebanov (1907–87) are two prominent Ukrainian composers.

UNITED ARAB EMIRATES

Dawlat Al-Amārat Al-'Arabiyya Al-Muttahida – United Arab Emirates

AREA – 83,600 sq. km approximately. Neighbours: Oman (north-east and east), Saudi Arabia (south and west), Qatar (north-west)
POPULATION – 2,654,000 (2001), of which 75 per cent are expatriates. The official language is Arabic, and English is widely spoken. The established religion is Islam
CAPITAL – ΨAbu Dhabi (population, 450,000)
CURRENCY – UAE dirham (Dh) of 100 fils
NATIONAL DAY – 2 December
NATIONAL FLAG – Horizontal stripes of green over white over black with vertical red stripe in the hoist
LIFE EXPECTANCY (years) – 75 (2001)
MORTALITY RATE (per 1,000 population) – 4 (2003)
INFANT MORTALITY (per 1,000 births) – 8 (2001)
HIV / AIDS ADULT PREVALENCE – 0.18 per cent (2001)
DEATH PENALTY – Yes
POPULATION GROWTH RATE – 2.5 per cent (1990–2001)
POPULATION DENSITY – 32 per sq. km (2001)

CLIMATE AND TERRAIN

The United Arab Emirates is situated in the south-east of the Arabian peninsula. Six of the emirates lie on the shore of the Gulf between the Musandam peninsula in the east and the Qatar peninsula in the west while the seventh, Fujairah, lies on the Gulf of Oman. Much of the inland terrain is desert, leading to the flat coastal plain and there are mountains in the east of the country. Elevation extremes range from 1,527 m (Jabal Yibir) at the highest point to 0 m (Persian Gulf) at the lowest. Average temperatures in Sharjah range between 12°C in January to 38°C in August.

HISTORY AND POLITICS

The United Arab Emirates (formerly the Trucial States) is composed of seven emirates which came together as an independent state on 2 December 1971 when they ended their individual special treaty relationships with the British government (Ras al-Khaimah joined the other six on 10 February 1972). On independence, the Union Government assumed full responsibility for all internal and external affairs apart from some internal matters that remained the prerogative of the individual emirates.

POLITICAL SYSTEM

Overall authority lies with the Supreme Council of the seven emirate rulers, each of whom also governs in his own territory. The president and vice-president are elected every five years by the Supreme Council from among its members. The president appoints the Council of Ministers. A 40-member Federal National Council, comprising eight members each from Abu Dhabi and Dubai, six each from Sharjah and Ras al-Khaimah and four each for Fujairah, Umm al-Qaiwain and Ajman, appointed by the rulers of each emirate, studies draft laws referred to it by the Council of Ministers.

The legal system consists of both secular and religious courts guided by the Islamic philosophy of justice. Individual emirates retain their own penal codes and courts alongside a federal court system and penal code.

FEDERAL STRUCTURE

Each emirate has its separate government, with Abu Dhabi having an executive council chaired by the Crown Prince. The Emirates are (population 2000 census): Abu Dhabi (1,186,000), Ajman (174,000), Dubai (913,000), Fujairah (98,000), Ras al-Khaimah (171,000), Sharjah (520,000), Umm al-Qaiwain (46,000).

HEAD OF STATE
President, HH Sheikh Zayed bin Sultan al-Nahyan *(Abu Dhabi), elected* 1971, *re-elected* 1976, 1981, 1986, 1991, 1996, December 2001
Vice-President, Prime Minister, HH Sheikh Maktoum bin Rashid al-Maktoum *(Dubai)*

SELECTED GOVERNMENT MEMBERS *as at July 2004*
Deputy Prime Minister, Sheikh Sultan bin Zayed al-Nahyan
Defence, HH Gen. Sheikh Mohammed bin Rashid al-Maktoum
Finance and Industry, HH Sheikh Hamdan bin Rashid al-Maktoum
Foreign Affairs, Rashid Abdullah al-Nuaimi
Interior, Lt.-Gen. Mohammed Saeed al-Badi

EMBASSY OF THE UNITED ARAB EMIRATES
30 Princes Gate, London SW7 1PT
T 020-7581 1281
Ambassador Extraordinary and Plenipotentiary, HE Easa Saleh al-Gurg, CBE, apptd 1991

BRITISH EMBASSIES
PO Box 248, Abu Dhabi
T (+971) (2) 610 1100
Ambassador Extraordinary and Plenipotentiary, HE Richard Makepeace, apptd 2003
PO Box 65, Dubai
T (+971) (4) 309 4444

BRITISH COUNCIL DIRECTOR, Peter Ellwood, OBE
Villa no. 7, Al-Nasr Street, Khalidiya, PO Box 46523, Abu Dhabi
T (+971) (2) 665 9300
E information@ae.britishcouncil.org

DEFENCE

The Army has 443 main battle tanks, 517 armoured personnel carriers and 430 armoured infantry fighting vehicles. The Navy has two frigates and 16 patrol and coastal vessels. The Air Force has 106 combat aircraft and 51 armed helicopters.
MILITARY EXPENDITURE – 4.0 per cent of GDP (2002)
MILITARY PERSONNEL – 50,500: Army 44,000, Navy 2,500, Air Force 4,000

ECONOMY AND TRADE

The UAE is the Gulf's third largest oil producer after Saudi Arabia and Iran, with oil reserves of 98,200 million barrels and gas reserves of 5,800 million cubic metres. Oil production in 2000 accounted for 33.9 per cent of GDP. Other important sectors of the economy are manufacturing (aluminium, cement, chemicals, fertilisers, pharmaceuticals, ship repair), government services, construction, transport, communications, financial services and tourism. Agricultural production has increased due to large-scale water desalination and irrigation projects. There is no personal or corporate taxation apart from on oil companies and foreign banks. There are several free zones, where overseas companies can trade tax-free.

Oil revenues over the past 30 years have enabled the government to invest heavily in education, health and social services, housing, transport and communications infrastructure, and agriculture.

GNI – US$49,205 million (1998); US$17,870 per capita (1998)
ANNUAL AVERAGE GROWTH OF GDP – 7.0 per cent (1998)

Trade with UK	*2002*	*2003*
Imports from UK	£1,612,780,000	£1,084,002,000
Exports to UK	783,980,000	2,080,595,000

TRANSPORT INFRASTRUCTURE

Roads total 1,088 km, all of which are surfaced, but the country has no railway system. There are 15 major ports, and six international airports.

EDUCATION

In 2000 there were 747 government schools, where education is free; and 426 private schools. There are five universities.
ILLITERACY RATE – (m) 25.9 per cent; (f) 21.1 per cent (2000)
ENROLMENT (percentage of age group) – primary 89 per cent (1997); secondary 80 per cent (1997); tertiary 12 per cent (1997)

MEDIA

Dubai is an important media hub and is home to pan-Arab satellite television channels and other international media organisations. UAE residents can receive several local and pan-Arab television and radio stations. There are three national newspapers, *Al-Bayan, Gulf News* and *Khaleej Times.*

UNITED STATES OF AMERICA

AREA – 9,159,000 sq. km. Neighbours: Canada (north), Mexico (south)
POPULATION – 285,926,000 (2001). The language is English. There is a significant Spanish-speaking minority
CAPITAL – Washington DC (population, 4,923,153, 2000 census). The area of the District of Columbia (with which the City of Washington is considered co-extensive) is 61 sq. miles, with a resident population (2000 census) of 572,059. The District of Columbia is governed by an elected mayor and City Council
MAJOR CITIES – ΨChicago; Dallas; ΨDetroit; ΨHouston; ΨLos Angeles; ΨNew York; ΨPhiladelphia; Phoenix; San Antonio; ΨSan Diego
CURRENCY – US dollar (US$) of 100 cents
NATIONAL ANTHEM – The Star-Spangled Banner
NATIONAL DAY – 4 July (Independence Day)
NATIONAL FLAG – Thirteen horizontal stripes, alternately red and white, with blue canton in the hoist showing 50 white stars in nine horizontal rows of six and five alternately (known as the Star-Spangled Banner)
LIFE EXPECTANCY (years) – 77 (2001)
MORTALITY RATE (per 1,000 population) – 8.44 (2003)
INFANT MORTALITY (per 1,000 births) – 7 (2001)
HIV / AIDS ADULT PREVALENCE – 0.6 per cent (2001)
DEATH PENALTY – Yes
POPULATION BELOW POVERTY LINE – 12.7 per cent (2001)

POPULATION GROWTH RATE – 1.0 per cent (1990–2001)
POPULATION DENSITY – 31 per sq. km (2001)
URBAN POPULATION – 77 per cent (2001)

CLIMATE AND TERRAIN

The coastline has a length of about 3,329 km on the Atlantic Ocean 12,268 km on the Pacific, 1,705 km on the Arctic, and 2,624 km on the Gulf of Mexico. The principal river is the Mississippi-Missouri-Red (5,970 km long), traversing the whole country to its mouth in the Gulf of Mexico. The chain of the Rocky Mountains separates the western portion of the country from the remainder. West of these, bordering the Pacific coast, the Cascade Mountains and Sierra Nevada form the outer edge of a high tableland, consisting in part of stony and sandy desert and partly of grazing land and forested mountains, and including the Great Salt Lake, which extends to the Rocky Mountains. In the eastern states large forests still exist, the remnants of the forests which formerly extended over all the Atlantic slope. The highest point is Mount McKinley (6,193 m) in Alaska, and the lowest point of dry land is in Death Valley (Inyo, California), 85 m below sea level. Temperatures vary dramatically and average temperatures in Washington DC range from 6°C in January to 27°C in June.

HISTORY AND POLITICS

The area which is now the USA was first inhabited by nomadic hunters who probably arrived from Asia *c.*30,000 BC. The first (failed) European colony was founded by Sir Walter Raleigh in 1585. By 1733 there were 13 British colonies, composed largely of religious non-conformists who had left Britain to escape persecution; the French and Spanish had also founded colonies. The War of Independence broke out in 1775 largely because of the colonists' objection to being taxed by, but having no representation in, the British Parliament. The forces of the British government were defeated with French, Spanish and Dutch assistance. The Declaration of Independence which inaugurated the United States of America was signed on 4 July 1776; Britain recognised American sovereignty in 1783. The first federal constitution was drawn up in 1787; ten amendments, termed the Bill of Rights, were added in 1791. The 13 original states of the Union ratified the constitution between 1787 and 1790. Vermont, Kentucky and Tennessee were admitted in the 1790s but most of the states acceded in the 19th century as the opening up of the centre and west led to the creation of new states and European or neighbouring countries ceded or sold their territories to the USA.

The Civil War (1861–5) was fought over the issue of slavery, which was integral to the economy of the southern states but was opposed by the northern states. The northern states defeated the Confederacy of southern states (South Carolina, Georgia, Alabama, Florida, Mississippi, Louisiana).

The USA emerged as a world economic and military superpower in the 20th century and played a decisive role in the two world wars. Its economic and military (including nuclear) supremacy has given the USA a key role in shaping the post-war world.

Presidential and legislative elections held on 7 November 2000 saw the Republican candidate George W. Bush win 47.9 per cent of the vote with the Republican Party securing 51 seats in the Senate. Presidential and legislative elections were scheduled for November 2004.

FOREIGN RELATIONS

Following the terrorist attacks in New York and Washington DC on 11 September 2001, responsibility for which was claimed by Osama bin Laden's Islamist group, al Qa'eda, the USA led a military operation against al Qa'eda and the Taliban in Afghanistan in October 2001 (*see* Afghanistan). Attempts to capture bin Laden and the Taliban leader, Mullah Omar have, to date, been unsuccessful.

Tensions rose between the USA and Iraq in 2002 over US concerns that Iraq was developing weapons of mass destruction. UN weapons inspections continued into 2003 but the situation deteriorated and on 20 March 2003 the USA began a military campaign (which included British military involvement) to remove the Iraqi president, Saddam Hussein, from power. This move to war created a rift in foreign policy between the European Union (with the exception of Spain), which was opposed to military action, and the United States. US forces advanced into central Baghdad in early April. On 1 May, US President George Bush declared the major part of the war in Iraq to be over. However, as of September 2004, US troops remained in Iraq to stabilise the country and continue to be the targets of sniper and bomb attacks.

In response to the threat of terrorist attacks on US soil a Department of Homeland Security was created in November 2002, in the biggest reorganisation of the federal government for more than 50 years.

THE STATES OF THE UNION

The United States of America is a federal republic consisting of 50 states and the federal District of Columbia and of organised territories. Of the present 50 states, 13 are original states, seven were admitted without previous organisation as territories, and 30 were admitted after such organisation.

State (with date and order of admission)	*Area sq. km*	*Population (2003 estimates)*	*Capital*	*Governor (end of term in office)*	
Alabama (AL) (1819) (22)	133,915	4,500,752	Montgomery	Robert Riley (R)	(2006)
Alaska (AK) (1959) (49)	1,530,694	648,818	Juneau	Frank Murkowski (R)	(2006)
Arizona (AZ) (1912) (48)	295,259	5,580,811	Phoenix	Janet Napolitano (D)	(2006)
Arkansas (AR) (1836) (25)	137,754	2,725,714	Little Rock	Mike Huckabee (R)	(2006)
California (CA) (1850) (31)	411,047	35,484,453	Sacramento	Arnold Schwarzenegger (R)	(2006)
Colorado (CO) (1876) (38)	269,595	4,550,688	Denver	Bill Owens (R)	(2006)
Connecticut (CT) § (1788) (5)	12,997	3,483,372	Hartford	M. J. Rell (R)	(2007)
Delaware (DE) § (1787) (1)	5,297	817,491	Dover	Ruth Ann Minner (D)	(2004)

State (with date and order of admission)	*Area sq. km*	*Population (2003 estimates)*	*Capital*	*Governor (end of term in office)*	
Florida (FL) (1845) (27)	151,939	17,019,068	Tallahassee	Jeb Bush (R)	(2006)
Georgia (GA) § (1788) (4)	152,576	8,684,715	Atlanta	Sonny Perdue (R)	(2006)
Hawaii (HI) (1959) (50)	16,760	1,257,608	Honolulu	Linda Lingle (R)	(2006)
Idaho (ID) (1890) (43)	216,430	1,336,332	Boise	Dirk Kempthorne (R)	(2006)
Illinois (IL) (1818) (21)	145,933	12,653,544	Springfield	Rod Blagojevich (D)	(2006)
Indiana (IN) (1816) (19)	93,719	6,195,643	Indianapolis	Joe Kiernan (D)	(2004)
Iowa (IA) (1846) (29)	145,752	2,944,062	Des Moines	Tom Vilsack (D)	(2006)
Kansas (KS) (1861) (34)	213,097	2,723,507	Topeka	Kathleen Sebelius (D)	(2006)
Kentucky (KY) (1792) (15)	104,661	4,117,827	Frankfort	Ernie Fletcher (R)	(2007)
Louisiana (LA) (1812) (18)	123,677	4,496,334	Baton Rouge	Kathleen Blanco (R)	(2007)
Maine (ME) (1820) (23)	86,156	1,305,728	Augusta	John Baldacci (D)	(2006)
Maryland (MD) § (1788) (7)	27,091	5,508,909	Annapolis	Robert Ehrlich(D)	(2006)
Massachusetts (MA) § (1788) (6)	21,455	6,433,422	Boston	Mitt Romney (R)	(2006)
Michigan (MI) (1837) (26)	151,584	10,079,985	Lansing	Jennifer Granholm (D)	(2006)
Minnesota (MN) (1858) (32)	218,600	5,059,375	St Paul	Tim Pawlenty (R)	(2006)
Mississippi (MS) (1817) (20)	123,514	2,881,281	Jackson	Haley Barbour (D)	(2007)
Missouri (MO) (1821) (24)	180,514	5,704,484	Jefferson City	Bob Holden (D)	(2004)
Montana (MT) (1889) (41)	380,848	917,621	Helena	Judy Martz (R)	(2004)
Nebraska (NE) (1867) (37)	200,349	1,739,291	Lincoln	Mike Johanns (R)	(2006)
Nevada (NV) (1864) (36)	286,352	2,241,154	Carson City	Kenny Guinn (R)	(2006)
New Hampshire (NH) § (1788) (9)	24,033	1,287,687	Concord	Craig Benson (R)	(2004)
New Jersey (NJ) § (1787) (3)	20,168	8,638,396	Trenton	James McGreevey (D)	(2005)
New Mexico (NM) (1912) (47)	314,925	1,874,614	Santa Fé	Bill Richardson (D)	(2006)
New York (NY) § (1788) (11)	127,189	19,190,115	Albany	George Pataki (R)	(2006)
North Carolina (NC) § (1789) (12)	136,412	8,407,248	Raleigh	Mike Easley (D)	(2004)
North Dakota (ND) (1889) (39)	183,117	633,837	Bismarck	John Hoeven (R)	(2004)
Ohio (OH) (1803) (17)	107,044	11,435,798	Columbus	Bob Taft (R)	(2006)
Oklahoma (OK) (1907) (46)	181,185	3,511,532	Oklahoma City	Brad Henry (D)	(2006)
Oregon (OR) (1859) (33)	251,418	3,559,596	Salem	Ted Kulongoski (D)	(2006)
Pennsylvania (PA) § (1787) (2)	117,347	12,365,455	Harrisburg	Edward Rendell (D)	(2006)
Rhode Island (RI) § (1790) (13)	3,139	1,076,164	Providence	Don Carcieri (R)	(2006)
South Carolina (SC) § (1788) (8)	80,582	4,147,152	Columbia	Mark Sanford (R)	(2006)
South Dakota (SD) (1889) (40)	199,730	764,309	Pierre	Mike Rounds (R)	(2006)
Tennessee (TN) (1796) (16)	109,153	5,841,748	Nashville	Phil Bredesen (D)	(2006)
Texas (TX) (1845) (28)	691,027	22,118,509	Austin	Rick Perry (R)	(2006)
Utah (UT) (1896) (45)	219,888	2,351,467	Salt Lake City	Olene R. Walker (R)	(2004)
Vermont (VT) (1791) (14)	24,900	619,107	Montpelier	James Douglas (R)	(2004)
Virginia (VA) § (1788) (10)	105,586	7,386,330	Richmond	Mark Warner (D)	(2005)
Washington (WA) (1889) (42)	176,479	6,131,445	Olympia	Gary Locke (D)	(2004)
West Virginia (WV) (1863) (35)	62,761	1,810,354	Charleston	Bob Wise (D)	(2004)
Wisconsin (WI) (1848) (30)	145,436	5,472,299	Madison	Jim Doyle (D)	(2006)
Wyoming (WY) (1890) (44)	253,324	501,242	Cheyenne	Dave Freudenthal (D)	(2006)
Dist. of Columbia (DC) (1791)	179	563384	–	Anthony Williams (D) (*Mayor*)	

OUTLYING TERRITORIES AND POSSESSIONS

	Area sq. km	*Population (2003 estimates)*	*Capital*	*Governor (end of term in office)*	
American Samoa	200	67,084*	Pago Pago	Togiola Tulafono (D)	(2004)
Guam	544	157,557*	Hagatna	Felix Perez Camacho (R)	(2006)
Northern Mariana Islands	464	74,612*	Saipan	Juan N. Babauta (R)	(2005)
Puerto Rico	8,875	3,878,532*	San Juan	Sila María Calderón (D)	(2004)
US Virgin Islands	346	122,211*	Charlotte Amalie	Charles Wesley Turnbull (D)	(2006)

§The 13 original states
D Democratic Party; I Independent; R Republican Party
* 2001 estimates

RESIDENT POPULATION BY RACE 2001 ESTIMATE
(Thousands)

White	211,461
Black	34,658
*American Indian	2,476
Asian	10,242
Native Hawaiian and other Pacific Islanders	399
†Hispanic origin	35,306
Other race	15,359
Two or more races	6,826
Total	316,727

*Includes Eskimo and Aleut
†Persons of Hispanic origin may be of any race

IMMIGRATION

From 1820 to 2000, 666,089,431 immigrants were admitted to the United States. The total number of immigrants in 2002 was 1,063,733. Five countries supplied 40 per cent of new immigrants: Mexico (219,380), India (71,105), the People's Republic of China (61,282), the Philippines (51,308), and Vietnam (33,627).

POLITICAL SYSTEM

By the constitution of 17 September 1787 (to which amendments were added in 1791, 1798, 1804, 1865, 1868, 1870, 1913, 1920, 1933, 1951, 1961, 1964, 1967, 1971 and 1992), the government of the United States is entrusted to three separate authorities: the executive (the President and Cabinet), the legislature (Congress) and the judicature. The President is indirectly elected by an electoral college every four years. There is also a Vice-President, who, should the president die, becomes President for the remainder of the term. The tenure of the presidency is limited to two terms. The President, with the consent of the Senate, appoints the Cabinet officers and all the chief officials. He makes recommendations of a general nature to Congress, and when laws are passed by Congress he may return them to Congress with a veto. But if a measure so vetoed is again passed by both Houses of Congress by two-thirds majority in each House, it becomes law, notwithstanding the objection of the President. The President must be at least 35 years of age and a native citizen of the United States.

PRESIDENTIAL ELECTIONS

Each state elects (on the first Tuesday after the first Monday in November of the year preceding the year in which the presidential term expires) a number of electors (members of the electoral college), equal to the whole number of Senators and Representatives to which the state may be entitled in the Congress. The electors for each state meet in their respective states on the first Monday after the second Wednesday in December following, and vote for a President by ballot. The ballots are then sent to Washington, and opened on 6 January by the President of the Senate in the presence of Congress. The candidate who has received a majority of the whole number of electoral votes cast is declared president for the ensuing term. If no one has a majority, then from the highest on the list (not exceeding three) the House of Representatives elects a president, the votes being taken by states, the representation from each state having one vote. A presidential term begins at noon on 20 January.

HEAD OF STATE

President of the United States, George Walker Bush, *born* 6 July 1946, *elected* 7 November 2000, *sworn in* 20 January 2001 (Republican)
Vice-President, Richard B. Cheney, *born* 30 January 1941

SELECTED GOVERNMENT MEMBERS *as at July 2004*

Defence, Donald Rumsfeld
Interior, Gale Norton
Secretary of State, Colin Powell
Treasury, John Snow

UNITED STATES EMBASSY

24 Grosvenor Square, London W1A 1AE
T 020-7499 9000
Ambassador Extraordinary and Plenipotentiary, HE William S. Farish, apptd 2001

BRITISH EMBASSY

3100 Massachusetts Avenue NW, Washington DC 20008.
T (+1) (202) 588 7800
Ambassador Extraordinary and Plenipotentiary, HE Sir David Manning, KCMG, apptd 2003

BRITISH COUNCIL DIRECTOR, Andy Mackay

(Cultural Attaché), c/o The British Embassy, 3100 Massachusetts Avenue NW, Washington DC 20008–3600
T (+1) (202) 588 7838
E enquiries@us.britishcouncil.org

THE CONGRESS

Legislative power is vested in two houses, the Senate and the House of Representatives. The Senate has 100 members, two Senators from each state, elected for the term of six years, and each Senator has one vote. The House of Representatives consists of 435 Representatives, directly elected in each state for a two-year term, a resident commissioner from Puerto Rico and a delegate each from American Samoa, the District of Columbia, Guam and the Virgin Islands, making a total of 440 members. Members of the 108th Congress were elected on 5 November 2002 and the elections were scheduled for November 2004. The 108th Congress is constituted as follows:

Senate Republicans 51; Democrats 48; Independent 1; 2 vacancies; total 100
House Republicans 229; Democrats 205; Independent 1; total 435
President of the Senate, The Vice-President
Senate Majority Leader, Bill Frist *(R), Tennessee*
Speaker of the House of Representatives, J. Dennis Hastert *(R), Illinois*

THE JUDICATURE

The federal judiciary consists of three sets of federal courts: the Supreme Court at Washington DC, consisting of a Chief Justice and eight Associate Justices, the United States Courts of Appeals, consisting of 168 circuit judges within 13 regional circuits and the 94 United States district courts served by 575 district court judges.

THE SUPREME COURT

US Supreme Court Building, Washington DC 20543
Chief Justice, William H. Rehnquist, *Arizona*, apptd 1986

DEFENCE

Each military department is separately organised and functions under the direction, authority and control of the

Secretary of Defence. The Air Force has primary responsibility for the Department of Defence space development programmes and projects. Under strategic command the USA has 432 submarine-launched ballistic missiles, 550 inter-continental ballistic missiles, 208 heavy nuclear-capable bombers and 60 strategic defence interceptor aircraft together with 75 multiple intelligence satellites, radars and early warning systems throughout the world. The Army has 7,620 main battle tanks, 6,719 armoured infantry fighting vehicles, 14,300 armoured personnel carriers, 282 aircraft and 1,132 armed helicopters.

The Navy has 72 strategic submarines, 54 tactical submarines, 12 aircraft carriers, 27 cruisers, 49 destroyers, 30 frigates, 21 patrol and coastal vessels, 40 amphibious and support ships, 1,705 combat aircraft and 693 armed helicopters. The Marine Corps has 403 main battle tanks and 1,321 amphibious armoured vehicles. The Air Force has 208 long-range strike aircraft, 2,928 tactical combat aircraft and 227 helicopters.

The major deployments of US personnel overseas are: Germany (73,500); South Korea (41,360); Japan (40,680); Italy (11,965); UK (11,097); Turkey (1,742).

MILITARY EXPENDITURE – 3.3 per cent of GDP (2002)

MILITARY PERSONNEL – 1,464,582: Army 485,000, Navy 400,000, Marine Corps 174,400, Air Force 367,600, Coast Guard 37,582; Paramilitaries 53,000

ECONOMY AND TRADE

In 2003 central government budget receipts totalled US$2,048 billion and outlays US$2,128 billion. The largest areas of expenditure were social security (US$472 billion), defence (US$368 billion), income security (US$319.3 billion), Medicare (US$234.5 billion), and health (US$234.3 billion). US$56.6 billion was allocated to veterans' affairs and services, and US$82.56 billion to education and social services.

By the end of 2003 the unified federal budget deficit was US$374.2 billion.

GNI – US$9,780,800 million (2001); US$34,280 per capita (2001)

ANNUAL AVERAGE GROWTH OF GDP – 5.0 per cent (2000)

INFLATION RATE – 3.4 per cent (2000)

UNEMPLOYMENT – 5.8 per cent (2002)

FOREIGN DIRECT INVESTMENT – US$850,036 million (1997–2000)

IMPORTS – US$1,202,433 million (2002)

EXPORTS – US$693,860 million (2002)

GROSS DOMESTIC PRODUCT BY INDUSTRY
2000 US$ billions

Private industries	8,656.5
Agriculture, forestry, fisheries	135.8
Mining	127.1
Construction	4463.6
Manufacturing	1,566.6
Transportation and public utilities	825.0
Wholesale trade	674.1
Retail trade	893.9v
Finance, insurance, and real estate	1,936.2
Services	2,164.6v
Government and government enterprises	1,216.4
Statistical discrepancy	−130.4
Total	9,227.3

AGRICULTURE

The total number of farms in 2003 was 2,126,860 with a total area of land in farms of 938,750,000 acres, and an average acreage per farm of 441 acres. Principal crops are maize for grain, soybeans, wheat, hay, cotton, tobacco, grain sorghums, potatoes, oranges and barley. Agricultural trade for the 2003 fiscal year saw exports rise to an estimated US$56.2 billion, with imports of US$41 billion.

MINERALS

The value of non-fuel raw mineral production in 2003 totalled an estimated US$40 billion. Mineral exports in 2003 were valued at US$40 billion, and imports at US$60 billion. In 2003 the following quantities of minerals were produced: iron ore 50,000,000 tonnes; marketable phosphate rock 300,000 tonnes; copper 1,120,000 tonnes; zinc 77,000 tonnes; lead 50,000 tonnes.

ENERGY

Production in 2002 was 70.92 quadrillion British Thermal Unit (BTU), principally coal, natural gas and crude oil. Petroleum accounted for almost half of energy exports of 3.65 quadrillion BTU. Net imports were 25.74 quadrillion BTU, of which crude oil was 19.90 quadrillion BTU, to meet consumption of 97.90 quadrillion BTU (quadrillion=10^{15}).

BALANCE OF PAYMENTS

Trade – US$479,380 million deficit (2002)

Current Account – US$480,859 million deficit (2002)

Trade with UK	*2002*	*2003*
Imports from UK	£28,379,876,000	£28,997,721,000
Exports to UK	26,040,615,000	23,691,622,000

TRANSPORT INFRASTRUCTURE

There are approximately 6.4 million km of roads, with surfaced roads and streets accounting for 64.7 per cent of the total. The USA has nearly 195,000 km of railway, and more than 41,000 km of waterways. Its main ports and harbours are at Anchorage, Baltimore, Boston, Charleston, Chicago, Duluth, Hampton Roads, Honolulu, Houston, Jacksonville, Los Angeles, New Orleans, New York, Philadelphia, Port Canaveral, Portland (Oregon), Prudhoe Bay, San Francisco, Savannah, Seattle, Tampa and Toledo. US domestic and international scheduled airlines in 2000 carried approximately 665,042,490 passengers over 692,008,214,000 revenue passenger miles.

EDUCATION

All the states have compulsory school attendance laws. In general, children are obliged to attend school from seven to 16 years of age. Most of the revenue for public elementary and secondary school purposes comes from federal, state and local governments. Less than three per cent comes from gifts and from tuition and transportation fees.

Among the better-known universities are: Harvard, founded in 1636, and named after John Harvard of Emmanuel College, Cambridge, England, who bequeathed to it his library and a sum of money in 1638; Yale, founded in 1701; Princeton, New Jersey, founded 1746.

ENROLMENT (percentage of age group) – primary 100 per cent (1997); secondary 97 per cent (1997); tertiary 81 per cent (1997)

MEDIA

The American media is vast and powerful both at home and abroad. American film (based in Hollywood) and television (via the major networks of ABC, CBS, NBC, CNN, Fox, MTV, HBO, and PBS) are exported all over the world. The USA has around 10,000 commercial radio stations, and more than 1,500 daily newspapers (including *USA Today*, *The Wall Street Journal*, *The Washington Post* and *The New York Times*).

CULTURE

The USA has perhaps the most diverse culture in the world. Notable writers include Mark Twain (1835–1910), Herman Melville (1819–91), William Faulkner (1897–1962), Henry David Thoreau (1803–82), John Berryman (1914–72), Sylvia Plath (1932–63) and Toni Morrison (b. 1931), winner of the Nobel Prize for Literature in 1993.

The Hollywood film industry is the most wide-reaching in the world and celebrated names include Orson Welles (1915–85), Frank Capra (1897–1991), Stanley Kubrick (1928–99), Martin Scorsese (b. 1942) and Francis Ford Coppola (b. 1939).

Modern art found a spiritual home in New York, and the Guggenheim and Metropolitan Museums of Art both house vast collections of famous works. Renowned artists include Edward Hopper (1882–1967), Roy Lichtenstein (1923–97), Andy Warhol (1928–1987) and Jackson Pollock (1912–1956).

US TERRITORIES, ETC

Responsibility within the federal government for the United States insular areas other than Puerto Rico and Kingman Reef lies with the United States Department of the Interior, either the Office of Insular Affairs (for American Samoa, Guam, the Northern Mariana Islands, the United States Virgin Islands, Navassa Island (7.8 sq. km), Palmyra Atoll (4 sq. km) and Wake Atoll (6.4 sq. km) (shared with the United States Army Space and Missile Defense Command)) or the United States Fish and Wildlife Service (for Baker Island (1.5 sq. km), Howland Island (2.5 sq. km) and Jarvis Island (4.2 sq. km), Midway Atoll (5.2 sq. km) and Johnston Atoll (2.5 sq. km) (shared with the Defence Special Weapons Agency)). Four of the eight populated insular areas are represented in the United States House of Representatives, Puerto Rico by a resident commissioner and American Samoa, Guam and the United States Virgin Islands each by one non-voting delegate. Although represented in the United States House of Representatives by a delegate, the District of Columbia was an incorporated territory for only three years, from 21 February 1871 to 20 June 1874.

THE COMMONWEALTH OF PUERTO RICO

AREA – 9,104 sq. km
POPULATION – 3,834,000 (2001). The majority of the inhabitants are of Spanish descent, and Spanish and English are the official languages
CAPITAL – ΨSan Juan, population of the municipality (2002 estimate), 433,412. Other major towns are: Bayamón; Carolina; ΨPonce

Puerto Rico (Rich Port) is an island of the Greater Antilles group in the West Indies and was discovered in 1493 by Columbus. It was a Spanish possession until 1898, when the USA took formal possession as a result of the Spanish–American War. The 1952 constitution establishes the Commonwealth of Puerto Rico with full powers of local government. The Legislative Assembly consists of two elected houses: the Senate of 27 members and the House of Representatives of 51 members. The term of the Legislative Assembly is four years. The Governor is popularly elected for a term of four years. Residents of Puerto Rico are US citizens. Puerto Rico is represented in Congress by a resident commissioner, elected for a term of four years, who has a seat in the House of Representatives but not a vote, although he has a right to vote on those committees of which he is a member.
Governor, Sila María Calderón

Trade with UK	*2002*	*2003*
Imports from UK	£257,605,000	£321,846,000
Exports to UK	615,579,000	486,244,000

GUAM

AREA – 545 sq. km
POPULATION – 160,000 (2001): 43 per cent Chamorro stock mingled with Filipino and Spanish blood. The Chamorro language belongs to the Malayo-Polynesian family, but with considerable admixture of Spanish. Chamorro and English are the official languages; most Chamorro residents are bilingual
CAPITAL – Hagatna (also known as Agana). Port of entry, ΨApra

Guam is the largest of the Mariana Islands, in the north Pacific Ocean. Guam was occupied by the Japanese in December 1941 but was recaptured by US forces in 1944. Under the Organic Act of Guam 1950, Guam has statutory powers of self-government, and any person born in Guam is a US citizen but cannot vote in a US presidential election. A 15-member unicameral legislature is popularly elected biennially. The Governor and Lieutenant-Governor are popularly elected. There is also a District Court of Guam, with original jurisdiction in cases under federal law. Guam's two main sources of revenue are tourism (particularly from Japan) and US military spending.
Governor, Felix Perez Camacho

AMERICAN SAMOA

AREA – 199 sq. km
POPULATION – 63,000 (1997 estimate)
CAPITAL – ΨPago Pago (population, 3,519)
NATIONAL DAY – 17 April (Flag Day)

American Samoa consists of the islands of Tutuila, Aunu'u, Ofu, Olesega, Ta'u, Rose and Swains Islands. Those born in American Samoa are US non-citizen nationals, but some have acquired citizenship through service in the United States armed forces or other naturalisation procedure. The constitution of 1966 grants American Samoa a measure of self-government, with certain powers reserved to the US Secretary of the Interior. There is a bicameral legislature of 21 seats, 20

elected, one appointed, with popularly elected representatives and 18 traditionally elected senators, and a popularly elected Governor.
Governor, Togiola Tulafono

THE UNITED STATES VIRGIN ISLANDS

AREA – 363 sq. km
POPULATION – 123,000 (2001)
CAPITAL – ΨCharlotte Amalie (population, 12,331, 1990), on St Thomas

The US Virgin Islands were purchased from Denmark and came under US sovereignty in 1917. There are three main islands, St Thomas, St Croix, St John and about 50 small islets or cays. Under the provisions of the Revised Organic Act of the Virgin Islands 1954, legislative power is vested in the Legislature, a unicameral body composed of 15 senators popularly elected for two-year terms. The Governor is popularly elected. Those born in the US Virgin Islands are US nationals.
Governor, Charles Wesley Turnbull

NORTHERN MARIANA ISLANDS

AREA – 477 sq. km
POPULATION – 77,000 (2001)
SEAT OF GOVERNMENT – Saipan (population, 52,706, 1995 census)

The USA administered the Northern Mariana Islands as part of a UN Trusteeship until the trusteeship agreement was terminated in 1986, bringing fully into effect a 1976 congressional law establishing the Northern Mariana Islands as a Commonwealth under US sovereignty. Most of the then residents became US citizens. Those born subsequently in the Northern Mariana Islands are US citizen nationals. There is a popularly elected bicameral legislature and a popularly elected Governor.
Governor, Juan N. Babauta

URUGUAY

República Oriental del Uruguay – Eastern Republic of Uruguay

AREA – 175,000 sq. km. Neighbours: Argentina (west), Brazil (north and east)
POPULATION – 3,361,000 (2001): predominantly of Spanish and Italian descent. Spanish is the official language. Many Uruguayans are Roman Catholics. There is no established church
CAPITAL – ΨMontevideo (population, 1,303,182, 1996)
MAJOR CITIES – Canelones; Melo; Mercedes; Minas; ΨPaysandú; Punta del Este; Rivera; Salto
CURRENCY – Uruguayan peso of 100 centésimos
NATIONAL ANTHEM – Orientales, La Patria O La Tumba (Uruguayans, The Fatherland Or Death)
NATIONAL DAY – 25 August (Declaration of Independence, 1825)
NATIONAL FLAG – Four blue and five white horizontal stripes surcharged with sun on a white ground in the top corner, next flagstaff
LIFE EXPECTANCY (years) – 75 (2001)
MORTALITY RATE (per 1,000 population) – 8.97 (2003)
INFANT MORTALITY (per 1,000 births) – 14 (2001)
HIV / AIDS ADULT PREVALENCE – 0.3 per cent (2001)
DEATH PENALTY – No (abolished 1907)
POPULATION BELOW POVERTY LINE – 6 per cent (1997)
POPULATION GROWTH RATE – 0.7 per cent (1990–2001)
POPULATION DENSITY – 19 per sq. km (2001)
URBAN POPULATION – 92 per cent (2001)
MILITARY EXPENDITURE – 1.8 per cent of GDP (2002)
MILITARY PERSONNEL – 24,000: Army 15,200, Navy 5,700, Air Force 3,100; Paramilitaries 920

CLIMATE AND TERRAIN

The country consists mainly of undulating grassy plains, with low hills. Elevation extremes range from 514 m (Cerro Catedral) at the highest point to 0 m (Atlantic Ocean) at the lowest. The principal river is the Rio Negro (with its tributary the Yi), flowing from north-east to south-west into the Rio Uruguay. Average temperatures in Montevideo range from 6°C in July and to 28°C in January.

HISTORY AND POLITICS

Uruguay (or the *Banda Oriental*, as the territory lying on the eastern bank of the Uruguay River was then called) formed part of Spanish South America from 1726 to 1814, when it was annexed by the Argentine Confederation and then Portugal, becoming a province of Brazil. In 1825, the country threw off Brazilian rule. Uruguay was declared an independent state in 1828 and was inaugurated as a republic in 1830.

General elections held in 1984 marked the return to civilian rule after 11 years of presidential and military rule. The first fully free presidential and legislative elections since 1971 were held in 1989, and were won by the National (*Blanco*) Party (NP).

The presidential election of 1999 was won by Jorge Batlle Ibáñez of the Colorado Party (CP). The legislative elections for both houses of the General Assembly, which were held simultaneously with the first round of the presidential election, resulted in the Progressive Encounter-Broad Front (EP-FA) winning seats, the others being won by the CP 33 seats, the NP 22 seats and the New Space party (NE) four seats in the House of Representatives, with the EP-FA winning 12 seats, the CP, the NP seven seats and the NE one seat in the Senate. A coalition government of the CP and the NP was formed.

Presidential and legislative elections were scheduled for late October 2004.

POLITICAL SYSTEM

Under the constitution the President (who may serve only a single term of five years) appoints a council of ministers and a Secretary (Planning and Budget Office), and the Vice-President presides over Congress. The Congress consists of a Chamber of 99 deputies and a Senate of 30 members (plus the Vice-President), elected for five years by proportional representation. The republic is divided into 19 Departments, each with an elected Governor and legislature.

HEAD OF STATE

President, Jorge Batlle Ibáñez, *elected* 28 November 1999, *took office* 1 March 2000
Vice-President, Luis Hierro López

SELECTED GOVERNMENT MEMBERS *as at August 2004*

Economy and Finance, Isaac Alfie
Foreign Relations, Didier Opertti
Interior, Guillermo Sterling
National Defence, Yamandu Fau

EMBASSY OF URUGUAY
2nd Floor, 140 Brompton Road, London SW3 1HY
T 020-7589 8835
Chargé d'Affairs, Carlos Osvaldo Bentancour

BRITISH EMBASSY
Calle Marco Bruto 1073, 11300 Montevideo (PO Box 16024).
T (+598) (2) 622 3650/3630
E bemonte@internet.com.uy
Ambassador Extraordinary and Plenipotentiary, HE John Everard, apptd 2001

ECONOMY AND TRADE

Beef, mutton and wool are produced and rice, wheat, barley, linseed and sunflower seed are cultivated. Other foodstuffs (citrus, wine, beer), fishing and textile industries are also of importance. Textiles, tyres, sheet-glass, three-ply wood, cement, leather-curing, beet-sugar, plastics, household consumer goods and edible oils are produced. Exploited minerals include clinker, dolomite, marble and granite. Much of the economy is in the hands of state monopolies and there has been only limited market liberalisation.

The economic problems of neighbouring Brazil and Argentina have had a negative influence on the Uruguayan economy. Inflation became a serious issue, and as a consequence both unemployment, and Uruguay's external debt burden, increased significantly. In 2003 the IMF extended Uruguay's existing standby credit facility, due to expire in March 2004, to March 2005. Repayments of loans amounting to about US$94 million were postponed until August 2004.

The major exports are meat, meat by-products and livestock, agricultural products and textiles. The principal imports are machinery and transport equipment and chemical products. Principal trading partners are Brazil, Argentina, the USA and Germany.

GNI – US$19,200 million (2001); US$5,710 per capita (2001)
ANNUAL AVERAGE GROWTH OF GDP – 1.3 per cent (2000)
INFLATION RATE – 4.8 per cent (2000)
UNEMPLOYMENT – 13.6 per cent (2000)
TOTAL EXTERNAL DEBT – US$8,196 million (2000)
FOREIGN DIRECT INVESTMENT – US$851 million (1997–2000)
IMPORTS – US$3,061 million (2001)
EXPORTS – US$2,060 million (2001)

BALANCE OF PAYMENTS
Trade – US$60 million surplus (2002)
Current Account – US$262 million surplus (2002)

Trade with UK	*2002*	*2003*
Imports from UK	£31,023,000	£31,723,000
Exports to UK	46,490,000	44,265,000

TRANSPORT INFRASTRUCTURE

There are nearly 9,000 km of roads, 8,000 km of which are surfaced, and over 2,000 km of railway in use. The international airport of Carrasco lies 19 km outside Montevideo. There are 1,600 km of waterways. The River Uruguay is navigable from its estuary to Salto, 200 miles north, and the Negro is also navigable as far as Mercedes. In December 1998, the Senate approved the construction of a 45 km bridge across the River Plate, linking Uruguay and Argentina. Uruguay's main ports are at Colonia, Fray Bentos, Juan La Caze, La Paloma, Montevideo, Nueva Palmira, Paysandú, Punta del Este, and Piriapolis.

EDUCATION

Primary and secondary education is compulsory and free, and technical and trade schools and evening courses for adult education are state controlled. The university at Montevideo (founded in 1849) has ten faculties and a new university has been built at Salto.

ILLITERACY RATE – (m) 2.6 per cent; (f) 1.8 per cent (2000)
ENROLMENT (percentage of age group) – primary 100 per cent (1997); tertiary 30 per cent (1997)

MEDIA

The constitution enshrines freedom of expression. There are more than 100 daily and weekly newspapers, all privately owned, and more than 100 radio stations, as well as 20 television channels. The government runs one television and one radio station.

CULTURE

The music of Uruguay has European origins, from which the local versions (of, for example, polkas and waltzes) have evolved. The literature and art of Uruguay is well developed and diverse, from the epic poetry of Juan Zorillo de San Martín (1855–1931) to the complex symbolist writing of Juan Herrera y Reissig (1875–1910). Celebrated painters include Juan Manual Blanes (1830–1901) and Joaquin Torres-García (1874–1949).

UZBEKISTAN

Ŭzbekiston Žumhurijati – Republic of Uzbekistan

AREA – 414,200 sq. km. Neighbours: Kazakhstan (north and west), Kyrgyzstan and Tajikistan (east), Afghanistan and Turkmenistan (south)
POPULATION – 25,257,000 (2001): 72 per cent Uzbek, 8 per cent Russian, 5 per cent Tajik and 4 per cent Kazakh, with smaller numbers of Tatars, Kara-Kalpaks, Koreans, Ukrainians and Kyrgyz. The predominant religion is Sunni Muslim. Islam is tolerated within strict bounds; it is allowed to play no part in politics. The official language is Uzbek (72 per cent); Russian (8 per cent), Tajik (5 per cent) and Kazakh (4 per cent) are also spoken. Uzbek is one of the Turkic group of languages. In 1994 the government approved a six-year programme for the transfer of the Uzbek language to a Latin script
CAPITAL – Tashkent (population, 2,142,700, 1998 estimate)
MAJOR CITIES – Samarkand, which contains the Gur-Emir (Tamerlane's Mausoleum); Bukhara, which contains the Samanid Mausoleum and the Ulughbek Madrassah
CURRENCY – Soum of 100 tiyin
NATIONAL DAY – 1 September (Independence Day)
NATIONAL FLAG – Three horizontal stripes of blue, white, green, with the white fimbriated in red; on the blue near the hoist a crescent and twelve stars, all in white
LIFE EXPECTANCY (years) – 69 (2001)
MORTALITY RATE (per 1,000 population) – 7.97 (2003)
INFANT MORTALITY (per 1,000 births) – 52 (2001)
DEATH PENALTY – Yes

POPULATION GROWTH RATE – 1.9 per cent (1990–2001)
POPULATION DENSITY – 61 per sq. km (2001)
URBAN POPULATION – 37 per cent (2001)
MILITARY EXPENDITURE – 2.9 per cent of GDP (2002)
MILITARY PERSONNEL – 55,000: Army 40,000, Air Force 15,000; Paramilitaries 20,000
CONSCRIPTION DURATION – 18 months
ILLITERACY RATE – (m) 6.6 per cent; (f) 15.3 per cent (2000)

CLIMATE AND TERRAIN

Uzbekistan occupies the south-central part of former Soviet Central Asia, lying between the high Tien Shan mountains and the Pamir highlands in the east and south-east and sandy lowlands in the west and north-west, in the basin of the Amu Darya and Syr Darya rivers. Uzbekistan consists of the Republic of Karakalpakstan and 12 regions: Andijan, Bukhara, Jizak, Fergana, Kashka-Darya, Khorezm, Namanghan, Navoi, Samarkand, Surhan-Darya, Syr-Darya and Tashkent. Elevation extremes range from 4,301 m (Adelunga Toghi) at the highest point to −12 m (Sariqarnish Kuli) at the lowest. Average temperatures in Tashkent range from −2°C in January to 33°C in June.

HISTORY AND POLITICS

In the 13th century the area that is now Uzbekistan became the centre of a great Muslim empire under Amir Timur (Tamerlane), with its capital at Samarkand. By the beginning of the 19th century three independent Khanates, Khiva, Kokand and Bukhara, existed in what is now Uzbekistan. These were annexed to the Russian Empire in the second half of the 19th century. In 1917 a Communist revolution broke out in Tashkent and by 1921, all of Uzbekistan had been absorbed into the Soviet Union. Under Soviet rule a massive land irrigation programme was implemented to allow the cultivation of cotton.

Uzbekistan declared its independence from the Soviet Union on 1 September 1991. Its independence was confirmed in a referendum and recognised internationally. Elections to the new *Oliy Majlis* were held in 1994 and won by the ruling People's Democratic Party (PDP) and its allies.

Despite the constitutionally guaranteed freedom of religion and thought, and respect for human rights and multiparty democracy, censorship is still widely used and little political opposition is tolerated. In 1995 President Karimov's term of office was extended to 2000 by a national referendum and he won a further five-year term in a presidential election held in 2000, gaining 91.9 per cent of the vote. The election result attracted criticism from the Organisation for Security and Co-operation in Europe, which claimed that no real opposition candidate had been allowed to stand. Legislative elections were held in December 1999; the People's Democratic Party and its allies won 123 seats. The remaining seats were won by independent candidates and citizens' groups.

The main opposition parties, Erk (Freedom) and Birlik (Unity) nationalist parties, had been banned since the introduction of the multiparty constitution in 1992, but Birlik held a congress openly for the first time in ten years in May 2003 and Erk held its first formal meeting for 11 years in June. Erk pledged to raise the party's political profile at future elections.

Legislative elections were due in December 2004.

INSURGENCIES
The Islamic Movement of Uzbekistan (IMU), which seeks to overthrow the government and establish an Islamic state, was founded in 1996. Whilst it has carried out car bombings in Tashkent, its activities have centred on the Fergana valley and it has clashed with Kyrgyz armed forces.

FOREIGN RELATIONS
Uzbekistan is a member of the UN, OSCE, UNESCO and the WHO. In 2002, a military agreement was signed with the USA over the anti-terrorist operation in Afghanistan, outlining future co-operation and more frequent contact between the two countries.

A final agreement demarcating the 2,240 km border with Kazakhstan was signed on in 2002. A previous border agreement signed in 2001 had left unresolved the issue of a number of settlements in northern Uzbekistan, populated by significant numbers of Kazakh citizens.

POLITICAL SYSTEM
A referendum held in 2002 approved constitutional amendments on the extension of the presidential term of office from five to seven years and the creation of a bicameral legislature. The amendments were then approved by parliament. A second legislative chamber was planned for December 2004, following the end of the 1999–2004 parliamentary term.

HEAD OF STATE
President, Islam Karimov, *elected* 29 December 1991, *elected by referendum for a five-year term* 26 March 1995, *re-elected* 9 January 2000

SELECTED GOVERNMENT MEMBERS *as at July 2004*
Chairman of the Supreme Council, Erkin Khalilov
Prime Minister, Shavkat Mirziyayev
Defence, Kadyr Ghulomov
Finance, Saidahmad Rahimov
Foreign Affairs, Sodyk Safaev
Interior, Zokirjon Almatov

EMBASSY OF THE REPUBLIC OF UZBEKISTAN
41 Holland Park, London W11 3RP
T 020-7229 7679
Ambassador Extraordinary and Plenipotentiary, HE Tukhtapulat Tursunovich Riskiev, apptd 2003

BRITISH EMBASSY
Ul. Gulyamova 67, UZ-700000 Tashkent
T (+998) (71) 1206451
Ambassador Extraordinary and Plenipotentiary, HE Craig Murray, apptd 2002

BRITISH COUNCIL DIRECTOR, Neville McBain
11 D. Kounaev Street, Tashkent
T (+998) (71) 120 6752
E bc-tashkent@britishcouncil.uz

ECONOMY AND TRADE

Uzbekistan's economy is based on intensive agricultural production. Cotton production is approximately 4 million tonnes per year, made possible by extensive irrigation schemes. Textile manufacture, silk production and leather goods are also important while wheat, potatoes and rice are widely grown. There are some agricultural and textile machinery plants and several chemical combines.

Uzbekistan possesses a wide range of mineral deposits including copper, uranium, oil, gold and many other metals. The Muruntao mine is the largest open-cast gold mine in the world; in 1998, 81 tons of gold were produced. Total gold reserves are estimated at more than 5,000 tons. In 1998 oil output was 8.0 million tons, and gas production was 55 billion cubic metres. Foreign direct investment exceeds US$9 billion. South Korea, the USA, Japan, Turkey and the UK are the main investors. Uzbekistan is a member of the Commonwealth of Independent States economic union.

GNI – US$13,800 million (2001); US$550 per capita (2001)

ANNUAL AVERAGE GROWTH OF GDP – 4.4 per cent (1998)

TOTAL EXTERNAL DEBT – US$4,340 million (2000)

FOREIGN DIRECT INVESTMENT – US$698 million (1997–2000)

Trade with UK	*2002*	*2003*
Imports from UK	£14,622,000	£18,225,000
Exports to UK	22,035,000	28,956,000

TRANSPORT INFRASTRUCTURE

Uzbekistan has 81,600 km of roads, 71,000 km of which are paved. It has nearly 4,000 km of railway, and 1,100 km of waterways.

MEDIA AND CULTURE

There is a mix of government-run and private television and radio stations in Uzbekistan. Almost all newspapers are produced by the state or by pro-government organisations. In both print and broadcast media, despite constitutional protection of free speech, the government strictly controls political content. *Khalq Sozi* is one of the major daily newspapers.

Many aspects of Uzbek culture reflect the country's Islamic heritage, notably the religious architecture and the decorative arts traditions of calligraphy and wood carving. The folk art of the region includes carpet weaving, embroidery and jewellery making. Oral tradition remains strong throughout rural Uzbekistan and includes the sung poems *Koshuk* and *Lapar*.

VANUATU

Ripablik blong Vanuatu/Republic of Vanuatu/République de Vanuatu

AREA – 12,189 sq. km

POPULATION – 192,910 (2001 estimate). About 95 per cent are Melanesian, the rest being mostly Micronesian, Polynesian and European. The national language is Bislama, but English and French are also official languages

CAPITAL – ΨPort Vila (population, 29,356, 1999 census), on Efate

MAJOR TOWN – Luganville, on Espiritu Santo

CURRENCY – Vatu of 100 centimes

NATIONAL ANTHEM – Nasonal Sing Sing Blong Vanuatu (National Anthem Of Vanuatu)

NATIONAL DAY – 30 July (Independence Day)

NATIONAL FLAG – Red over green with a black triangle in the hoist, the three parts being divided by fimbriations of black and yellow, and in the centre of the black triangle a boar's tusk overlaid by two crossed fern leaves

MORTALITY RATE (per 1,000 population) – 8.13 (2003)

DEATH PENALTY – No (abolished 1980)

POPULATION GROWTH RATE – 1.5 per cent (2004)

POPULATION DENSITY – 15 per sq. km (1999)

CLIMATE AND TERRAIN

Vanuatu is situated in the South Pacific Ocean. It includes 13 large and some 70 small islands, of coral and volcanic origin, including the Banks and Torres Islands in the north. The principal islands are Vanua Lava, Espiritu Santo, Maewo, Pentecost, Ambae, Malekula, Ambrym, Epi, Efate, Erromango, Tanna and Aneityum. Most islands are mountainous and there are active volcanoes on several. Elevation extremes range from 1,877 m (Tabwemasana) at the highest point to 0 m (Pacific Ocean) at the lowest. Vanuatu has a tropical climate and the average temperature is 29°C all year round.

HISTORY AND POLITICS

Some of the islands of Vanuatu have been inhabited for over 4,000 years. Europeans first arrived in the early 17th century, and Captain Cook named the islands the New Hebrides in 1774. Settlers began to arrive in Vanuatu in the second half of the 19th century. In 1906 Britain and France held joint sovereignty over the country which was only relinquished in 1980 when Vanuatu gained independence and became a republic within the Commonwealth.

Parliament consists of 52 members, directly elected for a term of four years. A Council of Chiefs advises on matters of custom. Executive power is held by the Prime Minister (elected from and by parliament) and a Council of Ministers who are responsible to parliament. The President is elected for a five-year term by the presidents of the six provincial governments and the members of parliament.

In the legislative elections of July 2004, the National United Party (NUP) won 10 of the 52 seats in parliament, thereby securing a majority. On 29 July 2004, Serge Vohor of the Union of Moderate Parties (UMP) was named as prime minister of a coalition government that included the NUP, the UMP and the Vanuaaki Pati (VP). Alfred Maseng was elected president in April 2004 but was removed from office on 10 May. His successor, Kalkot Matas Kelekele, was elected on 17 August 2004.

HEAD OF STATE
President, Kalkot Matas Kelekele, *elected* 17 August 2004

SELECTED GOVERNMENT MEMBERS *at August 2004*
Prime Minister, Public Services, Serge Vohor
Deputy Prime Minister, Home Affairs, Ham Lini
Finance and Economic Development, Moana Carcasses
Foreign Affairs, Barak Tame Sope
Internal Affairs, Health, Keasipai Song

BRITISH HIGH COMMISSION
KPMG House, Rue Pasteur, PO Box 567, Port Vila
T (+678) 23100
E bhcvila@vanuatu.com.vu
High Commissioner, HE Michael Hill, OBE, apptd 2000

ECONOMY AND TRADE

Most of the population is employed on plantations or in subsistence agriculture. Subsistence crops include yams, taro, manioc, sweet potato and breadfruit; principal cash crops are copra, cocoa and coffee. Cattle are kept on the plantations and beef is the second largest export. There is a small light industrial sector. Principal exports are copra, meat, timber and cocoa. The main trading partner is Japan. Tourism is a growing industry and the absence of direct taxation has led to growth in the finance and associated industries. Following a tightening up of the country's tax and regulatory systems in May 2003 the Organisation for Economic Co-operation and Development removed Vanuatu from its list of unco-operative tax havens.

GNI – US$212 million (2001); US$1,050 per capita (2001)
ANNUAL AVERAGE GROWTH OF GDP – 2.1 per cent (1998)
INFLATION RATE – 2.0 per cent (1999)
TOTAL EXTERNAL DEBT – US$69 million (2000)
IMPORTS – US$96 million (1999)
EXPORTS – US$26 million (1999)

BALANCE OF PAYMENTS
Trade – US$58 million deficit (2001)
Current Account – US$15 million deficit (2001)

Trade with UK	*2002*	*2003*
Imports from UK	£389,000	£121,000
Exports to UK	188,000	219,000

TRANSPORT INFRASTRUCTURE

Vanuatu has just over 1,000 km of roads, of which about one quarter is surfaced. The islands have no waterways or railways. The main ports are Forari, Port Vila and Santo.

MEDIA

The majority of media in Vanuatu is state owned. This includes one television station and one radio company. There are four newspapers, one of which is state-run.

VATICAN CITY STATE

Status Civitatis Vaticanae/Stato della Città del Vaticano – State of the Vatican City

AREA – 0.44 sq. km. Neighbour: Italy
POPULATION – 911 (2003 estimate). The languages are Latin and Italian
CAPITAL – Vatican City (population, 766, 1988)
CURRENCY – Euro (€) of 100 cents
NATIONAL ANTHEM – Inno E Marcia Pontificale (Hymn And Pontifical March)
NATIONAL DAY – 22 October (Inauguration of present Pontiff)
NATIONAL FLAG – Square flag; equal vertical bands of yellow (next staff), and white; crossed keys and triple crown device on white band
DEATH PENALTY – No (abolished 1969)
POPULATION DENSITY – 2,273 per sq. km (1997)
GDP – US$10 million (1998); US$20,659 per capita (1998)
ANNUAL AVERAGE GROWTH OF GDP – 1.3 per cent (1998)

HISTORY

The office of the ecclesiastical head of the Roman Catholic Church (Holy See) is vested in the Pope, the Sovereign Pontiff. For many centuries the Sovereign Pontiff exercised temporal power but by 1870 the Papal States had become part of unified Italy. The temporal power of the Pope was in suspense until the treaty of 1929, which recognised the full and independent sovereignty of the Holy See in the City of the Vatican.

Sovereign Pontiff, His Holiness Pope John Paul II (Karol Wojtyła), *born* at Wadowice (Kraków, Poland), 18 May 1920, *elected* Pope in succession to Pope John Paul I, 16 October 1978

SECRETARIAT OF STATE *as at July 2004*
Secretary of State, Cardinal Angelo Sodano, apptd December 1990
Assistant Secretary of State, Archbishop Leonardo Sandri
Secretary for Relations with States, Giovanni Lajolo

APOSTOLIC NUNCIATURE
54 Parkside, London SW19 5NE
T 020-8944 7189
Apostolic Nuncio, HE Archbishop Pablo Puente, apptd 1997

BRITISH EMBASSY TO THE HOLY SEE
91 Via dei Condotti, I-00187 Rome
T (+39) (06) 6992 3561
Ambassador Extraordinary and Plenipotentiary, HE Kathryn Colvin, apptd 2002

MEDIA AND CULTURE

There is one official television channel in Vatican City, and one official radio station (Vatican Radio), broadcasting seven channels. The Vatican Information Service is the state's official news service.

The city's architectural masterpiece, St Peter's Basilica, is famed for its domed roof and the Sistine Chapel ceiling, respectively designed and painted by Michelangelo. Much of the state's wealth is in a vast art collection.

VENEZUELA

República Bolivariana de Venezuela – Bolivarian Republic of Venezuela

AREA – 882,100 sq. km. Neighbours: Colombia (west), Guyana (east), Brazil (south)
POPULATION – 24,632,000 (2001): 67 per cent mestizo, 21 per cent white, 10 per cent black and 2 per cent Amerindian. The language is Spanish. 93 per cent of the population is Roman Catholic
CAPITAL – Ψ Caracas (population, 3,435,795, 2002 estimate)
MAJOR CITIES – Barquisimeto; ΨMaracaibo; Maracay; Valencia
CURRENCY – Bolívar (Bs) of 100 céntimos
NATIONAL ANTHEM – Gloria Al Bravo Pueblo (Glory To The Brave People)
NATIONAL DAY – 5 July
NATIONAL FLAG – Three horizontal stripes of yellow, blue, red with an arc of seven white stars on the blue stripe and a coat of arms on the upper hoist.
LIFE EXPECTANCY (years) – 73 (2001)
MORTALITY RATE (per 1,000 population) – 4.9 (2003)
INFANT MORTALITY (per 1,000 births) – 19 (2001)

HIV / AIDS ADULT PREVALENCE – 0.5 per cent (2001)
DEATH PENALTY – No (abolished 1863)
POPULATION BELOW POVERTY LINE – 47 per cent (1998)
POPULATION GROWTH RATE – 2.1 per cent (1990–2001)
POPULATION DENSITY – 28 per sq. km (2001)
URBAN POPULATION – 87 per cent (2001)
ILLITERACY RATE – (m) 6.9 per cent; (f) 7.8 per cent (2000)
ENROLMENT (percentage of age group) – primary 91 per cent (1997); secondary 40 per cent (1997)

CLIMATE AND TERRAIN

The mountains of Venezuela are the Eastern Andes and Maritime Andes, running south-west to north-east. The main range is known as the Sierra Nevada de Mérida and elevation extremes range from 5,007 m (Pico Bolivar) at the highest point to 0 m (Caribbean Sea) at the lowest. The principal river is the Orinoco. The upper waters of the Orinoco are united with those of the Rio Negro (a Brazilian tributary of the Amazon) by a natural river or canal, known as the Brazo Casiquiare. The coastal regions contain many lagoons and lakes including Maracaibo (area 13,351 sq. km), the largest lake in South America. Venezuela's wet season lasts from May to November and average temperatures in Caracas range from 16°C in January to 29°C in June.

HISTORY AND POLITICS

The first Spanish settlement was established at Cumaná in 1520 and Venezuela became part of the Vice royalty of New Granada in 1718. An Act of Independence was signed on 15 July 1811 but was followed by several years of struggle until troops led by Simón Bolivar defeated the Spanish at the battle of Carabobo in 1821. Independence from Great Colombia, into which Venezuela had been incorporated in 1819, was achieved in 1830.

In May 1999, a referendum on convening a constituent assembly to rewrite the constitution was passed and an election to decide the members of the constituent assembly was subsequently held in July. The new constitution was approved in a referendum and was proclaimed on 20 December. The National Congress was dissolved in early 2000, pending elections to the new National Assembly. In the presidential election held in July 2000, President Chávez was re-elected, winning 59 per cent of the vote. In the simultaneous election for the National Assembly, the Fifth Republic Movement (MVR) won nearly half of the seats; the other main parties represented were Democratic Action and Movement towards Socialism. Other parties won over a quarter of the seats. The National Assembly granted President Chávez the power to rule by decree in industrial and economic policy and matters concerning the civil service. An attempted military coup in April 2002 forced President Chávez to resign, but he was reinstated with his Cabinet two days later after popular protest.

In 2003 a deal, brokered by the Organisation of American States (OAS) between President Chávez and parts of the extra-parliamentary opposition, was finalised. This established the framework for a recall referendum to be held in August 2003 to ask the electorate if they wished to cut short Chávez's presidential term and hold immediate elections. A petition was delivered in August with more than three million signatures in favour of a referendum, but it was rejected by the electoral body. The referendum finally took place on 15 August 2004 and the result saw President Chávez remain in office.

POLITICAL SYSTEM

Under the 1999 constitution a unicameral legislature, the National Assembly, was created, and the post of Vice-President instituted. The President, who is directly elected, serves a six-year term, which is renewable once only. The Vice-President is appointed by the President. Legislative power is exercised by the 165-member *Asamblea Nacional* (National Assembly), which is directly elected for a five-year term.

HEAD OF STATE

President, Hugo Chávez Frías, *elected* 6 December 1998, *sworn in* 2 February 1999, re-elected 30 July 2000
Vice-President, José Vicente Rangel

SELECTED GOVERNMENT MEMBERS *as at July 2004*
Defence, Gen. Luis García Carneiro
Finance, Tobías Nóbrega Suarez
Foreign Relations, Jesús Pérez
Interior and Justice, Jesse Chacón

EMBASSY OF THE BOLIVARIAN REPUBLIC OF VENEZUELA
1 Cromwell Road, London SW7 2HR
T 020-7584 4206
Ambassador Extraordinary and Plenipotentiary, HE Alfredo Toro-Hardy, apptd 2001

BRITISH EMBASSY
Edificio Torre Las Mercedes (Piso 3), Avenida La Estancia, Chuao (Apartado 1246), Caracas 1061
T (+58) (212) 993 4111/4224
Ambassador Extraordinary and Plenipotentiary, HE Donald Lamont

BRITISH COUNCIL DIRECTOR, Barbara Wickham
Piso 3, Torre Credicard, Av. Principal El Bosque, El Bosque, Caracas
T (+58) (212) 952 9965
E bc-venezuela@britishcouncil.org.ve

DEFENCE

The Army has 81 main battle tanks, 290 armoured personnel carriers and seven attack helicopters. The Navy has two submarines, six frigates, six patrol and coastal vessels, three combat aircraft and nine armed helicopters at nine bases. The Air Force has 125 combat aircraft and 31 armed helicopters.
MILITARY EXPENDITURE – 1.3 per cent of GDP (2002)
MILITARY PERSONNEL – 82,300: Army 34,000, Navy 18,300, Air Force 7,000, National Guard 23,000
CONSCRIPTION DURATION – 30 months (selective)

ECONOMY AND TRADE

President Hugo Chávez pledged in 1998 that his government would cut public spending and tackle tax evasion and corruption. Agriculture comprises large-scale commercial farms together with subsistence farming. Land distribution is uneven, with 1 per cent of farms occupying 46 per cent of arable land and 250,000 smallholdings occupying less than 2 per cent of arable land. Products of the tropical forest region include orchids, wild rubber, timber, mangrove bark, balata gum and tonka beans. Agricultural products include corn, bananas, cocoa beans, coffee, cotton, rice, maize, sugar, sesame, groundnuts, potatoes, tomatoes, other vegetables, sisal and tobacco. There is an extensive beef and dairy farming industry. The principal industry is petroleum and gas, which together account for 78 per cent of exports. There are eight refineries.

Aluminium is abundant while iron ore deposits in eastern Venezuela have been exploited. Other industry includes a wide variety of manufacturing and component assembly, principally petrochemicals, gold, diamonds and foodstuffs.

A week-long national strike took place in October and December 2002 crippling the oil industry and leading to fuel shortages. Shops, factories and universities re-opened in February 2003.

Apart from oil, the main exports are bauxite, iron ore, agricultural products and basic manufactures. The main imports are machinery and transport equipment, chemicals and foodstuffs. The USA and Colombia are the major trading partners.

GNI – US$117,200 million (2001); US$4,760 per capita (2001)
ANNUAL AVERAGE GROWTH OF GDP – 3.2 per cent (2000)
INFLATION RATE – 16.2 per cent (2000)
UNEMPLOYMENT – 14.9 per cent (1999)
TOTAL EXTERNAL DEBT – US$38,196 million (2000)
FOREIGN DIRECT
INVESTMENT – US$17,173 million (1997–2000)
IMPORTS – US$11,840 million (2002)
EXPORTS – US$24,482 million (2002)

BALANCE OF PAYMENTS
Trade – US$13,939 million surplus (2002)
Current Account – US$7,711 million surplus (2002)

Trade with UK	*2002*	2003
Imports from UK	£233,242,000	£143,961,000
Exports to UK	191,431,000	115,360,000

TRANSPORT INFRASTRUCTURE

There are 96,155 km of roads, some 32,308 km of them surfaced. Road and river communications have made railways of negligible importance in Venezuela except for carrying iron ore in the south-east, though the government is expanding the network, and there are now some 682 km of railway lines. The Orinoco is navigable for ocean-going ships and Venezuela's major ports include Maracaibo and Caracas.

MEDIA AND CULTURE

There are six daily newspapers including the daily titles *El Mundo* and *El Nacional*. Radio and television services are a mixture of state and privately owned.

Rómulo Gallegos (1884–1969) and Arturo Pietri (1906–2001) are two of Venezuela's most celebrated writers.

VIETNAM

Công Hòa Xã Hôi Chu Nghĩa Viêt Nam – Socialist Republic of Vietnam

AREA – 325,500 sq. km. Neighbours: China (north), Laos and Cambodia (west)
POPULATION – 79,175,000 (2001). The language is Vietnamese. French, English and Khmer are also spoken
CAPITAL – Hanoi (population, 1,073,760, 1992 estimate)
MAJOR CITIES – ΨHaiphong; ΨHo Chi Minh City
CURRENCY – Dông of 10 ho or 100 xu
NATIONAL ANTHEM – Tien Quan Ca (The Troops Are Advancing)
NATIONAL DAY – 2 September
NATIONAL FLAG – Red, with yellow five-point star in centre
LIFE EXPECTANCY (years) – 69 (2001)
MORTALITY RATE (per 1,000 population) – 6.19 (2003)
INFANT MORTALITY (per 1,000 births) – 30 (2001)
HIV / AIDS ADULT PREVALENCE – 0.3 per cent (2001)
DEATH PENALTY – Yes
POPULATION BELOW POVERTY LINE – 37 per cent (1998)
POPULATION GROWTH RATE – 1.6 per cent (1990–2001)
POPULATION DENSITY – 243 per sq. km (2001)
ILLITERACY RATE – (m) 4.5 per cent; (f) 8.6 per cent (2000)
ENROLMENT (percentage of age group) – primary 100 per cent (1997); tertiary 7 per cent (1997)

CLIMATE AND TERRAIN

The terrain consists of flat delta in the north and south, divided by central highlands. The country is mountainous in the far north with elevation extremes ranging from 3,144 m (Ngoc Linh) at the highest point to 0 m (South China Sea) at the lowest. Vietnam has a humid climate dominated by a monsoon season that lasts from May to September in the north of the country, and from September to January in the south. Average temperatures in Hanoi range from 17°C in January to 29°C in June.

HISTORY AND POLITICS

Vietnam became a unified state at the end of the 18th century, with the assistance of France, whose influence on the region grew. In 1899 the Indo-Chinese Union was proclaimed, uniting Vietnam with Cambodia and Laos under French rule. Vietnam was under Japanese occupation from 1940 to 1945; insurrection by Communist, Nationalist and Revolutionary forces led to a French withdrawal in 1954 and the division of the country into Communist North Vietnam and non-communist South Vietnam. War broke out between the two countries in 1961, and lasted until 1975; the USA entered the war on the side of South Vietnam. North and South Vietnam were reunified in 1976 as the Socialist Republic of Vietnam. The national flag, anthem and capital of North Vietnam were adopted, and Saigon was renamed Ho Chi Minh City.

INSURGENCY

In March 2002 the office of the UN High Commissioner for Refugees (UNHCR) withdrew from a programme to repatriate about 1,000 Montagnard refugees to Vietnam from camps in Cambodia, after claiming that the

Vietnamese authorities were using unacceptable levels of coercion. However, this claim was rejected by the Vietnamese Foreign Ministry. A week later the Cambodian government announced that it would allow more than 900 refugees to be moved from the camps to the USA, and in June the first group of 50 refugees left the Cambodian capital Phnom Penh on their way to asylum in the USA.

POLITICAL SYSTEM
Effective power lies with the Vietnamese Communist Party (VCP), its highest executive body being the Central Committee, elected by a Party Congress on a national basis. The Politburo and the Secretariat of the Central Committee exercise the real power. The constitution of 1992 reaffirmed Communist Party rule but also formalised free market economic reforms. A new National Assembly *(Quoc-Hoi)* was elected on 19 May 2002; the VCP holds 449 of the 500 seats. The President is elected for a five-year term by the members of the National Assembly.

HEAD OF STATE
President, Tran Duc Luong, *elected* 25 September 1997
Vice-President, Truong My Hoa

SELECTED GOVERNMENT MEMBERS *as at July 2004*
Prime Minister, Phan Van Khai
Deputy Prime Ministers, Nguyen Tan Dzung; Vu Khoan; Pham Gia Khiem
Finance, Nguyen Sinh Hung
Foreign Affairs, Nguyen Dy Nien
Internal Affairs, Do Quang Trung
National Defence, Gen. Pham Van Tra

EMBASSY OF THE SOCIALIST REPUBLIC OF VIETNAM
12–14 Victoria Road, London W8 5RD
T 020-7937 1912
Ambassador Extraordinary and Plenipotentiary, HE Trinh Duc Du, apptd 2003

BRITISH EMBASSY
Central Building, 31 Hai Ba Trung, Hanoi
T (+84) (4) 936 0500
E behanoi@fpt.vn
Ambassador Extraordinary and Plenipotentiary, HE Robert Gordon, apptd 2003

BRITISH COUNCIL DIRECTOR, David Cordingley *(Cultural Attaché)*, 40 Cat Linh Street, Dong Da, Hanoi
T (+84) (4) 843 6780
E bchanoi@britishcouncil.org.vn

DEFENCE
The Army has 1,315 main battle tanks, 1,380 armoured personnel carriers and 300 armoured infantry fighting vehicles. The Navy has two submarines, six frigates and 42 patrol and coastal vessels at seven principal bases. The Air Force has 189 combat aircraft and 26 armed helicopters.
MILITARY EXPENDITURE – 7.1 per cent of GDP (2002)
MILITARY PERSONNEL – 484,000: Army 412,000, Navy 42,000, Air Force 30,000; Paramilitaries 40,000
CONSCRIPTION DURATION – Two to three years

ECONOMY AND TRADE
Vietnam experienced economic difficulties following the imposition of socialist reforms in the south after 1975. However, economic reforms, known as 'Doi Moi' liberalisation, were instituted in 1986 and have had significant success. The state's share of control has been greatly reduced in most sectors, leading to significant improvement in agricultural production, with Vietnam becoming a major rice exporter. Industry has grown and now contributes around 37 per cent of GDP. Building materials, chemicals, machinery and foodstuffs are the main products.

Foreign investment has been actively encouraged and was further boosted by Vietnam's accession to ASEAN in August 1995, but the level of foreign investment has begun to fall in response to the lack of economic reform and the difficult local business environment. A stock exchange was opened in July 2000. Oil production has increased and large natural gas reserves have been found offshore, though these are also claimed by China.

A bilateral trade agreement between Vietnam and the USA was signed in July 2000. In June 2001, the World Bank granted Vietnam a US$250 million poverty reduction loan and the EU announced that it would commit €2,600 million in aid.
GNI – US$32,800 million (2001); US$410 per capita (2001)
ANNUAL AVERAGE GROWTH OF GDP – 6.8 per cent (2001)
TOTAL EXTERNAL DEBT – US$12,787 million (2000)
FOREIGN DIRECT INVESTMENT – US$5,907 million (1997–2000)

BALANCE OF PAYMENTS
Trade – US$481 million surplus (2001)
Current Account – US$682 million surplus (2001)

Trade with UK	*2002*	*2003*
Imports from UK	£79,970,000	£100,640,000
Exports to UK	487,880,000	606,820,000

TRANSPORT INFRASTRUCTURE
Vietnam has 93,300 km of roads, nearly 70,000 km of which are unsurfaced. It has over 3,000 km of railway, and 17,700 km of waterways. Chief ports include Da Nang, Haiphong, and Ho Chi Minh City.

MEDIA
There are many local television stations and one national station; some satellite channels are also available, though these, like all other media, are closely controlled by the government. The state-run radio network operates several national stations. The Communist Party and the People's Army both publish a daily newspaper, and there are also newspapers published in English and French.

YEMEN

Al-Jumhūriyya Al-Yamaniyya – Republic of Yemen

AREA – 527,968 sq. km. Neighbours: Saudi Arabia (north), Oman (east)
POPULATION – 18,078,035 (2001 estimate). The language is Arabic
CAPITAL – Sana'a' (population, 1,590,624, 2001)
MAJOR CITIES – ΨAden ('Adan), the former capital of South Yemen; ΨAl-Hudaydah; Ta'izz

CURRENCY – Riyal of 100 fils
NATIONAL ANTHEM – Raddidi Ayyatuha Ad-Dunya Nashidi (Repeat, O World, My Song)
NATIONAL DAY – 22 May
NATIONAL FLAG – Horizontal bands of red, white and black
MORTALITY RATE (per 1,000 population) – 9 (2003)
HIV / AIDS ADULT PREVALENCE – 0.1 per cent (2001)
DEATH PENALTY – Yes
POPULATION GROWTH RATE – 3.4 per cent (2004)
POPULATION DENSITY – 33 per sq. km (1999)
ILLITERACY RATE – (m) 32.5 per cent; (f) 74.8 per cent (2000)
ENROLMENT (percentage of age group) – tertiary 4 per cent (1997)

Included in the state of Yemen are the offshore islands of Perim and Kamaran in the Red Sea, and Suqutra in the Gulf of Aden. The border with Saudi Arabia, except for the north-west corner, is unclear and is being delineated following an agreement between the two countries signed on 12 June 2000.

CLIMATE AND TERRAIN

A mountainous region divides the desert and the coastal regions of Yemen. Elevation extremes range from 3,760 m (Jabal an Nabi Shu'ayb) at the highest point to 0 m (Arabian Sea) at the lowest. The coastal area has high humidity, but rainfall throughout the country is unpredictable resulting in droughts and severe floods. Average temperatures in Aden range from 22°C in January to 37°C in June.

HISTORY AND POLITICS

The area around modern-day Yemen became part of the Ottoman Empire in the early 16th century. Independence from the Ottoman Empire was initiated by the Zaydi dynasty in the 17th century and Aden came under British rule in 1839.

Turkish occupation of North Yemen (1872–1918) was followed by the rule of the Hamid al-Din dynasty until a revolution in 1962 overthrew the monarchy and the Yemen Arab Republic was declared. The People's Republic of South Yemen was set up in 1967 when the British government ceded power to the National Liberation Front, bringing to an end 129 years of British rule in Aden and some years of protectorate status in the hinterland. Negotiations towards merging the two states began in 1979 and unification was proclaimed on 22 May 1990. The constitution was approved by referendum in 1991.

A power struggle between the former Northern and Southern Yemen élites led to civil war in 1994. However, Aden was quickly captured by victorious Northern forces on 7 July, bringing the war to an end.

After the war a coalition government of the General People's Congress and the Islamic Islah was formed and the constitution amended. Gen. Saleh was elected president by the House of Representatives for a five-year term. Multiparty democracy, a free market economy and Sharia law are enshrined in the constitution.

A general election in April 1997 was won by the ruling General People's Congress (GPC). President Ali Abdullah Saleh was re-elected in the first direct presidential election held in 1999, winning 96.3 per cent of the vote. Legislative elections took place in April 2003, in which the GPC held on to the presidency and a large majority in the House of Representatives, having won 238 of the 301 seats. Bajammal was re-appointed prime minister at the head of a re-shuffled cabinet.

POLITICAL SYSTEM

The 1991 constitution was amended following a referendum in 2001. The President is directly elected and serves a seven-year term which may be renewed once only. The unicameral legislature, the House of Representatives *(Majlis an-Nowab)*, has 301 directly-elected members, who serve a six-year term. In addition, there is an advisory Shura Council, which is appointed by the president and has 111 members.

HEAD OF STATE
President, Field Marshal Ali Abdullah Saleh, *took office* 22 May 1990, *elected* 1 October 1994, *re-elected* 23 September 1999
Vice-President, Gen. Abd Rabbah Mansur Hadi

SELECTED GOVERNMENT MEMBERS *as at July 2004*
Prime Minister, Abd al-Qadir Abd al-Rahman Bajammal
Deputy Prime Minister, Finance, Alawi Salih al-Salami
Deputy Prime Minister, Planning and International Co-operation, Ahmad Muhammad Abdallah al-Sufan
Defence, Maj.-Gen. Abdallah Ali Alywah
Foreign Affairs, Abu-Bakr Abdallah al-Qirdi
Interior, Rashad al-Alimi

EMBASSY OF THE REPUBLIC OF YEMEN
57 Cromwell Road, London SW7 2ED
T 020-7584 6607
Ambassador Extraordinary and Plenipotentiary, HE Dr Mutahar Abdullah Alsaeede, apptd 2001

BRITISH EMBASSY
129 Haddah Road, PO Box 1287, Sana'a'
T (+967) (1) 264 081/2/3/4
Ambassador Extraordinary and Plenipotentiary, HE Frances Guy, apptd 2001

BRITISH COUNCIL DIRECTOR, Aziz Al-Baar
3rd Floor, Administrative Tower, Sana'a' Trade Centre, Algiers Street, PO Box 2157, Sana'a'
T (+967) 1448 356/7
E britishcouncil@ye.britishcouncil.org

DEFENCE

The Army has 790 main battle tanks, 710 armoured personnel carriers and 200 armoured infantry fighting vehicles. The Navy has 11 patrol and coastal vessels at two bases. The Air Force has 76 combat aircraft and eight attack helicopters.
MILITARY EXPENDITURE – 5.7 per cent of GDP (2002)
MILITARY PERSONNEL – 66,700: Army 60,000, Navy 1,700, Air Force 5,000; Paramilitaries 70,000
CONSCRIPTION DURATION – Two years

ECONOMY AND TRADE

The civil war, although damaging much of Yemen's economy and transport infrastructure, had little effect on oil production. An agreement was signed with the French oil company Total in September 1995 for the exploitation of liquefied natural gas over a 25-year period and the construction of a gas liquefaction plant. The principal imports are machinery and transport equipment, raw materials, and foodstuffs and livestock. Agriculture is the main occupation of the inhabitants. This is largely of a subsistence nature, sorghum, sesame, millet, wheat and barley being the chief crops. Exports include cotton, coffee, fruit, vegetables and hides.

GNI – US$8,177 million (2001); US$450 per capita (2001)
ANNUAL AVERAGE GROWTH OF GDP – 3.1 per cent (2001)
INFLATION RATE – 7.9 per cent (1998)
TOTAL EXTERNAL DEBT – US$6,200 million (2002)
IMPORTS – US$2,310 million (2001)
EXPORTS – US$3,215 million (2001)

BALANCE OF PAYMENTS
Trade – US$1,609 million surplus (2000)
Current Account – US$1,862 million surplus (2000)

Trade with UK	*2002*	*2003*
Imports from UK	£74,044,000	£80,395,000
Exports to UK	39,769,000	9,062,000

TRANSPORT INFRASTRUCTURE

Yemen has 67,000 km of roads, of which 7,700 km are surfaced. Its main ports are at Aden, Al-Hudaydah, Al Mukalla, Al Salif, Ras Issa, Mocha and Nishtu.

MEDIA AND CULTURE

All broadcasting is state run. The government also funds some newspapers, and controls most of the printing. There are four newspapers in Yemen: *Al-Thawrah, Yemen Times, Yemen Observer* and *Al-Ayyam*.

Yemen is home to a multitude of historical and archaeological sites that include the Aban Masjid Mosque in the Crater district, Seira Castle and the ancient town of Aden.

ZAMBIA

Republic of Zambia

AREA – 743,400 sq. km. Neighbours: Democratic Republic of Congo and Tanzania (north), Malawi (east), Mozambique, Zimbabwe and Namibia (south), Angola (west)
POPULATION – 10,649,000 (2001). English is the official language; other languages spoken include Bemba, Kaonda, Lozi, Lunda, Luvale, Nyanja and Tonga
CAPITAL – Lusaka (population, 1,269,848, 1999)
MAJOR CITIES – Chingola; Kabwe; Kitwe; Luanshya; Mufulira; Ndola
CURRENCY – Kwacha (K) of 100 ngwee
NATIONAL ANTHEM – Stand And Sing Of Zambia, Proud And Free
NATIONAL DAY – 24 October (Independence Day)
NATIONAL FLAG – Green with three small vertical stripes, red, black and orange (next fly); eagle device on green above stripes
LIFE EXPECTANCY (years) – 42 (2001)
MORTALITY RATE (per 1,000 population) – 24.3 (2003)
INFANT MORTALITY (per 1,000 births) – 112 (2001)
HIV / AIDS ADULT PREVALENCE – 21.5 per cent (2001)
DEATH PENALTY – Yes
POPULATION BELOW POVERTY LINE – 86 per cent (1993)
POPULATION GROWTH RATE – 2.5 per cent (1990–2001)
POPULATION DENSITY – 14 per sq. km (2001)
MILITARY EXPENDITURE – 0.7 per cent of GDP (2001)
MILITARY PERSONNEL – 21,600: Army 20,000, Air Force 1,600; Paramilitaries 1,400
ILLITERACY RATE – (m) 14.8 per cent; (f) 28.6 per cent (2000)
ENROLMENT (percentage of age group) – primary 89 per cent (1997); secondary 27 per cent (1997); tertiary 3 per cent (1997)

CLIMATE AND TERRAIN

Zambia lies on the plateau of Central Africa and elevation extremes range from 2,361 m (Mafinga Hills) at the highest point to 321 m (Zambezi River) at the lowest. The climate is tropical with an average temperature of 28°C all year.

HISTORY AND POLITICS

Northern Rhodesia came under British rule in 1889. It achieved internal self-government when the Federation of Rhodesia and Nyasaland was dissolved in 1963, and became an independent republic within the Commonwealth on 24 October 1964 under the name of Zambia.

Zambia was a one-party state (the United National Independence Party) from 1973 until 1990, when pressure from opposition groups led to a new constitution (in August 1991) and multiparty legislative and presidential elections in October 1991. The Movement for Multiparty Democracy (MMD) won a majority of seats in the parliament, and the MMD candidate Frederick Chiluba defeated Kenneth Kaunda in the presidential election; Kaunda was later stripped of his Zambian citizenship.

Presidential elections held on 27 December 2001 were won by MMD candidate Levy Mwanawasa with 28.7 per cent of the vote. In simultaneous legislative elections the MMD won 69 of the 150 elected seats in the National Assembly; the United Party for National Development (UPND) won 49 seats; and other parties and independents won 32 seats. A new Cabinet composed of the MMD was appointed in early 2002. Vice-President Enoch Kavindele was dismissed in 2003, and was succeeded on the same day by Nevers Mumba.

HEAD OF STATE
President, Minister of Defence, Levy Mwanawasa, *elected* 27 December 2001, *sworn in* 2 January 2002
Vice-President, Nevers Mumba

HIGH COMMISSION FOR THE REPUBLIC OF ZAMBIA
2 Palace Gate, London W8 5NG
T 020-7589 6655
High Commissioner, HE Anderson Chibwa, apptd 2003

BRITISH HIGH COMMISSION
5210 Independence Avenue (PO Box 50050), 15101 Ridgeway, Lusaka
T (+ 260) (1) 251133
E brithc@zamnet.zm
High Commissioner, HE Timothy David, apptd 2002

BRITISH COUNCIL DIRECTOR, John Mitchell
Heroes Place, Cairo Road (PO Box 34571), Lusaka
T (+ 260) (1) 223 602/228 332
E info@britishcouncil.org.zm

ECONOMY AND TRADE

In 1991, the MMD government began the transition from a state-controlled economy to a free market system. Privatisation has been encouraged, foreign exchange controls have been removed and the Kwacha has been floated on international stock markets. Price subsidies and tariffs have been lowered or abolished, but increased imports have affected manufacturing. In 2001, 85 per cent of the workforce were engaged in agriculture, which accounted for 14.9 per cent of GDP that year. Principal agricultural products are maize, sugar, groundnuts, cotton, livestock, vegetables and tobacco. The principal exports are copper and cobalt. The principal imports are industrial goods, machinery and transport equipment, fuel and foodstuffs.

GNI – US$3,300 million (2001); US$320 per capita (2001)
ANNUAL AVERAGE GROWTH OF GDP – 4.9 per cent (2001)
INFLATION RATE – 24.8 per cent (1997)
TOTAL EXTERNAL DEBT – US$5,730 million (2000)
FOREIGN DIRECT INVESTMENT – US$505 million (1997–2000)
IMPORTS – US$819 million (1997)
EXPORTS – US$915 million (1997)

Trade with UK	*2002*	*2003*
Imports from UK	£19,075,000	£21,465,000
Exports to UK	10,741,000	15,983,000

MEDIA

Zambian broadcast media are dominated by the government-run television and radio networks. There are private radio stations (in contrast to television, where the only service is the state-run channel) but they do not provide much political content. Three of the four newspapers are state owned.

ZIMBABWE

Republic of Zimbabwe

AREA – 386,900 sq. km. Neighbours: Zambia (north), Mozambique (east), South Africa (south), Botswana and Namibia (west)
POPULATION – 12,852,000 (2001); 77 per cent Shona, 17 per cent Ndebele, 1.4 per cent Europeans. The official language is English, with Shona the largest indigenous language group
CAPITAL – Harare (population, 1,189,103, 1992)
MAJOR CITIES – Bulawayo, the largest town in Matabeleland; Chitungwiza
CURRENCY – Zimbabwe dollar (Z$) of 100 cents
NATIONAL ANTHEM – Ngaikomberarwe Nyika Ye Zimbabwe (Blessed Be The Country Of Zimbabwe)
NATIONAL DAY – 18 April (Independence Day)
NATIONAL FLAG – Seven horizontal stripes of green, yellow, red, black, red, yellow, green; a white, black-bordered, triangle based on the hoist containing the national emblem
LIFE EXPECTANCY (years) – 43 (2001)
MORTALITY RATE (per 1,000 population) – 22.02 (2003)
INFANT MORTALITY (per 1,000 births) – 76 (2001)
HIV / AIDS ADULT PREVALENCE – 33.7 per cent (2001)
DEATH PENALTY – Yes
POPULATION BELOW POVERTY LINE – 70 per cent (2002)
POPULATION GROWTH RATE – 2.1 per cent (1990–2001)
POPULATION DENSITY – 33 per sq. km (2001)
MILITARY EXPENDITURE – 3.4 per cent of GDP (2002)
MILITARY PERSONNEL – 29,000: Army 25,000, Air Force 4,000; Paramilitaries 21,800

CLIMATE AND TERRAIN

The country is divided into eight provinces: Manicaland, Mashonaland Central, Mashonaland East, Mashonaland West, Masvingo, Matabeleland North, Matabeleland South and Midlands. Zimbabwe's terrain is mainly high plateau with mountains in the east. Elevation extremes range from 2,592 m (Inyangani) at the highest point to 162 m (Runde River) at the lowest. Average temperatures in Harare range from 7°C in May to 29°C in November.

HISTORY AND POLITICS

Organised settlement of the region began at least 20,000 years ago and culminated in the establishment of a powerful settlement at Great Zimbabwe.

European colonisation of Zimbabwe began in 1890 when settlers forcibly acquired Shona lands, followed by the seizure of Ndebele lands in 1893. It became a self-governing colony under the name of Southern Rhodesia in 1923. A unilateral declaration of independence, under Prime Minister Ian Smith, in 1965 resulted in UN sanctions against the country, and was finally terminated in 1979. Following elections in February 1980, won by Robert Mugabe, the country became independent on 18 April 1980 as the Republic of Zimbabwe, a member of the British Commonwealth.

The independence constitution was amended in 1987, making the presidency an executive post. The President is popularly elected for a six-year term, he appoints the Cabinet and can veto parliamentary bills. The unicameral legislature, the House of Assembly, has 150 members: 120 elected, ten traditional chiefs and 20 others appointed by the president.

The most recent general election was held in June 2000. The Zimbabwe African National Union – Patriotic Front (ZANU-PF) won 62 of the 120 elective seats and the Movement for Democratic Change (MDC), a new opposition grouping formed by various civic groups and the Zimbabwe Congress of Trade Unions, won 57 seats. President Mugabe was re-elected in 2002 with 56.2 per cent of the vote, while Morgan Tsvangirai of the MDC gained 42.0 per cent. However, the integrity of the election was called into question by Tsvangirai who claimed that thousands of opposition supporters had been disenfranchised.

In June 2003 Tsvangirai was arrested and charged with treason.

LAND REFORM

Following independence, about 30 per cent of agricultural land remained in the possession of around 4,000 white farmers. They employed nearly 300,000 workers and accounted for about 70 per cent of the country's agricultural production and about a third of foreign currency earnings. A further 37 per cent of agricultural land was in the possession of 1.2 million black peasant farmers, mainly engaged in subsistence farming. Most of this land was located in less fertile, drought-prone regions. Land reform was designed to achieve a more equitable distribution of land. By 1997 the state had acquired 3.4 million hectares of land, but either left it fallow or distributed it to members of the government. The 1990 amendments to the 1980 constitution had made provision for the compulsory acquisition of farms, with compensation to be paid to the owners. The occupation of white-owned farms by protestors, led by former veterans of the war against the white minority regime, began in February 2000. The Supreme Court ordered the police to evict the black war veterans who had occupied around 600 white-owned farms. The police ignored the judgement with the support of President Mugabe. The House of Assembly then approved the Land Acquisition Act, which amended the constitution to enable the government to take over white-owned farms without compensation and redistribute them to landless blacks. A meeting of representatives of the British and Zimbabwean governments in April 2000 failed to resolve the crisis and in May the UK imposed an embargo on weapons sales to Zimbabwe, making financial support for land reform dependent on an end to the farm occupations.

The Supreme Court ruled late in 2000 that the compulsory land seizures were illegal and ordered the removal of squatters. The government rejected the ruling and accelerated the land acquisition programme. The Supreme Court then directed the President to produce a land distribution programme within six months and to protect white farmers whose land had been occupied by squatters. Following a Commonwealth meeting, Zimbabwe agreed to end the illegal land occupations and restore the rule of law in return for international assistance. But the Supreme Court, dominated by recent appointees of President Mugabe, issued an interim order reversing all previous rulings in order to allow the government to proceed with its fast-track land reform programme, and the government issued a decree that any farm given a 'notice of acquisition' would become state property immediately. The government would then be entitled to move settlers onto the land and the owner would be banned from conducting any farming on it. Mugabe ordered some 2,900 white farmers, whose farms had been earmarked to be seized and given to blacks under the government's 'fast-track land reform' programme, to cease work as of June 2002. In September the House of Assembly passed an amendment to the 1992 Land Acquisition Act reducing the time give to white farmers to vacate before being evicted from 90 days to 7. Zimbabwe was suspended from the Commonwealth in March 2002 and in September 2002 a Commonwealth committee, meeting to discuss Zimbabwe's political and economic crisis, failed to reach an agreement on new sanctions against President Mugabe. On 7 December 2003 Zimbabwe officially withdrew from the Commonwealth.

HEAD OF STATE
President, C.-in-C. of the Defence Forces, Transport and Energy, Robert Gabriel Mugabe, *elected* 30 December 1987, *re-elected* March 1990, March 1996, 11 March 2002
Vice-President, Joseph Msika

SELECTED GOVERNMENT MEMBERS *as at July 2004*
The President
Defence, Sidney Tigere Sekeramayi
Finance and Economic Development, Herbert Murerina *(acting)*
Foreign Affairs, Stanislaus Mudenge
Home Affairs, Kembo Mohadi
National Security, Nicholas Goche

HIGH COMMISSION OF THE REPUBLIC OF ZIMBABWE
Zimbabwe House, 429 Strand, London WC2R 0JR
T 020-7836 7755
High Commissioner, HE Simbarashe Simbanenduku Mumbengegwi, apptd 1999

BRITISH HIGH COMMISSION
Corner House, Samora Machel Avenue/Leopold Takawira Street (PO Box 4490), Harare
T (+263) (4) 772990/774700
High Commissioner, HE Brian Donnelly, CMG, apptd 2001

BRITISH COUNCIL DIRECTOR, Dr Marcus Milton
Corner House, Samora Machel Avenue, PO Box 664, Harare
T (+263) (4) 775 313/4
E general.enquiries@britishcouncil.org.zw

ECONOMY AND TRADE

The economy remains highly regulated and weak, unemployment is high and huge rises in the prices of basic commodities and fuel, caused by rampant inflation, have resulted in widespread strike action and protests. Agriculture accounted for 28 per cent of GDP in 1998 and two-thirds of the workforce are engaged in agriculture, but the activities of squatters and the government land acquisition campaign have had a dramatic effect on productivity at commercial farms, preventing the planting of many crops. Tobacco remains the most important crop in terms of export (Zimbabwe is the largest exporter in the world), and maize the most important for domestic consumption. Other crops include wheat, cotton, sugar, horticultural products, fruit and vegetables.

The manufacturing sector is very dependent on the agricultural sector for raw materials and on imports e.g. fuel oil, steel products and chemicals, as well as heavy machinery and items of transport. The mining sector, although contributing a relatively small portion to GDP, is important to the economy as a foreign exchange earner. Almost all mineral production is exported. Gold is the most important product; others are asbestos, diamonds, silver, nickel, copper, platinum, chrome ore, tin, iron ore and cobalt. There is a successful ferro-chrome industry and a substantial steel works which has been heavily subsidised by government. The main trading partners are South Africa and the UK.

GNI – US$6,200 million (2001); US$480 per capita (2001)
ANNUAL AVERAGE GROWTH OF GDP – 1.6 per cent (1999)
INFLATION RATE – 58.5 per cent (1999)
TOTAL EXTERNAL DEBT – US$4,002 million (2000)

FOREIGN DIRECT INVESTMENT – US$284 million (1997–2000)
IMPORTS – US$2,803 million (1996)
EXPORTS – US$2,406 million (1996)

Trade with UK	*2002*	*2003*
Imports from UK	£34,146,000	£29,294,000
Exports to UK	86,200,000	58,295,000

TRANSPORT INFRASTRUCTURE

Zimbabwe has at least 18,000 km of roads, over 8,500 km of which are surfaced. There are also 3,000 km of railways. Its main ports are at Binga and Kariba.

EDUCATION

Education is compulsory, and the language of instruction is English. Over 80 per cent of schools are government-aided. There are four universities; the University of Zimbabwe was founded in 1955.

ILLITERACY RATE – (m) 7.2 per cent; (f) 15.3 per cent (2000)
ENROLMENT (percentage of age group) – tertiary 7 per cent (1997)

MEDIA

The Zimbabwean government exercises strict control over the print and broadcast media, and some foreign journalists are prevented from reporting from within the country. The only television and radio stations are government controlled. There is one independent radio station that broadcasts in Zimbabwe. Two of the three daily newspapers are government run, they are *The Herald* and *The Chronicle.*

EXPLANATION OF TERMS

1. Ψ = seaport.
2. (m) = male; (f) = female.
3. Life expectancy figures are averages for males and females.
4. Infant mortality rate – total number of deaths of infants under one year old. Includes both male and female infants.
5. Paramilitaries are not included in the total military personnel figure for each country.
6. HIV/AIDS adult prevalence rate – this entry gives an estimate of the percentage of the total population of adults (aged 15–49) living with HIV/AIDS.
7. Population below poverty line – although strict definitions of poverty vary considerably between nations, this figure represents the percentage of the population whose income is less than US$1 a day.
8. Death Penalty:
No – abolished for all crimes (year in which death penalty was abolished in parenthesis). This also includes 'abolitionists in practice', i.e. countries that retain the death penalty but have not executed anybody in the last ten years.
Yes* – abolished but retained for exceptional circumstances (i.e. crimes under military law).
Yes – used as legal form of punishment.
9. Cabinet/Government listings: our listings contain heads of state and people in key government posts, e.g. those responsible for defence, home affairs, foreign affairs and finance, as well as Prime Ministers and deputies. For full government listings, visit www.peopleinpower.com.

Sources: Amnesty international; CIA World Factbook 2004; IMF International Financial Statistics Yearbook; People in Power; The Military Balance 2003–4.

UK OVERSEAS TERRITORIES

ANGUILLA

AREA – 37 sq. miles (96 sq. km)
POPULATION – 12,394 (1998 estimate)
CAPITAL – The Valley (population, 2,400, 1994)
CURRENCY – East Caribbean dollar (EC$) of 100 cents
FLAG – British blue ensign with the coat of arms and three dolphins in the fly
POPULATION GROWTH RATE – 6.7 per cent (1999)
POPULATION DENSITY – 134 per sq. km (1999)

CLIMATE AND TERRAIN

Anguilla is a flat coralline island in the Caribbean, and is the most northerly of the Leeward islands. The climate is tropical, modified by north-east trade winds, with temperatures ranging from 24°C to 30°C throughout the year. Elevation extremes range from 65 m (Crocus Hill) at the highest point to 0 m (Caribbean Sea) at the lowest.

HISTORY AND POLITICS

Anguilla has been a British colony since 1650. For much of its history it was linked administratively with St Kitts, but three months after the Associated State of Saint Christopher (St Kitts)-Nevis-Anguilla came into being in 1967, the Anguillans repudiated government from St Kitts. A Commissioner was installed in 1969 and in 1976 Anguilla was given a new status and separate constitution. Final separation from St Kitts and Nevis was effected in December 1980 and Anguilla reverted to a British dependency. A new constitution was introduced in 1982, providing for a Governor, an Executive Council comprising four elected Ministers and two ex-officio members (the Attorney-General and Deputy Governor), and a 12-member legislative House of Assembly, consisting of seven elected members, two nominated members, two ex-officio members (the Attorney-General and Deputy Governor) and presided over by a Speaker. The last general election was held in March 2000, with the next scheduled for June 2005.

Governor, HE Alan Huckle, *apptd* 2004
Deputy Governor, Roger Cousins, OBE, *apptd* 1997

ECONOMY

Low rainfall limits agricultural output and export earnings are mainly from sales of fish and lobsters. Tourism has developed rapidly in recent years and accounts for most of the island's economic activity.

GDP – US$95 million (1998); US$11,678 per capita (1998)
ANNUAL AVERAGE GROWTH OF GDP – 4.1 per cent (1998)

BALANCE OF PAYMENTS
Trade – US$64 million deficit (2001)
Current Account – US$35 million deficit (2001)

TRANSPORT INFRASTRUCTURE AND MEDIA

Highways total 105 km, of which 65 km are paved (1997). Ports and harbours include Blowing Point and Road Bay, and there are three airports. Around 12 radio stations and one television broadcast station serve the island.

BERMUDA

AREA – 20 sq. miles (52 sq. km)
POPULATION – 63,400 (2002 estimate)
CAPITAL – ΨHamilton (population, 2,277, 1994)
CURRENCY – Bermuda dollar of 100 cents
FLAG – British red ensign with the shield of arms in the fly
LIFE EXPECTANCY (years) – 77 (2001)
POPULATION GROWTH RATE – 1.7 per cent (1999)
POPULATION DENSITY – 1,231 per sq. km (2001)

CLIMATE AND TERRAIN

The climate is subtropical, regulated by the Gulf Stream, with an average temperature of 23°C. All the islands are volcanic in origin, with hilly interiors, surrounded by coral reefs. Elevation extremes range from 76 m (Town Hill) at the highest point to 0 m (Caribbean Sea) at the lowest.

HISTORY AND POLITICS

Internal self-government was introduced in 1968. There is a Senate of 11 members and an elected House of Assembly of 40 members. The Governor retains responsibility for external affairs, defence, internal security and the police, although administrative matters for the police service have been delegated to the Minister of Labour, Home Affairs and Public Safety. Independence from the UK was rejected in a referendum in August 1995. The last general election was held on 24 July 2003. The Progressive Labour Party won 22 of the 40 seats.

Governor and Commander-in-Chief, HE Sir John Vereker, KCB, *apptd* 2002

ECONOMY

The islands' economic structure is based on tourism and international company business, attracted by the low level of taxation and sophisticated telecommunications system.

Locally manufactured concentrates, perfumes, cut flowers and pharmaceuticals are the islands' leading exports.

Trade with UK	*2002*	*2003*
Imports from UK	£30,920,000	£41,983,000
Exports to UK	18,047,000	67,991,000

EDUCATION

Free elementary education was introduced in 1949. Free secondary education was introduced in 1965 for those children in the aided and maintained schools who were below the upper limit of the statutory school age of 18.

MEDIA

One daily and two weekly newspapers are published in Bermuda. Three commercial companies operate radio and television services, including a cable-television system.

BRITISH ANTARCTIC TERRITORY

AREA - 660,000 sq. miles (1,709,340 sq. km)
FLAG - British white ensign, without the cross of St George, with the coat of arms of the territory in the fly

CLIMATE AND TERRAIN

The British Antarctic Territory (BAT) consists of the areas south of 60°S. latitude and bounded by longitudes 20°W. and 80°W. The territory includes the South Orkney Islands, the South Shetland Islands, the mountainous Antarctic Peninsula (highest point Mount Jackson, 3,183 m above sea level) and all adjacent islands, and the land mass extending to the South Pole.

HISTORY AND POLITICS

Britain made its first territorial claim to part of the Antarctic in 1908. Since 1943, a permanent presence has been maintained which became the British Antarctic Survey (BAS) in 1962. In the same year, the BAT – originally administered as a Dependency of the Falkland Islands – became an Overseas Territory of the United Kingdom in its own right.

GOVERNMENT

The BAT is administered by the Foreign and Commonwealth Office (FCO), and has a full suite of laws, and legal and postal administrations. All activities are governed by the Antarctic Treaty of 1961, agreed with the objectives of keeping Antarctica demilitarised and to promote international scientific co-operation.

GOVERNMENT OF THE BRITISH ANTARCTIC TERRITORY
Polar Regions Unit, Overseas Territory Department, Foreign and Commonwealth Office, London SW1A 2AH
T 020-7008 3543
Commissioner (non-resident), Anthony Campbell Crombie, *apptd* 2004

BRITISH INDIAN OCEAN TERRITORY

AREA – 59 sq. km
FLAG – Divided horizontally into blue and white wavy stripes, with the Union Flag in the canton and a crowned palm-tree over all in the fly

CLIMATE AND TERRAIN

The British Indian Ocean Territory (BIOT) comprises an archipelago of 2,300 islands that covers some 54,400 sq. km of ocean. The islands have a land area of only 60 sq. km and 698 km of coastline.

HISTORY AND POLITICS

The British Indian Ocean Territory was established by an Order in Council in 1965 and included islands formerly administered from Mauritius and the Seychelles. The islands of Farquhar, Desroches and Aldabra became part of the Seychelles when it became independent in 1976; since then the Territory has consisted of the Chagos Archipelago only. Successive Mauritian governments have asserted a sovereignty claim to the islands, arguing that they were annexed illegally.

The Chagos Archipelago consists of six main groups of islands situated on the Great Chagos Bank. The largest and most southerly of the Chagos Islands is Diego Garcia, a sand cay with a land area of about 44 sq. km, used as a joint naval support facility by Britain and the USA. In 2003, Diego Garcia was populated by around 3,000 UK and US military personnel and civilian contract employees.

The other main island groups of the archipelago, Peros Banhos (29 islands with a total land area of 6.5 sq. km) and Salamon (11 islands with a total land area of 3.2 sq. km) are uninhabited.

The islands' former inhabitants (the Ilois) were expelled between 1967 and 1973 to allow for the construction of the naval base, most being resettled in Mauritius. Following legal action by representatives of the Ilois, in November 2000 the High Court overturned the ordinance that had required the Ilois to seek permission to visit the territory, effectively granting them the right of return.

Commissioner, Tony Crombie, *apptd* 2004

BRITISH VIRGIN ISLANDS

AREA – 153 sq. km
POPULATION – 21,000 (2001: Tortola 16,630; Virgin Gorda 3,063; Anegada 204; Jost Van Dyke 176; other islands 181)
CAPITAL – ΨRoad Town (population, 3,983, 2001 estimate)
CURRENCY – US dollar (US$)
FLAG – British blue ensign with the shield of arms in the fly
LIFE EXPECTANCY (years) – 76 (2001)
INFANT MORTALITY (per 1,000 births) – 20 (2001)
POPULATION GROWTH RATE – 2.9 per cent (1999)
POPULATION DENSITY – 134 per sq. km (2001)

CLIMATE AND TERRAIN

The principal islands are Tortola, Virgin Gorda, Anegada and Jost Van Dyke. Apart from Anegada, which is a flat coral island, the British Virgin Islands are hilly, being an extension of the Puerto Rico and the US Virgin Islands archipelago. The highest point of elevation is 1,780 m (Sage Mountain) while the lowest is 0 m (Caribbean Sea).

HISTORY AND POLITICS

Initially settled by the Arawak Indians from South America, the islands were named by Christopher Columbus on his second visit to the New World. Under the 1977 constitution the Governor, appointed by the Crown, remains responsible for defence and internal security, external affairs and the civil service but in other matters acts in accordance with the advice of the Executive Council. The Executive Council consists of the Governor as Chairman, one ex-officio member (the Attorney-General), the Chief Minister and four other ministers. The Legislative Council consists of a Speaker chosen from outside the Council, one ex-officio member (the Attorney-General), and 13 elected members returned from ten electoral districts.

Governor, HE Thomas Macan

ECONOMY

Tourism is the main industry but the offshore financial centre is gaining importance. Other industries include a rum distillery, three stone-crushing plants and factories manufacturing concrete blocks and paint. The major export items are fresh fish, gravel, sand, fruit and vegetables. Chief imports are building materials, machinery, cars and beverages.

Trade with UK	*2002*	*2003*
Imports from UK	£25,839,000	£13,944,000
Exports to UK	18,871,000	32,636,000

TRANSPORT INFRASTRUCTURE

The principal airport is on Beef Island, linked by bridge to Tortola, and an extended runway enables larger aircraft to call. There is a second airfield on Virgin Gorda and a third on Anegada. There are direct shipping services to the UK and the USA and fast passenger services connect the main islands by ferry.

CAYMAN ISLANDS

AREA – 264 sq. km
POPULATION – 44,144 (2003 estimate)
CAPITAL – ΨGeorge Town (population, 20,626, 1999 census)
CURRENCY – Cayman Islands dollar (CI$) of 100 cents
FLAG – British blue ensign with the arms on a white disc in the fly
LIFE EXPECTANCY (years) – 77 years (2003)
INFANT MORTALITY (per 1,000 births) – 4.8 (2003)
POPULATION GROWTH RATE – 2.6 per cent (2002)
POPULATION DENSITY – 163 per sq. km (2002)
GNI – US$43,703 per capita (2002)
ANNUAL AVERAGE GROWTH OF GDP – 1.7 per cent (2002)

CLIMATE AND TERRAIN

The Cayman Islands comprise Grand Cayman, Cayman Brac, and Little Cayman. About 241 km south of Cuba, the islands are divided from Jamaica, 289 km to the south-east, by the Cayman Trench, the deepest part of the Caribbean Sea.

HISTORY AND POLITICS

The colony derives its name from the Carib word for the crocodile, 'caymanas', which appeared in the log of an early English visitor to the islands, Sir Francis Drake. Permanent settlers followed the first land grant by Britain in 1734 and the islands were placed under direct control of Jamaica in 1863. When Jamaica became independent in 1962, the islands opted to remain under the British Crown.

The constitution provides for a Governor, a Legislative Assembly and a Cabinet, and allows a large measure of self-government. Unless there are exceptional reasons, the Governor accepts the advice of the Cabinet, which comprises three appointed official members and five ministers elected from the 15 elected members of the Assembly. The official members also sit in the Assembly. The Governor has responsibility for the police, civil service, defence and external affairs. The normal life of the Assembly is four years; a general election was scheduled for November 2004.

A constitutional review, begun in 2001, resulted in the Executive Council being renamed the Cabinet and the official appointments (incorporated in the Constitution for the first time) of a Leader of Government Business, Leader of the Opposition, and an Electoral Boundary Commission.

Governor, HE Bruce Dinwiddy, CMG, *apptd* 2002

CAYMAN ISLANDS GOVERNMENT OFFICE, 6 Arlington Street, London SW1A 1RE T 020-7491 7772
Government Representative, Jennifer Dilbert

ECONOMY

With a complete absence of direct taxation, the Cayman Islands has become successful as an offshore financial centre. At the end of 2003 there were 474 banks and trust companies. In addition, there were 672 licensed insurance companies, 68,078 registered companies, 4,820 registered mutual funds, and 735 listings on the stock exchange. Tourism, with an emphasis on scuba diving, has also been developed successfully.

Import duties and fees have provided revenue enabling the government to undertake investment in education, health, social programmes and infrastructure.

Trade with UK	*2002*	*2003*
Imports from UK	£8,969,000	£8,694,000
Exports to UK	4,477,000	3,754,000

TRANSPORT INFRASTRUCTURE

There are two main airports on the Cayman Islands and one small airfield on the island of Little Cayman. Georgetown is the main port and there are 785 km of surfaced roads.

FALKLAND ISLANDS

AREA – 4,700 sq. miles (12,173 sq. km)
POPULATION – 2,564 (2001 census)
CAPITAL – ΨStanley (population, 1,989, 2001 census)
CURRENCY – Falkland pound of 100 pence
FLAG – British blue ensign with the arms on a white disc in the fly
POPULATION GROWTH RATE – 2.4 per cent (2004)
URBAN POPULATION – 84.0 per cent (2001)

CLIMATE AND TERRAIN

The Falkland Islands consist of East Falkland (area 6,759 sq. km), West Falkland (5,413 sq. km) and over 700 small islands. Elevation extremes range from 705 m (Mt Usbourne) at the highest point to 0 m (Atlantic Ocean) at the lowest.

HISTORY AND POLITICS

The Falkland Islands have experienced a long history of occupation by European countries including France, Spain and the UK, which established its first settlement in 1766.

After Argentina declared independence from Spain, the Argentine government in 1820 proclaimed its sovereignty over the Falklands and a settlement was founded in 1826 but was subsequently destroyed by the USA in 1831. In 1833 occupation was resumed by the British for the protection of the seal-fisheries, and the islands were permanently colonised. Argentina continued to claim sovereignty over the islands (known to them as *las Islas Malvinas*), and invaded the islands in April 1982. A naval and military task-force dispatched from the UK recaptured the islands some seven weeks later on 14 June 1982. A British naval and military garrison of 1,265 personnel remains in the area.

Under the 1985 constitution, the Governor is advised by an Executive Council consisting of three elected members of the Legislative Council and two ex-officio members, the Chief Executive and the Financial Secretary. The Legislative Council consists of eight elected members and the same two ex-officio members.

Governor and Chairman of the Executive Council, HE Howard Pearce, CVO, *apptd* 2002

FALKLAND ISLANDS GOVERNMENT OFFICE, Falkland House, 14 Broadway, London SW1H 0BH T 020-7222 2542
Government Representative, Miss S. Cameron, MBE

ECONOMY

Since the establishment of an interim conservation and management fishing zone around the islands in 1987 and the consequent introduction of a licensing regime for vessels fishing within the 321 km zone, the economy has diversified. Income from the associated fishing activities, mainly for illex squid, is now the largest source of revenue. The increase in government revenue from fishing licences has led to the establishment of a substantial health, education and welfare system. Chief imports are provisions, alcoholic beverages, timber, clothing and hardware. In 2002, a consortium of oil companies, led by Global Petroleum, were awarded 10 exploration licences by the Falkland Islands Government. It is expected that substantial reserves of oil will be found within the next five years.

An EU-standard abattoir was opened in 2001, enabling the Falkland Islands to export meat to the European Union.

Trade with UK	*2002*	*2003*
Imports from UK	£17,223,000	£27,345,000
Exports to UK	5,454,000	8,979,000

TRANSPORT INFRASTRUCTURE

The islands have one international airport and the Falkland Islands Government Air Service (FIGAS) provides charter flights. There are some 440 km of roads, 50 km of which are paved. The main port is Stanley Harbour.

GIBRALTAR

AREA – 2.3 sq. miles (6 sq. km)
POPULATION – 28,000 (2001)
CAPITAL – ΨGibraltar
CURRENCY – Gibraltar pound of 100 pence
FLAG – White with a red stripe along the lower edge; over all a red castle with a key hanging from its gateway
POPULATION GROWTH RATE – 0.6 per cent (2000)
POPULATION DENSITY – 4,338 per sq. km (2001)
GNI – US$5,000 per capita (2001)

CLIMATE AND TERRAIN

Gibraltar is a rocky promontory which juts southwards from the south-east coast of Spain, with which it is connected by a low isthmus. It is about 32 km (20 miles) from the opposite coast of Africa.

HISTORY AND POLITICS

Gibraltar was captured in 1704, during the War of the Spanish Succession, by a combined Dutch and English force, and was ceded to Great Britain by the Treaty of Utrecht (1713). This treaty stipulates that if Britain ever relinquishes colonial rights over Gibraltar the colony would return to Spain.

The 1969 constitution makes provision for certain domestic matters to devolve on a local government of ministers appointed from among elected members of the House of Assembly. The House of Assembly consists of an independent Speaker, 15 elected members, the Attorney-General and the Financial and Development Secretary.

The Governor retains responsibility for external affairs, defence, internal security and financial security, while the local government is responsible for other domestic matters. The Gibraltar government has recently been pressing for more local autonomy especially in its relations with the EU, and this has led to tension with the UK and Spanish governments. Gibraltar is part of the EU (with the UK government responsible for enforcing EU directives affecting Gibraltar) but is not a full member and is exempt from the Common Customs Tariff and the Common Agricultural Policy. Value added tax is not applied. The last elections were held on 27 November 2003 and the Gibraltar Social Democrats won 51.5 per cent of the vote and secured 8 seats in the House of Assembly. A coalition of the Gibraltar Socialist Labour Party and the Liberal Party won 39.7 per cent and 7 seats in the Assembly. Talks between the UK and Spain on the future of Gibraltar resumed in July 2001, but have stalled since Gibraltar residents voted overwhelmingly by referendum in 2003 against a 'total shared sovereignty' arrangement.

Governor and Commander-in-Chief, HE Sir Francis Richards, KCMG, CVO, *apptd* 2003

GOVERNMENT OF GIBRALTAR, Arundel Great Court, 178–179 The Strand, London WC2R 1EL
T 020-7836 0777
Government Representative, A. Poggio

ECONOMY

Gibraltar has an extensive shipping trade and is a popular shopping centre and tourist resort. The chief sources of revenue are the port dues, the rent of the Crown estate in the town, and duties on consumer items. A financial services industry is expanding, based on Gibraltar's status as an offshore financial centre.

Trade with UK	*2002*	*2003*
Imports from UK	£128,339,000	£154,382,000
Exports to UK	22,615,000	25,757,000

TRANSPORT INFRASTRUCTURE

Gibraltar has one international airport and about 29 km of roads. There is also a regular ferry service from the island to Tangiers.

MONTSERRAT

AREA – 39 sq. miles (102 sq. km)
POPULATION – 9,245 (2004 estimate)
CAPITAL – ΨPlymouth
CURRENCY – East Caribbean dollar (EC$) of 100 cents
FLAG – British blue ensign with the shield of arms in the fly
POPULATION GROWTH RATE – 1.03 per cent (2004 estimate)
POPULATION DENSITY – 108 per sq. km (1999)

CLIMATE AND TERRAIN

Montserrat is a mountainous volcanic island with elevation extremes ranging from 914 m (Chances Peak) at the highest point to 0 m (Caribbean Sea) at the lowest.

The climate is tropical and the average temperature is 29°C.

HISTORY AND POLITICS

Discovered by Columbus in 1493, Montserrat became a British colony in 1632. The first settlers were predominantly Irish indentured servants from St Christopher. France and Britain fought over the island during the 17th and 18th centuries but Montserrat was finally assigned to Great Britain in 1783.

A ministerial system was introduced in Montserrat in 1960. The Executive Council is presided over by the Governor and is composed of four elected members (the Chief and three other Ministers) and two ex-officio members (the Attorney-General and the Financial Secretary). The four Ministers are appointed from the members of the political party or coalition holding the majority in the Legislative Council. The Legislative Council consists of the Speaker, two ex-officio members (the Attorney-General and the Financial Secretary) and nine elected members. Following elections in April 2001 the elected element of the legislature comprised the following parties: New People's Liberation Movement 7; National Progressive Party 2.

Two-thirds of the population fled the island following the resumption of volcanic activity in 1995 and a disastrous eruption of the Soufrière Hills volcano in 1997.

Acting Governor, HE Sir Howard Fergus *apptd* 2004

BRITISH HIGH COMMISSION
Lower Collymore Rock (PO Box 676), Bridgetown, Barbados
T (+1) (246) 430 7800

PITCAIRN ISLANDS

AREA – 2 sq. miles (4.5 sq. km)
POPULATION – 46 (2004). Since 1887 the islanders have generally been adherents of the Seventh-day Adventist Church. English and Pitkern are the official languages; the latter is a mixture of English and Tahitian and became an official language in 1997
CAPITAL – ΨAdamstown
CURRENCY – Currency is that of New Zealand
FLAG – British blue ensign with the arms in the fly

CLIMATE AND TERRAIN

Pitcairn is the chief of a group of islands situated about midway between New Zealand and Panama in the South Pacific Ocean. The other three islands of the group (Henderson, lying 168 km east-north-east of Pitcairn, Oeno, lying 120 km north-west, and Ducie, lying 470 km east) are all uninhabited. The climate is tropical, and the average temperature is 29°C

HISTORY AND POLITICS

Pitcairn became a British settlement under the British Settlement Act 1887 and was administered by the Governor of Fiji from 1952 until 1970, when the administration was transferred to the British High Commission in New Zealand and the British High Commissioner was appointed Governor. The local Government Ordinance of 1964 provides for a Council of ten members of whom six are elected.

Governor of Pitcairn, Henderson, Ducie and Oeno Islands, HE Richard Fell, CVO *(British High Commissioner to New Zealand)*

ECONOMY

The islanders live by subsistence gardening and fishing. Other than small fees charged for gun and driving licences there are no taxes and government revenue is derived almost solely from the sale of postage stamps and income from investments. Henderson Island, the largest of islands in the group, was declared a UNESCO World Heritage Site in 1988.

TRANSPORT INFRASTRUCTURE

There are 6.4 km of roads on the islands, none of which are paved. Communication with the outside world is maintained by cargo vessels travelling between New Zealand and Panama which call at irregular intervals.

SOUTH GEORGIA AND THE SOUTH SANDWICH ISLANDS

AREA – 1,580 sq. miles (4,092 sq. km)
POPULATION – No permanent population
CAPITAL – Ψ King Edward Point (Administrative Centre)
CURRENCY – Pound Sterling
FLAG – British blue ensign, with the shield of arms in the fly

CLIMATE AND TERRAIN

South Georgia is an island 1,390 km east-south-east of the Falkland Islands. More than half of the island is covered by permanent ice with many large glaciers reaching the sea at the head of fjords. The main mountain range is the Allardyce and elevation extremes range from 2,960 m (Mt Paget) at the highest point to 0 m (Atlantic Ocean) at the lowest. The South Sandwich Islands, lying some 750 km miles south-east of South Georgia, consist of a chain of 11 volcanic islands some 350 km long. Some of these islands are still active. The climate is wholly Antarctic, and in the late winter the Islands may be surrounded by pack ice.

HISTORY AND POLITICS

Britain annexed South Georgia and the South Sandwich Islands by Letters Patent in 1908 and since then they have been under continuous British occupation apart from a brief period during the Falklands war in 1982. Following the conflict, a small British Army garrison was maintained at King Edward Point on South Georgia, but this was withdrawn in March 2001. The population comprises the government's marine officer and the staff of the scientific research station operated by the British Antarctic Survey at King Edward Point, the curators of the museum at Grytviken and staff of the British Antarctic Survey at Bird Island, to the north-west of South Georgia.

The present constitution came into effect in 1985. It provides for a Commissioner who, for the time being, is the officer administering the government of the Falkland Islands.

Commissioner for South Georgia and the South Sandwich Islands, Howard Pearce, CVO, apptd 2002

ECONOMY

Some fishing takes place in adjacent waters, and there is a potential source of income from harvesting finfish and krill. In 1993 the UK government decreed an extension of Crown sovereignty and jurisdiction from 19 km around

South Georgia and the South Sandwich Islands to 321 km around each in order to preserve marine stocks.

The islands receive income from postage stamps produced in the UK, sale of fishing licences, and harbour and landing fees from tourist vessels. Tourism from specialised cruise ships is increasing.

ST HELENA AND DEPENDENCIES

AREA – 47 sq. miles (122 sq. km)
POPULATION – 7,417 (2004 estimate)
CAPITAL – ΨJamestown (population, 884, 1998)
CURRENCY – St Helena pound (£) of 100 pence
FLAG – British blue ensign with the shield of arms in the fly
POPULATION GROWTH RATE – 0.8 per cent (1998)
POPULATION DENSITY – 40 per sq. km (1998)
URBAN POPULATION – 39.2 per cent (1998)
ILLITERACY RATE – 3.6 per cent (1998)

CLIMATE AND TERRAIN

St Helena is situated in the South Atlantic Ocean, 1,500 km south of the Equator. The islands are 16.8 km long and around 10.5 km wide. Elevation extremes range from 2,060 m (St Mary's Peak on Tristan da Cunha) to 0 m (Atlantic Ocean). The climate is mild and the annual average temperature is 27°C.

HISTORY AND POLITICS

St Helena is believed to have been discovered by the Portuguese navigator João da Nova in 1502. It was used as a port of call for vessels of all nations trading to the East until it was annexed by the Dutch in 1633. It was never occupied by them, however, and the English East India Company seized it in 1659.

From 1815 to 1821 the island was lent to the British government as a place of exile for the Emperor Napoleon Bonaparte who died in St Helena on 5 May 1821, and in 1834 it was annexed to the British Crown. The Zulu Chief, Dinizulu, was exiled to the island in 1890 and up to 6,000 Boer prisoners were held there between 1900 and 1903.

The government of St Helena is administered by a Governor, with the aid of a Legislative Council, consisting of a Speaker, three ex-officio members (Chief Secretary, Financial Secretary and Attorney-General) and 12 elected members. Five committees of the Legislative Council are responsible for the overseeing of the activities of the five biggest government departments, and have in addition a wide range of statutory and administrative functions. The Governor is also assisted by an Executive Council of the three ex-officio members and the chairmen of the Council committees.

Governor, HE Michael Clancy, *apptd* 2004

ECONOMY

St Helena was intended as a maritime base, with an economy dedicated to the provision of supplies for shipping and the local garrison, rather than as a self-sufficient colony. St Helena still receives an annual grant from the UK, the only UK Overseas Territory to do so, with the exception of Montserrat. The only significant export is canned and frozen fish.

TRANSPORT INFRASTRUCTURE AND MEDIA

St Helena has 138 km of roads, most of which are single track. James's Bay, on the north-west of the island is the principal port.

Television programmes are received in St Helena via satellite and distributed by cable. The island also has one radio station.

ASCENSION ISLAND

AREA – 34 sq. miles (88 sq. km)
POPULATION – 980 (2001 census)
CAPITAL – ΨGeorgetown
CURRENCY – Currency is that of St Helena or the UK

CLIMATE AND TERRAIN

The small island of Ascension lies in the South Atlantic some 1,200 km north-west of St Helena. It is a rocky peak of purely volcanic origin. The highest point (Green Mountain), some 860 m, is covered with lush vegetation.

HISTORY AND POLITICS

Ascension is said to have been discovered by João da Nova in 1501 and two years later was visited on Ascension Day by Alphonse d'Albuquerque, who gave the island its present name. It was uninhabited until the arrival of Napoleon in St Helena in 1815 when a small British naval garrison was stationed on the island. As HMS *Ascension* it remained under the supervision of the Board of Admiralty until 1922, when it was made a dependency of St Helena.

The British Foreign Secretary appoints the Administrator who is responsible to the Governor resident in St Helena. There is a small police force, bank and post office. In August 2002, a plebiscite was held with residents to decide on a form of democratic self-government for the island, and an Island Council was formed as a result. A general election to appoint members to the Council took place in November. The Council consists of seven elected members plus the Director of Financial Services and the Attorney-General, and is chaired by the Governor, represented locally by the Administrator.

Administrator, Andrew Kettlewell, *apptd* 2002

ECONOMY AND TRADE

A new fiscal regime was introduced in 2002, and finance for public and common services is raised through taxation. Healthcare and schooling are provided free of charge to local tax payers.

TRANSPORT INFRASTRUCTURE

Ascension has 40 km of roads, and there is a monthly shipping service and a flight every five days by RAF Tristars which transit Ascension en route to the Falkland Islands.

TRISTAN DA CUNHA

AREA – 38 sq. miles (98 sq. km)
POPULATION – 277 (2003 estimate)
CAPITAL – ΨEdinburgh of the Seven Seas
CURRENCY – Currency is that of the UK
FLAG – Tristan da Cunha's own flag was raised on 18 November 2002 and the coat of arms reads: 'Our Faith is our Strength'.

CLIMATE AND TERRAIN

Tristan da Cunha is the chief island of a group of islands in the South Atlantic which lies some 2,333 km south-south-west of St Helena. All the islands are volcanic and steep-sided with cliffs or narrow beaches. The highest point of elevation is 2,060 m (Queen Mary's Peak) while the lowest is 0 m (Atlantic Ocean).

HISTORY AND POLITICS

Tristan da Cunha was discovered in 1506 by the Portuguese admiral Tristão da Cunha. In 1760 a British naval officer visited the islands and gave his name to Nightingale Island. In 1816 the group was annexed to the British Crown and a garrison was placed on Tristan da Cunha, but this force was withdrawn in 1817. Corporal William Glass remained at his own request with his wife and two children and this party, with two others, formed a settlement. In 1827 five women from St Helena, and afterwards others from Cape Colony, joined the party.

Due to its position on a main sailing route the colony thrived, with an economy based on trading with whalers, sealers and other passing ships. However, the replacement of sail by steam and the opening of the Suez Canal in the late 19th century led to decline.

In October 1961 a volcano, believed to have been extinct for thousands of years, erupted and the danger of further volcanic activity led to the evacuation of inhabitants to the UK. An advance party returned to Tristan da Cunha in 1963 and subsequently the main body of the islanders returned to the island.

GOVERNMENT

In 1938 Tristan da Cunha and the neighbouring islands of Inaccessible, Nightingale (both uninhabited) and Gough were made dependencies of St Helena. They are administered by the Governor of St Helena through a resident Administrator, with headquarters at Edinburgh. Under a constitution introduced in 1985, the Administrator is advised by an Island Council of eight elected members, of whom one must be a woman, and three appointed members. Elections are held every three years.
Administrator, Mike Hentley, *apptd* 2004

ECONOMY

The island is almost financially self-sufficient; UK government aid finances training scholarships and a resident medical officer at the hospital. The main industries are crayfish fishing, fish-processing and agriculture.

TRANSPORT INFRASTRUCTURE

Tristan da Cunha has 20 km of roads. Scheduled visits to the island are restricted to about six calls a year by fishing vessels from Cape Town and annual calls of the RMS *St Helena* and the SA *Agulhas*, also from Cape Town, which carry passengers, cargo and mail to and from the island.

TURKS AND CAICOS ISLANDS

AREA – 497 sq. km (191.2 sq. miles)
POPULATION – 20,014 (2001 census estimate)
CAPITAL – ΨGrand Turk (Cockburn Town; population, 3,691, 1994)
CURRENCY – US dollar (US$)
FLAG – British blue ensign with the shield of arms in the fly
POPULATION GROWTH RATE – 3.3 per cent (2004)
POPULATION DENSITY – 37 per sq. km (2001)

CLIMATE AND TERRAIN

The Turks and Caicos Islands are about 80 km south-east of the Bahamas, of which they are geographically an extension. There are over 30 islands, of which eight are inhabited, covering an estimated area of 430 sq. km. The principal island and seat of government is Grand Turk. Climate is marine tropical moderated by trade winds and the average annual temperature is 27°C.

HISTORY AND POLITICS

The islands were part of the UK's Jamaican colony until Jamaica's independence in 1962, when they assumed the status of a separate crown colony.

A constitution was introduced in 1988, and amended in 1993, which provides for an Executive Council and a Legislative Council. The Executive Council is presided over by the Governor and comprises the Chief Minister and five elected Ministers, together with the ex-officio Chief Secretary and Attorney-General.

At the general election of 24 April 2003, the People's Democratic Movement won seven seats and the Progressive National Party six seats in the Legislative Council.
Governor, HE Jim Poston, *apptd* 2002

ECONOMY

The most important industries are fishing, tourism and offshore finance. The islands were visited by 151,000 tourists in 2000, although tourism fell by 6 per cent in 2002.

Trade with UK	*2002*	*2003*
Imports from UK	£1,167,000	£1,514
Exports to UK	495,000	344,000

TRANSPORT INFRASTRUCTURE

The principal airports are on the islands of Grand Turk and Providenciales. Air services link Providenciales with London, Miami, Fort Lauderdale, Atlanta, Jamaica, the Bahamas, Haiti and the Dominican Republic. An internal air service provides a regular service between the principal islands. There are direct shipping services to the USA (Miami). The islands also have a total of 121 km of roads, 24 km of which are surfaced.

THE YEAR 2003–4

EVENTS OF THE YEAR

OBITUARIES

ARCHAEOLOGY

ARCHITECTURE

ART

BROADCASTING

BUSINESS AND FINANCE

CONSERVATION AND HERITAGE

DANCE

FILM

LITERATURE

MUSIC

OPERA

PARLIAMENT

SCIENCE AND DISCOVERY

THEATRE

WEATHER

SPORTS RESULTS AND RECORDS

EVENTS OF THE YEAR

BRITISH AFFAIRS

SEPTEMBER 2003

4. In Birmingham, the Bullring shopping centre was officially opened after 2½ years of construction and a total cost of £550 million, as part of the city's urban regeneration programme. The first phase of the Hutton Inquiry closed. **7**. A mock chemical attack was carried out at Bank underground station in London as a training exercise for the emergency services. **8**. Defence Secretary Geoff Hoon announced that 1,200 extra British troops would be sent to the south of Iraq. **9**. The Government published a White Paper on the future constitution of Europe which supported the appointment of a full-time chairman for the Council of Ministers and the use of Qualified Majority Voting (QMV) for EU business. **11**. Commander Richard Farrington and his officers were reprimanded after pleading guilty at a court martial in Portsmouth to a range of charges relating to £39 million of damage caused to *HMS Nottingham* when it ran aground on Wolf Rock, off the coast of Australia, in 2002. **14**. An investigation started on 30 June by the Office of Fair Trading (OFT) into alleged fee-fixing among four leading public schools was extended to include a further 700 independent schools. **15**. The Hutton Inquiry started a second round of witness-calling with Sir Richard Dearlove, the chief of MI6, and Greg Dyke, Director-General of the BBC, giving evidence. **16**. Six platforms at King's Cross station had to be closed during the morning rush hour after a train derailed at low speed in the station; no one was injured. **18**. *The Times* reported that the headmaster of Winchester College had admitted in a letter to parents that exchanging information on fees had been standard practice throughout the independent schools sector for many years, in a possible infringement of the 1998 Competition Act. Andrew Gilligan, the BBC reporter who interviewed Dr Kelly, was called to give further evidence to the Hutton Inquiry. **20**. Lord Williams of Mostyn, life peer, privy councillor and leader of the House of Lords died unexpectedly at his Gloucestershire home of a heart attack aged 62. **22**. The Liberal Democrat Party began its annual conference in Brighton. **23**. The Office of the Rail Regulator (ORR) approved a revised budget submitted by Network Rail to spend £24.5 billion over the next five years on the rail network. **25**. The Hutton Inquiry completed its main public proceedings. **30**. Tony Blair addressed the Labour Party Conference in Bournemouth, stating that there would be no reversal on the Party's schedule of reforms, including policies on foundation hospitals and tuition fees, and that he had no regrets over the conflict in Iraq.

OCTOBER 2003

1. A high court judge ruled that under European Law NHS patients on waiting lists could have surgery in European hospitals, refunded by the NHS, if they had faced an 'undue delay' receiving treatment in the UK. **2**. The Qualifications and Curriculum Authority announced major reforms for secondary education, including tailoring education to each individual's aptitude and ability and allowing pupils to study at their own speed, with courses such as GCSEs not having a pre-determined time span. **4**. Pope John Paul II held his first private audience with the Archbishop of Canterbury, Dr Rowan Williams, at the Vatican. The Strategic Rail Authority admitted that up to 500 new railway carriages, commissioned after legislation insisted on safer carriages, would have to be held in storage as there was not enough power to run them on the network. **5**. Allegations were made throughout the media that the Conservative leader Iain Duncan Smith improperly claimed allowances for 15 months for his wife, Betsy, after he became party leader. **10**. John Armitt, the Chief Executive of Network Rail, announced that it would take control of all three maintenance contracts surrendered by Jarvis, one of the main contractors used by Network Rail, effectively putting 40 per cent of the country's track back under public control. Lord Bach, Minister of Defence Procurement, admitted in a written parliamentary answer, that on 21 December 1990, three-and-a-half weeks before the 1991 Gulf War began, the MoD was told that tests on mice had produced serious side effects when anthrax and whooping cough vaccines were given together. Since the war thousands of soldiers had reported suffering from 'Gulf War Syndrome', believed to be caused by the vaccination programme. **15**. Parliamentary Standards Commissioner Sir Philip Mawer began a formal investigation into Iain Duncan Smith's employment of his wife as diary secretary. **19**. *The Times* reported a study by Datamonitor which found that 500 call centres in Britain had installed technology that filtered customers according to whether their postcodes represented 'poor' or 'wealthy' areas. The Prime Minister, Tony Blair, was admitted to Hammersmith Hospital in west London suffering from an irregular heartbeat, he was later discharged and returned home to rest. The second London underground derailment in 48 hours happened when a Northern Line train derailed at Camden station injuring seven passengers. **20**. NHS hospital consultants voted in favour of a new contract under which they would work a 40-hour week and receive a 20 per cent pay rise. **21**. The House of Lords again overturned the Government's attempt to ban fox hunting, with Peers voting 261 to 49 for a regulated system. Private correspondence of the late Diana, Princess of Wales, was published in *The Mirror*; the letters were obtained by the newspaper after it bought the serialisation rights to a book written by Paul Burrell, Diana's former butler. **22**. New guidelines were published by the National Institute for Clinical Excellence (NICE) on antenatal healthcare, aiming to standardise care across the country and offer earlier scans and Down's Syndrome screening to all pregnant women. **23**. The MP for Glasgow Kelvin, George Galloway, was expelled from the Labour Party after he was found guilty of four out of five charges of bringing the party into disrepute; including inciting British troops to disobey orders in Iraq. Dame Brenda Hale was appointed to Britain's highest court becoming the first female judge to be made a law lord, or *Lord of Appeal in Ordinary*. **24**. Concorde flew its last flight after being decommissioned by British Airways. Network Rail announced that it planned to take all remaining contracted-out track maintenance work back in-house by mid 2004. Prince William issued a statement asking Paul Burrell, the former butler to his late mother, to bring an end to the revelations regarding her private life. **29**. Iain Duncan Smith resigned as leader of the

Conservative Party after losing a vote of confidence by 90 votes to 75. **30**. Eighteen-year-old paratrooper, Christopher Finney, became the youngest serviceman to be awarded the George Cross for saving a comrade in a 'friendly-fire' incident in the war in Iraq. The MoD's annual report and accounts were published revealing losses of £1.7 billion; the Auditor-General, Sir John Bourne, stated that the losses were significant.

NOVEMBER 2003

1. Fifteen out of 73 postal areas in Britain were closed due to unofficial strike action by 30,000 members of the Communication Workers Union (CWU). **2**. Despite formal complaints and threats of schism within the Church, the consecration of the first openly gay bishop in the Anglican Communion took place in the US when Gene Robinson became Bishop of New Hampshire. **3**. At Durham Castle the Deputy Prime Minister, John Prescott, launched a Labour campaign to encourage electors to participate in three referendums to create three new regional assemblies for the North-East, the North-West and Yorkshire and Humberside. **5**. Michael Howard was elected leader of the Conservative Party. **6**. The House of Lords voted 150 to 100 against Labour plans to create Foundation Hospitals. **8**. The Countess of Wessex gave birth to a baby girl, Lady Louise Alice Windsor, eighth in line to the throne, at the NHS Frimley Park Hospital in Surrey. **18**. The US President, George W. Bush, arrived to begin his four-day state visit, the first state visit by a US President since Woodrow Wilson in 1918. **20**. Roger Short, the UK consul general in Turkey, was killed in a terrorist bomb blast at the UK consulate in Istanbul. **26**. The Government's 2003–4 legislative programme was delivered in the Queen's speech at the state opening of Parliament.

DECEMBER 2003

3. The Queen arrived in Nigeria to attend the Commonwealth summit, her first visit to the country since it became independent. **5**. The Independent Schools Council (ISC) issued a code of practice to all its 1,280 members banning the exchange of information on fees and costs between schools. **9**. Britain's first toll motorway, running for 27 miles around the edge of Birmingham, was officially opened to vehicles. **22**. Mark Henderson, a British tourist, was released alongside four Israelis, after being held hostage for 102 days in the Colombian jungle by Marxist guerrillas. The world's biggest passenger liner, the *Queen Mary 2*, set sail from its French shipyard after being handed over to its British owners, Cunard Line. **25**. Princess Alice, the Queen's aunt and oldest member of the British Royal family, celebrated her 102nd birthday. **26**. The Health Secretary John Reid announced that an additional £12 million was to be allocated to train medical staff working with the terminally ill. **28**. The Department for Transport made a joint announcement with the Home Office that armed, plain-clothes agents, or 'sky marshals', were to be deployed on British flights for the first time. **31**. British Airways flight 223 from Heathrow was escorted by fighter jets to a remote area of tarmac when it came to land at Dulles Airport in Washington following a security alert.

JANUARY 2004

1. New rules were introduced allowing the Driver and Vehicle Licensing Agency (DVLA) to automatically fine car owners who fail to renew their car tax within 6 weeks of date of expiry of their tax disc. British Airways flight 223 to Washington was cancelled as a security measure after British and US security forces received intelligence of a plot to hijack a BA airliner. **4**. On his way home from his Christmas break Tony Blair made a surprise visit to British forces stationed in Basra in southern Iraq; during his address he stated that it was expected that several thousand soldiers would remain in Iraq until at least 2006. **5**. A report published by the European Commission showed that more Britons were working longer than the weekly maximum of 48 hours than when the EU legislation was introduced 11 years ago. **6**. The Royal Coroner, Michael Burgess, opened two separate inquests into the deaths of Diana, Princess of Wales, and Dodi Fayed in a car crash on 31 August 1997 and asked the Metropolitan Police Commissioner Sir John Stevens to make enquiries into the incident. Two MPs, David Chidgey and Richard Ottaway, were cleared of contempt of Parliament after being accused of using prompts from a witness when questioning Dr Kelly at the Foreign Affairs Committee. Downing Street named Canon Stephen Cottrell as the Bishop of Reading after Canon Jeffrey John stood down in 2003 following objections within the church concerning his homosexuality. The National Executive Committee voted 22 to 2 in favour of re-admitting Ken Livingstone, Mayor of London, to the Labour Party so that he could become the party's official candidate for the Mayoral elections in June. **7**. US Officials announced that all British travellers to the USA with passports issued after 26 October 2004 would need a visa under new security measures imposed by the US Congress. **8**. It was announced in *The Times* that the Ministry of Defence had paid out its first compensation awards to the families of three men in Iraq who died after British troops allegedly tortured them whilst held in custody in Iraq. Pierre-Richard Prosper, the US Ambassador at Large for War Crimes, agreed that the nine British terrorist suspects held in Cuba could be repatriated, as long as they were 'managed' by British authorities. A new Higher Education Bill was published which would abolish the £1,125-a-year advance tuition fee by 2006 and allow universities to set their own fees of up to £3,000 a year. Students from the poorest 20 per cent of homes would be exempt from paying the first £1,200 of their fees and would also qualify for bursaries of at least £300 at universities charging the full £3,000. **12**. The Health Secretary John Reid announced that seven private companies had been awarded contracts to run 24 mobile specialist treatment centres in England; the centres would offer a limited range of treatments, including ophthalmology units offering cataract operations, and would travel to areas where waiting lists are longest. **22**. Steve Gough, also known as the 'naked rambler', completed his Land's End to John o' Groats solo nude hike; he was arrested 15 times and spent nearly five months in prison. The National Audit Office revealed that four defence projects, including the construction of three Astute submarines, the Eurofighter aircraft, Brimstone anti-armour missiles and 18 Nimrod MRAs, were running so late and over-budget that the total cost for the projects had risen by £2.7 billion. **23**. Charles Kennedy, leader of the Liberal Democrats, formally dismissed Dr Jenny Tonge from her position as party spokeswoman for international development, after she expressed sympathy to terrorists at a pro-Palestinian lobby on 21 January; she will stand down as MP for Richmond Park at the next election. The Health Secretary John Reid announced that patients infected with hepatitis C after receiving blood from the NHS would be eligible for compensation of

£20,000, with a further £25,000 available to patients with the more advanced stage of the disease. **27**. At a second reading, the Higher Education Bill was passed by the House of Commons by a majority of just five votes. **28**. Lord Hutton's report on the death of Dr David Kelly was published clearing Tony Blair and the Government of behaving duplicitously in revealing Dr Kelly's name to the media. The report strongly criticised BBC governance, stating that editorial control and complaints procedures were defective. It criticised the MoD for not informing Dr Kelly that he had been identified as the 'source' prior to publication and stated that BBC allegations that Downing Street had knowingly doctored an intelligence dossier were unfounded. The report concluded that Dr Kelly had killed himself after a 'severe loss of self esteem'. Gavyn Davies resigned as BBC chairman following the findings of the Hutton report. Snow fell throughout Britain with temperatures reaching −15°C in some parts of the country. **29**. Greg Dyke, the director-general of the BBC, resigned from his position following the results of the Hutton Inquiry. **30**. Andrew Gilligan, the journalist who originally made the claims on the BBC *Today* programme that the Government had 'sexed-up' a dossier on weapons of mass destruction resigned from the BBC, stating that the BBC had been served a grave injustice by the Hutton Inquiry.

FEBRUARY 2004

3. The Prime Minister, Tony Blair, set up an inquiry, to be led by Lord Butler of Brockwell, into the reliability of pre-war intelligence on Iraq's weapons of mass destruction. **6**. Nineteen Chinese migrant workers drowned while picking cockles at night in Morecambe Bay, 16 workers were rescued but it was not known how many were still missing. The RMT transport union voted 42 to 8 in favour of allowing union branches to affiliate to other parties if they felt they better represented their interests; five branches had already affiliated to the Scottish Socialist Party and two more had requested to do so. **7**. Labour took the unprecedented step of expelling the RMT transport union from the party following the union's decision to allow branches to affiliate to other political parties. **9**. The government announced plans for the formation of a new FBI-style police force combining the functions of the National Crime Squad (NCS), the National Criminal Intelligence Service (NCIS), the investigative arm of Customs and Excise and the Home Office's Immigration Service into one body: the Serious Organised Crime Agency. The Queen approved reforms put forward by Lord Falconer, the Lord Chancellor, to appoint a moderator and an additional body made up of three privy councillors to oversee Westminster Abbey and the five other *Royal Peculiars*, distancing the monarch from the role as sole authority. **10**. The Prime Minister, Tony Blair, met the Libyan Foreign Minister, Abdul Rahman Mohammad Shalgam, at Downing Street. **12**. The Health Minister, Rosie Winterton, announced that the cost of a NHS prescription would rise by 10p to £6.40 in England from 1 April 2004. **17**. All SAS One-Step pregnancy testing kits used by the NHS were recalled by the Medicines Healthcare Products Regulatory Agency (MHRA) after the Co. Durham and Darlington NHS Trust discovered abnormally high false negative readings during a routine quality control check. Estimates suggested that between 15,000 and 20,000 women could have been affected. **18**. The Chancellor Gordon Brown unveiled a national voluntary work scheme for young people which would allow school leavers to take a gap year to help their local communities; participants would receive help with basic living expenses and a possible contribution towards university or college fees. **19**. The Foreign Secretary Jack Straw announced that five British men held for more than two years without trial at the Guantanamo Bay camp in Cuba would be flown back to the UK. **23**. The Home Secretary David Blunkett announced that citizens of countries joining the EU on 1 May 2004 would be free to work in Britain, provided they registered their employment, but would not be eligible for benefits, apart from tax credits and housing benefit, until they had worked for at least a year. **25**. The Home Secretary David Blunkett announced that MI5's budget would rise by 50 per cent to £300 million to support a recruitment drive to expand staff numbers to around three thousand. **26**. The former International Development Secretary, Clare Short, alleged on the Radio 4 *Today* programme that Britain had spied on Kofi Annan, the Secretary-General of the UN prior to the war in Iraq. **27**. Snow and extreme temperatures spread across the country forcing more than 1,000 schools to close.

MARCH 2004

9. Five Britons arrived in Britain after being released from Camp X-Ray in Guantanamo Bay. The five men were taken to Paddington Green high-security police station and one man was released immediately after questioning. **10**. The remaining four detainees who arrived back in Britain from Guantanamo Bay were released without charge. **17**. In the 2004 Budget the Chancellor Gordon Brown announced detailed proposals based on Sir Michael Lyons' report of 15 March to cut 54,000 posts by 2008 from the Department for Work and Pensions, Inland Revenue and Customs and Excise in a move to reduce administration costs. During an adventure-training exercise in Mexico partly funded by the Armed Forces, 13 British cavers, including nine military personnel, became trapped 120ft underground by unseasonable floodwater. **25**. The Prime Minister, Tony Blair, met with Libyan leader Colonel Gaddafi in Libya after a 20-year deadlock in diplomatic relations between the two countries. In a six-hour operation, a team of British cavers were rescued, after being trapped underground by floodwater for eight days in Mexico. **26**. The Prime Minister, Tony Blair, called for the new constitution for Europe to be agreed within three months and, if possible, prior to the European elections on 10 June. **28**. It was announced that Network Rail, the not-for-profit company that owns and manages the UK's railways, had submitted a proposal to the Transport Secretary Alistair Darling requesting direct operational control of the train operating companies (TOCs). **29**. Iain Duncan Smith, the former Conservative leader, was cleared of deliberately misusing parliamentary funds to employ his wife as diary secretary in a report published by the Parliamentary Commissioner for Standards Sir Philip Mawer. **30**. The Home Secretary, David Blunkett, suspended all immigration applications from Romania and Bulgaria and promised an inquiry, following allegations that immigration officials were allowing bogus claims to be processed from these areas. **31**. The Higher Education Bill passed through to the House of Lords by a majority of 28 after a Labour back bench amendment to strike out the principle of varying fees was defeated by 316 votes to 288 in the House of Commons. The Civil Partnerships Bill was published to enable homosexual couples to register their partnerships in a civil ceremony and receive legal rights similar to those of a married couple. The first ten hospitals; Basildon and Thurrock; Bradford Teaching Hospital; Countess of Chester; Doncaster and Bassetlaw; Homerton University; Moorfields Eye Hospital; Peterborough & Stamford; Stockport; Royal Devon and Exeter and Royal Marsden assumed their status as Foundation Hospitals.

APRIL 2004

1. The Immigration Minister Beverley Hughes resigned after admitting that she had been warned over a year previously by Labour Deputy Chief Whip Bob Ainsworth that the Home Office was approving visa claims from eastern Europe backed by forged documents. The Prime Minister replaced Ms Hughes with Work and Pensions Minister Des Browne. **5**. Thames Trains was fined a record £2 million for its part in the 1999 Paddington rail disaster in which 31 people died. The judge ruled that the company had failed to limit the risk to passengers by not correcting faults with its driver-training programme. **17**. Research by the Audit Commission found there were at least 3.5 million excess names on GP lists in England alone, as practices receive NHS funds based on the number of patients registered, doctors were warned that they would face prosecution if they had deliberately failed to strike-off names. **19**. Tony Blair announced in the House of Commons that the British people would be given the chance to vote on whether to adopt a European constitution. **22**. On security advice from MI5, MPs voted in favour of spending £1.3 million on a permanent glass security barrier to be erected in the House of Commons between the public gallery and the rest of the chamber. **23**. Universities such as Durham, Nottingham, Warwick, Edinburgh, London and Bristol warned that thousands of candidates would face rejection due to unprecedented pressure on places due to an increase in the number of students achieving high grades. **25**. The car of French National Front leader, Jean-Marie Le Pen was pelted with eggs and rubbish by protesters after he left the launch of the British National Party's European election campaign at a hotel in Altrincham. **26**. A letter signed by 52 signatories including former ambassadors, high commissioners and governors was sent to the Prime Minister, Tony Blair, expressing concern regarding foreign policy on the Middle East and Iraq. **27**. Market analysts Mintel published figures showing that a quarter of seven to ten-year olds own mobile phones. The rail maintenance company Jarvis admitted joint liability with Network Rail for the Potters Bar rail crash, enabling compensation claims to proceed. **28**. New NHS guidelines developed in consultation with the National Institute for Clinical Excellence and the Collaborating Centre for Women's and Children's Health recommended that NHS doctors should not automatically arrange caesareans on request without legitimate medical reasons.

MAY 2004

2. Senior investigators from the Royal Military Police flew to Cyprus to interview soldiers from the Queen's Lancashire Regiment following claims that members of the regiment had been involved in mistreating Iraqi prisoners. **6**. The Government announced that John Scarlett, an MI6 intelligence officer and former head of the Joint Intelligence Committee, was to be the next chief of MI6 on the retirement of Sir Richard Dearlove in July 2004. Dr Jeffrey John was installed as the Dean of St Albans following his withdrawal from the post of Bishop of Reading in 2003 after protests concerning his homosexuality. **9**. Prime Minister, Tony Blair, apologised for the abuse of Iraqi prisoners in British custody and stated that those responsible would be punished according to Army disciplinary rules. **11**. Eight people were killed and more than 40 injured in Glasgow when a plastics factory collapsed following a huge explosion on the ground floor. A report leaked from the International Red Cross stated that officials within the US and UK armed forces had ignored its repeated and detailed complaints, regarding the abuse of prisoners held in custody in Iraq, throughout a period of many months. Figures published by Christian Research compiled on rural ministries showed that attendance at Anglican churches in the countryside had decreased by more than a third in the last ten years. **19**. Prime Minister Tony Blair was hit by a missile made of purple flour during Question Time in the House of Commons; the missile was thrown by two protesters in the public gallery who were there at the invitation of Lady Golding. A review of Commons security already underway by MI5 and Scotland Yard was accelerated following the incident. **24**. Britain and the USA tabled a draft United Nations Security Council resolution outlining their plans for the transfer of responsibility for all aspects of statehood in Iraq, excluding security, to an interim Iraqi government on 30 June. **29**. Some 20,000 people living in caravans on local authority sites won the same tenancy rights as council house tenants after a European court in Strasbourg ruled that summary evictions, without justification or the right to appeal, were against their human rights.

JUNE 2004

3. More than a thousand flights were delayed or cancelled when the computer system at West Drayton air traffic control centre failed. **6**. A BBC cameraman was killed and the BBC's security correspondent, Frank Gardner, was seriously injured in an attack blamed on islamist extremists in the Saudi Arabian capital, Riyadh. **10**. European parliamentary, local and London mayoral elections took place. In the London mayoral elections, Labour candidate Ken Livingstone, was re-elected for a second term, having completed his first term as an independent candidate. **11**. With three-quarters of the results declared in the local authority elections Labour had lost more than 400 seats with the Conservatives and the Liberal Democrats gaining more than 200 and 100 seats respectively. Turnout for the local elections was at 40 per cent, an increase from 31 per cent in 2003. **12**. The Queen's 2004 Birthday Honours List was published. Among those recognised were newsreader and presenter, Angela Rippon, who was awarded an OBE alongside bestselling author Jilly Cooper, poets Pam Ayres and Roger McGough and weather forecaster Michael Fish were awarded MBEs. **15**. Lord Goldsmith, the Attorney General, announced that four soldiers from the Royal Regiment of Fusiliers were to face a court martial on charges of abusing and sexually assaulting Iraqi civilians. **17**. The Fire Brigades Union (FBU) voluntarily disaffiliated from the Labour Party following a vote in which 250 delegates voted 35,105 to 14,611 in favour of leaving the Party. **23**. The Higher Education Minister, Alan Johnson, told the House of Commons that the Higher Education Bill, passed in January by five votes, would be amended to protect students opting for a gap year in 2005. Students completing their A-levels in 2005 who decided to take a gap year would pay the existing £1,125-a-year fee, capped for the duration of their studies. **24**. The Government announced, as part of its draft manifesto for the health service, that it would cut hospital waiting times (the time from GP referral to receiving hospital treatment) from 13 months to 18 weeks by 2008. The results of the first national education assessments for five-year-olds were published; the assessments known as Foundation Stage profile became compulsory in state schools in 2003. The tests had been widely criticised by teaching unions as well as the Chief Inspector of Schools, David Bell, as unreliable, unhelpful and time-consuming for teachers; initial results showed that more girls than boys were reaching or working beyond early learning goals. **29**. The RMT union began a 24-hour London Underground strike over pay; the union wanted a 35-hour, 4-day week and a minimum of £22,000 pa for all station staff. **30**. The London Underground strike continued; five tube lines were operating but with severe delays, many major roads were gridlocked.

JULY 2004

6. Prime Minister Tony Blair conceded for the first time, during a biannual appearance before the Commons Liaison Committee, that weapons of mass destruction might never be found in Iraq. **7**. *The Times* reported that doctors were treating record numbers of teenagers and young adults for mumps; the Health Protection Agency recorded 578 cases in the first three months of 2004, a 75 per cent increase over the first quarter in 2003. The UK was hit by severe storms with winds of up to 60mph recorded in some exposed places, an inch of rain fell across the Solent and 25ft-high waves were recorded in the English Channel forcing freighters to take shelter in emergency anchorages and ferries to be cancelled. **8**. Ian Gibson, Chairman of the Commons Science and Technology Committee, proposed that a joint committee of peers and MPs should be formed to re-consider the 1967 Abortion Act and the 1990 amendment, under which a foetus can be legally aborted for social reasons up to 24-weeks gestation. The Government's five-year plan for Education was published; the main reforms included the expansion of popular schools to increase admissions, financial independence for all schools from local authorities, the closure of failing schools and the introduction of more personalised learning for all children, such as the opportunity to learn a musical instrument or a foreign language at primary school level. **9**. The Department of Health announced that pilot 'fee-for-service' schemes would be introduced in 32 trusts in England in which doctors and other NHS staff will receive bonus payments for carrying out extra operations and treatments. **14**. Lord Butler of Brockwell's report into the reliability and quality of intelligence used to support the case for war with Iraq was published. Lord Butler surmised that the intelligence reports used to support the conflict were 'seriously flawed' although he cleared the Prime Minister Tony Blair of deliberately attempting to mislead the public and Parliament about the intelligence, finding no evidence to question Mr Blair's faith in the information he was given. Lord Butler reported that the Joint Intelligence Committee's warnings on the limitations of the intelligence were not made sufficiently clear in the dossier and that language used in the dossier and by the Prime Minister may have left readers with the impression that there was firmer intelligence than was the case. **15**. A new White Paper for the Rail Industry outlined proposals to abolish the Strategic Rail Authority and transfer its responsibilities to the Department for Transport. **16**. Health Secretary John Reid unveiled a plan to rescue NHS dentistry, promising to spend an extra £368 million on the service and recruit 1,000 extra dentists by October 2005. **19**. The Home Secretary David Blunkett announced plans for a five-year anti-crime drive, initiatives included on-the-spot fines for anti-social behaviour, the use of satellite tracking technology to keep track of offenders with an increase in the use of electronic tagging. Plans also included new border controls that would help to track criminals and terrorists, such as the introduction of photographic records for every traveller entering or leaving the UK. **20**. Transport Secretary Alistair Darling announced that the long-awaited £10 billion Crossrail scheme linking east and west London would go ahead. **22**. Culture Secretary Tessa Jowell, said in a statement to Parliament that the date for switching off analog television could be postponed until 2012; ministers had maintained that a 2010 deadline was possible but broadcasters said that not enough people would have access to digital television by then. **29**. Metropolitan Police, in partnership with Westminster Council, banned unaccompanied children under 16 from the West End of London after 9 p.m. **30**. The Home Office announced measures to increases police powers when dealing with animal rights extremists who orchestrate attacks on those working in the biotechnology and pharmaceutical industries.

AUGUST 2004

3. Severe flooding in London shut parts of the Underground and major road routes out of the capital. **12**. A human skeleton from the Iron Age was discovered almost intact on the island of Orkney; the body appeared to have been ritualistically buried with a set of antlers resting on its chest and a toe ring on each foot. **13**. The General Secretary of the train drivers' union ASLEF was dismissed for gross misconduct for allegedly failing to co-operate with an independent inquiry into the union's affairs. **15**. The Information Commissioner Richard Thomas voiced concerns over Government plans to introduce an identity card scheme and proposals by the Office for National Statistics for a population register, warning that civil liberties could be infringed. **16**. Torrential rain in Cornwall caused the River Valency to burst its banks resulting in a 10ft wall of water flooding the village of Boscastle. In total 108 people were rescued by the emergency services; there were no fatalities. **19**. A-level results showed that students gained a record 171,639 A-grades in the 2004 exams, representing 22.4 per cent of the total entry of 766,247. The overall pass rate increased for the 22nd consecutive year to 96 per cent. Scotland was hit by 24-hours of torrential rain, causing widespread flooding and mudslides. **22**. Paul Miller, chairman of the British Medical Consultants' Committee, warned that there could be a mass exodus of experienced consultants from the NHS due to the introduction of a new pension scheme. **25**. The 2004 GCSE exam results were published. The overall pass rate remained unchanged from 2003 with 97.6 per cent awarded A* to G grades with the proportion of entries awarded A* or A rising from 16.7 to 17.4 per cent.

NORTHERN IRELAND AFFAIRS

SEPTEMBER 2003

2. Sean Hoey, an alleged Real IRA bomb-maker, was arrested in Jonesborough, south Armagh, in connection with the 1998 Omagh bombing, and another man was arrested on suspicion of designing the 500lb car bomb. **4**.

Northern Ireland Secretary Paul Murphy announced the formation of the International Monitoring Commission, set up to monitor paramilitary cease-fires in Northern Ireland and to try and restore the Northern Ireland Assembly. **5**. Sean Hoey was charged with conspiracy to cause an explosion, possessing explosive substances with intent to endanger life, and membership of the Real IRA and was due to appear in court on 6 September. **8**. It was announced that paramilitaries being held in Northern Ireland's Maghaberry prison would be segregated to avoid attacks on prison officers and fights between republican and loyalist prisoners. **9**. Shadow Defence Minister Gerald Howarth called for a halt to the five-year Bloody Sunday inquiry due to it having cost £113 million. It was not due to reach a conclusion for 12 months. **10**. Paddy Ward, a former member of the IRA's youth wing, told the Saville inquiry that Martin McGuinness had arranged the supply of 16 detonators for nail bombs which the IRA had planned to use on Bloody Sunday. **18**. Four men and a woman were arrested in Strabane, Co Tyrone, after several Roman Catholic members of Northern Ireland's community policing boards received death threats; two members had their cars set alight and one member was sent a hoax bomb. **25**. General Sir Mike Jackson, the Chief of the General Staff, was recalled for further questioning by the Bloody Sunday inquiry to answer questions after it emerged that he was in possession of documents containing interviews with some of the soldiers who had fired shots on Bloody Sunday. **29**. Our Lady of Mercy Roman Catholic girls' secondary school in North Belfast was attacked by Protestants who set six cars on fire.

OCTOBER 2003

1. A former paratrooper, known as 'Soldier F' during the Saville Inquiry, who had been shown by forensic scientific evidence to have shot dead Michael Kelly on Bloody Sunday, told the Inquiry that he had complete memory loss about his actions on the day in 1972. He had previously admitted that he had shot three men during the demonstration in Londonderry. **2**. Northern Ireland Secretary Paul Murphy announced that a new law would be introduced by ministerial order to enable people to be more effectively prosecuted for committing 'hate crime', and would include a clause aimed specifically at dealing with anti-gay bigotry. 'Soldier F' admitted at the Saville Inquiry that he had shot dead Bernard McGuigan as he attempted to go to the aid of a dying man during the civil rights march on 30 January 1972. **7**. Martin McGuinness issued a statement to the Saville Inquiry denying that he had planned an IRA nail bomb attack hours before 13 people were shot dead on Bloody Sunday. **12**. Residents in Roslea, Co Fermanagh, were evacuated while army bomb experts carried out a controlled explosion on a crude car bomb containing 59kg of explosives, which had been left outside a police station. **17**. Five former members of the Provisional IRA submitted statements to the Saville inquiry in which they said that Martin McGuinness had not distributed nail bombs during the Londonderry peace march. **21** The Bloody Sunday inquiry moved from London to Londonderry after the total bill for its time in London came to £120 million. **24**. The IRA issued an apology to the families of the 'disappeared' men and women who were abducted and killed by the IRA in the 1970s and 80s, and said that they had begun an inquiry to locate the remains of those still missing.

NOVEMBER 2003

4. Seven suspected members of the Real IRA were arrested in a joint operation by Irish and French police in Dublin and Brittany after automatic weapons and ammunition were found in a forest near Dieppe. **5**. Martin McGuinness was threatened with legal action for refusing to co-operate with the Saville inquiry after he refused to reveal the names of IRA colleagues. **12**. A former member of the IRA, known as OIRA1, told the Saville Inquiry that he had shot at a soldier on Bloody Sunday and claimed that the soldier had previously wounded two civilians. **28**. The Revd Ian Paisley's Democratic Unionist Party won 30 seats in the elections to the National Assembly, the Ulster Unionist Party won 27 seats and Sinn Fein won 24 seats. The Democratic Unionist Party had previously promised to abolish the Good Friday agreement if it won the election.

DECEMBER 2003

1. The Revd Ian Paisley met the Northern Ireland Secretary Paul Murphy and told him that his party would not deal with republicans. **12**. Mitchell B. Reiss, a US government official, was selected as the special envoy to Northern Ireland in order to focus on issues of IRA decommissioning. **16**. Prime Minister Tony Blair held talks with the leader of the Democratic Unionist Party, Revd Ian Paisley, to attempt to break the political deadlock in Northern Ireland; Revd Paisley said there was 'no way' his party would share power with Sinn Fein. **17**. Charges against Fiona Farrelly, who had been accused of being part of an IRA spy ring that led to the collapse of the power-sharing Executive at Stormont, were dropped without explanation. **18**. Jeffrey Donaldson resigned from David Trimble's Ulster Unionist Party, saying that the party had 'abandoned its principles'.

JANUARY 2004

4. A 16-year-old boy was shot in both legs by three men who broke into a house in east Belfast and another 17-year-old youth was shot in both ankles by a man who broke into his home in west Belfast. **9**. Police in Northern Ireland published figures which showed that racist crimes in the predominantly loyalist areas of Belfast had soared from 25 in 1998 to 223 a year. **19**. The Police Ombudsman Nuala O'Loan announced that an investigation into the murder of Roman Catholic Sean Brown in 1997 had found that there had been 'significant failures' by the Royal Ulster Constabulary at the time. **25**. Around 100 former members of the Parachute Regiment were issued with handguns in Northern Ireland after police obtained information about the Provisional IRA gathering intelligence from the Bloody Sunday inquiry and other sources in order to kill those that gave evidence at the inquiry. **26**. Education Minister Jane Kennedy announced that all 71 grammar schools in Northern Ireland would be abolished and that the last 11-plus examinations would be held in 2008. **27**. It was announced that the Bloody Sunday Inquiry only had until 13 February 2004 to hear the evidence of around 900 witnesses, and that lawyers had a deadline of 12 March to hand in their written submissions. **29**. The Irish Prime Minister Bertie Ahern met Revd Ian Paisley, the leader of the Democratic Unionist Party, for talks at the Irish Embassy in London, a week before the opening of a review designed to revive the Good Friday agreement.

FEBRUARY 2004
4. Jaybe Ofrasio was arrested in Belfast on charges of making money and property available to terrorists in the Far East; he is believed to have links to the Bali nightclub bombing in October 2002. **17**. The funeral of 18-year-old Barney Cairns took place in the Ardoyne area of Belfast after he committed suicide as a result of being shot in the legs in 2002 for 'squaring up' to the Irish National Liberation Army; his friend Anthony O'Neill had committed suicide a week earlier after also being a victim of a 'punishment attack'. **22**. Alasdair McDonnell, a GP from south Belfast, was elected the new deputy leader of the nationalist SDLP party, replacing Brid Rodgers. **27**. The Police Service of Northern Ireland announced that punishment attacks had risen to a record high with 51 beatings and shootings carried out in 2004 by republican and loyalist groups who claim to be helping their communities to combat antisocial behaviour.

MARCH 2004
2. Seamus Daly, one of the leading suspects in the 1998 Omagh bombing, was jailed for three-and-a-half years at the Special Criminal Court in Dublin for being a member of the Real IRA. The Ulster Unionist leader, David Trimble, walked out on talks in Belfast aimed at restoring devolved government to Northern Ireland, in protest at the British government's failure to exclude Sinn Fein from the talks following the alleged abduction of dissident republican Bobby Tohill. **11**. The British government secured the right to prevent new investigations into alleged 'shoot to kill' deaths by security forces in Northern Ireland, after five Law Lords ruled that investigations into killings that occurred before the Human Rights Act 2002 came into force did not fall under the Act. **22**. A 46-year-old man was arrested in England and taken to Belfast in connection with the murder of 10-year-old Brian McDermott whose torso was found in the River Lagan in 1973. **27**. Ulster Unionist leader David Trimble urged his opponents to unite behind him after he secured a majority 448 votes during a leadership contest at a party meeting in Belfast.

APRIL 2004
8. Arthur Templeton, a member of the Democratic Unionists, was suspended by the Party after being found guilty at Belfast Magistrates' Court of harassing a gay colleague. **13**. A man was being questioned by police in connection with the murder of 16-year-old Megan McAlorum, whose body was found in woodland close to a quarry in west Belfast. **17**. Five prison officers, including one woman, were suspended after it was alleged that they had 'improper relations' with inmates at Maghaberry Prison in Co Antrim. **20**. The Independent Monitoring Commission in Northern Ireland issued a report condemning the Sinn Fein leaders, Gerry Adams and Martin McGuinness, for failing to use their influence to end violence by the IRA, which the commission claimed was still linked to the political party.

MAY 2004
12. Chief Constable Hugh Orde told the Northern Ireland Policing Board that loyalist and republican paramilitaries had carried out 1,700 punishment attacks in Northern Ireland since 1998. **26**. At Belfast Crown Court, Mr Justice Girvan ruled that the Real IRA could not be described as a proscribed group because the British Government had failed to list the organisation in the Terrorism Act 2000.

JUNE 2004
3. Kevin McAlorum, a former member of the Irish National Liberation Army, was shot dead outside Oakwood integrated primary school in Derriaghy, Belfast. **17**. Lt.-Gen. Sir Philip Trousdell, the General Officer Commanding Northern Ireland, announced that 1,200 members of the Devon and Dorset Regiment and the Queen's Dragoon Guards would leave Northern Ireland and revert to mainland command. **25**. Tony Blair announced that the IRA had until September 2004 to end its paramilitary activities and decommission its weapons, otherwise plans to reinstate the Northern Ireland Assembly could be abandoned. **29**. Donald Mullan, Brendan O'Connor, Sean Dillon and Kevin Murphy were cleared of plotting to murder police and troops in Northern Ireland at Belfast Crown Court after they were found with a rocket launcher outside Dungannon in 2002. **30**. The High Court in Belfast overturned the ruling by Justice Paul Girvan that the Real IRA is not an illegal terrorist organisation.

JULY 2004
12. Paratroopers came under attack after loyalists on the Orange Parade march were forbidden from returning along a route through the contentious Ardoyne area; it was reported that both republicans and loyalists were involved in the rioting. **22**. Mohammad Hossain, his wife and their five-year-old daughter escaped serious injury when their house in the Lisburn Road area, was petrol bombed. **27**. Workers at Belfast City Council went on strike in support of an ongoing civil service dispute over pay. **31**. Eight suspicious packages were discovered by Royal Mail staff at Mallusk. The packages were addressed to members of the Police Ombudsman and police board.

AUGUST 2004
1. The police ombudsman Nuala O'Loan announced that a report into a police raid on the Stormont offices of Sinn Fein in October 2002 found that it was not politically motivated, but a complaint from Sinn Fein that the scale of the search was excessive and disproportionate was upheld. **15**. Rita Restorick made a complaint to the Defence Secretary Geoff Hoon after the Northern Ireland police ombudsman Nuala O'Loan accused the Ministry of Defence of 'frustrating' her inquiry into the death of Mrs Restorick's son Stephen, who was shot dead in Ulster in 1997 whilst serving as a lance-bombardier in the Royal Horse Artillery. **29**. A memorial to 18 soldiers killed by the IRA 25 years ago at Narrow Water, Co Down, was vandalised two days after being unveiled.

ARTS AND THE MEDIA

SEPTEMBER 2003
2. ITN reported that Neil Armstrong's first steps on the moon was the most popular and frequently requested piece of news footage. **4**. The winners of the James Tait Black Memorial Prize were announced as Jonathan Franzen for his novel *The Corrections* in the fiction category, and *The Lunar Men: The Friends Who Made the Future* by Jenny Uglow, in the biography category. Anne Jones from Leicestershire won the title of the world's fastest reader after she read a 300-page novel in 47 minutes. **5**. Simon Beaufoy's budget film *This Is Not A Love Song* became the first to be officially premiered on the internet after it was released online. **7**. The director Andrey Zvyagintsev won the Venice Film Festival's

Golden Lion award for his film *The Return*. **8**. Religious groups objected to Damien Hirst's new exhibition *Romance in the Age of Uncertainty*, which contains reinterpretations of biblical themes using cows' heads and bloodied medical instruments. **9**. The 19-year-old rap artist Dizzee Rascal won the £20,000 Mercury Music Prize for his debut record *Boy In Da Corner*. **10**. The travel writer Bill Bryson was appointed a commissioner of English Heritage. It was reported that the opera *Carmen* would be performed outside the bullring and cigarette factory in Seville where the story of the opera unfolds. **16**. The Man Booker Prize shortlist was announced with the highest number of women novelists and the most debut novels in its history, only one well-known author, Margaret Atwood, was shortlisted. **17**. A pair of paintings by Robert Dodd, believed to be some of the earliest depictions of Lord Nelson's victory at Trafalgar, sold for a record sum of £270,650 at Bonhams. **18**. Dame Shirley Bassey was at Christie's in London for the sale of 50 of her gowns, which she had worn throughout her career; the sale raised £250,000 for charity and the highest price paid for one dress was £35,000. **21**. Hayley Westenra's classical album *Pure* set the record for being the fastest-selling debut album in the history of the British classical charts when it went straight to number one. **22**. Alexander McCall Smith, 55, won the £20,000 Saga Award for Wit, which rewards the most amusing book by an author over 50, for his detective thriller *The Full Cupboard of Life*. **24**. A signed copy of the Beatles *Revolver* album sold for £21,600 at Sotheby's in London. Six thousand stuffed animals were sold at Bonhams for £529,000; they had previously made up the Walter Potter Museum of Curiosities. **25**. It was reported that Damien Hirst had made £11 million within 15 days of the opening of his *Romance in the Age of Uncertainty* exhibition through sales of works on-show. Alexander McQueen was named the British Style Awards Designer of the Year. *The English Roses*, the debut children's novel by the singer Madonna, became the fastest-selling hardback children's picture book in British history after it sold more than 8,500 copies in its first week of release. **29**. The Royal Navy paid the Saatchi and Saatchi advertising agency £100,000 to 'refresh' their logo. **30**. A man found a small Roman vessel believed to date from the 2nd century AD in the Staffordshire Moorlands – it was valued at £100,000.

OCTOBER 2003

1. During a pop memorabilia sale at Christie's in London, a sculpture by John Lennon sold for £28,200, and a note from Lennon to his publicist Tony Bramwell telling him to keep quiet about the recording of *The Ballad of John and Yoko* until its release, sold for £19,975. A survey revealed that 71 per cent of Britons were not able to name Monet as the creator of the painting *Water Lilies*, 49 per cent could not name the painter of the *Mona Lisa*, and 85 per cent of respondents were unable to identify Edvard Munch as the artist who painted *The Scream*. **2**. The South African writer J. M. Coetzee was named the winner of the 2003 Nobel Prize for Literature, worth £900,000. The rock band *Radiohead* was voted the Best Act in the World by readers of *Q* music magazine. **7**. Students from Camberwell College of Art in London earned a place in *The Guinness Book of Records* after they assembled a 13ft statue of King Kong using 480,000 pieces of popcorn, in honour of the film's 70th anniversary. **8**. Ciaran Carson won the £10,000 Forward Poetry Prize for his work *Breaking News*. **9**. The actor Roger Moore was knighted by the Queen for his charity work. **10**. Ms Lesley Douglas was named as the new controller of BBC Radio 2, and was due to take over the £220,000 position in January 2004. One of the first coins minted in colonial America in the 17th century was found in the home of a deceased collector and was expected to fetch up to £25,000 at auction. **12**. The Zehetmair Quartet won the Record of the Year prize at the *Gramophone* Awards for its recording of String Quartets Number 1 and Number 3 by Schumann. **13**. The rap singer Ms Dynamite won the Capital Big Voice award at the Women of the Year Awards for speaking out against gun crime in urban areas. **14**. The £50,000 Man Booker Prize was awarded to DBC Pierre for his debut novel *Vernon God Little*. Philip Larkin's *The Whitsun Weddings* was voted Britain's favourite poem by over 800 visitors to poetry festivals; the top ten also included poems by Carol Ann Duffy, Seamus Heaney and Sylvia Plath. **15**. The Prince of Wales attended the Fashion Rocks event at the Albert Hall, which involved performances by key figures from the fashion and music industries in order to raise funds for the Prince's Trust charity. Gerhard Schulz was named Wildlife Photographer of the Year for his picture of a young boy watching a gorilla watching a photographer at Miami Metrozoo in Florida. **16**. The Channel 4 comedy sitcom *Peter Kay's Phoenix Nights* became the fastest-selling television DVD in Britain when it sold 160,000 copies in one week. **20**. Dame Diana Rigg won £38,000 for libel and breach of privacy after the *Daily Mail* and *Evening Standard* newspapers published articles claiming she had retired and was an 'embittered woman'. The *Saved!* exhibition containing 400 works of art by artists such as Picasso and Michelangelo, which were kept in Britain through the efforts of the National Art Collections Fund, opened at the Hayward Gallery in London. **22**. The London Film Festival opened with the British premiere of *In the Cut*, an erotic thriller starring Meg Ryan. Five police officers resigned after Mark Daly, an undercover reporter for the BBC, secretly filmed the officers making racist remarks and praising the Ku Klux Klan and Hitler as well as admitting to treating ethnic minorities differently whilst performing police duties. **27**. Elvis Presley was named as the highest earning dead celebrity in the Forbes rich list after the singer's estate made £24 million in the last year. **28**. Tony Blair presented Sir Trevor McDonald with a Special Recognition Award at the National Television Awards in honour of his 30 years in broadcasting. **29**. One of the largest dolls houses in Britain, Victorian Dingley Hall, was sold for £124,750 at Christie's to a toy museum near Hamburg.

NOVEMBER 2003

1. The creator of the Harry Potter novels, J. K. Rowling, became the highest-paid author in history after it was revealed that she earned £125 million in the past year, equivalent to receiving £388 for every word of her latest book *Harry Potter and the Order of the Phoenix*. **3**. The Independent Television Commission rejected complaints about a homosexual kiss that appeared in the soap *Coronation Street* and ruled that it had been suitable for family viewing. **4**. Stephen Frears's film *Dirty Pretty Things*, about asylum-seekers in London, won the Best British Film, Best Director and Best Actor awards at the British Independent Film Awards. **5**. A Victoria Cross, which had been awarded to Commander Daniel Beak for several acts of heroism on the Western Front during the First World War, sold at auction in London for a world record £178,250. Modigliani's *Reclining Nude (On Her Left Side)* was sold by the billionaire Steve Wynn for a record £16 million in New York. **9**. The Walt Disney Company paid £2.1 million for the rights to the unpublished novel *A Stolen Smile* by Jimmy Boyle, a former gangster from Glasgow who was jailed in 1967 for the murder of a rival. **12**. A plaque carrying William Wordsworth's poem *Composed Upon Westminster Bridge* was unveiled on London's Westminster Bridge, near the Houses of Parliament. **13**. Two cargo handlers at New York's John F. Kennedy airport were arrested for stealing *Painter's Garden* by Lucian Freud, worth £890,000. **14**. A Damien Hirst work entitled *Something Solid Beneath the Surface of All Creatures Great and Small*, consisting of animal skeletons, was sold to an anonymous bidder for a record price of £700,000 at a contemporary art auction in New York. **17**. *The Engagement between the Spanish Armada and the English Fleet off Calais*, the earliest known painting of Sir Francis Drake's fleet defeating the Spanish Armada, was discovered at Bonhams auction house when the owner of the painting took it to be valued; the owner's father paid £20 for the painting by an anonymous Dutch artist and it was valued at between £30,000 and £50,000. **19**. Lyrics to the Beatles song *Nowhere Man* in John Lennon's handwriting sold for £268,000 at a Christie's auction in New York. **21**. George Harrison's first guitar, given to him by his parents, sold at the annual Cooper Owen's Beatles sale for £276,000. **24**. *Jerry Springer – The Opera* won the Best Musical of the Year award at the *Evening Standard* Theatre awards. **26**. The poet Benjamin Zephaniah rejected an invitation to receive an OBE in protest at the Government's policies on the Iraq war and because of the order's 'legacy of colonialism'. **27**. The British Museum acquired a Babylonian terracotta relief of a naked woman for £1.5 million; it was thought to have hung as a sign outside a brothel 4,000 years ago. **30**. The low-budget New Zealand film *Whale Rider* won the Best Film award at the BAFTA Children's Awards, beating both *Harry Potter* and *Lord of the Rings*.

DECEMBER 2003

1. David Almond's *The Fire Eaters* was voted by 9 to 11-year-olds as their favourite novel and awarded the Nestle Smarties Book Prize Gold Medal. **2**. An unpublished account of the sinking of the *Titanic* by Second Officer Charles Lightoller was sold for £8,400 and a lunch menu from the ship was sold for £28,800 at an auction in London. **5**. Sir Christopher Frayling was appointed the new chairman of the Arts Council. Thirty-five Aboriginal stencils and paintings believed to be 11,000 years old, were discovered in a cave near Sydney, Australia. The handwritten manuscript of Beethoven's *Scherzo* from the String Quartet Op.127 in E Flat Major was sold for £1,181,600 at auction at Sotheby's in London. **7**. Transvestite artist Grayson Perry, whose work depicts images of child abuse scratched into the surfaces of ceramic vases, won the £20,000 Turner Prize. **9**. *Eats, Shoots and Leaves (The Zero Tolerance to Punctuation)* by Lynne Truss, became the fastest-selling book in Britain after it sold 67,287 copies in one week. **10**. At the British Comedy Awards Steve Coogan won the Best Comedy Actor award, David Walliams the Best Newcomer award, and Lenny Henry was given a Lifetime Achievement award. The father of the author J. K. Rowling sold four first editions of the Harry Potter books for £50,600, which had been inscribed by her and given to him as a Father's Day present. **11**. A Renaissance bronze roundel was sold for £7 million at auction in London after it was found in a cupboard under a staircase in Devon and thought to be worth only a few thousand pounds. **13**. *The Lord of the Rings* by J. R. R. Tolkien was voted Britain's favourite book after the BBC carried out a poll for its television programme *The Big Read*. **15**. Prime Minister Tony Blair announced that the British Museum would receive a grant of £500,000 in order to fund a five-year project aimed at building new links with African institutions. **18**. The pop star Michael Jackson was formally charged by prosecutors in California with performing lewd acts with a young boy. **19**. *The Return of the King*, the final film in the *Lord of the Rings* trilogy, recorded the biggest opening in British box office history after it made £3,029,176 in the first three days. **25**. *Gone With The Wind* was voted the greatest epic film by a poll of 6,500 customers of the *Blockbuster* video chain. **27**. *Grease* was voted the best musical in a poll for the Channel 4 programme, *100 Greatest Musicals*.

JANUARY 2004

5. It was reported by the Mobile Data Association that a record 111 million text messages were sent in Britain on New Year's Day. **8**. Mark Haddon won the Whitbread Novel Award 2004 for his book *The Curious Incident of the Dog in the Night-Time*, a popular children's book about an autistic boy. **9**. Michael Dixon was appointed the new director of the Natural History Museum and was due to take up the post in October 2004. **12**. The research company BLM reported that children watched an average of two-and-a-half hours of television every day while adults watched just over four hours per day. **14**. The British Museum paid £150,000 for a Roman drinking cup made from the mineral fluorspar; the Emperor Nero reportedly paid the equivalent of the wages of 830 soldiers for a year for one such fluorspar cup. The American company Kodak announced that it would halt production of traditional cameras in Europe and America and would only continue to produce digital cameras. **15**. The National Heritage Memorial Fund gave the Bodleian Library in Oxford £3 million to purchase a collection of Mary Shelley's manuscripts which include the original draft of *Frankenstein*. **16**. The BBC announced that the television presenter Robert Kilroy-Silk had left his morning chat-show 'Kilroy' after he had been suspended over an article he had written for the *Sunday Express* newspaper, expressing derogatory views about Arabs. **18**. Barry Joule, a friend of the late artist Francis Bacon, made a donation of more than 1,200 sketches by Bacon to the Tate Gallery, they were believed to be worth around £20 million. **19**. Don Paterson was awarded the T. S. Eliot Prize, worth £10,000, for his new collection of poetry *Landing Light*. **26**. Ricky Gervais, the British comedian who starred as David Brent in the comedy series *The Office*, was named Best Comedy Actor, and the programme Best TV Comedy, at the American Golden Globe awards. **27**. Mark Haddon's *The Curious Incident of the Dog in the Night-Time* was awarded the overall Whitbread prize; he received £25,000. **28**. The Culture Secretary Tessa Jowell announced that a greater role for 'decoding the media' would be introduced into the national curriculum so that children would be more 'active and informed' in decoding merchandising tie-ins in films.

FEBRUARY 2004

2. The Saudi Arabian Jameels family gave the Victoria and Albert Museum a donation of £5 million to house the museum's collection of Islamic art. **3**. One of Degas's 27 bronze sculptures belonging to his *Little Dancers* collection, was sold at Sotheby's for £5.04 million; it was the only sculpture exhibited by the artist during his lifetime. **6**. Frances Partridge, the last remaining member of the Bloomsbury set, died aged 103; she was best known for keeping journals in which she recounted conversations between people such as Virginia Woolf and E. M. Forster. **9**. A poll commissioned by the Mayor of London, Ken Livingstone, found that the nurse Mary Seacole was considered the greatest black Briton. The British rock band Coldplay won the Record of the Year prize at the Grammy Awards for their single *Clocks*. **13**. The National Gallery paid £35 million to the Duke of Northumberland, the owner of the Raphael masterpiece *Madonna of the Pinks*, in order to keep the painting in Britain. **15**. The final film in the *Lord of the Rings* trilogy, *The Return of the King*, was given the Best Film award at the BAFTA ceremony, while Bill Murray and Scarlett Johansson won Best Actor and Best Actress prizes for their respective roles in *Lost in Translation*. **16**. The Scottish Executive announced the appointment of Edwin Morgan as 'The Scots Makar', the Scottish equivalent of the English Poet Laureate. **17**. The British band *The Darkness* won three awards, Best British Album, Best British Group and Best British Rock Act, at the Brit Awards. **22**. At the Olivier Awards, Matthew Kelly was awarded the Best Actor prize for his role as Lenny in *Of Mice and Men* and *Jerry Springer – The Opera* was awarded three prizes including Best New Musical. **24**. A three-volume set of the first edition of *The Lord of the Rings* signed by J. R. R. Tolkien sold for more than £31,000 at Bonhams in London. **27**. T. E. Lawrence's working copy of *The Seven Pillars of Wisdom* was sold for a world record £51,400 at Christie's in New York.

MARCH 2004

1. Scottish Culture Minister Frank McAveety announced that the Scottish Executive would contribute £6.5 million to the National Library of Scotland to aid its bid to buy the John Murray Archive which contains 150,000 pieces of writing by authors including Jane Austen, Lord Byron and Charles Dickens. *The Lord of the Rings* films won 11 awards at the Oscars ceremony, including the Best Picture award; Sean Penn was awarded the Best Actor prize and Charlize Theron won Best Actress. **3**. The Film Distributors' Association released figures showing that only four out of the top 100 film successes of 2003 were British films. Letters from Robert Browning to Julia Wedgwood were sold for £83,650 at Christie's in London. **7**. The John Lennon album *Double Fantasy*, signed by him for his killer Mark Chapman, went on sale on the internet for £290,000. **8**. The Spitz Gallery in east London removed photographs of a naked five-year-old girl which formed part of an exhibit by the artist Betsy Schneider following an investigation by the Obscene Publications Unit and fears over paedophilia. **9**. The Archbishop of Canterbury, Dr Rowan Williams, recommended that school children study Philip Pullman's *His Dark Materials* trilogy to counter the 'inadequacies' of religious education. **11**. Five million people tuned in to hear the first gay kiss on long-running radio show *The Archers*. **12**. The Rijksmuseum in Amsterdam made its most expensive purchase ever when it paid £8.1 million for *The Burghermaster of Delft and his Daughter* by 17th century master Jan Steen. **14**. Disney paid £557,000 to supermarket manager Clive Woodall for the rights to his unpublished novel *One for Sorrow*, and planned to produce an animated film version of the story. **15**. Charles Saatchi purchased a portrait of schoolgirl Rachel Whitear, who died of a suspected heroin overdose and whose picture was used as part of an anti-drugs campaign, planning to display it as part of the *New Blood* show at the Saatchi Gallery. A panel acting for the Greater London Authority decided that a marble sculpture of an armless, naked pregnant woman by Marc Quinn and a 21-storey perspex tower entitled *Hotel for the Birds* by Thomas Schutte, would occupy the fourth plinth in Trafalgar Square. **16**. A survey of more than 400 people by the Mothers' Union found that the majority named Marge Simpson from *The Simpsons* cartoon as the best mother in public life. **19**. The BBC announced that the actor Christopher Eccleston would play the ninth Doctor Who in a new series of the television show. **22**. Emap, the publishers of *Just 17* magazine for teenage girls, announced that the magazine would be closed down and that the last edition would be published on 8 April. **25**. The British Museum and the Victoria and Albert Museum jointly paid £850,000 to acquire a 7th century Indian standing figure of the Buddha Sakyamuni from a European private collection. The Danish artist Marco Evaristti unveiled a red iceberg as his latest work of art off the coast of western Greenland. Sir Michael Atiyah and Professor Isadore Singer won the £475,000 Abel Prize for mathematics for developing the 'Atiyah-Singer index theorem'. **27**. Kate Long's debut novel *The Bad Mother's Handbook*, sold 18,000 copies in its first three weeks, outselling novels by established authors including John Grisham and Joanna Trollope. The British comedy *Only Fools and Horses*, was voted the best British sitcom in a poll commissioned by the BBC. **29**. Mel Gibson's *The Passion of the Christ*, became the fastest grossing subtitled film in Britain after making £2 million in its opening weekend. **30**. The Victoria and Albert Museum launched its biggest exhibition of the work of a British designer with its retrospective of the work of Vivienne Westwood. **31**. A 16th century coin featuring the face of Henry VIII was sold for a world record £34,500 at the coin auction specialist Spink in London. Linguistics experts at a conference at the University of Newcastle, announced that dialects in Britain are developing at record speed, mainly due to new immigrants to the country mixing the language of their host country with their native tongue.

APRIL 2004

1. Michael Grade was appointed Chairman of the BBC. **2**. It was announced that all 112,000 tickets for the Glastonbury music festival in June had sold out in 17 hours. **6**. The Royal Opera House announced that 100 of its most expensive seats would be available for £10 instead of £175 if bought 90 minutes before a performance on Monday; this had been made possible through a donation of £1 million from the foreign exchange specialist, Travelex. **7**. Canterbury City Council bought a £1 million portrait of Sir Basil Dixwell by Flemish painter Van Dyck to display at Canterbury's Royal Museum, after receiving more than £800,000 in lottery funding. The Royal Shakespeare Company announced that its new base would be the Whitehall Theatre following the company's controversial decision to leave the Barbican Centre. **11**. A survey for tesco.com found that men voted *Star Wars* their favourite film of all time and women preferred the 1987 film *Dirty Dancing*. **12**. Rachmaninov's Piano Concerto No 2 was voted Britain's favourite piece of classical music for the fourth consecutive year by listeners of Classic FM. **15**. A collection of 41 perforated snail shells, believed to have been strung together about 75,000 years ago, were discovered at Blombos Cave in South Africa, making them the oldest known example of jewellery. Sir Tim Berners-Lee, the inventor of the world wide web, won the €1 million Millennium Technology Prize, presented by the Finnish Technology Award Foundation. **16**. Deaf Jam, the first club night for deaf people, was held at Plastic People nightclub in east London. **18**. Julie Walters was named Best Actress for her role in BBC1s *The Wife of Bath* at the BAFTA awards and comedian Ricky Gervais won the Comedy Performance Prize for the third consecutive year for his performance in *The Office Christmas Special*. **19**. *The Singing Butler*, a painting by Jack Vettriano, fetched a record price for the Scottish painter of £750,000 at Sotheby's. **22**. A diary kept by Captain Scott's deputy, Captain Albert Armitage, was sold at Bloomsbury Auctions for £36,000 to a private collector. Andrew O'Hagan won the £3,000 James Tait Black Memorial Prize for Fiction for his second novel *Personality*. **25**. The founder of DreamWorks, David Geffen, bought the painting *Gray Numbers* by Jasper Johns for $40 million (£22.5 million), making it the most expensive picture by a living artist. **27**. Saskia Olde Wolbers won the £24,000 Beck's Futures Prize for *Interloper*, a video installation featuring a comatose hospital patient. **28**. The National Heritage Memorial Fund granted £1 million towards the erection of a 22ft high bronze sculpture by John Mills in remembrance of the seven million British women who contributed to the Second World War effort.

MAY 2004

5. Pablo Picasso's *Garcon à la pipe* fetched $93 million (£56 million) at Sotheby's in New York, making it the most expensive picture ever sold at auction. A signed copy of the 1962 contract between the Beatles and their manager Brian Epstein was sold for £122,850 at Christie's in London. The release of the film *Fahrenheit 9/11* by American documentary-maker Michael Moore, was blocked by Walt Disney, its American distributor because the company felt uncomfortable about the film linking President Bush with prominent Saudi families including that of Osama bin Laden. **10**. The European Audiovisual Observatory reported that screenings of European films beyond national boundaries attracted only 6.3 per cent of their total audience, down from 10 per cent the previous year. Jonny Hurst, a Birmingham City football club supporter, was awarded a bursary of £10,000 after he was picked to become the Premier League's first official Chant Laureate. **12**. Radio 4 was named Station of the Year at the Sony Radio Academy Awards in London. **14**. The editor of the *Daily Mirror* newspaper, Piers Morgan, was dismissed from his job after it was found that pictures printed in the newspaper alleged to have been of British soldiers abusing Iraqi prisoners, were fake. **16**. *The Poseidon Adventure* was voted the best disaster movie by film fans in a poll carried out by UCI Cinemas. **20**. *Total Film* magazine voted Janet Leigh's shower scene in Hitchcock's *Psycho* as the 'best movie death'; Slim Pickens' descent to atomic armageddon in *Dr Strangelove* came second. **23**. At the Cannes Film Festival, the Palme d'Or prize was awarded to *Fahrenheit 9/11*. **25**. A fire at a warehouse in Leyton, east London, destroyed numerous artworks worth millions of pounds including those belonging to Charles Saatchi: Tracey Emin's tent *Everyone I Have Ever Slept With* and *Hell* by Jake and Dinos Chapman. **26**. Daniel Hope was named Young British Classical Performer of the Year at the Classical Brit Awards in London. **28**. A dozen paintings by the Scottish artist Jack Vettriano sold at auction in Edinburgh for almost £1 million.

JUNE 2004

2. A new literary prize worth £60,000 was announced by John Carey, professor of English at Oxford University; the Man Booker International Prize is designed to 'celebrate English language fiction as a major cultural force in the modern world'. A 1940 photograph by Herbert Mason, of St Paul's Cathedral during the Blitz, was voted the most inspirational photograph of all time. **3**. Leontia Flynn, a post-graduate student at Queen's University, was picked by a panel chaired by Andrew Motion, the Poet Laureate, as one of 'the 20 most exciting poets of their generation' for her collection *These Days*. **8**. Andrea Levy won the £30,000 Orange Prize for Fiction for her novel *Small Island*. **10**. A 23-year-old man was arrested in connection with the east London warehouse fire which destroyed £20 million worth of art works. **14**. Bill Bryson won the £10,000 Aventis Prize for science books with his work *A Short History of Nearly Everything*. **15**. Anna Funder won the £30,000 Samuel Johnson Prize for non-fiction for her debut *Stasiland: Stories from Behind the Berlin Wall*. **17**. Richard Wallace, the former deputy editor of the *Sunday Mirror* was appointed editor of the *Daily Mirror* newspaper. *Two Figures Lying on a Bed with Attendants*, a painting worth around £5 million, by Francis Bacon, was put on display at Tate Britain after it had been locked away in the vaults of Teheran's Museum of Contemporary Art for 30 years; it was loaned to Tate Britain by the Iranian Museum. **21**. Stephen Shankland won the National Portrait Gallery's £25,000 BP Portrait Award for his painting of his wife and son *The Miracle*. **24**. Charles Saatchi paid £28,000 for *Beneath the Stride of Giants*, a 40ft boat by artist Brian Griffiths, made from bric-a-brac and waste items. **25**. Eric Clapton raised more than £4 million for a drugs and alcohol rehabilitation centre in the Caribbean after he auctioned 79 guitars at Christie's in New York – one of which became the most expensive guitar auctioned when it fetched £527,198. **29**. A 1795 letter written by Admiral Nelson, in which he offered to resign over accusations of bad leadership, fetched £7,170 at Bonhams.

JULY 2004

1. The painting *Portrait of Mrs Baldwin* by Joshua Reynolds became the most expensive work of art bought by the charitable foundation Littlewoods Pools when it was sold for £3,365,600 at Sotheby's in London. **6**. David Miliband, the School Standards Minister, announced the launch of the Government's 'Music Manifesto' which aimed to provide every child with the chance to learn a musical instrument. **7**. The painting *A Young Woman Seated at the Virginals* was sold for £16.2 million at a Sotheby's auction after only recently having been recognised as a work by the Dutch painter Johannes Vermeer. **8**. *Head of a Child*, a drawing by Raphael, fetched £179,200 at Sotheby's in London when it was bought by the millionaire Leon Black. An erotic letter from the writer James Joyce to his girlfriend Nora Barnacle was bought for £240,800 at Sotheby's in London. **9**. The American author Jennifer Donnelly won the Carnegie Medal for Children's Literature for her debut novel *A Gathering Light*. **12.** *Spider-Man 2* premiered in London after it was announced that it had already made £22 million in its first day in the USA, making it the highest-grossing opening in Hollywood history. **14.** A BBC documentary *The Secret Agent* claimed to expose racist behaviour within the British National Party (BNP) and had secretly recorded Nick Griffin, BNP chairman, telling supporters that their 'women' were under threat from Muslims and Islam. **25.** John Constable's great-great-great-granddaughter, Sasha Constable, presented her 'Peace of Art' project in Cambodia which involved sculptures made from weapons used during the Khmer Rouge genocide of the 1970s. **30.** It was announced that the Grade I listed West Pier in Brighton would be demolished after English Heritage reported that the structure was beyond repair.

AUGUST 2004

3. Cadbury's became the first company to give homeless *Big Issue* sellers a permanent pitch at its offices in Birmingham. English Heritage announced that it was searching for the first state jester since the post was abolished 350 years ago after the execution of Charles I. **5.** It was reported that Pink Floyd's 1979 album *The Wall* was being developed into a Broadway musical. **8.** *Portrait of a Londoner*, a lost essay by Virginia Woolf, was discovered by publisher Emma Cahill in a Bloomsbury antiquarian bookshop; the essay had never before been published and Ms Cahill planned to publish it alongside Woolf's five other essays on London, previously collected in the book *London Scene*. **12.** It was reported that Channel 4 had overtaken BBC2 in ratings for the first time in 10 years – this was largely due to BBC2's loss of the television show *The Simpsons*, which was bought by Channel 4 for £600,000 per episode. **16.** The singer Billy Bragg announced that he was rewriting the words to the hymn *I Vow To Thee My Country* after it was also criticised by the Right Revd Stephen Lowe, the suffragan Bishop of Hulme for being heretical with racist undertones. **21.** The Royal Shakespeare Company voted *Hamlet* the best play by William Shakespeare – *King Lear* came second and *Antony and Cleopatra* third. **22.** Armed robbers stole Edvard Munch's *The Scream* and *Madonna* paintings from the Munch Museum in Oslo. **24.** The former editor of the *Daily Mirror* Piers Morgan received £1.7 million in compensation from the newspaper after he was sacked for refusing to apologise for publishing pictures which purported to show British soldiers abusing Iraqi prisoners. **26.** A cleaner at Tate Britain mistook a bag of rubbish that was designed to be part of the 'recreation of the first public demonstration of auto-destructive art' for a bag of rubbish and threw it away.

CRIMES AND LEGAL AFFAIRS

OCTOBER 2003

1. A judge at the High Court in London ruled that the frozen embryos of Natallie Evans and Lorraine Hadley should be destroyed on the grounds that their former partners, who had fertilised the embryos but did not want the women to use them in future IVF treatment, had rights that should be respected. **5.** Eight police officers were suspended after an inquest into the death of Roger Sylvester in January 1999 found that he had been unlawfully killed. Mr Sylvester had been restrained by six police officers in a hospital and as a result slipped into a coma and died seven days later. **7.** Legal history was made when Margaret McTear began legal action against Imperial Tobacco for failing to warn her late husband, who died of lung cancer, of the dangers of smoking. She became the first person in Britain to bring a damages case against a cigarette manufacturer. The boy known as Boy C when he gave evidence at the Damilola Taylor murder trial was sentenced to 18 months in a young offenders institute for burglary. **8.** Audrey Hingston, 81, was charged with the murder of her husband Eric, who was found with a neck wound at their home on 29 August 2003. **9.** William Horncy and Peter Rees appeared at the Central Criminal Court charged with murdering the millionaire businessman Amarjit Chohan; both men denied the charges and were remanded in custody. A man and a woman were arrested by police in connection with the murder of seven-year-old Toni-Ann Byfield. **12.** Solicitor-General Harriet Harman made a plea to the Court of Appeal against a five-year jail sentence given to a man who regularly raped his sister-in-law over 18 months. The jail sentence was doubled to 10 years after the court found the original sentence to be 'unduly lenient'. **13.** More than 50 disabled people won the right to receive damages of more than £1 million from Buckinghamshire County Council after it was found that they were physically abused throughout the 1980s and 90s while resident at two care homes for people with learning difficulties. The police force in England was given the right to use anti-social behaviour orders to ban prostitutes from residential areas after two High Court judges overturned a ruling by a District judge who had refused to grant such an order against a prostitute operating in Preston. **15.** It was announced that Winston Silcott, the man convicted and later cleared on appeal of the murder of PC Keith Blakelock during riots on the Broadwater Farm Estate in 1985, would be released from prison after serving 17 years for the murder of another man, Anthony Smith, for which he had originally received a 14-year prison term. **16.** Five Law Lords ordered an independent public inquiry into the death of Zahid Mubarek after an independent hearing requested by Mr Mubarek's family was refused by the Home Office. Mr Mubarek was placed in a cell with a known racist at Feltham Young Offenders' Institute and was beaten to death by him on the day he was due to be released. Detectives investigating the murder of the boy code-named 'Adam', whose torso was found in the Thames in 2001, announced that traces of the poisonous calaber bean had been found in the boy's lower intestine; the bean is alleged to have been used in witchcraft rituals. **20.** Rafaqat and Tafarak Hussain were jailed for life for the 'honour killing' of their cousin, Sahjda Bibi, whom they stabbed to death on her wedding day because they disagreed with her marrying a divorcee. **21.** Twelve men were jailed at Liverpool Crown Court for smuggling more than £100 million worth of Class A drugs into Britain after the drugs ring was broken when a £15 million consignment was seized in the Channel Tunnel in May. **23.** Zhang Yong Hui, who headed an £11 million operation which smuggled more than 700 illegal immigrants into Britain, was jailed for seven years after it was found that he was torturing the immigrants and blackmailing their families in China in order to receive more money. **28.** The Court of Appeal quashed the conviction of George Kelly, who was executed in March 1950 after being found guilty for the murder of Leonard Thomas, on the grounds that police officers had withheld crucial evidence, including the fact that another man, Donald Johnson, had confessed to the crime. **30**. Michael Little was convicted of murdering Rachel Moran on 1 January 2003 after her body was found in a cupboard in his home with at least 20 stab wounds; he was sentenced to life imprisonment at Hull Crown Court.

NOVEMBER 2003

3. Mohammed Dica became the first person to be convicted of the crime of inflicting 'biological' grievous bodily harm after he knowingly infected two women with HIV by insisting on having unprotected sexual intercourse with them; he was jailed for eight years at the Inner London Crown Court. It was reported that a six-year-old girl, Makada Weaver, became one of the youngest victims of gun crime when she was shot on 2 November as she opened the door of her house in Liverpool to a gunman who then shot her brother and mother before a ricocheting bullet hit Makada in the arm; it was thought that the attack was connected to the murder of Clay Benjamin three years ago. **13**. Four men were charged with the murders of Charlene Ellis and Letisha Shakespeare, who were shot dead at a New Year party in Aston, Birmingham on 2 January 2003; one of the men charged with murder was Ms Ellis's half-brother Marcus Ellis. **14**. Benjamin Lewis and Scott Bower became the first people in Britain to be jailed for religious harassment after they were found guilty of conducting a three-month campaign of harassment against the Revd Christopher Rowberry and his family. A fifth man, Tafarwa Beckford, was charged with the murders of Charlene Ellis and Letisha Shakespeare. **16**. Lee Holbrook was charged with the murder of 18-year-old Alicia Eborne, whose body was found near Dartmoor. She had gone missing on 7 November from her home in Plymouth. **17**. A gang of five men known as the 'Prada Boys' were jailed at Harrow Crown Court for between seven and nine years after being found guilty of stealing more than £2 million of jewellery and cash from wealthy victims whom they targeted in the West End of London. **19**. Colin Waite, 42, was convicted of the rape and murder of 17-year-old Nicola Dixon, whose body was found on New Year's Day in 1997; Mr Waite was jailed for life at Warwick Crown Court. **20**. The Queen won a landmark ruling against a tabloid paper when the High Court imposed a temporary injunction on the *Daily Mirror* banning it from publishing photographs of private royal apartments taken by one of their reporters who had obtained a job as a footman at Buckingham Palace. **24**. Abdul Baset Ali al-Megrahi was sentenced at the High Court in Glasgow to at least 27 years in prison after he was convicted of killing 259 people in 1988 when a bomb went off on Pan Am flight 103 over Lockerbie, in Scotland. **25**. Anthony Hardy was given three life sentences at the Central Criminal Court after he was convicted of the murders of Sally Rose White, Elizabeth Valad and Brigitte Maclennan, whom he had strangled and dismembered. **27**. Police in London and the south-east of England arrested 11 Colombians suspected of controlling the distribution of £650 million worth of cocaine smuggled into Britain over the last four years. **30**. Cdr Janet Williams was appointed leader of Scotland Yard's Special Branch, becoming the first woman to lead the Branch in its 120-year history.

DECEMBER 2003

1. At the High Court in London, the Revd Joanna Jepson won the right to challenge West Mercia police force's decision not to prosecute doctors who aborted a 24-week-old baby with a cleft palate, an abortion which would normally be illegal unless there was a risk of 'serious handicap'. **3**. Police announced that they had opened a new investigation into the death of PC Keith Blakelock, who was hacked to death during the Broadwater Farm riots in 1985. **7**. Police announced that a woman jogger had been stabbed by a man on 5 December in Clissold Park in north east London; police believe she was attacked by the same man who murdered Margaret Muller while she was jogging in an east London park in February. **8**. Multimillionaire Nicholas van Hoogstraten was freed at the Central Criminal Court after serving 13 months of a 10-year prison sentence for the manslaughter of a business rival who was shot and stabbed on his doorstep. **10**. At the Court of Appeal, Angela Cannings had her conviction for murdering her three children quashed and was set free after spending 20 months in prison; she was the third woman in 11 months to have her conviction overturned after it was found that a key witness, the paediatrician Professor Sir Roy Meadow, had given 'wrong' evidence in many similar cases. Police found guns, machetes and drugs and 12 people were arrested in north London after one of the biggest co-ordinated armed raids was carried out to clamp down on organised crime gangs in the Turkish and Kurdish communities. **15**. Police arrested a 24-year-old man and a 15-year-old boy in connection with the murder of Margaret Muller and the stabbing of a female jogger on 5 December. **17**. Ian Huntley was convicted of the murders of Holly Wells and Jessica Chapman and was sentenced to two life sentences at the Central Criminal Court in London, while Maxine Carr was cleared of two charges of aiding an offender but convicted of conspiring to pervert the course of justice. **19**. Eight-year-old Matthew King was awarded £5.75 million in damages after an obstetric emergency at his birth was not dealt with properly; it was the highest award given for a child suffering from cerebral palsy. **31**. In Gateshead, police arrested an American man, David Francis Bieber, also known as Nathan Wayne Coleman, on suspicion of the murder of PC Ian Broadhurst and the attempted murder of PC Neil Roper after he shot the policemen on 26 December in the Oakwood area of Leeds.

JANUARY 2004

2. Paul Smith, 17, was arrested and charged with the murder of 10-year-old Rosie May Storrie after she was found dead by her parents at a family party on 28 December; she had been strangled. **7**. Two men aged 19 and 20 were arrested in connection with the death of Michael Howard on 6 January. Mr Howard was run over at Liverpool John Lennon Airport after thieves tried to steal his car as he was unpacking suitcases. **11**. Lincolnshire police announced that they would reinvestigate the death of 60-year-old Hugh Wallace, who was found dead in October 1999 by Ian Huntley, the man convicted of murdering Holly Wells and Jessica Chapman. **12**. Delroy 'the King' Lewis, also known as Antonio Kidd, who ran one of the biggest crack and heroin rings in Britain, was jailed for 16 years after being convicted of conspiracy to supply class A drugs and possessing a prohibited weapon. **13**. The serial killer Harold Shipman was found dead in his cell at Wakefield prison after hanging himself with his bed sheets. He had been convicted of the murder of 15 of his patients in January 2000 but was believed to have murdered at least 215 people during his 20 years as a doctor in Manchester. Gordon Park was arrested in connection with the murder of his wife, Carol Park, in 1976, who was known as 'The Lady in the Lake' after she was discovered in 1997 in Cumbria's Coniston Water. **16**. A 15-year-old boy was arrested and charged with the attempted murder of a female jogger who was stabbed on 5 December in Clissold Park, north London. **19**. Attorney-General Lord Goldsmith announced that the convictions of 258 parents charged with killing their children would be reviewed, making it the biggest inquiry into potential miscarriages of justice in British legal history. **28**. A 42-year-old man and his 41-year-old wife were arrested in Droitwich, Worcestershire, on suspicion of the murder of a six-month-old girl, whose body was found in a block of concrete 12 years ago. **29**. Cannabis was downgraded from a class B to a class C drug. **30**. The Crown Prosecution Service announced that the charge of rape against the Leeds United footballer Jody Morris and his friend Kristofer Dickie had been dropped as there was no 'realistic prospect' of securing a conviction.

FEBRUARY 2004

3. An appeal tribunal in Edinburgh decided that the Gulf War veteran Corporal Kenny Duncan would be awarded a pension for suffering from depleted uranium poisoning, making him the first person to receive such compensation. **4**. Graham Coutts was jailed for life at Lewes Crown Court for the murder of Jane Longhurst on 14 March 2003, whose body he had kept in a cardboard box for five weeks before he set it on fire in woodland near Pulborough in West Sussex. **6**. PCs Mark Witcher and Andrew Lang were arrested and charged with raping a 23-year-old woman whilst on duty. **7**. Police arrested five men in connection with a raid on the Menzies World Cargo depot at Heathrow airport, during which eight men stole £1.75 million after they tied up 15 workers on 6 February. **13**. Police smashed an international drugs ring after they raided an illegal drugs factory in Ovingdean near Brighton, and seized equipment and chemicals for making up to £4 million worth of amphetamines and LSD. **18**. Police charged Peter Bryan with murder after the dismembered body of a 45-year-old man was found in a flat in Walthamstow in London; police believe there may have been traces of human tissue in a frying pan at the property. **23**. Zaheer Ahmed was charged with murdering his wife Adeeba at Horseferry Road Magistrates' Court after her body was found in a suitcase on the banks of the River Thames. **24**. Stephen Soans-Wade was jailed for life at the Central Criminal court in London after he was found guilty of murdering Christophe Duclos on 13 September 2002 when he pushed Mr Duclos in front of a tube train at Mile End station in east London in order to be admitted to a psychiatric hospital; he had previously been told he was not mentally ill and turned away from various institutions by doctors. **27**. John Bale was jailed for five years at Taunton Crown Court after being found guilty of committing more than 320 burglaries and stealing cash and jewellery worth £260,000. **28**. Melanie Horridge, 25, was stabbed to death near her home in Chorley, Lancashire, as she was walking in an alleyway with her four-month-old son Oliver.

MARCH 2004

1. The Home Office released figures showing that police numbers in England and Wales had reached a record high of 138,000, with an addition of 6,000 new officers in 12 months being the largest yearly increase ever recorded. Thomas Titley was jailed for life at Wolverhampton Crown Court for sex attacks on two boys aged seven after he had previously served four-and-a-half years for similar offences. **2**. Sean Brown was sentenced to a minimum of 19 years in prison at Preston Crown Court after he pleaded guilty to the murder of his daughter Carry Ann – he deliberately crashed the car they were both in following revelations that he had impregnated her at the age of 13 and then made her abort the baby. **3**. PC Ian Tolmaer was jailed for 12 years after admitting to raping an 18-year-old woman and also filming and photographing her as she lay unconscious. **4**. Antoni Imiela was sentenced to seven life sentences at Maidstone Crown Court after he was convicted of raping four women and three girls between November 2001 and October 2002 in the south east of England. **8**. Peers in the House of Lords voted by 216 to 183 to block the Government's Constitutional Reform Bill, so that it would have to go before a select committee before it could be passed by the House of Commons. The Minister for Prisons, Paul Goggins, urged courts to make greater use of non-custodial sentences as the prisons population in England and Wales exceeded 75,000 for the first time. **12**. Audrey Hingston 81 became the oldest woman to be jailed in Britain after she was found guilty of stabbing her husband to death because she was unable to cope with his illness; she was jailed for two years at Plymouth Crown Court. **15**. The government announced the introduction of on-the-spot fines to be imposed on brewers, licensees and bar staff who serve alcohol to under-18s and drunks. **16**. Stephen King was jailed for seven years at Middlesex Guildhall Crown Court in London after admitting to 21 charges of paedophilia, including sex with a girl under the age of 13 and ten counts of indecent assault. **18**. The Court of Appeal ordered the release of a Libyan asylum seeker known as 'M' from prison after he had been detained for 16 months without being charged; the court ruled that the evidence against him was unfounded and rejected a Home Office appeal to keep him in jail. **19**. Police in Hertfordshire arrested a man in his sixties in connection with the murder of Colonel Robert Workman who was shot on his doorstep in January. **24**. Sallie-Anne Loughran was cleared of drowning her son at her home in 1991 after it was found that the police investigation drew on work by Sir Roy Meadow, whose evidence had in the past been successfully discredited in a number of court cases. **26**. A High Court judge in London ruled that families of children whose organs were removed after their death without their families' consent, had the right to seek compensation from the NHS. The Home Office announced that the number of England football fans subject to banning orders had risen to 2,083 and was expected to reach 2,100 by the start of the European 2004 Championship in June. **27**. Six men were arrested after police seized 200lb of heroin valued at £5 million in a lorry load of charcoal in Walthamstow, east London. **30**. Eight British men were arrested by MI5 agents and anti-terrorist officers after half a tonne of fertiliser was found in a west London storage unit; it was believed that the men planned to use the fertiliser to make a bomb and use it on a 'soft target' such as a shopping centre. All visa applications from Bulgarian and Romanian migrants wanting to enter Britain, were halted by the Home Secretary David Blunkett, following reports from embassy staff that many of the applicants were using forged papers. Following an appeal by John Hirst, serving a life sentence for manslaughter in Britain, the European Court of Human Rights ruled that a ban on convicted prisoners voting in local and general elections was a breach of their human rights. **31**. A survey by the charity Drugscope showed that one in five 11- to 15-year-olds had taken drugs during 2003.

APRIL 2004
1. A 22-year-old man was charged with the murder of Charlotte Pinkney, who was last seen near her home in Devon on 28 February 2004. **2**. Toby Studabaker, the former US Marine who groomed a 12-year-old British girl over the internet, was jailed by Manchester Crown Court for four-and-a-half years after he pleaded guilty to child abduction and to inciting a child to commit gross indecency. **6**. A third man, Kenneth Regan, was charged with the murder of the millionaire Amarjit Chohan after his body was found in the sea near Bournemouth and his wife's body was found in Poole Bay. **7**. A 15-year-old schoolboy was sentenced to six years in a young offenders' institution after being found guilty of raping two girls aged 15 and 17 near their school in Eastbourne. **8**. Anthony Garcia, Jawad Akbar, Omar Khyam, Waheed Mahmoud and Nabeel Hussain were charged with plotting to cause a terrorist explosion after homemade explosives were found in a storage Unit in Hanwell, west London. **13**. The senior Home Office pathologist, Michael Heath, was facing a disciplinary tribunal over alleged flaws in his work after independent experts reviewed two of his murder cases and told the Crown Prosecution Service of their concerns; if the tribunal were to find that Mr Heath had made errors, hundreds of criminal cases in which he was involved would be reviewed. **15**. A teenage boy appeared at Edinburgh Sheriff Court charged with the murder of Jodi Jones, who was stabbed to death in June 2003; the 15-year-old boy did not enter a plea. Ken Ralphs won £134,000 in compensation for a police blunder which resulted in his name being leaked after he had assisted detectives investigating a gangland killing. **16**. The body of Amanda Edwards was found buried at a building site in Wiltshire a week after she went missing and police had suspected she had been kidnapped; the body of the suspected kidnapper, Ian Cortis was also found dead – it was believed he had committed suicide. **17**. Daniel Archer was charged with the murder of Nasra Ismail, whose torso was found in a suitcase in a canal on 12 April in London. **21**. Brett Osborn was jailed for five years at Woolwich Crown Court for the manslaughter of Wayne Halling, who had forced his way into a flat and confronted Osborn in August 2003. Emma Last, Kerry Bauer and Steven Wood were jailed at Chelmsford Crown Court for the murder of Debra Carne after they were found guilty of setting Ms Carne alight in July 2002; Ms Last was ordered to be detained at Her Majesty's pleasure for a minimum of 20 years, Ms Bauer was jailed for life with a recommendation that she serve at least 17 years, and Mr Wood was jailed for eight years. **22**. Guy Beckett admitted that he had killed Laura Torn, whose body was found in Nottinghamshire in April 2003; he pleaded not guilty to murder but guilty to manslaughter at Hull Crown Court. A report by the TUC showed that unemployment among black and Asian people was two-and-a-half times worse than rates for whites. **23**. Gary Seabrook, a plumber, was jailed at Lewes Crown Court, for 30 months, for charging a 73-year-old woman £5,000 for unblocking a drain, which would normally cost around £107. Curtis Rowe was jailed for seven years at the Central Criminal Court after he was found guilty of killing his neighbour, Peter King, by stabbing him and setting him alight because he had 'made too much noise'. **28**. Lincoln White was jailed for 25 years at Kingston Crown Court for running an international drugs operation worth around £170 million.

MAY 2004
1. The new Sexual Offences Act came into force which allows juries to assume there was no consent if a rape victim was asleep, unconscious or disabled and also repeals offences of buggery and indecency between men which had previously criminalised certain homosexual activity. **2**. A survey carried out by the Local Authorities Co-ordinators of Regulatory Services showed that one in 29 civil weddings in Britain were fraudulent and a result of a multimillion-pound black market weddings industry. **4**. Brian Braker and Keith Hill were jailed for 11 and seven years respectively after police found 650,000 ecstasy pills with a street value of £2 million in their possession. **5**. Steven Poole, Daniel Poole and Richard Greyham from Derbyshire were all found guilty of murder at Nottingham Crown Court after they beat to death Matthew Murray because they believed him to be a paedophile. **14**. Feston Konzani was jailed for 10 years at Teesside Crown Court after he was found guilty on three counts of causing grievous bodily harm by attempting to deliberately infect three women with the HIV virus. **17**. Six men were arrested at Heathrow airport after an attempted armed robbery at a warehouse containing £40 million in gold bullion as well as £40 million in cash. The Constitutional Affairs Minister, David Lammy, announced a Criminal Defence Service Bill that outlined a £70 million decrease in the criminal legal aid budget; the Bill also proposed that the power to grant legal aid be taken from magistrates' courts and given to the Legal Services Commission. Nigel Da Costa was jailed for 20 years at Chelmsford Crown Court for the rape of two women after convincing them he was a member of the SAS and pretending to arrest them for being a 'security risk'. **18**. Humberside Police closed an inquiry into the death of the skydiver Stephen Hilder, after forensic evidence showed that he almost certainly killed himself. **21**. Moira Greenslade was jailed for two years at Leeds Crown Court for selling her unborn baby over the internet to three childless couples. **23**. A 48-year-old man was charged with the murder of Detective Constable Michael Swindells who was killed on 21 May in Birmingham whilst on duty. **24**. Six companies were fined £75,000 each for tricking people into ringing premium rate telephone numbers by sending unsolicited text messages logging a 'missed call'. **25**. Mahmood Siddiqui was awarded £178,000 in compensation for racial discrimination after hidden cameras proved that he routinely suffered racial abuse and bullying from colleagues at the Royal Mail sorting office in Harlow, Essex. **26**. Animal rights activists were barred for life from protesting outside Huntingdon Life Science laboratories at the High Court in London. **28**. Jason Ward was sentenced to life imprisonment at Nottingham Crown Court after raping and battering to death 87-year-old Gladys Godfrey at her home in Mansfield.

JUNE 2004
1. Douglas Mullings was shot dead during a dispute over parking in Tottenham, north London. **2**. The concert pianist Brian Parnell was jailed for two years after becoming the first person to be convicted under Britain's 'sex tourism' laws. **3**. Former police officer David Nutton was jailed for 18 months at Winchester Crown Court for gross misconduct in office after he passed on details from a police computer to a paedophile which enabled the man to continue abusing children. Scotland Yard announced that four men had been arrested in connection with the shooting of Douglas Mullings on 1 June. **4**. Iain Davis was found guilty of killing Ashley Keaton and Wayne Mowatt with one bullet at a New Year's Day party in 2002 and was sentenced to life imprisonment. **7**. Two 18-year-old men were arrested in Leeds for raping a woman and assaulting her boyfriend in the city's Chapel Allerton Park. **8**. A police doctor, Robert Wells, was jailed for 15 years at Winchester Crown Court for two rapes and three indecent assaults of an 11-year-old. **15**. Jonathan Rees-Williams, the Queen's former choirmaster was convicted at Reading Crown Court of 13 charges of indecent assault against children over a 14-year period. Shabina Begum, 15, lost her application for judicial review at the High Court in London following a decision that her human rights had not been infringed by Denbigh High School, after it refused to allow her to wear her jilbab, an Islamic gown covering her whole body except her hands and face. **18**. Barbara Salisbury, a nurse at Leighton Hospital in Crewe, was jailed for five years at Chester Crown Court for the attempted murder of two of her patients, May Taylor and Frank Owen. **21**. Law Lords ruled by a majority of four to one that the Human Rights Act required courts to read the phrase 'surviving spouse' in the Rent Act as including the survivor of a homosexual couple. **22**. Paul Dalton was charged with murder after the dismembered body of his wife, Tae Hui, was found at their home in London. **26**. Two 16-year-old boys and one 17-year-old boy were arrested in connection with the murder of 15-year-old Kieran Rodney-Davis, who was stabbed in the chest by three youths whilst on an errand for his mother near their home in Fulham, London, on 23 June.

JULY 2004
5. The House of Lords voted by 250 to 75 to reject an attempt to outlaw physical punishment of children by parents but backed a compromise proposal which removed the defence of 'reasonable chastisement' but still allowed parents to administer moderate punishment, as long as it did not result in visible marking on the skin for several hours afterwards. Dale Whittington was sentenced to eight years in prison at Southampton Crown Court after he was found guilty of arson with intent to endanger life when he was found to have disconnected three smoke alarms at a property housing asylum seekers before setting it alight. **6**. Kingsley Ojo from Nigeria admitted to six identity and trafficking offences at Southwark Crown Court and was due to be questioned by police in connection with the ritual killing of the boy known as 'Adam', whose torso was found in the River Thames in 2001. The first public inquiry into Gulf War Syndrome opened in London but the Ministry of Defence refused to co-operate with the investigation. **7**. Karen Parlour, the former wife of footballer Ray Parlour, won a landmark ruling at the High Court which secured her right to a third of Mr Parlour's future income. **8**. Bernard Heginbotham, 100, became the oldest man in Britain to be convicted of murder after he killed his wife, Ida, to spare her from dementia; he pleaded guilty to manslaughter on the grounds of diminished responsibility at Preston Crown Court and was ordered to complete a 12-month community rehabilitation order. **9**. Richard Jan was jailed for life at Middlesex Guildhall Crown Court for stalking around 200 people over a seven-year period between 1996 and 2003. **13**. The Court of Appeal ruled that nine Afghans who hijacked an airliner and forced it to land at Stansted Airport in 2000 could not be deported from the UK as their human rights would be infringed. The House of Lords voted by 240 to 208 to keep the post of Lord Chancellor; the government said it would use its majority to reinstate the measure into the Constitutional Reform Bill. **15**. Police launched an investigation after Noel White jumped from the top of a multi-storey car park with his five-year-old daughter Shanice in Wolverhampton – both were killed instantly. **16**. Sion Jenkins won a retrial after he was convicted in June 1998 of the murder of his step-daughter Billie-Jo; his conviction was quashed as unsafe due to scientific evidence being unavailable at his original trial. **21**. Nebojsa Denic was jailed for 15 years at the Central Criminal Court for conspiracy to rob and possessing a gun and using it to resist arrest after he helped steal £23 million worth of diamonds from Graff jewellers in Mayfair, London. **22**. The Department of Trade and Industry announced a new obligatory scheme for estate agents which would make it compulsory for all agents to sign up to an ombudsman scheme which would adjudicate on complaints from the public. Police announced a search for Mark Hobson as the main suspect for the murders of his girlfriend Claire Sanderson, her twin sister Diane Sanderson, and an elderly couple, James and Joan Britton, all of whom were found dead after having suffered violent deaths between 10 and 17 July. **23**. Dean Taylor and Craig Abbott were sentenced to seven-and-a-half-years in jail for the manslaughter of Michael Howard at Liverpool's John Lennon Airport on 6 January. **25**. Mark Hobson was captured by police at a petrol station on the A19 in Shipton, near York; he was first taken to a police station before being taken to Harrogate District Hospital. **26**. Andrew Wragg was arrested by Sussex police on suspicion of the murder of his son, Jacob, who had been suffering from Hunter syndrome and whose condition had deteriorated considerably; he died on 24 July at the family home. Kingsley Ojo was sentenced to four-and-a-half years in prison at Southwark Crown Court for running a trafficking ring thought to have brought the boy known as 'Adam' whose torso was found in the Thames, into Britain. **27**. The Association of Chief Police Officers announced that anyone working for the police force who chose to join the British National Party (BNP) would face dismissal. Alan Pennell was convicted of the murder of Luke Walmsley at Nottingham Crown Court and sentenced to a minimum of 12 years in prison after he was found guilty of stabbing him in the chest at Birkbeck School in Lincolnshire in November 2003. **28**. Shahajan Kabir was jailed for life at Carlisle Crown Court for slitting the throat of his one-year-old son Hassan Martin in October 2003 in front of Hassan's mother and grandmother because he faced being deported to Bangladesh. **30**. Figures published by the Department for Education and Skills showed that more than 10 children a day were expelled from schools in England for assaulting staff or fellow pupils during the summer term in 2003.

AUGUST 2004

2. Lee Holbrook was jailed for life at Plymouth Crown Court for the murder on 7 November 2003 of Alicia Eborne. **4**. A senior al-Qa'eda suspect was arrested followed by the arrest of a dozen other men on 13 August, suspected of plotting a terrorist attack in Britain. **5**. A 16-year-old boy was convicted of stabbing Monica Watts while she was jogging in Clissold Park in north London in December 2003. **6**. Mark Smith, a youth worker at Hammersmith and Fulham council, was jailed for eight years at the Central Criminal Court for conspiracy to sell or transfer prohibited weapons and of possessing them. Professor David Southall was banned by a General Medical Council tribunal from child protection work for three years for 'abusing his professional position' by accusing a father of murdering his two infant sons based on a 50-minute television documentary he had seen on the case. **9**. The Premiership footballer Lee Hughes was sentenced to six years in prison at Coventry Crown Court for killing Douglas Graham in a car crash in November 2003. **10**. George and Gwendoline Elliott, 75 and 72 respectively, were sentenced to one year in jail at Norwich Crown Court for allowing their son to hide heroin in their home. **13**. A 17-year-old boy, believed to be Britain's most prolific graffiti vandal, was sentenced to a 12-month referral order at Bath Youth Court after he admitted 10 counts of criminal damage. **15**. It was reported that MPs would be forced to declare their expense claims worth more than £100,000 a year when parliamentary accounts are published in order to comply with the Freedom of Information Act. Robert Boyer was arrested on suspicion of murdering Keith Frogson after Boyer was found hiding in Nottinghamshire woodland during a police search which involved 620 officers. **16**. Terry Rodgers was arrested for the murder of his daughter Chanel, who was found dead by her husband on 30 July. **17**. Joseph Mansoor was jailed for life at the Central Criminal Court for battering his wife, Yona, to death. **19**. James Raven, a 'covert operative' employed by the BBC and Channel 4, was jailed for life at Chester Crown Court for the murder of Brian Waters. **20**. Amelia Delagrange was murdered in Twickenham, south London; police believed she was the second victim of a serial killer after Marsha McDonnell was murdered in a similar way in the same area in February 2003. **22**. Tom Brown, a BBC archivist, was stabbed to death in an unprovoked attack in Southgate, north London.

ECONOMIC AND BUSINESS AFFAIRS

SEPTEMBER 2003

4. The Bank of England kept the base interest rate on hold at 3.5 per cent and the European Central Bank kept its key interest rate at 2 per cent. **8**. The Inland Revenue announced new legislation barring companies from claiming backdated tax refunds extending back more than six years with immediate effect. The new legislation was introduced after Deutsche Morgan Grenfell, part of Deutsche Bank, won the right in the High Court to seek a refund of tax payments made a decade ago. **9**. The Office of Fair Trading (OFT) announced that it was launching an inquiry into store cards offered by high street retailers, after MPs on the Commons Treasury Select Committee complained that research showed that the consumer arm of General Electric could own 70 per cent of the market share. **17**. Dick Grasso resigned as head of the New York Stock Exchange (NYSE) after a public outcry concerning his $187.5 million pay deal. He had previously returned $48 million, but in an emergency meeting the board of the NYSE voted 13 to 7 in favour of a motion proposing his resignation. **18**. The annual report of National Savings and Investments, the fundraising arm of the Treasury, revealed that funds had risen by £784 million to £63.1 billion due to record sales of premium bonds; sales topped £4.75 billion compared to £3.8 billion in 2002. **22**. A sharp fall in the value of the US dollar sparked a 2.5 per cent rise in the price of gold, which finished the day on the London market at $386 (£234) per troy ounce, continuing a three-year upward trend. **26**. Levi Strauss & Co, the American jeans label, announced it was to close its remaining US production plants and move its operation to South America and Asia making 2,000 employees redundant. **30**. Official figures published by the Office for National Statistics showed that inflation in the public sector was at its highest for 13 years: an average of 7.9 per cent over the first half of 2003. In a major cross-border deal in European aviation Air France agreed to an all-share takeover of Dutch airline KLM.

OCTOBER 2003

1. British Energy avoided bankruptcy after its creditors agreed to forfeit the £1.3 billion they were owed in return for £425 million worth of bonds and 97.5 per cent of the restructured energy company's equity. **2**. At the Labour Party conference the unions voted unanimously to make it compulsory for employers to contribute to employee pension schemes; Andrew Smith, Secretary of State for Work and Pensions, responded by saying that the Pension Commission would consider the case for greater compulsion. In his conference speech Mr Smith announced a pilot scheme with cash incentives to help single parents get back to work and plans for a more flexible state pension offering lump sums of up to £30,000 for people who defer their state pension for five years. **3**. The first UK outlet for the US brand Krispy Kreme doughnuts officially opened at Harrods. **6**. The Pension Credit replaced the pension Minimum Income Guarantee (MIG); the new system intended to ensure a minimum weekly income for everyone aged over 60 in the UK and was designed to reward those that had saved for their retirement via a system of monetary-linked credits. Robert Wiseman, managing director of Robert Wiseman Dairies, won the Ernst and Young UK Entrepreneur of the Year competition for his transformation of the company from a door step supplier to the country's third largest milk supplier with an annual turnover of £390 million. **7**. The two television companies Carlton and Granada merged in a £4 billion deal creating a single ITV. **8**. A British academic, Prof. Clive Granger from the University of California at San Diego was awarded the Nobel Economics Prize for his research techniques which have been used by the Bank of England and the Treasury for forecasting and monitoring the UK economy. **10**. The first week of electronic trading at the International Petroleum Exchange (IPE) in London ended with only 57 lots traded electronically compared to 147,000 lots traded traditionally on the floor by 'open outcry' after traders boycotted the new electronic system. **13**. Share prices surged to a 13-month high with the FTSE 100 index closing at 4431.6 points, its highest level since August 2002. **16**. Eddie Stobart announced that he was selling his haulage company to WA Developments, a real estate and railway infrastructure business, part-owned by his brother William Stobart. HSBC confirmed it would be moving 4,000 jobs to India, China and Malaysia. **19**. The British Retail Consortium reported the fourth consecutive month of solid sales growth in September, with like-for-like sales up 2.6 per cent and total sales up 5.5 per cent. A Valuation Tribunal ruled that individuals working from home would not have to pay business property rates on top of council tax after Eileen Tully who works for the Inland Revenue mounted a successful challenge against her employer's policy.

NOVEMBER 2003

3. Figures published by the Bank of England showed that during the first three-quarters of the year the number of businesses becoming bankrupt had increased by 11.1 per cent compared to the same period in 2002. **6**. The Bank of England's monetary policy committee raised the base interest rate by a quarter per cent to 3.75 per cent. **7**. Figures from the Department of Trade and Industry (DTI) showed that more than 9,000 Britons became bankrupt in the three months leading up to 30 September 2003; an increase of 17 per cent compared to the same period in 2002 and the highest number for 10 years. **13**. The price of gold soared to its highest level since March 1996, closing up $3 at $394 per troy ounce in London. **14**. The media group Hollinger International, the American parent company of the *Daily Telegraph* Group, revealed $32.5 million in payments to Hollinger executives had not been approved by the full board of directors or the audit committee. **19**. An 18-month joint undercover operation by the FBI, US Securities and Exchange Commission (SEC) and the US Attorney for the Southern District for New York into alleged fraudulent foreign exchange activities resulted in the arrests of 48 traders on Wall Street. Lord Black of Crossharbour announced his resignation as the chief executive of Hollinger International following the revelations concerning payments to Hollinger executives on the 14 November.

DECEMBER 2003

10. Chancellor Gordon Brown delivered his pre-budget report to the House of Commons in which he revealed that borrowing of up to £37.4 billion would be required in 2003–6 to meet government spending commitments. The price of platinum soared above $800 an ounce, the highest for 23-years, as concerns grew that not enough was being produced to satisfy demand. **18**. The price of platinum continued to rise closing at $840 an ounce, an all-time high. **31**. The US Securities and Exchange Commission started legal proceedings against Parmalat in a New York Court and sent investigators to Italy to liaise with prosecutors. Two executives at the Italian branch of Grant Thornton, auditors for Parmalat, were arrested on suspicion of fraudulent accounting practices. The FTSE 100 index of leading companies finished the year up for the first time since 1999 and the pound gained more than a cent against the dollar to finish at $1.7904.

JANUARY 2004

1. Citibank and HSBC Holdings became the first foreign bank to win approval to issue credit cards in China. The aerospace group Boeing was awarded a $1.6 billion (£900 million) extension from NASA to its contract to supply the International Space Station. **9**. Royal Dutch/Shell, the Anglo-Dutch oil company, revealed that it had overstated its oil and gas reserves by 20 per cent resulting in a drop in oil stocks world-wide. **12**. Figures from the Office of the Deputy Prime Minister showed that house price inflation was back into single figures after house prices dropped by 1.1 per cent in November 2003. **13**. Standard Life, one of the largest mutual insurance companies in Europe, stated that it was considering a stock market listing. **15**. The retailer Boots plc confirmed that it would be cutting 900 jobs at its head office in Nottingham. **18**. Sir David and Sir Frederick Barclay launched a bid to buy Lord Black of Crossharbour's 78 per cent stake in the Canadian-listed Hollinger Incorporated, which owns 30 per cent of the New York-listed Hollinger International's equity and controls 73 per cent of the voting shares. **19**. A resurgence in the stock market due to gains in insurance and oil shares raised the FTSE 100 index to its highest level for 18 months, closing up 30.2 points (0.7 per cent), at 4,518.1. **26**. The New York law firm, Milberg Weiss Bershad Hynes & Lerach, launched a lawsuit against Shell, the Anglo-Dutch oil company, on behalf of investors after the company's admission on 9 January that it had overstated its proven oil reserves by 20 per cent. Hollinger International filed a lawsuit to prevent the former chairman, Lord Black of Crossharbour, selling his controlling stake in the company to brothers Sir David and Sir Frederick Barclay. **27**. The media regulator Ofcom ruled that the operator of the *118 118* directory enquiry service had used the 'trademark' long hair, drooping moustache and red socks of the former 10,000-metre world record holder, David Bedford, without his permission in its £16 million advertising campaign. The Barclay brothers tabled a formal tender offer to buy Lord Black of Crossharbour's 30 per cent stake in Hollinger International for £259 million.

FEBRUARY 2004

3. The European Commission ruled that the Ryanair airline should repay more than £2 million in unlawful subsidies given by the Walloon regional government as an incentive for the airline to fly from Charleroi airport near Brussels. **5**. The Bank of England raised the base interest rate by 0.25 per cent to 4.0 per cent. **6**. Figures released by the Department of Trade and Industry showed the number of personal bankruptcies had risen by 29 per cent in the last four months of 2003 compared to the same period in 2002. A total of 36,328 people in England and Wales declared themselves personally insolvent in 2003, the highest figure for a decade. **7**. Tickets went on sale for a new European lottery organised and run by Camelot in partnership with its French and Spanish counterparts. **9**. The Treasury's annual assessment of European economic reform stated that EU spending should be capped at one per cent of gross national income and subjected to the same value-for-money assessment as spending by member states. **10**. The US dollar dropped to $1.86 against the pound sterling; its lowest level since Black Wednesday. **17**. The latest UK inflation data was published showing that the Consumer Prices Index was rising by an annual 1.4 per cent in January 2004, an increase from 1.3 per cent in December 2003. Italian police arrested the son and a daughter of Calisto Tanzi, founder of Parmalat, and six others, in connection with the investigation into suspected fraud and misappropriation of funds within the Parmalat group. **18**. The dollar continued to fall against the pound sterling, closing at $1.91 against the pound. **25**. Figures released by the Office for National Statistics showed an unchanged rate of economic expansion of 0.9 per cent for the fourth quarter, equivalent to a year-on-year 2.8 per cent increase in GDP for 2003. **26**. Lord Black of Crossharbour had his proposal to sell his controlling stake in Hollinger International to the Barclay brothers blocked after a judge in Delaware, USA, ruled that he had breached company law.

MARCH 2004

1. *The Times* newspaper reported that the Inland Revenue had written off more than £750 million in unpaid national insurance contributions after attempts to recover the money failed; the shortfall arose after the Inland Revenue failed to send out reminders for the five years (1996–2002) to those whose contributions fell short. The British retailer Marks & Spencer said that it would raise £400 million by issuing bonds to fund a £1 billion shortfall in its pension scheme funds. HSBC, the high-street bank announced record pre-tax profits of £7.8 billion, the biggest profit ever recorded by a British bank in a single year. **8**. Lord Penrose's report on the near-collapse of Equitable Life was published after two-and-a-half years. The report found that regulators failed to monitor the company adequately but blamed the company's former management as the direct cause of the losses suffered by policyholders, thereby ruling out the possibility of government compensation for the one million investors. **17**. The Chancellor Gordon Brown delivered the 2004 Budget to the House of Commons. Many taxes and duties were frozen but beer went up 1p a pint, wine up 4p a bottle and tax on cigarettes increased in-line with inflation. The inheritance tax threshold was increased to £263,000 and a £3,000 fine for late filing was introduced. Individual pension allowances were capped at £1.5 million under a new scheme to be introduced in 2006 with the allowance scheduled to rise to £1.8 million by 2010. Public spending plans included an annual 7.2 per cent increase in NHS funding until 2008 and an additional £6 billion allocated to fight terrorism. Overall the economy grew by 2.3 per cent in 2003, meeting Treasury forecasts, and growth forecasts remained at 3–3.5 per cent for 2004–5 and at 2.5–3 per cent for 2006. **18**. In Milan, prosecutors called for 29 people to strand trial in connection with the collapse of the Italian dairy firm, Parmalat. These included the company's founder, Calisto Tanzi, his son Stephano and his former financial chief, Fausto Tonna. The Anglo-Dutch business Shell admitted that revised figures issued in January for its proven oil and gas reserves, following revelations that it had overestimated stocks for 2003 by 20 per cent, were also too high. **22**. The European Commission fined Microsoft a record €497 million after ruling that Microsoft had abused its market position by not making its operating systems compatible with rival software. **24**. Figures published by the National Audit Office (NAO) showed that the Inland Revenue failed to collect £14 billion of tax for the financial year 2002–3; the missing debt included £4.9 billion in PAYE, £4.5 billion in self-assessment, £3.1 billion in corporation tax and £1.8 billion in other taxes. **29**. A survey published by Hometrack stated that house prices were continuing to rise at a high rate forecasting an eight per cent rise in 2004. The Post Office launched the first of a wide range of low-cost financial services products in collaboration with the Bank of Ireland.

APRIL 2004

8. The Bank of England kept the base interest rate on hold at four per cent despite much speculation that it would be raised by a quarter of a percentage point. **13**. The HSBC bank launched a new pension fund compliant with Shari'ah or Islamic law. **18**. *The Sunday Times Rich List* reported that Britain's richest people had seen their wealth increase by almost 30 per cent in the past 12 months, an increase of 15 times the rate of inflation. **19**. An investigation carried out on behalf of Royal Dutch Shell by US law firm, Davis, Polk and Wardwell, reported that former executives at the company had knowingly lied to investors about the true level of the company's oil and gas reserves for a number of years. **23**. Figures released by the Office for National Statistics showed that the UK economy grew by its fastest annual rate in almost three-and-a-half years in the first quarter of 2004, the growth was mainly from rapid expansion in the retailing, hotels and leisure sectors. The Financial Services Authority (FSA) confirmed that it had launched a formal investigation into Royal Dutch Shell, following the conclusion by its internal investigation. **26**. The US aerospace company, Boeing, announced it would start production of its new 7E7 *Dreamliner* jet after the Japanese airline All Nippon Airways ordered 50 of the jets in a deal worth about $6 billion. **29**. Figures released by the Nationwide Building Society showed that the value of the average home went up by almost £3,400 in a month to £145,918; overall, house prices had climbed seven per cent since January and 18.9 per cent in the past 12 months.

MAY 2004

2. Between 750 and 1,000 passengers were left stranded when a new airline, Duo, went into administration after only operating for seven months. **6**. The Bank of England raised the base interest rate by 0.25 per cent to 4.25 per cent. **10**. The FTSE-100 index dropped by 2.3 per cent, its sharpest one-day decline for a year, closing down 103.2 points at a five-week low of 4,395.2, amid fears of surging oil prices and a possible increase in US interest rates. **12**. From midnight British Airways added a £5 surcharge to its non-European fares due to an increase in oil prices. **16**. The Office of Fair Trading announced that British credit card companies were over-charging retailers for processing card payments and these costs were eventually borne by consumers. **24**. Oil prices continued to rise with the cost of a barrel of crude oil reaching $41.80, close to a 21-year high, on the New York Stock Exchange.

JUNE 2004

8. Carl Cushnie and Fred Clough, the former chairman and finance director of Versailles, the trade finance house which collapsed in 2000, were both convicted of conspiracy to defraud; Cushnie was convicted of defrauding £23 million from investors and Clough £19 million. **10**. The Bank of England raised the base interest rate by a quarter percentage point to 4.5 per cent. **16**. It was reported that UK inflation reached 1.5 per cent in May 2004, its highest level for more than one year. **21**. The Barclay twins, Sir David and Sir Frederick were successful, subject to regulatory approval, in their £665 million bid for the ownership of *The Daily Telegraph*.

JULY 2004

12. Chancellor Gordon Brown unveiled his 2004 Spending Review; public spending by government departments was forecast to rise from £279.3 billion in 2004–5 to £340.5 billion in 2007–8. NHS funding was to be increased from £69 to £92 billion by 2008, security spending to increase by 10 per cent annually (real-terms rise) with the Armed Forces budget to increase from £29.7 billion to £33.4 billion by 2008. Cutbacks included the loss of 84,150 civil service posts and plans to raise £30 billion from the sale of Government assets. **16**. Martha Stewart, former chief executive of Martha Stewart Living Omnimedia, was sentenced to five months in jail followed by five months house arrest, after being found guilty on 1 March of lying to the FBI and securities regulators; she was granted bail pending appeal. **22**. The British high street had its longest run of retail sales growth in at least two decades when sales rose for the thirteenth consecutive month in June. A warning from the Russian oil company Yukos, that a liquidity crisis could force it to cease export operations increased American crude oil prices to above $41 per barrel on the New York stock exchange. **25**. The board of Abbey agreed in principle to sell the high street bank to Santander Central Hispano, Spain's biggest finance group, for an estimated £8.5 billion. **28**. The price of American crude oil reached a 21-year high of $43.05 a barrel and London Brent oil reached a 14-year high of $39.60, after Siberian oil company Yukos received an order from the Russian Justice Ministry to halt all sales. Oil analysts believed the order to be a restraint aimed at stopping the company selling or changing the status of its assets, however, the Russian Justice Ministry failed to clarify the meaning of the order, resulting in shares in Yukos falling by 20 per cent.

AUGUST 2004

5. The Bank of England raised interest rates to 4.75 per cent, the highest level for almost three years. **6**. Analysts' concerns over the crude oil market subsided after the Moscow Arbitration Court ruled that seizure of a key production subsidiary of Russian oil company, Yukos, was illegal. **8**. Figures from the Land Registry showed that house prices in the three months to June were 17 per cent higher than in the same period in 2003; taking the average house price from just under £150,000 to more than £175,000 within a 12-month period. **20**. As the price of American crude oil reached nearly $50 a barrel and London Brent oil above $40 a barrel, fuel retailers across the UK began to raise prices with Total becoming the first chain to confirm a forecourt price increase of 0.6p a litre for petrol and diesel. **24**. Britain's largest gas and electricity supplier, British Gas, announced its highest single price increase since privatisation in 1996; gas would rise by 12.4 per cent and electricity by 9.4 per cent from 20 September 2004. British Gas blamed rises in the prices of wholesale energy and oil for the increase.

ENVIRONMENT AND SCIENCE

SEPTEMBER 2003

3. Scientists from the Weizmann Institute of Science in Israel developed a test to measure the activity of 8-oxoguanine DNA N-glycosylase (OGG), an enzyme responsible for DNA repair, and discovered that some people are better at repairing smoking-related damage to their DNA. **7**. NASA announced that Galileo space probe's 14-year mission to explore Jupiter and its moons would be brought to a close as the craft had run low on fuel; technicians put Galileo on course to disintegrate in the Jovian atmosphere. **10**. The Institute of Child Health in London identified a small fraction of the human genetic code that affects the part of the brain implicated in autism. Lord Winston warned of the possible long-term dangers of IVF treatment, stating that poorly researched fertility treatments were being used as a matter of course. He was particularly concerned with the long-term effects of freezing embryos and the use of intra-cytoplasmic sperm injection (ICSI), which involves directly injecting a sperm into an egg, increasing the risk of genetic defects being passed on. **15**. Prof. Alex Markham, chief executive of Cancer Research UK, said that a national screening programme for bowel cancer could save 5,000 lives a year but could not be implemented because the NHS did not have the capacity to treat the number of patients that such a programme would identify. **19**. It was reported in *The Times* that a complete fossil of a giant guinea-pig type creature, *Phoberomys pattersoni*, had been unearthed at Urumaco in Venezuela. The creature lived in South America eight million years ago and would have weighed about 700kg (110st), was 3m long and 1.3m high at the shoulder. **24**. Scientists reported that the largest ice shelf in the Arctic, the Ward Hunt ice shelf on the north coast of Ellesmere Island in Canada, had split into two main parts, each of which had cracked into many smaller pieces. Researchers stated that local warming of the climate was responsible. **30**. Cancer Research UK launched a 10-year study to test if the drug Arimidex anastrozole can reduce the risk of post-menopausal women developing breast cancer; initial studies had suggested that it could reduce the risk by up to 70 per cent.

OCTOBER 2003

1. The Met Office announced that September 2003 had been the sunniest September since sunshine records began in 1961, with an average of just over six hours of sunshine each day across England and Wales. **3**. Provisional figures released by the Office for National Statistics showed that the summer's exceptionally hot weather caused 2,045 more deaths compared to the averages for the previous five years. **6**. The Central Science Laboratory announced that wild boar were again breeding in the south east of England; government scientists estimated the numbers to be about 200, although farmers believed the numbers to be much higher. British physicist Sir Peter Mansfield and American scientist Paul Lauterbur from the University of Illinois jointly won the Nobel Prize for Medicine for developing magnetic resonance imaging (MRI), a technique for producing images of internal organs without using X-rays. **7**. Anthony Leggett, a British scientist and Professor of Physics at the University of Illinois, was honoured with the Nobel Prize for Physics for his work on superfluidity. **9**. A study by the Zoological Society of London and the University of Las Palmas in Gran Canaria reported that military sonar is confusing whales and dolphins by causing them to surface too quickly and suffer fatal attacks of decompression sickness. **14**. A team of scientists from Duke University in Durham, North Carolina reported they had successfully taught two rhesus macaque monkeys to control a cursor on screen via electrodes planted in the frontal and parietal lobes of their brains. **15**. The European Food Safety Authority confirmed its scientists had discovered the toxin semicarbazide, which can damage DNA and has been linked to a range of cancers in a variety of jarred food products, including baby food. China became the third nation to send a man into space after Lieutenant-Colonel Yang Liwei completed his mission. **21**. Microsoft launched a new range of software which allows users to send emails that can be ordered to 'self-destruct' at a date set by the sender. **23**. The first three-year phase of the 10-year marine life census recorded 15,304 species of fish and 210,000 marine species of all types. **29**. One of the most powerful solar storms on record hit Earth's atmosphere resulting in problems with aircraft navigational systems and a spectacular display of Northern Lights; the storm resulted from a massive gas cloud which erupted from the sun two days previously. **30**. The British award winning wildlife film-maker, Michael Linley, pleaded guilty in a Perth court to smuggling protected reptiles out of Australia; he was caught in October at Perth airport as he tried to leave with the protected species.

NOVEMBER 2003

4. A run of wild salmon were rescued from the waterfall at Cargill's Leap on the river Ericht in Perthshire after becoming too exhausted to leap upstream in shallow water. They were transported upstream to their spawning ground by the Tay District Salmon Fisheries. A new osteoporosis drug, the hormone derivative teriparatide, which increases the number of bone forming cells, was licensed for use in Britain for post-menopausal women. **14**. A possible new planet, named *Sedna*, located eight billion miles away from the sun, was sighted from the Palomar Observatory in California.

DECEMBER 2003

19. The *Beagle 2* Mars probe was successfully released from the nose cone of the European Space Agency's *Mars Express* spacecraft for the final part of its journey to the red planet where it was due to land on 25 December. **26**. The Jodrell Bank Radio Observatory in Cheshire failed to pick up a signal from the *Beagle 2* lander for a second night, the failure followed a second unsuccessful attempt at contact by the NASA *Mars Odyssey* orbiter.

JANUARY 2004

2. NASA successfully flew the *Stardust* space probe through the tail of the *Wild 2* comet where it took pictures of the comet's nucleus and was hoped to have successfully gathered a sample of comet dust. **4**. The first of two NASA exploration rovers successfully landed on Mars to begin a 90-day mission to establish if Mars was capable of sustaining life. **5**. The World Health Organisation confirmed that a new case of SARS had been identified in Guangdong, in south China. **7**. The *Mars Express* passed the landing site for the *Beagle 2*, but failed to pick up any radio signal from the missing probe. **12**. Research carried out by a team of scientists led by Philippa Darbre, a lecturer in cellular and molecular biology at Reading University, established the possibility of a link between the parabens contained in some anti-perspirants and breast cancer. **15**. The NASA *Spirit* rover successfully left its landing platform on Mars and drove three metres across the planet's surface. **21**. NASA lost contact with the *Spirit* Mars rover after it failed to send back expected scientific data and sent a simple signal instead. **22**. The Big Bird Race (The Ultimate Flutter) was launched in London by David Bellamy to raise money for the Conservation Foundation's work on seabird protection; gamblers could place bets on which one of 18 electronically tagged Tasmanian shy albatrosses would finish first on their 6,000-mile annual migration from Tasmania to South Africa. **23**. The European *Mars Express* transmitted a spectrometer image providing the first direct evidence that the Martian South Pole contained deposits of frozen water. **25**. NASA's second Mars rover *Opportunity* touched down in a shallow meteorite crater. **26**. The *Beagle 2* team announced that they accepted that the probe was probably lost and commenced an evaluation of what could have gone wrong. **29**. NASA re-established partial contact with the *Spirit* Mars rover which successfully transmitted an image back to Earth.

FEBRUARY 2004

11. A study published by the British Medical Association (BMA) aiming to consolidate medical evidence on the effects of smoking on fertility, pregnancy and childhood health concluded that smoking causes early menopause and reduces the chances of conceiving by approximately 40 per cent. **12**. The journal *Science* reported that a team of South Korean scientists had successfully produced human stem cells from cloned embryos as part of their research into therapeutic cloning. **13**. Microsoft called in the FBI to investigate the alleged theft of a 660-megabyte portion of the source code for the Windows 2000 and Windows NT 4 operating systems after they discovered the code was being traded over the internet. **16**. A study for the Global Initiative for Asthma reported that the asthma rate for British teenagers aged 13 to 14 years was the highest in the world, with 33.6 per cent suffering from the condition. **17**. A study reported in *The Times*, conducted by scientists at the University of Washington in Seattle, showed that long-term and regular users of antibiotics increased their risk of developing breast cancer by one-and-a-half times compared to those who had never taken antibiotics. **22**. The General Medical Council announced it was to investigate allegations that research by Dr Andrew Wakefield published in *The Lancet* in 1998, linking the MMR vaccine with autism, was fundamentally flawed due to a conflict of interests between Dr Wakefield's research projects at the time. **23**. The British Medical Association stated that if current trends in childhood weight gain and obesity continued, three million Britons would suffer from diabetes by 2010; twice the number recorded four years ago.

MARCH 2004

2. The European Space Agency's *Rosetta* spacecraft began a 12-year mission to land on Comet 67P/Churyumov-Gerasimenko in 2014 after an *Ariane-5* rocket carrying the probe was launched successfully from the Kourou spaceport in French Guiana. **3**. Ten of the 12 authors of the 1998 paper which linked autism with the MMR vaccine issued a retraction statement stating that while no causal link was established between the MMR vaccine and autism, the possibility of such a link had been raised. **9**. A study was published in the medical journal *The Lancet*, which announced that scientists at the Cornell University, New York, had for the first time successfully managed to conceive an embryo using tissue from a frozen human ovary. **24**. The Health Secretary John Reid announced a £1 million project to look into providing a 24-hour angioplasty service across the country, with the aim of offering patients the procedure, which unblocks arteries, within two hours of a heart attack. **28**. The world's first working 'scramjet', built by NASA, reached 5,000 mph (seven times the speed of sound) in its test flight; the flight lasted just 11 seconds and ended with a planned splashdown into the pacific ocean.

APRIL 2004

6. *The Times* reported that a study conducted by scientists in America and published in the US journal *Pediatrics* found that for every hour of television watched daily, children under two faced a 10 per cent increased risk of having attention problems by the age of seven. **16**. A team of scientists lead by Ian Bond of the Institute of Astronomy in Edinburgh announced the discovery of a planet 17,000 light years away orbiting a dwarf star in the constellation Sagittarius. **18**. A study by researchers from the University of Catania in Italy and the New York Medical College showed high concentrations of curcumin, which is present in tumeric, protected the brain against the progression of neurodegenerative diseases, such as Alzheimer's. **29**. Scientists at the Weizmann Institute in Israel, announced that they had built the world's smallest biological computer measuring just 100 nanometres across.

MAY 2004

3. Japanese car company Honda unveiled its new eco-friendly concept-car: the FCX car, which runs entirely on water-generated hydrogen gas and is completely soundless; the car looked like an ordinary car and had a top speed of 100mph. **7**. A report by Dutch scientist Jan Andries van Franeker concluded that the deaths of hundreds of seabirds on beaches along the North Norfolk coast in February were due to food shortages several months earlier; the bodies of up to 250 seabirds had been found daily mainly between Holkham and Cromer. **20**. A government-funded study published in the *Journal of Pathology* predicted that 3,800 people might be infected with vCJD. Pathologists found three cases of the prion protein responsible for vCJD in 12,500 specimens of tonsils and appendices and concluded that if this proportion was repeated throughout the country, about 3,800 people would be carrying the infective agent. **27**. It was reported in *The Times*, that a golden eagle had been successfully bred from frozen sperm via artificial insemination; the technique could be used to safeguard rare birds of prey.

JUNE 2004

1. Figures presented to Parliament by the Health Protection Agency indicated that the amount of teenagers with sexually transmitted diseases had increased. Cases of gonorrhoea in boys aged 13 to 19 more than tripled between 1995 and 2002, while cases in girls increased at almost the same rate. **8**. Between 6.19 a.m. and 12.23 p.m. the planet Venus could be seen moving across the face of the sun; the first visible 'transit' made by the planet since 6 December 1882. **9**. A well-preserved embryo of a pterosaur, dating back 121 million years, was discovered in a fossilised egg in north-eastern China. **11**. The first close-up pictures of Phoebe, one of Saturn's moons, were taken by the *Cassini* spacecraft when it flew within 2,000 km (1,240 miles) of the satellite. **18**. The first pictures of a comet taken by the *Stardust* probe, which passed within 149 miles of the nucleus of comet *Wild 2* on 2 January 2004, were published in the journal *Science*; the images showed the comet to be a rounded chunk of rock and ice, unexpectedly covered with craters, flat-topped hills and canyons. **21**. *SpaceShipOne* became the world's first manned vehicle to free itself from the Earth's gravitational pull and return to Earth immediately after it climbed to 340,000ft on gained momentum, before being steered back to Earth by 62-year old test pilot, Michael Mevill. **28**. The Government designated the New Forest as a National Park, covering an area of 220 sq. miles (571 sq. km) and with an estimated population of 38,000 it became England's first new National Park for almost half a century. **30**. It was reported in *The Times* that a 32-year old woman was 24-weeks pregnant after successfully undergoing a procedure to re-implant ovarian tissue removed and frozen prior to chemotherapy treatment for cancer which had rendered her infertile.

JULY 2004

1. The *Cassini* space probe successfully entered into a four-year orbit of Saturn. **12**. Six young red kites were freed in Tyneside as part of the £1 million Northern Kites project, led by the RSPB, to bring rare birds of prey into an urban environment. **19**. Following encouraging results from an initial clinical trial in Australia, a vaccine to treat melanoma was to be tested in Britain after the US Cancer Research Institute awarded a grant of $600,000 (£320,000) for trials to be carried out in Australia, New Zealand and Britain. **21**. At the International Conference on General Relativity and Gravitation held in Dublin Professor Stephen Hawking presented new calculations that suggest black holes are able to cast out their contents. Figures released by the Department of Health showed that abortions in England and Wales increased by 3.2 per cent in 2003 compared to 2002 figures; there were 181,600 terminations of which the majority (87 per cent) were carried out before 13 weeks. **27**. Figures released by the Health Protection Agency showed that cases of chlamydia rose by nine per cent between 2002 and 2003 while syphilis showed a 28 per cent increase, overall sexually transmitted infections rose by four per cent.

AUGUST 2004

11. The Human Fertilisation and Embryology Authority (HFEA) granted a one-year licence to a team of scientists at the University of Newcastle upon Tyne to enable them to clone human embryos for medical research into the use of embryonic stem cells for the treatment of disease. **19**. A team of scientists from the Royal Botanic Gardens at Kew and the Earthwatch Institute in Oxford published the findings of their 10-year project to catalogue and classify plant species in the forests of Cameroon. The scientists said the study had identified as many as 150 new species of which 50 had been independently scrutinised. The Government announced that an inquiry would be conducted by the Office for National Statistics in conjunction with the confidential inquiry into maternal and child health to establish why the number of stillbirths had risen for two years running after decades of decline. **26.** *The Lancet* reported that doctors at a hospital in Germany had successfully created a new jaw bone for a man – during a unique procedure. A titanium mesh was constructed from a mould of the patient's jaw and filled with bone minerals, protein and patient bone marrow which was then implanted under the patient's shoulder blade and left to grow for seven weeks.

SPORT

SEPTEMBER 2003

4. The International Skating Union (ISU) introduced a new scoring system at the annual Nebelhorn International in Oberstdorf, Germany; the new system used anonymous judging and each element of a skater's programme was scored against a base rate of difficulty. **6**. In football, England secured a 2–1 victory over Macedonia in the Euro 2004 qualifying tie, with Wayne Rooney becoming the youngest player, at 17 years and 317 days, to score a goal for England during a senior match. In tennis, Justine Henin-Hardenne reached the final of the US Open after defeating Jennifer Capriati, 4–6, 7–5, 7–6, in a gruelling three-hour match after which Henin-Hardenne was placed on a drip to recover. **8**. In cricket, England had a nine-wicket victory over South Africa at the Oval; the game was the last Test match for Alec Stewart who retired from Test cricket after the game. **9**. In athletics, Kelli White (US) was stripped of her 100 m and 200 m gold medals and $120,000 in prize-money after the International Association of Athletics Federations (IAAF) rejected her evidence in defence of a failed drugs test at the World Championships in August. **14**. Yetunde Price, the sister and personal assistant of tennis stars Venus and Serena Williams, was shot dead whilst driving through the suburb of Compton in Los Angeles. **18**. In cricket, Sussex won the county championships for the first time since the formal organisation of the championship by a governing body in 1890. **26**. Keith Mills, who devised the Air Miles programme and the Nectar loyalty card, was appointed chief executive of London's bid to host the 2012 Olympic Games. **28**. Paul Tergat (Kenya) set a new world record for the marathon when he won the Berlin Marathon in 2 hr 4 min 55 sec, taking 43 seconds off the previous record set by Khalid Khannouchi (USA) at the London Marathon in April 2002.

OCTOBER 2003

4. In horseracing, *Chivalry*, ridden by George Duffield and owned by Sir Mark Prescott, became the first horse this century to win the Tote Cambridgeshire without a previous run during the season. Paula Radcliffe won the World Half-Marathon at Vilamoura in Portugal after completing the 13.1-mile race in 1hr 7 min 35 sec; 51 seconds outside South African Elana Meyer's world best. **5**. In golf, Tiger Woods regained his position as top of the standings in the American Express World Championship after winning the final round in Atlanta, USA. **7**. In athletics, heptathlon champion Denise Lewis confirmed that she had dropped her controversial coach Dr Ekkart Arbeit, who was the head athletics coach for East Germany during the 1970s and 80s when the state practised systematic doping of its athletes. She reinstated her former coach Charles van Commence. **10**. The Rugby Union World Cup opened in Sydney, Australia. **11**. In football, England secured a place in the Euro 2004 finals in Portugal after winning a single point for a nil-nil draw with Turkey. **12**. England beat Georgia in their opening match in the Rugby World Cup. In motor racing, Michael Schumacher won the Formula One Driver's World Championship for a record-breaking sixth time, despite finishing eighth in the Japanese Grand Prix in Suzuka. **15**. Arsenal football club and five of its players pleaded guilty to Football Association misconduct charges relating to a game played against Manchester United on 21 September 2003. **19**. In golf, Ernie Els (Australia) won the World Matchplay Championship title for the fifth time at Wentworth. **20**. In football, Sir Alex Ferguson, the manager of Manchester United, received a touchline ban for two matches and a £10,000 fine from the Football Association after he was found guilty of two charges of improper conduct and insulting or abusing match officials. **22**. British sprinter Dwain Chambers was suspended pending a hearing by UK Athletics after it was alleged that he had tested positive for the banned steroid THG. In the Rugby Union World Cup in Australia, Scottish player Martin Leslie was banned from playing for 12 weeks after being found guilty of kneeing an opponent in the head during Scotland's game against the USA two days previously. **23**. In the Rugby Union World Cup England accidentally sent on Dan Luger as a substitute back for the injured Mike Tindall who had not left the field, resulting in 16 men being present for about 30 seconds during their 35–22 victory over Samoa. **30**. After a Rugby World Cup disciplinary hearing in Sydney the England team were fined £10,000 and received a two-match touchline ban for fitness coach Dave Reddin, who was found responsible for illegally substituting Dan Luger, causing England to play with 16 men in their match against Samoa on 23 October.

NOVEMBER 2003

2. Sir Ranulph Fiennes and Mike Stroud became the first men to run seven marathons in seven days when they both finished the New York Marathon in 5 hr 25 min. In tennis, Tim Henman won the Masters Series, placing him 14th in the Association of Tennis Professionals' world rankings. **3**. Frank Bruno made his first public appearance since being released from hospital after being sectioned under the Mental Health Act on 22 September, when he led out the 10-strong England amateur boxing team for their match against the United States at York Hall in Bethnal Green, London. **8**. The 37-time champion jockey Pat Eddery retired after 37 years race-riding. **9**. The Norwegian rally driver Peter Solberg, driving a Subaru, won the World Rally Championship after taking first place in the final placings for the Wales Rally. **11**. Keith Mills, the chief executive officer for London's 2012 bid to host the Olympic Games announced that the games would be centred on a 500-acre area near Stratford in east London. **22**. England beat Australia 20–17 in the Rugby Union World Cup final in Sydney, with fly-half Jonny Wilkinson winning the match with a drop goal in the last minute of extra time.

DECEMBER 2003

8. The England rugby team celebrated its World Cup win with a victory parade in central London attended by approximately three quarters of a million people. The team attended a private reception with the Queen at Buckingham Palace in the afternoon. **14**. England rugby fly-half, Jonny Wilkinson, won the 50th BBC Sports Personality of the Year, second place went to the England rugby captain, Martin Johnson and the 2002 winner, runner Paula Radcliffe, took third place. Rower Sir Steve Redgrave won the BBC Golden Personality award. Twenty-five-year-old Georgina Harland secured her first gold medal in a world cup final, after winning the Pentathlon world cup final in Athens. **16**. The Premiership football league agreed a deal with competition regulators in Brussels which would allow Premiership football to be screened live on terrestrial television for the first time in 10 years ending BSkyB's exclusivity deal. **19**. The Manchester United and England footballer Rio Ferdinand was given an eight-month suspension and fined £50,000 by the Football Association for failing to attend a routine drugs test on 23 September 2003. **26**. In horse racing, Jim Culloty won the Boxing Day King George VI Chase at Kempton Park on *Edredon Bleu* against odds of 25–1. **31**. In the New Year's Honours list the England Rugby coach Clive Woodward was awarded a knighthood with the rest of the team awarded MBEs; the captain, Martin Johnson, was promoted from OBE to CBE and Jonny Wilkinson, the record point-scoring fly-half, was awarded an OBE in addition to his MBE received on 10 December. The former boxer, Michael Watson, was also recognised with an MBE.

JANUARY 2004

1. Paula Radcliffe's times on road for the 10km, 20km and the London marathon in April 2003 were officially recognised as world records by the International Association of Athletics Federations. **2**. England cricketer Robert Croft announced his retirement from international cricket. **6**. The final Test match of the series between Australia and India was drawn, with Steve Waugh, Australia's captain, who retired from test cricket after the game, scoring 80 of the 357 runs of Australia's second innings. **8**. British tennis player Greg Rusedski confirmed that a sample he had provided for the Association of Tennis Professionals (ATP) had tested positive for a low concentration of nandrolone, a banned steroid. **11**. Fiona Thornewill, a 37-year-old recruitment consultant from Nottingham, completed the fastest unaided trek to the South Pole, becoming the first British woman to complete the journey alone. **13**. Former England goalkeeper David Seaman announced his retirement from football after 22 years in the game and stated that he would be leaving Manchester City immediately rather than at the end of the season due to a shoulder injury. **16**. London presented its bid to hold the 2012 Olympic Games. **17**. The England rugby captain, Martin Johnson, announced his retirement from international rugby with immediate effect; he confirmed that he would continue to play at club level for Leicester. **28**. Leeds United Football Club accepted an immediate payment of £1.5 million from Manchester United Football Club as final settlement on Rio Ferdinand's transfer, instead of £3.25 million in instalments, towards the £5 million needed by 5 p.m. on 30 January to satisfy creditors until the end of the season. **29**. Players at Leeds United Football Club agreed to have payment of 25 per cent of their wages deferred until the end of the season, raising £2.5 million towards a £5 million payment needed to stop the club from going into administration. Simon Murray, a 63-year-old British businessman became the oldest person to walk unaided to the South Pole. **31**. Belgian tennis player Justine Henin-Hardenne won the Australian Open title, her third Grand Slam title in seven months, beating Kim Cljisters 6–3, 4–6, 6–3.

FEBRUARY 2004

1. Swiss tennis player Roger Federer beat unseeded Russian, Marat Safin, in the final of the Australian Open, 7–6, 6–4, 6–2. **6**. Heavyweight boxer, Lennox Lewis, announced his retirement after 14 years in the game. **14**. The Italian former world cycling champion, 34-year-old Marco Pantani, was found dead in his hotel room in Rimini after a heart attack. **16**. The champion jockey, Tony McCoy, fractured his cheekbone in three places after a fall from his mount *Polar Red* in a novice chase at Plumpton. **20**. At the Norwich Union athletics Grand Prix in Birmingham, Kelly Holmes won the 1,000 metres, setting a new British and European record of 2 min 32.96 sec. **22**. In the football Premiership, Liverpool was defeated 1–0 by Portsmouth in their fifth round replay, forfeiting their chance to go through to the FA Cup quarter-finals. **23**. Arsenal Football Club announced that it had secured the funds to build a new £357 million, 60,000-seat stadium at Ashburton Grove. **24**. Sprinter Dwain Chambers was banned from competing for two years after he was found guilty by a UK Athletics disciplinary hearing of failing a drugs test; he tested positive for the banned steroid THG at a training camp in Germany on 1 August 2003 while preparing for the World Championships. **29**. In football, Middlesbrough won the Carling Cup beating Bolton Wanderers 2–1.

MARCH 2004

3. Nine Leicester City footballers on a five-day training break were arrested in Spain following allegations of sexual assault made by three German women; six were later released, three without charge and three on bail, while three were detained. **6**. In the rugby union Six Nations Tournament Ireland beat world champions England, 19–13 at Twickenham, ending England's 22-match winning run at the ground. **8**. Jockey Kieren Fallon received a 21-day suspension from the Jockey Club after being found guilty for failing to ride out for first place at Lingfield Park on 29 February. **10**. The tennis player Greg Rusedski was cleared of deliberately taking the banned stimulant nandrolone after he proved before a tribunal appointed by the Association of Tennis Professionals (ATP), that the drug was contained in supplements supplied by ATP trainers. In badminton, Briton Richard Vaughan, who had recently had a hip operation, produced the best win of his career when he beat the world champion, Xia Xuanze, at the Yonex All-England Open, 15–9, 7–15, 15–10. **12**. Three Leicester City footballers, Keith Gillespie, Frank Sinclair and Paul Dickov, arrested in Spain on 3 March, flew back to Britain on bail after spending seven nights in a Spanish jail on charges of serious sexual assault. **18**. In horse racing, *Best Mate* ridden by Jim Culloty won the Cheltenham Gold Cup for the third consecutive time matching *Arkle's* 1966 record. An appeal by footballer Rio Ferdinand to reduce his eight-month ban for failing to attend a routine drugs test was rejected by the Football Association. **23**. The British adventurer David Hempleman-Adams landed in a field in Colorado, USA, and claimed a new world altitude record of ascending more than eight miles (43,000 ft) in an open basket hot air balloon. **27**. In rugby union, France won a grand slam victory in the six nations championship following their defeat of England 24–21 in Paris. In swimming, the Australian 400-metre world champion, Ian Thorpe, considered an almost certain winner at the 2004 Athens Olympics, ruled himself out of the race under the international one-start rule after a false start at the Australian Olympic trials. **28**. The 150th University Boat Race was won by Cambridge: Oxford took an early lead in the race but a clash of oars with Cambridge which momentarily unseated their bow man allowed Cambridge to establish their lead. **29**. Sven-Goran Eriksson, the England Football coach, agreed a two-year contract extension until 2008 with the Football Association.

APRIL 2004

3. In horse racing, *Amberleigh House* with odds of 16–1, ridden by Graham Lee, won the Grand National making it the fourth time trainer Ginger McCain had won the event. **5**. American Steve Fossett and his multinational 12-man crew circumnavigated the globe in 58 days 9 hr 32 min 45 sec becoming the first sailors to complete the feat in less than 60 days. **11**. In golf, Phil Mickelson won the Masters championship by one stroke from Ernie Els. **12**. Brian Lara made cricketing history during the Fourth West Indies Test against England when he declared at 400 runs not out, reclaiming the record from Matthew Hayden (Australia) for the highest amount of runs scored in a test game. **14**. In cricket, England won the final match in Antigua in the four-match Test series against the West Indies, winning the series 3–0. **18**. In the London

Marathon, Tracey Morris, a 36-year optician from Leeds, who had never completed a marathon before, qualified for the Athens Olympics after completing the course in 2 hr 33 min 52 sec, coming 10th in the London women's race and the first British woman to finish. **21**. Ron Atkinson, the former Manchester United manager, sports broadcaster and newspaper columnist, resigned from ITV after a racist remark made following the European Cup semi-final between Chelsea and Monaco, was broadcast in parts of the Middle East from ITV footage not aired in the UK. **25**. In motor racing Jenson Button finished second at the San Marino Grand Prix, after losing his pole position to Michael Schumacher. **27**. Des Wilson resigned from the England and Wales Cricket Board after disagreeing with colleagues over the apolitical line taken by the International Cricket Council to the sport in Zimbabwe.

MAY 2004

2. William Fox-Pitt qualified his horse *Tamarillo* for the Olympic Games in Athens after taking first place at the Badminton Horse Trials. **3**. In snooker, Ronnie O'Sullivan won the £250,000 first prize in the Embassy World Championship at Sheffield's Crucible Theatre after defeating Graeme Dott 18–8. **4**. In Formula One motor racing, 10 team principals voted unanimously in favour of new rules put forward by the FIA, the sport's governing body, to outlaw high-technology cars by the beginning of the 2006 season; the move was expected to save the sport at least £300 million a year. **9**. In motor-racing, Michael Schumacher won the Spanish Grand Prix, his fifth successive victory of the season. **10**. The Zimbabwe Cricket Union (ZCU) terminated the contracts of 15 of its white cricketers following a disciplinary hearing regarding their protests against the political regime in Zimbabwe during the cricket World Cup in 2003. **15**. In football, Arsenal beat Leicester 2–1 completing an entire league season unbeaten. **18**. The International Olympic Committee announced that five cities, London, Madrid, Moscow, New York and Paris, had been short-listed to host the 2012 Olympic Games. **22**. In football, Manchester United won the FA Cup, their 11th FA Cup triumph. **21**. In cricket, Andrew Strauss scored a century in his Test debut at Lord's against New Zealand, becoming one of four batsmen in world cricket to achieve the feat. **25**. In the French Open, Fabrice Santoro defeated Arnaud Clément, 6–4, 6–3, 6–7, 3–6, 16–14, in six hours and 33 minutes, setting a record for the longest tennis match ever played. **26**. In football, Porto beat Monaco 3–0 to win the Champions League. **27**. The former England cricket captain, Nasser Hussein, announced his retirement from Test and first class cricket just three days after scoring a match winning century in the first Test against New Zealand at Lord's.

JUNE 2004

4. In tennis, Tim Henman reached the semi-final of the French Open where he was beaten 3–6, 6–4, 6–0, 7–5 by Argentinean Guilermo Coria. **6**. Guilermo Coria was defeated in the final of the French Open by fellow Argentinean Gaston Gaudio, ranked at number 44 in the world. **10**. The England Cricket Board (ECB) announced that England would go ahead with its one-day series against Zimbabwe in the autumn, despite the indefinite postponement of its Test matches. Failure to fulfil the three limited-overs matches would leave the ECB open to a fine of about £1.1 million and the possibility of suspension from the international game. **12**. In football, Greece beat host nation Portugal 2–1 in the opening game of the Euro 2004 championship. **14**. In England, more than 100 football fans were arrested and eight police forces had to call out reserve officers to curb rioting in towns and cities throughout England following England's defeat by France in the Euro 2004 championship; Portugese police reported no incidents. **16**. Eleven England football fans appeared in court in Albufeira, Portugal, after violent clashes between fans broke-out in the region. **17**. Ten England football fans arrived back in the UK after being voluntarily deported from Portugal following their court appearances on 16 June. In England's second match of the Euro 2004 championship, Wayne Rooney scored two goals for England resulting in a 3–0 win over Switzerland. **20**. Long-distance runner, Paula Radcliffe, returned to the track for the first time in almost two years in the European Cup women's 5,000 metres, winning the race in 14 min 29.11 sec; breaking her own British and Commonwealth record. **21**. England qualified for the quarter-finals of the Euro 2004 championship in Portugal after it beat Croatia 4–2. In tennis, Martina Navratilova, aged 47, beat Colombian, Catalina Castrano, 6–0, 6–1, on the first day of the Wimbledon tournament. **24**. England went out of the Euro 2004 championship defeated in extra time on penalties by the host nation Portugal; final score 2–2 (1–1 after 90 minutes, 6–5 on penalties). **30**. Tim Henman was defeated 7–6, 6–4, 6–2 in his eighth quarter-final of nine Wimbledon championship attempts by Croatian Mario Ancic.

JULY 2004

1. In football, a goal by Traianos Dellas in the first period of extra time secured a 1–0 win by Greece over the Czech Republic in the semi-final of the Euro 2004 Championship and took Greece into the final against the host nation Portugal. **3**. Maria Sharapova (Russia), beat Serena Williams (USA) to win the Wimbledon women's singles final, 6–1, 6–4, to become the second youngest winner of the championship. **4**. Greece won the Euro 2004 Football Championship, its first win in an international competition, beating favourites Portugal 1–0. In tennis, Roger Federer (Switzerland) defeated Andy Roddick (US) in four sets; 4–6, 7–5, 7–6, 6–4, to take his second Wimbledon men's title. **6**. Roads in Central London were closed to allow Formula One cars to race through the streets, an estimated 300,000 people turned out to watch the event and police had to turn away thousands more. The Mayor of London, Ken Livingstone announced a £20 million bid to stage the British Formula One Grand Prix in London in place of Silverstone in Northampton. **14**. St Lucia won the right to hold England's first-round matches in the 2007 Cricket World Cup; the England management team had identified St Lucia as its first choice to host the tournament because of its impressive facilities. **18**. In golf, Todd Hamilton (USA) won the Open Championship at Royal St George's, beating the world no. 2 and pre-tournament favourite, Ernie Els. **25**. Lance Armstrong set a new record when he rode into Paris to claim his sixth Tour de France victory.

AUGUST 2004

1. Mark Palios resigned as chief executive of the Football Association (FA) following allegations that he had a relationship with FA secretary Faria Alam and then had tried to cover-up the affair. In golf, Karen Stupples won her first major championship at the Weetabix Women's British Open at Sunningdale. **3**. Manchester United midfielder Paul Scholes announced his retirement from international football; he won 66 caps for England and scored 14 goals. **7**. The Irish Sports Council confirmed that distance runner, Cathal Lombard, who had qualified for the men's 5,000m and 10,000m at the Athens Olympics, had tested positive for the banned substance EPO. **8**. Six days away from completing a transatlantic crossing by rowing boat, four British oarsmen had to abandon ship when a rogue wave split their boat in half; the crew were rescued six hours later from their life-raft by a Danish cargo ship. The former French rugby captain, Marc Cécillon, was taken into custody after allegedly shooting his wife dead at a party attended by about 60 people at St Savin in central France. **14**. On the first day of the Olympic Games Britain's first medal was won by Leon Taylor and Peter Waterfield who took silver in the 10m synchronised diving. **18**. At the Olympics Great Britain's Helen Reeves won bronze in the canoeing, Alison Williamson became the first woman archer to win a medal since 1908, taking bronze and the Great Britain Equestrian team won a bronze medal in the three-day event. **19**. Great Britain won its first gold medal in the Olympic Games for sailing; Shirley Robertson's team won the title in the Yngling keelboat class. **20**. Chris Hoy secured Great Britain's second Olympic gold medal in the 1km cycling time trial. **21**. At the Olympics, Great Britain won four gold medals in eight hours; Matthew Pinsent's team took the rowing, Ben Ainslie Finn class sailing, Bradley Wiggins the 4,000 m cycling pursuit and Leslie Law in the individual equestrian competition after an appeal committee upheld penalties against Germany's Bettina Hoy. **22**. Runner Paula Radcliffe, Britain's favourite for a gold medal, failed to complete the Women's Olympic marathon after collapsing at 36 km. **23**. Kelly Holmes won the Olympic women's 800 m gold medal by five hundredths of a second, beating defending champion Maria Mutola. **25**. Amir Khan, aged 17, guaranteed himself and Britain a bronze medal in the Olympic lightweight boxing division after reaching the semi-finals in Athens. **27**. For the second time at the Olympic Games, runner Paula Radcliffe dropped out of a race when she failed to complete the 10,000 metres. **28**. Kelly Holmes secured her second Olympic Gold medal for Great Britain in the 1500 metres and became the third woman in Olympic history to win gold in both events. **29**. Britain's Amir Khan won Olympic Boxing silver after losing 30–22 to Cuban Mario Kindelan in the lightweight final on the final day of the 2004 Olympic Games in Athens.

INTERNATIONAL EVENTS

AFRICA

SEPTEMBER 2003

1. In Kenya, an estimated 300 tourists were evacuated from four blazing hotels in Mombasa. **2**. 243 Moroccan soldiers captured by the Polisario Front in the mid-1970s, were released. Zimbabwe's opposition Movement for Democratic Change (MDC) won a victory in local elections. **13**. At least 18 Somali asylum seekers drowned and 27 were missing after they were forced from their ship when it arrived off the coast of Yemen. **18**. The president of Guinea Bissau, Kumba Yala, resigned from his position. **26**. In Morocco, twin sisters aged 14 appeared in court charged with planning attacks against the king and royal family and of plotting to blow up parliament and a supermarket. **27**. In Côte d'Ivoire, at least 23 people were shot dead during a raid on a bank in the rebel stronghold of Bouake. It was unclear as to whether the dead were civilians or soldiers. It was announced that Algerian armed forces had killed 150 Islamic rebels during a two-week crackdown on the GSPC which is blamed for the kidnap of western tourists.

OCTOBER 2003

7. The United Nations announced that its peacekeeping troops in the north-eastern region of the Congo had uncovered a mass grave containing the bodies of 65 people, including 40 children. The victims were all from the Hema tribe and the UN believed that the rival Lendu tribe were behind the attack. A bush fire, believed to have been started by poachers, destroyed three quarters of Zimbabwe's Matopos National Park. **8**. Riot police arrested 40 trade unionists, including Lovemore Matombo, the president of the Zimbabwe Congress of Trade Unions, for demonstrating against high taxation and human rights abuses under President Robert Mugabe. **14**. South Africa's Constitutional Court passed a landmark judgement to restore ownership of ancestral lands and award compensation to the Richtersveld people, who were forcibly removed from their land by British colonial authorities; the diamond-rich territory is worth almost £1 billion.

NOVEMBER 2003

8. Maaoya Sid'Ahmed Ould Taya was re-elected president of Mauritania. **9**. The Sudanese army, also known as the Sudan Liberation Movement, announced that it had killed more than 60 people in attacks in the Darfur region of the country. **10**. Zimbabwe's first black president, Canaan Banana, died aged 67 after a long illness; he ruled the country between 1980 and 1987. **12**. Eugene Terre'Blanche, the leader of the South African white supremacist organisation, the Afrikaner Resistance Movement, was convicted of political crimes after he admitted ordering five bombings in the run-up to the first post-apartheid elections. **17**. Thirteen people were killed when a cargo plane exploded in the air near the city of Wau in southern Sudan. **25**. President Obasanjo of Nigeria announced that Zimbabwe's President Mugabe would not be allowed to attend the Commonwealth summit in Nigeria between 5–8 December. **27**. In the Congo, 163 people drowned after the *Dieu Merci* capsized during a storm on Lake Mai-Ndombe.

DECEMBER 2003

4. Interpol issued an international arrest warrant for the former Liberian President, Charles Taylor, on charges related to his support in the 1990s for the Sierra Leone rebels. **7**. President Mugabe of Zimbabwe announced that the country had unilaterally withdrawn from the Commonwealth after Commonwealth officials requested that Mr Mugabe's Zanu (PF) Party hold talks with the opposition Movement for Democratic Change Party. In Cairo, a western Sudanese rebel group claimed they had killed about 700 government troops in the Darfur region of the country. **16**. In Mogadishu, Somalia, around 34 people were killed and 80 wounded in clashes between the rival Dir and Marehan clans. **19**. Colonel Gaddafi signed an agreement that Libya would disclose and dismantle all weapons of mass destruction. **25**. Official results were published showing that President Conte of Guinea won 95.63 per cent of the vote and was elected for a third term following presidential elections on 21 December. In Benin, at least 82 people died when a passenger aircraft clipped a building after take-off and crashed into the sea. **28**. The former president of Mauritania, Mohamed Khouna Ould Haidallah, was given a five-year suspended jail sentence and fined £1,250 for plotting a coup to overthrow President Maaoya Sid'Ahmed Ould Taya during the elections.

JANUARY 2004

3. A Boeing 737, which had just taken off from the resort of Sharm el-Sheikh in Egypt, crashed into the Red Sea a few minutes after take-off, killing all 148 passengers and crew. **9**. Libya agreed to pay £1 million to each of the families of the people who died in 1989 when a bomb planted on a French airliner killed 170 people. **22**. Jean de Dieu Kamuhanda, a minister of the Rwandan Government during the 1994 ethnic genocide, was sentenced to life imprisonment by a UN court in Tanzania after he was found guilty of charges of crimes against humanity. **30**. South Africa's President Thabo Mbeki approved the new Land Rights Amendments Act, which allows the government to seize the land of white farmers from which black people were forcibly evicted by the former colonial and apartheid authorities. **31**. A ferry was destroyed by fire and 200 people were feared dead 280 miles from Kinshasa on the Congo River.

FEBRUARY 2004

3. Forty people drowned in western Uganda after a boat capsized on Lake Albert because of bad weather and overcrowding. **22**. In Uganda, the Lord's Resistance Army (LRA) from southern Sudan killed 192 people at a camp for displaced civilians in Ogur. **23**. Military officials from the Democratic Republic of Congo announced that around 100 civilians had been killed since January by peasant Mai Mai fighters. **24**. An earthquake killed around 600 people and injured around 300 more when it hit near the Moroccan city of al-Hoceima. **25**. Religious violence broke out in the town of Yelwa in central Nigeria and 48 Christians were killed by Muslims.

MARCH 2004

5. In Rwanda, nine people were sentenced to death and one to life in jail for the murder of Emile Ntahimana, who was killed to prevent him from giving evidence against suspects of the 1994 genocide. **6**. The White House announced that Libya had sent all its remaining nuclear arms equipment to the USA. **8**. Eighteen people died and around 50,000 were made homeless after cyclone Gafilo struck Madagascar. **21**. In Sudan, an Arab militia group executed 49 residents of the town of Korma in the Darfur region; 100 people died in a separate incident when rebels from the Sudan Liberation Movement fought with militia groups known as Janjaweed fighters. The Ugandan army announced that it had killed 52 Lord's Resistance Army rebels who had been killing and torturing civilians in northern Uganda. **25**. Tony Blair was the first British Prime Minister since Winston Churchill to visit Libya when he met Colonel Muammar Gaddafi in Tripoli to discuss the agreement to exchange intelligence information on terrorism. **28**. It was announced that more than 300 people had died in clashes between protesters and security forces during a rally against President Gbagbo in Cote d'Ivorie. Government forces defeated a coup by fighters loyal to Mobutu Sese Seko, against President Kabila of the Democratic Republic of Congo in Kinshasa, where fighting broke out at military bases and television headquarters.

APRIL 2004

8. It was reported that 63 people had died of starvation in one month in Zimbabwe's second largest city, Bulawayo. A cease-fire agreement was signed between representatives of the Sudanese government and rebel fighters from the western Darfur region of the country, allowing humanitarian agencies 45 days to reach a peace agreement. **9**. In Algeria, President Abdelaziz Bouteflika received 83 per cent of the vote during national elections and was given a second five-year term in office. **14**. In Zanzibar, parliament unanimously passed a bill to outlaw homosexuality, with jail terms of up to 25 years being passed on anyone involved in a gay male relationship. **27**. In South Africa, President Thabo Mbeki was sworn in for a second five-year term after his African National Congress party won its biggest ever landslide. The former prime minister of Guinea, Sidya Touré, was arrested for allegedly plotting to kill President Conté and overthrow the country's parliament. **30**. It was reported that around 120 Muslims and Christians had died in fighting in six farming villages in Nigeria.

MAY 2004

6. Kenya's police commissioner removed 57 senior officers from their positions following accusations of crime and corruption in the force; it was the largest reform of the police force since Kenya gained independence in 1963. **13**. In the northern Nigerian city of Kano, around 600 people were killed in riots between Christians and Muslims. **18**. The Ugandan army reported that its helicopter gunships had killed 54 members of the rebel Lord's Resistance Army.

JUNE 2004

1. At least 20 people were killed and 50 others wounded as clan militias fought for control of Beledhawo, a town on the border between Somalia and Kenya. **11**. In the Democratic Republic of Congo, Major Eric Lenge led a failed coup to overthrow President Kabila. **13**. The newly elected president of Malawi, Bingu wa Mutharika, appointed 20 ministers to his Cabinet, including members of opposition parties. **17**. At the United Nations International Criminal Tribunal for Rwanda in Tanzania, Sylvestre Gacumbitsi, a former district mayor in Rwanda, was sentenced to 30 years in jail for ordering the slaughter of 20,000 Tutsis during the 1994 Rwandan genocide.

JULY 2004

2. The Zimbabwean opposition leader, Morgan Tsvangirai, was attacked by supporters of President Robert Mugabe while he was giving a speech north of Harare. **18**. It was reported that around 1 million people had been displaced and at least 30,000 killed in the Darfur region of Sudan – pro-government Arab militias were being accused of ethnic cleansing and genocide in the region. **28**. The African Union announced that it planned to send peacekeeping troops into the Darfur region of Sudan.

AUGUST 2004

2. Sudan refused to co-operate with the UN's 30-day deadline for disarming the Janjaweed militia and announced that it would fight any foreign forces entering the country. **6**. Sudan's foreign minister Mustapha Osman Ismail announced that the country had accepted the United Nations resolution on Darfur to curb gunmen from the Janjaweed militia within 30 days. **8**. South Africa's National Party leader Marthinus van Schalkwyk announced that he would apply to join the African National Congress and that all other party members should do the same. **10**. Around 480 people in the Darfur refugee camps in Sudan were reported to have contracted hepatitis E. **14**. It was reported that around 159 Tutsi men, women and children were murdered during a raid on Gatumba refugee camp in Burundi – the country's Hutu rebel National Liberation Forces claimed responsibility. **15**. In Sudan, 150 Rwandans arrived as part of the African Union's mission to keep the peace in the Darfur region. **25**. Sir Mark Thatcher, the son of former prime minister Margaret Thatcher, was arrested at his home in Cape Town, South Africa, on suspicion of helping to fund a coup attempt in the state of Equatorial Guinea. **30**. In Somalia, the last 258 members of a new national assembly were sworn in.

THE AMERICAS

SEPTEMBER 2003

5. Hurricane Fabian battered Bermuda in the worst storm to hit the country in 50 years. **7**. A tape aired on Arabic television stated that there would be attacks on the US or US interests abroad on a more destructive scale than those of 11 September 2001. **11**. The names of people that died in the World Trade Centre on 11 September 2001 were read out by children who had lost a parent in the attacks, during a ceremony held at Ground Zero in Manhattan, New York. **14**. In Colombia, eight foreign tourists were kidnapped by left-wing rebels in a mountainous region in the north of the country. **17**. In Seattle, residents voted against a 10 per cent rise in tax on coffee. The tax was to be used to fund better child day-care for poor families. **21**. Seven people were killed near the Grand Canyon after their helicopter crashed. **24**. Matthew Scott, a Briton kidnapped in Colombia by anti-government forces, escaped and was taken to safety after wandering through rain forest for 12 days. Seven hostages remained in captivity.

OCTOBER 2003

2. A court in Alexandria, Virginia, ruled that Zacarias Moussaoui, the only person charged with being involved in the terrorist attacks of 11 September 2001, may not be executed. **8**. Arnold Schwarzenegger was elected governor of California after he received 48 per cent of the vote; the previous governor, Gray Davis received 45 per cent of the vote. The White House announced that it would be imposing economic and diplomatic sanctions on Syria after President George Bush said that the country was 'on the wrong side in the war on terrorism'. **9**. The US under-secretary of state, John Bolton, extended the members of America's 'axis of evil' to include Syria, Libya and Cuba, stating that all three countries were intent on developing weapons of mass destruction and were a threat to America and its allies. **12**. Twelve people were killed in Bolivia during riots in El Alto over the export of natural gas to Chile. **15**. Ten people were killed and dozens injured after a ferry smashed into the pier at Staten Island harbour in New York as it was docking; the boat's pilot had to undergo surgery after he fled to his home immediately after the crash and slit his wrists. **17**. The President of Bolivia, Sanches de Lozada, agreed to resign after weeks of protests over plans to sell natural gas to the US led to violence in La Paz and more than 80 people died in riots; Vice-President Mesa was sworn in as the new president. **19**. Foreign ministers at the Asia-Pacific Economic Co-operation forum meeting in Bangkok agreed to President Bush's plea to impose stricter controls on portable surface-to-air missiles, which are hampering the coalition reconstruction efforts in Iraq. **21**. The United States senate voted 64 to 34 in favour of banning a form of late-term abortion. **26**. Fires in southern California destroyed at least 650 homes and killed 11 people after powerful winds stoked a string of blazes across the state. **28**. Iyman Faris was jailed for 20 years at a court in Virginia for planning terrorist acts, including a plot to cut through cables supporting the Brooklyn Bridge.

NOVEMBER 2003

5. Gary Ridgway became America's most prolific serial killer after he pleaded guilty to the murders of 48 women between 1982 and 1998; he had originally pleaded not guilty to seven counts of murder but changed his plea after making a deal with prosecutors to escape the death penalty in return for guiding investigators to the remains of other victims. **12**. Five of Colombia's top policemen, including Teodoro Campo, the chief of Colombia's national police, lost their jobs after it was found that they had used government money to buy watches, works of art and other luxuries over a period of three years. **16**. The democrat Kathleen Babineaux Blanco was elected as the governor of Louisiana and became the first female governor of the state after she beat her Republican opponent Bobby Jindal. **25**. In Colombia, 850 members of the paramilitary group Bloque Cacique Nutibara surrendered their weapons to Luis Carlos Restrepo, the government's peace commissioner.

DECEMBER 2003

2. President Chavez of Venezuela rejected the results of a four-day petition by opposition leaders, which called for a recall referendum to remove him from power. **7**. In Managua, the former Nicaraguan President, Arnoldo Aleman, was jailed for 20 years after being found guilty of money-laundering, fraud, embezzlement and electoral crimes. **12**. Canadian Prime Minister Jean Chretien stepped down from his post after 10 years; the former finance minister Paul Martin was appointed to take over. **23**. In Virginia, Lee Malvo, 18, the accomplice of the 'Washington Sniper' John Muhammad, was sentenced to life imprisonment after being convicted of one charge of terrorism, one of murdering two people and one firearm charge. **29**. Oscar Berger of the Grand National Alliance won Guatemala's presidential elections with 54.1 per cent of the vote.

JANUARY 2004

4. In Quito, Ecuador, the senior commander in the Revolutionary Armed Forces of Colombia, Ricardo Palmera, was captured and charged with 59 crimes including kidnapping and murder. **12**. In Haiti, parliament was forced to close down after the mandate of MPs expired and government failed to hold new elections; President Jean-Bertrand Aristide refused calls to stand down.

FEBRUARY 2004

9. In Haiti, 40 people were killed as armed rebels belonging to the Artibonite Resistance Front took over nine towns in an attempt to drive out President Aristide. **19**. Argentina was brought to a standstill by more than 50,000 protesters who took to the country's main highways to demand the repudiation of the country's foreign debt after its economy collapsed in December 2001. The Canadian government agreed to pay £20 million compensation to 2,000 former soldiers exposed to mustard gas and other chemical weapons during the Second World War. **22**. In Haiti, more than 200 anti-government rebels captured the second largest city in the country, Cap-Haitien. Forty-two people died in north-eastern Brazil when the bus they were on veered off the road and plunged into a reservoir. **24**. The United States charged two men held at its Guantanamo Bay prison camp with conspiracy to commit war crimes; Ali Hamza Ahmed Sulayman al-Bahlul and Ibrahim Ahmed Mahmoud al-Qosi were the first men from the camp to be formally charged and were expected to be the first prisoners to face the special military tribunals created by President Bush. **26**. The United States lifted its ban on Americans travelling to Libya after Tripoli reaffirmed its guilt over the Lockerbie bombing. **29**. In Haiti, President Aristide fled the country after he resigned following violent civil unrest in the country; Louis Jodel Chamblain and his Rebel Army took control of most cities and towns in the country and President Bush announced that 500 US Marines were being sent to keep the peace.

MARCH 2004

2. Violent protests erupted across cities in Venezuela after the National Electoral Council announced that President Chavez would not be forced to submit to a referendum over his rule. **4**. Haiti's former President, Jean-Bertrand Aristide, was offered permanent asylum by the Central African Republic. **9**. The Washington sniper, John Allen Muhammad, was sentenced to death for the killing of Dean Harold Meyers on 9 October 2002. **10**. Lee Boyd Malvo, the teenager involved in the Washington sniper shootings, was sentenced to life imprisonment in court in Chesapeake, Virginia. **12**. Chile's parliament voted in favour of legalising divorce, making it the last country in the Western world to do so. **14**. Police in California announced that they had discovered nine dead bodies, eight of them children aged between 1 and 17, after searching the home of 57-year-old Marcus Wesson, who was believed to have fathered two of the victims with another of his daughters. **17**. Haiti's new government was sworn in by President Boniface Alexandre at Haiti's National Palace; Gerard Latortue was appointed Prime Minister. **24**. Baldwin Spencer became the new Prime Minister of Antigua and Barbuda following a landslide victory in elections for his United Progressive Party.

APRIL 2004

6. In Mexico, President Fox declared a state of emergency after flash floods in the town of Piedras Negras killed 31 people and left dozens more missing and without homes. **12**. The Canadian government approved the killing of 350,000 harp seals off the northern coast of Newfoundland after years of reduced quotas lead to an increase in the seal population of over 5 million; the cull was given backing in order to restore the cod population and to provide income to one of Canada's poorest regions.

MAY 2004

3. Martin Torrijos won Panama's first presidential election since the handover of the Panama Canal and the withdrawal of US troops in December 1999. **11**. A film was broadcast on the internet which showed Nick Berg, an American, identifying himself before being executed by militants with links to al-Qa'eda. **17**. Marriages between same-sex couples became legal in the American state of Massachusetts, the only US state to have introduced such legislation. A fire at a jail in San Pedro Sula, Honduras, killed 101 prisoners and injured 27 others. **26**. Terry Nichols was convicted of the murder of 161 people in the Oklahoma City bombing in April 1995 by a court in Oklahoma; he had previously been convicted of involuntary manslaughter and conspiracy in the deaths of eight federal law enforcement officials. Around 579 people were killed and 3,000 more left homeless in Haiti and the Dominican Republic after 10 days of flash floods.

JUNE 2004

1. Inmates at the Benfica Penitentiary in Rio de Janeiro murdered around 50 fellow prisoners following a week-long rebellion demanding increased visiting rights. **3**. The former prime minister of the Ukraine, Pavlo Lazarenko, was convicted by a court in San Francisco of using his position to extort money and launder it through Californian banks. **11**. The state funeral of former US president Ronald Reagan took place in Washington National Cathedral and was attended by Mikhail Gorbachev and Baroness Thatcher amongst others. **13**. Two shanty-town fires in Sao Paulo, Brazil, destroyed around 177 shacks and left 600 people homeless. **15**. In French Polynesia, the pro-independence Oscar Temaru, was elected leader of the island, replacing the conservative Gaston Flosse, who had held the position for 20 years. **29**. In Canada, the Liberals won 134 seats, while the Conservatives won 99 seats in the general election, leaving the Bloc Quebecois Party and the New Democratic Party as the ruling parties in parliament.

JULY 2004

14. The US Senate rejected President George W. Bush's appeal for constitutional amendment to ban same-sex marriage. **22**. The 9/11 Commission published its report into the September 11 attacks after 20 months of investigations. The report criticised both Bill Clinton's and George W. Bush's administrations for failing to combat the threat of terrorism as well as highlighting 10 missed opportunities to detect the September 11 plot, and concluded that there was no 'collaborative link' between Iraq and al-Qa'eda. **23**. The United States Congress declared that the killings in the Darfur region of Sudan were genocide stating that Khartoum's Arab regime was carrying out a genocidal campaign against the black African population; Congress also urged President George W. Bush to send military troops to the region.

AUGUST 2004

1. At least 236 people died and dozens were injured when a fire broke out in a supermarket in the Paraguayan capital of Asuncion. **3**. Lynndie England appeared before a military court in Fort Bragg, North Carolina on charges of abusing Iraqi prisoners in the Abu Ghraib prison in Baghdad – if convicted she faced up to 38 years in prison. **4**. Richard Smith pleaded guilty to manslaughter and to lying about his medical history after the Staten Island ferry he was operating hit a pier and killed 11 people in

October 2003. **12**. California's supreme court voided 4,000 same-sex marriages sanctioned by the mayor of San Francisco after it declared that legislation defined marriage as a union between man and woman. **13**. It was announced that President George W. Bush would order the withdrawal of 170,000 US troops and military staff from Europe and Asia. **14**. President George W. Bush declared a state of emergency in Florida after Hurricane Charley left at least 15 people dead and hundreds more missing and homeless. **16**. In Venezuela, President Hugo Chavez won more than 58 per cent of a ballot in a referendum on his rule. **22**. International observers endorsed the referendum results that gave Venezuelan President Hugo Chavez a victory following allegations that the elections were rigged. **26**. Chile's Supreme Court voted by nine to eight to lift General Augusto Pinochet's immunity from prosecution allowing victims of repression to take him to court. **29**. In New York, more than 120,000 protesters took part in demonstrations against President George W. Bush and his Republican Party who were arriving in the city for the Republican convention.

ASIA

SEPTEMBER 2003

3. In Afghanistan, an alleged al-Qa'eda suspect believed to be responsible for the suicide bombing of a German army bus, was captured in Kabul. **6**. In two incidents in Kashmir, at least six people died after a car bomb exploded at a market in Srinagar. **10**. More than 1,000 Nepalese pro-democracy protesters, including a former prime minister, were arrested in Kathmandu as police broke up a demonstration against the King. **18**. Ali Imron, responsible for the bombings in Bali of October 2002, was sentenced to life imprisonment. **22**. In India, Dara Singh, a Hindu extremist accused of killing an Australian missionary and his two young children in 1999, was sentenced to death by a court in Orissa. **25**. Two huge earthquakes hit northern Japan causing widespread damage and raised fears of tsunami. **27**. Aung San Suu Kyi, the Burmese opposition leader, was returned to house arrest after being discharged from hospital where she had undergone surgery. **29**. The world's oldest man died in southern Japan, aged 114.

OCTOBER 2003

2. Heavy fighting erupted in Afghanistan and Pakistan as Pakistan launched its largest offensive to date against al-Qa'eda near the Afghan border. The last of four main suspects in the Bali nightclub bombings of October 2002, Ali Ghufron, was sentenced to death. North Korea claimed that it had finished reprocessing 8,000 plutonium fuel rods. **7**. North Korea announced that it would bar Japan from any future negotiations on its nuclear programme in a move that threatened to undermine months of work aimed at disarming the country. **9**. In Indonesia, around 54 schoolchildren died when their coach crashed into a lorry in East Java. **12**. Families gathered on Kuta beach in Bali to mark the first anniversary of the terrorist attacks that killed 202 people. **15**. China became the third nation to send a man into space when the *Shenzhou 5* spacecraft lifted off from the Gobi Desert base at 9 a.m. and orbited the Earth 14 times in 21 hours before landing in Inner Mongolia. **17**. The world's tallest building, the Taipei 101 tower, was unveiled in Taiwan. Its full height is 1,671 ft (509 metres). **18**. Three people were jailed for 10 years in Karachi for carrying out an assassination attempt on President Pervez Musharraf. **22**. India announced that it would reverse its Kashmir policy and hold talks with the separatists for the first time in 13 years. **29**. Tomomasa Nakagawa, a senior member of the Aum Shinrikyo cult, was sentenced to death for his part in the murder of 24 people. **30**. Javed Hashmi, the leader of the Alliance for the Restoration of Democracy in Pakistan, was arrested on a charge of treason after he criticised the Pakistani military for failing to restore democracy. 'Tohir', one of the men wanted for the Bali bombing, was arrested by police near Jakarta in Cirebon as he was preparing to carry out another two suicide bombings. Prime Minister Datuk Seri Dr Mahathir Mohamad of Malaysia retired after 22 years in the post.

NOVEMBER 2003

3. A flash flood in Bukit Lawang, northern Sumatra, killed 71 people and 98 others were missing, feared dead. **5**. Sri Lankan President Chandrika Kumaratunga imposed a state of emergency after she suspended parliament and sacked the defence, interior and information ministers from the cabinet. **8**. In Myanmar, the pro-democracy campaigner Aung San Suu Kyi was released from house arrest but refused to accept liberty until 35 of her colleagues were released. **9**. In Japan, the governing coalition party, the Democratic Party of Japan, won the most votes in the general election and Junichiro Koizumi was re-elected Prime Minister. **14**. Norway pulled out of efforts to revive peace talks in Sri Lanka and said they would not be involved until the Sri Lankan Prime Minister and President settled their political differences. A gas explosion in a mine in Jiangxi province in eastern China killed 48 miners, bringing the death toll in Chinese mines up to 4,000 for the year. **23**. Zafarullah Khan Jamali, the Prime Minister of Pakistan, announced a cease-fire with India on the Line of Control, which separates the Himalayan region of Kashmir. **27**. In Taiwan, Parliament approved legislation to allow referendums to be held on constitutional change.

DECEMBER 2003

4. India's ruling party, the Bharatiya Janata Party, won over the Hindi states of Madhya Pradesh, Rajasthan and Chattisgarh from the Congress Party in state legislative elections. **9**. Japanese Prime Minister Junichiro Koizumi announced that 1,000 Japanese troops would be dispatched to Iraq making it the first military deployment since the Second World War. **14**. President Pervez Musharraf of Pakistan escaped an assassination attempt after a bomb exploded under a bridge over which his car had just passed. **25**. It was reported that 190 people had died in a natural gas explosion in south-western China on 23 December. President Pervez Musharraf of Pakistan survived a second assassination attempt after two trucks packed with explosives drove into the President's motorcade in Rawalpindi. **29**. In Pakistan, the Lower House approved constitutional changes to give the president the power to disband parliament and dismiss the prime minister.

JANUARY 2004

6. Sixteen people were killed in Afghanistan when two bombs exploded in the city of Kandahar near an army barracks. **14**. The World Health Organisation announced that avian flu could become deadlier than SARS after three people died from it in Vietnam and a further five possible cases were discovered. **22**. The Indian Deputy

Prime Minister, Lal Krishna Advani, and the Kashmiri separatist coalition, the All Party Hurriyat Conference, agreed that all violence in Kashmir should end and pledged to meet in March to agree terms. **25**. Indonesia reported cases of avian flu, making it the seventh country in Asia to have been infected; other countries that had confirmed the existence of avian flu included Thailand, Vietnam, Cambodia, Taiwan, South Korea and Japan. **26**. Afghanistan's new constitution became law, making it a democratic Islamic state with a two-chamber parliament. **27**. Indian Prime Minister Atal Behari Vajpayee and his Cabinet asked for parliament to be dissolved on 6 February in preparation for an early national election. **28**. In southern Thailand, more than 1,000 schools were closed and Buddhist monks evacuated temples after attacks by Muslim extremists left eight people dead.

FEBRUARY 2004

12. Kasitah Gaddam, Malaysia's Land Minister, was arrested on charges of corruption after he had been accused of accepting bribes in multimillion share deals. **15**. Fifty-three people died and more than 60 were injured in a fire at the Zhongbai Commercial Plaza in Jilin, and a further 39 people died in a fire at a Buddhist temple at Haining in Zhejiang province. **16**. In Bangladesh, violent clashes between the opposition Awami League and the government over crime control and allegedly looted public money, lead to 140 people being injured. **23**. The Indonesian Health Ministry announced that 227 people had died since the beginning of an outbreak of dengue fever on 1 January. **24**. In India, more than 2 million workers in banks and state-owned companies went on strike in protest at a Supreme Court order banning strikes. **27**. Shoko Asahara, the founder of the Aum Shinrikyo cult which carried out the sarin nerve gas attack on the Tokyo subway in 1995, was sentenced to death for multiple charges of murder at Tokyo District Court. In the Philippines, a ferry travelling from Manila to Bacolod caught fire following several explosions; 110 people were missing, feared dead.

MARCH 2004

2. In the Pakistani city of Quetta, armed men opened fire on hundreds of Shia worshippers taking part in a procession, and riots broke out after 40 people were killed and more than 150 wounded. **9**. Pakistan test-fired its long-range ballistic missile, Shaheen II. **12**. President Roh Moo Hyun of South Korea was voted out of power after deputies voted by 193 to 2 to impeach him. **16**. Pakistani troops killed 24 Islamic militants on the border with Afghanistan; eight Pakistani soldiers were killed and 15 wounded. **19**. Taiwan's President Chen Shui-bian and Vice-President Annette Lu were shot during an attempted assassination. **20**. Taiwan's President Chen Shui-bian was re-elected to government. **21**. More than 100 people were killed during fighting in western Afghanistan following the assassination of Mirwais Sadiq, the Aviation Minister. In Malaysia, Abdullah Badawi of the National Front coalition won the general election, driving the Pan-Malaysian Islamic Party from power in its heartland regional assemblies. The Nepalese military claimed to have killed 500 Maoist rebels during a 12-hour battle at Beni Bazar in the Mygdi district. **23**. President Chen of Taiwan agreed to a recount of all ballots cast in the election following protests held by more than 10,000 opposition supporters, who accused the ruling party of interfering with the vote count. **26**. The Niigata District Court in Japan ordered the Japanese government to compensate Chinese Second World War slave labourers. **28**. President Karzai of Afghanistan announced that national elections would be delayed until September 2004 in order to give the United Nations more time to organise the poll. **29**. In Uzbekistan, two female suicide bombers set off a series of explosions in a crowded bazaar in Tashkent, killing 19 people.

APRIL 2004

4. The Sri Lankan government suffered a defeat at the country's elections as the opposition alliance, lead by President Kumaratunga, won a majority of 105 seats in parliament. **5**. In Indonesia, the country's second democratic elections resulted in the ruling Indonesian Democratic Party of Struggle being given only 15 per cent of the 600 million votes, with the new Democratic Party winning the majority of votes in President Megawati Sukarnoputri's own ward. **9**. In Nepal, 25,000 protesters from a coalition of five political parties held a rally in Kathmandu against King Gyanendra, in protest at his dismissal of the elected government a year earlier. **13**. Aung Shwe and U Lwin of Burma's opposition party, the National League for Democracy, were released from house arrest; it was hoped that the party leader, Aung San Suu Kyi, would also be released. **15**. Hong Kong's Chief Executive, Tung Chee-hwa, ruled out full elections to choose his successor. A tornado destroyed several villages in northern Bangladesh, killing more than 70 people and injuring nearly 1,000. **16**. The Uri Party of South Korea won the national parliamentary election; the party supported President Roh Moo Hyun when the Grand National Party tried to impeach him. Police detained more than 1,000 pro-democracy protesters in the Nepalese capital Kathmandu, including the former prime minister, Sher Bahadur Deuba. **22**. North Korea declared a state of emergency after two fuel trains collided at Ryongchon station, 30 miles south of the border with China, killing up to 3,000 people. **25**. Japan's ruling Liberal Democratic Party retained all three seats contested in by-elections. **28**. Thai troops killed 34 militants and 132 Muslims died following a day of fighting in the southern provinces of Pattani, Yala and Songkhla.

MAY 2004

5. In Indonesia, a coalition government was planned after the Golkar party of former President Suharto won the election with 21.6 per cent of the vote while the ruling Indonesian Democratic Party of Struggle received 18.5 per cent of the vote. **9**. In Nepal, 34 people died and 22 Maoist rebels were shot in around four clashes between the rebels and police following the resignation of Prime Minister Surya Bahadur Thapa a week before. **13**. In the general election in India, the opposition Congress party, lead by Sonia Gandhi, won 217 seats and the governing Bharatiya Janata Party won 187. **14**. Roh Moo Hyun, the impeached South Korean President, regained power after a court overturned a vote to unseat him. **18**. Sonia Gandhi refused the post of prime minister of India after her Congress Party won the general election. **19**. Dr Manmohan Singh was appointed prime minister of India. **23**. The Commonwealth Secretary-General, Don McKinnon, announced the readmission of Pakistan into the Commonwealth after it had been suspended for five years following a coup.

JUNE 2004
2. King Gyanendra of Nepal re-appointed Sher Bahadur Deuba to the position of prime minister after his dismissal from the post in 2002. **9**. Twenty thousand people were evacuated after two volcanoes erupted in east Java province, near Jakarta, Indonesia. **14**. In Pakistan, at least 72 people were killed near the Afghan border following a five-day assault on al-Qa'eda hideouts. **20**. President Gloria Macapagal Arroyo of the Philippines was re-elected following a six-week count of votes; she had beaten Fernando Poe by 1.1 million votes. **24**. North Korea threatened to test a nuclear weapon despite an offer of aid from the US if it promised to scrap its weapons programme; North Korea demanded energy aid up front in exchange for freezing its nuclear programme. **26**. Chaudhry Shujaat Hussain was named as Pakistan's new prime minister after the resignation of Zafarullah Khan Jamali. **28**. The governing party of Mongolia, the Mongolian People's Revolutionary Party, lost its majority during elections, winning only 36 of 76 seats – the opposition Motherland Democratic Coalition also won 36 seats.

JULY 2004
11. Japan's ruling Liberal Democrat Party lost half of the 242 seats in the upper house of parliament to the opposition Democratic Party in elections. **15**. Maninder Pal Singh Kohli was arrested in Kalimpong in India on suspicion of raping and murdering the British teenager Hannah Foster in March 2003 near her home in Hampshire. Sultan Hassanal Bolkiah of Brunei announced that he would reconvene parliament – it had been 20 years since it last met. Cambodia's government was officially approved after more than 11 months of negotiations following a general election. **20**. The New York think tank Freedom House published its 2004 Freedom in the World survey which ranked Burma's regime as the worst in the world; Cuba and North Korea were also ranked as two of the worst regimes. **23**. The Constitutional Court in Jakarta declared that the terrorism legislation used to convict the 29 people involved in the Bali bombing was invalid as it was only passed into law months after the bombings. **25**. Severe monsoon floods across Bangladesh and parts of India and Nepal killed around 570 people in one month, forced millions from their homes and caused at least 10,000 Bangladeshis to suffer from various diseases. **26**. In Indonesia, it was announced that following a presidential election, Susilo Yudhoyono had received 33.5 per cent of the vote and the incumbent Megawati Sukarnoputri 26.6 per cent of the vote. **29**. Ahmed Khalfan Ghailani, one of the most-wanted leaders of al-Qa'eda, was arrested in the Pakistani city of Gujrat following a 12-hour gun battle with security forces.

AUGUST 2004
3. Pakistani authorities arrested eight al-Qa'eda terrorist suspects in the Punjab province. **10**. In Singapore, it was announced that the son of Prime Minister Lee Kuan Yew, Lee Hsien Loong would be sworn in as the new prime minister following his father's resignation. **25**. Thousands of people were evacuated from their homes in south-east China as Typhoon Aere approached the Fujian province – it had already killed at least 14 people in Taiwan and Japan and caused serious flooding. **27**. Shaukat Aziz was elected prime minister of Pakistan following Chaudhry Shujaat Hussain resignation on 26 June after having been in the post for only two months. **29**. The defence ministry in India said it had successfully tested a long-range missile capable of carrying a nuclear warhead off its eastern coast. In Thailand, the democrat Apirak Kosayodhin was elected governor of Bangkok.

AUSTRALASIA AND THE PACIFIC

SEPTEMBER 2003
2. The Australian government announced that a four-year jail sentence imposed on Abu Bakar Bashir, leader of Islamist group, Jemaah Islamiah was too lenient. **5**. The theft of two computers from an intelligence area at Sydney International Airport raised fears of terrorist interference as the 2nd anniversary of the attacks in New York and Washington drew close. **8**. Two men were jailed for life in Australia's worst serial murder case. John Bunting was found guilty of 11 and Robert Wagner of seven murders. **18**. A 1,800-mile railway line between Adelaide and Darwin was completed.

OCTOBER 2003
14. MPs in New Zealand voted to establish a Supreme Court of New Zealand, thereby abolishing appeals to the Privy Council in London and severing the last judicial link with Britain. **22**. Per Johan Adolfsson, a Swedish tourist, was jailed for two months at a court in Sydney after he had tried to smuggle eight baby snakes into Australia by strapping them to his legs on a flight from Bangkok to Sydney.

NOVEMBER 2003
5. The Australian government retrospectively removed Melville Island from the country's migration zone in order to prevent 14 Kurdish people, who arrived on the island in an Indonesian boat, from seeking asylum on the mainland; Australian law states that migrants are allowed to apply for refugee status once they have reached Australian mainland. **6**. Pauline Hanson, the former leader of the One Nation nationalist party in Australia, was released from jail after her conviction for electoral fraud was overturned by the Queensland Court of Appeal; her colleague David Ettridge was also freed. **10**. Bradley Murdoch was arrested at the South Australian District Court in Adelaide, after having been acquitted of separate rape and abduction charges, for the murder of the British tourist Peter Falconio and the unlawful detention of Joanne Lees, in the Northern Territory in July 2001.

DECEMBER 2003
1. Australia's opposition Labor Party voted in favour of Mark Latham taking over as leader of the party from Kim Beazley. **10**. The High Court in Canberra, Australia, ruled by a 4 to 3 majority that long-term British residents who have committed a crime in Australia can be deported back to Britain. **11**. Australia announced that it would be sending at least 230 armed police officers and 70 officials to Papua New Guinea in order to combat terrorism and criminal activity.

JANUARY 2004
30. The acclaimed British cosmologist, Will Saunders, was sentenced to nine months' weekend detention along with the Australian David Burgess, after they painted the words 'No War' in red paint across the highest 'sail' of the Sydney Opera House in protest at the war in Iraq.

FEBRUARY 2004

1. *The Ghan*, the first passenger train to run between the north and south of Australia, set off on its first journey between Adelaide and Darwin. **15.** Four people were arrested and 50 police officers were hurt during a nine-hour riot which broke out in the Aboriginal Redfern district of Sydney after 17-year-old Thomas Hickey died whilst allegedly being chased by police. **20.** The New Zealand Immigration Minister, Lianne Dalziel, resigned after it was found she had lied when she initially denied knowing how a letter about a Sri Lankan teenager, who was refused refugee status and deported, reached the media, but later admitted approving its release. **23.** Twenty-nine people died in Brisbane following a heatwave in Australia where temperatures reached 44.4C in Queensland and humidity rates rose to 70 per cent.

MARCH 2004

17. A plague of locusts devastated an area twice the size of England in eastern Australia as they devoured crops over 745 miles from south-west Queensland to central New South Wales; the infestation was a result of two years of drought followed by heavy rains. **25.** The leader of the Australian opposition Labor Party, Mark Latham, pledged to withdraw all 850 military personnel from Iraq if he were to win the next general election. David Kemp, the Australian Environment Minister, announced that from July 2004 fishing would be banned in 44,000 sq. miles of the coral reef along the coast of Queensland. **29.** In New Zealand, Maori Television (MT), set up to promote the Maori language and culture, went on air for the first time.

APRIL 2004

15. The Australian Prime Minister, John Howard, announced that he would be abolishing the country's Aboriginal and Torres Strait Islander Commission, and planned to appoint a panel of 'distinguished indigenous people' to advise on how to replace the Commission. **20.** Australia's leader of the opposition Labor Party, Mark Latham, announced that if his party won the upcoming elections, they would give Australians the opportunity to vote again on whether the country should become a republic.

MAY 2004

27. The Australian Prime Minister, John Howard, announced his intention to amend the 1961 Marriage Act in order to ban same-sex marriages and same-sex couples adopting children from overseas.

JUNE 2004

16. In Australia, the Human Rights and Equal Opportunity Commission reported that 99 per cent of Muslim women had suffered racist abuse or violence since the September 11 attacks in the US.

JULY 2004

1. The Great Barrier Reef became the world's largest protected marine reserve after the Australian government banned commercial fishermen from a third of the World Heritage listed site. **19.** Ivens Buffett, the deputy chief minister of Norfolk Island, was found shot dead in his office – it was only the second murder committed on the island in 150 years. **27.** The Australian government announced that it would send 300 police and officials to take up posts in the government of Papua New Guinea in order to stamp out corruption.

AUGUST 2004

8. The South Pacific nation of Tokelau announced that it would hold a referendum in 2005 on independence from New Zealand. **11.** In Australia, the New South Wales Farmers' Association released a warning to hikers about an aggressive new breed of half-dingo wild dog after the new 'super-dingoes' were found to have killed livestock and attacked walkers, horse riders and campers along the Great Dividing Range from Queensland through to Victoria. **29.** Australia's Prime Minister John Howard announced that the next general election would be held on 9 October 2004.

EUROPE

SEPTEMBER 2003

1. The Netherlands became the first country to introduce legislation permitting the medical use of cannabis when prescribed by a doctor as a painkiller. **2.** In Russia, President Vladimir Putin announced that elections for the *State Duma*, the lower chamber of the federal legislature, would be conducted on 7 December 2003. The Congress for Freedom and Democracy in Kurdistan (Kadek), the main militant Kurdish group in Turkey, announced they were ending their four-year unilateral cease-fire. **3.** In Stavropol, southern Russia, six people died and more than 40 were injured when two bombs exploded simultaneously beneath a crowded commuter train. **4.** In Spain, Prime Minister Jose Maria Aznar announced his successor of the right-wing People's Party (PP), with immediate effect, as the Deputy Prime Minister Mariano Rajoy Brey. **5.** In Italy, riot police used batons to beat back anti-globalisation protesters who tried to disrupt a meeting of EU foreign ministers. A riot took place in Kosovo's largest prison, killing five prisoners and injuring sixteen. **9.** In Slovenia, Prime Minister Anton Rop announced the abolition of obligatory military service stating that recruits would no longer be called-up. **10.** Swedish Foreign Minister Anna Lindh was stabbed and killed in a department store in central Stockholm by an unknown assailant. **16.** In Sweden, 35 year-old Per Olof Svensson was arrested on suspicion of the murder of Swedish Foreign minister Anna Lindh. In the Netherlands, the centre-right coalition government announced an austerity budget, which included cutting welfare benefits and increasing workers' premiums in a bid to comply with EU budget deficit guidelines. **18.** In France, new measures were announced giving the government the power to close mosques connected with fundamental islamicism and expel extremist Imams. **21.** In Germany, Chancellor Gerhard Schröder's Social Democrat Party was defeated in the Bavarian elections with the conservative Christian Socialist Union gaining the majority of seats in the state parliament. **23.** In Azerbaijan, a memorial to British servicemen who died defending the country's oilfields during the First World War was vandalised one week after it was erected. **24.** The Danish royal family announced that Crown Prince Frederick of Denmark would marry Australian estate agent, Mary Donaldson. Per Olof Svensson was cleared of all charges of the murder of Swedish Foreign Minister, Anna Lindh. **25.** Italian Prince Emmanuel-Filiberto, second in line to the Italian throne, married French actress, Clotilde Courau. **26.** In Germany, police claimed to have uncovered one of the world's biggest pornography rings: 530 men, including police officers and teachers had been identified as suspects. In France, a severely handicapped 22 year-old man at the centre of a debate over euthanasia died after his mother gave him an overdose. **28**. In Italy, a power cut plunged almost the entire country into darkness. Chechen Prime Minister Anatoli Povov was taken to hospital after what was believed to be an attempted assassination using poison. **30**. A member of al-Qa'eda, Nizar Trabelsi, was jailed for ten years by a Belgian court for planning to carry out a suicide bombing in the country just days after the terrorist attacks in America on 11 September 2001.

OCTOBER 2003

3. France's right-wing ruling party announced its intention to revoke the maximum 35-hour working week, following the suggestion by Economic Minister, Alain Lambert, that it was costing the state £11 billion per year. Lilla Freivalds was appointed as Sweden's new Foreign Minister. **5**. In southern Russia, the graves of 185 German soldiers who died during fighting with the Soviet Red Army between October and December 1942 were discovered in Diagara. **7**. Akhmed Kadyrov was elected president of Chechnya following a ballot that was widely believed to have been fixed. **12**. In the Ukraine, 30 people died at a mental hospital in Kozlovichi, when a man started a fire in the building. **15**. In Azerbaijan, Ilham Aliyev, won an overwhelming victory in the presidential elections. **17**. The lower house of the German parliament voted 306 to 291 in favour of new welfare reforms aimed at reviving the economy; the changes included cutting unemployment benefit and introducing legislation to make it compulsory for the long-term unemployed claiming benefits to accept any legal job offer. **19**. German Chancellor Gerhard Schröder ordered the first cut in pension benefits since the end of the Second World War; the cut was one of five measures agreed as a strategy to overcome an estimated €8 billion (£5.5 billion) shortfall in the state pay-as-you-go pension schemes. In Switzerland, the right-wing Swiss People's Party won a landslide victory in the general election. **23**. Hans Eichel, Germany's Finance Minister announced that Germany's public deficit had soared to €43 billion, its highest level since 1945, and warned that Germany was likely to breach the European single currency's Stability and Growth Pact for the third year in a row in 2004. **25**. In Russia, 33 of the 46 men trapped in the flooded Zapadnaya coal mine in Novoshakhtinsk were rescued. **27**. Russia's stock market plunged by 10 per cent (the RTS index of Russia's biggest stocks fell 59.86 points to 535.05) after the arrest of Russian oil billionaire Mikhail Khodorkovsky sparked fears amongst traders about the Government's commitment to economic reform. **29**. A further 11 of the 13 miners trapped in a deep shaft in the Zapadnaya coal mine in Russia were found alive after rescuers dug a 200ft tunnel from a neighbouring coal mine to get to the trapped men. **30**. Russian state prosecutors froze 44 per cent of shares in the country's leading oil company Yukos, following the arrest of its major shareholder, Mikhail Khodorkovsky. **31**. Ilham Aliyev was inaugurated as the new president of Azerbaijan replacing his father, Geider Aliyev, who had stood down due to serious illness after serving in the post since 1993.

NOVEMBER 2003

2. In Georgia parliamentary elections were held, the results were widely believed to have been rigged in favour of the President, Eduard Shevardnadze, who had been in office as President since 1992. **3**. Mikhail Khodorkovsky resigned as head of the Russian oil company Yukos following his detainment on tax evasion charges. In Lithuania, a special commission was established to investigate alleged links between President Rolandas Paksas and organised crime in Russia and a separate criminal investigation of Yuri Borisov, the Lithuanian-based Russian businessman at the centre of the allegations, began. **4**. In Azerbaijan, the Milli Majlis (the unicameral legislature) approved President Aliyev's proposal to appoint Artur Rasizade as prime minister. **11**. On the fourth day of protests in the Georgian capital Tbilisi, against the results of the parliamentary election, opposition leaders announced that they would not allow the new parliament to convene unless elections were re-held. **13**. In Germany, the Christian Democratic Union/Christian Social Union (CDU/CSU) coalition voted 195 to 28 in favour of the expulsion of CDU party member Martin Hohman, after he made anti-Semitic comments in October. **16**. In Serbia, presidential election results were declared null and void as turnout was below the required 50 per cent. **19**. In Serbia, the ruling coalition, the Democratic Opposition of Serbia (DOS), announced that the coalition would split up prior to the 28 December elections. **20**. In Turkey, two separate truck bombs exploded within five minutes of each other outside the headquarters of the HSBC bank and the UK consulate in Istanbul, the explosions killed at least 31 people, including the UK Consul-General Roger Short, and injured over 450 others. **23**. In Georgia, President Shevardnadze signed a statement of resignation in return for immunity from prosecution. Nino Burdjanadze, Speaker of the parliament, assumed all presidential powers pending fresh presidential and legislative elections. In Croatia, elections to the 152-seat Chamber of Representatives (the lower chamber of the bicameral legislature) the right-wing Croatian Democratic Union (HDZ) won a decisive victory, winning 66 seats. **29**. In Bulgaria, five defendants accused of the assassination of former prime minister Andrei Lukanov in 1996, were convicted and sentenced to life imprisonment in a court in Sofia.

DECEMBER 2003

2. Following heavy rainfall, southern France experienced extensive flooding which killed five people and forced the evacuation of more than 7,000 others; roads and rail lines were cut-off and the state electricity supplier was obliged to shut down four nuclear reactors. **4**. Ibon Fernandez, the alleged leader of the Basque separatist movement ETA, was rearrested in France near the border with Spain following his escape from prison in December 2002. In Poland, Prime Minister Leszek Miller was admitted to hospital with two fractured vertebrae after the helicopter in which he was travelling carried out an emergency landing near the town of Piaseczno, south of Warsaw. **5**. Thirty-two people were reported dead and dozens injured in an explosion on a commuter train between the towns of Mineralnye Vody and Kislovodsk in southern Russia near the Chechnya region; the Russian Ministry of Emergencies believed it was the result of a terrorist act. **7**. In Russia, President Putin's Unified Russia Party won nearly 38 per cent of the vote in the general election, resulting in a nearly two-thirds majority of the 300 seats in the State Duma (lower house). **11**. In France, a report by the commission on state secularism was published which recommended that the wearing of overt religious symbols in state educational institutions and public buildings should be banned. **12**. Geidar Aliyev, the former president of Azerbaijan, died aged 80 in Ohio, USA, where he had been undergoing treatment for heart and kidney problems. **19**. In Germany, Chancellor Gerhard Schröder secured parliamentary support for his Agenda 2010 package of economic and social reforms aimed at reviving the German economy. **23**. Turkey and Greece signed a deal in Ankara to build a gas pipeline between the two countries that would also carry gas to other parts of Europe; the project was expected to be completed in 2006 at a cost of £53.8 million. **24**. Spanish police foiled an attempt by Basque separatists to detonate two bombs at Madrid's main railway station; one man was arrested as he unloaded a suitcase containing 28kg of chemical explosives from his car and a further 20kg of explosives were found aboard a train en route to Madrid. **26**. In Serbia, the Bosnian Serb government set up a commission to investigate the 1995 Srebrenica massacre. In Turkey, the city governor for Istanbul announced that a cell of Turkish nationals linked to the al-Qa'eda network had orchestrated the November bombings of the UK Consulate, HSBC bank and two synagogues; 35 people had been charged in connection with the attacks. **28**. In Serbia, the Serbian Radical Party (SRS), whose leader was on trial for alleged atrocities committed in the Balkan wars of the 1990s, won the parliamentary elections taking 27.5 per cent of the vote and gaining 82 seats in the 250-member parliament.

JANUARY 2004

2. In Russia, the Defence Minister Sergei Ivanov approved President Putin's plans to end conscription and fill more than half of its one million-strong army with professional soldiers by 2007. **4**. In Georgia, Mikhail Saakashvili won a landslide victory in the presidential elections. **5**. In Lithuania, President Rolandas Paksas, stated that he would not appear before a parliamentary committee to consider whether he should be impeached as he had not been provided with full information on the charges against him. **7**. In Sweden, Mijailo Mijailovic was arrested in conjunction with the murder of Anna Lindh, the Swedish Foreign Minister who died after being stabbed in a Stockholm department store in September 2003. In Greece, Prime Minister, Kostas Simitis, announced his resignation as leader of the ruling party, the Panhellenic Socialist Movement (Pasok), and called for an early general election to be held on 7 March. **9**. In Spain, Prime Minister, José María Aznar, called a general election for 14 March. **11**. In the Turkish Republic of Northern Cyprus, Mehmet Ali Talat, leader of the pro-EU Republican Turkish Party agreed to form a coalition government with the anti-EU Democrat Party led by Serdar Denktash. **12**. In Russia, a Moscow court sentenced Adam Dekkushev and Yusef Krymshamkhalov to life imprisonment for their part in the 1999 Moscow and Volgodonsk bombings that killed 246 people. **14**. In the Turkish Republic of Northern Cyprus, President Serdar Denktash, leader of the Democrat Party approved the new cabinet, naming Ali Talat, leader of the Republican Turkish Party, as Prime Minister, with himself as Deputy Prime Minister and Foreign Minister. **15**. In Russia, former chief executive of the Yukos oil company, Mikhail Khodorkovsky, lost his appeal against continued detention in Moscow's Matrosskaya Tishina prison following the ruling on 23 December that he should stay in pre-trial detention until at least 25 March. **19**. A Norwegian cargo ship capsized in the Raune Fjord, just off the island of Bjoroey, 12 crew members were rescued, three bodies were recovered and the remaining 15 missing crew members were presumed dead. **25**. The new president of Georgia, Mikhail Saakashvili, was inaugurated on the steps of the parliament building in the capital Tibilisi. **28**. In France, the Cabinet approved a bill banning the wearing in state schools of symbols and clothing, which conspicuously display the religious affiliation of pupils; no banned items were specified in the bill which was left to the discretion of the teacher. In Turkey, the Grand National Assembly approved the proposal by Economy Minister, Ali Babacan to eliminate six zeros from the Turkish lira and rename it the 'new Turkish lira'; the old currency would remain in circulation, alongside the new currency, until its withdrawal on 30 December 2005.

FEBRUARY 2004

2. In the central Turkish city of Konya more than 100 people were feared dead after an 11-storey building collapsed. **3**. In France, Alain Juppé announced that he would remain Mayor of Bordeaux, an MP and president of the UMP despite being convicted on 30 January of organising illegal party funding; his prison sentence was suspended pending appeal. **6**. In Russia, a bomb was detonated on Moscow's underground rail system at 8:30 a.m. At least 39 people died and more than 120 were injured in the incident, which was believed to have been carried out by Chechyen separatists. German Chancellor Gerhard Schröder resigned as leader of the Social Democratic Party after internal criticism over his economic reform programme Agenda 2010. Herr Schröder stated that he would continue as chancellor and head of government but would hand the party leadership to the party's parliamentary group leader, Franz Münterfering. **10**. The Netherlands Government issued a deportation order for approximately 26,000 failed asylum-seekers that had arrived before the introduction of a new asylum regime in April 2001; the order constituted one of the biggest mass deportations in modern European history. **17**. The Dutch parliament voted in favour of the mass deportation of failed asylum seekers announced by the Government on 10 February 2004. **18**. In Lithuania, a parliamentary panel concluded that there were sufficient legal grounds for the impeachment of President Rolandas Paksas. In France, Jean-Marie Le Pen, the leader of France's far-right party was refused his application to stand in the April regional elections after election officials stated that he had not provided the necessary tax records to stand as a candidate in southern France. **21**. In France the terrorist group AZF directed French police to a bomb hidden beneath a railway line in Limoges after threatening that ten other such bombs hidden beneath railway lines throughout France would be detonated unless they received a £2.8 million ransom from the French government. **24**. In Russia, President Putin dismissed Prime Minister Mikhail Kasyanov and his entire Cabinet prior to the presidential election on 14 March 2004. **26**. Boris Trajkovski, President of Macedonia since 1999, died in an air crash in Bosnia. **29**. A terrorist attack on the Spanish capital, Madrid, was foiled when police intercepted a van containing more than 1,000lbs of explosives. In Germany, Chancellor Gerhard Schröder suffered a defeat when his party, the Social Democrats, took only 32 per cent of the vote in the Hamburg city-state elections; the Christian Democrats took the majority (46 per cent) and were set to secure 62 seats in the Hamburg State Parliament.

MARCH 2004

3. France's Senate voted 276 to 20 in favour of a law banning the wearing of overt religious symbols in state schools. In Belgrade, the new Serbian parliament voted in an 18-member, Conservative-led coalition cabinet led by Vojislav Kostunica, the former Yugoslav President and leader of the Democratic Party of Serbia (DSS). **4**. In France, more than 10,000 railway workers were deployed to search all 20,000 miles of railway track for bombs following the threat made by the terrorist group AZF on 21 February. **11**. In Spain, ten bombs exploded during the morning rush hour in Madrid; six bombs exploded on trains approaching central stations, three exploded at the Atocha terminus and one exploded at Santa Eugenia station. In total around 1,400 people were injured and 198 people killed in one of the worst terrorist attacks in Spain. Spanish Foreign Minister Ana Palacio said evidence appeared to indicate ETA as responsible for the attacks, although a London-based Arabic newspaper, Al-Quds, said it had received an email in which a group linked to al-Qae'da, the Abu Hafs al-Masri Brigades, claimed to have carried out the attacks. **13**. Spain's interior minister announced that al-Qa'eda had claimed responsibility for the terrorist attacks in Madrid, the claim was made on a video tape which had yet to be authenticated. **14**. In Russia, President Putin was re-elected for a second four-year term winning 71.2 per cent of the vote in the presidential elections. In the Spanish general election the Socialist Party won by a margin of 5 percent, winning 43 per cent of the votes. **17**. In the Serbian province of Kosovo ethnic Albanians carried out co-ordinated attacks against the Serbian minority; 14 people were killed and about 250 injured in the worst spate of violence seen in the region since the 1999 war. **18**. In Georgia, President Saakashvili, announced he was lifting the economic blockade imposed on the Adjaria region on 14 March following talks with the region's leader, Aslan Abashidze. **23**. In Sweden, Mijailo Mijailovic, was sentenced to life imprisonment for the murder of Anna Lindh, the Swedish Foreign Minister, after judges rejected his plea of insanity. **28**. In Georgia, President Saakashvili's National-Movement Democratic Party won 78.6 per cent of the vote in the parliamentary elections. **29**. In the Republic of Ireland, a smoking ban came into force in all places of work and public areas, including bars and restaurants. **31**. In Russia, the State Duma passed a government-drafted bill (294 votes for and 137 votes against) banning public protests near official buildings and pipelines and rallies that threaten 'public morality'.

APRIL 2004

1. The German state of Baden-Wûrttemberg, led by a coalition of the Christian Democratic Union and the liberal Free Democrats, became the first German state to ban the wearing of headscarves by Muslim teachers in schools. **2**. In Spain, a 26 lb bomb was found under a railway track at Mocejon near Toledo, the device was connected to a detonator but had not been fully assembled. **3**. In Spain, security forces traced the whereabouts of a terrorist cell linked to the 11 March Madrid bombings to a flat in the Madrid suburbs. While residents were being evacuated a gunman opened fire resulting in a two-hour siege which ended when the suspects detonated explosives killing themselves, a special forces police officer and injuring 11 officers from Spain's specialist anti-terrorist unit. **5**. Police in France broke up a suspected Islamic terrorist cell on the outskirts of Paris, arresting 15 people in connection with the suicide-bomb attacks in Morocco in 2003. **25**. In Austria, Heinz Fischer won the presidential elections with more than 53 per cent of the vote ahead of his Conservative rival Benita Ferrero-Waldner. In Rome, the Pope appointed Sister Enrica Rosanna, a Salesian nun, as under-secretary of the Congregation for the Consecrated Life, the highest appointment ever bestowed on a woman in the Roman Catholic Church. **30**. Macedonian police acknowledged that the killing of seven alleged Pakistani terrorists in March 2002 was staged to win US support and promote Macedonia as a player in the global fight against terrorism and admitted that the victims were actually illegal immigrants. Three former police commanders, two special officers and a businessman were charged with murder in connection with the incident.

MAY 2004

3. In Turkey, police foiled a plot by terrorists to assassinate President Bush at the NATO summit to be held in Istanbul in June; in total 24 suspected members of a militant group linked to al-Qa'eda were detained and guns, explosives and detonators seized. **5**. President Mikhail Saakashvili of Georgia arrived in Adjaria's regional capital Batumi and assumed direct rule of the province. In Greece, three bombs exploded outside a police station in the Kallithea area of Athens, injuring a policeman and damaging buildings and cars. **6**. Turkish Prime Minister Tayyip Erdogan visited Greece for talks with Greek Prime Minister Kostas Karamanlis. **7**. In Germany, Sven Jaschen, 18, was arrested and admitted responsibility for the 'sasser' internet worm; Jaschen was traced after acquaintances gave information to Microsoft's German office in return for a £139,000 reward. **9**. Chechen President, Akhmed Kadyrov, was killed and at least 30 others injured when a bomb exploded under the VIP stand at Grozny Dinamo Stadium where the President was attending a Victory Day parade marking the anniversary of the end of the Second World War. **23**. In France, five people were killed and four others injured, one seriously, when a large part of the roof of Terminal 2E at Charles de Gaulle Airport in Paris collapsed onto a waiting area just before 7a.m. In Germany, Horst Koehler, joint candidate of the Christian Democratic Union/ Christian Social Union and the Free Democratic Party was elected for the post of Federal President, defeating Gesine Schwan, the candidate of the ruling coalition of the Social Democratic Party and the Greens.

JUNE 2004

1. Spanish newspaper *El Mundo* published letters between two senior members of terrorist groups, al-Qa'eda and ETA, dating back to 2001. **8**. Italy announced that anti-terrorist police in Milan had arrested Osman Sayed Ahmed, who was believed to have played a key role in the 11 March Madrid bombings. **9**. Turkish state television made its first broadcast in the once banned language of Kurdish, the language of Turkey's largest minority. In Turkey, four former MPs, Leyla Zana, Orhan Dogan, Hatip Dicle and Selim Sadek, were released after 10 years following a ruling by the Turkish court of appeal that the State Security Court, which twice tried them for alleged membership of an armed separatist group, failed to give them a fair hearing at their original trial. **22**. In the Russian autonomous region of Ingushetia bordering Chechnya, insurgents seized an Interior Ministry building and attacked police posts throughout the region; 57 people were killed including the Interior Minister, Abukar

Kostoyev. **24**. In Turkey, three people were killed and more than a dozen injured when a bomb exploded on a busy Istanbul bus just two days prior to the arrival of world leaders for the NATO summit in the city. **30**. In Bosnia, Lord Ashdown of Norton-sub-Hamdon, the Chief International Envoy to Bosnia, sacked 60 senior Bosnian Serb officials, including Dragan Kalinic, Speaker of the Bosnian Serb parliament, and Zoran Djeric, the Bosnian Serb Interior Minister, for allegedly helping Radovan Karadzic and other indicted war criminals to evade capture.

JULY 2004

5. Italian Prime Minister, Silvio Berlusconi presented a package of expenditure reforms and special tax measures worth €4.5 billion (£5.25 billion) to ensure that Italy kept within the European single currency country deficit regulations. Prime Minister Silvio Berlusconi made the announcement in place of former Economy Minister, Giulio Tremonti, who resigned over the weekend. **19**. In Turkey, a taxi driver was jailed for 36 years for the murder of a British child who was caught in crossfire during a gunfight in the resort of Foca in July 2003. **20**. In Russia the Justice Ministry announced that bailiffs were to sell off the Yukos subsidiary, Yuganskneftegaz, to cover a £1.8 billion bill for back taxes from 2000 that Yukos failed to pay in June. **22**. In Turkey, at least 36 people were killed when a train travelling from Istanbul to the Turkish capital Ankara derailed.

AUGUST 2004

1. Italian police working undercover arrested three Italians and three Bulgarians after discovering a baby-selling ring in which Bulgarian women were brought to Italy to give birth and their children sold. One woman was arrested on leaving the hospital where she had just given birth and two infants were taken into care. **10**. In Austria, a tourist coach carrying mainly British passengers came off a road near the village of Bad Dürnberg and rolled 100ft down a mountain into a field, five passengers died and 20 were seriously injured in the accident. **10**. In Turkey two people died and eleven people were injured in simultaneous explosions in two hotels in Istanbul; the Islamic Abu Hafs al-Masri Brigades claimed responsibility for the blasts. **18**. Italian police discovered a bomb close to the Italian Prime Minister Silvio Berlusconi's villa in Sardinia just hours after Prime Minister Tony Blair and his wife Cherie had left following a private visit to Mr Berluscconi's Sardinian home. **22**. Russian president Vladimir Putin made a surprise visit to the region of Chechnya where he visited the grave of the late Chechen president Akhmed Kadyrov assassinated on 9 May. **24**. Two Russian airliners carrying more than 80 people simultaneously disappeared from Russian air traffic control radar screens. The first aircraft was en route from Moscow to Volgograd and wreckage was found near the village of Buchalki with no reports of survivors. The other aircraft remained missing after disappearing near the city of Rostov-on-Don about 600 miles south of Moscow en route from Moscow to the Black Sea resort of Sochi. **25**. The wreckage of the second plane that went missing in Russia on 24 August was discovered. **28**. The Russian Federal Security Service confirmed that traces of explosives had been found in the wreckage of both planes concluding that it was an act of terrorism that caused the destruction of the planes and the death of all passengers and crew.

EUROPEAN UNION

SEPTEMBER 2003

2. The European Commission rejected US demands for airlines to reveal passenger information as an anti-terrorist measure. **11**. The EU added Hamas to its blacklist of terrorist organisations in an attempt to reduce the flow of funds that support the group's campaign of suicide bombings against Israelis. **14**. A Swedish referendum voted overwhelmingly against joining the European single currency. Estonia voted to join the EU in a referendum. **18**. The International Monetary Fund criticised the economic performance of the countries in the European single currency. **20**. Latvia voted for EU membership during a referendum; 67 per cent of the 72.5 per cent turnout voted in favour of accession on 1 May 2004.

OCTOBER 2003

16. Twenty-eight European leaders met in Brussels to discuss a new constitution for Europe. It was envisaged that the constitution would create a full-time European president and foreign minister, make majority voting the norm in EU business and put the European Commission in charge of justice and home affairs. Britain ruled out holding a referendum on the new EU constitution, several other nations, including Spain, Portugal, the Netherlands, Denmark, Ireland and Luxembourg stated they were almost certain to hold referendums, whilst France, Italy and the Czech Republic were among those still considering the idea. **31**. Wim Duisenberg stepped down after five years in charge of the European Central Bank and handed over to his successor, Jean-Claude Trichet.

NOVEMBER 2003

25. EU finance ministers meeting in Brussels decided by a majority not to impose sanctions on France and Germany for breaching Euro budget deficit rules; effectively breaking the Stability and Growth Pact governing participation in the Euro single currency.

DECEMBER 2003

27. The President of the European Union, Romano Prodi, received a letter bomb, which he opened, at his home in Bologna, Italy. No-one was injured in the blast. **30**. A letter bomb was intercepted in the post room of Eurojust, an EU agency situated in the Hague, Netherlands; the bomb was the fourth device in as many days to be received by an EU institution.

JANUARY 2004

1. Irish Prime Minister, Bertie Ahern, assumed the EU's rotating presidency for a six-month term. **12**. In Rome, Italian police found a package containing bullet casings and firecrackers at the Bologna home of the European Commission President, Romano Prodi, the package contained a threatening letter claiming to be from an anarchist group in Sardinia. **13**. The European Commission announced that it would take legal action in the European Court of Justice to challenge the decision by EU finance Ministers on 25 November 2003 to suspend the rules of the Stability and Growth Pact governing participation in the euro single currency. **23**. The European Union imposed a ban on the import of all Thai chicken slaughtered after 1 January 2004 after an outbreak of avian flu in Thailand.

FEBRUARY 2004
18. German Chancellor Gerhard Schröder hosted a trilateral summit in Berlin attended by French President Jacques Chirac and Prime Minister Tony Blair to establish a joint line on key policy issues in an enlarged European Union.

MARCH 2004
23. Talks on a new constitution for the European Union were revived in Warsaw after Germany and Poland paved the way for an agreement to be reached by the end of June.

APRIL 2004
27. Libyan leader, Colonel Gaddafi, made his first visit to Europe for 15 years.

MAY 2004
1. Membership of the EU increased from 15 to 25 states with the formal admission of Cyprus, the Czech Republic, Estonia, Hungary, Latvia, Lithuania, Malta, Poland, Slovakia and Slovenia.

JUNE 2004
1. The Dutch Prime Minister, Jan Peter Balkenende, began the first day of his sixth-month EU presidency. **10**. European parliamentary elections took place across Europe. **11**. As part of the ongoing negotiations to create a European constitution, EU member states agreed to go ahead with the creation of a European Union diplomatic service, the *European External Action Service*, serving under an EU Foreign Minister. **15**. Final results for the UK in the European parliamentary elections showed that the Liberal Democrats increased their number of seats from 10 to 12, the UK Independence Party (UKIP) from 3 to 12 with Labour and the Conservatives losing ten and nine seats respectively. **17/18**. During a summit in Brussels European leaders agreed on a constitution for Europe which had to be ratified by all 25 member states within two years, either by parliamentary vote or national referendum; at least eight countries, including Britain, were set to hold referendums. **18**. EU Member States appointed José Manuel Barroso to take office as European Commission President on 1 November 2004, replacing Romano Prodi.

JULY 2004
14. In France, President Jacques Chirac announced that France would hold a national referendum on the new constitution of the European Union, qualifying that the vote will take place in the second half of 2005.

AUGUST 2004
12. President of the European Commission, José Manuel Barroso, named Hartlepool MP and former cabinet minister, Peter Mandelson, as the next European Union Trade Commissioner. **20**. The incoming 25-member European Commission held its first informal session under new president José Manuel Barroso.

INTERNATIONAL RELATIONS

SEPTEMBER 2003
4. The UN was forced to shut down all its famine relief field offices in Zimbabwe by the government. **12**. The UN Security Council voted to lift sanctions against Libya. **22**. In an attack on the UN offices in Baghdad one policeman was killed and 19 people were injured. **14**. The World Trade Organisation talks to further the Doha round of trade negotiations in Cancún, Mexico, collapsed after some 90 developing countries walked out following a late demand by the EU and Japan for immediate negotiations to take place on investment, competition rules, trade facilitation and transparency in Government procurement. **23**. The new president of the UN, Julian Hunte of St Lucia, opened the 58th session of the General Assembly of the UN.

OCTOBER 2003
3. The UN Secretary-General Kofi Annan challenged the draft US-British plan for Iraq stating that the occupation might not be sustainable for long enough to prepare a new constitution; he outlined a rival UN blueprint that would transfer sovereignty to the Iraqi people in three months. **23**. The UN General Assembly elected five non-permanent members to the Security Council for a two-year term; the new members are Algeria, Benin, Brazil, the Philippines and Romania. **24**. At the close of an international donor conference in Madrid, $33.75 billion (£20 billion) was pledged towards the reconstruction of Iraq; the amount fell short of the $56 billion (£33 billion) target.

NOVEMBER 2003
4. A new 16-member UN group was formed to review the role of the UN in the wake of the diplomatic failures in the run-up to the war against Iraq. The UN's envoy in Iraq and its global security chief were suspended pending the outcome of an investigation into the lapses of security that had preceded the bombing of the UN offices in Baghdad, Iraq on 19 August 2003. **15**. After two days of intensive talks with the US-appointed Iraqi governing council, US Ambassador Paul Bremer appeared to have reached an agreement for transferring power in Iraq to an elected Iraqi government by the end of 2005.

DECEMBER 2003
14. The US Army released photographs of Saddam Hussein's arrest and medical examination. **19**. Libya announced its decision to abandon its programme to develop weapons of mass destruction.

JANUARY 2004
5. The former Dutch Foreign Minister, Jaap de Hoop Scheffer, took up his post as NATO Secretary-General succeeding Lord Robertson of Port Ellen. **8**. The UN launched a multimillion dollar appeal to help fund relief efforts and reconstruction in Bam, south east Iran, after an earthquake devastated the area on 26 December 2003. **16–21**. Some 100,000 activists from around the world attended the anti-corporate globalisation World Social Forum (WSF) in Bombay, India. **21–25**. The World Economic Forum (WEF) took place in Davos, Switzerland and was attended by some 2,100 people from 94 countries. **23**. Dr David Kay, head of the Iraq survey group searching for Saddam Hussein's weapons of mass destruction for eight months, resigned saying that he believed Saddam Hussein had not possessed any such weapons for at least a decade. **28**. Milan Babic, a former Croatian Serb leader, was convicted of persecuting Croats between 1991–2 by the war crimes tribunal at The Hague. **30**. The UN Security Council adopted Resolution 1526 (2004), proposed by Chile, Russia and the USA, outling tougher sanctions and controls over people and entities associated with the al-Qa'eda network and the former ruling Afghan Taliban group.

FEBRUARY 2004

9–20. The seventh ordinary meeting of the Conference of the Parties to the UN Convention on Biological Diversity was held in Kuala Lumpur, Malaysia; 123 member states signed an agreement to ensure 'a significant' reduction of biodiversity loss by 2010. **15**. In Cyprus, decisive negotiations began in Nicosia on a UN blueprint to unite the island as a federation with a central government overseeing two largely autonomous areas. **25**. The UN General Assembly approved the nomination by UN Secretary-General, Kofi Annan of Canadian Louise Arbour as the new UN High Commissioner for Human Rights; Arbour was expected to begin her four-year term of office in June following her retirement from the Canadian Supreme Court.

MARCH 2004

4. In Germany, Mounir el Motassadeq, the only person to be convicted of involvement in the 11 September suicide hijackings won his appeal for a retrial. **15**. The new Spanish Prime Minister Jose Rodriguez Zapatero accused Tony Blair and President George W. Bush of dishonesty over the war in Iraq during a radio interview, and pledged to withdraw his country's 1,300 troops from Iraq. **18**. NATO made a request for 825 reserve troops from Britain, Italy and the US to reinforce the 17,500 German-led NATO force in Kosovo following fighting between ethnic Albanians and Serbs in the Serbian province on 17 March. **24**. UK Chancellor Gordon Brown used new anti-terrorist powers introduced after 11 September attacks in the US to freeze all assets held in British banks in the name of the new Hamas leader in Gaza, Abdel Aziz Rantisi. **31**. Kofi Annan, the UN Secretary-General, handed his final plan for the reunification of Cyprus to Greek, Turkish and Cypriot officials.

APRIL 2004

13. A number of European countries instructed their civilian workers to leave Iraq after a spate of civilian kidnappings in the country; Russia prepared to evacuate all of its 500 citizens while the French Foreign Ministry and the Czech Republic formally advised all non- military personnel to leave. **24**. In Cyprus, Greek Cypriots overwhelmingly rejected UN proposals to reunify the island, 75.8 per cent voted against the plan in a referendum, while in a separate poll the Turkish Cypriot community backed the proposals with 64.9 per cent voting in favour of the UN reunification plan.

MAY 2004

4. The UN Economic and Social Council elected 14 countries to serve on the 53-member UN Human Rights Commission for three-year terms starting from January 2005.

JUNE 2004

11. Turkish security services admitted bugging the telephone of the British Ambassador in Ankara in 2002; the admission was made in a letter submitted to a court by the Turkish National Intelligence Organisation as evidence in a trial of a journalist who published a transcript of a conversation between the ambassador and a senior EU official. **28/29**. The NATO summit took place in Istanbul, Turkey, amid tight security. **30**. In Qatar, two Russian intelligence agents were convicted of murdering former Chechen President Zelimkham Yandarbiyev and were sentenced to life imprisonment.

JULY 2004

1. In Iraq, the trial of former President Saddam Hussein for alleged crimes against humanity began.

AUGUST 2004

1. German Chancellor Gerhard Schröder marked the 60th anniversary of the start of the 1944 Warsaw Uprising by visiting the square where the rebellion began. **9**. In Afghanistan, Canada handed over control of the NATO force to Europe's five-nation defence force, Eurocorps, for a sixth month period. It was the Eurocorps first deployment outside Europe.

THE MIDDLE EAST

SEPTEMBER 2003

1. Iraq's Governing Council named the 25 ministers of the new cabinet that would form an interim administration. **3**. Polish forces took command of a multinational coalition division in Iraq, becoming the only nation apart from the US and Britain to assume control of a sector of the country. **6**. Palestinian Prime Minister, Mahmoud Abbas, resigned from his position. One of the reasons he gave was the apparent lack of Israeli willingness to adhere to the 'roadmap to peace process'. **8**. Ahmed Qureia became Prime Minister of Palestine, having earlier demanded guarantees of American and European support in negotiations with Israel. **9**. Two Palestinian suicide attacks took place within five hours of each other. The first bomb killed at least seven Israeli soldiers and wounded dozens more at a crowded bus stop near Tel Aviv and the second took place in a café in the German Colony neighbourhood, killing at least six more people. **10**. A suicide bomber killed himself and an Iraqi child and wounded more than 50 people in a car-bomb attack in the northern Kurdish city of Arbil. Israel launched an airstrike against the home of a leading Hamas member in response to the double suicide bombings of the day before. **20**. A leading Iranian cleric called for his country to consider withdrawing from the nuclear non-proliferation treaty which raised fresh fears that Iran would ignore an international deadline to curb its nuclear ambitions. **29**. Jordan announced that it would train 30,000 Iraqi police and troops in the first such pledge of aid from an Arab country in support of the American-led reconstruction effort in Iraq.

OCTOBER 2003

1. The Israeli cabinet announced that it had decided to go ahead with the building of a security fence around Jewish settlements in the West Bank. The fence was designed to keep Palestinian suicide bombers out of Jewish areas. **4**. A female suicide bomber detonated a bomb in a crowded restaurant in the Israeli city of Haifa, killing at least 19 people and wounding more than 40. **5**. Israel attacked what was believed to be a terrorist training camp for Islamic Jihad in Syria in response to the suicide bombing in Israel of the previous day. **6**. The Palestinian terrorist group Hamas vowed to take revenge against Israel for the militant attack in Syria against the group. **9**. Israel stated that it would call up 800 reserve soldiers in readiness for increased operations in the West Bank and Gaza Strip following the suicide bombing that killed 19 people on 4 November. **10**. Seven Palestinians were killed when Israeli tanks entered the Rafah refugee camp in southern Gaza. Some 10,000 Shia Muslim demonstrators congregated on the streets of Baghdad in protest against the US after a night of violence that left two Americans and two Iraqis dead. The lawyer and democracy activist Shirin Ebadi was named as the first Iranian and Muslim woman winner of the £800,000 Nobel Peace Prize. She had previously been imprisoned by the Iranian regime for representing certain clients in human rights cases. **12**. According to reports from the *Los Angeles Times*, Israel had acquired the capability of launching a nuclear strike from submarines. **13**. Saudi Arabia announced it would hold its first elections for municipal councils. **14**. Israel ordered the expulsion of 15 Palestinian prisoners from the West Bank to Gaza. The prisoners were being held without trial or charges and human rights groups claimed that the army was violating international law. A gun battle broke out in Karbala and at least one person was killed as followers of the cleric Moqtada al-Sadr fought for control of the Imam Hussein mosque, which is run by the cleric Ayatollah Ali al-Sistani. **15**. Thousands of people demonstrated against a rigged presidential election in Azerbaijan's capital Baku, after Ilham Aliyev, the son of the previous president, was declared the winner before the counting of votes had been completed. **19**. Three Israeli soldiers were shot dead east of Ramallah; the Al-Aqsa Martyrs' Brigades claimed responsibility for the killings. **20**. Ten people were killed and almost 100 injured after Israeli aircraft carried out five raids in Gaza. **21**. Iran announced that it would meet all of the key demands of the International Atomic Energy Agency in order to prove to the United Nations that it did not have plans to develop nuclear weapons under cover of a civil nuclear power project. **26**. Eight rockets were fired at the al-Rasheed hotel in Baghdad where coalition troops were staying; one American colonel died and 15 other soldiers were injured. Israeli forces demolished three tower blocks in the Gaza Strip and ordered 2,000 Palestinians out of their homes claiming that the towers had been used by militants planning attacks on nearby Jewish settlements. **27**. Suicide bombers in Baghdad killed 35 people and injured around 230 after car bombs were driven into the headquarters of the International Committee of the Red Cross and three separate police stations.

NOVEMBER 2003

2. A surface-to-air missile shot down a US Chinook helicopter near Baghdad; 15 American soldiers, about to take leave after months of serving in Iraq, were killed. **8**. Three bombs exploded in the Saudi capital Riyadh; 28 people were killed and around 100 more were injured. **9**. Iran announced that it was suspending uranium enrichment 'within days' to prove that it was not trying to make nuclear weapons. **9**. The Israeli cabinet voted 12 to 11 in favour of freeing 400 Palestinian and 20 Lebanese prisoners in exchange for the kidnapped Israeli businessman Elhanan Tannenbaum. **10**. Syria's former president, General Amin al-Hafez, returned to the country after spending 36 years in exile in Iraq. **12**. In Israel, the Palestinian Legislative Council ratified the new Palestinian cabinet 48 to 13, and Ahmed Qureia was announced as the new Palestinian Prime Minister. **15**. Twelve US servicemen were killed and nine injured after two American Black Hawk helicopters crashed into each other over the Iraqi city of Mosul. **17**. Six people were killed when American troops fired a 500 lb satellite-guided missile at a suspected guerrilla hideout south of Tikrit in Iraq. **22**. Two bombs were set off by suicide bombers outside police stations in Baghdad; 18 people were killed. **30**. A US military convoy was attacked in Samarra, Iraq, resulting in 46 Iraqis being killed by US tank fire.

DECEMBER 2003

9. Two suicide bombers blew themselves up at the gates of an American army base near the town of Fallujah in Iraq, wounding 58 soldiers. **13**. Economic and diplomatic sanctions were imposed on Syria by the US. In al-Maabar near Tikrit, American forces captured the former Iraqi leader Saddam Hussein; he had been hiding in a tiny underground shaft, known as a 'spider hole'. **15**. In Baku, thousands of people gathered for the funeral of the former President of Azerbaijan Heydar Aliyev; his son Ilham Aliyev took over the presidency. **18**. Iran signed an agreement to allow United Nations inspectors to make surprise visits to its atomic facilities. **26**. In Iran, an earthquake measuring 6.3 on the Richter scale killed an estimated 50,000 people and destroyed the city of Bam.

JANUARY 2004

9. Saddam Hussein was formally declared an enemy prisoner of war by Pentagon spokesman, Major Michael Shavers. **18**. Twenty people died and many people were injured when a suicide bomber detonated half a ton of explosives outside the headquarters of the coalition troops in Baghdad. **28**. Eight Palestinians were killed by Israeli troops when fighting broke out between them and around 200 Palestinian gunmen near the Jewish settlement of Netzarim in Israel.

FEBRUARY 2004

1. In Saudi Arabia, 244 people were trampled to death during the annual muslim pilgrimage to the Jamarat Bridge near Mecca for the stoning ritual which is part of the Eid al-Adha feast day of sacrifice. Two suicide bombers blew themselves up in the Kurdish city of Arbil in Iraq, killing 57 people, including the deputy governor of Arbil province and the city police chief. In Iran, 100 reformist MPs resigned in protest at the disqualification by the ruling Guardian Council of hundreds of reformist candidates from upcoming parliamentary elections. **2**. The Israeli Prime Minister Ariel Sharon announced his intention to begin the evacuation of 17 Jewish settlements in the Gaza Strip and said that he was working on the assumption that in the future there would be no Jews in Gaza. **10**. In Iraq, 55 people were killed near Baghdad after a 500 lb bomb exploded outside a police station; it was believed that al-Qa'eda had planted the bomb in order to provoke tensions between the majority Shia population and the Sunni minority. **18**. A train carrying fuel and chemicals derailed in north-east Iran, killing 295 people. **22**. The European Union and the US Administration criticised Iran's general election as 'undemocratic' after the Traditionalists won the election; 2,500 Reformists had been barred from standing at the election and many voters boycotted the elections.

MARCH 2004

2. Around 150 Shia muslims were killed and many more injured as five bombs exploded in Karbala and Baghdad. **15**. The International Atomic Energy Agency chief, Mohamed ElBaradei, announced that Iran had lifted its freeze on nuclear inspections and that they would resume on 27 March. **22**. In Israel, the founder of Hamas, Sheikh Ahmed Yassin, was assassinated outside his mosque by Israeli troops during a dawn missile attack, leading to 200,000 Palestinians protesting in the streets of Gaza City.

APRIL 2004

4. In Baghdad, nine American soldiers were killed and more than 24 wounded in fighting with Shia Muslims loyal to the radical Shia cleric, Hojatoleslam Moqtada al-Sadr; there was fighting in cities across Iraq in protest at the presence of the coalition forces in the country, resulting in more than 20 Iraqi deaths. **17**. The newly-appointed leader of the Palestinian group Hamas, Abdel Aziz al-Rantissi, was assassinated by Israeli forces after two Israeli helicopters fired rockets at his car. **18**. Hamas announced that the physician, Mahmoud Zahar, had been appointed as its new leader. **20**. In Iraq, a multiple mortar attack on the Abu Ghraib prison, west of Baghdad, killed 22 Iraqi inmates and injured almost 100 more. **21**. Four co-ordinated suicide bombings in the Iraqi city of Basra killed at least 68 people, including 17 schoolchildren, and injured a further 100 people. **27**. Two bombs exploded in the Syrian Capital Damascus and security forces fought gunmen in the Mezze suburb of the city; the attack was believed to have been carried out by a militant Muslim group. US forces in the Iraqi city of Najaf killed 64 Shia militiamen after they opened fire on an American patrol on the edge of the Kufa suburb. **29**. The American CBS television channel broadcast pictures taken in the Abu Ghraib prison outside Baghdad which depicted US troops abusing and humiliating Iraqi inmates; six soldiers faced charges of conspiracy, dereliction of duty, cruelty and maltreatment, assault and indecent acts and 11 others were suspended.

MAY 2004

4. An internal investigation by the US army reported that two Iraqi prisoners had been murdered by American soldiers and that there had been 35 criminal investigations into claims of prisoner abuse and deaths in Iraq and Afghanistan. **16**. The Kuwaiti cabinet approved a Bill to grant women the right to vote and stand for parliament. **17**. Abdel-Zahraa Othman, the president of the Iraqi Governing Council, was assassinated in Baghdad by a suicide car bomber at the headquarters of the American military. **19**. In Israel, 10 Palestinians were killed and more than 50 wounded when an Israeli tank fired into a crowd of unarmed demonstrators in the Gaza Strip. In Iraq, the US army killed around 40 members of a wedding party in the village of Maker al-Theeb after mistaking them for foreign fighters. **28**. An earthquake in the Mazandaran province of Iran killed 20 and injured 80 people. **30**. In Saudi Arabia, at least 22 people died after al-Qa'eda members launched kidnappings and attacks on Western targets.

JUNE 2004

6. Marwan Barghouti, the leader of the Palestinian intifada, was jailed by an Israeli court for attempted murder and membership of a terrorist organisation; he was sentenced to five life terms and 40 years in jail. **8**. Effi Eitam, the Israeli housing minister, and Yitzhak Levy, a deputy minister, resigned from Arial Sharon's coalition in protest at plans to withdraw from the Gaza Strip. **12**. Bassam Qubba, the Iraqi Deputy Foreign Minister was killed by gunmen while driving to work. **13**. In Iraq, the Cultural Affairs Officer, Kamal al-Jarrah, was shot dead outside his home. **17**. At least 35 Iraqis were killed and more than 130 wounded when a suicide bomber blew up a car outside the Iraqi army recruiting centre in Baghdad. **18**. Security officials in Saudi Arabia announced that they had killed three of the most-wanted al-Qa'eda members after they had made a broadcast on the internet claiming to have tortured and beheaded Paul Johnson, an aeronautical engineer from New Jersey. **22**. Iran state television showed three British servicemen blindfolded and apologising for their 'big mistake' after their patrol vessels strayed off course into Tehran's territorial waters. **24**. In Iraq, at least 62 people died and 220 were injured in car bombings in the northern city of Mosul. **27**. Israeli paratroopers killed six Palestinian militant leaders in a secret tunnel beneath a house in the city of Nablus, including Nayef Abu Sharkh, the commander of the militant group the Al-Aqsa Martyrs Brigades. **28**. The US and Britain handed over sovereignty to Iraq and officially ended the 15-month occupation two days earlier than expected. Iyad Allawi was named as the new Prime Minister of Iraq and a document containing the transfer of power was handed to him by Paul Bremer, the head of the Coalition Provisional Authority. **30**. In Israel, the Supreme Court ordered the Government to change the route of its security fence in the West Bank and to rip up a section already built in north Jerusalem as it caused unjustified hardship to around 35,000 Palestinians. Saudi Arabian security forces killed Abdullah al-Rooshood, believed to be al-Qa'eda's spiritual leader in the country, following a car chase in Riyadh.

JULY 2004

7. Iraq's prime minister Iyad Allawi signed in the new National Safety Law which would allow the interim government to declare an emergency in any area of the country deemed under threat from terrorism and would give security forces the power to search houses and detain suspects without an arrest warrant. **9**. Israel rejected a demand from the International Court of Justice to dismantle its security fence being built through occupied Palestinian territory after 14 out of 15 judges in the Hague voted that it breached international law. **13**. Khaled al-Harbi, a leading member of al-Qa'eda, gave himself up to Saudi Arabian authorities as part of a Saudi government amnesty which had recently been extended to terrorists. **22**. American marines in Iraq reported that they had killed 25 insurgents, wounded 17 and captured another 25 in a battle in the city of Ramadi after a US patrol came under attack from militants. **28**. At least 129 people were killed in Iraq by suicide bomb attacks in Baghdad, Ramadi, Fallujah and Balad-Ruz.

AUGUST 2004

6. Three hundred militants loyal to the cleric Moqtada al-Sadr were killed by US marines following fighting to regain control of the Iraqi city of Najaf. **8**. Palestine's justice minister, Nahed al-Reyes, and Nabil Qasis, the planning minister, announced their resignation from the Palestinian cabinet. **18**. The Iranian defence minister Ali Shamkhani warned America and Israel that it was ready to launch pre-emptive strikes to stop them attacking its nuclear facilities. In Israel, Prime Minister Ariel Sharon's Likud Party rejected proposals to enter a coalition with the Labour Party.

OBITUARIES

Aiken, Joan, children's author, aged 79 – *d.* 4 January 2004, *b.* 4 September 1924

Ainley, Anthony, actor, gained cult status for his role in Dr Who, the television series, aged 66 – *d.* 3 May 2004, *b.* 30 August 1937

Alcock, Vivien, children's author, aged 79 – *d.* 12 October 2003, *b.* 23 September 1924

Alison, Michael, Conservative MP for Barkston Ash (1964–83) and Selby (1983–97), minister of state at the Northern Ireland Office (1979–83) and parliamentary private secretary to Margaret Thatcher (1983–7), aged 77 – *d.* 28 May 2004, *b.* 27 June 1926

Aliyev, Heydar, president of Azerbaijan (1993–2003), aged 80 – *d.* 12 December 2003, *b.* 10 May 1923

Atkins, Babs, conservationist, owner and last inhabitant of the 22-acre St George's Island, Looe, aged 86 – *d.* 30 March 2004, *b.* 3 June 1917

Baldock, John, MBE, VRD, businessman, MP and founder of the Hollycombe Steam Collection, aged 87 – *d.* 3 October 2003, *b.* 19 November 1915

Bates, Sir Alan, actor, aged 69 – *d.* 27 December 2003, *b.* 17 February 1934

Batty, Sir William, former chairman and managing director of Ford in Britain, aged 90 – *d.* 31 October 2003, *b.* 15 May 1913

Berger, Vice-Adm. Sir Peter, KCB, LVO, DSC, aged 78 – *d.* 19 October 2003, *b.* 11 February 1925

Bertram, Elsie, MBE, book wholesaler, aged 91 – *d.* 26 October 2003, *b.* 2 June 1912

Blake, Lord, FBA, life peer, historian and provost of Queen's College, Oxford (1968–87), aged 86 – *d.* 20 September 2003, *b.* 23 December 1916

Blankers-Koen, Fanny, Dutch athlete who won four gold medals at the 1948 London Olympics and was voted the greatest female athlete of the 20th century by the IAAF in 1999, aged 85 – *d.* 25 January 2004, *b.* 26 April 1918

Blow, Prof. David, FRS, biophysicist, aged 72 – *d.* 8 June 2004, *b.* 27 June 1931

Boreham, Sir Leslie, High Court judge (1972–), aged 85 – *d.* 2 May 2004, *b.* 19 October 1918

Boyd, Prof. Sir Robert, CBE, FRS, space research scientist, professor of physics at the University of London (1962–83), aged 81 – *d.* 5 February 2004, *b.* 19 October 1922

Brando, Marlon, American actor, aged 80 – *d.* 1 July 2004, *b.* 3 April 1924

Brockhouse, Bertram, Canadian physicist, winner of the Nobel Prize for Physics (1994), aged 85 – *d.* 13 October 2003, *b.* 15 July 1918

Brown, Iona, violinist and conductor, aged 63 – *d.* 5 June 2004, *b.* 7 January 1941

Buck, Sir Antony, QC, Conservative MP for Colchester (1961–83) and for Colchester North (1983–92), aged 74 – *d.* 6 October 2003, *b.* 19 December 1928

Buckeridge, Anthony, OBE, schoolmaster and author of the 'Jennings' stories, aged 92 – *d.* 28 June 2004, *b.* 20 June 1912

Bullock, Lord, historian, founder of St Catherine's College, Oxford, created a life peer in 1976, aged 89 – *d.* 2 February 2004, *b.* 13 December 1914

Cameron of Lochiel, Col. Sir Donald, KT, CVO, TD, clan chief, appointed Knight of the Thistle in 1973, aged 93 – *d.* 26 May 2004, *b.* 12 September 1910

Campbell/Birkin, Judy, actress, aged 88 – *d.* 6 June 2004, *b.* 31 May 1916

Carr, Joe, golfer, aged 82 – *d.* 3 June 2004, *b.* 18 February 1922

Carrington, Joanna, artist, aged 72 – *d.* 13 November 2003, *b.* 6 November 1931

Cartier-Bresson, Henri, French photographer, aged 95 – *d.* 2 August 2004, *b.* 22 August 1908

Cartwright, Stephen, children's book illustrator, aged 57 – *d.* 12 February 2004, *b.* 28 December 1947

Cash, Johnny, country music singer, aged 71 – *d.* 12 September 2003, *b.* 26 February 1932

Causley, Charles, CBE, poet, aged 86 – *d.* 4 November 2003, *b.* 24 August 1917

Cavenagh, Prof. Winifred, OBE, criminologist, aged 95 – *d.* 7 May 2004, *b.* 12 November 1908

Charles, Pierre, prime minister of Dominica (2000–4), aged 49 – *d.* 6 January 2004 of a heart attack, *b.* 30 June 1954

Charles, John, CBE, Welsh footballer, aged 72 – *d.* 21 February 2004, *b.* 27 December 1931

Charles, Ray, American musician, aged 73 – *d.* 10 June 2004, *b.* 23 September 1930

Chilcott, Susan, opera singer, aged 40 – *d.* 4 September 2003, *b.* 8 July 1963

Coldstream, Sir George, KCB, KCVO, permanent secretary to the Lord Chancellor (1954–68), aged 96 – *d.* 19 April 2004, *b.* 20 December 1907

Constantine of Stanmore, Lord, CBE, AE, business and political activist, created a life peer in 1981, aged 93 – *d.* 13 February 2004, *b.* 15 March 1910

Cooke, Alistair, journalist and broadcaster, aged 95 – *d.* 29 March 2004, *b.* 20 November 1908

Crick, Francis, OM, FRS, biologist, joint recipient of the Nobel Prize for Medicine (1962) for the discovery of the structure of DNA, aged 88 – *d.* 28 July 2004, *b.* 8 June 1916

Daly, Lt.-Gen. Sir Tom, KBE, CB, DSO, Australia's chief of general staff (1966–71), aged 90 – *d.* 5 January 2004 in Sydney, Australia, *b.* 19 March 1913

Darling (2nd), Lord, aged 84 – *d.* 16 October 2003, *b.* 15 May 1919

Davis, Richard, cricketer, aged 37 – *d.* 29 December 2003, *b.* 18 March 1966

Devonshire (11th), Duke of, KG, MC, aged 84 – *d.* 3 May 2004, *b.* 2 January 1920

Diamond, Lord, PC, QC, former Labour MP, chief secretary to the Treasury (1964–70) and SDP leader in House of Lords (1982–8), aged 96 – *d.* 3 April 2004, *b.* 30 April 1907

Donaldson, Dame Mary, GBE, philanthropist, first woman to hold the office of Lord Mayor of London (1983–4), aged 82 – *d.* 4 October 2003, *b.* 29 August 1921

Doniach, Prof. Deborah, clinical immunologist, aged 91 – *d.* 1 January 2004, *b.* 6 April 1912

Dormand of Easington, Lord, MP for Easington (1970–87) and chairman of the Parliamentary Labour Party (1981–7), created a life peer in 1987, aged 84 – *d.* 18 December 2003, *b.* 27 August 1919

Downshire (8th), The Marquess of, aged 74 – *d.* 18 December 2003, *b.* 10 May 1929

Duffen, Leslie, teacher and pioneer in the teaching of Down's syndrome children, aged 79 – *d.* 8 May 2004, *b.* 14 November 1924

Dugdale, Lady, DCVO, lady-in-waiting to the Queen (1955–2002), aged 80 – *d.* 4 November 1923, *b.* 12 March 2004

Dumas, Charles, American athlete who became the first man to clear 7ft in the high jump in 1956, aged 66 – *d.* 5 January 2004, *b.* 12 February 1937

Dunboyne (28th), Lord, judge, aged 87 – *d.* 19 May 2004, *b.* 27 January 1917

Dunn, Air Marshal Sir Patrick, KBE, CB, DFC, aged 91 – *d.* 17 June 2004, *b.* 31 December 1912

Dunne, John Gregory, American journalist, novelist and screenwriter, aged 71 – *d.* 30 December 2003, *b.* 25 May 1932

Durkin, Air Marshal Sir Herbert, KBE, CB, aged 82 – *d.* 12 April 2004, *b.* 31 March 1922

Ederle, Gertrude, American swimmer, the first woman to swim the English Channel, aged 97 – *d.* 30 November 2003, *b.* 23 October 1906

Esher (4th), Viscount, CBE, architect and town planner, aged 90 – *d.* 9 July 2004, *b.* 18 July 1913

Fiennes, Lady Virginia, explorer, aged 56 – *d.* 20 February 2004, *b.* 9 July 1947

Fluss, Elfrieda, milliner, aged 89 – *d.* 8 January 2004, *b.* 16 November 1914

Foot, Paul, author and journalist, aged 66 – *d.* 18 July 2004, *b.* 8 November 1937

Forest, Antonia, children's author, aged 88 – *d.* 28 November 2003, *b.* 26 May 1915

Friedlander, Rabbi Dr Albert, spiritual leader and interfaith worker, aged 77 – *d.* 8 July 2004, *b.* 10 May 1927

Frost, Sir Terry, RA, artist, aged 87 – *d.* 1 September 2003, *b.* 13 October 1915

Fry, Tim, car designer and engineer, aged 68 – *d.* 17 May 2004, *b.* 25 August 1935

Geraint, Lord, Welsh politician, leader of the Welsh Liberal party (1979–85), created a life peer in 1992, aged 79 – *d.* 17 April 2004, *b.* 15 April 1925

Getting, Ivan, American scientist, aged 91 – *d.* 11 October 2003, *b.* 18 January 1912

Gibson, Sir Ralph, PC, QC, chairman of the Law Commission (1981–5) and Lord Justice of Appeal (1985–94), aged 81 – *d.* 30 October 2003, *b.* 17 October 1922

Gibson, Lord, chairman of the Arts Council (1972–7), the National Trust (1977–86) and the Pearson Group (1978–83), aged 88 – *d.* 20 April 2004, *b.* 5 February 1916

Gilmour, Sally, ballerina, aged 82 – *d.* 23 May 2004, *b.* 2 November 1921

Ginsberg, Jean, doctor and specialist in women's health, aged 77 – *d.* 8 April 2004, *b.* 19 October 1926

Golub, Leon, artist, aged 82 – *d.* 8 August 2004, *b.* 23 January 1922

Gordon, Nick, wildlife cameraman and film producer, aged 51 – *d.* 25 April 2004, *b.* 9 May 1952

Grandy, Marshal of the RAF Sir John, GCB, GCVO, KBE, DSO, chief of the Air Staff (1967–71), appointed Marshal of the Royal Air Force on his retirement in 1971, aged 90 – *d.* 2 January 2004, *b.* 8 February 1913

Grant Duff, Shiela, writer and reporter, aged 90 – *d.* 19 March 2004, *b.* 11 May 1913

Greene of Harrow Weald, Lord, CBE, life peer, general secretary of the National Union of Railwaymen (1957–75), aged 94 – *d.* 26 July 2004, *b.* 12 February 1910

Gregg, Hubert, composer, actor and broadcaster, aged 89 – *d.* 29 March 2004, *b.* 19 July 1914

Gunn, Thom, poet, aged 74 – *b.* 29 August 1929, *d.* 25 April 2004

Hampshire, Prof. Sir Stuart, philosopher and warden of Wadham College, Oxford (1970–84), aged 89 – *d.* 13 June 2004, *b.* 1 October 1914

Hardinge (6th), Viscount of, aged 47 – *d.* 18 January 2004, *b.* 25 August 1956

Hardy of Wath, Lord, Labour MP for Rother Valley (1970–83) and Wentworth (1983–97), created a life peer in 1997, aged 72 – *d.* 16 December 2003, *b.* 17 July 1931

Hayter (3rd), Lord, last family chairman of Chubb & Sons, Locksmiths, aged 92 – *d.* 2 September 2003, *b.* 25 April 1911

Hemmings, David, actor, director and producer, aged 62 – *d.* 3 December 2003, *b.* 18 November 1941

Henley, Sir Douglas, KCB, 14th comptroller and auditor-general at the Treasury (1976–81), aged 84 – *d.* 1 October 2003, *b.* 5 April 1919

Henniker (8th), Lord, KCMG, CMG, CVO, MC, diplomat, aged 88 – *d.* 29 April 2004, *b.* 19 February 1916

Hill-Norton, Admiral of the Fleet, Lord, GCB, GCVO, KBE, DSO, chief of Defence Staff (1971–3), chairman of the Military Committee of NATO (1974–7), aged 89 – *d.* 16 May 2004, *b.* 8 February 1915

Hobhouse of Woodborough, Lord, PC, QC, Lord of Appeal (1998–2004), created a life peer in 1998, aged 72 – *d.* 15 March 2004, *b.* 31 January 1932

Holland, Mary, journalist, aged 67 – *d.* 7 June 2004, *b.* 19 June 1936

Hounsfield, Sir Godfrey, CBE, FRS, scientist, winner of the Nobel Prize for Medicine (1979) for inventing the CAT (computerised axial tomography) scanner, aged 84 – *d.* 12 August 2004, *b.* 29 August 1919

Hurley, Denis, Archbishop of Durban (1952–92), aged 88 – *d.* 13 February 2004, *b.* 9 November 1915

Hurley, Dame Rosalinde, DBE, microbiologist and pathologist, chairman of the Medicines Commission (1982–93), aged 74 – *d.* 30 June 2004, *b.* 30 December 1929

Ishihara, Takashi, president (1977–85) and chairman (1985–92) of Nissan Motor Co., aged 91 – *d.* 31 December 2003, *b.* 3 March 1912

Islwyn, Lord, Labour MP for Newport (1966–83) and Newport East (1983–97), created a life peer in 1997, aged 78 – *d.* 19 December 2003, *b.* 9 June 1925

Izetbegovic, Alija, Bosnian politician, Muslim member of the joint presidency of Bosnia Hercegovina (1996–2000), aged 78 – *d.* 19 October 2003, *b.* 8 August 1925

Jenkins, Vivien, rugby player for Wales in the 1930s and later, sports journalist who retired in 1976, aged 92 – *d.* 5 January 2004, *b.* 2 November 1911

Jenkins of Putney, Lord, Labour MP for Wandsworth, Putney (1964–79), created a life peer in 1981, aged 95 – *d.* 26 January 2004, *b.* 27 July 1908

Jennings, Sir Robert, international lawyer, president of the International Court of Justice (1982–96), aged 90 – *d.* 4 August 2004, *b.* 19 October 1913

Jupp, Sir Kenneth, MC, judge of the High Court, Queen's Bench Division (1975–90), aged 86 – *d.* 15 March 2004, *b.* 2 June 1917

Kadyrov, Akhmad, president of Chechnya (2003–4), aged 53 – *d.* assassinated 9 May 2004, *b.* 23 August 1950

Kay, Sir John, PC, QC, Lord Justice of Appeal (2000–4), aged 60 – *d.* 2 July 2004, *b.* 13 September 1943

Keating, Caron, television presenter, aged 41 – *d.* 13 April 2004, *b.* 5 October 1962

Keith of Castleacre, Lord, merchant banker and industrialist, chairman of Rolls-Royce (1972–80), created a life peer in 1980, aged 88 – *d.* 1 September 2004, *b.* 30 August 1916

Kessel, Barney, American jazz guitarist, aged 80 – *d.* 6 May 2004, *b.* 17 October 1923

Landen, Dinsdale, actor, aged 71 – *d.* 29 December 2003, *b.* 4 September 1932

Langman, Mary, MBE, organic farmer, founder member of the Soil Association, aged 95 – *d.* 31 March 2004, *b.* 6 August 1908

Lauder, Estée, founder of the Estée Lauder cosmetics company, aged 97 – *d.* 24 April 2004, *b.* 1 July 1906

Leask, Lt.-Gen. Sir Henry, KCB, DSO, OBE, GOC, aged 90 – *d.* 10 January 2004, *b.* 30 June 1913

Lee, Air Chief Marshal Sir David, GBE, CB, military representative to NATO (1968–71), aged 91 – *d.* 13 February 2004, *b.* 4 September 1912

Lee, Anna, actress, aged 91 – *d.* 14 May 2004, *b.* 2 January 1913

Levin, Bernard, CBE, journalist, aged 75 – *d.* 7 August 2004, *b.* 19 August 1928

Lindh, Anna, Swedish politician and Foreign Minister, aged 46 – *d.* 11 September 2003, *b.* 19 June 1957

Livesay, Adm. Sir Michael, KCB, head of the Naval Advisory Group during the Falklands war, aged 67 – *d.* 6 October 2003, *b.* 5 April 1936

Lodge, David, actor, aged 82 – *d.* 18 October 2003, *b.* 19 August 1921

MacDougall, Sir Donald, CBE, economist, aged 91 – *d.* 22 March 2004, *b.* 26 October 1912

May, Sir Richard, presiding judge of the International Criminal Tribunal for the former Yugoslavia (1997–2004), aged 65 – *d.* 1 July 2004, *b.* 12 November 1938

Maynard Smith, John, FRS, biologist, aged 84 – *d.* 19 April 2004, *b.* 6 January 1920

McKechnie, Dame Sheila, DBE, director of Shelter, the housing charity, (1985–94) and the Consumers' Association (1995–2003), aged 55 – *d.* 2 January 2004 of cancer, *b.* 3 May 1948

McWhirter, Norris, CBE, co-founder of the *Guinness Book of Records* and contributor to *Whitaker's Almanack*, aged 78 – *d.* 19 April 2004, *b.* 12 August 1925

Mercer, The Rt. Revd Eric, Bishop of Exeter (1973–85), aged 85 – *d.* 8 November 2003, *b.* 6 December 1917

Metcalfe, Ben, journalist and founding member of Greenpeace, aged 84 – *d.* 16 October 2003, *b.* 27 November 1918

Monkhouse, Bob, entertainer, aged 75 – *d.* 29 December 2003, *b.* 1 June 1928

Morgan, Peter, sports car manufacturer, aged 83 – *d.* 20 October 2003, *b.* 3 November 1919

Mountgarret (17th), Viscount, aged 67 – *d.* 7 February 2004, *b.* 8 November 1936

Murray of Epping Forest, Lord, OBE, PC, trades unionist, general secretary of the TUC (1973–84), aged 81 – *d.* 20 May 2004, *b.* 2 August 1922

Neagu, Paul, Romanian sculptor, aged 66 – *d.* 16 June 2004, *b.* 22 February 1938

Newton, Helmut, photographer, aged 83 – *d.* 23 January 2004 in Los Angeles, USA, *b.* 31 October 1920

Nuttall, Jeff, painter, poet, author and performance artist, aged 70 – *d.* 4 January 2004, *b.* 8 July 1933

Palmer, Robert, rock singer, aged 53 – *d.* 25 September 2003, *b.* 19 January 1949

Pantani, Marco, former world cycling champion, aged 34 – *d.* 14 February 2004, Rimini, Italy, *b.* 13 January 1970

Partridge, Frances, CBE, author and last survivor of the 'Bloomsbury set', aged 103 – *d.* 5 February 2004, *b.* 15 March 1990

Paul, Sir John, GCMG, MC, governor-general of the Gambia (1961–6), the Bahamas (1972–3) and lieutenant-governor of the Isle of Man (1974–80), aged 88 – *d.* 31 March 2004, *b.* 29 March 1916

Pearce, Sir Austen, chairman of British Aerospace (1980–7), aged 82 – *d.* 21 March 2004, *b.* 1 September 1921

Pembroke (17th) and Montgomery (18th), Earl of, film and television director, aged 64 – *d.* 7 October 2003, *b.* 19 May 1939

Pike, Baroness Mervyn, DBE, Conservative MP for Melton (1956–74), chairman of the Women's Royal Voluntary Service (1974–81) and life peer, aged 85 – *d.* 11 January 2004, *b.* 16 September 1918

Pople, Anthony, musicologist, aged 48 – *d.* 10 October 2003, *b.* 18 January 1955

Pople, Sir John, KBE, FRS, quantum chemist, winner of the Nobel Prize for Chemistry in 1998, aged 78 – *d.* 15 March 2004, *b.* 31 October 1925

Quilley, Denis, actor, aged 75 – *d.* 5 October 2003, *b.* 26 December 1927

Ravensworth (8th), Lord, aged – *d.* 28 March 2004, *b.* 25 July 1924

Rayne, Lord, QC, property developer and philanthropist, made a life peer in 1976, aged 85 – *d.* 10 October 2003, *b.* 8 February 1918

Reagan, Ronald, actor and politician, president of the USA (1980–89), aged 93 – *d.* 5 June 2004, *b.* 6 February 1911

Reid, Gordon, television and theatre actor, aged 64 – *d.* 26 November 2003, *b.* 8 June 1939

Resnick, Milton, artist, aged 87 – *d.* 12 March 2004, *b.* 8 January 1917

Richardson, Lord, LVO, physician, president of the General Medical Council (1973–80), the British Medical Association (1970–1) and the Royal Society of Medicine (1969–71), created a life peer in 1979, aged 94 – *d.* 8 August 2004, *b.* 16 June 1910

Rossiter, Nick, BBC documentary-maker, aged 43 – *d.* 23 July 2004, *b.* 17 July 1961

Roxburgh, Vice-Adm. Sir John, KCB, CBE, DSO, DSC and Bar, aged 84 – *d.* 13 April 2004, *b.* 29 June 1919

Sackville (6th), Lord, aged 90 – *d.* 27 March 2004, *b.* 30 May 1913

Said, Edward, literary and political commentator, aged 67 – *d.* 24 September 2003, *b.* 1 November 1935

Sandilands, John, journalist, aged 72 – *d.* 15 March 2004, *b.* 19 July 1931

Scanlon, Lord, trade union leader, created a life peer in 1979, aged 90 – *d.* 27 January 2004, *b.* 26 October 1913

Scarbrough (12th), Earl of, aged 71 – *d.* 23 March 2004, *b.* 5 December 1932

Schott, Alberic, Belgian cyclist, aged 84 – *d.* 4 April 2004, *b.* 7 September 1919

Shapiro, Isaac Avi, literary scholar, aged 99 – *d.* 14 March 2004, *b.* 7 November 1904

Shenfield, Dame Barbara, DBE, sociologist, aged 85 – *d.* 17 June 2004, *b.* 9 March 1919

Shoenberg, Prof. David, MBE, physicist known for his work in the field of superconductivity, aged 93 – *d.* 10 March 2004, *b.* 4 January 1911

Short, Roger, diplomat, UK consul-general in Turkey, aged 58 – *d.* 20 November 2003, killed in a terrorist bombing, *b.* 9 December 1944

Skeet, Trevor, Conservative MP for Willesden East (1959–64) and Bedford, later Bedfordshire North (1970–97), aged 86 – *d.* 14 August 2004, *b.* 28 January 1918

Smart, Prof. Sir George, physician, endocrinologist and Director of the British Postgraduate Medical Federation (1971–8), aged 89 – *d.* 1 November 2003, *b.* 16 December 1913

Squire, Raglan, architect, aged 92 – *d.* 18 May 2004, *b.* 30 January 1912

Stacey, Margaret, sociologist, aged 81 – *d.* 10 February 2004, *b.* 27 March 1922

Stamper, John, aeronautical engineer and chief designer of the Buccaneer strike aircraft (1961), aged 77 – *d.* 15 November 2003, *b.* 12 October 1926

Stanbrook, Ivor, Conservative MP (1970–92), aged 80 – *d.* 18 February 2004, *b.* 13 January 1924

Steel, Sir David, DSO, MC, chairman of BP (1975–81), aged 87 – *d.* 9 August 2004, *b.* 29 November 1916

Steig, William, American cartoonist and children's author, aged 95 – *d.* 3 October 2003, *b.* 17 November 1907

Stockdale, Sir Noel, founding chairman of the ASDA supermarket chain, aged 83 – *d.* 2 February 2004, *b.* 25 December 1920

Tanner, John, CBE, director, RAF Museum (1963–88), aged 77 – *d.* 18 May 2004, *b.* 2 January 1927

Taylor, Lt.-Gen. Sir Allan, KBE, MC, deputy commander-in-chief, UK Land Forces (1973–6), aged 85 – *d.* 13 June 2004, *b.* 26 March 1919

Tidsdale, Bob, Irish athlete, gold medallist at the 1932 Los Angeles Olympics, aged 97 – *d.* 28 July 2004, *b.* 16 May 1916

Trajkovski, Boris, president of Macedonia (1999–2004), aged 47 – *d.* 26 February 2004, killed in an air crash in Bosnia, *b.* 25 June 1956

Trevor-Roper, Patrick, ophthalmologist and art historian, aged 87 – *d.* 22 April 2004, *b.* 7 June 1916

Tumim, Sir Stephen, lawyer and prison reformer, aged 73 – *d.* 8 December 2003, *b.* 15 August 1930

Ustinov, Sir Peter, actor, director and writer, aged 82 – *d.* 28 March 2004, *b.* 16 April 1921

Venables, Clare, theatre director, aged 60 – *d.* 17 October 2003, *b.* 17 March 1943

Vladimov, Georgi, Russian writer and political dissident, aged 72 – *d.* 19 October 2003, *b.* 19 February 1931

Walker of Doncaster, Lord, PC, Labour MP for 33 years, knighted in 1992 and created a life peer in 1997, aged 76 – *d.* 11 November 2003, *b.* 12 July 1927

Wallace of Coslany, Lord, Labour politician, aged 97 – *d.* 11 November 2003, *b.* 18 April 1906

Watson, Willie, cricketer, aged 84 – *d.* 24 April 2004, *b.* 7 March 1920

Wickham, Glynne, academic and drama teacher, aged 81 – *d.* 27 January 2004, *b.* 15 May 1922

Wigoder, Lord, QC, lawyer and Liberal peer, Liberal chief whip in the Lords (1977–84), aged 83 – *d.* 12 August 2004, *b.* 12 February 1921

Williams of Mostyn, Lord, PC, QC, barrister and politician, Lord President of the Privy Council and leader of the House of Lords, aged 62 – *d.* 20 September 2003, *b.* 5 February 1941

Wilson, Sir Geoffrey, KCB, CMG, lawyer and diplomat, vice-president of the World Bank (1961–6), aged 94 – *d.* 11 July 2004, *b.* 7 April 1910

Winter, Fred, CBE, jump jockey and trainer, aged 77 – *d.* 5 April 2004, *b.* 20 September 1926

Woodin, Michael, principal speaker of the Green Party (2001 and 2003–4), aged 38 – *d.* 9 July 2004, *b.* 6 November 1965

Ziegler, Anne, 1940s concert and variety performance singer, aged 93 – *d.* 13 October 2003, *b.* 22 June 1910

ARCHAEOLOGY

EARLY HOMINIDS IN BRITAIN

The discovery of *c.* 500,000-year-old hominid remains in a gravel quarry at Boxgrove near Chichester in Sussex in 1993 transformed views on when Britain was first inhabited by hominids by pushing the date backwards to a period before the great Anglian Glaciation of *c.* 450,000 BC. Now new research is pushing the date back much further: to a period before the two preceding glaciations (the so-called 'Cromerian Complex'), that is, to *c.* 700,000 BC.

This is one aspect of a major five-year project, Ancient Human Occupation of Britain (AHOB), set up in 2002 with a million-pound grant from the Leverhulme Trust, and involving the British Museum, the Natural History Museum and five universities. Key questions being tackled by AHOB include: 'Were there humans in Britain before Boxgrove? Was human occupation continuous, or were there periods of abandonment and recolonisation? How did early humans exploit the landscape, and what was the driving force for big changes in the Stone Age toolkit?' Answers are rapidly emerging. The oldest site, with remains possibly dating back 700,000 years, is Happisburgh in East Anglia, but other sites are more recent, with one of *c.* 600,000 BC, and another of *c.* 550,000 BC. The early human occupation of Britain was not likely to be continuous. In fact, even as late as *c.* 180,000–60,000 BC, during the Ipswichian Interglacial, there appears to have been another major abandonment.

Other work is revealing the way our forebears exploited their environment, a pattern that changed over time, no doubt in line with available resources. The chemical composition of human bones from Gough's and Sun Hole caves, for instance – datable to the Upper Palaeolithic (*c.* 35,000–8,000 BC) – had revealed people who were predominately meat-eaters, providing a new answer to the old question: 'Were early humans hunters, foragers or scavengers?'

As for changes in the toolkit, where previously it was thought that migrant groups introduced new techniques and implements, evidence now suggests that, in some cases at least, these developed in different places at the same time. An example would be the Levallois tradition of the Lower-Middle Palaeolithic transition (*c.* 300,000–180,000 BC), which involved preparing the core from which flakes were struck so that a wider range of specific tools could be produced. Africa and Europe seem to have developed this innovation in parallel. This provides a new answer to the old argument between 'diffusionists' (who see new ideas spreading out from an advanced centre) and 'evolutionists' (who see human societies in similar conditions coming up with the same solutions to the problems of development independently).

THE THORNBOROUGH HENGES

Neolithic archaeology faces a crisis in North Yorkshire. This revolves around the famous Thornborough Henges. These monuments are unique. There are three of them, almost identical in size and layout, and they are set in a row, extending across 1.7 km of landscape. Each is comprised of massive banks and ditches (the original uprights were made of wood and have not survived), and has a diameter of about 240 m. Only four British henges are larger – all in Wiltshire and Dorset. Hardly surprising, then, that the Thornborough Henges have been dubbed the 'Stonehenge of the North'.

Much of the appreciation of the henges, and their remarkable place in British prehistory, comes in the wake of a proposal by Tarmac Northern Ltd to extend quarrying into two new extraction sites within the 'archaeology zone' dominated by the three Thornborough Henges. This would destroy 111 acres of prehistoric archaeology. Already, test excavations have revealed evidence of ritual activity continuing around the henges over some 3,000 years. This includes human burials and three probable processional ways, two defined by banks and ditches (cursuses), one by a double-pit alignment. If the destruction of the henges' environs goes ahead, important information about the meaning of the henges will be lost; as at Stonehenge, the relationship between the ceremonial monuments and the sacred landscape in which they lie is essential to their interpretation. Heritage Action, The Friends of Thornborough and other local groups are campaigning to stop the quarrying.

BURIALS OF THE BEAKER ELITE

The 'Beaker' folk of the Early Bronze Age – named after their distinctive, decorated, red-coloured 'beakers', probably used for drinking mead – have featured heavily in recent discoveries. The 'Amesbury Archer' (excavated in 2002) was buried near Stonehenge in the late third millennium BC accompanied by five Beaker vessels, golden hair ornaments, three copper knives, a quiver full of arrows, and two stone wrist-guards to protect his left arm from the whiplash of the bowstring. Chemical analysis of his tooth enamel showed he came from the area around modern Switzerland. Was he part of a new metal-working elite that had arrived from the Continent? Was this evidence for an embryonic ruling class with the power to raise a great monument like Stonehenge? Then, from another site nearby, came the seven 'Boscombe Bowmen' (excavated 2003) – three adult males, a teenage male and three children in one normal-sized grave. Buried with them were eight Beaker vessels, five flint arrowheads, a boar's tusk, and an unusual bone toggle. Of the same date as the Amesbury Archer, the Boscombe Bowmen add to our impression that a new group had arrived or evolved in the Wessex region around the time Stonehenge was built.

New scientific results have quashed the idea that the Boscombe Bowmen also came from across the Channel; rather, chemical analysis of their teeth this time indicates they came from Wales. This is a stunning discovery, since the bluestones at Stonehenge – believed to have been rearranged at least four times between *c.* 2,400 and 2,000 BC – came from the Preseli Hills in Pembrokeshire, south-west Wales. Did the Boscombe Bowmen arrive with the stones? Are the three men among the builders of Stonehenge?

There was news of yet another new Beaker-age discovery, this time at Gayhurst in Northamptonshire near the M1 motorway. Bones from perhaps 600 cattle were buried in one of seven Beaker barrows excavated at the site between 1997 and 2002 by Northamptonshire Archaeology. Though the other six barrows had been ploughed flat in medieval times, the largest – 34 m in diameter – still survived as a low earthwork. The excavators found two ditches around the outside and a massive grave-pit in the middle – 3.5 m long and 1.45 m deep – which contained five successive burials. Piled over the barrow of the primary burial – an adult man in an oak lined chamber, buried in an extended position – were the cattle bones. Was this evidence of a huge funerary feast? The other four burials were placed above the roof of the burial chamber – after the feasting, and after the burial chamber had collapsed. Then the barrow seems to have been enlarged, and the second ditch was dug outside. Finally, two more cremations were made, dated between 2,100 and 1,900 BC. It seems the feasting was over, for there were no more cattle bones in the second ditch. A preliminary study of some of the cattle bones shows there was a preference for joints with high meat-yields; there are disproportionate quantities of upper-limb and pelvic bones. Was the meat of 600 animals all consumed in a single feast? Or was the feasting spread over many years? Either way, the first occupant of this Beaker barrow, the man in the oak-lined chamber, may have been another of the Early Bronze Age elite.

CHARIOTS OF THE WARLORDS, GOLD OF THE GODS

An Iron Age chariot-burial containing three surprises has been found by Oxford Archaeology at Ferrybridge in West Yorkshire, where the A1(M) motorway crosses the River Wharfe. Though the wooden parts had long since rotted, the iron tyres on the wheels remained. Several chariot fittings were also recovered, including the five bronze terret rings fixed to the wooden yoke to gather the reins.

The first surprise was that the chariot itself was intact and complete. Of the 20 Iron Age chariot-burials known, in most the vehicle had been dismantled; in only two or three other examples was this not the case. The second surprise was in the ditch surrounding the grave. There, archaeologists found bones from at least 250 cattle, mainly animals aged two to three years – the prime age for slaughtering meat. There were also a few pig bones, and single bones from a horse and sheep. Presumably these are the remains of funerary feasting, for which there is very little evidence elsewhere in the Iron Age. Thirdly, the Ferrybridge chariot-burial is in the wrong place. Though chariots were widely used in Late Iron Age Britain – they are recorded by classical writers like Caesar and Tacitus, and stray finds of chariot fittings are not uncommon – known chariot-burials have, until recently, been confined to East Yorkshire. Three were excavated on the prominent hill above the village of Wetwang Slack in 1984, and then another in the same place in 2001. But we now have one from Newbridge near Edinburgh (excavated in 2001), and another from Ferrybridge in West Yorkshire.

Chariots were costly and prestigious battle-carts for warrior elite. Burial with a chariot was an assertive display of rank and role. A practice once believed confined to a small area may in fact have been widespread in the centuries before the Roman Conquest. The funeral of a great British king – celebrated in Celtic style shortly after the Roman Conquest at the Folly Lane site just outside *Verulamium* (Roman St Albans) – included the burning of a chariot, along with many other rich offerings, as if this were an essential part of the traditional send-off.

Other new discoveries come from Sedgeford in north-west Norfolk, the area with the richest Iron Age hoarding in Britain. The neighbouring parish of Snettisham is famous for its fabulous hoards of gold, electrum, silver and bronze torcs (neck-rings), buried in 12 small pits. The Sedgeford team had set out to investigate an Anglo-Saxon village, but they suddenly found themselves digging gold – Iron Age gold. First they found a hoard of gold coins hidden inside an animal bone. They were Gallo-Belgic E gold staters, dated *c.* 60–50 BC, and at least 20 of them had been placed inside the shaft of a cow's front right humerus, while another 19 were found dispersed nearby. The bone and coins had been placed in a small pit, and round about was evidence for rituals involving pot smashing and horse sacrifice, as well as huge boundary ditches, apparently demarcating a sacred area at the base of a slope, close to a river, a natural spring and a possible area of marshland.

That was in the summer of 2003. The following Easter, the same team, working in another part of the parish, found the missing terminal from a broken gold torc that had been in the British Museum for 40 years. This extraordinary chance discovery has alerted archaeologists to the possibility of other Celtic ritual sites in the parish. A sacred landscape much wider in extent than the immediate vicinity of the famous Snettisham hoards is emerging to view. The latest news from the site (summer 2004) is that one of the boundary ditches near the coin hoard contained a small group of fineware pottery – a mixture of Late Iron Age and Early Roman vessels – probably dating to the mid 1st century AD, that is, to the time of the Icenian client-kingdom and the Boudiccan Revolt.

ROMANO-BRITISH TOWNS

Two towns have dominated recent work on Roman Britain: Canterbury and London. The Whitefriars Project in Canterbury, dubbed 'the Big Dig', which started in 1999 and finished in 2004, was a massive rescue dig to explore a large slice of the south-eastern part of the town between the ancient walls and the central zone, amounting to an astonishing 6 per cent of the old city. The exploration was spurred on by a rolling programme of demolition, earth-moving, pile-driving, and new building by the developers of a new shopping centre. So how much of the city's history has been changed by new discoveries?

Firstly, no real evidence was found to support the idea of Canterbury as an *oppidum* (a major political centre with perimeter defences) in the late Iron Age. Material of this date has only been found in a small central area where a Roman temple precinct later developed; there was very little Iron Age evidence at Whitefriars. Perhaps, then, Canterbury originally developed around a religious sanctuary beside a ford over the River Stour.

Secondly, the Whitefriars site seems to have straddled two urban zones in the Early Roman period, a more developed inner one close to the centrally-placed public buildings, and an outer one which remained largely open ground. Romano-British towns were not, perhaps, as built-up as we might have thought: urbanism was a rather fragile flower in ancient Britain. Thirdly, fuel has been added to the debate about 'the decline of the towns'. Whitefriars has evidence both for dilapidation and abandonment, and for new building and continuing commercial activity. But which is the dominant trend? A grand town-house was certainly refurbished, with new rooms added and floors re-laid, in the fourth century. But later, from the fifth-century evidence, we seem to have an apocalyptic vision of 'the end of civilisation': seven bodies dumped unceremoniously in a ditch beside a track running across an area of wasteground.

London continues to be of prime interest to Romanists for two reasons: the frenetic pace of redevelopment in the City and Southwark, where the Roman remains lie; and the high water-table, which means layers of waterlogged archaeology just beneath the surface, with rich hauls of preserved timber structures and wooden artefacts. In the space of a few months in 2001, for instance, London produced evidence of three, possibly four, bucket-chains for raising water from giant wells – discoveries that are unique in the Roman Empire, with both iron links *and* the wooden box-buckets preserved. A short while later, there was the spectacular discovery of an elaborate Roman bath-house beneath the American-themed 'Babe Ruth' diner in Shadwell in the East End. Was this evidence for a Late Roman port east of London, perhaps replacing the old port along the City waterfront after a defensive wall was built along the riverbank?

The bucket-chains from two sites in the City had revealed how Roman London was supplied with water. The Shadwell bath-house had pinpointed a hitherto unsuspected extramural settlement to the east. The Tabard Square site in Southwark has now yielded something equally remarkable: a monumental Roman inscription from the 2nd century – the oldest one known to mention London, or more accurately, *Londiniensium*, which means 'of the Londoners'. Excavation of the site by the PCA archaeological unit has now finished. Like Canterbury Whitefriars, it was a massive operation, the largest single dig in London's history, covering 1.25 ha. As well as the inscription, it also yielded another headline-grabbing discovery: an unopened pot of moisturising cream, into which the finger-marks of the last (Roman) user were deeply gouged. We can now report something of the context for these unusual finds.

The earliest settlement was of clay and timber buildings, probably shops, dating to the 1st century AD, but this was wiped away around AD 72. The character of the site then completely changed. Two small square buildings (11 m × 11 m), very probably Romano-Celtic temples, were built. About 50 m south ran a ditch, interpreted as a ritual boundary, owing to the numerous unusual small finds discovered therein: exquisite tiny brooches, seal boxes, and coins. Between temples and ditch was a high-status structure – interpreted as a pilgrims' inn – which appears to have been in the form of a winged corridor villa, 25 m long, 10 m wide, with a possible flight of steps to the first floor.

Tabard Square seems, then, to have been a ritual site. Except for the Mithras temple excavated in the 1950s and an inscription that refers to an Isis temple, there is very little evidence for religious activity in Roman London north of the river. Perhaps there was a division of space: administration and commerce concentrated in the 'Central Business District' to the north; religion and recreation on the South Bank.

TREASURES OF A CHRISTIAN KING?

In February 2004, the Museum of London Archaeology Service (MoLAS) made public the discovery of an Anglo-Saxon royal burial in Prittlewell, south-east Essex, that was fit to compare with Sutton Hoo. The body had completely rotted away, but the wooden burial chamber had been preserved by sand seeping through cracks to fill the air space, leaving artefacts still hanging on walls just where they had been placed at a funeral 1,400 years before.

Two gold-foil crosses indicate that the king – if he was indeed a king – may have been a Christian convert, but he was also equipped with everything he might need to resume a life of feasting and heroic display in a pagan underworld. Most of the 60 or so grave-goods in the burial chamber evoke that world of smoky halls, mead-swilling warriors and rich gift-exchange that we know mainly from *Beowulf*. Among the more exotic items were: a gold buckle; a flagon and bowl imported from the Byzantine Empire; a hanging bowl decorated with metallic strips and medallions; and two cauldrons, one small, the other huge, measuring 75 cm across. There were also two pairs of coloured glass vessels, eight wooden drinking cups with gilded mounts, and the remains of a large casket that may originally have contained textiles. An unusual item was the frame of a folding stool, perhaps from Asia Minor or Italy, while traces of gold braid and the presence of two Merovingian gold coins testify further to the rank of the grave's occupant. There was also a sword and a shield.

The dig had begun in October 2003 as part of a proposed road improvement on the site of a known Anglo-Saxon cemetery. Many of the objects uncovered were so delicate or ephemeral they had to be lifted by MoLAS conservators in a block with the soil surrounding them, to be 'excavated' later in the conservation laboratories of the Museum of London. By summer 2004, another fascinating object had emerged: a silver spoon, apparently placed with a few other items inside a wooden box. The spoon has an elongated handle, and etched upon its ovoid bowl is a Roman inscription. Only the letters *FAB*, and possibly *RONAM*, are readable. The letters may refer to a name, but the full meaning will probably never be known. Another noteworthy find was a lyre. When discovered, the lyre, which is of Sutton Hoo type, was just a dark patch on the ground. Nevertheless, the outline was complete – the first time we have ever seen this in Britain, since even at Sutton Hoo only the top half had survived.

The 'Prince of Prittlewell' was afforded one of the richest Anglo-Saxon burials known. The excavation of his grave is probably the most spectacular archaeological discovery of the year in Britain. But who was he? Preliminary study suggests an early 7th century date, broadly contemporary with Sutton Hoo. This provisional date, and the two gold-foil crosses found in the chamber, fit with the first two Christian kings of the East Saxons. One was King Saeberht, who was converted by St Mellitus, the third Archbishop of Canterbury, in AD 604. He was a contemporary of Raedwald, King of East Anglia, the man thought most likely to have been the occupant of the sumptuous Mound 1 ship-burial at Sutton Hoo. Because Saeberht's sons and heirs abandoned the faith, the second royal possibility is King Sigeberht, who reigned half a century later, converting in AD 653. Analysis of some of the finds, especially the two Merovingian coins, may in due course allow us to narrow down the date one way or the other.

WHARRAM PERCY: THE SKELETONS

Medieval archaeology has traditionally focused on manors, villages and parish churches. The classic medieval dig was the 40-year project based at the deserted medieval village of Wharram Percy in Yorkshire. Though the project ended in 1990, the work of English Heritage specialist Simon Mays on the 687 skeletons from the cemetery at Wharram has only just reached completion. There is now a raft of new evidence about child nutrition, the role of women, and the town/country divide in medieval England.

The churchyard at Wharram was in use from *c.* AD 950 to 1850, but the village itself was deserted by the early 16th century, so the great majority of the burials were of medieval peasants. Of the total, 15 per cent of the skeletons were of infants. This sizeable sample of babies made possible an investigation of infant nutrition. The technique used was nitrogen stable isotope analysis. Nitrogen compounds are found in high quantities in breast milk and become incorporated in the growing bones of a baby. Bone growth in the Wharram skeletons matches those of modern populations up to the age of about one year. In the second year, Wharram children begin to fall behind, and by 10 years they average a full 20 cm shorter than today's children. Clearly, 'breast was best', and this was known to grandmothers and midwives in medieval Wharram Percy.

Two other findings are interesting to note, though predictable. Women's lives were hard. Child-bearing and suckling must have dominated adult life, for otherwise, given the high mortality, the population could barely have sustained itself. Osteoporosis – loss of bone density in old age, especially in women, leading to brittleness and an increased risk of fractures, especially of hip and spine – is both a modern problem, and, it turns out, a medieval one; in the latter case, probably due in large part to repeated pregnancy and prolonged lactation by undernourished mothers. At other times, they were expected to work hard at domestic chores or out in the fields. Bones grow to support muscular strength, but there is no difference in this respect between men and women at Wharram. Female osteoarthritis, on the other hand, is concentrated in legs and back, and this, along with the frequency of 'squatting facets', indicates distinctive, gender-based activity like grinding and weaving.

Finally, there is some support for the idea of the rural idyll: comparisons with skeletons from urban cemeteries in nearby York shows that the people of medieval Wharram were generally healthier, less disease-ridden, and less likely to suffer violence. On the other hand, their immunities to infection were lower: York skeletons have a higher proportion of healed lesions; in other words, York people were more likely to recover from injury and infection than their country cousins.

METAL-DETECTORS: GOOD OR BAD?

Are we for or against metal-detectors? The issue has divided archaeologists for a generation. Some, like the late Tony Gregory in Norfolk and Kevin Leahy in Lincolnshire, pioneered good relations with local metal-detectorists in the 1970s and piloted successful recording systems. Their model has formed the basis of two major recent initiatives: a new Treasure Act (introduced in 1997) whose main purpose is to encourage finders to report all discoveries by offering a guaranteed reward; and the Portable Antiquities Scheme (launched in 1997), a network of county-based Finds Liaison Officers (FLOs) whose job it is to record finds and find-spots. There have been three developments over the last year.

First, the Treasure Act has been modified so that prehistoric base-metal – not just precious-metal – objects qualify as 'treasure' as long as there are at least two from the same spot. Thus, for instance, a hoard of Bronze Age axes would now count. Second, the Portable Antiquities Scheme has finally become fully operational, its network of FLOs now covering the whole country. Third, the BBC TV series *Hidden Treasure*, which featured a succession of spectacular metal-detected treasure finds, caused a storm of protest from archaeologists incensed that it emphasised commercial – rather than archaeological – values. The message, it was claimed, was 'buy yourself a metal-detector and get rich quick'. The series probably strengthened the ill-informed fear that some archaeologists allegedly have; that all metal-detectorists are irresponsible treasure-hunters. Nonetheless, a significant number of archaeologists now agree that 'responsible' metal-detecting should be supported, and that the new Treasure Act and the Portable Antiquities Scheme are powerful tools for ensuring that the data generated are properly recorded. Some would go further and argue that metal-detectorists are 'salvage archaeologists' rescuing threatened information about the past from the destructive processes in the plough-soil, and that plots of metal-detected finds are an exciting and fast-expanding resource for both researchers and heritage managers.

WHO OWNS OUR DEAD?

Archaeologists value human remains from all periods. In some countries, like Australia and the USA, there is fierce debate about the ancient remains of indigenous people. But in Britain, the strongest debate turns on how archaeologists deal with more recent remains. This is particularly true of World War I and II fatalities. However, government policy on this issue has not been consistent. Thus, in the 1960s and 1970s, virtually every accessible Battle of Britain site was picked over – by amateurs and experts alike – all with very little control, bar a 'Note of Guidance' issued by the Ministry of Defence (MoD) in the 1960s. Indeed, in 1973, the MoD stated that it had abandoned all claim to crashed planes from the world wars, and that rights to surviving wrecks fell to the landowners. But by the late 1970s, they reversed this position, issuing excavation guidelines in which they claimed title to all British and German wrecks.

Control has since become increasingly tight, and by 1986, the Protection of Military Remains Act was brought into force. It meant licences had to be sought before investigations were undertaken. Though this might appear to be a positive move, tighter control has meant, inevitably, that much less work has been undertaken on battlefield sites. Such work can, however, serve an important humanitarian role. Consider the case of Sgt Pilot 'Eddie' Egan, lost during the Battle of Britain – it was only after careful sifting of a plane crash site in a Kentish wood that archaeologists found a brass plate with the serial number of Egan's plane, proving this was his aircraft. Consequently, the Commonwealth War Graves Commission provided a grave with a headstone bearing Egan's name. The peace of mind and condolence this afforded his family cannot be underestimated.

Now, in 2004, the issue is again being debated in the Department of Culture, Media and Sport's *Care of Historic Remains* paper. Among other issues, the governmental report considers current laws relating to human remains kept in British museums, and claims for their repatriation. The document, jointly published with the Welsh Assembly, is based on the recommendations of the Working Group on Human Remains in a report published in November 2003. Four main points are under discussion. First, the report considers whether current laws relating to the holding of human remains by British museums are sufficient. At present, museums are prevented from returning human remains: the report recommends that they should be given the discretion to do so. Secondly, should museums holding human remains be subject to some form of code of practice or regulation? There is currently no licensing authority with the power to secure high standards of care for human remains held in museum collections – again, the report urges changes. Thirdly, do we need a 'Human Remains Advisory Panel' to mediate claims for repatriation? Fourthly, the report considers how museums should handle and deal with claims for restitution of human remains. As part of the solution, it recommends that there should be better information available to the claimant and researchers about the human remains kept in museum collections. Whichever way policy moves, we can be sure that the issues – far from black and white – will continue to be hotly debated.

ARCHITECTURE

OFFICE TOWER, 30 ST. MARY AXE, LONDON
Architect: Foster and Partners
With the completion of this radical new 40-storey tower for the Swiss Re insurance company, Norman Foster has irrevocably changed the London skyline, providing an instantly recognisable icon that has given the world of architecture a stunning exemplar for office design that opens new horizons environmentally, spatially, socially and structurally.

Its obvious point of departure from the conventional office towers that populate the City of London is its three-dimensional cigar-shaped form. Circular on plan throughout, the building rises from its paved plaza at a gently outward leaning angle to belly out smoothly around its mid-point before tapering elegantly to a conical top. It is totally glazed, and a powerful spiralling striped effect is derived from contrasting bands of glass which wind up and round the building's bulbous form. It has earned the popular soubriquet 'the Gherkin', and indeed the outer 'skin' is the most characteristic and inventive aspect of a building which in many other ways follows conventional office patterns.

Structural load-bearing elements are confined to the circular central core of lifts, stairs, duct shafts and lavatories, and the outer skin, leaving unobstructed interior floor spaces. These are not left as circular discs of space but are cut into with triangular voids to leave, on typical floors, six equal-sized areas of open plan office laid out on a 1.5 metre planning grid, for office tenants to fit out as required. The voids run up the facade of the building and are linked together either over two floors or six, to form tall narrow atria. Each successive floor plate, with its voids and 'spokes' of office space, rotates about the last by 5 degrees, so that the office floors, and their accompanying atrium spaces, rotate in a continuing upward spiral configuration that gives the exterior of the building its distinctive candy stripe appearance.

This creates an alternate overhanging, underlapping arrangement for the balcony edges of the individual office floor plates, and imbues the winding atrium spaces with movement and drama, heightened by the enormity of the views available through the glazed facade out over the city. The opportunity for penetration of daylight into the heart of the building is maximised, enabling reliance on artificial lighting to be reduced and thus aid economies in energy consumption.

The spiralling atria are part of a comprehensive programme of environmental measures aimed at making this building approximately 50 per cent more energy efficient than a conventional office of comparable quality. They were originally intended to provide a series of 'gardens in the sky', though this ambition is substantially unrealised in the finished building, but they play an important role in the reduction of air-conditioning and energy loads by assisting the introduction of natural ventilation at all levels of the building. This function is aided by the aerodynamic shape of the building, which encourages air to flow around it, rather than providing the resistance offered by a flat elevation. This minimises the impact of wind loads on the structure and cladding, and reduces the disturbing effects at ground level of deflected air movement. Wind tunnel tests indicate that conditions at the base of the tower affecting pedestrian comfort and safety are much improved over traditional forms.

The movement of air across the face of the building creates pressure differentials between different points on the surface. This acts as a driver for cross-ventilation between the lower two-storey atria and reinforces the natural stack effect that comes into play in the taller six-storey atria, to the extent that the designers envisage that the building could be naturally ventilated for at least 40 per cent of the year. Ventilation is achieved through the operation of motorised opening windows in the glazing to the spiralling light-wells, the lights being controlled by a series of perimeter weather stations in conjunction with internal sensors. The opening windows will also double up to provide natural smoke extraction in the event of fire, thus avoiding the need for mechanical smoke venting systems.

The external skin fully integrates the structure with the cladding, with the main structural diagrid frame occupying the zone between the double-glazed external envelope and, over the extent of the office areas, a secondary single-glazed inner screen. The substantial cavity is internally ventilated, drawing air out from the offices, and acts as a buffer zone, reducing the impact of solar gain in order to reduce the air-conditioning load. Solar control is also assisted by the introduction of blinds within the cavity. The light-wells by contrast have only the external skin, and utilise tinted solar glass with a high performance coating to control solar gain, hence the different colour when seen from the outside, compared with the office areas which utilise untinted clear glass.

The primary structure within this composite skin is a diagrid of simple straight circular steel sections linked to hexagonal welded steel nodes at alternate storey levels. The nodes are generated from three intersecting steel plates, two to the crossing diagonal columns and one to the horizontal perimeter floor beams, welded together at angles that vary according to the variable geometry derived from the tapering cylindrical form. The resulting structure derives great strength and rigidity from its three dimensional interlocking grid, with its inherent ability to transmit loads smoothly around the entire facade. The completed steel frame is hidden behind a substantial cladding of fire resistant boards, whose white finish reads through the glazed skin and emphasises the twisting diamond pattern of the structure.

From the 34th storey upwards, as the form tapers to its apex, the glazing reverts entirely to the darker grey colour of the spiralling light-wells, and the presence of three storeys of mechanical plant space is signalled by a double ring of metal guide rails for the mobile cleaning gantry. At level 38 there is a suite of private dining rooms, at level 39 a restaurant, and at the topmost level a spectacular bar. This is formed as a mezzanine level with its curving balcony set back from the facade to permit the full drama of the glazed conical roof to be enjoyed from both the restaurant and bar. Here the main structural frame terminates, leaving as a final cap only the slender diagonal glazing bars and transoms of the external glazing system meeting in a dramatic central oculus, while patrons enjoy an unrivalled 360 degree panoramic view over the City.

At the foot of the building the faceted glazed cladding is cut away to reveal the main entrance with its banks of clear glass revolving doors set back at an angle behind the huge exposed columns of the diagrid frame, with their faceted white cladding. These imposing struts rise directly from the ground plane at the point of intersection, the base of the V, as though the building were sitting on its knuckles, and form a rather daunting grille where one might have wished for a more welcoming portal. By its very nature the circular tapering form of the building releases a considerable amount of the site area for furnishing as a landscaped plaza, and also maximises the amount of sunlight penetrating down to the ground between the surrounding buildings.

From the immediate viewpoint of the plaza and surrounding streets, however, the soaring height and relatively slender proportions of the tower, evident in long range views, are not perceived. As the upper storeys gradually recede from view behind its middle section, the building seems much more bulbous and overpowering when seen from below. There is much more to say about this innovative design than can be summarised here. Its apparent grace and simplicity is, in part, a direct result of the application of very sophisticated parametric modelling techniques. Such techniques were originally developed by the automobile and aerospace industries for plotting, manipulating and rationalising complex curved surfaces and forms but have been further developed to enable precise dimensional and locational data to be transferred electronically directly into the manufacturing process. This is a huge step forward in office design and aims to utilise technology in an environmentally productive and energy efficient manner, while rising above the purely mechanical to produce an inspiring and creative piece of architecture for the 21st century.

MAGGIE'S CENTRE, NINEWELLS HOSPITAL, DUNDEE, SCOTLAND

Architect: Gehry and Partners
Executive Architect: James F. Stephen Architects

This small but instantly recognisable building, opened at the end of September 2003, is the latest in a nationwide series of support centres for cancer sufferers, and the third to open in Scotland. Conceived and inspired by Maggie Keswick Jencks, who died of cancer in 1995, the centres are intended to supplement the work and facilities of the hospitals to which they are attached, by providing opportunities for support, counselling and care for patients and their families in a manner and an environment not typically provided by the NHS.

Ninewells Hospital is located to the west of Dundee, set on high ground with views to the south over the Firth of Tay, and the architect has fully exploited this setting in the location of the centre. A short walk from the hospital's oncology unit, the building is approached through a grove of trees and sits on top of a steep bank overlooking the hospital approach road, enjoying views directly out over the estuary.

The brief for the building sought to provide both an environment in which a sense of community and support can be developed, and a range of spaces catering directly for patients' and carers' needs, whether it be a place to sit and relax, a space for remedial therapy and relaxation classes, or a small private room for counselling. Frank Gehry's design has all the imprints of the stylistic approach typical of his larger and more famous creations. Though modest in scale, its shape is characteristically complex and striking. It features a solid white rendered elliptical tower contrasting with and acting as a calm focus and point of anchorage for the quirky and irregularly folded planes of the surrounding roof, wrapping around the tower and extending beyond the walls of the centre in a series of exaggerated overhangs. With the exception of the tower, all the accommodation is at ground level. Planned around an open plan entrance lobby, reception and office area, the adjacent relaxation room and the dining/kitchen area are easily visible and read as part of an integrated sequence of spacers unified by the overriding and stunning 'roofscape' of timber framing exposed on the underside of the undulating folded roof planes. Therapy and retreat rooms, together with back-up storage and lavatory facilities, complete the accommodation.

The plan form is as organic as the section is geometric, with external and internal walls adopting varying degrees of curvature. This culminates in the tight concave and convex forms of the look-out tower projecting forwards on the south-west elevation adjacent to a projecting external seating area, which is suggestive of the spreading wings of a bird about to depart its perch. Internally the flooring throughout is of solid beech, while the staircase and internal joinery are made from fine-grained Douglas fir, so the warmth and texture of natural wood finishes are a predominant feature of the interior.

The roof structure, however, remains the single exceptional tour de force of the design, and a tribute to the craftsmanship of its fabricators, accounting for nearly half the cost of the building. The overall shape of the roof, and its relationship with the supporting walls, was developed with the aid of sophisticated computer programmes and 3D modelling techniques. It is formed from a series of intersecting and irregularly folded planes, like the pleats of a badly ironed skirt, rising and falling over the space below so that the timber structure is required to curve both on plan and in section. The primary ridge and valley beams are constructed from laminated veneer lumber, with treated softwood purlins spanning between them at varying centres and angles depending on the requirements of the geometry, all expressed internally beneath a double skin deck of plywood, which acts as the ceiling finish. The main beams are supported on a series of steel hollow section posts set within the external wall cavities.

The roof is covered with stainless steel shingles, 1,800 × 600 × 0.5 mm thick, which have been given an 'angel-hair' or brushed finish in order to cut down surface reflections and give the roof a silky sheen. At the perimeter the stainless steel roofing continues past the timber edge beam and terminates in a simple drip, sometimes as much as three metres beyond the face of the building. There are no gutters, at the express wish of the designer, and rainwater therefore cascades freely off the roof valleys to be collected in ground drains concealed beneath circles of pebbles. The lack of such visually intrusive features as gutters, brackets and down-pipes helps to establish a real sense of the elemental to the composition as a whole.

At £1.3 million for 255 sq. metres of accommodation, this is an expensive building and its cost was met by private donations. While practical and functional, it is also uplifting and inspirational, and its high public profile will help to focus greater attention on the needs of the people it serves and the desperately needed work on future developments being taken on by the inheritors of Maggie Jencks' ambitious legacy. The building received a commendation in the 2004 Royal Fine Art Commission Trust's Building of the Year Awards as a building 'of the highest social significance'.

THE BULLRING SHOPPING CENTRE AND SELFRIDGES DEPARTMENT STORE, BIRMINGHAM

Concept Architect (Bullring): Benoy
Executive Architect (Bullring): Chapman Taylor
Architect (Selfridges): Future Systems

The opening of the Bullring Shopping Centre on 4 September 2003 represents the culmination of over a decade of planning and design work. The Bullring Centre, comprising 110,000 m^2 of retail space for shops, cafés and restaurants, new housing and 3,000 car parking spaces, ranks as the largest inner-city regeneration project carried out in Europe in recent years, and promotes unimpeded pedestrian access through a series of interconnecting internal malls, streets and squares.

Where the site was previously cut off from the city centre by the inner ring road a new open square has been established, with the roadway downgraded and buried within a tunnel. This has enabled a new north-south pedestrian axis to be created providing a link between the end of the High Street at the top end of the site and the newly formed paved plaza around the gothic spire and pinnacles of St Martin's Church at the lower end. There is a substantial 19 metre drop down the site, but this has been handled as a broad continuous slope opening out towards the lower end into sweeping terraces framing a restored church.

The huge bulk of the development is split into two halves either side of this paved concourse, each half anchored to one of the major department stores. These are located at opposing ends of a wide two-level cross-mall that passes underneath the north-south axis at the lower level and at the upper level provides access direct to the paved concourse through tall glazed screens. The internal circulation is completed by two further multi-level malls which return from the node points at each end of the cross-mall back up to the entrances either side of the new open space at the end of High Street. The overall configuration is of a triangular layout of multi-level covered malls bisected by the north-south slope of the street.

Each of the resulting V-shaped mall spaces is roofed by a ceiling of sheer glass that is almost flat and passes clear over the lines of the internal facades fronting the malls. Each of these 'sky planes' is supported from above by a series of major triangulated steel trusses passing above the glass plane, which in turn support a system of secondary struts and bracing cables picking up the four point 'spider' fixings located at the junction of each set of panes. The glass roof is part of a deliberate design strategy aimed at passing off the malls as quasi external streets, and the elevations over the shop fronts are broken up into different architectural treatments as if to suggest individual building blocks. However, their detailing and the materials used do not really reflect the practicality required of proper external elevations and the malls consequently come across as rather 'odd ball' internal spaces, slightly aggressive in feel and lacking the finesse and elegance to be expected of a well designed interior.

A certain lack of elegance and proportion might equally apply to a judgement of the external architectural treatment of the mammoth development, whose huge height and volume in relation to the surrounding streets is neither effectively disguised nor dramatically exploited by the modelling and fenestration of the facade. However, these particular criticisms cannot be levelled at Selfridges, one of the two major anchor stores, which occupies the corner of the eastern block.

Compared with the somewhat banal post-modern language of the surrounding elevations, Selfridges is by contrast breathtakingly bizarre and unconventional. It is essentially a windowless box, in itself a perfectly rational solution to the problem of accommodating an entirely inward looking environment such as a department store. But here it is anything but a 'box', its form instead softened and massaged into the most exotically curvi-planar three dimensional 'blob'-like form that oozes away from its rather perfunctory vertical junction with the rest of the Bullring Centre.

The amorphous quality of the building is further emphasised by its snake-like 'skin' or outer covering, which comprises some 15,000 natural anodised aluminium discs, 600 mm in diameter with a slightly convex face, standing just proud of a rendered weathering surface that is painted a deep shade of blue. The discs are set out equidistantly in horizontal rows, slightly interlocking, and following the undulating angles of the sub-skin, thus generating a constantly changing and varied sequence of reflections that lend a disarmingly light and diaphanous quality to such a huge and otherwise largely blank volume. In keeping with the lack of formality in its shape, the store can be entered from a relatively large number of points, and at varying levels, both internally from the malls, and externally via free-form terraces and a cable suspended bridge link to the adjacent multi-storey car park, in the form of a curved glazed tube. External entrances are effected through the projecting lozenge-shaped glazed window elements that break through the facade. These overlap the rows of aluminium discs and their shape is accentuated by having the outer edges of the glazed surface treated with a pattern that helps to obscure the perimeter weatherproofing detailing, while helping them to read as the 'eyes' of some weird creature. The unique shape of the building has inevitably given rise to all manner of epithets, such as 'amoeba', 'alien cocoon', 'fish', 'snake', 'bloid' and 'predator'. Viewed from the curved frontages of the terraces overlooking St Martin's Church, the relationship of the shapes of the upper entrance 'eye' and the protruding 'beak' of the lower terrace as it wraps around a second mouth-shaped glazed entrance is uncannily suggestive of a whale. Internally, the free-form aesthetic continues. Apart from the floors and the escalators, there are few flat surfaces, straight lines and right-angled corners on the retail floors. Each floor has been designed individually and designers include Eldridge Smerin, Stanton Williams, Cibic and Partners with Lees Associates and Future Systems. Surfaces and shapes are curved and softened, particularly around the central voids, with their moulded and drooping bulkheads and curvy balustrades, and with the rounded soffits of the escalators criss-crossing the atrium spaces. This is not a building that serves easy comparison with other examples of its type, as it is such an unconventional and one-off design response to the usual constraints of the retail world: tight cost control, clear visibility, efficient pedestrian flow, and an unmistakable image to support the brand. But it cannot be argued that the commissioning chief executive at the time the building was conceived, Vittorio Radice, and the architect behind the design, Jan Kaplicky, have not achieved their ambition to create a building that would be instantly recognisable without signage. Birmingham now boasts the ultimate retail icon, a seductive and shimmering, if ultimately alien, presence in its newly configured and extended city centre.

GRADUATE CENTRE, LONDON METROPOLITAN UNIVERSITY, HOLLOWAY ROAD, LONDON
Architect: Studio Libeskind
The London Metropolitan University is the latest incarnation of an educational establishment that has been known previously as the Northern Polytechnic Institution, the Polytechnic of North London and the University of North London.

This lack of a consistent identity is reflected in the fabric of the campus, with its somewhat disorganised collection of buildings, which date from the Victorian era up to the last decade. The Graduate Centre is intended to imprint a greater sense of identity and quality on the campus and is part of a developing programme of new buildings and infrastructure being designed by well known architects.

The result of an architectural competition held in 2001, the £3.5 million centre caters for the University's 5,000 graduate students. The accommodation includes a large reception area entered via a small plaza off the street, two 50-seat lecture rooms, a multi-purpose gathering area and a 100-seat lecture theatre. All the spaces are accessible from a wide corridor running along the back of the building where it makes a direct abutment to the existing structure. The centre occupies a long narrow space in front of the existing University building and fronts directly onto Holloway Road, a typically busy, noisy, traffic-dominated north London street. The form of the building responds to its immediate urban context in an aggressive and uncompromising manner, expressed as a series of tumbling, interlocking geometric volumes that pay scant regard to the three dimensional norms of vertical and horizontal planes.

As a result of the precision of its modelling and its metallic finishes it has a crystalline or rock-like quality, though of a markedly random nature, as no two surfaces or lines seem to follow any other or adhere to any common organisational scheme. Conceived as three intersecting volumes, the building rises to a peak on its short north elevation, set at right angles to the road, its trapezoidal north- and west-facing elevations being slashed by a wildly asymmetric diagonally aligned window that wraps around the angled corner and illuminates both upper and lower foyer spaces. The two secondary elements, expressing the volumes of the lecture rooms at each floor level, continue the theme of irregular geometry, emerging from the dominant volume in a series of canted and splayed surfaces wrapping around the lower southern side, with irregularly shaped windows cut into the surfaces at seemingly random locations.

The building is clad with a rain-screen of stainless steel panels arranged in a regular diagonal grid, which encloses all the exposed elevations including the sloping roof planes. The triangular panels are embossed with a dimple pattern, and are all the same size and shape, except where the grid is arbitrarily terminated at one of the angled building corners and the panels are simply cut to shape as necessary. None of the diagonal grids correlate from one surface to the next across the building edges, so the gridding seems an entirely decorative statement rather than demonstrating any structural or internal logic. Even the window edges fail to observe any symmetry or alignment with the lines of the regular triangular panels. The disturbing 'leaning tower' geometry, and the wilful use of strange angles, is reflected no less powerfully in the interior, where there are no right-angled corners and no vertical walls, and where the effect of the apparently randomly placed and angular windows is all the more idiosyncratic.

The fact that there are few vertical walls in the building did nothing to simplify construction methods, which utilise cast in-situ concrete techniques as well as drywall construction, but inevitably the spaces generated are unique and memorable, if at times somewhat disturbing. The structure required exceptional temporary support works during construction, as the sloping planes and interconnecting elements only function as a structurally coherent design when the whole building is complete. Typical of the bizarre nature of the interiors is the main staircase, which is angular on plan, tapering to become narrower at its foot, and is set between concrete walls angled off the vertical, with each side wall set at a different angle.

Other spaces display an equally anarchic approach, with sloping and angled walls, sloping ceiling planes and canted irregular windows plunging past the floor or poking down from above. The internal finishes are simple and robust, the concrete walls being finished with a consistent translucent paint, and the ceilings displaying a series of randomly criss-crossing narrow bands in which are housed all the necessary services elements and down-lighters. It is a building in which the complexity of the spatial experience takes precedence over complexity of material, detail, texture or colour, and the building is remarkably coherent as a result, if a little ascetic.

The architect's pronouncements on the matter of symbolism and the initial creative impulse appear to place considerable emphasis on the Orion constellation and other features of the northern sky, but this seems fanciful and is not in the least bit evident from a study of the building as an object. Nevertheless it does stand as a remarkably effective and powerful symbol for the new campus, despite its relatively small size, its angular jagged geometry giving it an eye-catching presence and creating a point of reference in the generally confused and polyglot north London environment in which it sits. Hopefully the still-to-be-completed companion developments will help to play their part in tying together the currently disparate components of the University campus into a more coherent whole.

WALES MILLENNIUM CENTRE, CARDIFF
Architect: Percy Thomas Architects
The new Wales Millennium Centre lies to the south of the city and occupies a prominent and roughly triangular site overlooking Cardiff Bay, close by the site of the new National Assembly for Wales, currently under construction, and the recently infilled and landscaped Oval Basin, a former dock.

At the heart of the new building is a 1,900-seat auditorium that follows the traditional horseshoe plan shape for opera houses. This is designed to be acoustically appropriate for both operatic and amplified forms of music, thus enabling a whole range of performance events to be catered for.

Further accommodation includes large stage areas and two large rehearsal rooms, two smaller studio spaces and a wing for Urdd Gobaith Cymru, a Welsh youth movement, together with the usual ranges of backstage offices and support facilities. There are extensive public foyer and gallery areas with bars, some shops and a large public dining area.

The volume of the opera house, with its fly tower and adjoining secondary stages, is expressed in simple terms on the outside as a huge curved metal clad volume with a single over-arching curved roof plane, the sleek helmet-like shape surrounded and supported by a series of rugged, stepped and banded natural slate walls. The main approach to the Centre is on the axis of the auditorium, beneath the great sweeping overhang of the metal clad roof. Here the fronted facade is canted forward at a pronounced angle over a slightly concave soffit sloping down to the line of entrance doors.

The canted facade is inset with dramatic inscriptions, whose 2 metre-high letters are actually openings through the metal rain-screen, forming deep-set windows that illuminate the upper gallery levels as they sweep around the rear of the auditorium. The glazing to these huge letters is not itself cut to the shapes of the individual letters, but is formed from larger, double-glazed units that are masked out by the inner and outer skins of the wall construction, and mirrored in the cut-outs in the overriding metal rain-screen. The striking effect of the lettering is heightened by the use of tinted glass in colours ranging from blue to copper, casting coloured shafts of light over the interior surfaces.

The skin of the metal roof enclosure is constructed using an aluminium standing seam roof system. This is flexible enough to take the long gentle curves required to form the three-dimensional shapes and it also acts as the principal waterproofing element. A series of clips has been devised to provide the additional support required for further metal sections fixed at right angles to the standing seams, to which the sheet steel cladding panels are fixed. These are made from stainless steel with an embossed dimpled pattern and a light bronze coloured coating designed to resist the corrosive effects of the prevailing marine environment of Cardiff Bay. Designed to act only as a rain-screen, the panels are mounted so as to leave a clear gap between adjoining sheets, and each full-sized panel is secured by 32 fixings that remain visible and add a further fine grain to the sleek sheen of the panels.

The crisp lines and smooth surfaces of the bulbous enclosure to the auditorium stand in total contrast to the rugged natural appearance of the supporting fabric, which features a most unusual application of that most 'Welsh' of materials – slate. A series of stepped and curved stone walls wraps around the complex tying the building elements and the site together. To the south of the auditorium, three stepped bays define the public foyer and gallery spaces, with a fourth bay to the north of the auditorium, from whence the wall turns the corner and develops into a curved facade enclosing a substantial goods delivery and service yard. The return faces of the successive projecting bays are glazed to admit light to the interiors, and a further narrow horizontal window has been introduced at mid-height to break up the masses of stonework.

Far from being finely worked stonework, however, the elevations resemble more of a naturally fissured cliff face, or a very neatly constructed drystone wall, the material in question having been sourced from the off-cuts from a number of quarries in north Wales.

The supporting walls are constructed in reinforced concrete, each of the major bandings of material being built up in a traditional load-bearing manner from a projecting concrete toe, to the face of which is fixed a stainless steel shelf angle. The stones are prepared by being either sawn to a smooth finish or pillared (i.e. split or 'cleaved' at right angles to the usual cleavage plane) to create a rougher but regular face. Stones of many different sizes have been used, varying from a few centimetres to half a metre in length and in varying thicknesses, laid in random courses with the naturally riven face projecting downwards and the prepared face projecting outwards, for better weathering qualities. The walls are built in bands of contrasting colours, suggesting the variations to be found in natural rock strata, with some bands exposed and others recessed slightly, to form an unusually massive cavity wall construction. Recessed horizontal slivers of blue glass bricks have been inserted in the bands of slate to give an impression of the surprisingly intense colours that can be seen in some of the deeply stratified cliffs that characterise the Welsh coastline.

The sides of the auditorium facing the service yard maintain the horizontal stratified theme with deep bands of horizontal Norwegian spruce boarding, retaining its un-planed 'waney' edges to give a slightly rustic character, and long narrow strips of windows lighting the backstage offices and ancillary accommodation. The treatment of internal materials frequently picks up the prevailing theme of horizontal strata, as in the curving balustrades to the main public balconies which are clad in horizontal hardwood planking with a wide range of colour and texture, and also in the cladding to the auditorium walls, which utilises random cut glass gypsum tiles laid in narrow horizontal courses, reminiscent of the slate and timber finishes elsewhere, and pigmented in a strong red and orange hue. These are laid in random lengths and angled to achieve the desired acoustic performance by controlling the extent of resonance and reverberation.

AWARDS 2003–4

THE STIRLING PRIZE

Laban Centre, Deptford, London (Herzog and de Meuron)

THE STIRLING SHORTLIST

Great Court, British Museum, London (Foster and Partners)

Tiree Ferry Shelter, Scotland (Sutherland Hussey Architects with Jake Harvey, Donald Urquhart, Glen Onwin and Sandra Kennedy)

Theatre Royal, Plymouth (Ian Ritchie Architects)

30 Finsbury Square, London (Eric Parry Architects)

BedZed Housing Development, Wallington, Surrey (Bill Dunster Architects)

RIBA SPECIAL AWARDS

The Stephen Lawrence Prize (Buildings under £350k)

Think Tank, Skibbereen, West Cork (Gumuchdjian Architects)

RIBA Journal Sustainability Award

BedZed Housing Development, Wallington, Surrey (Bill Dunster Architects)

The Crown Estate Conservation Award

Newhailes House, Musselburgh (LDN Architects)

AJ First Building Award

No. 1 Centaur Street, London (De Rijke Marsh Morgan)

ADAPT Trust Access Award

The Space (Dance and Drama Centre), Dundee College (Nicoll Russell Studios)

RIBA Client of the Year

Manchester City Council

ART

On 26 May 2004 an estimated £60 million worth of art was destroyed in a warehouse fire in east London, damaging the reputation of art shipping company Momart (which had responsibility for the works in the 10,000 sq ft storage facility) and causing great loss to the modern art world. But it was the Young British Artists' most devoted patron, Charles Saatchi, who grabbed the headlines, after key pieces from his collection perished in the blaze, including Tracey Emin's *Everyone I have ever slept with from 1963 to 1995* and the Chapman Brothers' magnum opus, the toy soldier diorama, *Hell.* Despite losing over 100 works, Saatchi was not the only victim. Art dealer Leslie Waddington revealed that 150 works from his stockpile had gone up in smoke, and artists including Damien Hirst and Gillian Ayres lost considerable amounts of their own work. Sadly, a collection of pictures by Patrick Heron, who died in 1999 aged 79, was also doomed. The fact that Saatchi and the art world in general expressed devastation at the loss of so much modern art sparked heated debate between advocates of contemporary art and its naysaying opponents, who reacted with mirth on realising that 50 years of British art had been reduced to glowing embers.

It seemed at one stage that the general public's uneasiness with modern art may have been exacerbated by 10 Downing Street, despite the preponderance of 20th-century British art that is said to hang in its corridors. Cherie Blair reportedly vetoed an official portrait of her husband because she thought the work of Nicola Hicks, the artist chosen for the commission, was 'too scary'.

Widespread ignorance of art was revealed in a public poll conducted in October 2003 by the *Encyclopaedia Britannica.* It found that 7 per cent of people surveyed believed that Claude Monet's famous *Water Lilies* was painted by TV presenter Rolf Harris and that nearly half of those surveyed could not identify Leonardo Da Vinci as the creator of the *Mona Lisa.*

ART AND CELEBRITY

When it comes to celebrity endorsements of culture, pop star Sting and actor Mel Gibson may not spring to mind as the most devoted patrons of the arts. However, in July 2004, the pair pledged financial support to art preservation organisation, the Friends of Florence, to help restore 22 Michelangelo paintings and clean the revered sculpture *David.*

A famous name came to the Royal Academy's rescue in September 2003 when composer and theatre producer, Andrew Lloyd Webber, exhibited his extensive collection of Pre-Raphaelite and Victorian paintings in public for the first time following the cancellation of the Royal Academy's planned Egyptian art show. The exhibition attracted large crowds eager to experience Lord Webber's taste in art.

It has been suggested, however, that the Royal Academy put too much emphasis on famous names in 2003. Style really did supersede substance in an autumn show dedicated to the fashion guru Giorgio Armani to launch the Academy's new Burlington Gardens venue, formerly the premises of the Museum of Mankind. Despite exhibition director Norman Rosenthal's assurance that the show was not about commercial success but about 'the spirit of our times', the 400 Armani outfits on display succeeded in bringing in Hollywood's A-list to the opening parties.

By far the most bizarre art story of the year involved a celebrity collector, the actress Elizabeth Taylor, who launched legal proceedings against the descendants of a Jewish woman in May 2004 following a dispute concerning a work by Van Gogh. Taylor was at the height of her career in 1963 when her father paid £92,000 for the oil painting, *View of the Asylum and Chapel at Saint-Remy.* However, the great-grandchildren of Margarete Mauthner, who owned the painting in the 1930s, claimed it was looted by the Nazis and demanded its return or a share of the proceeds.

Tracey Emin made the headlines again in March 2004 when a north London school decided to sell a quilt that she had created with eight-year-old students as part of an art project. Emin demanded that the blanket be returned to her and threatened to refuse to authenticate the work as hers if Ecclesbourne primary school continued with its efforts to raise £35,000 from the sale. Another quilt appliquéd by Emin appeared in a theatre production of Jean Cocteau's play *Les Parents Terribles,* for which the artist was employed as set designer.

Although the Momart inferno created the biggest news of the art year, important world events also informed the works of a handful of artists. In October 2003, a group of Mancunian artists built an operational miniature version of the US internment camp at Guantanamo Bay, complete with mock prisoners, gates, guards and an interrogation centre. In the same month a new gallery, Hauser & Wirth, opened in central London with an exhibition by famed Los Angeles performer Paul McCarthy. His video featured actors frolicking while dressed in oversized rubber masks mimicking the Queen Mother, George W. Bush and Osama Bin Laden. The other big commercial gallery opening of the year was that of US dealer Larry Gagosian, whose Britannia Street venue became one of the largest in London and a significant addition to the up-and-coming King's Cross area.

THEFTS AND CAPERS

The biggest heist in recent memory took place in August 2003 when two thieves posing as tourists stole the Leonardo Da Vinci painting known as *Madonna of the Yarnwinder* from the Duke of Buccleuch's Drumlanrig Castle in Scotland. The £60 million picture had been subject to some suspicion in regard to its originality but experts agreed that the majority of the work had been painted by the 16th-century Italian master. *Madonna of the Yarnwinder* was one of very few such masterpieces to be privately owned and the Duke of Buccleuch's loss highlighted the potential security risks faced by all such art-owning estates.

In October 2003, street artist Banksy managed to sneak one of his works onto a wall at Tate Britain without anyone noticing. The picture, an oil painting covered in police incident tape, was only discovered when the glue used to hang the work gave way and it crashed to the floor.

AUCTION UPS AND DOWNS

The year 2004 was a good one for Sotheby's, in particular the evening of 5 May at its New York sales room, when a Picasso achieved the highest ever price for a work of art at $93 million (£56 million). The 1905 painting from Picasso's 'rose period' called *Garçon à la Pipe* was sold to an anonymous private buyer, thought most likely to be one of the Lauder brothers (heirs to the cosmetic fortune), the Las Vegas casino entrepreneur Steve Wynn or Microsoft's Bill Gates. Sotheby's good fortune continued in June 2004 when it enjoyed sales of Impressionist and Modern art totalling £61.47 million, the highest monthly total recorded in London in 15 years.

Despite Sotheby's successes, Christie's did not lose its traditionally dominant market position, and a record for post-war American painting was set a few days after the Picasso shocker when a Jackson Pollock sold in New York for $11.65 million (nearly £7 million). This was a welcome boost for Christie's which had attributed a drop in sales in the first half of 2003 (£589 million compared with £682 million in the same period in 2002) to the SARS epidemic and the war in Iraq. However, Christie's had no-one to blame but itself for two cases involving two works of art allegedly looted by Nazis from Jewish families in Germany and Austria. Despite a spirit of agreement within the international art fraternity that goods stolen in such circumstances should be handed back to heirs of the original owners, Christie's made no attempts to return the two paintings.

More embarrassment was heaped on Christie's when Taylor Thompson, the daughter of newspaper magnate Lord Thomson of Fleet, sued the auction house over a pair of urns bought a decade before, latterly believed to be fakes. The Louis XV gilt and bronze vases were bought for £1.9 million in 1994 but experts later declared them to be reproductions and so only worth £30,000. The court eventually ruled that the urns were more than likely to be real but that Christie's should have made it clear that there was a possibility they were copies.

MUSEUMS AND NEW SPACES

The Hayward Gallery, built in the late 1960s in the brutalist style of the surrounding concrete South Bank complex, received a facelift in 2003 with a new glass frontage, a café and a curved viewing pavilion. Designed by American artist Dan Graham, the work was entitled *Waterloo Sunset* after the famous song.

The Barbican was also given a makeover to celebrate its 20th anniversary and the gallery finally opened in April 2004 after a £1 million redevelopment that created an additional 140m^2 of display area. A new programme was also launched which mixed photography by Tina Modotti and Edward Weston with fine art by Helen Chadwick.

A grand old Warwickshire mansion, Compton Verney, became an exhibition venue in 2004 under the guidance of owner Sir Peter Moores, philanthropist and heir to the football pools millions. His eclectic collection includes some fine examples of 16th-century German art and antique Chinese bronzes as well as a smattering of modern art. The inaugural exhibition was installed by film director Peter Greenaway.

In the year under review, just three years after opening at a cost of £21 million in 2000, the New Art Gallery Walsall applied for further grants from the Arts Council. Visitor numbers fell from 250,000 in 2000 to just 110,000 in 2003 which was blamed on the failure to appoint a director for the first two years, followed by the closure of its spectacular top-floor restaurant.

Donations to US museums have always been incentivised with attractive tax breaks for private donors, so Sir Nicholas Goodison's recommendations to the Government in January 2004 concerning the possible introduction of similar measures in the UK were welcomed especially by museums whose grants have been consistently cut or frozen. 'We must find ways of encouraging more gifts from private owners and donors. In the United States private giving to public collections, with some encouragement from tax relief, is part of the country's culture. I want more people in the UK to discover the pleasure of giving in this way,' said Sir Nicholas.

In July 2004, it was announced that the Victoria and Albert Museum had failed to secure the £15 million lottery funding needed to build the Daniel Libeskind-designed extension, nicknamed the Spiral, putting the £80 million eight-year-old project into jeopardy. The V&A did, however, find anonymous funding for renovations to its central gardens, proving perhaps that it was the conservatism of the principal trustees, not a lack of funds, that thwarted the museum's most ambitious expansion plans.

On a similar theme, the National Gallery warned the Government that a £2.5 million grant reduction could result in galleries being closed to the public. In November 2003, the gallery's chairman had protested that the reduced funds also impacted on the institution's ability to prevent works of art such as Raphael's *Madonna of the Pinks* from being sold to overseas buyers.

The Tate's own funding crisis prompted Nicholas Serota to consider, for the first time, selling surplus works from the collection. This practice is heavily frowned upon in museum circles but was deemed necessary to bolster the Tate's limited funds for new acquisitions. An example of the museum's dwindling resources was witnessed in May 2004, when a major work by Francis Bacon, *Study for Velazquez*, was deemed too expensive, at £9.5 million, for the Tate to consider raising money to keep it in the country.

Also deemed too expensive was the entrance fee to Charles Saatchi's County Hall gallery on London's South Bank which, at £8.50, is second only to the Guggenheim Museum in New York in the list of the world's most expensive art attractions. Saatchi's gallery had hit the headlines once again in October 2003 following a dispute with County Hall landlord, Mac Okamoto, in which Okamoto ordered the closure of two of the gallery's rooms that were not in Saatchi's original lease.

FINDS AND ACQUISITIONS

In December 2003, an astronomer and self-styled art detective came up with the most spurious claim of the year by connecting the eruption of the volcano Krakatoa in 1883 with the blood red sky of Edvard Munch's *The Scream*. Donald Olson claimed he had pinpointed the exact spot where the painting was conceived by charting the stratospheric echo of the volcanic explosion and comparing it with reports that northern Europe experienced odd twilight glows.

Back on terra firma, the lengthy struggle to keep Raphael's *Madonna of the Pinks* in the UK finally ended in February 2004 when the Duke of Northumberland, then Britain's 108th richest man, sold the picture to the National Gallery for £35 million, a sum raised jointly by the Heritage Lottery Fund and the British public. The row over the huge amount of public money spent on the old masterpiece reached fever pitch when Tate director Sir Nicholas Serota exclaimed, 'we care too much for the past and not enough for the present and near-present.' The painting promptly went on a tour of galleries from Cardiff to Manchester and Durham but was scheduled to return to London for the National's Raphael exhibition in October 2004.

In January 2004, the Tate acquired an archive collection from the studio of Francis Bacon, one of the 20th-century's most important painters, thanks to the generous gift of Barry Joule, a friend of the artist. The Barry Joule Collection of material from Bacon's Reece Mews studio comprises over 1,200 items including many photographs and documents, as yet unstudied. Joule, a Canadian, became Bacon's neighbour and close friend in 1978.

SHOWS AND FAIRS

Annual visitor figures for art exhibitions once again revealed that London trails way behind other cultural cities such as New York, Paris and St Petersburg. London's highest visitor figures were achieved by the Victoria and Albert Museum's Art Deco display, which ranked 30th in the list of the world's most attended shows. More disturbing news was that touring shows are more popular abroad than in the UK. Max Beckmann's 2003 retrospective, for example, received an average of 1,042 visitors per day at the Tate Modern but 2,567 at the Pompidou in Paris.

On a more positive note, the Hayward Gallery was host to one of the biggest blockbusters of the year under review. *Saved!*, which was held from 23 October to 18 January 2004, was the centenary exhibition of the National Art Collections Fund (NACF) and among the 400 works were masterpieces such as Velazquez's *The Rokeby Venus* from the National Gallery in London. It was estimated that, throughout the 20th century, the NACF raised around £40 million in grants to buy works that would now command considerably higher prices. As part of its year-long celebrations, the NACF also helped to restore the Rodin's imposing sculpture *The Burghers of Calais* which stands in front of the Houses of Parliament.

Not only was Bill Viola's exhibition *The Passions* the first major showing of video art at the National Gallery (22 October–4 January 2004), surprisingly it was its first retrospective given to a contemporary artist. Cynics might have seen the exhibition as a ploy for a stuffy museum to get on the cutting-edge bandwagon but Viola's slow-moving quasi-religious figures glided across sleek plasma screens with grace reminiscent of a painting by an Old Master.

One of the greatest Old Masters, El Greco, received his first full retrospective in Britain at the National Gallery in 2004. First mounted by the Metropolitan Museum in New York, London's staging of the exhibition (12 February–23 May 2004) surveyed El Greco's early career as a painter of religious icons in Crete, his training in Italy and his mature career as painter to the court of Phillip II of Spain in Toledo.

While Spain celebrated the centenary of Salvador Dali in 2004, Scotland celebrated the 100th anniversary of the death of American artist James Whistler, albeit based on the slightly disingenuous link that he was widely collected by Scottish institutions and galleries. The famous painting of Whistler's mother was displayed following extensive restoration and cleaning.

Early 2004 saw the first annual Frieze Art Fair which was staged in a giant marquee in Regent's Park and immediately proved a commercial and critical success. Over 120 galleries came from as far afield as Brazil and the USA to exhibit and sell the best in cutting-edge art. Hot on its heels was a new photography fair, Photo London, which was held at the Royal Academy's Burlington Gardens in May 2004. More than 40 specialist dealers exhibited a broad range of work from 19th-century vintage and gelatin prints to contemporary works by artists such as Andreas Gursky and Cindy Sherman. Another photographic first was the Brighton Photo Biennial, which took place in October 2003.

PRIZES, COMMISSIONS AND SPONSORSHIP

For the duration of its run, October 2003–March 2004, the Tate Modern's annual £250,000 Unilever Turbine Hall commission attracted 750,000 visitors. Commonly likened to an artificial sun, *The Weather Project* by Icelandic–Danish artist Olafur Eliasson was constructed from 200 yellow lights shining through an artificial mist in the Tate's cavernous entrance hall. Bruce Norman was the next artist to be invited to fill the space and, as an innovator of video art, he intended to be the first artist to use sound rather than sculpture or light.

The Turner Prize glow may have dimmed in recent years but the exuberant transvestism of potter Grayson Perry brought a new lease of life to the 2003 award. Perry and his alter ego Claire, who wore a frilly dress custom-made for the occasion, pipped the Chapman Brothers to the £20,000 post with Perry's selection of traditionally shaped ceramics covered with figures, patterns and text that depict thought-provoking social themes. Shortlisted for the 2004 prize were video artists Jeremy Deller and Kutlug Ataman as well as sculptors Yinka Shonibare and Langlands and Bell.

A competition to fill the vacant fourth plinth in Trafalgar Square resulted in six unusual proposals that included two anti-war protests, two pieces that paid homage to the innumerable pigeons that populate the area, and a pair of Meccano skyscrapers. In 2005, Marc Quinn's marble statue of his physically disabled friend will be displayed on the plinth followed by Thomas Schütte's humorous *Hotel for the Birds* in 2006.

In December 2003, the annual Beck's Futures Prize for young artists working in Britain was awarded to a Dutch artist living in London, Saskia Olde-Wolbers. Her fantastical video narrative beat competitors including Turkish-born Haluk Akakce and Brazilian sculptor Tonico Lemos Auad for the top prize of £24,000.

A number of new art prizes have emerged in recent times. A young graduate of the Royal Academy Schools, Christian Ward, won the first £20,000 Lexmark Europe-wide painting prize and Manchester's inaugural attempt to found a rival to the Turner Prize was sponsored by the Comme Ca gallery, who awarded £10,000 to Liverpudlian video artist Paul Rooney. Most ambitious of all the new awards was the Artes Mundi Prize, with a shortlist of 11 international artists vying for a £40,000 cheque, one of the world's biggest individual prizes. The first winner of the biennial prize was the Chinese artist Xu Bing who made an installation using dust from the rubble of the World Trade Centre twin towers in New York.

COMINGS . . .

It was announced in December 2003 that Sir Christopher Frayling was to become the new chairman of Arts Council England. Passionate about design, architecture and film,

Frayling's diplomatic skills and extensive experience in the arts world made him the ideal successor to businessman Gerry Robinson. Culture Secretary, Tessa Jowell, was 'delighted that Sir Christopher has agreed to take on this key role in Arts Council England. He radiates a love for the arts and his skill at sharing that enthusiasm makes him the ideal choice for the job.'

Two major resignations were announced in July 2004, with Phillip Dodd stepping down after seven years as director of the Institute of Contemporary Arts and Susan Ferleger Brades announcing her resignation as director of the Hayward Gallery.

. . . AND GOINGS

London-born editor and photographer John Coplans died in August 2003 at the age of 83. Having discovered his true artistic course at the ripe age of 60, Coplans looked to the US for inspiration and moved to the west coast before settling in New York in 1971, co-founding and then taking up the editorship of *Artforum* magazine. After the pressures of publishing took their toll, Coplans withdrew into a melancholic style of self-portraiture in which he photographed his ageing, naked body in graphic detail.

Terry Frost, one of the remaining artists of the post-war St Ives generation passed away in September 2003. His abstract, colourful works were derived from his surroundings in Cornwall but he only received serious attention late in his career, with a retrospective at the Royal Academy in 2000 and a knighthood in 1998. At around the same time British artist Patrick Procktor died at the age of 67. A contemporary of David Hockney and Bridget Riley, Procktor never achieved the fame of his fellow painters and, by the time a fire destroyed the contents of his house in 1999, his reputation had all but waned.

The last surviving member of the original St Ives Group, Wilhelmina Barns-Graham died at the age of 91 in January 2004. She had been a relatively marginalised abstract painter until the Tate Gallery's 1985 St Ives show that renewed her confidence and resulted in many commercial shows and the award of a CBE in 2001.

Losses to the international art world included the death of Mario Merz, one of the original group of 1960s 'Arte Povera' artists from Italy. Merz used earth, glass, clay, wax and other everyday materials but developed a trademark in sculptural igloos and often used neon in his work.

In January 2004 the photography community mourned the loss of Helmut Newton, the German-born fashion photographer and portraitist, famed for his erotically charged black and white full-length nudes which depicted women as both objects of desire and dominatrices. Before he was killed in a car crash in Los Angeles at the age of 84, the '35mm Marquis de Sade', as he was jokingly known, was finalising plans to open his own photography foundation in Berlin.

BROADCASTING

TELEVISION

It is not unusual for the BBC to be attacked from all sides of the political spectrum, especially during times of national crisis, but the extraordinary series of events leading up to the resignation of the corporation's chairman and director-general in January 2004 were unprecedented. Without doubt the crisis was the gravest in the BBC's history. The root of the problem was a report broadcast the previous May by the defence correspondent of Radio 4's *Today* programme, Andrew Gilligan. His report claimed the government had deliberately inserted exaggerated claims, knowing them to be untrue, into an intelligence dossier in order to justify the invasion of Iraq. The trigger for the crisis at Broadcasting House was the findings of a report by Lord Hutton, commissioned by the Prime Minister following the assumed suicide of Gilligan's source for his story, government weapons scientist Dr David Kelly. Despite Hutton's harsh words, the BBC took comfort in the evidence of opinion polls conducted following the publication of his report which suggested that more people trusted the BBC than Tony Blair and his ministers. This was fortunate for the beleaguered national broadcaster because the process of government-led scrutiny, leading to the renewal of the BBC's Royal Charter in 2006, had begun in December.

If public trust in the Corporation's journalism looked robust, research unveiled in the spring by the new communication's regulator, Ofcom, suggested that viewers of all the main television channels thought that programme controllers should try harder in providing genuinely entertaining programmes. Audiences reckoned there was too much copycat programming screened at peak viewing periods, too little innovation and too little protection for children before the 9 p.m. watershed. People were also beginning to tire of the glut of reality shows, however, a lot of reality TV continued to attract big audiences during 2003–4. In the summer Channel 4's *Big Brother*, which the previous year looked like it was past its prime, staged a comeback thanks to a dose of those old TV staples – sex and violence. Elsewhere, reality shows like *I'm A Celebrity . . . Get Me Out of Here!* and *Hell's Kitchen* gave ITV some much-needed success.

The big broadcasting technology story of the year was the sustained success of the digital terrestrial Freeview service (in around four million homes by the summer). Overall, the spread of digital TV continued to grow, if not quite as fast as the government wanted it to; the target of switching off the analogue signal by 2010 began to look increasingly unlikely and 2012 emerged as a more likely date. Experts believed that Freeview's success had begun to undermine the growth of BSkyB's subscriber numbers as the company came under new management in the form of Rupert Murdoch's son, James.

LAST EXIT FOR DAVIES AND DYKE

Excluding any successful future move to privatise the BBC, the closing days of January 2004 will go down in history as the broadcaster's most bleak period. On 28 January Lord Hutton announced his coruscating verdict on the corporation's journalism and management style. He claimed both were 'defective' after examining the methods used by Gilligan to obtain the 'evidence' for his infamous *Today* report on 29 May, and how the teams, led by BBC director-general Greg Dyke and chairman Gavyn Davies, dealt with the complaints from Blair's then director of communications Alistair Campbell. The BBC's previous director-general, John Birt, agreed with Hutton. Speaking in the House of Lords, he declared: 'The root of this crisis was a slipshod piece of journalism.' Within hours of Hutton delivering his report, Davies resigned. With Davies gone, the board of governors refused to back Dyke and he quit the following day. 'It's remarkable how he (Hutton) has given the benefit of judgement to virtually everyone in the government and to no-one at the BBC,' fumed Dyke. Gilligan was next out of the revolving door, and months later the BBC's director of news at the time of the 'sexed up' dossier affair, Richard Sambrook, was moved sideways.

In the weeks following Hutton's withering verdict on the BBC, the Corporation, led initially by former World Service chief, Mark Byford, began quietly to distance itself from the law lord's findings. Fleet Street is traditionally hostile to the BBC, but much of the national press regarded Hutton's report as a 'whitewash'. Some newspaper commentators regarded the conclusion of the Butler inquiry – set up in February after widespread public concern over the veracity of pre-war intelligence that Iraq possessed weapons of mass destruction – as a partial vindication of Gilligan's original *Today* report.

Whatever the final verdict on this complex and long-running battle between Downing Street and Broadcasting House, one surprise development was the appointment of veteran TV executive and entertainment impresario Michael Grade as the BBC's new chairman. Like Dyke, Grade was regarded as a charismatic maverick in broadcasting circles and he, perhaps inevitably, rapidly appointed Mark Thompson as the new director-general. Thompson, an Oxford-educated Catholic, had spent the bulk of his career at the BBC prior to doing a two-year stint running Channel 4. He was the kind of journalistic heavyweight (he had edited both *Panorama* and *The Nine O'Clock News*) and strategic thinker needed to get the Corporation back on course.

Immediately the new BBC regime announced a sweeping set of changes, including moves to 'bullet proof' journalism, the implementation of a new complaints procedure, and a series of reviews designed to make the Corporation look more like a public service broadcaster and less like the entrepreneurial company that had begun to emerge under Dyke. These changes were aimed at securing the renewal of the charter in 2006 on favourable terms – in other words, a commitment to the long-term future of the licence fee, despite the onward march of pay-TV. The fact that the Government had given the chairman's job to a TV professional like Grade (who 20 years earlier ran the Corporation's flagship station, BBC1) was regarded by many as an attempt to improve relations between the Government and Broadcasting House. Grade moved quickly to show critics that under his leadership, the BBC's governors would be a thoroughly independent body holding the BBC's executive to account, rather than maintaining the somewhat cosy relationship evident under Davies and Dyke.

The BBC's annual report, published in July, reflected this new, more rigorous approach to running the organisation and the governors said the Corporation must 'extend the range and quality of its radio and television services'. The focus must be on 'broadcasting more high-impact, memorable programmes, particularly arts and current affairs.' BBC1 received lukewarm praise from the governors who announced an independent review of the channel following falling approval ratings.

REALITY COOKS UP A STORM

While all the main channels struggled to maintain their popularity as digital channels continued to proliferate, the easiest way to make an impact on audiences was to schedule more and more editions of existing hits (at times during the year ITV1's peak time schedule was virtually gridlocked by episodes of *Coronation Street*) or to plug into the vogue for reality TV. Even ITV's former director of television, David Liddiment, thought that ITV was guilty of soap overkill. Writing in *The Guardian*, he opined: 'A handful of big hitting shows have become absolutely vital to the terrestrial broadcasters who are desperately fighting to hold audiences as competition intensifies. But how much further can they be squeezed before the law of diminishing returns kicks in?'

As for the ever-expanding reality TV juggernaut, Channel 4 reaped the biggest harvest as shows like *Wife Swap*, *Supernanny*, and *Faking It* kept viewers coming back for more. In the summer the fifth series of *Big Brother* gave the station another big reality hit. For the first time in a British *Big Brother* two of the contestants, Michelle and Stuart, consummated their relationship as the cameras watched. There was no explicit sex as the couple 'performed' in private under 'a love shack' built beneath the dining room table, however, voyeurs were kept satisfied when a drunken brawl broke out one night in the house. Inevitably, ratings surged (the so-called 'sex' episode attracted more than six million viewers) but the show's producer, Endemol, and Channel 4 insisted 'the welfare and safety of the housemates is always our overriding concern.' Some commentators disagreed complaining that the producers were only concerned with revenue streams from advertising, text messaging and telephone voting.

Also on Channel 4 a new TV star emerged in the form of combative celebrity chef Gordon Ramsay, presenting *Ramsay's Kitchen Nightmares*. His liberal use of four-letter words was not to everyone's taste, but as more than five and a half million people tuned in to witness the confrontational cook proffer his advice to some of Britain's failing eateries and inept kitchen professionals, there was no doubt that the small screen had discovered a much needed, new larger-than-life personality; newspaper reports suggested that Channel 4 was determined to sign Ramsay to an exclusive contract.

Over on ITV1, Ramsay re-emerged, this time with a cast of middling celebrities who he attempted to drill into ace practitioners of the culinary arts in *Hell's Kitchen*. The show failed to repeat the success of the second series of *I'm A Celebrity . . . Get Me Out Of Here!* but as more than eight million tuned in, ITV's hunch that Ramsay could work for a mainstream audience paid off. Shown in February 2004, *I'm A Celebrity* . . . was easily the year's biggest reality TV hit. The secret? Deft presentation by Ant and Dec alongside a cast of celebrities, notably ex-Sex Pistol Johnny Lydon and model Jordan, ensured saturation coverage in the tabloids. Almost 15 million viewers watched the show's finale. By which time Lydon had stormed off the set, his walk out prompted, reportedly, by a craving for chocolate. *I'm A Celebrity* . . . took a significant slice of audience share prompting the *Financial Times* to note that such high viewing figures are not supposed to occur 'in the age of multi-channel TV and viewer fragmentation.'

If only television drama (soaps excluded) or situation comedy were still capable of creating audiences this big. Even the appeal of ITV1's long-running gentle moorland drama, *Heartbeat*, was starting to fade. In the winter of 2003 *Heartbeat*'s average audience was 12.8 million; a year later it had fallen to 11.1 million. Still, another lynchpin of ITV1's schedule, *A Touch Of Frost*, pulled in 12.9 million. ITV1 triumphed too with *Prime Suspect 6*, as Detective Superintendent Jane Tennison, portrayed to perfection by Helen Mirren, returned for the first time in seven years. Other well-received new ITV1 drama included a new vehicle for Tom Conti in the psychological thriller, *Donovan*, and writer Mike Bullen's follow-up to *Cold Feet*, *Life Begins*, starring Caroline Quentin. In spite of its glitzy cast – Helena Bonham Carter played Anne Boleyn – ITV1's much-anticipated attempt at re-telling the story of *Henry VIII* drew mixed notices. Most critics agreed that the main problem was the much-married monarch's (played by a typically energetic Ray Winstone) perplexing Cockney accent.

CHAUCER'S LESSON IN TV DRAMA

Few British actresses can be as depended upon as the highly versatile Julie Walters to bring some genuine magic to the small screen, but even by her own high standards, Walters' performance as *The Wife of Bath* (scripted by Sally Wainwright, creator of *At Home With the Braithwaites*) in BBC1's contemporary re-working of Chaucer's Canterbury Tales was a tour de force. Overall, reviewers hailed this series, in which this classic of English literature was updated for the 21st century, as one of the year's high spots; Billie Piper, critics agreed, was a revelation in *The Miller's Tale*. Another high-profile literary-inspired drama, based on Anthony Trollope's *He Knew He Was Right*, and adapted by the much-feted Andrew Davies also succeeded for the BBC. But having Davies' name on the credits of ITV1's *Boudica*, starring Alex Kingston as the warrior queen, failed to save it from a critical panning. TV drama never wanders far from the subject of crime and true to form the BBC provided audiences with one of the year's most rewarding new dramas in *The Long Firm*, starring Mark Strong as charismatic gang leader Harry Starks. Derek Jacobi also impressed in this unexpected summer treat from BBC2, set in the sixties and its immediate aftermath.

For contemporary drama, Paul Abbott's semi-autobiographical *Shameless*, the story of modern dysfunctional family life on a Manchester housing estate, was, according to some critics, the outstanding series of 2003–4. Channel 4's ability to back high quality small screen drama was also evident in Granada's *The Deal*, a one-off single drama directed by Stephen Frears dissecting the 20-year relationship between Tony Blair and Gordon Brown. Shown on the eve of the Labour Party conference, the *New Statesman* observed: 'As a record of the richly deserved death of Old Labour, *The Deal* was about as good, and probably as close, as television has yet got.' David Morrissey's performance as the future chancellor was highly acclaimed, not least by former Brown PR man, Charlie Whelan, who writing in *The Guardian* said: 'He was so good there were times when I forget I was watching an actor and really thought Gordon Brown was on the telly.'

The year witnessed the death of one of British television's greatest playwrights, Jack Rosenthal. He had begun his career as a *Coronation Street* scriptwriter before creating some of television's most human and enduring dramas such as *Spend, Spend, Spend, Bar Mitzvah Boy* and *Eskimo Day*. In the summer the BBC's digital channel, BBC4, devoted a short season to Rosenthal's work to commemorate his achievement. That almost half the country was unable to enjoy these repeats because they lacked the necessary digital equipment prompted a letter to *The Times* from a Mrs Deb Atkinson. She wanted to know why the Corporation was not broadcasting programmes of this quality on its terrestrial services, rather than what she insisted was the usual mix of lifestyle and makeover shows. 'We watched the programmes with our three children in their twenties,' observed Mrs Atkinson. 'Having barely had the opportunity to watch a play made for television they didn't really know what to expect, but after seeing *Eskimo Day, The Evacuees* and *Bar Mitzvah Boy* they were completely won over. If young people never get the chance to watch programmes like these, how are they going to know if they would enjoy them?' Hopefully, BBC2's new controller Roly Keating, who replaced the American-bound Jane Root in the spring, will encourage the return of single drama to BBC2.

Overall, comedy too struggled to match former glories, especially situation comedy, acknowledged as the most challenging of all small screen genres to get right. On Channel 4, the hugely popular *Friends* came to the end of its run, but two of its home grown programmes, the youth-friendly and deeply irreverent *Bo Selecta* and 'lads comedy' *Peep Show* starring David Mitchell and Robert Webb made an impact. *The Office* returned for its final bow as a Christmas special on BBC1 watched by seven million. This was thrown into perspective by the huge turnout – 16.4 million – for Del Boy and Rodney's traditional seasonal *Only Fools and Horses* appearance on the same channel.

Aware that Britain's black population remained an elusive audience for the Corporation, BBC1 attempted to redress the situation by screening its first-ever black situation comedy, *The Crouches*. Unfortunately, the show flopped. *New Nation*'s editor Michael Eboda said the programme was 'about as funny as being carjacked' and 'as patronising as a politician with a large minority'. Maybe it didn't help that a white writer, Glaswegian Ian Pattison, creator of *Rab C Nesbit*, wrote the show.

Infinitely more successful was *Little Britain*, created by and starring David Walliams and Matt Lucas, one of the year's cult comedy successes and firmly in the tradition of Monty Python; *Little Britain* transferred from BBC3 to BBC2. Two other subversive new BBC3 comedies made waves: *Nighty, Night*, a vehicle for Catherine Tate (who was also given her own show on BBC2) and the animation, *Monkey Dust*. Some audiences, however, considered their subject matter (terminal cancer, for example) too tough for comedy. Perhaps acknowledging that mass appeal situation comedy was a dying craft, BBC2 devoted a series to find Britain's best sitcom of all time; there was a certain inevitability about the winner, *Only Fools and Horses*. ITV1's recent record in comedy has been dismal, but a short series of animations created by Bristol's famed Aardman studios, *Creature Comforts*, suggested that its instincts for original comedy could still prevail.

WHATEVER HAPPENED TO SATURDAY NIGHT?

For the big terrestrial channels, Saturday night TV remained by and large a black hole, as Channel 4 made quite clear in July when it devoted an entire programme to the subject, *Who Killed Saturday Night TV?* Yet there were some notable successes. Veteran Bruce Forsyth returned to host *Strictly Come Dancing* giving BBC1 a surprise hit and *Pop Idol* continued to score for ITV1; the final of the second series was seen by almost 11 million viewers as more than ten million of them voted for the winning wannabe, Michelle McManus. One of the lynchpins of BBC1's Saturday night line-up, chat show king Michael Parkinson, announced in the spring that he was leaving after signing a contract with ITV. He was annoyed that *Match of The Day*'s return would have dislodged him from his usual 10 p.m. BBC1 slot. Parkinson's ITV1 show will debut in the autumn.

The year may have lacked a big new original entertainment hit, but one of the period's most interesting developments was the success of programmes that mixed different programme genres. It was hard to tell if Channel 4's *Operatunity* was an arts or a reality show. Undeniably it was successful TV as it offered members of the public the chance to sing a principal role with English National Opera and created two new divas, one a blind mother of two, the other a supermarket checkout operator. In ratings terms, the most successful of these hybrid shows was BBC1's *Pompeii – The Last Day* which blended science, drama, history and computer imagery to offer a gripping, if fictionalised account of what happened when Vesuvius erupted on that fateful day in August AD 79. Ten million viewers watched this original take on ancient history.

Two outstanding drama documentaries of 2003–4 were BBC2's *The Genius Of Mozart*, providing further evidence that the Corporation was once again taking its responsibilities to the arts seriously, and *Dunkirk* featuring actors recreating the great maritime evacuation of May 1940. A more traditional documentary that attracted praise was Channel 4's 10-parter *The First World War*, based on Huw Strachan's book, which put the conflict into a global context, rather than a European one. Another seminal 20th century event, the assassination of President Kennedy, was the subject of BBC2's *The Kennedy Assassination: Beyond Conspiracy*, a forensic examination of the evidence surrounding the shooting that finally vanquished the various conspiracy theories. The programme won the Broadcasting Press Guild's prize for best single documentary. A BBC expose of racism in Britain's police force, *The Secret Policeman*, was another of the year's important documentaries, in which reporter Mark Daly went undercover with Manchester police. 'What I found,' he reported, 'was a police service trying very hard – and failing – to put its house in order.'

RADIO

As digital technology continued to develop there were signs of even more radical shifts in how people consume radio in the period under review. 'The radio landscape is changing fundamentally,' noted the BBC in its annual report. 'There are strong new national digital stations. People are listening in new ways – via television, the internet or mobile phones. Some young music-lovers are turning from radio to downloading music online.'

Thirteen million people said they had listened to radio via the internet, according to the BBC. Furthermore, with the Corporation's radio output available online via its Radio Player service, allowing listeners the chance to replay any programme during the week following their original transmission, no longer did listeners need to be slaves to the programme schedules. The most popular programme for replay was one of BBC Radio's longest running shows – the veteran soap opera, *The Archers*.

Take-up of digital sets was encouraging. By the end of May, 600,000 digital radios had been sold in the UK and Virgin Radio gave hundreds of sets away in a Christmas competition. With prices poised to break the £50 barrier, growth was certain to accelerate in the near future. Dozens of digital stations were now available, but generally the number of regular listeners tuning into any one station remained low. The BBC's digital offerings were no exception and they had the benefit of being promoted on the Corporation's other services; in fact research suggested that some of the commercial networks, such as Kiss, Kerrang and Smash Hits, were doing better than the BBC's digital stations. Yet despite the growing competition, as far as analogue listening went, the BBC remained in pole position. Figures released in the summer of 2004 indicated that the BBC had actually strengthened its position in 2003–4 with a 53.1 per cent share of the market – up from 52.6 per cent the previous year.

WOGAN HITS 65

The ratings showed a surge in audience levels for Radio 2 (which remained Britain's most popular station) and Radio 4 in the year under review. Radio 2 added another 500,000 listeners in the March–June quarter. This gave the network its biggest ever audience; 13.4 million people tuned in every week. This was encouraging news for the service's new controller, Lesley Duncan, who had started work in January. Veteran presenter Terry Wogan added 250,000 new listeners to his breakfast show. Now 65, and with his contract due for renewal in 2005, there was speculation that he might be considering hanging up his headphones for good. However, Duncan, speaking to journalists in the spring, declined to be drawn on Wogan's future at the station. Remembering Jimmy Young's messy exit from Radio 2, Wogan was cryptic when he told *The Observer*: 'Will I have the guts to retire? What you have to avoid is leaving with bad taste, hanging on too long. But what is too long?' His radio listeners were loyal but TV viewers are more unforgiving and in the winter Channel 5 axed his mid-morning show, co-hosted with Gaby Roslin. Wogan was beaten to presenter of the year at the Sony awards in May by two unknowns – at least outside their Manchester transmission area – JK and Joel, presenters on local station, Key 103.

Another Radio 2 stalwart, Johnnie Walker, saw audiences for his show climb to a new high as more than five million people listened. Walker had returned to the network following treatment for cancer. His 40 years of service to British radio were recognised at the Sonys with a Gold Award. Jonathan Ross's Saturday morning show gained in popularity too. He had in excess of 3.5 million regular listeners, but not all of them were admirers. Gillian Reynolds, the *Daily Telegraph*'s veteran radio writer, was revolted by his show – her main complaint was Ross's obsession with body parts and the frequent sexual innuendo. 'If Jonathan Ross were on commercial radio, would his employer be as tolerant as the BBC?' she asked rhetorically. 'Does a man with so many awards (in May he added another Sony to his cache) really have to display quite so much angst about his penis?'

Jeremy Vine, a far less controversial broadcaster than Ross, continued to win plaudits for his new afternoon show; in July the BBC's governors expressed their admiration for Vine. They also applauded Radios 2's decision to extend its weekly arts show, from 90 minutes to two hours, and re-launched it as *The Green Room*. Meanwhile, the network's new controller indicated that she wanted to hear more seventies music on the station – Steve Harley's *Sounds of The Seventies* was singled out for praise – and more musical soundtracks, especially following the success of Radio 2's broadcasts of *Ball Over Broadway*, starring Michael Ball, and *Sunset Boulevard* featuring Ball and Petula Clark.

During 2003–4 the BBC's problems at Radio 1 showed few signs of being resolved. The broadcaster's weekly audience had fallen to 9.7 million from 10 million. But there was some encouraging news from the latest listening figures which indicated that the network's new breakfast show host, Chris Moyles, was attracting a substantial number of new loyal listeners; Moyles had replaced Sara Cox in January. Part of the problem for the network was that Radio 1's target audience of 15 to 24 year olds faced so many choices in their music listening, and their musical tastes were so varied, that it was harder than ever for the station to strike the right note. The BBC acknowledged that, following audience research, 'some aspects of Radio 1 were off-putting, for instance, its 'relentlessly single' image despite the fact that half of 25 to 30 year olds have children. Listeners wanted the station to be more relaxed and less intense about the music it played – and they also wanted older music.' Nevertheless, the BBC added, there was much that audiences liked. Evolutionary, not revolutionary changes were required. The station's critics were more outspoken. Asked by *The Guardian* in the spring for their opinion on Radio 1, a group of under-25s delivered a withering verdict. DJ Jo Whiley was described as the 'apex of awfulness' by 22-year-old Gary Ryan from Manchester. He added: 'Radio 1 wants credibility and listeners, but they'll find neither while clinging to the pub bores and backing presenters that don't interpret music in a fun, diverting way.'

HUMPHRYS IN A HUFF

Despite the waves created by the Hutton report, Radio 4 continued to shine as a station providing matchless news and current affairs coverage; for the second year running the network was voted station of the year at the Sony awards. During 2003–4 listening levels dipped slightly (commentators thought this was because the Iraq war was officially over), but by the summer Radio 4 had recovered; 9.5 million listeners were tuning in each week. Its most popular programme remained the *Today* show, where the row over the 'sexed up' dossier had begun. In the run-up to the publication of Lord Hutton's report in January, speculation centred on whether its combative presenter, John Humphrys, would leave the programme. But in December it emerged that he had signed a new three-year contract. It had certainly been an eventful year for the presenter. In the autumn of 2003 he had clashed with his editor when part of a pre-recorded interview with the Archbishop of Canterbury, Dr Rowan Williams, was cut from the programme in which the presenter asked the cleric if he thought the war in Iraq was 'immoral'. After a 12-second pause, Dr Williams replied that he would find 'it very hard to give unqualified support to the rightness of that decision'. Unbeknown to Humphrys the archbishop had complained to *Today*'s editor, Kevin Marsh, about the question, who had agreed to cut it from the interview. When Humphrys found out, he was furious and reportedly threatened to resign. 'I behaved in a most unprofessional manner, yes,' he told *The Times*. 'Well you shouldn't lose your temper, should you?'

During the Christmas period a number of guest celebrity editors, including Stephen Hawking and Radiohead singer Thom Yorke, accepted an invitation to edit the programme. Marsh said: 'Judging from the letters and emails I got, everybody thinks they can edit *Today*. Well, here's the chance for five of our better known listeners to prove it.' In the wake of Hutton's criticism of the BBC's journalism, there were suggestions that *Today* – and indeed the rest of the BBC's news machine – would adopt a more conservative approach to its reporting and avoid breaking exclusive stories. The new BBC chairman, Michael Grade, denied this would happen. Indeed *Today* took on extra staff to strengthen its investigative journalism. However, in an effort to reaffirm the BBC's commitment to impartial reporting Humphrys and several of his colleagues, including John Simpson and Andrew Marr, were forced to stop writing their regular newspaper columns. Prompted by the row over its Iraq coverage and the negotiations with the Government regarding the charter, Radio 4 sought to bring greater authority to its flagship news and current affairs programmes. In an effort to make the weekday afternoon programme, *PM*, as authoritative as *Today* and *The World At One*, presenter Eddie Mair was transferred from Sunday morning's *Broadcasting House* to host *PM*. His successor at *Broadcasting House* was Fi Glover, late of Radio 5 Live.

In March Radio 4's most distinguished broadcaster, Alistair Cooke, announced that due to failing health he would reluctantly be delivering his final *Letter From America*. In 58 years he had recorded 2,869 letters for the BBC. Signing off for the last time, Cooke told his listeners: 'I have had much enjoyment in doing these talks and hope that some of it has passed over to the listeners, to all of whom I now say thank you for your loyalty and goodbye.' Less than a month later Cooke, 95, was dead. Tony Blair led the tributes describing him as 'one of the greatest broadcasters of all time, and we shall feel his loss very, very heavily indeed'. Radio 4's controller, Helen Boaden, said she had no plans to replace Cooke. 'My instinct is that Alistair was unique.' Boaden herself was one of the first to benefit from the arrival of a new director-general at Broadcasting House. In the summer she was made the BBC's first female director of news. Applications were invited for a new Radio 4 controller.

ALL WRIGHT FOR RADIO 3

Radio 3 continued to plough an eclectic furrow. Some, including lobby group the Friends of Radio 3, accused the network of dumbing down. They were outraged when in the spring the annual BBC Statements of Programme Policy, which the previous year had pledged to put 'classical music at the heart of the schedule', was replaced by a less precise promise to a 'broad spectrum' of listening pleasures including jazz and world music. The network's controller, Roger Wright, interviewed by *The Financial Times* in July, was unrepentant. 'The fact is we're doing nothing that Radio 3 hasn't done before,' he said. 'We're not changing the format, or the priorities.' Wright pointed out that around 85 per cent of the schedule remained devoted to classical music. The Broadcasting Press Guild tended to agree. *In Tune* presenter Sean Rafferty was awarded the guild's prize for radio presenter of the year. This recognition of Radio 3's success was nothing, however, compared with Radio 5 Live's. It won seven honours at the Sony awards, including one for Jeremy Bowens' report of the capture of Saddam Hussein, plus an accolade to Ian Robertson for his coverage of England's victory in the Rugby World Cup.

It was a good year for Kelvin MacKenzie, chairman and chief executive of the Wireless Group, owner of TalkSport and 16 local stations, as the company reported its first full-year operating profit. The national sports station triumphed against his arch-enemy, the BBC, clinching the rights to England's cricket tour in the West Indies.

MacKenzie's battle with radio audience share analyst, RAJAR, was widely reported. If he wins his court case (he is claiming £66 million in damages because he claims RAJAR consistently underestimates TalkSport's popularity) the implications for the British radio industry would be enormous. One of the potential beneficiaries might be Virgin Radio, whose performance was consistent, if not spectacular during 2003–4. To persuade more people to tune in, Virgin announced in May that it had signed Madness singer Suggs to present a new Friday night show. 'This is going to be a great show – only Virgin Radio would be brave or stupid enough to let me loose on the airwaves to play whatever I fancy to the nation,' he told reporters.

In London, Britain's most competitive radio market, Capital 95.8FM continued to struggle as its audience dropped to the lowest level in its 30-year history. It was disappointing news for the station's new breakfast presenter, Johnny Vaughan, who replaced Chris Tarrant in April. Tarrant was a hard act to follow and Vaughan's show attracted almost 200,000 fewer listeners over a three month period than his predecessor. Capital remained London's most popular station, but only by a whisker, and it may not be long before a rival overtakes it. But it was not all bad news for Capital despite increasing rivalry from Heart and Classic FM – its sister station, the new music network Xfm, broadcasting nationally on digital frequencies, reported record growth.

BUSINESS AND FINANCE

After the long build-up to the war in Iraq, the end of 2003 and much of 2004, were dominated by fears surrounding the UK economy. The Bank of England implemented four quarter point interest rate rises between November 2003 and June 2004 in a bid to control property price rises and curb consumer spending. Initially, the rate rises did little to dampen high street sales, with the Confederation of British Industry (CBI) announcing that confidence among retailers was at its highest level in two years.

In contrast, oil prices reached US$40 a barrel amid fears that disruption to oil supply caused by the war in Iraq would increase oil companies' costs and threaten to restrict economic growth. It was also feared that rises in the price of oil would fuel inflation.

At the end of 2003, economists warned of worsening balance of trade figures. The UK's trade in oil was steadily moving from comfortable surplus to deficit, and slow economic growth in China and the USA was expected to hamper UK export growth in key markets. Meanwhile, the UK's appetite for imports remained voracious. In the short term, the trade figures were predicted to have only a modest downward effect on the pound and a negligible impact on both the stock market and interest rate expectations.

In the USA, the US Federal Reserve increased interest rates by a quarter point in July 2004, the first rate rise in four years, amid growing concern over inflationary pressures in the US economy.

The strengthening of the pound against the US dollar failed to dent a tentative recovery in UK manufacturing. Analysis by the CBI found demand and output picking up despite the gains in sterling. The strong pound failed to have a noticeable impact on export orders, although competition from cheaper imports put pressure on domestic prices.

In London, the FTSE 100 stock market index made strong gains in 2003 before setting into a 'consolidation' phase in the first half of 2004. The index peaked at just under 7,000 in late 1999, at the height of the dot-com bubble. It fell to a low of 3,250 in March 2003, then began a slow climb back, peaking at 4,575 in early 2004. Shares proved resilient in the face of a raft of negative factors. The FTSE 100 index ended the first half of 2004 down just 0.3 per cent on its closing level at the end of December 2003. Forecasters expected the market to show a more sustained rise in the second half of the year.

HIRING AND FIRING

Improving economic prospects fuelled an employment surge in the financial services sector, in particular within fund management companies, general insurers and building societies. The 'big four' accounting firms, which had made a number of redundancies and reduced graduate intake in preceding years, set about recruiting hundreds of accountants to cope with the buoyant economy and additional industry regulation. Strong business growth was forecast to continue into the latter months of 2004.

City firms were sent reeling by a wave of legal actions brought by former employees alleging sexism and unfair dismissal. Stephanie Villalba took Merrill Lynch to an industrial tribunal seeking record damages of £7.5 million and, in an exercise calculated to cause maximum embarrassment, Villalba portrayed Merrill Lynch as intensely hostile to women.

Elizabeth Weston, a former lawyer with Merrill Lynch, subsequently brought a claim against the firm for sex discrimination. She alleged that a senior lawyer had made 'lewd and disgusting' comments to her at a Christmas party and accepted a pay out estimated at £1 million. Merrill Lynch is no stranger to such scenarios. Since the late 1990s the company has paid out millions of dollars in compensation, including the settlement of a class action in the US in which 1,000 female brokers claimed the firm had a culture of bias against women.

MOVERS AND SHAKERS

UK boardrooms continued to feel the aftershocks of the corporate governance reforms of 2003, notably Sir Derek Higgs's review on board composition. The review championed the role of the senior non-executive director as a point of contact for investors, and sought to end boardroom cliques with the recommendation that a chief executive should not become chairman of the same company.

The reforms coincided with a number of boardroom reshuffles and departures. Sir Christopher Hogg, non-executive chairman of Reuters and GlaxoSmithKline (GSK), stepped down from both positions in 2004, complaining that Higgs's recommendation that no-one should hold two FTSE 100 chairmanships had made his position much more difficult. Sir Christopher had worked hard to improve relations with GSK investors after a damaging row in 2003 over a £22 million severance package for GSK's chief executive, J. P. Garnier. He was replaced at GSK by Sir Christopher Gent, formerly of Vodafone, and by Niall FitzGerald at Reuters, who stepped down as chairman of Unilever after eight years.

In another reshuffle, Martin Broughton, chairman of British American Tobacco, became non-executive chairman of British Airways, replacing Lord Marshall of Knightsbridge.

Big institutional investors continued to make their presence felt throughout 2003–4. In the wake of the GSK pay row, investors intervened in the proposed boardroom line-up following the merger of Carlton Communications, led by Michael Green, and Granada, fronted by Charles Allen. The plan was for Green to take the chairmanship, with Allen as chief executive but fund managers led by Anthony Bolton of Fidelity threatened to veto the arrangement, which they considered to be 'too cosy'. Faced with this backlash, Green stood aside to make way for Sir Peter Burt, former chief executive of Bank of Scotland. Bolton was henceforth known as 'the quiet assassin' for his influence in blocking Green's progress.

STORE WARS

Further hostilities erupted within J Sainsbury, the supermarket group, with shareholders angered by a long run of poor performance. Sainsbury's had been struggling to keep its head above water as Tesco and Waitrose increased in popularity and Safeway, which was bought by the William Morrison group after a protracted bidding campaign, launched a price war. Shares in Sainsbury's fell sharply as the company warned of lower profits for the latter months of 2003. Sir Peter Davis resigned as Sainsbury's chairman in July 2004 after the board reneged on an agreement to award him a £2.4 million bonus due to poor performance. He was replaced as chairman by Philip Hampton, a veteran of BT, Lloyds TSB and British Gas.

A boardroom shake-up at Marks & Spencer (M&S) paved the way for one of the biggest City showdowns in years. Luc Vandevelde stood down as chairman in May 2004, citing personal business commitments. His departure provided the cue for Philip Green, the owner of Bhs, to unveil his intention to bid for M&S.

M&S responded by appointing Stuart Rose, formerly with fashion group Arcadia, to replace former McKinsey consultant Roger Holmes as chief executive, and Paul Myners as interim chairman. The shake-up also saw the departure of Vittorio Radice, director of clothing, who had been poached from Selfridges in 2002 amid great fanfare.

Green's initial £8.7 billion offer was rebuffed by the M&S board, which said it undervalued the company. He returned with a £9 billion offer, but M&S refused to budge. It was better, M&S directors said, to allow Rose time to put reforms in place stating that M&S was profitable, but had lost direction. Dirty tactics ensued, with details leaked of share transactions made by Rose in the days before Green unveiled his bid. There were allegations that similar purchases were made by Michael Spencer, chief executive of brokerage firm ICAP, after he had lunch with Rose but both men denied wrongdoing and said they were the victims of a smear campaign. The Financial Services Authority launched an investigation into dealings in M&S shares and associated derivatives, including contracts for differences (CFDs) which are sometimes used in takeovers to quietly build up stakes. Rose was cleared of insider dealing in July 2004.

The battle abruptly fizzled out in mid-July 2004, when shareholders at M&S's annual general meeting made it clear that they were willing to give Rose time to prove himself. Green withdrew, threatening to take his revenge by luring M&S customers to his stores with better products.

SERIOUS FRAUD

One of the most high-profile fraud trials of recent years ended with guilty verdicts and long prison sentences for those charged. Carl Cushnie, lauded by Tony Blair as one of the UK's leading black entrepreneurs, was jailed for six years for defrauding investors who had handed over millions of pounds to Versailles, a trade finance company. Fred Clough, the former Versailles finance director, was also jailed for six years. Clough pleaded guilty ahead of the trial and gave evidence against his former colleague, who maintained his innocence throughout. Versailles was one of the stock market's high-fliers of the late 1990s, worth £630 million at its peak, but it emerged that bankers, accountants and the stock exchange had been misled as to its true value. The company appeared to be earning millions from trade finance fees when in fact Clough was writing cheques to himself. Versailles' accounts for 1999 showed turnover of £232 million, whereas actual turnover was less than £37 million. Clough was later ordered to repay £14 million in stolen funds or else have three years added to his jail sentence.

The Versailles case was a landmark victory for the Serious Fraud Office, which has had a patchy record of winning big cases. Its overall conviction rate fell to just 51 per cent in 2003–4 and of 39 defendants, 10 pleaded guilty, 10 were convicted and 19 were acquitted.

Another high-profile case saw an action for fraud brought against Joyti De-Laurey, a former personal assistant to senior bankers at Goldman Sachs. She was sentenced to seven years imprisonment for stealing £4.5 million from her employers. De-Laurey claimed the money was a reward given in recognition of her ultra-efficient organisation of the private and professional lives of Jennifer Moss, her husband Ron Beller and another executive, Scott Mead.

De-Laurey, who at one stage claimed to have cancer and wrote letters to God asking for help in getting 'what's mine', was arrested just weeks before she was due to start a new life in Cyprus where she had bought a £750,000 seafront villa. She had already spent nearly £400,000 on jewellery, and considerable sums on clothes, holidays and flying lessons. She was found to have forged signatures on cheques and other documents.

PENSIONS CHAOS

Underfunded pension funds continued to pose difficulties for companies in 2004. The scale of the problem was highlighted when Permira, a private equity firm, scheduled a £940 million takeover bid for WH Smith, the struggling high street retailer. Talks broke down after the trustees to the WH Smith pension fund insisted that Permira inject additional cash to plug the fund's £250 million pension deficit.

The bid coincided with a row over the new Pensions Bill, which was feared could force directors, shareholders and private equity firms to plug pension fund gaps in the companies they own or manage. Advisers warned that the Bill could deter potential bidders from WH Smith.

Stock market gains and increased pension contributions by companies saw the UK pension funds deficit narrow to £100 billion at the end of 2003 down from £160 billion in June 2003, according to the CBI. It estimated, however, that companies would still have to make additional contributions averaging £6 billion a year over the next three years. Pension deficits have ballooned under the new accounting standard FRS 17, which forces companies to account for pension assets and liabilities on the balance sheet.

The mis-selling of pensions and endowments continued to vex the Financial Services Authority and a further scandal surrounded split capital investment trusts, also known as split caps. The FSA spent two years investigating claims that split cap trust fund managers colluded in buying one another's shares, exposing investors to losses when stock markets collapsed. It demanded that the 21 firms involved in selling split caps should pay £350 million in compensation to the 50,000 investors who lost out. The firms were given until May 2004 to sign up to a compensation deal. In the event, they offered just £120 million for investors, leaving the FSA no choice but to force the miscreants into a collective settlement.

Sir Howard Davies, who had been chairman of the FSA since its inception in 2000, stepped down in 2003 to join the London School of Economics. Callum McCarthy succeeded him as chairman and John Tiner was appointed chief executive.

BCCI VERSUS BANK OF ENGLAND

Legal history was made in January 2004 when the liquidators of the Bank of Credit and Commerce International (BCCI) took the Bank of England to court seeking damages of £850 million. The BCCI was shut down by banking regulators in 1991 after it was found to be harbouring fraudulent activity. The BCCI was domiciled in Luxembourg but conducted most of its business in London, and the bank's liquidators argued that the Bank of England had shirked its responsibility to regulate and prevent instability in the financial industry. The Bank of England cannot be sued for negligence, since this would open it to a flood of claims so instead, the liquidators accused it of 'misfeasance in public office', alleging that 22 Bank of England officials had conspired to ignore the danger signs at the BCCI. Misfeasance is an ancient tort covering the actions of public officials.

The case looks set to run well into 2005. Gordon Pollock, QC, the lead barrister for the liquidators, outlined the case in an opening speech that lasted five months, reputedly the longest opening address in English legal history. Opening the case for the Bank of England, Nicholas Stadlen, QC, described the claim as 'fundamentally implausible', pointing out that only one case of misfeasance had succeeded in 300 years. He told the court: 'public officers who commit this tort, it seems, are rather like a number 31 bus. You wait 300 years for one to come along and then there are 22 of them all at once.'

Former Bank of England governors are expected to be called to give evidence in early 2005. Mervyn King, who succeeded Sir Edward George as Bank of England governor in 2003, voiced his frustration at the enormous legal fees in the BCCI case, which totalled more than £100 million after several years' preparation.

PROPERTY MARKET WARNING

Mervyn King saw his profile rise dramatically in June 2004 when he issued a stark warning about the overheated UK residential property market. He cautioned that property prices were 'now at levels which are well above what most people would regard as sustainable in the longer term.'

King said that first-time buyers and those seeking to move should think carefully, adding that 'anyone entering or moving within the housing market should consider carefully the possible future paths of both house prices and interest rates. After the hectic pace of price rises over the past year, it is clear that the chances of a fall in house prices are greater than they were.'

Surveys released through the summer of 2004 pointed to a cooling in the housing market, as buyers backed off and sellers began dropping prices to more realistic levels. Annual house price inflation hit 19.5 per cent in May 2004, according to the Nationwide Building Society. Accountancy firm PricewaterhouseCoopers forecast that prices could fall by 10 to 15 per cent over the next four to five years, wiping thousands of pounds off the price of an average property. It found that house prices were 20 to 40 per cent above their long-term averages relative to incomes and rents, although part of this apparent overvaluation could be explained by lower interest rates and housing supply constraints.

Figures released in July 2004 showed that the gulf between house prices in the north and south of Britain had shrunk to its lowest level in five years. Average house prices in the south were only 1.74 times higher than those in northern areas compared with a peak of 2.19 times higher in 2002. In the year ending June 2004, house prices in the north, the north-west and Wales had all risen by more than 30 per cent, while London prices had increased by less than 12 per cent.

HIGH COSTS AND JACKPOTS

Signs of confidence returned to the commercial property market in London. In May 2004, landlords in the West End increased rents for office suites for the first time in three years. The move raised hopes that the slump across the capital's commercial real estate market was over. Demand for office space was driven by hedge funds and private equity firms. A survey published in early 2004 found confidence returning in commercial property across the UK. The Midlands saw the greatest demand, followed by London and the south-east.

In the year under review the London skyline was transformed by the Swiss Re building in the City, dubbed the 'erotic gherkin', the first in a wave of new skyscrapers planned for the capital. Property entrepreneur Gerald Ronson was granted planning permission for the 730 ft Heron Tower in the City, while another developer, Irvine Sellar, got the go-ahead to erect a 1,000 ft building nicknamed the 'shard of glass' next to London Bridge station.

London was named the world's second most expensive city after Tokyo in a survey released in the summer of 2004 by Mercer, the consulting group, putting the capital ahead of Moscow and Geneva. Mercer based its rankings on the comparative cost of more than 200 items including housing, food, clothing, household goods and entertainment.

American casino operators targeted the UK ahead of the deregulation of the gaming industry, expected in 2005. In June 2003, Harrah's Entertainment announced a £550 million joint venture with Gala, the bingo and casino operator, to develop eight huge US-style casinos while MGM Mirage, the US gaming giant, signed an agreement with Earls Court and Olympia to turn the Olympia Two exhibition hall into a £150 million resort-style gaming complex.

Sol Kerzner, the tycoon behind South Africa's Sun City development, announced plans to turn the Millennium Dome in London's docklands into a giant casino and hotel complex. Deregulation brings with it the prospect of Las Vegas-style slot machines paying unlimited jackpots, however, the Government looks set to restrict these to the new 'mega' casinos, angering smaller existing operators.

Dame Shirley Porter, former leader of Westminster City Council, paid £12.3 million to settle the long-running 'homes for votes' case surrounding council flats sold off to prospective Conservative voters in the 1980s. Dame Shirley had been ordered to repay £42 million, the amount (swelled considerably by interest) that the council was deemed to have lost out by having homes sold on the cheap. She maintained that her housing policy was lawful, but finally settled the case in July 2004.

Laura Tyson, dean of the London Business School, led a taskforce investigating diversity in UK boardrooms. The Tyson Report built on the work of Derek Higgs, whose review concluded that boards were dominated by ageing white males and found that only seven per cent of non-executive directors were non-British nationals, six per cent were women and one per cent were from Britain's ethnic minorities. Tyson called for greater transparency in the recruitment process and training of non-executive directors.

TRIALS AND TRIBULATIONS

America was treated to a series of high-profile court cases, in the year under review. In March 2004, lifestyle guru Martha Stewart was convicted of obstructing justice and lying to investigators about the sale of shares in ImClone, a biotechnology company run by her friend, Sam Waksal. Waksal was sentenced to seven years in prison for perjury in June 2003. Stewart requested a retrial, claiming that one of the jurors had failed to disclose that he had a criminal record. This was denied and in July 2004 she was fined and sentenced to five months imprisonment to be followed by five months house arrest.

In May 2004, Frank Quattrone, a former banker with Credit Suisse First Boston (CSFB), was found guilty of obstructing justice. He had urged subordinates to destroy incriminating computer files before officials from the Securities and Exchange Commission, which was investigating CSFB's conduct during the dotcom boom, converged on CSFB's offices. Quattrone insisted that he was following company policy in destroying old paperwork.

John Rigas, the 79-year-old founder of Adelphia Communications, went on trial with his sons accused of defrauding the company of $3 billion. They were charged with the unauthorised borrowing of $2.3 billion of company money to spend on stock purchases and a string of luxury properties. Rigas was convicted, along with one of his sons, in July 2004.

Dennis Kozlowski, the former chief executive of US conglomerate Tyco, went on trial in April 2004 on charges of looting the company of more than $600 million. The trial collapsed after a member of the jury received a threatening letter and a new trial date was set for January 2005.

STOCK MARKET SUCCESS

The Year 2004 brought a renewed wave of UK companies floating on the stock market. They included Centaur Communications, publisher of *Marketing Week*, and M&C Saatchi, the advertising agency created by Maurice and Charles Saatchi following a split from their previous agency, Saatchi & Saatchi.

Sir Richard Branson returned to the UK stock market with the £800 million flotation of Virgin Mobile, his mobile telecommunications arm. The flotation price was reduced to make it more appealing to City investors. Branson's Virgin Group was listed in London in the mid-1980s but was privatised again after the shares did not perform as well as expected. Branson has, however, enjoyed considerable stock market success overseas. He made nearly £130 million floating Virgin Blue, his budget Australian airline, in December 2003.

NOT A BARREL OF LAUGHS

Deregulation of the UK's telephone directory enquiries services in late 2003 triggered aggressive advertising from a rash of new entrants to the market. An American operator, InfoNXX, ran a high-profile campaign featuring two 1970s-style athletes. David Bedford, an athlete famous in the 1970s, threatened legal action because he felt that the moustachioed runners featured in the advertisements were exploiting his image.

Matt Barrett, chief executive of Barclays, courted controversy in October 2003 when he told MPs that long-term borrowing on credit cards was 'too expensive' and that he would advise his children to avoid running up credit card debts. Barclays has more than nine million credit card customers in the UK and made profits of £450 million from its credit card business in 2002. MPs described Barrett's comments as an embarrassing gaffe.

Mikhail Khodorkovsky, head of Russian oil group Yukos, was arrested in October 2003 and charged with tax evasion and fraud. Yukos subsequently abandoned a merger with Sibneft, controlled by Roman Abramovich, the owner of Chelsea Football Club.

Shell, the Anglo-Dutch oil company, was rocked by a massive scandal which led to the ousting of Sir Philip Watts as chairman. Early in 2004, the company admitted to a large shortfall in its oil and gas reserves. It emerged that reserves had been overbooked by 20 per cent, or about 3.9 billion barrels. The disclosure also led to the resignation of Walter van de Vijver, chief executive of Shell's exploration and production business and Judy Boynton, chief financial officer.

In May 2004, Cazenove, the blue-blooded stockbroking firm, announced its intention to float on the stock market. No date was set, although Cazenove said plans were 'progressing', and the firm soon received several offers from rivals eager to acquire it. A float remained the preferred option, but the firm spent much of 2004 evaluating approaches from competitors.

Lord Black of Crossharbour, the Canadian media tycoon, lost control of the *Daily Telegraph* after a bitter seven-month battle. The newspaper was purchased in June 2004 by the reclusive Barclay brothers, who pipped rivals including venture capital firms and the *Daily Mail*, with a bid worth £665 million. Black's problems began in late 2003 when he was accused of receiving millions of dollars in unauthorised payments from Canadian media company, Hollinger. He denied wrongdoing.

AIRLINE UPS AND DOWNS

The airline industry began to emerge from the worst recession in its history in the year under review. Confidence continued to return after the trauma of the September 11 attacks in 2001, although 2003 brought the uncertainty of war in Iraq and the outbreak of SARS in China. Passenger traffic hit a low in May 2003 before slowly starting to recover and high oil prices continued to pose a threat to the industry.

In the UK, the low-cost airline sector suffered a series of setbacks. EasyJet saw £235 million wiped off its share price in May 2004, a fall of 20 per cent, after admitting that bookings had been hit by aggressive discounting by competitors. Full-service airlines like British Airways reduced fares to Europe in a bid to challenge no-frills operators.

Barbara Cassani, former head of low-cost airline Go, stepped down as chairman of the team fronting London's bid to host the Olympic Games in 2012. She was replaced by former athlete, Lord Coe.

CONSERVATION AND HERITAGE

THE NATURAL ENVIRONMENT

THE END OF ENGLAND'S INDEPENDENT WILDLIFE SERVICE

English Nature, the Government's wildlife watchdog, is to be merged with other countryside agencies to form a 'super-quango'. The Government's proposals follow Lord Haskin's review of Britain's countryside agencies, published on 11 November 2003, which criticised the present system as over-regulated, unco-ordinated and inefficient. The key recommendation is to create a single body responsible for nature conservation, amenity and regional development by abolishing the Countryside Agency and fusing English Nature with the Department for Food, Environment and Rural Affairs (DEFRA) Rural Delivery Service. This, it is hoped, will reduce bureaucracy and ensure that funding reaches those who need it. At the same time, Haskins argued, DEFRA's role should be restricted to broad policy issues, while the implementation of policy should be devolved to regional development agencies, with more involvement from local authorities.

There is anxiety that such a move could compromise English Nature's role as an independent wildlife watchdog. Haskins praised its work and considered 'there is a good case for using English Nature as the body on which to build the new agency', however, there is a perceived risk that nature conservation might become swamped in the work of an integrated super-agency that would also be responsible for landscape, natural resources, access and recreation. Some have argued that this has happened in Scotland and Wales, where devolved and integrated countryside bodies were set up in 1992.

On 22 July, DEFRA Minister, Margaret Beckett, presented the Government's rural strategy to Parliament, announcing her acceptance of the central recommendation of Lord Haskin's Report. English Nature is to merge with DEFRA's Regional Development Service and parts of the Countryside Agency to form a single body charged with 'the integrated management of our natural heritage'. At the same time, the multifarious funding schemes for countryside development and conservation are to be 'ruthlessly streamlined'. Nature conservation will form part of the Government's wider policy for sustainable land management. The Government plans to introduce legislation to establish the new body in 2005.

CONDITION OF SITES OF SPECIAL SCIENTIFIC INTEREST

Sites of Special Scientific Interest (SSSI) are areas of protected wildlife habitat or geological formations. Only a minority are publicly owned or managed for nature conservation goals. The rest are private land or commons used for agriculture, forestry or recreation, with various constraints on 'activities likely to damage the special interest'. Under an international agreement on biodiversity, the Government has committed itself to ensuring that 95 per cent of all SSSIs should be in 'favourable condition' by the year 2010. 'Favourable' is defined as 'the special habitat and species features being in a healthy state and being conserved for the future by appropriate management'.

In England, SSSIs are the responsibility of English Nature. In support of the Government's aims, English Nature has been monitoring the condition of all SSSIs in England. The results, published in 2003, make sober reading. Some 42 percent of SSSIs, covering 400,000 hectares, are judged to be in unfavourable condition, with 16 percent classed as 'unfavourable and declining'. The worst-hit SSSIs are rivers and streams (69 per cent), which are suffering from declining water quality exacerbated by drought and abstraction, and upland grasslands (60 per cent), which have been over-grazed by sheep. The best preserved sites are woodlands and the shore, especially rocky shores, shingle and sand-dunes, but even there up to a third of sites are in unfavourable condition.

Sites in currently 'unfavourable but improving' condition include many peat bogs, where the peat-cutting rights have been bought out and restoration work begun. Lowland heaths are also benefiting from scrub clearance and low-level grazing as part of a lottery-funded conservation plan. English Nature is optimistic that the Government's ambitious target is achievable. It proposes to work out a plan for restoring every SSSI to favourable condition, but admits that most of the necessary measures are outside its control. Only 'a combination of legislation, funding and policy can embed suitable and sustainable site management into the way we manage the countryside', says English Nature.

RETURN OF THE GREAT BUSTARD

With adult males reaching 20kg in weight, the Great Bustard is the world's heaviest flying bird. It was a resident British bird until the mid-nineteenth century, when it died out through a combination of shooting and agricultural changes. It is now threatened worldwide, with the largest remaining numbers in parts of Spain, Hungary and the former USSR. It is thought that the reintroduction of the species to Britain would not only boost the world population but would restore a spectacular breeding bird to its former glory and help create a wider public interest in bird-life. To this end, a project to establish a small breeding population in the wild has been initiated by the Great Bustard Consortium and academics at Stirling University.

With its combination of crop fields and natural grassland, high biodiversity and comparative remoteness, Salisbury Plain is considered an ideal habitat for Great Bustards. As part of the project, forty chicks collected from nests in the Saratov area of Russia will be held in a pen at Netheravon on the edge of Salisbury Plain and released over the next five to ten years. Genetic testing at Stirling University has shown that Russian Great Bustards are more closely related to the extinct British population, whereas the Spanish birds, though geographically nearer, are less genetically alike.

Great trouble has been taken to ensure that the birds develop a healthy fear of mankind. Anyone entering the bustard pen must wear a 'dehumanisation suit' and the chicks are to be fed with a glove puppet. Before release, the birds will undergo what is being called 'predator awareness training', with the help of a tame fox. The public will be able to watch the birds from a hide. Great bustards take five years to reach maturity, however, it is hoped that a small breeding population will be established in the wild by 2010.

SUDDEN OAK DEATH

A fungal disease related to potato blight has spread to Britain via garden centres and now threatens native trees. 'Sudden oak death' originated on the Pacific coast of North America where the disease earned its name by devastating the native black oaks and tan oaks. It is caused by the fungus, *Phytophthora ramorum*, unknown to science before 1995, and characteristic symptom is weeping lesions on the trunk, which quickly cause the death of the tree. The fungus spreads by spores carried in moist air or rainwater. The risk that it might spread to Britain led to an emergency ban on oak timber imports from the affected parts of America in 2002. However, a different strain of the same disease is already well-established on viburnums and rhododendrons in garden centres, and it has spread to gardens and other locations across Britain. In November 2003, it was detected on an oak for the first time, a planted American red oak, *Quercus falcata*. The following month it was found on four non-native holm oaks in Cornwall, as well as on a beech, a turkey oak and a horse chestnut.

There were fears that the disease could spread onto our native pedunculate and sessile oaks, and perhaps devastate parks and woods across Britain in a similar manner to Dutch elm disease in the 1970s. Fortunately, this has not yet happened. A Forestry Commission inspection pronounced our woods disease-free, and there is evidence to suggest that native oaks are resistant to the disease. Beech seems to be a more vulnerable species.

Fungal diseases, particularly those affecting trees, are increasing. For example, a mildew that whitens the leaves of horse chestnut and Norway maple trees has spread across England in the past few years. In some river valleys, alders and crack willows are succumbing to fungal diseases which attack both roots and branches. In gardens, azaleas and pelargoniums are vulnerable to fungi which have recently appeared from Japan and South Africa. Daisies now often exhibit the tell-tale white markings of a rust disease originating from Australia. Whether, in some cases, the spread is assisted by the changing climate, especially much milder winters, is uncertain.

NEW FOREST TO BE MADE A NATIONAL PARK

The Rural Affairs Minister, Alun Michael, has accepted the findings of a seven-month public inquiry, which closed in April 2003, and will designate the New Forest a National Park. It will become the first formal National Park to be designated in England for fifty years, and also the smallest, at 571 square kilometers (220 square miles) and with a population of 38,000. The minister agreed with the inspector's recommendation that some 38 square miles should be shaved off the boundary proposed by the Countryside Agency to exclude the towns of Ringwood and Lymington, and the Avon Valley. The Park will, however, include Fawley power station. There will be a further round of consultations before the Designation Order is made.

Responsibility for managing the New Forest as a recreation asset will pass from the Forestry Commission to a new National Park Authority. It will have to balance the needs of conservation and tourism with those of local communities, including the forest's commoners, who have time-honoured rights to graze cattle and ponies and allow pigs to forage for acorn and beech mast. The Authority will be expected to curb creeping suburban development, provide better incentives for environmentally-friendly land management and deal with the many pressures on the Forest and its wild inhabitants.

To the surprise of many, the Government turned down plans for a large container port at Dibden Bay, on the outskirts of the Forest, after a long-running public inquiry. Evidence submitted by English Nature that the port would worsen long-term coastal erosion in Southampton Water was taken into consideration, as was the value of the site for feeding shorebirds and other wildlife. The site for the new container port is now likely to be in East Anglia.

NEW NAMES FOR FUNGI

Being too small or obscure to be known by anyone except specialists, many organisms are known only by a technical Latin name. In the case of the larger fungi, including most mushrooms, toadstools and bracket fungi, the absence of an accepted English name may be due to our traditional suspicion of 'poisonous toadstools'. In many European countries, these species are known by common names in the same way as wild flowers.

In a bid to popularise fungi and make them more accessible, new names have been devised for nearly all the fungi which can be recognised without a microscope. This undertaking was sponsored by English Nature and Plantlife with the blessing of the British Mycological Society. A report including the new names was published in September 2003. The author, Elizabeth Holden, a professional mycologist based in Scotland, gave each species a name based on a specific character of the fungus, including shape, colour, texture or smell. Like Latin names, each consists of a group name and a species name. For example, the waxcap *Hygrocybe ovina*, which characteristically turns red when bruised, is now the Blushing Waxcap. A pleasantly-scented, trumpet-shaped species, *Clitocybe fragrans*, has been dubbed the Fragrant Funnel. Most existing names, like Fly Agaric and Horse Mushroom were retained. However, the Jew's Ear fungus has been renamed the Jelly Ear. It is hoped that the new names will become familiar with usage and by being adopted by field guides and other identification manuals. However, not everyone likes the new names. There is considerable opposition by a mycological 'old guard' which believes that anyone capable of spelling tyrannosaurus or rhododendron should have little trouble learning scientific names.

BUGLIFE

A new conservation charity dedicated to preserving the invertebrate world was launched in May 2004. Named Buglife, it will act as an umbrella body representing Britain's numerous specialist societies concerned with insects and other invertebrates, and encourage their conservation by contributing expertise and campaigning to save important sites for bugs. In short, it is to be for insects what the RSPB is for birds and Plantlife for wild plants. At the launch, Sir Robert May, President of the Royal Society, pointed out that half of Britain's 20,000 invertebrates are believed to be declining, and 230 species are probably extinct. Television presenter, Nick Baker, claimed 'we let so many of them disappear because they lack obvious charisma, fluff and wet, watery eyes'. Buglife's mission is to convince people of bugs' hidden charms and to that end it has helped launch the first nationwide survey of bumble-bees.

Buglife has pointed out that brownfield sites – industrial wasteground in cities – tend to be more important for insects than farmed countryside. It has chalked up an early success in saving one such site, formerly occupied by oil storage tanks, on Canvey Island, Essex, from development. The site, believed to boast more rare insects than any comparable area in the UK, is to be preserved. The fate of a peat bog at Auchennies Moss in Dumfries, destined to become a landfill site, but which is also the only Scottish home of the Bog Bush-cricket and Sorrel Pygmy moth, is uncertain.

A FUTURE FOR HORSESHOE BATS

The greater horseshoe bat is the largest and rarest of Britain's fifteen resident species of bat. It is believed to have declined by as much as 99 per cent over the past century, probably because of agricultural changes that have reduced numbers of large insects, especially cockchafers and dung beetles, which are its prey. Like other bats, it has also suffered from toxic chemicals used in timber treatments and agriculture. The bat is, however, easy to survey because the bats roost together in a small number of colonies in caves, mines and old buildings so it can be determined with some confidence that there are 5,700 adult greater horseshoe bats left, scattered among 14 colonies, all in south-west England and south Wales.

Against the odds, the Greater Horseshoe Bat Project, started in 1998, has claimed a success in raising bat numbers in the largest colony, in south Devon. Some of the bats were fitted with tiny radio transmitters which enabled researchers to find out exactly where the animals were hunting – entirely, it turned out, within four kilometers of their roosting site. Within that area, and working with English Nature and other bodies, the project has been instrumental in persuading farmers to use bat-friendly methods such as retaining hedges and field headlands, and, by scaling down the use of harmful chemicals like ivermectin, used to worm cattle, in giving the dung beetles a helping hand. One organic farmer made the headlines by selling 'bat-friendly milk'. The project aims to ensure that the 'ambitious' recovery target of a 25 per cent increase in Greater Horseshoe bats by the year 2010 will be met. Bat-friendly farming benefits other wildlife too, including hares, farmland birds and insects like grasshoppers and bumble-bees.

WILD FLOWERS FOR THE COUNTIES

Conservation bodies, led by Plantlife, have been eager to promote interest in field botany by inviting the public to choose a wild flower to represent their home county. The vote, originally timed to coincide with the Queen's Golden Jubilee, was carried over to a second year after too many counties opted for the same flower – the bluebell. The bluebell was therefore removed from the running and promoted to our 'national flower'. The final results were announced in June 2004.

The choices were often surprising. The popularity of flowers like cowslip and thrift were confirmed when several counties voted for them. Yorkshire adopted the harebell instead of the expected white rose, while voters in Greater London, with memories of postwar bomb sites in mind, opted for the rosebay willowherb. Sussex, less surprisingly, chose the blue round-headed rampion, known locally as the Pride of Sussex. The large number of rare, relatively obscure flowers chosen suggests that in some places the majority of votes came from knowledgeable botanists. But it also indicates the difficulty of finding flowers that represent one county more than another. Durham, for example, may have chosen spring gentian precisely because it doesn't grow anywhere outside the county. It is hoped that local authorities and other bodies will adopt and use the chosen flower as a symbol (for example, on car number plates), in the same way as the federal states of Canada, Australia and the United States have done.

GM CROPS SENT PACKING

The results of four years of intensive testing of genetically modified (GM) crops were announced in October 2003. Scientists monitored 273 field trials and sampled a million plants in addition to well over a million insects in what is claimed to be the most extensive field trial of GM crops. Its purpose was to investigate whether GM crops yielded environmental benefits, such as greater numbers of weeds and insects, compared with conventional crops.

The results showed that GM herbicide-resistant oilseed rape and sugar-beet were significantly less 'nature-friendly' than conventional crops, with fewer weeds, including less fat-hen, an important species for farm birds. Although it was not investigated, both rape and sugar-beet have wild counterparts which raise the possibility of interbreeding and genetic contamination, possibly resulting in aggressive 'super-weeds'. With GM maize, by contrast, there was more room for wildlife than conventional maize. The Government's advisory committee on releases to the environment concluded that GM maize would not have adverse environmental effects. However, any hope that this would give a green light for GM maize was cast into doubt by the Government's coincidental ban on atrazine, the main maize herbicide, on health and safety grounds.

With public opposition to GM crops as strong as ever, the GM industry has made up its own mind. Monsanto has already shelved its plans to launch GM wheat on the world market after resistance from American cereal farmers. In the UK, Bayer CropScience has given up attempts to grow GM wheat in Britain and the biggest biotechnology company working in Britain, Syngenta, announced it was transferring its GM project from Britain to the United States. For the moment at least, the future of GM crops in Britain seems bleak.

FRESHWATER CRAYFISH

The survival of the only native species of crayfish, one of Britain's largest invertebrates, is increasingly threatened through competition with imported species of crayfish which have escaped into ponds, rivers and reservoirs. Throughout much of England it has been replaced by the larger Signal crayfish, an American species. This species was farmed for food with the help of grants from the then Ministry of Agriculture, and, being able to move about on land as well as water, in addition to an ability to climb low walls and tunneling under wire netting, it inevitably escaped into the wild. Unfortunately the Signal Crayfish carries a fungal disease to which it seems immune, but which is fatal to native crayfish. The spores of the disease are also carried and spread on boots and fishing gear. 'mass mortalities' of native crayfish were a feature of many lowland rivers in the 1980s and early 90s. The American species also suffers from porcelain disease caused by a protozoan parasite.

The native crayfish is still widespread in the Midlands and northern England. However, only 12 river catchments are still free of the invaders, and, at the present rate of decline, the species will be extinct thirty years from now. Since 1996, crayfish farming has been belatedly licenced, and 'no-go areas' set up in areas where the native species still occurs. However this is somewhat academic since the industry, never very profitable in the UK, has declined from over 90 registered farms to just 5. The main hope for the native crayfish resides in the creation of 'crayfish arks' in isolated waters and catchments.

THE BUILT ENVIRONMENT

The Review of Heritage Protection (latterly renamed the Historic Environment Review), published in July 2003, aimed to reform the statutory protection of historic buildings and sites. It proposed, *inter alia*:

- That existing regime of protection (listing, scheduling and registration) should be combined to form a single list of historic sites and buildings.
- That the authority to list structures and sites should be removed from the Secretary of State and given to English Heritage (with a right of appeal and the formulation of strategic policy left to the former).
- That all proposals for the addition of sites and structures to the lists should be open to public consultation, something currently only embarked upon in respect of post-war structures.
- The preparation of a comprehensive instruction pack for owners of protected structures, including a possible requirement to maintain a 'log book' of repairs and alterations.
- That locally listed buildings should be given statutory protection. At present this sub-regime of listing is not fully effective.
- The preparation of 'Statements of Significance' relating to all listed sites and structures which outline the exact nature of protection (something that is only current practice for scheduling, the registration of gardens and for more recent listings).

The Review came to no firm conclusions on the possible reform of the existing system of grading listed sites and structures (Grade I, II* and II). There were, however, concurrent technical explorations of the possible introduction of a single consent that would add heritage controls to the need to seek planning permission. The resultant report to Government came down broadly in favour of this proposal. A re-examination of Planning Policy Guidance 15 and 16, which defines the Government policy relating to the protection of the historic environment, was started but delayed indefinitely.

The Government's response to the Review has so far been interim. However, the suggestion that there should be a single regime for listing apparently found favour among the 500 or so people that responded, and pilot projects have commenced in 15 areas where at present there are multiple regimes of protection. One such example is Holkham Hall in Norfolk where the main house is listed Grade I alongside myriad curtilage structures, listed garden buildings, buried and scheduled archaeological remains and a registered historic landscape.

ABOLITION OF CROWN EXEMPTION

Spring 2004 saw the passing into legislation of the Planning and Compulsory Purchase Act. While this was a broad attempt to reform the overall planning process, it abolished Crown Exemption from the panoply of heritage controls. However, more conservation driven is the Dealing in Cultural Objects (Offences) Act which came into force on 31 December 2003. This has been instrumental in the fight against the sale and export of stolen works of art or souvenirs chipped from ancient sites. The Government also announced that it was exploring the possibility of setting up a national database of stolen and unlawfully removed cultural objects.

Now that the Crown has lost its exemption from heritage controls, the only institutions that do not need to apply for building consent, conservation area consent or scheduled monument consent are places of worship belonging to the Church of England, the Church in Wales, the Baptist Union, the Roman Catholic Church, the United Reformed Church and the Methodist Church. However, this exemption is regarded as so exceptional that the arguments for and against are rehearsed on a regular basis in a formal review. The Welsh Assembly has decided to conduct the process through an individual reviewer, Peter Howell, but in England the Department for Culture, Media and Sport (DCMS) concluded that English Heritage should conduct the reviews in the future. The DCMS premised its report on the basis that the arguments in favour of the so-called Ecclesiastical Exemption could be accepted in principle. The suggestion was that future maintenance of the Exemption would be dependent upon the acceptance of 'a high level management agreement' where the broker on the State side would be English Heritage. In the meantime, the Church of England decided to reform its own procedures for dealing with redundant churches. The most obvious aspect of the reform was the proposed abolition, once legislation allowed, of the Advisory Board for Redundant Churches which has hitherto been the principal source of advice to the Commissioners on how to deal with churches that have fallen out of use. The General Synod approved the abolition in February 2004.

SAVE OUR CHURCHES

It has been widely recognised throughout the conversation movement that a serious plight faces historic churches in the short and medium terms. This view has been endorsed on several occasions by Dr Simon Thurley, Chief Executive of English Heritage. By way of assistance, the Government announced that from 1 April 2004, repairs to listed places of worship would be free from VAT. For the two years prior to that date, congregations had to find 5 per cent and before that, the full 17.5 per cent to meet the cost of repairs. Despite no longer being subject to VAT, listed churches continue to pass into redundancy, a problem which is exacerbated by budget constraints within the Churches Conservation Trust. The Grade I medieval church at Wintringham in Yorkshire, for example, was vested with the CCT but the Trust declared that its current funding would have limited effect. However, The Friends of Friendless Churches, the equivalent of the CCT in Wales, announced in the course of the year that it would assist the Grade I listed art nouveau church at Brithdir in Gwynedd designed in 1895–98 by Henry Wilson, following the formal confirmation of redundancy.

GROWTH OF LISTINGS

Currently, until any review proposals are introduced, the principal means of control is through listing. In England alone there are 470,000 listings and the total continues to expand by several thousand each year. Some of the newcomers in the 12 months under review reflect the breadth of vision given to the definition of 'architectural and historic interest'. These include: the late 18th-century pest house at Townland's Hospital in Henley-on-Thames, Oxfordshire which is attached to the workhouse where

Samuel Taylor Coleridge spent a miserable week in 1794; the barrage balloon workshop of 1938 at Pucklechurch in Gloucestershire; the 'Regional Seat of Government' at Cambridge built in the early 1950s to house staff who might survive an atomic bomb blast; the Barton Aerodrome at Eccles in Greater Manchester, 'the earliest municipal airport passenger terminal building in Britain' of 1930; Twiggs Barn, in Stevenage, Hertfordshire which retains high up in its rafters the coffin intended to house the earthly remains of the wealthy 18th-century Hertfordshire grocer, Henry Twigg, driven to this extreme by a paranoid fear of grave robbing; the Byker Estate in Newcastle-upon-Tyne, one of the North's most spectacular post-war housing estates designed by Ralph Erskine in the 1970s; 12–14 Broad Street, Wokingham, Berkshire which looks like a modest 19th-century property from the outside but in fact conceals much of the timberwork of a late medieval townhouse; the new Bodleian Library, Broad Street, Oxford of 1935 by Sir Giles Gilbert Scott; the cabman's shelter in Rosslyn Hill in Hampstead, designed in 1935 by Elizabeth Scott, architect of the Shakespeare Memorial Theatre at Stratford-on-Avon; the Crematorium Chapel at Whitley Bay in Tyne & Wear which, having previously been unlisted, now finds itself with Grade II* status because of the extraordinary rich plaster decoration by the master of that medium, George Bankart of 1913; the Owl House at Home Farm, Morton-on-the-Hill, Norfolk, a two-storey structure from 1830; and 35 Regent Parade, Harrogate, Yorkshire, the childhood home of W. P. Frith, the famous Victorian painter and the scene of a performance by the world famous violinist Paganini in 1833.

There are also various shadow lists. One was recently updated by CAMRA, the Campaign for Real Ale, which issued a national inventory of pub interiors of outstanding historic interest (covering some 248) and conducted a similar assessment of outstanding pub interiors and exteriors in London. It is hoped that regional inventories will eventually cover the whole country.

Inclusion on the statutory lists does not preclude a subsequent application to demolish or alter. In the full 12 months of 2003, 114 listed buildings in England and 14 in Wales were the subject of applications to demolish. The presumption is against grant of consent and the majority were refused, including the extraordinary proposal to demolish (or move) the Grade I listed church of St Lawrence and All Saints at Eastwood in Essex to allow the expansion of Southend Airport. Other controversial schemes also met with planning refusal: the proposed clearance of 350 Victorian houses in the East Lancashire town of Nelson; the projected redevelopment of a site known as 'The Eye of York' in the centre of the city overlooking Clifford's Tower; and the proposal for a 100-seat restaurant within the bailey of Cardiff Castle.

GRANTS AND REPAIRS

Other major cases in the year involved the reoccupation and extension of Toddington Manor in Gloucestershire, one of the great early Gothic revival houses; the proposed closure of a number of major churches within Brighton; the ejection of the pews from Wesley's New Rooms at Bristol; the demolition of much of Smithfield Market in the section facing Farringdon Road on the City of London/Islington borders; and the conservation of Apethorpe Hall, Northamptonshire. So concerned was English Heritage by the poor condition in which this major building had been kept since 1983 that it seconded a member of staff to shadow the case full time and initiate compulsory purchase proceedings through the Department for Culture, Media and Sport. Another case that caused a furore, and hit the national press, was the demolition without consent of the 1936 villa at Virginia Water known as Greenside. A Public Inquiry into the application to demolish was due to be held in November 2004.

Each of the State agencies in Britain – English Heritage, Historic Scotland, Cadw and the Department of the Environment for Northern Ireland – are empowered to offer grants towards the repair of historic structures. In the course of the year under review, English Heritage announced £2 million worth of grants towards the nation's cathedrals and relaunched its programme of assistance for war memorials to the tune of £60,000 a year. Other funding included: £879,000 for Godolphin House, near Helston in Cornwall, owned by the National Trust, and £500,000 for the three huge concrete 'listening ears' built in the 1920s at Greatstone on the Kent Coast. Even so, the generosity of English Heritage continued to be overwhelmed by the proceeds of the National Lottery. The Heritage Lottery Fund (HLF) has continued to allocate £300 million a year to conservation driven projects despite a slight blip in ticket sales and the Government's requirement that London's Olympic bid should be paid for in part by the Lottery.

A sum as large as £300 million will enable large-scale projects to be funded. For example: St Martin in the Fields in Trafalgar Square received £13.377m for repairs and to open up the undercroft to a further array of new activities, the London Transport Museum in Covent Garden received £9.47m; The Royal Observatory, Greenwich received £7.14m (Stage One Pass) to include the opening up of the extraordinary Victorian Altazimuth Pavilion; the Kibble Palace in Glasgow, one of the world's finest glasshouse structures received £3.49m (Stage One Pass); Wentworth Castle in Barnsley, South Yorkshire, now the home of the Northern College for Residential Adult Education, received £10.357m to finance urgent repairs; the Brading Roman Villa on the Isle of Wight received £2.13m to construct a new cover for its 4th-century mosaics; St George's, Bloomsbury received £2.37m (Stage One Pass); Kew Palace received £1.5m; Hardwick Park in County Durham received £4.05m (Stage One Pass) to retrieve landscape and 18th-century buildings from dilapidation; Fulham Palace received £3.3m (Stage One Pass) to begin the long term rescue of this former palace of the Bishops of London; Hylands Park in Chelmsford received £3.05m to conserve the 570-acre parkland designed by Humphry Repton in the 1820s that surrounds a house which had been the subject of an application to demolish in the 1980s; Braintree District Museum received £1.908m to permit the purchase of the Warner Archive of over 80,000 hand-woven fabrics and designs made between 1821 and 1971; Wollaton Hall in Nottingham received £4.5m (Stage One Pass) to repair and enhance one of Robert Smythson's great houses of the 1580s, now a Museum of Natural History; The Woodhall Colliery at Ashington, Northumberland received £10m to conserve the coalfield's buildings and re-house the County Records Office; The Victoria County History received £3.598m (Stage One Pass) for a five-year project allowing the production of 17 local history volumes covering ten English counties; Leeds City Museum received £19m to re-house the museum within the Grade II* listed Leeds Institute in the Millennium Square built 1865–68; Torre Abbey in Torquay, Devon received £4.9m to repair and reinvigorate one of the area's oldest buildings and its principal museum; Cowdray Park in Midhurst, Sussex received £2.9 million to conserve the ruins of the great house gutted by fire in 1793; The Museum of Bristol received £10.277m (Stage One Pass) to create a museum of that name on the site of the present Industrial Museum; Ashton Court in Bristol received £4.35m to rescue a 1783 Humphry Repton landscape; and Cobham Park in Kent received £4.98m.

Very rarely the HLF withdraws grants. Probably the year's most dramatic decision was to rescind an earlier promise to grant aid for the repair of Brighton's West Pier, one of only two piers with Grade I listing. Following a grant request of £15m at Stage Two, without any further commitment that there would not be demands for additional funds, Trustees felt they had to pull the plug. English Heritage publicly opposed the decision but there seemed an inevitability to it given that three fires and the ravages of weather had virtually destroyed all of the pier's superstructure, leaving only a few of the legs and the framing for the flat decking.

Fortunately, this is an unusual occurence and most grants lead to the completion of the project concerned. Other HLF-funded campaigns in the year under review include: the refurbishment and construction of the new south porch at the Albert Hall; the opening of Dilston Castle and Chapel near Corbridge in Northumberland; Sker House, Glamorgan, one of the country's most spectacular buildings in the 16th-century which would face almost certain collapse without HLF intervention; Manchester Art Gallery (total HLF grant £18.8m) which now has a brand new extension by Michael Hopkins; the fountain at Witley Court, Worcestershire, the centrepiece of the gardens by W. A. Nesfield, now operational with 120 separate jets following a grant of £727,000; Sheffield Botanical Gardens (HLF grant £5.8m) with greenhouses dating from 1837 now reopened with their original linking blocks; 78/80 Derngate in Northampton, interior by Charles Rennie Mackintosh, now open as a museum and study centre; Temple Newsam House near Leeds which reopened in the first half of 2003 with four further rooms to be reopened in 2004 after a major scheme of consolidation which involved the reinstatement of the 18th-century ground levels; The Jerwood Centre, next to the birthplace of William Wordsworth, in the Lake District was designed by Napper Architects to provide a centre for conservation and research with a space for poetry reading; and the Kings Library at the British Museum reopened in December 2003, justifying once again the description by the Museum's Historian Joe Mordaunt-Crook as 'one of the noblest rooms in London'.

Even so, there seems to be a growing trend for smaller, more fragile, museums to close their doors despite the existence of HLF grants. Local campaigns fought off cuts which would have closed museums for at least one day a week in Kingston-upon-Thames and Worthing, but Daventry Museum in Northamptonshire closed its doors completely in March 2004, whilst a similar threat hangs over the Folk Museum at Gloucester. Esoteric interests faced a further blow with the projected closure of the British Dovecote Society. The organisation known as 'Heritage Information', a clearing house for information on crafts, skills and other services for historic buildings repair, mentioned in the Review for 2004, failed to reach the critical mass of subscribers and is now de facto defunct. The quarrying of hydraulic lime, an essential ingredient in the repair of historic buildings, was also dealt a blow with the decision, following a public inquiry, to deny planning permission for the extension of the quarry at Appledoor in Somerset. This site had been described as 'the only supply of hydraulic building lime in the United Kingdom' and this blow means that virtually the only source of lime is from France. The decision was taken despite the endorsement of the extension by English Heritage, the Society for the Protection of Ancient Buildings (SPAB) and the UK Building Limes Forum.

SWINGS AND ROUNDABOUTS

If these were the roundabouts, there were many swings. Among them was *Restoration*, a BBC2 programme aired during 2003 and 2004. Viewers were invited to vote by telephone to save buildings and sites of their choice from continued dereliction and the threat of demolition. There were 30 to choose from in 2003 and 21 in 2004. Despite criticism that the choice was unrepresentative (there being no Church of England place of worship), the series was regarded as a great success by conservation professionals and BBC executives with some 4.5 million people tuning in to the last episode of 2003. The winner was the Victoria Baths in Manchester. An international network for traditional building was launched through the Prince's Foundation of the Prince of Wales at the same time as the National Heritage Training Group set itself the task of increasing the small number of people practising skills in traditional building conservation crafts. This is currently estimated to be a mere 40,000 worldwide.

A longstanding threat was averted with the relocation of Sir Christopher Wren's Temple Bar in the City of London following its expulsion in 1878 to the Hertfordshire wilds of Theobald's Park. Completion was scheduled for November 2004 and the new site is situated next to St Paul's Cathedral. English Heritage chose to offer absolute protection to the precious archaeological remains in Boxgrove Quarry, the site of the 1993 discovery of Boxgrove Man, by buying it for £100,000.

The conservation of country houses was dealt a tremendous blow with the sudden bankruptcy of the Country Houses Association (CHA). Founded in 1955 under as the Mutual Householders Association, the CHA, at the time of its demise owned eight substantial houses all of supreme importance, including Great Maytham Hall in Kent by Lutyens, Albury Park in Surrey and Aynhoe Park in Northamptonshire. By the time of writing six of the eight properties had been sold as going concerns. For the vast majority of historic buildings that have fallen into disuse, sensitive conversion remains the best solution. The year under review saw the biggest step forward yet in the campaign to save one of the greatest of all the Northern textile mills – Manningham Mills located in Bradford. The site has now been purchased by Tom Bloxham, founder of the company known as Urban Splash, which intends to convert the million square feet with the help of at least £6m of public money.

DANCE

A number of notable anniversaries were marked by the dance world in 2003–4. Dance Umbrella, the annual festival of contemporary dance, celebrated its 25th birthday in autumn 2003. In 2004 the centenaries of the births of two of the greatest choreographers of the 20th century, Sir Frederick Ashton and George Balanchine, were marked by classical companies all over the world, and the 75th anniversary of the death of the Russian impresario Serge Diaghilev inspired many tributes to his vision and artistic legacy.

Dance Umbrella was founded in 1978 by the former Royal Ballet dancer, Val Bourne, who is still its artistic director today. After its modest first season it gradually grew into a wide-ranging and impressive platform from which leading contemporary choreographers from overseas have been introduced to the UK and on which British choreographers have learnt and developed their craft. The anniversary was marked by a gala at Sadler's Wells Theatre on 28 September 2003 featuring work by British and American luminaries including Siobhan Davies, Matthew Bourne, Wayne McGregor, Trisha Brown, Bill T. Jones and Mark Morris. The season itself presented new work by choreographers including Michael Clark (*Oh My Goddess,* including a long solo for Clark himself set to songs by P. J. Harvey), Charles Linehan (the quartet *Disintegration Loops*) and Stephen Petronio (*The Island of Misfit Toys*), and was graced once more by the presence of the Merce Cunningham Dance Company, which gave a special week of Anniversary Events at the Turbine Hall at the Tate Modern. Ballett Frankfurt gave its last UK performances under the direction of William Forsyth, and Anna Teresa De Keersmaeker returned with her introspective work *Small Hands (out of the lie of no).* Jonathan Burrows and the composer Matteo Fargion presented their intriguing *Both Sitting Duet,* neatly described by a Belgian journalist after its première there in 2002 as 'an unspectacular spectacle'. A special anniversary programme featuring Siobhan Davies, Akram Khan, Sara Rudner, David Gordon and Valda Setterfield, Richard Alston Dance Company and others was given for two nights at the Queen Elizabeth Hall in October 2003 under the title *Silver Celebration.* In June 2004, Val Bourne was awarded a CBE for services to dance.

NEW WORKS

Other contemporary dance events of note during the year included Wayne McGregor's moving new work *AtaXia* for his Random Dance Company, which premièred at Sadler's Wells in June 2004 and was inspired by MacGregor's recent research into the interaction of the brain and the body. Michael Gordon's score, *Trance,* was played by Icebreaker and the work was designed by Lucy Carter. George Piper Dances continued to present strongly danced contemporary works interspersed with video diaries of their lives on the road, and featured in a Channel 4 series, *The Rough Guide to Choreography,* as well as touring to the USA for the first time. Lea Anderson's Cholmondeleys and Featherstonehaughs undertook a tour to celebrate the 20th anniversary of their formation in 1984. Richard Alston created two new works for his company during the season: *Overdrive,* an intricate and energetic work to a score by Terry Riley, and *Shimmer,* a quieter piece with unusually theatrical costumes (i.e. unusual for an Alston work) by the fashion designer Julien Macdonald. Alston also introduced a work by another choreographer, Martin Lawrance, into his company's repertoire for the first time when *Grey Allegro* was premièred in October 2003.

Nigel Hinds, chairman of Shobana Jeyasingh Dance Company and a member of the board of Dance Umbrella, was appointed director of The Place and will work with the rest of the Executive Team responsible for running the venue: Richard Alston (artistic director), John Ashford (theatre director) and Veronica Lewis (director, London Contemporary Dance School). The Place Prize for Dance, worth £25,000, was launched in January 2004 and will be awarded in the autumn. Another important centre for contemporary dance, the new Laban building at Creekside, south London, was awarded the 2003 Stirling Prize for architecture as the building which had made the greatest contribution to British architecture in the preceding year. Late in 2003, Laban and Trinity College of Music (now based in Greenwich) announced that they would merge by August 2004 to form a dedicated conservatoire for music and dance, the first of its kind in the UK.

Rambert Dance Company, Britain's largest contemporary dance company, continued its extensive programme of touring in the UK and also visited China, Hungary and Italy during the year. Mark Baldwin, installed as director in late 2002, commissioned works by Javier de Frutos, Fin Walker and Ian Spink for the 2003–4 season. The most ambitious and interesting of the new works was Spink's *A Tragedy of Fashion,* conceived as a centenary tribute to Ashton, whose first ballet, created in 1926, bore the same title but the choreography of which has been almost completely lost. Spink uses the original scenario concerning a suicidal couturier but expands and adapts it to fit a much larger work full of references to ideas and images that influenced Ashton and which abounds with in-jokes and entertaining puns. De Frutos's new work, *Elsa Canasta,* deliberately confounds the romantic music of Cole Porter by juxtaposing it with overtly sexy, crudely physical choreography, while Walker's *Reflection* is a repetitive work for two groups of five dancers to music by Ben Park.

RELAUNCH OF SCOTTISH BALLET

Scottish Ballet, in its first season under new director Ashley Page, is now perched somewhat uncomfortably on the fence between contemporary dance and classical ballet. Page presented works by leading contemporary choreographers Richard Alston, Siobhan Davies and Stephen Petronio as well as several of his own works and Balanchine's *The Four Temperaments.* He also mounted a new production of *The Nutcracker,* with the scenario updated to Weimar Germany and the beauty and poetry of the score largely ignored in the desire to be anti-traditional. It is not yet clear whether the company's dancers can rise to the technical challenges required of them in such a diverse repertoire, or whether Scottish audiences will continue to receive them with the enthusiasm and interest generated by this first season.

The Royal Ballet, in Monica Mason's first full season as director, elected to mark Balanchine's centenary and the 75th anniversary of Diaghilev's death in 2003–4, and Sir Frederick Ashton's centenary in 2004–5 (although it did take part in Ashton celebrations in California and New York in July 2004). Balanchine was born Georgiy Melitonovich Balanchivadze in St Petersburg in 1904 and joined Diaghilev's Ballets Russes in 1924 as a dancer. Diaghilev appointed him his chief choreographer in 1925, and after Diaghilev's death Balanchine stayed in Europe until he was invited to the USA by Lincoln Kirstein in 1934 to found the School of American Ballet. The New York City Ballet, officially founded in 1948, became the vehicle for the expression and development of Balanchine's radical style of neoclassicism until his death in 1983. (From 1958 he was ably assisted by the choreographer and ballet master John Taras, who died on 2 April 2004). Balanchine's work was represented in the Royal Ballet's repertoire during the year by performances of *Agon, The Prodigal Son, Symphony in C* and, perhaps his most significant masterpiece, *The Four Temperaments,* created to Hindemith's music in 1946 but still vibrant and exciting nearly 60 years later.

Diaghilev, who died in Venice in 1929, was instrumental in promoting the talents and careers of numerous other dancers, choreographers, musicians and artists, and through his Ballets Russes he ensured that ballet was presented and judged as a serious, expressive art form rather than as a merely decorative spectacle. The Royal Ballet mounted four works in tribute to him during the season: Ashton's *Daphnis and Chloë,* to the Ravel score commissioned by Diaghilev in 1912; *L'Après-midi d'un faune,* the first work choreographed by Vaslav Nijinsky, Diaghilev's star dancer, and here using the choreograher's own notation from 1915; *Le Spectre de la rose,* created by Mikhail Fokine for Diaghilev's company in 1911; and *Les Noces,* the powerful, austere evocation of a Russian peasant wedding to Stravinsky's music choreographed by Bronislava Nijinska for Diaghilev in 1923. Mason also invited five young choreographers to produce works inspired by Diaghilev and his legacy at the Linbury Studio Theatre at the Royal Opera House in June 2004.

ROYAL CREATIONS

The choreographic creativity that burgeoned under Diaghilev has been conspicuous by its absence from the Royal Ballet in recent years. Three new one-act works were presented in 2003–4. *Broken Fall* is a sterile, gymnastic piece by Russell Maliphant performed by the self-styled 'Ballet Boyz' (Michael Nunn and William Trevitt, both in their thirties) and Sylvie Guillem, once more showing us her remarkably flexible body. *Qualia* by Wayne McGregor is another example of how not to waste beautifully trained classical dancers. The most successful of the three works was an interesting and expressive *pas de deux* by William Tuckett, depicting a fragile relationship and stunningly danced by Adam Cooper and Zenaida Yanowsky. (The same dancers joined Matthew Hart and Will Kemp in Tuckett's highly successful production of *The Soldier's Tale* to Stravinsky's music and with designs by Lez Brotherston in the Linbury Studio Theatre in June 2004). The company also performed Christopher Wheeldon's *Polyphonia* for the first time; this was created in 2001 for New York City Ballet, and Balanchine's influence is evident in this as in much of Wheeldon's work; but it suffered badly from being programmed on the same bill as the vastly superior *The Four Temperaments.*

The company gave strong performances of a range of full-length works during the year, although a planned revival of MacMillan's *Isadora* was postponed at short notice. Ashton's 1948 production of *Cinderella* was performed in handsome new designs by Toer van Schayk and Christine Haworth, and outstanding performances of MacMillan's *Mayerling* were followed by a dismal revival of his *Anastasia* (in place of *Isadora*), the full-length version of which has not stood the test of time and has, in any case, been overtaken by the real-life revelation that Anna Anderson was not, in fact, the youngest daughter of the last Tsar.

Birmingham Royal Ballet marked Ashton's centenary by reviving two of his most popular full-length works, *La fille mal gardée* and *The Two Pigeons,* and the historic wartime work *Dante Sonata;* it also toured some of his smaller pieces to regional venues in April 2004. In July 2004 the company performed in New York as part of the Ashton centenary celebrations at the Metropolitan Opera House. Ashton and Balanchine were honoured by a gala, *Sir Fred and Mr B,* held at the Birmingham Hippodrome on 11 March 2004, and Balanchine's *Apollo* was brought into the repertoire at the beginning of the season.

BINTLEY'S BEAST

Unlike the Royal Ballet, the Birmingham company has seen no shortage of new works over the years, some supplied by its prolific director, David Bintley. In December 2003 he mounted a full-length production of *The Beauty and the Beast* to a score by Glen Buhr and with impressive designs by Philip Prowse. The cast worked hard but the ballet is over-complicated and choreographically weak; however it was well received by audiences. The other new work of the season was *Krishna,* a colourful but confused evocation of the life of the Hindu god by the kathak dancer and choreographer Nahid Siddiqui. Bintley's own far superior 1985 work, *The Sons of Horus,* based on Ancient Egyptian beliefs concerning death and the body, was introduced into the repertoire in September 2003.

English National Ballet dedicated its performances during the year to another dance pioneer whose centenary fell in July 2004 – Sir Anton Dolin, who was born in 1904 and died in 1983, and who danced under Diaghilev and de Valois and in the USA before co-founding the London Festival Ballet (now English National Ballet) with Dame Alicia Markova in 1950. The company appointed John Talbot as chairman in place of Angela Rippon in April 2004. Its repertoire during the year was heavily influenced by financial considerations and largely comprised two productions of *Swan Lake* joined by the ever-popular *Nutcracker* (albeit in the poor 2002 production by Christopher Hampson) and Michael Corder's stylish *Cinderella.*

Yet another *Swan Lake* was premièred by Northern Ballet Theatre in February 2004. Choreographed by the company's artistic director, David Nixon, it uses a score assembled by John Longstaff from various Tchaikovsky sources, and updates the action to 1912 New England while replacing the traditional scenario with a confused gay love story. More successful was Nixon's reworking of *A Midsummer Night's Dream,* mounted in September 2003 with stunning sets by Duncan Hayler and costumes by Nixon himself. Shakespeare's play is transposed to the late 1940s and the plot centres on a touring ballet company and the professional intrigues and romantic entanglements therein; the production was strongly performed and dramatically coherent as well as being an undoubted crowd-pleaser.

VISITORS

Visitors in 2003–4 included the first ever tour to the UK by the Royal New Zealand Ballet, which chose its first programme unwisely (a turgid triple bill of works by Christopher Hampson, Javier de Frutos and Mark Baldwin) but redeemed its season at Sadler's Wells with performances of Hampson's effective 2003 production of *Romeo and Juliet,* set in the 1960s. Other visitors came largely from across the Atlantic. The Martha Graham Company performed at Sadler's Wells for the first time in November 2003, and San Francisco Ballet appeared at the 2003 Edinburgh Festival. Dance Theatre of Harlem undertook a seven-week tour of the UK that opened at Sadler's Wells in March 2004. The Bill T. Jones/Arnie Zane company celebrated its 20th anniversary with a season at Sadler's Wells in June 2004 that was disappointing in the quality of both dancing and choreography. Other visitors included: the National Ballet of China; Ballet Preljocaj; the eminent Russian ballerina Nina Ananiashvili and her own Moscow Dance Theatre in a short season of sub-standard contemporary works at Sadler's Wells in March 2004; and the Bolshoi Ballet in a lengthy season (the first in London under its new director, Alexei Ratmansky) at the Royal Opera House in summer 2004.

In February 2004 a new national organisation was set up by the Arts Council of England and the Department for Education and Skills to support and promote young people in dance. The National Youth Dance Agency, based at the Royal Academy of Dance, is directed by Linda Jasper; it will identify the full range of dance activities available to young people and will seek to create new partnerships across the various sectors involved in order to maximise and co-ordinate the opportunities offered to the dancers of the future.

PARLIAMENTARY INQUIRY

In April 2004 the Culture, Media and Sport Committee of the House of Commons announced an inquiry into the development of dance in the UK. It invited information and views from interested parties based around questions concerning the dance economy, the effect of public investment on the dance sector, and young people and dance. The committee received more than 70 written submissions from individuals, dance companies, national dance agencies, dance critics, community and support organisations, and funding bodies. It also held an evidence session in May 2004. Its report, published in July 2004, outlined the challenges facing the dance sector in relation to children's experience of dance, funding, working conditions for dancers, the physical infrastructure, and the problem of low salaries in the profession. It concluded that it was very important for the Government to set out 'a clear, overarching policy for dance', describing how it intended to achieve its objectives: excellence, access and contribution to healthy living. The committee emphasised the importance of raising the profile of dance and its potential to contribute to different policy areas. The Government's resulting strategy for dance is due to be revealed in October 2004, and could have long-term effects on the development of the art form in the UK.

PRODUCTIONS

ROYAL BALLET

Founded 1931 as the Vic-Wells Ballet

Royal Opera House, Covent Garden, London WC2E 9DD

WORLD PREMIÈRES:

Proverb (William Tuckett), 3 December 2003. A *pas de deux.* Music, Steve Reich; design, Nicky Gillibrand. Dancers, Zenaida Yanowsky and Adam Cooper

Broken Fall (Russell Maliphant), 3 December 2003. A one-act work. Music, Barry Adamson. Danced by Sylvie Guillem, Michael Nunn and William Trevitt

Qualia (Wayne McGregor), 3 December 2003. A one-act work. Music, Scanner; design, Vicky Mortimer. Cast led by Leanne Benjamin, Jaimie Tapper, Laura Morera, Edward Watson and Ivan Putrov

COMPANY PREMIÈRE:

Polyphonia (Christopher Wheeldon, 2001), 15 November 2003. A one-act work. Music, Gyorgy Ligeti; design, Holly Hynes; cast led by Jonathan Cope, Leanne Benjamin and Alina Cojocaru

Full-length works from the repertoire: *La Bayadère* (Makarova after Petipa, 1980), *Romeo and Juliet* (MacMillan, 1965), *Cinderella* (Ashton, 1948, with new sets by Toer van Schayk and new costumes by Christine Haworth), *Giselle* (Petipa after Coralli/Perrot, prod. Wright 1985), *The Sleeping Beauty* (Petipa, prod. Makarova 2003), *Mayerling* (MacMillan, 1978), *Anastasia* (MacMillan, 1971), *Onegin* (Cranko, 1965).

One-act works from the repertoire: *The Four Temperaments* (Balanchine, 1946), *Sinfonietta* (Kylin, 1978), *Gong* (Mark Morris, 2001), *Agon* (Balanchine, 1957), *The Prodigal Son* (Balanchine, 1929), *Symphony in C* (Balanchine, 1947), *Daphnis and Chloë* (Ashton, 1951), *Le Spectre de la rose* (Fokine, 1911), *L'Après-midi d'un faune* (Nijinsky, 1912), *Les Noces* (Nijinska, 1923).

The company toured to the USA in July 2004, performing *Cinderella* and *Giselle* in Orange County, California, and *Scènes de Ballet* (Ashton, 1944), *Marguerite and Armand* (Ashton, 1963) and *pas de deux* by Ashton (the Awakening *pas de deux* from *The Sleeping Beauty, Voices of Spring, Thas pas de deux,* and *pas de deux* from *Ondine* and *Birthday Offering*) at the Metropolitan Opera House, New York, as part of a celebration of the works of Sir Frederick Ashton.

Dancers from the company performed in five new works at the Linbury Studio Theatre at the Royal Opera House in June 2004 commissioned to mark the 75th anniversary of the death of Diaghilev; the works were choreographed by Robert Garland *(Spring Rites),* Matjash Mrozewski *(World of Art),* Vanessa Fenton *(On Public Display),* Cathy Marston *(Venetian Requiem)* and Alistair Marriott *(Being and Having Been).*

BIRMINGHAM ROYAL BALLET

Founded 1946 as the Sadler's Wells Opera Ballet

Birmingham Hippodrome, Thorp Street, Birmingham B5 4AU

WORLD PREMIÈRES:

Krishna (Nahid Siddiqui), 24 September 2003. A one-act work. Music, Hariprasad Chaurasia; design, Kate Ford. Cast led by Tiit Helimet, Laëtitia Lo Sardo and Koshuke Yamamoto

Beauty and the Beast (David Bintley), 1 December 2003. A full-length work. Score, Glen Buhr; design, Philip Prowse. Cast led by Robert Parker, Asta Bazevicite,

Desmond Kelly, Marion Tait, Ambra Vallo and Michael Revie

COMPANY PREMIÈRES:
Apollo (Balanchine, 1928), 24 September 2003. A one-act work. Music, Stravinsky. Cast led by Robert Parker, Asta Bazevicite, Nao Sakuma and Molly Smolen

The Sons of Horus (David Bintley, 1985), 24 September 2003. Music, Peter McGowan; design, Terry Bartlett. A one-act work. Cast led by Molly Smolen

Full-length works from the repertoire: *Giselle* (Petipa after Coralli/Perrot, prod. Bintley and Samsova 1999), *Swan Lake* (Petipa/Ivanov, prod. Wright and Samsova 1981), *The Two Pigeons* (Ashton, 1961), *La fille mal gardée* (Ashton, 1960).

One-act work from the repertoire: *Dante Sonata* (Ashton, 1940). In addition to performances at the Birmingham Hippodrome Theatre, the full company toured to Plymouth (two seasons), Sunderland (two seasons), Salford and Bradford.

In April 2004 the company split into two sections, with half performing *Concerto Barocco* (Balanchine, 1941), *Five Brahms Waltzes in the Manner of Isadora Duncan* (Ashton, 1976), *Monotones II* (Ashton, 1966), *Tweedledum and Tweedledee* (Ashton, 1977) and *Five Tangos* (Van Manen, 1977) in Truro, Barnstaple and Yeovil, and the other half performing *Allegri Diversi* (Bintley, 1987), *Dante Sonata* and *Elite Syncopations* (MacMillan, 1974) in York, Durham and Middlesbrough.

The company staged a gala, *Sir Fred and Mr B*, to mark the centenaries of Sir Frederick Ashton and George Balanchine, at the Birmingham Hippodrome on 11 March 2004. Dancers from the company participated in An Evening of Music and Dance at the Symphony Hall, Birmingham, on 7 February 2004.

In July 2004 the company performed *Enigma Variations* (Ashton, 1968), *Dante Sonata, Five Brahms Waltzes in the Manner of Isadora Duncan,* and *The Two Pigeons* at the Metropolitan Opera House, New York, as part of a celebration of the works of Sir Frederick Ashton.

ENGLISH NATIONAL BALLET

Founded 1950 as London Festival Ballet
Markova House, 39 Jay Mews, London SW7 2ES
Full-length works from the repertoire: *Cinderella* (Corder, 1996), *The Nutcracker* (Hampson, 2002), *Swan Lake* (Petipa/Ivanov, prod. Deane 2000), *Swan Lake* (Petipa/Ivanov, prod. Deane 1997).

One-act works from the repertoire: *Drink To Me Only With Thine Eyes* (Morris, 1988), *Trapèze* (Hampson, 2003), *Melody on the Move* (Corder, 2003).

The full company toured to Manchester (two seasons), Bristol (three seasons), Oxford (two seasons), London (Apollo, Hammersmith and the Royal Albert Hall), Liverpool (two seasons) and Southampton.

In April 2004 the company toured to Spain, performing *Double Concerto* (Hampson, 2001), Act II of *Swan Lake* and *Melody on the Move* in Barcelona.

RAMBERT DANCE COMPANY

Founded 1926 as the Marie Rambert Dancers
94 Chiswick High Road, London W4 1SH

WORLD PREMIÈRES:
Elsa Canasta (Javier de Frutos), 24 September 2003. Music, Cole Porter; design, Jean-Marc Puissant

Reflection (Fin Walker), 3 March 2004. Score, Ben Park; design, Ben Maher

A Tragedy of Fashion (Ian Spink), 25 May 2004. Music, Elena Kats-Chernin; design, Antony McDonald and Juliette Blondelle. Cast led by Martin Lindinger

Works from the repertoire: *Visions Fugitives* (Van Manen, 1990), *Living Toys* (Armitage, 2003), *21* (Bonachela, 2003), *PreSentient* (McGregor, 2002), *Linear Remains* (Bonachela, 2001), *Five Brahms Waltzes in the Manner of Isadora Duncan* (Ashton, 1976).

The company performed in Salford, Norwich, Bristol, Milton Keynes, High Wycombe, Edinburgh, London (two seasons at Sadler's Wells Theatre), Plymouth, Truro, Sheffield, Isle of Man, Brighton, Mold, Birmingham, Oxford and Glasgow.

The company also visited China, performing *PreSentient, 21, Visions Fugitives* and *Living Toys* in Shanghai in November 2003 and in Beijing in January 2004. It also performed in Hungary (Budapest and Gyor) and at the Venice Biennale festival, Italy, in June 2004, with a repertoire of *Reflection, A Tragedy of Fashion* and *PreSentient.*

AWARDS 2003–4

CRITICS' CIRCLE NATIONAL DANCE AWARDS 2003
De Valois Award for Outstanding Achievement in Dance: Val Bourne (Dance Umbrella Artistic Director)
Best Male Dancer: Carlos Acosta (Royal Ballet)
Best Female Dancer: Zenaida Yanowsky (Royal Ballet)
Audience Award: Adam Cooper
Sunday Express Children's Award: Harry Walker
Dance UK Industry Award: Theresa Beattie (Director of Artist Development, The Place)
Committee Special Award: Lez Brotherston
Best Choreography (Classical): Michael Corder (English National Ballet)
Best Choreography (Modern): Akram Khan
Best Choreography (Musical Theatre): Adam Cooper for *On Your Toes*
Outstanding Female Artist (Modern): Ana Lujan Sanchez (Rambert Dance Company)
Oustanding Male Artist (Modern): Henry Montes (Siobhan Davies Dance Company)
Outstanding Female Artist (Classical): Oxana Panchenko (George Piper Dances)
Outstanding Male Artist (Classical): Robert Parker (Birmingham Royal Ballet)
Company Prize for Outstanding Repertoire (Classical): English National Ballet
Company Prize for Outstanding Repertoire (Modern): Scottish Dance Theatre
Best Foreign Dance Company: Paul Taylor Dance Company (USA)

LAURENCE OLIVIER AWARDS 2004 (DANCE)
Best Theatre Choreographer: Karen Bruce for *Pacific Overtures* at the Donmar Warehouse
Best New Dance Production: Broken Fall (a George Piper Dances commission in association with The Royal Ballet at the Royal Opera House)
Outstanding Acheivement in Dance: Thomas Edur and Agnes Oaks for their performances in English National Ballet's *2 Human* at Sadler's Wells

FILM

In 2003–4 the world of film was decidedly political. In November 2004, Austrian-born film star Arnold Schwarzenegger fronted the recall campaign against the Democrat incumbent Governor of California, Gray Davis, culminating in the Republican's landslide victory. Schwarzenegger was sworn in as the 38th Governor on 17 November 2003, just months after he'd topped the box-office charts with *Terminator 3*.

Whatever one thinks of Schwarzenegger's politics it was hard not to see this as a victory of celebrity over substance, and an alarming indication of voter frustration. For Arnie to follow the late Ronald Reagan's career path all the way to the White House would require an amendment to the US constitution (which states that the President must be US-born), but that is not inconceivable. First though, he will have to patch up some significant holes in the state budget and for now, at least, his movie career is on indefinite hold.

Satirist Michael Moore could only dream of a left-wing candidate with Arnie's popular appeal to take on George W. Bush, and his preferred choice, General Wesley Clark, quickly limped out of the presidential race. Perhaps Moore should have stood as a candidate himself? The Democrat Party may take a lot of convincing but many people thought that Moore's non-fiction film *Fahrenheit 9/11* mounted a better case against the President than John Kerry managed in six months of campaigning.

FAHRENHEIT 9/11

Against the backdrop of ongoing mayhem in Iraq this was always going to be a controversial film. Even then, it exceeded all expectations. In April, Moore publicly accused the Disney Corporation of refusing to distribute his movie for political reasons (*Fahrenheit 9/11* was financed by Miramax, a subsidiary of Disney). The story made front page news around the world, and sent Disney into a spin of damage limitation.

In May, the movie premiered at the Cannes film festival. Short on facts but long on opinion and innuendo, *Fahrenheit 9/11* was no conventional documentary. Rather, it was a polemical broadside aimed directly at Bush's re-election bid.

Contrary to popular opinion in the USA, Iraqis didn't have anything to do with the attack on the World Trade Centre – most of the terrorists were Saudis. In *Fahrenheit 9/11*, Moore duly recycles speculation that Saudi oil interests have bankrolled Bush since the early 1970s but fails to deliver any definitive evidence. This lack of evidence is the least impressive aspect of the film and Moore implies the war in Iraq was simply a diversion to spare the President's blushes – a thesis no more proven than Bush's contention that Saddam Hussein was in possession of weapons of mass destruction.

Moore is on safer ground satirising the President's syntactical infelicities, his leisurely style and his privileged background. Here, the selective use of archival footage is overtly provocative, and a legitimate corrective to the institutionalised distortions of the network news. Moore, for example, may be the first person to reveal the full extent of the protesting at Bush's inauguration. A section of footage showing the President's bewildered response to the breaking news of the destruction of the World Trade Centre is simply excruciating: caught on camera as he reads a children's book to pre-schoolers, Bush sits there for seven minutes apparently incapable of decisive action.

The movie's most substantial section addresses the so-called Patriot Act, and accuses the administration of fostering a climate of fear and paranoia – in effect, terrorising citizens while curtailing their civil liberties. Most of the second half of the film is dedicated to the fate of US troops in Iraq and Lila Lipscomb, a mother who proudly sent two of her children to Iraq, lost her son, and changed her mind about the validity of the war, emerges as the emotional core of the film. She subsequently became the focus for many Americans' scepticism and anger about the war, or about the film, depending on their politics.

In Cannes, the jury awarded *Fahrenheit 9/11* the Palme d'Or on 'aesthetic grounds'. Released in the USA in June 2004 by a coalition of independent distribution companies (including Miramax, whose troubled relationship with Disney may soon be terminated), *Fahrenheit 9/11* reached a far wider audience than had been expected, breaking the $100 million barrier to become the most successful documentary ever made (taking five times more than Moore's previous record-holder, *Bowling for Columbine*). Even then, the controversy continued, with singer Linda Ronstadt being booed and subsequently banned from a Las Vegas venue after she endorsed the film during one of her concerts.

Perhaps surprisingly, for a film calibrated to appeal directly to the middle-American voter (and which all but ignores Tony Blair), *Fahrenheit* also became the most successful documentary released in the UK.

STRANGER THAN FICTION

Fahrenheit 9/11 was inescapable but it wasn't the only prominent documentary to reach cinemas this year. Indeed, while television broadcasters are shying away from challenging non-fiction, documentary filmmakers are enjoying unprecedented success on the big screen.

In 2003 hits included *Etre et Avoir*, *Dogtown and Z Boys*, *The Kid Stays in the Picture* and *Spellbound*. In 2004, there was no shortage of equivalents. Stacy Peralta returned with *Riding Giants* and Jorgen Leth met Lars von Trier's challenges head-on in the post-modern *The Five Obstructions*, while Kevin Macdonald's *Touching the Void* recreated the white-knuckle drama of a near-fatal mountain climb. But in the same vein as *Fahrenheit 9/11*, many of 2004's documentaries had a more political orientation. Nick Broomfield looked at the case of multiple-murderer Aileen Wuornos in *Aileen: Life and Death of a Serial Killer* (coincidentally also the subject of *Monster*, for which Charlize Theron won an Academy Award), and suggested that she was wrongfully executed by Florida Governor Jeb Bush.

Errol Morris teased out fascinating ironies, confessions and evasions from the former US Secretary of State for Defence, Robert McNamara, in the Oscar-winning *The Fog of War*, and any parallels between Vietnam and Iraq were left to the viewers' discretion.

Morgan Spurlock took on fast food giant McDonalds in the witty but cautionary tale *Super Size Me*. Spurlock ate nothing but McDonalds for a month which played havoc with his health. It was a stunt, but an effective one, and McDonalds discontinued its Super Size Me option within a month of the film's successful US release.

And so it continued: *The Control Room* painted a sympathetic portrait of the al-Jazeera news network; *Outfoxed* highlighted the alleged right-wing bias of Rupert Murdoch's Fox News; and *The Corporation* charted the rise of the business institution as an invincible entity.

Provocative and unabashedly partisan, these documentaries showed that where Michael Moore led, others were keen to follow. None of them had anything like *Fahrenheit 9/11*'s commercial success (*Super Size Me* came closest with a domestic figure of about $10 million) but they all made waves and got people talking. Clearly there is an appetite for this kind of film-making which has not been stimulated before.

RETURN OF THE EPIC

In mainstream cinema, spectacle and escapism were the order of the day. In the year under review, the Academy Awards resembled a coronation, as Peter Jackson's *The Lord of the Rings: The Return of the King* was duly rewarded with eleven statuettes including Oscars for Best Picture and Best Director. This haul puts it on a par with the biggest ever winners, *Ben-Hur* (1959) and *Titanic* (1997).

A fundamentally moralistic war story, *The Lord of the Rings* trilogy resonated with events in Afghanistan and Iraq but Tolkien's mythology is ultimately hermetic, and the film's appeal is largely based on the wonder of its CGI (Computer Generated Imagery). Not surprisingly, advances in CGI, coupled with the box office bonanza unearthed by the trilogy (and *Gladiator* before it), has inspired a return to epic film-making. The year 2004 saw Brad Pitt and Peter O'Toole in *Troy*, Clive Owen and Keira Knightley in a pagan *King Arthur*, and Colin Farrell as the great *Alexander*. There are many more epics in the making, including four potential films about Iceni queen, Boudicca.

There was even some hope of a return for that once dominant, now dormant, genre, the Western. Viggo Mortensen (Aragorn in *Lord of the Rings*) had a minor success in *Hidalgo*, and Kevin Costner's *Open Range*, while not on a par with *Dances with Wolves*, was a welcome comeback. However, *The Missing* went AWOL at the box office, despite being a gripping piece of storytelling with a formidable performance from Cate Blanchett. Lastly, the revisionist version of *The Alamo* was a financial disaster for Disney, which saw an initial return of just $22 million on an investment of $95 million.

KILL BILL

On the subject of returns, 2004 saw the much anticipated return of writer-director Quentin Tarantino, seven years after *Jackie Brown*. His long-gestating martial arts extravaganza *Kill Bill* finally emerged in two feature-length instalments, *Kill Bill Vol. 1* and *Kill Bill Vol. 2*.

What at first looked like a panic measure (the combined running time would have put the film at more than four hours) turned out to be a master stroke. Critics raved about the panache and grace Tarantino brought to what is essentially a delirious sampler of great moments from American, Japanese and Chinese trash culture. *Kill Bill Vol. 1* is style for style's sake. Toying with his audience, Tarantino didn't even bother to explain the backstory to the film's revenge plot, as the Bride (Uma Thurman) tracks down and eliminates her former colleagues from the Deadly Viper Squad. Her quest climaxes in a showdown with a hundred bodyguards, whom she leaves bleeding, clutching at lost limbs, or dead on the floor.

Kill Bill Vol. 2 made its predecessor look like the longest trailer ever made. Here were the answers Tarantino had left hanging, the rhyme and reason, and emotions more complex than pure hatred. Neither film enjoyed *Pulp Fiction*-type success but enough to vindicate Tarantino and production company Miramax.

Tarantino, however, failed to feature at the Academy Awards and despite Peter Jackson's clean sweep, none of the cast of *Lord of the Rings* was nominated either. This left some elbow room for the handful of serious dramas Hollywood produced this year: Peter Weir's superbly fashioned mariners' tale, *Master and Commander: The Far Side of the World*; Anthony Minghella's civil war love story *Cold Mountain*; Alejandro Gonzales Inarritu's soul-searching *21 Grams*; Patty Jenkins' *Monster*; Vadim Perelman's gloomy *House of Sand and Fog*; and Clint Eastwood's *Mystic River*.

Along with Sofia Coppola's comic romance *Lost in Translation*, *Mystic River* was the best reviewed American film of the year. Neither would have been made but for the clout of their directors. Coppola went down the indie route, and shot her Tokyo story in less than 30 days. Eastwood persuaded enough stars to sign up (Sean Penn, Tim Robbins, Kevin Bacon, Laura Linney and Laurence Fishburne) that Warner had to relent, despite its misgivings: 'we're not in the business of making dramas anymore', one executive reportedly advised the astonished Eastwood. A depressing sign of the times. *Mystic River* features dark subject matter, including child abuse, but it is basically a suspense thriller, nothing more challenging than that. It was budgeted at $30 million, and made three times that at the US box office and if the studios aren't interested in this kind of film, what business are they in, exactly? The answer, probably, is either much more expensive films, or much cheaper, but preferably the former, because such juggernauts create their own momentum and the richest gravy train. *Mystic River* is not the kind of film to inspire marketing tie-ins, toys, or sponsorship deals.

HIT PARADE

The biggest hits of 2003 were *Finding Nemo*, *Pirates of the Caribbean*, *Lord of the Rings: The Return of the King*, *Matrix Reloaded*, *Bruce Almighty*, *X2*, *Elf*, *Terminator 3*, *Bad Boys 2*, and *Matrix Revolutions*. Apart from the comedies, they were all sequels, known brands, tried and tested. As one frustrated film-maker explained, 'the ideal studio movie is the sequel. The problem is, how to originate a sequel?'

With box-office returns for 2003 more or less flat, and audience figures down, the economics of the studios' approach would look shaky save for the DVD bonanza, which continues to boost everyone's profit margins. Last year's North American DVD revenue hit $17.5 billion, two-thirds of that in sales, one third rentals.

Take the case of *Finding Nemo*, the underwater tale of an anxious father who loses his son and has to cross the ocean to find him again. Another triumph from Pixar, who also made the *Toy Story* films, *Finding Nemo* generated $339 million in US cinemas but more than doubled that figure internationally, and then went on to sell eight million copies on the first day of its DVD release, heading for something in the region of another $400 million in home viewing revenue.

Not surprisingly, the problem on which the entertainment giants are focusing is not cutting back overheads, but cutting out digital piracy.

BRITISH FILM

In this high stakes business environment, how did the British film industry fare during 2003–4? Figures compiled by the UK Film Council paint a rosy picture: 173 films were made in Britain in 2003 (twice as many as in 2002), generating over $1 billion worldwide, and even taking a 5.7 per cent share of US ticket sales.

It should be noted that the UK Film Council claims the likes of *Tomb Raider 2* as a British production – it was filmed here but is a US/UK/Japanese/German co-production. Nevertheless, more people are going to the cinema in the UK on a regular basis than at any time over the past 30 years (admissions of 167.3 million were the second highest in that period), and British films constitute a relatively healthy 14.8 per cent of what we watch.

Home-grown hits included *Love Actually*, *Calendar Girls* and *Touching the Void*. The latest *Harry Potter* instalment, Richard Eyre's *Stage Beauty*, and Working Title's *Wimbledon* should keep the figures up through 2004 but these 'British' films have a distinctly trans-Atlantic feel to them: *Harry Potter and the Prisoner of Azkaban* is made by Warner and directed by Mexican Alfonso Cuaron; *Stage Beauty* stars Americans Billy Crudup and Claire Danes, is based on an American play, and is a US/GB co-production; and *Wimbledon* is financed through Universal, co-stars Paul Bettany (who is British) and Kirsten Dunst (who isn't), and is written by an American, Adam Brooks.

Of course, there are authentic British films being made. Ken Loach's *A Fond Kiss*, Pawel Pawelkowski's *My Summer of Love*, Richard Jobson's *Sixteen Years of Alcohol*, Roger Michell's *The Mother* and David Mackenzie's *Young Adam* all fit the bill. Often these British films look less to the USA than to Europe for inspiration but in so doing, they're falling outside of the mainstream and struggling to find an audience. As the Film Council has acknowledged, this is a significant challenge which needs to be addressed.

As for the fortunes of European films on British screens, the situation could scarcely be worse. The most successful foreign language film released in the UK in 2003 was the Brazilian *City of God* which was by no means a box office success. The most popular French film was the animation *Belleville Rendez-vous*, followed by Francois Ozon's *Swimming Pool* and *L'Homme du Train* (co-financed by the Film Council). None of these made it into the box office top 100.

THE PASSION OF THE CHRIST

One subtitled film sure to figure in the top ten box office lists for 2004 is Mel Gibson's, *The Passion of Christ* which was, in one sense at least, a labour of love. Financed entirely by the actor-director, who also co-wrote the film, it detailed Christ's last hours, from the Garden of Gethsemane to his crucifixion and resurrection.

Like *Fahrenheit 9/11*, *The Passion of Christ* became a news item well before anyone had seen the film. The source of the controversy, fears that Gibson (a devout Catholic and whose father is an alleged Holocaust-denier) was making an anti-semitic film. By inviting Catholic Church leaders but not their Jewish counterparts to preview the film, Gibson fuelled the fear. He also got an endorsement from the Pope, who reportedly declared, 'It is as it was.'

Reviews were overwhelmingly negative. Gibson's film is brutally and relentlessly violent. It begins with words from Isaiah, 'He was wounded for our transgressions, crushed for our iniquities. By his wounds we are healed.' This interpretation of the Christ's last hours is one of guilt and atonement. Gibson wants viewers to experience Jesus being beaten and tortured for two hours because in sharing his suffering we have to acknowledge our own sin. Some are more guilty than others, however. While Gibson claimed biblical integrity, to the extent he shot the film in Aramaic and Latin (the language of the traditional Catholic Church, but not the language of the Roman Empire of the time), he admitted to inserting details from other sources, notably *The Dolorous Passion of Our Lord Jesus Christ* by early nineteenth-century nun Anne Catherine Emmerich, and even claimed that 'the Holy Ghost worked through me' during the film's shooting.

Gibson's unhistorical interpretation relieves Pontius Pilate (and by extension the Romans) of their responsibility for the crucifixion, and lays the blame instead on the Jewish priests. The film does not make it clear that Jesus was himself Jewish. Unlike *The Last Temptation of Christ*, which religious groups picketed in 1988, *The Passion of the Christ* was embraced by the Catholic Church and evangelical Protestants, who accepted Gibson's evaluation that it was 'perhaps the best outreach opportunity in 2,000 years'. Despite (or because of) the violence, the subtitles, the bad reviews and the controversy, *The Passion of the Christ* enjoyed financial success, grossing $370 million in the US, £10 million in the UK, and much more in Catholic countries around the world.

AWARDS

BRITISH ACADEMY OF FILM AND TELEVISION FILM AWARDS 2004

Best Film: *The Lord of the Rings: The Return of the King*
Outstanding British Film of the Year: *Touching the Void*
Achievement in Direction: *Master and Commander: The Far Side of the World*
Original Screenplay: *The Station Agent*
Adapted Screenplay: *The Lord of the Rings: The Return of the King*
Best Actor: Bill Murray, *Lost in Translation*
Best Actress: Scarlett Johansson, *Lost in Translation*
Supporting Actor: Bill Nighy, *Love Actually*
Supporting Actress: Renée Zellweger, *Cold Mountain*
Cinematography: *The Lord of the Rings: The Return of the King*

THE 76TH ACADEMY AWARDS

Best Picture: *The Lord of the Rings: The Return of the King*
Best Actor: Sean Penn, *Mystic River*
Best Actress: Charlize Theron, *Monster*
Best Supporting Actor: Tim Robbins, *Mystic River*
Best Supporting Actress: Renée Zellweger, *Cold Mountain*
Animated Feature Film: *Finding Nemo*
Original Screenplay: *Lost in Translation*
Cinematography: *Master and Commander: The Far Side of the World*
Directing: Peter Jackson, *The Lord of the Rings: The Return of the King*
Foreign Language Film: *The Barbarian Invasions*

CANNES FILM FESTIVAL 2004

Palme d'Or: *Fahrenheit 9/11*, Michael Moore
Best Director: Tony Gatlif, *Exils*
Grand Prize: *Old Boy*, Park Chan-wook
Best Actor: Yuuya Yagira, *Nobody Knows*
Best Actress: Maggie Cheung, *Clean*
Best Screenplay: *Comme une Image*, Agnes Jaoui and Jean-Piérre Baer

LITERATURE

A book originally written as a children's book which was already one of the critical and commercial successes of 2003 went on to win a slew of prizes in 2004. Mark Haddon's *The Curious Incident of The Dog in the Night-Time* was acquired by children's publisher David Fickling, but taken up by sister imprint Cape and published in two editions, for adults and children. The children's edition was submitted for the Man Booker Prize, and chair of the judges, John Carey, confessed on television that he very much wanted it to be shortlisted, only to be thwarted, to his surprise, by others on the panel. Haddon's book, the narrative of a boy with Asperger's syndrome trying to solve the mystery of the murder of a neighbour's dog, nevertheless went on to win the novel (rather than the children's novel) category of the Whitbread Prize, then the overall Whitbread Book of the Year award, as well as both the literary novel and the children's novel categories at the book trade's British Book Awards, which take account of sales. It also won the Guardian Children's Fiction Prize and was shortlisted for the CILIP Carnegie Medal, the prestigious children's book prize chosen by librarians. The book sold 100,000 copies in hardback, with the adult edition outselling the children's by four to one.

BOOKER HIGHLIGHTS

The Man Booker Prize shortlist did have its surprises though. Alongside former winner Margaret Atwood's lauded vision of a futuristic dystopia, *Oryx and Crake* (Bloomsbury); *Brick Lane* (Doubleday), the acclaimed first novel by Monica Ali, selected in 2003 as one of Granta's Best of Young British novelists; and Zoe Heller's highly regarded *Notes on a Scandal*, were two works by lesser known authors, Damon Galgut's *The Good Doctor* (Atlantic), set in post-apartheid South Africa and a book from small, state-subsidised, Birmingham-based publisher Tindal Street Press, Clare Morrall's *Astonishing Splashes of Colour*, a narrative of a woman with an unresolved emotional history. There was also a first novel, *Vernon God Little* (Faber) written under the pseudonym DBC Pierre. When this book won, it caused a stir, not just for its style and subject – it is the story of a boy accused of a Columbine-style atrocity at a high school narrated in his own disaffected voice – but for the history of the author. The pseudonym was partly a joke: DBC stood for 'Dirty But Clean' and the author, Peter Finlay had a chequered past, which included substantial bad debts.

Two books by literary heavyweights Martin Amis and Peter Carey were unflatteringly reviewed – *Yellow Dog* (Cape) and *My Life as a Fake* (Faber) were missed off the Booker Prize shortlist. Tibor Fischer had livened up the silly season by trashing *Yellow Dog*. Fischer's own novel, *Voyage to the End of the Room* (Chatto), was published on the same day as Amis's; the online bookseller Amazon mischievously offered the two for sale together, at a saving of £7.

A Man Booker innovation for 2004 was the introduction of a specially programmed website to allow library users to select titles from the longlist using search terms defining their tastes. Categories included 'easy', 'disturbing', 'optimistic', and – one that ruled out several fancied candidates – 'no sex'.

Other Booker winners or shortlisted candidates of the past who had notable new novels out during the year were Peter Ackroyd with *The Lambs of London* (Chatto) about Charles and Mary Lamb and the discovery of a document by Shakespeare; J. G. Ballard with a story of middle-class revolution, *Millennium People* (Perennial); Pat Barker with her tale of a war-reporter from Afghanistan finding human brutality closer to home, *A Mind to Kill* (Penguin); J. M. Coetzee with *Elizabeth Costello* (Secker), about a tired author on the lecture circuit; and Jim Crace with *Six* (Viking), a riff on conception, relationships and birth, whose hero had fathered six children by different mothers. John Updike paid a rare visit to Britain and was the star guest at the Guardian Hay Festival in May.

Margaret Atwood's *Oryx and Crake* appeared again on the shortlist for the Orange Prize for Fiction, but the judging panel, chaired by novelist and broadcaster Sandi Toksvig, selected as the winner Andrea Levy's *Small Island*, prompting an immediate reprint by publisher Headline of 12,000 copies. *Small Island* sold modestly before the announcement, but so too did last year's winner, Valerie Martin's *Property* (Time Warner), which went on to sell 50,000 copies.

The literary theme of the year turned out to be Henry James, who appeared in novels by Colm Toibin (*The Master*, Picador, which followed five years of James's life), Alan Hollinghurst (*The Line of Beauty*, Picador, whose protagonist was a postgraduate studying James), David Lodge (*Author, Author*, Secker, which chronicled James's middle years) and Toby Litt (*Finding Myself*, Penguin, in which James had a bit part).

Among the notable biographies were the culmination of a decade of research in Peter Parker's definitive life of Christopher Isherwood (*Isherwood*, Picador), which was widely and favourably reviewed in tandem with John Sutherland's life of Isherwood's associate, *Stephen Spender, The Authorised Biography* (Viking). Autumn 2003 saw the first overview of the life and work of children's author and illustrator Raymond Briggs, *Blooming Books* (Cape) with copious samples of Briggs' work and text by Nicolette Jones. Autumn 2004 saw Robert McCrum writing on P. G. Wodehouse (Viking), John Coldstream on Dirk Bogarde (Weidenfeld), and Patrick Marnham on Mary Wesley (Bantam Press); Marnham's book, entitled *May I Borrow Your Husband for the Afternoon?*, was billed as including material that would be revelatory even to the author's family.

CELEBRITY MEMOIRS

Autumn 2003–4 saw a profusion of celebrity memoirs, notably *David Beckham: My Side*, written 'with' the former EastEnders actor Tom Watt, for which HarperCollins reportedly paid £2m. *My Side* sold more than 86,000 copies in the first two days of publication, and over 150,000 copies in the first fortnight.

Footballer Paul Gascoigne's autobiography *Gazza: My Story* (Headline), written 'with' Hunter Davies, was launched with a print run of 200,000 copies and an eight-day signing tour in June. It sold 18,759 copies in its first two days on sale and a total of 32,702 copies in the first week, outselling the memoirs of former US president Bill Clinton, whose *My Life* (Hutchinson) was published at the same time and sold 21,690 copies through bookshops in that week. Clinton came to the UK to promote his book in July.

Robson Books did not wait for Wayne Rooney to prove himself one of the most valuable football players in the world at Euro 2004. In autumn 2003 the publisher thought that the 18-year-old already had enough achievements under his belt to justify a 260-page biography by Harry Harris. A revised version was published to coincide with the nation's obsession with the world cup. Meanwhile John Blake signed up Sue Evison's *Wayne Rooney: England's Hero* which was published in mid-August.

Sporting autobiographies included England rugby captain Martin Johnson's (Headline), and, in autumn 2004, books by marathon runner Paula Radcliffe (Simon & Schuster), commissioned before her disappointment at the Athens Olympics; by England rugby coach Clive Woodward, who published *Winning!* (Hodder) just as his team started losing; by members of that rugby World Cup-winning team Jonny Wilkinson (Headline) and Will Greenwood (Century); and by England cricket captain Nasser Hussain (Michael Joseph) and golfer Nick Faldo (Headline).

Media personalities had plenty to say for themselves. The memoirs of journalist and television presenter Joan Bakewell, *The Centre of the Bed*, attracted widespread attention, revealing as they did details of her affair with Harold Pinter (Hodder). *The Success of Ricky*, by Ricky Tomlinson, an actor of humble origins who had achieved a substantial following with the television series *The Royle Family*, helped to justify Time Warner's advance of £850,000. Glamour model Jordan, whose real name is Katie Price, appeared at the London Book Fair with a jacket-only mock-up of her book-to-be, *Being Jordan* (published by John Blake), thereby giving the papers the opportunity to make jokes about her book having nothing in it. It was nevertheless one of the year's highest sellers.

Other celebrity memoirs included the singer and television presenter Cilla Black's record of her sustained career (*What's It All About?*, Ebury), radio presenter Sir Jimmy Young's autobiography *Forever Young* (Hodder), pop musician Sting's *Broken Music* (Simon & Schuster), and actress Martine McCutcheon's *Behind the Scenes – A Personal Diary* (HarperCollins). There were books too from Eastenders star Shane Richie (*From Rags to Richie*, Contender), TV presenter Graham Norton (*So Me*, Hodder), actress Sheila Hancock, about her husband (*The Two of Us: My Life with John Thaw*, Bloomsbury), and from broadcasters Jon Snow (*Shooting History*, HarperCollins) and Michael Buerk (*The Road Taken*, Hutchinson). Straight after his headline-grabbing resignation from his role as Director-General of the BBC in the wake of the Hutton report, Greg Dyke was signed up to write his memoirs (HarperCollins). Pamela Stephenson, the comedian whose biography, *Billy*, of her husband, fellow comedian Billy Connolly, published by HarperCollins in 2001, had sold more than a million copies, produced a sequel: *Bravemouth: A Year of Living with Billy Connolly* (Headline). Other slightly less triumphant follow-ups to earlier bestsellers included a second television spin-off offering sartorial advice, Susannah Constantine and Trinny Woodall's *What Not To Wear, Part 2* (Weidenfeld) and *Schott's Original Food and Drink Miscellany* (Bloomsbury), following the runaway success of *Schott's Original Miscellany*, a bijou collection of general knowledge and trivia.

RICHARD AND JUDY

The BBC's The Big Read, a promotion involving a series of programmes about the nation's favourite books, culminated in December 2003 in a vote predictably won by the bookmakers' favourite J. R. R. Tolkien's *The Lord of the Rings*. The Big Read gave rise to initiatives in libraries, schools and online, which enthused existing readers and enticed reluctant ones. Seventeen of the top 21 titles achieved combined extra sales of more than 750,000 copies. The biggest gainer was Daphne du Maurier's *Rebecca*, which moved to a new publisher, Time Warner, and improved its sales from 10,000 copies in 2002 to 95,000 copies in 2003.

Following this success, Channel 4's independently-made afternoon chat show *Richard and Judy*, whose distinguishing feature is that its presenters are married to each other, had an unexpectedly big impact on book sales. In January 2004 it launched its own book club, in the mould of Oprah Winfrey's which has been so successful in the USA, with a recommended list of ten titles. Each novel was featured on the show and one of the outstanding benefactors of the publicity was Joseph O'Connor's novel *Star of the Sea* (Vintage), which became a number one bestseller. Also included in the selection were *Toast*, a memoir by chef Nigel Slater (Fourth Estate), which doubled its sales in the week it was featured, and the novels *Lucia, Lucia* by Adriana Trigiani (Simon & Schuster), *Brick Lane* by Monica Ali (Doubleday), *The Lovely Bones* by Alice Sebold (Picador), Cecelia Ahern's *PS I Love You* (HarperCollins) and *Starter for Ten* by David Nicholls (Flame). Public libraries joined in the promotion of the Richard and Judy selections, and found the stock heavily borrowed. Viewers voted for a winner, presented in April at the British Book Awards; highlights from the awards dinner were broadcast on Richard and Judy. The first selection sold so well that the programme went on to choose a similar list of six paperbacks for summer reading.

Appearing in Richard and Judy's summer selection was American Jennifer Donnelly's remarkable novel *A Gathering Light*, which was originally published by Bloomsbury Children's Books for young adults but later issued in an adult edition. It told the story of a teenage farm girl in the Adirondacks in 1906 facing a timeless choice between career and family: a college education that would enable her to fulfil her ambitions as a writer or carrying out domestic duty to her father and her motherless siblings. After its Richard and Judy selection, *A Gathering Light* won the CILIP Carnegie Medal for children's fiction, beating to the prize not only Mark Haddon but former Whitbread winner David Almond, with his novel *The Fire-Eaters*, set at the time of the Cuban missile crisis and about a working-class Geordie boy going to grammar school (which went on to win a Smarties Prize gold award), and Children's Laureate Michael Morpurgo, whose *Private Peaceful*, a First World War tearjerker, was generally agreed to be one of his finest books to date, also with crossover appeal. *Private Peaceful* made the headlines because it concerned a soldier shot for cowardice: the 300 British soldiers to whom this happened have never been pardoned, despite flawed prosecutions and the evidence that what was then called cowardice was often shellshock. Morpurgo called, unsuccessfully, on the government to follow the example of other nations and issue posthumous pardons.

CELEBRITY KIDS' BOOKS

Just as a few years ago celebrities (Ivana Trump, Naomi Campbell) put their names to novels, and comedians (Ben Elton, Stephen Fry, Hugh Laurie, Adrian Edmondson, David Baddiel) wrote their own, so the fashionable genre of choice for celebs and comics alike became the children's book. After Madonna, whose first two of a series of six picture books were published in 2003, with the third, *Jakov and the Seven Thieves* out in 2004, Ricky

Gervais, star of the documentary-style sitcom The Office, was signed up by Faber to produce *Flanimals*, described as 'part Pokemon, part Dr Seuss, with a bit of Hilaire Belloc thrown in' for publication in autumn 2004. Paul McCartney also 'developed an idea' for Faber, *High in the Clouds*, in collaboration with author Philip Ardagh and illustrator Geoff Dunbar. Meanwhile, American thriller writer Elmore Leonard wrote his first children's book, *A Coyote's In the House*; Margaret Atwood and John Irving were signed up by Bloomsbury to write children's books for autumn 2004; journalist Julie Burchill wrote a novel for young adults with a lesbian theme, *Sugar Rush*; and former SAS serviceman Andy McNab followed his rival thriller writer Chris Ryan, author of the Alpha Force series for young readers, to sign up action adventure books for children, of which the first, *Young Blood*, is due to be published by Doubleday in spring 2005. Thriller writer Philip Kerr jumped on the J. K. Rowling bandwagon as P. B. Kerr, with a fantasy series called *The Children of the Lamp*, which sold film rights for seven figures to DreamWorks before publishers saw any written material and commanded a seven-figure advance for US and UK rights from Scholastic. The first volume, published in autumn 2004, was *The Akhenaten Adventure*.

Lynne Truss, novelist and journalist, produced an impassioned and entertaining volume about punctuation, *Eats, Shoots and Leaves*, which became an enormous and unexpected bestseller for independent publisher Profile Books, which began by printing 15,000 copies but had 100,000 copies in print within a fortnight, and went on to sell some three quarters of a million copies. The book was awarded the accolade Book of the Year at the British Book Awards in April 2004 and Truss's signings attracted round-the-block queues.

Penguin printed 300,000 copies of *A Royal Duty*, by Princess Diana's butler Paul Burrell. A court case accusing him of stealing some of Diana's possessions was called off at the last minute when the Queen recalled a conversation in which she was informed that Burrell had taken them for safekeeping. The book sold more than 77,000 in the first week, beaten only by *Harry Potter and the Order of the Phoenix* and David Beckham's *My Side*. Penguin is thought to have paid £1.3m for world rights in *A Royal Duty*, but the association with the book lost Penguin William Shawcross's authorised biography of the Queen Mother. Shawcross had signed a deal, reportedly for £1m, with Penguin, but took his project to Macmillan out of distaste for Burrell's book.

Penguin UK also signed up a book about the connections between the US Presidency and the Saudi Royal Family, *House of Bush, House of Saud*, by Craig Unger, but after legal advice decided not to publish. It was taken up by small publisher Gibson Square Books, but subsequently online bookseller Amazon took a decision not to stock it. The book went so far as to suggest that Americans turned a blind eye to Saudi complicity in the events of 9/11.

Transworld published *Forbidden Love*, the 'true' account of the honour killing of a Jordanian woman because of her relationship with a Catholic, written by her friend Norma Khouri. It was a bestseller and sold some 250,000 copies in the USA, before it came to light that not all the author's claims were true. Opinion was divided over whether the whole book was a dangerous fabrication suggesting that a sophisticated Islamic culture was barbaric; or whether it was merely an embellished account that usefully drew attention to an actual practice with victims around the world.

A non-fiction high seller of the year was *A Short History of Nearly Everything* by Bill Bryson (Black Swan), which won the Aventis Prize for Science Books and was shortlisted for the BBC Four Samuel Johnson Prize (it lost out to Anna Funder's *Stasiland: Stories from Behind the Berlin Wall*, Granta Books).

One of the fiction sensations of the year was Dan Brown's *The Da Vinci Code* (Corgi), a thriller concerned with a conspiracy in the Catholic church. Scottish author Alexander McCall Smith also struck a winning formula with his series of novels about a woman detective in Africa, Precious Ramotswe of the No. 1 Ladies' Detective Agency whose success earned McCall Smith the accolade Author of the year at the British Book Awards ('the Nibbies'). He was the third bestselling paperback author in British bookshops in 2003, behind only the international blockbusters John Grisham and James Patterson. In autumn 2004 he introduced a new heroine, Isabel Dalhousie, an Edinburgh philosopher and, like Precious Ramotswe, a crime fighter, in *The Sunday Philosophy Club* (Little, Brown). Robert Harris' bestselling novel *Pompeii* (Hutchinson) sold 18,000 copies in hardback in the first fortnight. Helen Fielding produced her first novel since Bridget Jones; the first print run of *Olivia Joules and the Overactive Imagination* (Picador) was 200,000 copies. 'Lad lit' author Tony Parsons aimed to show his sensitive side with his book *The Family Way* (HarperCollins), narrated by a woman. Meanwhile Jeffrey Archer's new paperback, *Sons of Fortune* (Pan), rose rapidly up the charts, despite declining sales of his books over the past few years.

Other high-selling commercial fiction included novels from Bernard Cornwell (*Heretic*, HarperCollins), Patricia Cornwell (*Blow Fly/Trace*, Little, Brown), James Patterson (*The Big Bad Wolf*, Headline), Terry Pratchett (*Monstrous Regiment/The Wee Free Men/A Hat Full of Sky*, Doubleday), Ian Rankin (*A Question of Blood*, Orion), Andy McNab (*Dark Winter*, Bantam Press), Marian Keyes (*The Other Side of the Story*, Michael Joseph), John Grisham (*The King of Torts*, Arrow/*The Last Juror*, Century), Frederick Forsyth (*Avenger* St Martin's Press), Jackie Collins (*Hollywood Divorces*, Pocket Books), Tom Clancy (*Teeth of the Tiger*, Penguin), James Herbert (*Nobody True*, Pan), Martina Cole (*The Know*, Headline), Ruth Rendell (*The Rottweiler*, Arrow), Stephen King (*The Dark Tower: Wolves of the Calla/Song of Susannah*, Hodder), and Michael Connolly (*Lost Light/The Narrows*, Orion).

Patricia Cornwell and Alexander McCall Smith were among the authors billed to feature in the trial run of a new code of practice for publication dates introduced by the book industry in September 2004, when a selection of lead titles were to hit bookshops on Mondays - and not before or after - thereby enjoying six days in the shops before the bestseller lists are compiled.

The fifth volume of J. K. Rowling's series, *Harry Potter and the Order of the Phoenix* (Bloomsbury), was published in paperback on 10 July 2004. By then, hardback sales had reached a total of 3.4 million copies, and the New England Journal of Medicine had identified 'Hogwarts Headache', a syndrome by which children experienced sore heads and necks as a result of reading the 766 pages too intensively. German children were even more at risk: their translation ran to more than 1,000 pages! After all this, the paperback sold like any other successful title. On its first day in the shops 37,000 copies were bought in adults' and children's editions, just failing to overtake the weekly sales of the two paperback editions, from Vintage and Red Fox, of Mark Haddon's *The Curious Incident of the Dog in the Night-time*.

MUSIC

CLASSICAL MUSIC

The £90 million refurbishment of the Royal Festival Hall (RFH) and its surroundings began in April 2004 with £71 million for the refurbishment of the RFH and £19 million for the renovation of the riverfront at ground level, as well as a new RFH extension building which will house cultural, staff and technical facilities. The extension building alongside Hungerford Bridge and the new river frontage of the RFH will be completed before the major refurbishment of the foyers and auditorium begins in July 2005. The hall will reopen to the public in late 2006 with the official opening of the auditorium in January 2007. The South Bank Centre aims to 'create a world-class venue for London, for artists and audiences for the 21st century'.

The year 2004 saw the inauguration of the South Bank Centre's major classical music festival, *Omaggio: A Celebration of Luciano Berio*. Devised in close consultation with Berio before his death in May 2003, the South Bank Centre, Royal Academy of Music and London Sinfonietta all collaborated on this festival which also featured the BBC Symphony Orchestra (BBCSO), the Philharmonia Orchestra and the Arditti Quartet. Homage was paid to Berio by presenting his music in the contexts he wanted, performed by the artists he chose. Highlights included all of Berio's music for string quartet (performed by the Arditti Quartet), plus the UK premiere of the Sequenza for solo cello, one of Berio's last works, written for Rohan de Saram, the cellist of the Quartet. Artists chosen by Berio and Royal Academy musicians performed all of his Sequenzas throughout the festival, and the UK premiere of Berio's last complete work, *Stanze*, for baritone and orchestra. The London Sinfonietta juxtaposed *Naturale* and *Folk Songs* with folk music from Sardinia, Armenia and the inimitable Kamkars from Kurdistan. There was also a 'Berio lounge' on the Ballroom floor, a major installation enabling people to experience and interact with Berio's music and work inspired by his legacy. The last filmed interview that Berio gave before his death, filmed by the South Bank Centre's education team, was also played.

In June 2004, in the presence of the Queen, Prince Philip and half the good burghers of the city, the London Symphony Orchestra presented the mother of all galas to celebrate its 100th birthday with a host of stars who have long associations with the Orchestra. A three-hour concert, broadcast live on BBC Radio and Television, featured 14 different items, exposing not only the history of the LSO but a list of past and present friends. Sir Colin Davis, the LSO's current music director, opened the concert with the last movement of Beethoven's Fifth, followed by Rostropovich conducting the 1st movement of Mozart's *Sinfonia Concertante* with Midori (violin) and Yuri Bashmet (viola). Michael Tilson Thomas continued with Sarasate's *Carmen Fantasy* and Ravel's *La Valse*, a show-stopper that demonstrated so palpably how the LSO loves the music it plays. Colin Matthew's *Fanfare: Bravo LSO!* opened the second half, conducted by Antonio Pappano, who then steered a breathtaking performance of Bernstein's 'Candide' Overture. Sir Colin was back with Mozart's rapturous *Ch'io mi scordi di te*, the voice of Susan Graham partnered by Alfred Brendel. In a switch of style Dave Brubeck performed a work by his brother Howard, conducted by Russell Gloyd. Film music has long provided a financial lifeline for the orchestra, and in Bliss's *Things to Come* and John T. Williams's *Star Wars* (conducted, respectively, by Richard Hickox and Daniel Harding), one could only marvel at the strength and energy of the playing. Quieter moments intervened, with John Williams caressing Rodrigo's *Concierto de Aranjuez* slow movement, and Hickox conducting a taste of Elgar's *Enigma Variations*. Britten's fugue from *The Young Person's Guide to the Orchestra* was a fitting finale.

The London Sinfonietta's continued their dynamic programming, bold thinking, and unparalleled commitment to uniting new music and new audiences in their 2003–4 season, which combined a world-class concert series at the Queen Elizabeth Hall with an exciting range of performances in festivals nationwide and abroad. Throughout the season the ensemble performed premieres of Elliot Carter's *Dialogues* (specially commissioned by BBC Radio 3, written for pianist Nicolas Hodges and the London Sinfonietta), Harrison Birtwistle's major new work, *Theseus Game* (co-commissioned by the London Sinfonietta, SBC and Ensemble Modern), and Brian Ferneyhough's eagerly awaited new work, *Seven 'Tableaux Vivants'*. Oliver Knussen also conducted new works by Mauricio Kagel and Silvina Milstein. In a day of performances and workshops led by the London Sinfonietta, Arditti Quartet and the Society for the Promotion of New Music (spnm), at the Queen Elizabeth Hall and other RFH spaces, the ensemble performed premieres from young composers, including a new work by Royal Philharmonic Society Composition Prizewinner, Brian Herrington, and the first results of the London Sinfonietta's Blue Touch Paper Project. As part of the Ether Festival at the RFH in March 2004, the ensemble joined forces with sound experimenters from the Warp record label, continuing their highly successful collaboration and exploring modern classics from the 20th-century avant-garde. The world premiere of an ambitious project by Jonathan Harvey was featured, a work which uses live electronic transformations on a scale never attempted before, with individual sonic manipulation for each musician in the ensemble, and sound design by Sound Intermedia.

In January 2004, the London Sinfonietta took part in the BBC Symphony Orchestra's 'John Cage Uncaged' weekend with pianist Joanna MacGregor, revisiting the radical compositional developments from 1950s New York: a packed weekend of concerts, talks, films and 'happenings' to celebrate the life, influences and legacy of this maverick musician, writer, artist, mushroom expert and cultural icon who died in 1992. The BBCSO gave the first orchestral performance in the UK of John Cage's seminal silent work *4′33″* in the opening concert which was broadcast live on BBC Radio 3 – the first broadcaster to risk airing nearly five minutes of ambient silence. BBC Radio 3's emergency backup systems, designed to cut in when there is apparent silence on air, were switched off.

The concert also featured work by musical pioneer Earle Brown, and other sonic collisions included Led Zeppelin's John Paul Jones playing a flashing bass guitar, members of the BBC Symphony Chorus having a dinner party on the foyer, amplified cacti (kindly lent to the BBC by Kew Gardens), one man playing five tubas connected by 16 feet of tubing and singers disguised as Barbican staff who sang information to the audience. Among the other highlights were an 18-hour performance of Erik Satie's marathon piano work *Vexations* given by more than 50 pianists from top classical performers and composers to jazz stars Django Bates and Julian Joseph. There was also a performance of material from Cage's *Songbooks* which involved sopranos Frances M. Lynch and Nicole Tibbels, along with pianist Rolf Hind, drinking gin, eating crisps, playing cards and having a party, as well as singing.

The Barbican's 80th-birthday tribute to Ligeti in October 2004, provided an orchestral showcase of Ligeti's four concertos, spanning 50 years of his creative career, with the London Sinfonietta conducted by George Benjamin, and a performance of his only full-length opera, *Le Grand Macabre*, with the BBC Symphony Orchestra under Alexander Rumpf. *Le Grand Macabre*, an opera about death and an end to the world that turns out to be not quite as final as everyone expects, is nearly a repertory work now, and certainly one of Ligeti's masterpieces. Gyorgy Ligeti's folk-inspired *Romanian Concerto* also received its UK premiere at the Barbican. Other season highlights included a weekend of concerts to mark Bernard Haitink's 75th birthday, in which the Barbican revisited some of his fondest associations with Europe's leading orchestras, the Berliner Philharmoniker, the Vienna Philharmonic Orchestra, the Royal Concertgebouw Orchestra of Amsterdam, the Dresden Staatskapelle and the LSO. The programme included some of his favourite orchestral repertoire, much of which he has recorded to great acclaim.

OUTSIDE LONDON

The Birmingham Contemporary Music Group (BCMG) 2003–4 season began with with the return of charismatic Scottish composer James MacMillan conducting BCMG in a concert of his own work and that of the visionary and reclusive Russian Galina Ustvolskaya. BCMG's *Sound Investment* scheme, through which BCMG's audiences have contributed nearly £100,000 towards new works, brought its 2003–4 series to a tumultuous close in May with the unveiling of two new commissions – the UK premiere of Mark-Anthony Turnage's *The Torn Fields* with renowned Canadian baritone Gerald Finley, and the World Premiere of a large-scale work by Philip Cashian. The concert, which was in association with BBC Radio 3, also featured Franco Donatoni's composition *Hot* with the celebrated jazz saxophonist John Harle as soloist. The big theatrical event of the season was Simon Holt's gripping chamber opera *Who put Bella in the Wych elm?* in which BCMG joined forces with Almeida Opera to revisit a Black Country mystery that has remained unanswered for over half a century: The tale of a woman's body found stuffed inside a tree in Hagley Woods. The opera, in a double-bill with Salvatore Sciarrino's *Infinito Nero*, also toured nationally.

Sonorities Festival of Contemporary Music in Belfast featured a visit by Karlheinz Stockhausen. The first weekend of the festival included three concerts of his electronic works traversing a creative span of nearly fifty years, from the pioneering Electronic Studies I & II of 1953–4 right up to the world premiere of the large-scale multichannel piece *Mittwochs-Gruss* written in the late 1990s. The second weekend focused on a celebration of Sonic Arts Network's (the UK's main organisation for promoting work at the cutting edge of music and technology) 25th anniversary, with a major concert featuring the work of leading UK composers over that period. The weekend also included a Cut & Splice event (co-promoted by SARC, the BBC and Sonic Arts Network) with international performance artists exploring the concept of 'grains and clouds' inspired by Xenakis. Other premieres included Sonorities commissions by Cort Lippe, Natasha Barrett, Ludger Brümmer and Denis Smalley.

The City of Birmingham Symphony Orchestra's (CBSO) 2003–4 season featured a rich mixture of music from Beethoven to Bollywood. In Sakari Oramo's sixth season as Music Director of the CBSO, he was joined by over 70 visiting artists and conductors. The major theme running through this season was the influence of South Asian (particularly Indian) music and cultures on Western classical music. In January the CBSO performed Messiaen's 'Turangalila' Symphony, alongside premieres of two scores by the British composer, John Foulds, whose dream was to fuse the music of Europe and India, plus performances of his rarely performed *Three Mantras*, and Holst's short opera *Savriti*. Also featured were the Bollywood soundtracks of A. R. Rahman, the world famous conductor and composer, perhaps best known to British audiences through his hit West End musical *Bombay Dreams*. In addition, the CBSO continued to attract new audiences with a night of classic silent movies in the Symphony Hall with a huge screen suspended over the stage.

The Liverpool Philharmonic Orchestra certainly had another successful year of Brahms, Beethoven and Shostakovich. The orchestra gave some passionate yet disciplined performances with a full-bodied sonority under the skilful direction of Kurt Masur.

FESTIVALS

With 14 world premieres, 34 UK premieres and three new commissions, the Huddersfield Contemporary Music Festival (HCMF) 2003 was again a remarkable success. Along with a number of overseas performers who made their UK debuts, HCMF welcomed visits by Sir Harrison Birtwistle, Simon Holt, Brian Ferneyhough, Judith Weir, Michael Finnissy and Gavin Bryars. Representing the younger generation of British composers and performers were Jonathan Powell, Bernard Hughes, Luke Stoneham, Hilary Robinson and Bryn Harrison. As ever, the festival balanced its international perspective by giving opportunities to the best and most creative British and international artists. Many of these composers were from the younger generation, and their fresh outlook on composition was inspiring. The festival presented a 60th birthday tribute to the California-based British composer Brian Ferneyhough, by making an important body of work by the leading figure of 'new complexity' available to British audiences, performed by some of the artists most closely associated with him, most notably the Arditti Quartet. Two concerts in the festival commemorated the life and works of Luciano Berio, who died on 27 May 2004. The Italian Ex Novo Ensemble performed *Sequenzas I* and *IV* in a programme of contemporary Italian music that also included works by Donatoni and rising star Emanuele Casale. The Neue Vocalsolisten Stuttgart, Europe's leading contemporary vocal ensemble, made a welcome return with a programme that included Berio's classic *A-Ronne.* A focus on new music for voices brought the UK debut of the 40-strong Tapiola Chamber Choir from Finland, with a programme of beautifully atmospheric Finnish and Estonian choral music, including UK premieres by Kaija Saariaho and Einojuhani Rautavaara. The young and dynamic EXAUDI Vocal Ensemble appeared followed by York-based ensemble Red Byrd who performed the world premiere of the HCMF-commissioned madrigals by Gavin Bryars, and the BBC Singers performed the UK premiere of James Dillon's *...residue*, a rare interpretation of Mauricio Kagel's *Rrrrrr...*, and the world premiere of a new commission by young composer Bernard Hughes.

The Edinburgh International Festival 2004 under the direction of Brian McMaster attracted audiences from far and wide with another popular programme of opera, music, theatre and dance. The music programme offered variety and diversity from Hanover Opera to a one-woman show from Beirut and from an in-depth look at the great choreographer Antony Tudor to Akram Khan's latest dance work. Music featured large-scale classical and choral concerts, intimate chamber music, traditional Gaelic song and contemporary music from around the world. Opening with Honegger's moving oratorio *Jeanne d'Arc au bûher*, and closing with the Bank of Scotland Fireworks Concert in September, in between there were visits from Ensemble Intercontemporain, The Cleveland Orchestra, Leipzig Gewandhaus Orchestra, London Philharmonic Orchestra and Dresden Staatskapelle, and some of the world's major singers, pianists and instrumentalists, including Richard Goode, Violeta Urmana, Elisabeth Leonskaja, Robert Holl, Leonidas Kavakos and Steven Osborne.

The 2004 series of Promenade Concerts in London, under the directorship of Nicholas Kenyon, remained one of the largest music festivals anywhere, with over 70 concerts. As well as being broadcast live on BBC Radio 3 every evening, each concert was audio-streamed onto the internet. In addition a selection of concerts were shown on BBC Television, on the BBC's digital TV channel BBC4, and video-streamed onto an interactive website. As always the Proms attracted some of the biggest names in the classical music world. This series saw appearances from bass-baritone Willard W. White, violinists Sarah Chang, Joshua Bell and Maxim Vengerov, pianist Alfred Brendel, percussionist Evelyn Glennie and conductors Sir Simon Rattle and Bernard Haitink. There was also a number of world premieres performed, including a new symphony by John Casken, Judith Bingham's *The Secret Garden*, and *League of Gentlemen* composer Joby Talbot's *Sneaker Wave*, all commissioned by the BBC. Each year the BBC Proms explores a different theme, as a way of bringing together music that spans many centuries and different styles. This year's main themes were 'Back to Bohemia', 'East meets West' and 'England in 1934'. The year 2004 marks the centenary of the death of the great Czech composer Dvorak, and the Proms offered a feast of music by Czech composers, including works by Martinu, Novak, Janacek, Biber, Zelenka, Vejvanovsky, Myslivecek, Eben and Smetana. A performance of Dvorak's lesser-known opera *Dimitrij* celebrated his centenary in style, as well as the popular *Cello Concerto* with Truls Mork and the BBC National Orchestra of Wales, and also four of his nine symphonies.

The year 1934 is a crucial date in the history of English music, the year in which three of the great patriarchs of the English musical renaissance, Elgar, Holst and Delius, died, and two of our most important and internationally celebrated living composers, Harrison Birtwistle and Peter Maxwell Davies, were born. 1934 also saw the sensationally successful premiere of the (still incomplete) First Symphony by the 32-year-old William Walton, and the completion of another symphony that was to be just as enthusiastically received when it was heard the following year, Vaughan Williams's Fourth – its violent modernism marking an invigorating new development for a composer already in his sixties. The Proms' East/West theme brought the charismatic cellist Yo-Yo Ma and his Silk Road Ensemble to the Proms for the first time, as well as new music by Chinese-American composers Tan Dun, Zhou Long and Bright Sheng. Many of the finest works of Western music by composers such as Britten, Debussy, Mahler, Messiaen and Ravel were also heard. Yo-Yo Ma and his Silk Road Ensemble explored yet more musical links between the Orient and the Occident. In a colourful and evocative programme including music and artists from China, India, Persia, Armenia and Kyrgyzstan, the extraordinary Indian tabla player Sandeep Das and Iranian spike-fiddle master Kayhan Kalhor feature in their own compositions, and Chinese pipa virtuoso Wu Man performed arrangements of Armenian folk songs and music of the Roma. The ensemble also performed a new quadruple concerto specially written for them by Chinese-American composer Bright Sheng. An expanded London Sinfonietta continued the survey of Messiaen's most monumental scores with his erotically-charged, Eastern-influenced 'Turangalia' Symphony.

AWARDS AND COMPETITIONS

Presented at the Dorchester Hotel on Wednesday 5 May 2004 by the celebrated bass John Tomlinson and hosted by BBC Radio 3's Stephanie Hughes, the Royal Philharmonic Society Awards honoured achievement and excellence during 2003. Winners included the Belcea Quartet in the Chamber Ensemble category for 'giving great performances of standard repertoire as well as showing a passionate commitment to contemporary music and to their creative educational programmes'. The award for Chamber scale composition went to Helmut Lachenmann for *Grido* – 'a radical and masterful contribution to the string quartet repertoire. The piece conjures a rich, poetic and sensual soundworld, and reveals the range and depth of Lachenmann's unique and uncompromising compositional language.' Also commended in this category were George Benjamin's *Shadowlines* and Jonathan Harvey's String Quartet no. 4. The Concert Series and Festivals award went to 'LSO: By George!' an extensive series where the LSO 'gave George Benjamin the rare opportunity to present his own works, juxtaposed with a range of composers whose music he most admires. These concerts were complemented by a wide variety of ancillary events, which drew large and enthusiastic audiences'. The Award for best Conductor went to Mariss Jansons for his final UK concerts with the Pittsburgh Symphony Orchestra at the Barbican and the BBC Proms. The jury commended him for the 'revelatory performances, innately truthful to the score yet continually animated with fresh insights and ideas, superlatively played by an orchestra totally at one with its conductor.'

Welsh National Opera's 'Max's Katerina Project' won the Education Award for its work in 'involving 500 children in Merthyr Tydfil, together with composer Ruth Byrchmore and librettist Alan Osborne, who developed and performed their own opera, inspired by the story of Katya Kabanova. Since then the project has forged partnerships with Denbighshire and Gwynedd County Councils, involved children and teachers from six primary schools, and demonstrated a true connection between the work of Welsh National Opera and the children's learning and performance.' Other winners included the West-Eastern Divan Orchestra and Daniel Barenboim for the Large Ensemble award, given 'to a unique orchestra for a single concert in the UK, whose influence far outweighs its singularity. The West-Eastern Divan Orchestra was courageously founded by conductor Daniel Barenboim and the late Edward Said, and formed from both Israeli and Palestinian musicians, who sit and play side by side. Their appearance at the Proms in 2003 acted as a powerful reminder that idealism and optimism are still very much alive, even in our jaded, violent and crisis-ridden times. Music making like this can and does change lives.'

The jury unanimously gave the Large-Scale Composition award to Harrison Birtwistle for his *The Shadow of Night,* inspired by a Dürer engraving, a Dowland lute-song and a poem by the Elizabethan George Chapman. The jury were drawn to 'this poised and eloquent work' which 'draws the listener into a world of extraordinary sonorities, haunting melody and interlocking mechanisms.' Mitsuko Uchida won the award for best instrumentalist, 'for the profound musicality and intellectual rigour which she pursues with such vigour and joy in a wide range of music-making, and in particular for her intense, questioning performances of the last Beethoven Sonatas and of Schubert's *Die Schöne Mullerin* with Ian Bostridge'. The Best Singer award went to Susan Chilcott 'for her searing vocal and dramatic performances, in particular in the role of Jenufa for Welsh National Opera. The Young Artist award went to the conductor, Ilan Volkov. 'The BBC Scottish Symphony Orchestra took a brave and far-sighted decision in appointing such a young chief conductor. This was his first season: he has vision and a huge desire to communicate, and is making bold and imaginative programmes: a truly exciting newcomer.'

The Audience Development Award went to *Operatunity* (English National Opera and Diverse Production for Channel 4) for a project which has 'caught the public imagination and gripped a mass audience. It demystifies the art form, captures the thrill of performance and gives a rare insight into the challenge of live music making'. Also shortlisted for this award were the Hallé and London Sinfonietta for the 3D Music and Warpworks projects, (collaborations with Braunarts and Warp Records and South Bank Centre respectively). The BBC Radio 3 Listeners Award went to Thomas Allen for 'superb recitals and a variety of brilliant stage roles, notably in *Die Fledermaus* at Glyndebourne and *Sweeney Todd* at the Royal Opera House'.

AWARDS

GRAMOPHONE AWARDS 2003

Record of the Year Chamber: Schumann, String Quartets 1 & 3. Zehetmair Quartett, ECM Records
Artist of the Year: Marin Alsop
Lifetime Achievement: Leontyne Price
Editor's Choice: Simon Trpceski
Classic FM Listener's Choice: Cecilia Bartoli
Special Achievement Award: Vernon Handley
Label of the Year: Harmonia Mundi

THE CLASSICAL BRIT AWARDS 2004

Female Artist of the Year: Cecilia Bartoli
Male Artist of the Year: Bryn Terfel
Album of the Year: Bryn Terfel, *Bryn*
Contemporary Music Award: Phillip Glass, *The Hours*
Young British Classical Performer: Daniel Hope
Ensemble/Orchestral Album of the Year: Sir Simon Rattle/VPO
Critics Award: Rattle/VPO, Beethoven/Complete Symphonies
Outstanding Contribution to Music Award: Renee Fleming

POP MUSIC

This year, music fans of a certain vintage could be forgiven for thinking it was 1984, not 2004, as two new British rock groups whose music and appearance owe much to that period in pop captured the record-buying public's imagination, heralding a return to fashion for guitar bands. Viewed by their detractors as a kitsch novelty act, Lowestoft quartet, The Darkness, combined clichéd rock'n'roll with histrionic crowd-pleasing performances, exemplified by singer and unlikely sex symbol Justin Hawkins' penchant for capes, catsuits and falsetto singing. Evoking the flamboyant stadium rock of Kiss, Marillion and Queen, The Darkness' debut album, *Permission To Land,* topped the charts, selling over 1.2 million copies in the UK. Their tongue-in-cheek festive single, *Christmas Time (Don't Let The Bells End)*, was kept from the number one spot by the year's best-selling British single, a version of Tears For Fears' *Mad World* performed by Michael Andrews and Gary Jules, belatedly lifted from the *Donnie Darko* film soundtrack. In February 2004, The Darkness won three BRIT Awards for Best British Group, Best Rock Act and Best Album, later winning a prestigious Ivor Novello Award for Songwriters Of The Year – which amused critics who had lampooned the band for their derivative music and insincere manner.

In contrast, critics adored Franz Ferdinand, a sharp-suited, charismatic four-piece from Glasgow whose infectious blend of upbeat angular rock and sexually ambiguous lyrics are reminiscent of The Smiths and cult Leeds band Gang Of Four. Even Morrissey, avuncular former The Smiths' singer who staged a comeback this year with his well-received album, *You Are The Quarry,* deigned to patronise his debonair disciples by offering them a support slot at one of his concerts in Manchester, presumably so he could bask in the reflected glory. Though pretentious and erudite, Franz Ferdinand rapidly became a mainstream concern when their second single *Take Me Out* and eponymous debut album both entered the top three in January, providing the decade-old independent record label Domino with its first million-selling release. Not since Oasis' unrivalled dominance of the mid-1990s during Britpop's heyday has a homegrown band so comprehensively captivated a nation.

Elsewhere, it proved another good year for Dido, the unassuming English MOR chanteuse. Her inescapable second album, *Life For Rent,* while seemingly indistinguishable from her last, *No Angel,* was the biggest-selling British long-player of 2003, shifting 2.2 million copies in its first three months. Encouraged by the success of contemporary easy listening artists such as Dido and dulcet American jazz vocalist Norah Jones, major record companies this year unveiled a new batch of talented telegenic young British performers aimed squarely at the solvent BBC Radio 2-listening demographic. Katie Melua's *Call Off The Search,* Jamie Callum's *Twentysomething,* Amy Winehouse's *Frank,* and *The Soul Sessions* by teenager Joss Stone were heavily marketed and sold respectably, leading to more lucrative acclaim across the Atlantic. Their generic music, which ranged from insipid ballads to polite dinner jazz, ersatz soul and Sinatra-style crooning, was the antithesis of modern pop, yet the rewards reaped assuaged a troubled industry ever wary of taking risks.

The two main reality TV pop series, ITV's *Pop Idol* and the BBC's *Fame Academy*, annual competitions that ruthlessly demystify the star-making process, both showed signs of fatigue this year as fickle audiences ultimately displayed indifference to the eventual winners. The controversial victor of *Pop Idol*'s second series, larger-than-life Scot Michelle McManus, scored an inevitable number one with her debut single, *All This Time*, in early January, but was forgotten by March when her album, *The Meaning Of Love*, limped into the shops. Alex Parks, the 19-year-old Cornish singer who triumphed on *Fame Academy 2*, reached number three with *Maybe That's What It Takes* immediately after her win in November, and her album of covers and original songs, *Introduction*, also sold well. Her profile in 2004 was negligible, however.

An 18-year-old from a deprived east London council estate won this year's Mercury Music Prize, now an established ceremony in its 12th year rewarding excellence in British music. *Boy In Da Corner* by newcomer Dizzee Rascal, the musical alias of Dylan Mills, was an innovative and vibrant example of UK garage or two-step, an aggressive style of dance music derived from US hip-hop and Jamaican dancehall, emanating almost exclusively from London. The record sold 250,000 copies in the UK, catapulting this daring electronic music into the mainstream and thrusting Mills reluctantly into the limelight. Similar musically to Dizzee Rascal, Londoner Mike Skinner's celebrated project, The Streets, returned this year with his widely acclaimed second album, *A Grand Don't Come For Free*, a concept record in which Skinner's search for mislaid cash provides an illuminating, meandering narrative. For one week in July, this quintessentially English act topped the UK albums chart (it sold 700,000 copies in four months) and the singles chart, with *Dry Your Eyes*.

THE US INFLUENCE

For the first time, US acts outperformed British artists in the UK album charts, according to figures for 2003 from the British Phonographic Industry (BPI). American artists sold 45.4 per cent of albums compared with the UK's 42.3 per cent. In 1997, the US share was only 28.4 per cent against the UK's 58.3 per cent. The rise could be attributed to the increasing prevalence of US hip-hop, R&B and pop acts on radio playlists, as well as on terrestrial TV programmes such as *Top Of The Pops* and myriad dedicated satellite music channels like MTV, MTV2, VIVA, VH1 and The Box. Although the British Academy of Songwriters lamented these statistics, voicing concern that not enough British music was being promoted in Britain, this trend is set to continue in tandem with the steady Americanisation of British cultural values and attitudes.

Glamorous American artists enjoying aspirational lifestyles were responsible for many of the year's defining pop moments. 'Urban' music, the media's questionable catch-all term for modern black music, encompassing hip-hop, soul and their fertile hybrid R&B, had an excellent 12 months. With 610,000 copies sold, *Where Is The Love?* by hip-hop collective Black Eyed Peas was 2003's biggest-selling single, while 21-year-old Beyoncé Knowles' ubiquitous *Crazy In Love* smash resulted in the former Destiny's Child singer winning a BRIT for Best International Female. Hard-boiled New York rapper 50 Cent, who has been shot nine times in his eventful life, took home a BRIT for International Breakthrough Artist. The protégé of Eminem and influential producer Dr Dre, 50 Cent's multi-million-selling *Get Rich Or Die Tryin'* album spawned the Top Ten singles *In Da Club* and *P.I.M.P.* His 'thugged-out' lifestyle, sluggish demeanour and routine endorsement of streetwear products, now standard in hip-hop, appealed to impressionable rap fans world-wide.

Fanciful Atlanta duo Outkast cemented their reputation as masters of the hip-hop/pop crossover with the addictive *Hey Ya!* single, taken from their double-album *Speakerboxx/The Love Below* (unusually, both members contributed one solo disc each) which sold nine million copies, 730,000 of those in the UK. One of the year's most downloaded tracks, *Hey Ya!*, included the line, 'Shake it like a Polaroid!', prompting a sudden upturn in sales of the camera, though the manufacturer insisted that shaking the photograph was not technically necessary. In a bizarre move, US hip-hop icon Jay-Z announced his retirement from the rap world following the November release of his supposedly final LP, *The Black Album*. Six months later he was coaxed out of retirement and appeared on stage at London's Earls Court, headlining the Prince's Trust Urban Music Foundation event before an audience that included Princes Charles, William and Harry. Meanwhile, underground New York hip-hop producer Dangermouse made headlines when he mixed elements of *The Black Album* with parts of The Beatles' classic *White Album*, creating a bootleg LP entitled *The Grey Album*, much to the chagrin of EMI, owners of the *White Album*'s copyright. While only 3,000 promotional vinyl copies were pressed, the album's availability online meant hundreds of thousands of curious fans were able to download it for free.

Other US hip-hop artists whose success at home translated into significant sales in the UK included Kanye West, a New York producer-turned-rapper whose likeable *College Dropout* debut addressed more thoughtful issues normally neglected in gangster rap's traditional mantra of girls, guns and drugs; and Pharrell Williams, the 31-year-old Virginia Beach, Virginia native, whose influence on pop music this century has been remarkable. Williams is the more media-friendly half of prolific production duo The Neptunes, which he formed with childhood friend Chad Hugo, who prefers to shun the spotlight. The pair produced cutting-edge yet accessible hit songs this year for stars such as Justin Timberlake, Kelis, Jay-Z, Britney Spears and Ludacris. They also released a successful multi-artist collaborative album, *The Neptunes Present . . . Clones*, and, with N*E*R*D, their rock-based studio project, sold 250,000 copies of their second album, *Fly Or Die*, in the UK alone. At one point during the summer of 2003, it was estimated that 20 per cent of all pop records played on British radio were produced by Williams and Hugo. Furthermore, Williams penned fast-food giant McDonalds' 'I'm lovin' it' global advertising jingle, sung by BRIT winner Justin Timberlake, whose *Justified* album was the second biggest selling LP of 2003. US rock acts, spearheaded by Detroit neo-blues duo The White Stripes and rejuvenated LA funk-pop veterans Red Hot Chili Peppers, found considerable success in Britain. The former's *Elephant* album sold 750,000 copies, the latter rounded off a fine year with two capacity summer shows in London's Hyde Park.

THE DIGITAL REVOLUTION

The arrival this year of legal digital download music services such as Apple's iTunes Music Store (ITMS) and Napster has revolutionised the way the global music industry sells, distributes and markets its products. These online shops, which in Apple's case offers 700,000 tracks available to download at 79p each (or £7.99 for LPs) using its iTunes software on to its popular portable iPod listening device, aimed to combat the dramatic increase in illegal downloading and physical piracy. In addition, they provided record companies with a new means of re-selling their valuable back catalogues. BPI figures stated that UK music piracy grew by 13 per cent in 2003, six times the growth in legal CD sales, and that illegal music sales in the UK reached £56.1 million, equivalent to 4.2 per cent of the legal market. Most culpable were the millions of internet users who freely swap MP3s of tracks via peer-to-peer file-sharing networks without the record labels' consent.

Launched in Europe in June 2004, Apple's ITMS was an instant success, selling 450,000 tracks in the UK in its first seven days, and more than 800,000 in Europe on what it calls 'the biggest jukebox in the world'. Prior to ITMS, the number of legal downloads sold in the first five months of 2004 was 500,000, according to figures from the Official UK Chart Company. Apple was the market leader primarily because its iPod, which is only compatible with iTunes, has sold over 3 million in the UK and has been hailed as the Walkman for the 21st century. Other electronics companies such as Sony are developing similar MP3-storage and listening devices. Apple's share is expected to decline as increased competition from sites operated by Coca-Cola, Napster and Microsoft muscle in on this lucrative market.

Major record companies were initially slow to embrace this new technology. While digital singles releases are now common, they are not yet standard. EastWest Records released the UK's best-selling legitimate download-only single of 2003 with *Stockholm Syndrome* by the rock band Muse, which sold 8,000 copies. However, the sheer volume of legal download sales this year lead to an official weekly Download Chart being set up in June by the Official UK Chart Company. Radio 1 began broadcasting this in September 2004. The first chart in June included Top Ten entrants by Outkast and Dido with tracks that were released up to nine months earlier.

A fortnightly chart compiling the 20 most popular downloaded musical mobile phone ringtones was also established this year. Compiled by accountancy firm KPMG using information supplied by mobile phone companies, the chart reflected the increasing popularity of downloadable ringtones, an estimated £70 million of which were sold in the UK in 2003, up from £40 million in 2002, according to the Mobile Data Association (MDA). According to the MDA, sales of ringtones were expected to rise by 60 per cent in 2004. Advances in mobile phone technology meant that samples of actual music, such as best-selling singles, rather than polyphonic synthesised sounds could be used as ringtones. Sites sell ringtones of pop hits for between £1.50 and £3.50. However, the BPI pointed out, record companies do not make money from ringtones as royalties are paid directly to music publishers. 'Record companies invest an enormous amount of money in creating recorded content. It's only fair that they have a right to decide how and where that content is used,' said a BPI spokesman.

AWARDS

BRIT AWARDS 2004

Best British Male: Daniel Bedingfield
Best British Female: Dido
Best British Group: The Darkness
Mastercard Best British Album: The Darkness, *Permission to Land*
Best British Breakthrough Artist: Busted
British Rock: The Darkness
British Single: Dido, *White Flag*
International Male: Justin Timberlake
International Female: Beyoncé
International Album: Justin Timberlake, *Justified*
International Group: The White Stripes
International Breakthrough Artist: 50 Cent
Outstanding Contribution to Music: Duran Duran
Best Urban Act: Lemar
Best Dance Act: Basement Jaxx
Best Pop Act: Busted

MERCURY MUSIC PRIZE 2003

Dizzee Rascal, *Boy In Da Corner*

NME AWARDS 2004

Best Radio Show: Zane Lowe, Radio 1
Best New Band: Kings Of Leon
Best Video: Radiohead, *There There*
Best Single: The White Stripes, *Seven Nation Army*
Best Live Band: Queens Of The Stone Age
Best International Band: Kings Of Leon
Best UK Band: The Libertines
Best Album: Radiohead, *Hail To The Thief*

OPERA

Co-productions are an economic fact of life in the opera world today. Of the nine so-called new productions presented by the Royal Opera this season, five had already been performed in other theatres, but the three finest, most interesting and original productions of the year originated in the Royal Opera, though two of them had, of necessity, co-producers. Possibly the best, and certainly the most overwhelming, was *Lady Macbeth of Mtsensk*, the original version of Shostakovich's opera, receiving its first production at Covent Garden, directed by Richard Jones. Conducted by the music director, Antonio Pappano, with Swedish soprano Katarina Dalayman in the title role, and bass John Tomlinson as Boris Ismailov, this was a magnificent experience, and notably, £75 was the top ticket price, with many tickets selling for £50 or less.

For the world premiere of *The Tempest* (with libretto based on Shakespeare's play) by Meredith Oakes and music by Thomas Adès, tickets were all £50 or less and six performances sold out. Adès, in his early thirties, conducted his brilliant score with great aplomb. Directed by Tom Cairns, the production vividly brought to life the 'enchanted isle' and its inhabitants. The performance was rightly dominated by baritone Simon Keenlyside's Prospero, while tenor Ian Bostridge as Caliban and high soprano Cyndia Sieden as Ariel both impressed with their amazing virtuosity at the top of their vocal ranges. Another treat of a somewhat different, and very much more expensive kind, was offered by David McVicar's new production of Gounod's *Faust*, conducted by Pappano and starring Roberto Alagno as Faust, Angela Gheorghiu as Marguerite and Bryn Terfel as Mephistophélès. By setting Goethe's legend in Paris at the time of the Franco-Prussian War and emphasising the theatrical nature of the plot, McVicar proved that there was still plenty of life in the much-loved work. It was televised and shown on the big screen in Covent Garden Piazza and at several other locations.

The season ended with the last revival of the 1964 production of *Tosca* originally directed by Franco Zeffirelli, with Maria Callas in the title role and Tito Gobbi as Scarpia. Staged by John Cox, with two casts that gave seven performances in eight days, the production gave pleasure that was not merely nostalgic. *Tosca* was also broadcast on the big screen in the Piazza and at Canary Wharf, Sherwood Forest Center Parc and the Botanical Gardens, Belfast. The final performance was the 242nd of the production.

In the Linbury Studio Theatre the Royal Opera presented a new production of Britten's *The Rape of Lucretia*, sung by members (and one ex-member) of the Vilar Young Artists. Music Theatre Wales (MTW) gave the British premiere of *Ion* by Parham Vir, born in India but now resident in England. His chamber opera is based on the play by Euripides, translated by David Lan, and has a rich, finely worked score for 17 players. Staged by Michael McCarthy and designed by Simon Banham, it was conducted by Michael Rafferty, MTW's music director.

After a short autumn season at the Barbican, using both the Theatre and the Hall, English National Opera (ENO) finally returned to its home, the London Coliseum, on 21 February 2004, when a concert was given for those who had been instrumental in restoring the theatre to its original glory. Opened in 1904, the Coliseum seems set for at least another hundred years of musical life. ENO has acquired two valuable new sponsors, Sky and Arts World, for the next three years, and communications company O_2 to help the company reach new audiences. The first new production was *The Rhinegold*, the beginning of Phyllida Lloyd's staging of Wagner's *Ring Cycle*, designed by Richard Hudson. Dramatically, this proved something of a disappointment, with the gods emulating an ordinary suburban family. In *The Valkyrie* matters improved greatly and Wotan turned out to be a god after all. Musically, both opeas were fine, with Andrew Shore's Alberich towering over *The Rhinegold* and Kathleen Broderick's magnificent Brunnhilde illuminating *The Valkyrie*.

Act III of *The Valkyrie* was performed by ENO at the Glastonbury Festival, the first operatic music ever heard there, and enjoyed a huge success. This was the first fruit of O_2's collaboration. The second should have been a complete performance of Puccini's *La Boheme* in Trafalgar Square, which was to be carpeted in astroturf for the occasion. Tickets were free and 6,500 had been distributed. Unfortunately, torrential rain and high winds prevented any performance in Trafalgar Square, but some ticket-holders were admitted to the Coliseum for an impromptu performance of *La Bohème*. Paul Daniel, the music director, conducted both these events. He also conducted the most enjoyable revival of the season, Robert Carsen's magical production of Britten's *A Midsummer Night's Dream*. A revival of John Adams's *Nixon in China*, which should have been the opening production at the Coliseum, unfortunately had to be cancelled, but was promised for future performance.

An attempt by the impresario Raymond Gubbay to inaugurate a low-price London opera company at the Savoy Theatre was unsuccessful and closed after two months because of poor ticket sales. The most expensive ticket was £49.50 but both the Royal Opera and English National Opera could offer cheaper seats. There was also the question of quality: the productions of the two operas staged, Rossini's *Barber of Seville* and Mozart's *Marriage of Figaro*, were judged as poor, although many singers received individual praise. There is no doubt that London would benefit from a company using a small theatre, perfect for the operas of Mozart and Rossini, as a training ground for young singers, but the Savoy Opera, unfortunately, did not fill the gap.

Opera North celebrated its 25th birthday with a most unusual season, Eight Little Greats, which consisted of eight short operas given in various combinations of two per performance. Opera-goers could attend only one if they preferred, at half the usual price, or they could buy four tickets for the price of three, or eight for the price of six. The eight productions, all new, had two directors, David Pountney and Christopher Alden, and one designer, Johan Engels. There was an ensemble of 21 singers. Only two of the operas were well known; Leoncavallo's *Pagliacci* and Puccini's *Il tabarro*. The others included Alexander Zemlinsky's *The Dwarf* (also known as *The Birthday of the Infanta*), Bizet's *Djamileh*,

Rachmaninov's *Francesca da Rimini,* and *La vida breve* by Manuel de Falla. The company brought the Eight Little Greats to Sadler's Wells Theatre in London at the end of June, where they attracted large audiences. Outstanding performances were given by baritone Jonathan Summers as Tonio in *Pagliacci* and Michele in *Il tabarro,* while Pountney's production of *The Dwarf,* in which the protagonist was the 'normal' person and the Infanta and her friends the 'monsters', was the most original.

Scottish Opera's *Ring Cycle* was nominated for the South Bank Show Award, and the Opera Award by the *Manchester Evening News,* the latter after the Company's visit to The Lowry, Salford. Sir Richard Armstrong, Scottish Opera's music director, who conducted the *Ring Cycle,* was both knighted and received the Royal Philharmonic Society Music Award in early 2004. He has renewed his contract with Scottish Opera until July 2005. Despite this great artistic and popular success, Scottish Opera was in dire financial trouble. The £4.5 million advanced by the Scottish Arts Council for 2003–4 was insufficient for the company to continue with its large-scale productions as well as its commitments to education and small-scale touring. In June 2004 Scottish Opera proposed a plan, accepted by the Scottish Executive, by which the latter would provide up to £7 million towards restructuring costs while the Company repays the Scottish Arts Council over four years. The number of personnel will be reduced from 208 to 120, with cuts mainly from the technical and administration departments, but also from the chorus. The orchestra will be retained.

Meanwhile *The Minotaur,* a children's opera with music by Julian Evans and libretto by Allan Dunn, based on the Greek myth of Theseus and the Minotaur, was successfully launched by Scottish Opera for All in May 2004 and toured five cities. Earlier, some 10,000 children from over one hundred schools across Scotland participated in a series of Scottish Opera for All workshops. By the time the children actually saw and heard *The Minotaur* in the theatre, they knew all about the story of Theseus, Ariadne and the Minotaur, as well as the mechanics of staging an opera. The opera itself was performed by seven singers and a dancer (as the Minotaur), with seven players in the orchestra. It was widely praised by local and national press.

Welsh National Opera's (WNO) splendid new production of *Eugene Onegin* was conducted by Tugan Sokhiev, the company's young Russian music director, who was obviously in perfect rapport with Tchaikovsky's opera. However, later in the season he attempted Verdi's *La traviata* (also a new production) with rather less success, and after one performance, relinquished the baton for the remaining performances. In August 2004 Sokhiev resigned as music director and WNO announced that Carlo Rizzi, music director from 1992–2001, would return for the next two seasons. WNO paid a very welcome visit to London's Sadler's Wells Theatre, where the repertory included *Eugene Onegin* and a revival of *Madama Butterfly,* originally directed by Joachim Hertz in 1978. WNO is due to move into its new home at the Wales Millennium Centre in Cardiff Bay in spring 2005. As Anthony Freud, General Director of WNO, declared at a press conference, 'The WMC . . . will allow us a firmer base from which to tour throughout the UK and internationally. With our rehearsal and administrative base, and a significant proportion of our technical production work, being contained within the WMC, we will be . . . at the heart of one of the most exciting arts buildings to have been created in Europe in decades.'

Glyndebourne Festival Opera offered two new productions in the 2004 season. First came Mozart's *Die Zauberflöte,* a perennial favourite with Sussex opera goers, staged by Adrian Noble, former artistic director of the Royal Shakespeare Company. The second novelty was a double bill with Rachmaninov's *The Miserly Knight* and Puccini's *Gianni Schicchi.* At first sight these two operas, one a 'little tragedy', as Pushkin's story, the basis of the libretto, is called, and the other a riotous black comedy, have little or nothing in common. However, they do share a theme, namely greed for money and power. Staged by Annabel Arden and conducted by music director Vladimir Jurowski (who also conducted *Die Zauberflöte*), these two fascinating variations on a theme were dominated by the singers of the title roles – Russian baritone Sergei Leiferkus in Rachmaninov and Italian baritone Alessandro Corbelli in Puccini – who provided a most rewarding evening's entertainment.

Other summer festivals also provided interesting and original work. At Aldeburgh there was the world premiere of Harrison Birtwistle's *The Io Passion* in June, repeated in London by Almeida Opera a month later. Almeida also presented a new opera, *Man and Boy: Dada* by Michael Nyman, on the passion for collecting bus-tickets and a fictitious friendship between the émigre German artist Kurt Schwitters and a young boy in WW2 London. Cheltenham, in July, offered Britten's *Death in Venice* and *The Turn of the Screw,* as well as the first performance of *Birds, Bones, Barks: a Trojan Trilogy* by Edward Rushton. At Grange Park during June and July, Tchaikovsky's *The Enchantress* was a welcome rarity, while Garsington offered an even rarer Tchaikovsky opera, *Cherevichki.* In July, Buxton put on an amusing production of Rossini's *Turk in Italy* as well as the first full staging of Will Todd's *The Blackened Man.* Holland Park Opera, running from early June to early August, performed Bellini's *Norma,* with a fine performance in the title role from Nelly Miriciou, Puccini's *La fanciulla del West* and Verdi's *Luisa Miller.* Most enterprising of all, Loughborough Festival staged a complete *Ring Cycle,* with Donald McIntyre, now 70 but still in excellent form, as Wotan.

At the 2004 Edinburgh Festival, Hanover State Opera brought productions of *Pelléas et Mélisande* and Luigi Nono's *Al gran sole carico d'amore,* as well as a concert performance of Strauss's *Capriccio.* There were also concert performances of Weber's three major operas, *Der Freischütz, Oberon* and *Euryanthe.* Operatic items in the Promenade Concerts at the Albert Hall, all broadcast by BBC Radio 3 and some televised, included Dvořák's *Dimitry,* in celebration of the centenary of the composer's death. Other Proms ranged from Britten's church-parable *Curlew River* to Wagner's *The Rhinegold,* played by the Orchestra of the Age of Enlightenment conducted by Simon Rattle, and from Holst's *Savitri* and Bartok's *Duke Bluebeard's Castle* to Glyndebourne's Rachmaninov/ Puccini double bill.

GONE BUT NOT FORGOTTEN

The great German bass-baritone Hans Hotter died on 6 December 2003 at the age of 94. The finest Wotan of his generation, he first appeared at Covent Garden in 1947 with the Vienna State Opera, singing the Count in *Le nozze di Figaro* and the title role of *Don Giovanni.* He returned the following year to sing with the fledgling Covent Garden Opera Company (later to become the Royal Opera) as Wotan *(Die Walkure),* Hans Sachs *(Die Meistersinger)* and Kurwenal *(Tristan und Isolde).* He continued to visit Covent Garden for many years and directed a *Ring Cycle* there. His roles included Amfortas and later Gurnemanz in *Parsifal*, and King Mark as well as Amfortas in *Tristan*. His career lasted well into his eighties, and Schigolch in Berg's *Lulu* became a favourite role. In sharp contrast, the career of British soprano Susan Chilcott, who died on 4 September 2003 aged only 40, was tragically short. She sang with all the British opera companies, making her debut at Covent garden in 2002 as Lisa in Tchaikovsky's *Queen of Spades*, opposite Placido Domingo as Hermann. She sang regularly in Europe and the USA, making her Metropolitan debut in New York as Helena, in Britten's *A Midsummer Night's Dream*, in 2002. Other roles she sang included Ellen Orford *(Peter Grimes)*, the Governess *(The Turn of the Screw)*, Fiordiligi *(Cosi fan tutte)*, Blanche (Poulenc's *Dialogues des Carmélites*) and the title roles of Dvořák's *Rusalka* and Janáček's *Jenufa*.

Julia Trevelyan Oman, British stage designer, died on 10 October 2003, aged 73. Her designs for opera included three very fine productions for Covent Garden: *Eugene Onegin* (1971); *La Bohème* (1974), which is still in the repertory, and; *Die Fledermaus* (1977). She also designed Richard Strauss's *Arabella* for Glyndebourne (1984). As a boy soprano, David Hemmings, the British actor who died aged 62 on 3 December 2003, created the role of Miles at the premiere in 1954 of Britten's *The Turn of the Screw* at the Teatro la Fenice in Venice. Norman Platt, founder and for twenty years artistic director of Kent Opera, died on 4 January 2004, aged 84. He started his career as a baritone singer at Sadler's Wells and with the English Opera Group. In 1969 he founded Kent Opera, which he successfully ran as a touring company, performing works by Monteverdi and Mozart that did not need very large orchestras. He employed Nicholas Hytner and Jonathan Miller in their first roles as opera directors, and in 1987 commissioned Judith Weir's *A Night at the Chinese Opera*, which was greatly admired. In 1989, Kent Opera's subsidy from the Arts Council was withdrawn, and the Company had to close.

Bernard Dickerson, the British tenor who died on 13 February 2004, aged 69, sang for many years with the English Opera Group, creating roles in Gordon Crosse's *Purgatory* (1966) and Thea Musgrave's *The Voice of Ariadne* (1974). He also sang in Britten's church-operas *The Prodigal Son* and *Curlew River*, and was a riotously funny Flute in *A Midsummer Night's Dream*. In 1973 he took the title role at the British premiere of Shostakovich's *The Nose* for the New Opera Company. He also sang at Glyndebourne, Covent Garden and with Opera North. William McAlpine, the Scottish tenor who died on 2 February 2004, aged 81, made his debut in 1952 at Covent Garden as Andres in the first British stage performance of Berg's *Wozzeck*. The following year he created the Spirit of the Masque in Britten's *Gloriana*. In 1955 he moved to Sadler's Wells, where he sang major roles for over a decade. At Glyndebourne he sang Idamante in *Idomeneo* and Bacchus in *Ariadne auf Naxos*. He returned to Covent Garden for the title role of *Les Contes d'Hoffmann*. Adele Leigh, the British soprano who died on the 25 May 2004, aged 76, joined Covent Garden Opera Company in 1948. Her first major role was Cherubino in *The Marriage of Figaro*. She later sang Susanna in that opera, Sophie and Octavian in *Der Rosenkavalier* and many other roles. In 1955 she created Bella in Michael Tippett's *The Midsummer Marriage*, scoring a great success. In 1963 she moved to Vienna to sing at the Volksoper.

PRODUCTIONS

In the summaries below, the dates in brackets indicate the year that the current production entered the repertory.

ROYAL OPERA
Founded 1946
Royal Opera House, Covent Garden, London WC2E 9DD

Productions from the repertory: *Don Giovanni* (2002), *Madama Butterfly* (2003), *Boris Godunov* (1983), *Les Contes d'Hoffmann* (1980), *Simon Boccanegra* (1991), *Samson et Dalila* (1981), *Der Rosenkavalier* (1984), *Ariadne auf Naxos* (2002), *Tosca* (1964).

NEW PRODUCTIONS:

Orlando (Handel), 6 October 2003. Conductor, Harry Bicket; director, Francisco Negrin; designer, Anthony Baker. Alice Coote (Orlando), Barbara Bonney (Angelica), Mejun Mehta (Medora), Camilla Tilling (Dorinda), Jonathan Lemalu (Zoroastro).

Aida (Verdi), 8 November 2003. Conductor, Antonio Pappano; director and set designer, Robert Wilson; costume designer, Jacques Reynaud. Norma Fantini (Aida), Ildiko Komlosi (Amneris), Johan Botha (Radames), Graeme Broadbent (King), Carlo Colombara (Ramfis), Mark Doss (Amonasro).

Lucia di Lammermoor (Donizetti), 29 November 2003. Conductor Evelino Pido; director Christoph Loy; designer, Herbert Murauer. Andrea Rost (Lucia), Marcelo Alvarez (Edgardo), Anthony Michaels-Moore (Enrico), Peter Auty (Arturo), John Relyea (Raimondo), Andrew Kennedy (Normanno), Ekaterina Gubanova (Alisa).

Sweeney Todd (Sondheim), 15 December 2003. Conductor, Paul Gemingnani; director, Neil Armfield; set designer, Brian Thomson; costume designer, Tess Schofield. Thomas Allen (Sweeney Todd), Felicity Palmer (Mrs Lovett), William Dazeley (Anthony Hope), Rebecca Evans (Johanna), Doug Jones (Tobias Ragg), Jonathan Veira (Judge Turpin), Robert Tear (The Beadle), Bonaventura Bottone (Pirelli), Rosalind Plowright (Beggar Woman), Matthew Rose (Jonas Fogg).

The Tempest (Thomas Adès), world premiere 10 February 2004. Conductor, Thomas Adès; director and set designer, Tom Cairns; set and costume designer, Moritz Junge. Simon Keenlyside (Prospero), Christine Rice (Miranda), Toby Spence (Ferdinand), Ian Bostridge (Caliban), Cyndia Sieden (Ariel), Philip Langridge (King of Naples), John Daszak (Antonio), Lawrence Zazzo (Trinculo), Gwynne Howell (Gonzalo).

Lady Macbeth of Mtsensk (Shostakovich), 1 April 2004. Conductor, Antonio Pappano; director, Richard Jones; set designer, John Macfarlane; costume designer, Nicky Gillibrand. Katarina Dalayman (Katerina Ismailova), John Tomlinson (Boris Ismailov), Stefan Margita (Zinovy Ismailov), Christopher Ventris (Sergei), Peter Bronder (Village Drunk), Maxim Mihailov (Priest), Roderick Earle (Police Inspector), Gwynne Howell (Old Convict), Christine Rice (Sonyechka).

The Rape of Lucretia (Britten), 28 April 2004 in Linbury Studio Theatre. Conductor, Alexander Briger; director and set designer, John Lloyd-Davis; costume designer, Suzanne Hubrich. Christine Rice (Lucretia), Matthew Rose (Collatinus), Grant Doyle (Tarquinius), Victoria Nava (Female chorus), Hubert Francis (Male Chorus), Ekaterina Gubanova (Bianca), Ha Young Lee (Lucia), Jared Holt (Junius).

Arabella (R. Strauss), 21 May 2004. Conductor,

Christoph von Dohnanyi; director, Peter Mussbach; set designer, Erich Wonder; costume designer, Andrea Schmidt-Futterer. Karita Mattila (Arabella), Barbara Bonney (Zdenka), Cornelia Kallisch (Adelaide), Diana Damrau (Fiakermilli), Thomas Hampson (Mandryka), Artur Korn (Waldner), Raymond Very (Matteo), John Daszak (Elemer), Quentin Hayes (Dominik), Iain Patterson (Lamoral).

Faust (Gounod), 11 June 2004. Conductor, Antonio Pappano; director, David McVicar; set designer, Charles Edwards; costume designer, Birgitte Reiffenstuel. Roberto Alagna (Faust), Bryn Terfel (Mephistopheles), Angela Gheorghiu (Marguerite), Simon Keenlyside (Valentin), Sophie Koch (Siebel).

Peter Grimes (Britten), 3 July 2004. Conductor, Antonio Pappano; director, Willy Decker; designer, John Macfarlane. Ben Heppner (Peter Grimes), Alan Opie (Captain Balstrode), Janice Watson (Ellen Orford), Jonathan Veira (Hobson), Matthew Best (Swallow), Quentin Hayes (Ned Keane), Ian Caley (Bob Boles), Anne Collins (Auntie), Alish Tynan (First Niece), Helen Williams (Second Niece), Sarah Walker (Mrs Sedley), Brian Galliford (Rector).

ENGLISH NATIONAL OPERA
Founded 1931
London Coliseum, St Martin's Lane, London WC2N 4BS

Productions from the repertory: *The Rape of Lucretia* (2001), *Tosca* (2002), *The Magic Flute* (1988), *The Mikado* (1986), *Carmen* (1995), *Ernani* (2000), *A Midsummer Night's Dream* (1995).

NEW PRODUCTIONS:

Così fan tutte (Mozart), 20 September 2003 at Barbican Theatre. Conductor, Mark Wigglesworth; director, Samuel West; designer, Alison Chitty; Mary Plazas (Fiordiligi), Victoria Simmons (Dorabella), Alison Roddy (Despina), Colin Lee (Ferrando), Toby Stafford-Allen (Guglielmo), Andrew Shore (Don Alfonso).

Twilight of the Gods (Wagner), 25 November 2003, semi-staged concert performance at Barbican Theatre. Conductor, Paul Daniel. Kathleen Broderick (Brunnhilde), Richard Berkeley-Steele (Siegfried), Gidon Saks (Hagen), Robert Poulton (Gunther), Claire Weston (Gutrune), Sara Fulgoni (Waltraute), Andrew Shore (Alberich).

The Rhinegold (Wagner), 27 February 2004. Conductor, Paul Daniel; director, Phyllida Lloyd; designer, Richard Hudson. Robert Hayward (Wotan), Andrew Shore (Alberich), Susan Parry (Fricka), Tom Randle (Loge), Claire Weston (Freia), Andrew Rees (Froh), Darren Jeffery (Donner), Iain Patterson (Fasolt), Gerald O'Connor (Fafner), John Graham Hall (Mime), Patricia Bardon (Erda).

The Valkyrie (Wagner), 8 May 2004. Conductor, Paul Daniel; director, Phyllida Lloyd; designer, Richard Hudson. Par Lindskog (Siegmund), Orla Boylan (Sieglinde), Clive Bayley (Hunding), Kathleen Broderick (Brunnhilde), Robert Hayward (Wotan), Susan Parry (Fricka).

OPERA NORTH
Founded 1978
Grand Theatre, 40 New Briggate, Leeds LS1 6NU

Productions from the repertory: *La traviata* (1999), *The Barber of Seville* (1986), *The Bartered Bride* (1998).

NEW PRODUCTIONS:

Rusalka (Dvořák), 4 October 2003. Conductor, Sebastian Lang-Lessing; director, Olivia Fuchs; designer Niki Turner. Giselle Allen (Rusalka), Stuart Skelton (The Prince), Susan Bickley (Jezibaba), Susannah Glanville (The Foreign Princess), Richard Angas (The Water Sprite), Sarah Cox (Kitchen Boy).

Manon (Massenet), 16 October 2003. Conductor, Grant Llewylyn; director, Daniel Slater; designer, Francis O'Connor. Malin Bystrom (Manon), Julian Gavin (Le Chevalier des Grieux), William Dazeley (Lescaut), Johnathan Best (Le Comte des Grieux).

Der Zwerg (Zemlinsky), 15 April 2004. Conductor, David Parry; director, David Pountney; set designer, Johan Engels; costume designer, Marie-Jeanne Lecca. Stefanie Krahnenfeld (Donna Clara), Majella Cullagh (Ghita), Paul Nilon (Dwarf), Graeme Broadbent (Don Estoban).

La vida breve (de Falla), 15 April 2004). Conductor, Martin Andre; director, Christopher Alden; set designer, Johan Engels; costume designer, Adam Silverman. Mary Plazas (Salud), Susan Gorton (La abuela), Kim-Marie Woodhouse (Carmela), Leonardo Capalbo (Paco), Mark Stone (Manuel), Graeme Broadbent (Uncle Salvador), Adrian Clarke (Singer).

Il tabarro (Puccini), 21 April 2004. Conductor, Martin Andre; director, David Pountney; set designer, Johan Engels; costume designer, Tom Pye. Nina Pavlovski (Giorgetta), Marie-Anne Owens (La Frugola), Leonardo Capalbo (Luigi), Jonathan Summers (Michele), Nicholas Sharratt (Tinca), William Mackie (Talpa).

L'occasione fa il ladro (Rossini), 21 April 2004. Conductor, David Parry; director, Christopher Alden; set designer, Johan Engels; costume designer, Tom Pye. Majella Cullagh (Berenice), Iain Paton (Count Alberto), Mark Stone (Don Parmenione), Kim-Marie Woodhouse (Ernestina), Adrian Clarke (Martino), Nicholas Sharratt (Don Eusebio).

Francesca da Rimini (Rachmaninov), 7 May 2004. Conductor, Martin Andre; director, David Pountney; set designer, Johan Engels; costume designer, Sue Wilmington. Nina Pavlovski (Francesca), Jeffrey Lloyd-Roberts (Paolo/Dante), Jonathan Summers (Malatesta/ Ghost of Virgil).

Pagliacci (Leoncavallo), 7 May 2004. Conductor, David Parry; director Christopher Alden; set designer, Johan Engels; costume designer, Sue Wilmington. Geraint Dodd (Canio), Majella Cullagh (Nedda), Jonathan Summers (Tonio), Iain Paton (Beppe), Mark Stone (Silvio).

Djamileh (Bizet), 14 May 2004. Conductor, David Parry; director, Christopher Alden; set designer, Johan Engels; costume designer, Sue Wilmington. Paul Nilon (Haroun), Mark Stone (Splendiano), Patricia Bardon (Djamileh).

The Seven Deadly Sins (Weill), 14 May 2004. Conductor, James Holmes; director, David Pountney; set designer, Johan Engels; costume designer, Marie-Jeanne Lecca. Rebecca Caine (Anna I), Beate Vollack (Anna II), Iain Paton (Tenor I), Nicholas Sharratt (Tenor II), Adrian Clarke (Father), Graeme Broadbent (Mother).

Performances were given at the Grand Theatre, Leeds and on tour in Newcastle, Hull, Nottingham, Salford Quay, Norwich and Sadler's Wells Theatre, London.

SCOTTISH OPERA
Founded1962
39 Elmbank Crescent, Glasgow G2 4PT

Productions from the repertory: *Das Rheingold* (2000), *Die*

Walküre (2001), *Siegfried* (2002), *Götterdämmerung* (2003), *The Magic Flute* (1992), *Aida* (1999).

NEW PRODUCTIONS:

La Bohème (Puccini), 28 April 2004. Conductor, Richard Farnes; director and designer, Stewart Laing. Peter Auty (Rodolfo), Rachel Hynes (Mimi), Rebecca von Lipinski (Musetta), Roderick Williams (Marcello), Roland Wood (Schaunard), Alessandro Guerzoni (Colline), Paul Anwyl (Benoit).

Performances were given at the Theatre Royal, Glasgow and on tour in Edinburgh, Salford Quay, Aberdeen, Inverness and Liverpool.

WELSH NATIONAL OPERA
Founded 1946
John Street, Cardiff CF1 4SP

Productions from the repertory: *Le nozze di Figaro* (2001), *Hansel and Gretel* (1998), *Madama Butterfly* (1978), *Carmen* (1997), *Katya Kabanova* (2001).

NEW PRODUCTIONS:

Parsifal (Wagner), 27 September 2003. Conductor Vladimir Jurowski; director and designer, Silviu Purcarete. Stephen O'Mara (Parsifal), Sara Fulgoni (Kundry), Alfred Reiter (Gurnemanz), Robert Hayward (Amfortas), Donald Maxwell (Klingsor), Iain Paterson (Titurel).

Il trovatore (Verdi), 3 October 2003. Conductor, Alberto Hold-Garrido; director; Peter Watson; designer, Tim Healy. Elena Lasovskaya (Leonore), David Rendall (Manrico), Yuri Nechaev (Count di Luna), Patricia Bardon (Azucena).

Eugene Onegin (Tchaikovsky). 14 February 2004. Conductor, Tugan Sokhiev; director, James Macdonald; designer, Tobias Hoheisel. Amanda Roocroft (Tatyana), Ekaterina Semenchuk (Olga), Suzanne Murphy (Mme Larina), Linda Ormiston (Filipovna), Marius Brenciu (Lensky), Vladimir Moroz (Onegin), Robert Tear (Monsieur Triquet), Brindley Sherratt (Prince Gremin).

La traviata (Verdi), 15 May 2004. Conductor, Tugan Sokhiev; directors, Patrice Caurier and Moshe Leiser; set designer, Christian Fenouillat; costume designer, Agostino Cavalca, Nuccia Focile (Violetta), Peter Wedd (Alfredo), Christopher Purves (Germont).

Performances were given at the New Theatre, Cardiff and on tour in Oxford, Llandudno, Birmingham, Swansea, Belfast, Liverpool, Bristol, Milton Keynes, Southampton, Plymouth and Sadler's Wells Theatre, London.

GLYNDEBOURNE FESTIVAL OPERA
Founded 1934
Glyndebourne, Lewes, East Sussex BN8 5UU

The Festival ran from 20 May to 29 August 2004. *Pelléas et Mélisande* (1999), *Rodelinda* (1998), *Carmen* (2002), *Jenufa* (1989) were revived.

NEW PRODUCTIONS:

Der Zauberflöte (Mozart), 20 May 2004. Conductor, Vladimir Jurowsky; director, Adrian Noble; designer, Anthony Ward. Pavol Breslik (Tamino), Lisa Milne (Pamina), Cornelia Götz (Queen of Night), Peter Rose (Sarastro), Gerd Grochowski (Speaker), Claire Ormshaw (Papagena), Tatiana Monogarova (First Lady), Juliane de Villiers (Second Lady), Romina Basso (Third Lady).

The Miserly Knight (Rachmaninov), 1 July 2004. Conductor, Vladimir Jurowski; director, Annabel Arden; set designer, Vicki Mortimer; costume designer, Nicky Gillibrand. Sergei Leiferkus (The Baron), Albert Schagidullin (The Duke), Richard Berkeley Steele (Albert), Viateschlav Voinarovski (The Money Lender), Maxim Mikhailov (The Servant).

Gianni Schicchi (Puccini), 1 July 2004. Conductor, Vladimir Jurowski; director, Annabel Arden; set designer, Vicki Mortimer; costume designer, Nicky Gillibrand. Alessandro Corbelli (Gianni Schicchi), Sally Matthews (Lauretta), Massimo Giordano (Rinuccio), Felicity Palmer (Zita), Luigi Roni (Simone), Adrian Thompson (Gherardo), Riccardo Novaro (Marco), Marie McLaughlin (La Ciesca), Olga Schalaeva (Nella), Maxim Mikhailov (Betto di Signa).

GLYNDEBOURNE TOURING OPERA

La Bohème (2000), *Die Zauberflöte* (2004), *Pelléas et Mélisande* (1999) were performed from 5 October to 11 December 2004 at Glyndebourne, Woking, Milton Keynes, Norwich, Plymouth, Stoke-on-Trent, Oxford and Wimbledon (*La Boheme* only).

GARSINGTON OPERA
Founded 1989
Garsington Manor, Garsington, Oxford OX44 9DH

The season ran from 12 June to 11 July 2004.

NEW PRODUCTIONS:

Cosí fan tutte (Mozart), 12 June 2004. Conductor Steuart Bedford; director, John Cox; designer, Robert Perdziola. Sarah-Jane Davies (Fiordiligi), Wendy Dawn Thompson (Dorabella), Edgaras Montvidas (Ferrando), Daniel Belcher (Guglielmo), Jonathan Best (Don Alfonso), Lillian Watson (Despina).

Cherevichki (Tchaikovsky), 15 June 2004. Conductor, Elgar Howarth; director, Olivia Fuchs; designer, Niki Turner. Adrian Dwyer (Vakula), Anne-Sophie Duprels (Oksana), Frances McCafferty (Solokha), Roderick Earle (The Devil), Leonid Zimnenko (Chub), Gerard O'Connor (The Mayor), Stuart Kale (The Schoolmaster), Blake Fischer (Panas), D'Arcy Bleiker (Potemkin).

ENGLISH TOURING OPERA
Founded 1980 as OPERA 80

Ariodante (Handel) and *The Turn of the Screw* (Britten) were toured to Richmond, Canterbury, King's Lynn, Snape Maltings, Lincoln, Tunbridge Wells, Cheltenham, Exeter and Bath between 15 October and 29 November 2003.

The Marriage of Figaro (Mozart) and *A Midsummer Night's Dream* (Britten) were toured to Hackney, Dartford, Buxton, Cambridge, Truro, Crawley, Snape Maltings, Malvern, Exeter, Poole, Yeovil, Sheffield, Wolverhampton, Coventry, Durham and Perth between 11 March and 29 May 2004.

PARLIAMENT

Prime Minister Tony Blair faced another turbulent year caused by the ramifications of the war with Iraq, the UK's close support for the USA and his perceived style of leadership. The issue of his handling of a possible new Constitution for Europe also brought his critics to the fore and he was even the subject of a flour bomb attack in the Chamber on 19 May (though this was to do with the campaign group Fathers 4 Justice). He survived the publication of two reports (Hutton and Butler) on the Iraq conflict and despite seeing his Commons majority reduced to just 5 on the second reading of the Higher Education Bill in January, having a difficult spring and early summer and losing a by-election in what should have been a safe Labour seat in Leicester South in July, he was in a strong enough position to see off the Opposition in a debate on the Butler report on 20 July and then nominate his close ally Peter Mandelson as Britain's choice for the next European Commissioner. This was despite widespread backbench dissent, just as Parliament went off for their summer break on 23 July. The Conservative stance on the conflict seemed to do no favours for the new Conservative leader Michael Howard (November 2003), who claimed in July that if he had known there were no Weapons of Mass Destruction (WMD) in Iraq he might not have voted for the war. Liberal Democrat leader Charles Kennedy was constant in his opposition to the war and criticism of the handling of the post conflict issues and this stance seemed to go down well with the electors in the July by-elections.

IRAQ AND THE MIDDLE EAST

It was this issue that continued to dominate British politics. Returning for the short pre-conference session of Parliament on 8 September 2003, Foreign Secretary Jack Straw updated MPs on developments in Iraq and the Middle East over the summer. Nine Britons had lost their lives in Iraq since he last spoke in the House on 17 July, but he claimed 'we are determined to work with the international community to establish peace and security across the whole region.' Conservative Foreign Affairs spokesman Michael Ancram supported the Government saying 'What we did in the war was right. What we must not do now is squander the peace for lack of political direction.' In an Opposition debate on the military Situation in Iraq on 9 September, Conservative Defence spokesman Bernard Jenkin felt 'the Government must convince the British people that the prize of democracy and prosperity for the Iraqi people are prizes worth the money, sweat and even the lives of the hard-pressed men and women of our armed forces.' Defence Secretary Geoff Hoon reiterated that 'our commitment to a stable, united and law-abiding Iraqi state, welcomed back into the international community and providing effective and representative government for its own people, remains constant.' Liberal Democrat Defence spokesperson Paul Keetch turned on the Conservative Party, as well as the Government, 'I find it surprising that the Conservatives, who supported the decision to go to war and were the only people more vociferous in their support for the US than the Government, should now complain so bitterly about its aftermath.' One of the leading backbench Labour critics of the war Alice Mahon stated 'we are right to concentrate on the misleading devices that were employed to get the country to go to war.' SNP Westminster leader Alex Salmond felt that the people 'deeply resent being gathered into a conflict on a trail of deception.'

On 12 November 2003 Secretary of State for International Development Hilary Benn made a statement on progress of reconstruction in Iraq, 'we must all remain committed to the economic and social reconstruction of Iraq and to a better life for its people.' Conservative International Development spokesman John Bercow felt, 'Is it not the truth that, whereas the Government, notably in the form of the Prime Minister, displayed courage and statesmanship in the conduct of war, the reality is that they have been guilty of dithering and abdication of responsibility in failing to prepare for the peace?'

On 20 November Jack Straw made a statement on the bomb explosion in Istanbul, which appeared to target British interests and confirmed that 'we shall stand united with the international community in the fight against this appalling global terrorism.'

On 11 December Geoff Hoon published the Defence White Paper – *Delivering Security in a Changing World*, and a separate report – *Operations in Iraq: Lessons for the Future.*

Returning after the Christmas Recess on 5 January 2004, Jack Straw made a statement on Libya and its decision, announced on 19 December to eliminate its weapons of mass destruction – 'an important step forward . . . to enhancing international peace and security.'

On 28 January Tony Blair made a statement on the publication of Lord Hutton's report into the death of Ministry of Defence special adviser Dr David Kelly, which the Government 'accepted in full.' 'Over the last six or more months, allegations have been made that go to the heart of the integrity of the Government, our intelligence services and me personally as Prime Minister . . . The allegation that I or anyone else lied to this House or deliberately misled the country by falsifying intelligence on WMD is itself the real lie. Lord Hutton concluded 'false accusations of fact impugning the integrity of others should not be made." Michael Howard also accepted the conclusions of the report but called for a full independent inquiry into the wider questions of the affair. He felt 'what will remain in people's minds is the blinding light that this inquiry has shed on the innermost workings of the Prime Minister and his Government.' Charles Kennedy commented, 'the Prime Minister cannot therefore dodge or escape profound questions about the basis on which his judgement (to go to war) was made.' Labour MP Gerald Kaufman (Manchester Gorton) posed the question that in light of the criticisms of the BBC in the report, 'how can the BBC continue as a public service broadcasting operation, funded by a tax, unless people are cleared out and a new regime appointed?'

On 2 February 2004 Culture Secretary Tessa Jowell answered an Urgent Notice Question from Labour MP David Winnick on the procedure for appointing a new Chair of the BBC Governors following the resignation of Gavyn Davies and the Director-General Greg Dyke over the Hutton report. 'We all want a strong BBC that is independent of government and anyone who cares about politics, standards in public life and the quality of our media knows just how much the BBC matters.' On 3 February Jack Straw made a statement on the setting up of a committee to review intelligence on weapons of mass destruction, to be composed of Privy Councillors and to report before the summer recess. The Committee would be chaired by Lord Butler and would include senior Labour backbench MP Ann Taylor and senior Conservative backbench MP Michael Mates. The Liberal Democrats had declined to support the inquiry and so would not be represented. Jack Straw stated, 'The decision that the House took 10 months ago to go to war was justified given the defiance of a regime that uniquely had used weapons of mass destruction and had refused for so long to comply with obligations unanimously imposed on it by the UN Security Council ... we cannot subcontract that responsibility to any inquiry ... but I believe Lord Butler ... will be able to perform a most valuable service to the House and to the country.' Michael Ancram welcomed the inquiry but was annoyed at the delay in setting it up, 'a considerable price has been paid for the Government's obstinacy ... not only to their own reputation but to that of the dedicated intelligence personnel who serve our country with commitment and distinction.' Menzies Campbell explained the Liberal Democrat decision not to participate was due to the narrow remit which the inquiry had been given, 'why can we not have a remit with sufficient breadth to allow the members of the Committee to examine the Attorney General's advice?' In a debate on Lord Hutton's report on 4 February, Tony Blair thought 'the report itself... is the best defence to the charges of Government whitewash.' The debate had to be suspended for 15 minutes following a disturbance by anti-war protestors in the public gallery. He concluded by addressing the close alliance with the USA, 'I think that America now understands and believes that the best and ultimate guarantee of its security is the spread of the values of freedom, democracy and rule of law. If America no longer takes an isolationist view of the world but considers that part of its job is to spread those values around the world, I for one am proud to be its friend and ally.' Michael Howard claimed that 'it is possible to support the war and to want to get at the truth' and concluded that 'the Hutton Report has been subjected to intense comment, some of it questioning, some of it critical and some of it more than a little incredulous ... unfortunately the initial opinion of the Prime Minister and his colleagues does not seem to be reflected in the more settled opinion of the public.' Charles Kennedy remained of the view that, 'given the situation at the time and for the reasons that were given, it was the wrong war, prosecuted at the wrong time for quite the wrong reason.' Father of the House and opponent of the war Tam Dalyell hoped the Butler inquiry would 'carry over into the question which many of our fellow citizens want to know: the justification of the war in the first place.'

On 24 February Jack Straw made a statement about the release of five of the nine UK detainees at Guantanamo Bay – 'our overall position remains that the detainees should either be tried in accordance with international standards or returned to the UK.' On 26 February Harriet Harman repeated a statement by the Attorney General in the House of Lords about the collapse of the prosecution of Katharine Gunn, who had been charged under Section 1 of the Official Secrets Act 1989 with passing on information about Iraq and whose defence lawyers had demanded the publication of the Attorney General's advice on the legality of the Iraq war.

On 1 April 2004 Jack Straw published a review of the Foreign and Commonwealth Office's travel advice given the threat from global terrorism, inviting comments from all interested parties. 'We all live with the threat of global terrorism. Our response must be not panic but commonsense precautions.'

Returning from the Easter Recess on 19 April, Tony Blair reported on his visit to the USA where he had discussed Iraq and the Middle East Peace Process with President George W. Bush and UN Secretary-General Kofi Annan. 'There is no doubt that the present situation in Iraq is very difficult ... but we should not lose sight of what is happening across the majority of the country.' There had been agreement that the UN should play a central role in the reconstruction of Iraq and Blair also welcomed the Israeli proposal to withdraw from Gaza and parts of the West Bank. 'All these issues need to be seen in a wider context, for they are all linked. We are firm in response to terrorism and states proliferating WMD but we must also be firm in tackling the breeding grounds of terrorism.' He did not mention his decision to hold a referendum on the proposed EU Constitutional Treaty after all (and it was rumoured that he did not consult many in his party either). Michael Howard 'welcomed this small u-turn by the Prime Minister (on UN involvement), just as we welcome his big u-turn to hold a referendum on the European constitution.' Charles Kennedy asked him to confirm or contradict the rumour that 'during the build up to the original decision to mount the war in Iraq, the Americans gave him the option of not participating.'

On 4 May 2004 Armed Forces Minister Adam Ingram came to the House following serious allegations about the conduct of British soldiers in Iraq in the light of photographs published in the *Daily Mirror*, appearing to show mistreatment of Iraqi prisoners. An inquiry had been launched immediately by the Royal Military Police and Mr Ingram stated 'would be wrong for me to speculate about the outcome.' On 10 May Geoff Hoon brought the House up-to-date in relation to the security situation in Iraq, with British forces, coalition allies and Iraqi police facing violent attacks in the south in more than 100 engagements. He also reported that the investigations into the Mirror photographs gave strong indications that they were not taken in Iraq. Full investigations were being carried out into all allegations of mistreatment, 'we are determined to see through the task in Iraq according to standards of behaviour set out in the Geneva Convention and international humanitarian law.'

On 27 May Geoff Hoon announced an increase of troop levels in Iraq to about 8,900. Conservative Defence spokesman Nicholas Soames felt, 'the Government need to show that they have reclaimed a grip on the drift on their policy in Iraq and prove that they are the master of their objectives and not merely the victim of events.'

Returning after the Whitsun Recess on 7 June 2004 Jack Straw updated MPs on political and diplomatic developments related to Iraq. Full authority would transfer from the occupying powers to a sovereign interim Iraqi government in three weeks (30 June) with elections being held by 31 January 2005. A UN Resolution was being drafted. 'There will be some difficult times ahead, but the path to a free and democratic Iraq is now clear and the British Government will remain committed to helping the Iraqi Government and people to achieve that historic goal.' Michael Ancram, after paying tribute to the late President Reagan ('he challenged the inevitable march of communism and won. We have lost a champion and a friend'), welcomed the progress but criticised 'the political incompetence of the Government and the instability that has flowed from their failure to plan adequately and early enough for the post-war reconstruction and return to democracy.'

On 14 June Tony Blair reported on the outcome of the G8 summit in Georgia the previous week. The summit had agreed that they 'will succeed in making Iraq a better place not just for Iraqis but for the wider region and the world.' On the final day six African states had joined the meeting and agreement had been reached on a new initiative to extend AIDS vaccine research and to increase the heavily indebted poor countries initiative, to break the cycle of famine and food insecurity in the Horn of Africa. He concluded 'The G8 was originally created to discuss economic issues . . . but increasingly the focus has moved towards issues of international solidarity. It is morally right that we extend democracy, cut poverty, remove the causes of conflict and instability, and bring the hope of advancement to all nations; but it is also now clearly in our enlightened self-interest. If global terrorism and the proliferation of chemical, biological and nuclear weapons are the new security threat we face, we recognise that it cannot be defeated by security measures alone. Political freedom and rising prosperity, as much as force of arms, will be our ultimate shield: this year's G8 recognised that reality. We look forward to deepening it under British chairmanship next year.'

On 30 June Tony Blair made a statement at the NATO summit in Istanbul and the special European Council in Brussels that followed immediately after. The issues of Iraq and Afghanistan had dominated the NATO meeting, 'even for those who passionately disagreed with our decision to go to war, the issues are now clear, the side we should be on without doubt, and the cause manifestly one worth winning. Succeeding in it would be a fitting way to reinvigorate the transatlantic alliance and heal its divisions.'

On 14 July 2004 Tony Blair came to the House to report on the publication of Lord Butler's report *Intelligence on Weapons of Mass Destruction.* In a very confident display he said, 'This report, the Hutton inquiry, the report of the Intelligence and Security Committee before it, and that of the Foreign Affairs Committee before that, found the same thing. No one lied. No one made up the intelligence. No one inserted things into the dossier against the advice of the intelligence services. Everyone genuinely tried to do their best in good faith for the country in circumstances of acute difficulty. That issue of good faith should now be at an end . . . for any mistakes made, as the report finds, in good faith, I of course take responsibility, but I cannot honestly say that I believe that getting rid of Saddam was a mistake at all. Iraq, the region and the wider world are better and safer places without him . . . This report will not end the arguments about the war, but in its balance and common sense, it should at least help to set them in a more rational light.' Michael Howard gave what was generally considered to be a poor performance in reply. He concluded, 'He has said that mistakes were made and he accepts responsibility, but it is not a question of responsibility, it is a question of credibility. I hope that we will not face in this country another war in the foreseeable future, but if we did and this Prime Minister identified the threat, would the country believe him?' Charles Kennedy summed up, 'Inevitably, Lord Butler and his colleagues have not been able to address the fundamental question that many of us wanted to have addressed from the start: what was the key reality of the political judgments that led us to this war? When the Prime Minister now says that the outcome was desirable, albeit arrived at by insufficient conclusions and methodology, surely that is not a satisfactory way to proceed.' Labour backbench critics such as former Foreign Secretary Robin Cook stated, 'I welcome the Prime Minister's frank acceptance that there were no stockpiles of weapons of mass destruction at the time of war. He is entitled to argue that that does not mean that there was no justification for the war, but it does surely mean that there was no urgent necessity for the war, because there was no imminent threat. Will he now recognise that there was time for Hans Blix to finish his job and to confirm through the process of UN weapons inspections that Saddam had no weapons of mass destruction and that, had he done so, we might have been spared the unavoidable conclusion from the content of the Butler report that we committed British troops to action on the basis of false intelligence, overheated analysis and unreliable sources?'

EUROPE

On 9 September 2003 Jack Straw made a statement to MPs on the publication of a White Paper on a New Constitutional Treaty for the European Union, prior to the October European Union Intergovernmental Conference in Rome to discuss the issue. 'To turn our backs on the Union at this historic time would not only betray our national interest but mark a profound lack of confidence in Britain and everything we stand for,' he said. Michael Ancram called it 'not so much a white paper as a white flag and the Government's docile surrender to the concept of a politically united Europe is a betrayal of trust.' He also criticised the Government's refusal to hold a referendum on the issue. Menzies Campbell agreed, feeling that 'a Government confident of its own position would be comfortable in seeking the endorsement of the people of the United Kingdom.'

Returning after the Conference Recess on 20 October 2003, Jack Straw reported back to the House on the outcome of the European Council meeting in Brussels the previous week. At this meeting the first substantive discussion of the draft constitutional treaty had taken place, 'the European constitutional treaty has to be based on independent sovereign nation states co-operating not on some federal super state.' Michael Ancram again demanded a referendum on the issue, 'why are the Government so frightened of the British people?'

On 15 December 2003 Tony Blair reported on the outcome of the European Council IGC meeting in Brussels, which had also discussed Iraq, following the capture of Saddam Hussein. The European leaders had discussed the imminent enlargement, the future of European defence and the draft constitutional treaty. Final agreement had not been possible over the issue of the relative weight of votes that member states would have in the enlarged Union but 'the negotiation was living proof that the European Union is and will remain an organisation of sovereign member states . . . we can either be on the touchline shouting our criticism or on the field as an active and successful player.' Michael Howard pressed again for a referendum on any future European Constitution insisting Government should 'trust the people', and Charles Kennedy reiterated Liberal Democrat support for such a constitution.

On 11 February 2004 Jack Straw made a statement on the Government's plans for enhancing the role of Parliament in European Union matters. Firstly the

Government would produce a White Paper every January looking a year ahead at the EU's legislative and other activities, setting out the Government's priorities and each July it would produce a Command Paper taking stock of progress. Secondly they would recommend the setting up of a new Committee system to cover the whole of the EU's work. Planning for the British EU presidency in the second half of 2005 was well underway.

Returning from the half-term recess on 23 February David Blunkett made a statement on the Government's approach to the free movement of workers from the ten accession countries to the European Union from 1 May 2004, announcing measures 'that will ensure that those who come here . . . but do not work will not be able to claim benefits' with a new workers registration scheme to replace work permits for accession nationals. David Davies thought the Government had 'come up with a bureaucratic solution that carries unnecessary risk.'

On 29 March 2004 Tony Blair reported back on the outcome of the European Council in Brussels over the weekend, in the aftermath of the Madrid bombing, and his visit to Libya on 25 March. On Libya he felt, 'if the change in Libya is real, we should support it.' On the Council which had negotiated a new constitutional treaty for the EU he commented, 'Britain will ensure that we keep control over our tax and social security systems, over our own criminal justice system and over defence and foreign policy as we said we would. Provided we do so, this treaty is right for Europe and right for Britain.' Michael Howard felt 'any proposal for a new constitution must be put to the British people. At least seven other member states of the EU are giving their people a say . . . the Prime Minister says, trust him; we say, trust the people.' Charles Kennedy thought, 'a referendum would be the right way to go.'

Tony Blair returned to the Commons on 20 April 2004 to make a statement on the forthcoming negotiation over the new European treaty, with the Foreign Secretary publishing a White Paper on Europe at the same time. 'Provided that the treaty embodies the essential British positions, we shall agree to it as a Government. Once agreed . . . Parliament should debate it in detail and decide upon it. Then, let the people have the final say.' Michael Howard 'welcomed the fact that the Prime Minister has, at long last, seen sense and decided to give the British people their say on a question of such fundamental importance, even though he could not bring himself to utter the word 'referendum'.' Charles Kennedy welcomed the 'confirmation that in due course there will be a referendum of the British people' and hoped, 'it will be based on an unloaded, unbiased question which will be subject to confirmation by the Electoral Commission, and that it is best decided after due Parliamentary consideration.'

On 21 June 2004 Tony Blair reported on the outcome of the European Council meeting in Brussels on 17/18 June, the first with 25 member states. They had agreed a new treaty for Europe setting out for the first time, in one single treaty, the powers, rights and duties of the European Union. 'Not a single Government of a single nation – either those in Europe now or those wanting to join – opposed this treaty. All welcomed it. All want it to work. In the end, the final say will be with the British people in a referendum. But in that debate, we will argue that this constitutional treaty represents a success for the new Europe that is taking shape, is a success for Britain.' Michael Howard opined, 'this constitution is bad for our democracy, bad for jobs and bad for Britain. The Prime Minister has said that we must separate myth from reality. The Prime Minister has hailed this constitution as a great success for Britain. In fact, only 27 of the 275 amendments submitted by the Government to the European Convention have been included in the final draft. That is one in 10 . . . the Prime Minister knows that he has no mandate whatever for this constitution. There was nothing in his manifesto on the constitution and the British people rejected it at the polls only 10 days ago.' Charles Kennedy welcomed the treaty but was concerned about the referendum, 'Will he (Tony Blair) acknowledge that a referendum campaign that is seen by the public in this country to be spun from No. 10 Downing street would not be won?

HIGHER EDUCATION BILL

Although the Government faced many defeats in the Lords over its legislative programme, opposition to the Higher Education Bill was the most widespread, even among traditional loyal backbench MPs. The Bill, which would introduce variable top-up fees of £3,000 per annum, was announced in the Queen's Speech on 26 November 2003. The fifth day of debate on the Speech (3 December) concentrated on education and the Government was reminded of the struggle it was to face. Education Secretary Charles Clarke defended the Bill saying 'the arguments rest on three pillars. Firstly that universities need more money; secondly that it is reasonable that graduates should make a contribution towards the education from which they benefit; thirdly that that contribution should be levied and repaid in a fair way.' Conservative spokesman Tim Yeo tabled an amendment 'regretting the violation of the Government's 2001 manifesto pledge not to introduce top-up fees.' Liberal Democrat spokesperson Phil Willis said the Government 'did not produce a shred of evidence to show how we will encourage students from less traditional backgrounds to aspire to university by charging the poorest students and by increasing the debt burden to mortgage-style amounts.' But it was from Labour's own backbenches that the most damning criticism came. Eric Illsley (Barnsley Central) said, 'I plead with my Government to think again. The cost of higher education should be spread more broadly. Everyone should pay for it and the cost should not just be dumped on future students.' Martin Caton (Gower) commented, 'I fear that top-up fees will act as a deterrent for people from lower and middle income families when they consider what courses to take and at what university.'

In an attempt to diffuse the situation, on the day the Bill was introduced in the Commons on 8 January 2004, Charles Clarke made a statement on the related matter of student support, promising an independent report on the new proposed system after three years, a vote on any proposal to increase the £3,000 limit, improved fee support, a grant for part-time students, and a promise to write off any student loan debts after 25 years. Tim Yeo thought, 'the Government are destroying the independence of universities, burdening future students with huge debts and wasting more taxpayers' money.' By the time of the second reading in the Commons on 27 January, there had been days of intense campaigning by Ministers (with Tony Blair staking his authority on winning the vote) and a great deal of arm twisting had been exerted by the Government Whips but the backbench opposition remained. Introducing the debate Charles Clarke promised to produce a report next year on the fees' impact on middle income homes and promised extra money. Although few Labour backbench objectors were called to speak in the debate, former Cabinet Minister Nick Brown, one of the unofficial leaders of campaign to scrap the fees, had four objections, 'the increase in the level of debt for graduates; the difficulties with regard to the current proposals for meeting the universities' funding gap; . . . the manifesto pledge and the potential introduction of a marketplace in higher education.' He had, however, been persuaded to switch his allegiance by the concessions offered by the Government. The vote on Second Reading was carried by 316 votes to 311, a majority for the Government reduced to just five (rather than the usual 161). 72 Labour MPs voted against the Government but with Nick Brown having been persuaded to switch his vote at the eleventh hour, former Higher Education Minister Robert Jackson voting with the Government and two others, Ian Taylor (Esher & Walton) and Scottish MP Peter Duncan abstaining, the Government scraped home.

The Government came in for further criticism when the nominations for the Standing Committee to carry out the detailed examination of the bill was announced and seemed not to reflect the close vote in the House – of the 16 Labour MPs on the 27-person committee, only one, George Mudie (Leeds East) voted against the government, with fellow MP Anne Campbell (Cambridge) abstaining. The Bill was not amended in Committee and returned to the Commons on 31 March. Rebel Labour MPs (organised by Ian Gibson) put down an amendment to stop universities introducing top-up fees – wanting to retain the rest of the legislation, ending up-front fees and bringing in a regulator to improve university access for poorer students but Ministers warned that they would withdraw the bill if the rebel amendment was passed. In the event, the amendment was defeated by 316 votes to 288, a majority of 28, with 57 Labour rebels voting against the Government and the Bill was then sent to the Lords.

Second reading in the Lords was on 19 April 2004 and whilst many peers spoke against the measure, by convention a major piece of legislation passed by the Commons is not put to the vote at Second Reading. Also many peers representing universities spoke in favour of the measure, such as Labour peer Baroness Warwick of Undercliffe, Chief Executive of Universities UK, who said 'it is I believe, a good piece of legislation . . . and is essential for the future health and strength of our universities.' On the first day of Report Stage on 8 June the House of Lords inflicted three defeats on the Government – by voting to defer the fees for those on gap years in 2005 (moved by Conservative peer Lord Forsyth of Drumlean, by 143 votes to 132), to limit fees to the first three years of a degree (moved by Conservative peer Lord Skelmersdale, by 156 votes to 139), and that state funding should not be cut (moved by Liberal Democrat peer Lord Phillips of Sudbury, by 98 votes to 88). On the second and final day of Report Stage, peers also inflicted a defeat on the Government when an amendment over the appointment of the Director of Fair Access to Higher Education moved by Conservative Baroness Perry of Southwark, was passed by 142 votes to 122.

The Government accepted that gap-year students would not be penalised and tabled their own amendments to that effect when the Commons considered the Lords' amendments on 23 June 2004. The other defeats were overturned and the Bill went on to get Royal Assent on 1 July.

OTHER ISSUES

Education Secretary Charles Clarke published the Children's Green Paper on 8 September 2003, 'to protect children and young people and to ensure that each child has the opportunity to fulfil their potential.' The Green Paper was published alongside the Government's detailed response to the Victoria Climbie inquiry report.

On 11 September the House of Commons agreed to suspend Labour MP Clive Betts from the House for seven days following a report into the circumstances in which he had employed a Brazilian national to work for him.

On 17 September Trade and Industry Secretary Patricia Hewitt made a statement about the fifth World Trade Organisation Ministerial Conference in Cancun saying, 'We are determined to do all we can to help to deliver a development round in line with the promises that we made at Doha.'

On 18 September the Minister for Constitutional Affairs Christopher Leslie made a statement about reforms of the House of Lords and the repeal of the Office of Lord Chancellor, which led to a major row over the lack of consultation, with Conservative spokesman Bill Cash saying 'anyone would think that the constitution of this country was the personal chattel of the Prime Minister and his cronies.'

On 21 October 2003 the Commons took the second reading of the European Parliament and Local Elections Bill in the Commons, which included plans for all-postal ballots in four regions in the local and European elections in June 2004. Passed by the Commons, the Bill moved to the Lords for Second Reading on 8 January 2004. During the passage of the Bill, peers agreed to all-postal ballots in Yorkshire and Humberside, the East Midlands and North-East England, but refused to include North-West England as the Government wished, with the Conservatives claiming that Labour wanted postal votes in its heartlands for political advantage. The vote was originally on an amendment moved by Conservative Baroness Hanham at Report Stage on 23 February 2004 and passed by 169 votes to 110. A further defeat was inflicted on the Government at that stage when an amendment moved by Liberal Democrat peer Lord Rennard to insist that each postal ballot was accompanied by a declaration of identity was passed a by 157 votes to 110. The Bill had to get through Parliament by the close of business on 1 April, when Parliament was due to rise for the Easter recess or it would have been too late to implement for the June elections. After a series of 'ping-pong' votes in March on this specific issue, MPs again endorsed the four-pilot plan on 29 March by 302 votes to 182, a Government majority of 120, and returned it to the Lords for a sixth time. Leader of the House Peter Hain announced that MPs would be given further time on the last day of sitting before the recess to resolve the issue if peers continued their opposition. He warned the situation was 'unprecedented', insisting, 'we have never been, according to the records we have been able to discover, in the situation where the House of Lords has disagreed this number of times.' The Lords did back down and the measure received Royal Assent on 1 April 2004.

On 22 October 2003 Northern Ireland Secretary Paul Murphy made a statement on political developments in Northern Ireland, with the breakdown of talks between the Ulster Unionists and Sinn Fein over the issue of decommissioning but concluding that elections should be held on 26 November 2003 as planned. 'I cannot hide my disappointment at the turn of events but I hope and believe that agreement can be reached so that the comprehensive acts of completion for which the Prime Minster called last October can be achieved and we can move to a stable and devolved Government for Northern Ireland.'

His deputy Jane Kennedy returned to the House on 27 October to answer a Private Notice Question from his Conservative counterpart, Quentin Davies, on the exact detail of what General de Chastelain had actually given to the two Government's the previous week about the level of the IRA decommissioning exercise but she was adamant that 'the Prime Minister did not deceive the House.' On 28 October Transport Secretary Alistair Darling made a statement about changes to the way that railway maintenance is carried out, following the announcement by Network Rail that it would take maintenance back in-house 'to bear down on cost and ensure that money is properly and effectively spent, as well as to improve performance.' On 29 October Charles Clarke made a statement on funding of schools for the next two years, guaranteeing schools an increase of at least a 4 per cent 'to help restore confidence in the school funding system and to increase stability in school budgets.'

On 3 November 2003 Environment Minister Elliot Morley had to respond to an Urgent Notice Question from Conservative Environment spokesman David Lidington on the role of the Environment Agency in approving the decommissioning of American ships by Able UK of Hartlepool. On 6 November the House of Commons agreed the recommendations of the Committee on Modernisation to continue the experiments on programming of Bills (by 232 votes to 87) and deferred divisions into the next session of Parliament (by 242 votes to 80).

On 10 November an amendment to the Water Bill at remaining stages to prohibit the fluoridation of water supplies moved by Plaid Cymru MP Simon Thomas was defeated by 284 votes to 181, on what was 'for the most part, a free vote.' On 11 November Home Secretary David Blunkett published an explanatory paper on identity cards with the Government beginning the process of building a base for a national compulsory identity card scheme – 'this is about asserting our sense of identity and belonging; about our citizenship; about reinforcing the balance between rights and responsibilities . . . no-one has anything to fear from being correctly identified, but everything to fear from having their identity stolen or misused.' Conservative Home Affairs spokesman David Davies felt 'the Government have failed to advance any convincing arguments as to why these cards should be introduced' and Liberal Democrat Home Affairs spokesperson Mark Oaten reiterated 'we are fundamentally opposed to identity cards.'

On 11 November Labour MP Clive Soley raised a point of order with the Speaker of the House (Michael Martin) suggesting that News International had used the editor of the Sun Newspaper to threaten him whilst carrying out a legitimate inquiry into the group's employment practices. Mr Martin did not believe 'that the correspondence raises any issues on which I can intervene.'

On 19 November David Blunkett, in replying to an Urgent Notice Question from David Davies about a serious breach of security at Buckingham Palace reported in the *Daily Mirror*, announced a thorough review of security by the Security Commission. The Minister for Local Government Nick Raynsford then announced the details of the Local Government Finance Settlement 2004–5, with a 6.5 per cent increase in total support from Government and concluded that 'it is vital that councils meet the expectations of their taxpayers and budget prudently to improve services at a reasonable cost.' For the Conservatives David Curry felt 'the settlement is quite simply bad news . . . the citizen has been stuffed.'

On 20 November Leader of the House Peter Hain moved a Sittings of the House motion, threatening to extend the Parliamentary session by two days if the Lords continued to block Government legislation. The motion was passed by 331 votes to 175 but in the event, the Lords backed down and the 2002–3 session of Parliament was concluded that night.

NEW SESSION

The 2003–4 Session of Parliament was opened by the Queen's Speech on 26 November, later than in previous years, and contained proposals for twenty three Bills for the session (plus two carried over from the previous session) and also mentioned seven Bills that would be introduced in draft.

On 9 December 2003 Tony Blair reported on the outcome of the Commonwealth Heads of Government meeting in Abuja, which had endorsed the decision that Zimbabwe should continue to be excluded from the Councils of the Commonwealth. On 10 December Gordon Brown presented his Pre-Budget Report in which he forecast economic growth of 2.1 per cent in 2003, with targets for 2004–5 at 3 to 3.5 per cent. His new borrowing forecast for 2003 was £37 bn, up £10 bn on the April Budget, with figures for 2004 of £31 bn, up from the £27 bn predicted in April. Debt in the UK this year and in future years would be well below 40 per cent, meeting one of Mr Brown's 'golden rules' and the UK was on course for meeting his 'golden rule' of balancing the current budget and he would even have a surplus of £14 bn over the economic cycle. He described the report as 'economic stability, enterprise and fairness and the strength to make the best long-term decisions for Britain.' Shadow Chancellor Oliver Letwin felt, 'there's very little sign that all this spending is delivering improvements on the scale that people want to see . . . all this report offers them is the prospect of paying now and paying more later.' Liberal Democrat Treasury spokesperson Vincent Cable accused the Chancellor of adding 'a long stream of complex new tax gimmicks to an already over-complicated tax system.'

On 16 December Alistair Darling published a White Paper on the future of air transport designed 'to support economic prosperity throughout the UK; to enable people to make flights at reasonable costs; and to control and mitigate the environmental impacts of aviation.' Conservative Transport spokesman Theresa May felt the announcement, 'is a fudge from an incompetent Government, which will deliver only blight and indefinite uncertainty to millions of people living around airports in the country.' Liberal Democrat Transport spokesperson John Thurso hoped the Government would accept 'that more could and should be done to manage demand as the essential tool for achieving sustainable growth for our aviation industry.' On 16 December Health Secretary John Reid made a statement about a blood transfusion incident involving new variant Creutzfeldt-Jakob Disease (vCJD), the first report anywhere in the world of the possible transmission of vCJD from person to person via blood. After this the Asylum and Immigration (Treatment of Claimants etc.) Bill was given a Second Reading in the Commons. A group of Labour MPs, led by Hilton Dawson (Lancaster and Wyre) tabled a wrecking amendment because 'the bill contains provision that would make children destitute.' The amendment was defeated by 287 votes to 78 – a majority of 209. Second Reading was passed by 412 votes to 72. Unamended in Committee, the Bill returned for Remaining Stages on 1 March, when the rebels again tabled two amendments. The first, again trying to protect the children of asylum seekers, was supported by 28 Labour backbench MPs but was defeated by 444 votes to 82, a Government majority of 362. Labour MP Bob Marshall-Andrews (Medway) felt, 'in all the dreary and depressing history of this administration's assaults on fundamental civil liberties this is, by a streak, the worst.' The second amendment, on appeals against asylum decisions, was supported by 35 Labour MPs, but was also defeated by 303 votes to 97, a Government majority of 206. Third Reading was passed by 304 votes to 65. Speaking at Second Reading in the Lords on 15 March, the Lord Chancellor announced that the Government would drop the plans to deny asylum seekers the right of a court appeal if their claims are rejected. At Report Stage on 7 June, the Government was defeated twice: first when an amendment moved by Lord Goodhart (Liberal Democrat) to double the time allowed for appeal to the new Asylum and Immigration Tribunal from five days to ten was passed by 143 votes to 94 and second when an amendment moved by Lord Kingsland (Conservative) to allow lay people to assess appeals alongside the judge heading the tribunals was passed by 151 votes to 98. The Bill received Royal Assent on 22 July.

On 6 January 2004 Alistair Darling answered a Private Notice Question from Theresa May on the introduction of sky marshals on flights from the UK. David Blunkett then made a statement on the Correctional Services Review as the next phase of improving the effectiveness of the criminal justice system, setting up a new National Offender Management Service. 'Our key objective is reducing offending by better protecting our communities, by punishing offenders more transparently and by equipping them to avoid a return to criminality.'

On 15 January the Speaker altered the business of the House to allow a debate on Privilege to be held, following the publication of a report by the Constitutional Affairs Committee into the case of Ms Judy Weleminsky and CAFCASS, who seemed to have been suspended from her job for giving evidence to the Committee. It was agreed to refer the matter to the Committee on Standards and Privileges.

On 19 January Alistair Darling made a statement on Britain's railways, promising to deliver 'the long-term commitment needed to rebuild the railways.' Theresa May thought this 'heralded the fifth change in the structure of the railways in seven years of this Labour government . . . and will do nothing in the next 18 months to make the lives of passengers any better.'

On 20 January the Solicitor General Harriet Harman replied to a Private Notice Question from Conservative Legal Affairs spokesman Dominic Grieve on the review of criminal cases resulting from the Court of Appeal decision in the case of Angela Cannings (Sudden Infant Death Syndrome). 258 convictions, covering ten years had been identified for review and the 54 where the convicted person was still in prison would be given priority for review.

On 26 January Secretary of State for Constitutional Affairs and Lord Chancellor, Lord Falconer, made a statement in the Upper House on judiciary-related functions of the office of Lord Chancellor. Following a consultation the previous summer, he confirmed that, as in the Queen's Speech the Government would be introducing legislation to establish a new way of appointing judges and creating of a new Supreme Court. 'With the approval of Parliament, the reforms I have set out will guarantee that the independence of the judiciary is protected for future generations. The reforms will clarify the relationship between the executive and judicial arms of the state, improve each arm's accountability, and promote and strengthen partnership, so as to serve the public better.' He was to find, however, that getting the approval of Parliament was not straightforward. The Constitutional Reform Bill (Lords) was introduced in the House of Lords on 24 February but at Second Reading on 8 March Conservative and Crossbench peers voted by 216 to 183 for a reasoned amendment moved by crossbench peer and former law lord Lord Lloyd, to send the Bill to a special Lords Select Committee for extra scrutiny. He said a closer look was needed at the costs of a supreme court, adding: 'It's not too late to save the office of Lord Chancellor – that's what I hope we shall do.' Government Leader of the Lords Baroness Amos said: 'Make no mistake, tonight's events have nothing to do with constitutional principle – and everything to do with political opportunism.' After scrutiny in the Special Committee, the bill resumed its progress through the Lords in July, making the possibility of it reaching the Statute Book in the Parliamentary session remote.

On 28 January Environment Minister Ben Bradshaw responded to an Urgent Notice Question from Liberal Democrat spokesman Andrew George on the outbreak of avian influenza in Thailand stating, 'the risk of the disease being transmitted to the UK poultry flock is low.'

On 9 February 2004 Environment Minister Alun Michael replied to an Urgent Notice Question from local Labour MP Geraldine Smith on the measures the Government intended to introduce to regulate the activities and operations of gangmasters following the tragedy in Morecambe Bay on 6 February 2004, where 19 Chinese cockle pickers died. The Government would be supporting the Private Member's Bill on Gangmasters (Licensing) already due to be introduced by Labour MP Jim Sheridan (West Renfrewshire) later that month.

On 11 February Charles Clarke published the Government's long term strategy for special educational needs, 'reaffirming our commitment to working in partnership to unlock the potential of the many children who may have difficulty learning but whose life chances depend upon high quality education.' A motion to approve the extension of the amnesty period for arms decommissioning in Northern Ireland for another year was passed by 446 votes to 16.

On 12 February Environment Secretary Margaret Beckett made a statement on Common Agricultural Policy (CAP) Reform in England. The reforms (decoupling subsidy paid and level of production) would mean that 'farmers' activities will no longer be dictated by what the subsidy regime requires them to produce – with all the costs and bureaucracy entailed – and frees them to farm in accordance with what the market wants.' Theresa May feared, 'far from minimising bureaucracy, the Government have changed one complexity for another.' Andrew George agreed it was 'the most significant change in agricultural support in a generation' but regretted that the House would not be able to debate the changes.

On 8 March 2004 Home Office Minister Beverley Hughes answered an Urgent Notice Question from David

Davies on the Immigration Service's operation of the European Communities association agreement, following a report from the Sheffield Office that rules were being ignored to lessen the impact of accession on 1 May. 'There was no question of staff being instructed to grant leave to those whom they believed to be fraudulent . . . Ministers were not consulted and I have ordered a full investigation into how this came about.' She saw no reason to resign and had the support of the Home Secretary. Mr Davies felt, 'whether there has been collusion, cover up or simple incompetence, the responsibility for this disgrace rests firmly with her and the Home Secretary.' She continued to refuse to resign, having the full support of the Prime Minster and the Home Secretary but on 1 April she came to the House to make a personal statement following her resignation, 'I am confident that at all times I have acted properly and in the best interests of the people of this country . . . none the less, it has become clear to me that, however unwittingly, I may have given a misleading impression in interviews.' Following this Financial Secretary to the Treasury Ruth Kelly announced the publication of Lord Penrose's report into the events at Equitable Life. As for the Government, 'we cannot underwrite each and every company whose managements and boards make fundamental mistakes and questionable decisions. In dealing with the issues, we have a responsibility to the needs of the taxpayer now and in the future.' For the Conservatives Howard Flight hoped the report 'will be the beginning of a process of that leads to the restoration of a trust (in the financial system) that has been sorely and dangerously diminished in recent years.'

On 9 March 2004 Margaret Beckett made a statement on the Government's approach to the technology of genetic modification, including its use in crops. Ministers had agreed in principle to the growing of a single variety of GM maize in England – 'there is no scientific case for a blanket approval of all uses of GM . . . however, it is less than honest to pretend, especially against a background of climate change, that GM does not have the potential to contribute to some solutions.' Andrew George called it 'a watershed decision' and again regretted the lack of consultation with MPs before the decision was made.

On 16 March John Reid made a further statement about the action the Government were taking following the blood transfusion incident involving vCJD in December. Taking the precautionary approach, all those who have previously received transfusions of whole blood components since January 1980 would be excluded from donating blood but he added the plea that 'people who can do so should continue to donate blood. Blood donation is a safe procedure.'

On 17 March Gordon Brown presented his eighth budget statement. He allocated extra cash for schools and pensioners but announced plans to cut 40,000 civil service jobs (with plans to relocate a further 20,000 civil servants from London to the regions, saving an estimated £2 bn over 15 years). He froze a range of taxes and claimed the UK was enjoying its longest period of economic growth since the Industrial Revolution. Measures included a one-off £100 to help people over 70 cope with council tax rises, while primary schools would each get £55,000 for school improvements and secondary schools would get £180,000. Taxes on cigarettes would go up by 8p a packet, beer by 1p a pint and wine by 4p a bottle. He would introduce a system of tax stamps on the Scotch whisky industry. The annual rise in fuel duty would be delayed for nearly six months. He admitted that the Government would have to borrow £37 bn in the year – £10 bn more than he predicted the previous year – and that borrowing would remain high for some years to come. He opened his speech claiming, 'the purpose of this Budget is to lock in for Great Britain the economic stability that can and will endure.' For the Liberal Democrats, Vincent Cable speaking in place of an ill Charles Kennedy said, 'the Budget simply avoids key decisions that must be made for the long-term future of the economy' and that Mr Brown had ducked tough choices on the economy, such as the Euro, until after the next election. The Labour Chairman of the Treasury Select Committee, John McFall, welcomed the Budget but raised a variety of concerns, notably about credit cards and debt. After four days' debate the Shadow Chancellor Oliver Letwin said, 'the Chancellor's plan is clear. Up to the election he proceeds entirely by stealth. There are, in fact, six extra stealth taxes in the Budget . . . that brings the number to 66. We have before us the clickety-click Chancellor'. The various Budget resolutions were approved in a two and a half hour session of voting, with the Opposition parties forcing separate votes on issues such as whisky tax stamps (approved by 309 votes to 205), petrol duties (approved by 311 votes to 205), VAT (approved by 358 votes to 146), corporation tax rates (approved by 290 votes to 191), construction industry scheme (approved by 341 votes to 127), income tax (property held by spouses) (approved by 334 votes to 130) and chargeable gains (gifts relief) (approved by 287 votes to 163). The Finance Bill, containing the Budget proposals was given a second reading in the Commons on 20 April and completed Committee consideration by 24 June (having had two extra sessions added to the timetable) with third reading on 7 July. The Lords Economic Affairs Sub-Committee on the Finance Bill produced their report on 25 June and the House of Lords considered the Bill in one day on 20 July. The Finance Act received Royal Assent on 22 July.

On 24 March 2004 Harriet Harman had to answer an Urgent Notice Question from Dominic Grieve on the Solicitor General's Department's wrongful disclosure of court papers to the Minister for Children, in a case involving a solicitor who happened to be her sister. Countering Mr Grieve's claim that, 'it is an extremely unfortunate state of affairs when the Law Officer's Department . . . does not know the rules governing contempt of court and the confidentiality of documents,' she maintained that she 'acted on legal advice.'

On 1 April 2004 Northern Ireland Secretary Paul Murphy made a statement on the outcome of the Cory Collusion Inquiry. 'Wrongdoers will be brought to justice. I firmly believe that the only way we can put the past behind us in Northern Ireland is by seeking to establish the truth.' For the Conservatives David Lidington thought 'it would be the greatest travesty of justice if we let the alleged actions of a few denigrate and besmirch the collective reputations of the RUC and the armed forces.' Ulster Unionist Party leader David Trimble found it 'most unfortunate that Justice Cory seems to have failed to understand the circumstances and background of the situation that he was dealing with.'

On 20 April Paul Murphy returned to the Commons to make a statement publishing the report he had received from the Independent Monitoring Commission concerning paramilitary activity in Northern Ireland which had found 'paramilitary activity is at a disturbingly high level on the part of both republican and loyalist groups' which had persuaded him 'that it would be right to block the financial assistance paid to Assembly parties in respect of both Sinn Fein and the Progressive Unionists.'

On 29 April Local Government Minister Nick Raynsford outlined the Government's proposals for dealing with those local authorities that have set excessive budgets for the current year, with the average council tax increase in England being 5.9 per cent. For the Conservatives Philip Hammond felt this was, 'a culmination of a sorry story of fiddled figures and broken promises . . . which will do nothing to address the underlying driver of soaring council taxes – fiddled local funding from Whitehall.' Edward Davey stated, 'the Government should not be capping council tax. They should be scrapping it all together.'

On 24 May 2004 Adam Ingram made a statement on the report of the Surrey police into four deaths at Deepcut Barracks and the actions taken by the Government in response to improve the initial training regime in the army. He had asked the Adult Learning Inspectorate to conduct independent inspection and oversight of the armed forces' training establishments.

On 9 June International Development Secretary Hilary Benn made a statement on the humanitarian emergency in Darfur, on his return from a visit to the region. More than 1 million people had to flee their homes and a further 130,000 refugees had crossed into Chad. He announced a further £15 m worth of aid for the region (bringing the total to £34 m) and called for an urgent deployment of an African Union cease-fire monitoring team, to which the UK had contributed a further £2 m.

On 22 June 2004 David Blunkett made a statement on Sir Michael Bichard's inquiry into the Soham murders, which had uncovered serious failures in recording and managing information. He had accepted Sir Michael's main recommendations and would act on them immediately. Due to the 'grave concerns raised about the senior management of Humberside police', he was also requiring Humberside Police Authority to suspend David Westwood as Chief Constable forthwith. The report was welcomed by all sides but both main Opposition parties expressed concern over the detail of Sir Michael's recommendations for registering those working with children and the implications for charities and voluntary groups.

On 22 June John Reid outlined progress on the NHS Improvement Plan, 'I can confirm one principle at the outset. We will not waver from the founding principle of the NHS. Under this Government, NHS care will continue to be provided according to need and not according to ability to pay. No one will suffer disadvantage through lack of means, and no one will gain unfair advantage in medical treatment because of their financial position. The comprehensiveness, and above all the fairness, of the NHS service are qualities that are already admired throughout the world and this Government will retain them.' Conservative Health spokesman Andrew Lansley called it a reiteration of 'Labour's pigheaded belief that setting a target is the same as getting things done.' Liberal Democrat Health spokesperson Paul Burstow welcomed the extra investment but felt, 'that investment will be wasted if innovation is stifled by ministerial meddling.'

On 6 July 2004 Tony Blair made the second of his six monthly appearances before the Commons Liaison Committee, composed of all the Committee chairmen. On the same day Alistair Darling made a short statement concerning new measures to encourage better use of the roads and the M6 between Birmingham and Manchester. The Highways Agency would be carrying out a feasibility study for trialling high occupancy vehicle or car pool lanes. He was also publishing a consultation on a proposal for a tolled expressway to run parallel with the M6 between Birmingham and Manchester, as an alternative to widening the existing road. Tim Yeo felt this was 'another attempt to con the media and the public into believing that decisions have been taken . . . all it contains is a commitment to start more consultations.'

On 8 July Charles Clarke made a statement on the Government's five-year strategy for education and skills and for children's services. The key points were to give more independence with collective responsibility, to encourage uniforms and house systems, to give all schools specialist or academy status, to allow popular schools to expand and to introduce three-year budgets. 'We have made our decision: for excellence, for opportunity, for choice, but, importantly, for all.' Conservative Education spokesman Tim Collins said, 'imitation is the sincerest form of flattery, in which case Conservatives should feel really flattered today.' Liberal Democrat Education spokesperson Phil Willis agreed, 'it is Tory policy being delivered by a Labour Government and I find that absolutely scandalous.'

On 12 July Gordon Brown delivered his long-awaited third Comprehensive Spending Review announcing that overall departmental spending would rise by £61 bn to £340 bn in 2007–8. Gross cuts of 84,150 civil service posts would be made by 2008 to free up resources for 'front line' investment, with a further 20,000 posts to be cut in Scotland, Wales, Northern Ireland and English local government, which, with other efficiency measures, would save £21.5 bn a year. He set a new target of selling off £30 bn worth of government assets by 2010. The defence budget would rise by £3.7 bn to £33.4 bn by 2007–8 – a real terms increase of 1.4 per cent; the total International Development budget to rise from 3.8bn to 5.3bn by 2007–8 – an average real terms increase of 9.2 per cent. Health spending would rise by 7.1 per cent over the next three years. Spending on local government would rise by 2.7 per cent a year above inflation for the next three years and local councils would get three-year budgets to help them plan ahead. The Transport budget would rise from £10.4 bn this year to £12.8 bn in 2008. Education spending would increase from £63 bn to £77 bn. 'All those investments are possible because I have rejected the proposals of those who would cut spending on important services: more investment, not less, now and into the next Parliament. We are rebuilding our communities; there is such a thing as society. Our prudence is for a purpose.' Oliver Letwin felt the Chancellor's plans were a recipe for 'fat government'. 'While ministers have been preaching about obesity, their departments have been getting fat on taxpayers' money,' he said. Vincent Cable felt somewhat differently, exaclaiming, 'we have the mock battle between the Conservatives' slash and burn versus the Chancellor's somewhat more cautious trim-and-singe approach to public spending. However, conceptually they are the same.' On the following day (13 July) Deputy Prime Minister John Prescott detailed the ODPM elements of the Spending Review Settlement stating that, 'providing affordable homes for those who need them most is a key element of our programme to create sustainable communities. By 2008 the Government will have more than doubled spending on new affordable housing since 1997: it will have reached £2.25 bn. We will provide an extra 10,000 homes a year for social rent.' Both the major Opposition parties wanted to know if the spending review meant that council tax would have to rise by 7 per cent or more in each of the next three years, as indicated in an ODPM release. On 15 July Alistair Darling returned to the House to publish a White Paper with the conclusions of the rail review he had announced earlier in the year. In particular, 'the Government will take charge of setting the overall strategy for the railways. It must be for Ministers, accountable to Parliament and to the electorate, to set the national strategy for the railways. It follows, therefore, that the Strategic Rail Authority will be wound up, and that the majority of its functions, including all its financial obligations, will be transferred to the Secretary of State. The Department for Transport will take responsibility for awarding train operating company franchises. The Department will be restructured to reflect its new responsibilities . . . Network Rail will be responsible for operating the network and track.'

On 19 July David Blunkett published the five-year strategic plan for the Home Office, *Confident Communities in a Secure Britain*. 'We will put the law-abiding citizen first. We will invest in the modernisation of policing and we will develop new forms of community engagement appropriate for the 21st century. We seek a partnership with all those willing to join in this critical task.' For the Conservatives James Paice said, 'The people of this country are fed up with units, targets and initiatives. They want a Government who do not confuse good intent with achievement.' On 20 July Alistair Darling made a statement on the five-year strategy for transport. 'There are no quick fixes for Britain's transport challenges. The long-term solution requires investment and a willingness to face up to difficult decisions. That is why we are making sustained high levels of investment and planning ahead to meet the needs of generations to come.' Tim Yeo feared, 'Given the fact that almost every promise made in the document published four years ago has now been broken and that almost every target has been missed, there can be little confidence that a fresh set of promises in this new document will be kept. Instead of a vision for our transport system, we are offered a muddle. Instead of decisions, we are offered debates.'

On 21 July Environment Secretary Margaret Beckett presented the Government's Rural Strategy as 'an ambitious set of policies for rural communities and the countryside, coupled with radical reforms to the delivery of our policies' with more funding for the Business Link network and the Rural Development Agencies. Tim Yeo felt the proposals lacked 'practical steps, without which her claims that the policy will protect the rural environment will ring very hollow indeed in many parts of the countryside.' Later Geoff Hoon detailed plans for Future Defence Capabilities outlined in a White Paper, setting out 'new plans to ensure that our armed forces can retain maximum effectiveness.' He concluded, 'For the third successive spending review, the Government have been able to announce real growth in the defence budget. Even with these additional funds, it is necessary to secure maximum benefit from efficiencies and make choices to ensure that our force structure matches the requirements of today's security environment. The plans that I have announced today show the Government's determination to make the choices necessary to ensure that the real growth in defence expenditure is targeted at what the armed forces require in the 21st century, rather than what they have inherited from the 20th. That will ensure that the armed forces are equipped and trained to continue to perform with success in the future the tasks that they have undertaken so admirably and successfully in recent years.' Nicholas Soames felt, 'however the Secretary of State tries to present it today, this announcement is essentially about cuts.' Paul Keetch said, 'There is more money but the Government are desperately trying to do more with less. I agree with the MOD that there is a need to look at the defence budget, but Labour seems to be looking in the wrong places.' On 22 July Nick Raynsford made a statement on Regional Assemblies, postponing two of the three referendums planned for 4 November 2004 (in the North-West and in Yorkshire and the Humber) despite the fact that the Commons had only approved the legislation for these referendums the day before. Conservative spokesman Bernard Jenkin said, 'the statement was quite incredible, completely unbelievable and utterly cynical. Only yesterday, he urged the House to support the principle of three referendums, but he has the gall and temerity to return within 24 hours to say that he has changed his mind. Only yesterday, he denied that he would do what I predicted'. Both Houses then rose for the summer recess, to return for a two week period in September before the conference season, returning again after that on 11 October 2004.

PUBLIC ACTS OF PARLIAMENT

This list of selected Public Acts received the Royal Assent after 31 August 2003. The date stated after each Act is the date on which it came into effect.

Fireworks Act 2003 c 22 (various dates, some to be appointed) Makes provision about fireworks and explosives.

National Lottery (Funding of Endowments) Act 2003 c 23 (18 September 2003) Makes provision about the funding of endowments from distributions of money out of the National Lottery Distribution Fund; and for connected purposes.

Human Fertilisation and Embryology (Deceased Fathers) Act 2003 c 24 (various dates) Makes provision about the circumstances in which a man is to be treated in law as the father of a child where the child has resulted from certain fertility treatment undertaken after the man's death; and for connected purposes.

Northern Ireland (Monitoring Commission etc.) Act 2003 c 25 (various dates) Makes provision in connection with the establishment under international law for an independent commission with monitoring functions in relation to Northern Ireland; about exclusion from Ministerial office in Northern Ireland; about reduction of remuneration of members of the Northern Ireland Assembly; and for other matters connected with Northern Ireland.

Local Government Act 2003 c 26 (various dates, some to be appointed) Makes provision in regard to the finance of local and certain other authorities; provides for changing the dates of local elections in 2004; amends the Audit Commission Act 1998; and for connected purposes.

Dealing in Cultural Objects (Offences) Act 2003 c 27 (30 December 2003) Creates an offence of acquiring, disposing of, importing or exporting tainted cultural objects, or agreeing or arranging so to do, and for connected purposes.

Legal Deposit Libraries Act 2003 c 28 (1 February 2004) Makes provision in place of s 15 of the Copyright Act 1911 relating to the deposit of printed and similar publications, including on- and off-line publications; and about the use and preservation of material deposited; and for connected purposes.

Household Waste Recycling Act 2003 c 29 (30 December 2003) Makes further provision regarding the collection, composting and recycling of household waste; and for connected purposes.

Sustainable Energy Act 2003 c 30 (various dates, some to be appointed) Makes provision about the development and promotion of sustainable energy policy; and amends the Utilities Act 2000; and for connected purposes.
Female Genital Mutilation Act 2003 c 31 (3 March 2004) Restates and amends the law relating to female genital mutilation; and for connected purposes.

Crime (International Co-operation) Act 2003 c 32 (various dates, some to be appointed) Makes provision for furthering co-operation with other countries; extends jurisdiction to deal with terrorist acts or threats outside the UK; amends the Forgery and Counterfeiting Act 1981, s 5; and makes corresponding provision for Scotland; and for connected purposes.

Waste and Emissions Trading Act 2003 c 33 (various dates, some to be appointed) Makes provision about waste and about penalties for non-compliance with regulatory schemes.

Arms Control and Disarmament (Inspections) Act 2003 c 34 (day to be appointed) Makes provision relating to the Treaty on Conventional Armed Forces in Europe.

European Union (Accessions) Act 2003 c 35 (13 November 2003) Makes provision concerning the accession of the Czech Republic, Estonia, Cyprus, Latvia, Lithuania, Hungary, Slovakia, Malta, Poland and Slovenia to the EU consequential to the treaty signed at Athens on 16 April 2003.

Fire Services Act 2003 c 36 (13 November 2003) Confers power to set or modify the conditions of service of members of fire brigades and to give directions to fire authorities.

Water Act 2003 c 37 (various dates, some to be appointed) Amends the Water Resources Act 1991 and the Water Industry Act 1991; makes provision with respect to compensation; provides for the establishment and functions of the Water Services Regulation Authority and the Consumer Council for Water; makes provision in connection with land and drainage and flood defence; repeals the Metropolis Act 1852, s 1.

Anti-social Behaviour Act 2003 c 38 (various dates, some to be appointed) Makes provision in connection with anti-social behaviour.

Courts Act 2003 c 39 (various dates, some to be appointed) Makes provision about the courts and their procedure and practice; about judges and magistrates; about fines and the enforcement processes of the courts; and about periodical payments of damages.

Ragwort Control Act 2003 c 40 (20 February 2004) Amends the Weeds Act 1959 by providing a code of practice to be made to prevent the spread of ragwort.

Extradition Act 2003 c 41 (1 January 2004) Makes provision about extradition.

Sexual Offences Act 2003 c 42 (various dates) Makes new provision about sexual offences, their prevention and the protection of children from harm from sexual acts; extends the definition of rape.

Health and Social Care (Community Health and Standards) Act 2003 c 43 (various dates, some to be appointed) Amends the law governing the NHS; makes provision about quality and standards in the provision of health and social care, including establishing the Commissions for Healthcare Audit and Inspection, and for Social Care Inspection; amends the law relating to the recovery of NHS costs from persons making compensation payments.

Criminal Justice Act 2003 c 44 (various dates, some to be appointed) Makes provision about criminal justice (including the powers and duties of the police) and about dealing with offenders; amends the law relating to jury service; amends the Crime and Disorder Act 1998 and the

Police Act 1997; and makes provision for civil proceedings brought by offenders.

Consolidated Fund (No 2) Act c 45 (17 December 2003) Authorises the use of resources for the service of the years ending 31 March, 2004 and 2005 and applies certain sums out of the Consolidated Fund to the same years.

Consolidated Fund Act 2004 c 1 (22 March 2004) Authorises the use of resources for the service of the years ending 31 March, 2003 and 2004 and applies certain sums out of the Consolidated Fund to the service of those years.

European Parliamentary and Local Election (Pilots) Act 2004 c 2 (1 April 2004) Makes provision for piloting in certain regions different methods of voting at the European elections in 2004 and at certain local elections held at the same time; and enables consequential alterations to be made to voting procedures at local elections.

National Insurance Contributions and Statutory Payments Act 2004 c 3 (day or days to be appointed) Makes provision relating to the payment and administration of National Insurance Contributions and the provision of information in connection with the payment of statutory sick pay and statutory maternity pay.

Justice (Northern Ireland) Act 2004 c 4 (day or days to be appointed) Amends the 2002 Act; makes further provision concerning the public prosecution service; imposes a new duty on certain criminal justice organisations in NI in relation to human rights standards; enables barristers in NI to enter into contracts for the provision of their services.

Planning and Compulsory Purchase Act 2004 c 5 (various dates, some to be appointed) Makes provision relating to spatial development and town and country planning, and the compulsory acquisition of land.

Child Trust Funds Act 2004 c 6 (various dates, some to be appointed) Makes provision about child trust funds; and for connected purposes.

Gender Recognition Act 2004 c 7 (various dates, some to be appointed) Makes provision for, and in connection with, change of gender.

Higher Education Act 2004 c 8 (various dates, some to be appointed) Makes provision about research in the arts and humanities and about complaints by students against institutions providing higher education; makes provision about fees payable by students in higher education; provides for the appointment of a Director of Fair Access to Higher Education; makes provision about grants and loans to students in higher or further education; and for connected purposes.

Appropriation Act 2004 c 9 (8 July 2004) Authorises the use of resources for the service for the year ending 31 March 2005 and applies certain sums out of the Consolidated Fund to the service of the year ending 31 March 2005; appropriates the supply authorised in this Session of Parliament; and repeals certain Consolidated Fund and Appropriation Acts.

Age-Related Payments Act 2004 c 10 (8 July 2004) Makes provision for payments by the Secretary of State to persons over the age of 70; and enables provision to be made for payments by the Secretary of State to persons over the age of 60.

Gangmasters (Licensing) Act 2004 c 11 (day or days to be appointed) Makes provision for the licensing of activities involving the supply or use of workers in connection with agricultural work, the gathering of wild creatures and wild plants, the harvesting of fish from fish farms, and certain processing and packaging; and for connected purposes.

Finance Act 2004 c 12 (22 July 2004) Grants certain duties, alters others, and amends the law relating to the National Debt and Public Revenue; and makes further provision in connection with finance. For example, it imposes new charges on benefits receivable under certain pension schemes and brings in further provisions in connection with the construction industry and subcontractors' registration.

Scottish Parliament (Constituencies) Act 2004 c 13 (22 July 2004) Replaces schedule 1 of the Scotland Act 1998 making new provision in relation to the constituencies for the Scottish Parliament.

Carers (Equal Opportunities) Act 2004 c 15 (day or days to be appointed) Places duties on local authorities and health bodies in respect of carers; and for connected purposes.

Traffic Management Act 2004 c 18 (day or days to be appointed) Makes provision for the designation of traffic officers and their duties; makes provision in relation to the management of road networks; makes new provision for regulating the carrying out of works and other activities in the street; amends Part 3 of the New Roads and Street Works Act 1991 and Parts 9 and 14 of the Highways Act 1980; makes new provision in relation to the civil enforcement of traffic contraventions; amends section 55 of the Road Traffic Regulation Act 1984; and for connected purposes.

Asylum and Immigration (Treatment of Claimants, etc.) Act 2004 c 19 (various dates, some to be appointed) Makes provision about asylum and immigration.

Energy Act 2004 c 20 (day or days to be appointed) Makes provision for the decommissioning and cleaning up of installations and sites used for, or contaminated by, nuclear activities; makes provision relating to the civil nuclear industry; makes provision about radioactive waste; makes provision for the development, regulation and encouragement of the use of renewable energy sources; makes further provision in connection with the regulation of the gas and electricity industries; makes provision for the imposition of charges in connection with the carrying out of the Secretary of State's functions relating to energy matters.

Fire and Rescue Services Act 2004 c 21 (various dates, some to be appointed) Makes provision about fire and rescue authorities and their functions; makes provision about employment by, and powers of employees of, fire and rescue authorities; makes provision about education and training and pension schemes; makes provision about the supply of water; makes provision about false alarms of fire; provides for the funding of advisory bodies; and for connected purposes.

WHITE PAPERS, REPORTS ETC

This section provides an outline of a selection of White Papers and Reports that have been published in the last year. For further information visit www.official-documents.co.uk or www.parliament.uk. Alternatively, visit the websites of individual government departments – details of these can be found in the Government Departments section.

Identity Cards, The Next Steps was presented to Parliament in November 2003 by the Secretary of State for the Home Department. This paper details the process of introducing a national identity card scheme in order to ensure more reliable means of authenticating a person's identity. The paper proposes a two-stage process: the establishment of a National Identity Register and introduction of biometric passports and driving licences at the first stage; and the introduction of a compulsory identity card scheme at the second stage. The paper points out that the move towards a compulsory identity card scheme would require full debate and a vote in both Houses of Parliament.

The *Draft Disability Discrimination Bill* was presented to Parliament in December 2003 by the Secretary of State for Work and Pensions and sets out major reforms of the Disability Discrimination Act 1995 (DDA). It includes new measures that would enhance disabled people's civil rights and bring into the scope of the DDA areas in which disabled people currently have no, or limited, rights. The draft Bill proposes to strengthen existing DDA rights in such areas as the definition of disability, transport services, renting premises and discriminatory job advertisements. The Bill also introduces a new duty on public bodies to promote equality of opportunity for disabled people.

Reforming the Coroner and Death Certification Service: A Position Paper was presented to Parliament by the Secretary of State for the Home Department in March 2004. This paper constitutes the Government's response to the Fundamental Review of Death Certification and Coroner Services and the Shipman Inquiry, and contains outline proposals for reform. The paper details how the existing system could be reorganised to deliver greater benefits to both bereaved families and public health policy, to reduce avoidable deaths and to detect or prevent medical malpractice and crime. The paper also addresses how reorganisation of the existing system would be judicially independent, have direct links to public health initiatives, incorporate a greater degree of medical expertise in scrutiny, training and accountability, and have an advisory Coronial Council.

Energy Efficiency: The Government's Plan for Action was presented to Parliament in April 2004 by the Secretary of State for the Department of Environment, Food and Rural Affairs. This paper details the Government's plans to make over 12 million tonnes of carbon savings through energy efficiency by 2010. The plan involves: the launch of the *EU Emissions Trading Scheme* in 2005; the introduction of tax allowances which ensure that energy intensive industries have strong incentives to reduce their emissions; working closely with local authorities, regional assemblies and regional development agencies to support the development of innovative approaches to energy efficiency; and the development of cost-effective products and technologies.

The *Draft Charities Bill* was presented to Parliament by the Secretary of State for the Home Department on 27 May 2004. This draft Bill aims to implement several changes to the regulation of charities and other not-for-profit organisations. *Inter alia*, the Bill aims to clarify the definition of a charity, address the regulation of charities and examine the funding of charities and their fundraising powers. The Bill also establishes the Charity Commission as the regulatory body for charities, gives recommendations for the creation of a tribunal to hear appeals against decisions made by the Charity Commission, and makes provision for the registration of charities.

Report on Child Poverty: Reply by the Government to the Second Report of the Work and Pensions Select Committee, Session 2003–4 was presented to Parliament by the Secretary of State for Work and Pensions in June 2004 in response to the Child Poverty Report published on 8 April 2004 by the Work and Pensions Select Committee. The paper outlines the key elements of the Government's strategy to tackle child poverty which includes: enabling poorer families to increase their income through participation in the labour market, education and training; supplementing the incomes of low income families; introducing new tax credits; and ensuring that schools equip children from poor families with skills that enable them to benefit from continued learning.

The *Draft Animal Welfare Bill* was presented to Parliament by the Secretary of State for Environment, Food and Rural Affairs and the Chief Secretary to the Treasury in July 2004. This Bill seeks to consolidate and update existing legislation relating to the welfare of farmed, domestic and captive animals, and aims to establish an Animal Welfare Bill. This Bill would include a radical overhaul of the Protection of Animals Act 1911 and bring about a higher number of prosecutions than under existing legislation. It also looks at adapting animal welfare law so that it is more pro-active, and suffering is prevented before it occurs. Other proposals include greater licensing controls and regulation of circuses, pet fairs and animal sanctuaries, and raising the minimum age at which an unaccompanied child can buy a pet from 12 to 16 years.

SCIENCE AND DISCOVERY

PLUTO DEBATE REOPENED

In March 2004, a team of astronomers from Caltech, led by Mike Brown, announced its November 2003 discovery of the most distant Solar System body known to date. Officially designated 2003VB12, the object has been given the provisional name Sedna, after the Inuit goddess of the sea.

Sedna was found with the 1.2m Oschin Schmidt telescope at Palomar Observatory during a continuing search for Kuiper Belt objects, which populate a region from the orbit of Neptune at 30 astronomical units (AU) to 50 AU from the Sun. 1 AU is equivalent to the mean Sun-Earth distance of nearly 150,000,000 km. At discovery, Sedna was located 90 AU away – clearly too distant to be a Kuiper Belt member.

Calculations show the new object to have a highly-elliptical orbit with perihelion (closest approach to the Sun) at a distance of 76 AU, and aphelion (its most distant) at a distance of approximately 860 AU. Sedna takes 10,200 years to complete its orbit, and will reach perihelion in 2075. Its unusual orbit suggests that Sedna may be a body derived from the Oort Cloud (a remote halo of cometary bodies surrounding the Sun to a distance perhaps half-way to the nearest star) early in the Solar System's history.

Observations indicate a maximum size of 1,800 km for Sedna, rivalling that of Pluto (2,390 km) and reopening the debate as to whether the latter truly merits its status as a planet. Many astronomers contend that Pluto is simply the largest-known of a whole population of icy bodies at the edge of the Solar System, and discoveries of further objects like Sedna, or the 1,200 km diameter Quaoar found in 2002, may further strengthen the case for Pluto's 'downgrading'.

CLOSE FLY-BY RECORD FALLS AGAIN

In the same week that the discovery of the Solar System's most distant body was announced, the Lincoln Near Earth Asteroid Research (LINEAR) facility in New Mexico discovered a fast-moving object which, on 18 March 2004, became the closest-known asteroid to fly by Earth. At a distance of 43,000 km the object, designated 2004FH, was approximately one-ninth of the Moon's distance from Earth at closest approach. The asteroid, which has a diameter of 30 metres, was not considered hazardous.

RAT GENOME SEQUENCED

The Norwegian brown rat *Rattus norvegicus* has been used in pharmacological studies, and the investigation of diseases such as diabetes and arthritis, for about a century. Its physiological similarity to humans makes it better suited than the mouse to such studies. An international Rat Genome Sequencing Consortium announced the completion of its work in the 1 April 2004 issue of *Nature,* and the results of this effort are expected to allow more effective use of the rat – which becomes the third mammal after human and mouse to have its genome fully sequenced – as an experimental model in the future.

The genome – the entire genetic complement – of a rat totals an estimated 2.75 billion basepairs (2.75 Gb) of DNA, compared with 2.9 Gb for a human and 2.6 Gb for a mouse. Of the roughly 30,000 genes encoded by the rat's genome, about 90 per cent are shared with humans. The 10 per cent of genes that are specific to the rat appear to be involved in immunological or reproductive function, or with, for example, olfaction. In common with the mouse, the rat has more detoxifying cytochrome P450 genes than the human – a finding which may have implications for pharmacological toxicity testing.

Comparative analysis shows the genomes of both the mouse and the rat to be more 'dynamic' than that of *Homo sapiens.* The rodents evolve about three times faster than humans and it is unclear whether this is a function of the rodents' shorter generation time, or whether there is an intrinsically higher mutation rate in mice and rats.

SEQUENCING THE HONEY BEE

Commercially important both for its honey and as a pollinator of many crop plants, the honey bee *Apis mollifera* has had its entire genome, about 300 million basepairs of DNA, sequenced by a team led by Richard Gibbs at Baylor College of Medicine in Houston, Texas. The project was completed in less than a year, and is expected to benefit many areas, not least of all agriculture. Comparison with previously sequenced insect genomes – the fruit fly and the mosquito – may prove particularly informative, and researchers also plan to compare the honey bee genetically with 'Africanised' wild bees which have invaded the southern United States. Analysis of the bee genome, published in draft in January 2004, suggests a complement of about 9,000 genes.

VOYAGER 1 NEARS INTERSTELLAR SPACE

Launched in 1977, the *Voyager 1* and *Voyager 2* spacecraft made ground-breaking discoveries as they passed the giant planets Jupiter and Saturn a few years later: *Voyager 2*'s trajectory was tailored to allow close fly-by of Uranus in 1986 and Neptune in 1989. Now heading out of the Solar System into interstellar space, the voyagers continue to provide valuable insights into the nature of the outermost parts of the heliosphere, the volume of space in which the Sun's magnetic field is a dominant influence. Data published in November 2003 offers strong suggestions that *Voyager 1* – by some way the more distant of the two spacecraft – is approaching the heliosphere's boundary (the heliopause), where the Sun's domain gives way to truly interstellar space.

Streaming radially outwards from the Sun is a supersonic solar wind which breezes past Earth at about 400 km/s. At a considerable distance from the Sun, theory predicts, the solar wind should be abruptly decelerated by interaction with the interstellar medium. A consequence of this deceleration is a shockwave, known as the termination shock, characterised by processes which accelerate energetic particles and ionise interstellar gas to produce so-called anomalous cosmic rays.

A team of scientists led by Stamatios Krimigis (Johns Hopkins University) believes measurements from *Voyager 1* indicate that the spacecraft encountered the termination shock in early August 2002, and experienced it for a further 200 days. Subsequently – perhaps in response to enhanced solar activity – the termination shock moved outwards from *Voyager 1*'s position (by then 87 AU from the Sun), and the spacecraft was again in the supersonic solar wind. It is likely that the termination shock will be further encountered as a result of varying solar activity.

Voyager 1 still has some way to go to reach the heliopause, thought to lie about 150 AU from the Sun. At its 3–4 AU per year velocity, the spacecraft will not reach that distance until about 2020, by which time the fuel in its thermonuclear generators will have run out.

Not all scientists accept that *Voyager 1* has reached the termination shock. An alternative interpretation from Frank McDonald (University of Maryland) and co-workers proposes that the observed increase in energetic particles is a precursor to an encounter which is still some years away.

HUGE SUNSPOTS AND GEOMAGNETIC STORMS

Closer to home, in October and November 2003, Earth was buffeted by strong solar activity, associated with the development of three remarkably large sunspot groups. The current sunspot cycle (number 23 in the modern series) reached its peak in 2000–1, and is on the decline towards minimum expected in 2006–7. However, the largest active regions (ARs) of the cycle erupted on the solar surface in October and AR 484, AR 486 and AR 488 each grew sufficiently vast to be visible with the suitably protected naked eye. At its greatest extent, on 30 October, AR 486 covered 0.26 per cent of the Sun's visible hemisphere, making it the largest sunspot group for 13 years.

Release of magnetic energy in the inner solar atmosphere above active regions produces solar flares and coronal mass ejections (CMEs) which hurl energetic particles into interplanetary space. Solar flares are detectable principally in the ultraviolet and x-ray parts of the spectrum, and are categorised on an ascending scale of intensity – A, B, C, M and X. M- and X-class flares have the potential to seriously affect the near-Earth space environment triggering geomagnetic storms. Energetic protons ejected during flares cause solar radiation storms that can damage spacecraft and are hazardous to space-walking astronauts. Over the two weeks during which these active regions were turned towards Earth, the orbital environment was particularly hostile. A total of 44 M-class, and 11 X-class flares was recorded between 19 October and 4 November, the total number of X-class events being greater than for the preceding 12 months. Most severe of these was a flare from AR 486 on 4 November as it rotated out of view over the Sun's western limb.

Earth-directed CMEs in late October triggered massive geomagnetic storms, with accompanying enhanced auroral activity visible at low latitudes on 29-30 and 30-31 October (these have become known as the 'halloween aurorae'). The giant spots returned, still active, in the third week of November, and a CME from AR 484 once again set off a major geomagnetic storm. Sky watchers as far south as Athens were treated, for the second time in four weeks, to displays of the northern lights (which typically occur once every decade at Mediterranean latitudes).

The giant sunspots gradually decayed as they crossed the visible solar hemisphere a second time, and the decline of cycle 23 towards minimum has resumed its steady progress (although July 2004 brought a further, brief revival in sunspot numbers and solar flare activity). Such late-cycle activity outbursts are not unusual, and the intensity of the late 2003 events is a reminder of how our Sun can occasionally disrupt the near-Earth space environment. International efforts to monitor and more accurately forecast 'space weather' continue, and scientists will study data collected during these storms for a long time to come.

FIRST FLIGHT DATE CONTESTED

The old red sandstone at Rhynie, Aberdeenshire in north-east Scotland has been a rich source of early invertebrate fossil finds, including an ancestral springtail *(Rhyniella praecursor)*, dating back to some 396 to 407 million years ago. Re-examination of another Rhynie fossil, stored since the 1920s at London's Natural History Museum, has provided new insight to the evolution of insects. *Rhyniognatha hirsti* was studied by Michael Engel (University of Kansas) and David Grimaldi (American Museum of Natural History, New York) using a compound microscope and their findings were reported in *Nature* in February 2004.

Although only parts of the insect's head have been preserved, the report's authors were able to conclude that the fossil represented the mandibles (mouth parts) of the earliest known insect. Furthermore, such dicondylic mandibles (with two points of articulation and movement limited to a single plane) are found only among flying insects. The short, triangular morphology of these mandibles is also typical of flying insects. Therefore, these findings place the development of insect flight some 80 million years earlier than had previously been estimated.

The previous oldest-known definite fossil insect, found in the US state of New York, dates back to 370 million years ago and was wingless.

Meanwhile, in Cowie Harbour near Stonehaven (also in Aberdeenshire), a centimetre-sized fossil millipede dating back 420 million years is believed to be the oldest-known air-breathing animal, predating the previous record-holder, a spider-like fossil, by 20 million years. The millipede has been given the name *Pseudodesmus*, and was reported in January 2004.

COMET ENCOUNTER

NASA's *Stardust* spacecraft, launched in 1999, made its long-awaited close fly-by of Comet 81P/Wild 2 on 2 January 2004. Passing within 236 km of the comet's 5 km diameter nucleus, *Stardust* became the third probe to undertake a close examination of such a body, following *Giotto* at 1P/Halley and *Deep Space 1* at 19P/Borrelly in 2001.

Comet Wild 2 is interesting because it has only recently become locked into its current short-period orbit. Passage close to Jupiter in 1974 shortened Wild 2's orbital period from 40 to 6 years, and scientists see this as a good opportunity to study a relatively pristine, unmodified comet nucleus starting to become active in terms of gas and dust emission. By contrast, the Halley and Borrelly nuclei have changed considerably due to repeated close passage to the Sun.

Stardust's cameras revealed a cratered, roughly spherical nucleus, from which jets of gas emerged. Steep cliffs and other topographic features could also be seen. In common with the previously studied nuclei, that of Comet Wild 2 has a very dark surface. The spacecraft recorded swarms of dust particles consistent with the break up of small chunks close to the nucleus, and distinct narrow streams of ejected dust. Spectroscopic analysis of the dust suggested it to be rich in organic molecules but not amino acids.

An important target of the mission was to capture samples of the comet's dust using an aerogel trap. It is estimated that this experiment succeeded in collecting over 3,000 particles in the size range greater than 15 microns. These will be brought to Earth for analysis, with the aerogel package being scheduled for retrieval over the Utah desert in January 2006.

Meanwhile, the European Space Agency's *Rosetta* mission was finally launched on 2 March 2004, after a year's delay. *Rosetta* will rendezvous with Comet 67P/Churyumov-Gerasimenko in 2014, and will monitor its changing activity as it moves towards the Sun during the following year. Ground-based observers had a couple of interesting comets to study in May 2004. Comet 2002 T7 LINEAR proved slightly less bright than expected, but Comet 2001 Q4 NEAT was, briefly, a faint naked eye object in the western evening sky.

HUBBLE'S DEEPEST VIEW

Between 24 September 2003 and 16 January 2004, instruments on the Hubble Space Telescope (HST) stared at a small patch of sky in the constellation Fornax to obtain the deepest ever view of the Universe. Penetrating even farther back than the Hubble Deep Fields of 1995 and 1998, the new set of images was obtained with the Advanced Camera for Surveys (ACS) and the Near Infrared Camera and Multi Object Spectrometer (NICMOS). Released on 9 March 2004, the Hubble Ultra Deep Field provides a view of the very early Universe, soon after the first stars began to shine following the 'Big Bang' moment of creation 13.7 billion years ago.

The ACS (optical) image shows around 10,000 galaxies to a 'look back time' of 800 million years after the Big Bang. The oldest galaxies in the infrared NICMOS image date back to 400 million years after the Big Bang. Preliminary analysis shows galaxies in the early Universe to be more chaotic than their relatively 'modern' counterparts, with mergers between spiral galaxies apparently common. Such mergers led to the formation of giant elliptical galaxies, and these findings favour a 'bottom up' model of galaxy evolution. Formation of the structures we see in the modern Universe came about from merging of smaller units, rather than a 'top down' fragmentation of larger ones.

Launched in 1990 with a projected 20-year operational lifetime, the HST faces a rather uncertain future. Following the accident involving *Columbia* in February 2003, the space shuttle servicing mission scheduled for 2006 has been cancelled, while NASA's future plans, announced by President George Bush in January 2004, call for a shift of emphasis towards lunar exploration in preparation for an eventual manned mission to Mars. To enable accuracy, the HST depends on having at least three of its six gyroscopes functioning or else the orbiting telescope's usefulness will be greatly impaired. Four gyroscopes are currently functioning but the HST's on-board batteries will soon require replacement.

Astronomers are lobbying hard for the reinstatement of the servicing mission, and alternatives, possibly involving robotic spacecraft to perform the necessary upgrades, are being actively investigated. Hubble is rated as having a 50 per cent chance of remaining operational until 2007, however, its eventual successor, the James Webb Space Telescope, is not scheduled for launch until at least 2011.

The Spitzer Telescope, a new orbital infrared facility, was successfully launched in August 2003. This has an 85 cm mirror and cryogenically-cooled detectors which allow the investigation of star-forming regions. Its detectors were used to measure thermal radiation from the newly-discovered Sedna in order to estimate its size in November 2003. To minimise thermal interference from the planet, the Spitzer Telescope has a unique Earth-trailing heliocentric orbit, and it is expected to operate for up to five years.

CASSINI REACHES SATURN

After a seven-year voyage, the *Cassini* spacecraft was finally launched into orbit around Saturn on 1 July 2004. Weighing 5,724 kg, and with dimensions of 6.7 × 4 m, *Cassini* is the largest planetary probe ever launched and is scheduled to conduct a four-year survey of the Saturn system, during which it will complete 76 orbits around the ringed planet and have 52 close encounters with seven of its 31 known satellites. Orbit was achieved by passage through a gap in the rings and an engine burn 20,000 km above Saturn's cloud-tops to slow *Cassini* down.

Early results from the mission have been spectacular. On its route to Saturn on 11 June 2004, *Cassini* passed within 2,068 km of Phoebe, revealing unprecedented detail on this outer satellite. The 220 km diameter moon was revealed to have a heavily cratered icy surface, covered to a depth of several hundred metres with dark material. Phoebe may be a gravitationally-captured comet nucleus.

Views of Saturn's rings have revealed density waves, and while most of the material in them appears to be icy in nature, the major gap (the Cassini Division – named, like the spacecraft, after the Italian-French astronomer who first observed it in 1675) is populated by 'dirt', perhaps similar to the material covering Phoebe.

Cassini will release the *Huygens* probe in late December for descent to Saturn's largest satellite, Titan, on 14 January 2005. Infrared imaging equipment on board *Cassini* has been able to penetrate Titan's smog to reveal some surface features, including probable craters, icy material and deposits of hydrocarbons.

The *Cassini* mission is a joint venture between NASA, ESA and the Italian Space Agency.

FAREWELL TO *GALILEO*

While *Cassini*'s main mission got underway, NASA's venerable *Galileo* spacecraft, in orbit around Jupiter since 1995, came to the end of its exploration. The probe was directed to crash into the giant planet's cloud-tops on 21 September 2003, avoiding the risk of contaminating Europa (one of Jupiter's large moons, which some scientists believe could have conditions suitable for the development of life) with terrestrial micro-organisms.

Galileo was enormously successful, despite problems with fully unfurling its main communications antenna. Over the course of its eight-year primary mission, it sent a probe into Jupiter's atmosphere, obtained high-resolution images of the planet's cloud features and main satellites, and measured the high-energy radiation environment around it. *Galileo* and *Cassini* operated in tandem during the 'Millennium Mission' as the latter passed close to Jupiter late in 2000 on its way to Saturn. En route to Jupiter, *Galileo* also became the first spacecraft to make a close fly-by of an asteroid, Gaspra, in 1989.

TUNGSTEN ISOTOPE STUDIES

Soon after its formation, Earth became differentiated in its internal structure, to have a dense, deep iron-nickel rich core, surrounded by the convective mantle, and thin outer continental crust. The extent to which material is exchanged between the core and the base of the mantle is a matter of continuing geophysical debate. Some studies, based on the relative abundance of osmium isotopes, show that plumes of magma originate from deep within the Earth, giving rise to volcanic hotspots such as the Hawaiian islands. Examination of lava emerging at such sites should reveal whether it contains any components indicative of origin from the core.

A study of Hawaiian basalts and material from South Africa by Anders Scherster and co-workers at the University of Bristol has focused on tungsten (W) isotope ratios. The ^{182}W isotope results from radioactive decay of ^{182}Hf (hafnium) with a geologically short half-life of 9 million years. As a siderophile ('iron-loving') element, tungsten should be found preferentially in Earth's core. The rapid process of differentiation within early Earth, with the core forming in the first 30 million years, however, resulted in significant amounts of radioactive ^{182}Hf remaining in the mantle. The subsequent decay of this has meant that the mantle is enriched in ^{182}W relative to the chondritic (stony) meteorites that provide examples of the primitive material from which the planet was formed 4.6 billion years ago.

Convective mixing in the mantle has led to a remarkably homogeneous distribution of ^{182}W, from which it can be predicted that where substantial mixing of mantle and core material might occur (as at a deep-seated magma plume, for example), this isotope should actually be relatively depleted. Studies of Hawaiian basalt show this not to be the case. Instead, the conclusion has to be that the core is isolated from the mantle, and there is no detectable mixing of material between the two.

These conclusions fit with data published in early 2003 that the observed osmium isotope ratios are consistent with plume material under the Azores containing recycled ancient mantle.

LOST ASTEROID RECOVERED

Discovered by Karl Reinmuth at Heidelberg on 28 October 1937, the asteroid *Hermes* caused a considerable stir when it passed only 800,000 km (slightly more than twice the Moon's distance) from Earth two days later. The first known 'Earth-crosser', *Hermes* was followed for only five nights before being lost.

Hermes remained lost until 15 October 2003 when it was detected by Brian Skiff of the Lowell Observatory Near Earth Object Search (LONEOS) programme. Skiff's detection was made with a 60 cm aperture Schmidt telescope at Anderson Mesa, near Flagstaff, Arizona. His measurements were relayed to the Minor Planet Center at Cambridge, Massachusetts, where Timothy B. Spahr was able to identify the suspect as the long-lost *Hermes*.

Back-tracking *Hermes*' movements is rendered difficult by its chaotic orbit, affected by frequent close passage to both Venus and Earth. Forward projections indicate that *Hermes* will not be a hazardous near-Earth asteroid in at least the next hundred years. At its closest pass on 4 November 2003, *Hermes* was a comfortable 7.2 million km away.

Radar observations with the 30.5 m dish at Arecibo in Puerto Rico have revealed *Hermes* to be a binary object, with two 400-metre bodies orbiting a common centre of gravity.

FOSSIL SKULLS CHALLENGE

It has long been assumed that North America's first human colonists came from north Asia, via the land bridge which connected Russia and Alaska during the ice age about 12,000 years ago. While fossil remains dating back to the end of the ice age 10,000 years ago are scarce, measurements of cranial and facial features of human skulls from this time show sufficient similarity (broad and short shape) to those of modern north Asians to confirm the link.

The idea of a single colonisation from north Asia has been challenged by results from a study by Rolando Gonzalez-Jose (University of Barcelona) and colleagues, who examined cranio-facial features of 33 skulls found at a site on the tip of the Baja Peninsula in Mexico. Dating back 2,500 years, these have a comparatively long and narrow shape, more akin to native inhabitants of south Asia and the Pacific rim. The Baja skulls are thought to be the remains of a population which became geographically isolated from other colonising groups as a result of post-ice age climatic change.

These findings suggest that the view of a single colonising migration from north Asia may be over-simplistic, and perhaps there were several independent human arrivals in prehistoric North America. The situation is further complicated by fossil discoveries in South America dating back 12,500 years which may push back the arrival date of humans on continental America by several thousand years.

A 'NEW' NEBULA IN ORION

The region of sky in the direction of the constellation Orion contains many nebulae in which new stars are forming. Best-known of these is the bright Orion Nebula M42, a little to the south of the Hunter's belt, and the brightest part of a huge complex of gas and dust in the next spiral arm out from our own in the home Milky Way Galaxy.

To the north-east of Orion's belt lies a further nebula, illuminated by reflected light from a couple of stars cocooned within its depths and known as M78. In the course of testing a newly-acquired small telescope during January 2004, Jay McNeil – an amateur astronomer based in Kentucky, USA – took some images of M78 and its environs with a CCD camera. On examining the results, McNeil was surprised to find a small patch of nebulosity, absent from reference images of this part of the sky obtained during the Palomar Observatory Sky Survey. Later searches through archival images did, however, turn up images of the 'new' object, which quickly become known as 'McNeil's Nebula'.

It is now understood that the object is a variable nebula, detected at a bright phase in early 2004 (though not recorded on images taken three months earlier). Other examples of such nebulae, changing in brightness and apparent shape in response to variable light output from young stars which illuminate them and/or as a result of shadowing by moving dust and gas clouds within them, are known in this general area of sky – among them Hubble's Variable Nebula in Monoceros, and Hind's Variable Nebula in Taurus.

McNeil's Nebula is illuminated by a previously unseen star, identified as the infrared source IRAS 05436-0007 by the Infrared Astronomical Satellite in 1983. The star has an estimated age of 100,000 years, and continued study of this object should improve astronomers' understanding of the behaviour of young stars settling in to their main nuclear-burning lifespan.

740,000 YEARS OF CLIMATE HISTORY

Snow falling on the Antarctic each year gradually becomes compacted into ice and the continental bedrock in some places has been covered by a gradually-thickening ice sheet for up to a billion years. Air bubbles trapped within the compacted ice provide a record of past atmospheric gas composition, while dust deposits are an indicator of temperature and aridity.

By drilling deep into the ice and analysing the core samples obtained, scientists can obtain a picture of past climatic conditions. Ice cores are paralleled by cores obtained from deep ocean-floor sediments, where deposition of foraminifera shells has preserved a record of temperature conditions, indicated by oxygen-isotope ratios. Samples from ice have the advantage of providing additional information on the atmospheric content of greenhouse gases such as carbon dioxide and methane.

June 2004 saw the publication of results from the European Project for Ice Coring in Antarctica (EPICA), a ten-country collaboration in which researchers from the British Antarctic Survey plays a major part. EPICA scientists are seeking to obtain two deep cores in East Antarctica, from Dronning Maud Land and Dome C. The Dome C drilling has penetrated to a depth of 3,190 m below the surface and the 2004 report discussed analysis of the top 3,139 m of this material which dates back 740,000 years. This interval embraces eight glacial cycles (ice ages), including four already studied in data from the Vostok ice core (dating back 400,000 years) obtained at a site 560 km away – there is excellent correspondence between the two.

The Dome C results show a rough 100,000 year periodicity in the last four glacial cycles, thought to relate to changes in Earth's elliptical orbit around the Sun. Periods of glaciation are separated by warmer interglacials. Dome C data shows that before about 500,000 years ago, interglacials were longer-lasting but less warm. Interglacials in the last 400,000 years have been short and typically lasted 6,000 years.

The current interglacial began about 12,000 years ago. Comparison with the most similar interglacial in the ice core record, dating back 400,000 years, shows that levels of greenhouse gases are significantly higher. The EPICA scientists conclude that interglacial conditions should be stable for a very long period but disturbance of the situation by industrial-age CO_2 emissions makes a stable long-term climate unlikely.

The Dome C EPICA drilling, for which field work began in 1996, is now thought to be within about 120 m of the Antarctic bedrock. Extracting the last portion - potentially extending the record back 960,000 years - will be technically challenging, as the ice at this depth is under enormous pressure and close to its melting temperature.

MODERN HUMANS IDENTIFIED?

A team of researchers from the University of Pennsylvania in Philadelphia has published an intriguing analysis of the human MYH16 gene, offering possible insight into a key moment in our evolutionary history. MYH16 encodes the heavy chain of myosin, an essential protein in skeletal muscle – specifically, the gene is expressed in jaw muscle. Monkeys and apes, with well-developed jaws for crunching tough foodstuffs, express the gene strongly, but in humans a mutation has led to production of a truncated, non-functional form of the protein.

Loss of MYH16 function, accompanied by a change of diet towards, for example, soft meat may have coincided with the development of bigger brains in ancestral species of *Homo*. Powerful jaw muscles demand, anatomically, a strong point of attachment to the skull, provided in monkeys and apes by a ridge of bone, the sagittal crest, on top of the cranium. In humans, this crest has been replaced by sutures, allowing development of a larger brain case. It is tempting to speculate that the loss-of-function mutation was a critical event in allowing human ancestors to develop larger brains and greater intelligence at the expense of a less powerful jaw.

The 'molecular clock' used to determine when the MYH16 mutation arose involved a comparison between the now-defunct human gene and its equivalents in the chimpanzee, orang-utan, macaque and dog. By assessing the number of 'silent' mutations (which do not alter the resulting protein sequence) relative to those which lead to insertion of a different amino acid at a given position in the protein, the researchers established that the loss-of-function mutation in human MYH16 occurred close to 2.4 million years ago. This is strikingly similar to the time at which the fossil record suggests development of the more human cranial form. The skulls of more direct human ancestors lack the bone structure to support powerful masticating muscles, although this is evident in the earlier *Australopithecus* and *Paranthropus* fossils.

CHIMPANZEE-HUMAN DATA COMPARED

Detailed comparisons between the chimpanzee (*Pan troglodytes*) genome and the human genome are expected to uncover further examples of the subtle mutations which distinguish our species from its close relatives. Patterns and regulation of gene expression, rather than the genes themselves, may prove to be the critical factors. An early draft version of the chimpanzee genome was published in December 2003 and a more complete sequence, removing gaps and ambiguities, was expected by the end of 2004.

An International Chimpanzee Chromosome 22 Consortium, with researchers based in Japan, Korea, China, Taiwan and Germany, obtained high quality sequence data for 33.3 Mb of DNA, for comparison with the equivalent human chromosome 21. The results indicate changes of nucleotide in 1.44 per cent of the sequence. Of 231 functional, protein-producing genes identified in the study as being common to chimpanzees and humans, 179 were found to be identical in the lengths of their amino acid chains, with 140 of these (73 per cent) showing one or more amino acid changes. Most of these changes probably have little or no effect on protein function. Of the remaining 52 genes, 47 (90 per cent) show more significant structural alterations.

About one-fifth of the genes in this study showed significant differences in expression levels between chimpanzees and humans in liver and brain tissue.

From the rough draft of the chimpanzee genome, an interesting finding is that the human genes for enzymes involved in amino acid breakdown (catabolism) have been under positive selection, perhaps lending weight to the idea that a diet including an increased proportion of meat (contrasting with chimpanzees' more herbivorous lifestyle) was linked to increasing brain size in humans' direct ancestors.

FORECASTING EL NINO

Under normal circumstances, climate and ocean circulation in the tropical Pacific are driven by westwards-blowing trade winds. These lead to accumulation of warm surface waters in the western Pacific, resulting in rainy conditions during the monsoon season. This normal pattern promotes the upwelling of cold, nutrient-rich water from deep waters on the eastern side of the Pacific Ocean, off the coast of South America.

During El Nino events, which occur at intervals of between three and seven years, the trade winds ease, bringing rainfall eastwards across the Pacific, and the efficiency of coastal upwelling is reduced, with drastic consequences for fisheries in countries such as Peru. The effects of an El Nino event can be far-reaching, causing flooding in the eastern Pacific, drought in the western Pacific, and suppression of hurricane development in the south-west Atlantic. Particularly severe El Nino conditions in 1982–83 and 1997–98 were linked to drought and bushfires in Australia and the forecasting of El Nino events has been a long-standing goal of meteorologists and oceanographers.

Studies of fossil corals at Palmyra Island by a team led by Kim Cobb from the Scripps Institute of Oceanography in California have provided some useful insights into El Nino behaviour in pre-industrial times, and may help in development of predictive models. Rather as trees develop growth rings, corals at Palmyra show annual banded growth. By measuring oxygen isotope ratios in these bands, it is possible to gauge ocean surface temperatures, which are elevated during El Nino years.

Cobb *et al* recovered beached coral heads, washed up by storms, providing a fragmentary record of ocean temperature extending back to the 10th century. Direct comparison is possible between these and modern corals. From its study, the team was able to conclude that the intensity of El Nino events has been highly variable over time – those in the 17th century, for example, were stronger and more frequent than in the 20th century.

An important finding was that El Nino events in pre-industrial times appeared not to be influenced by external factors. For example, neither the Maunder Minimum 'little ice age' which produced cold conditions over Europe from the 17th to 19th centuries or the 'Medieval Warm Period' of the 11th to 14th centuries is reflected in the coral El Nino record.

The lack of influence by external factors such as volcanic eruptions or climate variation in the northern hemisphere is important to a forecasting model developed by Dake Chen and co-workers. Chen *et al* take a model of El Nino driven by its internal dynamics, and refine the respective atmosphere–ocean and ocean–atmosphere interactions to predict the occurrence of events. Applied retrospectively to data covering the period from 1857 to 2003, this is successful in predicting the occurrence of El Nino events with a lead time of up to two years.

MOUSE WITH TWO MOTHERS

A team of researchers led by Tomohiro Kono at Tokyo University succeeded in creating a viable mouse by fusing the nuclei of unfertilised eggs (oocytes) from two females. Described by Kono *et al* as parthenogenetic, the progeny of this experiment differ from clones, where the nucleus of a mature cell is inserted to an empty oocyte which is then chemically activated to become an embryo.

In normal mammalian embryonic development, fertilisation of an egg by a sperm is followed by sequential expression of genes, governed by *imprinting* – some 30 critical genes are expressed only from their maternal or paternal copies. This imprinting was seen as a barrier to the successful generation of viable embryos from same-sex nuclei. An activated oocyte containing only the female gene set can only show limited development, since female-specific imprinting prevents expression of some genes which have to be provided in active form by the male.

To overcome the imprinting barrier, Kono and his co-workers had to first genetically modify one of the donor partners. By disabling the H19 gene (of which only the maternal copy is normally active), they were able to make one of the donors more like a sperm cell in terms of imprinting. The H19 gene product suppresses a second gene, Igf2 (usually expressed only in the paternal copy), which is required for early embryonic development. Removing this suppression therefore allows development to proceed.

The H19-deficient oocytes were fused with immature oocytes in which imprinting had not yet been established and the fusion products were then chemically activated to simulate fertilisation. The implanting of 26 surrogate mothers resulted in 24 pregnancies. Foetuses were recovered by autopsy at 19.5 days' gestation, with 18 dead and 10 live progenies (from a total of 371 implanted embryos).

Two apparently normal mouse pups were recovered. One was used for investigation of the pattern of gene expression, while the other – named Kaguya after a character in a Japanese fairytale – was successfully reared to adulthood and proved to be a reproductively-normal female, going on to have her own offspring.

The results of the experiment emphasise the importance of imprinting to successful foetal development in mammals. The success rate in producing viable embryos from same-sex parents is extremely low – even lower than for established cloning procedures – and the chances of such technology being applied to human reproduction, ethical objections notwithstanding, are essentially nil.

CLONED HORSE BORN IN ITALY

In August 2003, scientists led by Cesare Galli at the Laboratory of Reproductive Technology at Cremona, Italy announced success in cloning a horse. Nuclei of skin cells obtained from a mare were fused with anucleate (empty) equine egg cells to produce a total of 328 embryos, which were implanted in surrogate mothers. This resulted in four pregnancies, one of which was successful, producing the cloned foal called Prometea, born on 28 May 2003. The mother of the foal was, in fact, the mare whose skin cells were used in the experiment.

Some researchers believe that cloning technology will, in the future, allow propagation of successful racehorse lines, even from animals which have been gelded. There has, however, been some ethical opposition to this idea. The creation of Prometea means that the horse can be added to the growing list of cloned mammalian species, which includes sheep, goats, cattle, cats, mice, rabbits and pigs. Earlier in 2003, American scientists announced the successful delivery of Idaho Gem, the first cloned mule.

MAIZE MAPPED

Funded by the US National Science Foundation, the Maize Mapping Project completed its work in the autumn of 2003. A high-resolution genetic map of the genes in maize (*Zea mays*) showing the relative positions of its genes had been assembled a year earlier, and the final stage was to complete a physical map, relating the actual distances in the DNA between them. While there have been calls for maize to have its entire DNA sequence determined, the close similarity of its 2.5 Gb genomes – almost as large as the human genome – to that of rice suggests that such a project may not yield any particularly new information. There is also the problem that the maize genome abounds with repeated elements, which present major difficulties for sequencing. It is possible, however, that strategies which eliminate non-expressed DNA, concentrating on functional genes, may lead to a sequencing project in the future, driven by the commercial importance of maize as a food crop.

VIOLIN QUALITY LINKED TO THE SUN?

A climatic story with an interesting twist relates to the revered violins made in Cremona, Italy, in the late 17th and early 18th centuries by artisans including Antonio Stradivari (1644–1737). It has long been a mystery as to why these instruments have such unique tonal qualities. Some have suggested that the Cremonese violin makers used special seasoning techniques or chemical treatments to prepare their wood but the known histories of the surviving examples (over 600 Stradivarius instruments remain extant) indicate no common factor in the manufacturing process that could account for their quality.

An interesting new proposal, by Lloyd Burckle (Columbia University, New York) and Henri Grissino-Mayer (University of Tennessee), is that the climate of the so-called Maunder Minimum of 1645 to 1715 was a critical factor, favouring production of wood with the required characteristics. The Maunder Minimum was a period of decreased solar activity, during which sunspots were scarce, and appears correlated with an interval of colder weather over Europe. Summers were short and relatively cool, leading to restricted tree growth, and dendrochronological studies show the annual growth rings from this time to be narrow and closely-spaced. The authors made a study of tree rings at 16 sites in the European Alps, from which the Cremonese violin makers obtained their wood, finding a strong Maunder Minimum signal in growth rings from 1625 to 1720 in larch, spruce and pine trees.

The most-prized Stradivarius instruments come from a 'golden period' between 1700 and 1720, and were made from wood grown during the Maunder Minimum. Burckle and Grissino-Mayer propose that slow growth (narrow annual rings) producing dense spruce wood used in violin sounding boards at this time was a key factor in determining their quality.

TRANSIT OF VENUS

For the first time in nearly 122 years, Venus made a transit across the face of the Sun as seen from Earth on 6 June 2004. Appearing as a dark circular spot, the planet took 5h 30m to cross from the Sun's south-eastern limb to the south-western limb. Thousands of observers around the world were able to follow the event; only those in the western states of America, where the transit ended before sunrise, were denied a view. In the British Isles, good weather allowed many to follow the event from start (a couple of hours after sunrise) to finish (around noon BST). As for viewing eclipses, observers were required to take sensible precautions, avoiding direct viewing of the blinding solar disk through optical equipment. Many public viewing events were organised in the UK, and many members of the public saw the transit from the Old Royal Observatory at Greenwich.

Historically, transits of Venus were important in attempts to define the distance-scale of the Solar System. By determining the chord followed across the Sun's disk as seen from widely-separated geographical locations, astronomers in the 18th century hoped to obtain a parallax from which Earth-Sun distance could be found. These efforts were thwarted, however, by an optical illusion – the so-called black drop effect – whereby the limb of Venus appeared attached to that of the Sun, even when the planet was completely in silhouette on the solar disk. Part of this may have had its origins in earlier optical systems – most observations in 2004 did not show a pronounced black drop effect.

With the scale of the Solar System now established from radar measurements, observations of transits of Venus no longer have such great scientific significance but for many who witnessed the 2004 event there was the thrill of witnessing an astronomical phenomenon not previously seen by any living person. Transits of Venus occur in pairs, separated by eight years – the next is on 6 June 2012, but is rather unfavourable for viewing for much of the British Isles.

SPECTACULAR SCIENCE AT MARS

In a year when planetary scientists achieved many breakthroughs, Mars has dominated the headlines. The red planet's August 2003 opposition, when it came fractionally closer to Earth than at any time in the past 60,000 years and was a bright object in midnight skies, was met by concerted observing campaigns. Even amateur astronomers equipped with modest telescopes enjoyed splendid views of Mars' south polar cap and dark markings. On this occasion, the extensive obscuring dust storms which often conceal the plane's features around the time of its close approach did not materialise.

Spacecraft launched to explore Mars *in situ* have, since early 2004, provided many exciting results. ESA's *Mars Express* arrived just before Christmas, and was successfully placed in a polar mapping orbit around the planet. Europe's first dedicated planetary mission, *Mars Express* has among its instruments the High Resolution Stereo Camera (HRSC), which has sent back detailed images of the Martian surface, including the vast canyon system of the Valles Marineris. The OMEGA instrument on board *Mars Express* confirmed the presence of substantial deposits of water ice under the frozen carbon dioxide of the planet's south polar cap.

Rather less successful, alas, was the UK's *Beagle 2* lander, carried by *Mars Express* and released just before arrival for a landing on Isidis Planitia on Christmas Day 2003. No signal was received from the surface, and the lander is presumed destroyed.

The two NASA Mars Exploration Rovers were successfully landed on the surface, their final decent cushioned by airbags. First to arrive was *Spirit*, which landed in the 150 km diameter Gusev crater on 4 January 2004. Scientists believe that Gusev once contained a lake, making it an attractive target for the exploration of possible water-based physical and chemical traces. Following initial problems with computer memory, *Spirit* has functioned extremely well, travelling 3 km across Gusev's floor to reach a feature called the Columbia Hills by June.

The sister rover *Opportunity* landed three weeks later at Meridiani Planitia, a site selected for its previously-established abundance of hematite – an iron mineral formed in the presence of water. *Opportunity* landed close to an outcrop of exposed Martian bedrock and scientists have been excited by the possibility that this has a sedimentary nature consistent with origin in an aquatic environment. By June 2004, *Opportunity* was beginning exploration of a crater named Endurance and has found hematite-rich marble-like stones ('blueberries') whose terrestrial equivalents form where water leaches through sandstone.

The results from the six-wheeled, 1.5-m high rovers certainly point to an important role for water in past Martian geology. Operating well past their projected 90-day lifetimes, *Spirit* and *Opportunity* are expected to continue providing valuable science from the Martian surface until early 2005, provided they survive the harsh local winter conditions.

THEATRE

NATIONAL SUCCESS

There can be no doubt about who was the theatrical hero of the year. Nicholas Hytner, artistic director of the National Theatre, could do no wrong. Having taken over from Trevor Nunn in April 2003, Hytner went on to present a string of dynamic, popular productions. Susannah Clapp in *The Observer* pronounced that 'Overnight, London theatre has turned on its axis.' The New York Times was equally enthusiastic, declaring that the National is 'an exciting place to be – you feel as if you could camp out there for a week.'

When Hytner arrived, he made it clear that he intended to concentrate on the work. He was not interested in what he described as 'the fashionable insistence on judging an artistic enterprise by its ability to pull in the right crowd.' Rather he wanted 'to provoke investigation of what makes us tick as a nation and as individuals. I wasn't interested in playing the target game.' In fact, intentionally or not, he has achieved both. The audience at the National has been made up of a wide cross-section of people, and he has produced a range of provocative productions. Remarkably, three major new plays have been staged in the space of a year: Michael Frayn's *Democracy* was seen in the Cottesloe and the Lyttelton before transferring to the West End; Martin McDonagh's *The Pillowman* played in the Cottesloe; and Alan Bennett's *The History Boys* was presented in the Lyttelton, a rare occasion on which a new play opened on one of the National's two large stages. There was much more to enjoy. Revivals included: Chekhov's *Three Sisters;* Euripides' *Iphigenia in Tauris* with Ben Daniels; Eugene O'Neill's *Mourning Becomes Electra* with Helen Mirren; Marivaux's *The False Servant* with Charlotte Rampling; and Shakespeare's *Measure for Measure* with Paul Rhys. Reflecting a new interest in children's theatre throughout the profession, Hytner directed Nicholas Wright's adaptation of Philip Pullman's *His Dark Materials,* and political theatre was represented by *The Permanent Way.* Improbable Theatre, a leading experimental company, staged *Lifegame,* a show that explores the very nature of theatre, and for sheer good fun, most people agreed that there was very little to beat Edward Hall's production of *A Funny Thing Happened on the Way to the Forum* with Desmond Barrit. At a time when the price of tickets has become a major issue, many of these productions could be seen at the Olivier for only £10, a scheme supported once again by Travelex which helped fill seats in the summer when audiences are traditionally sparse. Even the two most flawed productions – *Tales from the Vienna Woods* and *Cyrano de Bergerac* in which Stephen Rea sported the famous nose – attracted respectable houses, many people visiting the building for the very first time.

Hytner is more of a collegiate director than his predecessor, and a strong team surrounds him. Nick Starr is his very experienced and dedicated executive director, Howard Davies is his extremely talented associate director, and Tom Morris has been appointed from Battersea Arts Centre, bringing with him his experience of non-script based theatre. There are also sixteen unsalaried 'associates' who include the director Katie Mitchell, playwrights Mark Ravenhill and Patrick Marber, and actor Alex Jennings.

Three major new plays in a period of less than twelve months is a terrific achievement for any theatre. Not even the Royal Court could compete, although in Conor McPherson's *Shining City,* it did produce one of the scarier new plays of the year with a ghostly twist. At the National, Michael Frayn's *Democracy* was an unlikely hit given that it is set in post-war Germany during the chancellorship of Willy Brandt – about which British people know very little – and that its subject matter is the complexity of decision-making. Frayn articulately depicts the relationship between the popular Brandt and Gunter Guillaume, the East German spy who managed to worm his way into Brandt's office and whose exposure led to Brandt's downfall in 1974. In Roger Allam's thoughtful performance, Brandt was revealed to be a complicated mix of integrity, intelligence, womanising and indecision. The play's energy and humour comes from the way that the smarmy Guillaume (Conleth Hill) avoids high-powered discussions at the Chancellery to report to his controller, Kretschmann, sitting at the side of the stage. At the end of Michael Blakemore's production, the set slowly collapsed, a reminder that Brandt's determination to achieve a rapprochement helped lead to the destruction of the Berlin Wall many years later.

In contrast with the subtlety and complexity of *Democracy,* Martin McDonagh's *The Pillowman* is more of a visceral thrill. McDonagh explores the survival of art and the responsibility of the artist as Katurian (David Tennant), a writer, is taken in for questioning by two blackly-comic and brutal interrogators (Jim Broadbent and Nigel Lindsay) representing an unspecified totalitarian state. Katurian's arrest is provoked by the murder of some local children whose grisly end resembles events in Katurian's own horrific fairy tales. In spite of his fear, he values his stories above his life and will do anything to see them survive. In John Crowley's exciting production, scenes from Katurian's unusual childhood were displayed in a series of Gothic tableaux using puppets and presented above the rest of the action. Comedy and violence proved a potent combination even if the meaning of McDonagh's play was not always clear.

The History Boys was Alan Bennett's first play for five years. The opening night did not bode well when a fire onstage meant that the performance had to be delayed for an hour but the quality of the drama proved more than capable of rising above such a setback. Bennett's play, overflowing with memorable and often hilarious epigrams, is an investigation of the purpose and nature of education set in the sixth form of a boys' grammar school in the 1980s. The boys are taught by three teachers: Mrs Lintott, who gives them a solid grounding in history; Irwin, who is brought in to sharpen them up for their

Oxbridge entrance; and Hector, for whom exams and education are very different beasts. They find themselves torn between Irwin who forces them to be controversial as a slick ploy to wake up tired examiners, and Hector, who passes on his passion for films, Shakespeare and Gracie Fields. The school sometimes seems more reminiscent of Bennett's own school days in the 1940s than the 1980s, but Hytner's magisterial production, which included filmed shots of life in a local school today, did its best to redress the balance.

In December 2003, Hytner directed Nicholas Wright's adaptation of Philip Pullman's epic fantasy *His Dark Materials* in a six-hour version divided into two shows. The challenge was both to compress the story and to find a theatrical way of presenting the many fantastical elements. The Olivier's drum worked overtime in order to present the numerous different locations, including the parallel universes through which the two main characters – Will and Lyra – pass at the stroke of a magic knife. The personal demons or spirits, possessed by all the inhabitants of Lyra's world, were represented by puppets manipulated by visible masked handlers in a similar fashion to *The Lion King*. It wasn't always the most spectacular effects that made the most impact, but rather the touching relationship between Anna Maxwell Martin's irrepressible Lyra and Dominic Cooper's more thoughtful Will. Also impressive was Howard Davies' revival of *Mourning Becomes Electra*, a once-in-a-lifetime opportunity to see Eugene O'Neill's intractable 1931 epic, which draws on both Greek tragedy and Freudian psychology. The relentless tale of retribution and guilt reveals the tragic consequences of Lavinia Mannon's determination to punish her mother's adultery and win her father's love. Davies' production managed to acknowledge the play's melodramatic qualities without detracting from the remorseless descent into tragedy. Paul Hilton as Orin, the anguished son, and Eve Best as the puritanical Lavinia, in particular, enhanced their already burgeoning reputations. Bob Crowley's magnificent set showed a porticoed verandah, its peeling ceiling painted with a representation of the Union flag, symbolising a world of privilege that was on the brink of extinction. Nicholas Hytner made it look easy to attract over 2,000 people nightly to the three stages at the National Theatre and the West End struggled to match the cornucopia on the South Bank.

WEST END FAILURES AND FORTUNES

The West End's theatres, admired in the past for the intimate relationship between audience and actors, seemed to be less and less appealing. Complaints have grown about lack of leg-room, inadequate loos, cramped bars, and bad sight lines as well as over-priced programmes, over-priced glasses of wine, and, as ever, the hated booking fee. In contrast with the National's Travelex season, seat prices in the West End were usually steep, although during the summer of 2004 tickets for almost all shows could be bought at the half-price ticket booth in Leicester Square. A report by the Theatre Trust suggested that West End theatres need £255 million of investment over the next 15 years to bring them up to scratch. Some theatre owners are optimistically hoping for help from the government, but Cameron Mackintosh has already embarked on an extensive programme of refurbishment using his own money. In June 2004, the Prince of Wales was the first of his theatres to reopen. Huge bars, elegant art deco fittings, extraordinarily comfortable seats, and great sight lines from all parts of the house have transformed one of London's most claustrophobic theatres. *Mamma Mia!* has moved there from the Prince Edward and it looks as though the Abba show will be happily coining 'Money, Money, Money' for many years to come.

West End producers floundered as they tried to second-guess public taste in an attempt to recoup their ever-increasing costs. *Life is Rhythm*, an Edinburgh transfer, particularly provoked despair among the critics, prompting Charles Spencer to say in the *Daily Telegraph* that 'the place is engulfed with brain-dead rubbish, stand-up comedians, back-catalogue compilation musicals, one woman shows and any amount of tacky tat'. Ben Elton's tribute to Rod Stewart *Tonight's the Night* rather proved Spencer's point. Perhaps most embarrassing was the return of Michael Barrymore. After a disastrous first night in which the comedian died a slow and excruciating death, the show was taken off a few nights later. Some productions never seemed suitable for the West End including *Coyote on a Fence, Sweet Panic, Rattle of a Simple Man*, and Imogen Stubbs' *We Happy Few*. Some needed better productions such as *The Secret Rapture, The Shape of Things* and *Les Liaisons Dangereuses*. Michael Hastings' *Calico*, about Joyce's daughter Lucia (played by Romola Garai), clearly needed a script doctor.

As if searching for something bankable, producers turned to films. *Chitty Chitty Bang Bang* was joined – albeit briefly – by *Thoroughly Modern Millie* with Amanda Holden flying the flag for modernity. *When Harry met Sally* came to the Haymarket with Luke Perry and Alyson Hannigan who proved a draw with audiences despite the drawbacks of an adaptation that lacked both the charm of the original and the New York scenery. *The Producers, Mary Poppins* and *Billy Elliott* are still to come.

It wasn't all rubbish, however. Trevor Nunn directed a modern *Hamlet* at the Old Vic with an exceptionally young cast. Twenty-three-year-old Ben Whishaw was a snivelling, skinny Hamlet in a beanie hat and Imogen Stubbs played a youthful Gertrude, making this production one to which young audiences could easily relate. Simon Gray's *The Holy Terror* quickly vanished, but he returned more successfully with *The Old Masters* directed by Harold Pinter in which Edward Fox as Bernard Berenson, the Renaissance art expert, and Peter Bowles as his dealer, Joseph Duveen, fiercely argued the attribution of a painting. Julia Stiles appeared in a revival of David Mamet's *Oleanna* with Aaron Eckhart. Michael Gambon and Lee Evans made an improbable pair in a production of *Endgame* that exploited the old-fashioned theatricality of the Albery and R. C. Sherriff's old stalwart *Journey's End* proved as moving as ever with David Haig as the stoical schoolmaster and Geoffrey Streatfield as Stanhope. As always, there was an injection of shows from elsewhere, the most successful of which came – once again – from the National: *Democracy, Anything Goes* and *Jerry Springer – The Opera*. The Almeida launched *The Goat or Who is Sylvia?*, Edward Albee's play about tolerance in which an architect, played by Jonathan Pryce, falls in love with a goat, to his wife's understandable distress. The Almeida also presented one of the great artistic achievements of the year, Rufus Norris's production of *Festen* adapted by David Eldridge from the film, which transferred in the autumn. Michael Grandage's production of *Suddenly Last Summer* transferred from the Sheffield Crucible with Diana Rigg and Victoria Hamilton. From the Watermill at Newbury came Edward Hall's highly enjoyable all-male production of *A Midsummer Night's Dream* and *Sweeney Todd*. The Tricycle, which had an excellent year, transferred *The Price* with Warren Mitchell and *Guantanamo: Honor Bound to Defend Freedom*. Shared Experience came into the Duke of York's with *After Mrs Rochester*, Polly Teale's fascinating exploration of the life of Jean Rhys.

ROYAL SHAKESPEARE COMPANY

The relationship between the National and the Royal Shakespeare Company (RSC) often resembles a seesaw – when one is up, the other is down. Artistic director Michael Boyd, who is widely admired, cut costs both off and on stage in order to whittle away at a massive deficit of £2.8 million. He has returned to the original idea of the RSC as an ensemble in which the actors work together over a long period of time. There is no longer talk of pulling the main house down in Stratford, but rather of radical refurbishment in order to improve sight lines and facilities backstage, both of which Boyd's predecessor insisted were impossible to achieve without totally demolishing the building. London remains the thorny problem. Actors involved in the 2003 season were shocked to discover that the RSC could not afford to bring any of the productions to London. The two hits of the season were Gregory Doran's production of *The Taming of the Shrew* and John Fletcher's little known riposte, *The Tamer Tamed*, written some twenty years later. In spite of having lost a reputed £1 million on the season of Jacobean and Elizabethan plays earlier in the year, West End producer Bill Kenwright was persuaded to step into the breach again and transfer *The Taming of the Shrew* and *The Tamer Tamed* to London. Alexandra Gilbreath played Kate and Jasper Britton played Petruchio while Rory Kinnear made his mark as an upwardly mobile Tranio. Later, Gregory Doran's admired production of *All's Well that Ends Well* transferred from the Swan in Stratford to the Gielgud. Returning to the company after many years, Judi Dench played the Countess, which guaranteed good audiences both in Stratford and London. As this production opened in the West End, Doran – one of the busiest directors of the year – was working on *Othello* in Stratford which eventually transferred to London's Trafalgar Studio. Antony Sher as Iago and Sello Maake ka-Ncube as Othello brought a South African flavour to the play.

These sporadic visits to the capital emphasised the RSC's need for a proper London home. The company runs the risk of losing a substantial part of its grant if it does not find one soon. While actors are always keen to be seen in London, audiences were beginning to get used to the company's absence from the capital. Tourists, in particular, are only too happy to go to Shakespeare's Globe instead. Boyd has announced that four tragedies seen in Stratford – *King Lear* with Corin Redgrave, *Hamlet* with Toby Stephens, *Macbeth* with Greg Hicks, and *Romeo and Juliet* – will play for a six month season at the Albery from autumn 2004 but this will again be a temporary home.

REALITY THEATRE

Political theatre proliferated in the year under review, undoubtedly influenced by 9/11 and the Iraq War, but also covering such topics as a siege in Hackney and the state of the railways. The Tricycle Theatre in Kilburn led the way in this field. Even before Lord Hutton had presented his report, Richard Norton-Taylor and Nicolas Kent presented their own edited, dramatised version of the tribunal, which was held to explore the events leading to the death of Dr David Kelly. Although much of the material was very detailed, the evening was notable for the audience's determination to sift through the evidence and understand its significance. Later in the year, the Tricycle returned to the fray with *Guantanamo: Honor Bound to Defend Freedom*, a play based on interviews with the family and solicitors of those held in Guantanamo Bay without trial. Both these productions were described as verbatim theatre, based on the actual words of those who were interviewed, or on the court transcriptions. This was taken to extremes in *Come Out Eli* at the Arcola Theatre which recounts, through pre-recorded witness accounts read by actors, how Eli Hall barricaded himself into a flat with a gun and a hostage in Hackney on Boxing Day 2002. The siege lasted sixteen days before the hostage escaped and Eli set fire to the flat and killed himself.

The Permanent Way, presented by Out of Joint, was also based on interviews, in this case with those involved in the privatisation of Britain's railways and the succession of disasters that followed at Southall, Ladbroke Grove and Potters Bar. The interviews were filtered through the imagination of playwright David Hare who built up a damning indictment of the separation of train and track management, a policy brought in during John Major's time as Prime Minister. Hare also criticised Tony Blair for attacking privatisation of the railways before the 1997 election and refusing to take them back into state ownership after the election. The production by Max Stafford-Clark attracted vast audiences round the country, especially in the railway town of York, and presented a devastating but also inspiring portrait of both the bereaved and the survivors, and of their determination to make sure that the Government learns from the disasters.

Elsewhere playwrights fought back with their imaginative responses to real-life events. Steve Waters' *World Music* at the Donmar Warehouse examined the West's response to the aftermath of war in Rwanda while David Edgar's hugely ambitious pair of plays, *Mothers Against* and *Daughters of the Revolution*, looked at a gubernatorial election in a US state from both sides of the political divide. In *Mothers Against*, the Republican candidate, a libertarian of the right, is coached for a forthcoming television debate and learns that he is expected to toe the moral line. *Daughters of the Revolution* concerns a left-wing activist who tries to discover who ruined his career many years ago. Edgar's depth of research and the intricacy of the links between the two plays were impressive, even if the play's detailed arguments were devoid of any real drama. There were more obvious political satires such as *The Madness of George Dubya* – an update of Dr Strangelove – by Justin Butcher at the Arts Theatre and Alastair Beaton's *Follow My Leader* at Birmingham Rep and Hampstead. Echoes of the Iraq War were frequently felt in classical revivals, especially Luc Bondy's production of *Cruel and Tender* at the Young Vic, and Katie Mitchell's production of Euripides' *Iphigenia at Tauris* at the National Theatre. In Simon McBurney's powerful production of *Measure for Measure*, also at the National, the prisoners were dressed in orange boiler suits and George Bush's face was flashed up on a screen. The war seemed to be on everyone's minds but, predictably, few supporters of Bush's policy in Iraq could be found.

REGIONAL HIGHS

Regional theatre continued to flourish largely because of the vast injection of £25 million from the Arts Council. Michael Grandage announced his departure from the Sheffield Crucible after a hugely successful run, which he combined with the artistic directorship of the Donmar Warehouse. Gemma Bodinetz presented Dael Orlandersmith's remarkable play about colour and prejudice at the Liverpool Playhouse. Jonathan Church massively increased the amount of work shown at Birmingham Rep. His production of *Of Mice and Men* with Matthew Kelly transferred to London. David Farr had a surprise hit with his adaptation of *Paradise Lost* at the Bristol Old Vic. Steven Pimlott directed a much admired adaptation of Bulgakov's *Master and Marguerita* at Chichester with Sam West and Michael Feast. Ian Brown created memorable collaborations with the touring companies Improbable and Kneehigh and, with the Newcastle Playhouse and Theatre Romea Barcelona, he presented an adaptation of George Orwell's *Homage to Catalonia* directed by controversial Catalan director Calixto Beito. The new confidence of these theatres showed in their artistic work but was also amply rewarded when figures revealed that Derby Playhouse contributed £3.9 million to the local economy and Sheffield Crucible an impressive £22 million.

THEATRE AWARDS 2003

CRITICS' CIRCLE
Best New Play – *Democracy* by Michael Frayn
Best Musical – *Jerry Springer – The Opera* by Richard Thomas and Stewart Lee
Best Director – Howard Davies for *Mourning Becomes Electra*
Best Designer – Bob Crowley for *Mourning Becomes Electra*
Best Actor – Michael Sheen for *Caligula*
Best Actress – Eve Best for *Mourning Becomes Electra*
Most Promising Playwright – Lucy Prebble for *The Sugar Syndrome*
Most Promising Newcomer – Lisa Dillon for *Iphigenia* and *The Master Builder*
Best Shakespearean Performance – Greg Hicks for *Coriolanus*

EVENING STANDARD
Best Play – *Democracy* by Michael Frayn
Best Actor – Michael Sheen for *Caligula*
Best Actress – Sandy McDade for *Iron*
Best Musical – *Jerry Springer – The Opera* by Richard Thomas and Stewart Lee
Most Promising Playwright – Kwame Kwei-Armah for *Elmina's Kitchen*
Best Director – Polly Teale for *After Mrs Rochester*
Best Designer – Christopher Oram for *Caligula*
Outstanding Newcomer – Tom Hardy for *Blood/In Arabia We'd All Be Kings*
Special Award – Max Stafford-Clark

LAURENCE OLIVIER
Best New Play – *The Pillowman* by Martin McDonagh
Best New Musical – *Jerry Springer – The Opera* by Richard Thomas and Stewart Lee
Outstanding Musical – *Pacific Overtures* by Stephen Sondheim/John Weidman/Hugh Wheeler
Best Revival – *Mourning Becomes Electra* by Eugene O'Neill
Best Entertainment – *C'est Barbican!* presented by Duckie
Best Director – Michael Grandage for *Caligula*
Best Designer – William Dudley for *Hitchcock Blonde*
Best Lighting Designer – Hugh Vanstone for *Pacific Overtures*
Best Sound Design – Mike Walker for *Jerry Springer – The Opera*
Best Choreography – Karen Bruce for *Pacific Overtures*
Best Costume Designer – Christopher Oram for *Power*
Best Actor – Matthew Kelly for *Of Mice and Men*
Best Actress – Eileen Atkins for *Honour*
Best Supporting Performance – Warren Mitchell for *The Price*
Best Actor in a Musical – David Bedella for *Jerry Springer – The Opera*
Best Actress in a Musical – Maria Friedman for *Ragtime*
Best Supporting Performance in a Musical – The Chorus in *Jerry Springer – The Opera*
Most Promising Newcomer – Debbie Tucker Green for *Born Bad*
Outstanding Achievement – The Young Vic
Special Award – Judi Dench

TMA THEATRE AWARDS 2003
Best Actor – Timothy West for *King Lear*, English Touring Theatre
Best Actress – Eileen McCallum for *If Only* at the Royal Lyceum, Edinburgh
Best Actress in a Supporting Role – Lyndsey Marshal for *A Midsummer Night's Dream* at the Bristol Old Vic
Best Actor in a Supporting Role – Andy Serkis for *Othello* at the Royal Exchange, Manchester
Best Director – David Farr for *A Midsummer Night's Dream* at the Bristol Old Vic
Best Designer – Julian Crouch, Phil Eddols, Colin Grenfell and Stephen Snell for *The Hanging Man* Improbable Theatre/West Yorkshire Playhouse
Best New Play – *The Breathing House* by Peter Arnott at the Royal Lyceum, Edinburgh
Best Touring Production – *A Midsummer Night's Dream* Propeller/Watermill Theatre, Newbury
Best Musical – *Sweet Charity* at the Crucible, Sheffield
Best Play for Children and Young People – *Tom's Midnight Garden* adapted by David Wood, Library, Manchester
Most Welcoming Theatre – Brunton, Musselburgh
Special Regional Theatre award – The Georgian Theatre Royal, Richmond, N. Yorks
Eclipse Award – New Wolsey Theatre, Ipswich

WEATHER

JULY 2003

From the 1st to the 3rd a depression in the North Sea brought a cool unsettled spell with rain and thundery showers in many places. From the 4th to the 11th the weather became mostly dry with rising temperatures and high pressure settled close by to the south. Atlantic fronts skirting northern districts on the 8th resulted in rain and drizzle. Most days saw long sunny periods and very warm or hot conditions were experienced in many parts during the 9th and 10th. A weak cold front passing later on the 10th introduced fresher air by the 11th. Wisley in Surrey reached 33.6°C on the 15th while Maidenhead had its hottest July day since 1976. The 16th to the 20th was more unsettled as Atlantic depressions encroached but it stayed mostly very warm or hot at first. There was widespread thundery rain, heavy at times during the 16th and 17th, as a low moved north-east across the region. St Athan in the Vale of Glamorgan had over 50mm of rain in 12hrs on the 17th. Western areas had more rain at times on the 18th, 19th and 20th, while eastern areas were relatively sunnier and drier. Residual hot air over the south-east and East Anglia on the 19th gave way that evening as thunderstorms broke out, some lasting to the early hours. The 21st to the 23rd saw a breezy spell with sunny periods and some scattered showers mostly in the west and north. From the 24th to the 26th Atlantic depressions to the north-west brought an unsettled spell, especially over south-west England, Wales and the Midlands. Cardinham in Cornwall received 58mm of rain in 12hrs. Thunder was reported from Lyneham in Wiltshire during the 26th. After some thunderstorms in the south-east and East Anglia early on 27th, further rain and showers and cooler temperatures affected many places. A small low moved eastwards over northern England during the 30th bringing heavy thundery showers to north-west England and eastern England down to East Anglia, with tornadoes reported from Sculthorpe in Norfolk.

AUGUST 2003

This was the driest and sunniest August since 1995 and the warmest since 1997. On the 1st and 2nd low pressure to the north-west brought a breezy start to the month with occasional rain and drizzle, however it became sunny and warm by the 2nd. The 3rd to the 13th saw a notable and record breaking heatwave especially in the Midlands, Central Southern and south-east England and East Anglia. Temperatures exceeded 35°C in many places on the 6th, 9th and 10th. There was some patchy hill and coastal fog mainly around south-west and western areas. The 5th and 6th saw a little thunder in the north, while rain affected the north-west on the 9th. Valley in Anglesey reached 33°C on the 5th, with 35°C recorded at Rocquaine on Jersey, both new weather station records. The 9th and 10th saw extreme heat across much of the region, particularly in south-east England on the 10th where 38.1°C was claimed by Gravesend, a new UK record. In contrast there were thunderstorms in north, west and central areas of the region, with severe outbreaks over north-east England. Carlton in Cleveland collected 48mm of rain in 15 mins and 2cms of hail on the ground, while Middlesborough had 30mm in a downpour. There was more thunder in west, north-west and north-east areas on the 11th. It continued mostly hot with a little thunder in the south-west on the 13th as a cold front moved south-east. From the 14th to the 18th it was changeable with occasional rain or showers in places, mainly in western and southern areas. It was cooler though still warm at times. There were good sunny periods generally, especially inland and in eastern areas. Developing low pressure to the north brought fresher air from the north-west during the 18th. The 19th to the 26th was dry and mostly warm with sunny periods at first but more breezy in the north on the 21st as a low tracked eastwards passing by north Scotland. Slow moving fronts gave light rain and drizzle in many places during the 21st and 22nd and in the north-east on the 23rd. High pressure then restablished itself over the UK but retreated to Iceland by the 25th allowing cloudier cooler conditions and a little rain and drizzle to spread in from the north-east. From the 27th to the 31st an anticyclone near Iceland and low pressure over Scandinavia fed markedly cooler air from the Arctic. The cold front stalled over southern districts on the 28th as a depression from Biscay moved east-north-east bringing much needed rain to these areas.

SEPTEMBER 2003

This was the sunniest and the driest September since 1997. From the 1st to the 4th high pressure migrated slowly across the UK from the Atlantic to the low countries bringing dry weather with good sunny periods and some warm temperatures later. The 5th to the 11th was a rather unsettled period with rain at times as secondary depressions and their associated fronts crossed the region. After a very warm start on the 5th the first band of thundery showers affected many parts on the 6th, with more rain spreading in on the 7th as a low approached southern areas from Biscay. It was wet in many places on 8th and 9th as more depressions tracked close by. A low near the Thames Estuary on the 10th gave rain in the north and east. More Atlantic fronts brought rain and drizzle to many places on the 11th, while western and northern areas were affected by hill and coastal fog. From the 12th to the 17th an anticyclone which formed over the UK drifted east to the near continent retaining the region under its influence. Dry, sunny and very warm or hot weather prevailed, with 28.4°C being recorded at Gravesend in Kent on the 17th. Patchy mist and fog in the morning cleared quickly. From the 18th to the 22nd a cold front became stalled over north Wales and northern England for much of the period, bringing rain to these parts, often heavy and prolonged. The cold front advanced south during the 22nd providing some heavy and desperately needed rain to the region. In the south-east temperature drops of ten degrees in less than an hour were noted in many places. From the 23rd to the 25th high pressure established itself again then drifted east maintaining sunny dry conditions. A number of places had air frost on the 24th, with –2.8°C being recorded at Redhill Airport in Surrey. At Boscombe Down in Wiltshire it was the coldest September night since 1931. The 26th to the 28th saw occasional showers and sunny periods as a cold front moved slowly down during the 26th. Most showers were in north-western areas, while the south-east and East Anglia had rain and showers as a small low hovered nearby. A depression near Iceland on the 29th transferred to the Bay of Biscay by the 30th bringing an unsettled spell especially to northern England and northern Wales. Valley on Anglesey reported 25mm of rain on the 29th.

OCTOBER 2003

This was the sunniest October on record and the coldest for ten years. From the 1st to the 2nd a depression over Biscay gave warm and changeable weather in the south, where some thundery rain broke out later. Saunton Sands in Devon reached 22.1°C on the 2nd. From the 3rd to the 10th the changeable theme continued as low-pressure systems tracked east-south-east from the Iceland area. There were outbreaks of rain and showers from time to time and the north-west in particular experienced regular soakings during the 4th, 5th and 6th. There were sunny spells between the showers however. Some thundery outbreaks affected south-eastern districts during the 4th and 5th. The 11th to the 19th was a mainly sunny dry period as high pressure exerted its influence. An anticyclone over Scandinavia migrated to Denmark by the 16th, then to the Greenland and Iceland areas by the 18th. Low pressure near Biscay drifted east bringing occasional rain or showers to the south-west from the 11th to 15th. Overnight mist and fog patches formed in places and later and it became chilly as easterly winds picked up. Temperatures dropped markedly everywhere by the end of the 19th as north-east winds transported air in from arctic regions. The 20th to the 25th was mostly unsettled and cold with outbreaks of thundery rain or showers in many places. A depression off southern Norway moved to Biscay by the 22nd and 23rd bringing freshening easterly winds. Snow lay early on the 20th over high parts of the north Pennines. Thundery rain fell over North Yorkshire and east coast counties during the 20th and 21st and later in east Kent overnight from the 20th to the 21st. Margate received 38mm of rain on the 21st. Southern areas bore the brunt of the thundery showers on the 22nd. Sleet and snow fell widely with Dartmoor having a covering above 1,000 feet. There was widespread frost on most nights and –6.9°C was registered at Shap in Cumbria on the 22nd. The 26th to the 27th was mainly dry and sunny, with overnight frost and some fog patches under transient high pressure. The 28th to the 31st was very unsettled and wet. After a frosty start on the 28th with some patchy mist and fog, bands of heavy rain and showers crossed the region. During the 30th a deep north Atlantic depression heading for Biscay brought very heavy rain to many places. The 31st saw outbreaks of rain, thundery near the south coast gradually die out.

NOVEMBER 2003

From the 1st to the 3rd depressions passing to the north brought frequent rain and showers, some of which were thundery. From the 4th to the 8th high pressure built up over the region and then transferred to Scandinavia. It was dry and mild or very mild with good sunny periods after early mist and fog patches cleared. Wisley in Surrey reached 19.2°C on the 6th. The 9th to the 12th was changeable as Atlantic fronts crossed the region. Temperatures were generally not far from normal but with rain at times. Central and eastern areas of England had extensive areas of mist and fog early on the 11th. There was some heavy rain at times especially in western areas later on the 11th and early on the 12th, with thunder being heard in south Wales. From the 13th to the 15th a deep depression moved north-east from southern Ireland to the North Sea. Bands of heavy rain and showers were carried on the gale force south-westerly winds. Mumbles in South Wales had gusts of up to 73kts. The 15th was quieter with occasional showers in western areas and the best of the sunshine in the south-east. The 16th to the 20th was changeable and mainly mild in a west-south-westerly airstream between low pressure to the north and high pressure to the south. Some rain and showers, heavy at times, broke out on the 17th, 19th and 20th, mainly in the west. A cold front became slow moving over south-east England later on 20th. From the 21st to the 23rd a low over Biscay caused weather fronts to stall over south-east England, bringing copious rainfall to the Kent, Surrey and Sussex areas. Redesdale in Northumberland fell to –6.2°C on the 23rd. The 24th to the 30th was mostly unsettled and wet after a quiet frosty start on the 24th. Vigorous Atlantic depressions to the north brought heavy rain and showers to all areas during the 25th and 26th and some showers turned thundery in the south-west later. After the clearance of some thundery rain near the south coast, the 27th and 28th provided a mainly dry sunny interlude, with overnight frost and fog patches. More mild wet and windy weather spread in from the North Atlantic during the 29th and the rain was heavy at times and turned showery later. Eastern counties had a sunny start on the 30th.

DECEMBER 2003

The 1st to the 2nd saw low pressure in the Channel and it was a very wet start to the month. However the rain gradually died out during the 2nd. From the 3rd to the 9th an anticyclone built up to the north with a significant cold front moving south on the 6th. The east Midlands and East Anglia were foggy on the 3rd and the north-east of England was affected on the 4th. It was cloudy at first becoming mainly sunny later with overnight patchy fog and frost. After some freezing fog at first in places on 10th, depressions passing to the north brought bands of rain and showers, heavy at times, especially in northern and western areas. It was mild in southern areas on the 11th, 12th and 13th before cooler north-westerly winds arrived later. Teignmouth in Devon reached 14.9°C on 11th. The 15th to the 19th saw high pressure return to the region which moved to north France by the 16th, then to the Balkans by the 18th but maintaining its influence throughout. Mist and fog patches were reported on the 17th and 18th in places and in the south on the 19th. From the 20th to the 22nd a deep depression formed over the UK bringing widespread heavy rain to most areas. The low moved to Denmark during the 21st bringing cold northerly winds and heavy wintry showers in its rear. High ground in the north and north-west including Wales received snow cover as did East Coast counties down to Lincolnshire in the evening. Early on the 22nd more snow fell in eastern counties. From the 23rd to the 26th low pressure to the north heralded the return of mild damp westerly winds. Although mostly dry at first, rain became more widespread over Christmas and Boxing day especially in north-west England and Wales, where showers turned thundery later. Rain totalling 80mm was recorded in 18 hours at Shap Fell in Cumbria on the 26th. From the 27th to the 31st low pressure transferred to Scandinavia and a colder north draught ensued. Southern counties were deluged from the 27th to the 29th as heavy rain, thundery at times affected the south coast. There was some sleet or snow later on adjacent high ground. Further north clearer skies allowed widespread frost, severe and persisting throughout the day in places on the 29th and 30th. Shap Fell in Cumbria registered –11.4°C overnight from the 30th to 31st.

JANUARY 2004

This was the wettest January since 1999. The month commenced rather cold and changeable, with some rain and drizzle and snow over high ground in the north. Redhill fell to –6.7°C early on the 3rd. The 4th to the 6th saw high pressure to the south gave mild conditions and some hill and coastal fog at first. Rain and drizzle on the 5th gave way to scattered showers later on the 6th. The 7th to the 13th was very unsettled and wet as vigorous depressions swept their associated fronts across the region, mostly mild or very mild at first. A low crossed the Borders on the 8th bringing gales to many places and a few thundery showers on the 9th. It reached 13.6°C at Teignmouth in Devon on the 10th. A deep depression brought gales, lowering temperatures and some thundery showers on the 11th with a waterspout observed in the Bristol channel. There was more rain and blustery showers on the 12th and 13th as another depression tracked close by. Snow fell in the Midlands and the north on the 14th, reaching up to 5cms deep in places, with as much as 15cms over high ground in Wales. Another deep depression crossed northern England during the 15th and 16th bringing widespread gales. Further snow fell over high ground in the north allowing 20cms to accumulate at Boltshope Park later on the 15th. From the 19th to the 25th it was mostly mild and changeable with rain at times as complex low pressure to the north of the UK pushed weak fronts across the region. It was mainly cloudy with some hill and coastal fog on the 21st and 23rd. The 22nd and 23rd were generally wet, however along the north coast of Wales at Colwyn Bay it reached 13.6°C on the 22nd. In contrast, the 24th and 25th brought long sunny periods, lower temperatures and a few showers. After a rather cold cloudy day on the 26th an arctic airstream brought snowfall to northern areas, affecting east coast counties and the south-east later on the 27th. During the 28th another snow band gathered strength over the Midlands as it migrated southwards. The passage of this front produced squalls, a sudden drop in temperature and a period of heavy snow which settled quickly, even in central London where 2 to 4cms fell. There were also many reports of lightning and thunder. north Wales, north-east England, the Wolds and parts of East Anglia had significant falls, with depths up to 15cms in places. Scampton in Lincolnshire recorded –8.0°C on the 28th. After a sunny cold start on the 29th, heavy rain and gales swept across the region from the west, with wet weather continuing for the remainder of the month.

FEBRUARY 2004

From the 1st to the 6th vigorous low pressure to the north and north-west brought very mild wet and windy weather to the region. The rain was often heavy especially in North Wales and Cumbria where severe local flooding occurred. Capel Curig registered 260mm of rain in 48 hours during the 3rd and 4th. Gravesend in Kent achieved 17.9°C on the 4th while central London reached 17.8°C, a record high for so early in the year. The 7th to the 10th saw a deep low near Faroes moved south-east to Denmark. After overnight frost at first on the 9th and 10th very mild air returned. From the 11th to the 15th it stayed mild as high pressure sat over the UK. There was some heavy rain at times in the north-east during the 14th. The 16th to the 21st was continuing anticyclonic and generally dry and mild at first, becoming colder later. There was a little rain on the 17th and a few showers on North Sea coasts on the 18th. Southern England had some snow flurries on the 20th, and rain in the south-west on the 21st. From the 22nd to the 25th it became colder with northerly winds as high pressure receded westwards and a deep depression from Greenland migrated to south Scandinavia. The 26th to the 29th saw bands of snow affecting Wales, north England and east coast areas including East Anglia at first, giving significant falls in places. Later on the 26th an area of moderate snow moved across central southern England, with 10–12cm depth reported from Bournemouth early on the 27th. Sennybridge in Powys fell to –10.9°C that same morning; overnight frost became widespread and severe in places. Persistent snow showers during the 27th and 28th gave further moderate accumulations over Wales, north England and north-east coastal areas. Some parts adjacent to the North Sea as far south as Kent also received a few centimetres and there were some odd reports of thunder too. Wintry showers also broke out over central southern England on the 28th. Boltshope Park in north England boasted 16cm of snow on the 29th, however rising pressure restricted snow showers to south-east England that day.

MARCH 2004

From the 1st to the 2nd high pressure brought good sunny periods and widespread overnight frost which was severe in places. A temperature of –11.7°C was noted at Redesdale in north England on the 1st. The 3rd to the 7th saw a changeable spell as Atlantic fronts crossed the region bringing occasional rain and showers. From the 8th to the 10th there was a recurrence of high pressure. A deep depression swept fronts north-east across the region during the 11th and 12th preceded by sleet and snow in many parts especially over high ground. There were several centimetres in a number of places early on the 12th and some thunder reported from south-west England. It was milder on 13th and 14th but with rain and showers especially in the west and showers turning thundery in the south-east on the 13th. The 15th to the 17th saw high pressure over Europe. There was occasional light rain in western areas. It became exceptionally warm with Cleethorpes in north east Lincolnshire reaching 18.7°C on the 16th and there were good sunny periods especially in the east and south-east. The 18th to the 25th was more unsettled as deep complex low pressure to the north drifted to Scandinavia. Winds veered slowly from westerly to northerly with severe gales affecting many areas during the 19th to the 21st especially on the 20th when Aberdaron in north Wales gusted to 87kts. Eastern areas became very warm on the 20th. Showers were fairly widespread at times from the 21st, some becoming heavy with hail and thunder. Generally it was rather cold later with some overnight frost and a little sleet or snow in places on the 25th. The 26th to the 29th was mostly dull with patchy mist and fog as a weak front moved very slowly south-east across the region. Some outbreaks of rain and drizzle gave way during the 29th to brighter drier conditions and warmer temperatures. Northolt in London reached 20.1°C on the 31st.

APRIL 2004

This was the warmest April since 1987. The 1st to the 7th saw low pressure to the west slowly moving east and north driving bands of rain and showers across the region. The 4th onwards saw showers often heavy and thundery with hail in many places. From the 8th to the 14th the Azores high extended a weak ridge across southern parts of the UK. It was chilly at first with some overnight frost and –4°C was registered at Sennybridge in Wales on the 9th. After a few showers on the 8th, and a little light rain on the 9th and 10th, mainly dry warm weather with good sunny periods prevailed. Northern areas were cloudy at times and some light rain spread in later on the 14th to north-west parts. The 15th to the 21st saw active depressions residing close to or over the UK bringing a second spell of unsettled weather, however it was dry and warm at first particularly in the south-east. Fronts made erratic progress eastwards during the 17th and 18th bringing lower temps and copious amounts of rain to many places. Further bands of rain and showers affected most areas from the 19th to the 21st, with hail and thunder mixed in. Reigate in Surrey experienced a violent thunderstorm on the 19th with heavy hail, sleet and snow. There were scattered light showers on the 22nd and very warm sunny weather arrived with 23.4°C reached in central London on the 24th. There was patchy hill and coastal fog in places and thunder later in the north on the 25th. The 26th to the 30th saw low pressure developing off southern England causing bands of thundery rain to affect many areas with numerous reports of local flooding and lightning strikes. On the 26th one band stretched from north-east England to the Seven estuary. There was 33mm of rain in an hour during a storm at Sheffield which caused local flooding. Overnight from the 26 to the 27th Worcestershire was hit by storms with many homes or businesses struck by lightning and affected by local flooding. Near Worcester, 43mm of rain fell in two hours. The south-east and East Anglia were visited later on the 27th with outbreaks in south-east London causing much disruption to rail services during evening rush hour. The 28th saw more outbreaks over the south-east and East Anglia and a particularly violent storm broke out around the South Downs and Sussex area during the late afternoon. It was warm at first but became colder on the 28th as north-north-easterly winds picked up. The 29th saw more rain heavy at times and again early on the 30th in the south.

MAY 2004

There were occasional thundery showers on the 1st becoming rather warm by the 2nd with scattered showers and sunny periods. Low pressure took up residence over the UK bringing heavy thundery showers to many places on the 3rd and 4th and in the north, Midlands and East Anglia during the 5th. It was rather cold or cold with sunny periods. From the 6th to the 10th the low centre drifted east allowing a northerly airstream to be established. Scattered thundery showers on the 6th became more widespread over the eastern half of England during the 7th. Temperatures were generally near normal; some thundery outbreaks affected the south-west, Wales and the Midlands on the 10th. From the 11th to the 18th a high from the Azores extended its influence after thundery outbreaks on the 11th died away. The exception was light showers in the Hampshire and Surrey areas during the evening of the 13th. There were long sunny periods after early morning patchy mist and fog cleared and it became warm or very warm from the 15th onwards. From the 19th to the 21st the high pressure receded westwards allowing a cold front to move slowly down. It was very warm and sunny in the south at first, 25.3°C being recorded in central London on the 19th, however some sea fog plagued parts of the south-west. Prone areas had a touch of air frost, with Shap in Cumbria falling to −2.4°C early on the 21st. High pressure was mostly dominant from the 22nd to the 27th and a dry sunny spell ensued. The 26th saw thundery outbreaks affecting a few places in south Wales and south England but these died out early the next day with most areas becoming very warm. The 28th to the 31st was changeable as low pressure to the west pushed Atlantic fronts erratically across the region bringing further outbreaks of rain and showers, some thundery, to some areas. The north-west received significant rain on the 28th. During the 29th scattered outbreaks of rain affected a number of locations. Central and north-eastern areas of England had thundery rain later on the 30th, while southern parts of the region reported scattered thundery showers.

JUNE 2004

From the 1st to the 6th a weak ridge of high pressure built across Wales and south-west England keeping these areas mostly dry, but weak fronts pushed down the North Sea to give some light rain at times over eastern counties of England. By the 7th the high pressure had drifted into central Europe allowing warm air to spill in from the Continent, as well as allowing a few thunderstorms to develop. The hottest day occurred on the 8th when several places in southern and eastern England reported over 30 °C, the highest being Cambridge with 31.5 °C. During the evening scattered thunderstorm occurred, with Leconfield recording 12.6 mm of rain. The high pressure maintained its influence until the 16th keeping many places dry and warm but scattered showers did occur in places. Temperatures reached 29 °C in Bournemouth on the 15th and 27 °C in Leicester on the 16th. On the 17th a cold front crossed the area bringing a change to much fresher weather with blustery west to north-westerly winds. On the 18th Scarborough and Leeds saw maximum temperatures of only 10 °C, and a frost was recorded at Shap Fell overnight as temperatures fell to –0.2 °C. The cool north to north-westerly airflow continued until the 21st. The main event of the month occurred on the 22nd and 23rd as a major depression swept across Wales and northern England. The central pressure at 6 a.m. on the 23rd was 982 hPa, making it one of the deepest depressions recorded in June over England and Wales. Many parts of Cornwall, Wales and Cumbria received over 25 mm of rain, Dunkeswell recording 34 mm of which 22.1 mm fell in just 2 hours. On the 23rd gale force winds along the English Channel coast gave gusts in excess of 50 kts, Dover reporting 58 knots. The low pushed out over the North Sea on the 24th but not before giving 47 mm of rain at Loftus and gusts of 40 to 50 knots over eastern England. The next depression on the 26th gave 22.8 mm of rain at Plymouth and as it cleared on the 27th, heavy showers and thunderstorms broke out in its wake. From the 28th to the 30th southern areas stayed mainly fine and dry but showers affected the north and west. Some heavy showers occurred over northern England on the 30th with totals of 7 mm in one hour at Manchester and Preston.

AVERAGE AND GENERAL MONTHLY VALUES 2003–2004 (JUNE)

	Rainfall (mm)				*Temperature (°C)*				*Bright Sunshine (hrs per day)*			
	1961–90	2002	2003	2004	1961–90	2002	2003	2004	1961–90	2002	2003	2004
ENGLAND AND WALES												
January	77	90	84	124	3.8	5.3	4.2	4.9	1.6	1.42	2.35	1.60
February	55	129	39	56	3.8	6.6	3.7	5.0	2.4	2.71	3.47	3.07
March	63	49	39	51	5.6	7.2	7.2	6.2	3.5	3.60	5.56	3.51
April	53	54	43	80	7.7	8.8	9.3	9.1	4.9	6.35	6.42	4.46
May	56	92	73	46	10.9	11.4	11.6	11.7	6.2	6.04	5.96	6.58
June	58	55	67	58	13.9	13.9	15.5	14.9	6.4	5.77	7.13	6.63
July	56	82	76		15.7	15.4	17.0		6.0	5.51	5.57	
August	68	67	18		15.6	16.5	17.7		6.0	5.29	6.70	
September	70	35	37		13.6	13.9	14.0		4.5	5.43	5.53	
October	77	134	58		10.7	9.8	8.9		3.2	3.16	4.20	
November	81	150	100		6.6	8.2	7.9		2.2	1.91	2.25	
December	82	131	100		4.7	5.4	4.8		1.5	1.16	1.68	
YEAR	796	1068	734		9.4	10.2	10.2		4.0	4.00	4.70	
SCOTLAND												
January	117	206	167	208	3.1	4.3	2.6	3.4	1.3	0.99	1.22	0.97
February	78	235	57	104	3.1	3.6	2.7	3.1	2.4	1.93	3.18	3.06
March	94	124	86	93	4.6	5.0	5.7	4.8	3.2	3.42	4.88	3.71
April	60	87	58	121	6.5	7.0	8.0	7.5	4.8	4.90	5.94	3.41
May	67	101	139	59	9.3	9.5	9.1	9.9	5.6	5.62	4.58	6.18
June	67	129	79	122	12.1	11.8	13.0	12.1	5.6	4.70	5.55	4.04
July	74	124	80		13.6	12.5	14.8		4.9	3.47	4.46	
August	92	87	46		13.5	14.0	14.4		4.9	4.11	5.88	
September	111	50	85		11.5	11.8	11.5		3.5	3.51	3.84	
October	120	182	78		9.1	6.8	6.8		2.6	2.49	3.44	
November	118	159	160		5.3	6.2	6.4		1.7	1.31	1.94	
December	115	68	168		3.9	3.5	3.2		1.0	0.79	1.03	
YEAR	1,113	1,552	1,203		7.9	8.0	8.2		3.5	3.10	3.80	

Source: Data provided by the Met Office

WIND FORCE MEASURES

The *Beaufort Scale* of wind force has been accepted internationally and is used in communicating weather conditions. Devised originally by Admiral Sir Francis Beaufort in 1805, it now consists of the numbers 0–17, each representing a certain strength or velocity of wind at 10 m (33 ft) above ground in the open.

Scale no.	*Wind Force*	*mph*	*knots*
0	Calm	1	1
1	Light air	1–3	1–3
2	Slight breeze	4–7	4–6
3	Gentle breeze	8–12	7–10
4	Moderate breeze	13–18	11–16
5	Fresh breeze	19–24	17–21
6	Strong breeze	25–31	22–27
7	High wind	32–38	28–33
8	Gale	39–46	34–40
9	Strong gale	47–54	41–47
10	Whole gale	55–63	48–55
11	Storm	64–72	56–63
12	Hurricane	73–82	64–71
13	–	83–92	72–80
14	–	93–103	81–89
15	–	104–114	90–99
16	–	115–125	100–108
17	–	126–136	109–118

TEMPERATURE, RAINFALL AND SUNSHINE

At selected climatological reporting stations, July 2003–June 2004 and calendar year 2003

Ht height (in metres) of station above mean sea level
°C mean air temperature
Rain total monthly rainfall
Sun monthy total (hours)
Source: Data provided by the Met Office

	Ht	*July 2003*			*August 2003*			*September 2003*			*October 2003*		
			Rain	*Sun*		*Rain*	*Sun*		*Rain*	*Sun*		*Rain*	*Sun*
	m	*°C*	*mm*	*hrs*	*°C*	*mm*	*hrs*	*°C*	*mm*	*hrs*	*°C*	*mm*	*hrs*
Lerwick	82	14.4.	39.5	169.0	13.9	59.4	174.8	11.4	114.6	124.2	7.4	125.4	105.8
Stornoway	15	15.0	48.4	115.5	14.7	46.2	140.5	12.2	77.2	87.2	8.3	68.0	102.1
Dyce	65	16.2	12.4	189.1	15.8	16.6	220.0	12.7	26.7	146.8	8.3	48.5	137.8
Eskdalemuir	242	14.9	166.1	120.6	15.0	33.6	205.6	11.5	83.4	114.1	6.8	60.2	124.5
Aldergrove	68	16.3	53.6	107.5	15.8	16.8	175.6	13.1	83.4	113.4	8.6	37.4	95.5
Bingley	64	16.2	74.4	–	16.1	12.0	–	13.1	39.6	–	7.9	29.8	–
Valley	10	16.5	39.4	117.6	17.0	16.4	140.6	14.5	108.1	113.9	9.9	66.1	87.9
Coleshill	–	17.6	35.8	–	18.5	16.2	–	14.8	31.6	–	8.9	62.6	–
Skegness	6	18.0	59.0	221.2	17.5	8.1	218.7	14.8	17.3	191.3	9.9	54.9	122.4
Bristol	42	18.0	76.0	157.6	19.2	7.4	191.3	15.2	8.8	175.0	9.7	48.0	111.5
St Mawgan	103	16.7	110.4	156.7	18.0	22.3	217.5	15.1	29.2	192.8	11.0	73.4	137.3
Hastings	45	18.3	52.3	288.3	19.6	29.8	286.4	16.2	11.2	243.3	10.9	37.7	169.3

	November 2003			*December 2003*			*The Year 2003*			*January 2004*			*February 2004*		
		Rain	*Sun*		*Rain*	*Sun*		*Rain*	*Sun*		*Rain*	*Sun*		*Rain*	*Sun*
	°C	*mm*	*hrs*	*°C*	*mm*	*hrs*	*°C*	*mm*	*hrs*	*°C*	*mm*	*hrs*	*°C*	*mm*	*hrs*
Lerwick	7.3	120.7	51.6	4.6	146.3	23.8	8.4	94.7	106	3.9	155.5	38.2	4.0	102.2	46.9
Stornoway	8.1	103.2	44.2	5.3	71.9	27.9	9.5	75.04	90.7	4.9	111.2	23.2	4.6	79.4	64.7
Dyce	6.9	74.5	71.1	4.1	89.3	43.1	9.25	45.9	142.9	4.0	77.4	46.2	4.2	38.3	92.3
Eskdalemuir	6.2	209.3	41.4	2.7	167.5	48.5	8.2	109.4	124.6	2.9	232.6	29.3	3.0	122.9	95.0
Aldergrove	7.5	89.4	74.1	5.3	108.2	51.9	9.75	61.4	117.4	4.7	90.8	36.4	4.5	21.4	107.9
Bingley	6.7	96.2	–	3.6	92.4	–	10.1	54.3	–	4.0	138.6	–	4.0	70.8	–
Valley	9.6	95.5	46.7	6.6	102.7	43.0	10	64.3	128	6.5	104.3	29.0	5.7	60.9	68.9
Coleshill	8.0	66.8	–	4.8	83.2	–	10.5	45.8	–	5.1	101.0	–	5.3	20.6	–
Skegness	8.6	56.0	65.8	5.3	72.2	51.0	–	–	–	5.0	71.8	43.3	5.6	30.5	60.4
Bristol	8.7	92.6	72.9	5.8	100.6	46.8	11.1	50	136	5.9	74.8	56.1	5.9	43.0	83.2
St Mawgan	10.0	76.2	102.5	7.5	116.2	60.0	11.4	70	161	7.5	131.2	67.3	6.4	55.0	110.6
Hastings	10.2	121.0	74.9	6.8	85.6	66.7	–	–	–	6.4	90.8	74.5	6.0	22.9	88.8

	March 2004			*April 2004*			*May 2004*			*June 2004*		
		Rain	*Sun*		*Rain*	*Sun*		*Rain*	*Sun*		*Rain*	*Sun*
	°C	*mm*	*hrs*	*°C*	*mm*	*hrs*	*°C*	*mm*	*hrs*	*°C*	*mm*	*hrs*
Lerwick	5.6	93.1	119.2	7.4	78.9	111.8	8.8	64.2	125.2	10.5	87.2	136.5
Stornoway	6.5	38.0	121.5	8.3	77.6	105.2	10.2	39.4	145.4	12.3	71.0	89.2
Dyce	5.4	42.1	124.4	8.6	115.5	117.0	10.9	22.6	198.6	13.7	85.8	170.6
Eskdalemuir	4.3	152.2	80.2	7.3	152.4	97.0	10.3	63.3	202.4	12.7	130.4	109.2
Aldergrove	6.3	67.8	122.8	8.7	61.8	137.8	11.2	23.6	182.2	14.5	57.2	130.0
Bingley	5.0	58.8	–	8.2	99.2	–	10.9	40.2	–	13.7	31.8	–
Valley	7.0	35.4	124.5	9.4	28.7	101.0	11.7	35.8	137.9	14.3	50.2	121.0
Coleshill	6.6	43.9	–	9.6	66.8	–	12.1	43.4	–	15.8	46.0	–
Skegness	6.7	27.8	109.6	9.6	55.9	134.2	11.2	46.7	217.5	–	–	–
Bristol	7.1	56.2	97.2	10.0	69.6	142.1	13.1	43.2	196.4	16.5	44.6	224.7
St Mawgan	7.3	67.5	163.0	9.5	54.9	176.7	12.4	27.0	268.0	15.3	61.0	254.3
Hastings	7.0	27.4	131.0	10.0	74.7	209.4	12.7	41.0	252.4	17.0	34.4	275.3

METEOROLOGICAL OBSERVATIONS LONDON (HEATHROW)

Temperature maxima and minima cover the 24-hour period 9 – 9 h; mean wind speed is 10 m above ground; rainfall is for the 24 hours starting on 9 h on the day of entry; sunshine is for the 24 hours. *Source:* Data provided by the Met Office

JULY 2003

Day	*Temperature* Max °C	Min °C	*Wind* knots	*Rain* mm	*Sun* hrs
1	20.3	13.8	7.3	1.2	1.2
2	20.4	14.4	6.4	5.6	1.5
3	19.8	13.6	7.3	0.4	0.2
4	22.1	11.5	7.8	0.0	3.1
5	19.4	11.9	5.5	0.0	4.7
6	23.2	15.0	5.7	0.0	7.7
7	22.0	12.1	7.0	0.0	9.6
8	25.0	13.8	6.6	0.0	1.4
9	28.3	16.1	5.0	0.0	8.4
10	29.3	16.2	8.4	0.0	11.5
11	23.9	14.4	8.9	0.0	12.9
12	26.7	12.3	4.2	0.0	15.1
13	28.5	14.8	8.5	0.0	15.4
14	n/a	15.6	9.7	0.0	15.3
15	32.8	17.0	7.7	trace	14.8
16	24.4	18.7	6.0	3.8	3.3
17	21.0	17.3	12.4	2.2	0.1
18	25.1	15.7	10.3	0.0	8.3
19	28.5	15.4	8.4	0.0	10.7
20	24.4	16.1	9.9	0.0	12.5
21	25.1	14.7	11.0	0.0	10.6
22	24.2	14.6	9.3	0.0	6.9
23	24.6	15.2	11.1	0.4	3.4
24	24.2	15.2	10.7	1.6	5.2
25	21.4	15.5	11.5	4.0	1.8
26	20.7	12.5	6.9	5.4	1.4
27	23.5	14.5	9.6	trace	9.4
28	23.1	11.8	10.2	0.4	7.4
29	21.4	16.1	10.8	2.8	0.2
30	24.8	15.9	9.2	0.0	7.9
31	23.1	15.0	8.4	1.0	2.0

AUGUST 2003

Day	*Temperature* Max °C	Min °C	*Wind* knots	*Rain* mm	*Sun* hrs
1	19.5	15.2	8.1	0.2	0.0
2	25.1	12.3	4.9	0.0	14.5
3	29.5	13.1	4.4	0.0	13.9
4	31.8	16.7	7.2	trace	12.0
5	32.2	18.7	9.0	0.0	10.0
6	35.2	20.3	6.1	0.0	12.7
7	29.7	18.0	6.8	0.0	12.9
8	30.7	18.8	4.8	0.0	12.3
9	35.0	18.3	4.9	0.0	13.0
10	37.9	20.1	6.3	0.0	12.5
11	33.7	20.0	7.3	0.0	10.4
12	30.1	18.7	6.3	0.0	8.6
13	28.5	17.5	7.5	0.0	10.5
14	25.1	15.5	8.0	0.0	13.5
15	24.5	13.4	7.7	0.6	12.6
16	24.0	14.8	8.1	0.0	3.7
17	27.0	15.0	7.6	0.0	7.1
18	25.3	16.9	8.8	0.4	5.7
19	23.2	11.4	7.2	0.0	7.3
20	23.4	10.6	5.8	0.0	13.0
21	23.7	14.0	10.2	trace	4.4
22	26.3	17.6	11.8	0.0	4.6
23	27.1	17.4	5.5	trace	4.2
24	25.4	19.7	7.8	0.0	8.1
25	21.3	15.0	8.8	0.0	0.1
26	23.1	14.6	6.3	0.0	1.8
27	23.2	16.8	6.7	0.0	2.2
28	18.8	15.5	7.2	8.2	0.3
29	19.2	12.8	10.4	1.0	1.0
30	19.5	9.1	7.5	0.0	12.5
31	20.5	8.4	5.6	0.0	9.9

SEPTEMBER 2003

Day	Max °C	Min °C	knots	mm	hrs
1	19.4	13.0	7.3	0.0	6.8
2	21.0	11.5	3.3	0.0	2.3
3	22.4	14.9	3.7	0.0	0.5
4	24.5	11.2	6.0	0.0	11.8
5	26.9	13.1	5.4	0.2	5.6
6	21.8	14.2	7.7	0.4	6.8
7	19.3	9.5	4.5	trace	2.8
8	22.1	10.3	5.6	0.0	5.4
9	20.8	13.1	9.4	2.0	6.9
10	21.9	12.1	9.7	0.2	4.0
11	18.5	10.5	5.3	0.2	1.1
12	20.9	12.8	6.3	0.0	8.7
13	23.9	10.5	5.0	0.0	11.4
14	26.0	11.3	4.3	0.0	11.1
15	26.1	11.1	4.2	0.0	9.8
16	27.0	11.9	4.1	0.0	10.8
17	27.9	11.8	6.4	0.0	11.3
18	21.7	12.2	8.6	0.0	3.2
19	23.5	12.1	7.5	0.0	7.1
20	27.0	11.1	4.5	0.0	9.6
21	26.8	13.1	6.3	0.0	7.8
22	21.9	16.1	11.3	4.2	3.5
23	14.9	6.7	9.0	0.0	9.9
24	17.3	4.0	3.7	0.0	10.7
25	19.7	5.7	4.5	0.0	10.7
26	20.4	7.3	5.9	1.2	5.7
27	17.6	10.5	5.2	0.0	2.6
28	16.1	8.9	6.8	0.0	4.4
29	18.8	5.4	5.8	0.0	10.1
30	20.8	9.0	8.6	0.0	4.3

OCTOBER 2003

Day	Max °C	Min °C	knots	mm	hrs
1	18.6	11.3	8.7	3.8	0.4
2	18.4	10.7	5.0	2.0	0.1
3	18.0	12.9	6.7	0.0	0.1
4	13.2	7.9	10.1	trace	2.4
5	13.3	3.8	10.8	0.0	9.8
6	15.3	6.9	14.0	trace	3.5
7	14.4	11.2	14.4	0.2	6.1
8	20.4	4.8	10.3	trace	2.5
9	18.7	11.2	10.7	0.0	7.5
10	19.3	13.0	12.0	1.4	2.0
11	18.3	7.7	3.5	0.0	9.5
12	17.0	8.4	9.8	0.0	5.1
13	17.1	10.0	9.2	0.0	2.9
14	16.5	10.5	11.3	0.0	6.3
15	15.8	8.2	11.8	0.0	9.3
16	15.7	7.5	10.3	0.0	9.4
17	15.0	6.9	9.7	0.0	9.4
18	16.0	4.4	8.8	0.0	6.8
19	13.2	6.3	11.9	0.0	3.7
20	12.2	6.1	12.4	0.0	5.9
21	11.3	1.3	4.9	4.6	6.4
22	9.2	3.4	9.1	0.6	0.0
23	11.1	6.5	12.0	trace	8.2
24	10.3	0.1	7.8	0.0	5.8
25	11.3	0.3	9.0	0.2	4.3
26	11.8	4.1	8.0	trace	7.6
27	12.0	0.8	3.2	0.0	8.8
28	12.2	0.4	5.4	3.0	7.4
29	10.3	4.3	6.6	6.0	1.0
30	10.4	3.3	9.0	11.6	4.7
31	12.6	5.4	6.2	0.6	3.8

NOVEMBER 2003

	Temperature Max °C	Min °C	Wind knots	Rain mm	Sun hrs
Day 1	12.1	6.6	9.7	4.4	6.5
2	14.6	6.9	13.0	6.2	1.1
3	15.4	8.4	13.8	0.2	7.0
4	15.4	4.4	6.8	0.2	6.3
5	15.7	9.7	8.7	0.0	7.2
6	18.4	7.4	5.0	0.0	4.7
7	13.9	8.2	8.6	trace	8.3
8	10.5	8.2	10.8	0.0	1.1
9	11.1	4.4	6.3	1.2	0.5
10	14.0	7.2	4.7	0.0	2.0
11	12.6	7.6	6.3	4.4	0.0
12	14.7	7.9	7.6	0.2	4.2
13	14.3	5.7	8.3	0.8	3.2
14	14.1	9.8	17.9	trace	5.1
15	13.3	8.9	8.1	0.0	3.9
16	10.5	5.3	6.6	trace	7.1
17	13.9	2.7	8.8	2.8	0.0
18	15.0	8.0	11.5	trace	0.0
19	14.7	12.2	9.3	0.2	0.0
20	13.1	10.9	8.6	5.8	0.0
21	9.9	9.1	4.6	12.4	0.0
22	8.8	8.1	7.8	27.0	0.0
23	7.5	6.6	11.5	18.2	0.0
24	9.7	6.2	7.1	0.2	1.6
25	12.5	2.5	9.8	16.4	0.4
26	9.8	8.4	11.7	2.6	3.1
27	9.1	1.9	3.5	0.2	4.2
28	11.0	-0.4	4.9	trace	6.5
29	12.2	2.7	11.5	3.0	0.0
30	10.4	5.5	5.3	7.4	4.2

DECEMBER 2003

	Temperature Max °C	Min °C	Wind knots	Rain mm	Sun hrs
Day 1	10.7	7.1	8.5	4.6	0.1
2	10.4	6.3	5.9	1.2	0.8
3	9.5	7.3	6.4	0.0	0.0
4	9.1	7.2	11.4	trace	0.0
5	8.9	8.2	6.0	0.2	0.0
6	9.0	2.2	7.3	0.2	0.0
7	6.0	0.9	8.4	0.0	7.4
8	8.0	-1.2	6.4	trace	2.9
9	9.1	0.2	4.1	0.0	6.3
10	9.8	2.5	3.8	5.2	0.0
11	11.7	1.4	7.9	1.2	0.0
12	13.4	3.1	8.2	8.2	0.0
13	14.1	6.0	14.8	1.4	0.0
14	9.9	6.1	12.3	trace	3.7
15	6.1	2.5	4.8	0.0	7.1
16	6.1	–3.1	3.5	0.0	2.1
17	8.4	–0.5	4.0	0.0	7.1
18	8.4	0.3	3.8	0.0	6.9
19	9.6	1.1	3.1	1.8	0.1
20	12.8	5.0	13.2	3.4	0.3
21	7.3	3.6	13.5	0.0	5.2
22	5.3	0.3	8.5	1.2	2.8
23	9.8	0.6	7.5	1.6	0.0
24	10.0	5.2	9.3	trace	0.0
25	11.4	9.2	12.1	0.2	0.0
26	10.7	9.2	14.2	1.6	0.0
27	8.1	3.4	10.1	2.2	2.7
28	5.8	2.6	10.7	2.6	2.5
29	3.7	1.0	5.2	8.8	0.0
30	5.0	1.8	3.0	1.2	0.0
31	5.7	0.9	4.5	4.6	0.0

JANUARY 2004

Day 1	8.0	0.6	9.4	1.2	0.0
2	4.7	4.4	6.4	trace	0.0
3	5.7	–2.4	5.4	1.0	0.0
4	8.0	–0.7	5.1	0.4	0.0
5	11.2	3.0	7.0	1.8	0.0
6	11.7	6.9	10.4	trace	3.1
7	10.4	6.6	10.4	7.4	0.9
8	11.9	7.9	14.8	2.8	2.1
9	9.5	4.7	10.8	0.4	3.1
10	12.1	3.7	8.3	7.6	0.0
11	11.5	8.7	14.8	5.8	2.8
12	10.5	4.2	9.1	7.6	1.7
13	9.2	6.1	18.2	1.8	3.2
14	7.1	4.1	10.0	2.0	0.4
15	9.3	1.1	10.9	6.6	3.0
16	8.4	3.2	16.3	0.0	3.6
17	6.5	–0.1	7.1	0.2	5.3
18	7.9	–0.2	6.6	trace	6.6
19	11.1	0.1	12.0	0.2	0.1
20	10.1	7.9	7.6	0.8	0.0
21	9.9	7.7	6.1	trace	0.4
22	8.5	6.5	7.3	5.4	0.0
23	8.9	5.8	6.3	3.8	0.0
24	10.0	4.0	7.2	0.2	7.3
25	7.3	–0.4	4.2	trace	5.4
26	5.4	1.3	8.3	trace	0.0
27	5.3	2.4	7.2	0.7	2.8
28	5.4	–0.8	11.9	4.0	3.8
29	4.4	–2.6	9.6	0.0	8.3
30	10.6	–1.0	10.4	4.8	0.1
31	12.4	4.0	22.1	5.4	0.0

FEBRUARY 2004

Day 1	12.9	9.3	14.5	7.6	2.0
2	14.3	9.6	15.5	trace	0.1
3	15.3	11.6	18.9	1.4	0.0
4	16.6	12.1	16.4	0.2	1.5
5	13.5	12.1	10.3	1.6	0.0
6	11.3	10.2	10.6	5.0	0.4
7	10.2	5.7	16.0	1.0	6.1
8	8.8	4.3	15.4	trace	5.8
9	6.2	-2.4	4.2	0.0	5.9
10	9.4	0.0	8.9	0.0	2.4
11	12.6	2.9	5.0	trace	0.0
12	11.1	7.9	3.5	0.0	0.0
13	9.6	7.4	4.1	0.8	0.0
14	10.0	6.7	4.0	1.4	2.9
15	9.0	5.3	4.0	0.4	0.1
16	7.8	5.6	3.4	trace	0.0
17	7.3	4.9	4.2	3.4	0.0
18	8.0	3.9	7.5	0.8	2.3
19	7.5	3.1	11.1	0.0	7.0
20	3.3	1.1	10.1	0.0	0.2
21	7.4	-0.2	10.8	trace	2.0
22	6.3	2.4	11.8	trace	1.4
23	5.9	0.1	7.5	0.0	7.0
24	6.3	-3.1	7.3	2.2	0.0
25	3.9	0.2	5.9	0.0	5.0
26	5.1	-3.6	6.6	trace	8.2
27	4.8	-4.8	6.9	0.0	1.0
28	3.2	-2.4	5.6	trace	0.4
29	5.7	-0.8	6.2	0.4	3.6

MARCH 2004

	Temperature Max °C	Min °C	*Wind* knots	*Rain* mm	*Sun* hrs
Day 1	6.6	−1.9	4.0	0.0	8.7
2	8.8	−3.8	5.3	0.0	8.9
3	10.9	−1.5	7.9	2.4	2.7
4	10.1	3.4	3.1	0.0	0.0
5	10.1	4.9	4.4	trace	1.3
6	9.6	4.2	5.5	1.2	0.2
7	7.8	3.7	6.1	0.8	1.5
8	9.5	2.3	6.8	0.0	3.3
9	8.1	2.7	8.7	trace	5.2
10	5.2	1.1	6.2	trace	3.9
11	6.5	1.9	10.6	4.5	1.9
12	7.0	0.3	8.0	5.6	0.0
13	12.5	2.4	11.5	2.4	6.4
14	11.2	6.6	16.2	2.0	0.0
15	13.3	8.8	13.4	0.2	0.1
16	17.4	10.8	11.7	0.0	5.8
17	14.7	6.9	5.2	trace	0.4
18	13.9	7.5	10.1	1.8	1.9
19	12.8	7.5	16.6	3.0	0.0
20	14.3	7.8	21.3	0.2	0.6
21	12.5	6.5	19.5	0.4	8.0
22	10.0	2.7	8.8	1.6	6.7
23	8.7	2.5	6.8	1.2	3.1
24	9.3	3.7	7.6	1.4	3.1
25	9.0	0.0	5.0	trace	3.7
26	9.4	1.6	5.4	0.8	5.8
27	8.4	5.0	4.8	trace	0.0
28	10.0	5.9	6.7	trace	0.0
29	13.8	6.9	4.5	0.0	1.2
30	15.3	4.8	8.8	0.0	10.8
31	19.4	5.7	7.7	trace	7.5

APRIL 2004

	Temperature Max °C	Min °C	*Wind* knots	*Rain* mm	*Sun* hrs
Day 1	16.4	9.6	9.0	3.4	3.4
2	15.4	9.8	7.5	trace	6.8
3	14.4	6.6	13.9	4.6	1.2
4	13.5	6.4	14.9	4.8	6.6
5	13.0	5.6	14.2	0.2	3.1
6	10.5	4.3	8.8	7.2	6.0
7	11.0	4.2	6.7	1.2	5.4
8	10.6	2.2	5.8	0.4	4.1
9	12.8	2.9	4.0	1.4	8.5
10	11.4	5.9	5.6	trace	0.3
11	12.4	2.6	2.7	0.0	0.9
12	16.2	4.1	2.5	trace	0.5
13	14.9	7.1	4.5	trace	3.2
14	16.6	5.2	6.8	0.0	10.4
15	15.1	4.1	7.7	0.0	0.3
16	19.1	7.2	6.8	trace	11.0
17	15.9	6.5	10.5	4.4	9.5
18	11.3	6.5	11.2	13.4	0.1
19	12.3	3.3	6.3	5.0	9.1
20	13.9	2.5	7.2	1.0	5.8
21	15.7	9.3	10.5	2.2	0.9
22	16.9	5.1	6.3	trace	11.2
23	19.3	5.3	3.5	0.0	13.2
24	21.5	8.6	3.5	0.0	13.3
25	20.2	9.5	3.7	0.0	5.0
26	20.8	8.8	3.5	0.0	10.3
27	18.5	11.3	6.8	13.4	4.9
28	13.8	10.1	9.4	0.4	0.0
29	9.5	7.3	8.0	3.0	0.0
30	12.6	7.5	7.6	3.4	0.0

MAY 2004

Day 1	13.3	9.1	3.8	trace	0.0
2	19.0	6.6	5.2	0.8	9.6
3	13.5	9.3	5.5	10.0	3.0
4	11.6	7.0	12.0	8.6	1.9
5	13.5	5.5	10.0	1.0	6.8
6	14.8	6.8	5.6	0.0	4.5
7	16.9	7.4	7.6	3.4	6.1
8	12.7	9.5	9.8	1.4	0.0
9	15.6	10.1	5.0	2.2	0.9
10	19.5	12.6	5.0	0.0	7.7
11	15.7	10.3	5.0	trace	4.2
12	13.6	8.6	5.7	0.0	0.0
13	18.0	8.5	3.7	0.0	5.2
14	20.3	8.4	4.0	0.0	9.9
15	21.9	11.1	3.9	0.0	11.1
16	22.6	12.3	4.2	0.0	7.3
17	24.5	10.6	3.9	0.0	12.5
18	23.3	13.3	4.3	0.0	13.5
19	23.9	11.2	5.5	0.0	14.2
20	21.7	14.7	5.3	5.2	6.4
21	15.3	9.2	7.5	0.0	5.5
22	15.8	5.3	6.4	0.0	14.7
23	18.9	6.0	4.3	0.0	12.6
24	20.4	8.3	3.9	0.0	11.6
25	19.6	10.7	4.8	0.0	6.8
26	18.4	11.1	7.3	1.6	3.7
27	17.7	9.4	7.0	0.0	5.8
28	20.1	7.3	8.2	trace	6.4
29	20.5	14.5	7.7	0.4	0.1
30	18.7	11.7	6.5	0.4	5.5
31	21.6	9.0	6.4	10.0	10.7

JUNE 2004

Day 1	17.0	12.0	6.2	0.2	0.0
2	20.5	11.3	6.3	0.0	11.5
3	20.6	11.4	5.1	0.2	5.1
4	23.3	15.2	7.6	trace	6.0
5	20.3	15.9	4.8	0.0	1.1
6	24.4	14.3	6.2	0.0	3.9
7	n/a	14.3	5.7	0.0	13.6
8	30.5	16.0	8.3	0.0	11.4
9	24.0	14.8	8.4	trace	5.4
10	24.6	14.7	8.9	0.0	6.6
11	22.1	13.5	11.3	0.0	10.8
12	21.7	11.5	8.5	trace	7.7
13	25.3	12.0	4.7	0.0	15.2
14	29.0	14.6	5.8	0.0	11.6
15	27.0	14.8	7.4	0.0	12.7
16	26.8	13.1	9.0	0.0	13.8
17	19.3	14.8	11.3	trace	4.7
18	18.4	14.0	8.5	trace	2.1
19	19.3	7.3	5.9	trace	9.9
20	16.9	7.4	7.9	8.2	6.2
21	19.4	7.8	5.5	13.8	8.3
22	20.3	9.8	7.7	10.0	6.6
23	16.6	13.9	19.4	1.0	0.2
24	19.7	11.9	17.1	0.2	14.0
25	21.5	9.5	7.8	trace	13.7
26	19.5	10.0	8.1	1.2	0.0
27	23.6	14.8	10.5	5.6	9.8
28	20.6	10.2	9.4	0.0	11.5
29	22.8	12.1	8.8	0.0	8.0
30	21.2	14.4	10.6	trace	4.6

SPORTS RESULTS

For 2005 sports fixtures, *see* pages 12–13

ALPINE SKIING

WORLD CUP 2003–4

MEN
Downhill: Stephan Eberharter (Austria), 831 points
Slalom: Rainer Schönfelder (Austria), 630 points
Giant Slalom: Bode Miller (USA), 410 points
Super Giant Slalom: Hermann Maier (Austria), 580 points
Overall: Hermann Maier (Austria), 1,265 points

WOMEN
Downhill: Renate Götschl (Austria), 680 points
Slalom: Anja Pärson (Sweden), 770 points
Giant Slalom: Anja Pärson (Sweden), 630 points
Super Giant Slalom: Renate Götschl (Austria), 467 points
Overall: Anja Pärson (Sweden), 1,561 points

AMERICAN FOOTBALL

AFC Championship 2003: New England Patriots beat Indianapolis Colts 24–14
NFC Championship 2003: Carolina Panthers beat Philadelphia Eagles 14–3
XXXVIII Superbowl 2004 (Houston, 1 February): New England Patriots beat Carolina Panthers 32–29

ANGLING

NATIONAL COARSE CHAMPIONSHIPS 2004
Division 1
Individual winner: S. Clark
Team winners: Barnsley & District

Division 2
Individual winner: M. Coleman
Team winners: Team Daiwa Trentmen

Division 3
Individual winner: G. West
Team winners: Thorne & District

Division 4
Individual winner: G. Callaghan
Team winners: Gerrards Cross

Ladies' Championship
Individual winner: Claire Dagnall
Team winners: Ashton A. S.

ASSOCIATION FOOTBALL

EUROPEAN CHAMPIONSHIP 2004

POOL A

	P	W	D	L	GF	GA	Pts
Portugal*	3	2	0	1	4	2	6
Greece*	3	1	1	1	4	4	4
Spain	3	1	1	1	2	2	4
Russia	3	1	0	2	2	4	3

Spain beat Russia 1–0; Greece beat Portugal 2–1; Greece drew with Spain 1–1; Portugal beat Russia 2–0; Portugal beat Spain 1–0; Russia beat Greece 2–1.

POOL B

	P	W	D	L	GF	GA	Pts
France*	3	2	1	0	7	4	7
England*	3	2	0	1	8	4	6
Croatia	3	0	2	1	4	6	2
Switzerland	3	0	1	2	1	6	1

Switzerland drew with Croatia 0–0; France beat England 2–1; England beat Switzerland 3–0; Croatia drew with France 2–2; England beat Croatia 4–2; France beat Switzerland 3–1.

POOL C

	P	W	D	L	GF	GA	Pts
Sweden*	3	1	2	0	8	3	5
Denmark*	3	1	2	0	4	2	5
Italy	3	1	2	0	3	2	5
Bulgaria	3	0	0	3	1	9	0

Denmark drew with Italy 0–0; Sweden beat Bulgaria 5–0; Denmark beat Bulgaria 2–0; Italy drew with Sweden 1–1; Italy beat Bulgaria 2–1; Denmark drew with Sweden 2–2.

POOL D

	P	W	D	L	GF	GA	Pts
Czech Rep.*	3	3	0	0	7	4	9
Holland*	3	1	1	1	6	4	4
Germany	3	0	2	1	2	3	2
Latvia	3	0	1	2	1	5	1

Czech Republic beat Latvia 2–1; Germany drew with Holland 1–1; Latvia drew with Germany 0–0; Czech Republic beat Holland 3–2; Holland beat Latvia 3–0; Czech Republic beat Germany 2–1.
* group winners and runners up

QUARTER FINALS
Lisbon (24 June 2004): Portugal drew with England 2–2 AET (Score at 90 mins: 1–1). Portugal won 6–5 on penalties.
Lisbon (25 June 2004): Greece beat France 1–0
Faro-Loule (26 June 2004): Sweden drew with Holland 0–0 AET. Holland won 5–4 on penalties.
Porto (27 June 2004): Czech Republic beat Denmark 3–0

SEMI FINALS
Lisbon (30 June 2004): Portugal beat Holland 2–1
Porto (1 July 2004): Greece beat Czech Republic 1–0 on the silver goal rule

FINAL
Lisbon (4 July 2004): Greece beat Portugal 1–0

LEAGUE COMPETITIONS 2003–4

ENGLAND AND WALES
Premiership
1. Arsenal, 90 points
2. Chelsea, 79 points
Relegated: Leicester City, Leeds United, Wolverhampton Wanderers

Division 1
1. Norwich City, 94 points
2. West Bromwich Albion, 86 points

Play-off winner and third promotion place: Crystal Palace
Relegated: Walsall, Bradford City, Wimbledon

Division 2
1. Plymouth Argyle, 90 points
2. Queen's Park Rangers, 83 points

Play-off winner and third promotion place: Brighton and Hove Albion
Relegated: Grimsby Town, Rushden and Diamonds, Notts County, Wycombe Wanderers

Division 3
1. Doncaster Rovers, 92 points
2. Hull City, 88 points
3. Torquay United, 81 points

Play-off winner and fourth promotion place: Huddersfield Town
Relegated: Carlisle United, York City

Football Conference
1. Chester, 92 points

Play off winner and second promotion place: Shrewsbury Town

League of Wales
1. Rhyl, 77 points
2. TNS, 76 points
3. Haverfordwest, 62 points

Women's Premier League National Division
1. Arsenal, 47 points
2. Charlton Athletic, 46 points
3. Fulham, 44 points

SCOTLAND
Premier Division
1. Celtic, 98 points
2. Rangers, 81 points

Relegated: Partick Thistle

Division 1
1. Inverness Caledonian Thistle, 70 points
2. Clyde, 69 points

Relegated: Ayr, Brechin

Division 2
1. Airdrie United, 70 points
2. Hamilton, 62 points

Relegated: East Fife, Stenhousemuir

Division 3
1. Stranraer, 79 points
2. Stirling, 77 points

Bottom: East Stirlingshire

NORTHERN IRELAND
Irish League Premier Division
1. Linfield, 73 points; 2. Portadown, 70 points; 3. Lisburn, 55 points

REPUBLIC OF IRELAND
Premier Division 2003
1. Shelbourne, 69 points; 2. Bohemians, 64 points; 3. Cork City, 53 points.

FRANCE
French League: 1. Lyon, 79 points; 2. Paris Saint Germain, 76 points; 3. Monaco, 75 points

GERMANY
German League: 1. Werder Bremen, 74 points; 2. Bayern Munich, 68 points; 3. Bayer Leverkusen, 65 points

ITALY
Italian League: 1. Milan, 82 points; 2. Roma, 71 points; 3. Juventus, 69 points

HOLLAND
Dutch League: 1. Ajax, 80 points; 2. PSV Eindhoven, 74 points; 3. Feyenoord, 68 points

SPAIN
Spanish League: 1. Valencia, 77 points; 2. Barcelona, 72 points; 3. Deportivo La Coruña, 71 points

CUP COMPETITIONS

ENGLAND
FA Cup final 2004: Manchester United beat Millwall 3–0
League Cup final 2004: Middlesbrough beat Bolton Wanderers 2–1
LDV Vans Trophy 2004: Blackpool beat Southend United 2–0
FA Vase final 2004: Winchester City beat Sudbury 2–0
FA Trophy final 2004: Hednesford Town beat Canvey Island 3–2
Community Shield 2004: Arsenal beat Manchester United 3–1

WOMEN
Women's FA Cup final 2004: Arsenal beat Charlton Athletic 3–0
Women's Premier League Cup Final 2004: Charlton Athletic beat Fulham 1–0
Women's Community Shield 2004: Charlton Athletic beat Arsenal 1–0

WALES
FA Wales Cup final 2004: Rhyl beat TNS 1–0
FA Wales Premier Cup final 2004: Wrexham beat Rhyl 4–1

SCOTLAND
Scottish Cup final 2004: Celtic beat Dunfermline 3–1
League Cup final 2004: Livingston beat Hibernian 2–0

NORTHERN IRELAND
Irish Cup final 2004: Glentoran beat Coleraine 1–0

EUROPE
European Champions' League final 2004: Porto beat Monaco 3–0
UEFA Cup final 2004: Valencia beat Marseille 2–0
European Super Cup final 2003: Milan beat Porto 1–0

WORLD FOOTBALLER OF THE YEAR
2003 – Zinedine Zidane (France)
2002 – Ronaldo (Brazil)
2001 – Luis Figo (Portugal)
2000 – Zinedine Zidane (France)
1999 – Rivaldo (Brazil)
1998 – Zinedine Zidane (France)
1997 – Ronaldo (Brazil)
1996 – Ronaldo (Brazil)

1995 – George Weah (Liberia)
1994 – Romario (Brazil)
1993 – Roberto Baggio (Italy)
1992 – Marco van Basten (Netherlands)

ATHLETICS

See also page 1205

IAAF WORLD ATHLETICS FINAL
Held at Monaco, 13–14 September 2003

MEN		min.	sec
100m	Bernard Williams (USA)		10.04
200m	J. J. Johnson (USA)		20.35
400m	Jerome Young (USA)		45.04
800m	Wilfred Bungei (Kenya)	1	45.97
1500m	Paul Korir (Kenya)	3	40.09
5000m	Eliud Kipchoge (Kenya)	13	23.34
3000m St	Saif Saeed Shaheen (Qatar)	7	57.38
110m H	Allen Johnson (USA)		13.11
400m H	Felix Sanchez (Dominica)		47.80

		metres
High Jump	Yaroslav Rybakov (Russia)	2.30
Pole Vault	Tim Lobinger (Germany)	5.91
Long Jump	Dwight Phillips (USA)	8.31
Triple Jump	Christian Olsson (Sweden)	17.55
Shot	Christian Cantwell (USA)	20.93
Discus	Virgilijus Alekna (Lithuania)	68.30
*Hammer**	Adrian Annus (Hungary)	82.10
Javelin	Sergei Makarov (Russia)	85.66

WOMEN		min	sec
100m	Chryste Gaines (USA)		10.86
200m	Kelli Whiye (USA)		22.31
400m	Ana Guevara (Mexico)		49.34
800m	Maria Mutola (Mozambique)	1	59.59
1500m	Sureyya Ayhan (Turkey)	3	57.72
3000m	Edith Masai (Kenya)	8	36.82
5000m	Elvan Abeylegesse (Turkey)	14	56.25
100m H	Gail Devers (USA)		12.45
400m H	Sandra Glover (USA)		53.65

		metres
High Jump	Hestrie Cloete (South Africa)	2.01
Pole Vault	Tatyana Polnova (Russia)	4.68
Long Jump	Eunice Barber (France)	7.05
Triple Jump	Tatyana Lebedeva (Russia)	15.13
Shot	Vita Pavlysh (Ukraine)	19.86
Discus	Vera Pospisilova (Czech Rep)	65.42
*Hammer**	Yipsi Moreno (Cuba)	73.42
Javelin	Tatyana Shikolenko (Russia)	64.47

* Held at Szombathely, Hungary 7 September 2003

EUROPEAN CROSS COUNTRY CHAMPIONSHIPS
Held at Edinburgh, 14 December 2003

SENIOR MEN (10095m)

Individual:	Sergei Lebid (Ukraine)	30m 47s
Team:	France	47 pts

JUNIOR MEN (6595m)

Individual:	Yevgeni Rybakov (Russia)	20m 52s
Team:	Russia	20 pts

SENIOR WOMEN (6595m)

Individual:	Paula Radcliffe (Great Britain)	22m 04s
Team:	Great Britain	25 pts

JUNIOR WOMEN (4520m)

Individual:	Inna Polushkina (Latvia)	15m 32s
Team:	Great Britain	32 pts

EUROPEAN INDOOR CUP
Held at Leipzig, 14 February 2004

MEN		min	sec
60m	Jason Gardener (Great Britain)		6.51
400m	Dimitri Forshev (Russia)		46.46
800m	Bram Som (Netherlands)	1	48.79
1500m	Mounir Yemmouni (France)	3	49.82
3000m	Gert-Jan Liefers (Netherlands)	7	49.70
60m H	Andrea Giaconi (Italy)		7.72
2000m Relay	Russia	4	12.26

		metres
Pole Vault	Bjorn Otto (Germany)	5.70
Triple Jump	Christian Olsson (Sweden)	17.31

Points: France 50; Russia 48; Germany 46; Italy 45; Netherlands 43; Great Britain 35; Poland 35; Sweden 29

WOMEN		min	sec
60m	Larisa Kruglova (Russia)		7.27
400m	Olesya Krasnomovets (Russia)		51.31
800m	Olga Raspopova (Russia)	2	00.41
1500m	Irina Lishchinska (Ukraine)	4	09.82
3000m	Yelena Zadorozhnaya (Russia)	8	53.45
60m H	Flora Redoumi (Greece)		7.97
2000m Relay	Russia	4	46.14

		metres
High Jump	Daniele Rath (Germany)	2.00
Long Jump	Irina Simagina (Russia)	6.72
Shot	Irina Khudoroshkina (Russia)	18.75

Points: Russia 82; Germany 64; Ukraine 46.5; Poland 41; Spain 39.5; Great Britain 35; Greece 33; France 28

ENGLISH NATIONAL CROSS COUNTRY CHAMPIONSHIPS
Held at Leeds, 21 February 2004

SENIOR MEN (12km)

Individual:	Glynn Tromans (Coventry Godiva)	41m 24s
Team:	Belgrave H	160 pts

JUNIOR MEN (9km)

Individual:	Phil McGlory (Liverpool H)	31m 17s
Team:	Aldershot, Farnham & District	74 pts

SENIOR WOMEN (8km)

Individual:	Birhan Dagne (Belgrave H)	32m 28s
Team:	Bristol	100 pts

JUNIOR WOMEN (5km)

Individual:	Faye Fullerton (Havering & Mayesbrook)	18m 47s
Team:	Aldershot, Farnham & District	126 pts

AAA INDOOR CHAMPIONSHIPS
Held at Sheffield 7–8 February 2004

MEN		min	sec
60m	Jason Gardener (Wessex)		6.41
200m	Paul Brizzel (Ireland)		20.98
400m	Robert Daly (Ireland)		46.68
800m	Ahmad Ismail (Sudan)	1	49.39
1500m	Michael East (Newham/Essex Beagles)	3	44.93
3000m	Andrew Graffin (Belgrave H)	8	06.59
60m H	Mohd Sillah-Freckleton (Blackheath)		7.68

		metres
High Jump	Ben Challenger (Belgrave H)	2.20
Pole Vault	Ashley Swain (Team Solent)	5.50
Long Jump	Chris Tomlinson (Newham/Essex Beagles)	7.80
Triple Jump	Julien Kapek (France)	16.32
Shot	Rutger Smith (Netherlands)	19.85

WOMEN		min	sec
60m	Joice Maduaka (Woodford Green)		7.37
200m	Ciara Sheehy (Ireland)		23.41
400m	Catherine Murpy (Woodford Green)		52.54
800m	Kelly Holmes (Ealing)	2	01.40
1500m	Jo Fenn (Woodford Green)	4	12.67
3000m	Jo Pavey (Exeter)	8	43.23
60m H	Sarah Claxton (Belgrave H)		8.11

		metres
High Jump	Susan Jones (Trafford)	1.87
Pole Vault	Tracey Grant (Guildford)	4.15
Long Jump	Fiona May (Italy)	6.68
Triple Jump	Trecia Smith (Jamaica)	14.13
Shot	Helena Engman (Sweden)	15.42

IAAF WORLD INDOOR CHAMPIONSHIPS
Held at Budapest, 5–7 March 2004

MEN		min	sec
60m	Jason Gardener (Great Britain)		6.49
200m	Dominic Demeritte (Bahamas)		20.66
400m	Alleyne Francique (Grenada)		45.88
800m	Mbulaeni Mulaudzi (South Africa)	1	45.71
1500m	Paul Korir (Kenya)	3	52.31
3000m	Bernard Lagat (Kenya)	7	56.34
60m H	Allen Johnson (USA)		7.36
4 × 400m	Jamaica	3	05.21

		metres
High Jump	Stefan Holm (Sweden)	2.35
Pole Vault	Igor Pavlov (Russia)	5.80
Long Jump	Savante Stringfellow (USA)	8.40
Triple Jump	Christian Olsson (Sweden)	17.83
Shot	Christian Cantwell (USA)	21.49
Heptathlon	Roman Sebrle (Czech Rep)	6438 pts

WOMEN		min	sec
60m	Gail Devers (USA)		7.08
200m	Anastasia Kapachinskaya (Russia)		22.78
400m	Natalya Nazarova (Russia)		50.19
800m	Maria Mutola (Mozambique)	1	58.50
1500m	Kutre Dulecha (Ethiopia)	2	06.40
3000m	Meseret Defar (Ethiopia)	9	11.22
60m H	Perdita Felicien (Canada)		7.75
4 × 400m	Russia	3	23.88

		metres
High Jump	Yelena Slesarenko (Russia)	2.04
Pole Vault	Yelena Isinbayeva (Russia)	4.86
Long Jump	Tatyana Lebedeva (Russia)	6.98
Triple Jump	Tatyana Lebedeva (Russia)	15.36
Shot	Vita Pavlysh (Ukraine)	20.49
Pentathlon	Naide Gomes (Portugal)	4759 pts

IAAF WORLD CROSS COUNTRY CHAMPIONSHIPS
Held at Brussels, 20–21 March 2004

SENIOR MEN (12km)

Individual:	Kenenisa Bekele (Ethiopia)	35m 52s
Team:	Ethiopia	14 pts

SENIOR MEN (4km)

Individual:	Kenenisa Bekele (Eithiopia)	11m 31s
Team:	Ethiopia	17 pts

JUNIOR MEN (8km)

Individual:	Meba Tadesse (Ethiopia)	24m 01s
Team:	Kenya	20 pts

SENIOR WOMEN (8km)

Individual:	Benita Johnson (Australia)	27m 17s
Team:	Ethiopia	26 pts

SENIOR WOMEN (4km)

Individual:	Edith Masai (Kenya)	13m 07s
Team:	Ethiopia	19 pts

JUNIOR WOMEN (6km)

Individual:	Meselech Melkamu (Ethiopia)	20m 48s
Team:	Ethiopia	10 pts

LONDON MARATHON
Held in London, 18 April 2004

		hr	min	sec
MEN	Evans Rutto (Kenya)	2	06	18
WOMEN	Margaret Okayo (Kenya)	2	22	35

IAAF WORLD RACE WALKING CUP
Held at Naumburg, Germany, 1–2 May 2004

MEN

20km		hr	min	sec
Individual:	Jefferson Perez (Ecuador)	1	18	42
Team:	China			18 pts
50km				
Individual:	Aleksei Voyevodin (Russia)	3	42	44
Team:	Russia			8 pts

WOMEN

20km				
Individual:	Yelena Nikolayeva (Russia)	1	27	24
Team:	China			18 pts

EUROPEAN CUP SUPER LEAGUE
Held at Bydgoszcz, Poland, 19–20 June 2004

MEN		min	sec
100m	Lukasz Chyla (Poland)		10.42
200m	Christian Malcolm (GBR)		20.56
400m	Tim Benjamin (GBR)		45.37
800m	Florent Lacasse (France)	1	45.19

		min	sec
1500m	Mehdi Baala (France)	3	49.13
3000m	Wolfram Muller (Germany)	8	04.37
5000m	John Mayock (GBR)	14	44.71
3000m St	Bouabdellah Tahri (France)	8	23.40
110m H	Robert Kronberg (Sweden)		13.58
400m H	Chris Rawlinson (GBR)		48.59
4 × 100m	Great Britain		38.67
4 × 400m	Germany	3	01.78

		metres
High Jump	Stefan Holm (Sweden)	2.32
Pole Vault	Romain Mesnil (France)	5.75
Long Jump	Chris Tomlinson (GBR)	8.28
Triple Jump	Christian Olsson (Sweden)	17.30
Shot	Carl Myerscough (GBR)	20.85
Discus	Michael Mollenbeck (Germany)	64.42
Hammer	Szymon Ziolkowski (Poland)	77.27
Javelin	Aleksandr Ivanov (Russia)	82.55

Points: Germany 107.5; France 105; Poland 104; Great Britain 102.5; Russia 99; Italy 72; Sweden 67; Netherlands 62

WOMEN		min	sec
100m	Christine Arron (France)		11.23
200m	Muriel Hurtis (France)		22.78
400m	Olga Kotlyarova (Russia)		50.09
800m	Olga Raspopova (Russia)	2	00.24
1500m	Zulema Fuents-Pila (Spain)	4	08.05
3000m	Gulnara Samitova (Russia)	8	49.48
5000m	Paula Radcliffe (GBR)	14	29.11
3000m St	Elodie Olivares (France)	9	41.81
100m H	Yelena Krasovskaya (Ukraine)		12.78
400m H	Fani Halkia (Greece)		54.16
4 × 100m	France		42.41
4 × 400m	Russia	3	26.04

		metres
High Jump	Yelena Slesarenko (Russia)	2.04
Pole Vault	Anzhela Balakhonova (Ukraine)	4.50
Long Jump	Irina Simigina (Russia)	6.91
Triple Jump	Anna Pyatykh (Russia)	14.85
Shot	Olga Ryabinkina (Russia)	18.92
Discus	Ekaterini Voggoli (Greece)	64.25
Hammer	Irina Sekachova (Ukraine)	71.91
Javelin	Aggeliki Tsiolakoudi (Greece)	62.80

Points: Russia 142; Ukraine 97; France 92.5; Germany 92; Poland 86.5; Greece 79; Spain 66; Great Britain 63

AAA CHAMPIONSHIPS
Held at Manchester 10–11 July 2004

MEN		min	sec
100m	Jason Gardener (Wessex & Bath)		10.22
200m	Chris Lambert (Belgrave)		20.94
400m	Tim Benjamin (Belgrave)		45.58
800m	Sam Ellis (Barnsley)	1	49.19
1500m	Chris Mulvaney (Border)	3	50.14
5000m	Chris Thompson (Aldershot, F & D)	13	42.10
10,000m*	Kamiel Maase (Netherlands)	27	51.99
3000m St	Justin Chaston (Belgrave)	8	33.69
110m H	Robert Newton (Sale)		13.72
400m H	Chris Rawlinson (Trafford)		50.04

		metres
High Jump	Ben Challenger (Belgrave)	2.23
Pole Vault	Tim Thomas (Cardiff)	5.45
Long Jump	Chris Tomlinson (Newham)	7.84
Triple Jump	Nathan Douglas (Oxford City)	16.95
Shot	Carl Myerscough (Blackpool & Fylde)	20.84
Discus	Emeka Udechuku (Woodford Green)	61.60
Hammer	Mick Jones (Belgrave)	72.04
Javelin	Steve Backley (Cambridge H)	81.25
*Decathlon***	Louis Evling-Jones (Belgrave)	7405 pts

WOMEN		min	sec
100m	Ayi Oyepitan (Shaftesbury Barnet)		11.54
200m	Joice Maduaka (Woodford Green)		23.16
400m	Christine Ohuruogu (Newham)		50.98
800m	Kelly Holmes (Ealing)	1	59.39
1500m	Hayley Tullett (Swansea)	4	07.24
5000m	Catherine Berry (Belgrave)	15	45.28
10,000m*	Kathy Butler (WSE Harrow)	31	36.90
3000m St	Tina Brown (Coventry Godiva)	10	13.19
100m H	Sarah Claxton (Belgrave)		13.21
400m H	Katie Jones (Trafford)		58.26

		metres
High Jump	Susan Jones (Trafford)	1.89
Pole Vault	Zoe Brown (Shaftesbury Barnet)	4.15
Long Jump	Jade Johnson (Herne Hill)	6.72
Triple Jump	Michelle Griffith (WSE Harrow)	13.43
Shot	Julie Dunkley (Shaftesbury Barnet)	16.03
Discus	Philippa Roles (Sale)	58.57
Hammer	Lorraine Shaw (Sale)	68.11
Javelin	Goldie Sayers (Sale)	60.85
*Heptathlon***	Caroline Pearce (Huntingdon)	5253 pts

* Held at Watford 12 June ** Held at Stoke 12–13 June

BADMINTON

ENGLISH NATIONAL CHAMPIONSHIPS 2004
Manchester, 31 January–2 February

Men's Singles: Aamir Ghaffar beat Colin Haughton 2–0
Ladies' Singles: Tracey Hallam beat Julia Mann 2–1
Men's Doubles: Anthony Clark and Nathan Robertson beat David Lindley and Kristian Roebuck 2–0
Ladies' Doubles: Ella Tripp and Jo Wright beat Liza Parker and Suzanne Rayappan 2–0
Mixed Doubles: Donna Kellogg and Simon Archer beat Liza Parker and Kristian Roebuck 2–0

SCOTTISH NATIONAL CHAMPIONSHIPS 2004
Perth, 30 January–1 February

Men's Singles: B. Flockhart beat D. Forbes 2–0
Ladies' Singles: Y. Wemyss beat F. Sneddon 2–0
Men's Doubles: D. Gilmour and C. Robertson beat A. Bowman and G. Smith 2–0
Ladies' Doubles: K. McEwan and Y. Wemyss beat H. Donnelly and S. Watt 2–0
Mixed Doubles: Y. Wemyss and C. Robertson beat K. McEwan and G. Smith 2–0

ALL-ENGLAND CHAMPIONSHIPS 2004
NIA Birmingham, 10–14 March

Men's Singles: Dan Lin (China) beat Peter Gade (Denmark) 2–1
Ladies' Singles: Ruina Gong (China) beat Mi Zhou (China) 2–0
Men's Doubles: Jens Eriksen and Martin L. Hansen (Denmark) beat Tan Fook Choong and Wan Wah Lee (Malaysia) 2–1
Ladies' Doubles: Ling Gao and Sui Huang (China) beat Wei Yang and Jiewen Zhang (China) by walkover
Mixed Doubles: Dong-Moon Kim and Kyung-Min Ra (Korea) beat Yong-Hyun Kim and Hyo-Jung Lee (Korea) 2–0

EUROPEAN CHAMPIONSHIPS 2004
Geneva, April

Men's Singles: Peter Gade (Denmark) beat Kenneth Jonassen (Denmark) 2–0
Ladies' Singles: Mia Audina (Netherlands) beat Pi Hongyan (France) 2–0
Men's Doubles: Jens Eriksen & Martin Lundgaard (Denmark) beat Nathan Robertson & Anthony Clark (England) 2–0
Ladies' Doubles: Mia Audina & Lotte Bruil (Netherlands) beat Ann-Lou Jørgensen & Rikke Olsen (Denmark) 2–0
Mixed Doubles: Gail Emms & Nathan Robertson (England) beat Rikke Olsen & Jonas Rasmussen (Denmark) 2–1

BASEBALL

American League Championship Series 2003: New York Yankees beat Boston Red Sox 4–3
National League Championship Series 2003: Florida Marlins beat Chicago Cubs 4–3
World Series 2003: Florida Marlins beat New York Yankees 4–2

BASKETBALL

BRITISH

MEN
BBL Championship Final 2004: Sheffield Sharks beat Chester Jets 86–74
BBL Trophy Final 2004: Chester Jets beat Brighton Bears 68–66
National Cup 2004: Sheffield Sharks beat Scottish Rocks 83–70
BBL Champions 2003–4: Brighton Bears, 60 points

WOMEN
EBL Division 1 2003–4: Rhondda Rebels
EBL Division 1 Play-off 2003–4: Sheffield Hatters beat Rhondda Rebels 72–61
National Cup 2003–4: Rhondda Rebels beat Nottingham Wildcats 65–48

NORTH AMERICA – NATIONAL BASKETBALL LEAGUE (NBA)
Eastern Conference final 2004: Detroit Pistons beat Indiana Pacers 4–2 (best of 7 series)
Western Conference final 2003: LA Lakers beat Minnesota Timberwolves 4–2 (best of 7 series)
NBA final 2004: Detroit Pistons beat LA Lakers 4–1 (best of 7 series)

BOWLS – OUTDOOR

BRITISH ISLES CHAMPIONSHIPS 2004
Ayr, June

Singles: Martin McHugh (Ireland) beat Gary Pitschou (Guernsey) 21–12
Pairs: England beat Wales 19–13
Triples: Scotland beat Jersey 19–12
Fours: England beat Guernsey 25–10

ENGLISH NATIONAL CHAMPIONSHIPS 2004
Worthing, August

MEN
Singles: Yorkshire 'A' beat Essex 'B' 21–17
Pairs: Norfolk 'B' beat Bedfordshire 'A' 19–16
Triples: Yorkshire 'B' beat Berkshire 'A' 29–6
Fours: Surrey 'A' beat Durham 'A' 22–14
Middleton Cup (Inter-County Championship) final 2004: Devon beat Surrey 116–110

WORLD CHAMPIONSHIPS 2004
Ayr, July–August

MEN
Singles: Australia beat Scotland 21–15
Pairs: Canada beat Ireland 19–15
Triples: Scotland beat New Zealand 15–11
Fours: Ireland beat Australia 19–18

BOWLS – INDOOR

WORLD CHAMPIONSHIPS 2004
Norfolk, January

Men's Singles: Alex Marshall (Scotland) beat Mark McMahon (Australia) 2–0
Women's Singles: Carol Ashby (England) beat Lynne Whitehead (England) 2–0
Men's Pairs: Jeremy Henry & Ian McClure (England) beat David Holt (New Zealand) & Chris Young (England) 2–0
Mixed Pairs: Amy Monkhouse (England) & Alex Marshall (Scotland) beat Carol Ashby & Andy Thomson (England) 2–1

BRITISH ISLES INDOOR BOWLS CHAMPIONSHIPS 2004
Perth, March

Singles: Billy Jackson (England) beat Jeremy Henry (Ireland) 21–11
Pairs: Scotland beat England 23–18
Triples: Scotland beat Wales 14–13
Fours: England beat Scotland 27–7

ENGLISH NATIONAL CHAMPIONSHIPS 2003
Melton Mowbray, April

Singles: John Rednall beat Nick Brett 21–17
Pairs: City of Ely beat Whiteknights 22–16
Triples: Cyphers beat Ipswich 16–11
Fours: City of Ely beat East Dorset 17–15
Liberty Trophy (Inter-County Championship) final: Durham beat Devon 134–87
Champion of Champions 2003–4: John Wells beat Robert Paxton 21–16

BOXING

PROFESSIONAL BOXING
as at 1 September 2004

WORLD BOXING COUNCIL (WBC) CHAMPIONS
Heavy: Vitali Klitschko (Germany)
Cruiser: Wayne Braithwaite (Guyana)
Light-heavy: Antonio Tarver (USA)
Super-middle: Cristian Sanavia (Italy)
Middle: Bernard Hopkins (USA)
Super-welter: Winky Wright (USA)
Welter: Cory Spinks (USA)
Super-light: Kostya Tszyu (Australia)
Light: Jose Luis Castillo (Mexico)
Super-Feather: Erik Morales (Mexico)
Feather: Injin Chi (Korea)
Super-bantam: Oscar Larios (Mexico)
Bantam: Veeraphol Sahaprom (Thailand)
Super-fly: Katsushuigi Kawashima (Japan)
Fly: Pongsaklek Wonjongkam (Thailand)
Light-fly: Jorge Arce (Mexico)
Straw: Eagle Akakura (Thailand)

WORLD BOXING ASSOCIATION (WBA) CHAMPIONS
Heavy: John Ruiz (USA)
Cruiser: Jean-Marc Mormeck (France)
Light-heavy: Fabrice Tiozzo (Italy)
Super-middle: Manny Siaca (Puerto Rico)
Middle: Bernard Hopkins (USA)
Super-welter: Winky Wright (USA)
Welter: Cory Spinks (USA)
Super-light: Vivian Harris (Guyana)
Light: Juan Diaz (USA)
Super-feather: Yodsanan Nanthachaitha (Thailand)
Feather: Juan Manuel Marquez (Mexico)
Super-bantam: Mahyar Monshipor (France)
Bantam: Johnny Bredahl (Denmark)
Super-fly: Alexander Muñoz (Venezuela)
Fly: Lorenzo Parra (Venezuela)
Light-fly: Rosendo Alverez (Nicaragua)
Straw: Yukata Niida (Japan)

WORLD BOXING ORGANISATION (WBO) CHAMPIONS
Heavy: Lamon Brewster (USA)
Cruiser: Johnny Nelson (England)
Light-heavy: Zsolt Erdei (Hungary)
Super-middle: Joe Calzaghe (Wales)
Middle: Oscar De La Hoya (USA)
Super-welter: Daniel Santos (Puerto Rico)
Welter: Antonio Margarito (Mexico)
Super-light: vacant
Light: Diego Corrales (USA)
Super-feather: Mike Anchondo (USA)
Feather: Scott Harrison (Great Britain)
Super-bantam: Joan Guzman (Dominican Republic)
Bantam: Ratanachai Sor Vorapin (Thailand)
Super-fly: Mark Johnson (USA)
Fly: Omar Narvaez (Argentina)
Light-fly: Nelson Dieppa (Puerto Rico)
Straw: Ivan Calderon (Puerto Rico)

INTERNATIONAL BOXING FEDERATION (IBF) CHAMPIONS
Heavy: Chris Byrd (USA)
Cruiser: Kelvin Davis (USA)
Light-heavy: Glengoffe Johnson (Jamaica)
Super-middle: vacant
Middle: Bernard Hopkins (USA)
Super-welter: Verno Phillips (USA)
Welter: Cory Spinks (USA)
Super-light: Kostya Tszyu (Australia)
Light: Julio Diaz (USA)
Super-feather: Erik Morales (Mexico)
Feather: Juan Manuel Marquez (Mexico)
Super-bantam: Isreal Vazquez (Mexico)
Bantam: Rafael Marquez (Mexico)
Super-fly: Luis Perez (Nicaragua)
Fly: Irene Pacheco (Colombia)
Light-fly: Jose Victor Burgos (Mexico)
Straw: Daniel Reyes (Colombia)

BRITISH CHAMPIONS
Heavy: Matt Skelton
Cruiser: Mark Hobson
Light-heavy: Peter Oboh
Super-middle: Tony Dodson
Middle: vacant
Light-middle: Jamie Moore
Welter: David Barnes
Light-welter: Junior Witter
Light: Graham Earl
Super-feather: vacant
Feather: Dazzo Williams
Super-bantam: Michael Hunter
Bantam: Nicky Booth
Fly: vacant

CHESS

FIDE World Champion 2004: Rustam Kasimdzhanov (Uzbekistan)
British Champion 2004: Jonathan Rowson (Scotland)

CRICKET

TEST SERIES

ENGLAND V. BANGLADESH
Dhaka (21–25 October 2003): England beat Bangladesh by 7 wickets. Bangladesh 203 and 255; England 295 and 164–3
Chittagong (29 October–2 November 2003): England beat Bangladesh by 329 runs. England 326 and 293–5; Bangladesh 152 and 138

ENGLAND V. SRI LANKA
Galle (2–6 December 2003): England drew with Sri Lanka. Sri Lanka 331 and 226; England 235 and 210–9
Kandy (10–14 December 2003): England drew with Sri Lanka. Sri Lanka 382 and 279–7; England 294 and 285–7
Colombo (18–22 December 2003): Sri Lanka beat England by an innings and 215 runs. England 265 and 148; Sri Lanka 628–8

ENGLAND V. WEST INDIES
Kingston (11–15 March 2004): England beat West Indies by 10 wickets. West Indies 311 and 47; England 339 and 20–0
Port of Spain (19–23 March 2004): England beat West Indies by 7 wickets. West Indies 208 and 209; England 319 and 99–3
Bridgetown (1–5 April 2004): England beat West Indies by 8 wickets. West Indies 224 and 94; England 226 and 93–2

St John's (10–14 April 2004): England drew with West Indies. West Indies 751–5; England 285 and 422–5

ENGLAND V. NEW ZEALAND

Lord's (20–24 May 2004): England beat New Zealand by 7 wickets. New Zealand 386 and 336; England 441 and 282–3

Headingley (3–7 June 2004): England beat New Zealand by 9 wickets. New Zealand 409 and 161; England 526 and 45–1

Trent Bridge (10–13 June 2004): England beat New Zealand by 4 wickets. New Zealand 384 and 218; England 319 and 284–6

ENGLAND V. WEST INDIES

Lord's (22–26 July 2004): England beat West Indies by 210 runs. England 568 and 325–5; West Indies 416 and 267

Edgbaston (29 July–1 August 2004): England beat West Indies by 256 runs. England 566–9 and 248; West Indies 336 and 222

Old Trafford (12–16 August 2004): England beat West Indies by 7 wickets. West Indies 395–9 and 165; England 330 and 231–3

Oval (19–23 August 2004): England beat West Indies by 10 wickets. England 470 and 4–0; West Indies 152 and 318

ONE-DAY INTERNATIONALS

ENGLAND V. BANGLADESH

Chittagong (7 November 2003): England beat Bangladesh by 7 wickets. Bangladesh 143; England 144–3

Dhaka (10 November 2003): England beat Bangladesh by 7 wickets. Bangladesh 134–9; England 137–3

Dhaka (12 November 2003): England beat Bangladesh by 7 wickets. Bangladesh 182; England 185–3

ENGLAND V. SRI LANKA

Dambulla (18 November 2003): Sri Lanka beat England by 10 wickets. England 88; Sri Lanka 89–0

Colombo (21 November 2003): Match abandoned without a ball bowled

Colombo (23 November 2003): Match abandoned without a ball bowled

ENGLAND V. WEST INDIES

Georgetown (18 April 2004): England beat West Indies by 2 wickets. West Indies 156–5; England 157–8

Port of Spain (24 April 2004): No result. West Indies 57–2

Port of Spain (25 April 2004): Match abandoned without a ball bowled

Grenada (28 April 2004): Match abandoned without a ball bowled

Gros Islet, St Lucia (1 May 2004): West Indies beat England by 5 wickets. England 281–8; West Indies 284–5

Gros Islet, St Lucia (2 May 2004): West Indies beat England by 4 wickets. England 280–8; West Indies 282–6

Bridgetown (5 May 2004): England beat West Indies by 5 wickets. West Indies 261–6; England 262–5

NATWEST SERIES

Old Trafford (24 June 2004): England v New Zealand. Match abandoned without a ball bowled

Edgbaston (26 June 2004): Match abandoned: no result. West Indies 122–4; England 97–2

Trent Bridge (27 June 2004): West Indies beat England by 7 wickets. England 147; West Indies 148–3

Riverside (29 June 2004): New Zealand beat England by 7 wickets. England 101; New Zealand 103–3

Headingley (1 July 2004): England beat West Indies by 7 wickets. West Indies 159; England 160–3

Sophia Gardens (3 July 2004): New Zealand beat West Indies by 5 wickets. West Indies 216; New Zealand 220–5

County Ground, Bristol (4 July 2004): New Zealand beat England by 6 wickets. England 237–7; New Zealand 241–4

Lord's (6 July 2004): West Indies beat England by 7 wickets. England 285–7; West Indies 286–3

Rose Bowl (8 July 2004): West Indies v New Zealand. Match abandoned without a ball bowled

Final: Lord's (10 July 2004): New Zealand beat West Indies by 107 runs. New Zealand 266; West Indies 159

NATWEST CHALLENGE

Trent Bridge (1 September 2004): England beat India by 7 wickets. India 170; England 171–3

The Oval (3 September 2004): England beat India by 70 runs. England 307–5; India 237

Lord's (5 September 2004): India beat England by 23 runs. India 204; England 181

ICC Champions Trophy: see Stop Press

ENGLAND AND WALES DOMESTIC COMPETITIONS 2004

County Championship: see Stop Press

National League: see Stop Press

C & G Trophy final: Gloucestershire beat Worcestershire by 8 wickets. Worcestershire 236–9; Gloucestershire 237–2

Twenty20 Cup final: Leicestershire beat Surrey by 7 wickets. Surrey 168–6; Leicestershire 169–3

OTHER INTERNATIONAL DOMESTIC CHAMPIONSHIPS

Australia: Pura Cup Final 2003–4: Victoria beat Queensland by 321 runs. Victoria 710 and 140–1; Queensland 275 and 254. *ING Cup Final 2003–4:* Western Australia beat Queensland by 4 wickets. Queensland 244; Western Australia 248–6

India: Irani Trophy 2003–4: Rest of India beat Mumbai by 3 wickets. Mumbai 297 and 244; Rest of India 202 and 340–7. *Ranji Trophy Elite Final 2003–4:* Mumbai drew with Tamil Nadu; Mumbai wins the trophy. Tamil Nadu 294 and 353–4; Mumbai 613. *Ranji Trophy One-Day Competition 2003–4:* Mumbai, 13 points. *Deodhar Trophy 2003–4:* East zone, 18 points. *Duleep Trophy Final 2003–4:* North Zone beat East Zone by 59 runs. North Zone 330 and 400. East Zone 322 and 349

New Zealand: State Championship Final 2003–4: Wellington drew with Canterbury; Wellington wins title. Canterbury 192 and 335–8; Wellington 301 and 182–6. *State Shield Final 2003–4:* Central Districts beat Canterbury by 99 runs. Central Districts 354–5; Canterbury 255

Pakistan: Quaid-e-Azam Trophy 2003–4: Faisalabad, 36 points. *Quaid-e-Azam Cup 2003–4:* Faisalabad, 20 points. *Patron's Trophy 2003–4:* Agricultural

Development Bank beat Water and Power Development Authority by 3 wickets. Water and Power Development Authority 308 and 147; Agricultural Development Bank 280 and 177–7. *Patron's Cup 2003–4:* Habib Bank beat Pakistan International Airlines by 131 runs. Habib Bank 266–7; Pakistan International Airlines 135

South Africa: SuperSport Series Final 2003–4: Western Province beat KwaZulu Natal by 108 runs. Western Province 217 and 315; KwaZulu Natal 187 and 237. *Standard Bank Cup Final 2003–4:* Gauteng beat Easterns by 7 wickets. Easterns 144; Gauteng 146–3. *Standard Bank Pro20 Series 2003–4:* Eagles beat Eastern Cape by 7 runs (D/L method). Eagles 131–6; Eastern Cape 108–9

Sri Lanka: Ten Sports Inter-Provincial Tournament 2003–4: Central Province beat North Central Province by 176 runs. Central Province 235 and 258; North Central Province 120 and 197. *Premier League Tournament 2003–4:* Moors Sports Club beat Chilaw Marians Cricket Club by 10 wickets. Chilaw Marians Cricket Club 91 and 223; Moors Sports Club 303 and 12–0. *Premier Limited Overs Tournament Final 2003–4:* Bloomfield Cricket and Athletic Club beat Colts Cricket Club by 189 runs Bloomfield Cricket and Athletic Club 299–7; Colts Cricket Club 110. *MCA Challenge Trophy 2003–4:* Sampath Bank beat Janashakthi Group by 2 wickets. Janashakthi Group 213–9; Sampath Bank 214–8

West Indies: Red Stripe Bowl Final 2003–4: Guyana beat Barbados by 27 runs (D/L method). Guyana 212–9; Barbados 156. *Carib Beer Cup Final 2003–4:* Barbados beat Jamaica by 84 runs. Barbados 142 and 315; Jamaica 258 and 115

Zimbabwe: Logan Cup 2003–4: Mashonaland, 78 points. *Inter-Provincial One-Day Competition 2003–4:* Mashonaland, 22 points

CURLING

EUROPEAN CHAMPIONSHIPS 2003
Courmayeur, Switzerland, December

Men's Final: Scotland beat Sweden 11–5
Women's Final: Sweden beat Switzerland 7–6

WORLD CHAMPIONSHIPS 2004
Gävle, Sweden, April

Men's Final: Sweden beat Germany 7–6
Women's Final: Canada beat Norway 8–4

CYCLING

BRITISH NATIONAL ROAD RACE CHAMPIONSHIPS 2003
Newport, June

MEN
Road Race: Roger Hammond

WOMEN
Road Race: Nicole Cooke

WORLD ROAD CYCLING CHAMPIONSHIPS 2003
7–12 October, Hamilton, Canada

MEN
Elite Time trial: David Millar (Great Britain) 51:17.29
Road race (260.4 km): Igor Astarloa (Spain) 6 hr 30:19

WOMEN
Elite Time trial: Joane Somarriba Arrola (Spain) 28:23.23
Road race (124 km): Susanne Ljungskog (Sweden) 3hr 16.06
Giro d'Italia 2004: Damiano Cunego (Italy)
Tour de France 2004: Lance Armstrong (USA)
Tour of Britain 2004: Mauricio Ardila (Colombia)
Tour of Spain 2004: *see* Stop Press

WORLD TRACK CHAMPIONSHIPS 2004
May, Melbourne

MEN
Points race: Franck Perque (France) 35 points
Olympic Sprint: France 44.394
1km Time Trial: Chris Hoy (Great Britain) 1:01.599
Individual Pursuit: Sergi Escobar Roure (Spain) 4:19.382
Scratch Race: Greg Henderson (New Zealand)
Keirin: Jamie Staff (Great Britain)
Team Pursuit: Australia (Peter Dawson, Ashley Hutchinson, Luke Roberts, Stephen Wooldridge) 4:00.322
Madison: Argentina (Juan Esteban Curuchet, Walter Perez) 7 points
Sprint: Theo Bos (Netherlands) Run 1, 10.752; Run 2, 10.715

WOMEN
Keirin: Clara Sanchez (France)
Individual Pursuit: Sarah Ulmer (New Zealand) 3:31.778
Points Race: Olga Slyusareva (Russia) 39 points
Sprint: Svetlana Grankovskaya (Russia) Run 1, 11.620; Run 2, 11.981
Scratch: Yoanka Gonzalez Perez (Cuba)
500m Time Trial: Anna Meares (Australia) 34.342

DARTS

BDO World Championship 2004: Andy Fordham (England) beat Mervyn King (England) 6–3
PDC World Championship 2004: Phil Taylor (England) beat Kevin Painter (England) 7–6

EQUESTRIANISM

Badminton Horse Trials 2004: William Fox-Pitt (Great Britain) on Tamarillo
British Open Horse Trials 2004 (Gatcombe Park): Ruth Friend (Great Britain) on Two Thyme
Burghley Horse Trials 2004: Andrew Hoy (Australia) on Moon Fleet

ETON FIVES

Amateur Championship (Kinnaird Cup) final 2004: R. A. Mason and T. R. Dunbar beat J. P. Toop and C. J. P. Cooley 3–1
Alan Barber Cup final 2004: Old Olavians beat Old Salopians 2–1
County Championship final 2004: Warwickshire beat Kent 2–1
Schools' Championship 2004: Shrewsbury 1 (T. D. Gerrard and T. W. P. Cox) beat Highgate 1 (A. Patel and J. O'Callaghan) 3–1
Preparatory Schools' Tournament 2004: Highgate 1 (S. C. Little and J. A Marks) beat Highgate 2 (N. J. Lindo and C. D. Ryan) 2–0

FENCING

WORLD CHAMPIONSHIP 2003
4–12 October, Havana, Cuba

MEN
Individual Foil: Peter Joppich (Germany)
Individual Epée: Fabrice Jeannet (France)
Individual Sabre: Vladimir Lukashenko (Ukraine)
Team Epée: Russia
Team Foil: Italy
Team Sabre: Russia

WOMEN
Individual Foil: Valentina Vezzali (Italy)
Individual Epée: Natalia Conrad (Ukraine)
Individual Sabre: Dorina Mihai (Romania)
Team Foil: Poland
Team Epée: Russia
Team Sabre: Italy

BRITISH CHAMPIONSHIPS 2004
July

MEN
Individual Foil: James Beevers
Individual Epée: Tom Cadman
Individual Sabre: Chris Farren
Team Foil: Sussex House 'A'
Team Epée: Haverstock 'A'
Team Sabre: Laszlo's Fencing 'A'

WOMEN
Individual Foil: Camille Datoo
Individual Epée: Jo Beadsworth
Individual Sabre: Louise Bond-Williams
Team Foil: Salle Paul 'A'
Team Epée: LTFC 'A'
Team Sabre: Laszlo's Fencing Angels

IPSWICH CUP 2004
(International Epée World Cup Series)
Magdalena Kumiet (Poland)

CORBLE CUP 2004
(International Sabre World Cup Series)
Men, Eun Seok Oh (Korea);
Women, Chrystall Nicoll (Great Britain))

GOLF (MEN)

THE MAJOR CHAMPIONSHIPS 2004
US Masters (Augusta, 8–11 April): Phil Mickelson (USA), 279
US Open (Shinnecock Hills, June): Retief Goosen (South Africa), 276
The Open (Royal St George's, July): Todd Hamilton (USA), 274
US PGA Championship (Whistling Straits, Wisconsin, August): Vijay Singh (Fiji), 280

WORLD RANKINGS
(as at 1 September 2004)

1. Tiger Woods (USA)
2. Vijay Singh (Fiji)
3. Ernie Els (South Africa)
4. Phil Mickelson (USA)
5. Davis Love (USA)

EUROPEAN TOUR ORDER OF MERIT
(as at 1 September 2004)

1. Ernie Els (South Africa); 2. Retief Goosen (South Africa); 3. Miguel Angel Jiménez (Spain); 4. Thomas Levet (Spain); 5. Vijay Singh (Fiji)

PGA EUROPEAN TOUR 2003
WGC Championship (Capital City Club, USA): Tiger Woods (USA), 274
Dutch Open (Hilversumsche): Maarten Lafeber (Netherlands), 267
Turespaña Mallorca Classic (Pula): Miguel Angel Jiménez (Spain), 204
World Match Play Championship (Wentworth): Ernie Els (South Africa)
Open de Madrid (Club de Campo): Ricardo Gonzalez (Argentina), 270
Volvo Masters Andalucia (Valderrama): Fredrik Jacobson (Sweden), 276
Seve Trophy (Parador El Saler): Great Britain and Ireland beat Continental Europe 15–13
WGC World Cup (Kiawah Island): South Africa

PGA EUROPEAN TOUR 2004
Hong Kong Open (Hong Kong GC): Padraig Harrington (Ireland), 269
South African Airways Open (Erinvale GC): Trevor Immelman (South Africa), 276
Dunhill Championship (Houghton GC, South Africa): Marcel Siem (Germany), 266
Johnnie Walker Classic (Alpine GC, Thailand): Miguel Angel Jiménez (Spain), 271
Heineken Classic (Royal Melbourne GC): Ernie Els (South Africa), 268
ANZ Championship (Horizons GC, Australia): Brian Davis (England), 44 points
Malaysian Open (Saujana): Thongchai Jaidee (Thailand), 274
WGC – Accenture Match Play (La Costa, California): Tiger Woods (USA) beat Davis Love (USA) by 3&2
Dubai Desert Classic (Emirates): Mark O'Meara (USA), 271
Qatar Masters (Doha): Joakim Haeggman (Sweden), 272
Caltex Masters (Laguna National, Singapore): Colin Montgomerie (Scotland), 272
Madeira Island Open (Santo da Serra): Christopher Hanell (Sweden), 284
Algarve Open de Portugal (Penina): Miguel Angel Jiménez (Spain), 272
Open de Sevilla (Real Club): Ricardo Gonzalez (Argentina), 274
Canarias Open de Espana (Fuerteventura): Christian Cévaër (France), 271
Italian Open (Castello di Tolcinasco): Graeme McDowell (Northern Ireland), 197
British Masters (Forest of Arden): Barry Lane (England), 272
Asian Open (Shanghai Pudong): Miguel Angel Jiménez (Spain), 274
Open of Europe (St Leon-Rot, Germany): Trevor Immelman (South Africa), 271
Volvo PGA Championship (Wentworth): Scott Drummond (Scotland), 269
Wales Open (Celtic Manor): Simon Khan (England), 267
Diageo Championship (Gleneagles): Miles Tunnicliff (England), 275

Aa St Omer Open (Aa St Omer):
Philippe Lima (France), 279
Open de France (Le Golf National): Jean-Francois Remesy (France), 272
European Open (K Club):
Retief Gooosen (South Africa), 275
Scottish Open (Loch Lomond): Thomas Levet (France), 269
Irish Open (Co Louth): Brett Rumford (Australia), 274
Scandinavian Masters (Barsebäck):
Luke Donald (England), 272
Dutch Open (Hilversumsche): David Lynn (England), 264
Russian Open (Le Meridien Moscow): Gary Emerson (England), 272
WGC NEC Invitational (Firestone):
Stewart Cink (USA), 269
BMW International Open (München Nord-Eichenried):
Miguel Angel Jiménez (Spain), 267
Omega European Masters (Crans-sur-Sierre): Luke Donald (England), 265
German Masters: (Gut Lärchenhof): Padraig Harrington (Ireland), 275
The Heritage: see Stop Press

RYDER CUP 2004
14–19 September, Oakland Hills USA
Europe beat USA 18½–9½

AMATEUR CHAMPIONSHIPS
British Amateur Championship 2004 (St Andrews): Stuart Wilson
English Amateur Championship 2004 (Hollinwell):
James Heath
Welsh Amateur Championship 2004 (Ashburnham):
Ryan Thomas
Scottish Amateur Championship 2004 (Gullane):
George Murray
Brabazon Trophy (English Open Strokeplay) 2004 (Royal Birkdale): Matthew Richardson, 279
Welsh Open Strokeplay 2004 (Royal Porthcawl): Heidar Bragason, 286
Scottish Open Strokeplay 2004 (Lundin):
Richie Ramsay, 269
Irish Amateur Open Championship 2004 (Carton House):
Craig Smith, 289
Lytham Trophy 2004 (Royal Lytham Golf Club):
James Heath, 266
Berkshire Trophy 2004 (The Berkshire):
Sam Osborne, 267
Irish Amateur Close Championship 2003 (Donegal):
Brian McElhinney

GOLF (WOMEN)

THE MAJOR CHAMPIONSHIPS 2004
Kraft Nabisco Championship (Mission Hills Country Club):
Grace Park (Korea) 277
US Women's Open (The Orchards):
Meg Mallon (USA) 274
McDonalds LPGA Championship (Dupont Country Club):
Annika Sorenstam (Sweden) 271
Weetabix Women's British Open (Sunningdale, England):
Karen Stupples (England), 269

EUROPEAN LPGA TOUR 2003
Biarritz Ladies' Classic (Biarritz): Marlene Hedblom (Sweden), 200
BT Ladies' Open (Warrenpoint, Northern Ireland): Sophie Gustafson (Sweden), 275
Wales WPGA Championship of Europe (Royal Porthcawl):
Shani Waugh (Australia), 286
European Tour Order of Merit 2003
1. Sophie Gustafson (Sweden); 2. Elisabeth Esterl (Germany); 3. Laura Davies (England); 4. Iben Tinning (Denmark); 5. Lynnette Brooky (New Zealand).

EUROPEAN LPGA TOUR 2004
ANZ Ladies' Masters (Royal Pines, Australia): Annika Sorenstam (Sweden), 269
Women's Australian Open (Concord Club, Australia): Laura Davies (England), 283
Tenerife Ladies' Open (Buenavista): Diana Luna (Italy), 279
Ladies' Open of Portugal (Aroeira I): Cecilia Ekelundh (Sweden), 206
Open de Espana Feminino Xacobeo (la Coruna): Stephanie Arricau (France), 279
Ladies Italian Open (Parco di Roma): Ana B Sanchez (Spain), 281
Open de France Dames (Le Golf d'Arras): Stephanie Arricau (France), 281
Dutch Ladies' Open (Kennemer): Elisabeth Esterl (Germany), 214
Ladies English Open (Chart Hills):
Maria Hjorth (Sweden), 197
Ladies Central European Open – Hungary (Old Lake):
Minea Blomqvist (Finland), 199
Evian Masters (Evian Masters, France): Wendy Doolan (Australia), 270
HP Open (Ullna, Sweden): Annika Sorenstam (Sweden), 275
Wales Ladies Open (Royal Porthcawl): Trish Johnson (England), 277

AMATEUR CHAMPIONSHIPS
British Open Championship 2004 (Gullane):
Louise Stahle (Sweden)
Ladies' British Open Amateur Strokeplay Championship 2004 (Alwoodley): Clare Queen (England), 294
Scottish Open Strokeplay Championship 2004 (Troon):
Emma Dugleby, 211
Scottish Ladies (Close) Amateur Championship 2004:
Anne Laing
English Close Amateur Championship 2004: Kerry Smith
English Strokeplay Championship 2004: Sian Reddick, 285
Curtis Cup 2004: USA beat Great Britain and Ireland 10–8

GREYHOUND RACING

The Laurels (Belle Vue): Knockeevan Magic (corrects last year's incorrect Farloe Verdict)
Milton Keynes Derby (Milton Keynes): Setemup Joe
Oaks (Wimbledon): Cooly Pantera
St Leger (Wimbledon): Shelbourne Star
Television Trophy (Wimbledon): Ericas Equity

GYMNASTICS

BRITISH WOMEN'S CHAMPIONSHIPS 2004
July, Guildford

Overall Champion: Elizabeth Tweddle
Individual Apparatus Champions
Floor: Elisabeth Tweddle
Beam: Vanessa Hobbs
Vault: Vanessa Hobbs
Assymetric Bars: Elisabeth Tweddle

BRITISH MEN'S CHAMPIONSHIPS 2004
November, Stoke-on-Trent

Overall Champion: Ross Brewer
Individual Apparatus Champions
Floor: Ross Brewer
Pommel Horse: Ross Brewer
Still Rings: David Massam
Vault: Darren Gerrard
Parallel Bars: Kanukai Jackson
High Bar: Ross Brewer

WOMEN'S EUROPEAN CHAMPIONSHIPS 2004
April–May, Amsterdam, Netherlands

Overall Champion: Alina Kozich (Ukraine)
Team Champions: Romania
Individual Apparatus Champions
Floor: Catalina Ponor (Romania)
Beam: Catalina Ponor (Romania)
Vault: Monica Rosu (Romania)
Assymetric Bars: Svetlana Khorkina (Russia)

MEN'S EUROPEAN CHAMPIONSHIPS 2004
April, Ljubljana, Slovenia

Overall Champion: Marian Dragulescu (Romania)
Team Champions: Romania
Individual Apparatus Champions
Floor: Marian Dragulescu (Romania)
Pommel Horse: Ioan Silviu Suciu (Romania)
Still Rings: Dimosthenis Tampakos (Greece)
Vault: Marian Dragulescu (Romania)
Parallel Bars: Roman Zozulia (Ukraine)
High Bar: Vlasios Maras (Greece)

HOCKEY

MEN
English Hockey League 2003–4: Premier Division: Cannock 43 points; Division One, Firebrands 40 points; Division Two, Old Georgians 52 points
English Hockey League Premiership final 2003–4: Reading beat Cannock 5–4 on penalties (1–1 draw AET)
English Hockey League Indoor Championship final 2004: Loughborough Students beat Beeston 9–4
County Championship final 2003: Essex beat Warwickshire 1–0

WOMEN
English Hockey League 2003–4: Premier Division: Hightown 40 points; Division One, Trojans 37 points; Division Two, University of Birmingham 37 points
English Hockey League Super Cup 2003–4: Hightown beat Chelmsford 4–3
English Hockey League Indoor Championship final 2004: Chelmsford beat Hightown 8–3

HORSE-RACING

THE FLAT

THE CLASSICS
ONE THOUSAND GUINEAS
(1814) Rowley Mile, Newmarket, for three-year-old fillies

Year	*Winner*	*Betting*	*Owner*	*Jockey*	*Trainer*	*No. of Runners*
2000	Lahan	14–1	Sheikh Hamdan Al Maktoum	R. Hills	J. Gosden	18
2001	Ameerat	11–1	Sheikh Ahmed Al Maktoum	P. Robinson	M. A. Jarvis	15
2002	Kazzia	14–1	Godolphin	L. Dettori	Saeed bin Suroor	17
2003	Russian Rhythm	12–1	Cheveley Park Stud	K. Fallon	Sir Michael Stoute	19
2004	Attraction	11–2	Duke of Roxburghe	K. Darley	M. Johnston	16

TWO THOUSAND GUINEAS
(1809) Rowley Mile, Newmarket, for three-year-olds

Year	*Winner*	*Betting*	*Owner*	*Jockey*	*Trainer*	*No. of Runners*
2000	King's Best	13–2	Saeed Suhail	K. Fallon	Sir Michael Stoute	27
2001	Golan	11–1	Lord Weinstock	K. Fallon	Sir Michael Stoute	18
2002	Rock of Gibraltar	9–1	Sir Alex Ferguson	J. Murtagh	A. O'Brien	22
2003	Refuse To Bend	9–2	Moyglare Stud Farms	P. Smullen	D. Weld	20
2004	Haafhd	11–2	Sheikh Hamdan Al Maktoum	B. Hills	R. Hills	14

THE DERBY
(1780) Epsom, 1 mile and about 4 f, for three-year-olds
The first winner was Sir Charles Bunbury's Diomed in 1780. The owners with the record number of winners are Lord Egremont, who won in 1782, 1804, 1805, 1807, 1826 (also won five Oaks); and the late Aga Khan, who won in 1930, 1935, 1936, 1948, 1952. Other winning owners are: Duke of Grafton (1802, 1809, 1810, 1815); Mr J. Bowes (1835, 1843, 1852, 1853); Sir J. Hawley (1851, 1858, 1859, 1868); the 1st Duke of Westminster (1880, 1882, 1886, 1899); and Sir Victor Sassoon (1953, 1957, 1958, 1960).
The Derby was run at Newmarket in 1915–18 and 1940–5.

Year	*Winner*	*Betting*	*Owner*	*Jockey*	*Trainer*	*No. of Runners*
2000	Sinndar	7–1	Aga Khan	J. Murtagh	J. Oxx	8
2001	Galileo	11–4	Mrs. J. Magnier	M. Kinane	A. O'Brien	12
2002	High Chaparral	7–2	Michael Tabor	J. Murtagh	A. O'Brien	12
2003	Kris Kin	6–1	Saeed Suhail	K. Fallon	Sir Michael Stoute	20
2004	North Light	7–2	Exors of the late Lord Weinstock	K. Fallon	Sir Michael Stoute	14

THE OAKS
(1779) Epsom, 1 mile and about 4 f, for three-year-old fillies

Year	*Winner*	*Betting*	*Owner*	*Jockey*	*Trainer*	*No. of Runners*
2000	Love Divine	9–4	Lordship Stud	T. Quinn	H. Cecil	18
2001	Imagine	3–1	Mrs. J. Magnier	M. Kinane	–	12
2002	Kazzia	100–30	Godolphin	L. Dettori	Saeed bin Suroor	14
2003	Casual Look	10–1	W. Farish III	M. Dwyer	A. Balding	15
2004	Ouija Board	7–2	Lord Derby	K. Fallon	E. Dunlop	7

ST LEGER
(1776) Doncaster, 1 mile and about 6 f, for three-year-olds

Year	*Winner*	*Betting*	*Owner*	*Jockey*	*Trainer*	*No. of Runners*
1997	Silver Patriarch	5–4	P. Winfield	P. Eddery	J. Dunlop	10
1998	Nedawi	5–2	Godolphin	J. Reid	Saeed bin Suroor	9
1999	Mutafaweq	11–2	Godolphin	R. Hills	Saeed bin Suroor	9
2000	Goggles	14–1	Mrs J. Powell	C. Rutter	H. Candy	22
2001	Milan	13–8	–	M. Kinane	A. O'Brien	10
2002	Bollin Eric	7–1	Sir Neil and Lady Westbrook	K. Darley	T. Easterby	8
2003	Brian Boru	5–4	Sir Neil and Lady Westbrook	J. Spencer	A. O'Brien	8
2004	Rule of Law	3–1	Godolphin	K. McEvoy	Saeed bin Suroor	9

RESULTS

CAMBRIDGESHIRE HANDICAP
(1839) Newmarket, 1 mile

2000 Katy Nowaitee (4y), J. Reid
2001 I Cried For You (6y), M. Fenton
2002 Beauchamp Pilot (4y), E. Ahern
2003 Chivalry (4y), G. Duffield

PRIX DE L'ARC DE TRIOMPHE
(1920) Longchamp, 1 mile, 4 f

2000 Sinndar (3y), J. P. Murtagh
2001 Sakhee (4y), L. Dettori
2002 Marienbard (5y), L. Dettori
2003 Dalakhani (3y), C. Soumillon

CESAREWITCH
(1839) Newmarket, 2 miles and about 2 f

2000 Heros Fatal (6y), G. Carter
2001 Distant Prospect, M. Dwyer
2002 Miss Fara, R. Moore
2003 Landing Light (8y), P. Eddery

CHAMPION STAKES
(1877) Newmarket, 1 mile, 2 f

2000 Kalanisi (5y), J. Murtagh
2001 Nayef (3y), R. Hills
2002 Storming Home (4y), M. Hills
2003 Rakti (4y), P. Robinson

BREEDERS CUP CLASSIC
(1984) Various tracks, USA, 1 mile and 2 f

2001 Tiznow (4y), C. McCarron
2002 Volponi (4y), J. Santos
2003 Pleasantly Perfect (5y), A. Solis

DUBAI WORLD CUP
(1957) Dubai, 1 mile and 2 f

2001 Captain Steve (4y), J. D. Bailey
2002 Street Cry (4y), J. D. Bailey
2003 Moon Ballad (4y), L. Dettori
2004 Pleasantly Perfect (6y), A. Solis

LINCOLN HANDICAP
(1965) Doncaster, 1 mile

2001 Nimello (5y), J. Fortune
2002 Nimello (6y), J. Fortune
2003 Pablo (4y), M. Hills
2004 Babodana (4y), P. Robinson

JOCKEY CLUB STAKES
(1894) Newmarket, 2 miles, 24 yds

2000 Millenary (4y), P. Eddery
2002 Marienbard (5y), J. Spencer
2003 Warrsan (5y), P. Robinson
2004 Gamut (5y), K. Fallon

PRIX DU JOCKEY CLUB
(1836) Chantilly, 1½ miles

2001 Anaba Blue, C. Soumillon
2002 Sulamani, T. Thulliez
2003 Dalakhani, C. Soumillon
2004 Blue Canari, T. Thulliez

ASCOT GOLD CUP
(1807) Ascot, 2 miles and about 4 f

2001 Royal Rebel (5y), J. P. Murtagh
2002 Royal Rebel (6y), J. P. Murtagh
2003 Mr Dinos (4y), K. Fallon
2004 Papineau (4y), L. Dettori

IRISH DERBY
(1866) Curragh, 1½ miles, for three-year-olds

2001 Galileo, M. Kinane
2002 High Chaparral, M. Kinane
2003 Alamshar, J. P. Murtagh
2004 Grey Swallow, P. Smullen

ECLIPSE STAKES
(1886) Sandown, 1 mile and about 2 f

2001 Medicean, K. Fallon
2002 Hawk Wing (3y), M. Kinane

2003 Falbrav (5y), D. Netherlands
2004 Refuse To Bend (4y), L. Dettori

KING GEORGE VI AND QUEEN ELIZABETH DIAMOND STAKES
(1952) Ascot, 1 mile and about 4 f

2000 Montjeu (4yr), M. Kinane
2001 Galileo (3y), M. Kinane
2002 Golan, K. Fallon
2003 Alamshar (3y), J. P. Murtagh
2004 Doyen (4y), L. Dettori

GOODWOOD CUP
(1812) Goodwood, about 2 miles

1999 Kayf Tara (5y), L. Dettori
2000 Royal Rebel (4y), M. Kinane
2001 Persian Punch (8y), T. Quinn
2002 Jardines Lookout (5y), M. Kinane
2003 Persian Punch (10y), M. Dwyer
2004 Darasim (6y), J. Fanning

STATISTICS

WINNING FLAT OWNERS 2003

K. Abdulla	£1,735,745
Hamdan Al Maktoum	£1,591,611
Cheveley Park Stud	£1,324,142
Sheikh Mohammed	£1,305,078
Saeed Suhail	£1,171,227
Godolphin	£903,691
Aga Khan	£853,246
Mrs J. Magnier	£829,907
Scuderia Rencati Srl	£700,236
J. C. Smith	£523,733

WINNING FLAT TRAINERS 2003

Sir Michael Stoute	£3,608,776
M. Johnston	£1,910,956
M. R. Channon	£1,855,922
R. Hannon	£1,571,095
B. W. Hills	£1,373,307
J. H. M. Gosden	£1,313,286
M. P. Tregoning	£1,312,178
A. P. O'Brien (Ireland)	£1,145,392
L. M. Cumani	£1,101,180
A. M. Balding	£1,080,126

WINNING FLAT SIRES 2003

	Races won	*Stakes*
Sadler's Wells by Northern Dancer	54	£1,823,440
Kris S by Roberto	15	£1,278,813
Green Desert by Danzig	50	£1,067,285
Cadeaux Genereux by Young Generation	60	£912,482
Kingmambo by Mr Prospector	26	£908,386
Indian Ridge by Ahonoora	57	£892,539
Danehill by Danzig	65	£890,558
Grand Lodge by Chief's Crown	60	£888,009
Royal Applause by Waajib	58	£859,433
Selkirk by Sharpen Up	56	£848,663

WINNING FLAT JOCKEYS 2003

	1st	*2nd*	*3rd*	*Unpl*	*Total mts*
K. Fallon	221	164	142	528	1055
D. Holland	157	136	109	588	990
K. Darley	125	114	98	531	868
R. Hughes	121	88	80	462	751
A. Culhane	112	106	89	555	862
Dane O'Neill	110	109	111	688	1018
S. Drowne	109	104	99	710	1022
E. Ahern	107	103	90	552	852
J. P. Spencer	102	96	62	337	597
S. Sanders	101	106	90	563	860

NATIONAL HUNT

HENNESSY GOLD CUP
(1957) Newbury, 3 miles and about 2½ f

2000 Kings Road (8y), J. Goldstein
2001 What's Up Boys, P. Flynn
2002 Gingembre (8y), A. Thornton
2003 Strong Flow (6y), R. Walsh

TINGLE CREEK CHASE
(1957) Sandown, 2 miles (held at Cheltenham in 2000)

2000 Flagship Uberalles (6y), R. Johnson
2001 Flagship Uberalles (7y), R. Widger
2002 Cenkos (8y), R. Walsh
2003 Moscow Flyer (9y), B. Geraghty

KING GEORGE VI CHASE
(1937) Kempton, about 3 miles

2000 First Gold, T. Dounan
2001 Florida Pearl (9y), A. Maguire
2002 Best Mate (7y), A. P. McCoy
2003 Edredon Bleu (11y), J. Culloty

CHAMPION HURDLE
(1927) Cheltenham, 2 miles and about ½ f

2001 cancelled due to foot and mouth crisis
2002 Hors La Loi III (7y), D. Gallagher
2003 Rooster Booster (9y), R. Johnson
2004 Hardy Eustace (7y), C. O'Dwyer

QUEEN MOTHER CHAMPION CHASE
(1959) Cheltenham, about 2 miles

2001 cancelled due to foot and mouth crisis
2002 Flagship Uberalles (8y), R. Johnson
2003 Moscow Flyer (9y), B. Geraghty
2004 Azertyuiop (8y), R. Walsh

CHELTENHAM GOLD CUP
(1924) 3 miles and about 2½ f

2001 cancelled due to foot and mouth crisis
2002 Best Mate (7y), J. Culloty
2003 Best Mate (8y), J. Culloty
2004 Best Mate (9y), J. Culloty

GRAND NATIONAL
(1837) Liverpool, 4 miles and about 4 f

2000 Papillon (9y), R. Walsh
2001 Red Marauder (11y), R. Guest
2002 Bindaree (8y), J. Culloty
2003 Monty's Pass (10y), B. Geraghty
2004 Amberleigh House (12y), G. Lee

BETFRED GOLD CUP
(known as Whitbread Gold Cup until 2002, and At the Races Gold Cup until 2004)
(1957) Sandown, 3 miles and about 5 f

2001 Ad Hoc (7y), R. Walsh
2002 Bounce Back, A. P. McCoy
2003 Ad Hoc (9y), R. Walsh
2004 Puntal (8y), D. Howard

STATISTICS

WINNING NATIONAL HUNT TRAINERS 2003–4

M. C. Pipe	£2,263,718
P. F. Nicholls	£2,078,144
J. J. O'Neill	£1,483,091
P. J. Hobbs	£1,440,312
N. J. Henderson	£1,145,939
Miss V. Williams	£877,137
Miss H. C. Knight	£819,486
N. A. Twiston Davis	£724,123
Mrs M. Reveley, Mrs S. J. Smith	£698,846
A. King	£475,233

WINNING NATIONAL HUNT JOCKEYS 2003–4

	1st	*2nd*	*3rd*	*Unpl.*	*Total mts*
A. P. McCoy	209	144	111	336	800
R. Johnson	186	158	107	440	891
G. Lee	94	87	68	376	625
A. Dobbin	89	61	45	304	499
A. Thornton	86	68	64	311	529
R. Thornton	73	59	70	319	521
C. Llewellyn	65	48	37	270	420
R. Walsh	62	66	41	125	294
J. Tizzard	61	69	54	286	470
J. Culloty	58	48	49	212	367

The above statistics have been provided by *Timeform*, publishers of the *Racehorses* and *Chasers and Hurdlers* annuals.

ICE HOCKEY

MEN'S WORLD CHAMPIONSHIPS 2004
May, Czech Republic
Final: Canada beat Sweden 5–3

WOMEN'S WORLD CHAMPIONSHIPS 2004
April, Canada
Final: Canada beat USA 2–0

DOMESTIC COMPETITIONS
Elite League Champions 2003–4: Sheffield Steelers
Play-off Champions 2004: Sheffield Steelers
Challenge Cup Final 2004: Nottingham Panthers beat Sheffield Steelers 4–3

NATIONAL HOCKEY LEAGUE
Eastern Conference Final 2003: Tampa Bay Lightning beat Philadelphia Fliers 4–3
Western Conference Final 2003: Calgary Flames beat San Jose Sharks 4–2
Stanley Cup Final Series 2004: Tampa Bay Lightning beat Calgary Flames 4–3

ICE SKATING

BRITISH FIGURE SKATING CHAMPIONSHIPS 2003
Sheffield, December

Men: Matthew Davies
Women: Jenna McCorkell
Ice Dance: Sinead Kerr and John Kerr

EUROPEAN CHAMPIONSHIPS 2004
February, Budapest, Hungary

Men: Brian Joubert (France)
Women: Julia Sebestyen (Hungary)
Pairs: Tatyana Totmyanina & Maxim Marinin (Russia)
Ice Dance: Tatyana Navka & Roman Kostomarov (Russia)

WORLD CHAMPIONSHIPS 2004
March, Dortmund, Germany

Men: Evgeni Plushenko (Russia)
Women: Shizuka Arakawa (Japan)
Pairs: Tatyana Totmyanina & Maxim Marinin (Russia)
Ice Dance: Tatyana Navka & Roman Kostomarov (Russia)

JUDO

EUROPEAN CHAMPIONSHIPS 2004
14–16 May, Bucharest

MEN
Heavyweight (100kg): Selim Tataroglu (Turkey)
Light-heavyweight (100kg): Ariel Zeevi (Israel)
Middleweight (90kg): Francesco Lepre (Italy)
Welterweight (81kg): Ilias Nikolaos Iliadis (Greece)
Lightweight (73kg): Kioshi Uematsu (Spain)
Junior Lightweight (66kg): Bektas Demirel (Turkey)
Bantamweight (60kg): Ludwig Paischer (Austria)

WOMEN
Heavyweight (over 78kg): Maryna Prokofyeva (Ukraine)
Light-heavyweight (78kg): Jenny Karl (Germany)
Middleweight (70kg): Edith Bosch (Netherlands)
Welterweight (63kg): Sara Alvarez (Spain)
Lightweight (57kg): Isabel Fernandez (Spain)
Junior lightweight (52kg): Ioana-Maria Aluas Dinea (Romania)
Bantamweight (48kg): Alina Alexandra Dumitru (Romania)

BRITISH OPEN CHAMPIONSHIPS 2003
17–18 April

MEN
Heavyweight (over 100 kg): Suren Balachinskiy (Russia)
Light-heavyweight (100 kg): Michele Monti (Italy)
Middleweight (90 kg): Mehedui Jhaldoun (France)
Welter (81 kg): Romann Wolska (France)
Lightweight (73 kg): Mark Van Der Ham (Netherlands)
Junior lightweight (66 kg): Mauel Mueller (Germany)
Bantamweight (60 kg): Pudwig Paischer (Austria)

WOMEN
Heavyweight (over 78 kg): Simone Callender (Great Britain)
Middleweight (70 kg): Karen Roberts (Great Britain)
Welter (63 kg): Daniela Krukower (Argentina)
Lightweight (57 kg): Valerie Degryse (Belgium)
Junior lightweight (52 kg): Caroline Lantoine (France)
Bantamweight (48 kg): Amel Bensemain (France)

MOTOR CYCLING

500CC GRAND PRIX 2003
Pacific (Motegi, Japan): Max Biaggi (Italy), Honda
Malaysian (Sepang): Valentino Rossi (Italy), Honda
Australian (Phillip Island): Valentino Rossi (Italy), Honda
Valencia (Valencia): Valentino Rossi (Italy), Honda

Riders' Championship 2003: 1. Valentino Rossi (Italy), Honda, 357 pts; 2. Sete Gibernau (Spain), Honda, 277 pts; 3. Max Biaggi (Italy), Honda, 228 pts

500CC GRAND PRIX 2004
South African (Phakisa Freeway): Valentino Rossi (Italy), Yamaha
Spanish (Jerez): Sete Gibernau (Spain), Honda
French (Le Mans): Sete Gibernau (Spain), Honda
Italian (Mugello): Valentino Rossi (Italy), Yamaha
Catalunyan (Barcelona): Valentino Rossi (Italy), Yamaha
Dutch (Assen): Valentino Rossi (Italy), Yamaha
Brazilian (Nelson Piquet): Makoto Tamada (Japan), Honda
German (Sachsenring): Max Biaggi (Italy), Honda
British (Donington Park): Valentino Rossi (Italy), Yamaha
Czech Republic (Brno): Sete Gibernau (Spain), Honda
Portugal (Estoril): Valentino Rossi (Italy), Yamaha
Japan (Motegi): Makoto Tamada (Japan), Honda

250CC GRAND PRIX 2003
Pacific (Motegi, Japan): Toni Elias (Spain), Aprilia
Malaysian (Sepang): Toni Elias (Spain), Aprilia
Australian (Phillip Island): Roberto Rolfo (Italy), Honda
Valencia (Valencia): Randy De Puniet (France), Aprilia

Riders' Championship 2003: 1 Manuel Poggiali (San Marino), Aprilia, 249 pts; 2. Roberto Rolfo (Italy), Honda, 235 pts; 3. Tony Elias (Spain), Aprilia 226 pts

250CC GRAND PRIX 2004
South African (Phakisa Freeway): Daniel Pedrosa (Spain), Honda
Spanish (Jerez): Roberto Rolfo (Italy), Honda
French (Le Mans): Daniel Pedrosa (Spain), Honda
Italian (Mugello) Sebastian Porto (Argentina), Aprilia
Catalunyan (Barcelona) Randy De Puniet (France), Aprilia

Dutch (Assen): Sebastian Porto (Argentina), Aprilia
Brazilian (Nelson Piquet): Manuel Poggiali (San Marino), Aprilia
German (Sachsenring): Daniel Pedrosa (Spain), Honda
British (Donington Park): Daniel Pedrosa (Spain), Honda
Czech Republic (Brno): Sebastian Porto (Argentina), Aprilia
Portugal (Estoril): Tony Elias (Spain), Honda
Japan (Motegi): Daniel Pedrosa (Spain), Honda

125CC GRAND PRIX 2003
Pacific (Motegi, Japan): Hector Barbera (Spain), Aprilia
Malaysian (Sepang): Daniel Pedrosa (Spain), Honda
Australian (Phillip Island): Andrea Ballerini (Italy), Honda
Valencia (Valencia): Casey Stoner (Australia), Aprilia

Riders' Championship 2003: 1 Daniel Pedrosa (Spain), Honda, 223 pts; 2. Alex De Angelis (San Marino), Aprilia, 166 pts; 3. Hector Barbera (Spain), Aprilia, 164 pts

125CC GRAND PRIX 2004
South Africa (Phakisa Freeway): Andrea Dovizioso (Italy), Honda
Spain (Jerez): Marco Simoncelli (Italy), Aprilia
France (Le Mans): Andrea Dovizioso (Italy), Honda
Italy (Mugello): Roberto Locatelli (Italy), Aprilia
Catalunya (Barcelona): Hector Barbera (Spain), Aprilia
Dutch (Assen): Jorge Lorenzo (Spain), Derbi
Brazilian (Nelson Piquet): Hector Barbera (Spain), Aprilia
German (Sachsenring): Roberto Locatelli (Italy), Aprilia
British (Donington Park): Andrea Dovizioso (Italy), Honda
Czech Republic (Brno): Jorge Lorenzo (Spain), Derbi
Portugal (Estoril): Hector Barbera (Spain), Aprilia
Japan (Motegi): Andrea Dorizioso (Italy), Honda

Senior TT 2004, Isle of Man: Adrian Archibad (Northern Ireland), Suzuki
Junior TT 2004, Isle of Man: John McGuinness (England), Yamaha

WORLD SUPERBIKES 2003
Italy (Imola): Race 1 – Ruben Xaus (Spain), Ducati; Race 2 – Ruben Xaus (Spain), Ducati
France (Magny Cours): Race 1 – Neil Hodgson (Great Britain), Ducati; Race 2 – Ruben Xaus (Spain), Ducati

Riders' World Championship 2003: 1 Neil Hodgson (Great Britain), 489 points; 2 Ruben Xaus (Spain), 386 points; 3. James Toseland (Great Britain), 271 points.

WORLD SUPERBIKES 2004
Spain (Valencia): Race 1 – James Toseland (Great Britain), Ducati; Race 2 – Noriyuki Haga (Japan), Ducati

Australia (Phillip Island): Race 1 – Régis Laconi (France), Ducati; Race 2 – Garry McCoy (Australia), Ducati
San Marino (Misano Adriatico): Race 1 – Régis Laconi (France), Ducati; Race 2 – Pierfrancesco Chili (Italy), Ducati
Italy (Monza): Race 1 – Régis Laconi (France), Ducati; Race 2 – Régis Laconi (France), Ducati
Germany (Oschersleben): Race 1 – Noriyuki Haga (Japan), Ducati; Race 2 – Régis Laconi (France), Ducati
Great Britain (Silverstone): Race 1 – Noriyuki Haga (Japan), Ducati; Race 2 – Chris Vermeulen (Australia), Honda
United States (Laguna Seca): Race 1 – Chris Vermeulen (Australia), Honda; Race 2 – Chris Vermeulen (Australia), Honda
European (Brands Hatch): Race 1 – Noriyuki Haga (Japan), Ducati; Race 2 – Noriyuki Haga (Japan), Ducati
Netherlands (Assen): James Toseland (Great Britain), Ducati; Race 2 – Chris Vermeulen (Australia), Honda
Italy (Imola): *see* Stop Press

MOTOR RACING

FORMULA ONE GRAND PRIX 2003
United States Grand Prix (Indianapolis) (28 September): Michael Schumacher (Germany), Ferrari
Japanese Grand Prix (Suzuka) (12 October): Rubens Barrichello (Brazil), Ferrari

Drivers' World Championship 2003: 1. Michael Schumacher (Germany), Ferrari, 93 points; 2. Kimi Räikkönen (Finland), McClaren, 91 points; 3. Juan Pablo Montoya (Colombia), Williams, 82 points.
Constructors' World Championship 2003: 1. Ferrari, 158 points; 2. Williams-BMW, 144 points; 3. McLaren-Mercedes, 142 points.

FORMULA ONE GRAND PRIX 2004
Australian (Melbourne, 7 March) Michael Schumacher (Germany), Ferrari
Malaysia (Sepang, 21 March) Michael Schumacher (Germany), Ferrari
Bahrain (Sakhir, 4 April) Michael Schumacher (Germany), Ferrari
San Marino (Imola, 25 April) Michael Schumacher (Germany), Ferrari
Spanish (Barcelona, 9 May) Michael Schumacher (Germany), Ferrari
Monaco (Monte Carlo, 23 May) Jarno Trulli (Italy), Renault
European (Nurburgring, 30 May) Michael Schumacher (Germany), Ferrari
Canadian (Montreal, 13 June) Michael Schumacher (Germany), Ferrari
United States (Indianapolis, 20 June) Michael Schumacher (Germany), Ferrari
France (Magny Cours, 4 July) Michael Schumacher (Germany), Ferrari
British (Silverstone, 11 July) Michael Schumacher (Germany), Ferrari
German (Hockenheim, 25 July), Michael Schumacher (Germany), Ferrari
Hungarian (Hungaroring, 15 August), Michael Schumacher (Germany), Ferrari
Belgian (Spa, 29 August), Kimi Räikkönen (Finland), McLaren
Italy (Monza, 12 September): Rubens Barrichello (Brazil), Ferrari
China (Shanghai, 26 September): *see* Stop Press

INDIANAPOLIS 500 2004
Buddy Rice (USA), Rahal-Letterman Argent/Pioneer

LE MANS 24-HOUR RACE 2004
Seiji Ara, Tom Kristensen and Rinaldo Capello (Audi Japan Team Goh)

MOTOR RALLYING

WORLD RALLY CHAMPIONSHIPS
2003
Italy: Sébastien Loeb (France), Citroën
France: Petter Solberg (Norway), Subaru
Spain: Gilles Panizzi (France), Peugeot
Great Britain: Petter Solberg (Norway), Subaru

Drivers' World Championship 2003: Petter Solberg (Norway), 72 points
Manufacturers' World Championship 2003: Citroën, 160 points

2004
Monte Carlo: Sébastien Loeb (France), Citroën
Sweden: Sébastien Loeb (France), Citroën
Mexico: Markko Martin (Estonia), Ford
New Zealand: Petter Solberg (Norway), Subaru
Cyprus: Sébastien Loeb (France), Citroën
Acropolis: Petter Solberg (Norway), Subaru
Turkey: Sébastien Loeb (France), Citroën
Argentina: Carlos Sainz (Spain), Citroën
Finland: Marcus Gronholm (Finland), Peugeot
Germany: Sébastien Loeb (France), Citroën
Japan: Petter Solberg (Norway), Subaru
Wales Rally GB: Petter Solberg (Norway), Subaru

BRITISH RALLY CHAMPIONSHIPS 2004
Pirelli International Rally: David Higgins (Great Britain), Hyundai
International Rally of Wales: Jonny Milner (Great Britain), Subaru
Scottish Rally: Jonny Milner (Great Britain), Subaru
Jim Clark Memorial Rally: Andrew Nesbitt (Great Britain), Subaru
Manx International: Jonny Milner (Great Britain), Subaru
Ulster Rally: Mark Higgins (Great Britain), Ford

DAKAR RALLY 2004
Cars: Stephane Peterhansel (France), Mitsubishi
Motorcycles: Nani Roma (Spain), KTM
Trucks: Vladimir Tchaguine (Russia), Kamaz

NETBALL

Inter-County Championship 2004: Essex Metropolitan
National Clubs League Championship 2004: Linden
English Counties League Championship 2004: Middlesex
Super Cup Final 2004: Team Bath beat Northern Thunder 49–43

NORDIC EVENTS

BIATHLON WORLD CHAMPIONSHIPS 2004
Oberhof, Germany

MEN
10km sprint: Raphael Poiree (France) 30min. 11.9sec.
12.5km pursuit: Ricco Gross (Germany) 38min. 53.82sec.
15km mass start: Raphael Poiree (France) 40min. 31.77sec.
20km individual: Raphael Poiree (France) 51min. 37.9sec.
4 × 7.5km relay: Germany 1hr. 17min. 50.39sec.

WOMEN
7.5km sprint: Liv Grete Poiree (Norway) 25min. 51.0sec.
10km pursuit: Liv Grete Poiree (Norway) 37min. 39.33sec.
12.5km mass start: Liv Grete Poiree (Norway) 39min. 46.10sec.
15km individual: Olga Pyleva (Russia) 49min. 43.0sec.
4 × 6km relay: Norway 1hr. 16min. 59.88sec.

BIATHLON WORLD CUP 2003–4

MEN
Overall: Raphael Poiree (France)

WOMEN
Overall: Liv Grete Poiree (Norway)

CROSS-COUNTRY WORLD CUP 2003–4

MEN
Rene Sommerfeldt (Germany), 956 points

WOMEN
Gabriella Paruzzui (Italy), 1,228 points

NORDIC-COMBINED WORLD CUP 2003–4
Hannu Manninen (Finland), 1,392 points

SKI-JUMPING WORLD CUP 2004
Janne Ahonen (Finland), 1,316 points

POLO

Prince of Wales Trophy final 2004: Azzura beat Geebung 9½–5
Queen's Cup final 2004: Labegorce beat Azzura 7–6
Warwickshire Cup 2004: Black Bears beat Foxcote Red 9–5
Gold Cup (British Open) final 2004: Azzura beat Dubai 17–9
Coronation Cup 2004: Chile beat England 10–7

RACKETS

Noel Bruce Cup 2003: Eton 1 beat Harrow 1 4–3
British Professional Singles Championship final 2004: Neil Smith beat Mark Hubbard 3–2
British Open Singles Championship final 2004: Alister Robinson beat Harry Foster 4–2
British Open Doubles Championship final 2004: Guy Barker and Alister Robinson beat James Male & John Prenn 4–1
Amateur Singles Championship final 2003: Guy Smith-Bingham beat Tim Cockroft 3–1
Amateur Doubles Championship 2004: Guy Barker & Alister Robinson beat Tim Cockroft and Guy Smith-Bingham 4–3
The Foster Cup final 2003 (public schools' singles championship): A. Brignall (Marlborough) beat J. Bone (Harrow) 3–2

REAL TENNIS

British Professional Singles Championship final 2004: Ben Ronaldson beat Craig Greenhalgh 2–0
British Professional Doubles Championship final 2004: Mike Gooding and Nick Wood beat Adam Phillips and Danny Jones 3–0
British Open Singles Championship final 2003: Robert Fahey beat Ruaraidh Gunn 3–0
British Open Doubles Championship final 2003: Robert Fahey and Ruaraidh Gunn beat Julian Snow and Adam Phillips 3–1
Henry Leaf Cup final 2004 (public schools' old boys' doubles championship): Canford 1 beat Canford 2 2–1
World Singles Championships 2004: Robert Fahey beat Tim Chisholm 7–1
Women's World Singles Championships 2004: Penny Lumley beat Charlotte Cornwallis 2–0
National League Final 2003: Seacourt 1 beat Oxford 1 3–0
Women's British Open Singles Championship final 2004: Penny Lumley beat Charlotte Cornwallis 2–0

ROWING

NATIONAL CHAMPIONSHIPS 2003
Nottingham, July

MEN
Coxless pairs: London RC 7:05.90
Coxed fours: Molesey BC 6:31.37
Coxless fours: London RC 6:36.12
Single sculls: Glasgow RC 7:31.39
Double sculls: Nottinghamshire County 7:10.54
Quad sculls: Leander Club 6:25.61
Eights: Imperial College/Molesey BC 6:05.98

WOMEN
Coxless pairs: Thames RC/Globe RC 8:05.72
Coxed fours: Thames RC 7:39.68
Coxless fours: City of Oxford RC 7:29.53
Single sculls: Glasgow RC 8:21.07
Double sculls: University of Sunderland 7:34.02
Quad sculls: University of London 7:13.32
Eights: Thames RC 6:54.42

THE 150TH UNIVERSITY BOAT RACE
Putney–Mortlake, 4 miles 1 f, 180 yd, 28 March 2004

Cambridge beat Oxford by 6 lengths; 18 min. 47 sec.

Cambridge has won 78 times, Oxford 71 and there has been one dead heat. The record time is 16 min. 19 sec., rowed by Cambridge in 1998.

HENLEY ROYAL REGATTA 2004
Grand Challenge Cup: Hollandia Roeiclub (Netherlands) beat Harvard University (USA) by ⅔ length
Ladies' Challenge Plate: Leander Club beat Harvard University (USA) by ¾ length
Thames Challenge Cup: London Rowing Club 'A' beat RC Reuss Luzern (Switzerland) by ½ length
Temple Challenge Cup: ASR Nereus (Netherlands) beat DSR Proteus-Eretes (Netherlands) by ¾ length
Princess Elizabeth Challenge Cup: St Paul's School, Concord (USA) beat Abingdon School by 1¼ lengths
Remenham Challenge Cup: Thames RC and University of London beat Princeton University, (USA) by 3 lengths
Stewards' Challenge Cup: Leander Club & Imperial College London beat Melbourne University & University Queensland (Australia) by 2 lengths
Queen Mother Challenge Cup: Ts.S.K.A. Ukraine (Ukraine) beat Leander Club and Molesey Boat Club by 1 length
Visitors' Challenge Cup: Oxford Brookes University & Oxford University beat Cambridge University 'A' by 2¼ lengths
Wyfold Challenge Cup: London Rowing Club 'A' beat Army Rowing Club by 1¼ lengths
Britannia Challenge Cup: Molesey Boat Club beat Nottingham & Union RC easily
Fawley Challenge Cup: Marlow R.C. & The Tideway Scullers' School beat Sydney Rowing Club (Australia) by ½ length
Silver Goblets and Nickalls' Challenge Cup: R. P. Di Clementé & D. Cech (South Africa) beat J. A. Livingston & R. C. E. C. Dunn by 4¼ lengths
Double Sculls Challenge Cup: P. Lorinczy & K. Szabó (Hungary) beat S. D. Goodbrand & G. B. Blanchard by 2¾ lengths
Diamond Challenge Sculls: M. Hacker (Germany) beat C. M. Smith easily
Princess Royal Challenge Cup: C. S. Bishop (USA) beat R. Geyser (South Africa) easily
Princess Grace Challenge Cup: Leander Club & University of London beat Ts.S.K.A, Ukraine (Ukraine) by 2¾ lengths
Men's Quadruple Sculls: Molesey Boat Club beat Commercial Rowing Club (Ireland) by ¼ length

OTHER ROWING EVENTS
Wingfield Sculls 2003: Ian Lawson (Leander)
Oxford Torpids 2004: Men, Oriel; Women, Merton
Oxford Summer Eights 2004: Men, Magdalen; Women, New College
Head of the River 2004: Men, Cancelled; Women, Imperial College/Marlow RC/Reading University/Rob Roy/Thames RC/University of London

RUGBY FIVES

National Open Singles Championship final 2003: J. P. Toop beat H. Buchanan
National Open Doubles Championship final 2004: H. Buchanan and R. Perry beat D. J. Hebden and I. P. Fuller
National Club Championship final 2004: Oxford Past beat Alleyn Old Boys
National Schools' Singles Champion 2004: A. Beverly (St. Paul's School)
National Schools' Doubles Champions 2004: J. Pendergrass and O. Santrakul (Loretto School)
Varsity Match 2004: Oxford beat Cambridge

RUGBY LEAGUE

Super League Grand Final 2003 (Old Trafford, 18 October): Bradford Bulls beat Wigan Warriors 25–12
World Club Challenge 2004 (Huddersfield, 13 February): Bradford Bulls beat Penrith Panthers 22–4
Challenge Cup final 2004 (Cardiff, 15 May): St Helens beat Wigan Warriors 32–16

AMATEUR RUGBY LEAGUE 2003–4
National Conference League Premier Division Grand Final Champions: Siddal; *Division One:* Wath Brow Hornets; *Division Two:* East Hull
National Cup: Wath Brow Hornets beat Oldham St Annes 25–19
Varsity Match 2004 (Richmond, 3 March): Oxford beat Cambridge 29–16

RUGBY UNION

RUGBY WORLD CUP 2003

POOL A

	P	W	L	D	Pts
Australia	4	4	0	0	18
Ireland	4	3	1	0	15
Argentina	4	2	2	0	11
Romania	4	1	3	0	5
Namibia	4	0	4	0	0

Australia beat Argentina 24–8; Ireland beat Romania 45–17; Argentina beat Namibia 67–14; Australia beat Romania 90–8; Ireland beat Namibia 64–7; Argentina beat Romania 50–3; Australia beat Namibia 142–0; Ireland beat Argentina 16–15; Romania beat Namibia 37–7; Australia beat Ireland 17–16

POOL B

	P	W	L	D	Pts
France	4	4	0	0	20
Scotland	4	3	1	0	14
Fiji	4	2	2	0	10
USA	4	1	3	0	6
Japan	4	0	4	0	0

France beat Fiji 61–18; Scotland beat Japan 32–11; Fiji beat USA 19–18; France beat Japan 51–29; Scotland beat USA 39–15; Fiji beat Japan 41–13; France beat Scotland 51–9; USA beat Japan 39–26; France beat USA 41–14; Scotland beat Fiji 22–20

POOL C

	P	W	L	D	Pts
England	4	4	0	0	19
South Africa	4	3	1	0	15
Samoa	4	2	2	0	10
Uruguay	4	1	3	0	4
Georgia	4	0	4	0	0

South Africa beat Uruguay 72–6; England beat Georgia 84–6; Samoa beat Uruguay 60–13; England beat South Africa 25–6; Samoa beat Georgia 46–9; South Africa beat Georgia 46–19; England beat Samoa 35–22; Uruguay beat Georgia 24–12; South Africa beat Samoa 60–10; England beat Uruguay 111–13

POOL D

	P	W	L	D	Pts
New Zealand	4	4	0	0	20
Wales	4	3	1	0	14
Italy	4	2	2	0	8
Canada	4	1	3	0	5
Tonga	4	0	4	0	1

New Zealand beat Italy 70–7; Wales beat Canada 41–10; Italy beat Tonga 36–12; New Zealand beat Canada 68–6; Wales beat Tonga 27–20; Italy beat Canada 19–14; New Zealand beat Tonga 91–7; Wales beat Italy 27–15; Canada beat Tonga 24–7; New Zealand beat Wales 53–37

QUARTER FINALS
Melbourne (8 November 2003): New Zealand beat South Africa 29–9
Brisbane (8 November 2003): Australia beat Scotland 33–16
Melbourne (9 November 2003): France beat Ireland 43–21
Brisbane (9 November 2003): England beat Wales 28–17

SEMI FINALS
Sydney (15 November 2003): Australia beat New Zealand 22–10
Sydney (16 November 2003): England beat France 24–7

THIRD PLACE PLAY OFF
Sydney (20 November 2003): New Zealand beat France 40–13

FINAL
Sydney (22 November 2003): England beat Australia 20–17

SIX NATIONS' CHAMPIONSHIP 2004

14 February	Paris	France 35, Ireland 17
	Cardiff	Wales 23, Scotland 10
15 February	Rome	Italy 9, England 50
21 February	Paris	France 25, Italy 0
	Edinburgh	Scotland 13, England 35
22 February	Dublin	Ireland 36, Wales 15
6 March	Rome	Italy 20, Scotland 14
	London	England 13, Ireland 19
7 March	Cardiff	Wales 22, France 29
20 March	Dublin	Ireland 19, Italy 3
	London	England 31, Wales 21
21 March	Edinburgh	Scotland 0, France 31

27 March	Cardiff	Wales 44, Italy 10
	Dublin	Ireland 37, Scotland 16
30 March	Paris	France 24, England 21

Final standings: 1. France, 10 points; 2. Ireland, 8 points; 3. England, 6 points; 4. Wales, 4 points; 5. Italy, 2 points; 6. Scotland, 0 points

EUROPEAN COMPETITIONS 2003–4
Heineken European Cup final 2004 (Twickenham, 23 May): Wasps beat Toulouse 27–20
Parker Pen Cup 2004: Harlequins beat Montferrand 27–26
Parker Pen Shield 2004: Montpellier beat Viadana 25–19

DOMESTIC COMPETITIONS 2003–4

ENGLAND
Zurich Premiership: Gloucester, 79 points
Championship final: Wasps beat Bath 10–6
National League: Division 1, Worcester, 125 points; *Division 2,* Sedgley Park 41 points; *Division 3* (North), Waterloo, 50 points; (South) Blackheath, 44 points
Powergen Cup final: Newcastle beat Sale 37–33
Challenge Shield final: Bristol beat Waterloo 53–24
Tetley's County Championship final: Devon beat Gloucestershire 43–14
Tetley's County Shield: North Midlands beat Eastern Counties 58–5
122nd Varsity Match: Cambridge drew with Oxford 11–11

CELTIC
Celtic League: Llanelli, 76 points
Celtic Cup Final: Ulster beat Edinburgh 27–21

SCOTLAND
Scottish Premier League: Division 1, Glasgow Hawks, 90 points; *Division 2,* Gala, 85 points; *Division 3,* Edinburgh Academicals, 92 points
Scottish Cup final 2004: Glasgow Hawks beat Dundee H. S. F. P. 29–17

WALES
Welsh Premiership: Newport, 82 points
Welsh National League: Division 1, Llanharan, 85 points
Konica Minolta Cup final (Cardiff, 8 May): Neath beat Caerphilly 36–13

IRELAND
All Ireland League: Division 1, Cork Constitution, 51 points; *Division 2,* Dublin University, 49 points; *Division 3,* Highfield, 58 points

SHOOTING

135TH NATIONAL RIFLE ASSOCIATION IMPERIAL MEETING
Bisley, July 2004

Queen's Prize: H. R. T. Jeens, 291.25 v-bulls
Grand Aggregate: T. L. W. Kidner, 696.80 v-bulls
Prince of Wales Prize: Tie for first place – J. M. Rankin; P. M. Hakim; C. N. Tremlett; C. P. Weeden, 75.13 v-bulls
St George's Vase: Lt N. J. Ball, 148.21 v-bulls
All Comers' Aggregate: C. P. Weeden, 373.49 v-bulls
Kolapore Cup: Great Britain, 1,188.158 v-bulls
Chancellor's Trophy: Cambridge University, 1,143.108 v-bulls
Musketeers Cup: University of London 'A', 573.58 v-bulls
County Long-Range Championship: East of Scotland, 579.58 v-bulls
Mackinnon Challenge Cup: England, 1,139.104 v-bulls
The Albert: C. M. Tremlett, 220.30 v-bulls
Hopton Challenge Cup: C. M. Tremlett, 1,004.124 v-bulls

SPEED SKATING

EUROPEAN CHAMPIONSHIPS 2004
January, Heerenveen, Netherlands

MEN
500 metres: Mika Poutala (Finland) 36.09sec.
1,500 metres: Mark Tuitert (Netherlands) 1min. 47.41sec.
5,000 metres: Carl Verheijen (Netherlands) 6min. 26.43sec.
10,000 metres: Carl Verheijen (Netherlands) 13min. 22.91sec.
Overall: Mark Tuitert (Netherlands) 151.691 points.

WOMEN
500 metres: Anni Friesinger (Germany) 39.28sec.
1,500 metres: Renate Groenewold (Netherlands) 1min. 57.81sec.
3,000 metres: Gretha Smit (Netherlands) 4min. 7.96sec.
5,000 metres: Gretha Smit (Netherlands) 6min. 58.34sec.
Overall: Anni Friesinger (Germany) 162.717 points.

WORLD CHAMPIONSHIPS 2004
March, Seoul, Korea

MEN
500 metres: Jeremy Wotherspoon (Canada) 70.790sec. (aggregate of two legs)
1,000 metres: Erben Wennemars (Netherlands) 1min. 10.66sec.
1,500 metres: Shani Davis (USA) 1min. 48.64sec.
5,000 metres: Chad Hedrick (USA) 6min. 34.37sec.
10,000 metres: Carl Verheijen (Netherlands) 13min. 37.15sec.

WOMEN
500 metres: Manli Wang (China) 76.880sec. (aggregate of two legs).
1,000 metres: Anni Friesinger (Germany) 1min. 17.82sec.
1,500 metres: Anni Friesinger (Germany) 2min. 0.48sec.
3,000 metres: Claudia Pechstein (Germany) 4min. 13.46sec.
5,000 metres: Clara Hughes (Canada) 7min. 10.66sec.

EUROPEAN SHORT TRACK CHAMPIONSHIPS 2004
Zoetermeer, Netherlands, January

MEN
500 metres: Nicola Franceschina (Italy) 42.845sec.
1,000 metres: Fabio Carta (Italy) 1min. 35.599sec.
1,500 metres: Nicola Rodigari (Italy) 2min. 23.483sec.
3,000 metres: Pieter Gysel (Belgium) 5min. 11.707sec.
5,000 metres relay: Italy 7min. 11.668sec.
Overall: Nicola Rodigari (Italy) 81 points.

WOMEN

500 metres: Evgenia Radanova (Bulgaria) 44.882sec.

1,000 metres: Evgenia Radanova (Bulgaria) 1min. 37.158sec.

1,500 metres: Evgenia Radanova (Bulgaria) 2min. 48.282sec.

3,000 metres: Tatiana Borodulina (Russia) 5min. 33.897sec.

3,000 metres relay: Russia 4 min. 26.687sec.

Overall: Evgenia Radanova (Bulgaria) 104 points.

WORLD SHORT TRACK CHAMPIONSHIPS 2004
Gothenburg, Sweden, March

MEN

500 metres: Suk-Woo Song (Korea) 42.599sec.

1,000 metres: Hyun-Soo Ahn (Korea) 1min 26.813sec.

1,500 metres: Hyun-Soo Ahn (Korea) 2min. 16.376sec.

3,000 metres: Hyun-Soo Ahn (Korea) 5min. 03.670sec.

5,000 metres relay: Korea 6min. 48.133sec.

Overall: Hyun-Soo Ahn (Korea) 102 points

WOMEN

500 metres: Meng Wang (China) 45.332sec.

1,000 metres: Eun-Kyung Choi (Korea) 1min. 34.724sec.

1,500 metres: Eun-Kyung Choi (Korea) 2min. 28.048sec.

3,000 metres: Chun-Sa Byun (Korea) 5min. 58.035sec.

3,000 metres relay: Korea 4min. 20.985sec.

Overall: Eun-Kyung Choi (Korea) 84 points

SNOOKER

2003–4

Welsh Open (Cardiff): Ronnie O'Sullivan (England) beat Steve Davis (England) 9–8

LG Cup (Preston): Mark J. Williams (Wales) beat John Higgins (Scotland) 9–5

British Open (Brighton): Stephen Hendry (Scotland) beat Ronnie O'Sullivan (England) 9–6

UK Championship (York): Matthew Stevens (Wales) beat Stephen Hendry (Scotland) 10–8

Masters (Wembley): Paul Hunter (England) beat Ronnie O'Sullivan (England) 10–9

European Open (Malta): Stephen Maguire (Scotland) beat Jimmy White (England) 9–3

Irish Masters (Dublin): Peter Ebdon (England) beat Mark King (England) 10–7

Players' Championship (Glasgow): Jimmy White (England) beat Paul Hunter (England) 9–7

World Championship (Sheffield): Ronnie O'Sullivan (England) beat Graeme Dott (Scotland) 18–8

WOMEN

European Championship 2004: Wendy Jans (Belgium) beat Reanne Evans (England) 6–3

SQUASH RACKETS

MEN

World Team Championship final 2003: Australia beat France 3–0

World Open 2003: Amr Shabana (Egypt) beat Thierry Lincou 3–1

British Open 2003: David Palmer (Australia) beat Peter Nicol (England) 3–0

British National Championship Final 2004: John White beat Lee Beachill 3–1

WOMEN

Netherlands

World Open 2003: Carol Owens (New Zealand) beat Cassie Jackman (England) 3–1

British Open 2003: Rachel Grinham (Australia) beat Cassie Jackman (England) 3–1

British National Championship Final 2004: Cassie Jackman beat Linda Charman 3–0

SWIMMING

BRITISH CHAMPIONSHIPS 2004
April, Sheffield

MEN

50 metres freestyle: Mark Foster, 22.47

100 metres freestyle: Matthew Kidd, 49.72

200 metres freestyle: Simon Burnett, 1:48.50

400 metres freestyle: Adam Faulkner, 3:49.97

1,500 metres freestyle: David Davies, 14:57.93

100 metres backstroke: Gregor Tait, 54.90

200 metres backstroke: Gregor Tait, 1:57.42

100 metres breaststroke: Darren Mew, 1:00.02

200 metres breaststroke: Ian Edmond, 2:11.87

100 metres butterfly: Todd Cooper, 52.46

200 metres butterfly: Stephen Parry, 1:56.16

200 metres medley: Robin Francis, 2:01.06

400 metres medley: Adrian Turner, 4:16.65

WOMEN

50 metres freestyle: Alison Sheppard, 25.23

100 metres freestyle: Melanie Marshall, 54.62

200 metres freestyle: Melanie Marshall, 1:57.51

400 metres freestyle: Joanne Jackson, 4:08.45

800 metres freestyle: Rebecca Cooke, 8:33.02

100 metres backstroke: Katy Sexton, 1:01.16

200 metres backstroke: Katy Sexton, 2:11.48

100 metres breaststroke: Kirsty Balfour, 1:09.94

200 metres breaststroke: Kirsty Balfour, 2:28.54

100 metres butterfly: Georgina Lee, 59.45

200 metres butterfly: Gergina Lee, 2:09.42

200 metres medley: Sophie Caul, 2:16.99

400 metres medley: Rebecca Cooke, 4:46.79

TABLE TENNIS

ENGLISH NATIONAL CHAMPIONSHIPS 2004
Sheffield, March

Men's Singles: Alan Cooke (Derbys) beat Terry Young (Berks) 4–0

Women's Singles: Andrea Holt (Lancs) beat Helen Lower (Staffs) 4–3

Men's Doubles: Alan Cooke and Bradley Billington (Derbys) beat Alex Perry (Devon) and Terry Young (Berks) 3–2

Women's Doubles: Helen Lower (Staffs) and Georgina Walker (Notts) beat Gemma Chapman (Bucks) Sarah Brown (Essex) 3–0

Mixed Doubles: Helen Lower (Staffs) and Alex Perry (Devon) beat Natalie Bawden (Essex) and Gareth Herbert (Bucks) 3–1

WORLD TEAM CHAMPIONSHIPS 2004
Doha, March

Men's Champions: China

Women's Champions: China

TENNIS

AUSTRALIAN OPEN CHAMPIONSHIPS 2004
Melbourne, 13–26 January

Men's Singles: Roger Federer (Switzerland) beat Marat Safin (Russia) 7–6, 6–4, 6–2
Women's Singles: Justine Henin-Hardenne (Belgium) beat Kim Clijsters (Belgium) 6–3, 4–6, 6–3
Men's Doubles: Michael Llodra (France) and Fabrice Santoro (France) beat Bob Bryan (USA) and Mike Bryan (USA) 7–6, 6–3
Women's Doubles: Virginia Ruano Pascual (Spain) and Paola Suarez (Argentina) beat Svetlana Kuznetsova (Russia) & Elena Likhovtseva (Russia) 6–4, 6–3
Mixed Doubles: Elena Bovina (Russia) and Nenad Zimonjic (Serbia and Montenegro) beat Martina Navratilova (USA) and Leander Paes (India) 6–1, 7–6

FRENCH OPEN CHAMPIONSHIP 2004
Paris, 14 May–6 June

Men's Singles: Gaston Gaudio (Argentina) beat Guillermo Coria (Argentina) 0–6, 3–6, 6–4, 6–1, 8–6
Women's Singles: Anastasia Myskina (Russia) beat Elena Dementieva (Russia) 6–1, 6–2
Men's Doubles: Xavier Malisse and Olivier Rochus (Belgium) beat Michael Llodra & Fabrice Santoro (France) 7–5, 7–5
Women's Doubles: Virginia Ruano Pascual (Spain) and Paola Suarez (Argentina) beat Svetlana Kuznetsova and Elena Likhovtseva (Russia) 6–0, 6–3
Mixed Doubles: Tatiana Golovin and Richard Gasquet (France) beat Cara Black and Wayne Black (Zimbabwe) 6–3, 6–4

ALL-ENGLAND CHAMPIONSHIPS 2004
Wimbledon, 23 June–4 July

Men's Singles: Roger Federer (Switzerland) beat Andy Roddick (USA) 4–6, 7–5, 7–6, 6–4
Women's Singles: Maria Sharapova (Russia) beat Serena Williams (USA) 6–1, 6–4
Men's Doubles: Jonas Bjorkman (Sweden) and Todd Woodbridge (Australia) beat Julian Knowle (Austria) and Nenad Zimonjic (Serbia and Montenegro) 6–1, 6–4, 4–6, 6–4
Women's Doubles: Cara Black (Zimbabwe) and Rennae Stubbs (Australia) beat Liezel Huber (South Africa) and Ai Sugiyama (Japan) 6–3, 7–6
Mixed Doubles: Cara Black and Wayne Black (Zimbabwe) beat Alicia Molik (Australia) and Todd Woodbridge (Australia) 6–3, 6–3

US OPEN CHAMPIONSHIPS 2004
New York, 30 August–12 September
see Stop Press

TEAM CHAMPIONSHIPS
Davis Cup final 2003: Australia beat Spain 3–1

WORLD ATHLETICS FINAL

Monaco, 18/19 September 2004

MEN

TRACK		*min*	*sec*
100m	Asafa Powell (Jamaica)		9.98
200m	Asafa Powell (Jamaica)		20.06
400m	Michael Blackwood (Jamaica)		44.95
800m	Youssef Saad Kamel (Bahrein)	1	45.92
1500m	Ivan Heshko (Ukraine)	3	44.92
3000m	Eliud Kipchoge (Kenya)	7	38.67
5000m	Sileshi Sihine (Ethiopia)	13	06.95
3000m St	Saif Saaeed Shaheen (Qatar)	7	56.94
100m H	Allen Johnson (USA)		13.16
400m H	Bershawn Jackson (USA)		47.86

FIELD		*metres*
High Jump	Stefan Holm (Sweden)	2.33
Pole Vault	Timothy Mack (USA)	6,01
Long Jump	Ignisious Gaisah (Ghana)	8.32
Triple Jump	Christian Olsson (Sweden)	17.66
Shot	Joachim Olsen (Denmark)	21.46
Discuss	Mario Pestano (Spain)	64.11
*Hammer**	Olli-Pekka Karjalainen (Finland)	81.43
Javelin	Breaux Greer (USA)	54.57

WOMEN

TRACK		*min*	*sec*
100m	Veronica Campbell (Jamaica)		10.91
200m	Veronica Campbell (Jamaica)		22.64
400m	Ana Guevara (Mexico)		50.13
800m	Hasna Benhassi (Morocco)	2	01.42
1500m	Kelly Holmes (GBR)	4	04.55
3000m	Meseret Defar (Ethiopia)	8	36.46
5000m	Elvan Abeylegesse (Turkey)	14	59.19
100m H	Joanna Hayes (USA)		12.58
400m H	Sandra Glover (USA)		54.57

FIELD		*metres*
High Jump	Yelena Slesarenko (Russia)	2.01
Pole Vault	Yelena Isinbayeva (Russia)	4.83
Long Jump	Irina Simigina (Russia)	6.74
Triple Jump	Francoise Mbango (Cameroon)	15.01
Shot	Nadyezda Ostapchuk (Belarus)	19.23
Discuss	Vera Pospisilova-Cechlova (Czech Rep)	65.86
*Hammer**	Olga Kuzenkova (Russia)	72.90
Javelin	Osleidys Menendez (Cuba)	66.20

* Held at Szombathely, Hungary, 5 September 2004

OLYMPIC GAMES

Athens, Greece 2004

Gold Medallists

ARCHERY

MEN
Individual: Marco Galiazzo (Italy)
Team: Korea

WOMEN
Individual: Sung Hyun Park (Korea)
Team: Korea

ATHLETICS

MEN

TRACK		*hr.*	*min.*	*sec.*
100m	Justin Gatlin (USA)			9.85
200m	Shawn Crawford (USA)			19.79
400m	Jeremy Wariner (USA)			44.00
800m	Yuri Borzakovski (Russia)		1	44.45

TRACK		hr. min. sec.
1500m	Hicham El Guerrouj (Morocco)	3 34.18
5000m	Hicham El Guerrouj (Morocco)	13 14.39
10,000m	Kenenisa Bekele (Ethiopia)	27 05.10
Marathon	Stafano Baldini (Italy)	2 10 55
3000m St	Ezekiel Kemboi (Kenya)	8 05.81
110m H	Liu Xiang (China)	12.91
400m H	Felix Sanchez (Dominican Rep)	47.63
4 × 100m Relay	Great Britain	38.07
4 × 400m Relay	United States	2 55.91
20km Walk	Ivano Brugnetti (Italy)	1 19 40
50km Walk	Robert Korzeniowski (Poland)	3 38 46

FIELD		metres
High Jump	Stefan Holm (Sweden)	2.36
Pole Vault	Tim Mack (USA)	5.95
Long Jump	Dwight Phillips (USA)	8.59
Triple Jump	Christian Olsson (Sweden)	17.79
Shot	Yuri Belonog (Ukraine)	21.16
Discus	Virgilijus Alekna (Lithuania)	69.89
Hammer	Koji Murofushi (Japan)	82.91
Javelin	Andreas Thorkildsen (Norway)	86.50
Decathlon	Roman Sebrle (Czech Republic)	8893 pts

WOMEN

TRACK		hr. min. sec.
100m	Yuliya Nesterenko (Belarus)	10.93
200m	Veronica Campbell (Jamaica)	22.06
400m	Tonique Williams (Bahamas)	49.41
800m	Kelly Holmes (Great Britain)	1 56.38
1500m	Kelly Holmes (Great Britain)	3 57.90
5000m	Meseret Defar (Ethiopia)	14 45.85
10000m	Xing Huina (China)	30 24.36
Marathon	Mizuki Noguchi (Japan)	2 26 20
100m H	Joanna Hayes (USA)	12.37
400m H	Fani Halkia (Greece)	52.82
4 × 100m Relay	Jamaica	41.71
4 × 400m Relay	United States	3 19.01
20km Walk	Athanasia Tsoumeleka (Greece)	1 29 12

FIELD		metres
High Jump	Yelena Slesarenko (Ukraine)	2.06
Pole Vault	Yelena Isinbayeva (Russia)	4.91
Long Jump	Tatyana Lebedeva (Russia)	7.07
Triple Jump	Francoise Mbango (Cameroon)	15.30
Discus	Natalya Sadova (Russia)	67.02
Hammer	Olga Kuzenkova (Russia)	75.02
Javelin	Osleidys Menendez (Cuba)	71.53
Heptathlon	Carolina Kluft (Sweden)	6952 pts

BADMINTON

MEN
Singles: Taufik Hidaya (Indonesia)
Doubles: Korea

WOMEN
Singles: Zhang Ning (China)
Doubles: China

Mixed Doubles: China

BASEBALL

MEN Cuba

BASKETBALL

MEN Argentina
WOMEN United States

BOXING

MEN
Light-fly: Yan Bhartelemy (Cuba)
Fly: Yuriorkis Gamboa (Cuba)
Bantam: Guillermo Rigondeaux (Cuba)
Feather: Alexei Tishchenko (Russia)
Light: Mario Kindelan (Cuba)
Light-welter: Manus Boonjumnong (Thailand)
Welter: Bakhtiyar Artayev (Kazakhstan)
Middle: Gaydarbek Gaydarbekov (Russia)
Light-heavy: Andre Ward (USA)
Heavy: Odlanier Solis (Cuba)
Super-heavy: Alexander Povetkin (Russia)

CANOEING

MEN

		min.	sec.
K1 500m	Adam van Koeverden (Canada)	1	37.919
K1 1000m	Erik Larsen (Norway)	3	25.897
K2 500m	Germany	1	27.040
K2 100m	Sweden	3	18.420
K4 1000m	Hungary	2	56.919
C1 500m	Andreas Dittmer (Germany)	1	48.383
C1 1000m	David Cal (Spain)	3	46.201
C2 500m	China	1	40.278
C2 1000m	Germany	3	41.802
K1 Slalom	Benoit Peschier (France)		187.96
C1 Slalom	Tony Estanguet (France)		189.16
C2 Slalom	Slovakia		207.16

WOMEN

		min.	sec.
K1 500m	Natasa Janics (Hungary)	1	47.741
K2 500m	Hungary	1	38.101
K4 500m	Germany	1	34.340
K1 Slalom	Elena Kaliska (Slovakia)		210.03

CYCLING

MEN

		hr. min. sec.
1km T/T	Chris Hoy (Great Britain)	1 00.711
Sprint	Ryan Bayley (Australia)	
Individual Pursuit	Bradley Wiggins (Great Britain)	4 16.304
Points Race	Mikhail Ignatyev (Russia)	93 pts
Keirin	Ryan Bayley (Australia)	
Team Sprint	Germany	
Team Pursuit	Australia	3 58.233
Madison	Australia	22 pts
Road-Mass start	Paolo Bettini (Italy)	5 41 44
Road-T/T	Tyler Hamilton (USA)	57 31.74
Mountain Bike	Julien Absalon (France)	2 15 02

WOMEN

		hr.	min.	sec.
500m T/T	Anna Meares (Australia)			33.952
Sprint	Lori-Ann Muenzer (Canada)			
Individual Pursuit	Sarah Ulmer (New Zealand)		3	23.537
Points Race	Olga Slyusaryeva (Russia)			20 pts
Road-Mass start	Sara Carrigan (Australia)	3	24	24
Road-T/T	Leontien Zijlaard-van Moorsel (Netherlands)	31	11	53
Mountain Bike	Gunn-Rita Dahle (Norway)	1	56	21

EQUESTRIAN

OPEN

Jumping-Team	Germany	
Jumping-Ind	Cian O'Connor (Ireland) on *Waterford Crystal*	
Dressage-Team	Germany	74.653
Dressage-Ind (Netherlands)	Anky van Grunsven on *Salinero*	79.273
Three Day-Team	France	140.40
Three Day-Ind	Leslie Law (Great Britain) on *Shear L'Eau*	44.40

FENCING

MEN

Foil-Ind	Brice Guyert (France)
Foil-Team	Italy
Epee-Ind	Marcel Fischer (Switzerland)
Epee-Team	France
Sabre-Ind	Aldo Montano (Italy)
Sabre-Team	France

WOMEN

Foil-Ind	Valentina Vezzali (Italy)
Epee-Ind	Timea Nagy (Hungary)
Epee-Team	Russia
Sabre-Ind	Mariel Zagunis (USA)

FOOTBALL

MEN	Argentina
WOMEN	United States

GYMNASTICS

MEN

Team	Japan	173.821 pts
Individual	Paul Hamm (USA)	57.823 pts
Floor	Kyle Shewfelt (Canada)	9.787 pts
Pommel	Haibin Teng (China)	9.837 pts
Rings	Dimosthenis Tampakos (Greece)	9.862 pts
Vault	Gervasio Deferr (Spain)	9.737 pts
Parallel Bars	Valeri Goncharov (Ukraine)	9.787 pts
Horizontal Bar	Igor Cassina (Italy)	9.812 pts
Trampoline	Yuri Nikitin (Ukraine)	41.500 pts

WOMEN

Team	Romania	114.283 pts
Individual	Carly Patterson (USA)	38.387 pts
Floor	Catalina Ponor (Romania)	9.750 pts
Vault	Monica Rosu (Romania)	9.656 pts
Asymmetric Bars	Emilie Lepennec (France)	9.687 pts
Balance Beam	Catalina Ponor (Romania)	9.787 pts
Trampoline	Anna Dogonadze (Germany)	39.600 pts
Rhythmic-Ind	Alina Kabaeva (Russia)	
Rhythmic-Team	Russia	51.100 pts

HANDBALL

MEN	Croatia
WOMEN	Denmark

HOCKEY

MEN	Australia
WOMEN	Germany

JUDO

MEN

60kg	Tadahiro Nomura (Japan)
66kg	Masato Uchishiba (Japan)
73kg	Won Hee Lee (Korea)
81kg	Ilias Iliadis (Greece)
90kg	Zurab Zviadauri (Georgia)
100kg	Ihar Makarau (Belarus)
100kg+	Keiji Suzuki (Japan)

WOMEN

48kg	Ryoko Tani (Japan)
52kg	Dongmei Xian (China)
57kg	Yvonne Boenisch (Germany)
63kg	Ayumi Tanimoto (Japan)
70kg	Masae Ueno (Japan)
78kg	Noriko Anno (Japan)
78kg+	Maki Tsukada (Japan)

MODERN PENTATHLON

MEN	Andrei Moiseyev (Russia)	5480 pts
WOMEN	Zsuzsanna Voros (Hungary)	5448 pts

ROWING

MEN

		min.	sec.
Single sculls	Olaf Tufte (Norway)	6	49.30
Pairs	Australia	6	30.76
Double sculls	France	6	29.00
Fours	Great Britain	6	06.98
Quad sculls	Russia	5	56.85
Eights	United States	5	42.48
L/weight double sculls	Poland	6	20.93
L/weight fours	Denmark	6	01.39

WOMEN

Single sculls	Katrin Rutschow-Stomporowski (Germany)	7	18.12
Pairs	Romania	7	06.55
Double sculls	New Zealand	7	01.79
Quad sculls	Germany	6	29.2
Eights	Romania	6	17.70
L/weight double sculls	Romania	6	56.05

SAILING

MEN

Mistral	Gal Fridman (Israel)	50 pts
470	United States	
Finn	Ben Ainslie (Great Britain)	
Star	Brazil	

WOMEN

Mistral	Faustine Merret (France)
470	Greece
Europe	Siren Sundby (Norway)
Yngling	Great Britain

OPEN

Tornado	Austria	
49-er	Spain	67 pts
Laser	Robert Scheidt (Brazil)	

SHOOTING

MEN

Rifle 50m Prone	Matthew Emmons (USA)	599
Rifle 50m 3-pos	Zhanbo Jia (China)	1264.5
Air Rifle 10m	Qinan Zhu (China)	702.7
Pistol	Mikhail Nestruyev (Russia)	565
Rapid Fire Pistol	Ralf Schumann (Germany)	694.9
Air Pistol	Yifu Wang (China)	690.0
Running Target	Manfred Kurzer (Germany)	682.4
Trap	Alexei Alipov (Russia)	149
Double trap	Ahmed Almaktoum (United Arab Emirates)	189
Skeet	Andrea Benelli (Italy)	149

WOMEN

Rifle 50m 3-pos	Lyubov Galkina (Russia)	688.4
Air Rifle	Li Du (China)	502.0
Pistol	Maria Grozdeva (Bulgaria)	688.2
Air Pistol	Olena Kostevych (Ukraine)	483.3
Trap	Suzanna Balogh (Australia)	88
Double Trap	Kimberley Rhode (USA)	146
Skeet	Diana Igaly (Hungary)	97

SOFTBALL

WOMEN	United States

SWIMMING

MEN

		min.	*sec.*
50m Free	Gary Hall Jr (USA)		21.93
100m Free	Pieter van den Hoogenband (Netherlands)		48.17
200m Free	Ian Thorpe (Australia)	1	44.71
400m Free	Ian Thorpe (Australia)	3	43.10
1500m Free	Grant Hackett (Australia)	14	43.40
100m Back	Aaron Peirsol (USA)		54.04
200m Back	Aaron Peirsol (USA)	1	54.95
100m Breast	Kosuke Kitajima (Japan)		60.08
200m Breast	Kosuke Kitajima (Japan)	2	09.44
100m Butterfly	Michael Phelps (USA)		51.25
200m Butterfly	Michael Phelps (USA)	1	54.04
200m Ind Medley	Michael Phelps (USA)	1	57.14
400m Ind Medley	Michael Phelps (USA)	4	08.26
4 × 100m Free	South Africa	3	13.17
4 × 200m Free	United States	7	07.33
4 × 100m Medley	United States	3	30.68

WOMEN

		min.	*sec.*
50m Free	Inge de Bruijn (Netherlands)		24.58
100m Free	Jodie Henry (Australia)		53.84
200m Free	Camelia Potec (Romania)	1	58.03
400m Free	Laure Manaudou (France)	4	05.34
800m Free	Ai Shibata (Japan)	8	24.54
100m Back	Natalie Coughlin (USA)		60.37
200m Back	Kirsty Coventry (Zimbabwe)	2	09.19
100m Breast	Xuejuan Luo (China)	1	06.64
200m Breast	Amanda Beard (USA)	2	23.37
100m Butterfly	Petria Thomas (Australia)		57.72
200m Butterfly	Otylia Jedrzejczak (Poland)	2	06.03
200m Ind Medley	Yana Klochkova (Ukraine)	2	11.14
400m Ind Medley	Yana Klochkova (Ukraine)	4	38.36
4 × 100m Free	Australia	3	35.94
4 × 200m Free	United States	7	53.42
4 × 100m Medley	Australia	3	57.32

DIVING

MEN

Springboard Indiv	Bo Peng (China)	787.38 pts
Platform Indiv	Hu Jia (China)	748.08 pts
Synchron Springboard	Greece	353.34 pts
Synchron Platform	China	383.88 pts

WOMEN

Springboard Indiv	Jingjing Guo (China)	633.15 pts
Platform Indiv	Chantelle Newbery (Australia)	590.31 pts
Synchron Springboard	China	336.90 pts
Synchron Platform	China	352.14 pts

WATER POLO

MEN	Hungary
WOMEN	Italy

SYNCHRONISED SWIMMING

WOMEN

Duet	Russia	99.833 pts
Team	Russia	99.501 pts

TABLE TENNIS

MEN

Singles	Seung Min Ryu (Korea)
Doubles	China

WOMEN

Singles	Yining Zhang (China)
Doubles	China

TAEKWONDO

MEN

58kg	Mu Yen Chu (Chinese Taipei)
68kg	Hadi Saei Bonehkohal (Iran)
80kg	Steven Lopez (USA)
80kg+	Moon Dae-Sung (Korea)

WOMEN

49kg	Shih Hsin Chen (Chinese Taipei)
57kg	Ji Won Jang (Korea)
67kg	Wei Luo (China)
67kg+	Chen Zhong (China)

TENNIS

MEN

Singles	Nicolas Massu (Chile)
Doubles	Chile

WOMEN

Singles	Justine Henin-Hardenne (Belgium)
Doubles	China

TRIATHLON

MEN	Hamish Carter (New Zealand)	1h 51m 07s
WOMEN	Kate Allen (Austria)	2h 04m 43s

VOLLEYBALL

MEN

Indoor	Brazil
Beach	Brazil

WOMEN

Indoor	China
Beach	United States

WEIGHTLIFTING

MEN

		kg.
56kg	Halil Mutlu (Turkey)	295
62kg	Zhiyong Shi (China)	325
69kg	Guozheng Zhang (China)	347.5
77kg	Tanir Sagir (Turkey)	375
85kg	George Asinidze (Georgia)	382.5
94kg	Milen Dobrov (Bulgaria)	407.5
105kg	Dmitri Berestov (Russia)	425
105kg+	Hossein Reza Zadeh (Iran)	472.5

WOMEN

		kg.
48kg	Nurcan Taylan (Turkey)	210
53kg	Udomporn Polsak (Thailand)	222.5
58kg	Yanging Chen (China)	237.5
63kg	Natalya Skakun (Ukraine)	242.5
69kg	Chunhong Liu (China)	275
75kg	Pawina Thongsuk (Thailand)	272.5
75kg +	Gonghong Tang (China)	305

WRESTLING

MEN

Freestyle

55kg	Mavlet Batirov (Russia)
60kg	Yandro Quintana (Cuba)
66kg	Elbrus Tedeyev (Ukraine)
74kg	Buvaysa Saytiev (Russia)
84kg	Cael Sanderson (USA)
96kg	Khadjimourat Gatsalov (Russia)
120kg	Artur Taymazov (Uzbekistan)

Greco-Roman

55kg	Istvan Majoros (Hungary)
60kg	Ji Hyun Jung (Korea)
66kg	Farid Mansurov (Azerbaijan)
74kg	Alexandr Dokturishvili (Uzbekistan)
84kg	Alexei Michine (Russia)
96kg	Karam Ibrahim (Egypt)
120kg	Khasan Baroev (Russia)

WOMEN

Freestyle

48kg	Irini Merleni (Ukraine)
55kg	Saori Yoshida (Japan)
63kg	Kaori Icho (Japan)
72kg	Xu Wang (China)

OLYMPIC MEDALS TABLE

COUNTRY	GOLD	SILVER	BRONZE	TOTAL
United States	35	39	29	103
China	32	17	14	63
Russia	27	27	38	92
Australia	17	16	16	49
Japan	16	9	12	37
Germany	14	16	18	48
France	11	9	13	33
Italy	10	11	11	32
Korea	9	12	9	30
Great Britain	9	9	12	30
Cuba	9	7	11	27
Ukraine	9	5	9	23
Hungary	8	6	3	17
Romania	8	5	6	19
Greece	6	6	4	16
Norway	5	0	1	6
Netherlands	4	9	9	22
Brazil	4	3	3	10
Sweden	4	1	2	7
Spain	3	11	5	19
Canada	3	6	3	12
Turkey	3	3	4	10
Poland	3	2	5	10
New Zealand	3	2	0	5
Thailand	3	1	4	8
Belarus	2	6	7	15
Austria	2	4	1	7
Ethiopia	2	3	2	7
Iran	2	2	2	6
Slovakia	2	2	2	6
Chinese Taipei	2	2	1	5
Georgia	2	2	0	4
Bulgaria	2	1	9	12
Jamaica	2	1	2	5
Uzbekistan	2	1	0	3
Morocco	2	1	0	3
Denmark	2	0	6	8
Argentina	2	0	4	6
Chile	2	0	1	3
Kazakhstan	1	4	3	8
Kenya	1	4	2	7
Czech Republic	1	3	4	8
South Africa	1	3	2	6
Croatia	1	2	2	5
Lithuania	1	2	0	3
Egypt	1	1	3	5
Switzerland	1	1	3	5
Indonesia	1	1	2	4
Zimbabwe	1	1	1	3
Azerbaijan	1	0	4	5
Belgium	1	0	2	3
Bahamas	1	0	1	2
Israel	1	0	1	2
Cameroon	1	0	0	1
Dominican Republic	1	0	0	1
Ireland	1	0	0	1
UAE	1	0	0	1
North Korea	0	4	1	5
Latvia	0	4	0	4
Mexico	0	3	1	4
Portugal	0	2	1	3
Finland	0	2	0	2
Serbia/Montenegro	0	2	0	2
Slovenia	0	1	3	4
Estonia	0	1	2	3
Hong Kong	0	1	0	1
India	0	1	0	1
Paraguay	0	1	0	1
Nigeria	0	0	2	2
Venezuela	0	0	2	2
Colombia	0	0	1	1
Eritrea	0	0	1	1
Mongolia	0	0	1	1
Syria	0	0	1	1
Trinidad/Tobago	0	0	1	1

THE OLYMPIC GAMES

Venues of the modern Olympic Games

SUMMER OLYMPIC GAMES

I	Athens, Greece	1896
II	Paris, France	1900
III	St Louis, USA	1904
*	Athens	1906
IV	London, Britain	1908
V	Stockholm, Sweden	1912
†VI	Berlin, Germany	1916
VII	Antwerp, Belgium	1920
VIII	Paris, France	1924
IX	Amsterdam, Netherlands	1928
X	Los Angeles, USA	1932
XI	Berlin, Germany	1936
†XII	Tokyo, Japan, then Helsinki, Finland	1940
†XIII	London, Britain	1944
XIV	London, Britain	1948
XV	Helsinki, Finland	1952
†§XVI	Melbourne, Australia	1956
XVII	Rome, Italy	1960
XVIII	Tokyo, Japan	1964
XIX	Mexico City, Mexico	1968
XX	Munich, West Germany	1972
XXI	Montreal, Canada	1976
XXII	Moscow, USSR	1980
XXIII	Los Angeles, USA	1984
XXIV	Seoul, South Korea	1988
XXV	Barcelona, Spain	1992
XXVI	Atlanta, USA	1996
XXVII	Sydney, Australia	2000
XXVIII	Athens, Greece	2004

WINTER OLYMPIC GAMES

I	Chamonix, France	1924
II	St Moritz, Switzerland	1928
III	Lake Placid, USA	1932
IV	Garmisch-Partenkirchen, Germany	1936
V	St Moritz, Switzerland	1948
VI	Oslo, Norway	1952
VII	Cortina d'Ampezzo, Italy	1956
VIII	Squaw Valley, USA	1960
IX	Innsbruck, Austria	1964
X	Grenoble, France	1968
XI	Sapporo, Japan	1972
XII	Innsbruck, Austria	1976
XIII	Lake Placid, USA	1980
XIV	Sarajevo, Yugoslavia	1984
XV	Calgary, Canada	1988
XVI	Albertville, France	1992
XVII	Lillehammer, Norway	1994
XVIII	Nagano, Japan	1998
XIX	Salt Lake City, USA	2002
XX	Turin, Italy	2006

* The Intercalated Games

† These Games were scheduled but did not take place owing to World Wars

§ Equestrian events were held in Stockholm, Sweden

SPORTS RECORDS

ATHLETICS WORLD RECORDS

AS AT SEPTEMBER 2004

All the world records given below have been accepted by the International Amateur Athletic Federation except those marked with an asterisk* which are awaiting homologation. Fully automatic timing to 1/100th second is mandatory up to and including 400 metres. For distances up to and including 10,000 metres, records will be accepted to 1/100th second if timed automatically, and to 1/10th if hand timing is used.

MEN'S EVENTS

TRACK EVENTS	hr.	min.	sec.
100 metres			9.78
Tim Montgomery, USA, 2002			
200 metres			19.32
Michael Johnson, USA, 1996			
400 metres			43.18
Michael Johnson, USA, 1999			
800 metres		1	41.11
Wilson Kipketer, Denmark, 1997			
1,000 metres		2	11.96
Noah Ngeny, Kenya, 1999			
1,500 metres		3	26.00
Hicham El Guerrouj, Morocco, 1998			
1 mile		3	43.13
Hicham El Guerrouj, Morocco, 1999			
2,000 metres		4	44.79
Hicham El Guerrouj, Morocco, 1999			
3,000 metres		7	20.67
Daniel Komen, Kenya, 1996			
5,000 metres		12	37.35
Kenenisa Bekele, Ethiopia, 2004			
10,000 metres		26	20.31
Kenenisa Bekele, Ethiopia, 2004			
20,000 metres		56	55.6
Arturo Barrios, Mexico, 1991			
21,101 metres (13 miles 196 yards 1 foot)	1	00	00.0
Arturo Barrios, Mexico, 1991			
25,000 metres	1	13	55.8
Toshihiko Seko, Japan, 1981			
30,000 metres	1	29	18.8
Toshihiko Seko, Japan, 1981			
Marathon			
Paul Tergat, Kenya, 2003	2	04	55
110 metres hurdles (3 ft 6 in)			
Colin Jackson, GB, 1993 and Liu Xiang, China, 2004			12.91
400 metres hurdles (3 ft 0 in)			46.78
Kevin Young, USA, 1992			
3,000 metres steeplechase		7	53.63
Saif Saaeed Shaheen, Qatar			

RELAYS	min.	sec.
4 × 100 metres		37.40
USA, 1992, 1993		
4 × 200 metres	1	19.11
Santa Monica TC, 1992		
4 × 400 metres	2	54.20
USA, 1998		
4 × 800 metres	7	03.89
GB, 1982		
4 × 1,500 metres	14	38.8
Federal Republic of Germany, 1977		

FIELD EVENTS	metres	ft	in
High jump	2.45	8	0½
Javier Sotomayor, Cuba, 1993			
Pole vault	6.14	20	1¾
Sergei Bubka, Ukraine, 1994			
Long jump	8.95	29	4½
Mike Powell, USA, 1991			
Triple jump	18.29	60	0¼
Jonathan Edwards, GB, 1995			
Shot	23.12	75	10¼
Randy Barnes, USA, 1990			
Discus	74.08	243	0
Jürgen Schult, GDR, 1986			
Hammer	86.74	284	7
Yuriy Sedykh, USSR, 1986			
Javelin	98.48	323	1
Jan Zelezny, Czech Rep., 1996			
Decathlon†	9,026 points		
Roman Sebrle, Czech Rep., 2001			

† Ten events comprising 100 m, long jump, shot, high jump, 400 m, 110 m hurdles, discus, pole vault, javelin, 1500 m

WALKING (TRACK)	hr.	min.	sec.
20,000 metres	1	17	25.6
Bernard Segura, Mexico, 1994			
29,572 metres (18 miles 660 yards)	2	00	00.0
Maurizio Damilano, Italy, 1992			
30,000 metres	2	01	44.1
Maurizio Damilano, Italy, 1992			
50,000 metres	3	40	57.9
Thierry Toutain, France, 1996			

WOMEN'S EVENTS

TRACK EVENTS	hr.	min.	sec.
100 metres			10.49
Florence Griffith-Joyner, USA, 1988			
200 metres			21.34
Florence Griffith-Joyner, USA, 1988			
400 metres			47.60
Marita Koch, GDR, 1985			
800 metres		1	53.28
Jarmila Kratochvilova, Czechoslovakia, 1983			
1,500 metres		3	50.46
Qu Yunxia, China, 1993			
1 mile		4	12.56
Svetlana Masterkova, Russia, 1996			
3,000 metres		8	06.11
Wang Junxia, China, 1993			
5,000 metres		14	24.68
Elvan Abeylegesse, Turkey, 2004			
10,000 metres		29	31.78
Wang Junxia, China, 1993			
Marathon	2	15	25
Paula Radcliffe, GB, 2003			
100 metres hurdles (2 ft 9 in)			12.21
Yordanka Donkova, Bulgaria, 1988			

400 metres hurdles (2 ft 6 in)		52.34*
Yulia Pechonkina, Russia, 2003		
3,000 metres steeplechase	9	01.59*
Gulnara Samitova, Russia, 2004		

RELAYS	*min.*	*Sec.*
4 × 100 metres		41.37
GDR, 1985		
4 × 200 metres	1	27.46*
USA, 2000		
4 × 400 metres	3	15.17
USSR, 1988		
4 × 800 metres	7	50.17
USSR, 1984		

FIELD EVENTS	*metres*	*ft*	*in*
High jump	2.09	6	10¼
Stefka Kostadinova, Bulgaria, 1987			
Pole vault	4.92*	16	1¾
Yelena Isinbayeva, Russia, 2004			
Long jump	7.52	24	8¼
Galina Chistiakova, USSR, 1988			
Triple jump	15.50	50	10¼
Inessa Kravets, Ukraine, 1995			
Shot	22.63	74	3
Natalya Lisovskaya, USSR, 1987			
Discus	76.80	252	0
Gabriele Reinsch, GDR, 1988			
Hammer	76.07	249	6
Mihaela Melinte, Romania, 1999			
Javelin (new implement in 1999)	71.54	234	8
Osleidys Menendez, Cuba, 2001			
Heptathlon†		7,291 points	
Jackie Joyner-Kersee, USA, 1988			

† Seven events comprising 100 m hurdles, shot, high jump, 200 m, long jump, javelin, 800 m

ATHLETICS NATIONAL (UK) RECORDS

AS AT SEPTEMBER 2004

Records set anywhere by athletes eligible to represent Great Britain and Northern Ireland

MEN

TRACK EVENTS	*hr.*	*min.*	*sec.*
100 metres			9.87
Linford Christie, 1993 and Dwain Chambers, 2002			
200 metres			19.87
John Regis, 1994			
400 metres			44.36
Iwan Thomas, 1997			
800 metres		1	41.73
Sebastian Coe, 1981			
1,000 metres		2	12.18
Sebastian Coe, 1981			
1,500 metres		3	29.67
Sebastian Coe, 1985			
1 mile		3	46.32
Steve Cram, 1985			
2,000 metres		4	51.39
Steve Cram, 1985			
3,000 metres		7	32.79
David Moorcroft, 1982			
5,000 metres		13	00.41
David Moorcroft, 1982			
10,000 metres		27	18.14
Jon Brown, 1998			
20,000 metres		57	28.7
Carl Thackery, 1990			
20,855 metres	1	00	00.0
Carl Thackery, 1990			
25,000 metres	1	15	22.6
Ron Hill, 1965			
30,000 metres	1	31	30.4
Jim Alder, 1970			
Marathon	2	07	13
Steve Jones, 1985			
3,000 metres steeplechase		8	07.96
Mark Rowland, 1988			
110 metres hurdles			12.91
Colin Jackson, 1993			
400 metres hurdles			47.82
Kriss Akabusi, 1992			

RELAYS	*min.*	*sec.*
4 × 100 metres		37.73
GB team, 1999		
4 × 200 metres	1	21.29
GB team, 1989		
4 × 400 metres	2	56.60
GB team, 1996		
4 × 800 metres	7	03.89
GB team, 1982		

FIELD EVENTS	*metres*	*ft*	*in*
High jump	2.37	7	9¼
Steve Smith, 1993			
Pole vault	5.80	19	0¼
Nick Buckfield, 1998			
Long jump	8.27	27	1¾
Chris Tomlinson, 2002			
Triple jump	18.29	60	0¼
Jonathan Edwards, 1995			
Shot	21.92	71	11
Carl Myerscough, 2003			
Discus	66.64	218	8
Perris Wilkins, 1998			
Hammer	77.54	254	5
Martin Girvan, 1984			
Javelin	91.46	300	1
Steve Backley, 1992			
Decathlon		8,847 points	
Daley Thompson, 1984			

WALKING (TRACK)	*hr.*	*min.*	*sec.*
20,000 metres	1	23	26.5
Ian McCombie, 1990			
30,000 metres	2	19	18
Christopher Maddocks, 1984			
50,000 metres	4	05	44.6
Paul Blagg, 1990			
26,037 metres (16 miles 315 yards)	2	00	00.0
Ron Wallwork, 1971			

WOMEN

TRACK EVENTS	*hr.*	*min.*	*sec.*
100 metres			11.10
Kathy Cook, 1981			
200 metres			22.10
Kathy Cook, 1984			
400 metres			49.43
Kathy Cook, 1984			
800 metres		1	56.21
Kelly Holmes, 1995			

1,500 metres Kelly Holmes, 2004		3	57.90
1 mile Zola Budd, 1985		4	17.57
3,000 metres Paula Radcliffe, 2002		8	22.20
5,000 metres Paula Radcliffe, 2004		14	29.11*
10,000 metres Paula Radcliffe, 2002		30	01.09
Marathon Paula Radcliffe, 2003	2	15	25
100 metres hurdles Angela Thorp, 1996			12.80
400 metres hurdles Sally Gunnell, 1993			52.74

RELAYS	*min.*	*sec.*
4 × 100 metres GB team, 1980		42.43
4 × 200 metres GB team, 1977	1	31.57
4 × 400 metres GB team, 1991	3	22.01
4 × 800 metres GB team, 1971	8	23.8

FIELD EVENTS	*metres*	*ft*	*in*
High jump Diana Elliott, 1982 Susan Jones, 2001	1.95	6	4¾
Pole vault Janine Whitlock, 2002	4.41	14	5¾
Long jump Beverley Kinch, 1983	6.90	22	7¾
Triple jump Ashia Hansen, 1997	15.15	49	8½
Shot Judy Oakes, 1988	19.36	63	6¼
Discus Margaret Ritchie, 1981	67.48	221	5
Hammer Lorraine Shaw, 2001	68.93	226	1
Javelin (new implement) Kelly Morgan, 2002	64.87	212	9
Heptathlon Denise Lewis, 2000	6,831 points		

*Awaiting ratification

SWIMMING WORLD RECORDS

AS AT SEPTEMBER 2004

MEN	*min.*	*sec.*
50 metres freestyle Alexander Popov, Russia		21.64
100 metres freestyle Pieter van den Hoogenband, Netherlands		47.84
200 metres freestyle Ian Thorpe, Australia	1	44.06
400 metres freestyle Ian Thorpe, Australia	3	40.08
800 metres freestyle Ian Thorpe, Australia	7	39.16
1,500 metres freestyle Grant Hackett, Australia	14	34.56
50 metres breaststoke Oleg Lisogor, Ukraine		27.18
100 metres breaststroke Brendan Hansen, USA		59.30
200 metres breaststroke Brendan Hansen, USA	2	09.04
50 metres butterfly Matt Welsh, Australia		23.43
100 metres butterfly Ian Crocker, USA		50.76
200 metres butterfly Michael Phelps, USA	1	53.93
50 metres backstroke Thomas Rupprath, Germany		24.80
100 metres backstroke Aaron Peirsol, USA		53.45
200 metres backstroke Aaron Peirsol, USA	1	54.74
200 metres medley Michael Phelps, USA	1	55.94
400 metres medley Michael Phelps, USA	4	08.26
4 × 100 metres freestyle relay South Africa	3	13.17
4 × 200 metres freestyle relay Australia	7	04.66
4 × 100 metres medley relay USA	3	30.68

WOMEN	*min.*	*sec.*
50 metres freestyle Inge de Bruin, Netherlands		24.13
100 metres freestyle Jodie Henry, Australia		53.52
200 metres freestyle Franziska van Almsick, Germany	1	56.64
400 metres freestyle Janet Evans, USA	4	03.85
800 metres freestyle Janet Evans, USA	8	16.22
1,500 metres freestyle Janet Evans, USA	15	52.10
50 metres breaststroke Zoe Baker, Great Britain		30.57
100 metres breaststroke Leisel Jones, Australia	1	06.37
200 metres breaststroke Amanda Beard, USA	2	22.44
50 metres butterfly Anna-Karin Kammerling, Sweden		25.57
100 metres butterfly Inge de Bruin, Netherlands		56.61
200 metres butterfly Otylia Jedrejczak, Poland	2	05.78
50 metres backstroke Sandra Volker, Germany		28.25
100 metres backstroke Natalie Coughlin, USA		59.58
200 metres backstroke Krisztina Egerszegi, Hungary	2	06.62
200 metres medley Wu Yanyan, China	2	09.72
400 metres medley Yana Klochkova, Ukraine	4	33.59
4 × 100 metres freestyle relay Australia	3	35.94
4 × 200 metres freestyle relay USA	7	53.42
4 × 100 metres medley relay Australia	3	57.32

TIME AND SPACE

ASTRONOMY

TIME MEASUREMENT AND CALENDARS

TIDAL PREDICTIONS

ASTRONOMY

The following pages give astronomical data for each month of the year 2005. There are four pages of data for each month. All data are given for 0h Greenwich Mean Time (GMT), i.e. at the midnight at the beginning of the day named. This applies also to data for the months when British Summer Time is in operation (for dates, *see* below).

The astronomical data are given in a form suitable for observation with the naked eye or with a small telescope. These data do not attempt to replace the *Astronomical Almanac* for professional astronomers.

A fuller explanation of how to use the astronomical data is given on pages 1273–7.

CALENDAR FOR EACH MONTH

The calendar for each month comprises dates of general interest plus the dates of birth or death of well-known people. For key religious, civil and legal dates *see* page 9. For details of flag-flying days *see* page 23. For royal birthdays *see* pages 23 and 24–5. Public holidays are given in italics. *See* also pages 10 and 11.

Fuller explanations of the various calendars can be found under Time Measurement and Calendars (pages 1283–1298).

The zodiacal signs through which the Sun is passing during each month are illustrated. The date of transition from one sign to the next, to the nearest hour, is given under Astronomical Phenomena.

JULIAN DATE

The Julian date on 2005 January 0.0 is 2453370.5. To find the Julian date for any other date in 2005 (at 0h GMT), add the day-of-the-year number on the extreme right of the calendar for each month to the Julian date for January 0.0.

SEASONS

The seasons are defined astronomically as follows:

Spring from the vernal equinox to the summer solstice
Summer from the summer solstice to the autumnal equinox
Autumn from the autumnal equinox to the winter solstice
Winter from the winter solstice to the vernal equinox

The seasons in 2005 are:

Northern Hemisphere

Vernal equinox	March 20d 13h GMT
Summer solstice	June 21d 07h GMT
Autumnal equinox	September 22d 23h GMT
Winter solstice	December 21d 19h GMT

Southern Hemisphere

Autumnal equinox	March 20d 13h GMT
Winter solstice	June 21d 07h GMT
Vernal equinox	September 22d 23h GMT
Summer solstice	December 21d 19h GMT

The longest day of the year, measured from sunrise to sunset, is at the summer solstice. The longest day in the United Kingdom will fall on 21 June in 2005.

The shortest day of the year is at the winter solstice. The shortest day in the United Kingdom will fall on 21 December in 2005.

The equinox is the point at which day and night are of equal length all over the world.

In popular parlance, the seasons in the northern hemisphere comprise the following months:

Spring	March, April, May
Summer	June, July, August
Autumn	September, October, November
Winter	December, January, February

BRITISH SUMMER TIME

British Summer Time is the legal time for general purposes during the period in which it is in operation (*see also* page 1275). During this period, clocks are kept one hour ahead of Greenwich Mean Time. The hour of changeover is 01h Greenwich Mean Time. The duration of Summer Time in 2005 is from March 27 01h GMT to October 30 01h GMT.

JANUARY 2005

FIRST MONTH, 31 DAYS. *Janus*, god of the portal, facing two ways, past and future

1	*Saturday*	John Le Carré b. 1931. King John of England d. 1216	1
2	*Sunday*	David Bailey b. 1938. Ovid d. AD17	2
3	*Monday*	J. R. R. Tolkien b. 1892. Pierre Larousse d. 1875	week 1 day 3
4	*Tuesday*	Augustus John b. 1878. T. S. Eliot d. 1965	4
5	*Wednesday*	Juan Carlos, King of Spain b. 1938. Catherine de Medici, Queen of France d. 1589	5
6	*Thursday*	Richard II b. 1367. Rudolf Nureyev d. 1993	6
7	*Friday*	Gerald Durrell b. 1925. Catherine of Aragon, d. 1536	7
8	*Saturday*	Wilkie Collins b. 1824. Paul Verlaine d. 1896	8
9	*Sunday*	The ocean liner Queen Elizabeth destroyed by fire 1972	9
10	*Monday*	Dame Barbara Hepworth b. 1903. Sinclair Lewis d. 1951	week 2 day 10
11	*Tuesday*	James Earl Jones b. 1931. Thomas Hardy d. 1928	11
12	*Wednesday*	John Singer Sargent b. 1856. Dame Agatha Christie d. 1976	12
13	*Thursday*	Jan van Goyen b. 1656. James Joyce d. 1941	13
14	*Friday*	Sir Cecil Beaton b. 1904. Lewis Carroll d. 1898	14
15	*Saturday*	The coronation of Queen Elizabeth I 1559	15
16	*Sunday*	Diane Fossey b. 1932. Léo Delibes d. 1891	16
17	*Monday*	Anne Brontë b. 1820. Ruskin Spear d. 1990	week 3 day 17
18	*Tuesday*	A. A. Milne b. 1882. Rudyard Kipling d. 1936	18
19	*Wednesday*	Paul Cézanne b. 1839. Patricia Highsmith, b. 1951	19
20	*Thursday*	Sir John Soane d. 1837. George V d. 1936	20
21	*Friday*	George Orwell d. 1950. Louis XVI, King of France d. 1793	21
22	*Saturday*	Lord Byron b. 1788. Queen Victoria d. 1901	22
23	*Sunday*	Édouard Manet b. 1832. Anna Pavlova d. 1931	23
24	*Monday*	Frederick the Great, King of Prussia b. 1712. Amadeo Modigliani d. 1920	week 4 day 24
25	*Tuesday*	Henry VIII and Anne Boleyn married in secret 1533	25
26	*Wednesday*	Mary Mapes Dodge b. 1831. Nelson Rockefeller d. 1979	26
27	*Thursday*	Wolfgang Amadeus Mozart b. 1756. Giuseppe Verdi d. 1901	27
28	*Friday*	Jackson Pollock b. 1912. Henry VIII d. 1547	28
29	*Saturday*	Germaine Greer b. 1939. George III d. 1820	29
30	*Sunday*	Anton Chekhov b. 1860. Charles I d. 1649	30
31	*Monday*	Franz Schubert b. 1797. A. A. Milne d. 1956	week 5 day 31

ASTRONOMICAL PHENOMENA

d	*h*	
2	00	Earth at perihelion (147 million km.)
4	01	Jupiter in conjunction with Moon. Jupiter 0°.3 N.
7	19	Mars in conjunction with Moon. Mars 3° N.
9	02	Mercury in conjunction with Moon. Mercury 5° N.
9	03	Venus in conjunction with Moon. Venus 5° N.
13	23	Saturn at opposition
14	03	Venus in conjunction with Mercury. Venus 0°.4 N.
19	23	Sun's longitude 300° ♒
24	09	Saturn in conjunction with Moon. Saturn 5° S.
31	10	Jupiter in conjunction with Moon. Jupiter 0°.8 N.

MINIMA OF ALGOL

d	*h*	*d*	*h*	*d*	*h*
1	07.6	12	18.8	24	06.1
4	04.4	15	15.7	27	02.9
7	01.2	18	12.5	29	23.8
9	22.0	21	09.3		

CONSTELLATIONS

The following constellations are near the meridian at

	d	*h*		*d*	*h*
December	1	24	January	16	21
December	16	23	February	1	20
January	1	22	February	15	19

Draco (below the Pole), Ursa Minor (below the Pole), Camelopardus, Perseus, Auriga, Taurus, Orion, Eridanus and Lepdus

THE MOON

Phases, Apsides and Node	*d*	*h*	*m*
☾ Last Quarter	3	17	46
● New Moon	10	12	03
☽ First Quarter	17	06	57
○ Full Moon	25	10	32
Perigee (356,569 km)	10	10	00
Apogee (406,458 km)	23	18	38

Mean longitude of ascending node on January 1, 28°

THE SUN

s.d. 16′.3

Day	Right Ascension			Dec. –		Equation of time		Rise 52°		Rise 56°		Transit		Set 52°		Set 56°		Sidereal time			Transit of first point of Aries		
	h	*m*	*s*	°	′	*m*	*s*	*h*	*m*	*h*	*m*	*h*	*m*	*h*	*m*	*h*	*m*	*h*	*m*	*s*	*h*	*m*	*s*
1	18	46	24	23	01	−3	26	8	08	8	31	12	04	15	59	15	36	6	42	58	17	14	12
2	18	50	49	22	56	−3	54	8	08	8	31	12	04	16	00	15	38	6	46	55	17	10	16
3	18	55	13	22	50	−4	22	8	08	8	31	12	05	16	02	15	39	6	50	51	17	06	20
4	18	59	37	22	44	−4	49	8	08	8	30	12	05	16	03	15	40	6	54	48	17	02	24
5	19	04	01	22	38	−5	16	8	07	8	30	12	05	16	04	15	42	6	58	45	16	58	28
6	19	08	24	22	31	−5	43	8	07	8	29	12	06	16	05	15	43	7	02	41	16	54	32
7	19	12	47	22	23	−6	09	8	06	8	28	12	06	16	07	15	45	7	06	38	16	50	36
8	19	17	09	22	15	−6	35	8	06	8	28	12	07	16	08	15	46	7	10	34	16	46	40
9	19	21	31	22	07	−7	00	8	05	8	27	12	07	16	09	15	48	7	14	31	16	42	44
10	19	25	52	21	58	−7	25	8	05	8	26	12	08	16	11	15	49	7	18	27	16	38	49
11	19	30	13	21	49	−7	49	8	04	8	25	12	08	16	12	15	51	7	22	24	16	34	53
12	19	34	33	21	40	−8	13	8	03	8	24	12	08	16	14	15	53	7	26	20	16	30	57
13	19	38	53	21	30	−8	36	8	03	8	23	12	09	16	15	15	55	7	30	17	16	27	01
14	19	43	12	21	19	−8	58	8	02	8	22	12	09	16	17	15	56	7	34	14	16	23	05
15	19	47	30	21	09	−9	20	8	01	8	21	12	10	16	18	15	58	7	38	10	16	19	09
16	19	51	47	20	57	−9	41	8	00	8	20	12	10	16	20	16	00	7	42	07	16	15	13
17	19	56	04	20	46	−10	01	7	59	8	19	12	10	16	22	16	02	7	46	03	16	11	17
18	20	00	20	20	34	−10	21	7	58	8	17	12	11	16	23	16	04	7	50	00	16	07	21
19	20	04	36	20	22	−10	39	7	57	8	16	12	11	16	25	16	06	7	53	56	16	03	25
20	20	08	50	20	09	−10	57	7	56	8	15	12	11	16	27	16	08	7	57	53	15	59	29
21	20	13	04	19	56	−11	15	7	55	8	13	12	11	16	28	16	10	8	01	50	15	55	34
22	20	17	17	19	42	−11	31	7	54	8	12	12	12	16	30	16	12	8	05	46	15	51	38
23	20	21	30	19	28	−11	47	7	53	8	10	12	12	16	32	16	14	8	09	43	15	47	42
24	20	25	41	19	14	−12	02	7	51	8	09	12	12	16	34	16	16	8	13	39	15	43	46
25	20	29	52	18	59	−12	16	7	50	8	07	12	12	16	35	16	18	8	17	36	15	39	50
26	20	34	02	18	44	−12	29	7	49	8	06	12	13	16	37	16	20	8	21	32	15	35	54
27	20	38	11	18	29	−12	42	7	47	8	04	12	13	16	39	16	22	8	25	29	15	31	58
28	20	42	19	18	14	−12	54	7	46	8	02	12	13	16	41	16	25	8	29	25	15	28	02
29	20	46	27	17	58	−13	05	7	44	8	00	12	13	16	43	16	27	8	33	22	15	24	06
30	20	50	33	17	41	−13	15	7	43	7	58	12	13	16	44	16	29	8	37	19	15	20	10
31	20	54	39	17	25	−13	24	7	41	7	57	12	13	16	46	16	31	8	41	15	15	16	14

DURATION OF TWILIGHT (in minutes)

Latitude	52°	56°	52°	56°	52°	56°	52°	56°
	1 January		*11 January*		*21 January*		*31 January*	
Civil	41	47	40	45	38	43	37	41
Nautical	84	96	82	93	80	90	78	87
Astronomical	125	141	123	138	120	134	117	130

THE NIGHT SKY

Mercury, magnitude −0.3, is visible as a morning object for the first week of the month. It is very close to Venus which should make the location of Mercury much easier. On the 1st Mercury will be 1.1 degrees above and 0.2 degrees to the right of Venus, while by the 7th these figures have changed gradually to 0.6 degrees above and 0.6 degrees to the right of Venus. If visibility is poor the glare from Venus may overpower the light from the much fainter innermost planet.

Venus is a brilliant object in the early morning sky, magnitude −3.9, and at the beginning of the month is visible very low in the east-south-eastern sky for nearly an hour before dawn.

Mars, magnitude +1.5, although technically a morning object, is continuing to move slowly southwards in declination, and this means that it will be a very difficult object to detect even with very clear conditions. It will be barely 10 degrees above the horizon one hour before sunrise for observers in southern England. Measured in ecliptic longitude Mars is 15 degrees from Venus at the beginning of the month: this distance increases to 32 degrees by the end of January.

Jupiter is a brilliant object in the morning sky, magnitude −2.1. By the end of the month it is visible in the east-south-eastern sky before midnight. Jupiter is in the constellation of Virgo. On the night of the 3rd–4th the Moon, at Last Quarter, passes about 1 degree south of the planet.

Saturn, magnitude −0.4, reaches opposition on the 13th, and therefore is visible throughout the hours of darkness, crossing the meridian around midnight. Saturn is retrograding slowly in the constellation of Gemini, some 7 degrees south of Pollux. The Full Moon will be seen near the planet around the 23rd–25th.

THE MOON

Day	RA		Dec.	Hor. par.	Semi-diam.	Sun's Co-long.	PA of Br. Limb	Ph.	Age	Rise				Transit		Set			
										52°		56°				52°		56°	
	h	m	°	′	′	°	°	%	d	h	m	h	m	h	m	h	m	h	m
1	10	49	+11.6	54.9	15.0	154	110	76	19.9	22	10	22	05	4	14	11	12	11	20
2	11	34	+6.2	55.4	15.1	166	112	67	20.9	23	24	23	24	4	55	11	23	11	26
3	12	18	+0.3	56.1	15.3	179	113	58	21.9	—	—	—	—	5	37	11	33	11	31
4	13	04	−5.6	56.9	15.5	191	113	47	22.9	0	41	0	46	6	20	11	45	11	37
5	13	52	−11.6	57.8	15.8	203	111	37	23.9	2	01	2	12	7	06	11	58	11	45
6	14	43	−17.2	58.8	16.0	215	107	27	24.9	3	27	3	45	7	57	12	16	11	56
7	15	40	−22.0	59.7	16.3	227	101	17	25.9	4	57	5	23	8	54	12	41	12	14
8	16	41	−25.7	60.5	16.5	239	93	9	26.9	6	27	7	01	9	56	13	20	12	45
9	17	48	−27.7	61.1	16.7	252	80	4	27.9	7	47	8	26	11	03	14	20	13	41
10	18	57	−27.6	61.5	16.7	264	51	1	28.9	8	47	9	23	12	11	15	41	15	06
11	20	05	−25.5	61.4	16.7	276	293	1	0.5	9	28	9	55	13	16	17	15	16	49
12	21	09	−21.5	61.1	16.6	288	265	4	1.5	9	54	10	13	14	16	18	51	18	33
13	22	08	−16.1	60.4	16.5	300	255	9	2.5	10	13	10	25	15	10	20	22	20	12
14	23	02	−10.0	59.6	16.2	312	250	17	3.5	10	27	10	33	15	59	21	48	21	44
15	23	53	−3.6	58.6	16.0	325	248	27	4.5	10	39	10	40	16	45	23	09	23	11
16	0	41	+2.8	57.6	15.7	337	247	37	5.5	10	50	10	46	17	30	—	—	—	—
17	1	28	+8.8	56.7	15.5	349	248	47	6.5	11	02	10	52	18	14	0	28	0	36
18	2	15	+14.3	55.9	15.2	1	251	57	7.5	11	16	11	00	18	59	1	46	1	59
19	3	03	+19.1	55.3	15.1	13	254	67	8.5	11	33	11	11	19	46	3	02	3	23
20	3	52	+23.0	54.7	14.9	25	259	76	9.5	11	55	11	27	20	35	4	18	4	45
21	4	43	+25.9	54.4	14.8	38	266	83	10.5	12	26	11	52	21	25	5	29	6	02
22	5	36	+27.5	54.1	14.7	50	273	90	11.5	13	08	12	30	22	16	6	33	7	10
23	6	30	+27.9	54.0	14.7	62	282	95	12.5	14	02	13	25	23	07	7	24	8	01
24	7	23	+27.1	53.9	14.7	74	295	98	13.5	15	07	14	35	23	57	8	03	8	36
25	8	15	+24.9	54.0	14.7	86	329	100	14.5	16	19	15	53	—	—	8	31	8	58
26	9	05	+21.7	54.2	14.8	98	69	100	15.5	17	33	17	14	0	45	8	52	9	12
27	9	52	+17.6	54.4	14.8	110	96	98	16.5	18	47	18	34	1	30	9	07	9	22
28	10	38	+12.7	54.7	14.9	123	105	94	17.5	20	01	19	53	2	13	9	20	9	29
29	11	23	+7.3	55.1	15.0	135	109	89	18.5	21	14	21	12	2	54	9	31	9	35
30	12	07	+1.6	55.6	15.1	147	112	82	19.5	22	28	22	32	3	35	9	41	9	40
31	12	51	−4.3	56.2	15.3	159	112	73	20.5	23	46	23	55	4	17	9	51	9	46

MERCURY

Day	RA		Dec.	Diam.	Phase	Transit		5° high			
								52°		56°	
	h	m	°	″	%	h	m	h	m	h	m
1	17	10	−21.3	6	69	10	28	7	10	7	41
3	17	20	−21.8	6	72	10	30	7	16	7	48
5	17	31	−22.2	6	76	10	32	7	23	7	56
7	17	42	−22.6	6	79	10	36	7	29	8	03
9	17	53	−22.9	6	81	10	39	7	36	8	11
11	18	05	−23.2	5	83	10	43	7	42	8	18
13	18	17	−23.4	5	85	10	48	7	48	8	25
15	18	30	−23.5	5	87	10	53	7	54	8	31
17	18	42	−23.6	5	89	10	57	7	59	8	37
19	18	55	−23.6	5	90	11	03	8	04	8	41
21	19	08	−23.5	5	91	11	08	8	08	8	45
23	19	22	−23.3	5	93	11	13	8	12	8	48
25	19	35	−23.0	5	94	11	19	8	15	8	50
27	19	48	−22.6	5	95	11	24	8	17	8	51
29	20	02	−22.2	5	96	11	30	8	19	8	51
31	20	16	−21.6	5	96	11	36	8	20	8	50

VENUS

Day	RA		Dec.	Diam.	Phase	Transit		5° high			
								52°		56°	
	h	m	°	″	%	h	m	h	m	h	m
1	17	13	−22.3	11	93	10	30	7	21	7	54
6	17	40	−22.8	11	94	10	38	7	33	8	08
11	18	07	−23.1	11	95	10	45	7	43	8	19
16	18	34	−23.1	10	95	10	53	7	50	8	26
21	19	02	−22.8	10	96	11	00	7	55	8	29
26	19	29	−22.2	10	97	11	08	7	57	8	30
31	19	55	−21.3	10	97	11	15	7	57	8	27

MARS

Day	RA		Dec.	Diam.	Phase	Transit		5° high			
								52°		56°	
	h	m	°	″	%	h	m	h	m	h	m
1	16	10	−20.9	4	96	9	26	6	06	6	35
6	16	24	−21.5	4	96	9	21	6	06	6	37
11	16	39	−22.1	4	96	9	16	6	05	6	38
16	16	54	−22.6	4	95	9	11	6	05	6	39
21	17	09	−23.0	4	95	9	07	6	04	6	39
26	17	24	−23.3	5	95	9	02	6	02	6	38
31	17	39	−23.5	5	94	8	58	5	59	6	37

SUNRISE AND SUNSET

	London 0° 05′	51° 30′	*Bristol* 2° 35′	51° 28′	*Birmingham* 1° 55′	52° 28′	*Manchester* 2° 15′	53° 28′	*Newcastle* 1° 37′	54° 59′	*Glasgow* 4° 14′	55° 52′	*Belfast* 5° 56′	54° 35′
	h m	*h m*	*h m*	*h m*	*h m*	*h m*	*h m*	*h m*	*h m*	*h m*	*h m*	*h m*	*h m*	*h m*
1	8 06	16 02	8 16	16 12	8 18	16 05	8 25	16 01	8 31	15 49	8 47	15 54	8 46	16 09
2	8 06	16 03	8 16	16 13	8 18	16 06	8 25	16 02	8 31	15 50	8 47	15 55	8 46	16 10
3	8 06	16 04	8 16	16 15	8 18	16 07	8 24	16 03	8 31	15 52	8 47	15 57	8 46	16 11
4	8 05	16 06	8 15	16 16	8 18	16 08	8 24	16 04	8 30	15 53	8 46	15 58	8 45	16 13
5	8 05	16 07	8 15	16 17	8 17	16 09	8 24	16 05	8 30	15 54	8 46	15 59	8 45	16 14
6	8 05	16 08	8 15	16 18	8 17	16 11	8 23	16 07	8 29	15 56	8 45	16 01	8 44	16 15
7	8 04	16 09	8 14	16 19	8 16	16 12	8 23	16 08	8 29	15 57	8 45	16 02	8 44	16 17
8	8 04	16 11	8 14	16 21	8 16	16 13	8 22	16 10	8 28	15 59	8 44	16 04	8 43	16 18
9	8 03	16 12	8 13	16 22	8 15	16 15	8 22	16 11	8 27	16 00	8 43	16 06	8 42	16 20
10	8 03	16 13	8 13	16 24	8 15	16 16	8 21	16 13	8 27	16 02	8 42	16 07	8 42	16 21
11	8 02	16 15	8 12	16 25	8 14	16 18	8 20	16 14	8 26	16 03	8 41	16 09	8 41	16 23
12	8 02	16 16	8 11	16 26	8 13	16 19	8 20	16 16	8 25	16 05	8 40	16 11	8 40	16 25
13	8 01	16 18	8 11	16 28	8 13	16 21	8 19	16 17	8 24	16 07	8 39	16 12	8 39	16 26
14	8 00	16 19	8 10	16 29	8 12	16 22	8 18	16 19	8 23	16 09	8 38	16 14	8 38	16 28
15	7 59	16 21	8 09	16 31	8 11	16 24	8 17	16 21	8 22	16 10	8 37	16 16	8 37	16 30
16	7 58	16 22	8 08	16 33	8 10	16 26	8 16	16 22	8 21	16 12	8 36	16 18	8 36	16 32
17	7 57	16 24	8 07	16 34	8 09	16 27	8 15	16 24	8 20	16 14	8 35	16 20	8 35	16 33
18	7 56	16 26	8 06	16 36	8 08	16 29	8 14	16 26	8 19	16 16	8 34	16 22	8 34	16 35
19	7 55	16 27	8 05	16 37	8 07	16 31	8 13	16 27	8 17	16 18	8 32	16 24	8 33	16 37
20	7 54	16 29	8 04	16 39	8 06	16 32	8 11	16 29	8 16	16 20	8 31	16 26	8 31	16 39
21	7 53	16 31	8 03	16 41	8 05	16 34	8 10	16 31	8 15	16 22	8 30	16 28	8 30	16 41
22	7 52	16 32	8 02	16 42	8 03	16 36	8 09	16 33	8 13	16 23	8 28	16 30	8 29	16 43
23	7 51	16 34	8 01	16 44	8 02	16 38	8 08	16 35	8 12	16 25	8 27	16 32	8 27	16 45
24	7 50	16 36	8 00	16 46	8 01	16 39	8 06	16 37	8 10	16 27	8 25	16 34	8 26	16 47
25	7 48	16 38	7 58	16 48	7 59	16 41	8 05	16 38	8 09	16 29	8 23	16 36	8 24	16 48
26	7 47	16 39	7 57	16 49	7 58	16 43	8 03	16 40	8 07	16 31	8 22	16 38	8 23	16 50
27	7 46	16 41	7 56	16 51	7 57	16 45	8 02	16 42	8 06	16 33	8 20	16 40	8 21	16 52
28	7 44	16 43	7 54	16 53	7 55	16 47	8 00	16 44	8 04	16 36	8 18	16 42	8 20	16 54
29	7 43	16 45	7 53	16 55	7 54	16 49	7 59	16 46	8 02	16 38	8 17	16 44	8 18	16 56
30	7 42	16 46	7 51	16 56	7 52	16 50	7 57	16 48	8 01	16 40	8 15	16 46	8 16	16 59
31	7 40	16 48	7 50	16 58	7 51	16 52	7 56	16 50	7 59	16 42	8 13	16 49	8 15	17 01

JUPITER

Day	*RA*		*Dec.*		*Transit*		*5° high*			
							52°		*56°*	
	h	*m*	°	′	*h*	*m*	*h*	*m*	*h*	*m*
1	13	05.7	–5	36	6	22	1	25	1	33
11	13	08.8	–5	52	5	46	0	50	0	58
21	13	10.9	–6	02	5	08	0	13	0	22
31	13	11.8	–6	04	4	30	23	31	23	40

Diameters – equatorial 38″ polar 35″

SATURN

Day	*RA*		*Dec.*		*Transit*		*5° high*			
							52°		*56°*	
	h	*m*	°	′	*h*	*m*	*h*	*m*	*h*	*m*
1	7	47.5	+21	08	1	04	8	23	8	39
11	7	44.1	+21	18	0	22	7	42	7	57
21	7	40.6	+21	27	23	35	7	00	7	16
31	7	37.3	+21	36	22	52	6	18	6	34

Diameters –equatorial 20″ polar 19″
Rings – major axis 46″ minor axis 18″

URANUS

Day	*RA*		*Dec.*		*Transit*		*10° high*			
							52°		*56°*	
	h	*m*	°	′	*h*	*m*	*h*	*m*	*h*	*m*
1	22	24.3	–10	46	15	39	19	30	19	11
11	22	25.9	–10	37	15	01	18	54	18	35
21	22	27.7	–10	26	14	24	18	17	17	59
31	22	29.7	–10	14	13	46	17	41	17	23

Diameter 4″

NEPTUNE

Day	*RA*		*Dec.*		*Transit*		*10° high*			
							52°		*56°*	
	h	*m*	°	′	*h*	*m*	*h*	*m*	*h*	*m*
1	21	05.4	–16	46	14	20	17	28	16	58
11	21	06.7	–16	40	13	42	16	51	16	21
21	21	08.2	–16	33	13	04	16	14	15	44
31	21	09.7	–16	27	12	26	15	37	15	08

Diameter 2″

FEBRUARY 2005

SECOND MONTH, 28 or 29 DAYS. *Februa*, Roman festival of Purification

1	*Tuesday*	Mary Shelley b. 1851. Piet Mondrian d. 1944	32
2	*Wednesday*	James Joyce b. 1882. James Joyce's *Ulysses* published in Paris 1922	33
3	*Thursday*	Felix Mendelssohn b. 1809. Buddy Holly d. 1959	34
4	*Friday*	Jaques Prévert b. 1900. Patricia Highsmith d. 1995	35
5	*Saturday*	Marquise de Sévigné b. 1626. Marianne Moore d. 1972	36
6	*Sunday*	Christopher Marlowe b. 1564. Gustav Klimt d. 1918	37
7	*Monday*	Charles Dickens b. 1812. King Hussein of Jordan d. 1999	week 6 day 38
8	*Tuesday*	John Ruskin b. 1819. Dame Iris Murdoch d. 1999	39
9	*Wednesday*	Alice Walker b. 1944. Fyodor Dostoevsky, d. 1881	40
10	*Thursday*	Berthold Brecht b. 1898. Aleksandr Pushkin d. 1837	41
11	*Friday*	William Henry Fox Talbot b. 1800. Sylvia Plath d. 1963	42
12	*Saturday*	Anna Pavlova b. 1881. Lady Jane Grey d. 1554	43
13	*Sunday*	Georges Simenon b. 1903. Richard Wagner d. 1883	44
14	*Monday*	Richard II d. 1400. P. G. Wodehouse d. 1975	week 7 day 45
15	*Tuesday*	Jeremy Bentham b. 1748. Mikhail Glinka d. 1857	46
16	*Wednesday*	Iain Banks b. 1954. Pierre-Paul Prud'hon d. 1823	47
17	*Thursday*	Ruth Rendell b. 1930. Molière d. 1673	48
18	*Friday*	Henri Laurens b. 1885. Balthus d. 2001	49
19	*Saturday*	Duke of York b. 1960. Georg Büchner d. 1837	50
20	*Sunday*	Dame Marie Rambert b. 1888. James I d. 1437	51
21	*Monday*	W. H. Auden b. 1907. Dame Margot Fonteyn d. 1991	week 8 day 52
22	*Tuesday*	Eric Gill b. 1872. Andy Warhol d. 1987	53
23	*Wednesday*	George Frideric Handel b. 1685. John Keats d. 1821	54
24	*Thursday*	Wilhelm Grimm b. 1786. Bobby Moore d. 1993	55
25	*Friday*	Anthony Burgess b. 1917. Tennessee Williams d. 1983	56
26	*Saturday*	Victor Hugo b. 1802. Frank Bridge b. 1879	57
27	*Sunday*	John Steinbeck b. 1902. John Evelyn d. 1706	58
28	*Monday*	Sir Stephen Spender b. 1909. Henry James d. 1916	week 9 day 59

ASTRONOMICAL PHENOMENA

d	*h*	
2	02	Jupiter at stationary point
3	19	Neptune in conjunction
5	13	Mars in conjunction with Moon. Mars 4° N.
8	01	Venus in conjunction with Moon. Venus 4° N.
8	15	Mercury in conjunction with Moon. Mercury 3° N.
14	11	Mercury in superior conjunction
18	14	Sun's longitude 330° ♓
20	12	Saturn in conjunction with Moon. Saturn 5° S.
25	07	Uranus in conjunction
27	14	Jupiter in conjunction with Moon. Jupiter 1° N.

MINIMA OF ALGOL

d	*h*	*d*	*h*	*d*	*h*
1	20.6	10	11.1	19	01.5
4	17.4	13	07.9	21	22.3
7	14.2	16	04.7	24	19.2

CONSTELLATIONS

The following constellations are near the meridian at

	d	*h*		*d*	*h*
January	1	24	February	15	21
January	16	23	March	1	20
February	1	22	March	16	19

Draco (below the Pole), Camelopardus, Auriga, Taurus, Gemini, Orion, Canis Minor, Monoceros, Lepus, Canis Major and Puppis

THE MOON

Phases, Apsides and Node	*d*	*h*	*m*
☾ Last Quarter	2	07	27
● New Moon	8	22	28
☽ First Quarter	16	00	16
○ Full Moon	24	04	54
Perigee (358,556 km)	7	22	05
Apogee (405,833 km)	20	04	51

Mean longitude of ascending node on February 1, 27°

THE SUN

s.d. 16′.2

Day	Right Ascension			Dec. –		Equation of time		Rise 52°		Rise 56°		Transit		Set 52°		Set 56°		Sidereal time			Transit of first point of Aries		
	h	m	s	°	′	m	s	h	m	h	m	h	m	h	m	h	m	h	m	s	h	m	s
1	20	58	44	17	08	−13	33	7	40	7	55	12	14	16	48	16	33	8	45	12	15	12	18
2	21	02	49	16	51	−13	41	7	38	7	53	12	14	16	50	16	35	8	49	08	15	08	23
3	21	06	52	16	33	−13	47	7	37	7	51	12	14	16	52	16	38	8	53	05	15	04	27
4	21	10	55	16	16	−13	54	7	35	7	49	12	14	16	54	16	40	8	57	01	15	00	31
5	21	14	57	15	58	−13	59	7	33	7	47	12	14	16	55	16	42	9	00	58	14	56	35
6	21	18	58	15	39	−14	04	7	32	7	45	12	14	16	57	16	44	9	04	54	14	52	39
7	21	22	58	15	21	−14	07	7	30	7	43	12	14	16	59	16	46	9	08	51	14	48	43
8	21	26	58	15	02	−14	10	7	28	7	41	12	14	17	01	16	49	9	12	48	14	44	47
9	21	30	57	14	43	−14	13	7	26	7	39	12	14	17	03	16	51	9	16	44	14	40	51
10	21	34	55	14	23	−14	14	7	24	7	36	12	14	17	05	16	53	9	20	41	14	36	55
11	21	38	52	14	04	−14	15	7	23	7	34	12	14	17	07	16	55	9	24	37	14	32	59
12	21	42	48	13	44	−14	15	7	21	7	32	12	14	17	09	16	57	9	28	34	14	29	03
13	21	46	44	13	24	−14	14	7	19	7	30	12	14	17	10	17	00	9	32	30	14	25	08
14	21	50	39	13	03	−14	12	7	17	7	27	12	14	17	12	17	02	9	36	27	14	21	12
15	21	54	33	12	43	−14	10	7	15	7	25	12	14	17	14	17	04	9	40	23	14	17	16
16	21	58	26	12	22	−14	06	7	13	7	23	12	14	17	16	17	06	9	44	20	14	13	20
17	22	02	19	12	01	−14	03	7	11	7	21	12	14	17	18	17	08	9	48	17	14	09	24
18	22	06	11	11	40	−13	58	7	09	7	18	12	14	17	20	17	11	9	52	13	14	05	28
19	22	10	02	11	19	−13	53	7	07	7	16	12	14	17	22	17	13	9	56	10	14	01	32
20	22	13	53	10	58	−13	47	7	05	7	13	12	14	17	23	17	15	10	00	06	13	57	36
21	22	17	43	10	36	−13	40	7	03	7	11	12	14	17	25	17	17	10	04	03	13	53	40
22	22	21	32	10	14	−13	33	7	01	7	09	12	13	17	27	17	19	10	07	59	13	49	44
23	22	25	21	9	52	−13	25	6	59	7	06	12	13	17	29	17	21	10	11	56	13	45	48
24	22	29	09	9	30	−13	16	6	57	7	04	12	13	17	31	17	24	10	15	52	13	41	53
25	22	32	56	9	08	−13	07	6	54	7	01	12	13	17	33	17	26	10	19	49	13	37	57
26	22	36	43	8	46	−12	57	6	52	6	59	12	13	17	34	17	28	10	23	46	13	34	01
27	22	40	29	8	23	−12	47	6	50	6	56	12	13	17	36	17	30	10	27	42	13	30	05
28	22	44	15	8	01	−12	36	6	48	6	54	12	13	17	38	17	32	10	31	39	13	26	09

DURATION OF TWILIGHT (in minutes)

Latitude	52°	56°	52°	56°	52°	56°	52°	56°
	1 February		*11 February*		*21 February*		*31 February*	
Civil	37	41	35	39	34	38	34	37
Nautical	77	86	75	83	74	81	73	80
Astronomical	117	130	114	126	113	124	112	124

THE NIGHT SKY

Mercury passes through superior conjunction on the 14th and is unsuitably placed for observation throughout the month.

Venus remains too close to the Sun for observation throughout the month.

Mars, magnitude +1.3, reaches its greatest southerly declination of −23.7 degrees during this month and despite its increasing elongation from the Sun observers in these latitudes will continue to have great difficulty in locating the planet. Observers in southern England may possibly be able to detect it as a difficult morning object low in the south-eastern sky, though only for a short while before the morning twilight inhibits observation, and only under exceptionally clear conditions.

Jupiter, magnitude −2.3, continues to be visible as a brilliant morning object, rising above the east-south-eastern horizon well before midnight. Jupiter reaches its first stationary point on the 2nd and then begins its slow retrograde motion, west of Spica, in the constellation of Virgo.

Saturn continues to be visible as a bright object in the southern sky in the evenings and in fact, for most of the night, magnitude −0.2. It is retrograding slowly in the constellation of Gemini, south of Castor and Pollux. On the 20th the waxing gibbous Moon passes 4 degrees north of the planet. The rings of Saturn present a beautiful spectacle to the observer with a small telescope. The rings were at their maximum opening in 2002. They will next appear edge-on in 2009. The diameter of the minor axis is now 18 arcseconds, almost exactly the same as the polar diameter of the planet itself.

Zodiacal Light. The evening cone may be observed stretching up from the western horizon, along the ecliptic, after the end of twilight, from the beginning of the month until the 10th and again after the 26th. This faint phenomenon is only visible under good conditions and in the absence of both moonlight and artificial lighting.

THE MOON

Day	RA		Dec.	Hor. par.	Semi-diam.	Sun's Co-long.	PA of Br. Limb	Ph.	Age	Rise				Transit		Set			
										52°		56°				52°		56°	
	h	m	°	′	′	°	°	%	d	h	m	h	m	h	m	h	m	h	m
1	13	37	−10.2	56.8	15.5	171	111	64	21.5	—	—	—	—	5	01	10	03	9	52
2	14	26	−15.8	57.6	15.7	183	109	53	22.5	1	07	1	22	5	49	10	19	10	01
3	15	19	−20.7	58.4	15.9	195	105	43	23.5	2	32	2	55	6	41	10	39	10	15
4	16	17	−24.7	59.2	16.1	208	99	32	24.5	4	00	4	31	7	39	11	10	10	38
5	17	20	−27.3	60.0	16.3	220	91	22	25.5	5	23	6	01	8	41	11	58	11	19
6	18	26	−28.1	60.6	16.5	232	82	13	26.5	6	31	7	09	9	47	13	06	12	29
7	19	34	−26.8	61.0	16.6	244	71	6	27.5	7	20	7	52	10	53	14	34	14	03
8	20	39	−23.5	61.2	16.7	256	55	1	28.5	7	52	8	16	11	55	16	10	15	48
9	21	41	−18.7	61.0	16.6	269	330	0	0.1	8	14	8	30	12	53	17	46	17	32
10	22	38	−12.8	60.5	16.5	281	262	1	1.1	8	31	8	40	13	46	19	17	19	10
11	23	31	−6.2	59.8	16.3	293	252	6	2.1	8	44	8	47	14	35	20	43	20	43
12	0	21	+0.4	58.9	16.0	305	249	13	3.1	8	56	8	53	15	22	22	06	22	12
13	1	10	+6.9	57.9	15.8	317	248	21	4.1	9	07	9	00	16	07	23	27	23	38
14	1	58	+12.8	57.0	15.5	330	249	30	5.1	9	20	9	07	16	53	—	—	—	—
15	2	47	+18.0	56.1	15.3	342	252	40	6.1	9	36	9	17	17	41	0	47	1	05
16	3	37	+22.2	55.4	15.1	354	257	50	7.1	9	57	9	31	18	29	2	05	2	29
17	4	29	+25.4	54.8	14.9	6	262	60	8.1	10	24	9	52	19	20	3	19	3	51
18	5	22	+27.4	54.4	14.8	18	268	69	9.1	11	02	10	25	20	11	4	26	5	03
19	6	15	+28.2	54.1	14.7	30	275	77	10.1	11	53	11	15	21	02	5	22	6	00
20	7	09	+27.6	54.0	14.7	42	282	85	11.1	12	55	12	21	21	53	6	05	6	39
21	8	01	+25.7	54.1	14.7	55	289	91	12.1	14	05	13	38	22	41	6	36	7	04
22	8	51	+22.7	54.2	14.8	67	296	95	13.1	15	20	14	59	23	27	6	58	7	20
23	9	40	+18.8	54.5	14.8	79	307	98	14.1	16	35	16	20	—	—	7	15	7	31
24	10	26	+14.0	54.8	14.9	91	351	100	15.1	17	49	17	40	0	11	7	28	7	39
25	11	11	+8.6	55.2	15.0	103	94	99	16.1	19	04	19	00	0	53	7	39	7	45
26	11	56	+2.9	55.6	15.2	115	108	97	17.1	20	18	20	20	1	35	7	49	7	50
27	12	41	−3.1	56.1	15.3	127	111	92	18.1	21	35	21	43	2	17	8	00	7	55
28	13	26	−9.1	56.6	15.4	140	112	86	19.1	22	55	23	09	3	00	8	11	8	01

MERCURY

Day	RA		Dec.	Diam.	Phase	Transit		5° high			
								52°		56°	
	h	m	°	″	%	h	m	h	m	h	m
1	20	22	−21.3	5	97	11	39	8	20	8	50
3	20	36	−20.6	5	97	11	44	8	20	8	48
5	20	50	−19.8	5	98	11	50	8	20	8	46
7	21	04	−18.9	5	99	11	56	8	19	8	44
9	21	17	−18.0	5	99	12	02	15	48	15	25
11	21	31	−16.9	5	100	12	08	16	02	15	41
13	21	45	−15.7	5	100	12	14	16	16	15	56
15	21	59	−14.4	5	100	12	20	16	30	16	13
17	22	13	−13.1	5	100	12	26	16	45	16	29
19	22	27	−11.6	5	99	12	32	17	00	16	46
21	22	41	−10.1	5	98	12	38	17	15	17	03
23	22	54	−8.5	5	97	12	44	17	30	17	20
25	23	08	−6.8	5	95	12	50	17	45	17	36
27	23	21	−5.0	5	92	12	55	18	00	17	53
29	23	34	−3.3	6	88	13	00	18	15	18	09
31	23	47	−1.5	6	83	13	05	18	28	18	24

VENUS

Day	RA		Dec.	Diam.	Phase	Transit		5° high			
								52°		56°	
	h	m	°	″	%	h	m	h	m	h	m
1	20	01	−21.1	10	97	11	16	7	56	8	26
6	20	27	−19.9	10	98	11	23	7	53	8	20
11	20	53	−18.5	10	98	11	29	7	49	8	13
16	21	18	−16.8	10	98	11	34	7	43	8	04
21	21	43	−15.0	10	99	11	39	7	35	7	54
26	22	07	−12.9	10	99	11	44	7	27	7	43
31	22	31	−10.8	10	99	11	48	7	18	7	31

MARS

Day	RA		Dec.	Diam.	Phase	Transit		5° high			
								52°		56°	
	h	m	°	″	%	h	m	h	m	h	m
1	17	42	−23.6	5	94	8	57	5	59	6	36
6	17	58	−23.7	5	94	8	52	5	56	6	33
11	18	13	−23.7	5	94	8	48	5	52	6	30
16	18	29	−23.7	5	93	8	44	5	47	6	25
21	18	44	−23.5	5	93	8	40	5	41	6	18
26	19	00	−23.3	5	92	8	36	5	35	6	11
31	19	15	−23.0	5	92	8	31	5	28	6	03

SUNRISE AND SUNSET

	London		*Bristol*		*Birmingham*		*Manchester*		*Newcastle*		*Glasgow*		*Belfast*	
	0° 05′	*51° 30′*	*2° 35′*	*51° 28′*	*1° 55′*	*52° 28′*	*2° 15′*	*53° 28′*	*1° 37′*	*54° 59′*	*4° 14′*	*55° 52′*	*5° 56′*	*54° 35′*
	h m	*h m*	*h m*	*h m*	*h m*	*h m*	*h m*	*h m*	*h m*	*h m*	*h m*	*h m*	*h m*	*h m*
1	7 39	16 50	7 48	17 00	7 49	16 54	7 54	16 52	7 57	16 44	8 11	16 51	8 13	17 03
2	7 37	16 52	7 47	17 02	7 47	16 56	7 52	16 54	7 55	16 46	8 09	16 53	8 11	17 05
3	7 35	16 54	7 45	17 04	7 46	16 58	7 50	16 56	7 53	16 48	8 07	16 55	8 09	17 07
4	7 34	16 55	7 44	17 06	7 44	17 00	7 49	16 58	7 52	16 50	8 05	16 57	8 07	17 09
5	7 32	16 57	7 42	17 07	7 42	17 02	7 47	17 00	7 50	16 52	8 03	16 59	8 05	17 11
6	7 30	16 59	7 40	17 09	7 41	17 04	7 45	17 02	7 48	16 54	8 01	17 02	8 03	17 13
7	7 29	17 01	7 39	17 11	7 39	17 05	7 43	17 04	7 46	16 56	7 59	17 04	8 02	17 15
8	7 27	17 03	7 37	17 13	7 37	17 07	7 41	17 06	7 44	16 58	7 57	17 06	8 00	17 17
9	7 25	17 05	7 35	17 15	7 35	17 09	7 39	17 08	7 42	17 01	7 55	17 08	7 58	17 19
10	7 23	17 06	7 33	17 17	7 33	17 11	7 38	17 10	7 40	17 03	7 53	17 10	7 56	17 21
11	7 22	17 08	7 32	17 18	7 31	17 13	7 36	17 12	7 37	17 05	7 51	17 13	7 53	17 23
12	7 20	17 10	7 30	17 20	7 30	17 15	7 34	17 14	7 35	17 07	7 48	17 15	7 51	17 25
13	7 18	17 12	7 28	17 22	7 28	17 17	7 32	17 16	7 33	17 09	7 46	17 17	7 49	17 27
14	7 16	17 14	7 26	17 24	7 26	17 19	7 30	17 18	7 31	17 11	7 44	17 19	7 47	17 30
15	7 14	17 16	7 24	17 26	7 24	17 21	7 27	17 20	7 29	17 13	7 42	17 21	7 45	17 32
16	7 12	17 17	7 22	17 27	7 22	17 23	7 25	17 22	7 27	17 15	7 39	17 23	7 43	17 34
17	7 10	17 19	7 20	17 29	7 20	17 24	7 23	17 24	7 24	17 17	7 37	17 26	7 41	17 36
18	7 08	17 21	7 18	17 31	7 18	17 26	7 21	17 26	7 22	17 20	7 35	17 28	7 38	17 38
19	7 06	17 23	7 16	17 33	7 16	17 28	7 19	17 28	7 20	17 22	7 32	17 30	7 36	17 40
20	7 04	17 25	7 14	17 35	7 13	17 30	7 17	17 29	7 18	17 24	7 30	17 32	7 34	17 42
21	7 02	17 26	7 12	17 37	7 11	17 32	7 15	17 31	7 15	17 26	7 28	17 34	7 32	17 44
22	7 00	17 28	7 10	17 38	7 09	17 34	7 12	17 33	7 13	17 28	7 25	17 36	7 29	17 46
23	6 58	17 30	7 08	17 40	7 07	17 36	7 10	17 35	7 11	17 30	7 23	17 39	7 27	17 48
24	6 56	17 32	7 06	17 42	7 05	17 38	7 08	17 37	7 08	17 32	7 20	17 41	7 25	17 50
25	6 54	17 34	7 04	17 44	7 03	17 39	7 06	17 39	7 06	17 34	7 18	17 43	7 22	17 52
26	6 52	17 35	7 02	17 45	7 01	17 41	7 04	17 41	7 04	17 36	7 16	17 45	7 20	17 54
27	6 50	17 37	7 00	17 47	6 58	17 43	7 01	17 43	7 01	17 38	7 13	17 47	7 18	17 56
28	6 48	17 39	6 58	17 49	6 56	17 45	6 59	17 45	6 59	17 40	7 11	17 49	7 15	17 58

JUPITER

Day	*RA*		*Dec.*		*Transit*		*5° high*			
							52°		*56°*	
	h	*m*	°	′	*h*	*m*	*h*	*m*	*h*	*m*
1	13	11.8	−6	04	4	26	23	27	23	36
11	13	11.4	−5	59	3	46	22	47	22	56
21	13	09.8	−5	47	3	05	22	05	22	13
31	13	07.2	−5	28	2	23	21	21	21	29

Diameters – equatorial 41″ polar 38″

SATURN

Day	*RA*		*Dec.*		*Transit*		*5° high*			
							52°		*56°*	
	h	*m*	°	′	*h*	*m*	*h*	*m*	*h*	*m*
1	7	37.0	+21	37	22	48	6	14	6	30
11	7	34.0	+21	45	22	05	5	32	5	49
21	7	31.5	+21	51	21	24	4	51	5	08
31	7	29.7	+21	56	20	43	4	11	4	27

Diameters – equatorial 20″ polar 18″
Rings – major axis 46″ minor axis 18″

URANUS

Day	*RA*		*Dec.*		*Transit*		*10° high*			
							52°		*56°*	
	h	*m*	°	′	*h*	*m*	*h*	*m*	*h*	*m*
1	22	29.9	−10	13	13	43	17	37	17	20
11	22	32.0	−10	01	13	05	17	02	16	44
21	22	34.1	−9	48	12	28	16	26	16	08
31	22	36.3	−9	35	11	51	15	50	15	33

Diameter 4″

NEPTUNE

Day	*RA*		*Dec.*		*Transit*		*10° high*			
							52°		*56°*	
	h	*m*	°	′	*h*	*m*	*h*	*m*	*h*	*m*
1	21	09.8	−16	26	12	23	9	12	9	41
11	21	11.4	−16	20	11	45	8	33	9	02
21	21	12.9	−16	13	11	07	7	55	8	23
31	21	14.3	−16	07	10	29	7	16	7	44

Diameter 2″

MARCH 2005

THIRD MONTH, 31 DAYS. *Mars*, Roman god of battle

1	*Tuesday*	Frédéric Chopin b. 1810. Girolamo Frescobaldi d. 1643	60
2	*Wednesday*	Horace Walpole d. 1797. D. H. Lawrence d. 1930	61
3	*Thursday*	Sir Henry J. Wood b. 1869. Robert Adam d. 1792	62
4	*Friday*	Antonio Vivaldi b. 1678. Nikolai Gogol d. 1852	63
5	*Saturday*	Henry II b. 1133. Sergey Prokofiev d. 1953	64
6	*Sunday*	Savinien Cyrano de Bergerac b. 1619. Elizabeth Barrett Browning b. 1806	65
7	*Monday*	Piet Mondrian b. 1872. Stevie Smith d. 1971	week 10 day 66
8	*Tuesday*	Kenneth Grahame b. 1859. Dame Ninette de Valois d. 2001	67
9	*Wednesday*	David Riccio, secretary to Mary Queen of Scots murdered d. 1566	68
10	*Thursday*	Earl of Wessex b. 1964. Mikhail Bulgakov d. 1940	69
11	*Friday*	Douglas Adams b. 1952. Erle Stanley Gardner d. 1970	70
12	*Saturday*	Vaslav Nijinsky b. 1890. Anne Frank d. 1945	71
13	*Sunday*	Sir Hugh Walpole b. 1884. John Middleton Murry d. 1957	72
14	*Monday*	Johann Strauss b. 1804. Karl Marx d. 1883	week 11 day 73
15	*Tuesday*	H. P. Lovecraft d. 1937. Dame Rebecca West d. 1983	74
16	*Wednesday*	Bernardo Bertolucci b. 1941. Aubrey Beardsley d. 1898	75
17	*Thursday*	Rudolf Nureyev b. 1938. Harold I (Harefoot) d. 1046	76
18	*Friday*	Nikolay Rimsky-Korsakov b. 1844. Wilfred Owen b. 1893	77
19	*Saturday*	Glenn Close b. 1947. Edgar Rice Burroughs d. 1950	78
20	*Sunday*	Henrik Ibsen b. 1828. Henry IV d. 1413	79
21	*Monday*	Johann Sebastian Bach b. 1685. Phyllis McGinley b. 1925	week 12 day 80
22	*Tuesday*	Sir Anthony Van Dyck b. 1599. Thomas Hughes d. 1896	81
23	*Wednesday*	Princess Eugenie of York b. 1990. Stendhal d. 1842	82
24	*Thursday*	William Morris b. 1834. Elizabeth I d. 1603	83
25	*Friday*	Béla Bartók b. 1881. Claude Debussy d. 1918	84
26	*Saturday*	Tennessee Williams b. 1911. Sir Noel Coward d. 1973	85
27	*Sunday*	Sir George Gilbert Scott b. 1878. James I (IV of Scotland) d. 1625	86
28	*Monday*	Maxim Gorky b. 1868. Virginia Woolf d. 1941	week 13 day 87
29	*Tuesday*	Sir William Walton b. 1902. George Seurat d. 1891	88
30	*Wednesday*	Anna Sewell b. 1820. Paul Verlaine b. 1844	89
31	*Thursday*	John Constable d. 1837. Charlotte Brontë d. 1855	90

ASTRONOMICAL PHENOMENA

d	*h*	
6	07	Mars in conjunction with Moon. Mars 4° N.
10	00	Venus in conjunction with Moon. Venus 2° N.
11	18	Mercury in conjunction with Moon. Mercury 3° N.
12	18	Mercury at greatest elongation E.18°
19	18	Saturn in conjunction with Moon. Saturn 5° S.
20	00	Mercury at stationary point
20	13	Sun's longitude 0° ♈
22	03	Saturn at stationary point
26	15	Jupiter in conjunction with Moon. Jupiter 0°.9 N.
27	02	Pluto at stationary point
29	16	Mercury in inferior conjunction
29	20	Venus in conjunction with Mercury. Venus 4° S.
31	03	Venus in superior conjunction

MINIMA OF ALGOL

d	*h*	*d*	*h*	*d*	*h*
2	12.8	14	00.1	25	11.4
5	09.6	16	20.9	28	08.2
8	06.5	19	17.7	31	05.0
11	03.3	22	14.6		

CONSTELLATIONS

The following constellations are near the meridian at

	d	*h*		*d*	*h*
February	1	24	March	16	21
February	15	23	April	1	20
March	1	22	April	15	19

Cepheus (below the Pole), Camelopardus, Lybx, Gemini, Cancer, Leo, Canis Minor, Hydra, Monoceros, Canis Major and Puppis

THE MOON

Phases, Apsides and Node	*d*	*h*	*m*
☾ Last Quarter	3	17	36
● New Moon	10	09	10
☽ First Quarter	17	19	19
○ Full Moon	25	20	58
Perigee (363,215 km)	8	03	32
Apogee (404,883 km)	19	22	50

Mean longitude of ascending node on March 1, 25°

THE SUN

s.d. 16′.1

Day	Right Ascension h m s	Dec. ° ′	Equation of time m s	Rise 52° h m	Rise 56° h m	Transit h m	Set 52° h m	Set 56° h m	Sidereal time h m s	Transit of first point of Aries h m s
1	22 48 00	−7 38	−12 25	6 46	6 51	12 12	17 40	17 34	10 35 35	13 22 13
2	22 51 45	−7 15	−12 13	6 44	6 49	12 12	17 42	17 36	10 39 32	13 18 17
3	22 55 29	−6 52	−12 01	6 41	6 46	12 12	17 43	17 38	10 43 28	13 14 21
4	22 59 13	−6 29	−11 48	6 39	6 44	12 12	17 45	17 41	10 47 25	13 10 25
5	23 02 56	−6 06	−11 35	6 37	6 41	12 11	17 47	17 43	10 51 21	13 06 29
6	23 06 39	−5 43	−11 21	6 35	6 39	12 11	17 49	17 45	10 55 18	13 02 33
7	23 10 22	−5 19	−11 07	6 32	6 36	12 11	17 51	17 47	10 59 15	12 58 38
8	23 14 04	−4 56	−10 53	6 30	6 34	12 11	17 52	17 49	11 03 11	12 54 42
9	23 17 45	−4 33	−10 38	6 28	6 31	12 11	17 54	17 51	11 07 08	12 50 46
10	23 21 27	−4 09	−10 23	6 26	6 28	12 10	17 56	17 53	11 11 04	12 46 50
11	23 25 08	−3 46	−10 07	6 23	6 26	12 10	17 58	17 55	11 15 01	12 42 54
12	23 28 49	−3 22	−9 51	6 21	6 23	12 10	17 59	17 57	11 18 57	12 38 58
13	23 32 29	−2 58	−9 35	6 19	6 21	12 09	18 01	17 59	11 22 54	12 35 02
14	23 36 09	−2 35	−9 19	6 17	6 18	12 09	18 03	18 02	11 26 50	12 31 06
15	23 39 49	−2 11	−9 02	6 14	6 15	12 09	18 05	18 04	11 30 47	12 27 10
16	23 43 29	−1 47	−8 45	6 12	6 13	12 09	18 06	18 06	11 34 44	12 23 14
17	23 47 08	−1 24	−8 28	6 10	6 10	12 08	18 08	18 08	11 38 40	12 19 18
18	23 50 48	−1 00	−8 11	6 07	6 07	12 08	18 10	18 10	11 42 37	12 15 23
19	23 54 27	−0 36	−7 54	6 05	6 05	12 08	18 12	18 12	11 46 33	12 11 27
20	23 58 06	−0 12	−7 36	6 03	6 02	12 07	18 13	18 14	11 50 30	12 07 31
21	0 01 44	+0 11	−7 18	6 00	6 00	12 07	18 15	18 16	11 54 26	12 03 35
22	0 05 23	+0 35	−7 00	5 58	5 57	12 07	18 17	18 18	11 58 23	11 59 39
23	0 09 01	+0 59	−6 42	5 56	5 54	12 07	18 18	18 20	12 02 19	11 55 43
24	0 12 40	+1 22	−6 24	5 53	5 52	12 06	18 20	18 22	12 06 16	11 51 47
25	0 16 18	+1 46	−6 06	5 51	5 49	12 06	18 22	18 24	12 10 12	11 47 51
26	0 19 56	+2 09	−5 47	5 49	5 46	12 06	18 24	18 26	12 14 09	11 43 55
27	0 23 35	+2 33	−5 29	5 46	5 44	12 05	18 25	18 28	12 18 06	11 39 59
28	0 27 13	+2 56	−5 11	5 44	5 41	12 05	18 27	18 30	12 22 02	11 36 04
29	0 30 51	+3 20	−4 53	5 42	5 38	12 05	18 29	18 32	12 25 59	11 32 08
30	0 34 30	+3 43	−4 34	5 39	5 36	12 04	18 30	18 34	12 29 55	11 28 12
31	0 38 08	+4 06	−4 16	5 37	5 33	12 04	18 32	18 36	12 33 52	11 24 16

DURATION OF TWILIGHT (in minutes)

Latitude	52°	56°	52°	56°	52°	56°	52°	56°
	1 March		*11 March*		*21 March*		*31 March*	
Civil	34	37	34	37	34	37	34	38
Nautical	73	80	73	80	74	81	75	84
Astronomical	112	124	113	125	115	128	120	135

THE NIGHT SKY

Mercury is at greatest eastern elongation (18 degrees) on the 12th and thus is visible in the evenings low in the western sky around the end of evening civil twilight during the first half of the month. It is best seen (because it is brighter) near the beginning of the month: by the 18th its magnitude has faded to +1.1. On the evening of the 11th, the New Moon, barely 1.5 days old, passes 4 degrees south of the planet. This evening apparition is the most suitable one of the year for observers in northern temperate latitudes, and, in fact, the only evening apparition for observers in the latitudes of the British Isles.

Venus passes through superior conjunction on the last day of the month and therefore remains too close to the Sun for observation.

Mars continues to be visible as a very difficult morning object, low above the south-eastern horizon for a short while before twilight renders observation impossible. Its magnitude is +1.1.

Jupiter, magnitude −2.4, continues to be visible as a brilliant object in the night sky, and by the end of the month may be seen rising above the east-south-eastern horizon soon after sunset. The Moon, near Full, will be seen close to the planet between the 25th and 27th.

Saturn continues to be visible as an evening object, magnitude 0.0. It reaches its second stationary point on the 22nd, and then resumes its direct motion, in the constellation of Gemini. On the early evening of the 19th the waxing gibbous Moon passes 4 degrees north of the planet.

Zodiacal Light. The evening cone may be observed, stretching up from the western horizon, along the ecliptic, after the end of twilight, from the beginning of the month until the 11th, and again after the 27th.

THE MOON

Day	RA		Dec.	Hor. par.	Semi-diam.	Sun's Co-long.	PA of Br. Limb	Ph.	Age	Rise 52°		Rise 56°		Transit		Set 52°		Set 56°	
	h	m	°	′	′	°	°	%	d	h	m	h	m	h	m	h	m	h	m
1	14	15	−14.7	57.1	15.6	152	110	78	20.1	—	—	—	—	3	46	8	24	8	09
2	15	06	−19.8	57.7	15.7	164	107	69	21.1	0	18	0	39	4	36	8	43	8	20
3	16	02	−24.0	58.3	15.9	176	102	58	22.1	1	44	2	13	5	31	9	09	8	39
4	17	01	−26.9	58.9	16.0	188	96	47	23.1	3	08	3	44	6	30	9	48	9	11
5	18	05	−28.2	59.4	16.2	200	88	36	24.1	4	20	5	00	7	33	10	46	10	06
6	19	10	−27.6	59.9	16.3	213	80	25	25.1	5	14	5	50	8	36	12	04	11	29
7	20	14	−25.1	60.2	16.4	225	72	16	26.1	5	51	6	19	9	38	13	35	13	09
8	21	15	−21.0	60.4	16.4	237	65	8	27.1	6	17	6	36	10	36	15	09	14	52
9	22	13	−15.5	60.3	16.4	249	57	3	28.1	6	35	6	47	11	31	16	42	16	31
10	23	07	−9.2	60.0	16.3	261	35	0	29.1	6	49	6	55	12	21	18	10	18	07
11	23	59	−2.4	59.4	16.2	274	261	1	0.6	7	01	7	01	13	09	19	36	19	39
12	0	49	+ 4.2	58.7	16.0	286	249	3	1.6	7	12	7	07	13	56	21	00	21	08
13	1	38	+10.6	57.9	15.8	298	248	9	2.6	7	25	7	14	14	43	22	22	22	37
14	2	28	+16.2	57.0	15.5	310	250	16	3.6	7	39	7	23	15	31	23	44	—	—
15	3	19	+21.0	56.2	15.3	322	253	24	4.6	7	58	7	35	16	21	—	—	0	06
16	4	11	+24.7	55.5	15.1	335	258	33	5.6	8	22	7	52	17	11	1	02	1	32
17	5	04	+27.1	54.9	15.0	347	264	42	6.6	8	56	8	20	18	03	2	14	2	50
18	5	58	+28.2	54.5	14.8	359	270	52	7.6	9	43	9	04	18	55	3	16	3	55
19	6	52	+28.0	54.2	14.8	11	276	61	8.6	10	41	10	05	19	46	4	04	4	41
20	7	45	+26.6	54.2	14.8	23	283	70	9.6	11	49	11	19	20	35	4	39	5	10
21	8	36	+23.9	54.2	14.8	36	288	79	10.6	13	03	12	39	21	22	5	04	5	28
22	9	25	+20.2	54.5	14.8	48	293	86	11.6	14	18	14	01	22	07	5	22	5	40
23	10	12	+15.6	54.8	14.9	60	297	92	12.6	15	33	15	22	22	50	5	36	5	49
24	10	58	+10.4	55.3	15.1	72	301	96	13.6	16	48	16	43	23	32	5	48	5	55
25	11	43	+ 4.6	55.8	15.2	84	307	99	14.6	18	04	18	04	—	—	5	58	6	00
26	12	28	−1.4	56.3	15.3	96	69	100	15.6	19	21	19	27	0	14	6	08	6	05
27	13	14	−7.5	56.8	15.5	109	111	99	16.6	20	41	20	53	0	57	6	19	6	11
28	14	02	−13.4	57.3	15.6	121	112	95	17.6	22	05	22	24	1	43	6	32	6	18
29	14	53	−18.8	57.8	15.7	133	110	89	18.6	23	32	23	58	2	33	6	48	6	28
30	15	48	−23.3	58.2	15.9	145	105	82	19.6	—	—	—	—	3	26	7	11	6	44
31	16	48	−26.5	58.6	16.0	157	99	72	20.6	0	57	1	32	4	24	7	46	7	11

MERCURY

Day	RA		Dec.	Diam.	Phase	Transit		5° high 52°		5° high 56°	
	h	m	°	″	%	h	m	h	m	h	m
1	23	34	−3.3	6	88	13	00	18	15	18	09
3	23	47	−1.5	6	83	13	05	18	28	18	24
5	23	59	+0.2	6	77	13	09	18	41	18	39
7	0	10	+1.9	6	69	13	12	18	53	18	51
9	0	20	+3.5	7	61	13	14	19	02	19	02
11	0	29	+4.9	7	53	13	14	19	09	19	10
13	0	36	+6.2	7	44	13	13	19	14	19	16
15	0	42	+7.2	8	35	13	10	19	15	19	18
17	0	45	+8.0	8	27	13	05	19	14	19	17
19	0	47	+8.4	9	20	12	58	19	08	19	12
21	0	46	+8.6	9	14	12	49	19	00	19	04
23	0	44	+8.5	10	8	12	39	18	48	18	52
25	0	41	+8.1	10	4	12	27	18	34	18	37
27	0	36	+7.5	11	2	12	15	18	17	18	20
29	0	31	+6.6	11	1	12	01	17	59	18	01
31	0	25	+5.7	11	1	11	48	5	54	5	52

VENUS

Day	RA		Dec.	Diam.	Phase	Transit		5° high 52°		5° high 56°	
	h	m	°	″	%	h	m	h	m	h	m
1	22	22	−11.7	10	99	11	46	7	22	7	36
6	22	45	−9.4	10	99	11	50	7	13	7	24
11	23	09	−7.1	10	100	11	54	7	03	7	13
16	23	32	−4.6	10	100	11	57	6	53	7	00
21	23	55	−2.1	10	100	12	00	6	43	6	48
26	0	17	+0.4	10	100	12	03	6	33	6	36
31	0	40	+2.9	10	100	12	07	6	23	6	24

MARS

Day	RA		Dec.	Diam.	Phase	Transit		5° high 52°		5° high 56°	
	h	m	°	″	%	h	m	h	m	h	m
1	19	09	−23.1	5	92	8	33	5	31	6	06
6	19	24	−22.7	5	92	8	29	5	23	5	57
11	19	40	−22.2	5	91	8	24	5	14	5	47
16	19	55	−21.7	5	91	8	20	5	05	5	36
21	20	10	−21.0	6	90	8	16	4	56	5	25
26	20	25	−20.3	6	90	8	11	4	45	5	13
31	20	40	−19.5	6	90	8	06	4	34	5	00

SUNRISE AND SUNSET

	London		*Bristol*		*Birmingham*		*Manchester*		*Newcastle*		*Glasgow*		*Belfast*	
	0° 05′	*51° 30′*	*2° 35′*	*51° 28′*	*1° 55′*	*52° 28′*	*2° 15′*	*53° 28′*	*1° 37′*	*54° 59′*	*4° 14′*	*55° 52′*	*5° 56′*	*54° 35′*
	h m	*h m*	*h m*	*h m*	*h m*	*h m*	*h m*	*h m*	*h m*	*h m*	*h m*	*h m*	*h m*	*h m*
1	6 45	17 41	6 55	17 51	6 54	17 47	6 57	17 47	6 56	17 42	7 08	17 51	7 13	18 00
2	6 43	17 42	6 53	17 53	6 52	17 49	6 54	17 49	6 54	17 44	7 06	17 54	7 11	18 02
3	6 41	17 44	6 51	17 54	6 50	17 51	6 52	17 51	6 51	17 46	7 03	17 56	7 08	18 04
4	6 39	17 46	6 49	17 56	6 47	17 52	6 50	17 53	6 49	17 48	7 01	17 58	7 06	18 06
5	6 37	17 48	6 47	17 58	6 45	17 54	6 47	17 54	6 47	17 50	6 58	18 00	7 03	18 08
6	6 35	17 49	6 45	18 00	6 43	17 56	6 45	17 56	6 44	17 52	6 55	18 02	7 01	18 10
7	6 32	17 51	6 42	18 01	6 40	17 58	6 43	17 58	6 42	17 54	6 53	18 04	6 58	18 12
8	6 30	17 53	6 40	18 03	6 38	18 00	6 40	18 00	6 39	17 56	6 50	18 06	6 56	18 14
9	6 28	17 55	6 38	18 05	6 36	18 01	6 38	18 02	6 37	17 58	6 48	18 08	6 54	18 16
10	6 26	17 56	6 36	18 06	6 34	18 03	6 36	18 04	6 34	18 00	6 45	18 10	6 51	18 18
11	6 23	17 58	6 33	18 08	6 31	18 05	6 33	18 06	6 32	18 02	6 43	18 12	6 49	18 20
12	6 21	18 00	6 31	18 10	6 29	18 07	6 31	18 08	6 29	18 04	6 40	18 14	6 46	18 22
13	6 19	18 02	6 29	18 12	6 27	18 09	6 28	18 10	6 27	18 06	6 37	18 16	6 44	18 24
14	6 17	18 03	6 27	18 13	6 24	18 10	6 26	18 11	6 24	18 08	6 35	18 19	6 41	18 26
15	6 14	18 05	6 24	18 15	6 22	18 12	6 24	18 13	6 21	18 10	6 32	18 21	6 39	18 28
16	6 12	18 07	6 22	18 17	6 20	18 14	6 21	18 15	6 19	18 12	6 30	18 23	6 36	18 30
17	6 10	18 08	6 20	18 18	6 17	18 16	6 19	18 17	6 16	18 14	6 27	18 25	6 34	18 32
18	6 08	18 10	6 18	18 20	6 15	18 17	6 16	18 19	6 14	18 16	6 24	18 27	6 31	18 34
19	6 05	18 12	6 15	18 22	6 13	18 19	6 14	18 21	6 11	18 18	6 22	18 29	6 29	18 35
20	6 03	18 14	6 13	18 24	6 10	18 21	6 11	18 22	6 09	18 20	6 19	18 31	6 26	18 37
21	6 01	18 15	6 11	18 25	6 08	18 23	6 09	18 24	6 06	18 22	6 16	18 33	6 24	18 39
22	5 58	18 17	6 08	18 27	6 06	18 25	6 07	18 26	6 04	18 24	6 14	18 35	6 21	18 41
23	5 56	18 19	6 06	18 29	6 03	18 26	6 04	18 28	6 01	18 26	6 11	18 37	6 19	18 43
24	5 54	18 20	6 04	18 30	6 01	18 28	6 02	18 30	5 59	18 28	6 09	18 39	6 16	18 45
25	5 52	18 22	6 02	18 32	5 58	18 30	5 59	18 32	5 56	18 30	6 06	18 41	6 13	18 47
26	5 49	18 24	5 59	18 34	5 56	18 32	5 57	18 33	5 53	18 32	6 03	18 43	6 11	18 49
27	5 47	18 25	5 57	18 35	5 54	18 33	5 54	18 35	5 51	18 34	6 01	18 45	6 08	18 51
28	5 45	18 27	5 55	18 37	5 51	18 35	5 52	18 37	5 48	18 36	5 58	18 47	6 06	18 53
29	5 43	18 29	5 53	18 39	5 49	18 37	5 50	18 39	5 46	18 38	5 55	18 49	6 03	18 55
30	5 40	18 30	5 50	18 40	5 47	18 39	5 47	18 41	5 43	18 40	5 53	18 51	6 01	18 57
31	5 38	18 32	5 48	18 42	5 44	18 40	5 45	18 43	5 41	18 42	5 50	18 53	5 58	18 59

JUPITER

Day	*RA*		*Dec.*		*Transit*		*5° high*			
							52°		*56°*	
	h	*m*	°	′	*h*	*m*	*h*	*m*	*h*	*m*
1	13	07.8	–5	33	2	32	21	30	21	38
11	13	04.4	–5	10	1	49	20	45	20	53
21	13	00.2	–4	43	1	06	19	59	20	07
31	12	55.6	–4	13	0	22	19	13	19	20

Diameters – equatorial 44″ polar 41″

SATURN

Day	*RA*		*Dec.*		*Transit*		*5° high*			
							52°		*56°*	
	h	*m*	°	′	*h*	*m*	*h*	*m*	*h*	*m*
1	7	30.0	+21	55	20	51	4	19	4	35
11	7	28.8	+21	59	20	10	3	39	3	55
21	7	28.3	+22	01	19	31	2	59	3	16
31	7	28.6	+22	01	18	52	2	20	2	37

Diameters – equatorial 19″ polar 18″

Rings – major axis 44″ minor axis 18″

URANUS

Day	*RA*		*Dec.*		*Transit*		*10° high*			
							52°		*56°*	
	h	*m*	°	′	*h*	*m*	*h*	*m*	*h*	*m*
1	22	35.9	–9	38	11	58	8	00	8	17
11	22	38.0	–9	25	11	21	7	21	7	38
21	22	40.1	–9	13	10	44	6	43	6	59
31	22	42.1	–9	01	10	07	6	04	6	21

Diameter 4″

NEPTUNE

Day	*RA*		*Dec.*		*Transit*		*10° high*			
							52°		*56°*	
	h	*m*	°	′	*h*	*m*	*h*	*m*	*h*	*m*
1	21	14.0	–16	08	10	37	7	24	7	52
11	21	15.4	–16	02	9	59	6	45	7	13
21	21	16.6	–15	57	9	21	6	06	6	34
31	21	17.7	–15	52	8	42	5	27	5	55

Diameter 2″

APRIL 2005

FOURTH MONTH, 30 DAYS. *Aperire*, to open; Earth opens to receive seed.

1	*Friday*	Eleanor of Aquitaine d. 1204. Max Ernst d. 1976	91
2	*Saturday*	Hans Christian Andersen b. 1805. C. S. Forester d. 1966	92
3	*Sunday*	Johannes Brahms d. 1897. Graham Greene d. 1991	93
4	*Monday*	Maya Angelou b. 1928. Oliver Goldsmith d. 1774	week 14 day 94
5	*Tuesday*	Jean-Baptiste Rousseau b. 1671. Allen Ginsberg, poet d. 1997	95
6	*Wednesday*	Andre Previn b. 1929. Igor Stravinsky d. 1971	96
7	*Thursday*	William Wordsworth b. 1770. El Greco d. 1614	97
8	*Friday*	Vaslav Nijinsky d. 1950. Pablo Picasso d. 1973	98
9	*Saturday*	François-Rabelais d. 1553. Dante Gabriel Rosetti d. 1882	99
10	*Sunday*	Joseph Pulitzer b. 1847. Evelyn Waugh d. 1966	100
11	*Monday*	John O'Hara d. 1970. Jaques Prévert d. 1977	week 15 day 101
12	*Tuesday*	Alan Ayckbourn b. 1939. William Kent d. 1748	102
13	*Wednesday*	Samuel Beckett b. 1906. Sir William Orchardson d. 1910	103
14	*Thursday*	George Frideric Handel d. 1759. Simone de Beauvoir d. 1986	104
15	*Friday*	Leonardo da Vinci b. 1452. Jean Paul Sartre d. 1980	105
16	*Saturday*	Sir Kingsley Amis b. 1922. Francisco de Goya d. 1828	106
17	*Sunday*	Nick Hornby b. 1957. Marquise de Sévigné d. 1696	107
18	*Monday*	Leopold Stokowski b. 1882. Dame Elizabeth Frink d. 1993	week 16 day 108
19	*Tuesday*	Richard Hughes b. 1900. Dame Daphne du Maurier d. 1989	109
20	*Wednesday*	Canaletto d. 1768. Bram Stoker d. 1912	110
21	*Thursday*	Elizabeth II b. 1926. Mark Twain d. 1910	111
22	*Friday*	Henry Fielding b. 1707. Vladimir Nabokov b. 1899	112
23	*Saturday*	J. M. W. Turner b. 1775. William Shakespeare d. 1616	113
24	*Sunday*	Anthony Trollope b. 1815. Daniel Defoe d. 1731	114
25	*Monday*	Walter de la Mare b. 1873. Anna Sewell d. 1878	week 17 day 115
26	*Tuesday*	Edward II b. 1284. Eugène Delacroix b. 1798	116
27	*Wednesday*	Cecil Day Lewis b. 1904. Mary Wollstonecraft Godwin b. 1759	117
28	*Thursday*	Edward IV b. 1442. Francis Bacon d. 1992	118
29	*Friday*	Jean-George Naverre b. 1727. Sir Thomas Beecham b. 1879	119
30	*Saturday*	Jaroslav Hašek b. 1883. Édouard Manet d. 1883	120

ASTRONOMICAL PHENOMENA

d	*h*	
3	16	Jupiter at opposition
4	00	Mars in conjunction with Moon. Mars 4° N.
7	16	Mercury in conjunction with Moon. Mercury 3° N.
8	21	Annular-Total eclipse of Sun
9	01	Venus in conjunction with Moon. Venus 1° S.
12	08	Mercury at stationary point
16	03	Saturn in conjunction with Moon. Saturn 5° S.
20	00	Sun's longitude 30° ♉
22	17	Jupiter in conjunction with Moon. Jupiter 0°.5 N.
26	16	Mercury at greatest elongation W.27°

MINIMA OF ALGOL

d	*h*	*d*	*h*	*d*	*h*
3	01.8	14	13.1	26	00.4
5	22.7	17	09.9	28	21.2
8	19.5	20	06.8		
11	16.3	23	03.6		

CONSTELLATIONS

The following constellations are near the meridian at

	d	*h*		*d*	*h*
March	1	24	April	15	21
March	16	23	May	1	20
April	1	22	May	16	19

Cepheus (below the Pole), Cassiopeia (below the Pole), Ursa Major, Leo Minor, Leo, Sextans, Hydra and Crater

THE MOON

Phases, Apsides and Node	*d*	*h*	*m*
☾ Last Quarter	2	00	50
● New Moon	8	20	32
☽ First Quarter	16	14	37
○ Full Moon	24	10	06
Perigee (368,462 km)	4	11	02
Apogee (404,344 km)	16	18	40
Perigee (368,995 km)	29	10	20

Mean longitude of ascending node on April 1, 24°

THE SUN

s.d. 16′.0

Day	Right Ascension			Dec. +		Equation of time		Rise 52°		Rise 56°		Transit		Set 52°		Set 56°		Sidereal time			Transit of First point of Aries		
	h	m	s	°	′	m	s	h	m	h	m	h	m	h	m	h	m	h	m	s	h	m	s
1	0	41	47	4	30	–3	58	5	35	5	31	12	04	18	34	18	38	12	37	48	11	20	20
2	0	45	26	4	53	–3	41	5	33	5	28	12	04	18	36	18	40	12	41	45	11	16	24
3	0	49	04	5	16	–3	23	5	30	5	25	12	03	18	37	18	42	12	45	41	11	12	28
4	0	52	43	5	39	–3	05	5	28	5	23	12	03	18	39	18	44	12	49	38	11	08	32
5	0	56	23	6	02	–2	48	5	26	5	20	12	03	18	41	18	46	12	53	35	11	04	36
6	1	00	02	6	24	–2	31	5	23	5	18	12	02	18	42	18	49	12	57	31	11	00	40
7	1	03	42	6	47	–2	14	5	21	5	15	12	02	18	44	18	51	13	01	28	10	56	44
8	1	07	21	7	10	–1	57	5	19	5	12	12	02	18	46	18	53	13	05	24	10	52	49
9	1	11	02	7	32	–1	41	5	17	5	10	12	02	18	48	18	55	13	09	21	10	48	53
10	1	14	42	7	54	–1	24	5	14	5	07	12	01	18	49	18	57	13	13	17	10	44	57
11	1	18	22	8	16	–1	09	5	12	5	05	12	01	18	51	18	59	13	17	14	10	41	01
12	1	22	03	8	38	–0	53	5	10	5	02	12	01	18	53	19	01	13	21	10	10	37	05
13	1	25	44	9	00	–0	37	5	08	5	00	12	00	18	54	19	03	13	25	07	10	33	09
14	1	29	26	9	22	–0	22	5	06	4	57	12	00	18	56	19	05	13	29	04	10	29	13
15	1	33	08	9	44	–0	08	5	03	4	54	12	00	18	58	19	07	13	33	00	10	25	17
16	1	36	50	10	05	+0	07	5	01	4	52	12	00	19	00	19	09	13	36	57	10	21	21
17	1	40	32	10	26	+0	21	4	59	4	49	12	00	19	01	19	11	13	40	53	10	17	25
18	1	44	15	10	47	+0	35	4	57	4	47	11	59	19	03	19	13	13	44	50	10	13	29
19	1	47	58	11	08	+0	48	4	55	4	44	11	59	19	05	19	15	13	48	46	10	09	34
20	1	51	42	11	29	+1	01	4	53	4	42	11	59	19	06	19	17	13	52	43	10	05	38
21	1	55	26	11	49	+1	13	4	50	4	40	11	59	19	08	19	19	13	56	39	10	01	42
22	1	59	10	12	09	+1	26	4	48	4	37	11	58	19	10	19	21	14	00	36	9	57	46
23	2	02	55	12	30	+1	37	4	46	4	35	11	58	19	11	19	23	14	04	33	9	53	50
24	2	06	41	12	49	+1	48	4	44	4	32	11	58	19	13	19	25	14	08	29	9	49	54
25	2	10	26	13	09	+1	59	4	42	4	30	11	58	19	15	19	27	14	12	26	9	45	58
26	2	14	13	13	29	+2	09	4	40	4	28	11	58	19	17	19	29	14	16	22	9	42	02
27	2	18	00	13	48	+2	19	4	38	4	25	11	58	19	18	19	31	14	20	19	9	38	06
28	2	21	47	14	07	+2	28	4	36	4	23	11	57	19	20	19	33	14	24	15	9	34	10
29	2	25	35	14	26	+2	37	4	34	4	21	11	57	19	22	19	35	14	28	12	9	30	14
30	2	29	23	14	44	+2	45	4	32	4	18	11	57	19	23	19	37	14	32	08	9	26	19

DURATION OF TWILIGHT (in minutes)

Latitude	52°	56°	52°	56°	52°	56°	52°	56°
	1 April		*11 April*		*21 April*		*31 April*	
Civil	34	38	35	39	37	42	39	44
Nautical	76	84	79	89	83	96	89	106
Astronomical	120	136	127	147	137	165	152	204

THE NIGHT SKY

Mercury is too close to the Sun for observation throughout the month, despite the facts that it (a) reaches greatest western elongation on the 26th, and (b) reaches aphelion only 5 days earlier.

Venus is not suitably placed for observation at first, but becomes visible during the last few days of the month as a brilliant object in the evening sky, magnitude –3.9. It may be seen low above the western horizon for a very short while just after sunset.

Mars is visible as a difficult morning object, low in the south-eastern sky for a short while before sunrise. Its magnitude brightens slowly during the month from +0.9 to +0.6. The slight reddish tinge in its colour is an aid to its identification.

Jupiter, magnitude –2.5, reaches opposition on the 3rd, and is visible throughout the hours of darkness. Jupiter is retrograding slowly in the constellation of Virgo. The nearly Full Moon is near the planet on the 21st to the 23rd. The four Galilean satellites are readily observable with a small telescope or even a good pair of binoculars provided that they are held rigidly. Time of eclipses and shadow transits of these satellites are given on page 1272.

Saturn, magnitude +0.2, continues to be visible as an evening object in the constellation of Gemini. The Moon, at First Quarter, is in the vicinity of the planet on the evenings of the 15th and 16th. The rings of Saturn present a beautiful spectacle to the observer with a small telescope. The rings were at their maximum opening in 2002. They will next appear edge-on in 2009. The diameter of the minor axis is now the same as the polar diameter of the planet itself (17 arcseconds).

THE MOON

Day	RA		Dec.	Hor. par.	Semi-diam.	Sun's Co-long.	PA of Br. Limb	Ph.	Age	Rise				Transit		Set			
										52°		56°				52°		56°	
	h	m	°	′	′	°	°	%	d	h	m	h	m	h	m	h	m	h	m
1	17	50	−28.2	58.9	16.1	169	92	62	21.6	2	13	2	53	5	26	8	37	7	57
2	18	54	−28.1	59.2	16.1	182	85	51	22.6	3	12	3	50	6	28	9	48	9	11
3	19	57	−26.1	59.4	16.2	194	78	39	23.6	3	53	4	24	7	29	11	13	10	44
4	20	57	−22.5	59.5	16.2	206	71	28	24.6	4	21	4	44	8	27	12	44	12	23
5	21	55	−17.5	59.5	16.2	218	66	18	25.6	4	40	4	56	9	21	14	15	14	02
6	22	48	−11.5	59.3	16.2	230	63	10	26.6	4	55	5	04	10	11	15	43	15	36
7	23	39	−5.1	59.1	16.1	243	61	4	27.6	5	07	5	10	10	59	17	08	17	08
8	0	29	+1.6	58.6	16.0	255	60	1	28.6	5	19	5	16	11	46	18	32	18	37
9	1	18	+8.1	58.1	15.8	267	253	0	0.1	5	31	5	23	12	32	19	55	20	07
10	2	08	+14.1	57.4	15.6	279	246	2	1.1	5	44	5	30	13	20	21	18	21	37
11	2	58	+19.3	56.7	15.5	291	249	5	2.1	6	00	5	40	14	10	22	39	23	05
12	3	51	+23.4	56.0	15.3	304	254	11	3.1	6	22	5	55	15	01	23	56	—	—
13	4	45	+26.4	55.4	15.1	316	259	18	4.1	6	52	6	18	15	53	—	—	0	30
14	5	39	+28.1	54.9	15.0	328	265	26	5.1	7	33	6	55	16	46	1	04	1	42
15	6	34	+28.3	54.5	14.9	340	272	35	6.1	8	27	7	49	17	38	1	58	2	37
16	7	28	+27.2	54.3	14.8	353	278	44	7.1	9	32	8	59	18	28	2	38	3	12
17	8	19	+24.9	54.2	14.8	5	284	54	8.1	10	44	10	17	19	15	3	07	3	35
18	9	09	+21.6	54.4	14.8	17	288	63	9.1	11	59	11	39	20	00	3	27	3	49
19	9	56	+17.3	54.6	14.9	29	292	72	10.1	13	13	13	00	20	44	3	43	3	58
20	10	42	+12.3	55.1	15.0	41	295	80	11.1	14	28	14	20	21	26	3	55	4	05
21	11	27	+6.7	55.6	15.2	54	296	88	12.1	15	43	15	41	22	08	4	06	4	10
22	12	12	+0.7	56.3	15.3	66	297	94	13.1	17	00	17	03	22	51	4	16	4	16
23	12	58	−5.4	56.9	15.5	78	295	98	14.1	18	20	18	29	23	36	4	26	4	21
24	13	46	−11.5	57.6	15.7	90	285	100	15.1	19	44	20	00	—	—	4	38	4	27
25	14	37	−17.2	58.2	15.9	102	121	100	16.1	21	12	21	36	0	25	4	54	4	36
26	15	32	−22.1	58.7	16.0	114	112	97	17.1	22	41	23	13	1	19	5	15	4	50
27	16	31	−25.8	59.1	16.1	127	105	92	18.1	—	—	—	—	2	17	5	45	5	12
28	17	34	−27.9	59.3	16.2	139	97	84	19.1	0	03	0	42	3	18	6	32	5	52
29	18	39	−28.2	59.4	16.2	151	89	75	20.1	1	09	1	48	4	22	7	37	6	59
30	19	43	−26.7	59.4	16.2	163	82	65	21.1	1	55	2	28	5	24	9	00	8	28

MERCURY

Day	RA		Dec.	Diam.	Phase	Transit		5° high			
								52°		56°	
	h	m	°	″	%	h	m	h	m	h	m
1	0	22	+5.1	11	1	11	41	5	50	5	49
3	0	17	+4.1	11	3	11	28	5	42	5	42
5	0	13	+3.0	11	5	11	16	5	35	5	36
7	0	09	+2.1	11	9	11	06	5	29	5	31
9	0	07	+1.3	11	12	10	56	5	23	5	26
11	0	07	+0.7	11	16	10	48	5	18	5	21
13	0	07	+0.2	10	20	10	41	5	13	5	16
15	0	09	−0.1	10	24	10	35	5	09	5	12
17	0	12	−0.2	10	28	10	30	5	04	5	08
19	0	16	−0.2	9	31	10	26	5	00	5	04
21	0	21	0.0	9	35	10	24	4	56	5	00
23	0	27	+0.3	9	38	10	22	4	52	4	55
25	0	33	+0.8	8	42	10	20	4	49	4	51
27	0	40	+1.4	8	45	10	20	4	45	4	47
29	0	48	+2.1	8	48	10	20	4	41	4	43
31	0	57	+2.9	7	51	10	21	4	38	4	39

VENUS

Day	RA		Dec.	Diam.	Phase	Transit		5° high			
								52°		56°	
	h	m	°	″	%	h	m	h	m	h	m
1	0	45	+3.4	10	100	12	07	17	54	17	54
6	1	07	+5.9	10	100	12	10	18	10	18	12
11	1	30	+8.3	10	100	12	14	18	26	18	29
16	1	54	+10.7	10	100	12	17	18	41	18	47
21	2	17	+12.9	10	100	12	21	18	57	19	05
26	2	41	+15.0	10	99	12	25	19	13	19	22
31	3	05	+17.0	10	99	12	30	19	28	19	40

MARS

Day	RA		Dec.	Diam.	Phase	Transit		5° high			
								52°		56°	
	h	m	°	″	%	h	m	h	m	h	m
1	20	43	−19.3	6	90	8	05	4	32	4	58
6	20	58	−18.4	6	89	8	00	4	21	4	45
11	21	13	−17.4	6	89	7	55	4	09	4	31
16	21	28	−16.4	6	88	7	50	3	57	4	17
21	21	42	−15.3	6	88	7	45	3	44	4	03
26	21	56	−14.2	7	88	7	40	3	32	3	49
31	22	10	−13.0	7	87	7	34	3	19	3	35

SUNRISE AND SUNSET

	London				*Bristol*				*Birmingham*				*Manchester*				*Newcastle*				*Glasgow*				*Belfast*			
	0°05′		*51°30′*		*2°35′*		*51°28′*		*1°55′*		*52°28′*		*2°15′*		*53°28′*		*1°37′*		*54°59′*		*4°14′*		*55°52′*		*5°56′*		*54°35′*	
	h	*m*	*h*	*m*	*h*	*m*	*h*	*m*	*h*	*m*	*h*	*m*	*h*	*m*	*h*	*m*	*h*	*m*	*h*	*m*	*h*	*m*	*h*	*m*	*h*	*m*	*h*	*m*
1	5	36	18	34	5	46	18	44	5	42	18	42	5	42	18	44	5	38	18	44	5	48	18	55	5	56	19	00
2	5	33	18	35	5	43	18	45	5	40	18	44	5	40	18	46	5	36	18	46	5	45	18	57	5	53	19	02
3	5	31	18	37	5	41	18	47	5	37	18	45	5	38	18	48	5	33	18	47	5	42	18	59	5	51	19	04
4	5	29	18	39	5	39	18	49	5	35	18	47	5	35	18	50	5	31	18	49	5	40	19	01	5	48	19	06
5	5	27	18	40	5	37	18	50	5	33	18	49	5	33	18	52	5	28	18	51	5	37	19	03	5	46	19	08
6	5	24	18	42	5	34	18	52	5	30	18	51	5	30	18	54	5	26	18	53	5	35	19	05	5	43	19	10
7	5	22	18	44	5	32	18	54	5	28	18	52	5	28	18	55	5	23	18	55	5	32	19	07	5	41	19	12
8	5	20	18	45	5	30	18	55	5	26	18	54	5	26	18	57	5	21	18	57	5	29	19	09	5	39	19	14
9	5	18	18	47	5	28	18	57	5	24	18	56	5	23	18	59	5	18	18	59	5	27	19	11	5	36	19	16
10	5	16	18	49	5	26	18	59	5	21	18	58	5	21	19	01	5	16	19	01	5	24	19	13	5	34	19	18
11	5	13	18	50	5	23	19	00	5	19	18	59	5	19	19	03	5	13	19	03	5	22	19	15	5	31	19	20
12	5	11	18	52	5	21	19	02	5	17	19	01	5	16	19	04	5	11	19	05	5	19	19	17	5	29	19	21
13	5	09	18	54	5	19	19	04	5	15	19	03	5	14	19	06	5	08	19	07	5	17	19	19	5	26	19	23
14	5	07	18	55	5	17	19	05	5	12	19	05	5	12	19	08	5	06	19	09	5	14	19	21	5	24	19	25
15	5	05	18	57	5	15	19	07	5	10	19	06	5	09	19	10	5	03	19	11	5	12	19	24	5	22	19	27
16	5	03	18	59	5	13	19	09	5	08	19	08	5	07	19	12	5	01	19	13	5	09	19	26	5	19	19	29
17	5	00	19	00	5	10	19	10	5	06	19	10	5	05	19	14	4	59	19	15	5	07	19	28	5	17	19	31
18	4	58	19	02	5	08	19	12	5	03	19	12	5	02	19	15	4	56	19	17	5	04	19	30	5	14	19	33
19	4	56	19	04	5	06	19	14	5	01	19	13	5	00	19	17	4	54	19	19	5	02	19	32	5	12	19	35
20	4	54	19	05	5	04	19	15	4	59	19	15	4	58	19	19	4	51	19	21	4	59	19	34	5	10	19	37
21	4	52	19	07	5	02	19	17	4	57	19	17	4	56	19	21	4	49	19	23	4	57	19	36	5	07	19	39
22	4	50	19	09	5	00	19	19	4	55	19	19	4	53	19	23	4	47	19	25	4	54	19	38	5	05	19	41
23	4	48	19	10	4	58	19	20	4	53	19	20	4	51	19	24	4	44	19	26	4	52	19	40	5	03	19	43
24	4	46	19	12	4	56	19	22	4	51	19	22	4	49	19	26	4	42	19	28	4	50	19	42	5	01	19	44
25	4	44	19	14	4	54	19	24	4	49	19	24	4	47	19	28	4	40	19	30	4	47	19	44	4	58	19	46
26	4	42	19	15	4	52	19	25	4	46	19	26	4	45	19	30	4	37	19	32	4	45	19	46	4	56	19	48
27	4	40	19	17	4	50	19	27	4	44	19	27	4	43	19	32	4	35	19	34	4	43	19	48	4	54	19	50
28	4	38	19	19	4	48	19	29	4	42	19	29	4	41	19	34	4	33	19	36	4	40	19	50	4	52	19	52
29	4	36	19	20	4	46	19	30	4	40	19	31	4	39	19	35	4	31	19	38	4	38	19	52	4	49	19	54
30	4	34	19	22	4	44	19	32	4	38	19	32	4	36	19	37	4	29	19	40	4	36	19	54	4	47	19	56

JUPITER

Day	*RA*		*Dec.*		*Transit*		*5° high*			
							52°		*56°*	
	h	*m*	°	′	*h*	*m*	*h*	*m*	*h*	*m*
1	12	55.2	−4	10	0	17	5	22	5	15
11	12	50.4	−3	41	23	29	4	41	4	34
21	12	45.9	−3	13	22	45	3	59	3	53
31	12	41.9	−2	49	22	02	3	18	3	12

Diameters – equatorial 44″ polar 41″

SATURN

Day	*RA*		*Dec.*		*Transit*		*5° high*			
							52°		*56°*	
	h	*m*	°	′	*h*	*m*	*h*	*m*	*h*	*m*
1	7	28.7	+22	01	18	48	2	16	2	33
11	7	29.9	+21	59	18	10	1	38	1	54
21	7	31.8	+21	56	17	32	1	00	1	17
31	7	34.4	+21	51	16	56	0	23	0	39

Diameters – equatorial 18″ polar 17″
Rings – major axis 41″ minor axis 17″

URANUS

Day	*RA*		*Dec.*		*Transit*		*10° high*			
							52°		*56°*	
	h	*m*	°	′	*h*	*m*	*h*	*m*	*h*	*m*
1	22	42.3	−9	00	10	03	6	00	6	17
11	22	44.1	−8	49	9	25	5	22	5	38
21	22	45.7	−8	40	8	48	4	43	4	59
31	22	47.1	−8	32	8	10	4	04	4	20

Diameter 4″

NEPTUNE

Day	*RA*		*Dec.*		*Transit*		*10° high*			
							52°		*56°*	
	h	*m*	°	′	*h*	*m*	*h*	*m*	*h*	*m*
1	21	17.8	−15	51	8	39	5	23	5	51
11	21	18.7	−15	47	8	00	4	44	5	12
21	21	19.4	−15	44	7	22	4	05	4	33
31	21	19.9	−15	42	6	43	3	26	3	54

Diameter 2″

MAY 2005

FIFTH MONTH, 31 DAYS. *Maia*, goddess of growth and increase

1	*Sunday*	Queen Victoria opened the Great Exhibition in Hyde Park 1851	121
2	*Monday*	Catherine II of Russia (The Great) b. 1729. Leonardo da Vinci d. 1519	week 18 day 122
3	*Tuesday*	Dodie Smith b. 1896. Thomas Hood d. 1845	123
4	*Wednesday*	Audrey Hepburn b. 1929. Sir Osbert Sitwell d. 1969	124
5	*Thursday*	Karl Marx b. 1818. Edward Young d. 1765	125
6	*Friday*	Henry David Thoreau d. 1862. Edward VII d. 1910	126
7	*Saturday*	Johannes Brahms b. 1833. Pyotr Ilyich Tchaikovsky b. 1840	127
8	*Sunday*	Francis Quarles b. 1592. Henri Laurens d. 1954	128
9	*Monday*	Sir James M. Barrie b. 1860. Alan Bennett b. 1934	week 19 day 129
10	*Tuesday*	Fred Astaire b. 1899. Hokusai d. 1849	130
11	*Wednesday*	Salvador Dalí b. 1904. Douglas Adams d. 2001	131
12	*Thursday*	Dante Gabriel Rosetti b. 1828. John Dryden d. 1700	132
13	*Friday*	Dame Daphne du Maurier b. 1907. John Nash d. 1835	133
14	*Saturday*	Thomas Gainsborough b. 1727. Jean Rhys d. 1979	134
15	*Sunday*	Mikhail Bulgakov b. 1891. Joseph Whitaker d. 1895	135
16	*Monday*	John Sell Cotman b. 1782. Charles Perrault d. 1703	week 20 day 136
17	*Tuesday*	Dennis Potter b. 1935. Sandro Botticelli d. 1510	137
18	*Wednesday*	Nicholas II, Tzar of Russia b. 1868. George Meredith d. 1909	138
19	*Thursday*	Ogden Nash d. 1971. Sir John Betjeman d. 1984	139
20	*Friday*	Honoré de Balzac b. 1799. Dame Barbara Hepworth d. 1975	140
21	*Saturday*	King Philip II of Spain b. 1527. Mikhail Glinka b. 1804	141
22	*Sunday*	Sir Arthur Conan Doyle b. 1859. Victor Hugo d. 1885	142
23	*Monday*	Edmund Rubbra b. 1901. Henrik Ibsen d. 1906	week 21 day 143
24	*Tuesday*	William Byrd b. 1543. Queen Victoria b. 1819	144
25	*Wednesday*	Sir Ian McKellen b. 1939. Gustav Holst d. 1934	145
26	*Thursday*	Isadora Duncan b. 1877. Samuel Pepys d. 1706	146
27	*Friday*	Julia Ward Howe b. 1819. John Calvin d. 1564	147
28	*Saturday*	Ian Fleming b. 1908. Anne Brontë d. 1849	148
29	*Sunday*	Charles II b. 1630. Sir W. S. Gilbert d. 1911	149
30	*Monday*	Christopher Marlowe d. 1593. Voltaire d. 1778	week 22 day 150
31	*Tuesday*	Walt Whitman b. 1819. Joseph Haydn d. 1809	151

ASTRONOMICAL PHENOMENA

d	*h*	
2	17	Mars in conjunction with Moon. Mars 2° N.
6	08	Mercury in conjunction with Moon. Mercury 3° S.
9	05	Venus in conjunction with Moon. Venus 3° S.
13	15	Saturn in conjunction with Moon. Saturn 5° S.
19	22	Jupiter in conjunction with Moon. Jupiter 0°.3 N.
20	00	Neptune at stationary point
20	23	Sun's longitude 60° ♊
31	10	Mars in conjunction with Moon. Mars 0°.5 N.

MINIMA OF ALGOL

Algol is inconveniently situated for observation during May

CONSTELLATIONS

The following constellations are near the meridian at

	d	*h*		*d*	*h*
April	1	24	May	16	21
April	15	23	June	1	20
May	1	22	June	15	19

Cepheus (below the Pole), Cassiopeia (below the Pole), Ursa Minor, Ursa Major, Canes Venatici, Coma Berenices, Bootes, Leo, Virgo, Crater, Corvus and Hydra

THE MOON

Phases, Apsides and Node	*d*	*h*	*m*
☾ Last Quarter	1	06	24
● New Moon	8	08	45
☽ First Quarter	16	08	57
○ Full Moon	23	20	18
☾ Last Quarter	30	11	47
Apogee (404,638 km)	14	13	44
Perigee (364,219 km)	26	10	50

Mean longitude of ascending node on May 1, 22°

THE SUN

s.d. 15′.8

Day	*Right Ascension*			*Dec.* +		*Equation of time*		*Rise* 52°		*Rise* 56°		*Transit*		*Set* 52°		*Set* 56°		*Sidereal time*			*Transit of first point of Aries*		
	h	*m*	*s*	°	′	*m*	*s*	*h*	*m*	*h*	*m*	*h*	*m*	*h*	*m*	*h*	*m*	*h*	*m*	*s*	*h*	*m*	*s*
1	2	33	12	15	02	+2	53	4	30	4	16	11	57	19	25	19	39	14	36	05	9	22	23
2	2	37	01	15	21	+3	00	4	28	4	14	11	57	19	27	19	41	14	40	02	9	18	27
3	2	40	51	15	38	+3	07	4	26	4	12	11	57	19	28	19	43	14	43	58	9	14	31
4	2	44	42	15	56	+3	13	4	25	4	09	11	57	19	30	19	45	14	47	55	9	10	35
5	2	48	33	16	13	+3	18	4	23	4	07	11	57	19	32	19	47	14	51	51	9	06	39
6	2	52	25	16	30	+3	23	4	21	4	05	11	57	19	33	19	49	14	55	48	9	02	43
7	2	56	17	16	47	+3	27	4	19	4	03	11	57	19	35	19	51	14	59	44	8	58	47
8	3	00	10	17	03	+3	31	4	17	4	01	11	56	19	36	19	53	15	03	41	8	54	51
9	3	04	04	17	20	+3	34	4	16	3	59	11	56	19	38	19	55	15	07	37	8	50	55
10	3	07	58	17	35	+3	36	4	14	3	57	11	56	19	40	19	57	15	11	34	8	46	59
11	3	11	52	17	51	+3	38	4	12	3	55	11	56	19	41	19	59	15	15	31	8	43	04
12	3	15	47	18	06	+3	40	4	11	3	53	11	56	19	43	20	01	15	19	27	8	39	08
13	3	19	43	18	21	+3	41	4	09	3	51	11	56	19	44	20	03	15	23	24	8	35	12
14	3	23	39	18	36	+3	41	4	08	3	49	11	56	19	46	20	05	15	27	20	8	31	16
15	3	27	36	18	50	+3	41	4	06	3	47	11	56	19	48	20	07	15	31	17	8	27	20
16	3	31	34	19	04	+3	40	4	05	3	45	11	56	19	49	20	09	15	35	13	8	23	24
17	3	35	31	19	18	+3	38	4	03	3	43	11	56	19	51	20	10	15	39	10	8	19	28
18	3	39	30	19	32	+3	36	4	02	3	42	11	56	19	52	20	12	15	43	06	8	15	32
19	3	43	29	19	45	+3	34	4	00	3	40	11	56	19	54	20	14	15	47	03	8	11	36
20	3	47	28	19	57	+3	31	3	59	3	38	11	57	19	55	20	16	15	51	00	8	07	40
21	3	51	29	20	10	+3	28	3	58	3	37	11	57	19	56	20	18	15	54	56	8	03	44
22	3	55	29	20	22	+3	24	3	56	3	35	11	57	19	58	20	19	15	58	53	7	59	48
23	3	59	30	20	33	+3	19	3	55	3	34	11	57	19	59	20	21	16	02	49	7	55	53
24	4	03	32	20	45	+3	14	3	54	3	32	11	57	20	01	20	23	16	06	46	7	51	57
25	4	07	34	20	56	+3	08	3	53	3	31	11	57	20	02	20	24	16	10	42	7	48	01
26	4	11	37	21	06	+3	02	3	52	3	29	11	57	20	03	20	26	16	14	39	7	44	05
27	4	15	40	21	17	+2	56	3	51	3	28	11	57	20	04	20	27	16	18	35	7	40	09
28	4	19	43	21	27	+2	49	3	50	3	27	11	57	20	06	20	29	16	22	32	7	36	13
29	4	23	47	21	36	+2	41	3	49	3	25	11	57	20	07	20	30	16	26	29	7	32	17
30	4	27	52	21	45	+2	33	3	48	3	24	11	58	20	08	20	32	16	30	25	7	28	21
31	4	31	57	21	54	+2	25	3	47	3	23	11	58	20	09	20	33	16	34	22	7	24	25

DURATION OF TWILIGHT (in minutes)

Latitude	*52°*	*56°*	*52°*	*56°*	*52°*	*56°*	*52°*	*56°*
	1 May		*11 May*		*21 May*		*31 May*	
Civil	39	44	41	48	44	53	46	57
Nautical	89	106	97	120	106	141	115	187
Astronomical	152	204	176	TAN	TAN	TAN	TAN	TAN

THE NIGHT SKY

Mercury is too close to the Sun to be visible in either the early evenings or early mornings during the month.

Venus, magnitude −3.9, is slowly beginning to move out of the long evening twilight, becoming a brilliant object. It may be seen low above the western horizon for a very short time after sunset.

Mars continues to brighten slowly during the month, its magnitude changing from +0.6 to +0.3. Mars is now moving northwards in declination and thereby slowly improving its visibility prospects, despite the lengthening twilight. By the end of the month it may be detected low above the east-south-eastern horizon by about 02h. Mars is in the constellation of Aquarius. On the last day of the month the Moon, just after Last Quarter, passes 1 degree south of the planet.

Jupiter, magnitude −2.3, continues to be visible as a brilliant object in the evening skies, and even at the end of the month can be seen in the south-western sky until well after midnight. Jupiter is in the constellation of Virgo. The waxing gibbous Moon passes 1 degree south of the planet on the evening of the 19th.

Saturn is still visible in the western sky in the evenings, magnitude +0.3, though no longer visible after midnight. Saturn passes 7 degrees south of Pollux at the end of the month. On the 13th the waxing crescent Moon will be seen in the vicinity of the planet.

THE MOON

Day	RA		Dec.	Hor. par.	Semi-diam.	Sun's Co-long.	PA of Bright Limb	Ph.	Age	Rise				Transit		Set			
										52°		56°				52°		56°	
	h	m	°	′	′	°	°	%	d	h	m	h	m	h	m	h	m	h	m
1	20	44	−23.4	59.3	16.2	175	75	53	22.1	2	26	2	51	6	22	10	29	10	06
2	21	41	−18.7	59.1	16.1	188	70	42	23.1	2	47	3	05	7	17	11	59	11	43
3	22	35	−13.1	58.9	16.0	200	67	31	24.1	3	03	3	14	8	07	13	26	13	17
4	23	25	−6.9	58.5	16.0	212	65	21	25.1	3	15	3	21	8	54	14	49	14	47
5	0	14	−0.4	58.2	15.8	224	65	13	26.1	3	27	3	26	9	40	16	11	16	15
6	1	02	+6.0	57.7	15.7	236	66	6	27.1	3	38	3	32	10	26	17	33	17	42
7	1	51	+12.1	57.2	15.6	249	72	2	28.1	3	50	3	39	11	12	18	55	19	10
8	2	40	+17.5	56.7	15.4	261	95	0	29.1	4	05	3	48	12	00	20	16	20	39
9	3	32	+22.1	56.1	15.3	273	235	0	0.6	4	24	4	00	12	51	21	36	22	06
10	4	25	+25.5	55.6	15.1	285	250	3	1.6	4	50	4	19	13	43	22	48	23	25
11	5	20	+27.6	55.1	15.0	298	259	7	2.6	5	27	4	50	14	36	23	49	—	—
12	6	15	+28.3	54.7	14.9	310	266	13	3.6	6	16	5	37	15	29	—	—	0	28
13	7	10	+27.7	54.4	14.8	322	273	20	4.6	7	17	6	42	16	20	0	35	1	11
14	8	02	+25.8	54.2	14.8	334	279	28	5.6	8	27	7	58	17	08	1	08	1	38
15	8	52	+22.7	54.2	14.8	347	285	37	6.6	9	41	9	18	17	54	1	31	1	55
16	9	40	+18.8	54.4	14.8	359	289	47	7.6	10	55	10	39	18	38	1	49	2	06
17	10	26	+14.0	54.7	14.9	11	292	56	8.6	12	08	11	58	19	20	2	02	2	14
18	11	11	+8.7	55.2	15.0	23	294	66	9.6	13	22	13	17	20	01	2	13	2	20
19	11	55	+2.9	55.8	15.2	35	295	75	10.6	14	37	14	38	20	43	2	23	2	25
20	12	40	−3.1	56.6	15.4	48	294	83	11.6	15	55	16	01	21	27	2	33	2	30
21	13	27	−9.2	57.4	15.6	60	292	90	12.6	17	17	17	29	22	14	2	44	2	36
22	14	16	−15.0	58.2	15.9	72	286	96	13.6	18	44	19	03	23	06	2	58	2	43
23	15	11	−20.3	58.9	16.1	84	273	99	14.6	20	14	20	42	—	—	3	16	2	55
24	16	09	−24.6	59.5	16.2	96	160	100	15.6	21	42	22	18	0	03	3	43	3	13
25	17	13	−27.4	60.0	16.3	108	110	98	16.6	22	57	23	37	1	05	4	23	3	46
26	18	19	−28.3	60.2	16.4	121	97	93	17.6	23	52	—	—	2	10	5	23	4	44
27	19	25	−27.2	60.2	16.4	133	87	86	18.6	—	—	0	28	3	15	6	43	6	08
28	20	29	−24.3	60.0	16.3	145	79	77	19.6	0	29	0	56	4	16	8	13	7	47
29	21	28	−19.8	59.6	16.2	157	73	67	20.6	0	53	1	13	5	13	9	45	9	27
30	22	23	−14.3	59.1	16.1	169	69	56	21.6	1	10	1	23	6	05	11	13	11	03
31	23	14	−8.2	58.6	16.0	182	67	44	22.6	1	24	1	30	6	53	12	38	12	33

MERCURY

Day	RA		Dec.	Diam.	Phase	Transit		5° high			
								52°		56°	
	h	m	°	″	%	h	m	h	m	h	m
1	0	57	+2.9	7	51	10	21	4	38	4	39
3	1	06	+3.8	7	54	10	22	4	34	4	35
5	1	15	+4.8	7	57	10	24	4	31	4	30
7	1	25	+5.8	7	60	10	26	4	28	4	26
9	1	36	+7.0	6	63	10	29	4	25	4	23
11	1	47	+8.2	6	67	10	33	4	22	4	19
13	1	59	+9.4	6	70	10	37	4	20	4	15
15	2	11	+10.7	6	73	10	41	4	17	4	12
17	2	24	+12.1	6	77	10	46	4	15	4	09
19	2	38	+13.4	6	80	10	52	4	14	4	06
21	2	52	+14.8	6	84	10	59	4	13	4	04
23	3	07	+16.2	5	87	11	06	4	12	4	02
25	3	23	+17.6	5	91	11	14	4	13	4	01
27	3	39	+18.9	5	94	11	23	4	14	4	01
29	3	56	+20.1	5	97	11	32	4	16	4	01
31	4	14	+21.3	5	99	11	42	4	19	4	03

VENUS

Day	RA		Dec.	Diam.	Phase	Transit		5° high			
								52°		56°	
	h	m	°	″	%	h	m	h	m	h	m
1	3	05	+17.0	10	99	12	30	19	28	19	40
6	3	30	+18.8	10	99	12	35	19	43	19	57
11	3	56	+20.3	10	98	12	41	19	58	20	13
16	4	21	+21.7	10	98	12	47	20	12	20	28
21	4	47	+22.8	10	97	12	53	20	25	20	43
26	5	14	+23.6	10	97	13	00	20	37	20	55
31	5	40	+24.1	10	96	13	07	20	47	21	06

MARS

Day	RA		Dec.	Diam.	Phase	Transit		5° high			
								52°		56°	
	h	m	°	″	%	h	m	h	m	h	m
1	22	10	−13.0	7	87	7	34	3	19	3	35
6	22	24	−11.8	7	87	7	28	3	05	3	20
11	22	38	−10.5	7	86	7	22	2	52	3	05
16	22	52	−9.3	7	86	7	16	2	39	2	50
21	23	05	−8.0	7	86	7	10	2	25	2	36
26	23	19	−6.6	8	86	7	04	2	12	2	21
31	23	32	−5.3	8	85	6	57	1	58	2	06

SUNRISE AND SUNSET

	London		*Bristol*		*Birmingham*		*Manchester*		*Newcastle*		*Glasgow*		*Belfast*	
	0° 05′	*51° 30′*	*2° 35′*	*51° 28′*	*1° 55′*	*52° 28′*	*2° 15′*	*53° 28′*	*1° 37′*	*54° 59′*	*4° 14′*	*55° 52′*	*5° 56′*	*54° 35′*
	h m	*h m*	*h m*	*h m*	*h m*	*h m*	*h m*	*h m*	*h m*	*h m*	*h m*	*h m*	*h m*	*h m*
1	4 32	19 24	4 42	19 34	4 36	19 34	4 34	19 39	4 26	19 42	4 33	19 56	4 45	19 58
2	4 30	19 25	4 40	19 35	4 34	19 36	4 32	19 41	4 24	19 44	4 31	19 58	4 43	20 00
3	4 28	19 27	4 39	19 37	4 33	19 38	4 30	19 42	4 22	19 46	4 29	20 00	4 41	20 01
4	4 27	19 29	4 37	19 38	4 31	19 39	4 28	19 44	4 20	19 48	4 27	20 02	4 39	20 03
5	4 25	19 30	4 35	19 40	4 29	19 41	4 26	19 46	4 18	19 50	4 25	20 04	4 37	20 05
6	4 23	19 32	4 33	19 42	4 27	19 43	4 25	19 48	4 16	19 51	4 23	20 06	4 35	20 07
7	4 21	19 33	4 31	19 43	4 25	19 44	4 23	19 50	4 14	19 53	4 20	20 08	4 33	20 09
8	4 20	19 35	4 30	19 45	4 23	19 46	4 21	19 51	4 12	19 55	4 18	20 10	4 31	20 11
9	4 18	19 37	4 28	19 46	4 22	19 48	4 19	19 53	4 10	19 57	4 16	20 12	4 29	20 13
10	4 16	19 38	4 26	19 48	4 20	19 49	4 17	19 55	4 08	19 59	4 14	20 14	4 27	20 14
11	4 15	19 40	4 25	19 50	4 18	19 51	4 15	19 56	4 06	20 01	4 12	20 16	4 25	20 16
12	4 13	19 41	4 23	19 51	4 17	19 52	4 14	19 58	4 04	20 03	4 10	20 17	4 23	20 18
13	4 12	19 43	4 22	19 53	4 15	19 54	4 12	20 00	4 02	20 04	4 08	20 19	4 22	20 20
14	4 10	19 44	4 20	19 54	4 13	19 56	4 10	20 01	4 01	20 06	4 07	20 21	4 20	20 21
15	4 08	19 46	4 19	19 56	4 12	19 57	4 09	20 03	3 59	20 08	4 05	20 23	4 18	20 23
16	4 07	19 47	4 17	19 57	4 10	19 59	4 07	20 05	3 57	20 10	4 03	20 25	4 16	20 25
17	4 06	19 49	4 16	19 59	4 09	20 00	4 05	20 06	3 55	20 11	4 01	20 27	4 15	20 27
18	4 04	19 50	4 14	20 00	4 07	20 02	4 04	20 08	3 54	20 13	3 59	20 28	4 13	20 28
19	4 03	19 52	4 13	20 02	4 06	20 03	4 02	20 10	3 52	20 15	3 58	20 30	4 12	20 30
20	4 02	19 53	4 12	20 03	4 04	20 05	4 01	20 11	3 51	20 16	3 56	20 32	4 10	20 32
21	4 00	19 54	4 10	20 04	4 03	20 06	4 00	20 13	3 49	20 18	3 54	20 34	4 08	20 33
22	3 59	19 56	4 09	20 06	4 02	20 08	3 58	20 14	3 48	20 20	3 53	20 35	4 07	20 35
23	3 58	19 57	4 08	20 07	4 01	20 09	3 57	20 16	3 46	20 21	3 51	20 37	4 06	20 36
24	3 57	19 59	4 07	20 08	3 59	20 11	3 56	20 17	3 45	20 23	3 50	20 39	4 04	20 38
25	3 55	20 00	4 06	20 10	3 58	20 12	3 54	20 18	3 43	20 24	3 48	20 40	4 03	20 39
26	3 54	20 01	4 05	20 11	3 57	20 13	3 53	20 20	3 42	20 26	3 47	20 42	4 02	20 41
27	3 53	20 02	4 03	20 12	3 56	20 15	3 52	20 21	3 41	20 27	3 46	20 43	4 00	20 42
28	3 52	20 04	4 03	20 13	3 55	20 16	3 51	20 23	3 39	20 29	3 44	20 45	3 59	20 44
29	3 51	20 05	4 02	20 15	3 54	20 17	3 50	20 24	3 38	20 30	3 43	20 46	3 58	20 45
30	3 50	20 06	4 01	20 16	3 53	20 18	3 49	20 25	3 37	20 32	3 42	20 48	3 57	20 46
31	3 50	20 07	4 00	20 17	3 52	20 19	3 48	20 26	3 36	20 33	3 41	20 49	3 56	20 48

JUPITER

Day	*RA*		*Dec.*		*Transit*		*5° high*			
							52°		*56°*	
	h	*m*	°	′	*h*	*m*	*h*	*m*	*h*	*m*
1	12	41.9	−2	49	22	02	3	18	3	12
11	12	38.7	−2	31	21	19	2	37	2	32
21	12	36.4	−2	19	20	38	1	57	1	51
31	12	35.2	−2	14	19	58	1	17	1	11

Diameters – equatorial 42″ polar 39″

SATURN

Day	*RA*		*Dec.*		*Transit*		*5° high*			
							52°		*56°*	
	h	*m*	°	′	*h*	*m*	*h*	*m*	*h*	*m*
1	7	34.4	+21	51	16	56	0	23	0	39
11	7	37.6	+21	44	16	20	23	42	0	02
21	7	41.3	+21	36	15	44	23	06	23	22
31	7	45.5	+21	27	15	09	22	30	22	46

Diameters – equatorial 17″ polar 16″
Rings – major axis 39″ minor axis 16″

URANUS

Day	*RA*		*Dec.*		*Transit*		*10° high*			
							52°		*56°*	
	h	*m*	°	′	*h*	*m*	*h*	*m*	*h*	*m*
1	22	47.1	−8	32	8	10	4	04	4	20
11	22	48.3	−8	25	7	32	3	26	3	41
21	22	49.2	−8	20	6	53	2	47	3	02
31	22	49.8	−8	17	6	14	2	08	2	23

Diameter 4″

NEPTUNE

Day	*RA*		*Dec.*		*Transit*		*10° high*			
							52°		*56°*	
	h	*m*	°	′	*h*	*m*	*h*	*m*	*h*	*m*
1	21	19.9	−15	42	6	43	3	26	3	54
11	21	20.3	−15	41	6	04	2	47	3	15
21	21	20.3	−15	40	25	2	2	08	2	35
31	21	20.2	−15	41	4	45	1	29	1	56

Diameter 2″

♊ JUNE 2005 ♋

SIXTH MONTH, 30 DAYS. *Junius*, Roman gens (family)

1	*Wednesday*	Sir David Wilkie d. 1841. Sir Hugh Walpole d. 1941	152
2	*Thursday*	Sir Edward Elgar b. 1857. Vita Sackville-West d. 1962	153
3	*Friday*	George V b. 1865. Georges Bizet d. 1875	154
4	*Saturday*	George III b. 1738. Kaiser Wilhelm II d. 1941	155
5	*Sunday*	Margaret Drabble b. 1939. Sir David Hare d. 1947	156
6	*Monday*	Aleksandr Pushkin b. 1799. Jeremy Bentham d. 1832	week 23 day 157
7	*Tuesday*	Paul Gauguin b. 1848. E. M. Forster d. 1970	158
8	*Wednesday*	Frank Lloyd Wright b. 1867. Thomas Paine d. 1809	159
9	*Thursday*	Peter I (The Great), Tzar of Russia 1682–1725 b. 1672. Charles Dickens d. 1870	160
10	*Friday*	Duke of Edinburgh b. 1921. Frederick Delius d. 1934	161
11	*Saturday*	John Constable b. 1776. Catherine Cookson d. 1998	162
12	*Sunday*	Anne Frank b. 1929. Dame Marie Rambert d. 1982	163
13	*Monday*	William Butler Yeats b. 1865. Alexander the Great d. 332BC	week 24 day 164
14	*Tuesday*	Maxim Gorky d. 1938. Henry Mancini d. 1994	165
15	*Wednesday*	Edward the Black Prince b. 1330. Edward Grieg b. 1843	166
16	*Thursday*	Russian ballet dancer Rudolf Nureyev defects to the West 1961	167
17	*Friday*	Edward I (Longshanks) b. 1239. Joseph Addison d. 1719	168
18	*Saturday*	Sir Paul McCartney b. 1942. Samuel Butler d. 1902	169
19	*Sunday*	Salman Rushdie b. 1947. Sir William Golding d. 1993	170
20	*Monday*	Catherine Cookson b. 1906. William IV d. 1908	week 25 day 171
21	*Tuesday*	Ian McEwan b. 1948. Prince William of Wales b. 1982	172
22	*Wednesday*	Jaques Delille b. 1738. Walter de la Mare d. 1956	173
23	*Thursday*	Anna Akhmatova b. 1889. Jean Anouilh b. 1910	174
24	*Friday*	Mary Tudor d. 1533. Warner d. 1986	175
25	*Saturday*	John Marston d. 1634. Margaret Oliphant d. 1897	176
26	*Sunday*	Laurie Lee b. 1914. Ford Madox Ford d. 1939	177
27	*Monday*	Louis XII, King of France b. 1462. Helen Keller b. 1880	week 26 day 178
28	*Tuesday*	Henry VIII b. 1491. Archduke Franz Ferdinand assassinated d. 1914	179
29	*Wednesday*	Elizabeth Barrett Browning d. 1861. Paul Klee d. 1940	180
30	*Thursday*	George Duhamel b. 1884. Nancy Mitford d. 1973	181

ASTRONOMICAL PHENOMENA

d	*h*	
3	09	Mercury in superior conjunction
5	07	Jupiter at stationary point
7	08	Mercury in conjunction with Moon. Mercury 3° S.
8	13	Venus in conjunction with Moon. Venus 4° S.
10	04	Saturn in conjunction with Moon. Saturn 5° S.
14	03	Pluto at opposition
14	23	Uranus at stationary point
16	07	Jupiter in conjunction with Moon. Jupiter 0°.4 N.
21	07	Sun's longitude 90° ♋
26	03	Saturn in conjunction with Venus. Saturn 1° S.
26	11	Saturn in conjunction with Mercury. Saturn 1° S.
27	19	Venus in conjunction with Mercury. Venus 0°.01 N.
29	02	Mars in conjunction with Moon. Mars 2° S.

MINIMA OF ALGOL

Algol is inconveniently situated for observation during June

CONSTELLATIONS

The following constellations are near the meridian at

	d	*h*		*d*	*h*
May	1	24	June	15	21
May	16	23	July	1	20
June	1	22	July	16	19

Cassiopeia (below the Pole), Ursa Minor, Draco, Ursa Major, Canes Venatici, Bootes, Corona, Serpens, Virgo and Libra

THE MOON

Phases, Apsides and Node	*d*	*h*	*m*
● New Moon	6	21	55
☽ First Quarter	15	01	22
○ Full Moon	22	04	14
☾ Last Quarter	28	18	23
Apogee (405,534 km)	11	06	18
Perigee (359,661 km)	23	11	53

Mean longitude of ascending node on June 1, 20°

THE SUN

s.d. 15′.8

Day	Right Ascension			Dec. +		Equation of time		Rise 52°		Rise 56°		Transit		Set 52°		Set 56°		Sidereal time			Transit of first point of Aries		
	h	*m*	*s*	°	′	*m*	*s*	*h*	*m*	*h*	*m*	*h*	*m*	*h*	*m*	*h*	*m*	*h*	*m*	*s*	*h*	*m*	*s*
1	4	36	02	22	02	+2	16	3	46	3	22	11	58	20	10	20	35	16	38	18	7	20	29
2	4	40	08	22	10	+2	07	3	45	3	21	11	58	20	11	20	36	16	42	15	7	16	33
3	4	44	14	22	18	+1	57	3	44	3	20	11	58	20	13	20	37	16	46	11	7	12	38
4	4	48	21	22	25	+1	47	3	44	3	19	11	58	20	14	20	38	16	50	08	7	08	42
5	4	52	28	22	32	+1	36	3	43	3	18	11	58	20	14	20	40	16	54	04	7	04	46
6	4	56	35	22	38	+1	26	3	42	3	17	11	59	20	15	20	41	16	58	01	7	00	50
7	5	00	43	22	44	+1	15	3	42	3	17	11	59	20	16	20	42	17	01	58	6	56	54
8	5	04	51	22	50	+1	03	3	41	3	16	11	59	20	17	20	43	17	05	54	6	52	58
9	5	08	59	22	55	+0	51	3	41	3	15	11	59	20	18	20	44	17	09	51	6	49	02
10	5	13	08	23	00	+0	40	3	41	3	15	11	59	20	19	20	45	17	13	47	6	45	06
11	5	17	16	23	05	+0	27	3	40	3	14	12	00	20	19	20	45	17	17	44	6	41	10
12	5	21	25	23	09	+0	15	3	40	3	14	12	00	20	20	20	46	17	21	40	6	37	14
13	5	25	34	23	12	+0	03	3	40	3	14	12	00	20	21	20	47	17	25	37	6	33	18
14	5	29	43	23	16	−0	10	3	40	3	13	12	00	20	21	20	48	17	29	34	6	29	23
15	5	33	53	23	18	−0	23	3	39	3	13	12	00	20	22	20	48	17	33	30	6	25	27
16	5	38	02	23	21	−0	35	3	39	3	13	12	01	20	22	20	49	17	37	27	6	21	31
17	5	42	12	23	23	−0	48	3	39	3	13	12	01	20	23	20	49	17	41	23	6	17	35
18	5	46	21	23	24	−1	01	3	39	3	13	12	01	20	23	20	50	17	45	20	6	13	39
19	5	50	31	23	25	−1	14	3	39	3	13	12	01	20	23	20	50	17	49	16	6	09	43
20	5	54	40	23	26	−1	27	3	40	3	13	12	02	20	24	20	50	17	53	13	6	05	47
21	5	58	50	23	26	−1	40	3	40	3	13	12	02	20	24	20	50	17	57	09	6	01	51
22	6	02	59	23	26	−1	53	3	40	3	13	12	02	20	24	20	51	18	01	06	5	57	55
23	6	07	09	23	26	−2	06	3	40	3	14	12	02	20	24	20	51	18	05	03	5	53	59
24	6	11	18	23	25	−2	19	3	41	3	14	12	02	20	24	20	51	18	08	59	5	50	03
25	6	15	27	23	24	−2	32	3	41	3	14	12	03	20	24	20	51	18	12	56	5	46	07
26	6	19	36	23	22	−2	44	3	41	3	15	12	03	20	24	20	51	18	16	52	5	42	12
27	6	23	46	23	20	−2	57	3	42	3	15	12	03	20	24	20	50	18	20	49	5	38	16
28	6	27	54	23	17	−3	09	3	42	3	16	12	03	20	24	20	50	18	24	45	5	34	20
29	6	32	03	23	14	−3	21	3	43	3	17	12	03	20	24	20	50	18	28	42	5	30	24
30	6	36	12	23	11	−3	33	3	44	3	18	12	04	20	23	20	49	18	32	38	5	26	28

DURATION OF TWILIGHT (in minutes)

Latitude	*52°*	*56°*	*52°*	*56°*	*52°*	*56°*	*52°*	*56°*
	1 June		*11 June*		*21 June*		*31 June*	
Civil	46	58	48	61	49	63	48	61
Nautical	116	TAN	124	TAN	127	TAN	124	TAN
Astronomical	TAN	TAN	TAN	TAN	TAN	TAN	TAN	TAN

THE NIGHT SKY

Mercury remains too close to the Sun for observation throughout June as it passes through superior conjunction on the 3rd.

Venus, magnitude −3.9, is a brilliant object in the evening sky, though only visible low above the west-north-western horizon for about half an hour after sunset.

Mars continues to be visible as a morning object in the south-eastern sky, its magnitude brightening during the month from +0.3 to 0.0. Mars is moving northeastwards, starting the month in Aquarius and ending it in Pisces, having passed through the extreme northwestern portion of Cetus on the way. On the morning of the 29th the Moon, at Last Quarter, passes 1 degree north of the planet.

Jupiter, magnitude −2.1, continues to be visible as an evening object in the south-western quadrant of the sky, though by the end of the month it is lost to view over the western horizon before midnight. It reaches its second stationary point on the 5th and then resumes its direct eastward motion towards Spica. The Moon, around First Quarter, is near Jupiter on the evenings of the 15th and 16th.

Saturn, magnitude +0.3, is a difficult object to detect, low above the west-north-western horizon, in the evenings. By the middle of the month it is lost to view in the long twilight. On the evenings of the 9th and 10th the waxing crescent Moon is near the planet.

THE MOON

Day	RA		Dec.	Hor. par.	Semi-diam.	Sun's Co-long.	PA of Br. Limb	Ph.	Age	Rise 52°		Rise 56°		Transit		Set 52°		Set 56°	
	h	m	°	′	′	°	°	%	d	h	m	h	m	h	m	h	m	h	m
1	0	03	−1.8	58.1	15.8	194	66	34	23.6	1	35	1	36	7	38	13	59	14	01
2	0	50	+4.6	57.5	15.7	206	67	24	24.6	1	46	1	42	8	23	15	19	15	26
3	1	38	+10.6	57.0	15.5	218	69	15	25.6	1	58	1	48	9	09	16	39	16	53
4	2	26	+16.2	56.5	15.4	231	74	9	26.6	2	11	1	56	9	55	18	00	18	20
5	3	17	+20.9	56.0	15.2	243	81	4	27.6	2	29	2	07	10	44	19	19	19	46
6	4	09	+24.6	55.5	15.1	255	98	1	28.6	2	52	2	24	11	35	20	34	21	08
7	5	03	+27.0	55.1	15.0	267	188	0	0.1	3	24	2	50	12	28	21	39	22	17
8	5	58	+28.2	54.7	14.9	280	249	1	1.1	4	09	3	30	13	21	22	30	23	07
9	6	53	+27.9	54.4	14.8	292	264	4	2.1	5	06	4	29	14	13	23	08	23	40
10	7	46	+26.3	54.2	14.8	304	273	9	3.1	6	13	5	42	15	02	23	34	—	—
11	8	37	+23.6	54.1	14.7	316	280	15	4.1	7	26	7	01	15	49	23	53	0	00
12	9	26	+19.9	54.1	14.7	329	285	22	5.1	8	39	8	21	16	33	—	—	0	13
13	10	12	+15.4	54.3	14.8	341	289	31	6.1	9	52	9	40	17	15	0	08	0	22
14	10	56	+10.3	54.6	14.9	353	292	40	7.1	11	05	10	58	17	56	0	20	0	28
15	11	39	+4.8	55.1	15.0	5	293	50	8.1	12	17	12	16	18	37	0	30	0	34
16	12	23	−1.1	55.8	15.2	17	294	59	9.1	13	32	13	36	19	18	0	40	0	38
17	13	08	−7.0	56.6	15.4	30	292	69	10.1	14	50	15	00	20	03	0	50	0	44
18	13	56	−12.9	57.5	15.7	42	290	78	11.1	16	13	16	29	20	52	1	02	0	50
19	14	47	−18.3	58.4	15.9	54	285	87	12.1	17	41	18	05	21	46	1	18	1	00
20	15	44	−23.0	59.3	16.2	66	277	93	13.1	19	11	19	44	22	46	1	40	1	14
21	16	46	−26.4	60.1	16.4	78	264	98	14.1	20	35	21	14	23	50	2	13	1	39
22	17	52	−28.1	60.6	16.5	91	209	100	15.1	21	41	22	19	—	—	3	04	2	25
23	19	00	−27.7	60.9	16.6	103	107	99	16.1	22	26	22	57	0	57	4	18	3	40
24	20	06	−25.4	60.9	16.6	115	88	95	17.1	22	56	23	18	2	02	5	48	5	18
25	21	09	−21.2	60.6	16.5	127	78	88	18.1	23	16	23	30	3	03	7	23	7	02
26	22	07	−15.8	60.1	16.4	139	72	80	19.1	23	31	23	39	3	59	8	56	8	43
27	23	00	−9.6	59.5	16.2	152	69	70	20.1	23	43	23	46	4	49	10	24	10	17
28	23	51	−3.1	58.7	16.0	164	67	59	21.1	23	54	23	51	5	36	11	47	11	47
29	0	39	+3.3	58.0	15.8	176	67	48	22.1	—	—	23	58	6	22	13	08	13	14
30	1	27	+9.5	57.2	15.6	188	68	37	23.1	0	06	—	—	7	07	14	28	14	40

MERCURY

Day	RA		Dec.	Diam.	Phase	Transit		5° high 52°		5° high 56°	
	h	m	°	″	%	h	m	h	m	h	m
1	4	23	+21.9	5	99	11	48	4	21	4	04
3	4	42	+22.8	5	100	11	58	4	25	4	08
5	5	01	+23.7	5	100	12	09	19	49	20	08
7	5	20	+24.3	5	98	12	21	20	04	20	24
9	5	39	+24.8	5	96	12	32	20	18	20	38
11	5	57	+25.1	5	93	12	42	20	30	20	51
13	6	16	+25.2	5	89	12	53	20	40	21	01
15	6	33	+25.2	5	86	13	02	20	49	21	09
17	6	50	+24.9	6	82	13	11	20	56	21	16
19	7	06	+24.6	6	78	13	19	21	01	21	21
21	7	22	+24.1	6	74	13	27	21	05	21	24
23	7	36	+23.5	6	70	13	33	21	07	21	25
25	7	50	+22.8	6	66	13	39	21	08	21	25
27	8	03	+22.0	6	62	13	43	21	08	21	24
29	8	15	+21.2	7	59	13	47	21	06	21	21
31	8	26	+20.3	7	55	13	50	21	04	21	18

VENUS

Day	RA		Dec.	Diam.	Phase	Transit		5° high 52°		5° high 56°	
	h	m	°	″	%	h	m	h	m	h	m
1	5	46	+24.2	10	96	13	08	20	49	21	08
6	6	13	+24.4	10	95	13	15	20	57	21	16
11	6	40	+24.3	10	95	13	23	21	03	21	22
16	7	06	+23.9	11	94	13	30	21	07	21	25
21	7	33	+23.2	11	93	13	36	21	08	21	26
26	7	59	+22.2	11	92	13	42	21	08	21	25
31	8	24	+21.0	11	91	13	48	21	06	21	21

MARS

Day	RA		Dec.	Diam.	Phase	Transit		5° high 52°		5° high 56°	
	h	m	°	″	%	h	m	h	m	h	m
1	23	35	−5.1	8	85	6	56	1	55	2	03
6	23	48	−3.7	8	85	6	49	1	42	1	48
11	0	01	−2.4	8	85	6	43	1	28	1	33
16	0	14	−1.1	9	84	6	36	1	14	1	18
21	0	26	+0.2	9	84	6	29	1	00	1	04
26	0	39	+1.5	9	84	6	22	0	47	0	49
31	0	51	+2.8	9	84	6	14	0	33	0	34

SUNRISE AND SUNSET

	London		*Bristol*		*Birmingham*		*Manchester*		*Newcastle*		*Glasgow*		*Belfast*	
	0°05′	*51°30′*	*2°35′*	*51° 28′*	*1°55′*	*52°28′*	*2° 15′*	*53°28′*	*1°37′*	*54°59′*	*4° 14′*	*55°52′*	*5°56′*	*54°35′*
	h m	*h m*	*h m*	*h m*	*h m*	*h m*	*h m*	*h m*	*h m*	*h m*	*h m*	*h m*	*h m*	*h m*
1	3 49	20 08	3 59	20 18	3 51	20 21	3 47	20 28	3 35	20 34	3 40	20 51	3 55	20 49
2	3 48	20 09	3 58	20 19	3 50	20 22	3 46	20 29	3 34	20 35	3 39	20 52	3 54	20 50
3	3 47	20 10	3 57	20 20	3 49	20 23	3 45	20 30	3 33	20 37	3 38	20 53	3 53	20 51
4	3 47	20 11	3 57	20 21	3 49	20 24	3 44	20 31	3 32	20 38	3 37	20 54	3 52	20 53
5	3 46	20 12	3 56	20 22	3 48	20 25	3 44	20 32	3 32	20 39	3 36	20 56	3 51	20 54
6	3 45	20 13	3 56	20 23	3 47	20 26	3 43	20 33	3 31	20 40	3 35	20 57	3 51	20 55
7	3 45	20 14	3 55	20 24	3 47	20 27	3 42	20 34	3 30	20 41	3 35	20 58	3 50	20 56
8	3 44	20 15	3 55	20 25	3 46	20 27	3 42	20 35	3 30	20 42	3 34	20 59	3 49	20 57
9	3 44	20 16	3 54	20 25	3 46	20 28	3 41	20 36	3 29	20 43	3 33	21 00	3 49	20 57
10	3 44	20 16	3 54	20 26	3 46	20 29	3 41	20 36	3 28	20 44	3 33	21 01	3 48	20 58
11	3 43	20 17	3 54	20 27	3 45	20 30	3 41	20 37	3 28	20 45	3 32	21 01	3 48	20 59
12	3 43	20 18	3 53	20 27	3 45	20 30	3 40	20 38	3 28	20 45	3 32	21 02	3 48	21 00
13	3 43	20 18	3 53	20 28	3 45	20 31	3 40	20 38	3 27	20 46	3 31	21 03	3 47	21 01
14	3 43	20 19	3 53	20 29	3 44	20 32	3 40	20 39	3 27	20 47	3 31	21 04	3 47	21 01
15	3 43	20 19	3 53	20 29	3 44	20 32	3 40	20 40	3 27	20 47	3 31	21 04	3 47	21 02
16	3 42	20 20	3 53	20 30	3 44	20 33	3 39	20 40	3 27	20 48	3 31	21 05	3 47	21 02
17	3 42	20 20	3 53	20 30	3 44	20 33	3 39	20 41	3 27	20 48	3 31	21 05	3 47	21 03
18	3 42	20 21	3 53	20 30	3 44	20 33	3 39	20 41	3 27	20 49	3 31	21 06	3 47	21 03
19	3 43	20 21	3 53	20 31	3 44	20 34	3 39	20 41	3 27	20 49	3 31	21 06	3 47	21 03
20	3 43	20 21	3 53	20 31	3 44	20 34	3 40	20 42	3 27	20 49	3 31	21 06	3 47	21 04
21	3 43	20 21	3 53	20 31	3 45	20 34	3 40	20 42	3 27	20 49	3 31	21 06	3 47	21 04
22	3 43	20 21	3 53	20 31	3 45	20 34	3 40	20 42	3 27	20 50	3 31	21 07	3 47	21 04
23	3 43	20 22	3 54	20 31	3 45	20 35	3 40	20 42	3 28	20 50	3 32	21 07	3 48	21 04
24	3 44	20 22	3 54	20 31	3 45	20 35	3 41	20 42	3 28	20 50	3 32	21 07	3 48	21 04
25	3 44	20 22	3 54	20 31	3 46	20 35	3 41	20 42	3 28	20 50	3 32	21 07	3 48	21 04
26	3 45	20 22	3 55	20 31	3 46	20 34	3 42	20 42	3 29	20 50	3 33	21 06	3 49	21 04
27	3 45	20 22	3 55	20 31	3 47	20 34	3 42	20 42	3 29	20 49	3 33	21 06	3 49	21 04
28	3 46	20 21	3 56	20 31	3 47	20 34	3 43	20 42	3 30	20 49	3 34	21 06	3 50	21 04
29	3 46	20 21	3 56	20 31	3 48	20 34	3 43	20 41	3 31	20 49	3 35	21 06	3 51	21 03
30	3 47	20 21	3 57	20 31	3 49	20 34	3 44	20 41	3 31	20 48	3 35	21 05	3 51	21 03

JUPITER

Day	*RA*		*Dec.*		*Transit*		*5° high*			
							52°		*56°*	
	h	*m*	°	′	*h*	*m*	*h*	*m*	*h*	*m*
1	12	35.2	−2	14	19	54	1	13	1	07
11	12	35.2	−2	17	19	14	0	33	0	28
21	12	36.3	−2	27	18	36	23	50	23	45
31	12	38.4	−2	43	17	59	23	11	23	06

Diameters – equatorial 38″ polar 36″

SATURN

Day	*RA*		*Dec.*		*Transit*		*5° high*			
							52°		*56°*	
	h	*m*	°	′	*h*	*m*	*h*	*m*	*h*	*m*
1	7	46.0	+21	26	15	05	22	26	22	42
11	7	50.6	+21	14	14	31	21	51	22	06
21	7	55.5	+21	02	13	56	21	15	21	30
31	8	00.7	+20	48	13	22	20	39	20	54

Diameters – equatorial 17″ polar 15″
Rings – major axis 38″ minor axis 14″

URANUS

Day	*RA*		*Dec.*		*Transit*		*10° high*			
							52°		*56°*	
	h	*m*	°	′	*h*	*m*	*h*	*m*	*h*	*m*
1	22	49.9	−8	16	6	11	2	04	2	19
11	22	50.2	−8	15	5	32	1	24	1	40
21	22	50.1	−8	16	4	52	0	45	1	01
31	22	49.8	−8	18	4	13	0	06	0	21

Diameter 4″

NEPTUNE

Day	*RA*		*Dec.*		*Transit*		*10° high*			
							52°		*56°*	
	h	*m*	°	′	*h*	*m*	*h*	*m*	*h*	*m*
1	21	20.2	−15	41	4	41	1	25	1	52
11	21	19.8	−15	43	4	01	0	45	1	13
21	21	19.3	−15	46	3	22	0	06	0	33
31	21	18.6	−15	49	2	42	23	22	23	50

Diameter 2″

JULY 2005

SEVENTH MONTH, 31 DAYS. *Julius* Caesar, formerly *Quintilis,* fifth month of Roman pre-Julian calendar

1	*Friday*	Harriet Beecher Stowe b. 1896. Erik Satie d. 1925	182
2	*Saturday*	Ernest Hemingway d. 1961. Vladimir Nabokov d. 1977	183
3	*Sunday*	Robert Adam b. 1728. Tom Stoppard b. 1937	184
4	*Monday*	Samuel Richardson d. 1761. Georgette Heyer d. 1974	week 27 day 185
5	*Tuesday*	Jean Cocteau b. 1889. Max Klinger d. 1920	186
6	*Wednesday*	Henry II d. 1189. Kenneth Grahame d. 1932	187
7	*Thursday*	Edward I (Longshanks) d. 1307. Sir Arthur Conan Doyle d. 1930	188
8	*Friday*	Percy Grainger b. 1882. Percy Bysshe Shelley d. 1822	189
9	*Saturday*	Dame Barbara Cartland b. 1901. David Hockney b. 1937	190
10	*Sunday*	Marcel Proust b. 1871. George Stubbs d. 1806	191
11	*Monday*	Robert I of Scotland (Bruce) b. 1274. George Gershwin d. 1937	week 28 day 192
12	*Tuesday*	Henry David Thoreau b. 1817. Amadeo Modigliani b. 1884	193
13	*Wednesday*	Sir George Gilbert Scott b. 1811. David Storey d. 1933	194
14	*Thursday*	Gustav Klimt b. 1862. Alphonse Mucha d. 1939	195
15	*Friday*	Inigo Jones b. 1573. Dame Iris Murdoch b. 1919	196
16	*Saturday*	Tsar Nicholas II d. 1918. Sir Stephen Spender d. 1995	197
17	*Sunday*	Erle Stanley Gardner b. 1889. James McNeill Whistler d. 1903	198
18	*Monday*	William Makepeace Thackeray b. 1811. Jane Austen d. 1817	week 29 day 199
19	*Tuesday*	Edgar Degas b. 1834. A. J. Cronin b. 1896	200
20	*Wednesday*	Erik Karlfeldt b. 1864. Bruce Lee d. 1973	201
21	*Thursday*	Ernest Hemingway b. 1899. Robert Burns d. 1796	202
22	*Friday*	James Whale b. 1893. Carl Sandburg d. 1967	203
23	*Saturday*	Raymond Chandler b. 1888. Domenico Scarlatti d. 1757	204
24	*Sunday*	Alphonse Mucha b. 1860. John Sell Cotman d. 1842	205
25	*Monday*	Eric Hoffer b. 1902. Samuel Taylor Coleridge d. 1834	week 30 day 206
26	*Tuesday*	George Bernard Shaw b. 1856. Aldous Huxley b. 1894	207
27	*Wednesday*	Alexandre Dumas fils b. 1824. Sir Anton Dolin b. 1904	208
28	*Thursday*	Beatrix Potter b. 1866. Johann Sebastian Bach d. 1750	209
29	*Friday*	Robert Schumann d. 1856. Vincent van Gogh d. 1890	210
30	*Saturday*	Emily Brontë b. 1818. Henry Moore b. 1898	211
31	*Sunday*	J. K. Rowling b. 1965. Franz Liszt d. 1886	212

ASTRONOMICAL PHENOMENA

d	*h*	
5	05	Earth at aphelion (152 million km.)
7	17	Saturn in conjunction with Moon. Saturn 5° S.
8	21	Venus in conjunction with Moon. Venus 3° S.
8	22	Mercury in conjunction with Moon. Mercury 5° S.
9	03	Mercury at greatest elongation E.26°
9	10	Venus in conjunction with Mercury . Venus 2° N.
13	18	Jupiter in conjunction with Moon. Jupiter 0°.7 N.
22	18	Sun's longitude 120° ♌
23	03	Mercury at stationary point
23	17	Saturn in conjunction
27	17	Mars in conjunction with Moon. Mars 4° S.

MINIMA OF ALGOL

d	*h*	*d*	*h*	*d*	*h*
3	19.9	15	07.2	26	18.4
6	16.7	18	04.0	29	15.2
9	13.6	21	00.8		
12	10.4	23	21.6		

CONSTELLATIONS

The following constellations are near their meridian at

	d	*h*		*d*	*h*
June	1	24	July	16	21
June	15	23	August	1	20
July	1	22	August	16	19

Ursa Minor, Draco, Coruna, Hercules, Lyra, Serpens, Ophiuchus, Libra, Scorpius and Sagittarius

THE MOON

Phases, Apsides and Node	*d*	*h*	*m*
● New Moon	6	12	02
☽ First Quarter	14	15	20
○ Full Moon	21	11	00
☾ Last Quarter	28	03	19
Apogee (406,379 km)	8	17	52
Perigee (357,154 km)	21	19	50

Mean longitude of ascending node on July 1, 19°

THE SUN

s.d. 15′.8

Day	Right Ascension			Dec. +		Equation of time		Rise 52°		Rise 56°		Transit		Set 52°		Set 56°		Sidereal time			Transit of first point of Aries		
	h	*m*	*s*	°	′	*m*	*s*	*h*	*m*	*h*	*m*	*h*	*m*	*h*	*m*	*h*	*m*	*h*	*m*	*s*	*h*	*m*	*s*
1	6	40	20	23	07	–3	45	3	44	3	18	12	04	20	23	20	49	18	36	35	5	22	32
2	6	44	28	23	03	–3	57	3	45	3	19	12	04	20	23	20	48	18	40	32	5	18	36
3	6	48	36	22	58	–4	08	3	46	3	20	12	04	20	22	20	48	18	44	28	5	14	40
4	6	52	44	22	53	–4	19	3	47	3	21	12	04	20	22	20	47	18	48	25	5	10	44
5	6	56	51	22	48	–4	30	3	47	3	22	12	05	20	21	20	46	18	52	21	5	06	48
6	7	00	58	22	42	–4	40	3	48	3	23	12	05	20	21	20	46	18	56	18	5	02	52
7	7	05	05	22	36	–4	50	3	49	3	24	12	05	20	20	20	45	19	00	14	4	58	57
8	7	09	11	22	29	–5	00	3	50	3	25	12	05	20	19	20	44	19	04	11	4	55	01
9	7	13	17	22	22	–5	09	3	51	3	27	12	05	20	19	20	43	19	08	07	4	51	05
10	7	17	22	22	15	–5	18	3	52	3	28	12	05	20	18	20	42	19	12	04	4	47	09
11	7	21	27	22	07	–5	26	3	53	3	29	12	06	20	17	20	41	19	16	01	4	43	13
12	7	25	31	21	59	–5	34	3	54	3	31	12	06	20	16	20	40	19	19	57	4	39	17
13	7	29	35	21	51	–5	42	3	56	3	32	12	06	20	15	20	39	19	23	54	4	35	21
14	7	33	39	21	42	–5	49	3	57	3	33	12	06	20	14	20	37	19	27	50	4	31	25
15	7	37	42	21	33	–5	55	3	58	3	35	12	06	20	13	20	36	19	31	47	4	27	29
16	7	41	44	21	23	–6	01	3	59	3	36	12	06	20	12	20	35	19	35	43	4	23	33
17	7	45	46	21	13	–6	06	4	00	3	38	12	06	20	11	20	33	19	39	40	4	19	37
18	7	49	48	21	03	–6	11	4	02	3	39	12	06	20	10	20	32	19	43	37	4	15	41
19	7	53	49	20	52	–6	15	4	03	3	41	12	06	20	09	20	30	19	47	33	4	11	46
20	7	57	49	20	41	–6	19	4	04	3	43	12	06	20	08	20	29	19	51	30	4	07	50
21	8	01	49	20	30	–6	22	4	06	3	44	12	06	20	06	20	27	19	55	26	4	03	54
22	8	05	48	20	18	–6	25	4	07	3	46	12	06	20	05	20	26	19	59	23	3	59	58
23	8	09	46	20	06	–6	27	4	08	3	48	12	06	20	04	20	24	20	03	19	3	56	02
24	8	13	44	19	54	–6	29	4	10	3	49	12	06	20	02	20	22	20	07	16	3	52	06
25	8	17	42	19	41	–6	29	4	11	3	51	12	07	20	01	20	21	20	11	12	3	48	10
26	8	21	39	19	28	–6	30	4	13	3	53	12	07	19	59	20	19	20	15	09	3	44	14
27	8	25	35	19	14	–6	29	4	14	3	55	12	06	19	58	20	17	20	19	06	3	40	18
28	8	29	31	19	01	–6	29	4	16	3	56	12	06	19	56	20	15	20	23	02	3	36	22
29	8	33	26	18	47	–6	27	4	17	3	58	12	06	19	55	20	13	20	26	59	3	32	26
30	8	37	20	18	32	–6	25	4	19	4	00	12	06	19	53	20	11	20	30	55	3	28	31
31	8	41	14	18	18	–6	23	4	20	4	02	12	06	19	51	20	09	20	34	52	3	24	35

DURATION OF TWILIGHT (in minutes)

Latitude	*52°*	*56°*	*52°*	*56°*	*52°*	*56°*	*52°*	*56°*
	1 July		*11 July*		*21 July*		*31 July*	
Civil	48	61	47	58	44	53	42	49
Nautical	124	TAN	117	TAN	107	146	98	123
Astronomical	TAN	TAN	TAN	TAN	TAN	TAN	182	TAN

THE NIGHT SKY

Mercury reaches greatest eastern elongation on the 9th but the long duration of twilight means that it is unsuitably placed for observation throughout the month.

Venus, magnitude –3.9, is a brilliant object in the evening sky, but only visible low above the western horizon for about half an hour after sunset. Under good conditions the thin crescent Moon, just over 2 days old, may be glimpsed nearly 3 degrees above Venus on the evening of the 8th.

Mars continues to brighten during the month, its magnitude changing from –0.1 to –0.5. Although technically a morning object, by the end of July it is visible low in the eastern sky before midnight, and will be seen high in the southern sky before dawn. Mars is moving east-north-eastwards in the constellation of Pisces. The Moon, at Last Quarter, passes 3 degrees north of the planet on the 27th.

Jupiter, magnitude –1.9, continues to be visible as a brilliant evening object in the south-western sky, in the constellation of Virgo. The Moon, near First Quarter, passes 1 degree south of Jupiter on the 13th.

Saturn passes through conjunction on the 23rd and therefore remains too close to the Sun for observation throughout the month.

Twilight. Reference to the section above shows that astronomical twilight lasts all night for a period around the summer solstice (i.e. in June and July), even in southern England. Under these conditions the sky never gets completely dark as the Sun is always less than 18 degrees below the horizon.

THE MOON

Day	RA		Dec.	Hor. par.	Semi-diam.	Sun's Co-long.	PA of Br. Limb	Ph.	Age	Rise				Transit		Set			
										52°		56°		52°		56°			
	h	m	°	′	′	°	°	%	d	h	m	h	m	h	m	h	m	h	m
1	2	15	+15.1	56.5	15.4	201	71	27	24.1	0	18	0	05	7	53	15	48	16	07
2	3	05	+20.0	55.9	15.2	213	76	19	25.1	0	34	0	15	8	41	17	07	17	33
3	3	56	+23.9	55.4	15.1	225	82	11	26.1	0	55	0	29	9	31	18	23	18	56
4	4	49	+26.6	55.0	15.0	237	91	6	27.1	1	24	0	52	10	23	19	31	20	09
5	5	44	+28.0	54.6	14.9	250	103	2	28.1	2	05	1	27	11	15	20	27	21	05
6	6	38	+28.1	54.3	14.8	262	135	0	29.1	2	58	2	20	12	07	21	08	21	42
7	7	32	+26.8	54.1	14.7	274	237	0	0.5	4	02	3	29	12	58	21	38	22	05
8	8	23	+24.3	54.0	14.7	286	268	2	1.5	5	14	4	47	13	45	21	59	22	20
9	9	12	+20.9	54.0	14.7	299	279	6	2.5	6	27	6	07	14	30	22	14	22	30
10	9	59	+16.5	54.0	14.7	311	285	11	3.5	7	40	7	26	15	13	22	27	22	37
11	10	43	+11.6	54.3	14.8	323	289	17	4.5	8	52	8	44	15	53	22	37	22	42
12	11	26	+6.2	54.6	14.9	335	292	25	5.5	10	04	10	01	16	33	22	47	22	47
13	12	09	+0.5	55.1	15.0	347	293	34	6.5	11	16	11	18	17	14	22	56	22	52
14	12	53	−5.3	55.7	15.2	360	293	44	7.5	12	31	12	38	17	56	23	07	22	58
15	13	39	−11.1	56.5	15.4	12	291	54	8.5	13	49	14	03	18	41	23	21	23	05
16	14	27	−16.6	57.4	15.6	24	288	64	9.5	15	13	15	33	19	31	23	39	23	17
17	15	21	−21.5	58.3	15.9	36	283	74	10.5	16	41	17	09	20	27	—	—	23	35
18	16	19	−25.3	59.3	16.2	49	276	83	11.5	18	07	18	44	21	29	0	05	—	—
19	17	23	−27.7	60.2	16.4	61	267	91	12.5	19	22	20	01	22	35	0	46	0	09
20	18	30	−28.2	60.8	16.6	73	254	97	13.5	20	17	20	52	23	41	1	49	1	09
21	19	38	−26.6	61.3	16.7	85	223	99	14.5	20	54	21	20	—	—	3	12	2	38
22	20	43	−23.1	61.4	16.7	97	106	99	15.5	21	18	21	36	0	46	4	49	4	24
23	21	44	−17.9	61.2	16.7	110	81	96	16.5	21	35	21	46	1	45	6	26	6	10
24	22	41	−11.8	60.6	16.5	122	72	90	17.5	21	49	21	54	2	39	7	59	7	51
25	23	34	−5.1	59.9	16.3	134	68	82	18.5	22	01	22	00	3	30	9	28	9	26
26	0	24	+1.6	59.0	16.1	146	67	73	19.5	22	12	22	06	4	17	10	52	10	56
27	1	13	+8.1	58.1	15.8	158	68	62	20.5	22	25	22	13	5	04	12	15	12	25
28	2	02	+14.0	57.2	15.6	171	70	52	21.5	22	40	22	22	5	50	13	37	13	53
29	2	52	+19.1	56.4	15.4	183	74	41	22.5	22	59	22	35	6	38	14	57	15	21
30	3	44	+23.3	55.7	15.2	195	78	31	23.5	23	26	22	54	7	28	16	15	16	45
31	4	37	+26.2	55.1	15.0	207	85	23	24.5	—	—	23	25	8	19	17	25	18	02

MERCURY

Day	RA		Dec.	Diam.	Phase	Transit		5° high			
								52°		56°	
	h	m	°	″	%	h	m	h	m	h	m
1	8	26	+20.3	7	55	13	50	21	04	21	18
3	8	36	+19.4	7	52	13	53	21	01	21	14
5	8	46	+18.5	7	49	13	54	20	56	21	09
7	8	55	+17.6	8	46	13	54	20	51	21	03
9	9	02	+16.6	8	42	13	54	20	46	20	56
11	9	09	+15.7	8	39	13	52	20	39	20	49
13	9	15	+14.8	9	36	13	50	20	32	20	41
15	9	19	+14.0	9	32	13	47	20	24	20	32
17	9	23	+13.2	9	29	13	42	20	16	20	23
19	9	26	+12.6	10	25	13	36	20	06	20	13
21	9	27	+12.0	10	22	13	30	19	56	20	03
23	9	27	+11.5	10	18	13	21	19	46	19	52
25	9	26	+11.1	11	14	13	12	19	35	19	41
27	9	24	+10.9	11	11	13	02	19	23	19	29
29	9	20	+10.8	11	8	12	50	19	12	19	17
31	9	16	+10.9	11	5	12	37	19	00	19	05

VENUS

Day	R.A.		Dec.	Diam.	Phase	Transit		5° high			
								52°		56°	
h	h	m	°	″	%	h	m	h	m	h	m
1	8	24	+21.0	11	91	13	48	21	06	21	21
6	8	49	+19.5	11	90	13	54	21	03	21	16
11	9	14	+17.8	11	89	13	58	20	57	21	09
16	9	38	+15.9	12	88	14	02	20	51	21	01
21	10	01	+13.8	12	86	14	06	20	43	20	51
26	10	24	+11.6	12	85	14	09	20	35	20	40
31	10	47	+9.3	12	84	14	12	20	25	20	29

MARS

Day	RA		Dec.	Diam.	Phase	Transit		5° high			
								52°		56°	
	h	m	°	″	%	h	m	h	m	h	m
1	0	51	+2.8	9	84	6	14	0	33	0	34
6	1	04	+4.0	10	84	6	07	0	19	0	19
11	1	16	+5.2	10	84	5	59	0	06	0	05
16	1	28	+6.3	10	84	5	51	23	49	23	47
21	1	39	+7.4	11	84	5	43	23	36	23	33
26	1	51	+8.4	11	84	5	35	23	22	23	18
31	2	02	+9.4	11	84	5	26	23	08	23	04

SUNRISE AND SUNSET

	London 0°05′	51°30′	*Bristol* 2°35′	51°28′	*Birmingham* 1°55′	52°28′	*Manchester* 2°15′	53°28′	*Newcastle* 1°37′	54°49′	*Glasgow* 4°14′	55°52′	*Belfast* 5°56′	54°35′
	h m	*h m*	*h m*	*h m*	*h m*	*h m*	*h m*	*h m*	*h m*	*h m*	*h m*	*h m*	*h m*	*h m*
1	3 47	20 21	3 58	20 30	3 49	20 33	3 45	20 41	3 32	20 48	3 36	21 05	3 52	21 03
2	3 48	20 20	3 58	20 30	3 50	20 33	3 45	20 40	3 33	20 48	3 37	21 04	3 53	21 02
3	3 49	20 20	3 59	20 30	3 51	20 33	3 46	20 40	3 34	20 47	3 38	21 04	3 54	21 02
4	3 50	20 19	4 00	20 29	3 52	20 32	3 47	20 39	3 35	20 46	3 39	21 03	3 55	21 01
5	3 50	20 19	4 01	20 29	3 52	20 32	3 48	20 39	3 36	20 46	3 40	21 02	3 56	21 00
6	3 51	20 18	4 02	20 28	3 53	20 31	3 49	20 38	3 37	20 45	3 41	21 02	3 57	21 00
7	3 52	20 18	4 02	20 28	3 54	20 30	3 50	20 37	3 38	20 44	3 42	21 01	3 58	20 59
8	3 53	20 17	4 03	20 27	3 55	20 30	3 51	20 37	3 39	20 44	3 43	21 00	3 59	20 58
9	3 54	20 16	4 04	20 26	3 56	20 29	3 52	20 36	3 40	20 43	3 45	20 59	4 00	20 57
10	3 55	20 16	4 05	20 25	3 57	20 28	3 53	20 35	3 41	20 42	3 46	20 58	4 01	20 56
11	3 56	20 15	4 06	20 25	3 58	20 27	3 54	20 34	3 42	20 41	3 47	20 57	4 02	20 55
12	3 57	20 14	4 07	20 24	4 00	20 26	3 55	20 33	3 44	20 40	3 48	20 56	4 04	20 54
13	3 58	20 13	4 09	20 23	4 01	20 25	3 57	20 32	3 45	20 39	3 50	20 55	4 05	20 53
14	4 00	20 12	4 10	20 22	4 02	20 24	3 58	20 31	3 46	20 37	3 51	20 53	4 06	20 52
15	4 01	20 11	4 11	20 21	4 03	20 23	3 59	20 30	3 48	20 36	3 53	20 52	4 07	20 51
16	4 02	20 10	4 12	20 20	4 04	20 22	4 00	20 29	3 49	20 35	3 54	20 51	4 09	20 50
17	4 03	20 09	4 13	20 19	4 06	20 21	4 02	20 28	3 51	20 34	3 56	20 49	4 10	20 49
18	4 04	20 08	4 15	20 18	4 07	20 20	4 03	20 26	3 52	20 32	3 57	20 48	4 12	20 47
19	4 06	20 07	4 16	20 17	4 08	20 19	4 05	20 25	3 54	20 31	3 59	20 47	4 13	20 46
20	4 07	20 06	4 17	20 15	4 10	20 17	4 06	20 24	3 55	20 29	4 00	20 45	4 15	20 44
21	4 08	20 04	4 18	20 14	4 11	20 16	4 07	20 22	3 57	20 28	4 02	20 43	4 16	20 43
22	4 10	20 03	4 20	20 13	4 13	20 15	4 09	20 21	3 58	20 26	4 04	20 42	4 18	20 41
23	4 11	20 02	4 21	20 12	4 14	20 13	4 10	20 20	4 00	20 25	4 05	20 40	4 19	20 40
24	4 12	20 00	4 23	20 10	4 15	20 12	4 12	20 18	4 02	20 23	4 07	20 39	4 21	20 38
25	4 14	19 59	4 24	20 09	4 17	20 11	4 13	20 16	4 03	20 22	4 09	20 37	4 23	20 37
26	4 15	19 58	4 25	20 07	4 18	20 09	4 15	20 15	4 05	20 20	4 11	20 35	4 24	20 35
27	4 17	19 56	4 27	20 06	4 20	20 07	4 17	20 13	4 07	20 18	4 12	20 33	4 26	20 33
28	4 18	19 55	4 28	20 04	4 21	20 06	4 18	20 12	4 08	20 16	4 14	20 31	4 28	20 32
29	4 20	19 53	4 30	20 03	4 23	20 04	4 20	20 10	4 10	20 15	4 16	20 30	4 29	20 30
30	4 21	19 51	4 31	20 01	4 24	20 03	4 21	20 08	4 12	20 13	4 18	20 28	4 31	20 28
31	4 22	19 50	4 33	20 00	4 26	20 01	4 23	20 07	4 14	20 11	4 20	20 26	4 33	20 26

JUPITER

Day	*RA*		*Dec.*		*Transit*		*5° high*			
							52°		*56°*	
	h	*m*	°	′	*h*	*m*	*h*	*m*	*h*	*m*
1	12	38.4	−2	43	17	59	23	11	23	06
11	12	41.5	−3	05	17	23	22	33	22	27
21	12	45.5	−3	33	16	48	21	56	21	49
31	12	50.3	−4	06	16	13	21	18	21	11

Diameters – equatorial 35″ polar 33″

SATURN

Day	*RA*		*Dec.*		*Transit*		*5° high*			
							52°		*56°*	
	h	*m*	°	′	*h*	*m*	*h*	*m*	*h*	*m*
1	8	00.7	+20	48	13	22	20	39	20	54
11	8	06.0	+20	34	12	48	20	04	20	19
21	8	11.4	+20	18	12	14	19	28	19	43
31	8	16.8	+20	02	11	40	18	53	19	07

Diameters – equatorial 16″ polar 15″
Rings – major axis 37″ minor axis 13″

URANUS

Day	*RA*		*Dec.*		*Transit*		*10° high*			
							52°		*56°*	
	h	*m*	°	′	*h*	*m*	*h*	*m*	*h*	*m*
1	22	49.8	−8	18	4	13	0	06	0	21
11	22	49.2	−8	22	3	33	23	22	23	38
21	22	48.4	−8	27	2	52	22	43	22	58
31	22	47.3	−8	34	2	12	22	03	22	19

Diameter 4″

NEPTUNE

Day	*RA*		*Dec.*		*Transit*		*5° high*			
							52°		*56°*	
	h	*m*	°	′	*h*	*m*	*h*	*m*	*h*	*m*
1	21	18.6	−15	69	2	42	23	22	23	50
11	21	17.8	−15	53	2	01	22	42	23	10
21	21	16.8	−15	58	1	21	22	03	22	31
31	21	15.8	−16	03	0	41	21	23	21	51

Diameter 2″

AUGUST 2005

EIGHTH MONTH, 31 DAYS. *Augustus*, formerly *Sextilis*, sixth month of Roman pre-Julian calendar

1	*Monday*	Herman Melville b. 1819. Queen Anne d. 1714	week 31 day 213
2	*Tuesday*	Thomas Gainsborough d. 1788. Carlos Chavez d. 1978	214
3	*Wednesday*	Sir Joseph Paxton b. 1801. P. D. James b. 1920	215
4	*Thursday*	Percy Bysshe Shelley b. 1792. Hans Christian Andersen d. 1874	216
5	*Friday*	Guy de Maupassant b. 1850. Friedrich Engels d. 1895	217
6	*Saturday*	Alfred, Lord Tennyson b. 1809. Ben Jonson d. 1637	218
7	*Sunday*	Emil Nolde b. 1867. Rabindranath Tagore d. 1941	219
8	*Monday*	Princess Beatrice of York b. 1988. James Tissot d. 1902	week 32 day 220
9	*Tuesday*	Ruggero Leoncavallo d. 1919. Dmitry Shostakovich d. 1975	221
10	*Wednesday*	Ferdinand VI d. 1759. Alan Ramsay d. 1784	222
11	*Thursday*	Enid Blyton b. 1897. Jackson Pollock d. 1956	223
12	*Friday*	William Blake d. 1827. Ian Fleming d. 1964	224
13	*Saturday*	H. G. Wells b. 1866. Sir John Everett Millais d. 1896	225
14	*Sunday*	John Galsworthy b. 1867. Bertolt Brecht d. 1956	226
15	*Monday*	Sir Walter Scott b. 1771. The Princess Royal b. 1950	week 33 day 227
16	*Tuesday*	Ted Hughes b. 1930. Margaret Mitchell d. 1946	228
17	*Wednesday*	Frederick the Great d. 1786. Ludwig Mies van der Rohe d. 1969	229
18	*Thursday*	William Henry Hudson d. 1922. Honoré de Balzac d. 1850	230
19	*Friday*	John Dryden b. 1631. Sergey Diaghilev d. 1929	231
20	*Saturday*	H. P. Lovecraft b. 1890. Leon Trotsky, d. 1940	232
21	*Sunday*	William IV b. 1765. Aubrey Beardsley b. 1872	233
22	*Monday*	Claude Debussy b. 1862. Richard III d. 1485	week 34 day 234
23	*Tuesday*	Louis XVI, King of France b. 1754. Willy Russell b. 1947	235
24	*Wednesday*	George Stubbs b. 1724. Jean Rhys b. 1890	236
25	*Thursday*	Leonard Bernstein b. 1918. Frederick Forsyth b. 1938	237
26	*Friday*	Albert, Prince Consort to Queen Victoria b. 1819	238
27	*Saturday*	C. S. Forester b. 1899. Le Corbusier d. 1965	239
28	*Sunday*	Johann Wolfgang von Goethe b. 1749. Leigh Hunt d. 1859	240
29	*Monday*	Jean Ingres b. 1780. Joseph Wright d. 1797	week 35 day 241
30	*Tuesday*	Mary Shelley b. 1797. Cleopatra d. 30BC	242
31	*Wednesday*	Henry V d. 1422. Henry Moore d. 1986	243

ASTRONOMICAL PHENOMENA

d	*h*	
4	06	Saturn in conjunction with Moon. Saturn 5° S.
5	06	Mercury in conjunction with Moon. Mercury 9° S.
6	00	Mercury in inferior conjunction
8	05	Venus in conjunction with Moon. Venus 1° S.
8	16	Neptune at opposition
10	07	Jupiter in conjunction with Moon. Jupiter 1° N.
16	04	Mercury at stationary point
23	01	Sun's longitude 150° ♍
23	23	Mercury at greatest elongation W.18°
25	04	Mars in conjunction with Moon. Mars 5° S.
31	19	Saturn in conjunction with Moon. Saturn 4° S.

MINIMA OF ALGOL

d	*h*	*d*	*h*	*d*	*h*
1	12.0	12	23.3	24	10.5
4	08.8	15	20.1	27	07.3
7	05.7	18	16.9	30	04.1
10	02.5	21	13.7		

CONSTELLATIONS

The following constellations are near their meridian at

	d	*h*		*d*	*h*
July	1	24	August	16	21
July	16	23	September	1	20
August	1	22	September	15	19

Draco, Hercules, Lyra, Cygnus, Sagitta, Ophiuchus, Serpens, Aquila and Sagittarius

THE MOON

Phases, Apsides and Node	*d*	*h*	*m*
● New Moon	5	03	05
☽ First Quarter	13	02	39
○ Full Moon	19	17	53
☾ Last Quarter	26	15	18
Apogee (406,630 km)	4	22	04
Perigee (357,398 km)	19	05	43

Mean longitude of ascending node on August 1, 17°

THE SUN

s.d. 15′.8

Day	Right Ascension			Dec. +		Equation of time		Rise 52°		Rise 56°		Transit		Set 52°		Set 56°		Sidereal time			Transit of first point of Aries		
	h	m	s	°	′	m	s	h	m	h	m	h	m	h	m	h	m	h	m	s	h	m	s
1	8	45	08	18	03	–6	19	4	22	4	04	12	06	19	50	20	07	20	38	48	3	20	39
2	8	49	01	17	48	–6	16	4	23	4	06	12	06	19	48	20	05	20	42	45	3	16	43
3	8	52	53	17	32	–6	11	4	25	4	08	12	06	19	46	20	03	20	46	41	3	12	47
4	8	56	44	17	16	–6	06	4	26	4	10	12	06	19	45	20	01	20	50	38	3	08	51
5	9	00	35	17	00	–6	01	4	28	4	11	12	06	19	43	19	59	20	54	35	3	04	55
6	9	04	26	16	44	–5	55	4	30	4	13	12	06	19	41	19	57	20	58	31	3	00	59
7	9	08	15	16	27	–5	48	4	31	4	15	12	06	19	39	19	55	21	02	28	2	57	03
8	9	12	05	16	10	–5	40	4	33	4	17	12	06	19	37	19	53	21	06	24	2	53	07
9	9	15	53	15	53	–5	32	4	34	4	19	12	05	19	36	19	50	21	10	21	2	49	11
10	9	19	41	15	36	–5	24	4	36	4	21	12	05	19	34	19	48	21	14	17	2	45	16
11	9	23	29	15	18	–5	15	4	38	4	23	12	05	19	32	19	46	21	18	14	2	41	20
12	9	27	15	15	00	–5	05	4	39	4	25	12	05	19	30	19	44	21	22	10	2	37	24
13	9	31	02	14	42	–4	55	4	41	4	27	12	05	19	28	19	41	21	26	07	2	33	28
14	9	34	47	14	24	–4	44	4	42	4	29	12	05	19	26	19	39	21	30	04	2	29	32
15	9	38	32	14	05	–4	32	4	44	4	31	12	04	19	24	19	37	21	34	00	2	25	36
16	9	42	17	13	46	–4	20	4	46	4	33	12	04	19	22	19	34	21	37	57	2	21	40
17	9	46	01	13	27	–4	08	4	47	4	35	12	04	19	20	19	32	21	41	53	2	17	44
18	9	49	44	13	08	–3	55	4	49	4	37	12	04	19	18	19	29	21	45	50	2	13	48
19	9	53	27	12	49	–3	41	4	50	4	39	12	04	19	16	19	27	21	49	46	2	09	52
20	9	57	10	12	29	–3	27	4	52	4	41	12	03	19	13	19	25	21	53	43	2	05	56
21	10	00	52	12	09	–3	12	4	54	4	43	12	03	19	11	19	22	21	57	39	2	02	01
22	10	04	33	11	49	–2	57	4	55	4	45	12	03	19	09	19	20	22	01	36	1	58	05
23	10	08	15	11	29	–2	42	4	57	4	47	12	03	19	07	19	17	22	05	33	1	54	09
24	10	11	55	11	09	–2	26	4	59	4	49	12	02	19	05	19	15	22	09	29	1	50	13
25	10	15	36	10	48	–2	10	5	00	4	50	12	02	19	03	19	12	22	13	26	1	46	17
26	10	19	15	10	27	–1	53	5	02	4	52	12	02	19	00	19	10	22	17	22	1	42	21
27	10	22	55	10	06	–1	36	5	04	4	54	12	01	18	58	19	07	22	21	19	1	38	25
28	10	26	34	9	45	–1	19	5	05	4	56	12	01	18	56	19	05	22	25	15	1	34	29
29	10	30	13	9	24	–1	01	5	07	4	58	12	01	18	54	19	02	22	29	12	1	30	33
30	10	33	51	9	03	–0	43	5	08	5	00	12	01	18	52	19	00	22	33	08	1	26	37
31	10	37	30	8	41	–0	25	5	10	5	02	12	00	18	49	18	57	22	37	05	1	22	41

DURATION OF TWILIGHT (in minutes)

Latitude	52°	56°	52°	56°	52°	56°	52	56°
	1 August		*11 August*		*21 August*		*31 August*	
Civil	41	49	39	45	37	42	35	40
Nautical	97	121	90	107	84	97	79	90
Astronomical	179	TAN	154	210	139	168	128	148

THE NIGHT SKY

Mercury is unsuitably placed for observation at first, since it passes through inferior conjunction on the 5th. For the last ten days in the month it may be seen as a morning object, magnitude +0.5 to –0.9, low above the east-north-east horizon at the beginning of morning civil twilight.

Venus, magnitude –4.0, continues to be visible as a brilliant object in the evening skies, though only visible for about half an hour after sunset, low above the western horizon. Under good conditions the thin crescent Moon may be seen about 4 degrees to the right of Venus on the evening of the 7th and 8th. On the following evening the Moon will be seen about 6 degrees to the left of the planet.

Mars has now become a conspicuous object in the night sky, its magnitude brightening during the month from –0.5 to –1.0. By the end of August it is easily located in the eastern sky before 22h. Mars is in the constellation of Aries. During the night of the 24th–25th the gibbous Moon passes about 5 degrees north of the planet.

Jupiter is still a bright evening object, magnitude –1.8. It is moving towards the Sun and only visible for a short time in the south-western sky before it sets. By the end of the month it is a difficult object to detect in the gathering twilight. The waxing crescent Moon is in the vicinity of the planet on the evenings of the 9th and 10th.

Saturn, magnitude +0.3, slowly becomes visible during the second half of the month, low above the eastern horizon in the early mornings before it is lost in the pre-dawn twilight. The waning crescent Moon will be seen about 8 degrees above the planet on the morning of the 31st.

Neptune is at opposition on the 8th, in the constellation of Capricornus. It is not visible to the naked-eye since its magnitude is +7.8.

Meteors. The maximum of the famous Perseid meteor shower occurs on the 12th, and will be best seen from the late evening onwards.

THE MOON

Day	RA		Dec.	Hor. par.	Semi-diam.	Suns Co-long.	PA of Br. Limb	Ph.	Age	Rise				Transit		Set			
										52°		56°				52°		56°	
	h	m	°	′	′	°	°	%	d	h	m	h	m	h	m	h	m	h	m
1	5	31	+27.9	54.7	14.9	219	92	15	25.5	0	02	—	—	9	11	18	24	19	03
2	6	25	+28.3	54.3	14.8	232	100	9	26.5	0	51	0	13	10	03	19	09	19	45
3	7	19	+27.3	54.1	14.7	244	109	4	27.5	1	53	1	18	10	54	19	42	20	12
4	8	11	+25.1	54.0	14.7	256	124	1	28.5	3	03	2	34	11	43	20	05	20	28
5	9	00	+21.8	53.9	14.7	268	179	0	29.5	4	16	3	54	12	28	20	22	20	39
6	9	47	+17.6	54.0	14.7	281	267	1	0.9	5	30	5	14	13	12	20	35	20	46
7	10	32	+12.7	54.1	14.7	293	283	3	1.9	6	42	6	32	13	53	20	45	20	52
8	11	16	+7.4	54.4	14.8	305	289	7	2.9	7	54	7	49	14	33	20	55	20	57
9	11	58	+1.7	54.7	14.9	317	292	13	3.9	9	06	9	06	15	13	21	04	21	01
10	12	41	–4.0	55.2	15.0	330	293	20	4.9	10	18	10	24	15	53	21	14	21	07
11	13	26	–9.8	55.7	15.2	342	292	29	5.9	11	34	11	46	16	37	21	26	21	13
12	14	12	–15.3	56.4	15.4	354	290	39	6.9	12	54	13	12	17	24	21	41	21	22
13	15	03	–20.2	57.2	15.6	6	286	49	7.9	14	18	14	44	18	15	22	03	21	36
14	15	58	–24.3	58.1	15.8	19	281	60	8.9	15	43	16	17	19	12	22	36	22	01
15	16	58	–27.2	59.0	16.1	31	274	70	9.9	17	02	17	41	20	15	23	26	22	46
16	18	02	–28.4	59.8	16.3	43	266	80	10.9	18	05	18	43	21	20	—	—	—	—
17	19	09	–27.7	60.6	16.5	55	257	89	11.9	18	49	19	20	22	24	0	39	0	01
18	20	14	–24.9	61.1	16.6	67	247	95	12.9	19	18	19	40	23	26	2	09	1	39
19	21	17	–20.4	61.3	16.7	79	230	99	13.9	19	38	19	53	—	—	3	47	3	26
20	22	16	–14.5	61.3	16.7	92	113	100	14.9	19	54	20	01	0	23	5	24	5	11
21	23	12	–7.9	60.8	16.6	104	75	98	15.9	20	06	20	08	1	17	6	57	6	52
22	0	04	–0.9	60.2	16.4	116	69	93	16.9	20	18	20	14	2	07	8	26	8	27
23	0	55	+5.9	59.3	16.2	128	67	85	17.9	20	30	20	21	2	55	9	52	10	00
24	1	46	+12.3	58.4	15.9	140	68	77	18.9	20	44	20	29	3	43	11	17	11	31
25	2	36	+17.8	57.4	15.6	153	71	67	19.9	21	02	20	40	4	32	12	41	13	02
26	3	29	+22.4	56.5	15.4	165	75	57	20.9	21	26	20	57	5	22	14	02	14	31
27	4	22	+25.8	55.7	15.2	177	81	46	21.9	21	59	21	23	6	14	15	17	15	52
28	5	17	+27.8	55.1	15.0	189	87	37	22.9	22	45	22	06	7	06	16	20	17	00
29	6	12	+28.5	54.6	14.9	201	94	28	23.9	23	43	23	06	7	59	17	10	17	48
30	7	06	+27.8	54.3	14.8	214	100	20	24.9	—	—	—	—	8	51	17	46	18	18
31	7	58	+25.8	54.1	14.7	226	107	13	25.9	0	51	0	19	9	40	18	11	18	37

MERCURY

Day	RA		Dec.	Diam.	Phase	Transit		5° high			
								52°		56°	
	h	m	°	″	%	h	m	h	m	h	m
1	9	13	+11.0	11	4	12	31	18	54	19	00
3	9	08	+11.4	11	2	12	17	18	42	18	48
5	9	02	+11.8	11	1	12	04	18	31	18	38
7	8	56	+12.4	11	1	11	50	5	20	5	13
9	8	50	+13.0	11	2	11	37	5	04	4	56
11	8	46	+13.7	10	5	11	25	4	48	4	40
13	8	43	+14.4	10	8	11	15	4	34	4	25
15	8	42	+15.0	10	12	11	06	4	21	4	12
17	8	42	+15.5	9	18	10	59	4	11	4	01
19	8	44	+16.0	9	24	10	54	4	04	3	53
21	8	49	+16.3	8	31	10	51	3	59	3	48
23	8	55	+16.5	8	39	10	50	3	57	3	46
25	9	04	+16.4	7	47	10	51	3	57	3	47
27	9	14	+16.2	7	55	10	53	4	01	3	50
29	9	25	+15.8	6	64	10	57	4	07	3	57
31	9	38	+15.2	6	71	11	02	4	15	4	06

VENUS

Day	RA		Dec.	Diam.	Phase	Transit		5° high			
								52°		56°	
h	h	m	°	″	%	h	m	h	m	h	m
1	10	51	+8.8	12	83	14	13	20	23	20	27
6	11	13	+6.3	13	82	14	15	20	13	20	14
11	11	35	+3.8	13	81	14	17	20	02	20	01
16	11	56	+1.3	13	79	14	19	19	50	19	48
21	12	18	–1.3	14	78	14	20	19	39	19	34
26	12	39	–3.9	14	76	14	22	19	27	19	20
31	13	00	–6.4	15	75	14	23	19	15	19	05

MARS

Day	RA		Dec.	Diam.	Phase	Transit		5° high			
								52°		56°	
	h	m	°	″	%	h	m	h	m	h	m
1	2	04	+9.6	11	84	5	25	23	06	23	01
6	2	15	+10.5	12	85	5	16	22	52	22	46
11	2	25	+11.4	12	85	5	06	22	38	22	32
16	2	35	+12.2	13	85	4	56	22	24	22	17
21	2	44	+12.9	13	86	4	46	22	09	22	02
26	2	52	+13.6	13	86	4	35	21	55	21	47
31	3	00	+14.2	14	87	4	23	21	39	21	31

SUNRISE AND SUNSET

	London				*Bristol*				*Birmingham*				*Manchester*				*Newcastle*				*Glasgow*				*Belfast*			
	0°05′		*51°30′*		*2°35′*		*51°28′*		*1°55′*		*52°28′*		*2°15′*		*53°28′*		*1°37′*		*54°59′*		*4°14′*		*55°52′*		*5°56′*		*54°35′*	
	h	*m*	*h*	*m*	*h*	*m*	*h*	*m*	*h*	*m*	*h*	*m*	*h*	*m*	*h*	*m*	*h*	*m*	*h*	*m*	*h*	*m*	*h*	*m*	*h*	*m*	*h*	*m*
1	4	24	19	48	4	34	19	58	4	27	19	59	4	25	20	05	4	15	20	09	4	21	20	24	4	34	20	24
2	4	25	19	47	4	36	19	56	4	29	19	58	4	26	20	03	4	17	20	07	4	23	20	22	4	36	20	23
3	4	27	19	45	4	37	19	55	4	31	19	56	4	28	20	01	4	19	20	05	4	25	20	20	4	38	20	21
4	4	29	19	43	4	39	19	53	4	32	19	54	4	30	19	59	4	21	20	03	4	27	20	18	4	40	20	19
5	4	30	19	41	4	40	19	51	4	34	19	52	4	31	19	57	4	22	20	01	4	29	20	15	4	41	20	17
6	4	32	19	40	4	42	19	50	4	35	19	50	4	33	19	55	4	24	19	59	4	31	20	13	4	43	20	15
7	4	33	19	38	4	43	19	48	4	37	19	49	4	35	19	54	4	26	19	57	4	33	20	11	4	45	20	13
8	4	35	19	36	4	45	19	46	4	39	19	47	4	36	19	52	4	28	19	55	4	35	20	09	4	47	20	11
9	4	36	19	34	4	46	19	44	4	40	19	45	4	38	19	50	4	30	19	53	4	37	20	07	4	49	20	08
10	4	38	19	32	4	48	19	42	4	42	19	43	4	40	19	48	4	32	19	51	4	39	20	05	4	51	20	06
11	4	39	19	30	4	50	19	40	4	44	19	41	4	42	19	46	4	34	19	48	4	41	20	02	4	52	20	04
12	4	41	19	29	4	51	19	38	4	45	19	39	4	43	19	43	4	35	19	46	4	42	20	00	4	54	20	02
13	4	43	19	27	4	53	19	36	4	47	19	37	4	45	19	41	4	37	19	44	4	44	19	58	4	56	20	00
14	4	44	19	25	4	54	19	35	4	49	19	35	4	47	19	39	4	39	19	42	4	46	19	55	4	58	19	58
15	4	46	19	23	4	56	19	33	4	50	19	33	4	49	19	37	4	41	19	40	4	48	19	53	5	00	19	55
16	4	47	19	21	4	57	19	31	4	52	19	31	4	50	19	35	4	43	19	37	4	50	19	51	5	01	19	53
17	4	49	19	19	4	59	19	29	4	54	19	29	4	52	19	33	4	45	19	35	4	52	19	48	5	03	19	51
18	4	51	19	17	5	01	19	27	4	55	19	27	4	54	19	31	4	47	19	33	4	54	19	46	5	05	19	49
19	4	52	19	15	5	02	19	24	4	57	19	24	4	55	19	28	4	48	19	30	4	56	19	44	5	07	19	46
20	4	54	19	12	5	04	19	22	4	59	19	22	4	57	19	26	4	50	19	28	4	58	19	41	5	09	19	44
21	4	55	19	10	5	05	19	20	5	00	19	20	4	59	19	24	4	52	19	26	5	00	19	39	5	11	19	42
22	4	57	19	08	5	07	19	18	5	02	19	18	5	01	19	22	4	54	19	23	5	02	19	36	5	12	19	39
23	4	59	19	06	5	09	19	16	5	04	19	16	5	02	19	19	4	56	19	21	5	04	19	34	5	14	19	37
24	5	00	19	04	5	10	19	14	5	05	19	14	5	04	19	17	4	58	19	18	5	06	19	31	5	16	19	35
25	5	02	19	02	5	12	19	12	5	07	19	11	5	06	19	15	5	00	19	16	5	08	19	29	5	18	19	32
26	5	03	19	00	5	13	19	10	5	09	19	09	5	08	19	13	5	02	19	14	5	10	19	26	5	20	19	30
27	5	05	18	58	5	15	19	08	5	10	19	07	5	09	19	10	5	03	19	11	5	12	19	24	5	22	19	27
28	5	06	18	55	5	17	19	05	5	12	19	05	5	11	19	08	5	05	19	09	5	14	19	21	5	23	19	25
29	5	08	18	53	5	18	19	03	5	14	19	02	5	13	19	06	5	07	19	06	5	16	19	19	5	25	19	23
30	5	10	18	51	5	20	19	01	5	15	19	00	5	15	19	03	5	09	19	04	5	18	19	16	5	27	19	20
31	5	11	18	49	5	21	18	59	5	17	18	58	5	16	19	01	5	11	19	01	5	19	19	14	5	29	19	18

JUPITER

Day	*RA*		*Dec.*		*Transit*		*5° high*			
							52°		*56°*	
	h	*m*	°	′	*h*	*m*	*h*	*m*	*h*	*m*
1	12	50.8	−4	09	16	10	21	14	21	08
11	12	56.4	−4	46	15	36	20	37	20	30
21	13	02.6	−5	26	15	03	20	01	19	53
31	13	09.3	−6	09	14	30	19	24	19	15

Diameters – equatorial 33″ polar 31″

SATURN

Day	*RA*		*Dec.*		*Transit*		*5° high*			
							52°		*56°*	
	h	*m*	°	′	*h*	*m*	*h*	*m*	*h*	*m*
1	8	17.3	+20	00	11	37	4	24	4	10
11	8	22.6	+19	44	11	03	3	52	3	38
21	8	27.8	+19	27	10	29	3	19	3	06
31	8	32.7	+19	11	9	54	2	47	2	33

Diameters – equatorial 16″ polar 15″

Rings – major axis 37″ minor axis 13″

URANUS

Day	*RA*		*Dec.*		*Transit*		*5° high*			
							52°		*56°*	
	h	*m*	°	′	*h*	*m*	*h*	*m*	*h*	*m*
1	22	47.2	−8	35	2	08	21	59	22	15
11	22	45.9	−8	43	1	27	21	19	21	35
21	22	44.5	−8	52	0	47	20	39	20	56
31	22	43.0	−9	01	0	06	20	00	20	16

Diameter 4″

NEPTUNE

Day	*RA*		*Dec.*		*Transit*		*5° high*			
							52°		*56°*	
	h	*m*	°	′	*h*	*m*	*h*	*m*	*h*	*m*
1	21	15.6	−16	03	0	37	3	50	3	22
11	21	14.6	−16	08	23	52	3	09	2	41
21	21	13.5	−16	13	23	12	2	28	2	00
31	21	12.5	−16	18	22	32	1	47	1	18

Diameter 2″

SEPTEMBER 2005

NINTH MONTH, 30 DAYS. *Septem* (seven), seventh month of Roman pre-Julian calendar

1	*Thursday*	Edgar Rice Burroughs b. 1875. Francois Mauriac d. 1970	244
2	*Friday*	Henri Rousseau d. 1910. J. R. R. Tolkien d. 1973	245
3	*Saturday*	Joseph Wright b. 1734. E. E. Cummings d. 1962	246
4	*Sunday*	Edvard Grieg d. 1907. Georges Simenon d. 1989	247
5	*Monday*	Louis XIV b. 1638. Victorien Sardou b. 1831	week 36 day 248
6	*Tuesday*	James II d. 1701. John Clavell d. 1994	249
7	*Wednesday*	Elizabeth I b. 1533. Dame Edith Sitwell b. 1887	250
8	*Thursday*	Richard I (The Lionheart) b. 1157. Antonín Dvorák b. 1841	251
9	*Friday*	Leo Tolstoy b. 1828. William I (The Conqueror) d. 1087	252
10	*Saturday*	Sir John Soane b. 1753. Mary Wollstonecraft Godwin d. 1797	253
11	*Sunday*	D. H. Lawrence b. 1885. Jessica Tandy d. 1994	254
12	*Monday*	Louis MacNeice b. 1907. Peter Mark Roget d. 1869	week 37 day 255
13	*Tuesday*	Dante Alighieri d. 1321. Leopold Stokowski d. 1977	256
14	*Wednesday*	Princess Grace of Monaco d. 1982. Isadora Duncan d. 1927	257
15	*Thursday*	Dame Agatha Christie b. 1890. Prince Henry of Wales b. 1984	258
16	*Friday*	Henry V b. 1387. Louis XVIII, King of France d. 1824	259
17	*Saturday*	Sir Frederick Ashton b. 1904. William Henry Fox Talbot d. 1871	260
18	*Sunday*	Dr Samuel Johnson b. 1709. William Hazlitt d. 1830	261
19	*Monday*	Sir William Golding b. 1911. Jeremy Irons b. 1948	week 38 day 262
20	*Tuesday*	Stevie Smith b. 1902. Jean Sibelius d. 1957	263
21	*Wednesday*	H. G. Wells b. 1866. Sir Walter Scott d. 1832	264
22	*Thursday*	Fay Weldon b. 1931. Irving Berlin d. 1989	265
23	*Friday*	Ferdinand VI, King of Spain b. 1713. Pablo Neruda d. 1973	266
24	*Saturday*	Horace Walpole b. 1717. F. Scott Fitzgerald b. 1896	267
25	*Sunday*	Mark Rothko b. 1903. Dimitry Shostakovich b. 1906	268
26	*Monday*	George Gershwin b. 1898. Béla Bartók d. 1945	week 39 day 269
27	*Tuesday*	Ariel Sharon b. 1928. Edgar Degas d. 1917	270
28	*Wednesday*	Herman Melville d. 1891. Sir Robert Helpman d. 1986	271
29	*Thursday*	W. H. Auden d. 1973. Roy Lichtenstein d. 1997	272
30	*Friday*	Truman Capote b. 1924. Patrick White d. 1990	273

ASTRONOMICAL PHENOMENA

d	*h*	
1	03	Uranus at opposition
2	00	Jupiter in conjunction with Venus. Jupiter 1° N.
2	11	Pluto at stationary point
2	12	Mercury in conjunction with Moon. Mercury 3° S.
6	22	Jupiter in conjunction with Moon. Jupiter 2° N.
7	09	Venus in conjunction with Moon. Venus 0°.6 N.
18	03	Mercury in superior conjunction
22	04	Mars in conjunction with Moon. Mars 6° S.
22	22	Sun's longitude 180° ♎
28	08	Saturn in conjunction with Moon. Saturn 4° S.

MINIMA OF ALGOL

d	*h*	*d*	*h*	*d*	*h*
2	00.9	13	12.2	24	23.4
4	21.8	16	09.0	27	20.2
7	18.6	19	05.8	30	17.0
10	15.4	22	02.6	17	

CONSTELLATIONS

The following constellations are near their meridian at

	d	*h*		*d*	*h*
August	1	24	September	15	21
August	16	23	October	1	20
September	1	22	October	16	19

Draco, Cepheus, Lyra, Cygnus, Vulpecula, Sagitta, Delphinus, Equuleus, Aquila, Aquarius and Capricornus

THE MOON

Phases, Apsides and Node	*d*	*h*	*m*
● New Moon	3	18	45
☽ First Quarter	11	11	37
○ Full Moon	18	02	01
☾ Last Quarter	25	06	41
Apogee (406,192 km)	1	02	46
Perigee (360,418 km)	16	13	59
Apogee (405,275 km)	28	15	26

Mean longitude of ascending node on September 1, 15°

THE SUN

s.d. 15′.9

Day	Right Ascension			Dec.		Equation of time		Rise 52°		Rise 56°		Transit		Set 52°		Set 56°		Sidereal time			Transit of first point of Aries		
	h	*m*	*s*	°	′	*m*	*s*	*h*	*m*	*h*	*m*	*h*	*m*	*h*	*m*	*h*	*m*	*h*	*m*	*s*	*h*	*m*	*s*
1	10	41	07	+8	19	−0	06	5	12	5	04	12	00	18	47	18	54	22	41	02	1	18	46
2	10	44	45	+7	58	+0	13	5	13	5	06	12	00	18	45	18	52	22	44	58	1	14	50
3	10	48	22	+7	36	+0	33	5	15	5	08	11	59	18	43	18	49	22	48	55	1	10	54
4	10	51	59	+7	14	+0	52	5	17	5	10	11	59	18	40	18	47	22	52	51	1	06	58
5	10	55	36	+6	51	+1	12	5	18	5	12	11	59	18	38	18	44	22	56	48	1	03	02
6	10	59	12	+6	29	+1	32	5	20	5	14	11	58	18	36	18	41	23	00	44	0	59	06
7	11	02	49	+6	07	+1	52	5	21	5	16	11	58	18	33	18	39	23	04	41	0	55	10
8	11	06	25	+5	44	+2	13	5	23	5	18	11	58	18	31	18	36	23	08	37	0	51	14
9	11	10	01	+5	22	+2	33	5	25	5	20	11	57	18	29	18	33	23	12	34	0	47	18
10	11	13	36	+4	59	+2	54	5	26	5	22	11	57	18	26	18	31	23	16	31	0	43	22
11	11	17	12	+4	36	+3	15	5	28	5	24	11	57	18	24	18	28	23	20	27	0	39	26
12	11	20	47	+4	13	+3	36	5	30	5	26	11	56	18	22	18	26	23	24	24	0	35	31
13	11	24	23	+3	50	+3	57	5	31	5	28	11	56	18	19	18	23	23	28	20	0	31	35
14	11	27	58	+3	27	+4	19	5	33	5	30	11	56	18	17	18	20	23	32	17	0	27	39
15	11	31	33	+3	04	+4	40	5	35	5	32	11	55	18	15	18	18	23	36	13	0	23	43
16	11	35	08	+2	41	+5	02	5	36	5	34	11	55	18	12	18	15	23	40	10	0	19	47
17	11	38	43	+2	18	+5	23	5	38	5	35	11	54	18	10	18	12	23	44	06	0	15	51
18	11	42	18	+1	55	+5	45	5	39	5	37	11	54	18	08	18	10	23	48	03	0	11	55
19	11	45	53	+1	32	+6	06	5	41	5	39	11	54	18	05	18	07	23	52	00	0	07	59
20	11	49	29	+1	08	+6	27	5	43	5	41	11	53	18	03	18	04	23	55	56	0	04	03
21	11	53	04	+0	45	+6	49	5	44	5	43	11	53	18	01	18	02	23	59	53	0	00	07
22	11	56	39	+0	22	+7	10	5	46	5	45	11	53	17	58	17	59	0	03	49	23 23	56 52	11 16
23	12	00	15	−0	02	+7	31	5	48	5	47	11	52	17	56	17	56	0	07	46	23	48	20
24	12	03	50	−0	25	+7	52	5	49	5	49	11	52	17	54	17	54	0	11	42	23	44	24
25	12	07	26	−0	48	+8	13	5	51	5	51	11	52	17	51	17	51	0	15	39	23	40	28
26	12	11	02	−1	12	+8	34	5	53	5	53	11	51	17	49	17	48	0	19	35	23	36	32
27	12	14	38	−1	35	+8	54	5	54	5	55	11	51	17	47	17	46	0	23	32	23	32	36
28	12	18	14	−1	58	+9	14	5	56	5	57	11	51	17	44	17	43	0	27	28	23	28	40
29	12	21	51	−2	22	+9	34	5	57	5	59	11	50	17	42	17	40	0	31	25	23	24	44
30	12	25	27	−2	45	+9	54	5	59	6	01	11	50	17	40	17	38	0	35	22	23	20	48

DURATION OF TWILIGHT (in minutes)

Latitude	*52°*	*56°*	*52°*	*56°*	*52°*	*56°*	*52°*	*56*
	1 September		*11 September*		*21 September*		*31 September*	
Civil	35	39	34	38	34	37	34	37
Nautical	79	89	76	85	74	82	73	80
Astronomical	127	147	120	136	116	129	113	125

THE NIGHT SKY

Mercury continues to be visible in the mornings but only for the first 4 or 5 days of the month, magnitude −1.1, low above the east-north-eastern horizon, around the time of beginning of morning civil twilight. On the morning of the 2nd the old crescent Moon, barely 1.5 days before New, passes 2 degrees north of the planet.

Venus, magnitude −4.1, is a brilliant object in the early evening sky, but still only visible for about half an hour after sunset, low above the south-western horizon. Under good conditions the four-day old crescent Moon will be seen about 5 degrees to the left of Venus on the evening of the 7th.

Mars is a conspicuous object, its magnitude brightening from −1.0 to −1.7 during the month. By the end of September it becomes visible low in the eastern sky shortly after the end of evening astronomical twilight. During the month Mars moves from Aries into Taurus. During the night of the 21st–22nd the waning gibbous Moon passes 5 degrees north of the planet.

Jupiter, although technically an evening object, is lost in the gathering twilight and will not be seen again until it reappears in the morning skies in November.

Saturn, magnitude +0.3, continues to be visible as a morning object in the south-eastern quadrant of the sky. Saturn is in the constellation of Gemini. On the morning of the 1st the thin, waning crescent Moon, less than 3 days before New, may be detected about 6 degrees to the left of, and 2 degrees lower than the planet.

Uranus is at opposition on the 1st, in the constellation of Aquarius. Uranus is barely visible to the naked eye as its magnitude is +5.7, but it is readily located with only small optical aid.

Zodiacal Light. The morning cone may be seen reaching up from the eastern horizon along the ecliptic, before the beginning of morning twilight, from the 3rd to the 16th.

THE MOON

Day	RA		Dec.	Hor. par.	Semi-diam.	Sun's Co-long.	PA of Br. Limb	Ph.	Age	Rise 52°		Rise 56°		Transit		Set 52°		Set 56°	
	h	m	°	′	′	°	°	%	d	h	m	h	m	h	m	h	m	h	m
1	8	48	+22.8	54.0	14.7	238	113	7	26.9	2	04	1	39	10	26	18	30	18	49
2	9	36	+18.7	54.0	14.7	250	120	3	27.9	3	18	3	00	11	10	18	43	18	57
3	10	21	+14.0	54.2	14.8	263	133	1	28.9	4	31	4	20	11	52	18	54	19	03
4	11	05	+8.7	54.4	14.8	275	246	0	0.2	5	44	5	38	12	33	19	04	19	08
5	11	48	+3.0	54.7	14.9	287	287	1	1.2	6	56	6	55	13	13	19	13	19	12
6	12	31	−2.8	55.0	15.0	299	292	5	2.2	8	09	8	13	13	53	19	23	19	17
7	13	15	−8.6	55.5	15.1	312	293	10	3.2	9	24	9	34	14	36	19	34	19	22
8	14	01	−14.2	56.0	15.3	324	292	16	4.2	10	42	10	58	15	21	19	48	19	30
9	14	50	−19.2	56.6	15.4	336	289	25	5.2	12	04	12	27	16	10	20	06	19	42
10	15	43	−23.5	57.2	15.6	348	284	34	6.2	13	27	13	59	17	04	20	34	20	01
11	16	40	−26.7	57.9	15.8	0	278	45	7.2	14	47	15	26	18	03	21	15	20	36
12	17	42	−28.4	58.7	16.0	13	271	56	8.2	15	55	16	35	19	05	22	17	21	36
13	18	46	−28.3	59.4	16.2	25	264	67	9.2	16	44	17	19	20	08	23	38	23	04
14	19	50	−26.3	60.0	16.3	37	256	77	10.2	17	18	17	44	21	09	—	—	—	—
15	20	52	−22.5	60.5	16.5	49	249	86	11.2	17	41	17	59	22	07	1	11	0	45
16	21	51	−17.2	60.8	16.6	61	243	94	12.2	17	58	18	09	23	01	2	47	2	30
17	22	47	−10.9	60.8	16.6	74	237	98	13.2	18	11	18	16	23	53	4	21	4	12
18	23	41	−4.0	60.6	16.5	86	190	100	14.2	18	23	18	22	—	—	5	52	5	50
19	0	33	+3.0	60.0	16.4	98	69	99	15.2	18	35	18	28	0	42	7	21	7	25
20	1	24	+9.8	59.3	16.2	110	66	95	16.2	18	49	18	36	1	31	8	48	8	59
21	2	16	+15.9	58.4	15.9	122	68	89	17.2	19	05	18	45	2	21	10	15	10	33
22	3	09	+21.0	57.5	15.7	134	72	81	18.2	19	26	19	00	3	12	11	40	12	06
23	4	04	+24.9	56.6	15.4	147	77	72	19.2	19	56	19	22	4	04	13	01	13	34
24	4	59	+27.4	55.8	15.2	159	83	63	20.2	20	37	19	58	4	58	14	11	14	50
25	5	55	+28.5	55.2	15.0	171	89	53	21.2	21	32	20	53	5	52	15	07	15	46
26	6	50	+28.2	54.7	14.9	183	96	43	22.2	22	37	22	03	6	45	15	48	16	22
27	7	43	+26.6	54.3	14.8	195	102	34	23.2	23	49	23	22	7	35	16	16	16	44
28	8	34	+23.8	54.1	14.7	208	107	25	24.2	—	—	—	—	8	23	16	37	16	58
29	9	23	+20.0	54.1	14.7	220	112	17	25.2	1	04	0	43	9	07	16	52	17	07
30	10	09	+15.4	54.2	14.8	232	115	11	26.2	2	18	2	04	9	50	17	03	17	14

MERCURY

Day	RA		Dec.	Diam.	Phase	Transit		5° high 52°		5° high 56°	
	h	m	°	″	%	h	m	h	m	h	m
1	9	44	+14.8	6	75	11	05	4	20	4	11
3	9	58	+13.9	6	82	11	11	4	31	4	23
5	10	12	+12.8	6	87	11	17	4	44	4	36
7	10	27	+11.5	5	91	11	24	4	57	4	51
9	10	41	+10.2	5	95	11	30	5	11	5	06
11	10	56	+8.8	5	97	11	37	5	25	5	21
13	11	10	+7.3	5	99	11	43	5	39	5	36
15	11	24	+5.7	5	99	11	49	5	53	5	51
17	11	38	+4.2	5	100	11	55	6	06	6	07
19	11	51	+2.6	5	100	12	00	17	39	17	37
21	12	04	+1.0	5	100	12	06	17	36	17	33
23	12	17	−0.6	5	99	12	10	17	32	17	28
25	12	29	−2.1	5	99	12	15	17	29	17	23
27	12	42	−3.7	5	98	12	19	17	25	17	18
29	12	54	−5.2	5	97	12	24	17	21	17	13
31	13	06	−6.7	5	96	12	28	17	17	17	07

VENUS

Day	RA		Dec.	Diam.	Phase	Transit		5° high 52°		5° high 56°	
h	h	m	°	″	%	h	m	h	m	h	m
1	13	05	−6.9	15	74	14	24	19	12	19	02
6	13	26	−9.4	15	73	14	26	19	00	18	48
11	13	48	−11.8	16	71	14	27	18	48	18	33
16	14	09	−14.2	16	70	14	30	18	36	18	18
21	14	32	−16.3	17	68	14	32	18	24	18	03
26	14	54	−18.4	17	66	14	35	18	12	17	48
31	15	17	−20.3	18	64	14	38	18	02	17	33

MARS

Day	RA		Dec.	Diam.	Phase	Transit		5° high 52°		5° high 56°	
	h	m	°	″	%	h	m	h	m	h	m
1	3	02	+14.3	14	87	4	20	21	36	21	28
6	3	09	+14.8	15	88	4	07	21	21	21	12
11	3	15	+15.3	15	89	3	54	21	04	20	55
16	3	19	+15.7	16	90	3	39	20	47	20	37
21	3	23	+16.0	17	91	3	23	20	29	20	19
26	3	25	+16.3	17	92	3	05	20	10	20	00
31	3	26	+16.5	18	93	2	47	19	50	19	40

SUNRISE AND SUNSET

	London		*Bristol*		*Birmingham*		*Manchester*		*Newcastle*		*Glasgow*		*Belfast*	
	0°05′	*51°30′*	*2°35′*	*51°28′*	*1°55′*	*52°28′*	*2°15′*	*53°28′*	*1°37′*	*54°59′*	*4°14′*	*55°52′*	*5°56′*	*54°35′*
	h m	*h m*	*h m*	*h m*	*h m*	*h m*	*h m*	*h m*	*h m*	*h m*	*h m*	*h m*	*h m*	*h m*
1	5 13	18 47	5 23	18 57	5 19	18 56	5 18	18 59	5 13	18 59	5 21	19 11	5 31	19 15
2	5 14	18 44	5 25	18 54	5 20	18 53	5 20	18 56	5 15	18 56	5 23	19 08	5 33	19 13
3	5 16	18 42	5 26	18 52	5 22	18 51	5 22	18 54	5 16	18 54	5 25	19 06	5 34	19 10
4	5 18	18 40	5 28	18 50	5 24	18 49	5 23	18 51	5 18	18 51	5 27	19 03	5 36	19 08
5	5 19	18 38	5 29	18 48	5 25	18 46	5 25	18 49	5 20	18 49	5 29	19 01	5 38	19 05
6	5 21	18 35	5 31	18 45	5 27	18 44	5 27	18 47	5 22	18 46	5 31	18 58	5 40	19 03
7	5 22	18 33	5 32	18 43	5 29	18 42	5 29	18 44	5 24	18 44	5 33	18 55	5 42	19 00
8	5 24	18 31	5 34	18 41	5 30	18 39	5 30	18 42	5 26	18 41	5 35	18 53	5 44	18 58
9	5 26	18 29	5 36	18 38	5 32	18 37	5 32	18 39	5 28	18 39	5 37	18 50	5 45	18 55
10	5 27	18 26	5 37	18 36	5 34	18 35	5 34	18 37	5 30	18 36	5 39	18 48	5 47	18 53
11	5 29	18 24	5 39	18 34	5 35	18 32	5 36	18 34	5 31	18 33	5 41	18 45	5 49	18 50
12	5 30	18 22	5 40	18 32	5 37	18 30	5 37	18 32	5 33	18 31	5 43	18 42	5 51	18 48
13	5 32	18 19	5 42	18 29	5 39	18 27	5 39	18 30	5 35	18 28	5 45	18 40	5 53	18 45
14	5 34	18 17	5 44	18 27	5 40	18 25	5 41	18 27	5 37	18 26	5 47	18 37	5 55	18 43
15	5 35	18 15	5 45	18 25	5 42	18 23	5 43	18 25	5 39	18 23	5 49	18 34	5 56	18 40
16	5 37	18 12	5 47	18 22	5 44	18 20	5 44	18 22	5 41	18 21	5 51	18 32	5 58	18 38
17	5 38	18 10	5 48	18 20	5 45	18 18	5 46	18 20	5 43	18 18	5 52	18 29	6 00	18 35
18	5 40	18 08	5 50	18 18	5 47	18 16	5 48	18 17	5 44	18 16	5 54	18 26	6 02	18 33
19	5 42	18 06	5 52	18 16	5 49	18 13	5 49	18 15	5 46	18 13	5 56	18 24	6 04	18 30
20	5 43	18 03	5 53	18 13	5 50	18 11	5 51	18 12	5 48	18 10	5 58	18 21	6 06	18 27
21	5 45	18 01	5 55	18 11	5 52	18 08	5 53	18 10	5 50	18 08	6 00	18 18	6 07	18 25
22	5 46	17 59	5 56	18 09	5 54	18 06	5 55	18 08	5 52	18 05	6 02	18 16	6 09	18 22
23	5 48	17 56	5 58	18 06	5 55	18 04	5 56	18 05	5 54	18 03	6 04	18 13	6 11	18 20
24	5 50	17 54	6 00	18 04	5 57	18 01	5 58	18 03	5 56	18 00	6 06	18 11	6 13	18 17
25	5 51	17 52	6 01	18 02	5 59	17 59	6 00	18 00	5 57	17 58	6 08	18 08	6 15	18 15
26	5 53	17 49	6 03	17 59	6 00	17 57	6 02	17 58	5 59	17 55	6 10	18 05	6 17	18 12
27	5 54	17 47	6 04	17 57	6 02	17 54	6 04	17 55	6 01	17 52	6 12	18 03	6 18	18 10
28	5 56	17 45	6 06	17 55	6 04	17 52	6 05	17 53	6 03	17 50	6 14	18 00	6 20	18 07
29	5 58	17 43	6 08	17 53	6 05	17 49	6 07	17 50	6 05	17 47	6 16	17 57	6 22	18 05
30	5 59	17 40	6 09	17 50	6 07	17 47	6 09	17 48	6 07	17 45	6 18	17 55	6 24	18 02

JUPITER

Day	*RA*		*Dec.*		*Transit*		*5° high*			
							52°		*56°*	
	h	*m*	°	′	*h*	*m*	*h*	*m*	*h*	*m*
1	13	10.0	−6	14	14	27	19	21	19	12
11	13	17.2	−6	59	13	55	18	44	18	35
21	13	24.7	−7	45	13	23	18	08	17	58
31	13	32.6	−8	32	12	52	17	32	17	21

Diameters – equatorial 31″ polar 29″

SATURN

Day	*RA*		*Dec.*		*Transit*		*5° high*			
							52°		*56°*	
	h	*m*	°	′	*h*	*m*	*h*	*m*	*h*	*m*
1	8	33.2	+19	09	9	51	2	43	2	30
11	8	37.8	+18	53	9	16	2	10	1	57
21	8	42.0	+18	39	8	41	1	36	1	23
31	8	45.8	+18	25	8	05	1	02	0	49

Diameters – equatorial 17″ polar 15″
Rings – major axis 38″ minor axis 12″

URANUS

Day	*RA*		*Dec.*		*Transit*		*10° high*			
							52°		*56°*	
	h	*m*	°	′	*h*	*m*	*h*	*m*	*h*	*m*
1	22	42.8	−9	02	0	02	4	04	3	48
11	22	41.3	−9	10	23	17	3	22	3	06
21	22	39.9	−9	19	22	36	2	41	2	24
31	22	38.6	−9	27	21	56	1	59	1	42

Diameter 4″

NEPTUNE

Day	*RA*		*Dec.*		*Transit*		*10° high*			
							52°		*56°*	
	h	*m*	°	′	*h*	*m*	*h*	*m*	*h*	*m*
1	21	12.4	−16	18	22	28	1	43	1	14
11	21	11.5	−16	22	21	47	1	03	0	33
21	21	10.7	−16	26	21	07	0	22	23	49
31	21	10.0	−16	29	20	27	23	38	23	08

Diameter 2″

♎ OCTOBER 2005 ♏

TENTH MONTH, 31 DAYS. *Octo* (eighth), eighth month of Roman pre-Julian calendar

1	*Saturday*	Henry III b. 1207. Sir Edwin Landseer d. 1873	274
2	*Sunday*	Richard III b. 1452. Graham Greene b. 1904	275
3	*Monday*	William Morris d. 1896. Jean Anouilh d. 1987	week 40 day 276
4	*Tuesday*	Jean Francois Millet b. 1814. Rembrandt d. 1669	277
5	*Wednesday*	Václav Havel b. 1936. Joachim Patinir d. 1524	278
6	*Thursday*	Le Corbusier b. 1887. Lord Tennyson d. 1862	279
7	*Friday*	James Whitcomb Riley b. 1849. Edgar Allen Poe d. 1849	280
8	*Saturday*	John Cowper Powys b. 1872. Henry Fielding d. 1754	281
9	*Sunday*	Giuseppe Verdi b. 1813. André Maurois d. 1967	282
10	*Monday*	James Clavell b. 1924. Harold Pinter b. 1930	week 41 day 283
11	*Tuesday*	Francois Mauriac b. 1885. Jean Cocteau d. 1963	284
12	*Wednesday*	Edward VI b. 1537. Ralph Vaughan Williams b. 1872	285
13	*Thursday*	Alan Ramsay b. 1713. Margaret Thatcher b. 1925	286
14	*Friday*	Harold II d. 1066. Leonard Bernstein d. 1990	287
15	*Saturday*	Sir P. G. Wodehouse b. 1881. James Tissot b. 1836	288
16	*Sunday*	Oscar Wilde b. 1854. Marie-Antoinette d. 1793	289
17	*Monday*	Georg Büchner b. 1813. Frédéric Chopin d. 1849	week 42 day 290
18	*Tuesday*	Canaletto b. 1697. Charles Babbage d. 1871	291
19	*Wednesday*	Leigh Hunt b. 1784. Jean-George Navarre d. 1810	292
20	*Thursday*	Sir Christopher Wren b. 1632. Thomas Hughes b. 1822	293
21	*Friday*	Samuel Taylor Coleridge b. 1772. Jack Kerouac d. 1969	294
22	*Saturday*	Franz Liszt b. 1811. Paul Cézanne d. 1906	295
23	*Sunday*	Robert Bridges b. 1844. Michael Crichton b. 1942	296
24	*Monday*	Luciano Berio b. 1925. Jane Seymour d. 1537	week 43 day 297
25	*Tuesday*	Pablo Picasso b. 1881. Geoffrey Chaucer d. 1400	298
26	*Wednesday*	Domenico Scarlatti b. 1685. William Hogarth d. 1764	299
27	*Thursday*	Dylan Thomas b. 1914. Sylvia Plath b. 1932	300
28	*Friday*	Francis Bacon b. 1909. Ted Hughes d. 1998	301
29	*Saturday*	Joseph Pulitzer d. 1911. Sir Kenneth Macmillan d. 1992	302
30	*Sunday*	Ezra Pound b. 1885. Robert Volkmann d. 1883	303
31	*Monday*	John Evelyn b. 1626. Augustus John d. 1961	week 44 day 304

ASTRONOMICAL PHENOMENA

d	*h*	
1	22	Mars at stationary point
3	10	Annular eclipse of Sun
4	11	Mercury in conjunction with Moon. Mercury 0°.8 N.
4	15	Jupiter in conjunction with Moon. Jupiter 2° N.
5	22	Jupiter in conjunction with Mercury. Jupiter 1° N.
7	06	Venus in conjunction with Moon. Venus 1° N.
17	12	Partial eclipse of Moon
19	11	Mars in conjunction with Moon. Mars 5° S.
22	13	Jupiter in conjunction
23	08	Sun's longitude 210° ♏
25	19	Saturn in conjunction with Moon. Saturn 4° S.
26	23	Neptune at stationary point

MINIMA OF ALGOL

d	*h*	*d*	*h*	*d*	*h*
3	13.9	15	01.1	26	12.4
6	10.7	17	21.9	29	09.2
9	07.5	20	18.7		
12	04.3	23	15.5		

CONSTELLATIONS

The following constellations are near their meridian at

	d	*h*		*d*	*h*
September	1	24	October	16	21
September	15	23	November	1	20
October	1	22	November	15	19

Ursa Major (below the Pole), Cepheus, Cassiopeia, Cygnus, Lacerta, Andromeda, Pegasus, Capricornus, Aquarius and Piscis Austrinus

THE MOON

Phases, Apsides and Node	*d*	*h*	*m*
● New Moon	3	10	28
☽ First Quarter	10	19	01
○ Full Moon	17	12	14
☾ Last Quarter	25	01	17
Perigee (365,473 km)	14	14	07
Apogee (404,455 km)	26	09	35

Mean longitude of ascending node on October 1, 14°

THE SUN

s.d. 16′.1

Day	Right Ascension			Dec. –		Equation of time		Rise 52°		Rise 56°		Transit		Set 52°		Set 56°		Sidereal time			Transit of first point of Aries		
	h	*m*	*s*	°	′	*m*	*s*	*h*	*m*	*h*	*m*	*h*	*m*	*h*	*m*	*h*	*m*	*h*	*m*	*s*	*h*	*m*	*s*
1	12	29	04	3	08	+10	14	6	01	6	03	11	50	17	37	17	35	0	39	18	23	16	52
2	12	32	42	3	32	+10	33	6	03	6	05	11	49	17	35	17	33	0	43	15	23	12	56
3	12	36	19	3	55	+10	52	6	04	6	07	11	49	17	33	17	30	0	47	11	23	09	01
4	12	39	57	4	18	+11	10	6	06	6	09	11	49	17	30	17	27	0	51	08	23	05	05
5	12	43	36	4	41	+11	29	6	08	6	11	11	48	17	28	17	25	0	55	04	23	01	09
6	12	47	14	5	04	+11	46	6	09	6	13	11	48	17	26	17	22	0	59	01	22	57	13
7	12	50	54	5	27	+12	04	6	11	6	15	11	48	17	24	17	20	1	02	57	22	53	17
8	12	54	33	5	50	+12	21	6	13	6	17	11	48	17	21	17	17	1	06	54	22	49	21
9	12	58	13	6	13	+12	38	6	14	6	19	11	47	17	19	17	14	1	10	51	22	45	25
10	13	01	53	6	36	+12	54	6	16	6	21	11	47	17	17	17	12	1	14	47	22	41	29
11	13	05	34	6	59	+13	10	6	18	6	23	11	47	17	15	17	09	1	18	44	22	37	33
12	13	09	15	7	21	+13	25	6	20	6	25	11	46	17	12	17	07	1	22	40	22	33	37
13	13	12	57	7	44	+13	40	6	21	6	27	11	46	17	10	17	04	1	26	37	22	29	41
14	13	16	39	8	06	+13	54	6	23	6	29	11	46	17	08	17	02	1	30	33	22	25	46
15	13	20	22	8	28	+14	08	6	25	6	31	11	46	17	06	16	59	1	34	30	22	21	50
16	13	24	05	8	50	+14	21	6	26	6	33	11	46	17	04	16	57	1	38	26	22	17	54
17	13	27	49	9	12	+14	34	6	28	6	35	11	45	17	02	16	54	1	42	23	22	13	58
18	13	31	33	9	34	+14	46	6	30	6	38	11	45	16	59	16	52	1	46	20	22	10	02
19	13	35	19	9	56	+14	58	6	32	6	40	11	45	16	57	16	49	1	50	16	22	06	06
20	13	39	04	10	18	+15	09	6	33	6	42	11	45	16	55	16	47	1	54	13	22	02	10
21	13	42	51	10	39	+15	19	6	35	6	44	11	45	16	53	16	45	1	58	09	21	58	14
22	13	46	38	11	00	+15	28	6	37	6	46	11	44	16	51	16	42	2	02	06	21	54	18
23	13	50	25	11	22	+15	37	6	39	6	48	11	44	16	49	16	40	2	06	02	21	50	22
24	13	54	14	11	43	+15	45	6	41	6	50	11	44	16	47	16	37	2	09	59	21	46	26
25	13	58	03	12	03	+15	53	6	42	6	52	11	44	16	45	16	35	2	13	55	21	42	31
26	14	01	53	12	24	+15	59	6	44	6	54	11	44	16	43	16	33	2	17	52	21	38	35
27	14	05	43	12	44	+16	05	6	46	6	56	11	44	16	41	16	30	2	21	49	21	34	39
28	14	09	34	13	05	+16	11	6	48	6	59	11	44	16	39	16	28	2	25	45	21	30	43
29	14	13	27	13	25	+16	15	6	49	7	01	11	44	16	37	16	26	2	29	42	21	26	47
30	14	17	19	13	44	+16	19	6	51	7	03	11	44	16	35	16	24	2	33	38	21	22	51
31	14	21	13	14	04	+16	22	6	53	7	05	11	44	16	33	16	21	2	37	35	21	18	55

DURATION OF TWILIGHT (in minutes)

Latitude	*52°*	*56°*	*52°*	*56°*	*52°*	*56°*	*52°*	*56*
	1 October		*11 October*		*21 October*		*31 October*	
Civil	34	37	34	37	34	38	35	39
Nautical	73	80	73	80	74	81	75	83
Astronomical	113	125	112	124	113	124	114	126

THE NIGHT SKY

Mercury remains too close to the Sun for observation throughout the month.

Venus, magnitude −4.3, continues to be a brilliant object in the early evenings, low above the south-western horizon for a short while after sunset. This interval increases slightly during October so that by the end of the month Venus is visible for almost an hour. Under good conditions the waxing crescent Moon will be seen about 6 degrees to the left of the planet on the evening of the 7th.

Mars reaches its first stationary point on the 1st, and then moves retrograde from Taurus back into Aries during the month. Its magnitude is still brightening (from −1.7 to −2.3) during October as it approaches opposition next month. Due to the eccentricity of its orbit the closest approach of Mars to the Earth during this apparition (69 million kilometres) occurs on the last day of October, one week before opposition. Mars is already visible for most of the night and by the end of the month may be seen rising in the east about an hour after sunset. The Moon, just past Full, is near the planet around the 19th–20th.

Jupiter passes through conjunction on the 22nd and thus remains too close to the Sun for observation throughout the month.

Saturn, magnitude +0.3, continues to be visible in the eastern sky in the early mornings. It is noticeably brighter than the nearby bright stars in Gemini, Castor and Pollux, which are of magnitude +1.9 and +1.1 respectively. The Moon, around Last Quarter, is near the planet on the mornings of the 25th and 26th.

THE MOON

Day	*RA*		*Dec.*	*Hor. par.*	*Semi-diam.*	*Sun's Co-long.*	*PA of Br. Limb*	*Ph.*	*Age*	*Rise*				*Transit*		*Set*			
										52°		*56°*				*52°*		*56°*	
	h	*m*	°	′	′	°	°	%	*d*	*h*	*m*	*h*	*m*	*h*	*m*	*h*	*m*	*h*	*m*
1	10	53	+10.3	54.5	14.8	244	118	6	27.2	3	31	3	22	10	31	17	13	17	18
2	11	36	+4.6	54.8	14.9	256	120	2	28.2	4	43	4	40	11	11	17	23	17	23
3	12	19	−1.2	55.2	15.0	269	123	0	29.2	5	56	5	59	11	52	17	32	17	27
4	13	03	−7.1	55.6	15.2	281	296	0	0.6	7	11	7	19	12	34	17	42	17	33
5	13	49	−12.9	56.1	15.3	293	295	3	1.6	8	30	8	44	13	19	17	55	17	40
6	14	38	−18.1	56.6	15.4	305	292	7	2.6	9	51	10	13	14	07	18	12	17	50
7	15	31	−22.7	57.1	15.6	318	288	13	3.6	11	15	11	45	15	00	18	37	18	06
8	16	27	−26.1	57.6	15.7	330	282	21	4.6	12	37	13	14	15	57	19	13	18	35
9	17	27	−28.2	58.1	15.8	342	275	31	5.6	13	48	14	29	16	57	20	07	19	26
10	18	29	−28.5	58.6	16.0	354	268	41	6.6	14	42	15	20	17	59	21	20	20	43
11	19	32	−27.1	59.0	16.1	6	261	52	7.6	15	20	15	49	18	59	22	47	22	18
12	20	33	−23.9	59.5	16.2	18	254	64	8.6	15	45	16	07	19	56	—	—	23	59
13	21	32	−19.2	59.8	16.3	31	249	75	9.6	16	03	16	17	20	50	0	19	—	—
14	22	27	−13.4	60.0	16.3	43	245	84	10.6	16	17	16	25	21	41	1	51	1	39
15	23	20	−6.8	60.0	16.3	55	243	92	11.6	16	30	16	31	22	30	3	21	3	16
16	0	11	+0.1	59.8	16.3	67	244	97	12.6	16	41	16	37	23	18	4	49	4	50
17	1	02	+7.0	59.4	16.2	79	250	100	13.6	16	54	16	44	—	—	6	16	6	24
18	1	54	+13.4	58.8	16.0	91	56	100	14.6	17	08	16	52	0	08	7	44	7	58
19	2	47	+19.0	58.1	15.8	104	65	97	15.6	17	27	17	04	0	58	9	11	9	33
20	3	41	+23.5	57.4	15.6	116	71	92	16.6	17	53	17	22	1	51	10	36	11	06
21	4	38	+26.6	56.6	15.4	128	77	86	17.6	18	30	17	52	2	46	11	53	12	30
22	5	35	+28.3	55.8	15.2	140	84	78	18.6	19	19	18	40	3	41	12	57	13	37
23	6	31	+28.5	55.2	15.0	152	91	69	19.6	20	22	19	45	4	35	13	45	14	22
24	7	26	+27.3	54.7	14.9	164	97	60	20.6	21	33	21	03	5	27	14	18	14	49
25	8	18	+24.8	54.4	14.8	177	103	51	21.6	22	47	22	24	6	16	14	41	15	05
26	9	07	+21.3	54.2	14.8	189	108	41	22.6	—	—	23	44	7	02	14	58	15	16
27	9	54	+17.0	54.2	14.8	201	111	32	23.6	0	01	—	—	7	45	15	11	15	23
28	10	39	+12.0	54.4	14.8	213	114	24	24.6	1	14	1	03	8	27	15	22	15	29
29	11	22	+6.5	54.7	14.9	225	115	16	25.6	2	26	2	21	9	07	15	31	15	33
30	12	05	+0.7	55.2	15.0	238	115	9	26.6	3	39	3	39	9	48	15	40	15	38
31	12	49	−5.2	55.7	15.2	250	113	4	27.6	4	54	4	59	10	29	15	50	15	43

MERCURY

Day	*RA*		*Dec.*	*Diam.*	*Phase*	*Transit*		*5° high*			
								52°		*56°*	
	h	*m*	°	″	%	*h*	*m*	*h*	*m*	*h*	*m*
1	13	06	−6.7	5	96	12	28	17	17	17	07
3	13	18	−8.1	5	95	12	32	17	13	17	02
5	13	29	−9.5	5	94	12	35	17	09	16	56
7	13	41	−10.9	5	93	12	39	17	05	16	51
9	13	52	−12.2	5	92	12	42	17	00	16	45
11	14	04	−13.5	5	91	12	46	16	56	16	39
13	14	15	−14.7	5	89	12	49	16	52	16	33
15	14	26	−15.9	5	88	12	53	16	47	16	27
17	14	37	−17.0	5	86	12	56	16	43	16	21
19	14	49	−18.0	5	85	12	59	16	39	16	15
21	15	00	−19.0	5	83	13	02	16	35	16	09
23	15	10	−20.0	6	81	13	05	16	31	16	03
25	15	21	−20.8	6	79	13	08	16	27	15	58
27	15	32	−21.6	6	76	13	11	16	24	15	52
29	15	42	−22.3	6	73	13	13	16	20	15	47
31	15	52	−22.9	6	70	13	15	16	17	15	41

VENUS

Day	*RA*		*Dec.*	*Diam.*	*Phase*	*Transit*		*5° high*			
								52°		*56°*	
h	*h*	*m*	°	″	%	*h*	*m*	*h*	*m*	*h*	*m*
1	15	17	−20.3	18	64	14	38	18	02	17	33
6	15	40	−21.9	19	62	14	41	17	51	17	19
11	16	03	−23.4	20	60	14	44	17	42	17	05
16	16	26	−24.6	21	58	14	48	17	35	16	53
21	16	50	−25.6	22	56	14	52	17	29	16	41
26	17	13	−26.4	23	54	14	55	17	25	16	32
31	17	36	−26.9	24	51	14	59	17	23	16	27

MARS

Day	*RA*		*Dec.*	*Diam.*	*Phase*	*Transit*		*5° high*			
								52°		*56°*	
	h	*m*	°	″	%	*h*	*m*	*h*	*m*	*h*	*m*
1	3	26	+16.5	18	93	2	47	19	50	19	40
6	3	26	+16.6	18	95	2	26	19	29	19	18
11	3	23	+16.6	19	96	2	04	19	07	18	56
16	3	20	+16.6	19	97	1	41	18	43	18	33
21	3	15	+16.6	20	98	1	16	18	19	18	08
26	3	09	+16.4	20	99	0	51	17	54	17	43
31	3	02	+16.2	20	100	0	24	17	28	17	18

SUNRISE AND SUNSET

	London		Bristol		Birmingham		Manchester		Newcastle		Glasgow		Belfast	
	0°05′	51°30′	2°35′	51°28′	1°55′	52°28′	2°15′	53°28′	1°37′	54°59′	4°14′	55°52′	5°56′	54°35′
	h m	h m	h m	h m	h m	h m	h m	h m	h m	h m	h m	h m	h m	h m
1	6 01	17 38	6 11	17 48	6 09	17 45	6 11	17 46	6 09	17 42	6 20	17 52	6 26	18 00
2	6 03	17 36	6 13	17 46	6 10	17 42	6 12	17 43	6 11	17 40	6 22	17 50	6 28	17 57
3	6 04	17 33	6 14	17 43	6 12	17 40	6 14	17 41	6 13	17 37	6 24	17 47	6 30	17 55
4	6 06	17 31	6 16	17 41	6 14	17 38	6 16	17 38	6 15	17 35	6 26	17 44	6 32	17 52
5	6 08	17 29	6 18	17 39	6 16	17 35	6 18	17 36	6 16	17 32	6 28	17 42	6 33	17 50
6	6 09	17 27	6 19	17 37	6 17	17 33	6 20	17 34	6 18	17 30	6 30	17 39	6 35	17 47
7	6 11	17 24	6 21	17 34	6 19	17 31	6 21	17 31	6 20	17 27	6 32	17 37	6 37	17 45
8	6 13	17 22	6 23	17 32	6 21	17 29	6 23	17 29	6 22	17 25	6 34	17 34	6 39	17 42
9	6 14	17 20	6 24	17 30	6 23	17 26	6 25	17 27	6 24	17 22	6 36	17 31	6 41	17 40
10	6 16	17 18	6 26	17 28	6 24	17 24	6 27	17 24	6 26	17 20	6 38	17 29	6 43	17 37
11	6 18	17 16	6 28	17 26	6 26	17 22	6 29	17 22	6 28	17 17	6 40	17 26	6 45	17 35
12	6 19	17 13	6 29	17 23	6 28	17 20	6 30	17 20	6 30	17 15	6 42	17 24	6 47	17 33
13	6 21	17 11	6 31	17 21	6 30	17 17	6 32	17 17	6 32	17 12	6 44	17 21	6 49	17 30
14	6 23	17 09	6 33	17 19	6 31	17 15	6 34	17 15	6 34	17 10	6 46	17 19	6 51	17 28
15	6 24	17 07	6 34	17 17	6 33	17 13	6 36	17 13	6 36	17 08	6 48	17 16	6 53	17 25
16	6 26	17 05	6 36	17 15	6 35	17 11	6 38	17 10	6 38	17 05	6 50	17 14	6 55	17 23
17	6 28	17 03	6 38	17 13	6 37	17 08	6 40	17 08	6 40	17 03	6 52	17 11	6 56	17 21
18	6 29	17 01	6 39	17 11	6 38	17 06	6 42	17 06	6 42	17 00	6 54	17 09	6 58	17 18
19	6 31	16 59	6 41	17 09	6 40	17 04	6 43	17 04	6 44	16 58	6 56	17 07	7 00	17 16
20	6 33	16 56	6 43	17 07	6 42	17 02	6 45	17 01	6 46	16 56	6 58	17 04	7 02	17 14
21	6 35	16 54	6 45	17 05	6 44	17 00	6 47	16 59	6 48	16 53	7 00	17 02	7 04	17 11
22	6 36	16 52	6 46	17 02	6 46	16 58	6 49	16 57	6 50	16 51	7 02	16 59	7 06	17 09
23	6 38	16 50	6 48	17 00	6 47	16 56	6 51	16 55	6 52	16 49	7 05	16 57	7 08	17 07
24	6 40	16 48	6 50	16 58	6 49	16 54	6 53	16 53	6 54	16 46	7 07	16 55	7 10	17 05
25	6 42	16 46	6 51	16 56	6 51	16 52	6 55	16 51	6 56	16 44	7 09	16 52	7 12	17 02
26	6 43	16 44	6 53	16 55	6 53	16 50	6 57	16 48	6 58	16 42	7 11	16 50	7 14	17 00
27	6 45	16 43	6 55	16 53	6 55	16 48	6 59	16 46	7 00	16 40	7 13	16 48	7 16	16 58
28	6 47	16 41	6 57	16 51	6 57	16 46	7 00	16 44	7 02	16 38	7 15	16 45	7 18	16 56
29	6 49	16 39	6 59	16 49	6 58	16 44	7 02	16 42	7 04	16 35	7 17	16 43	7 20	16 54
30	6 50	16 37	7 00	16 47	7 00	16 42	7 04	16 40	7 06	16 33	7 19	16 41	7 22	16 52
31	6 52	16 35	7 02	16 45	7 02	16 40	7 06	16 38	7 08	16 31	7 21	16 39	7 24	16 50

JUPITER

Day	*RA*		*Dec.*		*Transit*		*5° high*			
							52°		*56°*	
	h	*m*	°	′	*h*	*m*	*h*	*m*	*h*	*m*
1	13	32.6	−8	32	12	52	8	11	8	22
11	13	40.7	−9	19	12	20	7	44	7	56
21	13	48.9	−10	06	11	49	7	17	7	30
31	13	57.2	−10	52	11	18	6	51	7	04

Diameters – equatorial 31″ polar 29″

SATURN

Day	*RA*		*Dec.*		*Transit*		*5° high*			
							52°		*56°*	
	h	*m*	°	′	*h*	*m*	*h*	*m*	*h*	*m*
1	8	45.8	+18	25	8	05	1	02	0	49
11	8	49.0	+18	14	7	29	0	27	0	15
21	8	51.7	+18	05	6	53	23	48	23	35
31	8	53.7	+17	58	6	15	23	11	22	59

Diameters – equatorial 18″ polar 16″

Rings – major axis 40″ minor axis 12″

URANUS

Day	*RA*		*Dec.*		*Transit*		*10° high*			
							52°		*56°*	
	h	*m*	°	′	*h*	*m*	*h*	*m*	*h*	*m*
1	22	38.6	−9	27	21	56	1	59	1	42
11	22	37.5	−9	33	21	15	1	18	1	01
21	22	36.5	−9	38	20	35	0	37	0	20
31	22	35.9	−9	42	19	55	23	53	23	36

Diameter 4″

NEPTUNE

Day	*RA*		*Dec.*		*Transit*		*10° high*			
							52°		*56°*	
	h	*m*	°	′	*h*	*m*	*h*	*m*	*h*	*m*
1	21	10.0	−16	29	20	27	23	38	23	08
11	21	09.6	−16	31	19	48	22	58	22	28
21	21	09.3	−16	32	19	08	22	18	21	48
31	21	09.3	−16	32	18	29	21	39	21	09

Diameter 2″

NOVEMBER 2005

ELEVENTH MONTH, 30 DAYS. *Novem* (nine), ninth month of Roman pre-Julian calendar

1	*Tuesday*	Naomi Mitchison b. 1897. Ezra Pound d. 1972	305
2	*Wednesday*	Marie-Antoinette b. 1755. George Bernard Shaw d. 1950	306
3	*Thursday*	Karl Baedeker b. 1801. Henri Matisse d. 1954	307
4	*Friday*	Felix Mendelssohn d. 1847. Wilfred Owen d. 1918	308
5	*Saturday*	Sam Shepard b. 1943. Maurice Utrillo d. 1955	309
6	*Sunday*	Pyotr Ilyich Tchaikovsky d. 1893. Kate Greenaway d. 1901	310
7	*Monday*	Albert Camus b. 1913. Steve McQueen d. 1980	week 45 day 311
8	*Tuesday*	Margaret Mitchell b. 1900. John Milton d. 1674	312
9	*Wednesday*	Edward VII b. 1841. Dylan Thomas d. 1953	313
10	*Thursday*	William Hogarth b. 1697. Oliver Goldsmith b. 1730	314
11	*Friday*	Fyodor Dostoevsky b. 1821. Sir Edward German d. 1936	315
12	*Saturday*	Auguste Rodin b. 1840. Cnut the Great d. 1035	316
13	*Sunday*	Robert Louis Stevenson b. 1850. Camile Pissarro d. 1903	317
14	*Monday*	Dame Elizabeth Frink b. 1930. Prince of Wales b. 1948	week 46 day 318
15	*Tuesday*	Marianne Moore b. 1887. George Romney d. 1802	319
16	*Wednesday*	Clarke Gable d. 1960. Henry III d. 1272	320
17	*Thursday*	Catherine II (The Great) of Russia d. 1796. Auguste Rodin d. 1917	321
18	*Friday*	Sir David Wilkie b. 1785. Marcel Proust d. 1922	322
19	*Saturday*	Charles I b. 1600. Franz Schubert d. 1828	323
20	*Sunday*	Leo Tolstoy d. 1910. Queen Alexandra d. 1925	324
21	*Monday*	Voltaire b. 1694. Henry Purcell d. 1695	week 47 day 325
22	*Tuesday*	Benjamin Britten b. 1913. C. S. Lewis d. 1963	326
23	*Wednesday*	James Thomson b. 1834. Roald Dahl d. 1990	327
24	*Thursday*	Laurence Sterne b. 1713. Henri de Toulouse-Lautrec b. 1864	328
25	*Friday*	Upton Sinclair d. 1968. Sir Anton Dolin d. 1983	329
26	*Saturday*	Tina Turner b. 1939. Isabella I d. 1504	330
27	*Sunday*	Alexander Dumas d. 1895. Eugene O'Neill d. 1953	331
28	*Monday*	Nancy Mitford b. 1904. Enid Blyton d. 1968	week 48 day 332
29	*Tuesday*	Louisa May Alcott b. 1832. Giacomo Puccini d. 1924	333
30	*Wednesday*	Mark Twain b. 1835. Oscar Wilde d. 1900	334

ASTRONOMICAL PHENOMENA

d	*h*	
1	10	Jupiter in conjunction with Moon. Jupiter 3° N.
3	16	Mercury at greatest elongation E.24°
3	19	Venus at greatest elongation E.47°
3	23	Mercury in conjunction with Moon. Mercury 1° N.
5	19	Venus in conjunction with Moon. Venus 1° N.
7	08	Mars at opposition
14	06	Mercury at stationary point
15	05	Mars in conjunction with Moon. Mars 3° S.
16	00	Uranus at stationary point
22	05	Saturn in conjunction with Moon. Saturn 4° S.
22	05	Sun's longitude 240° ♐
22	09	Saturn at stationary point
24	16	Mercury in inferior conjunction
29	06	Jupiter in conjunction with Moon. Jupiter 3° N.
30	15	Mercury in conjunction with Moon. Mercury 6° N.

MINIMA OF ALGOL

d	*h*	*d*	*h*	*d*	*h*
1	06.0	12	17.2	24	04.5
4	02.8	15	14.1	27	01.3
6	23.6	18	10.9	29	22.1
9	20.4	21	07.7		

CONSTELLATIONS

The following constellations are near their meridian at

	d	*h*		*d*	*h*
October	1	24	November	15	21
October	16	23	December	1	20
November	1	22	December	16	19

Ursa Major (below the Pole), Cepheus, Cassiopeia, Andromeda, Pegasus, Pisces, Acquarius and Cetus

THE MOON

Phases, Apsides and Node	*d*	*h*	*m*
● New Moon	2	01	25
☽ First Quarter	9	01	57
○ Full Moon	16	00	58
☾ Last Quarter	23	22	11
Perigee (370,046 km)	10	00	28
Apogee (404,331 km)	23	06	16

Mean longitude of ascending node on November 1, 12°

THE SUN

s.d. 16′.2

Day	Right Ascension h m s	Dec. – ° ′	Equation of time m s	Rise 52° h m	Rise 56° h m	Transit h m	Set 52° h m	Set 56° h m	Sidereal time h m s	Transit of first point of Aries h m s
1	14 25 08	14 23	+16 24	6 55	7 07	11 44	16 32	16 19	2 41 31	21 14 59
2	14 29 03	14 43	+16 25	6 57	7 09	11 44	16 30	16 17	2 45 28	21 11 03
3	14 32 59	15 01	+16 26	6 59	7 11	11 44	16 28	16 15	2 49 24	21 07 07
4	14 36 56	15 20	+16 25	7 00	7 13	11 44	16 26	16 13	2 53 21	21 03 11
5	14 40 54	15 39	+16 24	7 02	7 16	11 44	16 24	16 11	2 57 18	20 59 16
6	14 44 52	15 57	+16 22	7 04	7 18	11 44	16 23	16 09	3 01 14	20 55 20
7	14 48 51	16 15	+16 19	7 06	7 20	11 44	16 21	16 07	3 05 11	20 51 24
8	14 52 52	16 32	+16 16	7 08	7 22	11 44	16 19	16 05	3 09 07	20 47 28
9	14 56 53	16 49	+16 11	7 09	7 24	11 44	16 18	16 03	3 13 04	20 43 32
10	15 00 54	17 07	+16 06	7 11	7 26	11 44	16 16	16 01	3 17 00	20 39 36
11	15 04 57	17 23	+16 00	7 13	7 28	11 44	16 15	15 59	3 20 57	20 35 40
12	15 09 01	17 40	+15 53	7 15	7 30	11 44	16 13	15 57	3 24 53	20 31 44
13	15 13 05	17 56	+15 45	7 16	7 32	11 44	16 12	15 55	3 28 50	20 27 48
14	15 17 10	18 12	+15 37	7 18	7 35	11 44	16 10	15 54	3 32 47	20 23 52
15	15 21 16	18 27	+15 27	7 20	7 37	11 45	16 09	15 52	3 36 43	20 19 56
16	15 25 23	18 42	+15 17	7 22	7 39	11 45	16 07	15 50	3 40 40	20 16 01
17	15 29 30	18 57	+15 06	7 23	7 41	11 45	16 06	15 49	3 44 36	20 12 05
18	15 33 39	19 12	+14 54	7 25	7 43	11 45	16 05	15 47	3 48 33	20 08 09
19	15 37 48	19 26	+14 41	7 27	7 45	11 45	16 03	15 45	3 52 29	20 04 13
20	15 41 58	19 40	+14 27	7 29	7 47	11 46	16 02	15 44	3 56 26	20 00 17
21	15 46 09	19 53	+14 13	7 30	7 49	11 46	16 01	15 43	4 00 22	19 56 21
22	15 50 21	20 06	+13 58	7 32	7 51	11 46	16 00	15 41	4 04 19	19 52 25
23	15 54 34	20 19	+13 42	7 33	7 53	11 46	15 59	15 40	4 08 16	19 48 29
24	15 58 47	20 31	+13 25	7 35	7 54	11 47	15 58	15 38	4 12 12	19 44 33
25	16 03 01	20 43	+13 07	7 37	7 56	11 47	15 57	15 37	4 16 09	19 40 37
26	16 07 16	20 55	+12 49	7 38	7 58	11 47	15 56	15 36	4 20 05	19 36 41
27	16 11 32	21 06	+12 30	7 40	8 00	11 48	15 55	15 35	4 24 02	19 32 46
28	16 15 49	21 17	+12 10	7 41	8 02	11 48	15 54	15 34	4 27 58	19 28 50
29	16 20 06	21 27	+11 49	7 43	8 04	11 48	15 54	15 33	4 31 55	19 24 54
30	16 24 24	21 37	+11 28	7 44	8 05	11 49	15 53	15 32	4 35 52	19 20 58

DURATION OF TWILIGHT (in minutes)

Latitude	*52°*	*56°*	*52°*	*56°*	*52°*	*56°*	*52°*	*56*
	1 November		*11 November*		*21 November*		*31 November*	
Civil	36	40	37	41	38	43	40	45
Nautical	75	84	78	87	80	90	82	93
Astronomical	115	127	117	130	120	134	123	138

THE NIGHT SKY

Mercury, although it reaches greatest eastern elongation on the 3rd and later passes through inferior conjunction on the 24th, is unsuitably placed for observation throughout the month.

Venus, magnitude −4.5, is still visible as a brilliant object in the early evenings, low above the south-western horizon after sunset. Under good conditions the four-day old crescent Moon will be seen nearly 3 degrees below the planet on the evening of the 5th. Venus is at greatest eastern elongation (47 degrees) on the 3rd and during the month is gradually becoming visible for a little longer each evening until by the end of the month it may be seen for almost two hours after sunset, from southern England, and for about an hour and a half from Scotland.

Mars reaches opposition on the 7th, and is visible throughout the hours of darkness. Its magnitude then is −2.3, and for a few weeks around opposition is actually brighter than Jupiter. Mars is in the constellation of Aries. The Full Moon is in the vicinity of the planet on the 15th and 16th.

Jupiter, magnitude −1.7, becomes visible as a bright morning object after the first week of the month, low above the south-eastern horizon for a short while before sunrise. Jupiter is moving slowly eastwards, a few degrees east of Spica, in Virgo. On the morning of the 29th, the thin waning crescent Moon, only 2 days before New, passes 4 degrees south of the planet.

Saturn, magnitude +0.2, is moving very slowly direct in the constellation of Cancer: it reaches its first stationary point on the 22nd, when it starts to retrograde. It is now rising in the east about three hours before midnight. The gibbous Moon, just before Last Quarter, is near the planet around the 21st to the 23rd.

Meteors. Although the Leonids do not usually produce a brilliant display there has been considerable activity during the last few years. The peak of any activity will occur around the 17th but is not likely to produce a spectacular display.

THE MOON

Day	RA		Dec.	Hor. par.	Semi-diam.	Sun's Co-long.	PA of Br. Limb	Ph.	Age	Rise 52°		Rise 56°		Transit		Set 52°		Set 56°	
	h	m	°	′	′	°	°	%	d	h	m	h	m	h	m	h	m	h	m
1	13	35	−11.1	56.3	15.3	262	106	1	28.6	6	11	6	23	11	14	16	02	15	49
2	14	23	−16.6	56.9	15.5	274	36	0	29.6	7	33	7	52	12	01	16	18	15	58
3	15	16	−21.5	57.4	15.6	286	301	1	0.9	8	58	9	25	12	54	16	40	16	13
4	16	12	−25.3	57.9	15.8	299	290	4	1.9	10	23	10	58	13	51	17	13	16	37
5	17	12	−27.8	58.3	15.9	311	281	10	2.9	11	40	12	20	14	51	18	02	17	21
6	18	15	−28.5	58.7	16.0	323	273	18	3.9	12	40	13	19	15	53	19	10	18	31
7	19	18	−27.5	58.9	16.1	335	265	27	4.9	13	22	13	54	16	54	20	33	20	02
8	20	20	−24.7	59.1	16.1	347	258	38	5.9	13	50	14	14	17	51	22	03	21	41
9	21	18	−20.3	59.2	16.1	360	252	49	6.9	14	10	14	26	18	45	23	33	23	19
10	22	13	−14.9	59.3	16.1	12	248	61	7.9	14	25	14	34	19	35	—	—	—	—
11	23	05	−8.7	59.2	16.1	24	246	71	8.9	14	37	14	41	20	23	1	01	0	53
12	23	55	−2.0	59.1	16.1	36	245	81	9.9	14	48	14	47	21	10	2	27	2	25
13	0	44	+4.7	58.8	16.0	48	247	89	10.9	15	00	14	53	21	58	3	51	3	56
14	1	35	+11.1	58.5	15.9	60	251	95	11.9	15	13	15	00	22	47	5	17	5	28
15	2	26	+16.9	58.0	15.8	72	261	99	12.9	15	30	15	10	23	38	6	43	7	01
16	3	20	+21.8	57.5	15.7	85	337	100	13.9	15	52	15	25	—	—	8	08	8	35
17	4	16	+25.5	56.9	15.5	97	61	99	14.9	16	24	15	50	0	32	9	30	10	04
18	5	13	+27.7	56.2	15.3	109	75	96	15.9	17	08	16	29	1	27	10	41	11	20
19	6	10	+28.5	55.6	15.2	121	84	91	16.9	18	06	17	28	2	23	11	36	12	15
20	7	06	+27.7	55.1	15.0	133	92	84	17.9	19	15	18	42	3	17	12	16	12	49
21	8	00	+25.7	54.7	14.9	145	98	76	18.9	20	29	20	03	4	08	12	44	13	10
22	8	51	+22.5	54.4	14.8	157	104	68	19.9	21	43	21	24	4	55	13	03	13	23
23	9	38	+18.4	54.2	14.8	170	108	59	20.9	22	56	22	44	5	40	13	17	13	31
24	10	23	+13.6	54.3	14.8	182	111	49	21.9	—	—	—	—	6	22	13	29	13	38
25	11	07	+8.3	54.5	14.8	194	113	40	22.9	0	08	0	01	7	02	13	38	13	43
26	11	49	+2.7	54.9	15.0	206	114	31	23.9	1	20	1	18	7	42	13	48	13	47
27	12	32	−3.1	55.4	15.1	218	113	22	24.9	2	33	2	36	8	22	13	57	13	52
28	13	17	−9.0	56.1	15.3	230	111	15	25.9	3	48	3	57	9	05	14	08	13	57
29	14	04	−14.6	56.8	15.5	243	107	8	26.9	5	08	5	23	9	51	14	22	14	05
30	14	56	−19.8	57.5	15.7	255	99	3	27.9	6	32	6	55	10	42	14	41	14	17

MERCURY

Day	RA		Dec.	Diam.	Phase	Transit		5° high 52°		5° high 56°	
	h	m	°	″	%	h	m	h	m	h	m
1	15	57	−23.2	6	68	13	16	16	15	15	39
3	16	06	−23.7	7	65	13	17	16	12	15	34
5	16	14	−24.1	7	60	13	17	16	09	15	30
7	16	22	−24.4	7	55	13	16	16	06	15	26
9	16	28	−24.5	7	49	13	14	16	03	15	22
11	16	33	−24.5	8	43	13	11	16	00	15	19
13	16	36	−24.4	8	36	13	05	15	56	15	16
15	16	36	−24.1	9	28	12	57	15	51	15	13
17	16	34	−23.6	9	20	12	46	15	45	15	09
19	16	29	−22.9	9	12	12	32	15	38	15	04
21	16	21	−22.0	10	5	12	16	15	30	14	59
23	16	11	−20.9	10	1	11	58	8	37	9	05
25	16	00	−19.7	10	0	11	40	8	09	8	35
27	15	50	−18.5	10	3	11	22	7	43	8	07
29	15	41	−17.6	9	8	11	06	7	21	7	43
31	15	36	−16.9	9	16	10	53	7	03	7	24

VENUS

Day	RA		Dec.	Diam.	Phase	Transit		5° high 52°		5° high 56°	
	h	m	°	″	%	h	m	h	m	h	m
1	17	40	−26.9	24	51	14	59	17	23	16	26
6	18	03	−27.1	26	48	15	02	17	24	16	26
11	18	25	−27.0	27	46	15	04	17	27	16	31
16	18	45	−26.7	29	43	15	05	17	32	16	39
21	19	05	−26.1	31	40	15	04	17	38	16	48
26	19	22	−25.4	33	36	15	02	17	44	16	59
31	19	38	−24.5	36	33	14	58	17	48	17	08

MARS

Day	RA		Dec.	Diam.	Phase	Transit		5° high 52°		5° high 56°	
	h	m	°	″	%	h	m	h	m	h	m
1	3	00	+16.2	20	100	0	19	7	09	7	19
6	2	53	+16.0	20	100	23	46	6	40	6	51
11	2	45	+15.7	20	100	23	19	6	12	6	22
16	2	39	+15.5	19	100	22	53	5	45	5	55
21	2	33	+15.3	18	99	22	28	5	18	5	28
26	2	28	+15.2	18	98	22	04	4	53	5	03
31	2	25	+15.1	17	97	21	41	4	30	4	40

SUNRISE AND SUNSET

	London *0°05'*	*51°30'*	*Bristol* *2°35'*	*51°28'*	*Birmingham* *1°55'*	*52°28'*	*Manchester* *2°15'*	*53°28'*	*Newcastle* *1°37'*	*54°59'*	*Glasgow* *4°14'*	*55°52'*	*Belfast* *5°56'*	*54°35'*
	h m	*h m*	*h m*	*h m*	*h m*	*h m*	*h m*	*h m*	*h m*	*h m*	*h m*	*h m*	*h m*	*h m*
1	6 54	16 33	7 04	16 43	7 04	16 38	7 08	16 36	7 10	16 29	7 24	16 37	7 26	16 48
2	6 56	16 31	7 06	16 42	7 06	16 36	7 10	16 34	7 12	16 27	7 26	16 35	7 28	16 46
3	6 57	16 30	7 07	16 40	7 08	16 34	7 12	16 32	7 14	16 25	7 28	16 32	7 30	16 44
4	6 59	16 28	7 09	16 38	7 09	16 32	7 14	16 31	7 16	16 23	7 30	16 30	7 32	16 42
5	7 01	16 26	7 11	16 36	7 11	16 31	7 16	16 29	7 18	16 21	7 32	16 28	7 34	16 40
6	7 03	16 25	7 13	16 35	7 13	16 29	7 18	16 27	7 20	16 19	7 34	16 26	7 36	16 38
7	7 04	16 23	7 14	16 33	7 15	16 27	7 20	16 25	7 22	16 17	7 36	16 24	7 38	16 36
8	7 06	16 21	7 16	16 31	7 17	16 25	7 21	16 23	7 24	16 15	7 38	16 22	7 40	16 34
9	7 08	16 20	7 18	16 30	7 19	16 24	7 23	16 22	7 27	16 13	7 41	16 20	7 42	16 32
10	7 10	16 18	7 20	16 28	7 20	16 22	7 25	16 20	7 29	16 12	7 43	16 18	7 44	16 30
11	7 12	16 17	7 21	16 27	7 22	16 21	7 27	16 18	7 31	16 10	7 45	16 17	7 46	16 29
12	7 13	16 15	7 23	16 25	7 24	16 19	7 29	16 17	7 33	16 08	7 47	16 15	7 48	16 27
13	7 15	16 14	7 25	16 24	7 26	16 18	7 31	16 15	7 35	16 06	7 49	16 13	7 50	16 25
14	7 17	16 12	7 27	16 22	7 28	16 16	7 33	16 14	7 36	16 05	7 51	16 11	7 52	16 24
15	7 18	16 11	7 28	16 21	7 29	16 15	7 35	16 12	7 38	16 03	7 53	16 10	7 54	16 22
16	7 20	16 10	7 30	16 20	7 31	16 13	7 36	16 11	7 40	16 01	7 55	16 08	7 56	16 20
17	7 22	16 08	7 32	16 18	7 33	16 12	7 38	16 09	7 42	16 00	7 57	16 06	7 58	16 19
18	7 23	16 07	7 33	16 17	7 35	16 11	7 40	16 08	7 44	15 58	7 59	16 05	8 00	16 17
19	7 25	16 06	7 35	16 16	7 36	16 09	7 42	16 06	7 46	15 57	8 01	16 03	8 02	16 16
20	7 27	16 05	7 37	16 15	7 38	16 08	7 44	16 05	7 48	15 56	8 03	16 02	8 04	16 15
21	7 28	16 04	7 38	16 14	7 40	16 07	7 45	16 04	7 50	15 54	8 05	16 00	8 05	16 13
22	7 30	16 02	7 40	16 13	7 41	16 06	7 47	16 03	7 52	15 53	8 07	15 59	8 07	16 12
23	7 32	16 01	7 42	16 12	7 43	16 05	7 49	16 01	7 54	15 52	8 09	15 57	8 09	16 11
24	7 33	16 00	7 43	16 11	7 45	16 04	7 51	16 00	7 56	15 50	8 11	15 56	8 11	16 10
25	7 35	15 59	7 45	16 10	7 46	16 03	7 52	15 59	7 57	15 49	8 13	15 55	8 13	16 08
26	7 36	15 59	7 46	16 09	7 48	16 02	7 54	15 58	7 59	15 48	8 14	15 54	8 14	16 07
27	7 38	15 58	7 48	16 08	7 50	16 01	7 56	15 57	8 01	15 47	8 16	15 53	8 16	16 06
28	7 39	15 57	7 49	16 07	7 51	16 00	7 57	15 56	8 03	15 46	8 18	15 51	8 18	16 05
29	7 41	15 56	7 51	16 06	7 53	15 59	7 59	15 55	8 04	15 45	8 20	15 50	8 19	16 04
30	7 42	15 55	7 52	16 06	7 54	15 58	8 00	15 55	8 06	15 44	8 21	15 49	8 21	16 04

JUPITER

Day	*RA*		*Dec.*		*Transit*		*5° high*			
							52°		*56°*	
	h	*m*	°	′	*h*	*m*	*h*	*m*	*h*	*m*
1	13	58.0	−10	57	11	15	6	48	7	02
11	14	06.3	−11	41	10	44	6	21	6	36
21	14	14.4	−12	23	10	13	5	54	6	10
31	14	22.4	−13	03	9	41	5	27	5	43

Diameters – equatorial 31″ polar 29″

SATURN

Day	*RA*		*Dec.*		*Transit*		*5° high*			
							52°		*56°*	
	h	*m*	°	′	*h*	*m*	*h*	*m*	*h*	*m*
1	8	53.9	+17	57	6	11	23	07	22	55
11	8	55.2	+17	54	5	33	22	29	22	17
21	8	55.7	+17	53	4	55	21	50	21	38
31	8	55.4	+17	56	4	15	21	10	20	

Diameters – equatorial 19″ polar 17″
Rings – major axis 42″ minor axis 13″

URANUS

Day	*RA*		*Dec.*		*Transit*		*10° high*			
							52°		*56°*	
	h	*m*	°	′	*h*	*m*	*h*	*m*	*h*	*m*
1	22	35.8	−9	42	19	51	23	49	23	32
11	22	35.5	−9	43	19	11	23	09	22	52
21	22	35.5	−9	43	18	32	22	30	22	13
31	22	35.8	−9	41	17	53	21	51	21	34

Diameter 4″

NEPTUNE

Day	*RA*		*Dec.*		*Transit*		*10° high*			
							52°		*56°*	
	h	*m*	°	′	*h*	*m*	*h*	*m*	*h*	*m*
1	21	09.3	−16	32	18	25	21	35	21	05
11	21	09.6	−16	31	17	46	20	56	20	26
21	21	10.0	−16	29	17	07	20	17	19	48
31	21	10.7	−16	26	16	28	19	39	19	10

Diameter 2″

DECEMBER 2005

TWELFTH MONTH, 31 DAYS. *Decem* (ten), tenth month of Roman pre-Julian calendar

1	*Thursday*	Queen Alexandra b. 1844. Henry I d. 1135	335
2	*Friday*	George Seurat b. 1859. Marquis de Sade d. 1814	336
3	*Saturday*	Robert Louis Stevenson d. 1894. Pierre Renoir d. 1919	337
4	*Sunday*	Wassily Kandinsky b. 1866. Benjamin Britten d. 1976	338
5	*Monday*	Wolfgang Amadeus Mozart d. 1791. Claude Monet d. 1926	week 49 day 339
6	*Tuesday*	Sir Osbert Sitwell b. 1892. Anthony Trollope d. 1882	340
7	*Wednesday*	Lord Darnley b. 1545. Robert Graves d. 1985	341
8	*Thursday*	Mary Queen of Scots b. 1542. Jean Sibelius b. 1865	342
9	*Friday*	John Milton b. 1608. Sir Anthony Van Dyck d. 1641	343
10	*Saturday*	Emily Dickinson b. 1830. Otis Redding d. 1967	344
11	*Sunday*	Hector Berlioz b. 1803. Sir Kenneth Macmillan d. 1992	345
12	*Monday*	Edvard Munch b. 1863. Robert Browning d. 1889	week 50 day 346
13	*Tuesday*	Dr Samuel Johnson b. 1784. Wassily Kandinsky d. 1944	347
14	*Wednesday*	George VI b. 1895. Albert, Prince Consort to Queen Victoria d. 1861	348
15	*Thursday*	George Romney b. 1734. Johannes Vermeer d. 1851	349
16	*Friday*	Sir Arthur C. Clarke b. 1917. Wilhelm Grimm d. 1859	350
17	*Saturday*	Ford Madox Ford b. 1873. Dorothy L. Sayers d. 1957	351
18	*Sunday*	Archduke Franz Ferdinand of Austria-Hungary b. 1863. Paul Klee b. 1879	352
19	*Monday*	Emily Brontë d. 1848. J. M. W. Turner d. 1851	week 51 day 353
20	*Tuesday*	James Hilton d. 1954. John Steinbeck d. 1968	354
21	*Wednesday*	Dame Rebecca West b. 1892. F. Scott Fitzgerald d. 1940	355
22	*Thursday*	Giacomo Puccini b. 1858. Samuel Becket d. 1989	356
23	*Friday*	Alexander I, Tsar of Russia b. 1777. Peggy Guggenheim d. 1979	357
24	*Saturday*	CHRISTMAS EVE. William Makepeace Thackeray d. 1863	358
25	*Sunday*	CHRISTMAS DAY. Maurice Utrillo b. 1883	359
26	*Monday*	BOXING DAY. Thomas Gray b. 1716	week 52 day 360
27	*Tuesday*	Marlene Dietrich b. 1901. Charles Lamb d. 1834	361
28	*Wednesday*	Mary II d. 1694. Maurice Ravel d. 1937	362
29	*Thursday*	Thomas Becket is killed by soldiers in Canterbury Cathedral 1170	363
30	*Friday*	Rudyard Kipling b. 1865. Richard Rogers, American composer d. 1979	364
31	*Saturday*	John Denver b. 1943. Henri Matisse b. 1869	365

ASTRONOMICAL PHENOMENA

d	*h*	
4	02	Mercury at stationary point
4	19	Venus in conjunction with Moon. Venus 2° N.
9	13	Venus at greatest brilliancy
10	04	Mars at stationary point
12	05	Mars in conjunction with Moon. Mars 1° S.
12	13	Mercury at greatest elongation W.21°
16	04	Pluto in conjunction
19	12	Saturn in conjunction with Moon. Saturn 4° S.
21	19	Sun's longitude 270° ♑
24	10	Venus at stationary point
27	01	Jupiter in conjunction with Moon. Jupiter 4° N.
29	23	Mercury in conjunction with Moon. Mercury 5° N.

MINIMA OF ALGOL

d	*h*	*d*	*h*	*d*	*h*
2	19.0	14	06.2	25	17.5
5	15.8	17	03.0	28	14.3
8	12.6	19	23.9	31	11.1
11	09.4	22	20.7		

CONSTELLATIONS

The following constellations are near their meridian at

	d	*h*		*d*	*h*
November	1	24	January	1	20
December	16	21	December	1	22
November	15	23	January	16	19

Ursa Major (below the Pole), Ursa Minor (below the Pole), Cassiopeia, Andromeda, Perseus, Triangulum, Aries, Taurus, Cetus and Eridanus

THE MOON

Phases, Apsides and Node	*d*	*h*	*m*
● New Moon	1	15	01
☽ First Quarter	8	09	36
○ Full Moon	15	16	16
☾ Last Quarter	23	19	36
● New Moon	31	03	12
Perigee (367,392 km)	5	04	24
Apogee (404,978 km)	21	02	45

Mean longitude of ascending node on December 1, 11°

THE SUN

s.d. 16′.3

Day	Right Ascension			Dec. –		Equation of time		Rise 52°		Rise 56°		Transit		Set 52°		Set 56°		Sidereal time			Transit of first point of Aries		
	h	m	s	°	′	m	s	h	m	h	m	h	m	h	m	h	m	h	m	s	h	m	s
1	16	28	42	21	47	+11	06	7	46	8	07	11	49	15	52	15	31	4	39	48	19	17	02
2	16	33	02	21	56	+10	43	7	47	8	09	11	49	15	51	15	30	4	43	45	19	13	06
3	16	37	22	22	05	+10	20	7	48	8	10	11	50	15	51	15	29	4	47	41	19	09	10
4	16	41	42	22	13	+9	56	7	50	8	12	11	50	15	50	15	29	4	51	38	19	05	14
5	16	46	03	22	21	+9	31	7	51	8	13	11	51	15	50	15	28	4	55	34	19	01	18
6	16	50	25	22	29	+9	06	7	52	8	15	11	51	15	50	15	27	4	59	31	18	57	22
7	16	54	47	22	36	+8	41	7	54	8	16	11	52	15	49	15	27	5	03	27	18	53	26
8	16	59	09	22	42	+8	15	7	55	8	17	11	52	15	49	15	26	5	07	24	18	49	30
9	17	03	32	22	48	+7	48	7	56	8	19	11	52	15	49	15	26	5	11	21	18	45	35
10	17	07	56	22	54	+7	21	7	57	8	20	11	53	15	49	15	26	5	15	17	18	41	39
11	17	12	20	22	59	+6	54	7	58	8	21	11	53	15	48	15	25	5	19	14	18	37	43
12	17	16	44	23	04	+6	26	7	59	8	22	11	54	15	48	15	25	5	23	10	18	33	47
13	17	21	08	23	08	+5	58	8	00	8	23	11	54	15	48	15	25	5	27	07	18	29	51
14	17	25	33	23	12	+5	30	8	01	8	24	11	55	15	48	15	25	5	31	03	18	25	55
15	17	29	58	23	16	+5	02	8	02	8	25	11	55	15	49	15	25	5	35	00	18	21	59
16	17	34	24	23	19	+4	33	8	03	8	26	11	56	15	49	15	25	5	38	56	18	18	03
17	17	38	49	23	21	+4	04	8	03	8	27	11	56	15	49	15	25	5	42	53	18	14	07
18	17	43	15	23	23	+3	34	8	04	8	28	11	57	15	49	15	25	5	46	50	18	10	11
19	17	47	41	23	25	+3	05	8	05	8	29	11	57	15	50	15	26	5	50	46	18	06	15
20	17	52	08	23	26	+2	35	8	05	8	29	11	58	15	50	15	26	5	54	43	18	02	20
21	17	56	34	23	26	+2	05	8	06	8	30	11	58	15	50	15	27	5	58	39	17	58	24
22	18	01	00	23	26	+1	36	8	06	8	30	11	59	15	51	15	27	6	02	36	17	54	28
23	18	05	27	23	26	+1	06	8	07	8	31	11	59	15	52	15	28	6	06	32	17	50	32
24	18	09	53	23	25	+0	36	8	07	8	31	12	00	15	52	15	28	6	10	29	17	46	36
25	18	14	19	23	24	+0	06	8	07	8	31	12	00	15	53	15	29	6	14	25	17	42	40
26	18	18	46	23	22	–0	24	8	08	8	32	12	01	15	54	15	30	6	18	22	17	38	44
27	18	23	12	23	20	–0	53	8	08	8	32	12	01	15	54	15	31	6	22	19	17	34	48
28	18	27	38	23	17	–1	23	8	08	8	32	12	02	15	55	15	32	6	26	15	17	30	52
29	18	32	04	23	14	–1	52	8	08	8	32	12	02	15	56	15	33	6	30	12	17	26	56
30	18	36	30	23	11	–2	21	8	08	8	32	12	03	15	57	15	34	6	34	08	17	23	00
31	18	40	55	23	06	–2	50	8	08	8	31	12	03	15	58	15	35	6	38	05	17	19	04

DURATION OF TWILIGHT (in minutes)

Latitude	*52°*	*56°*	*52°*	*56°*	*52°*	*56°*	*52°*	*56*
	1 December		*11 December*		*21 December*		*31 December*	
Civil	40	45	41	47	41	47	41	47
Nautical	82	93	84	96	85	97	84	96
Astronomical	123	138	125	141	126	142	125	141

THE NIGHT SKY

Mercury is at its greatest western elongation (21 degrees) on the 12th and thus is visible in the mornings for about 12 days either side of that date, magnitude +0.9 to –0.5. It may be seen low above the east-south-eastern horizon around the time of beginning of morning civil twilight. This morning apparition is the most suitable one of the year for observers in the latitudes of the British Isles.

Venus is still a magnificent object in the early evening sky, reaching its greatest brilliancy, magnitude –4.7, on the 9th. It is visible low above the south-western horizon for about two hours after sunset. On the evening of the 4th the three-day old crescent Moon will be seen about 4 degrees below the planet. Observers with telescopes can witness the decreasing crescent phase during the month (falling from 33 to 6 per cent illuminated) while the apparent diameter increases from 36 to 57 arcseconds.

Mars reaches its second stationary point on the 10th, when it resumes its direct motion, in the constellation of Aries. Its brightness decreases noticeably during the month, from a magnitude of –1.6 to –0.6, though still noticeably brighter than Aldebaran, some 30 degrees to the east. The waxing gibbous Moon is near the planet on the 11th and 12th.

Jupiter, magnitude –1.8, is a brilliant morning object, in the south-eastern sky. By the end of the month it is crossing the meridian at about the same time as sunrise. On the morning of the 27th the waning crescent Moon, 4 days before New, passes 5 degrees south of the planet. Jupiter moves from Virgo into Libra early in the month.

Saturn, magnitude 0.0, is now well placed for observation as it becomes visible in the eastern sky from the latter part of the evening onwards. Saturn is in the constellation of Cancer. The waning gibbous Moon will be seen near the planet around the 18th to the 20th.

Meteors. The maximum of the well-known Geminid meteor shower occurs on the late evening of the 13th though observation will be seriously affected by bright moonlight.

THE MOON

Day	RA		Dec.	Hor. par.	Semi-diam.	Sun's Co-long.	PA of Br. Limb	Ph.	Age	Rise				Transit		Set			
										52°		56°				52°		56°	
	h	m	°	′	′	°	°	%	d	h	m	h	m	h	m	h	m	h	m
1	15	51	−24.1	58.2	15.9	267	77	1	28.9	7	59	8	30	11	38	15	10	14	38
2	16	52	−27.1	58.8	16.0	279	319	0	0.4	9	22	10	00	12	39	15	53	15	14
3	17	55	−28.4	59.3	16.2	291	285	3	1.4	10	31	11	11	13	43	16	56	16	17
4	19	00	−27.8	59.6	16.2	304	272	8	2.4	11	20	11	55	14	46	18	18	17	44
5	20	04	−25.4	59.7	16.3	316	263	15	3.4	11	53	12	19	15	46	19	48	19	24
6	21	04	−21.3	59.6	16.2	328	256	24	4.4	12	16	12	34	16	41	21	20	21	04
7	22	00	−16.0	59.5	16.2	340	251	34	5.4	12	32	12	43	17	33	22	49	22	39
8	22	53	−9.9	59.2	16.1	352	248	46	6.4	12	45	12	50	18	21	—	—	—	—
9	23	43	−3.4	58.8	16.0	4	246	57	7.4	12	56	12	56	19	08	0	14	0	11
10	0	32	+3.2	58.5	15.9	17	247	68	8.4	13	07	13	02	19	54	1	37	1	40
11	1	21	+9.6	58.0	15.8	29	249	77	9.4	13	20	13	09	20	41	3	00	3	09
12	2	11	+15.4	57.6	15.7	41	253	86	10.4	13	35	13	17	21	30	4	24	4	40
13	3	03	+20.5	57.1	15.6	53	259	92	11.4	13	55	13	30	22	22	5	48	6	11
14	3	57	+24.4	56.6	15.4	65	269	97	12.4	14	22	13	50	23	17	7	10	7	41
15	4	53	+27.1	56.2	15.3	77	293	99	13.4	15	01	14	23	—	—	8	25	9	02
16	5	50	+28.3	55.7	15.2	89	37	100	14.4	15	54	15	15	0	12	9	26	10	05
17	6	47	+28.0	55.2	15.0	102	77	98	15.4	16	59	16	24	1	07	10	12	10	47
18	7	42	+26.3	54.8	14.9	114	90	95	16.4	18	11	17	43	1	59	10	44	11	13
19	8	34	+23.5	54.5	14.8	126	98	89	17.4	19	26	19	05	2	48	11	06	11	29
20	9	22	+19.6	54.2	14.8	138	104	83	18.4	20	40	20	25	3	34	11	22	11	39
21	10	08	+15.0	54.1	14.8	150	109	75	19.4	21	52	21	43	4	17	11	35	11	46
22	10	52	+9.9	54.2	14.8	162	111	67	20.4	23	03	22	59	4	57	11	45	11	51
23	11	34	+4.4	54.4	14.8	174	113	58	21.4	—	—	—	—	5	37	11	54	11	55
24	12	16	−1.3	54.8	14.9	187	113	48	22.4	0	14	0	15	6	16	12	03	12	00
25	13	00	−7.0	55.4	15.1	199	112	39	23.4	1	26	1	33	6	57	12	13	12	05
26	13	45	−12.6	56.1	15.3	211	110	29	24.4	2	43	2	55	7	41	12	26	12	12
27	14	34	−17.9	56.9	15.5	223	106	20	25.4	4	03	4	22	8	28	12	42	12	21
28	15	27	−22.5	57.8	15.8	235	100	13	26.4	5	29	5	56	9	21	13	05	12	37
29	16	25	−26.0	58.7	16.0	247	91	6	27.4	6	54	7	29	10	20	13	41	13	05
30	17	28	−28.1	59.5	16.2	260	76	2	28.4	8	11	8	51	11	23	14	35	13	55
31	18	34	−28.2	60.1	16.4	272	17	0	29.4	9	11	9	48	12	29	15	51	15	14

MERCURY

Day	RA		Dec.	Diam.	Phase	Transit		5° high			
								52°		56°	
	h	m	°	″	%	h	m	h	m	h	m
1	15	36	−16.9	9	16	10	53	7	03	7	24
3	15	33	−16.5	9	25	10	43	6	50	7	11
5	15	33	−16.4	8	34	10	36	6	43	7	03
7	15	35	−16.5	8	43	10	31	6	39	7	00
9	15	40	−16.9	7	51	10	28	6	38	7	00
11	15	46	−17.4	7	58	10	27	6	41	7	03
13	15	54	−18.0	7	64	10	27	6	45	7	08
15	16	03	−18.7	6	69	10	28	6	51	7	16
17	16	12	−19.3	6	74	10	30	6	58	7	24
19	16	23	−20.0	6	78	10	33	7	06	7	33
21	16	34	−20.7	6	81	10	36	7	14	7	43
23	16	45	−21.3	6	84	10	40	7	23	7	54
25	16	57	−21.9	5	86	10	44	7	32	8	04
27	17	09	−22.5	5	88	10	48	7	41	8	14
29	17	22	−22.9	5	90	10	53	7	49	8	25
31	17	35	−23.4	5	91	10	58	7	58	8	35

VENUS

Day	RA		Dec.	Diam.	Phase	Transit		5° high			
								52°		56°	
	h	m	°	″	%	h	m	h	m	h	m
1	19	38	−24.5	36	33	14	58	17	48	17	08
6	19	52	−23.5	39	29	14	51	17	51	17	15
11	20	03	−22.4	42	25	14	42	17	52	17	19
16	20	10	−21.3	46	20	14	30	17	48	17	19
21	20	14	−20.1	50	16	14	13	17	41	17	14
26	20	14	−19.0	54	11	13	53	17	28	17	04
31	20	09	−18.0	57	7	13	28	17	11	16	48

MARS

Day	RA		Dec.	Diam.	Phase	Transit		5° high			
								52°		56°	
	h	m	°	″	%	h	m	h	m	h	m
1	2	25	+15.1	17	97	21	41	4	30	4	40
6	2	23	+15.2	16	96	21	19	4	09	4	18
11	2	22	+15.3	15	95	20	59	3	49	3	59
16	2	23	+15.5	14	94	20	41	3	31	3	41
21	2	25	+15.8	14	93	20	23	3	15	3	25
26	2	28	+16.1	13	93	20	07	3	00	3	11
31	2	32	+16.5	12	92	19	51	2	47	2	58

SUNRISE AND SUNSET

	London				*Bristol*				*Birmingham*				*Manchester*				*Newcastle*				*Glasgow*				*Belfast*			
	0°05′		*51°30′*		*2°35′*		*51°28′*		*1°55′*		*52°28′*		*2°15′*		*53°28′*		*1°37′*		*54°59′*		*4°14′*		*55°52′*		*5°56′*		*54°35′*	
	h	*m*	*h*	*m*	*h*	*m*	*h*	*m*	*h*	*m*	*h*	*m*	*h*	*m*	*h*	*m*	*h*	*m*	*h*	*m*	*h*	*m*	*h*	*m*	*h*	*m*	*h*	*m*
1	7	44	15	55	7	54	16	05	7	56	15	58	8	02	15	54	8	07	15	43	8	23	15	49	8	23	16	03
2	7	45	15	54	7	55	16	04	7	57	15	57	8	03	15	53	8	09	15	42	8	25	15	48	8	24	16	02
3	7	46	15	54	7	56	16	04	7	58	15	56	8	05	15	53	8	11	15	42	8	26	15	47	8	26	16	01
4	7	48	15	53	7	58	16	03	8	00	15	56	8	06	15	52	8	12	15	41	8	28	15	46	8	27	16	01
5	7	49	15	53	7	59	16	03	8	01	15	55	8	08	15	51	8	14	15	40	8	29	15	46	8	28	16	00
6	7	50	15	52	8	00	16	03	8	02	15	55	8	09	15	51	8	15	15	40	8	31	15	45	8	30	16	00
7	7	51	15	52	8	01	16	02	8	04	15	55	8	10	15	51	8	16	15	39	8	32	15	44	8	31	15	59
8	7	53	15	52	8	02	16	02	8	05	15	54	8	11	15	50	8	18	15	39	8	34	15	44	8	32	15	59
9	7	54	15	52	8	04	16	02	8	06	15	54	8	13	15	50	8	19	15	39	8	35	15	44	8	34	15	58
10	7	55	15	51	8	05	16	02	8	07	15	54	8	14	15	50	8	20	15	38	8	36	15	43	8	35	15	58
11	7	56	15	51	8	06	16	01	8	08	15	54	8	15	15	50	8	21	15	38	8	37	15	43	8	36	15	58
12	7	57	15	51	8	07	16	01	8	09	15	54	8	16	15	50	8	22	15	38	8	38	15	43	8	37	15	58
13	7	58	15	51	8	08	16	01	8	10	15	54	8	17	15	49	8	23	15	38	8	39	15	43	8	38	15	58
14	7	59	15	51	8	09	16	01	8	11	15	54	8	18	15	49	8	24	15	38	8	40	15	43	8	39	15	58
15	8	00	15	51	8	09	16	02	8	12	15	54	8	19	15	50	8	25	15	38	8	41	15	43	8	40	15	58
16	8	00	15	52	8	10	16	02	8	13	15	54	8	20	15	50	8	26	15	38	8	42	15	43	8	41	15	58
17	8	01	15	52	8	11	16	02	8	13	15	54	8	20	15	50	8	27	15	38	8	43	15	43	8	42	15	58
18	8	02	15	52	8	12	16	02	8	14	15	54	8	21	15	50	8	28	15	39	8	44	15	43	8	42	15	58
19	8	02	15	52	8	12	16	03	8	15	15	55	8	22	15	51	8	28	15	39	8	45	15	44	8	43	15	59
20	8	03	15	53	8	13	16	03	8	15	15	55	8	22	15	51	8	29	15	39	8	45	15	44	8	44	15	59
21	8	04	15	53	8	13	16	04	8	16	15	56	8	23	15	51	8	30	15	40	8	46	15	44	8	44	15	59
22	8	04	15	54	8	14	16	04	8	16	15	56	8	23	15	52	8	30	15	40	8	46	15	45	8	45	16	00
23	8	05	15	54	8	14	16	05	8	17	15	57	8	24	15	53	8	30	15	41	8	47	15	46	8	45	16	01
24	8	05	15	55	8	15	16	05	8	17	15	57	8	24	15	53	8	31	15	41	8	47	15	46	8	46	16	01
25	8	05	15	56	8	15	16	06	8	18	15	58	8	24	15	54	8	31	15	42	8	47	15	47	8	46	16	02
26	8	06	15	56	8	15	16	07	8	18	15	59	8	25	15	55	8	31	15	43	8	48	15	48	8	46	16	03
27	8	06	15	57	8	16	16	07	8	18	16	00	8	25	15	55	8	31	15	44	8	48	15	49	8	46	16	04
28	8	06	15	58	8	16	16	08	8	18	16	00	8	25	15	56	8	32	15	45	8	48	15	50	8	46	16	04
29	8	06	15	59	8	16	16	09	8	18	16	01	8	25	15	57	8	32	15	46	8	48	15	51	8	46	16	05
30	8	06	16	00	8	16	16	10	8	18	16	02	8	25	15	58	8	32	15	47	8	48	15	52	8	46	16	06
31	8	06	16	01	8	16	16	11	8	18	16	03	8	25	15	59	8	31	15	48	8	48	15	53	8	46	16	08

JUPITER

Day	*RA*		*Dec.*		*Transit*		*5° high*			
							52°		*56°*	
	h	*m*	°	′	*h*	*m*	*h*	*m*	*h*	*m*
1	14	22.4	−13	03	9	41	5	27	5	43
11	14	30.1	−13	40	9	10	4	59	5	16
21	14	37.4	−14	14	8	38	4	31	4	48
31	14	44.1	−14	44	8	05	4	01	4	19

Diameters – equatorial 32″ polar 30″

SATURN

Day	*RA*		*Dec.*		*Transit*		*5° high*			
							52°		*56°*	
	h	*m*	°	′	*h*	*m*	*h*	*m*	*h*	*m*
1	8	55.4	+17	56	4	15	21	10	20	58
11	8	54.4	+18	02	3	35	20	30	20	17
21	8	52.7	+18	10	2	54	19	48	19	35
31	8	50.4	+18	21	2	12	19	05	18	53

Diameters – equatorial 20″ polar 18″
Rings – major axis 45″ minor axis 14″

URANUS

Day	*RA*		*Dec.*		*Transit*		*10° high*			
							52°		*56°*	
	h	*m*	°	′	*h*	*m*	*h*	*m*	*h*	*m*
1	22	35.8	−9	41	17	53	21	51	21	34
11	22	36.4	−9	37	17	14	21	13	20	56
21	22	37.4	−9	31	16	36	20	35	20	18
31	22	38.6	−9	23	15	58	19	58	19	41

Diameter 4″

NEPTUNE

Day	*RA*		*Dec.*		*Transit*		*10° high*			
							52°		*56°*	
	h	*m*	°	′	*h*	*m*	*h*	*m*	*h*	*m*
1	21	10.7	−16	26	16	28	19	39	19	10
11	21	11.6	−16	22	15	50	19	01	18	32
21	21	12.6	−16	18	15	12	18	23	17	54
31	21	13.8	−16	12	14	33	17	46	17	17

Diameter 2″

RISING AND SETTING TIMES

TABLE 1. SEMI-DIURNAL ARCS (HOUR ANGLES AT RISING/SETTING)

Dec.	*Latitude* 0°	10°	20°	30°	40°	45°	50°	52°	54°	56°	58°	60°	*Dec.*
	h m	*h m*	*h m*	*h m*	*h m*	*h m*	*h m*	*h m*	*h m*	*h m*	*h m*	*h m*	
0°	6 00	6 00	6 00	6 00	6 00	6 00	6 00	6 00	6 00	6 00	6 00	6 00	0°
1°	6 00	6 01	6 01	6 02	6 03	6 04	6 05	6 05	6 06	6 06	6 06	6 07	1°
2°	6 00	6 01	6 03	6 05	6 07	6 08	6 10	6 10	6 11	6 12	6 13	6 14	2°
3°	6 00	6 02	6 04	6 07	6 10	6 12	6 14	6 15	6 17	6 18	6 19	6 21	3°
4°	6 00	6 03	6 06	6 09	6 13	6 16	6 19	6 21	6 22	6 24	6 26	6 28	4°
5°	6 00	6 04	6 07	6 12	6 17	6 20	6 24	6 26	6 28	6 30	6 32	6 35	5°
6°	6 00	6 04	6 09	6 14	6 20	6 24	6 29	6 31	6 33	6 36	6 39	6 42	6°
7°	6 00	6 05	6 10	6 16	6 24	6 28	6 34	6 36	6 39	6 42	6 45	6 49	7°
8°	6 00	6 06	6 12	6 19	6 27	6 32	6 39	6 41	6 45	6 48	6 52	6 56	8°
9°	6 00	6 06	6 13	6 21	6 31	6 36	6 44	6 47	6 50	6 54	6 59	7 04	9°
10°	6 00	6 07	6 15	6 23	6 34	6 41	6 49	6 52	6 56	7 01	7 06	7 11	10°
11°	6 00	6 08	6 16	6 26	6 38	6 45	6 54	6 58	7 02	7 07	7 12	7 19	11°
12°	6 00	6 09	6 18	6 28	6 41	6 49	6 59	7 03	7 08	7 13	7 20	7 26	12°
13°	6 00	6 09	6 19	6 31	6 45	6 53	7 04	7 09	7 14	7 20	7 27	7 34	13°
14°	6 00	6 10	6 21	6 33	6 48	6 58	7 09	7 14	7 20	7 27	7 34	7 42	14°
15°	6 00	6 11	6 22	6 36	6 52	7 02	7 14	7 20	7 27	7 34	7 42	7 51	15°
16°	6 00	6 12	6 24	6 38	6 56	7 07	7 20	7 26	7 33	7 41	7 49	7 59	16°
17°	6 00	6 12	6 26	6 41	6 59	7 11	7 25	7 32	7 40	7 48	7 57	8 08	17°
18°	6 00	6 13	6 27	6 43	7 03	7 16	7 31	7 38	7 46	7 55	8 05	8 17	18°
19°	6 00	6 14	6 29	6 46	7 07	7 21	7 37	7 45	7 53	8 03	8 14	8 26	19°
20°	6 00	6 15	6 30	6 49	7 11	7 25	7 43	7 51	8 00	8 11	8 22	8 36	20°
21°	6 00	6 16	6 32	6 51	7 15	7 30	7 49	7 58	8 08	8 19	8 32	8 47	21°
22°	6 00	6 16	6 34	6 54	7 19	7 35	7 55	8 05	8 15	8 27	8 41	8 58	22°
23°	6 00	6 17	6 36	6 57	7 23	7 40	8 02	8 12	8 23	8 36	8 51	9 09	23°
24°	6 00	6 18	6 37	7 00	7 28	7 46	8 08	8 19	8 31	8 45	9 02	9 22	24°
25°	6 00	6 19	6 39	7 02	7 32	7 51	8 15	8 27	8 40	8 55	9 13	9 35	25°
26°	6 00	6 20	6 41	7 05	7 37	7 57	8 22	8 35	8 49	9 05	9 25	9 51	26°
27°	6 00	6 21	6 43	7 08	7 41	8 03	8 30	8 43	8 58	9 16	9 39	10 08	27°
28°	6 00	6 22	6 45	7 12	7 46	8 08	8 37	8 52	9 08	9 28	9 53	10 28	28°
29°	6 00	6 22	6 47	7 15	7 51	8 15	8 45	9 01	9 19	9 41	10 10	10 55	29°
30°	6 00	6 23	6 49	7 18	7 56	8 21	8 54	9 11	9 30	9 55	10 30	12 00	30°
35°	6 00	6 28	6 59	7 35	8 24	8 58	9 46	10 15	10 58	12 00	12 00	12 00	35°
40°	6 00	6 34	7 11	7 56	8 59	9 48	12 00	12 00	12 00	12 00	12 00	12 00	40°
45°	6 00	6 41	7 25	8 21	9 48	12 00	12 00	12 00	12 00	12 00	12 00	12 00	45°
50°	6 00	6 49	7 43	8 54	12 00	12 00	12 00	12 00	12 00	12 00	12 00	12 00	50°
55°	6 00	6 58	8 05	9 42	12 00	12 00	12 00	12 00	12 00	12 00	12 00	12 00	55°
60°	6 00	7 11	8 36	12 00	12 00	12 00	12 00	12 00	12 00	12 00	12 00	12 00	60°
65°	6 00	7 29	9 25	12 00	12 00	12 00	12 00	12 00	12 00	12 00	12 00	12 00	65°
70°	6 00	7 56	12 00	12 00	12 00	12 00	12 00	12 00	12 00	12 00	12 00	12 00	70°
75°	6 00	8 45	12 00	12 00	12 00	12 00	12 00	12 00	12 00	12 00	12 00	12 00	75°
80°	6 00	12 00	12 00	12 00	12 00	12 00	12 00	12 00	12 00	12 00	12 00	12 00	80°

TABLE 2. CORRECTION FOR REFRACTION AND SEMI-DIAMETER

	m	*m*	*m*	*m*	*m*	*m*	*m*	*m*	*m*	*m*	*m*	*m*	*m*
0°	3	3	4	4	4	5	5	5	6	6	6	7	0°
10°	3	3	4	4	4	5	5	6	6	6	7	7	10°
20°	4	4	4	4	5	5	6	7	7	8	8	9	20°
25°	4	4	4	4	5	6	7	8	8	9	11	13	25°
30°	4	4	4	5	6	7	8	9	11	14	21	—	30°

NB: Regarding Table 1. If latitude and declination are of the same sign, take out the respondent directly. If they are of opposite signs, subtract the respondent from 12h.

Table 1 gives the complete range of declinations in case any user wishes to calculate semi-diurnal arcs for bodies other than the Sun and Moon.

Example:

Lat.	Dec.	Semi-diurnal arc
+52°	+20°	7h 51m
+52°	–20°	4h 09m

SUNRISE AND SUNSET

The local mean time of sunrise or sunset may be found by obtaining the hour angle from Table 1 and applying it to the time of transit. The hour angle is negative for sunrise and positive for sunset. A small correction to the hour angle, which always has the effect of increasing it numerically, is necessary to allow for the Sun's semi-diameter (16′) and for refraction (34′); it is obtained from Table 2. The resulting local mean time may be converted into the standard time of the country by taking the difference between the longitude of the standard meridian of the country and that of the place, adding it to the local mean time if the place is west of the standard meridian, and subtracting it if the place is east.

Example– Required the New Zealand Mean Time (12h fast on GMT) of sunset on May 23 at Auckland, latitude 36° 50′ S. (or minus), longitude 11h 39m E. Taking the declination as +20°.6 (page 1235), we find

		h	*m*
New Zealand Standard Time	+	12	00
Longitude	–	11	39
Longitudinal Correction	+	0	21
Tabular entry for Lat. 30° and Dec. 20°, opposite signs	+	5	11
Proportional part for 6° 50′ of Lat.	–		15
Proportional part for 0°.6 of Dec.	–		2
Correction (Table 2)	+		4
Hour angle		4	58
Sun transits (page 1235)		11	57
Longitudinal correction	+		21
New Zealand Mean Time		17	16

MOONRISE AND MOONSET

It is possible to calculate the times of moonrise and moonset using Table 1, though the method is more complicated because the apparent motion of the Moon is much more rapid and also more variable than that of the Sun.

TABLE 3. LONGITUDE CORRECTION

X / *A*	*40m*	*45m*	*50m*	*55m*	*60m*	*65m*	*70m*
h	*m*	*m*	*m*	*m*	*m*	*m*	*m*
1	2	2	2	2	3	3	3
2	3	4	4	5	5	5	6
3	5	6	6	7	8	8	9
4	7	8	8	9	10	11	12
5	8	9	10	11	13	14	15
6	10	11	13	14	15	16	18
7	12	13	15	16	18	19	20
8	13	15	17	18	20	22	23
9	15	17	19	21	23	24	26
10	17	19	21	23	25	27	29
11	18	21	23	25	28	30	32
12	20	23	25	28	30	33	35
13	22	24	27	30	33	35	38
14	23	26	29	32	35	38	41
15	25	28	31	34	38	41	44
16	27	30	33	37	40	43	47
17	28	32	35	39	43	46	50
18	30	34	38	41	45	49	53
19	32	36	40	44	48	51	55
20	33	38	42	46	50	54	58
21	35	39	44	48	53	57	61
22	37	41	46	50	55	60	64
23	38	43	48	53	58	62	67
24	40	45	50	55	60	65	70

The parallax of the Moon, about 57′, is near to the sum of the semi-diameter and refraction but has the opposite effect on these times. It is thus convenient to neglect all three quantities in the method outlined below.

Notation

ϕ	= latitude of observer
λ	= longitude of observer (measured positively towards the west)
T_{-1}	= time of transit of Moon on previous day
T_0	= time of transit of Moon on day in question
T_1	= time of transit of Moon on following day
δ_0	= approximate declination of Moon
δ_R	= declination of Moon at moonrise
δ_S	= declination of Moon at moonset
h_0	= approximate hour angle of Moon
h_R	= hour angle of Moon at moonrise
h_S	= hour angle of Moon at moonset
t_R	= time of moonrise
t_S	= time of moonset

Method

1. With arguments ϕ, δ_0 enter Table 1 on page 1266 to determine h_0 where h_0 is negative for moonrise and positive for moonset.

2. Form approximate times from
 $t_R = T_0 + \lambda + h_0$
 $t_S = T_0 + \lambda + h_0$

3. Determine δ_R, δ_S for times t_R, t_S respectively.

4. Re-enter Table 1 on page 1266 with
 (*a*) arguments ϕ, δ_R to determine h_R
 (*b*) arguments ϕ, δ_S to determine h_S

5. Form $t_R = T_0 + \lambda + h_R + AX$
 $t_S = T_0 + \lambda + h_S + AX$

 where $A = (\lambda + h)$

 and $X = (T_0 - T_{-1})$ if $(\lambda + h)$ is negative
 $X = (T_1 - T_0)$ if $(\lambda + h)$ is positive

 AX is the respondent in Table 3.

Example – To find the times of moonrise and moonset at Vancouver (ϕ = +49°, λ = +8h 12m) on 2005 August 24. The starting data (page 1248) are

T_{-1} = 2h 55m
T_0 = 3h 43m
T_1 = 4h 32m
δ_0 = +15°

1. h_0 = 7h 12m
2. Approximate values
 t_R = 24d 03h 43m + 8h 12m + (–7h 12m)
 = 24d 04h 43m
 t_S = 24d 03h 43m + 8h 12m + (+7h 12m)
 = 24d 19h 07m
3. δ_R = +13°.4
 δ_S = +16°.7
4. h_R = – 7h 04m
 h_S = +7h 20m
5. t_R = 24d 03h 43m + 8h 12m + (–7h 04m) + 2m
 = 24d 04h 53m
 t_S = 24d 03h 43m + 8h 12m + (+7h 20m) + 31m
 = 24d 19h 46m

To get the LMT of the phenomenon the longitude is subtracted from the GMT thus:

Moonrise = 8d 06h 40m – 8h 12m = 7d 22h 28m
Moonset = 8d 22h 29m – 8h 12m = 8d 14h 17m

ECLIPSES AND OCCULTATIONS 2005

ECLIPSES

During 2005 there will be three eclipses, two of the Sun and one of the Moon. (Penumbral eclipses are not mentioned in this section as they are so difficult to observe).

1. An annular-total eclipse of the Sun on April 8 is visible as a partial eclipse from North Island (New Zealand), the Pacific Ocean, southern North America, Central America, South America (except for eastern Brazil and south of about S.35), the Caribbean and Bermuda. The partial phase begins at 17h 51m and ends at 23h 20m. The path of the central line is annular at the beginning of the track, but is total over most of the Pacific Ocean. It again becomes annular before crossing Panama and Columbia. The annular eclipse ends in Venezuela. Annularity begins at 18h 53m and ends at 22h 18m. The maximum duration of totality (42 seconds) occurs in the middle of the Pacific Ocean.

2. An annular eclipse of the Sun on October 3 is visible as a partial eclipse from the Arctic Ocean, Greenland, Iceland, the eastern North Atlantic Ocean, Africa (except the southern tip), Europe (including the British Isles), west and south Asia, and the Indian Ocean, including Madagascar. The partial phase begins at 07h 35m and ends at 13h 28m. The path of annularity starts in the eastern North Atlantic Ocean, crosses northern Portugal, Spain, northern Algeria, Tunisia, Libya, north-east Chad, Sudan, south-west Ethiopia, north-east Kenya, and the extreme south of Somalia before ending in the Indian Ocean. Totality begins at 08h 41m and ends at 12h 23m. The maximum duration is 4m 31s. At Greenwich the partial phase begins at 7h 49m and ends at 10h 18m, with 66 per cent of the Sun obscured at maximum. From Edinburgh the corresponding times are 7h 53m and 10h 13m, with a maximum obscuration of the Sun of 58 per cent.

3. A partial eclipse of the Moon on the October 17 is visible from the Arctic Ocean, North and Central America, western South America, the Pacific Ocean, Asia, Australasia, the Indian Ocean and the Southern Ocean. The eclipse begins at 11h 34m and ends at 12h 32m. At maximum only 7 per cent of the moon is obscured.

LUNAR OCCULTATIONS

Observations of the times of occultations are made by both amateur and professional astronomers. Such observations are later analysed to yield accurate positions of the Moon; this is one method of determining the difference between terrestrial time and universal time.

Many of the observations made by amateurs are obtained with the use of a stop-watch which is compared with a time-signal immediately after the observation. Thus an accuracy of about one-fifth of a second is obtainable, though the observer's personal equation may amount to one-third or one-half of a second.

The list on page 1269 includes most of the occultations visible under favourable conditions in the British Isles. No occultation is included unless the star is at least 10° above the horizon and the Sun sufficiently far below the horizon to permit the star to be seen with the naked eye or with a small telescope. The altitude limit is reduced from 10° to 2° for stars and planets brighter than magnitude 2.0 and such occultations are also predicted in daylight.

The column Phase shows (i) whether a disappearance (D) or reappearance (R) is to be observed; and (ii) whether it is at the dark limb (D) or bright limb (B). The column headed 'El. of Moon' gives the elongation of the Moon from the Sun, in degrees. The elongation increases from 0° at New Moon to 180° at Full Moon and on to 360° (or 0°) at New Moon again. Times and position angles (*P*), reckoned from the north point in the direction north, east, south, west, are given for Greenwich (lat. 51° 30′, long. 0°) and Edinburgh (lat. 56° 00′, long. 3° 12′ west).

The coefficients *a* and *b* are the variations in the GMT for each degree of longitude (positive to the west) and latitude (positive to the north) respectively; they enable approximate times (to within about 1m generally) to be found for any point in the British Isles. If the point of observation is $\Delta\lambda$ degrees west and $\Delta\phi$ degrees north, the approximate time is found by adding $a.\Delta\lambda+b.\Delta\phi$ to the given GMT.

Example: the disappearance of ZC465 on March 14 at Coventry, found from both Greenwich and Edinburgh.

	Greenwich		Edinburgh	
		°		°
Longitude		0.0		+3.2
Long. of Coventry		+1.5		+1.5
$\Delta\lambda$		+1.5		−1.7
Latitude		+51.5		+56.0
Lat. of Coventry		+52.4		+52.4
$\Delta\phi$		+0.9		−3.6
	h	*m*	*h*	*m*
GMT	21	32.4	21	22.3
$a.\Delta\lambda$		+0.3		+0.2
$b.\Delta\phi$		−2.3		+7.6
	21	30.4	21	30.1

If the occultation is given for one station but not the other, the reason for the suppression is given by the following code:

N = star not occulted
A = star's altitude less than 10° (2° for bright stars and planets)
S = Sun not sufficiently below the horizon
G = occultation is of very short duration

In some cases the coefficients *a* and *b* are not given; this is because the occultation is so short that prediction for other places by means of these coefficients would not be reliable.

LUNAR OCCULTATIONS 2005

						GREENWICH					EDINBURGH				
Date		*ZC*	*Mag.*	*Phase*	*El. of Moon*	*UT*		*a*	*b*	*P*	*UT*		*a*	*b*	*P*
						h	*m*	*m*	*m*	°	*h*	*m*	*m*	*m*	°
Jan.	17	319	7.6	DD	97	22	10.1	−0.9	−2.8	111	21	57.5	−0.9	−1.7	92
	18	325	7.4	DD	98	0	18.2	G		5	N				
	18	416	5.4	DD	106	16	50.9	+0.2	+3.2	5	N				
	18	429	6.9	DD	108	20	18.6	G		129	20	01.7	−1.7	−1.1	102
	18	433	5.6	DD	108	21	11.3	−1.5	−1.4	95	21	02.8	−1.3	−0.5	78
	18	432	5.9	DD	108	21	24.0	G		7	N				
	19	563	6.9	DD	120	23	28.2	−1.0	−0.3	57	23	24.8	−1.0	+0.3	42
	19	566	5.9	DD	121	23	43.0	−0.4	−4.4	135	23	25.8	−0.8	−2.7	115
	20	582	5.8	DD	122	N					3	11.5	G		155
	20	703	6.3	DD	131	22	16.8	−1.5	−1.5	104	22	07.3	−1.4	−0.6	88
	22	844	5.7	DD	143	1	12.4	−0.2	−3.5	141	0	57.2	−0.5	−2.8	127
Feb.	13	264	7.0	DD	64	18	46.3	−1.4	−1.9	101	18	36.1	−1.2	−0.9	82
	19	1067	7.2	DD	132	20	15.3	−1.7	−3.7	153	20	00.4	−1.5	−1.1	130
	20	1088	5.6	DD	134	2	02.5	−0.2	−1.8	104	1	53.4	−0.4	−1.8	100
	20	1105	6.5	DD	136	A					4	32.3	+0.1	−1.3	68
	21	1206	5.9	DD	145	0	30.5	−2.2	+0.5	53	0	28.0	G		39
	21	1211	6.2	DD	145	0	54.5	−0.8	−1.9	113	0	43.6	−0.9	−1.7	107
Mar.	14	465	4.5	DD	57	21	32.4	+0.2	−2.5	116	21	22.3	−0.1	−2.1	103
	15	611	7.0	DD	70	A					23	44.0	+0.2	−1.4	87
	17	890	4.5	DD	91	22	28.3	−0.4	−2.0	109	22	18.0	−0.5	−1.9	101
	18	909	6.1	DD	93	A					1	47.8	+0.2	−1.3	80
	18	1035	6.8	DD	102	21	19.2	−1.2	−1.6	102	21	09.4	−1.2	−1.1	92
	19	1056	7.0	DD	104	2	23.3	+0.3	−1.2	82	2	18.1	+0.2	−1.4	80
	20	1169	5.4	DD	114	0	29.3	+0.2	−2.5	144	0	18.5	0.0	−2.5	140
	20	1270	6.1	DD	123	19	53.6	−2.1	+2.2	62	20	02.7	G		37
	22	1393	6.7	DD	136	0	31.3	G		37	N				
	22	1479	6.3	DD	145	19	45.5	−1.1	−0.9	142	19	40.0	−1.0	−0.1	128
Apr.	12	683	7.3	DD	48	19	29.5	G		146	S				
	12	698	7.6	DD	49	21	52.5	−0.7	+0.4	26	21	53.7	G		10
	13	812	7.8	DD	59	19	31.8	G		17	N				
	14	979	7.7	DD	71	20	44.6	−1.4	−0.1	51	20	40.7	−1.6	+0.6	39
	15	1108	6.9	DD	82	20	58.4	−0.4	−2.6	134	20	45.9	−0.6	−2.3	127
	16	1131	7.2	DD	84	A					1	05.3	+0.7	−1.9	152
	17	1251	5.9	DD	95	1	22.8	+0.4	−1.6	111	1	16.3	+0.2	−1.7	111
	17	1348	7.7	DD	104	21	09.7	−1.3	−1.4	103	20	59.9	−1.3	−1.1	97
	19	1462	7.4	DD	117	1	30.2	−0.4	−1.5	71	1	21.6	−0.5	−1.6	71
	20	1645	6.6	DD	137	20	44.7	−0.8	−1.6	155	20	36.1	−0.8	−1.1	147
	20	1648	7.0	DD	138	21	43.1	−1.7	−0.5	100	21	36.5	−1.6	−0.1	95
May	10	780	6.8	DD	30	A					21	26.5	+0.9	−2.4	146
	12	1067	7.2	DD	52	20	54.6	0.0	−1.9	114	S				
Jun.	19	2237	5.1	DD	149	22	26.0	−1.3	−0.6	126	22	20.0	−1.1	−0.4	126
Jul.	2	465	4.5	RD	310	2	47.5	0.0	1.7	254	S				
	11	1644	4.1	DD	59	21	53.3	−0.1	−1.6	82	21	45.1	−0.2	−1.8	81
Sep.	14	3032	7.2	DD	135	21	44.3	−0.9	+0.3	41	A				
	15	3175	4.8	DD	148	20	06.5	G		349	N				
	22	472	5.0	RD	233	3	17.2	−1.6	+0.1	265	3	11.4	−1.7	−0.4	283
	24	890	4.5	RD	266	22	39.9	+0.7	+2.0	218	22	50.5	+0.6	+1.8	228
Oct.	12	3130	5.5	DD	117	20	41.3	−1.5	−0.3	84	20	36.3	−1.2	−0.1	75
	14	3421	5.1	DD	146	22	55.9	−0.5	+1.1	20	23	00.8	0.0	+1.5	2
Nov.	9	3228	6.5	DD	99	19	10.1	−1.5	0.0	80	19	06.1	−1.2	+0.2	71
	12	81	6.6	DD	139	20	20.3	−0.6	+1.8	21	20	27.5	−0.2	+2.0	8
Dec.	5	3032	7.2	DD	54	16	36.5	−1.7	−0.6	101	A				
	6	3191	7.6	DD	69	18	39.2	−1.4	−1.0	92	18	31.6	−1.1	−0.6	79
	7	3327	6.8	DD	82	18	31.5	−1.5	−0.3	82	18	26.6	−1.2	0.0	70
	9	38	7.9	DD	107	16	42.7	−1.0	+1.5	64	16	46.8	−0.8	+1.6	57
	9	50	6.0	DD	109	21	21.8	−0.5	+1.2	21	21	28.1	0.0	+2.2	359
	11	309	7.9	DD	135	22	18.7	−1.1	+0.8	46	22	20.4	−0.8	+1.4	28
	12	326	6.0	DD	137	1	55.8	−0.4	−0.5	56	1	52.8	−0.5	−0.2	41

MEAN PLACES OF STARS 2005.5

Name	*Mag.*	*RA* h	m	*Dec.* °	′	*Spectrum*
α And *Alpheratz*	2.1	0	08.7	+29	07	A0*p*
β Cassiopeiae *Caph*	2.3	0	09.5	+59	11	F5
γ Pegasi *Algenib*	2.8	0	13.5	+15	13	B2
β Mensae	2.9	0	26.0	−77	13	G0
α Phoenicis	2.4	0	26.6	−42	17	K0
α Cassiopeiae *Schedar*	2.2	0	40.8	+56	34	K0
β Ceti *Diphda*	2.0	0	43.9	−17	57	K0
γ Cassiopeiae*	Var.	0	57.0	+60	45	B0*p*
β Andromedae *Mirach*	2.1	1	10.0	+35	39	M0
δ Cassiopeiae	2.7	1	26.2	+60	16	A5
α Eridani *Achernar*	0.5	1	37.9	−57	13	B5
β Arietis *Sheratan*	2.6	1	54.9	+20	50	A5
γ Andromedae *Almak*	2.3	2	04.2	+42	21	K0
α Arietis *Hamal*	2.0	2	07.5	+23	29	K2
α Ursae Minoris *Polaris*	2.0	2	38.2	+89	17	F8
β Persei *Algol**	Var.	3	08.5	+40	59	B8
α Persei *Mirfak*	1.8	3	24.7	+49	53	F5
η Tauri *Alcyone*	2.9	3	47.8	+24	07	B5*p*
α Tauri *Aldebaran*	0.9	4	36.2	+16	31	K5
β Orionis *Rigel*	0.1	5	14.8	−8	12	B8*p*
α Aurigae *Capella*	0.1	5	17.1	+46	00	G0
γ Orionis *Bellatrix*	1.6	5	25.4	+6	21	B2
β Tauri *Elnath*	1.7	5	26.6	+28	37	B8
δ Orionis	2.2	5	32.3	−0	18	B0
α Leporis	2.6	5	33.0	−17	49	F0
ε Orionis	1.7	5	36.5	−1	12	B0
ζ Orionis	1.8	5	41.0	−1	56	B0
κ Orionis	2.1	5	48.0	−9	40	B0
α Orionis *Betelgeuse**	Var.	5	55.5	+7	24	M0
β Aurigae *Menkalinan*	1.9	5	59.9	+44	57	A0*p*
β CMa *Mirzam*	2.0	6	22.9	−17	58	B1
α Carinae *Canopus*	−0.7	6	24.1	−52	42	F0
γ Geminorum *Alhena*	1.9	6	38.0	+16	24	A0
α Canis Majoris *Sirius*	−1.5	6	45.4	−16	43	A0
ε Canis Majoris	1.5	6	58.8	−28	59	B1
δ Canis Majoris	1.9	7	08.6	−26	24	F8*p*
α Germinorum *Castor*	1.6	7	35.0	+31	53	A0
α CMi Procyon	0.4	7	39.6	+5	13	F5
β Geminorum *Pollux*	1.1	7	45.7	+28	01	K0
ζ Puppis	1.7	8	03.8	−40	01	Od
γ Velorum	1.8	8	09.7	−47	21	Oa*p*
ε Carinae	1.9	8	22.6	−59	32	K0
δ Velorum	2.0	8	44.9	−54	44	A0
λ Velorum *Suhail*	2.2	9	08.2	−43	27	K5
β Carinae	1.7	9	13.3	−69	44	A0
ι Carinae	2.2	9	17.2	−59	18	F0
κ Velorum	2.6	9	22.3	−55	02	B3
α Hydrae *Alphard*	2.0	9	27.9	−8	41	K2
α Leonis *Regulus*	1.3	10	08.7	+11	56	B8
γ Leonis *Algeiba*	1.9	10	20.3	+19	49	K0
β Ursae Majoris *Merak*	2.4	11	02.2	+56	21	A0
α Ursae Majoris *Dubhe*	1.8	11	04.1	+61	43	K0
δ Leonis	2.6	11	14.4	+20	30	A3
β Leonis *Denebola*	2.1	11	49.3	+14	32	A2
γ Ursae Majoris *Phecda*	2.4	11	54.1	+53	40	A0
γ Corvi	2.6	12	16.1	−17	34	B8
α Crucis	1.0	12	26.9	−63	08	B1
γ Crucis	1.6	12	31.5	−57	09	M3
γ Centauri	2.2	12	41.8	−48	59	A0
γ Viriginis	2.7	12	41.9	−1	29	F0
β Crucis	1.3	12	48.0	−59	43	B1
ε Ursae Majoris *Alioth*	1.8	12	54.3	+55	56	A0*p*
α Canum *Venaticorum*	2.9	12	56.3	+38	17	A0*p*
ζ Ursae Majoris *Mizar*	2.1	13	24.1	+54	54	A2*p*
α Virginis *Spica*	1.0	13	25.5	−11	11	B2
ε Centauri	2.6	13	40.2	−53	30	B1
η Ursae Majoris *Alkaid*	1.9	13	47.8	+49	17	B3
β Centauri *Hadar*	0.6	14	04.2	−60	24	B1
θ Centauri	2.1	14	07.0	−36	24	K0
α Bootis *Arcturus*	0.0	14	15.9	+19	09	K0
α Centauri *Rigil Kent*	0.1	14	40.0	−60	51	G0
ε Bootis	2.4	14	45.2	+27	03	K0
β UMi *Kochab*	2.1	14	50.7	+74	08	K5
γ Ursae Minoris	3.1	15	20.7	+71	49	A2
α CrB *Alphecca*	2.2	15	34.9	+26	42	A0
β Trianguli *Australis*	3.0	15	55.6	−63	27	F0
δ Scorpii	2.3	16	00.7	−22	38	B0
β Scorpii	2.6	16	05.8	−19	49	B1
α Scorpii *Antares*	1.0	16	29.7	−26	27	M0
α Trianguli Australis	1.9	16	49.3	−69	02	K2
ε Scorpii	2.3	16	50.5	−34	18	K0
α Herculis†	Var.	17	14.9	+14	23	M3
λ Scorpii	1.6	17	34.0	−37	06	B2
α Ophiuchi *Rasalhague*	2.1	17	35.2	+12	33	A5
θ Scorpii	1.9	17	37.7	−43	00	F0
κ Scorpii	2.4	17	42.9	−39	02	B2
λ Draconis	2.2	17	56.7	+51	29	K5
ε Sgr Kaus *Australis*	1.9	18	24.5	−34	23	A0
α Lyrae Vega	0.0	18	37.1	+38	47	A0
σ Sagittarii	2.0	18	55.6	−26	17	B3
β Cygni *Albireo*	3.1	19	30.9	+27	58	K0
α Aquilae *Altair*	0.8	19	51.1	+8	53	A5
α Capricorni	3.8	20	18.4	−12	32	G5
γ Cygni	2.2	20	22.4	+40	16	F8*p*
α Pavonis	1.9	20	26.1	−56	43	B3
α Cygni *Deneb*	1.3	20	41.6	+45	18	A2*p*
α Cephei *Alderamin*	2.4	21	18.7	+62	37	A5
ε Pegasi	2.4	21	44.5	+9	54	K0
δ Capricorni	2.9	21	47.3	−16	06	A5
α Gruis	1.7	22	08.6	−46	56	B5
δ Cephei†	3.7	22	29.4	+58	27	†
β Gruis	2.1	22	43.0	−46	51	M3
α PsA *Fomalhaut*	1.2	22	58.0	−29	36	A3
β Pegasi *Scheat*	2.4	23	04.0	+28	07	M0
α Pegasi *Markab*	2.5	23	05.0	+15	14	A0

*γ Cassiopeiae, 2004 mag. 2.6. β Persei, mag. 2.1 to 3.4.
α Orionis, mag. 0.1 to 1.2.
†α Herculis, mag. 3.1 to 3.9.
δ Cephei, mag. 3.7 to 4.4, spectrum F5 to G0.

The positions of heavenly bodies on the celestial sphere are defined by two co-ordinates, right ascension and declination, which are analogous to longitude and latitude on the surface of the Earth. If we imagine the plane of the terrestrial equator extended indefinitely, it will cut the celestial sphere in a great circle known as the celestial equator. Similarly the plane of the Earth's orbit, when extended, cuts in the great circle called the ecliptic. The two intersections of these circles are known as the First Point of Aries and the First Point of Libra. If from any star a perpendicular is drawn to the celestial equator, the length of this perpendicular is the star's declination. The arc, measured eastwards along the equator from the First Point of Aries to the foot of this perpendicular, is the right ascension. An alternative definition of right ascension is that it is the angle at the celestial pole (where the Earth's axis, if prolonged, would meet the sphere) between the great circles to the First Point of Aries and to the star.

The plane of the Earth's equator has a slow movement, so that our reference system for right ascension and declination is not fixed. The consequent alteration in these quantities from year to year is called precession. In right ascension it is an increase of about 3 seconds a year for equatorial stars, and larger or smaller changes in either direction for stars near the poles, depending on the right ascension of the star. In declination it varies between +20″ and −20″ according to the right ascension of the star.

A star or other body crosses the meridian when the sidereal time is equal to its right ascension. The altitude is then a maximum, and may be deduced by remembering that the altitude of the elevated pole is numerically equal to the latitude, while that of the equator at its intersection with the meridian is equal to the co-latitude, or complement of the latitude.

Thus in London (lat. 51° 30′) the meridian altitude of Sirius is found as follows:

	°	′
Altitude of equator	38	30
Declination south	16	43
Difference	21	47

The altitude of Capella (Dec. +46° 00′) at lower transit is:

Altitude of pole	51	30
Polar distance of star	44	00
Difference	7	30

The brightness of a heavenly body is denoted by its magnitude. Omitting the exceptionally bright stars Sirius and Canopus, the twenty brightest stars are of the first magnitude, while the faintest stars visible to the naked eye are of the sixth magnitude. The magnitude scale is a precise one, as a difference of five magnitudes represents a ratio of 100 to 1 in brightness. Typical second magnitude stars are Polaris and the stars in the belt of Orion. The scale is most easily fixed in memory by comparing the stars with Norton's *Star Atlas*. The stars Sirius and Canopus and the planets Venus and Jupiter are so bright that their magnitudes are expressed by negative numbers. A small telescope will show stars down to the ninth or tenth magnitude, while stars fainter than the twentieth magnitude may be photographed by long exposures with the largest telescopes.

MEAN AND SIDEREAL TIME

Acceleration						Retardation					
h	*m*	*s*	*m*	*s*	*s*	*h*	*m*	*s*	*m*	*s*	*s*
1	0	10	0	00	0	1	0	10	0	00	0
2	0	20	3	02	1	2	0	20	3	03	1
3	0	30	9	07	2	3	0	29	9	09	2
4	0	39	15	13	3	4	0	39	15	15	3
5	0	49	21	18	4	5	0	49	21	21	4
6	0	59	27	23	5	6	0	59	27	28	5
7	1	09	33	28	6	7	1	09	33	34	6
8	1	19	39	34	7	8	1	19	39	40	7
9	1	29	45	39	8	9	1	28	45	46	8
10	1	39	51	44	9	10	1	38	51	53	9
11	1	48	57	49	10	11	1	48	57	59	10
12	1	58	60	00		12	1	58	60	00	
13	2	08				13	2	08			
14	2	18				14	2	18			
15	2	28				15	2	27			
16	2	38				16	2	37			
17	2	48				17	2	47			
18	2	57				18	2	57			
19	3	07				19	3	07			
20	3	17				20	3	17			
21	3	27				21	3	26			
22	3	37				22	3	36			
23	3	47				23	3	46			
24	3	57				24	3	56			

The length of a sidereal day in mean time is 23h 56m 04s.09. Hence 1h MT = 1h+9^{s}.86 ST and 1h ST = 1h−9^{s}.83 MT.

To convert an interval of mean time to the corresponding interval of sidereal time, enter the acceleration table with the given mean time (taking the hours and the minutes and seconds separately) and add the acceleration obtained to the given mean time. To convert an interval of sidereal time to the corresponding interval of mean time, take out the retardation for the given sidereal time and subtract.

The columns for the minutes and seconds of the argument are in the form known as critical tables. To use these tables, find in the appropriate left-hand column the two entries between which the given number of minutes and seconds lies; the quantity in the right-hand column between these two entries is the required acceleration or retardation. Thus the acceleration for 11m 26s (which lies between the entries 9m 07s and 15m 13s) is 2s. If the given number of minutes and seconds is a tabular entry, the required acceleration or retardation is the entry in the right-hand column above the given tabular entry, e.g. the retardation for 45m 46s is 7s.

Example – Convert 14h 27m 35s from ST to MT

	h	*m*	*s*
Given ST	14	27	35
Retardation for 14h		2	18
Retardation for 27m 35s			5
Corresponding MT	14	25	12

For further explanation, *see* pages 1275–1276.

ECLIPSES AND SHADOW TRANSITS OF JUPITER'S SATELLITES 2005

GMT *d*	*h*	*m*	*Sat.*	*Phen.*
January				
1	07	04	II	Sh.I
3	02	05	II	Ec.D
7	06	15	I	Sh.I
8	03	22	I	Ec.D
9	01	59	III	Sh.E
9	02	55	I	Sh.E
10	04	40	II	Ec.D
12	01	35	II	Sh.E
15	05	15	I	Ec.D
16	02	36	I	Sh.I
16	03	08	III	Sh.I
16	04	48	I	Sh.E
16	05	55	III	Sh.E
17	07	15	II	Ec.D
19	01	27	II	Sh.I
19	04	08	II	Sh.E
22	07	08	I	Ec.D
23	04	29	I	Sh.I
23	06	42	I	Sh.E
23	07	05	III	Sh.I
24	01	37	I	Ec.D
25	01	10	I	Sh.E
26	04	01	II	Sh.I
26	06	41	II	Sh.E
30	06	23	I	Sh.I
31	03	30	I	Ec.D
February				
1	00	51	I	Sh.I
1	03	03	I	Sh.E
2	06	34	II	Sh.I
3	01	07	III	Ec.D
3	03	54	III	Ec.R
4	01	42	II	Ec.D
7	05	23	I	Ec.D
8	02	44	I	Sh.I
8	04	56	I	Sh.E
8	23	51	I	Ec.D
9	23	24	I	Sh.E
10	05	04	III	Ec.D
11	04	17	II	Ec.D
13	01	06	II	Sh.E
15	04	37	I	Sh.I
15	06	49	I	Sh.E
16	01	44	I	Ec.D
16	23	06	I	Sh.I
17	01	18	I	Sh.E
18	06	51	II	Ec.D
20	00	59	II	Sh.I
20	03	40	II	Sh.E
20	22	56	III	Sh.I
21	01	39	III	Sh.E
22	06	31	I	Sh.I
23	03	37	I	Ec.D
24	00	59	I	Sh.I
24	03	11	I	Sh.E
27	03	34	II	Sh.I
27	06	15	II	Sh.E
28	02	53	III	Sh.I
28	05	36	III	Sh.E
28	22	43	II	Ec.D
March				
2	05	31	I	Ec.D
3	02	52	I	Sh.I
3	05	04	I	Sh.E
3	23	59	I	Ec.D
4	23	33	I	Sh.E
6	06	08	II	Sh.I
8	01	17	II	Ec.D
9	22	07	II	Sh.E
10	04	46	I	Sh.I
11	01	53	I	Ec.D
11	23	14	I	Sh.I
12	01	26	I	Sh.E
15	03	52	II	Ec.D
16	22	00	II	Sh.I
17	00	42	II	Sh.E
18	00	55	III	Ec.D
18	03	47	I	Ec.D
19	01	07	I	Sh.I
19	03	19	I	Sh.E
19	22	15	I	Ec.D
20	21	48	I	Sh.E
24	00	36	II	Sh.I
24	03	17	II	Sh.E
25	04	53	III	Ec.D
25	05	41	I	Ec.D
26	03	01	I	Sh.I
26	05	13	I	Sh.E
27	00	09	I	Ec.D
27	21	29	I	Sh.I
27	23	41	I	Sh.E
28	21	23	III	Sh.E
31	03	11	II	Sh.I
April				
1	22	17	II	Ec.D
2	04	55	I	Sh.I
3	02	03	I	Ec.D
3	04	16	I	Ec.R
3	23	23	I	Sh.I
4	01	35	I	Sh.E
4	22	43	III	Sh.I
4	22	44	I	Ec.R
5	01	20	III	Sh.E
5	20	04	I	Sh.E
9	03	32	II	Ec.R
10	21	47	II	Sh.E
11	01	17	I	Sh.I
11	03	29	I	Sh.E
12	00	39	I	Ec.R
12	02	42	III	Sh.I
12	19	46	I	Sh.I
12	21	57	I	Sh.E
17	21	42	II	Sh.I
18	00	23	II	Sh.E
18	03	11	I	Sh.I
19	02	33	I	Ec.R
19	21	40	I	Sh.I
19	23	51	I	Sh.E
20	21	02	I	Ec.R
22	23	23	III	Ec.R
25	00	19	II	Sh.I
25	03	00	II	Sh.E
26	21	57	II	Ec.R
26	23	34	I	Sh.I
27	01	45	I	Sh.E
27	22	56	I	Ec.R
28	20	14	I	Sh.E
30	03	21	III	Ec.R
May				
2	02	55	II	Sh.I
4	00	31	II	Ec.R
4	01	28	I	Sh.I
5	00	51	I	Ec.R
5	22	08	I	Sh.E
10	21	08	III	Sh.E
12	21	31	II	Sh.E
12	21	51	I	Sh.I
13	00	02	I	Sh.E
13	21	15	I	Ec.R
17	22	35	III	Sh.I
18	01	06	III	Sh.E
19	21	28	II	Sh.I
19	23	45	I	Sh.I
20	00	08	II	Sh.E
20	01	56	I	Sh.E
20	23	10	I	Ec.R
27	00	05	II	Sh.I
27	01	40	I	Sh.I
28	01	05	I	Ec.R
28	21	31	II	Ec.R
28	22	19	I	Sh.E
June				
4	22	03	I	Sh.I
4	23	12	III	Ec.R
5	00	05	II	Ec.R
5	00	13	I	Sh.E
5	21	29	I	Ec.R
11	23	57	I	Sh.I
12	23	24	I	Ec.R
13	21	18	II	Sh.E
20	21	17	II	Sh.I
20	22	31	I	Sh.E
20	23	55	II	Sh.E
27	22	15	I	Sh.I
28	21	43	I	Ec.R
29	22	30	III	Sh.I
July				
15	21	05	II	Sh.E
21	21	57	I	Ec.R
22	21	05	II	Sh.I
31	20	40	II	Ec.R
November				
24	06	26	II	Sh.I
26	06	05	I	Ec.D
December				
4	07	19	I	Sh.E
8	06	22	III	Ec.R
10	05	56	II	Ec.D
11	07	02	I	Sh.I
19	05	57	II	Sh.E
19	06	13	I	Ec.D
20	05	34	I	Sh.E
26	05	56	II	Sh.I
27	05	18	I	Sh.I
27	07	28	I	Sh.E

Jupiter's satellites transit across the disk from east to west, and pass behind the disk from west to east. The shadows that they cast also transit across the disk. With the exception at times of Satellite IV, the satellites also pass through the shadow of the planet, i.e. they are eclipsed. Just before opposition the satellite disappears in the shadow to the west of the planet and reappears from occultation on the east limb. Immediately after opposition the satellite is occulted at the west limb and reappears from eclipse to the east of the planet. At times approximately two to four months before and after opposition, both phases of eclipses of Satellite III may be seen. When Satellite IV is eclipsed, both phases may be seen.

The times given refer to the centre of the satellite. As the satellite is of considerable size, the immersion and emersion phases are not instantaneous. Even when the satellite enters or leaves the shadow along a radius of the shadow, the phase can last for several minutes. With Satellite IV, grazing phenomena can occur so that the light from the satellite may fade and brighten again without a complete eclipse taking place.

The list of phenomena gives most of the eclipses and shadow transits visible in the British Isles under favourable conditions.

Ec. = Eclipse
Sh. = Shadow transit
D = Disappearance
R = Reappearance
I = Ingress
E = Egress

EXPLANATION OF ASTRONOMICAL DATA

Positions of the heavenly bodies are given only to the degree of accuracy required by amateur astronomers for setting telescopes, or for plotting on celestial globes or star atlases. Where intermediate positions are required, linear interpolation may be employed.

Definitions of the terms used cannot be given here. They must be sought in astronomical literature and textbooks.

A special feature has been made of the times when the various heavenly bodies are visible in the British Isles. Since two columns, calculated for latitudes 52° and 56°, are devoted to risings and settings, the range 50° to 58° can be covered by interpolation and extrapolation. The times given in these columns are Greenwich Mean Times for the meridian of Greenwich. An observer west of this meridian must add his/her longitude (in time) and vice versa.

In accordance with the usual convention in astronomy, + and – indicate respectively north and south latitudes or declinations.

All data are, unless otherwise stated, for 0h Greenwich Mean Time (GMT), i.e. at the midnight at the beginning of the day named. Allowance must be made for British Summer Time during the period that this is in operation.

PAGE ONE OF EACH MONTH

The calendar for each month is explained on page 1217.

Under the heading Astronomical Phenomena will be found particulars of the more important conjunctions of the Sun, Moon and planets with each other, and also the dates of other astronomical phenomena of special interest.

Times of Minima of Algol are approximate times of the middle of the period of diminished light.

The Constellations listed each month are those that are near the meridian at the beginning of the month at 22h local mean time. Allowance must be made for British Summer Time if necessary. The fact that any star crosses the meridian 4m earlier each night or 2h earlier each month may be used, in conjunction with the lists given each month, to find what constellations are favourably placed at any moment. The table preceding the list of constellations may be extended indefinitely at the rate just quoted.

The principal phases of the Moon are the GMTs when the difference between the longitude of the Moon and that of the Sun is 0°, 90°, 180° or 270°. The times of perigee and apogee are those when the Moon is nearest to, and farthest from, the Earth, respectively. The nodes or points of intersection of the Moon's orbit and the ecliptic make a complete retrograde circuit of the ecliptic in about 19 years. From a knowledge of the longitude of the ascending node and the inclination, whose value does not vary much from 5°, the path of the Moon among the stars may be plotted on a celestial globe or star atlas.

PAGE TWO OF EACH MONTH

The Sun's semi-diameter, in arc, is given once a month.

The right ascension and declination (Dec.) is that of the true Sun. The right ascension of the mean Sun is obtained by applying the equation of time, with the sign given, to the right ascension of the true Sun, or, more easily, by applying 12h to the Sidereal Time. The direction in which the equation of time has to be applied in different problems is a frequent source of confusion and error. Apparent Solar Time is equal to the Mean Solar Time plus the Equation of Time. For example, at 12h GMT on August 8 the Equation of Time is –5m 36s and thus at 12h Mean Time on that day the Apparent Time is 12h – 5m 36s = 11h 54m 24s.

The Greenwich Sidereal Time at 0h and the Transit of the First Point of Aries (which is really the mean time when the sidereal time is 0h) are used for converting mean time to sidereal time and vice versa.

The GMT of transit of the Sun at Greenwich may also be taken as the local mean time (LMT) of transit in any longitude. It is independent of latitude. The GMT of transit in any longitude is obtained by adding the longitude to the time given if west, and vice versa.

LIGHTING-UP TIME

The legal importance of sunrise and sunset is that the Road Vehicles Lighting Regulations 1989 (SI 1989 No. 1796) make the use of front and rear position lamps on vehicles compulsory during the period between sunset and sunrise. Headlamps on vehicles are required to be used during the hours of darkness on unlit roads or whenever visibility is seriously reduced. The hours of darkness are defined in these regulations as the period between half an hour after sunset and half an hour before sunrise.

In all laws and regulations 'sunset' refers to the local sunset, i.e. the time at which the Sun sets at the place in question. This common-sense interpretation has been upheld by legal tribunals. Thus the necessity for providing for different latitudes and longitudes, as already described, is evident.

SUNRISE AND SUNSET

The times of sunrise and sunset are those when the Sun's upper limb, as affected by refraction, is on the true horizon of an observer at sea-level. Assuming the mean refraction to be 34′, and the Sun's semi-diameter to be 16′, the time given is that when the true zenith distance of the Sun's centre is 90°+34′+16′ or 90° 50′, or, in other words, when the depression of the Sun's centre below the true horizon is 50′. The upper limb is then 34′ below the true horizon, but is brought there by refraction. An observer on a ship might see the Sun for a minute or so longer, because of the dip of the horizon, while another viewing the sunset over hills or mountains would record an earlier time. Nevertheless, the moment when the true zenith distance of the Sun's centre is 90° 50′ is a precise time dependent only on the latitude and longitude of the place, and independent of its altitude above sea-level, the contour of its horizon, the vagaries of refraction or the small seasonal change in the Sun's semi-diameter; this moment is suitable in every way as a definition of sunset (or sunrise) for all statutory purposes. (For further information, *see* footnote on page 1274.)

TWILIGHT

Light reaches us before sunrise and continues to reach us for some time after sunset. The interval between darkness and sunrise or sunset and darkness is called twilight. Astronomically speaking, twilight is considered to begin or end when the Sun's centre is 18° below the horizon, as no light from the Sun can then reach the observer. As thus defined twilight may last several hours; in high latitudes at the summer solstice the depression of 18° is not reached, and twilight lasts from sunset to sunrise.

The need for some sub-division of twilight is met by dividing the gathering darkness into four stages.

(1) *Sunrise or Sunset*, defined as above

(2) *Civil twilight*, which begins or ends when the Sun's centre is 6° below the horizon. This marks the time when operations requiring daylight may commence or

must cease. In England it varies from about 30 to 60 minutes after sunset and the same interval before sunrise

(3) *Nautical twilight*, which begins or ends when the Sun's centre is 12° below the horizon. This marks the time when it is, to all intents and purposes, completely dark

(4) *Astronomical twilight*, which begins or ends when the Sun's centre is 18° below the horizon. This marks theoretical perfect darkness. It is of little practical importance, especially if nautical twilight is tabulated

To assist observers the durations of civil, nautical and astronomical twilights are given at intervals of ten days. The beginning of a particular twilight is found by subtracting the duration from the time of sunrise, while the end is found by adding the duration to the time of sunset. Thus the beginning of astronomical twilight in latitude 52°, on the Greenwich meridian, on March 11 is found as 06h 23m − 113m = 04h 30m and similarly the end of civil twilight as 17h 58m + 34m = 18h 32m. The letters TAN (twilight all night) are printed when twilight lasts all night.

Under the heading The Night Sky will be found notes describing the position and visibility of the planets and other phenomena.

PAGE THREE OF EACH MONTH

The Moon moves so rapidly among the stars that its position is given only to the degree of accuracy that permits linear interpolation. The right ascension (RA) and declination (Dec.) are geocentric, i.e. for an imaginary observer at the centre of the Earth. To an observer on the surface of the Earth the position is always different, as the altitude is always less on account of parallax, which may reach 1°.

The lunar terminator is the line separating the bright from the dark part of the Moon's disk. Apart from irregularities of the lunar surface, the terminator is elliptical, because it is a circle seen in projection. It becomes the full circle forming the limb, or edge, of the Moon at New and Full Moon. The selenographic longitude of the terminator is measured from the mean centre of the visible disk, which may differ from the visible centre by as much as 8°, because of libration.

Instead of the longitude of the terminator the Sun's selenographic co-longitude (Sun's co-long.) is tabulated. It is numerically equal to the selenographic longitude of the morning terminator, measured eastwards from the mean centre of the disk. Thus its value is approximately 270° at New Moon, 360° at First Quarter, 90° at Full Moon and 180° at Last Quarter.

The Position Angle (PA) of the Bright Limb is the position angle of the midpoint of the illuminated limb, measured eastwards from the north point on the disk. The Phase column shows the percentage of the area of the Moon's disk illuminated; this is also the illuminated percentage of the diameter at right angles to the line of cusps. The terminator is a semi-ellipse whose major axis is the line of cusps, and whose semi-minor axis is determined by the tabulated percentage; from New Moon to Full Moon the east limb is dark, and vice versa.

The times given as moonrise and moonset are those when the upper limb of the Moon is on the horizon of an observer at sea-level. The Sun's horizontal parallax (Hor. par.) is about 9″, and is negligible when considering sunrise and sunset, but that of the Moon averages about 57′. Hence the computed time represents the moment when the true zenith distance of the Moon is 90° 50′ (as for the Sun) minus the horizontal parallax. The time required for the Sun or Moon to rise or set is about four minutes (except in high latitudes). *See also* page 1267 and footnote below.

The GMT of transit of the Moon over the meridian of Greenwich is given; these times are independent of latitude but must be corrected for longitude. For places in the British Isles it suffices to add the longitude if west, and vice versa. For other places a further correction is necessary because of the rapid movement of the Moon relative to the stars. The entire correction is conveniently determined by first finding the west longitude λ of the place. If the place is in west longitude, λ is the ordinary west longitude; if the place is in east longitude λ is the complement to 24h (or 360°) of the longitude and will be greater than 12h (or 180°). The correction then consists of two positive portions, namely λ and the fraction $\lambda/24$ (or $\lambda°/360$) multiplied by the difference between consecutive transits. Thus for Christchurch, New Zealand, the longitude is 11h 31m east, so λ = 12h 29m and the fraction $\lambda/24$ is 0.52. The transit on the local date 31 May 2005 is found as follows:

		d	*h*	*m*
GMT of transit at Greenwich	May	30	06	05
λ			12	29
0.52 × (6h 53m − 6h 05m)				25
GMT of transit at Christchurch		30	18	59
Corr. to NZ Standard Time			12	00
Local standard time of transit	May	31	06	59

As is evident, for any given place the quantities λ and the correction to local standard time may be combined permanently, being here 24h 29m.

Positions of Mercury are given for every second day, and those of Venus and Mars for every fifth day; they may be interpolated linearly. The diameter (Diam.) is given in seconds of arc. The phase is the illuminated percentage of the disk. In the case of the inner planets this approaches 100 at superior conjunction and 0 at inferior conjunction. When the phase is less than 50 the planet is crescent-shaped or horned; for greater phases it is gibbous. In the case of the exterior planet Mars, the phase approaches 100 at conjunction and opposition, and is a minimum at the quadratures.

Since the planets cannot be seen when on the horizon, the actual times of rising and setting are not given; instead, the time when the planet has an apparent altitude of 5° has been tabulated. If the time of transit is between 00h and 12h the time refers to an altitude of 5° above the eastern horizon; if between 12h and 24h, to the western horizon. The phenomenon tabulated is the one that occurs between sunset and sunrise. The times given may be interpolated for latitude and corrected for longitude, as in the case of the Sun and Moon.

SUNRISE, SUNSET, MOONRISE AND MOONSET

The tables have been constructed for the meridian of Greenwich and for latitudes 52° and 56°. They give Greenwich Mean Time (GMT) throughout the year. To obtain the GMT of the phenomenon as seen from any other latitude and longitude in the British Isles, first interpolate or extrapolate for latitude by the usual rules of proportion. To the time thus found, the longitude (expressed in time) is to be added if west (as it usually is in Great Britain) or subtracted if east. If the longitude is expressed in degrees and minutes of arc, it must be converted to time at the rate of 1° = 4m and 15′ = 1m. A method of calculating rise and set time for other places in the world is given on pages 1266 and 1267

The GMT at which the planet transits the Greenwich meridian is also given. The times of transit are to be corrected to local meridians in the usual way, as already described.

PAGE FOUR OF EACH MONTH

The GMTs of sunrise and sunset for seven cities, whose adopted positions in longitude (W.) and latitude (N.) are given immediately below the name, may be used not only for these phenomena, but also for lighting-up times (*see* page 1273 for a fuller explanation).

The particulars for the four outer planets resemble those for the planets on Page Three of each month, except that, under Uranus and Neptune, times when the planet is 10° high instead of 5° high are given; this is because of the inferior brightness of these planets. The diameters given for the rings of Saturn are those of the major axis (in the plane of the planet's equator) and the minor axis respectively. The former has a small seasonal change due to the slightly varying distance of the Earth from Saturn, but the latter varies from zero when the Earth passes through the ring plane every 15 years to its maximum opening half-way between these periods. The rings were last open at their widest extent (and Saturn at its brightest) in 2002; this will occur again in 2017. The Earth passed through the ring plane in 1995–6 and will do so again in 2009.

TIME

From the earliest ages, the natural division of time into recurring periods of day and night has provided the practical time-scale for the everyday activities of the human race. Indeed, if any alternative means of time measurement is adopted, it must be capable of adjustment so as to remain in general agreement with the natural time-scale defined by the diurnal rotation of the Earth on its axis. Ideally the rotation should be measured against a fixed frame of reference; in practice it must be measured against the background provided by the celestial bodies. If the Sun is chosen as the reference point, we obtain Apparent Solar Time, which is the time indicated by a sundial. It is not a uniform time but is subject to variations which amount to as much as a quarter of an hour in each direction. Such wide variations cannot be tolerated in a practical time-scale, and this has led to the concept of Mean Solar Time in which all the days are exactly the same length and equal to the average length of the Apparent Solar Day.

The positions of the stars in the sky are specified in relation to a fictitious reference point in the sky known as the First Point of Aries (or the Vernal Equinox). It is therefore convenient to adopt this same reference point when considering the rotation of the Earth against the background of the stars. The time-scale so obtained is known as Apparent Sidereal Time.

GREENWICH MEAN TIME

The daily rotation of the Earth on its axis causes the Sun and the other heavenly bodies to appear to cross the sky from east to west. It is convenient to represent this relative motion as if the Sun really performed a daily circuit around a fixed Earth. Noon in Apparent Solar Time may then be defined as the time at which the Sun transits across the observer's meridian. In Mean Solar Time, noon is similarly defined by the meridian transit of a fictitious Mean Sun moving uniformly in the sky with the same average speed as the true Sun. Mean Solar Time observed on the meridian of the transit circle telescope of the Royal Observatory at Greenwich is called Greenwich Mean Time (GMT). The mean solar day is divided into 24 hours and, for astronomical and other scientific purposes, these are numbered 0 to 23, commencing at midnight. Civil time is usually reckoned in two periods of 12 hours, designated a.m. (*ante meridiem*, i.e. before noon) and p.m. (*post meridiem*, i.e. after noon), although the 24 hour clock is increasingly being used.

UNIVERSAL TIME

Before 1925 January 1, GMT was reckoned in 24 hours commencing at noon; since that date it has been reckoned from midnight. To avoid confusion in the use of the designation GMT before and after 1925, since 1928 astronomers have tended to use the term Universal Time (UT) or Weltzeit (WZ) to denote GMT measured from Greenwich Mean Midnight.

In precision work it is necessary to take account of small variations in Universal Time. These arise from small irregularities in the rotation of the Earth. Observed astronomical time is designated UT0. Observed time corrected for the effects of the motion of the poles (giving rise to a 'wandering' in longitude) is designated UT1. There is also a seasonal fluctuation in the rate of rotation of the Earth arising from meteorological causes, often called the annual fluctuation. UT1 corrected for this effect is designated UT2 and provides a time-scale free from short-period fluctuations. It is still subject to small secular and irregular changes.

APPARENT SOLAR TIME

As mentioned above, the time shown by a sundial is called Apparent Solar Time. It differs from Mean Solar Time by an amount known as the Equation of Time, which is the total effect of two causes which make the length of the apparent solar day non-uniform. One cause of variation is that the orbit of the Earth is not a circle but an ellipse, having the Sun at one focus. As a consequence, the angular speed of the Earth in its orbit is not constant; it is greatest at the beginning of January when the Earth is nearest the Sun.

The other cause is due to the obliquity of the ecliptic; the plane of the equator (which is at right angles to the axis of rotation of the Earth) does not coincide with the ecliptic (the plane defined by the apparent annual motion of the Sun around the celestial sphere) but is inclined to it at an angle of 23° 26′. As a result, the apparent solar day is shorter than average at the equinoxes and longer at the solstices. From the combined effects of the components due to obliquity and eccentricity, the equation of time reaches its maximum values in February (−14 minutes) and early November (+16 minutes). It has a zero value on four dates during the year, and it is only on these dates (approximately April 15, June 14, September 1 and December 25) that a sundial shows Mean Solar Time.

SIDEREAL TIME

A sidereal day is the duration of a complete rotation of the Earth with reference to the First Point of Aries. The term sidereal (or 'star') time is a little misleading since the time-scale so defined is not exactly the same as that which would be defined by successive transits of a selected star, as there is a small progressive motion between the stars and the First Point of Aries due to the precession of the Earth's axis. This makes the length of the sidereal day shorter than the true period of rotation by 0.008 seconds. Superimposed on this steady precessional motion are small oscillations (nutation), giving rise to fluctuations in apparent sidereal time amounting to as much as 1.2 seconds. It is therefore customary to employ Mean Sidereal Time, from which these fluctuations have been removed. The conversion of GMT to Greenwich sidereal time (GST) may be performed by adding the value of the GST at 0h on the day in question (page two of each month) to the GMT converted to sidereal time using the table on page 1271.

Example – To find the GST at August 8d 02h 41m 11s GMT

	h	*m*	*s*
GST at 0h	21	06	24
GMT	2	41	11
Acceleration for 2h			20
Acceleration for 41m 11s			7
Sum = GST =	23	48	02

If the observer is not on the Greenwich meridian then his/her longitude, measured positively westwards from Greenwich, must be subtracted from the GST to obtain Local Sidereal Time (LST). Thus, in the above example, an observer 5h east of Greenwich, or 19h west, would find the LST as 4h 48m 59s.

EPHEMERIS TIME

An analysis of observations of the positions of the Sun, Moon and planets taken over an extended period is used in preparing ephemerides. (An ephemeris is a table giving the apparent position of a heavenly body at regular intervals of time, e.g. one day or ten days, and may be used to compare current observations with tabulated positions.) Discrepancies between the positions of heavenly bodies observed over a 300-year period and their predicted positions arose because the time-scale to which the observations were related was based on the assumption that the rate of rotation of the Earth is uniform. It is now known that this rate of rotation is variable. A revised time-scale, Ephemeris Time (ET), was devised to bring the ephemerides into agreement with the observations.

The second of ET is defined in terms of the annual motion of the Earth in its orbit around the Sun (1/31556925.9747 of the tropical year for 1900 January 0d 12h ET). The precise determination of ET from astronomical observations is a lengthy process as the requisite standard of accuracy can only be achieved by averaging over a number of years.

In 1976 the International Astronomical Union adopted Terrestrial Dynamical Time (TDT), a new dynamical time-scale for general use whose scale unit is the SI second (*see* Atomic Time, below). TDT was renamed Terrestrial Time (TT) in 1991. ET is now of little more than historical interest.

TERRESTRIAL TIME

The uniform time system used in computing the ephemerides of the solar system is Terrestrial Time (TT), which has replaced ET for this purpose. Except for the most rigorous astronomical calculations, it may be assumed to be the same as ET. During 2005 the estimated difference TT – UT is about 65 seconds.

ATOMIC TIME

The fundamental standards of time and frequency must be defined in terms of a periodic motion adequately uniform, enduring and measurable. Progress has made it possible to use natural standards, such as atomic or molecular oscillations. Continuous oscillations are generated in an electrical circuit, the frequency of which is then compared or brought into coincidence with the frequency characteristic of the absorption or emission by the atoms or molecules when they change between two selected energy levels. The National Physical Laboratory (NPL) routinely uses clocks of high stability produced by locking a quartz oscillator to the frequencies defined by caesium or hydrogen atoms.

International Atomic Time (TAI), established through international collaboration, is formed by combining the readings of many caesium clocks and was set close to the astronomically-based Universal Time (UT) near the beginning of 1958. It was formally recognised in 1971 and since 1988 January 1 has been maintained by the International Bureau of Weights and Measures (BIPM). The second markers are generated according to the International System (SI) definition adopted in 1967 at the 13th General Conference of Weights and Measures: 'The second is the duration of 9,192,631,770 periods of the radiation corresponding to the transition between the two hyperfine levels of the ground state of the caesium-133 atom.'

Civil time in almost all countries is now based on Co-ordinated Universal Time (UTC), which was adopted for scientific purposes on 1972 January 1. UTC differs from TAI by an integer number of seconds (determined from studies of the rate of rotation of the Earth) and was designed to make both atomic time and UT accessible with accuracies appropriate for most users. The UTC time-scale is adjusted by the insertion (or, in principle, omission) of leap seconds in order to keep it within ±0.9 s of UT. These leap seconds are introduced, when necessary, at the same instant throughout the world, either at the end of December or at the end of June. All leap seconds so far have been positive, with 61 seconds in the final minute of the UTC month. The time 23h 59m 60s UTC is followed one second later by 0h 0m 00s of the first day of the following month. Notices concerning the insertion of leap seconds are issued by the International Earth Rotation Service (IERS) at the Observatoire de Paris.

RADIO TIME-SIGNALS

UTC is made generally available through time-signals and standard frequency broadcasts such as MSF in the UK, CHU in Canada and WWV and WWVH in the USA. These are based on national time-scales that are maintained in close agreement with UTC and provide traceability to the national time-scale and to UTC. The markers of seconds in the UTC scale coincide with those of TAI.

To disseminate the national time-scale in the UK, special signals are broadcast on behalf of the National Physical Laboratory from the BT radio station at Rugby (call-sign MSF). The signals are controlled from a caesium beam atomic frequency standard and consist of a precise frequency carrier of 60 kHz which is switched off, after being on for at least half a second, to mark every second. The first second of the minute begins with a period of 500 ms with the carrier switched off, to serve as a minute marker. In the other seconds the carrier is always off for at least one tenth of a second at the start and then it carries an on-off code giving the British clock time and date, together with information identifying the start of the next minute. Changes to and from summer time are made following government announcements. Leap seconds are inserted as announced by the IERS and information provided by them on the difference between UTC and UT is also signalled. Other broadcast signals in the UK include the BBC six pips signal, the BT Timeline ('speaking clock'), the NPL Truetime service for computers, and a coded time-signal on the BBC 198 kHz transmitters which is used for timing in the electricity supply industry. From 1972 January 1 the six pips on the BBC have consisted of five short pips from second 55 to second 59 (six pips in the case of a leap second) followed by one lengthened pip, the start of which indicates the exact minute. From 1990 February 5 these signals have been controlled by the BBC with seconds markers referenced to the satellite-based US navigation system GPS (Global Positioning System) and time and day referenced to the MSF transmitter. Formerly they were generated by the Royal Greenwich Observatory. The BT Timeline is compared daily with the National Physical Laboratory caesium beam atomic frequency standard at the Rugby radio station. The NPL Truetime service is directly connected to the national time scale.

Accurate timing may also be obtained from the signals of international navigation systems such as the ground-based Omega, or the satellite-based American GPS or Russian GLONASS systems.

STANDARD TIME

Since 1880 the standard time in Britain has been Greenwich Mean Time (GMT); a statute that year enacted that the word 'time' when used in any legal document relating to Britain meant, unless otherwise specifically stated, the mean time of the Greenwich meridian. Greenwich was adopted as the universal meridian on 13 October 1884. A system of standard time by zones is used world-wide, standard time in each zone differing from that of the Greenwich meridian by an integral number of hours, either fast or slow. The large territories of the USA and Canada are divided into zones approximately 7.5° on either side of central meridians.

Variations from the standard time of some countries occur during part of the year; they are decided annually and are usually referred to as Summer Time or Daylight Saving Time.

At the 180th meridian the time can be either 12 hours fast on Greenwich Mean Time or 12 hours slow, and a change of date occurs. The internationally recognised date or calendar line is a modification of the 180th meridian, drawn so as to include islands of any one group on the same side of the line, or for political reasons. The line is indicated by joining up the following co-ordinates:

Lat.	*Long.*	*Lat.*	*Long.*
60° S.	180°	48° N.	180°
51° S.	180°	53° N.	170° E.
45° S.	172.5° W.	65.5° N.	169° W.
15° S.	172.5° W.	75° N.	180°
5° S.	180°		

Changes to the date line would require an international conference.

BRITISH SUMMER TIME

In 1916 an Act ordained that during a defined period of that year the legal time for general purposes in Great Britain should be one hour in advance of Greenwich Mean Time. The Summer Time Acts 1922 and 1925 defined the period during which Summer Time was to be in force, stabilising practice until the Second World War.

During World War 2 the duration of Summer Time was extended and in the years 1941 to 1945 and in 1947 Double Summer Time (two hours in advance of Greenwich Mean Time) was in force. After the war, Summer Time was extended each year in 1948–52 and 1961–4 by Order in Council.

Between 1968 October 27 and 1971 October 31 clocks were kept one hour ahead of Greenwich Mean Time throughout the year. This was known as British Standard Time.

The most recent legislation is the Summer Time Act 1972, which enacted that 'the period of summer time for the purposes of this Act is the period beginning at two o'clock, Greenwich mean time, in the morning of the day after the third Saturday in March or, if that day is Easter Day, the day after the second Saturday in March, and ending at two o'clock, Greenwich mean time, in the morning of the day after the fourth Saturday in October.'

The duration of Summer Time can be varied by Order in Council and in recent years alterations have been made to bring the operation of Summer Time in Britain closer to similar provisions in other countries of the European Union; for instance, since 1981 the hour of changeover has been 01h Greenwich Mean Time.

The duration of Summer Time in 2005 is:

March 27 01h GMT to October 30 01h GMT

MEAN REFRACTION

Alt. °	Ref. ′	′	Alt. °	Ref. ′	′	Alt. °	Ref. ′	′
1	20		3	12		7	54	
		21			13			6
1	30		3	34		9	27	
		20			12			5
1	41		4	00		11	39	
		19			11			4
1	52		4	30		15	00	
		18			10			3
2	05		5	06		20	42	
		17			9			2
2	19		5	50		32	20	
		16			8			1
2	35		6	44		62	17	
		15			7			0
2	52		7	54		90	00	
		14						
3	12							

The refraction table is in the form of a critical table (*see* page 1271)

ASTRONOMICAL CONSTANTS

Solar parallax	8″.794
Astronomical unit	149597870 km
Precession for the year 2005	50″.291
Precession in right ascension	$3^s.075$
Precession in declination	20″.043
Constant of nutation	9″.202
Constant of aberration	20″.496
Mean obliquity of ecliptic (2005)	23° 26′ 20″
Moon's equatorial hor. parallax	57′ 02″.70
Velocity of light in vacuo per second	299792.5 km
Solar motion per second	20.0 km
Equatorial radius of the Earth	6378.140 km
Polar radius of the Earth	6356.755 km
North galactic pole (IAU standard)	RA 12h 49m (1950.0). Dec. +27°.4 N.
Solar apex	RA 18h 06m Dec. +30
Length of year (in mean solar days)	
Tropical	365.24219
Sidereal	365.25636
Anomalistic (perihelion to perihelion)	365.25964
Eclipse	346.62000

Length of month (mean values)	*d*	*h*	*m*	*s*
New Moon to New	29	12	44	02.9
Sidereal	27	07	43	11.5
Anomalistic (perigee to perigee)	27	13	18	33.2

ELEMENTS OF THE SOLAR SYSTEM

Orb	*Mean distance from Sun* (Earth = 1)	km 10^6	*Sidereal period days*	*Synodic period days*	*Incl. of orbit to ecliptic* ° ′	*Diameter km*	*Mass (Earth = 1) days*	*Period of rotation on axis*
Sun	—	—	—	—	—	1,392,530	332,946	25–35*
Mercury	0.39	58	88.0	116	7 00	4,879	0.0553	58.646
Venus	0.72	108	224.7	584	3 24	12,104	0.8150	243.019*r*
Earth	1.00	150	365.3	—	—	12,756*e*	1.0000	0.997
Mars	1.52	228	687.0	780	1 51	6,794*e*	0.1074	1.026
Jupiter	5.20	778	4,332.6	399	1 18	142,984*e* / 133,708*p*	317.89	0.410*e*
Saturn	9.54	1427	10,759.2	378	2 29	120,536*e* / 108,728*p*	95.18	0.426*e*
Uranus	19.18	2870	30,684.6	370	0 46	51,118*e*	14.54	0.718*r*
Neptune	30.06	4497	60,191.0	367	1 46	49,528*e*	17.15	0.671
Pluto	39.80	5954	91,708.2	367	17 09	2,302	0.002	6.387

e equatorial, *p* polar, *r* retrograde, * depending on latitude

THE SATELLITES

Name		*Star mag.*	*Mean distance from primary km*	*Sidereal period of revolution d*
EARTH				
I	Moon	—	384,400	27.322
MARS				
I	Phobos	11	9,378	0.319
II	Deimos	12	23,459	1.262
JUPITER				
XVI	Metis	17	127,960	0.295
XV	Adrastea	19	128,980	0.298
V	Amalthea	14	181,300	0.498
XIV	Thebe	16	221,900	0.675
I	Io	5	421,600	1.769
II	Europa	5	670,900	3.552
III	Ganymede	5	1,070,000	7.155
IV	Callisto	6	1,883,000	16.689
XIII	Leda	20	11,165,000	240.92
VI	Himalia	15	11,460,000	250.57
X	Lysithea	18	11,717,000	259.20
VII	Elara	17	11,741,000	259.64
XII	Ananke	19	21,276,000	629.77*r*
XI	Carme	18	23,404,000	734.17*r*
VIII	Pasiphae	17	23,624,000	743.68*r*
IX	Sinope	18	23,939,000	758.90*r*
SATURN				
XVIII	Pan	20	133,583	0.575
XV	Atlas	18	137,640	0.602
XVI	Prometheus	16	139,353	0.613
XVII	Pandora	16	141,700	0.629
XI	Epimetheus	15	151,422	0.695
X	Janus	14	151,472	0.695
I	Mimas	13	185,520	0.942
II	Enceladus	12	238,020	1.370
III	Tethys	10	294,660	1.888
XIII	Telesto	19	294,660	1.888
XIV	Calypso	19	294,660	1.888
IV	Dione	10	377,400	2.737
XII	Helene	18	377,400	2.737
V	Rhea	10	527,040	4.518
VI	Titan	8	1,221,850	15.945

Name		*Star mag.*	*Mean distance from primary km*	*Sidereal period of revolution d*
SATURN				
VII	Hyperion	14	1,481,100	21.277
VIII	Iapetus	11	3,561,300	79.330
IX	Phoebe	16	12,952,000	550.48*r*
URANUS				
VI	Cordelia	24	49,750	0.335
VII	Orphelia	24	53,760	0.376
VIII	Bianca	23	59,170	0.435
IX	Cressida	22	61,780	0.464
X	Desdemona	22	62,660	0.474
XI	Juliet	21	64,360	0.493
XII	Portia	21	66,100	0.513
XIII	Rosalind	22	69,930	0.558
XIV	Belinda	22	75,260	0.624
XV	Puck	20	86,000	0.762
V	Miranda	16	129,900	1.413
I	Ariel	14	190,900	2.520
II	Umbriel	15	266,000	4.144
III	Titania	14	426,300	8.706
IV	Oberon	14	583,600	13.463
XVI	Caliban	22	7,231,000	579.93
XX	Stephano	24	9,608,400	677.36
XVII	Sycorax	21	12,179,000	1,288.30
XVIII	Prospero	23	16,256,000	1,978.29
XIX	Setebos	23	17,418,000	2,225.21
NEPTUNE				
III	Naiad	25	48,230	0.294
IV	Thalassa	24	50,070	0.311
V	Despina	23	52,530	0.335
VI	Galatea	22	61,950	0.429
VII	Larissa	22	73,550	0.555
VIII	Proteus	20	117,650	1.122
I	Triton	13	354,760	5.877
II	Nereid	19	5,513,400	360.136
PLUTO				
I	Charon	17	19,600	6.387

Currently the total number of satellites of the outer planets are: Jupiter 63, Saturn 31, Uranus 28, Neptune 13, Pluto 1.

THE EARTH

The shape of the Earth is that of an oblate spheroid or solid of revolution whose meridian sections are ellipses not differing much from circles, whilst the sections at right angles are circles. The length of the equatorial axis is about 12,756 km, and that of the polar axis is 12,714 km. The mean density of the Earth is 5.5 times that of water, although that of the surface layer is less. The Earth and Moon revolve about their common centre of gravity in a lunar month; this centre in turn revolves round the Sun in a plane known as the ecliptic, that passes through the Sun's centre. The Earth's equator is inclined to this plane at an angle of 23.4°. This tilt is the cause of the seasons. In mid-latitudes, and when the Sun is high above the Equator, not only does the high noon altitude make the days longer, but the Sun's rays fall more directly on the Earth's surface; these effects combine to produce summer. In equatorial regions the noon altitude is large throughout the year, and there is little variation in the length of the day. In higher latitudes the noon altitude is lower, and the days in summer are appreciably longer than those in winter.

The average velocity of the Earth in its orbit is 30 km a second. It makes a complete rotation on its axis in about 23h 56m of mean time, which is the sidereal day. Because of its annual revolution round the Sun, the rotation with respect to the Sun, or the solar day, is more than this by about four minutes (*see* page 1275). The extremity of the axis of rotation, or the North Pole of the Earth, is not rigidly fixed, but wanders over an area roughly 20 metres in diameter.

TERRESTRIAL MAGNETISM

The Earth's main magnetic field corresponds approximately to that of a very strong small bar magnet near the centre of the Earth, but with appreciable smooth spatial departures. The origin of the main field is generally ascribed to electric currents associated with fluid motions in the Earth's core. As a result not only does the main field vary in strength and direction from place to place, but also with time. Superimposed on the main field are local and regional anomalies whose magnitudes may in places approach that of the main field; these are due to the influence of mineral deposits in the Earth's crust. A small proportion of the field is of external origin, mostly associated with electric currents in the ionosphere. The configuration of the external field and the ionisation of the atmosphere depend on the incident particle and radiation flux from the Sun. There are, therefore, short-term and non-periodic as well as diurnal, 27-day, seasonal and 11-year periodic changes in the magnetic field, dependent upon the position of the Sun and the degree of solar activity.

A magnetic compass points along the horizontal component of a magnetic line of force. These lines of force converge on the 'magnetic dip-poles', the places where the Earth's magnetic field is vertical. These poles move with time, and their present approximate adopted mean positions are 83.3° N., 118.7° W. and 64.5° S., 137.8° E.

There is also a 'magnetic equator', at all points of which the vertical component of the Earth's magnetic field is zero and a magnetised needle remains horizontal. This line runs between 2° and 12° north of the geographical equator in Asia and Africa, turns sharply south off the west African coast, and crosses South America through Brazil, Bolivia and Peru; it re-crosses the geographical equator in mid-Pacific.

Reference has already been made to secular changes in the Earth's field. The following table indicates the changes in magnetic declination (or variation of the compass). Declination is the angle in the horizontal plane between the direction of true north and that in which a magnetic compass points. Similar, though much smaller, changes have occurred in 'dip' or magnetic inclination. Secular changes differ throughout the world. Although the London observations suggest a cycle with a period of several hundred years, an exact repetition is unlikely.

London		*Greenwich*	
1580	11° 15′ E.	1900	16° 29′ W.
1622	5° 56′ E.	1925	13° 10′ W.
1665	1° 22′ W.	1950	9° 07′ W.
1730	13° 00′ W.	1975	6° 39′ W.
1773	21° 09′ W.	1998	3° 32′ W.
1850	22° 24′ W.		

In order that up-to-date information on declination may be available, many governments publish magnetic charts on which there are lines (isogonic lines) passing through all places at which specified values of declination will be found at the date of the chart.

In the British Isles, isogonic lines now run approximately north-east to south-west. Though there are considerable local deviations due to geological causes, a rough value of magnetic declination may be obtained by assuming that at 50° N. on the meridian of Greenwich, the value in 2005 is 1° 45′ west and allowing an increase of 14′ for each degree of latitude northwards and one of 27′ for each degree of longitude westwards. For example, at 53° N., 5° W., declination will be about 1°45′ + 42′ + 135′, i.e. 4° 42′ west. The average annual change at the present time is about 11′ decrease.

The number of magnetic observatories is about 180, irregularly distributed over the globe. There are three in Great Britain, run by the British Geological Survey: at Hartland, north Devon; at Eskdalemuir, Dumfries and Galloway; and at Lerwick, Shetland Islands. The following are some recent annual mean values of the magnetic elements for Hartland.

Year	*Declination West* ° ′	*Dip or inclination* ° ′	*Horizontal intensity nanoTesla (nT)*	*Vertical intensity nT*
1960	9 58.8	66 43.9	18707	43504
1965	9 30.1	66 34.0	18872	43540
1970	9 06.5	66 26.1	19033	43636
1975	8 32.3	66 17.0	19212	43733
1980	7 43.8	66 10.3	19330	43768
1985	6 56.1	66 07.9	19379	43796
1990	6 15.0	66 09.7	19539	43896
1995	5 33.2	66 07.3	19457	43951
2000	4 43.6	66 06.9	19508	44051
2003	4 14.4	66 06.8	19545	44134

As well as navigation at sea, in the air and on land by compass the oil industry depends on the Earth's magnetic field as a directional reference. They use magnetic survey tools when drilling well-bores and require accurate estimates of the local magnetic field, taking into account the crustal and external fields.

MAGNETIC STORMS

Occasionally, sometimes with great suddenness, the Earth's magnetic field is subject for several hours to marked disturbance. During a severe storm in October 2003 the declination at Eskdalemuir changed by over 5° in six minutes. In many instances such disturbances are accompanied by widespread displays of aurorae, marked changes in the incidence of cosmic rays, an increase in the reception of 'noise' from the Sun at radio frequencies, and rapid changes in the ionosphere and induced electric currents within the Earth which adversely affect satellite operations, telecommunications and electric power transmission systems. The disturbances are caused by changes in the stream of ionised particles which emanates from the Sun and through which the Earth is continuously passing. Some of these changes are associated with visible eruptions on the Sun, usually in the region of sun-spots. There is a marked tendency for disturbances to recur after intervals of about 27 days, the apparent period of rotation of the Sun on its axis, which is consistent with the sources being located on particular areas of the Sun.

ARTIFICIAL SATELLITES

Since the beginning of the Space Age, *Whitaker's Almanack* has given details of every successful satellite launch. This edition gives details of all successful launches that have taken place since the last edition. To consider the orbit of an artificial satellite, it is best to imagine that one is looking at the Earth from a distant point in space. The Earth would then be seen to be rotating about its axis inside the orbit described by the rapidly revolving satellite. The inclination of a satellite orbit to the Earth's equator (which generally remains almost constant throughout the satellite's lifetime) gives at once the maximum range of latitudes over which the satellite passes. Thus a satellite whose orbit has an inclination of 53° will pass overhead all latitudes between 53° S. and 53° N., but would never be seen in the zenith of any place nearer the poles than these latitudes. If we consider a particular place on the earth, whose latitude is less than the inclination of the satellite's orbit, then the Earth's rotation carries this place first under the northbound part of the orbit and then under the southbound part of the orbit, these two occurrences being always less than 12 hours apart for satellites moving in direct orbits (i.e. to the east). (For satellites in retrograde orbits, the words 'northbound' and 'southbound' should be interchanged in the preceding statement.) As the value of the latitude of the observer increases and approaches the value of the inclination of the orbit, so this interval gets shorter until (when the latitude is equal to the inclination) only one overhead passage occurs each day.

OBSERVATION OF SATELLITES

The regression of the orbit around the Earth causes alternate periods of visibility and invisibility, though this is of little concern to the radio or radar observer. To the visual observer the following cycle of events normally occurs (though the cycle may start in any position): invisibility, morning observations before dawn, invisibility, evening observations after dusk, invisibility, morning observations before dawn, and so on. With reasonably high satellites and for observers in high latitudes around the summer solstice, the evening observations follow the morning observations without interruption as sunlight passing over the polar regions can still illuminate satellites which are passing over temperate latitudes at local midnight. At the moment all satellites rely on sunlight to make them visible, though a satellite with a flashing light has been suggested for a future launching. The observer must be in darkness or twilight in order to make any useful observations. (For durations of twilight, and sunrise and sunset times, *see* page two of each month.)

Some of the satellites are visible to the naked eye and much interest has been aroused by the spectacle of a bright satellite disappearing into the Earth's shadow. The event is even more interesting telescopically as the disappearance occurs gradually as the satellite traverses the Earth's penumbral shadow, and during the last few seconds before the eclipse is complete the satellite may change colour (in suitable atmospheric conditions) from yellow to red. This is because the last rays of sunlight are refracted through the denser layers of our atmosphere before striking the satellite.

Some satellites rotate about one or more axes so that a periodic variation in brightness is observed. This was particularly noticeable in several of the Soviet satellites.

Satellite research has provided some interesting results, including a revised value of the Earth's oblateness (1/298.2), and the discovery of the Van Allen radiation belts.

LAUNCHINGS

Apart from their names, e.g. Cosmos 6 Rocket, the satellites are also classified according to their date of launch. Thus 1961 α refers to the first satellite launching of 1961. A number following the Greek letter indicated the relative brightness of the satellites put in orbit. From the beginning of 1963 the Greek letters were replaced by numbers and the numbers by roman letters e.g. 1963–01A. For all satellites successfully injected into orbit the following table gives the designation and names of the main objects, the launch date and some initial orbital data. These are the inclination to the equator (i), the nodal period of revolution (P), and the apogee and perigee heights.

Although most of the satellites launched are injected into orbits less than 1,000 km high, there are an increasing number of satellites in geostationary orbits, i.e. where the orbital inclination is zero, the eccentricity close to zero, and the period of revolution is 1436.1 minutes. Thus the satellite is permanently situated over the equator at one selected longitude at a mean height of 35,786 km. This geostationary band is crowded. In one case there are six television satellites (Astra 2, 5, 6, 7, 1H and 2C) orbiting within a few tens of kilometres of each other. In the sky they appear to be separated by only a few arcminutes.

In 1997 a number of *Iridium* satellites were launched into high inclination orbits. These are owned by the mobile telephone company Cellnet. For visual observers, these satellites have the interesting characteristic that the large aerials they carry can, when in exactly the right orientation with respect to the Sun and the observer, give off a 'flare' in brightness which can on occasion attain a magnitude of −6, much brighter than Venus. The flare can be visible to the naked eye for nearly a minute.

The Russian Space Station, Mir, 1986–17A, which was launched in 1986 was successfully de-orbited on March 23 2001. The re-entry was carried out in several stages, the first small burn to lower the orbit occurring at 00h 33m. The main de-orbit burn began at 05h 07m, which lowered the perigee height to <80km. At 05h 50m observers in Fiji saw multiple bright re-entry bodies in the sky. The impact area was at about W. 160°, S. 40°. During its 15 years in orbit it had been visited by 111 spacecraft. The record for the longest spaceflight was set by Valeriy Polyakov in 1994–5 who spent 437 days in Mir.

The new International Space Station ISS, 1998–67A, is currently being assembled in an orbit of similar size and inclination to Mir. It will become even brighter as more parts are added to it. When passing over Britain it can appear to be almost as bright as Jupiter on favourable transits, though only visible for four or five minutes on each pass.

ARTIFICIAL SATELLITE LAUNCHES

Desig-nation	*Satellite*	*Launch date*	*P*	*i*	*Apogee*	*Perigee*
2003–			*m*	°	*km*	*km*
001	CORIOLIS, rocket	Jan. 6	95.9	98.7	841	279
002	ICESAT, CHIPSAT, rocket, DPAF	Jan. 13	96.5	94.0	594	586
003	STS 107	Jan. 16	90.1	39.0	287	271
004	SORCE, rocket	Jan. 25	97.3	40.0	649	609
005	NAVSTAR 51 (USA 166), rocket, rocket XSS 10	Jan. 29	720.7	55.1	20345	20155
006	PROGRESS M-47, rocket	Feb. 2	92.3	51.6	390	382
007	INTELSAT 907, rocket	Feb. 15	1431.2	0.1	35748	35634
008	USA 167, rocket, IABS	Mar. 11	No elements available			
009	IGS 1A, IGS 1B	Mar. 28	94.3	97.3	490	484
010	NAVSTAR 52 (USA 168), rocket, rocket	Mar. 31	717.9	55.0	20376	19984
011	MOLNIYA 1–92, platform, rocket, rocket	Apr. 2	736.4	62.9	40643	625
012	USA 169, rocket	Apr. 8	1436.1	4.2	35774	35759
013	INSAT 3A, Galaxy XII, rocket	Apr. 9	645.9	2.0	35881	867
014	ASIASAT 4, rocket	Apr. 12	871.3	27.3	47506	174
015	CONGLOMERATE, rocket, platform	Apr. 24	1443.0	2.3	35927	35917
016	SOYUZ TMA-2, rocket	Apr. 26	90.6	51.6	358	254
017	GALEX, rocket	Apr. 28	98.7	29.0	699	691
018	GSAT 2, rocket	May 8	626.6	19.2	35601	157
019	MUSES C, rocket	May 9	No elements available			
020	HELLAS-SAT 2, rocket	May 13	1793.9	17.0	84650	404
021	BEIDOU 1C, rocket	May 24	1436.1	0.3	35822	35752
022	MARS EXPRESS, rocket	June 2	88.0	51.8	177	177
023	COSMOS 2398, rocket	June 5	105.0	83.0	1015	971
024	AMC-9, BREEZE M	June 6	1334.4	0.8	35690	31852
025	PROGRESS M1–10, rocket	June 8	90.8	51.6	319	305
026	THURAYA 2, rocket	June 10	650.5	6.3	35777	1203
027	MARS EXPLORER ROVER A, rocket, rocket	June 10	No elements available			
028	B-SAT 2C, OPTUS C1, rocket	June 11	1427.2	0.0	35796	35430
029	MOLNIYA 3–53, rocket, platform, rocket	June 19	736.3	62.9	40635	629
030	ORBVIEW 3, rocket	June 26	92.5	97.3	429	365
031	MONITOR-E/SL-19, MIMOSA, DTUSAT, MOST, CUTE-1, QUAKESAT, AAU CUBESAT, CANX-1, CUBESAT XI-IV	June 30	100.1	98.7	834	694
032	MARS EXPLORER ROVER B, rocket, rocket	July 8	87.8	29.4	175	155
033	RAINBOW 1, rocket	July 17	1436.2	0.0	35796	35782
034	ECHOSTAR 9 (TELSTAR 13), rocket	Aug. 8	1436.1	0.0	35810	35764
035	COSMOS 2399, rocket	Aug. 12	89.8	64.9	326	202
036	SCISAT 1, rocket	Aug. 13	97.7	73.9	655	641
037	COSMOS 2400, COSMOS 2401, rocket	Aug. 19	115.6	82.5	1501	1469
038	SIRTF, rocket	Aug. 25	87.7	31.5	163	161
039	PROGRESS-M 48, rocket	Aug. 28	92.2	51.6	387	377
040	USA 170, rocket, IABS	Aug. 29	No elements available			
041	USA 171, rocket	Sep. 9	No elements available			
042	MOZHAYETS 2, RUBIN 4/SL-8 NIGERIASAT 1, UK-DMC BILSAT 1, LARETS, KAISTSAT, rocket	Sep. 27	98.5	98.2	696	676
043	ARIANE 5 rocket, E-BIRD, SMART 1, INSAT 1E	Sep. 27	644.4	7.1	36006	666
044	HORIZONS 1 (GALAXY 13), rocket	Oct. 1	673.5	0.0	35751	2397
045	SHENZHOU 5, rocket, module	Oct.15	91.2	42.4	336	332
046	IRS P6, rocket	Oct. 17	101.7	98.7	875	803
047	SOYUZ, rocket	Oct. 18	89.9	51.6	274	268
048	DMSP-16	Oct. 18	101.9	98.9	852	844
049	OBJECTS A,B,C, rocket	Oct. 21	99.9	98.5	765	739
050	UNK, rocket	Oct. 30	105.1	99.5	1016	984
051	FSW-3 1, rocket	Nov. 3	88.9	62.9	265	177

ARTIFICIAL SATELLITE LAUNCHES

Desig-nation	*Satellite*	*Launch date*	*P*	*i*	*Apogee*	*Perigee*
2003–			*m*	°	*km*	*km*
052	ZHONGXING 20, rocket	Nov. 14	1436.0	0.3	35797	35771
053	CONGLOMERATE, platform, rocket	Nov. 24	649.8	49.3	36736	208
054	USA 137, rocket	Dec. 2	107.5	63.4	1209	1011
055	GRUZOMAKET, rocket	Dec. 5	93.7	67.1	461	453
056	COSMOS 2402–4, rocket	Dec. 10	672.0	65.1	19104	18970
057	UFO 11 (USA 174), rocket	Dec. 18	No elements available			
058	NAVSTAR 53, rocket, rocket	Dec. 21	356.1	39.0	20349	181
059	AMOS-2, rocket	Dec. 27	714.4	23.6	35778	4410
060	EXPRESS AM-22, rocket platform	Dec. 28	633.4	48.6	35863	243
061	?	Dec. 29	No elements available			
2004–						
001	ESTRELA DU SOL-TELSTAR14, rocket	Jan. 11	641.1	0.1	35757	747
002	PROGRESS-M1 11, rocket	Jan. 29	88.6	51.7	234	178
003	AMC-10 (GE-10)	Feb. 5	858.2	4.0	35710	11364
004	USA 176, rocket, rocket, rocket	Feb. 14	No elements available			
005	COSMOS 2405, rocket, rocket, platform	Feb. 18	735.5	62.8	40600	624
006	ROSETTA, rocket	Mar. 2	No elements available			

TIME MEASUREMENT AND CALENDARS

MEASUREMENTS OF TIME

Measurements of time are based on the time taken by the earth to rotate on its axis (day); by the moon to revolve round the earth (month); and by the earth to revolve round the sun (year). From these, which are not commensurable, certain average or mean intervals have been adopted for ordinary use.

THE DAY

The day begins at midnight and is divided into 24 hours of 60 minutes, each of 60 seconds. The hours are counted from midnight up to 12 noon (when the sun crosses the meridian), and these hours are designated a.m. *(ante meridiem)*; and again from noon up to 12 midnight, which hours are designated p.m. *(post meridiem)*, except when the 24-hour reckoning is employed. The 24-hour reckoning ignores a.m. and p.m., numbering the hours 0 to 23 from midnight.

Colloquially the 24 hours are divided into day and night, day being the time while the sun is above the horizon (including the four stages of twilight defined in the Astronomy section). Day is subdivided into morning, the early part of daytime, ending at noon; afternoon, from noon to about 6 p.m.; and evening, which may be said to extend from 6 p.m. until midnight. Night begins at the close of astronomical twilight (*see* the Astronomy section) and extends beyond midnight to sunrise the next day.

The names of the days are derived from Old English translations or adaptations of the Roman titles.

Sunday	Sun	Sol
Monday	Moon	Luna
Tuesday	Tiw/Tyr (god of war)	Mars
Wednesday	Woden/Odin	Mercury
Thursday	Thor	Jupiter
Friday	Frigga/Freyja (goddess of love)	Venus
Saturday	Saeternes	Saturn

THE MONTH

The month in the ordinary calendar is approximately the twelfth part of a year, but the lengths of the different months vary from 28 (or 29) days to 31.

THE YEAR

The equinoctial or tropical year is the time that the earth takes to revolve round the sun from equinox to equinox, i.e. 365.24219 mean solar days, or 365 days 5 hours 48 minutes and 45 seconds.

The calendar year usually consists of 365 days but a year containing 366 days is called bissextile (*see* Roman calendar) or leap year, one day being added to the month of February so that a date 'leaps over' a day of the week. In the Roman calendar the day that was repeated was the sixth day before the beginning of March, the equivalent of 24 February.

A year is a leap year if the date of the year is divisible by four without remainder, unless it is the last year of the century. The last year of a century is a leap year only if its number is divisible by 400 without remainder, e.g. the years 1800 and 1900 had only 365 days but the year 2000 has 366 days.

THE SOLSTICE

A solstice is the point in the tropical year at which the sun attains its greatest distance, north or south, from the Equator. In the northern hemisphere the furthest point north of the Equator marks the summer solstice and the furthest point south the winter solstice.

The date of the solstice varies according to locality. For example, if the summer solstice falls on 21 June late in the day by Greenwich time, that day will be the longest of the year at Greenwich though it may be by only a second, but it will fall on 22 June, local date, in Japan, and so 22 June will be the longest day there. The date of the solstice is also affected by the length of the tropical year, which is 365 days 6 hours less about 11 minutes 15 seconds. If a solstice happens late on 21 June in one year, it will be nearly six hours later in the next (unless the next year is a leap year), i.e. early on 22 June, and that will be the longest day.

This delay of the solstice does not continue because the extra day in leap year brings it back a day in the calendar. However, because of the 11 minutes 15 seconds mentioned above, the additional day in leap year brings the solstice back too far by 45 minutes, and the time of the solstice in the calendar is earlier, in a four-year pattern, as the century progresses. The last year of a century is in most cases not a leap year, and the omission of the extra day puts the date of the solstice later by about six hours too much. Compensation for this is made by the fourth centennial year being a leap year. The solstice has become earlier in date throughout the last century and, because the year 2000 was a leap year, the solstice will get earlier still throughout the 21st century.

The date of the winter solstice, the shortest day of the year, is affected by the same factors as the longest day.

At Greenwich the sun sets at its earliest by the clock about ten days before the shortest day. The daily change in the time of sunset is due in the first place to the sun's movement southwards at this time of the year, which diminishes the interval between the sun's transit and its setting. However, the daily decrease of the Equation of Time causes the time of apparent noon to be continuously later day by day, which to some extent counteracts the first effect. The rates of the change of these two quantities are not equal or uniform; their combination causes the date of earliest sunset to be 12 or 13 December at Greenwich. In more southerly latitudes the effect of the movement of the sun is less, and the change in the time of sunset depends on that of the Equation of Time to a greater degree, and the date of earliest sunset is earlier than it is at Greenwich, e.g. on the Equator it is about 1 November.

THE EQUINOX

The equinox is the point at which the sun crosses the Equator and day and night are of equal length all over the world. This occurs in March and September.

DOG DAYS

The days about the heliacal rising of the Dog Star, noted from ancient times as the hottest period of the year in the northern hemisphere, are called the Dog Days. Their incidence has been variously calculated as depending on the Greater or Lesser Dog Star (Sirius or Procyon) and their duration has been reckoned as from 30 to 54 days. A generally accepted period is from 3 July to 15 August.

CHRISTIAN CALENDAR

In the Christian chronological system the years are distinguished by cardinal numbers before or after the birth of Christ, the period being denoted by the letters BC (Before Christ) or, more rarely, AC *(Ante Christum)*, and AD (*Anno Domini* – In the Year of Our Lord). The correlative dates of the epoch are the fourth year of the 194th Olympiad, the 753rd year from the foundation of Rome, AM 3761 in Jewish chronology, and the 4714th year of the Julian period. The actual date of the birth of Christ is somewhat uncertain.

The system was introduced into Italy in the sixth century. Though first used in France in the seventh century, it was not universally established there until about the eighth century. It has been said that the system was introduced into England by St Augustine (AD 596), but it was probably not generally used until some centuries later. It was ordered to be used by the Bishops at the Council of Chelsea (AD 816).

THE JULIAN CALENDAR

In the Julian calendar (adopted by the Roman Empire in 45 BC) all the centennial years were leap years, and for this reason towards the close of the 16th century there was a difference of ten days between the tropical and calendar years; the equinox fell on 11 March of the calendar, whereas at the time of the Council of Nicaea (AD 325), it had fallen on 21 March. In 1582 Pope Gregory ordained that 5 October should be called 15 October and that of the end-century years only the fourth should be a leap year.

THE GREGORIAN CALENDAR

The Gregorian calendar was adopted by Italy, France, Spain and Portugal in 1582, by Prussia, the Roman Catholic German states, Switzerland, Holland and Flanders on 1 January 1583, by Poland in 1586, Hungary in 1587, the Protestant German and Netherland states and Denmark in 1700, and by Great Britain and Dominions (including the North American colonies) in 1752, by the omission of eleven days (3 September being reckoned as 14 September). Sweden omitted the leap day in 1700 but observed leap days in 1704 and 1708, and reverted to the Julian calendar by having two leap days in 1712; the Gregorian calendar was adopted in 1753 by the omission of eleven days (18 February being reckoned as 1 March). Japan adopted the calendar in 1872, China in 1912, Bulgaria in 1915, Turkey and Soviet Russia in 1918, Yugoslavia and Romania in 1919, and Greece in 1923.

In the same year that the change was made in England from the Julian to the Gregorian calendar, the beginning of the new year was also changed from 25 March to 1 January.

THE ORTHODOX CHURCHES

Some Orthodox Churches still use the Julian reckoning but the majority of Greek Orthodox Churches and the Romanian Orthodox Church have adopted a modified 'New Calendar', observing the Gregorian calendar for fixed feasts and the Julian for movable feasts.

The Orthodox Church year begins on 1 September. There are four fast periods and, in addition to Pascha (Easter), twelve great feasts, as well as numerous commemorations of the saints of the Old and New Testaments throughout the year.

THE DOMINICAL LETTER

The dominical letter is one of the letters A–G which are used to denote the Sundays in successive years. If the first day of the year is a Sunday the letter is A; if the second, B; the third, C; and so on. A leap year requires two letters, the first for 1 January to 29 February, the second for 1 March to 31 December.

EPIPHANY

The feast of the Epiphany, commemorating the manifestation of Christ, later became associated with the offering of gifts by the Magi. The day was of great importance from the time of the Council of Nicaea (AD 325), as the primate of Alexandria was charged at every Epiphany feast with the announcement in a letter to the churches of the date of the forthcoming Easter. The day was also of importance in Britain as it influenced dates, ecclesiastical and lay, e.g. Plough Monday, when work was resumed in the fields, fell on the Monday in the first full week after Epiphany.

LENT

The Teutonic word *Lent*, which denotes the fast preceding Easter, originally meant no more than the spring season; but from Anglo-Saxon times at least it has been used as the equivalent of the more significant Latin term Quadragesima, meaning the 'forty days' or, more literally, the fortieth day. Ash Wednesday is the first day of Lent, which ends at midnight before Easter Day.

PALM SUNDAY

Palm Sunday, the Sunday before Easter and the beginning of Holy Week, commemorates the triumphal entry of Christ into Jerusalem and is celebrated in Britain (when palm is not available) by branches of willow gathered for use in the decoration of churches on that day.

MAUNDY THURSDAY

Maundy Thursday is the day before Good Friday, the name itself being a corruption of *dies mandati* (day of the mandate) when Christ washed the feet of the disciples and gave them the mandate to love one another.

EASTER DAY

Easter Day is the first Sunday after the full moon which happens on, or next after, the 21st day of March; if the full moon happens on a Sunday, Easter Day is the Sunday after.

This definition is contained in an Act of Parliament (24 Geo. II c. 23) and explanation is given in the preamble to the Act that the day of full moon depends on certain tables that have been prepared. These tables are summarised in the early pages of the Book of Common Prayer. The moon referred to is not the real moon of the heavens, but a hypothetical moon on whose 'full' the date of Easter depends, and the lunations of this 'calendar' moon consist of twenty-nine and thirty days alternately, with certain necessary modifications to make the date of its full agree as nearly as possible with that of the real moon, which is known as the Paschal Full Moon.

A FIXED EASTER

In 1928 the House of Commons agreed to a motion for the third reading of a bill proposing that Easter Day shall, in the calendar year next but one after the commencement of the Act and in all subsequent years, be the first Sunday after the second Saturday in April. Easter would thus fall on the second or third Sunday in April, i.e. between 9 and 15 April (inclusive). A clause in the Bill provided that before it shall come into operation, regard shall be had to any opinion expressed officially by the various Christian churches. Efforts by the World Council of Churches to secure a unanimous choice of date for Easter by its member churches have so far been unsuccessful.

ROGATION DAYS
Rogation Days are the Monday, Tuesday and Wednesday preceding Ascension Day and from the fifth century were observed as public fasts with solemn processions and supplications. The processions were discontinued as religious observances at the Reformation, but survive in the ceremony known as 'beating the parish bounds'. Rogation Sunday is the Sunday before Ascension Day.

EMBER DAYS
The Ember Days at the four seasons are the Wednesday, Friday and Saturday *(a)* before the third Sunday in Advent, *(b)* before the second Sunday in Lent, and *(c)* before the Sundays nearest to the festivals of St Peter and of St Michael and All Angels.

TRINITY SUNDAY
Trinity Sunday is eight weeks after Easter Day, on the Sunday following Pentecost (Whit Sunday). Subsequent Sundays are reckoned in the Book of Common Prayer calendar of the Church of England as 'after Trinity'.

Thomas Becket (1118–70) was consecrated Archbishop of Canterbury on the Sunday after Whit Sunday and his first act was to ordain that the day of his consecration should be held as a new festival in honour of the Holy Trinity. This observance spread from Canterbury throughout the whole of Christendom.

MOVABLE FEASTS TO THE YEAR 2035

Year	*Ash Wednesday*	*Easter*	*Ascension*	*Pentecost (Whit Sunday)*	*Advent Sunday*
2005	9 February	27 March	5 May	15 May	27 November
2006	1 March	16 April	25 May	4 June	3 December
2007	21 February	8 April	17 May	27 May	2 December
2008	6 February	23 March	1 May	11 May	30 November
2009	25 February	12 April	21 May	31 May	29 November
2010	17 February	4 April	13 May	23 May	28 November
2011	9 March	24 April	2 June	12 June	27 November
2012	22 February	8 April	17 May	27 May	2 December
2013	13 February	31 March	9 May	19 May	1 December
2014	5 March	20 April	29 May	8 June	30 November
2015	18 February	5 April	14 May	24 May	29 November
2016	10 February	27 March	5 May	15 May	27 November
2017	1 March	16 April	25 May	4 June	3 December
2018	14 February	1 April	10 May	20 May	2 December
2019	6 March	21 April	30 May	9 June	1 December
2020	26 February	12 April	21 May	31 May	29 November
2021	17 February	4 April	13 May	23 May	28 November
2022	2 March	17 April	26 May	5 June	27 November
2023	22 February	9 April	18 May	28 May	3 December
2024	14 February	31 March	9 May	19 May	1 December
2025	5 March	20 April	29 May	8 June	30 November
2026	18 February	5 April	14 May	24 May	29 November
2027	10 February	28 March	6 May	16 May	28 November
2028	1 March	16 April	25 May	4 June	3 December
2029	14 February	1 April	10 May	20 May	2 December
2030	6 March	21 April	30 May	9 June	1 December
2031	26 February	13 April	22 May	1 June	30 November
2032	11 February	28 March	6 May	16 May	28 November
2033	2 March	17 April	26 May	5 June	27 November
2034	22 February	9 April	18 May	28 May	3 December
2035	7 February	25 March	3 May	13 May	2 December

NOTES
Ash Wednesday (first day in Lent) can fall at earliest on 4 February and at latest on 10 March
Mothering Sunday (fourth Sunday in Lent) can fall at earliest on 1 March and at latest on 4 April
Easter Day can fall at earliest on 22 March and at latest on 25 April
Ascension Day is forty days after Easter Day and can fall at earliest on 30 April and at latest on 3 June
Pentecost (Whit Sunday) is seven weeks after Easter and can fall at earliest on 10 May and at latest on 13 June
Trinity Sunday is the Sunday after Whit Sunday
Corpus Christi falls on the Thursday after Trinity Sunday
Sundays after Pentecost – there are not less than 18 and not more than 23
Advent Sunday is the Sunday nearest to 30 November

EASTER DAYS AND DOMINICAL LETTERS 1500 TO 2035

Dates up to and including 1752 are according to the Julian calendar. For dominical letters in leap years, *see* note below

		1500–1599	1600–1699	1700–1799	1800–1899	1900–1999	2000–2035
March							
d	22	1573	1668	1761	1818		
e	23	1505/16	1600	1788	1845/56	1913	2008
f	24		1611/95	1706/99		1940	
g	25	1543/54	1627/38/49	1722/33/44	1883/94	1951	2035
A	26	1559/70/81/92	1654/65/76	1749/58/69/80	1815/26/37	1967/78/89	
b	27	1502/13/24/97	1608/87/92	1785/96	1842/53/64	1910/21/32	2005/16
c	28	1529/35/40	1619/24/30	1703/14/25	1869/75/80	1937/48	2027/32
d	29	1551/62	1635/46/57	1719/30/41/52	1807/12/91	1959/64/70	
e	30	1567/78/89	1651/62/73/84	1746/55/66/77	1823/34	1902/75/86/97	
f	31	1510/21/32/83/94	1605/16/78/89	1700/71/82/93	1839/50/61/72	1907/18/29/91	2002/13/24
April							
g	1	1526/37/48	1621/32	1711/16	1804/66/77/88	1923/34/45/56	2018/29
A	2	1553/64	1643/48	1727/38	1809/20/93/99	1961/72	
b	3	1575/80/86	1659/70/81	1743/63/68/74	1825/31/36	1904/83/88/94	
c	4	1507/18/91	1602/13/75/86/97	1708/79/90	1847/58	1915/20/26/99	2010/21
d	5	1523/34/45/56	1607/18/29/40	1702/13/24/95	1801/63/74/85/96	1931/42/53	2015/26
e	6	1539/50/61/72	1634/45/56	1729/35/40/60	1806/17/28/90	1947/58/69/80	
f	7	1504/77/88	1667/72	1751/65/76	1822/33/44	1901/12/85/96	
g	8	1509/15/20/99	1604/10/83/94	1705/87/92/98	1849/55/60	1917/28	2007/12
A	9	1531/42	1615/26/37/99	1710/21/32	1871/82	1939/44/50	2023/34
b	10	1547/58/69	1631/42/53/64	1726/37/48/57	1803/14/87/98	1955/66/77	
c	11	1501/12/63/74/85/96	1658/69/80	1762/73/84	1819/30/41/52	1909/71/82/93	2004
d	12	1506/17/28	1601/12/91/96	1789	1846/57/68	1903/14/25/36/98	2009/20
e	13	1533/44	1623/28	1707/18	1800/73/79/84	1941/52	2031
f	14	1555/60/66	1639/50/61	1723/34/45/54	1805/11/16/95	1963/68/74	
g	15	1571/82/93	1655/66/77/88	1750/59/70/81	1827/38	1900/06/79/90	2001
A	16	1503/14/25/36/87/98	1609/20/82/93	1704/75/86/97	1843/54/65/76	1911/22/33/95	2006/17/28
b	17	1530/41/52	1625/36	1715/20	1808/70/81/92	1927/38/49/60	2022/33
c	18	1557/68	1647/52	1731/42/56	1802/13/24/97	1954/65/76	
d	19	1500/79/84/90	1663/74/85	1747/67/72/78	1829/35/40	1908/81/87/92	
e	20	1511/22/95	1606/17/79/90	1701/12/83/94	1851/62	1919/24/30	2003/14/25
f	21	1527/38/49	1622/33/44	1717/28	1867/78/89	1935/46/57	2019/30
g	22	1565/76	1660	1739/53/64	1810/21/32	1962/73/84	
A	23	1508	1671		1848	1905/16	2000
b	24	1519	1603/14/98	1709/91	1859		2011
c	25	1546	1641	1736	1886	1943	

No dominical letter is placed against the intercalary day 29 February but since it is still counted as a weekday and given a name, the series of letters moves back one day every leap year after intercalation. Thus, a leap year beginning with the dominical letter C will change to a year with the dominical letter B on 1 March

HINDU CALENDAR

The Hindu calendar is a luni-solar calendar of twelve months, each containing 29 days, 12 hours. Each month is divided into a light fortnight (Shukla or Shuddha) and a dark fortnight (Krishna or Vadya) based on the waxing and waning of the moon. In most parts of India the month starts with the light fortnight, i.e. the day after the new moon, although in some regions it begins with the dark fortnight, i.e. the day after the full moon.

The new year begins in the month of Chaitra (March/April) and ends in the month of Phalgun (March). The twelve months, Chaitra, Vaishakh, Jyeshtha, Ashadh, Shravan, Bhadrapad, Ashvin, Kartik, Margashirsh, Paush, Magh and Phalgun, have Sanskrit names derived from twelve asterisms (constellations). There are regional variations to the names of the months but the Sanskrit names are understood throughout India.

Every lunar month must have a solar transit and is termed pure (shuddha). The lunar month without a solar transit is impure (mala) and called an intercalary month. An intercalary month occurs approximately every 32 lunar months, whenever the difference between the Hindu year of 360 lunar days (354 days 8 hours solar time) and the 365 days 6 hours of the solar year reaches the length of one Hindu lunar month (29 days 12 hours).

The leap month may be added at any point in the Hindu year. The name given to the month varies according to when it occurs but is taken from the month immediately following it. There is no leap month in 2005.

The days of the week are called Raviwar (Sunday), Somawar (Monday), Mangalwar (Tuesday), Budhawar (Wednesday), Guruwar (Thursday), Shukrawar (Friday) and Shaniwar (Saturday). The names are derived from the Sanskrit names of the Sun, the Moon and five planets, Mars, Mercury, Jupiter, Venus and Saturn.

Most fasts and festivals are based on the lunar calendar but a few are determined by the apparent movement of the Sun, e.g. Sankranti and Pongal (in southern India), which are celebrated on 14/15 January to mark the start of the Sun's apparent journey northwards and a change of season.

Festivals celebrated throughout India are Chaitra (the New Year), Raksha-bandhan (the renewal of the kinship bond between brothers and sisters), Navaratri (a nine-night festival dedicated to the goddess Parvati), Dasara (the victory of Rama over the demon army), Diwali (a festival of lights), Makara Sankranti, Shivaratri (dedicated to Shiva), and Holi (a spring festival).

Regional festivals are Durga-puja (dedicated to the goddess Durga (Parvati)), Sarasvati-puja (dedicated to the goddess Sarasvati), Ganesh Chaturthi (worship of Ganesh on the fourth day (Chaturthi) of the light half of Bhadrapad), Ramanavami (the birth festival of the god Rama) and Janmashtami (the birth festival of the god Krishna).

The main festivals celebrated in Britain are Navaratri, Dasara, Durga-puja, Diwali, Holi, Sarasvati-puja, Ganesh Chaturthi, Raksha-bandhan, Ramanavami and Janmashtami.

For dates of the main festivals in 2005, *see* page 9.

JEWISH CALENDAR

The story of the Flood in the Book of Genesis indicates the use of a calendar of some kind and that the writers recognised thirty days as the length of a lunation. However, after the diaspora, Jewish communities were left in considerable doubt as to the times of fasts and festivals. This led to the formation of the Jewish calendar as used today. It is said that this was done in AD 358 by Rabbi Hillel II, though some assert that it did not happen until much later.

The calendar is luni-solar, and is based on the lengths of the lunation and of the tropical year as found by Hipparchus (*c.*120 BC), which differ little from those adopted at the present day. The year AM 5765 (2004–2005) is the 8th year of the 304th Metonic (Minor or Lunar) cycle of 19 years and the 25th year of the 206th Solar (or Major) cycle of 28 years since the Era of the Creation. Jews hold that the Creation occurred at the time of the autumnal equinox in the year known in the Christian calendar as 3760 BC (954 of the Julian period). The epoch or starting point of Jewish chronology corresponds to 7 October 3761 BC. At the beginning of each solar cycle, the Tekufah of Nisan (the vernal equinox) returns to the same day and to the same hour.

The hour is divided into 1080 minims, and the month between one new moon and the next is reckoned as 29 days, 12 hours, 793 minims. The normal calendar year, called a Regular Common year, consists of 12 months of 30 days and 29 days alternately. Since 12 months such as these comprise only 354 days, in order that each of them shall not diverge greatly from an average place in the solar year, a 13th month is occasionally added after the fifth month of the civil year (which commences on the first day of the month Tishri), or as the penultimate month of the ecclesiastical year (which commences on the first day of the month Nisan). The years when this happens are called Embolismic or leap years.

Of the 19 years that form a Metonic cycle, seven are leap years; they occur at places in the cycle indicated by the numbers 3, 6, 8, 11, 14, 17 and 19, these places being chosen so that the accumulated excesses of the solar years should be as small as possible.

A Jewish year is of one of the following six types:

Minimal Common	353 days
Regular Common	354 days
Full Common	355 days
Minimal Leap	383 days
Regular Leap	384 days
Full Leap	385 days

The Regular year has alternate months of 30 and 29 days. In a Full year, whether common or leap, Marcheshvan, the second month of the civil year, has 30 days instead of 29; in Minimal years Kislev, the third month, has 29 instead of 30. The additional month in leap years is called Adar I and precedes the month called Adar in Common years. Adar II is called Adar Sheni in leap years, and the usual Adar festivals are kept in Adar Sheni. Adar I and Adar II always have 30 days, but neither this, nor the other variations mentioned, is allowed to change the number of days in the other months, which still follow the alternation of the normal twelve.

These are the main features of the Jewish calendar, which must be considered permanent because as a Jewish law it cannot be altered except by a great Sanhedrin.

The Jewish day begins between sunset and nightfall. The time used is that of the meridian of Jerusalem, which is 2h 21m in advance of Greenwich Mean Time. Rules for the beginning of sabbaths and festivals were laid down for the latitude of London in the 18th century and hours for nightfall are now fixed annually by the Chief Rabbi.

JEWISH CALENDAR 5765–6

AM 5765 (765) is a Minimal Leap year of 13 months, 55 sabbaths and 383 days.

Month (first day)	AM 5765	AM 5766
Tishri 1	16 September 2004	4 October 2005
Marcheshvan 1	16 October	3 November
Kislev 1	14 November	2 December
Tebet 1	13 December	
Shebat 1	11 January 2005	
**Adar* 1	9 February	
†*Adar* II	11 March	
Nisan 1	10 April	
Iyar 1	9 May	
Sivan 1	8 June	
Tammuz 1	7 July	
Ab 1	6 August	
Elul 1	4 September	

*Known as Adar Rishon in leap years
†Known as Adar Sheni in leap years

JEWISH FASTS AND FESTIVALS

For dates of principal festivals in 2005, *see* page 9.

Tishri 1–2	Rosh Hashanah (New Year)
Tishri 3	*Fast of Gedaliah
Tishri 10	Yom Kippur (Day of Atonement)
Tishri 15–21	Succoth (Feast of Tabernacles)
Tishri 21	Hoshana Rabba
Tishri 22	Shemini Atseret (Solemn Assembly)
Tishri 23	Simchat Torah (Rejoicing of the Law)
Kislev 25	Chanucah (Dedication of the Temple) begins
Tebet 10	Fast of Tebet
†*Adar* 13	§Fast of Esther
†*Adar* 14	Purim
†*Adar* 15	Shushan Purim
Nisan 15–22	Pesach (Passover)
Sivan 6–7	Shavuot (Feast of Weeks)
Tammuz 17	*Fast of Tammuz
Ab 9	*Fast of Ab

*If these dates fall on the sabbath the fast is kept on the following day
†Adar Sheni in leap years
§This fast is observed on Adar 11 (or Adar Sheni 11 in leap years) if Adar 13 falls on a Sabbath

THE MUSLIM CALENDAR

The Muslim era is dated from the *Hijrah,* or flight of the Prophet Muhammad from Mecca to Medina, the corresponding date of which in the Julian calendar is 16 July AD 622. The lunar *hijri* calendar is used principally in Iran, Egypt, Malaysia, Pakistan, Mauritania, various Arab states and certain parts of India. Iran uses the solar *hijri* calendar as well as the lunar *hijri* calendar. The dating system was adopted about AD 639, commencing with the first day of the month Muharram.

The lunar calendar consists of twelve months containing an alternate sequence of 30 and 29 days, with the intercalation of one day at the end of the twelfth month at stated intervals in each cycle of 30 years. The object of the intercalation is to reconcile the date of the first day of the month with the date of the actual new moon.

Some adherents still take the date of the evening of the first physical sighting of the crescent of the new moon as that of the first of the month. If cloud obscures the moon the present month may be extended to 30 days, after which the new month will begin automatically regardless of whether the moon has been seen. (Under religious law a month must have less than 31 days.) This means that the beginning of a new month and the date of religious festivals can vary from the published calendars.

In each cycle of 30 years, 19 years are common and contain 354 days, and 11 years are intercalary (leap years) of 355 days, the latter being called *kabisah*. The mean length of the Hijrah years is 354 days 8 hours 48 minutes and the period of mean lunation is 29 days 12 hours 44 minutes.

To ascertain if a year is common or kabisah, divide it by 30: the quotient gives the number of completed cycles and the remainder shows the place of the year in the current cycle. If the remainder is 2, 5, 7, 10, 13, 16, 18, 21, 24, 26 or 29, the year is kabisah and consists of 355 days.

MUSLIM CALENDAR 1425–26

Hijrah 1425 AH (remainder 15) is a common year, 1426 AH (remainder 16) is a kabisah year. Calendar dates below are estimates based on calculations of moon phases.

Month Length	1426 *(1425)* AH
Dhu'l-Qa'da (30)	13 December
Dhu'l-Hijjah (29 or 30)	12 January
Muharram (30)	10 February
Safar (29)	12 March
Rabi' I (30)	10 April
Rabi' II (29)	10 May
Jumada I (30)	8 June
Jumada II (29)	8 July
Rajab (30)	6 August
Sha'ban (29)	5 September
Ramadân (30)	4 October
Shawwâl (29)	3 November

MUSLIM FESTIVALS

Ramadan is a month of fasting for all Muslims because it is the month in which the revelation of the *Qur'an* (Koran) began. During Ramadan Muslims abstain from food, drink and sexual pleasure from dawn until after sunset throughout the month.

The two major festivals are *Id al-Fitr* and *Id al-Adha*. Id al-Fitr marks the end of the Ramadan fast and is celebrated on the day after the sighting of the new moon of the following month. Id al-Adha, the festival of sacrifice (also known as the great festival), celebrates the submission of the Prophet Ibrahim (Abraham) to God. Id al-Adha falls on the tenth day of Dhul-Hijjah, coinciding with the day when those on *hajj* (pilgrimage to Mecca) sacrifice animals.

Other days accorded special recognition are:

Muharram 1	New Year's Day
Muharram 10	Ashura (the day Prophet Noah left the Ark and Prophet Moses was saved from Pharaoh (Sunni), the death of the Prophet's grandson Husain (Shi'ite))
Rabi'u-l-Awwal (Rabi' I) 12	Mawlid al-Nabi (birthday of the Prophet Muhammad)
Rajab 27	Laylat al-Isra' wa'l-Mi'raj (The Night of Journey and Ascension)
Ramadân One of the odd-numbered nights in the last 10 of the month	Laylat al-Qadr (Night of Power)
Dhu'l-Hijjah 10	Id al-Adha (Festival of Sacrifice)

THE SIKH CALENDAR

The Sikh calendar is a lunar calendar of 365 days divided into 12 months. The length of the months varies between 29 and 32 days.

There are no prescribed feast days and no fasting periods. The main celebrations are Baisakhi Mela (the new year and the anniversary of the founding of the Khalsa), Diwali Mela (festival of light), Hola Mohalla Mela (a spring festival held in the Punjab), and the Gurupurabs (anniversaries associated with the ten Gurus).

For dates of the major celebrations in 2005, *see* page 9.

THAI CALENDAR

Thailand adopted the Suriyakati calendar, a modified version of the Gregorian calendar (Suriyakati) during the reign of King Rama V in 1888, using 1 April as the first day of the year. In 1940, the date of the new year was changed to 1 January. The years are counted from the beginning of the Buddhist era (BE), which is calculated to have commenced upon the death of the Lord Buddha, which is taken to have occurred in BC 543, so AD 2005 is BE 2548. The Chinese system of associating years with one of twelve animals is also in use in Thailand. The Chantarakati lunar calendar is used to determine religious holidays; the new year begins on the first day of the waxing moon in November or, if there is a leap month, in December.

CIVIL AND LEGAL CALENDAR

THE HISTORICAL YEAR

Before 1752, two calendar systems were used in England. The civil or legal year began on 25 March and the historical year on 1 January. Thus the civil or legal date 24 March 1658 was the same day as the historical date 24 March 1659; a date in that portion of the year is written as 24 March 165 8/9, the lower figure showing the historical year.

THE NEW YEAR

In England in the seventh century, and as late as the 13th, the year was reckoned from Christmas Day, but in the 12th century the Church in England began the year with the feast of the Annunciation of the Blessed Virgin ('Lady Day') on 25 March and this practice was adopted generally in the 14th century. The civil or legal year in the British Dominions (exclusive of Scotland) began with Lady Day until 1751. But in and since 1752 the civil year has begun with 1 January. New Year's Day in Scotland was changed from 25 March to 1 January in 1600.

Elsewhere in Europe, 1 January was adopted as the first day of the year by Venice in 1522, German states in 1544, Spain, Portugal and the Roman Catholic Netherlands in 1556, Prussia, Denmark and Sweden in 1559, France in 1564, Lorraine in 1579, the Protestant Netherlands in 1583, Russia in 1725, and Tuscany in 1751.

REGNAL YEARS

Regnal years are the years of a sovereign's reign and each begins on the anniversary of his or her accession, e.g. regnal year 54 of the present Queen begins on 6 February 2005.

The system was used for dating Acts of Parliament until 1962. The Summer Time Act 1925, for example, is quoted as 15 and 16 Geo. V c. 64, because it became law in the parliamentary session which extended over part of both of these regnal years. Acts of a parliamentary session during which a sovereign died were usually given two year numbers, the regnal year of the deceased sovereign and the regnal year of his or her successor, e.g. those passed in 1952 were dated 16 Geo. VI and 1 Elizabeth II. Since 1962 Acts of Parliament have been dated by the calendar year.

QUARTER AND TERM DAYS

Holy days and saints days were the usual means in early times for setting the dates of future and recurrent appointments. The quarter days in England and Wales are the feast of the Nativity (25 December), the feast of the Annunciation (25 March), the feast of St John the Baptist (24 June) and the feast of St Michael and All Angels (29 September).

The term days in Scotland are Candlemas (the feast of the Purification), Whitsunday, Lammas (Loaf Mass), and Martinmas (St Martin's Day). These fell on 2 February, 15 May, 1 August and 11 November respectively. However, by the Term and Quarter Days (Scotland) Act 1990, the dates of the term days were changed to 28 February (Candlemas), 28 May (Whitsunday), 28 August (Lammas) and 28 November (Martinmas).

RED-LETTER DAYS

Red-letter days were originally the holy days and saints days indicated in early ecclesiastical calendars by letters printed in red ink. The days to be distinguished in this way were approved at the Council of Nicaea in AD 325.

These days still have a legal significance, as judges of the Queen's Bench Division wear scarlet robes on red-letter days falling during the law sittings. The days designated as red-letter days for this purpose are:

Holy and saints days
The Conversion of St Paul, the Purification, Ash Wednesday, the Annunciation, the Ascension, the feasts of St Mark, SS Philip and James, St Matthias, St Barnabas, St John the Baptist, St Peter, St Thomas, St James, St Luke, SS Simon and Jude, All Saints, St Andrew.

Civil calendar (for dates, *see* page 9)
The anniversaries of The Queen's accession, The Queen's birthday and The Queen's coronation, The Queen's official birthday, the birthday of the Duke of Edinburgh, the birthday of the Prince of Wales, St David's Day and Lord Mayor's Day.

PUBLIC HOLIDAYS

Public holidays are divided into two categories, common law and statutory. Common law holidays are holidays 'by habit and custom'; in England, Wales and Northern Ireland these are Good Friday and Christmas Day.

Statutory public holidays, known as bank holidays, were first established by the Bank Holidays Act 1871. They were, literally, days on which the banks (and other public institutions) were closed and financial obligations due on that day were payable the following day. The legislation currently governing public holidays in the UK, which is the Banking and Financial Dealings Act 1971, stipulates the days that are to be public holidays in England, Wales, Scotland and Northern Ireland.

Certain holidays (indicated by * below) are granted annually by royal proclamation, either throughout the UK or in any place in the UK. The public holidays are:

England and Wales
*New Year's Day
Good Friday
Easter Monday
*The first Monday in May
The last Monday in May
The last Monday in August
26 December, if it is not a Sunday
27 December when 25 or 26 December is a Sunday

Scotland
New Year's Day, or if it is a Sunday, 2 January
2 January, or if it is a Sunday, 3 January
Good Friday
The first Monday in May
*The last Monday in May
The first Monday in August
Christmas Day, or if it is a Sunday, 26 December
*Boxing Day – if Christmas Day falls on a Sunday, 26 December is given in lieu and an alternative day is given for Boxing Day

Northern Ireland
*New Year's Day
17 March, or if it is a Sunday, 18 March
Easter Monday
*The first Monday in May
The last Monday in May
*12 July, or if it is a Sunday, 13 July
The last Monday in August
26 December, if it is not a Sunday
27 December if 25 or 26 December is a Sunday

For dates of public holidays in 2005 and 2006, *see* pages 10–11.

CHRONOLOGICAL CYCLES AND ERAS

SOLAR (OR MAJOR) CYCLE

The solar cycle is a period of twenty-eight years in any corresponding year of which the days of the week recur on the same day of the month.

METONIC (LUNAR, OR MINOR) CYCLE

In 432 BC, Meton, an Athenian astronomer, found that 235 lunations are very nearly, though not exactly, equal in duration to 19 solar years and so after 19 years the phases of the Moon recur on the same days of the month (nearly). The dates of full moon in a cycle of 19 years were inscribed in figures of gold on public monuments in Athens, and the number showing the position of a year in the cycle is called the golden number of that year.

JULIAN PERIOD

The Julian period was proposed by Joseph Scaliger in 1582. The period is 7980 Julian years, and its first year coincides with the year 4713 BC. The figure of 7980 is the product of the number of years in the solar cycle, the Metonic cycle and the cycle of the Roman indiction (28 × 19 × 15).

ROMAN INDICTION
The Roman indiction is a period of fifteen years, instituted for fiscal purposes about AD 300.

EPACT
The epact is the age of the calendar Moon, diminished by one day, on 1 January, in the ecclesiastical lunar calendar.

CHINESE CALENDAR
A lunar calendar was the sole calendar in use in China until 1911, when the government adopted the new (Gregorian) calendar for official and most business activities. The Chinese tend to follow both calendars, the lunar calendar playing an important part in personal life, e.g. birth celebrations, festivals, marriages; and in rural villages the lunar calendar dictates the cycle of activities, denoting the change of weather and farming activities.

The lunar calendar is used in Hong Kong, Singapore, Malaysia, Tibet and elsewhere in south-east Asia. The calendar has a cycle of 60 years. The new year begins at the first new moon after the sun enters the sign of Aquarius, i.e. the new year falls between 21 January and 19 February in the Gregorian calendar.

Each year in the Chinese calendar is associated with one of 12 animals: the rat, the ox, the tiger, the rabbit, the dragon, the snake, the horse, the goat or sheep, the monkey, the chicken or rooster, the dog, and the pig.

The date of the Chinese new year and the astrological sign for the years 2005–2008 are:

2005	9 February	Chicken or Rooster
2006	29 January	Dog
2007	18 February	Pig
2008	7 February	Rat

COPTIC CALENDAR
In the Coptic calendar, which is used in parts of Egypt and Ethiopia, the year is made up of 12 months of 30 days each, followed, in general, by five complementary days. Every fourth year is an intercalary or leap year and in these years there are six complementary days. The intercalary year of the Coptic calendar immediately precedes the leap year of the Julian calendar. The era is that of Diocletian or the Martyrs, the origin of which is fixed at 29 August AD 284 (Julian date).

INDIAN ERAS
In addition to the Muslim reckoning, other eras are used in India. The Saka era of southern India, dating from 3 March AD 78, was declared the national calendar of the Republic of India with effect from 22 March 1957, to be used concurrently with the Gregorian calendar. As revised, the year of the new Saka era begins at the spring equinox, with five successive months of 31 days and seven of 30 days in ordinary years, and six months of each length in leap years. The year AD 2005 is 1927 of the revised Saka era.

The year AD 2005 corresponds to the following years in other eras:

Year 2062 of the Vikram Samvat era
Year 1412 of the Bengali San era
Year 1181 of the Kollam era
Vedanga Jyotisa year 1 of the five-yearly cycle (387th cycle of Paitamah Siddhanta)
Year 6006 of the Kaliyuga era
Year 2547 of the Buddha Nirvana era

JAPANESE CALENDAR
The Japanese calendar is essentially the same as the Gregorian calendar, the years, months and weeks being of the same length and beginning on the same days as those of the Gregorian calendar. The numeration of the years is different, based on a system of epochs or periods, each of which begins at the accession of an Emperor or other important occurrence. The method is not unlike the British system of regnal years, except that each year of a period closes on 31 December. The Japanese chronology begins about AD 650 and the three latest epochs are defined by the reigns of Emperors, whose actual names are not necessarily used:

Epoch
Taishō 1 August 1912 to 25 December 1926
Shōwa 26 December 1926 to 7 January 1989
Heisei 8 January 1989

The year Heisei 17 begins on 1 January 2005.

The months are known as First Month, Second Month, etc., First Month being equivalent to January. The days of the week are Nichiyōbi (Sun-day), Getsuyōbi (Moon-day), Kayōbi (Fire-day), Suiyōbi (Water-day), Mokuyōbi (Wood-day), Kinyōbi (Metal-day), Doyōbi (Earth-day).

THE MASONIC YEAR
Two dates are quoted in warrants, dispensations, etc., issued by the United Grand Lodge of England, those for the current year being expressed as *Anno Domini* 2005–*Anno Lucis* 6005. This *Anno Lucis* (year of light) is based on the Book of Genesis 1:3, the 4000-year difference being derived, in modified form, from *Ussher's Notation*, published in 1654, which places the Creation of the World in 4004 BC.

OLYMPIADS
Ancient Greek chronology was reckoned in Olympiads, cycles of four years corresponding with the periodic Olympic Games held on the plain of Olympia in Elis once every four years. The intervening years were the first, second, etc., of the Olympiad, which received the name of the victor at the Games. The first recorded Olympiad is that of Choroebus, 776 BC.

ZOROASTRIAN CALENDAR
Zoroastrians, followers of the Iranian prophet Zarathushtra (known to the Greeks as Zoroaster) are mostly to be found in Iran and in India, where they are known as Parsees.

The Zoroastrian era dates from the coronation of the last Zoroastrian Sasanian king in AD 631. The Zoroastrian calendar is divided into twelve months, each comprising 30 days, followed by five holy days of the Gathas at the end of each year to make the year consist of 365 days.

In order to synchronise the calendar with the solar year of 365 days, an extra month was intercalated once every 120 years. However, this intercalation ceased in the 12th century and the New Year, which had fallen in the spring, slipped back to August. Because intercalation ceased at different times in Iran and India, there was one month's difference between the calendar followed in Iran (Kadmi calendar) and that followed by the Parsees (Shenshai calendar). In 1906 a group of Zoroastrians decided to bring the calendar back in line with the seasons again and restore the New Year to 21 March each year (Fasli calendar).

The Shenshai calendar (New Year in August) is mainly used by Parsees. The Fasli calendar (New Year, 21 March) is mainly used by Zoroastrians living in Iran, in the Indian subcontinent, or away from Iran.

THE ROMAN CALENDAR

Roman historians adopted as an epoch the foundation of Rome, which is believed to have happened in the year 753 BC. The ordinal number of the years in Roman reckoning is followed by the letters AUC *(ab urbe condita)*, so that the year 2005 is 2758 AUC (MMDCCLVIII). The calendar that we know has developed from one said to have been established by Romulus using a year of 304 days divided into ten months, beginning with March. To this Numa added January and February, making the year consist of 12 months of 30 and 29 days alternately, with an additional day so that the total was 355. It is also said that Numa ordered an intercalary month of 22 or 23 days in alternate years, making 90 days in eight years, to be inserted after 23 February.

However, there is some doubt as to the origination and the details of the intercalation in the Roman calendar. It is certain that some scheme of this kind was inaugurated and not fully carried out, for in the year 46 BC Julius Caesar found that the calendar had been allowed to fall into some confusion. He sought the help of the Egyptian astronomer Sosigenes, which led to the construction and adoption (45 BC) of the Julian calendar, and, by a slight alteration, to the Gregorian calendar now in use. The year 46 BC was made to consist of 445 days and is called the Year of Confusion.

In the Roman (Julian) calendar the days of the month were counted backwards from three fixed points, or days, and an intervening day was said to be so many days before the next coming point, the first and last being counted. These three points were the Kalends, the Nones, and the Ides. Their positions in the months and the method of counting from them will be seen in the table below. The year containing 366 days was called *bissextillis annus*, as it had a doubled sixth day *(bissextus dies)* before the March Kalends on 24 February – *ante diem sextum Kalendas Martias*, or a.d. VI Kal. Mart.

Present days of the month	*March, May, July, October have thirty-one days*		*January, August, December have thirty-one days*		*April, June, September, November have thirty days*		*February has twenty-eight days, and in leap year twenty-nine*	
1	Kalendis		Kalendis		Kalendis		Kalendis	
2	VI		IV	ante	IV	ante	IV	ante
3	V	ante	III	Nonas	III	Nonas	III	Nonas
4	IV	Nonas	pridie Nonas		pridie Nonas		pridie Nonas	
5	III		Nonis		Nonis		Nonis	
6	pridie Nonas		VIII		VIII		VIII	
7	Nonis		VII		VII		VII	
8	VIII		VI	ante	VI	ante	VI	ante
9	VII		V	Idus	V	Idus	V	Idus
10	VI	ante	IV		IV		IV	
11	V	Idus	III		III		III	
12	IV		pridie Idus		pridie Idus		pridie Idus	
13	III		Idibus		Idibus		Idibus	
14	pridie Idus		XIX		XVIII		XVI	
15	Idibus		XVIII		XVII		XV	
16	XVII		XVII		XVI		XIV	
17	XVI		XVI		XV		XIII	
18	XV		XV		XIV		XII	
19	XIV		XIV		XIII		XI	
20	XIII		XIII		XII	ante Kalendas	X	ante Kalendas
21	XII		XII	ante Kalendas	XI	(of the month	IX	Martias
22	XI	ante Kalendas	XI	(of the month	X	following)	VIII	
23	X	(of the month	X	following)	IX		VII	
24	IX	following)	IX		VIII		*VI	
25	VIII		VIII		VII		V	
26	VII		VII		VI		IV	
27	VI		VI		V		III	
28	V		V		IV		pridie Kalendas Martias	
29	IV		IV		III			
30	III		III		pridie Kalendas (Maias, Quinctilis, Octobris, Decembris)			
31	pridie Kalendas (Aprilis, Iunias, Sextilis, Novembris)		pridie Kalendas (Februarias, Septembris, Ianuarias)					

* (repeated in leap year)

CALENDAR FOR ANY YEAR 1780–2040

To select the correct calendar for any year between 1780 and 2040, consult the index below

*leap year

1780 N*	1813 K	1846 I	1879 G	1912 D*	1945 C	1978 A	2011 M
1781 C	1814 M	1847 K	1880 J*	1913 G	1946 E	1979 C	2012 B*
1782 E	1815 A	1848 N*	1881 M	1914 I	1947 G	1980 F*	2013 E
1783 G	1816 D*	1849 C	1882 A	1915 K	1948 J*	1981 I	2014 G
1784 J*	1817 G	1850 E	1883 C	1916 N*	1949 M	1982 K	2015 I
1785 M	1818 I	1851 G	1884 F*	1917 C	1950 A	1983 M	2016 L*
1786 A	1819 K	1852 J*	1885 I	1918 E	1951 C	1984 B*	2017 A
1787 C	1820 N*	1853 M	1886 K	1919 G	1952 F*	1985 E	2018 C
1788 F*	1821 C	1854 A	1887 M	1920 J*	1953 I	1986 G	2019 E
1789 I	1822 E	1855 C	1888 B*	1921 M	1954 K	1987 I	2020 H*
1790 K	1823 G	1856 F*	1889 E	1922 A	1955 M	1988 L*	2021 K
1791 M	1824 J*	1857 I	1890 G	1923 C	1956 B*	1989 A	2022 M
1792 B*	1825 M	1858 K	1891 I	1924 F*	1957 E	1990 C	2023 A
1793 E	1826 A	1859 M	1892 L*	1925 I	1958 G	1991 E	2024 D*
1794 G	1827 C	1860 B*	1893 A	1926 K	1959 I	1992 H*	2025 G
1795 I	1828 F*	1861 E	1894 C	1927 M	1960 L*	1993 K	2026 I
1796 L*	1829 I	1862 G	1895 E	1928 B*	1961 A	1994 M	2027 K
1797 A	1830 K	1863 I	1896 H*	1929 E	1962 C	1995 A	2028 N*
1798 C	1831 M	1864 L*	1897 K	1930 G	1963 E	1996 D*	2029 C
1799 E	1832 B*	1865 A	1898 M	1931 I	1964 H*	1997 G	2030 E
1800 G	1833 E	1866 C	1899 A	1932 L*	1965 K	1998 I	2031 G
1801 I	1834 G	1867 E	1900 C	1933 A	1966 M	1999 K	2032 J*
1802 K	1835 I	1868 H*	1901 E	1934 C	1967 A	2000 N*	2033 M
1803 M	1836 L*	1869 K	1902 G	1935 E	1968 D*	2001 C	2034 A
1804 B*	1837 A	1870 M	1903 I	1936 H*	1969 G	2002 E	2035 C
1805 E	1838 C	1871 A	1904 L*	1937 K	1970 I	2003 G	2036 F*
1806 G	1839 E	1872 D*	1905 A	1938 M	1971 K	2004 J*	2037 I
1807 I	1840 H*	1873 G	1906 C	1939 A	1972 N*	2005 M	2038 K
1808 L*	1841 K	1874 I	1907 E	1940 D*	1973 C	2006 A	2039 M
1809 A	1842 M	1875 K	1908 H*	1941 G	1974 E	2007 C	2040 B*
1810 C	1843 A	1876 N*	1909 K	1942 I	1975 G	2008 F*	
1811 E	1844 D*	1877 C	1910 M	1943 K	1976 J*	2009 I	
1812 H*	1845 G	1878 E	1911 A	1944 N*	1977 M	2010 K	

A

	January	*February*	*March*
Sun.	1 8 15 22 29	5 12 19 26	5 12 19 26
Mon.	2 9 16 23 30	6 13 20 27	6 13 20 27
Tue.	3 10 17 24 31	7 14 21 28	7 14 21 28
Wed.	4 11 18 25	1 8 15 22	1 8 15 22 29
Thur.	5 12 19 26	2 9 16 23	2 9 16 23 30
Fri.	6 13 20 27	3 10 17 24	3 10 17 24 31
Sat.	7 14 21 28	4 11 18 25	4 11 18 25

	April	*May*	*June*
Sun.	2 9 16 23 30	7 14 21 28	4 11 18 25
Mon.	3 10 17 24	1 8 15 22 29	5 12 19 26
Tue.	4 11 18 25	2 9 16 23 30	6 13 20 27
Wed.	5 12 19 26	3 10 17 24 31	7 14 21 28
Thur.	6 13 20 27	4 11 18 25	1 8 15 22 29
Fri.	7 14 21 28	5 12 19 26	2 9 16 23 30
Sat.	1 8 15 22 29	6 13 20 27	3 10 17 24

	July	*August*	*September*
Sun.	2 9 16 23 30	6 13 20 27	3 10 17 24
Mon.	3 10 17 24 31	7 14 21 28	4 11 18 25
Tue.	4 11 18 25	1 8 15 22 29	5 12 19 26
Wed.	5 12 19 26	2 9 16 23 30	6 13 20 27
Thur.	6 13 20 27	3 10 17 24 31	7 14 21 28
Fri.	7 14 21 28	4 11 18 25	1 8 15 22 29
Sat.	1 8 15 22 29	5 12 19 26	2 9 16 23 30

	October	*November*	*December*
Sun.	1 8 15 22 29	5 12 19 26	3 10 17 24 31
Mon.	2 9 16 23 30	6 13 20 27	4 11 18 25
Tue.	3 10 17 24 31	7 14 21 28	5 12 19 26
Wed.	4 11 18 25	1 8 15 22 29	6 13 20 27
Thur.	5 12 19 26	2 9 16 23 30	7 14 21 28
Fri.	6 13 20 27	3 10 17 24	1 8 15 22 29
Sat.	7 14 21 28	4 11 18 25	2 9 16 23 30

EASTER DAYS

March 26	1815, 1826, 1837, 1967, 1978, 1989
April 2	1809, 1893, 1899, 1961
April 9	1871, 1882, 1939, 1950, 2023, 2034
April 16	1786, 1797, 1843, 1854, 1865, 1911 1922, 1933, 1995, 2006, 2017
April 23	1905

B (LEAP YEAR)

	January	*February*	*March*
Sun.	1 8 15 22 29	5 12 19 26	4 11 18 25
Mon.	2 9 16 23 30	6 13 20 27	5 12 19 26
Tue.	3 10 17 24 31	7 14 21 28	6 13 20 27
Wed.	4 11 18 25	1 8 15 22 29	7 14 21 28
Thur.	5 12 19 26	2 9 16 23	1 8 15 22 29
Fri.	6 13 20 27	3 10 17 24	2 9 16 23 30
Sat.	7 14 21 28	4 11 18 25	3 10 17 24 31

	April	*May*	*June*
Sun.	1 8 15 22 29	6 13 20 27	3 10 17 24
Mon.	2 9 16 23 30	7 14 21 28	4 11 18 25
Tue.	3 10 17 24	1 8 15 22 29	5 12 19 26
Wed.	4 11 18 25	2 9 16 23 30	6 13 20 27
Thur.	5 12 19 26	3 10 17 24 31	7 14 21 28
Fri.	6 13 20 27	4 11 18 25	1 8 15 22 29
Sat.	7 14 21 28	5 12 19 26	2 9 16 23 30

	July	*August*	*September*
Sun.	1 8 15 22 29	5 12 19 26	2 9 16 23 30
Mon.	2 9 16 23 30	6 13 20 27	3 10 17 24
Tue.	3 10 17 24 31	7 14 21 28	4 11 18 25
Wed.	4 11 18 25	1 8 15 22 29	5 12 19 26
Thur.	5 12 19 26	2 9 16 23 30	6 13 20 27
Fri.	6 13 20 27	3 10 17 24 31	7 14 21 28
Sat.	7 14 21 28	4 11 18 25	1 8 15 22 29

	October	*November*	*December*
Sun.	7 14 21 28	4 11 18 25	2 9 16 23 30
Mon.	1 8 15 22 29	5 12 19 26	3 10 17 24 31
Tue.	2 9 16 23 30	6 13 20 27	4 11 18 25
Wed.	3 10 17 24 31	7 14 21 28	5 12 19 26
Thur.	4 11 18 25	1 8 15 22 29	6 13 20 27
Fri.	5 12 19 26	2 9 16 23 30	7 14 21 28
Sat.	6 13 20 27	3 10 17 24	1 8 15 22 29

EASTER DAYS

April 1	1804, 1888, 1956, 2040
April 8	1792, 1860, 1928, 2012
April 22	1832, 1984

C

	January	*February*	*March*
Sun.	7 14 21 28	4 11 18 25	4 11 18 25
Mon.	1 8 15 22 29	5 12 19 26	5 12 19 26
Tue.	2 9 16 23 30	6 13 20 27	6 13 20 27
Wed.	3 10 17 24 31	7 14 21 28	7 14 21 28
Thur.	4 11 18 25	1 8 15 22	1 8 15 22 29
Fri.	5 12 19 26	2 9 16 23	2 9 16 23 30
Sat.	6 13 20 27	3 10 17 24	3 10 17 24 31

	April	*May*	*June*
Sun.	1 8 15 22 29	6 13 20 27	3 10 17 24
Mon.	2 9 16 23 30	7 14 21 28	4 11 18 25
Tue.	3 10 17 24	1 8 15 22 29	5 12 19 26
Wed.	4 11 18 25	2 9 16 23 30	6 13 20 27
Thur.	5 12 19 26	3 10 17 24 31	7 14 21 28
Fri.	6 13 20 27	4 11 18 25	1 8 15 22 29
Sat.	7 14 21 28	5 12 19 26	2 9 16 23 30

	July	*August*	*September*
Sun.	1 8 15 22 29	5 12 19 26	2 9 16 23 30
Mon.	2 9 16 23 30	6 13 20 27	3 10 17 24
Tue.	3 10 17 24 31	7 14 21 28	4 11 18 25
Wed.	4 11 18 25	1 8 15 22 29	5 12 19 26
Thur.	5 12 19 26	2 9 16 23 30	6 13 20 27
Fri.	6 13 20 27	3 10 17 24 31	7 14 21 28
Sat.	7 14 21 28	4 11 18 25	1 8 15 22 29

	October	*November*	*December*
Sun.	7 14 21 28	4 11 18 25	2 9 16 23 30
Mon.	1 8 15 22 29	5 12 19 26	3 10 17 24 31
Tue.	2 9 16 23 30	6 13 20 27	4 11 18 25
Wed.	3 10 17 24 31	7 14 21 28	5 12 19 26
Thur.	4 11 18 25	1 8 15 22 29	6 13 20 27
Fri.	5 12 19 26	2 9 16 23 30	7 14 21 28
Sat.	6 13 20 27	3 10 17 24	1 8 15 22 29

EASTER DAYS

March 25	1883, 1894, 1951, 2035
April 1	1866, 1877, 1923, 1934, 1945, 2018, 2029
April 8	1787, 1798, 1849, 1855, 1917, 2007
April 15	1781, 1827, 1838, 1900, 1906, 1979, 1990, 2001
April 22	1810, 1821, 1962, 1973

E

	January	*February*	*March*
Sun.	6 13 20 27	3 10 17 24	3 10 17 24 31
Mon.	7 14 21 28	4 11 18 25	4 11 18 25
Tue.	1 8 15 22 29	5 12 19 26	5 12 19 26
Wed.	2 9 16 23 30	6 13 20 27	6 13 20 27
Thur.	3 10 17 24 31	7 14 21 28	7 14 21 28
Fri.	4 11 18 25	1 8 15 22	1 8 15 22 29
Sat.	5 12 19 26	2 9 16 23	2 9 16 23 30

	April	*May*	*June*
Sun.	7 14 21 28	5 12 19 26	2 9 16 23 30
Mon.	1 8 15 22 29	6 13 20 27	3 10 17 24
Tue.	2 9 16 23 30	7 14 21 28	4 11 18 25
Wed.	3 10 17 24	1 8 15 22 29	5 12 19 26
Thur.	4 11 18 25	2 9 16 23 30	6 13 20 27
Fri.	5 12 19 26	3 10 17 24 31	7 14 21 28
Sat.	6 13 20 27	4 11 18 25	1 8 15 22 29

	July	*August*	*September*
Sun.	7 14 21 28	4 11 18 25	1 8 15 22 29
Mon.	1 8 15 22 29	5 12 19 26	2 9 16 23 30
Tue.	2 9 16 23 30	6 13 20 27	3 10 17 24
Wed.	3 10 17 24 31	7 14 21 28	4 11 18 25
Thur.	4 11 18 25	1 8 15 22 29	5 12 19 26
Fri.	5 12 19 26	2 9 16 23 30	6 13 20 27
Sat.	6 13 20 27	3 10 17 24 31	7 14 21 28

	October	*November*	*December*
Sun.	6 13 20 27	3 10 17 24	1 8 15 22 29
Mon.	7 14 21 28	4 11 18 25	2 9 16 23 30
Tue.	1 8 15 22 29	5 12 19 26	3 10 17 24 31
Wed.	2 9 16 23 30	6 13 20 27	4 11 18 25
Thur.	3 10 17 24 31	7 14 21 28	5 12 19 26
Fri.	4 11 18 25	1 8 15 22 29	6 13 20 27
Sat.	5 12 19 26	2 9 16 23 30	7 14 21 28

EASTER DAYS

March 24	1799
March 31	1782, 1793, 1839, 1850, 1861, 1907 1918, 1929, 1991, 2002, 2013
April 7	1822, 1833, 1901, 1985
April 14	1805, 1811, 1895, 1963, 1974
April 21	1867, 1878, 1889, 1935, 1946, 1957, 2019, 2030

D (LEAP YEAR)

	January	*February*	*March*
Sun.	7 14 21 28	4 11 18 25	3 10 17 24 31
Mon.	1 8 15 22 29	5 12 19 26	4 11 18 25
Tue.	2 9 16 23 30	6 13 20 27	5 12 19 26
Wed.	3 10 17 24 31	7 14 21 28	6 13 20 27
Thur.	4 11 18 25	1 8 15 22 29	7 14 21 28
Fri.	5 12 19 26	2 9 16 23	1 8 15 22 29
Sat.	6 13 20 27	3 10 17 24	2 9 16 23 30

	April	*May*	*June*
Sun.	7 14 21 28	5 12 19 26	2 9 16 23 30
Mon.	1 8 15 22 29	6 13 20 27	3 10 17 24
Tue.	2 9 16 23 30	7 14 21 28	4 11 18 25
Wed.	3 10 17 24	1 8 15 22 29	5 12 19 26
Thur.	4 11 18 25	2 9 16 23 30	6 13 20 27
Fri.	5 12 19 26	3 10 17 24 31	7 14 21 28
Sat.	6 13 20 27	4 11 18 25	1 8 15 22 29

	July	*August*	*September*
Sun.	7 14 21 28	4 11 18 25	1 8 15 22 29
Mon.	1 8 15 22 29	5 12 19 26	2 9 16 23 30
Tue.	2 9 16 23 30	6 13 20 27	3 10 17 24
Wed.	3 10 17 24 31	7 14 21 28	4 11 18 25
Thur.	4 11 18 25	1 8 15 22 29	5 12 19 26
Fri.	5 12 19 26	2 9 16 23 30	6 13 20 27
Sat.	6 13 20 27	3 10 17 24 31	7 14 21 28

	October	*November*	*December*
Sun.	6 13 20 27	3 10 17 24	1 8 15 22 29
Mon.	7 14 21 28	4 11 18 25	2 9 16 23 30
Tue.	1 8 15 22 29	5 12 19 26	3 10 17 24 31
Wed.	2 9 16 23 30	6 13 20 27	4 11 18 25
Thur.	3 10 17 24 31	7 14 21 28	5 12 19 26
Fri.	4 11 18 25	1 8 15 22 29	6 13 20 27
Sat.	5 12 19 26	2 9 16 23 30	7 14 21 28

EASTER DAYS

March 24	1940
March 31	1872, 2024
April 7	1844, 1912, 1996
April 14	1816, 1968

F (LEAP YEAR)

	January	*February*	*March*
Sun.	6 13 20 27	3 10 17 24	2 9 16 23 30
Mon.	7 14 21 28	4 11 18 25	3 10 17 24 31
Tue.	1 8 15 22 29	5 12 19 26	4 11 18 25
Wed.	2 9 16 23 30	6 13 20 27	5 12 19 26
Thur.	3 10 17 24 31	7 14 21 28	6 13 20 27
Fri.	4 11 18 25	1 8 15 22 29	7 14 21 28
Sat.	5 12 19 26	2 9 16 23	1 8 15 22 29

	April	*May*	*June*
Sun.	6 13 20 27	4 11 18 25	1 8 15 22 29
Mon.	7 14 21 28	5 12 19 26	2 9 16 23 30
Tue.	1 8 15 22 29	6 13 20 27	3 10 17 24
Wed.	2 9 16 23 30	7 14 21 28	4 11 18 25
Thur.	3 10 17 24	1 8 15 22 29	5 12 19 26
Fri.	4 11 18 25	2 9 16 23 30	6 13 20 27
Sat.	5 12 19 26	3 10 17 24 31	7 14 21 28

	July	*August*	*September*
Sun.	6 13 20 27	3 10 17 24 31	7 14 21 28
Mon.	7 14 21 28	4 11 18 25	1 8 15 22 29
Tue.	1 8 15 22 29	5 12 19 26	2 9 16 23 30
Wed.	2 9 16 23 30	6 13 20 27	3 10 17 24
Thur.	3 10 17 24 31	7 14 21 28	4 11 18 25
Fri.	4 11 18 25	1 8 15 22 29	5 12 19 26
Sat.	5 12 19 26	2 9 16 23 30	6 13 20 27

	October	*November*	*December*
Sun.	5 12 19 26	2 9 16 23 30	7 14 21 28
Mon.	6 13 20 27	3 10 17 24	1 8 15 22 29
Tue.	7 14 21 28	4 11 18 25	2 9 16 23 30
Wed.	1 8 15 22 29	5 12 19 26	3 10 17 24 31
Thur.	2 9 16 23 30	6 13 20 27	4 11 18 25
Fri.	3 10 17 24 31	7 14 21 28	5 12 19 26
Sat.	4 11 18 25	1 8 15 22 29	6 13 20 27

EASTER DAYS

March 23	1788, 1856, 2008
April 6	1828, 1980
April 13	1884, 1952, 2036
April 20	1924

G

	January	February	March
Sun.	5 12 19 26	2 9 16 23	2 9 16 23 30
Mon.	6 13 20 27	3 10 17 24	3 10 17 24 31
Tue.	7 14 21 28	4 11 18 25	4 11 18 25
Wed.	1 8 15 22 29	5 12 19 26	5 12 19 26
Thur.	2 9 16 23 30	6 13 20 27	6 13 20 27
Fri.	3 10 17 24 31	7 14 21 28	7 14 21 28
Sat.	4 11 18 25	1 8 15 22	1 8 15 22 29

	April	May	June
Sun.	6 13 20 27	4 11 18 25	1 8 15 22 29
Mon.	7 14 21 28	5 12 19 26	2 9 16 23 30
Tue.	1 8 15 22 29	6 13 20 27	3 10 17 24
Wed.	2 9 16 23 30	7 14 21 28	4 11 18 25
Thur.	3 10 17 24	1 8 15 22 29	5 12 19 26
Fri.	4 11 18 25	2 9 16 23 30	6 13 20 27
Sat.	5 12 19 26	3 10 17 24 31	7 14 21 28

	July	August	September
Sun.	6 13 20 27	3 10 17 24 31	7 14 21 28
Mon.	7 14 21 28	4 11 18 25	1 8 15 22 29
Tue.	1 8 15 22 29	5 12 19 26	2 9 16 23 30
Wed.	2 9 16 23 30	6 13 20 27	3 10 17 24
Thur.	3 10 17 24 31	7 14 21 28	4 11 18 25
Fri.	4 11 18 25	1 8 15 22 29	5 12 19 26
Sat.	5 12 19 26	2 9 16 23 30	6 13 20 27

	October	November	December
Sun.	5 12 19 26	2 9 16 23 30	7 14 21 28
Mon.	6 13 20 27	3 10 17 24	1 8 15 22 29
Tue.	7 14 21 28	4 11 18 25	2 9 16 23 30
Wed.	1 8 15 22 29	5 12 19 26	3 10 17 24 31
Thur.	2 9 16 23 30	6 13 20 27	4 11 18 25
Fri.	3 10 17 24 31	7 14 21 28	5 12 19 26
Sat.	4 11 18 25	1 8 15 22 29	6 13 20 27

EASTER DAYS

March 23	1845, 1913
March 30	1823, 1834, 1902, 1975, 1986, 1997
April 6	1806, 1817, 1890, 1947, 1958, 1969
April 13	1800, 1873, 1879, 1941, 2031
April 20	1783, 1794, 1851, 1862, 1919, 1930, 2003, 2014, 2025

H (LEAP YEAR)

	January	February	March
Sun.	5 12 19 26	2 9 16 23	1 8 15 22 29
Mon.	6 13 20 27	3 10 17 24	2 9 16 23 30
Tue.	7 14 21 28	4 11 18 25	3 10 17 24 31
Wed.	1 8 15 22 29	5 12 19 26	4 11 18 25
Thur.	2 9 16 23 30	6 13 20 27	5 12 19 26
Fri.	3 10 17 24 31	7 14 21 28	6 13 20 27
Sat.	4 11 18 25	1 8 15 22 29	7 14 21 28

	April	May	June
Sun.	5 12 19 26	3 10 17 24 31	7 14 21 28
Mon.	6 13 20 27	4 11 18 25	1 8 15 22 29
Tue.	7 14 21 28	5 12 19 26	2 9 16 23 30
Wed.	1 8 15 22 29	6 13 20 27	3 10 17 24
Thur.	2 9 16 23 30	7 14 21 28	4 11 18 25
Fri.	3 10 17 24	1 8 15 22 29	5 12 19 26
Sat.	4 11 18 25	2 9 16 23 30	6 13 20 27

	July	August	September
Sun.	5 12 19 26	2 9 16 23 30	6 13 20 27
Mon.	6 13 20 27	3 10 17 24 31	7 14 21 28
Tue.	7 14 21 28	4 11 18 25	1 8 15 22 29
Wed.	1 8 15 22 29	5 12 19 26	2 9 16 23 30
Thur.	2 9 16 23 30	6 13 20 27	3 10 17 24
Fri.	3 10 17 24 31	7 14 21 28	4 11 18 25
Sat.	4 11 18 25	1 8 15 22 29	5 12 19 26

	October	November	December
Sun.	4 11 18 25	1 8 15 22 29	6 13 20 27
Mon.	5 12 19 26	2 9 16 23 30	7 14 21 28
Tue.	6 13 20 27	3 10 17 24	1 8 15 22 29
Wed.	7 14 21 28	4 11 18 25	2 9 16 23 30
Thur.	1 8 15 22 29	5 12 19 26	3 10 17 24 31
Fri.	2 9 16 23 30	6 13 20 27	4 11 18 25
Sat.	3 10 17 24 31	7 14 21 28	5 12 19 26

EASTER DAYS

March 29	1812, 1964
April 5	1896
April 12	1868, 1936, 2020
April 19	1840, 1908, 1992

I

	January	February	March
Sun.	4 11 18 25	1 8 15 22	1 8 15 22 29
Mon.	5 12 19 26	2 9 16 23	2 9 16 23 30
Tue.	6 13 20 27	3 10 17 24	3 10 17 24 31
Wed.	7 14 21 28	4 11 18 25	4 11 18 25
Thur.	1 8 15 22 29	5 12 19 26	5 12 19 26
Fri.	2 9 16 23 30	6 13 20 27	6 13 20 27
Sat.	3 10 17 24 31	7 14 21 28	7 14 21 28

	April	May	June
Sun.	5 12 19 26	3 10 17 24 31	7 14 21 28
Mon.	6 13 20 27	4 11 18 25	1 8 15 22 29
Tue.	7 14 21 28	5 12 19 26	2 9 16 23 30
Wed.	1 8 15 22 29	6 13 20 27	3 10 17 24
Thur.	2 9 16 23 30	7 14 21 28	4 11 18 25
Fri.	3 10 17 24	1 8 15 22 29	5 12 19 26
Sat.	4 11 18 25	2 9 16 23 30	6 13 20 27

	July	August	September
Sun.	5 12 19 26	2 9 16 23 30	6 13 20 27
Mon.	6 13 20 27	3 10 17 24 31	7 14 21 28
Tue.	7 14 21 28	4 11 18 25	1 8 15 22 29
Wed.	1 8 15 22 29	5 12 19 26	2 9 16 23 30
Thur.	2 9 16 23 30	6 13 20 27	3 10 17 24
Fri.	3 10 17 24 31	7 14 21 28	4 11 18 25
Sat.	4 11 18 25	1 8 15 22 29	5 12 19 26

	October	November	December
Sun.	4 11 18 25	1 8 15 22 29	6 13 20 27
Mon.	5 12 19 26	2 9 16 23 30	7 14 21 28
Tue.	6 13 20 27	3 10 17 24	1 8 15 22 29
Wed.	7 14 21 28	4 11 18 25	2 9 16 23 30
Thur.	1 8 15 22 29	5 12 19 26	3 10 17 24 31
Fri.	2 9 16 23 30	6 13 20 27	4 11 18 25
Sat.	3 10 17 24 31	7 14 21 28	5 12 19 26

EASTER DAYS

March 22	1818
March 29	1807, 1891, 1959, 1970
April 5	1795, 1801, 1863, 1874, 1885, 1931, 1942, 1953, 2015, 2026, 2037
April 12	1789, 1846, 1857, 1903, 1914, 1925, 1998, 2009
April 19	1829, 1835, 1981, 1987

J (LEAP YEAR)

	January	February	March
Sun.	4 11 18 25	1 8 15 22 29	7 14 21 28
Mon.	5 12 19 26	2 9 16 23	1 8 15 22 29
Tue.	6 13 20 27	3 10 17 24	2 9 16 23 30
Wed.	7 14 21 28	4 11 18 25	3 10 17 24 31
Thur.	1 8 15 22 29	5 12 19 26	4 11 18 25
Fri.	2 9 16 23 30	6 13 20 27	5 12 19 26
Sat.	3 10 17 24 31	7 14 21 28	6 13 20 27

	April	May	June
Sun.	4 11 18 25	2 9 16 23 30	6 13 20 27
Mon.	5 12 19 26	3 10 17 24 31	7 14 21 28
Tue.	6 13 20 27	4 11 18 25	1 8 15 22 29
Wed.	7 14 21 28	5 12 19 26	2 9 16 23 30
Thur.	1 8 15 22 29	6 13 20 27	3 10 17 24
Fri.	2 9 16 23 30	7 14 21 28	4 11 18 25
Sat.	3 10 17 24	1 8 15 22 29	5 12 19 26

	July	August	September
Sun.	4 11 18 25	1 8 15 22 29	5 12 19 26
Mon.	5 12 19 26	2 9 16 23 30	6 13 20 27
Tue.	6 13 20 27	3 10 17 24 31	7 14 21 28
Wed.	7 14 21 28	4 11 18 25	1 8 15 22 29
Thur.	1 8 15 22 29	5 12 19 26	2 9 16 23 30
Fri.	2 9 16 23 30	6 13 20 27	3 10 17 24
Sat.	3 10 17 24 31	7 14 21 28	4 11 18 25

	October	November	December
Sun.	3 10 17 24 31	7 14 21 28	5 12 19 26
Mon.	4 11 18 25	1 8 15 22 29	6 13 20 27
Tue.	5 12 19 26	2 9 16 23 30	7 14 21 28
Wed.	6 13 20 27	3 10 17 24	1 8 15 22 29
Thur.	7 14 21 28	4 11 18 25	2 9 16 23 30
Fri.	1 8 15 22 29	5 12 19 26	3 10 17 24 31
Sat.	2 9 16 23 30	6 13 20 27	4 11 18 25

EASTER DAYS

March 28	1880, 1948, 2032
April 4	1920
April 11	1784, 1852, 2004
April 18	1824, 1976

K

	January	*February*	*March*
Sun.	3 10 17 24 31	7 14 21 28	7 14 21 28
Mon.	4 11 18 25	1 8 15 22	1 8 15 22 29
Tue.	5 12 19 26	2 9 16 23	2 9 16 23 30
Wed.	6 13 20 27	3 10 17 24	3 10 17 24 31
Thur.	7 14 21 28	4 11 18 25	4 11 18 25
Fri.	1 8 15 22 29	5 12 19 26	5 12 19 26
Sat.	2 9 16 23 30	6 13 20 27	6 13 20 27

	April	*May*	*June*
Sun.	4 11 18 25	2 9 16 23 30	6 13 20 27
Mon.	5 12 19 26	3 10 17 24 31	7 14 21 28
Tue.	6 13 20 27	4 11 18 25	1 8 15 22 29
Wed.	7 14 21 28	5 12 19 26	2 9 16 23 30
Thur.	1 8 15 22 29	6 13 20 27	3 10 17 24
Fri.	2 9 16 23 30	7 14 21 28	4 11 18 25
Sat.	3 10 17 24	1 8 15 22 29	5 12 19 26

	July	*August*	*September*
Sun.	4 11 18 25	1 8 15 22 29	5 12 19 26
Mon.	5 12 19 26	2 9 16 23 30	6 13 20 27
Tue.	6 13 20 27	3 10 17 24 31	7 14 21 28
Wed.	7 14 21 28	4 11 18 25	1 8 15 22 29
Thur.	1 8 15 22 29	5 12 19 26	2 9 16 23 30
Fri.	2 9 16 23 30	6 13 20 27	3 10 17 24
Sat.	3 10 17 24 31	7 14 21 28	4 11 18 25

	October	*November*	*December*
Sun.	3 10 17 24 31	7 14 21 28	5 12 19 26
Mon.	4 11 18 25	1 8 15 22 29	6 13 20 27
Tue.	5 12 19 26	2 9 16 23 30	7 14 21 28
Wed.	6 13 20 27	3 10 17 24	1 8 15 22 29
Thur.	7 14 21 28	4 11 18 25	2 9 16 23 30
Fri.	1 8 15 22 29	5 12 19 26	3 10 17 24 31
Sat.	2 9 16 23 30	6 13 20 27	4 11 18 25

EASTER DAYS

March 28	1869, 1875, 1937, 2027
April 4	1790, 1847, 1858, 1915, 1926, 1999, 2010, 2021
April 11	1819, 1830, 1841, 1909, 1971, 1982, 1993
April 18	1802, 1813, 1897, 1954, 1965
April 25	1886, 1943, 2038

L (LEAP YEAR)

	January	*February*	*March*
Sun.	3 10 17 24 31	7 14 21 28	6 13 20 27
Mon.	4 11 18 25	1 8 15 22 29	7 14 21 28
Tue.	5 12 19 26	2 9 16 23	1 8 15 22 29
Wed.	6 13 20 27	3 10 17 24	2 9 16 23 30
Thur.	7 14 21 28	4 11 18 25	3 10 17 24 31
Fri.	1 8 15 22 29	5 12 19 26	4 11 18 25
Sat.	2 9 16 23 30	6 13 20 27	5 12 19 26

	April	*May*	*June*
Sun.	3 10 17 24	1 8 15 22 29	5 12 19 26
Mon.	4 11 18 25	2 9 16 23 30	6 13 20 27
Tue.	5 12 19 26	3 10 17 24 31	7 14 21 28
Wed.	6 13 20 27	4 11 18 25	1 8 15 22 29
Thur.	7 14 21 28	5 12 19 26	2 9 16 23 30
Fri.	1 8 15 22 29	6 13 20 27	3 10 17 24
Sat.	2 9 16 23 30	7 14 21 28	4 11 18 25

	July	*August*	*September*
Sun.	3 10 17 24 31	7 14 21 28	4 11 18 25
Mon.	4 11 18 25	1 8 15 22 29	5 12 19 26
Tue.	5 12 19 26	2 9 16 23 30	6 13 20 27
Wed.	6 13 20 27	3 10 17 24 31	7 14 21 28
Thur.	7 14 21 28	4 11 18 25	1 8 15 22 29
Fri.	1 8 15 22 29	5 12 19 26	2 9 16 23 30
Sat.	2 9 16 23 30	6 13 20 27	3 10 17 24

	October	*November*	*December*
Sun.	2 9 16 23 30	6 13 20 27	4 11 18 25
Mon.	3 10 17 24 31	7 14 21 28	5 12 19 26
Tue.	4 11 18 25	1 8 15 22 29	6 13 20 27
Wed.	5 12 19 26	2 9 16 23 30	7 14 21 28
Thur.	6 13 20 27	3 10 17 24	1 8 15 22 29
Fri.	7 14 21 28	4 11 18 25	2 9 16 23 30
Sat.	1 8 15 22 29	5 12 19 26	3 10 17 24 31

EASTER DAYS

March 27	1796, 1864, 1932, 2016
April 3	1836, 1904, 1988
April 17	1808, 1892, 1960

M

	January	*February*	*March*
Sun.	2 9 16 23 30	6 13 20 27	6 13 20 27
Mon.	3 10 17 24 31	7 14 21 28	7 14 21 28
Tue.	4 11 18 25	1 8 15 22	1 8 15 22 29
Wed.	5 12 19 26	2 9 16 23	2 9 16 23 30
Thur.	6 13 20 27	3 10 17 24	3 10 17 24 31
Fri.	7 14 21 28	4 11 18 25	4 11 18 25
Sat.	1 8 15 22 29	5 12 19 26	5 12 19 26

	April	*May*	*June*
Sun.	3 10 17 24	1 8 15 22 29	5 12 19 26
Mon.	4 11 18 25	2 9 16 23 30	6 13 20 27
Tue.	5 12 19 26	3 10 17 24 31	7 14 21 28
Wed.	6 13 20 27	4 11 18 25	1 8 15 22 29
Thur.	7 14 21 28	5 12 19 26	2 9 16 23 30
Fri.	1 8 15 22 29	6 13 20 27	3 10 17 24
Sat.	2 9 16 23 30	7 14 21 28	4 11 18 25

	July	*August*	*September*
Sun.	3 10 17 24 31	7 14 21 28	4 11 18 25
Mon.	4 11 18 25	1 8 15 22 29	5 12 19 26
Tue.	5 12 19 26	2 9 16 23 30	6 13 20 27
Wed.	6 13 20 27	3 10 17 24 31	7 14 21 28
Thur.	7 14 21 28	4 11 18 25	1 8 15 22 29
Fri.	1 8 15 22 29	5 12 19 26	2 9 16 23 30
Sat.	2 9 16 23 30	6 13 20 27	3 10 17 24

	October	*November*	*December*
Sun.	2 9 16 23 30	6 13 20 27	4 11 18 25
Mon.	3 10 17 24 31	7 14 21 28	5 12 19 26
Tue.	4 11 18 25	1 8 15 22 29	6 13 20 27
Wed.	5 12 19 26	2 9 16 23 30	7 14 21 28
Thur.	6 13 20 27	3 10 17 24	1 8 15 22 29
Fri.	7 14 21 28	4 11 18 25	2 9 16 23 30
Sat.	1 8 15 22 29	5 12 19 26	3 10 17 24 31

EASTER DAYS

March 27	1785, 1842, 1853, 1910, 1921, 2005
April 3	1825, 1831, 1983, 1994
April 10	1803, 1814, 1887, 1898, 1955, 1966, 1977, 2039
April 17	1870, 1881, 1927, 1938, 1949, 2022, 2033
April 24	1791, 1859, 2011

N (LEAP YEAR)

	January	*February*	*March*
Sun.	2 9 16 23 30	6 13 20 27	5 12 19 26
Mon.	3 10 17 24 31	7 14 21 28	6 13 20 27
Tue.	4 11 18 25	1 8 15 22 29	7 14 21 28
Wed.	5 12 19 26	2 9 16 23	1 8 15 22 29
Thur.	6 13 20 27	3 10 17 24	2 9 16 23 30
Fri.	7 14 21 28	4 11 18 25	3 10 17 24 31
Sat.	1 8 15 22 29	5 12 19 26	4 11 18 25

	April	*May*	*June*
Sun.	2 9 16 23 30	7 14 21 28	4 11 18 25
Mon.	3 10 17 24	1 8 15 22 29	5 12 19 26
Tue.	4 11 18 25	2 9 16 23 30	6 13 20 27
Wed.	5 12 19 26	3 10 17 24 31	7 14 21 28
Thur.	6 13 20 27	4 11 18 25	1 8 15 22 29
Fri.	7 14 21 28	5 12 19 26	2 9 16 23 30
Sat.	1 8 15 22 29	6 13 20 27	3 10 17 24

	July	*August*	*September*
Sun.	2 9 16 23 30	6 13 20 27	3 10 17 24
Mon.	3 10 17 24 31	7 14 21 28	4 11 18 25
Tue.	4 11 18 25	1 8 15 22 29	5 12 19 26
Wed.	5 12 19 26	2 9 16 23 30	6 13 20 27
Thur.	6 13 20 27	3 10 17 24 31	7 14 21 28
Fri.	7 14 21 28	4 11 18 25	1 8 15 22 29
Sat.	1 8 15 22 29	5 12 19 26	2 9 16 23 30

	October	*November*	*December*
Sun.	1 8 15 22 29	5 12 19 26	3 10 17 24 31
Mon.	2 9 16 23 30	6 13 20 27	4 11 18 25
Tue.	3 10 17 24 31	7 14 21 28	5 12 19 26
Wed.	4 11 18 25	1 8 15 22 29	6 13 20 27
Thur.	5 12 19 26	2 9 16 23 30	7 14 21 28
Fri.	6 13 20 27	3 10 17 24	1 8 15 22 29
Sat.	7 14 21 28	4 11 18 25	2 9 16 23 30

EASTER DAYS

March 26	1780
April 2	1820, 1972
April 9	1944
April 16	1876, 2028
April 23	1848, 1916, 2000

GEOLOGICAL TIME

The earth is thought to have come into existence approximately 4,600 million years ago, but for nearly half this time, the Archean era, it was uninhabited. Life is generally believed to have emerged in the succeeding Proterozoic era. The Archean and the Proterozoic eras are often together referred to as the Precambrian.

Although primitive forms of life, e.g. algae and bacteria, existed during the Proterozoic era, it is not until the strata of Palaeozoic rocks is reached that abundant fossilised remains appear.

Since the Precambrian, there have been three great geological eras:

PALAEOZOIC ('ancient life')
c. 550–*c.* 248 million years ago

Cambrian – Mainly sandstones, slate and shales; limestones in Scotland. Shelled fossils and invertebrates, e.g. trilobites and brachiopods appear, as do the earliest known vertebrates (jawless fish)
Ordovician – Mainly shales and mudstones, e.g. in north Wales; limestones in Scotland. First fishes
Silurian – Shales, mudstones and some limestones, found mostly in Wales and southern Scotland
Devonian – Old red sandstone, shale, limestone and slate, e.g. in south Wales and the West Country
Carboniferous– Coal-bearing rocks, millstone grit, limestone and shale. First traces of land-living life
Permian – Marls, sandstones and clays. First reptile fossils

There were two great phases of mountain building in the Palaeozoic era: the Caledonian, characterised in Britain by NE–SW lines of hills and valleys; and the later Hercyian, widespread in west Germany and adjacent areas, and in Britain exemplified in E.–W. lines of hills and valleys.

The end of the Palaeozoic era was marked by the extensive glaciations of the Permian period in the southern continents and the decline of amphibians. It was succeeded by an era of warm conditions.

MESOZOIC ('middle forms of life')
c. 245–*c.* 65 million years ago

Triassic – Mostly sandstone, e.g. in the West Midlands; primitive mammals appear
Jurassic– Mainly limestones and clays, typically displayed in the Jura mountains, and in England in a NE–SW belt from Lincolnshire and the Wash to the Severn and the Dorset coast
Cretaceous – Mainly chalk, clay and sands, e.g. in Kent and Sussex

Giant reptiles were dominant during the Mesozoic era, but it was at this time that marsupial mammals first appeared, as well as *Archaeopteryx lithographica*, the earliest known species of bird. Coniferous trees and flowering plants also developed during the era and, with the birds and the mammals, were the main species to survive into the Cenozoic era. The giant reptiles became extinct.

CENOZOIC ('recent life')
from *c.* 65 million years ago

Palaeocene, *Eocene* – The emergence of new forms of life, including existing species; primates appear
Oligocene – Fossils of a few still existing species
Miocene – Fossil remains show a balance of existing and extinct species
Pliocene – Fossil remains show a majority of still existing species
Pleistocene – The majority of remains are those of still existing species
Holocene– The present, post-glacial period. Existing species only, except for a few exterminated by man.

In the last 25 million years, from the Miocene through the Pliocene periods, the Alpine-Himalayan and the circum-Pacific phases of mountain building reached their climax. During the Pleistocene period ice-sheets repeatedly locked up masses of water as land ice; its weight depressed the land, but the locking-up of the water lowered the sea-level by 100–200 metres. The glaciations and interglacials of the Ice Age are difficult to date and classify, but recent scientific opinion considers the Pleistocene period to have begun approximately 1.64 million years ago. The last glacial retreat, merging into the Holocene period, was 10,000 years ago.

HUMAN DEVELOPMENT

Any consideration of the history of mankind must start with the fact that all members of the human race belong to one species of animal, i.e. *Homo sapiens*, the definition of a species being in biological terms that all its members can interbreed. As a species of mammal it is possible to group man with other similar types, known as the primates. Amongst these is found a sub-group, the apes, which includes, in addition to man, the chimpanzees, gorillas, orang-utans and gibbons. All lack a tail, have shoulder blades at the back, and a Y-shaped chewing pattern on the surface of their molars, as well as showing the more general primate characteristics of four incisors, a thumb which is able to touch the fingers of the same hand, and finger and toe nails instead of claws. The factors available to scientific study suggest that human beings have chimpanzees and gorillas as their nearest relatives in the animal world. However, there remains the possibility that there once lived creatures, now extinct, which were closer to modern man than the chimpanzees and gorillas, and which shared with modern man the characteristics of having flat faces (i.e. the absence of a pronounced muzzle), being bipedal, and possessing large brains.

There are two broad groups of extinct apes recognised by specialists. The ramapithecines, the remains of which, mainly jaw fragments, have been found in east Africa, Asia, and Turkey. They lived about 14 to 8 million years ago, and from the evidence of their teeth it seems they chewed more in the manner of modern man than the other presently living apes. The second group, the australopithecines, have left more numerous remains amongst which sub-groups may be detected, although the geographic spread is limited to south and east Africa. Living between 5 and 1.5 million years ago, they were closer relatives of modern man to the extent that they walked upright, did not have an extensive muzzle and had similar types of pre-molars. The first australopithecine remains were recognised at Taung in South Africa in 1924 and named *Australopithecus africanus*, dating to 2.8 to 2.3 million years ago. The most impressive discovery was made at Hadar, Ethiopia, in 1974 when about half a skeleton of *Australopithecus afarensis*, known as 'Lucy', was found. Some 3.2 million years ago, 'Lucy' certainly walked upright.

Also in east Africa, especially at Olduvai Gorge in Tanzania, between 1.9 and 1.8 million years ago, lived a hominid group which not only walked upright, had a flat face, and a large brain case, but also made simple pebble and flake stone tools. On present evidence these habilines seem to have been the first people to make tools, however crude. This facility is related to the larger brain size and human beings are the only animals to make implements to be used in other processes. These early pebble tool users, because of their distinctive characteristics, have been grouped as a separate sub-species, now extinct, of the genus *Homo* and are known as *Homo habilis*.

The use of fire, again a human characteristic, is associated with another group of extinct hominids whose remains, about a million years old, are found in south and east Africa, China, Indonesia, north Africa and Europe. Mastery of the techniques of making fire probably helped the colonisation of the colder northern areas and in this respect the site of Vertesszollos in Hungary is of particular importance. *Homo ergaster* in Africa and *Homo erectus* in Asia are the names given to this group of fossils and they relate to a number of famous individual discoveries, e.g. Solo Man, Heidelberg Man, and especially Peking Man who lived at the cave site at Choukoutien which has yielded evidence of fire and burnt bone.

The well-known group Neanderthal Man, or *Homo neanderthalensis*, is an extinct form of man who lived between about 230,000 and 28,000 years ago, thus spanning the last Ice Age. Indeed, its ability to adapt to the cold climate on the edge of the ice-sheets is one of its characteristic features, the remains being found only in Europe, Asia and the Middle East. Complete neanderthal skeletons were found during excavations at Tabun in Israel, together with evidence of tool-making and the use of fire. Distinguished by very large brains, it seems that neanderthal man was the first to develop recognisable social customs, especially deliberate burial rites. Why the neanderthals became extinct is not clear but it may be connected with the climatic changes at the end of the Ice Ages, which would have seriously affected their food supplies; possibly they became too specialised for their own good.

The shin bone of Boxgrove Man found in 1993 – *Homo heidelbergensis* – and the Swanscombe skull are the best known human fossil remains found in England. Some specialists see Swanscombe Man (or, more probably, woman) as best grouped together with the Steinheim skull from Germany, seeing both as a separate sub-species. There is too little evidence as yet on which to form a final judgement.

Modern Man, *Homo sapiens* had evolved to our present physical condition and had colonised much of the world by about 40,000 years ago. There are many previously distinguished individual specimens, e.g. Cromagnon Man, which may now be grouped together as *Homo sapiens*. It was modern man who spread to the American continent by crossing the landbridge between Siberia and Alaska and thence moved south through North America and into South America. Equally it is modern man who over the last 40,000 years has been responsible for the major developments in technology, art and civilisation generally.

One of the problems for those studying fossil man is the lack in many cases of sufficient quantities of fossil bone for analysis. It is important that theories should be tested against evidence, rather than the evidence being made to fit the theory. The Piltdown hoax of 1912 (and not fully exposed until the 1970s) is a well-known example of 'fossils' being forged to fit what was seen in some quarters as the correct theory of man's evolution.

The discovery of the structure of DNA in 1953 has come to have a profound effect upon the study of human evolution. For example, it was claimed in 1987 that a common ancestor of all human beings was a person who lived in Africa some 200,000 years ago, thus encouraging the 'out of Africa' theory of hominid migration from east Africa to the Middle East and then throughout the world. There is no doubt that the studies based on DNA have vast potential to elucidate further the course of human evolution.

CULTURAL DEVELOPMENT

The Eurocentric bias of early archaeologists meant that the search for a starting point for the development and transmission of cultural ideas, especially by migration, trade and warfare, concentrated unduly on Europe and the Near East. The Three Age system, whereby pre-history was divided into a Stone Age, a Bronze Age and an Iron Age, was devised by Christian Thomsen, curator of the National Museum of Denmark in the early 19th century, to facilitate the classification of the museum's collections. The descriptive adjectives referred to the materials from which the implements and weapons were made and came to be regarded as the dominant features of the societies to which they related. The refinement of the Three Age system once dominated archaeological thought and remains a generally accepted concept in the popular mind. However, it is now seen by archaeologists as an inadequate model for human development.

Common sense suggests that there were no complete breaks between one so-called Age and another, any more than contemporaries would have regarded 1485 as a complete break between medieval and modern English history. Nor can the Three Age system be applied universally. In some areas it is necessary to insert a Copper Age, while in Africa south of the Sahara there would seem to be no Bronze Age at all; in Australia, Old Stone Age societies survived, while in South America, New Stone Age communities existed into modern times. The civilisations in other parts of the world clearly invalidate a Eurocentric theory of human development.

The concept of the 'Neolithic revolution', associated with the domestication of plants and animals, was a development of particular importance in the human cultural pattern. It reflected change from the primitive hunter/gatherer economies to a more settled agricultural way of life and therefore, so the argument goes, made possible the development of urban civilisation. However, it can no longer be argued that this 'revolution' took place only in one area from which all development stemmed. Though it appears that the cultivation of wheat and barley was first undertaken, together with the domestication of cattle and goats/sheep in the Fertile Crescent (the area bounded by the rivers Tigris and Euphrates), there is evidence that rice was first deliberately planted and pigs domesticated in south-east Asia, maize first cultivated in Central America and llamas first domesticated in South America. It has been recognised in recent years that cultural changes can take place independently of each other in different parts of the world at different rates and different times. There is no need for a general diffusionist theory.

Although scholars will continue to study the particular societies which interest them, it may be possible to obtain a reliable chronological framework, against which the cultural development of any particular area may be set. The development and refinement of radio-carbon dating and other scientific methods of producing absolute chronologies is enabling the cross-referencing of societies to be undertaken. As the techniques of dating become more rigorous in application and the number of scientifically obtained dates increases, the attainment of an absolute chronology for prehistoric societies throughout the world comes closer to being achieved.

GEOLOGICAL TIME

Era	*Period*	*Epoch*	*Date began**	*Evolutionary stages*
Cenozoic	Quaternary	Holocene	0.01	Man
		Pleistocene	1.64	
	Tertiary	Pliocene	5.2	
		Miocene	23.3	
		Oligocene	35.4	
		Eocene	56.5	
		Palaeocene	65.0	
Mesozoic	Cretaceous		145.6	
	Jurassic		208.0	First birds
	Triassic		248.0	First mammals
Palaeozoic	Permian		290.0	First reptiles
	Carboniferous		362.5	First amphibians and insects
	Devonian		408.5	
	Silurian		439.0	
	Ordovician		510.0	First fishes
	Cambrian		550.0	First invertebrates
Precambrian			4,600.0	First primitive life forms e.g. algae and bacteria

* Millions of years ago

TIDAL PREDICTIONS

CONSTANTS

The constant tidal difference may be used in conjunction with the time of high water at a standard port shown in the predictions data below to find the time of high water at any of the ports or places listed.

These tidal differences are very approximate and should be used only as a guide to the time of high water at the places below. More precise local data should be obtained for navigational and other nautical purposes.

All data allow high water time to be found in Greenwich Mean Time: this applies to data for the months when British Summer Time is in operation and the hour's time difference should be allowed for. Ports marked * are in a different time zone and the standard time zone difference also needs to be added/subtracted to give local time.

EXAMPLE

Required time of high water at Stranraer at 2 January 2005

Appropriate time of high water at Greenock

Afternoon tide 2 January	1633hrs
Tidal difference	– 0020hrs
High water at Stranraer	1613hrs

The columns headed 'Springs' and 'Neaps' show the height, in metres, of the tide above datum for mean high water springs and mean high water neaps respectively.

Port		*Diff.* h	m	*Springs* m	*Neaps* m
Aberdeen	*Leith*	–1	19	4.4	3.4
*Antwerp (Prosperpolder)	*London*	+0	50	5.8	4.8
Ardrossan	*Greenock*	–0	15	3.2	2.6
Avonmouth	*London*	–6	45	12.2	9.8
Ayr	*Greenock*	–0	25	3.0	2.5
Barrow (Docks)	*Liverpool*	0	00	9.3	7.1
Belfast	*London*	–2	47	3.5	3.0
Blackpool	*Liverpool*	–0	10	8.9	7.0
*Boulogne	*London*	–2	44	8.9	7.2
*Calais	*London*	–2	04	7.2	5.9
*Cherbourg	*London*	–6	00	6.4	5.0
Cobh	*Liverpool*	–5	55	4.2	3.2
Cowes	*London*	–2	38	4.2	3.5
Dartmouth	*London*	+4	25	4.9	3.8
*Dieppe	*London*	–3	03	9.3	7.3
Douglas, IoM	*Liverpool*	–0	04	6.9	5.4
Dover	*London*	–2	52	6.7	5.3
Dublin	*London*	–2	05	4.1	3.4
Dun Loaghaire	*London*	–2	10	4.1	3.4
*Dunkirk	*London*	–1	54	6.0	4.9
Fishguard	*Liverpool*	–4	01	4.8	3.4
Fleetwood	*Liverpool*	0	00	9.2	7.3
*Flushing	*London*	–0	15	4.7	3.9
Folkestone	*London*	–3	04	7.1	5.7
Galway	*Liverpool*	–6	08	5.1	3.9
Glasgow	*Greenock*	+0	26	4.7	4.0
Harwich	*London*	–2	06	4.0	3.4
*Le Havre	*London*	–3	55	7.9	6.6
Heysham	*Liverpool*	+0	05	9.4	7.4
Holyhead	*Liverpool*	–0	50	5.6	4.4
*Hook of Holland	*London*	–0	01	2.1	1.7
Hull (Albert Dock)	*London*	–7	40	7.5	5.8
Immingham	*London*	–8	00	7.3	5.8
Larne	*London*	–2	40	2.8	2.5
Lerwick	*Leith*	–3	48	2.2	1.6
Londonderry	*London*	–5	37	2.7	2.1
Lowestoft	*London*	–4	25	2.4	2.1
Margate	*London*	–1	53	4.8	3.9
Milford Haven	*Liverpool*	–5	08	7.0	5.2
Morecambe	*Liverpool*	+0	07	9.5	7.4
Newhaven	*London*	–2	46	6.7	5.1
Oban	*Greenock*	+5	43	4.0	2.9
*Ostend	*London*	–1	32	5.1	4.2
Plymouth	*London*	+4	05	5.5	4.4
Portland	*London*	+5	09	2.1	1.4
Portsmouth	*London*	–2	38	4.7	3.8
Ramsgate	*London*	–2	32	5.2	4.1
Richmond Lock	*London*	+1	00	4.9	3.7
Rosslare Harbour	*Liverpool*	–5	24	1.9	1.4
Rosyth	*Leith*	+0	09	5.8	4.7
*Rotterdam	*London*	+1	45	2.0	1.7
St Helier	*London*	+4	48	11.0	8.1
St Malo	*London*	+4	27	12.2	9.2
St Peter Port	*London*	+4	54	9.3	7.0
Scrabster	*Leith*	–6	06	5.0	4.0
Sheerness	*London*	–1	19	5.8	4.7
Shoreham	*London*	–2	44	6.3	4.9
Southampton (1st high water)	*London*	–2	54	4.5	3.7
Spurn Head	*London*	–8	25	6.9	5.5
Stornoway	*Liverpool*	–4	16	4.8	3.7
Stranraer	*Greenick*	–0	20	3.0	2.4
Stromness	*Leith*	–5	26	3.6	2.7
Swansea	*London*	–7	35	9.5	7.2
Tees (River Entrance)	*Leith*	+1	09	5.5	4.3
Tilbury	*London*	–0	49	6.4	5.4
Tobermory	*Liverpool*	–5	11	4.4	3.3
Tyne River (North Shields)	*London*	–10	30	5.0	3.9
Ullapool	*Leith*	–7	40	5.2	3.9
Walton-on-the-Naze	*London*	–2	10	4.2	3.4
Wick	*Leith*	–3	26	3.5	2.8
Zeebrugge	*London*	–0	55	4.8	3.9

PREDICTIONS

The following data are daily predictions of the time and height of high water at London Bridge, Liverpool, Greenock and Leith. The time of the data is Greenwich Mean Time; this applies also to data for the months when British Summer Time is in operation and the hour's time difference should be allowed for. The datum of predictions for each port shows the difference of height, in metres from Ordnance data (Newlyn).

JANUARY 2005 *High Water* GMT

	LONDON BRIDGE *Datum of Predictions 3.20m below				LIVERPOOL *Datum of Predictions 4.93m below				GREENOCK *Datum of Predictions 1.62m below				LEITH *Datum of Predictions 2.90m below			
	hr	*ht m*	*hr*	*ht m*	*hr*	*ht m*	*hr*	*ht m*	*hr*	*ht m*	*hr*	*ht m*	*hr*	*ht m*	*hr*	*ht m*
SA 1	04 41	6.4	17 23	6.4	02 19	8.3	14 36	8.5	03 58	3.0	15 52	3.4	05 58	4.8	18 06	4.9
SU 2	05 20	6.3	18 05	6.4	03 01	8.0	15 19	8.3	04 41	3.0	16 33	3.4	06 41	4.7	18 48	4.8
M 3	06 03	6.2	18 52	6.2	03 47	7.8	16 08	8.1	05 27	2.9	17 18	3.3	07 29	4.6	19 37	4.7
TU 4	06 54	6.1	19 46	6.1	04 42	7.6	17 05	7.9	06 16	2.8	18 09	3.2	08 23	4.5	20 36	4.6
W 5	07 55	5.9	20 49	5.9	05 46	7.6	18 10	7.9	07 10	2.8	19 08	3.1	09 24	4.6	21 45	4.6
TH 6	09 06	5.9	21 59	6.0	06 54	7.7	19 17	8.1	08 17	2.8	20 19	3.1	10 29	4.6	22 55	4.7
FR 7	10 19	6.0	23 07	6.2	08 00	8.1	20 23	8.4	09 34	2.9	21 37	3.1	11 32	4.8	—	—
SA 8	11 29	6.3	—	—	09 01	8.6	21 26	8.8	10 37	3.1	22 43	3.2	00 01	5.0	12 30	5.0
SU 9	00 08	6.5	12 31	6.7	09 56	9.1	22 23	9.1	11 29	3.3	23 42	3.3	01 02	5.2	13 24	5.3
M 10	01 03	6.7	13 28	6.9	10 48	9.5	23 17	9.4	—	—	12 16	3.5	01 57	5.5	14 13	5.5
TU 11	01 54	6.9	14 22	7.1	11 39	9.7	—	—	00 38	3.4	13 03	3.6	02 48	5.7	15 01	5.7
W 12	02 43	6.9	15 14	7.2	00 08	9.5	12 29	9.9	01 33	3.4	13 49	3.8	03 38	5.8	15 49	5.7
TH 13	03 31	6.9	16 05	7.2	00 59	9.5	13 18	9.9	02 25	3.4	14 34	3.8	04 27	5.8	16 37	5.7
FR 14	04 18	6.9	16 54	7.1	01 47	9.4	14 05	9.7	03 14	3.4	15 18	3.8	05 17	5.6	17 26	5.6
SA 15	05 04	6.8	17 42	7.0	02 33	9.1	14 52	9.4	04 00	3.3	16 03	3.8	06 08	5.3	18 18	5.4
SU 16	05 49	6.7	18 30	6.7	03 19	8.7	15 39	9.0	04 44	3.3	16 49	3.6	07 00	5.0	19 12	5.2
M 17	06 34	6.5	19 19	6.4	04 07	8.2	16 29	8.4	05 28	3.2	17 37	3.5	07 55	4.8	20 11	4.9
TU 18	07 24	6.3	20 11	6.1	05 01	7.7	17 27	7.9	06 13	3.1	18 29	3.2	08 52	4.5	21 13	4.7
W 19	08 22	6.1	21 09	5.8	06 05	7.4	18 36	7.6	07 02	3.0	19 30	3.0	09 53	4.4	22 19	4.5
TH 20	09 29	5.9	22 10	5.7	07 20	7.3	19 50	7.5	08 03	2.9	21 08	2.9	10 58	4.4	23 28	4.5
FR 21	10 38	5.8	23 13	5.8	08 28	7.6	20 54	7.7	09 31	2.9	22 28	2.9	—	—	12 04	4.5
SA 22	11 42	6.0	—	—	09 22	7.9	21 46	8.0	10 36	3.1	23 22	3.0	00 34	4.5	13 01	4.7
SU 23	00 11	6.0	12 40	6.2	10 07	8.3	22 30	8.3	11 24	3.2	—	—	01 27	4.7	13 46	4.9
M 24	01 02	6.2	13 28	6.4	10 47	8.6	23 08	8.5	00 08	3.0	12 06	3.3	02 09	4.8	14 24	5.0
TU 25	01 45	6.4	14 10	6.5	11 23	8.8	23 44	8.6	00 49	3.0	12 42	3.4	02 45	5.0	14 58	5.1
W 26	02 21	6.5	14 46	6.6	11 57	8.9	—	—	01 26	3.0	13 14	3.4	03 17	5.1	15 29	5.2
TH 27	02 53	6.4	15 19	6.5	00 17	8.7	12 31	9.0	01 59	3.0	13 45	3.5	03 48	5.1	16 01	5.3
FR 28	03 23	6.4	15 51	6.5	00 50	8.7	13 04	9.0	02 29	3.0	14 18	3.5	04 21	5.1	16 32	5.3
SA 29	03 52	6.4	16 25	6.6	01 23	8.7	13 37	9.0	03 00	3.0	14 52	3.5	04 55	5.1	17 04	5.2
SU 30	04 23	6.5	17 00	6.6	01 57	8.7	14 12	8.9	03 32	3.0	15 29	3.5	05 31	5.0	17 37	5.1
M 31	04 58	6.5	17 39	6.6	02 32	8.5	14 48	8.7	04 06	3.0	16 06	3.4	06 09	4.9	18 14	5.0

FEBRUARY 2005 *High Water* GMT

	LONDON BRIDGE				LIVERPOOL				GREENOCK				LEITH			
TU 1	05 38	6.5	18 21	6.4	03 10	8.3	15 30	8.5	04 41	3.0	16 45	3.3	06 51	4.8	18 56	4.9
W 2	06 24	6.4	19 10	6.2	03 57	8.0	16 22	8.1	05 20	2.9	17 29	3.2	07 38	4.6	19 48	4.7
TH 3	07 19	6.1	20 07	5.9	04 57	7.7	17 28	7.8	06 05	2.8	18 22	3.0	08 35	4.5	20 57	4.5
FR 4	08 26	5.9	21 15	5.7	06 11	7.5	18 44	7.7	07 06	2.7	19 30	2.9	09 46	4.4	22 24	4.5
SA 5	09 43	5.8	22 34	5.7	07 31	7.7	20 05	7.9	08 50	2.7	21 10	2.9	11 01	4.5	23 45	4.7
SU 6	11 07	5.9	23 49	6.0	08 46	8.2	21 18	8.4	10 19	2.9	22 36	3.0	—	—	12 12	4.8
M 7	—	—	12 21	6.4	09 47	8.9	22 18	8.9	11 16	3.2	23 40	3.1	00 54	5.1	13 13	5.1
TU 8	00 51	6.4	13 22	6.8	10 40	9.4	23 10	9.4	—	—	12 05	3.4	01 50	5.4	14 04	5.5
W 9	01 44	6.8	14 14	7.1	11 29	9.9	23 58	9.6	00 35	3.2	12 53	3.6	02 39	5.7	14 50	5.7
TH 10	02 31	7.0	15 03	7.3	—	—	12 15	10.1	01 27	3.3	13 38	3.8	03 25	5.8	15 34	5.9
FR 11	03 16	7.1	15 49	7.3	00 42	9.7	13 00	10.1	02 14	3.4	14 21	3.8	04 10	5.8	16 19	5.9
SA 12	03 58	7.1	16 32	7.3	01 25	9.6	13 42	10.0	02 55	3.4	15 02	3.9	04 54	5.6	17 03	5.8
SU 13	04 38	7.1	17 13	7.1	02 06	9.3	14 23	9.6	03 32	3.4	15 42	3.8	05 39	5.4	17 48	5.5
M 14	05 16	7.0	17 52	6.8	02 44	8.9	15 04	9.1	04 07	3.3	16 20	3.7	06 23	5.0	18 35	5.2
TU 15	05 53	6.8	18 28	6.5	03 23	8.4	15 45	8.4	04 43	3.3	17 00	3.4	07 10	4.7	19 25	4.8
W 16	06 32	6.5	19 05	6.1	04 06	7.8	16 34	7.7	05 22	3.1	17 42	3.1	08 01	4.4	20 25	4.5
TH 17	07 19	6.1	19 51	5.7	05 01	7.2	17 41	7.1	06 05	3.0	18 31	2.9	09 00	4.2	21 33	4.2
FR 18	08 23	5.6	20 57	5.3	06 23	6.9	19 13	6.9	06 58	2.8	19 38	2.6	10 08	4.1	22 52	4.1
SA 19	09 58	5.4	22 32	5.3	07 57	7.1	20 33	7.2	08 11	2.8	22 20	2.6	11 28	4.2	—	—
SU 20	11 19	5.6	23 44	5.6	09 01	7.6	21 29	7.7	10 12	2.9	23 12	2.8	00 16	4.3	12 41	4.5
M 21	—	—	12 19	6.0	09 49	8.1	22 13	8.1	11 06	3.1	23 54	2.9	01 14	4.5	13 29	4.7
TU 22	00 39	6.1	13 08	6.4	10 29	8.5	22 51	8.5	11 47	3.2	—	—	01 55	4.8	14 07	5.0
W 23	01 24	6.4	13 49	6.6	11 05	8.8	23 25	8.7	00 33	3.0	12 23	3.3	02 27	5.0	14 39	5.1
TH 24	02 02	6.5	14 25	6.7	11 38	9.0	23 57	8.9	01 09	3.0	12 53	3.3	02 56	5.1	15 09	5.3
FR 25	02 35	6.5	14 57	6.7	—	—	12 10	9.1	01 40	3.0	13 22	3.4	03 26	5.2	15 39	5.4
SA 26	03 05	6.5	15 29	6.6	00 28	8.9	12 41	9.2	02 07	3.0	13 54	3.4	03 56	5.3	16 08	5.4
SU 27	03 32	6.5	16 01	6.6	00 59	9.0	13 13	9.2	02 32	3.0	14 29	3.4	04 29	5.3	16 38	5.4
M 28	04 02	6.6	16 35	6.7	01 31	9.0	13 45	9.1	03 00	3.1	15 04	3.5	05 03	5.2	17 11	5.3

MARCH 2005 *High Water* GMT

	LONDON BRIDGE * Datum of Predictions 3.20m below				LIVERPOOL * Datum of Predictions 4.93m below				GREENOCK * Datum of Predictions 1.62m below				LEITH * Datum of Predictions 2.90m below			
	hr	ht m	hr	ht m	hr	ht m	hr	ht m	hr	ht m	hr	ht m	hr	ht m	hr	ht m
TU 1	04 37	6.7	17 12	6.6	02 03	8.9	14 21	9.0	03 30	3.1	15 40	3.4	05 39	5.1	17 48	5.2
W 2	05 17	6.7	17 53	6.5	02 39	8.6	15 01	8.6	04 02	3.0	16 17	3.3	06 19	4.9	18 31	5.0
TH 3	06 02	6.5	18 38	6.2	03 23	8.2	15 51	8.1	04 37	2.9	16 59	3.1	07 04	4.7	19 24	4.7
FR 4	06 54	6.2	19 31	5.8	04 21	7.7	16 59	7.5	05 20	2.8	17 51	2.9	07 59	4.5	20 36	4.5
SA 5	07 59	5.8	20 39	5.4	05 42	7.3	18 28	7.3	06 19	2.7	19 00	2.7	09 15	4.3	22 10	4.4
SU 6	09 21	5.5	22 10	5.4	07 16	7.4	20 03	7.6	08 16	2.6	21 11	2.7	10 43	4.4	23 39	4.7
M 7	11 02	5.7	23 38	5.8	08 38	8.1	21 16	8.2	10 06	2.9	22 39	2.9	—	—	12 01	4.7
TU 8	—	—	12 17	6.3	09 38	8.8	22 10	8.9	11 03	3.2	23 36	3.1	00 48	5.1	13 02	5.1
W 9	00 40	6.3	13 13	6.9	10 27	9.5	22 56	9.4	11 51	3.4	—	—	01 40	5.4	13 50	5.5
TH 10	01 30	6.8	14 01	7.3	11 13	9.9	23 39	9.7	00 26	3.2	12 37	3.6	02 25	5.7	14 32	5.8
FR 11	02 13	7.1	14 45	7.4	11 55	10.1	—	—	01 11	3.3	13 21	3.7	03 06	5.7	15 14	5.9
SA 12	02 54	7.2	15 26	7.4	00 19	9.7	12 36	10.1	01 51	3.3	14 02	3.8	03 46	5.7	15 55	5.9
SU 13	03 32	7.2	16 04	7.2	00 58	9.6	13 15	9.8	02 26	3.4	14 40	3.8	04 27	5.5	16 37	5.7
M 14	04 09	7.2	16 39	7.0	01 34	9.3	13 53	9.4	02 58	3.4	15 16	3.7	05 07	5.3	17 19	5.5
TU 15	04 44	7.1	17 11	6.8	02 09	8.9	14 29	8.9	03 30	3.4	15 51	3.5	05 47	5.0	18 02	5.1
W 16	05 19	6.9	17 43	6.5	02 43	8.4	15 07	8.2	04 04	3.3	16 28	3.3	06 29	4.7	18 50	4.7
TH 17	05 58	6.5	18 17	6.2	03 21	7.9	15 50	7.5	04 40	3.2	17 08	3.0	07 16	4.4	19 45	4.3
FR 18	06 42	6.0	18 59	5.7	04 09	7.3	16 52	6.9	05 23	3.0	17 56	2.7	08 12	4.2	20 50	4.1
SA 19	07 38	5.5	19 54	5.3	05 27	6.8	18 36	6.6	06 14	2.8	19 00	2.5	09 21	4.0	22 07	4.0
SU 20	09 08	5.2	21 38	5.1	07 19	6.8	20 04	6.9	07 22	2.7	22 00	2.5	10 42	4.1	23 44	4.1
M 21	10 50	5.4	23 12	5.5	08 30	7.3	21 01	7.5	09 33	2.7	22 48	2.7	—	—	12 06	4.3
TU 22	11 52	5.9	—	—	09 20	7.9	21 45	8.0	10 36	2.9	23 28	2.8	00 47	4.4	12 59	4.6
W 23	00 10	6.0	12 40	6.4	10 01	8.4	22 22	8.4	11 17	3.1	—	—	01 26	4.7	13 37	4.9
TH 24	00 56	6.3	13 20	6.7	10 37	8.7	22 56	8.7	00 05	2.9	11 52	3.2	01 58	5.0	14 09	5.1
FR 25	01 34	6.5	13 56	6.8	11 10	9.0	23 28	8.9	00 39	3.0	12 21	3.2	02 27	5.1	14 40	5.3
SA 26	02 08	6.6	14 29	6.7	11 41	9.1	23 59	9.1	01 09	3.0	12 53	3.3	02 56	5.3	15 09	5.4
SU 27	02 38	6.5	15 02	6.7	—	—	12 13	9.2	01 34	3.0	13 27	3.3	03 27	5.4	15 40	5.5
M 28	03 08	6.6	15 35	6.7	00 31	9.1	12 47	9.3	02 00	3.1	14 04	3.4	04 00	5.4	16 13	5.5
TU 29	03 41	6.7	16 11	6.7	01 04	9.1	13 22	9.2	02 28	3.1	14 41	3.4	04 35	5.3	16 50	5.4
W 30	04 19	6.8	16 48	6.6	01 39	9.0	14 00	9.0	02 59	3.2	15 18	3.4	05 12	5.2	17 31	5.2
TH 31	05 01	6.7	17 29	6.4	02 18	8.7	14 43	8.5	03 32	3.2	15 57	3.2	05 54	5.0	18 19	5.0

APRIL 2005 *High Water* GMT

	LONDON BRIDGE				LIVERPOOL				GREENOCK				LEITH			
FR 1	05 47	6.5	18 14	6.1	03 04	8.2	15 36	7.9	04 09	3.0	16 41	3.0	06 41	4.7	19 17	4.7
SA 2	06 42	6.1	19 07	5.7	04 05	7.7	16 50	7.3	04 54	2.9	17 37	2.8	07 39	4.5	20 34	4.4
SU 3	07 50	5.7	20 21	5.3	05 32	7.3	18 28	7.1	06 00	2.7	19 03	2.6	09 02	4.3	22 06	4.5
M 4	09 23	5.5	22 02	5.4	07 08	7.5	19 58	7.6	08 16	2.6	21 21	2.6	10 32	4.4	23 30	4.7
TU 5	10 58	5.9	23 21	5.9	08 23	8.1	21 02	8.3	09 48	2.9	22 30	2.9	11 47	4.8	—	—
W 6	—	—	12 03	6.5	09 20	8.8	21 51	8.9	10 43	3.2	23 21	3.1	00 34	5.1	12 44	5.2
TH 7	00 19	6.5	12 55	7.1	10 07	9.4	22 35	9.3	11 30	3.4	—	—	01 23	5.4	13 29	5.5
FR 8	01 06	6.9	13 39	7.3	10 51	9.7	23 15	9.5	00 05	3.2	12 15	3.5	02 04	5.5	14 10	5.7
SA 9	01 48	7.2	14 20	7.4	11 31	9.8	23 52	9.5	00 45	3.2	12 58	3.6	02 42	5.6	14 51	5.8
SU 10	02 28	7.2	14 59	7.2	—	—	12 10	9.7	01 21	3.3	13 38	3.6	03 20	5.5	15 32	5.7
M 11	03 06	7.2	15 34	7.0	00 28	9.3	12 47	9.5	01 53	3.3	14 15	3.5	03 59	5.4	16 13	5.5
TU 12	03 42	7.1	16 05	6.8	01 02	9.1	13 23	9.1	02 25	3.4	14 50	3.5	04 37	5.2	16 54	5.3
W 13	04 17	6.9	16 35	6.6	01 36	8.8	13 58	8.6	02 57	3.4	15 25	3.3	05 15	5.0	17 36	5.0
TH 14	04 54	6.7	17 07	6.5	02 09	8.4	14 34	8.1	03 31	3.4	16 02	3.1	05 54	4.7	18 22	4.6
FR 15	05 33	6.4	17 43	6.2	02 46	7.9	15 17	7.4	04 07	3.2	16 44	2.9	06 38	4.5	19 13	4.3
SA 16	06 17	6.0	18 26	5.8	03 32	7.4	16 13	6.9	04 48	3.0	17 35	2.6	07 32	4.2	20 12	4.1
SU 17	07 10	5.6	19 18	5.4	04 38	6.9	17 48	6.6	05 41	2.8	18 41	2.5	08 39	4.1	21 21	4.0
M 18	08 22	5.3	20 34	5.2	06 28	6.8	19 20	6.8	06 47	2.7	20 31	2.4	09 54	4.1	22 38	4.1
TU 19	10 04	5.4	22 25	5.4	07 45	7.2	20 20	7.3	08 11	2.7	22 04	2.6	11 10	4.2	23 51	4.3
W 20	11 10	5.8	23 29	5.8	08 38	7.7	21 05	7.9	09 41	2.8	22 48	2.8	—	—	12 09	4.5
TH 21	—	—	12 01	6.3	09 21	8.2	21 44	8.3	10 29	3.0	23 25	2.9	00 38	4.6	12 53	4.8
FR 22	00 17	6.2	12 43	6.6	09 58	8.6	22 19	8.7	11 06	3.1	—	—	01 15	4.9	13 30	5.1
SA 23	00 57	6.4	13 21	6.8	10 33	8.9	22 53	8.9	00 00	3.0	11 42	3.2	01 49	5.1	14 04	5.3
SU 24	01 34	6.6	13 58	6.8	11 08	9.1	23 27	9.1	00 31	3.0	12 20	3.2	02 23	5.3	14 38	5.4
M 25	02 09	6.7	14 34	6.8	11 44	9.2	—	—	01 01	3.1	13 00	3.3	02 57	5.4	15 13	5.5
TU 26	02 45	6.8	15 11	6.8	00 03	9.2	12 23	9.2	01 31	3.2	13 41	3.3	03 32	5.4	15 52	5.5
W 27	03 24	6.8	15 50	6.7	00 41	9.2	13 04	9.1	02 03	3.3	14 22	3.3	04 10	5.4	16 34	5.4
TH 28	04 07	6.8	16 31	6.6	01 22	9.1	13 48	8.8	02 38	3.3	15 03	3.3	04 51	5.2	17 21	5.2
FR 29	04 53	6.7	17 14	6.3	02 07	8.7	14 37	8.4	03 14	3.3	15 47	3.1	05 36	5.0	18 14	5.0
SA 30	05 44	6.4	18 02	6.0	02 59	8.3	15 36	7.8	03 55	3.1	16 39	2.9	06 28	4.8	19 17	4.7

MAY 2005 *High Water* GMT

	LONDON BRIDGE * Datum of Predictions 3.20m below				LIVERPOOL * Datum of Predictions 4.93m below				GREENOCK * Datum of Predictions 1.62m below				LEITH * Datum of Predictions 2.90m below			
	hr	*ht m*	*hr*	*ht m*	*hr*	*ht m*	*hr*	*ht m*	*hr*	*ht m*	*hr*	*ht m*	*hr*	*ht m*	*hr*	*ht m*
SU 1	06 44	6.1	19 01	5.7	04 05	7.9	16 52	7.4	04 46	3.0	17 50	2.7	07 33	4.6	20 34	4.6
M 2	07 58	5.8	20 23	5.5	05 28	7.6	18 20	7.4	06 04	2.8	19 29	2.6	08 56	4.5	21 55	4.6
TU 3	09 24	5.9	21 46	5.7	06 49	7.8	19 36	7.8	08 01	2.8	21 03	2.7	10 16	4.6	23 09	4.8
W 4	10 37	6.3	22 53	6.2	07 57	8.3	20 35	8.3	09 21	3.0	22 05	2.9	11 24	4.9	—	—
TH 5	11 36	6.7	23 49	6.6	08 53	8.8	21 25	8.7	10 16	3.2	22 53	3.0	00 09	5.0	12 19	5.1
FR 6	—	—	12 27	7.1	09 42	9.1	22 08	9.0	11 05	3.3	23 36	3.1	00 58	5.2	13 06	5.3
SA 7	00 37	6.9	13 12	7.2	10 26	9.3	22 48	9.1	11 50	3.4	—	—	01 39	5.3	13 48	5.4
SU 8	01 22	7.1	13 53	7.1	11 07	9.3	23 25	9.1	00 14	3.2	12 33	3.4	02 18	5.4	14 30	5.5
M 9	02 03	7.1	14 32	7.0	11 45	9.2	—	—	00 50	3.2	13 13	3.3	02 56	5.3	15 12	5.4
TU 10	02 43	6.9	15 06	6.7	00 00	9.0	12 22	9.0	01 24	3.3	13 51	3.3	03 34	5.3	15 53	5.3
W 11	03 21	6.8	15 37	6.6	00 34	8.9	12 57	8.7	01 57	3.4	14 28	3.2	04 11	5.1	16 34	5.1
TH 12	03 58	6.6	16 07	6.5	01 08	8.7	13 32	8.4	02 31	3.4	15 04	3.1	04 48	5.0	17 15	4.9
FR 13	04 35	6.5	16 41	6.4	01 43	8.4	14 10	8.0	03 05	3.4	15 43	3.0	05 26	4.8	17 57	4.6
SA 14	05 14	6.3	17 18	6.2	02 22	8.0	14 53	7.6	03 41	3.3	16 28	2.8	06 08	4.6	18 44	4.4
SU 15	05 58	6.0	18 00	6.0	03 07	7.6	15 44	7.1	04 22	3.1	17 20	2.7	06 58	4.4	19 36	4.3
M 16	06 46	5.8	18 49	5.7	04 03	7.3	16 51	6.9	05 11	2.9	18 21	2.6	07 57	4.2	20 34	4.2
TU 17	07 44	5.6	19 52	5.4	05 18	7.1	18 15	6.9	06 11	2.8	19 28	2.5	09 04	4.2	21 37	4.2
W 18	08 55	5.5	21 13	5.4	06 38	7.2	19 22	7.2	07 19	2.8	20 42	2.6	10 09	4.3	22 40	4.3
TH 19	10 09	5.8	22 29	5.7	07 40	7.6	20 14	7.7	08 28	2.8	21 47	2.7	11 09	4.5	23 37	4.6
FR 20	11 10	6.1	23 27	6.0	08 29	8.0	20 58	8.2	09 29	2.9	22 36	2.8	12 00	4.7	—	—
SA 21	12 00	6.5	—	—	09 13	8.4	21 39	8.6	10 20	3.0	23 17	2.9	00 26	4.8	12 46	5.0
SU 22	00 15	6.4	12 45	6.7	09 55	8.7	22 18	8.9	11 05	3.1	23 54	3.0	01 09	5.1	13 28	5.2
M 23	01 00	6.6	13 28	6.9	10 37	9.0	22 58	9.1	11 50	3.2	—	—	01 49	5.2	14 09	5.3
TU 24	01 42	6.8	14 09	6.9	11 20	9.1	23 40	9.3	00 31	3.1	12 36	3.3	02 29	5.4	14 52	5.5
W 25	02 26	6.9	14 52	6.9	—	—	12 05	9.2	01 09	3.2	13 23	3.3	03 09	5.4	15 37	5.5
TH 26	03 12	6.9	15 36	6.7	00 25	9.3	12 53	9.1	01 47	3.3	14 10	3.3	03 52	5.4	16 24	5.5
FR 27	04 00	6.9	16 21	6.6	01 13	9.1	13 44	8.8	02 26	3.4	14 59	3.2	04 37	5.3	17 15	5.4
SA 28	04 52	6.8	17 09	6.4	02 04	8.9	14 37	8.5	03 08	3.4	15 52	3.1	05 26	5.2	18 11	5.2
SU 29	05 47	6.5	18 02	6.2	03 00	8.6	15 36	8.1	03 54	3.3	16 53	2.9	06 22	5.0	19 13	4.9
M 30	06 47	6.3	19 02	6.0	04 02	8.3	16 43	7.8	04 52	3.1	18 02	2.8	07 27	4.9	20 22	4.8
TU 31	07 55	6.2	20 11	6.0	05 10	8.2	17 54	7.7	06 05	3.0	19 14	2.8	08 41	4.8	21 32	4.7

JUNE 2005 *High Water* GMT

	LONDON BRIDGE				LIVERPOOL				GREENOCK				LEITH			
W 1	09 03	6.3	21 18	6.1	06 19	8.1	19 02	7.8	07 30	3.0	20 24	2.8	09 51	4.8	22 38	4.8
TH 2	10 06	6.5	22 19	6.3	07 24	8.2	20 02	8.0	08 45	3.1	21 26	2.9	10 54	4.9	23 38	4.9
FR 3	11 03	6.7	23 16	6.6	08 23	8.4	20 55	8.3	09 46	3.2	22 18	3.0	11 52	5.0	—	—
SA 4	11 55	6.8	—	—	09 15	8.6	21 41	8.5	10 39	3.2	23 04	3.0	00 30	5.0	12 43	5.1
SU 5	00 08	6.7	12 44	6.9	10 02	8.7	22 23	8.7	11 27	3.2	23 46	3.1	01 16	5.1	13 30	5.1
M 6	00 57	6.8	13 28	6.8	10 45	8.7	23 01	8.8	—	—	12 12	3.1	01 57	5.1	14 14	5.1
TU 7	01 43	6.8	14 09	6.7	11 24	8.7	23 37	8.7	00 24	3.2	12 54	3.1	02 36	5.2	14 56	5.1
W 8	02 27	6.7	14 45	6.5	—	—	12 02	8.6	01 00	3.3	13 34	3.0	03 14	5.1	15 37	5.1
TH 9	03 07	6.6	15 18	6.4	00 12	8.7	12 38	8.5	01 35	3.3	14 12	3.0	03 50	5.1	16 16	5.0
FR 10	03 45	6.4	15 49	6.4	00 48	8.6	13 14	8.3	02 10	3.4	14 50	2.9	04 26	5.0	16 54	4.9
SA 11	04 21	6.4	16 22	6.3	01 25	8.4	13 52	8.1	02 45	3.4	15 30	2.9	05 04	4.9	17 33	4.7
SU 12	04 58	6.3	16 58	6.3	02 04	8.2	14 32	7.9	03 21	3.3	16 14	2.8	05 43	4.8	18 15	4.6
M 13	05 38	6.2	17 38	6.1	02 46	8.0	15 16	7.6	04 00	3.2	17 01	2.7	06 27	4.6	19 01	4.5
TU 14	06 21	6.1	18 22	6.0	03 33	7.8	16 06	7.4	04 44	3.1	17 52	2.7	07 15	4.5	19 50	4.4
W 15	07 10	5.9	19 13	5.8	04 26	7.6	17 05	7.3	05 34	2.9	18 43	2.7	08 10	4.4	20 46	4.4
TH 16	08 06	5.8	20 16	5.7	05 27	7.5	18 10	7.3	06 31	2.9	19 37	2.6	09 10	4.4	21 44	4.4
FR 17	09 10	5.8	21 26	5.7	06 29	7.6	19 12	7.6	07 31	2.8	20 37	2.7	10 11	4.5	22 43	4.5
SA 18	10 17	6.0	22 34	5.9	07 30	7.9	20 09	8.0	08 36	2.9	21 41	2.7	11 09	4.6	23 39	4.7
SU 19	11 18	6.3	23 35	6.2	08 26	8.2	21 00	8.4	09 39	3.0	22 37	2.9	—	—	12 05	4.8
M 20	—	—	12 12	6.6	09 20	8.5	21 49	8.8	10 35	3.1	23 25	3.0	00 32	4.9	12 58	5.1
TU 21	00 30	6.6	13 02	6.8	10 12	8.8	22 36	9.1	11 28	3.2	—	—	01 21	5.1	13 48	5.3
W 22	01 22	6.8	13 50	6.9	11 04	9.0	23 25	9.3	00 10	3.2	12 20	3.2	02 07	5.3	14 38	5.5
TH 23	02 12	7.0	14 37	6.9	11 55	9.1	—	—	00 54	3.3	13 13	3.2	02 52	5.4	15 27	5.6
FR 24	03 03	7.1	15 25	6.8	00 15	9.4	12 47	9.1	01 37	3.4	14 07	3.2	03 39	5.5	16 16	5.6
SA 25	03 55	7.0	16 14	6.8	01 06	9.4	13 39	9.1	02 21	3.5	15 02	3.2	04 27	5.5	17 08	5.5
SU 26	04 47	7.0	17 03	6.7	01 58	9.4	14 31	8.9	03 06	3.5	15 56	3.1	05 17	5.4	18 01	5.4
M 27	05 40	6.9	17 53	6.6	02 50	9.2	15 23	8.6	03 54	3.5	16 50	3.1	06 11	5.3	18 58	5.1
TU 28	06 35	6.7	18 45	6.5	03 44	8.9	16 17	8.2	04 46	3.4	17 44	3.0	07 10	5.2	19 58	4.9
W 29	07 32	6.6	19 42	6.4	04 40	8.5	17 16	7.9	05 44	3.2	18 36	2.9	08 13	5.0	20 59	4.7
TH 30	08 31	6.4	20 41	6.3	05 41	8.2	18 21	7.7	06 48	3.1	19 30	2.9	09 18	4.9	22 01	4.6

JULY 2005 *High Water* GMT

	LONDON BRIDGE * Datum of Predictions 3.20m below				LIVERPOOL * Datum of Predictions 4.93m below				GREENOCK * Datum of Predictions 1.62m below				LEITH * Datum of Predictions 2.90m below			
	hr	*ht m*	*hr*	*ht m*	*hr*	*ht m*	*hr*	*ht m*	*hr*	*ht m*	*hr*	*ht m*	*hr*	*ht m*	*hr*	*ht m*
FR 1	09 30	6.3	21 42	6.3	06 46	8.0	19 25	7.7	08 01	3.0	20 32	2.8	10 22	4.8	23 02	4.6
SA 2	10 27	6.3	22 42	6.2	07 50	7.9	20 25	7.8	09 15	3.0	21 38	2.9	11 24	4.7	—	—
SU 3	11 23	6.3	23 42	6.3	08 50	8.0	21 18	8.1	10 18	3.0	22 35	2.9	00 01	4.7	12 25	4.8
M 4	—	—	12 17	6.4	09 43	8.2	22 04	8.3	11 12	3.0	23 23	3.0	00 55	4.8	13 18	4.8
TU 5	00 38	6.4	13 07	6.5	10 29	8.3	22 45	8.5	12 00	3.0	—	—	01 41	4.9	14 05	4.9
W 6	01 29	6.5	13 52	6.5	11 11	8.4	23 22	8.6	00 05	3.2	12 45	2.9	02 22	5.0	14 46	5.0
TH 7	02 15	6.6	14 31	6.5	11 49	8.4	23 58	8.7	00 44	3.2	13 26	2.9	03 00	5.1	15 23	5.0
FR 8	02 56	6.5	15 05	6.4	—	—	12 24	8.4	01 20	3.3	14 04	2.9	03 35	5.1	15 58	5.0
SA 9	03 32	6.5	15 36	6.4	00 33	8.7	12 59	8.4	01 53	3.3	14 40	2.8	04 09	5.1	16 33	5.0
SU 10	04 05	6.4	16 07	6.4	01 09	8.6	13 34	8.3	02 27	3.3	15 16	2.8	04 43	5.1	17 09	4.9
M 11	04 38	6.4	16 39	6.4	01 45	8.5	14 10	8.2	03 01	3.3	15 53	2.8	05 19	5.0	17 46	4.8
TU 12	05 14	6.4	17 14	6.3	02 22	8.4	14 47	8.1	03 37	3.3	16 31	2.8	05 56	4.9	18 27	4.7
W 13	05 52	6.3	17 53	6.3	03 01	8.2	15 27	7.9	04 16	3.2	17 12	2.8	06 36	4.8	19 10	4.6
TH 14	06 35	6.2	18 36	6.1	03 44	8.1	16 14	7.7	04 58	3.1	17 55	2.8	07 19	4.7	19 58	4.5
FR 15	07 24	6.0	19 30	6.0	04 35	7.9	17 10	7.5	05 46	3.0	18 41	2.7	08 10	4.6	20 53	4.5
SA 16	08 23	5.9	20 34	5.8	05 35	7.7	18 16	7.5	06 41	2.9	19 36	2.6	09 13	4.5	21 55	4.5
SU 17	09 29	5.8	21 46	5.8	06 41	7.7	19 24	7.7	07 48	2.8	20 49	2.7	10 23	4.5	22 59	4.6
M 18	10 39	6.0	23 00	6.0	07 50	7.9	20 30	8.1	09 04	2.9	22 05	2.8	11 33	4.7	—	—
TU 19	11 44	6.3	—	—	08 57	8.2	21 29	8.6	10 15	3.0	23 04	3.0	00 02	4.8	12 38	5.0
W 20	00 08	6.4	12 43	6.6	09 58	8.6	22 23	9.1	11 16	3.1	23 54	3.2	01 00	5.0	13 36	5.3
TH 21	01 08	6.8	13 35	6.8	10 54	9.0	23 14	9.5	—	—	12 13	3.1	01 52	5.3	14 28	5.6
FR 22	02 02	7.1	14 25	7.0	11 47	9.2	—	—	00 42	3.4	13 10	3.2	02 40	5.5	15 16	5.8
SA 23	02 54	7.2	15 13	7.0	00 04	9.7	12 38	9.4	01 28	3.5	14 04	3.2	03 26	5.7	16 04	5.8
SU 24	03 44	7.3	16 00	7.0	00 54	9.8	13 26	9.4	02 14	3.6	14 55	3.2	04 13	5.8	16 52	5.7
M 25	04 33	7.2	16 45	7.0	01 42	9.8	14 12	9.2	02 58	3.7	15 42	3.2	05 01	5.8	17 41	5.5
TU 26	05 21	7.1	17 30	7.0	02 29	9.6	14 57	8.9	03 41	3.7	16 25	3.2	05 50	5.6	18 31	5.2
W 27	06 08	6.9	18 13	6.8	03 16	9.2	15 43	8.5	04 25	3.6	17 06	3.2	06 41	5.4	19 24	5.0
TH 28	06 56	6.6	19 00	6.6	04 04	8.7	16 32	8.0	05 11	3.4	17 48	3.1	07 38	5.1	20 20	4.7
FR 29	07 48	6.3	19 53	6.3	04 58	8.1	17 30	7.5	06 02	3.2	18 33	2.9	08 41	4.8	21 20	4.5
SA 30	08 45	6.0	20 57	6.0	06 03	7.6	18 43	7.3	07 00	2.9	19 24	2.8	09 47	4.6	22 24	4.4
SU 31	09 47	5.8	22 09	5.8	07 19	7.4	19 58	7.4	08 36	2.7	20 41	2.8	10 58	4.4	23 33	4.5

AUGUST 2005 *High Water* GMT

	LONDON BRIDGE				LIVERPOOL				GREENOCK				LEITH			
M 1	10 51	5.8	23 20	5.9	08 31	7.5	20 59	7.7	10 11	2.8	22 11	2.9	—	—	12 10	4.5
TU 2	11 53	6.0	—	—	09 28	7.7	21 49	8.1	11 08	2.8	23 06	3.0	00 38	4.6	13 11	4.6
W 3	00 22	6.2	12 48	6.3	10 16	8.1	22 32	8.5	11 55	2.9	23 51	3.2	01 29	4.8	13 57	4.8
TH 4	01 15	6.5	13 35	6.5	10 58	8.3	23 09	8.7	—	—	12 37	2.9	02 10	5.0	14 34	5.0
FR 5	02 00	6.6	14 15	6.6	11 34	8.5	23 44	8.8	00 30	3.2	13 17	2.9	02 46	5.1	15 07	5.0
SA 6	02 39	6.7	14 50	6.6	—	—	12 08	8.5	01 05	3.3	13 52	2.9	03 18	5.2	15 37	5.1
SU 7	03 13	6.6	15 20	6.5	00 17	8.9	12 40	8.6	01 35	3.3	14 23	2.9	03 48	5.3	16 08	5.1
M 8	03 43	6.5	15 48	6.4	00 49	8.8	13 11	8.6	02 05	3.3	14 52	2.9	04 20	5.3	16 41	5.1
TU 9	04 13	6.5	16 16	6.4	01 21	8.8	13 42	8.5	02 37	3.3	15 21	2.9	04 51	5.2	17 16	5.0
W 10	04 45	6.5	16 46	6.5	01 53	8.7	14 14	8.4	03 11	3.3	15 53	3.0	05 24	5.1	17 53	4.9
TH 11	05 20	6.5	17 22	6.5	02 27	8.6	14 49	8.3	03 47	3.3	16 27	2.9	05 59	5.0	18 32	4.8
FR 12	05 59	6.4	18 04	6.4	03 05	8.4	15 31	8.0	04 24	3.2	17 03	2.9	06 39	4.9	19 16	4.7
SA 13	06 44	6.1	18 53	6.2	03 53	8.0	16 23	7.7	05 06	3.1	17 45	2.8	07 26	4.7	20 08	4.5
SU 14	07 38	5.9	19 55	5.9	04 54	7.7	17 32	7.4	05 57	2.9	18 39	2.7	08 29	4.5	21 13	4.4
M 15	08 44	5.6	21 08	5.7	06 07	7.4	18 53	7.5	07 05	2.8	20 00	2.6	09 51	4.4	22 28	4.5
TU 16	10 03	5.6	22 33	5.8	07 30	7.6	20 12	7.9	08 40	2.7	21 44	2.8	11 14	4.6	23 42	4.7
W 17	11 23	5.9	23 56	6.2	08 49	8.0	21 18	8.6	10 10	2.9	22 50	3.0	—	—	12 27	5.0
TH 18	—	—	12 28	6.4	09 52	8.6	22 13	9.2	11 15	3.1	23 41	3.3	00 46	5.1	13 26	5.4
FR 19	00 59	6.7	13 22	6.8	10 45	9.1	23 02	9.7	—	—	12 10	3.2	01 39	5.4	14 15	5.7
SA 20	01 52	7.2	14 10	7.1	11 34	9.5	23 49	10.0	00 28	3.5	13 02	3.3	02 24	5.7	15 01	5.9
SU 21	02 40	7.4	14 54	7.2	—	—	12 19	9.6	01 14	3.7	13 50	3.3	03 08	5.9	15 45	5.9
M 22	03 26	7.5	15 37	7.3	00 34	10.1	13 03	9.6	01 58	3.8	14 34	3.4	03 52	6.0	16 29	5.8
TU 23	04 10	7.4	16 18	7.3	01 18	10.0	13 45	9.4	02 40	3.8	15 12	3.4	04 37	6.0	17 13	5.6
W 24	04 52	7.2	16 58	7.2	02 01	9.7	14 25	9.0	03 19	3.8	15 48	3.4	05 23	5.8	17 59	5.3
TH 25	05 32	6.9	17 37	7.0	02 42	9.2	15 04	8.5	03 58	3.6	16 23	3.3	06 10	5.4	18 46	4.9
FR 26	06 11	6.6	18 16	6.7	03 25	8.5	15 47	8.0	04 37	3.4	17 01	3.2	07 02	5.0	19 38	4.6
SA 27	06 50	6.1	19 01	6.2	04 14	7.8	16 38	7.4	05 20	3.1	17 44	3.1	08 04	4.6	20 38	4.4
SU 28	07 37	5.7	20 03	5.7	05 19	7.2	17 57	7.0	06 10	2.8	18 33	2.9	09 13	4.3	21 46	4.3
M 29	08 52	5.4	21 37	5.4	06 53	6.9	19 33	7.1	07 21	2.6	19 38	2.8	10 30	4.2	23 03	4.3
TU 30	10 19	5.4	23 00	5.6	08 14	7.1	20 41	7.6	10 09	2.7	21 49	2.9	11 56	4.3	—	—
W 31	11 29	5.7	—	—	09 11	7.6	21 31	8.1	11 00	2.8	22 48	3.1	00 18	4.5	12 59	4.6

SEPTEMBER 2005 *High Water* GMT

	LONDON BRIDGE * Datum of Predictions 3.20m below				LIVERPOOL * Datum of Predictions 4.93m below				GREENOCK * Datum of Predictions 1.62m below				LEITH * Datum of Predictions 2.90m below			
	hr	*ht m*	*hr*	*ht m*	*hr*	*ht m*	*hr*	*ht m*	*hr*	*ht m*	*hr*	*ht m*	*hr*	*ht m*	*hr*	*ht m*
TH 1	00 03	6.1	12 25	6.2	09 57	8.0	22 12	8.5	11 41	3.0	23 32	3.2	01 11	4.8	13 41	4.8
FR 2	00 54	6.5	13 11	6.5	10 36	8.4	22 49	8.8	—	—	12 18	3.0	01 51	5.0	14 14	5.0
SA 3	01 37	6.8	13 51	6.7	11 11	8.6	23 22	9.0	00 09	3.3	12 55	3.0	02 23	5.2	14 43	5.1
SU 4	02 14	6.8	14 25	6.6	11 43	8.7	23 53	9.0	00 42	3.3	13 27	3.0	02 53	5.3	15 11	5.2
M 5	02 46	6.7	14 55	6.5	—	—	12 13	8.8	01 10	3.3	13 55	3.0	03 22	5.4	15 40	5.3
TU 6	03 15	6.6	15 21	6.4	00 22	9.0	12 42	8.8	01 39	3.4	14 19	3.1	03 51	5.4	16 11	5.3
W 7	03 44	6.6	15 47	6.5	00 51	9.0	13 11	8.8	02 10	3.4	14 45	3.1	04 22	5.4	16 44	5.2
TH 8	04 14	6.6	16 18	6.6	01 22	8.9	13 42	8.7	02 44	3.4	15 14	3.1	04 54	5.3	17 20	5.1
FR 9	04 48	6.6	16 55	6.6	01 55	8.8	14 16	8.5	03 19	3.4	15 46	3.1	05 30	5.1	17 58	5.0
SA 10	05 26	6.4	17 37	6.5	02 33	8.5	14 56	8.2	03 55	3.3	16 20	3.0	06 11	5.0	18 41	4.8
SU 11	06 09	6.2	18 27	6.2	03 21	8.0	15 50	7.7	04 34	3.1	16 59	2.9	07 02	4.7	19 34	4.6
M 12	07 00	5.8	19 28	5.8	04 25	7.5	17 04	7.3	05 24	2.9	17 54	2.8	08 08	4.5	20 42	4.4
TU 13	08 06	5.5	20 43	5.5	05 51	7.2	18 37	7.3	06 36	2.7	19 26	2.7	09 36	4.4	22 09	4.5
W 14	09 33	5.4	22 22	5.6	07 27	7.4	20 04	7.9	08 40	2.7	21 31	2.9	11 04	4.7	23 28	4.7
TH 15	11 08	5.8	23 49	6.2	08 45	8.0	21 07	8.7	10 14	2.9	22 34	3.2	—	—	12 17	5.1
FR 16	—	—	12 13	6.4	09 41	8.8	21 58	9.4	11 11	3.1	23 24	3.4	00 31	5.2	13 12	5.5
SA 17	00 47	6.9	13 04	6.9	10 29	9.3	22 44	9.9	11 59	3.3	—	—	01 21	5.6	13 57	5.8
SU 18	01 35	7.3	13 48	7.2	11 13	9.6	23 27	10.2	00 10	3.6	12 44	3.4	02 04	5.9	14 39	5.9
M 19	02 19	7.5	14 29	7.4	11 55	9.7	—	—	00 54	3.8	13 25	3.4	02 45	6.1	15 20	5.9
TU 20	03 01	7.5	15 09	7.4	00 09	10.2	12 35	9.6	01 37	3.8	14 03	3.5	03 28	6.1	16 01	5.8
W 21	03 41	7.4	15 48	7.3	00 51	9.9	13 13	9.4	02 16	3.8	14 37	3.5	04 11	6.0	16 43	5.5
TH 22	04 18	7.1	16 26	7.2	01 30	9.5	13 50	9.0	02 54	3.8	15 10	3.5	04 56	5.7	17 26	5.3
FR 23	04 53	6.8	17 03	7.0	02 08	9.0	14 26	8.5	03 30	3.6	15 45	3.5	05 42	5.3	18 10	4.9
SA 24	05 25	6.5	17 42	6.6	02 48	8.3	15 04	8.0	04 07	3.4	16 22	3.4	06 32	4.9	18 59	4.6
SU 25	05 59	6.1	18 26	6.1	03 33	7.6	15 52	7.4	04 47	3.1	17 04	3.2	07 30	4.5	19 58	4.4
M 26	06 38	5.7	19 22	5.6	04 37	6.9	17 10	6.9	05 37	2.8	17 55	3.0	08 39	4.2	21 08	4.2
TU 27	07 35	5.3	21 04	5.2	06 25	6.6	19 02	6.9	06 47	2.6	19 00	2.9	09 56	4.1	22 27	4.3
W 28	09 44	5.2	22 33	5.5	07 48	7.0	20 12	7.4	09 52	2.7	21 06	2.9	11 27	4.3	23 46	4.5
TH 29	10 58	5.6	23 34	6.0	08 44	7.5	21 02	8.0	10 36	2.9	22 18	3.1	—	—	12 31	4.6
FR 30	11 54	6.1	—	—	09 28	8.0	21 43	8.5	11 13	3.1	23 02	3.2	00 39	4.8	13 12	4.8

OCTOBER 2005 *High Water* GMT

	LONDON BRIDGE				LIVERPOOL				GREENOCK				LEITH			
SA 1	00 24	6.5	12 40	6.5	10 06	8.5	22 19	8.8	11 49	3.1	23 38	3.3	01 19	5.1	13 43	5.1
SU 2	01 06	6.8	13 19	6.6	10 40	8.7	22 52	9.0	—	—	12 22	3.2	01 51	5.3	14 11	5.2
M 3	01 41	6.8	13 53	6.6	11 11	8.9	23 21	9.1	00 08	3.3	12 54	3.2	02 21	5.4	14 39	5.3
TU 4	02 13	6.8	14 23	6.6	11 41	9.0	23 51	9.1	00 38	3.4	13 20	3.2	02 51	5.5	15 09	5.4
W 5	02 43	6.7	14 51	6.5	—	—	12 10	9.0	01 09	3.4	13 44	3.2	03 21	5.5	15 40	5.4
TH 6	03 13	6.7	15 21	6.6	00 21	9.1	12 41	9.0	01 43	3.4	14 12	3.3	03 53	5.5	16 14	5.4
FR 7	03 45	6.6	15 56	6.6	00 55	9.0	13 15	8.9	02 19	3.5	14 42	3.3	04 29	5.4	16 50	5.3
SA 8	04 20	6.6	16 36	6.7	01 32	8.8	13 52	8.6	02 56	3.4	15 15	3.3	05 09	5.2	17 30	5.1
SU 9	04 59	6.5	17 21	6.5	02 14	8.4	14 36	8.2	03 33	3.3	15 50	3.2	05 56	5.0	18 16	4.9
M 10	05 43	6.2	18 13	6.2	03 05	7.9	15 34	7.8	04 15	3.1	16 32	3.1	06 51	4.8	19 11	4.6
TU 11	06 34	5.8	19 16	5.8	04 15	7.3	16 52	7.4	05 08	2.9	17 31	2.9	08 01	4.6	20 26	4.5
W 12	07 42	5.4	20 38	5.5	05 48	7.1	18 28	7.5	06 35	2.7	19 19	2.8	09 29	4.5	21 55	4.6
TH 13	09 21	5.4	22 19	5.8	07 22	7.5	19 48	8.1	08 47	2.8	21 11	3.0	10 52	4.8	23 11	4.9
FR 14	10 48	5.9	23 32	6.4	08 30	8.2	20 48	8.8	10 03	3.0	22 12	3.3	12 00	5.2	—	—
SA 15	11 48	6.5	—	—	09 22	8.9	21 37	9.4	10 53	3.2	23 01	3.6	00 10	5.3	12 52	5.5
SU 16	00 26	7.0	12 37	7.0	10 07	9.3	22 22	9.8	11 37	3.4	23 47	3.7	00 58	5.6	13 35	5.7
M 17	01 12	7.4	13 21	7.3	10 48	9.6	23 04	10.0	—	—	12 17	3.5	01 41	5.9	14 15	5.8
TU 18	01 54	7.5	14 02	7.4	11 28	9.6	23 44	9.9	00 30	3.8	12 55	3.5	02 22	6.0	14 54	5.8
W 19	02 33	7.4	14 42	7.3	—	—	12 05	9.5	01 13	3.8	13 30	3.6	03 05	5.9	15 34	5.7
TH 20	03 11	7.2	15 21	7.2	00 23	9.6	12 42	9.3	01 52	3.7	14 04	3.6	03 48	5.8	16 14	5.5
FR 21	03 45	6.9	15 59	7.0	01 01	9.2	13 17	8.9	02 29	3.7	14 38	3.7	04 33	5.5	16 55	5.2
SA 22	04 17	6.7	16 38	6.7	01 38	8.7	13 53	8.5	03 05	3.5	15 14	3.6	05 18	5.2	17 37	5.0
SU 23	04 48	6.4	17 18	6.4	02 17	8.1	14 31	8.0	03 43	3.3	15 51	3.5	06 06	4.8	18 24	4.7
M 24	05 22	6.2	18 02	6.0	03 01	7.5	15 17	7.5	04 25	3.1	16 33	3.4	07 00	4.5	19 21	4.4
TU 25	06 02	5.8	18 55	5.6	03 59	6.9	16 23	7.1	05 17	2.8	17 24	3.2	08 01	4.2	20 29	4.3
W 26	06 54	5.4	20 10	5.3	05 38	6.6	18 11	7.0	06 28	2.6	18 27	3.0	09 10	4.1	21 41	4.3
TH 27	08 27	5.2	21 47	5.4	07 05	6.9	19 27	7.3	08 56	2.7	19 49	3.0	10 26	4.2	22 53	4.4
FR 28	10 12	5.4	22 52	5.8	08 03	7.4	20 21	7.8	09 52	2.9	21 22	3.1	11 37	4.5	23 51	4.7
SA 29	11 11	5.8	23 43	6.2	08 49	7.9	21 04	8.3	10 33	3.1	22 15	3.2	—	—	12 24	4.7
SU 30	11 59	6.2	—	—	09 28	8.4	21 41	8.6	11 10	3.2	22 54	3.3	00 35	5.0	13 00	5.0
M 31	00 25	6.5	12 40	6.5	10 03	8.7	22 15	8.9	11 45	3.3	23 29	3.3	01 12	5.2	13 32	5.2

NOVEMBER 2005 *High Water* GMT

	LONDON BRIDGE * Datum of Predictions 3.20m below				LIVERPOOL * Datum of Predictions 4.93m below				GREENOCK * Datum of Predictions 1.62m below				LEITH * Datum of Predictions 2.90m below			
	hr	*ht m*	*hr*	*ht m*	*hr*	*ht m*	*hr*	*ht m*	*hr*	*ht m*	*hr*	*ht m*	*hr*	*ht m*	*hr*	*ht m*
TU 1	01 03	6.7	13 16	6.6	10 36	8.9	22 47	9.1	—	—	12 16	3.3	01 46	5.3	14 04	5.3
W 2	01 38	6.8	13 50	6.6	11 08	9.1	23 21	9.2	00 03	3.4	12 45	3.3	02 19	5.5	14 37	5.4
TH 3	02 12	6.8	14 24	6.7	11 41	9.2	23 57	9.2	00 41	3.4	13 14	3.4	02 54	5.5	15 12	5.5
FR 4	02 47	6.8	15 01	6.7	—	—	12 17	9.1	01 20	3.5	13 46	3.5	03 31	5.5	15 48	5.4
SA 5	03 23	6.7	15 42	6.8	00 36	9.1	12 57	9.0	02 00	3.5	14 20	3.5	04 12	5.4	16 27	5.3
SU 6	04 01	6.6	16 27	6.7	01 19	8.8	13 41	8.8	02 40	3.4	14 56	3.5	04 57	5.3	17 10	5.2
M 7	04 43	6.4	17 16	6.5	02 07	8.4	14 30	8.4	03 22	3.3	15 35	3.4	05 47	5.1	18 00	5.0
TU 8	05 28	6.2	18 11	6.2	03 03	8.0	15 31	8.1	04 11	3.1	16 22	3.3	06 46	4.9	18 59	4.8
W 9	06 22	5.8	19 17	5.9	04 13	7.6	16 45	7.8	05 15	2.9	17 29	3.1	07 56	4.7	20 14	4.7
TH 10	07 36	5.6	20 38	5.8	05 38	7.4	18 08	7.9	06 48	2.8	19 08	3.1	09 16	4.7	21 37	4.8
FR 11	09 07	5.7	21 58	6.1	06 58	7.7	19 20	8.3	08 25	2.9	20 39	3.2	10 30	4.9	22 46	5.0
SA 12	10 18	6.1	23 02	6.5	08 03	8.2	20 20	8.8	09 33	3.1	21 43	3.4	11 34	5.1	23 44	5.3
SU 13	11 16	6.6	23 56	6.9	08 56	8.7	21 12	9.2	10 24	3.3	22 35	3.5	—	—	12 26	5.3
M 14	—	—	12 07	6.9	09 41	9.1	21 58	9.4	11 08	3.4	23 23	3.6	00 34	5.5	13 11	5.5
TU 15	00 44	7.2	12 54	7.1	10 23	9.3	22 41	9.5	11 48	3.5	—	—	01 20	5.6	13 51	5.5
W 16	01 27	7.2	13 38	7.2	11 03	9.3	23 22	9.4	00 08	3.6	12 26	3.5	02 03	5.7	14 31	5.6
TH 17	02 07	7.1	14 20	7.1	11 40	9.3	—	—	00 51	3.6	13 02	3.6	02 47	5.6	15 11	5.5
FR 18	02 45	6.9	15 01	6.9	00 00	9.2	12 16	9.1	01 31	3.5	13 38	3.7	03 31	5.5	15 51	5.4
SA 19	03 19	6.7	15 42	6.7	00 38	8.9	12 52	8.9	02 10	3.5	14 14	3.7	04 15	5.3	16 30	5.2
SU 20	03 50	6.5	16 21	6.5	01 15	8.6	13 29	8.6	02 47	3.3	14 50	3.7	04 58	5.0	17 10	5.0
M 21	04 21	6.4	17 01	6.3	01 54	8.2	14 09	8.3	03 27	3.2	15 28	3.6	05 42	4.8	17 53	4.8
TU 22	04 57	6.2	17 42	6.1	02 37	7.7	14 53	7.9	04 11	3.1	16 09	3.5	06 29	4.6	18 43	4.6
W 23	05 37	6.0	18 29	5.8	03 27	7.3	15 47	7.5	05 03	2.9	16 56	3.3	07 21	4.4	19 43	4.4
TH 24	06 24	5.7	19 22	5.6	04 32	7.0	16 55	7.3	06 04	2.8	17 52	3.1	08 19	4.3	20 47	4.4
FR 25	07 24	5.5	20 27	5.5	05 53	6.9	18 15	7.3	07 11	2.8	18 54	3.1	09 20	4.3	21 50	4.4
SA 26	08 47	5.4	21 40	5.6	07 04	7.2	19 20	7.6	08 27	2.8	20 01	3.1	10 20	4.4	22 48	4.6
SU 27	10 06	5.6	22 44	5.9	07 58	7.6	20 11	7.9	09 33	3.0	21 07	3.1	11 17	4.6	23 41	4.8
M 28	11 05	5.9	23 36	6.3	08 43	8.1	20 55	8.3	10 23	3.1	22 02	3.2	—	—	12 07	4.8
TU 29	11 54	6.2	—	—	09 23	8.5	21 36	8.7	11 04	3.2	22 49	3.3	00 27	5.0	12 51	5.0
W 30	00 22	6.6	12 39	6.5	10 01	8.8	22 16	8.9	11 40	3.3	23 33	3.3	01 11	5.2	13 32	5.2

DECEMBER 2005 *High Water* GMT

	LONDON BRIDGE				LIVERPOOL				GREENOCK				LEITH			
TH 1	01 05	6.8	13 21	6.7	10 40	9.1	22 58	9.1	—	—	12 15	3.4	01 52	5.3	14 10	5.4
FR 2	01 46	6.9	14 03	6.8	11 20	9.2	23 41	9.2	00 17	3.4	12 51	3.5	02 33	5.4	14 49	5.5
SA 3	02 27	6.9	14 48	6.9	—	—	12 02	9.3	01 02	3.4	13 28	3.6	03 16	5.5	15 29	5.5
SU 4	03 08	6.8	15 34	6.9	00 26	9.1	12 48	9.3	01 48	3.4	14 07	3.6	04 01	5.5	16 12	5.4
M 5	03 51	6.7	16 24	6.8	01 15	8.9	13 37	9.1	02 34	3.4	14 48	3.6	04 49	5.4	16 59	5.3
TU 6	04 37	6.5	17 16	6.6	02 06	8.7	14 29	8.9	03 23	3.3	15 32	3.6	05 41	5.3	17 50	5.2
W 7	05 25	6.3	18 12	6.4	03 01	8.4	15 26	8.7	04 18	3.1	16 24	3.5	06 37	5.1	18 47	5.1
TH 8	06 20	6.1	19 13	6.3	04 02	8.1	16 28	8.4	05 21	3.0	17 26	3.4	07 41	4.9	19 55	5.0
FR 9	07 27	6.0	20 20	6.2	05 10	7.8	17 35	8.3	06 30	3.0	18 39	3.3	08 51	4.8	21 08	4.9
SA 10	08 38	6.1	21 26	6.3	06 21	7.8	18 44	8.3	07 40	3.0	19 57	3.3	09 59	4.8	22 15	5.0
SU 11	09 43	6.2	22 28	6.4	07 28	8.0	19 48	8.5	08 48	3.1	21 09	3.3	11 02	4.9	23 17	5.1
M 12	10 43	6.4	23 24	6.6	08 27	8.3	20 46	8.7	09 48	3.2	22 10	3.4	11 58	5.0	—	—
TU 13	11 38	6.6	—	—	09 18	8.6	21 38	8.8	10 38	3.3	23 03	3.4	00 13	5.2	12 49	5.1
W 14	00 15	6.7	12 31	6.7	10 03	8.8	22 24	8.9	11 23	3.4	23 51	3.4	01 05	5.2	13 34	5.2
TH 15	01 03	6.7	13 20	6.8	10 44	9.0	23 06	8.9	—	—	12 03	3.5	01 52	5.3	14 16	5.3
FR 16	01 47	6.7	14 06	6.7	11 23	9.0	23 45	8.8	00 37	3.3	12 42	3.6	02 37	5.3	14 56	5.3
SA 17	02 27	6.6	14 50	6.6	12 00	9.0	—	—	01 20	3.3	13 20	3.6	03 20	5.2	15 35	5.3
SU 18	03 02	6.5	15 31	6.5	00 23	8.7	12 37	8.9	02 00	3.2	13 56	3.7	04 00	5.1	16 12	5.2
M 19	03 33	6.4	16 08	6.4	01 00	8.5	13 14	8.8	02 38	3.2	14 33	3.7	04 39	5.0	16 49	5.1
TU 20	04 05	6.3	16 44	6.3	01 38	8.3	13 52	8.6	03 17	3.1	15 10	3.6	05 18	4.9	17 27	5.0
W 21	04 39	6.3	17 21	6.3	02 17	8.1	14 32	8.3	03 57	3.1	15 48	3.5	05 59	4.7	18 09	4.8
TH 22	05 16	6.2	18 00	6.2	02 58	7.8	15 15	8.1	04 41	3.0	16 29	3.4	06 42	4.6	18 55	4.7
FR 23	05 57	6.1	18 44	6.0	03 44	7.6	16 03	7.8	05 28	2.9	17 14	3.3	07 29	4.5	19 47	4.5
SA 24	06 44	5.9	19 33	5.9	04 38	7.3	16 59	7.6	06 18	2.9	18 04	3.2	08 22	4.4	20 44	4.5
SU 25	07 40	5.7	20 31	5.8	05 41	7.2	18 01	7.5	07 11	2.8	18 59	3.1	09 19	4.4	21 45	4.5
M 26	08 49	5.6	21 37	5.8	06 47	7.4	19 05	7.7	08 12	2.8	20 01	3.0	10 18	4.4	22 46	4.5
TU 27	10 01	5.7	22 44	6.0	07 49	7.7	20 05	8.0	09 21	2.9	21 10	3.0	11 16	4.6	23 45	4.7
W 28	11 07	6.0	23 44	6.3	08 43	8.1	21 01	8.3	10 21	3.0	22 14	3.1	—	—	12 12	4.8
TH 29	—	—	12 06	6.4	09 32	8.6	21 52	8.7	11 10	3.2	23 09	3.2	00 40	4.9	13 03	5.0
FR 30	00 37	6.6	12 59	6.7	10 19	9.0	22 42	9.0	11 53	3.3	—	—	01 32	5.2	13 50	5.2
SA 31	01 26	6.8	13 49	6.9	11 06	9.3	23 32	9.2	00 01	3.3	12 35	3.5	02 20	5.4	14 34	5.4

GENERAL REFERENCE

WEIGHTS AND MEASURES

SI UNITS

The Système International d'Unités (SI) is an international and coherent system of units devised to meet all known needs for measurement in science and technology. The system was adopted by the eleventh Conférence Générale des Poids et Mesures (CGPM) in 1960. A comprehensive description of the system is given in *SI The International System of Units* (HMSO). The British Standards describing the essential features of the International System of Units are *Specifications for SI units and recommendations for the use of their multiples and certain other units* (BS 5555:1993) and *Conversion Factors and Tables* (BS 350, Part 1:1974).

The system consists of seven base units and the derived units formed as products or quotients of various powers of the base units. Together the base units and the derived units make up the coherent system of units. In the UK the SI base units, and almost all important derived units, are realised at the National Physical Laboratory and disseminated through the National Measurement System.

BASE UNITS

metre (m) = unit of length
kilogram (kg) = unit of mass
second (s) = unit of time
ampere (A) = unit of electric current
kelvin (K) = unit of thermodynamic temperature
mole (mol) = unit of amount of substance
candela (cd) = unit of luminous intensity

DERIVED UNITS

For some of the derived SI units, special names and symbols exist; those approved by the CGPM are as follows:

hertz (Hz) = unit of frequency
newton (N) = unit of force
pascal (Pa) = unit of pressure, stress
joule (J) = unit of energy, work, quantity of heat
watt (W) = unit of power, radiant flux
coulomb (C) = unit of electric charge, quantity of electricity
volt (V) = unit of electric potential, potential difference, electromotive force
farad (F) = unit of electric capacitance
ohm (Ω) = unit of electric resistance
siemens (S) = unit of electric conductance
weber (Wb) = unit of magnetic flux
tesla (T) = unit of magnetic flux density
henry (H) = unit of inductance
degree Celsius (°C) = unit of Celsius temperature
lumen (lm) = unit of luminous flux
lux (lx) = unit of illuminance
becquerel (Bq) = unit of activity (of a radionuclide)
gray (Gy) = unit of absorbed dose, specific energy imparted, kerma, absorbed dose index
sievert (Sv) = unit of dose equivalent, dose equivalent index
radian (rad) = unit of plane angle
steradian (sr) = unit of solid angle

Other derived units are expressed in terms of base units. Some of the more commonly used derived units are the following:

Unit of area = square metre (m^2)
Unit of volume = cubic metre (m^3)
Unit of velocity = metre per second ($m\ s^{-1}$)
Unit of acceleration = metre per second squared ($m\ s^{-2}$)
Unit of density = kilogram per cubic metre ($kg\ m^{-3}$)
Unit of momentum = kilogram metre per second ($kg\ m\ s^{-1}$)
Unit of magnetic field strength = ampere per metre ($A\ m^{-1}$)
Unit of surface tension = newton per metre ($N\ m^{-1}$)
Unit of dynamic viscosity = pascal second (Pa s)
Unit of heat capacity = joule per kelvin ($J\ K^{-1}$)
Unit of specific heat capacity = joule per kilogram kelvin ($J\ kg^{-1}\ K^{-1}$)
Unit of heat flux density, irradiance = watt per square metre ($W\ m^{-2}$)
Unit of thermal conductivity = watt per metre kelvin ($W\ m^{-1}\ K^{-1}$)
Unit of electric field strength = volt per metre ($V\ m^{-1}$)
Unit of luminance = candela per square metre ($cd\ m^{-2}$)

SI PREFIXES

Decimal multiples and submultiples of the SI units are indicated by SI prefixes. These are as follows:

multiples	*submultiples*
yotta (Y) × 10^{24}	deci (d) × 10^{-1}
zetta (Z) × 10^{21}	centi (c) × 10^{-2}
exa (E) × 10^{18}	milli (m) × 10^{-3}
peta (P) × 10^{15}	micro (μ) × 10^{-6}
tera (T) × 10^{12}	nano (n) × 10^{-9}
giga (G) × 10^{9}	pico (p) × 10^{-12}
mega (M) × 10^{6}	femto (f) × 10^{-15}
kilo (k) × 10^{3}	atto (a) × 10^{-18}
hecto (h) × 10^{2}	zepto (z) × 10^{-21}
deca (da) × 10	yocto (y) × 10^{-24}

METRIC UNITS

The metric primary standards are the metre as the unit of measurement of length, and the kilogram as the unit of measurement of mass. Other units of measurement are defined by reference to the primary standards.

MEASUREMENT OF LENGTH

Kilometre (km) = 1000 metres
Metre (m) is the length of the path travelled by light in vacuum during a time interval of 1/299 792 458 of a second
Decimetre (dm) = 1/10 metre
Centimetre (cm) = 1/100 metre
Millimetre (mm) = 1/1000 metre

MEASUREMENT OF AREA

Hectare (ha) = 100 ares
Decare = 10 ares
Are (a) = 100 square metres
Square metre = a superficial area equal to that of a square each side of which measures one metre
Square decimetre = 1/100 square metre

Square centimetre = 1/100 square decimetre
Square millimetre = 1/100 square centimetre

MEASUREMENT OF VOLUME
Cubic metre (m^3) = a volume equal to that of a cube each edge of which measures one metre
Cubic decimetre = 1/1000 cubic metre
Cubic centimetre (cc) = 1/1000 cubic decimetre
Hectolitre = 100 litres
Litre = a cubic decimetre
Decilitre = 1/10 litre
Centilitre = 1/100 litre
Millilitre = 1/1000 litre

MEASUREMENT OF CAPACITY
Hectolitre (hl) = 100 litres
Litre (l or L) = a cubic decimetre
Decilitre (dl) = 1/10 litre
Centilitre (cl) = 1/100 litre
Millilitre (ml) = 1/1000 litre

MEASUREMENT OF MASS OR WEIGHT
Tonne (t) = 1000 kilograms
Kilogram (kg) is equal to the mass of the international prototype of the kilogram
Hectogram (hg) = 1/10 kilogram
Gram (g) = 1/1000 kilogram
*Carat (metric) = 1/5 gram
Milligram (mg) = 1/1000 gram

* Used only for transactions in precious stones or pearls

METRICATION IN THE UK
The European Council Directive 80/181/EEC, as amended by Council Directive 89/617/EEC, relates to the use of units of measurement for economic, public health, public safety or administrative purposes in the member states of the European Union. The provisions of the directives were incorporated into British law by the Weights and Measures Act 1985 (Metrication) (Amendment) Order 1994 and the Units of Measurement Regulations 1994; these instruments amended the Weights and Measures Act 1985. Parallel statutory rules amending Northern Ireland weights and measures legislation were made in May 1995.

The general effect of the 1994 and 1995 legislation is to end the use of imperial units of measurement for trade, replacing them with metric units – *see* below for timetable for UK metrication. Imperial units can, however, be used in addition to metric units, as supplementary indications.

IMPERIAL UNITS

The imperial primary standards are the yard as the unit of measurement of length and the pound as the unit of measurement of mass. Other units of measurement are defined by reference to the primary standards. Most of these units are no longer authorised for use in trade in the UK – *see* below.

MEASUREMENT OF LENGTH
Mile = 1760 yards
Furlong = 220 yards
Chain = 22 yards
Yard (yd) = 0.9144 metre
Foot (ft) = 1/3 yard
Inch (in) = 1/36 yard

MEASUREMENT OF AREA
Square mile = 640 acres
Acre = 4840 square yards
Rood = 1210 square yards
Square yard (sq. yd) = a superficial area equal to that of a square each side of which measures one yard
Square foot (sq. ft) = 1/9 square yard
Square inch (sq. in) = 1/144 square foot

MEASUREMENT OF VOLUME
Cubic yard = a volume equal to that of a cube each edge of which measures one yard
Cubic foot = 1/27 cubic yard
Cubic inch = 1/1728 cubic foot

MEASUREMENT OF CAPACITY
Bushel = 8 gallons
Peck = 2 gallons
Gallon (gal) = 4.54609 cubic decimetres
Quart (qt) = 1/4 gallon
*Pint (pt) = 1/2 quart
Gill = 1/4 pint
*Fluid ounce (fl oz) = 1/20 pint
Fluid drachm = 1/8 fluid ounce
Minim (min) = 1/60 fluid drachm

MEASUREMENT OF MASS OR WEIGHT
Ton = 2240 pounds
Hundredweight (cwt) = 112 pounds
Cental = 100 pounds
Quarter = 28 pounds
Stone = 14 pounds
*Pound (lb) = 0.453 592 37 kilogram
*Ounce (oz) = 1/16 pound
*†Ounce troy (oz tr) = 12/175 pound
Dram (dr) = 1/16 ounce
Grain (gr) = 1/7000 pound
Pennyweight (dwt) = 24 grains
Ounce apothecaries' = 480 grains
Drachm (ʒ1) = 1/8 ounce apothecaries'
Scruple (℈1) = 1/3 drachm

* Units of measurement still authorised for use for trade in the UK
† Used only for transactions in gold, silver or other precious metals, and articles made therefrom

PHASING-OUT OF IMPERIAL UNITS IN THE UK
Since 1965 the United Kingdom has been adopting metric weights and measures in response to the adoption of metric units as the international system of measurement. Since 1 January 2000, goods sold loose by weight (mainly fresh foods) are required to be sold in grams and kilograms. Retailers can continue to display the price per imperial unit alongside the price per unit in metric unit. Consumers can continue to express in ounces and pounds the quantity they wish to buy. Retailers will weigh out the equivalent quantity in grams and kilograms. The Weights and Measures Units of Measurement Regulations 1995 (Statutory Instrument 1995 No. 1804) require that metric units should be used for all economic, public health, public safety and administrative purposes.

Units of measurement authorised for use in specialised fields are:

Unit	*Field of application*
Fathom	Marine navigation
Fluid ounce, Pint	Beer, cider, water, lemonade, fruit juice
Ounce, Pound	Goods for sale loose from bulk
Therm	Gas supply

Units of measurement authorised for use in specialised fields from 1 October 1995, without time limit

Unit	*Field of application*
Inch, Foot, Yard, Mile	Road traffic signs, distance and speed measurement
Pint	Dispense of draught beer or cider in returnable containers
Acre	Land registration
Troy ounce	Transactions in precious metals

MEASUREMENT OF ELECTRICITY

Units of measurement of electricity are defined by the Weights and Measures Act 1985 as follows:

ampere (A) = that constant current which, if maintained in two straight parallel conductors of infinite length, of negligible circular cross-section and placed 1 metre apart in vacuum, would produce between these conductors a force equal to 2 x 10^{-7} newton per metre of length
ohm (Ω) = the electric resistance between two points of a conductor when a constant potential difference of 1 volt, applied between the two points, produces in the conductor a current of 1 ampere, the conductor not being the seat of any electromotive force
volt (V) = the difference of electric potential between two points of a conducting wire carrying a constant current of 1 ampere when the power dissipated between these points is equal to 1 watt
watt (W) = the power which in one second gives rise to energy of 1 joule
kilowatt (kW) = 1000 watts
megawatt (MW) = one million watts

WATER AND LIQUOR MEASURES

1 cubic foot = 62.32 lb
1 gallon = 10 lb
1 cubic cm = 1 gram
1000 cubic cm = 1 litre; 1 kilogram
1 cubic metre = 1000 litres; 1000 kg; 1 tonne
An inch of rain on the surface of an acre (43560 sq. ft) = 3630 cubic ft = 100.992 tons
Cisterns: A cistern 4 × 2½ feet and 3 feet deep will hold brimful 186.963 gallons, weighing 1869.63 lb in addition to its own weight

WATER FOR SHIPS
Kilderkin = 18 gallons
Barrel = 36 gallons
Puncheon = 72 gallons
Butt = 110 gallons
Tun = 210 gallons

BOTTLES OF WINE
Traditional equivalents in standard champagne bottles:
Magnum = 2 bottles
Jeroboam = 4 bottles
Rehoboam = 6 bottles
Methuselah = 8 bottles
Salmanazar = 12 bottles
Balthazar = 16 bottles
Nebuchadnezzar = 20 bottles

A quarter of a bottle is known as a *nip*
An eighth of a bottle is known as a *baby*

ANGULAR AND CIRCULAR MEASURES

60 seconds (″) = 1 minute (′)
60 minutes = 1 degree (°)
90 degrees = 1 right angle or quadrant
Diameter of circle × 3.1416 = circumference
Diameter squared × 0.7854 = area of circle
Diameter squared × 3.1416 = surface of sphere
Diameter cubed × 0.523 = solidity of sphere
One degree of circumference × 57.3 = radius*
Diameter of cylinder × 3.1416; product by length or height, gives the surface
Diameter squared × 0.7854; product by length or height, gives solid content

*Or, one radian (the angle subtended at the centre of a circle by an arc of the circumference equal in length to the radius) = 57.3 degrees

MILLION, BILLION, ETC.

Value in the UK		
Million	thousand × thousand	10^6
*Billion	million × million	10^{12}
Trillion	million × billion	10^{18}
Quadrillion	million × trillion	10^{24}

Value in the USA		
Million	thousand × thousand	10^6
*Billion	thousand × million	10^9
Trillion	million × million	10^{12}
Quadrillion	million × billion US	10^{15}

* The American usage of billion (i.e. 10^9) is increasingly common, and is now universally used by statisticians

NAUTICAL MEASURES

DISTANCE
Distance at sea is measured in nautical miles. The British standard nautical mile was 6080 feet but this measure has been obsolete since 1970 when the international nautical mile of 1852 metres was adopted by the Hydrographic Department of the Ministry of Defence. The cable (600 feet or 100 fathoms) was a measure approximately one-tenth of a nautical mile. Such distances are now expressed in decimal parts of a sea mile or in metres.

Soundings at sea were recorded in fathoms (6 feet). Depths are now expressed in metres on Admiralty charts.

SPEED

Speed is measured in nautical miles per hour, called knots. A ship moving at the rate of 30 nautical miles per hour is said to be doing 30 knots.

Knots	*m.p.h.*	*knots*	*m.p.h.*
1	1.1515	9	10.3636
2	2.3030	10	11.5151
3	3.4545	15	17.2727
4	4.6060	20	23.0303
5	5.7575	25	28.7878
6	6.9090	30	34.5454
7	8.0606	35	40.3030
8	9.2121	40	46.0606

TONNAGE

Under the Merchant Shipping Act 1854, the tonnage of UK-registered vessels was measured in tons of 100 cubic feet. The need for a universal method of measurement led to the adoption of the International Convention on Tonnage Measurements of Ships 1969, which measures, in cubic metres, all the internal spaces of a vessel for the gross tonnage and those of the cargo compartments for the net tonnage. The convention has applied since July 1982 to new ships, ships which needed to be remeasured because of substantial alterations, and ships whose owners requested remeasurement. On 18 July 1994 the convention became mandatory.

DISTANCE OF THE HORIZON

The limit of distance to which one can see varies with the height of the spectator. The greatest distance at which an object on the surface of the sea, or of a level plain, can be seen by a person whose eyes are at a height of five feet from the same level is nearly three miles. At a height of 20 feet the range is increased to nearly six miles, and an approximate rule for finding the range of vision for small heights is to increase the square root of the number of feet that the eye is above the level surface by a third of itself. The result is the distance of the horizon in miles, but is slightly in excess of that in the table below, which is computed by a more precise formula. The table may be used conversely to show the distance of an object of given height that is just visible from a point on the surface of the earth or sea. Refraction is taken into account both in the approximate rule and in the table.

Height in feet	*range in miles*
5	2.9
20	5.9
50	9.3
100	13.2
500	29.5
1,000	41.6
2,000	58.9
3,000	72.1
4,000	83.3
5,000	93.1
20,000	186.2

TEMPERATURE SCALES

The SI (International System) unit of temperature is the kelvin, which is defined as the fraction 1/273.16 of the temperature of the triple point of water (i.e. where ice, water and water vapour are in equilibrium). The zero of the Kelvin scale is the absolute zero of temperature. The freezing point of water is 273.15 K and the boiling point (as adopted in the International Temperature Scale of 1990) is 373.124 K.

The Celsius scale (formerly centigrade) is defined by subtracting 273.15 from the Kelvin temperature. The Fahrenheit scale is related to the Celsius scale by the relationships:

temperature °F = (temperature °C × 1.8) + 32
temperature °C = (temperature °F − 32) ÷ 1.8

It follows from these definitions that the freezing point of water is 0°C and 32°F. The boiling point is 99.974°C and 211.953°F.

The temperature of the human body varies from person to person and in the same person can be affected by a variety of factors. In most people body temperature varies between 36.5°C and 37.2°C (97.7–98.9°F).

Conversion between scales

°C	°F	°C	°F	°C	°F
100	212	60	140	20	68
99	210.2	59	138.2	19	66.2
98	208.4	58	136.4	18	64.4
97	206.6	57	134.6	17	62.6
96	204.8	56	132.8	16	60.8
95	203	55	131	15	59
94	201.2	54	129.2	14	57.2
93	199.4	53	127.4	13	55.4
92	197.6	52	125.6	12	53.6
91	195.8	51	123.8	11	51.8
90	194	50	122	10	50
89	192.2	49	120.2	9	48.2
88	190.4	48	118.4	8	46.4
87	188.6	47	116.6	7	44.6
86	186.8	46	114.8	6	42.8
85	185	45	113	5	41
84	183.2	44	111.2	4	39.2
83	181.4	43	109.4	3	37.4
82	179.6	42	107.6	2	35.6
81	177.8	41	105.8	1	33.8
80	176	40	104	*Zero*	32
79	174.2	39	102.2	−1	30.2
78	172.4	38	100.4	−2	28.4
77	170.6	37	98.6	−3	26.6
76	168.8	36	96.8	−4	24.8
75	167	35	95	−5	23
74	165.2	34	93.2	−6	21.2
73	163.4	33	91.4	−7	19.4
72	161.6	32	89.6	−8	17.6
71	159.8	31	87.8	−9	15.8
70	158	30	86	−10	14
69	156.2	29	84.2	−11	12.2
68	154.4	28	82.4	−12	10.4
67	152.6	27	80.6	−13	8.6
66	150.8	26	78.8	−14	6.8
65	149	25	77	−15	5
64	147.2	24	75.2	−16	3.2
63	145.4	23	73.4	−17	1.4
62	143.6	22	71.6	−18	0.4
61	141.8	21	69.8	−19	−2.2

PAPER MEASURES

Printing Paper

516 sheets = 1 ream
2 reams = 1 bundle
5 bundles = 1 bale

Writing Paper

480 sheets = 1 ream
20 quires = 1 ream
24 sheets = 1 quire

INTERNATIONAL PAPER SIZES

The basis of the international series of paper sizes is a rectangle having an area of one square metre, the sides of which are in the proportion of $1:\sqrt{2}$. The proportions $1:\sqrt{2}$ have a geometrical relationship, the side and diagonal of any square being in this proportion. The effect of this arrangement is that if the area of the sheet of paper is doubled or halved, the shorter side and the longer side of the new sheet are still in the same proportion $1:\sqrt{2}$. This feature is useful where photographic enlargement or reduction is used, as the proportions remain the same.

Description of the A series is by capital A followed by a figure. The basic size has the description A0 and the higher the figure following the letter, the greater is the number of sub-divisions and therefore the smaller the sheet. Half A0 is A1 and half A1 is A2. Where larger dimensions are required the A is preceded by a figure. Thus 2A means twice the size A0; 4A is four times the size of A0.

SUBSIDIARY SERIES

B sizes are sizes intermediate between any two adjacent sizes of the A series. There is a series of C sizes which is used much less. A is for magazines and books, B for posters, wall charts and other large items, C for envelopes particularly where it is necessary for an envelope (in C series) to fit into another envelope. The size recommended for business correspondence is A4.

Long sizes (DL) are obtainable by dividing any appropriate sizes from the two series above into three, four or eight equal parts parallel with the shorter side in such a manner that the proportion of $1:\sqrt{2}$ is not maintained, the ratio between the longer and the shorter sides being greater than $\sqrt{2}:1$. In practice long sizes should be produced from the A series only.

It is an essential feature of these series that the dimensions are of the trimmed or finished size.

A SERIES

	mm		*mm*
A0	841 × 1189	A6	105 × 148
A1	594 × 841	A7	74 × 105
A2	420 × 594	A8	52 × 74
A3	297 × 420	A9	37 × 52
A4	210 × 297	A10	26 × 37
A5	148 × 210		

B SERIES

	mm		*mm*
B0	1000 × 1414	B6	125 × 176
B1	707 × 1000	B7	88 × 125
B2	500 × 707	B8	62 × 88
B3	353 × 500	B9	44 × 62
B4	250 × 353	B10	31 × 44
B5	176 × 250		

C SERIES		**DL**	
	mm		*mm*
C4	324 × 229	DL	110 × 220
C5	229 × 162		
C6	114 × 162		

CONVERSION TABLES FOR WEIGHTS AND MEASURES

Bold figures equal units of either of the columns beside them; thus: 1 cm = 0.394 inches and 1 inch = 2.540 cm

LENGTH			AREA			VOLUME			WEIGHT (MASS)		
Centimetres		*Inches*	*Square cm*		*Square in*	*Cubic cm*		*Cubic in*	*Kilograms*		*Pounds*
2.540	**1**	0.394	6.452	**1**	0.155	16.387	**1**	0.061	0.454	**1**	2.205
5.080	**2**	0.787	12.903	**2**	0.310	32.774	**2**	0.122	0.907	**2**	4.409
7.620	**3**	1.181	19.355	**3**	0.465	49.161	**3**	0.183	1.361	**3**	6.614
10.160	**4**	1.575	25.806	**4**	0.620	65.548	**4**	0.244	1.814	**4**	8.819
12.700	**5**	1.969	32.258	**5**	0.775	81.936	**5**	0.305	2.268	**5**	11.023
15.240	**6**	2.362	38.710	**6**	0.930	98.323	**6**	0.366	2.722	**6**	13.228
17.780	**7**	2.756	45.161	**7**	1.085	114.710	**7**	0.427	3.175	**7**	15.432
20.320	**8**	3.150	51.613	**8**	1.240	131.097	**8**	0.488	3.629	**8**	17.637
22.860	**9**	3.543	58.064	**9**	1.395	147.484	**9**	0.549	4.082	**9**	19.842
25.400	**10**	3.937	64.516	**10**	1.550	163.871	**10**	0.610	4.536	**10**	22.046
50.800	**20**	7.874	129.032	**20**	3.100	327.742	**20**	1.220	9.072	**20**	44.092
76.200	**30**	11.811	193.548	**30**	4.650	491.613	**30**	1.831	13.608	**30**	66.139
101.600	**40**	15.748	258.064	**40**	6.200	655.484	**40**	2.441	18.144	**40**	88.185
127.000	**50**	19.685	322.580	**50**	7.750	819.355	**50**	3.051	22.680	**50**	110.231
152.400	**60**	23.622	387.096	**60**	9.300	983.226	**60**	3.661	27.216	**60**	132.277
177.800	**70**	27.559	451.612	**70**	10.850	1147.097	**70**	4.272	31.752	**70**	154.324
203.200	**80**	31.496	516.128	**80**	12.400	1310.968	**80**	4.882	36.287	**80**	176.370
228.600	**90**	35.433	580.644	**90**	13.950	1474.839	**90**	5.492	40.823	**90**	198.416
254.000	**100**	39.370	645.160	**100**	15.500	1638.710	**100**	6.102	45.359	**100**	220.464

Metres		*Yards*	*Square m*		*Square yd*	*Cubic m*		*Cubic yd*	*Metric tonnes*		*Tons (UK)*
0.914	**1**	1.094	0.836	**1**	1.196	0.765	**1**	1.308	1.016	**1**	0.984
1.829	**2**	2.187	1.672	**2**	2.392	1.529	**2**	2.616	2.032	**2**	1.968
2.743	**3**	3.281	2.508	**3**	3.588	2.294	**3**	3.924	3.048	**3**	2.953
3.658	**4**	4.374	3.345	**4**	4.784	3.058	**4**	5.232	4.064	**4**	3.937
4.572	**5**	5.468	4.181	**5**	5.980	3.823	**5**	6.540	5.080	**5**	4.921
5.486	**6**	6.562	5.017	**6**	7.176	4.587	**6**	7.848	6.096	**6**	5.905
6.401	**7**	7.655	5.853	**7**	8.372	5.352	**7**	9.156	7.112	**7**	6.889
7.315	**8**	8.749	6.689	**8**	9.568	6.116	**8**	10.464	8.128	**8**	7.874
8.230	**9**	9.843	7.525	**9**	10.764	6.881	**9**	11.772	9.144	**9**	8.858
9.144	**10**	10.936	8.361	**10**	11.960	7.646	**10**	13.080	10.161	**10**	9.842
18.288	**20**	21.872	16.723	**20**	23.920	15.291	**20**	26.159	20.321	**20**	19.684
27.432	**30**	32.808	25.084	**30**	35.880	22.937	**30**	39.239	30.481	**30**	29.526
36.576	**40**	43.745	33.445	**40**	47.840	30.582	**40**	52.318	40.642	**40**	39.368
45.720	**50**	54.681	41.806	**50**	59.799	38.228	**50**	65.398	50.802	**50**	49.210
54.864	**60**	65.617	50.168	**60**	71.759	45.873	**60**	78.477	60.963	**60**	59.052
64.008	**70**	76.553	58.529	**70**	83.719	53.519	**70**	91.557	71.123	**70**	68.894
73.152	**80**	87.489	66.890	**80**	95.679	61.164	**80**	104.636	81.284	**80**	78.737
82.296	**90**	98.425	75.251	**90**	107.639	68.810	**90**	117.716	91.444	**90**	88.579
91.440	**100**	109.361	83.613	**100**	119.599	76.455	**100**	130.795	101.605	**100**	98.421

Kilometres		*Miles*	*Hectares*		*Acres*	*Litres*		*Gallons*	*Metric tonnes*		*Tons (US)*
1.609	**1**	0.621	0.405	**1**	2.471	4.546	**1**	0.220	0.907	**1**	1.102
3.219	**2**	1.243	0.809	**2**	4.942	9.092	**2**	0.440	1.814	**2**	2.205
4.828	**3**	1.864	1.214	**3**	7.413	13.638	**3**	0.660	2.722	**3**	3.305
6.437	**4**	2.485	1.619	**4**	9.844	18.184	**4**	0.880	3.629	**4**	4.409
8.047	**5**	3.107	2.023	**5**	12.355	22.730	**5**	1.100	4.536	**5**	5.521
9.656	**6**	3.728	2.428	**6**	14.826	27.276	**6**	1.320	5.443	**6**	6.614
11.265	**7**	4.350	2.833	**7**	17.297	31.822	**7**	1.540	6.350	**7**	7.716
12.875	**8**	4.971	3.327	**8**	19.769	36.368	**8**	1.760	7.257	**8**	8.818
14.484	**9**	5.592	3.642	**9**	22.240	40.914	**9**	1.980	8.165	**9**	9.921
16.093	**10**	6.214	4.047	**10**	24.711	45.460	**10**	2.200	9.072	**10**	11.023
32.187	**20**	12.427	8.094	**20**	49.421	90.919	**20**	4.400	18.144	**20**	22.046
48.280	**30**	18.641	12.140	**30**	74.132	136.379	**30**	6.599	27.216	**30**	33.069
64.374	**40**	24.855	16.187	**40**	98.842	181.839	**40**	8.799	36.287	**40**	44.092
80.467	**50**	31.069	20.234	**50**	123.555	227.298	**50**	10.999	45.359	**50**	55.116
96.561	**60**	37.282	24.281	**60**	148.263	272.758	**60**	13.199	54.431	**60**	66.139
112.654	**70**	43.496	28.328	**70**	172.974	318.217	**70**	15.398	63.503	**70**	77.162
128.748	**80**	49.710	32.375	**80**	197.684	363.677	**80**	17.598	72.575	**80**	88.185
144.841	**90**	55.923	36.422	**90**	222.395	409.137	**90**	19.798	81.647	**90**	99.208
160.934	**100**	62.137	40.469	**100**	247.105	454.596	**100**	21.998	90.719	**100**	110.231

FACTS, FIGURES AND LISTS

This section contains a selection of listings that could come in handy for a variety of crosswords and quizzes.

LANGUAGE, ALPHABETS AND CODES

PHOBIAS

Acrophobia	fear of heights
Agoraphobia	fear of open spaces
Ailurophobia	fear of cats
Algophobia	fear of pain
Androphobia	fear of men
Anthophobia	fear of flowers
Anthropophobia	fear of people
Apiphobia	fear of bees
Arachnaphobia	fear of spiders
Ataxiaphobia	fear of untidiness
Bogyphobia	fear of goblins
Brontophobia	fear of thunder
Carcinomaphobia	fear of cancer
Catoptrophobia	fear of mirrors
Chaetophobia	fear of hair
Cheimaphobia	fear of cold
Chorophobia	fear of dancing
Chronophobia	fear of time
Cibophobia	fear of food
Clinophobia	fear of going to bed
Cynophobia	fear of dogs
Demophobia	fear of crowds
Dentophobia	fear of dentists
Ergasiophobia	fear of work
Gamophobia	fear of marriage
Gerascophobia	fear of ageing
Gynaephobia	fear of women
Hemaphobia	fear of blood
Herpetophobia	fear of reptiles
Hormephobia	fear of shock
Hydrophobia	fear of water
Iatrophobia	fear of doctors
Kenophobia	fear of empty rooms
Lachanaphobia	fear of vegetables
Methyphobia	fear of alcohol
Mysophobia	fear of dirt
Necrophobia	fear of death, corpses
Nosocomephobia	fear of hospitals
Oenophobia	fear of wine
Olfactophobia	fear of smells
Ommatophobia	fear of eyes
Ophidiophobia	fear of snakes
Peladophobia	fear of baldness
Pharmacophobia	fear of drugs
Philemaphobia	fear of kissing
Photophobia	fear of light
Pogonophobia	fear of beards
Pyrophobia	fear of fire
Rhytiphobia	fear of getting wrinkles
Sciophobia	fear of shadows
Scopophobia	fear of being looked at
Selenophobia	fear of the moon
Soceraphobia	fear of parents-in-law
Stasiphobia	fear of standing
Taphephobia	fear of being buried alive
Thaasophobia	fear of the sea
Tocophobia	fear of childbirth
Tomophobia	fear of surgery
Trypanophobia	fear of injections
Venustaphobia	fear of beautiful women
Xenophobia	fear of foreigners
Xerophobia	fear of dryness
Zelophobia	fear of jealousy

MORSE CODE

The International Morse Code was formulated in 1852. The spoken code enables radio operators to send messages with their own voices, using the expressions 'dah' and 'di' or 'dit' instead of keying in dashes and dots on their transmitters.

A	. —	di-dah
B	— . . .	dah-di-di-dit
C	— . — .	dah-di-dah-dit
D	— . .	dah-di-dit
E	.	dit
F	. . — .	di-di-dah-dit
G	— — .	dah-dah-dit
H	. . . .	di-di-di-dit
I	. .	di-dit
J	. — — —	di-dah-dah-dah
K	— . —	dah-di-dah
L	. — . .	di-dah-di-dit
M	— —	dah-dah
N	— .	dah-dit
O	— — —	dah-dah-dah
P	. — — .	di-dah-dah-dit
Q	— — . —	dah-dah-di-dah
R	. — .	di-dah-dit
S	. . .	di-di-dit
T	—	dah
U	. . —	di-di-dah
V	. . . —	di-di-di-dah
W	. — —	di-dah-dah
X	— . . —	dah-di-di-dah
Y	— . — —	dah-di-dah-dah
Z	— — . .	dah-dah-di-dit

Dash = dah
Dot = di or dit

BOOKS OF THE BIBLE

The following list gives the commonly used abbreviations for the books of the Bible.

Old Testament

Genesis	Gen.
Exodus	Exod.
Leviticus	Lev.
Numbers	Num.
Deuteronomy	Deut.
Joshua	Josh.
Judges	Judg.
Ruth	Ruth
1 Samuel	1 Sam.
2 Samuel	2 Sam.
1 Kings	1 Kgs.
2 Kings	2 Kgs.

1 Chronicles	1 Chr.
2 Chronicles	2 Chr.
Ezra	Ezra
Nehemiah	Neh.
Esther	Esther
Job	Job
Psalms	Ps.
Proverbs	Prov.
Ecclesiastes	Eccles.
Song of Solomon	S. of S.
Isaiah	Isa.
Jeremiah	Jer.
Lamentations	Lam.
Ezekiel	Ezek.
Daniel	Dan.
Hosea	Hos.
Joel	Joel
Amos	Amos
Obadiah	Obad.
Jonah	Jon.
Micah	Mic.
Nahum	Nah.
Habakkuk	Hab.
Zephaniah	Zeph.
Haggai	Hag.
Zechariah	Zech.
Malachi	Mal.
Apocrypha	
1 Esdras	1 Esd.
2 Esdras	2 Esd.
Tobit	Tobit
Judith	Judith
Rest of Esther	Rest of Esth.
Wisdom of Solomon	Wisd.
Ecclesiasticus	Ecclus.
Baruch with the Epistle of Jeremy	Baruch and Ep. of Jer.
Song of the Three Holy Children	S. of III Ch.
History of Susanna	Sus.
Bel and the Dragon	Bel & Dr.
Prayer of Manasses	Pr. of Man.
1 Maccabees	1 Macc.
2 Maccabees	2 Macc.
New Testament	
Matthew	Matt.
Mark	Mark
Luke	Luke
John	John
Acts	Acts
Romans	Rom.
1 Corinthians	1 Cor.
2 Corinthians	2 Cor.
Galatians	Gal.
Ephesians	Eph.
Philippians	Phil.
Colossians	Col.
1 Thessalonians	1 Thess.
2 Thessalonians	2 Thess.
1 Timothy	1 Tim.
2 Timothy	2 Tim.
Titus	Titus
Philemon	Philem.
Hebrews	Heb.
James	Jas.
1 Peter	1 Pet.
2 Peter	2 Pet.
1 John	1 John
2 John	2 John
3 John	3 John
Jude	Jude
Revelation	Rev.

INTERNATIONAL RADIO ALPHABET

A	Alpha
B	Bravo
C	Charlie
D	Delta
E	Echo
F	Foxtrot
G	Golf
H	Hotel
I	India
J	Juliet
K	Kilo
L	Lima
M	Mike
N	November
O	Oscar
P	Papa
Q	Quebec
R	Romeo
S	Sierra
T	Tango
U	Uniform
V	Victor
W	Whiskey
X	X-Ray
Y	Yankee
Z	Zulu

COMMON LATIN PHRASES

a priori	from what was before
ad hoc	for this special purpose
ad infinitum	without limit
annus horribilis	a bad year
annus mirabilis	a wonderful year
ars gratia artis	art for art's sake
compos mentis	sane
de facto	in fact
de jure	by right
dramatis personae	the list of characters in a play
in absentia	while absent
in extremis	near death
in flagrante delicto	in the act of committing an offence
in loco parentis	in place of a parent
in memoriam	in memory
in situ	in its original situation
in vino veritas	in wine there is truth
in vitro	the living body and in an artificial environment
inter alia	among other things
ipso facto	by that very fact
magna cum laude	with great honour or distinction
mea culpa	by my fault
mens rea	guilty mind
mens sana in corpore sano	a sound mind in a sound body
modus operandi	the manner of working
mutatis mutandis	the necessary changes being made
non sequitur	it does not follow
per capita	by the head
persona non grata	a non-acceptable person
post mortem	after death

prima facie	on the face of it
quid pro quo	something for something
quod erat demonstrandum	which was to be proved
sine qua non	an indispensible condition
sub judice	before a court
tempus fugit	time flies
terra firma	dry land
terra incognita	unknown land
vade mecum	a constant companion
verbatim	exactly as said
vox populi	voice of the people

ROMAN NUMERALS

1	I	30	XXX
2	II	40	XL
3	III	50	L
4	IV	60	LX
5	V	70	LXX
6	VI	80	LXXX
7	VII	90	XC
8	VIII	100	C
9	IX	200	CC
10	X	300	CCC
11	XI	400	CD
12	XII	500	D
13	XIII	600	DC
14	XIV	700	DCC
15	XV	800	DCCC
16	XVI	900	CM
17	XVII	1000	M
18	XVIII	1500	MD
19	XIX	1900	MCM
20	XX	2000	MM

Examples

43	XLIII
66	LXVI
98	XCVIII
339	CCCXXXIX
619	DCXIX
988	CMLXXXVIII
996	CMXCVI
1674	MDCLXXIV
1962	MCMLXII
1998	MCMXCVIII

PEOPLE

PRESIDENTS OF THE USA

Year inaugurated	
1789	George Washington (1732–99), Federation
1797	John Adams (1735–1826), Federation
1801	Thomas Jefferson (1743–1826), Republican
1809	James Madison (1751–1836), Republican
1817	James Monroe (1758–1831), Republican
1825	John Quincy Adams (1767–1848), Republican
1829	Andrew Jackson (1767–1845), Democrat
1837	Martin Van Buren (1782–1862), Democrat
1841	William Harrison (1773–1841) (died in office), Whig
1841	John Tyler (1790–1862) (elected as Vice-President), Whig
1845	James Polk (1795–1849), Democrat
1849	Zachary Taylor (1784–1850) (died in office), Whig
1850	Millard Fillmore (1800–1874) (elected as Vice-President), Whig
1853	Franklin Pierce (1804–69), Democrat
1857	James Buchanan (1791–1868), Democrat
1861	Abraham Lincoln (1809–65) (assassinated in office), Republican
1865	Andrew Johnson (1808–75) (elected as Vice-President), Republican
1869	Ulysses Grant (1822–85), Republican
1877	Rutherford Hayes (1822–93), Republican
1881	James Garfield (1831–81) (assassinated in office), Republican
1881	Chester Arthur (1830–86) (elected as Vice-President), Republican
1885	Grover Cleveland (1837–1908), Democrat
1889	Benjamin Harrison (1833–1901), Republican
1893	Grover Cleveland (1837–1908), Democrat
1897	William McKinley (1843–1901) (assassinated in office), Republican
1901	Theodore Roosevelt (1858–1919) (elected as Vice-President), Republican
1909	William Taft (1857–1930), Republican
1913	Woodrow Wilson (1856–1924), Democrat
1921	Warren Harding (1865–1923) (died in office), Republican
1923	Calvin Coolidge (1872–1933) (elected as Vice-President), Republican
1929	Herbert Hoover (1874–1964), Republican
1933*	Franklin Roosevelt (1882–1945) (died in office), Democrat
1945	Harry Truman (1884–1972) (elected as Vice-President), Democrat
1953	Dwight Eisenhower (1890–1969), Republican
1961	John Kennedy (1917–63) (assassinated in office), Democrat
1963	Lyndon Johnson (1908–73) (elected as Vice-President), Democrat
1969	Richard Nixon (1913–94), Republican
1974†	Gerald Ford (1913–), Republican
1977	James Carter (1924–), Democrat
1981	Ronald Reagan (1911–2004), Republican
1989	George Bush (1924–), Republican
1993	William Clinton (1946–), Democrat
2000	George W. Bush, (1946–), Republican

* Re-elected 5 November 1940, the first case of a third term; re-elected for a fourth term 7 November 1944

†Appointed under the provisions of the 25th Amendment

NOBEL PRIZE WINNERS

For prize winners for the years 1901–2000, *see* earlier editions of *Whitaker's Almanack*.

The Nobel Prizes are awarded each year from the income of a trust fund established by the Swedish scientist Alfred Nobel, the inventor of dynamite, who died on 10 December 1896 leaving a fortune of £1,750,000. The prizes are awarded to those who have contributed most to the common good in the domain of:

Physics – awarded by the Royal Swedish Academy of Sciences
Chemistry – awarded by the Royal Swedish Academy of Sciences
Physiology or Medicine – awarded by the Karolinska Institute
Literature – awarded by the Swedish Academy of Arts
Peace – awarded by a five-person committee elected by the Norwegian Storting
Economic Sciences (instituted 1969) – awarded by the Royal Swedish Academy of Sciences

The prizes are awarded every year on 10 December, the anniversary of Nobel's death. The first awards were made on 10 December 1901. The Trust is administered by the board of directors of the Nobel Foundation, Stockholm, consisting of five members and three deputy members.

The Swedish Government appoints a chairman and a deputy chairman, the remaining members being appointed by the awarding authorities.

The awards in the last three years have been distributed as follows:

	2001	2002	2003
Physics	Eric A. Cornell *(USA)*, Wolfgang Ketterle *(Germany)*, Carl E. Wieman *(USA)*	Raymond Davis Jr. *(USA)*, Masatoshi Koshiba *(Japan)*, Riccardo Giacconi *(USA)*	Alexei A. Abrikosov *(USA and Russia)*, Vitaly L. Ginzburg *(Russia)*, Anthony J. Leggett *(UK and USA)*
Chemistry	William S. Knowles *(USA)*, Ryoji Noyori *(Japan)*, K. Barry Sharpless *(USA)*	John B. Fenn *(USA)*, Koichi Tanaka *(Japan)*, Kurt Wüthrich *(Switzerland)*	Peter Agre *(USA)*, Roderick MacKinnon *(USA)*
Physiology or Medicine	Leland H. Hartwell *(USA)*, Tim Hunt *(UK)*, Sir Paul Nurse *(UK)*	Sydney Brenner *(UK)*, H. Robert Horvitz *(USA)*, John E. Sulston *(UK)*	Paul C. Lauterbur *(USA)*, Sir Peter Mansfield *(UK)*
Literature	V. S. Naipaul *(UK)*	Imre Kertész *(Hungary)*	J. M. Coetzee *(South Africa)*
Peace	United Nations, Kofi Annan *(Ghana)*	Jimmy Carter *(USA)*	Shirin Ebadi *(Iran)*
Economics	George A. Akerlof *(USA)*, A. Michael Spence *(USA)*, Joseph E. Stiglitz *(USA)*	Daniel Kahneman *(USA and Israel)*, Vernon L. Smith *(USA)*	Robert F. Engle *(USA)*, Clive W. J. Granger *(UK)*

ARCHBISHOPS OF CANTERBURY

Year appointed			
1533	Thomas Cranmer	1768	Frederick Cornwallis
1556	Reginald Pole	1783	John Moore
1559	Matthew Parker	1805	Charles Manners-Sutton
1576	Edmund Grindal	1828	William Howley
1583	John Whitgift	1848	John Bird Sumner
1604	Richard Bancroft	1862	Charles Longley
1611	George Abbot	1868	Archibald Campbell Tait
1633	William Laud	1883	Edward White Benson
1660	William Juxon	1896	Frederick Temple
1663	Gilbert Sheldon	1903	Randall Davidson
1678	William Sancroft	1928	Cosmo Lang
1691	John Tillotson	1942	William Temple
1695	Thomas Tenison	1945	Geoffrey Fisher
1716	William Wake	1961	Michael Ramsey
1737	John Potter	1974	Donald Coggan
1747	Thomas Herring	1980	Robert Runcie
1757	Matthew Hutton	1991	George Carey
1758	Thomas Secker	2002	Rowan Williams

SPORT

FA CUP WINNERS SINCE 1950

First held 1872

Year	Winner
1950	Arsenal
1951	Newcastle United
1952	Newcastle United
1953	Blackpool
1954	West Bromwich Albion
1955	Newcastle United
1956	Manchester City
1957	Aston Villa
1958	Bolton Wanderers
1959	Nottingham Forest
1960	Wolverhampton Wanderers
1961	Tottenham Hotspur
1962	Tottenham Hotspur
1963	Manchester United
1964	West Ham United
1965	Liverpool
1966	Everton
1967	Tottenham Hotspur
1968	West Bromwich Albion
1969	Manchester City
1970	Chelsea
1971	Arsenal
1972	Leeds United
1973	Sunderland
1974	Liverpool
1975	West Ham United
1976	Southampton
1977	Manchester United
1978	Ipswich Town
1979	Arsenal
1980	West Ham United
1981	Tottenham Hotspur
1982	Tottenham Hotspur
1983	Manchester United
1984	Everton
1985	Manchester United
1986	Liverpool
1987	Coventry
1988	Wimbledon
1989	Liverpool
1990	Manchester United
1991	Tottenham Hotspur
1992	Liverpool
1993	Arsenal
1994	Manchester United
1995	Everton
1996	Manchester United
1997	Chelsea
1998	Arsenal
1999	Manchester United
2000	Chelsea
2001	Liverpool
2002	Arsenal
2003	Arsenal
2004	Manchester United

WORLD CUP WINNERS

First held 1930

Year	Venue	Winner
1930	Uruguay	Uruguay
1934	Italy	Italy
1938	France	Italy
1950	Brazil	Uruguay
1954	Switzerland	West Germany
1958	Sweden	Brazil
1962	Chile	Brazil
1966	England	England
1970	Mexico	Brazil
1974	West Germany	West Germany
1978	Argentina	Argentina
1982	Spain	Italy
1986	Mexico	Argentina
1990	Italy	West Germany
1994	USA	Brazil
1998	France	France
2002	Korea/Japan	Brazil

THE PERIODIC TABLE OF ELEMENTS

6	atomic number
Carbon	name of element
C	chemical number
12.01	atomic mass

Alkali metals: I A. Alkaline earth metals: II A. Transition metals: III B – II B. Non-metals: III A – VII A. Noble gases.

	I A	II A	III B	IV B	V B	VI B	V II		VIII		I B	II B	III A	IV A	V A	VI A	VII A	Noble gases
1	1 Hydrogen **H** 1.01																	2 Helium **He** 4.00
2	3 Lithium **Li** 6.94	4 Beryllium **Be** 9.01											5 Boron **B** 10.81	6 Carbon **C** 12.01	7 Nitrogen **N** 14.01	8 Oxygen **O** 16.00	9 Fluorine **F** 19.00	10 Neon **Ne** 20.18
3	11 Sodium **Na** 22.99	12 Magnesium **Mg** 24.31											13 Aluminium **Al** 26.98	14 Silicon **Si** 28.09	15 Phosphorus **P** 30.97	16 Sulphur **S** 32.07	17 Chlorine **Cl** 35.45	18 Argon **Ar** 39.95
4	19 Potassium **K** 39.10	20 Calcium **Ca** 40.08	21 Scandium **Sc** 44.96	22 Titanium **Ti** 47.88	23 Vanadium **V** 50.94	24 Chromium **Cr** 52.00	25 Manganese **Mn** 54.95	26 Iron **Fe** 55.85	27 Cobalt **Co** 58.93	28 Nickel **Ni** 58.70	29 Copper **Cu** 63.55	30 Zinc **Zn** 65.39	31 Gallium **Ga** 69.72	32 Germanium **Ge** 72.61	33 Arsenic **As** 74.92	34 Selenium **Se** 78.96	35 Bromine **Br** 79.904	36 Krypton **Kr** 83.80
5	37 Rubidium **Rb** 85.47	38 Strontium **Sr** 87.62	39 Yttrium **Y** 88.91	40 Zirconium **Zr** 91.22	41 Niobium **Nb** 92.91	42 Molybdenum **Mo** 95.94	43 Technetium **Tc** 97.91	44 Ruthenium **Ru** 101.07	45 Rhodium **Rh** 102.91	46 Palladium **Pd** 106.4	47 Silver **Ag** 107.87	48 Cadmium **Cd** 112.41	49 Indium **In** 114.82	50 Tin **Sn** 118.71	51 Antimony **Sb** 121.74	52 Tellurium **Te** 127.60	53 Iodine **I** 126.9045	54 Xenon **Xe** 131.29
6	55 Caesium **Cs** 132.91	56 Barium **Ba** 137.33	Lanthanide series (*see* below)	72 Hafnium **Hf** 178.49	73 Tantalum **Ta** 180.94	74 Tungsten **W** 183.85	75 Rhenium **Ru** 186.21	76 Osmium **Os** 190.23	77 Iridium **Ir** 192.22	78 Platinum **Pt** 195.08	79 Gold **Au** 196.97	80 Mercury **Hg** 200.59	81 Thallium **Tl** 204.38	82 Lead **Pb** 207.2	83 Bismuth **Bi** 208.98	84 Polonium **Po** 209	85 Astatine **At** 210	86 Radon **Rn** 222.02
7	87 Francium **Fr** 223.02	88 Radium **Ra** 226.03	Actinide series (*see* below)	104 Rutherfordium **Rf** 261.12	105 Dubnium **Db** 262.11	106 Seaborgium **Sg** 236.12	107 Bohrium **Bh** 262	108 Hassium **Hs** 265	109 Meitnerium **Mt** 266	110 Darmstadtium **Ds** 269	111 Unununium **Uuu** 272	112 Ununbium **Uub** 277		114 Ununquadium **Uuq** 289				

Rare earth elements—Lanthanide series	57 Lanthanum La 138.91	58 Cerium Ce 140.12	59 Praeseodymium **Pr** 140.91	60 Neodymium **Nd** 144.24	61 Promethium **Pm** 144.91	62 Samarium **Sm** 150.36	63 Europium **Eu** 151.96	64 Gadolinium **Gd** 157.25	65 Terbium **Tb** 158.93	66 Dysprosium **Dy** 162.50	67 Holmium **Ho** 164.93	68 Erbium **Er** 167.26	69 Thulium **Tm** 168.93	70 Ytterbium **Yb** 173.04	71 Lutetium **Lu** 174.97
Actinide series	89 Actinium Ac 227.03	90 Thorium Th 232.04	91 Protactinium **Pa** 231.04	92 Uranium **U** 238.03	93 Neptunium **Np** 237.05	94 Plutonium **Pu** 244.06	95 Americium **Am** 243.06	96 Curium **Cm** 247.07	97 Berkelium **Bk** 247	98 Californium **Cf** 251.08	99 Eisteinium **Es** 252.08	100 Fermium **Fm** 257.10	101 Mendelevium **Md** 258.10	102 Nobelium **No** 259.10	103 Lawrencium **Lr** 260.11

The Periodic Table arranges the elements into horizontal rows (periods) and vertical columns (groups) according to their atomic number. The elements in a group all have similar properties; across each period, atoms are electropositive (form positive ions) to the left and electronegative to the right. The earliest version of the periodic table was devised in 1869 by Dmitriy Mendeleyev, who predicted the existence of several elements from gaps in the table.

ABBREVIATIONS AND ACRONYMS

Ψ = seaport

A

AA	Alcoholics Anonymous
	Automobile Association
AAA	Amateur Athletic Association
ABA	Amateur Boxing Association
abbr(ev)	abbreviation
ABM	Anti-ballistic missile
abr	abridged
ac	alternating current
a/c	account
AC	*(Ante Christum)* Before Christ
	Companion, Order of Australia
ACAS	Advisory, Conciliation and Arbitration Service
ACT	Australian Capital Territory
AD	*(Anno Domini)* In the year of our Lord
ADB	Asian Development Bank
ADC	Aide-de-Camp
ADC (P)	Personal ADC to The Queen
Adj	Adjective
Adj	Adjutant
ad lib	*(ad libitum)* at pleasure
Adm	Admiral
	Admission
Adv	Adverb
AE	Air Efficiency Award
AEM	Air Efficiency Medal
AFC	Air Force Cross
AFM	Air Force Medal
AG	Adjutant-General
	Attorney-General
AGM	air-to-ground missile
	annual general meeting
AH	*(Anno Hegirae)* In the year of the Hegira
AI	Artificial intelligence
AIDS	Acquired immune deficiency syndrome
AIM	Alternative Investment Market
Alt	Altitude
a.m.	*(ante meridiem)* before noon
AM	*(Anno mundi)* In the year of the world
	amplitude modulation
amp	ampere
	amplifier
AMU	Arab Maghreb Union
ANC	African National Congress
anon	anonymous
ANZAC	Australian and New Zealand Army Corps
AO	Air Officer
	Officer, Order of Australia
AOC	Air Officer Commanding
AONB	Area of Outstanding Natural Beauty
APEC	Asia Pacific Economic Co-operation
APR	annual percentage rate
AS	Anglo-Saxon
ASA	Advertising Standards Authority
	Amateur Swimming Association
asap	as soon as possible
ASEAN	Association of South East Asian Nations
ASH	Action on Smoking and Health
ASLEF	Associated Society of Locomotive Engineers and Firemen
ASLIB	Association for Information Management
ATC	Air Training Corps
AUC	*(ab urbe condita)* In the year from the foundation of Rome
	(anno urbis conditae) In the year of the founding of the city
AUT	Association of University Teachers
AV	Audio-visual
	Authorised Version *(of Bible)*
AVR	Army Volunteer Reserve
AWOL	Absent without leave

B

b	born
	bowled
BA	Bachelor of Arts
BAA	British Airports Authority
	British Astronomical Association
BAF	British Athletics Federation
BAFTA	British Academy of Film and Television Arts
BAS	Bachelor in Agricultural Science
	British Antarctic Survey
BBC	British Broadcasting Corporation
BBSRC	Biotechnology and Biological Sciences Research Council
BC	Before Christ
	Borough Council
	British Columbia
BCH (D)	Bachelor of (Dental) Surgery
BCL	Bachelor of Civil Law
BCOM	Bachelor of Commerce
BD	Bachelor of Divinity
BDA	British Dental Association
BDS	Bachelor of Dental Surgery
BED	Bachelor of Education
BEM	British Empire Medal
BENG	Bachelor of Engineering
BFI	British Film Institute
BFPO	British Forces Post Office
BLITT	Bachelor of Letters *or* of Literature
BM	Bachelor of Medicine
	British Museum
BMA	British Medical Association
BMUS	Bachelor of Music
BNFL	British Nuclear Fuels Ltd
BOTB	British Overseas Trade Board
Bp	Bishop
BPHARM	Bachelor of Pharmacy
BPHIL	Bachelor of Philosophy
bpm	beats per minute
Br(it)	Britain
	British
Brig	Brigadier
BSC	Bachelor of Science
BSE	Bovine spongiform encephalopathy
BSI	British Standards Institution
BST	British Summer Time
Bt	Baronet
BTEC	Business and Technology Education Council
Btu	British thermal unit
BVMS	Bachelor of Veterinary Medicine and Surgery

C

c	*(circa)* about
C	Celsius
	Centigrade
	Conservative
CA	Chartered Accountant *(Scotland)*
CAA	Civil Aviation Authority
CAB	Citizens' Advice Bureau
CADW	Ancient Monuments Board for Wales
Cantab	(of) Cambridge
Cantuar:	of Canterbury *(Archbishop)*
CAP	Common Agricultural Policy
Capt	Captain
Caricom	Caribbean Community and Common Market
Carliol:	of Carlisle *(Bishop)*
CB	Companion, Order of the Bath
CBE	Commander, Order of the British Empire
CBI	Confederation of British Industry
CBSS	Council of the Baltic Sea States
CC	Chamber of Commerce
	Companion, Order of Canada
	City Council
	County Council
	County Court
CCC	County Cricket Club
CCF	Combined Cadet Force
CCTA	City Colleges for Technology and the Arts
CCHEM	Chartered Chemist
CD	Civil Defence
	compact disc
	Corps Diplomatique
Cdr	Commander
Cdre	Commodore
CDS	Chief of the Defence Staff
CE	Christian Era
	Civil Engineer
CENG	Chartered Engineer

CERN	European Organisation for Nuclear Research
Cestr:	of Chester *(Bishop)*
CET	Central European Time Common External Tariff
cf	*(confer)* compare
CF	Chaplain to the Forces
CFC	Chlorofluorocarbon
CGC	Conspicuous Gallantry Cross
CGEOL	Chartered Geologist
CGI	Computer generated imagery
CGM	Conspicuous Gallantry Medal
CGS	Centimetre-gramme-second *(system)* Chief of General Staff
CH	Companion of Honour
CHB/M	Bachelor/Master of Surgery
CI	Channel Islands The Imperial Order of the Crown of India
CIA	Central Intelligence Agency
CICA	Conference on International and Confidence Building Measures in Asia Criminal Injuries Compensation Authority
CICAP	Criminal Injuries Compensation Appeals Panel
Cicestr:	of Chichester *(Bishop)*
CID	Criminal Investigation Department
CIE	Companion, Order of the Indian Empire
cif	cost, insurance and freight
C-in-C	Commander-in-Chief
CIPFA	Chartered Institute of Public Finance and Accountancy
CIS	Commonwealth of Independent States
CJD	Creutzfeld-Jakob disease
CLJ	Commander, Order of St Lazarus of Jerusalem
CM	*(Chirurgiae Magister)* Master of Surgery
CMG	Companion, Order of St Michael and St George
CND	Campaign for Nuclear Disarmament
c/o	care of
CO	Commanding Officer
C of E	Church of England
COI	Central Office of Information
Col	Colonel
Con	Conservative
cons	consecrated
Cpl	Corporal
CPM	Colonial Police Medal
CPRE	Council for the Protection of Rural England
CPS	Crown Prosecution Service
CPVE	Certificate of Pre-Vocational Education
CRE	Commission for Racial Equality
CSA	Child Support Agency
CSI	Companion, Order of the Star of India
CTC	City Technology College
CVO	Commander, Royal Victorian Order

D

d	*(denarius)* penny
DBE	Dame Commander, Order of the British Empire
dc	direct current
DC	District Council District of Columbia
DCA	Department for Constitutional Affairs
DCB	Dame Commander, Order of the Bath
D CH	*(Doctor Chirurgiae)* Doctor of Surgery
DCL	Doctor of Civil Law
DCM	Distinguished Conduct Medal
DCMG	Dame Commander, Order of St Michael and St George
DCMS	Department for Culture, Media and Sport
DCVO	Dame Commander, Royal Victorian Order
DD	Doctor of Divinity
DDS	Doctor of Dental Surgery
DDT	dichlorodiphenyl trichloroethane
del	*(delineavit)* he/she drew it
DEFRA	Department of the Environment, Food and Rural Affairs
DFC	Distinguished Flying Cross
DfES	Department for Education and Skills
DFID	Department for International Development
DFM	Distinguished Flying Medal
DfT	Department for Transport
DG	*(Dei gratia)* By the grace of God
DHA	District Health Authority
DIP ED	Diploma in Education
DIP HE	Diploma in Higher Education
DIP TECH	Diploma in Technology
DJ	Disc jockey
DL	Deputy Lieutenant
DLITT	Doctor of Letters *or* of Literature
DM	Deutsche Mark
DMUS	Doctor of Music
DNA	deoxyribonucleic acid
DNB	*Dictionary of National Biography*
do	*(ditto)* the same
DoH	Department of Health
DOS	Disk operating system
DP	Data processing
DPH or DPHIL	Doctor of Philosophy
DPP	Director of Public Prosecutions
Dr	Doctor
DRC	Disability Rights Commission
DSC	Doctor of Science
DSC	Distinguished Service Cross
DSM	Distinguished Service Medal
DSO	Companion, Distinguished Service Order
DTI	Department of Trade and Industry
DTP	Desk-top publishing
Dunelm:	of Durham *(Bishop)*
DV	*(Deo volente)* God willing
DVD	Digital Versatile Disc
DVLA	Driver and Vehicle Licensing Agency
DWI	Drinking Water Inspectorate
DWP	Department for Work and Pensions

E

E	East Email
Ebor:	of York *(Archbishop)*
EBRD	European Bank for Reconstruction and Development
EC	European Community
ECG	Electrocardiogram
ECGD	Export Credits Guarantee Department
ECOWAS	Economic Community of West African States
ECSC	European Coal and Steel Community
ECU	European Currency Unit
ED	Efficiency Decoration
EEC	European Economic Community
EEG	Electroencephalogram
EFA	European Fighter Aircraft
EFTA	European Free Trade Association
eg	*(exempli gratia)* for the sake of example
EIB	European Investment Bank
EMS	European Monetary System
EMU	European Monetary Union
EOC	Equal Opportunities Commission
EPSRC	Engineering and Physical Sciences Research Council
ER	*(Elizabetha Regina)* Queen Elizabeth
ERM	Exchange Rate Mechanism
ERNIE	Electronic random number indicator equipment
ESA	European Space Agency
ESP	Extra-sensory perception
ESRC	Economic and Social Research Council
ETA	*Euzkadi ta Askatasuna* (Basque separatist organisation)
et al	*(et alibi)* and elsewhere *(et alii)* and others
etc	*(et cetera)* and the other things/and so forth
et seq	*(et sequentia)* and the following
EU	European Union
Euratom	European Atomic Energy Commission
Exon:	of Exeter *(Bishop)*

F

f	*(forte)* loud
F	Fahrenheit Fax Fellow of
FA	Football Association

FANY	First Aid Nursing Yeomanry
FAO	Food and Agriculture Organisation *(UN)*
	For the attention of
FAQ	Frequently asked question
FBA	Fellow, British Academy
FBAA	Fellow, British Association of Accountants and Auditors
FBI	Federal Bureau of Investigation
FBU	Fire Brigades Union
FCO	Foreign and Commonwealth Office
FIMGT	Fellow, Institute of Management
FBS	Fellow, Botanical Society
FC	Football Club
FCA	Fellow, Institute of Chartered Accountants in England and Wales
FCCA	Fellow, Chartered Association of Certified Accountants
FCGI	Fellow, City and Guilds of London Institute
FCIA	Fellow, Corporation of Insurance Agents
FCIARB	Fellow, Chartered Institute of Arbitrators
FCIB	Fellow, Chartered Institute of Bankers
	Fellow, Corporation of Insurance Brokers
FCIBSE	Fellow, Chartered Institution of Building Services Engineers
FCII	Fellow, Chartered Insurance Institute
FCIPS	Fellow, Chartered Institute of Purchasing and Supply
FCIS	Fellow, Institute of Chartered Secretaries and Administrators
FCIT	Fellow, Chartered Institute of Transport
FCMA	Fellow, Chartered Institute of Management Accountants
FCO	Foreign and Commonwealth Office
FD	*(Fidei Defensor)* Defender of the Faith
FE	Further Education
fec	*(fecit)* made this
ff	*(fecerunt)* made this *(pl)*
	folios following
ff	*(fortissimo)* very loud
FFA	Fellow, Faculty of Actuaries *(Scotland)*
	Fellow, Institute of Financial Accountants
FFAS	Fellow, Faculty of Architects and Surveyors
FFCM	Fellow, Faculty of Community Medicine
FFPHM	Fellow, Faculty of Public Health Medicine
FGS	Fellow, Geological Society
FHS	Fellow, Heraldry Society
FHSM	Fellow, Institute of Health Service Management
FIA	Fellow, Institute of Actuaries
FIBIOL	Fellow, Institute of Biology
FICE	Fellow, Institution of Civil Engineers
FICS	Fellow, Institution of Chartered Shipbrokers
FIEE	Fellow, Institution of Electrical Engineers
FIERE	Fellow, Institution of Electronic and Radio Engineers
FIFA	International Association Football Federation
FIM	Fellow, Institute of Metals
FIMM	Fellow, Institution of Mining and Metallurgy
FINSTF	Fellow, Institute of Fuel
FINSTP	Fellow, Institute of Physics
FIQS	Fellow, Institute of Quantity Surveyors
FIS	Fellow, Institute of Statisticians
FJI	Fellow, Institute of Journalists
fl	*(floruit)* flourished
FLA	Fellow, Library Association
FLS	Fellow, Linnaean Society
FM	Field Marshal
	frequency modulation
fo	folio
FO	Flying Officer
fob	free on board
FPHS	Fellow, Philosophical Society
FRAD	Fellow, Royal Academy of Dancing
FRAES	Fellow, Royal Aeronautical Society
FRAI	Fellow, Royal Anthropological Institute
FRAM	Fellow, Royal Academy of Music
FRAS	Fellow, Royal Asiatic Society
	Fellow, Royal Astronomical Society
FRBS	Fellow, Royal Botanic Society
	Fellow, Royal Society of British Sculptors
FRCA	Fellow, Royal College of Anaesthetists
FRCGP	Fellow, Royal College of General Practitioners
FRCM	Fellow, Royal College of Music
FRCO	Fellow, Royal College of Organists
FRCOG	Fellow, Royal College of Obstetricians and Gynaecologists
FRCP	Fellow, Royal College of Physicians, London
FRCPATH	Fellow, Royal College of Pathologists
FRCPE *or* FRCPED	Fellow, Royal College of Physicians, Edinburgh
FRCPI	Fellow, Royal College of Physicians, Ireland
FRCPSYCH	Fellow, Royal College of Psychiatrists
FRCR	Fellow, Royal College of Radiologists
FRCS	Fellow, Royal College of Surgeons of England
FRCSE *or* FRCSED	Fellow, Royal College of Surgeons of Edinburgh
FRCSGLAS	Fellow, Royal College of Physicians and Surgeons of Glasgow
FRCSI	Fellow, Royal College of Surgeons in Ireland
FRCVS	Fellow, Royal College of Veterinary Surgeons
FRECONS	Fellow, Royal Economic Society
FRENG	Fellow, Royal Academy of Engineering
FRGS	Fellow, Royal Geographical Society
FRHISTS	Fellow, Royal Historical Society
FRHS	Fellow, Royal Horticultural Society
FRIBA	Fellow, Royal Institute of British Architects
FRICS	Fellow, Royal Institution of Chartered Surveyors
FRMETS	Fellow, Royal Meteorological Society
FRMS	Fellow, Royal Microscopical Society
FRNS	Fellow, Royal Numismatic Society
FRPHARMS	Fellow, Royal Pharmaceutical Society
FRPS	Fellow, Royal Photographic Society
FRS	Fellow, Royal Society
FRSA	Fellow, Royal Society of Arts
FRSC	Fellow, Royal Society of Chemistry
FRSE	Fellow, Royal Society of Edinburgh
FRSH	Fellow, Royal Society of Health
FRSL	Fellow, Royal Society of Literature
FRTPI	Fellow, Royal Town Planning Institute
FSA	Fellow, Society of Antiquaries
	Financial Services Authority
	Food Standards Agency
FSS	Fellow, Royal Statistical Society
FSVA	Fellow, Incorporated Society of Valuers and Auctioneers
FT	*Financial Times*
FTI	Fellow, Textile Institute
FTII	Fellow, Chartered Institute of Taxation
FZS	Fellow, Zoological Society

G

GATT	General Agreement on Tariffs and Trade
GBE	Dame/Knight Grand Cross, Order of the British Empire
GC	George Cross
GCB	Dame/Knight Grand Cross, Order of the Bath
GCC	Gulf Co-operation Council
GCHQ	Government Communications Headquarters
GCIE	Knight Grand Commander, Order of the Indian Empire

GCLJ	Knight Grand Cross, Order of St Lazarus of Jerusalem
GCMG	Dame/Knight Grand Cross, Order of St Michael and St George
GCSE	General Certificate of Secondary Education
GCSI	Knight Grand Commander, Order of the Star of India
GCVO	Dame/Knight Grand Cross, Royal Victorian Order
GDP	Gross Domestic Product
Gen	General
GHQ	General Headquarters
GLA	Greater London Authority
GM	George Medal genetically modified
GMB	General, Municipal, Boilermakers and Allied Trades Union
GMT	Greenwich Mean Time
GNI	Gross National Index
GNP	Gross National Product
GNVQ	General National Vocational Qualification
GOC	General Officer Commanding
GP	General Practitioner
Gp Capt	Group Captain
GSA	Girls' Schools Association
GST	Greenwich Sidereal Time

H

HAC	Honourable Artillery Company
HB	His Beatitude
HBM	Her/His Britannic Majesty('s)
HCF	Highest common factor Honorary Chaplain to the Forces
HE	Her/His Excellency Higher Education His Eminence
HGV	Heavy Goods Vehicle
HH	Her/His Highness Her/His Honour His Holiness
HIM	Her/His Imperial Majesty
HIV	Human immunodeficiency virus
HJS	*(hic jacet sepultus)* here lies buried
HM	Her/His Majesty('s)
HMAS	Her/His Majesty's Australian Ship
HMC	Headmasters' Conference
HMI	Her/His Majesty's Inspector
HML	Her/His Majesty's Lieutenant
HMS	Her/His Majesty's Ship
HMSO	Her/His Majesty's Stationery Office
HNC	Higher National Certificate
HND	Higher National Diploma
Hon	Honorary Honourable
hp	horse power
HP	Hire purchase
HQ	Headquarters
HR	Human resources
HRH	Her/His Royal Highness
HRT	hormone replacement therapy
HSE	Health and Safety Executive *(hic sepultus est)* here lies buried
HSH	Her/His Serene Highness
HST	Hubble Space Telescope
HWM	High water mark

I

I	Island
IAAS	Incorporated Association of Architects and Surveyors
IAEA	International Atomic Energy Agency
IATA	International Air Transport Association
ibid	*(ibidem)* in the same place
IBRD	International Bank for Reconstruction and Development
ICAO	International Civil Aviation Organisation
ICBM	Inter-continental ballistic missile
ICFTU	International Confederation of Free Trade Unions
ICJ	International Court of Justice
ICRC	International Committee of the Red Cross
id	*(idem)* the same
IDA	International Development Association
IDD	International direct dialling
ie	*(id est)* that is
IEA	International Energy Agency
IFA	Independent Financial Advisor
IFAD	International Fund for Agricultural Development
IFC	International Finance Corporation
ILO	International Labour Office/Organisation
ILR	Independent local radio
IMF	International Monetary Fund
IMO	International Maritime Organisation
Inc	Incorporated
incog	*(incognito)* unknown, unrecognised
INLA	Irish National Liberation Army
in loc	*(in loco)* in its place
Inmarsat	International Maritime Satellite Organisation
INRI	*(Iesus Nazarenus Rex Iudaeorum)* Jesus of Nazareth, King of the Jews
inst	*(instant)* current month
Intelsat	International Telecommunications Satellite Organisation
Interpol	International Criminal Police Organisation
IOC	International Olympic Committee
IOM	Isle of Man
IOU	I owe you
IOW	Isle of Wight
IQ	Intelligence quotient
IRA	Irish Republican Army
IRC	International Red Cross
Is	Islands
ISA	Individual Savings Account
ISBN	International Standard Book Number
ISO	Imperial Service Order International Organisation for Standardisation International Standards Organisation
ISSN	International Standard Serial Number
IT	Information Technology
ITN	Independent Television News
ITU	International Telecommunication Union
ITV	Independent Television
IVF	in vitro fertilisation

J

J	Judge Justice
JP	Justice of the Peace

K

KBE	Knight Commander, Order of the British Empire
KCB	Knight Commander, Order of the Bath
KCIE	Knight Commander, Order of the Indian Empire
KCLJ	Knight Commander, Order of St Lazarus of Jerusalem
KCMG	Knight Commander, Order of St Michael and St George
KCSI	Knight Commander, Order of the Star of India
KCVO	Knight Commander, Royal Victorian Order
KG	Knight of the Garter
KGB	*(Komitet Gosudarstvennoi Bezopasnosti)* Committee of State Security *(USSR)*
kHz	kiloHertz
KLJ	Knight, Order of St Lazarus of Jerusalem
ko	knock out *(boxing)*
KP	Knight, Order of St Patrick
KStJ	Knight, Order of St John of Jerusalem
Kt	Knight
KT	Knight of the Thistle
kV	Kilovolt
kW	Kilowatt
kWh	Kilowatt hour

L

L	Liberal
Lab	Labour
Lat	Latitude
lbw	leg before wicket
lc	lower case *(printing)*
LCJ	Lord Chief Justice
LCM	Least/lowest common multiple
LD	Liberal Democrat

LDS	Licentiate in Dental Surgery
LEA	Local Education Authority
LHD	*(Literarum Humaniorum Doctor)* Doctor of Humane Letters/Literature
Lib	Liberal
Lic	*(Licenciado)* lawyer *(Spanish)*
Lit	Literary
Lit Hum	*(Literae Humaniores)* Faculty of classics and philosophy, Oxford
LITT D	Doctor of Letters
LJ	Lord Justice
LLB	Bachelor of Laws
LLD	Doctor of Laws
LLM	Master of Laws
LMS	Local management in schools
LMSSA	Licentiate in Medicine and Surgery, Society of Apothecaries
loc cit	*(loco citato)* in the place cited
log	Logarithm
Londin:	of London *(Bishop)*
Long	Longitude
LRT	London Regional Transport
LS	*(loco sigilli)* place of the seal
LSA	Licentiate of Society of Apothecaries
LSC	Learning and Skills Council Legal Services Commission
Lsd	*(Librae, solidi, denarii)* pounds, shillings and pence
LSE	London School of Economics and Political Science
LST	Local Sidereal Time
Lt	Lieutenant
LTA	Lawn Tennis Association
Ltd	Limited (liability)
LVO	Lieutenant, Royal Victorian Order
LW	long wave
LWM	Low water mark

M

M	Member Monsieur
MA	Master of Arts
Maj	Major, majority
max	Maximum
MB	Bachelor of Medicine
MBA	Master of Business Administration
MBC	Metropolitan Borough Council
MBE	Member, Order of the British Empire
MBO	Management Buy-out
MC	Master of Ceremonies Military Cross
MCC	Marylebone Cricket Club
MCH(D)	Master of (Dental) Surgery
MD	Managing Director Doctor of Medicine
MDS	Master of Dental Surgery
ME	Middle English Myalgic Encephalomyelitis
MEC	Member of Executive Council
MED	Master of Education
mega	one million times
MEP	Member of the European Parliament
MFH	Master of Foxhounds
Mgr	Monsignor
MI	Military Intelligence
micro	one-millionth part
milli	one-thousandth part
min	Minimum
MLA	Member of Legislative Assembly
MLC	Member of Legislative Council
MLITT	Master of Letters
Mlle	Mademoiselle
MLR	Minimum lending rate
MM	Military Medal
Mme	Madame
MN	Merchant Navy
MO	Medical Officer/Orderly
MoD	Ministry of Defence
MoT	Ministry of Transport
MP	Member of Parliament Military Police
mph	miles per hour
M PHIL	Master of Philosophy
MR	Master of the Rolls
MRC	Medical Research Council
MS	Master of Surgery Manuscript *(pl* MSS*)* Multiple Sclerosis
MSC	Master of Science
MSP	Member of Scottish Parliament
Mus B/D	Bachelor/Doctor of Music
MV	Merchant Vessel Motor Vessel
MVO	Member, Royal Victorian Order
MW	medium wave
MWA	Member of the Welsh Assembly

N

N	North
n/a	not applicable not available
NAAFI	Navy, Army and Air Force Institutes
NAFTA	North American Free Trade Agreement
NASA	National Aeronautics and Space Administration
NASUWT	National Association of Schoolmasters/Union of Women Teachers
NATO	North Atlantic Treaty Organisation
NB	New Brunswick *(nota bene)* note well
NCIS	National Criminal Intelligence Service
NCO	Non-commissioned officer
NDPB	Non-departmental public body
NEB	New English Bible
nem con	*(nemine contradicente)* no one contradicting
NERC	Natural Environment Research Council
nes	not elsewhere specified
NESTA	National Endowment for Science, Technology and the Arts
NFT	National Film Theatre
NFU	National Farmers' Union
NHS	National Health Service
NI	National Insurance Northern Ireland
No	*(numero)* number
non seq	*(non sequitur)* it does not follow
Norvic:	of Norwich *(Bishop)*
NP	Notary Public
NRA	National Rifle Association
NS	New Style *(calendar)* Nova Scotia
NSPCC	National Society for the Prevention of Cruelty to Children
NSW	New South Wales
NT	National Theatre National Trust New Testament Northern Territory
NUJ	National Union of Journalists
NUM	National Union of Mineworkers
NUS	National Union of Students
NUT	National Union of Teachers
NVQ	National Vocational Qualification
NWT	Northwest Territory
NZ	New Zealand

O

OAP	old age pension(er)
OAPEC	Organisation of Arab Petroleum Exporting Countries
OAS	Organisation of American States
OAU	Organisation of African Unity
Ob *or* obit	Died
OBE	Officer, Order of the British Empire
OC	Officer Commanding
ODA	Overseas Development Administration
ODPM	Office of the Deputy Prime Minister
OE	Old English omissions excepted
OECD	Organisation for Economic Co-operation and Development
OED	*Oxford English Dictionary*
Ofcom	Office of Communications
Ofgem	Office of Gas and Electricity Markets
OFM	Order of Friars Minor *(Franciscans)*
Ofreg	Office for the Regulation of Electricity and Gas
Ofsted	Office for Standards in Education
OFT	Office of Fair Trading
Ofwat	Office of Water Services
OHMS	On Her/His Majesty's Service
ohp	overhead projector

OIC	Organisation of the Islamic Conference
OM	Order of Merit
ono	or near offer
ONS	Office for National Statistics
op	*(opus)* work
OP	Opposite prompt side *(of theatre)*
	Order of Preachers *(Dominicans)*
	out of print *(books)*
op cit	*(opere citato)* in the work cited
OPEC	Organisation of Petroleum Exporting Countries
OPRAF	Office of Passenger Rail Franchising
OPS	Office of Public Service
ORR	Office of the Rail Regulator
OS	Old Style *(calendar)*
	Ordnance Survey
OSA	Order of St Augustine
OSB	Order of St Benedict
OSCE	Organisation for Security and Co-operation in Europe
O St J	Officer, Order of St John of Jerusalem
OT	Old Testament
OTC	Officers' Training Corps
Oxon	(of) Oxford
	Oxfordshire

P

p	Page
p	*(piano)* softly
PA	Personal Assistant
	Press Association
	Public address (system)
PAYE	Pay as You Earn
pc	*(per centum)* in the hundred
PC	personal computer
	Police Constable
	politically correct
	Privy Counsellor
PDA	Personal digital assistant
PDSA	People's Dispensary for Sick Animals
PE	Physical Education
Petriburg:	of Peterborough *(Bishop)*
PFI	Private Finance Initiative
PG	Parental Guidance
PGA	Professional Golfers Association
PGCE	Postgraduate Certificate of Education
PHD	Doctor of Philosophy
PHLS	Public Health Laboratory Service
PIF	Pacific Islands Forum
pl	Plural
PLA	Port of London Authority
PLC	Public Limited Company
PLO	Palestine Liberation Organisation
p.m.	*(post meridiem)* after noon
PM	Prime Minister
	Post mortem
PMRAFNS	Princess Mary's Royal Air Force Nursing Service
PO	Petty Officer
	Pilot Officer
	Post Office
	postal order
POW	Prisoner of War
pp	Pages
	(per procurationem) by proxy
PPARC	Particle Physics and Astronomy Research Council
PPS	Parliamentary Private Secretary
PR	Proportional representation
	Public relations
PRA	President of the Royal Academy
Pres	President
Pro tem	*(pro tempore)* for the time being
Prox	*(proximo)* next month
PRS	President of the Royal Society
PRSE	President of the Royal Society of Edinburgh
PS	*(postscriptum)* postscript
PSBR	Public sector borrowing requirement
psc	passed Staff College
PSV	Public Service Vehicle
PTA	Parent-Teacher Association
Pte	Private
PTO	Please turn over
PVC	Polyvinyl chloride

Q

QARANC	Queen Alexandra's Royal Army Nursing Corps
QARNNS	Queen Alexandra's Royal Naval Nursing Service
QB(D)	Queen's Bench (Division)
QC	Queen's Counsel
QED	*(quod erat demonstrandum)* which was to be proved
QGM	Queen's Gallantry Medal
QHC	Queen's Honorary Chaplain
QHDS	Queen's Honorary Dental Surgeon
QHNS	Queen's Honorary Nursing Sister
QHP	Queen's Honorary Physician
QHS	Queen's Honorary Surgeon
Qld	Queensland
QMG	Quartermaster General
QPM	Queen's Police Medal
QS	Quarter Sessions
QSO	Quasi-stellar object (quasar)
	Queen's Service Order
quango	quasi-autonomous non-governmental organisation
qv	*(quod vide)* which see

R

R	*(Regina)* Queen
	(Rex) King
RA	Royal Academy/Academician
	Royal Artillery
R&B	rhythm and blues
R&D	research and development
RAC	Royal Armoured Corps
	Royal Automobile Club
RADA	Royal Academy of Dramatic Art
RADC	Royal Army Dental Corps
RAE	Royal Aerospace Establishment
RAEC	Royal Army Educational Corps
RAES	Royal Aeronautical Society
RAF	Royal Air Force
RAM	Random-access memory
	Royal Academy of Music
RAMC	Royal Army Medical Corps
RAN	Royal Australian Navy
RAOC	Royal Army Ordnance Corps
RAPC	Royal Army Pay Corps
RAVC	Royal Army Veterinary Corps
RBG	Royal Botanic Garden
RBS	Royal Society of British Sculptors
RC	Red Cross
	Roman Catholic
RCM	Royal College of Music
RCN	Royal Canadian Navy
RCT	Royal Corps of Transport
RD	Refer to drawer *(banking)*
	Royal Naval and Royal Marine Forces Reserve Decoration
	Rural Dean
RDI	Royal Designer for Industry
RE	Religious Education
	Royal Engineers
REM	rapid eye movement
REME	Royal Electrical and Mechanical Engineers
Rep	Representative
	Republican
Rev(d)	Reverend
RFU	Rugby Football Union
RGN	Registered General Nurse
RGS	Royal Geographical Society
RHA	Regional Health Authority
RHS	Royal Horticultural Society
RI	Rhode Island
	Royal Institute of Painters in Watercolours
	Royal Institution
RIBA	Royal Institute of British Architects
RIP	*(Requiescat in pace)* May he/she rest in peace
RIR	Royal Irish Regiment
RL	Rugby League
RM	Registered Midwife
	Royal Marines
RMA	Royal Military Academy
RMN	Registered Mental Nurse
RMT	National Union of Rail, Maritime and Transport Workers
RN	Royal Navy
RNIB	Royal National Institute for the Blind
RNID	Royal National Institute for the Deaf
RNLI	Royal National Lifeboat Institution
RNMH	Registered Nurse for the Mentally Handicapped
RNR	Royal Naval Reserve
RNVR	Royal Naval Volunteer Reserve
RNXS	Royal Naval Auxiliary Service
RNZN	Royal New Zealand Navy

Ro	*(Recto)* on the right-hand page
ROC	Royal Observer Corps
Roffen:	of Rochester *(Bishop)*
ROI	Royal Institute of Oil Painters
ROM	Read-only memory
RoSPA	Royal Society for the Prevention of Accidents
RP	Royal Society of Portrait Painters
RPA	Rural Payments Agency
rpm	revolutions per minute
RRC	Lady of Royal Red Cross
RSA	Royal Scottish Academician Royal Society of Arts
RSC	Royal Shakespeare Company
RSCN	Registered Sick Children's Nurse
RSE	Royal Society of Edinburgh
RSM	Regimental Sergeant Major
RSPB	Royal Society for the Protection of Birds
RSPCA	Royal Society for the Prevention of Cruelty to Animals
RSV	Revised Standard Version *(of Bible)*
RSVP	(Répondez, s'il vous plaît) Please reply
RSW	Royal Scottish Society of Painters in Watercolours
Rt Hon	Right Honourable
RTPI	Royal Town Planning Institute
RU	Rugby Union
RUC	Royal Ulster Constabulary
RV	Revised Version *(of Bible)*
RWS	Royal Water Colour Society
RYS	Royal Yacht Squadron

S

s	second *(solidus)* shilling
S	South
SA	Salvation Army South Africa South America South Australia
SAARC	South Asian Association for Regional Co-operation
SAD	Seasonal affective disorder
SAE	stamped addressed envelope
Salop	Shropshire
Sars	Severe Acute Respiratory Syndrome
Sarum:	of Salisbury *(Bishop)*
SAS	Special Air Service
SBS	Special Boat Service Small Business Service
ScD	Doctor of Science
SCM	State Certified Midwife
SDLP	Social Democratic and Labour Party
SEAQ	Stock Exchange Automated Quotations system
SEN	Special Educational Needs State Enrolled Nurse
SERPS	State Earnings Related Pension Scheme
SFO	Serious Fraud Office
SHMIS	Society of Headmasters and Headmistresses of Independent Schools
SI	*(Système International d'Unités)* International System of Units Statutory Instrument
Sic	so written
Sig	Signature Signor
SJ	Society of Jesus *(Jesuits)*
SLD	Social and Liberal Democrats
SMP	Statutory Maternity Pay
SNP	Scottish National Party
SOE	Special Operations Executive
SOS	Save Our Souls *(distress signal)*
Sp	*(sine prole)* without issue
Spgr	specific gravity
SRN	State Registered Nurse
SRO	Self Regulating Organisations
SS	Saints Steamship
SSC	Solicitor before Supreme Court *(Scotland)*
SSN	Standard Serial Number
SSP	Statutory Sick Pay
SSSI	Site of special scientific interest
STD	*(Sacrae Theologiae Doctor)* Doctor of Sacred Theology Subscriber trunk dialling
STI	Sexually transmitted infection
Stet	let it stand *(printing)*
Stp	Standard temperature and pressure
STP	*(Sacrae Theologiae Professor)* Professor of Sacred Theology
Sub Lt	Sub-Lieutenant
SVQ	Scottish Vocational Qualification

T

T	Telephone
TA	Territorial Army
TB	Tuberculosis
TCCB	Test and County Cricket Board
TD	Territorial Efficiency Decoration
TEC	Training and Enterprise Council
TEFL	Teaching English as a foreign language
temp	Temperature temporary employee
TES	*Times Educational Supplement*
T&G	Transport and General Workers' Union
THES	*Times Higher Education Supplement*
TLS	*Times Literary Supplement*
TNT	trinitrotoluene *(explosive)*
trans	Translated
trs	transpose *(printing)*
TRH	Their Royal Highnesses
TT	Tourist Trophy *(motorcycle races)* Tuberculin tested
TUC	Trades Union Congress

U

U	Unionist
UAE	United Arab Emirates
uc	upper case *(printing)*
UC	Unitary Council
UCAS	Universities and Colleges Admissions Service
UCATT	Union of Construction, Allied Trades and Technicians
UCL	University College London
UDA	Ulster Defence Association
UDI	Unilateral Declaration of Independence
UDR	Ulster Defence Regiment
UEFA	Union of European Football Associations
UFF	Ulster Freedom Fighters
UFO	Unidentified flying object
UHF	ultra-high frequency
UKAEA	UK Atomic Energy Authority
UN	United Nations
UNESCO	United Nations Educational, Scientific and Cultural Organisation
UNHCR	United Nations High Commissioner for Refugees
UNICEF	United Nations Children's Fund
UNIDO	United Nations Industrial Development Organisation
Unita	National Union for the Total Independence of Angola
UNPO	Unrepresented Nations and Peoples Organisation
UPU	Universal Postal Union
US(A)	United States (of America)
USDAW	Union of Shop, Distributive and Allied Workers
USM	Unlisted Securities Market
USSR	Union of Soviet Socialist Republics
UTC	Co-ordinated Universal Time system
UVF	Ulster Volunteer Force

V

v	*(versus)* against
VA	Vicar Apostolic Victoria and Albert Order
VAD	Voluntary Aid Detachment
V&A	Victoria and Albert Museum
VAT	Value added tax
VC	Victoria Cross
VCR	video cassette recorder
VD	Venereal disease Volunteer Officers' Decoration
VDU	Visual display unit
Ven	Venerable
VHF	very high frequency
VIP	Very important person
Vo	*(Verso)* on the left-hand page
VRD	Royal Naval Volunteer Reserve Officers' Decoration
VSO	Voluntary Service Overseas
VTOL	Vertical take-off and landing *(aircraft)*

W

W	Website West
WCC	World Council of Churches
WEA	Workers' Educational Association
WEU	Western European Union
WFTU	World Federation of Trade Unions
WHO	World Health Organisation
WI	West Indies Women's Institute
Winton:	of Winchester *(Bishop)*
WIPO	World Intellectual Property Organisation
WMD	Weapons of mass destruction
WMO	World Meteorological Organisation
WO	Warrant Officer
WRAC	Women's Royal Army Corps
WRAF	Women's Royal Air Force
WRNS	Women's Royal Naval Service
WRVS	Women's Royal Voluntary Service
WS	Writer to the Signet
WTO	World Trade Organisation
WWW	World Wide Web

Y

YMCA	Young Men's Christian Association
YWCA	Young Women's Christian Association

INDEX

E

J

O

X

Y

Z

STOP-PRESS

CHANGES SINCE PAGES WENT TO PRESS

PARLIAMENT

A by-election for Hartlepool was held on 30 September 2004 following the resignation of Peter Mandelson. Labour candidate Iain Wright won with 12,752 votes, a majority of 2,033.

PUBLIC OFFICES

HM REVENUE AND CUSTOMS

3 September 2004 – Steve Lamey was appointed as Chief Information Officer.

REGIONAL GOVERNMENT

NORTHERN IRELAND

16–18 September, Leeds Castle – Talks between British Prime Minister Tony Blair and Irish Prime Minister Bertie Ahern on the re-wording of the Good Friday Agreement, to ensure full decommissioning of IRA weapons, ended without a deal being reached.

21–22 September, Stormont – Northern Ireland Secretary Paul Murphy and Irish Minister of State Tom Kitt met with representatives of Northern Ireland's political parties, however the talks broke down on 22 September.

POLICE

5 July 2004 – Sir John Stevens confirmed he would retire as Commissioner of the Metropolitan Police on 31 January 2005.

EVENTS OF THE YEAR – SEPTEMBER 2004

BRITISH AFFAIRS

13. A *Fathers 4 Justice* protester trespassed the perimeter walls of Buckingham Palace and climbed up the front of the building. Metropolitan Police Commissioner, Sir John Stevens, demanded a full report into the security breach. **15.** A pro-hunting demonstration in Parliament Square ended in violent clashes between protesters and police. Five protesters managed to enter the House of Commons during a debate of the Hunting Bill.

ENVIRONMENT AND SCIENCE

8. A £153 million NASA mission to collect particles of the sun ended in disaster when the probe carrying the samples crashed into the Utah desert after two parachutes failed to open; scientists hoped that some of the sample could still be salvaged if the pod remained sealed.

THE AMERICAS

12. Hurricane Ivan passed directly over the Cayman Islands, causing flash flooding and mudslides. Across the Caribbean sixty people had already been killed as a result of the storm. **19.** Floodwaters tore through Haiti in the wake of tropical storm Jeanne, submerging the entire northern coastal city of Gonaives and killing at least 250 people.

ASIA

9. A British couple was shot dead by an off-duty policeman in Thailand following an argument in a restaurant near the River Kwai. **12.** It was reported that a large explosion causing a two-mile-wide mushroom cloud had occurred in North Korea near the Chinese border.

EUROPE

1. Twenty Chechen terrorists took hundreds of adults and children hostage in a school in Beslan, southern Russia, as the children returned after the summer break. The terrorists threatened to blow-up the school if the Russian Government did not withdraw its troops from Chechnya and release prisoners captured after recent Chechen attacks on the neighbouring region of Ingushetia. **2.** The siege of the school in Beslan continued; fifteen children and eleven women were released following negotiations. **3.** The siege of the school in Beslan ended after two explosions, followed by gunfire from within the school, forced Russian special forces to storm the building. **4.** Official figures were released stating that 323 people had died during the Beslan school siege. More than 600 people were injured.

THE MIDDLE EAST

18. In Iraq, terrorists from the Tawhid wal Jihad group released video footage of three hostages (a British engineer and two Americans) stating that they would be beheaded unless demands for the release of Iraqi women prisoners were met within 48 hours. **20.** Video footage was released by Tawhid wal Jihad showing that one of the American hostages had been beheaded. **21.** The Tawhid wal Jihad group announced that the second American hostage had been killed. **22.** Baghdad police retrieved the body of the second American hostage. A video of the final hostage, Briton Kenneth Bigley, was released in which he made a direct plea to Prime Minister Tony Blair to intervene and requested him to meet the demands of the hostage-takers and free the female prisoners held in Iraqi jails.

OBITUARIES

Ramone, Johnny (John Cummings), guitarist, aged 55 – *d.* 15 September 2004, *b.* 8 October 1948

Clough, Brian, footballer and manager, aged 69 – *d.* 20 September 2004, *b.* 21 March 1935

SPORTS RESULTS

CRICKET

County Championship Cricket 2004: Division 1, Warwickshire, 220 points; *Relegated,* Worcestershire, 161 points; Lancashire, 154 points; Northamptonshire, 134 points
Division 2, Promoted, Nottinghamshire, 252 points; Hampshire, 228 points; Glamorgan, 196.5 points

National League 2004: Division 1, Glamorgan, 44 points; *Relegated,* Warwickshire, 30 points; Kent, 24 points, Surrey 22 points
Division 2, Promoted, Middlesex, 48 points, Worcestershire, 48 points, Nottinghamshire, 46 points

ICC Champions' Trophy, Oval (25 September 2004): West Indies beat England by 2 wickets. England 217; West Indies 218–8

CYCLING

Tour of Spain 2004: Roberto Heras (Spain)

GOLF

The Heritage: Henrik Stenson (Sweden), 269

MOTOR CYCLING

World Superbikes 2004, Italy (Imola): Race 1 – Régis Laconi (France), Ducati; Race 2 – Régis Laconi (France), Ducati

MOTOR RACING

China Grand Prix (Shanghai), 26 September: Rubens Barrichello (Brazil), Ferrari

TENNIS

US OPEN CHAMPIONSHIPS 2004

New York, 30–12 September

Men's Singles: Roger Federer (Switzerland) beat Lleyton Hewitt (Australia) 6–0, 7–6, 6–0

Ladies' Singles: Svetlana Kuznetsova (Russia) beat Elena Dementieva (Russia) 6–3, 7–5

Men's Doubles: Marl Knowles (Bahamas) and Daniel Nestor (Canada) beat Leander Paes (India) and David Rikl (Czech Republic) 6–3, 6–3

Ladies' Doubles: Virginia Ruano Pascual (Spain) and Paola Suarez (Argentina) beat Svetlana Kuznetsova (Russia) and Elena Likhovtseva (Russia) 6–4, 7–5

Mixed Doubles: Vera Zvonareva (Russia) and Bob Bryan (USA) beat Alicia Molik (Australia and Todd Woodbridge (Australia) 6–3, 6–4

COUNTRIES OF THE WORLD

KAZAKHSTAN

Legislative Elections 19 September 2004 – President Nazarbayev's Otan party secured 42 per cent of the vote while the main opposition, the Asar party, won 19 per cent.